AFRICANA

The Encyclopedia of the African and African American Experience

To the memory of
William Edward Burghardt Du Bois and
in honor of Nelson Rolihlahla Mandela

William Edward Burghardt Du Bois

AFRICANA

The Encyclopedia of the African and African American Experience

Editors

Kwame Anthony Appiah, *Harvard University*
Henry Louis Gates, Jr., *Harvard University*

A Member of the Perseus Books Group

A Member of the Perseus Books Group

 For information, address Basic *Civitas* Books, 10 East 53rd Street, New York, NY 10022-5299.

FIRST EDITION

Library of Congress Cataloging-in-Publication Data
Africana : the encyclopedia of the African and African American experience / editors, Kwame Anthony Appiah, Henry Louis Gates.
p. cm.
"A member of the Perseus Books Group."
Includes bibliographical references
ISBN 0-465-00071-1
1. Africa — Civilization Encyclopedias. 2. Blacks Encyclopedias. 3. African diaspora Encyclopedias. 4. African-Americans Encyclopedias. I. Appiah, Anthony. II. Gates, Henry Louis.

DT14.A37435 1999
909'.0496'003 — dc21 99-37834
CIP

This paper meets the requirements of NSI/NISO Z39.48.1992 (Permanence of Paper).

Advisory Board

Publishing, Editorial, and Production Staff

CHAIRMAN,
PERSEUS BOOKS GROUP
Frank H. Pearl

PUBLISHER
Jack McKeown

MARKETING DIRECTOR
Elizabeth Carduff

SALES DIRECTOR
Matthew Goldberg

PRODUCTION DIRECTOR
Della R. Mancuso

SUBJECT EDITORS
Rafael de la Dehesa
Susanne Freidberg
Leyla Keough
Richard Newman
Mark O'Malley
Francisco Ortega
Ben Penglase
Patricia Sullivan

EDITORIAL CONSULTANT
Charles Van Doren

EXECUTIVE EDITOR
Karen C. C. Dalton

MANAGING EDITOR
Peter T. Glenshaw

PROJECT EDITORS
Pat Jalbert
Kate Tuttle

MANUSCRIPT EDITORS
Jamie Carter
Toni Rosenberg

PROOFREADER
Amy Finch

TEXT PREPARATION
Jaman Greene
Kevin Rabener

DESIGN
Dynamic Diagrams

DESIGN DIRECTOR
Krzysztof Lenk

ART DIRECTOR
Elaine Froehlich

DESIGNERS
Lynn Faitelson
Sarah Von Dreele

INFORMATION DESIGNERS
Chin-lien Chen
Kerry Fishback
Chihiro Hosoe

PROGRAMMING CONSULTANT
David Durand

DESIGN COORDINATION
X Bonnie Woods

CARTOGRAPHER
MAGELLAN Geographix/
maps.com
Bryan E. Conant

PRINTER AND BINDER
R. R. Donnelly & Sons Co.
Willard, Ohio

COLOR SEPARATOR
Color Associates
St. Louis, Missouri

DUST JACKET PRINTER
Coral Graphic Services
Hicksville, New York

Table of Contents

Introduction: An Encyclopedia of the African Diaspora

Between 1909 and his death in 1963, W. E. B. Du Bois, the Harvard-trained historian, sociologist, journalist, and political activist, dreamed of editing an "Encyclopædia Africana." He envisioned a comprehensive compendium of "scientific" knowledge about the history, cultures, and social institutions of people of African descent: of Africans in the Old World, African Americans in the New World, and persons of African descent who had risen to prominence in Europe, the Middle East, and Asia. Du Bois sought to publish nothing less than the equivalent of a black *Encyclopaedia Britannica*, believing that such a broad assemblage of biography, interpretive essays, facts, and figures would do for the much denigrated black world of the twentieth century what *Britannica* and Denis Diderot's *Encyclopédie* had done for the European world of the eighteenth century. These publications, which consolidated the scholarly knowledge accumulated by academics and intellectuals in the Age of Reason, served both as a tangible sign of the enlightened skepticism that characterized that era of scholarship, and as a basis upon which further scholarship could be constructed. These encyclopedias became monuments to "scientific" inquiry, bulwarks against superstition, myth, and what their authors viewed as the false solace of religious faith. An encyclopedia of the African diaspora in Du Bois's view would achieve these things for persons of African descent.

But a black encyclopedia would have an additional function. Its publication would, at least symbolically, unite the fragmented world of the African diaspora, a diaspora created by the European slave trade and the turn-of-the-century "scramble for Africa." Moreover, for Du Bois, marshalling the tools of "scientific knowledge," as he would put it in his landmark essay, "The Need for an Encyclopedia of the Negro" (1945), could also serve as a weapon in the war against racism: "There is need for young pupils and for mature students of a statement of the present condition of our knowledge concerning the darker races and especially concerning Negroes, which would make available our present scientific knowledge and set aside the vast accumulation of tradition and prejudice which makes such knowledge difficult now for the layman to obtain: A Vade mecum for American schools, editors, libraries, for Europeans inquiring into the race status here, for South Americans, and Africans."

The publication of such an encyclopedia, Du Bois continued, would establish "a base for further advance and further study" of "questions affecting the Negro race." An encyclopedia of the Negro, he reasoned, would establish both social policy and "social thought and discussion... upon a basis of accepted scientific conclusion."

Du Bois first announced his desire to edit an "Encyclopædia Africana" in a letter to Edward Wilmot Blyden, the Pan-Africanist intellectual, in Sierra Leone in 1909: "I am venturing to address you on the subject of a Negro Encyclopædia. In celebration of the 50th anniversary of the Emancipation of the American Negro, I am proposing to bring out an Encyclopædia Africana covering the chief points in the history and condition of the Negro race." Du Bois sent a similar letter to dozens of other scholars, white and black, including William James, Hugo Munsterberg, George Santayana, Albert Bushnell Hart (his professors at Harvard), President Charles William Eliot of Harvard, Sir Harry Johnston, Sir Flinders Petrie, Giuseppe Sergi, Franz Boas, J. E. Casely-Hayford, John Hope, Kelly Miller, Benjamin Brawley, Anna

Jones, Richard Greener, Henry Ossawa Tanner, and several others, all of whom — with the sole exception of President Eliot — agreed to serve on his editorial board. Du Bois sought to create a board of "One Hundred Negro Americans, African and West Indian Scholars," as he put it in a letter, and a second board of white advisors. Du Bois, in other words, sought the collaboration of the very best scholars of what we would call today African Studies and African American Studies, as well as prominent American and European intellectuals such as James and Boas.

Nevertheless, as he put it to Blyden, "the real work I want done by Negroes." Du Bois, admitting that this plan was "still in embryo," created official stationery that projected a publication date of the first volume in 1913 — "the Jubilee of Emancipation in America and the Tercentenary of the Landing of the Negro." The remaining four volumes would be published between 1913 and 1919.

Despite the nearly unanimous enthusiasm that greeted Du Bois's call for participation, he could not secure the necessary funding to mount the massive effort necessary to edit an encyclopedia of the black world. But he never abandoned the idea. At the height of the Great Depression, the idea would surface once again.

Anson Phelps Stokes, head of the Phelps-Stokes Association, a foundation dedicated to ameliorating race relations in America, called a meeting of 20 scholars and public figures at Howard University on November 7, 1931, to edit an "Encyclopedia of the Negro," a Pan-African encyclopedia similar to Du Bois's 1909 project. Incredibly, neither Du Bois nor Alain Locke, a Harvard trained Ph.D. in philosophy and the dean of the Harlem Renaissance, nor Carter G. Woodson (like Du Bois, a Harvard Ph.D. in history and the founder of the Association for the Study of Negro Life and History) was invited to attend. Du Bois protested, angrily, to Phelps Stokes. A second meeting was convened on January 9, 1932, at which Du Bois was unanimously elected editor-in-chief. Between 1932 and 1946, Du Bois would serve as "Editor-in-Chief" of the second incarnation of his project, now named "The Encyclopædia of the Negro," and housed at 200 West 135th Street in New York City.

Du Bois planned a four-volume encyclopedia, each volume comprising 500,000 words. Just as he had done in 1909, he secured the cooperation of an impressive array of scholars, including Charles Beard, Franz Boas, John R. Connors, Edith Abbott, Felix Frankfurter, Otto Klineburg, Carl Van Doren, H. L. Mencken, Roscoe Pound, Robert E. Park, Sidney Hook, Harold Laski, Broadus Mitchell, "and scores of others," as Du Bois put it in a letter to the historian Charles Wesley. Du Bois's "Encyclopædia of the Negro" would require a budget of $225,000. It would be written by a staff of between "25 and 100 persons" hired to be "research aides," to be located in editorial offices to be established in New York, Chicago, Atlanta, and New Orleans. They would prepare bibliographies, collect books and manuscripts, and gather and write "special data" and shorter entries. Black and white scholars, primarily located in Europe, America, and Africa, would write longer interpretive entries.

Du Bois tells us that his project was interrupted by the Depression for three years. But by 1935, he was actively engaged in its planning full-time, time made available by his forced resignation from his position as editor of the *Crisis* magazine, the official organ of the National Association for the Advancement of Colored People, which Du Bois had held since its first publication in 1910. Du Bois had written an editorial advocating the development of independent Negro social and economic institutions, since the goal posts of the Civil Rights Movement appeared to be receding. The NAACP's board of directors was outraged and demanded his resignation. Du Bois obliged. Du Bois sought funding virtually everywhere, including the Works Progress Administration and the Federal Writers' Project, to no avail, despite the fact that Phelps Stokes had pledged, on a matching basis, half of the needed funds. He continued to write to hundreds of scholars, soliciting their cooperation. E. Franklin Frazier, the great black sociologist, declined Du Bois's overture, citing in a letter dated November 7, 1936, the presence of too many "politicians," "statesmen," "big Negroes," and "whites of good will" on Du Bois's editorial board. Throw out the table of contents, fire the board of editors, replace them with scholars, Frazier wrote, and he would consider joining the project.

A few months before this exchange, Du Bois was viciously attacked by Carter G. Woodson in the black newspaper the *Baltimore Afro-American*. On May 30, 1936, a page-one headline blared the news that Woodson "Calls Du Bois a Traitor if He Accepts Post," with a subtitle adding for good measure: "He Told Ofays, We'd Write Own History." Woodson charged that Du Bois had stolen the idea of *The Encyclopedia of the Negro* from him and that his project was doomed to failure because Du Bois was financed by, and his editorial board included, white people. Du Bois was embarrassed and sought to defend himself in letters to potential contributors and board members. Between his enemies at the NAACP and his intellectual rivals such as Woodson and Frazier, Du Bois faced an enormous amount of opposition to his encyclopedia project. In this swirl of controversy, in the midst of the Depression, funding appeared increasingly elusive.

Du Bois's assistant editor, Rayford Logan, like Du Bois, Woodson, and Charles Wesley a Harvard-trained Ph.D. in history, told a poignant story about the failure of this project to receive funding. By 1937, Du Bois had secured a pledge of $125,000 from the Phelps-Stokes Fund to proceed with his project — half of the funds needed to complete it. He applied to the Carnegie Corporation for the remaining half of his budget, with the strong endorsement of Phelps Stokes and the president of the General Education Board, a group of four or five private foundations that included the Rockefeller Foundation. So convinced was Du Bois that his project would finally be funded, that he invited Logan to wait with him for the telephone call that he had been promised immediately following the Carnegie board meeting. A bottle of vintage champagne sat chilling on Du Bois's desk in a silver bucket, two cut crystal champagne flutes resting nearby.

The phone never rang. Persuaded that Du Bois was far too "radical" to serve as a model of disinterested scholarship, and lobbied by Du Bois's intellectual enemies, such as the anthropologist Melville J. Herskovits, the Carnegie Corporation rejected the project.

Nevertheless, Du Bois stubbornly persisted, even publishing two putative "entries" from the *Encyclopædia* in *Phylon* magazine in 1940, one on Robert Russa Moton, the principal of Tuskegee Institute between 1915 and 1935, the other on Alexander Pushkin. He even was able to publish two editions in 1945 and 1946 of a *Preparatory Volume with Reference Lists and Reports of the Encyclopædia of the Negro*. But the project itself never could secure adequate backing.

David Levering Lewis, Du Bois's biographer, tells us what happened to Du Bois's promised funding. The executive committee of the General Education Board rejected the proposal early in May 1937. "In his conference a few days later with Carnegie Corporation president Frederick Keppel, GEB's Jackson Davis paradoxically pleaded for favorable Carnegie consideration of the project. 'Dr. Du Bois is the most influential Negro in the United States,' Davis reminded Keppel. 'This project would keep him busy for the rest of his life.' Predictably, Carnegie declined. Within a remarkably short time, the study of the Negro (generously underwritten by the Carnegie Corporation) found a quite different direction under a Swedish scholar then unknown in the field of race relations, one whose understanding of American race problems was to be distinctly more psychological and less economic than was Du Bois's.... When the president of the Phelps Stokes Fund wrote Du Bois in 1944 at the time of the publication of *An American Dilemma: [The Negro Problem and Modern Democracy]* that 'there has been no one who has been quite so often quoted by [Gunnar] Myrdal than yourself,' Du Bois must have savored the irony."

Adding insult to injury, in 1948 the General Education Board, along with the Dodd Mead publishing company, approached Frederick Patterson, the president of Tuskegee Institute, to edit a new incarnation of the project, to be entitled *The Negro: An Encyclopedia*. Then in 1950, the historian Charles Wesley wrote to Du Bois, informing him that in the wake of Carter Woodson's death, the Association for the Study of Negro Life and History had decided to resurrect *The Encyclopedia Africana* project, reminding him of Woodson's claims to have conceived of it in 1921. Du Bois wished him well, but cautioned him in a postscript that "there is no such thing as a cheap encyclopedia." Everyone, it seemed, wanted to claim title to the encyclopedia, but no one wanted Du Bois to serve as its editor. For black scholars, *Africana* had become the Grail. Its publication, as Du Bois put it "would mark an epoch."

Long after Du Bois had abandoned all hope of realizing his great ambition, an offer of assistance would come quite unexpectedly from Africa. On September 26, 1960, Du Bois announced that Kwame Nkrumah, the president of the newly independent Republic of Ghana, had invited him to repatriate to Ghana, where he would serve as the editor-in-chief of *The Encyclopædia Africana*. Du Bois accepted, moving in 1961. On December 15, 1962, in his last public speech before his death on the eve of the March on Washington in August 1963, Du Bois addressed a conference assembled expressly to launch — at last — his great project.

He wanted to edit "an Encyclopædia Africana based in Africa and compiled by Africans," he announced, an encyclopedia that is "long overdue," referring no doubt to his previously frustrated attempts. "Yet," he continued with a certain grim satisfaction, "it is logical that such a work had to wait for independent Africans to carry it out [because] the encyclopedia is concerned with Africa as a whole." Citing his own introductory essay in the *Preparatory Volume* of 1945, Du Bois justified this project by railing against "present thought and action" that "are all too often guided by old and discarded theories of race and heredity, by misleading emphasis and silence of former histories." After all of these centuries of slavery and colonialism, on the eve of the independence of the Continent, "it is African scholars themselves who will create the ultimate *Encyclopædia Africana.*" Eight months later Du Bois would be dead, and with him died his 54-year-old dream of shepherding a great black encyclopedia into print. Nevertheless, the Secretariat of the *Encyclopædia Africana*, based in Accra, Ghana, which Du Bois founded, eventually published three volumes of biographical dictionaries, in the late seventies and early eighties, and has recently announced plans to publish an encyclopedia about the African continent in 2009, which is welcome news.

We first became enamored of this project as students at the University of Cambridge. One of us, Henry Louis Gates, Jr., was a student of Wole Soyinka, the great playwright who in 1986 became the first African to receive the Nobel Prize for Literature. The other, Kwame Anthony Appiah, was an undergraduate studying philosophy. Though we came from very different backgrounds — in rural West Virginia and in urban Asante, in Ghana — we both already had, like Soyinka, a sense of the worlds of Africa and her diaspora as profoundly interconnected, even if, as we learned ourselves, there were risks of misunderstanding that arose from our different origins and experiences. The three of us represented three different places in the black world, and we vowed in 1973 to edit a Pan-African encyclopedia of the African diaspora, inspired by Du Bois's original objective formulated in 1909. Du Bois's later conception of the project was, we felt, too narrow in its scope, and too parochial in its stated desire to exclude the scholarly work of those who had not had the good fortune, by accident of birth, to have been born on the African continent. (Du Bois himself, had this rule been literally applied, would have been excluded from his own project!) Instead, we sought to edit a project that would produce a genuine compendium of "Africana."

Our own attempts to secure the necessary support were in vain too until four years ago when, first, Quincy Jones and Martin Payson, and then Sonny Mehta and Alberto Vitale at Random House, agreed to fund the preparation of a prototype of a CD-ROM encyclopedia of the African diaspora, to be edited by us, with Soyinka serving as the chair of an international and multiethnic board of editors. Two years later we secured the support for a 2-million-word encyclopedia from Frank Pearl, the CEO of a new publisher called Perseus Books, and from the Microsoft Corporation. Modifying the editorial structure that Du Bois planned to use to complete *The Encyclopædia of the Negro*, we deployed a staff of some three dozen writers and editors, and we solicited about 400 scholars to write longer, interpretive articles.

Du Bois's own idea, although he did not admit this, probably arose at least in part out of the publication of the *Encyclopædia Judaica* in 1907, as well as black encyclopedia antecedents such as James T. Holly, who published *The Afro-American Encyclopedia* in 1895, Alexander W. Wayman's *Cyclopedia of African Methodism* (1882), Charles O. Boothe's *The Cyclopedia of the Colored Baptists of Alabama* (1895), and Revels Adams's *Cyclopedia of African Methodism in Mississippi* (1902). Other unpublished projects patterned after Du Bois's 1909 proposal included Daniel Murray's monumental "Historical and Biographical Encyclopædia of the Colored Race Throughout the World," which was to have been published in 1912 in six volumes and, later, Edward Garrett's self-written "A Negro Encyclopedia," consisting of 4000 entries, and completed on the eve of World War II. Both encyclopedias exist in manuscript form, but tragically were never published. All told, more than two dozen black encyclopedias have been published in the past century with limited distribution, but none has explored in a single compass both the African continent and the triumphs and the tragedies of Africa's people and their descendants around the globe.

That continent is where human prehistory begins. It was in Africa, as biologists now believe, that our species evolved, and so, in a literal sense, every modern human being is of African descent. Indeed, it was probably only about 100,000 years ago that the first members of our species left Africa, across the Suez Peninsula, and set out on an adventure that would lead to the peopling of the whole earth.

It is important to emphasize that Africa has never been separate from the rest of the human world. There have been long periods and many cultures that knew nothing of life in Africa. For much of African history, even in Africa, most Africans were unaware of other peoples in their own continent, unaware, in fact, that they shared a continent at all (just as most people in Europe, Asia, Australasia, and the Americas would have been astonished to learn that they were Europeans, Asians, Australasians, or Americans!). But the Straits of Gibraltar and the Suez Peninsula were always bridges more than obstacles to travel; the Mediterranean was already a system of trade long before the founding of Rome; the Sahara Desert, which so many people imagine as an impenetrable barrier, has a network of trade routes older than the Roman Empire. Starting some 2000 or so years ago, in the area of modern day Cameroon, Bantu-speaking migrants fanned out south and east into tropical Africa, taking with them the knowledge of iron smelting and new forms of agriculture. And so, when Greek and Arab travelers explored the East Coast of Africa in the first millennium C.E., or European explorers began to travel down the West African coast toward the equator in the fifteenth century, they were making direct contact with cultures with which their ancestors had very often been in remote and indirect contact all along.

The first European scholars to write about Africa in the modern period, which begins with the European Age of Discovery, knew very little of Africa's history. They did not know that their ancestors, thousands of generations ago, had also lived in Africa. If they had read Herodotus, they might have noticed his brief discussion of the civilizations of the upper Nile, and so they might have realized that Egypt was in touch with other African societies. However, it would probably not have occurred to them that, since those societies were also in touch with still others, Egypt was in touch with Central Africa as well. So they thought of much of Africa as being outside the human historical narrative they already knew.

These first scholars were also obviously struck by the physical differences between Africans and themselves — especially of skin color and hair — and by the differences between the customs back home and the ones the European explorers found on the Guinea coast. And so they thought of Africans as different in kind from themselves, wondering, sometimes, whether they were really also descendants of Adam and Eve.

Attitudes like these already distorted Western understandings of Africa from the fifteenth century on. Worse yet, as the transatlantic slave trade developed, so did an increasingly negative set of ideas about African peoples and their capacities. It became normal to think of black Africans as inferior to Europeans, and many Europeans found in that inferiority a rationalization for the enslavement of Africans. As a result, much of the writing about Africans and about people of African descent in the New World was frankly derogatory. Because modern Africans were educated in European colonies, they too inherited a distorted and dismissive attitude toward Africa's past and African capacities, and one of the first tasks of modern African intellectuals has been to try to frame a sense of the world and our place in it that is freed from these sad legacies.

There have been many skirmishes in the battle to find a just representation of Africa and her peoples. But in the course of this century — and more especially in the last 30 or 40 years — a more objective knowledge of Africa has gradually emerged, both in Africa and elsewhere. Anthropologists began to describe the rich religious, artistic, and social life of African peoples. African historians have learned to interpret oral histories, passed down in Africa's many traditions, crosschecking them against archæological and documentary evidence to produce a rich picture of the African past. Economists and political scientists, literary critics and philosophers, scholars of almost every discipline in the social sciences and the humanities have contributed to this new knowledge. And it has been the work of scholars on every continent, Africans prominent among them. Work in African American Studies has led to new understandings of the culture of slaves and of the role of people of African descent in shaping the New World's language, religion, agriculture, architecture, music, and art. As a result, it is now possible to comb through a great library of material on African history and on the peoples of Africa and her diaspora, and to offer, in a single volume, a compendium of facts and interpretations.

An encyclopedia cannot include everything that is known about its subject matter, even everything that is important. So we have had to make choices. (And, alas, some of the most interesting questions are as yet unanswered.) But we have sought to provide a broad range of information and so to represent the full range of Africa and her diaspora. About two-fifths of the text of the encyclopedia has to do exclusively, or almost so, with the African continent: the history of each of the modern nations of Africa and what happened within their territories before those nations developed; the names of ethnic groups, including some that were formerly empires and nations, and their histories; biographies of eminent African men and women; major cities and geographical features: rivers, mountains, lakes, deserts; forms of culture: art, literature, music, religion; and some of Africa's diverse plant and animal life. Another third deals mostly with Latin America and the Caribbean, focusing on the influence of African cultures and people of African descent in shaping those portions of the New World. Slightly less than a third of the material deals with North America in the same way. And the rest is material of cross-cultural significance or has to do with the African presence in Europe, Asia, or the rest of the world.

Our main focus has been on history—political and social—and on literature and the arts, including music, to which African and African American contributions have been especially notable in modern times. Our aim has been to give a sense of the wide diversity of peoples, cultures, and traditions that we know about in Africa in historical times, a feel for the environment in which that history was lived, and a broad outline of the contributions of people of African descent, especially in the Americas, but, more generally, around the world.

It is natural, faced with a compendium of this sort, to go looking first for what we know already and to be especially pleased with ourselves if we find something missing! But in setting out to make an encyclopedia in a single volume, we had to make choices all the time about what to include, and we did so in the light of our own best judgments, in consultation with many scholars from around the world. It has been one of the great satisfactions of compiling a work with so many colleagues with so many different specialized areas of knowledge, that we have been able to fill in some of our own many areas of ignorance. That, we believe, is the great pleasure of this new encyclopedia: it not only answers many questions that you knew you wanted to ask, it invites you to ask questions that you had not dreamed of asking. We hope you will find, as we have, that the answers to these unfamiliar questions are as amazing and as varied as Africa, her peoples, and their descendants all around the globe.

We mentioned earlier some of the many encyclopedias of various aspects of African and African American life that have been published in the past. The publication of *Africana: The Encyclopedia of the African and African American Experience* as a one-volume print edition aspires to belong in the grand tradition of encyclopedia editing by scholars interested in the black world on both sides of the Atlantic. It also relies upon the work of thousands of scholars who have sought to gather and to analyze, according to the highest scholarly standards, the lives and the worlds of black people everywhere. We acknowledge our indebtedness to these traditions of scholarly endeavor—more than a century old—to which we are heirs, by dedicating our encyclopedia to the monumental contribution of W. E. B. Du Bois.

Kwame Anthony Appiah
Henry Louis Gates, Jr.

Acknowledgments

Building an encyclopedia requires the labor and support of hundreds of individuals and many institutions. In addition to the contributors, who are acknowledged elsewhere in this book, the editors wish to express their profound gratitude to the following persons:

Sharon Adams, Rachel Antell, Bennett Ashley, Robbie Bach, Tim Bartlett, Craig Bartholomew, John Blassingame, William G. Bowen, Peggy Cooper Cafritz, Elizabeth Carduff, Albert Carnesale, Jamie Carter, Sheldon Cheek, Chin-lien Chen, Coureton C. Dalton, Karen C. C. Dalton, the late Charles T. Davis, Rafael de la Dehesa, John Donatich, David Du Bois, Joseph Duffy, Olawale Edun, Richard Ekman, Lynn Faitelson, Amy Finch, Henry Finder, Lisa Finder, Kerry Fishback, Susanne Freidberg, Elaine Froehlich, Tony Gleaton, Peter Glenshaw, Lisa Goldberg, Matthew Goldberg, Jaman Greene, Holly Hartman, Pete Higgins, Jessica Hochman, Chihiro Hosoe, Pat Jalbert, Mary Janisch, Quincy Jones, Paul Kahn, Leyla Keough, Jeremy Knowles, Joanne Kendall, Harry Lasker, Todd Lee, Krzysztof Lenk, Erroll McDonald, Jack McKeown, Della R. Mancuso, Nancy Maull, Sonny Mehta, Joel W. Motley III, Richard Newman, Peter Norton, Mark O'Malley, Jennifer Oppenheimer, Francisco Ortega, Martin Payson, Frank Pearl, Ben Penglase, Kevin Rabener, Toni Rosenberg, Daryl Roth, Michael Roy, Neil Rudenstine, Kelefa Sanneh, Carrie Seglin, Keith Senzel, Bill Smith, Wole Soyinka, Patti Stonesifer, Patricia Sullivan, Carol Thompson, Larry Thompson, Lucy Tinkcombe, Kate Tuttle, Charles Van Doren, Robert Vare, Michael Vazquez, Alberto Vitale, Sarah Von Dreele, Philippe Wamba, Carrie Mae Weems, and X Bonnie Woods.

Contributors

Rosanne Adderley, *Tulane University*
Marian Aguiar, *Amherst, Massachusetts*
Emmanuel Akyeampong, *Harvard University*
Suzanne Albulak, *Cambridge, Massachusetts*
Samir Amin, *Director of the Forum Tiers Monde, Dakar, Senegal*
George Reid Andrews, *University of Pittsburgh*
Abdullahi Ahmed An-Na'im, *Emory University*
Rachel Antell, *San Francisco, California*
Kwame Anthony Appiah, *Harvard University*
Jorge Arce, *Boston Conservatory of Music*
Alberto Arenas, *University of California at Berkeley*
Paul Austerlitz, *Brown University*
Karen Backstein, *City University of New York, College of Staten Island*
Anthony Badger, *University of Cambridge*
Lawrie Balfour, *Babson College*
Marlyse Baptista, *University of Georgia*
Robert Baum, *Iowa State University*
Stephen Behrendt, *Harvard University*
Patrick Bellegarde-Smith, *University of Wisconsin at Milwaukee*
Eric Bennett, *Iowa City, Iowa*
Suzanne Preston Blier, *Harvard University*
Juan Botero, *Former Executive Director, Instituto de Ciencia Politica, Bogota, Colombia*
Keith Boykin, *Washington, D.C.*
Esperanza Brizvela-Garcia, *London, England*
Diana DeG. Brown, *Bard College*
Eva Stahl Brown, *University of Texas at Austin*
Barbara Browning, *New York University*
Eric Brosch, *Cambridge, Massachusetts*
John Burdick, *Syracuse University*
Andrew Burton, *London, England*
Alida Cagidemetrio, *University of Udine, Italy*
Chloe Campbell, *London, England*
Sophia Cantave, *Tufts University*
Yvonne Captain, *George Washington University*
Judy Carney, *University of California at Los Angeles*
Vincent Carretta, *University of Maryland at College Park*
Clayborne Carson, *Editor, Martin Luther King, Jr., Papers Project, Stanford University*
Odile Cazenave, *University of Tennessee*
Alistair Chisholm, *London, England*
Jace Clayton, *Cambridge, Massachusetts*
Patricia Collins, *University of Cincinnati*
Nicola Cooney, *Harvard University*
Belinda Cooper, *New School for Social Research*
Frederick Cooper, *University of Michigan at Ann Arbor*
Juan Giusti Cordero, *Universidad de Puerto Rico*
Thomas Cripps, *Morgan State University*
Selwyn R. Cudjoe, *Wellesley College*
Carlos Dalmau, *San Juan, Puerto Rico*
Darién J. Davis, *Middlebury College*
James Davis, *Howard University*
Martha Swearington Davis, *University of California at Santa Barbara*
Cristobal Diaz-Ayala, *Independent Scholar*
Rafael Diaz-Diaz, *Pontificia Universidad Javeriana, Bogota, Colombia*
Quinton Dixie, *Indiana University*
Andrew Du Bois, *Cambridge, Massachusetts*
Christopher Dunn, *Tulane University*
Anani Dzidzienyo, *Brown University*
Jonathan Edwards, *Belmont, Massachusetts*
Roanne Edwards, *Arlington, Massachusetts*
Joy Elizondo, *Cambridge, Massachusetts*
Robert Fay, *Medford, Massachusetts*
Martine Fernández, *Berkeley, California*
Paul Finkelman, *Harvard Law School*
Victor Figueroa, *Harvard University*
Gerdes Fleurant, *University of California at Santa Barbara*
Juan Flores, *Hunter College and City College of New York Graduate Center*
Paul Foster, *Chicago, Illinois*
Baltasar Fra-Molinero, *Bates College*
Gregory Freeland, *California Lutheran University*
Susanne Freidberg, *Dartmouth College*
Nina Friedemann, *Pontifica Universidad Javeriana, Bogota, Colombia*
Rob Garrison, *Boston, Massachusetts*
Henry Louis Gates, Jr., *Harvard University*
John Gennari, *University of Virginia*
Danielle Georges, *New York, New York*
Peter Gerhard, *Independent Scholar*
Mark Gevisser, *Editor of* Defiant Desire: Gay and Lesbian Lives in South Africa
Patric V. Giesler, *Gustavus Adolphus College*
Peter Glenshaw, *Belmont, Massachusetts*
Matthew Goff, *Chicago, Illinois*
Flora González, *Emerson College*
Mayda Grano de Oro, *San Juan, Puerto Rico*
Sue Grant Lewis, *Harvard University*
Roderick Grierson, *Independent Scholar*
Barbara Grosh, *New York, New York*
Gerard Gryski, *Auburn University*
Betty Gubert, *Former Head of Reference, Schomburg Center for Research in Black Culture, New York Public Library*
Michelle Gueraldi, *San José, Costa Rica*
Stuart Hall, *The Open University, London*
Michael Hanchard, *Northwestern University*
Julia Harrington, *Banjul, The Gambia*
Elizabeth Heath, *San Francisco, California*
Andrew Hermann, *Former Literary Associate, Denver Center Theatre Company*
Evelyn Brooks Higginbotham, *Harvard University*
Jessica Hochman, *New York, New York*
Cynthia Hoehler-Fatton, *University of Virginia*
Peter Hudson, *Toronto, Canada*
Michelle Hunter, *Cambridge, Massachusetts*
Abiola Irele, *Ohio State University*
David P. Johnson, Jr., *Boston, Massachusetts*
Bill Johnson-González, *Cambridge, Massachusetts*
André Juste, *New York, New York*
Chuck Kapelke, *Boston, Massachusetts*
Ketu Katrak, *University of California at Irvine*
Robin Kelley, *New York University*
R. K. Kent, *University of California at Berkeley*
Leyla Keough, *Cambridge, Massachusetts*
Muhonjia Khaminwa, *Boston, Massachusetts*
David Kim, *Cambridge, Massachusetts*
Martha King, *New York, New York*
Franklin W. Knight, *Johns Hopkins University*
Peter Kolchin, *University of Delaware*
Corinne Kratz, *Emory University*
Modupe Labode, *Iowa State University*
Peter Lau, *New Brunswick, New Jersey*
Claudia Leal, *Former Assistant Director, Socioeconomic Area of the Biopacific Project, Bogota, Colombia*
René Lemarchand, *University of Florida*
W. T. Lhamon, Jr., *Florida State University*
Margit Liander, *Belmont, Massachusetts*
David Levering Lewis, *Rutgers University*
Marvín Lewis, *University of Missouri at Columbia*
Lorraine Anastasia Lezama, *Boston, Massachusetts*
Kevin MacDonald, *University of London*
Marcos Chor Maio, *Rio de Janeiro, Brazil*
Mahmood Mamdani, *University of Cape Town*
Lawrence Mamiya, *Vassar College*
Patrick Manning, *Northeastern University*
Peter Manuel, *John Jay College of Criminal Justice*
Dellita Martin-Ogunsola, *University of Alabama at Birmingham*
Waldo Martin, *University of California at Berkeley*
J. Lorand Matory, *Harvard University*
Felix V. Matos Rodriguez, *Northeastern University*
Marc Mazique, *Seattle, Washington*

José Mazzotti, *Harvard University*
Elizabeth McHenry, *New York University*
Jim Mendelsohn, *New York, New York*
Gabriel Mendes, *Annandale, New York*
Claudine Michel, *Wellesley College*
Georges Michel, *Military Academy of Haiti, Port-au-Prince, Haiti*
Gwendolyn Mikell, *Georgetown University*
Zebulon Miletsky, *Boston, Massachusetts*
Irene Monroe, *Harvard Divinity School*
Sally Falk Moore, *Harvard University*
Judith Morrison, *Inter-American Foundation at Arlington, Virginia*
Gerardo Mosquera, *Independent Scholar*
Luis Mott, *Federal University of Bahia, Brazil*
Salikoko S. Mufwene, *University of Chicago*
Edward Mullen, *University of Missouri at Columbia*
Kurt Mullen, *Seattle, Washington*
Stuart Munro-Hay, *Independent Scholar*
Aaron Myers, *Cambridge, Massachusetts*
Abdias do Nascimento, *Former Senator, Brazilian National Congress, Brasilia*
Ari Nave, *New York, New York*
Marcos Natalí, *University of Chicago*
Okey Ndibe, *Connecticut College*
Nick Nesbitt, *Miami University (Ohio)*
Richard Newman, *W. E. B. Du Bois Institute for Afro-American Research, Harvard University*
Liliana Obregón, *Harvard Law School*
Kathleen O'Connor, *Cambridge, Massachusetts*
Tejumola Olaniyan, *University of Virginia*
Mark O'Malley, *Cambridge, Massachusetts*
Yaa Pokua Afriyie Oppong, *London, England*
Carmen Oquendo-Villar, *Cambridge, Massachusetts*
Kenneth O'Reilly, *University of Alaska at Anchorage*
Carlos L. Orihuela, *University of Alabama at Birmingham*
Francisco Ortega, *Harvard University*
Juan Otero-Garabis, *Universidad de Puerto Rico*
Deborah Pacini Hernandez, *Brown University*
Carlos Parra, *Harvard University*
Ben Penglase, *Cambridge, Massachusetts*
Pedro Pérez-Sarduy, *London, England and Havana, Cuba*
Julio Cesar Pino, *Kent State University*
Donald Pollock, *State University of New York at Buffalo*
Angelina Pollak-Eltz, *Univesidad Catolice A. Bella*
Paulette Poujol-Oriol, *Port-au-Prince, Haiti*
Richard J. Powell, *Duke University*
Jean Muteba Rahier, *Florida International University*
João José Reis, *Federal University of Bahia, Brazil*
Carolyn Richardson Durham, *Texas Christian University*
Alonford James Robinson, Jr., *Washington, D.C.*
Lisa Clayton Robinson, *Washington, D.C.*
Sonia Labrador Rodrigués, *University of Texas at Austin*
Gordon Root, *Cambridge, Massachusetts*
Aninydo Roy, *Colby College*
Sarah Russell, *Cambridge, England*
Marveta Ryan, *Indiana University (Pennsylvania)*
Ali Osman Mohammad Salih, *University of Khartoum*
Lamine Sanneh, *Yale University*
Jalane Schmidt, *Cambridge, Massachusetts*
Charles Schmitz, *Sonoma State University*
Brooke Grundfest Schoepf, *Harvard University*
LaVerne M. Seales-Soley, *Canisius College*
James Clyde Sellman, *University of Massachussetts at Boston*
Thomas Skidmore, *Brown University*
James Smethurst, *University of North Florida*
Paulette Smith, *Tufts University*
Suzanne Smith, *George Mason University*
Barbara Solow, *Associate of the W. E. B. Du Bois Institute for Afro-American Research, Harvard University*
Doris Sommer, *Harvard University*
Thomas Stephens, *State University of New Jersey*
Jean Stubbs, *London, England and Havana, Cuba*
Patricia Sullivan, *Harvard University*
Carol Swain, *Princeton University*
Katherine Tate, *Univerity of California at Irvine*
Richard Taub, *University of Chicago*
April Taylor, *Boston, Massachusetts*
Christopher Tiné, *Cambridge, Massachusetts*
Richard Turits, *Princeton University*
Kate Tuttle, *Cambridge, Massachusetts*
Timothy Tyson, *University of Wisconsin*
Charles Van Doren, *Former Vice President/ Editorial, Encyclopædia Britannica Inc.*
Alexandra Vega-Merino, *Harvard University*
Joëlle Vitiello, *Macalester College*
Peter Wade, *University of Manchester*
James W. St. G. Walker, *University of Waterloo*
Phillipe Wamba, *Cambridge, Massachusetts*
William E. Ward, *Harvard University*
Salim Washington, *Boston, Massachusetts*
Christopher Alan Waterman, *University of California at Los Angeles*
Richard Watts, *Tulane University*
Harold Weaver, *Independent Scholar*
Norman Weinstein, *State University of New York at New Paltz*
Amelia Weir, *New York, New York*
Tim Weiskel, *Harvard University*
Alan West, *Northern Illinois University*
Cornel West, *Harvard University*
Norman Whitten, *University of Illinois at Urbana*
Andre Willis, *Cambridge, Massachusetts*
Deborah Willis, *Center for African American History and Culture, Smithsonian Institution*
William Julius Wilson, *Harvard University*
Barbara Worley, *Cambridge, Massachusetts*
Eric Young, *Washington, D.C.*
Gary Zuk, *Auburn University*

Charts, Maps, and Tables

Charts

Maps: Geopolitical

Maps: Thematic

Tables

Articles

b

d

i

j

k

l

m

n

O

P

q

r

t

U

V

W

x

y

z

AFRICANA

The Encyclopedia of the African and African American Experience

a

Africa

Aardvark

Aardvark (Afrikaans for "earth pig"), common name for a burrowing, ant-eating mammal. The aardvark is found throughout much of Africa, from the southern part of EGYPT to the Cape of Good Hope. A primarily nocturnal animal, it lives in burrows and feeds on ants and termites, occasionally eating other insects, the fat mouse, and a species of wild ground cucumber.

The aardvark is up to 2.3 m (7.5 ft) long, including the fleshy, tapering tail, which it uses to throw earth backward when it burrows. It has an arched back, a tubular snout, and large, upright ears. The aardvark uses its specialized, chisel-shaped claws to break open the hard clay of termite nests; then it uses its sticky tongue to capture the insects in the nest. Unlike the animals known as anteaters, which are toothless, the aardvark has 20 cylindrical, rootless teeth that grow continually throughout its lifetime.

The female gives birth to one or occasionally two offspring, which can dig their own burrows at the age of six months. Although timid, the aardvark will fight when it cannot flee or burrow to safety; it defends itself with its powerful claws or by striking with its tail or shoulders.

Scientific classification: the aardvark makes up the order Tubulidentata. It is classified as *Orycteropus afer.*

North America

Aaron, Henry Louis (Hank)

Aaron, Henry Louis (Hank) (b. February 5, 1934, Mobile, Ala.), African American baseball player, broke Babe Ruth's record for career home runs in 1974.

The third of eight children, Henry Aaron was raised in Mobile, Alabama, by Estella and Herbert Aaron. His first experience with professional baseball came in the NEGRO LEAGUES, as he moved up through the ranks with the Pritchett Athletics, the Mobile Black Bears, and the Indianapolis Clowns. In 1952 Aaron received his first opportunity to play in the newly integrated major leagues as a shortstop with the Milwaukee Braves' farm team. Moving from Eau Claire, Wisconsin, to Jacksonville, Florida, Aaron made it to the major leagues in 1954, playing for the Milwaukee Braves (now the Atlanta Braves).

Aaron is considered by some the best baseball player in history. Over his 23-year Major League baseball career, Aaron compiled more batting records than any other player in baseball history. He holds the record for runs batted in with 2297, and was a Gold Glove Winner in 1958, 1959, and 1960. Aaron's most acclaimed accomplishment came on April 8, 1974. At the age of 40, he hit a 385-foot home run against the Los Angeles Dodgers, thus surpassing Babe Ruth's record of 714 career home runs. He ended his career with 755 home runs.

After retiring, Aaron returned to the Atlanta Braves as a vice president for player development. In 1989 he was promoted to senior vice president. Aaron currently serves as corporate vice president of community relations for Turner Broadcasting Systems, Inc. (TBS) and is a member of the Sterling Committee of Morehouse College. He is also the founder of the Hank Aaron Rookie League program. He was inducted into the Baseball Hall of Fame in 1982.

Alonford James Robinson, Jr.

SEE ALSO

Baseball in the United States.

Africa

Abacha, Sani

Abacha, Sani (b. September 20, 1943, Kano, Nigeria; d. June 8, 1998, Abuja, Nigeria), military dictator of NIGERIA.

Sani Abacha attended primary and secondary school in his home state of Kano and then joined the army in 1962. As a soldier he attended the Nigerian Military Training College in Kaduna (1962-1963), and then went to England for further military schooling.

Abacha achieved steady promotions as a soldier and by the mid-1980s had entered Nigeria's military elite. In 1983 he was among those who overthrew Shehu Shagari, leader of the Second Republic, in a coup that led to the military rule of Muhammadu Buhari. In 1985 Abacha participated in a second coup, which replaced Buhari with General Ibrahim Babangida. As head of state, Babangida announced that free elections would be held in the early 1990s. In 1993, however, after Babangida nullified the results of these belated free elections, Abacha staged a third coup and ousted his former ally.

Once in power, Abacha dissolved all of Nigeria's democratic institutions, from local governments to the national assembly and the constitution. He replaced state governors with military officers and banned the country's two political parties. Abacha also began imprisoning and executing most of his opposition. Among the long list of people imprisoned under Abacha were OLUSEGUN OBASANJO, a former Nigerian head of state; Moshood K. O. Abiola, the presumed winner of the 1993 elections; numerous human rights lobbyists; and several journalists. Obasanjo's vice president, Shehu Musa Yar'Adua, died in prison in 1997, and environmental activist and writer Ken Saro-Wiwa was jailed, then executed in 1995. Abiola died in prison in July 1998, shortly after Abacha's death.

Abacha even imprisoned his own second-in-command, Oladipo Diya, in December 1997. His regime was characterized by a concern with security that verged on paranoia. In addition to maintaining a large personal guard, Abacha employed plainclothes policemen to flush out dissenters. Although his image was plastered everywhere, Abacha himself rarely appeared in public.

Abacha scheduled elections for August 1998, but months beforehand all five legal parties nominated him as their "consensus candidate." As the election approached, Abacha used the military and police to break up pro-democracy demonstrations. In June 1998 Abacha died unexpectedly of a heart attack.

Eric Bennett

See Also
Babangida, Ibrahim Gbadamosi; Kano, Nigeria; Saro-Wiwa, Kenule Beeson; Abiola, Moshood Kashimawo Olawale.

Latin America and the Caribbean

Abakuás, all-male secret societies created by African slaves living in Cuba during the mid-nineteenth century.

In the first half of the nineteenth century, thousands of African slaves were involuntarily brought from the Calabar region of southwestern Nigeria to Cuba in order to labor on the sugar plantations. In Cuba, these enslaved people reconstructed aspects of their language (Ibo) and religious rituals in *Abakuás*, all-male organizations with closely guarded religious, musical, and dance traditions. The prototype for Cuba's Abakuás can be found in Calabar's leopard societies, groups of highly respected, accomplished men who adopted the leopard as a symbol of masculinity. Today as in the past, Abakuás are found predominantly in the city of Havana and the province of Matanzas and are united by a common African mythology and ritual system.

Abakuás preserve African traditions through performative ceremonies, a complex system of signs, and narratives in the Ibo language. Customarily led by four leaders and eight subordinate officers, members of the Abakuás seek to protect themselves from misfortune and harm through a spiritual alliance. Abakuás also constitute a financial support system in which members, who are required to pay monthly dues, can borrow money in times of need.

The Abakuá ceremonies of worship combine music, song, dance, and costume. The traditional instrumentation features a lead conga-like drum and several smaller drums held under the arm. Two bells attached by a curved metal rivet and a type of friction drum may also be included. Members clap their hands and sing in a chorus-response format. Some Abakuá members don a checked outfit, fringed with hay-like raffia and topped with a conical hood, and dance in veneration of ancestral spirits known as *iremés* or *ñáñigos*. These ceremonies reenact aspects of the mythology surrounding the group's origins in Africa and often involve spirit possession and animal sacrifice. Although most of the ceremonies take place in a clandestine, sacred setting known as a *fambá*, others, such as funerals, take the form of a public procession.

Abakuás' exclusion of women is explained by the myths that provide the basis for their rituals. The two individuals central to Abakuá mythology are Tanze, the ancient king of Ejagham (part of the Calabar region in southwest Nigeria) and the founding father of leopard societies; and Sikán, a powerful princess of Efut, a region to the south of Ejagham. Members of Abakuás believe that when Tanze died his soul became a fish that was later captured by Sikán. By coming into possession of Tanze's soul, Sikán came into possession of the secrets of his leopard society, some of which she revealed to the world. This episode, which ends in the death of Sikán, accounts for the general mistrust of women among members of Abakuás.

The story of Tanze and Sikán also informs the Abakuás' symbolic language, known as *anaforuana*. The central symbol of the Abakuás is a geometric form divided into quartered areas, each of which contains a small circle. The small circles are interpreted individually as the eyes of Tanze and Sikán, and the whole form is interpreted as the fusion of their powers, since by capturing his soul Sikán essentially became the bride of Tanze. It is a symbol of spiritual communication and enlightenment. The theme of four eyes is a reoccurring motif among some 500 sacred symbols used by members of Abakuás to communicate with one another and with the divine.

Since their inception in the early to mid-eighteenth century, Abakuás have frequently been misunderstood and repressed by the dominant segment of Cuban society. While some refer to Abakuá members as ñáñigos, after the spirits they worship, others have labeled them *diablitos*, or little devils. Their reputation among light-skinned Cubans as bloodthirsty and cannibalistic is implied in sayings such as "Pórtense bien porque si no se los lleva el ñáñigo" (Behave yourself or else the ñáñigo will get you).

Although Abakuás initially only admitted blacks, over time some mulatto and white Cubans have gained entrance into the secret societies, giving way to religious syncretism. Some parallels in the practices of Abakuás and Catholics include a set of commandments (Abakuás tend to have seven rather than ten) and an altar complete with candles, holy water, and incense. Abakuás, however, continue to be predominantly black and centered on maintaining spiritual connections with an African past.

Aaron Myers

See Also
Matanzas, Cuba; Catholic Church in Latin America and the Caribbean.

Europe

Abbott, Diane (b. September 27, 1953, London, Great Britain), the first black woman to be elected a member of Parliament (MP) in Great Britain.

Diane Abbott, a working-class Cambridge University graduate, made history on June 11, 1987, by becoming the first black female member of the British Parliament. Her outspoken criticism of racism and her commitment to progressive politics have made her a controversial figure in Great Britain's Labour Party.

Diane Abbott was born in 1953 in the working-class London neighborhood of Paddington. Her mother (a nurse) and father (a welder) had moved there in 1951 from Jamaica. Later they moved to lower-middle-class Harrow, where Abbott was the only black student at the Harrow County School for Girls. Graduating among the top in her class, she applied and was accepted into Newnham College at Cambridge University, despite a high school teacher's comment that attendance there would give her ambitions that were above her social status.

She began work after graduation at the home office, a government department responsible for a broad range of domestic policies. Eighteen months later she left to become the first black staff member at the National Council for Civil Liberties. She left claiming she disliked the "hypocrisy of making a living out of race." Abbott then tried her hand at television reporting. Later, she became a public relations officer for the Greater London Council, the city's metropolitan government.

Abbott joined the Labour Party at age 18 and has been active in politics ever since. Her political career began in 1982. She won a Westminster city council seat, and learned to maneuver in what has been described as the "bare-knuckled, gibe-and-jeer politics of England's elected neighborhood councils." This experience prepared her for parliamentary battles.

After a failed election bid in 1985, Abbott won a Parliament seat in the district of Hackney North. In winning, Abbott joined the 4 percent of members of Parliament (MPs) who are women. In the 1987 election just two other blacks, Bernie Grant and Paul Boateng, won seats.

In her first speech to Parliament, Abbott denounced the racism of Great Britain's immigration policies. In 1988, to the dismay of the Labour leadership who sought unity within the party, Abbott attempted to create a black caucus similar to that in the United States Congress. However, Abbott was the only black MP to show up at the caucus's first meeting. Despite this and other setbacks, she continues to voice often contentious views.

In Parliament she has not only had to defend her views on racism in Great Britain; she has needed to justify her status as a single mother with a career. Many conservatives blame single mothers for the breakdown of family and the subsequent rise in poverty and crime. Abbott married Ghanaian David Thompson in 1991 and had a child, James, but divorced soon after. She believes that her experience as a single mother has helped to prepare her for parliamentary battles. She stated, "First I can manage with very little sleep. Second, I am very flexible. . . .

And third... I can put up with a lot of childish babble."

During the 1990s, the centrist policies of Prime Minister Tony Blair's New Labour alienated left-wing MPs such as Abbott. Before the 1997 election, Blair reprimanded Abbott for her public criticism of Labour Party campaign contribution and election practices. After winning the election, the Labour government dismissed Abbott from Parliament's Treasury Committee because she disagreed with Blair's fiscally conservative policies. Reassigned to the Foreign Affairs Committee, Abbott has criticized the lack of democracy in Hong Kong since it was handed over to China in 1997, and has opposed British military action in Iraq in 1998. Abbott remains a blunt critic of policies she considers unethical or racist, and continues to advocate social policies to help poor immigrant and minority populations.

Leyla Keough

See Also
Great Britain; Congressional Black Caucus.

North America

Abbott, Robert Sengstacke

(b. November 28, 1868, Frederica, Ga.; d. February 22, 1940, Chicago, Ill.), African American founder, editor, and publisher of the *Chicago Defender*.

Robert S. Abbott was the son of Thomas and Flora (Butler) Abbott, both former slaves. From 1892 to 1896 he attended Hampton Institute, where he learned the printing trade. Abbott moved to Chicago to attend Kent College of Law, graduating in 1898. He practiced law for a few years but changed careers to become a journalist.

Abbott founded the *Chicago Defender*, a weekly newspaper, on May 6, 1905. He started the paper with $25, and at first operated it out of his kitchen. Under his direction, the *Defender* became the most widely circulated African American newspaper of its time and a leading voice in the fight against racism. Abbott cultivated a controversial, aggressive style, reporting on such issues as violence against blacks and police brutality. The *Defender* raised eyebrows with its antilynching slogan, "If you must die, take at least one with you"; its opposition to a segregated Colored Officers Training Camp in Fort Des Moines, Iowa, in 1917; and its condemnation of Marcus Garvey's Universal Negro Improvement Association (UNIA). Through the *Defender*, Abbott also played a major role in the Great Migration of many African Americans from the South to Chicago.

In addition to his journalistic leadership, Abbot also actively participated in several civic and art organizations in Chicago. He served as a member of the Chicago Commission on Race Relations, which published the study *The Negro in Chicago* (1922). Abbott developed tuberculosis in 1932 and died in Chicago of Bright's disease. The *Defender* continued under the control of Abbott's nephew, John H. Sengstacke, who began publishing it as a daily in 1956.

Robert Fay

See Also
Antilynching Movement; *Chicago Defender*; Garvey, Marcus Mosiah; Great Migration, The; Universal Negro Improvement Association.

Abd al-Kadir. Please see Abd al-Qadir

Abdallah ibn Yacin. Please see 'Abd Allah ibn Yasin

Africa

'Abd Allah ibn Yasin

[also known as Abdullah b. Yasin al-Gazuli and Abdallah ibn Rasin] (b.?, Morocco; d. 1059?), an Islamic scholar and one of the founders of the Almoravid movement.

The Almoravid movement of 'Abd Allah ibn Yasin conquered parts of northwestern Africa and later Spain during the eleventh and twelfth centuries, and converted the defeated populations to Malekite (Maliki) Sunni Islam. Little is known of 'Abd Allah ibn Yasin's life prior to 1035 B.C.E., when as a student he was visited by a Sanhadja Berber chieftain and invited to return home with him to teach his people the true faith of Islam.

A devout Muslim, 'Abd Allah ibn Yasin was scandalized by the Sanhadja Berbers' lax and immoral practices. He had them convert to Malekite Sunni Islam, imposing a strict interpretation of Koranic law. Eventually he even restructured the Berbers' troops to conduct *jihads* (holy wars) in accordance with the Koran. By 1041, however, the Berber chieftains resented the religious scholar's rule, and sent him away. 'Abd Allah ibn Yasin and a group of followers spent a year at a coastal *ribat* (religious retreat), then returned and launched a series of attacks on Berber communities, marking the beginning of the Almoravid movement.

Under 'Abd Allah ibn Yasin, the Almoravid movement conquered the Gadala, Lemtuna, and Messufa Berber clans in the southern part of present-day Morocco, and brought Islam to the ancient kingdom of Ghana. It also took over several important Saharan market towns, such as Aoudaghost and Sijilmasa. In 1059 'Abd Allah ibn Yasin was killed in battle against Gadala Berbers. He was succeeded by Abu Bakr ibn Omar and his cousin Yousuf ibn Tasfin, who led the movement throughout Morocco and into northern Spain.

Elizabeth Heath

See Also
Ghana, Early Kingdom of; Sahara Desert; Almoravids; Islamic Fundamentalism: An Interpretation.

Africa

Abd al-Qadir

(b. May 26, 1807; d. 1883), Algerian religious and military leader credited with unifying Algerian territory into a state through his campaign against French colonization.

Considered a hero of anticolonial resistance by many contemporary Algerians, Abd al-Qadir created an Arab-Berber alliance to oppose French expansion in the 1830s and 1840s. He also organized an Islamic state that, at one point, controlled the western two-thirds of Algeria's inhabited land.

Abd al-Qadir's ability to unite Arabs and Berbers owed in part to the legacy of his father, the head of the Hashim tribe in Mascara and leader of the *Qadirayya* regional political body, which opposed the Turkish sultanate. In 1826 Abd al-Qadir and his father made a pilgrimage, or *hajj*, to Mecca in Saudi Arabia, the birthplace of the prophet Muhammad, founder of Islam. Upon his return in 1828, Abd al-Qadir's own reputation as an Islamic religious and cultural leader grew, and Arabs and Berbers alike looked to him to lead the resistance against the French after their 1830 invasion of Algiers.

As the French expanded westward, in 1832 Abd al-Qadir led attacks on French-occupied Oran, taking the city within six months. He signed a treaty with France in 1834 that permitted French occupation of western coastal cities, but resumed fighting after a new French military leader attempted to organize tribal resistance against him. Through military and diplomatic triumphs over both the French and rival local groups, Abd al-Qadir expanded and consolidated his rule over the territory in the surrounding Oran. As emir, he governed a hierarchical, theocratic state integrating tribal traditions and promoted commerce and education. In 1837 France signed the Treaty of Tafna with Abd al-Qadir, acknowledging his sovereign authority over an area encompassing two-thirds of Algeria.

The French abandoned the policy of "limited occupation" when General Thomas-Robert Bugeaud came to power. Using "scorched earth" tactics, the French systematically destroyed the Algerian means of livelihood, including villages, crops, livestock, and forests, and reportedly trapped surrendering Muslims in caves and burned them. In 1843 the emir was forced into exile in Morocco, but when former allies there turned on him, he returned to Algeria to lead resistance efforts. His last retreat to Morocco in July 1846 ended in complete loss of Moroccan support, and in 1847 he returned to Algeria and surrendered to French authorities. The French broke promises of safe conduct and imprisoned him for four years in France, until Emperor Napoleon III released him to permanent exile.

In 1852 Abd al-Qadir went to Damascus, in present-day Syria, where he wrote about politics and studied science. During the anti-Christian riots of 1860 in Damascus and Lebanon, he gathered several hundred followers to rescue more than 12,000 Christians from their attackers. Napoleon III awarded him the Grand Cross of the Legion of Honor.

In Algeria, Abd al-Qadir's legacy remained an inspiration through the War of Independence (1954-1962). In 1968 the newly independent nation erected a monument to Abd al-Qadir in the place where a French monument to General Bugeaud had stood, and took up his green and white standard as its flag.

Marian Aguiar

See Also
Algeria; Algiers, Algeria; Berber.

North America

Abdul-Jabbar, Kareem

(b. April 16, 1947, Harlem, N.Y.), African American Basketball player, widely considered to be one of the greatest National Basketball Association (NBA) players in history.

Kareem Abdul-Jabbar, the highest scorer in NBA history, was born Ferdinand Lewis Alcindor Jr. in Harlem, New York. Raised in a middle-class household and educated at Catholic schools in Manhattan, he was introduced to basketball at age nine and played competitively throughout elementary and high school. He was 6 ft, 8 in (2.05 m) tall by the time he was 14 and became a star center for Power Memorial Academy, leading the high school to two city championships. He continued his dominant play at the University of California Los Angeles (UCLA), where the team won three National Collegiate Athletic Association championships and lost only two games during his college career. An outspoken political activist who was influenced by the Black Power movement, he changed his name from Alcindor to Kareem Abdul-Jabbar in 1971 after converting to Islam. A popular NBA star from 1969 to 1989, he thwarted opponents with his "skyhook" shot and became professional basketball's most imposing offensive threat. In his 20-year professional career, Abdul-Jabbar played on 18 All Star teams and claimed six championships, six most valuable player awards, and numerous other NBA records.

In 1996 Abdul-Jabbar authored *Black Profiles in Courage: A Legacy of African-American Achievement.*

Robert Fay

See Also
Harlem, New York.

Africa

Abé (also known as the Abbe or Abbey), ethnic group of Côte d'Ivoire.

The Abé, numbering around 180,000, live in the Agboville region of Côte d'Ivoire. They speak a Niger-Congo language. Linguistically and culturally, they belong to the Akan group.

See Also
Côte d'Ivoire; Languages, African: An Overview.

Africa

Abeokuta, Nigeria, the capital of Ogun State, in southwestern Nigeria.

The Egba leader Sodeke founded Abeokuta around 1830 as a settlement for a group of refugees from the collapse of the Oyo Kingdom. *Abeokuta* translates as "under the rocks," or "refuge among rocks," and refers to the city's location on the craggy east bank of the Ogun River. The early city comprised four Egba subgroups, the Ake, Gbagura, Oke-Ona, and Owu, each in a separate ward. (The Egba are themselves a subgroup of the Yoruba.) In the 1840s missionaries and freed Egba slaves introduced Christianity and secular European influences to Abeokuta. The subsequent arrival of Sierra Leone Creoles further diversified the town.

In the mid-nineteenth century, the people of Abeokuta warred with the neighboring kingdom of Dahomey (in present-day Benin) and then with Ibadan. Abeokuta maintained an alliance with Great Britain during this war and the later Yoruba civil wars (1877-1893). Consequently, when Great Britain asserted its control over the region in 1893, it granted Abeokuta and the surrounding Egba region a degree of autonomy. Abeokutans protested their city's incorporation into British Nigeria in 1914.

Today Abeokuta serves as a market town for the surrounding agricultural region, which produces staple crops, fresh produce, cotton, and palm products. It lies on the main rail line from Lagos to Ibadan and the interior, and highways link it to surrounding cities, including Ketou in Benin. Abeokutans are known for their traditional *adire*, cotton cloth dyed with locally grown indigo. Small-scale local industries include fruit canning, brewing, saw milling, and the manufacture of plastic and aluminum products. In 1984 the University of Lagos established an Abeokuta campus, which focuses on science, technology, and agriculture. The city's population is approximately 400,000.

Eric Bennett

See Also
Dahomey, Early Kingdom of; Ibadan, Nigeria; Lagos, Nigeria; Oyo, Early Kingdom of.

North America

Abernathy, Ralph David

(b. March 11, 1926, Linden, Ala.; d. April 17, 1990, Atlanta, Ga.), American minister and civil rights leader who organized nonviolent resistance to segregation and succeeded Martin Luther King Jr. as president of the Southern Christian Leadership Conference (SCLC).

Ralph Abernathy was born on March 11, 1926, in Linden, Alabama, to William and Louivery Abernathy. He earned a B.S. from Alabama State College and was ordained a Baptist minister in 1948. In 1951 he received an M.A. in sociology and became pastor of the First Baptist Church in Montgomery, Alabama. He and Martin Luther King Jr. led the successful boycott of the Montgomery bus system in 1955, protesting segregated public transportation.

In 1957 Abernathy helped King found the Southern Christian Leadership Council (SCLC) to coordinate nonviolent resistance to segregation. After King's assassination in 1968, Abernathy served as SCLC president until he resigned in 1977.

Robert Fay

See Also
King, Martin Luther, Jr.; Montgomery Bus Boycott; Southern Christian Leadership Conference.

Africa

Abidjan, Côte d'Ivoire,

the former capital and largest city of the Côte d'Ivoire.

The administrative, cultural, and economic center of the Côte d'Ivoire, Abidjan surrounds the Ebrié Lagoon on the Atlantic Ocean's Gulf of Guinea. It is believed that people founded settlements on the site in the early sixteenth century. Later in that century three Ebrié fishing villages existed in the area – Locodjo, Anoumabo, and Cocody. The area was briefly explored by Portuguese traders in the seventeenth century, after which it was largely ignored by Europeans until French colonization. In 1903 the French chose the area as the endpoint for a railway connecting Upper Volta (now Burkina Faso) to the coast, and a small town soon developed around the train station; but without a viable port, it grew slowly at first.

In 1934, shortly after the completion of the rail link to the Upper Volta city of Bobo-Dioulasso, the French moved the colonial capital from nearby Bingerville to Abidjan and began building a series of bridges between the mainland and the lagoon islands. The completion of the Vridi Canal in 1950, followed by the construction of a port on the barrier island of Petit Bassam, made Abidjan the colony's center of industry and shipping. The opening of the port also dramatically increased the city's wealth and population, and Abidjan has since become the most populous city in the Côte d'Ivoire. Today, it has an estimated population of more than 2 million, a fact that helped prompt the government of Félix Houphouët-Boigny to move the capital to Houphouët-Boigny's hometown, Yamoussoukro, in 1983.

A series of islands centered on a Manhattan-like business center called the Plateau, Abidjan is considered one of the most cosmopolitan (and expensive) African cities, sometimes referred to as "the Petit Paris of Africa." Its glass-walled skyscrapers house the headquarters of numerous international firms and agencies, and shopping centers and French restaurants cater to a sizable population of European expatriates. Most of the city's African residents – many of whom are migrants from Burkina Faso, Mali, and other West African countries – live in neighborhoods such as Treichville and Adjamé, both centered on huge outdoor markets.

Abidjan is home to the country's largest port as well as to factories that process the country's main exports – cocoa, coffee, and palm oil. Although these industries have contributed to the city's prosperity, its population is still sharply divided economically, and many of the neighborhoods beyond the Plateau are extremely poor, crowded, and inadequately serviced. In recent years the government has attempted to counteract urban poverty by training the unemployed as farmers and then giving them land in the country's interior. Although some of these "back to the land" programs have had a measure of success, overpopulation and underemployment remain significant problems in Abidjan.

Elizabeth Heath

See Also

Bobo-Dioulasso, Burkina Faso; Colonial Rule; New York, New York; Yamoussoukro, Côte d'Ivoire.

Africa

Abiola, Moshood Kashimawo Olawale (b. August 24, 1937, Abeokuta, Nigeria; d. July 7, 1998, Abuja, Nigeria), Nigerian businessman, presidential candidate, and political prisoner.

On June 12, 1993, the popular businessman Moshood Kashimawo Olawale Abiola won a long-awaited presidential election in Nigeria, only to have the country's military leader, Gen. Ibrahim Babangida, annul the election results. When Abiola declared himself the country's legitimate leader a year later, Babangida's successor, Gen. Sani Abacha, jailed him for treason. As a political prisoner, Abiola became the rallying symbol for Nigerians' democratic aspirations.

Abiola was born into a poor, polygamous household of Yoruba-speaking Muslims. None of his parents' first 22 children had survived past infancy, so Abiola, the 23rd, was given the middle name Kashimawo, meaning "Let's see if he will survive." Growing up in the ancient Yoruba town of Abeokuta, he first attended the Islamic Nawar Ud-Deen School, then transferred to the Christian-run African Central School. As an indigent student at the Baptist Boys' High School, Abiola sold firewood to pay for his books. He was so poor that he did not eat his first egg until he was 19 years old. He organized a traveling orchestra that performed at public events, often for food. A slight stammerer, Abiola had questionable musical talent but tremendous determination.

After leaving high school, Abiola worked briefly as a bank clerk and a civil servant, then won a scholarship to Glasgow University to study accounting. A bright student, he graduated with several awards in 1965. Returning to Nigeria, he worked as an accountant for the Lagos University Teaching Hospital. He then became divisional controller for the pharmaceutical company Pfizer Products. In 1968 he joined International Telephone and Telegraph (ITT), a corporation that was owed a considerable debt by the Nigerian army. After securing the recovery of the debt, Abiola was named the company's chairman in Nigeria and its vice president for Africa and the Middle East.

In 1974 Abiola launched his own company, Radio Communications of Nigeria. Abiola started accumulating wealth rapidly. At his death, Abiola's business interests spanned 60 countries and included firms engaged in banking, shipping, oil prospecting, agriculture, publishing, air transportation, and entertainment. His Nigerian companies alone employed close to 20,000 workers.

Abiola's philanthropy was famous throughout Nigeria. He supported education, sports, and numerous social and political causes. He called for reparations from the West to compensate African peoples for the transatlantic slave trade. He married at least five wives and fathered, by some accounts, more than 50 children.

Abiola's public life was full of paradoxes. As a businessman, he received large contracts from his military friends, yet he became an outspoken opponent of the military dictatorship. Abiola's political career was cut short by two such friends: Babangida, who annulled Abiola's presidential victory, and Abacha, who threw him in jail.

Abiola was the first presidential candidate from the southern part of the country who won a majority of votes even in the predominantly Hausa north. Hopes for his release from prison soared after Sani Abacha died suddenly in June 1998 and his successor, Gen. Abdulsalam Abubakar, announced the release of many other political prisoners. However, Abiola, who had suffered from heart problems for several years, fell ill on July 7, 1998, while meeting with United States diplomats to discuss the terms of his release. He died several hours later, apparently of a heart attack. Abiola's death in detention sparked anger and violence in parts of Nigeria.

Okey Ndibe

See Also

Abeokuta, Nigeria; Babangida, Ibrahim Gbadamosi; Education in Africa; Lagos, Nigeria; Abacha, Sani; Islam and Tradition: An Interpretation.

Latin America and the Caribbean

Abolition and Emancipation in Latin America and the Caribbean

In light of the complex process of deferral, legal disregard, and noncompliance with international treaties that characterized the abolition movement, slaves' own pursuit of emancipation became decisive. In other words, slave resistance, in the context of the abolitionist phenomenon, developed into the principal means by which the abolition of slavery would be hastened, bit by bit, from the bottom up. The cases of Brazil, Cuba, Haiti, and Jamaica are perhaps the most representative. Violent protests and revolts, collective escapes, individual reactions, presumed submission, destruction of property, cane fields set alight: all figure among the actions slaves took to gain their freedom.

In this sense, enslaved men and women cannot be said to have been simple spectators or passive subjects who would leave the determination of their freedom in the hands of the slaveholding elite. To imagine, for instance, that the news, laws, incidents, and arguments common to an evolving abolitionist sentiment did not reach slaves' ears is not to acknowledge reality. Sooner or later, whether through public channels or through the passing whispers of group conversation, slaves would get news of the tortuous juridical/political, military, and economic course of abolition. Among the slave huts, on the plantation, in the house in the city, on the country estate, in the mines – in all these places bands of workers traded views on the Haitian Revolution, the debates in the Assembly of Cádiz or in the British Parliament. Thus stirred by the rumors of abolitionism, there were few slaves who did not sense in these events that liberty lay close by, a

30°
Mexico
1829
Bahama
Islands
Haiti
1803
Puerto Rico
1878
North
Atlantic
Ocean
Cuba
1886
Jamaica
Guyana
(British)
1834
Central
American
Federation
1824
Venezuela
1854
Surinam
(Dutch)
1863
Colombia
and
Panama
1850
French Guiana
1794 - 1802 and 1848
(See Note on French Caribbean)
Galapagos
Islands
Equator
Ecuador
1852
Peru
1855
Brazil
1888
Bolivia
1861
Pacific Ocean
Paraguay
1870
30°
Chile
1823
Argentine
Republic
1853
Uruguay
1846
Dates of Abolition of Slavery
in Latin America and the Caribbean
1834 - Slavery Abolished in British Caribbean Holdings
1863 - Slavery Abolished in Dutch Caribbean Holdings
1794 - Slavery Abolished in French Caribbean Holdings
but reinstated by Napolean in 1802, except in Haiti,
which achieved independence in 1803; abolished
definitively in remaining French colonies in 1848
0
800 km
0
800 mi
South
Atlantic
Ocean
Falkland
Islands
South
Georgia
90°
60°

fact that not only exposed slavery as an anachronistic institution but that also aggravated the tense relationship between masters and slaves.

The slave uprising on the island of Santo Domingo in 1791 is considered one of the most representative incidents in a chain of events leading to abolition and emancipation. Events such as the defeat dealt to the Spanish and English by Dominican blacks, and the triumph of the black and mulatto rebellion against the French that brought about the first black republic in Haiti, decided the course of a history that would soon lead to the abolition of slavery. Yet these events have not always been recognized or legitimized as manifestations of how slaves could gain liberty acting by and for themselves, outside the operations of metropolitan ideology or the political ideas of whites and CREOLES.

From the Haitian Revolution onward, though in earlier periods as well, slave resistance revealed itself to be the bluntest demonstration of the system of slavery's delegitimization. Massive waves of black and mulatto resistance in Haiti provoked the French National Convention, an outgrowth of the French Revolution, to declare the abolition of slavery throughout the French colonies in 1794. Black leader Toussaint L'Ouverture's political and military effectiveness played an essential role in this decision. In his negotiations with the British and the French, L'Ouverture reminded them that he knew how to fight just as well as the maroons in the forests of Jamaica, thereby bringing to light the networks of information that escaped slaves had maintained in certain areas of the Caribbean islands since the end of the seventeenth century.

When Napoleon rose to power in France he not only restored slavery in 1802 but was also able to bring the forces of Spain and Great Britain together in an attempt to quell the rebellion in Haiti. On the island of GUADELOUPE, a French colony, blacks and mulattos rose up against slavery's reinstatement but were defeated by an invasion of French troops. Meanwhile, in Haiti, L'Ouverture's mistakes and indecision when faced with the extraordinary French invasion force – some 20,000 troops in the first phase alone – prompted a change in the leadership of the Negro uprising, with Dessalines, a black military officer, taking command. A regrouping of rebel forces, the knowledge of the restoration of slavery in MARTINIQUE and Guadeloupe, and the participation of the mulatto general Pétion, were determining factors in the defeat of an invading army of more than 60,000 men and the subsequent declaration of Haitian independence on December 31, 1803. Some 12 years later, Bolívar, seeking political and logistical support, turned to Pétion, promising the abolition of slavery in return.

English abolitionists were alarmed by the slave revolution in Santo Domingo and Haiti and mindful of the abolition of slavery in French colonies by the National Convention of 1794, when they ruled out any action, whether in recognition or favor of the slave revolt, which might have served as a means to apply the definitive pressure needed to achieve the abolition of slavery. They preferred to maintain a passive and distant attitude toward the slaves, believing instead that the abolitionist process should adapt itself to the exclusive procedures of empire.

The slaves in the British West Indies did not, of course, share the same view. There, the tendency to react, to flee, to rebel, began to rise from the outset of the nineteenth century, especially among Creoles, born on colonial soil. Jamaica's case is perhaps the most famous. More and more slaves began to reject the harsh and inhuman work conditions on plantations and fled as often as they could, establishing *palenques*, or communities of escaped slaves, in the inhospitable forests and rural surroundings. The spirit of defiance came to a head in 1831, when the Jamaican maroons revolted en masse. Although the rebellion was put down four months later, it precipitated the British Parliament's drafting a law for the abolition of slavery in colonies throughout the British Empire.

Underlying the movements for emancipation and abolition was the matter of the social conditions and treatment of slaves. "The whip," said a powerful Jamaican slaveholder in 1834, "is the great symbol of slavery in the West Indies," adding that slaves would consider its abolition "the abolition of slavery itself." This statement indicates to what degree the repressive, inhuman treatment of slaves, and the more general social conditions of the slaves' existence, were central to the pursuit of the abolition of slavery. For the most part, slaveholders in the colonies resisted abiding by the standards issued by the metropolis, which were designed to better slaves' day-to-day existence. The Black Codes, or laws governing slavery, meant to be applied in Spanish colonies in 1789 as a mechanism for improving the slaves' conditions, brought such opposition from slaveholders, who saw their interests, property rights, and relations with slaves jeopardized, that application of the Black Code came to be viewed as dangerous. The measure never took effect.

A direct relationship existed between increased production in the colonies and the decline in slaves' social conditions. In Cuba, during the first half of the nineteenth century, economic exploitation of the slave population (*see* SLAVERY IN LATIN AMERICA AND THE CARIBBEAN) increased, largely because of a notable increase in sugar production. This led to more frequent slave rebellions in the provinces of Havana (1809), Matanzas (1825), and Güira (1826). In addition, there were major uprisings in many sugar refineries between 1842 and 1843. All these movements were brutally suppressed. Fear of reprisals drove many of the Matanzas slaves to suicide between 1843 and 1844. Nevertheless, such rebellion demonstrated not only the slaves' resolve but also the participation and collaboration of sectors of the free population, especially blacks, mulattos, *mestizos,* and some whites.

Colonial slaveholders' opposition to measures that sought a partial improvement of the conditions in slave communities corresponded to a fear of emancipatory reactions among slaves, who for their part interpreted these attitudes as owners' betrayal of regulations issued by the metropolitan powers. This standoff intensified the crisis that would ultimately delegitimize slavery as an institution and social practice. For similar reasons, slave owners historically violated the regulations referring to the slaves' evangelization. Undoubtedly, the crisis of slavery was accompanied by theological processes and juridical conversations that no longer guaranteed, nor convincingly justified, whites' and colonists' right to keep fellow human beings in the condition of slavery. With increasing frequency, slaves expressed their opinion in a number of ways, thereby openly defying the legality of slavery. As a New Grenadine (Colombia) slave from Mompox put it: "There are enslaved men only in the legal codes."

Slaves' resistance to, and adaptive capacity within, the slavery dynamic rendered groundless the racist nineteenth-century images of the unproductive slave and of the slave as lacking in social and economic personality. Not only did the "unproductiveness" of slaves arise from, among other things, acts of resistance such as disobedience or destruction of economic goods, but slaves had also been able to consolidate their "own" economy as cultivators of their goods and merchants of their agricultural products in regional markets. Thus, slaves began to participate actively in various economic dynamics through sheer initiative.

In slave societies throughout the Americas, the reactions of the elite to slave revolts, to slaves' emancipatory ideas, and to the proposed abolition of slavery were expressed through the mechanisms of gradual abolition. This process strove to protect slaveholders' property rights above all, while at the same time safeguarding their investments in the buying and selling of slaves. But such an attitude was, for many owners, also due to a pathetic phenomenon, central to slavery in the Americas: whites' disdainful attitudes toward work and their economic dependence on slaves. Furthermore, the gradual emancipation of slaves itself was conceived on the basis of eminently racist assumptions, whose common basis was a belief in the slaves' inability to adapt to living free in society, given their supposed social and cultural inferiority. Gradual abolition, then, produced a group of regulations concerning rights of free birth and slave owner compensation, the creation of the Juntas de Manumisión (Manumission Committees), and the mechanisms that regulated systems of *coartización*, an arrangement by which slaves could purchase their freedom through apprenticeship and *patronato*. Each was a new form of labor control, which tied slaves in the process of emancipation to centers of economic production. In reality, what this meant for those concerned was the prolonged development of a "second horizon of slavery," that is, the setting in motion of a process of reenslavement.

It was to be expected, then, that this would constitute another point of resistance for many slaves, since they watched as the liberty they so ardently pursued was postponed in order to protect their masters' interests. In fact, since the second decade of the nineteenth century in Spanish colonies, and since the third in the French and British, slaveholders made manifest that they would grant liberty to slaves only if they were compensated for doing so, and/or if it was legislated that slaves were to remain under their control as apprentices or *coartados* (slaves working to buy their freedom) during a period that could span 5 to 20 years. In the new Hispanic republics, particularly VENEZUELA, Ecuador, PERU, and COLOMBIA, regulations concerning the laws of free birth instituted both slaveholder compensation and the requirement that slaves remain in the direct service of their masters.

The slaves in the British colonies most actively rejected this system of compulsory labor; they protested measures to such a degree that by 1838, obligatory apprenticeship and patronato ceased to be enforced. A decade later, France and Holland suspended the implementation of coartización, thanks mostly to slave opposition. In 1863 the Dutch colony of SURINAME encountered a similar environment of slave opposition, rendering impossible the application of controls limiting recently liberated slaves' movement between territories. In Spain and Cuba, promulgation in 1870 of the Moret Law, which regulated the gradual abolition of slavery, could not contain an insurrection of Creoles, slaves, and freedpeople that would escalate into the TEN YEARS' WAR of 1868-1878.

Brazil offers perhaps the best example of an important, widespread social movement fiercely opposed to the procedures of the gradual abolition of slavery. Portuguese America's independence in 1822 gave birth to a period of radical confrontation between slavery and the monarchy over slave revolts tied to abolitionist movements and separatist regional forces. Between 1820 and 1850, actions by the monarchic state and the plantation owners were able to neutralize, at least temporarily, the development of armed rebellions. However, during the middle of the nineteenth century, abolitionist activity again intensified in the face of the war with PARAGUAY, which laid bare the state's weaknesses. As a result, slaves renewed their acts of disobedience, escape campaigns, and attacks against the agents of slavery (masters, overseers, and so on). In 1871, Brazilian abolitionism gained its first triumph, albeit partial, with the enactment of the Rio Branco Law, or Law of Free Birth. Slaveholders capitalized on its effects, spurred by a rally in coffee production and the consequent climb in the price of slaves.

In the 1880s, slaves in Brazil began to mount increasingly collective escape campaigns, often shielded in their flight by free men and women. At the same time, JOAQUIM NABUCO, Rui Barbosa, and others applied political pressure to end slavery tied to owner compensation. The province of Ceará resolved to abolish slavery, adding momentum to the abolitionist movement in the national arena. Under these circumstances, networks of political agitation linked to illegal action arose, sanctioning the flight of slaves and the burning of the cane fields. A few years before slavery would be entirely abolished, a substantial contingent of men and women prevented the military breakup of Jabaguara's *quilombo* (maroon community) in Santos. By the beginning of 1888, Brazilian slavery faced outright and irreversible collapse, which materialized on May 13, 1888, with the declaration of the abolition of slavery without the possibility of slaveholder compensation. This final resolution in the last country in the Americas to uphold the institution of slavery was made possible only through the combined action of slave revolts and abolitionist organizations.

While slaves held firmly to their decision to advance toward liberty, risking even their lives, white Western society and its offshoots in the American colonies demonstrated not only tremendous fear at the thought of liberating those whom they had enslaved but also a growing political and social incapacity to coexist with the newly liberated men and women in a society free of slaves. Such an incapacity arose from the high degree of dependence on slaves to which masters had grown accustomed. Slaveholders' political power was undoubtedly a factor that reduced the abolitionist movement's potential in the major cities.

In 1776 David Hartley was one of the first in the British House of Commons to condemn the TRANSATLANTIC SLAVE TRADE. Quakers and other abolitionists, including GRANVILLE SHARP and Thomas Clarkson, founded the Abolitionist Society in 1787, with the support of William Wilberforce, who would from then on distinguish himself as a spokesperson for English abolitionism. At the outset, abolitionists mistakenly believed it unnecessary for their campaign to consider the ideas and perceptions about abolition held by the slaves themselves. Because of this, and due to white colonists' harsh opposition to prohibition of the trade, the Society decided in 1788 that it would not fight for the abolition of slavery. Abolitionists also struggled against an English monarchy and aristocracy that had strong economic ties to the slave trade, a fact that would delay its prohibition in England for some 20 years. Given these conditions, it is hardly unexpected that it would take a long and tortuous century for England to eliminate slavery. From the end of the eighteenth century and into the nineteenth, the idea advanced by English, French, and Spanish colonists – that the normal and growing supply of slaves was vital for the colonial economies and that an abrupt elimination of slavery would shatter the peaceful existence of colonial societies – remained constant. Proslavery ideas and fear gained momentum in light of the slave uprisings on the island of Santo Domingo, which made it difficult for those who advocated the declaration of the slave trade's illegality. Starting in 1804, abolitionist activity was renewed, by virtue of the notable upturn in sugar production and its consequent increase in the supply of slaves, the subsequent saturation of British sugar market, and the overproduction of sugar. Faced with these excesses, slaveholders in the British colonies became disposed to the abolition of the slave trade, at least for a time, to stem the flow of slaves to other sugar-producing areas such as Cuba and Brazil.

British colonists and slaveholders feared that their economy teetered on the brink of bankruptcy. In 1806 the rise of a new British government – a coalition of Grenville and his Foxite allies – more inclined to the abolition of the slave trade, resulted in an 1807 declaration that it would henceforth be prohibited to off-load slaves in the British colonies. In January of 1808, the U.S. Congress outlawed the importation of slaves in a motion passed in such a way that Southern slaveholders and other sectors of U.S. society with strong interests in the TRANSATLANTIC SLAVE TRADE would remain relatively unaware of the change.

As a result of the ban, Jamaican landowners stepped up their opposition to the final elimination of the slave trade. In fact, from 1808 on, the relations between colony and metropolis became increasingly strained as London continued to demand improvements in the situation of slave society as a whole.

After the legal suspension of the slave trade had been achieved, the British Abolitionist Society, with Wilberforce at its head, reiterated its decision not to count the abrogation of slavery among its objectives. Instead, they dedicated their efforts to the resolution of the problem of slaves smuggled aboard British ships flying other nations' flags. The illegal traffic in slaves, by no means a novel practice on the Atlantic, swelled to a grand scale through schemes, shared among English, Portuguese, Spanish, and French traffickers and colonists, which were designed to outmaneuver the new regulations. In 1811 smuggling was classified as a crime and would later be considered piracy. However, the rules against smuggling promoted the illegality of slave commerce by failing to consider fraudulent the trading of slaves among colonies. In an attempt to remedy the situation, a procedure was implemented to register periodically the number of slaves per owner and per hacienda. Once again, this became the object of systematic abuses, permitted by, if not perpetrated by, slaveholders and functionaries. In Trinidad, for instance, of the 25,000 slaves registered in 1812, 5,000 had been registered fraudulently.

In 1817 British and American members of the industrial and financial classes who were heavily invested in sugar, coffee, and cotton interests in Cuba, Brazil, and the United States began to withdraw their support for measures against the slave trade, because they wanted to maintain the supply of slaves in their colonial economies. Thus, the North American, Brazilian, and Cuban economies emerged as the leaders of the illegal market in slaves. Moreover, the United States would remain reluctant to allow the registry of its ships by the British. Around 1830 a great number of slave ships sailed under the American flag.

Even while international legislation that restricted the commercialization of slaves may have regularly diminished the volume of trade, it was no less true that the flow of slaves into slaveholding colonies remained active, especially until the middle of the nineteenth century. Spain, for example, having decreed in 1820 the slave trade's illegality, made little effort to follow through on the agreement, since Cuba was continuously supplied with an ample number of slaves until 1860. The same situation held true in Brazil, where plantation owners continued to import slaves even though the slave trade had been declared illegal in 1831. Between 1800 and 1855, even under the sway of abolitionism, approximately 1,250,000 slaves embarked for Brazilian shores.

Ultimately, a number of consequences and effects of the antislavery movement turned out to be historically negative and damaging for the African continent, since the abolition of slavery in Latin America and the Caribbean resulted in the commencement of another period of slavery and colonial domination throughout Africa. European colonialists in Africa at the end of the nineteenth century, even imbued with an abolitionist spirit, began to doubt as never before the Africans' capacity to govern themselves. European abolitionist ideology extended its collaboration to the foundation of a new colonialist ideology brought to bear on the "Black Continent."

Rafael Diaz-Diaz

SEE ALSO

Colonial Rule; Great Britain; France; Maroonage in the Americas; Netherlands, The; Portugal; Spain; Abolitionism in the United States; Dominican Republic; Matanzas, Cuba; Barbosa, Rui; Dessalines, Jean-Jacques; Pétion, Alexandre; Toussaint L'Ouverture, François Dominique; Slave Rebellions in Latin America and the Caribbean; Punishment of Slaves in Colonial Latin America and the Caribbean; White Abolitionists in Brazil; Black Codes in Latin America.

North America

Abolitionism in the United States, a major American reform movement that sought to eradicate slavery in the United States by means of a wide range of tactics and organizations; the antislavery crusade mobilized many African Americans and a small minority of whites, who saw their goal realized during the Civil War.

During the three decades that preceded the Civil War in the United States, abolitionism was a major factor in electoral politics. Most historians use the term *abolitionism* to refer to antislavery activism between the early 1830s, when William Lloyd Garrison began publishing the *Liberator*, and the Civil War. Historians also commonly distinguish abolitionism, a morally grounded and uncompromising social reform movement, from political antislavery – represented, for example, by the Free Soil and Republican parties – which advocated more limited political solutions, such as keeping slavery out of the western territories, and were more amenable to compromise.

Abolitionists played a key role in setting the terms of the debate over slavery and in making it a compelling moral issue. Yet abolitionists had remarkably little influence in the North. Very few Northerners were abolitionists, and many regarded abolitionists as dangerous fanatics. What made their case telling was the South's violent reaction. Extreme Southern responses appeared to confirm abolitionist warnings about a conspiratorial "Slave Power." By the 1850s, however, the escalating sectional conflict had largely taken on a momentum of its own, one that owed less and less to abolitionism.

Abolitionism was never a self-contained or singular movement. It encompassed a bewildering array of national, state, and local organizations, contradictory tactics, and clashing personalities. Abolitionists are commonly portrayed as benevolent white people deeply concerned with the well-being of enslaved blacks, epitomized by such activists as Garrison and Harriet Beecher Stowe, the author of UNCLE TOM'S CABIN (1852). In fact, a great number of abolitionists, including FREDERICK DOUGLASS and SOJOURNER TRUTH, were African American. Free blacks in the North were stalwart in their dedication to the cause and provided a disproportionate share of the movement's financial support, including a large majority of the *Liberator*'s early subscribers.

Whether black or white, most abolitionists found inspiration in two key strains of American thought: republicanism, the intellectual legacy of the AMERICAN REVOLUTION, and Protestant Christianity, especially an emotionally charged evangelicalism. Yet like their nonabolitionist contemporaries, many white abolitionists were convinced of the racial inferiority of blacks. Abolitionists acted forthrightly to correct what they perceived as a grievous wrong, but they could not wholly separate themselves from the assumptions and limitations of their time.

Although later observers have noted glaring inconsistencies and obvious shortcomings in abolitionists' efforts, it is more remarkable that so many were inspired to challenge an institution deeply entrenched in American society. During the nineteenth century reformers could rely upon familiar arguments in condemning slavery. That critical language, by and large, emerged during the preceding century. Opposition to slavery increased dramatically during the antebellum years, but its roots lay in the last half of the eighteenth century. During these years a number of individuals sought to transform slavery from an unquestioned part of the status quo to a significant problem. The principal challenge facing these eighteenth-century activists was arousing a conviction that slavery was wrong.

THE SOCIETY OF FRIENDS AND RELIGIOUS OPPOSITION TO SLAVERY IN THE COLONIAL ERA

In the United States today human slavery is regarded not simply as wrong but as utterly indefensible and an affront to humanity. This powerful consensus makes it hard to appreciate the significance of taking an antislavery stance in the eighteenth century. It was not easy to come to abolitionist principles. Eighteenth- and early nineteenth-century abolitionists had to wrench themselves free of institutions and attitudes that had been accepted for centuries. The Bible,

Frederick Douglass began his career as an abolitionist orator in 1841. This photograph of the powerful speaker was made between 1847 and 1860. *CORBIS/Bettmann*

viewed by many as a compendium of social as well as religious truth, did not condemn slavery. The ancient Greek democracies and the Roman republic, which provided political inspiration during the revolutionary era, practiced and accepted slavery.

Although it is hard to imagine, white society did not see slavery as a moral or philosophical problem until a small number of outspoken individuals made it a problem. Beginning in the 1750s members of the Society of Friends, or Quakers, took the lead in challenging the institution. The most important Quaker antislavery activists were New Jersey Quaker John Woolman, author of the pamphlet *Some Considerations on the Keeping of Negroes* (1754), and Philadelphia Quaker Anthony Benezet. During the mid-eighteenth century Woolman traveled widely in British North America, appealing to Friends to free their slaves.

Woolman and other antislavery Friends were unique in basing their opposition to slavery on their sympathy for enslaved African Americans. In the nineteenth century Friends would be at the vanguard of a wide range of reforms aimed at bettering American society. During the eighteenth century, however, they turned their attention inward, focusing on their own religious society. In 1775 Benezet and Woolman played a leading role in founding the first American antislavery organization, the Pennsylvania Society for the Abolition of Slavery. After long discussion and debate, the Society of Friends reached consensus on the issue and became the first institution in the United States to condemn slavery as a moral wrong.

By 1784 every yearly Quaker meeting in the United States had forbidden its members to own slaves. In 1797 the Philadelphia Yearly Meeting resolved that members should be admitted "without regard to colour." At the time, this was truly a radical stance. In 1790 the Society of Friends presented Congress with the first petition calling for emancipation. Friends remained active in their opposition to slavery. But American Protestantism as a whole did little to challenge the institution until well into the nineteenth century.

The American Revolution and the Problem of Slavery

During the eighteenth century the most significant opposition to slavery was secular rather than religious. The political discourse of American radicals emphasized the degradation of slavery and the need to defend liberty. Revolutionary agitators such as Samuel Adams warned that the British government aimed to "enslave" the American colonists. Patriots declared that liberty was a fundamental human quality and intrinsic to natural law. Patrick Henry of Virginia declaimed, "Give me liberty or give me death!"

Most patriot leaders did not linger on the contradiction of a slaveholder such as Thomas Jefferson proclaiming that liberty was an "unalienable right." But some extended their political principles more widely. In 1764, for example, Massachusetts lawyer James Otis Jr. asked, if all people were born free and equal, how could it be "right to enslave a man because he is black?" In 1773 Philadelphia patriot Dr. Benjamin Rush portrayed slavery as a "vice which degrades human nature."

In the North, revolutionary idealism resulted in a series of political challenges to the institution of slavery. During the war, African Americans in New Hampshire and Connecticut petitioned their respective state legislatures, unsuccessfully, for their freedom, using the language of republican liberty. Vermont, which had almost no slaves or African Americans, abolished slavery in 1777. In 1780 Pennsylvania followed suit. During the 1780s Massachusetts courts ruled that the commonwealth's 1780 constitution had, in effect, outlawed the institution. Between 1784 and 1804 the states of Rhode Island, Connecticut, New York, and New Jersey all adopted plans for gradual emancipation. The United States Constitution set a date of 1807 for cessation of the African slave trade (*see* Transatlantic Slave Trade).

Neither the Revolution nor the Constitution solved the problem of slavery in the United States. But perhaps just as important, they helped create the problem of slavery. During the colonial era, very few whites considered slavery to be a major social problem. During the first six decades of the nineteenth century, very few could deny that it was. The Revolution created the problem of slavery in two ways. First, having accepted liberty as a fundamental political tenet, Americans could no longer view slavery with equanimity. It became a troubling inconsistency in America's democratic society. In response, a number of states and territories organized abolition societies, including Rhode Island (1785), New York (1785), Illinois (1785), Delaware (1788), Maryland (1789), Connecticut (1790), and New Jersey (1793). In 1794 the American Convention of Abolition Societies was established in Philadelphia to unite the various state societies.

Second, once revolutionary idealism resulted in immediate or gradual emancipation throughout the North, slavery became an exclusively Southern institution. The debate over slavery now had potent sectional overtones, and it quickly emerged as the most divisive topic in national politics. At the start of the century, however, opponents of slavery had no intention of sharpening sectional controversy. Most early nineteenth-century abolitionists invoked moderation rather than militancy. They shared two key assumptions: that emancipation would be gradual, and that the freed slaves would not remain in the United States but should be colonized in Africa.

Gradual Emancipation and Colonization

Prior to the 1830s most antislavery activists focused on gradual emancipation. Most of these activists were Southern whites, who thought that the institution would gradually whither away. Only black abolitionists, whose numbers were relatively few, demanded an immediate end to slavery. Most white – and a considerable number of black – opponents of slavery viewed colonization as intrinsic to any planned emancipation. In 1776, the year in which he wrote the Declaration of Independence, Thomas Jefferson also formulated a proposal for the African colonization of American blacks. Jefferson was a slaveholder who deplored slavery; yet he – like many other whites – believed in the absolute inferiority of blacks.

Jefferson was far from alone in concluding that the two groups could not live together beyond the constraints of slavery. For those who held such views, colonization seemed to offer a congenial solution: African Americans would be freed and returned to Africa – where, colonizationists insisted, they belonged – leaving the United States to whites. The most important advocate of colonization was the American Colonization Society (ACS), founded in 1816 by a group of Presbyterian ministers gathered in Washington, D.C. The ACS's initial goal was to encourage free blacks to immigrate to Africa.

The ACS attracted such illustrious supporters as former American presidents James Madison and James Monroe, Supreme Court justice John Marshall, and Kentucky senator and slaveholder Henry Clay. In 1821 the ACS purchased a colony for African American settlement. The colony, soon christened Liberia, was located south of Sierra Leone in West Africa. During the nineteenth century the ACS sent an estimated 12,000 to 20,000 African Americans to Africa.

One of the first prominent black advocates of colonization was the Massachusetts ship owner and Quaker Paul Cuffe. In 1815 he carried a group of African American settlers to Sierra Leone. Although most free blacks despised the ACS, Cuffe supported the organization. Other important black advocates of colonization were Martin Robison Delany, Alexander Crummell, and Rev. Henry Highland Garnet, who in the early 1850s was president of the newly formed African Civilization Society, an organization that advocated a black return to Africa.

African Americans as a whole remained aloof from colonization schemes, although many free blacks were active in assisting runaway slaves and in raising money for legal challenges to the enslavement of individual blacks. They also formed black organizations that combined antislavery activism and self-defense. For example, the New York Vigilance Committee, founded in 1835 by David Ruggles, helped more than 1000 runaway slaves avoid being recaptured and returned to the South. Following passage of the Fugitive Slave Law of 1850, which made African Americans much more vulnerable to claims that they were runaway slaves and to kidnapping by so-called slave catchers, many free blacks moved to Canada. But in most cases, flight to Canada was a practical means of protection rather than an endorsement of emigration.

The high point of colonization was during the 1820s. In 1821 white abolitionist Benjamin Lundy, an advocate of colonization, began publishing the *Genius of Universal Emancipation*. Eight years later, a young William Lloyd Garrison joined him as an associate editor. But Garrison grew in creasingly critical of Lundy on the issue of colonizing freed slaves, and in 1831 he began publishing his own radical antislavery journal, the *Liberator*, which was adamant in rejecting colonizationist arguments. Garrison's proslavery opponents and many of his one-time reform allies condemned him as an intemperate extremist. In the first issue of the *Liberator*, he met their challenges head on: "I am aware that many object to the severity of my language; but is there not cause for severity? I *will be* as harsh as truth, and as uncompromising as justice. On this subject, I do not wish to think, or speak, or write, with moderation.... I am in earnest – I will not excuse – I will not retreat a single inch – AND I WILL BE HEARD." Garrison helped to usher in a new era in abolitionism, but he was not alone in setting abolitionism on a more radical tack.

The Sources of Radical Abolitionism

Abolitionism in its radical form dates from about 1830. A series of developments at about this time served to discredit gradualist approaches to emancipation. Southerners became more adamant in defending slavery, and antislavery activists became more radical in their attacks on the institution. The radical approach to abolitionism is termed *immediatism*, as opposed to gradualism. The term immediatism is usually associated with Garrison, but black abolitionists had for years demanded an immediate end to slavery.

In 1829, two years before Garrison commenced the *Liberator*, black abolitionist David Walker published a far more inflammatory work, *Walker's Appeal... to the Colored Citizens of the World* (1829). Walker urged slaves to rise up against their masters and take their freedom by force. In August 1831 Nat Turner instigated a slave revolt in Southampton County, Virginia, that resulted in the deaths of 57 white men, women, and children and more than 100 slaves. Southern whites charged that the "fanaticism" of Walker, Garrison, and other immediatists was the direct cause of Turner's Rebellion.

Antislavery supporters were radicalized not only as a result of the increasing vehemence of their proslavery opponents, but also because colonization was discredited as a viable option. The proslavery Virginian Thomas R. Dew, who was later president of William and Mary College, played an important part in this effort. During the winter of 1831-1832 the Virginia legislature debated the question of abolishing slavery in the state through gradual emancipation and colonization. Dew's report of those debates, published as the *Review of the Debate in the Virginia Legislature of 1831 and 1832* (1832), argued persuasively that colonization was unworkable.

Dew used census figures to show that the growth of the black population outstripped the passenger-carrying capacity of the nation's merchant fleet. Perhaps the most surprising aspect of the Virginia debates, which followed Turner's Rebellion by only a few months, was that they took place at all. The legislators decided against ending slavery, but the vote (73-58) was remarkably close. It would, however, be the last time that any Southern state would voluntarily consider emancipation.

Radical abolitionists like Garrison also worked tirelessly to counter the advocates of colonization. Garrison's widely distributed *Thoughts on African Colonization* (1832) offered an uncompromising attack on the idea, in part by citing blatantly racist and proslavery statements of various leading colonizationists. Although the idea of colonization continued to appeal to many whites – Abraham Lincoln was for years a colonizationist – after 1830 it was clearly embattled.

The most important source of the radicalizing of abolitionism was evangelical Protestantism. Beginning in the late 1790s, a major religious revival, the Second Great Awakening, had spread across the United States. The revival was based in evangelicalism, a fervent and intensely personal form of Christianity. Evangelicals viewed themselves and the world as being in a constant battle against the temptations of sin; yet evangelicalism was an optimistic faith. Both the individual and the larger society could be saved. Salvation required putting oneself in God's hands and trying to live by Jesus' example, but it also required the concerted efforts of the faithful. Evangelicals who righted society's wrongs were thus doing God's work on earth.

At the height of the Second Great Awakening, in the two decades after 1820, the United States entered an age of reform. Reformers took up a wide variety of social problems. They promoted temperance and discouraged prostitution. Some advocated women's rights; others proposed improvements in public education or in prison conditions. Aside from temperance, abolitionism was the principal focus for antebellum reformers. Not all evangelicals became abolitionists; nor were all abolitionists evangelicals, but during the 1830s and 1840s the effort to eradicate slavery took on a new energy and radicalism due to the many evangelicals who joined the crusade.

Abolitionist Organizations and Activities

The new phase of abolitionism after 1830 unfolded through new antislavery institutions and new forms of activism. In 1832 Garrison and ten others formed the New England Anti-Slavery Society. In 1833 Garrison and two wealthy New York City businessmen and philanthropists, Arthur and Lewis Tappan, played key roles in establishing the American Anti-Slavery Society (AASS). Also in 1833 black and white women of Boston organized the interracial Boston Female Anti-Slavery Society, and women established a similarly constituted organization in Philadelphia. Many other local and state societies appeared during these years. By 1837 Massachusetts had 145 different antislavery societies; New York had 274; and Ohio, 214. Abolitionist sentiment was strongest in New England, New York, and their cultural hinterlands across the upper Midwest. By 1838 the AASS claimed nearly 250,000 members and 1350 affiliated societies.

During the 1830s antislavery societies effectively made slavery a social issue. They sent out massive mailings of antislavery literature, much of it directed to the South. In 1835 alone the AASS mailed 1.1 million abolitionist tracts. The campaign led President Andrew Jackson to propose legislation that would prohibit mailing antislavery literature. Slave narratives, former slaves' graphic, first-person accounts of their experiences under slavery, were an especially effective form of abolitionist propaganda. During the antebellum years, abolitionists published some 70 fugitive slave narratives, the most celebrated being Douglass's *Narrative of the Life of Frederick Douglass* (1845).

Abolitionist speakers also carried the antislavery message throughout the North. Other notable black abolitionist speakers were Sarah Mapps Douglass, William Wells Brown, William and Ellen Craft, and Frances Ellen Watkins Harper. These traveling orators were impassioned and willing to debate their opponents. They were also courageous – abolitionist views were not popular and could elicit hostile responses.

During the 1830s and 1840s abolitionists encountered almost as much resistance in the North as they did in the slaveholding South. Many Northerners feared not simply that the abolitionists would unsettle national politics and worsen sectional conflict, but also that, if successful, they would upset the North's racial balance as hordes of freed slaves fled the South to join the tiny number of free blacks already residing in the North. Anti-abolitionist mobs in the North attacked abolitionist speakers and destroyed abolitionist presses. In 1837, for example, abolitionist editor Elijah P. Lovejoy died defending his press against a mob in Alton, Illinois. Five years later, Frederick Douglass had his hand broken by a stone-throwing mob in Pendleton, Indiana. These mobs were by no means simply rowdies or social rabble. They were organized and often led, in the phrase of the time, by "gentlemen of property and standing."

The Depression of 1837-1843 seriously undermined the abolitionist campaign by reducing its financial resources and by drawing Northern attention to more pressing economic concerns. Almost as severe an impediment was the so-called Gag Rule, a procedural rule of the House of Representatives, adopted annually between 1836 and 1844, which automatically tabled any petition or letter on the subject of slavery. Yet the Gag Rule also provided abolitionists with a new tactic. Beginning in 1837 the AASS began mounting antislavery petition drives. By 1838 it had inundated Congress with more than 400,000 signatures. Abolitionists rightly pointed out that the Gag Rule violated their First Amendment right to petition their elected representatives. In this struggle, they gained many nonabolitionist allies, the most important of whom was Massachusetts representative and former president John Quincy Adams, who opposed the Gag Rule and in 1844 saw it defeated.

Frustrated by their political leaders' general reluctance to confront slavery, more and more abolitionists turned to direct action and civil disobedience. In 1832 Theodore Dwight Weld was forced out of Cincinnati's Lane Theological Seminary for encouraging students to debate the merits of colonization. In 1833 Weld began teaching at Oberlin College, which became a hotbed of abolitionist sentiment and was soon an important stop on the Underground Railroad.

The Underground Railroad, a secret network of activists who aided fugitive slaves in their journey to freedom, was the most important example of abolitionist direct action. A system for assisting escaped slaves existed as early as 1786, but the network did not spread throughout the North until after 1830. More than 3200 individuals are known to have been active in the Underground Railroad, and they aided perhaps as many as 50,000 escaped slaves in their journey to freedom. Among the best known of those active in the Underground Railroad are Harriet Tubman and Indiana Quaker Levi Coffin. Douglass, Delany, Garnet, and many other African Americans were also involved. Following the passage of the federal Fugitive Slave Law of 1850, abolitionists became even more militant in their efforts to assist runaway slaves. In 1851, for example, a Boston mob rescued a fugitive slave from a U.S. marshal and helped him safely reach Canada.

Abolitionist Divisions and Slavery in the Territories

Although historians disagree on its political impact, abolitionism unquestionably helped define slavery as a pressing moral problem. During the 1840s, however, internal and external developments decreased the movement's significance. In 1840 the AASS split into two factions. Garrison and his radical followers retained control over the original organization; the Tappan brothers, Weld, and their followers formed the more conservative American and Foreign Antislavery Society.

There were numerous other fallings-out among abolitionists in subsequent years. In 1843 Douglass, a Garrisonian advocate of nonviolence, prevented the publication of a fiery speech by Garnet that called for slave insurrection. Garrison relied on moral suasion as the means to gain emancipation. He dismissed politics and declined to vote, and he was convinced that nonviolence was the proper means of combating slavery. In 1851 Douglass decided that political action was essential to the antislavery struggle and that violence might be needed as well. During the 1850s a number of white abolitionists, including Theodore Parker and Thomas Wentworth Higginson, similarly concluded that to emancipate the slaves might require violent acts of resistance.

By the mid-1840s America's territorial expansion was far more important than abolitionists in shaping the debate over slavery. The Mexican-American War (1846-1848) brought the United States a vast new area of land, which since it lay south of the Missouri Compromise line of 36 degrees, 30 minutes, would be open to slavery. Slavery was already well established in Texas, a large part of this new territory, because of its mainly Southern settlers. The South, as a section, was eager for new land in which to expand its social and economic system. But the North was reluctant to see the extension of slavery into new territories because Northern whites feared being unable to compete with Southern plantation slavery and, in large

measure, because of their racial prejudice. Rather than the moral appeals of abolitionism, it was the practical question of slavery in the territories that drove a wedge between the North and South.

The issue of slavery in the territories made political antislavery the dominant form of abolitionism from the mid-1840s to the Civil War. In 1839 the antislavery Liberty Party nominated former slaveholder and abolitionist James G. Birney as its first presidential candidate. In 1848 the Liberty Party dissolved and joined in forming the new Free Soil Party. In 1854 the Free Soil Party, along with many former Whigs, antislavery Northern Democrats, and supporters of the nativist American Party, created the Republican Party. For Free Soilers and Republicans, the primary issue was the nonextension of slavery, in other words, keeping slavery out of the western territories.

That issue lay at the heart of the most divisive political controversies of the era, including the Wilmot Proviso (1847), the Compromise of 1850, the Kansas-Nebraska Act (1854), and the Supreme Court's Dred Scott decision (1857). During these years, abolitionists increasingly found themselves in the position of reacting to outside developments, rather than setting an agenda of their own. Two important exceptions were Harriet Beecher Stowe and John Brown.

Harriet Beecher Stowe, John Brown, and the Coming of the Civil War

It is difficult to imagine a greater contrast between two abolitionists than that between Stowe and Brown. Stowe was deeply committed to moral persuasion. Brown, in essence, was an antislavery terrorist who committed reprisal killings and organized attacks on federal government installations. Brown was one of the only abolitionists who left his mark with a gun; Stowe, a better representative of the crusade, made the pen her weapon of choice. Stowe's sentimental antislavery novel Uncle Tom's Cabin became the most popular novel of the nineteenth century.

Uncle Tom's Cabin was quickly adapted for the stage, and touring theatrical companies presented versions of the story throughout the North. The novel's characters were, to a considerable extent, unflattering stereotypes, and the theatrical performances relied upon the demeaning racial caricatures of nineteenth-century minstrelsy. Yet

Uncle Tom's Cabin played a crucial part in turning Northerners against slavery and against the South. When he met Stowe during the Civil War, President Lincoln reportedly declared, "So this is the little woman who wrote the book that started this great war!"

In 1856 JOHN BROWN led four of his sons and two other followers on a murderous spree in Kansas that culminated in the execution-style killings of five unarmed proslavery Kansas settlers. Three years later, he masterminded a bloody, misguided raid on the federal armory at Harpers Ferry, Virginia. Brown secured financial backing from half a dozen New England and New York abolitionists and expected to instigate a massive slave uprising. Black abolitionists such as Garnet, Tubman, and Douglass admired Brown's zeal, but by the time he made his raid, they had all carefully distanced themselves from him. Neither did Virginia's slaves rise up in response to his raid. Within 36 hours, Brown and his surviving followers were captured.

During his trial and execution Brown remained calm and dignified. His demeanor won the admiration even of those Northerners who condemned his actions. Many Northerners regarded him as a principled martyr. By contrast, Southerners viewed Brown's Northern defenders – and the revelations of his abolitionist backers – as proof that the North was actively conspiring to subvert slavery. Northerners were equally convinced of the threat posed by a conspiratorial Southern "Slave Power" bent on extending its dominion over the entire nation, North as well as South.

With the 1860 election of Republican presidential candidate Abraham Lincoln, these suspicions provided the tripwires for secession and war. Abolitionists doggedly continued trying to influence events. Douglass and Delany advocated the enlisting of African American soldiers for the Union army (*see* MILITARY, BLACKS IN THE AMERICAN). Even more momentous, Douglass was prominent in imploring Lincoln to transform the war from its limited goal of restoring the Union into a full-fledged crusade against slavery. Both goals were realized in 1863, when Lincoln signed the Emancipation Proclamation and the Union army began accepting black recruits. Yet each of these decisions reflected larger political consideration as much as abolitionist appeals.

By the start of the Civil War, abolitionists were increasingly marginal to unfolding events. Although they had speeded the process of emancipation, the actual demise of slavery did not come according to their plans. Nonetheless, the abolitionists made lasting historical contributions. They were notable for their principled advocacy of unpopular ideas. They also insisted that American political and religious principles should apply to all. In particular, they provided a powerful model for later social movements. From the nineteenth-century women's rights movement to the twentieth-century Civil Rights, gay rights, and anti-abortion or right-to-life movements, American reformers have drawn upon the idealism and, in many cases, the specific tactics that are a central part of the abolitionists' legacy.

James Clyde Sellman

SEE ALSO
American Anti-Slavery Society; Civil Rights Movement; Civil War, American; Craft, Ellen and William; Dred Scott v. Sanford; Garnet, Henry Highland; Thirteenth Amendment of the United States Constitution and the Emancipation Proclamation; Tubman, Harriet Ross.

Africa

Abrahams, Peter (b. March 19, 1919, Vrededorp, South Africa), expatriate South African novelist.

The son of an Ethiopian father and a mother of French and African descent, Peter Abrahams was considered "Coloured" in the South African racial classification scheme. He grew up outside Johannesburg and began working at the age of nine, never having attended school. He later enrolled, however, after he was inspired by hearing *Othello* read to him by a co-worker. As a teenager Abrahams discovered works by African American writers such as W. E. B. Du Bois, COUNTEE CULLEN, LANGSTON HUGHES, CLAUDE MCKAY, and JEAN TOOMER in the library at the Bantu Men's Social Centre.

Abrahams began publishing his own poems in local newspapers while studying at a teachers' training college. While enrolled at St. Peter's Secondary School – a fertile political environment – Abrahams became a member of the SOUTH AFRICAN COMMUNIST PARTY. After his failed attempt to start a school for poor African children in Cape Town, Abrahams left South Africa in 1939, taking a job as a stoker on a steamship. Two years later he settled in England.

Though he never again lived in South Africa, Abrahams wrote six of his seven novels about his home country. *Song of the City* (1945) and *Mine Boy* (1946) explore the racial injustices of a rapidly industrializing and urbanizing South Africa. Abrahams also wrote a historical novel about South Africa's Afrikaners, *Wild Conquest* (1950), and another about African-Indian solidarity, *A Night of Their Own* (1965).

In the 1950s Abrahams wrote for the London *Observer* and the New York *Herald Tribune;* an assignment in JAMAICA led him to move his family there in 1956. *This Island Now* (1966) deals with political struggles in a fictional Caribbean setting. Abrahams worked as a radio journalist and eventually became chairman of Radio Jamaica, but he resigned in 1964 to concentrate on writing. By then Abrahams was known as a novelist of ideas whom some critics considered didactic, but in whom many readers found provocative and idealistic theories. Abraham's travel books, which include *Jamaica: An Island Mosaic* (1957), and the two memoirs *Return to Goli* (1953) and *Tell Freedom* (1954) are among his most widely praised works.

Kate Tuttle

SEE ALSO
Afrikaner; Cape Coloured; Cape Town, South Africa; Ethiopia; Indian Communities in Africa; Johannesburg, South Africa; Great Britain; South Africa; Du Bois, William Edward Burghardt (W. E. B.).

Africa

Abron (also known as Abrong, Bron, Brong, Bono, and Tchaman), ethnic group of West Africa.

The Abron inhabit the borderlands of CÔTE D'IVOIRE, GHANA, and BURKINA FASO. They speak a Niger-Congo language and are part of the larger AKAN cultural and linguistic group. Their ancestors, the Bono, founded the first known Akan kingdom during the fourteenth century. Approximately 100,000 people identify themselves as Abron.

SEE ALSO
Languages, African: An Overview.

North America

Abu-Jamal, Mumia (b. April 24, 1954, Philadelphia, Pa.), African American activist and militant journalist whose death-sentence conviction for the alleged murder of a police officer became a cause célèbre.

Born Wesley Cook in Philadelphia, Mumia Abu-Jamal was a political activist from adolescence. At the age of 14 he was arrested and beaten for demonstrating against segregationist presidential candidate George Wallace. He was a founding member of the Philadelphia chapter of the BLACK PANTHER PARTY in 1968 and worked on the party's newspaper in California during the summer of 1970.

Returning to Philadelphia, Abu-Jamal became a radio journalist with the Corporation for Public Broadcasting and had his own talk show on station WUHY. He was highly critical of Philadelphia's police department and of the city's "law and order" mayor, Frank Rizzo. He provided coverage of the police treatment of MOVE, a Philadelphia black militant group, which further alienated the authorities. Forced to leave his position as a journalist, Abu-Jamal took a job as a taxi driver.

While Abu-Jamal was driving his cab

on the night of December 9, 1981, a police officer, Daniel Faulkner, was fatally shot during an altercation with Abu-Jamal's brother, William Cook. Faulkner wounded Abu-Jamal, who had arrived on the scene moments before. When other officers arrived to investigate, they assumed that Abu-Jamal was the shooter and arrested him after reportedly beating him severely. Despite witnesses who claimed they saw Faulkner's killer flee on foot and despite irregularities during the trial, Abu-Jamal was convicted of murder in the first degree and sentenced to death.

Abu-Jamal has remained on death row while his case has drawn increasing worldwide attention. The conviction is considered by some to be a racist miscarriage of justice, but appeals to the Pennsylvania and United States Supreme Courts have been unsuccessful. Finally allowed to write, Abu-Jamal has produced two books of essays, *Live from Death Row* (1995) and *Death Blossoms* (1996), as well as articles for the *Yale Law Review* and other periodicals. National Public Radio commissioned a series of radio commentaries from Abu-Jamal in 1994, but they were cancelled under pressure from Republican senator Robert Dole and the Fraternal Order of Police.

April Taylor

See Also
Philadelphia, Pennsylvania.

Africa

Abuja, Nigeria, the official capital of Nigeria.

The town of Abuja was founded by the Hausa Zazzua Dynasty and conquered by the Fulani during their early eighteenth-century *jihad* (holy war). Abuja is also home to numerous smaller ethnic groups, making it one of the more ethnically "neutral" cities in Nigeria. Its population is expected to soon exceed 1 million residents.

Relative ethnic parity was one of several reasons that the Nigerian government chose Abuja as the capital. Other factors included its central location – almost exactly in the middle of the country – and its comfortable climate, low population density, and potential for expansion. Abuja is located on the grassy, rolling Chukuku Hills, at an elevation of 360 m (1,180 ft).

Plans for Abuja's development were drafted in 1976, and construction, slowed by Nigeria's debt, took place over several years. In 1991 Abuja officially replaced congested Lagos as the capital. The city's central zone contains government buildings, including the National Assembly, as well as cultural institutes; residential and commercial areas lie at the periphery.

Electricity from Shiroro Dam, 74 km (46 mi) to the southwest on the Niger River, powers Abuja. Expressways connect the city to other parts of the country, and an airport services international flights.

Eric Bennett

Africa

Abyssinia. Former name of Ethiopia.

North America

Accommodationism in the United States,

a conciliatory approach to racial issues in the late nineteenth and early twentieth centuries that was personified by Booker Taliaferro Washington.

See Also
Washington, Booker Taliaferro.

Africa

Accra, Ghana, the capital, transportation hub, and largest city of Ghana.

The political, economic, and cultural center of Ghana, Accra occupies a flat, level plain on the Atlantic coast. Originally the site of several villages of the Ga people, Accra developed after the Europeans established three fortified trading posts in the vicinity. In 1650 the Dutch built Fort Crevecoeur, which was later renamed Ussher Fort. The Danes constructed Christiansborg Castle in 1661 at nearby Osu, while the British erected Fort James in 1673. Three towns, Danish Christiansborg (or Osu), the Dutch Accra (or Ussher Town), and the British Accra (or James Town), developed around the forts as trade increased. Gradually the entire area became known as Accra, a corruption of *nkran*, the Akan word for the black ants common in the area. Accra quickly became an important center in the gold and slave trades. During the eighteenth century traders from Asante traveled to Accra to deal with Ga and European coastal traders. The region developed a distinctive urban and mercantile – and predominantly Ga – culture.

In 1850 the Danish relinquished their Gold Coast possessions, including Christiansborg, to the British. The Dutch left in 1872. Accra became the capital of the British Gold Coast Crown Colony in 1877. The Accra Town Council was formed in 1898. During the 1920s, after workers completed a rail line linking Accra to Kumasi and interior cocoa-growing regions, the city's commercial economy expanded. By the 1930s Accra boasted polo fields and a number of British colonial governmental buildings. On March 6, 1957, the Gold Coast became the independent nation of Ghana, with Accra its capital. Ghana's first president, Kwame Nkrumah, declared Accra a city in 1961.

Today Accra is a sprawling metropolis with a population of at least 2 million. Migrants from rural areas continue to pour into Accra looking for work, giving the city a 4.3 percent annual growth rate. If growth remains unchecked, the World Bank predicts Accra's population will soar to over 4 million by 2020. Unplanned population growth has clogged streets and increased water pollution and sanitation problems. Since many people are unable to find employment, more than half of Accra's residents live below the World Bank's absolute poverty threshold. Impoverished shantytowns contrast with the skyscrapers of the city's commercial center.

A 1987 survey determined that 32 percent of Ghana's manufacturing takes place in or near Accra. Industries include auto assembly plants, food-processing facilities, distilleries, breweries, textile manufacturing, lumber exporting, and aluminum plants. A hydroelectric dam nearby provides electricity. Three major markets provide food and other goods. Accra has an international airport, while railroads and paved roads link it with Ghana's interior.

Christiansborg Castle has been renamed The Castle and is now the seat of government. Pan-African leaders W. E. B. Du Bois and George Padmore are buried there. Other notable Accra institutions include the Kwame Nkrumah Conference Centre, National Archives, National Museum, Korle Bu General Hospital, Ghana Medical School, and University of Ghana. A variety of clubs, bars, and theaters provide a vibrant nightlife.

David P. Johnson, Jr.

See Also
Gold Trade; Kumasi, Ghana; Du Bois, William Edward Burghardt (W. E. B.).

Latin America and the Caribbean

Acea, Isidro (b.?; d. November 12, 1912, Güira de Melena, Cuba), Afro-Cuban hero of the independence war of 1895-1898.

Isidro Acea was greatly respected for his bravery and unceremonious nature. He was described as a very outspoken man and a charismatic leader, qualities that helped him gain a position as colonel in the Liberation Army under Gen. Máximo Gómez and Antonio Maceo y Grajales.

Acea lived during a period of Cuban history when the society was highly politicized around the issue of race, particularly after the independence war (*see* Spanish-Cuban-American War). Afro-Cubans were frustrated by the Cuban administration, United States military occupation, and Spanish migration, all of which exacerbated social inequity for people of African descent in the nation. Acea, like some other Afro-Cuban veterans, attempted to connect with the community and gain support by entering the political arena on a pro-black platform in the early 1900s. The platform lacked patronage particularly because of U.S.-imposed restrictions on male suffrage that required literacy and ownership of property, thus limiting access by Afro-Cuban voters. Not only did Acea lack the desired support but he was arrested for allegedly instigating a black rebellion in Güira de Melena. Many Afro-Cubans had joined the Partido Independiente de Color (Independent Party of Color), a political party founded in 1908 to fight for racial equality, political representation, and social reform. Although not a leader in the organization, Acea played a major role in the party's struggle for equality.

The party was outlawed in 1910, but many of its members rejected the act and staged an armed protest in May 1912. Acea and two other black veterans were accused of mobilizing Afro-Cubans to extend black protest, referred to as Cuba's "race war," from the Havana province into western Cuba. The men were arrested and subsequently freed for lack of evidence. Acea was reportedly assassinated a few months later. Information regarding the life, as well as the death, of Isidro Acea is not well documented and requires further investigation.

Rob Garrison

See Also
Cuba; Havana, Cuba.

Africa

Achebe, Chinua

(b. November 16, 1930, Ogidi, Nigeria), Nigerian author whose novel *Things Fall Apart* (1958) is one of the most widely read and discussed works of African fiction.

Chinua Achebe once described his writing as an attempt to set the historical record straight by showing "that African people did not hear of culture for the first time from Europeans; that their societies were not mindless but frequently had a philosophy of great depth and value and beauty; that they had poetry and, above all, they had dignity." Achebe's works portray Nigeria's communities as they pass through the trauma of colonization into a troubled nationhood. In bringing together the political and the literary, he neither romanticizes the culture of the indigenous nor apologizes for the colonial.

Achebe's own upbringing spanned the indigenous and colonial worlds. He was born Albert Chinualumogu Achebe to an Igbo (Ibo) family active in the Christian church, and grew up in the rural village of Ogidi, in eastern Nigeria. At a young age he received a coveted scholarship to Government College in Umuahia, where he studied alongside some of Nigeria's future political and cultural leaders. After receiving a bachelor's degree from University College, Ibadan, he worked for the Nigerian Broadcasting Corporation, ultimately acting as director of the radio program *Voice of Nigeria* in Lagos.

After moving to London in 1957 to attend the British Broadcasting Corporation staff school, Achebe decided to publish the fiction he had been writing for several years. He was inspired, in part, by a need to respond to the racist portrayals of Africa in the work of prominent European writers. In his first novel, *Things Fall Apart,* Achebe retold the history of colonization from the point of view of the colonized. The novel depicted the first contact between the Igbo people and European missionaries and administrators (*see* Christianity: Missionaries in Africa). Since its publication, *Things Fall Apart* has generated a wealth of literary criticism grappling with Achebe's unsentimental representations of tradition, religion, manhood, and the colonial experience. Immediately successful, the novel secured Achebe's position both in Nigeria and in the West as a preeminent voice among Africans writing in English.

Achebe subsequently wrote several novels that spanned more than a century of African history. Although most of these works deal specifically with Nigeria, they are also emblematic of what Achebe calls the "metaphysical landscape" of Africa, "a view of the world and of the whole cosmos perceived from a particular position." *No Longer at Ease* (1960) tells the story of a young man sent by his village to study overseas, who then returns to a government job in Nigeria only to find himself in a culturally fragmented world. As the young man sinks into materialism and corruption, Achebe represents a new generation caught in a moral and spiritual conflict between the modern and the traditional. *Arrow of God* (1964) returns to the colonial period of 1920s Nigeria. In this novel, Achebe focuses on a theme that underscores all of his work: the wielding of power and its deployment for the good or harm of a community. *A Man of the People* (1966), a work Achebe has characterized as "an indictment of independent Africa," is set in the context of the emerging African nation state. Representing a nation thought to be based on Nigeria, Achebe portrays the vacuum of true leadership left by the destruction of the governance provided by the traditional village. Achebe's critical political commentary continues in *Anthills of the Savannah* (1987), in which he uses a complex mythical structure to depict an African nation passing into the shadow of a military dictatorship.

During the 20-year gap between *A Man of the People* and *Anthills of the Savannah,* Achebe was a prolific writer and speaker. He helped found a publishing company in Nigeria with poet Christopher Okigbo and in 1971 was a founding editor for the prominent African literary magazine *Okike.* In addition, he published award-winning poetry collections and children's books.

Achebe taught literature at the University of Nigeria in the 1970s, a period when Nigeria was shaken by a series of military coups. After the start of the Nigerian Civil War, he traveled throughout Europe and North America on behalf of the Biafra state, which had split off from Nigeria. Many of his lectures and essays from this period have been published in *Morning Yet on Creation Day* (1975), *The Trouble with Nigeria* (1983), and *Hopes and Impediments* (1988). In addition to discussing the contemporary political situation in Nigeria, Achebe's nonfiction works address such topics as the role of the writer in the postcolonial African nation, literary depictions of Africa, and the debate over language choice by African writers. Responding to critics such as Ngugi wa Thiongo, who point to the political and cultural implications of writing in the colonial language, Achebe has defended his use of English, asserting that as a "medium of international exchange," the language is a lingua franca that will connect the communities of Africa.

"Art is man's constant effort to create for himself a different order of reality from that which is given to him," Achebe wrote in his essay "The Truth of Fiction." Achebe, who now teaches in the United States, has used his position as one of the most widely read African writers to comment on the crisis situation in contemporary Nigeria. It is still fiction, however, that provides for Achebe "the weapon for coping with [threats to integrity], whether they are found within our problematic and incoherent selves or in the world around us."

Marian Aguiar

See Also
Lagos, Nigeria; Fiction, English-Language, in Africa; Ngugi wa Thiong'o; Nigeria.

Africa

Acholi, also Acoli, Gang, or Shuli, an ethnic group living primarily along the border of Uganda and Sudan.

The Acholi people live mostly in the Acholi district of Uganda, a 28,000-sq-km (11,000-sq-mi) savanna plateau. While 43 percent of Acholi clans trace descent from Nilo-Saharan-speaking Luo groups, who migrated from present-day Sudan during the sixteenth and seventeenth centuries, others trace descent from the Lango, Karamojong, Mandi, and Bari ethnic groups. Thus the Acholi represent an emergent ethnic identity, forged among a number of distinct groups who have come to share a homeland as well as a language and certain cultural traditions. Contemporary population estimates fall in the range of 600,000 to 800,000 individuals.

Most Acholi live in small hamlets organized into patrilineal clans. Several clans constitute a chiefdom, or *kaka mandit*. The Acholi distinguish between "royal" lineages, most of which claim to be of Luo origin, and "commoners," but they have not historically recognized a centralized political authority. Like many neighboring groups, the Acholi have traditionally farmed (staple foods include MILLET, sorghum, maize, and various legumes) as well as raised livestock; cattle are particularly valued as a symbol of wealth.

Precolonial Acholi chiefdoms often raided each other for cattle. With the arrival of Arab traders in the area during the nineteenth century, they also began raiding neighboring groups for slaves. Exchanging captives and ivory for firearms, some clan leaders were able to acquire considerable wealth and regional political power.

Although British colonization during the late nineteenth century put an end to the most powerful Acholi chiefs' expansionist ambitions, it otherwise had relatively little initial impact on Acholi society. Colonial administrators perceived the Acholi as excellent warriors and recruited them into the colonial army and police force, but showed little interest in the Acholi region, which had neither great strategic importance nor especially valuable natural resources. In addition, the Acholi's relatively decentralized political organization appeared less threatening to colonial authority than kingdoms such as Buganda. The colonial regime only began to intervene seriously in the Acholi region in the early twentieth century, when it imposed a poll tax, confiscated weapons, and altered the spheres of control of some chiefs. It also strongly encouraged cotton cultivation, which many households undertook in order to pay their taxes.

The colonial administration's official designation of the Acholi as a "tribe" contributed to the development of a distinct Acholi identity, as did missionary efforts to transcribe the Acholi language and create a written version of their history. After Uganda achieved independence in 1963, such categories came to shape political alliances and conflicts. While the Bantu-speaking Baganda of southern Uganda were the largest ethnic group, the Acholi and their traditional enemies, the Lango, both northerners, dominated the military. When the first Ugandan prime minister, MILTON OBOTE, was ousted by IDI AMIN in 1971, soldiers and civilians from both groups faced severe persecution, including summary execution and torture. When Amin in turn was forced from office in 1979, Acholi members of the army and security forces sought retribution, killing many people of Amin's ethnic group, the Kawka. Obote later relied heavily on Acholi soldiers to fight Yoweri Museveni's National Resistence Army (NRA) during the early 1980s.

After Museveni came to power in 1986, the Acholi again found themselves out of favor with the Ugandan government, which has concentrated economic development efforts in the south of the country. The impoverished Acholi region provided fertile soil for the rise of the insurgent "Holy Spirit" group in 1986, led by self-proclaimed prophet Alice Lakwena, who guaranteed her followers magical protection against bullets when combating the NRA. Museveni's troops, whose bullets failed to turn to water in response to Lakwena's magic, imposed heavy casualties on the Acholi. Betty Bigombe, an Acholi member of Museveni's government, has begun to make some headway in improving the conditions of the Acholi in recent years.

Ari Nave

SEE ALSO
Buganda, Early Kingdom of; Ivory Trade; Slavery in Africa.

Africa

Adangbe, also known as the Adangme, Adampa, Dangme, and KROBO, ethnic group of southeastern GHANA.

The Adangbe live primarily along Ghana's coast and in the hills of the Accra Plain. They speak a Niger-Congo language closely related to GA. Approximately 500,000 people identify themselves as Adangbe.

SEE ALSO
Languages, African: An Overview.

North America

Adderley, Julian Edwin ("Cannonball")

(b. September 15, 1928, Tampa, Fla.; d. August 8, 1975, Gary, Ind.), African American alto saxophonist who explored bebop, modal, and soul-fusion styles.

Adderley was introduced to music by his father, a cornetist, and was performing in bands by the time he was 14. He played in local and army bands (he enlisted in 1950) and taught music before moving to New York to join his brother, Nat, in 1955. He immediately found success on the New York JAZZ scene, joining the bands of OSCAR PETTIFORD and, later, Miles Davis.

The recordings Adderley made with Davis – which included John Coltrane on tenor saxophone, Paul Chambers on bass, and Wynton Kelly on piano – are some of the most celebrated of the 1950s. In 1959 Adderley and his brother, Nat, formed their own quintet and built on the influence of Davis and Charlie Parker. During its 15 years, the quintet played soul jazz style, fusion, and mainstream post-bop, earning critical and popular acclaim and a reputation for drawing heavily on blues and gospel. Some critics hailed Adderley as the "new Bird," noting his style's debt to Parker. At times, Adderley doubled on soprano saxophone. An important innovator on his horn, Adderley also taught and lectured on jazz. Some of his finest performances appear on *Something Else Cannonball and Coltrane*, Miles Davis's *Kind of Blue*, and the popular Adderley quintet album *Mercy, Mercy, Mercy! Live at "the Club"* (1966).

Julian Adderley earned the nickname "Cannonball," a corruption of "cannibal," for his huge appetite. He died of a stroke while onstage in 1975.

Andre Willis

SEE ALSO
Blues, The; Coltrane, John William; Davis, Miles Dewey, III; Gospel Music; Parker, Charles Christopher ("Bird").

Africa

Addis Ababa, Ethiopia, the capital and largest city in ETHIOPIA.

Addis Ababa is Ethiopia's political, commercial, manufacturing, and cultural center. Located at the approximate geographical center of Ethiopia, it is the hub of the country's highway network and contains its international airport and the inland terminus of its only railroad. Its manufacturing sector produces consumer goods and building materials. In addition, the city houses Addis Ababa University and other cultural institutions. Addis Ababa is also the headquarters of the ORGANIZATION OF AFRICAN UNITY and the United Nations Economic Commission for Africa, both of which are located in Africa Hall.

While Emperor Menilek II was away on a military campaign in 1886, his wife, Empress Taitu, founded Addis Ababa, Amharic for "New Flower," on the site of hot springs. The center of the early city was the royal palace and the surrounding aristocratic residences and military encampments. A French firm completed a railroad linking the city to the Red Sea port of Djibouti in 1917. The rail link promoted trade and population growth. The government planted Australian acacia trees around the city as a source of firewood, and many remain today to provide shade and greenery along the streets of the city.

Between 1935 and 1941, officials of the Italian occupation oversaw a program of modernization, including paved roads, a modern water supply, a hydroelectric plant, and a central district, known as the Piazza, built using European-style architecture. The Italians relocated the Mercato, one of the largest open-air markets in Africa, outside the city center. The city has continued to grow rapidly in recent decades, as rural refugees have fled Ethiopia's war-ravaged countryside in search of jobs and security. In 1997 Addis Ababa was home to approximately 3.5 million residents.

Robert Fay

See Also
Djibouti, Djibouti.

Africa

Ade, King Sunny

(b. September 22, 1946, Ondo, Nigeria), popular Nigerian vocalist and guitarist, innovator of juju music.

Sunday Anthony Ishola Adeniyi Adegeye, known internationally to African music fans as King Sunny Ade, was raised in a home where Christian and Yoruba religious and cultural perspectives were thoroughly intermingled. Ade's father was a church organist. Ade attended missionary schools, then dropped out of college in the 1960s to pursue a career as a drummer in juju bands. Juju, a form of Nigerian pop music first developed by Yoruba musicians in the 1920s, was just beginning to gain an international audience. Ade's chief musical inspiration was I. K. Dairo, though Ade's later song lyrics drew more inspiration from his Christian education.

The early 1970s marked the birth of Ade's reputation as an African superstar with an international audience. Ade deviates from the Dairo legacy through a series of innovations. He expands the juju band lineup from a single electric guitarist to as many as six, played with at least that number of drummers, and introduces both the pedal steel guitar (previously identified with American country music) and the synthesizer. This augmented instrumentation creates a massive and complex soundscape, made all the more imposing through the recording studio technology that Ade utilizes. Studio effects include altering the sounds of his band's instruments through the intensive use of echo and reverb, a technique known as "dub" in Jamaican reggae. Another of Ade's innovations, one known only to concert-goers, has been his choreography dramatizing his soft vocals, perhaps a borrowing from American R&B and soul entertainers. As Ade's electric guitar playing is an extension of his singing, so are his stage dances.

Ade's recordings – over 110 currently – break new ground in two other arenas. Juju music lyrics before Ade relied almost entirely upon Yoruba folkloric sayings. Ade's first hit recording in Nigeria, by way of contrast, was a newsy account of soccer. Although vocals, guitar lines, and drum patterns are still based on traditional Yoruba speech, proverbs, and metaphors, Ade's song topics have included local and world politics, the dishonest nature of the music industry, and a Christian interpretation of the world's end. Ade's other innovation involves song length. He expands the length of songs to a half-hour or more, turning them into intricately layered drum and guitar jams.

However imposing his number of recordings, Ade gained renown with international music fans primarily through a single album, *Juju Music* (1982), released on the Island label. This was intended to become the first juju music recording to win the genre an international audience, and it did exactly that. Although some Nigerian music critics find the recording a dilution of Ade's talent, there is no question that fans of African music outside Africa find the recording to be a revelation. Heavily laced with studio dub effects and emotionally expressive pedal steel guitar colors, the studio recording replicates the feel of a live Nigerian party. No Ade recording since has achieved such international sales and acclaim, although Ade continues an active schedule of international touring and recording with an 18-piece band.

Norman Weinstein

See Also
Soul Music; Dub Poetry; Rhythm and Blues; Jamaica; Christianity: Missionaries in Africa.

Africa

Adja, also known as Aja, ethnic group of West Africa.

The Adja primarily inhabit southern Benin and Togo. They speak a Niger-Congo language. The western Adja belong to the Ewe cultural and linguistic group. Approximately 500,000 people identify themselves Adja Ewe. "Adja" is sometimes also used as an umbrella term to include all Ewe- and Fon-speaking peoples.

See Also
Languages, African: An Overview.

Africa

Afar, also known as Danakil, Denakil, and Adal, ethnic group of the Horn of Africa.

The Afar primarily inhabit a region known as the Afar Triangle, an area including parts of Ethiopia, Eritrea, and Djibouti. They speak an Afro-Asiatic language (*see* Languages, African: An Overview). Approximately 800,000 people identify themselves as Afar.

Africa

Afars and Issas, French Territory of the.

Former name of Djibouti.

North America

Affirmative Action, policies used in the United States to increase opportunities for minorities by favoring them in hiring and promotion, college admissions, and the awarding of government contracts.

Depending on the situation, "minorities" might include any underrepresented group, especially one defined by race, ethnicity, or gender. Generally, affirmative action has been undertaken by governments, businesses, or educational institutions to remedy the effects of past discrimination against a group, whether by a specific entity, such as a corporation, or by society as a whole.

Until the mid-1960s legal barriers prevented blacks and other racial minorities in the United States from entering many jobs and educational institutions. While women were rarely legally barred from jobs or education, many universities would not admit them and many employers would not hire them. The Civil Rights Act of 1964 prohibited discrimination in public accommodations and employment. A section of the act known as Title VII, which specifically banned discrimination in employment, laid the groundwork for the subsequent development of affirmative action. The Equal Employment Opportunity Commission (EEOC), created by the Civil Rights Act of 1964, and the Office of Federal Contract Compliance became important enforcement agencies for affirmative action.

The term *affirmative action* was first used by President Lyndon B. Johnson in a 1965 executive order. This order declared that federal contractors should "take affirmative action" to ensure that job applicants and employees "are treated without regard to their race, color, religion, sex, or national origin." While the original goal of the Civil Rights Movement had been "color-blind" laws, simply ending a long-standing policy of discrimination did not go far enough for many people. As President Johnson explained in a 1965 speech, "You do not take a person who for years has been hobbled by chains and… bring him up to the starting line of a race and then say, 'you are free to compete with all the others' and still justly believe that you have been completely fair."

President Richard Nixon was the first to implement federal policies designed to guarantee minority hiring. Responding to continuing racial inequalities in the work force, in 1969 the Nixon administration developed the Philadelphia Plan, requiring that contractors on federally assisted projects set specific goals for hiring minorities. Federal courts upheld this plan in 1970 and 1971.

Controversy

From its beginnings in the United States in the mid-1960s, affirmative action has been highly controversial. Critics charge that affirmative action policies, which give preferential treatment to people based on their membership in a group, violate the principle that all individuals are equal under the law. These critics argue that it is unfair to discriminate against members of one group today to compensate for discrimination against other groups in the past. They regard affirmative action as a form of reverse discrimination that unfairly prevents whites and men from being hired and promoted.

Advocates of affirmative action respond that discrimination is, by definition, unfair treatment of people because they belong to a certain group. Therefore, effective remedies must systematically aid groups that have suffered from discrimination. Supporters contend that affirmative action policies are the only way to ensure an integrated society in which all segments of the population have an equal opportunity to share in jobs, education, and other benefits. They argue that numerical goals for hiring, promotions, and college admissions are necessary to integrate fields traditionally closed to women and minorities because of discrimination.

Legislation and Supreme Court Rulings

The scope and limitations of affirmative action policy have been defined through a series of legislative initiatives and decisions by the Supreme Court of the United States. In *Griggs* v. *Duke Power* (1971) the Supreme Court held that Title VII bans "not only overt discrimination but also practices that are fair in form but discriminatory in operation." In order to avoid discrimination lawsuits under Title VII, public and private employers began to adopt hiring policies designed to recruit more minorities. The Equal Opportunity Act of 1972 expanded Title VII protections to educational institutions, leading to the extension of affirmative action to colleges and universities.

In later cases the Supreme Court upheld the constitutionality of affirmative action but placed some restrictions on its implementation. The Supreme Court's ruling in *Regents of the University of California* v. *Bakke* (1978) declared that it was unconstitutional for the medical school of the University of California at Davis to establish a rigid quota system by reserving a certain number of places in each class for minorities. However, the ruling upheld the right of schools to consider a variety of factors when evaluating applicants, including race, ethnicity, gender, and economic status. In *United Steelworkers* v. *Weber* (1979) the Court ruled that a short-term voluntary training program that gave preference to minorities was constitutional. The Court reasoned that a temporary program designed to remedy specific past discriminatory practices did not unduly restrict the advancement of whites. In *Fullilove* v. *Klutznick* (1980) the Supreme Court upheld a provision of the Public Works Employment Act of 1977, which provided a 10 percent "set-aside" for hiring minority contractors on federally funded public works projects. The majority of the justices believed that

Jesse Jackson, *left*, San Francisco supervisor Mabel Teng, and San Francisco mayor Willie Brown lead a march across the Golden Gate Bridge to protest California's Proposition 209, which voters approved in 1996 to end affirmative action. *Reuters/Lou Dematteis/Archive Photos*

the Congress of the United States has special powers to remedy past and ongoing discrimination in the awarding of federal contracts.

Conservative justices appointed to the Supreme Court by Republican presidents in the 1980s and 1990s attempted to limit the scope of affirmative action. Although sharply divided on the issue, the Court has struck down a number of affirmative action programs as unfair or too broad in their application. In *Wygant* v. *Jackson Board of Education* (1986) the Supreme Court struck down a plan to protect minority teachers from layoffs at the expense of white teachers with greater seniority. In *Richmond* v. *J. A. Croson Co.* (1989) the Court rejected a local set-aside program for minority contractors, ruling that local governments do not have the same power as Congress to enact such programs. The Supreme Court's ruling in *Ward's Cove Packing Company* v. *Antonio* (1989) revised the standards established by the 1971 *Griggs* decision. The *Ward's Cove* decision required that employees filing discrimination lawsuits demonstrate that specific hiring practices had led to racial disparities in the workplace. Even if this could be shown, these hiring practices would still be legal if they served "legitimate employment goals of the employer."

These rulings did not signal the end of affirmative action. In *Metro Broadcasting* v. *Federal Communications Commission* (1990) the Court upheld federal laws designed to increase the number of minority-owned radio and television stations. Meanwhile, Congress responded to a number of conservative rulings by the Supreme Court by passing the Civil Rights Act of 1991, which strengthened antidiscrimination laws and largely reversed the *Ward's Cove* decision.

Recent Developments

In the 1990s affirmative action became a highly charged legal and political issue. In *Adarand Constructors* v. *Peña* (1995) the Supreme Court examined a federal statute that reserved "not less than 10 percent" of funds provided for highway construction for small businesses owned by "socially and economically disadvantaged individuals." The Court's majority opinion, written by Sandra Day O'Connor, overturned the statute and declared that even federal affirmative action programs are constitutional only when they are "narrowly tailored" to serve a "compelling government interest." In April 1998 a federal appeals court eliminated a Federal Communications Commission program designed to increase opportunities for minorities in broadcasting.

Affirmative action has been controversial in local politics as well. Under pressure from Governor Pete Wilson, the regents of the University of California voted in 1995 to end all affirmative action in hiring and admissions for the entire state university system. In 1996 the Fifth U.S. Circuit Court barred the University of Texas Law School from "any consideration of race or ethnicity" in its admissions decisions. Since these rulings have been enacted, both institutions have seen a dramatic drop not only in the admissions of black and Hispanic students but also in the number of minority applicants.

In 1996 voters in California endorsed Proposition 209, called the Civil Rights Initiative by its supporters, ending all state-sponsored affirmative action programs. At that time, commentators predicted a wave of similar state rulings barring race and gender preferences. However, efforts failed in Ohio, Colorado, and Florida to collect signatures for a similar ballot initiative. Bills modeled on Proposition 209 have been introduced in 13 state legislatures and none has been successful. In November 1997 Houston, Texas, voters defeated a ballot measure that would have repealed the city's race- and gender-based hiring programs.

With legislatures, the public, and the courts divided over the issue, the status of affirmative action remains uncertain.

Paul Finkelman

Africa

Afonso I (also known as Afonso I and Alfonso I) (b. ?; d. 1543, São Salvador, present-day Democratic Republic of the Congo), king of the Kongo kingdom, the first Kongo king to embrace Catholicism and European trade relations.

Born Nzinga Mbemba, Afonso I ascended the throne in 1506 after the death of his father, Nzinga a Nkuwu. Unlike his father, who had rejected Catholicism and limited contact with the Portuguese explorers, Afonso immediately proclaimed Catholicism the state religion and established a strong trade alliance with the Portuguese Crown.

Eager to acquire European goods and to educate and Christianize his people, Afonso asked King Manuel of Portugal to send him priests, craftsmen, and military supplies. In return, Afonso supplied the monarch with ivory and slaves, two things for which the Portuguese seemed to have an unlimited appetite. This demand ultimately strained relations between the Portuguese and Kongo; Portuguese traders soon sidestepped Afonso's authority and acquired ivory and slaves from Kongo villagers. Realizing the threat to his power, Afonso asked Manuel to send a representative to enforce his kingdom's laws. In 1515 the representative arrived with a plan to recreate the kingdom on the Portuguese model, a service that the Portuguese would render in return for large amounts of slaves, ivory, and copper. Afonso rejected the offer.

In order to reestablish his authority, Afonso tried to limit slave trading in the Kongo kingdom. But he could do little to stop the Portuguese, who were now determined to procure not only slaves but also the kingdom's alleged mineral wealth. Tensions escalated as Afonso tried to control the traders and denied the existence of the mythical gold mines, but even after the Portuguese attempt to assassinate the Kongo king in 1540, he maintained relations with the Europeans in the hope that they would eventually send more missionaries. At the time of his death in 1545, however, no missionaries had arrived. Although some Kongolese later claimed that Afonso's contacts with the Portuguese ultimately led to the breakup of the kingdom, others, such as the famous prophetess Dona Beatrice, looked back at Afonso's reign as the golden age of the Kongo.

Latin America and the Caribbean

Afoxés/Blocos Afros, black Carnival organizations in Salvador, Bahia, Brazil that parade annually with costumes, music, and songs, using African and Afro-Brazilian themes; they also function as community service organizations.

During the 1960s and 1970s, influenced by the Civil Rights and Black Power movements in the United States and nationalist movements in Africa, Afro-Brazilians experienced a surge in black pride. This heightened black consciousness was also prompted by denouncements of racism and praises to "Mother Africa" heard in Jamaican reggae, increasingly popular in Brazil during the 1970s. As a result, black Brazilians, especially those in cities such as Rio de Janeiro, São Paulo, and Salvador, reaffirmed their connection with Africa and became more vocal about problems facing their community, particularly racial discrimination. This process was accelerated by the *abertura* (opening) – the gradual return to democratic rule that began in 1979 and loosened restrictions on free speech. In Salvador, this newfound black pride reinvigorated the old and waning *afoxés* and gave birth to a new type of black Carnival organization, the *bloco Afro*.

Afoxés emerged in the late nineteenth century. Historically, most afoxé members have been practitioners of Candomblé. For devotees of Candomblé, afoxés represent a way to incorporate the worship of the *orixás* into the festivities of Carnival. The prominent rhythm of the afoxés is called *ijexá*. It is a slow, hypnotic rhythm that is derived from the ceremonial music of Candomblé. Ijexá is played on three different-sized *atabaques* (long cylindrical drums) – *lê* (high), *rumpi* (middle), and the *rum* (low) – accompanied by *xequerês* (a hand-held gourd covered with a net of beads), *gonguês* (a double-pronged bell), and *ganzás* (a tubular metal shaker). During their Carnival procession, afoxé members perform the choreography of the orixás and sprinkle perfume over the crowd for purification. Filhos de Gandi (est. 1949) is the most famous afoxé in Salvador.

Afoxés are the predecessors of the blocos Afros, which appeared during the mid-1970s. In part, blocos Afros were a black response to the *trios elétricos*, predominantly white musical ensembles riding on large trucks equipped with numerous amplifiers, which had come to dominate the Carnival scene. Blocos Afros rival the trios elétricos with hundreds of drums and thousands of paraders. Their names often come from a West African language such as YORUBA. Some examples are OLODUM (after Olodumaré, the Yoruban deity), ILÊ AIYÊ (the house of life), and Aru Ketu (people of Ketu).

Compared to the religious-oriented afoxés, blocos Afros tend to explore a much broader range of themes. These themes are related to the historical and contemporary struggle for black liberation in Brazilian, African, Caribbean, and American (used here in the sense of the diaspora) contexts. For example, Ilê Aiyê's 1993 Carnival theme was "Black America – the African Dream" and featured floats in honor of Martin Luther King Jr., MALCOLM X, and the Black Panthers.

Blocos Afros also tend to use a wider array of instruments. In addition to the core percussion section of large *surdo* bass drums and smaller high-pitched *repique* drums, they may include horns, synthesizers, and even guitars. The principal rhythm played by blocos Afros is *samba-reggae*, pioneered by the famous bloco Afro Olodum. More upbeat than the ijexá rhythm, samba-reggae uses the repique drums to accent the offbeat.

In response to the growing popularity of the blocos Afros, some of the emergent afoxés in the late 1970s and early 1980s began to modify their Carnival presentations. Badauê (est. 1978) is considered to be the first modern afoxé because of its use of a sound truck, floats, women in leading roles, and original music compositions that spoke to contemporary Afro-Brazilian issues. Afoxés such as Badauê may still play the ijexá rhythm of the more traditional afoxés, yet they sometimes combine it with other musical genres or play other rhythms, such as *frevo*. By 1980 this type of experimentation led to a hybrid rhythm called *reggae-ijexá*. While their foundation is religious, modern afoxés do not limit themselves to Candomblé-related themes. In this sense, the more modern afoxés occupy a middle ground between the older, more traditional afoxés and the blocos Afros.

While previously many afoxés and blocos Afros were exclusively black, most have recently allowed a limited number of whites to join. Ara Ketu (est. 1980) claims to be the first bloco Afro to open itself to all classes, races, and religious affiliations. Olodum has also admitted some people of European descent. Ilê Aiyê, on the other hand, admits only blacks, which has led some critics to label the group racist. Ilê Aiyê has, however, established an alternative bloco that whites can join for a fee.

In contrast to afoxés, blocos Afros have reached out to the black community in Salvador by establishing schools and creating community uplift programs. Ilê Aiyê, for example, founded a public school called Mãe Hilda for underprivileged black children, who make up the majority of the 20 percent of Brazilian youth who cannot read or write. Beyond learning basic skills and subjects, the students learn about African and Afro-Brazilian history so that, in the words of the school's director, "they will value being black." The students are rewarded for good grades and attendance with music and dance classes. Almost all of the school's students graduate and go on to secondary school, as compared to the 40 percent

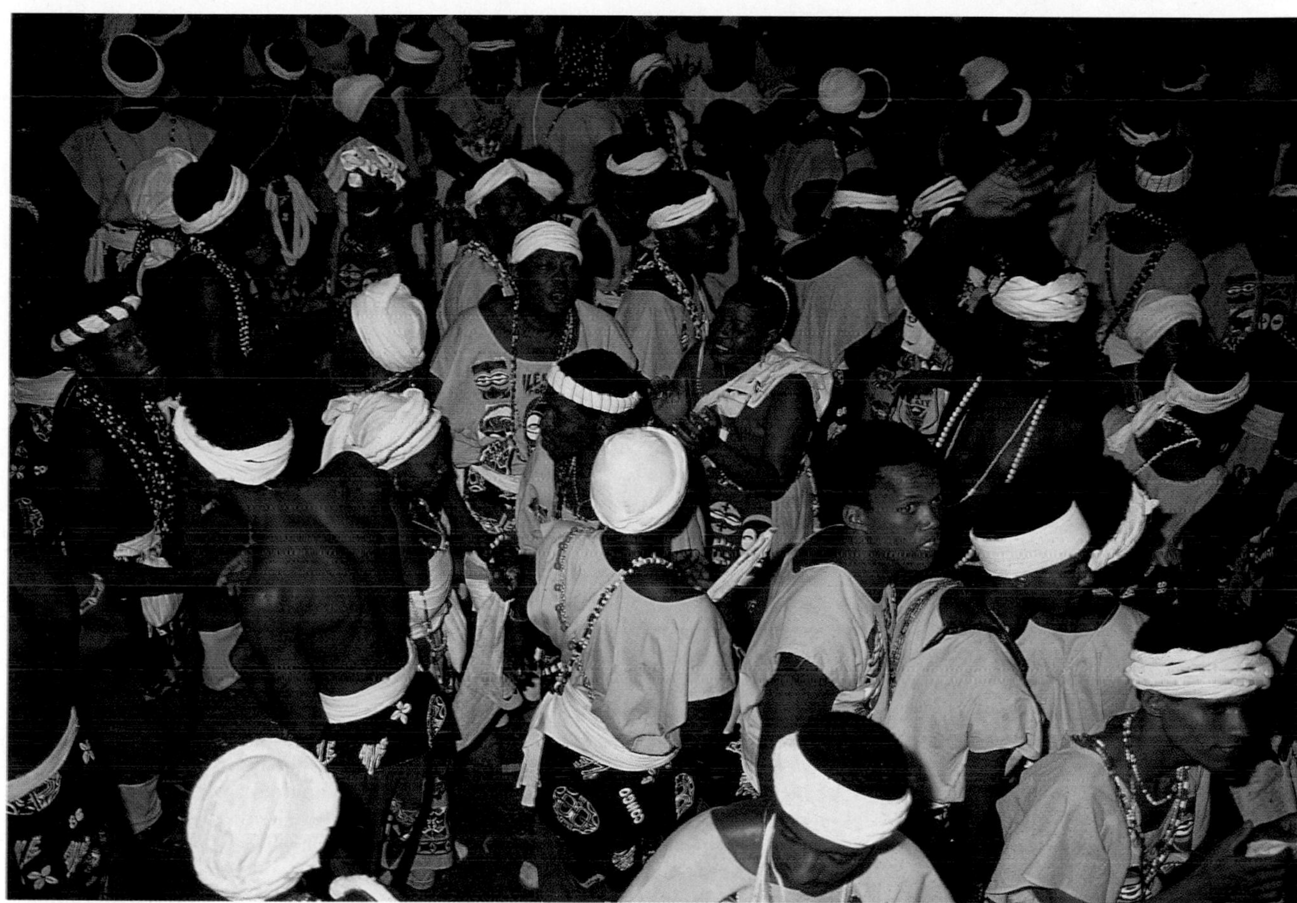

Since 1974 the *bloco Afro* Ilê Aiyê has been a distinguishing part of Salvador's annual Carnival celebration. Members parade through the streets in African inspired clothing playing drums of various sizes. *Vantoen Pereira, Jr./Contexto*

who do so nationally. Olodum has similar programs.

Thus, blocos Afros have had an immediate and positive impact on the blacks in Salvador both through their music and their community outreach programs. They have also influenced contemporary popular music in Bahia. As a result of the growing popularity of the afoxés and blocos Afros, words in African languages, especially Yoruban, and numerous references to Africa have become more common in Brazilian music. Today, afoxés and blocos Afros are the most distinguishing elements of Salvador's Carnival, annually involving over 100,000 people; they continue the African tradition of transmitting history and knowledge through performance and music.

Aaron Myers

See Also

Nationalism in Africa; Festivals in the United States; Black Panther Party; Civil Rights Movement; King, Martin Luther, Jr.; Filhos de Gandhi; Rio de Janeiro, Brazil; Jamaica; Salvador, Brazil.

African American Women's Club Movement. Please see Black Women's Club Movement

African American Women Writers. Please see Women Writers, Black, in the United States

North America

African Blood Brotherhood

(1919-1925), militant African American organization dedicated to self-defense.

Founded by West Indian radical Cyril Valentine Briggs in 1919 in New York, in response to the summer's increase in race riots and lynchings, the African Blood Brotherhood (ABB) promoted armed defense for blacks as a means of protecting and professing their rights. Claiming 50,000 members and 150 branches (numbers that cannot be substantiated due to the secretive nature of enlistment in the group), the ABB was aligned with the Communist Party of the U.S.A. (CPUSA) and remained underground for most of its existence.

Organized like a fraternal order on the model of the Irish Republican Brotherhood and committed to revolutionary tactics, the ABB was blamed by the mainstream press for a race riot in Tulsa in 1921. Although active throughout its existence, by the mid-1920s the ABB was dissolved by the CPUSA when the larger organization moved its activities above ground.

Alonford James Robinson, Jr.

See Also

Lynching; Tulsa Riot of 1921; Communist Party USA, African Americans and the.

Africa

African Cup of Nations,

a biennial tournament among African national football (soccer) teams.

The African Cup of Nations was founded to be not only a sporting event, but also a means of promoting African sovereignty and unity. Despite religious and linguistic differences among member nations and periods of political instability, both the number and quality of competitors in the African Cup have steadily increased since its founding over 40 years ago. Because of the skill they have exhibited at the tournaments, African soccer players are now highly sought by leagues around the world.

The African Cup of Nations began in February 1957 when representatives from Sudan, Egypt, Ethiopia, and South Africa met in the Sudanese capital of Khartoum to form the governing body of African football, the Confédération Africaine de Football (CAF), and to plan a continental international football tournament. Newly independent Sudan was picked to host the first tournament, for which only three teams competed – Sudan, Ethiopia, and the eventual winner, Egypt. By the time of its 21st meeting in Burkina Faso in 1998, the tournament featured 36 entrants, only 16 of which qualified for the tournament finals. By winning in 1998, Egypt tied Ghana for the most cup wins, with four. Winning the tournament is a source of national pride; some national leaders have been known to offer houses to their players in exchange for a victory.

The history of the African Cup of Nations has been marred by political conflict on several occasions. South Africa, which refused to allow its white players to play with its black players, was disqualified from the inaugural African Cup, leaving just three participants, Egypt, Ethiopia, and Sudan. While Ghana, Nigeria, and Uganda had achieved independence and had become CAF members by the time of the 1959 African Cup, they declined to participate, leaving the same three teams to compete in the second tournament. The African Cup slated for 1961 was delayed until 1962 because of general political instability in many newly independent nations.

More recently, criticism by South African president Nelson Mandela regarding Nigerian leader Gen. Sani Abacha led to Nigeria's withdrawal from the 1998 African Cup. Though Nigeria claimed it feared for its players' safety while traveling in a "hostile country," the CAF responded by banning the Nigerian national team from cup competition for two years.

Monetary problems have also plagued the cup's hosts and participants. Kenya once had to decline the opportunity to host the tournament for lack of funds. Burkina Faso, a country much poorer than Kenya, managed to find the funds to run the 1998 African Cup, but many people believed that money problems were behind the withdrawal of the national teams from Chad and the Comoros.

Nevertheless, the African Cup is still considered by its supporters – including Mandela – to be the continent's premier sporting event and a showcase for its increasingly talented football players. Numerous scouts from European professional leagues make a biennial pilgrimage to the tournament, hoping to discover the latest African talent.

Robert Fay

See Also

Khartoum, Sudan; Mandela, Nelson Rolihlahla.

Latin America and the Caribbean

African Ethnic Groups in Latin America and the Caribbean

Any discussion of African ethnic groups in the Americas must begin with certain caveats concerning the nature of African "ethnic groups" in the areas of West, west central, and southeastern Africa, from which African diasporic populations in the Americas and the Caribbean originated. First, scholars and other observers have rightly pointed out the cultural similarities and shared histories of large groups of people whom they have termed ethnic groups. However, among African people themselves, before the age of European colonialism in the nineteenth century, such labels affiliating large groups of people held little everyday meaning. That is to say, an Ibo woman in a village in West Africa did not necessarily attach great importance – or any importance at all – to belonging within a larger Ibo collective of tens of thousands of people.

Second, within all such ethnic groups, there exist literally countless local and regional subgroups with various cultural and historical distinctions of their own. Thus to identify someone as a Yoruba, for example, has only limited meaning, and by no means implies uniformity or even a shared sense of belonging among the hundreds of thousands of people who might have accurately shared that label in the eighteenth or nineteenth century.

Finally, one should not consider African ethnic groups as timeless or immutable identities, even when confronted with African cosmologies and foundation myths that attribute primordial or supernatural origins to a particular ethnicity. Like all social categorizations, African ethnic groups developed out of historical circumstances in which groups of people over long periods of time shared experiences out of which they created common or similar cultural

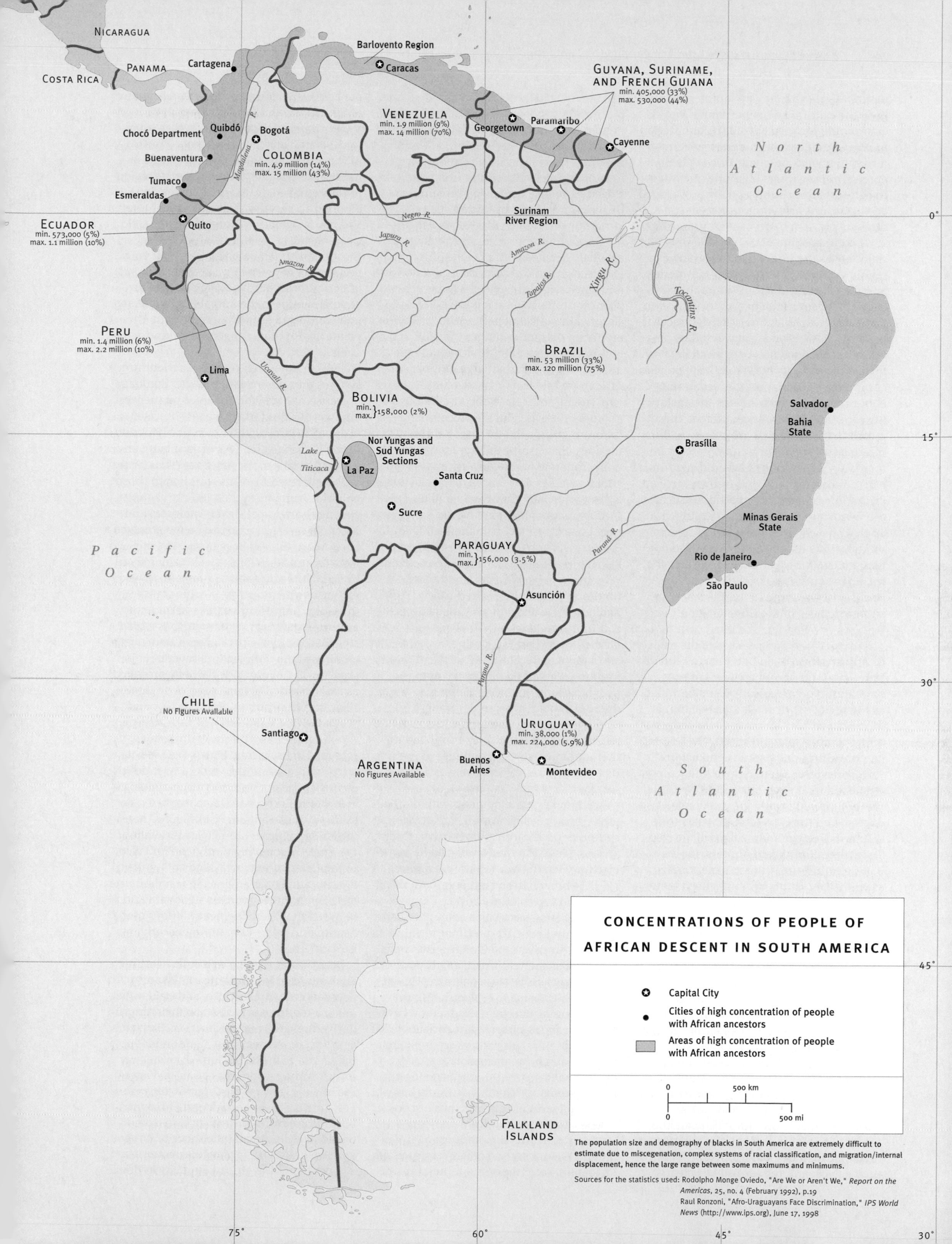

The population size and demography of blacks in South America are extremely difficult to estimate due to miscegenation, complex systems of racial classification, and migration/internal displacement, hence the large range between some maximums and minimums.

Sources for the statistics used: Rodolpho Monge Oviedo, "Are We or Aren't We," *Report on the Americas*, 25, no. 4 (February 1992), p.19
Raul Ronzoni, "Afro-Uruguayans Face Discrimination," *IPS World News* (http://www.ips.org), June 17, 1998

practices and shared ways of interpreting both the natural and supernatural worlds. One should above all avoid the temptation to conceptualize ethnic groups as exotic or regard them as a uniquely African phenomenon. Similar caveats about the meaning of cultural labels apply equally to Western ethnic groups and nationalities despite their greater familiarity to Western readers.

Of course, some concerns do apply uniquely to the understanding of African ethnic groups dispersed in Latin America and the Caribbean as a result of the slave trade. First, for much of their evidence on this subject, scholars must rely on records generated by European slave traders or other European actors who generally had neither the capacity nor the desire to provide complete or sophisticated information about the ethnic identities of the enslaved Africans whom they encountered. These records have serious shortcomings in terms of accuracy, specificity, and reliability. In many cases historians have information which indicates only that Africans arrived from some broad geographic locale such as the Windward Coast, a vast area stretching approximately from modern SENEGAL to modern LIBERIA; the Gold Coast, roughly modern GHANA; or ANGOLA, a large area that includes southern parts of the modern country of the same name as well as southern parts of the Congo region (*see* DEMOCRATIC REPUBLIC OF THE CONGO).

In other cases, Europeans used the names of African ports of embarkation as substitutes for ethnic identifications. For example, large numbers of Africans were identified as having come from Ouidah or Elmina, former slave ports in the modern countries of BENIN and Ghana, respectively. Scholars can obviously draw some conclusions through examination of the ethnic groups who lived near such ports. However, this method provides only imperfect analysis, as enslaved Africans often traveled long distances from interior regions to the coast. To further complicate matters, for the 350-year duration of the TRANSATLANTIC SLAVE TRADE, Europeans often used many different names to identify a single port, region, or cultural group. For example, enslaved Africans from the port of Ardra in the eighteenth-century kingdom of Dahomey appear in slave trade era records by at least half a dozen different names, such as Arada, Allada, Arara, Rara, and so forth.

With such confusion in the perceptions and descriptions of African ethnic groups during the years of transatlantic slave trading, one might be tempted to view as futile any effort to study the nature of ethnicity among populations of the African diaspora in Latin America and the Caribbean. However, people of both European and African descent in the Americas continued to use African ethnic terminology among themselves, and the terms have clearly had meaning in the lives of people up to the present day. Indeed, several scholars have argued that some of the very broad ethnic designations – such as YORUBA and KONGO – took on especially strong meaning in the Americas precisely because immigrant enslaved Africans faced displacement from their narrower bases of identity, such as their kin groups or home villages.

One cannot draw a comprehensive or minutely detailed portrait of the distribution of African ethnic groups in Latin America and the Caribbean. One can, however, point to some general patterns that had significant consequences in the formation of African diasporic cultures throughout the region. The transatlantic slave trade did indeed thrust together large numbers of African people from diverse ethnic groups who might never have encountered one another otherwise. But the process of mixing different groups did not occur entirely at random. Slave ships did not move haphazardly from one part of the African coast to another. Rather they tended to trade in those areas with which they were familiar. This usually meant areas where agents of their particular country – principally England, FRANCE, Holland, or PORTUGAL – had established forts or other trading contacts. These same traders likewise did not do business randomly with colonies in the New World. Traders of specific nations supplied specific colonies (not always their own) during different time periods. During the sixteenth and seventeenth centuries Dutch and British traders supplied the Spanish colonies of mainland Latin America. For example, during the mid-nineteenth century traders from Spain, the United States, Portugal, and the recently independent Brazil supplied the then booming sugar economies of both BRAZIL and CUBA (*see* SLAVERY IN LATIN AMERICA AND THE CARIBBEAN).

Additionally, developments within Africa itself – most notably wars – meant that during certain periods captives from some ethnic groups arrived in the New World in particularly large numbers. Knowledge of these kinds of broad trading patterns, combined with social and cultural evidence from New World societies, has yielded many persuasive conclusions about African ethnic identities in the Latin American and Caribbean diaspora. This kind of analysis is particularly powerful for these regions because unlike the United States, which came to replenish its enslaved population by natural reproduction, Latin American and Caribbean slave societies relied upon continuous African imports until their various dates of emancipation (*see* ABOLITION AND EMANCIPATION IN LATIN AMERICA AND THE CARIBBEAN). The following are some of the major ethnic distributions discerned.

One of the best-known demographic patterns concerns the presence of large numbers of ASANTE and other Akan-speaking Africans among the slave populations of the British Caribbean and the Dutch colony of SURINAME. Until the nineteenth century the Portuguese, Dutch, and English fought for hundreds of years over trade control of the so-called Gold Coast area around modern-day Ghana, the approximate region inhabited by Akan-Asante peoples. In the eighteenth century the British and Dutch had many significant footholds on the Gold Coast at the same time that their own Caribbean SUGAR colonies were enjoying their height of prosperity. This state of affairs, of course, was hardly coincidental. For centuries prior to the mid-1600s Europeans had conducted significant trade with Africa primarily for material goods or minerals such as gold.

However, once slave-based agricultural systems took off in the New World, European powers competed for footholds on the West and west Central African coast precisely in order to maximize their own participation in the lucrative business of supplying enslaved Africans to the Americas. Thus many of the enslaved Africans supplied to those colonies came from these ethnic groups. During the years of slavery, planters and other observers commented on the presence of people of this ethnicity in colonies such as JAMAICA and Suriname, usually calling them by variations of the name Coromantee, which in fact referred to a fort (Koromantin) on the Gold Coast. Europeans asserted, for example, that the Coromantee possessed so-called warlike temperaments, and in fact credited them with leading several major slave revolts, particularly those that resulted in the formation of large runaway (maroon) slave communities in both Jamaica and Suriname (*see* MAROONAGE IN THE AMERICAS).

Evidence of significant Akan-Asante presence in British and Dutch slave societies also emerges from the work of twentieth-century scholars on African cultural forms in formerly British and Dutch territories. For example, the Asante trickster figure Anansi the spider appears in folktales throughout the English-speaking Caribbean and also in the Dutch-speaking islands of ARUBA, Bonaire, and Curaçao. Similarly, many scholars have commented upon aesthetic similarities between the wood-carving traditions of the Asante and those of maroon descendants in Suriname.

Similar and equally well-known ethnic analyses exist for the African diasporic populations of Brazil, Cuba, and Haiti, where much attention has focused on their African-derived religions of CANDOMBLÉ, SANTERÍA, and VODOU, respectively. Candomblé in Brazil and Santería in Cuba draw heavily from Yoruba pantheons of spirits. Vodou, meanwhile, draws most significantly from FON spirits. These Yoruba and Fon contributions are by no means exclusive, and particularly in Brazil influences of Kongo and Angola groups are regularly present.

Understanding African ethnicity in Brazil

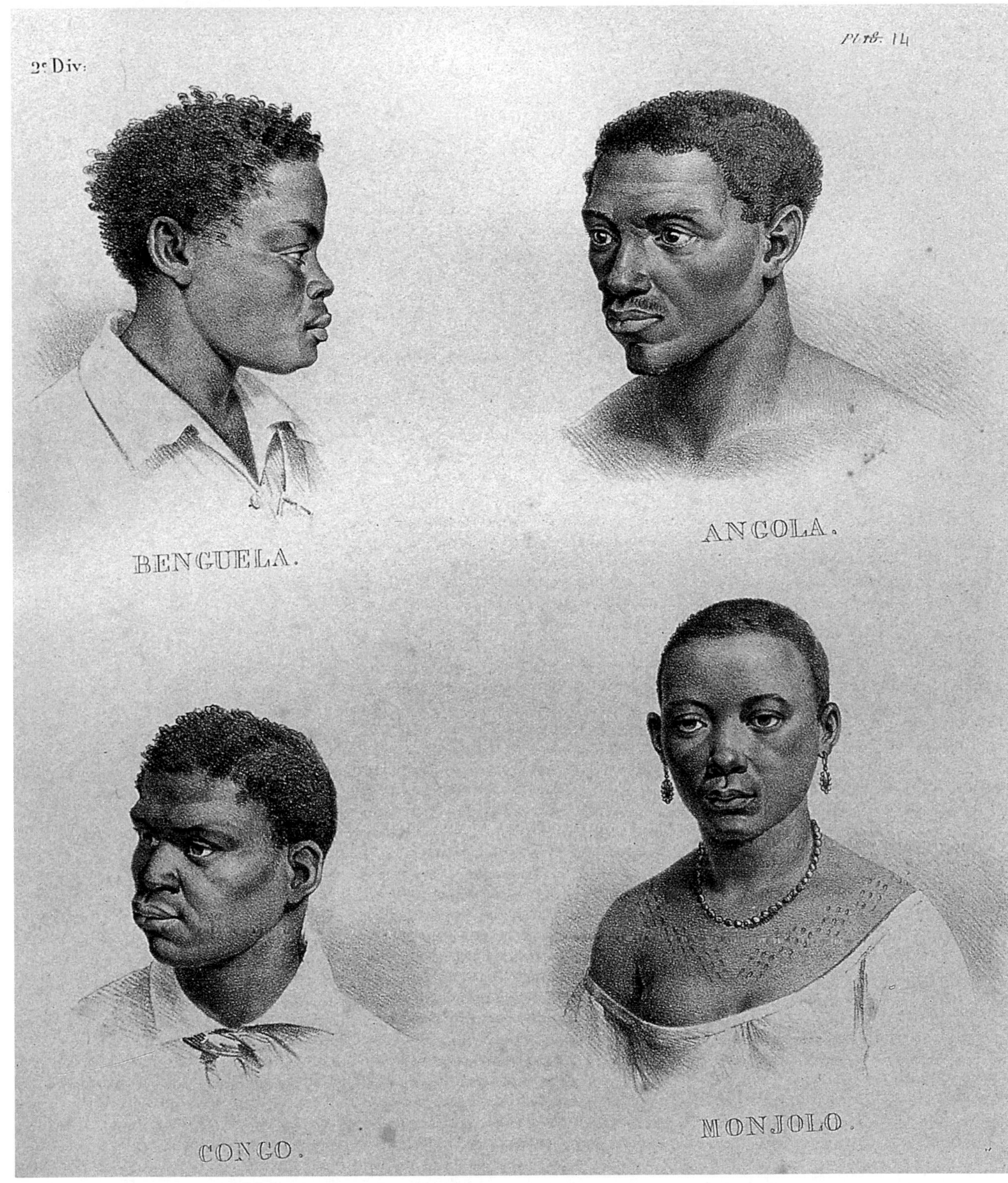

German artist Johann Moritz Rugendas depicted in his *Voyage pittoresque dans le Brésil* (1835) these individuals from four of the principal African "nations" transported to slavery in Brazil. *By permission of the Houghton Library, Harvard University*

is most fascinating and perhaps most complicated because, of all New World territories, Brazil had the largest and longest enduring slave trade. Portugal had long established footholds in west Central Africa, which explains the Kongo and Angola presence. It also had a significant and long-standing presence on the so-called Slave Coast around modern NIGERIA and Benin, regions inhabited by large numbers of Yoruba. Yoruba and Kongo peoples became especially important in the last half century of the transatlantic trade, during which Cuba and Brazil received enslaved Africans, between approximately 1820 and 1870. During this period particularly disruptive wars among both Kongo and Yoruba peoples pushed enormous numbers of captives into the transatlantic slave trade. Kongo and Yoruba peoples together accounted for roughly two-thirds of the mid-nineteenth-century trade, most of which went to Cuba and Brazil.

Cuba and Brazil highlight another important aspect of understanding African

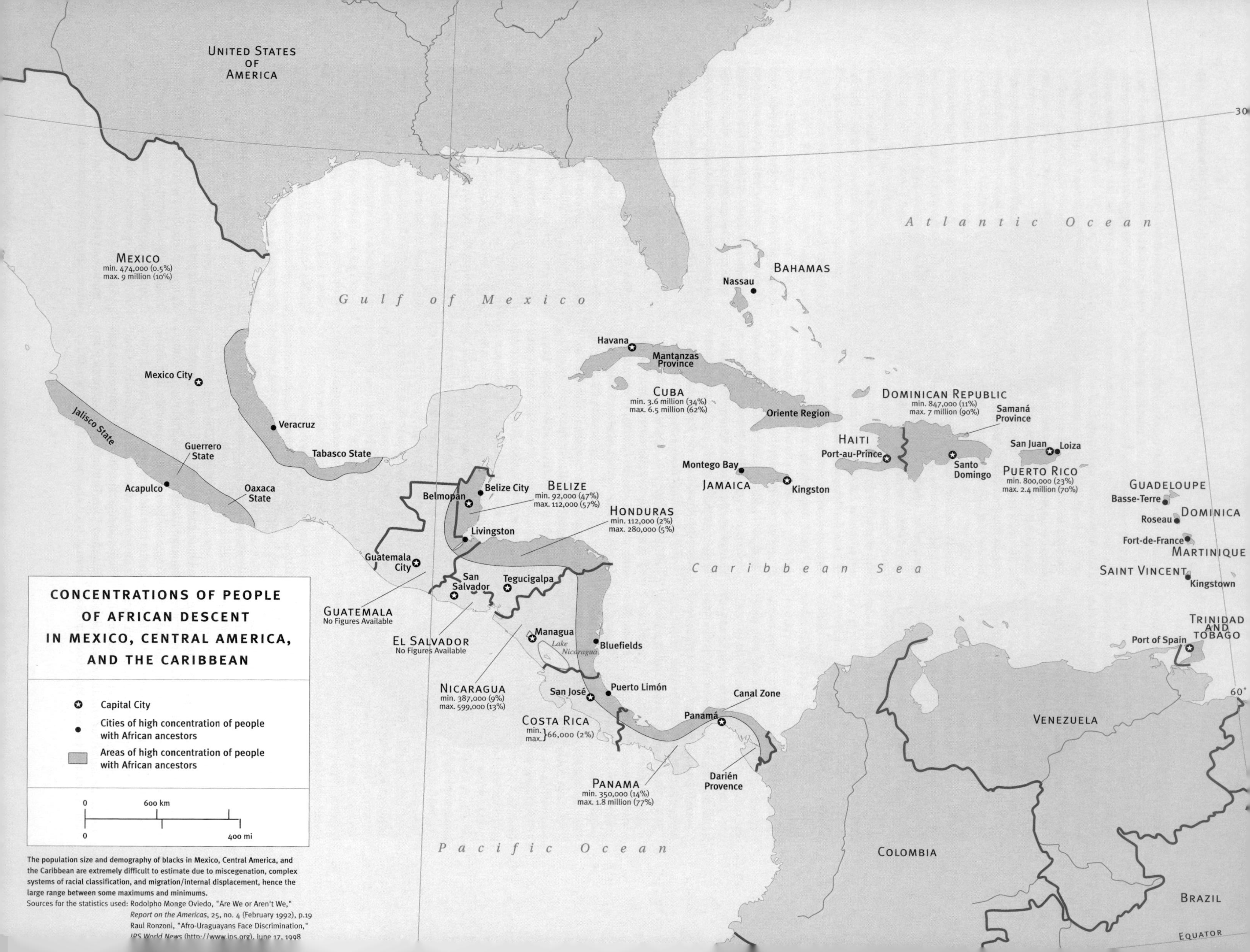
CONCENTRATIONS OF PEOPLE OF AFRICAN DESCENT IN MEXICO, CENTRAL AMERICA, AND THE CARIBBEAN
Capital City
Cities of high concentration of people with African ancestors
Areas of high concentration of people with African ancestors
0
600 km
0
400 mi
United States of America
Mexico
min. 474,000 (0.5%)
max. 9 million (10%)
Mexico City
Jalisco State
Guerrero State
Acapulco
Oaxaca State
Veracruz
Tabasco State
Gulf of Mexico
Atlantic Ocean
Bahamas
Nassau
Havana
Mantanzas Province
Cuba
min. 3.6 million (34%)
max. 6.5 million (62%)
Oriente Region
Dominican Republic
min. 847,000 (11%)
max. 7 million (90%)
Samaná Province
Haiti
Port-au-Prince
Santo Domingo
San Juan
Loiza
Puerto Rico
min. 800,000 (23%)
max. 2.4 million (70%)
Montego Bay
Jamaica
Kingston
Guadeloupe
Basse-Terre
Roseau
Dominica
Fort-de-France
Martinique
Saint Vincent
Kingstown
Trinidad and Tobago
Port of Spain
Belize
min. 92,000 (47%)
max. 112,000 (57%)
Belize City
Belmopan
Livingston
Honduras
min. 112,000 (2%)
max. 280,000 (5%)
Guatemala City
San Salvador
Tegucigalpa
Guatemala
No Figures Available
El Salvador
No Figures Available
Managua
Lake Nicaragua
Bluefields
Nicaragua
min. 387,000 (9%)
max. 599,000 (13%)
San José
Puerto Limón
Costa Rica
min. max. 66,000 (2%)
Canal Zone
Panamá
Darién Provence
Panama
min. 350,000 (14%)
max. 1.8 million (77%)
Caribbean Sea
Pacific Ocean
Venezuela
Colombia
Brazil
Equator
30°
60°
The population size and demography of blacks in Mexico, Central America, and the Caribbean are extremely difficult to estimate due to miscegenation, complex systems of racial classification, and migration/internal displacement, hence the large range between some maximums and minimums.
Sources for the statistics used: Rodolpho Monge Oviedo, "Are We or Aren't We," Report on the Americas, 25, no. 4 (February 1992), p.19
Raul Ronzoni, "Afro-Uraguayans Face Discrimination," IPS World News (http://www.ips.org), June 17, 1998

ethnicity in the diaspora. Just as Europeans in Africa developed various substitute or proxy terms for different African ethnicities, so too did both Africans and Europeans in the Americas. Thus in Brazil, the word "Nagô" – formerly a reference to one particular Yoruba subgroup – became the most common term for all people of reputed Yoruba ancestry. Likewise in Cuba the term "Lucumi" – derived from a Yoruba phrase which translates roughly as "my friend" – became a similar new label for all Yoruba people.

In the case of Haiti or Saint-Domingue, French slave traders supplying their own Caribbean colony had major African trading connections both on the Windward Coast around modern-day Senegal and on the Slave Coast, particularly with the eighteenth-century kingdom of Dahomey, or approximately modern Benin. The presence of Fon peoples in this latter region explains the presence of Fon peoples in Haiti, and the presence of Fon spirits in Haitian Vodou. Similarly, the presence of WOLOF peoples in the Senegal region explains their presence in Haiti, and also explains the presence of a hyena trickster figure from Wolof culture in Haitian folktales. The Haitian hyena bears the name Ti Bouki, combining a Haitian Creole term of affection, "Ti," meaning roughly "uncle," with a Wolof word for hyena.

The strong similarities (and in some cases, sameness) between the mostly Fon-derived spirits of Haitian Vodou and the mostly Yoruba-derived spirits of Brazilian Candomblé and Cuban Santería lead to an especially important insight. One might be tempted to explain such similarities merely by pointing to the arrival of Yoruba as well as Fon peoples in all three territories during the years of slavery. This would be an accurate observation. More important, however, in Africa itself the neighboring ethnic communities of Yoruba and Fon shared similar spirit pantheons and belief systems long before encountering one another in the transatlantic slave trade diaspora. Their experience provides a glaring illustration of the fallacy of thinking of African ethnic groups in rigid terms. Fon and Yoruba peoples in West Africa developed similar cosmologies over long, related historical experience. Their descendants in the New World began similar processes of cultural development, with the new complications of radical geographic displacement, encounters with numerous other African ethnic groups, and the shared experience of New World slavery. One can, with reasonable exactitude, point to larger numbers of Fon people in one colony and larger numbers of Yoruba in another. This step, however, constitutes only a beginning. The project of understanding African ethnic identities in Latin America and the Caribbean must entail a complex cultural and sociohistorical mapping process rather than an artificially simple exercise of demographic patterning.

Rosanne Adderley

SEE ALSO
Dahomey, Early Kingdom of; Yoruba; Haiti.

North America

African Free School, (1787-1834), a primary school in New York City that preceded the establishment of public education for African Americans.

The African Free School (AFS) was founded in 1787 in a private home in New York City by the Anglican and Quaker New York Manumission Society. The school was opened after the abolition of slavery in several Northern states. The AFS became an essential vehicle for the primary education of African Americans in New York City for almost 50 years.

Most African American schools were privately funded in the nineteenth century. Along with other charitable schools in New York, the AFS received assistance from the city beginning in 1796 and from both the city and county in 1813. In 1809 the AFS was the largest school in the city (141 students), by 1814 had educated over 2300 black students.

As in other schools, the curriculum of the AFS stressed reading, writing, and arithmetic, but it also provided specialized training in navigation to encourage seafaring as potential employment for blacks. In addition to teaching students basic skills, the black faculty of the AFS provided moral and religious instruction to its students, some of whom became prominent in the black community. Among this influential group were James McCune Smith, IRA ALDRIDGE, Peter Williams Jr., and ALEXANDER CRUMMELL.

In 1830 Samuel Cornish, editor of *Freedom's Journal*, doubled the school's enrollment, and two years later he opened four more schools to accommodate the growing student body. Despite financial strain, the AFS continued to provide first-rate primary education for black pupils until 1834 when the New York State Public School Society assumed control of it.

Alonford James Robinson, Jr.

SEE ALSO
Abolitionism in the United States; *Freedom's Journal*; Manumission Societies; New York, New York; Williams, Peter, Jr.

Africa

African Hunting Dog, small, wild dog found in Africa south and east of the Sahara; also known as the African wild dog or Cape hunting dog.

The African hunting dog belongs to the Canidae family of carnivores, and is classified as *Lycaon pictus*. The black-skinned, long-legged dog weighs up to 23 kg (about 50 lbs) and is covered with short, sparse fur in a wide range of black, yellow, and white patterns. The large ears are rounded, and each paw has only four toes. The animal lives and travels in packs numbering from a few to more than 50 individuals. Packs range up to 3900 sq km (about 1500 sq mi) in their search for food, but they greatly restrict their range when pups are young and unable to follow the pack. One of Africa's most successful hunters, with a kill rate of 70 percent (lions kill about 50 percent of their intended prey), the dogs hunt by pack, moving slowly after their prey and gradually increasing the pace as the victim moves away. Once the pack has selected a victim, it rarely wavers, sometimes following prey up to several kilometers. The dogs usually hunt small game, such as hares, rodents, ANTELOPE, and Thomson's gazelle, but a large pack can bring down large animals, such as lions.

The dogs exhibit complex social patterns. Unlike most social species, males make up the majority of a group. The dominant male and female usually are the only breeding pack members. After a gestation period of approximately 80 days, six to 16 young are born. The parents primarily care for the young, who learn much about hunting and game-trail patterns from the older dogs in the pack, although all members of the pack contribute to their upbringing. Any pack member (parents as well as male and female subadults) can feed young pups regurgitated meat after returning to the den from a hunt.

Although the animals are extremely adaptive to different habitats – they have been observed in deserts, high rainfall regions, open savanna, woodlands, and even on the snow caps of Mount Kilimanjaro – experts estimate that only 2000-3000 African hunting dogs exist in the wild. The dog's main threat has been its undeserved reputation as a bloodthirsty killer, the response to which has been attempted extermination. Hunters shot 3404 African hunting dogs in Zimbabwe between 1956 and 1975.

The dogs are threatened by human encroachment on their habitat, which has restricted their hunting grounds and isolated remaining packs from each other. Formerly, packs mixed considerably, which helped to increase genetic variation. Isolation has resulted in more interbreeding, a potential threat to genetic viability.

Despite laws against hunting, and programs aimed at reintroducing populations into games preserves, the African hunting dog is extinct in over 19 African countries. In nine additional countries, numbers are so low (below 100 individuals) that scientists do not consider those populations genetically viable.

Robert Fay

SEE ALSO
Kilimanjaro; Sahara Desert.

North America

African Meeting House, oldest extant African American church building in America.

Built by African Americans in 1806 on Joy Street in Boston, Massachusetts, the African Meeting House (AMH) served as the focal point for the political, social, religious, and educational activities of the black community throughout New England. The AMH also served as a place for speeches by such leading abolitionists as Frederick Douglass, William Lloyd Garrison, and Maria Stewart. Over the years, the AMH has had several names, including the First African Baptist Church, the Abolition Church, and the Black Faneuil Hall.

Using funds raised by the Free African Society, a black organization dedicated to providing financial assistance to the needy, the African Meeting House was erected first and foremost as a place of worship for blacks who were not accepted as full and equal members in Boston's white Baptist congregations. The building also contained an apartment for the minister and a schoolroom for black children in the basement.

By the late 1820s the church had 150 members. Rev. Thomas Paul, a black Baptist, led the church in its abolitionist activities. On January 6, 1832, the white abolitionist William Lloyd Garrison founded the New England Anti-Slavery Society in a meeting at the AMH. In 1964, under the leadership of Sue Bailey Thurman and Howard Thurman, the Museum of Afro-American History was founded in Boston. The museum succeeded in making the AMH a National Historic Landmark in 1974.

Alonford James Robinson, Jr.

See Also

Abolitionism in the United States.

North America

African Methodist Episcopal Church, independent African American Methodist organization dedicated to black self-improvement and Pan-Africanist ideals.

In November 1787 Richard Allen and a number of other black Methodists arrived at St. George's Methodist Episcopal Church in Philadelphia, Pennsylvania, to attend Sunday services. They were directed toward a newly built seating gallery and mistakenly sat in its "white" section. During a prayer, white ushers pulled the black worshipers to their feet and demanded that they sit in the "proper" section. Humiliated, Allen – a former slave from Delaware who had joined the Wesleyan movement because of its work against slavery and who eventually became a licensed Methodist preacher – and several others left the church at the prayer's end. "They were no more plagued with us in the church," he later said dryly.

The gap between black and white Methodists was also created, according to theologian Will B. Gravely, by "incidents of white pastors refusing to take black infants into their arms to christen them... of blacks having to wait until all whites were served the Lord's Supper before being admitted to the table... [and] of conflicts over access to burial grounds."

In response to such discrimination, African American Methodists in Baltimore, Maryland, and Philadelphia began holding separate prayer meetings as early as 1786, two years after the founding of American Methodism. With the support of other black Methodists Allen tried to buy a separate building for such meetings, but abandoned his plan in the face of white hostility. Recognizing the importance of black self-reliance, Allen, Absalom Jones, and others had formed the Free African Society – a benevolent organization whose commitment to abolition and the aiding of blacks in times of need became a model for other societies nationwide. But they were still dependent on dominant Methodist institutions.

By 1794 Philadelphia's black Methodists had raised enough money to build their own church, which a majority of the congregation voted to align with the Episcopalians rather than the Methodists. They named it the St. Thomas African Episcopal Church. Allen, however, believing that "no religious sect or denomination would suit the capacity of the colored people as well as the Methodists, for the plain and simple gospel suits best for any people," purchased that year a blacksmith shop with his own money and converted it into a storefront church. Methodist bishop Frances Asbury named it the Bethel African Methodist Episcopal (AME) Church.

By 1816 black Methodists, still facing persistent discrimination, had come to believe that separate churches were not enough. In April, 16 representatives from five congregations met at Bethel, Philadelphia, to discuss their legal independence from the main body of the Methodist church. Voting to organize under the name the African Methodist Episcopal Church, they then successfully sued for independence before the Supreme Court of Pennsylvania. Richard Allen became the first AME bishop after the elected bishop Daniel Coker declined the position.

The new AME Church was not greatly different from the original Methodist Church. Baptism and communion practices were much the same and hymn singing during worship remained prominent. But cultural practices distinct to African Americans assumed greater importance. AME services were "hot": spirituals and spontaneous praying and shouting distinguished them from the more tepid white Methodist services.

The AME Church was also distinguished by its commitment to political agitation and social activism in the United States and throughout the African diaspora. It followed the precedent set by the uplift projects of the Free African Society, and was influenced by the emergent philosophies of Black Nationalism and Pan-Africanism. In the nineteenth century, its political commitment and retention of vernacular cultural traditions fueled the church's expansion in both the United States and the rest of the world. In the South, its ranks were bolstered by evangelization among black soldiers during the Civil War. Later, AME clergy ran for and won numerous political offices in the Reconstruction South.

The church sent Scipio Bean as a missionary to Haiti in 1827, but it was not until later in the century that the evangelical efforts of AME clergy internationalized the church. British Methodist Episcopal (BME) congregations in Canada, Bermuda, and South America, originally part of the AME, rejoined the church in 1884. Bishop Henry McNeal Turner, a supporter of African American repatriation to Africa, established annual conferences in West Africa, oversaw the development of congregations in Cuba and Mexico, and accepted the membership of the Ethiopian Church of South Africa. Internally, there has been criticism of these internationalization efforts. Some members have argued that the AME should concentrate on improving the conditions of black people within the United States. Nevertheless, the church has congregations today in more than 20 African countries, as well as Jamaica, Guyana, Haiti, the Dominican Republic, Suriname, the Virgin Islands, the Windward Islands, Canada, and England.

During the twentieth century, the AME Church has been active in the Civil Rights Movement and in attending to the needs of African Americans dislocated in the northern exodus of the Great Migration. Through a pragmatic, activist gospel, the church addressed housing, welfare, and unionization issues for new immigrants to northern cities. At mid-century, AME pastors filed suits against public school segregation, which culminated in the *Brown* v. *Board of Education of Topeka, Kansas* (1954) decision. This interest in education dated back to 1863, when Bishop Daniel Alexander Payne encouraged the founding of the Wilberforce University, the first of numerous colleges founded by the AME, and the first black college to be founded by blacks.

In the 1960s AME-trained theologians James H. Cone and Cecil W. Cone pioneered the development of Black Theology. AME member Jacqueline Grant made significant contributions to feminist theology. Grant was one of many women to be involved in the church throughout its history. Although women were not ordained until 1960, unordained women had worked as church activists and evangelists since Richard Allen approved Jarena Lee to work as an adviser in 1819.

Peter Hudson

See Also

Abolitionism in the United States; *Brown v. Board of Education*; Civil War, American; Cone, James Hal; Great Migration, The; Payne, Daniel Alexander; Philadelphia, Pennsylvania; Turner, Henry McNeal; Dominican Republic; Virgin Islands (United States and British); Black Nationalism in the United States.

North America

African Methodist Episcopal Zion Church,

an American Methodist denomination known for its strong abolitionist roots and its evangelical work throughout the diaspora that emerged in reaction to the Methodists' segregationist policies.

Since Methodism first emerged in colonial America, it has consistently attracted African American adherents. According to religion scholar Alfred J. Raboteau, "the direct appeal, dramatic preaching, and plain doctrine of the Methodists, their conscious identification with the 'simpler sort,' and especially their antislavery beliefs" drew blacks to the church. Indeed, African Americans had been members of New York City's John Street Methodist Church since its founding in 1768. By 1793 black membership increased to 40 percent of John Street's congregation.

Still, African Americans within the John Street Church – and within American Methodism in general – were treated as second-class citizens. They were denied ordination, forced to sit in segregated pews, and limited in their access to the Methodist itinerant clergy and the Communion Table. Frustrated by this treatment two black John Street members, Peter Williams and William Miller, in 1796 founded the African Chapel. The chapel was later renamed the Zion Church and its members became known as the Zionites. In 1801, with the help of Rev. John McClaskey – a white minister who had opposed the independence efforts of Richard Allen's African Methodist Episcopal Church (AME) in Philadelphia, Pennsylvania – the Zion Church was incorporated as the African Methodist Episcopal Church of the City of New York. James Varick was its first pastor, later becoming the first black African Methodist Episcopal Zion (AMEZ) bishop.

Although the new congregation stipulated that its trustees would be limited to people of African descent, the church property was still controlled by the white Methodist authority. Conflicts within the white Methodist organization, however, soon changed this. When the Methodist church took legal action to centralize control of church properties in 1820, William Stillwell, the white pastor in charge of the African Methodist Church of the City of New York, resigned in protest.

Left without a pastor, the Zionites were free to pursue even greater autonomy. At their first annual conference on June 21, 1821, they voted to separate from the white-controlled Methodist Episcopal Church, which insisted on ultimate control of the church's leadership and property. They also decided against affiliating with the AME Church in Philadelphia. To distinguish between the two African Methodist Episcopal organizations, as well as to honor their original congregation, in 1848 the New York Methodists voted to add Zion to their name.

Before the American Civil War, the AMEZ Church enjoyed limited growth in the northeastern United States. Although membership was small, the church included such prominent abolitionists as Sojourner Truth, Frederick Douglass, Harriet Tubman, and Jermain Loguen. After the Civil War, the AMEZ Church competed with the AME Church and other independent black Methodist and Baptist organizations to recruit the millions of emancipated African American men and women. Between 1821 and 1900, membership increased from 1400 to 350,000. At the turn of the century, women began entering the AMEZ clergy. Although it was not until the 1980s that significant numbers of women were ordained, in the 1890s Mary Julia Small became the first female elder in any American Methodist denomination, and Julia Foote, an author, evangelist, and supporter of the Holiness Movement, was also ordained.

Like other independent African American denominations during the late nineteenth and early twentieth centuries, the AMEZ was influenced by the development of Black Nationalism and Pan-Africanism and their emphasis on black political and economic autonomy. Driven by an ideology that linked the spiritual and material uplift of peoples of African descent, the AMEZ embarked on evangelical missions to Nova Scotia, England, South America, the Caribbean, and Africa. Although the Bureau of Evangelism was founded in 1920 to coordinate missionary efforts, AMEZ evangelization beyond the United States began in the 1870s.

While the intentions of these missions may have been well-meaning, they were often rooted in a belief that Africans were pagans living in ignorance, in need of the liberating doctrines of Christianity. Nevertheless, there are currently more than 1.3 million members of the AMEZ Church in the United States and 100,000 overseas, primarily in Africa and the Caribbean.

Peter Hudson

See Also

Abolitionism in the United States; African Methodist Episcopal Church; Allen, Richard; Tubman, Harriet Ross; Black Nationalism in the United States.

Africa

African National Congress,

South African antiapartheid organization, now the country's leading political party.

In the history of South Africa, no group is more identified with the struggle against apartheid than the African National Congress (ANC). Many groups participated in the country's antiapartheid movement, but it was the ANC's Nelson Mandela who, through negotiations with the ruling National Party, finally brought about apartheid's demise. And in South Africa's first free elections in 1994, it was the ANC that won the majority of legislative seats and the presidency.

Since its founding in 1912 by middle-class, college-educated black South Africans, the ANC has changed with the times. Although the organization has undergone periods of considerable internal dissent, it has proven capable of compromise and growth, and has consistently embraced a vision of multiracial equality.

Colonial South Africa had been stratified by race ever since the establishment of the Dutch Cape Colony in 1652. After Great Britain's colonies and the Afrikaner republics were brought together in the Union of South Africa in 1910, however, the "color bar" was further institutionalized by a wide range of restrictive race-based policies. In response, a group of mostly foreign-educated Africans, including Pixley ka Izaka Seme, Sol Plaatje, and John Dube, formed the South African Native National Congress (renamed the African National Congress in 1923). They hoped to fight racist laws by building solidarity among South Africa's diverse and sometimes warring African societies. Seme's speech to the founding convention, in which he addressed "chiefs of royal blood and gentlemen of our race," suggested the aristocratic nature of the group's original leadership.

The ANC intially fought the color bar through legal and constitutional means – mostly petitions, speeches, and publicity drives. These efforts accomplished relatively little, but for several years the ANC membership resisted a more radical approach. In 1930 it did not re-elect its president, J. T. Gumnede, because he advocated cooperation with the South African Communist Party. More an intellectual movement than a political or popular force, the ANC was almost completely inactive for the next decade.

During the 1940s, a period of unprecedented trade union activism in rapidly industrializing South Africa, the ANC was revived. Its new president, Dr. Alfred Xuma, worked with a committee of distinguished colleagues to draft a set of demands, including full political rights for Africans. He also organized protests against the hated pass laws, but his overall caution disappointed a new generation of activists. In 1943 young

ANC members, including Nelson Mandela, Oliver Tambo, Walter Sisulu, and Anton Lembede, formed the ANC Youth League (ANC-YL). Their passion and political savvy drove the ANC for the next 50 years.

In 1949, a year after the newly elected National Party government began implementing its apartheid policies, the ANC-YL took over the ANC leadership. Influenced by the principles of nonviolent action and passive resistance pioneered by Indian nationalist leader Mohandas K. Gandhi, in 1952 the ANC drafted the "Defiance Campaign against Unjust Laws." The campaign's acts of civil disobedience did not result in any legislative reforms, but they did help swell the ANC membership from about 7000 to 100,000 members within a few months. In addition, the campaign ushered in a new era of cooperation with antiapartheid groups representing other racial constituencies, such as the Coloured People's Congress, the South African Indian Congress, and the white Congress of Democrats.

These groups, together with the ANC, formed the Congress Alliance, which convened a large "Congress of the People" that adopted the Freedom Charter on June 26, 1955. The charter called for multiracialism, economic equality, and full democratic rights for all South Africans, and was adopted by the ANC as its official program in 1956. Even as the ANC's membership and alliances grew, however, the organization faced new challenges. Increased harassment by the government resulted in treason charges against 156 members and helped provoke the defection of several ANC leaders, who subsequently founded the more militant Pan-Africanist Congress (PAC) in 1959.

The struggle against apartheid intensified after March 21, 1960, when police opened fire on a group of unarmed protesters at a PAC anti-pass demonstration in Sharpeville, a black township south of Johannesburg. Sixty-nine people were killed, shot in the back as they fled. Riots ensued, and the government banned both the PAC and the ANC. In May 1961, operating underground, Mandela and other ANC leaders concluded that the time had come to meet government violence with armed resistance. Mandela, Tambo, and longtime ANC associate and Communist Party leader Joe Slovo informed ANC president Albert Luthuli of their plan to form a separate paramilitary organization. Umkhonto we Sizwe, "the spear of the nation," was launched in December 1961.

Although Umkhonto primarily committed acts of sabotage against symbols of apartheid, such as the Bantu Administration Offices, and against South African industry and infrastructure, in 1962 its leaders began planning a guerrilla war, hoping to inspire a popular uprising that would topple the apartheid government. These plans were foiled when police raided Umkhonto's South African headquarters at Rivonia. Evidence found there was used to convict Mandela and others of treason. Mandela, already in prison for inciting strikes, was given a life sentence and sent to Robben Island. Slovo, out of the country at the time of the raid, went into exile.

With most of its leaders either exiled or imprisoned, in the 1960s the ANC entered a period of internal turmoil. Factions disputed the role of economic versus political liberation. Beginning in the 1970s, however, the ANC, now led by Oliver Tambo, was reenergized by both the student-led Black Consciousness movement and South Africa's increasingly militant labor unions. The Soweto uprising of June 1976, sparked by a police massacre of protesting students, helped unite disparate antiapartheid elements and heal the generational rifts that had dogged the ANC. At the same time, the defeat of white-ruled regimes in Angola and Mozambique brought new hope that the battle against apartheid could be won.

The government responded to the ANC's growing strength with harassment, detentions, torture, and assassination. But the crackdown only solidified the ANC's standing as the most viable alternative to apartheid rule. As international pressure grew in the 1980s, the South African government began secretly negotiating with Mandela and others. When F. W. De Klerk succeeded P. W. Botha as president in 1990, he freed Mandela from his 27-year imprisonment and lifted the ban on the ANC.

Three years later, talks among more than 20 organizations – but dominated by the ANC and the ruling National Party – led to a transitional government, new constitution, and plans for the country's first democratic election in April 1994. The electoral power of black South Africans, exercised for the first time, swept the ANC into a commanding legislative majority, and Nelson Mandela into the presidency.

Since becoming the nation's ruling party, the ANC has faced the challenge of retaining and broadening its appeal with considerable success. Under the leadership of Nelson Mandela, the ANC has crafted an image of pragmatism over militancy that attracts liberal capitalists and continues to be popular with labor, socialists, and women's groups. Even potentially damaging testimony about Umkhonto activities before the Truth and Reconciliation Commission, which investigated South Africa's apartheid-era crimes, did not significantly erode the ANC's popularity. In the 1999 elections Thabo Mbeki, who assumed ANC leadership in December 1997, was the ANC candidate and the winner.

Kate Tuttle

See Also

Dube, John Langalibalele; Johannesburg, South Africa; Mandela, Nelson Rolihlahla; Race: An Interpretation; Sharpeville, South Africa; Soweto, South Africa; Plaatje, Solomon Tshekisho; Black Consciousness in Africa; Botha, Pieter Willem; De Klerk, Frederik Willem.

Cross Cultural

African Orthodox Church,

an international religious body founded in the United States in 1921 by George Alexander McGuire as a religious arm of the Garvey Movement.

George Alexander McGuire (1866-1934) was an Antiguan ordained in the Episcopal Church in the United States who responded enthusiastically to the Black Nationalism of Marcus Garvey. McGuire envisioned an autonomous black church in the Episcopal tradition as a dimension of the Garvey Movement, much as the Anglican Church served as an international aspect of the British Empire. In 1921 he founded the African Orthodox Church (AOC) in New York. It attracted primarily West Indians sympathetic to Anglicanism, but also some Episcopalians and Roman Catholics who saw little future for blacks in American churches.

Garvey himself never joined the AOC, and in fact warned against both religious divisiveness and competing loyalties to his Universal Negro Improvement Association. McGuire spoke out strongly for a racially identified faith, creating nationalist liturgies and calling for the image of a black Christ. Unable to secure consecration to the bishopric from recognized authorities, he became an "Old Catholic" bishop. In this role, he turned from black militancy to defending the legitimacy of his ecclesiastical orders, which are generally considered valid but irregular. The AOC spread to Canada and the West Indies but began to wane following McGuire's death in 1934.

In 1927 McGuire consecrated Daniel William Alexander, a Coloured South African churchman who had left the Anglican Church to join an independent body. Alexander's impact throughout the continent was extraordinary. He ordained Africans in Kenya who became leaders of the Mau Mau movement; he built a thriving denomination in South Africa; and he was instrumental in establishing culturally nationalistic churches in Uganda, Zimbabwe, and Ghana. Despite the question of orders, the Greek Orthodox Church has identified with the African AOC, which claims hundreds of thousands of members. McGuire's dream of a racial church with its own bishops, a blend of Ethiopianism and Pan-Africanism, became a reality in ways he did not anticipate.

Richard Newman

See Also

Mau Mau Rebellion; Garvey, Marcus Mosiah; New York, New York.

Africa

African Religions: An Interpretation

African peoples have created hundreds of distinct religions that, despite centuries of contact with Islam and Christianity, remain important in Africa and to followers in the Americas and in Europe. Approximately half of Africa's current population identify themselves as Muslim. A smaller number identify themselves as Christian or as followers of indigenous African religions, and smaller groups (under 1 million each) identify themselves as Jewish or Hindu. This essay focuses on those religions created by African peoples south of the Sahara. While there is considerable diversity in African religions, this essay will emphasize their similarities.

Western Views of African Religions

Any discussion of African religions must consider how Western observers have described them. It is fair to say that African religions have been subjected to the most negative stereotyping of any religious tradition. Beginning in the sixteenth century Westerners attempted to justify the enslavement of African peoples by claiming that Africans lacked a sense of both history and religion. In the nineteenth century this alleged deficiency was used to justify the colonization of the African continent (*see* Colonial Rule). Europeans initially claimed that the slave trade and then colonization would bring Africans into history and, through missionary activity, into religion. Europeans assumed that "religion" happened in buildings and in reference to sacred scriptures. Their categories excluded Africa.

In the late nineteenth and twentieth centuries European administrators, travelers, missionaries, and anthropologists became increasingly aware that African cultures possessed something that corresponded to what Europeans regarded as "religion." Still, they could take comfort in the general absence of sacred written texts and what appeared to be a lack of focus on a supreme being, both of which stood in sharp contrast to the three monotheistic traditions of the West. African religions became relegated to a special category, labeled at various times as primitive, animist, fetishist, oral, traditional, and so on – essentially as living museums for a distant religious past. When missionaries sought to preach in African communities and to translate prayers and scriptures into African languages, they realized that most African religions have a term for the supreme being. Still, they insisted that this was not an active god, like that of Western religions. It was a god who began the act of creation and then stepped back. It became what they called a *deus otiotus*, a remote god, rarely invoked in African religions, which focused their attention on lesser spirits and ancestors and the rituals designed to supplicate them.

Western scholars have also characterized African societies as resistant to change. This view has even been accepted by some of the leading African scholars of religion, who argued that African religious change prior to colonial conquest was so slow as to be imperceptible. As John Mbiti has described it: "Human life is relatively stable and almost static. A rhythm of life is the norm and any radical change is either unknown, resented or so slow that it is hardly noticed."

While it is true that Africans do not have a word equivalent to the term *religion*, there are a number of terms in African languages that describe activities, practices, and a system of thought that corresponds with what most Westerners mean by religion. African religions are often closely associated with African peoples' concepts of ethnic identity, language, and culture. They are not limited to beliefs in supernatural beings or to ritual acts of worship, but govern all aspects of life, from farming to hunting, from travel to courtship. Like most religious systems, African religions focus on the eternal question of what it means to be human: What is the meaning of life, and what are the correct relations among humans, between humans and spiritual powers, and with the natural world? African religious systems seek to explain the persistence of evil and suffering, and they seek to portray the world as operating with some degree of order and predictability. They uphold certain types of ethical behavior, which their followers see as influencing their status in the afterlife. These ideas are expressed in sacred oral traditions, handed down from generation to generation through the performance of rituals and through intensive periods of education, including rites of passage.

Supreme Beings

While every African religious tradition has an idea of a supreme being who began the process of creating the universe and who created lesser spirits, they vary in how they worship these supreme beings and in how they perceive their involvement in people's daily lives. Most Western scholars see African supreme beings as somewhat remote, based on the relative lack of shrines devoted to such beings; on the fact that African ritual life typically focuses on lesser spirits; and also on the many African myths describing a supreme being who was active in the initial stages of world history, but then withdrew.

For example, the Dinka of Sudan describe a time when the supreme being hovered just over the earth and provided humans with a grain of millet a day, which was sufficient for all their food needs. According to one version of this myth, one day a woman decided to plant more than the one grain allotted to her. When she raised her hoe in the air to plant it, she poked the supreme being, Nhialic, in the eye. Nhialic withdrew into the sky, and death and hardship became forces in Dinka life. It withdrew because of a woman's greed, and because she invented agriculture. One could argue, however, that the supreme being was simply too close, and humans needed some distance to carve out an area for their own initiative. A proverb told by the Igbo of southeastern Nigeria also illustrates this sense of distance and the belief that the supreme being should be approached only on matters of major importance: "God is like a rich man. You approach him through his servants." According to this view, the supreme being remains in charge of major concerns, like rain, but is relatively uninvolved in the minor events of daily life.

These images of a remote supreme being, however, do not tell the whole story. Among

As part of a divination ritual, two Dogon men of Mali examine prints left in the sand by a jackal.
CORBIS/Charles & Josette Lenars

the Igbo and the SHONA of ZIMBABWE, the supreme being is said to speak to humans through spiritual mediums when they enter a state of possession. These mediums are usually women, though it is men who interpret the supreme being's message. Among the JOLA of SENEGAL, 50 men and women have claimed to be prophets of the supreme being; they spread their teachings throughout their communities on such topics as warfare between neighboring villages, the introduction of new forms of rain rituals, and the introduction of a day of rest for the land. Among the AKAN-speaking peoples of GHANA and CÔTE D'IVOIRE, daily rituals are performed to honor the supreme being, Nyame. In most African religions, the supreme being is both the bestower of life and the judge of human conduct after death. Thus, for the YORUBA of Nigeria and BENIN, OLORUN (also known as Olodumare) breathes life into a newborn and gives it a destiny. When a person dies, it is Olorun who decides whether that person will become an ancestor and will eventually be reborn, or whether it will go to the place of broken pots, where those who led destructive lives rest for all eternity. It is a hot place, heated not with fire but with West African peppers. These are not the actions of a remote deity, but one who plays a vital role in African views of the universe.

LESSER SPIRITS

As the Igbo proverb suggests, the supreme being has assistants who help humans to resolve particular concerns. Among the Yoruba these lesser spirits are known as *orishas*. There are said to be 401 *orishas*, each with a distinct character, special powers, and appropriate rituals. The most important of these include Obatalá, who was sent by Olorun to create the universe but got drunk on palm wine before he could finish creating human beings; Oduduwa, who completed Olorun's task, and descended to earth to become the first king (oni) of IFE; Changó, the god of thunder; Oshún, a goddess associated with the rivers and with feminine ideals of beauty; and Ifá, the god of divination. These deities are also worshiped in the African-inspired religious traditions of VODOU, SANTERÍA, and CANDOMBLÉ in the New World.

Among the peoples of East, Central, and southern Africa, many of the lesser spirits once lived as human beings, often as kings. This is especially true of the Buganda of UGANDA and the Shona. Elsewhere, the lesser spirits are associated with particular forces of nature or human activities. In other cases, the lesser spirits do not have such elaborate biographies, but are associated with particular forces of nature or with particular types of issues. Thus, among the DOGON of MALI, the Nommo are associated with the life-giving properties of water. The Jola have lesser spirits associated with rain, fishing, blacksmithing, community governance, women's fertility, and male initiation, among other things. It is not uncommon to have lesser spirits associated with rivers, the ocean, particular caves or springs, and other places in the natural world.

In all of these cases, however, the lesser spirits derive their powers from the supreme being. Much as Yoruba kings are said to reign rather than to rule (they delegate their authority to various types of councils and advisers at their courts), so Olorun delegates much of his power to the orishas. This is equally true of the NUER and Dinka of Sudan, who regard most of the spirits as creations of the supreme being. In some parts of Africa, these lesser spirits make their presence known through spirit possession. Among the FON of Benin and the Yoruba, the spirit enters into the body of the devotee and is said to ride him or her like a horse. The possessed person speaks and moves in the manner of the spirit and communicates its desires to an assembled congregation. In other areas of Africa, lesser spirits communicate through dreams and visions but do not possess their devotees. Spirits who fail to communicate with their devotees or to respond to their prayers are abandoned, and their cults forgotten.

In a separate but closely related category are the spirits of the ancestors. In some cases, such as the Yoruba and the Jola, this category is limited to the spirits of people who led benevolent lives. They continue to help the living by appearing to their descendants in dreams and visions and providing them with advice and warnings. In southern and Central Africa, the ancestors are not necessarily benevolent. They often seize

TOP: Many members of the Gurage ethnic group of southwestern Ethiopia continue to practice traditional religious rituals, such as the dance these men perform near the Omo River. *CORBIS/Jonathan Blair*
ABOVE: A Mungonge initiation ceremony in the Democratic Republic of the Congo. *CORBIS/Studio Patellani*

Men from the Dogon ethnic group perform a ritual dance in Mali. This ceremony, known as the Sigi, not only retells the Dogon's creation myth but also ensures the continued support of ancestors, seen as protectors in the Dogon cosmology. *CORBIS/Charles & Josette Lenars*

people with illnesses to punish them for neglecting ritual obligations or obligations to the extended family.

Finally, African religions recognize powers that circulate in the universe and originated from the supreme being. The Dogon, for example, worship a supreme being called Amma, whose vital force, which circulates throughout the universe, is known as *nyama*. For the Igbo the supreme being is known as Chiukwu or Chineke, and the life force that circulates in the world and governs people's destiny is known as *chi*.

African religions' lesser spirits show clearly how the religions themselves have changed. For example, in the Yoruba creation myth about Oduduwa's completing the making of human beings after Obatalá became drunk on palm wine, historians see a symbolic account of the rise of Ife and its god Oduduwa, who conquers or displaces the indigenous population who worshiped Obatalá. Both orishas find their way into a Yoruba pantheon, even though Obatalá's origins may not be Yoruba. With the growing importance of agriculture in Africa over the last 8000 years, one can trace the development of earth goddess cults like Ala among the Igbo and Asase Ya among the ASANTE. The increasing importance of cults associated with iron, like that of Ogun among the Yoruba, may well have reflected the growing importance of iron. Among the KONGO and related peoples of Central Africa and among the Jola of Senegal, new cults of lesser spirits emerged in relation to the development of the trans-atlantic slave trade. Similarly, the European conquest of Africa catalyzed a variety of new religious movements, which aimed to interpret the experience of conquest and offer a solution to the challenges of COLONIAL RULE. Like most religious systems, African religions have been influenced by disruptive events such as conquest, famines, droughts, and epidemics, all of which challenge their ability to explain the world and reassure adherents of its predictability and order.

African Religious Expression and Instruction

African religious thought is expressed in the recitation of myth and oral traditions, and through discussion both among elders and between generations. It is also expressed through ritual, which often involves making offerings in order to attract a spirit's power or win its benevolence. One reason that ritual offerings are seldom made to the supreme being, according to many traditions, is that the supreme being already owns everything in the world. Ritual offerings are often accompanied by libations of palm wine, millet beer, or water, which are seen to increase the power of the spoken word. Animal sacrifice may be used in order to release the life force of the animal, which combines with the force of the libation and of the spoken word, and thus further increases the ritual's power. Usually, the participants consume the meat of the sacrifice and the beverage of the libations, thereby binding the congregation, its priest, and the spirit being supplicated to work toward the fulfillment of their prayers.

Many African art forms are used primarily in religious ritual. In most of Africa, masks and costumes are used to impersonate the lesser spirits. Among the Yoruba, Igbo, Fon, and EWE of West Africa, wearing a mask and costume invites the presence of a god into one's body. Such impersonations and masking traditions are never done for the supreme being, whose physical image is also not represented in statuary. Lesser spirits are often represented in statues, but these are not idols; they are intended only to symbolize or attract the spirits portrayed.

Dance is also an important part of ritual activity. Dances invite the presence of particular spirits, depict the history of particular cults, or honor the dead. Among the !Kung of southern Africa, dance is a particularly important part of healing rituals. The dance itself heats up a spiritual power within the dancer, allowing him or her to enter an altered state of consciousness and heal other people. Dance is also a powerful means of prayer, both to the supreme being and to lesser spirits.

While several African countries, including Nigeria and the DEMOCRATIC REPUBLIC OF THE CONGO, have established formal schools devoted to African healing systems and African religions, most forms of religious instruction occur within the family. More formal occasions for religious instruction are often associated with rites of passage. Boys often endure an initiation school just before or after puberty, during which they are taught about their religious and social responsibilities as men. Such initiations into manhood may or may not be accompanied by circumcision, though usually

The religious traditions of Dahomey (present-day Benin) were among those that became the foundation of Vodou in Haiti. In this ceremony in Benin a practitioner dances as an Egungun, or resurrected ancestor. *CORBIS/Caroline Penn*

some sort of physical ordeal is involved. Girls are often initiated around the age of menarche. In some cases mothers instruct daughters in small groups; in other cases female initiation is more formal, with a period of ritual seclusion comparable to that of male initiation.

Religious Views of Evil and Suffering
African explanations of evil and suffering focus on disruptive spirits, often called tricksters, and on humans who use life-destroying powers for personal gain or to harm others. One trickster among the Yoruba is the messenger god Exú, who dislikes an overly orderly world. Exú often changes messages offered in prayer to see how events will unfold. While mistakenly identified as the Devil by early missionaries, Exú does not work to advance evil, but fully embraces life's incertitude, passion, and beauty. For the Dogon, the trickster – variously identified as the Pale Fox or as the Jackal – is a solitary figure who creates chaos in his efforts to find his natural companion. In both cases, these trickster gods make communication with the supreme being and with lesser spirits an uncertain enterprise, and help to explain the failure of even the most carefully prepared ritual.

But supernatural beings are not the only cause of suffering. Some humans are said to be able to separate their souls from their bodies and send them in the night to attack other people or other people's goods. These attacks are said to be the source of many illnesses, deaths, and other calamities. In troubled times, societies have often blamed witchcraft and undertaken elaborate witch-finding rituals. But identifying witches is particularly difficult because their activities, occurring entirely in the spiritual realm, are not visible to ordinary people. Sorcerers, on the other hand, use medicines and rituals for personal gain or to harm others. They also cause human suffering, but their use of material objects makes them more readily identifiable than witches. Witchcraft accusations greatly increased in number and frequency during the European conquest of Africa, as people searched for the spiritual significance of their loss of freedom.

While the overwhelming majority of North Africans as well as substantial minorities in East and West Africa now embrace Islam, African religions continue to command a substantial following in most of sub-Saharan Africa. Despite nearly a thousand years of contact with Islam and nearly five centuries of contact with Christianity, African religions continue to address the spiritual needs of their adherents. They have also influenced the practice of Islam and Christianity in Africa itself (*see* Christianity: Independent and Charismatic Churches in Africa). In addition, African religions are practiced by communities across the Americas, as well as in Europe. It appears that African religions will continue to play an important role in Africa and in the Western world in the twenty-first century.

Robert Baum

See Also

Art and Architecture, African; Buganda, Early Kingdom of; Christianity, African: An Overview; Dance in Sub-Saharan Africa; Ethnicity and Identity in Africa: An Interpretation; Jewish Communities in North Africa; Transatlantic Slave Trade; Shango; Anthropology in Africa; Christianity: Missionaries in Africa; Female Circumcision in Africa; Islam and Tradition: An Interpretation; Religions, African, in Latin America and the Caribbean.

Africa

African Socialism, a political philosophy popular in Africa from the 1950s through the 1970s, proposed as an African alternative to both Western capitalism and European and Chinese socialism.

During the independence era, some of Africa's most prominent statesmen supported a political philosophy that they labeled African socialism. Among the proponents of this philosophy were Léopold Senghor of Senegal, Sékou Touré of Guinea, Julius Nyerere of Tanzania, Kwame Nkrumah of Ghana, and Modibo Keita of Mali. These leaders advocated African socialism as a means of promoting rapid economic development in independent Africa without generating the inequality and injustice characteristic of Western capitalism.

Principles of African Socialism

The term *African socialism* actually encompassed a range of different views and approaches to economic and political development. African socialism lacked a basic theoretical work such as *Capital*, by Karl Marx, which helped to define European socialism. Instead, the principles of different forms of African socialism appeared in the writings and speeches of its proponents. Most forms of African socialism started from the idea that precolonial African lineages, or extended families – "traditionally" the basic social unit – were, in effect, socialist collectives within which all members shared the burdens of providing food, shelter, and clothing. African socialists argued that through cooperation and a commitment to the common good, precolonial African lineages prospered and all members' needs were met. African socialism aimed to revive these "traditions" in the modern context in order to achieve prosperity, secure economic independence from colonialist powers, and build a sense of nationhood (*see* Nationalism in Africa).

Proponents of African socialism claimed that it was distinct from European socialism because it derived from ancient, uniquely African traditions. In addition, some adherents of African socialism claimed that unlike European socialism, it was not a response to class conflict, which they felt was basically absent within modern African societies. Instead, African socialism was an attempt to modernize traditional collectivism and apply it to contemporary society. Nkrumah, the former president of Ghana, frequently argued that Africans possess an innate sense of inward dignity, integrity, and value. For Nkrumah, these attributes formed the basis for a cooperative society in which able-bodied members willingly provided for those who could not support themselves, including orphans, the elderly, and the sick. Many saw communal ownership of land in precolonial African societies as a further sign of traditional collectivism. As Kenyan Tom Mboya argued, "We are all sons and daughters of the soil."

African Socialism in Action

During the first three decades of African independence, from the mid-1950s through the mid-1980s, African leaders made several attempts to implement African socialism in the context of modern nation-states. These attempts shared a variety of common features. Usually governments nationalized the major industries and thereby assumed control over industrial production and management. African socialists also tried to improve the quality of life by improving access to education and health care. Frequently, socialist states provided incentives to students by guaranteeing them employment after graduation from high school or college, or both. In several cases, governments strove to increase agricultural production by introducing new farming methods and tools and by implementing national land reform policies. Governments hoped to use the profits from agriculture to invest in the industrial sector.

Nyerere initiated one of the best-known socialist experiments in Africa in Tanzania in 1967. The program, outlined in Nyerere's famous Arusha Declaration, attempted to develop the Tanzanian economy through rural land-reform and development projects, including the creation of collective farm villages, based on the principle of *ujamaa*, or familyhood. Nyerere believed that moving peasants from scattered homesteads (until then the prevailing settlement pattern in rural Tanzania) into larger villages would give the population better access to government services and agricultural assistance. At the same time, he believed, the collective organization would help prevent the emergence of poverty or profit-driven greed among individuals. Nyerere argued that these villages and farms would provide an engine for economic and social development and at the same time build a self-sufficient, debt-free, and classless society.

Between 1969 and 1980 the Tanzanian government forced millions of peasants to abandon their rural homesteads and move into ujamaa villages. By 1977 more than 80 percent of the population had been settled in the villages. Although the program did improve the quality of life in some ways – rural populations had better access to clean water, health care, and schools – it caused considerable human hardship and failed to increase agricultural productivity. In fact, agricultural production decreased during this period because the surrounding lands could not support the large numbers of farmers in the villages using intensive farming practices. By the late 1970s it was evident that ujamaa had failed, and Tanzania, like many other nations that experimented with socialist programs, had to borrow heavily from foreign lenders in order to support the failing economy.

Criticisms of African Socialism

African socialism has faced several major criticisms. Many observers have questioned the claim that socialism is an African tradition. Critics, including African scholars and some who sympathize with the goals of African socialism, have argued that few precolonial African societies really exhibited the broad-based equality and solidarity claimed by proponents of African socialism. Precolonial African societies, particularly those ruled by centralized states, critics argue, possessed both social classes and a concept of private property. According to critics' arguments, even those societies that once might have been more egalitarian had invariably lost these qualities as a result of colonialism and incorporation into global markets. Thus, virtually all modern African societies already incorporate class divisions and capitalist market values. Some critics have urged African leaders to define African socialism less as a return to doubtful traditions and more as a response to European capitalist imperialism. Finally, some critics argue that African socialism should embrace the influence of Marxist European socialism, particularly in its humanist and liberatory ideals.

The most biting critique of African socialism, however, stems from the fact that no African state has been able to develop a sustainable economy based on African socialist ideals. Although numerous countries, including Tanzania, Benin, Ethiopia, Mali, Ghana, Liberia, and Mauritania, experimented with socialism at some time between 1960 and 1990, none did so successfully. In almost every case, socialist regimes undermined their countries' economies and eventually had to borrow heavily from foreign lenders. Ultimately, these countries were forced to seek assistance from the International Monetary Fund, which granted loans on the condition that their governments undertake structural adjustment reforms – particularly economic liberalization and privatization of national industries – that reversed African socialist policies. By the mid-1980s almost every African state that had implemented a socialist program had to abandon it.

Elizabeth Heath

See Also

Nyerere, Julius Kambarage; Structural Adjustment in Africa.

Africa

Afrikaner, South African ethnic group whose 2.6 million members claim descent from seventeenth-century Dutch settlers.

In 1652 the Dutch East India Company established a colony on the Cape of Good Hope. The purpose of this settlement was to provision company ships sailing between Europe and Asia. The colony's first Dutch settlers built Cape Town and farmed in the surrounding countryside. Over the next few decades Germans and Huguenots arrived – many of them fleeing religious persecution in Europe – and intermarried with the Dutch settlers. The descendants of this population forged the Afrikaner ethnic identity, characterized by adherence to Calvinism and the Afrikaans language, which is closely related to Dutch.

From its early years the Cape Colony relied on slaves imported from India, Indonesia, Madagascar, and later, Mozambique. The colonialists imported slaves because they considered the Khoikhoi pastoralists an unsuitable labor force. Attempts of Afrikaner farmers (also known as Boers) to take over land occupied by the Khoikhoi led to two wars, in 1659-1660 and 1673-1677. The Boers' firepower, plus a smallpox epidemic in 1813, nearly eliminated the Khoikhoi population.

In 1806 the British took over the Cape Colony, principally to protect trade ships passing the Cape of Good Hope en route to India. The Afrikaners resented the imposition of the English language and culture, and above all the abolition of slavery in 1834. In response, in 1835 more than 12,000 Boers (approximately one-tenth of the colony's white population) began what Afrikaners later called their Great Trek out of the Cape Colony. As their ox-drawn wagons moved inland, the trekkers clashed with ZULU and NDEBELE groups. A trekker community would often draw its wagons into a circle, or laager; later the laager became a metaphor for the Afrikaners' sense of persecution and the need for community cohesion. After two years the Afrikaners had traveled beyond the Orange River, where they established the Orange Free State, also known as the South African Republic.

Afrikaner political independence did not last long. The 1867 discovery of diamonds near the Orange River sparked an expansionist drive by the British Cape Colony which, despite the claims made by the Orange Free State, annexed the diamond mine area in 1871, calling it Griqualand West. The British also took over the South African Republic in 1877, but then relinquished it after an Afrikaner rebellion in 1881, at which point the republic was renamed the Transvaal. The discovery of gold at Witwatersrand in 1886, however, ultimately brought an end to Transvaal independence. Thousands of immigrant prospectors, mainly British, began to arrive in search of fortune. Soon *Uitlanders*, or foreigners, outnumbered Afrikaners in the goldmining region. When the British sent troops to protect Uitlander interests in 1899, the Transvaal declared war. The so-called Anglo-Boer War lasted less than three years and was followed by the British takeover of the Afrikaner colonies. In 1910 these colonies joined the Cape Colony and Natal in the Union of South Africa.

During the early twentieth century, as South Africa underwent industrialization and urbanization, many rural Afrikaners migrated to cities such as Johannesburg and Pretoria, where they typically took low-paying manual labor or civil service jobs. In the countryside, Afrikaners whose farms depended on cheap African labor were among those who sought restrictions on Africans' access to land. This demand, coupled with demands for racial segregation in general, became part of the platform of the NATIONAL PARTY, formed in 1914. In 1948 the National Party came to power and instituted the APARTHEID policies that endured in South Africa until the 1990s. Since the election of Nelson Mandela and his AFRICAN NATIONAL CONGRESS-dominated government in 1994, however, the National Party has lost even many of its former white supporters, and relatively few civil service jobs now go to Afrikaners. Some Afrikaners (who altogether account for about 7 percent of the national population) have joined up with Afrikaner nationalist groups such as the Afrikaner Volksfront, who continue to call for a separate Afrikaner state. Most, however, are in the process of adjusting to life in a majority-controlled South Africa where they are frequently identified with the brutal oppression of the apartheid years.

Ari Nave

SEE ALSO

Cape Town, South Africa; Gold Trade; Johannesburg, South Africa; Mandela, Nelson Rolihlahla; Pretoria, South Africa; South Africa; Urbanism and Urbanization in Africa; Slavery in Africa.

Cross Cultural

Afro-Atlantic Culture: On the Live Dialogue Between Africa and the Americas

When Africa is regarded as part of the cultural and political history of the African diaspora, it is usually recognized only as an origin – as a "past" to the African American "present," as a source of "survival" in the Americas, as the "roots" of African American branches and leaves, or, at the most dialectical, as a concept conjured up by New World blacks as a trope of racial unity.

Yet, in truth, the cultures of both Africa and the Americas have shaped each other through a live dialogue that continued beyond the end of the slave trade. In ways easily documented since the eighteenth century, travel by free Africans and African Americans (by which I mean people of African descent throughout the Americas) has continued to shape political identities and cultural practices in North and South America, the Caribbean, and Africa.

Since the eighteenth century enslaved or free black seamen have woven a living web of links among the most diverse points around the Atlantic perimeter, transporting ideas, practices, and people between diaspora and homeland and among diaspora locales. Black seamen were especially cosmopolitan in their reflections on the black experience, which they freely spread among Providence, New York, Charleston, New Orleans, Havana, Kingston, Port-au-Prince, Rio de Janeiro, Cape Town, London (*see* LONDON, BLACKS IN: AN INTERPRETATION), and Lagos. So it is no accident that, for example, seamen wrote the first six autobiographies published in English by blacks, all before 1800, or that Denmark Vesey used his network of black sailors to spread his revolutionary doctrine. Massachusetts shipper PAUL CUFFE (1759-1817) is considered by some to be the father of Black Nationalism. Through such black mariners, the inhabitants of Lagos and Cape Town were never far removed from political and cultural developments surrounding Port-au-Prince and New York. Nor were the inhabitants of Rio and Havana out of touch with developments in Lagos or FREETOWN, SIERRA LEONE. Likewise, for centuries, free and slave sailors made Rio and Luanda into twin cities, while Cape Verdean seamen and ship owners linked networks of kin stretching from Rhode Island and Massachusetts to GUINEA-BISSAU, ANGOLA, and MOZAMBIQUE.

Hence, not all of these transatlantic links were transitory. Many were kin networks or the foundations of international political movements. For example, thousands of English-speaking blacks from JAMAICA, the United States, and CANADA immigrated to Freetown in the late eighteenth and nineteenth centuries, while thousands from the United States immigrated to LIBERIA in the nineteenth century. Similarly, from the eighteenth to the late nineteenth century, thousands of Spanish- or Portuguese-speaking blacks emigrated from CUBA and BRAZIL to the Gulf of Guinea coast, between Lagos, in what is now NIGERIA, and Accra, now in GHANA. Hence, from Monrovia to Lagos, returnees formed a culturally hybrid bourgeoisie with extensive international links, on the basis of which they also established the cultural and the ideological foundations of the nation-states that would later emerge in the coastal West Africa. Many Afro-Latin returnees continued to travel back and forth, trading in slaves and merchandise between the Guinea Coast and BAHIA, Brazil. They tended to maintain ties among relatives, former owners, slaves, and friends on multiple continents.

As we shall see, Afro-Latin travelers such as Martiniano do Bonfim of Bahia and Adechina of Cuba profoundly influenced African American religiosity through the ideas they bore among Afro-Atlantic locales. English-speaking travelers like the Saint Thomas-born EDWARD WILMOT BLYDEN revolutionized black political thought not only in the United States, the greater West Indies, and West Africa but, through Afro-Latin travelers in Lagos, in Bahia as well. Over the past century these religious and political streams have converged in various YORUBA-affiliated politico-religious movements in Nigeria, Brazil, Cuba, and the United States.

Missionaries, traveling entertainers, and audio recordings from the African diaspora have also profoundly reshaped African popular culture and politics. In turn, free Africans who immigrated to the Americas have deeply influenced African American popular cultures. Some Africans who had never been slaves chose freely to immigrate to Brazil or the Caribbean in the nineteenth century. Indeed, some of the founding figures in the Afro-Brazilian CANDOMBLÉ religion are said to have entered Brazil as free persons. King Christophe is said to have recruited 4000 free Dahomeans into the police force of postrevolutionary HAITI, and over 15,000 free West and Central Africans, some of them rescued from slave ships by the British Royal Navy, were settled in the British West Indies after abolition in 1834. One such immigrant built an important temple to the Dahomean Vodun gods on the Caribbean island of Trinidad. A few of these immigrants returned to Africa in the 1840s, sharing their berths with freed Afro-Cubans, also en route to the ancestral motherland. These examples illustrate the antiquity and scope of a live dialogue that continues to constitute both African homeland and diaspora well into the late twentieth century.

Neither then nor now has the effect of this dialogue always been harmony or unity. Returnees from the African diaspora regularly organized themselves socially, economically, and politically as a distinct class of intermediaries between Africans and Europeans. In the most shocking case, the Americo-Liberians set themselves up as a distinct and oppressive caste, unapologetically dominating the indigenous peoples of Liberia for a century and a half. More recently, African immigrants to the United States in the late twentieth century have in turn tended to emphasize their distinctness from native-born African Americans, lest they be treated like members of a native-born caste regularly despised by the dominant group in North American society. Yet African merchants and hairdressers in the United States often take advantage of their comparative advantage in the sale of the symbols of Afrocentric identity, such as African clothing and hairstyles. By contrast, the nineteenth-century Afro-Latin returnees to Lagos have been integrated seamlessly into Lagosian society, and, though contemporary African American residents of South Africa are sometimes resented as interlopers, black South African education, politics, and culture generally are deeply influenced by black North American models that were warmly embraced from the 1890s to the 1920s. Thus, this live dialogue between Africa and its American diaspora has produced, if not always harmony, then a set of new, hybrid discourses of self-expression and identity. This article will illustrate the historical and ongoing influence of this dialogue on the political identities, cultural practices, and, in particular, the religious practices of Africans and African Americans.

TRANSATLANTIC DIALOGUES OVER POLITICAL IDENTITY

Since the nineteenth century, free Africans and African Americans have interacted in ways less notable for their large numbers than for their momentous influence on subsequent political developments at and around the sites of that interaction. The circumstances and outcomes of such interactions have varied, but all have been affected by the emergence of the idea of territorial nationalism in eighteenth-century FRANCE and its subsequent imitation all over the globe. Moreover, this black transatlantic dialogue has occurred amid the specific rise of the British, French, and U.S. empires over their Portuguese and Spanish predecessors, as well as the peculiar racial ideas and policies propagated by GREAT BRITAIN, France, and the United States.

Twentieth-century Africa has hosted several major settler colonies, including ALGERIA, Kenya, and RHODESIA (present-day Zimbabwe). Better integrated into the Atlantic system, three other settler colonies have also lasted much longer. Sierra Leone, Liberia and SOUTH AFRICA border on the Atlantic Ocean and have maintained pivotal, long-running, and mutually transformative dialogues with the African diaspora. Sierra Leone and Liberia were first colonized by blacks from England and the United States seeking political independence from white oppression. These returnees thus founded novel Creole societies held together by alliance, patronage, oppression, commerce, and reciprocal emulation between Africans and Westernized black settlers. South Africa's geographical location and its mineral wealth made it a major commercial hub of the Atlantic world. Most of South Africa's colonial settlers were white, creating a racially hierarchical system akin to, and in dialogue with, such systems in the Americas. All three of these settler colonies have long hosted influential missionaries, scholars, sailors, diplomats, and entertainers from the diaspora, while sending students and other visitors in return. Moreover, Africa's Atlantic settler colonies have been an important theme in African Americans' reflections on their own political identity and potentials, just as the activities and writings of African Americans have powerfully shaped Liberian, Sierra Leonean, and South African politics.

Recently freed people from England, called the Black Poor, first colonized Sierra Leone in 1787 (*see* LONDON'S BLACK POOR AND THE SIERRA LEONE SETTLEMENT PLAN). These overseas returnees were joined by another sizable group of ex-captives. Over the next decade and a half, they were joined by 1190 Nova Scotian blacks (British Loyalists who had fled slavery in the rebellious 13 colonies) and 550 maroons, former fugitive slaves from Jamaica (*see* MAROONAGE IN THE AMERICAS). As part of Britain's efforts to enforce legislation against the slave trade, the Royal Navy rescued over 50,000 Africans from slave ships over the next seven decades and settled them in Freetown, the future capital of Sierra Leone. Many of these "recaptives" had come from the Oya kingdom in what is now Yorubaland, in Nigeria.

Though a British "divide-and-conquer" strategy initially sowed dissent among these groups, their intermarriage and embrace of missionary education welded them into a community known as Creole, or in their own hybrid language, Krio. Their equally hybrid culture reflected both their Western education and their diverse African and diasporic origins. Not only did the Krios provide the core of what would become the national language, culture, and early leadership of Sierra Leone, but they exported their Creole culture. Oya-born missionaries trained in Sierra Leone combined Oya language with a variety of neighboring dialects and coinages from the diaspora, giving form for the first time to the language that came to be called "standard Yoruba." They then reduced this composite to writing. While missionizing the hinterland of Lagos, they introduced "standard Yoruba" and its texts, including a translation of the Bible, which became foundations of an emergent Yoruba identity and of the fame that followed its progressive reinterpretation in the African-inspired religions of Brazil, Cuba, Trinidad, and the United States.

The "Yoruba" identity is not the only one in Africa that appears to have postdated the dispersion of its would-be bearers. Many of the black ethnic groups, or "nations," to which the slaves of Cuba, Brazil, Trinidad, and Haiti belonged – and the religious "nations," or denominations to which many of their descendants still belong – had not existed in ancient Africa but were instead labels imposed by slave traders. These ethnic labels reflected the captives' port of embarkation rather than any cultural, linguistic, or political category recognized by Africans in the homeland. However, labels like "Rada" in Haiti, "Lucumí" in Cuba, "Mina" in Louisiana, and "Jeje" in Brazil were often institutionalized through American religious brotherhoods, secret societies, denominations, work crews, and rebel armies.

Much as the "Yoruba" identity was confabulated by Western-educated exiles in Sierra Leone and only then introduced into the Lagos hinterland to refer collectively to a score of disparate linguistic and political units, the "Jeje" identity was constructed and labeled as such in Brazil, and only then introduced as an identity into the African ancestral home of its Brazilian bearers. Even though the speakers of the sometimes mutually comprehensible EWE, Gen, Aja, and Fon language varieties (*see* LANGUAGES, AFRICAN: AN OVERVIEW) were exported to Brazil in the greatest numbers before 1800, I have found no written mention of the name "Jeje" in the Gulf of Guinea region before 1864, after the effective end of the slave trade. On the other hand, the term Jeje appears in Brazilian documents as early as 1739, 125 years earlier than its first appearance in Africa. In Brazil, the origin of this ethnonym is subject to much speculation, but the leading lexicographer of Fon, Segurola, denies that the term originates in that language, even though the FON people were once among its primary referents. The term may have had some prior referent in West Africa now lost to memory, but it could not have referred to the entire Ewe-Gen-Aja-Fon dialect cluster and then gone unnoticed by the many European and American travelers who published accounts of their visits to the Gulf of Benin between the seventeenth and nineteenth centuries. Thus, it appears that Brazil, its slave-traders, and its former slaves are the most likely source of the Jeje ethnonym in Africa.

However obscure the origins of this term, its use in Africa after 1864 reveals much about the transatlantic history of African ethnicity and nationality. From the 1830s onward, hundreds, perhaps thousands, of Brazilian Jejes returned to the Gulf of Benin – to Lagos, Porto-Novo, Ouidah, Grand-Popo, Petit-Popo, Agoué, and Porto-Seguro (this last having been founded by the returnees themselves). It was evidently these travelers who applied the name Jeje to all the Africans whom they considered their compatriots, despite the fact that these "compatriots" had probably never previously identified themselves in these terms.

We know of these developments through the writings of the priests of the French Society of African Missions who, as guests of the prosperous Afro-Brazilian returnees, missionized this region in the late 1800s. These priests were the first to designate Ewe, Gen, Aja, and Fon as the same language, and the first Europeans to call this language and all its speakers "Jeje." Though after 1889 this ethnic label described only the speakers of these language varieties in the city of Porto-Novo, the term continued to be used until the 1930s to distinguish the alleged "natives" of colonial southern Dahomey (now Benin Republic) from the Yoruba, whose British commercial and cultural connections made them threatening to French colonialists. By choosing to ignore the reality that Yoruba ancestors had lived in this land for centuries, the French thereby implied that the British-influenced Yoruba were foreigners to French territory. Thus, the British not only prepared the ground on which "Yoruba" became a major African ethnic identity but the French, in an effort to naturalize and secure their domain against British influence, subsidized the "Jeje" identity introduced by the Afro-Brazilian returnees. Eventually, the "Jeje" identity in West Africa gave way to categories such as "Fon" and "Goun." What remains clear is the powerful role of the European-dominated Atlantic political economy in creating the conditions of the black Atlantic dialogue over collective identity.

The changing political conditions of Anglo-America propelled North American and Anglophone West Indian blacks headlong into this transatlantic dialogue as well. Since the time of the American Revolution, black North American leaders reflected on blacks' exclusion from the rights of citizenship in the new republic. The many who had lost hope in the United States dreamed of immigration to Africa, Haiti, Brazil, or elsewhere as places to form a community and live out their collective black identity as a territorial nation. The West African nation of Liberia resulted from the most successful emigrationist project in U.S. history. Though advocacy by the white-dominated AMERICAN COLONIZATION SOCIETY put off many potential emigrants, about 16,000 U.S. blacks and 400 Afro-West Indians settled in Liberia between 1822 and 1900. By 1846 the Americo-Liberian repatriates had achieved their own political and commercial independence from the American Colonization Society, well in advance of Sierra Leone's liberation from the British colonizers in 1961. Much like the rulers of Haiti, the Americo-Liberians barred whites from citizenship and land ownership in their black republic.

In the nineteenth and early twentieth centuries, some of the most quoted figures in black North American debates over collective identity and political strategy – such as Martin R. Delany, Edward Wilmot Blyden, and W. E. B. Du Bois – were equally often quoted in Liberian, Sierra Leonean, and Lagosian debates over the proper shape of their own emergent national societies. Many returnees to Liberia had envisioned themselves not only achieving personal freedom but enlightening a benighted, heathen Africa. However, in their ambivalent regard for Africa, they often behaved oppressively toward indigenous Liberians. There are doubts about accusations that the Americo-Liberians enslaved their African neighbors, but, if they are true, Americo-Liberians would join the company of the many Sierra Leonean settlers and Afro-Latin returnees on the Gulf of Benin coast who did undoubtedly capture and sell African people during the decades after the British had outlawed the trade. Many of these repatriates from the African diaspora indeed modeled their lifestyles on those of their Euro-American former masters. In turn, the Creole cultures they produced, including the forms of transatlantic racial identity that they propagated, became objects of both resentment and imitation by their indigenous neighbors around the Gulf of Guinea.

It is well known that important leaders of West African independence movements in the 1950s and 1960s, such as Nnamdi Azikiwe of Nigeria and KWAME NKRUMAH of Ghana, had reversed the direction of African American "return" and gone to the United States for training in historically black colleges. Nkrumah, for example, studied at the historically black Lincoln University during the 1930s and joined the Beta Sigma fraternity, the same fraternity to which Alain Locke, Booker T. Washington, JAMES WELDON JOHNSON, GEORGE WASHINGTON CARVER, and future president William Tubman of Liberia belonged. Nkrumah also studied the writings of Jamaican-American emigrationist and Pan-Africanist Marcus Garvey. Subsequently, Nkrumah became not only the first president of Ghana but the most committedly Pan-Africanist head of state in Africa's history (*see* PAN-AFRICANISM). It is difficult to avoid the conclusion that these leaders' experience of JIM CROW and of black North Americans' ideology of racial unity and struggle helped to shape their later resolve to struggle against British colonialism.

What is less often recognized is the age of African Americans' dialogue with black South Africa's political leadership and the centrality of its enduring effects. For example, in the early 1890s a small group of African Americans and Africans in Port Elizabeth, South Africa, established an interregional economic union, the goal of which was job creation, management training for black-owned businesses, and the promotion of black unity and racial uplift. They hoped to use a capitalist economic base to gain political power locally. John Dube, president of the South African National Congress, the forerunner of Nelson Mandela's African National Congress (ANC), had been influenced by Booker T. Washington and had even visited Tuskegee Institute. Therefore, during the first third of the twentieth century, he was known as the "Booker Washington of South Africa." At the turn of the century, as black South African churches sought independence from white missionary denominations, they hosted a visit from HENRY MCNEAL TURNER, bishop of the black North American AFRICAN METHODIST EPISCOPAL CHURCH (AME). His visit also inspired future ANC president James Thaele to seek training at Wilberforce, another historically black college in the United States. Thaele was in turn responsible for introducing Garveyism to the ANC. Both Garveyism and the ideas of W. E. B. Du Bois were well known in South Africa from the 1920s to the 1940s. Another ANC president, Alfred Bitini Xuma, who served until 1949, visited the United States, married a black North American, and endorsed the NATIONAL ASSOCIATION FOR THE ADVANCEMENT OF COLORED PEOPLE (NAACP) as a model for the ANC. In the 1970s, the Black Consciousness movement, best known for the martyrdom of its spokesman STEPHEN BIKO, embraced the influence of Eldridge Cleaver's *Soul on Ice* (1967), Alex Haley's *The Autobiography of Malcolm X* (1965), Charles Hamilton and STOKELY CARMICHAEL'S *Black Power* (1967), the theology of James Cone, and FRANTZ FANON'S *The Wretched of the Earth* (1963). Hence, both its place in the Atlantic economy and its political similarities with the American settler colonies have placed South Africa in sustained dialogue with the black Americas.

In the 1980s, as black North Americans seemed more besieged and less unified than they had in decades, one issue that appeared to invite no controversy in the divided black political class was the "Free South Africa" movement. The persistence and success of Randall Robinson's TRANSAFRICA lobby is a rare example of African American success at shaping U.S. foreign policy in the interest of black people globally. In the democratic South Africa of the 1990s, African American immigrants and businesspeople have perhaps sentimentalized this history and over-estimated the degree to which black South Africans would welcome their arrival. Whereas many African Americans expect to be "welcomed home," many South Africans regard them as interlopers, too anxious to claim the credit for South Africa's democratization and too ready to take corporate jobs that black South Africans feel rightfully belong to them. In South Africa, as in many parts of the continent, African American visitors, with their varied complexions and Western ways, are hardly recognized as "black," much less as long-lost African brothers and sisters. Such identifications have been negotiated and renegotiated over time according to the circumstances – no less in the Americas – (where, for example, light-skinned people have not everywhere and always been considered "black") – than in Africa. And the dialogue continues.

Indeed, African immigrants often report that they had not identified themselves as "black" until they emigrated to the United States or Britain. Few Africans in Africa outside Kenya, ZIMBABWE, and South Africa had had any reason to do so. In the daily lives of most Africans, blackness constitutes neither a barrier nor an admission pass to any particular social rights, and it signals no salient political or cultural identity. In the Americas, the social stigma attached to blackness and the rebellious conduct identified with black Americans in fact became a reason for African immigrants to demand recognition as being different from the native blacks. In the United States, this option has become more possible for all immigrant groups of African descent since the official desegregation of housing and educational institutions in the 1950s, 1960s, and 1970s.

On the other hand, some African immigrants to the United States have been leaders in the articulation of Pan-African identity. First, though they are often ill informed about Africans of other national origins, many Africans in the United States vocalize a sense of cultural unity and social camaraderie with the entire community of immigrants from Africa. For example, many North American universities host an African students' organization. Second, not only African merchants and hairdressers but African priests and professors profitably supply the goods and information that many African Americans have, in the past 20 years, come to embrace as signs of their ancestral roots. Thus, peddlers of *kente* cloth, itinerant diviners, and scholars of African art have a newly vested interest in Pan-Africanist and culturally nationalist forms of black identity.

Several factors have combined to make Lagos and New York City into international epicenters of black identity-formation and reaction to racism. First, these were prosperous cities that beckoned black immigrants from far and wide. Black-led rebellions were crushed in Brazil in 1835 and in Cuba in 1844, leading to deportations and general oppression. Many of the black victims fled to Lagos, where they enjoyed British protection from reenslavement and from the expropriation of their belongings by African rulers. Beginning in the 1860s and 1870s, whites in the U.S. South reacted violently to the civil rights gains of blacks during RECONSTRUCTION, thus accelerating the flight of blacks to Harlem, New York, and other Northern cities, as well as the eastward immigration of smaller numbers to Liberia. New York City's prosperity and temporarily liberal U.S. immigration laws also drew numerous West Indians and black Latin Americans, as well as a small but influential coterie of Africans, into the city in the 1900s and 1910s.

Lagos emerged as a capital of black identity for a second reason as well. Late nineteenth-century U.S. racism had its parallel in British West Africa. Since the early nineteenth century Western-educated Africans (including those who had returned from servitude in England or the Americas and those rescued from slave ships by the British Royal Navy) enjoyed, by and large, the respect and cooperation of British colonialists and missionaries. However, racial discrimination against the black bourgeoisie of British West Africa appeared to increase sharply in the 1880s and 1890s, when improvements in tropical medicine enabled increasing numbers of whites to immigrate and compete with blacks for the best jobs. Subject to a sudden upsurge in racial discrimination, these highly Western-educated Africans who had thoroughly identified with the British colonial project felt compelled to turn the tools of their rescuers in their own defense. Thus, culturally Creole Lagos became the hotbed of an ingenious cultural nationalism.

These multiregional and multicultural convergences of privileged and elite blacks in prosperous cities, unified by the shared experience of racial marginality but relatively safe from the coordinated violence suffered by their kin elsewhere, inspired lively literary and cultural movements in both Lagos and New York City. In the 1890s Lagos hosted a cultural renaissance that at once opposed British racism, endorsed the virtue of black racial purity, and canonized an emergent, internationally inspired Yoruba culture as the paramount exemplar of black racial dignity. The elites of Lagos thus produced a black literary and cultural explosion without parallel in its day. Both in the texts they produced and in person, they influenced generations of Afro-Latin Americans and Afro-Latin Americanists, who have judged the Yoruba superior to other Africans. Where Afro-Latin Americans in Cuba and Brazil have embraced the value of African cultural and racial purity, they appear to do so under the influence of the Lagosian cultural renaissance of the 1890s.

From around 1914 to 1920 Jamaican immigrant Marcus Garvey led the largest mass organization in black North American history, boasting an estimated 8 million members at its height. Though headquartered in New York City, Garvey's UNIVERSAL NEGRO IMPROVEMENT ASSOCIATION had branches all over the black world. His plan to repatriate blacks to Africa failed, but hardly any subsequent black nationalist movement has escaped the influence of his ideology and iconography. In the 1920s the culturally diverse immigrants who converged on Harlem, New York, produced another culturally and racially nationalist explosion of political, literary, and musical creativity – namely the HARLEM RENAISSANCE. Together, Garveyism and the Harlem Renaissance made black New York the inspiration, epicenter, and model for similarly racially nationalist cultural movements all around the Atlantic perimeter in the 1920s and 1930s, including the AFROCUBANISMO of NICOLÁS GUILLÉN and others, the Haitian cultural nationalism of JEAN PRICE-MARS and François Duvalier, and the NÉGRITUDE that, through MARTINIQUE'S AIMÉ CÉSAIRE and SENEGAL'S Léopold Senghor, captivated the whole black Francophone world. In turn, the ideas and the vocabulary of Négritude have lately been taken up in the Spanish- and Portuguese-speaking Americas, while the influence of the North American BLACK POWER Movement of the 1960s, in many ways the successor to the Harlem Renaissance, has been felt in Trinidad's Black Power Movement and South Africa's Black Consciousness movement in the 1970s as well.

It can be no accident that these most influential cultural renaissance movements arose in cities where cosmopolitan, culturally diverse, and culturally hybrid populations were compelled by racism to articulate and rationalize a cultural basis for their political unity. Nor is it an accident, in an age of increasing Anglo-Saxon military and economic dominance, that the most influential sites of such movements were Anglophone. Over the two centuries under consideration, the English language and the English-language publishing industry have afforded unparalleled media access to black Atlantic leaders who could write, record, or broadcast in English.

In general, both African Americans' experience of racially marked oppression in the lands of their birth and contemporary Africans' sojourns outside the continent have sparked unprecedented reflections on the collective nature of black experience and political identity. It is no surprise, then, that the best-documented and most influential Pan-Africanist dialogues have taken place in European or Euro-American metropolises, where the diverse black subjects of Britain, France, and the United States in particular have conferred over their shared values and conditions of struggle. From 1900 to 1945 a sequence of Pan-African Congresses brought together the leading intellectuals and politicians of the black Atlantic world in London, Paris, Lisbon, New York, and Manchester. Thus, in the formative years of the African and West Indian independence movements, North Americans like W. E. B. Du Bois and William Monroe Trotter came to know the Senegalese BLAISE DIAGNE, while Ghana's Kwame Nkrumah and Nigeria's Nnamdi Azikiwe came to know the likes of Trinidad's GEORGE PADMORE and Kenya's JOMO KENYATTA. Far more than the African American emigration and colonization movements of the nineteenth century, the Pan-African congresses of the twentieth century occasioned a dialogue among far-flung peers and a novel consensus among the elites of the Afro-Atlantic world that their constituencies shared a common spirit, political interest, and destiny. Though Pan-Africanism had begun in the Americas, this series of congresses demonstrated that, by 1945, it was no longer the dream of African Americans alone. In contrast to the paternalistic and missionizing aspirations of the nineteenth-century emigrationists, the new Pan-Africanists of the 1945 congress condemned Christianity for its exploitation of West African peoples. The diverse black peoples of the Atlantic perimeter surely shared numerous traditions, conventions, and political aspirations before the nineteenth- and twentieth-century dialogue among such free people began, but the changing investments of the black Atlantic political and intellectual classes shaped new and powerfully centripetal standards of Afro-Atlantic education, entertainment, worship, and other cultural symbolism. These are the subject of the next section.

TRANSATLANTIC DIALOGUES OVER CULTURAL PRACTICES

Education and popular culture around the black Atlantic clearly share deep ancestral roots, but they have also been transformed over the past two centuries of transoceanic dialogue and debate among free Africans and African Americans. In the nineteenth century black North American missionaries in Africa inspired generations of young Africans to seek higher education in the United States, very often at predominantly black, church-related institutions. Booker T. Washington and his successors at Tuskegee Institute initiated various agricultural, educational, and economic development projects in Liberia, German TOGO, and British West Africa during the first half of the twentieth century and found powerful advocates in educator Dr. James Aggrey of Ghana and HARRY THUKU of Kenya, as well as European colonial governments themselves. The ideas of W. E. B. Du Bois were also known and debated in West Africa during the first third of the century. This transoceanic dialogue thus helped to inspire the founding of both Tuskegee-style industrial-training institutes and liberal arts colleges in Africa. In turn, Tuskegee Institute president Robert R. Moton (1915-1935) acquired fame as a spokesperson for African affairs and integrated the aim of acquainting black North American students with African affairs into the Tuskegee project. This dialogue on education is imbued with the history and the ambiguous motives of African Americans' nineteenth-century project to "uplift" Africa, which was premised on a degree of accommodation to Western and white dominance and, by and large, on a sense of African cultural inferiority. However, the dialogue with those who had been most brutally enslaved by the West ultimately provided Africans with models of resistance to cultural assimilation and political domination as well. As we have seen, a number of the West African protagonists in this dialogue led their own countries to independence.

Black South African cultural leaders in the late nineteenth and twentieth centuries found these models similarly attractive. A major secessionist movement swept through the black churches of South Africa between 1892 and 1894, when Rev. Magena M. Mokone left the white-dominated Wesleyan Methodist denomination and founded the Ethiopian Church. The movement of cultural, political, educational, and religious autonomy that he inspired thus came to be known as "Ethiopianism." Soon thereafter, in 1896, Bishop Henry McNeal Turner of the U.S.-based AME Church visited South Africa, whereupon many "Ethiopian" churches in South Africa attached themselves to this African American denomination. Many leaders of the Ethiopianist movement traveled to the United States to study in historically black colleges, until the "Ethiopian" churches themselves founded Fort Hare University in South Africa in 1916.

Simultaneously, in the realm of entertainment, missionized South African Christians were creating an urban identity modeled on British colonial high society, which, in South Africa, had itself embraced American-style blackface MINSTRELSY as the dominant form of musical and theatrical entertainment. By the 1850s, soon after the first minstrel shows were performed in New York, they became popular among South African whites and, like those in New York, regularly featured made-up white performers. Black South Africans much more readily embraced performances by visiting African American sailors, adventurers, and professional performers who arrived late in the century. Coloured performers in Cape Town were particularly impressed with the music and dance styles of visiting black North Americans and West Indians. In the 1890s Cape Coloureds and the nascent African middle class witnessed performances of the FISK JUBILEE SINGERS and McAdoo's Jubilee Singers, who inspired much local imitation. Thereafter, local minstrel shows increasingly featured black religious music from the southern United States. Visiting African American performers helped black South African performers to recognize the commercial potential of their own musical creativity, through which a richly hybrid South African musical style has emerged and been reexported by such contemporary groups as LADYSMITH BLACK MAMBAZO. Yet Ladysmith Black Mambazo is not the first African group to speak back to America. In the mid-1890s a black South African minstrel troupe called the African Native Choir toured the United States. When the troupe ran out of funds in the midwestern United States, the AME Church stepped in and offered educational opportunities, whereby eight members of the troupe eventually earned bachelor's degrees at the historically black Wilberforce and Lincoln universities. Their own cultural work continued when they returned to urban South Africa imbued with black North American ideas about education and racial progress. For example, during and after their tour, African Native Choir member Charlotte Manye continued to cultivate contacts between the AME Church and the growing number of independent African clergymen.

Thus, at the turn of the century, music, religion, and education dovetailed in the genesis of urban black South African identity just as they did in the genesis of black North American identity. The Fisk Jubilee Singers, for example, sang the sacred music of African American slaves in a manner adapted to the concert hall. Their project was both a statement about the dignity of African Americans in an age of Jim Crow and a fund-raising venture for black higher education. The consequence has been a permanent and widespread transformation of black North American musical tradition. The songs now honored as "Negro spirituals" are far closer to the adaptations of the Fisk Jubilee Singers than they are to the antecedent improvisational folk genre of the same name. It is understandable, then, that music played such an important and enduring role in the emergence of black South African identity during the same period and that African American performers found such a willing interlocutor in black South Africa. Yet, in the first half of this century, the colonial Gold Coast (now Ghana, West Africa) also hosted a tradition of blackface minstrelsy, African American spirituals, and humorous plantation songs. Its continued influence in Ghana is, however, less evident.

West Africa engaged actively in the transoceanic musical dialogue in other ways. Since the early nineteenth century Afro-Latin returnees to the Gulf of Benin coast and the troops of the British West India regiments were introducing urban West Africa to the syncretic musical styles of the African diaspora, and Brazilian returnees to Lagos exercised a particularly profound influence on the popular music of Lagos. Moreover, in the early twentieth century European firms began importing gramophone discs into West Africa. The most influential of these were recordings of Afro-Cuban groups such as Septeto Habanero and Trio Matamoros. The importation of Afro-Cuban recordings and instruments, such as maracas, congas, and bongos, grew lively after World War II, further inspiring the growth of highlife music, which integrated the influence of black North American vaudeville and Trinidadian calypso as well. "As incredible as it may seem to Africans today," writes critic Wolfgang Bender, "the gradual re-Africanization [of urban African music] proceeded in a roundabout way via Afro-American percussion instruments." Bender makes a similar point about the fabulous growth of Afro-Cuban-inspired rumba music in Zaire (now the Democratic Republic of the Congo, or Congo-Kinshasa) since the 1950s and its "re-Africanization" (i.e., the increase in rhythmic elements) under the influence of recordings by black North Americans like JAMES BROWN and Aretha Franklin in the mid-1960s. Since the 1950s hardly any region of western Africa – from Senegal to Congo-Kinshasa – has been exempt from the influence of Afro-Cuban music or, since the 1960s, from the influence of soul, REGGAE, and disco.

As in the case of Afro-Atlantic music, much of the shared vocabulary of Afro-Atlantic dance is a shared ancestral legacy. However, some African dance performances, such as Bumba-Meu-Boi, were introduced to the Gulf of Benin coast by Afro-Brazilian returnees, and some Brazilian dance performances, such as that of the Egungun masquerade, are said to have been introduced to Brazil by free immigrants from West Africa.

Not all cultural legacies are continuous and none is primordial. Anthropologist Melville J. Herskovits, I think, correctly intuited the endurance of certain intergenerationally learned African bodily habits among the peoples of the African diaspora. However, the meanings given to them and the performances in which they are structured sometimes follow patterns that are hardly reducible to passive cultural inheritance. And, most important for the present argument, Africans and African Americans share many forms of movement and meaning, but many of them are products of a recent, transoceanic dialogue.

In fact, the politically inspired and government-sponsored dialogue between Africans and African Americans has played an important role in creating a number of national dance traditions on the Atlantic perimeter. Since the 1940s, Trinidadian PEARL PRIMUS and black North Americans KATHERINE DUNHAM, ALVIN AILEY, and JUDITH JAMISON – perhaps the most famous dance professionals in the black Atlantic world – have all traveled extensively in contemporary Africa, with the support of the U.S. government or foundations, and have collaborated with African governments and artists to establish an unprecedented tradition of Afro-Atlantic concert dance.

Katherine Dunham and Pearl Primus were the founders of black North American concert dance as we know it, and, as long as we have known it, its roots have been cosmopolitan. Choreographer and anthropologist Pearl Primus (1919-1994) combined African and West Indian ritual, music, and movement in her choreography and introduced these into black North American concert dance. In 1949 she received a Rosenwald Fellowship to make the first of several journeys to Africa – this time, for 18 months in Gold Coast/Ghana, Angola, CAMEROON, Liberia, Senegal, and the Belgian Congo/Congo-Kinshasa. In 1959 President William Tubman of Liberia, himself an Americo-Liberian, appointed Dunham director of the National Dance Company of Liberia and head of the African Performing Arts Center in Monrovia.

Dance anthropologist Katherine Dunham (b. 1910) traveled and performed many times in Africa, after similar stints in Jamaica and Haiti. Her choreographic style integrates African and Afro-Caribbean myths and dance techniques with modern dance. By her efforts, not only African dance but Haitian dance has become canonical in the black North American concert dance. During her first audience with Senegalese president Léopold Senghor, she was told that her work "had caused a cultural revolution" and that various sub-Saharan African heads-of-state "had been encouraged by her formula and format.... Dunham's presence in Africa thus opened a new vista for blacks" and "aided in spearheading Africa's cultural revolution." Senghor appointed her a technical and cultural adviser and teacher at Senegal's National Dance Company.

In the 1960s and 1970s Alvin Ailey and Judith Jamison also traveled extensively in Africa (under U.S. government sponsorship), collaborated with African artists, and integrated urban Africa dances they saw into their choreography. In particular, Ailey collaborated with South African jazz trumpeter Hugh Masekela, himself a frequent sojourner in the United States, in a work that was ostensibly about South African apartheid but, according to one of Ailey's dancers, was intended to evoke the U.S. South as well. "Cry," one of Ailey's most highly praised works, dramatizes the auctioning off of an African American slave woman and, according to Judith Jamison, features dance moves that Jamison and Ailey "had seen on tour in a club in Zaire." Jamison recounts that in Zaire, "we found ourselves in the middle of a war," and one night in a club, "Alvin and I saw movements that would eventually become the last steps in 'Cry.'"

It should not be forgotten that Ailey's and Jamison's travels placed them directly in dialogue with anthropologist, cultural nationalist, and Kenyan president Jomo Kenyatta, as well as Négritude poet, romanticist of black dance, and Senegalese president Léopold Senghor. As the successive directors of the most popular black dance company in the United States, Ailey and Jamison have done more than any other artists to establish the Pan-African character of black North American concert dance. Yet, in this tradition, they are disciples of Primus and Dunham. By the appointment of early African presidents, aesthetic Pan-Africanists Primus and Dunham have even participated in setting the standards of national dance performance in a number of African countries. Hence, by their efforts, the folklorics that are now staged as representations of emergent African national identities and those staged to represent the Pan-African identity of Anglophone New World blacks have emerged from a set of choreographers in close communication with each other. The New-World Anglophone choreographers have not only borrowed models of folkloric dance from the black Francophone world (e.g., Congo-Kinshasa, Haiti, and Sengal) but demonstrated influential forms of cultural nationalism resistant to Francophone black elites' usual drift toward European aesthetic models.

Perhaps the most famous cultural nationalism of the black Atlantic world is Négritude, which had its very beginnings in a transatlantic dialogue and, like the dialogue concerning dance, bridged the gap between Francophone and Anglophone in the Atlantic world. Long before he became the president of Senegal, Léopold Sédar Senghor was a student in Paris, where, in 1931, he met Martinican poet, eventual mayor of Fort-de-France, and member of the French national legislature, Aimé Césaire. At this early stage in their careers, both men "had begun to feel dissatisfied with their total immersion in French culture, and had grown curious about Africa." Through the numerous African American intellectuals who sojourned in Paris, Senghor and Césaire learned about the Harlem Renaissance, a cultural and literary movement in the 1920s that celebrated and scrutinized black culture worldwide. Under this inspiration, the Francophone Antilleans and Africans who founded *La Revue du Monde Noir* published articles on the black world, including extensive commentaries on blacks in the United States, Tuskegee Institute, the black colonizers of Liberia, and the poetry of Afro-American LANGSTON HUGHES and Jamaican-American CLAUDE MCKAY. In the 1930s Senghor read the work of other African American poets, as well as that of W. E. B. Du Bois and Carter G. Woodson. He read journals such as the NAACP's the *Crisis* and the Urban League's *Opportunity*, and Alain Locke's famous edited volume *The New Negro* (1925) – a book that also deeply influenced Nigerian nationalist politician Nnamdi Azikiwe. The title of Locke's volume so impressed Senghor that he used its translation, *Le nègre nouveau*, to identify the new man and the new attitudes he hoped to see in French-speaking blacks. Through the hybrid cultural and literary movement they founded, Césaire and Senghor endeavored to recognize and validate the shared spirit of the world's black cultures and thereby redeem it from the image of inferiority and undermine the contempt that so often divided Africans from France's black Antillean subjects. These were the transatlantic and cross-linguistic roots of Négritude, the most enduring literary expression of Pan-Africanism in Atlantic history.

Yet the forms of unity envisaged in political Pan-Africanism and of spiritual commonality imagined in Négritude are seldom fully realized where Africans and African Americans meet in person. For the most seemingly common of experiences sometimes evoke profoundly different meanings for the two groups. For example, African American visits to the coastal slave forts have, in recent decades, become an increasingly important dimension of tourism in West African countries such as Ghana and Senegal. Though no other sites better typify the African American link to Africa, they are the foci of clashing interpretations. For African American tourists, filmmakers, tour guides, and other culture brokers, Ghana's Elmina Castle, to give one example, is a somber place – "sacred ground not to be desecrated." Ghanaians, however, have a much more complex relationship with the fort that extends beyond its uses as a slave market. Hence, Ghanaian visitors, merchants, and government officials envisage a redeveloped Elmina as a festive place and often regard the African American tourists as "too emotional." Hence, rather than preserving the fort as it is, Ghanaian planners wish to convert it into a bustling commercial center. These differences of thought and feeling reinforce the sense that African Americans, like their white counterparts, are foreigners to Africa, even as African Americans understand themselves to be "coming home."

On the other hand, Kwame Nkrumah's prime ministership (1960-1966) cast a long shadow over public opinion in Ghana, where, perhaps more than in any other African country, African Americans are publicly recognized as Pan-African "brothers" and "sisters." Even if slave fort tourism has not yet created an interpretive consensus, it has enhanced Ghanaians' interest in their own cultural history and linked diverse black Atlantic populations in projects of local West African development and in the movement to secure reparations for the descendants of those victimized by the slave trade. Among the greatest sponsors of the REPARATIONS movement was the late president-elect of Nigeria, Moshood Abiola. The Gambian government, for its part, has made moves to develop Alex Haley's ancestral town, Juffure, in order to attract African American tourists. A representative of Gambia's National Council for Art and Culture even presented the outlines of this effort for discussion at a North American conference on diaspora research. Though relatively few black North Americans' ancestors may have embarked from Elmina or any Nigerian coastal site, Ghanaians and Nigerians have now joined Senegalese and African Americans in forging new political alliances and validating new focal symbols of their shared cultural history.

Under many circumstances, the will to unity has inspired many Africans and African Americans to undo their differences and search for the terms of similarity. Throughout the history of black North Americanist anthropology and folklore studies, both foes and advocates of African American dignity have looked for African "survivals" in black North American lifeways. "Should some weird, archaic, Negro doctrine be brought to his attention," writes Newbell Niles Puckett of one common interpretive error, the average white man "considers it a 'relic of African heathenism,' though in four cases out of five it is a European dogma from which only centuries of patient education could wean even his own ancestors."

Melville J. Herskovits led many subsequent generations of scholars and other culture brokers, such as dancer Katherine Dunham, in the study of Africa's positive contributions to African American cultures, though many equally well-intentioned scholars, such as E. Franklin Frazier, have preferred to attribute any cultural differences between black and white North Americans to the effects of oppression and deprivation on the blacks. The GULLAH people of the Georgia Sea Coast Islands have long been the focus of scholarly investigation into what remains culturally African about black North Americans, despite what all agree is their generally high degree of acculturation in Western ways. Geographical isolation long kept the speech and lifeway of the Sea Coast Islanders somewhat distinctive. Various scholars have sought to explain that distinctiveness as a debt to the cultures of what are now Sierra Leone and Liberia. In the second half of the eighteenth century, the rice farmers of the Sea Coast Islands drew many of their workers from the rice-growing regions of Sierra Leone and Liberia, and the term *Gullah* might derive from the ethnonym of Sierra Leone's Gola people. On the other hand, African captives had come to these islands from many other regions as well, and students of the local Creole language, known as Gullah or Geechee, have identified an extremely diverse set of African origins in its lexicon and in its justly famous basket-making tradition. Indeed, some identify the term *Angola* as the more likely source of the term *Gullah*.

As African Americans have grown more willing to embrace Africa as a cultural model and emblem of collective identity, the decline of Gullah language and crafts has been reversed. Indeed, the "Africanness" of Gullah basketry has become its major selling point and a means of livelihood for many craftswomen in coastal South Carolina. However, it was the intervention of Joseph Opala, anthropologist and former member of the Peace Corps in Sierra Leone, that established the local conviction that Sierra Leone in particular was the source of the islanders' Africanness and the appropriate target of their "return" to the motherland. Indeed, the interest in this ahistorically specific tie was reciprocal. President Joseph Saidu Momoh of Sierra Leone paid a highly public visit to the Sea Coast Islands in 1986 and encouraged the islanders to visit their "ancestral homeland," which a score of them did in 1989. President Momo continued the American tradition of attributing the islanders' linguistic distinctiveness to their African roots and identified Gullah's similarities to Sierra Leonean Krio, or Creole, as proof. In fact, both language varieties are predominantly English in their lexicon, since Krio resulted largely from the interaction of African American returnees, British-educated recaptives, British administrators, and Anglophone missionaries in Freetown. Thus, the similarity of condition between Gullah and Krio is highly ambiguous evidence of the Gullah people's African roots. Yet a complex politically, economically, and academically shaped dialogue made the highly creolized Gullah dialect into the grounds of a powerful new kinship – of a "family across the sea."

Contemporary New York City is the site of an equally complex and identity-transforming dialogue. Whereas the Harlem Renaissance of the 1920s and the Black Power Movement of the 1960s extensively involved Afro-Caribbean immigrants in the reformulation of African American collective identity, the more recent Yoruba renaissance and Afrocentrism have, since the 1980s, increasingly involved African priests, scholars, and merchants as well. Itinerant African priests, such as Wande Abimbola, Afolabi Epega, and Sikiru Salami, have begun initiating Yoruba priests in the New World and have introduced a new standard of authenticity into already-well-established American religions like Brazilian Candomblé, Cuban SANTERÍA, and Trinidadian SHANGO. As African civilization has come to be regarded as the classical origin of African American cultures, African academics have become increasingly prominent interpreters of that classical legacy in art history and Afro-American studies departments. Finally, African hairstylists and merchants of cloth, leatherware, and sculpture are now the chief suppliers of the African blazonry of popular Afrocentrism in the United States. African clothing, jewelry, wood carvings, and braids are now found in virtually every black North American home. Much to these merchants' profit, they have integrated not only wares from African ethnic groups far beyond their own but also imagery of American origin, such as MALCOLM X t-shirts.

The role of African merchants in cobbling together and supplying a Pan-African imagery of black North American identity has not, however, created a Pan-African uniformity of political opinion. For example, when New York City officials forcibly removed Harlem's "African Market" from its existing location in 1992, African American merchants tended to blame the eviction on white racism, while African merchants tended to blame a plot by the Black Muslims.

The Transatlantic Dialogue over Religious Practices

A staple of the Herskovitsian literature on Haiti, SURINAME, Brazil, and the United States, as well as that of Brazilian and Cuban folklore studies generally, has been the "survival" of African religious forms in the Americas. On the other hand, African American missionaries and others imbued with the missionary zeal to "redeem" Africa have played significant roles in Africa's cultural history, above all in West Africa and South Africa. Since the mid-1970s, when reggae music became popular in English-speaking West Africa, some young West African Christians have adopted Rastafarian ideals and symbols, such as ganja-smoking, dreadlocks, and "Dread talk." The influence of this religion has increased at the hands of Jamaican and Anglo-Jamaican missionaries, who set up communities in West Africa in the 1970s, and of West African travelers who met Jamaican Rastas in London and Amsterdam.

Much American religious culture that is thought to have "survived" slavery was in fact introduced, sustained, or deeply modified by free migrants from Africa to the Americas. The Brazilian Candomblé, for example, is often identified as an exemplary, if not the most exemplary, survival of African culture in the Americas. Yet the oral history identifies many of the founders of its leading institutions as voluntary immigrants from Africa. For example, Otampê Ojarô, founder of the Alakêtu temple; Marcos Pimentel, a nineteenth-century chief priest of the Mocambo temple on the island of Itaparica; and, most important, Iya Naso, founder of the ancient Casa Branca temple, are all identified as free immigrants from Africa. Iya Naso's mother is said to have secured her own manumission in Bahia and returned to Africa but voluntarily moved to Bahia to found this first of the three most famous Candomblé temples in Brazil. Her successor, Marcelina, is said to have gone from Africa to Bahia, Brazil, voluntarily, and then returned to Africa for an extended sojourn before returning finally to Bahia to assume the leadership of the Casa Branca temple. Verger reports that it was Marcelina who first brought to Bahia the famous Bamgbose, babalaô diviner from Oya and founder of Brazil's most illustrious line of male priests.

Similarly, in Cuba, the famous African-born Adechina is said to have been enslaved in Cuba but to have returned to Africa for initiation as a babalaô diviner, later returning to Cuba. The oral history also identifies a free-born African woman named Efunche (also Efunsetan or La Funche) who traveled as a free person to Cuba and there reformed Afro-Cuban religion in the nineteenth century.

These reports are made largely credible by archives documenting the return of thousands of Afro-Brazilians and Afro-Cubans to the West African coast. Moreover, in the lamentably incomplete Bahian archives of return voyages from Lagos, I have counted dozens of ships and hundreds of free Africans traveling from Lagos to Bahia or through Bahia to Rio or the State of Pernambuco, Brazil, between 1855 and 1898. Journalistic, epistolary, and ethnographic evidence reveals repeated journeys of another score of African-Brazilian travelers up to the 1930s. Many of them carried British passports, and most appear to have engaged in commerce, selling ethnically marked Brazilian merchandise (such as salted meat and Afro-Brazilian religious paraphernalia) to returnees in West Africa and "authentically African" merchandise (such as the cola nuts and woven cloth used in the Candomblé) to their black customers in Brazil. Thus, under British protection and motivated by their own commercial interests, a generation of back-and-forth travelers consolidated a set of novel, religiously based, and transnational identities unprecedented before the slave trade and as yet fragmentary before the nineteenth-century return of Afro-Brazilians and Afro-Cubans to Africa. These were the "Yoruba" and "Jeje" identities.

As these identities blossomed in early twentieth-century Brazil, they displayed not only the "memory" of religious icons, myths, and practices from the Africa that preceded the slave trade but the effects of the radical ideological transformations of late nineteenth-century Yoruba ethnogenesis, which occurred primarily after the end of the slave trade. The interaction of Westernized African recaptives and returnees in Sierra Leone and Lagos in the nineteenth century had produced, for the first time, a self-ascribed "Yoruba" identity that embraced the diverse peoples of Oya, EKITI, IJEBU, EGBA, Egbado, Ilesa, and so forth. Their Western education gave the returnee advocates of this identity privileged access to international markets and to the emergent colonial administrations of British and French West Africa. Moreover, their literacy allowed them an unparalleled opportunity to articulate their own vision of their culture and history. Thus, at the British-dominated crossroads of African/African American interaction, the Yoruba acquired a highly publicized reputation for superiority to other Africans. This reputation for superiority was useful in the 1880s and 1890s, as the bourgeois black Lagosians faced new forms of economic disadvantage and racial discrimination. Their reaction was a literary and cultural movement extensively documenting Yoruba "traditional" religion, advocating racial and cultural purity, and popularizing the adoption of African names in lieu of the European ones with which many returnees and recaptives had grown up. On the contrary, the cultures of the Guinea Coast, including the forbears of Yoruba culture, had long embraced the virtues of interethnic marriage and cultural hybridity. The dominant culture of nineteenth-century Brazil was highly Eurocentric, and, though the movement of independence from Portugal appeared to valorize the Indian as a symbol of Euro-Brazilian autonomy, the sizable African presence in Brazil tended to be regarded as polluting. From the 1930s onward, Brazilian nationalist culture embraced the virtue of a cultural hybridity that blended African, European, and native Brazilian blood and culture into one new and uniquely beautiful amalgam. In sum, neither Brazil nor pre-nineteenth-century West Africa appears to be the origin of the extraordinary value that the dignitaries and advocates of the Brazilian Candomblé religion have, since the early twentieth century, placed on black racial and religious purity. These values seem to be rooted in the racial and cultural nationalism of the Lagosian renaissance in the 1890s, during and after which time Afro-Brazilians were traveling back and forth between Lagos and Bahia. Long after that time, letters, newspapers, and Lagosian renaissance-inspired writings on "Yoruba traditional religion" and its alleged superiority continued to cross the Atlantic. At least one priestly traveler who sojourned in late nineteenth-century Lagos appears to have used his readings to justify the invention of a new category of priests – the *obás,* or *ministros,* of Xangô – in what is still described as Brazil's most "purely African" Candomblé temple, Ilê Axé Opô Afonjá.

Ironically, beyond the marked prestige and pursuit of purity articulated in this transatlantic religious culture, a most persistent set of its shared institutions and motifs derives from a British institution – Freemasonry. Freemasonry took its modern form as a male fraternal order and speculative philosophy, rather than an association of craftsmen, in the early eighteenth century. Over the next two centuries, it spread beyond England to other parts of Europe and to Europe's overseas colonies, where membership often became a highly prestigious marker of bourgeois status or an equally prestigious context of conspiracy against European rule, as it became in the British North American colonies. Avowedly based on pre-Christian philosophical and religious principles and parallel to many Afro-Atlantic religions in its fraternal secrecy, Freemasonry and its iconography have proved inviting to numerous West Africans, Afro-Brazilians, Afro-Cubans, Haitians, and black North Americans. Thus, tens of thousands of black men around the Atlantic perimeter are united by their shared membership in this British-founded fraternity.

Moreover, Freemasonry has inspired several neo-traditional spinoff organizations, such as the Reformed Ogboni Fraternity and the Aborigine Ogboni Fraternity of Nigeria, while the Masonic compass, the All-Seeing Eye, and the secret handshakes turn up in the apparently "traditional" religions of Nigerian villages, Haitian Vodou temples, the Afro-Cuban Palo Mayombe order, and at least one Afro-Brazilian diviner's office.

And there is a further irony. Americans have helped to re-Africanize religious policies of African nation-states through bank, civil service, and school holidays. On the one hand, West African nation-states in the twentieth century have tended to marginalize non-Christian and non-Islamic religions. For example, only Christian and Islamic religious holidays tend to be recognized through civil service and school vacations. On the other hand, the West African-inspired religions of the African diaspora have grown exponentially in wealth and membership since the 1960s. In Brazil, Cuba, Trinidad, and the Cuban-American and African American communities of the United States – not to mention Haiti, where it occurred well before the 1960s – these religions have become emblems of national identity. In Brazil, military dictators and democratic politicians alike have sought popular support through the temples of Afro-Brazilian religion.

During the past 40 years, the Brazilian government, the United Nations (UNESCO), and various U.S. corporate foundations have repeatedly sponsored Brazil's exchange of priests, professors, and museum exhibitions with state institutions in Nigeria and the People's Republic of Benin. These exchanges have highlighted the Yoruba and Ewe-Gen-Aja-Fon religious legacy that Brazil shares with Africa. Brazil's official support appears to be motivated partly by its desire for political and commercial leadership in the "non-aligned" world. Whatever Brazil's public relations motives might be, the Brazilian government established African-diaspora religion as a medium of transatlantic diplomacy and helped pave the way for numerous subsequent transoceanic priestly exchanges, involving Haitians, U.S. Latinos, Trinidadians, and black North Americans as well. Thus, New World governments, foundations, and priests have now inspired changes in the official cultural policies of at least one African government. The Beninese government has now reversed the pattern among African states and established an official and annual holiday for the Vodun gods, on January 10.

Hence, the cultural history that unites African and African American religions consists of much more than pre-slave-trade African origins and American "survivals." Much that appears to be primordial in so-called African "traditional" religion is in fact the product of a live Afro-Atlantic dialogue, and much that appears to "survive" of African religion in the Americas is in fact shaped by an African cultural politics that long postdated the slave trade. No less than the dialogue over political identity, the dialogue that has produced the most African of Afro-Atlantic religions is often mediated through European languages, colonial and postcolonial capitals, European institutions, and texts published in Roman script. For example, in the twentieth century, texts such as Col. A. B. Ellis's *The Yoruba-Speaking Peoples of the Slave Coast of West Africa* (1890), Samuel Johnson's *The History of the Yorubas* (1921), Melville J. Herskovits's *The Myth of the Negro Past* (1941), Robert Farris Thompson's *Flash of the Spirit* (1983), and John Mason's *Orin Orisà* (1912), have all exercised a momentous influence on African Americans' conception of their religion and cultural identities generally. Even more important, these transatlantic cultural politics demonstrate the overwhelming role of black volition in reshaping inherited and imposed cultural realities.

Conclusion

Melville J. Herskovits is correct in observing that intergenerational learning of belief, practice, and bodily habits continues to link contemporary African Americans to the African cultures of their ancestors. On the other hand, Paul Gilroy (author of *The Black Atlantic,* 1993) is also correct in observing the numerous "discontinuous" forms of communication by which locales in the African diaspora have influenced each other's culture and politics. This essay is intended to illustrate the further point that the diaspora and Africa itself are united by "discontinuous" and mutually influential dialogue that has continued long beyond the end of the slave trade. The dialogue between Africans and African Americans has not always produced the harmony and unity dreamed of by Pan-Africanists, but it has produced significant transformations of political identity, religious practice, and culture generally in both Africa and its diaspora. Thus, the conventional narrations of cultural history that identify the roots of African American culture in Africa and trace their "survival," "syncretization," or gradual dissolution in the Americas tell only part of the story. Not unlike other diasporas and their homelands – Jewish, Chinese, Irish, South Asian, and Lebanese – the African diaspora in the Americas reflects the effects of an enduring dialogue and a dialectic of mutual transformation over time.

J. Lorand Matory

See Also

Accra, Ghana; Azikiwe, Benjamin Nnamdi; Cape Town, South Africa; Cape Verde; Congo, Democratic Republic of the; Dahomey, Early Kingdom of; Dube, John Langalibalele; Kenya; Lagos, Nigeria; Luanda, Angola; Mandela, Nelson Rolihlahla; Masekela, Hugh Ramopolo; Monrovia, Liberia; Soul Music; Transatlantic Slave Trade; Senghor, Léopold Sédar; Duvalier, François; Porto-Novo, Benin; Tubman, William Vacanarat Shadrach; Pan-African Congress of 1919; Black Consciousness in the United States; Cleaver, Eldridge Leroy; Cone, James Hal; *Crisis, The*; Delany, Martin Robison; Denmark Vesey Conspiracy; Du Bois, William Edward Burghardt (W. E. B.); Franklin, Aretha Louise; Frazier, Edward Franklin; Garvey, Marcus Mosiah; Haley, Alexander Palmer (Alex); Harlem, New York; Locke, Alain Leroy; Moton, Robert Russa; National Urban League; New Orleans, Louisiana; New York, New York; *Opportunity: Journal of Negro Life*; Tuskegee University; Washington, Booker Taliaferro; Wilberforce University; Rio de Janeiro, Brazil; Kingston, Jamaica; Rastafarians; Trinidad and Tobago; Port-au-Prince, Haiti; Spirituals, African American; Abolition and Emancipation in Latin America and the Caribbean; UNESCO Race Relations Project; Abiola, Moshood Kashimawo Olawale; Havana, Cuba; West Indies; Black Nationalism in the United States; St. Thomas and Prince Islands.

Africa

Afro-Beat, genre of contemporary African music.

The Nigerian musicians Fela Anikulapo Kuti, popularly known as Fela, and Orlando Julius Ekemode both claim to have coined the term *Afro-Beat* to describe their fusion of highlife, soul, JAZZ, and traditional Nigerian musical styles, including JUJU and fuji, during the late 1960s and early 1970s. The music of JAMES BROWN and other African American artists contributed heavily to the Afro-Beat style. While the early recordings of Ekemode, such as his hit "Juagua Nana," show the elements of Afro-Beat, most recognize Fela's band, Africa '70, as the definitive Afro-Beat band. Their 1971 recording "Why Black Men Dey Suffer" defined the Afro-Beat style, incorporating call-and-response vocals with a unique beat and tempo.

Afro-Beat's popularity stemmed, in part, from Fela's courageous stance against political corruption and economic injustice in Nigeria. This made him a role model for the Nigerian urban underclass and intelligentsia. Writing lyrics in "pidgin" English rather than Yoruba to reach the urban masses throughout Anglophone Africa, he recounted stories of police brutality and government persecution. The 1978 album *Coffin for Head of State*, for example, blames Nigeria's leader at the time, Olusegun Obasanjo, for the death of Fela's mother. His 82-year-old mother died of injuries sustained when the army and police raided Fela's compound and threw her from a window.

Africa '70 was an entourage of talented musicians playing rhythm guitar, electric bass, drum, congas, percussion sticks, gourd rattlers, tenor sax, baritone sax, and two trumpets, as well as 20 backup singers. In the 1980s Fela began to experiment with longer and more complex compositions, including elements of polytonality, when he expanded his band, renamed Egypt '80. However, at his death in 1997, he was still the recognized king of Afro-Beat.

Ari Nave

See Also
Nigeria; Soul Music; Kuti, Fela.

Cross Cultural

Afrocentrism, the study of Africa and its history from a non-European perspective.

Molefi Kete Asante first coined the term *Afrocentrism* in 1976, although it has its roots in Pan-Africanism. At its most moderate, Afrocentrism means rediscovering African and African American achievement; restoring Africa's rightful place in history; and establishing its importance on a par with European history, culture, and accomplishment. Afrocentrists believe that African Americans and non-African Americans would gain from efforts made toward restoring pride and dignity in African heritage, viewing people of African descent as actors in history rather than "objects," and expanding school curricula to include diverse perspectives. These efforts include, in part, acknowledging the role that Africa played in shaping European culture by exploring such issues as how classical Greek society was influenced by ancient Egyptian society, for example.

Another example of Afrocentric scholarship is the study of the ancient kingdom of Kush in Nubia, where the civilization rivaled that of ancient Egypt, even ruling Egypt for almost 100 years. Many believe, however, that European scholars have ignored this distinctly black African empire because of the long-held belief in the "inferiority" and "backwardness" of Africans.

Afrocentrism's harshest critics have chosen to emphasize Afrocentrists who hold extreme and, some would say, questionable views, such as Professor Leonard Jeffries of the City University of New York. Critics of Jeffries claim he has used the term *Afrocentric* to promote anti-Semitism and to further his belief – based on pseudoscience – in the inherent superiority of black people. Jeffries claimed, for example, that Jews in large part financed the slave trade and that blacks are inherently superior to whites because blacks possess larger amounts of the skin pigment melanin than whites. At the same time, many of Afrocentrism's critics have concentrated on the more questionable ideas surrounding Afrocentrism to depict it as reverse racism based on capricious scholarship. Most scholars, however, agree that providing a realistic portrait of Africa and African history is necessary and overdue.

Robert Fay

See Also
Kush, Early Kingdom of.

Latin America and the Caribbean

Afrocubanismo, an artistic and literary movement founded in Cuba during the late 1920s and 1930s; the movement's representatives looked to Cuba's urban black culture both as a basis for new art forms and as a symbol of Cuban national identity.

Afrocubanismo, an expression of Cuba's national identity in the arts, arose during the late 1920s and the 1930s. Afro-Cubanist representatives, such as the composer Amadeo Roldán and the poet Nicolás Guillén, sought to recognize and promote the value of popular black musical, artistic, and literary forms. They also depicted Cuban blacks as central to the Cuban nation and a symbol of exploited Cubans in general. White Creole novelist Alejo Carpentier thus merged Afro-Cuban traditions with European avant-garde literary techniques to decry the social and political marginalization of Afro-Cubans in his first novel, *Ecué-Yamba-O* (1933). Afro-Chinese artist Wifredo Lam, used cubist techniques in paintings inspired by Afro-Caribbean religions.

In their creative work, these artists focused on Cuba's urban black music and culture, which also became a source of inspiration for many middle-class white composers, such as Ernesto Lecuona. As a result, Afro-Cuban music, which had gained tremendous popularity abroad, finally won acceptance in educated Cuban society. Although a reaction to Afrocubanismo developed among the musical elite during the 1940s, as composers again turned to European classical music for inspiration, mainstream Cuban culture has remained profoundly influenced by the movement. Indeed, Robin Moore, author of *Nationalizing Blackness*, states that Afro-Cubanist music, dance, literature, and art "served as the conceptual foundation of modern Cuban culture."

Afrocubanismo found its inspiration in the tremendously rich Afro-Cuban cultural and organizational life that flourished in the nineteenth and early twentieth centuries. Mutual aid societies and social clubs grew throughout the country during this period. The cultural life of Afro-Cubans developed in a context of segregation and racism, in which, more than in other Latin American countries, blacks and mulattos alike were classified and dismissed by the white elite as a single "race of color."

This marginalization paradoxically fostered closer ties and greater organizational strength among Afro-Cubans, and thus provided a parallel space for cultural expression. An early precursor to the Afrocubanismo movement can be found in the *teatro vernáculo*, the comic theater established as early as the 1860s. According, again, to Robin Moore, the comic theater was the first form of commercial entertainment "in which working-class Afro-Cuban music and dance were prominently represented, and the first to (occasionally) address issues of racial discrimination." It was thus, Moore explains, "crucial in the formation of a new cultural identity for the nation that accepted African-influenced expression as Cuban." At the same time, popular theater – performed almost entirely by white Cubans reflected the racial prejudices toward blacks, and stereotypes of them, prevalent in nineteenth-century Cuba. In this sense, popular theater, which attracted audiences from various classes, provided a space in which Afro-Cuban culture began to be defined in the national consciousness; it was also a means through which Cuban blacks became increasingly associated with the national struggle against colonialism.

The popularization of Afro-Cuban art forms in the 1920s was a direct response to Cuba's wavering national identity and the economic and cultural dominance of the United States in the Caribbean basin. Under the terms of the Platt Amendment to the country's 1901 constitution, Cuba had become a protectorate of the United States in that same year. The amendment gave the United States the power to intervene in Cuba to maintain "public order" and limited the island's ability to contract treaties with other nations. North American capital flowed into Cuba and into its growing sugar industry, and the landowning classes prospered. Yet as Moore observes, "The true oligarchs were North American investors who owned half of all farmland, in addition to virtually all railroads, utilities, construction companies, and other key interests." The United States presence in Cuba led to the further solidification of a racist social order: Cuban history was rewritten to avoid reference to Afro-Cuban leaders, and blacks were excluded from positions of power. Afro-Cubans were also excluded from elite venues for artistic, literary, and musical life – cultural spheres dominated largely by white middle-class artists, who looked down on black and working-class forms of expression.

By the late 1920s Cuba was rife with national tensions, due to a protracted economic crisis and a surge in political repression under the rule of Gerardo Machado (1924-1933). Prominent scholars like Emilio Roig de Leuchsenring and Fernando Ortiz began openly to protest U.S. dominance in the region, considered by many Cubans to have contributed to their economic depression. These factors led to an upsurge in Cuban nationalism and a renewed effort by Cuba's artists and intellectuals to develop a distinctive Cuban culture. Some middle-class artists and writers turned to Cuban *guajiro* (Hispanic folk) and Indian themes as national symbols; a larger number sought inspiration in popular Afro-Cuban musical forms, including the conga, RUMBA, and SON. Afro-Cuban culture was promoted in national festivals and scholarly research, particularly the work of Ortiz, who in 1936 founded the Sociedad de Estudios Afrocubanos (Society of Afro-Cuban Studies).

Paradoxically, the U.S. presence in Cuba facilitated a cultural exchange between Cuba's black artists and writers and some of America's leading black representatives of the Harlem Renaissance – a development that significantly influenced Afrocubanismo. For example, in 1929 Guillén interviewed the African American poet Langston Hughes in Havana. Guillén deeply admired Hughes, who became a lifelong friend. He felt that Hughes, more than any other poet, had succeeded in bringing black popular music, such as blues and jazz, into American literature. Ian Isidore Smart, author of *Nicolás Guillén*, notes that "Langston Hughes had a most transcendental impact on Guillén; in fact he literally triggered Guillén's turning to the *son* as the vehicle for his most original poetic expression."

The proliferation in Cuba of Afro-Cuban music and dance during the 1920s also inspired a number of avant-garde poets known as the *negrista* poets, most of whom were from white middle-class families. The negrista movement, occurring at the same time as Afrocubanismo, appropriated elements of Afro-Cuban culture, which it decontextualized and exoticized for consumption by a white, elite audience. Central figures in this group included Alfonso Hernández Catá, Emilio Ballagas, and José Zacarias Tallet. Their poetry, which they collected and published in anthologies such as *Órbita de la poesia afrocubana 1928-1937* and *Antología de la poesía negra hispano-americana*, draws heavily on the exotic, sensual appeal of black dance. In Tallet's poem "La rumba," for example, two black dancers, a male and a female, seethe with sexual passion: "Frenetic, the Negro hurls himself in assault / and, silk handkerchief in his hands, / gets ready to put his mark on Tomasa, / who challenges him insolently." In the same poem, Tomasa "boldly offers her rotund breasts / that oscillate from right to left / and dazzle Chepe Cachon."

In some negrista poetry, blacks were stereotyped as grotesque, subversive, and frivolous. In the poem "Rumba," Cata highlighted blacks' "crude beefsteak lips" and "spattered" noses. Both Tallet and Ballagas played on an association between blacks and devil worship. Ballagas's poem "Comparsa habanera" contains these lines: "The blood-brother devils / are lit up in rum and sunshine!" At times Tallet and Ballagas used nonsensical phrases in their poems that imitate the Yoruba and Carabali languages. Indeed, Tallet's "La rumba" was the result of a friend's challenge to incorporate the meaningless "Mambimba, mabomba, mabomo y bombo" into a poem. Although the negrista poets played a major role in incorporating Afro-Cuban themes into Cuban national identity, their cult of the exotic did nothing to promote a healthy respect for blacks in Cuban society. On the contrary, their poems reaffirmed the racial prejudices of the white intellectual elites who read them.

It is this exaggerated, even caricatured exoticism that constitutes the principal distinction between the negrista movement and Afrocubanismo. In contrast to the Afro-Cuban poet Nicolás Guillén, for instance, the negrista poets showed no concern for the social conditions under which Cuban blacks lived, choosing instead to objectify them as symbols of sensuality. There is some debate as to the extent to which Afrocubanismo itself mirrored Afro-Cuban culture or reflected a selective appropriation of Afro-Cuban themes, albeit in a more progressive discourse. It was partly for this reason that many Afro-Cubans took little interest in Afrocubanismo.

The popularity of Afro-Cuban cultural forms did not engender a social acceptance of Afro-Cubans themselves. Although some elements of black popular culture won acceptance in Cuban society, they did so largely because most Cuban composers and artists continued to adhere to European, middle-class styles. Moreover, until the Cuban Revolution of 1959, Cuban blacks remained subject to widespread segregation and job discrimination. It seemed to many blacks that white Cubans were more interested in them as cultural symbols than as equal participants in Cuban society.

Roanne Edwards

SEE ALSO

Lecuona, Ernesto.

Latin America and the Caribbean

Afro-Latin America, Research on

Afro-Latin America encompasses a broad geographical, cultural, and linguistic area of Latin America – from BRAZIL in South America to the Caribbean islands of CUBA, PUERTO RICO, and Hispaniola, which is shared by the DOMINICAN REPUBLIC and HAITI; and Guatemala, Honduras, Nicaragua, BELIZE, and MEXICO in CENTRAL AMERICA. There is no agreement among scholars or other observers about which countries may be correctly designated as Afro-Latin American. A generally accepted yardstick emphasizes the presence of people of African descent from the time of the TRANSATLANTIC SLAVE TRADE to the present. How many Afro-Latin Americans there are today is a difficult question to answer. Throughout Latin America, definitions of race, color, and origin are extremely varied. In Brazil, for example, the four official racial categories are black, brown (or *pardo*), yellow, and white. Yet census takers in 1980 counted some 140 terms used by respondents to describe their racial background. If we use African origins as the determining factor, the size of the Afro-Latin American population dramatically increases to include all members of the black and brown categories: thus, of the 43 percent of Colombians who are of African descent, 14 percent are pure black; of the 75 percent of Brazilians of African descent, 33 percent are black; and in the Dominican Republic the count is even more complicated.

Early research into Afro-Latin America focused on the survival of African culture, religion, and tradition, both during and after the time of slavery, primarily in Brazil, Cuba, Colombia, the Dominican Republic, Haiti, and VENEZUELA. In contrast to the rest of Latin America, these more visibly "African" societies received large numbers of slaves from Africa and experienced more profoundly, in their culture, art, and religious lives, the impact of the African presence. Of interest to researchers has been the push to attract European immigrants who would act as a kind of civilizing force meant to expunge what was seen as the taint of African and Indian roots from a newly independent Latin America (*see* WHITENING). For the offending groups, all visible reminders of their origins were accorded neither honor nor prestige.

Since the late 1970s scholars, artists, and writers have brought fresh perspectives to the often complex realities of Afro-Latin American studies. Their reconsiderations of specific events – like the attempts of nineteenth-century Afro-Latin Americans to win their freedom and analyses of present-day civil liberties organizations – increasingly acknowledge Afro-Latin America as part of a larger hemispheric reality that includes both the United States and Latin America.

Researchers have looked at the Cuban struggle for independence from Spain, which occurred from 1895 to 1898, and have seen that thousands of Afro-Cubans fought with nationalist forces in the hope of gaining full citizenship (*see* CUBA). After the war, political mobilization included the formation of the Independent Party of Color in 1908, the subsequent banning of political parties based on color, the outbreak of a racial war in 1912, and strong repressive measures unleashed against the Afro-Cuban community. Researchers have analyzed how these events point to miserably dashed hopes and the marginalization of Afro-Cubans, which would have far-reaching consequences.

Brazil, by virtue of its large population of blacks – exceeded only by NIGERIA – has been a principal focus of study in this area. In the first three decades of the twentieth century, Afro-Brazilians established sociocultural and political entities and published newspapers and magazines whose columns discussed the special problems of the community and its place within the larger Brazilian society. The press focused on the lack of employment opportunities, racial discrimination in public places, police harassment, and suggestions for general enhancement of the community and its members. Events in the larger black world – in the United States, Africa, and the Caribbean – were followed intently. One newspaper was even named after former emperor Menilek of Ethiopia. In 1944 the founding of the TEATRO EXPERIMENTAL DO NEGRO (the Black Experimental Theater) offered Afro-Brazilians a means of cultural expression that would present their view of what it meant to be Afro-Brazilian in contemporary Brazil. The emergence of the short-lived FRENTE NEGRA BRASILEIRA (the Black Brazilian Front), which was registered as a political party during this period, is perhaps the clearest signal that Afro-Brazilians as an organized group would raise an alternative voice in the political life of Brazil.

The Republic of Haiti and the Dominican Republic, uneasy neighbors on their shared island, provide one of the more complex issues in Afro-Latin American studies. Following the successful slave rebellion in the French colony of Saint-Domingue at the end of the eighteenth century and the establishment of the Haitian republic at the beginning of the nineteenth, Haiti occupied the Dominican Republic, which has the distinction of being the only Latin American country that gained its independence not from Spain but from a black republic (*see* HAITI and DOMINICAN REPUBLIC). Haiti, in the minds of Dominicans, came to symbolize blackness and African cultural and religious values, the antithesis of the value system of the European-minded elite.

Regional migrations in the nineteenth and twentieth centuries from English- and French-speaking Caribbean countries account for the increased presence of people of African descent in Costa Rica, Venezuela, PANAMA, Cuba, and even Brazil, and have important sociocultural, economic, and political consequences for Afro-Latin American research.

PERU, viewed principally as a country of Indians, *mestizos*, and whites, is also home to a community of blacks whose origins may be traced to the relatively small number of African slaves who had been absorbed into the general population by the 1830s. Despite its near invisibility, the Afro-Peruvian community has spawned an institute for Afro-Peruvian research, civil rights organizations, and a host of cultural groups. In the 1960s and early 1970s, NICOMEDES SANTA CRUZ, a self-identified Afro-Peruvian poet and cultural activist, wrote of the struggles of black South Africans to end racial oppression.

Recent research has shown the presence in nineteenth-century ARGENTINA of a black community whose visibility within Buenos Aires province and the rest of the nation ended after 1900. Findings from Colombia and ECUADOR point to the importance of regional concentrations in the study of Afro-Latin America. In Colombia, the Pacific coast (the Chocó region, where blacks are dominant) and the Atlantic coast (in Barranquilla and Cartagena, which have significant black communities) have Afro-Latin American populations with different relations to the structures of power and prestige in the dominant society. Urban areas have been shown to offer Afro-Latin American residents a space for organizing religious, cultural, and political activities. This phenomenon can be seen in Brazil in nineteenth-century Salvador, BAHIA, among African slaves, Brazil-born descendants of slaves, and free Afro-Brazilians; in Buenos Aires (Argentina); and in Lima (Peru). In Brazil, Rio de Janeiro, Salvador, and São Paulo, there are to this day centers of activity for Afro-Brazilians.

From the earliest research to the inquiries of present-day scholars, the African-derived religions of Latin America – CANDOMBLÉ, Macumba, and SANTERÍA – have been a major focus of Afro-Latin American studies (*see* RELIGIONS, AFRICAN, IN LATIN AMERICA AND THE CARIBBEAN). The blending of aspects of Catholicism and traditional African religions that began during slavery – most notably the identification of Catholic saints with African deities – shows the creative survival of a people and the endurance of institutions once deemed barbarous by the dominant society. Indeed, one can no longer assume that the practitioners of Candomblé, for example, are predominantly people of African descent: Afro-Brazilian religious traditions have crossed the border into purportedly Eurocentric Argentina. Afro-Latin Americans today may be adherents of Catholicism, Protestantism, or religions of Asian derivation, and the number of those who adhere to the traditions of their ancestors is not easily determined. That they exist reminds us that the study and appreciation of Latin American culture continues to have an important Afro component.

That Afro-Latin Americans, as individuals and in groups, articulate views that reflect a deeper connection to the global black world often challenges the widely accepted image of a Latin America that has managed to escape racial antagonism, racially segregated public spaces, and racially based inequalities among its citizens (*see* BLACKNESS IN LATIN AMERICA AND THE CARIBBEAN: AN INTERPRETATION and MYTH OF RACIAL DEMOCRACY IN LATIN AMERICA AND THE CARIBBEAN: AN INTERPRETATION). By articulating a connection with the global black diaspora, Afro-Latin Americans are implying that the situation in Latin America might not be unique, and that racism and racial inequalities exist in Latin America as they do elsewhere. The underrepresentation of Afro-Latin Americans in education, politics, business, and the centers of prestige and power is but a vivid reminder of a persistent inequity and moves the object of inquiry well beyond a focus on the celebrated few who have achieved success.

Throughout the nineteenth century, the specter of the Haitian Revolution and blacks rising en masse to end slavery and racial domination fueled the anxieties of Latin American societies. Today, Afro-Latin American activists, in spite of language barriers, struggle to keep abreast of developments in Africa and the United States. In the process they raise keen suspicion among the dominant sectors, who see such interest as both a betrayal of national identity and a possible move toward the violent patterns of North American race relations. Afro-Latin Americans, in their own defense, sometimes adopt a superpatriotic identity.

Required proclamations of national loyalties have posed no obstacle to some Afro-Latin Americans. The Black Brazilian Front found inspiration and example in Marcus Garvey's UNIVERSAL NEGRO IMPROVEMENT ASSOCIATION of the late 1910s and 1920s, and other activists looked to the movements to liberate Africa from European colonialism and the struggle to end APARTHEID in South Africa.

The United States has, since the mid-1960s, seen steady growth in the number of Latin American immigrants, which translates into complex research questions (*see* Afro-Latino Cultures in the United States). For example, to what extent does common nationality take precedence over the traditional black-white racial division in the United States? In other words, on which side of the hyphen does the Afro-Latin American's primary identity lie? Is the recent push for adding a mixed-race category to the United States census a reflection of the Latin Americanization of race relations in the United States? And, in turn, does the experience of Latin Americans, of all races, in the United States pave the way for the greatly feared North Americanization of race relations, with race defined in bipolar black or white terms in Latin America itself?

The pioneering research of Roger Bastide (from France), FERNANDO ORTIZ (Cuba), GILBERTO FREYRE (Brazil), Melville J. Herskovits (United States), and Manoel Querino (Brazil), and the writings of Adalberto Ortíz (Ecuador), MANUEL ZAPATA OLIVELLA (Colombia), and Ramon Diaz Sánchez (Venezuela) laid the groundwork for subsequent research on Afro-Latin America. The titles of recent works are a fine reflection of the state of current research: *No Longer Invisible: Afro-Latin Americans Today* (1995); *Our Rightful Share: The Afro-Cuban Struggle for Equality, 1886-1912* (1995); *Blackness and Race Mixture: The Dynamics of Racial Identity in Colombia* (1993); *Slave Rebellion in Brazil: The Muslim Uprising of 1835 in Bahia* (1993); *Castro, the Blacks, and Africa* (1988); *The Making of the African Diaspora in the Americas* (1987); *The Afro-Argentines of Buenos Aires, 1800 to 1900* (1980); *Black Writers in Latin America* (1979); and *The African Experience in Spanish America, 1512 to the Present Day* (1976).

The increasing visibility of Afro-Latin Americans who consciously assert an awareness of their African heritage argues for further research into their achievements and continuing struggles. The aim would be to bring Afro-Latin America closer to general discussions of the multiple dimensions of Africa in the Americas.

Anani Dzidzienyo

SEE ALSO

South Africa; Garvey, Marcus Mosiah; Haitian Revolution; Afro-Latino Cultures in the United States; Cartagena de Indias, Colombia; Pacific Coast of Colombia; Ortiz, Adalberto; Querino, Manoel Raimundo; Rio de Janeiro, Brazil; Catholic Church in Latin America and the Caribbean; Religions, African, in Latin America and the Caribbean; Protestant Church in Latin America and the Caribbean.

Children in Miami's Little Havana section. Once dominated by Cuban immigrants, later influxes of people from Honduras, Nicaragua, and El Salvador prompted the area's officially being renamed the city's "Latin Quarter." *© 1983 José Azel/Aurora*

Cross Cultural

Afro-Latino Cultures in the United States

The presence of Afro-Latino culture spans the history of the United States, and its earliest manifestations may predate the first English settlements and the very founding of the United States.

If by the term we are referring broadly to the cultural experience of Spanish-speaking black people in what has become the territory of the United States, then their role in the settlement of San Augustín, Florida, in 1565, and later in building the city's Castle of San Marcos (1672-1695) and Fort Mose (1702) places Afro-Latinos at the threshold of American history. Or perhaps, given the foundational symbolism of Jamestown (1620) and Plymouth (1607), those initial Afro-Latino experiences in Spanish Florida are more the antechamber, the less ceremonious advance contact between European invaders and indigenous peoples. As buffers and cannon fodder, as reconnaissance scouts and militiamen, as intermediaries, and, of course, as attendants and slaves, Afro-Latinos have been implicated in the forging of the North American story, made to comply with, and at the same time be themselves subject victims of, its inhuman excesses. Afro-Latino culture thus not only enriches but also points up the limits and exclusions of the hegemonic Anglo-American culture and its history.

The first Afro-Latino historical personage, immortalized in the memorable *Relación* of Cabeza de Vaca, was the famed ESTEBANICO the Black Man. Estebanico, along with the chronicler Cabeza de Vaca himself, was one of the four survivors of the ill-starred voyage of the Spanish explorer Pánfilo de Narvaez along the Florida coast in 1528. After many years of captivity among the Indian tribes of Florida, Estebanico then joined Cabeza de Vaca on the long trek across the continent, traversing what is now Texas and northern MEXICO. But Estebanico's unique historical role actually occurs in the years following those recounted by Cabeza de Vaca, which saw him joining the 1539 expedition of Fray Marcos de Niza to the legendary city of Cíbola (New Mexico) and providing indispensable reconnoitering and intermediary services to the campaign. It is said that to the native Puebla people he assumed magical and extrahuman qualities and, by now referred to as "the Black Mexican," was revered for his healing powers. Though Estebanico may appear an isolated and idiosyncratic instance of Afro-Latino presence in U.S. history, his most distinctive cultural features – his blackness and his Spanish language, and how they figure in the Anglo-Indian-African interaction that was to shape U.S. history – clearly prefigure those of subsequent Afro-Latino generations. His dilemma, too, of a black man serving as advance guard in the exploratory incursions of the white man, also remains a recurrent one in U.S. racial and cultural relations to the present.

While this prototypical positioning of the Afro-Latino first came into view in the sixteenth century, and in northern Mexico (now the American Southwest), the history of the group actually transpired in the nineteenth and twentieth centuries and in the eastern part of the country. Afro-Latinos in the United States are preponderantly of Hispanic Caribbean origins, emigrating in largest numbers from CUBA, PUERTO RICO, the Dominican Republic, Panama, and the coastal areas of COLOMBIA and VENEZUELA. The mid-nineteenth century initiated the formative period, which witnessed both the centrality of black-Latino historical relations in the war with Mexico – especially in the debates over the extension of slavery to Mexican territories – and the beginnings of the long-term experience of black Cubans in southern Florida. The burgeoning cigar industry brought thousands of Cubans, along with some Puerto Ricans, Spaniards, and Italians, to the cities of Tampa, Key West, and Ybor City, the majority of the cigar workers being Afro-Cubans (the owners and overseers were mostly white Cubans and Spaniards). After the turn of the century, and especially after the decline of the cigar industry by 1920, the population waned significantly, but between 1870 and 1940 the first sizable Afro-Latino community experienced the collective triumphs and hardships of prolonged group life in U.S. society. The Key West area was felt to be an extension of Havana, as many of the workers moved back and forth with frequency, establishing the kind of cross-border cultural dynamism so characteristic of later Afro-Latino peoples in times closer to our own. They enjoyed differential relations with other nationalities, most complex yet perhaps most significant with white Cubans on the one hand and African Americans on the other. Historical accounts show that while in the earlier period there existed a strong cultural and political unity among all Cubans and "Latinos" along national and linguistic lines, the impact of post-Reconstruction and JIM CROW conditions escalated the antiblack racism and increased the need for solidarity with other blacks. Ample testimony as to this unique Afro-Latino predicament remains available in the periodical literature and organizational documents of this historically important but largely unexplored community experience.

In the course of the twentieth century, the main locus of Afro-Latino cultural life has shifted from Florida to New York City, and from the Cuban to the Puerto Rican diaspora. Prior to the SPANISH-CUBAN-AMERICAN WAR and 1898 the two groups converged and united in their common struggle against Spanish colonialism, as represented in the Partido Revolucionario Cubano and its Puerto Rican section and the joint leadership of figures of the stature of JOSÉ MARTÍ, Eugenio María de Hostos, and Sotero Figueroa. During this later nineteenth-century period, the famous black Cuban general Antonio Maceo took on immense symbolic importance in Cuba and the United States; his name resonates in the frequently used first name Maceo (usually pronounced MAY-see-o) among African Americans. Though proclamations of racial equality were integral to the abolitionist and anticolonial rhetoric of the movement, evidence exists of the relegation and subordination of black members, as well as the absence and nonencouragement of any distinctive black cultural or political agenda.

With the U.S. occupation of Cuba and Puerto Rico and the ever growing migratory presence of both populations in New York and other northeastern cities, the central cultural concern of Afro-Latinos in the United States becomes their relationship with African Americans, and more generally with an African-descendant diasporic world. This new perspective is embodied most prominently by Arturo Alfonso Schomburg, a black Puerto Rican who took active part in the anti-Spanish liberation struggle, serving as secretary in the highly important Club Dos Antillas under the leadership of José Martí. Schomburg's Caribbean and Latino background has unfortunately been eclipsed by his subsequent accomplishments as a seminal figure in the HARLEM RENAISSANCE and as one of the foremost collectors and bibliophiles of the Africana experience, culminating in the founding of today's Schomburg Center for Research in Black Culture in New York City. Given his immense educational contribution to knowledge about the black world, which continued to include a special interest in the Caribbean, Latin America, and SPAIN, Schomburg may be considered the most illustrious and self-conscious of all Afro-Latinos in the United States, as well as the one whose aspirations and ambiguities seem the most deeply exemplary of Afro-Latino social experience. Furthermore, his involvement in both worlds is exemplified in his role as a bridge between Afro-Latino and African American writers and artists, most notably between the major poets NICOLÁS GUILLÉN and LANGSTON HUGHES.

By mid-century Puerto Ricans were already outnumbering Cubans as the largest Latino group in New York City, and the composition and nature of the Cuban migrations after the revolution in 1959 contributed further to this demographic change. While Cubans remained the archetype, and the stereotype, of Afro-Latino culture in the increasingly important U.S. mass culture, it was Puerto Ricans who made up the most sizable and vocal community of U.S. Afro-Latinos. The black Puerto Rican journalist and long-time Communist militant JESÚS COLÓN provided memorable depictions of life as a black Latino in his newspaper columns and sketches collected in *A Puerto Rican in New York* (1961). Furthermore, the 1960s saw an outburst of literary and cultural expression give voice and perspective to the particular position of young people who are both Puerto Rican and black. Most notable among these works is the autobiographical novel *Down These Mean Streets* (1967) by the young black Puerto Rican author PIRI THOMAS. Here we find nothing short of a psychological

Spanish Harlem, New York, also known as "El Barrio," is a center of Latin American culture in the United States. *Gerd Ludwig*

anatomy of the black Latino paradox, and the tortuous struggle to affirm both identities in the binary black-white U.S. racial formation.

In a similar vein, the so-called "Nuyorican" poets of the 1970s like Pedro Pietri, Sandra María Esteves, Felipe Luciano, and Victor Hernández Cruz incorporate a strong sense of black cultural identity in their proclamations of a U.S.-based Puerto Rican reality. Collaborations between these poets and such primarily African American ensembles as THE LAST POETS and the Third World Revelationists attest to the strong cultural bonds felt by Afro-Latinos with their African American contemporaries. Slightly more recent poets like Tato Laviera, Louis Reyes Rivera, and Willie Perdomo deepen these cross-cultural insights even further.

While religion, sports, food, language, and literature are all of vital importance in documenting and interpreting Afro-Latino culture in the United States, it is in the area of music that Afro-Latinos have had their most visible and clearly traceable cultural presence in North America. The legendary Jelly Roll Morton once said that you can't play JAZZ if you don't understand that "Spanish tinge," indicating the essential, constitutive role of Afro-Caribbean music in forging and developing a distinctively "American" musical idiom. Starting with the strong Haitian social and musical presence in New Orleans since the early nineteenth century, and embodied in the 1850s in the Caribbean-tinged trajectory of "America's first composer," the Creole prodigy Louis Moreau Gottschalk, the national music of the United States was born and has grown under the continual and profound influence of Afro-Caribbean styles and practices.

The twentieth century has witnessed a seemingly endless string of musical fads and crazes such as the TANGO, the RUMBA, the BOSSA NOVA, the conga, and the MAMBO – all dilutions of Afro-Latino traditions, mostly of Cuban and Brazilian provenance. In the late 1940s the fusion between Afro-Cuban and African American musics reached a new depth and complexity with the collaboration of Cuban innovators Mario Bauzá, Frank Grillo ("Machito"), and conga player Chano Pozo with jazz luminaries Dizzy Gillespie, Charlie Parker, and many others. The resulting "Cubop" then set the stage for the multiple interactions between these musical traditions under the names of Latin jazz and salsa. This rich cross-cultural mingling between Afro-Latino and African American traditions has found continuity in recent years with the varied styles and genres of hip hop, with Afro-Latinos playing a central though often obscured role in founding styles in RAP, graffiti, and breakdancing.

Juan Flores

SEE ALSO

Breakdancing; Gillespie, John Birks ("Dizzy"); Graffiti Art; Hip Hop in the United States; New York, New York; Parker, Charles Christopher ("Bird"); Reconstruction; Schomburg, Arthur Alfonso; Latin America, Blacks in; Jazz, Afro-Latin; Bauza, Mario; Dominican Republic; Maceo y Grajales, Antonio; Machito; Panama; Pietri, Pedro Juan; Pozo y González, Luciano (Chano); Salsa Music; Brazil; Music, Afro-Caribbean Secular; Baseball in Latin America and the Caribbean; Haiti; Colonial Latin America and the Caribbean; Havana, Cuba.

Africa

Afusari (also known as Afusare, Izere, Jari, Jarawa, Feserek, Afizarek, Fezere, Jarawan Dutse and Fizere), ethnic group of NIGERIA.

The Afusari primarily inhabit the Kadima, Plateau, and Bauchi States of Nigeria. They speak a Niger-Congo language. Approximately 200,000 people consider themselves Afusari.

SEE ALSO

Languages, African: An Overview.

Africa

Afwerki, Isaias (b. February 2, 1946, Asmara, Eritrea), leader of Eritrean fight for independence from Ethiopia and president of Eritrea since 1993.

As leader of the largest rebel force in Eritrea's independence struggle, Isaias Afwerki strove to unify peoples of diverse cultures and religious beliefs. Since assuming office, he has been widely praised for his pragmatism and modesty, and for maintaining a regime free of corruption. Like Rwanda's PAUL KAGAME, Uganda's Yoweri Museveni, and Ethiopia's MELES ZENAWI, Afwerki belongs to what has been called Africa's "new generation" of leaders, all of whom are known for their military backgrounds and for their tactical rather than ideological approach to leadership.

Isaias Afwerki was born at a time when the fate of the former Italian colony of Eritrea was in limbo. By the time he graduated from the elite Prince Makonnen Secondary School in Asmara in 1965, Ethiopia had annexed Eritrea, and Eritrean opponents to the despotic rule of Emperor Haile Selassie were preparing for all-out warfare. But like many TIGRINYA youth, Afwerki still went to Haile Selassie University in Addis Ababa, ETHIOPIA, where he studied engineering. After only a year, however, he was gripped by the revolutionary fervor sweeping through the Eritrean student body, and he quit school to join the Eritrean Liberation Front (ELF).

Afwerki rose through the ranks to become a deputy division commander for the ELF but soon clashed with the organization's Muslim-dominated leadership. A few years later he helped found the Eritrean People's Liberation Front (EPLF). Like the ELF, the EPLF described itself as a Marxist organization, and Afwerki was among those who went to China for training in guerrilla warfare. By the time the Ethiopian regime fell in 1991, the EPLF had moderated its previous positions, and Afwerki was the clear choice to become independent Eritrea's first leader. He served as acting president until the country gained official independence on May 24, 1993, and was formally elected president by the National Assembly shortly thereafter. Since then he has generally enjoyed broad popular support.

David P. Johnson, Jr.

SEE ALSO

Addis Ababa, Ethiopia; Asmara, Eritrea; Ethiopia; Museveni, Yoweri; Rwanda; Uganda; Gebrselassie, Haile.

Agadja. Please see FON

Africa

Agaja

(b. 1673, present-day BENIN; d. 1740, present-day Benin), king of Dahomey.

Agaja succeeded his brother, Akaba, in 1708 to become the third ruler of the Dahomey Kingdom. Agaja was a shrewd and powerful king, expanding the kingdom and making it one of the most powerful in West Africa. He spent much of his early reign instituting administrative reforms that centralized and strengthened the kingdom: he created an elite corps of female guards, enlarged the royal army, and employed military spies who acquired information about neighboring groups. These innovations proved crucial to his victorious conquest of the Allada and Whydah Kingdoms in the 1720s. The acquisition of these coastal kingdoms gave the previously landlocked Dahomey access to the sea and, consequently, European trade.

Agaja's ambition to control the TRANSATLANTIC SLAVE TRADE that flowed through these ports brought him into rivalry with the neighboring YORUBA kingdom of Oyo, whose attacks on Dahomey forced Agaja to surrender in 1730 and agree to pay tribute. Some believe that Agaja had hoped to replace the transatlantic slave trade with a domestic slave economy so that his kingdom could reap the economic benefits of slave labor (*see* SLAVERY IN AFRICA). But Europeans showed little interest in his invitation to establish slave plantations in Dahomey, and instead the kingdom, seeking to finance the purchase of firearms and other goods from the Europeans, became one of the biggest slave suppliers on the Slave Coast. Agaja's attempt to monopolize the slave trade, angered independent Dahomean slave traders, and by 1735 Agaja's kingdom faced serious internal unrest. Two years later he acquiesced to the independent traders' demands for access to the lucrative slave trade. Nevertheless, the kingdom of Dahomey reemerged as a dominant supplier of slaves after the death of Agaja in 1740. His conquests and internal reforms buttressed Dahomey's strength and prosperity, which endured for more than a century.

Elizabeth Heath

See Also
Dahomey, Early Kingdom of; Oyo, Early Kingdom of.

Africa

Agaw (also known as the Agau and Agew), ethnic group of the Horn of Africa.

The Agaw primarily inhabit central and northern Ethiopia and Eritrea. They speak an Afro-Asiatic language in the Cushitic cluster, suggesting that their ancestors lived in the region for thousands of years before the arrival of speakers of Semitic languages, such as the Amhara and Tigre. There are approximately 200,000 people identify themselves as Agaw.

See Also
Languages, African: An Overview.

Cross Cultural

Agriculture, African, in the Americas: An Interpretation

Lost Crops of Africa, a 1996 book by the National Research Council, draws attention to the potential of the continent's little-known indigenous crops for improving regional and global food supplies. Featured prominently among the 2000 native grains, roots, and fruits utilized as food staples is African rice (*Oryza glaberrima*), "the great red rice of the hook of the Niger." Yet, despite its potential, there are other compelling reasons for a research focus on glaberrima.

This overview of rice history in the Americas raises several issues that bear on prevailing conceptions of the "Columbian Exchange," the period of unparalleled crop exchanges from the sixteenth through eighteenth centuries. Scholarship on the Columbian Exchange has long emphasized the economically viable crops of American, Asian, and European origin; the role of Europeans in their global dispersal; and thus, the diffusion of crops to, rather than from, Africa. The slight attention accorded African crops in this scholarship is related to two factors: (1) the minor role of African domesticates like okra, cowpeas, yams, pearl millet, and sorghum in food and plantation economies; and (2) the long-standing belief that rice was solely of Asian origin.

Recent historical research on the beginnings of rice cultivation in the United States South, however, challenges the view that Africa contributed little more than labor to the agricultural history of the Americas. In extending the emphasis on rice history to Latin America, through a preliminary integration of botanical and historical materials, this essay lends additional support to the argument that glaberrima and slaves played a crucial role in the expansion of rice cultivation in the Americas during the early period of the transatlantic slave trade. In so doing, this article also engages broader issues of technology transfer, indigenous knowledge, and the active role of slaves in adapting a preferred dietary staple to diverse New World environments.

This essay is divided into four parts. The first section addresses botanical scholarship on rice origins, with emphasis on the discovery during the twentieth century that rice domestication occurred in West Africa independently of Asia, long viewed as the sole center of the plant's domestication. The next section shifts to the United States, where historical and historical-geographical research from the 1970s first claimed African agency in adjusting rice cultivation to the South Carolina swamps, the crop that sustained the South's most lucrative plantation economy. The role of the Cape Verde Islands as a pioneering agricultural experiment station for African crops and as an entrepôt for the diffusion of rice to Brazil is the focus of the third section. The last section presents the botanical and historical evidence for an early presence of glaberrima rice in the Americas.

Botanical Scholarship on African Rice

Domestication of African rice occurred more than 3000 years ago in the region from Senegal to the Côte d'Ivoire, long before any navigator from Java or Arabia could have introduced rice to Madagascar or the East African coast. From the eighth to the sixteenth century Arab and European commentaries mention rice cultivation along the inland delta of the Niger River and West African coast as well as the frequent purchases of surpluses by Portuguese mariners. During the transatlantic slave trade rice surpluses contributed to provisioning slave ships bound for the Americas. Yet, despite numerous commentaries on West African rice from the earliest period of contact, well into the twentieth century scholars routinely assigned rice an Asian origin, its diffusion to Africa attributed to Arab and Portuguese traders. As a result of the bias in scholarship, researchers failed to consider the indigenous knowledge base of African rice-production systems and its potential linkage to the cereal's appearance in the Americas.

African Agency in Establishing Rice Cultivation in South Carolina

Until historian Peter Wood's pathbreaking research on the evolution of the rice plantation system in colonial South Carolina, there was no hint that rice cultivation in the United States might owe its genesis to African slaves. Noting the appearance of rice cultivation in tandem with slavery from the earliest settlement period (1670-1730), the unfamiliarity of the colony's English and French Huguenot planters with cultivation techniques, and glaberrima domestication in West Africa, Wood attributed the crucial skills involved in the plantation rice system to West African slaves already familiar with its planting. Rice formed the dietary staple of millions swept into the transatlantic slave trade, and the Africa rice region contributed more than 40 percent of the slaves delivered to colonial South Carolina.

Scholar D. C. Littlefield advanced Wood's hypothesis by drawing attention to the antiquity of rice production in West Africa, European interest in the techniques of its cultivation during the transatlantic slave trade, and planter preference for slaves with rice-growing experience. He identified as of African origin the floodplain rice cultivation system found along the Upper Guinea Coast, where groups like the Baga perfected methods to desalinate fertile mangrove soils for rice cultivation. By enclosing plots with earthen palisades or embankments and constructing small canals, the Baga could retain water on the fields or remove it through gravity flow at low tides. As analogous techniques developed on Carolina floodplains, Littlefield showed that a rice system long attributed to planter ingenuity formed in fact an important part of the agronomic heritage of slaves from the West African rice region.

The absence of transplanting on Carolina floodplains was typical of rice cultivation in Africa, but not Asia. Also evident were parallel techniques of production like water control by sluices constructed from hollowed tree trunks, a comprehensive understanding of tidal ebb and flow to prevent field over-flooding while enabling cultivation in areas occasionally menaced by saltwater intrusion, and the widespread use of long-handled hoes for land preparation (still used in African rice farming).

But rice could become a valued export crop only when it was processed to remove the indigestible hulls. Until the advent of water-driven mills during the second half of the eighteenth century, rice milling was performed by hand in the African manner with a wooden mortar and pestle. The hulls were removed through winnowing the cereal in fanner baskets, woven in the same way as those for analogous purposes in the Senegambian rice area of West Africa.

The Cape Verde Islands and African Rice

From the mid-fifteenth century, settlement of the Cape Verde Islands, and especially Santiago, unfolded amid an active trade with

West African coastal peoples for waxes, hides, indigo, foodstuffs, salt, and slaves. Since the ninth century the littoral and offshore islands of the Upper Guinea Coast from Guinea Bissau to SIERRA LEONE had served as an important crossroads for the long-distance trade in salt. Wet rice cultivation supported this vast trading network, but the crop only emerged as an important trade good with the arrival of the Portuguese. By 1479 the principal ethnic groups of the region – the Baga, JOLA, BALANTA, Bullom/Sherbro, and Temne – were already marketing their dietary staple to the Portuguese. Their prominence in initial African-Portuguese trading networks, however, was not to endure; by the closure of the eighteenth century hundreds of thousands of wet rice farmers had become captives of the transatlantic slave trade.

At the onset of the sixteenth century, Valentim Fernandes, drawing upon earlier mariner accounts, ascribed the introduction of both rice and cotton cultivation in Santiago to the wet rice area of the Guinea Coast. The emergence of a sugar cane and grazing economy on the island during this period proceeded in tandem with the cultivation of African domesticates like yams, sorghum, millet, and rainfed and swamp rice.

Thus, by the sixteenth century, the initial period of the Columbian Exchange, the Cape Verde Islands were already serving as an ex officio agricultural research station for plant experimentation. European ships regularly provisioned there on outbound and inbound voyages to the Americas, these voyages serving to introduce American cultivars like maize and manioc to West Africa. But the American cultivars were preceded by an active rice trade, well in place by 1514. Rice appears on cargo lists of ships departing Cape Verde in 1513-1515. In 1530, just 30 years after Cabral claimed Brazil for Portugal, a ship left Santiago for Brazil, carrying rice seed in its cargo.

This voyage was followed in subsequent decades by other vessels that delivered seed rice to the state of BAHIA, an important locus for the sugar plantation system in Brazil's northeast. In 1587 the Bahian planter Gabriel Soares de Sousa noted the important role of the Cape Verde Islands for animal and crop introductions to Brazil. He attributed the widespread cultivation of rainfed and swamp rice to seed rice brought from Cape Verde, while noting slave preference for YAMS and foods of African origin, the mortar and pestle for food processing, and the triumph of African dietary preferences among the slave population.

THE DIFFUSION OF RICE CULTIVATION TO THE AMERICAS

Documents pertaining to Brazil prior to the mid-eighteenth century make frequent reference to rice, especially a red-hulled species, over a broad area from the northeast to the Amazon. Red rice again surfaces in commentaries during the second half of the eighteenth century, when a rice plantation system developed in the eastern Amazon with backing from metropolitan capital. The objective was to develop Amazonian exports to Portugal and thereby reduce dependency on Carolina rice imports as the American colonies headed into the Revolutionary War. This led to the implementation from the 1760s of tidal-irrigated rice plantations in the Amazonian states of Amapá, Pará, and Maranhão; the introduction of high-yielding "Carolina white" rice seed (a sativa variety); water mills for rice processing; the import of more than 25,000 slaves (many from the rice-growing region of Guinea Bissau); and, in 1767, the first exports of milled rice to Portugal.

But the continued cultivation of red rice aroused official concern. In a 1772 decree the Portuguese administration mandated a year's jail sentence and fine to whites planting the red rice and two years of imprisonment for slaves and Indians who did. While the reasons for this legal action remain unclear, it may suggest that the red variety was a glaberrima, which breaks more easily in milling and, when mixed with the improved variety, would have resulted in a higher percentage of broken rice and thus lower prices in European markets.

African rice may also figure in discussions of early varieties planted in the United States South. "Guinea rice" is listed among the varieties grown by slaves in their gardens in South Carolina, the toponym suggesting a West African origin. A cultivated red rice is recorded by J. Lawson in 1709 and in 1731. In another area of plantation slavery, SURINAME, the Dutch governor noted in 1750 the advantages of rice varieties cultivated there compared to one type found in South Carolina: "the rice in Essequibo has not the red husk which gives so much trouble in Carolina to get off." This may well indicate the advantages of sativa over glaberrima varieties in milling. Certainly by the mid-eighteenth century, rice export markets were based on Asian varieties. The high-yielding Carolina "white" and "gold" that made the colony's production world famous and introduced to the Amazon were sativa varieties.

Glaberrima was certainly introduced to Georgia in 1790 by Thomas Jefferson, whose request for rainfed rice varieties from slave merchants resulted in a shipment of seed rice from Guinea-Conakry. Jefferson asked for rainfed varieties, hoping to stimulate upland rice planting, which would reduce the death toll of slaves exposed to malarial floodplain cultivation. The merchants' descriptions of the African upland rice systems echo those of Dutch geographer Olfert Dapper, who noted 150 years earlier similar features and the short-duration characteristics that distinguish glaberrima rice.

The significance of rice as a food staple among maroon communities of the Guianas was already evident during the eighteenth century, when European mercenaries were sent to recapture them; maroons frequently cultivated rice, in forest clearings and inland swamps. The cereal's importance in maroon history is captured in legends by their descendants. In the area of Cayenne where Vaillant found the Baga varieties, the maroons claimed that rice originally came from Africa, brought by female slaves who smuggled the grains in their hair.

Yet, despite the crop's early association in the Guianas with slaves and maroons, little is known about the initial history of rice cultivation in the region. Several books mention that rice was being planted by ex-slaves prior to the arrival of the Javanese and Indian indentured laborers, who established it as a cash crop between the 1870s and 1930s, but little else is said. A great deal more archival research is needed on the food systems of plantation economies.

CONCLUSIONS

Eighteenth-century observers of plantation economies attributed the cultivation and diffusion of sorghum (*Sorghum vulgare*) and African oil palm (*Elaeis guineensis*) in the Americas to introduction by slave ships, thereby drawing importance to the role of commerce and scientific societies for the delivery of economically useful plants. However, less explored are the accounts that claim that African slaves directly introduced crops like okra (*Abelmoschus esculentus*), cowpeas or black-eyed peas (*Vigna unguiculata*), and yams (*Dioscorea cayenensis*) to the Americas. These crops, initially established in slave provision gardens, provided the locus for the survival of many African crops among black populations of the Americas. A research focus then on the networks that enabled slaves to obtain seeds of their favored dietary staples would undoubtedly improve our understanding of the role of African crops and its peoples in establishing their food staples in the Americas.

Judy Carney

SEE ALSO

Conakry, Guinea; Cape Verde; Guinea-Bissau; Portugal; Salt Trade; American Revolution; French Guiana.

Latin America and the Caribbean

Aguirre Beltrán, Gonzalo

(b. Veracruz, Mexico, 1918; d. Veracruz, Mexico, 1995), one of Mexico's most influential historians and anthropologists, who almost single-handedly revived interest in the history and contemporary lives of Afro-Mexicans.

Gonzalo Aguirre Beltrán received his primary and secondary schooling in Veracruz, where there was a strong African influence, before studying medicine in Mexico City. In the 1920s and 1930s intellectuals such as José

Vasconcelos undertook pioneering studies of Indians in Mexico, whose culture and history had largely been viewed with disdain until then. The studies resurrected a degree of interest in and dignity for Indian heritage. Although Vasconcelos argued that much of indigenous culture should be subsumed in a larger Mexican culture, Aguirre Beltrán believed that indigenous cultures were worthy of study for their own sake. After graduating from the University of Mexico with a medical degree, Aguirre Beltrán returned to Veracruz, where he held a post in public health that further sparked his interest in Indian ethnicity and history. In 1940 he published two studies on the ethnohistory of colonial and pre-colonial Indians in Mexico, *El señorío de Cuauhtochco* and *Luchas agrarias en México durante el Virrenato* (*see* LATIN AMERICA, BLACKS AND INDIANS IN: AN INTERPRETATION).

Aguirre Beltrán then turned his focus to Afro-Mexicans. Although Africans had played a vital role in early Mexico, and although hundreds of thousands of modern Mexicans are descended from Africans – most of whom were brought to Mexico as slaves – modern Mexico largely denied the existence of both historic and contemporary Afro-Mexicans before Aguirre Beltrán published his groundbreaking work. In *La población negra de México*, published in 1946, Aguirre Beltrán undertook an exhaustive study of black ethnicity and history that detailed the origins in Africa of Mexico's blacks, the routes they traveled to Mexico, their settlement patterns once there, and their treatment by Spanish colonists. Aguirre Beltrán convincingly established that early Afro-Mexicans far outnumbered Spanish colonists. He was also one of the first historians to shed light on the rigid caste system that the Spanish church and state created and maintained in Mexico. This system stigmatized blacks, who received better treatment if they could claim they were *mestizo*, or biracial. Aguirre Beltrán argued that centuries of intermarriage among blacks, Indians, and whites, combined with the caste stigma, led to the gradual disappearance of full-blooded Afro-Mexicans and the decline of Afro-Mexican culture. His conclusions drew praise from those who valued his "rediscovery" of black Mexicans and hostility from those who continued to see Mexico's black heritage as a stain. Half a century after Aguirre Beltrán's pioneering study, however, Mexico's government officially acknowledged this black "third root" as a part of the country's heritage no less integral than Mexico's Indian and European roots.

Although Aguirre Beltrán supplemented his original study with later articles, he spent most of the rest of his life working to ease the plight of poor and disenfranchised Indians. In several works, he argued that in former colonies like Mexico, large native populations were still subjected to what was essentially colonial domination by the white elite long after colonization had ended. In the 1960s Aguirre Beltrán was named the director of Mexico's National Indian Institute. He used the post to extend programs for education, health, and development to rural, mostly Indian, Mexico. When his policies came under attack in the late 1960s, he retired from the Indian Institute and returned to ethnohistorical studies.

SEE ALSO
Mexico; Colonial Latin America and the Caribbean.

Africa

Ahanta, ethnic group of GHANA.

The Ahanta primarily inhabit the coast of western Ghana. They speak a Niger-Congo language and are considered part of the larger AKAN ethnolinguistic group. Approximately 150,000 people identify themselves as Ahanta.

SEE ALSO
Languages, African: An Overview.

Africa

Ahidjo, El Hajj Ahmadou

(b. August 1924, Garoua, French Cameroun [present-day CAMEROON]; d. November 30, 1989, Dakar, SENEGAL), nationalist leader and president of Cameroon from 1960 to 1982.

Born and raised as a Muslim in the northern administrative center of Garoua, Ahmadou Ahidjo attended secondary school and college in Yaoundé. After working for several years as a radio operator, Ahidjo turned to politics. His 1949 election to the Cameroun representative assembly was followed by election in the 1950s to the territorial and union assemblies. He built a strong power base among the northern elite, comprised of Fulbé notables and HAUSA merchants. As head of the northern Union Camérounaise (UC), Ahidjo became vice prime minister in the preindependence coalition government with the Union of the Population of Cameroun (UPC). When the coalition collapsed in 1958, Ahidjo formed a new government, calling for immediate independence while reassuring FRANCE that close ties would be maintained.

On the first day of 1960, Cameroon became independent, with Ahidjo as president. He ruled Cameroon for the next 22 years. Realizing the divisiveness of ethnic, regional, religious, and linguistic identities, Ahidjo focused on building national unity. Through a 1961 plebiscite Ahidjo reunified British Cameroons and French Cameroun. He also capitalized on his popular appeal as the "father" of the nation to carry out authoritarian measures. Ahidjo centralized the government and incorporated associations representing women, youth, and labor into the sole legal party, the Cameroon National Union (CNU). Security forces, with French assistance, suppressed the vestiges of political opposition, particularly the UPC, which continued to wage a low-level insurgency war. The media were heavily censored.

Infrastructure projects both encouraged economic growth and centralized authority in the capital, Yaoundé. By the time Ahidjo replaced the federation with a republic in 1972, he faced no significant political opposition. He further solidified his control by balancing ethnic representation in the cabinet and national assembly, and by dispensing patronage to supporters in the government bureaucracy, the military, and the business community. This created a situation in which, as one Cameroonian saying goes, "the politics of the belly" predominated. Ahidjo's tight control over the economy and close relations with France made it possible for him to maintain an apparently stable if fairly repressive regime, and to assure Cameroonians a fairly high national standard of living.

On November 4, 1982, Ahidjo resigned, claiming exhaustion, and handed over power to PAUL BIYA, his chosen successor and then prime minister. Ahidjo did not, however, leave the political scene altogether, and as head of the CNU he tried to run the country from behind the scenes. Biya resisted, and conflicts between the two men led Ahidjo Loyalists in the Republican Guard to mount a bloody uprising. But the uprising failed and Ahidjo retired to France where, in absentia, he was tried, convicted, and condemned to death in 1984. President Biya commuted the death sentence, and Ahidjo spent time primarily in Senegal and France until his death in 1989.

Eric Young

SEE ALSO
Dakar, Senegal; Ethnicity and Identity in Africa: An Interpretation; Yaoundé, Cameroon.

Africa

Ahmad Baba (b. October 26, 1556, Arawan [near Tombouctou], present-day Mali; d. April 22, 1627, Tombouctou), Islamic scholar, writer, and jurist.

Ahmad Baba was one of the best-known Islamic scholars and writers of his time. Born into the prestigious Aqit family near Tombouctou (Timbuktu) in 1556, he was educated in Islamic theology and law. After completing his studies, he began writing books and treatises on theology, Islamic jurisprudence, history, and Arabic grammar. Over the course of his life he wrote more than 56 works. More than half of these are still in existence, and several are still used by West African *ulama* (scholars). Ahmad Baba also was a great collector of books; he amassed a library containing thousands of volumes. At this time, Tombouctou, ruled by the Songhai Empire, was renowned throughout the Islamic world as a center of learning.

In 1591 the sultan of MOROCCO invaded Tombouctou. Ahmad Baba and other scholars refused to serve the Moroccan rulers and, by some accounts, instigated a 1593 rebellion against the invaders. Because of their resistance, the Moroccans arrested Ahmad Baba and other prominent literati and deported them to Marrakech in 1594. The Moroccans also confiscated several of the scholars' private libraries. Ahmad Baba reportedly lost nearly 1600 volumes.

In Morocco, Ahmad Baba continued to write and was even allowed to teach and practice law. During this period he wrote the famous *Kifayat al-Muktaj*, a biographical dictionary of Maliki legal scholars and jurists. After the death of the Moroccan sultan in 1607, he was allowed to return to Tombouctou. Upon his return, he wrote a catalogue of Islamic and pagan peoples of the Sudan. This text was later used by USMAN DAN FODIO. Ahmad Baba also wrote a text on Arabic grammar, which is still used in some areas of northern Nigeria.

Elizabeth Heath

SEE ALSO

Marrakech, Morocco; Songhai Empire; Tombouctou, Mali.

Africa

Aidid, Mohammad Farrah

(b. 1934, Italian Somaliland; d. August 1, 1996, Mogadishu, Somalia), leader of the Somali organization that overthrew President MUHAMMAD SIAD BARRE.

Mohammad Farrah Aidid was born in Italian Somaliland and trained in the military in Rome and Moscow. After returning to independent SOMALIA, Aidid served in the army under Gen. Muhammad Siad Barre. When Siad Barre assumed the presidency in 1969, he appointed Aidid chief of staff of the army. Later that year, however, he began to suspect Aidid's loyalties, and imprisoned him without trial for seven years on charges of treasonous conspiracy.

In 1977 Siad Barre released Aidid and welcomed him back to the administration, no doubt seeking his help for the ongoing border war against ETHIOPIA. The loyalties of Aidid to his former jailer are unclear, but he served Siad Barre's military administration until the late 1980s. In 1989 Aidid broke with Siad Barre and joined the United Somali Congress (USC), an organization dominated by the Hawiye clan. The USC was one of several groups seeking the overthrow of the government. Aidid headed the USC capture of Mogadishu, a key victory that led to the ultimate ouster of Siad Barre. Shortly afterward, a rift within the USC between Aidid and Ali Mahdi Mohamed, who had been appointed interim president, turned into a full-scale war between subclans. The country, already suffering from the violence of the military regime, was thrown into complete civil war, with paramilitary groups fighting each other for whatever resources remained.

Both men were declared president by their supporters within the Hawiye clan. In the ensuing power struggle, the factions not only destroyed much of Mogadishu but impeded the distribution of famine relief during one of the worst droughts in Somalia's history. The United Nations sent peacekeeping troops, at first to deliver food aid but later to try to end the war. The United States viewed the "warlord" Aidid as the primary threat to peace, particularly after he was accused of inciting riots against foreign intervention and ambushes that killed 24 Pakistani soldiers and wounded 59. After an unsuccessful attempt by United States soldiers to capture Aidid left 300 Somali and 18 Americans dead, the United States withdrew in 1994, and the United Nations left a year later.

Aidid took the town of Baidoa in 1995, holding international aid workers hostage for several days and confiscating their equipment. A coalition fought against Aidid for power in southern Mogadishu, but he held onto power until his death in August 1996 of complications from a bullet wound. His son Hussein Mohammed, a former U.S. Marine, succeeded him as head of the clan's faction and in 1998 controlled part of Mogadishu.

Marian Aguiar

SEE ALSO

Mogadishu, Somalia; United Nations in Africa.

Africa

Aidoo, Ama Ata **(b. 1942?, Abeadzi Kyiakor, Ghana), writer whose plays, novels, and poetry examine the traditional roles assigned to African women.**

Christina Ama Aidoo was born into a FANTE family she once characterized as "a long line of fighters." Encouraged by her liberal-minded father, Aidoo pursued an English degree at the University of GHANA in Legon. As a student, she won a short story prize, but her interests centered on drama as a means of bringing to life the rich oral traditions of the Fante. She worked closely with Efua Sutherland, a leading Ghanaian dramatist, and became familiar with a Fante dramatic style that blossomed in the 1930s.

Aidoo's first play, *The Dilemma of a Ghost* (1965), was staged in 1964 by the Student's Theatre at the University of Ghana. With this play, Aidoo earned her lasting reputation as a writer (*see* Women Writers in English-Speaking Africa) who examines the traditional African roles of wife and mother. The play, like many of her later works, also demonstrated her willingness to grapple with complex and controversial issues. *The Dilemma of a Ghost* tells the story of an African man who returns to his village from abroad with his African American wife. While the young wife struggles as an outsider among the village women, her Westernized husband attempts to reconcile his inherited traditions with his adopted views. Ultimately, the wife bears the brunt of the couple's decisions, particularly the decision not to have children. Critics of the play noted Aidoo's compelling portrayal of relationships between women.

After receiving a creative writing fellowship at Stanford University in California, Aidoo spent two years traveling. Her next play, *Anowa* (1970), reworked a traditional legend she had learned as a song from her mother. Set in the late nineteenth century, *Anowa* tells the story of a strong-willed woman who refuses an arranged marriage and instead marries a man of her choice, who later makes her miserable. As Anowa's husband becomes a slaveholder, the play also confronts the fact of African participation in the slave trade (*see* TRANSATLANTIC SLAVE TRADE). Speaking about *Anowa* in an interview, Aidoo cited the importance of dealing with the uncomfortable history of African slavery as a key to resolving Africa's future.

Aidoo's next work, *No Sweetness Here* (1970), was a collection of short stories that undertook a number of complicated themes, including the divide between men and women and between rural and urban societies. In these stories, Aidoo brought a sense of the oral to the written word through the use of elements such as African idioms.

Aidoo described her *Our Sister Killjoy; or Reflections from a Black-Eyed Squint* (1977) as fiction in four episodes. In this dense work Aidoo used an experimental form, interspersing the prose narrative with poetry. The story follows a young African woman as she travels from Africa to Europe in the late 1960s, reflecting on the different yet intertwined histories of the two continents. In *Our Sister Killjoy*, which examines underdevelopment, racism, and the exoticizing of Africans, and includes a scene in which the main character rejects the sexual advances of a white woman, Aidoo again showed a willingness to deal with controversial issues.

In 1982 Aidoo was appointed Ghana's minister of education. She left the country a year later for Zimbabwe, where she continued to teach as well as write poems, published in the collection *Someone Talking to Sometime* (1985), and two children's books.

The 1991 novel *Changes* explores the possibilities of self-determination for contemporary women. The story narrates a woman's experience of a polygamous marriage, and her ultimate decision to leave her husband. For Aidoo, who once proclaimed that, given the seriousness of Africa's political problems, she could not imagine herself writing something so frivolous as an African love story, the novel was a realization that "love or the workings of love is also political." It later won her the Commonwealth Writers Prize for African writers. She followed this novel with a second volume of poetry, *An Angry Letter in January* (1992), and a short-story collection, *The Girl Who Can and Other Stories* (1997).

In a recent interview, Aidoo cited the development of African literature as a central concern for her work: "I still believe that one day, when Africa comes into her own, the dynamism of orality might be something that Africa can give to the world."

Marian Aguiar

See Also
Women Writers in English-Speaking Africa; Zimbabwe (Ready Reference).

Africa

AIDS in Africa: An Interpretation

Acquired immune deficiency syndrome (AIDS) is a fatal disease that emerged by the late 1970s in Africa and the United States. The slow-acting human immunodeficiency virus (HIV) that causes AIDS spread silently across the globe during the 1980s until AIDS became pandemic, or widespread. Some areas of the world were already significantly affected by HIV in the late 1990s, but in other parts of the world, the epidemic was just beginning. The virus was first identified in 1981 in the United States and France among homosexual men. Different transmission patterns have predominated in different parts of the world and among different populations within countries; these patterns have also changed over time.

HIV, which causes immune system damage leading to the illnesses classified as AIDS, is transmitted through sexual intercourse, contact with HIV-infected blood, and from mother to infant. Globally, experts believe that roughly 70 percent of infections have occurred during sexual intercourse that was unprotected by condoms. The sharing of syringes by injection drug users has also constituted a significant source of HIV infection in some countries. Some people have received HIV in emergency transfusions of unscreened blood. Mothers infected with HIV have also transmitted the virus to unborn children in the womb, during delivery, or through breast milk.

AIDS poses a threat to the survival of millions, especially in the Third World, where health and social infrastructures weakened by prolonged economic crises cannot bear the heavy burden of this new disease. Ninety percent of the more than 40 million people who had contracted HIV/AIDS by 1998 lived in less developed countries; more than two-thirds of the total, some 35 million, were Africans. Nearly half of those infected were female.

Sexual transmission of HIV/AIDS between heterosexual partners predominates in Africa. Adolescent girls are especially biologically and socially vulnerable to sexual infection by older men, and up to six times more girls are infected than boys of the same age. As in poverty-stricken United States urban areas, AIDS is the leading cause of death in youth and young adults in Africa. Because of a lack of funding in Africa for effective screening of the blood supply, transfusions for victims of acute malaria, hemorrhage in childbirth, or traffic accidents carry a significant risk of HIV infection. Since over half of infected Africans are females of childbearing age, many children – about 10 percent of the total number of those infected – acquire HIV in the womb, at birth, or during breast feeding. Countries with intravenous drug use can expect that shared syringes will become an additional source of HIV infection.

The period between infection with HIV and the onset of disease symptoms is lengthy and varies among individuals, apparently depending on their genetic makeup and the makeup of the virus. The viral strain predominant in high-prevalence areas of East and southern Africa, HIV-1 type E, is readily transmissible in heterosexual intercourse and accounts for an estimated 80 to 90 percent of infections. In addition, an untreated sexually transmitted disease (STD) such as syphilis or gonorrhea increases the likelihood of sexual transmission of HIV. Most Africans do not have access to effective antibiotic treatment for STDs. Together, these facts help to explain high rates of HIV transmission. The so-called opportunistic infections that characterize AIDS include tuberculosis, pneumonia, severe diarrhea, forms of cancer, blindness, and brain disorders. Effective treatment is costly and inaccessible to the poor majority in Africa.

Since people who carry the virus appear and feel healthy for some years, and since HIV testing is not widely available in Africa, most people who are infected do not know it. Therefore, most do not protect sexual partners from infection. A major challenge for prevention is to encourage people to accept the possibility that they may have been infected and, in that case, that they need to use condoms regularly, except when conception is desired, to decrease the risk of transmission. Another major challenge is to persuade or empower youth to delay sexual activity, to use condoms, and to avoid sexual promiscuity.

The prolonged disease process is extremely painful in its later stages, and the sick require extensive care. Much of the burden of care falls upon women who may be sick themselves and without resources. Ninety percent of deaths occur among adults aged 20 to 49, the prime working years; more than half of those infected are 15 to 24. HIV and AIDS exacerbate tuberculosis, a leading cause of death for young African women. Deaths of productive adults leave orphaned children and isolated elders who had once depended upon the now-deceased individual. By the year 2000, an estimated 10 million children under the age of 15 will have lost their mothers or both parents to AIDS. Some eight million of these children will be in Africa, where poverty will make them vulnerable to HIV as well. Gains made by child survival programs have been reversed in high prevalence areas, where AIDS has increased the mortality rate in infants and children under age five by two to three times. More African children now die from AIDS than from either malaria or measles, formerly the major killers.

In the United States, before new disease-delaying drugs became available in 1995, about half of those infected with HIV developed AIDS symptoms within ten years. Expensive new drug combinations can suppress viral replication and delay disease onset, but the rapidly mutating virus develops drug resistance. To date, no person with HIV has recovered a healthy immune system. Most may be expected to progress to AIDS eventually. In Africa, where sophisticated drugs and medical monitoring are not widely available, death generally occurs within two years following the onset of AIDS. Neither a cure nor effective vaccines are likely to emerge in the near future, and if they do become available, most people's access will be blocked by inability to pay, especially in poor regions such as Africa. Despite price reductions offered by pharmaceutical companies seeking African subjects for vaccine and drug testing, the poor or middle classes will not generally be able to afford these drugs.

Many epidemiologists underestimated the potential magnitude of HIV and AIDS in Africa, believing that the heterosexual epidemic could be contained by focusing prevention efforts on convincing the "core transmitters" – people such as sex workers and truck drivers known to have multiple sex partners – to use condoms. AIDS was seen as a technical disease-control problem. Because public health authorities perceived AIDS as an urban phenomenon, they believed that the majority of Africans lived in "traditional" rural areas and hence would be spared. Many social scientists, however, saw the coming catastrophe: first, few people anywhere have only a single lifetime sex partner, and rural areas are neither isolated nor unchanging. As infection levels rise, the chance that any one partner will be free of HIV infection decreases. Second, even if condoms can be made available very cheaply and on a regular basis, a variety of political, social, and cultural obstacles discourage their use. Third, harsh economic conditions have divided families, increased disparities in wealth and power, and changed behavioral standards in both rural and urban areas. These economic hardships have fueled the epidemic by increasing the number of vulnerable youths and young adults.

Since the mid-1970s, increasing millions of Africans have lived in abject poverty, their survival precarious, deprived of hope for the future. The deepening economic crisis and structural adjustment programs of the 1980s fell hardest on the poor: peasant incomes and wages declined sharply, and governments were forced to greatly reduce funding for public services, including education and health care. Dwindling government jobs and deindustrialization raised unemployment levels. Wars and military occupation brought civilian deaths, rapes, and mass population displacements. These conditions set the stage for sex with multiple partners and led to ever more widespread dissemination of HIV.

Poor people's survival strategies include migration in search of paid work, carrying goods long distances to urban markets, smuggling, and trading sex for food and shelter. Mines, plantations, trading towns, fishing camps, and ports attract job seekers in large numbers. Most are youths and men who come without their families; girls, divorced women, and widows also provide low-cost migrant labor and are vulnerable to sexual exploitation. Workers' camps are visited by girls and women who arrive on paydays, often traveling long distances. Poor women have few income-earning opportunities that pay as well as sex; often they must support dependents as well as provide for themselves. Poverty and pervasive gender inequality make it especially difficult for girls and women to avoid unsafe sex – even within marriage. Sexual violence – on the rise with deteriorating social conditions – further increases the risk of contracting HIV.

Responses to AIDS have political dimensions in Africa, as elsewhere. Public health action takes place in an environment in which differences in understanding and unequal power relationships prevail. AIDS is not just another disease; the HIV virus is not just one among many new microorganisms affecting humans. The biological processes involved are complex and difficult for lay people to understand. Linked to reproduction and death, AIDS in Africa carries a heavy emotional and symbolic charge. Some cultures stigmatize diseases associated with AIDS, such as tuberculosis, dementia, sexually transmitted diseases (STDs), and even skin rashes. Because it is sexually transmitted and incurable, some may blame AIDS on moral transgressions and unseen forces; a woman is often blamed for a man's infection.

AIDS often provokes fear and hostility toward the afflicted. Husbands may abandon wives. Families unable to hide the nature of the illness may find themselves isolated. AIDS orphans may be shunned and left to roam the streets, where they are particularly vulnerable to HIV infection. With many people falling sick and others overworked and demoralized by so much death around them, the impact on all economic activities in the affected areas is severe. AIDS particularly disrupts seasonally labor-intensive agriculture, food processing, and family life. Blaming others allows people to deny risk and to avoid taking realistic steps toward protecting themselves and others. Where people believe that AIDS is caused by women or by unseen forces, scapegoating, witch hunts, and social unrest compound socioeconomic disruption.

Effective prevention involves enabling large numbers of people to change sexual practices that are widely considered to be natural and essential to health. Children are highly valued, and they may allow a woman to hold a steady partner and gain community respect. Condoms are not popular among men, many of whom employ a double standard to rationalize their relations with numerous, often younger, sex partners while they strictly control their wives' sexuality. Condoms have been widely stigmatized by association with prostitutes and STDs. Even men who wish to use condoms may fear that their lover will berate them with accusations of mistrust, and so they may avoid the subject. Few women, married or single, can refuse to service a steady partner, even if they suspect that he may be infected, nor can most suggest condom protection. Penalties for doing so might include beatings or abandonment.

In many countries, powerful interest groups have treated AIDS, like other STDs, as a moral issue rather than a health issue. This makes it difficult for some governments to conduct rational prevention campaigns. Many adults believe that sex education and condoms will increase sexual activity (seen as immorality) among youth, although research carried out in numerous settings shows that this is not the case. Many men believe that access to condoms will lead wives to become unfaithful. Most wives who become infected, however, are infected by their husbands. Where national, non-governmental and community organization leaders share a moralistic perspective, this stance inhibits effective prevention campaigns. In Uganda, Tanzania, and Senegal strong resistance to effective prevention by religious leaders and community elders continued into the early 1990s. Alarmed governments nevertheless instituted safer-sex education and made STD treatment and condoms widely available and acceptable, especially among young people. The incidence of new infections apparently began to decline in these countries in 1996. Elsewhere, the virus continues to spread, not only in cities where the epidemic was well established in the 1980s, but also to rural areas and to countries that once had very low levels or were free of HIV.

In sum, an epidemic such as AIDS is an essentially social process, shaped by political economy and culture. Today, several economic processes fuel the spread of the epidemic. These include a global economy that relegates Africa to production of a few agricultural and mineral exports and distorted domestic economies inherited from colonialism. These circumstances result in unfavorable terms of trade, massive foreign debt, landlessness, unemployment, and widening disparities in wealth exacerbated by repressive politicians who siphon wealth from public funds. All of these processes, combined with the continued subordination of women, lead Africans to act out of desperation in ways that promote the spread of AIDS, while persistent poverty leaves most Africans without access to effective treatment.

Africa is the first but not the only continent to experience the effects of a prolonged, complex AIDS crisis. A major new center of HIV infection lies in South and Southeast Asia, home to well over a billion people. Despite its rapid industrial development, economic crisis in Southeast and East Asia can be expected to increase the spread of the AIDS pandemic, which is already rampant in the sex "industry," among the military, and among intravenous drug users. Within the United States, new infections are disproportionately concentrated among poor people of color. In the future, the pandemic will be even more heavily concentrated among poor populations than it is at present. While the burdens of care for the sick and orphaned mount, wealthy nations may become complacent and efforts to stem the pandemic may slacken. This was the case in the recent past with more easily preventable and treatable diseases such as tuberculosis, malaria, cholera, and STDs such as syphilis and gonorrhea that are now pandemic among the world's poor.

Limiting sexual transmission requires empowering substantial numbers of people to change highly valued behaviors or to cease activities that enhance people's short-term survival. HIV and AIDS prevention requires alleviating the problems faced by people at risk, rather than simply relaying prevention instructions or messages. Empowerment strategies that incorporate a deep understanding of local cultures and social group dynamics have the potential to bring about changes in sexual behavior and in the social environment in which sex occurs. Community groups can seek to identify problems faced by vulnerable populations not only to overcome obstacles to condom use, but also to address broader issues of poverty and inequality. Male dominance can be examined and more egalitarian behaviors can be modeled within a context of social action in support of democracy and development. It may be this potential for social change that makes many governments reluctant to deploy community-based consciousness-raising response to AIDS.

The components of sustainable development, which must incorporate both long-term economic growth and social justice, are well known. Sustainable development must include an agrarian strategy that supports food production by small farmers instead of large export-oriented farms and corporations. Sustainable development also requires support for rural nonfarm production, for development of regional import substitution industries, and for export diversification. Finally, sustainability entails the development of human capacities through broad access to education and training. The international community must provide the conditions necessary for this development, including debt forgiveness, increased aid for human needs, and policies that avoid the illusion that market capitalism can create bright futures for the poor.

Policymakers have not generally accepted the understanding on which this perspective is based or the need for global redistribution of power and wealth that follows. Instead, they tend to seek simple solutions – limited interventions that appear to offer a hope of interrupting the epidemic without threatening vested interests. Unless policies address the underlying struggles of millions to survive the consequences of poverty, powerlessness, and hopelessness, however, HIV infection will continue to spread among the world's poor. Since social structures limit the choices people make, stopping AIDS requires eliminating the barriers that deprive women of control over their sexual interactions, and poor men, women, and youth of control over their lives.

Brooke Grundfest Schoepf

See Also

Structural Adjustment in Africa.

North America

AIDS in the United States, a

highly infectious disease, acquired immune deficiency syndrome (AIDS) poses a health risk to American society in general; during the 1980s and 1990s the disease spread rapidly among minorities, and particularly among African Americans.

AIDS is caused by the human immunodeficiency virus (HIV), which slowly attacks its victim's immune system. AIDS is rarely fatal in itself: deaths usually result from opportunistic infections and cancers (collectively known as AIDS related complex [ARC]), which devastate the body's weakened immune system. HIV is transmitted through direct exchange of body fluids – such as blood or blood products, semen, and vaginal secretions – mainly during sexual intercourse or the sharing of needles by intravenous drug users. AIDS is considered the last stage of HIV infection.

Participants at a 1998 conference held by Harvard University's W. E. B. Du Bois Institute declared AIDS and HIV to be black America's "public enemy number 1." Reported cases of HIV infection and AIDS declined among white Americans in the 1990s, but the caseload was "skyrocketing" among African Americans. Experts dispute the reasons for this discrepancy. Some argue that AIDS-prevention education campaigns have not adequately targeted African Americans. Others note that many African Americans lack access to proper health care. Still others observe that, until recently, many African American community organizations have ignored the extent of this problem, perhaps because the news media have often presented AIDS as a disease primarily affecting white gay men.

By 1998, however, African Americans, who constituted only approximately 12 percent of the United States population, accounted for approximately 40 percent of all AIDS cases and 60 percent of newly diagnosed cases. By 1997 AIDS had become the leading killer of African Americans between the ages of 25 and 44. Experts expected these numbers to rise by the year 2000, projecting that as many as 50 percent of reported AIDS cases will affect African Americans.

In the late 1990s no cure for AIDS existed, and experts placed great emphasis on behavior modification to prevent spreading the disease, including safer-sex practices (including condom use), safer intravenous drug use (no sharing of needles), or abstinence from sex or drug use entirely. For those who are infected, early treatment is the most promising option. While no cure exists, in recent years scientists have developed effective treatments that center on inhibiting HIV's ability to replicate. Usually taken in combination with protease inhibitors, first introduced in the mid-1990s, have been effective – although long-term study of their use has not been completed – in lowering the viral amounts to undetectable levels. Unfortunately, the most effective treatments for AIDS are extremely expensive. Thus, African Americans, who face higher rates of poverty than white Americans, have not benefited as widely from these drugs as have other populations. However, during the 1990s African American community organizations devoted increasing attention to this growing problem. Their contribution to educational campaigns targeting black communities may help to prevent the further spread of this deadly disease among African Americans.

Robert Fay

North America

Ailey, Alvin (b. January 5, 1931, Rogers, Texas; d. December 1, 1989, New York, N.Y.),

African American dancer and choreographer who founded the Alvin Ailey American Dance Theater (AAADT) and incorporated African American styles and themes into dance performance.

Alvin Ailey grew up in a single-parent household headed by his mother, Lula Elizabeth Cooper. As a boy, he helped her pick cotton. In 1942 they moved to Los Angeles, where she found employment in the World War II aircraft industry. Ailey attended George Washington Carver Junior High School and Jefferson High School, primarily black schools. He went on to study literature at the University of California at Los Angeles (UCLA).

Ailey's dancing career began in 1949 when a high school friend, Carmen DeLavallade, introduced him to Lester Horton, his first dance instructor at the Lester Horton Dance Theater. When Horton died in 1953, Ailey became the director of the company. The following year Ailey moved to New York City, where he joined DeLavallade in the Broadway dance production *House of Flowers*. While appearing in other stage performances, Ailey continued his studies under Martha Graham, Charles Weidman, Doris Humphrey, Hanya Holm, and Karel Shook.

In 1958 Ailey assembled his own dance company, the Alvin Ailey American Dance Theater. Ailey himself stopped dancing in 1965 and reduced his choreographic assignments during the 1970s in order to seek more funding for his growing dance enterprise. The company toured the United States and the world so extensively that by 1989, the year that Ailey died, they had performed for an estimated 15 million people in 48 states and 45 countries on six continents. Two of the most significant awards Ailey received for his achievements in dance were the National Association for the Advancement of Colored People's prestigious Spingarn Medal (1976) and the Samuel H. Scripps American Dance Festival Award (1987).

The AAADT devotes itself to the performance of modern dance classics as well as the creations of Ailey and younger artists. The Alvin Ailey Dance Center School, founded in 1969, is dedicated to educating dance students in the history and art of both modern dance and ballet. The school's curriculum includes courses in choreography, dance technique, music for dancers, and theatrical design. Pursuing Ailey's goal of preserving and building upon great ballets, both classic and contemporary, the AAADT by 1989 had performed 150 ballets by 50 choreographers. In addition to having created over 50 dances for his own company, Ailey choreographed for others: the American Ballet Theater, the London Festival Ballet, the Robert Joffrey Ballet, the Paris Opera Ballet, and the Royal Danish Ballet.

Ailey's own works, whose style is founded on the techniques of modern dance, ballet, and jazz dance, draw upon African American themes, many of which are rooted in his boyhood experiences. Two of his major pieces, *Blues Suite* (1958) and *Revelations* (1960), for example, were inspired by a bar in Texas named the Dewdrop Inn and the Mount Olive Baptist Church he attended as a boy. *Revelations*, the AAADT's most celebrated number, explores the different facets of black religious worship and is performed to a series of spirituals and gospel music selections. His 1971 ballet *Cry*, a tribute to African American women, is dedicated to his mother.

Beyond the stage, Ailey's vision has been preserved by such people as Kelvin Rotardier,

Alvin Ailey's American Dance Theatre, pictured here in a performance of *Revelations*, seeks to blend elements of classical ballet with modern, jazz, and African American dance influences. *Alvin Ailey Dance Theater Foundation Archives/Photo © Zoe Dominic*

who in 1984 created the Alvin Ailey Student Performance Group, and by organizations such as Dance Foundation, Inc., which initiated the Ailey Camps in 1989. These programs aim to enrich the lives of inner-city youth through lectures, demonstrations, and dance instruction. In addition to his performances, the community outreach programs Ailey inspired constitute a contribution to twentieth-century dance.

Aaron Myers

See Also

World War II and African Americans; Gospel Music; Los Angeles, California; New York, New York; National Association for the Advancement of Colored People; Spirituals, African American.

North America

Ai Ogawa, Florence

(b. October 21, 1947, Albany, Tex.), African American poet and creative writer whose work investigates personal as well as societal questions of ethnicity and class.

Ai Ogawa was born in Albany, Texas, and raised in Tucson, Arizona. She graduated from the University of Arizona in 1969 and received a master of fine arts from the University of California at Irvine in 1971. In 1973 she published *Cruelty*, her first book of poetry, and her next book, the award-winning *Killing Floor* (1979), received critical acclaim. Her later works include *Sin* (1985) and *Fate* (1991).

Through her poetry, Ai gives people from all walks of life – including prostitutes, killers, poor farmers, and famous leaders – the same moral authority. This desire for equality of perspective also manifests itself in her quest for recognition of her multiethnic identity. Given her mixed race (black, Irish, Dutch, Native American, and Japanese), Ai (a self-chosen name that means "love" in Japanese) was unable to fit into predefined racial categories and social roles, and much of her poetry speaks to this tension.

Andre Willis

Africa

Akan, a cluster of ethnic groups living in southern Ghana and adjacent parts of Côte d'Ivoire and Togo.

The broad Akan grouping includes a number of separate ethnic groups. The Akan speak a group of closely related languages belonging to the Kwa branch of the Niger-Congo family (*see* Languages, African: An Overview). The Akan peoples share several cultural traits, but each has its own history and customs. In modern Ghana, the term *Akan* also refers to the country's most widely spoken indigenous language – also known as Twi – which is shared by the Asante, the Fante, and several other Ghanaian peoples. However, the "Akan" language of Ghana is but one of several languages in the larger Akan grouping. The main Akan ethnicities include the Akyem, Akwamu, Asante, Brong, Denkyira, Fante, Nzima, Sefwi, and Wassa of Ghana, and the Baule and Anyi of Côte d'Ivoire. Linguistic and archaeological evidence suggests that ancestors of the Akan have inhabited a heartland in south central Ghana for at least 2000 years. However, migrants from the north, including Mande merchants who arrived as early as the eleventh century, may have intermarried with the Akan and contributed to the development of Akan kingdoms.

The early Akan lived in agricultural villages raising yams, plantains in forest regions, and millet and sorghum in the north. Many Akan also hunted, worked metals such as iron and gold, and wove baskets and cloth. In ancient times, headmen governed rural villages, although some scholars say that even small units had queen mothers and kings who ruled with the assistance of a council of elders.

Traditionally, Akan societies trace descent, including inheritance, succession and kinship ties, matrilineally, or through the mother's line, though spiritual attributes and certain offices may pass patrilineally, or through the father's line. All Akan societies comprise seven or eight matrilineal clans, or *abusua*. Patrilineal groupings, the *ntoro*, also control certain taboos and rituals. Traditionally, Akan peoples worship a supreme being, Nyame. His children or creations form a secondary group of lesser deities, *abosom*, which inhabit everyday objects. Priests derive their power from the third level of supernatural entities, the talismans.

During the fourteenth century, the Brong were the first Akan people to form a powerful kingdom, known as Bono. Bono grew rich by controlling the gold trade with the north. Bono introduced standard gold weights made of brass, later adopted by other Akan nations, for use in the gold trade. By 1500 trade in gold and cola nuts probably fostered the development of larger Akan kingdoms throughout the Akan heartland.

With the arrival of Portuguese on the coast

during the late fifteenth century, Akan groups began to expand south toward the coast to trade directly with the Europeans. The period of major state formation, 1650 to 1750, also marked the rise of the slave trade. The Fante federation, Akwamu, and Denkyira traded gold and slaves in exchange for guns and other products from the Europeans. However, it was the Asante who built the strongest Akan state, which dominated most of what is now Ghana from about 1700 until the British finally conquered it in 1900. The Baule ruled much of modern Côte d'Ivoire from about 1750 until the French conquest around 1900.

The British policy of indirect rule (*see* COLONIAL RULE) left power in the hands of Akan chiefs and lineage heads . For instance, the exiled Asante king was allowed to return in 1924. Christian missionaries arrived in greater numbers after the French and British imposed colonial rule over the Akan. Many Akan today retain traditional beliefs, but Christianity is a major force in Akan society, especially in the south. Muslim influence is stronger in the north. Under colonial rule, gold extraction continued in Akan lands, but many Akan turned to the production of cash crops, especially COCOA, to purchase manufactured goods and meet colonial tax obligations.

Today Akan peoples number more than 10 million, almost half of Ghana's population, and one of the larger groupings in Côte d'Ivoire. They are primarily agriculturalists, farming cash crops such as cocoa and coffee along with subsistence crops such as yams and plantains. They have occupied prominent political offices in both countries. Ghana's first president, KWAME NKRUMAH, was an Akan of Nzima origin, and Côte d'Ivoire's independence leader, FÉLIX HOUPHOUËT-BOIGNY, was a Baule.

David P. Johnson, Jr.

SEE ALSO

Iron in Africa; Cola; Christianity: Missionaries in Africa.

Africa

Akposo (also known as the Akposso), ethnic group of West Africa.

The Akposo primarily inhabit central TOGO and adjacent eastern GHANA. They speak a Niger-Congo language, and are believed to have been among the indigenous population of Togo before EWE speakers migrated into the area from the east. Approximately 100,000 people consider themselves Akposo.

SEE ALSO

Languages, African: An Overview.

Africa

Aksum, an ancient kingdom that ruled parts of present-day Ethiopia and Eritrea from the first to the tenth century C.E.

"Pride of the entire universe and jewel of kings," Aksum ruled an ancient Ethiopian kingdom in a time remembered as a golden age of African civilization (*see* ANCIENT AFRICAN CIVILIZATIONS). This was true in a very literal sense: Aksumite kings issued a splendid gold coinage at a time when few other economies needed such a sophisticated currency or could have afforded it. The kings also marked their tombs with magnificent stone pillars, or *stelae*. The tallest of these were the largest stone monuments erected in the ancient world, surpassing in height even the obelisks of the Egyptian pharaohs.

The site of Aksum offered access to important international trade routes, as well as to the basic essentials of water and agricultural land. The city rose to power by using wealth gained from the control of trade to conquer other peoples who lived on the Ethiopian plateau, as far as the seacoast in ERITREA. By the end of the first century C.E., when Aksum first appears in the historical record, the state was the most powerful in the region. The system of government was imperial, with the *negusa nagast* (the king of kings) ruling over a number of subordinate states whose rulers paid tribute. Royal inscriptions from the fourth century C.E. describe Aksumite campaigns against "rebels" in various parts of the country and across the Red Sea in South Arabia (present-day Yemen) as well. One Aksumite expedition conquered the NUBIAN kingdom of Meroe in present-day SUDAN. The titles of the kings indicate claims to rule over Saba and Himyar, two important Arabian kingdoms, as well as over the Beja, Kasu, and Noba in Africa. The last two names refer to Kush and Nubia.

The inscriptions of the kings, their coinage, and the occasional mention of Aksum in Greek, Latin, and Arabic texts preserve only a limited amount of information. However, two kings stand out as exceptional. Scholars have often described Ezana, who ruled in the middle of the fourth century, as "the Constantine of Ethiopia" after his contemporary, the powerful Roman emperor who made Christianity the imperial religion. His inscriptions and coins record that he converted to Christianity from the traditional worship of the gods Astar, Beher, Meder, and Mahrem. One of his inscriptions refers to the Father, the Son, and the Holy Spirit, and during his reign, the Christian cross replaced the disk and crescent of the old religion. He was the first Christian king to employ the cross in this way, before even the emperors of Rome. The Latin church historian Rufinus corroborates the evidence of Ezana's coins and inscriptions by recording that the patriarch of Alexandria appointed the first Ethiopian metropolitan bishop at this time (*see* ETHIOPIAN ORTHODOX CHURCH and African Christianity). There is no indication that Ezana or his successors ever returned to pre-Christian religions.

During the sixth century, the Aksumite king Kaleb led a military expedition to South Arabia to crush a Jewish king who had killed the Christian community at Najran. This event caused a sensation throughout the Christian world, and is consequently well documented. Kaleb defeated the Jewish king Dhu Nuwas and installed a viceroy, but after a short time an Aksumite named Abreha deposed the viceroy. Abreha began to govern Yemen in defiance of Kaleb and refused to pay tribute to the king of kings. In Surah 105 of the Koran, there is an account of Abreha leading an expedition against Mecca in what is called "the Year of the Elephant," perhaps a reference to the use of African elephants in battle. Early Islamic historians also record that disciples of the Prophet, including his wife Umm Habiba, took refuge in Aksum when Muhammad was being persecuted in Arabia.

With the rise of Islamic power in Arabia during the seventh century, the kings of Aksum began to retreat from the Red Sea. There may also have been changes in climate, and the land around the city of Aksum may have been farmed too intensively to support its people, but once Arabians took control of the Red Sea trade, Aksum began to decline. Aksum suffered its final defeat at the hands of rebels during the tenth century.

In addition to the stelae and the coinage, accomplished styles of pottery making, ivory carving, and glassware production, and metalwork in gold, silver, bronze, and iron all attest to the skill of Aksumite craftsmen and the luxury and sophistication of their capital. The remains of palaces and royal tombs confirm the complete mastery of granite by Aksumite masons, whose decorative motifs were copied on the famous churches at Lalibela.

Roderick Grierson and Stuart Munro-Hay

SEE ALSO

Christianity, African: An Overview; Ethiopia; Egypt, Ancient Kingdom of; Kush, Early Kingdom of; Alexandria, Egypt.

Africa

Akuapem (also known as Akwapim), ethnic group of GHANA.

The Akuapem primarily inhabit the eastern region of Ghana. They speak a Niger-Congo language and belong to the larger AKAN cultural and linguistic group. Approximately 500,000 people consider themselves to be Akuapem.

SEE ALSO

Languages, African: An Overview.

Africa

Akunakuna,
ethnic group of West Africa.

The Akunakuna primarily inhabit the Cross River State of NIGERIA and western CAMEROON. They speak a Bantu language and are related to the Efiks and Ibibios, also of Nigeria. Approximately 350,000 people consider themselves Akunakuna.

SEE ALSO
Bantu: Dispersion and Settlement; Languages, African: An Overview; Ibibio; Efik.

Africa

Akyem (also known as Akem), ethnic group of GHANA.

The Akyem primarily inhabit the eastern region of Ghana. They comprise three major subgroups: the Abuakwa, the Bosume, and the Kotoku. They speak a Niger-Congo language and belong to the AKAN cultural and linguistic group. Approximately 500,000 people consider themselves Akyem.

SEE ALSO
Languages, African: An Overview.

Latin America and the Caribbean

Albizu Campos, Pedro
(b. June 29, 1893, Ponce, Puerto Rico; d. April 21, 1965, San Juan, Puerto Rico), Afro-Puerto Rican nationalist leader of African descent, considered by many to be the foremost advocate of Puerto Rico's independence and one of the most controversial figures in political and social struggles of the twentieth century.

A passionate speaker and outspoken critic of United States imperialism and the 1898 invasion and occupation of Puerto Rico, Pedro Albizu Campos spent many years in prison for his role in the pro-independence nationalist movement, during the turbulent years of the 1930s through the 1950s. He opposed PUERTO RICO's association with the United States, which started when the island was ceded by the Spanish after the SPANISH-CUBAN-AMERICAN WAR. For Albizu, Puerto Ricans – ethnically mixed and culturally different – were not, and should not be, Americans. Independence was the only legitimate and anti-imperialist solution to the island's status.

From an early age Albizu stood out as an excellent student. He grew up in Ponce, a municipality in southern Puerto Rico, where he received a grant that gave him the opportunity to study chemical engineering at the University of Vermont. He later graduated from Harvard Law School, where he received a scholarship for his outstanding achievements. During this time, he showed a great sympathy for the independence movements in Ireland and India.

Albizu, who had inherited his mother's dark skin color, was a victim of the institutionalized racism in the United States. As an army private, he was assigned to a segregated Negro battalion. He later visited the South and witnessed the discrimination against and mistreatment of blacks in that part of the United States. Upon his return to Puerto Rico, he also confronted the racial prejudice of the dominant Creole class, which resented his intellectual and social achievements and the fact that he was proud of his humble origins.

Shortly after returning to Puerto Rico, Albizu entered the Nationalist Party. From 1927 to 1929, he visited the Dominican Republic, Haiti, Cuba, Mexico, Peru, and Venezuela, promoting the cause of Puerto Rican independence. Drawing on the experiences of nineteenth-century patriots such as RAMÓN EMETERIO BETANCES, JOSÉ MARTÍ, and Simón Bolívar, who had struggled against Spanish colonialism, Albizu argued that Puerto Rico's independence was a necessary step toward the liberation of Latin America from United States imperialism. For Albizu, independence was not merely a desirable goal, it was a moral imperative. His political convictions were influenced by his Catholic religious conception of the world.

Upon his return to Puerto Rico, Albizu was elected president of the Nationalist Party in 1930. After his party lost in the 1932 polls, he adopted a radical political stance that welcomed nonelectoral means, including violence, in order to end the colonial status of Puerto Rico. As a result of a series of violent clashes between nationalists and the police, Albizu was incarcerated by United States federal authorities for conspiring to overthrow the government by force. He spent six years in a federal prison in Atlanta (1937-1943), followed by four years on probation in New York. In 1947 he returned to Puerto Rico and was received by many as a hero.

In October 1950 the military faction of the Nationalist Party started an ill-fated insurrection in different parts of Puerto Rico, known as the Revolt of 50. The United States National Guard promptly put an end to the revolt. Simultaneously, two nationalists made an attack on the life of President Truman at Blair House in Washington, D.C. Although Albizu did not participate directly in these events, he was arrested under Puerto Rico's "gag laws" (laws prohibiting antigovernment inflammatory speech) for having incited the insurrection through his public speeches, and was sentenced to 53 years in prison. In 1953, after three years in solitary confinement in a local prison, Albizu received an executive pardon due to his declining health.

In 1954 four nationalists opened gunfire at the House of Representatives of the United States, wounding five congressmen. Albizu

Afro-Puerto Rican nationalist leader Albizu Campos talks to reporters following his unsuccessful "Revolt of 50." *CORBIS/Bettmann*

was immediately arrested in his house in Puerto Rico; his pardon was revoked, and he was jailed in the same prison that he had left only a few months earlier. His health deteriorated dramatically during this last period of imprisonment, which he spent between prison and hospital admissions (1955-1964). Suffering from arteriosclerosis and a delicate heart condition, he was finally released from prison. He died on April 21, 1965. More than 100,000 attended his burial in San Juan.

Albizu's uncompromising quest for independence is for some Puerto Ricans the highest possible example of dignity and courage. For them, "Don Pedro" is one of the fathers of Puerto Rican national identity. For others, he was plainly wrong in trying to achieve independence for the island. Despite the controversy, Pedro Albizu Campos remains one of the towering figures of Puerto Rican history.

Carlos Dalmau

Latin America and the Caribbean

Albornoz, Bartolomé de.
See COLONIAL CRITICS OF SLAVERY.

Africa

Alcohol in Africa

Alcoholic beverages have played an important role in the religious, political, economic, and social history of sub-Saharan Africa. As early as the eleventh century C.E., historical records mention the presence of alcoholic drinks in the Sahelian kingdom of Ghana. Alcohol is a cultural artifact, a ritual object, an economic good, and a social marker. As a cultural artifact, its production, distribution, and consumption were circumscribed by rules in the precolonial era. Perceived as a sacred fluid in many cultures, it facilitated communication among the living, the ancestors, and the gods. Through the ritual of libation – the pouring of an alcoholic drink on the ground accompanied by prayer – alcohol played a key role in rites of passage and festivals. It was a valuable commodity, and its possession conferred status and wealth. Alcoholic drinks were coveted, and male elders monopolized the consumption of alcohol. As a marker of inclusion and exclusion, control over alcohol informed age, gender, and status conflicts. It is then not surprising that alcohol would become a major item in the trade among Europe, the Americas, and Africa. European missionary societies condemned this liquor traffic to Africa, and they hoped European COLONIAL RULE would end the slave trade and liquor traffic. Indeed, colonial rule did abolish the slave trade, but colonial governments found liquor revenues too valuable to abrogate the liquor trade. In postcolonial Africa, breweries and distilleries often have been the cornerstone of industrialization projects.

INDIGENOUS BEERS IN SUB-SAHARAN AFRICA

Indigenous beers have been prepared for generations in African societies from malted sorghum, MILLET, or maize. The resultant opaque beer was brownish in color with an alcoholic content of between three and five percent per volume. It had a heavy body because of the large quantities of particles and yeast suspended in it. Referred to as *dolo* or *pito* in parts of West Africa and as *utshwala* in SOUTH AFRICA, it was an important dietary component. Women brewed beer as an extension of domestic chores. A fermented banana drink was popular among Bantu speakers in East Africa. Palm wine has been obtained from the oil palm and the raffia palm in forested regions of sub-Saharan Africa and from the coconut palm along the African coast. Although young men may have tapped the wine, they had little control over its consumption.

The economic value of these cereals, palm trees, and bananas made them indices of wealth controlled by male elders. Among the AKAN of GHANA, it was taboo for a woman to climb an oil palm tree. This appears to have been an attempt to ensure male control over the valuable oil palm. Among the Giriama of KENYA, wine and copra prepared from coconuts have been central to accumulation and social mobility in the twentieth century. All these indigenous beers have a short shelf life and have to be consumed in a day or two. This meant that drinking was irregular, but large amounts may have been drunk at a time.

ALCOHOL, RITUAL, AND SOCIALIZATION IN PRECOLONIAL AFRICA

Alcohol's intoxicating quality seems to have infused it with some element of spirituality. Akan folktales about the first experience with palm wine emphasize the puzzling sequence of intoxication, deep slumber, and reawakening, comparing it with a journey to the land of the dead and back. Palm wine was used in naming, marriage, and funeral rites among the Akan. Akan perception of family and society encompassed the living, the ancestors, and those yet unborn. Any gathering important to the visible and invisible members of the family or community warranted the use of alcohol in libation. It bound the family or community and cemented their relations with the supernatural world of spirits. In preliterate African societies, the exchange of drinks and the pouring of libation served as a seal in legal transactions. Alcohol was also crucial to social life, and the beer party was the spice of rural life. Among the Kofyar of NIGERIA, the beer-brewing cycle even determined the structure of the week. The meaning and importance of beer were central to the philosophy of the ITESO of UGANDA and Kenya.

The European liquor traffic was inserted into this cultural context. Before the transatlantic trade in the fifteenth century, distilled spirits were virtually unknown in sub-Saharan Africa. Dutch and German traders monopolized the trade in gin and schnapps, while New England traders brought rum to West Africa. Brandy and whiskey were popular among Europeans in West Africa but not with the West Africans. Among the Akan, rum was incorporated into ritual by the seventeenth century. The higher cost and potency of European liquor made it a valuable offering to the ancestors and gods. In southern Nigeria, cases of gin were in use as currency in the nineteenth century. Trade spirits were attractively packaged, had an unlimited shelf life, and were in great demand. Gin fulfilled the functions of money. Individuals and social groups that profited from the Euro-African trade viewed the consumption of European liquor as a mark of their social distinction. For young men who had migrated from villages to participate in European coastal commerce, liquor was the symbol of their new independence from the control of rural elders.

Mention must be made of the West African savanna belt and the SWAHILI COAST, where Islamic influence has been growing since the eighth century C.E. Islam proscribes alcohol for believers.

ALCOHOL IN COLONIAL AFRICA

European trade extended the purview of European influence even before the formal onset of colonialism. Gifts of alcoholic drinks featured prominently in Euro-African protocol. European merchants used liquor and other European goods to induce some African chiefs to sign treaties of protection. These agreements would become important when the Berlin Conference (1884-1885) required treaties as evidence of protectorate relations and the basis of colonial rule. European missionaries denounced the havoc European liquor wreaked on the "less-civilized" peoples of Africa. In the 1880s, the Native Races and Liquor Traffic United Committee would emerge among missionary interests in England to champion the abolition of liquor traffic to Africa. European missionaries assumed that colonialism would end liquor traffic. Indeed, this assumption had partly motivated their support for colonial imposition. But colonies were designed to benefit colonial powers, and economic self-sufficiency was the minimum requirement of colonies. Liquor revenues and liquor legislation became crucial to colonial policy. In West Africa, where European settlement was minimal because of the mosquito and TSETSE FLY, colonial powers exploited the existing demand for liquor as a source of revenue. Import tariffs were imposed on liquor imports, enabling colonial governments to circumvent direct taxation in the early years of colonial rule. Between 1892 and 1903, import duties on liquor contributed over 55 percent of the total revenue of the colony of Lagos. The corresponding figure for the Gold Coast between 1910 and 1913 was 38 percent. Missionary interests felt betrayed and refused to be pacified by the findings of the Liquor Commissions of Inquiry in Southern Nigeria (1909) and the Gold Coast (1930) that these colonies had no liquor problems. Sometimes in partnership with African chiefs, missionary interests forged temperance organizations in African colonies.

In East and South Africa, strict liquor laws regulated even the consumption of indigenous beer to protect white settlers. These liquor laws reflected the insecurities of early colonial rule and were repealed or modified – as in the case of Kenya – with the consolidation of colonial rule. The discovery in South Africa of diamonds in Kimberley in the 1870s and of gold on the Witwatersrand in the 1880s, and the subsequent transformations in race relations, bequeathed a complex legacy to the social history of alcohol. Alcohol became entwined in labor issues, as it constituted bait in the attraction of migrant labor. The strategy posed problems, however, for a drinking labor force is potentially unproductive. Mine owners on the Witwatersrand successfully lobbied for prohibition at the beginning of this century, but the failure of prohibition foreshadowed the American experiment in the 1930s.

For migrant male workers in African cities, drinking was an important social activity. Male migrants often perceived migration as temporary and thus migrated as individuals. Bereft of family and kinship networks, they forged new social networks in the drinking bars and *shebeens* (neighborhood taverns) of South Africa. The indispensability of alcohol to town life encouraged municipalities in South Africa to establish beer halls for migrant workers. The proceeds would finance APARTHEID. Migrant labor weakened rural economies, making rural families dependent on remittances from migrant workers. The brunt of rural production fell on women, and overburdened widows, abandoned wives, and divorcees, gradually made their way into the towns. Deprived of economic opportunities in the male-oriented colonial economy, women commercialized beer brewing and inserted an old domestic chore into the urban economy.

International Liquor Conventions and Africa

Missionary pressure was partly responsible for securing the implementation of international liquor conventions to regulate the European liquor traffic to Africa. In 1890 an international convention in Brussels prohibited European liquor from areas in Africa without a previous history of liquor consumption. A wide belt in the interior of Africa, between latitudes 20 degrees north and 22 degrees south, was subject to this potential ban on European liquor. The next significant convention was passed at St. Germain-en-Laye (France) in September 1919. This convention banned the traffic in "trade spirits" in Africa, defined loosely as cheap spirits imported clearly for African consumption. An import duty of 800 francs (about 80 pounds sterling in the early 1920s) was imposed on every hectoliter (about 22 gallons) of pure alcohol, and the distillation of spirits was explicitly forbidden in colonial Africa. These stipulations would come under nationalist attack during the general assault on colonial rule.

Alcohol and Nationalist Politics

Liquor revenues and liquor legislation became contested arenas as African nationalists challenged the legitimacy of colonial rule from the 1930s on. To criticize liquor revenue was to assail the edifice of colonial rule. Liquor legislation, and colonial law in general, underscored the loss of African independence. The emergence of popular culture in African towns in the early twentieth century – drinking bars, dance bands, popular music, comic opera, "dressing up," soccer, romance – elevated the relevance of alcohol. Popular culture provided an antiestablishment ideology, and drinking bars in particular became the forum for political discussion. In southern Rhodesia (Zimbabwe), educated Africans agitated for the repeal of legislation that forbade European wine and spirits to Africans. Decolonization, and the introduction of general elections through universal adult suffrage, emphasized the importance of popular culture, as the African political elite needed mass support. Politicians promised to abolish restrictive liquor legislation. Political parties adopted specific brands of beer and extended patronage to particular drinking establishments. It may have seemed incongruous on the eve of independence for African politicians to be discussing access to alcohol, but alcohol was central to the culture of power in African societies, and it could not be disassociated from the processes of colonization and decolonization.

Alcohol in Independent Africa

Independent African governments quickly came to appreciate the value of alcohol revenues and the use of alcohol as a form of social control. Independence was achieved mostly in the 1950s and 1960s, and every African country yearned to modernize its economy. Breweries and distilleries would be part of this endeavor. Corporate Western capital entered the southern African market, developing the sorghum beer technology of South Africa for mass manufacture in the subregion. In West Africa, international giants such as Heineken, Holstein, and Guinness have established breweries and partnerships in Ghana, Nigeria, and Cameroon. Dividends, excise duties, and sales taxes from the alcohol industry contributed to government coffers. The importance of the alcohol industry increased for African governments as world market prices for African exports – minerals and unprocessed cash crops – declined in the decades after independence. The *Washington Post* reported on July 14, 1991, that alcohol sales generated between 7 and 15 percent of government revenue in many Third World countries, including Kenya, Tanzania, and Zimbabwe.

As dictatorial governments became the norm and economies declined in Africa in the 1970s and 1980s, governments ensured an abundance of alcoholic drinks internally to distract attention from political and economic failure, and to divide the nation by gender and class conflicts. South African youth attacked beer halls during the Soweto riots of 1976 because, in their view, the elders, with their alcohol-soaked minds had become politically quiescent, and the proceeds from the beer halls had built the migrant-labor hostels that perpetuated apartheid. As Zambia's economy declined with the collapse of the price for copper, the trucks that delivered beer became the major symbol of government presence in some rural areas. In 1980 the Kenneth Kaunda government admitted the existence of an alcohol problem in Zambia, and a program was implemented in conjunction with the World Health Organization to redress the situation. For many independent African governments, the challenge is to find a balance between the economic desirability of alcohol revenues and the social costs of alcoholism.

Alcohol's multiple uses, its ability to bridge the gap between the physical and supernatural worlds, and its place in the culture of power explains its endurance over the centuries of Africa's history. In contemporary Africa, old uses and meanings of alcohol persist in new contexts. A wealthy Akan would still consider the two bottles of schnapps as essential to his daughter's marriage rites but would specify that they be J. H. Henkes (imported from Holland) and not a local manufacture. The presence of the youth in drinking bars also underscores the changing face of alcohol.

Emmanuel Akyeampong

See Also

Bantu: Dispersion and Settlement; Music, African; Decolonization in Africa: An Interpretation; Ghana, Early Kingdom of; Gold Trade; Lagos, Nigeria; Nationalism in Africa; Transatlantic Slave Trade; Soweto, South Africa; Sahel; Islam and Tradition: An Interpretation; Christianity: Missionaries in Africa; Berlin Conference of 1884-1885.

North America

Aldridge, Ira (b. 1807, New York, N.Y.; d. 1867, Lodz, Poland), the most highly esteemed African American actor of the nineteenth century.

Ira Aldridge earned international recognition as one of his era's finest actors for his moving theatrical performances throughout England, Scotland, Ireland, Europe, and the United States. Though born free in New York City, the son of a slave turned Calvinist preacher, Aldridge saw limited theatrical opportunities in the United States and, after training at the African Free School in New York City, left the United States for England in 1824. Intent on pursuing an acting career, he studied drama at the University of Glasgow for more than a year.

Debuting onstage at the Royal Coburg in London in 1825, Aldridge won widespread praise for his portrayal of Othello, a role that became his trademark, as well as his renditions of other leading characters during the six-week theatrical run. After this success, he performed in the Theater Royal in Brighton, then went on to tour England, Scotland, and Ireland for the next six years. He mastered both black and white characters throughout dramatic literature and was hailed from city to city as an actor of great genius, best known for his portrayals of Shakespeare's *Othello*, Thomas Southerne's *Oroonoko*, Thomas Norton's *The Slave*, and characters from Matthew Gregory Lewis's *The Castle Spectre*, Isaac Bickerstaff's *The Padlock*, and Edward Young's *The Revenge*.

For many, the mounting claims that Aldridge was the greatest actor of his day seemed to be confirmed when he filled in as Othello for the renowned English thespian Edmund Kean, who fell ill during a performance at London's Covent Garden in 1833. Though some critics grumbled at Kean's having been eclipsed by the young upstart, the 24-year-old Aldridge received immense public acclaim for his portrayal of the Moor, and his fame spread throughout Europe.

In 1852 Aldridge toured Europe performing Shakespearean tragedies, and was so successful that he was invited to play Othello at the prestigious Lyceum Theater in London in 1858, and was offered the same role by the

This portrait of Ira Aldridge, painted by Henry Perronet Briggs in about 1830, depicts the great Shakespearean tragedian in his role as Othello. *National Portrait Gallery, Smithsonian Institution/ Art Resource, NY*

Haymarket in 1865. In 1867, at the height of his career, he died of respiratory failure while on tour in Lodz, Poland, and was buried in that city.

Aldridge was married twice, first to an Englishwoman and then to a wealthy Swede, and had four children. He not only left a rich legacy of drama, voice, and rhetoric, but he marked the beginning of the tradition of polished African American artists who would do most of their work outside the United States because of American racism.

Andre Willis

See Also
New York, New York.

North America

Alexander, Clifford L., Jr.

(b. September 3, 1933, New York, N.Y.), African American lawyer, political administrator, and management consultant who served as secretary of the army during the Carter administration.

After graduating from Harvard University in 1955 and Yale Law School in 1958, Clifford Alexander worked on a number of community development initiatives in Harlem before being appointed to a series of political positions in Washington, D.C., in the 1960s and 1970s. His influence culminated in his appointment as secretary of the army by President Jimmy Carter in 1977. The first African American to direct a military department, Alexander sought to hasten the army's desegregation and improve its preparedness. He held the post until 1981, when he returned to the private sector.

Prior to his appointment by Carter, he served as a National Security Council foreign affairs officer under President Kennedy in 1963 and was appointed to three high-ranking advisory positions between 1964 and 1967, including deputy special counsel to the president, by President Lyndon B. Johnson. In 1967 Johnson named Alexander chairman of the Equal Employment Opportunities Commission (EEOC), a position he filled until Richard Nixon took office in 1969.

After a brief return to private practice in Washington, D.C., Alexander quickly resumed a role in public life as host and producer of a television show about racial issues from 1971 to 1974. In 1974 he made an unsuccessful bid for the Washington mayoral office.

Andre Willis

See Also
Harlem, New York; Television and African Americans.

North America

Alexander, Raymond Pace

(b. October 13, 1898, Philadelphia, Pa.; d. November 23, 1974, Philadelphia, Pa.), lawyer, politician, and judge; the first African American to hold a position on the Common Pleas Court of Philadelphia.

Born and raised in Philadelphia, Raymond Pace Alexander graduated from the University of Pennsylvania in 1920 and Harvard Law School in 1923, at a time when very few African Americans gained admittance to Ivy League schools. He enjoyed a successful career in private practice, directly challenging racism and discrimination and helping to end segregation in a number of Philadelphia institutions, before becoming counsel for the National Association for the Advancement of Colored People (NAACP).

Between 1933 and 1935 Alexander served as president of the National Bar Association and sought a federal appointment. Though the prevailing racial climate made it difficult for Alexander to break into national politics, he was appointed honorary consul to the Republic of Haiti in 1938. He was considered for an ambassadorship to Ethiopia in 1951, but though he had President Truman's support, he was not confirmed. From 1951 to 1958 Alexander committed himself to city politics, serving on the Philadelphia city council.

Andre Willis

See Also
National Association for the Advancement of Colored People; Philadelphia, Pennsylvania.

North America

Alexander, Sadie Tanner Mossell

(b. January 1, 1898, Philadelphia, Pa.; d. November 1, 1989, Philadelphia, Pa.), American lawyer and civil rights activist, the first African American woman to earn a Ph.D. in economics, and an important advocate for social justice.

Sadie Mossell Alexander was born in 1898 to a prominent black Philadelphia family. Her father, Aaron Mossell, was the first African American to receive a law degree from the University of Pennsylvania. Her grandfather, Benjamin Tucker Tanner, edited America's first black scholarly journal, the *A.M.E. Church Review*.

Mossell received her doctorate from the University of Pennsylvania in 1921. She worked as an actuary in North Carolina, then left to marry Raymond Pace Alexander, a graduate of Harvard Law School. With her husband's encouragement, Sadie Alexander returned to the University of Pennsylvania, earning her law degree in 1927. The two entered law practice together. Their civil rights work began in 1935, when they fought to end racial segregation in Philadelphia, Pennsylvania. The Alexanders visited segregated city theaters, hotels, and restaurants to demand rightful admittance under law, and agitated for the legal prosecution of violators.

Sadie Alexander worked to integrate the American military, and served on President Harry S. Truman's Commission to Study the Civil Rights of All Races and Faiths in 1946. In 1963 President John F. Kennedy appointed her to the Lawyers' Committee for Civil Rights under Law. She chaired President Jimmy Carter's White House Conference on Aging in 1979 and 1980. In addition to fulfilling these appointments, Sadie Alexander also maintained a private legal practice from 1959 through 1983, when she retired at the age of 85.

See Also
Military, Blacks in the American.

Africa

Alexandria and Grecian Africa: An Interpretation

Alexandria flourished for over a thousand years as the intellectual and cultural center and was the greatest city of the ancient Mediterranean world. It was the prime conduit for the passage of African images and ideas into Europe and European images and ideas into Africa. This article deals primarily with the role of Alexandria in the development of Grecian Africa in ancient times. (For a history of the city up to modern times, see the entry on Alexandria, Egypt).

Ancient Egypt

For the early Greeks, Egypt was the oldest, the wisest, and the richest of all nations. The Greeks were new to civilization; when they first visited Egypt they discovered a civilization that was already more than 2000 years old. Temples and monuments loomed in the desert, their origins lost in the mists of time. The Great Sphinx looked down upon the newcomers with its benign, unfathomable gaze, as it had for 20 centuries or more. Confronted by the splendors of the Egyptian past, Greeks like the historian Herodotus (who visited Egypt in the middle of the fifth century B.C.E.) were overcome with a kind of religious awe.

Egyptian civilization was not only the oldest in the world, it was also astonishingly stable, at least when compared to every other nation known to the early Greeks. The concept of *ma'at*, or social order, ruled every aspect of Egyptian life. Greeks were iconoclasts; they constantly tested their laws and traditions, always seeking improvement, or at least novelty. Egyptians clung to their unimaginably ancient traditions; in their eyes, change was always dangerous and never desirable, as it was to the Greeks, for its own sake.

The agricultural economy of Egypt was based on the annual floods of their great river. Each year, in late summer, the river rose, bringing with it a flux of mud and silt that spread over the lands of the Nile Delta like a blanket of rich fertilizer. Farmers planted their fields, and the harvest was nearly always bountiful. A portion of the wealth brought by the river went to the king, or pharaoh, and to the priests who supported him and interpreted his will and that of the gods. But almost always there was enough for all, and over the centuries the national wealth had also become unimaginable.

For more than two millennia, from about 3500 to about 1500 B.C.E., Egypt was content with the unchanging existence it had chosen. In the second millennium B.C.E. it began to reach out, north into Palestine, Lebanon, and Syria, east into Arabia, south into Nubia and present-day Sudan. During the fifteenth century B.C.E., under Thutmose III, an Egyptian empire expanded over most of northeastern Africa and much of the Near East as well. Inevitably, these aggressive moves provoked a response. Slowly at first and then more rapidly, the nation was forced back within its ancient borders. A time of troubles ensued, with frequent revolts and rival claimants to the throne. Always there was the threat of Persia and other Asiatic powers. Vast wealth and innumerable artistic treasures remained, but when Alexander arrived with his army in 330 B.C.E. he was able to conquer the Old Kingdom without a battle. He was proclaimed pharaoh and king, and as a symbol of his triumph, in 332 B.C.E., he established a new city near the west branch of the Nile Delta and named it after himself.

Alexander the Great

Alexander was born in 365 B.C.E. in a small country in northern Greece called Macedonia, of which his father, Philip, was the king. From age 13 to 16, he was tutored by the philosopher Aristotle, who was brought from Athens by Philip. Alexander was more interested in warfare than in philosophy. Philip was assassinated in 336 B.C.E., and the Macedonian nobles and army accepted Alexander as their new king.

Philip had defeated a large force of allied Greek city-states before his death; now Alexander set about confirming Macedonian power in Greece. This took less than two years, whereupon he embarked on the adventure he had dreamed of since a child, namely, the conquest of Greece's perennial enemy, the Persian Empire. By now, Persia was the largest and richest nation in the world; its military prowess was legendary, its wealth almost mythical, its size and population many times greater than Greece, to say nothing of little Macedonia. Undaunted, Alexander set out on the Persian expedition in the spring of 334 B.C.E. with an army of 30,000 men and 5000 cavalry, plus at least an equal number of surveyors, engineers, architects, scientists, court officials, historians, and, of course, women. He let it be known that he intended to conquer not only Persia but the entire world.

He headed east, stopped at Troy to pay his respects to Achilles, and then turned south along the eastern coast of the Mediterranean Sea, defeating every Persian and other army that stood in his way. In Gordium, a city in Asia Minor, he was shown a famous knot that no one had ever untied; the man who could untie it, he was told, was fated to be the ruler of Asia. Alexander said nothing but drew his sword and cut the Gordian knot in twain. Within three years he was the undisputed lord of Asia, having conquered all of Persia and having been acclaimed as the Great King. He was then 25 years old.

Alexander founded half a dozen Alexandrias in various parts of Asia and India, but the Egyptian city was always his favorite. Choosing the site carefully, he endowed the new town with riches gleaned from his victories. He departed after two years to complete his conquest of the entire world as he knew it, but it seems he always intended to return. He did so, but only after his death, which occurred in Babylon in his

A stone relief thought to represent the legendary Cleopatra (69 B.C.E.-30 B.C.E.), the last independent ruler of Ancient Egypt. *Werner Forman/Art Resource, NY*

thirty-third year. His body was carried to Alexandria and buried in a coffin of solid gold that has long been sought but never found.

The Ptolemies

After his death, Alexander's vast empire, which he had hoped to unify and make permanent, was soon broken up and shared among his generals. One of the most capable of these was Ptolemy Soter, who had been left in charge of the Egyptian city. Ptolemy, who founded a dynasty that bore his name, was a man of parts. A brilliant military strategist and a cunning politician (cunning being an indispensable virtue of the times), he was also deeply curious and, a true Greek, tolerant of new ideas.

Eleven different Ptolemies in the direct line ruled Egypt from the death of Alexander to the conquest of the country by Rome, in 80 B.C.E., but of these only the first three, Ptolemy I Soter (r. 323-282 B.C.E.), Ptolemy II Philadelphus (r. 282-246 B.C.E.), and Ptolemy III Euergetes (r. 246-221 B.C.E.), were enlightened and effective monarchs. Father, son, and grandson, they ruled their city for a difficult 100 years, maintaining it as the center of a commercial and cultural sphere of influence extending from the Straits of Gibraltar to the shores of India.

The ups and downs of Egyptian political and military power during this period are too complex to discuss here; in any case, the achievements of the first Ptolemies in other realms were more important and enduring. At the head of these were two great institutions. Intended to rival and surpass Plato's Academy and Aristotle's Lyceum at Athens, the *Mouseion* (or Museum) was founded around 300 B.C.E. as a kind of research university and institute for advanced study. It occupied a large site near the king's palace on which were erected a number of structures, connected to one another by colonnades winding among beautiful gardens, each of which was devoted to the study of a different branch of knowledge. A faculty of experts in every field was paid by the king (later by the Roman emperors), who also funded scholarships that brought prominent poets, historians, and scientists from all over the Hellenic world to Alexandria, which soon became universally recognized as *the* place to live and work.

Among the famous scholars who studied and wrote in Alexandria's Mouseion during those halcyon years were Euclid, Archimedes, Aristarchus the astronomer, and Hipparchus, all famous mathematicians and physicists, and, in later years, Strabo the geographer and Ptolemy (not a member of the royal family) the astronomer. Ptolemy's geocentric theory of the universe prevailed for over 1000 years before it was displaced by the heliocentric theory of Copernicus, Galileo, and Newton. (Ironically, Aristarchus the astronomer, while at Alexandria, had also proposed a heliocentric theory.) Among the poets were Callimachus and Theocritus. The former was, after Homer, the most oft-cited poet of the later classical world. The latter had even greater influence, for his delicate, lovely verses about nature and country things were the foundation of the pastoral school of poetry, among whose practitioners have been Virgil, Wordsworth, Milton, and Robert Frost, as well as a host of others.

The other renowned Ptolemaic institution was a library, the largest in the ancient world and one of the most important in history. Founded by Ptolemy I Soter as part of the Mouseion, it provided employment as well as a place to work for many scholars. At its most extensive, around the time of Christ, it was said to contain more than 500,000 volumes. Sadly, this magnificent source of knowledge and scholarship did not survive the tumultuous years of the early first millennium C.E.

UPPER RIGHT: Bas reliefs depict the deities Horus and Hathor on the temple built for their worship by the Ptolemies at Kom Ombo. *CORBIS/Roger Wood*

UPPER LEFT: Egyptian relief shows Cleopatra VII, last ruler in the Macedonian dynasty of the Ptolemies. *CORBIS/Bettmann*

ABOVE: Sunken reliefs adorn the great pylon of this Temple of Horus, built at Edfu in Egypt by Ptolemy II Euergetes. *CORBIS/Roger Wood*

Often desecrated, the great library of Alexandria was finally burned toward the end of the third century C.E.; nothing is known to have survived. Not a single classical scholar of the last 500 years has failed to bemoan this terrible loss, perhaps the greatest in Western intellectual history.

The Ptolemies were Greeks; they spoke, read, and wrote Greek and looked to the land of their ancestors as the ultimate source of scientific and artistic ideas. But they were also Egyptians, and as such also Africans. Ptolemy I Soter was aware of the need to be, or at least to seem to be, Egyptian, especially in religion, and he established a new cult of the god Sarapis that combined Greek and Egyptian religious elements. Based in the ancient Egyptian capital city of Memphis, the cult spread all over the Mediterranean world and influenced Greek religious practices in Athens and other cities.

Cleopatra and Antony

Julius Caesar was assassinated in the Roman Senate on the Ides of March (March 15) in the year 44 B.C.E. After Caesar's death the fierce final phase ensued to the civil war that had been brewing for nearly a century. The two main factions were led by Octavian, named Caesar's successor in his will, and Mark Antony, who had been the dead man's closest associate. Octavian was a brilliant, handsome, and ruthlessly cold young man; he was 18 when Caesar died. Antony was a violent and passionate man of 36 who was adored by his soldiers and by many women.

One woman adored him more than any other, and he adored her with a passion that endured until their deaths. She was CLEOPATRA, queen of Egypt, who had seduced Caesar when he had visited her country a few years before and she now undertook to seduce the man she assumed would succeed him. How she did so is, thanks to Plutarch and Shakespeare, the stuff of legend. In Shakespeare's play (act 2, scene 2), Antony's lieutenant, Enobarbus, tells his friend Agrippa how "when she first met Mark Antony, she pursed up his heart, upon the river of Cydnus." Agrippa is astounded by the splendor of this famous meeting; nevertheless, he declares, Antony must leave Cleopatra if he is to succeed. Enobarbus replies:

Never! He will not.
Age cannot wither her, nor custom stale
Her infinite variety. Other women cloy
The appetites they feed, but she makes hungry
Where most she satisfies (II, ii, 239).

And so it was. Antony divorced his wife (who happened to be Octavian's sister) to marry Cleopatra. Spending too little time in Rome, he spent too much in Alexandria. He was generous and open, but his gifts were interpreted by the calculating Octavian as the excesses of a wastrel and a slave to love. Such a man, Octavian whispered, was not worthy to be the ruler of all Rome.

In the end, love and spectacle could not prevail over hard, practical politics. Too many Romans, even Antony's followers, believed Octavian was right. The last battle of the long civil war was fought at Actium, on the coast of Greece. The combined fleets of Antony and Cleopatra were soundly beaten and the lovers fled to Alexandria, where, abandoned and alone, they committed suicide. Octavian, henceforth unopposed and supported by all the Roman armies, became the man we know as Augustus, the first Roman emperor.

What if Antony and Cleopatra Had Won the Battle of Actium?

It is a good question, although there can be no certain answer. Paris and London are monopole cities; they are the artistic, intellectual, financial, *and* political capitals of their countries. Italy today has two capitals: Milan for business and finance, Rome for political administration. The financial and artistic capital of the United States is New York, while the national government is based in Washington, D.C. Both systems work, though in different ways.

Ruins of the Ptolemaic Temple of Isis, which stands on the island of Philae in the Nile River.
CORBIS/Adam Woolfitt

After Actium, Alexandria continued for centuries as the center of intellectual and artistic life of the Mediterranean, and one of the most important financial centers as well. But it had no political power beyond its minor role as the capital of the Roman province of Egypt. Lacking power, it was spared the political tumult that made life in Rome so dangerous. At the same time, Alexandria was starved for support, although the emperors made efforts to support the Mouseion and its library. Augustus was a Roman and a northern Italian; he had little interest in Africa. Alexandria continued to be a conduit for African products, men, and ideas under his rule, but the stream did not flow so richly as it had under the Ptolemies.

Mark Antony was a Roman, but he was the son and grandson of soldiers and had lived all over the world. His first allegiance was probably to Greece, not Rome; he tried for years to institute a Greco-Roman alliance that would include Egypt in an alliance of countries of the eastern Mediterranean. And he loved Cleopatra.

Augustus proclaimed, after spending millions of his people's money, that he had "found Rome brick and left it marble." The diversion of revenues from outlying provinces had made this possible. If Antony had won, the funds that rebuilt Rome might have rebuilt the ancient cities of the Nile and made Alexandria a glittering and better fortified imperial capital that might, because of its position on the African coast, have held off the barbarian invasions that inaugurated the Dark Ages.

Antony, Greek in spirit, was curious about new ideas. As emperor, he would have sought them out, even in that relatively unknown world beyond and below the Sahara. Under Augustus, the Roman Empire tended steadily northwest and east. Under Antony, guided by Cleopatra, it could have moved south and west. That difference would have changed almost everything.

As one example of what might have happened, note that slavery was rare in Egypt; it was endemic in Italy and Greece. The classical world was founded on the economic institution of slavery, without which, most Romans agreed, society could not endure. Aristotle had observed that if machines could do the work of men, then slaves would not be needed. A certain Greek, Hero of Alexandria, invented the steam engine, but the Augustans ignored its possibilities; the Antonians might have seen how to exploit it to replace slave labor. Taking these and other things into account, is it possible that Antony and Cleopatra, if they had won, might have established another kind of empire, based on the ideas of human equality instead of inequality, and freedom instead of slavery? And if so, might the Roman Empire, instead of being destroyed by Christianity (as Gibbon wrote), have made an early peace with it that changed not only the empire but Christianity as well?

Cleopatra's Nose

These speculations may seem absurd, or at the least misguided and illegitimate. Indeed, there is some truth in that judgment. Whatever happened in the past was the result of a long line of causes, not just one, and thus was more or less inevitable; at any rate, a single event could not be said to have determined the entire future. Thus the great changes that were occurring around the end of the first millennium B.C.E. – the collapse of the Roman Republic and its replacement by something like the Roman Empire, the advent of Christianity, and, later, the gradual movement of the center of Western civilization from the shores of the Mediterranean north and west to Germany, to France, to Great Britain (to use the modern names for those parts of Europe) – were probably going to occur anyway, whatever the outcome of a single battle.

We may remember, however, that famous remark of a great philosopher, Blaise Pascal, a remark that has teased schoolboys, if not professional historians, for over 300 years. "Cleopatra's nose," he wrote, "if it had been shorter, the whole course of history would have changed." Presumably, if Cleopatra's nose had been shorter, she would not have been so beautiful, Mark Antony would not have fallen in love with her, and he and Octavian would have reached some sort of reconciliation.

We should remember something else. History is always written by the winners. The irresponsibility of Cleopatra, the bad character of Mark Antony, are at least in part the creation of the Augustans. They had good reason to sully the reputations of their defeated foes, and they did so.

Perhaps it is not misguided or illegitimate, then, to imagine a past that was different than it actually was, and a present that is consequently different from what it actually is. At the least, if Antony and Cleopatra had won, the role played by Africa in the history of the last 2000 years would have been different. And the world we live in might be a good deal better than it is.

Charles Van Doren

See Also

Egypt, Ancient Kingdom of; Nile River; Alexandria, Egypt.

Africa

Alexandria, Egypt, the main port and second-largest city in Egypt.

Occupying more than 40 km (about 25 mi) of the Nile Delta's western edge on the Mediterranean Sea, the city of Alexandria is one of modern Egypt's most important economic and industrial centers. Now overshadowed by the Egyptian capital of Cairo, 183 km (114 mi) away, Alexandria dates back more than 2000 years, and was once considered the Western world's greatest city. Intending it to be a naval base and the capital of his Egyptian province, Alexander the Great founded Alexandria in 332 B.C.E. He entrusted its planning and construction to his personal architect, Dinocrates, and he left Egypt under the command of a general named Ptolemy Soter. But Alexander never saw his city completed, and when he died in 323, his empire disintegrated.

Ptolemy Soter built an empire based at Alexandria, and under his descendants, the Greek-speaking Ptolemies, the city reached what many consider to be its golden age. A network of canals linking it to the Nile and the Red Sea made the city a major commercial center. It was also a center of scholarship and science, boasting such residents as Euclid, Archimedes, Plotinus, and Ptolemy and Eratosthenes, who studied at the Mouseion, a center of higher learning. Some believe that Jewish scholars translated the Hebrew Bible into Greek in Alexandria. The city's famous library had the largest collection in the ancient world. (For a discussion of the place of Alexandria in the ancient Mediterranean, *see* Alexandria and Grecian Africa: An Interpretation.)

The Roman Empire gained control of the city in 30 B.C.E. and Alexandria became the capital of the Roman province of Egypt. Under Roman rule, Alexandria became important to the development of Christianity. Saint Mark, the attributed author of the second canonic Christian Gospel, is said to have preached in Alexandria in the mid-first century C.E. The city also played a key role in theological debates. Many Alexandrians embraced Monophysite Christianity, the doctrine that Jesus had a single divine nature. The Western Church (including the forerunners of the present-day Eastern Orthodox, Catholic, and Protestant Churches) rejected this doctrine and insisted on the dual human and divine nature of Jesus at the Council of Chalcedon in 451 C.E. Alexandrians and other Egyptian Christians (along with the Christians of Ethiopia) subsequently broke with the Western Church to form the Coptic Orthodox Church, still a substantial minority in modern Egypt.

Alexandria suffered a number of setbacks under Roman rule. The Romans massacred the city's Jewish population in 116 C.E. and its male population in 215 C.E. for opposing Roman rule. In the fourth century, Constantinople, the new capital of the Eastern Roman Empire (later known as the Byzantine Empire), eclipsed Alexandria as the political, economic, and cultural center of the eastern Mediterranean.

The decline of the Byzantine Empire, which had succeeded Rome in Egypt, left Alexandria vulnerable to the Arabs, who met no opposition when they sacked the city during the 640s. The Arabs established their Egyptian capital at al-Fustat, today a part of Cairo. Alexandria remained important as a naval base and commercial center, especially for the lucrative spice trade, which was dominated by the Egyptians until the sixteenth century, when Europeans discovered a route to Asia around southern Africa. After the Ottoman Turks took control of Egypt in 1517, Alexandria's importance dwindled further. The canal linking it with the Nile filled with silt, and the city became only a minor port.

In 1805, as part of his effort to modernize Egypt, Pasha Muhammad 'Ali ordered the al-Mahmudiyah Canal built to restore the city's access to the Nile. Cotton became a principal export and source of wealth, particularly during the cotton shortage caused by the United States Civil War in the 1860s. The opening of the Suez Canal in 1869 furthered Alexandria's prosperity, but also attracted greater interest in the region from British colonialists. After the British bombarded Alexandria in 1882, the city surrendered to British forces; thus began the British occupation of Egypt.

Although it never recaptured the cultural luster it once had, Alexandria has remained an important commercial center. The city now accounts for one-third of Egypt's industrial output. Its economic activities include banking, shipping, warehousing, and textile manufacturing. The majority of Egypt's foreign trade travels through Alexandria, particularly its modern Western port, including all cotton and oil exports. The city is also Egypt's most cosmopolitan, with large communities of expatriates from European and other Middle Eastern countries.

Robert Fay

See Also

Roman Africa: An Interpretation; Ethiopian Orthodox Church; Jewish Communities in North Africa; Nile River; Civil War, American; Cairo, Egypt.

Latin America and the Caribbean

Alexis, Jacques Stéphen

(b. April 22, 1922, Gonaives, Haiti; d. 1961, Haiti), Haitian novelist whose politically committed works made a profound impact on Haitian letters.

Jacques Stéphen Alexis was born into one of Haiti's literary families. His father, Stéphen Alexis, was the author of *Le Nègre masqué* (1933) and wrote a work on the history of Haiti. After finishing his studies at the

Saint-Louis de Gonzague Institute, the son studied medicine in both Port-au-Prince and Paris. Returning to Haiti after receiving his degree, he participated in the revolt of 1946. Alexis soon fled Haiti for fear of political persecution. From that point forward, he spent most of his time traveling, visiting the countries of the MIDDLE EAST and Russia and China, before settling in CUBA. But the lure of his native Haiti was strong, and he returned clandestinely to the northwest part of the island in 1961, in spite of reservations regarding the Duvalier regime. He was arrested and is believed to have died in captivity shortly thereafter.

Alexis's literary works, published over the course of a few productive years, capture the essence of a period in his country's history. His first two novels, *Compère Général Soleil* (1955) and *Les arbres musiciens* (1957) cover the tumultuous period from 1934 to 1942 (the United States occupied Haiti from 1934 to 1957) and paint a complex picture of the psychological, social, and political life of the people of the island. He also expressed his own political convictions through these novels. The Communist characters in *Compère Général Soleil* are portrayed in an utterly sympathetic light, while the *Arbres musiciens* constitutes a sustained attack on the Haitian bourgeosie. It should not be surprising that his works were widely translated throughout the Soviet Union during the 1960s.

The third novel, *L'Espace d'un cillement* (1959), moves away from the heroic narratives of the first two. It recounts the story of a Port-au-Prince prostitute who, after a life of virtual enslavement, seeks the freedom and authentic love that her work never permitted her to have. In her tragic end, it is possible to consider this story as a fitting allegory of the Haitian condition. Alexis's last published work, the collection of short stories *Romancero aux Etoiles* (1960), contains works of Haitian folklore as well as original works by the author. It is here that he most effectively expresses the complex synthesis of Haiti's linguistic, cultural, and political influences. Two unpublished manuscripts were found after his death: *L'Eglantine* and *Dans le blanc des yeux*.

Alexis stated that "we must expand Voltaire's language, enrich it with new words, and adapt it to the dimensions of the universe of the French language." His works reflect this effort of expansion, with their mixture of Creole and French and of coarse and elevated language. Although he was never a prose stylist in the mold of JACQUES ROUMAIN, Alexis's later works attain a level of stylistic refinement missing from the first two novels. Still, his importance lies in his vibrant evocation of the island's past and in his hope for a brighter future for its people.

Richard Watts

SEE ALSO

Duvalier, François; Literature, French Language, in Caribbean.

Latin America and the Caribbean

Algarín, Miguel

(b. September 11, 1941, Santurce, Puerto Rico), Afro-Puerto Rican educator, author, playwright, and a founder of the urban-based *Nuyorican* literary genre that emerged in the late twentieth century.

Miguel Algarín's family emigrated from PUERTO RICO to the Lower East Side of Manhattan, New York, when he was nine years old. The Lower East Side's Latin urban landscape served as the foundation for his literary career. Algarín obtained his B.A. in romance languages from the University of Wisconsin in 1963 and his M.A. in English literature from Pennsylvania State University in 1965. He completed his doctoral studies in comparative literature at Rutgers University. He served as an instructor at Brooklyn College and New York University before becoming an assistant professor and chair of the Puerto Rican Studies department at Rutgers University.

While Algarín is a popular educator, he is best known as one of the most active authors in the Puerto Rican poetic movement that flourished in New York City in the 1960s and 1970s. The poetry combined English and Spanish vernacular. Its content focused on the poets' daily lives and explored the Puerto Rican/American dichotomy. In 1975 Algarín established the Nuyorican Poets Café in order to provide an outlet for poetry and a host of other literary and performance genres.

He has published several books, including *Mongo Affair* (1978), *On Call* (1980), and *Times Now/Ya es tiempo* (1984). He has also edited two anthologies: *Nuyorican Poets Café: An Anthology of Puerto Rican Words and Feelings* (1975) and *Aloud: Voices from the Nuyorican Poets Café* (1994), which won the American Book Award. He has written several collaborative plays, including *Olu Clements* (1973), *Apartment 6-d* (1974), *The Murder of Pito* (1976), and *Blue Heaven* (1976), and his work appears in various literary anthologies.

SEE ALSO

New York, New York.

Alger, Algeria. Please see ALGIERS, ALGERIA

Africa

Algeria,

republic of western North Africa; bounded on the north by the Mediterranean Sea; on the east by Tunisia and Libya; on the south by Niger, Mali, and Mauritania; and on the west by Morocco.

To many outside observers, Algeria has been a preeminent symbol of postcolonial independence, a nation that waged a highly visible war against a European colonial power, France, in the mid-twentieth century, and won an independent secular state. The electoral success during the early 1990s of the ISLAMIC SALVATION FRONT (FIS), considered by many to be an Islamic fundamentalist group, was all the more startling. This apparent inconsistency revealed a complexity that stems from the fact that Algeria spans the traditions of the Berber, Arab, and European worlds. For the people of Algeria, Islam has been central to the culture since the seventh century. Within its history are many other strands as well, including the uneasy integration of BERBER-dominated territories, the experience of women at the forefront of the independence struggle, the socialist strategies of the newly independent state, and the capitalist vision of economic development that supplanted it.

EARLY HISTORY

The Berber people, who call themselves *Imazighen*, or "free men," historically have made up the majority of the population in the area that later became Algeria. From 208 to 148 B.C.E. the North African coastal kingdom Numidia encompassed portions of this region. After the destruction of Carthage (146 B.C.E.), Rome colonized the territory, transforming the vassal state into a major provider of grain for the empire and bringing Christianity to parts of the region. Later conquerors included the Vandals in the fifth century and a coastal presence of the Byzantine Empire in the sixth century. Certain areas, however, historically remained under independent Berber confederacies, particularly the Aurès and Kabylia, maintaining a distinct cultural status within the region that would become Algeria.

Islam spread through North Africa in the seventh century, brought at first by raids and later by immigration by Arabs to the area of northwest Africa known as the Maghreb, or "the land of the setting sun." The Berber population gradually converted to Islam, despite militant resistance in strongholds of Berber political rule. The extent to which the Berber culture and language were Arabized during this time in Algeria is a question still debated by historians. A series of Islamic dynasties spread over the Maghreb for the next few centuries, encompassing the area of present-day Algeria. The rule of the Berber Dynasty, ALMOHADS, brought the region into a prosperous alliance with the rest of the Maghreb and Muslim Spain. These dynasties marked the region culturally as well as politically, linking it to a heterogeneous Islamic world and facilitating the influx of peoples displaced by the Christian reconquest, including the Andalusian Muslims and Jews. Cities such as Constantine, Tlemcen, Annaba (Bône), Bejaïa (Bouie), and Algiers flourished as centers of learning and commerce.

The sixteenth century brought Spain to North Africa in a military campaign that was both a crusade against Muslim power in North Africa and an attempt to dominate the Mediterranean region. The Algerian coastal

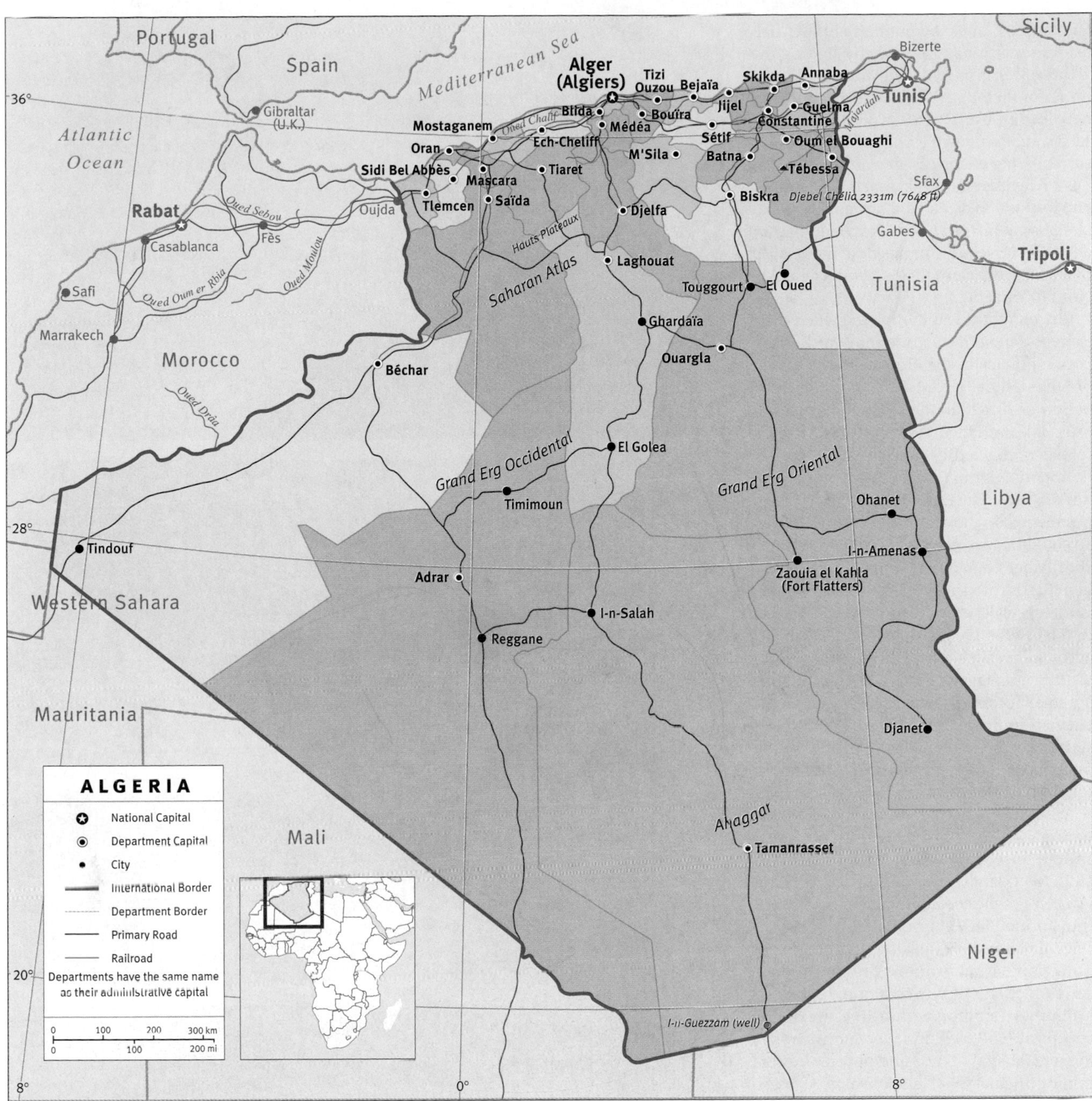

cities, including Algiers and Oran, were taken as strategic locations for the lucrative occupations of sea trade and piracy. After the death of Ferdinand of Castile of Spain in 1516, the Turkish "Barbarossa" brothers Aruj and Khayr al-Din intervened – ostensibly putting the region under the protection of an Islamic power, the Ottoman sultan, but also serving their own ambitions for trade and piracy in the Mediterranean region. Some scholars mark this intervention as the origin of Algeria as a political entity.

After the Spanish withdrew in 1541, Algeria entered the period known as the Regency. Historians have described the political state as an "Algerian Ottoman Republic," operating autonomously despite official allegiance to the Ottoman Empire. With a fertile countryside, thriving artisan trade communities, and an economy enriched by piracy, the area around Algiers developed over the next few centuries into a viable cosmopolitan center that was highly attractive to the French.

French Colonization

By the nineteenth century, France was trading extensively with merchants in the Algiers region, but the Bourbon government's refusal to honor a debt owed to an Algerian exporting firm signaled a shift toward more confrontational relations. In 1827 the French king Charles X ordered a blockade, ostensibly because an Algerian official slapped the French consul with a fly whisk, but also to display his military clout in a time of waning French support for his regime. On June 14, 1830, Gen. Louis de Bourmont landed at Sidi Fredj, west of Algiers. Within a month, the French had captured Algiers, defeating Turkish and allied Berber forces. Charles's successor, Louis-Philippe, who saw in colonization an opportunity to capture new markets and strategic military sites as well as to expand the reach of French civilization, helped secure the French position with the invasion of Constantine in 1837.

The population actively and persistently resisted French colonial occupation. Islam provided one nexus for an anticolonial alliance. One of the most prominent early anticolonial leaders was Abd al-Qadir, who organized an Islamic state in the west that at one point controlled two-thirds of Algeria's inhabited land. Considered a strategic genius, Abd al-Qadir consolidated his position as leader of Berber confederacies, and attempted to gain diplomatic recognition from England

and Spain. France did grant the influential leader territorial autonomy by signing the Treaty of Tafna in 1837. But when land ambitions conflicted, the French army, under a new leader, General Bugeaud, used massacres and "scorched earth" tactics – burning surrendering enemies alive and systemically destroying Algerian villages, crops, livestock, and forests – to defeat Abd al-Qadir ten years later. Some historians have argued that Abd al-Qadir planted the first seeds of nationalism by uniting the Berbers and Arabs against "infidel" invaders.

The conquest was completed when the French defeated the independent Berber confederacies in the Kabylia in 1857. The French military paved the way for an influx of European settlers, a population originally only half French and mostly poor. The interests of the settlers and the military-dominated administration were not always harmonious. The European settlers' political power grew as their population swelled from 10,000 settlers in 1834 to more than 1 million shortly before independence in 1962. They benefited from the confiscation of Algerian land, especially after the unsuccessful Kabylia Revolt in 1871. From 1830 to 1940, 8.64 million acres were taken over. During this period settlers campaigned for civilian rule and then colonial autonomy, and even waged an insurrection in 1898. Two years later, the settlers secured nominal administrative and financial autonomy from France, but maintained a governor general office.

As settlers took over the countryside, the region's peasant-based agrarian economy shifted to settler-owned, large-scale agricultural and industrial enterprises, and large expanses of the cereal producing lands were transformed into vineyards for wine export. The effects were devastating for the indigenous population: warfare, famine, and a series of plagues reduced a population of 3 million to 1 million within 40 years of the conquest. The traditional economy was no longer viable. With war and poverty undermining original tribal relationships, Algerians turned to a vision of national resistance to colonization.

TOP: Sand breaks protect the trees and structures of this oasis in the Algerian desert. *CORBIS/Tiziana and Gianni B*
MIDDLE: Algerian women march in support of independence from France as voting proceeds during the nationwide referendum in 1962. *Archive Photos*
RIGHT: The mosque and university at al-Karawiyyin, a complex of Islamic worship and learning that was begun in 859 by Fatima al-Fihri, the daughter of a wealthy merchant. Expansions throughout the next five centuries made al-Karawiyyin the largest mosque in North Africa, capable of accommodating 22,000 worshipers. *CORBIS/The Purcell Team*

An Algerian woman prepares couscous, a staple North African food made from semolina wheat. *A. Bordes, Explorer*

Struggle for National Independence

During the early twentieth century Algerian intellectuals, including the "Young Algerians," or *évolués*, educated at European universities, and Algerians holding official positions, such as Emir Khalid, a captain in the Algerian army and grandson of Abd al-Qadir, spoke out against the inequity of the colonial relationship and proposed reforms to equalize French and Muslim status. Algerian sacrifices during World War I had won them a degree of respect in France, and following the war Premier Georges Clemenceau introduced measures to ensure full citizenship for Muslims. Settler groups violently opposed these measures, creating a rift in the alliance between the settler population and its military and civil foundation, the colonial government. Settler opposition to reform created a fissure between France and European-Algerians that would tear open during the struggle for Algerian independence.

As settlers resisted early reform efforts and France capitulated, more of the indigenous population turned toward a goal of national liberation. During the 1930s a nationalist alliance emerged, bringing together anticolonialist leaders such as Ferhat Abbas and Messali Hadj, and Islamic leaders, notably Shaykh abd al-Hamid ibn Badis (Ben Badis). In the 1943 Manifesto of the Algerian People, Ferhat Abbas called for an independent Algeria, and a year later organized the Association des Amis de la Manifest (AML). The first Congress of the AML elected Messali as its leader and made clear that French leader Charles de Gaulle's appeasing gesture, the Ordinance of March 1944, did not meet their demands for autonomy. When Messali was then quickly deported, the Algerian people demonstrated their outrage with riots in Sétif and Guelma.

Nationalists formed the outlawed Organisation Speciale (OS), which was succeeded by the Comité Révolutionnaire pour l'Unité et l'Action (CRUA) and later the Front de Libération Nationale (FLN). The FLN became the force of the revolution, aiming, as its 1954 statement said, for "national independence through the restoration of the Algerian state, sovereign, democratic and social, within the framework of the principles of Islam." Its leaders, such as Ahmed Ben Bella, Mohamed Boudiaf, Rabah Bitat, and Hocine Ait Ahmed, would become synonymous with the struggle for independence. Political theorist Frantz Fanon's writings about the struggle captured the world's attention as well as the support of prominent European intellectuals such as Jean-Paul Sartre. The nationalist army, Armée de Libération (ALN), waged a fierce guerrilla campaign for decolonization, while the French army responded with equally ruthless counterinsurgency tactics, including torture. Settlers organized the vigilante army Organisation de l'Armée Secrète (OAS).

The Soummam Conference of FLN members still within Algeria marked a decisive point in the coalition of nationalist forces, as the FLN developed a framework for a future state and accelerated the urban guerrilla campaign. The campaign catapulted Algerian women into key roles in the struggle as weapons couriers and spies in French quarters. In 1958 the FLN formed a Provisional Government of the Algerian Republic (GPRA). As France under Charles de Gaulle began preparing for decolonization, a faction of the army joined the settler OAS to resist, targeting the French as well as the Algerians with bombs.

Independent Algeria

In March 1962 a cease-fire was finally arranged between government and FLN representatives at Evian, France. In the long-awaited referendum, held the following July, Algeria voted overwhelmingly for independence. The settlers began a mass evacuation; before the end of the year most of them had left the country.

A number of different groups had come forward to take leadership positions during the war for independence, often filling the void as other organizations were forced to disband or leaders were sent into exile. As Algeria began the task of building a new nation, the euphoria of independence gave way to a bitter struggle for leadership between the FLN and GPRA, and within the GPRA itself. In September 1962, after fratricidal battles, an elected Algerian Assembly appointed Ferhat Abbas as president and

Ahmed Ben Bella as prime minister. Once in office, Ben Bella outlawed opposition parties, making the FLN the only legal party. Bella's power-mongering tactics furthered the divisiveness between former leaders of the nationalist struggle.

Bella's regime chose a socialist path to rebuild a society ravaged by years of violent war and the huge repatriation of Europeans with wealth and professional skills. Algeria maintained tenuous links with France, bargaining military sites for technical and educational services.

After a bloodless coup d'état in 1965, Houari Boumedienne assumed the leadership of Algeria, filling a new governing body, the Council of the Revolution, with civilian technocrats and military supporters. Under Boumedienne, Algeria gained a reputation as a socialist nation determined to sidestep the pitfalls of foreign dependence. Concentrating his power through the suppression of political rivals, Boumedienne attempted to build an economically independent Algerian state through "superindustrialization," inaugurating a four-year plan to subsidize Algerian development through hydrocarbons export. After Boumedienne's death in 1978, Chadli Benjedid assumed power, reversing the socialist strategies of his predecessors by privatizing state-held agricultural land and opening the country to foreign investment.

Despite these moves, during the 1980s Algeria faced a rising Islamic populism, Berber unrest, and a severe shortage of consumer goods. In addition, intellectuals, proponents of women's rights, and advocates of free speech attacked the government for its repressive political and social constraints. These conditions prompted massive riots in October 1988. In an attempt to save the FLN from its deteriorating reputation as a front for corrupt politicians, Chadli implemented a series of reforms. In July 1989 the FLN legalized opposition parties, including the Islamic Salvation Front (FIS), lifted press restrictions, and scheduled Algeria's first free multiparty elections for the following year.

In June 1990 the FIS party won the majority of first-round local elections. Some observers read this victory as an Algerian mandate for Islamic fundamentalism, others as a sign of disillusionment with Chadli's government. Declaring Algeria to be under a state of siege, President Chadli halted the elections, and in January 1992 dissolved the National People's Assembly. The new High Council of State forced Chadli's removal, and Mohamed Boudiaf, along with a group of military leaders, assumed control of the country.

Boudiaf was assassinated in June 1992, and Algeria since has been in a declared state of emergency. With massacres and random killings leaving tens of thousands dead, Algeria has once again become a battlefield. The Islamic movement splintered, producing various factions of Islamic nationalists. Many attribute the terrorist attacks to the Groupes Islamiques Armés (GIA) because the banned FIS has distanced itself from the violence – in September 1997 the FIS called for its followers to lay down their arms. During this time, the military-backed government under President Liamine Zeroual has created internment camps and made massive arrests, reportedly using torture to flush out suspected FIS members and sympathizers. The people of Algeria, wary of the violence that follows in the wake of the military, have formed independent groups for protection that keep 24-hour watch over towns. A military victory in an October 1997 election has been contested by a range of groups, including socialists and supporters of the FIS.

Marian Aguiar

See Also

African Socialism; Algiers, Algeria; Fanon, Frantz; Front de Libération Nationale; Kabylia.

Africa

Algeria (Ready Reference)

Official Name: Democratic and Popular Republic of Algeria
Area: 2,381,741 sq km (919,595 sq mi)
Location: Northern Africa; bordering the Mediterranean Sea, Morocco, Tunisia, Libya, Mali, Mauritania, Niger, and the Western Sahara
Capital: Algiers (population 1,687,579 [1987 estimate])
Other Major Cities: Oran (population 916,000), Constantine (662,330 [1987 estimate])
Population: 29,852,000 (1998 estimate)
Population Density: 12 persons per sq km (about 31 persons per sq mi)
Population Below Age 15: 38 percent (male 5,923,087; female 5,709,814 [1998 estimate])
Population Growth Rate: 2.14 percent (1998 estimate)
Total Fertility Rate: 3.38 children born per woman (1998 estimate)
Life Expectancy at Birth: Total population: 68.93 years (male 67.78 years; female 70.12 years [1998 estimate])
Infant Mortality Rate: 45.44 deaths per 1000 live births (1998 estimate)
Literacy Rate (age 15 and over who can read and write): Total population: 61.6 percent (male 73.9 percent; female 49 percent [1995 estimate])
Education: Primary education is free and compulsory for all children between the ages of six and 15. In the early 1990s some 4.6 million pupils attended primary schools, 2.3 million were enrolled in secondary schools, and another 147,418 attended vocational schools. By the mid-1990s nearly 300,000 were pursuing higher education.
Languages: Arabic is the official language and is spoken by about 83 percent of the population; most of the remainder speak Berber. French, the colonial language, is still widely read and spoken by many educated Algerians.
Ethnic Groups: Arabs, Berbers, or people of mixed Arab-Berber ancestry make up 99 percent of the population; Europeans constitute less than 1 percent.
Religions: Sunni Islam is the state religion and is practiced by 99 percent of the population; 1 percent of the population are Christians or Jews.
Climate: The Tell region in the north has warm, dry summers and mild, rainy winters, with an annual rainfall of between 400 and 1000 mm (16 to 39 in). During the summer an exceedingly hot, dry dust and sand-filled wind, the *sirocco* (known locally as the *Chehili*), blows north from the Sahara. To the south the climate becomes increasingly dry, with an annual rainfall in the High Plateau and Saharan Atlas from about 200 to 400 mm (about 8 to 16 in). The Sahara is a region of daily temperature extremes, wind, and great aridity; annual rainfall is less than 130 mm (5 in) in all places.
Land, Plants, and Animals: The Tell region, between the northern Mediterranean coast and the mountainous Tell Atlas area, contains most of Algeria's arable land. The country's principal river, the Chelif (725 km/450 mi long), flows from the Tell Atlas to the Mediterranean Sea. Lying to the south and southwest is the High Plateau, a level, sparsely vegetated highland region. During rainy periods, basins collect water, forming large, shallow lakes that become salt flats, called *chotts*, or *shotts*, during dry seasons. The mountains of the Saharan Atlas lie south of this region. More than 90 percent of the country's total area lies in the Algerian Sahara, covered mostly by gravel with vast regions of sand dunes. Rising above the desert to the south are the Ahaggar Mountains, with Mount Tahat (3003 m/9852 ft), the highest peak in Algeria.

Remnants of forests exist in a few areas of the higher Tell and Saharan Atlas. Scattered plant life in the Sahara consists of drought-resistant grasses, acacia, and jujube trees. Wildlife includes scavengers, such as jackals, hyenas, and vultures, as well as antelope, hares, gazelles, and reptiles.
Natural Resources: Petroleum, natural gas, iron ore, phosphates, uranium, lead, zinc
Currency: The Algerian dinar
Gross Domestic Product (GDP): $15.38 billion (1994 estimate)
GDP per Capita: $4000 (1997 estimate)
GDP Real Growth Rate: 2.5 percent (1997 estimate)
Primary Economic Activities: Mineral production (primarily crude petroleum and natural gas), agriculture, fishing. Since the late 1960s the government has instituted major industrialization programs.
Primary Crops: Wheat, barley, potatoes, tomatoes, melons, grapes, dates, olives, tobacco

Industries: Petroleum, light industries, natural gas, mining, electricity production, petrochemical, food processing
Primary Exports: Petroleum and natural gas make up 97 percent of export revenues. Other exports include iron ore, vegetables, tobacco, phosphates, fruit, cork, and hides.
Primary Imports: Machinery, textiles, sugar, cereals, iron and steel, coal, gasoline
Primary Trade Partners: Italy, France, United States, Germany, Spain, Japan
Government: Under the constitution adopted in February 1989, Algeria is a socialist republic, and a president is elected to a five-year term by universal adult suffrage. A unicameral National People's Assembly of 295 members was elected in 1987. In January 1992, the assembly was suspended to prevent the Islamic Salvation Front (FIS), a Muslim fundamentalist party, from gaining a legislative majority. Since then, Algeria has been governed by the High Council of State, headed by President Liamine Zeroual, with Prime Minister Ahmed Ouyahia appointed by the president.

Marian Aguiar

Africa

Algiers, Algeria, capital city of Algeria, located on the northern coast of the country along the Mediterranean Sea.

Algiers was built through multiple conquests, and layers of different cultures can be found in its architecture and social character. Legend has it that the ancient city of Icosium, founded by 20 companions of Hercules, lies beneath the foundations of the modern city. Romans, Berbers, Vandals, Byzantines, and Arabs all left their mark on the site, but it was not until the mid-tenth century that the Berber emir Bulkkin built the harbor town into an important North African trading center, al-Jaza'ir.

For several hundred years a series of Islamic Maghreb rulers claimed the city as their seat of power. For the most part, the region operated as an independent city-state under dynastic rule, but at several points, al-Jaza'ir was governed by its own citizens. During the early sixteenth century, the city also became home to persecuted Andalusian Muslims, or Moors, and Jews, displaced by Christian reconquests in southern Europe. Spain followed closely on the heels of the fleeing Muslims and Jews, taking the islet Peñon in the bay of Algiers in 1511 as its base. For the next five years, Spain vied with the Ottoman Turks for control of the city, considered a prime location for lucrative sea trade and piracy.

After the Turkish "Barbarossa" brothers Aruj and Khayr al-Din gained control of the city in 1516, Algiers thrived as a relatively independent city under the nominal control of the Ottoman Empire. The Ottomans and the Turkish-Algerian rulers who succeeded them transformed the city's architectural character, constructing mosques similar to those in Asia Minor and erecting the famous white-washed military fortification, the Casbah.

Epidemics, famine, and declining trade undermined the vitality of the city during the early nineteenth century. France took Algiers in 1830, using it as a base for colonial occupation. Over the next 132 years, the French colonial administration developed the port, built wide boulevards, and constructed an opera house and several cathedrals. The city served as a military base during World War II, and even briefly as the provisional capital of France. By the mid-1950s, nearly half the population was European.

Algiers was also home to many prominent Algerian intellectual and political figures, and it became a center for the anticolonial movement, and eventually for the guerrilla campaigns of the Algerian nationalist Armée de Libération (ALN). As Algerians planted bombs in European neighborhoods and French soldiers scoured the streets for revolutionaries, the city suffered ten years of urban warfare, known as the Battle of Algiers.

Since independence in 1962, the capital city of Algiers has grown into the most important Mediterranean shipping center of northwest Africa. The population has grown to more than 3 million, and expansive suburbs surround the busy downtown.

Algiers also remains a center of ongoing political and social upheaval. In October 1988, residents of Algiers rioted to protest the scarcity of basic necessities. Violence filled the streets again after the 1991 elections were cancelled to forestall a potential victory by the Islamic Salvation Front (FIS). Since then, terrorist attacks and military reprisals waged as part of the conflict between the military-backed government and militant Islamic groups have repeatedly struck Algiers and its suburbs.

Marian Aguiar

See Also
Roman Africa: An Interpretation; Berber; Jewish Communities in North Africa; World War II and African Americans.

Africa

Al-Hajj Umar Tal, (also known as Umar ibn Siid Tal and al-Hajj Umar), (b. 1794?, Halwar [present-day Senegal]; d. February 12, 1864, near Hamdalahi [present-day Mali]), Muslim cleric and founder of the Tukulor empire of present-day Mali.

Al-Hajj Umar Tal's religious movement popularized the Tijaniya Sufi order and influenced religious reformers throughout nineteenth-century West Africa. The son of a prominent Tukulor cleric, Umar was influenced by the teachings of the Tijaniya brotherhood at an early age. In 1826 he made a pilgrimage to Mecca and on his return home visited several West African Islamic states, including the Sokoto Caliphate in northern Nigeria, then ruled by Mohammed Bello. He moved to the Fouta Djallon region after Bello's death in 1837.

For the next decade, Umar divided his time between religious and commercial pursuits. Having already accumulated considerable wealth abroad, he acquired firearms by selling non-Muslim captives to the French. He also gained renown as a religious scholar. Umar's greater ambition, however, was to convert the non-Muslim Bambara and Mandinka, and to unite the peoples of the region into one empire – not unlike the Sokoto Caliphate – based on the tenets of Tijaniya Sufism. In 1852 Umar mobilized his followers and launched the first of several *jihads* (holy wars) in the Senegal and Niger River valleys.

Umar's early campaigns easily conquered some of the smaller city-states and kingdoms, which he united under the rule of his sons. In the late 1850s, however, he met opposition from the French, who viewed the cleric's growing empire as a threat to French trade and future colonization. After a series of clashes Umar and the French signed a treaty in 1860. Ultimately, Umar was defeated by the Bambara kingdom of Ségou, once the kingdom allied with other rival forces from Tombouctou (Timbuktu). Umar died in a fire that was set by his enemies. After Umar's death, his empire quickly disintegrated; most of the territory between the Senegal and Niger Rivers was later colonized by the French.

Elizabeth Heath

See Also
Bello, Muhammad; Transatlantic Slave Trade; Sufism; Tombouctou, Mali.

Ali Farke Toure. Please see Touré, Ali Farka

Ali, Mohamed. Please see Ali, Muhammad

North America

Ali, Muhammad (b. January 17, 1942, Louisville, Ky.), African American heavyweight prizefighter, convert to Islam, antiwar protester, and international ambassador of goodwill.

As the dominant heavyweight boxer of the 1960s and 1970s, Muhammad Ali won an Olympic gold medal, captured the professional world heavyweight championship on three separate occasions, and successfully defended his title 19 times. Ali's extroverted, colorful style, both in and out of the ring, heralded a new mode of media-conscious athletic celebrity. Through his bold assertions of black pride, his conversion to the Muslim faith, and his outspoken opposition to the VIETNAM WAR, Ali became a highly controversial symbol of the turbulent 1960s.

Ali's 1981 retirement from boxing did not diminish his status in international public culture. Despite suffering from Parkinson's disease, he remained on the world stage as an adherent of the NATION OF ISLAM, an advocate of children and war victims, and a proponent of international understanding. Ali has been described as "the most recognizable human being on earth."

The Louisville Years

Muhammad Ali was born Cassius Marcellus Clay, the son of Marcellus Clay, a sign painter, and Odessa (Grady) Clay, a domestic worker. He was named for white Kentucky abolitionist Cassius M. Clay. He began boxing at the age of 12 under the tutelage of white Louisville policeman Joe Martin. Enraged one day to discover that his bicycle was missing, Ali resolved to "whup whoever stole it." Martin, wary of the problem of undisciplined adolescent belligerence in Ali's tough neighborhood, convinced the young Ali that such verbal boasts were best complemented by a mastery of the principles of boxing.

An indifferent student who graduated 376th in his high school class of 391, Cassius Clay passionately devoted himself to amateur boxing, appearing in 108 bouts between 1955 and 1960. He won six Kentucky Golden Glove titles, two National Amateur Athletic Union (AAU) championships, two National Golden Glove crowns, and the gold medal in the light heavyweight division in the 1960 Summer Olympic Games in Rome, Italy.

Returning triumphantly from Rome to Louisville, he was bitterly disappointed at not being welcomed as an American hero in his segregated hometown. According to one story, after being refused service at a Louisville diner while wearing the Olympic medal around his neck, he threw it into the Ohio River.

Professional Boxing Career

Cassius Clay's professional debut as a heavyweight came in October 1960 with a six-round decision over Tunny Hunsaker. He won his next 18 fights, 15 by knockouts. On February 25, 1964, in Miami Beach, Florida, he waged his first challenge for the heavyweight championship in a match against Sonny Liston. Though Liston was thought by many boxing experts to be invincible, the brash 22-year-old Clay spent the weeks leading up to the fight entertaining reporters and fans with colorfully worded promises of his impending victory. In one of the most stunning upsets in boxing history, he delivered on his promise, knocking Liston out in the seventh round.

Shortly after the fight, Cassius Clay startled the sports world by announcing that he had joined the Nation of Islam and had changed his name to Muhammad Ali. He defended his heavyweight crown in nine matches over the next two years. His title was revoked in 1967 when, citing his Islamic faith, he refused induction into the United States military and was sentenced to a five-year prison term.

Ali started fighting again in 1970, though the U.S. Supreme Court did not officially reverse his conviction for draft evasion until 1971. Knockout victories over Jerry Quarry and Oscar Bonaven earned Ali a chance to regain his heavyweight crown. But on March 8, 1971, he dropped a 15-round decision to Joe Frazier, the first loss of his career.

Ali regained the heavyweight championship on October 30, 1974, in Kinshasa, Zaire (present-day DEMOCRATIC REPUBLIC OF THE CONGO), with an eighth-round knockout of George Foreman. Ali defended his title ten times over the next four years, most famously in a 15-round victory over Joe Frazier on October 1, 1975, in the Philippines. Ali relinquished the crown to Olympic champion LEON SPINKS in a 15-round decision on February 15, 1978, in Las Vegas, Nevada. He regained the championship, however, on September 15, 1978, prevailing in a 15-round decision over Spinks in their rematch at the Superdome in New Orleans, Louisiana, thus becoming the only fighter ever to win the heavyweight crown three times.

Ali announced his retirement from boxing on June 27, 1979, but within a year he challenged the new heavyweight champion LARRY HOLMES for his crown. On October 2,

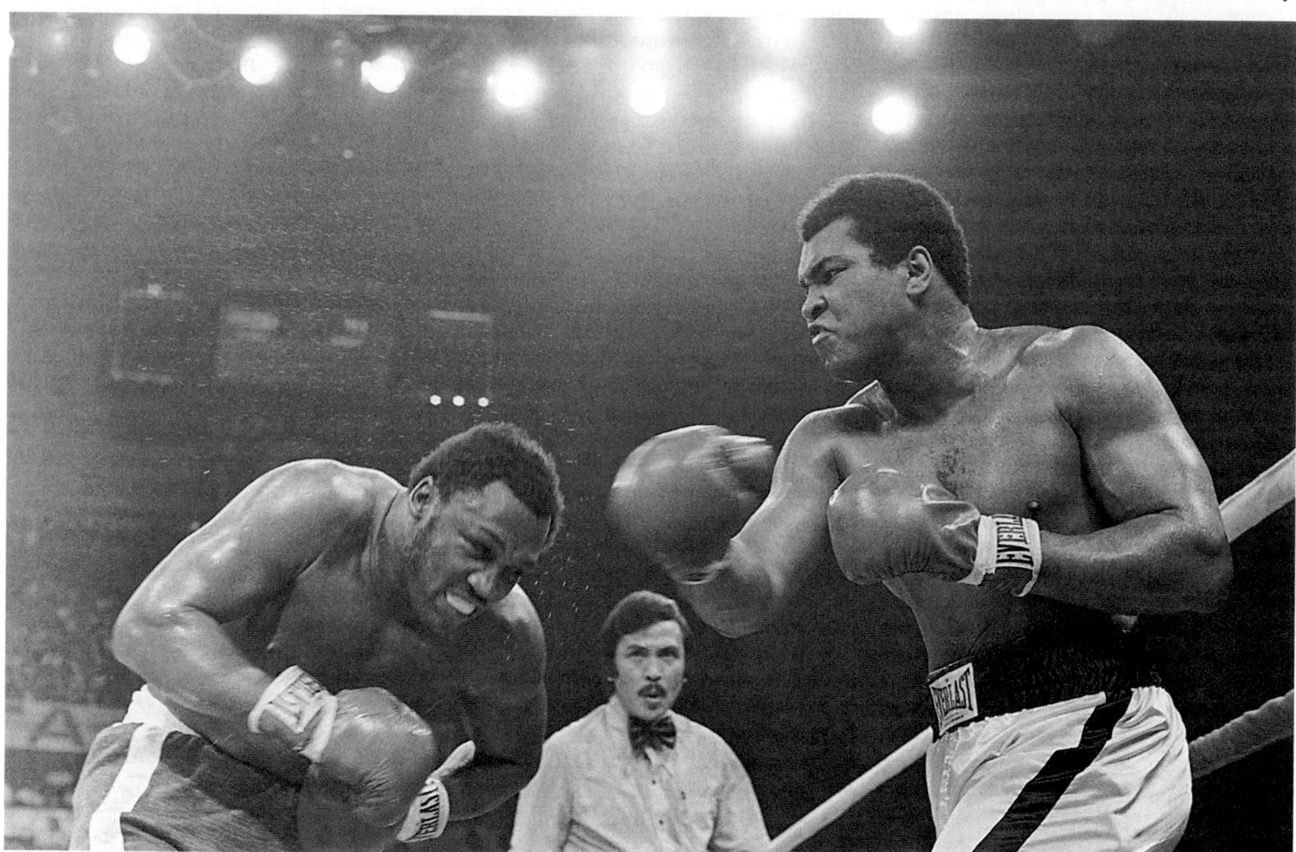

Muhammad Ali connects with challenger Joe Frazier during their 1975 heavyweight title fight in Manila, Philippines. *CORBIS/Bettmann*

1980, in Las Vegas, Nevada, Holmes dealt Ali the worst defeat of his career, physically punishing the former champion before delivering a knockout blow in the 11th round. Ali retired permanently in December 1981 after losing a ten-round decision to Trevor Berbick.

Ali as Performer and Cultural Hero

Ali's skills as a fighter included lightning-quick hands, a razor-sharp jab, agile footwork, and (especially evident in the later part of his career) the ability to absorb punches from bigger and stronger opponents. As important as these physical skills were to Ali's success, what distinguished him as an athletic performer was his use of the boxing ring as a public stage. "It is Ali," suggested Bartlett Giamatti, "who brought to the surface the actor in every athlete." A brilliant showman and provocateur, Ali enlisted the media – especially television – as an integral part of his competitive strategy.

While it was Jack Johnson, the first African American heavyweight champion, who introduced boasting and the taunting of one's opponent into the culture of boxing, Ali elevated the language of ridicule into an art form. Master of rhyming insult and a seminal contributor to the African American tradition of "signifying" or "playing the dozens," Ali transformed the prefight weigh-in from a procedural formality into the occasion for a display of creative verbal warfare.

In the days leading up to his championship match against George Foreman in 1974, Ali regaled the international press corps on hand in Zaire with this exercise in matching couplets: "Float like a butterfly, sting like a bee. His hands can't hit what his eyes can't see. Now you see me, now you don't. George thinks he will, but I know he won't." In the fight itself, Ali flustered the physically imposing, harder-punching Foreman with a stealthy defensive maneuver he dubbed the "rope-a-dope."

Ali's celebrity status and instincts as a performer did not diminish his religious convictions or defiant independence. His affiliation with the Nation of Islam came at a time when many Americans, and many of his fans, considered the Black Muslims a subversive and dangerous organization. Yet he frankly explained the motivation behind his refusal to serve in the American military: "I have searched my conscience," he said, "and I find I cannot be true to my belief in my religion by accepting such a call." Similarly he recited: "Keep asking me, no matter how long / On the war in Viet Nam, I sing this song / I ain't got no quarrel with them Viet Cong."

Such sentiments led some critics to portray Ali and the Black Muslim faith as anti-American. In the sports arena, Ali's self-promotion and flamboyance challenged a traditional unwritten code under which black athletes were expected to be dutiful, modest, and respectful of white authority.

Triumphs and Tribulations

Since retiring from the ring, much of the attention focused on Ali has centered on his physical condition. Ali suffers from Parkinson's syndrome, a neurological affliction that causes tremors, loss of balance, memory lapses, and confusion. Doctors have asserted that Ali's symptoms were brought on by the repeated blows to the head he endured in the latter part of his boxing career, a diagnosis that has prompted medical organizations and other civic groups to lobby for the elimination of boxing or for the use of head gear.

The young Ali was practically untouchable: Sonny Liston could land only two punches in their 1965 rematch. But in his late fights against the hard-hitting Joe Frazier, Leon Spinks, and Larry Holmes, Ali took several hundred punches in every match; in the punishing 1980 loss to Holmes, Ali took 125 punches in the ninth and tenth rounds alone.

Ali's neurological disorder is essentially a motor-skills problem; he has retained his wit, and his thought processes are clear. He has remained an important figure on the world stage. In November 1990 Ali traveled to Iraq to meet with Saddam Hussein in a bid to forestall war in the Persian Gulf. In late 1996 Ali acted as a spokesperson for Operation USA in war-torn Rwanda.

Earlier that year, Ali lit the flame to open the Olympic Games in Atlanta, Georgia. He has been honored for creating the Muhammad Ali Community and Economic Development Corporation, an organization that teaches job skills to low-income public housing residents in Chicago.

In 1987 *The Ring* named him the greatest heavyweight champion of all time. Ali was inducted into the International Boxing Hall of Fame in 1990, and into the U.S. Olympic Hall of Fame in 1983. In 1994 *Sports Illustrated* ranked Ali first on its "40 for the Ages List." The Muhammad Ali Museum opened in Louisville, Kentucky in 1995.

John Gennari

See Also

Kinshasa, Democratic Republic of the Congo; Boxing; Dozens, The; Foreman, George Edward; Frazier, Joseph William (Joe); Johnson, John Arthur (Jack); Liston, Charles ("Sonny"); Louisville, Kentucky.

North America

Ali, Noble Drew (b. January 8, 1886, Simpsonbuck County, N.C.; d. July 20, 1929, Chicago, Ill.), American religious leader who urged African Americans to reject racial labels given by European Americans and to define themselves.

Born Timothy Drew, Noble Drew Ali received little formal education. At 16, he began performing as a circus magician and traveled the world, during which time he was influenced by Eastern religions, especially Islam, with its racial inclusivity. He concluded that American blacks were Moors, that they had descended from the Moabites of Canaan, and that their true home was Morocco. Ali also believed that before the American Revolution, blacks had been free. Only at the Continental Congress of 1779, he thought, had blacks been forced into slavery and stripped of their Moorish identity.

In 1913, based on these principles, he founded the Moorish Science Temple of America in Newark, New Jersey, and published the Holy Koran of the Moorish Holy Temple of Science, as a catechism. Membership requirements were the acceptance of Moorish identity and a one-dollar contribution. By the mid-1920s temples had been established in Detroit, Pittsburgh, New York, Philadelphia, and Chicago, the organization's new headquarters. Because of its rapid growth, Ali could no longer manage the organization alone, and he appointed several associates, some of whom exploited the rank-and-file membership by selling Old Moorish Healing Oil and Moorish Purifier Bath Compound. Ali sought to regain control, firing the business manager, Claude D. Green. Green was killed in March 1929, and Ali, though not in Chicago at the time of the killing, was arrested for the murder. He died while in jail awaiting trial, and it was commonly believed that he was beaten to death.

Robert Fay

See Also

Chicago, Illinois; Detroit, Michigan; New York, New York; Philadelphia, Pennsylvania; Pittsburgh, Pennsylvania.

Latin America and the Caribbean

Alí, Pablo (b. ?; d. 1844, Dominican Republic), Afro-Dominican military leader.

Like many slaves from Saint-Domingue (present-day Haiti) during the Haitian Revolution (1791-1804), Pablo Alí crossed the border to serve in the Spanish colonial army of Santo Domingo (present-day Dominican Republic) as a means of obtaining his freedom. In 1795 Spain ceded Santo Domingo to France. Alí subsequently participated in the War of Reconquest, in which French troops were defeated and Santo Domingo was reunited with Spain (1809). In 1811 the Spanish throne named him first colonel and granted him a gold medal in recognition of his service to the Crown.

In 1820 Alí served as colonel of the Batallón de Morenos (Black Battalion) in Santo Domingo. In 1821, after learning that his application for Spanish citizenship had been denied, Alí pledged his loyalty to the insurrectionists, led by José de Núñez Cáceres, and served as their chief military commander. In 1821 these insurrectionists succeeded in winning the independence of Santo Domingo and established the state of Spanish Haiti. Independence proved short-lived, however, as Haitian forces occupied the territory in 1822. On February 9, 1822, Haitian president JEAN-PIERRE BOYER (1818-1843) emancipated slaves in Santo Domingo. During the Haitian occupation of Santo Domingo (1822-1844), Alí served as commander of the Batallion of Free Blacks and Batallion 32, composed of slaves who had been freed in the territory after the occupation. By 1843 Alí was commander of arms in Santo Domingo. He supported the reform movement that followed the ouster of Boyer but opposed the independence movement, which succeeded in ending the Haitian occupation in 1844. Alí died in 1844.

North America

Allen, Richard

(b. February 14, 1760, Philadelphia, Pa.; d. March 26, 1831, Philadelphia, Pa.), African American religious leader, founder, and first bishop of the African Methodist Episcopal (AME) Church.

Born a slave in PHILADELPHIA, PENNSYLVANIA, Richard Allen grew up during the AMERICAN REVOLUTION, an era characterized by the advocacy of individual rights, the growth of denominational Christianity, and the inception of the antislavery movement. Around 1768 Allen's owner, a Philadelphia lawyer named Benjamin Chew, sold him, his three siblings, and his parents to Stokely Sturgis, a plantation owner in Delaware.

With the permission of Sturgis, Allen began to attend Methodist meetings, and around 1777 he was converted to Methodism. In the second half of the eighteenth century, Methodism proliferated in Delaware, Maryland, and Pennsylvania. This Christian denomination emphasized a simple set of virtues that included honesty, modesty, and sobriety. Following his conversion, in 1780 Sturgis agreed to let Allen hire himself out in order to earn money to purchase his freedom for $2000. In addition to doing manual labor, Allen began to preach at Methodist churches in Delaware and neighboring states. In 1786 Allen paid his last installment to Sturgis and became free.

That same year, Allen accepted an invitation to preach at St. George's Church in Philadelphia, a mixed-race congregation of Methodists. Within a short time, St. George's black membership dramatically increased, and the building could no longer accommodate the growing congregation. White elders at St. George rejected Allen's request for a separate place of worship for African American members and chose instead to construct separated seating within the church by installing a balcony. In 1787, discouraged by the fact that the black worshipers who had helped construct the balcony would be relegated to sitting there, Allen joined the Reverend Absalom Jones in founding the FREE AFRICAN SOCIETY, a nondenominational religious association and mutual aid organization. Allen's Methodist fervor, however, drove him to leave the Free African Society after two years because of the organization's nondenominational orientation. Allen's commitment to Methodism also compelled him to stay at St. George's despite the segregated seating arrangement.

Richard Allen was the founder and first bishop of the African Methodist Episcopal Church.
Archive Photos

One Sunday morning in 1792, Jones challenged St. George's segregated seating arrangement by sitting downstairs. In the middle of the opening prayer two white trustees forced Jones to leave. Allen and other black members who had been seated in the balcony then walked out of St. George's. Until this incident, few black Methodists had been receptive to Allen's call for the establishment of an independent black church. On August 12, 1794, members of the Free African Society founded the African Church of Philadelphia. Because of the Methodists' discriminatory treatment of blacks, the church was consecrated as part of the Protestant Episcopal Church and Jones became the denomination's first black priest.

Allen, however, remained faithful to Methodism and used his own savings to buy a former blacksmith's shop and transplant it onto a plot of land he had previously purchased in Philadelphia. After renovations, Bethel African Church opened on April 9, 1794, and Allen was ordained its deacon. After Bethel was officially initiated at the 1796 Methodist Conference, white Methodist officials attempted to gain control over Allen's church, but a Pennsylvania Supreme Court ruling in 1807 declared that the black Methodist congregation owned the property on which they worshiped and that they could determine who would preach there.

Following Allen's example, many black Methodists formed African Methodist Churches in northeastern cities. Because all experienced similar challenges from white Methodists, Allen organized a convention of black Methodists in 1816 to address their shared problems. The leaders decided to unite their churches under the name of the African Methodist Episcopal (AME) Church. Accordingly, they gained control over the governance of their churches and placed themselves beyond white ecclesiastical jurisdiction. Attendants elected Allen bishop of the new denomination, a position he held until his death in 1831.

The AME Church immediately became a center of black institutional life. As its leader, Allen created the Bethel Benevolent Society and the African Society for the Education of Youth. He also published articles in *Freedom's Journal* attacking slavery and organizations such as the AMERICAN COLONIZATION SOCIETY. Because Allen believed enslaved and free black Americans could be best served through education and religious instruction, he opposed organizations that advocated the migration of black Americans to Africa.

Although the AME Church initiated missionary efforts in such countries as HAITI and CANADA during the late 1820s, Allen kept the church focused on elevating black Americans, especially those in the South. As he said, "We will never separate ourselves voluntarily from the slave population in this country; they are our brethren and we feel there is more virtue in suffering privations with them than fancied advantage for a season." The AME Church proliferated in the South after the Civil War and today has a membership of more than 1.2 million.

Aaron Myers

SEE ALSO
Abolitionism in the United States; African Methodist Episcopal Church; Civil War, American; *Freedom's Journal*; Jones, Absalom.

North America

Allensworth, Allen

(b. April 1842, Louisville, Ky.; d. September 14, 1914, Monrovia, Calif.), African American minister who founded the first all-black community in California.

In an era when African Americans saw many of the gains of RECONSTRUCTION overturned, one former delegate to the Republican National Convention created a town that he hoped would serve as a living model for black self-reliance. Upon his retirement from the army in 1906, Lt. Col. Allen Allensworth, who had been born a slave, began seeking residents for an all-black town in his adopted state of California. Advertising in black newspapers and in his own newsletter, Allensworth appealed to black veterans to realize their dream "to have a home, classic, beautiful, with perfect congenial environment." In this vision, Allensworth was inspired by Booker T. Washington's message that African Americans should "get a bank account. Get a home.... Get some property."

By 1912 more than 100 people had settled in Allensworth, California, which was located on farmland leased from a white-owned agriculture company in rural Tulare County, north of Bakersfield. Because Allensworth was a stop on the Los Angeles-San Francisco rail line, the town's residents thrived in a number of trades, including farming, shopkeeping, and carpentry. With its free library, prosperous churches, and Children's Glee Club, Allensworth attracted national attention from black newspapers.

But the town the *Los Angeles Times* dubbed "an ideal Negro settlement" soon buckled under a series of crises. First, the Santa Fe Railroad rerouted its line, slowing the town's economic pulse. Then Allensworth's landlord reneged on its water contract, which was of crucial importance in dusty central California. Finally, Allen Allensworth himself, the town's founder and first citizen, died mysteriously in a 1914 accident.

Over the following decades, Allensworth declined. By the 1940s it had become a ghost town. In 1976 California designated the 900-acre town site a state historical park. That Allen Allensworth ultimately failed to realize his dream is less important, argues historian B. Gordon Wheeler, than that "the attempt was made."

Kate Tuttle

See Also

Los Angeles, California; San Francisco and Oakland, California; Washington, Booker Taliaferro.

Africa

Almohads (Arabic *al-muwahhid* "who proclaim the unity of God"), Berber Muslim reform movement and dynasty established in North Africa and Spain during the twelfth and thirteenth centuries.

The origin of the movement is traced to Muhammad ibn Tumart, an Arab reformer in Morocco who preached moral reform and the doctrine of the unity of divine being. He gathered a large following of Arabs and Berbers and in 1121 was proclaimed Al-Mahdi ("the Rightly Guided"). The founder of the dynasty was the Berber Abd al-Mumin, who succeeded Ibn Tumart and took the title of caliph. He conquered Morocco (1140-1147) and other parts of North Africa, thus putting an end to the previous dynasty of the Almoravids. By 1154 he also ruled Islamic Spain and part of Portugal. Notable among successive Almohad rulers was Yakub al-Mansur, who ruled in Spain from 1184 until his death. He aided the sultan Saladin against the Crusaders and was responsible for the construction of numerous architectural monuments such as the the Hassan Tower (a 55-m/180-ft minaret) in Rabat, Morocco.

The Almohads incorporated Berber traditions of rule, such as representative government and tribal councils, into their centralized Islamic theocracy. They fostered a renaissance of Islamic scholarship in northwestern Africa and Andalusian (southern) Spain, sponsoring philosophers and scientists such as Ibn Bajja (Avempace), Ibn Tufayl, Ibn Rushd (Averroës), as well as the great explorer, Ibn Battutah. The Almohad Dynasty flourished until 1212, when the united kings of Castile, Aragón, and Navarre defeated the Almohad forces in the Battle of Navas de Tolosa. After that defeat, the power of the Almohads declined and finally came to an end in Spain in 1232 and in Africa in 1269.

See Also

Berber; Crusades.

Africa

Almoravids, Berber dynasty that ruled in Africa and Spain in the eleventh and twelfth centuries C.E.

Between 1053 and 1061, a large part of northwestern Africa was under the rule of a dynasty that began as an Islamic religious movement espousing a return to a more ascetic form of Islam. Leadership of the movement in the western Maghreb passed to Yusuf ibn Tashfin, a Berber chieftain. After enlarging their domain in northwestern Africa, the Almoravids invaded Spain in 1086. During the next four years, they conquered the area between the Tagus (Tajo) and Ebro rivers and set up viceroys in Seville and Granada. Upon returning from Spain, Yusuf ibn Tashfin was declared emir by councils of the eastern and western regions of the dynasty. In 1146 the dynasty was overthrown by the Almohads, another Muslim reform movement.

See Also

Nation of Islam.

North America

Alston, Charles Henry (b. November 28, 1907, Charlotte, N.C.; d. April 27, 1977, New York, N.Y.), African American artist and teacher whose popular work depicts the experiences of the African American family.

The art editor for his high school's annual magazine, Charles Alston earned both his undergraduate and M.A. from Columbia University. He gained popular recognition for his cover illustrations for *The New Yorker* and *Collier's*. In the 1930s Alston taught at the Harlem Art Workshop, where he was a proponent of muralism as a black art form, and from 1935-1936 he directed the Harlem Hospital murals for the Federal Arts Project. In 1950 he became the first African American teacher at the Art Students League in New York. His best known works are the paintings *Family* and *Walking*, which are noted for their figurative content, sculptural form, brilliant color, and their portrayal of the experiences of African American families in the 1950s and 1960s.

Robert Fay

See Also

Harlem, New York.

Africa

Alur, ethnic group of East Africa.

The Alur primarily inhabit the northern shores of Lake Albert, both in western Uganda and northeastern Congo-Kinshasa. They speak a Nilo-Saharan language and belong to the Western Nilotic cultural and linguistic cluster. Approximately 500,000 people consider themselves Alur.

See Also

Congo, Democratic Republic of the; Languages, African: An Overview.

Africa

Amadi, Elechi (b. May 12, 1934, Aluu, Nigeria), Nigerian novelist whose works describe the folklore and spirituality of traditional village life.

A member of the Igbo ethnic group, Elechi Amadi was born in a small southeastern Nigerian village near Port Harcourt. In 1959 he graduated with a degree in physics and mathematics from the University College of Ibadan, a prestigious college attended by other well-known Nigerian writers, such as Chinua Achebe, John Pepper Clark, Wole Soyinka, and Christopher Okigbo. After working as a land surveyor, Amadi taught science for three years at missionary schools in Ahoada and Oba. In 1963 he joined the Nigerian Army; he taught the Ikwerri dialect of Igbo at a military school in Zaria.

His first book, *The Concubine*, blended acute psychological detail and precise observation to tell the story of a young village woman's battle with spiritual forces. The book's publication in 1966 coincided with the proclamation of an independent state – Biafra – in Igbo-dominated southeastern Nigeria. Amadi's steady allegiance to the Federal side in the conflict put him virtually alone among Igbo writers. Steadfastly refusing to write political novels, which he called "a prostitution of literature," Amadi did not detail his wartime experiences until 1973, when he published *Sunset in Biafra: A Civil War Diary*. His novels *The Great Ponds* (1969) and *The Slave* (1978) completed what is thought of as Amadi's trilogy of the mythical in village life.

After the war, Amadi became dean of arts at the Rivers State College of Education (1985-1986) and, later, commissioner for education for Rivers State (1988-1989). In 1986 he published *Estrangement*, a departure from his earlier work in both its urban setting and its exploration of the effects of war on Nigeria's survivors. In addition, Amadi has published four plays – *Peppersoup* (1973), *Isiburu* (1973), *The Road to Ibadan* (1973), and *Dancer of Johannesburg* (1979) – and a scholarly work, *Ethics in Nigerian Culture* (1982).

Kate Tuttle

See Also
Ibadan, Nigeria; Nigeria.

Africa

Amazon, a division of the precolonial Dahomean army that was composed solely of women soldiers.

While the term Amazon most commonly refers to a female warrior society described in Greek mythology, it is also applied to an army of female soldiers in the precolonial kingdom of Dahomey. Originally called the *ahosi*, or "king's wives," the female troops were first called Amazons by Europeans, and then by the Dahomeans themselves.

Although the origins of the Amazons are uncertain, European explorers such as Sir Richard Burton, who visited the Dahomean king Agaja in 1720, reported that the king employed a small troop of women as night time palace guards. Recruited from the king's harems and wives, these women enabled Agaja to maintain his security while adhering to the royal dictate that "no man [shall] sleep within the wall of any of [my palaces] after sunset but myself." Amazons also participated in select activities outside the palace, such as ceremonial parades, but it is unlikely that they were employed as a branch of the regular army until the reign of King Ghezo (1818-1859).

Ghezo came to power in a coup d'état and immediately increased the size of the Amazon forces in an effort to prevent his own overthrow. Later in his reign, the imperialistic Ghezo began training Amazons as soldiers. According to Dahomean histories, nearly 8000 women served in the Amazon forces, and they played a crucial role in many important battles against the Yoruba as well as in the victorious war against the Mahi in 1847. European accounts from explorers such as John Duncan attest to the Amazons' bravery and skill: "They are far superior to the men in every thing – in appearance, dress, in figure, in activity, in their performances as soldiers, and in bravery." But there is also evidence that the Amazons consistently suffered the heaviest battlefield fatalities, and by the time of the first Franco-Dahomean war in 1890, the Amazon division was only half its original size. The force was essentially destroyed during the 1890 war; this loss contributed to the defeat of the Dahomean army during their second war against the French in 1892.

Elizabeth Heath

See Also
Agaja; Dahomey, Early Kingdom of.

AME Church. Please see African Methodist Episcopal Church

North America

Amenia Conference of 1916, meeting of African American leaders, organized by W. E. B. Du Bois, which established the preeminence of the National Association for the Advancement of Colored People (NAACP) in the black movement.

As a sign of respect for Booker T. Washington, who died in 1916, the NAACP canceled its annual meeting, despite the fact that his accommodationist views differed from the NAACP activist stance. To unify adherents of both approaches, NAACP leaders Du Bois and Joel E. Spingarn organized a conference, held August 24-26, 1916, at Spingarn's estate near Amenia, New York. The attendants agreed upon a "Unity Platform" written by Du Bois, which outlined goals of political freedom. While not entirely successful, the conference helped reconcile divergent factions under the auspices of the NAACP.

See Also
Du Bois, William Edward Burghardt (W. E. B.); National Association for the Advancement of Colored People; Washington, Booker Taliaferro.

North America

Amenia Conference of 1933, meeting organized by the National Association for the Advancement of Colored People (NAACP) to find solutions to the economic problems facing African Americans in the Great Depression.

Joel E. Spingarn, president of the NAACP in 1932, called for a conference at his Troutbeck estate near Amenia, New York, which assembled black leaders to restructure the NAACP's civil rights platform to accommodate economic issues. The conference met August 18-22, 1933. It called for the NAACP to criticize the New Deal for not addressing blacks and to bring black and white workers into a new labor union alliance. The conference did not produce a plan for implementing its goals, and, while important symbolically, was essentially ineffective.

See Also
Labor Unions in the United States; National Association for the Advancement of Colored People.

North America

American Anti-Slavery Society, an antislavery society founded in 1833 that brought a new energy and radicalism to the antislavery campaign and during the 1830s and 1840s helped to make slavery the most pressing issue confronting the United States.

After 1830 antislavery activism was marked by a new militancy (*see* Abolitionism in the United States). The American Anti-Slavery Society was one of the principal organizations responsible for this new phase of abolitionism. The story of the American Anti-Slavery Society begins with a small group of activists in New England and New York. In 1832 reform activist William Lloyd Garrison, editor of the *Liberator*, a Boston-based abolitionist periodical, and ten others founded the New England Anti-Slavery Society. A year later, in Philadelphia, Garrison and two wealthy New York City businessmen and philanthropists, Arthur and Lewis Tappan, were instrumental in the founding of the American Anti-Slavery Society. From 1843 to 1865 Garrison served as president of the society.

The organization had its greatest impact during the mid- to late 1830s. In these years the American Anti-Slavery Society played a significant role in making slavery a political issue of the first order. The society sent a large number of abolitionist speakers on tours across the North and printed and distributed large quantities of antislavery literature, including slave narratives. The society published and circulated a vast number of antislavery pamphlets, which between 1834 and 1835 increased from approximately 100,000 pieces to fully 1.1 million.

In 1836 the House of Representatives adopted what became known as the gag rule, which ordered the immediate tabling of any petition or constituent letter on the subject of slavery. The gag rule, which violated the First Amendment right to "petition the government for a redress of grievances," gave the society a further catalyst for action, resulting in massive petition campaigns in Northern states. But a nationwide depression that lasted from 1837 to 1843 significantly hampered the society's activities, depriving the organization of financial support and distracting Americans from social reform issues.

In 1840, however, conflicts over style and tactics divided more conservative abolitionists, such as the Tappans and Theodore Dwight Weld, and the radical Garrison, which resulted in a schism in the organization. In 1838 Garrison and his allies, known as Garrisonians, had advocated passive resistance rather than force. Garrison also endorsed a wide range of controversial social issues, including women's suffrage and civil rights for blacks in the North. When the two factions split, the Garrisonians retained control of the original society. Weld, the Tappans, and their allies established a smaller, less significant rival organization, the American and Foreign Anti-Slavery Society.

Other abolitionists broke with Garrison because of his single-minded reliance on moral suasion – rather than any sort of political activism – in the struggle against slavery. In 1844, for example, the former secretary of the American Anti-Slavery Society, James G. Birney, ran for president as candidate of the antislavery Liberty Party. During the 1850s, as slavery and sectional conflict came to dominate American politics, the American Anti-Slavery Society found its position increasingly marginal (*see* AMERICAN CIVIL WAR). The group continued to lobby for emancipation and for black suffrage during and after the war (*see* THIRTEENTH AMENDMENT OF THE UNITED STATES CONSTITUTION AND THE EMANCIPATION PROCLAMATION). Following the 1870 ratification of the Fifteenth Amendment, the American Anti-Slavery Society disbanded, viewing its work as finished.

Alonford James Robinson, Jr.

SEE ALSO

Boston, Massachusetts; Fifteenth Amendment to the United States Constitution; Philadelphia, Pennsylvania; New York, New York.

North America

American Colonization Society, founded December 28, 1816, Washington, D.C.; promoted the emigration and colonization of free African Americans along the coast of West Africa.

Initially called the American Society for Colonizing the Free People of Color in the United States, the American Colonization Society (ACS) was formed in 1816 by a group of Presbyterian ministers. The organization's chief objective was to encourage free blacks (and later manumitted slaves) to emigrate to West Africa.

To its audience of free blacks, the organization depicted emigration as an opportunity for African Americans to introduce education and Christianity to their African brethren. In contrast, to Southern whites reading its official newsletter, the *African Repository* (1825-1909), the ACS portrayed black emigration as a solution to the growing prevalence of free blacks, a population which many Southern whites feared would disrupt the system of slavery. As the ACS grew, the prominence of its members and supporters also grew. Among them were presidents Abraham Lincoln, James Madison, and James Monroe, and United States Supreme Court justice Bushrod Washington, who was also the organization's first president.

Most black leaders believed that the ACS was a racist and proslavery organization, and that black emigration was a ploy to strengthen the grip of slavery. However, there were African American leaders who embraced black emigration while rejecting the ACS. Black nationalists such as Martin Delany and PAUL CUFFE encouraged emigration, and organizations such as the African Civilization Society, established in 1858, pressed for a separate black nation. Although black separatism appealed to many, most blacks did not favor emigration, despised the ACS, and challenged its arguments for colonization.

As black support waned, the ACS turned its attention to its proslavery proponents. In 1819 the U.S. Congress authorized President Monroe to provide $100,000 to the ACS effort to purchase a suitable location in Africa for the colonization of America's free blacks. On December 15, 1821, the ACS purchased an area approximately 360 km (225 mi) south of Sierra Leone, an English colony established in 1787 for the colonization of British blacks. In 1822 the colony was named Liberia, and its capital, Monrovia, in honor of American President James Monroe.

Disputes within the ACS over financial mismanagement and accusations by several Southern states that the organization had become pro-emancipation led colonizationists in New York, Pennsylvania, Mississippi, Louisiana, and Maryland to establish their own colonies along the coast of West Africa. Despite such large-scale dissatisfaction with the organization, it is estimated that the ACS sponsored the emigration of between 12,000 and 20,000 African Americans during the nineteenth century.

The abolition of slavery and the Thirteenth, Fourteenth, and Fifteenth Amendments to the U.S. Constitution eventually weakened the ACS and slowed the numbers of black emigrants to a trickle. By the turn of the century, the ACS had limited interactions with Liberia and existed largely on a formal basis. After leading the effort to separate free blacks and manumitted slaves from whites in the nineteenth century, the ACS was finally terminated on March 22, 1963. The organization's assets were transferred to the Phelps-Stokes Fund, which supports African and African American education.

Alonford James Robinson, Jr.

SEE ALSO

Nationalism in Africa; Delany, Martin Robison.

North America

American Electoral Politics, Blacks in

In a 1965 article entitled "From Protest to Politics: The Future of the Civil Rights Movement," civil rights activist BAYARD RUSTIN predicted that the 1965 Voting Rights Act would transform the CIVIL RIGHTS MOVEMENT into formal, institutionalized party politics. Although the strategies and thrust of the movement would change, blacks, he argued, would still be engaged in a movement radically oriented toward social change. The new electoral phase of black politics would function as the "second stage" of the black Civil Rights Movement. Writing in the aftermath of the landslide election of President Lyndon B. Johnson in 1964, Rustin also predicted that an alliance between progressive groups, blacks, labor, and liberals would emerge within the Democratic Party and that conservatives would align themselves with the minority Republican Party.

While Rustin had correctly predicted the electoral mobilization of blacks, his hope for a liberal majority, which would then work through the Democratic Party, never materialized. Blacks, indeed, are a growing part of the American electorate, casting 7 percent of the presidential vote in 1966 and 11 percent by 1996. During this same time frame, the number of black elected officials would skyrocket from an estimated 500 or so to 8000 and more by 1993. And as Rustin expected, after the 1964 presidential election, the vast majority of blacks had become Democrats. Up until 1963 only 50 to 60 percent of blacks identified themselves as Democrats in surveys. As of 1996, over 80 percent of blacks called themselves Democrats.

Yet the massive entry of blacks into the American electorate has not, as Rustin had hoped, aided progressive politics, but rather coincided with and perhaps provoked the rise of conservative politics. Southern whites rallied to massively resist the implementation of the new civil rights laws, while Northern whites grew more conservative in response to the urban riots and black militancy and as race issues moved from the South to the North in the form of busing and affirmative action. With the exception of Jimmy Carter's one term as president from 1976 to 1980, Republicans would occupy the White House from 1968 until 1992. Rather than serve as an opposition party to the Republicans, Democrats strategically moved to the center ground of politics and abandoned the Left in an effort to win back votes. Thus by the 1980s, instead of belonging to a liberal-progressive coalition within the Democratic Party, as Rustin had predicted, blacks found themselves constituting a political minority, isolated and increasingly marginal within the Democratic Party and in national politics in general.

The conservatism that rebounded at the end of the Civil Rights Movement nevertheless ignited blacks politically. Since 1965 differences in black and white registration and turnout rates have diminished considerably. In 1984, during the conservative Reagan years, the gap between black and white voter registration rates was the smallest ever recorded – 2.2 percentage points compared to 9.2 percentage points in 1968. In 1984 more blacks turned out to vote in a collective effort to defeat Ronald Reagan. Blacks' feelings of political efficacy grew especially during the early civil rights years, 1954 to 1962. Since 1964 Americans have become more distrustful of government and more skeptical of their ability to be heard and influence government. However, this loss of confidence in government was less apparent in the black community. Although blacks are still somewhat more likely than whites to feel that they have "no say in government" and that "government officials don't care," racial differences have diminished mostly because larger percentages of whites now distrust government and have less faith in their ability to influence government.

Black mobilization during the Reagan years was greatly facilitated by the Reverend Jesse Jackson's two bids for the presidency in 1984 and in 1988. The Jackson campaigns gave "voice" to black dissatisfaction with the rightward drift of the Democratic Party. Millions of blacks supported both his bids. His campaigns were structured as a bargaining vehicle for black Democratic voters. In the end, while they stimulated black interest in political campaigns and mobilized new black voters, Jackson's candidacies did not enhance the effectiveness of the black vote. The record-high black turnout in 1984 did not affect the outcome of the Reagan-Mondale presidential race, and some have argued that Jackson's bids may have exacerbated blacks' political problems, pushing blacks further into a marginal and politically impotent corner of the party and in national politics in general.

While blacks mobilized but remained outside the national political scene during the 1980s, in 1992 they became part of the governing coalition in Washington. Contrary to Rustin's expectations, rather than liberalizing American politics, the incorporation of blacks has moderated their politics. Blacks have not only moved away from intraparty insurgent politics, but their political views have become more conservative. A number of factors explain blacks' move away from insurgent politics within the party. First, Bill Clinton's election in 1992 and his support within the black community have moderated black politics at the national level. Clinton had an 87 percent approval rating among blacks in 1996, and those who strongly approved of Clinton's performance in the White House were most likely to think that a third Jackson bid for the presidency in 1996 would have been "a very bad idea." Second, Jesse Jackson did little to resurrect the ideological divisions in the party that he capitalized on in his 1984 and 1988 presidential bids. In fact, Jackson's 1996 convention speech differed radically from his past three speeches insofar as there was little of his own political agenda in it and little criticism of the party. This speech was pointedly directed toward unifying the party. Finally, the majority of blacks came to believe that the Republican Party was hostile to their group's interests during the Reagan years, and Newt Gingrich's leadership of the new Republican majority in the U.S. House of Representatives beginning in 1994 did little to erase this image of the GOP as antiblack. In fact, more blacks felt in 1996 that the Republican Party does not work hard on issues blacks care about than in 1984 during the Reagan administration. The Republican Party has apparently not profited from growing black political conservatism. Democratic identification among blacks remained as strong in 1996 as it had been in 1984.

ABOVE: **David Dinkins, with his hand on the Bible, is sworn in as the first black mayor of New York City by Judge Fritz Alexander. New York Governor Mario Cuomo stands behind Dinkins.** *CORBIS/Bettmann*
LEFT: **Congressman John Lewis speaks with the press from his Atlanta, Georgia, home in 1985.** *CORBIS/Flip Schulke*

Blacks have also become more politically conservative. This was evident as early as the late 1980s, as the percentage of blacks opposing the idea of a federally guaranteed job program quadrupled from 7 percent in 1972 to 28 percent in 1988. Black opposition to federal assistance for minorities and blacks shot up during this period as well, from 6 percent in 1970 to 26 percent in 1988. Data from a national telephone survey of blacks in 1996 showed that fewer blacks favored government assistance to blacks and minorities than had in 1984.

When asked whether federal spending on defense, crime, food stamps, and Medicare should be increased, decreased, or kept about the same, more blacks in 1996 said spending should be decreased except in the area of crime. On crime, 63 percent in 1996 said that spending should be increased, in contrast to 56 percent in 1984. The growth in the proportion of blacks favoring an expansion of federal efforts on crime corresponds with other attitudinal shifts in the black community. More blacks in 1996 than in 1984 viewed crime as the single most important problem in the black community relative to unemployment or discrimination. In 1996 a large plurality (40 percent) of blacks ranked crime first and unemployment and discrimination second and third, respectively. In 1984 only 17 percent had placed crime above the other two problems; crime, in fact, came in third for half of the sample.

One of the most striking pieces of evidence that blacks have become more conservative is reflected in their attitudes toward welfare. In 1984 nearly half of the blacks polled felt that spending on food stamps should be increased, while only 10 percent thought it should be decreased. Twelve years later, however, that near-majority was cut down to 28 percent, while a nearly matching proportion thought that funds for this program should be cut. There was a less dramatic but still significant drop in the proportion of blacks who felt that federal spending on Medicare should be increased. Whereas 78 percent of

TOP: Richard Arrington, the first black mayor of Birmingham, Alabama, waves to supporters celebrating his 1983 election to a second term. *UPI/CORBIS-Bettmann*

ABOVE: California Assemblyman Willie Brown talks to reporters about the 1995 election in which he defeated the incumbent to become mayor of San Francisco. *Reuters/Lou Dematteis/Archive Photos*

RIGHT: Harold Washington hugs a baby during his 1983 campaign for mayor of Chicago, Illinois. Washington was the first African American mayor of Chicago. *CORBIS/Jacques M. Chenet*

BELOW RIGHT: Charlotta Bass, 1952 Progressive Party candidate for vice president, tells reporters that the United States should negotiate in Korea. *CORBIS/Bettmann-UPI*

blacks thought more money should go to Medicare in 1984, only 68 percent did in 1996. As in the case of food stamps, most in the black community felt that the spending levels for Medicare should remain where they are.

Black attitudes on welfare reform in 1996 matched their attitudes on spending levels for welfare programs. A solid majority (67 percent) in the black community favored the new law limiting welfare receipts to five years of benefits over the course of a recipient's life; only 30 percent opposed it. Blacks were divided, however, on the family cap policy that states enacted under waivers from the Clinton administration. Under this new policy, welfare payments are not increased for welfare recipients who have additional children while on welfare. About half (48 percent) favored such a policy, while 46 percent opposed it.

The 1996 National Black Election Study established that blacks today remain highly race conscious, and increasingly so. A higher percentage of blacks in 1996 believed their individual fates were linked to that of their group. More blacks in 1996 than in 1984 reflected on the meaning of their identities as blacks in this country. In 1984 blacks in a national telephone survey were asked whether or not blacks in this country would ever achieve full social and economic equality. More than one-third (36 percent) said no, that blacks would never win equality with whites in this country. The ranks of the pessimists have increased; nearly half (49 percent) of those surveyed in 1996 said that blacks are never going to obtain equality in this country. Finding blacks to be more race conscious in the 1990s than in the 1980s and yet more conservative is puzzling, given the strong impact of black solidarity in promoting political liberalism.

The political incorporation of blacks into mainstream politics represented one of the most important outcomes of the Civil Rights Movement. Yet although blacks remain strongly race conscious, the new electoral phase of black politics has not functioned as the second stage of the Civil Rights Movement as Rustin had hoped. Black voters have not been able to facilitate the rise of progressive politics; instead, their incorporation has resulted in the moderation of their politics. This is not entirely unexpected, given the nature of the American political system, which favors compromise and moderation as opposed to conflict and ideological purity. The American political system tends to support interests that favor the status quo or those who believe in incremental change. As participants in such a system, blacks' policy views and their political behavior have accordingly moderated. Furthermore, blacks in 1996 were highly satisfied with the centrist policy representation in Washington after decades of conservative Republican rule. This is not to argue that the potential for radical progressive politics no longer exists in the black community. Race remains a dominant issue on the political landscape. Nevertheless, in order to mount such a movement, blacks would have to move beyond the form of electoral politics that currently exists in the United States.

Katherine Tate

SEE ALSO

Jackson, Jesse Louis.

North America

American Federation of Labor and Congress of Industrial Organizations, **new American labor union formed in 1955 by a merger of two leading unions, which instituted civil rights resolutions but was criticized for the "Jim Crow" practices of its affiliate unions.**

When the American Federation of Labor (AFL) and the Congress of Industrial Organizations (CIO) merged in 1955 and became the AFL-CIO, one of the new union's first actions under the leadership of George Meaney was to set up a Committee on Civil Rights and to announce that "the merged labor movement would not tolerate racial or religious discrimination." Vowing to lead a crusade to secure equality of employment opportunity, the AFL-CIO publicly committed itself to supporting the desegregation of public facilities, advocating the prosecution of LYNCHING as a federal crime, and abolishing the poll tax for voting.

The swiftness with which the newly formed union made these statements revealed the troubled history of the relationship between blacks and unions in the United States. Throughout the early twentieth century blacks had been caught in a double bind, excluded from unions because of their color but reviled as strike breakers when they agreed to work for lower pay than unionized workers. Previous attempts to integrate unions had met with some success in the United States, but there was almost always a gap between the rhetoric of union leaders, who wished to unionize the growing black work force, and the actions of affiliate unions, who practiced both overt and subtle forms of discrimination. In 1955, despite its statement supporting civil rights, the AFL-CIO, too, refused to adopt the policy of ejecting any affiliate that practiced racial discrimination.

Prior to their merger, the AFL and the CIO had already begun the process of integration. In 1935 the Brotherhood of Sleeping Car Porters (BSCP) became the first black union to be granted an international charter by the AFL. The CIO, a year later, began a large-scale organizing campaign with an open-door policy on race. Yet both unions were conglomerates of smaller affiliates that continued to practice discrimination openly or by tacit consent, despite statements by union leadership. The African American union organizer A. Philip Randolph, representing the BSCP in the 1940s, challenged this behavior, demanding in the "Randolph Resolution" that the AFL censure the practices of its affiliates. Pressure mounted on the union leadership during the CIVIL RIGHTS MOVEMENT of the 1950s as the national awareness of discrimination increased and black workers became a more organized force in the labor movement.

In 1959, four years after the AFL-CIO's announcement supporting civil rights, Randolph made a series of charges at the union's Constitutional Convention. Declaring that the statement omitted punitive measures by which these principles would be enforced, he called for the new union to stop exclusionary practices by ejecting affiliates that practiced racial exclusion. Randolph also noted that blacks were often excluded from training programs, and argued that the national federation had a responsibility to help black workers get training for more highly skilled jobs.

By the late 1960s 2 million out of 14 million of the country's workers were black, a fact that drew increased attention to the labor movement from organizations such as the National Association for the Advancement of Colored People (NAACP). In 1964 the last segregated affiliate of the AFL-CIO integrated. Organized black representation within the union increased, with the Negro American Labor Council (NALC) formed in 1960 and the Coalition of Black Trade Unionists organized in 1972. Black membership in the AFL-CIO grew steadily, and by 1968 the union had become the most integrated public institution in the United States.

Over the years, the AFL-CIO's concerns have shifted from opening union ranks to black membership to the participation of African Americans in union leadership and the eradication of discriminatory practices in hiring and promotion.

Marian Aguiar

SEE ALSO

Brotherhood of Sleeping Car Porters; Jim Crow; National Association for the Advancement of Colored People; Labor Unions in the United States; Randolph, Asa Philip; Negro American Labor Council.

North America

American Indians, **native populations of the Western Hemisphere with whom Africans had a historical relationship of both cooperation and confrontation.**

Upon arriving in the Americas, Europeans first enslaved Indians, introducing Africans to the Americas only after calculating the difficulty of coercing large numbers of Native Americans into their labor systems. Nicolas de Ovando, governor of Hispaniola, first mentioned African and Indian interaction in a report, in about 1503, in which he stated that Africans commingled with Indians to avoid capture. Indians who escaped generally knew the surrounding areas, avoided capture, and returned to help free enslaved Africans.

Europeans feared an Indian-African alliance regardless of where slavery existed. The first slave rebellion occurred in Hispaniola in 1522, while the first on future United States soil (North Carolina) occurred in 1526. Both rebellions were organized and executed by coalitions of Africans and Indians. Europeans especially feared communities of escaped Africans, known as maroons, or *quilombos*, in frontier areas. The largest of these communities, the "Republic of Palmares," originated in the 1600s and at its peak had a population of approximately 11,000. This community, composed primarily of Africans but including Indians, contained three villages, churches, and shops and operated under its own legal system. Its army repelled European military attacks until 1694, when it fell to an army that contained 6000 Christianized Indians.

White reaction to such communities was extreme despite their limited numbers. The Europeans sought to keep the two peoples separated and, if possible, mutually hostile. They taught Africans to fight Indians and bribed Indians to hunt escaped Africans, promising lucrative rewards. Indians who captured escaped Africans received 35 deerskins in Virginia or three blankets and a musket in the Carolinas. Further sowing division, whites introduced African slavery into the Five Civilized Nations in the United States.

The U.S. government ended slavery among Indians by the time of the Revolutionary War. From pre-Revolutionary times to the Civil War, the government negotiated treaties with Indian tribes that included promises by the Indians to return escaped slaves. However, while many tribes who had such clauses in their treaties with the American government harbored many slaves, they returned none.

The most powerful African-Indian alliance linked escaped Africans who had settled in Florida with Seminoles (a word that means "runaway"), who were fleeing the Creek federation. The Africans taught the Indians rice cultivation, and the groups formed an agricultural and military alliance. In 1816 a U.S. soldier reported that prosperous plantations existed for 50 miles along the banks of the Apalachicola River in northwestern Florida. The African-Seminole forces repeatedly repelled U.S. slaveholders' posses and the U.S. Army. The Second Seminole War resulted in 1600 dead and cost over $40 million. The purchase of Florida from Spain was the U.S. government's attempt to eliminate it as a refuge for runaways.

Before the Civil War, many Native American nations on the eastern seaboard of the United States became biracial communities. African Americans were well represented in the Trail of Tears. By 1860 the Five Civilized Nations in the Indian Territory consisted of 18 percent African Americans. The Seminoles appointed six BLACK SEMINOLES members of its governing council. After the Civil War the BUFFALO SOLDIERS, six regiments of African American U.S. Army troops, helped to end Indian resistance to U.S. control. The most significant African-Native American was JOHN HORSE, a Black Seminole chief who negotiated a treaty with the U.S. government in 1870. Today, many African Americans can trace their ancestry in part to an Indian tribe.

Robert Fay

See Also
Civil War, American.

North America

American Negro Academy,

founded in 1897, first African American learned organization.

The American Negro Academy (ANA) was founded on March 5, 1897, in Washington, D.C. as a learned society for African American men of letters, arts, and science. Under the leadership of abolitionist and Episcopal minister Alexander Crummell, scholars such as W. E. B. Du Bois, Carter G. Woodson, and Alain Locke joined this academy. The goals of the ANA were to ensure recognition of African American advances in science, art, and literature. In addition, the organization sought to challenge and refute the circulation of racist and erroneous misinformation about African American life and culture. The organization embodied Du Bois's doctrine of "the talented tenth"; this stance, along with other philosophical differences regarding education, kept Booker T. Washington, one of the era's most powerful African American leaders, from ever joining the ANA.

ANA activities included conferences, meetings, research, data collection and youth outreach. Between 1897 and 1924, 22 Occasional Papers were presented at academy meetings disseminating the thinking of leading African American intellectuals on a wide range of issues. Academy members were instrumental in the formation of similar activities and organizations throughout the country. Alain Locke played an integral role in the Harlem Renaissance, W.E.B. Du Bois led the Niagara Movement and helped form the National Association for the Advancement of Colored People (NAACP), and Carter Woodson founded the Association for the Study of Negro Life and History (later the Association for the Study of Afro-American Life and History). Before its demise in 1928, the ANA had become an active organization that publicized African American intellect and achievement and provided a model for the many organizations that would follow.

Alonford James Robinson, Jr.

See Also
Du Bois, William Edward Burghardt (W. E. B.); Locke, Alain Leroy; National Association for the Advancement of Colored People; Washington, Booker Taliaferro; Woodson, Carter Godwin.

North America

American Negro Theatre,

pioneering African American theater company and school in which several hundred black actors, writers, and technicians began their careers.

The Academy Award-winning actor Sidney Poitier, the actor and singer Harry Belafonte, and the actress Ruby Dee are three of the prominent African American actors who were affiliated with the American Negro Theatre (ANT). The theater was founded in Harlem in 1940 by black writer Abram Hill and black actor Frederick O'Neal, who wanted to create a company that would provide opportunities for African American artists and entertainment for African American audiences that were unavailable downtown on Broadway. Over the next nine years, 50,000 people attended American Negro Theatre productions.

Hill and O'Neal felt that the mainstream professional theater provided only limited opportunity for African Americans and that it encouraged a "star system," under which actors constantly competed to be in the one breakthrough hit. Hill and O'Neal were more interested in the potential for local black community theaters, where directors, writers, and technicians would be as important as actors, and where black artists would be able to develop their talents. They sent postcards inviting other local writers and actors to join them, and in June 1940, 18 artists met to form the American Negro Theatre. These members' stated mission was "to break down the barriers of Black participation in the theater; to portray Negro life as they honestly saw it; [and] to fill in the gap of a Black theater which did not exist."

The company emphasized a cooperative spirit and chose the name in part for its acronym, ANT. Members wanted the abbreviation to signify that, like ants, they would all be true workers. ANT was also a financial cooperative: members shared expenses or profits, and members who performed outside ANT were required to deposit 2 percent of their salaries to ANT's account. Until the company received a $22,500 Rockefeller grant, in 1944, no one actually received a salary, but the financial arrangements symbolized the members' dedication to the company.

ANT was not meant to be a segregated organization, although its members were committed to a theater that would reflect the Harlem community. Most of the original members were African American actors and writers, including Dee. Performances were held in a converted lecture room at Harlem's 135th Street Library, which seated 125 people and had been used by several earlier black theater groups. As the playwright and novelist Alice Childress later said, "We thought we were Harlem's theater."

The company's first major production was Abram Hill's *On Striver's Row,* a satire about African American social climbing. It was well reviewed and well attended, and the new company was described by one critic as "a healthy experimental theater, one that at all costs strives to avoid conventional Broadway-bound clichés.... It remains firmly on the ground, using themes about everyday people, staged and played with originality and imagination." In 1942 ANT added its Studio Theatre, a training program for young artists. Poitier and Belafonte, two of the Studio Theatre's early graduates, went on to become internationally known actors.

Between 1940 and 1949 ANT produced 19 plays, including 12 original scripts. But its 1944 production of *Anna Lucasta,* by the white author Philip Yordan, proved to be a turning point. The play originally had been written about a Polish-American family, but after white companies rejected it, ANT revised it extensively and made it suitable for a black cast. It was an immediate success, and after five weeks it was moved to Broadway.

What should have been a tremendous achievement for ANT, however, instead brought problems. The production ran for two years on Broadway and eventually spawned a national tour and a movie, but ANT received royalties of less than 2 percent for the Broadway show and none at all for the tour or the film. The unfavorable financial arrangements understandably caused bitterness among company members. More important, however, the production undermined some of ANT's initial conceptions of itself as a community theater.

When *Anna Lucasta* went to Broadway, the new production retained only a few ANT actors. Despite ANT's hope that it would provide an alternative to the professional star system, the Broadway connection revived old grievances: actors who had not been chosen to go to Broadway were bitter, and new actors came to ANT seeking their chance to make it to the Broadway stage. The success of *Anna Lucasta* also brought about a new level of professional attention, and the company felt compelled to respond by changing the aim of its productions. Instead of continuing to encourage community-based writers, ANT after 1945 produced only plays by established white playwrights. As a result of these changes, ANT lost much of the creativity and community support that had sustained it.

The company did send three more productions to Broadway, but none was financially successful. In 1945 ANT became the first black theater company to produce a weekly radio series, but the radio show's success did not lessen the theater's difficulties. By the early 1950s, it stopped production.

Despite its eventual decline, however, ANT had played a crucial role in bringing an awareness of black theater to the rest of the American theater scene. As the actor Lofton Mitchell later put it, "There was a great social revolution underway, the plays of protest, the plays of social meaning, and this was the kind of theater we were trying to develop.... We were trying to say something. We were trying to say it within the black media, with the rhythm and quality of excitement."

Lisa Clayton Robinson

SEE ALSO
Belafonte, Harold George (Harry); Harlem, New York.

North America

American Revolution

(1775-1783), conflict between GREAT BRITAIN and 13 of its North American colonies, resulting in independence for the colonies and in the formation of the United States of America. African Americans were involved in every aspect of this war, and the ideology of freedom espoused during the revolution became the rallying cry for those who would fight for the abolition of slavery.

Espousing views of Enlightenment thinkers who argued that every person had an inherent right to life, liberty, and property, 13 British colonies along the eastern seaboard of North America rebelled against their mother country and fought for their freedom and liberty. By 1770 one-fifth of the population in these colonies was of African ancestry, and almost 95 percent of these were slaves. With the coming of the revolution the black population was militarily vital to both sides.

In the 1760s the conflict between Great Britain and its colonies was escalating as Parliament passed laws that the colonists declared unjust and refused to obey. The Stamp Act (1765) and the Townshend Acts (1767) are notorious examples. As the conflict escalated, Massachusetts became a hotbed of colonial resistance. When Boston citizens rioted in March of 1770, British troops fired into the crowd, killing five men. Among the Boston Massacre's dead was a sailor named CRISPUS ATTUCKS, who had escaped from slavery as a young man.

The conflict continued to escalate until it broke into open warfare with the battles of Lexington and Concord in April 1775. Blacks in the Massachusetts colony fought in these first battles and in the June 1775 Battle of Bunker Hill. PETER SALEM and Salem Poor were black men who fought in these battles and continued to fight with the Continental Army throughout the revolution. Gen. George Washington initially persuaded the Continental Congress to ban the enlistment of black soldiers in the Continental Army (*see* MILITARY, BLACKS IN THE AMERICAN). However, in 1777, faced with desperate shortages of manpower, Washington was forced to open the ranks to free black men. Some colonies allowed slaves to win their freedom by serving in the military, but colonies in which agricultural success depended on slave labor did not allow slaves to serve. Nonetheless, by the end of the war, African Americans had fought at Trenton, Brandywine, Saratoga, and in other battles. By the war's end at least 5000 blacks had served on the side of the colonists. Some, like Cornelius Lenox Remond, Barzillai Lew, Cuff Whitmore, Tack Sisson, and Prince Whipple, won distinction in their military service. Other blacks, like James Forten, served with the Continental Navy.

During the revolution many African Americans sided with the British. Particularly for enslaved blacks in the South, there was little guarantee that they would have any more freedom under the rule of the colonists than they did under the rule of the British. Indeed, in November 1775 Lord Dunmore, the royal governor of Virginia, issued a proclamation that any slaves who fled to his lines and assisted in suppressing the revolt would be given their freedom. This was a more enticing offer than the colonists had made, as the Southern colonies generally would not recruit slaves to fight. Over 2000 slaves joined Dunmore and became his Ethiopian Regiment. When the fighting moved south in 1779, thousands of slaves ran away from their masters and fled to the British lines. There they were often pressed into service as laborers, building fortifications around Charleston and Savannah.

By the end of the war blacks had served in many capacities. Many slaves who served in the military in Northern colonies were immediately freed. Many who had fled to the British or served with them were removed to Nova Scotia, and these "Black Loyalists," finding Nova Scotia inhospitable, emigrated to SIERRA LEONE. In the South some slaves who had served with a verbal promise of freedom were later freed, while others were returned to slavery.

The American Revolution raised a fundamental contradiction that America's founding fathers could not seem to reconcile. The foundational principles of the revolution were life, liberty, property, and equality; yet in the colonies nearly one-fifth of the population was denied these rights. Most Northern colonies ended slavery soon after the revolution. Vermont banned slavery in 1777 and a Massachusetts judge declared slavery unconstitutional in 1783. In the South, agriculture was far more dependent on slave labor. A few plantation owners, imbued with the revolutionary spirit, freed their slaves and resettled them in the Northwest Territory either upon the war's end or upon their death. For the most part, however, Southern plantation owners simply imported more slaves to replace those who ran away, and slavery continued as America's basic contradiction.

Paul Foster

SEE ALSO
Abolitionism in the United States.

North America

American West, Blacks in the,

African American explorers, settlers, cowboys, mountain men, and pioneers who played significant roles in the history of the American West.

The history of America is one of a constantly shifting frontier. The first outsiders to explore (and later settle) the land formerly occupied only by Native Americans traveled mostly on the coasts, gradually moving inland. From the 13 original colonies, white American settlers in the seventeenth century looked to the west and saw unknown territory in what is now America's Midwest. With the Louisiana Purchase and the acquisition of land previously owned by the Spanish, the frontier again edged west, to the Great Plains and Rocky Mountains and beyond. Even more than its practical meaning as the edge of European settlement, the frontier has had symbolic importance in American popular culture, peopled by mythical figures like trailblazers, cowboys, and pioneers. Often overlooked or omitted from this legend, though, are the African Americans who lived and worked on the American frontier.

From its earliest nonindigenous history, the American West was traveled by people of African descent. Estebanico, who was part of a 500-person Spanish expedition to the Gulf of Mexico in the 1520s, was born in MOROCCO. When disease and starvation claimed most of the party, ESTEBANICO was one of four survivors. His skills at negotiating with Native Americans and learning their languages helped the four survive and explore for eight more years. When the whites returned to Spain, Estabanico remained and helped the Spanish viceroy in his search for gold. Though he was eventually killed in an Indian massacre, Estebanico's affinity with the Native Americans he encountered – he lives on in Zuñi legend to this day – prefigured the often close ties between blacks and Indians in the early years of the United States.

Others of African descent helped explore what Europeans called the New World. Jean Baptiste Pointe Du Sable, the Haitian son of a French father and African slave mother, established a fur-trading post at the mouth of the Chicago River in 1779, thereby founding one of America's great cities. Other blacks in the fur trade, known as MOUNTAIN MEN, blazed trails throughout the West. California's Beckwourth Pass, the most important passage through the Sierra Nevada Mountains, is named for James P. Beckwourth, a former slave turned fur trapper.

In the early 1800s, while most of the African American population was still enslaved in the South, thousands of African Americans escaped slavery through the UNDERGROUND RAILROAD, some forming black settlements in the early frontier. Other African Americans accompanied white settlers as slaves, traveling with wagon trains that pushed farther west. Later in the century some of their descendants worked alongside whites as cowboys in the great cattle drives.

Throughout the colonial period and early republic the relationships among Native Americans, white settlers, and blacks, both free and slave, were varied. During the Florida SEMINOLE WARS, in the early to mid-1800s, a coalition of escaped slaves and Indians fought against white United States army forces. But in the 1870s along the western frontier, BUFFALO SOLDIERS – members of the Ninth and Tenth Cavalry, so named by Native Americans for their curly black hair – helped the government carry out its campaign against the Native Americans. White attitudes toward black-Indian relations are reflected in Col. Stephen Bull's order to "establish a hatred between Negroes and Indians," lest their affinity, already reflected in many marriages and the Native American tendency to spare black lives in battle, threaten white power.

Slavery, outlawed in much of the West, nonetheless existed there. African American Californians such as Biddy Mason and Mary Ellen "Mammy" Pleasant fought against the Fugitive Slave Act of 1850 and helped many establish their freedom through writs of habeas corpus. In particular, the black newspapers of the West, of which there were more than 60 by 1900, helped African Americans in the quest for full civil rights and economic equality.

After the Civil War black western migration increased. Thousands of "EXODUSTERS" left the South for Kansas, and black communities were established in Oklahoma and other western states. Black pioneers helped the African American populations of the Rocky Mountain states increase 13-fold in the years between 1870 and 1910. California, Oregon, and Washington experienced less startling but still significant growth in their black communities.

The early twentieth century was, as historians like B. Gordon Wheeler have noted, a time of disappointment for African Americans nationally and in the West. Fighting the then-popular pseudo-science of EUGENICS, which argued that blacks were genetically inferior to whites, men like ALLEN ALLENSWORTH tried to create BLACK TOWNS, havens of African American prosperity and respectability. But such efforts seldom succeeded completely, the twin forces of white racism and lack of black financial strength dooming them from the beginning.

As the West grew beyond its frontier status in the twentieth century, western African Americans faced the same triumphs and defeats as those in the rest of the country. They saw black soldiers, segregated into separate units during World War I, begin to be integrated with white forces by the end of World War II. The wars wrought another change, with blacks as well as whites streaming into the western states seeking war-related manufacturing jobs. Though they faced employment discrimination in such efforts, by 1944 about 100,000 African Americans worked in the aircraft industry, based mostly in the West. These wartime employment gains vanished when white soldiers returned from the war.

In recent years western blacks have faced economic inequality and a growing white backlash against AFFIRMATIVE ACTION, the first example of which was the 1978 case of *Bakke v. University of California*. In 1996 California voters approved Proposition 209, which many African Americans saw as an attack on their dreams of equal educational opportunity.

Also in California, the Watts Riot of 1965 was the first of what would be dozens of race riots in which African Americans expressed their outrage over lack of jobs and justice. Nearly 30 years later, in 1992, Los Angeles again exploded into angry violence following the acquittal of four police officers who had been videotaped savagely beating Rodney King, a black motorist.

For years worldwide popular culture has propagated an image of an all-white American West. Black faces among the nation's cowboys, pioneers, mountain men, and businesspeople have been either ignored or glossed over. But a true picture of this region – most representative of America's freewheeling, independent, contradictory, and democratic self-image – includes faces of color.

Kate Tuttle

SEE ALSO

Slavery in the United States; World War I and African Americans; World War II and African Americans; American Indians; Beckwourth, James Pierson; Black Cowboys; Civil War, American; Fugitive Slave Laws; Los Angeles Watts Riot of 1965; Mason, Biddy Bridget; Pleasant, Mary Ellen ("Mammy").

Africa

Americo-Liberians, descendants of the African American settlers who founded the African nation of LIBERIA and for many years held most of the country's political and economic power.

The roots of Americo-Liberian society can be traced to modern Liberia's settlement by free American blacks. From their arrival on the coast of West Africa in 1821, the settlers and their sponsors at the American Colonization Society (ACS), a white abolitionist group, had a complex relationship with the people who were already living there. The settlers brought with them American social, political, and economic values (as expressed in the first constitution of the Commonwealth, later the Republic, of Liberia). They were also strongly influenced by the ACS's ties to the Christian missionary movement. The motives of both white abolitionists and African American colonizers were challenged by critics such as the nineteenth-century African American writer Martin Delany, who charged that the ACS, in "deporting" free blacks, was helping to sustain the practice of slavery in America. Furthermore, these critics noted, the black settlers were establishing a caste system as unfair as the one they had only recently been subject to themselves.

Seeking to "civilize" as well as "save" the indigenous inhabitants of what would become Liberia, the Americo-Liberian settlers established laws that in fact discriminated against indigenous Africans in education, housing, employment, and political representation. Unlike other African colonies, however, no color bar separated the native inhabitants from the colonizers, and thus more movement between the two groups was possible. Not only did some indigenous Liberians "pass" as Americo-Liberians, but the Americo-Liberians intermarried and had children with native-born Liberians. In addition, many settlers in Liberia's interior arranged informal adoptions of indigenous children – educating them or leaving them land – as part of cooperative treaties with local leaders. Also included in the Americo-Liberian community, which grew from some 80 original settlers to more than 13,000 by the late 1860s, were former slaves from BARBADOS as well as Africans freed from slave ships by the English and American navies. Today, it is estimated that less than 5 percent of the Liberian population is Americo-Liberian.

Relations between indigenous peoples and Americo-Liberians have at times been contentious, beginning in 1822 with a pitched battle for control of the land that is now Monrovia, Liberia's capital. In addition, the Americo-Liberians faced a series of revolts by indigenous groups demanding autonomy and freedom, such as the Kru Confederation in 1856 and the G'debo Kingdom in 1875. Even after these uprisings, indigenous Liberians held only lower-class citizenship rights until 1945, when President William V. S. Tubman granted all male Liberians the right to vote (he extended suffrage to women in the following year).

The Americo-Liberian population produced all of Liberia's presidents until 1980. Joseph J. Roberts, the first nonwhite governor of the Liberian colony, became the independent republic's first president when it was founded in 1847. In 1870 the settler's True Whig Party (TWP) elected its first president, Edward James Roye, who was succeeded by TWP presidents for more than a century. In 1980 army officer Samuel K. Doe, an ethnic Krahn, overthrew President William Tolbert and went on to become the first non-Americo-Liberian head of state.

Kate Tuttle

SEE ALSO

Doe, Samuel Kanyon; Tolbert, William Richard, Jr.; Monrovia, Liberia; Slavery in the United States;

Tubman, William Vacanarat Shadrach; American Colonization Society; Delany, Martin Robison; Free Blacks in the United States, 1619 to 1863; Christianity: Missionaries in Africa.

AME Zion Church. Please see African Methodist Episcopal Zion Church

Africa

Amhara, an ethnic group of Ethiopia.

The Amhara, one of the two largest ethnic groups of Ethiopia, occupy central and western Ethiopia. Traditionally, the Amhara have been the country's dominant people – all but one of the Ethiopian emperors were Amhara – and their language, Amharic, a Semitic language like Hebrew or Arabic, has been the country's official language. Amhara's political dominance has created tensions between them and other ethnic groups, including the Tigre and the Oromo. Historically, the Amhara belonged to the Ethiopian Orthodox Church, which was the Ethiopian state religion until the overthrow of Emperor Haile Selassie I in 1974.

The origins and early history of the Amhara remain the subject of some speculation. Archaeological evidence suggests that sometime before 500 B.C.E. a Semitic-speaking people, from whom the Amhara are descended, migrated from present-day Yemen to the area of northern Ethiopia that would become Aksum. These Himyarites, as they have come to be called, intermarried with indigenous speakers of Cushitic languages, such as Agaw, and gradually spread south into the present-day homeland of the Amhara. Their descendants spoke Ge'ez, an ancient Semitic tongue that is no longer spoken but remains the official language of the Ethiopian Orthodox Church. They developed a civilization that made use of dams, cisterns (one of which was still operating in the 1950s), and other irrigation techniques; stone houses; and a unique form of writing (*see* Ethiopic Script and Language). According to the traditional account contained in the national epic *Kebra Negast* (Ge'ez for "The Glory of the Kings"), the Amhara and related groups such as the Tigrinya are descended from the Israelite king Solomon and the Queen of Sheba. Therefore, each Ethiopian emperor held the title "Lion of Judah." Christianity spread to Ethiopia during the fourth century C.E., and religion played a central role in shaping Amharic society.

The Amhara created a highly stratified feudal society. At the top sat the emperor, who was considered the head of the state, the army, and the church. Under the emperor was a class of landed nobility and clergy. Below this class were various classes of farmers and merchants, and lower-class peddlers, merchants, and weavers. Slaves were considered beneath this class structure entirely. Status was tied to land ownership. The more land a man owned, the more important he was. A wealthy man who owned no land had little status among the Amhara. Under the imperial system, the emperor granted title to lands to nobles in exchange for military service. Tenants farmed the land and paid the owner tribute.

For many Amhara, the Ethiopian Orthodox Church defines their identity. They tend to look down on surrounding Muslim peoples. Traditionally, the Amhara have considered many of the church's tenets laws; this remains true in the rural areas where roughly 90 percent of Amhara still live. Priests serve as examples by their holy lives, offer spiritual guidance and recite the Ge'ez liturgy, but typically they do not preach.

Most Amhara base their livelihood on subsistence agriculture. The most important crop is *teff,* a cereal unique to the Ethiopian highlands that is grown as a staple food. They also grow maize (known as corn in the United States), wheat, and other grains, as well as a variety of legumes and vegetables. Many Amhara raise cattle, sheep, chickens, and other livestock. Coffee is the major cash crop. The Amhara trace descent along both the father's and mother's lines, though most scholars agree that the father's line was traditionally considered more important. Kinship and descent historically provided the basis for land inheritance. Extended families, the descendants of a common ancestor along with their spouses, lived in their own hamlets, farmed their own land, and acknowledged the authority of a council of elders.

The Amhara imperial dynasty lasted from roughly 1270 to 1974, when a military council overthrew the regime of Emperor Haile Selassie I and a Marxist government, led by Haile Mariam Mengistu, took power. The Mengistu regime revolutionized traditional Amhara society by eliminating the feudal hierarchy and landholding patterns and by ending Amhara political dominance. Amhara still predominated in civil service and university teaching positions, however. In 1993 a long-running Tigrean rebellion against the Mengistu regime, led by Meles Zenawi, overthrew Mengistu. Tigreans (mostly members of the Tigrinya ethnic group) began to occupy prominent government positions, a situation that many Amhara resented. A new constitution established a federal structure and divided the country into ethnically defined regions. It permitted regions to secede, and Eritrea declared its independence in 1993. Many Amhara believed that the new constitution was put in place to ensure Tigrean ascendancy, and tensions persisted during the late 1990s. The Amhara numbered between 12 million and 15 million in 1997.

Robert Fay

See Also
Haile Selassie I.

Africa

Amin, Idi (b. 1925, Koboko, Uganda), president of Uganda from 1971 to 1979.

Self-titled "his Excellency President for Life Field Marshal Al Hadji Dr. Idi Amin, VC, DSO, MC, Lord of All the Beasts of the Earth and Fishes of the Sea and Conqueror of the British Empire in Africa in General and Uganda in Particular," Idi Amin also made a name for himself as one of the most despotic and brutal rulers in postcolonial Africa. Born near Koboko of Muslim parents, Idi Amin is a member of the Kakwa ethnic group. After receiving a missionary school education, he joined the King's African Rifles (KAR), the African unit of the British Armed Forces, in 1946. He served in Somalia, Uganda, and Kenya during the suppression of the Mau Mau and earned a reputation as a skilled and eager soldier. But early in his career his excessive tendencies were already apparent; one commanding officer described him as "overzealous" during a campaign to suppress cattle stealing in the north of Uganda.

No less combative off the battlefield, Amin won his country's light heavyweight boxing championship in 1951 and retained the title for nine years.

When Uganda achieved independence in 1962, Amin was one of only two African officers in the Ugandan armed forces. Amin had been an early political supporter of Milton Obote, the first prime minister of independent Uganda. The two were accused of selling smuggled gold and ivory out of the Democratic Republic of the Congo during the early 1960s, gold intended to purchase arms for Patrice Lumumba's troops led by General Olenga. The cabinet suspended Amin from his position as colonel until an investigation could be conducted, but Obote had five of these ministers arrested and subsequently suspended the 1962 constitution, declaring himself executive president.

In 1968 Obote promoted Amin to major general and commander of the armed forces. Soon afterward the president began to lose control over Amin, who was supplying arms to rebels in southern Sudan and cultivating ties with British and Israeli agents. Shortly after an assassination attempt on Obote, Amin's rival, Brig. Gen. Pierino Okoya, was murdered. A suspicious Obote placed the military commander under house arrest in 1970.

In January of the following year, Amin ousted Obote while the president was in Singapore. Ugandans, disillusioned with the corrupt Obote, initially welcomed Amin, as did the international community. But the new president's brutality quickly dampened his popularity within Uganda.

Among Amin's first targets were the ethnic Acholi and Lango, who dominated the Ugandan army. He began liquidating these former supporters of Obote and replacing them with ethnic Kakwa and soldiers from

Sudan and Zaire (present-day Democratic Republic of the Congo). After Obote attempted an unsuccessful countercoup in 1972 from TANZANIA, Amin retaliated by bombing Tanzanian towns and stepping up his campaign to terrorize Acholi and Lango, killing civilians as well as soldiers.

Amin dealt a severe blow to the Ugandan economy. In 1972 he declared an "Economic War" on the country's large Asian population, which dominated the trade and manufacturing sectors and also played an essential role in the civil service (*see* INDIAN COMMUNITIES IN AFRICA). After giving the 70,000 holders of British passports three months to leave the country, Amin distributed ownership of thousands of abandoned businesses to his cronies. In addition, he nationalized all British holdings in the country – some 85 firms – after the former colonial power severed diplomatic ties.

Paranoid and volatile, Amin frequently reorganized his army and security forces as well as his diplomatic alliances. After initially close ties with Israel – where he had once received paratrooper training – he later turned to LIBYA and the USSR for political and military support. In an about-face, he expelled Israeli diplomats in 1972, invited the Palestine Liberation Organization (PLO) to occupy the former Israeli embassy, and reportedly sent a cable to Golda Meir lamenting Hitler's failure to exterminate the Jews. He is also believed to have invited Palestinian hijackers to force an Air France plane full of Israelis to land at Entebbe in 1977. The hostages were freed by Israeli paratroopers, who at the same time killed the hijackers and Ugandan troops and destroyed Amin's fleet of fighter jets.

Amin is thought to have orchestrated the murders of numerous prominent Ugandans, including the Anglican archbishop of Uganda, the chief justice, the chancellor of Makerere College, and the governor of the Bank of Uganda. Tens of thousands of lesser-known Ugandans were abducted, tortured, and killed by the notorious State Research Bureau and Public Safety Unit. Not even Amin's family members escaped the violence. His first wife, Kay Amin, left him, and was later arrested, released, and ultimately found murdered. After his second wife, Mama Miriam, was also arrested and fined, Amin divorced his third wife, Nora, and battered his fourth, Madina, sending her to the hospital with a broken jaw. A brother-in-law who served briefly as foreign minister was found dead and mutilated on the banks of the Nile two weeks after his dismissal from office.

Rumored to have engaged in cannibalism as well as traditional Kakwa blood rituals, Amin came to be viewed by many as both sadistic and irrational. Some have attributed Amin's behavior to hypomania, a form of manic-depression characterized by erratic emotional outbursts and extremely rapid thinking. At the same time, the president's charisma and humorous antics in front of the international press enabled him to cultivate an image abroad as a populist leader defying the imperialist neocolonial forces.

In 1978 Amin's megalomaniac ambitions finally led to his fall from power. In October of that year he attempted to annex the Kagera Salient, a part of Tanzania. The Tanzanian president, Julius Nyerere, responded by sending troops into Uganda. The Tanzanian army, supported by rebel Ugandan forces, captured Kampala in April 1979, and Amin fled to Libya shortly afterward. He has remained exiled in Saudi Arabia ever since.

Ari Nave

SEE ALSO

Gold Trade; Indian Communities in Africa; Ivory Trade; Kampala, Uganda; Mau Mau Rebellion; Nyerere, Julius Kambarage.

North America

Amistad Mutiny (July 1839, off the northern coast of Cuba), rebellion of Africans held captive aboard the slave ship *La Amistad.*

Although England and Spain had signed a treaty in 1817 prohibiting the slave trade, a group of African MENDE were captured in an area near SIERRA LEONE in April 1839 and forced onto a Portuguese slave ship bound for Havana. To avoid prosecution for breaking international law, the captives were smuggled onto the island at night when the ship reached CUBA. While in Havana, 53 Africans (49 adult males, 3 girls, and 1 boy) were sold to two Spaniards, José Ruiz and Pedro Montes, who intended to use them as slaves on Cuban plantations. On June 28, 1839, the Africans were loaded aboard the Spanish schooner *La Amistad* as it set sail along the Cuban coast for Puerto Príncipe.

On the *Amistad's* fourth day at sea, a few of the captives were allowed to come on deck for exercise. One of them, JOSEPH CINQUE, found a nail and smuggled it back below with

Commissioned by black abolitionist Robert Purvis and painted by Nathaniel Jocelyn, this portrait of Joseph Cinque, or Singbe, leader of the 1839 mutiny aboard *La Amistad*, was intended to inspire support for the freedom-seeking Africans. *William K. Sacco/ Courtesy of The New Haven Colony Historical Society*

him. Using the nail to force open their chains and shackles, Cinque and his comrades seized cane knives and initiated the rebellion.

Along with the ship's captain and cook, ten Africans were killed. Ruiz and Montes were captured, and, with translation provided by a slave cabin boy named Antonio, instructed to sail the ship back to Africa. Cinque and the others were able to use the rising sun to ensure that the ship headed eastward during the day. However, unable to navigate by the stars, the Africans were tricked by Ruiz and Montes into sailing northwest at night.

The *Amistad* zigzagged through the waters for two months, finally landing near Culloden Point, Long Island, New York, on August 24, 1839. When Cinque sent a group to find water and food on shore, Lt. Thomas R. Gedney of the United States Navy seized the ship and arrested the Africans for murder and piracy.

Three New York abolitionists, Lewis Tappan, Joshua Leavitt, and Simeon Jocelyn, formed a committee called Friends of the Amistad to help defend the African captives. On March 9, 1841, the U.S. Supreme Court ruled that President Martin Van Buren did not have the right to return the Africans to Cuba, and that the Africans were never slaves under international law and should be granted their freedom. Despite their victory in court, only 35 of the original 53 Africans survived to board the ship *Gentleman* that set sail for Africa on November 27, 1841. Arriving in Sierra Leone in January 1842, three years from the start of their voyage, these Africans regained their freedom.

Alonford James Robinson, Jr.

See Also
Transatlantic Slave Trade; Abolitionism in the United States.

The television version of *Amos 'n' Andy* starred, *left*, Alvin Childress as Amos, Tim Moore as Kingfish, and Spencer Williams as Andy. *The Everett Collection*

Europe

Amo, Anton Wilhelm

(b. 1703?, Akonu, Gold Coast [present-day Ghana]; d. 1754?, Gold Coast), scholar and state councilor, one of the first prominent blacks in Germany.

Anton Wilhelm Amo, brother of a slave, was brought to Germany from the Gold Coast in 1707 as a gift from the Dutch West India Company to the dukes August Wilhelm and Ludwig Rudolf von Wolfenbüttel. Although it was the fashion at the time in Europe to make blacks servants or clowns, the dukes raised and educated Amo as a nobleman. They then sent him to the university in Halle, where he became acquainted with Enlightenment thinkers such as Christian Wolff, Christian Thomasius, John Locke, and René Descartes. His first work, published in 1729 and now lost, concerned the rights of Africans in Europe. Amo received his doctorate in 1734 with a thesis on the duality of body and soul and made his mark as a lecturer in philosophy at the universities in Halle, Wittenberg, and Jena. At a time when many Europeans believed that Africans were racially inferior, Amo proved that they could be the equals of Europeans in abilities and achievements. He was also appointed a Prussian government councilor in Berlin. By the 1740s, however, Amo had lost the support of his mentors, the dukes, who were caught up in the Austro-Prussian war (1866). He returned to the Gold Coast in 1747, apparently disenchanted by the racism that he had experienced in Germany. He worked as a goldsmith in Africa, where he died in 1754. In 1965 the University of Halle, in the former East Germany, erected a statue in his honor.

Belinda Cooper

North America

Amos 'n' Andy, popular American radio and television series based on racist and exaggerated stereotypes of black life. As a radio series, it ran from 1928 to 1960.

The "Sam 'n' Henry" radio show, as it was first called, was created in 1926 in Chicago by two white entertainers, Freeman Gosden and Charles Correll. The show portrayed its two African American characters in full racial stereotype, complete with broken English. In 1928 the characters were renamed Amos and Andy and were crafted to reflect white stereotypes of African American life and culture in Harlem in the years immediately following the Great Migration. While Amos was portrayed as weak and submissive, Andy was lazy and pretentious. Together, they were bumbling fools. When the National Broadcasting Company (NBC) acquired the radio program in 1929, they became a national comic sensation.

Due to its great popularity, the show was played on the radio in many of the country's bars, hotels, and restaurants. Controversy erupted in 1931 when the *Pittsburgh Courier*, an African American weekly newspaper, gathered 750,000 signatures calling for the show's cancellation. Despite protests by the National Association for the Advancement of Colored People (NAACP), the Central Broadcasting System (CBS) purchased the television rights to the show in 1951. Large audiences of both whites and blacks made the first all-black television show a huge hit in its first year (*see* Television and African Americans). Declining ratings forced the show's cancellation after only two years, but it remained in syndication on local stations until 1966. The "Amos 'n' Andy" show was an essential part of the American minstrel tradition, which served to reaffirm white stereotypes of African American life and culture.

Alonford James Robinson, Jr.

See Also
Chicago, Illinois; Great Migration, The; Harlem, New York; Minstrelsy; National Association for the Advancement of Colored People; *Pittsburgh Courier*.

North America

Amsterdam News, New York City's largest black-owned newspaper and the oldest black-owned newspaper in the United States.

Founded by entrepreneur James H. Anderson in 1909, the *New York Amsterdam News* presents news and events by and for the African American community, which historically have been underreported by the mainstream white press. The *Amsterdam News* has featured the writing of many important black journalists and leaders, including Cyril V. Briggs, T. Thomas Fortune, Adam Clayton

Powell Jr., W. E. B. Du Bois, and Roy Wilkins. During World War II, the paper was criticized for its coverage of sensational subjects such as murder and gambling rings, but it also protested segregation in the armed forces, sought to ally blacks with Jews, and argued for racial equality.

Although the *Amsterdam News* struggled financially during World War II, it flourished in the postwar era with a weekly circulation of 100,000. But increased competition from mainstream newspapers, which in the 1960s began to cover black-oriented stories, eroded its base, and by 1996 its circulation had fallen to 27,938.

Wilbert Tatum, the paper's principal stockholder since 1984, returned the paper to profitability but was criticized for his controversial stances, such as publishing the name of a rape victim, and for what critics described as his willingness to forsake journalistic objectivity for "black boosterism." In December 1997 Tatum promoted his daughter Elinor to the position of publisher and editor-in-chief. She endeavored to keep the paper a vital voice in New York's African American community by cutting production costs, creating an online presence, and targeting a younger audience.

Robert Fay

See Also
World War II and African Americans; Briggs, Cyril Valentine; New York, New York; Du Bois, William Edward Burghardt (W. E. B.); Wilkins, Roy Ottoway; Powell, Adam Clayton, Jr.

Africa

Ana (also known as Atakpamé), ethnic group of West Africa.

The Ana primarily inhabit central Togo and neighboring regions of Benin. They speak a Niger-Congo language and are considered part one of the Yoruba peoples. There are approximately 150,000 people who consider themselves Ana.

See Also
Languages, African: An Overview.

North America

An American Dilemma: The Negro Problem and Modern Democracy, first published in 1944, was the largest social study of the position of African Americans ever conducted in the United States, shaping the way social scientists thought about race relations for the next 20 years.

Gunnar Myrdal, the Swedish economist, was selected by the Carnegie Corporation to lead a study of race in America because, as a citizen of "a non imperialistic country with no background of domination of one race over another," the organization felt he would "approach the situation with an entirely fresh mind." Myrdal assembled a team of scholars that included a number of African Americans: Ralph Bunche, Allison Davis, St. Clair Drake, E. Franklin Frazier, Charles S. Johnson, and Kenneth Clark. He also sought advice from W. E. B. Du Bois.

An American Dilemma's major contribution involves three interconnected themes. The first posits that what was called "the Negro problem" is actually a white problem. Myrdal relates that when he began the project, he thought he would be studying African Americans, which is what such investigations usually did. But he quickly realized "that in their basic human traits, Negroes are inherently not much different from other people" and that blacks' enforced subordination to a lower caste was a consequence of the beliefs and actions of white people, who held "practically all the economic, social and political power."

The second theme identifies a conflict between white Americans' ideals and their behavior toward black people. The American creed encompasses equality before the law, participation in government, and the right to the pursuit of happiness. To the significant extent that African Americans are systematically treated in ways that negate these ideals, there has to be conflict within white people themselves. To improve race relations, then, is to highlight this tension and, through education, to help white America bring its attitudes and actions into line with the American creed. This position was later articulated by Martin Luther King Jr. and the Civil Rights Movement.

The study's third contribution is the concept of the "vicious circle." This means that "[w]hite prejudice and discrimination keep the Negro low in standards of living, health, education, manners and morals. This in turn gives support to" white prejudice, which points to the low standards and claims that blacks are inferior. According to Myrdal, the goal should be to reduce white prejudice enough to allow African Americans to make some educational and social gains, gains that would then diminish racism further.

Because so many important sociologists and anthropologists worked on *An American Dilemma*, its presuppositions and conclusions became the ruling ideas of a whole generation of scholars. Appearing just at the end of World War II, the study reflects the ideas of freedom and democracy that had been the goals of the war, a war in which African Americans had fought gallantly. It also reflects the optimism of the postwar world.

The Myrdal study was generally welcomed, but it did contain several weaknesses. The emphasis on attitudes and prejudice led to research interest in the nature of prejudice rather than to efforts to reduce it. To the extent that prejudice was the focus, the hard economic and political constraints on African Americans did not receive adequate attention. The belief that reducing prejudice would substantially reduce the problems of low income, limited education, and lack of political power naively underestimated the tenacity of American racism. Finally, Myrdal undervalued the potential of black leadership and community strength. Nevertheless, by focusing sharply on white attitudes and their role in keeping black people oppressed, *An American Dilemma* represented a substantial step forward, while also helping to train a generation of black and white social scientists.

Richard Taub

See Also
World War II and African Americans; Bunche, Ralph Johnson; Clark, Kenneth Bancroft; Du Bois, William Edward Burghardt (W. E. B.); Frazier, Edward Franklin; Johnson, Charles Spurgeon; King, Martin Luther, Jr.

Latin America and the Caribbean

Anancy Story, type of tale told and sung throughout the Caribbean.

During the period of slavery, Asanti slaves from the African Gold Coast brought the narrative form to the Caribbean. These original tales were interspersed with song, and depicted a wily spider character who used his wits and cunning to survive. Today, Anancy stories include many other types of tales as well, from African beast fables to fairy tales (*see* Theater in the Caribbean).

Africa

Anang (also known as the Anaang and the Annang), ethnic group of Nigeria.

The Anang primarily inhabit the Cross River State of Nigeria. They speak a Niger-Congo language and are closely related to the Ibibio people. Approximately 800,000 people consider themselves Anang.

See Also
Languages, African: An Overview.

Latin America and the Caribbean

Anastacia, a semimythical nineteenth-century slave woman who is worshiped by many in Brazil for her ability to provide miraculous cures.

The worship of Anastacia emerged in Brazil in the early 1970s. The devotion to her centers upon a striking portrait of a young black woman with piercing blue eyes, wearing a face-iron, an iron face mask that slaves were made to wear as a form of punishment. Legend has it that Anastacia was tortured with the face-iron when she refused to submit to the lust of her master. Legend also has it that before she died, she forgave her master and cured his child of a fatal disease. Although the Catholic Church denounces the devotion to her as superstition at best and heresy at worst, millions of Brazilians of all colors are deeply devoted to this woman, whom they regard as possessing, in death, unparalleled supernatural powers. Many of her devotees wear a small medallion of her image around their neck; others keep a card with her image tucked in their pocket or purse; still others make periodic pilgrimages to one of her shrines near Rio de Janeiro. To all of these devotees, Anastacia is a powerful healer to whom they may turn at any time for miraculous cures.

It is thus perhaps not surprising that activists in Brazil's black consciousness movement mistrust Anastacia, for they sense that miraculous cures produce strong emotions that easily flood out race-based meanings. In their view, Anastacia simply is not a reliable source of militant black identity. As far as symbols of political struggle go, they far prefer ZUMBI, the great leader of Palmares, the seventeenth-century runaway slave community. Though Zumbi cannot cure anyone, at least he embodies (albeit in a male form) the collective resistance to slavery and oppression of Afro-Brazilian people.

To some extent political mistrust of Anastacia may be warranted. Anastacia's cures are, after all, intensely personal and individual, not always conducive to associating her with collective meanings. Furthermore, those of Anastacia's black devotees who do think of her in collective terms do not necessarily connect her to black identity. Some, for example, find in her a symbol of the suffering of women in general, faced by the abuse of dominant men. Others find in her the embodiment of pure Christian forgiveness, charity, and hope.

And yet, research on Anastacia's black female devotees has revealed that for many of them her racial symbolism is unmistakable. For many of them she personifies the deep dignity and honor of all black women who had the courage to stand up to their oppressors and were willing to pay the ultimate price. This meaning has led some of her black devotees to translate their love for her into social action of various kinds. One longtime devotee founded the Slave Anastacia Women's Group, a small, neighborhood-based consciousness-raising group dedicated to educating rural black women about their bodies and health. Another black woman, inspired by Anastacia, started a small literacy program for poor black children in her neighborhood. Yet another woman founded and named a hair salon after the slave healer, which specializes in valorizing Afro-Brazilian women's natural beauty. Recognizing such connections, the black pastoral of the progressive Catholic Church has broken with the position of the bishops and embraced Anastacia as offering a potential symbol of hope and pride for poor black women. The extent to which this potential may be fulfilled has yet to be seen.

John Burdick

SEE ALSO

Palmares: An African State in Brazil; Slavery in Latin America and the Caribbean; Rio de Janeiro, Brazil; Catholic Church in Latin America and the Caribbean.

Africa

Ancient African Civilizations

Kevin MacDonald

A colossus of the Nubian pharaoh Aspelto who ruled Egypt and Nubia between 600 and 580 B.C.E. The two rearing cobras on his forehead were royal symbols. *Museum Expedition/Courtesy, Museum of Fine Arts, Boston*

The great chiefdoms, states, and empires of Africa were some of the last great civilizations of antiquity to come to the attention of the Western world. Before the fifteenth century, when the coasts of Africa fell increasingly within the European trading sphere, the states of the African interior were known in Europe only through frail rumors received at one remove from the Arabic world. By the time Europeans finally achieved the interior vastness of the continent in the nineteenth century, many of its great polities had been reduced by internal dissension or had withered away, leaving only their ruins. Oral traditions also remained, but for many years they went unheard or uncredited by the ear of the colonizer. Since the last few decades of the colonial era, much has been reconstructed about the vanished African past, through the use of oral traditions, a few textual sources (mostly in Arabic), historical linguistics, and – most of all – archaeological research.

Virtually every new program of field research provides alterations to the status quo of African prehistory. However, outside southeastern Africa, interdisciplinary studies incorporating oral histories, linguistics, and comparative ethnography are still very rare. Thus, it must be remembered that any synthesis in this rapidly changing field is imminently liable to augmentation. Despite this, it is possible to highlight the salient features of our current knowledge of the first African states.

In their distribution, the ancient complex societies of Africa clustered around the great water bodies of the continent. The Niger and Nile river basins both figured prominently in the rise of African states, as did the CONGO RIVER and the shores of the Red Sea and the Indian Ocean. It will be observed in the earliest state formations of Saharan and sub-Saharan Africa that two factors played central roles: livestock wealth and interregional trade, with the latter eclipsing the former in importance over time. Although much was made in the first postcolonial African histories of the role of external trade in the formation of African states, archaeological research has indicated that extensive internal, rather than external, trade webs formed the principal impetus for the formation of African complex societies.

AFRICA AND EGYPT

Much has been written in recent years about the connections of EGYPT and the African interior. Whether concerning Egypt in Africa or Africa in Egypt, the fountainhead of this new literature was the work of the late Cheikh Anta Diop. Embraced by the public, and uncomfortably ignored by professional scholars, Diop's radical tenets posited that all original early Holocene (c. 10,000-4000 B.C.E.) inhabitants of North Africa were black, and that they alone were responsible for the predynastic culture of Egypt and for all of the early dynasties. During the Old Kingdom it was thought that small-scale Caucasoid incursions from the Levant lightened the skin tone of the original Egyptians, with subsequent "invasions" from Persia, Greece, and Rome further transforming the physical characteristics of the Egyptians. Needless to say, this

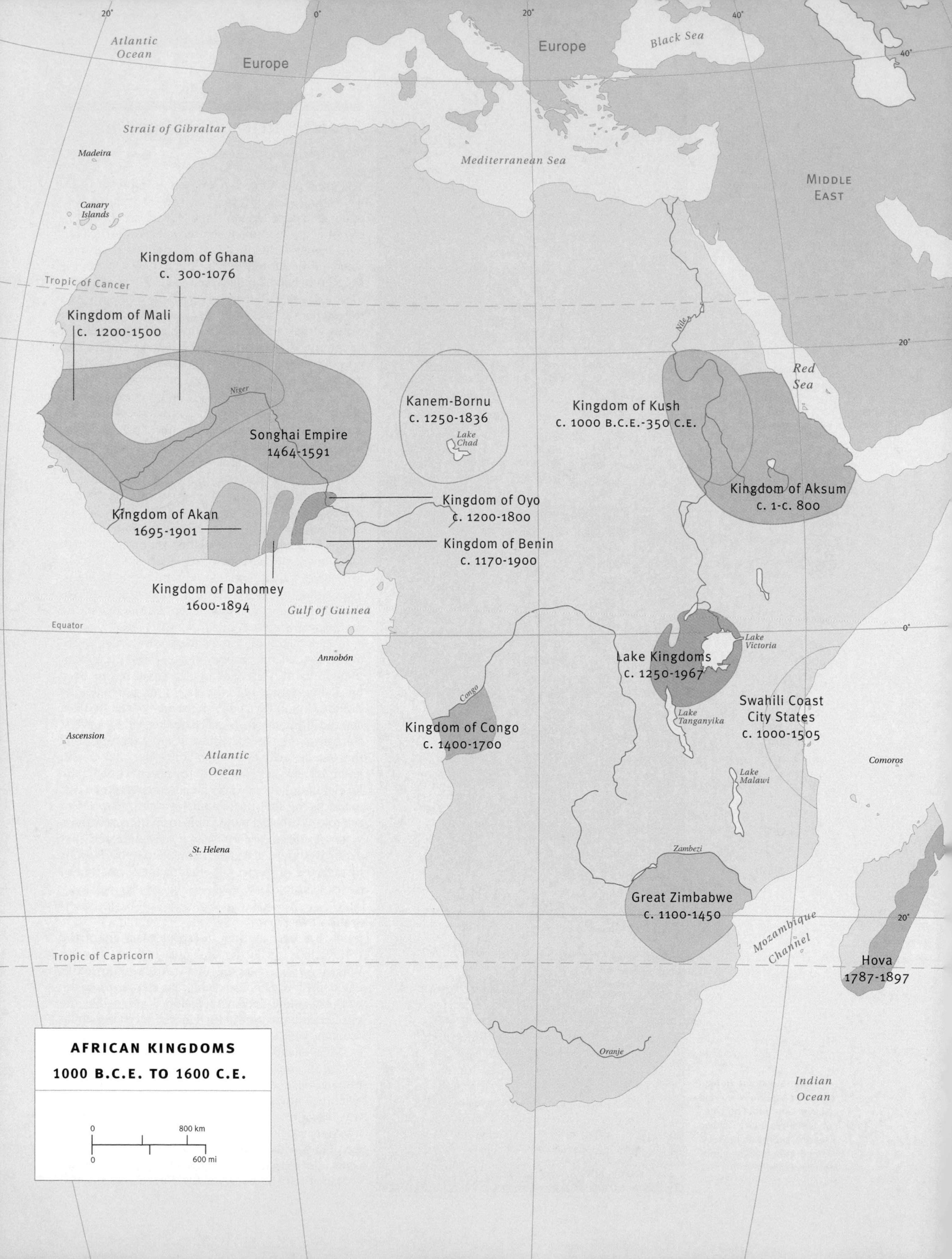

AFRICAN KINGDOMS
1000 B.C.E. TO 1600 C.E.
Atlantic Ocean
Europe
Europe
Black Sea
Strait of Gibraltar
Madeira
Mediterranean Sea
Middle East
Canary Islands
Kingdom of Ghana
c. 300-1076
Tropic of Cancer
Kingdom of Mali
c. 1200-1500
Nile
Red Sea
Niger
Kanem-Bornu
c. 1250-1836
Lake Chad
Kingdom of Kush
c. 1000 B.C.E.-350 C.E.
Songhai Empire
1464-1591
Kingdom of Aksum
c. 1-c. 800
Kingdom of Oyo
c. 1200-1800
Kingdom of Akan
1695-1901
Kingdom of Benin
c. 1170-1900
Kingdom of Dahomey
1600-1894
Gulf of Guinea
Equator
Annobón
Lake Victoria
Lake Kingdoms
c. 1250-1967
Congo
Swahili Coast City States
c. 1000-1505
Lake Tanganyika
Ascension
Kingdom of Congo
c. 1400-1700
Atlantic Ocean
Comoros
Lake Malawi
St. Helena
Zambezi
Great Zimbabwe
c. 1100-1450
Mozambique Channel
Tropic of Capricorn
Hova
1787-1897
Oranje
Indian Ocean
0
800 km
0
600 mi

King Ezana, who ruled Aksum in the mid-4th century, converted to Christianity about 343. After that time Aksumite coins, including this gold one, displayed both Ezana's profile and Christian symbolism. *The British Museum*

in-mixing of foreigners was thought to be linked to the decline of Egypt, with the best of Egyptian ideas being responsible for the grandeur of Greece and subsequent European civilization. This is not the place to enter into a point-by-point debate on Diop's claims and those of his numerous intellectual descendants. At their best they do much to redress the anti-African bias inherent in early Egyptology; at their worst they recreate in reverse the oblique racism inherent in the hyperdiffusionistic school of Grafton Elliot-Smith in the 1930s. Modern consensus sees Egypt, from its beginnings, as a multi-racial civilization, with African cultural aspects particularly coming from Egypt's Nubian corridor to Africa.

The great civilization of Egypt developed between Mediterranean and African spheres of influence out of a long tradition of incipient stratified social systems, already boasting well-organized agro-pastoral economies, ceremonial architecture, and sailing craft (the pre dynastic, 5500-3100 B.C.E). Between 3100 and 331 B.C.E, Egyptian dynasties would profoundly influence socioeconomic developments in northeast Africa and southwest Asia, and forever alter the landscape of Egypt with some of the most impressive monuments known to humanity. Throughout this time Egypt's NUBIAN neighbors possessed their own unique cultural institutions and political structures. These southern polities sometimes cooperated and sometimes contested the power of their northern neighbor.

Kerma, possibly the first Nubian state, prospered between the third and fourth cataracts of the Nile from roughly 2500 to 1500 B.C.E. During Kerma's earliest development, its cultural influences were undoubtedly from the African SAHEL, manifested in round-hut dwellings and ceremonial structures, as well as distinctive burial practices and circular tumuli featuring livestock sacrifices. Over time, however, the cultural proximity of Egypt becomes increasingly visible in linear-walled, fired mud-brick architecture; more elaborate burial practices; and prestige goods imported from the lower Nile (Middle to Final Kerma, c. 2050-1500 B.C.E). Kerma's economy appears to have been based upon external trade in ivory, diorite, and gold to the north, with its subsistence base founded upon pastoralism and an as yet unverified grain component. From 1550 B.C.E onward, Egypt began a period of violent conflict with Kerma, which culminated in the fall and burning of Kerma sometime around 1500 B.C.E.

After the collapse of Kerma, following a period of Egyptian domination, other Nubian states would arise in the same region. The most notable of these were Napata (c. 860-270 B.C.E) and Meroe (c. 270 B.C.E.-350 C.E.). Napata formed around a reemergent upper Nubian elite, with a heartland situated south of Kerma, during a time of dissension in Egypt. Its first rulers were buried in a monumental cemetery at Kurru, with later rulers being inhumed near Napata. With Egypt fragmented into approximately 11 competing polities in the early first millennium B.C.E, Napata was able to push its influence northward, ruling Egypt as a pharaonic dynasty from 750 to 660 B.C.E. Egypt then reunited under an indigenous dynasty, and Napata's sphere of influence contracted to its original center.

From the declining Napatan state, Meroe arose and endured for more than 500 years (c. 270 B.C.E-350 C.E.). Its center was the royal court at Meroe, although it was eventually to stretch as a mercantile empire into lower Nubia and the frontiers of Ptolemaic Egypt. William Adams, the first great synthesist of Nubian archaeology, wrote that both Ptolemaic Egypt and Meroe were "provincial expressions of a world civilization." In other words, they were both cultural outposts of Hellenistic Greece. Even the most fervent Africanists would be hard-pressed to argue against this sentiment. From Classic Kerma onward there is a progressive cultural trend in Nubia of looking away from Africa, and toward the Mediterranean world.

However, Meroe did retain some of its own gods – most notably the lion-headed Apedemack. Meroe also developed its own hieroglyphic-derived script, which unfortunately is as yet untranslatable. Meroe is also famed for its massive iron production, the first large-scale industry of its kind in the Nile Valley. But the technology of this industry is essentially Roman, rather than sub-Saharan. Indeed, although sub-Saharan animals, both as living circus animals or as animal products, continued to flow through Nubia, the region had by this time become more of a cul-de-sac and less of a corridor, seeking its luxuries and ideals from the Greco-Roman world.

CATTLE AS CAPITAL: EARLY COMPLEX SOCIETIES OF THE SAHARA AND SAHEL

By the third millennium B.C.E., a broad swath of cultures economically dominated by pastoralism stretched across the African Sahel, from modern SUDAN to MAURITANIA. At that time the Sahara was much moister than it is today, being carpeted with grasslands and crisscrossed by seasonally filled waterways and ponds. Its vast expanse was also populated with linguistically and culturally diverse groups that had both pastoral and hunter-gatherer ways of life. The small stone and earthen tumuli and monuments left in the wake of the early pastoral cultures attest to a degree of social ranking in the former – probably based around the accumulation of livestock and widely traded polished stone objects (beads, arm rings, axes, etc.).

The origins of these mobile, complex societies extend almost to the beginnings of cattle-keeping in Africa, possibly as early as 7000 B.C.E. in the northeastern corner of the continent. From a relatively early date, these cultures were constructing small stone monuments of a communal nature, including a circle of standing stones (built between 5000 and 4000 B.C.E., near Nabta Playa, Egypt), and small tumuli for cattle "sacrifices" or lineage bulls (c. 5000 B.C.E., NIGER and

CHAD). Soon, however, monuments of a more individualistic nature would appear across the central Sahara. Stone tumuli, alignments, and burial complexes, singling out the elites of these societies for special treatment, are well documented from 4000 B.C.E. until the virtual abandonment of the gradually desiccating region during the first millennium B.C.E. In two places, environmental and external social factors crystallized these mobile societies into more sedentary and complex polities, such as those known from Kerma and Dhar Tichitt.

Around 1500 B.C.E., far in the west of the continent, the first substantial masonry structures in Africa outside the Nile Valley were being built. Along the escarpments of Dhar Tichitt and Dhar Oualata, in modern Mauritania, a pristine chiefdom developed in a deteriorating environment where arable land and pasturage were at a premium. Remote sensing has revealed a four-tier settlement hierarchy, with the largest regional centers exceeding 90 hectares (220 acres) in area. The evolution of Tichitt-Oualata society remains unclear, with competing hypotheses of long-term local development, rapid evolution, or immigration from elsewhere being obscured by thin stratigraphy at deflated settlement sites.

By the mid-second millennium B.C.E., however, it is clear that pastoral peoples living in this zone had started to become more sedentary, building dry-stone masonry structures and cultivating millet. From this time onward, the presence of large stone-walled corral areas and numerous granary foundations points to the importance of mixed farming, with clear evidence of domestic millet, cattle, sheep, and goats. Inorganic wealth resided in the same objects valued by contemporary Sahelian pastoral cultures: carnelian and amazonite beads, polished stone bracelets, and a plethora of ax types, from large functional varieties to miniature tokens. Unfortunately, none of this region's many tumuli has yet been excavated. It would appear that the collapse of Tichitt-Oualata between 800 and 500 B.C.E. was brought about both by continually shrinking local ponds and grasslands and increasing harassment from BERBER interlopers from farther north.

THE EMPIRES OF GHANA AND MALI

During the first millennium B.C.E. the advent of metallurgy added further impetus to the growth of complex societies south of the Sahara. Indeed, gold would play a key role in international trade between West Africa and the Mediterranean world throughout the late first and early second millennia C.E. At a more regional level, iron and copper figured as crucial sources for both practical and prestige objects. Coupled with ivory and the slave trade, the control of metallurgical commodities supplanted mere subsistence as the power basis of African elites from the beginning of the first millennium C.E.

By the time Arab geographers began to write of West Africa in the eighth century C.E., the empire of Ghana – described as a "land of gold" – was already in existence. The origins of Ghana, and even its precise extent, remain unclear. But we do know that it was situated within the modern states of Mauritania and MALI. It should be noted that the modern state of GHANA was named after the empire because of possible historical connections, even though geographically there is no relationship.

It was not until the tenth and eleventh centuries C.E. that travelers and compilers of travelers' tales began to assemble a more complete written record of Ghana – an empire reaching the end of its existence by that time. Most notable among them were Ibn Hawkal, a late-tenth-century traveler, and the great geographical synthesist al-Bakri, whose masterwork was completed in 1068. Only eight years after this, the Almoravid Berbers completed their invasion of Ghana and captured its capital (Koumbi Saleh). It would appear that this act laid waste to the power structure of the state and marked its effective dissolution.

In their writings, Ibn Hawkal and al-Bakri paint a picture of a powerful and wealthy state able to "put 200,000 warriors in the field, more than 40,000 of them being armed with bow and arrow." The king, it was said, controlled the traffic of all gold out of his kingdom to the north, and the flow of salt from the Sahara to the south.

The ruins of Ghana's last capital, Koumbi Saleh, lie in southeastern Mauritania; yet the most substantive settlement clusters known from the first millennium C.E. rest within the bounds of the middle Niger in the neighboring Republic of Mali. Earlier scholarly thought placed Ghana as a puppet state founded by Arab traders, but recent research has emphasized the indigenous development of regional trade webs by the Soninke people, long before the Arab conquest of North Africa (c. 750 C.E.).

There is thus an unknown Ghana, the Ghana that existed before the first written accounts. There is a tantalizing reference in the *Tarikh as-Sudan*, a compilation of oral traditions written in Tombouctou (Timbuktu) in about 1650 C.E. It states that there were 21 kings of Ghana before the beginning of the Muslim era (622 C.E.) and 21 kings after that. If we accept this as anything more than an exercise in symmetry, then it would seem to place the origins of Ghana sometime before 300 C.E.

Archaeologically, if we move the center of gravity southward toward the inland Niger Delta, much evidence exists to support this claim. The substantial settlements that have been excavated along the middle Niger were all in existence by this time. At some sites, such as Tongo Maaré Diabal, permanent mud architecture has been present from 250 C.E. Certainly the high point of middle Niger civilization in terms of maximum settlement growth would date to the period between 400 and 800 C.E., well before the textually recorded Ghana. Was this the early Ghana eluded to in the *Tarikh as-Sudan?* On current evidence, it would appear likely. It is expected that future work will confirm the view that the heart of the empire of Ghana, like that of the MANDINKA empire of Mali, lay not in its trade entrepôts in the Sahara, but closer to the resource centers of the middle Niger.

The inland Niger Delta's best-excavated sequence is that of Djenné-Djeno (250 B.C.E. to 1400 C.E.), a 33-hectare (82-acre) mud-brick settlement mound. From its foundation, the inhabitants of the site fished, cultivated rice and sorghum, and had domestic livestock. Trade with adjoining regions brought in commodities such as copper, iron, and sandstone. By 450 C.E., local craft specialization, the building of a monumental city wall, and a regional site hierarchy centered on Djenné-Djeno point to an urban status for the site. It must be stressed, however, that Djenné-Djeno is only one of more than a dozen settlements of comparable size now known from the middle Niger, and, if one were to consider smaller settlement mounds, only one of

The ancient urban center of Djenné-Djeno developed a tradition of pottery sculpture. This warrior or hunter was probably made between the eleventh and sixteenth centuries. *Werner Forman/ Art Resource, NY*

thousands. The occupation of such sites continued through the time of Ghana's Islamic successor states, the empire of Mali (1250-1600) and the empire of Songhai (1375-1600).

With the conquest of Ghana by the Islamic Almoravid movement, and the subsequent rapid disintegration of this movement, there came a brief period of small feudal states in this region of West Africa. These successor kingdoms included those of Soso, in the north of ancient Ghana, and Kangaba, located in the modern Mali-GUINEA frontier zone. Kangaba had developed out of a grouping of local Mandinka chiefdoms and stateless societies, probably as a response to slave raiding during the time of the late empire of Ghana.

In the early thirteenth century animistic Soso, under the rule of Sumanguru Kante, began to expand. It raided the territories of the Mandinka and blocked their way to commerce in the north. Around 1240, SUNDIATA KEITA, or Mari-Diata, the young ruler of Kangaba, defeated the army of Sumanguru, conquered the north, and gained total control of the West African gold trade routes. With this conquest, Keita founded the empire later known as Mali. Mali was to become the first great Muslim empire of West Africa, eventually controlling much of modern SENEGAL, Mauritania, Guinea, and Mali. By 1312 Mali's greatest ruler, Mansa Musa, took the throne. He ruled for 25 years, making an elaborate pilgrimage to Mecca in 1324, during which the gold he lavished on Cairo was to have the effect of ruining the local gold standard. During his reign several monumental mosques were constructed within the territory of modern Mali. However, Mali did not last as long as Ghana, enduring as an empire for less than 200 years. Its short life may have been due to the instability created by its rapid expansion through conquest and its consequent ethnic diversity and potential for internal dissension.

The stelae of Aksum are among the largest monolithic monuments ever created by humans. The towers, created during the late fourth-early fifth centuries B.C.E., marked the tomb sites of Aksumite kings. *Werner Forman/ Art Resource, NY*

Unfortunately, archaeologically we know very little about Mali. Excavations at its putative capital of Niani (in modern Guinea) showed substantial occupations dating to before and after the time of Mali, but very little during its epoch. It is likely that Mali had many capitals, with the capital moving with each new successor to the throne. Much archaeology remains to be done in the Mali-Guinea border region, both to understand better the origins of the Sundiata's power base and to locate the later centers of Malian rule.

IGBO-UKWU, IFE, AND BENIN: GRANDEUR IN THE WEST AFRICAN FOREST

The first complex societies of the West African forest probably took root sometime in the first millennium C.E. Limited excavations have only begun to hint at the political organization of these societies during the late first millennium C.E., but their richness and artistic expertise have been well demonstrated at the site of Igbo-Ukwu (NIGERIA), dated to about 900 C.E. From this site, a regal burial and a storehouse of regalia have been excavated, both holding superb brass castings made by the "lost wax" method, and thousands of glass trade beads. The presence of such wealth hints at a well-organized system of trade, craft specialists, and a wealthy elite; but we know little of settlements in the region until the emergence of the state of Ife around 1100.

The tropical West African state of Ife does not benefit from the weight of textual records available for its contemporaries in the savanna and Sahel. However, a good deal of effort has been put into its archaeology, which is a compensating factor. Initial archaeological inquiries at Ife began as long ago as 1910, when the German anthropologist Leo Frobenius visited a shrine at the living holy city of Ife, and there acquired a series of naturalistic bronze and terracotta busts for £6 and some alcohol. He was later apprehended by the colonial authorities and the bronzes were returned, but seven terracottas found their way into European museums. As a result there was much speculation as to who could have created this magnificent lifelike sculpture. Frobenius, on stylistic grounds, asserted that ancient Ife was a lost Greek colony founded around 1300 B.C.E. and abandoned by 800 B.C.E. We now know that this is not even remotely true. The ancient art of Ife was entirely African in its origin, and dated instead to the earlier part of the second millennium C.E. The YORUBA city of Ife is itself an object of wonder. It is surrounded by high earthworks arranged in rings around the town, with the outer ring being 11.6 km (7.2 mi) in circumference. The date of these earthworks is not yet precisely known, but it is assumed that at least some of them correspond with the apogee of Ife as a political center.

Archaeological work at Ife and other sites in its vicinity has been driven primarily by accidental discoveries during building activities, as much of its ancient expanse remains covered with habitations, businesses, and public buildings. Excavations have generated a series of radiocarbon dates that allow the reconstruction of a rudimentary cultural sequence. Finds from between 500 and 950 C.E. are mainly of poor grave pits concentrated near the center of the town. However, for the period dating from 950 to 1300, there are rich graves, numerous ritual structures, and a distribution of finds throughout, and even beyond, the vast area enclosed by the earthworks. Most of the terracotta portrait busts have been thermoluminescence-dated to c. 1200-1300.

This late sixteenth- to early seventeenth-century brass plaque, decorated with a figure of an oba, or king, wearing ceremonial dress and carrying weapons, adorned the Oba palace of Benin. *Werner Forman/ Art Resource, NY*

In some sculptures, personages are depicted richly adorned in ceremonial regalia. Shrines featuring such depictions may point to a form of divine kingship that is known to have existed historically in the region.

Perched at the edge of Nigeria's tropical forest, Ife is thought to have come to prominence by the control of local products (ivory, gold, pepper, cola nuts, and slaves) in the external trade to Niger River civilizations. By 1300 its walled capital was at the peak of its wealth, with many shrines featuring elaborate potsherd pavements and sculptures scattered throughout the city. To support this large elite and artisanal population, Ife's subsistence base appears to have been yams, oil-palm products, and small livestock. Surrounding Ife there was likely to have been a continuous hinterland of farmsteads. Around 1500 the city of Ife declined, and the region's center of power shifted to Benin, without any appreciable break in cultural tradition, despite the fact that Benin City was founded by a different ethnic group (Edo instead of Yoruba).

The rise of Benin and its eclipse of Ife (fifteenth century) corresponds to the beginning of contacts with the Portuguese and a shift to coastal rather than riverine trade. The first of the great kings of Benin was Oba Euware (1440). He is said in oral traditions to have captured 201 towns and made them render regular tribute to him. He is also said to have been the builder of the walls and ditches of Benin, as well as external road networks. From the time of Oba Euware on, there were further innovations in bronze (or more properly brass) casting, with the advent of brass plaques showing the exploits of kings, and with brass pendant plaques being worn by local rulers and functionaries as badges of rank. The walls of Benin are even more spectacular than those of Ife, earning a spot in the *Guinness Book of World Records* as the world's largest earthwork. Benin City continued to flourish until the advent of the colonial era, when a British punitive expedition sacked the capital in 1897.

Pre-Aksumite and Aksumite Civilization in Ethiopia

Like Meroe, which was more linked to Egypt than Africa, we find in Aksum another outwardly looking state, wedded to the trading sphere of the Red Sea and southern Arabia rather than the African interior. Although there has been some debate concerning the cultural origins of Aksum, it is most likely that there was in fact an undifferentiated Ethiopian South Arabian cultural sphere from the late first millennium B.C.E. into the first millennium C.E. Unfortunately, the epoch most likely to shed important light on this matter, the pre-Aksumite period (500 B.C.E.-100 C.E.), has barely been studied. Indeed, little has been well documented save several religious and funerary shrines bearing South Arabian inscriptions. The best preserved of these are known from the site of Yeha, where there is a pre-Aksumite temple dedicated to the South Arabian moon god Alouqah. In addition, it can be noted that the distribution of pre-Aksumite material culture more or less equates to that of later Aksum: the northern Ethiopian/Eritrean highlands. Thus, Aksum has been viewed as the successor to this earlier complex society. The last few centuries of the pre-Aksumite period are sometimes referred to as the Intermediate Period. During this time inscriptions in South Arabian script decline, being replaced by a local script based upon the Ge'ez language.

Classic Aksumite civilization prospered between 100 and 600 C.E. The first textual mentions of Aksum may be found in the *Periplus of the Erythraean Sea*, an Alexandrian Greek trading guide published in the late first century C.E. The guide makes reference to a metropolis called "Axomite." There is also a mention in Ptolemy's *Geography* that would lead us to expect a city and a king's palace at Aksum in the mid-second century C.E. Archaeologically, during this early Aksumite period, the first stellae are known to have been installed in the funerary park of the city of Aksum. Textual records from South Arabian temples indicate that by the third century C.E., Aksumite armies were fighting with success in southern Arabia, were allied with local rulers, and were being led in person by the Aksumite king Gadarat. By 270 Aksum was minting its own coinage, marked with a distinctive disk and crescent symbol and the head of the ruler (in the first case, King Endybis). Between 200 and 330, Aksum's greatest monuments were erected. These include the underground chambered tombs of Nefas Mawcha and the Tomb of the Brick Arches, as well as the great stellae of Aksum (the largest being 30 m [98 ft] in height and weighing 517 tons). These stellae were carved from single blocks of stone, with low-relief sculpture on their surfaces representing multistoried structures with doors, windows, and beams. We know that by this time Aksum was supplying African luxury goods (particularly ivory and animal skins) to the Red Sea trade, receiving in return precious metals, glass, cloth, wine, and spices.

Aksum's most celebrated king, Ezana, came to power around 330 C.E. During his reign Aksum was sovereign over Ethiopia as well as parts of Yemen and Sudan. Ezana converted to Christianity in 333. There followed a trend toward simpler burial traditions, and the replacement of the disk and crescent with the cross on Aksumite coinage.

From 600 onward, Aksum began to decline. Aksum ceased to be the state's capital in 619. At this time the kingdom also lost its one seaport of Adulis, as a result of internal dissension. Aksum was one of the world's first Christian states, and its successors were to retain their religion in the wake of the Islamic expansion of the late first millennium C.E.

The Swahili Coast and the East African Interior

Along the East African littoral during the first millennium C.E., coastal trade was to play an important role in the elaboration of local social hierarchies, just as trans-Saharan trade was doing in the west. Likewise, for many years the Swahili civilization – a chain of semiautonomous city-states dotting the East African coast – was thought to be the direct result of Arabian colonization. Its cities were viewed as the very edge of the Islamic world – wealthy trading posts perched on the edge of a foreboding interior from which trade goods would "appear" in exchange for cloth and beads. However, the past few decades of research have exposed the indigenous African roots of the Swahili culture and their eventual synergy with incoming Arabian-Islamic culture.

Although *Periplus of the Erythraean Sea* cites the presence of a trading city (Rhapta) along the coast of KENYA or TANZANIA, little substantial archaeological evidence exists for East African trading societies until the ninth century. However, there is some encouraging recent evidence from the site of Unjuja Ukuu (situated at the southern tip of the island of ZANZIBAR, Tanzania). There, local ceramics have been found in stratigraphy with fragments of Egypto-Roman pottery, with the whole assemblage radiocarbon-dated to 400-550 C.E. This at least attests to coastal trade with Roman Egypt by that time, and hints that Rhapta may not be a myth.

By 800, Swahili trading cities dotted the East African coast, fusing Islamic religion and architecture with indigenous sociopolitical organization and commercial acumen. Trading settlements, of which 170 are known, eventually extended from southern Somalia to MOZAMBIQUE. From these towns the Indian Ocean acted as a trade corridor to the Far East, with lateen and square-rigged dhows stocking the menageries of Chinese emperors and carrying silks and porcelain to Swahili merchants and their sultans. At an incipient level, it is now apparent that Swahili civilization arose out of coastal agro-pastoral societies, whose gradual mastery of the sea lanes made them ideal intermediaries with foreign mariners. At the well-studied site of Shanga (Tanzania), mud and thatch indigenous architecture in the eighth and ninth centuries gives way to a local mutation of Islamic mortar and stone buildings in the tenth century; evidence for long-distance trade is present throughout the site's sequence.

At its apex, however, the Swahili coast packed a lavish Islamic veneer, with impressive palaces and mosques distributed among sites such as Kilwa and Gedi. Indeed, by 1331 the great traveler IBN BATTUTAH would write, "Kilwa is one of the most beautiful and well-constructed towns in the world." The eventual downfall of the Swahili trading network and its days of glory was brought about by the arrival of Portuguese mariners in the first years of the sixteenth century. They sacked Kilwa in 1505 and rapidly constructed a chain of stone and wood forts along the eastern seaboard, and the east coast trade soon lost its efficiency. The Portuguese, unlike the Arab traders, did not integrate well into the existing trading community.

During the time of the Swahili civilization, numerous complex societies and states grew in the interior, often as trade-item consolidators for the coastal trade. Farthest from the coast were the wealthy societies of the Democratic Republic of the Congo's Upemba Depression, the neighboring Kisalian and Katotian polities (c. 700-1300). Both are known for their sumptuous graves, with those of the Kisalian suggesting wealth deriving from an intra-African trade (copper, iron, and ivory), and those from the Katotian suggesting firmer links with Indian Ocean commerce (cowries, conus shells, glass beads). The successor to the Kisalian polity was the historic kingdom of LUBA.

Great Zimbabwe (and Its Predecessor Mapungubwe)

Farther to the south, trading states developed where Bantu agro-pastoralists had already established transient chiefdoms based upon the manipulation of livestock wealth. The first of these states, Mapungubwe (c. 1000-1200), grew up in the South African Limpopo River basin. Here, an intermediary role in the coastal trade fossilized existing, and otherwise transient, social hierarchies based upon cattle wealth. Glass trade beads, cowries, and copper ingots came in from the coast to the Mapungubwe hill settlement in exchange for ivory, animal skins, and locally mined gold. From 1075 it is apparent that artisanal specialists existed at the site, including metal, ivory, and bone workers, as well as spinners of cotton thread. These items would have been of use in both local and external trade.

A further elaboration of such hierarchies, but over

a greater zone of influence, can be seen in the state of GREAT ZIMBABWE (c. 1100-1450). Famed for the towering, dry-stone masonry architecture of its impressive central settlement, the Great Zimbabwe tradition, like Mapungubwe, consolidated the gold and animal product wealth of its hinterland as a powerful bargaining chip in the competitive coastal trade.

It is interesting to note that Great Zimbabwe, like Ife, was once perceived by colonialists as an outpost of peoples foreign to the African continent. Great Zimbabwe first became known to Europeans through Portuguese contacts. By 1506 there were rumors of a "King Mwene Motapa," who ruled a series of lands ranging from the Kalahari Desert to the Indian Ocean. However, in the seventeenth century, Portuguese missionaries and historians, who by now had seen the abandoned ruins of the interior, began to cast doubt upon the African origins of the stone structures, interpreting them instead as the remains of the vanished Christian kingdom of Prester John, or King Solomon's mines. The first archaeological investigations at the site in the late nineteenth century set out merely to determine the nature of Great Zimbabwe's external origins. Such work was supported by CECIL RHODES, who saw in Great Zimbabwe an ancient Phoenician trading settlement, mirroring the then current British marine hegemony. At this time, much of the site was mined for its valuables by treasure hunters.

As the twentieth century dawned, a series of professional archaeologists, including Keith Robinson and Gertrude Caton-Thompson, demonstrated through excavations that there was no evidence for a foreign presence at the site, with local (proto-SHONA) pottery, art, and architectural styles present throughout. Despite this, wrangles over the site's origins continued until a comparatively recent period, with the site figuring as an important propaganda tool in the Zimbabwean struggle for independence.

RIGHT: Built by the ancestors of today's Shona people, the granite walls of Great Zimbabwe were erected between the eleventh and fifteenth centuries. *CORBIS/David Reed*

BELOW: This photo shows the circular enclosure at the Great Zimbabwe palace and fortress. *CORBIS/MIT Collection*

The site of Great Zimbabwe is only one of over 50 other masonry settlements of its type scattered throughout Zimbabwe and northern BOTSWANA, although it is without doubt the most grandiose. It is now known that Great Zimbabwe was founded in the eleventh century C.E. as a relatively small-scale trading and herding center, consisting only of Daga (mud) huts dotting the local hills and valleys. But from 1085 on, profound changes began to take place. First the labyrinthine Hill Ruin was constructed. This high-walled, multiroom structure is accessed only by a precipitous stone stairway winding along the side of the hill. It has been interpreted as royal residence and a spiritual-ritual center. Later the Valley Ruin, with its much-photographed cyclopean Elliptical Building, was constructed. With its narrow, three-story-tall entrance passageway and central court featuring two circular stone towers, it has been interpreted by some as a later king's residence and by others as a women's area, perhaps a dwelling for the king's wives or a noblewomen's initiation center.

From 1085 to 1450 Daga huts continued to dot the plains around the stone complexes, taking in almost 100 hectares (250 acres) in area. At its height in the thirteenth century, Great Zimbabwe's capital was home to as many as 18,000 people. Subsistence to support such population concentrations remained crucial, and it is likely that cattle and agricultural surplus continued to play a highly visible role in the maintenance of power.

Contemporary with Great Zimbabwe there is evidence for regional centers subordinate to the central site. The best documented of these is Ingombe Ilede on the ZAMBEZI RIVER. There, the fifteenth-century graves of local rulers have been excavated. They were adorned with necklaces of local gold and imported glass beads and wrapped in fine cloth burial shrouds, of which traces remain. As was the case elsewhere in Africa, these local nodes of power served to consolidate goods for the external trading center of Great Zimbabwe (for example, ivory, rhinoceros horn, animal skins, gold, and slaves). Undoubtedly Great Zimbabwe owed much of its wealth to international trade, but it was also part of a long-term internal development, with its power based as much upon cattle wealth and military power as upon foreign riches.

The collapse of the Great Zimbabwe occupation is dated to the mid- to late fifteenth century, when most of the site was abandoned. Reasons posited for the collapse of Great Zimbabwe have included the possible exhaustion of local gold, arable land, or water resources and the disruption of the Indian Ocean trading sphere by the Portuguese. Majestic successor states such as Khami, located farther in the interior, soon sprang up, but none ever achieved the power of Great Zimbabwe.

SEE ALSO

Benin, Early Kingdom of; Congo, Democratic Republic of the; Eritrea; Ethiopia; Ghana, Early Kingdom of; Ivory Trade; Djenné-Djeno, Mali; Mansa Musa I; Iron in Africa; Niger River; Nile River; Nubia; Sahara Desert; Salt Trade; Somalia (Ready Reference); Songhai Empire; Soninké; South Africa; Swahili Coast; Swahili People; Tombouctou, Mali; Cola; Zimbabwe; Almoravids; Cairo, Egypt; Alexandria and Grecian Africa: An Interpretation; Trans-Saharan and Red Sea Slave Trade; Mali Empire.

North America

Anderson, Eddie ("Rochester")

(b. September 18, 1905, Oakland, Calif.; d. February 28, 1977, Los Angeles, Calif.), American actor best known for his comic portrayal of the character Rochester on the Jack Benny radio show.

The humor and energy between Jack Benny and Eddie Anderson led to the development of a 20-year collaboration that delighted radio, television, and film audiences. The relationship between Anderson and Benny, for all of its sarcasm, wit, and camaraderie, was typical of the "Uncle Tomism" of the era (Anderson's trademark line to Benny became "What's that, Boss?"), yet blacks not only appreciated the comedy, but were also pleased that the character was played by a black actor instead of a white actor attempting to imitate black expression.

Anderson's parents performed in vaudeville, and he began acting when he was eight. His formal show business career began in 1919 when he appeared in a Negro revue and continued when he and his older brother, Cornelius, toured as a two-man music and dance team. After appearing in his first film, *Green Pastures* (1936), Anderson was invited to play the role of Rochester, a Pullman porter on the Jack Benny radio show. Though it was only intended to be a one-show deal, Anderson struck such a chord with audiences that he was offered a permanent spot in the cast.

In addition to teaming up with Benny in the classic films *Man About Town* (1939), *Buck Benny Rides Again* (1940), and *Love Thy Neighbor* (1940), Anderson also acted in numerous films without Benny, including *Jezebel* (1938), *Gone With the Wind* (1939), *Birth of the Blues* (1941), and the "race" films *Stormy Weather* (1943) and *Cabin in the Sky* (1943), now recognized as Negro "classics." In the 1950s and 1960s, Anderson appeared regularly on television, at times with Benny and in many other small roles.

Andre Willis

See Also

Television and African Americans; Film, Blacks in American.

North America

Anderson, Marian

(b. 1900?, Philadelphia, Pa.; d. 1993), American singer and first African American to perform at the Metropolitan Opera.

Marian Anderson was born in Philadelphia, Pennsylvania, around 1900, the first of three daughters of John Berkeley Anderson, an ice and coal peddler, and Anna D. Anderson, who, though trained as a teacher, took in laundry. Throughout her childhood, Anderson's family was poor. When she was 12, her father died from injuries he received at work, and the family's financial situation worsened further. Anderson had an urge to make music from an early age, and was clearly talented. When she was six years old, she joined the junior choir at the church to which her father belonged, Union Baptist, and became known as the Baby Contralto. In addition, she taught herself to play the piano, eventually playing well enough to accompany herself during her singing concerts.

Anderson joined the church's senior choir at age 13. She began singing professionally and touring during high school to earn money for her family. After graduating from South Philadelphia School for Girls in 1921, she earned enough to help her family purchase a home. In 1924, however, Anderson gave a Town Hall concert in New York that was so poorly received by critics that she temporarily stopped performing. She returned to singing, and in 1925 won the opportunity to appear at Lewisohn Stadium with the New York Philharmonic Orchestra. Between

After the Daughters of the American Revolution refused to allow her to perform in Constitution Hall in Washington, D.C., Marian Anderson was invited by Secretary of the Interior Harold Ickes, Jr., to sing at the Lincoln Memorial. Her performance drew 75,000 people. *CORBIS*

1925 and 1935, Anderson studied and toured in Europe, and her career began to develop. Her repertoire expanded to comprise over 100 songs in various languages.

In 1939 the Daughters of the American Revolution (DAR) denied Anderson's request to perform at its Constitution Hall in WASHINGTON, D.C., because she was African American. Eleanor Roosevelt, wife of President Franklin D. Roosevelt, resigned from the DAR in protest. Reacting to the outrage the DAR inspired, the secretary of the interior, Harold Ickes, arranged an open-air concert at the Lincoln Memorial on Easter Sunday, which was attended by 75,000 people. Anderson performed once more from the steps of the Lincoln Memorial, as part of the March on Washington in 1963, a key event in the CIVIL RIGHTS MOVEMENT.

In 1955 Anderson became the first African American to perform at the Metropolitan Opera, singing the role of Ulrica in Verde's *Un Ballo in Maschera.* In 1958 President Dwight D. Eisenhower appointed her to the United States delegation to the United Nations, where she spoke on behalf of African independence. Anderson retired in 1965 and spent the bulk of her time on a farm in Danbury, Connecticut, which she and her husband, Orpheus Hodge Fisher, purchased shortly after their marriage in 1943. She received numerous awards, including the Spingarn Medal in 1939, the highest award conferred by the NATIONAL ASSOCIATION FOR THE ADVANCEMENT OF COLORED PEOPLE; the Bok Award in 1941; and the Page One award. She sang at President Eisenhower's inauguration, and in 1977, President Jimmy Carter presented her with a Congressional gold medal bearing her profile.

Robert Fay

SEE ALSO
New York, New York; Philadelphia, Pennsylvania.

Latin America and the Caribbean

Andes, Blacks During Colonial Times in the, the history of people of African descent in the former Spanish viceroyalty of Peru (present-day COLOMBIA, ECUADOR, PERU, CHILE, and BOLIVIA) during colonial times (1532-1820s).

The presence of Africans in the Andean region was recorded as early as the first expedition of the Spanish explorer Francisco Pizarro, which departed from PANAMA in 1524. Spanish chroniclers point out that even before Pizarro arrived at the empire of the Incas (in present-day Ecuador and Peru), an African slave saved the life of Diego de Almagro, one of Pizarro's partners, during an attack by natives from the western coast of what is today Colombia. When Pizarro returned to SPAIN in 1529 after his second expedition, the Spanish king Charles V granted him the title of governor of Peru, along with a license to import 50 African slaves ("at least a third female") to the newly conquered lands (*see* SLAVERY IN LATIN AMERICA AND THE CARIBBEAN).

Pizarro managed to capture Atahualpa, the last ruling Inca, in the northern Incan city of Cajamarca on November 16, 1532, during his third and last expedition. One of the four scouts sent by Pizarro to the royal Incan city of Cuzco to collect the ransom of gold and silver promised by the native ruler was a black slave. Far from assuming a purely subservient role, this slave was charged with overseeing one of the valuable envoys sent from the Andean city of Jauja.

Africans played an important role in the conquest of the Andes, although they were always subject to their Spanish masters. Their number is uncertain. Most of the slaves who accompanied the conquerors were born in Spain or northern Africa. They belonged to Moorish groups and were classified under the general denomination of *ladinos.* These slaves were generally light-brown-skinned and worked as personal servants of the soldiers, fighting for their masters when necessary. Once Pizarro and his brother Hernando had occupied the Incan capital of Cuzco in 1533, they each received a license to import 100 slaves. Such licenses were not only granted to the principal captains, but were used more generally to increase the profits of the conquerors, who could then become involved with the African slave trade.

The Spanish military also formed small batallions of slaves to fight in the recurrent civil wars. One Spanish rebel, Gonzalo Pizarro, included 600 African troops in his campaigns against the Spanish Crown between 1544 and 1548. Indeed, it was a black slave who beheaded Viceroy Núñez Vela, Pizarro's enemy, after the battle of Iñaquito in 1546. Another Spanish rebel, Francisco Hernandez Giron, managed to train 300 slaves to fight against the Spanish Crown in 1554, promising their freedom if his rebellion succeeded. The rebellion, however, did not succeed and though it is not clear what happened to all of the slaves, some suffered severe punishments, others remained captives under the victors, and yet another group went to work the mines (*see* GARRIDO, JUAN: A BLACK CONQUISTADOR IN MEXICO).

In the period 1560 to 1650 two clearly different groups of black slaves emerged. After the 1530s slaves from west central Africa started to arrive in the Andean region. These were the so-called *bozales,* who on arrival did not speak Spanish and were not trained in any of the colonial society's traditional occupations such as shoemaking or blacksmithing. On the other hand, slaves born in Spain, the WEST INDIES, or Peru were called *criollos* (CREOLES) and tended to speak more Spanish, have more marketable skills, and hence be better off than bozales.

Black criollos and bozales eventually became two clearly differentiated groups in colonial Peru. In one study of 7000 slaves sold in Lima during the period 1560-1650, the records reveal a majority of bozales. The predominance of bozales during this period reflects the growing demand for coerced labor in the mining and agricultural sectors of the colonial economy. This demand resulted in a marked increase in slaves from ANGOLA and MOZAMBIQUE, as an active illegal trade was established between Portuguese merchants and Spanish traders in the port of Buenos Aires in present-day ARGENTINA. Greater profits could be culled from this more direct route between west Central Africa and eastern South America, because the trade avoided the surveillance of Spanish authorities in the official northern port of Cartagena de Indias (present-day Colombia). The loyalty of the growing slave population was always suspect in the eyes of colonial officials. And with good reason. In 1579, for example, when Sir Francis Drake approached the coast of Lima, a group of slaves hid the breaks and bridles of the Spanish horses in order to help the British corsair prevail and presumably win their own freedom. Sadly for the slaves, Drake never attacked the city.

Andean indigenous observers also distinguished black bozales from the more socially advantaged criollos. The Indian chronicler Guamán Poma de Ayala, for example, wrote in about 1615 that "bozales make saints, while criollo Negroes are unruly, liars, robbers, gamblers, drunken, rapists and of bad habits." This perception was common within indigenous communities, since criollo slaves were typically charged with administering groups of tributary Indians for their Spanish masters. The skilled criollos often exploited the Indians, holding an intermediate albeit paradoxical position between the free Indians and their own Spanish masters.

There did exist some isolated groups of runaway slaves who managed to form their own small, independent states. Though there were some long-lasting maroon settlements in the area close to Lima, such as the Huachipa settlement (1712-1792) led by Francisco Congo (c. 1713), they were more common in the northern part of the viceroyalty of Peru, along the Pacific Ocean in what are today the regions of Chocó, Colombia, and ESMERALDAS, Ecuador (*see* MAROONAGE IN THE AMERICAS). Despite these courageous efforts to break their chains, most black slaves remained on the coast, forced to work in personal service and on cotton and SUGAR plantations. By 1615 blacks formed the largest segment of the population on the coast. A census from that period indicates that in Lima alone there were 10,386 blacks, 9360 whites, and some 5000 Indians. Included in this numerous black population was a small number of freedpeople who generally earned their living as artisans. Lima, the most important city of South America, was predominantly black throughout the seventeenth century and for part of the eighteenth century. In the highlands, in contrast, the Indian population constituted at least 85 percent of the total.

Criollos, bozales, and freedpeople formed an integral part of Andean social life. They participated in public celebrations and Carnivals like the one described by Francisco de Carvajal y Robles in his *Fiestas de Lima* (Celebrations in Lima) in 1632. Possibly the most important of these public events was the procession of the Señor de los Milagros (Our Lord of the Miracles), an important religious ceremony that originated in the eighteenth century and still takes place in Lima every October. Though the procession now attracts various social classes and ethnic groups, it was originally restricted to Afro-Peruvians, and its religious practices and beliefs reflect the influence of African culture in Peru. Notable individuals of African descent who formed part of Peruvian official religious and artistic life were SAN MARTÍN DE PORRES in the seventeenth century, the mystic poet JOSÉ MANUEL VALDÉS in the eighteenth century, and the mulatto painters Pancho Fierro and Gil de Castro in the nineteenth century (*see* ART IN LATIN AMERICA AND THE CARIBBEAN). Blacks formed part of the Spanish military, helping to defeat indigenous revolts and foreign interlopers. Blacks also participated in both the royalist and insurgent armies during the Wars of Independence (1815-1824), which brought the colonial period to an end.

The principal ethnic groups of Africans in the Andes had diverse origins. They arrived from CAPE VERDE, parts of western Africa (São Tomé), and from southern Africa (Angola, Mozambique), along with the criollos from Spain, Portugal, the West Indies, and those born in Peru. Although there existed an imposed relationship between white and black, the contributions of Africans and their descendants in music, dance, food, and language were vital to Andean coastal culture throughout the colonial period. The racial intermingling that formed the *castas*, groups of mulattos (white and black), *zambos* (black and Indian), and several other ethnic mixtures, infused a great variety of cultural manifestations that rarely resulted in a Peruvian or Andean national melting pot. In fact, peoples of African and Indian descent continue to suffer discrimination from upper-class whites, who generally enjoy a greater economic and social position and who all too often continue to consider themselves culturally superior.

José Mazzotti

SEE ALSO

Cartagena de Indias, Colombia; Pacific Coast of Colombia.

Latin America and the Caribbean

Andrada e Silva, José Bonifácio de

(b. June 13, 1763, Santos, São Paulo, Brazil; d. April 6, 1838, Niterói, Brazil), the first prime minister of independent BRAZIL, an early advocate of the abolition of the slave trade and the gradual emancipation of slaves (*see* ABOLITION AND EMANCIPATION IN LATIN AMERICA AND THE CARIBBEAN).

José Bonifácio de Andrada e Silva is best known for helping Brazil achieve independence in 1822. It is less often recognized that the year after independence he authored a plan for "the slow emancipation of the blacks." In this plan he stated: "It is time, and more than time, for us to put a stop to a traffic so barbaric and butcherlike, time too for us to eliminate gradually the last traces of slavery among us, so that in a few generations we may be able to form a homogeneous nation, without which we shall never be truly free, respectable, and happy."

Andrada e Silva argued that slavery was morally wrong and economically inefficient: a violation of God's laws and the laws of justice, and a corrupt influence over Brazil's inhabitants. Slave labor, he believed, resulted in the slaveholders' idleness, and gave Brazilians little incentive to develop industry or agriculture.

Andrada e Silva's abolition project was intended to become part of independent Brazil's new constitution. It would have granted slaves the right to purchase themselves at market price, provided free persons of color with land grants, and regulated slave work conditions. But before these articles could be debated, Emperor Pedro I dissolved the Congress. Notoriously impatient, Andrada e Silva turned against the throne and was exiled from Brazil.

To Andrada e Silva, independence was incomplete without plans to abolish slavery. He returned to Brazil in 1829 and regained the support of Pedro II, but soon fell from favor. Despite this, Andrada e Silva was celebrated by Brazilian abolitionists of the 1880s, who built upon many of his arguments.

Aaron Myers

North America

Andrews, Benny (b. Nov. 13, 1930, Madison, Ga.), African American artist known for creative use of media from Xerox to stencils.

Born in Madison, Georgia, Benny Andrews served four years in the United States Air Force before beginning his formal art training. Since he had displayed promise drawing cartoons at a very young age and had demonstrated a deep interest in art, he decided to attend the Art Institute of Chicago following his military service. Graduating with a B.F.A. in 1958, Andrews moved to New York City to pursue his art career. In addition to his artistic efforts, he sought to confront the racial politics of museums and tried to help minority artists enlarge their exhibition opportunities. He has exhibited at many galleries across the United States; has taught and lectured; and has been active in organizing art programs and working with museums in the New York City area.

Andrews' major contributions and their diverse media include *Janitors at Rest* (1957), appropriately constructed with paper towels and toilet paper; *Autobiographical Series* (1966), ink drawings depicting black Southern life; *Did the Bear Sit Under the Tree?* (1969), a painting that highlights political and racial conditions; *Women I've Known* (1976), a collage of spray paint through stencils and folded paper; and *Flight* (1981), a mural in the Hartman International Airport in Atlanta, Georgia.

Andre Willis

SEE ALSO

Atlanta, Georgia; New York, New York.

Africa

Anga (also known as Nnga and Kerang), ethnic group of NIGERIA.

The Anga primarily inhabit the Plateau State of Nigeria. They speak an Afro-Asiatic language belonging to the Chadic group. Approximately 200,000 people consider themselves Anga.

SEE ALSO

Languages, African: An Overview.

North America

Angelou, Maya (b. April 4, 1928, St. Louis, Mo.), American writer and actress who was the featured poet at President Bill Clinton's 1993 inauguration.

The wit, wisdom, and power of Maya Angelou's work have made her one of the most beloved contemporary American writers. Maya Angelou was born Marguerite Johnson; the name she chose to use combines her childhood nickname (Maya) with a version of her first husband's last name (Angelos). Her family moved to California soon after her birth, but her parents divorced when she was three, and she was sent to Stamps, Arkansas, to be raised by her paternal grandmother. When Angelou was seven, she was raped by her mother's boyfriend. The trauma of this experience rendered Angelou mute for five years, and it was during this period that she began to read extensively.

Angelou returned to California during high school and took drama and dance lessons. As a teenager, she became San Francisco's first female streetcar conductor. She gave birth at age 16 to her only child, Guy Johnson. To support herself and her son she took a variety of jobs, working as a cook, a waitress, and a madam to two prostitutes. At 22, she married her first husband. After their divorce a few years later, she became a professional dancer and made a 1954 tour of Europe and Africa in *Porgy and Bess*.

Angelou was active in the Civil Rights Movement, and from 1960 to 1961 she served as the Northern coordinator for the Southern Christian Leadership Conference (SCLC). In 1961 she moved to Africa with Vusumzi Make, a South African freedom fighter. She spent the next five years in Egypt and Ghana, working as a journalist and a university professor.

After her return to the United States, Angelou joined the Harlem Writers Guild. James Baldwin's editor at Random House was impressed by her poetry and her life story and asked her to consider writing an autobiography. The result was *I Know Why the Caged Bird Sings*, which was published in 1970 and became a best-seller.

In 1971 Angelou's first published book of poetry, *Just Give Me a Cool Drink of Water 'fore I Diiie*, was nominated for a Pulitzer Prize. Since then she has published five other volumes of poetry. The other volumes of her prose autobiography are *Gather Together in My Name* (1974), *Singin' and Swingin' and Gettin' Merry Like Christmas* (1976), *The Heart of a Woman* (1981), and *All God's Children Need Traveling Shoes* (1986). In 1993 she published a collection of essays, *Wouldn't Take Nothing for My Journey Now*, and *On the Pulse of Morning*, the poem she read at President Bill Clinton's 1993 inauguration.

Angelou has had a distinguished career in film and television as well. In 1971 her *Georgia, Georgia* was the first movie screenplay by a black woman to be produced. She was nominated for a Tony Award in 1973 for her performance in *Look Away* and for an Emmy Award in 1977 for her performance in *Roots*. She has received numerous honorary degrees and was named Reynolds Professor of American Studies at Wake Forest University in Winston-Salem, North Carolina.

Throughout her diverse career, Angelou has often broken new ground. In her words, "Humility says that there were people before me who found the path. I'm a road builder. For those who have yet to come, I seem to be finding the path and they will be road builders. That keeps one humble. Love keeps one humble." Yet despite her humility, Maya Angelou's determined road building and her willingness to share herself in her work have earned her widespread admiration, respect, and love.

Lisa Clayton Robinson

See Also

South Africa; Baldwin, James; Literature, African American; San Francisco and Oakland, California; Southern Christian Leadership Conference; Television and African Americans; Film, Blacks in American.

Africa

Anglo-Egyptian Sudan. Former name of Sudan, Republic of the.

See Also

Sudan.

Africa

Angola, a country on the southwest coast of Africa.

Few African countries have seen their natural and human potential as underutilized and thoroughly ravaged by violence as Angola. In precolonial southern Africa the area was home to some of the continent's richest kingdoms, which welcomed European merchants and missionaries in the fifteenth century, only to be corrupted and ultimately destroyed by the transatlantic slave trade in the sixteenth century. The abolition of the trade – a politically and economically destabilizing event – was followed by the repressive taxation and forced labor regimes of Portuguese colonialism. Although much of the rest of the continent underwent rapid decolonization in the 1960s, the armed struggle for independence in Angola took nearly 15 years and perpetuated internal divisions that turned into a two-decade-long civil war fed by cold war superpower rivalries. Only recently has fighting ceased. Although Angola's vast natural resources hold great promise, immense obstacles to development remain, particularly landmines and a shattered infrastructure.

Precolonial Kingdoms and the Slave Trade

Small groups of hunter-gatherer Khoikhoi people were the first to inhabit the region of present-day Angola, but late in the first millennium Bantu-speaking people migrated to the area from the north, pushing some Khoikhoi farther south and incorporating others. The Bantu speakers brought with them iron-smelting skills, agricultural practices, and cattle, all of which they used to establish some of the largest and most centralized kingdoms in Central Africa. In the mid-thirteenth or fourteenth century, Kongo kings organized the mostly matrilineal agricultural settlements surrounding the mouth of the Congo River into provinces, collected taxes, and established an official currency of shells. South of the Kongo, in the early sixteenth century, the centralized Ndongo controlled the trade in salt and iron. Later in the century the Lunda formed a kingdom in the grasslands of the upper Kasai River.

Iron work, weaving, and extensive trade took place in these and other inland kingdoms, especially the Matamba and Kasanje to the east, the Bié, Bailundu, and Ciyanda on the eastern plateau, and the Kwanhama in the south. Most of the kings held divine powers. The coastal kingdoms tended to be centralized and agricultural, capturing slaves and extracting people and natural resources, including ivory and gold, from the interior. The interior kingdoms, by contrast, were less centralized and more heterogeneous, and supported themselves through hunting and fishing. Over time, patterns of migration among the kingdoms produced the major ethnolinguistic groups of Angola, including the Bakongo, Mbundu, and Ovimbundu, as well as smaller groups such as the Nganguela, Lunda-Chokwe, Herero, Nyaneka-Humbe, and Ambo.

Portuguese explorer Diogo Cão, the first European to visit the region, sailed into the mouth of the Congo River in 1483. Portuguese missionaries soon followed and some kingdoms, including the Kongo, adopted Catholicism as the official religion. Initially the Portuguese maintained peaceful relations with the Kongo, trading goods with such leaders as King Alfonso in exchange for slaves. But as they moved farther south into the Ndongo kingdom, Portuguese slave traders became more intrusive and violent, while Africans, such as Queen Nzinga, resisted. When they began to meet resistance from the Bakongo, many of whom considered the trade contradictory to Christianity, the Portuguese monarchy sent troops to Angola.

During the first major military campaign (1574-1594), conquistadors established forts and a system of vassalage, setting a pattern that would be replicated throughout the region. The Portuguese recognized African chiefs, or *sobas*, in exchange for their subservience. In their effort to move into the interior of Angola, the Portuguese found tropical diseases, African hostility, and land that was unsuitable for agriculture. It was not until the middle of the seventeenth century that the major coastal kingdoms had been subjugated. Portuguese officials taxed the African kings in the use of porters and ivory, but predominantly for slaves.

Slavery and a local trade in slaves existed in some form in most of Angola's kingdoms. The transatlantic slave trade, however, was unsurpassed in scale and impact. It is estimated that between the late sixteenth century and 1836, when Portugal officially abolished slave trafficking, over 4 million people from the region were captured and sent across the Atlantic, though only about 3.5 million made it to the New World. As many as 2 million slaves were shipped to Brazil, and the rest went to plantations in the Caribbean. Slave-trading agents, or *pombeiros* – some Portuguese, most African or Afro-Portuguese *mestiços* – bought slaves from local chiefs in exchange for cloth, guns, and other European goods.

Although the slave trade made some chiefs enormously wealthy, it ultimately undermined local economies and political stability as villages' vital labor forces were

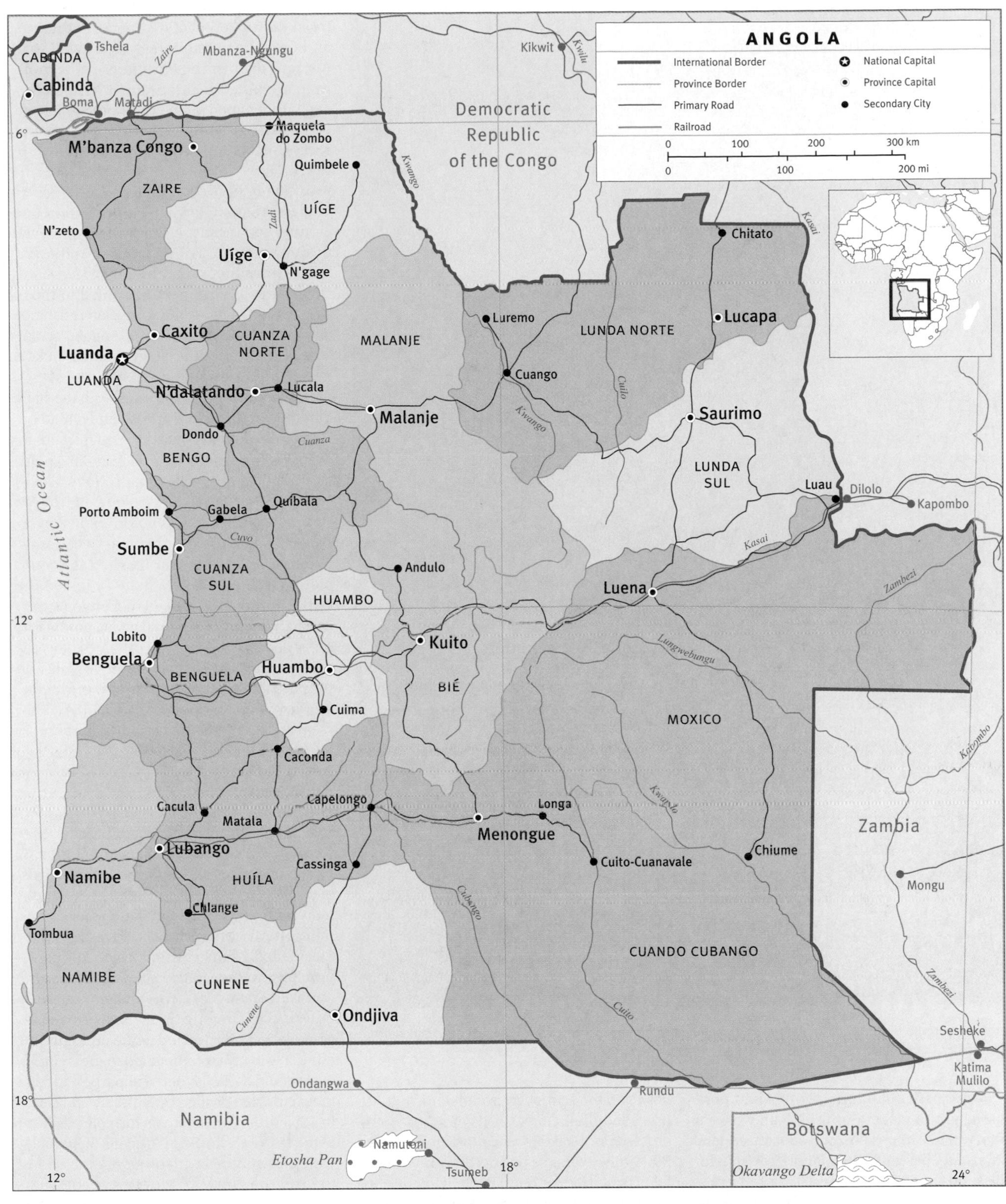

shipped overseas and slave raids and civil wars became commonplace. Demand for slaves was slowed, but not stopped, by the official ban on the trade. The transatlantic trade had made slavery an integral part of the economy and social structure in Angola that continued after Portugal abolished slavery there in 1858, as Portuguese settlers sustained labor laws that forced Africans to work on agricultural estates.

Portuguese Settlers and the "Overseas Province"

After the slave trade officially ended, Portugal sought other means to exact revenue and labor from Angola. In addition to raising port customs and imposing a higher hut tax, beginning in the 1830s Portugal launched a military expansion into the Angolan interior. But these costly campaigns met opposition from both Africans and other European powers, especially the British and Afrikaners. Eventually the Portuguese retreated to their coastal settlements at Luanda and Benguela, where they mixed with the local African population, creating a class of mestiços. Although there was little racial segregation, whites clearly dominated the social and economic hierarchy, despite the fact that many of these Portuguese emigrants were social outcasts, deserters, and criminals.

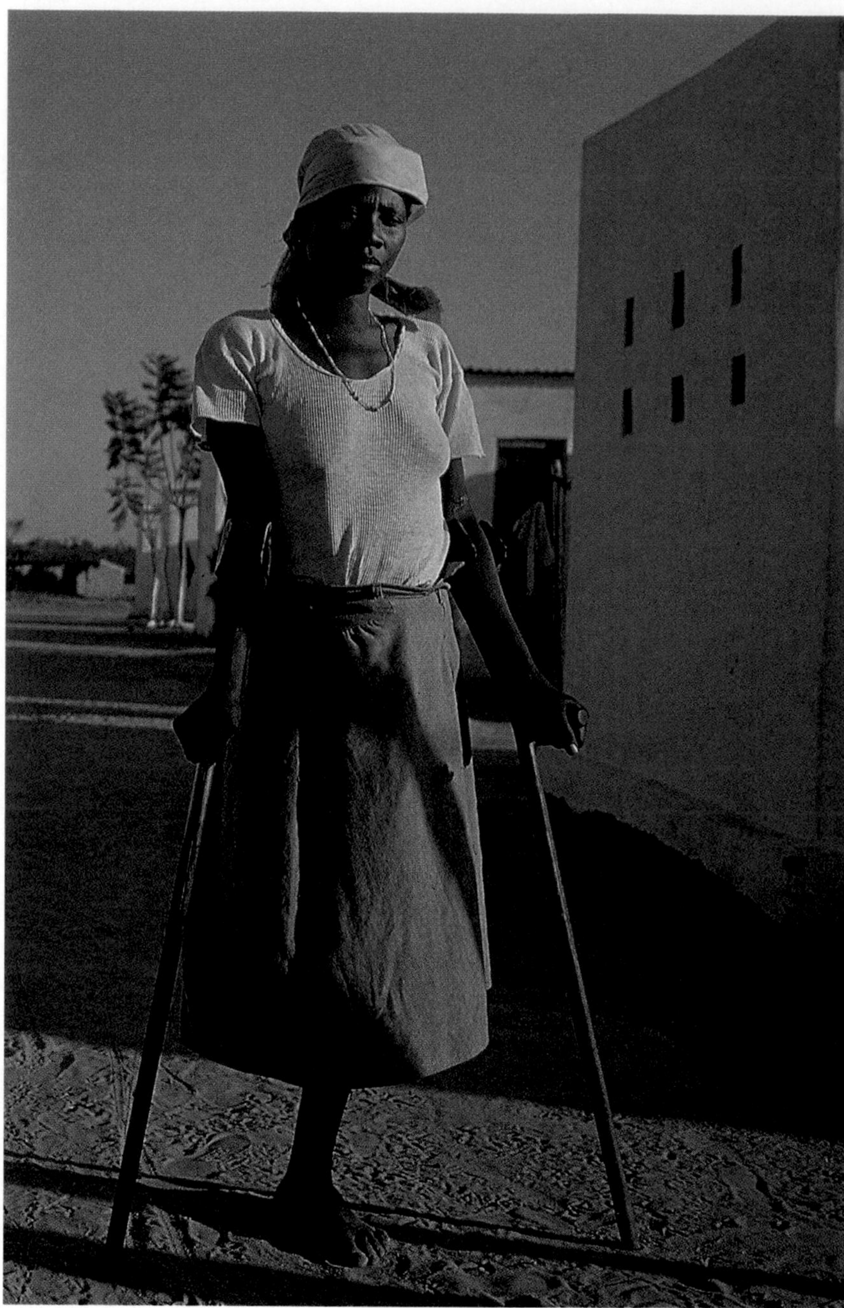

According to the United Nations, Angola has among the highest percentage of amputees in the world, the result of landmines used in the country's long and bitter civil war. *CORBIS/Baci*

Portuguese plantation owners had perennial problems retaining African workers, even with the imposition of labor conscription laws. Laws passed in 1878 and 1899 upheld the status of *liberto*, or freed slave, but introduced vagrancy laws that enabled Portuguese officials to force Africans to work on government projects and plantations in need of labor. Despite a growth in agriculture production – particularly coffee, SUGAR, and rubber – that generated significant revenue, the economy of Angola stagnated as a result of a lack of capital to develop the infrastructure. For most Africans, the *sertanejo*, or trader, was the most visible evidence of the Portuguese presence. In the latter half of the nineteenth century, however, the European expansionism that preceded the BERLIN CONFERENCE OF 1884-1885 led Portugal to occupy more of Angola. Portuguese soldiers and settlers, unsuccessful in acquiring the Shire River highlands (in present-day MALAWI) and the south bank of the Congo River, did retain Cabinda, a small enclave on the north bank of the river. At the turn of the century Portugal occupied one-tenth of the land that today comprises Angola.

Throughout the nineteenth century and until the military campaigns ended in 1930, many sectors of Angolan society resisted domination by the Portuguese monarchy. Kings, especially the well-educated leaders of the Kongo, invoked historical treaties to resist Portuguese dictates, and Protestant and Catholic missionaries often sided with Africans against the Portuguese governor-general in Angola. European settlers, soldiers, and businessmen periodically took advantage of the weak government in Lisbon to attempt secession from Portugal or unification with Brazil. Other vocal critics of Portuguese rule included *assimilados*, those Africans who had assimilated Portuguese education and culture, and mestiços, many of whom held positions in the civil service and military.

The introduction of the *Estado Novo*, or New State, to Portugal in 1926 led to the suppression of indigenous Angolan resistance and the institutionalization of Angola's social stratification. New legislation made assimilado a legal rather than social status and suppressed many rights of Africans, with the claim that they were not "advanced" and had to be "civilized" through education and religion. In 1950 31,000 out of 4 million Angolans held assimilado status. The Estado Novo also changed the status of Angola itself from a "colony" to an even less autonomous "overseas province." The "province's" economy boomed after World War II, when the completion of the Benguela Railway linked the fertile, mineral-rich Belgian Congo to the coast. Diamond mining and coffee production expanded rapidly, and the Portuguese government encouraged emigration to Angola and the purchase of land. But this new prosperity was fragile, dependent on a cheap and increasingly volatile African labor force.

African Nationalism and the War for Independence

The postwar era saw an explosion of nationalist political activity. Although heavily censored by colonial authorities, more than 60 parties and associations formed in the 1940s and 1950s to protest Portuguese policies, representing the old assimilado associations, militant Africans, ethnic separatists, and Europeans. Many cultural associations, prophets, and separatist religious groups also opposed Portuguese colonialism, but little unity existed among them. Resentment of assimilation policies and white immigration, especially in urban centers, led to the creation of several nationalist political parties, though they remained divided by ethnicity and class. In 1953 urban intellectuals formed the Party of the United Struggle of Africans of Angola, which later joined with other organizations to form the POPULAR MOVEMENT FOR THE LIBERATION OF ANGOLA, or MPLA, under the leadership of AGOSTINHO NETO. Meanwhile, Bakongo nationalists formed the Union of Angolan People, or UPA, which later became the National Front for the Liberation of Angola, or FNLA.

In 1961 rebellions in the north were joined by MPLA actions in Luanda. Colonial policemen crushed the rebellions, massacring thousands of civilians; in response, UPA insurgents in the north massacred settlers and mestiços. These atrocities roused the opposition groups but did not unite them. Throughout the early and mid-1960s, the FNLA and MPLA disagreed over ideology, strategy, and leadership. Because both movements faced overwhelming Portuguese military superiority, each concentrated on building their fighting forces in camps in neighboring countries. Instability in the Congo reinvigorated the war as the superpowers competed for influence in the region while the Eastern Bloc supported the Mbundu-dominated and socialist-leaning MPLA. The West backed the Bakongo-dominated and populist FNLA. China, and then the United States and South Africa, supported the Ovimbundu-dominated NATIONAL UNION FOR THE TOTAL INDEPENDENCE OF ANGOLA (UNITA), a breakaway faction led by Jonas Savimbi that professed little coherent ideology.

The war for independence continued until 1975. It became increasingly conventional as the militaries grew, but the nationalist groups fought each other as much as they did the Portuguese, while the civilian population suffered. Ultimately it was the effort of simultaneously fighting three insurgency wars – in MOZAMBIQUE and GUINEA-BISSAU as well as in Angola – that sapped the strength of the Portuguese military and helped precipitate the overthrow of the Caetano government in Lisbon in April 1974. A month before Angolan independence, SOUTH AFRICA invaded on the pretext of assisting the FNLA-UNITA, and in response the MPLA received additional military aid from the Soviet Union and assistance from Cuba. This international involvement did not, however, produce a clear victor, and on November 11, 1975, Portugal ceded independence to the people of Angola. The MPLA declared victory and the MPLA leader became president, though in fact the party controlled little of the country and fighting between the factions continued.

THE CIVIL WAR AND A FRAGILE PEACE

The South African invasion, Cuban intervention, and Soviet and American assistance internationalized the Angolan conflict. The FNLA and UNITA allied to form an alternative government based in the southern town of Huambo. Although the FNLA ceased to exist in 1976, UNITA, benefiting from extensive South African military assistance as well as United States aid and a lucrative diamond smuggling industry, built a formidable fighting force of around 40,000 soldiers. For nearly two decades a civil war raged between UNITA guerrillas and the MPLA government, killing more than 1.1 million civilians, mostly in the rural areas, where over 80 percent of the population lives.

The MPLA, a Marxist-Leninist vanguard party since 1977, expanded educational opportunities and the health care system and nationalized industries deserted by Portuguese settlers and foreign corporations. But its state-owned farms and inefficient bureaucracies only made life more difficult in the countryside, where roads deteriorated and small farmers were left without access to markets or agricultural inputs. President Neto and Jose Eduardo dos Santos, who succeeded Neto in 1979, both pursued pragmatic economic policies, permitting private ownership and cooperating with Western oil companies in exploiting Angola's rich reserves off the coast of Cabinda. The enclave had become one of the largest oil-producing regions in Africa, and Cabinda separatists continue to fight the Angolan government for their independence. Much – if not all – of the $400 million annual oil revenues were spent on the war effort, as defense accounted for 40 percent of annual government expenditures.

Not until the civil war was clearly stalemated and the cold war ended were genuine international efforts made to end the fighting in Angola. In 1988 negotiations between the warring factions and their international sponsors resulted in the withdrawal of Cuban and South African troops from Angola. This slow and uneven peace process culminated in 1992 in a ceasefire, military demobilization, and elections. Refusing to participate in runoff elections, Savimbi and UNITA withdrew from the peace process, and fighting resumed. In 1994 the international community pressured Savimbi into a second peace accord that resulted in UNITA representatives as-

TOP: Angolan government troops on the front line at Luena in 1993. *CORBIS/Baci*

LEFT: A boy watches from the side of the road as the Portuguese army prepares to retreat before the granting of independence to Angola in 1975. *CORBIS/Francoise de Mulder*

TOP: Boys play across the harbor from Luanda Port in Angola. Luanda's port is one of the busiest in the world. *CORBIS/Francoise de Mulder*
ABOVE: Masks and masquerades are important elements in many African ceremonies. On the border between Angola and Zambia, three men prepare to play the roles of an old man, an old woman, and a sorcerer in an initiation ritual. *CORBIS/Charles Lenars*

suming several posts and parliamentary seats in a government of national unity. Although international sanctions on UNITA have kept them in the peace process, these sanctions have also permitted the government of Angola, now highly militarized, to become more involved in regional affairs. In 1997 the Angolan military supported LAURENT-DÉSIRÉ KABILA in the DEMOCRATIC REPUBLIC OF THE CONGO and DENIS SASSOU-NGUESSO in the Republic of the Congo, and may have backed a coup attempt in ZAMBIA.

Angola, a country ruined by war, desperately needed economic recovery in the 1990s. The country needed to rebuild its infrastructure to benefit from its rich natural resources, including gold, diamonds, timber, fish, and agricultural products. More than 100,000 active landmines hidden throughout the countryside, however, continued to impede economic development. Angola also faced the burden of rehabilitating the approximately 70,000 landmine victims.

During 1998 escalating political and military tension between the Angolan government and UNITA threatened to flare again into a full-scale civil war. In September 1998 UNITA representatives were expelled from the Angolan unity government on the grounds that UNITA had not disarmed, as required by the 1994 peace accords. UNITA troops still occupy about one-third of Angola's territory, including diamond-mining areas that provide UNITA with a steady source of income. Their alliance with Tutsi-led rebels seeking to oust President Laurent-Désiré Kabila of the Democratic Republic of the Congo prompted the Angolan government to intervene to support Kabila. Meanwhile, there was consensus building within the 14-nation Southern African Development Community (SADC) that UNITA posed a threat to regional stability and should be crushed. An SADC military operation against UNITA could turn the Angolan civil war into a broader regional conflict that would further postpone Angola's recovery from years of conflict.

Eric Young

SEE ALSO

Afrikaner; Dos Santos, José Eduardo; Khoisan; Iron in Africa; Savimbi, Jonas Malheiro; World War II and African Americans; Popular Movement for the Liberation of Angola.

Africa

Angola (Ready Reference)

Official Name: Republic of Angola
Former Name: People's Republic of Angola
Area: 1,246,700 sq km (498,680 sq mi)
Location: Southern Africa, bordering the South Atlantic Ocean, between NAMIBIA and the DEMOCRATIC REPUBLIC OF THE CONGO
Capital: Luanda (population 1.2 million [1988 estimate])
Other Major Cities: Huambo (population 203,000), Benguela (155,000), Lobito (150,000), Lubango (105,000 [1983 estimate])
Population: 10,864,512 (1998 estimate)
Population Density: 9 persons per sq km (about 23 persons per sq mi)
Population Below Age 15: 45 percent (male 2,393,009; female 2,327,186 [1997 estimate])
Population Growth Rate: 2.84 percent (1998 estimate)
Total Fertility Rate: 6.2 children born per woman (1998 estimate)
Life Expectancy at Birth: Total population: 47.86 years (male 45.6 years; female 50.23 years [1998 estimate])
Infant Mortality Rate: 132.44 deaths per 1000 live births (1998 estimate)
Literacy Rate (age 15 and over who can read and write): 42 percent (male 56 percent; female 28 percent [1998 estimate])
Education: Officially compulsory for children age 7 to 15, but the majority of the population is rural and poor. Educational reforms enacted in the 1990s have produced an increase in primary school enrollment to 1.3 million students in 1993. Angola's only university is Agostinho Neto University, founded in 1976 in Luanda.
Languages: Portuguese is the official language. More than 90 percent of the population speaks Bantu languages. The most commonly spoken include Kimbundu, Umbundu, and Kikongo.
Ethnic Groups: Ovimbundu 37 percent, Kimbundu 25 percent, Bakongo 13 percent, *mestiço* (of indigenous and European descent) 2 percent, European 1 percent, other 22 percent
Religions: Indigenous beliefs 47 percent, Roman Catholic 38 percent, Protestant 15 percent

Climate: Angola is a tropical country. It is semiarid in the south and along coast to Luanda; the north has cool, dry season (May to October) and hot, rainy season (November to April). Annual rainfall ranges from 50 mm (about 2 in) near the Namibe desert to 1500 mm (about 60 in) in the central plateau.
Land, Plants, and Animals: Angola is the seventh largest country in Africa. The majority of the land comprises meadows, pastures, forests, and woodlands. Less than 3 percent of the land is arable. The primary rivers, the Cuanza and Cunene, drain to the Atlantic Ocean. Angola has no major lakes.
Natural Resources: Petroleum, diamonds, iron ore, phosphates, copper, feldspar, gold, bauxite, uranium, manganese
Currency: The new kwanza
Gross Domestic Product (GDP): $8.2 billion (1996 estimate)
GDP per Capita: $800 (1996 estimate)
GDP Real Growth Rate: 9 percent (1996 estimate)
Primary Economic Activities: Subsistence agriculture provides the main livelihood for 80 to 90 percent of the population but accounts for less than 15 percent of the GDP. Oil production and the supporting activities are vital to the economy, contributing about 50 percent to the GDP.
Primary Crops: Coffee, cassava, bananas, sugar cane, sisal, corn, cotton, manioc (tapioca), tobacco
Industries: Mining of petroleum, diamonds, iron ore, phosphates, feldspar, bauxite, uranium, gold; fish processing; food processing; brewing; tobacco processing; sugar; textiles; cement; basic metal products
Primary Exports: Oil, diamonds, refined petroleum products, gas, coffee, sisal, fish and fish products, timber, cotton
Primary Imports: Capital equipment (machinery and electrical equipment), food, vehicles and spare parts, textiles and clothing, medicines, substantial military deliveries
Primary Trade Partners: United States, European Union (Portugal especially), Brazil
Government: Angola currently has a transitional government and is nominally a multiparty democracy with a strong presidential system. Universal suffrage begins at age 18. The legislative branch is unicameral, and the National Assembly (Assembleia Nacional) seats 223. The president appoints the judges of the Supreme Court (Tribunal da Relação) and the Council of Ministers. Major political parties include the Popular Movement for the Liberation of Angola (MPLA) and the National Union for the Total Independence of Angola (UNITA). National independence was achieved on November 11, 1975 (from Portugal). President Jose Eduardo Dos Santos (since September 21, 1979) was originally elected without opposition under a one-party system and stood for election in Angola's first multiparty elections on September 29-30, 1992. He received 49.6 percent of the total vote, making a runoff election necessary between him and second-place Jonas Savimbi; the runoff was not held and Savimbi's UNITA party disputed the results of the first election; the civil war was resumed. As of mid-1998, a fragile ceasefire prevailed.

Alonford James Robinson, Jr.

SEE ALSO

Dos Santos, José Eduardo; Gold Trade; Luanda, Angola; Savimbi, Jonas Malheiro.

Latin America and the Caribbean

Anguilla, a British dependent territory located in the Caribbean at the northern end of the Leeward Islands.

Anguillan tradition holds that Christopher Columbus himself named the narrow island Anguilla – which is Spanish for "eel" – during one of his early trips to the Caribbean at the end of the fifteenth century. But many historians now believe that it was probably French explorers, passing the island en route from DOMINICA to Florida in the middle of the sixteenth century, who established the first European contact with it. Whenever Europeans may have reached Anguilla, its indigenous Amerindian population had probably lived there since at least 1300 B.C.E. By the time Columbus first reached the Caribbean in 1492, substantial communities of Arawak Indians were living across Anguilla, which they called Malliouhana. But within decades of the first European settlement of Anguilla, the island's entire Amerindian population had all but disappeared, victims of both enslavement and European diseases.

English colonists established the first settlement in 1650. Despite attempted attacks by the French, the Irish, and Carib Amerindians from nearby Dominica, Anguilla was one of the only Caribbean islands that remained under the control of a single power throughout the colonial period. The British used Anguilla in the same manner in which they exploited holdings throughout the Caribbean: planters quickly established estates, which were worked by slaves from West Africa. Since it was a small island, with less fertile soil than some nearby islands, Anguilla did not develop the same large-scale plantation economy that many of its neighbors established. Instead it became a small-scale slave society, and most contemporary Anguillans are descendants of those first slaves.

The "jollification," an important ritual in one contemporary cultural festival, represents Anguillans' slave roots. In the annual February tradition, men and women, dressed in field workers' clothing, proceed along a public route, then gather to plant a field. As they sing traditional Afro-Caribbean songs and spirituals, they commemorate the communal harvest gatherings and celebrations that began on the plantations. Even after the abolition of slavery in all British territories in 1834, most of Anguilla's black majority continued to work in agriculture or fishing, although salt mining eventually emerged as another common occupation.

Because Anguilla's population was small, Great Britain decided in the early 1800s to administer it jointly with St. Kitts, instead of continuing a separate Anguillan government. In 1871 Anguilla, St. Kitts, and Nevis were officially made a single colony, an artificial political union that would last almost a hundred years. For much of this time most Anguillans felt that they had very little political representation at all – the government of the three islands was controlled exclusively by white planters and British appointees, and it was located in St. Kitts, at a distance of 113 km (70 mi). It was not until the middle of the twentieth century, after a series of labor riots and protests had swept the Commonwealth Caribbean, that Great Britain began gradually to introduce universal adult suffrage in the islands. When Anguilla's black majority finally gained the vote, they decided that separate administration from the one in St. Kitts – which they felt too often ignored their tiny island's interests – was a political priority.

In the 1960s Robert Webster emerged as the leader of Anguilla's first political party, the People's Progressive Party (PPP), and a leader in the fight for Anguillan separation from St. Kitts and Nevis. Ironically, these conflicts arose just as St. Kitts and Nevis were fighting for independence from Great Britain, but Anguillans were convinced that it was better for them to become a separate dependent British territory than to become part of an independent country that included St. Kitts and Nevis. When St. Kitts-Nevis-Anguilla was granted associated statehood within the United Kingdom in 1967, the first step toward independence, Webster and the PPP led an Anguillan rebellion. In a famously ironic confrontation, British forces invaded Anguilla in 1969 to end the rebellion, only to find Anguillans embracing them with open arms, since continued affiliation with Great Britain was their main goal.

In 1971 Anguilla was returned to Crown colony status within Great Britain, as its citizens wished. A new constitution adopted in 1976 placed most of the island's affairs in the hands of the elected ministers and assembly, and political issues on the island have since been much more subdued. Today, Anguilla is slowly developing a reputation as a tourist destination, but the government is making efforts to ensure that the island remains underdeveloped to retain most of its natural beauty. The traditional Caribbean Carnival, popular boat races, and the Anguilla Cultural Festival are just a few of the shared celebrations that Anguillans take part in throughout the year. In the words of one locally published history of the island, Anguillans regard themselves as contentedly holding on to their own piece of "English heaven."

Lisa Clayton Robinson

See Also
St. Kitts and Nevis; Abolition and Emancipation in Latin America and the Caribbean; Carnivals in Latin America and the Caribbean.

Africa

Annan, Kofi (b. April 8, 1938, Kumasi, Gold Coast [present-day Ghana]), secretary general of the United Nations (UN).

The first person from sub-Saharan Africa to head the United Nations, Kofi Annan is also the first secretary general to have risen through the ranks of that organization. A lifelong diplomat, Annan assumed the UN's top post in January 1997 to serve a term ending December 31, 2001. Annan impressed the international diplomatic community while serving as undersecretary general for peacekeeping, a job in which he coordinated efforts to help such tortured areas as Rwanda, Somalia, and the former Yugoslavia. He began his term as secretary general under pressure to reform the large and economically troubled UN bureaucracy. Following his appointment, Annan pledged to improve the effectiveness of UN programs in poor countries, saying, "Economic development is not merely a matter of projects and statistics. It is, above all, a matter of people – real people with basic needs: food, clothing, shelter, and medical care."

Annan was born into one of Ghana's most prominent families. His father was both a hereditary chief of the Fante people and a high-ranking civil servant. Annan took advantage of the educational opportunities presented to him. After studying science and technology in Ghana, in 1959 he traveled to the United States to study at Macalester College in St. Paul, Minnesota. "It was an exciting period," says Annan. Two years earlier, Ghana had claimed its independence, and in America the Civil Rights Movement was gaining momentum. He graduated from Macalester in 1961 with a degree in economics, saying that his American years had taught him that "you [should] never walk into a situation and believe that you know better than the natives."

It was a lesson Annan would apply often during his diplomatic career. After graduate studies in economics in Geneva, Switzerland, Annan took his first UN job at the World Health Organization (WHO). After more than a decade of diplomatic work, he took a break to serve from 1974 to 1976 as director of the Ghana Tourist Development Company (*see* Tourism in Africa). Four years later, he received his first high-level UN post, as deputy director of administration and head of personnel at the office of the UN high commissioner for refugees. He worked there until 1983, when he became director of budget in the office of financial services. By 1990 he had risen to the office of assistant secretary general for program planning, budget, and finance.

In 1997 Kofi Annan became the first person from sub-Saharan Africa to serve as secretary general of the United Nations. *CORBIS/AFP*

Annan's 1993 appointment to the head of peacekeeping operations made him one of the UN's most visible and potentially controversial leaders. UN peacekeeping missions in Somalia and the former Yugoslavia had recently provoked widespread criticism and raised doubts about the agency's future. According to an American official quoted in the *New York Times*, Annan was "the only top official of the UN who came out of the Bosnia experience with dignity and without having harmed the organization or relations with any one of the great powers. That's what a great diplomat's about." He gained an international reputation not only for shrewd diplomacy but also for his candor and personal charm. When the United States publicly campaigned against a second term for then-secretary general Boutros Boutros-Ghali, it was Annan to whom the UN turned.

Given that Annan was expected to scale down the UN administration while simultaneously making it more responsive to member nations, it is not surprising that he has faced criticism in the early years of his secretariat. In particular, his preference for coalition-building and compromise over quick decision-making irritated some in the United States government, whose support – and repayment of its massive UN debt – is seen by many as crucial for Annan's success. At the same time, other member nations accused Annan of currying favor with America, to which he replied that he would "devote the same attention to any country that pays 25 percent of the dues and owes $1.3 billion." Annan silenced many of his critics, however, by his successful resolution of the first major diplomatic test of his leadership. In February 1998 his negotiations with Iraqi president Saddam Hussein averted what looked like a very likely war, further burnishing Annan's reputation as a devoted peacemaker.

Annan, whose first marriage ended in divorce, lives in the secretary general's residence in New York City with his wife, Nane Annan, a Swedish lawyer-turned-artist. The couple have three children from previous marriages.

Kate Tuttle

See Also
Ghana; United Nations in Africa.

Africa

Antaisaka (also known as the Taisaka and the Tesaki), ethnic group of Madagascar.

The Antaisaka primarily inhabit southeastern Madagascar, around the city of Farafangana. They speak a Malayo-Polynesian language and belong to the Malagasy cultural and linguistic group. Approximately 650,000 people consider themselves Antaisaka.

See Also
Madagascar, Ethnicity in; Languages, African: An Overview.

Africa

Antananarivo, Madagascar, the capital of Madagascar.

Antananarivo is located in the central highland province of the same name. The city is inhabited by approximately 1 million people, and while the province is dominated by the Merina, the largest ethnic group, Antananarivo, popularly referred to as Tana, is ethnically diverse.

Antananarivo was founded in the seventeenth century by the Merina king Andrianjaka. Originally named Analamànga (the "Blue Forest"), the high plateau site was selected for its defensive character and proximity to nearby wetlands, where rice could be cultivated. The settlement quickly grew into the largest city in the Merina territory.

In a campaign to consolidate Merina fiefdoms, Andrianampoinimerina, the king of nearby Ambohimanga, took control of Antananarivo in 1794, overthrowing his uncle after several previous attempts. As the Merina empire grew under the tenure of Andrianampoinimerina's son Radama, so did the city, becoming the capital of Imerina (the territory of the Merina people). An estimated 15,000 people inhabited the city by the close of the eighteenth century.

When the French colonized Madagascar in 1895, they named the city Tananarive. By this time the city's population had grown to between 50,000 and 75,000, the majority of whom were slaves. European influence can be found in the urban architecture, particularly the many two-story brick buildings. The city gained a reputation in Europe for its exquisite beauty.

Today 10 percent of the country's entire population inhabits the capital, which spans a dozen steep hills, crowned by the Rova, the royal palace. The city is larger than the population of the five province capitals combined, and continual urban migration only amplifies the domination of Antananarivo.

Although Madagascar remains a predominantly agrarian society, the country's main industries, which constitute 13.8 percent of the country's GDP and employ about 3 percent of the work force, are centered in Antananarivo. These include food and tobacco processing, brewing, soap production, and textile and leather manufacturing. Economic stagnation has hit residents of Antananarivo particularly hard, since they are more dependent on market forces than are subsistence farmers in rural areas. The number of jobs has declined while the number of job-seekers has risen. Austerity measures introduced as part of a structural adjustment program have also caused a significant decline in the standard of living for urban dwellers, increasing inflation and taxes while eliminating subsidies.

Ari Nave

See Also
Structural Adjustment in Africa.

Africa

Antandroy (also known as the Tandroy or Tandruy), ethnic group of Madagascar.

The Antandroy primarily inhabit southern Madagascar between the Mandrare and Menara Rivers. They speak a Malayo-Polynesian language and belong to the larger Malagasy cultural and linguistic group. Approximately 600,000 people consider themselves to be Antandroy, over half of them members of the Antanosy sub-group.

See Also
Languages, African: An Overview.

Africa

Antelope, common name applied to a large group of hollow-horned ruminants belonging to the same family as cattle, goats, and sheep.

The group comprises about 150 species, most of which are found in Africa and the remainder in Asia. Antelope range in size from the tiny royal antelope, which stands about 25 cm (about 10 in) high at the shoulder, to the eland, sometimes about 1.8 m (about 5.9 ft) in height and weighing up to about 680 kg (about 1500 lb). The corkscrew horns of the kudu, a large African antelope grow to about 1.5 m (about 5 ft) in length. Unlike the deer, which they resemble in body and in habits, antelope have unbranched, hollow horns that are never shed. Antelope are generally swift, and some species are the fastest of the quadrupeds, attaining speeds of 97 km/hr (60 mph). Antelope are often brilliantly colored and may live in open plains, marshes, deserts, or forests, according to the species. Some are solitary, but many species travel in herds.

Scientific classification: Antelope belong to the family Bovidae.

North America

Antelope Case, 1825 U.S. Supreme Court case that recognized the international trade in slaves.

On June 29, 1820, a United States Treasury cutter captured the Spanish vessel the *Antelope* off the coast of northern Florida, bringing it to port in Savannah, Georgia. Over 280 Africans were discovered chained in the ship's hold. The U.S. district attorney for Georgia argued that the captives were free under the 1807 legislation prohibiting the slave trade. Spanish and Portuguese slave traders claimed the Africans as property captured by pirates.

The case went to the Supreme Court, where an 1825 decision by Chief Justice John Marshall weakened the antislave trading laws. The court determined that the slave trade was recognized by international law and that the property rights of foreign nationals holding slaves were thus protected. Of the Africans still alive on the *Antelope*, 120 were sent to Liberia and 39 remained enslaved.

Marian Aguiar

See Also
Transatlantic Slave Trade.

Africa

Anthropology in Africa

Early Days

What was known about Africa before there were serious academic studies was sparse and variable in credibility. Anthropology, as a formal academic subject, was a late-nineteenth-century Anglo-Euro-American academic invention. It began as the comparative study of little-known non-Western societies, but very soon broadened into the study of all human societies. After some tentative starts, by the 1920s Africa had become a major area of serious research. Colonial administration made access easy, and the objective of achieving a greater understanding of the peoples of Africa attracted scholars, missionaries, and officials alike.

Inevitably, the first project was to identify who the peoples of Africa were, where they were situated geographically, and what their way of life might be. The task of information gathering was daunting. Hundreds of languages and dialects were spoken by as many groups of people, each of which identified itself as having a distinct history and culture. There also were numerous communities where a plurality of peoples were intermixed. Since there was no indigenous African form of writing, the absence of written records made recovering local history very difficult. The contemporary picture was obviously complex, and the past remained to be reconstructed.

Fieldwork: The Anthropological Method of Research

From the 1920s on, social anthropology became committed to the method of research that has characterized it ever since. Information is collected through fieldwork, the close study of a group of people and the context of their lives through firsthand contact. From the 1930s into the 1950s and beyond, British social anthropologists were dominant in African studies. They produced the major ethnographic and comparative work during that era. They approached this work with a basic theoretical presupposition. They assumed that there was an underlying coherent logic in the customs and ideas of each African society, in their sociocultural structure. The anthropologist's job, as they saw it, was to figure out what that logic was and explain it. No doubt, the British colonial policy of indirect rule, the policy of governing through indigenous institutions, stimulated an emphasis on political structure, but it could scarcely account for the passionate broader interest anthropologists had in everything from kinship to ritual.

The fieldwork standard of these British anthropologists was set by Bronislaw Malinowski, who became a prominent teacher in the field. He showed that the method of study he developed while living in a Trobriand village (in the Pacific) for two years could be applied anywhere. His detailed picture of everyday life in the Trobriands also carried a theoretical message. The thesis, which he called functionalism, argued that preindustrial society was in all its facets – economy, religion, kinship, politics, and law – a single integrated system in which every element of cultural practice had a function that complemented and reinforced the others.

Many Africanists attended Malinowski's seminars at the London School of Economics and were deeply influenced by him, including Jomo Kenyatta, later to become president of Kenya. Malinowski wrote the introduction to Kenyatta's ethnography of the Kikuyu, *Facing Mount Kenya* (1938). Many Africans studied in England in that period, and their presence enhanced the interest in Africanist anthropology. Major monographs resulted. These provided a high level of detailed description about local affairs.

As anthropologists collected information on more and more particular peoples, they realized that there was a bewildering range of variation among them in kinship organization, in other features of culture, in economy, and in politics. There were sophisticated kingdoms and rulerless nomadic groups. There were herders and agriculturalists. As the monographs accumulated, the possibility of broad comparative analysis opened. The need to classify became an imperative of the field, to make order in the aggregation of diverse information culled from fieldwork, and to understand the logic of similarities and differences.

The Comparison of Reconstructed "Traditional" Systems

One of the first anthropological classifiers of African societies was an American, Melville Herskovits, who was ultimately to become the doyen of African studies in the United States. He founded a center for African studies at Northwestern University, and in 1957 was one of the founders of the African Studies Association in the United States. In 1938 he published a history of the kingdom of Dahomey. But more than a decade before that, in his dissertation (1926), he applied to Africa a mode of classification that had been used by Clark Wissler to map the cultures of the indigenous peoples of the Americas, namely the "culture area." Herskovits divided Africa into six areas, classifying them into two categories: the dominantly pastoral and the dominantly agricultural.

Although this simplification omitted important matters, it was a significant step forward. Firmly grounded on known economic criteria, it was a departure from nineteenth-century tendencies to classify societies in terms of some unsteady yardstick of evolutionary advancement, or later efforts to explain the differences and similarities among societies in terms of geographical diffusion of cultural traits by conjecturing where particular cultural ideas and practices originated and where they spread.

From its outset the French research method and criteria of classification were very different from the British and American methods. Marcel Griaule, the leading French Africanist of the 1930s, based his categories on the different "modes of thought" of different peoples. He worked in West Africa among the Dogon people in what is now Mali, and studied their "modes of thought" through the information given him by a learned Dogon who explicated local philosophical precepts, myths, and rituals in elaborate detail. This use of a single informant who was interrogated largely about philosophical and symbolic matters was very different from the direct observation of daily life.

Generalizing very broadly from the Dogon material, and making a few comparisons, Griaule expanded his ideas to the point where he constructed his own version of "the African," a generic personage having a philosophical outlook distinct from the Christian European but who was his philosophical equal. On the basis of very limited comparative data regarding distributions of symbols, myths and rituals, technologies and aesthetics, he constructed a geographical typology of three variants, characterized by three African epistemological fields, three forms of knowledge.

Parallel in time to Herskovits and Griaule, with their work extending over several decades, was the group of British social anthropologists alluded to earlier. They worked in an entirely different manner, living among the people, observing and discussing mundane life, in all its facets, as it unfolded from day to day. They assembled very careful and vivid descriptions of work, of politics, of kinship and ritual, and of the life cycle of individuals and groups. On their return from Africa, they often met at seminars and symposia, heard each other's papers, read each other's books, and compared their approaches and findings.

This ready-made audience enriched the whole enterprise, so that by the time Malinowski left the scene and was replaced as a theoretical leader in 1937 by A. R. Radcliffe-Brown, at Oxford, their intellectual circle was well established. Radcliffe-Brown had also not worked in Africa, but rather in Australia. His principal contribution to African studies was to produce an elaborated theoretical framework, structural functionalism, that went beyond Malinowski's simple, functional notions of institutional and societal coherence.

Radcliffe-Brown posed specific questions about the way in which particular practices were related to each other, customs which on first sight did not seem at all connected. He wanted to turn anthropology into a general science of social laws. To do any such thing, even to approach such an ambition, he needed detailed ethnographies he could compare. At that time, the Africanists were able to supply the information required by such an approach. Under his aegis a major comparative volume was edited by E. E. Evans-Pritchard and Meyer Fortes called *African Political Systems* (1940). It classified the political systems of Africa into two kinds, polities with a centralized form of rule and "headless systems." In the acephalous systems the political order depended on the competitions and balances between groups, between segmentary lineages, not on the rule of chiefs or kings. This was a major step toward understanding how different types of political structures worked, and that the same patterns of political structure could appear in very different cultural milieus that had no connection with one another. Another major contribution was *African Systems of Kinship and Marriage*, published in 1950, edited by Radcliffe-Brown and Daryll Forde. In that volume Radcliffe-Brown tried to produce general laws regarding the logic of kinship nomenclatures (terms for relatives) and practices. Needless to say, there have been subsequent critiques and refinements of many of the contentions in these volumes, but these were the ones that broke the ground.

In all of these early theoretical works, the units of comparison were indigenous systems, whole societies and the way they functioned. Comparisons were made, typologies were developed. The theorizing was about the way these societies operated in the precolonial period, a reconstruction of the past that edited out colonial changes. The colonial period was not theoretically interesting at that stage. Only the great variety of reconstructed but putatively authentic and "pure" African cultures were useful for the kind of theorizing that was done at the time.

The Changing Anthropology of a Changing Africa

"Traditional" African systems – the way they "must have been" in precolonial times – were reconstructions from observed evidence. But this kind of holistic, tradition-oriented structural functional anthropology was carried on at the same time as anthropologists were actually seeing and experiencing an Africa that was deeply affected by colonial rule, and was changing rapidly. Anthropologists not only took note of this, they wrote about it. Thus, parallel to the academic concern with reconstructed past structures, there was a strong practical interest in what was going on in Africa at the time. The same anthropologists who wrote monographs about the "traditional" reported on current matters in very different papers and books. They wrote on rural economies and the effects of cash cropping. They wrote on labor migration. They were interested in the changes in political organization and law effectuated by the colonial authorities. At first, these matters were not treated as a serious object of theorizing. They were treated as reports of current history.

Thus there were two Africanist anthropologies in the British high period, one concerning the reconstructed past and all that remained of it, particularly in the countryside, and the other anthropology, which was occupied with change itself, with the new cities and the mix of migrants from many ethnic groups who peopled them. The anthropology of change included the study of the mining townships and the commercial towns and the altered countryside from which out-migration took place and into which cash cropping was installed, and to which missionaries and teachers and medical personnel and agricultural and veterinary officers sometimes came.

As long as structural functionalism prevailed, changing Africa was not the object of any theorizing subtlety in anthropology. Crude contrasts between "traditional" society and "modern" were the elements of the basic model. Africa was seen as caught between the two, neither traditional nor modern, in transition, its holistic traditions disrupted but its intimations of a coherent modernity not fully realized.

But from the mid-century on new forms of research were appearing to which the old techniques and totalizing concepts could not be applied, and gradually those were abandoned. Studies of urban situations in which Africans from many different ethnic groups were living and working next to each other did not lend themselves to the old methods. Network studies of the connections of individuals to other individuals emerged, with labor organization and neighborhood and ethnicity and kinship all in the mix. Extended case studies followed unfolding situations. Some were microhistories of conflicts, others noted changing patterns of marriage and divorce, still others the formation of ethnic ties without kinship ties underpinning them.

The change in perspective marked by these studies in Africa was of major theoretical significance to anthropology. Not only were the elements of time, history, and change incorporated into the anthropological canon but individual agency was a decisive feature of these accounts. Africa was now being treated as part of the historical time of those who were observing it.

A Topically Specialized Anthropology: Present-Awareness and the Historical Moment

Many new theoretical initiatives followed those of the mid-century. Two major influences in French anthropology had wide international influence in the 1960s and 1970s: (1) Marxist interpretations of African society, and (2) studies of systems of symbolic patterning, using the ideas of Claude Lévi-Strauss about a grammar of culture. But other themes were also focal. Thus, with the advent of independence and the primacy of the nation-building project in Africa, the political importance of ethnic pluralism became the object of anthropological study and debate. In the 1970s a rich international literature accumulated on the new religions of Africa, the indigenized and reimagined versions of world religions (*see* Islam and Tradition: An Interpretation and Christianity: Independent and Charismatic Churches in Africa). There also were studies of ethnic and class-specific religious practices, and the political meanings of these, most notably in South Africa. Studies of African elites and class differences appeared, studies of African servants, and, of course, studies of African commerce and class. Medical anthropology emerged, with its focus on indigenous theories of disease and curing. The studies of women's lives increased in number and kind. Feminist studies emerged. An interest in African law that began in the colonial period was carried forward in new dimensions, including national legal institutions, international human rights, and local "customary" practices.

It is obvious that the intellectual approaches of anthropology changed radically in the late colonial period and thereafter. This was partly a response to changes in the world, not the least in Africa itself, but partly because the questions with which anthropology became preoccupied were very different from those of earlier generations of scholars. Once differentiated only by their interests in particular geographical regions and ethnic groups, social anthropologists further divided themselves into numerous large thematic subspecialties, economic, political, semiotic-symbolic, historical, and others. Within these frameworks, specialized monographs are now written on such varied topics as economic development projects, ideas and practices relating to illness, law, human rights, music, art, agriculture, environment, land tenure, popular culture, religion, education, gender, refugees, colonial history, film, and numerous others.

Once an Anglo-Euro-American monopoly, Africanist anthropology is now completely internationalized, with professional specialists found all over the world, scattered everywhere from Japan to Africa itself. Today there are enough African anthropologists for a Pan-African Association of Anthropologists to have been established, and many African social scientists also contribute to the publications of CODESRIA, the Council for the Development of Social Science Research in Africa, whose headquarters are in Dakar.

As one of the first and one of the most active academic disciplines concerned with studying African affairs, anthropology has had much to do with dispelling the mythic notions of an Africa that did not exist except in the minds of outsiders. There remains much to learn about Africa's ever-changing present, both in its local and national forms and in its global connections. The old ethnographies are now read critically, but they remain valued for their content as close observations of a time long gone. The focus of anthropological interest has changed as Africa has changed. But the basic methodological commitment to fieldwork continues. There is no substitute for the firsthand observations of a trained researcher, and for the way he or she hears what it all means from African people themselves.

Sally Falk Moore

See Also

Art and Architecture, African; Colonial Rule; Dahomey, Early Kingdom of; Dakar, Senegal; Education in Africa; Environmental Movements in Africa; Ethnicity and Identity in Africa: An Interpretation; Languages, African: An Overview; Pastoralism; African Religions: An Interpretation; Christianity: Missionaries in Africa; Cinema, African; Human Rights in Africa.

Africa

Antiapartheid Movement, the people and organizations who fought to end apartheid in South Africa.

In 1990 the South African government reversed its long ban on organizations such as the African National Congress (ANC), the Pan-Africanist Congress (PAC), and the South African Communist Party (SACP). It also freed Nelson Mandela, the ANC leader who had been imprisoned since 1962, and began negotiations that eventually replaced white minority rule with electoral democracy and equal rights for all South Africans. As dramatic as these events were, they represented not a sudden reversal but rather the results of a long, complicated history of many individuals and groups that fought against South Africa's official policy of apartheid.

Apartheid – the name comes from the Dutch word expressing "apartness" – refers to the vast web of laws and regulations that restricted the rights and opportunities of South Africa's black majority, as well as its "nonwhite" minorities. It was imposed in the years after the National Party first came to power in South Africa in 1948. All South Africans were subjected to racial classification and designated as white, "Coloured" (people of mixed ethnic background), Asian (which included people of Indian descent), or black (people of African descent, also called native, Bantu, or – offensively – kaffir). Under apartheid, blacks were denied the right to vote, own land, or even live outside of strictly regulated rural "bantustans" or urban "locations" or townships. They were treated as second-class citizens whose inferior educational and occupational opportunities doomed them to lives of poverty and powerlessness. Asians and "coloured" South Africans faced similar, but less severe, forms of discrimination.

Although apartheid was only officially imposed in the mid-twentieth century, racial inequality had been part of South Africa's history since the arrival of Europeans nearly three centuries earlier. Africans had long fought white domination, but some of the earliest modern resistance to segregation and other racist policies came from the Indian community. Founded in 1894 by Mohandas K. Gandhi – who would later lead India to independence – the Natal Indian Congress pioneered strategies of mass demonstrations, civil disobedience, and passive resistance to arrest. These nonviolent tactics would be employed by a variety of groups in the early history of the antiapartheid movement.

The African National Congress, which would become the most powerful of these groups, was founded in 1912 as the South African Native National Congress. Initially it was fairly limited in size and scope, composed mostly of educated, bourgeois blacks intent on seeking reform through petitions and other legal channels. Its vision of a multiracial resistance movement was an important first step. The South African Communist Party, founded in 1921, eventually became a close though controversial ally of the ANC. The Communists saw segregation and later full-scale apartheid in the context of a capitalist system that exploited all workers, but black workers most of all. They sought to fight this racist system with a multiracial, class-based movement.

Black workers were excluded from trade unions during South Africa's industrial revolution at the turn of the century, but after the 1920 formation of the Industrial and Commercial Workers' Union of Africa (ICU), labor demands and actions became a central part of the resistance movement. Although the ICU itself was short-lived, black unions in the 1940s waged repeated strikes to protest labor policies that subjected African workers to the most dangerous, unhealthy, and poorly paid jobs. The African Mine Workers' Union was one of several unions that helped the antiapartheid movement grow beyond its bourgeois roots.

The 1940s were also a fertile time for the ANC, especially after the young lawyers Nelson Mandela and Oliver Tambo helped found the ANC's Youth League in 1943. The Youth League rejected the ANC's traditionally tame tactics, and instead called for strikes, demonstrations, and mass civil disobedience campaigns. By the late 1940s, membership rose to nearly 100,000 and the ANC was soon cooperating with a wide range of groups. In 1955 the Congress Alliance – consisting of the ANC, South African Indian Congress, Coloured Peoples' Congress, and the Congress of Democrats (a white organization) – drafted the Freedom Charter, which called for self-government, legal equality, human rights, and economic justice.

The postwar era was also an important time for the role of women in the fight against racial inequality. Black women had demonstrated against the hated pass laws, which required blacks to carry identification proving they had legal rights to reside and work in the city, as early as the second decade of the twentieth century. But sexual discrimination kept women in general, and black women in particular, from exerting much political power during the first half of the century. At the time of its founding, women were excluded from the ANC and relegated to the Bantu Women's League, a group that initially did little more than cater the men's meetings. Other early women's groups, such as the National Council of African Women, concerned themselves mostly with social welfare and charity work. Many of the most active women in the antiapartheid movement came out of the Communist Party or the trade unions. Communist Party members included middle-class white women such as Ruth First. During World War II increasing numbers of black women joined both the industrial work force and the labor movement. The Federation of South African Women (FSAW) was founded in 1954 by a multiracial group of women active in the Congress Alliance. Its campaigns against pass laws and in favor of racial and sexual equality attracted attention and government intimidation throughout the 1950s.

ABOVE: Randall Robinson speaks at a 1988 press conference called to announce a boycott of Shell Oil Company for its involvement in South Africa. *UPI/CORBIS-Bettmann*

LEFT: A popular figure among radical black militants of the anti-apartheid movement, Chris Hani became secretary general of the South African Communist Party in 1991. *REUTERS/CORBIS-Bettmann*

BELOW LEFT: Nelson Mandela, *center right*, sings with supporters and others of those accused during their 1956 treason trial in Johannesburg, South Africa. Mandela and the other accused were acquitted after a four-and-a-half-year trial. *Peter Magubane/AP*

During this period, the National Party government not only passed apartheid legislation, but also increasingly harassed those who opposed it. In 1956 Mandela and SACP leader Joe Slovo, along with 156 antiapartheid activists, were charged with treason; after a four-year trial they were finally acquitted. In response to the government's increasing repression, more militant antiapartheid activists formed new groups, among them the Pan-Africanist Congress, founded in 1959 by Robert Sobukwe and others. The PAC saw the fight against apartheid in terms of Black Nationalism, not class struggle, and sought to win an "Afrika for Africans." A demonstration against pass laws, sponsored by the PAC, led to a police massacre in Sharpeville in which 69 protesters were killed.

In the wake of rioting that followed Sharpeville, the South African government banned both the PAC and ANC, arrested more than 2000 activists, and declared martial law. (The Communist Party was already outlawed, and many antiapartheid leaders were already imprisoned, exiled, or banned from political activity.) The increased government repression ushered in a new era of antiapartheid activism. Rejecting the nonviolence they had embraced for so long, the ANC and SACP jointly founded Umkhonto we Sizwe ("the spear of the nation," often abbreviated as MK), an armed paramilitary wing. Overseen by exiled leaders such as Slovo and Tambo, MK carried out acts of sabotage against selected government targets such as military bases and pass offices.

As the struggle intensified in the 1960s and 1970s, new antiapartheid groups emerged, including many inspired by the Black Consciousness Movement. The South African Students' Organization (SASO), founded in 1968 by STEPHEN BIKO and others, grew out of the National Union of South African Students, a multiracial students' group. Influenced by independence movements throughout Africa, the philosophy of NÉGRITUDE, and the BLACK POWER Movement in the United States, Black Consciousness groups sought to empower black people to escape the "slave mentality" caused by centuries of oppression. The South African Students' Movement, an independent group of primary and secondary students, helped launch the school boycotts and protests that led to the 1976 uprisings in Soweto, the country's largest black township. As in Sharpeville, mostly peaceful protests led to massive police violence, ending in 575 deaths.

Divisions among antiapartheid groups had always been present: some felt apartheid was a class-based evil best fought by multiracial solidarity; others believed that it was primarily a racial matter in which blacks needed to reject the aid of concerned white liberals and forge their own victory. But after Soweto, conflicts within the antiapartheid movement multiplied. The South African government increasingly exploited political rivalries in an attempt both to weaken the opposition and to portray the urban violence as "tribal" warfare. Some groups that had initially fought apartheid, such as Gatsha Buthelezi's Inkatha movement, were accused of helping the government undermine the ANC. Murders of suspected government collaborators and informants grew common, as did violence at the increasingly frequent funerals of antiapartheid activists who were killed in police custody or under mysterious circumstances. Yet the 1983 founding of the United Democratic Front brought together some 575 different organizations, including women's and students' groups as well as less political bodies such as sports clubs, into an allied fight against apartheid.

By the early 1980s the situation in South Africa was attracting massive international attention. Antiapartheid demonstrations on college campuses and in cities around the world pressured businesses to divest their South African investments and called on governments to tighten economic sanctions against the country. Already banned from international sports competitions (*see* OLYMPICS, AFRICANS AND THE) and boycotted by most foreign entertainers, South Africa was becoming a pariah nation. In the mid-1980s President P. W. Botha instituted small reforms, but succeeded only in alienating his right-wing constituency. Soon after replacing Botha in 1989, President F. W. De Klerk released Mandela and removed the ban on major antiapartheid organizations. Long and difficult negotiations produced a transitional government, and a new constitution that dismantled apartheid. Following South Africa's first free elections in 1994, many of the leaders of the antiapartheid movement won offices in President Nelson Mandela's government.

Kate Tuttle

SEE ALSO

Cape Coloured; Indian Communities in Africa; Mandela, Nelson Rolihlahla; Sharpeville, South Africa; Soweto, South Africa; Inkatha Freedom Party; South Africa; Black Consciousness in Africa; Buthelezi, Mangosutho Gatsha; Botha, Pieter Willem; De Klerk, Frederik Willem; South African Communist Party.

Latin America and the Caribbean

Antigua and Barbuda,

a country comprising three islands that lie in the eastern arc of the Lesser Antilles, approximately 650 km (404 mi) southeast of PUERTO RICO, between the Atlantic Ocean and the Caribbean Sea.

In 1988 writer JAMAICA KINCAID published an acclaimed but honest and critical history of her childhood home, Antigua, entitled *A Small Place.* Antigua – a country consisting of the Antigua, Barbuda, and the tiny uninhabited Redonda islands – is indeed a small place. But its strategic location at the edge of the Caribbean Islands, its high rates of sugar production, and its tourist appeal have made it a valuable country. As Kincaid points out, however, this economic value – with profits concentrated in the hands of a few and labor spread out over the backs of many – has not enriched most Antiguans' lives. In recent decades Antigua's challenge has been to take advantage of its natural beauty and resources without continuing to do so at the expense of its people.

Like many of the Caribbean Islands, Antigua's earliest inhabitants were Ciboney Meso-Indians who began settling Antigua by about 2400 B.C.E. They were followed by people who have often been classified as Arawaks – a pastoral, agricultural people who introduced corn, sweet potatoes, indigo, cotton, and other familiar Antiguan crops. By about 1100 C.E. the Arawaks were displaced by the Caribs, who chose to use Antigua as a foundation for planting and gathering provisions. But none of these changes could compare to the 1493 arrival of Christopher Columbus and his men, who became the first Europeans to see Antigua during Columbus's second voyage to the Caribbean Islands.

Columbus named the island in honor of Santa Maria de la Antigua of Seville. The island's lack of fresh water and the active resistance of the Caribs discouraged the Spanish explorers from settling there. Consequently, Antigua was able to remain in the hands of its indigenous population for another hundred years. But the Europeans, who were busy colonizing the entire Caribbean during that time, did not forget Antigua, and in 1632 a group of English settlers from nearby St. Kitts established a colony on Antigua and claimed the island for GREAT BRITAIN. Except for a few months under French control, Antigua remained a British dependency for the next 350 years.

The earliest English settlers used Antigua as a base to produce crops such as tobacco and indigo for export. When Christopher Codrington established the first SUGAR plantation on Antigua in 1674, it changed the island's economy and population dramatically. Other planters quickly realized the potential Antigua could have as a profitable sugar producer and recognized the need for extra labor, which was required of large sugar-growing plantations. Within four years, half of Antigua's population consisted of African slaves who had been stolen from their homes and brought to Antigua to provide that labor.

Many of these slaves came from what is now called GUINEA, but they were also brought from other places along Africa's western coast and they became the ancestors of the overwhelming majority of today's Antiguans. In 1685 the British government granted the Codrington family the lease for Barbuda in exchange for "one fat pig per year if asked." The lease continued until 1870, and it assured the development of Antigua and Barbuda as related territories: the Codringtons used Barbuda to grow supplies and breed slaves that they then transferred to their Antiguan plantations.

For white slaveholders, Antigua's sugar plantations were a tremendous success. By the time of the AMERICAN REVOLUTION, Antigua's slaves produced three times more wealth for Great Britain than all of the New England colonies combined. Antigua's location at the edge of the Caribbean Islands also made it a valuable commercial and strategic gateway to the major sailing routes, to and from the rest of the Caribbean. But for black Antiguans, slavery on the sugar plantations was harsh. Antiguan slaves led revolts in 1702, 1736, and 1831, and the 1834 abolition of slavery in all British territories brought new hope to the 29,500 Antiguans who were slaves at that time (*see* ABOLITION AND EMANCIPATION IN LATIN AMERICA AND THE CARIBBEAN).

That hope, however, was slowly realized. Among the British colonies, Antigua was alone in declaring full emancipation in 1834, instead of the four-year apprenticeship program that most British islands followed. In that sense Antiguans became the first truly free black population in the British Caribbean (*see* APPRENTICESHIP IN THE BRITISH CARIBBEAN). Contemporary Antiguan Carnival celebrations still commemorate this historic landmark. But Antiguan planters had made that choice because they realized it would be less expensive for them to pay the former slaves extremely low wages than to continue to clothe and feed them. As a result, emancipation actually brought a period of extreme poverty and continued exploitation of black labor that lasted for many decades.

Slaves living in Barbuda found themselves in an even more precarious position. Because Barbuda was privately leased, the English government ruled that the legal emancipation of all British slaves did not apply to Barbudans, leaving them in limbo until Antigua legally annexed Barbuda in 1860. But white leaseholders continued to be allowed to lease the island, and thus control the population's labor, until 1898. When Barbuda finally became a parish of Antigua that year, its residents found that prevailing conditions for Antiguan workers were still not that much better than their own.

The demand for sugar had begun to decline in the nineteenth century, but there was no comparable industry in Antigua ready to incorporate the sugar workers. As a result, many Antiguans, including large numbers of underage children, continued to work on sugar estates under restrictive contracts and for very low wages. By the 1920s and 1930s, the combination of the Great Depression and a series of droughts brought the sugar industry and corresponding working conditions to a new low. The average daily wage for a sugar worker in 1936 was less than a shilling, a figure actually lower than the salary during emancipation one hundred years earlier, when workers were paid a shilling and sixpence. It was clear that, for the majority of the Antiguan population, conditions needed to be changed, and black workers came together to make those changes happen.

The Antigua Trades and Labor Union (ATLU) was founded in January 1939, and within two years the union began receiving major concessions from the white planters: increasing pay and bonuses, reducing work hours, and phasing out child labor. But as with labor unions and movements across the Caribbean, the ATLU recognized that its main goal needed to be much larger than even these accomplishments: Antiguan workers were ready for a complete overhaul of the country's political structure. In 1946 the union formed a political wing, the Antigua Labour Party (ALP), its goal being to give working class Antiguans more rights.

Agricultural workers tend the fields at a melon farm in Antigua. *Wolmuth/Hutchison*

In 1951 the ALP achieved one of its first main goals: universal adult suffrage, without property or literacy restrictions. As a result of this law, the ALP quickly won a majority in Parliament. When the position of chief minister was created in 1961, it went to ALP leader Vere Cornwall Bird Sr. As chief minister, Bird began to push for Antiguan independence. In 1966 Bird led a delegation to London to petition for Antiguan independence, and in February 1967 Antigua became an associated state of the British Commonwealth, with Barbuda and Redonda as dependencies. There was a separate push by Barbudans for their independence, but neither the Antiguan nor the British government supported this movement. Antigua and Barbuda became a single, fully independent nation in 1981.

At that time, Bird became the country's first prime minister. In the decades leading up to full independence, Antiguans saw positive changes in their country, including improvements in the educational system and infrastructure. Tourism replaced sugar production at the base of the country's economy, bringing with it a new set of industries that provided an increased variety in employment opportunities. But Antigua also continued to face challenges. V. C. Bird Sr. was succeeded as prime minister by his son Lester, meaning that the ALP and the Bird family have been in control of the government for nearly 35 of the last 40 years. V. C. Bird Sr. is revered by many as the "father of the nation," but others feel more ambivalent about the apparent monopoly of power, and the Bird administrations have faced stiff opposition and charges of government corruption. The tourist-based economy also makes Antigua vulnerable to any downturns in the world tourism market, and for a small country with few natural resources, economic diversification has been a difficult process.

But Antigua and Barbuda are entering the twenty-first century also as an independent nation finally ruled by its black majority – the descendants of the people who made Antigua's sugar plantations profitable for so long. A visitor to Antigua today can tour the restored sugar mill at Betty's Hope for a glimpse of what Antigua and Barbuda have been in the past. This in turn emphasizes the tremendous progress made by the current generation of Antiguans and Barbudans.

Lisa Clayton Robinson

SEE ALSO

Spain; St. Kitts and Nevis; Carnivals in Latin America and the Caribbean; Bird, Vere Cornwall.

Latin America and the Caribbean

Antilles, term applied to the whole of the West Indies except the Bahamas.

The Greater Antilles include Cuba, Jamaica, Haiti, the Dominican Republic, and Puerto Rico. The Lesser Antilles, extending in an arc from Puerto Rico to the northeastern coast of South America, include the Virgin Islands, Windward Islands, Leeward Islands, southern group of the Netherlands Antilles, and, usually, Barbados and Trinidad and Tobago (*see* WEST INDIES).

North America

Antilynching Movement,

the effort in the United States from the late nineteenth to the mid-twentieth century to halt the extralegal killing by mob violence of alleged lawbreakers, particularly African Americans.

Arthur F. Raper, in his classic 1933 study *The Tragedy of Lynching*, found that lynching rates were "highest in the newer and more sparsely settled portions of the South" and that poorer counties contributed a disproportionate share of such incidents. This study helped to reinforce the common view that lynchings were the product of an economically marginal lower class. However, current scholarship emphasizes the direct complicity of the prosperous and socially prominent, who in most cases condoned if they did not in fact take part in such incidents. Lynching thus served to unite whites of different classes and reinforced the subordinate status not only of blacks but also of Southern white women, whose lives were circumscribed due to their supposed irresistibility to black rapists. Given such circumstances, it is not surprising that African Americans were the first to take initiative against these attacks.

The origins of the antilynching movement lie in the single-minded efforts of one individual, the black journalist and political activist Ida B. Wells-Barnett. Three years before her marriage to Ferdinand L. Barnett, Wells launched her antilynching crusade in 1892 after the killing of three black businessmen in her hometown of MEMPHIS, TENNESSEE. Wells investigated the incident and concluded that the accusations of rape that served to justify the killings were baseless. The three men lost their lives, she declared, because they were in competition with white-owned businesses. Shortly after Wells's newspaper, the *Memphis Free Speech*, published her exposé, a white mob ransacked the newspaper's offices and destroyed the press.

Wells fled Memphis, taking a job with the *New York Age*, an African American newspaper in New York City, but she continued her antilynching campaign with undiminished zeal. In addition to newspaper stories, Wells wrote a number of pamphlets, including "Southern Horrors: Lynch Law in All Its Phases" (1892) and "A Red Record... Lynchings in the United States, 1892-1893-1894" (1895), which offered the first systematic statistical analysis of lynching in the United States. Her work attracted the attention of America's leading black activist, FREDERICK DOUGLASS, and the aging agitator joined her in his last crusade. Douglass's "Lynch Law in the South" appeared in the July 1892 issue of the *North American Review*. A year later, in his capacity as commissioner for the Republic of Haiti's exhibit at the World Columbian Exhibition in Chicago, Douglass provided Wells with a desk in the Haitian pavilion from which to distribute thousands of copies of her latest antilynching pamphlet.

Over the years the antilynching movement had two main goals. It sought to shake the American public out of its passivity on the subject of lynching, and since Southern state courts would not punish the participants, it lobbied for legislation that would make lynching a federal crime. African Americans had some success with the former goal but found themselves stymied with respect to the latter. Thus in 1901 Ida B. Wells-Barnett met with President William McKinley and pressed for the passage of antilynching legislation. But McKinley provided no assistance, and his successor, Theodore Roosevelt, did no better.

In the early twentieth century, the NATIONAL ASSOCIATION FOR THE ADVANCEMENT OF COLORED PEOPLE (NAACP) emerged as the key antilynching organization. The NAACP attempted to keep national statistics on lynchings and investigated many specific incidents. It published pamphlets such as "Thirty Years of Lynching in the United States, 1889-1918" (1919) and a book-length study of the problem by future NAACP executive director Walter F. White, entitled *Rope and Faggot: A Biography of Judge Lynch* (1929). Federal antilynching legislation remained one of the NAACP's highest priorities, a goal it came close to achieving three times, in 1922, 1937, and 1940. Indeed during the NEW DEAL of the 1930s such legislation seemed within grasp, but despite vigorous NAACP lobbying, neither Congress nor President Franklin D. Roosevelt proved willing to embrace such a measure, because of the opposition of Southern Democrats.

The NAACP was not the only organization that actively opposed lynching, nor did such opposition imply a particular political leaning. Liberals in the American Civil Liberties Union, Southern conservatives – black as well as white – in the Commission on Interracial Cooperation, and the radicals of the Communist Party of the United States of America (CPUSA) all played a role in the antilynching campaign. The CPUSA was particularly visible in these years, directly or through so-called Communist-front organizations in which it was the leading force. During the 1930s, for example, the SOUTHERN NEGRO YOUTH CONGRESS, a broad-based coalition with strong Communist ties, organized antilynching protests as part of its civil rights activism. The CPUSA was also prominent in responding to a wave of lynchings that followed World War II.

Yet another source of antilynching activism were white, middle-class Southern women, as exemplified by Jessie Daniel Ames's Association of Southern Women for the Prevention of Lynching, founded in 1930. Ames sought to challenge the underlying rationale for lynching among Southern whites, distilled in South Carolina Democrat "Cotton Ed" Smith's remark in a 1935 Senate filibuster that lynching was necessary to preserve "the sanctity of our firesides and the virtue of our women." It was generally assumed that an accusation of rape lay behind virtually every Southern lynching of an African American. In fact, less than a fifth of all blacks lynched between 1889 and 1918 were accused of rape. Even when these incidents are combined with those lynchings that followed other alleged attacks on women, the total amounts to only 28 percent of all blacks lynched. The most common justification for lynching was the charge of murder, which was leveled in 36 percent of all lynchings of African Americans during this 30-year period.

The various antilynching organizations often squabbled and worked at cross-purposes. For example, Jessie Daniel Ames emphasized the need for educational approaches at the state and local levels rather than coercive federal legislation, contending that education alone could end the social acceptance of lynching. Ames thus stubbornly opposed the NAACP's legislative campaign, taking such behind-the-scenes actions as meeting with Eleanor Roosevelt in a fruitless effort to turn the First Lady against the NAACP strategy. Likewise when PAUL ROBESON, W. E. B. Du Bois, and white liberal Bartley Crum called in 1946 for an "American crusade against lynching," NAACP executive director Walter White opposed them because he feared it might produce a new Communist-front antilynching organization. The staunchly anticommunist White complained privately to Robeson that the gathering would duplicate ongoing NAACP efforts, and he refused to have any part in it.

By the 1950s, however, lynching was clearly on the wane. Part of the explanation for the decline lies in growing opposition to the practice, inside as well as outside the South. In particular, the CIVIL RIGHTS MOVEMENT of the 1950s and 1960s both mobilized the Southern black population and secured the passage of important new federal legislation. Although no federal law addressed lynching per se, the Civil Rights Act of 1968 included provisions making it a federal offense to deprive individuals of their civil rights. Though not without deficiencies, the new federal law was successfully applied to racially motivated assaults. Moreover, in recent years Southern states have demonstrated a greater willingness to punish racially based killings. For example, more than three decades after the 1963 murder of black civil rights activist Medgar W. Evers, the state of Mississippi successfully convicted longtime suspect Byron De La Beckwith.

Yet changes in the law and its enforcement do not account for the marked drop in lynching that began much earlier. Indeed this decline seems less a product of antilynching activism than of profound changes taking place in Southern society. During the 1940s and 1950s migration shifted the center of the African American population from the South to the North and West. Urbanization, industrial growth, and the emergence of stronger institutions of government all served to make the South more and more like the rest of the nation. In 1955 there were only three lynchings in the entire United States, all of them in Mississippi, and the NAACP had already ceased to regard lynching as a high-priority issue.

James Clyde Sellman

See Also

World War II and African Americans; Du Bois, William Edward Burghardt (W. E. B.); Evers, Medgar Wylie; New York, New York; Wells-Barnett, Ida Bell; White, Walter Francis; Haiti; Communist Party USA, African Americans and the.

Antislavery in the United States. Please see Abolitionism in the United States

Latin America and the Caribbean

Anton, the first leader of the *zambo* society that developed in the Ecuadorian coastal province of Esmeraldas during the mid-1550s and endured through the mid-1700s. (A zambo is a person of mixed African and Indian ancestry.)

In 1553 Anton and 22 other slaves embarked from Cartagena de Indias, Colombia, as part of merchandise bound for the Peruvian port of Callao. The ship wrecked off the coast of Esmeraldas, and the 23 slaves killed their Spanish captors and escaped into the forest.

At that time various small indigenous groups inhabited central Esmeraldas: the Niguas, Yumbos, Campaces, Lachas, and Malabas. The first contact of the maroons was with the Niguas and the Yumbos (*see* Maroonage in the Americas). As the groups clashed, the maroons enjoyed an advantage in combat, owing to the surprise provoked by their arrival and the firearms they had liberated from the shipwreck. Anton was nicknamed "the big sorcerer," and his witchcraft skills were also a decisive factor in instilling fear into the Niguas and gaining their respect.

Through Anton's leadership the maroons increasingly dominated the indigenous communities. Sebastian Alonso de Illescas gradually established himself as Anton's successor. The zone of influence of what became the zambo society was limited to the central part of the province of Esmeraldas (*see* Ecuador).

Jean Muteba Rahier

See Also

Cartagena de Indias, Colombia; Illescas, Sebastián Alonso de.

Africa

Anuak (also known as the Anyuak or the Annuak), ethnic group of Sudan and Ethiopia.

The Anuak primarily inhabit a stretch of the Blue Nile River in western Ethiopia and eastern Sudan. They speak a Nilo-Saharan language and are closely related to the Shilluk people. Approximately 100,000 people consider themselves Anuak.

See Also

Languages, African: An Overview.

Africa

Anyi (also known as the Agni, the Bini, the Kotoko, and the Ton), ethnic group of West Africa.

The Anyi primarily inhabit southeastern Côte d'Ivoire and southwestern Ghana. They speak a Niger-Congo language and belong to the Akan cultural and linguistic group. Approximately 700,000 people consider themselves Anyi.

See Also

Côte d'Ivoire; Languages, African: An Overview.

Africa

Apartheid, social and political policy of racial segregation and discrimination enforced by white minority governments in South Africa from 1948 to 1994.

The term *apartheid* (from the Afrikaans word for "apartness") was coined in the 1930s and used as a political slogan of the National Party in the early 1940s, but the policy itself extends back to the beginning of white settlement in South Africa in 1652. After the primarily Afrikaner Nationalists came to power in 1948, the social custom of apartheid was systematized under law.

The implementation of the policy, later referred to as "separate development," was made possible by the Population Registration Act of 1950, which put all South Africans into three racial categories: Bantu (black African), white, or Coloured (of mixed race). A fourth category, Asian (Indians and Pakistanis), was added later. The system of apartheid was enforced by a series of laws passed in the 1950s: the Group Areas Act of 1950 assigned races to different residential and business sections in urban areas, and the Land Acts of 1954 and 1955 restricted nonwhite residence to specific areas. These laws further restricted the already limited right of black Africans to own land, entrenching the white minority's control of over 80 percent of South African land. In addition, other laws prohibited most social contacts between the races; enforced the segregation of public facilities and the separation of educational standards; created race-specific job categories; restricted the powers of nonwhite unions; and curbed nonwhite participation in government.

The Bantu Authorities Act of 1951 and the Promotion of Bantu Self-Government Act of 1959 furthered these divisions between the races by creating ten African "homelands" administered by what were supposed to be reestablished "tribal" organizations. The Bantu Homelands Citizenship Act of 1970 made every black South African a citizen of one of the homelands, effectively excluding blacks from South African politics. Most of the homelands, lacking natural resources, were not economically viable and, being both small and fragmented, lacked the autonomy of independent states.

Though the implementation and enforcement of apartheid was accompanied by tremendous suppression of opposition, continual resistance to apartheid existed within South Africa. A number of black political groups, often supported by sympathetic whites, opposed apartheid using a variety of tactics, including violence, strikes, demonstrations, and sabotage – strategies that often met with severe reprisals by the government. Apartheid was also denounced by the international community: in 1961 South Africa was forced to withdraw from the British Commonwealth by member states who were critical of the apartheid system, and in 1985 the governments of the United States and Great Britain imposed selective economic sanctions on South Africa in protest of its racial policy.

As antiapartheid pressure mounted within and outside South Africa, the South African government, led by President F. W. de Klerk, began to dismantle the apartheid system in the early 1990s. The year 1990 brought a National Party government dedicated to reform and also saw the legalization of formerly banned black congresses and the release of imprisoned black leaders. In 1994 the country's constitution was rewritten and free general elections were held for the first time in its history, and with Nelson Mandela's election as South Africa's first black president, the last vestiges of the apartheid system were finally outlawed.

Alonford James Robinson, Jr.

See Also

Afrikaner; Mandela, Nelson Rolihlahla; De Klerk, Frederik Willem.

TOP: A black girl stands under a sign indicating, in English and Afrikaans, the way to a segregated women's restroom. Racial separation of this kind was the essence of apartheid, a strict policy of segregation enforced by the South African government from 1948 until the early 1990s. *G. Boutin, Explorer*
ABOVE: Nelson Mandela stares out the window from his former cell in Robben Island prison. Convicted of sabotage for actions taken against apartheid, Mandela spent 18 of his 27 years in prison on the island. *CORBIS/David Turnley*

North America

Apollo Theater, the most influential African American popular theater.

The Apollo Theatre, located at 253 West 125th Street in central Harlem, was the most important venue in black show business from the 1930s through the 1970s, when waning popularity caused it financial problems. With live broadcasts that featured the Duke Ellington and Count Basie orchestras, the Apollo became a mecca for JAZZ bands in the 1930s and 1940s. By the 1950s the theater was the nation's top stage for established black artists. Its famous Amateur Night, in which unknown performers had their talent assessed by the notoriously raucous Harlem audience, had become a springboard for numerous careers. ELLA FITZGERALD, SARAH VAUGHAN, and PEARL BAILEY, for example, were all early Amateur Night winners, and later acts like the Jackson 5 and STEVIE WONDER also enjoyed their first major exposure at the Apollo. As musical styles changed, the theater evolved with the times, booking RHYTHM AND BLUES, gospel, FUNK, soul and hip hop acts, and hosting landmark performances by artists like JAMES BROWN.

The theater itself began its life in 1913 as Hurtig and Seamon's Music Hall, a venue frequented by white vaudeville acts that entertained predominantly white crowds until the 1930s. Sidney Cohen purchased the theater in 1933 and renamed it the Apollo, replacing the vaudeville fare with black entertainment. The Apollo's first show in 1934, "Jazz a la Carte," featured Benny Carter's big band and helped to solidify the theater's new role as the city's primary African American performance venue, overshadowing the Lincoln and Lafayette theaters.

During the 1970s the Apollo steadily lost money, forcing its closure in 1977. Its declaration as a national historic landmark in 1983 secured the building's survival, but efforts to make it a viable performance house throughout the 1980s largely failed. The theater was taken on by a nonprofit organization in 1991, which intended to make it a significant part of Harlem's 125th Street renewal.

Marian Aguiar

SEE ALSO
Soul Music; Basie, William James ("Count"); Gospel Music; Harlem, New York; Hip Hop in the United States; Jackson, Michael, and the Jackson Family; Lafayette Theatre; Lincoln Theater; Ellington, Edward Kennedy ("Duke").

Latin America and the Caribbean

Aponte, José Antonio (b. ?; d. April 9, 1812, Havana, Cuba), Afro-Cuban revolutionary who organized a large-scale revolt that took place in 1812.

José Antonio Aponte, a free black man, worked as a carpenter and a wood carver in Havana, Cuba, before taking the role of revolutionary leader. Like many other Afro-Cubans in the early 1800s, he was discontented with the continuation of slavery and Spanish dominance that kept blacks from freedom. Afro-Cubans had already supported an unsuccessful independence movement in 1810, and had their hopes raised when Spanish courts briefly considered ending slavery. Once this proposal was rejected, blacks knew that freedom could be achieved only through their own means. Aponte seized this opportunity and proceeded to gather both the free and enslaved blacks of Havana in 1811 to form the Central Revolutionary Junta. The group quickly expanded and established smaller units throughout Cuba. Aponte solicited the help of Haitian general Jean François, who promised support for the proposed revolt.

Aponte's intention was not only to end Afro-Cuban bondage, but to also destroy the economic system that perpetuated slavery. He assumed that if the Cuban economy were turned away from reliance on sugar and coffee production, slavery would come to a quick demise. His plan entailed the destruction of plantations, and with this the elimination of the cash sources that bought slaves. Without slavery, the white Cuban-born landowners would no longer control the country's economy.

Before the revolt began, Aponte's plan was discovered by Captain General Someruelos, who arrested him along with eight of his principal collaborators in February 1812. Even without the revolutionary leader, the planned uprising occurred through the coordination of the juntas throughout the country. In the provinces of Puerto Principe, Holguín, Bayamo, Trinidad, Baracoa, and Havana, as well as other areas, slaves burned sugar and coffee plantations and killed white overseers. The uprising did not encompass the whole nation because the military and the militia of white planters intervened.

Once the revolt was brought to an end, Aponte and the other initiators were sentenced to death. After Aponte and three others were hanged on the morning of April 9, 1812, their bodies were dismembered and their heads were placed on public display in different parts of Havana. Local authorities hoped that such extreme displays would deter further revolts.

Aponte's legacy continued in Afro-Cuban history with the founding of the Havana Club Aponte, a *sociedad de color* (mutual aid society in Cuba) that offered safe haven for political activism and supported the Afro-Cuban struggle for equality.

Rob Garrison

See Also
Cuba.

North America

Apostolic Movement, an outgrowth of African American Pentecostal churches that now includes over 1.5 million members.

The Apostolic Movement represents a broad cross section of African American Christianity comprising many semi-independent churches. Many Apostolic denominations, such as the Church of Our Lord Jesus, Church of the Apostolic Faith, the Church of the Lord Jesus Christ Apostolic, and the United Churches of Jesus Apostolic, arose from schisms caused by doctrinal disputes.

The Apostolic Movement began with the Azusa Street Revival of 1906-1909 in Los Angeles, California, which was led by William J. Seymour. Seymour leased a small empty building at 312 Azusa Street in a poor black neighborhood. Within several days, over a thousand people daily were coming to experience the spirit baptism, glossolalia (ecstatic speaking in tongues), and the passion of Seymour's services. His followers were multiracial and working class, primarily black female domestic workers. While Apostolic congregations often have a female majority, the leadership is usually male.

Religious leaders from across the country came to Azusa Street. One was Charles Mason, founder of the Church of God in Christ, who quickly spread the Apostolic faith. Seymour founded the Pacific Apostolic Faith Movement, appointed himself its bishop, and, due to racial conflicts with white Pentecostals, decreed that every succeeding bishop would be a man of color. However, when Seymour died in 1922, a woman of color, his wife, Jennie Seymour, assumed control of the mission.

Along with Seymour, one of the early Apostolic leaders was Garfield T. Haywood (1880-1931), who became bishop of the Pentecostal Assemblies of the World in 1925. Another prominent Apostolic leader was Robert Clarence Lawson, who founded the Church of Our Lord Jesus Church of the Apostolic Faith, after a dispute with Haywood. The most prominent Apostolic leader in the Civil Rights Movement, Smallwood E. Williams, founded the Bible Way Church of Our Lord Jesus Christ World Wide in 1957 and was the head of the pivotal civil rights organization the Southern Christian Leadership Conference (SCLC).

As in most Pentecostal churches, worship in Apostolic churches is characterized by revivalism and is often "leader-centered," meaning that the charisma of the minister, conveyed through a dynamic, expressive preaching style, often determines the success and reputation of a church. Apostolic leadership is also important because of the church's informal institutional structure.

Music plays an integral role in Apostolic church services. The congregation's enthusiastic singing and hand clapping along with the church choir is a standard feature of Apostolic worship.

All Apostolic churches share a theological emphasis on the centrality of baptism by the Holy Ghost, a concept derived from the New Testament Book of Acts. Apostolics believe that glossolalia (speaking in tongues) is the chief criterion for a person's baptism in spirit. Apostolic churches reject the traditional Christian Trinity and favor instead an exclusive focus on Jesus Christ. For this reason, they do not baptize using the standard Trinitarian formula ("in the name of the Father, the Son, and the Holy Ghost"). Instead, they invoke only Jesus's name. Apostolic churches are thus often called "Jesus only" or "Jesus's name" churches.

See Also
Mason, Charles Harrison; Pentecostalism; Seymour, William Joseph.

Latin America and the Caribbean

Apprenticeship in the British Caribbean, a system imposed by the British Parliament in 1834 as an intermediate step between slavery and full emancipation.

In 1807 the British Parliament voted to end British participation in the international slave trade. In 1834 it ended slavery entirely, promising freedom to more than a million slaves in the Caribbean (*see* Abolition and Emancipation in Latin America and the Caribbean). In an effort to soften the effects of emancipation on white slaveholders, the British Parliament decided to implement a program known as apprenticeship. Under this program all slaves under six years of age, and those born after August 1, 1834, were freed. But praedials (field workers) were required to work for their current owners for a period of six years, and nonpraedials for a period of four years. After this period all slaves would be emancipated.

The apprenticeship program was so overloaded with rules and restrictions that special magistrates had to be appointed to monitor it. Slaves worked 40 hours per week in exchange for food, clothing, and shelter. They were permitted to spend the remaining time working as wage laborers on local farms and in surrounding towns. In exchange for their participation in the program, white planters throughout the British Empire were reimbursed in cash, a sum totaling £20 million.

Implementation of the apprenticeship program was a major challenge. Most white planters feared that a decline in the labor force would mean an end to their plantations. During the first year of the program, whites tried unsuccessfully to bring European indentured servants to the island. They also turned to importing workers from India and China. More than 30,000 Indians and 5000 Chinese were brought to Jamaica between 1834 and 1917. For the most part, the fear held by white plantation owners that emancipated slaves would abandon the estates proved to be untrue. They simply could not. On most islands the only work available was found on the sugar estates. Still, despite the continuing supply of labor, the apprenticeship program suffered from mismanagement. Enforcing the lengthy regulations proved extremely difficult for the special magistrates. Confusion and conflict plagued the program, and by 1837 it was clear that it had to be dismantled.

By 1837 the apprenticeship program could not save the planters from their demise. That year, declining sugar prices forced more than 100 plantations to close. The following year the British Parliament – responding to pressure from antislavery groups – ended the apprenticeship program. More than 1.5 million slaves were fully emancipated, nearly 300,000 in Jamaica alone.

Alonford James Robinson, Jr.

See Also
Transatlantic Slave Trade.

Latin America and the Caribbean

Argentina, second largest country in South America after BRAZIL, forming the southern tip of the South American continent; Argentina enjoys a great many natural resources, including the pampas (fertile plains) made famous by gauchos (cowboys) who are immortalized in the national literature.

Bordered by BOLIVIA, Brazil, CHILE, PARAGUAY, URUGUAY, and the Atlantic Ocean, Argentina comprises 35.8 million people, over 85 percent of whom are of white European descent. Another 15 percent of the population is of indigenous or *mestizo* (European and indigenous) origin. Though traditionally known for its early Spanish and nineteenth-century Italian and German heritage, Argentina had a large black population during much of the colonial and independence periods. Today the Afro-Argentine population is estimated at a few thousand and is often remembered as part of the country's folklore: Afro-Argentines have been incorporated in independence celebrations as soldiers, or in traditional dances called *candombes.* Scholarly research about this group has been limited to the colonial period and the slave trade, or to songs, portraits, and folklore studies from the 1950s. Though the Indian has become a mythical symbol incorporated by nationalistic discourse in *indigenismo* (a literary and artistic movement that appropriated indigenous culture and images) and *mestizaje* (racial mixing), black contributions to Argentina's history have attracted little interest until fairly recently.

THE OFFICIAL HISTORY

First occupied in 1536, Buenos Aires was soon abandoned by Spanish settlers; the port city was not permanently settled until 1580. Since the city lay within the viceroyalty of PERU, trade was restricted by the Spanish Crown, as it was not a designated port of entry for Spanish goods. Buenos Aires remained a kind of backwater throughout much of the colonial period. Criollo (native-born, white) leaders, with the help of Gen. José de San Martín, declared independence in 1810; independence was finalized in 1816. For a century and a half one military takeover led to another, and this period was marked by the dictatorship of Juan Manuel Rosas (1835-1852). Unitarians, who promoted centralized power and free trade, struggled with Federalists, who emphasized more evenly distributed power among the provinces as well as protectionist measures. The constitution of 1853, still in effect, established the Republic of Argentina. The province of Buenos Aires, however, claimed its independence, and it was only after a series of conflicts and with the election of President Bartolomé Mitre in 1862 that the country was unified.

In the late nineteenth and early twentieth centuries an elite democracy consolidated itself in Argentina, and the country enjoyed economic growth of over 5 percent per year. This prosperity was driven largely by exports of beef and grain and was based to a great extent on foreign investment. The Argentine economy was particularly dependent on international markets, and the worldwide depression of 1929 precipitated a severe economic crisis in the country. The presidencies of Juan Domingo Perón (1946-1955, 1973-1974) forwarded nationalist and populist measures, establishing a base in the labor movement. Perón's third wife, Maria Estela Martinez de Perón, succeeded him as president after his death in 1974, but her tenure was cut short the following year by a military coup. After the military government launched an unsuccessful invasion of the disputed Islas Malvinas (Falkland Islands), democracy was restored in 1983.

The leftist Radical Civic Union coalition and the (Peronist) Justicialist Party have since contested political power. Though Argentina has experienced extreme economic recessions, hyperinflation, and foreign debt since the 1980s, its economy stabilized in the 1990s and the country possesses vast natural resources and a diversified industrial base. A member of the Mercosur trade bloc, Argentina has also attracted expanded foreign and domestic investment.

CONQUEST AND THE COLONIAL PERIOD

The present-day Argentine capital of Buenos Aires was officially denied trade with SPAIN, other European powers, and other Spanish colonies until 1776. With neither a supply of minerals nor a tropical climate that could produce exotic exports, the port city's economic potential paled in comparison to that afforded by the precious metals of Potosí (in present-day Bolivia) and the former Inca capital of Cuzco (in present-day PERU). Buenos Aires also lacked the sugar, coffee, and tobacco of the Caribbean. Thus, despite the city's strategic port – used as a threat to ward off possible Portuguese advances – it was virtually ignored by the Spanish during much of the colonial period. The principal economic activity between 1603 and 1655 was the barter trade of agricultural products: hides, tallow wheat, and *cecina* (salted beef).

A large indigenous population occupied Argentina's interior provinces. Indians of the coastal area were nomadic. Despite a brief period of trade, colonizers soon began enslaving natives, who fled south. Slaving expeditions were formed, but the Indians' frequent attempts to flee left *porteños* (residents of Buenos Aires) without a stable labor force. Smallpox epidemics also decimated most of the Indian populations in the early decades of the seventeenth century. In part due to an uprising in 1604, native labor was imported in 1610 from Chile, Peru, and Tucumán. By 1612 such importation was prohibited. Settlers eventually dubbed the coastal Indians "unsuitable" for agricultural labor. Beginning in 1740 expeditions against the pampa Indians lasted into the next century. During these expeditions, most Native Americans were either killed or placed in reservations, a process that culminated in the late 1870s with the so-called Conquest of the Desert. This military engagement was led by Gen. Julio Roca, who subsequently became president (1880-1886, 1898-1904).

Throughout the seventeenth and eighteenth centuries the city gradually became known for a flourishing illicit trade. The city and province prospered despite legal restrictions against their products: smuggled goods that evaded colonial taxes found profitable markets in the interior, Paraguay, Chile, and Bolivia. According to sources, "During the 1620s, a major share of the income of the Caja Real of Buenos Aires came from confiscated contraband." Illicit trade likewise extended to the importation of slaves, the first of whom arrived as early as 1587. Silver was illegally shipped from Buenos Aires in payment for goods and slaves. A series of *asientos*, or contracts to provide slaves, was granted primarily to Portuguese traders from 1595 until 1616, but at other times slave importation through Buenos Aires was prohibited. Dutch and English smugglers also took part in unlawful trade. Russell Edward Chace asserts that "contraband slaving... quite possibly supplied more blacks than did legitimate commerce." Some of these slaves stayed on in Buenos Aires, but the majority were taken into the interior, to Chile, Upper Peru (now Bolivia), and Peru.

SLAVE TRADE AND OCCUPATIONS IN THE SEVENTEENTH AND EIGHTEENTH CENTURIES

Throughout the seventeenth century, Portuguese slavers dominated the trade. Between the 1620s and 1630s approximately 1500 slaves (10 percent of the Africans taken from Angola) headed for Buenos Aires. This movement was stopped in the 1640s, however, as Portugal focused on protecting its claims in Brazil from Dutch expansionists and on winning independence from Spain in Europe. By 1680, however, 22,892 black slaves had been legally imported.

In the eighteenth century, first the French (1701) and then the British (1713) were granted asientos. The Real Compañía Francesa de Guinea brought slaves from the Mina coast (present-day CAPE VERDE and SENEGAL) and the kingdom of Ardre. Between 1702 and 1714, 3745 slaves were legally imported. The British South Sea Company was to introduce 4800 slaves per year for 40 years; 1200 of these stayed in Buenos Aires. Slaves imported by the English came from the Gold Coast and the bays of Biafra and Benin. Chace states that most slaves imported through Buenos Aires came from Bantu-populated Angola-Congo regions.

In 1776 Spain established the new viceroyalty of la Plata, with Buenos Aires as its seat of government and authorized port. In 1778 the Crown opened all the colonies to free trade with Spanish allies, but Buenos Aires had already developed long-standing illicit trade relationships with both the English and the Portuguese. Both of these connections would have a lasting impact on the slave trade in Argentina. After 1789 "free" slave trade lifted restrictions on trade for American subjects. Slaves then came from Portuguese factories in Angola (they were called Congos, Angolas, Benguelas, and Luandas) and from Mozambique. Between 1750 and 1810 approximately 45,000 slaves were imported by both legal and illegal means, according to Sergio Villalobos. Chace claims that this traffic, along with the decline of silver production in Potosí, "appears to have been an important factor in pushing Buenos Aires to a position of economic and, eventually, political hegemony in Argentina." Though the constituent assembly of the United Provinces officially banned the entry of new slaves into the nation in 1813, the slave trade continued until a pact with Britain in 1840 effectively ended it. Traders such as the British South Sea Company representative in Buenos Aires, Felipe Sarratea, got rich from the trade (*see* Transatlantic Slave Trade).

Early slaves worked primarily as agricultural laborers and domestic servants. As many *estancieros* (ranchers) could not afford them, slaves were a status symbol in both urban and rural areas. Many were transported inland to Upper Peru to work in the silver mines. The major period of slave importation in Argentina lasted from 1742 to 1806. By the late 1700s nearly 50 percent of the population in the interior of the country was black, and between 30 and 40 percent of the population of Buenos Aires was black or mulatto, according to one source. By 1836 only 25 percent of Buenos Aires was black, and the percentage would continue to decline throughout the nineteenth century. In the early 1800s slaves who stayed in the province of Buenos Aires worked mostly in urban occupations and under the dictator Rosas (1835-1852); they eventually became apprenticed as cobblers, tailors, barbers, hat makers, and so on (*see* Slavery in Latin America and the Caribbean).

Cofradías, Naciones, and Mutual Aid Societies

Slaves and slowly increasing numbers of free persons of color formed religious and social groups throughout the colonial period. *Cofradías* (religious lay brotherhoods) played an important role in Afro-Argentine life, supporting the Roman Catholic Church by collecting alms, maintaining church buildings, paying priests for masses, and preparing celebrations for patron saints (*see* Catholic Church in Latin America and the Caribbean). Though they were strictly regulated by the particular religious orders and priests, these were the first separate organizations of Afro-Argentines. Andrews identifies the cofradía of San Baltasar, founded in 1772, as the first black organization of this type in Buenos Aires.

At the end of the eighteenth century the *naciones* (ethnic associations begun both by free persons of color and slaves) emerged. The naciones were independent social and cultural organizations. They worked to buy freedom for members who were still slaves, make loans to members to buy houses, pay for members' funeral expenses, and sponsor public dances and cultural activities. During the early 1800s women assumed increasingly important roles in the naciones, as vast numbers of black and mulatto men were either fighting or killed in military battles (the skirmish with Great Britain in 1806-1807, the wars for independence from 1810 to 1816, the civil wars throughout the 1820s, and wars against Brazil and the Indian population). Mutual aid societies, which developed later, placed less emphasis on ethnic origins and more on black Argentine unity.

Independence, Abolition, and Emancipation

Independence from Spain was declared in 1810, but it was not completely won until 1816. As early as 1806 slaves served in civic militias, where they received military instruction to ward off possible attacks by other European colonial powers. A few notable recruits gained their freedom in 1807 after successfully warding off British assaults on Buenos Aires. From 1810 to 1815 Spanish slave owners were required to contribute slaves on a massive scale to the armies of Gen. San Martín. The legal status of the drafted slaves was changed to *liberto* (indicating an intermediate position between slavery and freedom), and black soldiers were promised freedom after five years of service in black regiments. With independence – an effective transfer from Spanish to Creole (native-born white) rule – came opportunity for emancipation.

Abolition, like independence, was only achieved after a long and arduous process. As in many of the former Spanish colonies, in Argentina a series of laws and proclamations that first restricted trade and then gradually emancipated slaves staggered over decades. There were three legal statuses for blacks in the nineteenth century: slave, liberto, and free. Slaves won their freedom either by manumission or, more frequently, by *coartación* (self-purchase), as they did throughout much of Latin America. Libertos were for the most part men who agreed to serve at least five years in the military; many men joined military regiments to fight in wars of independence from the Spanish Crown. Women, particularly urban slaves, most often bought their freedom through coartación. Those who worked as domestics sometimes enjoyed greater access to limited informal economic opportunities: although some sold food or mended and washed clothing to supplement their masters' incomes, others were allowed to save for their freedom.

In 1813 the law of the free womb was passed, freeing all slaves born after January 31, 1813. However, subsequent restrictions curtailed the measure. For example, a number of years of servitude came to be required for freedom (similar in principle to the service exacted from military libertos). According to Andrews, in 1810, 22.6 percent of the black population was free. In 1827, 54.8 percent was free. Slavery as an institution was not abolished, however, until 1853 in Argentina, and in 1861 in Buenos Aires, when the Unitarians realized their dream of a united nation under the hegemony of Buenos Aires (*see* Abolition and Emancipation in Latin America and the Caribbean).

Between 1830 and 1860 large numbers of blacks continued to serve in the regular national army, taking different sides in the various Unitarian-Federalist civil wars that lasted into the 1840s. Blacks fought in the Indian extermination campaigns of the 1830s and 1840s, seeking the social and economic mobility promised by politicians like Rosas. Black officers such as José Maria Morales and Domingo Sosa rose to prominence during this time.

Nineteenth-Century Postabolition and the Present Situation

Marta Goldberg shows that conditions for persons of color were, according to national census figures, often worse after abolition. Their life expectancies plunged as infant mortality rose. Artisan slaves had been well cared for because of their revenue-producing potential, whereas free black persons were now competing with poor whites and an increasing influx of unskilled labor from Europe. Chace writes, "... manumission meant little more than the actual release from the bonds of servitude, because free blacks were accorded much the same treatment as slaves." Blacks were excluded from education, religious orders, and many government positions. In some of the more rural regions, blacks, whites, and Indians intermarried and formed the multiracial gaucho class. Later a symbol of Argentine nationalism in literature and popular accounts, the gaucho's image would be gradually whitened.

Most freed urban slaves stayed in urban areas, working as apprentices in the trades mentioned above. By this time well-established community organizations had taken root; these were descended from the colonial cofradías, naciones, and mutual aid societies that flourished through most of the century. A healthy black press produced a number of literary journals. Yet by the 1850s a cultural move toward integration meant that, as Andrews points out, young people exhibited little interest in continuing the traditions of the naciones: the dances, meetings, and so forth. Young Afro-Argentines preferred to dance to waltzes and other European music.

After the 1850s the percentage of Afro-Argentines in the population precipitously declined, as mentioned earlier. The causes of the population decline were various: a rash of nineteenth-century wars in which blacks heavily participated, racial intermarriage motivated in part by the shortage of black men and the possibility of social mobility for children of mixed blood, high mortality rates specifically due to yellow fever, and the decline of the slave trade after 1813. More important, however, were official efforts to pattern Argentina after European nations. These attempts to whiten the population (*see* Whitening) were reflected in policies to attract European immigrants as well as the campaigns to exterminate the Native American populations. Intellectuals such as Domingo Faustino Sarmiento, Carlos Octavio Bunge, and José Ingenieros advanced theories of scientific racism, providing a justification for such measures. Creole elites had written for years about plans to attract European immigrants to temper the "degenerate" qualities of Argentina's diminishing black and decimated indigenous populations. By the second decade of the twentieth century, approximately one-third of the country's population was foreign-born.

While a number of countries in Latin American pursued policies of racial whitening, Argentina stands out for its "success" in this area. Goldberg cites a few cases of discrimination and some historians interested in black Argentines, but concurs with most scholars and popular accounts that Afro-Argentines have virtually disappeared. Andrews mentions "a small trickle of black immigration from Portuguese Africa, particularly from the Cape Verde Islands" as well as blacks who continue to migrate to the capital from the interior, called *cabecitas negras* (literally, "little black heads"). Certainly the earlier distinction between *pardos* ("mulattos") and *morenos* ("blacks") seems to have disappeared, according to Andrews. He mentions that some forms of popular entertainment have featured Afro-Argentine themes; two such dramatic productions are the 1940 musical *Candombe de San Baltasar* and a 1947 play, *Cuando había reyes* (When There Were Kings), which recounts the lives of a black community under Rosas. Some candombes have also survived and are performed in festivals by both black and white Argentines. Andrews states that one remnant of the Afro-Argentine community in Buenos Aires as of 1976 was the Shimmy Club, "a group that has no activities other than sponsoring occasional dances… in a working-class area near Congress." Many mixed couples dance to a tango orchestra and to "an electric Brazilian-tropical band."

Overall, however, the substantially reduced numbers of Afro-Argentines – by some accounts the population totals only a few thousand – have enabled Argentina to deny the historic relevance of blacks and portray theirs as a white nation free of racism. An article appearing in the *Montreal Gazette* in 1998 quotes a Buenos Aires museum director's response to the possibility of an Afro-Argentine exhibit: "We have too many important events and personalities to show. We can't waste space putting things that don't have any relevance to our history." The country's self-image coexists with continued manifestations of racism. The same article explains that when the Argentine soccer team was to play either the Brazilian or Nigerian team in the Olympic finals, a sports newspaper ran the headline, "Bring on the Monkeys," eliciting protests from the governments of both potential opponents. As of the late 1990s scholars like Andrews, Goldberg, Chace, and others sought to confront such persistent racism and ensure that the historic significance of Afro-Argentines is not forgotten.

Joy Elizondo

See Also

Morales, José María.

Latin America and the Caribbean

Aristide, Jean-Bertrand

(b. July 15, 1953, Port-Salut, Haiti), president of Haiti from February 1991 to September 1991 and from October 1994 to February 1996.

Jean-Bertrand Aristide rose from the role of country priest to the presidency of Haiti. He was born in a rural area far removed from the modern amenities of the city. Soon after he was born his father died, and with his mother and sister he moved to urban Port-au-Prince. At age 5 he became a student in a Roman Catholic school run by the order of the Salesian Brothers. There he learned to speak French, long officially preferred to Haitian Creole, as well as Latin, Greek, English, Spanish, and Italian. At age 14 Aristide began preparation for the priesthood at the Notre Dame secondary school.

In 1974, following graduation from the seminary, Aristide left Haiti to spend a year in the Dominican Republic. Returning to Port-au-Prince, he enrolled at National University in 1979, where he completed a degree in psychology. During the 1970s he also began reading several Latin American theologians who were developing and advancing what they called a theology of liberation. This theology, which preaches active participation by the Church in social issues affecting the poor, melded well with Aristide's own beliefs.

To further develop his theological philosophy, Aristide traveled to Israel, where he studied the Bible as well as Hebrew and Arabic. On July 3, 1982, he was ordained to the priesthood. His first assignment was to the parish of St. Joseph in the poor section of Port-au-Prince. After three months the Salesians sent Aristide to pursue graduate studies at the University of Montreal, where he received a master's degree in biblical theology. He continued his readings in liberation theology, and took a study tour to Greece before returning to Haiti on January 5, 1985.

Following his return Aristide taught biblical theology in Port-au-Prince's Salesian seminary and at the same time taught at a Salesian school in Les Cayes, Haiti. In September 1985 he was appointed master of studies at the National School for Arts and Crafts in St. Jean Bosco, a parish on the edge of a large slum in Port-au-Prince known for helping the poorest youth.

This is when Aristide's political activities became well known, particularly his staunch support of democracy and his devotion to improving the lives of Haiti's poor. Shortly after arriving at his new post, he organized thousands of young people in the Solidarité Ant Jen (or "Solidarity Among Youth") committee to press for democracy, the end of Haitian dictator Jean-Claude Duvalier's rule, and better conditions for Haiti's poor. By the end of 1985 St. Jean Bosco had a reputation as a center for political organizing. As a result, Aristide also attracted the government's hatred: on January 31, 1986, Aristide survived the first of several assassination attempts, when a gunman entered the church of St. Jean Bosco yet failed to kill him.

As Aristide became known for his personal bravery and his commitment to Haiti's poor, both his popularity and his congregation grew. At the same time popular resistance to the rule of Duvalier led to his resignation on February 7, 1986. Duvalier's exit did not put a halt to Aristide's political cause or religious conviction. However, his commitment to political activity compelled the Salesian Brothers, in May 1986, to ask that he refrain from political activities. Aristide complied temporarily but by November began to organize again, playing a key role in several demonstrations. The harassment carried out against Aristide during the Duvalier regime continued, now carried out by forces under the command of Duvalier's successor, Gen. Henri Namphy.

Opposition from the Roman Catholic Church continued as well. The Vatican had supported or ignored liberation theology and its practitioners in the 1960s and 1970s, but it was now an active critic. In August 1987 a Superior was sent from Rome, and Aristide was transferred from Port-au-Prince to the less politically visible city of Croix-des-Maisons, known as a center of support for the Tonton Macoutes, the secret police established under the rule of the Duvaliers. Young protesters, who occupied the national cathedral in Port-au-Prince and staged dramatic hunger strikes, were so determined to prevent Aristide's departure that the Church rescinded the transfer order.

Because of his activism, Aristide was seen as a threat by the United States government, which referred to him in diplomatic cables as a "radical firebrand." More important, Aristide survived two more assassination attempts. A particularly dramatic one occurred in August 1987 in the town of Pont-Sondé. There a gunman opened fire on a crowd listening to Aristide deliver a sermon. Then the gunman walked up to Aristide and fired at him from a distance of 20 paces but missed. A third attempt on Aristide's life occurred that same night.

As Aristide's popularity continued to grow, opposition to his activities from both the military and the Roman Catholic Church grew as well. With the end of Duvalier's reign in February 1986, elections were being held; international pressure on Haiti's military had forced the post-Duvalier military regime to attempt a transfer of power to a democratically elected government. Aristide campaigned for democracy and criticized the military while predicting that violence was inevitable under the prevalent political conditions and that the results of the elections would matter little. Indeed, during the campaign there were numerous disruptions; the feared Tonton Macoutes actively disrupted meetings of the opposition parties and harassed and threatened their supporters. The offices of the Comité Electoral Provisoire, the civilian organization charged with supervising the elections, were burned to the ground. Party members who expressed opposition to the military faced constant death threats; some were brutally murdered. On November 29, 1987, a number of voters and onlookers were gunned down at a Port-au-Prince polling station. The clear involvement of Haiti's military in this incident finally led the United States to assert that it would cut off aid to Haiti. The military, in turn, declared the elections invalid and instituted outright military rule, eventually under the command of Gen. Prosper Avril.

Pressure on Aristide also mounted. In the most shocking incident, on September 11, 1988, a group of armed thugs attacked the St. Jean Bosco Church as Aristide was delivering morning mass. They broke into the church, killed 13 parishioners, looted the church, and set it on fire. Finally, in December 1988, Aristide was expelled from the order of the Salesian Brothers. Nonetheless he continued his work among the poor. On October 18, 1990, he took the ultimate step in political participation by announcing his candidacy for the presidency. He ran as spokesperson for the Lavalas ("the Flood"), a loose coalition of grass-roots movements supported by the poor of Haiti.

Despite tremendous odds and harassment, on December 16, 1990, Aristide won the presidency of Haiti in a landslide with 67 percent of the vote. His overwhelming support astonished many outside observers, who had predicted that the pro-United States candidate, Marc Bazin, a former World Bank official, would easily triumph. After a last-minute unsuccessful coup attempt in January 1991 by Roger Lafontant, a former head of the Tonton Macoute during Duvalier's rule, Aristide was sworn in on February 7, 1991. In a symbolically powerful gesture, Aristide included parables in Haitian Creole in his inauguration speech, and during the ceremony hugged four boys from the orphanage that he had helped run. In his speech he stated: "It took 200 years to arrive at our second independence. At our first independence we cried 'Liberty or Death!' We must now shout with all our strength, 'Democracy or Death!'"

However, Aristide's policies, tinged with socialism and liberation theology, met with severe criticism, especially within the military. During his first seven months in office he proposed raising the minimum wage, dismantling the repressive rural section chief system, and instituting literacy campaigns. The human rights situation in Haiti also improved dramatically. But on September 30, 1991, Aristide was toppled from office by a military coup led by Brig. Gen. Raoul Cedras. Aristide went initially to VENEZUELA, then spent most of the years 1992 to 1994 in the United States, where he wrote and gave speeches before numerous groups.

Calls for Aristide's reinstatement as the Haitian president gathered significant support both in the United States and internationally. But the period of Aristide's ouster saw severe political turbulence in Haiti. Two of Aristide's top supporters – Justice Minister Guy Malary and Father Jean-Marie Vincent – were killed. Finally, in September 1994, after intense pressure by the United States and the United Nations, and negotiations spearheaded by former president Jimmy Carter, Gen. Colin Powell, and Sen. Sam Nunn, the Haitian military agreed to step down. On September 19, U.S. military forces began a virtual occupation of Haiti, eventually coming to number more than 20,000. At the culmination of this effort, Aristide resumed his presidency on October 15, 1994. Returning to Haiti with U.S. secretary of state Warren Christopher, Rev. Jesse Jackson, and members of the CONGRESSIONAL BLACK CAUCUS, Aristide vowed to restore democracy and urged reconciliation and forgiveness for supporters of the military regime. His return was met with countrywide celebrations. The agreement that restored him to office stipulated that he serve only two years, and in the next election René Préval was sworn in as Haiti's new president on February 7, 1996. Aristide now lives as an ex-president, but his popularity continues to be strong among the people.

Gregory Freeland

SEE ALSO

Duvalier, Jean-Claude; Jackson, Jesse Louis; Powell, Colin Luther; Port-au-Prince, Haiti; Catholic Church in Latin America and the Caribbean.

Africa

Armah, Ayi Kwei

(b. 1939), Ghanaian novelist and journalist.

Born in the western region of GHANA, Ayi Kyei Armah's career has taken him to three continents. Attending local schools and receiving his secondary education at Achimota College near Accra, Armah came to the United States in 1959 and received a degree in sociology from Harvard University. Shortly after, he moved to Algiers and began working for the weekly *Révolution Africaine* as a translator. Later returning to Ghana, Armah taught English and wrote for Ghana Television. In 1967 he enrolled in the Graduate Writing Program at Columbia University. He subsequently joined the staff of *Jeune Afrique* but soon left Paris in 1968, accepting professorships first in the United States and then in TANZANIA. He has spent much of his later life in Senegal.

Known for his novels, short stories, and poems, Armah is famed for his venomous attacks on the leaders of Ghana, particularly Prime Minister and later first president KWAME NKRUMAH, for what Armah saw as Nkrumah's corrupt and abusive practices. He is also known for the force and sweep of his prose, a sturdy complement to the power of his polemic. Best known for his three novels, *The Beautyful Ones Are Not Yet Born* (1968), *Fragments* (1970), and *Why Are We So Blest?* (1971), Armah critically examines the political and social consequences of colonialism in Ghana, leaving readers with little optimism about future change. Armah's later novels, *Two Thousand Seasons* (1973) and *The Healers* (1978), are much more allegorical and less dependent on realistic detail, a shift from his earlier work.

SEE ALSO

Accra, Ghana; Algiers, Algeria.

Latin America and the Caribbean

Armenteros, Alfredo "Chocolate"

(b. April 4, 1928, Ranchuelo, Santa Clara, Las Villas Province, CUBA), Afro-Cuban trumpeter, composer, and arranger, a master of Cuba's brass-led septeto and conjunto styles who helped shape AFRO-LATIN JAZZ and SALSA MUSIC.

Virtuoso trumpet and flügelhorn player Alfredo "Chocolate" Armenteros is the last surviving master of Cuba's distinctive septeto style, performed by a small ensemble featuring a trumpet backed by stringed instruments and percussion. He has played in many Latin American musical genres, including Afro-Latin jazz big bands, small-group Cuban *descargas* (jam sessions), and salsa music. On *Knockdown Calypsoes* (1979), he convincingly re-created the sound of Trinidad's 1930sand 1940s-era CALYPSO bands. In Latin music, Armenteros's trumpet playing is instantly recognizable. Rather than seeking harmonic complexity or intricate rapid-fire melodies, which have characterized JAZZ trumpet playing since the bop era, he projects a sound that is bold, brassy, and confident. His playing and arranging feature lyrical melodies, catchy riffs, and, above all, the rhythmic drive that epitomizes Afro-Cuban jazz.

Armenteros began playing trumpet at about the age of ten. In 1949 he made his recording debut as a member of Conjunto Los Astros, a band under the leadership of singer René Alvarez. In the early 1950s he joined innovative bandleader ARSENIO RODRÍGUEZ, whose expanded Conjunto – which added a second (and sometimes a third) trumpet, piano, and conga drum to the standard septeto format – helped lay the foundations for salsa music. From 1953 to 1956 he took charge of the brass section in BENY MORÉ's big band. He first performed in New York City during the late 1950s and was featured on singer Nat "King" Cole's album *Cole Español* (1958). In 1960, following the Cuban Revolution, he relocated permanently to New York and quickly established himself as one of the city's top-rated Latin musicians.

Armenteros has performed and recorded with many prominent Latin musicians, including Afro-Cuban jazz pioneer MACHITO, Afro-Cuban conga player Mongo Santamaria, Puerto Rican timbales player Tito Puente, and Dominican flutist JOHNNY PACHECO. From 1968 to 1978 he appeared regularly on Latin jazz pianist Eddie Palmieri's recordings. In 1994 he was featured on Afro-Cuban bassist Israel "Cachao" López's Grammy Award-winning album *Master Sessions, Vol. I.*

James Clyde Sellman

SEE ALSO

Cole, Nat ("King"); New York, New York; López, Israel ("Cachao"); Puente, Ernesto Antonio (Tito); Son; Santamaría, Ramón ("Mongo"); Trinidad and Tobago.

North America

Armstrong, Lillian Hardin (Lil)

(b. Feburary 3, 1898, Memphis, Tenn.; d. August 27, 1971, Chicago, Ill.), American jazz singer, pianist, and composer; worked with her husband, Louis Armstrong, in the bands Hot Five and Hot Seven.

Lillian Hardin's career as a JAZZ musician began with a job in a Chicago music store. She met Louis Armstrong while they were both with King Oliver's Creole Jazz Band in Chicago; they married in 1924 and divorced in 1938. Armstrong worked with her husband in the Hot Five and Hot Seven bands, and went on to appear in two Broadway shows, record under her own name, work as a house pianist for Decca Records, and sustain a long solo career. She died onstage at a Louis Armstrong memorial concert.

Lisa Clayton Robinson

SEE ALSO

Armstrong, Louis ("Satchmo"); Chicago, Illinois.

North America

Armstrong, Louis ("Satchmo")

(b. August 4, 1901, New Orleans, La.; d. July 6, 1971, New York, N.Y.), African American trumpet player and vocalist; the most significant soloist in the history of JAZZ.

LOUIS ARMSTRONG, JAZZ, AND AMERICAN POPULAR CULTURE

More than anyone else, Louis Armstrong was responsible for legitimizing and popularizing jazz for a wider public. A much-admired jazz trumpeter and gravel-voiced vocalist, Armstrong was also a consummate entertainer, steadily expanding his career from instrumentalist to popular singer, to film and television personality, and, ultimately, to cultural icon. He acquired many nicknames throughout his life, including Dippermouth, Pops, and Satchelmouth – the latter often contracted to Satchmo. As Satchmo, he was instantly identifiable around the world, decades before PRINCE, Madonna, or Sting. The international appeal of his music in effect made Armstrong the American goodwill ambassador to the world.

Armstrong transformed jazz in two profoundly important ways. Early jazz was characterized by freewheeling group improvisation, but Armstrong, by his virtuosity and lyricism, almost single-handedly elevated the individual soloist to preeminence. In addition, his relaxed phrasing catalyzed a shift away from the staccato and jerky rhythms of early jazz to the even, four-beat swing that still characterizes most jazz today.

Armstrong was above all a soloist, in much the same sense as tenor saxophonist Coleman Hawkins and alto saxophonist Charlie Parker. Unlike Duke Ellington, the other great jazz figure to emerge in the 1920s, Armstrong revealed little distinction as a composer, arranger, or bandleader. Armstrong's most successful ensembles were small – for example, his Hot Five and Hot Seven, which were strictly studio bands that never made regular public appearances. As was apparent in his big-band recordings of the early 1930s, Armstrong had an astonishing ability to transcend the limits of mediocre and sloppy accompaniment, which was a sign not only of his self-sustaining inspiration, but also of his casual attitude toward the quality of his sidemen.

THE TROUBLING LEGACY OF ARMSTRONG'S PERSONA

Armstrong was not known as a "race man." He recorded a hit version of the popular song "Shine" (1931), evidently not put off by its demeaning lyrics. He played the same song – while standing ankle-deep in soap bubbles and outfitted as an African warrior clad in a leopard skin – as part of the Hollywood short film *Rhapsody in Black and Blue* (1932). For much of his career, he offered no direct challenge to racial discrimination other than the indictment that was implicit in his own vast talent. Otherwise, he made his peace with the status quo. In light of the harsh racial environment of the early decades of the twentieth century, his attitude made practical sense. But it is worth remembering that not all black musicians of that era chose, as Armstrong did, to project a smiling acquiescence in the midst of racism. Clarinet and soprano saxophone player Sidney Bechet, one of Armstrong's foremost rivals as a jazz instrumentalist in the 1920s, responded very differently. His volatile temperament and willingness to challenge racial slights also ensured that he would not find widespread acceptance among whites until he settled in France following World War II.

Unfortunately, Armstrong's happy-go-lucky disposition and good humor provided a convenient reinforcement for the racial prejudices of many white listeners. Jazz musicians of the bop generation, who came to maturity in the 1940s and early 1950s, including trumpeters Dizzy Gillespie and Miles Davis, later condemned Armstrong for "Tomming" – in other words, for being an Uncle Tom, the uncomplaining "good" slave character in Harriet Beecher Stowe's UNCLE TOM'S CABIN (1852). Gillespie criticized his "plantation image," that "public image of him, handkerchief over his head, grinning in the face of white racism." Such comments suggest the vast difference between Armstrong's experiences and those of a younger generation of black musicians. Despite such criticisms, however, Armstrong clearly demonstrated his ability to take a stand during the late 1950s and the 1960s. For much of his career, however, he revealed few political convictions.

HIS EARLY YEARS

Armstrong was a poor boy who made good. He grew to adulthood in a time and place – the early twentieth-century American South – that offered African Americans few opportunities or prospects of any kind. He was born to a 15- or 16-year-old prostitute, Mary Albert, in a New Orleans neighborhood so tumbledown and violent that it was known as the Battlefield. His father, William Armstrong, abandoned the two soon after Louis's birth, and for the next five years Louis was raised by his grandmother.

In 1913 after a New Year's Eve prank involving his stepfather's .38-caliber pistol and six blanks fired into the air, he was remanded to the Colored Waif's Home. There he joined the brass band, first playing the tambourine, then graduating to a variety of brass instruments, including the alto horn and the

Louis Armstrong's studio ensemble in Chicago in 1925. The Hot Five are, *left to right*, Johnny Dodds, Armstrong, Johnny St. Cyr, Kid Ory, and Lil Hardin.
Frank Driggs/Archive Photos

trumpet. When Armstrong left the Waif's Home in 1914, he found work as a musician in the various honky-tonks and urban jook joints of his Perdido Street neighborhood. During these years he caught the eye of the city's most respected cornet player, Joe "King" Oliver, who repeatedly helped to advance his career. From 1918 to 1921 Armstrong also worked on steamboats that traveled the Mississippi River, in particular, in the band of pianist Fate Marable.

His Move North and Early Recordings

In 1922 King Oliver, who had moved to Chicago four years earlier, invited Armstrong to join him there to play second cornet in his Creole Jazz Band. Black migrants were then filling Chicago's raucous South Side, and white mobsters were busily opening bars, clubs, and speakeasies that featured the new jazz music. In 1923 the Creole Jazz Band traveled to Richmond, Indiana, and made a number of recordings for Gennett Records that remain profoundly important; jazz scholar James Lincoln Collier views them as "one of the root stocks of jazz." The group played in classic New Orleans jazz style, employing elaborate, collectively improvised polyphony, but a number of the brief instrumental breaks – such as Armstrong's two choruses on "Chimes Blues" (1923), his first recorded solo – pointed the way to the future. Armstrong's playing already displayed a loose, easy swing quite at odds with the stiff, RAGTIME-derived rhythms of many of his contemporaries.

Armstrong remained with Oliver only until 1924, when he left for New York City at the invitation of bandleader Fletcher Henderson and at the urging of his wife, pianist Lil Hardin, who wanted Armstrong to strike out on his own. During his brief stint with the Henderson big band, Armstrong had an impact on every jazz musician who heard him. By late 1925 he returned to Chicago, where he organized his most important band – the Hot Five, later expanded to the Hot Seven – and commenced a memorable series of recordings for Okeh Records. On such songs as "Cornet Chop Suey" (1926), "Struttin' with Some Barbecue" (1927), and above all "West End Blues" (1928), Armstrong played solos of breathtaking beauty and technical brilliance.

"West End Blues," in particular, amazed fellow jazz musicians. Armstrong's bravura open horn projected a bell-toned and brassy assurance. He entered on a high B-flat that he held out for four long, tension-building measures before falling away in a precisely articulated flurry of notes. Although there were general precedents for his "West End Blues" solo – most notably Bubber Miley's playing on Duke Ellington's "Black and Tan Fantasy" (1927) for Victor Records – no other jazz musician of the day could match Armstrong's technique and spontaneous lyricism.

The Defining Qualities of Armstrong's Trumpet Playing

Armstrong projected a clear tone, whatever his register, and whether he was playing high notes or low. His articulation was clean, and when he held out notes, he concluded by adding a slow vibrato, a slight quaver or alteration of the pitch, that was soon much imitated. It was different from the fast vibrato favored by most of his New Orleans contemporaries, including Bechet. Armstrong's melodic ideas were distinctive, classically balanced, and memorable, so much so that his style of improvising inspired countless imitators, including virtually every trumpet player to emerge during the 1920s and 1930s. He also had what was, for that period, an astonishing range.

Like many other self-taught brass players, Armstrong reached high notes by pulling the cornet or trumpet forcefully against his mouth to raise the pitch of his vibrating lips, rather than using the muscles of his mouth and cheeks to change the pitch. Photographs reveal that by the early 1930s Armstrong had already permanently scarred his lips. Over the years, his reckless and competitive nature – sometimes he played 50 or 100 high Cs in succession, topped by a high F – took an inevitable toll on his trumpet playing. His biographer James Lincoln Collier described the results of an April 26, 1933, recording session: "On the last tune of the day, 'Don't Play Me Cheap,' toward the end of his final chorus we are brought almost to tears as he writhes up to the climactic high note that he felt he had to give his audience. He was by this point jamming the sharp circle of steel of the mouthpiece deep into the flesh of his lips to give them enough support to reach the high notes." Victor Records and Johnny Collins, then respectively Armstrong's record company and manager, held him to a grueling pace, and Armstrong, always eager to please, did not refuse them.

During this period, however, Armstrong began to change his style by simplifying it. He continued to strive for high notes, but he began playing more slowly, using fewer notes per measure and leaving more open space. He improvised melodies that were more flowing, and he played longer phrases. Collier concluded that these changes were not simply an evolution in Armstrong's style; they were a way of sparing his lips. His need to lessen the wear and tear on his embouchure may also help explain his growing reliance upon vocals.

Armstrong as a Vocalist and Entertainer

By the early 1930s Armstrong's gravelly voice and swinging delivery had gained popularity with audiences regardless of race, and record companies urged him to sing more, and better, material. Armstrong was one of the first vocalists to use the technique known as scat singing – that is, singing nonsense syllables and improvised melodies instead of the actual lyrics and written melody. His phrasing had a powerful impact on virtually every jazz and popular vocalist to begin singing after 1930, including Cab Calloway, Billie Holiday, Ella Fitzgerald, Bing Crosby, and Frank Sinatra. Crosby declared categorically that Armstrong was "the beginning and the end of music in America."

Armstrong emerged as a certified star during the 1930s. He helped usher in the swing era as the featured soloist and front man of a number of early 1930s big bands. He traveled widely, including his first journeys abroad, to England in 1932 and to Europe in 1933-1934, which foreshadowed his post-World War II globetrotting. He began to appear in Hollywood films, including *Pennies from Heaven* (1936) and *Cabin in the Sky* (1943).

Although Armstrong developed a great popular following, jazz listeners increasingly viewed him as old-fashioned. Nonetheless, he continued to play music that was successful both commercially and artistically. In the post-World War II years, he enjoyed a series of hit recordings, including "Blueberry Hill" (1949), "Mack the Knife" (1955), and "Hello, Dolly" (1963). "What a Wonderful World" (1967) hit the charts – fully 17 years after his death – after its inclusion in the soundtrack of the film *Good Morning, Vietnam* (1988).

Beginning in 1947 Armstrong returned to small-group formats, something he had not done regularly since 1929. He organized the All Stars, which initially included his "West End Blues" collaborator Earl Hines on piano and other first-rate jazz musicians. The group continued through various personnel changes until the late 1960s. Armstrong's playing declined after a 1959 heart attack, although he recorded some of his finest late-career work in collaboration with the Duke Ellington Orchestra, resulting in two 1961 albums, *Together for the First Time* and *The Great Reunion*.

Social Critic and Ambassador to the World

During the 1950s Armstrong moved easily into his final and almost ubiquitous role as America's goodwill ambassador to the world. Beginning in 1949 he toured regularly overseas, most memorably including several trips to Africa (1956, 1960, and 1964) and a tour of Eastern Europe (1960). During his 1956 African tour, a crowd of more than 100,000 people turned out for him in Accra, Ghana.

Despite his reputation for "Tomming," Armstrong voiced trenchant criticisms of American racial injustices during the late 1950s and the 1960s. In 1957 he was slated to make a groundbreaking tour of the Soviet Union, but he stirred up controversy with his reaction to the Little Rock crisis, declaring that "the way they are treating my people in the South, the government can go to hell." In response, the United States State Department excluded Armstrong from the upcoming cultural mission, instead sending the less outspoken white clarinetist Benny Goodman.

Similarly, in 1965, after the violent beatings of civil rights demonstrators in Selma, Alabama, Armstrong remarked, "They would beat Jesus if he was black and marched." In 1968 he refused to take part in the Academy Awards telecast after the assassination of Martin Luther King Jr. Significantly, he spoke out not because of any personal affront or conflict, but rather in response to injuries inflicted on others.

During the 1960s jazz fans and the wider public gradually stopped thinking of Armstrong in terms of stylistic categories and musical fashions. He was beloved as a popular entertainer and revered as a jazz giant. In 1969 a second major heart attack virtually halted his trumpet playing, although still, on occasion, he could not resist taking up his horn. Following another hospitalization in 1971, Armstrong died in his sleep shortly before his 70th birthday.

James Clyde Sellman

See Also

Accra, Ghana; World War II and African Americans; Armstrong, Lillian Hardin (Lil); Bechet, Sidney Joseph; Calloway, Cabell (Cab); Chicago, Illinois; Civil Rights Movement; Davis, Miles Dewey, III; Gillespie, John Birks ("Dizzy"); Hawkins, Coleman Randolph; Henderson, Fletcher Hamilton, Jr.; Hines, Earl Kenneth ("Fatha"); New Orleans, Louisiana; King, Martin Luther, Jr.; Miley, James Wesley ("Bubber"); New Orleans, Louisiana; New York, New York; Oliver, Joseph ("King"); Parker, Charles Christopher ("Bird").

North America

Arnett, Benjamin William, Jr.

(b. March 6, 1838, Brownsville, Pa.; d. October 9, 1906, Green County, Ohio), African American religious and political activist, bishop of the African Methodist Episcopal Church, and influential black leader during William McKinley's presidency.

Benjamin William Arnett Jr. was entirely self-taught. After working as a waiter and a dockworker, he became certified as a teacher in Brownsville, Pennsylvania, in 1864. Soon thereafter he moved to Washington, D.C., and decided to become a minister in the African Methodist Episcopal (AME) Church. After receiving his license to preach in 1865, he was assigned his first pastorate near Cincinnati, Ohio, in 1867 (in Walnut Hills), where he also taught school. First ordained as a deacon in the AME Church in 1868, he became an elder in 1870. He served the AME General Conference as its secretary in 1876 and its financial secretary in 1880. In addition, he established close connections to the AME Church's center for learning, Wilberforce University.

During the Civil War, Arnett had worked with Frederick Douglass's National Equal Rights League as a Republican committed to equal rights. Later, he campaigned for Ohio Republicans, served as the chaplain for the Ohio legislature in 1879, and provided religious direction for the National Republican Convention in 1896. Because of his political connections and his ties to Wilberforce, he was urged, in 1885, to run for the Ohio legislature in order to secure money for Wilberforce. During his brief tenure, he was successful not only in gaining funding for the university, but also in working to secure rights for blacks in Ohio.

Andre Willis

See Also

African Methodist Episcopal Church; Civil War, American; Douglass, Frederick.

Africa

Aro, ethnic group of Nigeria.

The Aro of Nigeria speak a Niger-Congo language and are one of the Igbo peoples. Approximately 700,000 people consider themselves Aro.

See Also
Languages, African: An Overview.

Latin America and the Caribbean

Arozarena, Marcelino

(b. March 10, 1912, Havana, Cuba), Afro-Cuban poet, teacher, and journalist, considered one of the founders of *poesía negra*, or black poetry, in the Caribbean.

Marcelino Arozarena published his first poems in the 1920s in the Havana literary journal *La Palabra*. The journal was directed by Communist leader Juan Marinello. In his most famous poem, entitled "Caridá," Arozarena asks why a mulatto woman (of African and European descent) named Caridad has not shown up at a dance. Here, he employs typical *negrista* techniques (*see* Negrista Poets), such as mimicking musical rhythms and using *jitanjáfora* (onomatopoeic words) and folkloric depictions of Afro-Cuban music and dance.

Arozarena was among the first wave of negrista ("blackist") poets, including fellow Cubans Ramón Güirao, Alejo Carpentier, Regino Pedroso; Puerto Rican poet Palés Matos; and Mexican poet José Zacarías Tallet. Together with these authors, he helped spark a literary movement that embraced the cultural contributions made by black people throughout Latin America, particularly in his native Cuba. A few years later, Cuban poets Emilio Ballagas and especially Nicolás Guillén expanded the experimental boundaries of the movement still further: Ballagas by publishing a key anthology, *Mapa de la poesía negra americana* (1946; Map of Black Poetry in the Americas), and Guillén with his famous book of poems, *Motivos de son* (1930; Son Motifs), rhythmically based on the Afro-Cuban musical form son (*see* Afrocubanismo).

Like Guillén and Ballagas, Arozarena insisted on the universal value of what is today known as "black poetry." The title of his 1966 collection of poems, *Canción negra sin color* (Colorless Black Song), aptly expresses this view. He hoped "to see a day when this poetry would stop being considered racial poetry," according to critic Leslie Wilson. In 1983 he published his second collection of poems, *Habrá que esperar* (Having to Wait). Arozarena is a member of the Society for Afro-Cuban Studies founded by Fernando Ortiz in 1937 and is a founding member of Cuba's National Union of Journalists and its National Union of Writers and Artists.

See Also
Palés Matos, Luis; Music, Afro-Caribbean Secular; Dance in Latin America and the Caribbean; Havana, Cuba.

North America

Art, African American, painting, sculpture, graphic arts, and crafts developed by peoples of African descent in the United States and thematically and stylistically informed by African American culture.

The term *African American art* means different things to different people. For some it designates a largely racial phenomenon, describing all artistic products – paintings, sculptures, graphic arts, crafts, architecture, and so on – created by North Americans of African descent. For others the preceding definition fails to take into account the cultural, in addition to the racial, implications of the term. For this latter group African American art refers to the artistic and visual products not just of North Americans of African descent but of many peoples whose work has been shaped thematically, stylistically, formally, and theoretically by the confluence of black Atlantic cultures – folkways and traditions formed as a result of the transatlantic slave trade – and further developed during alternating periods of colonialism, emancipation, discrimination, and self-assertion. For our purposes, the concept of African American art moves freely between these two definitions, providing readers with both the breadth of such an idea and the possibilities for an object-centered and culturally informed definition.

Arts and Crafts during the Colonial, Federalist, and Antebellum Years

During America's infancy (in the period between the 1600s and the early 1800s), what one could describe as African American art indeed embraced a range of forms and definitions. A small drum, several wrought-iron figures, dozens of ceramic "face" vessels, and a few examples of domestic architecture found among enslaved black communities in the Southern United States have been singled out for their similarities with comparable crafts, functional objects, and structures in West and Central Africa. In contrast, black artisans like the New England-based engraver Scipio Moorhead and the Baltimore portrait painter Joshua Johnson created art that, despite occasional portrayals of black subjects, was conceived in a thoroughly Western European fashion. Other workshop- or academically-trained African American artists prior to the Civil War – New Yorkers Patrick Reason and William Simpson, Philadelphian Robert Douglass, and the New Orleans- and Paris-based brothers Daniel and Eugene Warburg – also created works of art that were indistinguishable from those of white printmakers, painters, and sculptors.

From the Civil War Years through the Post-Reconstruction Period

The tensions between an art that referred to people's social conditions and an art that transcended race and class politics are represented by the works of two artists active during the 1860s and 1870s: sculptor Edmonia Lewis and landscape painter Robert S. Duncanson. Lewis – who studied art at Oberlin College, independently in Boston, Massachusetts, and among American and British expatriates in Italy – used the artistic conventions of neoclassicism to create powerful marble statuary on the subjects of black American emancipation, female oppression, and Native Americans. Duncanson – working in Cincinnati, Ohio, and in the Great Lakes region near the state of Michigan – painted dreamy, pastoral scenes that recalled Hudson River aesthetics rather than overtly racial and political themes. Yet the racially tinged ordeals that both of these artists grappled with at various points in their careers gave even their most apolitical portrait busts and landscape allegories a social dimension, thus justifying the African American designation of their work.

A similar political-apolitical bifurcation is present in the work and lives of artists working between 1865 and 1900. First against a social backdrop of enfranchisement and hope and later against one of disenfranchisement and despair, landscape painters like Edward Mitchell Bannister and William Harper created moody, Barbizon School-like scenes, bereft of the political jockeying and white-on-black violence that characterized African American lives at the end of the century. For painter Henry Ossawa Tanner the pressures of American racism and the burdens of representing his race were too great. His 1893 move to Paris, France, encouraged his interest in painting mostly biblical scenes in a part academic, part symbolist manner. In contrast, the Athens, Georgia, seamstress Harriet Powers, oblivious to the world of art galleries and exhibitions, created at least two powerful Bible quilts that bore strong similarities to West African textile arts, especially to the cloth appliqués from the Akan and Fon peoples.

Increasingly, heroic and uplifting portrayals of African Americans appeared in paintings and sculpture in the first two decades of the twentieth century. Artist Edwin A. Harleston was renowned for his paintings of distinguished (and affluent) black Americans. Sculptors Isaac Scott Hathaway and May Howard Jackson also dedicated much of their careers to creating portrait busts of African American notables past and present. In the pages of the journal *The Voice of the Negro* artist John Henry Adams Jr. created dozens of African American portraits: finely drawn and idealized in the manner of the white illustrator Charles Dana Gibson but informed by an emerging racial consciousness. In the more symbolic and allegorical works of the sculptor Meta Warrick Fuller, a black cultural

Sharecropper, a 1968 color lithograph by Elizabeth Catlett, illustrates her skillful blending of African and Mexican elements.

cognizance manifested itself in important nineteenth-century topics such as emancipation and in pieces that foreshadowed several themes that would be important for artists and intellectuals in subsequent years (the African past, a black cultural rebirth, etc.).

The Harlem Renaissance

The social and political anxieties that many African Americans felt just after World War I were alleviated, in part, by mass migrations to the urban North. Northern cities offered a respite from the repressive attitudes and mandates of the old Southern order. The new racial compositions of cities like Washington, D.C, Philadelphia, New York, Pittsburgh, Detroit, Chicago, and St. Louis, in combination with a heightened social consciousness and a seemingly unbounded desire for leisure and escape, conspired to help create the cultural phenomenon known as the New Negro Arts Movement. Part social engineering and part spontaneous expression, this Harlem Renaissance (as the cultural movement later became known) was realized by a mix of American movers and shakers: social reformers, political activists, cultural elites, progressives in public policy and education, and, of course, artists. Although each of these constituencies had its own reasons for promoting African American achievements in the literary, musical, visual, and performing arts, the collective result of these endeavors was an unprecedented, broad-based focus on African Americans, their art, and the connections to a larger, modernist vision.

Visual artists played a key role in creating depictions of the "New Negro." Alongside their counterparts in literature, music, and theater, painters Palmer C. Hayden, Malvin Gray Johnson, and Laura Wheeler Waring, among others, exhibited bold, stylized por-

TOP LEFT: ***I Baptize Thee*, an oil-on-burlap painting by William H. Johnson (1901-1970), is one of several Southern rural scenes the artist painted in the early 1940s.** *National Museum of American Art, Washington, D.C./Art Resource, NY*
LEFT: ***Can Fire in the Park*, an oil on canvas by Beauford Delaney (1902-1979), dates from 1946. This work is one of many New York street scenes the artist painted before emigrating to Paris in 1953.** *National Museum of American Art, Washington, D.C. /Art Resource, NY*
TOP: In his painting *The Janitor Who Paints* (1939-1940), Palmer C. Hayden portrays both African American life and the struggle of African American artists. *National Museum of American Art, Washington D.C./Art Resource, NY*
ABOVE: Henry Ossawa Tanner (1859-1937), who pursued his successful career as an artist in France, painted *The Banjo Player* in 1893. *Hampton University Museum, Hampton, Virginia*

traits of African Americans during this period, as well as scenes of black life from a variety of perspectives. Sculptors RICHMOND BARTHÉ, SARGENT JOHNSON, and Augusta Savage used clay, wood, and bronze to create comparable representations.

Book and magazine publishers of the 1920s and 1930s also helped to disseminate Harlem Renaissance imagery. Published in the pages of the *Crisis, Opportunity,* and *New Masses* were the blockprint illustrations of James Lesesne Wells, the etchings and drawings of ALBERT ALEXANDER SMITH, and the illustrations and jacket covers of one of the period's most prolific artists, AARON DOUGLAS.

THE DEPRESSION AND WORLD WAR II YEARS

As the debates among artists and intellectuals around a "racially representative art" shifted to discussions about social responsibility and a "folk" identity, artists like Aaron Douglas increasingly turned to the public arena as a means of addressing art and life in the 1930s. Douglas's murals for schools, libraries, and YMCAs exemplified this shift toward the social, as did the colorful, compositionally rhythmic easel paintings of Archibald J. Motley Jr. Many artists in the 1930s who had begun their careers during the Harlem Renaissance and under the aegis of philanthropic organizations like the William E. Harmon Foundation now made art under the auspices of the Federal Arts Projects of the WORKS PROGRESS ADMINISTRATION. These artists, like ALLAN ROHAN CRITE, Ernest Crichlow, and

Dox Thrash, embraced a visually conservative but politically radical figurative art in which the themes of poverty, racial discrimination, and a growing social consciousness took center stage.

This newfound fascination in the art world with "the masses" resulted in an expanded appreciation for those artists, black *and* white, who had not attended art school, whose art was often unsophisticated, and who functioned on the margins of the art scene proper. One of these so-called folk artists, the Nashville, Tennessee, stone carver William Edmondson, was honored in 1937 with a one-person exhibition at New York's Museum of Modern Art; he was the first African American artist to receive that distinction.

In the final years of the Federal Arts Projects several painters emerged from obscurity into national prominence. The most celebrated in this group was the painter Jacob Lawrence. His multipaneled series on such topics as the eighteenth-century Haitian revolutionary Toussaint L'Ouverture, the African American migration experience, and Harlem struck an emotional chord among art aficionados in the 1940s. Paintings by the intuitive artist Horace Pippin on the lives of Abraham Lincoln and John Brown and other paintings inspired by biblical verses were also critically acclaimed and highly sought after. Other painters of the late 1930s and early 1940s – like William H. Johnson, Charles Sebree, and Eldzier Cortor – achieved a measure of success in the larger world of art as well, often fusing the style preferences of the day (color abstraction, figural expressionism, and surrealism) with the artists' affinities for selected African American subjects.

This silkscreen print from Jacob Lawrence's *Migration Series* (1940-1941) is entitled *The Migrants Cast Their Ballots.* *The Newark Museum/Art Resource, NY*

Abstraction and Realism during the Postwar Years

This balancing act between a race consciousness in art and visual assimilation into the white cultural mainstream – exemplified most emphatically in a nonfigurative, abstract art – was undermined by several artists in the post-World War II years. The work of these artists – decidedly abstract and expressionistic yet at times referential to Africa, black America, and the evolving civil rights struggle – necessitated an altogether different definition of what was then described as "modern Negro art." At the forefront of this new paradigm was Hale Woodruff, whose integration of African-design motifs into his colorful, large-scale canvases stood alongside an enigmatic and symbol-laden painterly abstraction in works by other painters. Similarly, a 1950s brand of New York School abstraction was defined in part by the "all-over" compositions of painter Norman Lewis. A master of visual wit, irony, and critique, Lewis figured in contradistinction to another abstractionist, Beauford Delaney, who wavered between completely nonillusionistic, gestural canvases and thickly painted, expressive portraits.

In the midst of this moment, when abstract art was considered the status quo, several figurative artists, among them Hughie Lee-Smith and Charles White, achieved broad recognition. Lee-Smith painted desolate, urban landscapes inhabited by solitary people of different ages and sexes and across the racial spectrum. White, whose career dated back to the 1930s, reappeared in the 1950s with a series of monumental crayon and ink drawings of idealized African American figures. These works, when thematically framed by the news reports of civil rights bus boycotts, lunch-counter sit-ins, and attacks on black protesters by angry whites, took on an even greater power than their abstract counterparts in explicitly communicating something about African American aspirations and dreams. James Hampton and Minnie Evans, although far removed from the New York art scene in their respective communities of Washington, D.C., and Pender County, North Carolina, created powerful artistic statements during this period that not only reintroduced so-called folk elements into the art world but added a spiritual dimension to black visual culture.

Bob Thompson and Romare Bearden, working around the 1960s, may be considered to have formed a bridge between the visual past and a visual future for African American art. The visual past was represented by the omnipresent black figure, overtures to visual modernism, and the need to acknowledge the politics of race. A visual future seemed to involve artistic singularity over racial unity, narrational/perceptual simultaneity, and the interjecting of class, gender, and sexuality into art.

The colorful, silhouetted, and enigmatic figures in Thompson's paintings, derived from

Meta Vaux Warrick Fuller (1877-1968) created *Ethiopia Awakening* in 1914. Drawing on Egyptian sculpture and themes, this bronze statue recalls the African heritage of black Americans. *Schomburg Center for Research in Black Culture, Art & Artifacts Division, The New York Public Library, Astor, Lenox and Tilden Foundations*

the works of the old masters of European painting and the "new young lions" of jazz, introduced a whole new set of options in African American visual culture. Similarly, the cut-up, collaged, and reconstituted images of Afro-America that Bearden introduced to the public in 1964 inaugurated an expanded and progressive view of art and art-making: a picture that reflected ambiguity, complexity, nuance, and affirmation in black culture.

The Black Arts Movement, Abstraction, and Beyond

Art's capacity to endow the artist, viewer, and others with self-affirmation and a sense of cultural authority became the benchmark for the Black Arts Movement of the late 1960s and early 1970s. During this period African American writers, performing artists, and visual artists made black culture and the political struggles of black peoples worldwide their raison d'être. Slogans like "Black Is Beautiful" and Black Power as well as jazz and "soul" music became the soundtrack for works by painter Murry DePillars, mixed-media artist Ben Jones, and muralist Dana Chandler. Jeff Donaldson, a cofounder of the Chicago-based black artist collective AFRI-COBRA, not only added to this milieu with his own African textile-inspired, mixed-media works, but also wrote influential art manifestos and helped organize international expositions of black artists in Africa and North America.

Many artists whose careers extended back to the 1930s and 1940s resurfaced with a renewed sense of racial solidarity and political insurgency during the Black Arts Movement. Painters Lois Mailou Jones and John Biggers and sculptor and printmaker Elizabeth Catlett all aligned themselves with the younger generation of black artists, creating works that underscored their shared interest in African design sensibilities, the black figure, and the continuing struggle for civil rights.

For many abstract artists like Frank Bowling, Sam Gilliam, Richard Hunt, Barbara Chase-Riboud, and Raymond Saunders, critical and commercial success provided evidence that black artists were capable of overcoming racial obstacles and taking their rightfully earned places within the contemporary scene. These advancements were made all the more emphatic by the achievements of artists like the Washington painter Alma Thomas, who, at the age of 80, was the first African American woman to have a solo exhibition at New York's Whitney Museum of American Art in 1972. Artists who subscribed to a black nationalist agenda argued that Thomas (along with the other well-known black abstractionists) created works that did not challenge the aesthetic sensibilities of the white cultural mainstream. In response, abstractionists like Al Loving, Ed Clark, Joe Overstreet, Jack Whitten, and William T. Williams felt that this line of thinking showed how pervasive more conservative approaches to the visual arts were in African American communities. Both positions demonstrated how difficult it was for even the most sophisticated art connoisseurs to glean cultural elements out of abstract works. The same myopia often existed in interpretations of works by folk artists like Clementine Hunter and the evangelist-turned-painter Sister Gertrude Morgan.

As artists and audiences grew more conversant in the diverse ways that one could express black culture, the 1970s and 1980s ushered in a variety of artists and artworks all comfortably operating under the rubric of Afro-American art. From the photo-realism of painter Barkley L. Hendricks and "neo-mannerist" stylizations of painter Ernie Barnes to the cloth-and-canvas accretions of mixed-media artist Benny Andrews and altar-like installations of sculptor Beyte Saar, African American art could no longer be contained in neat, stylistic categories. The important exhibitions of past and present African American art organized by curators David C. Driskell and Edmund B. Gaither and the definitive histories and art publications of Elsa Honig Fine, Samella Lewis, and Ruth Waddy helped educate the experts and uninformed public alike on all that might constitute an African American art.

African American Art and Postmodernism

By the mid- to late 1980s earlier definitions of African American art were supplanted by the postmodernist tenets of cultural relativity, art-as-performance, critical inquiries of art and society through one's work, and interrogations of identity, geography, and history. Several artistic precursors to this new generation had already begun to exhibit these more provocative, postmodernist characteristics in their work. For example, by 1975 artist David Hammons was already creating sculptures from black cultural detritus (hair, food, artifacts, etc.) that ironically commented on black identity. Around the same time Robert Colescott was making outlandish, cartoonlike paintings that poked fun at the art establishment, cultural conservatives, and ethnocentrism. In contrast, conceptual artist Adrian Piper countered the reigning avant-garde of her day with performances that placed racism at the center of art matters. Also at this time artist Houston Conwill wrestled with the notion of African American space, initially through site-specific earthworks and later through culturally informed diagrams and signs.

These pioneers of an African American visual postmodernism helped put into motion a different set of visual criteria in contemporary art: models that, in turn, have engendered an innovative group of artists. This inventive group includes sculptors Alison Saar and Renee Stout and photographers Albert Chong and Lyle Ashton Harris, who explore concepts of objecthood and fetishism; visual artists like Jean Michel Basquiat, Glenn Ligon, and Lorna Simpson, for whom issues of gender and language are central in art; photographers Dawoud Bey, Renee Cox, and Lorraine O'Grady and painters Kerry James Marshall and Howardena Pindell, each of whom presents the black body as a site of theoretical warfare, social research, and desire; and conceptualists like Gary Simmons, Kara Walker, and Fred Wilson who, through installation art, have problematized American history and the psychology of racism so that display and spectatorship can no longer be viewed as purely innocent acts.

Richard Powell

See Also

World War I and African Americans; Basquiat, Jean-Michel; Chase-Riboud, Barbara Dewayne; Chicago, Illinois; Civil War, American; Colescott, Robert H.; Detroit, Michigan; Driskell, David; Evans, Minnie Jones; Fuller, Meta Vaux Warrick; Great Migration, The; Harlem, New York; Hunter, Clementine Clemence Rubin; Johnson, William Henry; Lawrence, Jacob Armstead; New York, New York; Philadelphia, Pennsylvania; Saar, Betye Irene; Savage, Augusta Christine Fells; Washington, D.C.; Woodruff, Hale Aspacio; Toussaint L'Ouverture; François Dominique.

Africa

Art and Architecture, African,

in general, those works created by historical or contemporary African artists living south of the Sahara.

African artists belong to a wide variety of cultures, each of which is characterized by its own language, traditions, and artistic forms. Although the immense Sahara serves as a natural barrier within the continent, evidence has shown a considerable dissemination of influences through trade routes that traversed the continent from early times. Today, for example, many Islamic art and architectural forms of North African inspiration appear among cultures south of the Sahara. In addition, research has pointed to concurrent influences of sub-Saharan African arts and cultures on northern African areas closer to the Mediterranean. Egypt, one of the most resplendent of African civilizations, can also be seen as having important ancient artistic and cultural parallels with sub-Saharan African civilizations.

The arts of Africa illuminate the rich histories, philosophies, religions, and societies of the inhabitants of this vast continent. African artworks, in addition to their inherent significance to the peoples who produced them, also have inspired some of the most important artistic traditions emerging in Europe and America in the modern age. Western artists of this century have admired both the African artists' emphasis on abstraction and their freedom from naturalism.

The history of art in Africa spans many centuries. Among the most ancient of these arts are the rock paintings and engravings from Tassili and Ennedi in the Sahara (6000 B.C.E.-first century C.E.). Other examples of early arts include the terracotta sculptures modeled by Nok artists in central Nigeria between 500 B.C.E. and 200 C.E., the decorative bronze works of Igbo Ukwu (ninth century to tenth century C.E.), and the extraordinary bronze and terracotta sculptures from Ife (twelfth to fifteenth century C.E.). The technical expertise and naturalistic qualities of these latter arts led early viewers to assume erroneously that they must have been of classical Greek inspiration. Today rich African traditions continue, with artists working both within the traditional modes of expression and in nontraditional genres.

THE AFRICAN ARTISTIC HERITAGE

African artists have developed diverse traditions of sculpture (figures and masks), architecture (principally domestic structures), furniture, pottery, textiles, and jewelry. In addition, body decoration (coiffure and cicatrization, or decorative scarring) and painting (on building, textile, and human surfaces) are also part of the African artistic heritage.

Materials

The most commonly employed materials include wood, fiber, metal (especially iron, bronze, and gold), ivory, clay, earth, and stone. The forms of representation within each medium vary from relative naturalism to general abstraction, with art styles conforming to the aesthetic tradition established within a particular cultural area. In African art, considerable concern is given both to the maintenance of traditional artistic forms within a culture and to the encouragement of creativity and innovation within the parameters of each artistic tradition.

A young Samburu woman wears traditional bead necklaces. *CORBIS/The Purcell Team*

BELOW: An artist of the Senufo people paints delicate animal figures on fabric. *CORBIS/Fulvio Roiter*
BELOW LEFT: Phillip Mabala carves complex designs into an ivory tusk in Lebowa, South Africa. *CORBIS/Anthony Bannister; ABPL*
BELOW RIGHT: A Dogon man of Mali wears a traditional monkey mask. *CORBIS/Charles & Josette Lenars*

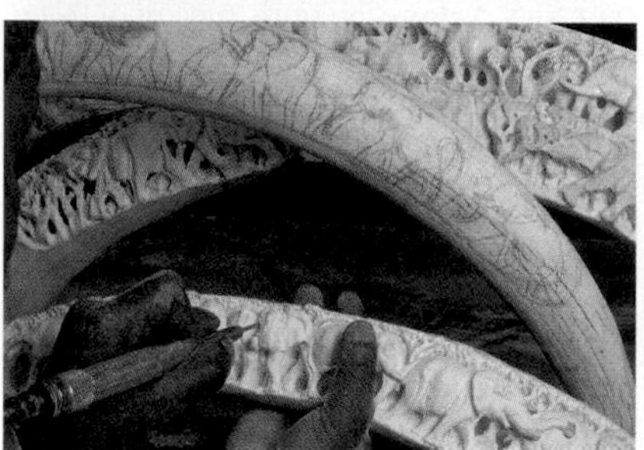

Artists

African artists generally work as specialists, receiving their training from established artists living in the community or wider area. In some old kingships, such as that of Benin in Nigeria, active guild systems controlled the training of young artists. Among the nearby Yoruba, important schools of artists were developed at local family compound centers. Often the artistic profession was seen as hereditary, with talent being passed from generation to generation, and with creativity and success often linked to a divine ancestral endowment. Among the Dogon and Bambara (or Bamana) of Mali, for this reason, sculptors were all selected from an ancient endogamous (intermarried by custom) group of blacksmiths. The place of work and the materials employed were also important to the artist during the creative process. Often these were controlled by religious proscriptions.

Aesthetics

Community criticism was an essential part of artistic traditions in many African cultures. Studies of the aesthetic canons followed by artists and critics in Africa indicate a deliberate concern for abstraction in the design process. Thus, for example, among the Yoruba of Nigeria, the criteria for sculptural beauty consist of a number of specifically non-representational elements. These include visibility, even if this necessitates proportional distortion; straightness, which implies youth and good health; symmetry, to the exclusion of more natural poses or postures; ephebism, the depiction of each person at an idealized youthful age; smoothness, suggesting again youth and health without natural body imperfections; and hypermimesis, an emphasis on general resemblance rather than on exact representation.

In some African cultures correct aesthetic canons were intentionally distorted in order to portray characters whose behavior was antisocial. The Igbo and Ibibio of Nigeria, for example, carve masks with diseased, horrific, monstrous, or asymmetrical features to represent characters who were unruly, evil, or dangerous. In Igbo and Ibibio masquerade performances, such masks are often contrasted with other, more beautifully featured and aesthetically pleasing masks that are worn to portray persons who were orderly, good, or peaceful.

Patronage

Patronage, like aesthetics, plays an important role in the creation of African artworks. Kings and their courts are of particular significance in this regard because of their artistic requirements for the mounting of state pageants, the performance of religious ceremonies, and the manufacture of charismatic personal displays. In architecture, the palaces of kings such as those who lived in Nigeria (Yoruba, Benin), Ghana (Akan), the Cameroons (Bamileke, Bamum), and Zaire (now the Democratic Republic of the Congo), (Quba, Mangbetu) rank among the most elaborate and richly decorated structures in Africa. The expensive materials available to these rulers – ivory, bronze, gold, glass beads, and plush raffia velours – are amply displayed in the arts produced at these royal courts.

Important types of art made for such regal patronage include staffs of office, thrones, state swords, crowns, royal memorial sculptures, drinking vessels, and serving containers.

Other important sources of art patronage in Africa included the various associations of men and women formed within many communities for social and political as well as religious control. The still-active Poro men's associations of the Dan and their neighbors in LIBERIA and CÔTE D'IVOIRE are characteristic examples of this type of patronage association. Poro members commissioned many of the masks and figural sculptures found in this region.

Associations that united community members by age and occupation were also important African art patrons. Examples of artworks commissioned by such associations are found among the Bambara (Mali) and among the Ibo and Ejagham (Nigeria), among others. Often each age group or occupationally linked section of the association had its own distinctive representations or masquerade themes. Among the Ejagham, animal forms characterized the masks of hunting societies, and themes of human deformity were often found in conjunction with warfare masks; images of women were commonly employed for the headdresses of the women's clubs or ancestral associations.

Traditional religious and cult organizations were also important as sources of art patronage in Africa. Artworks were not only a central component of many traditional shrines and chapels but also played a critical role in the diverse religious pageants. Among the Yoruba of Nigeria, cults linked with the principal deities – Shango (thunder), Obatala (creativity), Oshun (water), Ifa (knowledge), Yemoja (sorcery), Eshu (examination), and Odudua (earth) – had a vast array of associated art forms, including figures, masks, pottery, textiles, and jewelry. Here, as elsewhere in Africa, the artworks used in conjunction with each particular cult were often identifiable through their iconography, materials, styles, and modes of manufacture.

THE ROLE OF ART IN AFRICAN SOCIETY

The multiple roles that art plays in African communities are as diverse as their forms of patronage. These include social, political, economic, historical, and therapeutic functions.

SOCIAL ROLE

One of the most important functions of African art is distinctly social. In fulfilling this role, African art frequently depicts women as mothers, usually nursing or cradling their young. Men, on the other hand, are often presented both as elders, the traditional community leaders, and as successful warriors, appearing on horseback or with armaments. Social themes are prevalent in many African masquerade performances as well. In these masquerades, animal and human characters, in appropriate masks and garb, assume a variety of roles in demonstrating proper and improper forms of societal behavior. In performances of the Ijo and southern Ibo of Nigeria are found such diverse antisocial characters as the miser, the greedy person, the prostitute, the incompetent physician, and the unscrupulous lawyer. In the Egungun performances of the nearby Yoruba, the gossip, the glutton, and the strange-mannered foreigner have key parts as negative social models.

POLITICAL ROLE

Political control is another major concern displayed through art in Africa. Among the Dan (Liberia), Pende (Democratic Republic of the Congo) Kota (Gabon), and others, special masks are worn by persons acting as community judges and policemen. The Kwele Gon maskers of Gabon are a particularly good example of this type of masked community official. Because of their anonymity and special powers, these Gon masked figures are able to break normal societal codes and proscriptions as a means of redistributing scarce food and animals at times of great community need. A different type of social control is achieved by certain African figures and architectural motifs. The reliquary figures of the Kota, Sogo, and FANG of GABON, for example, are used as guardian images to protect the sacred ancestral relics of the community from theft or harm. The Dogon of Mali and the SENUFO of the Côte d'Ivoire carve elaborate doors that ritually protect the community food supplies and sacred objects in the same way.

Traditional East African shields. *CORBIS/The Purcell Team*

ECONOMIC ROLE

Art in Africa also fulfills an important economic role. The elegant wooden Chi Wara antelope headdresses of the Bambara of Mali are worn in planting and harvest ceremonies. Chi Wara, the mythical Bambara inventor of agriculture, is said to have buried himself in the earth as an act of self-sacrifice. The dance of the Chi Wara maskers on the agricultural fields (Chi Wara's grave) serves both to honor this great being and to remind the young Bambara farmers of the arduous sacrifice that they in turn must make each year. Among the Senufo of Côte d'Ivoire, delicately carved figures are used in a similar way to encourage farmers in their difficult work. Here *daleu* staffs, with bird or female imagery, are secured in the ground at the end of cultivation rows. These staffs serve as goals, markers, and trophies for the field-planting competitions.

HISTORICAL ROLE

An important historical role is also fulfilled in African art through its memorialization of important persons and events of the past. With this in mind, the Dogon of Mali have carved numerous images of their legendary ancestors, the Nommo, who descended from the sky at the beginning of time. Such Nommo figures (some of which have upraised hands pointing to the sky and their village of origin) are found on granary doors, cave paintings, and sacred architectural supports.

TOP: **All mural paintings among the southern Transvaal Ndebele of South Africa are created by women. Mothers pass their knowledge of wall decoration and beadwork to their daughters.** *CORBIS/Charles O'Rear*
ABOVE: **Pottery from Rukuba on display at the Museum of Jos, Nigeria.** *CORBIS/Paul Almasy*

In the powerful kingdom of Benin in Nigeria, elaborate relief plaques cast in bronze similarly carried images of important persons and events of the past, including the meetings of foreign dignitaries, battle scenes, court pageants, nobles in state dress, religious ceremonies, and musicians.

Therapeutic Role

Traditional African therapies have also required special forms of art. Divination, the means by which problems and their potential resolutions could be determined, was particularly important in the production of artworks. Yoruba (Nigeria) Ifa diviners, for example, used elaborately sculpted divination boards, bowls, and tappers as an essential part of their ritual equipment. Similarly, the Baule of Côte d'Ivoire used elaborately sculptured divination vessels for oracular purposes. Among the Kongo of the Democratic Republic of the Congo, powerful wooden fetish figures (stuck through with iron nails) were employed therapeutically as a means of repelling personal danger and trauma.

REGIONAL DISTINCTIONS

The widely differing cultures of sub-Saharan Africa are more readily comprehended if grouped by geographic regions, in view of the diversity in climate, topography, and social organization within this vast area. Although some of these cultures have disappeared, much of their art remains; other cultures have survived and continue to produce their traditional art.

Arts of the Western Savanna

Among the best known of the traditional western savanna arts are those of the Dogon, Bambara, Mossi, Bobo, and Tamberma living in the dry, grassy plains of Mali, Burkina Faso, and Togo. The arts of the Dogon, one of the most isolated of these peoples, have been especially well researched. The Dogon have a rich and complex philosophical foundation on which their arts are based. The Dogon village plan, for example, is seen to have the form of a human, representing the Nommo, the first humans created by the Dogon sun and creator god. Important parts of the Dogon village physiognomy include its head (the smithy and men's house), chest (the houses of lineage leaders), hands (women's houses), genitals (a mortar and altar), and feet (shrines). Dogon masks, carved for the men's association, Awa, represent in their totality the Dogon image of the world with the animals and people that inhabit it. The antelope, the bird, the hare, Fulani women, and Samana men are some of the characters who appear in the funerary performances of this association. Other masks presented at such times depict more abstract philosophical concepts. One mask, the 9 m (30 ft) long serpentine "Great Mother" mask, recalls the origin of death. Another, the roughly cruciform Kanaga mask, recreates, in its wearer's dance motions, the origin of the world.

Farther east, among the linguistically related Tamberma of Togo, house architecture has reached an apex of beauty and symbolic complexity. The two-story earthen "castles" of these people serve not only as their domiciles but also as their fortresses, cathedrals, theaters, and cosmological diagrams. The name that these people call themselves, Batammariba, or the "people who are the architects," bears out the importance of architecture among this group. Like the Dogon village, each Tamberma house is said to be distinctly human. Accordingly, its outer surfaces are scarified with the same patterns incised on women. Appropriate body parts are also found in the house, for example, the door "mouth," the window "eyes," the grinding stone "teeth," and so on.

The Western Forests

The great forested West Atlantic coast – often called the Guinea Coast – incorporates the diverse cultures and arts of Guinea, Sierra Leone, Liberia, and Côte d'Ivoire on the west and Ghana, Togo, Benin, and Nigeria on the east. In the western coastal forests, the dominant art patrons are associations of men and women such as Sandé and Poro. The women's Sandé society of the Mende (Sierra Leone) has a particularly important masquerade tradition. Sandé masks, which are polished a deep black to reflect the richness and beauty of the sea, are worn by female association leaders during the initiation ceremonies of young women in the community. The most beautiful of these masks reflect, in their form, the features that the Mende admire in themselves: a high, smooth forehead, an elaborate coiffure, and an elegant, strong neck.

Poro, the parallel men's association, has elaborate masking traditions as well. Dan, Kran, and Guere Poro members from Liberia and nearby Côte d'Ivoire present in their association performances a diverse cast of players. These include, among others, the judge, the singer, and the runner. Elegance of form, shiny black facial surfaces, and complex woven coiffures are featured in these masks. When not being worn, the masks are secured in a special sacred *go* (*ge*) house under the guardianship of the *go*-master. The wife of this important man has her own special art form, a decorated spoon that she displays in feasts for the community.

From the eastern Atlantic coast region that encompasses the countries of Ghana, Togo, Benin, and Nigeria are found some of the most important aristocratic arts of Africa. Perhaps the most famous of the kingships is the Benin Dynasty in Nigeria. The royal city of Benin (not be be confused with the recently named neighboring country of Benin) was at its height in the seventeenth and eighteenth centuries and was compared by travelers to the great contemporaneous cities of the Netherlands. The palace of the king, or *oba*, as he was called, was especially impressive. At one time its walls were covered with beautifully cast bronze plaques that were said to shimmer like gold. The three main buildings at the palace were each surmounted by immense turrets supporting giant bronze birds and pythons. On the royal palace altars, bronze memorial heads and sculptures were displayed for private and state festivities.

Central, South, and East Africa

In the thick equatorial forests and drier savanna regions running from Gabon through the Republic of the Congo, the Democratic Republic of the Congo, and various countries to the east and south, still other artistic forms are emphasized. In the matrilinear cultures of southern Democratic Republic of the Congo, female figures are particularly important. The Pende chief's house, for example, often bears a full-scale image of a woman at the apex of the roof. This figure sometimes holds a child (the symbol of the family line and future heirs) as well as an ax (the symbol of power).

Among the relatively isolated Gato, Bongo, and Konso of Sudan and Ethiopia, memorial figures of wood were set up in prominent positions in the village to survey its entrance and the tombs of its important ancestors. In most other East African cultures, monumental sculpture was rare. Instead, body decoration became an important focus of the arts. The Masaai of Kenya and the Zulu of South Africa are particularly noted for their beaded jewelry. Circular forms such as one finds in the jewelry of the Masaai are also emphasized in Bantu village planning in this area. The great elliptical stone building (circa 1200) of the ancient Monomotapa culture near Fort Victoria in Zimbabwe is conceptually part of this circular design and architectural tradition.

Contemporary African Art

Many of the so-called traditional arts of Africa are still being commissioned, carved, and used in active traditional contexts. As in all art periods, important innovations as well as significant retentions of established styles and modes of expression coexist. In recent years, with the changes in transportation and mass communications within the continent, a number of art forms have been disseminated widely among diverse African cultures. Today, for example, some Nigerian-style masks are being used in Ghanaian and other coastal centers on the eastern Guinea Coast.

In addition to distinctly African influences, a number of changes have originated from the outside. For example, Islamic architecture and design motifs can be seen in many of the arts of the northern regions of Nigeria, Mali, Burkina Faso, and Niger. East Indian print motifs have similarly found their way into sculptures and masks of the Ibibio and Efik artists living along the southern coast of Nigeria. Christian themes have also been taken up by some contemporary artists in their designs for panels, doors, and baptismal fonts for Africa's Christian churches and cathedrals. In recent years artists have also found important sources of patronage for various art forms in the banks, commercial establishments, government offices, and courts of the new nations. Tourists have been responsible for still other art demands, particularly for decorative masks and ornamental African sculptures made of ebony or ivory.

The development of schools of art and architecture in sub-Saharan African cities has pushed artists to work in new mediums such as cement, oil and other paints, ink, stone, aluminum, and a variety of graphic modes. The images and designs they have created reflect a vibrant union of African and contemporary Western traditions. Artists such as Twins Seven-Seven and Ashira Olatunde of Nigeria and Nicholas Mukomberanwa of Zimbabwe are among the most successful practitioners of these novel creative forms.

Suzanne Preston Blier

See Also

Gold Trade; Iron in Africa; Sahara Desert; Tourism in Africa; African Religions: An Interpretation.

Latin America and the Caribbean

Artel, Jorge

(b. April 27, 1909, Cartagena de Indias, Colombia; d. August 19, 1994, Barranquilla, Colombia), Afro-Colombian poet, lawyer, journalist, and diplomat; Artel, whose real name was Agapito de Arcos, was one of the most representative poets of Négritude in South America.

Jorge Artel was born in Colombia, in the colonial city of Cartagena de Indias, once the major entryway for slaves into the Spanish colonies in South America. He grew up surrounded by the drumbeats of the cumbia music, slavery's violent legacies, and the history of resistance embodied in the many maroon communities that dotted the city's borders (*see* Palenque de San Basilio). In his poetry he evokes those images, especially, as Lawrence Prescott has noted, using the symbol of the drum as the unifying thread essential to the black experience in the Americas. Like other black poets in Spanish America, such as the Cuban Nicolás Guillén (1902-1989) and the Afro-Peruvian Nicomedes Santa Cruz (1925-1992), Artel did not single out race alone as the defining element that shaped his life and his aesthetic vision. For him as for the others, class and economic exploitation were as important, and this awareness allowed them to express strong feelings of commitment toward the various other struggles faced by their fellow countrymen.

Artel obtained a law degree from the University of Cartagena in 1945 and published his dissertation on criminal law and popular culture the same year. The 1948 assassination of presidential candidate and progressive political leader Jorge Eliecer Gaitán in Bogota, along with the subsequent social explosion that resulted in the civil war Colombians know as La Violencia (the Violence, 1948-1962), left an indelible mark on Artel. Like Arnoldo Palacios (b. 1924) and Manuel Zapata Olivella (b. 1920), two other Afro-Colombian authors, Artel bore witness to these tragedies through his writings. Fearful for his life and having spent 3 months in jail as a political prisoner, he left Colombia and spent 23 years in exile. Five of these years Artel spent in the United States, mostly lecturing in various universities (including Princeton and Columbia) and living in New York. He later recounted this experience in the poem "Palabras a la ciudad de Nueva York" (Words to the City of New York). He also spent some time in MEXICO and 11 years in Panama City, where he taught at the University of PANAMA.

Artel published three books of poetry: *Tambores en la noche* (1940, Drums in the Night); *Poemas con botas y banderas* (1972, Poems with Boots and Flags); and the 1987 *Sinú, riberas de asombro jubiloso* (Sinu, Riverbanks of Joyful Wonder). In 1979 and again in 1986 he published revised anthologies of his poetry. *Tambores en la noche*, published at a time when other important black Spanish American authors such as ADALBERTO ORTIZ (b. 1914), PILAR BARRIOS (1899-1974), and JUAN PABLO SOJO (1908-1948) were issuing their first publications, was probably written during the 1930s in Cartagena. It is considered to be one of the first poetic interpretations of the modern Afro-Hispanic experience. Drawing on the poetic legacies of CANDELARIO OBESO (1849-1884), Artel sometimes used colloquial speech and often explored themes characteristic of the NÉGRITUDE movement, such as music and dance, Africa, and the question of identity (*see* Afro-Latin American and Afro-Caribbean Identity: An Interpretation).

Artel also published a novel, *No es la muerte, es el morir* (1979, It Is Not Death, It Is the Dying), that sympathetically portrays the guerrillas in a civil war that has devastated Colombia. In 1986 Jorge Artel was declared a national poet, but he remains relatively unknown both in Colombia and abroad.

Francisco Ortega

SEE ALSO

Maroonage in the Americas; Slavery in Latin America and the Caribbean; New York, New York; Cartagena de Indias, Colombia; Dance in Latin America and the Caribbean.

Latin America and the Caribbean

Art in Latin America and the Caribbean, the influence of African-derived themes and artists of African descent in the region's art, emphasizing nineteenth- and twentieth-century painting and sculpture and focusing on the artistic traditions of Jamaica, Cuba, and Brazil.

Because art is such a broad topic and Latin America and the Caribbean is such a diverse region, this article will largely focus on the media of painting and sculpture. With a few exceptions in the field of architecture, the following discussion will not explore the contributions of black artists in other genres, such as the graphic arts and photography. Although they constitute a large and important part of artistic production by blacks in Latin America and Caribbean, festival arts, such as the costumes or floats produced for such African-based celebrations as Carnival, and sacred arts, such as altars or ceremonial accessories used in various African-derived religions, including VODOU, SANTERÍA, and CANDOMBLÉ, are also beyond the scope of this article.

The discussion is divided into three sections, focusing on three countries in Latin America and the Caribbean where blacks have played a central role in defining the national art: JAMAICA, CUBA, and BRAZIL. HAITI boasts perhaps the most famous and deeply rooted legacy of black art, which is discussed in an independent entry (*see* HAITIAN ART). This article concludes by mentioning various artists of African descent, past and present, from elsewhere in the region. Much of the art by black artists in Latin America and the Caribbean has been and continues to be classified as "primitive" or "naïve," but these terms are limited in their capacity to describe the diversity and sophistication of artistic production by artists of African descent in this region.

JAMAICA

The Spanish occupied Jamaica for more than a century and a half, from Christopher Columbus's initial landing in 1494 until the British took possession in 1670. Under Spanish rule, the Taino Indian population was virtually wiped out, and only a few examples of Taino art survived. During the prosperous sugar-producing era (seventeenth and eighteenth centuries), Jamaica's Spanish and English colonizers relied on Europe for artistic commissions and prohibited African slaves from making art of any kind, especially ritual objects. Thus, although Africans and their descendants have historically constituted the majority of the island's population, no examples of Afro-Jamaican art survive from the era of slavery (from the sixteenth to the mid-nineteenth century) that would otherwise suggest a continuity of African art traditions in Jamaica.

According to many art historians, Jamaican art began in the 1930s, a decade characterized by labor protests and racial activism on the island. Marcus Garvey, who was in Jamaica from 1927 to 1935, promoted his form of Black Nationalism, and the religion Rastafarianism won many devotees among the poor, predominantly black working class. Taken together, these movements gave birth to an Afrocentric cultural nationalism in Jamaica that manifested itself through artwork that celebrated the black working class and through a proliferation of African-style sculpture.

The undisputed icon of Jamaican cultural nationalism is *Negro Aroused* (1935), one of a series of wood sculptures created by the British artist Edna Manley (1900-1987). Of European ancestry, Manley spearheaded Jamaican art. After arriving on the island in 1922, she became an important organizer for the arts in Jamaica. In 1940 she started free classes at the Institute of Jamaica, and in 1950 she helped found the Jamaican School of Art, which became the center of a coherent artistic community, referred to here as the Institute Group.

Some of the prominent members of the Institute Group were Albert Huie (b. 1920), David Pottinger (b. 1911), Ralph Campbell (1921-1985), and Henry Daley (1919-1951). Working in a post-impressionist style, many of these artists looked to local Jamaican settings and people for inspiration. For example, Huie painted rural scenes and activities, and Pottinger depicted aspects of daily life in Kingston's working-class neighborhoods.

Since the 1930s Jamaica's art history has also featured many independent, untrained artists, often referred to as the "intuitives," a term coined by Jamaican art historian David Boxer. They include John Dunkley (1891-1947), Carl Abrahams (b. 1913), William "Woody" Joseph (b. 1919), and Sidney McLaren (b. 1895). Dunkley, considered to be one of Jamaica's greatest painters, painted dark, mysterious landscapes populated by a strange assortment of animals. Joseph carved masks, animals, and human figures, sometimes combining elements from all three.

Some Jamaican artists, after growing up on the island, sought artistic training abroad, in Europe or North America, and later returned to Jamaica to develop their art. Sculptor Ronald Moody (1900-1984) studied in Britain and France, and his encounters with Egyptian sculpture while in Europe are reflected in his work after he returned to Jamaica. Namba Roy (Roy Atkins, 1910-1961) grew up in Accompong, previously a maroon (escaped slave) settlement, and studied art in GREAT BRITAIN, where he discovered African sculpture and began creating neo-African carvings in ivory. Rather than seek out African art in Europe, Kofi Kayiga (Ricardo Wilkins, b. 1943) traveled directly to KENYA, TANZANIA, and UGANDA. His vibrant abstract works were inspired by his experiences in African as well as by Jamaican folklore and religious themes.

After Jamaica achieved its independence in 1962, Rastafarianism gained wider public acceptance and became a major source of inspiration for several Jamaican artists. Painter and sculptor Everald Brown (b. 1917) won international renown for his synthesis of Rastafarian and Ethiopian Orthodox-derived religious imagery. Other artists, such as the painter Albert Artwell (b. 1942), have expressed the more militant, political dimension of Rastafarianism, asserting an African supremist view.

Although less influential than Rastafarianism, the Afro-Protestant religious tradition of Revivalism has inspired some of Jamaica's art. Some of the relief carvings of Osmond Watson (b. 1934) are based on Revivalism. The sculptor and painter Mallica "Kapo" Reynolds (1911-1989), perhaps the most famous Revivalist artist, produced a vast body of Revivalist-inspired sculpture from 1948 to 1967 that embodies the rhythm, movement, and emotional character of Revivalist rituals.

In Jamaica, the growth of cultural nationalism inspired a new interest in African sculpture. Like Edna Manley, sculptor Alvin Marriot (1902-1992) depicted black labor-related themes. In the 1960s, David Miller Jr. (1903-1977) executed a series of carved heads that display a strong sense of black consciousness and NÉGRITUDE. David Miller Sr.'s (1872-1969) works exhibit a spiritual sensibility and kinship with African art. His *Talisman* (1940), for example, has four faces, a characteristic found in KONGO art.

Jamaica, like Haiti, is one of the few Caribbean islands that have recognized and supported artists as ambassadors of culture and that have founded art schools and museums to foster the growth of the plastic arts. The 1960s witnessed the establishment of several private galleries, and in 1974 the National Gallery of Jamaica was founded. These institutions continue to nurture the growth of Jamaican art.

Two painters stand in front of their mural portraying the people of Choiseul, St. Lucia. *CORBIS/Bob Krist*

CUBA

As in Jamaica, the documentation of African contributions to the development of art in Cuba is limited to the twentieth century. During the nineteenth century a Cuban school of painting based on French and Spanish academicism emerged around Havana's San Alejandro Academy (established 1817), but in this era there were apparently no painters of African descent. However, the social and political changes that followed Cuba's late-nineteenth-century struggle for independence led to the revival of African traditions, paving the way for increased participation of black artists in the plastic arts.

Beginning in 1906 the Cuban anthropologist and political activist FERNANDO ORTIZ published several studies on Afro-Cuban culture, which he discussed as an integral part of Cuban national culture. His work had a strong impact on the vanguard artists who emerged during the 1920s and 1930s, a period of increased political and cultural activism. Although diverse in work and interests, these artists focused on indigenous Cuban images and themes, including Afro-Cuban traditions. Their efforts were part of a larger movement known as AFROCUBANISMO.

At first, Afrocubanismo in art referred to the romanticized representation of Afro-Cuban subjects. During the 1940s and 1950s abstract expressionism became a popular idiom, and references to Afro-Cuban subjects became more conceptual and indirect. The artist who redefined Afrocubanismo and the direction of Cuban art during these years was Wifredo Lam (1902-1982).

Lam was an academically trained painter of Afro-Chinese descent, and his work reflects his deep interest in Afro-Cuban history and traditions. He explained the motivating force behind his painting by saying, "I wanted with all of my heart to paint the drama of my country, but by thoroughly expressing the Negro spirit, the beauty of the plastic art of the blacks." In his masterwork, *The Jungle* (1943), he simultaneously invokes the exploitation and resistance of the slaves by merging human forms with sugar cane and dense foliage. Other Lam paintings such as *The Chair* (1943) are related to the Afro-Cuban religion SANTERÍA, which was an important part of his childhood environment. Lam cultivated an interest in Afro-Cuban subjects and themes in Cuba's younger generation of artists, including Roberto Diago (1920-1957). Lam's followers sought to learn and communicate through their work the ideological significance of Afro-Cuban traditions and not just use them as a source of picturesque indigenous subject matter, as the early Cuban vanguard had done.

Other Cuban artists of African descent who delved into Afro-Cuban traditions for subjects and ideas for their own artwork include Mateo Torriente (1910-1966), Augustín Cárdenas (b. 1927), and Manuel Mendive (b. 1944). Mateo Torriente was a mulatto sculptor who, after focusing on female figures, depicted animal forms and musical instruments with an increasingly abstract approach from the 1950s until his death. Augustín Cárdenas was an academically trained sculptor of African descent who merged African designs, especially those of the DOGON people, with abstraction to create a new aesthetic. His example was followed by Rogelio Rodríguez Cobas (b. 1926) and Ramón Haití (b. 1932), both wood sculptors of African descent. Manuel Mendive is an academically trained Cuban artist of African descent who is an initiate of both Santería and Mayombe and interprets contemporary events through the mythology of these religions.

Over the course of the twentieth century, Santería and Palo Monte have witnessed the increased participation of people of European descent. As a result, some white Cuban artists who are initiates of these Afro-Cuban religions have incorporated related images and themes into their work. These artists include Juan Francisco Elso (1956-1988), JOSÉ BEDIA (b. 1959), and Santiago Rodríguez Olazábal (b. 1955).

Black and mulatto female artists have been an integral part of the exploration of Afro-Cuban traditions. Ironically, artists such as ANA MENDIETA (1948-1985) and Belkis Ayón (b. 1967) have used the myths and iconography of all-male secret societies called ABAKUÁS to assert their identity as black and female and to comment on the patriarchal order of society. Representations of Abakuás, in particular the *irmes* – costumed members of the society who accompany Abakuá processions and Carnival – date to nineteenth-century Cuban *costumbrista* art. The irme has become a national symbol of Cuba and often appears in the work of such white artists as René Portocarrero (1912-1985).

Since the emergence of the Cuban vanguard in the 1930s, both black and white artists have explored Afro-Cuban culture. Today, Afrocubanismo continues to be one of the most important trends in Cuban art.

BRAZIL

Africans and their descendants have contributed to the development of the plastic arts in Brazil since the sixteenth century. They were initially apprentices or assistants working alongside other artists on the construction of churches and religious monuments. Afro-Brazilians carved religious images and embellished church interiors with paint and gold. They sometimes subverted the efforts to replicate the art and architecture of Catholic Portugal by introducing their own images and aesthetic preferences. This included transforming grapes (symbolizing

UPPER LEFT: Cubist image *Figura Abstracta* is a colorful pastel on paper laid down on canvas made in 1948 by René Portocarrero. *Christie's Images*
LOWER LEFT: *Trabajo de la Tierra y Preparación de Alimentos-Civilización Tolteca* by Diego Rivera shows Toltec people growing and preparing food. *Oronoz*
ABOVE: The painting *Cortadores de Cana* by Mario Carreno portrays the work of cutting sugar cane as a heroic struggle. *Christie's Images*

wines and the blood of Christ) into pineapples and depicting traditionally white virgins and cherubs as mulatto or black.

Brazilian artists of African descent individually distinguished themselves from the eighteenth century through the second part of the nineteenth century. During the eighteenth century, the major Brazilian artists were blacks or mulattos who often belonged to fraternities that drew up the contracts for carving images, painting cathedral ceilings, and so on. Among these Afro-Brazilian artists were Valentim Fonesca e Silva (1750-1813), also known as Mestre Valentim; the painter José Theophilo de Jesus (1770?-1847); Francisco das Chagas (active late 1700s), also known as Chagas o Cabra (the "He-Goat"); and the sculptor Manuel da Costa Athaide (1762-1830). The most famous Afro-Brazilian artist of this era was the sculptor and architect Antonio Francisco Lisboa (1738-1814), also known as Aleijadinho (the "Little Cripple"). All these painters and sculptors applied their talents to religious art. They left many examples of their work in the urban centers of Minas Gerais, Bahia, Pernambuco, and Rio de Janeiro.

Afro-Brazilian participation in the arts decreased with the advent of neoclassicism in the nineteenth century. Some art historians have interpreted Dom João VI's decision in 1816 to invite French artists to educate Brazilian artists as an attempt to "whiten" Brazilian art. This led to the establishment of French art academies in Brazil in the mid-nineteenth century. Although the institutionalization of art made artistic training less accessible to Afro-Brazilian artists, some, such as Firmino Monteiro (1855-1888), Estêvão Silva (1845?-1891), and Rafael Pinto Bandeira (1863-1896), entered the ranks of the artistic elite, where they often encountered racism.

In spite of being untrained in a formal sense, some Afro-Brazilians continued to make a living as artists. During the late nineteenth century Mestre Manoel Friandes (1823-1904), an Afro-Muslim architect, designed several secular and ecclesiastical buildings, including the Ordem Terceira de São Francisco and the Igreja de Lapinha, in Salvador, Bahia. One of Brazil's most famous vernacular artists, Francisco Biquiba de LaFuente Guarany (1884-1985) carved over 100 *carrancas* ("figureheads") for boats traveling on the São Francisco River over the course of a career spanning nearly 80 years. Heitor dos Prazeres (1889-1966) was a painter of Guarany's generation whose work reflects life in Rio de

Janeiro, including the emerging SAMBA scene of which he was a part.

The arrival of a large number of European and Asian immigrants in Brazil during the late nineteenth and early twentieth centuries effected a shift in Brazilian art to modernism. Using modern idioms such as cubism, many members of this next generation of artists explored CANDOMBLÉ-related themes. Deoscoredes M. de Santos (b. 1917), better known as Mestre Didi, is a sculptor of Yoruban ancestry whose multimedia works celebrate a number of orixás, the African divinities from the Candomblé religion, and are assembled using materials and colors associated with those gods. Terciliano Jr. (b. 1939) attempts to manifest the qualities and spiritual power of the orixás in his abstract paintings, in which the wooden offering bowl known as the *gamela* is a recurrent motif. The angular, abstract sculpture of Emanoel Araujo (b. 1940) attempts to capture in a minimal, nonrepresentational manner the movements and rhythms of the orixás, especially Exú and Ogun. The sculpture and painting of Rubem Valentim (b. 1922) evokes the symbols of the orixás through symmetrical compositions

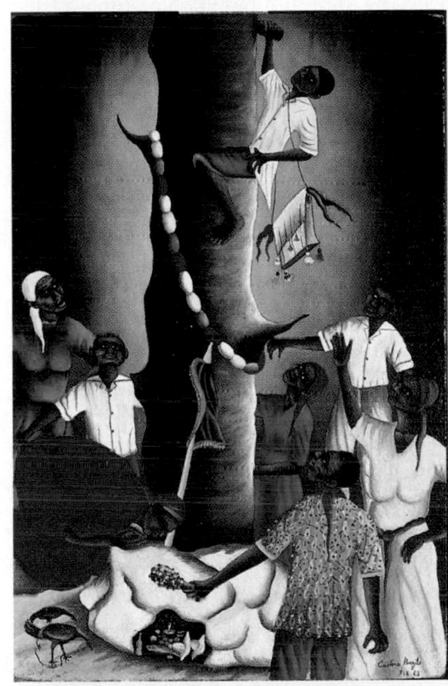

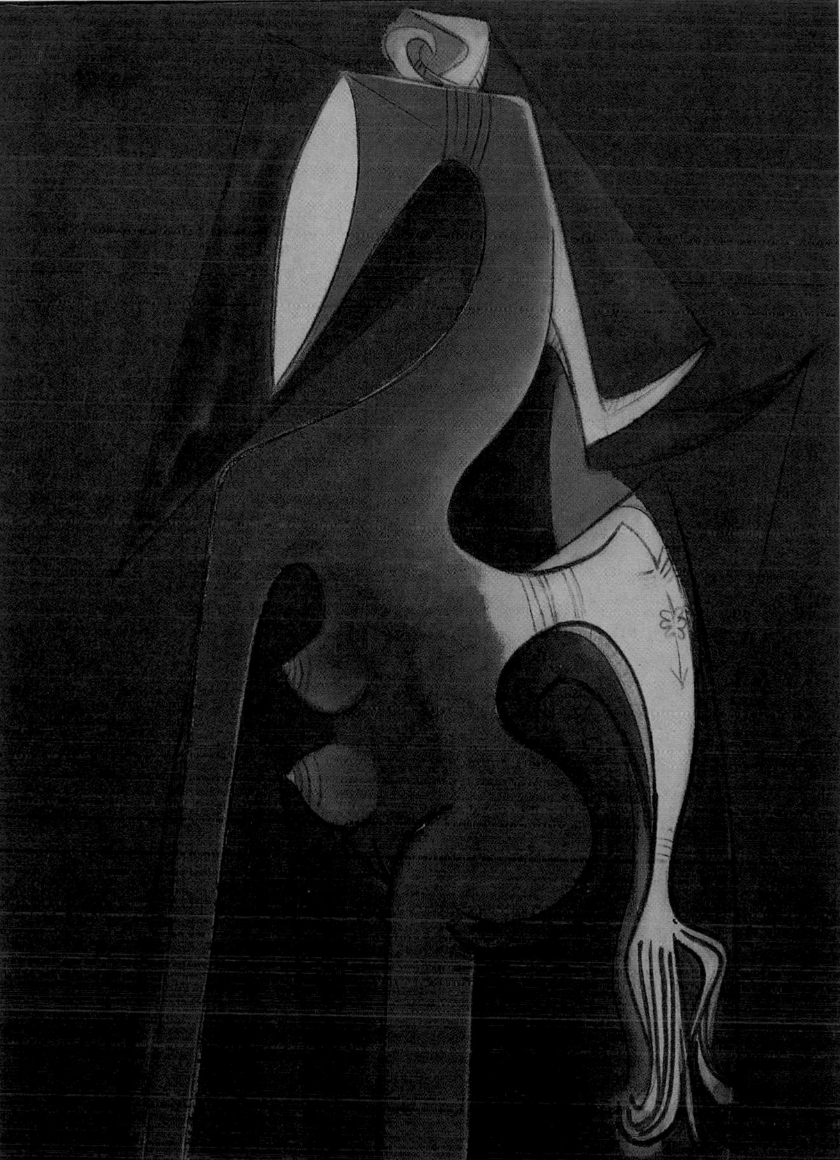

TOP LEFT: *Ceremonie sous Mapou*, a 1962 oil painting by the Haitian artist Castera Bazile (1923-1966), depicts a Vodou ceremony. *Christie's Images*
ABOVE: The "horse-woman" in *The Siren of the Niger* from 1950 by Afro-Cuban painter Wifredo Lam (1902-1982) combines ideas and imagery from the African-based religion Santería with European traditions. *Hirshhorn Museum and Sculpture Garden, Smithsonian Institution, Gift of Joseph H. Hirshhorn, 1972*
LEFT: Jamaican painter and sculptor Everald Brown (b. 1917) often uses images drawn from Rastafarianism, as in his painting *Ethiopian Apple* (1970) in which the central figure is both an Otaheite apple and a symbol of the sacred oneness of humanity and nature. *National Gallery of Jamaica, Kingston/Photograph © Maria LaYacona/Courtesy of Everald Brown*

A native of Puerto Rico, Francisco Oller (1833-1917) worked in a realist style influenced by his studies in Europe, but his subjects were often Puerto Rican, as in this 1893 oil painting *El Velorio* (The Wake). *From the collection of the Museum of History, Anthropology and Art of the University of Puerto Rico*

of bold, unmodulated colors and combined geometric forms.

Other Afro-Brazilian artists, especially those in the field of sculpture, have adhered to a more figurative approach. Some sculptors use abstraction and distortion in such a way that endows their sculpture with features often found in African art (larger head, geometric facial features, etc.). These artists include Agnaldo Manoel dos Santos (1926-1962), Boaventura Silva Filho Louco (b. 1932), and Maurino de Araujo (b. 1949).

Contemporary Afro-Brazilian art is eclectic, both in its subject matter and materials. Some works refer directly to Afro-Brazilian beliefs and practices, others only allude to them, and still others concern themselves with more universal issues. As they have since the seventeenth century, Afro-Brazilian artists continue to play an important part in shaping Brazil's national art.

Other Artists of African Descent

During the nineteenth century a number of artists of African descent gained prominence in other areas of Latin America and the Caribbean. José Gil de Castro (1785-1841), known as El Mulato Gil, was a portrait painter in Lima, Peru, and was the first artist to paint the heroes of Independence. Pancho Fierro (1810-1879) was another Afro-Peruvian artist from Lima who was one of the leading costumbristas, depicting in watercolors nineteenth-century customs and people in Peru. Notable Afro-Caribbean artists include José Campeche (1751-1809) and Michel-Jean Cazabon (1813-1888). Campeche was a mulatto Puerto Rican painter best known for his religious images and portraits of the Puerto Rican elite. He also inaugurated the depiction of African subjects in Puerto Rican visual art. Cazabon was also mulatto and, after studying in Paris, distinguished himself as a landscape painter in Trinidad and Martinique. There are a host of notable twentieth-century artists of African descent, among them Geoffery Holder (active late 1900s) of Trinidad and Amos Ferguson (b. 1920) of the Bahamas.

While this article has focused on individual black artists, there is at least one example of a collective black artistic tradition in Latin America and the Caribbean. The Bush Negroes of Suriname have preserved a distinctively African wood-carving tradition dating to the seventeenth and eighteenth centuries. They are the descendants of maroons who formed communities in the jungle and negotiated their independence with the Dutch in the late eighteenth century. In relative seclusion, they reconstructed many aspects of the West African cultures, including an eclectic wood-carving tradition. Thus, while many artists of African descent have asserted their identity within European artistic traditions and informed the character of their country's national art, Latin America and the Caribbean are not without an independent African artistic tradition.

Aaron Myers

See Also

Art and Architecture, African; Ethiopian Orthodox Church; Maroonage in the Americas; Yoruba; Garvey, Marcus Mosiah; Lam, Wifredo; Lisboa, Antônio Francisco ("Aleijadinho"); Rio de Janeiro, Brazil; Rastafarians; Trinidad and Tobago; Carnivals in Latin America and the Caribbean; Orishas; Whitening.

North America

Artis, William Ellisworth

(b. February 2, 1914, Washington, N.C.; d. 1977?), African American sculptor who applied traditional style to African American subjects.

William Ellisworth Artis was born February 2, 1914, in Washington, North Carolina, to Elizabeth Davis and Thomas Migget. In 1926 he went to live with his mother and her husband, George Artis, in New York City. Artis's artistic education took him through a number of institutions, including the Art Students League, Pennsylvania State University, Chadron State College in Nebraska, and Syracuse University. He also studied under the Harlem Renaissance sculptor Augusta Savage. Artis won the Metropolitan Scholarship award for creative sculpture in 1933 and the Outstanding Educator of America and Outstanding Afro-American Artist awards in 1970. His sculptures are singular in their treatment of human life and their vitality of form. Later in his career, Artis taught at Nebraska State Teacher's College and the Harlem Young Men's Christian Association (YMCA).

Andre Willis

See Also

Harlem, New York; New York, New York; Savage, Augusta Christine Fells.

Latin America and the Caribbean

Aruba, an island in the Caribbean Sea 32 km (19 mi) north of Venezuela.

Aruba is one of the few Caribbean Islands whose people are still largely descended from an original indigenous population. This is partly because Aruba was never the site of plantation slavery and so was never home to the large numbers of African slaves who are the ancestors of most other contemporary Caribbean islanders. Over 85 percent of Arubans are of mixed Arawak Indian and European ancestry (*see* Indigenous Cultures in the Caribbean). A majority of the remaining 15 percent are black immigrants from other Caribbean Islands who have come to Aruba to fill some of the many available jobs in thriving tourist and oil industries.

Aruba's earliest inhabitants were Caiquetios Arawaks, who migrated from South America approximately 2000 years ago. The first European contact with the island came in 1499, when explorer Alonso de Ojeda claimed Aruba for Spain. But Aruba was soon declared an *isla inútil* ("useless island") because of its barren soil, and Spain concentrated on settling more fertile lands. The Dutch gained control of the island in 1636, but they also chose not to settle immediately, sending colonists and slaves to nearby Curaçao instead (*see* Netherlands Antilles). The Dutch colonists who did eventually settle on Aruba used the island only to raise horses and sheep that were sent to the other Dutch Caribbean Islands; only a small number of African slaves were brought to colonial Aruba, and these generally worked as house servants.

Aruba became a more desirable place to settle in the nineteenth century when gold was discovered in parts of the island and the dry climate proved ideal for growing the profitable aloe plant. The island's population, however, was still largely descended from the Indians and Europeans who had lived there together since the mid-1600s. After oil was discovered in nearby VENEZUELA in the 1920s, the first large oil refinery in Aruba was built in 1929. The oil industry then dominated the country's economy for most of the twentieth century. In 1985 the refineries were shut down because of a worldwide petroleum surplus, but Aruba quickly rebounded with a new emphasis on tourism becoming one of the most popular tourist destinations in the Caribbean. Revenue from the tourism industry, combined with that of the refining industry (resumed in 1991), has made Aruba one of the wealthiest nations in the Caribbean.

Today Aruba is a truly multicultural country. Its mixed-race population is descended from over 40 nationalities, and one-third of contemporary Arubans were not born on Aruba. The local language, Papiamento, is a Creole dialect that incorporates elements of Dutch, Spanish, English, French, and Portuguese in addition to the Arawak Indian language and several African languages. Aruba became an autonomous state within the kingdom of the Netherlands in 1986, but the island's formal political and educational structures still connect the country to its Dutch colonial heritage. Annual traditions such as Carnival and Aruba's outstanding Jazz and Latin Music Festival display the country's strong cultural connections to its neighbors in South America and the Caribbean.

Lisa Clayton Robinson

SEE ALSO
Carnivals in Latin America and the Caribbean; Languages, Creole, in the Caribbean.

Africa

Arusha People (also known as the Warusha), ethnic group of TANZANIA.

The Arusha primarily inhabit the region adjacent to the Burka River in Tanzania. They speak a Nilo-Saharan language and are closely related, both linguistically and culturally, to the MAASAI. Approximately 120,000 people consider themselves Arusha.

SEE ALSO
Languages, African: An Overview.

Africa

Arusi (also known as the Arisi, the Arssi, and the Arsi), ethnic group of ETHIOPIA.

The Arusi primarily inhabit Bale Province in Ethiopia. They speak an Afro-Asiatic language and belong to the OROMO cultural and linguistic group. Approximately 300,000 people consider themselves Arusi.

SEE ALSO
Languages, African: An Overview.

Africa

Asante, dominant ethnic group of a powerful nineteenth-century empire and today one of Ghana's leading ethnic groups, with more than 2 million members concentrated in south-central Ghana.

The Asante are members of the AKAN cluster of ethnic groups. Their language, variously known as Asante or Twi, is also often called Akan, but is actually one of a number of separate Akan languages, all of which belong to the Kwa subgroup of the Niger-Congo language family (*see* LANGUAGES, AFRICAN: AN

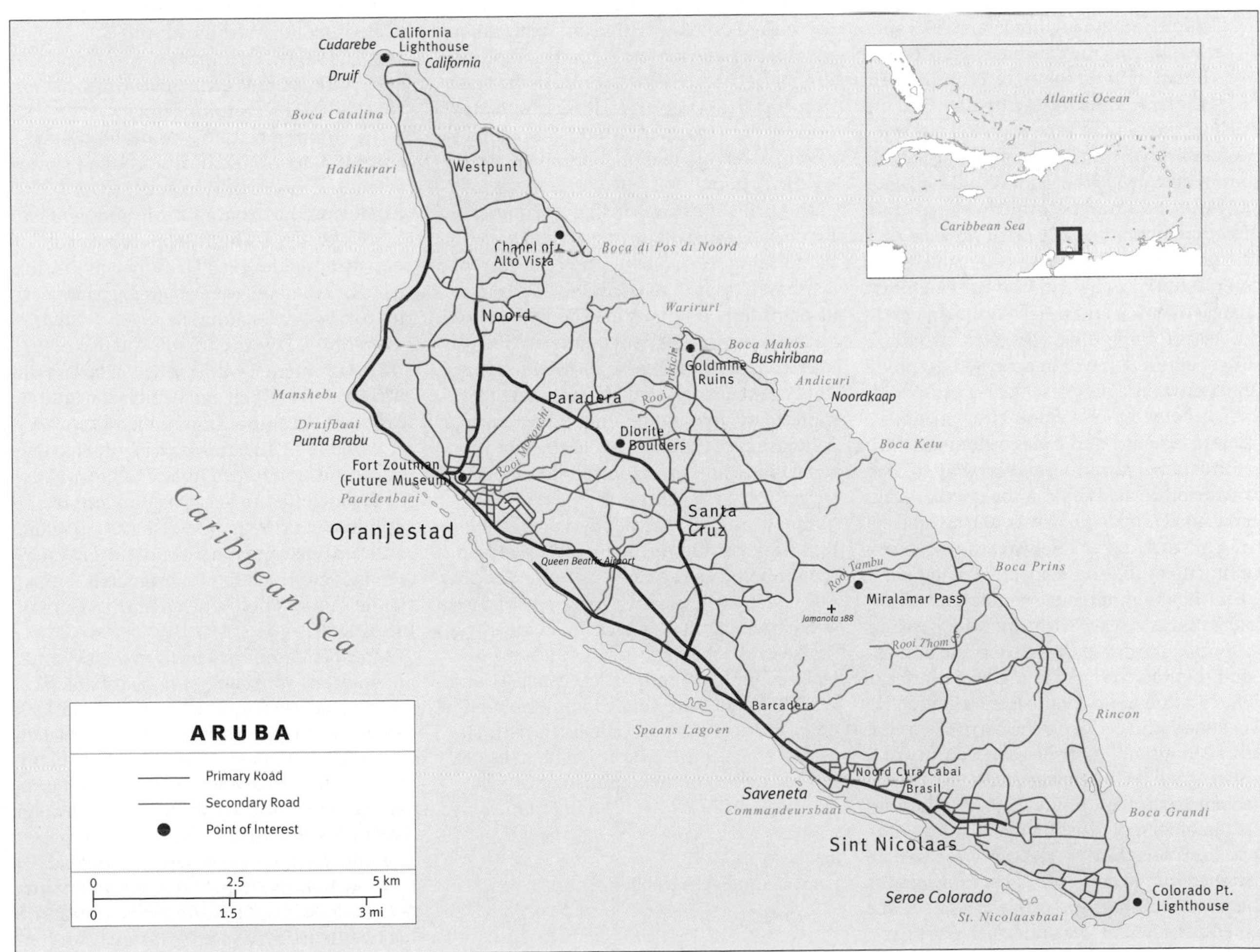

Overview). The Asante are often considered the custodians of the nation's culture because of the power, artistic splendor, and duration of their empire, which covered nearly all of present-day Ghana by 1800.

Asante oral accounts of the group's origin vary. According to one version, their ancestors are descended from the rulers of the ancient Ghana empire, far to the north in present-day Mali and Mauritania. This account forms the basis for the name of the modern nation. Other accounts claim that their ancestors emerged from the ground in their present homeland. Linguistic and archaeological evidence suggests that ancestors of the Asante have lived in their present homeland for at least 2000 years. With the expansion of gold production and trade in the fourteenth and fifteenth centuries, kingships began to emerge among the Akan. The further expansion of trade in the sixteenth and seventeenth centuries, following the arrival of Europeans along the coast, spurred the development of powerful states in the Asante region. By the early seventeenth century, the Denkyira kingdom had conquered the independent Asante clans.

The political, military, and spiritual foundations of the Asante nation date to the first Asante king, Osei Tutu. He forged the Asante Union by bringing together several subgroups from roughly 1670 to the 1690s. He also built a capital, Kumasi; created the legend of the Golden Stool to legitimize his rule; and began celebrating the Odwira, or yam festival, as a symbol of national unity. From 1698 to 1701, the united Asante army defeated the Denkyira people. Over the course of the eighteenth century, Asante conquered most of the surrounding peoples, including the Dagomba.

By the early nineteenth century, Asante territory covered nearly all of present-day Ghana, including the coast, where the Asante could trade directly with the British. In exchange for guns and other European goods, the Asante sold gold and slaves, usually either captured in war or accepted as tribute from conquered peoples. As they prospered, Asante culture flourished. They became famous for gold and brass craftsmanship, wood carving, furniture, and brightly colored woven cloth, called *kente*. Although the Asante maintained traditional beliefs, Muslim traders and Christian missionaries won some converts among them to their respective religions.

During the nineteenth century, Asante fought several wars with the British, who sought to eliminate the slave trade and expand their control in the region. A series of defeats at the hands of the British gradually weakened and reduced the territory of the Asante kingdom. After nearly a century of resistance to British power, Asante was finally declared a Crown Colony in 1902 following the uprising known as the Yaa Asantewa War.

Before long, however, Asante reemerged to contribute to the nationalist movement that would help shape modern Ghana. The exiled Asante king was allowed to return to Kumasi in 1924, and the British recognized the Asante Confederacy as a political entity in 1935. Today, most Asante live in the Asante Region of Ghana. They are primarily farmers, growing cocoa for export and yams, plantains, and other produce for local consumption. The Golden Stool, the Asante imperial palace, and artifacts at the Museum of National Culture in Kumasi have become enduring symbols of Ghana's illustrious past.

David P. Johnson, Jr.

See Also

Asantewa, Yaa; Ghana; Ghana, Early Kingdom of; Gold Trade; Kumasi, Ghana; Transatlantic Slave Trade.

Africa

Asantewa, Yaa

(b. 1850?, Besease, Asante [present-day Ghana]; d. 1921, Seychelles Islands), Asante heroine who led the Asante in the Third British-Asante War.

An indomitable aristocrat who led her people's last stand against incorporation into the British Empire in 1900, Yaa Asantewa is a much-loved figure in Asante history.

In 1896 the British occupied the Asante capital, Kumasi, and sent King Prempeh I and several chiefs and elders to exile in the Seychelles Islands in the Indian Ocean. Among them was Yaa Asantewa's grandson, Kwasi Afrane II, chief of Edweso, one of the states in the Asante Union. As queen mother of Edweso, Yaa Asantewa used her position to organize Asante leaders behind an attack on the British.

In April 1900 the British governor Sir Frederick Hodgson outraged the Asante by demanding the Golden Stool, the sacred symbol of Asante nationhood. Hodgson also announced that the exiled king would be assessed interest payments on his war indemnity and never be allowed to return. The Asante leaders, led by Yaa Asantewa, responded by demanding Prempeh's return, a restoration of the slave trade, an end to conscript labor, and the expulsion of foreigners from Kumasi.

Yaa Asantewa commanded the rebellion that broke out in April, an uprising often remembered as the Yaa Asantewa War. The siege of the British garrison trapped Hodgson and his wife until they escaped in June. The British broke the siege in July, but some resistance continued into 1901. Yaa Asantewa and other leaders were sent to join Prempeh in exile. She died in the Seychelles in 1921. The British annexed the Asante kingdom in 1902; it is today part of the Republic of Ghana.

David P. Johnson, Jr.

See Also

Kumasi, Ghana; Seychelles.

Ashanti. Please see Asante

North America

Ashe, Arthur Robert, Jr. **(b. July 10, 1943, Richmond, Va.; d. February 6, 1993, New York, N.Y.), African American tennis player, number one ranked player in the world in 1975, vocal critic of racial intolerance and historian of African American sports.**

Arthur Robert Ashe Jr. was born July 10, 1943, in Richmond, Virginia, to Mattie and Arthur Robert Ashe Sr. He began playing tennis at the age of ten under the guidance of Dr. Robert Walter Johnson, a prominent coach of African American youth from Charlottesville, Virginia. Under Johnson, Ashe won three American Tennis Association (ATA) Boys' Championships, becoming the first African American junior to be ranked by the United States Lawn Tennis Association (USLTA).

Between 1960 and 1963, Ashe won three ATA Men's Singles titles, became the first African American on the United States Junior Davis Cup team, and the first African American to win a USLTA national title in the South. His achievements earned him a full scholarship to the University of California at Los Angeles, where he received a bachelor's degree in business administration in 1966. While in college Ashe won the U.S. intercollegiate singles championship, leading UCLA to the National Collegiate Athletic Association (NCAA) team championship.

The summer of 1967 was disappointing for Ashe. Not only did he lose both his singles matches in the Davis Cup, but the U.S. team was defeated by Spain, Brazil, and Ecuador. He recovered from his disappointment, however, winning the 1968 U.S. Open in the first year that amateurs were allowed to compete. He turned professional in 1969.

Over his 11-year career, Ashe played in 304 tournaments, winning 51, including the 1970 Australian Open and Wimbledon in 1975. He was the number one ranked player in the world in 1975. Although a life-threatening heart condition forced him to retire in 1980, Ashe continued to serve as the nonplaying captain of that year's U.S. Davis Cup team. In 1985 he became the second African American inducted into the International Tennis Hall of Fame. The first was Althea Gibson in 1971.

After his career in tennis, Ashe became an eloquent spokesperson against racial intolerance. He was a critic of South Africa's racist system of apartheid, and in the United States he created tennis programs to benefit inner-city youth. He wrote a three-volume history of the African American athlete titled *A Hard Road to Glory* (1988).

In 1992 Ashe announced that he had contracted human immunodeficiency virus (HIV) from a blood transfusion during one of his two heart bypass operations. After his

Arthur Ashe holds up his trophy after winning the men's singles title at Wimbledon in 1974.
Allsport/Hulton Deutsch

announcement, he became an active leader in the fight to raise awareness of acquired immune deficiency syndrome (AIDS) and to increase funding for AIDS research. Suffering complications from AIDS, Ashe died in New York on February 6, 1993.

Alonford James Robinson, Jr.

See Also
AIDS in the United States; South Africa.

North America

Ashford, Evelyn (b. April 15, 1957, Shreveport, La.), African American sprinter, four-time winner of Olympic gold medal.

Born in Shreveport, Louisiana, Evelyn Ashford grew up in Roseville, California. She attended the University of California at Los Angeles (UCLA) on a scholarship. She participated in four Olympic Games (1976, 1984, 1988, 1992), winning a total of four gold medals and one silver medal. In 1979 she set a world record in the 200-meter dash. Ten years later she received the Flo Hyman Award from the Women's Sports Foundation. In 1992 the United States Olympic team asked Ashford to carry the U.S. flag during the opening ceremonies in Barcelona. She retired in 1993 at the age of 36.

Alonford James Robinson, Jr.

Africa

Askia Muhammad (b. ?; died 1538), king of Songhai (1493-1528) who ruled the empire at its greatest extent.

A governor under Sunni Ali, Askia Muhammad rebelled against Sunni Ali's son and successor and in 1493 ascended the throne. Two years later he went on a prolonged pilgrimage to Mecca that became legendary both in Europe and the Middle East for its pomp and ostentation. On his return, Muhammad set out not only to enlarge his empire but to transform the previously African state into an Islamic kingdom. Although he failed in that effort, he restored Tombouctou (Timbuctu) as a center of faith and learning and favored Muslim scholars with grants of land and high posts in government. Refining the administrative machinery inherited from Ali, he established directorial positions – similar to those of modern cabinet ministers – for finance, justice, agriculture, and other affairs. Although more a statesman than a warrior, he also added vast territories to his realm, extending his influence as far west as the Atlantic Ocean. In 1528 Muhammad was overthrown by his son, and he spent most of his remaining years in banishment on an island in the Niger River.

See Also
Songhai Empire; Tombouctou, Mali.

Africa

Asmara, Eritrea, capital and largest city of Eritrea.

Asmara is located in a highland region of Eritrea that was settled roughly 700 years ago. It is believed to have been the site of four small, feuding villages, which, under pressure from the villages' women inhabitants, finally made peace and united around 1515. The name "Asmara" comes from "Arbate Asmara," which in the Tigrinya language means "the four villages of those [women] who brought harmony." Sixteenth-century Italian sources describe Asmara as a caravan trading center.

Shortly afterward, Asmara was sacked by Islamic warriors and went into decline. Few historical records even mention Asmara again until the late nineteenth century, when the Italians began their colonial conquest of the region. After occupying Aseb in 1882 and Massawa in 1885, the Italians pushed into the highlands, where they encountered resistance. However, in exchange for weapons Ethiopian emperor Menilek II signed a treaty in 1889 acquiescing to Italian control of the highlands. Asmara became the colonial capital of Eritrea in 1900. It grew rapidly during the 1930s, as rural Eritreans and immigrant Italians alike sought work in new industries, among them textiles and food processing. Residential areas in Asmara at this time were strictly segregated.

In 1941 British troops occupied Asmara. The city slumped following Eritrea's federation with Ethiopia in 1951. No longer an administrative capital, Asmara soon lost its industrial base as well. Ethiopian emperor Haile Selassie had factories dismantled and moved to Addis Ababa.

During Eritrea's 30-year war for independence, from 1963 to 1993, Asmara's residents suffered through periods of siege, but the city itself emerged relatively undamaged. Since 1993 Asmara has been the national capital. With a population of approximately 450,000, it is a city known for its Italian architecture, tiled sidewalks, cafés, and mild climate. The National Musuem and the University of Asmara are located there, as are most of the nation's industries. Asmara has an international airport, and rail links to the port city of Massawa are being rebuilt.

David P. Johnson, Jr.

See Also
Addis Ababa, Ethiopia; Massawa, Eritrea; Haile Selassie I.

Latin America and the Caribbean

Asociación de Negros Ecuatorianos, an organization founded in 1988 to confront racism in Ecuador.

Africa

Assin (also known as the Asen), ethnic group of Ghana.

The Assin primarily inhabit the central region of Ghana. They speak a Niger-Congo language and belong to the Akan cultural and linguistic group. Approximately 140,000 people consider themselves Assin.

See Also
Languages, African: An Overview.

North America

Association for the Study of Afro-American Life and History, founded as a national organization to popularize and promote African American history.

The Association for the Study of Negro Life and History (ASNLH) was founded by historian Carter G. Woodson in Washington, D.C., on September 9, 1915, partially in response to the release of D. W. Griffith's racist film, The Birth of a Nation (1915). As a black alternative to the unofficially segregated American Historical Association (established by white historians in 1884), the ASNLH was dedicated to using scholarship to refute racist and erroneous ideas about African American life and history.

Originally run by Woodson and colleagues George Cleveland Hall, Alexander L. Jackson, and James E. Stamps, the ASNLH encouraged and supported African American historical research and provided important publication outlets for black scholars, including the *Journal of Negro History*, created in 1916, and the popular *Negro History Bulletin*, founded in 1937. Through these publications and other activities, the association was instrumental in influencing white public opinion.

In 1926 Woodson established an annual Negro History Week, seven days in February (the birth month of Abraham Lincoln and FREDERICK DOUGLASS) devoted to the celebration of black history and culture. After Woodson's death in 1950, the ASNLH struggled with funding problems, but the leadership of MARY MCLEOD BETHUNE (president from 1936 to 1951) and CHARLES HARRIS WESLEY (president in 1951 and executive director from 1965 to 1972) ensured the association's survival. In 1972 the organization's name was changed to the Association for the Study of Afro-American Life and History (ASALH), and in 1976, under the guidance of executive director J. Rupert Picott, Negro History Week was expanded to Black History Month.

Alonford James Robinson, Jr.

SEE ALSO

Black History Month/Negro History Week; *Journal of Negro History*, The; Woodson, Carter Godwin.

Africa

Aswan High Dam, dam in southern EGYPT that impounds the waters of the NILE RIVER in Lake Nasser, the world's second-largest artificial lake.

Located near the city of Aswan, the Aswan High Dam provoked controversy even before it was constructed. The United States had promised funds to Egyptian leader Gamal Abdal Nasser to underwrite the construction of the dam. Egypt claimed nonalignment during the cold war – that is, it allied with neither the Union of Soviet Socialist Republics (U.S.S.R.) nor the United States. However, while seeking funding for the dam, Egypt completed an arms deal with the U.S.S.R. In retaliation, the United States withdrew the funding offer, whereupon Nasser nationalized the SUEZ CANAL, claiming that revenue from the canal would offset the dam's construction costs. This provoked an international conflict over control of the canal.

Nasser, meanwhile, secured funds from the U.S.S.R. for one-third of the dam's construction costs, the total of which exceeded $1 billion. The dam was an important part of Nasser's vision for Egypt. He sought it to provide inexpensive power and irrigation to the Nile Valley, even in times of drought. Although construction lasted from 1960 to 1970, by 1964 the dam was storing water, and it produced hydroelectric power by 1968. The dam was formally inaugurated in 1971. It was an impressive engineering feat. Egypt had an expanse of concrete 111 m (about 365 ft) tall and 1000 m (about 3280 ft) wide. This massive barrier created Lake Nasser – 300 ft deep, 14 mi wide, and with a holding capacity of 168,900,000,000 cubic m (about 136,927,000 acre-ft), or the volume of the Nile's entire flow for roughly two years.

The Aswan High Dam has provided economic benefits to Egypt. The lake has brought an additional 324,000 hectares (about 1250 sq mi) under cultivation and converted 283,000 hectares (1093 sq mi) from flooded land to useful farmland. A treaty grants Egypt's southern neighbor, SUDAN, one-third of the water impounded, while Egypt has rights to the remaining two-thirds. (In fact, economic difficulties have prevented Sudan from claiming its full share, and Egypt has consumed more than its share.) The annual Nile flood is now controlled, the dam provides hydroelectric power, and Lake Nasser supports a fishing industry.

The dam has caused a number of problems, however. The creation of Lake Nasser forced the Egyptian government to relocate an ancient Egyptian temple at Abu Simbel that would have otherwise been submerged and destroyed. Other archaeological sites were lost. Egypt also had to relocate 90,000 Egyptians and Nubians, including some in Sudan, from lands that were flooded or submerged. In addition, massive amounts of water evaporate from Lake Nasser, which is surrounded by a hot and arid desert. This reduces the amount of water available for irrigation or the generation of electricity, and it increases the river's salinity.

The dam has severely reduced the deposits of fertile silt that the floodwaters once brought to the valley floodplain and Nile Delta. Consequently, Egyptian farmers have had to increase the use of chemical fertilizers. Meanwhile sediment accumulates at the bottom of the reservoir, which gradually reduces the reservoir's volume.

The lack of sedimentation downstream from the dam has had other harmful effects, such as erosion of the riverbanks. More ominously, with the loss of the silt that once regenerated the delta, erosion has led to flooding in the delta caused by the encroachment of salty sea water. A projected rise in global sea levels could submerge large areas of the delta, the site of two-thirds of Egypt's crowded farmland. The loss of silt has also damaged the ecology of the eastern Mediterranean Sea. This silt once nourished algae and plankton that in turn fed sardines, shrimp, and other sea creatures. Since the opening of the Aswan High Dam, the fish and shrimp catches have declined significantly.

Robert Fay

SEE ALSO

Nasser, Gamal Abdel.

Africa

Athletes, African, Abroad, the hundreds of African athletes who compete in soccer, running, basketball, boxing, and other sports around the world.

Africa has a long tradition of competitive sports, particularly in wrestling, athletics, and canoe racing. During the colonial era, European missionaries and educators encouraged a variety of sports in Africa to promote discipline. Since independence, African countries have participated in the Olympic Games, World Championships, Commonwealth Games, and other major international sporting events, while individuals have competed at both the professional and amateur levels throughout the world. Foreign universities and sports clubs often recruit young athletes from secondary schools and clubs in major African cities.

Soccer, by far the most popular sport in Africa, is also one in which Africans have excelled abroad. Africans have played soccer overseas since the 1920s, and some have recently ranked among the world's top international players, including GEORGE WEAH of LIBERIA, Abedi Pele of GHANA, and Roger Milla of CAMEROON (*see* CAMEROON LIONS). Approximately 350 Africans play professionally on teams in Asia, Europe, the Middle East, and North and South America. In Europe, African players charged other players with using racist epithets during competitions in the sport in the mid-1990s.

Africans have also won international recognition in track-and-field events. Since the 1960s African runners, particularly Kenyans and Ethiopians, have trained and raced in Europe and the United States. Runners such as Said Abouita of MOROCCO, Kipchoge Keino of Kenya, and HAILE GEBRSELASSIE of Ethiopia have dominated the middle-distance events, while Kenyans Moses Tanui and TEGLA LOROUPE and Ethiopians Fatima Roba and ABEBE BIKILA have taken top prizes in long-distance races. More recently, sprinters such as Mozambique's Maria Mutola and NAMIBIA's FRANKIE FREDRICKS have also performed well. In the late 1990s, many of Africa's top-finishing professional road runners – especially Kenyans – faced a backlash from American race officials, who were seeking to restrict winnings available to Africans and other international athletes.

In the United States, a number of Africans currently participate in professional BASKETBALL, football, and BOXING. Among the most prominent professional basketball players are HAKEEM OLAJUWON, Dikembe Motumbo, and Manute Bol. Many college teams also include African students. Christian Oke of NIGERIA is a standout among a handful of African players in the National Football League.

Africans have boxed at the international level since the colonial era, when in 1922

Louis Faal of Senegal became the first African to win a world title. Other Africans to win boxing titles abroad include Nigerian Dick Ihetu, in the 1940s, and Ghanaian Azumah Nelson, in the 1980s and 1990s.

African countries have also produced top international athletes and teams in golf (Ernie Els, GARY PLAYER, and Nick Price), rugby (SOUTH AFRICA), tennis (ZIMBABWE), field hockey (Kenya), cricket (Kenya, Zimbabwe, and South Africa), handball (Kenya and TANZANIA), and swimming (South Africa). Many of these, as well as various white South African athletes, lived and competed abroad during the APARTHEID years.

Eric Young

SEE ALSO

Olympics, Africans and the; Ethiopia; Kenya; Mozambique; Track and Field in the United States; Football, Professional; Ihetu, Dick ("Tiger").

North America

Atkins, Cholly (b. September 30, 1913, Birmingham, Ala.), African American choreographer, dancer, and dance coach best known for his team tap dancing with the great Charles "Honi" Coles.

Cholly Atkins was born in Birmingham, Alabama, and raised in Buffalo, New York, where he displayed a talent for the stage early on. He began performing at the age of ten, when he won a Charleston contest, and he learned basic jazz and soft shoe steps while in high school. He began his formal career as a singing waiter in 1929 and soon teamed up with William Porter, a dancing waiter, to form the Rhythm Pals, a vaudeville song and dance team. After ten years with Porter, Atkins left the Rhythm Pals to begin dancing and choreographing for the Cotton Club Boys, a tap troupe that toured with Cab Calloway's band and performed with Bill "Bojangles" Robinson in a swing musical, *The Hot Mikado*, at the World's Fair in New York City. A partnership with Dotty Saulters followed but was interrupted when Atkins was drafted into the army in 1943.

After serving in the military, Atkins joined forces with Charles "Honi" Coles, and they soon became one of the best known black tap duos of the late 1940s. From 1946 to 1950, they toured Europe and the United States (headlining at venues like Harlem's APOLLO THEATER) and often performed with the bands of Billy Eckstine, Count Basie, the MILLS BROTHERS, and Louis Armstrong. They also appeared on Broadway in *Gentlemen Prefer Blondes* (1949-1952).

In 1952 Atkins took a brief respite from live performing and began teaching tap at the KATHERINE DUNHAM School of Arts and Research in New York City. From 1955 to 1961 he reunited with Coles, performing dates in Las Vegas and with PEARL BAILEY, but the pair never repeated the success of the 1940s. With interest in tap waning, Atkins gave up performance in favor of choreography, creating dance routines for the Supremes, the Temptations, GLADYS KNIGHT and the Pips, and the O'Jays as a staff choreographer for Motown Records from 1965 to 1971. He also applied his talents to Broadway musicals, winning a Tony Award for his choreography work on *Black and Blue* in 1989.

Andre Willis

SEE ALSO

Armstrong, Louis ("Satchmo"); Basie, William James ("Count"); Calloway, Cabell (Cab); Eckstine, William Clarence (Billy); Motown; New York, New York; Supremes, The; Tap Dance; Temptations, The.

North America

Atlanta Compromise, (September 18, 1895, Atlanta, Ga.), speech by Booker T. Washington advocating black self-help and accommodation to segregation and disenfranchisement.

The period in American history known as RECONSTRUCTION (1863-1877) gave emancipated slaves the opportunity to participate in American society in an unprecedented fashion. Opportunities were opened in education, race relations, public facilities, and employment. Perhaps most important, African American men were given the right to vote and hold public office. By 1877, during the period referred to as Retrenchment, Southern whites had begun to wipe away many of these newfound freedoms, including the franchise. By 1895, 32 years after Emancipation, African Americans were faced with virtual elimination of their freedoms along with new challenges in the struggle for justice and equality.

In this context Booker T. Washington, the founder of Tuskegee Institute (now Tuskegee University), addressed the Atlanta Exposition in 1895. Formerly known as the Cotton States and International Exposition, the Atlanta Exposition provided Washington the opportunity to address one of the most urgent dilemmas facing the nation. Washington's remarks received widespread approval among white Americans, who then saw him as the leading spokesperson for the African American community.

Speaking with regard to the conflict between the white demand for segregation and African American insistence on civil and political equality, Washington offered a compromise. He urged African Americans to replace the quest for civil and political equality with black economic empowerment, claiming that "the agitation of questions of social equality is the extremist folly." Addressing the whites in the audience, he proclaimed, "In all things that are purely social we can be as separate as the fingers, yet one as the hand in all things essential to mutual progress." Turning to the African American section of the audience, he urged them to "Cast down your bucket where you are. Cast it down in agriculture, in mechanics, in commerce, in domestic service, in the professions." Washington's remarks were warmly received by many in the audience.

The Atlanta Compromise formed the basis of what became Washington's ideology of black self-reliance. He urged African Americans to abandon the struggle for civil rights, and instead, to work for economic power. It was an argument for African Americans to help themselves and to stop looking for help from white Americans. Critics called the compromise accommodationist, but supporters saw it as empowering. One of Washington's most severe critics, W. E. B. Du Bois, later challenged the self-help philosophy in his essay on Washington in *Souls of Black Folk* (1903).

Where Washington advocated the right of African Americans to build schools to promote segregated developments in agriculture and industry, Du Bois pointed to the inability of African Americans to participate in the very institutions that made America a "democracy." This debate was essential to the development of African American civil rights strategy and placed Booker T. Washington at the forefront of the debate on American race relations.

Alonford James Robinson, Jr.

SEE ALSO

Du Bois, William Edward Burghardt (W. E. B.); Tuskegee University; Washington, Booker Taliaferro.

Atlanta Exposition. Please see ATLANTA COMPROMISE

North America

Atlanta, Georgia

Before the Civil War, the African American presence in Atlanta was smaller than in other Southern cities. Its population was overwhelmingly made up of slaves who arrived between 1850 and 1860. Dispersed throughout Atlanta, they lacked a substantial community.

A postwar migration transformed the city. By 1870 African Americans composed 46 percent of 21,700 residents, a proportion they maintained for the remainder of the nineteenth century. The community lacked political strength, however. In 1870, when the "Radical" forces of RECONSTRUCTION were at their peak in Atlanta, only two city councilmen were African Americans – William Finch and George Graham, from the predominantly black third and fourth wards. One year later, the Georgia State legislature effectively ended black political representation when it changed city elections in Georgia from a ward to an at-large selection process. After 1875 white hostility in Atlanta reached levels that many considered the greatest in the South.

The African American community turned

inward, establishing its own institutions and cultural life. In the 1870s and 1880s it founded lodges of the Colored Odd Fellows, a library, and three black newspapers. As Atlanta grew, a black middle class developed around prominent black churches. The Summer Hill subdivision in south Atlanta and the Green's Ferry Street neighborhood were two such "respectable black communities." On the western side of the city, an unparalleled center of black colleges and universities developed with the founding of Atlanta University (where W. E. B. Du Bois taught from 1897 to 1910), Atlanta Baptist College (Morehouse), Clark University, Spelman Seminary for Women, and Morris Brown College – all between 1865 and 1881.

Despite these developments, as of the 1890s most African Americans were not well off. In Atlanta, archetype of the "New South," 90 percent of the unskilled labor force were African Americans, and 92 percent of all working black women were in domestic service. An 1892 law decreed that only white males could vote in primary elections, and by the turn of the century segregation extended into public transportation. Booker T. Washington's response to black discontent and white hostility in the South formed the basis of his ATLANTA COMPROMISE speech of 1895.

In 1906 a race riot engulfed Atlanta. Provoked by sensational news stories of black men menacing white women, 10,000 white men attacked African Americans in the downtown area and invaded black neighborhoods. The riot led to a modest effort at racial cooperation but a greater commitment from white politicians to exclude blacks from the political process. In 1915 the Ku Klux Klan was reborn, with Atlanta as its headquarters. The Klan's membership in Atlanta reached 15,000 by 1923. Hostility and restrictive housing codes condensed the African American community into neighborhoods on the near eastern and western sides of the city while many black businesses moved east from integrated Peachtree Street to form a black business district on Auburn Avenue.

Modest improvements in race relations followed World War I. The Commission on Interracial Cooperation was created in 1919, and the first city-funded, all-black high school was established on the booming west side. Meanwhile, the Auburn Avenue business and cultural district became very prosperous, increasing the influence of the black business and church elite in Atlanta.

African American political strength grew after World War II. Just as the war ended, the state legislature repealed the poll tax and the federal courts outlawed the all-white Democratic primary. African Americans registered 18,000 new voters to participate in the 1946 primary elections, and formed the bipartisan Atlanta Negro Voters League. The effects of this larger black electorate appeared in the early 1950s, when African American leaders were able to bargain – peacefully – for increased land, low-income housing, and the gradual elimination of all JIM CROW laws.

Atlanta remained substantially segregated, however. By 1959 African Americans represented 30 percent of the population but occupied 16 percent of the land. Four white high schools integrated in 1961, but restaurants, department stores, and many other businesses remained segregated. Organizing sit-ins and boycotts, black university students became more confrontational, which placed them in conflict with the older black leaders of Atlanta. A generational shift in black activism was under way, which eventually forced Martin Luther King Jr. – often a leader of nonviolent demonstrations – to mediate between students and a black elite, which included his father.

In 1962 the city tried to prevent African Americans from further integrating a neighborhood in southwest Atlanta. The "Peyton Road barricades" received national attention, galvanized local black activism and, at least officially, ended segregation in housing. A profound demographic change followed. Whites in south and east Atlanta moved to the suburbs, while blacks migrated to the city. By 1970 African Americans composed a majority of the city population; three years later, Maynard Jackson was elected the first African American mayor. Since then, Atlanta has elected two more black mayors, ANDREW YOUNG and Bill Campbell, who was elected to a second term in 1997. While there remains a significant interracial presence in the city, greater Atlanta continues to be effectively segregated into white suburbs and a black city.

Jim Mendelsohn

SEE ALSO

World War I and African Americans; World War II and African Americans; Atlanta Riot of 1906; Civil War, American; Du Bois, William Edward Burghardt (W. E. B.); Jackson, Maynard Holbrook, Jr.; King, Martin Luther, Jr.; Morehouse College; Spelman College; Washington, Booker Taliaferro.

North America

Atlanta Life Insurance Company, a successful American black-owned insurance company founded in Atlanta, Ga., in 1905.

The Atlanta Mutual Insurance Association was founded in 1905 by Alonzo Herndon, a former slave who owned and operated a successful Atlanta barbershop. Herndon, a close associate of both W. E. B. Du Bois and Booker T. Washington, was influenced by Washington's emphasis on black economic progress and sought to establish an African American entrepreneurial empire, dabbling in real estate development as well as insurance. Though Atlanta was home to a growing black middle class in the early 1900s, Herndon's new company served a largely impoverished clientele, and at first only offered industrial insurance for weekly premiums of just a few cents each. Despite early difficulties, by taking a grassroots approach to winning clients (company agents ventured into black communities selling insurance like door-to-door salesmen), and by pushing a "buy black" promotional campaign, Atlanta Life experienced swift growth. By 1906 the company had attracted almost $400,000 in new policies; and by 1921, when the company expanded into stocks and was retitled the Atlanta Life Insurance Company, its insurance holdings were valued at nearly $10 million.

In the late 1920s Atlanta Life was hurt by the GREAT DEPRESSION and by clients who felt more secure investing with larger, white-owned corporations. It continued to grow, however, by acquiring smaller African American insurance companies. Norris Herndon took over the company after his father's death in 1927, and when he retired in 1973, the company had expanded into 11 states and accrued $346 million insurance in force. This made Atlanta Life the second-largest African American-owned insurance company in the United States until the 1950s (the largest was the North Carolina Mutual Life Insurance Company). By the 1990s Atlanta Life had $2.5 billion insurance in force and $158 million in total assets.

Lisa Clayton Robinson

SEE ALSO

Du Bois, William Edward Burghardt (W. E. B.); Washington, Booker Taliaferro.

North America

Atlanta Riot of 1906 (September 22, 1906), a riot leading to the murder of African Americans and the destruction of black sections of the city by a white mob.

During the late nineteenth and early twentieth centuries, African American communities throughout the South fell victim to campaigns of violence and terror at the hands of white mobs, which were often aided by the local police. Eyewitness accounts described the climate in and around Atlanta on the eve of the riot as tense and volatile. The "race-baiting" gubernatorial campaign of Hoke Smith, a white politician, and an inflammatory newspaper editorial alleging that white women were being raped by African American men contributed to racial animosity.

On September 22 a white mob gathered on Decatur Street and began destroying African American businesses on nearby Auburn Street. The mob killed five African Americans, burned hundreds of homes, and destroyed vibrant sections of the city. Reports by survivors indicate that when the state militia arrived the following night, they offered little protection. Instead, the mob was allowed to move to Brownsville, a middle-class black suburb inhabited largely by college students. With the aid and support of the local white police force, the mob destroyed Brownsville, looting African American businesses and burning African American homes.

The Atlanta riot lasted five nights, leaving 25 African Americans dead, hundreds injured, and over 1000 homeless. Under the aegis of Booker T. Washington, black leaders gathered in New York City at the Carnegie Hall Conference of 1906 to generate ideas for rebuilding the community. Although many elite whites had encouraged and participated in the rioting, others were inspired by the violence to join forces with moderate black leaders to prevent future violence. As further amelioration, the Southern Sociological Congress instituted annual meetings to discuss race relations in 1912. These meetings led to the formation of the Commission on Interracial Cooperation in 1919.

The rioting in and around Atlanta led many African Americans to question seriously and challenge the so-called New South and its resolve for racial tolerance and racial healing. Many also questioned the usefulness of self-help philosophies of leaders like Booker T. Washington. Returning to his family in Atlanta just days after the riot, scholar W. E. B. Du Bois captured his anger and despair in a poem entitled "The Litany of Atlanta":

A city lay in travail, God our Lord, and from her loins sprang twin Murder and Black Hate. Red was the midnight; clang, crack and cry of death and fury filled the air and trembled underneath the stars when church spires pointed silently to Thee. And all this was to sate the greed of greedy men who hide behind the veil of vengeance!

Bend us Thine ear, O Lord!

The Atlanta riot of 1906 revealed a disturbing picture of the devastating implications of white racism and violence. It also symbolized the inability of African Americans to protect themselves from violence that was aided by the local police. The Atlanta riot was one of many similar riots, and in 1997, black film director John Singleton released *Rosewood* to educate later generations about this long, tragic, and concealed history.

Alonford James Robinson, Jr.

See Also

Atlanta, Georgia; New York, New York; Du Bois, William Edward Burghardt (W. E. B.); Washington, Booker Taliaferro; Film, Blacks in American.

Africa

Atlas Mountains, mountain system in northwestern Africa consisting of several distinct ranges and extending between Tunisia and Morocco, a distance of about 2400 km (about 1500 mi).

The Atlas Mountains are an extension of the Alpine system of Europe. The highest range, called the High, or Grand, Atlas, is in southwestern Morocco. Toubkal, with an elevation of 4165 m (13,665 ft), is the highest known peak in this range. Lying to the north in central Morocco is the next highest range, the Middle Atlas, with a maximum elevation of about 3350 m (about 11,000 ft). Other prominent ranges of the system include the Anti-Atlas (maximum elevation about 2060 m/6750 ft), south of and parallel to the High Atlas; the Saharan Atlas, extending from eastern Morocco into Algeria, with a maximum elevation of 2328 m (7638 ft) at Jebel Chelia; and the Tell, or Maritime, Atlas, averaging about 1520 m (about 5000 ft) in elevation and extending along the coast of the Mediterranean Sea from a point near the eastern end of the Strait of Gibraltar to Cape Bon in Tunisia. Jebel Musa (ancient *Abila* or *Abyla*), a promontory (846 m/2775 ft) marking the western extremity of the Little Atlas, and the Rock of Gibraltar, on the European side of the strait, are called the Pillars of Hercules.

The Atlas system is traversed by numerous passes that provide routes between the coast and the Sahara. The northern slopes of the High Atlas and the northern and southern slopes of the Middle Atlas are densely forested; cedar, pine, cork, and oak are the predominant species of trees. Fertile valleys and extensive tracts of pasturage lie in these ranges and other sections of the system. The ranges contain a wide variety of mineral deposits, including gold, silver, lead, zinc, iron, manganese, antimony, phosphates, and petroleum, but these resources are only slightly exploited.

The Atlas Mountains are the traditional territory of the Berbers, who were driven inland to the mountains by the Arabs in the seventh century C.E. Sections of the system, chiefly in the coastal areas, were known to the Europeans of antiquity, but not until the second half of the nineteenth century did systematic exploration of the various ranges begin.

See Also

Berber; Sahara Desert.

Attorney William Kunstler tells inmates involved in the Attica uprising that he will defend them, as members of the negotiating committee and prisoners occupying a guardhouse look on.
UPI/CORBIS-Bettmann

North America

Attica Uprising, a 1971 prison revolt in upstate New York by mostly black inmates that ended when police stormed the prison, indiscriminately killing 39 inmates and hostages.

Inmates at the state prison in Attica, New York, had several grievances before their uprising on September 9, 1971. In the summer of 1970 several hundred inmates went on strike over low wages for prison labor – about 30 cents per day – and the high cost of goods in the prison commissary. The strike, however, had little effect. Inmates repeatedly complained in 1970 of severe overcrowding, but also with little result. Toward the end of the year, several prisoners filed petitions in federal court accusing guards of brutally beating them. The guards, nearly all of whom were white, were also accused of censoring black publications (more than half of the inmates were black) and of treating members of the Nation of Islam especially harshly. The complaints produced few changes.

In the summer of 1971 several prisoners published a list of their demands for better conditions, including higher pay, better medical treatment, and an end to censorship.

PRISONERS IN THE U.S. UNDER STATE OR FEDERAL JURISDICTION, 1985-1991, BY RACE

Region and Jurisdiction	1985 Prisoner Population	1985 Black	1985 Percent Black	1991 Prisoner Population	1991 Black	1991 Percent Black
U.S. TOTAL	**502,376**	**227,137**	**45.2**	**824,133**	**395,245**	**48.0**
Federal	40,223	13,066	32.5	71,608	22,727	31.7
State	462,153	214,071	46.3	752,525	372,518	49.5
NORTHEAST	**75,706**	**38,036**	**50.2**	**131,866**	**66,442**	**50.4**
Connecticut	6,149	2,765	45.0	10,977	5,144	46.9
Maine	1,226	15	1.2	1,579	37	2.3
Massachusetts	5,390	1,849	34.3	9,155	3,036	33.2
New Hampshire	683	14	2.0	1,533	80	5.2
New Jersey	11,335	7,483	66.0	23,483	15,005	63.9
New York	34,712	17,497	50.4	57,862	39,151	50.4
Pennsylvania	14,227	8,035	56.5	23,388	13,090	56.0
Rhode Island	1,307	378	28.9	2,771	899	32.4
Vermont	667	–	–	1,118	–	–
MIDWEST	**95,585**	**43,534**	**45.6**	**155,917**	**79,217**	**50.8**
Illinois	18,634	11,132	59.7	29,115	18,306	62.9
Indiana	9,904	3,464	35.0	13,008	4,971	38.2
Iowa	2,832	568	20.1	4,145	904	22.7
Kansas	4,732	1,678	35.5	5,903	2,145	36.3
Michigan	17,755	10,076	56.8	36,423	20,985	57.6
Minnesota	2,343	502	21.4	3,472	1,051	30.3
Missouri	9,796	3,918	40.0	15,897	7,317	46.0
Nebraska	1,814	553	30.5	2,495	830	33.3
North Dakota	422	5	1.2	492	4	0.8
Ohio	20,864	9,553	45.8	35,744	19,311	54.0
South Dakota	1,047	22	2.1	1,374	32	2.3
Wisconsin	5,442	2,072	38.1	7,849	3,325	42.4
SOUTH	**202,100**	**109,663**	**54.3**	**301,866**	**181,341**	**60.1**
Alabama	11,015	6,560	59.6	16,760	10,793	64.4
Arkansas	4,611	2,264	49.1	7,766	4,437	57.1
Delaware	2,553	1,443	56.5	3,717	2,449	65.9
District of Columbia	6,404	6,232	97.3	10,455	10,237	97.9
Florida	28,600	14,142	49.4	46,533	27,185	58.4
Georgia	16,014	9,531	59.5	23,644	15,931	67.4
Kentucky	4,975	1,592	32.0	9,799	3,123	31.9
Louisiana	13,890	10,032	72.2	20,003	14,834	74.2
Maryland	13,005	9,370	72.0	19,291	14,638	75.9
Mississippi	6,392	4,324	67.6	8,904	6,410	72.0
North Carolina	17,344	9,341	53.9	18,903	11,522	61.0
Oklahoma	8,330	2,434	29.2	13,340	4,652	34.9
South Carolina	10,510	6,326	60.2	18,269	12,120	66.3
Tennessee	7,127	3,153	44.2	11,474	5,503	48.0
Texas	37,532	15,548	41.4	51,677	24,520	47.4
Virginia	12,073	7,111	58.9	19,829	12,769	64.4
West Virginia	1,725	260	15.1	1,502	218	14.5
WEST	**88,762**	**22,829**	**25.7**	**162,876**	**45,518**	**27.9**
Alaska	2,329	218	9.4	2,706	339	12.5
Arizona	8,531	1,362	16.0	15,415	2,633	17.1
California	50,111	16,954	33.8	101,808	35,205	34.6
Colorado	3,369	705	20.9	8,392	1,937	23.1
Hawaii	2,111	102	4.8	2,700	155	5.7
Idaho	1,344	32	2.4	2,143	32	1.5
Montana	1,129	16	1.4	1,478	20	1.4
Nevada	3,771	1,240	32.9	5,503	1,719	31.2
New Mexico	2,313	239	10.3	3,119	316	10.1
Oregon	4,454	503	11.3	6,732	923	13.7
Utah	1,633	149	9.1	2,625	222	8.5
Washington	6,909	1,273	18.4	9,156	1,966	21.5
Wyoming	758	36	4.7	1,099	51	4.6

Source: *Encyclopedia of African-American Culture and History* (1996): "Prisoners Under State or Federal Jursidiction, 1985 and 1991" (Table 4.3).

While this round of demands was lingering, prison guards in California killed George Jackson, a nationally known inmate and activist for prisoners' rights – further escalating tensions at Attica. The morning after Jackson's death, Attica prisoners refused to eat breakfast and wore makeshift armbands in commemoration.

Two weeks later, on September 8, Attica guards tried to break up what they believed to be a fight between two inmates in the prison yard. Both inmates protested (by some accounts, they were playing football), and a swarm of other prisoners encircled the guards. The guards withdrew but that night removed the two prisoners from their cells. When the two inmates again resisted, prisoners in nearby cells pelted guards with objects. One guard was injured by broken glass, and the prisoner who had thrown the glass was taken from his cell. The next morning, several prisoners refused to go to breakfast until he was released. While a prison official tried to mediate, inmates waiting in a nearby hallway overran the area, releasing the prisoner who had thrown the glass and storming other guards. In a short time, a large group of inmates controlled the entire prison.

The inmates released several guards who were injured during the rioting but held more than 30 others as hostages. They also elected a small group from their ranks to negotiate with the state government. In addition to their demands from earlier in the summer, they sought religious and political freedom, more programs for rehabilitation and education, and immunity from prosecution and beatings after they surrendered the hostages. They also invited doctors and reporters to the prison, both to verify that the hostages were in good health and to broadcast the events across the country.

State negotiators met with prisoners for several days, but New York governor Nelson Rockefeller turned down the inmates' request to visit Attica. His commissioner of prisons agreed to meet many of the inmates' demands but refused to guarantee immunity from prosecution. On September 13 Rockefeller cancelled negotiations and sent a large contingent of state troopers and prison guards into the prison. For several minutes, troopers fired at the prisoners, who did not have firearms, and at the hostages, many of whom were dressed in convicts' clothing.

Twenty-nine prisoners and 10 hostages were killed; another 85 prisoners and 3 hostages were wounded. (Three prisoners and a guard had already died from the initial riot.) Although ambulances were waiting for wounded hostages, provisions for prisoners were less forthcoming, which contributed to several needless deaths. Prison guards immediately and cruelly beat the surviving prisoners.

State authorities explained that Rockefeller ordered the raid because prisoners were mutilating the hostages. They also reported, falsely, that prisoners had killed the ten hostages who died during the raid. Autopsies and later investigations, however, proved both claims to be untrue: there was no mutilation, and the bullets that killed the hostages matched bullets fired by state troopers. State officials tried to explain the bullets by claiming that the prisoners had built homemade guns. This claim, however, was also proven to be untrue.

For months after the revolt, guards subjected prisoners to savage beatings. On December 1, 1971, a federal court found that guards had conducted an "orgy of brutality" and issued an injunction against further abuse. Coupled with the state's cover-up, the reports of brutality made Attica a symbol of the poor treatment of blacks and other people of color in United States prisons. As a result, Congress and several state legislatures passed minor reforms in the treatment of prisoners.

See Also

Jackson, George Lester.

Africa

Attié (also known as the Atié, Akié, and the Akyé), ethnic group of Côte d'Ivoire.

The Attié primarily inhabit the area directly north of Abidjan, Côte d'Ivoire. They speak a Niger-Congo language and belong to the Akan cultural and linguistic group. Approximately 350,000 people consider themselves Attié.

See Also

Abidjan, Côte d'Ivoire; Côte d'Ivoire; Languages, African: An Overview.

North America

Attucks, Crispus

(b. 1723?; d. March 5, 1770, Boston, Mass.), American patriot and the first martyr of the American Revolution.

Information on the birth and early childhood of Crispus Attucks is inconclusive, but historians believe that he was part African and part Native American (*see* American Indians) and was once the slave of William Brown of Framingham, Massachusetts. In November 1750, Attucks escaped. For the next 20 years, he worked on whaling ships docked in ports

A lithograph by American patriot and engraver Paul Revere shows British troops firing on and killing five unarmed colonists in the 1770 event that became known as the Boston Massacre. Among those killed was African American Crispus Attucks, a protest leader. *CORBIS/Bettmann*

throughout New England.

His fame is attributable largely to a single fateful day in Boston, March 5, 1770, when anticolonial patriot Samuel Adams urged dockworkers and seamen in Boston to protest the presence of British troops guarding the customs commissioners. Attucks was among an estimated 50 men who gathered that night to confront the British, and is alleged to have rallied his comrades by declaring, "Don't be afraid" as he led the ranks. When British soldiers fired on the protesters, Attucks was the first of five men killed in what became known as the Boston Massacre.

The colonial protesters carried Attucks's body to Faneuil Hall in downtown Boston, where it rested for three days before he and the other four victims were given a public funeral attended by an estimated 10,000 people. At an ensuing trial, Attucks was blamed by the defense for inciting the riot, and the British troops who fired into the crowd were acquitted. Nonetheless, American patriots hailed Attucks's heroism in the skirmish, and perceived it as the incident that sparked the AMERICAN REVOLUTION.

For more than a century, March 5 was celebrated as Crispus Attucks Day by blacks living in Boston. A monument commemorating the historic night and honoring Attucks and the other four martyrs was erected in Boston Common in 1888. Attucks's symbolic importance is exemplified by the many schools and institutions throughout the country that bear his name. African American leaders throughout the century have unsuccessfully lobbied the government to create a national holiday on March 5.

Alonford James Robinson, Jr.

Africa

Augustine, Saint

(b. November 13, 354, Thagste, Numidia; d. August 28, 430, Hippo Regius), Catholic saint from North Africa whose doctrinal innovations influenced much subsequent Christian theology.

One of the most famous theologians of his time, Augustine was raised in a mixed household: his mother was Christian but his father, an official of the Roman empire, was pagan. He spent his early years in what is today called Souk-Ahras, in ALGERIA. Despite the piety of his mother, Augustine abandoned Christianity at an early age, attracted instead by Manichaeism, a system of material dualism that claimed the human soul was like light imprisoned by darkness. A precocious learner, Augustine considered Christian Scripture intellectually crude. Inspired by *Hortensius*, a now-lost text by Cicero, he mastered rhetoric and, while still in his teens, held a professional chair of rhetoric in CARTHAGE.

Ever questioning the nature of things, Augustine discarded Manichaeism for Academic Skepticism, and, later, Neoplatonism. At the age of 28, he left Carthage for the Roman capital of Milan in search of better-disciplined students. In Milan, Augustine was profoundly impressed by Saint Ambrose, the preeminent Roman churchman of the time, and converted to Christianity. Saint Ambrose baptized Augustine, who thereafter returned to Africa and passed the remainder of his life deep in Christian thought. In contrast to his youthful agnosticism, the repentant Augustine decided that faith was the first and most essential step toward wisdom. He was ordained as an assistant priest in Hippo Regius in 391, and became the bishop of Roman Africa five years later.

Augustine's famous autobiography, *The Confessions*, showcases the tormented self-deprecation that underpins Augustine's theology and that flavored 1500 years of Christian faith. Augustine's most influential works include his philosophy of creation and of time, his philosophy of history, and his theory of salvation.

In contrast to Greek notions of eternal substance, Augustine believed that, as the Bible said, God created the world from absolute nothingness. Augustine also claimed that God was outside of time, existing always, and always the same. He posited that past and future were constructs of the human mind, ever-present sensations of memory and expectation.

In *The City of God*, Augustine created what was perhaps the first philosophy of history. Here he proclaimed that two cities – that of earth and that of heaven – are combined in this world. At the end of this world, however, these cities shall be divided into their true forms: the elect and the reprobate, the saved and the damned, heaven and hell. Augustine claimed that the Church was the only means by which people could attempt to enter the City of God. By doing this, he set the stage for the struggle between emperors and popes that characterized Western European history until the Protestant Reformation.

Although his work affected Western Europe more than it did Africa, Augustine was part of an imperial order that suppressed the Donatists, African Christians who often contested the Catholic establishment for economic and social as well as religious reasons.

Augustine died on August 28, 430, as Vandals were besieging the city of Hippo; August 28 has since become the day on which Catholics honor him.

Eric Bennett

SEE ALSO

Roman Africa: An Interpretation.

Africa

Aushi

(also known as Ushi), ethnic group of south central Africa.

The Aushi primarily inhabit the southeastern tip of Congo-Kinshasa and northern ZAMBIA. They speak a Bantu language and belong to the BEMBA cultural and linguistic group. Approximately 200,000 people consider themselves Aushi.

SEE ALSO

Bantu: Dispersion and Settlement; Congo, Democratic Republic of the.

North America

Aviators, African American,

African American pilots who operate aircraft for sport as well as military or commercial purposes.

At the beginning of the twentieth century, the dream of flying became a reality and the nation's expectations of the new technology were enormous – some thought it would even eliminate warfare. African Americans hoped to enter this new arena, in part to put to rest society's deeply held belief that blacks were an inferior race. In 1992, however, the Organization of Black Airline Pilots stated that only 600 of the nation's 70,000 commercial airline pilots were African American. The number rises only slightly when private and military pilots are considered.

The earliest African American pilot is thought to have been Charles Wesley Peters in 1911. Eugene J. Bullard (1894-1961) was the only black fighter pilot in World War I, having flown for the French. The first black woman to obtain a license (in 1921) was BESSIE COLEMAN (1892-1926); she, too, had to learn to fly in France. Other early black aviators include William J. Powell (1899-1942), who opened a flying school in Los Angeles, and Thomas C. Allen (1907-1989) and J. Herman Banning (1900-1933), who flew across the United States in 1932.

Chicago became the hub of black aviation. Black aviators there included John C. Robinson (1903-1954), Janet H. Waterford (1907-1993), Cornelius J. Coffey (1903-1994), Willa B. Brown (1906-1992), and Chauncey Spencer (b. 1906). Robinson replaced Hubert Julian, a Trinidadian, as aviation adviser to Haile Selassie of ETHIOPIA during the Italian invasion. Coffey and Brown ran an aviation school.

About 1000 African American men were trained at Tuskegee Airfield in Alabama during World War II. Nearly 500 of them saw action. Gen. Benjamin O. Davis Jr. (b. 1912) was the commander of the TUSKEGEE AIRMEN. Gen. Daniel "Chappie" James Jr. (1920-1978) became the first black four-star general. James Lincoln Holt Peck (1921-1996) flew in the Spanish Civil War in 1937 and became a prolific writer on aviation topics. Astronauts who are also pilots are Robert H. Lawrence (1935-1967), Guion S. Bluford Jr. (b. 1943), and Frederick D. Gregory (b. 1941). In 1983 Bluford became the first black American in space.

Betty Gubert

See Also
Haile Selassie I; World War I and African Americans; World War II and African Americans; Bluford, Guion Stewart (Guy), Jr.; Chicago, Illinois; Davis, Benjamin O., Jr.; Gregory, Frederick Drew; James, Daniel ("Chappie"), Jr.

Africa

Awoonor, Kofi,

(b. 1935, Wheta, Ghana), Ghanaian poet and novelist. His works in English focus on life in Ghana following independence from Great Britain in 1957, but they also draw heavily from the traditional literature of the Ewe culture in which he grew up.

Born in the coastal town of Wheta, Kofi Awoonor published his first work under the name George Awoonor-Williams. Since the late 1960s he has used his birth name. After receiving his B.A. in English from the University of Ghana at Legon (near Accra) in 1960, he served as managing editor of the Ghana Film Corporation.

In 1968 Awoonor went to the United States, earning his Ph.D. in comparative literature from the State University of New York at Stony Brook in 1972. He later taught there and at the University of Texas at Austin. Shortly after returning to Ghana in 1975 to teach in the English department at the University of Cape Coast, Awoonor was arrested and imprisoned by the military government, which he opposed. After his pardon and release in 1976, he returned to the university. Beginning in the 1980s he held a number of diplomatic positions, most notably as Ghana's ambassador to the United Nations in the early 1990s.

Awoonor has established himself as one of the most significant contemporary African writers, primarily through his poetry. He is a lyric poet in essence, with a strong sense of engagement with political and cultural concerns. Awoonor's first two books of verse, *Rediscovery* (1964) and *Night of My Blood* (1971), show a progression from fascination with his roots to a synthesis of traditional and Western ideas. His first novel, *This Earth, My Brother... : An Allegorical Tale of Africa* (1971), remains his most widely read work. In it he writes of a young lawyer's coming to terms with postcolonial West African society. As in his early poetry, Awoonor employs rhythms and motifs from traditional Ewe dirges to express the alienation and anguish that demand a restructuring, refocusing, and revitalizing of individual and communal order in contemporary Africa.

In his next poetry collection, *Ride Me, Memory* (1973), Awoonor reflects on his sojourn in America, often following the patterns of traditional African praise and abuse poetry. The title of his next collection, *The House by the Sea* (1978), alludes to the place where he was imprisoned, and in the poems he transforms the personal experience of imprisonment into a collective statement about his people. In his second novel, *Comes the Voyager at Last* (1991), Awoonor examines the process of an African American coming to Africa and finding his roots. *The Latin American and Caribbean Notebook, Volume I* (1992) is a collection of poems reflecting on global relations during Awoonor's years as an ambassador.

See Also
Accra, Ghana.

Latin America and the Caribbean

Axé Music, **Afro-Brazilian musical form that developed in the state of Bahia (*see* Contemporary Afro-Brazilian Music).**

Latin America and the Caribbean

Axé Opô Afonjá, **one of the oldest *terreiros*, or temples, of the Afro-Brazilian religion of Candomblé, established by the famous *ialorixá*, or Candomblé priestess, Mãe Aninha.**

Africa

Azande, **a major ethnic group of southern Sudan, northeastern Congo-Kinshasa, and the southeastern Central African Republic.**

In the early nineteenth century the Bandia people formed kingdoms that ruled over the Vungara, whose language they adopted, in the savannas of what is today the southeastern Central African Republic. The two groups merged to form the Azande people. Each Azande king directly administered the central province of his kingdom and delegated authority in outlying areas to his sons, nobles, or occasionally to particularly talented commoners. Each province had a court that served as an administrative as well as a social center, and each provincial governor collected tribute on behalf of the king.

With the king's death, however, a power struggle began that did not end until one of the king's sons came to dominate the bulk of his father's territory. The sons who lost their authority in this struggle frequently sought to establish kingdoms of their own in neighboring regions. By this means, the Azande expanded rapidly eastward and northward during the early nineteenth century toward the Bahr al-Ghazal and Nile rivers; their subjects, though, included many non-Azande. Because the Azande were divided in rival kingdoms, they could not develop a united front against foreign invaders. The raids of northern Sudanese slave traders checked the northward expansion of the group in the mid-nineteenth century.

Since precolonial times Azande have resolved disputes by consulting oracles with the guidance of ritual specialists. The community often considered misfortune, disease, and disaster to be the result of witchcraft. (The Azande believed that witches attacked the spiritual essence of their victims, not with medicines or charms, but through the ability of the witches' souls to attack other people at night.) Sorcery, which was also practiced in Azande communities, involved the ritual manipulation of objects, medicines, or the spoken word to achieve the perpetrator's personal goals.

During the Scramble for Africa, France, Belgium, and the Anglo-Egyptian Sudan each claimed a portion of the Azande homeland, and the Azande have remained divided among three different states since then. Although the Anglo-Egyptian administration left the Azande hierarchy intact by imposing a system of indirect rule through the aristocracy, the wealth of the royal and provincial courts fell sharply when the government hindered their ability to collect tribute. In fact, impoverished conditions have been common to the Azande in Sudan, Congo-Kinshasa, and the Central African Republic.

After World War II (1939-1945) the British developed a project known as the Zande Scheme to promote cotton cultivation in southern Sudan in a last-minute effort to bring that region's level of development up to that of northern Sudan. This effort largely failed. Because their homeland is so isolated – far from ports and in regions lacking good transportation infrastructure – the Azande's opportunities for trade have been limited, and an ongoing civil war in Sudan has compounded the difficulties of the Azande in that country. To compensate for their isolation and enhance their economic opportunities, many Azande who once lived in dispersed homesteads have migrated to towns along major roads in all three countries, often at the prompting of government authorities. The Azande continue to hunt and farm millet, sorghum, and corn as they have done for centuries. Although they once produced considerable amounts of cotton cloth, today the Azande farm cassava and peanuts as cash crops.

See Also
Colonial Rule; Congo, Democratic Republic of the; Nile River.

Africa

Azania, **the name used during the era of apartheid, or forced segregation, in South Africa in reference to a country of the future, independent and ruled by blacks.**

The term *azania,* meaning "the land of the blacks," was the name Arab traders gave the eastern coast of Africa beginning in the first century B.C.E. In the 1970s Azania was adopted by militant black South Africans, including the Pan-Africanist Congress (PAC), as a more authentic name for their country.

Organizations that were part of the Black Consciousness Movement also used the name. The South African government banned Black Consciousness organizations in 1977, but in 1978 the Azanian People's Organization (AZAPO) was founded. Like Black Consciousness organizations, AZAPO advocated a liberated Azania under black rule. The African National Congress (ANC), on the other hand, never supported Azania as a future name for South Africa.

In 1990 the South African government lifted its ban on antiapartheid groups. Black Consciousness organizations put forward the Azanian Manifesto in June 1993 in opposition to the ANC's statement of purpose, called the FREEDOM CHARTER. The manifesto stood as an alternative to nonracial strategies like those of the ANC and discouraged any collaboration with the former white oppressors. The ANC, however, had been holding negotiations with the ruling NATIONAL PARTY, and in 1994 South Africa held its first multiracial, democratic, national elections. The ANC won a majority of the vote and formed a new government. The name Azania fell out of use after South Africa achieved majority rule.

SEE ALSO
Black Consciousness in Africa; African National Congress.

Latin America and the Caribbean

Azeredo, Albuino, Afro-Brazilian engineer and successful businessman who was elected governor of the state of Espírito Santo in 1991, becoming, along with ALCEU COLLARES of the state of Rio Grande do Sul, one of the first black governors to be elected in Brazil.

As a politician, Albuino Azeredo ran for governor of the state of Espírito Santo in 1991 as a member of the Democratic Labor Party (PDT). Though Espírito Santo has an Afro-Brazilian population that counts for around 50 percent of the overall electorate, election patterns have not indicated that voters in Brazil vote along racial lines. But the PDT has an active and militant tradition of speaking about racial issues as part of its political platform. In 1982, for example, the PDT's electoral campaign emphasized its commitment to the black population. In addition, influential black leaders have been prominent members of the PDT, including famous black activist Professor Abdias do Nascimento.

During the 1991 campaign Azeredo's opponents emphasized the fact that he is black, but he did not base his campaign on his racial identity. He did work actively to demobilize the eminently racist opposition that formed against his candidacy. Azeredo defeated his opponent, José Ignácio Ferreira, by twice the number of votes, embarrassing then president Fernando Collor de Melo, who was of the same party.

A few months after Azeredo was elected, in August 1991, South African antiapartheid leader Nelson Mandela met with him in the city of Vitória, the capital of Espírito Santo. Even though Azeredo was Brazil's only black governor at the time, the meeting with Mandela was included in the tour only at the last minute and was not part of the Brazilian Foreign Ministry's official programme for the African National Congress (ANC) leader.

During his tenure as governor, Azeredo denounced the increasing number of murders of children and adolescents in the state of Espírito Santo, saying he had "no doubts that those instigating these murders belong to the groups that wield economic power." At a press conference in Rio de Janeiro, Azeredo said that his "fundamental concern" was to combat death squads, which usually comprise policemen, private security guards, and common delinquents. "If the country's recession continues, we'll always be up against a mortal enemy who believes that exterminating youngsters is the way to solve our public security problems," he stated. He also criticized the previous local and federal governments' economic policies and said that they had led to rising crime and delinquency.

In his personal life, Azeredo has suffered the tensions of racism in Brazil. Married to a white woman for more than two decades, he has encountered the scorn still faced by mixed couples. In 1994 his daughter, Ana Flavia, then 17 years old, was verbally attacked and hit in the face by a white woman and her son when she was trying to use the "social elevator" in an apartment building. Brazilian apartment buildings commonly have two elevators: a "social" one, for residents, and a "service" elevator for deliveries and for use by maids and servants.

Liliana Obregón

SEE ALSO
Mandela, Nelson Rolihlahla; Brazil, Blacks and Politics in: An Interpretation; African National Congress.

Africa

Azikiwe, Benjamin Nnamdi, (b. 1904, Nigeria), the first president of independent NIGERIA.

An Igbo from western Nigeria, Benjamin Nnamdi Azikiwe was educated at mission schools in Lagos. He clerked briefly for the treasury at Lagos but left Nigeria in 1925, a stowaway on a ship bound for the United States. In the United States he studied history and political science while supporting himself as a coal miner, casual laborer, dishwasher, and even as a boxer. While a graduate student at the University of Pennsylvania, he became acquainted with Marcus Garvey and the Back to Africa movement.

Azikiwe published *Liberia in World Affairs* in 1934, when he moved to GHANA and became editor of the *Africa Morning Post*. He returned to Nigeria in 1937, joined the Nigerian Youth Movement's executive committee, and started a chain of newspapers, including the *West African Pilot* and four other journals. Azikiwe was appointed secretary-general of the Nigerian National Council in 1944 and was later appointed its president.

As the nationalist political movement gained strength, Azikiwe figured prominently. He was unanimously elected the first president of Nigeria when the country became a republic in 1963. In 1966 he was removed from office by a military coup, but he returned to Nigeria after the fall of the Biafran state to serve as chancellor of the University of Lagos. Azikiwe's other publications include *Renascent Africa* (1937).

SEE ALSO
Lagos, Nigeria; Nationalism in Africa; Garvey, Marcus Mosiah.

b

Latin America and the Caribbean

Babalâo.

Priest in some Afro-Brazilian and Afro-Cuban religions (*see* Religions, African, in Latin America and the Caribbean).

Africa

Babangida, Ibrahim Gbadamosi

(b. August 17, 1941, Minna, Niger State, Nigeria), president of Nigeria from 1985 to 1993.

Ibrahim Gbadamosi Babangida was born to Muslim parents in northern Nigeria. His long education eventually placed him among Nigeria's military elite. After primary school Babangida studied at the government college in Bida (1957-1962) and the Nigerian Military Training College in Kaduna (1962-1963); abroad with the Indian Military Academy (1964), the Royal Armoured Center in Great Britain (1966-1967), and the United States Army (1972); and back home at the Command and Staff College in Jaji (1977) and the Nigerian Institute for Policy and Strategic Studies in Kuru (1979-1980). Well before he finished his studies, however, he began his active military duty.

Babangida graduated from the Training College and was a lieutenant by 1966. During the Biafran War (1967-1970) he commanded the 44th Infantry Battalion, known as The Rangers, and won recognition as a capable leader. In 1974 the army promoted him to lieutenant colonel, and in the next year appointed him head of the armored corps. In 1976 Babangida led forces that successfully resisted a coup to overthrow the government, and by the early 1980s he had established himself as a low-profile leader of the highest caliber.

In 1983, after his promotion to major general and appointment as chief of army staff, he led a coup that overthrew Shehu Shagari, the civilian leader of Nigeria's Second Republic (1979-1983). Although it was Muhammadu Buhari who assumed power in Shagari's stead, Bagangida ousted Buhari in 1985, ostensibly on the grounds of the latter's failure to revive Nigeria's failing economy. Inside observers suggested that a truer motive might have been the political conflict between Buhari and a majority of the Supreme Military Council (SMC), which Bagangida dominated.

Faced with a debt-ridden economy as well as Muslim-Christian conflict in the north, Babangida had usurped a troubled office. On the day of the coup he appeared on television, announcing his plans to liberalize the economy, revoke press restrictions, and protect human rights. Despite this initial decree, however, Babangida's regime proved at least as repressive as earlier dictators', and it was largely unsuccessful in its efforts to promote economic growth and stability.

Although Babangida initially refused to go along with economic reforms recommended by the International Monetary Fund (IMF), he did introduce austerity measures that caused high inflation and widespread deprivation. When students and labor unions protested these measures in 1988, Babangida closed the universities and dissolved the executive committee of the National Labour Council.

Early in his term Babangida announced that the transition to civilian rule would be completed by October 1990, a date he then pushed back to 1992 and later delayed again until 1993. The two-party democracy he described would exclude military leaders who had held office in earlier regimes, including himself. But Babangida then proceeded to quash free speech. He eventually chose the two presidential candidates himself, banning all other contenders. When faced with the victory of his less favored pick, businessman Moshood Abiola, Babangida nullified the elections and installed an interim government. This provoked enough dissent that Gen. Sani Abacha, Babangida's chief of staff, staged an easy coup three months later.

Eric Bennett

See Also

Human Rights in Africa.

Africa

Babimbi,

ethnic group of Cameroon.

The Babimbi primarily inhabit southern Cameroon. They speak a Bantu language and are related to the Bassa and Bakoko. Approximately 150,000 people consider themselves Babimbi.

See Also

Bantu: Dispersion and Settlement; Languages, African: An Overview; Bassa of Cameroon.

Africa

Baboon,

common name applied to certain large African monkeys and sometimes to the closely related gelada. Baboons generally are adapted to life on the ground and avoid forests; they range in large herds, called troops, over rocky, open lands and wooded areas of Africa and Arabia.

Powerful and aggressive animals about the size of a large dog, baboons have strong, elongated jaws, large cheek pouches in which they store food, and eyes close together. They have overhanging brows and strong limbs. Baboons can distinguish colors and have a keen sense of smell. They have large, often brightly colored, hairless areas on their buttocks, and thick, sturdy legs. The tail is generally short and is carried high in an arch.

Baboons eat various worms, eggs, insects, reptiles, crabs, mollusks, small mammals, fruits, and young shoots. Their troops are often composed of 30 to more than 100 members. Baboons have several different calls, many of which have specific meanings. After a gestation period of about six months, a female usually bears a single offspring, which clings to its mother's underside. In rare instances, a female will have twins.

The largest of the baboons is the chacma of southern Africa. Known also as the pig-tailed baboon, it is grayish-brown with a green tint along the back. The adult male may weigh up to 41 kg (90 lb) and is a formidable fighter against the troop's enemies.

The olive baboon is found in the sub-Saharan savanna region extending from MALI to ETHIOPIA and northern TANZANIA and also in several mountainous regions of the SAHARA DESERT. It has a darker brown coat than that of the chacma.

The yellow baboon is native to western, central, and eastern Africa, south to Mashonaland in ZIMBABWE. The several subspecies of these baboons all have light yellow coats and blackish faces.

Another well-known species is the North African hamadryas baboon of North Africa and the southwestern Arabian Peninsula. It is known as the sacred baboon because it was deified by the ancient Egyptians. It has a pink face and a long snout, and males have a long mane covering the neck and shoulders.

The mandrill, a large baboon of western Africa, has an enormous head, crested and bearded, and almost no forehead. Another western African species is the drill, somewhat smaller than the mandrill, but similar in its lack of aggressive behavior. The gelada, the only true primate grazer, sleeps in the cliffs of gorges in central Ethiopia.

Scientific classification: Baboons belong to the family Cercopithecidae. The chacma is classified as *Papio ursinus,* the olive baboon as *Papio anubis,* the yellow baboon as *Papio cynocephalus,* the hamadryas baboon as *Papio hamadryas,* the mandrill as *Papio sphinx,* the drill as *Papio leucophaeus,* and the gelada as *Theropithecus gelada.*

SEE ALSO
Egyptian Mythology.

Latin America and the Caribbean

Baca, Susana (b. 1954, Lima, Peru), Afro-Peruvian composer, vocalist, and ethnomusicologist, one of the leading performers and researchers of Afro-Peruvian music.

Susana Baca has become one of PERU's leading specialists of Afro-Peruvian music. Since the 1960s she has explored the distinctive rhythms, tempos, and instruments of the small but influential Afro-Peruvian community that has been sequestered for nearly 500 years along Peru's Pacific coast. Her research culminated in the path-breaking 1995 album, *The Soul of Black Peru,* which presented the traditions of Afro-Peruvian music to an international audience for the first time.

Baca leads the new generation of musicians who interpret the Afro-Peruvian traditions that were first explored in the 1950s by the renowned ethnomusicologist NICOMEDES SANTA CRUZ. She includes in her performances such Afro-Peruvian rhythms as the *lando* and *festejo,* which date back to the seventeenth century. She has also made use of indigenous instruments, including the Andean panpipes and the *cajon,* a wooden box which, when rhythmically struck with the hand, produces a variety of unusual timbres. Baca characterizes the songs she performs as a "mestizo music": "There are songs where the beat is African, the melody is Andean, and the words are Spanish," she told the *Boston Globe* in October 1997. "It is a sweet music, very melodious."

Baca grew up in the black coastal area of Chorrillos, near Lima. As a teenager she began exploring Afro-Peruvian culture by recording the songs and memories of her grandparents. As a scholar, she has continued to focus on her Afro-Peruvian cultural heritage – a considerably challenging task because Peru's black culture has been isolated for centuries and at times suppressed by the Peruvian authorities. Moreover, black elders have tended to retain only fragments of songs, often associated with the period of slavery. "I think it's that they don't want to remember the hard times that the black community has gone through," Baca told the Minneapolis *Star Tribune* in 1997. "Maybe forgetting the past and the years of slavery was a way of trying to move to a new era."

Since 1995 Baca has toured widely in Europe and the United States, where music critics have acclaimed her rich, soulful contralto voice. Her repertoire includes both traditional folk and contemporary songs. Describing Baca's October 1997 performance at New York City's New School of Social Research, Jon Pareles of the *New York Times* wrote: "Ms. Baca sang about hard work, dancing, love, and black pride, in a voice that has a halo of breathiness around a core of gentle determination... she gradually shed layers of refinement, dancing barefoot and breaking out of Western tuning to sing in the rawer tones of her ancestors." Baca's recent recordings include her debut solo album *Susana Baca* (1997) and *Del Fuego y del Agua: Black Contribution to the Formation of Peruvian Popular Music* (1997).

Roanne Edwards

SEE ALSO
Slavery in Latin America and the Caribbean.

Africa

Bade (also known as the Bede and the Bedde), ethnic group of West Africa.

The Bade primarily inhabit southeastern BURKINA FASO, southwestern NIGER, northwestern NIGERIA, and northern BENIN. They speak an Afro-Asiatic language belonging to the Chadic group. Approximately 100,000 people consider themselves Bade.

SEE ALSO
Languages, African: An Overview.

Latin America and the Caribbean

Baez, Buenaventura (1810-1882), mulatto president of the Dominican Republic (1849-1853, 1856-1857, 1865-1866, 1868-1873, 1876-1878) (*see* DOMINICAN REPUBLIC).

Africa

Baga, ethnic group of GUINEA.

The Baga primarily inhabit coastal Guinea between Rio Nunez and Conakry. They traditionally spoke a Niger-Congo language belonging to the Senegambian cluster of Western Atlantic languages, though today many speak Soso. Approximately 100,000 people consider themselves Baga.

SEE ALSO
Languages, African: An Overview.

Africa

Bagaza, Jean-Baptiste (b. August 29, 1946, Murambi, Ruanda-Urundi [present-day Burundi]), senior army officer and former president of BURUNDI.

Born into a Tutsi-Hima family in southern Urundi, now Burundi, Jean-Baptiste Bagaza attended a local Catholic school before entering the army. After Burundi achieved independence in 1962, he attended the officer school and military school in Belgium. In September 1971 Bagaza returned to Burundi to become assistant to the chief of staff. A kinsman of President MICHEL MICOMBERO, in 1972 Bagaza was placed in charge of logistics as the Tutsi-dominated army carried out genocide throughout the country, killing between 100,000 and 200,000 Hutu. His particular role in the genocide is unclear, but at its conclusion he was promoted to colonel and chief of staff of the military.

In November 1976, with dissatisfaction growing in the military, Colonel Bagaza overthrew President Micombero in a bloodless coup, claiming that "clans of self-interested politicians" used their positions for personal gain. He established a Supreme Revolutionary Council of military officers, but promised to return Burundi to civilian rule. Initially promising national reconciliation as well, he introduced agrarian reforms and a new constitution. He also held elections in 1984, which he won with 99.63 percent of the vote. Bagaza forbade politicians to use the terms "Tutsi" and "Hutu," fearing that they would again incite violence, and peace prevailed during his term in office. But for reasons still unclear, the increasingly autocratic president embarked upon a campaign against the Catholic Church, forcing foreign missionaries to leave, closing church-run schools, and banning church activities. His autocratic style upset the military, among others, and in September 1987 Maj. Pierre Buyoya overthrew Bagaza, who fled to Belgium. From exile in LIBYA, Bagaza was accused of participation in a coup d'état that overthrew the elected president Melchoir Ndadaye, though he denied the charges. In 1996, with the return to power of his successor, Pierre Buyoya, Bagaza assumed the leadership of hard-line Tutsi groups opposed to democratic change and negotiations with Hutu rebels. In 1997 he was arrested for stockpiling weapons for a purported overthrow of Buyoya.

Eric Young

SEE ALSO
Hutu and Tutsi; Buyoya, Pierre.

Africa

Baggara (also known as the Seleim, the Mesiriya, the Ta'aisha, and the Rashaida), ethnic group of SUDAN.

The Baggara primarily inhabit the DARFUR and Kordofan regions of Sudan. They speak Arabic and are one of the Juhayna Arab peoples. Approximately 1 million people consider themselves Baggara.

SEE ALSO
Languages, African: An Overview.

Latin America and the Caribbean

Baghio'o, Jean Louis (b. 1910, Sainte Anne, GUADELOUPE), novelist and poet whose works render the complex racial and cultural legacy of French colonialism in the Caribbean.

The novels of Jean Louis Baghio'o, (pseudonym for Jean-Louis Victor), unlike the more revolutionary works of his contemporaries and friends Léon-Gontran Damas, LÉOPOLD SÉDAR SENGHOR, and Jacques Rabemananjara, explore the lives of the mulatto bourgeoisie.

Baghio'o's most important work to date, *Le flamboyant à fleurs bleues* (1973; The Blue Flame-Tree), evokes four centuries of such a family's life on Guadeloupe, focusing on the nineteenth century, when the family acquires land and enters into direct rivalry with its former masters, the white plantation owners. Baghio'o uses this family, with its mixture of Africans, East Indians, Carib Indians, and Europeans, as a metaphor for the Creole culture of Guadeloupe, a culture that must fight to preserve its complex identity.

Baghio'o pursues the story of this same family in the recent *Choutoumounou* (Paris: 1995), placing the action and characters in present-day Paris. The travails of the two protagonists, the twins Pampou and Choutoumounou, illustrate the alienation of the Guadeloupean "of color" in Paris today.

Baghio'o's island narratives have been criticized for pandering to readers' taste for the "exotic," but his serious engagement with the history of these Francophone Caribbean islands has earned him the respect of MARYSE CONDÉ (who wrote a preface to the second edition of *Le flamboyant à fleurs bleues*), among others.

Baghio'o has also published another novel, *Le colibri blanc* (1980), and a collection of poems, *Les jeux du soleil* (1960).

Richard Watts

SEE ALSO
Creoles; East Indian Communities in the Caribbean.

Cross Cultural

Baha'i Faith, founded in Persia in 1863 by Mirza Husayn Ali (1817-1892), who believed he was a messenger of God.

Mirza Husayn Ali was an Iranian who became known within the faith he founded as Baha Ullah following his secession from Bab, a sect of Islam. While imprisoned by the Islamic government of the Ottoman Empire for blasphemy, Ali wrote the principal body of Baha'i scriptures.

Baha'i is centered on social and ethical reform and teaches the unity of humankind. The sexes are equal, and all racial, religious, and political prejudices are shunned. Private prayer, an annual fasting period, pilgrimage to various Baha'i holy sites, and monetary contributions are among the key rituals of the faith. Baha'i is strongly pacifist and envisions world peace through its message of unity and equality. In Baha'i, God is an unknowable being, and immortality is assured. The faith eschews ceremonial leaders.

Baha'i spread from its spiritual center in Acre, Palestine, through significant missionary work, spreading its message of social reform to America around 1894. Baha'i followers spread knowledge of the religion throughout the rural American South, adding thousands of African Americans to its corps of believers. Many converts responded to Baha'i's mission to end racism and to heal ethnic divisions within society. Since the 1960s, Baha'i has gained popularity in less developed countries, especially in sub-Saharan Africa, India, and South America.

Latin America and the Caribbean

Bahamas, a country comprising an archipelago of about 700 flat, low-lying islands, 30 of them inhabited, in the western Atlantic Ocean, extending for 1250 km (750 mi) between a point south-east of Palm Beach, Florida, and a point off the eastern tip of CUBA.

The Bahamas may be best known as the setting for one of the most charged events in history: the "discovery" of the New World by the Old. The exact place that Columbus first landed in the Americas has long been debated. Many sources have long believed it to be Long Bay; other possible sites may be San Salvador Island, Cat Island, Samana Cay, or one of several other Bahama islands. But historians agree that Columbus and his crew were in the waters of the Bahamas when they came ashore at 7:00 in the morning on Friday, October 12, 1492. In this way, the Bahamas became the backdrop for the cultural encounter that would eventually bring Europeans, Africans, and Asians to inhabit the Americas and the Caribbean.

The first known inhabitants of the Bahamas were the Lucayans, an Arawak people who appear to have settled several islands between 500 and 600 C.E. Although some historians have hypothesized that the name Bahamas comes from the Spanish *baja mar* ("shallow sea"), it appears to reflect a much older Lucayan word for what is now Grand Bahama Island. Like many Arawaks, the Lucayans supported themselves with subsistence agriculture and fishing and were known as a peaceful people. In 1559 the Spanish explorer and theologian BARTOLOMÉ DE LAS CASAS wrote that the Lucayans had outshone all other nations "in gentleness, simplicity, humility, peaceful disposition, tranquillity and in other virtues." But the Lucayan population, like many other indigenous groups in the Caribbean, was completely destroyed within 50 years of its first contact with Columbus and the outside world.

A journal entry Columbus made within days of first landing in the Bahamas betrays his intentions toward the people who already lived there. He noted that "when your Highnesses so command, they can all be carried off to Castile or held captive in the island itself, since with fifty men they would all be kept in subjection and forced to do whatever may be wished." Instead of enslaving the Lucayans in the islands that were already their homes, the Spanish government approved a plan to relocate these "idle people" to the Spanish colony at Hispaniola (now HAITI and the DOMINICAN REPUBLIC). The Bahamas' first inhabitants were eventually wiped out through a combination of the new European diseases to which they were exposed and the harsh treatment they received as Spanish slaves.

The Spanish kept their colonial claim to the Bahamas, but they did not view the islands as useful enough to establish a separate colony. Instead they focused on islands with greater mineral wealth.

Puritan migrants from the English colony at Bermuda established the first European colony in the Bahamas on Eleuthera in 1649. These colonists were seeking the same religious freedom as the Puritan settlers in Massachusetts, and chose the name Eleuthera after the Greek word for freedom. A second settlement followed in 1666 on another island, which the new migrants named New Providence. After several battles over the territory with Spain, England's rights to the Bahamas were upheld, and the Bahamas remained a British Crown colony until the late twentieth century.

The earliest English Bahamians were generally small farmers, occasionally supplementing their farming income by looting shipwrecks and piracy. (The islands were known as a key base for Bluebeard and other pirates through the first decades of the eighteenth century.) Most of these white colonists were not large landowners, so African slavery developed more slowly in the Bahamas than in several nearby islands. But it did develop, gradually changing the Bahamas into a majority-black population.

The first black Bahamians were free immigrants who arrived when Bermuda decided to banish all of its free blacks, nd some of its more "troublesome" slaves, to Eleuthera. As late as 1788, the black population on Eleuthera was still mostly free. But in other parts of the islands, most of the earliest black Bahamians were Yoruba, Congo, Ibo, Mandingo, Fulani, and Hausa West Africans and their descendants who had been stolen from their homes to serve as slaves for the English planters. By 1734 more than a third of Bahamians were black slaves, and another 5 percent were free people of color. The first Bahamian slave laws had been passed in 1723, restricting the mobility and rights of black Bahamians. In the text of those laws the terms "Negroes," "Negroes and Indians," and "slaves" were all used interchangeably, indicating clearly that even black Bahamians who were not enslaved were also not completely free.

In the late 1700s the Bahamas became a popular refuge for British Loyalists from the American colonies who chose to flee as the revolution approached. Many of these were Southern slaveholders who brought their slaves with them, and as a result, the black presence in the Bahamas also grew rapidly. By the 1780s blacks formed the majority of the Bahamian population.

While some early visitors described what they felt was the comparatively decent treatment of Bahamian slaves, black Bahamians were certainly no more "content" to be slaves than any other enslaved individuals. The persistence of advertisements for runaway slaves, and the existence of maroon settlements (*see* Maroonage in the Americas) designed to harbor those ex-slaves safely, make this clear. The first Bahamian slaves often served as domestic or farm help for their owners, who usually could afford only one or two slaves. But by the beginning of the nineteenth century there were several white Bahamians wealthy enough to own hundreds of slaves, sometimes spread out over several farms. The great majority of Bahamian slaves continued to serve as domestic and field workers, with smaller numbers employed as salt mine workers, mariners, tradesmen, or midwives.

The abolition of slavery in all British territories in 1834 freed 10,000 black Bahamians, who were thus ready to find a new role in Bahamian society (*see* Abolition and Emancipation in Latin America and the Caribbean). During the period of apprenticeship that lasted until 1838, former slaves were obligated to remain on their former owners' land in return for some form of payment that was agreed to individually. Even after apprenticeship had ended, many black Bahamians chose to remain employed as farmers and fishermen, the occupations most Bahamians had traditionally pursued. Those who were able to learn a craft or receive a higher education were quick to take advantage of these opportunities as well. In this way, some newly emancipated slaves were able to lay the foundation for the black middle class of tradesmen, teachers, ministers, doctors, and lawyers that would continue to grow.

In the 1860s, during the American Civil War, the economy of the Bahamas experienced a short windfall when the islands became a key strategic site for the Confederate States, which avoided President Lincoln's blockade of their own ports by diverting activity through the Bahamas instead. By this time, the town of Nassau on the island of New Providence had emerged as the Bahamas' key city and port, and it was there that the activity was centered. The bulk of the fortune made from the blockade running went to a small group of white Nassau merchants and ship owners, but some blacks did benefit from the boon as workers in the warehouses and at the docks. Once the war ended, however, many Bahamians returned to agricultural occupations. By the 1890s the most important economic activities for most Bahamians were sponge fishing and sisal farming. Sponging, in particular, became the mainstay of the country's economy, and going "on the mud" to collect the sponges became the primary occupation of thousands of Bahamian men.

By the turn of the century a new economic trend had begun to change the fabric of Bahamian society. The advent of the railroad in southeastern Florida led to a tremendous economic boom in that region, and with work so plentiful, between 10,000 and 12,000 people emigrated to Miami between 1900 and 1920 – approximately one of every five Bahamians. The trend slowed somewhat after new United States laws placed quotas on the number of immigrants who could come from the Caribbean, but even so, this migration created a permanent connection between the Bahamas and the United States. From this point on, there would also be cultural, economic, and psychological differences within many Bahamian families between those who chose to live abroad and those who chose to stay at home.

Even at home, similar divisions arose between Bahamians who chose to remain on more rural islands and those who migrated to New Providence and Nassau to seek better economic opportunities. In the 1920s another temporary economic boon flowed from the United States to Nassau. Just as Confederate blockade runners had used Nassau in the 1860s, so Prohibition runners used the port to circumvent the 1919 law that had made alcohol illegal in the United States, once again creating a demand for labor in a host of related industries. When the U.S. law was repealed in 1933, economic growth dried up once again and many Bahamians returned to sponging. But this time, a series of hurricanes, the effects of overfishing, and finally a deadly bacterial disease that spread through the sponge beds led to the sudden demise of the country's most stable industry. Within a few years tourism replaced sponging as the basis of the Bahamian economy.

The development of the tourist industry in the 1940s and 1950s led to even more urban employment for black Bahamians. As hotels, restaurants, airports, and casinos were built in Nassau and the newer city of Freeport, new jobs opened up for taxi drivers, porters, cooks, domestics, and waiters. Yet these positions only heightened the basic inequalities that remained in the Bahamian social system: black Bahamians served white tourists in facilities they were forbidden to use themselves, and in a style that most of the country could never afford. These social inequalities stemmed largely from the political inequalities that still existed.

The Bahamas were ruled internally by a House of Assembly composed of elected representatives. While the Bahamas were 80 to 85 percent black long before the middle of the twentieth century, they were still governed by the same small group of white elites who had always been in power. This group of politicians was nicknamed the Bay Street Boys, after the Nassau thoroughfare where many of them owned businesses. The islands' political districts were drawn in such a way that white voters were represented in disproportionately large numbers, but it was

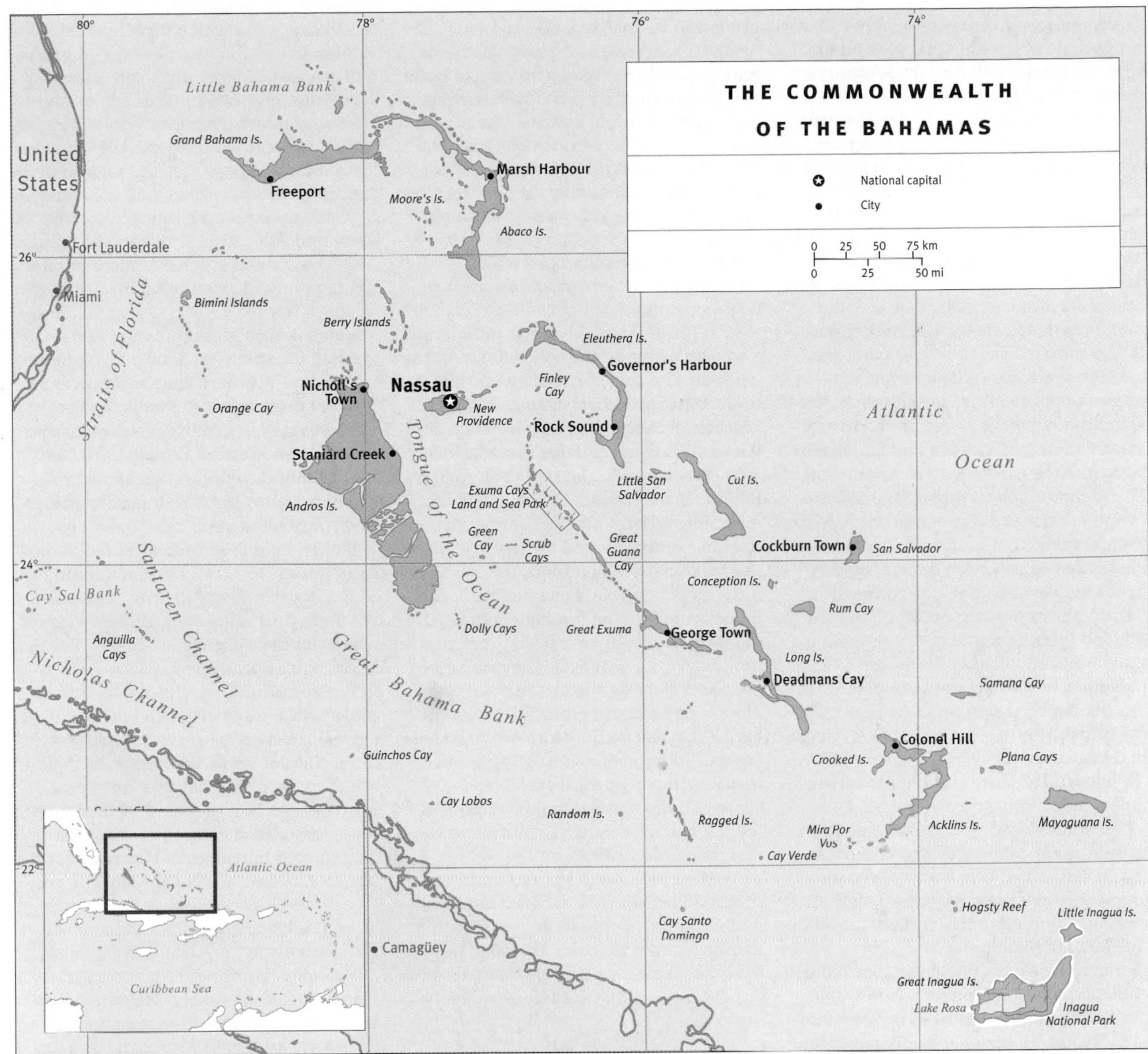

also true that black Bahamians had never organized a viable political challenge to the existing leadership. This changed in 1953 with the formation of the Progressive Liberal Party (PLP).

The PLP modeled itself after the Peoples National Party in JAMAICA and the SOUTHERN CHRISTIAN LEADERSHIP CONFERENCE in the United States. Like them, its primary goals were to ensure equal representation, economic opportunities, and rights for black Bahamians. Lyden O. Pindling, a London-educated lawyer, quickly became the party's first leader, and in 1956 the PLP won six seats in the House of Assembly. That same year, with the PLP's influence, the assembly passed an Anti-Discrimination Resolution forbidding segregation in public places – a major step forward in the Bahamian political struggle, and the first mark of the PLP's influence.

In 1958 Nassau hotel owners granted a white-owned tour company a contract to carry all of the passengers traveling between the airport and hotels. When black taxi drivers called for a work stoppage in protest, many blacks in other tourist industries chose to stop work in support of the strike. The result was a general strike that shut down the entire tourist industry for 19 days and that ended in victory for the taxi drivers. The PLP had supported the strike, and the effort was a powerful sign to black Bahamians of just how much power they could hold.

The passage of the law granting women the right to vote in 1961 gave blacks even more hope as the size of their electorate doubled. But when the next general election was held in 1962, even though the PLP won 44 percent of the vote, it won only 8 of the 33 available seats as a result of the unfair districting. It became clearer than ever that the time for equal representation for black Bahamians was long overdue.

The issue reached a dramatic crescendo on Black Tuesday – April 27, 1965. On that day, a debate on the redistricting question in the House of Assembly had again ended with white representatives stating that they were unwilling to consider reapportioning the seats fairly. Lynden Pindling, by then one of the PLP's assembly members, rose at the end of the debate to state that he did not want to be part of a government that did not represent its people fairly. Declaring that the true authority belonged outside with the people, Pindling took the wooden mace that had been the symbol of parliamentary authority in the Bahamas for 165 years and threw it out the window, where it broke in half in the middle of the crowd that had gathered outside. The act was predictably met with shock and charges of blasphemy by white assembly members, but the drama reflected the changing tide in Bahamian politics. Two years later a new redistricting act was finally approved, and when the PLP finally won a majority in the April 1968 general election, Pindling became the country's first black prime minister.

With an elected black leader, the new government moved quickly to increase educational and other spending in black areas and to limit the role of foreign capital and labor in the country. In 1971 Pindling also announced that the government of the Bahamas would seek independence from the United Kingdom within the next two years, following the example already set by many other West Indian nations. This idea was met with hesitation by some white Bahamians, many of whom both cherished their symbolic ties with Britain and also were fearful that black Bahamians had not had enough experience to be capable of self-government. The island of Abaco, the only part of the country that was not predominantly black, went as far as to unsuccessfully petition Parliament to let Abaco remain an independent Crown colony. But for most Bahamians, it was clear that the time to petition for independence had come. In a general election held in September 1972, Bahamians voted to support a petition for independence, and in May and June 1973 the British House of Commons and House of Lords, respectively, voted to accept it. On July 10, 1973, the Bahamas became an independent country.

The three decades since independence have brought challenges and advances for the Bahamas. The country's reputation as a tourist paradise has grown, and currently about 3 million visitors travel to the Bahamas each year. But even the vital tourist industry is unable to support the entire country, and in an economy that has few other robust industries, unemployment has often hovered as high as 25 percent. In the 1980s the Bahamas were affected by increases in drug addiction and crime that were connected to an increase in illegal drug trafficking through Bahamian ports, a problem that reached even the highest levels of government.

Pindling, often praised for his charismatic leadership, continued to win reelection throughout the 1970s and 1980s. But his image was irrevocably tarnished after a 1983 investigation charged his administration with corruption related to the drug trade. The PLP managed to hang on to power in the 1987 election, but in 1992 the Free National Movement (FNM) came to power, and Hubert Ingraham became prime minister. Ingraham and the FNM were reelected in 1997.

Despite political and economic problems, the last 30 years have been key in forming a strong national Bahamian identity. National traditions such as the junkanoo festival celebrate the country's connection with its slave and African past (for similar celebrations, *see* CARNIVALS IN LATIN AMERICA AND THE CARIBBEAN). Many contemporary writers and artists are choosing to embrace their specifically Bahamian and African cultural legacies. The foreword to the 1973 *Bahamian Anthology* describes Bahamian literature as a combination of "the lexicon of Europe, the tonal textures of Africa and the syntax and special peculiarities of the Caribbean and the Americas." Noted black Bahamian playwright Winston V. Saunders describes the new consciousness of Bahamian identity in this way: "Culture in the Bahamas today is an amalgam of our British heritage, our African heritage, and the effects of our closeness to North America. Our language is English.... Our courts follow the English system.... We wear [English and European fashions] with consistency.... Marry the above with the practice of obeah, the gyrating movements of the ring-play, the pulsating rhythm of junkanoo and the goatskin drum, the hand-clapping jumpers, the use of bush medicine... and you almost have a Bahamian. The final touches come in the form of the American jerry curl, the American afro, American television."

As Saunders says later, "Our paintings, our Sunday sermon oratory, our plays and our batik fashions, our straw-works and our Smokey Joe stories, our brightly painted homes and our satirical cartoonists – all these and more attest to the vibrancy of the Bahamian people." The Bahamas that met the world in 1992, on the 500th anniversary of Columbus's landing, was a country filled with just such vibrant, richly multicultural citizens, ready to display their pride in what one Bahamian poet has called their "beautiful and blessed land."

Lisa Clayton Robinson

Latin America and the Caribbean

Bahia, a state in northeastern BRAZIL, considered the cradle of Afro-Brazilian culture.

Of all the states in Brazil, Bahia has maintained the strongest ties with Africa and African culture. During the first two centuries of the colonial era, Bahia absorbed most of the slaves who were imported to Brazil. At this time, the slaves came to constitute a majority of Bahia's population and exerted a proportional effect on the developing character of the state. Today, Bahia's traditions and customs are living testimony to the enormous influence of Africans and their descendants.

BAHIA: AN OVERVIEW

Bahia is divided into three distinct regions: the *recôncavo*, the *sertão*, and the *litoral*. The recôncavo is the hot, humid area surrounding the Baía de Todos os Santos (Bay of All Saints), on which the city of Salvador is located. Its principal cities are Cachoeira, Santo Amaro, Maragojipe, and Nazaré, formerly the sugar and tobacco centers that brought wealth to Salvador during the seventeenth and eighteenth centuries. The sertão is a vast, dry stretch of land in the state's interior. It is sparsely populated by cattle raisers and farmers, who are sometimes forced by droughts to migrate. The litoral is the expansive cocoa-producing region to the south of the Baía de Todos os Santos.

Bahia is a state of more than 12.5 million inhabitants. Nearly 60 percent of the population is urban. People of African descent predominate in Bahia and are concentrated in urban centers along the coast. There are also more than 10,000 native Indians representing almost 20 different tribes, most residing on government-protected land.

Bahia's capital, Salvador, was the colonial capital from 1549 to 1763 and the center of the sugar industry that sustained the country's prosperity through the late eighteenth century. During the colonial period, it was one of the most important ports in the New World, carrying on a prosperous trade with Europe, Asia, and Africa. Today, Salvador is Bahia's most important and most populous city, with some 2.5 million inhabitants. Eighty percent are of African descent.

The historic district of the city was constructed in two levels – the *cidade alta* (upper city) and the *cidade baixa* (lower city). In the cidade alta, the neighborhood known as Pelourinho contains some of the finest examples of colonial architecture in all of South America, in addition to many art galleries, where African-style art flourishes. It is the home of the famous Afro-Brazilian Carnival groups OLODUM and FILHOS DE GANDHI as well as the black brotherhood of Nossa Senhora do Rosario dos Pretos, a church constructed by slaves in the eighteenth century. In colonial times, slaves were sold and publicly punished an open, steeply inclined part of the neighborhood known as the Largo do Pelourinho.

The seventeenth and eighteenth centuries were Bahia's golden age. With the growing international market for sugar, Bahia's sugar industry expanded and the state prospered. The cultivation of tobacco, often traded for slaves in Africa, also contributed to the province's wealth. The growth of agriculture stimulated the settlement of the interior, where cattle ranching developed on the sertão. In the late eighteenth century, coffee cultivation flourished in Rio de Janeiro and São Paulo, which displaced Bahia as the center of Brazil's economy. As a result of this shift, a significant number of slaves in Bahia were sold to coffee growers in these southeastern states.

The discovery of gold and diamonds in 1822 in Lençóis, part of the region today known as the Chapada Diamantina, briefly boosted Bahia's economy. In the late nineteenth century, however, Bahia's economy declined suddenly due to the collapse of the mining industry and the abolition of slavery in 1888. Bahia's economy was later reinvigorated by the introduction of the cocoa crop into the litoral region surrounding the city of Ilhéus. In recent years, the federal organization Superintendence for the Development of the Northeast (SUDENE) has focused on ways to develop industry in that part of the country. Despite these efforts and the existence of sizable oil deposits in northeastern states, the region continues to be characterized by a high level of poverty.

Black History in Colonial Bahia

Salvador was the principal point of entry for African slaves from the sixteenth through the late eighteenth century. The first slaves were brought from Guinea in 1538. Statistical information on the importation of slaves to Bahia is incomplete for some years and can only be estimated by looking at a variety of slave trade records collectively. According to this information, some 1.1 million to 1.3 million slaves entered Bahia between the sixteenth century and 1850, the year the slave trade was effectively abolished. This number represents about one-quarter of all the slaves imported to Brazil. It is estimated that 20,000 were imported in the sixteenth century; 205,000 in the seventeenth century; 655,000 in the eighteenth century; and 425,000 between 1800 and 1850. During the sixteenth century, the slaves brought to Bahia came principally from the Guinea region, including the present-day countries of Cape Verde, Senegal, and the Gambia. During the seventeenth century, they came primarily from the Angola region, including the countries of the Republic of the Congo and former Zaire (now the Democratic Republic of the Congo). From the eighteenth century through 1850, they came primarily from the Mina Coast and the Gulf of Benin, including Togo, Benin, and Nigeria.

Most of Bahia's slaves were concentrated in the coastal regions of Bahia, principally on the *engenhos* (sugar mills) and *fazendas* (plantations) of the sugar- and tobacco-growing recôncavo region, where they constituted the majority. With the exception of the mining regions, where return profits were great enough to justify investing in slaves, slaves were not dispersed into the interior. The sertão was not conducive to plantation agriculture, and cattle ranching was not lucrative enough to enable ranchers to purchase slaves. Indians, less expensive to purchase and with an intimate knowledge of the land, were more often used as slaves by people living in the sertão.

In Bahia, as in the rest of Brazil, enslaved and free blacks played an active role in the defense of the nation. In the early colonial period, African slaves fought against the indigenous populations on Bahia's coast. Later, they helped put an end to the Dutch invasion of Bahia, which lasted from 1624 to 1625. Blacks from Bahia also participated in the Paraguayan War (1865-1870). While some were forced to fight in these wars against their will, others voluntarily enlisted, as military service offered an escape from bondage and an opportunity to win freedom.

Although blacks in Bahia contributed to the cause of the state or nation as soldiers, they more often rebelled against their own enslavement. During the colonial era, most of Brazil's slave revolts (*see* Slave Rebellions in Latin America and the Caribbean) took place in the state of Bahia, where the concentration of slaves was greatest. In particular, the first half of the nineteenth century witnessed a high incidence of uprisings in Salvador and the surrounding recôncavo region.

In 1798 enslaved and free blacks in Bahia mounted a rebellion known as the *Conjuração Baiana/Revolução dos Sastres* (Conspiracy of the Tailors). Inspired by the ideas of the French Revolution and the *Inconfidência Mineira* (unsuccessful rebellion in the state of Minas Gerais, 1788-1789), the insurgents issued a manifesto calling for the establishment of an independent republic, the end of slavery, and a free market economy. Colonial authorities repressed their uprising and either exiled or executed the participants.

Muslim Hausa slaves referred to as Malês in Bahia repeatedly revolted during the early years of the nineteenth century. The most notorious of their uprisings occurred in 1835 in Salvador. Their plan to abolish slavery and take over the government was revealed to local police, who quelled the insurrection in its early stage. Fearing that similar rebellions could potentially establish a black republic, as had happened in Haiti in 1804, colonial officials sentenced many of the insurgents to death.

Afro-Brazilians also participated in the Sabinada Rebellion in Salvador, which lasted from November 17, 1837, to March 16, 1838. Led by the mulatto Francisco Sabino Álvares da Rocha Viera, this rebellion was a reaction against the centralization of power in Rio de Janeiro. Large numbers of slaves escaped bondage and joined the rebel army, which seized control of the city in 1837. Restorationist forces, however, cut off food supplies to Salvador and defeated the rebels the following year.

A woman at a street stall in Bahia sells acarajé, traditional Afro-Brazilian dried bean fritters stuffed with dried peppered shrimp. *Errington/Hutchison*

Another form of resistance exercised by slaves in Bahia was the creation of escaped slave communities called *quilombos* or *mocambos* (*see* Maroonage in the Americas). Although quilombos flourished throughout Bahia, they were especially prevalent in the litoral and recôncavo regions, where the geography was conducive to flight. Typically consisting of fewer than 100 members, quilombos first appeared in these regions in the late sixteenth century and continued to be cited in records through the first part of the nineteenth century. They were typically located near population centers, towns, or large villages, in a strategic position to conduct raids for food, supplies, and women, but some established friendly trade relations with nearby communities. Because quilombos posed a threat to the economic and social stability of colonial society, military expeditions were repeatedly sent to eliminate them. The escaped slaves who were captured were usually either killed or reenslaved.

The African Legacy in Contemporary Bahia

African slaves brought to Brazil preserved their traditions in a hostile environment characterized by political and social oppression and economic exploitation. The African traditions that developed in Brazil were the result of cultural negotiation between slaves of various ethnic backgrounds and the dominant Portuguese class. This process occurred both on the fazendas and in the quilombos. In the religious practices of the slaves in Bahia, Yoruban divinities and rituals predominated (*see* Yoruba). After being converted to Catholicism, slaves preserved their African deities, known as *orixás*, by identifying them with Catholic saints. This resulted in the creation of Candomblé, a religion in which members worship the orixás through African-based music, song, and dance.

Salvador, and Bahia in general, is often referred to as the *Terra de Todos os Santos*, or *Terra dos Orixás* (Land of All Saints or Land of African Gods). Although a popular saying holds that Salvador has 365 churches, one for every day of the year, the city is home to hundreds more *terreiros* ("houses of Candomblé"), arguably making Candomblé Salvador's principal religion. The oldest and most celebrated terreiros in Salvador include Casa Branca, which is over 450 years old; Gantois; and Axé Opô Afonjá.

While there are many monuments and historic places of significance to black Brazilians in Bahia, it is the vibrancy of living African-based traditions that distinguishes the state. For example, Salvador annually celebrates a number of festivals, most of which are a blend of European and African traditions. Several of these festivals are rooted in Candomblé and usually involve a religious service, a mass procession, a cleansing ritual, and a celebration complete with music, food, and drink.

First on the calendar of celebrations, the Lavagem do Bomfim occurs on the second Thursday of January. This event is attended by many *mães* and *filhas de santo* (Candomblé priestesses and initiates) who, clothed in flowing white dresses, bring clay vases filled with water and flowers to wash the Bomfim church. The Festival de São Lázaro, which is dedicated to the Candomblé orixá Omulú (the African god of disease and epidemics, who is often symbolized by Saint Lazarus), is another important occasion and is celebrated on the last Sunday in January. The biggest Candomblé-related festival is the Festa de Iemanjá. Thousands of people gather on the beach in the early hours of February 2 to honor Iemanjá, the queen of the ocean, by tossing baskets of flowers and perfumes into the sea. If their offerings are accepted

Right: **A boy walks down a residential street in Setiro Dias, Bahia.** *CORBIS/Stephanie Maze*
Below: **Slaves were sold and publicly punished in the Largo do Pelourinho neighborhood in Salvador, capital of the Brazilian state of Bahia. The state is considered the center of Afro-Brazilian culture.** *Alex Braga/Contexto*

ABOVE: Family in Santo Amara, Bahia. *CORBIS/Jan Butchofsky-Houser*
RIGHT: During the colonial era slaves constituted a majority of the population in Bahia, a state in northeast Brazil. Today Bahia is a center of Afro-Brazilian culture and maintains closer ties to Africa than the rest of the country. *Sue Cunningham/SCP*

by Iemanjá and carried out to sea, they can expect good fortune for the rest of the year. To ensure that their offerings are not rejected and do not float back to the shore, some people carry them far out to sea. Iemanjá is also honored during the Festa de Nossa Senhora da Conceição (Our Lady of Conception, the saint identified with Iemanjá) on December 8.

Candomblé celebrations are not exclusive to Salvador. In Cachoeira, for example, members of the *Irmandade da Boa Morte* (Sisterhood of Good Death) host the Festa da Nossa Senhora de Boa Morte, a three-day festival in mid-August that is attended by numerous black Brazilians and Candomblé members. Candomblé celebrations, however, are not exclusive to people of African descent or Candomblé members, but are attended by all races and social classes. In Bahia, it is not uncommon to see people of European descent recognizing Candomblé customs, such as the wearing of white on Fridays in honor of Oxalá, the African deity of procreation and the harvest, who is sometimes symbolized by Jesus Christ. This is only one example of the way in which African traditions have permeated the social fabric of Bahia.

Although many of Bahia's holidays have a syncretic character, the African traditions have exerted the strongest influence. This is reflected in Bahia's most famous festival, the annual Carnival celebration from February 15 to 21. The city of Salvador is the center of the Bahian Carnival, which features numerous predominantly black Carnival organizations whose members develop costumes, music, and floats around African and Afro-Brazilian themes. These African groups include the *blocos Afros* and the *afoxés*. The blocos Afros emerged during the *abertura*, Brazil's transition to democracy in the mid-1970s that facilitated the creation of black political organizations. The most famous blocos Afros are Ilê Aiyê (the first bloco Afro, established in 1974) and Olodum. The 1994 Carnival theme for Ilê-Aiyê was Black America – The African Dream. Members of the group were dressed as Malcolm X, Martin Luther King Jr., Marcus Garvey, and Fannie Lou Hamer.

Afoxés are the oldest black organizations to parade in Bahia's Carnival, dating to the end of the nineteenth century. Closely tied to Candomblé and the African religious traditions in Brazil, the afoxés sing and dance to African-derived rhythms such as *ijexá* in celebration of the orixás. Filhos de Gandhi is the most traditional and most famous afoxé. While some blocos Afros and afoxés parade in the historic district of Salvador, others, such as Ilê-Aiyê, perform in Liberdade, Salvador's largest black district.

The African slaves brought to Bahia, especially those of the Bantu ethnic group, developed numerous musical and dance traditions. Most originated in the recôncavo region during the colonial era and are still practiced today. Some, such as samba and capoeira, have gained international popularity. The *samba-de-roda* is a dance done by soloists in the center of a circle. Capoeira is an intricate dance-martial art created by slaves for the purpose of defending themselves. It is performed within a circle, which its participants enter in pairs, to the rhythm of a bow-like instrument called the *berimbau*. Closely related to capoeira is *maculelê*, an acrobatic warrior dance. In maculelê people dance in pairs, cross-striking either sugar canes or machetes to the beat of the *atabaque* (a long cylindrical drum).

Finally, Bahia is also known for its African-derived culinary tradition. Slaves introduced new ways of cooking and seasoning meat, fish, and chicken. Bahian food is usually cooked with peppers, spices, and the dark oil of the dendê palm tree. One example is *acarajé*, a fried bean fritter stuffed with dried, peppered shrimp. Women known as *baianas* sell acarajé on street corners throughout Bahia. Other dishes of African origin include *carurú*, *moqueca*, and *vatapá*. Carurú is a mix of broiled okra and onions, shrimp, and pepper that is traditionally served with fried fish such as grouper. Moqueca is a type of stew that usually contains fish, shrimp, oyster, or crab cooked in dendê oil and coconut milk. Perhaps the most famous dish of African origin in Bahia is vatapá, a seafood dish served in a thick manioc-based sauce.

African-derived traditions have long been Bahia's source of vitality. Historically, however, they have been repressed by state and federal governments. Afro-Brazilian practices such as Candomblé and capoeira were not widely accepted and embraced until the 1970s. At that time, Bahia was "re-Africanized" through a surge of black pride influenced by the black freedom movements in the United States and Africa. The afoxés and blocos Afros that emerged in the 1970s in Bahia organized blacks not only to celebrate African and Afro-Brazilian history, but to work for political change. While blacks in Bahia still lag behind other segments of the state's population in a host of socioeconomic categories, their mobilization around issues of race is creating conditions for improving the lives of people of African descent throughout Brazil.

Aaron Myers

See Also

Bantu: Dispersion and Settlement; Congo, Republic of the; Garvey, Marcus Mosiah; King, Martin Luther, Jr.; Afoxés/Blocos Afros; Rio de Janeiro, Brazil; Abolition and Emancipation in Latin America and the Caribbean; Art in Latin America and the Caribbean; Carnivals in Latin America and the Caribbean; Catholic Church in Latin America and the Caribbean; Orishas; Slave Laws in Colonial Spanish America.

North America

Bailey, Pearl **(b. March 29, 1918, Newport News, Va.; d. August 17, 1990, Philadelphia, Pa.), African American singer, actress, and entertainer known for her comedic timing and charm, honored for her service to American troops, and named as special delegate to the United Nations.**

Pearl Bailey was born in Newport News, Virginia on March 29, 1918, but soon moved to WASHINGTON, D.C., and then to PHILADELPHIA, PENNSYLVANIA. Her stage singing debut came when she was 15 years old. Bailey's brother Bill was beginning his own career as a tap dancer, and at his suggestion, she entered an amateur contest at Philadelphia's Pearl Theater, where she won first prize. Several months later, she won a similar contest at Harlem's famous APOLLO THEATER, and she decided to pursue a career in entertainment.

Bailey began by singing and dancing in Philadelphia's African American nightclubs in the 1930s, and soon started performing in other parts of the East Coast. In 1941, during World War II, she toured the country with the United Service Organizations (USO), performing for American troops. After the tour, she settled in New York. Her solo successes as a nightclub performer were followed by acts with such entertainers as Cab Calloway.

In 1946 Bailey made her Broadway debut in *St. Louis Woman* and won the Donaldson Award for most promising newcomer of the year. As an actress, she was known for her mix of charm and comedic timing. She went on to appear onstage in *Arms and the Girl* (1950), *House of Flowers* (1954), and *Bless You All* (1954). In 1947 Bailey made her film debut in *The Variety Girl.* She followed that screen appearance with larger roles in *Isn't It Romantic?* (1948), *Carmen Jones* (1955), *That Certain Feeling* (1956), *St. Louis Blues* (1958), *Porgy and Bess* (1959), and *All the Fine Young Cannibals* (1960).

Bailey continued to tour and record albums in between her stage and screen performances. She also appeared regularly on television variety shows, such as the Ed Sullivan and Perry Como shows, throughout the 1950s and 1960s. After a brief first marriage, Bailey was married to John Randolph Pinkett Jr. from 1948 to 1952. They had a son and a daughter. In 1952 she married white performer Louis Bellson.

In 1967 Bailey returned to Broadway with the title role in an all-black production of *Hello, Dolly!* She won a Tony Award for that role in 1968. That same year, President Richard Nixon named her the Ambassador of Love. In 1969 the USO named her Woman of the Year in recognition of her continuing service to American troops. She was also named a special delegate to the United Nations under the Ford, Reagan, and Bush administrations.

Through all of these honors, Bailey continued to perform. In 1971 she hosted her own ABC-TV variety show. She announced her retirement from show business in 1975 but still continued to appear in film roles and in television sitcoms, commercials, game shows, and specials. In 1975 she received the Britannica Life Achievement Award. While in her sixties, Bailey decided to complete her education, and in 1985 she received a B.A. in Theology from Georgetown University. In 1988 President Reagan awarded her the Presidential Medal of Freedom. Pearl Bailey died in Philadelphia on August 17, 1990.

Lisa Clayton Robinson

SEE ALSO
Calloway, Cabell (Cab); Harlem, New York; Tap Dance; Television and African Americans.

Africa

Baka, **ethnic group of north Central Africa.**

The Baka primarily inhabit southwestern SUDAN, the eastern CENTRAL AFRICAN REPUBLIC, and northern UGANDA. They speak a Nilo-Saharan language and belong to the MADI cultural and linguistic group. Approximately 100,000 people consider themselves Baka.

SEE ALSO
Languages, African: An Overview.

Africa

Bakèlè, **an ethnic group (also known as Kalai, Akèlè, Bongom, or Bougom) of Gabon and EQUATORIAL GUINEA.**

The Bakèlè speak an Equatorial Bantu language. Although they call themselves the Bongom or Bougom, outsiders have generally followed their Myènè-speaking neighbors in calling them the Bakèlè. Historians are unsure when the Bakèlè arrived in the north-central area of the country presently known as GABON. Historically they have maintained amicable relations with the Babongo "pygmies," who probably preceded them in the region. Traditionally, the Bakèlè were farmers and hunters, traveling widely in search of elephants and other game. The Bakèlè participated in the regional expansion of trade during the nineteenth entury. They obtained goods such as ivory from the FANG, which they traded to coastal groups such as the MPONGWE, who in turn traded with the Europeans. On the Ogooué and other rivers they controlled trade more directly by taxing passing traders.

To meet the increasing demand for slaves from the mid-eighteenth to the mid-nineteenth century, the Bakèlè became prominent slave raiders and slave traders (*see* TRANSATLANTIC SLAVE TRADE). They undertook large raids to obtain slaves from their neighbors, and they also sold their own village outcasts as slaves. The Bakèlè prospered in the trade. As the slave trade came to an end, the migrating Fang gradually drove the Bakèlè south toward the Gabon Estuary and the Ogooué Valley, where the Bakèlè engaged in the rubber, ivory, and dyewood trades.

The Bakèlè's seminomadic lifestyle and lack of hierarchy hindered French colonization and American missionary efforts in the late 1800s. The Bakèlè have played only a minor role in the early French colonial administration or in national politics since independence. Today the Bakèlè number around 40,000 in Gabon and Equatorial Guinea.

Eric Young

SEE ALSO
Colonial Rule; Elephant; Ivory Trade; Pygmy.

North America

Baker, Augusta **(b. April 1, 1911, Baltimore, Md.; d. February 23, 1998, Columbia, S.C.), African American librarian, educator, and storyteller, the first black to hold an administrative position in the New York Public Library system.**

In her 1970 article "My Years as a Children's Librarian," Augusta Baker summed up what she had learned in her long career: "Library work with children has had a great past and has a still greater future. Young black men and women have an opportunity to be part of this exciting future and for the sake of their children they should be." From her appointment as assistant children's librarian in the New York Public Library system in 1937 to her retirement in 1974, Baker pursued a career of library service to children with enthusiasm, vision, and leadership. During the 1940s, while working at the library's 135th Street branch, she spearheaded the creation of the JAMES WELDON JOHNSON Memorial Collection, whose purpose, she wrote, was "to bring together books for children that give an unbiased, accurate, well rounded picture of Negro life in all parts of the world."

The only child of teachers Winfort J. and Mabel Braxton, Baker was instilled from an early age with a love of learning. She had a close relationship with her grandmother, a former slave who recounted folk tales from her plantation days. Baker enrolled at the University of Pittsburgh at the age of 16. She later married a fellow student and the couple moved to Albany, New York. Baker applied for admission to the Albany State Teachers College, which was reluctant to admit her because of her color, but Eleanor Roosevelt, whose husband was then governor of New York, was instrumental in advancing her application. However, she decided not to pursue a teaching career, and received a bachelor's degree in library science in 1934.

Like her grandmother, Baker became an artful storyteller. After 16 years as a library assistant in the COUNTEE CULLEN Branch of the New York Public Library in Harlem, in 1953 she was promoted to the position of assistant coordinator of children's services and storytelling specialist. She directed the New York Public Library system's storytelling program for eight years, teaching and lecturing on oral narration and gathering folk tales from different cultures, a pursuit that culminated in the notable story collections *The Talking Tree* (1960) and *The Golden Lynx and Other Tales* (1960).

From 1961 until her retirement in 1974, Baker held the position of coordinator of children's services, managing children's services in 82 branch libraries and ensuring that the collections reflected the diversity of their readership. In 1971 she published a bibliography entitled *The Black Experience in Children's Books*, widely considered a benchmark guide for librarians in creating minority representation in their collections. During this period, she also worked as a consultant to *Sesame Street*, initiated a series of radio broadcasts called *The World of Children's Literature*, lectured at universities across the United States, and held senior positions at the American Library Association, including chair of the Newberry/Caldecott Awards Committee.

In 1974 Baker retired to Columbia, South Carolina, where she became storyteller-in-residence at the University of South Carolina. Baker died in 1998 at the age of 86, five years after the American Library Association cited her for a Distinguished Services Award, its highest tribute to a member.

Roanne Edwards

SEE ALSO

Harlem, New York.

North America

Baker, Ella J. (b. December 13, 1903, Norfolk, Va.; d. December 13, 1986, New York, N.Y.), social justice activist who was instrumental in the founding the Student Nonviolent Coordinating Committee.

The granddaughter of slaves, Ella Baker began her career as an activist early. As a student at Shaw University in Raleigh, North Carolina, Baker challenged school policies that she found demeaning. After graduating from Shaw as class valedictorian in 1927, she moved to New York City.

Baker responded to the suffering she saw in Harlem during the GREAT DEPRESSION by joining a variety of political causes. In 1930 she joined the Young Negroes Cooperative League and was elected as its first national director a year later. The league, which was founded by writer George Schuyler, aimed to develop blacks' economic power through collective planning. Baker also became involved with several women's organizations and, as an employee of the WORKS PROGRESS ADMINISTRATION, offered literacy and consumer education to workers while educating herself about radical politics.

The year 1940 marked the beginning of Baker's affiliation with the National Association for Advancement of Colored People (NAACP). After working as a field secretary, Baker served as director of branches from 1943 to 1946. Her efforts to expand the reach of the NAACP throughout the South helped create the grassroots network that provided a base for the CIVIL RIGHTS MOVEMENT in the following decades. At the same time, Baker fought to make the NAACP itself more democratic by shifting the organization's emphasis away from legal battles and toward community-based activism. Although Baker resigned from the NAACP staff in 1946, she stayed on as a volunteer and, as the first woman to head the New York branch, led its fight to desegregate New York City public schools.

In 1956 Baker, BAYARD RUSTIN, and Stanley Levison established In Friendship, an organization dedicated to raising money to support the Southern struggle. She moved to Atlanta the following year to organize Martin Luther King Jr.'s newly formed Southern Christian Leadership Conference (SCLC) and to run the Crusade for Citizenship, a voter registration campaign. Baker stayed at SCLC for two years, but she never accepted its policy of favoring strong central leadership over local, grassroots politics.

When a group of students in Greensboro, North Carolina, touched off a sit-in campaign, Baker left SCLC. Determined to assist the fledgling student movement, she took a job at the Young Women's Christian Association (YWCA). She invited sit-in leaders to attend a conference at Shaw University in April 1960. From that conference, the STUDENT NONVIOLENT COORDINATING COMMITTEE (SNCC) was born the following October. Unlike older civil rights groups, SNCC was a decentralized organization that stressed direct-action tactics and encouraged women, the young, and the poor to take leadership positions. Among SNCC's achievements was its role in founding the Mississippi Freedom Democratic Party. Baker was a key player in the party's attempt to replace the all-white delegation from Mississippi at the 1964 Democratic party convention.

Baker returned to New York in 1964 and fought for human rights until her death. Called an "unsung hero" of the Civil Rights Movement, Baker has inspired a range of political organizations, including the Black Panthers, Students for a Democratic Society, and feminist groups.

Lawrie Balfour

SEE ALSO

Black Panther Party; Harlem, New York; King, Martin Luther, Jr.; National Association for the Advancement of Colored People; New York, New York; Schuyler, George S.; Sit-Ins; Southern Christian Leadership Conference.

North America

Baker, Josephine (b. June 3, 1906, St. Louis, Mo; d. April 12, 1975, Paris, FRANCE), African American expatriate dancer, singer, and entertainer.

For many people, Josephine Baker's name will always evoke a familiar, controversial image: the "black Venus" naked onstage, except for a string of bananas around her waist, dancing to African drums before her white Parisian audiences. It was this image that first made Baker a star, one whose international fame lasted for five decades. But the picture of the exotic dancer does not fully capture the complexity of the woman who was one of the first black performers to transcend race and appeal to audiences of all colors from around the world.

Baker was born Freda Josephine MacDonald (the name Baker came from her second husband). Her parents were not married; her father was a drummer in a local band, and her mother, a washerwoman, rarely had enough money to support Baker and her three younger half-siblings. At age 8, Baker began working as a maid in white homes, and by age 14 she had left home, married and separated from her first of five husbands, and begun working with a traveling vaudeville troupe. Her first break came when she was featured in *Shuffle Along*, Broadway's first black musical, in 1921.

Originally rejected from the show for being too young, too thin, and too dark, she eventually won the role of the comic "end girl" in the chorus line – the one too confused to keep up with the moves – and wound up stealing the show. Four years later she was offered the opportunity to go to Paris and perform in *La Revue Nègre*. By then her teenaged body had fully matured, and her show-stopping finale, "Danse sauvage" – in which she danced the Charleston wearing nothing but a girdle of feathers – made her an overnight sensation.

FAR LEFT: Josephine Baker opens her first Broadway engagement in 15 years, at the Strand Theater in New York City in 1951. *CORBIS/Bettmann*
LEFT: Josephine Baker appears in minstrel blackface in Paris, France, in 1927. *CORBIS/Bettmann*
BELOW: Josephine Baker, *La Joséphine,* as the French called her, first danced in her witty but risqué banana costume in April 1926 at the Folies-Bergère in Paris. Paul Colin's colored lithograph records both the costume and Baker's movements. *Image of the Black Project, Harvard University*

Baker became the living embodiment of everything European audiences found exotic and provocative about black women's sexuality.

Similar stage and film roles across Europe soon followed. Baker's act was most notorious for its nudity, but its innovative techniques also introduced many popular African American dance styles to European audiences. The unique blend of comedy, sensuality, passion, and exuberance present in her JAZZ-inspired performances also spilled over into her personal life. Baker and her leopard, Chiquita, were a common sight on Paris streets. Her stable of animals also included dogs, monkeys, birds, rabbits, snakes, a turkey, and a pig named Albert. Christian Dior designed her clothing; her admirers included Ernest Hemingway (who called her the most beautiful woman he had ever seen) and Pablo Picasso; and she was known for her many lovers, both male and female.

In the midst of all this adulation, however, American audiences were still cool. Baker returned to the United States to appear with the Ziegfeld Follies in 1936 and received terrible reviews. Her stage show had evolved by then into a more glamorous, refined act, and white America did not seem ready to see a sophisticated black star on stage. In 1937, after returning to Paris, Baker legally became a French citizen. During World War II she served as an intelligence liaison and an ambulance driver for the French Resistance and was awarded the Medal of the Resistance and the Legion of Honor.

Soon after the war Baker toured the United States again, and this time she won respect and praise from African Americans for her support of the CIVIL RIGHTS MOVEMENT. She refused to play to segregated audiences or stay in segregated hotels during a 1951 American tour, and as a result the NATIONAL ASSOCIATION FOR THE ADVANCEMENT OF COLORED PEOPLE (NAACP) named her its Most Outstanding Woman of the Year. She also participated in the 1963 March on Washington, and later that year gave a benefit concert at Carnegie Hall for the NAACP, the Student Nonviolent Coordinating Committee, and the CONGRESS OF RACIAL EQUALITY.

By then, she had taken on another of her most important roles, that of mother. Baker was forced to undergo an emergency hysterectomy that almost took her life after the 1942 birth of a stillborn child, and she never had biological children. But between 1954 and 1965 she adopted ten sons and two daughters of various races and nationalities – the family she called her Rainbow Tribe. Baker planned to retire from show business to raise her children at Les Milandes, her French chateau, but her savings were not enough to support the entire family in the style to which she was accustomed. The expenses eventually sent her into deep debt, and when her beloved chateau was seized in 1969, the family was forced to move into a much smaller villa given to them by Princess Grace of Monaco.

The last five years of her life were marked by an ironic mix of public adoration and personal poverty. At home in France, she was sometimes reduced to begging on the streets for her children – unrecognizable without her makeup, wig, and costumes. Her health also began to decline, and she suffered two heart attacks and a stroke. But she continued to perform, and onstage she was as glamorous as ever. A 1973 tour of the United States brought widespread acclaim, although some African American audiences were upset by Baker's condemnation of the Black Power Movement (which she saw as too separatist). In 1974 she starred in a Monaco production of *Josephine,* a show based on her life, and the performances were so successful that the show came to Paris in April 1975.

That year marked the fiftieth anniversary of her arrival in Paris, and on April 8 there was a huge gala in a Paris hotel to celebrate both that anniversary and *Josephine*'s opening night. Four days later, however, Baker suffered a fatal cerebral hemorrhage during a nap. Twenty thousand people attended her Paris funeral in a massive show of devotion to an African American performer whose boldness and unconventional style had taken France and the world by storm.

Lisa Clayton Robinson

See Also
Student Nonviolent Coordinating Committee (SNCC); March on Washington, 1963; Black Power.

Africa

Bakoko, ethnic group of Cameroon.

The Bakoko primarily inhabit southern Cameroon. They speak a Bantu language and are related to the Bassa and Babimbi, also of southern Cameroon. Approximately 200,000 people consider themselves Bakoko.

See Also
Bantu: Dispersion and Settlement; Bassa of Cameroon; Babimbi.

Africa

Bakossi (also known as Kossi), ethnic group of Cameroon.

The Bakossi primarily inhabit western Cameroon. They speak a Bantu language and belong to the Bassa-Bokoko cultural and linguistic group. Approximately 100,000 people consider themselves Bakossi.

See Also
Bantu: Dispersion and Settlement.

Africa

Bakota, an ethnic group of northeastern Gabon and northwestern Republic of the Congo.

With around 125,000 members, the Bantu-speaking Bakota are one of the largest ethnic groups of Gabon. The Bakota migrated to the area from the northwest during the nineteenth century, fleeing a Bakouélé invasion known as the War of Poupou. The Bakouélé themselves were fleeing the Fang expansion farther north. The Bakota finally settled near the confluence of the Ivindo and Ogooué rivers, where they were able to ward off additional Bakouélé invasions. The oncoming Fang eventually divided the Bakota into two groups, one in the east and one in the west. The eastern group became particularly known for ironwork, including the high-quality weapons they used to defend themselves.

The Bakota earned their livelihood from farming and trade, exchanging ivory and rubber with the Europeans for weapons and cloth. In the 1890s a French concessionary company took control of the area and expanded the rubber and ivory trade by forcing Bakota to labor as porters. The settlement of Booué subsequently became the commercial center for the Bakota region. But the Bakota benefited little from the colonial and missionary educational systems, which remained concentrated outside their territory on the coast. As a result, the Bakota played a minor role in the colonial administration and remain largely outside the formal political structures of independent Gabon and the Republic of the Congo. Today, many Bakota work in the iron ore mines of the region.

Eric Young

See Also
Colonial Rule; Ivory Trade; Iron in Africa.

Africa

Bakweri (also known as the Bakwere and the Bakwiri), ethnic group of Cameroon.

The Bakweri live on the slopes of Mount Cameroon and the surrounding regions of South West Province. They speak a Bantu language and comprise several subgroups, including the Isuwu, the Kpe, the Moboko, and the Wovea. The Bakweri number over 100,000.

See Also
Bantu: Dispersion and Settlement.

Latin America and the Caribbean

Balaguer, Joaquín

(b. September 1, 1907, Villa Bisono, Dominican Republic), president of the Dominican Republic (1960-1962, 1966-1978, 1986-1996).

Joaquín Balaguer studied law in Santo Domingo and earned a doctorate at the University of Paris. In 1930 he became involved in the conspiracy involving former Secretary of Foreign Relations Rafael Estrella Ureña against President Horacio Vásquez, which culminated in Rafael Leónidas Trujillo seizing the presidency. Balaguer served in various ambassadorial posts abroad during the Trujillo regime (1930-1961) and also served as minister of education and vice president (1957-1960). Balaguer began his first term as president as one of a series of puppet leaders while Trujillo continued to pull the strings. Trujillo's assassination in 1961 left Balaguer as president but facing massive popular protests for a return to democratic rule. In 1962 a general strike forced Balaguer from power. He spent the next three years in exile in New York City.

Those years were a period of dashed hopes for many in the Dominican Republic. In 1962 social reformer Juan Bosch, leader of the Partido Revolucionario Dominicano (PRD), was elected president only to be deposed the following year. When Bosch supporters took to the streets to reinstate the constitutional government, the United States sent marines to put a stop to what the Lyndon Johnson administration saw as another Cuban revolution in the making (*see* Cuba). During the United States occupation of the island in 1965, Balaguer returned to the Dominican Republic. A favorite of both the U.S. and Dominican elite, he was elected president, defeating Bosch, in 1966. He ran under the Reformist Party (PR), which he had founded in 1963 during his years in exile. The elections were marked by intimidation, and Bosch was not allowed out of his house, on threat of death by the military.

Balaguer's 12-year tenure (1966-1978) has been labeled "Trujillismo without Trujillo." Thousands of Dominicans who opposed Balaguer were killed, many by the paramilitary group La Banda, which he organized (*see* Human Rights in Latin America and the Caribbean). Balaguer encouraged foreign investment through tax incentives, removing restrictions on foreign ownership of land, as well as the creation of duty-free zones. Between 1969 and 1974, the country's economy grew on average over 10 percent per year. Massive aid from the United States and the rise in world sugar prices also spurred the economic boom. The distribution of this wealth, however, was highly inequitable, and foreign investment went largely to capital-intensive industries, creating few jobs. Protest against these conditions was stifled. Balaguer's second presidential term ended in 1978, as the economic situation began to deteriorate. As the nationally televised vote counting for the presidential race showed PRD candidate Antonio Guzmán in the lead, armed officers entered to interrupt the procedure. International outcry following this blatant attempt to subvert the election forced Balaguer to concede the race.

After losing two elections (1978, 1982), Balaguer won again in 1986, this time under the banner of the Reformist Social Christian Party (PRSC). In 1986 the Dominican Republic, like other countries in Latin America, was in the midst of a debt crisis, exacerbated by falling prices for Dominican exports. Balaguer pursued a number of construction programs to boost the economy and create jobs. These benefits, however, were dissipated as the country fell deeper into debt and faced greater inflation. Balaguer was elected again in 1990 and 1994. The 1994 election was so marred by fraud and irregularities, however, that national and international condemnation forced Balaguer, then blind and in his eighties, to hold early elections in 1996 with a promise not to compete.

Like many of the Dominican elite who supported his presidency, Balaguer highlighted the Dominican Republic's Hispanic roots while undervaluing its African heritage. In 1992 some criticized Balaguer's ostentatious celebration of the 500th anniversary of Columbus's arrival in the New World for its embrace of the Spanish conquest. The commemoration included the construction of a multimillion-dollar lighthouse as a monument to Columbus, which involved displacing residents from slums where the lighthouse was to stand.

Himself Afro-Dominican, Balaguer's racial discourse, following a long tradition in the country, was often voiced as anti-Haitian rather than antiblack. Haiti is closely and negatively associated with Africa and in particular with the Afro-Haitian religion Vodou (*see* Dominican-Haitian Relations). In his book *La isla revés: Haiti y el destino dominicano* (The Island in Reverse: Haiti and the Dominican Destiny; 1983), Balaguer expressed concern over the Haitianization of the island as well as the "fecundity characteristic of the Negro." His 1994 campaign against the darker-skinned José Francisco Peña Gómez (PRD) included attacks on the candidate for his alleged loyalties to Haiti. In the 1996 election former Balaguer supporters made similar attacks on Peña Gómez, though this time in support of the ultimately victorious candidate, Lionel Fernández. Although no longer president, Balaguer continued to be an influential political figure in his party and in Dominican politics.

See Also

Trujillo, Rafael.

Africa

Balanta, ethnic group of Guinea-Bissau and Senegal.

The Balanta, meaning literally "those who resist," are the largest ethnic group of Guinea-Bissau, representing more than one-quarter of the population. But despite their numbers, they have remained outside the colonial and postcolonial state because of their social organization. The Balanta can be divided into four subgroups, the largest of which are the Balanta Brassa.

Archaeologists believe that the people who became the Balanta migrated to northern present-day Guinea-Bissau in small groups between the tenth and fourteenth century c.e. During the nineteenth century they spread throughout the area that is presently Guinea-Bissau and southern Senegal in order to resist the expansion of the Kaabu kingdom.

Chiefs occasionally governed some Balanta groups, but in general egalitarianism prevailed among the rice-cultivating Balanta. Consequently, the Portuguese colonialists found it difficult to govern them. In the late nineteenth and early twentieth centuries, Portugal mounted "pacification" campaigns against the resistant Balanta and subjected them to appointed Fulbe chiefs. Because of this Portuguese repression, the Balanta enlisted as soldiers in great numbers in the nationalist struggle during the 1960s and 1970s. However, when the nationalists assumed power after independence, they found it difficult to establish village committees and other organizations among the Balanta because of their decentralized social organization. Many Balanta resented their exclusion from the government; their prominence in the military spurred a series of Balanta-led coup attempts in the 1980s.

Eric Young

See Also

Colonial Rule; Fulani; Nationalism in Africa; Kaabu, Early Kingdom of; Plena and Bomba.

North America

Baldwin, James (b. August 2, 1924, Harlem, N.Y.; d. December 1, 1987, St.-Paul-de-Vence, France), African American novelist, essayist, playwright, and poet known especially for his astute commentary on American race relations.

"We are responsible for the world in which we find ourselves, if only because we are the only sentient force which can change it." In this statement from his collection of essays, *No Name in the Street,* James Baldwin sums up a philosophy that drove much of his work. Baldwin was continually conscious of the hypocrisies and injustices in the world around him, and as a writer, he strove to make his audiences aware of the possibility that people could do, and be, better. An expatriate most of his adult life, Baldwin nevertheless wrote tirelessly about the contradictions inherent in American identity, and especially about the state of American race relations. He came to be respected as one of the sagest intellectuals in the Civil Rights Movement and as a leading figure in the African American literary tradition.

Baldwin was born in Harlem in 1924. Shortly after his out-of-wedlock birth his mother married David Baldwin, a factory worker and Pentecostal minister, and Baldwin was raised in their home along with seven younger half-siblings. His troubled relationship with his strict, domineering stepfather colored much of his childhood, and he turned to reading as a means of escape. At Frederick Douglass Junior High School Baldwin edited the school paper and belonged to the literary club, whose adviser was poet Countee Cullen. At 14, his literary career was temporarily challenged by a new vocation when he became a junior minister at a Harlem storefront church, drawing crowds bigger than his stepfather's. Three years later he decided to leave the church and Christianity, but throughout his career he was described as a prophet, and his work is ripe with biblical cadences and imagery.

After his high school graduation in 1942, Baldwin took a series of odd jobs in New Jersey. But when his stepfather's death and the Harlem riots occurred during the same 24-hour period in the summer of 1943, the trauma of the two events spurred him to return to New York, where he settled in Greenwich Village, determined to concentrate on his writing. During the winter of 1944-1945 he met the celebrated black writer Richard Wright, who became a mentor and father figure to him and who recommended him for the Eugene Saxton Fellowship that he received in 1945. Until that time Baldwin had been working only on an unpublished draft of a novel, but in 1946 he published his first essay in the *Nation.* He soon became well known as an essayist, publishing in the *New Leader, Commentary,* and *Partisan Review.* In 1948 Baldwin was awarded a Rosenwald Fellowship and used the prize money to buy a one-way ticket to Paris. He left New York on November 11, 1948.

As an openly gay African American, Baldwin had long felt stifled by the prevailing racial and sexual prejudices in the United States. The 1948 trip marked the beginning of his career as an expatriate writer, and while his writing often returned to American subjects, he was based abroad for most of the next 40 years. In Paris, though he lived as a struggling artist, his friends included French writers Jean-Paul Sartre and Simone de Beauvoir and fellow American expatriates Saul Bellow, Truman Capote, BEAUFORD DELANEY, and Wright. Baldwin's 1949 essay "Everybody's Protest Novel" and 1951 essay "Many Thousands Gone," however, both of which criticized Wright's *Native Son,* created a lasting break in that friendship. But by then Baldwin was well on his way to establishing his own identity as a writer.

Baldwin finished his long-awaited first book, *Go Tell it on the Mountain,* during a stay in his companion's Swiss hometown, and published it in 1953. The novel, a largely autobiographical account of his teenage years, received critical acclaim, but his next two novels caused controversy. *Giovanni's Room* (1956) and *Another Country* (1962) featured characters struggling to define sexual, racial, and national identities, and the matter-of-fact depictions of gay relationships in both books surprised many readers. During the same period, however, Baldwin also published three collections of essays, and it was the nonfiction books – *Notes of a Native Son* (1955), *Nobody Knows My Name* (1961), and *The Fire Next Time* (1963) – that secured his reputation as an important American writer and social critic.

Through his essays, Baldwin developed a reputation for being a shrewd and prophetic commentator on American culture, particularly on racial identity. As one critic explains, these three books – each of which sold more than a million copies at publication – "won Baldwin a popularity and acclaim as the 'conscience of the nation,' who brought to racial discourse a passion and honesty that demanded notice.... Baldwin's knife-edged criticism of the failed promises of American democracy, and the consequent social injustices, is unrelenting and demonstrates a piercing understanding of the function of blacks in the white racial imagination."

During this period, Baldwin's trips to the United States became more frequent. He visited the American South for the first time in 1957, and during the 1960s was one of the most public intellectuals in the Civil Rights Movement, lecturing and speaking out at such forums as a meeting he arranged between Attorney General Robert Kennedy and black celebrities including Harry Belafonte, LENA HORNE, and LORRAINE HANSBERRY. It was *The Fire Next Time,* whose publication coincided with the 1963 March on Washington and the hundredth anniversary of the Emancipation Proclamation, that earned Baldwin his national reputation as a prophet. Baldwin took the book's title from the lines of an old spiritual – "God gave Noah the rainbow sign / No more water, the fire next time" – as he argued that American race relations were in danger of reaching violent conclusions. Many readers interpreted the riots that occurred in American cities throughout the late 1960s as the fulfillment of Baldwin's warnings.

But Baldwin had concluded that essay on a hopeful note, suggesting that "if we [blacks and whites] do not falter in our duty now, we may be able... to end the racial nightmare, and achieve our country, and change the history of the world." This optimism about the possibility of reconciliation in American race relations had been expressed even more strongly in some of his earlier essays, and it created a rift between Baldwin and many younger African Americans – most notably black nationalists such as Eldridge Cleaver and the more militant black writers who were associated with the BLACK ARTS MOVEMENT. But even as his politics began to be criticized, Baldwin kept writing.

Baldwin's 1955 play *The Amen Corner* and 1964 play *Blues for Mr. Charlie* were both successfully produced on Broadway. Baldwin's other publications in the 1960s included *Going to Meet the Man* (1965), a collection of short stories, and the novel *Tell Me How Long the Train's Been Gone* (1968). In the 1970s his books included the essay collection *No Name in the Street* (1972) and the novels *If Beale Street Could Talk* (1974) and *Just Above My Head* (1979). By then, Baldwin was again recognized and embraced as a major figure in African American literature, and he lectured and taught at several American colleges and universities between the late 1970s and mid-1980s. In 1985 he published *The Evidence of Things Not Seen,* a collection of essays on the 1980-1981 Atlanta child murders, and *The Price of the Ticket: Collected Nonfiction, 1948-1985.*

When Baldwin died in France of stomach cancer on December 1, 1987, he was at work on a play and a biography of Martin Luther King Jr. Baldwin's memorial service at the Cathedral of St. John the Divine in New York City drew thousands of mourners, and writers from MAYA ANGELOU to TONI MORRISON spoke of his profound impact on their own work. As AMIRI BARAKA said in his eulogy, "This man traveled the earth like history and its biographer. He reported, criticized, made beautiful, analyzed, cajoled, lyricized, attacked, sang, made us think, made us better, made us consciously human."

The writer James Baldwin (1924-1987), photographed in Paris in 1986. *CORBIS/Peter Turnley*

Lisa Clayton Robinson

SEE ALSO

Belafonte, Harold George (Harry); Cleaver, Eldridge Leroy; Harlem Riots of 1943; Harlem, New York; King, Martin Luther, Jr.; Thirteenth Amendment of the United States Constitution and the Emancipation Proclamation; March on Washington, 1963.

North America

Baldwin, Maria Louise

(b. September 13, 1856, Cambridge, Mass.; d. January 9, 1922, Boston, Mass.), African American educator who lectured widely on issues dealing with women and African Americans.

The daughter of Mary E. and Peter L. Baldwin, Maria Baldwin was educated in Cambridge, Massachusetts, and also taught there, at the Agassiz Grammar School, where she became principal in 1889.

In 1897 Baldwin was the first black woman to address the Brooklyn Institute of Arts and Sciences, where she delivered her well-known speech, "The Life and Services of the Late Harriet Beecher Stowe." She lectured around the country on both women's suffrage and notable African Americans. While giving an address in Boston in 1922, Baldwin collapsed and died from heart failure.

SEE ALSO
Boston, Massachusetts.

Balente. Please see BALANTA

Africa

Balewa, Abubakar Tafawa

(b. 1912, Bauchi State, Nigeria; d. January 15, 1966), first prime minister of independent NIGERIA.

Unlike other members of the northern Nigerian elite that he was to join, Alhaji Abubakar Tafawa Balewa was born into a low-status, non-FULANI family. He attended primary and secondary school in Bauchi State and then enrolled at Katsina Higher College. In 1933 he became a schoolmaster and in 1934 his novel, *Shaihu Umar*, was published.

Balewa's political career began in 1943 when he cofounded the Bauchi General Improvement Union, a group that promoted modernization and criticized British colonialism in Nigeria. Less radical than his cohorts, Balewa won election in 1946 to the Northern Legislature and became vice president of the Northern People's Congress (NPC). The government appointed him minister of works in 1952 and minister of transport in 1954. In September 1957 Balewa became the prime minister of Nigeria under British control, a position he held until 1959. In 1960 he was knighted in England.

When Nigeria gained independence in 1960, Balewa served a second term as prime minister. Although he could act independently, Balewa's power depended on the support of a stronger politician, AHMADU BELLO, a traditional leader of northern Nigeria in Sokoto. Presiding over a new, volatile, and deeply divided political landscape, Balewa espoused moderate positions that probably saved Nigeria from disintegration during its early years. Despite his diligence and integrity, Balewa was assassinated on January 15, 1966, during a coup.

Eric Bennett

SEE ALSO
Sokoto Caliphate.

North America

Ball, James Presley

(b. 1825, Virginia; d. 1905, Hawaii), African American daguerreotypist and photographer.

Born free in Virginia, James Ball operated short-lived businesses in Cincinnati, Ohio, in 1845, 1847, and 1849, and two years later opened his first successful photography studio, which prospered until the early 1870s. Active in the abolitionist movement, he commissioned a 216 sq m (2400 sq ft) antislavery painted panorama, *Ball's Splendid Mammoth Pictorial Tour of the United States Comprising Views of the African Slave Trade; of Northern and Southern Cities; of Cotton and Sugar Plantations; of the Mississippi, Ohio and Susquehanna Rivers, Niagara Falls, & C* (1855).

In 1887 Ball became the official photographer for a celebration of the 25th anniversary of the Emancipation Proclamation in Minneapolis, Minnesota. After his move to Helena, Montana, that same year, he was elected to several local political and civic positions. Ball moved to Seattle, Washington, in around 1900 and opened Globe Studios, which he operated until 1904, when rheumatism necessitated a move to a warmer climate. Ball moved to Hawaii and died the following year.

SEE ALSO
Abolitionism in the United States; Cincinnati, Ohio; Thirteenth Amendment of the United States Constitution and the Emancipation Proclamation; Photography, African American.

North America

Baltimore, Maryland

African Americans fought on both sides of the Revolutionary War in Baltimore, after which many freed slaves settled there, beginning the development of a free black community that, in size, was unusual for a proslavery city. By 1850 there were 2946 slaves but 25,442 free blacks, constituting 15 percent of Baltimore's population.

In 1789 Baltimore Quakers organized an abolitionist movement that was led in the nineteenth century by both whites – notably Benjamin Lundy and William Lloyd Garrison – and free blacks such as William Watkins. A strong, sometimes outspoken African American community developed around black religious institutions. Daniel Coker and his colleagues organized the African Methodist Episcopal Conference (1816), while other black leaders established St. James Episcopal Church (1827) and founded the first black women's Catholic order, the Oblate Sisters of Providence (1829). Intent upon educating all African Americans, free or enslaved, black Methodists founded the African Academy in 1802, and in 1829, the Oblate order started the first black girls' school in the United States. Such belief in empowering freedom through education was shared by FREDERICK DOUGLASS, who in the 1830s escaped slavery while a caulker in the Baltimore shipyards. It also inspired poet and antislavery crusader Frances Ellen Harper, who was graduated from Baltimore schools.

Immediately after the Civil War ended, African Americans continued to develop black institutions. They established the Frederick Douglass Institute – a cultural center – and the Centenary Biblical Institute, later Morgan State University. Isaac Myers lobbied for public education for blacks and helped to organize the Colored National Labor Union, which was especially important because of black-white labor conflicts that developed as Baltimore industrialized. In 1885 Henry Johnson founded the Baltimore Mutual United Brotherhood of Liberty, a precursor to the NATIONAL ASSOCIATION FOR THE ADVANCEMENT OF COLORED PEOPLE (NAACP) for its reliance on the courts to pursue civil rights. By the end of the century, a black elite had formed around Druid Hill Avenue in Northwest Baltimore. Harry S. Cummings became the first black city councilor in 1890, and in 1892, the *Baltimore Afro-American*, one of the oldest operating black newspapers in the United States, began publishing.

After 1900 JIM CROW laws mandated and expanded de facto segregation that lasted 50 years. Confined to crowded, substandard housing, Baltimore's black community suffered a devastating tuberculosis epidemic in the 1920s. Yet West Baltimore, especially Pennsylvania Avenuc, became a flourishing center of black life through the 1930s, producing Baltimore musicians Eubie Blake, BILLIE HOLIDAY, and Chick Webb.

In the 1930s LILLIE MAE CARROLL JACKSON developed the Baltimore branch of the NAACP into the second largest chapter in the country, an important center of a new civil rights strategy. Her daughter, Juanita Jackson Mitchell, was youth director and later a civil rights lawyer; Baltimore native THURGOOD MARSHALL, who later became the first African American Supreme Court justice, led judicial challenges to segregated schools and universities. After World War II, African American migration to the city increased, and so did racial tension. A 1942 shooting of a black man by a white police officer led to street demonstrations and eventually produced the political momentum that ended some discriminatory hiring practices and secured city jobs for many African Americans.

Then came a series of rapid, irreversible changes and demographic shifts. A 1952 decision to admit a dozen black schoolchildren into Polytechnic High School began the dismantling of segregation. Many whites responded by moving to the suburbs. By 1958 the Baltimore school population was 50 percent African American, and the city tax base began shrinking. Two years later, Morgan State students led sit-ins at Baltimore restaurants that hastened the integration of public facilities.

But inequality persisted, and in the wake of Martin Luther King Jr.'s assassination in 1968, Baltimore erupted into a four-day race riot. In the 1970s and 1980s the middle class continued to flee to the suburbs, reproducing de facto racial and economic segregation. By the mid-1970s Baltimore had a black majority. Parren Mitchell was elected to the United States Congress in 1970, and when he retired, KWEISI MFUME – now executive director of the NAACP – was elected. In 1987 Kurt Schmoke became Baltimore's first black mayor. Since many industries relocated elsewhere, high unemployment and crime have significantly increased in the African American community.

Jim Mendelsohn

SEE ALSO

World War II and African Americans; American Revolution; Blake, James Hubert ("Eubie"); Harper, Frances Ellen Watkins; King, Martin Luther, Jr.

Africa

Bamako, Mali, the capital and largest city of MALI.

The administrative, economic, and cultural center of Mali, Bamako lies on the left bank of the NIGER RIVER in the southwestern part of the country. Little is known about Bamako before the eleventh century, when it achieved prominence as a center of Islamic scholarship in the MALI EMPIRE. After the fall of Mali in the sixteenth century, the BAMBARA occupied the town, which became a fishing and trading center. In 1806 Scottish explorer Mungo Park (*see* EXPLORERS IN AFRICA SINCE 1800) estimated Bamako's population to be less than 6000. By 1880 the town had fallen under the domination of the MANDINKA warrior SAMORY TOURÉ, whose kingdom covered an expanse of territory to the south.

In 1883 French lieutenant colonel Gustave Borgnis-Desbordes occupied Bamako and used it as a base for military campaigns against Touré. Bamako took on new importance under the French, who valued the town's position on the navigable portion of the Niger River, an asset that had long facilitated Bamako's trade with other towns along the river. The French planned a railroad to connect the town with the navigable section of the SENEGAL RIVER and Dakar. After securing the region, the French completed the railroad as far as Kayes in 1904. In 1908 the French moved the capital of French Sudan from Kayes to Bamako.

Since the colonial era Bamako has served as a regional crossroads; it connects many of the country's smaller towns with the Atlantic coast and Dakar. Roads fan out from the city to every province of Mali and to the ports of Conakry, Guinea, and Monrovia, LIBERIA. Bamako is also an important trade center for the gold mined in the west and the cola nuts and rice crops of the south and east. It is Mali's primary shipping port for its major exports – cotton, peanuts, livestock, and fish – and it is the country's main financial and administrative center. The economy of Bamako includes manufacturing plants that produce motor vehicles, textiles, and pharmaceuticals.

In recent years the city's prosperity has attracted many migrants from rural areas. As a result, the city has been expanding to accommodate the influx and has recently absorbed some of the small villages on the right bank of the Niger River. Despite the influences of colonialism, Bamako has retained much of its precolonial structure. It is distinct among West African capitals for the mud-brick architecture of its residential areas. Today, Bamako has an estimated population of 880,000.

Elizabeth Heath

SEE ALSO

Conakry, Guinea; Colonial Rule; Dakar, Senegal; Gold Trade; Guinea; Monrovia, Liberia; Cola.

Africa

Bâ, Mariama (b. 1929, Dakar, Senegal; d. 1981), Senegalese writer whose work highlighted the social inequities facing women.

Mariama Bâ was born into a highly educated Muslim family, the daughter of SENEGAL's first minister of health. Bâ's father had a strong belief in the value of education and, ignoring traditional prohibitions, insisted that his daughter pursue higher education. Bâ attended a prestigious French boarding school near Dakar, passing the entrance examination with the highest marks of all candidates in West Africa that year.

While still a student, Bâ began writing essays for local journals and newspapers. Her writing revealed her to be an articulate and political young woman: one essay, for example, attacked assimilation, a French policy encouraging Africans to adopt French identity and culture. An active participant in women's organizations (*see* FEMINISM IN AFRICA: AN INTERPRETATION; WOMANISM), the young Bâ found her voice as a spokesperson for African women facing new troubles in the traditional institution of marriage. Later, as a mother of nine, Bâ would confront these difficulties in her own life, when her marriage to a Senegalese politician ended in divorce.

Bâ's first and best-known novel, *Une si longue lettre* (1980; So Long a Letter), articulates the social inequities facing women in contemporary Senegalese society, particularly the practice of polygamy. The Noma Prize-winning novel takes the form of a letter from Ramatoulaye, whose husband has just died, to her friend Aïssatou. Both women have suffered from their marriages, and the fact that they are highly educated and married for love does not protect them from the oppression experienced by their mothers. In her letter Ramatoulaye tells how both marriages unraveled as their husbands took other, younger brides. The story of a third woman, Jaqueline, unfolds around the challenge of a cross-cultural relationship between a Muslim Senegalese man and a Christian woman from CÔTE D'IVOIRE. By showing the conflict between individual desires and obligations to the extended family, the novel renders the oppression of women without apology or sentimentalism. Abiola Irele characterized *Une si longue lettre* as "the most deeply felt presentation of the female condition in African fiction."

Bâ followed the success of her first novel with *Le chant écarlate* (1981; Scarlet Song), also an examination of cross-cultural relationships. The novel traces how a marriage between a white French woman and a Senegalese man collapses under the strain of conflicting worldviews and pressures from the extended family. But the story also depicts another, successful interracial relationship, leaving open the possibility of transcending a cultural gap through compromise and sacrifice. The novel was Bâ's final work; she passed away shortly before its publication.

Marian Aguiar

SEE ALSO

Dakar, Senegal.

Africa

Bambara, African ethnolinguistic group.

The million or so Bambara (sometimes called Bamana), who speak languages of the Manding group, live primarily in Mali beside the Niger River. They are descendants of the people of Ancient Mali, who founded both the Segu and Kaarta kingdoms. Bambara means "unbeliever" or "infidel," the name the group acquired in the course of resisting Islam after it was introduced in 1854 by the Tukulor conqueror el-Hajj Umar.

Religion and agriculture for the Bambara are intertwined: for example, the high god of the Bambara is represented as a grain from which the whole of creation is born. The Bambara recognize one god, Bemba or Ngala, as the creator of all things, a being who cannot be perceived by humans through the usual senses, but whose existence is manifested as an immaterial force, often as a whirlwind or a thought. Many of their religious beliefs are symbolized in their famous masks and carvings, which often feature the antelope, who they believe taught men to grow crops. Although many present-day Bambara are Muslim, they still make masks, mostly to sell to tourists.

The traditional social organization of the Bambara is the large united clan, a group of families descended from a common ancestor. Family heads are obligated to obey the village chief, who not only organizes the village for religious activities but also acts as mediator for the chief of the earth spirits. Although the Bambara are linked by clan, there has long been a great deal of intermingling among ethnic groups in this region, and so there is no strong centralized Bambara political authority.

Traditionally cultivators of MILLET and guinea corn, the Bambara now also grow crops such as peanuts, rice, and cotton, and many now live in BAMAKO, MALI and/or migrate seasonally to work on the cocoa and coffee plantations of GHANA and CÔTE D'IVOIRE.

SEE ALSO
Tourism in Africa; Mali Empire.

North America

Bambara, Toni Cade

(b. March 25, 1939, New York, N.Y.; d. December 9, 1995, Philadelphia, Pa.), African American novelist, short story writer, and social activist whose work emphasizes the importance of community, history, and social engagement.

Toni Cade was born in New York City in 1939. She began writing as a child and published her first short story in 1959, the year she received a B.A. from Queens College. She received an M.A. in American literature from the City College of New York in 1963. Her diverse careers included teaching, social work, documentary filmmaking, and community activism in addition to writing.

When Cade discovered "Bambaba" as a signature in her grandmother's sketchbook, she added it to her name. In 1970 Bambara edited the anthology *The Black Woman.* This work was partially a response to the civil rights and women's movements, and included works by Nikki Giovanni, Audre Lorde, PAULE MARSHALL, and ALICE WALKER. In 1971 she edited a second anthology, *Tales and Stories for Black Folks.* Bambara's first collection of short stories, *Gorilla, My Love,* was published in 1972, and her second, *The Sea Birds Are Still Alive,* in 1977. Her novel *The Salt Eaters* was published in 1980 and won the American Book Award in 1981. She began writing and editing documentary films in the 1980s, and in 1986 won the Best Documentary Academy Award for Louis Massiah's *The Bombing of Osage Avenue* (see MOVE).

Bambara stated often that art needed to reflect social commitment, and her fiction emphasized the importance of community and social activism. Her own activism included participation in women's groups, particularly those supporting women of color. She continued her work with writers' workshops and community groups until her death in 1995.

Lisa Clayton Robinson

SEE ALSO
Literature, African American; Women Writers, Black, in the United States; Civil Rights Movement; Giovanni, Yolande Cornelia ("Nikki"); Lorde, Audre Geraldine; New York, New York; Film, Blacks in American.

Africa

Bamiléké, a term commonly used to refer to several ethnic groups of CAMEROON.

The name Bamiléké comes from the phrase *mba lekeo,* or "the people who live over there," which was used by people of the western grasslands of Cameroon to describe their neighbors to the east. European travelers to the region corrupted the word into "Bamiléké" and used it to describe the people of the eastern highlands, including such Bantu-speaking groups as the Babadju, Bafoussam, Bagam, Baham, Banjoun, and Bangu. At the end of the nineteenth century, the population of the Bamiléké was estimated at 1.8 million, though more recently the numbers have been revised to less than 1 million. The Bamiléké were not indigenous to the eastern grasslands but fled there from the north, primarily during the eighteenth century, to escape the slave raids of the FULANI. They mixed with the indigenous inhabitants of the area and reestablished highly stratified dynasties, loosely based on a conception of divine kingship that had been adopted from various Sudanic empires. Subchiefs often formed their own chiefdoms.

The Bamiléké chiefdoms did not share a unified ethnic or national identity, though many Bamiléké groups have similar social structures and cultural practices. Historically, most have been agrarian peoples, cultivating maize and peanuts, though in contemporary Cameroon they have excelled in business as well. They are also accomplished carvers of wood and ivory; their elaborate masks are used in the elephant masquerades held by men's societies and in public ceremonies and funerals. Customary political structures revolve around kinship, which the Bamiléké define by dual descent: patrilineal ties typically determine village residence and rights to land, but matrilineal ties define ritual obligations and the inheritance of movable property. Although Islam penetrated some Bamiléké groups, most of the people have retained their animist religious beliefs.

The grasslands long held high population densities, but since the colonial era many Bamiléké have migrated to urban centers, especially Douala, as a result of their business aspirations and increasing pressures for land. After Cameroon was divided between the French and British colonial mandates, many Bamiléké began working on French-owned agricultural plantations, but over time they came to own land and be involved in commerce and transportation. Some scholars discern the emergence of a rural bourgeoisie in this process, though many Bamiléké were also recruited into the colonial administration and banking. They formed agricultural cooperatives, and after World War II they supported the leading, though ultimately unsuccessful, nationalist party, the Union of the Peoples of Cameroon (UPC).

During the anticolonial insurgency the Bamiléké area was the site of much of the violence, which was exacerbated by resentment of their economic success. The hopes of many Bamiléké to benefit politically and economically from independence have often not been fulfilled, and anti-Bamiléké sentiments have often flared. At the same time, the Bamiléké, because of their migration between east and west, have come to symbolize the unification of southern Cameroon with the rest of the country.

Eric Young

SEE ALSO
Nationalism in Africa; Sudan; Douala, Cameroon; African Religions: An Interpretation.

Africa

Banda, the largest ethnic group of the CENTRAL AFRICAN REPUBLIC; they also occupy adjacent parts of CAMEROON and the DEMOCRATIC REPUBLIC OF THE CONGO.

The Banda number almost 1.5 million. They are the largest ethnic group in the Central African Republic and inhabit the central part of that country. The Banda speak a Niger-Congo language. Though they have a tradition of migration in the early 1800s from the Darfur in the SUDAN to their present homeland, their language suggests a longer presence in the region. During the nineteenth century, the Banda resisted slave raids from the kingdoms of Wadai and Darfur and later resisted conquest by RABIH (*see* SLAVERY IN AFRICA).

The Banda traditionally worked iron and grew crops such as peanuts, corn, and sweet potatoes. Women traditionally gathered wild foods and farmed, while men hunted and fished on the many rivers of the area. Families could be polygamous, and marriage required payment of a bride price, often in the form of iron tools. They lived in dispersed homesteads loosely governed by a headman. During times of crisis, such as slave raids and warfare, the people would select a war chief.

Today, in addition to food crops, the Banda cultivate cotton as a cash crop. They are perhaps best known for their craftsmanship, especially their large slit drums, typically carved in the shape of animals. Historically, Banda in homesteads and villages used the drums in order to communicate in times of crisis and celebration. The demands of a market economy and modern life have brought an end to many Banda traditions, such as polygamy.

Eric Young

See Also
Iron in Africa.

Africa

Banda, Ngwazi Hastings Kamuzu

(b. May 14, 1906 [1898?], outside Kasungu, British Central African Protectorate; d. November 26, 1997, Johannesburg, South Africa), president of Malawi from 1966 until the first multiparty elections in 1994.

Known as the Lion of Malawi, Ngwazi Hastings Kamuzu Banda was also known as the dictator who showed so little appreciation for his country's people and culture that he was sometimes suspected of being an American impostor. Kamuzu Banda was born to Chewa peasants in a village near Kasungu, Nyasaland (present-day Malawi). No birth records were kept at the time; while his official year of birth is 1906, other sources cite 1898. As a child, Banda left the household of his maternal grandmother and entered a newly established school built by Church of Scotland missionaries. Influenced by his uncle, Hanock Phiri, Banda converted to Christianity and adopted the surname of missionary John Hastings.

Shortly after completing primary school, Banda traveled with his uncle to South Africa (supposedly walking the 1667 km [1,000 mi]), where they initially worked in a coal mine in Dundee, Natal. Upon reaching Johannesburg, he again worked as a clerk for a mining company and continued his secondary schooling in the evenings. Banda joined the black separatist African Methodist Episcopal Church, which arranged for him to continue his education at the church-sponsored Wilberforce University in Ohio. He later attended Indiana University, transferred to the University of Chicago, and completed a degree in history and political science in 1931, and then attended medical school at Meharry Medical College in Nashville, Tennessee.

In 1937 Banda traveled to Scotland, intending to qualify as a physician so he could return to Nyasaland to practice medicine. But both the Church of Scotland and the colonial administration refused to allow Banda to practice medicine in Nyasaland, reportedly for racial reasons, so he opened a general practice in Liverpool. After World War II he moved his practice to London, where he met African nationalist leaders such as Jomo Kenyatta and Kwame Nkrumah. Despite his geographical distance from Malawi, Banda kept in contact with members of the nationalist Nyasaland African Congress (NAC), and used earnings from his thriving medical practice to provide the NAC with financial support.

In 1953 Kwame Nkrumah asked Banda to come to the Gold Coast, and Banda agreed, settling in Kumasi. For unknown reasons, Banda was suspended from his medical practice by the Ghanaian Ministry of Health in 1957. Although his suspension was ultimately reversed, Banda abandoned his practice and returned to Nyasaland, where he had been invited to lead the NAC's struggle for independence.

Banda's maturity, education, and professionalism earned him great respect among the colony's young nationalists. As the newly elected NAC president, he immediately embarked on a program of Fabian resistance to the colonial authorities, instigating a movement that became increasingly violent and demanding. This resulted in his arrest in March 1959, along with the banning of the NAC. After 13 months in prison, Banda was released, only to take charge of the newly formed Malawi Congress Party (MCP), which replaced the NAC. By then Great Britain had agreed to the country's independence, and, in the general elections held in 1963, Banda became Malawi's first prime minister. In 1966 he was elected president.

Banda's ruthless authoritarianism soon became apparent. His primary political challenge had originally come from opposition leader Dunduza Chisiza, who died in 1962 in a suspicious car accident. Once in power, Banda moved quickly to eradicate any remaining political opposition. Many dissidents fled the country, while others mysteriously disappeared or died. Within his own government ranks, Banda relied heavily on expatriate experts and bureaucrats, who posed less of a challenge to his power than Malawian intellectuals. Toward Malawian citizens, Banda adopted an overtly paternalistic attitude, referring to them as his "children" and dictating laws on everything from skirt length to hairstyle. He banned the Simon and Garfunkel song "Cecilia" in deference to Malawi's Official Hostess, Mama CeceliaKadzamira, with whom he had been living for over 30 years.

Even while Banda denounced Western miniskirts and pop songs as immoral, he himself preferred Western culture, and his economic policies were staunchly pro-Western and anticommunist. His foreign policy was equally paradoxical; officially nonaligned, he maintained relations with South Africa despite international sanctions, but he supported the anticolonial struggle of the Front for the Liberation of Mozambique (FRELIMO), by allowing resistance fighters to enter Malawi.

Despite his dictatorial governance and disregard for human rights, Banda nurtured bonds with international financial institutions such as the World Bank and the International Monetary Fund, and he encouraged foreign investment. Consequently, Malawi developed a high credit rating in the international finance sector. Despite this, the country has developed little industry. Malawi also has extreme disparities between the poor masses and the rich elite. Banda himself accounted for much of this disparity, as he owned "as trustee for the nation" Press Holdings, a holding corporation composed of companies that earned 40 percent of the entire country's gross domestic product.

For many years rumors have circulated that the real Kamuzu Banda died in the United States and that Malawi's ruler was in fact an imposter, perhaps one Richard Armstrong, a roommate of Banda's during medical school. As evidence, subscribers to this theory point out that Banda could not speak his native Nayanja. In fact, he could, although his fluency had diminished and he used out-of-date phrases, because he had been out of the country for so long. This rumor reflected the alienation that many Malawians felt toward their leader, who was both so remote and so completely "Europeanized" – as seen, for example, in his taste for homburgs (formal Continental-style hats) and his distaste for Malawian food – that he seemed indistinguishable from the colonial administrators he replaced.

Pressured by international human-rights monitoring organizations and newly emerging opposition parties, in 1992 Banda agreed to hold a referendum on the reinstatement of multiparty politics. When the electorate returned an overwhelming vote in favor of multiparty elections, Banda acquiesced. He was reportedly becoming increasingly senile. In 1993 he underwent brain surgery after suffering a cranial hemorrhage. During the following year he was deposed in the first multiparty elections. Later he was tried for and acquitted of the murders of three cabinet members and a parliament member. He died of pneumonia in a South African hospital in 1997 and was given a state funeral.

Ari Nave

See Also
Front for the Liberation of Mozambique; Ghana; Johannesburg, South Africa; Kumasi, Ghana; Nationalism in Africa; World War II and African Americans.

Africa

Bangui, Central African Republic, the capital and largest city of the Central African Republic.

Sited on the northwest bank of the Oubangui River, Bangui is both a major trading center and the national capital. The French first established a military post nearby in 1889, at the confluence of the Oubangui and Mpoko Rivers. Two years later they moved the post upstream to the present site of Bangui, at the base of several rapids on the Oubangui. Local inhabitants initially resisted the French presence and killed two chiefs-of-post. In 1906 the post became the administrative center of the Oubangui-Chari territory of French Equatorial Africa. It grew slowly as an administrative and trading center, fanning northwest from its administrative hub, bounded by a large hill to the east and the river to the south, until World War II. As the country's economy boomed during the war, the city expanded rapidly.

As the capital of the independent Central African Republic (CAR), Bangui has witnessed the coronation of Emperor Bokassa in 1977, the demonstrations and bloody massacre that led to his downfall two years later, and, more recently, street fighting between President Agne-Félix Patassé and opposition groups.

Bangui has a soap-making factory, breweries, and other light industries but is primarily a commercial and trading center. A network of roads connects the city with most parts of the Central African Republic. Bangui's docks ship cotton, timber, coffee, and sisal downriver to Brazzaville, where a rail line provides connections to ocean-going commerce. A ferry runs to Zongo, across the river in the Democratic Republic of the Congo.

Today Bangui has a population of more than 500,000, divided between the expatriate and elite, who live in the center, and the majority, who live in sprawling suburbs, or *kodros*, to the north and west, most of which are ethnically homogeneous. The most important and vibrant kodro is Kilometre Cinq, which houses a vast marketplace, bars, and dance halls as well as the city's largest mosque. In the past two years of continuing unrest, unemployment has doubled to nearly 60 percent, and there are widespread shortages of fuel and food.

Eric Young

See Also

Bokassa, Jean-Bédel; Brazzaville, Republic of the Congo; France; Patassé, Ange-Félix.

Bani Hilal and Bani Sulaim. Please see Banu Hilal and Banu Sulaim

Africa

Banjul, the Gambia, the capital and largest city of the Republic of the Gambia.

Shortly after Britain outlawed the trans-atlantic slave trade in 1804, it began seeking a means of patrolling illegal slave trading in the coastal areas of Senegambia. Rather than rebuild the port at James Island, which had been destroyed by the French in the early 1780s, the British decided to establish a new settlement on a small, strategically located island near the mouth of the Gambia River. In 1816 Capt. Alexander Grant purchased the island, which was known by its Mandinka name of Banjul, and named it after Lord Henry Bathurst, who was then Great Britain's secretary of state.

Wolof traders settled in Bathurst in the 1820s and 1830s and were soon joined by small groups of Jola, Mandinka, and Aku (liberated slaves and their descendants from Sierra Leone). Throughout the colonial period Bathurst served as the Gambia's administrative center, maritime port, and military base, though epidemics of yellow fever, cholera, and other diseases slowed the growth of the city, earning one particularly hard-hit neighborhood the nickname "Half Die." By 1850 the city had become the center of the colony's peanut and palm oil trades. In the early twentieth century, it was home to a small peanut-shelling and peanut-oil-processing industry and to most of the colony's few schools.

In 1965 the Gambia achieved independence, and eight years later Bathurst was officially given the name Banjul, which had long been used by local Mandinka and other African communities. Although Banjul remains the administrative and maritime capital of the Gambia, it has outgrown the two square kilometers of land it once occupied, and much of its commercial activity has been moved to the nearby towns of Serrekunda, Bakau, and Fajara. In 1989 its population was estimated at 150,000.

Robert Baum

See Also

Gambia, The.

North America

Banks, Ernest (Ernie)

(b. January 31, 1931, Dallas, Tex.), American professional baseball player who established a major league record in 1955 by hitting five grand-slam home runs in a single season.

Ernie Banks was the first player in the National League (NL) to be named most valuable player two years in a row (1958, 1959). The shortstop and first baseman played all of his 19 major league seasons (1953-1971) with the Chicago Cubs and earned the nickname "Mr. Cub."

As a child, Banks excelled in high school baseball, basketball, and track and field. He pursued baseball, signing with the Kansas City Monarchs of the Negro American League in 1950. After a stint in the army from 1951 to 1953, Banks finished the 1953 season with the Monarchs. He then signed a contract with the Chicago Cubs, making him that team's first black player. In Chicago Banks became a favorite among fans when he hit 44 home runs in 1955, a major-league record for a shortstop. Three years later he broke his own record by hitting 47 home runs. For four consecutive years (1957-1960) he hit more than 40 home runs, ending his career with a total of 512.

Banks was also among the best defensive baseball players. In 1959 his fielding average set a National League (NL) season record for shortstops. In 1969 (having moved to first base in 1962) his fielding average led all NL first basemen. A popular figure among fans, Banks possessed an infectious enthusiasm for the game and was known for his favorite saying, "Let's play two today!" He was elected to the Baseball Hall of Fame in 1977.

See Also

Track and Field in the United States; Baseball in the United States; Negro Leagues.

North America

Banneker, Benjamin

(b. November 9, 1731, Baltimore County, Md.; d. October 9, 1806, Baltimore, Md.), African American self-taught astronomer and mathematician who built a clock out of wood, planned the survey for the establishment of Washington, D.C., and published important almanacs.

Benjamin Banneker was one of several children born to Robert, a freed slave from Guinea, and Mary Banneker. Mary's mother, Molly Welsh, came to the American colonies as an indentured servant from England and later married one of her slaves, an African of royal descent named Bannaka or Banneky. Banneker and his sisters were born free and grew up on a self-sufficient 100-acre tobacco farm. Banneker received the equivalent of an eighth-grade education at a local integrated school and also was tutored by his grandmother. In his early years, he spent much of his free time devising and solving mathetical puzzles. He took over the farm after his father's death in 1759.

In the eighteenth century, clocks and watches were rare devices constructed in metal by skilled artisans. At the age of 22, Benjamin Banneker created a working

Benjamin Bannaker's
PENNSYLVANIA, DELAWARE, MARY-
LAND, AND VIRGINIA
ALMANAC,
FOR THE
YEAR of our LORD 1795;
Being the Third after Leap-Year.

PHILADELPHIA:
Printed for WILLIAM GIBBONS, Cherry Street

Astronomer and mathematician Benjamin Banneker appears on the title page of his *Almanac* for the year 1795. *CORBIS/Bettmann*

clock from wood after studying a watch that belonged to a friend. Having no metal at his disposal, he meticulously carved each component from wood with a pocketknife. It took him two years to finish the clock, which kept accurate time in hours, minutes, and seconds.

After his retirement from farming at the age of 59, Banneker began to study astronomy through borrowed books, becoming a man of science and mathematics through unassisted experimentation and close observation of natural phenomena. Banneker employed his knowledge of astronomy and mathematics to help plan the city of WASHINGTON, D.C. He became interested in astronomy through a local surveyor named George Ellicott, who loaned him astronomy books. In February 1791 George Washington commissioned George Ellicott and French engineer Pierre L'Enfant to help plan the construction of the nation's capital on a 26 sq km (10 sq mi) area of land in Virginia and Maryland. Ellicott invited Banneker to be his assistant. A dispute between some Americans and Frenchmen on the project led L'Enfant to abandon it and take the drafted plans with him. Over the course of two days, Banneker reproduced the intricate plans from memory, preventing a major delay. For this reason, some historians refer to Banneker as "the man who saved Washington, D.C."

Shortly after returning to his farm in April 1791, Banneker issued the first of some ten annual almanacs, which were published by several printers and sold widely in both England and the United States. Banneker charted the movement of heavenly bodies and successfully predicted several solar eclipses. Farmers and navigators relied on this important information. Banneker also reproduced road maps, conversion charts, and literature in his almanacs.

On August 19, 1791, Banneker sent a copy of his first almanac to Thomas Jefferson, then secretary of state under President George Washington, in an effort to dispute Jefferson's belief that blacks were intellectually inferior to whites and in order to protest slavery. Jefferson congratulated Banneker on his publication and expressed his wish for more proof "that nature has given to our [black] brethren talents equal to that of other colors of men." Jefferson forwarded a copy of Banneker's almanac to the Academy of Sciences in Paris, one of the world's leading scientific societies in the eighteenth century.

Aaron Myers

See Also
Slavery in the United States; Free Blacks in the United States, 1619 to 1863.

North America

Bannister, Edward Mitchell

(b. November 1826, St. Andrews, New Brunswick, Canada; d. January 9, 1901, Providence, R.I.), one of the first African Americans to receive national recognition as a painter and the only major black artist of the nineteenth century who did not travel to Europe to study art.

Edward Mitchell Bannister was the first of two sons born to Edward and Hannah Alexander Bannister. His father was from BARBADOS; his mother, who was probably of Scottish descent, was a native of St. Andrews, New Brunswick, and fostered her older son's love of drawing. His father died when Bannister was six; his mother died in 1844. The two boys were sent to live with a wealthy white lawyer, Harris Hatch, and his family. They worked on the Hatches' farm but had access to the Hatches' library, which was filled with books and with paintings that Bannister copied incessantly.

Following the path of many young men who lived in coastal communities, Bannister went to sea, working on fishing boats and schooners. He settled in Boston in 1848, laboring at menial jobs before he learned the skilled trades of barbering and women's hair styling. He also began to study painting at the Boston Studio Building and the Lowell Institute. At Lowell he attended the anatomy lessons of William Rimmer, a well-known sculptor.

Another artist who had a considerable influence on Bannister was William Morris Hunt, who had studied in Europe. A landscape painter of poetic pastoral scenes, Hunt often exhibited in Boston. He himself had been influenced by the French Barbizon School, which included the landscape artists Corot and Millais. The Barbizon School's theme of the sacredness of nature meshed with Bannister's own feelings of reverence for the beauty of trees, clouds, and water. Bannister also became interested in a recently developed novelty that combined art and technology: photography. He became skilled at tinting photographs and worked at this trade for a year in New York.

In 1857 Bannister married Christiana B. Carteaux, who was born in 1822 in North Kingston, Rhode Island. She was the owner of fashionable and successful hairdressing salons in Boston and Providence. Bannister had been her employee, but at their marriage she encouraged him to give up the trade and concentrate on his painting. He shared a studio and participated in group exhibitions at the Boston Art Club and Museum, showing works of biblical themes, portraits, landscapes and seascapes, and genre scenes. Most of these early works are now lost, and known only from written descriptions.

Boston was a cultural center for both black and white society. Bannister joined the Crispus Attucks Choir, in which he sang tenor, and both he and his wife participated in a drama group. The Bannisters were ardent and active abolitionists in the city's strong black antislavery movement. In 1864 Christiana Bannister organized a fair to raise money for the families of black Civil War soldiers, since their pay was less than that of white troops. Bannister contributed a full-length portrait of Col. Robert Gould Shaw, *Our Martyr*, the white officer who was in charge of the famous black Massachusetts Fifty-fourth Regiment and who had been killed at the attack on Fort Wagner. The portrait is now lost.

In the same year Bannister was commissioned by his fellow abolitionist Robert Johnson to paint a portrait of Johnson's mother-in-law, Prudence Nelson Bell. It is Bannister's only extant work of 1864, and the portrait was donated by family members in 1998 to Boston's Museum of Afro-American History.

In 1870 the Bannisters moved to Providence, where they easily fit into artistic and professional circles. Bannister joined the group of artists who had studios in the Woods Building, among them John Nelson Arnold, an old friend. In 1876 Bannister's painting *Under the Oaks* took the first prize medal at the Philadelphia Centennial Exposition, although the judges tried to withhold the award when they discovered that he was black. The painting has since been lost, along with the sketches for it and the medal. The prize certificate, however, is in the archives of the Providence Art Club.

The Providence Art Club was founded in 1880, following a meeting in Bannister's studio, to bring together artists, both professional and amateur, as well as art collectors and civic leaders. It remains in existence today. Among Bannister's later works are *Moon Over a Harbor* (1868), *Newspaper Boy* (1869), *Oak Trees* (1876), *Approaching Storm* (1886), and *Sabin Point, Narragansett Bay* (1885). His works are currently held by Brown University, the National Museum of American Art, the Rhode Island School of Design, and the Schomburg Center for Research in Black Culture.

Betty Gubert

See Also

Boston, Massachusetts; Civil War, American; Fifty-fourth Regiment of Massachusetts Volunteer Infantry; Schomburg Library.

Africa

Bantu: Dispersion and Settlement, the spread of Bantu-speaking peoples across sub-Saharan Africa.

Linguistic and genetic evidence suggests that groups of Bantu speakers originating in what is today eastern Nigeria and adjoining areas of Cameroon spread across a vast area of central, southern, and eastern Africa over the course of 2000 years. In the past the dispersion of Bantu speakers was associated with the spread of iron working, agriculture, and a unique pottery style collectively known as the Early Iron Age Complex. Although agriculture and the use of iron do seem to have disseminated together, recent linguistic analysis confidently places the initial wave of Bantu expansion well before the Early Iron Age.

Bantu Origins

The Bantu language is a member of the Benue-Congo branch of the Niger-Congo family of languages, spoken widely across West Africa and as far east as southern Sudan. Speakers of the Benue-Congo branch of this family live almost exclusively within eastern Nigeria and adjoining areas of southern Cameroon – with the exception, of course, of the expansive Bantu (*see* Languages, African: An Overview). The word *bantu*, literally translated, means "people." By approximating the time it would take for Bantu languages to differentiate from a common ancestor, a technique known as glottochronology, linguists estimate that proto-Bantu speakers began to spread throughout the tropical rain forests and the adjoining savanna margins that straddle the equator approximately 4000 years ago.

The proto-Bantu were probably shifting cultivators of yam and oil palm, as well as riverine fishers, given the antiquity of related Bantu words. In contrast, there were no proto-Bantu words for iron or iron working, as one would expect if the invention predated their dispersion. Eastern and western branches of Bantu languages do share related words that refer to iron foraging. Thus, iron technologies were probably adapted after the proto-Bantu had dispersed throughout the tropical rain forest but before the secondary dispersion farther east and south.

Bantu Expansion

As early as 1500 B.C.E. the proto-Bantu speakers had settled on the Gabon coast. Linguistic patterns suggest that from there they migrated along two distinct routes beginning around 1000 B.C.E. One group moved south to Angola, forming the Western Bantu Group. The Eastern Bantu Group expanded to the east and southeast. Initially it was believed that the iron working led to the sudden rapid expansion east and south. Revisionist theories, however, place more emphasis on the adaptation of new crops, such as the grain millet, a practice that likely diffused from Sudanic and Cushitic-speaking people with whom the Bantu came into contact as they moved eastward into more arid regions. The exact reasons for the Bantu expansion, however, remain unclear.

By the time the Eastern Bantu reached Urewe in the Great Lakes Region during the last millennium B.C.E., words for iron working were widespread. From Urewe the Eastern Bantu spread rapidly to the south and farther to the east, reaching the east coast by the second century B.C.E. Likewise the Western Bantu Group had moved as far as the Democratic Republic of the Congo by about 400 B.C.E. Genetic and linguistic evidence suggests that as the Eastern Bantu moved south and west

POSSIBLE SPREAD OF BANTU SPEAKERS 3000 B.C.E. - 1100 C.E.
1 Homeland, 3000 B.C.E.
2 Eastern and Western Groups by 500 B.C.E.
3 East African Coast by 100 B.C.E.
4 About 400 C.E.
Flow of Migration
0 800 km
0 600 mi
Benue R.
Ubangi R.
Congo R.
Kasai R.
Cunene R.
Zambezi R.
Limpopo R.
Orange R.
Juba R.
Tana R.
Lake Turkana (Rudolf)
Lake Kyoga
Lake Albert
Lake Kivu
Lake Victoria
Lake Tanganyika
Mweru
Kisale
Lake Bangweulu
Lake Malawi
Lake Kariba
Atlantic Ocean
Indian Ocean
Mozambique Channel
TROPIC OF CAPRICORN
KARA-MOJONG
TURKANA
HIMA
LUO
Urewe
LUO
KIKUYU
SHUNGWAYA
TUTSI
SEGEJU
CHAGGA
KONGO
JAGA
ANGOLA
LUBA
LUNDA
CHOKWE
KATANGA
BEMBA
BISA
Kilwa
ZIMBA
CHOKWE
Tete
MUTAPA
Sena
TORWA
CHANGAMIRE
Zimbabwe
Sofala
20°
40°

of LAKE TANGANYIKA, they came into contact with already established Western Bantu, leading to the intermixing of both people and ideas.

No single element can explain the rapid Bantu drive southward and eastward, although a number of possibilities have been suggested. Much of the early Bantu migration may simply have resulted from swidden agriculturists encroaching on the lands of hunter-gatherers who were more mobile and lived at lower population densities, pushing populations of Khoisan-speakers into increasingly marginal environments. Other scholars have suggested that the continued desiccation of the Sahara until the mid-third millennium B.C.E. resulted in the loss of wooded savanna and rain forest, aggravating the need to clear new tracts of forest.

However, the Bantu expansion proceeded in a number of fits and starts, suggesting that multiple forces influenced the dispersion. For example, the introduction or invention of iron may have contributed to the more rapid expansion of Bantu speakers after the first millennium B.C.E., enabling them to clear land more readily for agriculture as well as providing more effective weapons. The diffusion of bananas and Asian yams has also been posited as a factor leading to the Bantu dispersion in moister climates.

Bantu populations also absorbed Nilo-Saharan speakers as they moved east and south. By between 500 and 1000 C.E. most of the Bantu dispersion had taken place. However, through intermarriage and diffusion, the Bantu language and culture continued to spread, assimilating people in other populations, such as among the Khoikoi speakers in southern Africa and Dahalo speakers in East Africa. Today Bantu speakers live in a wide range of ecosystems and have adapted numerous subsistence strategies, from sedentary agriculture to fishing.

Ari Nave

SEE ALSO
Gabon; Iron in Africa; Sahara Desert.

Africa

Banu Hilal and Banu Sulaim, Bedouin ethnic groups that migrated into North Africa.

In the eleventh century the Banu Hilal and the Banu Sulaim, Arabic-speaking nomadic tribes originally from the central Arabian plateau, began to migrate westward from Upper EGYPT to the land called Ifriqiyah (present-day TUNISIA and eastern ALGERIA). They settled in the regions now constituting LIBYA, ALGERIA, TUNISIA, and MOROCCO. Historians mark the movement of the Hilalians, as they were collectively known, as a critical moment in the "Arabization" of North Africa. The migration of around 200,000 Bedouin herders reached places that had maintained distinct BERBER identities even during the period of Roman rule, transforming the people, the language, and the land.

Arabic historical accounts place the Hilalian migration in the context of an eleventh-century power struggle between the Fatimids, then based in Egypt, and the Berber Zirid Dynasty. The Fatimids had left the Zirids in power over their western holdings in Ifriquiya, and when the Zirids claimed autonomy, the Fatimids sent the Banu Hilal to invade the west – or, at least, the Fatimids allowed the Hilalians to pass beyond the Nile without challenge.

Historians disagree on the impact of the Hilalian's westward migration. Until recently it was portrayed as a pillaging, destructive so-called invasion of the Berber countryside. This account is based partly on the Arabic historian Ibn Khaldun's description of the Banu Hilal as a swarm of locusts who sacked villages, burned farms, and filled wells. However, some historians have now challenged the dual portrayal of the Hilalians as destructive nomads and the Berbers as civilized settlers. These historians point out that the region had a long history of intra-Berber conflict between sedentary and nomadic groups.

In any case, the Hilalians occupied the land in huge numbers. The Banu Salim migration stopped for some time in Libya, and the Banu Hilal continued west, settling Algeria and Tunisia, and by the mid-twelfth century, Morocco. Some Berber groups fled into remote mountainous regions, where they maintained a distinct Berber identity and language.

Two hundred years later, another large Hilalian migration moved west through North Africa. In the thirteenth century, the Banu Sulaim traveled from the regions of Tripolitania and Cyrenaica in present-day Libya to Tunisia. They were encourage by the Tunisian Hafsid Dynasty, which sought to undermine growing Banu Hilal power. Using incentives such as land rewards and official positions, the Hafsids placed the Banu Sulaim in bureaucratic and military positions over the Banu Hilal.

Although Islam had already made its mark in North Africa, Arab culture had for the most part remained the culture of the urban elite, communicated through the classical Arabic language and literary traditions. Both the Banu Hilal and the Banu Sulaim, however, brought Arab culture to the countryside, including the colloquial Arabic language of their oral traditions.

The definition of "Arab" is tricky in North Africa; after all, the Banu Hilal and Banu Sulaim had left the central Arabian plateau at the beginning of the eleventh century, and the migration lasted through the thirteenth century. The migration produced a hybrid culture, and the historical observer may characterize the change brought by this migration as either the Arabization of the Berber population or the assimilation of new North African traditions into the Berber identity.

Marian Aguiar

SEE ALSO
Nile River; Khaldun, Ibn.

Africa

Baobab Tree, a large African tree found primarily in semi-arid regions, where it is highly valued by many African peoples.

The baobab tree, classified as *Adansonia digitata*, grows only to the height of a large maple tree (about 15 m or 50 ft), but the trunk sometimes attains a diameter of 9 m (30 ft), making it one of the world's largest trees. Only the sequoia and the eucalyptus have greater trunk diameters. The branches, frequently as thick as the trunks of other large trees, form a hemispherical mass of foliage often 45 m (150 ft) in diameter. Both the large diameter of the trunk and the tree's lower limbs are adaptations that allow the tree to store large amounts of water. A similar adaptation is that, during the dry season, baobabs lose their leaves, eliminating much of the water loss that would normally occur through transpiration.

The baobab provides food and shelter for many animals. People also eat the baobab fruit, commonly called monkey bread, which is about the size of a grapefruit. Pulp from the tree is used in the preparation of cooling drinks. In addition, the bark of the tree yields a strong cordage fiber.

The baobab holds spiritual significance for some peoples living in the Sudanic savanna region of West Africa, including the Serer, the WOLOF, and the MANDINKA. Their griots – community oral historians, storytellers, and praise singers – have traditionally been buried in baobab trunks because they are believed too sacred to be buried in the ground. The Jola people of SENEGAL revere baobabs because of the spirits that are said to live inside them. They also believe that baobabs are harbingers of the rainy season, because they produce leaves just before the rain arrives.

Robert Fay

North America

Baptists

The origins of the black Baptist movement are rooted in the intellectual and moral incongruity of the late colonial period. The Enlightenment ideals of liberty, justice, freedom, and equality that fueled the colonial passion for independence in the 1770s stood in stark contrast to the commodification of African bodies. Only a few early Americans felt that reason demanded the emancipation of enslaved Africans; most were willing to compromise and settle for the liberation of African souls from the bondage of sin. It is during the 1770s that we find the earliest extant evidence of black inclusion in the Baptist fold.

The institution of slavery in New England towns did not require the intensive labor found in the Southern plantation economy. As a result, the number of blacks residing in New England communities remained relatively low throughout the eighteenth century. Since the minute African presence did not pose much of a psychological and social threat, the earliest black participants in the Baptist movement were members in mixed-race (albeit segregated) congregations. By 1772 the First Baptist churches of Boston and Providence, Rhode Island, listed Africans among their members. Initially, the same held true in the South. However, the larger African presence in the South challenged white slaveholders to either tacitly commit to the idea of racially mixed worship or support the development of a separate institutional structure for blacks. They chose the latter.

The first institution that was established for black Baptists in North America was the role of the slave preacher. This individual had the awesome responsibility of negotiating between the master's spiritual and political expectations and those of his own people. Some slave preachers were adept at employing the arts of resistance, giving the master just enough of what he wanted in order to thwart suspicion, while other slave preachers displayed an uneasy allegiance to the slavocracy. In both instances, though, the slave preacher was the spiritual guide for enslaved Africans on Southern plantations.

Over time, as the number of African converts to the Baptist faith began to swell, slave preachers were largely responsible for the establishment of independent black Baptist congregations. George Liele (c. 1750-1820) was one such preacher. Licensed in the early 1770s by his master's congregation to minister to the slaves on plantations in and around Buck County, Georgia, Liele assembled one of the first black Baptist congregations in North America at Yama Craw, near Savannah. Among those to whom Liele witnessed were David George (c. 1742-1810) and Andrew Bryan (1737-1812). George lived on a plantation near Silver Bluff, South Carolina, about 20 km (12 mi) from Augusta, Georgia. With the encouragement of his master and other slaves, he preached to slaves in a mill on the plantation, and by 1775, he and his followers had established the first African American Baptist Church. Bryan converted to Christianity in 1777 after hearing Liele preach. In 1782, when Liele accompanied British troops to Jamaica, Bryan reconstituted the congregation at Yama Craw as the First African Baptist Church of Savannah.

Black Baptists continued to organize congregations and associations of their own throughout the first half of the nineteenth century. Like their white counterparts, African American Baptists basically grouped themselves into two types of organizations: single-purpose entities (societies) and multipurpose entities (conventions/denominations). Whether societal or conventional, most black Baptist organizations prior to the Civil War were regionally based. A primary aim for the development of single-purpose organizations was the evangelization of Africa. Like other African American Protestant movements, black Baptists felt a unique obligation to bring the "good news" to the African continent. In fact, some attempted to rationalize the enslavement of Africans as part of God's plan of redemption for the Dark Continent. Regardless of their motivation, black Baptists played a significant role in the African American story of African missions. Institutional efforts to missionize Africa began in 1815 with the organization of the African Baptist Missionary Society (ABMS). Located at Richmond, the ABMS formally supported Virginia native Lott Carey when he set sail for Liberia in 1821.

The creation of multipurpose organizations beyond the local level began in 1840, when black Baptists in the northeastern states organized the American Baptist Missionary Convention (ABMC) at Abyssinian Baptist Church in New York. Under the leadership of Abyssinian's pastor, Sampson White, the organization took a strong stand against slavery, refusing to engage in fellowship with any Baptists who owned slaves. The group's membership was open to all antislavery Baptists, but it maintained a mostly regional base throughout its existence.

About 20 years later, in 1864, another regional convention was organized by black Baptists. The Northwestern and Southern Baptist Convention (NWSBC) took place in St. Louis and was the reconstitution of the Western Colored Baptist Convention. The latter group convened regularly from 1853 to 1859, but the outbreak of the Civil War interrupted its work between 1859 and 1864. The NWSBC's membership comprised churches from Indiana, Illinois, Missouri, Ohio, Arkansas, Mississippi, Louisiana, and Tennessee. It also shared the antislavery and missionary interests of the ABMC, electing former missionary William P. Newman as its president.

After the Civil War black Baptists entered the mission field at home with the same zeal that they had previously expressed for foreign missions. While both the ABMC and the NWSBC recognized the opportunities that the war provided, they also saw the need for a more united effort. NWSBC president William Newman envisioned an all-black organization that would transcend regional barriers. Unfortunately, his death just weeks before the union commission convened prevented him from witnessing the moment he had longed for. Nonetheless, the two groups met in Richmond in late August 1867 and formed the Consolidated American Baptist Missionary Convention (CABMC).

The CABMC became the organization responsible for both home and foreign missions among freedpeople for the next decade and a half. Although it was realistically a loose conglomeration of regional entities, the group sought to represent black Baptist interests on a national level. After measures had been instituted to make the organizations more efficient and fiscally responsible, however, regional rifts began to resurface. No one seemed to want a strong denominational apparatus for fear that local control and interest would have to give way to the national will. By 1879 the CABMC's effort to become "a Church with the soul of a nation" had collapsed, and at its meeting in Cincinnati the convention voted to disband.

Most national Baptists date their organizational history from 1880, the year in which the Baptist Foreign Mission Convention (BFMC) was founded. Despite the word "convention" in its name, it was organized along the societal model, with foreign missions as its only institutional function. A full-fledged attempt at forming an organization on the convention model began in 1886 with the founding of the American National Baptist Convention (ANBC). The other major national organization founded by black Baptists around the time of the ANBC was the National Baptist Educational Convention (NBEC), established in 1892. This organization grew out of the education committee of the ANBC, and its charge was to establish a national Baptist university for the development of an educated black Baptist clergy.

These three groups – the BFMC, ANBC, and NBEC – often held their annual meetings in the same city so that those who held membership in more than one organization could attend meetings without increasing the financial burden. In 1895 the three groups met in Atlanta and merged into the National Baptist Convention (NBC).

While the creation of the NBC may be seen as the first full-fledged denominational enterprise among black Baptists, it was by no means the last. In 1897 the convention experienced its first schism. Black Baptists from state conventions along the East Coast complained about three things: the

The Dexter Avenue Baptist Church in Montgomery, Alabama, where Rev. Martin Luther King, Jr. was pastor from 1954 to 1960. *CORBIS/Raymond Gehman*

relocation of the headquarters of the foreign mission board (FMB) from Richmond to Louisville; the financial structure of the FMB; and the weak presentation of Sunday school material by the National Baptist Publishing Board. These Baptists, particularly those in Virginia, had a rather high stake in foreign missions, and they did not want to see the seat of power moved so far away. They perceived this as an attempt to pull the work out of their hands, which they greatly resented. Moreover, they thought that the relocation of the FMB to Southern soil, as well as the establishment of an independent publishing house, was a sign of ungratefulness for all that Northern Baptists (white) had done for blacks. These "cooperationists," as they were called, pulled away from the NBC and formed the single-purpose Lott Carey Foreign Mission Convention.

In 1915 another break occurred in the organization. A discussion of the possible incorporation of the NBC led to a fight among several black Baptist factions. Some opposed incorporation on theological grounds. They felt that incorporation of the national body was inconsistent with the New Testament understanding of church. Furthermore, they found it to be inconsistent with their understanding of Baptist polity. The national office, they argued, had no business to conduct between sessions. Its business was carried out by the boards. Advocates of incorporation argued that if the denomination was going to own property (a national university), then it needed to be able to legally represent the interests of black Baptists. Advocates of incorporation also wanted to exert greater control over the affiliated boards, which were acting more like independent entities than like instrumentalities of the convention.

The National Baptist Publishing Board was becoming a major problem for the convention. It had incorporated in 1898 under the laws of Tennessee as a private business venture, not as an NBC instrumentality. In 1902 the National Baptist Educational Board incorporated in Washington, D.C., and the Benefit Board followed suit in 1913. What was at stake was the war between a convention model and a societal model. Black Baptists were caught in between, with a convention structure (similar to that of the Southern Baptists) that functioned as a confederation of societies (similar in scope to the Northern Baptist societies). When R. H. Boyd became convinced that incorporation of the NBC was an attempt to claim his property (the National Baptist Publishing Board), he led an exodus of black Baptists away from the convention in 1915, under the guise of opposition to incorporation. The result was the National Baptist Convention of America, Unincorporated, and the National Baptist Convention, U.S.A., Incorporated.

Another major division in the black Baptist family took place in 1960, when a group of ministers challenged NBC president Joseph H. Jackson to use the organization as a vehicle for change in the Civil Rights Movement. Gardner C. Taylor, pastor of the Concord Baptist Church of Christ in Brooklyn, New York, ran against Jackson. He was supported by Martin Luther King Jr. and other Baptist clergymen involved in King's Southern Christian Leadership Conference. Taylor and the Progressives, as they were called, were defeated and in September 1961 formed the Progressive National Baptist Convention.

Quinton Dixie

See Also

Boston, Massachusetts; Civil War, American; King, Martin Luther, Jr.

Africa

Bara, ethnic group of MADAGASCAR.

The Bara primarily inhabit the southern highlands of Madagascar. They speak MALAGASY, a Malayo-Polynesian language, and comprise several subgroups, including the Barobe and the Imamono. Approximately 400,000 people consider themselves Bara.

SEE ALSO
Languages, African: An Overview.

North America

Baraka, Amiri (b. October 7, 1934, Newark, N.J.), African American writer, playwright, and political activist.

Amiri Baraka is a prolific writer who has worked across a range of genres: poetry, drama, the novel, JAZZ operas, and nonfiction. He also played a crucial role as an organizer, editor, and promoter of the avant-garde movements of the New American Literature in the 1950s and early 1960s and the BLACK ARTS MOVEMENT in the late 1960s and early 1970s.

Born Everett Leroy (later LeRoi) Jones, Baraka attended Newark public schools and studied chemistry at HOWARD UNIVERSITY before turning to literature and philosophy. In 1954 he left Howard and joined the United States Air Force, where he became increasingly interested in literature, immersing himself in the work of American poet Ezra Pound, Irish novelist James Joyce, and other modernists.

Discharged from the Air Force in 1957 for possessing allegedly Communist literary journals, Baraka moved to Greenwich Village in New York City and established relationships with members of the avant-garde Beat, Black Mountain, and New York School movements. He published his acclaimed book of poetry, *Preface to a Twenty Volume Suicide Note* (1961), and co-edited the poetry journals *Yugen* and *Floating Bear* with his then-wife Hettie Jones and poet Diane Di Prima, respectively.

Baraka began distancing himself from the bohemian literary scene after a trip to CUBA. Influenced by the artists of the newly revolutionary country, and by the CIVIL RIGHTS MOVEMENT and black political figures such as MALCOLM X, his work became more politically and socially committed. His plays *Dutchman* and *The Slave* (both 1964) combined the nonrealistic staging of early-1960s experimentalist theater with militant and often violent assertions of black pride. The poems collected in *The Dead Lecturer* (1964) are similar; their violent imagery and fragmentary style and syntax provide a vivid record of the black intellectual and artist in torment and transformation.

Baraka was also influenced by musicians such as ORNETTE COLEMAN, John Coltrane, Cecil Taylor, and SUN RA – New Jazz players of the late 1950s and early 1960s who demonstrated that it was possible for black artists to produce avant-garde art rooted in African American cultural traditions. A series of shorter essays that helped introduce the New Jazz to a wider audience was collected in *Black Music* (1968). His history of jazz, *Blues People* (1963), was one of the first books to trace the social and political development of African American music.

While Baraka became increasingly involved with militant political organizations in the mid-1960s, it was the assassination of Malcolm X in 1965 that led to his final break with the predominantly white bohemian world. Shortly thereafter, Baraka abandoned his family and moved to Harlem, where he was instrumental in creating the Black Arts Repertory Theatre, whose impetus was to create a well-defined black aesthetic. Though short-lived, it provided the blueprint for similar theaters across the country and helped develop the cultural corollary to black nationalism, the Black Arts Movement.

Though Baraka left Harlem after a year for his native Newark, he continued to serve as a Black Arts Movement and BLACK POWER leader. With poet Larry Neal, Baraka edited the important nationalist-tinged anthology of African American writing, *Black Fire* (1968). Baraka's poetry, while often retaining something of his earlier fragmentary style, was crucial in establishing a connnection between African American vernacular forms and literature.

In addition to his importance as an artist, Baraka figured in national African American political events, such as the 1972 Black Political Convention in Gary, Indiana, as well as in local Newark politics, where he was active in the campaign of the first black mayor, Kenneth Gibson, in 1970. Heavily influenced by the cultural nationalist Maulana Karenga (from whom he received the name Amiri Baraka), Baraka was an advocate of an Afrocentric doctrine of separatism, self-determination, and communual African American cultural and economic self-development. Seeing the weaknesses of Black Nationalism, in the early 1970s he adopted Marxism-Leninism, which he felt better addressed the interrelated problems of racism, national oppression, colonialism, and neocolonialism. *The Motion of History* (1978), *Reggae or Not!* (1981), *Daggers and Javelins* (1984), and *The Autobiography of LeRoi Jones* (1984) were published during this time.

Baraka has taught at Yale and Columbia universities and the State University of New York at Stony Brook and continues to write.

Jim Smethurst

SEE ALSO
Literature, African American; Black Aesthetic, The; Black Vernacular English; Coltrane, John William; Harlem, New York; New York, New York; Newark, New Jersey; Communist Party USA, African Americans and the.

Latin America and the Caribbean

Barbados, a former British colony that was given the nickname "Little England" because British culture is highly visible throughout the island. Barbados is located between the Caribbean Sea and the North Atlantic Ocean, northeast of VENEZUELA in an island chain known as the Windward Islands of the Lesser Antilles.

Barbados has been described as the Caribbean's most "British" island. Blacks in Barbados speak with a British accent, play the traditionally British sport of cricket, and adhere to British custom in their legal and political affairs. Great Britain has indeed been an important force in the nation's development. But standard accounts of the history of Barbados have often focused on its British character at the expense of its African heritage. Some historians have emphasized the British role in creating the institutions that govern Barbados today. Similarly, its educational system, sports industry, and economy have all been tied to Great Britain. However, British culture has not necessarily played the most important role in the historical emergence of Barbados as a free and democratic society.

Many historians now acknowledge that slavery was perhaps the defining institution in Barbados and that African slaves are essential players in the island's history. In fact, the African roots of contemporary Barbadian society are evident in its music, literature, and poetry. On an equally compelling note, the history of this island country offers a fitting introduction to the rise and fall of European colonialism. Slavery and the sugar plantation were first perfected in the seventeenth century by British planters in Barbados.

The economic role that Barbados played in the development of European capitalism is vital to an understanding of both the history of slavery and its demise in the Western world. Barbados was a colony founded entirely on slave labor. As early as the seventeenth century black slaves outnumbered whites by nearly four to one, culminating in the creation of legal and political institutions that dominated and subjugated the island's black majority for more than 300 years. The authoritarian style with which the white minority ruled Barbados was admired and emulated by white colonists throughout the Caribbean (*see* COLONIAL RULE). By the mid-seventeenth century Barbados was the prototype for European colonialism, and the demise of that system on the island bears vivid testimony to the ability of African slaves to overcome enormous obstacles on the road to freedom (*see* Abolition and Emancipation in Latin America and the Caribbean).

Amerindian Presence

The earliest inhabitants on Barbados were Native American nomads whom most historians refer to as Amerindians. The island was a temporary stopping ground for three successive waves of Amerindian migrants moving north toward North America. The first wave, a group known as the Saladoid-Barrancoid, migrated by canoe from South America around 350 c.e. They were farmers, fishermen, and ceramists. Many of their customs and languages resembled those of the Arawak, who were among the largest indigenous groups in the Caribbean in the first century c.e. The Arawak, also known as the Lokono, constituted the second wave of Amerindian migrants, arriving in Barbados from South America around 800 c.e. Some of the more famous extant Arawak settlements include Stroud Point, Chandler Bay, St. Luke's Gully, and Mapp's Cave. The Arawak lived relatively isolated from other Amerindian groups until the thirteenth century, when the Carib arrived from South America, representing the third wave. Within a few years the Carib had displaced both the Arawak and the Salodoid-Barrancoid populations.

For centuries the Carib lived in isolation on the island. However, that peaceful existence was disrupted in the first decade of the sixteenth century when Spanish conquistadors began enslaving Amerindians throughout the Caribbean, forcing them to work as slaves on plantations throughout the region. The Carib on Barbados were among those seized by Spanish conquistadors. Scholars believe that those Carib who managed to avoid enslavement did so by emigrating to nearby islands. Both of these forces – the enslavement and subsequent emigration – left the island uninhabited by the time the first British ship arrived in 1625.

British Colonization

Although Barbados was well known to Spanish and Portuguese sailors at least a century earlier, Great Britain did not become acquainted with the island until the seventeenth century. On May 14, 1625, a ship led by the British captain John Powell stopped to explore the island. After verifying that it was uninhabited, Powell returned to England to formalize the plan to establish a permanent settlement on Barbados. Two years later, on February 17, 1627, a British ship carrying 10 African slaves and more than 80 British colonists landed on the western side of the island, at a site later named Holetown Village.

There were few colonists who could afford to purchase slaves, so most had to work the land themselves. But even though the slave population was small – according to the records of a British merchant there were less than 50 in 1629 – they occupied a central position in the Barbadian economy from the onset. African and Amerindian slaves were forced to perform some of the most physically demanding work, such as constructing colonial buildings and clearing land for colonial homes. Their status as the property of white settlers was formalized in 1636 when colonial officials passed a law declaring all slaves who were brought into Barbados – both Amerindian and African – to be enslaved for life. This law was extended to include the offspring of slaves. During this period there were only 22 free people of color on the island – Amerindian farmers from the Guianas brought in to teach the settlers new agricultural techniques.

European indentured servants were the primary source of labor during most of the island's history throughout the seventeenth century. Poor, uneducated laborers were recruited in England, Scotland, and throughout Europe to work on tobacco and cotton plantations. Although they could not be enslaved under law, indentured servants during this period were considered tenants at will. They could not own the land they worked and were unable to leave the plantation without permission in the form of a pass from their employer. The harsh conditions of indentured servitude made it increasingly difficult for Barbadian tobacco and cotton planters to recruit white labor. As the labor supply dwindled, so did the capacity of the island's tobacco and cotton producers to compete with their international competitors. A drop in world tobacco prices in the early 1640s further weakened the island's economy.

The Emergence of the Sugar Industry

For years Barbadian planters had searched avidly for alternatives to tobacco and cotton as sources of revenue. In 1642 Dutch merchants introduced them to a far more lucrative crop – sugar cane. Before 1642 sugar was used in Barbados mainly as fuel, in the production of rum, and to feed livestock. By 1644 large sugar cane plantations were producing sugar exports across the island. The political infrastructure of Barbados drew wealthy landowners; with political participation tied to landowning, they reigned supreme. The planter elite, or so-called plantocracy, excluded all nonwhites and most poor whites from participation in government affairs. In the words of historian Hilary Beckles: "Partly because of these political and constitutional developments, Barbados emerged in the mid-1640s as perhaps the most attractive colony in the English New World." Land values doubled and tripled in the 1640s as wealthy British capitalists flocked to Barbados to commence the operation of sugar plantations.

Escalation of the Slave Trade

Throughout the seventeenth and eighteenth centuries slaves from various parts of West Africa, including the Gold Coast (present-day Ghana) and Benin, were packed in crowded European vessels bound for the Caribbean. The transatlantic slave trade carried between 10 and 20 million African slaves to colonial plantations throughout the world. By the mid-seventeenth century Barbados was already a leading participant in the slave trade and one of the most In 1645 there were an estimated 5680 African slaves in Barbados. In 1685, 40 years later, their numbers had soared to nearly 60,000. Historian Philip Curtin estimates that by 1700 there were 134,500 African-born slaves in Barbados.

Seventeenth-Century Slave Society

Slaves in Barbados spoke a variety of languages and represented various ethnic groups, including the Igbo, Asante, Fante, Ga, Fon, and Yoruba. Most were forced to work on sugar plantations, where they cut and processed sugar cane. The highly labor-intensive work was performed in conditions of severe heat. One of the most physically demanding aspects of sugar production was grinding the cane, which slaves were forced to do by hand.

Despite the 4-to-1 ratio of slaves to whites in Barbados as early as 1685, the thriving slave trade of the late seventeenth and early eighteenth centuries had an even more dramatic effect on the demographic landscape. As the African presence increased in Barbados, white indentured servants, who at one time had been the primary source of labor, began to question their place in the island's future. At the turn of the eighteenth century white indentured servants began leaving Barbados in waves.

More than 30,000 whites emigrated to neighboring islands throughout the first half of the eighteenth century. The racial imbalance created by this "white flight" placed the colony's white plantation owners in an uncomfortable position. They were intimidated by the sheer size of the slave labor force and its potential for rebellion, but they were dependent on the cheap and seemingly inexhaustible supply of African slaves. Colonial officials responded to the racial imbalance by institutionalizing white hegemony.

Black Codes

Officials began by reemphasizing, and in some cases, strengthening the island's slave codes, that is, laws regulating the behavior of slaves. Colonial officials had already passed a series of slave codes in

1661, 1676, 1682, and 1688, creating one of the most repressive political and economic systems in the slaveholding Caribbean. By the mid-eighteenth century Barbadian law prohibited slaves from leaving their plantations without permission from their owners and barred them from beating drums, blowing horns, or playing other loud instruments – tools enabling slaves who spoke different languages to communicate with each other (*see* Stono Rebellion).

Barbados enacted its own version of the Fugitive Slave Law by requiring all whites to return runaway slaves to colonial officials. The law was lenient toward a master who intentionally killed a slave, requiring him only to pay a fine of $15. Those who killed their slaves "unintentionally" often escaped with no fine. The Barbadian Slave Codes served as models for other slave colonies in the Caribbean, including Jamaica and Antigua, which passed similar laws in 1664 and 1702, respectively.

Slave Resistance

Attempts to use these laws to intimidate slaves and to discourage them from resisting did not succeed. Though they met with defeat, slaves undertook three major rebellions in Barbados in 1649, 1675, and 1692. The first insurrection involved two plantations and was sparked by anger over the inadequate food supplies being allocated to slaves. This uprising did little damage and was suppressed almost immediately.

Plans for the second rebellion were uncovered in 1675 when a female slave named Fortuna betrayed the organizers. The revolt had reportedly been devised over a three-year period and involved plantations throughout the island. Colonial officials arrested more than 100 alleged conspirators and tortured them until they named others. The court found nearly 50 slaves guilty of rebellion and sentenced them to be executed. At least 6 were burned alive; 11 more were beheaded and their bodies dragged through the streets of Speightstown. Five slaves committed suicide before they could be executed.

Plans for the third rebellion were discovered in 1692. An estimated 200 to 300 slaves were arrested, including the principal conspirators, and 93 slaves were executed for their alleged involvement.

There are no records of any armed slave insurrections occurring in Barbados between 1702 and 1815, a fact that scholars attribute to the presence of a powerful colonial militia that had been assembled on the island by the beginning of the eighteenth century. Moreover, British military ships frequently stopped at the island to purchase supplies, probably an indication to most slaves that armed rebellion was an unrealistic option.

Armed resistance also lost its appeal as the proportion of Barbadian-born slaves (known as Creoles), mulattos or coloreds (persons of African and European ancestry), and free blacks increased. Scholars of slave resistance cite evidence that African-born slaves who had experienced freedom at some point in their lives were more likely to engage in overt acts of defiance. The perception held by many white slave owners in Barbados was that Creole slaves were more docile than their African-born counterparts. Plantation owners often tried to widen these divisions by appointing Creoles to positions of power over African-born slaves.

Free Blacks and Free Coloreds in the Eighteenth Century

By most historical accounts the number of free blacks and free coloreds on Barbados remained quite small throughout the eighteenth century. According to official records there were only 78 free blacks and free coloreds on the island in 1773. Most were treated little better than slaves. Free blacks could not vote, hold public office, or testify against whites in court. Most lived in towns and worked as tradesmen and innkeepers.

Free coloreds were placed under the same political restrictions as free blacks. Since they represented 75 percent of the free nonwhite population in eighteenth-century Barbadian society, free coloreds occupied an important place in the social hierarchy. Many of them reacted to racial discrimination by distancing themselves from free blacks, embracing British culture, and in some cases even accepting many tenets of white supremacy, including the notion that blacks were intellectually incapable of being productive citizens. Many in the free colored community distanced themselves even more from their African ancestry by favoring those with European features, such as light skin and straight hair, and by embracing British customs.

The Plantocracy

White Barbadian society experienced its own demographic shift in the late eighteenth century. The enormous profits accumulated by white plantation owners in Barbados made the island a haven for the European elite. Since most of them were sugar and tobacco planters, they became known as the white plantocracy – a planter elite that controlled the economic, legislative, and political affairs of the island. During the eighteenth century the Barbadian plantocracy solidified its power, and in the process perpetuated the racial and class-based distinctions in Barbados. Ownership of land became concentrated in the hands of fewer than 100 of the colony's elite families, in contrast to the more than 700 landowning families in 1667. Members of the plantocracy firmly controlled the House of Assembly and the Legislative Council. They lived on a grand scale, building elaborate estates like Drax Hall and Nicholas Abbey, which still exist. They promoted slave reproduction in an effort to avoid dependence on the importation of slaves. By the beginning of the nineteenth century Barbados was the only island in the British Caribbean that was no longer dependent on slave imports. The British Parliament met with little resistance from Barbadian planters when it abolished the international slave trade in 1807.

Easter Rebellion

The 1807 ban posed no immediate threat to Barbadian planters, but it sent a glimmer of hope to slaves throughout the Caribbean. In the meantime slaves in Barbados were closely following the Haitian Revolution, the presence of abolitionist missionaries on Barbados, and antislavery debates in England and the United States. Their desire to be free culminated in the Easter Rebellion of 1816. Also known as Bussa's Insurrection, because it was led by an African-born slave named Bussa, the revolt began on Sunday, April 14, and engulfed the southern half of the island for more than three days.

The Easter Rebellion is considered the first large-scale slave insurrection in the British Caribbean. Between 500 and 1000 slaves were killed in the fighting; more than 140 slaves were executed; and 123 were forcibly removed from the colony. Frightened by the uprising and hoping to avoid future insurrections, officials in London insisted that the colonists implement reforms to ease the burdens of slavery. This policy, known then as amelioration, met with fierce resistance from Barbadian planters. But after a tumultuous debate the policy was approved by the Barbadian legislature. The 1825 Consolidated Slave Law, as the new legislation was called, established three "rights" for slaves: the right to own property; the right to testify in all court cases; and a reduction of the fees charged for manumission (a strategy used in the past to discourage white slaveholders from emancipating their slaves).

Emancipation and Apprenticeship

The 1816 insurrection and the Consolidated Slave Law advanced the crusade for freedom more than any other events in Barbadian history. Slaves became more defiant, and British abolitionists increased their pressure on Parliament, frequently citing the severity and repressiveness of slavery on the island. These factors, combined with two other major slave insurrections – in Demerara in 1823 and Jamaica in 1832 – moved the British Parliament to reconsider abolition. In 1833 it voted to abolish slavery in all British territories, including Barbados, where an estimated 83,150 slaves were emancipated.

To ease the burden of abolition on white planters, Great Britain imposed a program known as apprenticeship, which required slaves to enter into labor contracts as indentured servants for varying periods of time. In Barbados apprenticeship was implemented in a particularly cruel fashion. The 12-year tenure of labor contracts there was the longest in the British Caribbean. Black and colored laborers were paid just 9 to 11 pence per day, the lowest wages of all indentured workers in the region; were charged exorbitant rents; and were barred from participating in the island's educational systems. Great Britain repealed apprenticeship in 1838, but in 1838 and 1840 the Masters and Servant Act, also known as the Contract Law, institutionalized discrimination against black and colored workers in Barbados. Little changed over the next 60 years. Black and colored workers were confined to laboring on sugar plantations, and few earned enough to purchase their own land.

Black Empowerment

Toward the end of the nineteenth century, black and colored workers began to unite within a self-help movement inspired by

black activists throughout the Caribbean, including Marcus Garvey in Jamaica. The beginning of the twentieth century witnessed the emergence of "friendly societies" that provided insurance to the families of black workers who fell ill or died. Weekly dues, or premiums, were collected and deposited in the National Savings Bank of Barbados. These groups became so popular that in 1905 the plantocracy prohibited individual societies from holding more than one acre of land. By 1910 there were 110 friendly societies. Thirty-six years later there were 161 groups across the island, worth close to $130,217 and with more than 97,000 dues-paying members. In addition to the friendly societies, voluntary neighborhood associations (known as landships) and revivalist churches worked to empower blacks in Barbados during the first two decades of the twentieth century.

In 1919 a radical wing of the black empowerment movement emerged with the formation of the Barbados Labour Union. In that same year the *Barbados Herald*, a weekly newspaper representing the black working class, was founded. Five years later the Democratic League (DL) became the first political party in Barbados. Led by black activist Charles Duncan O'Neale, the DL fought during the 1920s and 1930s to end child labor and provide compulsory education for black youth. Black workers also contributed to the self-help movement by establishing the Workingmen's Association, the union arm of the DL, in 1926.

White planters reacted to the emergence of black political and economic consciousness by consolidating their political and economic power. Although a few blacks and coloreds from the DL held positions within the legislature, in the 1930s the government was still dominated by wealthy whites. A further challenge to black advancement came in 1934, when white sugar planters united to form the Barbados Produce Exporters Association (BPEA). The organization secretly agreed to lower wages, thus weakening the emerging strength of black labor. Black workers in Barbados, like their counterparts throughout the Caribbean during this period, responded in 1937 with a strike. The demonstrations were met with violent resistance from the police, leaving 14 strikers dead and 47 wounded.

A. Brunias pinx.t et sculp.t

THE BARBADOES MULATTO GIRL

This Plate is Dedicated to John Geo. Felton Esq.r by his most Obliged and devoted Serv.t A. Brunias.

LEFT: ***The Barbadoes Mulatto Girl*, a 1779 engraving by Agostino Brunias, depicts the mixture of indigenous peoples, Africans, and Europeans that still exists on Barbados.** *Image of the Black Project, Harvard University*

ABOVE: **More than eighty percent of Barbadians are of African descent.** *CORBIS/Dave B. Houser*

ABOVE: A man cycles along a street in St. Michael Parish, Barbados. *CORBIS/Tony Arruza*
RIGHT: Workers roll barrels along a loading dock at a rum refinery in Barbados. *CORBIS/Tony Arruza*

INDEPENDENCE

In 1938 black activist Grantley Adams and others institutionalized the demands of black labor by forming the Barbados Progressive League (later renamed the Barbados Labour Party). Working with the Democratic League, they registered black voters who could meet the government's income and property requirements. They achieved their greatest victory when the government announced in 1946 that it would introduce limited reforms. Another milestone was reached four years later when the government granted universal adult suffrage. Reforms continued throughout the 1950s, and in 1961 Barbados was granted self-rule. It became an independent state on November 30, 1966.

POST-INDEPENDENCE

Since 1966 Barbados has been a member of the British Commonwealth of Nations and has assumed a leadership role in the CARIBBEAN COMMUNITY (CARICOM). It has enjoyed a stable democratic society in which the Barbados Labour Party and the Democratic Labour Party have continued to share power peacefully. In 1986 Errol Barrow, leader of the Democratic Labour Party, was elected prime minister, but he died in 1987 and was replaced by Erskine Sandiford. In 1994 Sandiford was removed from power by a no-confidence vote in the House of Assembly and was replaced by Owen Arthur, a member of the Barbados Labour Party.

Barbados has fused two worlds, the African and the British, to create a vibrant nation and popular tourist destination. It still relies on its sugar cane exports, and labor remains a powerful political force. Education has been an important tool in empowering the island's black majority; Barbados boasts a literacy rate of 98 percent – one of the highest in the world. But not all Barbadians are beneficiaries of the island's political and economic stability; poverty is still a persistent problem for some.

Alonford James Robinson, Jr.

SEE ALSO

Netherlands Antilles; Slavery in Latin America and the Caribbean; Fugitive Slave Laws; Garvey, Marcus Mosiah; Apprenticeship in the British Caribbean; Black Codes in Latin America.

Europe

Barber, Francis (b. 1745, Jamaica; d. January 1801, Great Britain), Jamaican-born servant of Samuel Johnson in Great Britain.

Born in Jamaica around 1745, Francis Barber was baptized, educated, and brought to England by a West Indian slave owner, Colonel Bathurst, in 1752. Bathurst died shortly after their arrival, but not before freeing Barber. Bathurst's son found Barber work with the English author Samuel Johnson, who opposed the slave trade. At a time when black pages in their twenties were commonly deported because it was unfashionable to employ them after adolesence, it was particularly unusual that Johnson and Barber sustained a long and affectionate relationship.

Johnson, who had no children of his own, treated Barber as a son. From 1767 to 1772, he sent Barber to school, where he proved himself bright and articulate. Barber served Johnson for nearly 30 years, acting as his manservant and receiving and answering Johnson's letters. Barber left the Johnson household only twice: once to work for a pharmacy and once to run off to sea. This second time, in 1758, Johnson became distraught; admitting his "tenderness" for Barber, he called for his return.

Barber had an active social life with working-class blacks and whites, and in 1762 he married a white woman named Elizabeth. Together they had three children and continued to live in the Johnson household. The marriage of Barber to a white woman caused a scandal among Johnson's society friends, who accused Elizabeth of being a prostitute and derided Johnson for permitting them to live with him.

Johnson died in 1782, leaving Barber a generous inheritance of £70 per year. Johnson also gave Barber control over some of his manuscripts and artifacts, an act that outraged some of Johnson's admirers, particularly his first biographer, Sir John Hawkins. After Johnson's death, the Barbers moved out of the household, but found it difficult to live on their inheritance and suffered from poverty and poor health. Barber's son, Samuel, became a Methodist lay minister; after Barber's death, Elizabeth and their daughter, Anne, set up a school to support themselves.

Leyla Keough

See Also

Transatlantic Slave Trade.

North America

Barber, Jesse Max (b. July 5, 1878, Blackstock, S.C.; d. Sept. 20, 1949, Philadelphia, Pa.), African American journalist, managing editor of *Voice of the Negro*, and radical thinker who argued for black civil rights.

Jesse Max Barber was the son of former slaves. He trained as a teacher in Columbia, South Carolina, at Benedict College. His literary career began as editor of the *University Journal* at Virginia Union University in Richmond, Virginia.

Immediately after his graduation from Virginia Union in 1903, Barber began a literary career as managing editor of a new black journal, *Voice of the Negro*, founded in Atlanta in January 1904. While the *Voice* initially sought a moderate position between accommodationists and activists, Barber made the journal a progressive forum. He was known at the time as a politically aware, radical thinker who sided with his friend W. E. B. Du Bois against Booker T. Washington. Writers for the *Voice* included Pauline Hopkins, Du Bois, Washington, Charles W. Chesnutt, and Paul Laurence Dunbar, as well as Barber. Barber used his journal to argue for black civil rights and to chronicle historical events so that, in his words, "it will become a kind of documentation for the coming generations."

Relocated to Chicago after the Atlanta race riots of September 1906, the *Voice* ceased publication in 1907. Barber subsequently entered the dentistry profession but remained committed to social activism, serving on the executive committee of the National Association for the Advancement of Colored People from 1919 to 1921. Barber continued his journalism and published in the magazine *Abbott's Monthly* between 1930 and 1933.

See Also

Atlanta Riot of 1906; Chesnutt, Charles Waddell; Chicago, Illinois; Du Bois, William Edward Burghardt (W. E. B.); Hopkins, Pauline Elizabeth; Richmond, Virginia; Washington, Booker Taliaferro.

Latin America and the Caribbean

Barbosa, José Celso (b. 1857, Bayamón, Puerto Rico; d. 1921, Santurce, Puerto Rico), Afro-Puerto Rican doctor, politician, and legislator who struggled for the island's autonomy from Spain and defended the annexation to the United States after the Spanish-Cuban-American War in 1898. He played a key role in the politics of this transitional period, denouncing the Creoles' political aspirations. He also represented the complexities and contradictions confronted by black Puerto Ricans of his time regarding race issues.

José Celso Barbosa's achievements were not typical of blacks in Puerto Rico at the turn of the century. He represented the self-made man who came from humble origins. He had the opportunity to study at the only institution of secondary education in the island, thanks to the determination of his aunt. He completed his studies in the Jesuit seminary before going to the University of Michigan Medical School in Ann Arbor, where he graduated in 1880. His experience in the United States made him an admirer of republican democratic ideals for social equality and justice.

Upon his return to Puerto Rico, Barbosa started his medical practice and became a member of a Masonic lodge, which played an important role in the development of subversive political activities on the island. He was one of the founders of the Cooperativists Movement in 1893 and a writer for local newspapers. He also served as delegate in the constitution of the Autonomist Party in 1887. Due to ideological differences with the party, in 1897 he founded the Partido Autonomista Ortodoxo (Autonomist Orthodox Party).

The Spanish Cuban American war of 1898 marked a turning point in the island's history when Spain ceded Puerto Rico to the United States. Barbosa, who first believed that Puerto Rico had to be independent from Spanish colonial rule, then defended the idea that the island should become a state. In 1900 he founded the Puerto Rican chapter of the United States Republican Party and was appointed as a member of the executive council by U.S. president William McKinley.

His ideals were often questioned because he was black and defended the island's annexation to an openly racist country. Many considered him a traitor to his race. This juxtaposition is emblematic of the contradictions concerning race definitions and relations in Puerto Rico.

In writings that appeared mostly in the party's newspaper, *El Tiempo,* from 1915 to 1920, Barbosa defended his political beliefs and opinions. He thought there was no color problem in Puerto Rico. For him, racial and class prejudices were mostly an individual issue, not a social problem that existed during the Spanish regime as well. Barbosa believed that superiority came from intellectual and moral preparation and the environment in which an individual and society developed, not from the color of one's skin. At the same time, he praised African Americans for overcoming prejudice and repression in their struggle for equality.

Mayda Grano de Oro

Latin America and the Caribbean

Barbosa, Rui (b. November 5, 1849, Salvador, Bahia, Brazil; d. March 1, 1923, Petrópolis, Rio de Janeiro, Brazil), Brazilian politician, jurist, and journalist; a prominent abolitionist who ultimately destroyed many of the government's records of the slave trade.

Born in Salvador, BAHIA, Rui Barbosa de Oliveira studied at the law academies of Recife and São Paulo, where he met Antônio de Castro Alves, the "Poet of the Slaves," and future abolitionist JOAQUIM NABUCO. Barbosa's abolitionist campaign began in 1869, when he organized a conference titled *O Elemento Servil* (The Servile Element). Although the slave trade had been outlawed on November 7, 1831, slaves who had entered BRAZIL before that time remained in bondage, and many Africans had since been illegally enslaved. At the *Elemento Servil* conference, Barbosa condemned slavery on legal grounds by invoking the 1831 law.

In the following years Barbosa frequently challenged the proslavery Conservative Party. During the provincial elections of 1874 he criticized the Free Womb Law, which freed the children of all female slaves, as "a superficial improvement." In 1884 he joined a reform cabinet led by Manoel Dantas that outlined steps to gradually end slavery. The resultant Dantas Bill called for the freeing of slaves age 60 or older with no monetary compensation for their owners. Dantas's cabinet was defeated by Conservatives and dissident Liberals in 1885 and replaced by a cabinet headed by José Antônio Saraiva. The new administration radically revised the Dantas Bill in favor of slaveholders' interests. For example, it provided for the freeing of elderly slaves but only after an unpaid service period of three years (or until they reached the age of 65). Barbosa called the revised bill "a surrender to slaveocrats" and compared part of it, which made aiding runaway slaves a crime subject to high fines and imprisonment, to the American Fugitive Slave Act. Despite criticism from Barbosa and other abolitionists, the bill became the Saraiva-Cotegipe Law on September 28, 1885.

Over time, Barbosa's abolitionism became increasingly radical. In 1881, for example, he declared that his "position [would] always be… with the emancipation movement." His antislavery stance thwarted his political career, and he increasingly turned to the press to advance his abolitionist views. Working with Castro Alves and Nabuco, he published articles in the journal *Radical Paulistano*. Thereafter, he contributed numerous articles to the Liberal Party's *Diário da Bahia*, his own journal *O País*, and the *Jornal do Comércio*.

Early in 1891, three years after the abolition of slavery in Brazil, Barbosa, as minister of finance for the provisional government of the first republic (1889-1891), ordered that the principal slave-trade archives in the *Tesouro Nacional* be burned. Some historians have seen this as part of the *branqueamento* program, which aimed to help Brazil forget its African past and make it a "whiter" nation. Others argue that Barbosa burned the records to prevent slaveholders from claiming compensation for the loss of their slaves. Despite his contributions to Brazil's abolitionist movement, Barbosa is more often remembered negatively for this destruction of invaluable historical information about Brazilian slavery.

Aaron Myers

SEE ALSO

Slavery in Latin America and the Caribbean; Fugitive Slave Laws; Abolition and Emancipation in Latin America and the Caribbean; Whitening; White Abolitionists in Brazil.

Latin America and the Caribbean

Barcala, Lorenzo (1775-1835), known as the Black Caballero for the leading role he played in the Viceroyalty of la Plata's war of independence from Spain. Barcala was named colonel for his leadership. Barcala was born a slave in Mendoza, Argentina, and was freed in 1813 (*see* URUGUAY).

Africa

Barghash ibn Said (b. 1834; d. March 27, 1888, ZANZIBAR), sultan of Zanzibar.

The sultan of Zanzibar at the height of its prosperity, Sayyid Barghash ibn Said ultimately saw his realm humbled and partitioned by European colonialists. After his father, SA'ID SAYYID IBN SULTAN, died in 1856, Barghash tried to usurp the throne from his older brother, Majid ibn Sa'id. His attempt failed, and Barghash was exiled to Bombay. He returned to Zanzibar two years later and ascended the throne peacefully after his brother's death in 1870.

In 1872 a hurricane destroyed Zanzibar's navy and many of the island's valuable clove and coconut plantations. To aid recovery from this disaster, Barghash allied himself with British forces in the region and signed antislavery treaties in exchange for funding and military equipment. This support enabled Barghash to consolidate his hold on the coastal mainland. By the late 1870s the tariffs and tributes he had collected from mainland possessions substantially increased his revenue and compensated for the loss of the slave trade. Although his power never extended far inland, agreements with Arab-Swahili traders such as TIPPU TIP enabled the sultan to acquire valuable goods, such as ivory and rubber, which he sold to Europeans.

By 1882 the Europeans, particularly the Germans, began to challenge Barghash's territorial claims. Heavily dependent on the British, his supposed allies, the sultan believed that they would help defend his territory. But he was mistaken. In 1886 the British secretly met with the Germans and divided the sultanate's possessions between themselves. Thereafter, the sultanate consisted solely of the island of Zanzibar, which became a British protectorate after the death of Barghash in 1888.

Elizabeth Heath

SEE ALSO

Ivory Trade.

Africa

Bari, ethnic group of north Central Africa.

The Bari primarily inhabit the region just east of the Mountain Nile in southern SUDAN and northern UGANDA. They speak a Nilo-Saharan language. Approximately 100,000 people consider themselves Bari.

SEE ALSO

Languages, African: An Overview; Nile River.

Africa

Bariba (also known as the Borgawa, the Bargu, and the Batonun), ethnic group of West Africa.

The Bariba primarily inhabit northern BENIN, southeastern BURKINA FASO, northestern NIGERIA, and northern TOGO. They speak a Niger-Congo language belonging to the Voltaic group and comprise two distinct groups: the BUSA of Nigeria and the Nikki of Benin. Approximately 700,000 people consider themselves Bariba.

SEE ALSO

Languages, African: An Overview.

Latin America and the Caribbean

Barnet, Miguel (b. 1940), Cuban writer and ethnologist; author of *Biografía de un cimarrón* (Autobiography of a Runaway Slave, 1966), which recounts Esteban Montejo's accounts of his life as a runaway slave in Cuba and as a soldier in the Spanish-Cuban-American War (1895-1898). Other works by Barnet include *Canción de Raquel* (Rachel's Song, 1969), *Mapa del tiempo* (Map of Time, 1989); and *Oficio de angel* (Angel's Craft, 1989) (*see* ESTEBAN MONTEJO).

North America

Barnett, Claude Albert (b. 1889, Sanford, Fla.; d. August 2, 1967, Chicago, Ill.), founder of the Associated Negro Press (ANP), which distributed news to black newspapers for half a century.

Claude Albert Barnett left Florida at an early age when he was sent to live with his grandparents and other relatives in suburban Chicago. He returned to the South to study engineering at Alabama's Tuskegee Institute, from which he graduated in 1906. Back in Chicago, working as a postal clerk, he saw a wide range of advertising journals and decided to make a career in advertising. In 1913 he produced a series of photographs of famous blacks, which he succeeded in selling through the mail and which increased his interest in business.

Five years later Barnett and several other entrepreneurs formed the Kashmir Chemical Company, which sold cosmetics. Barnett left the post office, took the job of advertising manager at Kashmir, and toured the country selling cosmetics as well as his photographs of famous blacks. In each town he visited the black newspaper, hoping to bargain for advertising space. These forays earned only mild success for Kashmir, but Barnett discovered that the newspapers, too poor to afford newswire services, were hungry for national news. He returned to Kashmir and persuaded its board of directors to fund a black news service. In 1919, the ANP began operation.

The ANP, like its model the Associated Press, was a cooperative: newspapers paid a fee to join and in turn contributed articles about important local events. Barnett oversaw a small staff in Chicago who collected, edited, and two or three times weekly mailed articles to the ANP's subscribers. Most of the articles focused on news affecting blacks, often stories that the white press had overlooked. After several years of steady growth, the ANP maintained a few of its own reporters in major American cities and foreign countries.

By World War II about 200 black newspapers subscribed to the ANP. During the war, Barnett and other blacks pressured the federal government to accredit black journalists as war correspondents, partly to cover the war but also to cover race relations in the armed services. After the war, the ANP expanded its distribution service to Africa, where it offered articles in both French and English.

Influenced by his years at Tuskegee, Barnett also worked to improve the condition of black tenant farmers and sharecroppers in the South. In the early 1940s he offered to serve, and was accepted, as a consultant to the United States Department of Agriculture (USDA). For the next decade, he advocated policies that would give poor farmers a chance to own their land and the credit to develop it. His efforts, however, did little to improve the condition of Southern farmers. In 1953, with the inauguration of Republican president Dwight Eisenhower, Barnett was dismissed.

As the power of black newspapers waned in the 1960s, so too did the ANP. By the time Barnett died of a cerebral hemorrhage in 1967, the ANP's subscribers had dwindled to about 100, and the organization ceased altogether shortly after his death.

See Also
Chicago, Illinois; Tuskegee University.

North America

Barnett, Etta Moten (b. November 24, 1902, San Antonio, Tex.), African American singer, actress, and activist for women's issues.

The daughter of a minister, Etta Moten Barnett married at 17 and had three children before divorcing six years later. After her marriage ended, she attended the University of Kansas and in 1931 received a B.F.A. in music. Her senior college recital led to an invitation to join the Eva Jessye Choir in New York.

In New York, Barnett appeared in the Broadway musicals *Fast and Furious* (1931), *Zombie* (1932), *Sugar Hill* (1932), and *Lysistrata* (1933). She also sang on the soundtracks of several films and appeared in the movies *Gold Diggers of 1933* (1933) and *Flying Down to Rio* (1934).

In 1934 she married Claude Barnett, founder of the Associated Negro Press. During the next several years, Etta Moten Barnett gave concerts and lectures throughout the country, including a private White House concert for President and Mrs. Franklin D. Roosevelt and their guests.

In 1942 Barnett joined the Broadway production of *Porgy and Bess*. During the next two decades, she traveled to Africa with her husband on several diplomatic trips. Barnett also became active in international women's issues as a member of Alpha Kappa Alpha, the Links, the National Association for the Advancement of Colored People (NAACP), and the National Council of Negro Women.

Lisa Clayton Robinson

See Also
National Association for the Advancement of Colored People.

Latin America and the Caribbean

Barreto, Ray, (b. 1929), percussionist and bandleader, renowned for his contributions to Latin jazz and salsa. Born in New York of Puerto Rican heritage, Barreto joined Tito Puente's big band in the 1950s. In the 1960s he established the Ray Barreto Orchestra, which recorded under the Fania label. In 1992 he established the jazz band New World Spirit (*see* Salsa).

See Also
Salsa Music.

Latin America and the Caribbean

Barrios, Pilar (b. 1889, Montevideo, Uruguay; d. 1974), Afro-Uruguayan poet and longtime contributor to *Nuestra Raza*, one of the most prestigious black newspapers in South America.

Dubbed by the literary critic Richard Jackson the "dean of Afro-Uruguayan poets," Pilar Barrios was a key figure in the development of the Uruguayan black press. He got his start writing poetry for *Nuestra Raza*, the longest-running black periodical in Uruguay, founded by his sister Maria Esperanza Barrios in 1917. Thanks to their efforts; those of another contributing brother, Ventura; and a host of illustrious black writers like Elemo Cabral, Juan Julio Arrascaeta, and Virginia Brindis de Salas, the journal defended black intellectual potential and achievements in art, music, and science. The same motive would continue to dominate Barrios's own poetry throughout his lifetime.

With the help of *Nuestra Raza*, Barrios began to publish books of poetry. The first, titled *Piel negra* (1947; Black Skin), focused on a variety of themes, including "black pride, liberty, equality, fraternity... antiwar sentiments, a hatred of injustice and tyranny," as Jackson points out. Many of the poems are directed to black youth and black women, encouraging their intellectual and creative endeavors. He was likewise keenly aware of black heroes of the diaspora, dedicating poems to both Langston Hughes (1902-1967), with whom he had corresponded, and Nicolás Guillén (1902-1989), whom he had met during Guillén's visit to Uruguay. Despite such progressive motifs, Barrios stuck to the traditional, established versification that typified turn-of-the-century poetry, and tended to shy away from formal avant-garde techniques.

His second book, *Mis cantos* (My Songs), was published two years later in 1949. While his previous poetry tended to focus mostly on black pride and intellectual achievements, this second volume took a more universal turn. Earlier, he had confronted racial discrimination outright; in *Mis cantos* he softened his tone, invoking "brotherhood" with whites and aligning himself with more dominant national and continental concerns.

Campo afuera (Outside Country), published in 1959, represented a significant departure from his first two works, as it was devoted entirely to *gaucho* (Argentinian and Uruguayan cowboys or frontiersmen) poetry, and was written in that dialect. In the view of some critics, Barrios had forsaken the black colloquial speech and consciousness that characterized some of his earlier production to adopt the gaucho, the regional symbol par excellence of a white identity in the entire Rio de la Plata area (Argentina and Uruguay). However, as Jackson points out, there are poems in *Campo afuera*, such as "Yo opino así" (I Think This Way), which continue to insist on issues of black identity.

Politically, Barrios was an active member of the Partido Autóctono Negro (the Indigenous Black Party), the first black Uruguayan political party, until its demise in 1937 after a disheartening loss at the national polls. He also helped found CIAPEN (Círculo de Intelectuales Artistas Perodistas y Escritores Negros – Circle of Black Intellectuals, Artists, Journalists, and Writers), an early professional organization that fostered lively intellectual and cultural debates within the community. Though relatively little has been written about his work, every source available hails him as a key founder of an Afro-Uruguayan literary culture, imbued with a deep social consciousness, committed to making itself seen and heard both on a national and international scale.

Joy Elizondo

North America

Barry, Marion Shepilov, Jr.

(b. March 6, 1936, Itta Bena, Miss.), four-time mayor of Washington, D.C., and founding member of the Student Nonviolent Coordinating Committee.

Marion Barry's 1994 election to a fourth term as mayor of WASHINGTON, D.C., three years after his conviction for cocaine possession, was yet another twist in the turbulent career of the sharecropper's son from the Mississippi Delta. Born near the small town of Itta Bena, he moved to MEMPHIS, TENNESSEE, at the age of five and grew up amid poverty, segregation, and racism. Despite these circumstances, he excelled academically and became the first member of his family to attend college. At LeMoyne College, a racially mixed institution in Memphis, Barry joined the campus chapter of the National Association for the Advancement of Colored People (NAACP), becoming its president his senior year.

Barry received his bachelor's degree in chemistry in 1958, and that fall began postgraduate study at the historically black FISK UNIVERSITY in Nashville. He organized the campus's first NAACP chapter and helped stage nonviolent SIT-INS at Nashville restaurants. At a Southern Christian Leadership Conference (SCLC) gathering in 1960, Barry first heard the Reverend Martin Luther King Jr. speak and was impressed by the "new kind of leadership" King offered. Shortly afterward, Barry helped found and became the first chairman of the STUDENT NONVIOLENT COORDINATING COMMITTEE (SNCC).

For the next several years, Barry continued to work for civil rights in the Deep South, abandoning his doctoral studies in 1964 to devote more time to SNCC. In 1965 Barry moved to Washington, D.C., where he organized a massive boycott of the city's transit system, and a year later founded the Free D.C. movement in an effort to gain political control for the city's residents, long ruled by Congress in a quasicolonial system. Proclaiming that it was time for African Americans to concentrate on "economic and political power," in 1967 Barry resigned from SNCC and founded Youth Pride, a nonprofit organization devoted to finding jobs for young African Americans. After its initial success, he expanded into profit-making ventures with Pride Economic Enterprises.

Barry served three terms on the city's school board before running for city council in 1974. He served two terms on the council before running for mayor, an office that had, with the advent of home rule, increased in political and financial power. In 1978, still recuperating from a gunshot wound received when terrorists raided the city council building, Barry won a narrow victory, with many observers citing the support of white voters as the decisive factor. Barry depended on the loyalty of the city's black majority for his reelection in 1982, following a first term marred by fiscal disaster and increasing crime rates. Barry's second and third terms, despite some successes in economic growth and job creation, were characterized by scandal and accusations of wrongdoing, including rumors of illegal drug use.

In January 1990 FBI agents, after offering Barry crack cocaine, videotaped the mayor smoking the drug in the hotel room of a former girlfriend. Despite charges of entrapment, Barry was convicted of misdemeanor possession and sentenced to six months in prison. Following his release in 1991, Barry began his political comeback with reelection to the city council in 1992, this time representing the city's poorest neighborhoods. Two years later, crediting Narcotics Anonymous for his rehabilitation and invoking themes of redemption, Marion Barry defeated incumbent Sharon Pratt Kelly to win a fourth term as the city's mayor.

Kate Tuttle

SEE ALSO

King, Martin Luther, Jr.; National Association for the Advancement of Colored People; Southern Christian Leadership Conference.

North America

Barthé, Richmond

(b. January 28, 1901, Bay Saint Louis, Miss.; d. March 6, 1989, Altadena, Calif.), a sculptor of the HARLEM RENAISSANCE era whose sculptures and busts defied universal negative representations of African Americans and other individuals of African descent. Barthé introduced such themes as balance, rhythm, grace, and beauty to the image of his subjects.

Richmond Barthé grew up in Bay Saint Louis, Mississippi, and NEW ORLEANS, LOUISIANA. His father died at the age of 22, one month after Barthé's birth. His mother, Marie Clementine Roboteau, raised him alone, nurturing his interest in the arts. He also received encouragement from fellow townspeople and the nuns at his parochial school. In early childhood, Barthé began drawing and painting watercolor scenes. When he was 12 years old, Barthé's work was exhibited at the Mississippi County Fair.

In 1915 Barthé moved to New Orleans, where he painted and worked as a butler. At the age of 18, he won the blue ribbon for his submission to a parish contest. During the nine years that Barthé spent in New Orleans, he attempted to enter art school but his admission was denied because he was black. Lyle Saxon of the *Times-Picayune* wielded his influence to gain entry for Barthé into a New Orleans art school, but his efforts failed.

Eventually, Barthé focused his interest on schools within the Chicago area. With the help of Father Harry Kane, a Catholic priest who was impressed by Barthé's paintings, Barthé entered the Chicago Art Institute in 1924 with the intention of becoming a painter. As he followed the curriculum for painting majors, two occurrences shaped his interest in sculpting. The first was an assignment for his anatomy professor, Charles Schroeder; the second was his participation in Negro Week.

As part of an assignment intended to enhance his understanding of anatomy, Barthé designed two clay heads. The final result of these two pieces showcased his deep understanding of three-dimensional pieces. Barthé viewed the successful reception of these works as an incentive to launch a sculpting career, which he did by participating in the exhibition mounted in Chicago during Negro Week in 1927.

Barthé graduated from the Chicago Art Institute in February 1929 and moved to New York City that same year. The time after his relocation to New York proved to be prosperous for him; his work was widely honored and exhibited. For example, in 1932 he sculpted *Blackberry Woman*, and *African Dancer* in 1933. The Whitney Museum of American Art purchased these two pieces in 1935. The Caz Delbo Galleries granted Barthé his first solo show in 1934, and he also gained greater recognition after his 1939 exhibit at the Arden Galleries in New York. As a result, he was nominated for and accepted a Guggenheim Fellowship in 1940 and 1941.

He captured the complexities of movement in *The Boxer* (1943), and in 1946 he commemorated such African American achievers as George Washington Carver and Booker T. Washington. The bust of Booker T. Washington was created for the Hall of Fame of New York University. Barthé also modeled a portrait of Othello after the actor Paul Robeson for the Actors Equity. His other commissions included a bas-relief of Arthur Brisbane for New York's Central Park. He designed a large frieze, *Green Pastures: The Walls of Jericho*, for the Harlem River Housing Project, and the General Toussaint L'Ouverture Monument for Port-au-Prince, Haiti.

In 1947, at the apex of his career, when such phrases as "leading moderns of American art" were used in connection with his name, Barthé relocated to Jamaica, West Indies. He exchanged the accelerated pace of city life for the tranquillity of the Jamaican countryside, where he resided until 1969. After he left Jamaica, Barthé lived in Europe. There, in addition to spending time with friends, he studied the art and culture of the masters of the Italian Renaissance such as Donatello and Michelangelo. He returned to the United States in 1976, stayed for a brief time in Queens, New York, and then settled permanently in Altadena, California.

Richmond Barthé's career spanned more than 60 years. The art world consistently responded to his work with acclaim. It recognized him for his impressive bronzes and immense statues by electing him to the National Academy of Arts and Letters in 1915; he was the first black sculptor to receive this honor. His work has also been incorporated into the collections of the Metropolitan Museum of Art, the Pennsylvania Museum of Art, the Virginia Museum of Fine Arts, and the Museum of the Art Institute of Chicago.

Ironically, despite Barthé's fame, he never achieved the financial success that often complements such visibility. Rather, the hardships of his final days were alleviated by the assistance of actors James Garner and Esther Jones. Upon Barthé's death in 1989, Garner donated Barthé's remaining works to the Museum of African Art in Los Angeles and the Schomburg Center in New York City.

See Also
Chicago, Illinois; Washington, Booker Taliaferro; Schomburg Library.

Africa

Barth, Heinrich **(b. 1821, Hamburg, Germany; d. 1865, Berlin, Germany), German explorer of western and northern Africa.**

During the mid-nineteenth century Heinrich Barth traveled widely in northern Africa and the central Sudan, and authored some of the earliest and most comprehensive works on North and West African history. The son of a German businessman, Barth earned a degree in classics and linguistics at the University of Berlin. He completed his studies in 1845 and subsequently spent two years traveling in northern Africa, where he perfected his Arabic and kept a detailed diary of his trip. After a disappointing experience teaching in Germany, he accepted an offer to join a British expedition to the central Sudan.

At first led by James Richardson, the expedition left Tripoli in 1850. Within a year Richardson died and Barth assumed command. During the next four years Barth led the group through present-day Chad, Cameroon, Nigeria, Niger, and Mali and visited all of the major towns, including Zinder, Sokoto, Tombouctou (Timbuktu), and Kano. The group returned to England in 1855, where Barth recorded his memoirs of the journey. This work provided the basis for a five-volume series, *Travels and Discoveries in North and Central Africa*, chronicling the history and linguistics of the areas he visited. Although some of his remarks on the Sokoto Caliphate have recently been challenged, Barth's work remains an invaluable resource for African scholars.

Elizabeth Heath

See Also
Sokoto Caliphate; Tombouctou, Mali; Tripoli, Libya; Zinder, Niger.

Latin America and the Caribbean

Baseball in Latin America and the Caribbean, **a sport that has become a popular pastime.**

In June 1866 sailors from the United States who were importing sugar from Cuba invited local Cuban dockworkers to play baseball. Thus began the Caribbean's initiation to the game, less than 30 years after its North American inception (*see* Baseball in the United States). In the next few years baseball was pushed to the fore of Cuban consciousness by visiting North American businessmen, United States Marines, and wealthy Cuban students who had played at U.S. schools. By decade's end the development of a local talent pool was under way, and with the emerging political turmoil in the Caribbean around the turn of the century, both migrating Cubans and occupying Marines took the new pastime across the Caribbean basin.

At first baseball was played by Cuba's wealthy class, lending it the exclusivity of polo, cycling, cricket, soccer, and other European sports that had taken root in the clubs of the Caribbean's urban elite. But it quickly spread to all classes in both rural and urban Cuba, due in part to its accessibility: the poor were easily able to improvise baseball fields, gloves, bats, and balls. It now seems a matter of course that baseball became a "game for the masses."

From the outset baseball carried political undertones for imperialist Spain and colonial Cuba. As tensions rose during the first decade of Cuban baseball play, the sport became "racially mixed," with both "light" and "dark-skinned" participants playing together and often uniting in solidarity against Spain, from which Cuba sought independence. It had even become popular in the camps of the *mambises*, the predominantly black and mulatto guerrilla fighters who aggressively fought for Cuba's independence (*see* Cuba). This crossing of baseball and politics was no less fortunate than in the case of Emilio Sabourín, a professional who played in the first formal Cuban ball game in 1868, and who was later caught donating baseball proceeds to the independence movement. In so doing he incurred the wrath of Spanish officials and was jailed for life. Subsequently, the Spanish attempted to ban the new pastime from the island.

But these troubles only stimulated baseball's spread. Cuba's first fight for independence, the Ten Years' War (1868-1878), prompted Cubans to take refuge in neighboring regions. Sharing a common language and other cultural similarities, these exiles were well suited to teach the game to other Caribbeans and Latin Americans. Julio Santana, a former sportswriter in the Dominican Republic, underscored the Cuban contribution, as quoted by writer and historian Rob Ruck in his book *The Tropic of Baseball* (1991): "It is much the same as that which happened with Christianity. Jesus could be compared to the North Americans, but the apostles were the ones that spread the faith, and the apostles of baseball were the Cubans. They went out into the world to preach the gospel of baseball. Even though the Dominican Republic and Puerto Rico were occupied by the

North Americans, the Cubans brought baseball here first, and to Mexico and Venezuela, too."

As a result of the Ten Years' War, several thousand Cubans migrated to the Dominican Republic. Two of the many legacies they brought were their ability to grow sugar cane and their love of baseball. In 1891 Ignacio and Ubaldo Aloma, two well-established iron-working Cuban brothers, formed several teams in Santo Domingo. That year they played the first organized game, using a ball procured from a sailor aboard a nearby North American ship. The clubs comprised mostly Cubans, but the rosters included a few Dominicans who, like the first ball players in Cuba, hailed predominantly from wealthy families and from U.S. schools. The progeny of the lower classes, however, were not far behind. Their emulation of the Cubans only kindled their enthusiasm for the sport. Around this time another Cuban, Dr. Samuel Mendoza y Ponce de Leon, was at work in the country's interior, where he organized another pair of clubs. Cubans and Dominicans of all classes soon created a more sophisticated system of teams and tournaments. In 1907 Dominicans saw the establishment of their first professional league.

By then baseball had made its way across the Caribbean basin. It went to Mexico via U.S. railroad workers, who played with their counterparts as early as the 1880s. Though that country's chief pastime remains soccer, baseball still predominates in the Yucatán Peninsula, where players learned the game from Cubans. According to legend, the origins of baseball in the Yucatán are traced to a June day in 1890 when three Cuban brothers – Juan Francisco, Fernando, and Eduardo Urzáiz Rodriguez – stepped off a boat in Mérida on the peninsula and started playing ball in the street. Cubans also introduced the game to Venezuela, when Emílio Cramer brought it to Caracas in 1895. Santana was correct in saying that Cubans ushered baseball into Puerto Rico, but only partially. In 1898 a Spanish diplomat who had learned to play on a previous assignment in Cuba brought baseball to the island.

After the Spanish-Cuban-American War (1895-1898), contact with baseball-playing U.S. Marines became, for most of the Caribbean, inevitable. Between 1898 and 1933 Marines landed in ten different Caribbean-basin nations a total of 34 times. To help morale during longer occupations, soldiers often played baseball. In the four countries where Cubans played a primary role in teaching the game, U.S. troops helped to shape its development. In the Dominican Republic, for example, games among Dominicans were frequent and high spirited. For the Dominicans the competition became a means of expression: beating the Marines, the representatives of neocolonialism, held a distinct, patriotic significance. In this regard Marines left their imprimatur on the island, for when they vacated after an eight-year stay, baseball was wending its way into Dominican culture.

The tumultuous political and economic situation of the first decades of the twentieth century left Caribbean and Latin ball players with few other career options. At the same time, both Caribbeans and Latin Americans were barred, like their African American counterparts, from the game's most exclusive league – Major League Baseball (MLB). But during the opening decades of the twentieth century, professional leagues arose in Puerto Rico, Mexico, Colombia, Nicaragua, Panama, and Venezuela. These leagues were typically closely associated with particular industries – a Nicaraguan coffee manufacturer, a Cuban rum company, a Dominican sugar refinery, for example – which compensated players with work, if not with money. As the game generated more gate revenue, the leagues grew independent of industry. Inter-Caribbean competition ensued, yielding intense nationalistic rivalries among the players and the spectators of the respective countries.

Caribbean teams began "barnstorming," or playing exhibition games, around the turn of the century. Making regular trips across the Caribbean, Latin America, and Central America, the players further increased the sport's popularity. In 1905 the Cuban Stars were the first team to tour the United States. The Stars played in mostly black-inhabited areas and proved to be a popular success. In 1920, when Andrew "Rube" Foster, a ball player-turned-entrepreneur, formed his Negro Leagues, he welcomed the Stars. He also formally assimilated their contemporaries, the New York Cubans. Foster, said to be a shrewd businessman, knew that the Cubans would continue to be a popular draw with the African American community. He also knew that they would play for little pay.

When the Negro Leagues closed for the season, the best players usually signed with Caribbean winter league teams. "Winterball," as it is still called today, is played from November to February in most Caribbean countries, wherever baseball is played – Puerto Rico, the Dominican Republic, Colombia, Venezuela, Mexico, Honduras, and Nicaragua. Winterball has secured an important place in baseball history, for during the first half of the twentieth century it was the only racially integrated baseball. Major league owners claimed that black ball players could not compete with whites, but winters in the Caribbean proved a cogent counterpoint. For a few months each year, the Caribbean leagues received an influx of the best black and white U.S. baseball players. From the major leagues came Carl Hubbel, Ty Cobb, Tris Speaker, Christy Mathewson, and other future Hall of Famers, all seizing the opportunity to supplement their salaries and hone their skills during the major league off-season. They often found a higher caliber of competition than they were accustomed to.

Most black players could not afford to pass up the opportunity to play during the winter. Barred from the major leagues but competitive with its best players in "winterball" were such stars of the Negro Leagues and barnstorming circuit stars as Josh Gibson, James "Cool" Papa Bell, Satchel Paige, and Cuba's legendary Martín Dihigo. For many, the Caribbean offered an opportunity to compete for enthusiastic fans, play for money, and be free of the racism that pervaded their lives in the United States.

After the Cuban Revolution in 1959, North American players stopped traveling to Cuba. More players spent winters in the Dominican Republic and Puerto Rico, which hosted the strongest leagues. The leagues sustained their significance, and during the 1960s – long after the American major leagues were racially integrated – stars such as Juan Marichal, Felipe Alou, and Mateo Alou returned to the Dominican to play before their hometown fans. The Dominican season began on October 2, the birthday of Gen. Rafael Trujillo, the Dominican dictator, and lasted until February, when the winner of the playoffs vied with other Caribbean winter league teams for the Caribbean championship. During the 1960s and 1970s the caliber of play stayed very high as North American players, both black and white, continued to embrace the concept of playing year-round. Notables included Frank Howard, Willie Stargell, Phil Niekro, Dave Parker, and Gaylord Perry.

The leagues' makeup changed considerably during the 1980s, however, when major league owners began to offer greater pay and asked their players to rest during the MLB off-season. This posed a difficult situation for Caribbean players in the United States, who were expected to play for their homeland. They were often torn between an allegiance to their country and the pressure from the major league teams that paid them. The stress proved so great for Marichal that one winter he stayed in San Francisco in order to avoid criticism from his Dominican fans. The leagues continue today but with a different purpose. Where Hall of Fame players once competed, the leagues now feature mostly up-and-coming Caribbeans, U.S. minor leaguers, and young Japanese prospects.

In the United States, Caribbean ball players played on either side of the racial divide created by segregation, depending on the color of their skin. The first

Caribbean to play professionally was Esteban Bellàn, a Cuban who debuted with the Troy Haymakers in 1871. Reportedly of African descent, Bellàn played before professional baseball imposed its all-white standard. For baseball, official segregation came around the turn of the century. But between Bellàn's debut and the year 1946, 49 Caribbeans "passed" for white – most were Cubans. Most of these careers were short-lived. The first to succeed Bellàn was Luis Castro, a Colombian who, like Bellàn, attended school in the United States. He played only part of the summer of 1902 on Connie Mack's Philadelphia Athletics. The first Caribbean players of any talent came nine years later when two Cubans, Rafael Almeida and Armando Marsans, signed with the Cincinnati Reds. In retrospect, their appearance in the league helps to illuminate the confusion the white press faced during segregation in identifying the Caribbean players' racial background. One Cincinnati newspaper presented Almeida and Marsans as "Castilian," meaning that they were descended from Castile, a region of Spain, so as not to offend the city's racial sensibilities.

The most successful segregation-era player was perhaps Adolfo Luque, a Cuban pitcher who played 20 major league seasons. He had his best season in 1923 when he pitched for the Cincinnati Reds. He led the National League with 27 wins and a 1.93 earned run average. In 1933 he shut out the Washington Senators in relief in the seventh game of the World Series. The Senators' owner, Clark Griffith, quickly deployed Joe "Papa Joe" Cambria, a Negro League and winterball star-turned-scout, to Cuba. He signed several Cubans to contracts with the Senators. Like Almeida, Marsans, and Luque, these players were primarily light-skinned.

In 1947 Jackie Robinson broke the MLB color barrier. Though this led to the demise of the Negro Leagues, the transfer of talent came slowly. In the year of Robinson's debut, only two Caribbeans played in the MLB – Fermín Guerra of Cuba and Jesse Flores of Mexico. The first Caribbean to begin his career "post-Robinson" was the Cuban Orestes "Minnie" Minosa, in 1949.

By the 1960s, however, the U.S. leagues were actively recruiting Caribbean and Latin players. The Caribbean-basin immigrant population in the United States was growing and represented a new baseball audience. For that matter, their countrymen in the major leagues may have represented, in microcosm, the plight of the Caribbean minority in the United States. Team owners, rather than pay these players as much as their white contemporaries, enjoyed an influx of cheap talent. Between 1950 and 1955, 54 Caribbean basin players – 43 of whom were Cuban – started in the major leagues. And, with an eye on the future, scouting efforts were extended through Central America, Puerto Rico, the Dominican Republic, and Venezuela.

In the 1960s the Venezuelan Luís Aparicio, the Dominican Republic's Marichal, and Puerto Ricans Vic Power and Roberto Clemente were some of the more dominant players in the league. Clemente played an important role not only in right field for the Pittsburgh Pirates, but as spokesman for all Caribbean ball players. He was joined by Orlanda Cepeda and Felipe Alou, and the three publicly argued against white owners and the media. The owners, they felt, were still paying Caribbeans and Latin Americans less than their major league counterparts. Moreover, they believed that the media still paid little attention to the Spanish-speaking players.

If at first they did not receive the accolades the white players enjoyed, their careers were closely watched at home. Clemente was a national hero in Puerto Rico, where he returned each year for winterball, and where he was renowned for his generosity and endeavors in philanthropy. In the Dominican Republic, Juan Marichal's pitching exploits for the San Francisco Giants were copiously documented in Dominican newspapers. The players may have argued against the owners' inclination to pay deferentially to white ball players, but their young fans at home were beginning to view the major leagues as a way out of the same poor upbringings from which their idols, Marichal and Clemente and the rest of the growing population of Caribbean-basin players in the major leagues, originated.

This perceived "way out" had two effects on the young Latin American or Caribbean players. While it fanned youthful dreams of fame and fortune, it also left the players open to exploitation. For those whose hopes were realized, many found life in the United States a cruel paradox. Not only did Caribbeans and Latin Americans of African descent face racism in the United States, they faced further problems of acculturation. A Caribbean player unable to communicate could very well be sent to play minor league ball in Kansas, Indiana, Nebraska, or any other predominantly white and isolated area of the country. There, they would often encounter overt bigotry.

While the language barrier posed obvious everyday problems, for the ball player it also prevented desired recognition; English speakers naturally made easier interview subjects. Moreover, the Spanish-speaking players often sent a portion of their meager salaries home to impoverished families. Caribbean and Latin American players were frequently stereotyped, usually as good fielders who could not hit or as temperamental "hotheads" who threatened the unity of the clubhouse. Ironically, the 1947 Dodgers organization had been close to signing Silvio García, a talented Afro-Cuban infielder, instead of Robinson. According to one story, the Dodgers' front office believed that the Cuban did not have the temperament for the controversial role of being the first to desegregate major league baseball. But another story puts the Dodgers organization at a loss to locate García when it came time to sign him. The "hothead" stereotype was no stronger than in 1965, when Marichal fought with Dodgers catcher John Roseboro and severely lacerated his head with a bat in front of a national television audience.

Since integration, players from the Dominican Republic, Puerto Rico, Cuba, Venezuela, Panama, Colombia, Nicaragua, Mexico, and the Bahamas have taken the field in the major leagues. After 1961, when the United States and Cuba broke diplomatic ties, only a few defecting Cubans would play in America. Cuba continues to be a powerhouse in amateur play, but has been replaced as the deepest source of major league talent by Puerto Rico, Venezuela, and, most notably, the Dominican Republic. Intra-Caribbean baseball has been highly competitive; Cuba, the Dominican Republic, Nicaragua, Venezuela, and Colombia have all won the World Series of Amateur Baseball at least once. The Dominican Republic has sent the most players to the major leagues. Remarkably, the city of San Pedro de Macorís alone has contributed nearly a third of the Dominican major leaguers. Puerto Rico and Venezuela are well represented too. While Mexico is larger than any of these countries, most of its players remain in Mexico and play its well-developed professional league.

Between 1954 and 1988 Caribbean players won six Most Valuable Player Awards, seven Rookie of the Year Awards, three Cy Young trophies, and 17 batting championships. The five Caribbean-basin players in the Hall of Fame are Aparicio, Clemente, Marichal, Rod Carew and – though he never had the chance to play in the major leagues – Cuba's Martín Dihigo, who was inducted for his play in the Negro Leagues.

Kurt Mullen

See Also

Gibson, Joshua; Negro Leagues; Paige, Leroy Robert ("Satchel"); Central America; Panama.

North America

Baseball in the United States

Question: "Just tell me, why do you think there is still that much prejudice in baseball today?"

Answer: "No, I don't believe it's prejudice. I truly believe that they may not have some of the necessities to be, let's say, a field manager or perhaps a general manager."

Guess the year those words were uttered. Would you guess 1930? 1950? 1970? Well, it was *1987*. The further irony is that the context was a late-night talk show commemorating the 40th anniversary of the day JACKIE ROBINSON shattered the color barrier in Major League Baseball (MLB). On top of that, the man who answered the question was Al Campanis, who at the time was vice president of the Los Angeles Dodgers. Campanis was interviewed because he had played and roomed with Robinson and on many occasions actually defended him against racial onslaughts. Campanis was fired the day after his astonishing comment. The event was a stunning reminder of the perhaps more subtle yet still pernicious underbelly of discrimination in the national pastime. In the contemporary era the dominant issue had switched from opportunities for African Americans as players to their inclusion as managers and executives.

THE EARLY YEARS AND THE NEGRO LEAGUES

In the middle of the nineteenth century an impermeable wall separated the races in virtually all areas of American society, yet there were a number of rather remarkable parallels in the maturation of baseball for both races. The first baseball governing board (white) was the National Association of Base Ball Players (NABBP). Formed in 1858, it foundered during the Civil War and its aftermath and was resuscitated in 1867. While there are unconfirmed reports that two African American teams played each other as early as 1861, in Brooklyn, the first officially recorded occurrence was "the championship of colored baseball" between the Uniques of Brooklyn and the Excelsiors of Philadelphia in 1867. A few months later the Philadelphia Pythians applied for membership to the NABBP but were rejected on the grounds that "If colored clubs were admitted there would be in all probability some division of feeling, whereas, by excluding them no injury could result to anyone." From that emanated a "gentleman's agreement" among white owners that would bar African Americans from major league baseball for decades.

In a rather ironic historical footnote, major league baseball was almost integrated – albeit surreptitiously – in 1902, when the legendary Baltimore Orioles manager John J. McGraw signed Charlie Grant. Grant had a light complexion, straight hair, and high cheekbones, so McGraw claimed that he was a Native American, Charlie Tokohama. Grant played all spring but was banned from the major leagues before the start of the season when the cover-up was discovered by Chicago White Sox owner Charlie Comiskey.

While denied the chance to play major league baseball, African Americans could still play baseball, and so emerged the illustrious NEGRO LEAGUES. The first all-black professional team, comprising employees of the Argyle Hotel in New York and organized by headwaiter Frank Thompson, was formed in 1885, bought later in the year by a New Jersey businessman, and officially named the Cuban Giants. In 1886 the Southern League of Colored Base Ballists became the first Negro league. Various Negro leagues foundered during the early years, primarily for financial reasons, and it was not until 1920 that an organized African American league (the Negro National League) survived a full season. With the exception of the GREAT DEPRESSION era, from that point on the Negro leagues flourished. The second league formed in 1923 (Eastern Colored League), and the following year the Kansas City Monarchs defeated the Philadelphia Hilldales in the first "colored" World Series.

LEFT: In 1973 baseball legend Roberto Clemente was inducted into the Baseball Hall of Fame, capping a stellar career for the Puerto Rican native. *CORBIS/Bettmann*

OPPOSITE: Dominican baseball great Juan Marichal winds up for the pitch. *CORBIS/Bettmann*

Many great teams played in the Negro Leagues, with perhaps the Homestead Grays, Pittsburgh Crawfords, and Kansas City Monarchs being the most remembered. So, too, did many superstars grace the playing field. Some students of baseball, for example, consider James "Cool Papa" Bell the smoothest and fleetest outfielder ever to play the game. Others would argue that Josh Gibson, who batted .362 over his 16-year career, was the best hitter of all time. In fact during his career he had over 60 at-bats against major league pitchers – including Dizzy Dean and Johnny Vander Meer – and hit .426, with five home runs. Of course no list could be complete without the legendary pitcher Leroy "Satchel" Paige, unquestionably the greatest pitcher of the Negro Leagues. His career spanned five decades, and some of his many accomplishments include 64 consecutive scoreless innings, 21 straight wins, and a 31-4 record in 1933. No one knows how many games he pitched, but including winterball in the Caribbean (*see* Baseball in the Latin America and the Caribbean) it is estimated that he pitched in over 2000 games in the 1930s and 1940s alone, not counting innumerable exhibitions. He was also the ultimate showman. Folklore has it that he would have his outfielders sit behind the mound while he struck out the side, intentionally walk the bases full so that he could pitch to Josh Gibson, and throw 20 straight pitches across a chewing gum wrapper that was used for home plate. In 1948 he realized his dream when he signed to play with the major league Cleveland Indians. At 59 he became the oldest player to pitch in a major league game, and in 1971 he was inducted into the Hall of Fame, the first player elected from the Negro Leagues. Joe DiMaggio called him "the best and fastest pitcher I've ever faced." Other former Negro League players who went on to star in the major leagues include Willie Mays, Henry Aaron, Roy Campanella, Ernie Banks, Junior Gilliam, Don Newcombe, and Joe Black.

The promotion of Jackie Robinson to the Brooklyn Dodgers in 1947 not only opened the doors for other African American players, it also signaled the beginning of the end of the Negro Leagues. More than in any other sport, baseball fans and mavens relish an argument over who was the best hitter, pitcher, or fielder of all time.

Comparisons across historical periods are obviously tenuous. Perhaps the biggest tragedy for Negro League players is that segregation made it impossible for their greatest to play against the greatest in the major leagues. As a consequence, Negro Leagues stars do not receive enough consideration in arguments over who was the best.

The Modern Era

The Dodgers were the first to integrate, and the Boston Red Sox were the last, 12 years later, with infielder "Pumpsie" Green. Ironically, Robinson had a tryout, arranged by a black sportswriter, with the Red Sox at Fenway Park in April 1945. While Robinson strutted his skills on the field, a man reportedly affiliated with the Red Sox yelled, "Get those niggers off the field." Four years later the Red Sox passed on an 18-year-old outfield prospect playing with the Birmingham Black Barons of the Negro Leagues – Willie Mays.

Robinson was born in Cairo, Georgia, on January 31, 1919. He was a three-sport star at UCLA (also football and track), and in 1945 he signed a minor league contract to play for the Montreal Royals for $600 per month. Robinson was a man possessed of extraordinary athletic ability and incomparable inner strength. Branch Rickey, the Dodger executive who brought Robinson to the major leagues, once remarked that he chose Robinson for the historic breakthrough because, even though at the time there were a few better African American ball players, it was Robinson who had the heart of a lion. He would need it for all that he had to endure: not being able to eat or sleep with his team in certain cities, vicious verbal barrages from fans and opposing players (and more than once even from players on his own team), and cheap physical assaults from opposing players on the field.

Through it all Robinson persevered, suffering along with his family the enormous emotional costs that left their scars years after his egress from baseball. After baseball he was a successful business executive, but he died in 1972 at the premature age of 53. Over his ten-year career he batted .311, was named National League Rookie of the Year in 1947 and Most Valuable Player in 1949, played in six consecutive All Star games, six World Series, and was inducted into the Hall of Fame in 1962.

The next milestone occurred in 1975, when the Cleveland Indians appointed Frank Robinson as the first African American manager in baseball history. Robinson was Rookie of the Year with the Cincinnati Reds in 1956, winner of the Triple Crown (most home runs, runs-batted-in, and highest batting average) in 1966, and the only player to win the Most Valuable Player Award in both the American and National Leagues. He was inducted into the Hall of Fame in 1982. Before his first game as player-manager Robinson said: "My feelings are that this is the end of a long road, but the sacrifices were worthwhile to get here. My only regret is that Jackie couldn't be alive to see this happen."

The last piece of the integration puzzle in major league baseball is that of including African Americans in "the front office." Here, of course, the focus shifts from sheer physical ability to baseball and business acumen. In the weeks following the Al Campanis debacle, Commissioner of Baseball Peter Ueberroth hired African American consultants to devise a plan to increase minority recruitment. Within four years African Americans held 9 percent of front office jobs, up from almost nothing. Bill White, a 13-year veteran with a solid but not distinguished career, was appointed president of the National League, and the number of African American managers rose to four. Diversification in the front office remains a muffled concern as major league baseball enters the twenty-first century. The fact persists that while there are 30 major league teams, representation for African Americans in the front office remains low – even lower for Latinos, who now are the second largest block of players in the major leagues, after whites – and every team is owned by whites.

TOP: Chicago Cub great Ernie Banks receiving the National League's Most Valuable Player award in 1960. *CORBIS/Bettmann*
ABOVE: All-time home run leader Henry "Hank" Aaron hits his 700th in a 1973 game. *CORBIS/Bettmann*
LEFT: Hall of Famer Willie Mays sliding into home in a 1964 game against the New York Mets. *CORBIS/Bettmann*

Records and Distinctions

Baseball is a team game, but individual achievements are chronicled meticulously. In this regard, Henry Louis "Hammerin' Hank" Aaron is the beacon of African American major leaguers. Born in 1934 in Mobile, Alabama, he had a singular 23-year career. On April 8, 1974, he hit his 715th home run, which shattered the record established by Babe Ruth. Aaron ended his career with 755 homers. After retiring as a player, he became an executive with the Atlanta Braves, and with that stature was able to address the nagging racial injustices in baseball. He once said: "Jackie Robinson gave all of us – not only black athletes, but every black person in this country – a sense of our own strength. I think my style in the early days was similar to Jackie's. In order for people to listen to you, you have to have done something." In the Baseball Hall of Fame in Cooperstown, New York, only two players are honored by having exclusive rooms dedicated to displaying their extraordinary contributions to baseball – Babe Ruth and Henry Aaron. Aaron was inducted into the Hall of Fame in 1982 and, amazingly, holds the following lifetime records: most home runs, most runs-batted-in, most total bases, most extra-base hits; at-bats (2nd), hits (3rd).

TOP: Members of the New York Black Yankees, a Negro League baseball team, pictured in 1942. *CORBIS/Bettmann*

ABOVE: Panamanian baseball player Rod Carew, playing for the Minnesota Twins, gets a hit in a game with the New York Yankees in 1974. *CORBIS/Bettmann*

The individual achievements of African American major leaguers abound. Here is a listing of just a few of them (and keep in mind that the "clock" begins only in 1947).

Inducted into the Hall of Fame:
Henry Aaron, Ernie Banks, James "Cool Papa" Bell,* Lou Brock, Roy Campanella, Rod Carew, Oscar Charleston,* Roberto Clemente, Roy Dandridge,* Leon Day,* Martín Dihigo,* Larry Doby, Andrew "Rube" Foster, Bill Foster,* Bob Gibson, Josh Gibson,* Monte Irvin,* Reggie Jackson, Ferguson Jenkins, Judy Johnson,* Buck Leonard,* John Henry Lloyd,* Juan Marichal, Willie Mays, Willie McCovey, Joe Morgan, Satchel Paige,* Jackie Robinson, Frank Robinson, Wilbur "Bullet" Rogan, Willie Stargell, Willie Wells, Billy Williams (* indicates based on performance in the Negro Leagues).

Most Valuable Player Awards:
Jackie Robinson, Roy Campanella (three times in a career that was abbreviated by a near-fatal car accident), Don Newcombe, Henry Aaron, Ernie Banks (twice), Frank Robinson (twice), Maury Wills, Elston Howard, Willie Mays, Bob Gibson, Willie McCovey, Joe Morgan (twice), George Foster, Dave Parker, Vida Blue, Dick Allen, Reggie Jackson, Willie Stargell, Willie McGee, Andre Dawson, Jim Rice, Don Baylor, Rickey Henderson, Kevin Mitchell, Barry Bonds (twice) Terry Pendleton, Barry Larkin, Frank Thomas (twice), Mo Vaughn.

Cy Young Award (for best pitcher):
Don Newcombe, Bob Gibson (twice), Ferguson Jenkins, Vida Blue, Dwight Gooden.

Rookie of the Year:
Jackie Robinson, Don Newcombe, Sam Jethroe, Willie Mays, Joe Black, Jim Gilliam, Frank Robinson, Willie McCovey, Billy Williams, Dick Allen, Tommy Agee, Earl Williams, Chris Chambliss, Al Bumbry, Jon Matlock, Gary Matthews, Bake McBride, Eddie Murray, Andre Dawson, Lou Whitaker, Darryl Strawberry, Dwight Gooden, Vince Coleman, Jerome Walton, David Justice.

Other Achievements:
In addition to the career marks of Henry Aaron and others noted above, Willie Mays ranks third on the all-time career home run list and Frank Robinson is fourth; Lou Brock broke Ty Cobb's lifetime stolen base record, and Rickey Henderson later surpassed Brock; Lee Smith holds the major league record for most saves by a relief pitcher.

Gerard Gryski

See Also

Aaron, Henry Louis (Hank); Banks, Ernest (Ernie); Civil War, American; Gibson, Joshua; Mays, Willie Howard; Paige, Leroy Robert ("Satchel").

North America

Basie, William James ("Count")

(b. August 21, 1904, Red Bank, N. J.; d. April 26, 1984, Hollywood, Calif.), African American piano player and big-band leader from the mid-1930s to the 1980s, whose band made hard-swinging Kansas City jazz popular across the United States.

Though white clarinetist Benny Goodman was proclaimed the "King of Swing," by all rights the title belonged to Count Basie. For nearly half a century, with the exception of a brief interruption between 1949 and 1952, Basie headed one of the finest big bands in JAZZ, one that has enjoyed an unrivaled longevity. No other jazz orchestra has continued so long under the same leadership. In fact, Basie led two distinct bands, which some critics designate the Old Testament and New Testament bands. The Old Testament band was Basie's aggregation from the mid-1930s through the 1940s; the New Testament band encompasses the Basie band since the early 1950s.

The earlier band played a hard-swinging, rough-around-the-edges Kansas City jazz and often used head arrangements rather than written charts. It featured brilliant musical stylists, including tenor saxophonist Lester Young, trumpeters Buck Clayton and Harry "Sweets" Edison, vocalist Jimmy "Mr. Five by Five" Rushing, drummer Jo Jones, and Basie himself on piano. Basie's later band – although it featured such soloists as trumpeters Thad Jones and Joe Newman, tenor saxophonists Frank Foster and Frank Wess, and vocalist Joe Williams – was above all an arranger's orchestra, skillfully performing the arrangements of Frank Foster, Neal Hefti, Quincy Jones, and Ernie Wilkins. The one constant in the Basie band was Basie himself.

As a boy, Basie dreamed of becoming a drummer, but watching future Duke Ellington drummer Sonny Greer convinced him that he should choose another instrument. Though always modest about his abilities, he was performing locally from the time he left junior high school. In 1924 he went to New York City to try his luck and fell under the influence of the three great Harlem stride pianists, James P. Johnson, Willie "the Lion" Smith, and Thomas

"Fats" Waller. Waller, who also played the organ at the Lincoln Theater in Harlem, gave Basie his first instruction in that instrument while the day's movies were shown, helping to inspire his long-standing interest in organ playing.

Basie is rightly known as a pianist, and his playing remained rooted in the stride tradition of 1920s Harlem. Stride piano essentially divides the piano keyboard into three ranges. The pianist's left hand covers the two lower ranges, alternating single bass notes at the bottom with chord clusters struck higher up. The style takes its name from the characteristic bouncing "oom-pah, oom-pah" produced by the pianist's "striding" left hand. While the left hand establishes a propulsive beat and outlines the tune's harmonic structure, the pianist's right hand plays the melody, adds ornamentation, and improvises solo lines.

William James "Count" Basie, seen here at the piano, delighted nightclub and concert audiences with Kansas City jazz for 50 years. *Culver Pictures*

In 1924 and 1925 Basie toured with *Hippity Hop*, a burlesque show on the Columbia Circuit, which took the young pianist as far afield as Montreal, Canada; Omaha, Nebraska; and Kansas City, Missouri. On his second visit to Kansas City, Basie had more time to take part in the night life. Years later, he remembered the experience vividly: "[E]verywhere you went, there was at least a piano player and somebody singing, if not a combo or maybe a jam session. There was so much going on that I couldn't believe my eyes or my ears.... There we were, way out there in the middle of nowhere... and wham... the action was greater than anything I'd ever heard."

In 1926 and 1927 Basie signed on with a vaudeville show on the Theater Owners Booking Association (TOBA), the nationwide circuit of blacks-only theaters. But when the financially strapped TOBA dissolved, Basie's show was stranded and broke up in Kansas City.

As a jazz musician, Basie could not have asked for a better spot to be marooned. Soon he joined a territory band, Walter Page's Blue Devils, out of Oklahoma City, Oklahoma. After two years he became part of Benny Moten's Kansas City Orchestra. Basie played with Moten from 1929 to 1932, including a famed 1932 Victor recording session highlighted by a classic version of "Blue Room" that prefigured the swing sound that Goodman would make famous in 1935. When Moten died in 1935, his band broke up and Basie formed his own, mainly comprising members of the Blue Devils and Moten's band. It was initially known as the Barons of Rhythm.

In 1936 a small group of Basie band members recorded one of the most important sessions in jazz history for producer John Hammond. For legal reasons, the Basie-led group was identified as Jones-Smith Incorporated. It brilliantly captured the smooth sound and subtle interplay of Kansas City jazz. Years later Hammond would recall the date as "one of the only perfect sessions I ever had." It was also noteworthy for being Lester Young's first recording session. All four sides, especially Young's lyrical solos on "Shoe Shine Boy" and "Oh, Lady Be Good," were superb. According to musicologist Gunther Schuller, Young's two choruses on the latter demonstrate a "harmonic freeing up of the language of jazz" that was essential to all subsequent developments in jazz history.

Between 1937 and 1939 the Basie band made a memorable series of recordings for Decca Records, including "One O'Clock Jump," "Jumpin' at the Woodside," and "Sent for You Yesterday." These recordings clearly demonstrate the unrivaled swing of Basie's rhythm section, which consisted of Basie (piano), Walter Page (bass), Freddie Greene (rhythm guitar), and Jo Jones (drums). That rhythm section propelled the shouting unison passages, cushioned the soloists, and drove the music forward both gently and relentlessly. Indeed it was so strong that Basie began to simplify his piano style, deemphasizing the instrument's timekeeping role and concentrating on brief treble fills and punctuations. In so doing, he prepared the way for the more radical transformations that would be wrought by modern jazz pianists Thelonious Monk and Earl "Bud" Powell.

In 1939 the Basie band began a long association with Columbia Records. By the late 1940s, however, the big-band era was nearly over, and like many other groups, Basie's folded around the end of the decade. Basie spent three years touring with small groups that ranged in size from sextets to nonets, but in 1952, disregarding the conventional wisdom, he decided to re-form his big band. He signed his new band with Verve Records (1952-1957) and Roulette (1957-1962) and made some of the most successful recordings of his career, in particular the Verve albums *Count Basie Swings, Joe Williams Sings* (1955), and *April in Paris* (1956).

After a series of less memorable recordings in the 1960s, the band joined Pablo Records in 1972, an association that continued until the leader's death. Although Basie performed and recorded in many musical contexts besides his big band, that band unquestionably constitutes his lasting legacy. It is fitting, then, that since Basie's death, his band has maintained its creativity and financial health. Indeed, it is the only such "ghost" band – one that keeps on performing after the death of its leader – that continues to play new music of undiminished vitality.

James Clyde Sellman

See Also
Young, Lester Willis ("Prez"); Harlem, New York; Jones, Quincy Delight, Jr.; Kansas City, Missouri; Monk, Thelonious Sphere; New York, New York; Powell, Earl ("Bud"); Rushing, Jimmy; Smith, Willie ("the Lion"); Waller, Thomas Wright ("Fats"); Ellington, Edward Kennedy ("Duke").

North America

Basketball, a team sport that has been transformed by the presence of African Americans and, as such, has been an important signifier of the cultural, political, and social changes in the United States for more than 100 years.

In December 1891 Canadian-American physical education teacher James Naismith, of the School for Christian Workers (now Springfield College) in Springfield, Massachusetts, was instructed to invent a new game to entertain the school's athletes during the winter season. With an ordinary soccer ball, Naismith assembled his class of 18 young men, appointed captains of two 9-player teams, and introduced them to the game of "Basket Ball."

Since its creation in 1891, and particularly since African Americans entered the ranks of professional players in the 1950s, basketball has become one of the most popular and exciting games in the world. Players in the National Basketball Association (NBA), including Michael Jordan and Shaquille O'Neill, have helped to transform what was once a rigid and formal game into a billion-dollar industry. African American women such as Sheryl Swoopes and Lisa Leslie have expanded the game beyond its traditional male purview, and the long-standing tradition of women's collegiate basketball has inspired the creation of professional leagues for women, including the American Basketball League (ABL) and the Women's National Basketball Association (WNBA). The game has also become an important signifier of fashion: the logos of American basketball teams can be found on the clothing of children from South Africa to China. But although the elegance and power of black athleticism has now captured the respect and admiration of the world, for years it was forced to evolve in isolation, as segregation split America along racial lines.

Early Black College Programs

After being exposed to the game during a summer at Harvard University, Coach Edwin B. Henderson introduced basketball to a physical education class at Howard University in 1905. By 1910 basketball was one of the most popular sports among young African Americans. The game could be played on almost any surface, and it required little or no equipment. It was promoted largely in Young Men's Christian Associations (YMCAs) located in black neighborhoods, and basketball courts were soon constructed outdoors, in parks and on playgrounds. By 1915 African Americans were playing basketball on college and university squads, in high school physical education classes, and on club teams representing major urban cities. Some of the first predominantly black universities to form basketball squads included Hampton, Lincoln (Pennsylvania), Wilberforce (Ohio), and Virginia Union. In 1916 the all-black Central Interscholastic Athletic Association (CIAA) was formed, uniting the universities of Virginia Union, Shaw, Lincoln (Pennsylvania), and Howard in competition. Four years later the all-black Southeastern Athletic Conference was established, and by 1928 there were four all-black regional conferences.

Regional competition produced a flurry of excitement as black squads battled on college campuses, in city parks, and on high school varsity teams. In several states, tournaments allowed high school teams to compete for the title of state champion. At the collegiate level, athletes such as Paul Robeson at Rutgers, Wilbur Woods at Nebraska, and Charles Drew at Amherst became basketball stars. Several college basketball programs stood out. Xavier University won 67 games and lost only 2 between 1934 and 1938, and Alabama State, Lincoln University in Missouri, Morgan State in Maryland, and Wiley College in Texas all produced exceptional basketball teams.

Basketball in American Cities

While basketball was becoming institutionalized in colleges and in high schools throughout the United States, it was also being dramatically altered by African American club teams. Basketball in the city became a game of innovation and style. Some of the earliest all-black club teams, such as the Smart Set Athletic Club of Brooklyn, New York, the St. Christopher's Club of New Jersey, and the Loendi Club from Pittsburgh, produced high-scoring, action-packed games. Club teams in New York, New Jersey, Washington, D.C., and Philadelphia dazzled crowds. Two of the most famous African American club teams are the Renaissance Big Five (or "Rens") and the Savoy Big Five (or "Harlem Globetrotters"). Playing in Harlem, the Rens dominated club play for 16 years. Between 1923 and 1939 they won more than 1500 games and lost fewer than 240. The squad, which featured such players as Charles "Tarzan" Cooper, William "Pop" Gates, Clarence "Puggy" Bell, and William "Wee Willie" Smith, won the first black professional tournament. Despite their tremendous success and popularity, however, the Rens were no match for the legendary Harlem Globetrotters.

Harlem Globetrotters

Although not a single player came from Harlem and the team was based in Illinois, the Harlem Globetrotters began as the Savoy Big Five, playing in Chicago's Savoy ballroom; in 1927 team owner Abe Saperstein changed their name to the Harlem Globetrotters. They were one of the most innovative teams in basketball history. Led by players such as Marques Haynes, Willie "Sweet Willie" Oliver, Al "Runt" Pullins, and Reece "Goose" Tatum, for decades the Globetrotters excelled in club play, becoming so dominant that they began to experiment with new ways of winning. They became master ball handlers and deceptive passers. Haynes embarrassed opposing players with his dribbling skills and Tatum followed by humiliating them with comedic performances. In 1952 Meadowlark "Lemon" and "Curly" Neal joined the team, along with Wilt Chamberlain and Connie Hawkins, two future professional stars. After more than 70 years the Globetrotters have played in more than a hundred countries and in front of more than 60 million fans.
In 1985 Lynette Woodard became the first woman to play for the Globetrotters.

The Early Years of Women in Basketball

During the first half of the twentieth century, gender discrimination prevented most women from participating in areas reserved for men, and basketball was no exception. Among the earliest all-black, all-female basketball clubs were the Philadelphia Tribune Girls, founded in 1931 and led by Ora Washington, and the Chicago Romas. The Romas, who played against both male and female teams, never lost a game after World War II. Corinne Robinson, Mignon Burns, Lillian Ross, Virginia Willis, Lola Porter, and Isadore Channels were among the Roma standouts. Although black women continued to play basketball throughout the 1930s and 1940s, they were unable to enjoy many of the opportunities that the game afforded black men, including national recognition and significant monetary compensation.

Interracial Competition

By contrast, African American men could learn basketball as adolescents and play in organized leagues through high school and college, and, more important, they could look forward to a professional career. Although they could not play on teams with white men, they did compete against them. Interconference leagues fostered intense competition between all-black and all-white squads, and the stakes often went beyond numbers in the win-loss column. For instance, in 1951 the city of Indianapolis, Indiana, was riveted by a semifinal high school game between the all-white Anderson Indians and the all-black Crispus Attucks Tigers. Anderson was the city favorite and the school hoped to win its fourth state title. But the Tigers forced the game down to the wire, and a last minute shot by Bailey "Flap" Robertson brought the Anderson Indians to their knees and the black community in Indianapolis to their feet. The victory spoke to much more than the final score of 81-80. The game was a symbolic dialogue between blacks and whites, constituting a small part of the larger Civil Rights Movement beginning in the 1950s that took place throughout the United States. Integrated competition displayed the beauty and the creativity of African American athleticism and inspired the NBA to admit black players.

Early Black Stars in the NBA

After Chuck Cooper joined the Boston Celtics in 1951, becoming the first African American player in the NBA, black players took what was once a highly mechanical and rigid game and developed it into a spontaneous and artistic forum for self-expression. Bill Russell, and Wilt "the Stilt" Chamberlain – who both stood close to 2.13 m (7 ft) tall – elevated the game with their thunderous slam dunks and graceful lay-ups. In college Russell led the University of California at San Francisco to two national titles and as a professional helped to lead the Boston Celtics to nine straight NBA titles. Chamberlain played 14 years in the NBA (1959-1973) and was an all-star for 13 of those years. He set a single game scoring record in 1962 when he scored 100 points against the New York Knickerbockers. Chamberlain amassed more than 31,000 points and 23,000 rebounds during his career, second only to Kareem Abdul-Jabbar.

While Russell and Chamberlain set new standards for the position of center, players such as Elgin Baylor and Oscar Robertson introduced speed and agility to the NBA. Baylor, a 1958 graduate of Seattle University, led the Los Angeles Lakers to the 1968 finals and scored 71 points in a single game. Robertson, who graduated from the University of Cincinnati and played on the 1960 gold-medal-winning U.S. Olympic basketball team, became an all-star in the NBA and had almost 10,000 assists during his career.

The success of these professionals and the growing strength of the Civil Rights Movement opened new doors for young black athletes as predominantly white schools rushed to attract the best high school stars. Soon young black men were being recruited from inner-city high schools in New York, Baltimore, Philadelphia, and Washington, D.C. In 1966 James Cash became the first black player at Texas Christian University and Perry Wallace was the first black to be recruited by the Southeast Conference in 1967. Billy Jones followed Wallace, integrating the Atlantic Coast Conference a year later. The University of California at Los Angeles won ten national titles from 1964 to 1975, largely because of black players such as Lew Alcindor (Kareem Abdul-Jabbar). Alcindor, standing more than 2.13 m (7 ft) tall, was so dominant at UCLA that league officials had to outlaw the slam dunk while he was in school.

Integration and Its Effect on the Game

Integration opened the door for African American players to attend basketball programs with better equipment, larger gyms, and a wider national audience. These opportunities produced stronger and faster athletes, and ultimately, more successful college programs. But the most dramatic effect of integration was an increase in the number of players from urban environments. Inner-city playground competitions, such as the Baker League in Philadelphia and the Rucker Tournament in New York City, introduced promising young black players to professional and college scouts. These players possessed a unique style of play that some call street basketball. The influence of street basketball was evident most clearly during the 1970s as the NBA welcomed an impressive array of players from urban backgrounds. Earl "the Pearl" Monroe, Julius "Dr. J." Erving, and Kareem Abdul-Jabbar pushed the game into a fast-paced, high-scoring frenzy.

Monroe, a dynamic dribbler and prolific passer, was named Rookie of the Year after his first season with the Baltimore Bullets. Julius Erving led the New York Nets of the American Basketball Association (ABA) to consecutive titles in 1974 and 1975 before joining the Philadelphia 76ers in the NBA. "Dr. J," as Erving was known, was one of the most creative players in the league. He patented the finger-roll, a move characterized by gently guiding the ball over the opponent's outstretched hand. Dr. J was considered a fierce competitor and a graceful athlete; today he is a professional sports television commentator.

Kareem Abdul-Jabbar left a successful college career for the NBA in 1969. A conscientious and innovative athlete, he easily dunked the ball over his opponents and developed a new and virtually unstoppable move known as the "sky hook." He helped lead the Los Angeles Lakers to five NBA titles during his 25-year career and set the standard for contemporary centers such as Shaquille O'Neal, Patrick Ewing, and Hakeem Olajuwon. Other standouts of this era included Willis Reed, who played with a broken leg during the seventh game of the 1970 NBA finals; his teammate Walt Frazier; and Elvin Hayes of the Washington Bullets – each of whom was a product of street basketball. Together they helped to bring new energy, excitement, and confidence to professional basketball.

By the late 1980s basketball was dominated by African American players from urban centers, and celebrity players such as Earvin "Magic" Johnson and Michael "Air" Jordan were captivating fans. Johnson, a sophomore guard, led Michigan State University to an NCAA title in 1979. At 2.04 m (6 ft, 6 in) tall, he was an unusually gifted ball handler and a deceptive passer. Johnson left college after his sophomore year to join the Los Angeles Lakers, and during his rookie season played a pivotal role as the Lakers closed the season as NBA champions. He and fellow teammates Kareem Abdul-Jabbar, James Worthy, and Byron Scott led the Lakers to five NBA titles. In 1991 Johnson was forced to retire from professional basketball at the pinnacle of his career after he was diagnosed with the human immunodeficiency virus (HIV).

ABOVE: An informal, or pick-up, game of basketball. *CORBIS/Tony Arruza*

OPPOSITE: Shown here in 1989, Michael Jordan is widely considered basketball's greatest player ever. *CORBIS/Bettmann*

Like Johnson, Michael Jordan was a superstar at the University of North Carolina, and after leading them to an NCAA title in 1983, Jordan also left college early to join the Chicago Bulls. He is described by many as the best basketball player of all time. His energy, enthusiasm, and last-minute heroics have produced six NBA crowns in Chicago. Magic Johnson and Michael Jordan are immensely popular throughout the world and are widely considered cultural icons.

Exploitation or Opportunity?
Today, professional basketball is a major vehicle for young African American men seeking to escape the hardships of urban life. Although it is relatively rare, some players elect not to attend college in hopes of turning professional immediately after high school. Critics contend that African American athletes have been exploited for their athletic prowess by professional, collegiate, and, in some cases, high school basketball programs. Some, including author John Hoberman, argue that "the cult of black athleticism continues a racist tradition that has long emphasized the motor skills and manual training of African Americans." Hoberman and others suggest that the enormous salaries of today's professional athletes send the wrong signal to young children about the value of sports.

But many disagree, including black basketball coaches who argue that basketball should be seen as a legitimate and viable vehicle for young, poor African Americans seeking a better life. A coach can play a major role in the athletic and personal development of young basketball players, ensuring that the desire for a professional sports career is moderated by the necessity of education. Some African American coaches have worked throughout their careers to teach young players the value of education and the importance of becoming a well-rounded individual, including two of the most respected coaches in basketball, Clarence "Big House" Gaines and Lenny Wilkens. Gaines was a coach at Winston Salem State University and is the "winningest coach" in Division II history. After his one-thousandth victory in 1996, Lenny Wilkens became the "winningest" coach in NBA history. Other outstanding African American coaches include John Thompson, John Chaney, K.C. Jones, Clem Haskins, George Raveling, and Nolan Richardson.

Women's Professional Basketball
Although professional and collegiate basketball programs have opened doors for men, it is only within the last 20 years that women's basketball has gained national backing. In the mid-1990s, after years of success by women's collegiate and Olympic basketball teams, public interest in women's basketball convinced a group of entrepreneurs to form the American Basketball League (ABL). The eight teams of the ABL began play in 1996, and in March 1997 the Columbus Quest defeated the Richmond Rage in a five-game series to win the inaugural league championship. The NBA also formed an eight-team women's league, the Women's National Basketball Association (WNBA), which began play in June 1997. The ABL was disbanded in December 1998.

Both leagues recruited the top women basketball stars in college, including former U.S. Olympic stars Lisa Leslie and

Sheryl Swoopes. The 2.04 m (6 ft, 5 in) tall Lisa Leslie is a member of the Los Angeles Sparks (WNBA). She is considered one of the top shot blockers and rebounders in the league. Swoopes, a 1996 Olympic champion and member of the Houston Comets in the WNBA, is the first woman to have a shoe named after her, the Air Swoopes. African American women, like their male counterparts, have brought innovation and style to the game of basketball. They have opened new doors for young women and in turn have made remarkable contributions to the struggle to empower women throughout the world.

Basketball Today

Basketball has always been about much more than guiding a ball through a hoop. The history of American basketball tells a compelling story about athletic competition in a nation struggling to live up to its ideals of freedom and democracy. Segregation forced African American basketball players to develop a unique game that is distinctly urban, relentlessly innovative, and always stylistic. Today basketball is about the head fake and the swagger, the finger roll and the sky hook; it is about the jump shot and the cross-over dribble. Basketball is also about wearing the latest sneakers and sporting the sleekest haircut. It is about playing the game "above the rim," a phrase that has come to symbolize not just whether or not points are scored, but the way in which it is done. Basketball is a sport transformed by the presence of African Americans, and as such, a signifier of the cultural, political, and social changes in the United States.

Alonford James Robinson, Jr.

See Also

AIDS in the United States; Chamberlain, Wilton Norman (Wilt); Erving, Julius ("Dr. J"); Hampton University; Harlem, New York; Johnson, Magic; Jordan, Michael Jeffrey; Lincoln University (Missouri); Lincoln University (Pennsylvania); New York, New York; O'Neal, Shaquille; Philadelphia, Pennsylvania; Russell, William Fenton (Bill); Television and African Americans; Wilberforce University.

TOP: Earvin "Magic" Johnson, one of basketball's greatest stars, in a 1987 game. *CORBIS/Neal Preston*
ABOVE LEFT: Kareem Abdul-Jabbar, the National Basketball Association's all-time leading scorer, pictured in a 1962 game. *CORBIS/Jerry Cooke*
ABOVE: Boston Celtic Bill Russell guards Philadelphia Warrior Wilt Chamberlain. The two big men dominated professional basketball in the 1960s. *CORBIS/Bettmann*

Latin America and the Caribbean

Basora, Santiago, Afro-Dominican military leader of the African Batallion; Basora was born in Africa.

Santiago Basora served as a captain in the African Battalion during the Haitian occupation of Santo Domingo (present-day Dominican Republic), which lasted from 1822 to 1844 (see Dominican-Haitian Relations). He was put in charge of a regiment at Pajarito Fort (in present-day Villa Duarte). Initially, Haiti's abolition of slavery in Santo Domingo won the support of the Afro-Dominican majority and the enmity of its elite. In time, however, broader opposition to occupation coalesced, in part due to the imposition of high taxes and its disruption of traditional patterns of land tenure.

In February 1844, when the Santo Domingo *independentistas,* led by Juan Pablo Duarte and the group of conspirators known as La Trinitaria, declared independence from Haiti, the black and mulatto population grew concerned, given the pro-Spanish sentiments of many elite members in the ranks of the independence forces. Spain still enslaved Africans in its colonies of Cuba and Puerto Rico, and people of color in Santo Domingo feared that Haiti's abolition of slavery would be reversed. Shortly after the declaration of independence, Afro-Dominicans in Monte Grande, led by Basora, revolted, demanding guarantees that slavery not be reinstituted as well as the integration of Basora into the government. In response to their demands, on July 17, 1844, the new Dominican government published a law that outlawed slave trafficking of any kind and declared that enslaved individuals entering the Dominican Republic would immediately gain their freedom. Following these assurances, the African Batallion joined the independence forces. Its military campaigns, which took place in the southern part of the country, culminated in many successes against the retreating Haitian forces.

Basora was forced into exile in 1849 due to his support for President Manuel Jiménez, who had been deposed by political rival Gen. Pedro Santana earlier that year.

North America

Basquiat, Jean-Michel

(b. December 22, 1960, Brooklyn, N.Y.; d. August 12, 1988, Brooklyn, N.Y.), American painter, initially a street artist, whose graffiti-inspired work won international acclaim during the 1980s.

Born to a Haitian father and a first-generation Puerto Rican-American mother, Jean-Michel Basquiat grew up in Brooklyn. As a child, he created drawings inspired by comic books and television cartoons. His early interest in art was nurtured by his mother, who often took him to local art museums.

In May 1968, Basquiat was hit by a car. He suffered a broken arm and his spleen had to be removed. While he was hospitalized, his mother gave him a copy of *Gray's Anatomy,* a book that inspired many of his later works as well as the name of the noise band he co-founded in 1979, Gray. After his parents separated in 1968, Basquiat and his two sisters lived with their father, including two years in Puerto Rico. At the age of 17, Basquiat dropped out of high school and lived, by choice, on the streets and with various friends.

Basquiat's career as an artist began in 1977 when he began to spray-paint New York City streets and subways with one of his high school classmates, Al Diaz. The works were signed SAMO, an acronym for "same old shit," and consisted of short poetic phrases such as "Plush safe he think; SAMO." They strategically placed these street texts in SoHo and the East Village, where they were more likely to be seen by people in influential artistic circles. In December 1978, the *Village Voice* published an article about the SAMO writings. While working on the SAMO project, which ended in 1979, Basquiat sold hand-painted postcards and T-shirts to make money.

Basquiat's art was publicly exhibited for the first time in the 1980 Times Square Show. Art critics responded positively to his debut and in May 1981, after being included in several group shows, he had his first solo exhibition in Modena, Italy. His first one-man show in the United States took place in March 1982 at the Annina Nosei Gallery. Basquiat's work began to be shown internationally in prominent art galleries. In June 1982, the 21-one-year-old Basquiat was the youngest of 176 artists participating in the international exhibition Documenta 7 in Germany.

Basquiat was also featured in the 1983 Biennial Exhibition at the Whitney Museum of American Art in New York, becoming the youngest artist ever to be included. Between 1983 and 1985, Basquiat produced 31 works in collaboration with Andy Warhol. Basquiat was devastated by the death in 1987 of Warhol, who had been his close friend and mentor. A year later, at the age of 27, Basquiat died of a drug overdose in his New York apartment.

Within the span of eight years, Jean-Michel Basquiat went from being an anonymous tag-writer to an internationally celebrated artist. His large, colorful works combine GRAFFITI ART with abstract expressionism. Some of Basquiat's paintings celebrate African American JAZZ musicians and boxers, while others address issues such as mortality, racism, and commercialism. The three-pointed crown and the circled *c* of the copyright symbol are recurrent images in his paintings. Basquiat's work is characterized by the inclusion and canceling out of words, which he explained by saying, "I cross out words so you will see them more; the fact that they are obscured makes you want to read them." Basquiat's rhythmic juxtaposition of words and images constitutes one of his most distinctive contributions to twentieth-century painting.

Aaron Myers

Known first as a graffiti artist and later as a leading avant-garde painter in New York City, Jean-Michel Basquiat (1960-1988) posed for photographer James VanDerZee in 1982. Basquiat in turn painted VanDerZee after this sitting. *James VanDerZee/©Donna VanDerZee*

SEE ALSO
New York, New York.

Africa

Bassa of Cameroon, ethnic group of CAMEROON.

The Bassa primarily inhabit southern Cameroon. They speak a Bantu language and are related to the BAKOKO and BABIMBI, also of Cameroon. More than 200,000 people consider themselves Bassa in Cameroon.

SEE ALSO
Bantu: Dispersion and Settlement.

Africa

Bassa of Liberia, also known as the Basa, the Basso, and the Gbasa, ethnic group of LIBERIA.

The Bassa primarily inhabit Grand Bassa County, Liberia. They speak a Niger-Congo language belonging to the KRU group and are divided into several distinct subgroups. Approximately 400,000 people consider themselves Bassa in Liberia.

SEE ALSO
Languages, African: An Overview.

North America

Bass, Charlotta Spears

(b. October 1880, S.C.; d. April 29, 1969, Los Angeles, Calif.), publisher, editor, and the first black woman to campaign for the vice presidency of the United States.

Charlotta Spears Bass was the sixth of 11 children of Hiram and Kate Spears. At the age of 20, she left South Carolina to live with an older brother in Providence, Rhode Island, where she worked for ten years at a local newspaper. Suffering exhaustion, she moved to Los Angeles to recuperate but soon ran out of money and began collecting subscriptions for the *Eagle*, the oldest black newspaper on the West Coast.

By 1912 she was the newspaper's managing editor. She renamed it the *California Eagle* and transformed it into a tool for publicizing and attacking racial discrimination. In 1912 she also met her future husband, John Bass, who had founded the *Topeka Plaindealer* and who had recently been named editor of the *California Eagle*.

The Basses won widespread attention for their assault on *Birth of a Nation*, D. W. Griffith's 1915 film glorifying the Ku Klux Klan. They were also among the main promoters of the "Don't Buy Where You Can't Work" campaign. Largely due to their efforts, job discrimination at the Los Angeles General Hospital, the Los Angeles Rapid Transit Company, and the Southern California Telephone Company was ended. In 1934 John Bass died, and Charlotta continued her work alone.

A longtime member of the party of Abraham Lincoln, Bass was the Western director of Republican Wendell Wilkie's 1940 presidential campaign. She was later chosen by city representatives to run for a seat on the Los Angeles city council; she lost but succeeded in uniting black businesses and voters. In 1948 she broke with the Republicans, whom she viewed as negligent concerning race relations, and four years later was nom-inated as the vice-presidential candidate of the Progressive Party. Together with presidential nominee Vincent Hallinan, a white civil liberties lawyer, she argued for an end to the Korean War and a greater emphasis on civil rights. "Win or lose," Bass said of the campaign, "we win by raising the issues." The Progressives won less than 1 percent of the vote. Bass continued her political and editorial work, publishing her autobiography in 1960.

See Also
Birth of a Nation, The.

Africa

Basutoland. **Former name of Lesotho.**

North America

Bates, Clayton ("Peg Leg")

(b. October 11, 1907, Fountain Inn, S.C.), American tap dancer who performed in Harlem nightclubs and appeared on the Ed Sullivan television show.

Clayton Bates was born on October 11, 1907 in Fountain Inn, South Carolina. He lost his leg in a cotton-seed mill accident at age 12, but decided to tour the country with a homemade wooden leg at the age of 15, working as a minstrel in racially integrated vaudeville circuits. He later danced in Harlem nightclubs, and frequently appeared on the Ed Sullivan television show. In 1952 Bates opened the Peg Leg Bates Country Club in New York, the largest black-owned and -operated resort in America until it was sold in the late 1980s.

Alonford James Robinson, Jr.

See Also
Harlem, New York; Minstrelsy; Tap Dance; Television and African Americans.

North America

Bates, Daisy Lee Gatson

(b. 1920, Huttig, Ark.), African American civil rights activist who coordinated the integration of Central High School in Little Rock, Arkansas.

Daisy Lee Gatson Bates barely knew her parents. Her mother was killed by three white men after she resisted their sexual advances; her father left town, fearing reprisals if he sought to prosecute those responsible. Orlee and Susie Smith, friends of her parents, adopted her. In 1941 she married L. C. Bates, a journalist. They moved to Little Rock, Arkansas, and established a newspaper, the *Arkansas State Press;* it became the leading African American newspaper in the state and a powerful voice in the Civil Rights Movement.

It was as president of the Arkansas state conference of the National Association for the Advancement of Colored People that Bates coordinated the efforts to integrate Little Rock's public schools after the Supreme Court's Brown v. Board of Education decision outlawed segregated public schools in 1954. Nine African American students, the "Little Rock Nine," were admitted to Little Rock's Central High School for the 1957-1958 school year.

Violent white reaction to integration forced President Dwight D. Eisenhower to order 1000 army paratroopers to Little Rock to restore order and protect the children. Bates was the students' leading advocate, escorting them safely to school until the crisis was resolved. She continued to serve the children, intervening with school officials during conflicts and accompanying parents to school meetings. In 1962 Bates published her memoir of the Little Rock crisis, *The Long Shadow of Little Rock.*

Robert Fay

Latin America and the Caribbean

Batista, Fulgencio

(b. January 16, 1901, Oriente Province, Cuba; d. August 6, 1973, Guadalmira, Spain), Afro-Cuban dictator and president ousted by Fidel Castro.

Fulgencio Batista y Zaldivar was a controversial Cuban leader who dominated much of the country's politics for three decades. Born in 1901 to a rural farming family in the Oriente province, Batista was orphaned at age 13 and left school to become a tailor's apprentice. He joined the military at age 20.

On September 4, 1933, Batista led the Sergeants' Rebellion, which culminated in the appointment of President Ramón Grau San Martín and the ousting of President Manuel de Céspedes. Grau's revolutionary policies incurred the disfavor of the United States, which refused to recognize the government. In 1934, with United States support, Batista forced Grau's resignation. Batista ruled through a series of puppet presidents and was himself elected in 1940, defeating his rival, Grau. As president from 1940 to 1944, Batista passed a number of reforms governing the areas of health, welfare, and labor. He also legalized the Communist Party.

Constitutionally prohibited from running a consecutive term as president, Batista moved to Florida, returning to Cuba in 1948 with a senate seat and his own political party, called Unitary Action. In March 1952 Batista ran for his second presidential term but preempted the election by launching another coup. He was sworn in as president on April 4, 1952, with the support of foreign governments and the Cuban economic elite. In 1954 he won in a rigged election in which none of the major parties participated. Batista's second administration was noted for the growth of gambling and tourism and was notorious for government corruption.

In the 1950s Cuba was relatively prosperous among Latin American countries, ranking second in per capita gross domestic product, fourth in literacy, and first in the number of televisions and radios per capita. Nonetheless, Cuban society was tremendously inequitable. Afro-Cubans, in particular, were socially and economically marginalized, excluded from private beaches and social venues and discriminated against in employment and education. Batista himself was a mulatto, but he did nothing to address these racial disparities. It was these social tensions as well as Batista's refusal to abdicate power that led to his overthrow by Fidel Castro in 1959. After the Cuban Revolution, Batista lived in exile in Europe. He died in 1973 in Spain.

Judith Morrison

See Also
Cuba.

North America

Battey, Cornelius M. **(b. 1873, Augusta, Ga.; d. 1927), African American photographer known for his portraiture technique; established the photography department at Tuskegee Institute.**

By the age of 27, Cornelius Battey was well known for his photographic portraiture in New York City and Cleveland. At his popular portrait studio on New York's Mott Street, he photographed such celebrities as Frederick Douglass and President Calvin Coolidge. In 1914 he set up a photography department at Tuskegee Institute and headed it from 1914 until his death in 1927. As an artist he created picture postcards of major African American figures, which were sold nationwide. Between 1915 and 1927 his photographs were featured on the covers of the *Crisis, Messenger,* and *Opportunity* magazines.

See Also
Crisis, The; *Messenger, The*; New York, New York; *Opportunity: Journal of Negro Life*; Tuskegee University.

North America

Battle, Kathleen (b. August 13, 1948, Portsmouth, Ohio), African American soprano in international OPERA.

Kathleen Battle began singing in church as a child and received bachelor's and master's degrees in music from the University of Cincinnati College Conservatory of Music. She made her professional debut as an opera singer at the 1972 Spoleto Festival in Italy.

Battle debuted at New York's Metropolitan Opera in 1977 and became internationally known within a few years. In addition to singing soprano roles in opera houses and with symphony orchestras, her repertoire has expanded to include spirituals and the work of George Gershwin and Duke Ellington. Battle has received many honors for her work, including three Grammy Awards and a Candace Award from the National Coalition of 100 Black Women.

Lisa Clayton Robinson

See Also
New York, New York; Ellington, Edward Kennedy ("Duke").

Latin America and the Caribbean

Batuque, a religion practiced in Belém, a city in Brazil, which combines elements of rural "caboclo" religions with the more African-derived Tambor de Mina religion. Batuque is also commonly used as a generic term for any type of Afro-Brazilian religion or religious ritual.

See Also
Religions, African, in Brazil.

Africa

Baule, the largest ethnic group in the Côte d'Ivoire.

According to oral tradition, the Baule were originally part of the powerful ASANTE Confederation, based in what is present-day GHANA, but a violent succession struggle forced the group to break from the confederation. Led by Queen Aura Pokou, the sister of one of the slain contenders, the Baule migrated west in the late eighteenth century. During the journey they absorbed members of the many smaller DYULA, KRU, and Voltaic groups they encountered. The Baule also established profitable trade connections with several of the larger groups, with whom they exchanged the luxurious cloth produced by Baule women for guns, salt, and grain. They eventually settled in the valley between the Comoé and Bandama rivers, in the central region of what is now the CÔTE D'IVOIRE, and established trade connections between the coastal and savanna peoples. By the mid-nineteenth century the Baule had become prosperous from a lucrative north-south trade in gold, cloth, palm oil, and slaves.

The Baule were originally a highly centralized and hierarchical society, but their experience of migration and relocation gradually undermined their authority structures. By the time FRANCE attempted to colonize the Côte d'Ivoire in the late nineteenth century, the Baule state had broken into decentralized village clusters, bound only by kinship and commerce. Although village chiefs typically led these groups, successful traders with connections to other powerful clusters occasionally seized control. Internal rivalries, however, were fairly rare, and were generally limited to trade groups vying for commercial profits. It was this antagonism that the French attempted to exploit during the early twentieth century in their efforts to subdue the Baule populations.

Although the Baule welcomed commercial relations with the French, they were much less receptive to French troops passing through their homeland en route to conquests farther north, especially because the French demanded the use of Baule slaves as porters. In 1893 their attacks on French troops delayed a military campaign against the warrior-chief SAMORY TOURÉ. In the following years they accumulated guns and ammunition; when the French finally defeated Touré in 1898, they found the Baule stronger than before and just as unwilling to accept COLONIAL RULE.

In 1900 the French began a series of military campaigns against the Baule, but they proved no match for the Baule's guerrilla warfare tactics. Attempts to tax Baule merchants' trade also met with strong resistance. In 1908 the governor of the Côte d'Ivoire, Gabriel Angoulvant, announced a campaign of "pacification," ordering colonial troops to "search and destroy" all rebels as well as their crops and villages. The French administration also attempted to play rival trade groups off each other. Although these tactics were at first only partially successful, the destruction of crops caused famines that, by 1911, ultimately destroyed organized Baule resistance.

Throughout the colonial era the Baule remained wary of the French, though many were educated at missionary schools and went on to become high-ranking civil servants and wealthy plantation owners. The Baule exercised considerable influence within the colonial Côte d'Ivoire, helping Ivoirians vocalize their demands for decolonization in the 1940s. The Baule people's most famous nationalist leader, FÉLIX HOUPHOUËT-BOIGNY, led the country to independence in 1960. Houphouët-Boigny ruled the country for the next 30 years, during which the Baule became the most influential and richest ethnic group in the Côte d'Ivoire. In 1993 he was succeeded by another Baule, HENRI-KONAN BÉDIÉ, whose administration has continued to promote the concerns of Baule plantation owners.

Elizabeth Heath

See Also
Slavery in Africa.

Latin America and the Caribbean

Bauza, Mario (b. April 28, 1911, Havana, CUBA; d. July 11, 1993, New York, N.Y.), Afro-Cuban trumpet player, bandleader, and arranger who had a key role in the creation of Afro-Cuban jazz.

Mario Bauza was a talented multi-instrumentalist whose greatest musical achievement lay in his prominent role in the founding of AFRO-LATIN JAZZ. Prior to his 1930 departure for New York City, Bauza had concentrated on classical music, playing oboe and clarinet in the Havana Philharmonic. But in the United States he found his true calling as a JAZZ musician. In 1932, while working in Noble Sissle's band, Bauza began to perform on trumpet, and he went on to serve as a trumpet player and the musical director for Chick Webb's big band (1933-1938). While working with Webb, Bauza helped convince the initially skeptical bandleader of Ella Fitzgerald's great potential as a vocalist.

Later Bauza played trumpet with bandleaders Don Redman (1938-1939) and Cab Calloway (1939-1941). Bauza played a major role in convincing Calloway to hire the brash young trumpeter Dizzy Gillespie, whom Bauza had met two years earlier during his stint with Webb. In his autobiography, Gillespie declared that Bauza "was the first to impress me with the importance of Afro-Cuban music.... With Mario Bauza in the band, I really became interested in bringing Latin and especially Afro-Cuban influences into my music." Particularly impressed by the surging polyrhythms of Cuban conga drummers, Gillespie resolved that if he ever organized his own band, he would make sure to include a conga drummer.

At that time Gillespie's notion was a radical one. Although most big bands had at least one so-called Latin number in their books, swing-era jazz remained closed off from authentic Afro-Latin music. "In those days," Bauza recalled in an interview, "those American musicians didn't have the slightest idea about Latin music. The rhythms were too complicated for them." This situation began to change during the 1940s, an era of musical experimentation best remembered for the rise of bop, or modern jazz. Gillespie organized a big band, and in 1947 kept his resolution to add a conga drummer. He turned to Bauza for suggestions, and Bauza introduced him to Luciano "Chano" Pozo.

Bauza was a capable section player but had no illusions about his limited improvisational abilities. However, he quickly revealed his talents as an arranger during a long stint (1941-1976) as musical director for his brother-in-law Frank "Machito" Grillo's Afro-Cuban band. Bauza played a key role in the Afro-Cubans' successful merging of Cuban music – and above all Afro-Cuban rhythms – with African American jazz. His dynamic arrangements helped formalize Afro-Cuban jazz, and he urged Machito to incorporate jazz solos into the band's performances. Bauza also encouraged Machito to feature prominent American jazz musicians as guest artists with the band, including Charlie Parker, Dizzy Gillespie, and Cannonball Adderley, whose performances helped confirm the legitimacy of Latin jazz.

Despite his seminal role, Bauza remained virtually unknown to the wider jazz public, having been overshadowed for so many years by Machito, the Afro-Cubans' bandleader and front man. At last, in the 1980s, Bauza organized his own big band, the Afro-Cuban Orchestra. The band released three albums of Bauza's compositions and arrangements, the last of which was recorded just two months before his death. These albums gained him a measure of well-deserved critical and popular acclaim.

James Clyde Sellman

SEE ALSO

Adderley, Julian Edwin ("Cannonball"); Calloway, Cabell (Cab); Fitzgerald, Ella; Gillespie, John Birks ("Dizzy"); New York, New York; Parker, Charles Christopher ("Bird"); Sissle, Noble; Machito; Pozo y González, Luciano (Chano).

Baya. Please see GBAYA

Latin America and the Caribbean

Bayano, King, sixteenth-century slave leader of a maroon community in the San Blas Mountains in the area of present-day Panama (*see* PANAMA).

SEE ALSO

Maroonage in the Americas.

American artist Romare Bearden experimented with many materials and styles in depicting the African American experience. This 1988 collage is called *Family*. *National Museum of American Art, Washington, D.C./Art Resource, NY*

North America

Bearden, Romare (b. September 2, 1912, Charlotte, N.C.; d. March 12, 1988, New York, N.Y.), African American artist famous for his collages, which capture the daily rhythms of black life.

Romare Bearden was inspired by the work of such European artists as Pablo Picasso, Henri Matisse, and Joan Miró, who, in the early twentieth century, championed a collage aesthetic. These artists painted or pasted onto canvas elements from various sources, creating images with stylistic and spatial distortions. Bearden was also inspired by the CIVIL RIGHTS MOVEMENT, and he assembled a group of African American artists in the early 1960s to create artwork in celebration of the movement. When they rejected his suggestion that collage be the official medium of the group, Bearden began to create collages on his own.

Bearden became famous for his collage work of the 1960s. The works from this period combine acrylic or oil paints, or both, with images from magazines, newspapers, and photographs. Bearden drew on these various pictorial sources to construct African American people and their surroundings.

Most of Bearden's collages are informed by his childhood memories from Pittsburgh, Charlotte, and Harlem in the 1920s. His collages depict African Americans engaged in everyday activities in both street and interior settings. *Evening 9:10, 461 Lenox Avenue* (1964), for example, shows an apartment in which three people are involved in a card game. One of Bearden's outdoor scenes is *Watching the Trains Go By* (1964), in which one of the people waiting for a train strums a guitar to pass the time.

Bearden's collages are uniquely African American. He occasionally juxtaposed African masks with contemporary black American figures in his compositions. Art critic Hilton Kramer interpreted this juxtaposition as the "morphology of certain forms that derive originally from African art, then passed into modern art by way of cubism, and are now being employed to evoke a mode of African American experience." The African American character of these collages also derives from their connection with JAZZ music. Growing up in Harlem, Bearden regularly attended the cabarets and nightclubs where jazz was played. His mother's work as a social activist and a New York editor for the *Chicago Defender* brought young Bearden into contact with many of the Harlem Renaissance's most celebrated musicians, painters, and writers.

Bearden's creation of collages entailed a process of deconstruction and reconstruction that paralleled the creation of jazz music. He often tore away sections of his works and relayered them with new images. Of this technique, Bearden said, "Well, it's like jazz: you do this and then you improvise." The abrupt juxtapositions resulting from this process mirror the creatively disjunctured sounds of jazz music. One of Bearden's collages, *1930s, Chicago Jazz* (1964), is dedicated to the African American form of music that inspired his artwork.

Some critics have interpreted the fragmented character of Bearden's collages and jazz music as representative of African American history. The writer RALPH ELLISON, a close friend of Bearden, drew an analogy between Bearden's collages and "the sharp breaks, leaps in consciousness, distortions, paradoxes, reversals, telescoping of time and surreal blending of styles, value, hopes and dreams which characterize much of Negro American history."

Inspired by E. Simms Campbell, an African American cartoonist for *Esquire* magazine, Bearden began his art career as a cartoonist. While a student at New York University from 1931 to 1935, Bearden created cartoons for the *Medley*, the school's humor magazine, as well as the *Baltimore Afro-American*, *Collier's*, and the *Saturday Evening Post*. In the late 1930s Bearden attempted his first paintings, genre scenes of black city life executed in the then-popular style of social realism. He was influenced to pursue a more socially conscious art while studying at the Art Students League under the German satirical and social artist George Grosz.

After serving in the army during World War II, Bearden began painting in an abstract mode inspired by the cubism of Pablo Picasso. The works from this period are rich in geometrically rendered figures with bold contours and vibrant colors arranged in stained-glass-like patterns. The figures are derived largely from epic literary sources such as Homer's *Iliad* and the Bible. One such work is *He Is Risen* (1945), which treats the figure of Christ in a triangular fashion. From 1945 to 1948 Bearden regularly exhibited his paintings with those of other avant-garde artists at the gallery of Samuel M. Koontz. In the 1950s Bearden studied painting at the Sorbonne in Paris and tried his hand at songwriting before embarking on collage work.

Bearden once stated, "I have chosen to paint the life of my people as I know and feel it – passionately and dispassionately." This is an important statement in light of the fact that Bearden was from a well-educated, middle-class family and was light-skinned enough to pass for being white, yet chose to live as black. He added, "It is important that the artist identify with the self-reliance, hope, and courage of the people around him, for an art must always go where energy is."

Aaron Myers

SEE ALSO
World War II and African Americans; *Chicago Defender*; Harlem Renaissance; Harlem, New York; Pittsburgh, Pennsylvania; Art, African American.

North America

Beasley, Delilah Isontium

(b. September 9, 1872, Cincinnati, Ohio; d. August 18, 1934, San Leandro, Calif.), African American journalist and historian, campaigned to stop the use of derogatory racial terms in newspapers and chronicled the presence of African Americans in California history.

Delilah Beasley was born on September 9, 1872, in Cincinnati, Ohio, to Margaret and Daniel Beasley. She began her career in journalism by writing for the *Cleveland Gazette* at the age of 12; by 15, she had a regular column in the Sunday *Cincinnati Enquirer*. After her parents' deaths while she was still a teenager, Beasley had to find another full-time job to support herself, and she pursued a career as a trained masseuse. In 1910, after she followed a client to California, Beasley resumed her original interest in journalism.

Beasley wrote a weekly column for the Sunday *Oakland Tribune* called "Activities among Negroes" for the next 20 years. She spoke out against racial stereotyping and discrimination throughout her career. One of her most significant contributions to journalism was her campaign to stop the use in mainstream newspapers of such derogatory terms as "darky" and "nigger" to refer to African Americans.

Beasley also studied history informally at the University of California at Berkeley and by searching research archives and collecting oral histories across the state. In 1919 she published *The Negro Trail-Blazers of California*, which chronicled the presence of African Americans in California history.

Beasley was active in the Oakland community, and was a member of several organizations, including the National Association for the Advancement of Colored People (NAACP), the League of Nations Association of Northern California, and the League of Women Voters. Delilah Beasley died of heart disease in San Leandro, California on August 18, 1934.

Lisa Clayton Robinson

SEE ALSO
National Association for the Advancement of Colored People; Racial Stereotypes; San Francisco and Oakland, California.

Africa

Beatrice, Dona

(b. 1682?, Kongo Kingdom [present-day Democratic Republic of the Congo, or Congo-Kinshasa]; d. July 2, 1706, São Salvador, present-day Congo-Kinshasa), seventeenth-century KONGO prophet who preached the reunification of the Kongo Kingdom.

During a period of instability and fragmentation within the Kongo Kingdom, a young woman named Kimpa Vita (later baptized Beatrice and known as Dona Beatrice) led a religious movement to restore the empire to its former glory. Beatrice began her movement, later called Antonianism, in 1704, when she claimed to have a near-death vision of Saint Anthony. She said the popular Portuguese saint appeared to her as an African, after which she died and came back to life as the saint. Soon afterward she began preaching a religious message that combined an anti-Catholic Christianity with Kongo culture, through which she hoped to reunite the Kongo Kingdom.

Within months Beatrice established a church in the Kongo capital of São Salvador. Her church was frequently filled with followers who identified with her popular message; although the message was based on Christian theology, Beatrice preached that the founders of the Christianity were Africans, Kongo was the Holy Land, and that Christ had been born in São Salvador. Later, she tried to reenact the beginnings of Christianity by giving birth to a son she claimed was immaculately conceived. In addition, Beatrice renounced fetishes (including crosses, because they were the instrument of Christ's death), witchcraft, and European clothing. According to Beatrice, these were the correct tenets of Christianity and through their adherence the Kongo people would redeem themselves before God and pave the way for heaven on earth – the reformation of the Kongo Kingdom as it was during the rule of Afonso I.

As Beatrice became increasingly popular, however, Catholic missionaries tried to find ways to destroy her. At the same time, Pedro IV, the ruler of the Kimbangu clan, was looking to solidify his power over the Kongo Kingdom. Claiming Beatrice to be the supporter of a rival clan, the missionaries convinced Pedro to arrest her, which he did in 1706 after the birth of her son raised doubts about her saintliness. She was tried before the royal council and sentenced to death. On July 2, Beatrice and her son were burned at the stake as heretics.

Elizabeth Heath

See Also

Christianity, African: An Overview; Portugal.

North America

Beavers, Louise (b. March 18, 1902, Cincinnati, Ohio; d. 1962), African American film actor best known for her 1934 portrayal of the mother in *Imitation of Life*.

Born in Cincinnati, Ohio, on March 18, 1902, and raised in Los Angeles, Louise Beavers began her career in the silent film *Uncle Tom's Cabin* (1927). She appeared in over 120 motion pictures, always typecast as a Southern mammy or a source of comic relief. Although her portrayal of the mother in *Imitation of Life* (1934) was called the finest film performance of 1934 and established her career, her acting potential was never allowed to develop. Her notable roles included Pearl, Mae West's sassy maid in *She Done Him Wrong* (1933), Robinson's mother in *The Jackie Robinson Story* (1950), and the title role in the popular ABC television series *Beulah* (1952-1953).

See Also

Cincinnati, Ohio; Los Angeles, California.

North America

Bechet, Sidney Joseph, (b. May 14, 1897, New Orleans, La.; d. May 14, 1959, Paris), African American clarinet and soprano saxophone player who was, along with Louis Armstrong, the greatest jazz soloist of the 1920s.

Although well known to jazz listeners and critics, Sidney Bechet has never enjoyed the reputation of his only peer, cornet and trumpet player Louis Armstrong. Yet in recent years Bechet has gained greater recognition, at least from jazz scholars and critics. For example, Barry Singer, in a 1997 *New York Times* article, described him as an "intrepid musical pioneer who was not merely Louis Armstrong's contemporary but in every way his creative equal."

In many respects, the two men shared much: they were near contemporaries, born and raised in New Orleans, and both were virtuosos on their chosen instruments. Both were known above all as improvisers, as soloists rather than bandleaders, composers, or arrangers. Various factors help account for Armstrong's greater renown. His clarion-like trumpet moved even nonmusicians, while Bechet's facility on woodwinds was less visceral in effect. Armstrong found his greatest popularity as a vocalist; Bechet had no illusions about his limited singing ability. In the post-World War II years, Bechet settled in France and was largely absent from the American jazz scene.

At heart, however, the divergent reputations of the two men reflect profound differences in personality and background. Throughout his long career, from the pinched social world of the Jim Crow South to international acclaim, Armstrong always projected a happy-go-lucky demeanor. Bechet, on the other hand, fought to contain a powerful temper and seething rage toward racial injustice.

Armstrong, a poor black orphan, discovered in music a means of escape, a way up and out of poverty. Bechet grew up in a middle-class, land-owning Creole family, racially mixed and light-skinned. The musical tradition of New Orleans Creoles was formal and schooled; many Creoles disdained the blues-based, improvised jazz of the black community. Bechet's decision to throw his lot with jazz thus took him across a key racial boundary.

Bechet, who was four years Armstrong's senior, repeatedly achieved musical successes, only to be eclipsed by the younger and more charismatic trumpeter. During the 1910s Bechet won acclaim throughout New Orleans as an instrumentalist. He left the South for Chicago in 1917, five years before Armstrong, in the first wave of the Great Migration of blacks out of the South, and quickly dominated the Chicago jazz scene. In 1919 he joined Will Marion Cook's orchestra for a European tour.

Bechet remained in Europe until late in 1922. His playing inspired the first piece of serious jazz criticism, an essay by the Swiss conductor Ernest Ansermet, who praised him as "an extraordinary clarinet virtuoso who is, so it seems, the first of his race to have composed perfectly formed blues on the clarinet.... [T]heir form was gripping, abrupt, harsh, with a brusque and pitiless ending like that of Bach's second Brandenburg Concerto. I wish to set down the name of this artist of genius; as for myself, I shall never forget it, it is Sidney Bechet." It was by no means the last time that Bechet found himself better appreciated by Europeans than by Americans.

While in London, Bechet bought a soprano saxophone, the instrument for which he would be best remembered. He quickly mastered the difficult instrument, which poses significant problems of intonation, especially in its upper register. Soon Bechet played it with no less facility than he did the clarinet. Prior to his taking up the soprano saxophone, musicians and the listening public had generally regarded saxophones as comic instruments best reserved for novelty effects. Bechet's virtuosity on the soprano, like Coleman Hawkins's tenor playing later in the decade, gave the saxophone musical legitimacy.

In 1923 Bechet became the first major jazz soloist to record, beating Armstrong by several months. In 1924 he joined Armstrong on several recordings, including "Texas Moaner Blues" (1924), recorded by pianist Clarence Williams's Blue Five, and "Cake Walkin' Babies" (1924), by the Red Onion Jazz Babies. These recordings reveal Bechet and Armstrong in the act of transforming jazz from collective improvisation – the essence of the New Orleans style – to a focus on the improvising soloist.

Bechet's next trip abroad, in 1925, included lengthy stays in France and the Soviet Union. While sailing to Cherbourg aboard the Cunard liner *Berengaria*, Bechet had a shipboard romance with Josephine Baker, the 19-year-old singer and dancer who was just beginning her ascent to stardom.

But while Armstrong found success as a singer, bandleader, and entertainer in films and on radio programs, Bechet remained obscure. In 1932 he teamed up with trumpeter Tommy Ladnier in a recording session for RCA Victor, but work dried up during the Great Depression, and Bechet and Ladnier opened a tailor shop in 1933-1934. During the 1930s, Bechet's fortunes gradually improved. He joined Noble Sissle's band from 1934 to 1938. The French jazz writer and producer Hugues Panassie reunited him with Ladnier for a notable 1938 session that produced the classic "Really the Blues." The following year Bechet had his first (though minor) hit, a memorable rendition of "Summertime" that gave the fledgling Blue Note Records its first commercial success.

Bechet played with a pronounced vibrato. To produce a vibrato, the musician alters the pitch of a note by slightly changing his or her embouchure – that is, the position and pressure of the mouth on the instrument's mouthpiece – making the note waver above and below its true pitch. During the 1920s most jazz musicians favored a rapid vibrato, but during the 1930s, swing-era musicians preferred a slower vibrato. Since the 1940s jazz musicians have largely dispensed with it altogether, except on held-out notes or phrase endings, especially in slow-tempo ballads.

Bechet, however, never changed his sound or style: he always used a rapid, wide vibrato. He was a confident and inventive improviser, both in individual solos and in the collective improvisation that characterized New Orleans jazz. He was also highly competitive, and vied with the trumpet or cornet player for the lead in collective improvisation.

Some of Bechet's best playing occurred in ensembles with trumpet players who would simply get out of his way and give him the room to improvise freely; for example, in an innovative piano-less quartet that recorded eight selections in 1940. Besides Bechet, the group featured Muggsy Spanier on cornet, Welman Braud on bass, and Carmen Mastren on guitar. The quartet played timeless jazz that was exceptional for its light, driving swing and for giving Bechet ample room in which to solo, exemplified by his superb rendition of "China Boy."

Sidney Bechet, one of the greatest jazz musicians of the 1920s, is shown here later in life. A true musical innovator, Bechet played clarinet and soprano saxophone. *The Everett Collection*

During the bop revolution of the 1940s Bechet again fell on hard times, but when he appeared at a 1949 jazz festival in Paris, he met with such a warm reception that he decided to remain in France. He performed for enthusiastic audiences in Europe and made occasional return visits to the United States until shortly before his death from cancer in 1959.

James Clyde Sellman

See Also

World War II and African Americans; Armstrong, Louis ("Satchmo"); Blues, The; Chicago, Illinois; Great Migration, The; Hawkins, Coleman Randolph; New Orleans, Louisiana.

Africa

Bechuanaland. Former name of Botswana.

North America

Beckwourth, James Pierson

(b. April 26, 1798, Fredericksburg, Va.; d. January 22, 1866, Laramie Plains, Wyoming Territory), legendary American Western mountain man, trapper, warrior, Indian chief, and trailblazer.

James P. Beckwourth, born of mixed-race parentage, escaped an apprenticeship to a St. Louis blacksmith and went west, taking a job with the Rocky Mountain Fur Company. He became an experienced trapper and fighter in the sparsely settled western territories. In 1824, the Crow Indian tribe adopted Beckwourth, who then married the daughter of the chief and earned such renown in battle that he was renamed Bloody Arm. Though he left the tribe after several years, and after earning honorary chief status, he continued a lifelong friendship with the Crows.

Criss-crossing the western and southern frontiers, Beckwourth worked as a guide, prospected for gold, served as an army scout during the third Seminole War, and was a rider for the Pony Express. He also worked with California's Black Franchise League in an effort, unsuccessful at the time, to repeal a law barring blacks from testifying in a court of law. In 1850 he discovered a pass through the Sierra Nevada mountains, enabling pioneers to reach California more quickly and safely. Beckwourth Pass is still used by the Pacific Railroad and the United States Interstate Highway system.

Beckwourth died in 1866, leaving behind an autobiography described by one critic as "the gaudiest, goriest book in our literature." He was almost as well known for his wild stories as for his true exploits, but his contribution to western expansion – the discovery of Beckwourth Pass – secured his place in the history of western trailblazers.

Kate Tuttle

See Also

American Indians; Mountain Men; Seminole Wars.

Latin America and the Caribbean

Bedia, José (b. 1959, Havana, Cuba), Cuban artist of Spanish ancestry.

José Bedia pursued his formal artistic education at Havana's Academia de Artes Plásticas San Alejandro and at the Instituto Superior de Arte. He served his military term in Angola. Following his departure from Cuba in 1991 and a relatively brief sojourn in Mexico, the artist established himself in Miami in 1992. Bedia's work – drawings on paper; oil paintings on canvas; works in ink, acrylic, charcoal, and oil crayons; and installations – derives most of its power from Cuba's African heritage, sometimes bringing to mind Kongo cosmograms (geometric designs that carry religious meanings) and Abakuá (Afro-Cuban all-male secret societies) ideographic writing. Texts in Spanish, Yoruba, or Bantu accompany many of his pieces. Despite the deep presence of African art in his work, and because it does not pretend to be a reenactment of original African art, Cuban critic Gerardo Mosquera has labeled it postmodern Kongo art.

Bedia's adherence to localist attitudes does not prevent him from establishing a dialogue between African American, Amerindian, Asian, and Euro-American cultures. He has pondered his artistic project in the following manner: "I am a person with Western training who, through a voluntary, conscious, premeditated system of an intellectual order, attempts an approach to 'primitive' cultures to experience their influences in a transcultural manner. Both of us are thus midway between modernity and primitiveness, between the civilized and the savage, between western and not western.... From this recognition, and on this boundary line that tends to break, comes my work." This deviation, or dialogue with the primitivistic appropriations embraced by the European modernists, has made Bedia an heir to Cuban artist of Afro-Chinese ancestry Wifredo Lam.

Bedia's interest in non-Western aboriginal cultures led to a residency with the Dakota Sioux in 1985, where he worked with icons from the Sioux pictographs. In his earliest body of work (1976-1978) he produced formal portraits with the accompanying accouterments placed below. These portraits incorporate several elements, including figures and photocopies taken from nineteenth-century photographs of the Amerindian people and, in some cases, cut-and-pasted pictures of animals, bullets, and feathers. A complex relationship between representation and reproduction is thus elaborated in these pieces.

Between 1978 and 1983 Bedia produced a series of works on paper that again drew on books about indigenous people of the Americas. In these drawings he recreated the world of indigenous America, including that of the inhabitants of Cuba prior to the Spanish conquest.

Since 1984, upon his initiation into Palo Monte (an Afro-Cuban religion), his engagement with Afro-Cuban culture has increased. Incorporating frequent visual images of the nonmaterial world of spirits and deities, some of his pieces are reminiscent of Afro-Cuban altars. It should be noted, however, that, while Bedia admits that his religious beliefs and practices influence his art, the difference between the two is very clear in his mind. He is "incapable of placing a sacred element of his religion in a secular art installation." In these installations, he does not seek a reproduction of original religious intentions or outcomes; rather he tends to incorporate both ritual-like artifacts and kitsch elements. Insofar as his work emphasizes the constructed nature of both the "original" image and the artist's, some critics have labeled him a postmodern anthropologist archaeologist or even a cosmographer.

Although Bedia is not known for being militantly opposed to the Cuban government, the political hardships he faced as an installation artist on the island made him leave Cuba. Though immigration themes had already surfaced in pieces that predated his exile, since that time they have appeared with greater frequency in his work. Geographic distance notwithstanding, Bedia's artistic production has maintained an intense cultural dialogue with his island of origin.

Carmen Oquendo-Villar

See Also

Bantu: Dispersion and Settlement; Abakuás; Regla de Palo.

Africa

Bédié, Henri-Konan (b. 1934, Dadiékro, Côte d'Ivoire), president of Côte d'Ivoire since 1993.

Henri-Konan Bédié was born in Dadiékro, in central Côte d'Ivoire. A member of the Baule ethnic group, which has dominated the nation's politics and cocoa interests since independence, he attended schools in Côte d'Ivoire and France before completing a doctoral degree in economics at the University of Poitiers in France. He entered the civil service of Côte d'Ivoire in 1960 during its final months as a French colony, serving as diplomatic counselor at the French Embassy in the United States. From 1961 to 1966 he was Côte d'Ivoire's first ambassador to the United States. In January 1966 he returned home to accept an appointment as minister delegate for financial affairs. He was soon promoted to minister of economy and finance. At the same time he acted as a governor of the International Monetary Fund and administrator for the International Bank for Reconstruction and Development (also known as the World Bank). In June 1977, after being dismissed from his ministry following the bankruptcy of six state-owned sugar factories, Bédié became special adviser for African affairs to the president of the International Finance Corporation of the World Bank in Washington, D.C.

Returning home in December 1980, Bédié, a member of the Democratic Party of Côte d'Ivoire, was elected president of the new National Assembly. Having been reelected assembly president in 1986, he became acting president of Côte d'Ivoire in 1993, following the death of President Félix Houphouët-Boigny. In October 1995 Bédié won election to a five-year term as president. He has been credited with reducing violent crime in Côte d'Ivoire but has been accused of persecuting journalists who have criticized him.

Africa

Bedouin, Arabs who live in the deserts of the Middle East and North Africa and who have traditionally practiced nomadic pastoralism.

The Bedouin are Arab nomads who traditionally controlled caravan trade routes through the Arabian and Saharan deserts and played a substantial role in the politics and economy of the Middle East and North Africa. Proud of their strict ethical codes and their nomadic lifestyle, the Bedouin helped introduce Islam to Africa.

The Bedouin originated in the Arabian Peninsula, where their ancestors lived in a number of distinct tribes before the emergence of Islam during the seventh century C.E. The Bedouin have remained divided into numerous tribal groups, and, with one brief exception, never formed a coherent state. They unified briefly under the leadership of the prophet Muhammad and his successors during the mid-seventh century to embrace Islam. Indeed, the first Muslims were primarily the Bedouin. By 642 C.E., Muslim, largely Bedouin, armies conquered much of the Middle East, including Egypt. During the late seventh and the eighth centuries Bedouin armies brought Islam to the remainder of North Africa. They initially settled in garrison cities, which then served as bases for further Arab expansion.

Throughout the following centuries the Bedouin competed with Berber nomads such as the Tuareg for control of the Saharan desert trade routes. The Bedouin were important figures in the Arabization of North Africa. In the eleventh through the thirteenth centuries the Bedouin tribes of Banu Hilal and the Banu Sulaim migrated west from Egypt and Libya, respectively, bringing Arab culture, language, and traditions to Algeria, Tunisia, and Morocco.

The traditional Bedouin economy centered on animal husbandry and trade. Most North African Bedouin groups raised camels, while some raised horses, donkeys, sheep, goats, and cattle. Living in tents, the Bedouin migrated seasonally in search of pasture. In summer they often settled in camps near villages where they exchanged animal products for manufactured goods and some foods. They also acted as transporters of products between the countryside and towns. Bedouins provided caravans passing through their desert oasis camps with shelter, animals, guides, and guards. Caravans that refused to pay tolls to the Bedouin were sometimes subject to raiding.

Because of the harsh desert conditions in which they lived, the erratic nature of their nomadic lifestyle, and their economic dependence on raiding, the Bedouin have developed a culture defined by disciplined group solidarity and loyalty. Traditionally Bedouins have valued courage and bravery and maintained rigorous codes of honor, revenge, loyalty, and hospitality. Their customary organization has been tribes made up of several clans or extended families that are strictly patriarchal, led by a *shaykh* and a group of male leaders. Clans have traditionally migrated together, shared pastures, and united to defend or avenge their members.

The Bedouin in Africa continued to fulfill a vital role in trans-Saharan trade until the late nineteenth century. However, the Bedouins' independence and their resistance to the boundaries, taxes, and trade restrictions imposed by modern states made them an obstacle to colonialism during this period. During the early twentieth century British and French colonialists sought to force the Bedouin to settle by converting their chiefs into landlords and building trains and roadways across the Sahara to render camels obsolete. In the early part of the twentieth century Italians colonized Libya, where they attempted to seize Bedouin land. But the Bedouin of Libya – largely united in the reformist and purist Sufi sect, the Sanusiya – resisted Italian rule, and Libya gained independence in 1951.

During the twentieth century the Bedouin lost control of the desert. Modern-day national borders have blocked the Bedouins' traditional freedom of movement and trade. Government wells have violated tribal rights to water preserves in the desert. Cars, trucks, and planes have reduced the value of camels as a form of transportation. While a few North African Bedouin struggle to maintain their traditional lifestyle despite these obstacles, many have turned to wage labor even though Bedouin culture has historically looked down on the dependence entailed in working for a wage.

Today many Bedouin drive trucks rather than camels or work in North Africa's oil industry. Nevertheless, the romantic ideal of the traditional Bedouin lifestyle, symbolic of the purest Arab values, persists. Bedouin poetry, glorifying great journeys, martyrs of love and war, and proud and honorable deeds, remains popular among Arabs of both the desert and city. Though it is impossible to state an exact population figure for the Bedouin, between 1 and 4 million live in North Africa, including Mauritania, Western Sahara, Morocco, Algeria, Mali, Libya, Tunisia, Chad, Egypt, and Sudan. A few million more live in Saudi Arabia and surrounding countries.

Leyla Keough

See Also
Camel; Sahara Desert; Sufism; Banu Hilal and Banu Sulaim; Islam and Tradition: An Interpretation; Trans-Saharan and Red Sea Slave Trade.

Africa

Beira, Mozambique, major city of central Mozambique.

Named after a province of northern Portugal, Beira is the second largest city in Mozambique and is located at the mouth of the Pungue and Buzi rivers on the Indian Ocean. Although the Portuguese explorer Pero da Covilha anchored near present-day Beira in 1487, it was not until 1891 that the Mozambique Company founded Beira as its headquarters. In 1941 the colonial state of Portuguese East Africa acquired Beira from the company. Under company and colonial control, Beira served as a major port for Indian Ocean trade. Beira became a busy international commercial entrepôt during the colonial period due to the construction of road and rail links to present-day Malawi, Zimbabwe, Zambia, and the Democratic Republic of the Congo.

Portuguese colonialists exported agricultural products from Beira and built a light-manufacturing sector in the city. After Mozambique achieved independence in 1975, the government pursued a policy of rapid industrialization, some of which took place in Beira's suburbs. However, the city suffered in the 1980s as a result of the war between the government of Mozambique and the Mozambican National Resistance (RENAMO) insurgents.

Today the port at Beira provides a vital outlet to the sea for Malawi and Zimbabwe. The road and rail route to Zimbabwe, called the Beira Corridor, has recently attracted considerable investment to the region. Beira has few amenities for tourists, although there are beautiful beaches nearby and the town provides access to the Gorongosa National Park. Beira's population is approximately 300,000.

Eric Young

See Also
Colonial Rule; Mozambican National Resistance.

Beit Israel. Please see Ethiopian Jews

Africa

Beja (also known as Bega), ethnic group of northeastern Africa.

The Beja primarily inhabit eastern Sudan, western Eritrea, and southeastern Egypt. During the 1970s and 1980s the violence of the Eritrean succession struggle forced many Beja in the region to flee to Sudan. They speak an Afro-Asiatic language and comprise numerous distinct subgroups, including Beni Amer, the Bisharin, and the Halanga. Approximately 2 million people consider themselves Beja.

See Also
Languages, African: An Overview.

North America

Belafonte, Harold George (Harry) (b. March 1, 1927, New York, N.Y.), African American singer, actor, producer, and activist who has used his position as an entertainer to promote human rights worldwide.

Harry Belafonte waves to Martin Luther King Jr. after walking in the 1965 Selma-to-Montgomery civil rights march. Actor Tony Perkins, behind Belafonte, was another of the celebrities who participated in the march. *UPI/CORBIS-Bettmann*

Harry Belafonte may be best known to American audiences as the singer of the "Banana Boat Song" (known popularly as "Day-O"), but it is his commitment to political causes that inspired scholar Henry Louis Gates Jr.'s comment that "Harry Belafonte was radical long before it was chic and remained so long after it wasn't."

Harold George Belafonte was born in Harlem, New York, to West Indian parents. The family moved to Jamaica in 1935 but returned five years later. Struggling with dyslexia, Belafonte dropped out of high school after the ninth grade and, at the age of 17, joined the U.S. Navy. Although the work was menial – scrubbing the decks of ships in port during World War II – naval service introduced Belafonte to African Americans who awakened Belafonte's political consciousness and introduced him to the works of radical black intellectual W. E. B. Du Bois.

In 1948 Belafonte settled in New York City and, after working a variety of odd jobs, found a calling in acting. As a member of the American Negro Theatre in Harlem, he earned his first leading role in *Juno and the Paycock* and met Paul Robeson, his hero, and Sidney Poitier, who became his lifelong friend.

Belafonte's performance as the only black member of the cast of John Murray Anderson's *Almanac* earned him a Tony award in 1953. A year later he starred with Dorothy Dandridge in *Carmen Jones*, a movie remake of Bizet's opera that brought widespread attention to Belafonte's sensual good looks. His other early films include *Island in the Sun* (1957) and *The World, the Flesh, and the Devil* (1959). In addition, for his work in "Tonight with Belafonte," in 1960 he became the first African American to receive an Emmy Award.

As Belafonte began to achieve success as an actor, he stumbled into the singing career that made him one of the most popular entertainers of the late 1950s. In 1949 a performance at an amateur night at the Royal Roost nightclub in New York led to an RCA recording contract. Belafonte's 1956 album *Calypso* became the first record to sell more than a million copies and started a craze for his husky voice and for the infectious rhythm of such songs as "Matilda," "Brown Skin Girl," and "Jamaica Farewell."

To critics who charged that a singer who had never visited Trinidad could not claim to know calypso, Belafonte offered no apologies. Not only did he make his version of Caribbean music accessible to a mainstream American audience but, in the dozens of albums that followed *Calypso*, he also performed songs such as "Cotton Fields" that conveyed the pain of the black African American experience.

Belafonte's appeal to white audiences did not, however, protect him from racial segregation. As a result, he refused to perform in the South from 1954 until 1961, and he became deeply involved in the CIVIL RIGHTS MOVEMENT. In 1956 Belafonte met Martin Luther King Jr. in Montgomery, Alabama, and they quickly became close friends. Belafonte was also a friend of Attorney General Robert F. Kennedy and frequently served as a liaison between King and policymakers in Washington, D.C.

It was Belafonte who sent the money to bail King out of the Birmingham City Jail and who raised thousands of dollars to release other jailed protesters, financed the Freedom Rides, and supported voter-registration drives. He joined BAYARD RUSTIN in leading the youth march for integrated schools from New York to Washington, D.C., in 1958 and helped to organize the March on Washington five years later.

Belafonte continues to use his power as an entertainer in the struggle for civil rights. His production company, Harbel, formed in 1959, produces movies and television shows by and about black Americans. Belafonte's idea for the hit song "We Are the World" generated more than 70 million dollars to fight famine in Ethiopia in 1985. Two years later he became the second American to be named UNICEF Goodwill Ambassador. A long-time antiapartheid activist, Belafonte recorded an album of South African music, *Paradise in Gazankulu*, in 1988 and chaired the welcoming committee for Nelson Mandela's visit to the United States in 1990.

Lawrie Balfour

SEE ALSO

Antiapartheid Movement; Mandela, Nelson Rolihlahla; World War II and African Americans; Military, Blacks in the American; Du Bois, William Edward Burghardt (W. E. B.); King, Martin Luther, Jr.; New York, New York; Trinidad and Tobago; March on Washington, 1963.

Africa

Belgian Congo. **Former name of DEMOCRATIC REPUBLIC OF THE CONGO.**

Latin America and the Caribbean

Belgrave, Valerie, **Afro-Trinidadian novelist whose best-known work is *Ti Marie* (1989). Belgrave is also a visual artist who has exhibited her dyed works in Trinidad and Canada (*see* LITERATURE, ENGLISH LANGUAGE, CARIBBEAN).**

Latin America and the Caribbean

Belize, **country in northeastern Central America, bounded on the north and northwest by MEXICO, on the east by the Caribbean Sea, and on the south and west by Guatemala. Known until 1973 as British Honduras, Belize became independent in 1981 and is a member of the Commonwealth of Nations.**

In a region dominated by the Spanish Empire, Belize was conquered by England and has long been an unusual country in the context of CENTRAL AMERICA. It is the only country in the region in which blacks have constituted a majority of the population for most of the twentieth century, in which English is the official language, and in which Caribbean culture predominates. In 1981 it became the last country in Central America to achieve independence from its European colonizer (*see* COLONIAL LATIN AMERICA AND THE CARIBBEAN). For all these reasons and more, few of the generalizations that apply to other Afro-Central American histories and cultures apply to Belize.

BELIZE BEFORE AFRICANS

The area now known as Belize has been occupied by a succession of native peoples, including the Maya, since at least 9000 B.C.E. The Maya were subjected to Spanish domination in the mid-1500s. In 1638 they rebelled against the Spanish system of *encomienda*, by which Indian labor and land were granted to Spanish conquerors, and drove the Spaniards from most of Belize. The Spaniards did not return until 1695.

During this interlude, probably in the late 1630s, English buccaneers settled in an area that is probably along the Cockscomb coast and began harvesting logwood trees. At the time logwood was prized chiefly for its role in the production of dark-colored dyes. In 1670, after a century of wars, England and Spain signed the Treaty of Madrid, which vaguely acknowledged English rights in the Caribbean but failed to specifically recognize the English settlement in Belize, to which Spain had laid claim. Consequently, the baymen, as England's logcutters were known, were under constant attack from the Spanish provincial government of the Yucatán Peninsula, to the north of Belize. Several times the baymen were forced to abandon and recolonize the territory.

ARRIVAL OF AFRICAN SLAVES

Although harvesting logwood required less labor than other forms of forestry, the baymen nonetheless imported African slaves to hasten the logging. The first slaves arrived by at least 1724, when a Spanish missionary noted that British settlers had imported slaves from JAMAICA and BERMUDA. Although most of the slaves were brought from the WEST INDIES, they had typically been born in Africa, probably around the BIGHT OF BENIN and the REPUBLIC OF THE CONGO. Many were apparently of IGBO origin: a section of Belize City was known as Eboe Town for several decades. At first the slaves clung closely to their African heritage, and the arrival of new slaves helped to maintain this connection. Over time, the Africans, West Indians (i.e., Jamaicans and Bermudans), and Europeans gradually created a Creole (or mixed) culture.

Cutting wood was seasonal work. A settler would take one or two male slaves, set up camp along the Belize River, and cut logwood for several months before the rainy season. When the rains came, the wood would be floated down the river, processed in Belize City, and loaded onto boats bound for England. Until the dry season came again, the slaves and their owners would live in Belize City. Thus many slave families endured a cycle of separation and reunion throughout the years.

In 1763 England and Spain signed another treaty, part of which gave a measure of legitimacy to the settlement in Belize. While Spain continued to maintain sovereignty over the land, it conceded the right of English settlers to harvest and export wood and to establish "temporary" settlements needed for the harvesting. To ensure that such settlements were temporary, the treaty specifically forbade plantation agriculture and other forms of more permanent commerce. In practice, the treaty gave the English settlers more time to strengthen their hold on the region, and thus a stronger claim to the land. The treaty's guarantees also made it possible to shift from small-scale logwood harvesting to large-scale mahogany harvesting.

Mahogany harvesting brought more changes to slave life in Belize, which already varied significantly from slavery in the rest of the Anglophone Caribbean as well as in Spanish America, where large plantations and mines were the norm. Mahogany harvesting was a large operation that exploited vast tracts of land, so slaves were required to venture farther and farther inland with less and less supervision than slaves in mines, towns, or plantations were subjected to. Slaves had several roles in the mahogany venture. Skilled and highly prized slaves known as huntsmen searched forests for mahogany trees. On finding them, they reported back to the axmen, or teams of slaves who felled the trees. The trees were then transported by oxen, overseen by another group of slaves, to a river where they could be floated down to the coast.

It is generally thought that Afro-Belizean slaves had more independence than their counterparts elsewhere in the New World and that the whip-bearing slave driver was more common in farm than forest. However, many early historians erred in believing that this freedom allowed the slaves of

Belize a much more humane experience. Revisionists such as Belizean scholar Assad Shoman now give more credence to the many reports of the seventeenth through nineteenth centuries recording the cruelties inflicted on slaves. These included severe beatings for failing to meet production targets, torture and maiming for escape attempts, and in some cases the same for little or no provocation (*see* PUNISHMENT OF SLAVES IN COLONIAL LATIN AMERICA AND THE CARIBBEAN).

Many slaves provided their own commentary on their condition by using the cover of the forest to escape north to the Yucatán, west to Guatemala, or south to Honduras. Most such escapees (*see* MAROONAGE IN THE AMERICAS) were forced to abandon their families in Belize City to obtain their freedom. Once free, some mixed with Spanish and Mayan communities, while others established their own villages and offered refuge to new escapees. One such settlement, on the Sibun River, grew in size to a modest town. Still other slaves attested to the horrors of slavery with suicide, abortion, or revolt. Colonial Belize experienced a string of slave rebellions between 1765 and 1773. A colonial government report on the last major slave revolt, led by two slaves named Will and Sharper in 1820, concluded that the slaves had been treated cruelly and had "certainly good grounds" for rebelling.

The focus on slavery in Belize has centered mainly on the men who worked the mahogany forests. However, enslaved women and children were also widely used in colonial Belize, mainly for domestic chores and small-scale farming and mostly in Belize City. Occasionally they were sent to the timber camps to perform similar chores. Others were taken as concubines by their white masters. A few slaves, principally men but occasionally women, became artisans – blacksmiths, woodworkers, and so on – but these were exceptions.

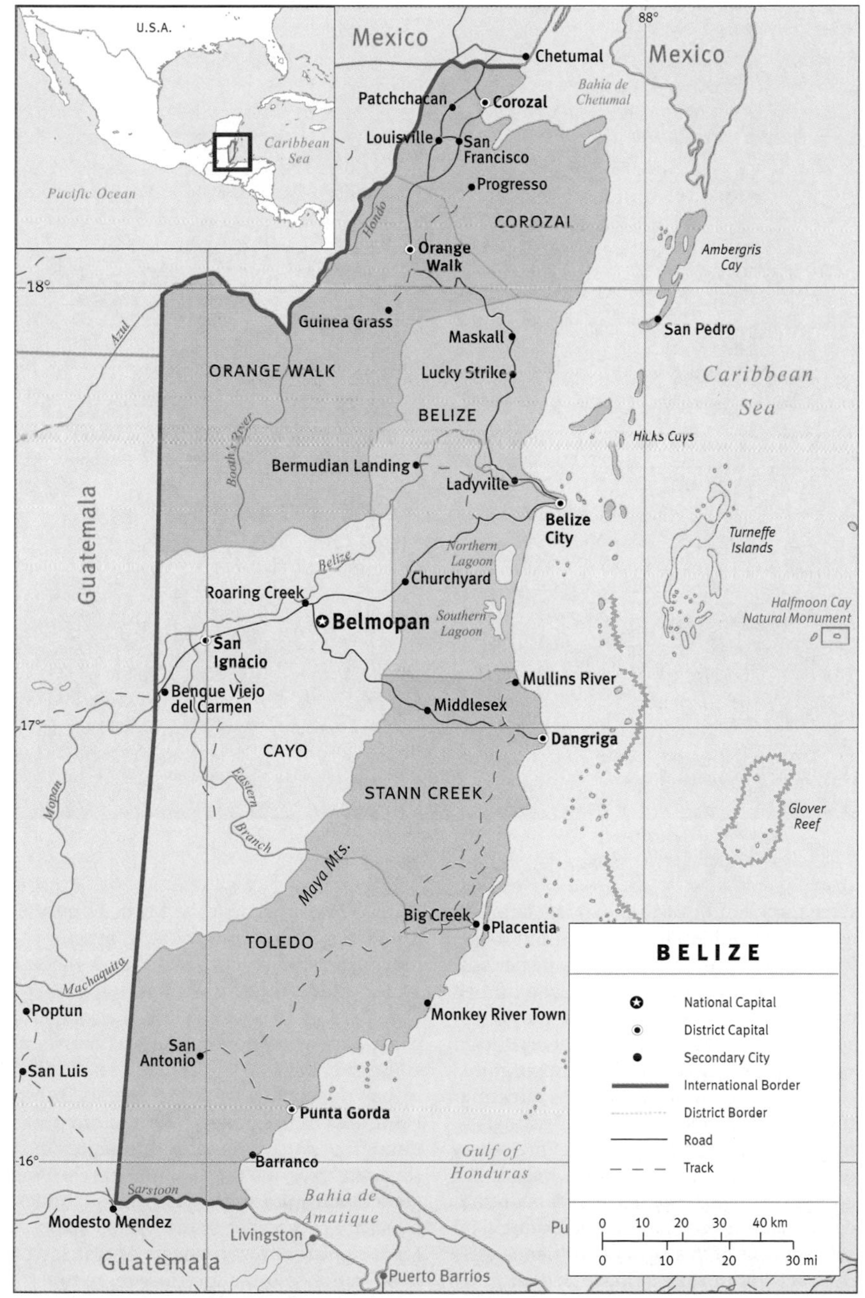

FREE BLACKS IN BELIZE

Whites have always been a minority in Belize. In the early 1780s settlers numbered about 500, while slaves numbered 3000. (There are few accurate estimates of the Mayan population, since few Mayans settled in Belize City or the nearby district.) As the slave population grew, so too did the population of black CREOLES who either moved from other parts of the West Indies, where they were already free, or who were granted their freedom by their masters after one or more generations in Belize. A rigid social stratification soon emerged in which the white minority held all political and economic power, and free blacks – who, like whites, were also numerically inferior to the slaves – were granted limited privileges. Free black Creoles suffered from economic and social discrimination, but their precarious position, one rung above their enslaved kinsmen, served to keep most of them quiescent.

In 1798 Spanish forces made a last effort to dislodge the British colony. Off the coast of Belize, near St. George's Caye, a small number of white settlers, slaves, and free blacks rebuffed the Spaniards. The Battle of St. George's Caye marks the assurance of sovereignty by British settlers and thus the birth of the period in which Belize was known as British Honduras, though diplomatic problems would delay the formal declaration of the area as a British colony until 1892. The battle also played a large part in creating the myth that blacks and whites have long cooperated in Belize, when in fact at that time free blacks mostly cooperated with whites because their weak economic and political status left them little choice.

In the early 1800s the Garifuna arrived in British Honduras. The Garifuna were previously residents of the Caribbean island of St. Vincent, where shipwrecked Africans mixed with Indian Caribs and created a culture known as the Black Caribs, or Garifuna. The Garifuna often challenged English authority and in 1797 were deported en masse to the Bay Islands off the coast of what is now Honduras. Most Garifuna eventually migrated to mainland Honduras and the southern coast of British Honduras.

In 1833 Great Britain nominally abolished slavery in its colonies (*see* ABOLITION AND EMANCIPATION IN LATIN AMERICA AND THE CARIBBEAN). As elsewhere in the British Empire, slaves in British Honduras had to wait through the five-year apprenticeship, during which time they were forced to work without wages for their owners, before gaining their freedom. Even after emancipation was complete in 1838, many free blacks were forced, by lack of employment, to continue working for their masters.

Emancipation reserved other hardships for the freedpeople as well. Despite the numerical superiority of free black Creoles, the tiny white elite of British Honduras continued its tight grip on political power. Equally important, they also held virtually all of the colony's accessible and arable land, forcing blacks who wished to work to do so where and when the white minority chose, and at meager wages. Typically, most blacks worked in the forest industry and were made further dependent on whites through a system of wage advances, which put them in debt with their employers before their wages were paid. Black workers were also forced to buy food and goods in company stores at exorbitant prices. People of African descent continued to face rigid restrictions on farming, which was generally forbidden, and settlement, which was generally under the control of whites, as a further means of limiting their independence – even though the colony had large tracts of unsettled land. Nonetheless, because blacks made up such a large part of the colony's population, some free black Creoles were able to rise to a modest prosperity as minor tradespeople and merchants.

Economy in Decline

The nineteenth-century economy of British Honduras peaked in 1846, when exports of mahogany reached 13.7 million feet. Timber companies, however, had been rapacious in their extraction of mahogany, so by mid-century most of the easily accessible trees had been cut and a large number of the young trees had been harvested as well. As a result, the country's timber stands could not replenish themselves on a pace with extraction, and foresters were pushed deeper inland to find new timber. The difficulty of harvesting more remote trees slowed production and thus profits. Making matters worse, mahogany prices in Europe were declining. By 1870 total mahogany exports from British Honduras had declined to 2.8 million feet, and many black Creoles were forced out of work. Exports climbed again to 11 million feet in 1906, but these levels proved unsustainable for long periods.

The economic hardships forced timber companies to consolidate, and as they did so they became highly dependent on British capital. Thus, many of the most important economic and political decisions affecting the colony's residents were increasingly made by whites in London. The managers of the largest of these London-based companies were guaranteed seats on the colony's appointed Legislative Council. The epitome of this London influence was the decision in 1826 to make British Honduras subordinate to Jamaica. Only in 1884 did British Honduras become an independent Crown colony. When black Creole elites requested in 1890 that some of the seats be opened to election (as had happened in New Zealand and Canada), the council, fearing the large numbers of black Creoles, refused. A few years later, the colony's governor appointed a small number of blacks to the council as a token gesture to quiet protesters. The power of the black councilors, however, was minimal.

At the turn of the century, more than 30,000 people lived in British Honduras: perhaps 12,000 to 15,000 of these were black Creoles, most of whom lived in and around Belize City. Another 10,000 were Spanish or *mestizo* (of indigenous and European descent), most of whom lived in northern British Honduras near the Mexican border. About 4000 were Amerindians, mostly Mayans who lived in the country's western and southern interior; and perhaps 3000 were Garífuna, who lived along the southern coast. The white population was between 1000 and 2000.

Fishing is an important economic activity in Belize. *John Curtis/DDB Stock Photo*

A few blacks in turn-of-the-century British Honduras found employment in the production of *chicle,* the latex drained from sapodilla trees and used for making chewing gum. Chicle was exported in great quantities, mostly to companies in the United States. Most *chicleros* however, were Mayans, who lived in the colony's interior where the sapodilla trees were more numerous. Chicle production at any rate declined after synthetic substitutes became widespread. More common for nonurban blacks was work on fruit plantations. As in other parts of Central America, bananas were harvested in increasingly large quantities in the early twentieth century, until disease crippled most of the crop in 1913. Devastating hurricanes in 1931, 1955, and 1961 blew down large numbers of trees and assured that the banana plantations never fully recovered. Black Creoles were thus left to seek work mostly in and around the Belize City district, where they provided services for the white elite and for other Creoles or became fishermen. Some also participated in small-scale subsistence farming. The Garífuna, more removed from whites in their southern coastal communities, relied largely on fishing and turtling for their livelihood.

The few black Creoles who nonetheless prospered created a base for future political and economic power. Robert Turton was the chicle buyer for Wrigley's of Chicago and, as such, the commander of some wealth in the early twentieth century. Henry Melhado, another black Creole, used his connections in the United States to export vast stores of bootleg liquor there during America's Prohibition Era. The work of such entrepreneurs gradually shifted the focus of the economy from Great Britain to the United States, where it remains today.

Toward Independence

In the 1920s Great Britain's Colonial Office proposed opening the Legislative Council in British Honduras to elections, with the provision that the governor retain powers to veto the council in exceptional circumstances. The Legal Council in British Honduras refused even this modest change, but it could not hold off all reforms. Several labor unions and black advocacy groups continued agitating for representation. In 1927 Britain forced the Legal Council to replace most of the white landowners, who had long been guaranteed seats on the council, with black businessmen.

On September 10, 1931, with the colony already reeling from the Great Depression, a hurricane leveled Belize City, leaving more than 1000 people dead. Great Britain used the disaster to tighten its control of the colony and give the governor greater power, much to the distress of the black middle class, which had finally gained representation on the Legislative Council. These grievances, combined with crushing unemployment, prompted protests by poor blacks and mestizos in the mid-1930s. Although the protests wrested only minor relief from the governor, they set in motion powerful political changes. Black Creoles sympathetic toward labor won seats on the Belize town board in the late 1930s, and labor unions, like the General Workers Union, were legalized and formed in the early 1940s. Both bodies would play a crucial role in winning independence.

In 1949 British Honduras faced a scandal when the governor sharply devalued the colony's currency despite previous promises that he would do nothing of the sort. Angered by the arbitrariness of the governor's power and by the higher price of goods, black Creoles in labor and other parts of society coalesced behind George Price. Price was a member of the black elite and the town board who had earlier made a name for himself when he condemned a British proposal to federate its Caribbean colonies. Under Price, black Creoles formed what would eventually become the People's United Party (PUP). The PUP, which grew largely from the General Workers Union, demanded several reforms to the colony's Constitution, including universal adult suffrage, an elected Legislative Council, the creation of a ministerial government, and an end to several of the governor's more extraordinary powers.

The governor responded by abolishing the town board and by sentencing the publishers of the PUP's newspaper to a year of hard labor. A few reforms nonetheless passed the Legislative Council, including elections for some of the council seats. In elections held in April 1954 the PUP won eight of the nine elected seats, bringing the issues of complete constitutional reform to the forefront. The issue of decolonization was not long in coming.

Great Britain was initially adamant in its refusal to decolonize, but independence movements were sweeping the remnants of colonial empires in the late 1950s and early 1960s, giving Britain little choice but to relinquish its stronghold. In 1961 Britain announced its intention to decolonize, and by 1964 it had restricted its duties in British Honduras mostly to defense and foreign affairs.

In the end, the chief obstacle to a complete withdrawal turned out to be less Britain than Guatemala. Guatemala had long maintained that Britain was an illegal occupant of Central America, and thus British Honduras was properly a department of Guatemala. Britain, and to a large degree the inhabitants of British Honduras, feared a Guatemalan invasion if Britain departed. Although negotiations between Britain, Guatemala, and British Honduras failed to resolve the issue, local leaders during the 1960s and 1970s won support for independence in the international community. They also convinced important Latin American allies to condemn a possible Guatemalan invasion. In 1981 British Honduras finally achieved independence and officially became Belize, with Britain maintaining a small defensive force in the country.

In the late 1990s Belize was one of the most ethnically diverse countries in Central America. A 1995 census found Afro-Belizeans to be the largest ethnic group in the population, constituting 45 percent of Belize's 200,000 people. More than four-fifths of Afro-Belizeans are black Creoles, who continue to live mostly in and around Belize City. The remainder are Garifuna, who populated the southern coast. Mestizos, who totaled only 33 percent in 1980, were 44 percent of the population by 1995; many of the new mestizo arrivals were fleeing civil war and poverty in their Guatemalan homeland for the unsettled areas of western Belize. Their presence has strained already precarious relations with Belize's blacks and mestizos, with their contrasting languages and cultures. Amerindians make up another 11 percent of the population and live chiefly in the western and southern interior. The white population totals less than 1 percent.

A girl sells watermelon in Belize, a Central American nation in which people of African descent constitute the largest ethnic group.
Steve Chenn Photography, A.G.E. Fotostock

Blacks in Belize straddle several cultures. Black Creoles typically speak both English and Creole. Black Creoles also increasingly speak Spanish, as business and cultural ties with mestizos become more important. Among black Creoles, the Anglican religion of Britain dominates, though other forms of Protestantism are not unusual and many black Creoles are Catholic. Black Creole life has been explored by several contemporary Belizean writers and artists. One of these is Zee Edgell, whose novel *Beka Lamb* (1982) focuses on the contribution of black Creole women to the Belizean independence movement. The Garifunas have retained much more of their African heritage than the Creoles. Their Carib language, for example, blends African and Amerindian languages, while their religion contains elements of animism derived from their African ancestors.

See Also

Decolonization in Africa: An Interpretation; Great Britain; Slavery in Latin America and the Caribbean; Spain; Chicago, Illinois; Creoles; Central America; Garifuna; St. Vincent and the Grenadines; Languages, Creole, in the Caribbean; Slave Rebellions in Latin America and the Caribbean.

Latin America and the Caribbean

Bellegarde, Dantès

(b. May 18, 1877, Port-au-Prince, Haiti; d. June 14, 1966), Haiti's best-known diplomat in the twentieth century; an educator, social thinker, and historian who wrote 19 books and numerous articles.

Dantès Bellegarde was born in Port-au-Prince in 1877. His family had long been at the center of Haitian politics. His mother was Marie Boisson; his father was Jean-Louis Bellegarde. His maternal great-grandfather, Jacques Ignace Fresnel, was named judge by Jean-Jacques Dessalines, a leader of the Haitian Revolution, who became the first leader of the independent state in 1804 and soon proclaimed himself Emperor Jean-Jacques I. This same great-grandfather was also later minister of justice under President Jean-Pierre Boyer, who ruled Haiti from 1818 to 1843. Bellegarde's paternal grandfather, Jean-Louis de Bellegarde, was a duke and marshal in Haiti's second empire during the rule of Faustin Soulouque, who declared himself emperor and ruled from 1847 to 1859. Bellegarde's aunt, Argentine Bellegarde (1842-1901), was a noted educator and an early feminist. Bellegarde married Cécile Savain (1875-1965) in 1902, and they had seven children.

Bellegarde's activities and interests ranged from diplomacy to education and historical writing. In 1898 he helped create La Ronde, Haiti's greatest literary movement up to that time, which sought to move away from a slavish imitation of French literary genres and establish a truly national literature. He entered government service in 1904 and remained a prominent member of numerous administrations until retirement at the age of 81, in 1957. His lengthy and prestigious diplomatic career began in 1920, when he was named to the Permanent Court of Arbitration (also known as the Hague Court). In 1921 he represented Haiti in France, at the League of Nations, and at the Vatican. That year he also attended the second Pan-African Congress, organized by W. E. B. Du Bois, as an honorary president. He was a special guest at the fourth Pan-African Congress in 1927.

Bellegarde returned to his diplomatic posts in Paris and Geneva in 1930 but was transferred to the United States and the Pan-American Union in 1931. In the next three decades, he represented Haiti at various international conclaves throughout Latin America, was widely acclaimed as a public speaker, and was decorated by governments of the region. Bellegarde returned as Haiti's ambassador to Washington in 1946. In 1951 he was elected president of Haiti's Constitutional Assembly. His diplomatic career resumed shortly thereafter, and between 1951 and 1953 he went to the United Nations as his country's representative and fulfilled additional functions for the secretary-general. In 1957 he was named Haiti's ambassador to the United States and to the Organization of American States.

During much of Bellegarde's career Haiti was occupied militarily by the United States (the United States occupation lasted from 1915 to 1934; *see* Haiti). During this period Bellegarde became the leader of the "pro-French" and "pro-Western" forces, while his friend Jean Price-Mars (1876-1969) led the "pro-African" forces as represented in the Indigenism and Négritude movements the latter had helped create. The reality, though, was always more complex than implied by these dichotomies. Despite their divergences both men were believers in the philosophy of Auguste Comte and the positivist movement Comte created, and also followed Henri Bergson in their philosophical outlook.

The historian Duraciné Vaval wrote in 1933 that Bellegarde was the "quasi-official" ideologue of the Haitian state. In 1926 W. E. B. Du Bois gave him the title "international spokesman of the Negroes of the world." The historian Edner Brutus wrote in 1948 that Bellegarde was one of the most outstanding ministers of education in Haitian history. Poet and Minister of Foreign Affairs Léon Laleau wrote in 1966 that Bellegarde gave a "decisive direction to our foreign policy."

Patrick Bellegarde-Smith

See Also

Du Bois, William Edward Burghardt (W. E. B.); Haitian Revolution.

Africa

Bello, Ahmadu

(b. 1910, in Rabbah, near Sokoto, Nigeria; d. 1966), traditional Islamic leader as well as Nigerian regional premier and power broker during the first years of independence.

Ahmadu Bello was a descendant of royal blood: his grandfather, Atiku na Rabah, was the seventh sultan of Sokoto in the years 1873-1877; his great-great-grandfather, Usman dan Fodio (1744-1817), founded and ruled the Sokoto caliphate. Throughout his life, Bello relied on his illustrious ancestry as a source of political power.

Bello studied at the Sokoto provincial school and then trained as a teacher at Katsina College. He received less Western education than did other prominent Nigerian politicians. Nevertheless, his status and family connections smoothed his ascent to power. Although his cousin Abubakar beat him out for the highest traditional position, the sultanate of Sokoto, Abubakar granted Bello the high position of sardauna, or military commander of the caliphate.

As regional adminstrator and sardauna, Bello achieved considerable power during the 1940s. His most significant advance, however, came with his membership in the Northern People's Congress (NPC) in 1951. Shortly after its founding, the NPC became the dominant power in Nigerian politics. By rising through its ranks, Bello advanced in the national power structure; by assuming the position of premier of the Northern Region, as he did in 1954, Bello became the virtual leader of Nigeria.

Although Bello was Nigeria's preeminent politician until 1966, his primary interest lay in the Northern Region. By lauding his ancestors, remaining in the northern city of Kaduna (unlike other regional premiers, who frequented Lagos), and allowing Abubakar Tafawa Balewa of the NPC to become prime minister, Bello revealed his commitment to customary rule, which is based on tradition rather than on written law or contract.

Bello focused on advancing the interests of the Northern Region. Aware that southerners tended to be better educated, he established programs to train his constituency for public service and the armed forces. Bello also implemented rules that made it difficult for southerners to receive civil service jobs, extending preference to northerners first, to Europeans second, and only then to workers from the south. This spurred southern resentment, as did Bello's Islamic zealotry, because he proselytized among followers of indigenous religions and supported a foreign policy that denigrated Israel.

Bello's policies won him passionate support in the north and considerable animosity in the south. He was assassinated in the 1966 coup. His death was mourned in the north and celebrated in some parts of the south.

Eric Bennett

See Also

Lagos, Nigeria; Nigeria; Sokoto Caliphate.

Africa

Bello, Muhammad

(b. 1781, Gobir, present-day Nigeria; d. 1837, Sokoto, present-day Nigeria), military leader and ruler of the Sokoto Caliphate.

Muhammad Bello helped his father, Usman dan Fodio, overthrow the Hausa states and build the powerful Sokoto Caliphate, which ruled over the northern half of present-day Nigeria. In the early nineteenth century Bello's father, a Fulani Muslim religious leader, called on the rulers of the Hausa states to abandon their corrupt ways. He organized a popular movement among the Fulani and among Hausa peasants and merchants, advocating a purer form of Islam and the application of the *Shari'a*, or Islamic law. Usman first tried peaceful means, but his peaceful movement only provoked repression from the Hausa rulers. In 1804 Usman and his followers called for a *jihad*, or holy war, to overthrow resistant rulers. Among those who led the military campaign was Usman's 23-year-old son, Muhammad Bello. A capable military leader and administrator, Bello was crucial to the defeat of the states of Gobir, Kebbi, Zamfara, Zaria, Katsina, and Kano, which later became emirates within a single large Islamic empire, the Sokoto Caliphate.

In 1812, after most of the fighting had subsided, Usman divided the caliphate between Bello and Bello's uncle, Abdullahi, and retired to religious life. Bello oversaw the eastern emirates and built the new capital of Sokoto for the caliphate. Upon his father's death in 1817, Bello assumed overall leadership of the caliphate as "commander of the faithful." During his reign Bello consolidated the empire and soothed internal conflicts between the Hausa and the Fulani leadership by constructing an impartial justice system, reinstating some Hausa leaders, and improving access to education. He also commissioned a network of fortresses for the caliphate's defense along the border with the Kanem-Bornu empire. Under Bello, Sokoto's forces raided and enslaved peoples to the south (*see* SLAVERY IN AFRICA). These slaves provided the agricultural labor that generated much of the caliphate's revenue. The resolution of internal conflict enabled Bello to extend the empire to include Nupe and YORUBA territory. Sokoto's power and stability under Bello supported a thriving economy. By the time of Bello's death the Sokoto Caliphate was the largest state in sub-Saharan Africa, with a population of almost 10 million. When Bello died in 1837, he was succeeded by his brother Abubakar Atiku.

Elizabeth Heath

SEE ALSO
Hausa; Kano, Nigeria.

Africa

Bemba, the dominant ethnic group in ZAMBIA.

The Bemba are a Central Bantu-speaking people, numbering roughly 1.25 million, or more than one-ninth of Zambia's population in 1995. However, more than one-third of Zambia's population speak the Bemba language, Cibemba (or chiBemba), which is the prevailing language in Zambia's populous Copperbelt and, increasingly, the lingua franca for the country as a whole. Though many have migrated to the Copperbelt and other parts of Zambia, the Bemba homeland lies in Zambia's Northern and Luapula provinces. Additionally, more than 120,000 Bemba live in the DEMOCRATIC REPUBLIC OF THE CONGO, and 39,000 inhabit TANZANIA.

The exact origins of the Bemba are unclear. Oral histories record that during the eighteenth century, LUBA migrants from the Congo Basin arrived in what is now northeastern Zambia. They settled along the banks of the Kalungu River among a group (probably of earlier Bantu-speaking immigrants) known as the Bemba. The newcomers adopted Bemba cultural traits but maintained the Luba institution of chief-ship. Over time the two groups fused into a single ethnic group. Although multiple distinct chiefdoms existed, all leaders deferred to a senior chief called the Chitimukulu, after the great leader, Chiti. The Chitimukulu were believed to possess divine powers, though they had little real power over the various chiefs. Members of a matrilineal royal lineage filled the more powerful chiefships.

A highly centralized Bemba kingdom emerged in the nineteenth century. The Bemba preyed upon more loosely organized neighbors, including the Bisa, whom the Bemba absorbed and raided to acquire slaves for trade. Traditionally, the Bemba were considered excellent hunters and fierce warriors. In the past their ability to hunt elephants and harvest ivory for trade formed the basis of their wealth, as did their military proficiency. Under the leadership of two great Chitimukulus, Chileshye and Chitapankwa, the Bemba expanded their sphere of influence to control the commodities important in the Indian Ocean trade, namely, slaves, ivory, and copper. This expansion resulted in the wide adoption of the Cibemba language and Bemba culture by other ethnic groups. Although native Cibemba speakers, known as Babemba, share a high degree of cultural homogeneity, 18 different Babemba ethnic groups can be differentiated, only one of which is the "Bemba proper."

Major demographic changes occurred when the British occupied Central Africa, ended the slave trade, and developed copper mines in the Copper Belt. Large numbers of Bemba, forced to pay a "hut tax" to the colonial government, migrated to the Copper Belt and sought employment in the mines to earn currency. Consequently, within the cities and towns of Zambia – particularly those of the Copper Belt – Cibemba emerged as the lingua franca. The Babemba continue to dominate the Northern Province, where they mainly practice shifting cultivation of finger millet and manioc. Because of the prevalence of the TSETSE FLY in this region, there is no tradition of cattle herding. Poor soils still spur the Babemba to migrate to Zambia's cities.

The Bemba took a central role in both the African labor movement, beginning in the 1930s, and the nationalist movements that led to Zambian independence. Nationalist leaders such as Vice President Simon Kapwepwe hailed from the Bemba ethnic group. Today, the Babemba continue to dominate the politics of Zambia. Although President Kenneth Kaunda's parents are Malawian, he is also a native Cibemba speaker, having been raised at Lubwe. Indeed, Cibemba speakers hold most of the seats in the national legislature.

Ari Nave

SEE ALSO
Ivory Trade; Kaunda, Kenneth; Nationalism in Africa; Slavery in Africa.

Africa

Bena, ethnic group of TANZANIA.

The Bena primarily inhabit the Iringa Plateau and the Ulanga Plains of south-central Tanzania. They speak a Bantu language. The Sowe and the Vemba, also of Tanzania, are sometimes considered Bena subgroups. Approximately 500,000 people consider themselves Bena.

SEE ALSO
Bantu: Dispersion and Settlement.

Africa

Ben Bella, Ahmed

(b. December 25, 1919, Maghnia, ALGERIA), founding member of an Algerian national independence revolutionary organization and first president of Algeria.

After fighting for the French during World War II, Ahmed Ben Bella came home to witness the colonial administration's crackdown on the Algerian population, during which the French bombed Muslim villages and killed thousands of Muslims in response to the 1945 anticolonial riots in the Sétif region. Inspired to join the growing Algerian independence movement, Ben Bella worked with several illegal revolutionary groups until he was arrested and imprisoned by the French in 1950.

After escaping from prison in 1952, Ben Bella joined other exiled anticolonial leaders, including Mohamed Boudiaf and Hocine Aït Ahmed, in Cairo. Together they helped found the main revolutionary party, the Algerian National Liberation Front (Front de Libération Nationale, or FLN). Ben Bella was an arms procurer for the FLN in 1956 when he was captured aboard a plane and imprisoned in France.

Ben Bella was released from prison at the end of the war of independence, only to find his position as preeminent revolutionary leader assumed by others who had stayed in Algeria throughout the struggle. He fought his way into his home country, joining up with military commander HOUARI BOUMEDIENNE to defeat his political rival Yusuf Ben Kheddha for leadership of the newly independent Algeria.

As Algeria's first prime minister (1962-1963) and first elected president of the Algerian Republic (1963-1965), Ben Bella charted a socialist path for the new country, which had suffered severe economic losses from the war and the subsequent flight of colonial resources. Under the leadership of Ben Bella and Vice President Boumedienne, Algeria gained a reputation as a self-reliant nation and a proponent of Third World anticolonial struggles. At home, Ben Bella used strong-arm tactics to secure his power and suppress dissent.

In 1965 Vice President Boumedienne overthrew Ben Bella, then placed him under house arrest for the next 14 years. Upon his release in 1980, Ben Bella left for France, where he formed an opposition party calling for a multiparty democratic Algerian government. He returned to Algeria ten years later, and although he ran for president in 1991, he has never regained his original status.

Marian Aguiar

See Also
African Socialism; World War II and African Americans; Front de Libération Nationale.

Europe

Benedict of Palermo, Saint

(b. 1526, San Fratello, Italy; d. April 4, 1589, Palermo, Italy), Franciscan lay brother who was one of the first Africans to be canonized and is known as the patron saint of Negroes of North America.

Saint Benedict the Moor, as he became known, was born in Sicily to Christopher and Diane Manasseri, who named him Benedetto. His parents had been transported as slaves from Africa to Sicily, where they converted to Christianity. Benedetto worked on a farm until he gained his freedom as a teen. He continued to work as a laborer. Sharing his wages with the poor and healing the sick, he became known as "the black saint."

Benedetto joined a group of hermits who chose him as their leader. In 1562 he became a lay brother. Stories began to circulate about his saintliness and miraculous deeds; for example, he is said to have resurrected a young boy. Church accounts report that people of all classes in Sicily sought his prayers and his counsel. In 1578, though he was neither a priest nor literate, he was chosen to lead a Palermo friary. Under his charge, the monastery became famous and prosperous. Toward the end of his life he requested leave from his duties at the friary to work as a cook. According to church accounts, he died of a severe illness the exact hour he had predicted.

Upon his death a cult arose around him. He became very popular in Brazil, particularly among Afro-Brazilians. The Church canonized Benedetto in 1807, and church sources refer to him as "the patron saint of the Negroes of North America."

Leyla Keough

See Also
Italy.

Africa

Beni Amer

(also known as Amer and Nabtab), ethnic group of northeastern Africa.

The Beni Amer primarily inhabit eastern Sudan and northwestern Ethiopia. They speak an Afro-Asiatic language and are one of the Beja peoples. Approximately 100,000 people consider themselves Beni Amer.

See Also
Languages, African: An Overview.

Africa

Benin,

West African country bordered by Togo, Burkina Faso, Niger, Nigeria, and the Atlantic Ocean.

Benin, formerly Dahomey, is a country better known by its past than its present. Along its narrow tropical coast, precolonial kingdoms grew wealthy through participation in the transatlantic slave trade. Developing rich religious traditions, such as Vodou, they also built formidable armies, which for years resisted French conquest. But during the colonial era Dahomey, a small palm oil exporter known for frequent uprisings, found itself on the periphery of France's West African empire. In the years that followed independence in 1960, Dahomey maintained its reputation for political volatility while doing little to invigorate an economy still heavily dependent on palm oil exports. Since democratic reforms in the early 1990s, however, Benin's political climate and economy have both improved considerably. Observers are now waiting to see if this progress continues after the 1996 reelection of former dictator Mathieu Kérékou.

Precolonial History

The early histories of northern and southern Benin are markedly different. Although both regions were controlled by powerful kingdoms, they had little interaction until the period of European colonialism that began in the 1890s. The northern region was primarily inhabited by the Bariba. Little is known about the precolonial Bariba except that they were reputed to have killed every European explorer who crossed their borders. According to oral histories, the Bariba Kingdom was founded by a Persian warrior, Kisra, during the seventh century. She led the group from what is now Sudan to the present-day Borgou province, where they settled between the Niger River and the Atacora Mountains and divided into four main smaller states – Bussa, Illo, Nikki, and Wawa. Bussa was the ruling state, but Nikki was the largest and possessed the strongest army.

Numerous smaller, semiautonomous states such as Bikki, Kanì, Kouande, and Parakou formed the base of the kingdom's hierarchy. In each the landed nobility, called *wasangari*, ruled over Fulani herdsmen and *gando*, slaves who had been acquired through conquests and slave raids. The Bariba's economy was based primarily on agriculture and trade, mostly with trans-Saharan merchants and neighboring Hausa and Fulani states, including the Sokoto Caliphate. Although some trade occurred with the southern kingdom of Dahomey during the eighteenth century, it was relatively infrequent and was limited to slave trading.

The history of southern Benin, home of the Dahomey, Allada, Houéda, and Gun Kingdoms, is much better recorded. These kingdoms were founded by Adja peoples who migrated to the area from Tado (in present-day Togo) during the fifteenth and sixteenth centuries. By the late sixteenth century the Fon (or Agadja) had created the Dahomey Kingdom near Abomey in the southern interior, while the Allada, Houéda, and Gun established their kingdoms closer to the Atlantic coast, where they built ports at Cotonou, Ouidah (or Wydah), and Porto-Novo. All paid tribute to the more powerful Yoruba Oyo Empire. In the late seventeenth century these kingdoms began to use their ports to trade slaves for firearms with European merchants, particularly the Portuguese and French. In the 1720s this lucrative trade came almost entirely under the control of King Agaja of Dahomey, after he conquered the Allada and Houéda.

The Dahomey Kingdom's participation in the transatlantic slave trade dramatically transformed the region's economy and political relations. Although Dahomean armies had always raided neighboring peoples for slaves to be used in the royal court, on the king's plantations, and as sacrificial victims in the Annual Custom religious ceremonies, the booming European demand for slaves led Dahomean rulers to devote more time and people to raids and wars of conquest. The firearms they obtained from the Europeans facilitated their military exploits, but many historians argue that Dahomean reliance on the slave trade ultimately weakened the kingdom. On the other hand, Dahomey managed to cast off Oyo domination in 1818, and successfully weathered the Europeans' formal abolition of the transatlantic slave trade in the early 1800s by switching the kingdom's economic focus to palm oil. Produced on the king's plantations by the king's slaves, palm oil had a fairly stable market in France but generated smaller profits than slave trading. In the 1860s and 1870s, the Dahomean king Ghezo attempted to earn additional revenue by leasing ports such as Cotonou to the French. But as the European conquest of the continent gained momentum, France used these leases to gain a foothold in coastal West Africa. Ultimately it was disputes between

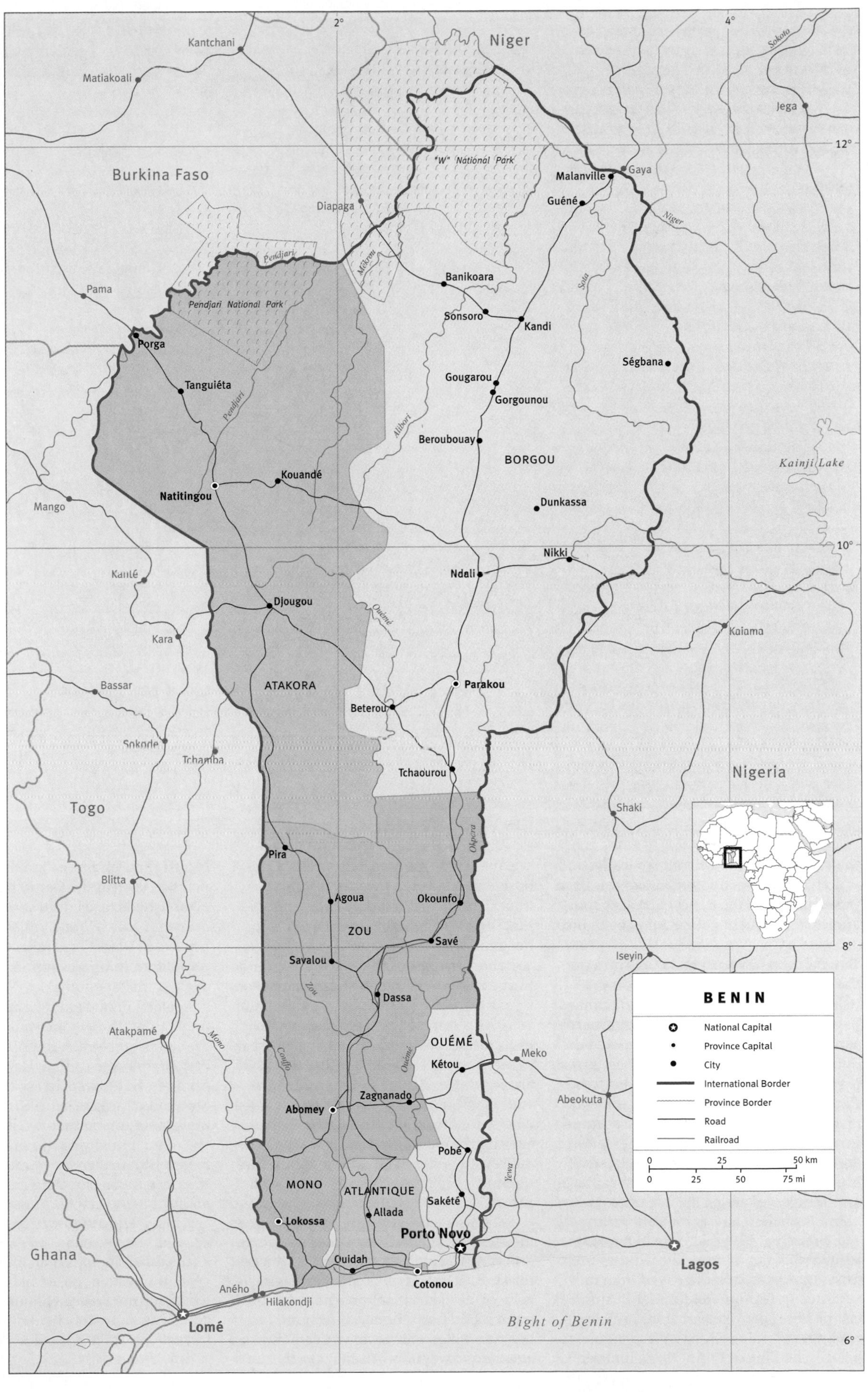
BENIN
National Capital
Province Capital
City
International Border
Province Border
Road
Railroad
Niger
Burkina Faso
Togo
Ghana
Nigeria
"W" National Park
Pendjari National Park
BORGOU
ATAKORA
ZOU
OUÉMÉ
MONO
ATLANTIQUE
Porto Novo
Cotonou
Lomé
Lagos
Malanville
Kandi
Natitingou
Djougou
Parakou
Abomey
Lokossa
Bight of Benin
Kainji Lake

Women examine goods for sale at the market in Cotonou, Benin. *Betty Press*

the French and the Dahomean leadership, rather than the economic loss of the slave trade, that led to the defeat of the kingdom and its subsequent colonization by France.

The Franco-Dahomean Wars and the Fall of the Kingdom of Dahomey
Relations between Dahomey and France began to sour in 1889, when King Ghezo's successor, Glele, refused the proposal by the lieutenant governor of French West Africa, Jean Bayol, to allow France to improve the Cotonou port and recoup the costs by imposing its own tariffs on all goods shipped through it. Glele died shortly thereafter, and his successor, Behanzin, declared all previous treaties regarding the port illegal and sent Bayol a long list of complaints about French behavior on Dahomean soil. The French government urged Bayol to resolve the dispute quickly, while French missionaries, citing the use of human sacrifice in Dahomean Annual Customs, claimed the Fon were barbarous heathens who needed to be Christianized and "civilized." The king of Porto-Novo, himself seeking respite from Dahomean attacks, also beseeched Bayol to take decisive action. In early 1890 the lieutenant governor did just that: he blockaded the coastline and declared war on Dahomey.

Behanzin mobilized his army, including the fierce Amazon troops, and for more than a year deflected the attacks. By the end of 1891, the French appeared resigned to Dahomean sovereignty. But Behanzin, seeking to prepare his army for future attacks, arranged to exchange slaves for firearms with German and Portuguese merchants, who would then ship the slaves to the colonies of the Congo Free State (present-day Democratic Republic of the Congo), Kamerun (present-day Cameroon), and Sao Tomé and Príncipe.

The deals ultimately strained the Dahomey Kingdom, which was suffering a severe drought. The king's subjects were reluctant to export slaves when their labor was desperately needed not only to tend to the king's palm plantations, but also to counteract the crop failures that were threatening the kingdom's food supply. In addition, the deals forced the Dahomey to raid neighboring peoples, such as the Gun, who had by then established close connections with the French. Finally, French missionaries used reports of these slave raids to rally French popular opinion in support of retaliation against the kingdom.

Retaliation came in 1892 after the Dahomey raided the Whéme valley, by then a French protectorate. It took two years for French troops to capture Dahomey's capital, Abomey, but Behanzin escaped into the bush; from there he led an armed resistance movement for another two years. In 1894 the French finally captured Behanzin and forced him to sign a peace treaty, ceding the Dahomean coastline and roads and abolishing the kingdom's custom of human sacrifice, before allowing him to leave for exile in Martinique. The French installed a successor, Agboli-Agbo, but within six years they had deposed him as well. Soon afterward the French conquered the Bariba kingdoms in the north and by 1900 had formal control of the colony of Dahomey.

TOP: **Villagers pole skiffs past houses on stilts in a Benin fishing village.** *CORBIS/Caroline Penn*
ABOVE: **A group of children in Ouidah, Benin.** *CORBIS/Owen Franken*

French Colonial Rule

Although united under a single administration, northern and southern Dahomey experienced colonialism very differently. In the southern region, the transition to French COLONIAL RULE was fairly smooth. There the French had a limited military presence and took full advantage of the Dahomean administrative structure, delegating the duties of tax collection and labor recruitment to local chiefs.

In the north, however, the French faced a much greater challenge. The Bariba Kingdom had essentially disintegrated when the French abolished domestic slavery. Instantly, the ruling wasangaris lost their primary source of income and status, and the former gandos formed "freedom" villages, in which their small farms produced barely enough for subsistence, much less for trade. Hostilities between the two groups were soon superseded by resentment toward the heavy taxes and compulsory labor service imposed by the colonial administration. These resentments escalated during World War I, when forced military conscription became known in Dahomey as the "blood tax." During this time, resistance leaders such as Bio Guera and Gaba mobilized popular discontent to wage strikes and revolts throughout the region. The French managed to subdue the north after World War I, but by then unrest was spreading throughout the south.

In 1923 major demonstrations broke out in Porto-Novo and neighboring areas. Although the French authorities blamed intellectuals, such as LOUIS HUNKANRIN, and Islamic religious leaders, these figures had simply articulated the underlying causes of popular discontent: poverty compounded by harsh taxes. Even while Dahomey suffered depressed commodity prices after World War I, the administration of French West Africa funneled much of the colony's revenue to its seat in Dakar, where it was used to support France's less profitable colonies in Central Africa. What little revenue remained in Dahomey was used primarily to run the administration and support the colony's French businesses. During World War II, the Dahomey colonial administration used land and conscripted labor – previously devoted to the palm oil industry – to produce maize and other crops for export to France. After the war ended, Dahomey's export sector was in disarray, and the colony grew increasingly dependent on aid from France.

While war undermined the economy, it also sparked new political initiative among army veterans and mission-educated intellectuals in Dahomey, many of whom joined the nationalist organization, the Union Progressiste Dahoméene (UPD). Under pressure from the UPD and other groups, in 1946 France granted Dahomey direct representation in the French National Assembly as well as its own territorial council. Because voting rights had initially been limited to French citizens and a handful of African civil servants, few formal political parties formed until 1956, when the French enacted the Loi Cadre, which universalized the franchise only weeks before territorial assembly elections.

Faced with little time to develop either a platform or a base of supporters, candidates for these elections resorted to clientelism, a strategy employed by the emerging political classes throughout decolonizing Africa. Candidates promised goods and services, such as a new school or pay increase, in return for votes from large groups such as labor unions, merchant communities, and ethnic and regional coalitions. In Dahomey the most successful politicians were members of major ethnic groups, such as Fon politician Tometin Justin Ahomadegbe; civil servants in influential positions, such as former teacher Huber Maga; and candidates from major cities, such as Sorou-Migan Apithy from Porto-Novo, who also gained the support of preexisting national organizations, including the UPD. In 1958 Dahomey won internal self-rule, and the government's new members sought to secure their positions by offering supporters valuable state resources, such as civil service employment. By the time France formally granted Dahomey independence in 1960, clientelism was firmly ingrained in Dahomean politics.

Independence

For the first three years after independence, President Hubert Maga and his team of French advisers appeared to have firm control over the government, despite outspoken criticism from his opponents Apithy and Ahomadegbe. In October 1963, however, news that a National Assembly delegate had evaded a trial on murder charges provoked massive protests from student and civil servant unions throughout the southern region, where Dahomeans saw the so-called Bohiki Affair as evidence of their leadership's corruption and lack of accountability. With the purported aim of restoring peace to the riot-torn country, Gen. Christophe Soglo seized control of the government. His coup d'état would be the first of many: during the next nine years Dahomey went through six military coups and 12 different governments.

In 1972 a group of junior army officers with broad popular support, especially from students, overthrew the government of Ahomadegbe. One of the officers, Maj. Mathieu Kérékou, moved quickly to the forefront: within a year he had restructured the army and dismissed senior army officers over the age of 40, imprisoned the three former presidents – Maga, Apithy, and Ahomadegbe – and channeled his student support into one "official" student organization. In 1973 Kérékou named himself president and began guiding Dahomey on a radically different course.

The People's Republic of Benin

In 1974 Kérékou declared Marxist-Leninism the official state ideology and renamed the country the People's Republic of Benin. Shortly thereafter he strengthened diplomatic relations with China, North Korea, and Russia and threatened to cut ties with France. In addition, Kérékou took steps to consolidate his power by weakening potential opposition in the countryside. Kérékou disguised his intentions as a campaign to remove "traditional rulers" such as village chiefs, who Kérékou claimed were taking cuts from local taxes. Toward this goal he installed "revolutionary committees" in each village and town to take responsibility for local administration and taxation. He later announced an "anti-feudalism" campaign, barring many landowners from holding local government positions. When these programs failed to sufficiently reduce the influence of rural chiefs, Kérékou tried a more radical policy: a crusade to eliminate witchcraft.

Because many chiefs were also Vodou priests, Kérékou believed that he could unseat them by declaring witchcraft illegal. At first, all went smoothly; only village headmen and chiefs whom Kérékou wanted eliminated were named sorcerers. Within weeks, however, the accusations increased exponentially. Villagers began using the campaign to accuse their enemies and to avenge vendettas. Public confessions, many of which were coerced by the military, aggravated the situation. During the next few months, accusations divided villages and families. Many innocent people were executed or imprisoned, and others fled the country in fear. Although Kérékou ended the campaign in 1975 after its devastating effects became apparent, in many areas it took years to recover from the divisions that remained.

At this point Kérékou turned his attention to economic reforms, beginning with a program to collectivize agriculture. Villagers were required to join cooperatives and work on collective fields, while the state took over the trade in agricultural commodities. Yet despite support from foreign donors, Kérékou's rural development programs did not make farming a more attractive livelihood to the many Beninese who enrolled in school with the hope of obtaining employment in the burgeoning state bureaucracies.

Benin's already fragile economy was devastated by the end of Nigeria's oil boom in the global recession of the early 1980s. Nigeria expelled almost 100,000 migrant workers and closed its borders. The effects for Benin were overwhelming; not only did Nigeria end all trade between the two countries, it sent thousands of laid-off Beninese and other migrant laborers across the border to Benin, where there were few jobs to be found. In 1985 the debt-ridden government of Benin stopped regular salary payments to its employees; two years later, state-owned banks began to collapse. In 1988 international donors, concerned that Benin would default on its loans, pressured Kérékou to adopt new austerity measures. But government social service and payroll cuts immediately provoked student and union protests, and Kérékou, fearing a coup d'état, agreed to demands for democratic reforms, including a new constitution and free elections. In 1991 economist and former director of the International Bank for Reconstruction and Development NICÉPHORE SOGLO received 67 percent of the vote and became president of Benin.

At first Soglo enjoyed broad support both in the National Assembly and among the public. His determination to adhere to the conditions of World Bank structural adjustment measures, however, provoked another wave of widespread demonstrations in 1992, which Soglo met with a military crackdown. As unrest continued, foreign firms, whose investments in manufacturing and construction were vital to Soglo's plans to reinvigorate and diversify the national economy, began to pull out of the country.

In early 1994 the 50 percent devaluation of the currency used through much of French-speaking West Africa, the CFA, led to rampant inflation, further undermining Soglo's popularity. Not surprisingly, he was defeated in the 1996 elections by his old opponent, Kérékou. In his second term Kérékou has largely abandoned his socialist vision, instead pursuing policies of economic liberalization. Although the economy is now the strongest it has been since independence, many believe that the president's continuing legitimacy will depend on his ability to spread the benefits of economic growth among Benin's citizens, most of whom have yet to recover from years of austerity.

Elizabeth Heath

SEE ALSO

African Socialism; Dahomey, Early Kingdom of; Dakar, Senegal; Nigeria; France; Oyo, Early Kingdom of; Porto-Novo, Benin; Portugal; São Tomé and Príncipe; Structural Adjustment in Africa; Cotonou, Benin.

Africa

Benin (Ready Reference)

Official Name: Republic of Benin
Former Name: Dahomey
Area: 112,620 sq km (43,483 sq mi)
Location: West Africa, bordering the Atlantic Ocean, BURKINA FASO, NIGERIA, NIGER, and TOGO.
Capital: Porto-Novo (population 164,000 [1984 estimate])
Other Major Cities: Cotonou (population 533,212 [1992 census]) and Parakou (92,000 [1984 estimate])
Population: 6,100,799 (1998 estimate)
Population Density: 52 persons per sq km (about 136 persons per sq mi)
Population Below Age 15: 48 percent (1998 estimate)
Population Growth Rate: 3.31 percent (1998 estimate)
Total Fertility Rate: 6.48 children born per woman (1998 estimate)
Life Expectancy at Birth: Total population: 53.61 years (male 51.56 years; female 55.72 years [1998 estimate])
Infant Mortality Rate: 100.22 deaths per 1000 live births (1998 estimate)
Literacy Rate (age 15 and over who can read and write): Total population 37 percent (male 48.7 percent; female 25.8 percent [1995 estimate])
Education: In 1975 Benin made education free and compulsory. However, literacy rates have increased only to 37 percent, and only 61 percent of all primary-school-age children are enrolled in schools.
Languages: French is the official language, but most people speak an African language. YORUBA and FON are the most common languages in the south, and at least six major languages are spoken in the north.
Ethnic Groups: At least 42 different ethnic groups are represented in Benin's population. The Fon, or the Dahomeans, and the closely related ADJA group account for at least 59 percent of the total population, and they are the major ethnic groups in the south. In the north the BARIBA and SOMBA (together about 15 percent of total population) are the largest ethnic groups. The Yoruba (9 percent of total population) predominate in the southeast.
Religions: About 70 percent of the population adhere to indigenous beliefs. Christians and Muslims each account for 15 percent of the population.
Climate: Tropical in the south, semi-arid in the north. The south receives about 1300 mm (about 51 in) of rainfall a year, mostly between March and July and between October and November. The average temperatures in the south range from 20°C (68°F) to 34°C (93°F). The temperatures in the north are nearly the same. In the north the rainy season occurs between May and September and annual rainfall averages 890 mm (about 35 in).
Land, Plants, and Animals: Benin is mostly flat to undulating plains, with some hills and low mountains. At one time dense tropical forest covered much of the land near Benin's coast. Most of this forest has been cleared, except near the rivers. Palm trees now dominate the south. Central Benin is covered by woodlands, and northern Benin is savanna. Animals found in Benin include elephants, buffalo, ANTELOPE, panthers, monkeys, crocodiles, and wild ducks.
Natural Resources: Offshore oil deposits, limestone, marble, and timber
Currency: The CFA franc
Gross Domestic Product (GDP): $11.3 billion (1997 estimate)
GDP Per Capita: $1900 (1997 estimate)
GDP Real Growth Rate: 5.8 percent (1997 estimate)
Primary Economic Activities: Agriculture employs 60 percent of the labor force. The

remainder are engaged mostly in small-scale trade and manufacturing.
Primary Crops: Corn, sorghum, cassava (tapioca), yams, beans, rice, cotton, palm oil, peanuts, and livestock
Industries: Textiles, cigarettes, beverages, food, construction materials, and petroleum.
Primary Exports: Cotton, crude oil, palm products, and COCOA
Primary Imports: Foodstuffs, beverages, tobacco, petroleum products, capital goods, and light consumer goods
Primary Trade Partners:
France, Thailand, the Netherlands, the United States, and China
Government: Benin is a republic under multiparty democratic rule. The executive branch is led by President MATHIEU KÉRÉKOU and the Executive Council, which he appoints. The legislative branch is the elected 83-member National Assembly.

Elizabeth Heath

SEE ALSO
Crocodile; Dahomey, Early Kingdom of; Elephant.

Africa

Benin Bronzes, sculptures from the Benin empire, among the most prized examples of African art.

The Benin bronzes – full-scale portraits or heads, statues of people and animals, small devotional objects, and bas-relief placques – date back hundreds of years, some as far back as the thirteenth century, when startlingly advanced processes of metalworking and casting were introduced into BENIN from elsewhere in NIGERIA. (The Benin bronzes imitated the great sculptural works of the Ife people, who pioneered a kind of figural realism centuries before the Europeans.)

Benin, today the principal city of the Edo people of southern Nigeria, was the capital of the Benin Kingdom, which flourished from the thirteenth to the seventeenth centuries. At the height of its power in the fifteenth century, it was the greatest empire in the Gulf of Guinea. In 1897, after a period of long decline, the city was torched by the British, who ransacked its cultural treasures and returned to Europe with numerous works of bronze and ivory.

The appearance of Benin bronze surprised and amazed the Europeans; some were incredulous as to the age and style of the pieces, as well as the advanced metalworking techniques employed in their production. The appearance of the Benin bronze castings heralded the full-scale importation of African art into European culture in the twentieth century.

Africa

Benin, Early Kingdom of, medieval African empire centered in the Edo state of contemporary NIGERIA.

The early kingdom of Benin gained prominence in the fifteenth century under the rule of Ewuare, the oba, or king, of Benin. Ewuare established the empire's political organization and consolidated its territory by conquering YORUBA territory to the west and Igbo land to the east. Despite the arrival of Portuguese merchants in the late fifteenth century, the kingdom maintained independence from European control, and under Oba Eware, as well as under the next two obas, relations between the people of Benin and the Portuguese were largely peaceful and cooperative.

In the sixteenth century, under the rule of Oba Esigie, the empire grew. Like many of the great African empires, Benin was intimately involved in the slave trade; various border conflicts and civil disturbances were exploited to send large numbers of non-Benin Africans to the Americas. The empire's power waned throughout the eighteenth and nineteenth centuries as neighboring Yoruba states, especially the Oyo Empire, gained prominence. In 1897 the city of Benin was taken by the British, forcing Oba Ovonramwen into exile and effectively ending the independence of Benin. In 1900 Benin was incorporated into British colonial administration within the protectorate of Southern Nigeria. Although the position of oba is not obsolete, the present-day Benin oba has only an advisory role in the government. The story of the defeat of the Benin Empire is told in *Ovonramwen Nogbaisi* (1973), a tragic drama by the Nigerian playwright and director Olawale Rotimi.

SEE ALSO
Transatlantic Slave Trade; Oyo, Early Kingdom of.

Africa

Benjedid, Chadli (b. 1929, Bouteldja, Algeria), third president of ALGERIA.

Chadli Benjedid grew up in the Annaba region of colonial Algeria, then joined the military wing of the national liberation group, the Front de Libération Nationale (FLN). Moving quickly through the ranks, he became a rebel commander in 1960. After Algeria's independence he helped oversee the withdrawal of French troops.

While in the rebel army, Benjedid earned the trust of chief of staff HOUARI BOUMEDIENNE, whom he later supported in the 1965 coup d'état against President AHMED BEN BELLA. Under President Boumedienne, Benjedid held high positions in the military and served on the ruling Revolutionary Council.

Within the FLN Benjedid gained a reputation as an even-handed leader, and for this reason he was sought as the presidential candidate to heal divisions within the party after Boumedienne's death. In 1979 Benjedid was elected president and began a tenure that lasted through two reelections. During his 13 years as president, he took steps to liberalize the state-controlled economy and to develop regional relations.

In the 1980s Benjedid faced increasing pressure from groups critical of the FLN's exclusive hold on power. Hoping to appease pro-Islamic groups, Benjedid signed the National Charter, which affirmed Algeria's Arab and socialist identity. Despite these gestures, Benjedid continued to draw criticism, particularly as the national economy floundered in the late 1980s. In 1988 the military killed over 500 citizens following

FAR LEFT: One of the Benin bronzes that first introduced African art to the rest of the world, this piece illustrates a hunting scene. *Werner Forman/Art Resource, NY*

LEFT: Dating to the seventeenth or eighteenth century, this sculpture of an *oba* (king) now sits in the Museum für Völkerkunde in Vienna. *Werner Forman/Art Resource, NY*

a riot over food shortages. In the aftermath of this incident, popular outrage forced Benjedid to make concessions such as the legalization of the ISLAMIC SALVATION FRONT (FIS) and other banned parties.

Although Benjedid was reelected president in 1989, the Islamic Salvation Front won municipal elections in 1990. In 1991 Benjedid resigned as the head of the FLN, as support for the FIS grew. Shortly after, he was deposed by a coup and placed under house arrest.

Marian Aguiar

SEE ALSO

African Socialism; Front de Libération Nationale; Islamic Fundamentalism: An Interpretation.

Latin America and the Caribbean

Benjor, Jorge

[Jorge Duílio Lima Menezes] (b. March 22, 1942, Rio de Janeiro, BRAZIL), a leading Afro-Brazilian pop music innovator known best for his upbeat hybrids of SAMBA, FUNK, soul, and other diasporic rhythms.

Jorge Duílio Lima Menezes began his music career in the early 1960s using the stage name Jorge Ben, taken from the surname of his Ethiopian mother, who gave him his first guitar. He divided his energies between rock 'n' roll and bossa nova, the sophisticated new style based on samba rhythms and JAZZ harmonies. In 1963 he recorded his first LP album, *Samba Esquema Novo,* followed by *Sacudim Ben Samba* and *Ben é Samba Bom* in 1964. He scored an international hit with "Mas que nada," which inspired versions by Sérgio Mendes, South African diva Miriam Makeba, and Hugh Masekela.

In the late 1960s his music was embraced by the innovative tropicalist movement led by GILBERTO GIL and Caetano Veloso, who celebrated his electric fusions of international black popular music, while others criticized him for deviating from "authentic" Brazilian samba. His 1969 recording *Jorge Ben,* which features "País Tropical," "Que Pena," and "Charles Anjo 45," evinces a strong affinity for soul music and the black counterculture of the United States. During this period, he participated in the annual International Song Festival of Rio de Janeiro, winning several awards for his compositions.

In 1975 Benjor recorded with Gilberto Gil *Gil e Jorge,* a magnificent acoustic album that explores their common Afro-Brazilian heritage. In 1976 he recorded "XICA DA SILVA," the theme song for a popular film by CARLOS DIEGUES about the powerful and shrewd black mistress of a Portuguese diamond merchant and slaveholder. This song was later recorded by Miriam Makeba.

Benjor's popularity declined sharply during the Brazilian rock boom of the 1980s. In 1989, when he changed his name to Jorge Benjor, he released an acclaimed recording, *Benjor.* The subsequent release of a popular compilation of Brazilian music, *Beleza Tropical,* which included his irresistible soccer anthems "Fio Maravilha" and "Ponta de Lança Africano," boosted his international renown. In 1994 he enjoyed a massive comeback in Brazil with the album *23.*

Christopher Dunn

SEE ALSO

Makeba, Miriam Zenzi; Masekela, Hugh Ramopolo; Soul Music; Rio de Janeiro, Brazil; Tropicália; Soccer in Latin America and the Caribbean.

North America

Bennett, Lerone, Jr.

(b. October 17, 1928, Clarksdale, Mo.), American editor of *Ebony* magazine who popularized African American history.

After graduating from MOREHOUSE COLLEGE in 1949, Lerone Bennett began his career as a reporter at the *Atlanta Daily World.* In 1953 he became an associate editor at John H. Johnson's *Jet* magazine in Chicago. In 1954 he became an associate editor at Johnson's *Ebony* magazine, becoming its first senior editor in 1957. He was named executive editor of *Ebony* in 1987. Through his positions at *Ebony* and *Jet,* Bennett encouraged the popularization of African American history. Despite being a popular magazine, *Ebony* included articles on historical subjects, many of which were written by Bennett.

Bennett has published several books on historical and contemporary subjects. His first book, *Before the Mayflower: A History of the Negro in America, 1619-1962* (1962), was a bestseller with numerous editions. His other books include *What Matter of Man,* a 1964 biography of Rev. Dr. Martin Luther King Jr.; *Confrontation: Black and White* (1965); *The Challenge of Blackness* (1972); and *Wade in the Water* (1979) (reprinted as *Great Moments in Black American History*). Bennett also collaborated on John H. Johnson's memoirs, *Succeeding Against the Odds* (1989). In 1978 Bennett's work was recognized with the Literature Award from the American Academy of Arts and Letters, and in 1993 he was appointed to the National Panel on the Arts and Humanities by President Bill Clinton.

Lisa Clayton Robinson

SEE ALSO

Chicago, Illinois; *Ebony*; *Jet*; Johnson Publishing Company; King, Martin Luther, Jr.

Latin America and the Caribbean

Bennett, Louise

(b. September 7, 1919, Kingston, Jamaica), Jamaican writer, performer, and folklorist who helped popularize the literary use of dialect.

While Louise Bennett is not the first writer to use Jamaican dialect, the facility with which she reproduces it in her writing and performances has marked her as a pioneer. She is the daughter of Augustus Cornelius Bennett, a baker who died when Louise was seven years old, and dressmaker Kerene Robinson. "Miss Lou," as she was called, studied social work and Jamaican folklore at Friends' College in Highgate, Jamaica, in 1943, and in 1945 received a British Council Scholarship to the Royal Academy of Dramatic Arts in London.

Bennett began writing in dialect in the late 1930s, inspired by the language she heard spoken by Jamaicans on the streets of Kingston. Soon after she began writing, she staged public performances of her poems. In 1942 her first collection of poetry, *Dialect Verses,* was published. Starting in 1943, Bennett contributed a weekly column to the *Daily Gleaner.*

Bennett traveled through rural Jamaica, visiting village festivals where her poetry was dramatized. These trips, as well as later ones as drama officer for the Jamaica Social Welfare Commission in the mid-1950s, increased her knowledge of Jamaican language and folklore, and provided the raw material for her writing and performance.

Bennett gained a reputation as a popular radio and television performer and comedian, and garnered considerable attention from literary critics. Her published work, including the collections of poetry *Verses in Jamaican Dialect* (1942), *Laugh with Louise* (1952), *Jamaica Labrish* (1966), and *Selected Poems* (1982), and the folktales *Anancy and Miss Lou* (1979), is all written in dialect and "celebrates Jamaican culture, often incorporating the metaphoric richness and wisdom of Jamaican proverbs." Bennett's work has drawn criticism, however, from those who feel that dialect is a corruption of standard English, that it is unfit for literature and lends credence to negative stereotypes of Jamaican culture.

Bennett has had a profound influence on the development of the national cultures in the English-speaking Caribbean. Her recognition of the unique cultural practices of Jamaica has served as an important aesthetic stimulant to the region's postcolonial independence movements. She has received numerous awards for her work, including the Norman Manley Award for Excellence in the Arts (1972), the Order of Jamaica (1974), and the Musgrave Gold Medal of the Institute of Jamaica (1978). Bennett and Jamaican radio impresario

Coverly have been married since 1954 and reside in Toronto.

Peter Hudson

See Also

Dialect Poetry; Jamaica; Kingston, Jamaica.

Africa

Berber, a large and widely dispersed ethnic group in North and West Africa.

The origins of the name Berber are uncertain. Some have claimed that it means outcast, or barbarian, or those from the land of Ber, who was the son of the biblical figure Ham. The name refers to several disparate groups who speak related languages and share certain historical experiences.

Berbers have lived in North Africa since at least 3000 B.C.E.; today the largest populations of the estimated 15 million people of Berber heritage are found in Algeria and Morocco, but significant populations also exist in Tunisia, Libya, Egypt, Mauritania, Mali, Burkina Faso, Nigeria, and Niger. Many Berbers call themselves the *Imazinghan*, the "free people," and indeed in North Africa the Carthaginians, Romans, Vandals, Byzantines, Arabs, and French all encountered Berber resistance. Famous Berbers include Goliath, Septimius Severus, and Saint Augustine.

Some of the larger Berber groups include the nomadic Tuareg, Rif, Kabylia, Shawia, Haratin, Shluh, and Beraber. Although their languages are distinct, all belong to the Berber branch of the Afro-Asiatic language family. Some employ a writing system called *tifinagh*, which is based on an ancient Libyan script. In addition to linguistic variations, historians have typically distinguished between Berber groups according to whether they are nomadic or sedentary, urban or rural.

Centuries of migration, assimilation, and Islamization in North and West Africa have both broadened and blurred the borders of Berber identity. Many Berber confederacies in North Africa resisted Arab rule; the revolt led by the Berber queen Kahina in the seventh century was just one of the best known. Other Berber confederacies entered semiautonomous alliances with Islamic rulers, maintaining a decentralized tradition of rule. The mass migrations through the region of Arabs (particularly the Banu Hilal), which began in the ninth century, led to the gradual conversion of most Berbers to Islam. Many Berbers also began to speak Arabic. Although Berber groups' experiences with Islam have varied widely, it may be said that Berber tradition remade Islam in North Africa as Islam remade the Berbers. North African Islamic dynasties, including the Almoravids, the Almohads, and the Marinids, were led by Berbers, and some incorporated elements of Berber confederate leadership, such as succession based on female kinship. As these Islamic empires conquered portions of southern Spain, Berber influence traveled throughout the Mediterranean.

In the nineteenth century, many Berber confederacies resisted the French presence in North Africa, but tensions between them played into the hands of the French. One of the more formidable Berber opponents to French colonial rule was Abd el-Krim, who in the early twentieth century founded the Rif Republic, a Berber state on the northeast edge of Morocco. Given the Berbers' long history in North Africa, the French viewed them as anti-Arab and created a cultural stereotype of a "Berber race," a somewhat contradictory characterization of Berbers as "honest," "free," "nonblack," and "friendly" but also "shifty" and "xenophobic." Under the Berber Policy, the French institutionalized their vision of the Berbers as potential allies against Islamic resistance, particularly after they began conquering predominantly Berber areas in 1913. Like many of the colonial-era "native policies" implemented south of the Sahara, this policy endorsed Berber customary law while calling for a vigorous Christianizing campaign (*see* Law in Africa: Colonial and Contemporary). French rule had a profound impact on Berber self-identity, as well as on the outside world's conception of the Berbers. The tensions that developed between groups who identified as Berber and those who identified more closely with Islam continue to be felt today.

Following independence, Berbers in North Africa became increasingly integrated into Arabic-speaking, mixed-ancestry national populations. Some of the nomadic Berber groups living in the Sahara and the Sahel, such as the Tuareg, have maintained relatively distinct identities. Most Berbers identify themselves as Islamic, but some continue to honor pre-Islamic religious traditions, such as the traditional celebration of "the King of the Devils." Although many North African Berbers live in mountainous rural areas or in the desert, they are also a significant presence in cities, and migrant laborers have carried Berber traditions into Europe. Political protests, such as a 1994 strike in Algeria for official recognition of the Berber Tamazight language, show that in some locations, the distinctive Berber identity remains vital.

Marian Aguiar

See Also

Haratine; Sahara Desert; Banu Hilal and Banu Sulaim.

Latin America and the Caribbean

Berbice Slave Revolt. *See* Guyana.

Africa

Beri (also known as Kige and Pari), ethnic group of north Central Africa.

The Beri primarily inhabit western Sudan and eastern Chad. They speak a Nilo-Saharan language and comprise two major subgroups: the Zaghawa and the Bideyat. Approximately 400,000 people consider themselves Beri.

See Also

Languages, African: An Overview.

Beriberi. Please see Kanuri

Latin America and the Caribbean

Berimbau, an Afro-Brazilian musical instrument.

The *berimbau* is a musical bow that is most often associated with capoeira, an Afro-Brazilian martial art and dance. It consists of a wooden stick about 1.2-1.5 m (4-5 ft) long, which is strung tight with a metal wire to form a bow. A hollow gourd resonator is attached to the lower end of the bow with a piece of string. The open end of the gourd faces the musician's stomach and chest, and the wire faces away from the musician. The berimbau is played by striking the wire with a thin stick, called a *vaqueta*. As the player strikes the wire, a coin or stone (called a *dobrão*) is placed against the wire to produce different pitches, and the gourd is moved on or off the musician's belly to produce different tones. A rattle (called a *caxixí*) is also held in one hand.

The origins of the berimbau are a subject of debate, but many experts trace it to the Kongo people, who were brought to Brazil as slaves. Though the instrument was probably modified and elaborated in Brazil, there are several similar instruments in present-day southwestern Africa, and there are reports from the nineteenth century of similar instruments in the parts of Africa from which Kongo slaves were brought to Brazil. Some scholars also trace the word "berimbau" to the Kimbunda word *mbirimbau*, while others point out that the word *urucungu*, sometimes used as a synonym for "berimbau," has its origins among the Kongo.

The instrument's existence in Brazil was first documented in the early nineteenth century, most prominently by the French traveler Jean-Baptiste Debret. In the 1830s he described and painted an old, blind slave, whom he called an "African troubadour," playing the instrument. When and how it became associated with capoeira is unclear, but it may have been used to disguise the martial art, which was practiced by slaves and free blacks, as a dance. It has long been traditional to practice capoeira to the sounds of three berimbaus: the bass *gunga*, the mid-tone *médio*, and the higher-pitched *viola*. The berimbau was also often used as a percussion instrument to accompany traditional Afro-Brazilian musical forms such as the *samba de roda*, a precursor to the current form of SAMBA music. More recently, in the hands of musicians such as NANÁ VASCONCELOS, it has become a common element in many other forms of Brazilian music.

Ben Penglase

SEE ALSO
Mbundu; Slavery in Latin America and the Caribbean.

Africa

Berlin Conference of 1884-1885, conference at which the major European powers negotiated and formalized claims to territory in Africa.

The Berlin Conference of 1884-1885 marked the climax of the European competition for territory in Africa, a process commonly known as the SCRAMBLE FOR AFRICA. During the 1870s and early 1880s European nations such as GREAT BRITAIN, FRANCE, and GERMANY began looking to Africa for natural resources for their growing industrial sectors as well as a potential market for the goods these factories produced. As a result, these governments sought to safeguard their commercial interests in Africa and began sending scouts to the continent to secure treaties from indigenous peoples or their supposed representatives. Similarly, Belgium's King Leopold II, who aspired to increase his personal wealth by acquiring African territory, hired agents to lay claim to vast tracts of land in Central Africa. To protect Germany's commercial interests, German chancellor Otto von Bismarck, who was otherwise uninterested in Africa, felt compelled to stake claims to African land.

Inevitably, the scramble for territory led to conflict among European powers, particularly among the British and French in West Africa; EGYPT, the Portuguese, and British in East Africa; and the French and King Leopold II in Central Africa. Rivalry between Great Britain and France led Bismarck to intervene, and in late 1884 he called a meeting of European powers in Berlin. In the subsequent meetings, Great Britain, France, Germany, Portugal, and King Leopold II negotiated their claims to African territory, which were then formalized and mapped. During the conference the leaders agreed to allow free trade among the colonies and established a framework for negotiating future European claims in Africa. Neither the Berlin Conference itself nor the framework for future negotiations provided any say for the peoples of Africa over the partitioning of their homelands.

The Berlin Conference did not initiate European colonization of Africa, but it did legitimate and formalize the process. In addition, it sparked new interest in Africa. Following the close of the conference, European powers expanded their claims in Africa to such an extent that by 1900, European states had claimed nearly 90 percent of African territory.

Elizabeth Heath

SEE ALSO
Leopold II.

Latin America and the Caribbean

Bermuda, a British dependent territory that consists of an archipelago of about 150 islands in the Atlantic Ocean, 117 km (70 mi) off the coast of South Carolina in the United States.

Bermuda's reputation as a tropical paradise leads many outsiders to mistakenly identify it as part of the Caribbean Islands. In fact, Bermuda is closer to New York and New England than to Florida and the Caribbean, and as far from the Caribbean as Washington, D.C., is from Dallas, Texas. As a dependent territory of Great Britain, it shares a common legacy of colonialism and slavery with countries in the British Caribbean. But Bermuda was actually part of British North America, and its history is connected to the early British colonies in Virginia.

The name "Bermuda" is used in the singular to describe a country of nearly 150 islands. The principal island is St. George's. Most Bermudans live on one of seven islands; the other islands are uninhabited. Bermuda was first discovered by the Spanish sailor Juan de Bermudez in 1503. By 1510 maps of the area referred to the islands as La Bermuda. None of the islands were inhabited when Bermudez first saw them, and Spain chose not to settle them. They remained uninhabited and isolated until 1609, when the British ship *Sea Venture* was shipwrecked on one of the reefs as it carried English colonists to Virginia. The survivors were impressed by the islands' beauty, and their stories were carried back to England – Shakespeare's play *The Tempest* was reputedly inspired by their accounts. British emigrants became interested in the islands, and by 1612 Bermuda had become a separate colony.

Four years later, records for the ship *Edwin* showed that the cargo included "an Indian and a negar [sic]" – the first known black Bermudan. By the mid-1600s African slavery was common across Bermuda. The islands' soil was not fertile enough to support a large-scale plantation economy, but slaves were still used as field hands, fishermen, and tradesmen. There were several recorded revolts. In 1730 a group of slaves were accused of plotting to kill their masters, and slave Sarah Bassett was burned at the stake for leading the insurrection. Thirty years later, between 600 and 700 slaves were accused of planning a much larger mutiny; many of them were tried and executed. Slavery was not abolished in Bermuda and all other British territories until 1834 (*see* ABOLITION AND EMANCIPATION IN LATIN AMERICA AND THE CARIBBEAN).

Throughout the seventeenth and eighteenth centuries, most Bermudans worked in the shipbuilding, tobacco, fishing, or salt mining business. Abolition took effect just as these industries were beginning to die out, so black and white Bermudans found themselves in search of new livelihoods. The AMERICAN CIVIL WAR (1861-1865) brought temporary prosperity to Bermuda. With the North's blockade of Southern ports, the nearby Southern states turned to Bermuda as an alternative port. Goods and guns were smuggled between Europe and the South via boats based in Bermuda. But when the war ended, so did Bermuda's short-lived prosperity.

For the next several decades Bermudans turned their attention to agriculture. Eventually crops such as Easter lilies, Bermuda onions, and potatoes became so successful that many planters chose to use indentured laborers from Portugal to supplement their work force. By the 1920s tourism began to replace agriculture as the islands' economic foundation. The United States military base at Kindley Field, established during World War II, boosted the local economy for 50 years before it was shut down in 1995. In recent decades financial services and offshore banking have become key components of the economy, and all of these factors together have brought Bermuda one of the highest per capita incomes in the world.

Their prosperity under the current political arrangement may be one reason most Bermudans do not favor independence from Great Britain. Bermuda is the oldest colony in the British Commonwealth. For most of its first 300 years as a British colony, the local government was made up exclusively of wealthy white landowners or white appointees of the British Crown. Black Bermudans protested, and in 1963 universal adult suffrage was finally introduced for the first time (although property owners were still given two votes). In 1968 a new constitution gave the elected government complete autonomy over local affairs. But when the British government recommended in 1978 that Bermuda become independent, most Bermudans rejected the proposal. About 20 years later, sentiments on the islands were the same; 73 percent of Bermudans voted against independence in a 1995 referendum.

It is clear that Bermudans currently do not want full independence, but the strength of their ties to Britain is a controversial issue that is split along party and racial lines. The United Bermuda Party (UBP), in control of the government since 1968, is often associated with the white business community, while the primary opposition party, the Progressive Labour Party (PLP), is identified with the unions and the black working class. The PLP strongly opposes any attempts to strengthen ties with Britain, and in the 1993 elections it won 18 seats to the UBP's 22. But how – if at all – Bermuda's close relationship with Britain will change remains to be seen.

Today Bermuda is a multicultural country in which cricket is as popular as CALYPSO. It has more people per square mile than most other countries, and more places of worship and more golf courses per square mile than anywhere else in the world. Its native residents are joined every year by about 2100 non-Bermudan workers, often from the Caribbean, and by half a million tourists, mostly from North America. But in recent decades, the government of Bermuda has limited new construction in order to keep the country from becoming too overcrowded. Even with the crowds, however, Bermuda retains its reputation as a friendly and relaxing place to work and live.

Lisa Clayton Robinson

North America

Berry, Charles Edward Anderson (Chuck)

(b. October 18, 1926, St. Louis, Mo.), American singer, songwriter, and guitarist, a founding figure of rock 'n' roll.

Few performers have had a more profound effect on American popular music than Chuck Berry. The staccato guitar cadenzas with which he opened songs like "Johnny B. Goode" and "Maybellene" helped define the new guitar idiom of rock 'n' roll. His lyrics, celebrating teen freedom, music, dancing, and the pleasures of automobiles, gave substance to the rock genre. Berry's influence shaped the work of later musicians from the Beatles and the Rolling Stones to artists of the present.

Berry's earliest exposure to music came when the choir of his parents' Baptist church gathered to rehearse in the front room of his childhood home. An avid fan of the blues, Berry took up guitar as a hobby at age 14. He worked in an automobile factory and as a hairdresser before turning to his guitar playing and singing as a source of income.

By 1955 Berry had developed enough confidence in his songwriting abilities to travel to Chicago, where he came to the attention of blues singer MUDDY WATERS. Waters recommended Berry to the president of Chess Records. Berry's first single on Chess, "Maybellene," became a national sensation. A string of hits followed until the end of the 1950s, including "School Days" and "Sweet Little Sixteen." Berry toured relentlessly. He impressed audiences with his trademark "duck walk," a crouching, locomotive dance step that carried him across stage in time to the picking of his guitar.

Berry's most famous compositions captured the remembered pleasures of his freewheeling youth, as well as his pride in making music. "Roll Over Beethoven" and "Rock 'n' Roll Music" hailed the triumph of rock over the stodginess of classical music and the complexity of modern JAZZ. "Johnny B. Goode" told the autobiographical story of an ordinary boy who rose to stardom because of his natural talent for playing the guitar. Bands as disparate as the Beatles, the Jimi Hendrix Experience, Living Colour, and the Grateful Dead interpreted Berry's songs on records and in live performances.

Rock 'n' roll pioneer Chuck Berry, shown performing in Portsmouth, Virginia, in 1959. *CORBIS/Bettmann*

The success of Berry's early period was interrupted in 1962 when federal prosecutors convicted him on a morals charge for trans-porting a 14-year-old girl across state lines. The singer spent two years in a penitentiary in Terre Haute, Indiana. After his release, Berry resumed his recording career and scored successes in both America and England with new hits like "No Particular Place to Go." In 1968 he opened an entertainment complex in Wentzville, Missouri. At a performance in Manchester, England, in 1972, he recorded the novelty single "My Ding-a-Ling," which became his first number one hit in America.

In the decades that followed, Berry continued to tour and perform. He also continued to encounter trouble from police and prosecutors. He served three months in jail in 1979 for tax evasion. He escaped charges of child abuse and drug possession in 1990 because of the prosecutors' misconduct. In 1986 he became a member of the Rock and Roll Hall of Fame. In 1987 the publication of his autobiography and the release of the concert film *Hail! Hail! Rock 'n' Roll* framed the artist's achievements and imperfections for a new generation of fans.

SEE ALSO
Blues, The; Chicago, Illinois; Hendrix, Jimi.

Latin America and the Caribbean

Berry, James (b. 1924?, Jamaica), Jamaican-British poet and short story writer.

Born in a Jamaican village, James Berry worked in America as a teenager but moved to London in 1948. He worked in the International Telegraphs Department of the Post Office from 1951 until 1977, when the award of a C. Day Lewis Fellowship allowed him to write full-time. His work reflects the transcultural insecurity of being "black British," on the one hand rehabilitating West Indian folklore and dialect, on the other graphically describing the immigrant experience. In *Lucy's Letter and Loving* (1982), the speaker, Lucy, is an uneducated Jamaican woman who feels alienated in Britain. *Chain of Days* (1985) was written, it seems, in the spirit of the younger performance and "dub" poets who followed in Berry's wake, but he had long been a powerful reader of his work on its own, generally more restrained, terms.

Other volumes of Berry's verse include *Fractured Circles* (1979) and *When I Dance* (1988). His short stories are collected in *A Thief in the Village* (1987) and *Anancy-Spiderman* (1989). In 1981 he won the National Poetry Competition for his poem "Fantasy of an African Boy." He is also the editor of two anthologies, *Bluefoot Traveller: An Anthology of West Indian Poets of Britain* (1976) and *News for Babylon* (1984).

SEE ALSO
London, Blacks in: An Interpretation.

North America

Berry, Leon Brown ("Chu")

(b. September 13, 1908, Wheeling, W. Va.; d. October 30, 1941, Conneaut, Ohio), American tenor saxophonist who played swing music with JAZZ greats such as BESSIE SMITH, Count Basie, and BILLIE HOLIDAY.

Leon "Chu" Berry's family taught him piano as a child, and he learned alto saxophone in high school. After three years at West Virginia State College, Berry left in 1929, when he was hired by Edwards' Collegians in West

Virginia. He later worked with Sammy Stewart's orchestra in Columbus, Ohio.

In 1930 Berry moved to New York with the Stewart Orchestra. He made his first recordings with Benny Carter's orchestra in 1932, and he played on the esteemed Spike Hughes 1933 recordings. Other significant connections that year included his work with Charlie Johnson and playing on Bessie Smith's final recording session. Performing with Teddy Hill's orchestra from 1933 to 1935, Berry met Roy Eldridge, who became his close friend. Hired by Cab Calloway in 1937, Berry appeared as featured soloist on recordings such as "Ghost of a Chance" (1940). Berry also led his own small group swing sessions, recording with leading swing soloists and singers, including Count Basie. "Indiana" (1937), "46 West 52nd Street" (1938), "Oh! Lady Be Good!" (1939), and "Blowin' Up a Breeze" (1941) were produced in some of these sessions.

Berry later played with Lionel Hampton, Billie Holiday, Benny Goodman, Mildred Baitly, Gene Krupa, and Wingy Manone. He is remembered as one of the period's most influential swing soloists, celebrated for his warm tone and energetic sense of swing. Berry died at the height of his musical talents in an automobile accident.

See Also
Basie, William James ("Count"); Calloway, Cabell (Cab); Carter, Bennett Lester (Benny); Hampton, Lionel Leo.

North America

Berry, Mary Frances

(b. February 17, 1938, Nashville, Tenn.), American historian, civil rights activist, attorney, and the first African American woman to chair the United States Commission on Civil Rights.

The second of three children born to George and Frances Berry, Mary Frances Berry grew up in Nashville, Tennessee, and experienced the racial discrimination of the segregated South. Economic struggle led her parents to send her and her older brother, George Jr., to an orphanage temporarily, a period Berry likened to a "horror story."

Despite her considerable intellect, Berry remained an indifferent student until gaining the attention and support of Minerva Hawkins, one of only three black teachers at Nashville's segregated Pearl High School. According to Berry, Hawkins exhorted her to develop her intellectual gifts, telling her that she could do "all the things I would have done if it had been possible for me." Thus heartened, Berry applied herself to her studies and gained a deep interest in a broad range of subjects. She attended Nashville's Fisk University, studying philosophy, history, and chemistry before transferring to Howard University in Washington, D.C. She earned a bachelor's degree in 1961 and a master's degree in history in 1962. She then pursued a Ph.D. at the University of Michigan, focusing on United States history, with a concentration on constitutional history.

After receiving a Ph.D. in 1966, Berry taught history at Central Michigan University while simultaneously attending the University of Michigan's law school. She later taught at Eastern Michigan University, then at the University of Maryland. After earning her law degree, Berry accepted a professorship at the University of Maryland and the University of Michigan – both full-time positions.

Berry quickly established her reputation as a first-rate scholar, producing such books as *Black Resistance/White Law: A History of Constitutional Racism* (1971), in which she explored how racism influenced interpretation of the U.S. Constitution; *Military Necessity and Civil Rights Policy: Black Citizenship and the Constitution, 1861-1868* (1977); *Stability, Security, and Continuity: Mr. Justice Burton and Decision-Making in the Supreme Court, 1945-1958* (1978); *Long Memory: The Black Experience in America* (coauthored with John W. Blassingame, 1982); *Why ERA Failed* (1986); and *The Politics of Parenthood: Child Care, Women's Rights, and the Myth of the Good Mother* (1993). She added to her reputation by publishing regularly in scholarly journals.

Berry has also enjoyed success as an educational administrator, first at the University of Maryland as its director of Afro-American Studies, and later as interim chairperson and provost of the Division of Behavioral and of the University of Colorado, the first African American woman to hold that post at a major research university. In 1980 she accepted a professorship at Howard University and later at the University of Pennsylvania, where she became the Geraldine R. Segal Professor of Social Thought and Professor of History.

Berry's most visible contribution has been in the arena of civil rights. In 1980 President Jimmy Carter appointed her to the U.S. Commission on Civil Rights, an independent agency that was created in 1957 to investigate discrimination. Berry's political views differed from those of President Ronald Reagan, who sought to fire her in 1984. Her characterization in the press of Reagan's intentions – that he wanted to transform the agency from a "watchdog of civil rights" to a "lapdog for the administration" – summed up their differences. It also signaled her willingness to fight the president, which she did, in court, successfully blocking Reagan's attempt to unseat her. She continued to serve on the commission and in 1992 was named its chair by President Bill Clinton.

Berry has also participated in other civil rights activism, most notably as a founding member of the Free South Africa Movement, which gained notoriety on Thanksgiving in 1984 by protesting Apartheid at the South African Embassy.

Peter Glenshaw

See Also
South Africa.

Africa

Berti, ethnic group of north Central Africa.

The Berti primarily inhabit Darfur Province, Sudan. They once spoke a Nilo-Saharan language, although today they speak Arabic. Some ethnologists consider the Berti part of the larger Shilluk ethnic cluster. Approximately 100,000 people consider themselves Berti.

See Also
Darfur; Languages, African: An Overview.

Latin America and the Caribbean

Betances, Ramón Emeterio

(b. April 8, 1827, Cabo Rojo, Puerto Rico; d. September 16, 1898, Neuilly, France), Puerto Rican abolitionist and one of the principal leaders of the independence movement in the Spanish Antilles.

Although he was officially considered white, Ramón Emeterio Betances proudly affirmed that he was of African descent. Born to a well-to-do family, Betances was sent to study in Toulouse, France, at the age of ten. He later moved to Paris and in 1855 graduated from medical school.

In 1856 Betances returned to Puerto Rico. At that time an epidemic of cholera hit the island and killed more than 30,000 people from all social strata of the population. The plague lasted more than a year and Betances was exceptionally compassionate in looking after poor patients, including slaves. His medical service to the underprivileged and oppressed during the plague caused him to become known as "doctor of the poor."

The colony's political and social problems concerned Betances as much as the health of his patients. Convinced that slavery was the cruelest institution of the colonial regime (*see* Colonial Rule), Betances was instrumental in spearheading the antislavery movement in Puerto Rico. He founded a secret abolitionist society comprising a small group of *criollos* (people of European descent born in the Americas). The group liberated the newborn children of slaves by buying their freedom upon baptism. The society's goal was to reduce the number of new slaves to a minimum. As a consequence of his abolitionist activity, Betances was forced into exile by the colonial authorities.

After a few years in Europe, Betances returned to Puerto Rico in 1865 and immediately resumed his liberation campaign. Betances also collaborated with members of Cuba's independence movement. He concluded that since SPAIN was not willing to end slavery and to grant democratic rights to its colonies, the only solution was to fight for independence. He proposed the creation of the Antilles Confederation of independent Cuba, Santo Domingo, and Puerto Rico. In 1867 Betances was again forced to leave the island after the government received information about his plans to organize a revolt against Spain.

From exile in 1868 Betances headed El Grito de Lares, the first military attempt to overthrow the Spanish government in Puerto Rico. The colonial army suppressed the insurrection in a matter of days. However, the patriotic gesture of the rebellious criollos stood as the first nationalist act against colonial oppression in the history of Puerto Rico.

The attempted revolution put additional pressure on Spain to end slavery. On March 22, 1873, slavery was finally abolished in Puerto Rico. Betances continued his struggle for the independence of the Caribbean and provided important intellectual support to the Cuban war of independence. Although Betances did not meet his goal of liberating Puerto Rico, his life and political thought had a significant impact on the development of the Puerto Rican national identity. He died in Paris in 1898, a few months after Puerto Rico was ceded to the United States as a result of the Spanish-Cuban-American War.

Carlos Dalmau

SEE ALSO
Slavery in Latin America and the Caribbean; Spanish-Cuban-American War, African Americans in the; Cuba; Abolition and Emancipation in Latin America and the Caribbean.

Africa

Bété, an ethnic group of CÔTE D'IVOIRE.

One of the largest groups of KRU speakers, the Bété number more than 600,000 people, most of whom live near the cities of Daloa, Soubre, and Gagnoa in southwestern Côte d'Ivoire. According to Bété history, the group migrated to the area in the seventeenth century after warfare (perhaps connected with the expansion of the MALI empire) drove them out of their home in the savanna to the northwest. They displaced the Gagu, Dida, and Guro people who had formerly occupied the region and practiced hunting and gathering. The Bété fiercely resisted French COLONIAL RULE into the early twentieth century. After a final rebellion in 1906, the French army incorporated Bété territory into the Côte d'Ivoire colony.

Surprisingly, the group quickly embraced both Christianity and cash-crop farming – the mainstay of the colonial economy – and soon constituted one of the largest groups of plantation workers in the colony. According to some historians, the term *Bété* took on a pejorative meaning during the colonial era because of their affiliation with plantation work, which was considered degrading; at times the term was used indiscriminately to refer to any plantation worker. Since independence in 1960, however, members of the Bété group have made a concerted effort to redefine Bété ethnicity and to affirm their own cultural importance. Today the Bété constitute a substantial percentage of coffee and COCOA farmers in the southern regions of Côte d'Ivoire, though many have also migrated to the capital of Abidjan.

Elizabeth Heath

SEE ALSO
Abidjan, Côte d'Ivoire.

North America

Bethune, Mary McLeod

(b. July 10, 1875, near Mayesville, S.C.; d. May 18, 1955, Daytona Beach, Fla.), African American civil rights leader, educator, and government official who founded the National Council of Negro Women (NCNW) and Bethune-Cookman College, and who had significant influence in Franklin D. Roosevelt's New Deal government.

Mary McLeod was born July 10, 1875, near Mayesville, South Carolina. In 1885 she enrolled at Trinity Presbyterian Mission School. With the aid of her mentor, Emma Jane Wilson, she moved on to Scotia Seminary in 1888, a missionary school in Concord, North Carolina. There she was given a "head-heart-hand" education, which emphasized not only academic but religious and vocational training as well. Because McLeod's dream was to become a missionary to Africa, she entered the missionary training school now known as Moody Bible Institute. After a year of study, she applied for service but was rejected because Presbyterian policy did not permit African Americans to serve in Africa.

Following this rejection McLeod began teaching, first at Haines Institute in Augusta, Georgia in 1896, and a year later at the Presbyterians' Kendall Institute in Sumter, North Carolina. In 1900 Bethune moved to Palatka, Florida where she established two schools. In 1904 she relocated to Daytona, Florida and opened the Daytona Educational and Industrial Institute. The Daytona Institute initially consisted of five African American girls in a rented house, but eventually the school expanded to include a farm, a high school, and a nursing school. After merging with Cookman Institute, the school became the coeducational Bethune-Cookman College in 1929 and reached the status of fully accredited college in 1943. Bethune's achievement as the school's founder and president won her the NATIONAL ASSOCIATION FOR THE ADVANCEMENT OF COLORED PEOPLE's prestigious Spingarn Medal in 1935.

Mary McLeod Bethune (1875-1955), founder of Bethune-Cookman College, with a group of students. *CORBIS*

Through the Daytona Institute, Bethune proved her abilities not only as an educator but also as an organizer, fundraiser, and as one adept at negotiating between black and white communities. She also employed these skills as president and founder of several black women's organizations, which culminated in her establishment of the National Council of Negro Women (NCNW) in 1935. By the end of her presidency in 1949, the NCNW had coordinated the activities of many black women's organizations, presenting a unified voice to the federal government to secure greater equity for African Americans in social welfare programs.

Bethune had significant influence in Franklin D. Roosevelt's New Deal government. From 1936 to 1945 Bethune held the informal position of the federal administration's "race leader at large," and she was one of the influential black leaders who organized the Federal Council on Negro Affairs, known as the Black Cabinet. Bethune also became the Director of Negro Affairs for the National Youth Administration, a title she held from 1939 to 1943. This made her the highest-ranking black woman in government at that time. As director she fought for racial equality in the distribution of funds to young people and she secured state and local government positions for African Americans.

In her work Bethune emphasized an internationalism that advocated the unity of humanity. In the early 1940s the United States House Committee on Un-American Activities labeled her a Communist, which damaged her reputation. Still, Bethune's support for civil rights was unfaltering: she participated in the New Negro Alliance's picket line in 1939 and she joined A. Philip Randolph's March on Washington Movement in 1941. Bethune was honored with awards for her work as a civil and women's rights leader throughout her life; she suffered a heart attack and died May 18, 1955.

Leyla Keough

See Also

Black Cabinet; Randolph, Asa Philip; Communist Party USA, African Americans and the.

Africa

Beti, ethnic group of Cameroon.

The Beti inhabit primarily Centre Province, Cameroon. They speak a Bantu language, and comprise several distinct sub-groups, including the Bulu, the Buku, the Bane, the Eton, and the Ewindo. The Beti are considered part of the larger Fang-Pahouin ethnolinguistic group. Approximately 800,000 people consider themselves Beti.

See Also

Bantu: Dispersion and Settlement.

Africa

Beti, Mongo (b. June 30, 1932, Mbalmayo, Cameroon), Cameroonian novelist and political essayist whose works examine Africa's transition from a traditional to a modern society with specific attention to the ongoing effects of colonial policies in his country.

Born Alexandre Biyidi-Awala in Mbalmayo, a town near Yaoundé, he adopted the pen name Eza Bota with his first work and thereafter used the pseudonym Mongo Beti. Educated in Catholic mission schools and then at a French lycée in Yaoundé, Beti went to France in 1951 to study literature at the University of Aix-en-Provence. He published his first novel, *Ville cruelle* (Cruel City), in 1954. This work sets up the major themes of his early writing: the social disorientation caused by colonialism and the African's revolt against traditional village life, especially its patriarchy.

With his second novel, *Le pauvre Christ de Bomba* (1956; The Poor Christ of Bomba, 1971), Beti established himself as an important Francophone (French-language) writer. The novel was banned in Cameroon, however, because it presumes a complicity between missionaries and the government in maintaining colonialism. Written in the form of a diary, it traces the journey of a naive young man as he follows a European priest on his missionary circuit and learns how destructive missionaries can be despite good intentions. *Mission Terminée* (1957; Mission to Kala, 1958) tells of a young man who has just failed the baccalaureate examination. He returns home to be greeted as a hero because of the Western education his people believe he has. He subsequently learns that he can adapt neither to the colonial order nor to the traditional society.

Beti put aside his writing for more than a decade but returned to his craft in the 1970s with a political book, *Main basse sur le Cameroun* (Rape of Cameroon, 1972). The work clearly marked a new phase in his writing in which he focused on denouncing the government of Cameroon for its neocolonial policies that allowed France to maintain its influence. His first novel of this period, *Perpétue et l'habitude du malheur* (1974; Perpetua and the Habit of Unhappiness, 1978), is an allegory in which a woman represents both an Africa conquered by European nations and the victims of neocolonialism. *Les deux mères de Guillaume Ismaël Dzewatama, futur camionneur* (The Two Mothers of Guillaume Ismaël Dzewatama, Future Truck Driver, 1982) tells of a mixed marriage between a French woman and a Cameroonian man.

Beti remained in France after completing his education and taught literature at a lycée in Rouen beginning in the late 1950s. In the early 1990s he returned to Cameroon and ran a bookstore.

See Also

Yaoundé, Cameroon.

Africa

Betsileo, ethnic group of Madagascar.

The Betsileo (*see* Madagascar, Ethnicity in) primarily inhabit the Central Highlands of Madagascar. They speak Malagasy, a Malayo-Polynesian language, and comprise four subgroups: the Arindrano, the Halangina, the Isandra, and the Manadriana. Approximately 1.5 million people consider themselves Betsileo.

See Also

Languages, African: An Overview.

Africa

Betsimisaraka, ethnic group of Madagascar.

The Betsimisaraka (*see* Madagascar, Ethnicity in) primarily inhabit the east coast of Madagascar. They speak Malgasy, a Malayo-Polynesian language. Approximately 1.5 million people consider themselves Betsimisaraka, including members of the Betanmena subgroup.

See Also

Languages, African: An Overview; Malagasy.

North America

Beulah, fictional black domestic servant on American radio and television programs from 1940 to 1953, who became famous for her comic wisdom and abiding loyalty to her white employers.

Beulah Brown, a black domestic servant in radio and television comedies, carried on a long tradition of white stereotyping of African Americans. An updated version of the faithful Mammy figure, Beulah subordinated her own life and needs to serve as mother figure, therapist, and problem-solver to her employers – in the NBC television program, a white New York lawyer and his family.

Whenever a member of the white upper-middle-class Henderson family faced a crisis, the maid hurried to the rescue with the cry, "Somebody bawl fo' Beulah?" Beulah also opened each episode by sharing some observation or bit of folksy wisdom that would frame the evening's story; for example, "If marriages are made in heaven, my guardian angel's sho' been loafin' on the job. Ha, ha, ha, ha, ha." Despite the demeaning nature of such material, the program – along with the televised version of Amos 'n' Andy (1951-1953) on CBS – did give work to a considerable number of African American actors.

Paradoxically, however, in the first seven years of the character's existence, she was not even portrayed by an African American actor. Beulah Brown was first heard during 1940 on the NBC radio musical program *Show Boat.* Four years later Beulah joined the popular comedy series *Fibber McGee and Molly* and in 1945 received a much more prominent role in a spin-off series, *The Marlin Hunt and Beulah Show,* later shortened to simply *Beulah.* Only in 1947, when Academy Award-winner HATTIE MCDANIEL (1895-1952) took the radio role for several seasons, was Beulah finally played by an African American. In 1950 *Beulah*'s move to television, for what would be a three-season run, provided greater opportunities for African American actors, both in the title role and in several supporting parts as well.

On television, three distinguished black actors played Beulah. Singer and Oscar-nominee ETHEL WATERS (1896-1977) took the part for the first two seasons. McDaniel was slated to take Waters's place, but, due to ill health, appeared in only a few episodes. The role then passed to LOUISE BEAVERS (1908-1962), best known for her portrayal of the maternal and long-suffering Delilah in *Imitation of Life* (1934). Important actors in supporting roles included Butterfly McQueen, forever typecast after taking her chirping portrayal of Prissy in *Gone With the Wind* (1939), and Dooley Wilson, most memorable in the role of the piano-playing Sam in *Casablanca* (1943).

The program was still earning high ratings when it went off the air in 1953, the same year in which protests by the NATIONAL ASSOCIATION FOR THE ADVANCEMENT OF COLORED PEOPLE led CBS to cancel *Amos 'n' Andy.* NBC denied any connection between the two events, attributing the cancellation of *Beulah* to Louise Beavers' decision to leave the show.

James Clyde Sellman

SEE ALSO

McQueen, Thelma ("Butterfly"); New York, New York; Television and African Americans; Wilson, Eric Arthur ("Dooley").

North America

Bibb, Henry Walton

(b. May 10, 1815, Ky.; d. 1854), author and emigrationist who founded and edited Canada's first black newspaper.

The son of a Kentucky plantation slave and a state senator, Henry Walton Bibb was born a slave. His repeated attempts to escape bondage were successful in 1842 when he fled to Detroit. By then his first wife, whom he married in 1833 and with whom he had a daughter, had been sold again. Bibb turned his energies to abolitionism.

In 1850 he published his autobiography, *Narrative of the Life and Adventures of an American Slave,* the same year Congress passed the Fugitive Slave Act, which forced him to flee with his second wife to CANADA. A leader of the African American community there, Bibb founded the first black newspaper in Canada, *Voice of the Fugitive,* in 1851. He died in 1854 at the age of 39.

SEE ALSO

Abolitionism in the United States; Detroit, Michigan; Fugitive Slave Laws; Slave Narratives.

Latin America and the Caribbean

Bigaud, Wilson

(b. January 29, 1931, Port-au-Prince, Haiti), one of the most prominent of the early Haitian artists, who achieved greatest recognition for his work in the 1940s and 1950s.

Wilson Bigaud was introduced to so-called naive painting by HECTOR HYPPOLITE, one of HAITI's most famous artists. Bigaud's exceptional but tragically short career was plagued by deep melancholy and depression. His famous canvas *Paradis terrestre,* recognized as one of the purest masterpieces of Haitian art, has single-handedly exported the magic of his vision of a black Adam to a broad international audience.

Bigaud's artistic talent was proclaimed to equal Brueghel's when he produced his *Noces de Cana* (Miracle of Cana), the famous 528-square-foot fresco decorating the Episcopal Cathedral of Port-au-Prince. Bigaud's impressive self-portrait (1958) reveals best his brush's precision and the artist's desire to perfectly control his surroundings. In the painting he depicts himself in the apparel of the *arrivé* (a Haitian term meaning "the one who made it"), wearing a distinguished panama hat and elegantly dressed in his upper-class finery. His figure is framed by a home built of brick and wrought iron, rather than the more realistic thatch or mud wall on an earthen ground. This pose strangely foreshadows his mental collapse soon thereafter, at the pinnacle of his mastery and grandeur.

Because of the strong African influence on Haitian culture, some have been tempted to look to naive paintings for pure representations of ancient African motifs. As René Depestre indicates, however, naive painters do not impose constraints on themselves by reproducing primitive effects. Rather, the subjects of naive art often stress the adaptation and transformation of African sources against a new background and on new soils.

This synthesis can be seen in several of Bigaud's canvases. While African spirits and Haiti's African-derived Vodou religion make their influence felt, they coexist with Roman Catholic and European elements or with deities that were developed in Haiti itself (*see* VODOU and RELIGIONS, AFRICAN, IN LATIN AMERICA AND THE CARIBBEAN).

For example, in *Le Serment sur la montagne* (Sermon on the Mount), an imposing triptych, Bigaud depicts hell alongside paradise. Irreverent with regard to religious doctrine, or perhaps making a commentary on the tense and sometimes contradictory relationships between Christianity and Vodou, Bigaud includes within his sacred paintings sharply cut tree trunks. These suggest that the refuges of loas, or deities, who are known to hide themselves in trees, have been broken asunder and scattered freely within his Christian vision. In *Le Portement de Croix* (Carrying of the Cross), Christ wears the colors of the Haitian flag, and in *La Veillée* (The Wake), he welcomes saints and loas at the same door. Bigaud was often present at Vodou ceremonies, which furnished his favorite themes. He also attended *raras,* or popular Mardi Gras festivities; these were a source for the maliciously playful twist seen in some of his paintings, such as his lively *Rara in a Far Out Village* (1952).

Bigaud's paintings have been displayed in countless expositions worldwide. Many tourists, journalists, and local and foreign art critics crowded Port-au-Prince galleries to see them in the 1950s. His work has the merit of having popularized the Indigenist School, a literary movement of the 1930s and 1940s that stressed a return to Haitian culture after the destabilizing effects of foreign occupation. To this day, Bigaud's paintings are so many windows offering insight into Haitian cultural identity and mores. The artist himself suffered a series of nervous breakdowns in the late 1950s that have interrupted his career.

Paulette Smith

SEE ALSO

Port-au-Prince, Haiti.

North America

Biggers, John

(b. April 13, 1924, Gastonia, N.C.), African American artist known for his murals and community-based visual style.

John Biggers was one of seven children whose father, Paul Biggers, was a school principal, preacher, and basket maker. Biggers studied at Hampton Institute in Virginia, where he resolved to become an artist. During his time at Hampton, Biggers served in the United States Navy from 1943 to 1946, and in 1944 he painted a mural for the U.S. Naval Training School at Hampton. He subsequently attended Pennsylvania State University, where he received B.S., M.S., and Ph.D. degrees. He founded and chaired the art department at Texas Southern University, where he implemented progressive art programs that involved local communities.

Biggers is known for his murals, a form he began to master while at Hampton. Many of his early works no longer exist, because they were painted directly on buildings that were later destroyed or altered. His works demonstrate his personal interest in the concrete spiritual symbolism of Africa. This fascination is apparent in his mural, *The Rites of Passage*, which incorporates themes of life cycles and transitions. In his later works Biggers addressed the African American heritage, using iconic, domestic symbols such as a washboard, an anvil, and a three-legged wash pot to suggest the daily lives and heritages of African Americans.

His awards include a UNESCO fellowship in 1957, and his work is exhibited in the collections of the Houston Museum of Fine Arts, the Dallas Museum of Fine Arts, Howard University, and Pennsylvania State University.

See Also
Hampton University; Art, African American.

Africa

Bight of Benin, bay in West Africa, forming the western part of the Gulf of Guinea.

The Bight of Benin extends from the mouth of the Volta River to the mouth of the Niger River and measures about 720 km (about 450 mi) in length. It is fed by the Mono, Donga, Ogun, and Benin rivers. Principal ports include Accra, Ghana; Lomé, Togo; Porto-Novo and Cotonou, Benin; and Lagos, Nigeria. The coast is characterized by rough surf and low offshore islands that protect shallow anchorages.

Throughout the eighteenth century the Bight of Benin was known as the Slave Coast, when Badagri (in Nigeria) and Ouidah (in Benin) were major slaving ports. Between 1711 and 1810 about 1 million people were captured along the Bight of Benin, most of them from the Yoruba ethnic group in southwest Nigeria and some from the Hausa and Nupe groups living north of the Niger (*see* Transatlantic Slave Trade).

See Also
Accra, Ghana; Lagos, Nigeria; Lomé, Togo; Porto-Novo, Benin; Cotonou, Benin.

Latin America and the Caribbean

Biguine, orchestral dance music of Martinique and Guadeloupe popular from the 1940s to the 1960s.

The two principal types of biguine – *biguine classique*, ballroom dance music in the French Caribbean islands, and *biguine vidé*, heard mostly at Carnival there – reflect their African heritage in the emphasis on the call and response between the soloist and chorus, the prominence of rhythm over melody, and the vital importance of percussion. Biguine classique of the 1940s is more directly related to American big band and New Orleans music, from the nature of the rhythm (carried by guitar and drums) to the use of wind instruments for the melody. Jazz also influenced later biguine classique, most notably in trumpet, clarinet, and saxophone improvisation heard in many compositions.

In the mid-1950s biguine integrated components from more local musical forms. Elements of Cuban *guaguancó*, or mambo, became part of the biguine vernacular through the introduction of the tumba rhythmic figure and the addition of the piano. The borrowing of the high-hat (foot-operated cymbals) from Trinidadian calypso led to another such modification of the biguine classique and to the creation of a hybrid musical form known as biguine calypso. Biguine vidé, characterized by a faster tempo and a simpler song structure than biguine classique, reflects few of these outside influences.

As with the zouk style of music, the word "biguine" refers as much to an occasion for music as it does to the music itself. Biguine classique is closely linked with the popular ballroom dances of the period in Martinique and Guadeloupe. As very few people had phonographs, biguine orchestras of the 1940s such as Fairness Jazz, Esperanza Jazz, and El Calderón regularly performed at balls where *gens biens* (literally "good people," a term that referred to anyone who held a job) would get together to dance the night away in their best clothes. These dances became less class- and status-conscious in the 1950s and 1960s, with all strata of Martinican and Guadeloupean society participating.

If biguine classique filled the dance halls, biguine vidé served as the live outdoor soundtrack to parades during Carnival season. (This helps explain its stripped-down form, since it is easier for Carnival participants to repeat the refrain of a song continuously than it is for them to try to memorize the more complicated couplets.) Contests were organized to determine the best biguine composition of that year's festivities and the winner was a celebrity, at least until he was unseated the following year. The decline in the 1970s of both types of biguine can be linked in large part to competition from recorded music, as well as to the diminishing importance of organized dances. Nonetheless, its adherents maintain that biguine's rhythms live on in today's zouk.

Richard Watts

See Also
New Orleans, Louisiana; Mambo; Trinidad and Tobago; Carnivals in Latin America and the Caribbean.

Africa

Bijagó, an ethnic group of Guinea-Bissau.

The people of the Bijagó ethnic group inhabit the Guinea-Bissau archipelago of the same name. For years they fiercely resisted foreign domination. Anthropologists believe that the Bijagó are related to mainland ethnic groups such as the Papeis and Nalus, who migrated to the region between the tenth and fourteenth centuries. Retaining their animist religious beliefs, the Bijagó lived in small chiefdoms. They fished, cultivated a variety of crops (especially rice), produced palm wine, and built canoes that were able to hold up to 70 people.

The Bijagó's canoes enabled them to conduct raids on slave traders and trading outposts that were involved in the transatlantic slave trade. Many Bijagó also participated in the transatlantic trade. During the early nineteenth century, Portugal tried unsuccessfully to suppress the Bijagó. Successive Portuguese military campaigns finally suppressed them in 1936. Colonial rule on the islands was harsh because of past Bijagó resistance and isolation from mainland scrutiny. Portuguese-appointed chiefs, or *regulos*, collected young men for forced labor on palm oil plantations. Many Bijagó evaded forced labor and taxes, and the Portuguese collectively punished the evaders' family members.

Many Bijagó participated in the independence war, but the war on the islands was one-sided from the start because of the lack of a Portuguese presence. Today there are approximately 25,000 Bijagó, many of whom are involved in palm oil production and fishing. Recently, international nongovernmental organizations have been working with the Bijagó to create a national park in the archipelago.

Eric Young

See Also
Colonial Rule.

Africa

Bikila, Abebe (b. August 7, 1932, Mout, Ethiopia; d. October 25, 1973, Addis Ababa, Ethiopia), Ethiopian two-time Olympic gold medalist in the marathon.

Before competing as a runner, Abebe Bikila was a member of the imperial bodyguard of Haile Selassie I, the Ethiopian emperor. The marathon at the 1960 Olympic Games in Rome, Italy, was only Bikila's third race at this distance, but he set a new world best time of 2 hours, 15 minutes, 16.2 seconds, and also attracted attention by running barefoot. (The designation *world best* is used instead of *record* because marathon courses differ greatly and comparison of finish times is difficult.)

At the 1964 Olympic Games in Tokyo, Japan, Bikila, no longer competing barefoot, became the first runner to win the Olympic marathon twice, finishing with a new world best time of 2 hours, 12 minutes, 11.2 seconds (his previous mark had been broken several times between the Olympic Games). Bikila competed in the marathon at the 1968 Olympic Games in Mexico City, but he dropped out after about 16 km (about 10 mi) because of injury; his Ethiopian teammate Mamo Wolde went on to win the race. In 1969 an automobile accident left Bikila paralyzed below the waist, and he died of a brain hemorrhage four years later.

During his career Bikila won 12 of the 15 marathons he entered, an outstanding accomplishment. Since then, many Ethiopian distance runners have followed in his record-breaking footsteps, including Fatima Roba, who in 1996 became the first Ethiopian woman to win an Olympic gold medal in the Olympic marathon. Bikila's career marked the beginning of a period of excellence by Ethiopian runners at longer distances.

See Also
Olympics, Africans and the; Ethiopia.

Africa

Biko, Stephen **(b. December 18, 1946, Tarkastad, South Africa; d. September 12, 1977, Port Elizabeth, South Africa), founder of the South African Students' Organisation and leader of the Black Consciousness Movement.**

Steve Biko's death at the age of 30 robbed South Africa of one of its most popular and effective antiapartheid activists and gave the movement its most famous martyr. Memorialized in the 1987 film *Cry Freedom*, Biko became an international symbol of the brutal repression facing those who fought racial injustice in South Africa.

The third of four children, Biko grew up in the all-black Ginsberg area of King William's Town, in the Eastern Cape. He was only 4 when his father, a policeman, died. When Biko was 16 the town raised money to send him to the Lovedale Institution, the school that his older brother Khaya attended. Shortly after Biko arrived, Khaya was arrested on suspicion of belonging to the banned Pan-Africanist Congress (PAC). Although Khaya was later acquitted, both brothers were expelled. Biko finished his studies at St. Francis' College, a Catholic boarding school in Natal Province, and graduated in 1965.

The next year Biko entered the University of Natal to study medicine. There he joined the National Union of South African Students (NUSAS), a multiracial antiapartheid student group. By 1967 international events had led Biko to question his commitment to a nonracial approach. Much of Africa had only recently won independence from years of white colonial rule, and in the United States the Black Power Movement was on the rise.

Resolving that it was time to reject the help of white liberals and form an all-black antiapartheid organization, Biko and other members of NUSAS and the University Christian Movement (UCM) founded the South African Students' Organisation (SASO) in 1968. As SASO's first president, Biko traveled throughout South Africa training students to lead their own SASO chapters. In his SASO newsletter column "I Write What I Like," he expressed his views on Black Consciousness, the belief that black South Africans could overcome injustice only by first defeating the mentality of oppression. Even after stepping down as president in 1970 – SASO's bylaws provided for a new president every year – he continued to function as the organisation's heart and soul. His studies suffered, and in 1972 he left the university without receiving his medical degree.

Biko went to work for the newly formed Black Community Programmes (BCP), helping to organize youth groups aimed at building skills and self-esteem among its members. He also continued to serve as publicity director for SASO and began a correspondence course in law. In addition, Biko helped found the Black Peoples' Convention (BPC), which sought to expand SASO's work beyond the student population. In 1973 the South African government placed banning orders on Biko and seven other SASO leaders. Confined to King William's Town, Biko founded and ran an Eastern Cape branch of the BCP until 1975.

By that time Biko was looking to increase SASO and BPC cooperation with the banned African National Congress (ANC) and PAC. But after the 1976 Soweto student uprising, the government increased its harassment of Biko, one of the few leading figures in the antiapartheid movement who had not been imprisoned or exiled. He was detained twice under the Terrorist Act, and then on August 18, 1977, he was once again taken into police custody, where he was stripped naked and beaten for refusing to cooperate. Less than a month later, his naked, manacled body was found in a Pretoria jail cell.

An official investigation into Biko's death cleared the police, and in October 1977 the government banned all Black Consciousness Movement organizations. For years, the South African police denied responsibility for his death, first claiming that he had starved while on a hunger strike, then that he had smashed his own head into a wall, fatally fracturing his skull. In 1997 testimony before the Truth and Reconciliation Commission and the public, including Biko's widow, Nontsikelelo, the officers involved finally admitted to having tortured and murdered Biko 20 years earlier. Biko, who was eulogized by then Bishop Desmond Tutu, left behind three young children.

Kate Tuttle

See Also
Antiapartheid Movement; Soweto, South Africa; Pretoria, South Africa; Black Consciousness in Africa; Tutu, Desmond Mpilo; Black Power.

Africa

Bilin **(also known as Bilen, Belen, Bogo, and Gabra Tarqwe Qur), ethnic group of the Horn of Africa.**

The Bilin primarily inhabit western Eritrea and the Tigray Province of Ethiopia. Large numbers of Bilin refugees also settled in Sudan during the Eritrean secession wars of the 1970s and 1980s. They speak an Afro-Asiatic language and are one of the Agaw peoples. Approximately 200,000 people consider themselves Bilin.

See Also
Languages, African: An Overview.

Africa

Bimoba **(also known as Bimawba, B'Moba, Moab, and Moba), ethnic group of West Africa.**

The Bimoba primarily inhabit northern Ghana and northern Togo. They speak a Niger-Congo language and belong to the Gurma cultural and linguistic group. Approximately 200,000 people consider themselves Bimoba.

See Also
Languages, African: An Overview.

Africa

Biogeography of Africa, **the distribution of plant and animal life on the continent of Africa.**

Due to its tectonic history, weather patterns, and sheer longitudinal sprawl (7918 km [4920 mi] from Tunis, Tunisia, to Cape Town, South Africa), Africa contains an extraordinary range of habitats. As a result, measurements of species diversity, average biomass, and "primary productivity" (how much energy plants photosynthesize) vary immensely. In addition, the flora and fauna of Africa have evolved and adapted according to specific local and regional conditions, which have in turn been influenced by global patterns and epochal changes; thus the climate and geomorphology of Africa play primary roles in the determination of biological diversity.

Although the complexity of life in Africa limits the use of simple categories, the continent may be roughly divided into a small number of *biomes*. Scientists use biomes to classify large regions of relative uniformity, where soil, plants, animals, and weather suggest a continuity of condition. A biome

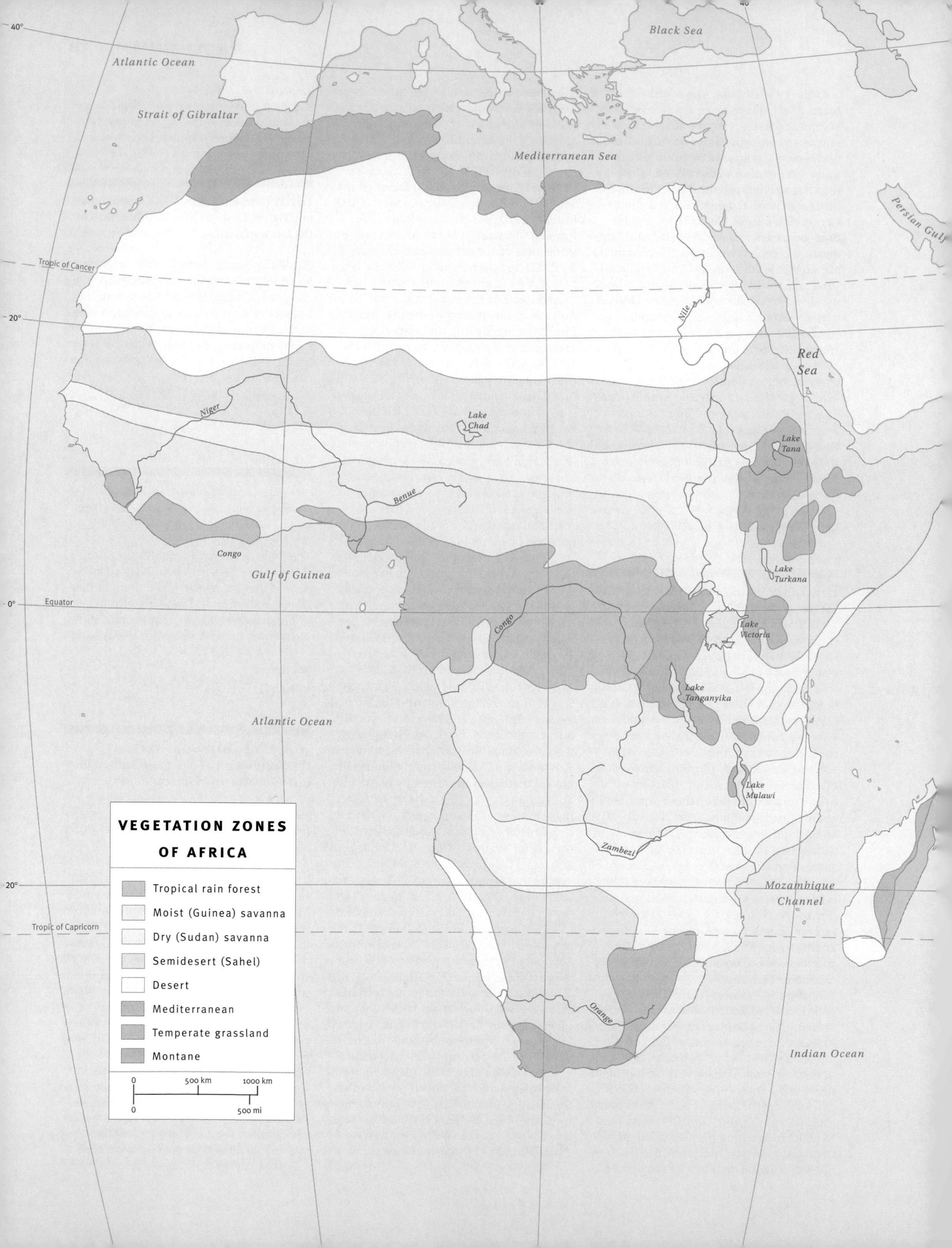
VEGETATION ZONES OF AFRICA
Tropical rain forest
Moist (Guinea) savanna
Dry (Sudan) savanna
Semidesert (Sahel)
Desert
Mediterranean
Temperate grassland
Montane
0
500 km
1000 km
0
500 mi
40°
20°
0°
20°
Tropic of Cancer
Equator
Tropic of Capricorn
Atlantic Ocean
Strait of Gibraltar
Black Sea
Mediterranean Sea
Persian Gulf
Red Sea
Nile
Niger
Lake Chad
Lake Tana
Benue
Congo
Gulf of Guinea
Lake Turkana
Lake Victoria
Congo
Lake Tanganyika
Atlantic Ocean
Lake Malawi
Zambezi
Mozambique Channel
Orange
Indian Ocean

most often takes the name of the predominant vegetation within it.

Biomes in Africa appear to radiate concentrically from the equator, as those to the south mirror those to the north. Biogeographers often divide Africa into at least seven biomes, but main variations may be characterized in five. Tropical rain forests cut the middle of the continent; savannas spread outward from these; deserts emerge from the savanna at higher latitudes; and Mediterranean conditions prevail on the southern tip as well as the northern coast of the continent. In addition, mountainous regions, also called Afromontane biomes, are scattered throughout.

Tropical Rain Forest

In Africa, four distinct rain forest regions exist, all close to the equator: the Congolian Rain Forest belt, which sprawls across Gabon, Republic of the Congo, Democratic Republic of the Congo, and western Tanzania; the smaller Upper Guinean belt, which extends from Guinea to Ghana; and two narrow coastal strips, one abutting the ocean in Mozambique, Tanzania, and Kenya, and the other covering east Madagascar.

The Congolian and Guinean belts display numerous biotic similarities, including year-round high temperatures and rainfall (at least 1400 mm [55 in] annually, and over 5000 mm [200 in] in some areas) and rich species diversity. Together they are thought to contain more than 8000 plant species, most of them native to the region. The forests on the east coast and Madagascar receive less rain and host fewer species of flora.

Rain forest flora commonly assume a three-level structure, with a few exceptionally tall trees (up to 50 m [165 ft]), a denser middle canopy of interlocking treetops (25 to 35 m [80 to 115 ft]), and a bottom tier of small trees (15 m [50 ft]). In its most developed form, the rain forest allows little forest-floor vegetation, since the middle canopy blocks out a great deal of sunlight. Where trees have fallen or been cut or burned, undergrowth may proliferate in the exposed patches. Broad-leafed evergreen trees, including palms, predominate in African rain forests, especially in the wetter regions. In drier, semideciduous belts, such as those of the east coast, the canopy is thinner and the undergrowth typically more dense.

A great diversity of bird species populate Africa's rain forests, along with many higher primates. Despite the upper-strata richness of life in these regions, however, rain forest soil often contains little organic matter, in part because of rapid bacterial breakdown. Farmers in rain forest regions typically practice "shifting" cultivation, in which they relocate their plots every two or three years, thereby allowing tired soils to regain fertility.

Although rain forests cover only about 7 percent of sub-Saharan Africa, they contain more than 50 percent of Africa's native species. Within the biome, biologists have identified at least eight distinct subcategories according to moisture, soil, and elevation. Compared with the rain forests of Asia and the Amazon, African rain forests lack biodiversity. They do, however, face similar threats, especially from logging companies that export high-value tropical hardwoods.

Savanna

Savannas stretch across Africa, both to the north and to the south of the Congolian and Guinean rain forest belts. The Sudanian savanna in the Northern Hemisphere and the Zambezian savanna in the Southern Hemisphere are the largest savanna biomes.

The term *savanna* connotes grassland but can also refer to regions with abundant trees. "Moist" or "Guinea" savannas, in fact, contain large woodland areas. Compared to the grasslands in Australia and South America, the savannas of Africa include a high number of trees and tree species.

Unlike the rain forest regions, the African savannas have distinct dry and rainy seasons, which influence patterns of plant growth and animal migration. In the drier zones many grasses and trees, such as baobabs

UPPER LEFT: A male silverback gorilla sits on the jungle floor. *CORBIS/Tony Wilson-Bligh; Papilio*
UPPER RIGHT: Lions, like most of the large African fauna, inhabit the grassy savanna. *CORBIS/Brian Vikander*
RIGHT: On the Kenyan savanna, this giraffe stretches to graze from an acacia tree. *CORBIS/Jim Zuckerman*

ABOVE: **A few drought-adapted trees grow on the edge of sand dunes in the desert of Namibia.** *CORBIS/Francesc Muntada*
LEFT: **Mt. Kilimanjaro, the highest mountain in Africa, rises to 5,895 meters (19,340 feet). The vegetation on the slopes of Kilimanjaro is typical of afromontane biomes.** *CORBIS/© Kennan Ward*

and acacias, have evolved to resist fires and droughts. Africa's famous large fauna, such as lions and zebras, elephants and rhinoceroses, roam the savannas in migratory patterns that reflect the seasonal rains.

Desert and Semi-Desert

Savanna vegetation dwindles on the edges of Africa's deserts. The largest of these are the Sahara, in the north; the Kalahari, primarily in Botswana; and the Namib, which lies along the southwestern coast. In the semiarid regions bordering the deserts, such as the Sahel, immediately south of the Sahara, plants tend to be perennials and succulents, and all animal life is sparse. Many of the people living in these regions practice nomadic pastoralism and migrate throughout the year to find adequate water and fodder for their livestock.

Like the savannas, transitional desert regions exhibit numerous variations. The border areas of the Namib, for instance, display a far wider diversity of flora than the Sahel. In all three deserts, patches of vegetation grow around oases or sprout after occasional torrential rains. In general, biological proliferation is an "event-driven" affair in arid regions. Life happens when rain falls. Sometimes deserts receive as little as 20 mm [1 in] of rain annually, and even semi-arid regions seldom get more than 500 mm [20 in]. Although aridity is typically accompanied by extremely high daytime temperatures (sometimes over 40° C [104° F]), at night temperatures can drop precipitously, often to near 0° C [32° F].

Mediterranean

Due to the moderating effect of the South Atlantic, a zone of Mediterranean-like conditions exists on the southern tip of Africa as well as along the Mediterranean Sea. Warm dry summers and cool rainy winters characterize both regions, though rainfall averages often resemble those of semi-arid zones.

Floral diversity far exceeds faunal diversity in the Mediterranean biomes. Native plant species display drought-resistant adaptations such as long dormancy periods and thick spiny leaves. The relatively temperate climate of these regions also supports diverse forms of agricultural production, ranging in South Africa, for example, from grain and yam farming to vineyards and orchards.

Afromontane

Afromontane vegetation occurs in high-altitude areas throughout the continent, including the Cameroon and Guinea highlands of West Africa; the Ethiopian, Kenyan, Tanzanian, and Albertine Rift highlands of East Africa; and the Drakensberg highlands in the Southeast. Vegetation in such regions often occurs in vertical belts, reflecting gradients in temperature and precipitation. Montane forests cover the lower areas (1200 to 2500 m [3900 to 8200 ft]), and at higher levels (3000 m [10,000 ft] and above) vegetation thins out, due to the great fluctuation between daytime and nighttime temperatures. Mountain forests in the equatorial zone are noted for their towering heath and heathlike flora. Elsewhere, evergreens predominate.

In the Afromontane biomes, windward slopes often catch precipitation that leeward slopes miss, causing mountains to develop lopsided patterns of vegetation. Precipitation often freezes at the highest elevations, as evinced by the snows of Kilimanjaro and Mount Kenya. Because highland regions tend to have relatively fertile soils, they are among the most intensively farmed areas of Africa.

Eric Bennett

See Also

Baobab Tree; Climate of Africa; Elephant; Ethiopia; Geomorphology, African; Kalahari Desert; Lion; Namib Desert; Rhinoceros; Sahara Desert; Tunis, Tunisia; Zebra.

Latin America and the Caribbean

Biohó, Benkos

(b. late 1500s, Guinea-Bissau, West Africa; d. March 16, 1621, Cartagena, Colombia), an African slave who allegedly became one of the first organizers, founders, and leaders of a maroon community in the Americas. Known also as Domingo Benkos Biohó, Dionisio Biohó, Rey (King) Benkos, Rey de la Matuna, and Biohó Rey, he is recognized for his rebellious leadership and for founding one of the longest-surviving communities of escaped Africans in Spanish America.

Benkos Biohó was enslaved in his native Africa and taken to the South American slave port of Cartagena de Indias. In 1596 he was sold to Spanish colonizer Alonso del Campo, who baptized him Domingo (or Dionisio). In 1599 Biohó, claiming to have been a king in Africa, escaped, along with several male and female slaves, into the neighboring forests and marshlands known as the Matuna. There he founded one of the first *palenques* (rebel slave communities) in the Americas.

Biohó's leadership earned him the title Benkos, or "king." He became renowned for his skill in administering the rebel community and for his efforts to free slaves. He wanted to become the head of an independent black republic. To further this dream, he planned an attack on the cities of Cartagena, Panama, and Mompox, with the goal of liberating slaves and organizing them under his rule. Upon receiving word of Biohó's plan, Alonso Sotomayor, the governor of Panama, ordered the murder of many African slaves.

In 1603, after many failed Spanish expeditions against the maroon settlement,

Benkos Biohó secured the autonomy of the Matuna palenque through a peace treaty with Cartagena's governor Gerónimo Suazo. A decade later, another governor, Diego Fernández de Velasco, offered amnesty and freedom to all *palenqueros* who would abandon their refuge. Though some did, in 1619 another slave revolt in the city led authorities to recognize the continued leadership of Biohó and the fact that the palenqueros were not yet to be defeated.

Some historians maintain that on one of his excursions, Biohó founded the settlement that would later be known as PALENQUE DE SAN BASILIO. Today San Basilio is famous for conserving many African traditions and for being the birthplace of palenquero Creole, a language still spoken in this region of COLOMBIA. Other historians, however, dispute the association of this palenque with Biohó, arguing that the Palenque de San Basilio appears in the historical record much later.

On March 16, 1621, Biohó was executed after being captured near the walls of Cartagena. His wife, Wiwa, daughter, Orika, and son, Sando, went on to establish the palenques of San Miguel and Sierra María. Seventy years after the death of Benkos Biohó, on August 23, 1691, the king of Spain issued a decree that recognized the independence and autonomy of the palenqueros and acknowledged their "comprehensive and absolute" liberty.

Judith Morrison

SEE ALSO
Maroonage in the Americas; Cartagena de Indias, Colombia.

Latin America and the Caribbean

Biquiba de La Fuente Guarany, Francisco (1882-1985), Brazilian folk artist who carved numerous figureheads for boats on the San Francisco River (*see* ART IN LATIN AMERICA AND THE CARIBBEAN).

Latin America and the Caribbean

Bird, Vere Cornwall (b. 1909), political leader of Antigua and Barbuda.

Vere Cornwall Bird began his political career in 1939 as a member of the newly created Antigua Trade and Labor Union. Within this labor organization, he founded the Antigua Labor Party (ALP). Prior to independence from Britain, Bird was first elected to the Legislative Council, the governing body of the island, in 1945. He held the posts of chief minister (1960-1967) and premier (1967-1971). After a five-year hiatus, Bird again came to power in 1976. In 1981, when the country gained its independence from Britain, Bird became its first prime minister, a post which he held until he retired in 1994.

SEE ALSO
Antigua and Barbuda.

Africa

Birifor (also known as Birifo and Malba), ethnic group of West Africa.

The Birifor primarily inhabit northern GHANA, southern BURKINA FASO, and northern Côte d'Ivoire. They speak a Niger-Congo language and belong to the Mole-Dagbane linguistic and cultural group. Approximately 200,000 people consider themselves Birifor.

SEE ALSO
Côte d'Ivoire; Languages, African: An Overview.

Africa

Birom (also known as Berum, Borom, Kibo, Gbang, Afango, and Kibyen), ethnic group of NIGERIA.

The Birom primarily inhabit the Jos Plateau of Nigeria. They speak a Niger-Congo language and comprise three distinct subgroups: Western Birom, Southern Birom, and Eastern Birom. Approximately 200,000 people consider themselves Birom.

SEE ALSO
Languages, African: An Overview.

North America

Birth of a Nation, The, American director D. W. Griffith's silent film about the rise of the Ku Klux Klan, one of the most controversial films of all time because of its demeaning portrayal of blacks.

First released on February 8, 1915, *The Birth of a Nation*'s depictions of blacks as idling and brutish sparked a massive wave of protests from thousands of African Americans. The explosive controversy set off by the film revealed Hollywood's power to reflect and shape public attitudes about race, while setting the stage for what would be a decades-long struggle to improve the portrayal of blacks on film.

Unprecedentedly long – three hours (and 12 reels of film) – *The Birth of a Nation* chronicles the fall of the South during the Civil War and the reemergence of white political domination over the interracial state governments of the Reconstruction era. In the film's final scenes, the Ku Klux Klan, described in a *New York Times* review as "a company of avenging spectral crusaders sweeping along... moonlit roads," takes revenge for the attempted rape of two white women by black men. The film, based on the racist novels of Thomas Dixon, *The Leopard's Spots* and *The Clansmen*, rushes through visually striking Civil War panoramas and melodramatic episodes about the plight of Southern soldiers and depicts the rise of the Klan as heroic, all the while portraying blacks as lazy and weak or violent and dangerous.

Griffith's innovative filmmaking techniques delighted critics and drew a national audience deeply enmeshed in a culture of lynchings, Jim Crow segregation, and widespread antiblack sentiment. In its first 11 months in New York City alone, the film sold an estimated 3 million tickets. On Thanksgiving night in 1915, 25,000 Klansmen paraded through the streets of Atlanta to celebrate the movie's opening. And when Griffith, the son of a Confederate soldier, presented his work to President Woodrow Wilson (reportedly the first screening of a feature film in the White House), the president allegedly declared, "It is like writing history with lightning. And my only regret is that it is all so terribly true."

Black groups, while aware that a public controversy would only boost ticket sales, were quick to react to the film's blatant racism. The National Association for the Advancement of Colored People (NAACP) sent copies of a scathing *New Republic* review to more than 500 newspapers, issued strong warnings that screening the film could spark rioting, and even managed to have deleted some of the movie's harshest moments, including a scene proposing that blacks be sent back to Africa as a remedy for the nation's ills.

But the efforts of the black organizations were drowned out by the film's runaway box-office success. Perhaps the protesters' biggest victory lay in rallying African Americans around a common cause and in increasing awareness of the recently created NAACP and other black political groups. While the film is still praised by critics as a cinematic masterpiece, it has also become an important object lesson in how the relationship of popular media to public opinion can perpetuate RACIAL STEREOTYPES.

SEE ALSO
Atlanta, Georgia; Civil War, American; Jim Crow; Lynching; National Association for the Advancement of Colored People; New York, New York; Reconstruction; Film, Blacks in American.

Africa

Bisa, ethnic group of ZAMBIA.

The Bisa primarily inhabit eastern Zambia. They speak a Bantu language and belong to the larger BEMBA cultural and linguistic group. Approximately 200,000 people consider themselves Bisa.

SEE ALSO
Bantu: Dispersion and Settlement.

Africa

Bisharin, ethnic group of Sudan and Eritrea.

The Bisharin inhabit northeastern Sudan and neighboring Eritrea. They speak an Afro-Asiatic language and are one of the larger Beja peoples. Approximately 100,000 people consider themselves Bisharin.

See Also

Languages, African: An Overview.

Latin America and the Caribbean

Bishop, Maurice (b. May 29, 1944, Aruba; d. October 19, 1983, St. George's, Grenada), revolutionary leader who became prime minister of Grenada in a 1979 coup but was killed by his opponents in 1983.

Maurice Bishop became the prime minister of Grenada in a 1979 coup and rose to prominence as one of the most controversial figures in the Caribbean. He was born in Aruba in 1944, but his parents, both native Grenadians, moved the family back to Grenada in 1950. He was educated at Catholic schools in St. George's and in 1963 won a scholarship to attend university in England. Bishop studied at Gray's Inn, London University's Holborn College of Law, and King's College. During this time, he became involved in the Black Power Movement and was influenced by such leaders as Malcolm X, Martin Luther King Jr., Kwame Nkrumah, and Walter Rodney.

On his return to Grenada in 1970 Bishop went into private legal practice and co-founded a discussion group of young radical intellectuals and professionals. The group evolved into the Movement for Assemblies of the People (MAP), a political organization whose members were committed to protesting the corruption and apathy they saw under the government of long-time leader Eric Gairy. In 1973 MAP joined forces with the Joint Endeavour for the Welfare, Education and Liberation of the People (JEWEL), and Bishop became the leader of the new organization, the New Jewel Movement (NJM).

The NJM began staging large protests against the Gairy government and soon became a target of the administration's ire. In 1974 six of the NJM's leaders, including Bishop, were jailed, and Bishop's father, Rupert, was killed during a police attack at an NJM protest. These actions only brought renewed support and sympathy for the NJM, but when the 1976 elections were held, Gairy's party prevailed and Bishop became the minority leader in Grenada's government.

The NJM believed that they had won the election and that Gairy's party had retained control through fraud. On March 13, 1979, Bishop and the NJM took control of Grenada's government in a bloodless coup, staged when Gairy was out of the country. The new administration was called the People's Revolutionary Government (PRG), and Bishop was named its first prime minister. The PRG immediately declared its determination to provide better jobs, housing, health care, and education for the Grenadian people; as a result, the new administration met with widespread popular support.

Bishop and the PRG chose to pattern their new government after Fidel Castro's Cuba. Bishop had admired Castro since childhood, and Castro became a key ally, sending Cuban doctors, teachers, and other workers into Grenada. Cuba, the Soviet Union, and several other countries also gave the new government substantial loans. But the United States, its most powerful neighbor, was very suspicious of the PRG's Communist ties. The United States imposed political and economic sanctions on Grenada, and as loans from other countries began drying up, the ensuing financial crisis led to a split within the PRG.

Bishop supported private industry as a solution and even traveled to the United States in an attempt to win American support for his government. But a radical faction within his government disapproved of these moves and began to demand that Bishop share power with Deputy Prime Minister Bernard Coard. Bishop refused and was placed under house arrest on October 13, 1983. Six days later a crowd of demonstrators freed Bishop and several ministers who had been detained with him, but he was immediately rearrested by the pro-Coard military police. At 2:00 on the afternoon of October 19, Bishop and ten of his supporters were executed.

The United States chose to use the assassinations and the government's instability as an opportunity to reestablish its influence in the region. Less than a week after Bishop's death, on October 25, the United States led a military invasion of Grenada, which effectively ended the PRG's regime. New elections occurred in 1984, and a peacekeeping mission remained on the island until 1985. Coard, his wife, and several of his supporters were eventually convicted and sentenced to death (although their case remained on appeal as of late 1998) for their role in Maurice Bishop's murder.

Lisa Clayton Robinson

See Also

King, Martin Luther, Jr.; Black Power.

North America

Bishop, Sanford

(b. February 4, 1947, Mobile, Ala.), Democratic member of the United States House of Representatives from Georgia (1993-).

Born in Mobile, Alabama, Sanford Bishop received a bachelor's degree in 1968 from Morehouse College in Atlanta. After graduating from Emory Law School in Atlanta in 1971, he practiced civil rights law in Columbus, Georgia. He built his reputation as a member of the Georgia State House of Representatives from 1977 to 1991 and then as a member of the Georgia Senate from 1991 to 1993. In 1992 Bishop ran against incumbent representative Charles Hatcher for the U.S. House seat representing the Second Congressional District. Bishop won easily and was returned to office in subsequent elections.

Bishop represents Georgia's Second Congressional District, located in the southwest region of the state. This district has been one of three districts in the state where blacks compose the majority of the population. Its urban areas are home to two army bases and considerable industry; the rural areas also tend to be Democratic. Georgia's redistricting in December 1995, however, not only reduced the district's black majority but made Bishop a resident of the state's Third Congressional District. For the 1996 elections, Bishop relocated to within the new borders of the Second District, which, while no longer having a black majority, still contains most of the district he had originally represented. In the 105th Congress (1997-1999), Bishop sat on the Agriculture Committee and the Select Intelligence Committee and is a member of the Congressional Black Caucus.

Bissago. Please see Bijagó

Africa

Bissau, Guinea-Bissau, capital of Guinea-Bissau and major port city.

When Portuguese explorers first anchored in the Geba River estuary, on the central coast of present-day Guinea-Bissau, in the late 1450s, they found the Papei people living on its shores. European influence in the region remained limited, and it was Afro-Portuguese slave traders who first established a base at Bissau in the late fifteenth century, on an island that has since become a peninsula in the river. With the intensification of the transatlantic slave trade in the seventeenth century, European activity on the island increased. Its economic importance was second to that of Cacheu, and Portugal's hold was tenuous. In 1753, after abandoning the island for several years, the Portuguese, alarmed at French inroads into the area, returned in force to build a fortress at Bissau. The Papei occasionally attacked the Portuguese, although the Portuguese paid the Papei for the right to remain in the area.

The end of the slave trade in the early 1800s nearly destroyed Bissau's economy, but slowly the town recovered and in 1869 it became a district capital, with a population of 573. Until the mid-twentieth century, Bissau remained a minor colonial town, subject to disease and continued resistance from the Papei. However, in 1941 Bissau became the capital of Portuguese Guinea, and Africans began to migrate to the city. In 1959 the killing of Bissau dockworkers sparked the independence war, which drove refugees into the city and increased the population from 25,000 to 80,000.

Guinea-Bissau became independent in 1974, with Bissau as its capital. Today the population of Bissau is just over 200,000, or 20 percent of the country's population. Bissau remains the economic hub of the country, but Guinea-Bissau's poverty has stunted Bissau's development since independence despite this rapid population growth.

Eric Young

See Also
Transatlantic Slave Trade; Portugal; Cacheu, Guinea-Bissau.

Africa

Biya, Paul (b. February 13, 1933, Mvomeka, French Cameroon), president of Cameroon from 1982 to the present.

Paul Biya was born to poor parents of the Bulu ethnic group in southern French Cameroun. After his primary education, Biya briefly entered the seminary, but ultimately attended a French secondary school in Yaoundé. Later, he studied in France at the Sorbonne, the Institut des etudes politique, and the Institut des Hautes Etudes d'Outre Mer. Returning to Cameroon in 1962, he began serving in administrative positions in the office of the presidency. Biya held a variety of administrative and cabinet posts until President Amhadou Ahidjo appointed him minister of state in 1970. Five years later, Ahidjo named him prime minister.

In November 1982 Ahidjo resigned and Biya became the second president of Cameroon. Ahidjo, however, retained his position of head of the sole legal party. Conflict ensued as Biya moved away from the autocratic style of his predecessor, but in 1983 Biya prevailed. He later formed a new party, seeking to further distinguish himself from Ahidjo.

Biya outlined his philosophical principles in his book *Communal Liberalism* (1987), in which he called for greater "rigor" and "moralization" in politics and society. In Biya's conception, communal liberalism would allow for personal freedom and democracy, but emphasize national unity above all. This scenario, Biya claimed, would require a strong party and state to avoid regional, ethnic, and religious fragmentation. But progress was slow, and Biya's rule was marked by authoritarianism, even after he held and narrowly won elections in 1992. In the 1997 elections Biya ran unopposed, and won another seven-year term.

Eric Young

See Also
Ahidjo, El Hajj Ahmadou; Yaoundé, Cameroon.

North America

Black Aesthetic, The, an expression of the Black Power Movement's principles and aspirations in literature, in which its proponents challenged artists and writers to establish new standards of beauty and judgment based on African American values in opposition to Western aesthetic ideals, and to forge a sense of black cultural pride and nationalism.

The term *black aesthetic* was used informally during the 1960s and adopted as a theoretical concept in 1971 with the publication of Addison Gayle's *The Black Aesthetic*, a collection of essays on the characteristics of the black aesthetic in literature and music. The black aesthetic encompasses a body of oral and written nonfiction and fiction that asserts the equality, uniqueness, and sometimes the superiority of African American modes of perception and expression; a set of political principles opposing inequality; and ethical and artistic criteria outlining what is valid and invalid writing by black Americans. One of the main expectations for a black aesthetic work is that it be politically engaged and socially uplifting.

According to critic Reginald Martin, a black aesthetic has existed since the earliest writings by African Americans, and its evolution can be divided into three chronological phases. The first phase began with David Walker's *Appeal* (1829) and ran through Frederick Douglass's *Narrative* (1881). During this interval, the fundamental works of the black aesthetic were written by slave or former slave authors who called for physical resistance to white oppression and listed their demands from whites. The second phase was framed by Booker T. Washington's "Atlanta Exposition Address" (1895) and the assassination of President John F. Kennedy (1963), an event that many civil rights activists saw as the end of black-white negotiations. The most important publications of this phase were *The Souls of Black Folk* (1903) by W. E. B. Du Bois and *The New Negro* (1925) by Alain Locke. Common to these writings were educational demands, negotiation for better social conditions, divergent black intellectual views on issues central to blacks, and colloquial language. The third division spanned only six years, from Martin Luther King Jr.'s "I Have a Dream" speech (1963) to Clarence Major's introduction to *New Black Poetry* (1969). In this final stage, artists emphasized blackness as a metaphysical concept, prose with a folk-sermon structure, the expression of pent-up emotions, black self-reliance, and black self-love. In the 1970s critical writings by Houston Baker Jr., Amiri Baraka, Hoyt Fuller, and Dudley Randall further defined the black aesthetic.

Aaron Myers

See Also
Du Bois, William Edward Burghardt (W. E. B.); King, Martin Luther, Jr.; Locke, Alain Leroy; Randall, Dudley Felker; Washington, Booker Taliaferro; Black Power.

North America

Black Arts Movement (1965-1975), a Black Nationalist African American arts movement focusing on music, literature, drama, and the visual arts.

The Black Arts Movement was a loose network of Black Nationalist African American artists and intellectuals during the mid-1960s to the mid-1970s. In many respects, the Black Arts Movement was the cultural wing of the Black Power Movement. Like the Black Power Movement, its participants held a variety of political beliefs, ranging from revolutionary Marxism to versions of what was understood as the cultures and ideologies of traditional precolonial Africa. Despite this range of often conflicting beliefs, there was a generally shared concept of African American liberation and of the right of African Americans to determine their own destiny. There was also usually some common notion of the development or recovery of an authentic national black culture that was linked to an existing African American folk or popular culture.

It is difficult to date precisely the beginning of the Black Arts Movement. One possibility is 1965, when Amiri Baraka and other black cultural activists founded the Black Arts Repertory Theatre/School (BARTS) in Harlem. However, a number of important forerunners to BARTS helped make the larger movement possible. For example, Umbra, a seminationalist group of African American writers in the Lower East Side of New York City in the early 1960s, provided a training ground for a number of influential Black Arts activists, including Ishmael Reed, Lorenzo Thomas, David Henderson, Calvin Hernton, and Askia Muhammad Touré. The influence of the Nation of Islam on many African American jazz musicians in the 1950s and early 1960s also helped prepare the way for a Black Nationalist arts movement. The journals The Liberator and *Negro Digest* (later *Black World*) offered important outlets and encouragement for emerging literary and artistic nationalists in the early 1960s. Baraka's pre-BARTS drama, particularly *Dutchman* (1964) and *The Slave* (1964), were crucial in shaping the form and direction that African American nationalist drama would take in the late 1960s and early 1970s.

It is after 1965, however, that one can talk about a Black Arts Movement in a cohesive sense. Though there often existed sharp conflict between participants in the movement about politics and aesthetics, there was enough common ground to produce national conferences, journals (such as *Black Dialogue*, *Journal of Black Poetry*, and *Black World*), organizations, and widely read anthologies (such as Amiri Baraka and Larry Neal's seminal *Black Fire* [1968]). Unlike earlier groupings of African American artistic production, the Black Arts Movement flourished in a wide range of locations. Virtually every sizable African American community and many college campuses saw the rise of new black theaters and organizations of nationalist-minded visual artists, writers, dancers, and musicians. Some of these organizations and institutions are the Association for the Advancement of Creative Music, the Organization of Black American Culture, and the African Commune of Bad Relevant Artists, all in Chicago, Illinois; Spirit House, in Newark, New Jersey; the Black Arts Group, in St. Louis, Missouri; the Watts Writer's Workshop, in Los Angeles, California; and Broadside Press, in Detroit, Michigan.

Music (particularly avant-garde or "free" jazz), poetry, and drama were the artistic genres that dominated the Black Arts Movement. In part this was due to the movement's close connection to the political movement of Black Power: music, poetry, and drama were easily performed at street rallies, demonstrations, political meetings, and other communal events. These genres also lent themselves to the multimedia productions, combining spoken, visual, and musical elements, that characterized the movement. Another important art form of the period was the public wall mural, which engaged whole communities in its creation and viewing.

Amiri Baraka is considered the leading figure of the era. Baraka's Black Arts poetry, drama, music criticism, and social commentary were apocalyptic, antiwhite, and often misogynist, anti-Semitic, and homophobic, projecting a powerful vision of a utopian unity of African Americans that proved tremendously important in defining the discussion of a "black aesthetic." Other significant writers of the Black Arts Movement include poet and essayist Larry Neal, poet Sonia Sanchez, poet Don L. Lee (Haki Madhubuti), poet Nikki Giovanni, playwright Ed Bullins, and novelist Toni Morrison. Such critics, scholars, and editors as Addison Gayle Jr. (editor of the anthology of criticism *The Black Aesthetic* [1971]), Harold Cruse (author of the study *The Crisis of the Negro Intellectual* [1967]), and Hoyt Fuller (editor of the journal *Black World*) played prominent roles in promoting and shaping the conversations and debates that took place among Black Arts artists and intellectuals.

Jazz musicians such as Archie Shepp, Sun Ra, and Richard Muhal Abrams were among the most powerful and most visible artists of the movement. Many African American popular musicians were heavily influenced by Black Power and Black Arts, producing best-selling songs such as Curtis Mayfield and the Impressions's "Keep On Pushing" and James Brown's "Say It Loud (I'm Black and I'm Proud)," which became anthems of the period.

Like its beginning, the ending of the Black Arts Movement is hard to pinpoint. In general, as the activities and the organizations of the Black Power Movement, such as the Black Panther Party and Maulana Karenga's US Organization, dwindled or disappeared in the early and mid-1970s, the Black Arts Movement did so also. Nonetheless, the impact of the movement lasted far beyond its perceived end. On some writers, such as Alice Walker and Sherley Anne Williams, the influence was largely negative, as they reacted against what they saw as the sexism and homophobia of the movement. Others, notably Amiri Baraka and Sonia Sanchez, who both moved away from nationalism toward a "Third World Marxism," acknowledged a positive Black Arts legacy while critiquing its limitations. Still other artists, such as Toni Morrison, continued to embrace what was essentially a Black Arts stance in their work after 1975. Similarly, present-day editors have assembled anthologies of African American writing, such as Keith Gilyard's *Spirit and Flame* (1996), which look back to the key Black Arts anthologies, particularly *Black Fire*, for inspiration.

Another lasting influence of the Black Arts Movement is found in institutions, such as African American Studies departments (and the field of African American Studies itself) as well as African American-oriented publishers, book imprints, academic book series, art galleries, and theaters, which would not have existed without the explosion of African American nationalist-influenced artistic activity in the 1960s and 1970s. Finally, the movement made a considerable impression on artists and intellectuals too young to remember its events firsthand. For example, much rap music owes a large debt to the militancy, urgent tone, and multimedia aesthetics of the Black Arts Movement.

James Smethurst

See Also

Black World/Negro Digest; Brown, James; Bullins, Edward (Ed); Cruse, Harold Wright; Giovanni, Yolande Cornelia ("Nikki"); Harlem, New York; Williams, Sherley; Black Power.

Latin America and the Caribbean

Black Autochthonous Party,

black political party founded in Uruguay in 1937 that sought to advance the cause of social justice and equity for Afro-Uruguayans. After a poor showing in the 1938 election, its activities diminished and it finally disbanded in 1944 (*see* Uruguay).

North America

Black Cabinet,

an informal network of African American public policy advisers in the administration of President Franklin Delano Roosevelt.

With the Great Depression at its worst, in 1933 President Franklin D. Roosevelt launched the New Deal, a major economic recovery program that dramatically expanded the role of the federal government in American life. Several groups and individuals recognized the vital importance of ensuring that black interests be represented within the Roosevelt administration. Prior to 1933 no African Americans had formally served as policy advisers within a presidential administration.

During the early days of the Roosevelt administration, the National Association for the Advancement of Colored People (NAACP) and the Julius Rosenwald Fund were among the groups that lobbied administration officials to appoint black advisers to federal agencies and New Deal

"Black Cabinet" member Robert C. Weaver sits at his desk at the United States Housing Authority. In 1940 Weaver was appointed assistant to the head of President Franklin Delano Roosevelt's Defense Commission. *UPI/CORBIS-Bettmann*

programs. Meanwhile, in the summer of 1933, shortly after hearings began on the New Deal's National Recovery Administration (NRA), Robert C. Weaver, a young black economist, and John P. Davis, a recent graduate of Harvard Law School, established themselves as the Negro Industrial League. Its main purpose was to represent the interests of black workers at NRA hearings on Capitol Hill.

First Lady Eleanor Roosevelt and some progressive New Dealers were sympathetic to black demands, but they feared that the appointment of African Americans to policy positions would alienate powerful Southern Democrats in Congress. Secretary of Interior Harold Ickes, a former president of the Chicago branch of the NAACP, volunteered to appoint an adviser on Negro affairs, a position to be paid for by the Rosenwald Fund. But Ickes appointed Clark Foreman, a white Southerner. While black civil rights activists acknowledged Foreman's demonstrated commitment to racial equality, there was nearly unanimous opposition on the part of the NAACP, black newspapers, and others to the appointment of a white man to serve as an advocate for black America. Foreman supported this protest. When Ickes still refused to appoint a black adviser, Foreman proposed a compromise: that Robert C. Weaver be appointed as an assistant adviser, and that he take over Foreman's position when Ickes judged political circumstances to be more favorable. Ickes agreed, as did Weaver, who became Foreman's assistant and succeeded him as adviser on Negro affairs in the Interior Department in 1935.

Once established at the Department of the Interior, Ickes, Foreman, and Weaver determined to work throughout the government to gain equal treatment for blacks. Their initial progress was minimal, because most of the black advisers whose appointments they arranged did little to monitor the administration; they had been hired in part for their pro-Roosevelt politics. Early in 1934 Roosevelt approved Ickes's plan to create the Interdepartmental Group Concerned with the Special Problems of Negroes. For six months the group met regularly with white representatives of the National Recovery Administration, the Civilian Conservation Corps, the Agriculture Department, and the military, but disbanded after encountering resistance and accomplishing nothing.

Still, more black advisers received appointments in the Roosevelt administration, and by mid-1935, 45 African Americans were working in many of the cabinet offices and New Deal agencies. They included James C. Evans, Frank S. Horne, Rayford Logan, William J. Tent Jr., and Ralph Bunche. In 1936 the group began to call itself the Federal Council on Negro Affairs, although the press referred to it as the Black Cabinet or the Black Brain Trust. The members, who usually assembled on Friday evenings at the home of Mary McLeod Bethune, quickly became a bridge between the New Deal and the Civil Rights Movement. For example, during the 1936 presidential campaign, civil rights leaders and the Black Cabinet often shared information and coordinated strategies. During Roosevelt's second term, black leaders like Walter White, Channing Tobias, John P. Davis, and A. Philip Randolph frequently corresponded with Black Cabinet members to arrange protests against heel-dragging New Deal officials and to remain abreast of government developments.

The Black Cabinet brought issues of racial equity into the corridors of the federal government; had some success in ending job discrimination in certain government agencies; and helped expand the number of government jobs available to blacks in Washington. Through their presence and their individual efforts, they helped to increase black interest in politics and worked to encourage black participation in New Deal programs. Mary McLeod Bethune and Robert Weaver, who served for more than a decade in Washington, were especially effective in working with white progressives in creating biracial political coalitions that linked the interests of blacks and whites around issues of economic justice and social welfare. Indeed, the members of the Black Cabinet worked in tandem with the massive crossover of black voters into the Democratic Party in the presidential election of 1936, giving form to a "New Deal coalition" built upon black voters, labor, and liberals.

Robert Fay

See Also

Bunche, Ralph Johnson; Randolph, Asa Philip; Tobias, Channing Heggie; White, Walter Francis; Weaver, Robert Clifton.

Mary McLeod Bethune shown with Eleanor Roosevelt and Aubrey Williams, executive director of the National Youth Association (NYA), in 1937. *CORBIS/Bettmann*

North America

Black Church, The, a simplified way of referring to the more than 65,000 Christian churches that have a predominance of African American members and black clerical leadership; the Black Church has served as a major institutional foundation of African American spiritual and community life.

The Black Church emerged from the period of slavery as the most stable and dominant institutional sphere in black communities in the United States. This centrality of religion was achieved through a gradual historical process that involved several factors. First, prior to and during the rise of the transatlantic slave trade, the traditional worldviews and societies of the Africans themselves were permeated by religion, with no division between sacred and secular, especially between religion and politics. The Africans who were brought as slaves to the New World came as human beings who were already socialized in their own African traditions and values. It is estimated that between 10 and 15 percent of the slaves came from Muslim-dominated parts of Africa or areas that were undergoing the transition to Islam.

Early Influences

While there has been a debate about how much of the traditional African religious culture or African Islam survived in the New World, especially in the United States, there has also been a consensus that a homegrown, indigenous African American culture, a fusion of elements from Africa, Europe, and the United States, was created during the several centuries of slavery and the period of Jim Crow segregation that followed it.

White Protestantism and Slavery

A second important factor in the development of the institutional centrality of black churches involved the great ambivalence among white colonists toward religion and toward the conversion of slaves. Most of the early colonies were founded by religious groups like the Puritans, who were seeking the freedom to practice their religion without persecution. Although Native Americans and Africans were viewed as subhuman, various groups were pressing toward their conversion. As early as 1667 the Virginia colony passed laws, which other colonies followed, that permitted the baptism and conversion of African slaves without setting them free. In 1701 the Anglican Society for the Propagation of the Gospel in Foreign Parts began their missionary efforts among the slaves and Native Americans (*see* American Indians). But it was not until the early decades of the nineteenth century, during the Second Great Awakening, or national religious revival, that many of the slaves became converted. While some slaves were converted to Christianity in the North during the First Awakening (1740-1760), it was the Second Awakening (1790-1830) that swept through the plantations of the South, bringing with it an emotional, evangelical form of Protestant piety that became embodied among Baptists and Methodists. But for most whites, Christianity was largely viewed as an instrument of social control, to produce "obedient and docile" slaves.

Slave Religion: "The Invisible Institution"

While the social-control aspects of Christianity were quite effective when intermeshed with other constraints such as laws and black codes, illiteracy, and an omnipresent threat of extermination, religion became the only institutional area in which African slaves exercised a measure of freedom, despite the many efforts to hinder or control their religious life. Sometimes stealing off to the backwoods and bayous of Southern plantations, or meeting clandestinely in the slave quarters, and at times even openly in services with whites present, they performed their own rituals, songs, and other cultural forms of religious worship. They also developed their own leaders so that the "invisible institution" – the underground slave religion – could effectively merge with the rise of institutional black churches in the latter half of the eighteenth and the early nineteenth centuries.

As a consequence of these historical factors, religion among black people became the only institutional area that was permitted to develop to any significant degree. During several centuries of slavery, political, economic, educational, and other cultural and social institutions were deemed illegal and remained relatively undeveloped. Finally, as the only significant social institution other than the black family, the Black Church took on multiple roles and burdens that differed from those of its white counterpart.

The First Black Churches: Baptist Churches in the South

Emerging from the "invisible institution" of slave religion, the first known black churches arose before the American Revolution, with the African Baptist or "Bluestone" Church on the William Byrd plantation near the Bluestone River in Mecklenburg, Virginia, in 1758, and the Silver Bluff Baptist Church on the South Carolina bank of the Savannah River, founded sometime between 1750 and 1775. These first churches were of Baptist origin, which meant that they believed that only adult baptism and baptism by total immersion in water were doctrinally correct. They also supported a congregational polity that asserted the autonomy of a congregation to choose its own pastor and to make its decisions independently of any larger association. Early Baptist preachers George Liele, Andrew Bryan, and Jesse Peters (also called Jesse Galphin) were instrumental in founding the Springfield Baptist Church of Augusta, Georgia, and the First African Baptist and First Bryan Baptist churches of Savannah, Georgia. Liele became a missionary to Jamaica in 1783 and established the first Baptist churches there.

Philadelphia's "New African" Churches

While the Baptists founded the first black churches, it was the Methodists who organized the first black denominations, which also became the first national associations for African Americans. In 1787 former slaves Richard Allen and Absalom Jones established the Free African Society of Philadelphia, a mutual aid and benevolent society that assumed both secular and religious functions. Allen, Jones, and several black worshipers withdrew from the St. George's Methodist Episcopal Church in Philadelphia after being pulled from their knees during worship in a gallery they did not know was closed to black Christians. In protest, "All went out of the church in a body," according to Allen, "and they were no more plagued with [us] in that church." Two black churches arose out of the Free African Society. In 1790 Richard Allen founded the "African Church," which eventually was called the Mother Bethel African Methodist Episcopal Church, while Absalom Jones became the rector of the St. Thomas African Episcopal Church in 1794.

New York's First Black Church

In New York City, similar incidents of racism and segregation during worship, where blacks were forced to sit in the upper galleries or in back pews, led black members to withdraw from the John Street Methodist Episcopal Church near Wall Street. Peter Williams Sr. and Francis Jacobs of New York City and James Varick of Newburgh, New York, helped to establish a new African church. Jealousy and competition for new members resulted in the inability of both black Methodist movements on the East Coast to unite in one body.

TOP: In the evangelical tradition of many black churches, a man proselytizes at a Philadelphia block party. *CORBIS/Ted Spiegel*
ABOVE: Choirs such as this one serve an important role in the Black Church. *CORBIS/Jules T. Allen*

Methodist Churches: African Methodist Episcopal and African Methodist Episcopal Zion Churches

The central questions of the full ordination of black preachers as clergy, the election of blacks as bishops (episcopacy), the desire to worship in their own cultural style, and the issues of black independence and control of their own religious institutions finally led to the establishment of two black Methodist denominations. The "Allenites" of Philadelphia and Baltimore established the African Methodist Episcopal Church (AME) as a denomination in 1816 and elected Richard Allen as its first bishop. The Reverend Daniel Coker became the first AME missionary to Africa in 1820. The New Yorkers founded the African Methodist Episcopal Zion Church (AMEZ) in 1821, led by Bishop James Varick. Both denominations became the institutional base of an incipient black middle class of free Negroes.

TOP: This man, a member of the Holiness Pentacostal Church, has just been baptized in a lake. *CORBIS/Kevin Fleming*
ABOVE: A Baptist congregation at prayer in Beaufort, South Carolina. *CORBIS/Jules T. Allen*

The AME Church distinguished itself in the field of education with the founding of WILBERFORCE UNIVERSITY in 1857 by Bishop Daniel Payne, its first president. While the AME also participated in the abolitionist movement, with Richard Allen using Mother Bethel as a hiding place for escaped slaves in the UNDERGROUND RAILROAD, it was the Zionites who became the leaders of abolitionism. Long known as the Freedom Church, AME Zion claimed such abolitionary luminaries as SOJOURNER TRUTH, Harriet Tubman, the Reverend Jermain Loguen, Catherine Harris, the Reverend Thomas James, and FREDERICK DOUGLASS, who was licensed as a local AME Zion preacher in Rochester, New York. The Zion denomination was also the first of all Christian denominations, black or white, to extend the vote and full clerical ordination to women in 1898.

Although both the AME Church and the AME Zion Church originated as Northern black denominations, during the Civil War they sent missionaries to follow the Union army's march through the South and recruit blacks and their churches to their fold. As a result, South Carolina has the most AME churches and North Carolina has emerged as the AME Zion stronghold.

CHRISTIAN METHODIST EPISCOPAL CHURCH

In 1844 the issue of slavery split the Methodist Episcopal Church into Northern and Southern branches. In 1866 the General Conference of the Methodist Episcopal Church, South – in response to the twin pressures of blacks who wanted autonomy and whites who wanted to dispense with the black membership – made arrangements for the eventual withdrawal of its black constituents at their petition. The third black Methodist denomination, the Colored Methodist Episcopal Church in America, was founded in 1870 by bishops William H. Miles and Richard H. Vanderhorst. Headquartered in Jackson, Tennessee, the denomination replaced the word "Colored" with "Christian" in 1954.

BAPTIST CHURCHES

Although they had the earliest churches and the largest constituency of African American congregants, the black Baptists did not organize a national denomination until 1895, when the National Baptist Convention, USA, Inc. (NBC, USA) was established. Its first president was the Reverend E. C. Morris. However, the principle of congregational autonomy, combined with the charismatic force of strong-willed pastors, led to denominational schisms. In 1897 the Lott Carey Foreign Missionary Convention broke away. Two schisms occurred in the twentieth century, once in 1915 with the formation of the National Baptist Convention of America in a dispute over the control and ownership of a publishing house in Nashville, Tennessee, and again in 1961 with the organizing of the Progressive National Baptist Convention (PNBC).

The PNBC arose out of disagreement over the proclaimed "lifetime tenure" of President J. H. Jackson and the denomination's participation in the Civil Rights Movement. Led by the Reverend Dr. Gardner Taylor, the supporters of Dr. Martin Luther King Jr. challenged the status quo of the NBC, USA, and eventually withdrew to form their own more politically progressive denomination.

PENTECOSTAL MOVEMENTS

In his last memoirs, John Wesley, the founder of Methodism, claimed that the attainment of "spiritual perfection" is possible in this life.

This belief fueled the quest of the Holiness/Pentecostal movement among blacks and whites that arose in 1867 with the National Camp Meeting Association for the Promotion of Holiness. Holiness members believed that a second blessing of the Holy Spirit, or experience of "sanctification," was required beyond the act of individual salvation, or "being saved." This blessing was manifested in a cathartic emotional experience that left some believers rolling in spasms on the floor, or "falling out," while others engaged in the uncontrollable movements of the "holy dance." In the quest to become more holy, a rigid and disciplined lifestyle evolved. Among African Americans, the Holiness/Pentecostal movement also became the major carrier of black folk cultural practices that middle-class Baptists and Methodists attempted to discard in their desire to achieve the "order and decorum" found in worship services of their white counterparts. More foot stomping, hand clapping, tambourine banging, and shouting occurred in the emotional cauldrons of the "sanctified people."

The massive black urban migrations of the twentieth century also gave rise to numerous sanctified church storefronts in Northern cities, with names such as the Fire Baptized Holiness Church. Since the sanctified churches allowed horns, guitars, drums, and other musical instruments into their services, they became the musical training grounds for many African American blues and jazz musicians. There was a dynamic interaction between the storefront church and the nightclub. For example, learning to play the piano in church, Thomas Dorsey, or Georgia Tom as he was known on the nightclub circuit, eventually brought the blues back to the churches in the form of gospel music in the 1920s.

The modern Pentecostal movement in the United States, inclusive of both black and white people, dates from the Azusa Street Revival held in Los Angeles from 1906 to 1909 under the leadership of William J. Seymour, a black Holiness preacher. Pentecostalism, in turn, as suggested by Seymour's background, had roots in the Holiness movement of the late nineteenth century. Pentecostalists believed in the need for a "third work of grace" called the "baptism of the Holy Ghost," which is manifested in glossolalia, or speaking in tongues. Although the line between Holiness and Pentecostal churches increasingly blurred in the late twentieth century, there are some Holiness groups that do not accept the need for speaking in tongues. After attending the Azusa Street Revival in 1907, Charles Harrison Mason, a black preacher from Memphis, Tennessee, led his Holiness group into Pentecostalism. Bishop Mason became the founder of the largest black Pentecostal denomination, the Church of God in Christ. Pentecostalism has become the fastest-growing sector of Christianity in the world, especially in the United States among African Americans and Latinos and in Third World countries in Africa, Asia, and Latin America. From a few hundred members in 1907, the Church of God in Christ has increased to more than 5 million members.

The Church and Community Development: Political Leadership
As the most educated and best trained in leadership skills, black clergy emerged as the prime leaders of black communities nationwide in the eighteenth and nineteenth centuries, not only in religious matters but also in the secular spheres of politics, economics, education, and sociocultural activities. During the period of slavery, efforts at liberation and abolitionism were often led by religious leaders, as exemplified by the three largest slave revolts in American history, led by Gabriel Prosser in 1801 in Richmond, Virginia; Denmark Vesey in 1822 in Charleston, South Carolina; and Nat Turner in 1831 in Southampton County, Virginia. Black churches were not only used as secret meeting places to plot slave

TOP: African American photographer Gordon Parks captured this scene in a Washington, D.C., church in 1942. *CORBIS*
RIGHT: Black Philadelphian Richard Allen (1760-1831), a staunch Methodist dismayed by the racist treatment he encountered at a mostly white church, bought the building that became the Bethel African Church in 1794; in 1816, it was the site of the founding of the American Methodist Episcopal (AME) Church. *Archive Photos*

uprisings, but also served as Underground Railroad stops for abolitionists. With the end of the black franchise in Southern states in the late nineteenth century, black people continued to vote in their churches, electing bishops, preachers, deacons, and other church officers. During the RECONSTRUCTION period, the phenomenon of the "preacher-politician" arose with the election of the first black senator, the Reverend Hiram Revels of Mississippi, and the first black congressman, the Reverend Richard Cain of Georgia. The pattern of the preacher-politician continued throughout the twentieth century, for example, with the election of such notable figures as congressmen Adam Clayton Powell Jr., William Gray, JOHN LEWIS, and Floyd Flake and the Reverend Jesse Jackson's presidential campaigns in 1984 and 1988. Both black and white politicians have discovered the value of speaking at political forums at black churches during election campaigns to mobilize the black vote. During the mid-century civil rights period (1954-1968), black churches provided many of the leaders, such as Dr. Martin Luther King; they also served as the location for members to mobilize for the movement, because the church buildings were the only ones large enough to accommodate mass meetings in the highly segregated urban and rural areas of the South.

ECONOMIC DEVELOPMENT

Black churches have long been involved in economic development enterprises and in creating economic institutions. As W. E. B. Du Bois wrote in 1907, the study of "economic cooperation among Negroes must begin with the Church group." Beyond the economic cooperation required in building the churches themselves, other projects were created. In 1866 five lay leaders of the Bethel AME Church in Baltimore pooled their funds to develop the first black-owned dry dock company and joint stock institution after black ship caulkers were fired because whites had protested their job competition. After the collapse of the Freedman's Savings and Trust Company in 1874, which resulted in the loss of the bounties paid to black Civil War soldiers and the savings accounts of many black people, the churches helped to develop some 50 black-owned banks beginning in 1888 and lasting until the GREAT DEPRESSION of the 1930s.

Together with the financial resources of fraternal lodges and mutual aid and burial societies, the churches also helped create the first black life insurance companies, such as North Carolina Mutual, Atlanta Life Insurance Company, and the Afro-American Industrial Insurance Society of Jacksonville, Florida. A highly segregated society resulted in the creation of parallel institutions by African Americans. In the late twentieth century black churches became the largest builders and sponsors of housing, pooling federal, state, and private funds. The 5000 single-family, mixed-income dwellings of the Nehemiah Houses of East Brooklyn are one example.

EDUCATION

Even more than economic projects, black clergy and churches have always viewed education as the key to upward mobility in American society. Churches have often doubled as schools, beginning with church school on Sunday morning for children and adults. The first lessons in reading and writing often occurred in Sunday school. MOREHOUSE COLLEGE began as a school in the basement of the Springfield Baptist Church in Augusta, Georgia, while SPELMAN COLLEGE was founded in the basement of the Friendship Baptist Church of Atlanta. Tuskegee Institute also started as a school in the basement of the AMEZ Church in Tuskegee, Alabama. Just as Harvard and Yale universities, were founded for the education of the clergy, the curricula of many of the best black colleges, like Fisk and Howard universities, were steeped in religious and moral instruction. All of the black denominations founded their own schools and seminaries.

Besides serving as places of worship, black churches have performed other functions. The first black newspaper in the United States, Freedom's Journal, was started by the Reverend Samuel Cornish in 1827. The first speeches or musical recitals in public for black children occurred in the sanctuaries of black churches. Black artists often exhibited their work in the dining halls of the churches because the public art museums and private galleries were closed to them. However, the true genius of the Black Church resides in the fact that it has given status, dignity, and respect to common people who were often invisible in American society.

Lawrence Mamiya

SEE ALSO

Slavery in the United States; Baltimore, Maryland; Baptists; Black Codes in the United States; Civil War, American; Denmark Vesey Conspiracy; Du Bois, William Edward Burghardt (W. E. B.); Fisk University; *Freedom's Journal*; Gabriel Prosser Conspiracy; Gray, William Herbert, III; Great Migration, The; Howard University; Jackson, Jesse Louis; Williams, Peter, Sr.; King, Martin Luther, Jr.; Memphis, Tennessee; New York, New York; North Carolina Mutual Life Insurance Company; Payne, Daniel Alexander; Pentecostalism; Powell, Adam Clayton, Jr.; Revels, Hiram Rhoades; Seymour, William Joseph; Taylor, Gardner Calvin; Tubman, Harriet Ross; Tuskegee University; Jackson, Joseph Harrison.

Latin America and the Caribbean

Black Codes in Latin America,

a comprehensive and methodically organized set of seventeenth-century French and late eighteenth-century Spanish colonial laws that sought to impose a system of social, religious, and property relations upon African slaves and the European and Creole population.

The Black Codes comprise an elaborate set of principles, rules, and procedures that were designed to protect plantation economies and prevent slaves from running away. But because they conflicted with the slaveholders' actual interests and practices – the codes specified minimal standards for slaves' food and clothing, restrictions on punishments, and means of achieving manumission – they were rarely implemented. Nevertheless, the codes give insight into the working conditions, economic interests, and social practices of the French Caribbean and Spanish American slave societies they addressed. These laws contrast with those relating to slavery in the Portuguese colony of BRAZIL; the Brazilian laws were never codified, though compilations were published to instruct slaveholders on their rights and responsibilities.

FRENCH CODE NOIR, VERSAILLES, 1685

The first formal codification of slave laws in the Americas was issued in 1685 in Versailles, by the French king Louis XIV. The *Code Noir* (Black Code) was intended to regulate the "discipline and the commerce of blacks and slaves" in the French islands of America. At the time, the sugar-producing Antilles was France's most prized colony. The king and his powerful minister Jean-Baptiste Colbert, director of other influential legal reforms and codes, concluded that it was necessary to develop a comprehensive slave system in order to increase efficiency and maximize profits.

Legal historians debate the origins of the Code Noir. Some claim that many of the articles were taken from previous ordinances and edicts originally issued on the islands of St. Christophe, GUADELOUPE, and MARTINIQUE. Others trace their origins to seventeenth-century Spanish slave laws and Roman law. A few believe that the code was entirely a local production.

The Code Noir comprises 60 articles organized in thematic sections. The first 8 articles of the code determined that slaves could not practice any religion other than Roman Catholicism, under which they should be baptized, married, and buried. A second section specified security measures in order to control theft and prevent slave assemblies and revolts. A third set of articles regulated minimum food and clothing rations, farming by slaves, and care for sick slaves. The code specified that the weekly ration of food for slaves between 10 and

60 years of age should be approximately two pounds of starches (manioc, cassavas, or the equivalent) and two or three pounds of meat (salted beef or fish). "Two outfits of linen" were the yearly rations of clothing to be supplied by the owner.

The section "On Crimes, Penalties and Punishments" is the longest in the code and deals with crimes such as "striking the master," "insolent or violent behavior toward whites," and escaping (maroonage). The punishment for slave crimes was both private – whipping – and public, in the form of physical mutilation, including the cutting of ears, branding with a fleur-de-lis (the emblem of the French monarchy), severing of hamstrings, and/or death. The last articles in the code disqualified slaves as witnesses in civil and criminal cases and denied them any rights to property or to the possibility of being parties in civil law actions.

Despite these controls and restrictions, many agree that the Code Noir was relatively liberal compared to British colonial and later United States slave law. For example, according to Article 59, slaves could buy their own freedom or be freed as a gift from their owner. It was not unheard of that plantation owners would free slaves, especially the offspring of male owners and female slaves. In Caribbean societies, this produced a mixed population with various race and class strata among people of African descent.

French Code For Louisiana, 1724

By 1724 the possibility of freedom for slaves established in the Code Noir had proven too liberal for the white population, which was concerned by the increase of free blacks. Although the Louisiana French Code essentially paralleled the 1685 Code Noir, it did incorporate a few changes. Slaves could no longer be freed unless they had written permission from the governor general and the intendant; the age for manumitters was raised to 25 years; and manumitted slaves, free-born blacks, and slaves were no longer allowed to receive any kind of donations from whites. By making slaves unable to acquire property or wealth, the law effectively denied slaves the means to purchase freedom for themselves or others.

Códigos Negros Españoles (Spanish Black Codes)

In the sixteenth and seventeenth centuries, royal *cédulas* (legislation, issued by the Spanish king, that took precedence over orders by the Council of Indies) regulated a variety of issues related to slaves in the New World – not only the commercial aspects of the trade, but the behavior of the slaves. In the late eighteenth century, the Spanish king Carlos III initiated a series of reforms in Spanish colonial policies as well as in the law. The king, in the hope of becoming competitive with the grand plantations of the French Antilles and Brazil, intended to use slave labor to expand agricultural production. The Spanish Crown attributed the economic success of the French Indies in part to the fact that their slaves were under legal control. King Carlos believed that a more intensive importation of slaves required systematically organized and updated legislation. For this purpose, at different times he assigned lawyers and government officials to develop codes.

For sources in modeling the Spanish Black Codes, their authors used several sources, including the French Code Noir; the thirteenth-century Spanish compilation of laws known as the *Siete Partidas;* colonial compendiums of laws from 1567 and 1680; ordinances on slaves from Hispaniola dating as far back as 1528; Roman law; and slave laws from other colonies. The Black Codes of 1768, 1769, and 1784, as well as the later instruction of 1789 and regulations of Puerto Rico and Cuba from 1826 and 1842, are all linked by the objective of controlling and repressing slaves and preventing maroonage through minimal guarantees for subsistence. But even the minor requirements of food and clothing rations and controlled punishments were protested and disregarded by most slaveholders in the Americas.

First Code: Santo Domingo, 1768

The first Spanish Black Code was written for the city of Santo Domingo in 1768 by local authorities who wished to "prevent black slave desertion and to subject and assist them." This code had 41 articles and was organized around three areas: control of slaves, prevention of maroonage, and repression of disobedience. The code regulated rations and punishment in a form similar to the Code Noir and sixteenth-century Spanish ordinances. The document was sent back and forth among colonial officials for more than a decade and was finally archived, never receiving final approval from the Spanish Crown for its implementation.

Second Code: Louisiana, 1769

Spain received Louisiana in 1766 from the king of France as compensation for its losses in the wars with Great Britain. Since 1724, slaves in French Louisiana had been under the rule of a version of the Code Noir. In 1769 the Spanish governor of Louisiana, Alejandro O'Reilly, ordered the French code to be "observed with exactitude" and translated into Spanish. The code was in place until 1800, when Spain lost Louisiana. Curiously, it was the only one of the Spanish Black Codes that was officially issued.

The code was an important political instrument in controlling the enormous slave population, despite the fact that it contradicted much of the Spanish legislation in the Indies. For example, the first article ordered the displacement and extermination of American Indians in Louisiana, who were "declared enemies of the Christian faith." This proclamation was inconsistent with the papal orders, which had justified Spanish colonization through the evangelization of American Indians.

The Louisiana code also declared that slaves should be considered material goods, or property that could be inherited or distributed. This law contradicted the principle in the Siete Partidas, which deemed that some persons could rightly be enslaved even if they had been born free. Another difference was that the Louisiana code did not allow slaves to own property, buy their freedom, or be freed without official consent. A 1526 Spanish cédula, however, had permitted slaves to obtain manumission by buying their freedom, and the Siete Partidas had allowed owners to free their slaves voluntarily under certain conditions.

In addition, Spanish Louisiana prohibited interracial marriage and cohabitation as well as marriage among slaves, a custom that was widespread and not yet regulated in the rest of the Spanish colonies. Finally, this second code determined that the offspring of female slaves and their white male owners had to be donated to hospitals and would never be eligible to obtain their freedom. This was also different from the Spanish colonies, where mixed-race children were not separated from their mothers.

The Louisiana code reintroduced the use of bodily mutilations and branding, forms of punishment that had been removed from the Spanish code of 1768. It was particularly severe on fugitive slaves. If caught, an escaped slave could have his "ears cut off and a fleur-de-lis branded on his back the first time… if reinciding would have an arm cut off and a flower branded on his side… and the third time would be punished with death."

Third Code: Código Negro Carolino, Santo Domingo, 1784

The third Spanish Code was titled *Code of Legislation for the Moral, Political and Economic Government of Slaves on the Spanish Island* and was known as the Código Negro Carolino. It was written by a colonial government official, Augustín de Emparán y Orbe. The code was finished in December 1784 and approved by the *audiencia* (the regional high court) of Santo Domingo in 1785. It continued to circulate among colonial officials until the "Instructions on Slaves for all of the Indies" was issued in 1789, after which it was forgotten and archived, never having been implemented.

The Código Negro Carolino was written with the expectation that the island would receive a great number of slaves from the newly acquired Spanish territories, and as a result become as powerful as its French neighbor, Saint-Domingue (present-day Haiti). The importance of the code lies in its underlying objectives, as outlined in the preface: (1) to regenerate black Dominicans from their "horrible past" of "shameful laziness, independent spirit, arrogance... theft and disorder"; (2) to manage free blacks and slaves in agricultural production and categorize them by class and race in order "to administer and define the work each one should do"; (3) to obtain the "perfect subordination and respect [of blacks] toward their master, and in general, toward all white people"; (4) to prize "good service and conduct" in order to motivate the continuing servitude of blacks; and (5) to place them under a corrective law so that their enslavement would be "easier to endure."

These objectives reflect the complex content of the code. The code is divided into 37 chapters and subdivided into nearly 200 articles that reflect Emperán's theories on race, economics, law, religion, and assorted issues relevant to the daily life of free blacks and slaves. It was intended not only to control the slave population but to map out a socioeconomic reorganization of Spanish Santo Domingo (present-day Dominican Republic). As the primary basis for these changes, the code was emphatic in stating that Catholic indoctrination of slaves was fundamental in order to "assure internal and external security of the island because [religion's] powerful influence has preserved Spanish Colonies in the past." According to the second chapter of the code, Africans were "superstitious and fanatics, easily giving in to seduction and revenge, inclined to the poisonous arts, which they have dangerously used in other colonies.... Therefore it is necessary to remove such strong native inclinations and substitute for them the love of the Spanish Nation, the recognition and gratefulness toward their masters, subordination toward all whites... and other social graces toward which education should be inclined."

A system of color division that correlated to specific tasks and classes was another of the code's strategies for reorganizing Dominican society. Chapter 3 of the code divides blacks into two categories: free and slave. Free blacks are then divided into three groups: blacks, mulattos, and pardos (according to the shade of blackness). Their offspring are then subdivided (according to the degree of mixture with whites) into *tercerones, cuarterones,* and *quinteros* (thirds, fourths, and fifths). Based on these chromatic divisions, Emparán proposed a class system. In the first class were free blacks and slaves; in the second (and preferred class) were the mulattos, pardos, and their offspring. The second class was again subdivided into several groups. According to this racial and class division, the code assigned a "distribution and regulation of civil rights," labor, and punishments. Throughout the code, Emparán was emphatic about restricting the positions that blacks of all shades had obtained in Dominican society. Emparán wanted the code to impose a system of segregated education in which only those in the preferred class could go to school, but without mixing with whites, as they had in the past. He also sought to eliminate the climate of tolerance in which, as he said, "blacks and freedpeople, even slaves, exercised all sorts of arts, professions and mechanical tasks, taking away jobs for the white and light colored population."

Real Cédula: Instructions on Slaves, Aranjuez, 1789

Soon after the death of King Charles III, in February 1789 a *real* (royal) cédula that promoted the free trade of slaves was issued in Aranjuez, Spain. This cédula was an attempt to encourage agricultural production by promoting the importation of more slaves. The *Instructions for the Education, Treatment and Occupations of Slaves in all of the Indies and Philippine Islands* was a temporary provision, written in a record time of two months in order to prepare for an anticipated abundance of slaves. Although the document is actually a set of instructions intended to regulate slave labor and recognize minimum rights for slaves, some historians have called it a Spanish Black Code. The new legislation selected and adopted norms from previous codes and ordinances and presented them in a generalized form. Copies were sent to all of the Spanish government centers (Mexico, Lima, Santafé de Bogotá, Santo Domingo, Caracas, Buenos Aires, Cuzco, Charcas, Chile, Quito, Guatemala, Guadalajara, and Manila), and for this reason it is the best-known slave legislation of the colonial period.

The instructions have 14 chapters. Many of these were taken from previous codes but with minor variations on such subjects as religious indoctrination; food and clothing rationing; division of labor according to age, gender, and strength; permitted celebrations and festivities; slave marriages; separation of rooms by sex; and care for the elderly and disabled.

Chapters 8 and 13, however, provoked a strong reaction from slaveholders. Chapter 8 allowed only prescribed correctional punishment by the owner for minor acts of misconduct. It also stated that owners could be held accountable for excesses. Punishment was limited to imprisonment or striking the slave with "a chain or whip, but not by hanging them from the head, or hitting them more than 25 times, with a gentle instrument which should not cause them serious bruising or bleeding." This punishment was minor compared to the dismemberment and 200 to 300 floggings permitted by previous codes.

Under this new legislation, if the slave committed a major crime he or she was entitled to a trial, and only the official government could determine a sentence of mutilation or death. The owner who did not obey these instructions could be fined and even charged for a crime as if the slave were a free person. An official "protector for slaves" could intervene and overview the process when the master committed excesses or the slave was insulted, hit, or killed by a third party.

Chapter 13 allowed for priests to denounce any bad treatment of slaves they might observe while visiting a plantation. It also provided for the assignation of officials who would visit each plantation three times a year so that the government might determine whether instructions were being followed.

Slaveholders and government officials throughout the Americas responded with outrage, claiming that such lax punishment would surely cause poverty, chaos, violence, misery, the destruction of all crops, and a general slave insurrection (in the manner of the Haitian Revolution of 1791). The owners tried to assure the Spanish government that slaves were happy and well treated and had to be under strict control because they were naturally prone to "anguish, revolts, theft, drunkenness, laziness, perversity and... all sorts of vices." Moreover, they claimed that the only recourse available to the owners was the threat of absolute authority and control over punishment, because "over such immature people, it is more effective to threaten than to implement." Facing such generalized opposition and criticism to the law, in 1795 the Spanish Crown issued an order that "suspended in its effects" the instructions of 1789. In actual terms, the law was never implemented in any of the colonies.

Reglamento: Puerto Rico, 1826

Although other countries were abolishing slavery and the Spanish Crown formally declared an end to the slave trade in 1820, Puerto Rico's governor continued to grant licenses to slave traders that allowed for an enormous increase in the importation of "illegal" slaves. After the amount of imported slaves increased to an unmanageable level, in 1826 the local government reenacted the 1789 instructions to control the slave revolts that were then erupting on the island. This 1826 *Reglamento,* a set of slave rules for Puerto Rico, was created by copying the 1789 instructions and adapting them to local conditions. A few previous norms from earlier codes and ordinances were added. The Reglamento continued to be in effect until the abolition of slavery in 1873, though historians question its actual application.

Reglamento: Havana, Cuba, 1842

After the institution of slavery had almost disappeared in the Western world, Cuba decided to promote its *Reglamento de Esclavos* to control the country's enormous slave population as well as continuing revolts and maroonage. In the early 1840s Cuba was at its peak of importing slaves and exporting sugar and other agricultural products, such as coffee and tobacco, that required slave

BLACK CODES IN THE UNITED STATES

State	Codes	Example
Alabama	Acts of the General Assembly, 1865, 1866, Montgomery. The Code of Alabama..., 1852, Montgomery. Constitution and Ordinances of the Convention Which Assembled September 12, 1865..., Montgomery. Journal of the House, 1865-66, 1866-67, Montgomery. Journal of Proceedings of the Convention Which Assembled September 12, 1865..., Montgomery. The Penal Code of Alabama...1866, Montgomery.	"any free person of color, found in company with any slave in any kitchen, or house, or negro quarter, without a written permission from the owner, or overseer of such slave, must, for every such offence, receive fifteen lashes; which may be inflicted by the owner, or overseer of the slave, or by any officer or member of any patrol company" (sec.1035).
Arkansas	Acts of the General Assembly, 1858-59, 1862-1866-67, Little Rock. Journal of the House, 16th, 17th sessions, Little Rock: 1870. New Constitution, with acts of April 16-June 2, 1864; November 7, 1864-January 3, 1865, April 3-22, Little Rock: Unconditional Union Print, 1865.	"AN ACT to legalize marriages of persons of color."
Delaware	Laws of the General Assembly, 1865, Dover. Revised Statutes of the State of Delaware to the Year 1852, Dover.	"No free Negro, or free mulatto, shall be admitted as a witness to charge a white man with being the father of a bastard child" (c.107, sec.4).
Florida	Acts and Resolutions of the General Assembly, 1865, 1866, Tallahassee. Journal of the House, 2nd session of the 14th sesssion, Tallahassee. Journal of Proceedings of the Convention of Florida, Begun and Held... October 25th, 1865, Tallahassee. Journal of the Senate, 14th session, 2nd session of the 14th session, Tallahassee. A manual or Digest of the Statute Law of the State of Florida of a General and Public Character in Force... on the Sixth Day of January, 1847. By Leslie A. Thompson. Boston: Charles C. Little and James Brown, 1847.	"If any negro or mulatto, bond or free, shall at any time use abusive and provoking language to, or lift his hand... and extended the permissible punishing lashes to thirty-nine" (title 4, c.1, sec.2).
Georgia	Acts of the General Assembly, 1865-66, 1866, Milledgeville. The Code of the State of Georgia, Atlanta, 1861. A Digest of the Laws of the State of Georgia... to the Year 1798, Inclusive, and the Principle Acts of 1799. By Robert and George Watkins. Philadelphia: R. Aitken, 1800. Journal of the House, 1865-66, Milledgeville. Journal of the Senate, 1865-66, 1866, Milledgeville.	"any person may take up any negroes that shall be found out of the plantation or place where they belong, or incorporated town where they reside, acting unlawfully, or under suspicious circumstances, and if found with an offensive weapon shall take same away, and if the negro is insolent, or refuses to answer, may whip said negroes..." (sec.1368).
Kentucky	Acts of the General Assembly 1865, Frankfort. Journal of the Senate, 1865, Frankfort.	
Louisiana	Acts of the General Assembly, 1865, 1866, 1867, New Orleans. Debates in Convention for Revision and Amendment of the Constitution, Assembled... April 6, 1864, New Orleans. Journal of the House, 1865, 1866, New Orleans. Journal of the Senate, 1865, 1866, New Orleans. Official Journal of Proceedings of Louisiana, compiled by U.B. Phillips under the Direction of a Joint Committee of the Legislature, New Orleans.	"If any slave or free colored person shall willfully and maliciously burn or destroy...any grain or other produce of this State,...he shall, on conviction thereof, be punished at the discretion of the court" (sec. 11).
Maryland	The Maryland Code. Public General Laws, compiled by Otho Scott and Hiram McCullough. Adopted... January, 1860, Baltimore: John Murphy and Co., 1860.	"all negroes or other slaves shall serve durante vita." Maryland Archives, I, pp. 526-33 (cited by James Curtis Ballagh, *A History of Slavery in Virginia* [Baltimore: Johns Hopkins Press, 1902], p.34).
Mississippi	Constitution as Amended, with Ordinances and Resolutions, Adopted by the Constitutional Convention, August, 1867, Jackson. Journal of the House, 1865, 1866, Jackson. Jounal of the Senate, 1865, 1866, Jackson. Laws of the Legislature, 1838, 1859. 1865, 1866,1867, Jackson. The Revised Code of the Laws of Mississippi...as Were in Force at the End of the Year 1823, Natchez.	"to kill all dogs owned and kept by negroes" (1824-38), An Act amendatory of an act, entitled "an act to alter and amend an act, or reduce into one, the several acts concerning patrols" (sec.4).
North Carolina	Acts and Resolutions of the General Assembly... Passed in Secret Session, Raleigh, 1865. Journal of the House, 1865, 1865-66, 1866, Raleigh. Journal of the Senate, 1865, 1865-66, 1866, Raleigh. Private Laws of the General Assembly, 1864-65, 1865, 1866, 1867, Raleigh. Public Laws of the General Assembly, 1864-65, 1865, 1866, 1867, Raleigh. Public Laws of the General Assembly...Passed by the General Assembly at the 1865-1866, and 1861-62-63 and 1864 [Sessions], together with Important Ordinances Passed by the Convention of 1866, Raleigh. Revised Code of North Carolina, Enacted by the General Assembly at the Session of 1854; together with other Acts of a Public and General Nature, Passed at the Same Session, By Bartholomey F. Moore and Asas Biggs, Boston: Little, Brown and Co., 1855.	"where the punishment of a white person might be imprisonment, the court may sentence the free negro to be both whipped and imprisoned" (c.107).
South Carolina	Acts of the General Assembly, 1864-65, Extra Session of 1866, Regular Session of 1866, Columbia. Constitution of the State of South Carolina and the Ordinances, Reports and Resolutions Adopted by the Convention of the People,...1865, Columbia. Journal of the House, Extra Session of 1865, Regular Session of 1865, Extra Session of 1866, Regular Session of 1866, Columbia. Journal of the Senate, Extra Session of 1865, Regular Session of 1865, Extra Session of 1866, Regular Session of 1866, Columbia.	"be protected against the fraud and violence of the artful and the lawless... [but], they must be restrained from theft, idleness, vagrancy and crime, and taught the absolute necessity of strictly complying with their contracts for labor" (1865, reg. session, p.17).

State	Codes	Example
Tennessee	Acts of the General Assembly, 1865, 1865-66, 1866-67, Nashville. The Code of Tennessee, Enacted by the General Assembly of 1857-58, Nashville. Journal of the House, 1865, 1865-66, 1867, Nashville. Journal of the Senate, 1865, 1865-66, 1866-67, Nashville.	"to repeal all laws in relation to slaves" (pp. 177, 218).
Texas	The Constitution, as Amended and Ordinances of the Convention of 1866, ... and the General Laws of the Regular Session of the Eleventh Legislature of the State of Texas, Austin. Journal of the House, 1866, Austin. Journal of the Senate, 1866, Austin.	"All criminal prosecutions against them shall be conducted in the same manner as prosecution for like offenses against the white race, and they shall be subject to like penalties" (art.8).
Virginia	Acts of the General Assembly, 1865, 1865-66, 1866-67, Richmond. The Code of Virginia, Second Edition, Including Legislation to the Year 1860, Richmond. A Collection of All Such Acts of the General Assembly of Virginia, of a Public and Permanent Nature, as Are Now in Force, Richmond, 1803. An Exact Abridgement of All the Acts of Assembly of Virginia in Force and Use, January, 1758. By John Mercer. Glasgow: Printed by John Brye and David Paterson, 1759. Journal of the House, 1865-66, 1865, 1866-67, Richmond. Journal of the Senate, 1865, 1865-66, 1866-67, Richmond. The Statutes at Large; Being a Collection of all the Laws of Virginia, 1619-1792. Edited by William Waller Hening, 13 vols., Richmond, 1809-1823 (cited as Hening).	"for the prevention of that abominable mixture and spurious issue, which may hereafter increase in this dominion ...Whatever white man or woman being free shall intermarry with a negroe, mulatto, or Indian man or woman, bond or free, shall within three months after such marriage be banished and removed from this dominion for ever" (I, p.552r).

Source: Theodore Branter Wilson, *The Black Codes of the South* (Tuscaloosa, AL: University of Alabama Press, 1965).

labor. Therefore, in 1842 the Cuban colonial government copied the Puerto Rican rules and adopted them to the Cuban situation.

The Cuban version had its own peculiarities, though it was better synthesized and less elaborate than the previous legislation from the neighboring island. It contained 48 articles and actually made conditions for slaves harsher than the Puerto Rican version. It reduced some of the clothing rations, incremented work hours, eliminated certain privileges for slave women and children, omitted incentives for those who had worked for more than 35 years, and removed the obligation of supervisory visits by judges to the plantations as well as the possibility of denouncing bad treatment of slaves.

Like previous slave laws, the Cuban Reglamento was devised to increase repression and control and was not in fact enforced. Nevertheless, it remained in place until the abolition of slavery in 1873.

Liliana Obregón

See Also

France; Maroonage in the Americas; Slavery in Latin America and the Caribbean; Spain; Miscegenation; Abolition and Emancipation in Latin America and the Caribbean; Slave Laws in Colonial Spanish America; Punishment of Slaves in Colonial Latin America and the Caribbean.

North America

Black Codes in the United States, **legal statutes that curtailed the rights of African Americans during the early years of Reconstruction in the United States.**

Similar in both character and content to the Slave Codes, Black Codes were instituted by Southern legislative bodies in 1865 and 1866 in order to eviscerate civil rights legislation of the Reconstruction and reestablish control over the 4 million newly emancipated African Americans. Just as the Slave Codes denied African Americans any legal status besides that of property, Black Codes defined the freedpeople as legally subordinate to whites.

Faced with a rapidly transformed political and economic structure in the postbellum South, states such as Mississippi and South Carolina began passing laws in 1865 to limit the freedom of African Americans in many ways. Laws were instituted forcing black men and women to work or face imprisonment. Often the result was that freed men and women returned to work for their former slave owners or on nearby plantations. The termination of a contract was made illegal for "any freedman, free Negro or mulatto" with the consequence, again, of imprisonment or hard labor.

In order to restrict the movement and resettlement of ex-slaves, laws forbade blacks to own or rent farmland. Ironically, African Americans were given the new status of being allowed *some* legal responsibility; this had been absent during slavery. The rights to marry each other, sue each other, and own minimal property were written into the Codes. The purpose of the Black Codes, however, was the maintenance of a white-dominated hierarchy after the Civil War.

In 1865 Alabama and Louisiana joined Mississippi and South Carolina in the creation of laws that were, in spirit, attempts to reenslave African Americans. By 1866 all the states of the former Confederacy, except North Carolina, had enacted laws that echoed the Slave Codes. These Southern states passed laws that permitted the imprisonment or hiring out of vagrants, with vagrancy defined as black persons who were unemployed or possessed no contract with a white employer. Further, children who were orphans, or whose parents were impoverished, were turned over to the state and forced into apprenticeships with white private businessmen. Statutes requiring African American skilled laborers and artisans to pay exorbitant licensing fees made it rare for freedpeople to be anything besides wage laborers. Outrage over this virtual reenslavement led Northern journalists in such newspapers as the *New York Times* and the *Chicago Tribune* to print protests.

An important aspect of the Black Codes was their unequal system of punishment. The codes sanctioned the whipping of black workers by white employers, and a minor offense such as stealing food could bring physical brutality and forced servitude. Blacks found "unlawfully assembling themselves together either in the day or nighttime" were subject to immediate imprisonment. Whites could rarely be held culpable for any crime that they committed against an African American. Thus, intimidation and attacks upon freedpeople by white individuals and groups such as the Ku Klux Klan were commonplace, and blacks had no form of legal redress for their mistreatment.

Gabriel Mendes

See Also
Civil War, American; Free Blacks in the United States, 1619 to 1863.

North America

Black Collectibles,

African American objects and memorabilia, usually acquired as a hobby.

Black collectibles comprise any objects created by or about African Americans. Traditionally this has meant the "higher" categories of books and art, but the term now also refers to the vernacular material of popular culture, including items that perpetuate negative stereotypes, such as Aunt Jemima cookie jars or postcard views of black children eating watermelon.

Attitudes vary regarding the collection of these racist images. Some believe that they should be acquired in order to be destroyed; others think that representative samples should be preserved as documentation of everyday American racism; still others maintain that possessing these offensive objects, especially their ownership by African Americans, gives the collector a certain power that nullifies their damage. Despite the debate, black memorabilia has become scarcer in the marketplace and prices continue to rise, often dramatically, as the hobby gains popularity.

Richard Newman

See Also
Racial Stereotypes.

Africa

Black Consciousness in Africa,

ideology stressing black self-reliance in the fight against apartheid in South Africa.

Unlike more established antiapartheid groups such as the African National Congress (ANC), the South African Communist Party (SACP), or the Pan-Africanist Congress (PAC), South Africa's Black Consciousness Movement was not a single party. It was instead a philosophy, both political and intellectual, that spawned a loose federation of organizations. Drawing inspiration from independence movements throughout Africa, the postcolonial philosophy of Négritude, and the Black Power Movement in the United States, Black Consciousness was one of the more powerful influences in the 1976 Soweto uprisings and in subsequent resistance to South Africa's apartheid system.

For their purposes, Black Consciousness leaders defined "black" to include not only black Africans but also people of Indian or "coloured" descent. "The way to the future," Black Consciousness Movement leader Barney Pityana wrote, "is not through a directionless multiracialism but through a positive unilateral approach." Movement leaders believed that only by working without help from white liberals would black people escape the "slave mentality" created by white domination and achieve the pride and dignity they would ultimately need to end white minority rule. In addition, they called for an economy based on "black communalism," in which private enterprise would coexist with state-sponsored communal villages.

The Black Consciousness Movement had its roots in the South African Student Organisation (SASO), which was founded in 1968 by Pityana, Steve Biko, and others. Frustrated by what they saw as the paternalism of white liberals in the National Union of South African Students, these black students sought a movement that would unite only those directly oppressed by apartheid. Although most previous racially exclusive student groups had failed, SASO, which drew support and publicity from the University Christian Movement (itself founded by black students in 1967), sought "not black visibility but real black participation."

To spread its message, SASO established Formation Schools that provided leadership training seminars for black students and solicited their ideas. The avoidance of centralized power or rigid hierarchies was an important part of SASO's philosophy, and no person served more than one year as the organization's president. Nevertheless, Biko was clearly its most important leader. After his term as president, he stayed on as publicity director, speaking and writing about Black Consciousness until his death in 1977 at the hands of South African police.

Many other groups incorporated Black Consciousness into their work. The South African Students' Movement (SASM), founded in Soweto in 1968, operated independently of SASO but shared many of its principles. Black Community Programmes, an organization Biko helped to run, promoted skills training and self-esteem among black teenagers. In 1972 SASO formed the Black Peoples' Convention (BPC) to spread Black Consciousness thinking beyond the student population. The Black Allied Workers' Union, established after the Durban strikes of 1972-1973, rejected traditional movement tactics in favor of training inspired by the Black Consciousness Movement.

Students, including those in secondary school, remained the most active proponents of Black Consciousness, sometimes with tragic consequences. In 1976 police threw tear gas and then opened fire on an SASM-organized demonstration in Soweto against laws mandating teaching in Afrikaans, which was then considered the language of the white oppressor; three days of rioting followed. Biko, already banned from political action, was arrested repeatedly after the Soweto uprisings, and murdered while in police custody in September 1977. Some historians attribute the government's harsh treatment of Biko to its fears about planned cooperation between the BPC and the historically more moderate ANC. Regardless, a month later the South African government banned all groups related to the Black Consciousness Movement. Although there were attempts to revive the movement in exile, internal disagreements doomed such efforts to failure.

Kate Tuttle

See Also
Afrikaner; Antiapartheid Movement; Biko, Stephen; Cape Coloured; Indian Communities in Africa; Soweto, South Africa; Durban, South Africa; South Africa.

Latin America and the Caribbean

Black Consciousness in Brazil

On May 11, 1988, two days before the hundredth anniversary of the abolition of Brazilian slavery, 5000 people marched under a punishing sun through downtown Rio de Janeiro. At the head of the march, Frei Davi, the fiery leader of Rio de Janeiro's Commission of Black Religious, Seminarians, and Priests, bellowed through a megaphone: "They say the good white masters gave us our freedom! Nonsense!" The true importance of the anniversary, he thundered, was that it reminded Brazilian blacks that they had yet to be liberated. "One hundred years without abolition!" the crowd chanted. "We are still enslaved! Racial democracy is a lie!"

Brazil's Black Consciousness Movement, a loosely linked collection of nearly 600 organizations, is now active in almost every state in the country. Their goal: to teach the younger generation of black Brazilians (or *negros*) that their history and the very terms they use to describe themselves have been distorted by whites. These organizations include lay associations established by the Catholic Church, university-associated research centers, tightly run political bodies, and informal clusters of activists.

The Pastoral of the Negro in Duque de Caxias, a Rio suburb, was established by the progressive bishop Dom Mauro Morelli in 1986 and is led by two priests and a dozen activists who organize workshops, disseminate literature, and run discussion groups. The aim, as one organizer put it, is "to get *negros* to think differently about themselves." The first step is to teach that abolition was not a gift of the master; the second, to convince all those who call themselves *"mulato"* or *"moreno"* (brown) to call themselves *"negro"* instead. As another explained, "We see that for every 100 negros, 70 reject their identity. So we must convince the negro to reject the ideology of 'whitening.' And the way to start is for him call himself a negro."

Some organizations present racism as primarily a cultural problem, to be solved through the development of black identity, based on the rediscovery of one's slave and African "roots." In São Paulo, for instance, the Afro-Brazilian Research Dance Company offers training in SAMBA music, an art form derivative of African rhythms. Similarly, São Paulo's Center of Negro Culture and Art has tried to promote Black Consciousness through classes in CAPOEIRA, an Afro-Brazilian martial art.

Other Black Consciousness organizations, however, including the São Paulo-based Group of Black Women, the Group Nzinga, and the Group of Unity and Black Consciousness, believe that the struggle against racism must seek to change economic, social, and political structures. By far the largest (and, as it happens, oldest) of the more explicitly political groups is the São Paulo-based Unified Negro Movement (MNU), founded in 1978, with roughly 6000 members. The MNU is currently the closest the black movement comes to having a national organization. MNU's platform embraces socialism and states that blacks constitute an underclass whose labor maintains the wealth and power of the white elite.

MNU's activists do not deny the value of raising consciousness about "roots." Their priority, however, is contemporary racial politics. They have demonstrated against police violence and fought in the courts for the enforcement of existing laws against discrimination in the workplace. They also provide logistical support to struggles for better health care and support the rights of prostitutes, battered women, and street children. During the writing of Brazil's current constitution in 1986-1988, MNU activists were instrumental in calling for a National Convention of Blacks for the Constitution, which promoted debates on the constitutional process in hundreds of towns and cities. Along with the direct pressure of Carlos Alberto Oliveira and BENEDITA DA SILVA, two black members of Congress elected in 1986, the grassroots debates undoubtedly helped bring about the inclusion of a constitutional amendment that outlawed racial discrimination.

The vocal presence of groups like MNU has persuaded a number of political parties, from left to center, to place antiracist planks in their platforms and create commissions on racial issues, as well as nominate blacks to run for office. In 1982 São Paulo's governor, Franco Montoro of the centrist Brazilian Democratic Movement Party (PMDB), created the Council for Participation and Development of the Black Community. His equally centrist successor, Orestes Quercia, appointed several *negros* to highly visible posts and set up an office to eliminate racist hiring practices. Similarly, the desire to steal MNU's thunder prompted the federal government in 1986 to create Palmares National Park, in Alagoas state, commemorating the great seventeenth-century community of runaway slaves (*see* MAROONAGE IN THE AMERICAS).

At first glance such gestures appear to be garden-variety cooptation; but they offer the first (admittedly limited and tentative) state-sanctioned acknowledgment that "racial democracy" is a myth. The new agencies also use their position inside the government to gain access to important resources. They have pressured the state census bureau in São Paulo to gather data on black employment, income, and education, to publicize racial issues, and to disseminate information about blacks in newspapers, booklets, and videotapes. In 1987 São Paulo's Council for Black Participation ran Project ZUMBI, an extensive program of lectures, concerts, exhibits, and public debates publicizing the historical importance of the leader of Palmares.

Despite the willingness of mainstream political parties to curry black favor, in 1982 only 2 of the 54 black candidates who ran in São Paulo were elected, and currently there are only a handful of blacks in Congress. Because of this, and to avoid dilution of their message, many black militants have called for distance from white-dominated parties: indeed, in 1982 the MNU adopted this position formally.

Still, many *negro* activists continue to seek alliances with progressive parties, such as the Worker's Party (PT), led by Luiz Inácio da Silva (Lula). The PT succeeded in sending two *negros* to the Constituent Assembly, including the only black woman ever elected to national office, Benedita da Silva. Black militants are, however, wary of the PT's tendency to regard racial discrimination as the result of class oppression. In 1982, for example, the party published a pamphlet in which it denounced racism primarily as a device to maintain an army of cheap reserve labor.

Put off by this kind of analysis (which they regard as denying the primacy and specificity of the race issue), many black leaders have been attracted instead to Leonel Brizola's social democratic, populist Democratic Worker's Party (PDT), which lacks the sectarianism of the Left and has one of the best-oiled patronage machines in the country. As governor of Rio de Janeiro, Brizola placed blacks in prominent positions and, in a gesture that earned him the undying affection of Rio's (mainly black) domestic workers, he prohibited employers from requiring maids to use separate stairwells and elevators. Soon thereafter, MNU firebrand ABDIAS DO NASCIMENTO went to Brasília as a congressman on the PDT ticket, as did black singer Timóteo Agnaldo.

The black movement is currently far from being the mass political phenomenon to which its militants aspire. "Ninety percent of all negros in Brazil," Frei Davi stated, "don't acknowledge their blackness; they want to forget their slave past. That is what we're up against." Even optimistic observers concede that the movement has a fairly narrow social base. Recent estimates place the number of *negro* organizers throughout Brazil at only 25,000 active followers, out of an Afro-Brazilian population that the movement estimates at over 70 million. The large number of organizations is a bit misleading. In Goiás state, for example, the movement musters no more than a few dozen activists. And the 5000 marchers who protested the centennial of abolition are less impressive compared to the 20,000 Brizola can muster at a moment's notice, or the half million that gathered in Rio to call for direct presidential elections in 1984.

Black Consciousness groups comprise primarily professionals, intellectuals, and upwardly mobile students, a pattern that has characterized the movement from the start. In the late 1960s the dictatorship's policy of subsidizing private universities allowed an unprecedented number of young blacks and mulattos to enter college. By the early 1970s they faced the bitter realization that even a college degree could not outweigh the color of their skin on the job market. Among these students were many, such as well-known activist and journalist Hamilton Cardoso, who turned their frustration into an organized challenge to the myth of racial democracy and its underlying institutionalized racism.

Middle-class blacks who see racial politics as their primary concern sometimes find themselves talking past black workers for whom race occupies a secondary (though important) place. "The guy came here all hot," remarked one young black worker about the visit to this town of an MNU militant. "'You must assume your black identity,' he said. OK, fine. I assumed it, long ago. What does that get me? Does that help feed my family?" Undoubtedly such sentiments help explain why the few black candidates in São Paulo elected in 1982 and 1986 did not run on race-based platforms, but rather emphasized working-class issues.

Typically, the audiences for the movement's "culturalist" activities are students, professionals, journalists, and middle-class artists, rather than the art form's usual consumers – the inhabitants of the FAVELAS or urban periphery. In Rio de Janeiro, the Institute of Research on Negro Culture produces video documentaries on and recreates the musical instruments and songs of the slave quarters, then shows these at its downtown headquarters and at art galleries. The way the Instituto Senghor in Porto Alegre exhorts Afro-Brazilians not to forget their ancestry is by publishing "African" poetry read primarily by university students.

Not surprisingly, the little systematic evidence available suggests that the working class is largely unaware of the movement. In one study of working-class black voters, most had no opinion about the Black Consciousness Movement, many had not even heard of its existence, and 90 percent could not name a contemporary black political figure.

Not only is the leadership of the black movement primarily middle class; it also appears to be dominated by Afro-Brazilians with comparatively light skin. In the town of Duque de Caxias, among 24 activists, no fewer than 20 admitted that before becoming involved in the movement, they had identified themselves not as *negro* or *preto* (black), but as *mulato* or *moreno* (brown). Confronted with this fact, they cheerfully accepted it, explaining that their about-face was simply proof of the movement's success in raising consciousness.

Both the causes of the mulatto monopoly on leadership and the tensions inherent in it are evident in the *negro* organization led by the progressive Catholic Church. Mulattos, given greater opportunities than their darker-skinned brothers and sisters, achieve institutional positions in the Church. But then they often find themselves treated as second-class citizens. Mariana, a nun who used to call herself *morena,* explained, "I thought that by becoming a nun I would wipe away that blemish. But I found out that no one would let me forget it. Who do you think made coffee for visitors? That disgusted me."

Translating this disgust into action, Mariana joined Frei Davi in his commission. Already literate, educated, and well placed institutionally, Mariana "returned" to her "black identity" in the role of leader. Her return is typical of mulattos who, discriminated against in the white world, try to resolve the ambiguity of their status by embracing black identity while insisting on being compensated with a higher status in the black realm.

This author's research showed that very few dark blacks participated in Catholic consciousness-raising programs near Rio. One dark-skinned black said, "Look, mulattos have always tried to run away from us. How could they have our culture? They want to use what we have.... They don't know what they are." Another commented, "They say they are negros, but they aren't. They haven't suffered.... Mulattos still think they are better than us. They think the black man still needs to look to them as masters."

Poor and working-class blacks are not immune to the myth of racial democracy, reinforced as it is by schoolbooks, the media, and state-sponsored rituals. But the relative scarcity of working-class Negros in the contemporary Black Consciousness Movement does not mean that such people have little "consciousness." An extraordinary variety of popular cultural practices among the black working class keep an alternative, subversive interpretation of Brazilian history and race relations alive.

In the early 1970s large numbers of young, uneducated, underemployed youths living in Rio de Janeiro's favelas began crowding into all the nightclubs to dance to the music of JAMES BROWN, Isaac Hayes, and Aretha Franklin. They filled movie houses to see films like *Wattstax, Claudine, Superfly,* and *Shaft.* Within a few years, the phenomenon had developed its own lexicon of English-language phrases and its own paraphernalia of colorful clothes and elaborate handshakes.

Though many dismissed this "soul" movement as simply cultural imperialism, it revealed acute disillusionment with elements of traditional Afro-Brazilian culture. Young blacks felt keenly what scholars had observed for some time: that traditional practices of the black community such as samba and capoeira had been coopted by white society. SOUL MUSIC, on the other hand, was perceived as the incontrovertible patrimony of North American blacks.

Anything which suggested that blacks in Brazil, where racial harmony supposedly prevails, might have something in common with angry North American blacks could not fail to be a highly charged political phenomenon. The "soul" movement thus struck at the very heart of the myth of racial democracy by proclaiming a transnational "pan-black" community of suffering, symbolized by the youths' clenched-fist black power salutes.

Religion is another rich vehicle for Black Consciousness. UMBANDA is, along with PENTECOSTALISM, one of the fastest growing religions in Brazil today. In literally thousands of small ritual centers throughout the country, blacks, mulattos, and whites come together to become possessed by, and seek advice from, a range of distinctively Brazilian spirits, including deceased slaves and Indians.

The most well-known version of Umbanda situates the slave at the bottom beneath the Indian and white in the hierarchy of spirits. But this version is adhered to mainly by whites and mulattos. Blacks in Umbanda worship a spirit unrecognized by either whites or mulattos: Zumbi, one of the chiefs of Palmares, the great maroon society that survived for almost century in the backlands of Alagoas until it was finally destroyed by the Portuguese in 1694.

Catholicism, too, provides *negros* with martyrs and saints, including ANASTACIA, an eighteenth-century Brazilian slave, not yet canonized, who enjoys a large following among older black women. As recounted by these elderly *negras,* the jealous wife of a slave owner unjustly accused the virgin slave Anastacia of seducing her husband, and forced her to wear a face-iron for the rest of her life. Anastacia's legend embodies a sharp critique of the master class, and stands as a popular rebuttal to claims that Brazilian slave owners were kindly and paternal.

The music, dance, and lyrics of samba are rich with the history and experience of Afro-Brazilians. In the shantytowns of large Brazilian cities on Saturday afternoons and evenings, one often encounters small groups of young men under the awnings of corner bars, beating a drum, singing, and dancing a sliding four-step. The music the men are singing is samba, and the small gathering is most likely a delegation from a far larger group, known as a samba "school," which organizes a major parade during Carnival. Thousands of favela dwellers are members of these schools, rehearsing and practicing year-round the sambas they perform during the last Tuesday before Lent.

The music and its accompanying dance originated in slaves' melodic calls to African gods, asking them to descend into spirit mediums. In classic samba, a circle of people sing and clap their hands while someone in the center improvises quatrains about everyday life. These improvisations provide the vehicle for subtle, ironic commentaries on race relations and society in general. Even under the military dictatorship, the samba schools commented on hyperinflation, police violence, corruption, low wages, and foreign debt. Most significant, they have dealt head-on with the issue of race. In 1988 the Mangueira samba school sang:

Can it be...
The dawn of liberty,
Or was it all just illusion?
Can it be...
That the dreamed of Golden Law
Signed so long ago
Was not the end of slavery?
In the real world today,
Where is freedom?
Where is it? I don't see it.

I dreamed...
That Zumbi of Palmares returned.
The blacks' misery ended:
It was a new redemption.

The Black Consciousness Movement is certainly contributing in important ways to the cause of racial justice in Brazil. Still, Frei Davi's claim that "we are casting light into all dark corners of Brazil" seems overstated. The important question may not be the accuracy of the claim, but whether the casting of light should ever be one way. Many leaders of the black movement have already begun to realize that profound change in the racial status quo will occur only when they allow the masses to shed a little light on *them.*

John Burdick

See Also
Palmares: An African State in Brazil; Franklin, Aretha Louise; Samba Schools; Brazil; Movimento Negro Unificado; Rio de Janeiro, Brazil; Abolition and Emancipation in Latin America and the Caribbean; Catholic Church in Latin America and the Caribbean; Religions, African, in Latin America and the Caribbean; Education in Latin America and the Caribbean; Myth of Racial Democracy in Latin America and the Caribbean: An Interpretation.

North America

Black Consciousness in the United States

One of the most important aspects of the Civil Rights (1945-1965) and Black Power (1966-1975) Movements, or simply put, the Movement, was the increasing awareness among contemporary Negroes of the centrality of a positive racial identity. "Black Consciousness" here refers to how and with what consequences peoples of African descent in the United States have defined themselves as a people.

Since the creation of the American nation, and especially since emancipation in the Civil War and Reconstruction years, each generation of Negroes has consistently endeavored to build upon the struggles of its forbears. Black Consciousness crystallizes this enduring sensibility of struggle – both failure and achievement. Consequently, it includes how they have collectively viewed their history and culture. Black Consciousness also reflects the relationship between Africans in Africa and those spread throughout the African diaspora, in this case African Americans in the United States.

Black succeeded *Negro* as the major term of self-definition during the Black Power years. In the late 1980s, in the aftermath of a smaller cultural nationalist moment, *African American* superseded *black* as a preferred term of self-reference. On the cusp of the twenty-first century, *black* and *African American* are often used synonymously. Historically, the group, or race, has encompassed both Africans and Africans mixed with other groups, notably Europeans and indigenous Americans. Stretching back to the arrival of Africans in America, the ongoing melding of a diversity of African peoples and experiences into a singular group and experience was a profound historical and cultural development. Variously defined as Negroes, coloreds, and blacks, most Africans in America by the nineteenth century were born in the United States. As a result, their consciousness as a unique people evolved simultaneously with the notion that they, like whites or Caucasians, were not only a race, but inherently American as well. These two allegiances – to the Negro race and the American nation – have decisively shaped Black Consciousness in its various modes.

While it is readily conceded today that there is no scientific or biological basis for the idea of race, the historical and cultural impact of race continues to be widespread and profound. Indeed, in the modern world, race is often seen as a basis for peoplehood or nationhood. The enduring black freedom struggle has exemplified this complicated – at bottom paradoxical – development. Blacks and their allies have fought to create a world where race does not matter. Unfortunately, in spite of their best efforts, race still matters. It continues to frame group consciousness and affect American life in large and small ways.

During the Movement it was not enough to replace the social, political, and economic structures of Jim Crow with a fully desegregated environment. Attitudes, behaviors, and institutions among all Americans had to reflect and build upon racial equality. Indeed, racial egalitarianism was seen as both interwoven with and fundamental to the Movement in its entirety. Basic to the struggle was the related assumption that true freedom and equality demanded that Negroes feel good about themselves, their culture, and their history.

Among Negroes themselves, the Southern, church-based, grassroots social movement between 1945 and 1965 revealed a growing sense of group affiliation and pride. The widespread Negro commitment during World War II to fight for democracy at home as well as abroad characterized this intensifying group-based spirit. Negro membership in the National Association for the Advancement of Colored People (NAACP), the major civil rights organization of the modern era, grew exponentially. Further evidence of the more assertive wartime Negro mentality was the 1941 March on Washington movement, led by A. Philip Randolph. Indeed, President Franklin Delano Roosevelt created the Fair Employment Practices Committee, intended to alleviate racial discrimination in wartime industrial employment, in order to prevent the threatened mass march on the capital.

The same increasingly assertive Negro mentality thus sustained the modern Negro freedom struggle, from the principal local campaigns like the Montgomery Bus Boycott (1955-1956) and the 1963 Birmingham campaign to the inspiring leadership of Martin Luther King Jr. and Ella Baker. That very struggle intensified an expanding group-based commitment to a culturally and historically rooted sense of separateness. That sense of Negro nationhood, of cultural uniqueness, of historical distinctiveness, increasingly contributed to a race-based brand of cultural nationalism that emphasized the importance of an affirmative Negro identity. Race pride and a full commitment to the ongoing Negro freedom struggle were absolutely imperative to that evolving identity.

The full spectrum of the historical experiences and cultural development of Negro Americans – from the period of enslavement to the present – had to be critically yet sympathetically comprehended. This resounding and ever-widening emphasis on truthful yet uplifting resolutions to questions of Negro identity, self-concept, and self-esteem abounded. Taking root and flowering in the soil of the revitalized freedom struggle, the growing awareness of the significance of the cultural dimension of that struggle gave added emphasis to the belief that the realization of Negro freedom was as much mental, emotional, and psychological as structural, material, and physical.

Black Power was the historical moment in which cultural nationalism assumed unprecedented urgency and impact. Blackness signified the need to create an ever more positive and empowering group identity, thus alleviating the negativity associated with past representations of group identity, Negroness in particular. As revealed in the militant politics of community empowerment of the Oakland-based Black Panther Party and the valiant efforts to create independent black political parties, Black Consciousness was an aggressive escalation of the ongoing black freedom struggle. As reflected in practices such as African styles of dress, African-inflected naming practices, and the creation of Kwanzaa as an African-based alternative to Christmas, Black Consciousness meant acceptance of the Africanness of blacks, another important component of the liberation struggle. As captured in King's last effort – the Poor People's Campaign – and the growing awareness of economic justice as crucial to racial justice, Black Consciousness mirrored an increasingly challenging radical politics. Black Consciousness thus represented a desire for black self-definition and greater black autonomy over a black nation within a nation, or black communities. According to this perspective, black lives, black institutions, and black spirit necessitated a militant commitment to the interests of the group. Once blacks had achieved power commensurate with an equal and fair stake in the American dream and they were truly respected as a people, a realistic merger of Black Consciousness with American consciousness and Black Power with American Power might be possible. Regardless, the omnipresence of race as a factor in American life at the end of the twentieth century ensures the necessity and viability of Black Consciousness in the foreseeable future.

Waldo Martin

See Also
World War II and African Americans; Baker, Ella J.; Civil Rights Movement; Civil War, American; King, Martin Luther, Jr.; Poor People's Washington Campaign; Randolph, Asa Philip.

North America

Black Cowboys, legendary American figures who drove great cattle herds across the early West.

Idealized in movies, television, and books, the cowboy serves as the great American icon, representing courage, hardiness, and independence. Yet images of black cowboys have been scarce in popular culture, giving the false impression that African Americans were not among the men and women who settled the West. In fact, by the time the huge cattle drives of cowboy legend ended, at least 5000 black men had worked as cowboys.

The word "cowboy" refers to the men who drove herds of cattle from ranchland in Texas over hundreds of miles of rough and dangerous terrain to the stockyards in the North, a trip taking two to three months. A typical crew consisted of one trail chief, eight cowboys, a wrangler to take care of the horses, and the cook. One historian estimates that an average crew would have included two or three black cowboys.

Black cowboy Nat Love earned the nickname Deadwood Dick for his cattle-roping skill. *CORBIS/Bettmann*

African Americans came to cattle country most often as slaves, brought by white landowners who hoped to take advantage of the fertile Texas soil to grow cotton. Once there, many whites began ranching, often selling or trading their slaves for livestock. By the start of the Civil War, Texas had over 180,000 black inhabitants and close to 4 million head of cattle. When the war ended, ranching, with its dependence on cowboys, became the dominant industry.

Though black cowboys seldom became trail chiefs or owned their own stock – although some did, usually those who had been free men before the war – they encountered less discrimination along the cattle trail than in most other occupations at the time. While riding herd, black and white cowboys depended upon each other. They lived, ate, and slept together. The demands of the trail, which included dangerous snakes and wolves, treacherous rivers and mountains, and the threat of attack from Native Americans, made most cowboys transcend their prejudices. One black cowboy, Nat Love (also known as DEADWOOD DICK), summed up the cowboy code: "There a man's work was to be done, and a man's life to be lived, and when death was to be met, he met it like a man."

If life on the trail was arduous, life in the cattle market towns, like Dodge City, Kansas, and Cheyenne, Wyoming, was wide open and lawless. Despite the efforts of marshals like Wyatt Earp and Bat Masterson, thieves, rustlers, and gunslingers were abundant. Though most black cowboys, like the majority of whites, were tough but law-abiding, there were a few famous black outlaws. One, known as Cherokee Bill, was as bloodthirsty as Billy the Kid and was hanged before his 20th birthday.

By around 1890 the cowboy's world had changed. Railroad lines had rendered long drives unnecessary, and barbed-wire fences now blocked the legendary Chisholm and Western trails. Some old cowboys, like Nat Love, found work as Pullman porters. Others continued to work on ranches as bronco busters who tamed wild mustangs. Still others, like BILL PICKETT, put their riding, roping, or shooting skills to use on the RODEO and vaudeville circuits.

Kate Tuttle

SEE ALSO

Slavery in the United States; American Indians; Civil War, American.

North America

Black Entertainment Television, a Washington, D.C.-based entertainment company that primarily targets black consumers through original programming on its three cable television channels and through its magazine, clothing, and cosmetic ventures.

Black Entertainment Television Holdings, Inc. (BET Holdings) was founded in 1979 by former cable industry lobbyist Robert Johnson. The company's primary business is its 24-hour cable channel, Black Entertainment Television Cable Network (BET). The BET Cable Network has an estimated 45 million subscribers nationwide. Its predominantly black viewing audience has transformed this once struggling company into a powerful social and economic force in the media industry.

BET began by broadcasting music videos in 1980 and 11 years later became the first black-controlled company listed on the New York Stock Exchange (NYSE). Since then BET has diversified its holdings by moving into the publishing industry. The company publishes several magazines targeting black readers, including *Emerge*, *BET Weekend*, and *Heart & Soul*. It has also acquired three other cable channels, including a cable jazz channel (BET on Jazz) and the BET Movies/Starz!3 channel. In 1994 BET established a radio network to provide news and information to radio stations located in urban markets around the country.

Two years later the company formed a partnership with Microsoft to form MSBET, an online service that offers up-to-date information on concerts, entertainers, movies, and cable programming. BET has continued to expand its cable television programming by offering a public affairs show, a weekly show for teenagers, and broadcasts of town hall meetings that address contemporary issues facing the African American community.

Alonford James Robinson, Jr.

North America

Black History Month/Negro History Week, American designation of February as a time of emphasis on black history.

When historian Carter G. Woodson first conceived of the idea of a Negro History Week, he envisioned a celebration of black history and achievement as well as an educational medium. With the support of the Association for the Study of Negro Life and History, he organized the first annual celebration in 1926 to be held during the second week in February, in honor of the birthdays of FREDERICK DOUGLASS and Abraham Lincoln. The event grew in popularity, promoted by schools, women's clubs, and the white as well as black press. Negro History Week provided an opportunity for lectures, performances, written materials, and photographs of black history to reach wide audiences. In the early 1970s the Association for the Study of Negro Life and History (later the ASSOCIATION FOR THE STUDY OF AFRO-AMERICAN LIFE AND HISTORY) expanded the February celebration, renaming it Black History Month.

Marian Aguiar

SEE ALSO

Press, Black, in the United States; Black Women's Club Movement; Woodson, Carter Godwin.

North America

"Black Manifesto," declaration authored by American James Forman demanding reparations for African American enslavement and oppression.

Service was disrupted at New York's Riverside Church on May 4, 1969, when black nationalist James Forman strode to the pulpit before a predominantly white congregation and demanded that white churches and synagogues pay $500 million in reparations for the history of black enslavement and oppression. With the Black Manifesto, Forman implicated white religious institutions in this history, citing the church as part of "the vast system of controls over black people and their minds."

In 1969 civil rights activist James Forman demanded that American religious institutions pay $500 million in reparations for black slavery.
UPI/CORBIS/Bettmann

The Black Manifesto was the product of an organized effort that had its origins a month earlier at the National Black Economic Development Conference (NBEDC). Frustrated by the slow progress of reform projects in minority communities, Forman led the NBEDC in drafting a statement demanding money for a Southern land bank, four television networks, and a black university. With the support of the League of Black Revolutionary Workers and Forman leading the way, the NBEDC organized a series of church disruptions to announce the demands.

Despite the short-lived nature of the demonstration and the lack of support by the Student Nonviolent Coordinating Committee (SNCC), the Black Manifesto did raise a half a million dollars for African American projects. Ironically, very little of the money went to the NBEDC, which was under investigation by the FBI and Justice Department. Instead, the funds ended up with the very reform projects Forman had criticized. With the money it did receive, the NBEDC established the Detroit publishing house Black Star Publications.

Marian Aguiar

See Also
New York, New York; Television and African Americans.

North America

Black Mural Movement, The, an urban movement in which African American artists worked in teams to create large-scale public paintings on the walls of predominantly black neighborhoods.

The Black Mural Movement developed out of the 1960s Black Arts Movement and embraced the political creed of the black aesthetic. The founding work of the Black Mural Movement, *Wall of Respect* (1967), by Chicago-based William Walker and other artists, drew on a long-standing tradition of African American mural painting. In the 1930s the Federal Art Project of the Works Progress Administration helped such African American artists as Aaron Douglas, Charles White, and Hale Woodruff complete murals that documented African American history. These monumental works, done in a style best described as social realism, were executed on the interior walls of public buildings.

Students and professors continued to create murals with black themes throughout the 1940s and 1950s. From the 1930s through the Black Mural Movement, African American muralists drew inspiration from the work of Mexican muralists such as Diego Rivera, Jose Clemente Orozco, and David Alfaro Siquieros, who created murals that portrayed and celebrated Mexican history during the 1920s and 1930s.

Murals done before and during the Black Mural Movement commonly celebrated black historical figures, promoted black pride and racial solidarity, and emphasized the importance of education. Two things distinguish most of the murals of the 1960s and 1970s from their predecessors: (1) they were painted on exterior walls, where they could be viewed by a wider, more varied audience, and (2) they were conceived and funded by members of the African American community at the grassroots level, as opposed to large government or corporate organizations outside the African American community.

The success of *Wall of Respect* led to commissions for Walker and his team of artists and sparked similar projects in other African American as well as Hispanic neighborhoods throughout the country. In 1968 Walker and other Chicago muralists went to Detroit to assist in the painting of three murals in neighborhoods that had been devastated by the 1967 Detroit riots. At the same time, Dana Chandler and Gary Rickson coordinated the creation of several murals in the Roxbury section of Boston, Massachusetts. The African American citizens of Compton and Oakland, California, initiated a mural program, although urban California emerged as the center of Latino mural production. Chicago remained at the center of the Black Mural Movement.

The emergence of public-art agencies followed the proliferation of community-initiated murals. These organizations work to secure private, corporate, and government funding for mural projects through which African American artists continue to portray their past and present experiences.

Aaron Myers

See Also
Black Aesthetic, The; Chicago, Illinois; Detroit Riot of 1967; San Francisco and Oakland, California; *Wall of Respect, The*; Woodruff, Hale Aspacio.

North America

Black Nationalism in the United States, the set of beliefs or the political theory that African Americans should maintain social, economic, and political institutions separate and distinct from those of whites.

Black Nationalism, also known as black separatism, is a complex set of beliefs emphasizing the need for the cultural, political, and economic separation of African Americans from white society. Comparatively few African Americans have embraced thoroughgoing separatist philosophies. In his classic study *Negro Thought in America, 1880-1915*, August Meier noted that the general black attitude has been one of "essential ambivalence." On the other hand, nationalist assumptions inform the daily actions and choices of many African Americans.

Over the course of the nineteenth and twentieth centuries, Black Nationalists have agreed on two defining principles: black pride and racial separatism. Black Nationalism calls for black pride and seeks a unity that is racially based rather than one grounded in a specific African culture or ethnicity. Thus the basic outlook of Black Nationalism is premised upon Pan-Africanism. Historian Sterling Stuckey argued that this Pan-African perspective emerged as an unintended byproduct of the institution of slavery. Slaveholders deliberately mixed together slaves of diverse linguistic and tribal backgrounds in order to minimize their ability to communicate and make common cause. In response, African slaves were forced "to bridge ethnic differences and to form themselves into a single people to meet the challenge of a common foe.... "

Those espousing nationalist or separatist philosophies have envisioned nationalism in quite different ways. For some, Black Nationalism demanded a territorial base; for others, it required only separate institutions within American society. Some have perceived nationalism in strictly secular terms; others, as an extension of their religious beliefs. Black Nationalists also differ in the degree to which they identify with Africa and African culture.

During the late eighteenth and the nineteenth centuries African Americans showed an increased level of racial pride and solidarity. African American leaders sought to highlight black accomplishments. For example, black ship owner Paul Cuffe of Massachusetts hired only black seamen to crew his ships so as to demonstrate their ability to a skeptical world. Boston's free blacks made Crispus Attucks – the black seaman killed in the Boston Massacre – a symbol of the African American role in the American Revolution, and for decades they celebrated March 5 as Crispus Attucks Day.

Nineteenth-century free blacks established separate religious organizations, such as the Free African Society, founded in 1787 by Philadelphians Richard Allen and Absalom Jones, and Boston's African Meetinghouse. In 1816 Allen played a leading role in the formation of the African Methodist Episcopal Church (AME).

Black pride has also involved an insistence on distinctly black standards of beauty (*see* Hair and Beauty Culture). Black Nationalist Marcus Garvey, founder of the Universal Negro Improvement Association (UNIA), deplored black acceptance of white standards of beauty, for example, in preferring straight hair or a lighter skin color. During the 1920s he refused to place advertisements for hair straighteners or purported skin whiteners in *Negro World*, the UNIA newspaper. In the 1960s Black Nationalists embraced the political slogan Black Power, but they also proclaimed that "black is beautiful."

In many respects Black Nationalism represented a response to the overt hostility of white society. During the antebellum era David Walker's *Appeal... to the Colored People of the World* (1829) epitomized the demand for a united black defense. According to Stuckey, Walker's trenchant arguments earned him recognition as the "father of Black Nationalist theory in America." During the 1850s Martin Delany and the Reverend Henry Highland Garnet emerged as the most forceful nationalists. In the late nineteenth century AME bishop Henry McNeal Turner gained prominence as a nationalist leader. Booker T. Washington did not endorse Black Nationalism, but at Tuskegee Institute he insisted on the need for black economic independence and self-help, views that many separatists found congenial.

The most consistent proponents of Black Nationalism were those who advocated emigration or colonization. Delany, Garnet, Turner, and Alexander Crummell all endorsed colonization and insisted that African Americans' greatest hope lay in the establishment of all-black settlements or colonies, most often planned for Africa. Emigration or colonization entailed blacks leaving the United States to establish an African American settlement abroad, often in the hope of creating an independent black state.

In 1815, for example, Paul Cuffe led a group of 38 African Americans to found a settlement in Sierra Leone, which the British government planned to use for the repatriation of slaves freed in its colonies. Free African Society founders Richard Allen and Absalom Jones endorsed Cuffe's plan. Garvey's UNIA was the most powerful back-to-Africa movement of the twentieth century. But emigrationists differed among themselves over an appropriate destination and, in the case of emigration to Africa, in their attitudes toward the African people with whom they intended to settle.

Advocates of emigration diverged sharply in their perceptions of African culture. Delany, for example, contended that African ethical values were inherently superior to those of European Christians, who appeared to be driven by an insatiable lust for power and material gain. Turner and Garnet justified a return to Africa in terms of the opportunity it provided in bringing what they felt were the benefits of Christianity and economic progress to "savage and backward" Africans. Others stressed the opportunity that colonization would offer to demonstrate the extent of African American accomplishment when unencumbered by racial discrimination and prejudice. Some envisioned a black colony as an African American homeland to which all African Americans should return – in much the same way that twentieth-century Zionists call upon Jews to return to Israel.

Black Nationalists seek racial separation but differ on the degree and nature of that separation. Some have sought a specific territory that could be reserved for and controlled by blacks. Others have advocated separate black social, religious, economic, or political institutions within the existing white society. Territorial nationalists have differed on an appropriate location. Those calling for a return to Africa have most commonly suggested the territories of such present-day West African nations as Liberia, Sierra Leone, and Nigeria.

Others proposed creating a separate black nation in the Americas, often viewing Haiti as a likely possibility. Still others believed that a part of the United States should be set aside as a separate black state. In the late 1920s white radicals of the Communist Party of the United States of America (CPUSA) viewed African Americans as an internal colony of American imperialism and demanded recognition for a Negro Nation that would be located within the Black Belt counties of Mississippi, Alabama, and Georgia.

Many African Americans implicitly acted on nationalist principles. In the 1870s, for example, black Exodusters fled the South to found all-black settlements in Kansas. African Americans established other all-black towns, including Eatonville, Florida, the childhood home of Zora Neale Hurston. Hurston and such prominent African Americans as Paul Robeson and W. E. B. Du Bois also expressed attitudes that at times resembled or drew upon Black Nationalism. Hurston's writing, notably *Their Eyes Were Watching God* (1938), portrayed a black world in which whites rarely intruded and mattered little.

Singer and activist Robeson was never a Black Nationalist, but he held views that were, to some extent, compatible with nationalism. He believed that African Americans were fundamentally African people and insisted that they must be "proud of being black." He believed that African peoples were more spiritually attuned and more community-oriented than their white American or European counterparts. He studied several African languages and worked to end Europe's colonial domination of the African continent. Yet Robeson rejected separatism and never abandoned his vision of a racially integrated society. Moreover, in all of his extensive travels, he never visited sub-Saharan Africa.

W. E. B. Du Bois – one of America's foremost black intellectuals and a leading figure in the founding of the National Association for the Advancement of Colored People (NAACP) – had strong ties to Africa. In 1919 he organized the first Pan-African Congress. During the 1920s he traveled to Africa. Yet for most of his life, Du Bois rejected Black Nationalism. In the 1920s he opposed Marcus Garvey and the UNIA. During the 1930s, as Du Bois grew more radical, he turned to socialism and internationalism rather than to Black Nationalism. But during the harsh anticommunism of the cold war era, Du Bois lost his faith in American society. In 1961 he abandoned the United States and settled in Ghana, where he died two years later, shortly after taking Ghanaian citizenship.

From the 1930s through the 1950s Black Nationalists maintained a low profile. In 1935 Garvey failed to resurrect the UNIA, despite the hardships that many blacks endured during the Great Depression. Apart from Elijah Muhammad, the Nation of Islam's relatively obscure leader, there was no Black Nationalist who could supplant Garvey. Although Hurston, Robeson, and Du Bois were significant figures, they were not principled separatists.

The decade of the 1960s, by contrast, was a high point for Black Nationalist thought. In some respects, it became a radical extension of the Civil Rights Movement. Many blacks grew impatient with the slow pace of change and broke with the movement's principles of passive nonviolence. The STUDENT NONVIOLENT COORDINATING COMMITTEE (SNCC) contributed an important expression of Black Nationalism through its slogan Black Power. SNCC leader STOKELY CARMICHAEL (Kwame Ture) and political scientist Charles Hamilton wrote *Black Power* (1967) to elaborate that slogan into a philosophy and political program.

In 1966 BOBBY SEALE and Huey Newton founded the BLACK PANTHER PARTY, which advocated militant self-defense and Black Nationalism. The Black Panther Party, like SNCC Black Power advocates, embraced a Black Nationalism that was primarily secular and political. By contrast, Nation of Islam leaders Elijah Muhammad and the charismatic MALCOLM X grounded their goals of racial separation in religious precepts. Black Muslims sought to establish separate economic enterprises, finding a religious justification for a racially separate business life.

As of the late 1990s African American attitudes and beliefs continued to reveal the significance of Black Nationalism, although less as a political philosophy than as a cultural attitude. It is difficult to weigh this cultural impact, but its manifestations can be seen throughout African American society. For example, a growing number of black parents give their children African names. Since the 1970s African-style clothing has been a recurring feature in black fashion. Likewise, the celebration of KWANZAA emphasizes African Americans' distinctly African heritage.

Kwanzaa, however, is not a traditional African celebration. It is an invented tradition that was developed and promoted by the Black Nationalist Maulana Ron Karenga. Contemporary RAP music, while not embracing African culture, emphasizes themes of black pride. Finally, the ubiquitous presence of Malcolm X suggests how broadly Black Nationalism has been disseminated throughout black culture. But few would argue that Malcolm X posters or X insignias on caps or sweaters represent a coherent outlook or set of principles. At the dawn of the twenty-first century, the most telling assessment remains that of August Meier: African Americans continue to view Black Nationalism with an essential ambivalence.

James Clyde Sellman

SEE ALSO

Ghana; Slavery in the United States; Pan-African Congress of 1919; African Methodist Episcopal Church; Boston, Massachusetts; Delany, Martin Robison; Du Bois, William Edward Burghardt (W. E. B.); Free Blacks in the United States, 1619 to 1863; Garvey, Marcus Mosiah; Nation of Islam; Newton, Huey P.; Philadelphia, Pennsylvania; Tuskegee University; Universal Negro Improvement Association; Washington, Booker Taliaferro.

Latin America and the Caribbean

Blackness in Latin America and the Caribbean: An Interpretation

Whether or not black Africans or black Iberians reached the New World with Columbus in either of his first two voyages is not clear. Nor is it clear whether Africans reached the New World prior to Columbus. We do know, however, that with the first serious European settlement on the island of Hispaniola (now the DOMINICAN REPUBLIC and HAITI), the African diaspora in the Americas began with a seminal moment of self-liberation.

"With the fleet of Governor Ovando, bound for Hispaniola in 1502 to reinvigorate the faltering colony that Columbus had left behind the previous year, sailed a few Negroes brought by their masters," wrote historian Carlos Federico Guillot. "Among them was the first Afro-American maroon, an anonymous slave who escaped to the Indians [Taíno Arawaks] in the mountainous interior soon after setting foot in the New World."

In western Hispaniola, where the French established colonial St. Domingue, and in the interior of the Spanish territory that eventually became the Dominican Republic, "maroonage" (flight from servitude) sustained an atmosphere of liberation (*see* MAROONAGE IN THE AMERICAS). "From the first years of slavery on the island," wrote Michel S. Laguerre, "Indians and slaves had run away to inaccessible mountains, and throughout the colonial period, every mountain in Haiti was used at one time or another by fugitive slaves."

In the first indigenous and black revolution on the island of PUERTO RICO, two Taíno Arawak chiefs and their people allied with black *ladinos* (Spaniards of African descent) to fight against the representatives of the Spanish Crown in 1514. A second major uprising 17 years later that involved the enslaved black population represented a greater threat to the colonizers because the number of "blacks" had grown, while the "white" population had decreased. In retaliation, the Church and Crown in Puerto Rico accused freed and enslaved black men and women of sorcery and witchcraft.

In 1522 black people revolted in Santo Domingo, the major city of Hispaniola. According to Leslie B. Rout Jr., "Some 40 slaves working at the sugar mill on the plantation of the governor, Admiral Diego Columbus (a son of the explorer), conspired with other blacks working on nearby establishments." Thereafter, revolt was ubiquitous in the Caribbean and mainland South and Central America. Wherever slavery existed, self-liberation began.

Writing about Haiti, Laguerre says: "Maroonage was a central fact in the life of the colony, not only because of maroon military power and the number of slaves who constantly joined them, but also because of the danger inherent in expeditions to destroy revolutionary centers of these fugitive slaves... [W]herever there were slaves, there were also maroons.... Living in free camps or on the fringes of port cities, they were a model for the slaves to imitate, embodying the desires of most of the slaves. What the slaves used to say in *sotto voce* on the plantations, they were able to say aloud in the maroon settlements."

Ethnographer Richard Price writes: "For more than four centuries, the communities formed by such runaways dotted the fringes of plantation America, from BRAZIL to the southeastern United States, from PERU to the American Southwest. Known variously as *palenques*, *quilombos*, *mocambos*, *cumbes*, *ladeiras*, or *mambises*, these new societies ranged from tiny bands that survived less than a year to powerful states encompassing thousands of members and surviving for generations or even centuries. Today their descendants still form semi-independent enclaves in several parts of the hemisphere, remaining fiercely proud of their maroon origins and, in some cases at least, faithful to unique cultural traditions forged during the earliest days of Afro-American history."

Although few twentieth-century scholars have taken time to document such information, self-liberation in the midst of war, pestilence, and death is thoroughly embedded in the dynamic history of African American people hemisphere-wide. Out of this creative process emerged most of the region's prominent black areas: among them, various parts of Brazil; the Yungas of BOLIVIA; the northwest coast of ECUADOR; the Pacific and Atlantic coasts and Cauca Valley of COLOMBIA; the Venezuelan Llanos and northern coastal crescent; the interior of PANAMA; the Mosquitía of Honduras and Nicaragua; the Atlantic coast of Guatemala, Belize, Honduras, and Nicaragua (*see* CENTRAL AMERICA); the mountains of HAITI and the Dominican Republic; the Jamaican Blue Mountains and Red Hills; and the Oriente of eastern CUBA.

The term *black*, according to *Webster's*, is an adjective derived from the Latin cognate meaning, in a literal sense, "sooted, smoke black from flame." Its first meaning today is "opposite to white." The "sooted" (darkened, blackened) concept has an earlier (or deeper) etymology from the Latin *flagrare*, "flame," "burn" and, by association, "flagrant." A theme running through the history of black America is the dialectic between, on the one hand, the darkening influences of white domination in the African diaspora and, on the other, the illuminated creativity produced and reproduced in the eternal fires of black rebellion.

To discuss "communities," "regions," or "societies" in the New World where blackness is an important criterion for social categorization and interaction is to plunge into contradictory ideologies of "races," and to chart the moral topographies of deeply held religious and aesthetic feelings about racial separation and racial mixture. The plunge deepens where "blackness" expands, and the process of immersion brings surprising revelations of the richness of cultural experience among New World peoples who are called, or call themselves, black, Negro, mulatto, *negro, zambo, moreno, trigueño, mulato, pardo, negre, preto, cafuso, noire, nengre* – or *libre* (free), as in the El Chocó region on the Pacific coast of Colombia.

Black people of the Pacific lowlands of Panama, Colombia, and Ecuador – who constitute 90 percent or more of the population there – emphatically deny an African diaspora. They reject concepts that suggest that they are lost souls separated from a distant homeland. Rather they insist that they are possessors of their own homeland, the coastal and riverine sectors of this tropical rain forest. There, they say, their ancestors seized their freedom, asserted their culture, and made the productive land "theirs." Like the maroons in the interior of SURINAME and FRENCH GUIANA, their collective notion of history is alive with events establishing their own communities in their own territory by their own creative volitions.

This firm sense of black selfhood and social history developed under the shadow of enduring racism. In the Cauca Valley of Colombia, with a history characterized by increasingly white wealth, oppression of black yeomanry, and destruction of indigenous people, black people are viewed as morally "darkened" by history, geography, and descent. For whites and *mestizos* in the valley, *negro* refers to "lazy" and "dangerous" migrants from a "jungle" littered with African "superstitions." Such racism stems from the legacies of slavery and black self-liberation, in concert with the later white tradition of importing black laborers from the adjacent Pacific lowlands. It is also rooted in a deep-seated white and mestizo fear of the free black people who have long resided there.

Writing of the descendants of the self-liberated black *cimarrones* there in the 1880s, Michael Taussig says: "... these black peasants were outlaws – free peasants and foresters who lived by their wits and weapons rather than by legal guarantees to land citizenship. The fearful specter of a black state was not lost on some observers. 'In the woods that enclose the Cauca Valley,' wrote the German traveler Friedrich von Schenk in 1880, 'vegetate many blacks whom one could equate with the maroons of the West Indies.' They sought solitude in the woods, 'where they regress once again slowly to the custom of their African birthplace as one commonly sees in the interior of Haiti.... These people are tremendously dangerous, especially in times of revolution when they get together in gangs and enter the struggle as valiant fighters in the service of whatever hero of liberty promises them booty.'"

The blacks of Colombia do not accept the position of ethnic disadvantage that whites assign them, nor do they describe themselves as whites do. Blacks turn such stigmatization on its head through narrative modes too often strung together and published as "folklore" – that constitute a rich embodiment of enlightened and insightful black representation of the entwined stories of conquest, domination, and self-liberation. As Taussig puts it: "From the represented shall come that which overturns the representation."

"Race" is a powerful ideological concept in modern Latin America and the Caribbean (*see* RACE IN LATIN AMERICA). In Spanish-, Portuguese-, and French-speaking republics today we find two nationalist ideologies of racial culture: *mestizaje* (racial mixture) and NÉGRITUDE (blackness). Mestizaje, the ideology of racial intermingling, is an explicit master symbol of the nation in all Latin American countries. Négritude is a concept that denotes the positive features of blackness among "black" people. In the Americas only Haiti has adopted an explicit nationalist ideology of Négritude.

Challenges to dominant racialist ideologies often come from what Clifford Geertz calls "ethnic-blocs." The power of identity within an ethnic bloc can derive from ethnic exclusion, as when indigenous people or black people are ethnically disfranchised from full participation in the dominant society. Or it can come from a collective inner sense of the oneness of a people, in contradistinction to nationalist racialist hegemony. Black-based ethnic blocs in the Americas often adopt the ideology of Négritude and, in doing so, are perceived as a threat to the sovereignty and territoriality of the official "nation."

Competing with Négritude in black communities is another master symbol of ideology: *blanqueamiento* – somatic, cultural, or ethnic lightening to become increasingly acceptable to those classified and self-identified as "white." Although not often recognized as such, the ideology of "whitening" is an unconscious psychological process that accompanies the economic state of underdevelopment in the twentieth century. Essentially, blanqueamiento accepts the implicit hegemonic rhetoric of the United States with regard to "white supremacy," and often blames those classed as black and indigenous for the worsening state of the nation.

From the beginning of the African diaspora in Europe and the Americas, "whitening" and "darkening" have been dual symbolic processes of classification and identity. Though dominant in nationalist rhetoric, mestizaje is not viewed positively in black communities and regions, where nevertheless, lightness is often considered superior to darkness. "Mulatto" often signifies "free black" as well as "lightened black." In some areas, however, it may mean "darkened white," or just plain "darkened." With the abolishment of slavery between the mid- and late nineteenth century (*see* ABOLITION AND EMANCIPATION IN LATIN AMERICA AND THE CARIBBEAN), the terminology became "mulatto/black" in black regions, and "white/mulatto" in regions dominated by peoples of lighter skin color. Extended occupation by United States troops in several areas (among them, Nicaragua, Haiti, and Puerto Rico) facilitated this process.

In many black regions and communities, the word "mestizo" may refer to "black blood" (meaning, "darkening" – *negreando*) with no connotation of "lightening." Such is the case with the Portuguese term *mestiço* ("darkening" or "darkened"), as in many parts of Brazil, and the French *métissage* in parts of the French-speaking Caribbean. The process of darkening is called *mutalización* in Cuban communities in Cuba and Miami.

The interplay between the discourses and practices of "white culture" and "darkened people" has produced a myriad of racial concepts and codes. Columbus, on his first voyage, was struck by one feature of the Taino Arawak (and later, other) indigenous people whom he encountered: they did not wear clothes. Rather, they presented their sense of individual and collective identity by such means as body and face painting, hair dressing, stone adornments in lips and cheeks, and nasal and ear adornments of precious metals (gold and *guanín*). One of the codes of the Old World to be immediately imposed on the New World was to "clothe" the subjugated Native Americans and black Africans in European garb. Significantly, then, in Dutch Guiana, which was to become Suriname, as elsewhere, one of the first things that self-liberated slaves did was to shed their European clothes. Equally telling, perhaps, is the call of dark people in the Caribbean, as elsewhere, when beginning the English game of cricket: "Put on your whites!"

In non-Anglophone America today, Colombia-Ecuador and Haiti constitute polar nationalist opposites. In the former, the colonial dream of overcoming the barriers of racial classification that limit economic opportunities became transformed into a nationalist, democratic ideology of "racial mixture." In the latter, blackness inundated a formative New World gene pool to create, in the revolution of 1791-1804, the first self-liberated democratic island republic in the Americas with collective, self-conscious roots in its African and European past (*see* HAITIAN REVOLUTION).

Black Haiti, the nation occupying the western portion of the island of Hispaniola, abuts Cuba's black Oriente region to the west, where Fidel Castro launched his revolutionary movement in 1956 from the Sierra Maestra Mountains. To the east of Haiti, on the same island, lies the Dominican

Republic, where, according to some scholars, the 1844 independence movement stressed the European, Catholic, "civilized" culture of the Dominicans over the African and "barbarous" Haitians.

South of Haiti lie Venezuela and Colombia, lands also governed by mestizaje ideology. But in the coastal areas, the people are predominantly black. In the wars of liberation against European colonialism (between 1813 and 1822) led by Simón Bolívar, black troops from revolutionary Haiti helped overthrow colonial governments in the territories that became the Republic of Gran Colombia: from the Orinoco River in today's Venezuela to the Pacific coast, and from what is now northern Peru to Panama. As Creole nationalist spirits rose, so too did ethnic unity among the black communities that marched with Bolívar and continued their struggles after independence had been won.

Racialist ideologies influencing the complementary processes of nationalism and ethnic-bloc formation became tightly intertwined. For example, the oft-raised possibility that Bolívar had black ancestors was (and is) viewed as a positive trait in Haiti, but as a negative one in the territory of Gran Colombia and among his white and mestizo biographers, who are clearly uneasy about the blackness within the mestizo "mixture." Paradoxically, Bolívar himself feared the worst for elite whites and mixed Creoles if the energies manifest in black cultures were unleashed. Indeed, when black soldiers of liberation began to rally around one of his black Haitian generals, he had the general shot.

This same uneasiness about blackness is evident in the images of Haiti held by many white and mestizo people living in the Spanish Caribbean and adjacent Spanish Main, and in Ecuador and Peru. Within the cultural ideologies of these regions, those who self-identify as "white" or "light" often associate with Haiti the idea of brutal impoverishment and a revolution out of control. This imagery suggests a racialist revulsion and spiritual awe of the power of blackness within mestizaje.

Even within Haiti, somatic and/or cultural categories are also prey to the ideological specter of "lightening." An urban mulatto elite has separated itself from the rural black masses of poor people. Moreover, in downtown Port-au-Prince a "black ghetto" has come into being due to the historical flow of power away from the black poor.

The phenomenon of "lightening" is well known in Venezuela, Colombia, and Ecuador, where people classed as mestizo usually refer to themselves as *blanco* (white). Those seeking to become "whiter" view their "whiteness" in cultural terms. They aspire to be more civilized and "conscious" than "darker" black and indigenous peoples. "Blacks" and "Indians" are considered people without consciousness (*a quien les falta consciencia*) and hence un-self-reflective and stupid (*see* Latin America, Blacks and Indians in).

Mestizaje is a powerful force of exclusion of both black and indigenous communities in the Americas today. As a consequence, black and indigenous awareness of exclusion and continuous struggle for ethnic power will remain prominent.

These processes are especially evident in the largest vestige of U.S. colonialism in the Caribbean: Puerto Rico. *Puertorriqueños* clearly regard their island as a *nación* and are as "nationalist" about their identity as are Colombians, Ecuadorians, Venezuelans, Jamaicans, Cubans, or Haitians. Emergent Puerto Rican nationalism under Spanish rule embraced the ideology of mestizaje in which the *jíbaro* (Puerto Rican peasant) was the bearer of a nascent Puerto Rican identity and culture. The "mixture" emphasized Spanish-indigenous heritage, with privilege accorded to the former.

Although in many areas jíbaros vary in skin color from brown to black, there is little, if any, "national" emphasis on the African component of Puerto Rican heritage. The 1898 invasion by U.S. troops and subsequent enforced segregation gave impetus to the nationalist ideology of mestizaje and especially to its dimension of blanqueamiento. This was further reinforced by the view that the paternalist social order of the plantation contributed to racial integration.

Today black Puerto Ricans, who have maintained their autonomy since the formation of maroon groupings on the island, are challenging the official interpretation of Puerto Rico's ethnic heritage. Migration to and from the mainland United States has intensified the multifaceted debate by infusing it with features of the U.S. Black Power Movement and the official U.S. categorization of Puerto Ricans as "minorities" and "people of color."

In countries undergoing an intensive process of building national identity, the term *ethnic* comes to mean something at variance with what nationalist ideologues proclaim is "traditional" to the nation's "authentic past." The case of the black people who hold territorial sovereignty in the interior of Suriname demonstrates how black governance challenges the broader nation-state.

In the interior of Suriname and French Guiana, six nations of self-liberated black people – the Saramaka, Matawai, Kwinti, Djuka, Paramaka, and Aluku – emerged from the creativity of African American ethnogenesis. These peoples are collectively called *bushenenge*, "forest blacks," by Dutch-speaking outsiders and "Bush Negroes" by English-speakers searching for "lost Africans."

Each of these peoples fought for more than a hundred years against the Dutch to win their independence. Then, in the mid-1980s, as Suriname entered a phase of avowed socialist nationalism, the sheer existence of peaceful and autonomous black people in a "plural" nation seemed to threaten the sovereignty and territoriality of an increasingly bloodthirsty and oppressive military state. The consequence was a civil war, news of which scarcely reached beyond Suriname's borders.

In the 1970s the Saramaka people had cautiously told ethnographers Richard and Sally Price about customs they no longer practiced except in times of collective crisis, because these were associated with "First Time," a real, historical period of war and rebellion which, if discussed, would "kill people." Using many techniques of sophisticated communication, they told of battles, rituals, and powerful artifacts while withholding specific details.

In *Alabi's World*, published in 1990, Richard Price gives moving testimony to the strength of Saramaka tradition, sustained through historical lore and prominent in the continuing struggle against dominion. "In 1978, the Saramaka elder Peleki voiced the greatest fear of all maroons, prophesying that those times – the days of war and slavery – shall come again," Price wrote. "In 1986, after two centuries of peace, they did. Great war *obias* [spirits] that had lain dormant since the eighteenth century were dug from the earth and revivified. The blood of hundreds of maroons – men, women, and children – as well as that of other Surinamers has once again stained the ground."

Anthropological understanding of black cultures and traditions in the New World has often bogged down in debates about how to scale Africanisms against Europeanisms in such areas as aesthetics, ritual, play theater, folklore, cosmology, music, dance, religion, and ideology. Some scholars have even stewed over the relationships between Native American cultures and black cultures, holding learned conferences on "Black Indians." But cultural traditions may come from any source and may change radically for a variety of reasons. Black Bermudans' fondness for English cricket is no less "theirs" in the late twentieth century than white Mississippians' taste for okra (which blacks brought to the Americas from Africa).

Yet patterns do suggest relationships to the past and trajectories toward the future. Traditional African American arts and rituals, for example, exist as material objects (sculpture, carving, painting, quilting, weaving, pottery) or cultural forms (storytelling, jokes, poetry, myths, historic narrative, worship, dance, mime, music, theater) that certain peoples take to be part of their own heritage and identity.

These cultural forms may also exist in the living memory of people who no longer engage in them. Absence of ongoing practice is not necessarily evidence of "culture loss" or "acculturation," because talk of past customs may become a vehicle for cultural continuity. And such contemporary discourses may reveal far more about black or indigenous history and identity than reified inscriptions in learned volumes about "genuine" (but "disappearing") Africans and Indians in the New World.

At the First Congress on Black Culture of the Americas, held in Cali, Colombia, in 1977, a prominent Ecuadorian folklorist presented a paper based on his extensive research on Afro-Ecuadorian "beliefs and superstitions." In his presentation he used the proverb, "*Lo que no tiene de inga tiene de mandinga*" ("that which is not of [the] Inca is of [the] mandinga"). This popular saying in Ecuador and Peru is a pejorative reference to the darkening of national history, implying essentially: "We are in this plight because of our Indian and African blood."

Ecuadorian blacks in attendance said that they deeply resented the use of this figure of speech as a way of asserting the mestizo character of Ecuadorian popular culture. They pointed to the lack of the Spanish article (*la*) before both Inca and Mandinga. This, they argued, demeaned the indigenous cultures of the Americas (bound up in the word "inga") and indigenous cultures of Africa (bound up in the word "mandinga") as something "vernacular," worthy of study only by folklorists, not by historians in the Latin American civilization. Still worse, *cultura negra*, or black culture in the Americas, is viewed as unrefined, inchoate, fragmented, and static, studied only to find "Africanisms" as scattered traits, reinterpretations, or syncretisms that suggest a bit of Africa retained and an enormous amount of "culture lost."

At the Cali congress, black people, well aware of these stereotypes and the power of racist symbols, insisted on using the term *la cultura negra:* sophisticated, existential, experiential, and adaptable black culture, in which entwined processes of tradition, history, and modernity spur ever higher levels of black civilization. "La cultura negra" comes from black people in black communities, but is the polar opposite of "popular culture." Blackness, they asserted, in all its flagrant dimensions, is to be cultivated and understood, not "studied" as a set of scattered artifacts.

In the "Black Americas" – from the Pacific lowlands of Colombia and Ecuador to Brazil, to Haiti, Cuba, and Puerto Rico – illuminating ethnic power often arises in mythical and religious contexts, taking the form of two forces derived from African deities: Ogún is iron; Shangó is fire. When united as male and female these images form a symbol of imminent transformation. If we are to understand the meanings of "blackness" in the African diaspora and elsewhere, we must sharpen our critical perspectives on cherished paradigms that were forged over the past five centuries on the anvil of Euro-American racism and in the fires of black liberation. In words from Puerto Rican lore: "At last, Ogún's machete that severs the heads of old myths has as his ally these times we are living, this convulsive new era when everything can be questioned, when to build the better societies to which we aspire we turn our sights toward the past, critically, vividly – cutting the brush from our way when necessary – to forge, firmly and forcefully, the future."

Norman Whitten

See Also

Pacific Coast of Colombia; Venezuela; Jamaica; Shango; Transculturation, Mestizaje, and the Cosmic Race: An Interpretation; Latin America, Blacks and Indians in: An Interpretation; Whitening; Black Power; Bermuda; Ogum.

North America

Black Panther Party, a militant black political organization originally known as the Black Panther Party for Self-Defense.

The Black Panther Party (BPP) was founded in Oakland, California, by Huey Newton and Bobby Seale in October 1966. Newton became the party's defense minister and Seale its chairman. The BPP advocated black self-defense and restructuring American society to make it more politically, economically, and socially equal.

Newton and Seale articulated their goals in a ten-point platform that demanded, among other items, full employment, exemption of black men from military service, and an end to police brutality. They summarized their demands in the final point: "We want land, bread, housing, education, clothing, justice, and peace." They adopted the black panther symbol from an independent political party established the previous year by black residents of Lowndes County, Alabama.

Both Newton and Seale were influenced by the black Muslim leader Malcolm X, who called on black people to defend themselves. They also supported the Black Power Movement, which stressed racial dignity and self-reliance. The BPP established patrols in black communities in order to monitor police activities and protect the residents from police brutality. The BPP affirmed the right of blacks to use violence to defend themselves and thus became an alternative to more moderate civil rights groups. Their militancy quickly attracted the support of many black residents of Oakland. Newton, who had studied law, objected strongly when police engaged in brutality, conducted illegal searches, and otherwise violated the civil rights of black citizens.

The BPP combined elements of socialism and Black Nationalism, insisting that if businesses and the government did not provide for full employment, the community should take over the means of production. It promoted the development of strong, black-controlled institutions, calling for blacks to work together to protect their rights and to improve their economic and social conditions. The BPP also emphasized class unity, criticizing the black middle class for acting against the interests of other, less fortunate blacks. The BPP welcomed alliances with white activists, such as the Students for a Democratic Society (SDS) and later the Weather Underground, because they believed that all revolutionaries who wanted to change United States society should unite across racial lines. This position differed from the views of many black organizations of the late 1960s, such as the Student Nonviolent Coordinating Committee (SNCC), which excluded white members after 1966.

The party first attracted attention in May 1967 when it protested a bill to outlaw carrying loaded weapons in public. Reporters quickly gathered around the contingent of protesters, who had marched on the California state capital in Sacramento armed with weapons and wearing the party's distinctive black leather jackets and black berets. After Seale read a statement, police arrested him and 30 others. News coverage of the incident attracted new recruits and led to the formation of chapters outside the San Francisco Bay Area. The BPP grew throughout the late 1960s and eventually had chapters all around the country.

Among those arrested in Sacramento was Eldridge Cleaver, a former convict who had recently published a book of essays called *Soul on Ice* (1967). Cleaver's influence in the party increased when Newton was arrested in October 1967 and charged with murder in the death of an Oakland police officer. Cleaver was a powerful speaker who took the lead in building the Free Huey Movement to defend Newton.

As part of this effort, Cleaver and Seale contacted Stokely Carmichael, the former chairman of SNCC and a nationally known proponent of Black Power. Carmichael agreed to become prime minister of the party and speak at Free Huey rallies during February 1968. The Free Huey movement allowed the BPP to expand its following nationally, particularly after it recruited well-known figures such as Carmichael and other SNCC members. The campaign on behalf of Newton saved him from the death penalty, but in September 1968 he was convicted of voluntary manslaughter and sentenced to 2 to 15 years in prison. This conviction was appealed and was overturned in 1970 due to procedural errors.

The SNCC-Panther alliance began to disintegrate in the summer of 1968 for a variety of reasons. Carmichael and other SNCC representatives had hoped to guide the less experienced Panthers but soon found that

Cleaver and Seale were forceful leaders who were not easily led. In addition, Carmichael wanted to end all ties with white activists because he believed that they stood in the way of black self-reliance and equality. He eventually broke with Panther leaders over the issue of white support. The BPP also had differences with followers of the southern California black nationalist Maulana Karenga, leader of a group called US. Panther leaders saw themselves as revolutionary nationalists who wanted all revolutionaries, regardless of race, to unite. They disparaged Karenga as a cultural nationalist who placed too much emphasis on racial unity. The escalating verbal battles between the two groups culminated in a gun battle in January 1969 at the University of California at Los Angeles that left two Panthers dead.

As racial tension increased around the country, the Federal Bureau of Investigation (FBI) blamed the Black Panthers for riots and other incidents of violence. The bureau launched a program called COINTELPRO (short for counterintelligence program) designed to disrupt efforts to unify black militant groups such as SNCC, BPP, and US. FBI agents sent anonymous threatening letters to Panthers, infiltrated the group with informers, and worked with local police to weaken the party. In December 1969 two Chicago leaders of the party, Fred Hampton and Mark Clark, were killed in a police raid. By the end of the decade, according to the party's attorney, 28 Panthers had been killed and many other members were either in jail or had been forced to leave the United States in order to avoid arrest. In 1970 Connecticut authorities began an unsuccessful effort to convict Seale and other Panthers of the murder of a Panther who was believed to have been a police informant. In New York, 21 Panthers were charged with plotting to assassinate police officers and blow up buildings. Chief of staff David Hilliard awaited trial on charges of threatening the life of President Richard Nixon. Cleaver left the United States for exile in CUBA to avoid returning to prison for parole violations.

After Newton's conviction was reversed, he sought to revive the party and reestablish his control by discouraging further police confrontations, calling instead for the development of survival programs in black communities to build support for the BPP. These programs provided free breakfasts for children, established free medical clinics, helped the homeless find housing, and gave away free clothing and food. In 1973 Seale also tried to build popular support for the party by running for mayor of Oakland. He was defeated but received over 40 percent of the vote.

This attempt to shift the direction of the party did not prevent further external attacks and internal conflicts, and the party continued to decline as a political force. Newton and Seale broke with Cleaver, who continued to support black revolution instead of community programs. Newton became debilitated by his increasing use of cocaine and other drugs, and in 1974 he fled to Cuba to avoid new criminal charges of drug use. In that same year, Seale resigned from the party.

After the departure of Newton and Seale, the party's new leader, Elaine Brown, continued to emphasize community service programs. These programs were frequently organized and run by black women, who were a majority in the party by the mid-1970s. By then most of the party's original leaders had left or had been expelled from the group. The BPP lost even more support after newspaper reports appeared describing the illicit activities of party leaders, including extortion schemes directed against Oakland merchants. By the end of the 1970s, weakened by external attacks, legal problems, and internal divisions, the BPP was no longer a political force.

TOP: Black Panther Party members at the Alameda County Courthouse in July 1968, as the murder trial of Panther leader Huey Newton begins. Newton was accused of killing an Oakland, California, policeman. *UPI/CORBIS-Bettmann*

ABOVE: Huey Newton, *center*, leader of the Black Panther Party, at a 1971 press conference following his meeting with Chinese leader Chou En-Lai. *CORBIS/Bettmann*

See Also
Cleaver, Eldridge Leroy; Newton, Huey P.; San Francisco and Oakland, California; Black Power.

North America

Black Power,

political movement expressing a new racial consciousness among blacks in the United States in the late 1960s. Black Power represented both a conclusion to the decade's Civil Rights Movement and a reaction against the racism that persisted despite the efforts of black activists during the early 1960s. Black Power was influential mainly in the late 1960s.

The meaning of Black Power was debated vigorously while the movement was in progress. To some it represented blacks' insistence on racial dignity and self-reliance, which was usually interpreted as economic and political independence, as well as freedom from white authority.

These themes had been advanced most forcefully in the early 1960s by Malcolm X, the articulate and controversial black Muslim leader. He argued that blacks should focus on improving their own communities rather than striving for complete integration, and that blacks had the right to retaliate against violent assaults. The publication of *The Autobiography of Malcolm X* (1965) created further support for the idea of black self-determination and had a strong influence on the emerging leaders of the Black Power Movement.

Other interpreters of Black Power emphasized the cultural heritage of blacks, especially the African roots of black identity. This view encouraged study and celebration of black history and culture. In the late 1960s black college students requested curricula in black studies that explored their distinctive culture and history. Led by the cultural critic Harold Cruse and the poet Amiri Baraka, some black intellectuals called for a cultural-nationalist perspective on literature, art, and history in the belief that blacks had separate values and ways of living. Blacks often expressed a sense of cultural nationalism by wearing loose, bright-colored African garments, called dashikis, and the natural "Afro" hairstyle.

Still another view of Black Power called for a revolutionary political struggle to reject racism and imperialism in the United States, as well as throughout the world. This interpretation encouraged the unity of nonwhites, including Hispanics and Asians, against their perceived oppressors. Revolutionary nationalists like Stokely Carmichael, later known as Kwame Turé, first advocated a worldwide Marxist revolution but later emphasized Pan-Africanism, the political and cultural unity of all people of African origins.

Black Power as a political idea originated with the Student Nonviolent Coordinating Committee (SNCC) in the mid-1960s. By 1965 many SNCC workers, frustrated at Southern whites' continued resistance to black civil rights, believed that any future progress could come only through independent black political power. When that faction took over the organization in 1966, with Carmichael leading the way, whites were ejected from SNCC membership.

Widespread use of the term *Black Power* started in June of 1966 during a protest march through Mississippi begun by James Meredith, who had been the first black to attend the University of Mississippi. Meredith was wounded by a sniper during the march and had to be hospitalized. Leaders of several civil rights organizations, including Carmichael and Martin Luther King Jr., took up the march. Along the route, Carmichael and SNCC activists exhorted marchers by demanding, "What do you want?" and then leading the response, "Black Power!"

The national media began to report on Black Power, which immediately drew condemnation from whites for its racially separatist message. Leaders of several black organizations, including the National Association for the Advancement of Colored People (NAACP), the National Urban League, and the Southern Christian Leadership Conference (SCLC), also denounced Black Power. As head of the SCLC, King, who many people viewed as the leader of blacks in the United States, voiced his disapproval of the threatening, antiwhite message often associated with Black Power. While encouraging blacks to be proud of their race and to appreciate their heritage, King advised them to "avoid the error of building a distrust for all white people."

From 1966 to 1969 SNCC and the Congress of Racial Equality (CORE), a New York-based civil rights organization, were dominated by Black Power. In 1966 and 1967 Carmichael and his successor as chairman of SNCC, H. Rap Brown, became well known as national spokespeople for Black Power. Brown once said, "Violence is as American as apple pie." Such statements were condemned by many whites and some blacks as efforts to instigate racial division and violence.

Opposition to Black Power became much stronger in 1968 when the Black Panther Party, which had been founded in Oakland, California, in 1966, became the most prominent organization advocating Black Power. Black Panthers battled with police departments in several major American cities between 1968 and 1970, and several of the group's leaders were killed, imprisoned, or made fugitives from the police. The party split in 1972, with some of its leaders favoring peaceful means to achieve its goals and others still urging revolution. Although Black Power as a movement largely disappeared after 1970, the idea remained a powerful one in the consciousness of black Americans.

See Also
Brown, Hubert G. ("H. Rap"); Cruse, Harold Wright; King, Martin Luther, Jr.; Meredith, James H.; San Francisco and Oakland, California.

Cross Cultural

Black Seminoles,

a Native American nation comprising Creek refugees and both free and enslaved blacks. For more information, *see* John Horse.

North America

Black Swan Records,

the first black-owned recording company specializing in "race records" – popular music, especially blues, recorded for a black audience.

In 1921 music publisher Harry Pace founded the Pace Phonographic Corporation. Black Swan Records, the division responsible for releasing Pace's records, was named for the nineteenth-century opera singer Elizabeth Taylor Greenfield, who was known as "the black swan." Pace hired up-and-coming bandleader Fletcher Henderson as recording director and composer William Grant Still as arranger and music director, and in May 1921 Black Swan released its first record. The success of Black Swan's early recordings, most notably "Down Home Blues," sung by Ethel Waters, led to the formation of the Black Swan Troubadours, a group led by Henderson and Waters that toured the South to promote the Black Swan label.

Pace purchased the Olympic Disc Record Corporation in 1922 to market music by black

Labels and record jackets from Black Swan specified that Black Swan records were made entirely by black people and featured only black voices. *Archive Photos*

BLACK TONY AWARD WINNERS

Year	Recipient	Category	Performance
1962	Diahann Carroll	Best Actress in a Musical	*No Strings*
1968	Leslie Uggams	Best Actress in a Musical	*Hallelujah, Baby!*
	Lillian Hayman	Best Supporting Actress in a Musical	*Hallelujah, Baby!*
	Pearl Bailey	Special Award	
1969	James Earl Jones	Best Actor in a Dramatic Play	*The Great White Hope*
	The Negro Ensemble Company	Special Award	
1970	Cleavon Little	Best Actor in a Musical	*Purlie*
	Melba Moore	Best Supporting Actress in a Musical	*Purlie*
1974	Virginia Capers	Best Actress in a Musical	*Raisin*
	Producer: The Negro Ensemble Company	Best Play	*The River Niger*
		Best Musical	*Raisin*
1975	John Kani & Winston Ntoshona	Best Actor in a Dramatic Play	*Sizwe Banzi Is Dead* and *The Island*
	Dee Dee Bridgewater	Best Supporting Actress in a Musical	*The Wiz*
	Ted Ross	Best Supporting Actor in a Musical	*The Wiz*
		Best Musical	*The Wiz*
1977	Trazana Beverly	Best Actress in a Featured Role in a Dramatic Play	*For Colored Girls Who Have Considered Suicide*
		Most Innovative Production of a Revival	*Porgy and Bess*
	Diana Ross	Special Award	
1978		Best Musical	*Ain't Misbehavin'*
	Nell Carter	Outstanding Performance by an Actress in a Featured Role in a Musical	*Ain't Misbehavin'*
1982	Jennifer Holiday	Outstanding Performance by an Actress in a Musical	*Dreamgirls*
	Cleavant Derricks	Outstanding Performance by a Featured Actor in a Musical	*Dreamgirls*
	Ben Harney	Outstanding Performance by an Actor in a Musical	*Dreamgirls*
1983	Charles "Honi" Coles	Outstanding Performance by a Featured Actor in a Musical	*My One and Only*
1987	James Earl Jones	Best Actor in a Play	*Fences*
1989	Ruth Brown	Best Actress in a Musical	*Black and Blue*
1991	Hinton Battle	Outstanding Actor in a Featured Role in a Musical	*Miss Saigon*
1992	Gregory Hines	Best Actor in a Musical	*Jelly's Last Jam*
	Laurence Fishburne	Outstanding Featured Actor in a Play	*Two Trains Running*
	Tonya Pinkins	Outstanding Featured Actress in a Play	*Jelly's Last Jam*

and white artists. Many African American patrons were disappointed by Pace's decision because it seemed to contradict his earlier declaration that Black Swan would have only African American stockholders, employees, and artists. Outmaneuvered by larger, white-owned recording companies such as Paramount and Okeh, which recognized the market potential of race records, Black Swan went bankrupt in 1923. In 1924 Paramount took over the Black Swan catalogue.

Aaron Myers

See Also
Blues, The.

North America

Black Theatre Alliance,

an association of small African American commercial theaters in New York City.

The Black Theatre Alliance (BTA) was founded in 1971 in New York City to support the artistic and financial development of small commercially owned African American theater companies. The alliance was formed partly as a result of the burgeoning African American commercial theater scene in the late 1960s, which had begun to flourish during the Black Arts Movement. Plays written in this period attempted to capture the frustration and anger felt by many African Americans by depicting whites' exploitation of blacks and seeking to create a strong black aesthetic in American theater.

Founded by playwrights Delano Stewart, Hazel Bryant, and Roger Furman, the Black Theatre Alliance initially comprised seven theater companies. To nurture the growth of these theaters, the alliance provided technical equipment, graphics, funds, resources, information, and touring assistance. The alliance compiled the *Black Theatre Resources Directory,* listing noncommercial black theater operations in the United States, theater technicians, administrators, artistic directors, and works by black playwrights. In 1972 the BTA began publishing a newsletter titled *Black Theatre Alliance* to encourage collaboration and to promote the activities of member theaters. In the mid-1970s, the BTA began admitting dance companies as members.

Zebulon Miletsky

See Also
New York, New York.

North America

Black Towns, **African American settlements in the United States.**

Although residential segregation is often considered one of the more harmful effects of racism in the United States, some African Americans in the nineteenth century chose to form their own racially separate communities. Unlike the ghettos and rural enclaves where many blacks at the time were forced to live, black towns were established to promote economic independence, self-government, and social equality for African Americans. More than 80 such towns were settled in the 50 years after the Civil War. A few, such as New Philadelphia, Illinois, were formed even before the Civil War, but it was not until after Emancipation that the population of free blacks was large enough to supply settlers for the new towns.

The first great wave of black migration began as Reconstruction ended in 1877. When federal troops withdrew from the

BLACK TOWNS
Black Towns still in existence
Black Towns no longer in existence
State Capital
0
300 km
Canada
Ottawa
Mexico
Cuba
Havana
Bahamas
Pacific Ocean
Atlantic Ocean
Gulf of Mexico
Lake Winnipeg
Lake Superior
Lake Michigan
Lake Huron
Lake Ontario
Lake Erie
Missouri
Columbia
Snake
Colorado
Ohio
Mississippi
Rio Grande
120°
105°
90°
75°
45°
30°
WASHINGTON
Olympia
OREGON
Salem
CALIFORNIA
Sacramento
Allensworth (now a state park)
Victorville
NEVADA
Carson City
IDAHO
Boise
MONTANA
Helena
WYOMING
Cheyenne
UTAH
Salt Lake City
COLORADO
Denver
ARIZONA
Phoenix
NEW MEXICO
Santa Fe
NORTH DAKOTA
Bismarck
SOUTH DAKOTA
Pierre
NEBRASKA
Lincoln
KANSAS
Nicodemus
Topeka
OKLAHOMA
Booker
Langston (Langston University)
Oklahoma City
Boley
Porter
Taft
Clearview
TEXAS
Austin
Kendleton
MINNESOTA
St. Paul
IOWA
Des Moines
MISSOURI
Jefferson City
ARKANSAS
Little Rock
LOUISIANA
North Shreveport
Grambling
Baton Rouge
WISCONSIN
Madison
ILLINOIS
Robbins
Brooklyn
Springfield
MICHIGAN
Lansing
INDIANA
Indianapolis
OHIO
Columbus
Urbancrest
KENTUCKY
Frankfort
TENNESSEE
Nashville
MISSISSIPPI
Mound Bayou
Jackson
ALABAMA
Montgomery
GEORGIA
Atlanta
FLORIDA
Tallahassee
Richmond Heights
SOUTH CAROLINA
Columbia
NORTH CAROLINA
Raleigh
VIRGINIA
Richmond
WEST VIRGINIA
Charleston
Washington, D.C.
MD.
Annapolis
Fairmont Heights and Glenarden
DELAWARE
Dover
PENNSYLVANIA
Harrisburg
NEW JERSEY
Trenton
Lawnside (originally named Free Haven)
Whitesboro
NEW YORK
Albany
CONN.
Hartford
R.I.
Providence
MASS.
Boston
VT.
Montpelier
N.H.
Concord
MAINE
Augusta

BLACK TOWNS IN THE TRANS-APPALACHIAN WEST

State	Town
Alabama	Cedarlake Greenwood Village Hobson City Plateau Shepherdsville
Arkansas	Edmondson Thomasville
California	Abila Allensworth Bowles Victorville
Colorado	Dearfield
Illinois	Brooklyn Robbins
Iowa	Buxton
Kansas	Nicodemus
Kentucky	Camp Nelson New Zion
Louisiana	Grambling North Shreveport
Maryland	Fairmount Heights Glenarden Lincoln City
Michigan	Idlewind Marlborough
Mississippi	Expose Mound Bayou Renova
Missouri	Kinloch
New Jersey	Lawnside Gouldtown Springtown Whitesboro
New Mexico	Blackdom
Ohio	Lincoln Heights Urbancrest
Oklahoma	Arkansas Colored Bailey Boley Booktee Colored Canadian Chase Clearview Ferguson Forman Gibson Station Grayson Langston City Lewisville Liberty Lima Mantu Marshalltown North Fork Colored Overton Porter Redbird Taft Tatum Tullahassee Vernon Wellston Colony Wybark Two unnamed towns in the Seminole Nation
South Carolina	Bennetaville
Tennessee	Hortense New Bedford
Texas	Andy Board House Booker Independence Heights Kendleton Mill City Oldham Roberts Union City
Virginia	Lloyd Place Pleasant Hill Saratoga Place
West Virginia	Institute

Source: K.M Hamilton, *Black Towns and Profit: Promotion and Development in the Trans-Appalachian West, 1877-1915* (1991)

South, many blacks feared that the civil and political rights they had recently acquired would disappear as well. In addition, most African Americans in the South faced limited educational and economic opportunities. Many heeded the call of Benjamin "Pap" Singleton, a former slave and UNDERGROUND RAILROAD "conductor" whose publicity tours and promotional posters helped inspire what historians call the Kansas Fever of the late 1870s.

Tens of thousands of African American EXODUSTERS left their homes bound for Singleton's Cherokee County colony or Nicodemus, in Graham County, Kansas. Nicodemus was founded in 1877 by a corporation of seven members, six of whom were black. Circulars promoting the town as the "Promised Land" were posted throughout the South (particularly in Tennessee, Kentucky, and Mississippi), and founders hosted visits by potential settlers. By 1879 the town's population stood at about 700. After enduring a decade of harsh weather and bad crops, the town's residents were crushed by the 1887 announcement that the Union Pacific Railroad would bypass Nicodemus. In a fate shared by most black towns that failed to attract a rail line, Nicodemus soon dwindled and died.

Founded in 1904, Boley, Oklahoma, escaped the trouble that had doomed Nicodemus. Railroad access and arable land helped Boley – one of at least 20 black towns in Oklahoma – to thrive. By 1907 it had at least 1000 residents, and twice that many farmers settled outside of town. In addition, Boley boasted several businesses and churches and an industrial school. Booker T. Washington, who played an important role in the success of another black town, MOUND BAYOU, MISSISSIPPI, praised Boley as a paragon of black self-help. Its boom soon ended, however, as the Democratic Party gained control in Oklahoma, which achieved statehood in 1907. With the imposition of JIM CROW segregation and discrimination, Boley's residents found themselves effectively disfranchised and their town at the mercy of a hostile state government.

Most black towns were founded for the same reasons that white or biracial towns were – to exploit natural resources, provide opportunities for settlers, and make money for speculators. Black towns, however, shared certain unique characteristics. Black settlers sought not only to find economic and social freedom but to embody ideals of racial uplift. Established in 1908, Allensworth, California, was billed as a "model city," a "school of citizenship" to showcase African American respectability, industry, and initiative. Allensworth's charter, like that of many black towns, prohibited prostitution, gambling, and the sale of alcohol. Such goals, seen as accommodationist, were criticized by some African American leaders, such as Ida B. Wells. But black towns were also a nurturing environment, shielding residents from the everyday racism of white society and offering them opportunities not available in more diverse environments.

Kate Tuttle

SEE ALSO
Slavery in the United States; Allensworth, Allen; Civil War, American; Singleton, Benjamin ("Pap"); Thirteenth Amendment of the United States Constitution and the Emancipation Proclamation; Washington, Booker Taliaferro; Wells-Barnett, Ida Bell.

North America

Black Vernacular English,

a dialect of spoken English characteristic of segments of the African American population; a distinctive, orally based language with roots in African and African American history and culture.

Black vernacular English, or Black English, is fundamentally a spoken language. In fact, it is several distinct languages, encompassing the vernacular speech of blacks in the United States, the Caribbean, Great Britain, and elsewhere. Each of these black vernacular languages emerged within a particular racial and cultural context. Most significant, the roots of Black English lie in the experience of slavery and in the cultural collision between a panoply of African languages and an English-speaking dominant culture. This essay focuses on the spoken English of blacks in the United States, which since the 1960s has been the subject of increased attention and occasional controversy.

Black English is not substandard English – it is *nonstandard* English. Grounded in an oral tradition and subject to continuous innovation, it is not easily codified or reduced to formal rules. Yet as linguist William Labov made clear in a groundbreaking series of essays during the mid-1960s and early 1970s – in particular, *Language in the Inner City: Studies in the Black English Vernacular* (1972) – Black English has its own linguistic structure and its own rules of usage. As linguist Geneva Smitherman explained in *Talkin and Testifyin* (1986), the "main structural components" of Black English are "based on African language rules." She noted a number of rules of usage that are shared by West African languages and Black English, including:

Repetition of noun subject with pronoun: My father, he work there

Same form of noun for singular and plural: one boy; five boy

Same verb form for all subjects: I know; you know; he know; we know; they know

The best known characteristic of Black English is its treatment of the verb "to be," especially the lack of verb conjugation in the present tense – I be, you be, he be, we be, they be.

In addition, some African Americans retained more substantial elements of African languages into the twentieth century. This was true of the GULLAH dialect of the Sea Islands off the Georgia and South Carolina coast, an area distinguished by its black majority and relative isolation. But in *The Origin of American Black English* (1996), Traute Ewers concluded on the basis of quantitative linguistic analysis of black use of the verb "to be" that Black English probably did not originate in the Gullah or some other Creole language. What remains unclear are the actual processes by which Black English did take form.

In part, however, Black English would appear to reflect a process of cultural diffusion among African slaves, speaking many different tongues, trapped within a predominantly English-speaking culture. Thus, some African expressions filtered into the usage of the majority culture. For example, the term *jook* (or "juke") – as in jook (or juke) joint or juke box – derives from the *juke* or *joog* of the Gullah dialect. Originally a West African word – as in the Wolof *dzug* or the Bambara *dzugu* – it connoted a disreputable or wicked way of living, an apt description of the wild and raucous jook joints, rural Southern roadhouses where African Americans gathered to listen to music, dance, drink, and have a good time.

When African Americans first arrived in the New World, they came as slaves under the power of white owners who, in furthering their control, often tried to prevent the use of African speech by intermixing slaves who spoke different languages and by insisting on the use of English. Not surprisingly, then, what distinguishes Black English is not its maintenance of African languages but rather its distinctive adaptation of English. Yet Black English is more than the linguistic adjustments made by African individuals newly introduced into Anglo-American culture.

One of the constant and determinative qualities of Black English, from the days of slavery to the present, is its oppositional nature. From the first, African Americans confronted the reality of white power and the need to avoid or subvert white domination. Slaveholders and other whites, constantly fearful of slave rebellions, maintained ongoing surveillance of the African American population, attempting to prevent unauthorized gatherings of blacks and listening in on slave conversations.

Anthropologist James Scott has noted that slaves circumvented this scrutiny by using "linguistic codes, dialects, and gestures" that were "opaque to the masters and mistresses." Black English continues to reflect these power realities and sharply delineates those who are within and those who lie without the group boundaries. In mid-twentieth-century black slang, whites were "ofays," pig latin for foes. As linguist Roger D. Abrahams observed, many African Americans believe that "Black English has been maintained... because whites cannot understand it."

Black English also took shape as a critique of white society, although its protest was of necessity indirect. In the early twentieth century, ZORA NEALE HURSTON noted that the language patterns of African Americans "were characterized by indirect, veiled social comment and criticism, a technique appropriately described as hitting a straight lick with a crooked stick." More recently, comedian Richard Pryor remarked, "Niggers just have a way of telling you stuff and not telling you stuff. Martians would have a difficult time with Niggers. They be translating words, saying a whole lot of things underneath you, all around you." Similarly, linguist Claudia Mitchell-Kernan found that "some element of indirection" was the key feature of "signifying," a large class of verbal interplay that was important in shaping African American vernacular.

Black slang is inventive, continually creating new words and phrases. During the 1930s, for example, a person who was attuned to the latest developments in JAZZ was termed a "hep cat" or a "hepster." By the mid-1940s "hepster" had given way to "hipster," and a decade later, black hipsters had become "cats" and had coined a derisive term for white hangers-on to the jazz life, "hippies," which would later be appropriated by white culture and put to a very different use. Roger Abrahams noted that one explanation for the rapid turnover in black slang was this constant white borrowing or raiding. Black English reveals sharp spatial as well as temporal variations. Abrahams observed that the same ritual of competitive insults that was termed "jiving" in mid-1960s Philadelphia was to an older generation "jitterbugging" or "bugging," and on the West Coast was called "shucking."

During the 1930s and 1940s black slang was known as jive, and jazz musicians were among the most inventive sources for the jive lexicon. In 1938 band leader Cab Calloway published the *Hepster's Dictionary*, which the New York Public Library long employed as its official reference work on jive. Tenor saxophonist Lester Young, whose lyrical playing had a profound influence on the shape of jazz improvisation, had an equally fertile mind for language. He gave singer BILLIE HOLIDAY her nickname, Lady Day. To Young, heroin addicts were "needle dancers," and anything depressing or downbeat was "von Hangman." His general term for whites was "grey boys"; African Americans were "oxford greys." When he encountered bigoted or racist attitudes, he would remark, "I feel a draft." Although many of Young's expressions gained currency in the 1930s and 1940s, none continues in use today.

Besides having a characteristic grammar and a changing vocabulary, Black English is marked by its distinctive approach to rhythm. In contemporary America the most important shapers of Black English are hip hop culture and RAP music. Rap, in particular, exemplifies the close links between African American language and rhythm. But the rhythmic qualities of Black English long antedate the hip hop beat; the root or source of this distinctive rhythmic approach lies in the cultures of West Africa. In America this influence has been particularly evident in the Black Church and in African American conventions of phrasing and delivery in preaching, praying, and, singing. Since the 1960s a number of African American comedians, including Dick Gregory, Richard Pryor, and EDDIE MURPHY, acquainted a larger white audience not only with African American expressions but also with the distinctive rhythms of black humor.

These comics have drawn upon a rich tradition of black male street talk that shares much with stand-up comedy, including an expectation of playing to an audience and an emphasis on fast-paced and humorous verbal repartee. A distinctive rhythmic quality can be seen in such African American folk traditions as toasts, which are often rhymed as well as metrically ordered verbal performances, or the "dozens." The dozens is a competitive exchange of insults directed toward the participants' mothers and occasionally toward other members of the opponents' families.

Historian Lawrence Levine noted that the dozens serves two large purposes – it sharpens verbal skills and it tests self-discipline. It emerged, Levine argued, "at a time when black Americans were especially subject to insults and assaults upon their dignity to which they could not safely respond," and it served to hone "the ability to control emotions and anger; an ability which was often necessary for survival." Levine also suggested that if during the past few decades the dozens "has become more exclusively a vehicle for adolescents and juveniles," this shift may reflect the "expansion of opportunities for black adults to express their discontent in a variety of ways." The dozens may someday come to resemble the nursery rhymes of the white population, which once conveyed significant political commentary but now give amusement to toddlers.

Since the 1960s Black English has existed on three different levels: as an aspect of black American culture; as a topic of voluminous research by linguists, educators, and other academics; and as a controversial public policy issue. The policy aspect of Black English was made prominent in the heated 1996 debate over the proposed teaching of "ebonics," or Black English, in the Oakland, California, public schools. This conflict pitted advocates of Black English, and those favoring multicultural approaches in general, against those who insisted upon standard English as a necessary source of cultural homogeneity.

In the end, the Oakland school system chose not to mandate Black English as part of its curriculum and conceded that that the primary role of public schools is to teach standard English. At the same time, the Oakland controversy served as a reminder that at least some African Americans harbor doubts as to whether the public schools truly understand and respect the linguistic backgrounds of all their students.

In any case, formal instruction is unlikely to have much impact on black vernacular speech. Several significant factors sustain a distinct African American vernacular. It offers a positive source of identity and pride to many African Americans. It grows out of underlying cultural and political realities that over the past generation have not greatly changed. Black English will continue to have a functional role as long as there are racially based differences in power and access to the benefits of American society. Above all, the continued vitality of Black English seems assured by the emergence since 1980 of rap music and hip hop culture. As long as African Americans continue to live in their own communities, attend their own churches, seek out their own forms of music, entertainment, and recreation, and value the expressiveness of their own linguistic voice, Black English is certain to endure.

James Clyde Sellman

See Also

Calloway, Cabell (Cab); Young, Lester Willis ("Prez"); Dozens, The; Gregory, Richard Claxton "Dick"; Hip Hop in the United States; Pryor, Richard Franklin Lenox Thomas; San Francisco and Oakland, California; Slave Rebellions in Latin America and the Caribbean.

North America

Blackwell, Unita

(b. March 18, 1933, Lula, Miss.), American civil rights activist and politician who advocated affordable housing for African Americans and became the first African American woman mayor in Mississippi.

Unita Blackwell, the daughter of sharecroppers, was born March 18, 1933, in Lula, Mississippi. Although she never attended high school, Blackwell eventually earned a master's degree in regional planning from the University of Massachusetts-Amherst. She began her civil rights work in the early 1960s in Mayersville, Mississippi. At that time she supported herself by chopping cotton for three dollars a day. When civil rights workers came to Mayersville encouraging voter registration among African Americans, Blackwell was one of the first to register. She was fired shortly thereafter for urging others to register.

Blackwell then began working for the Student Nonviolent Coordinating Committee (SNCC), registering voters, leading boycotts and protests, and initiating civil proceedings to stop discriminatory practices in the state. The most notable case was the landmark *Blackwell* v. *Board of Education* in 1965 and 1966, which furthered school desegregation. Blackwell was also a founding member of the Mississippi Freedom Democratic Party (MFDP), which protested the Democratic Party's seating of Mississippi's all-white delegation at the 1964 Democratic National Convention in Atlantic City, New Jersey.

Through her civil rights work, Blackwell became an expert on rural housing and development, about which she lectured and launched projects to gain home ownership for low-income families. In 1976 she worked successfully to incorporate the town of Mayersville. Later that year she was elected mayor, becoming the first African American woman mayor in Mississippi – in a town where she was formerly prohibited from voting. She held this position until 1993. After serving as a town alderman, she was reelected mayor of Mayersville in 1997. She was also elected chair of the National Conference of Black Mayors in 1989, and in 1992 received a MacArthur Foundation Fellowship.

Robert Fay

See Also

Civil Rights Movement.

North America

Black Women's Club Movement

clubs, associations, and sororities that African American women have founded, many of which emphasize public service and promote social, racial, and gender equality.

For nearly 200 years clubs, mutual aid societies, sororities, and organizations established by African American women have played active and positive roles in communities across the United States and throughout the diaspora. In 1818 members of the Colored Female Religious and Moral Society of Salem, Massachusetts, declared that they had formed their organization to "be charitably watchful over each other." This phrase captures the spirit of cooperative work that has characterized most of these organizations, which often made available needed social services to black women, children, and families. At the same time, members of these organizations have frequently been middle- and upper-middle-class women seeking to provide role models and opportunities for less fortunate sisters – in the words of one well-known slogan, "Lifting As We Climb."

The Salem Society was one of many small local associations that existed during the nineteenth century. Most of the earliest ones were located in free black communities in northeastern cities – Philadelphia alone had 27 by 1830 (*see* Early African American Women's Organizations). Some of these early organizations were mutual-relief associations that allowed members to pool their small resources. Others were benevolent societies, in which women who belonged worked to help people in their communities. Still others were literary societies, where women wrote poetry and essays to share with one another, often giving them a rare forum to express their political opinions.

The clubs grew in importance after Reconstruction, when the few social services that the government had begun providing for ex-slaves were eliminated. At the same time, black women were quickly realizing that the gains the Fourteenth and Fifteenth Amendments had brought to black men did not extend to them, and that the clubs were some of the only places where women could become leaders and speak out for change. In 1895, after a white Southern journalist wrote a widely publicized letter accusing activist Ida B. Wells-Barnett in particular and black women in general of "having no sense of virtue and of being altogether without character," another purpose for the black women's groups began to emerge: to defend black womanhood.

Women from across the country responded to this letter by calling a conference in Boston to discuss ways to combine their efforts. Their 1895 meeting led to the founding of the National Association of Colored

Women (NACW), the first national black organization. The new prominence of the clubwomen's movement and the corresponding surge in public activity and activism by black women helped define the 1890s as the Woman's Era in African American history. In addition to Wells-Barnett, such clubwomen as Josephine St. Pierre Ruffin, Mary Church Terrell, and Margaret Murray Washington reached national audiences with their messages of social responsibility and racial uplift.

New types of women's organizations began to appear just after the turn of the century. The Associations for the Protection of Negro Women (later the National League for the Protection of Colored Women), founded in 1904, helped black Southern women migrants find decent jobs and safe housing in the North. Alpha Kappa Alpha, the first black sorority, was founded at Howard University in 1908, and soon Delta Sigma Theta, Zeta Phi Beta, and Sigma Gamma Rho were added to the spectrum of black women's clubs (*see* Fraternities and Sororities, Black, in the United States). By this point, the club movement was solidly defined as middle class, and professional organizations began to spring up alongside the college sororities. But most clubs, including the sororities, continued to emphasize a commitment to service.

In the mid-twentieth century, activist Mary McLeod Bethune changed the clubs' scope yet again as she began to explore their potential for influencing real political change. After serving as president of the NACW during the 1920s, in 1935 she founded the National Council of Negro Women (NCNW), a new umbrella organization that emphasized political activism. The NCNW immediately began lobbying for domestic and international causes, such as the founding of the Federal Employment Practices Commission and the establishment of the United Nations. Under president Dorothy I. Height, it has become an international organization that works to support black women across the diaspora.

The network of black women's clubs, sororities, and professional societies remains strong today. The NACW, now the National Association of Colored Women's Clubs, celebrated its 100th anniversary in 1996, and like the NCNW has branches across the country. Modern clubs and sororities provide college scholarships to young women, run women's employment resource centers, and sponsor preschools and health clinics in underserved areas. They also continue to provide African American women with an important space for networking, supporting, and fellowshiping with one another as they work together toward common goals, still inspired to lift as they climb.

Lisa Clayton Robinson

See Also

Fifteenth Amendment to the U.S. Constitution; Fourteenth Amendment to the U.S. Constitution; Free Blacks in the United States, 1619 to 1863; Height, Dorothy; National Council of Negro Women; Ruffin, Josephine Saint Pierre; Terrell, Mary Eliza Church; Wells-Barnett, Ida Bell.

North America

Black World/Negro Digest,

the first successful black-owned general interest magazine and the foundation publication of Johnson Publishing Company.

While working for an insurance company, college student John H. Johnson prepared a summary of news about the African American community for distribution among the company's upper managers. Believing that this same news could be marketed to African Americans, who had been largely ignored by the mainstream press, Johnson began publishing *Negro Digest*. The first issue reached newsstands in 1942.

Similar in format to *Reader's Digest*, *Negro Digest* initially reprinted articles, mostly general-interest pieces about African American life, from other periodicals. Soon, however, the magazine began publishing original articles and essays, including the popular feature "If I Were a Negro," which featured pieces by famous white people, including First Lady Eleanor Roosevelt. By the end of 1943, *Negro Digest* had a weekly circulation of 50,000. The magazine's success led Johnson, whose initial one-man operation had grown to become the Johnson Publishing Company, to develop other magazines, including the short-lived *Copper Romance*, *Tan Confessions*, and *Black Stars* and the successful and enduring *Ebony* and *Jet*. *Negro Digest*'s popularity dwindled, however, and the company ceased publishing it in 1951.

Ten years later Johnson resumed publication of *Negro Digest*, hiring Hoyt W. Fuller to serve as managing editor. During the 1960s Fuller gradually changed the publication's editorial focus, transforming it from a general-interest, racially integrationist magazine into a literary periodical that explored Black Nationalism. Editorials examined the connection between literature and politics, and the magazine featured the work of both famous and lesser-known African American writers, making it a major voice in the debate about the direction of African American literature, culture, and politics. But much of this revolutionary attitude among blacks waned during the mid-1970s, and the magazine, which had been renamed *Black World* in 1970, declined in popularity and profitability. Its last issue was published in April 1976.

Robert Fay

See Also

Ebony; *Jet*.

North America

Blake, James Hubert ("Eubie")

(b. February 7, 1883, Baltimore, Md.; d. February 12, 1983, New York, N.Y.), African American jazz pianist and composer.

Eubie Blake was the son of John Sumner Black and Emily Johnston Black, both former slaves. He began organ lessons at age six and was playing ragtime piano professionally in Baltimore bordellos and saloons just ten years later. Around this time he composed "Charleston Rag." In his early twenties he began playing in Atlantic City, New Jersey, where he composed another of his popular songs, "Tricky Fingers."

After his introduction to legendary ragtime and stride piano players Willie "the Lion" Smith, Luckey Roberts, and James P. Johnson, Blake's piano playing matured as he combined a melodic ragtime style with waltzes and comic operas of the time. His playing was noted for its broken-octave parts, sophisticated chord progressions, and altered blues chords. Both Johnson and Fats Waller later used Blake's songs extensively in their repertoires.

In 1916 James Reese Europe, leader of the popular World War I 369th Infantry Band, advised Blake and singer Noble Sissle to collaborate. They became a piano and vocalist team called the Dixie Duo, performing in vaudeville shows and writing music together. In 1921 they joined with the comedy duo of Flournoy Miller and Aubrey Lyles to write a Broadway show, *Shuffle Along*, which was so popular that three separate companies toured the United States simultaneously performing it. This show ran continuously on Broadway until 1928.

In 1924 Sissle and Blake teamed with Lew Payton to create *In Bamville*, later renamed *The Chocolate Dandies*. The show lasted until 1925, when Sissle and Blake returned to the vaudeville stages of the United States, Great Britain, and France. In 1927 the partnership ended when Blake returned to the United States while Sissle remained in Europe. Though he wrote and produced a number of shows in the 1930s, none ever attained the success of *Shuffle Along* or *Chocolate Dandies*.

Blake also had a successful career as a band leader. In 1919, after James Reese Europe's death, Blake took over his band. During World War II, Blake and his band performed extensively for United States troops in USO shows. While Harry Truman campaigned for president in 1948, Blake's song, "I'm Just Wild About Harry," which he wrote for *Shuffle Along*, became popular. In 1946 he began to study formal composition in semi-retirement, although he appeared in several ragtime revival shows in the 1950s.

In 1969 Blake released a recording, *The Eighty-Six Years of Eubie Blake*, and was once again in demand. He spent much of his time

FAR LEFT: American jazz composer and pianist James Hubert "Eubie" Blake, age 98, at the Songwriters Hall of Fame in New York in 1980. *Tim Boxer/Archive Photos*

LEFT: American drummer and bandleader Art Blakey was a major exponent of the intense style of jazz known as hard bop. *Tim Boxer/Archive Photos*

lecturing at colleges and playing concerts and JAZZ festivals. To preserve piano rags and the songs of the 1920s, he formed his own recording company in 1972. In all, Blake wrote over 300 songs, among which are the popular "Tickle the Ivories," "Memories of You," "Chevy Chase," "Loving You the Way I Do," and "Love Will Find a Way." In 1978 *Eubie!*, a revue-style show based on his life, was performed on Broadway.

In addition to the numerous honorary degrees and awards Blake received throughout his life, he was awarded the Presidential Medal of Freedom in 1981. Eubie Blake died on February 12, 1983, five days after his 100th birthday.

Robert Fay

See Also

World War II and African Americans; Waller, Thomas Wright ("Fats").

North America

Blakey, Art (b. October 11, 1919, Pittsburgh, Pa.; d. October 16, 1990, New York, N.Y.), African American JAZZ musician, innovator of bop drumming, and leader of the Jazz Messengers.

As a drummer and bandleader, Art Blakey had a profound impact on the shape of modern jazz. During the late 1940s, along with Kenny Clarke and Max Roach, he was one of the creators of modern jazz drumming. His long-standing group, the Jazz Messengers (1955-1990) – together with Miles Davis's quintet with John Coltrane, the Max Roach-Clifford Brown quintet, and the Horace Silver quintet – popularized the style known as hard bop. Hard bop draws equally on the harmonic and rhythmic complexity of bebop and on the visceral sounds and simpler rhythms that characterize THE BLUES and GOSPEL MUSIC. In an interview published in the *Black Perspective in Music,* Blakey summed up his approach simply, declaring that he wanted to play music that would "wash away the dust of everyday life."

Blakey was also one of the great talent scouts of jazz. During his 35 years as leader of the Jazz Messengers, he nurtured countless young jazz musicians, many of whom later became leaders in their own right. His discoveries included trumpeters WYNTON MARSALIS, Lee Morgan, and Freddie Hubbard; saxophonists Wayne Shorter, Jackie McLean, and Branford Marsalis; trombonist Curtis Fuller; and pianists Bobby Timmons, Cedar Walton, and Keith Jarrett.

Blakey was working in a Pittsburgh-area steel mill when he first began his musical career, playing the piano in small local clubs. But he gave up the piano after hearing Erroll Garner, who was then a local jazz pianist, and turned instead to playing the drums. In 1939 he briefly toured with Fletcher Henderson's big band, and he rejoined Henderson in 1943-1944. When Blakey arrived in New York City in the early 1940s, pianist Thelonious Monk took him in and introduced him to the city's jazz scene. In 1947 Blakey joined Monk on some of the pianist's early recordings. Blakey first gained notice as a bop innovator during his stint from 1944 to 1947 with singer Billy Eckstine's orchestra, which featured such bop luminaries as saxophonists Charlie Parker and Dexter Gordon and trumpeters Dizzy Gillespie, Miles Davis, and Fats Navarro.

Like many musicians of the era, Blakey developed an interest in Islam. During the late 1940s he led a modern jazz big band, Art Blakey and the Seventeen Messengers, composed primarily of Muslim musicians. In 1947 Blakey recorded with a nine-piece band that was drawn, in part, from the larger ensemble. His interest in Islam resulted in a 1948 journey to West Africa, where he studied Islamic religion and culture as well as African drumming. Eventually, he took the Islamic name Abdullah Ibn Buhaina, from which came his nickname, "Bu." Following his sojourn, Blakey incorporated a variety of African drumming techniques into his music, including the pressing of one elbow on the drumhead to alter the drum's pitch and the use of polyrhythms.

In 1955 Blakey was part of the quintet known as the Jazz Messengers. In addition to Blakey on drums, it featured Horace Silver on piano, Kenny Dorham on trumpet, Hank Mobley on tenor saxophone, and Doug Watkins on bass. The group had many different members over the years; yet despite these changes, it retained its identity through Blakey's constant presence and forceful leadership. Jackie McLean told *New York Times* jazz critic Peter Watrous that of the many leaders he had worked with – including the formidable Miles Davis and Charles Mingus – Blakey had taught him the most, "[n]ot just [about] how to be a musician, but about being a man and keeping a sense of responsibility."

James Clyde Sellman

See Also

Coltrane, John William; Davis, Miles Dewey, III; Eckstine, William Clarence (Billy), Gillespie, John Birks ("Dizzy"); Gordon, Dexter Keith; Henderson, Fletcher Hamilton, Jr.; Mingus, Charles, Jr.; Monk, Thelonious Sphere; New York, New York; Parker, Charles Christopher ("Bird"); Roach, Maxwell Lemuel (Max).

North America

Bland, Bobby ("Blue") (b. January 27, 1930, Rosemark, Tenn.), African American bluesman and songwriter.

Born in rural Rosemark, Tennessee, Bobby "Blue" Bland gravitated to Memphis as a teen, at a time when RHYTHM AND BLUES was beginning to gain popularity. Bland sang with the Pilgrim Travelers, a gospel group, before joining the Beale Streeters, a loose ensemble of R&B pioneers that included Johnny Ace and B. B. King. In his early recordings on Modern Records, Bland imitated the sounds of King as well as those of Nat King Cole.

Bland served in the United States Army from 1952 to 1954, a tour of duty that slowed his career. When he returned to Memphis, he found that his old friends were already prospering as musicians. Slowly he returned to the scene, recording his best work between the mid-1950s and the early 1960s on the Duke Records label. Hits from the time included "Cry Cry Cry" and "Turn On Your Lovelight." Bland developed a distinctive sound, blending big-band influences, Memphis blues, and smooth vocals redolent of Frank Sinatra.

After scoring 37 R&B hits during the 1960s, Bland was outshone by a new generation of performers, and his incorporation of disco in the 1970s met with limited success. Although he succeeded in refreshing his career with a 1983 release, *Here We Go Again*, his most important contributions to popular music remain the ones that he made 40 years earlier.

Eric Bennett

See Also

Blues, The; Cole, Nat ("King"); Gospel Music; King, Riley B. ("B. B."); Memphis, Tennessee.

Blanqueamiento. Please see Whitening

North America

Blaxploitation Films, popular film genre of the 1970s that depicted African American heroes defying an oppressive system.

In the early 1970s an American film genre began to crystallize from different elements in the American political and cultural scene. At the center of the new genre was a new kind of hero: a black, urban, poor male striking back at a system that had denied him basic rights and respect. Set in the dense urban landscape of black America, these films gave a vision of America different from the one typically portrayed by mainstream Hollywood cinema.

The term *blaxploitation* was first coined to describe Gordon Parks Jr.'s *Superfly* (1972). Two earlier films are frequently cited as forerunners of the genre: Melvin Van Peebles's *Sweet Sweetback's Baadasssss Song* (1971), and Gordon Parks Sr.'s *Shaft* (1971). Throughout the 1970s it is estimated that some 150 films were made within the blaxploitation genre.

Drawing upon both the mainstream marketability of action films and the growing Black Power Movement, blaxploitation films were popularly well-received, if not always critically acclaimed. In these films, the black hero fought back and won, often against overwhelming odds. Filled with fast-paced action, the plot usually involved a male hero, or antihero, who found it necessary to renounce the system and resort to violence. These films portrayed a virile black male sexuality that had been missing in both mainstream and African American cinema up to that point. A few films, such as *Coffy* (1973) with Pam Grier, featured female protagonists.

Blaxploitation films drew criticism for resorting to formulas and portraying unrealistic scenarios, and were actively opposed by a coalition that included the National Association for the Advancement of Colored People (NAACP). Many critics felt that the films were too simplistic to offer any kind of viable model for African American resistance to an oppressive system. Others noted that the character development, particularly of women, was limited. Some, such as black psychiatrist Alvin Poussaint, saw the films as dangerous for their glorification of criminal life and machismo, and as ultimately destructive to the black community.

For director Melvin Van Peebles, however, this was not the point. The blaxploitation film's attraction was that "the black audience finally gets a chance to see some of their own fantasies acted out – [it's] about rising out of the mud and kicking ass."

The films were oriented specifically toward black urban audiences, who made the blaxploitation film a lucrative business. Made on low budgets, the films were proven financial successes for the studios, with *Shaft* making more than $16 million for MGM. Inner-city youth imitated the fashions and hairstyles worn in the films, and soundtracks, such as Curtis Mayfield's score for *Superfly*, achieved wide popularity.

Although most critics place the term *blaxploitation* within the 1970s, the genre had a noted effect on later films. Major film studios continued to produce "against the odds" action-packed films. Later works by John Singleton and Mario Van Peebles, Melvin's son, were influenced by the political concerns of blaxploitation, and continued to portray African American life in the inner city.

Marian Aguiar

See Also

Mayfield, Curtis; Parks, Gordon, Jr.; Parks, Gordon, Sr.; Poussaint, Alvin Francis; Van Peebles, Melvin; Film, Blacks in American.

North America

Bledsoe, Julius C. (Jules) (b. December 29, 1898, Waco, Tex.; d. July 14, 1943, Hollywood, Calif.), African American baritone who originated the role of Joe in *Show Boat*.

Julius Bledsoe received bachelor's degrees in history, composition, and piano in 1918 from Bishop College. He continued his study of voice in the United States and Europe, and made his professional debut at Aeolian Hall in New York in 1924.

In 1927 Bledsoe originated the role of Joe in Jerome Kern's *Show Boat*. Over the next decade and a half, he performed throughout the United States and Europe. He was also a composer, and his position on the music staff of the Roxy Theater made him the first African American to be continually employed by a Broadway theater.

Lisa Clayton Robinson

See Also

New York, New York.

Africa

Blondy, Alpha (b. January 1, 1953, Dimbokro, Côte d'Ivoire), popular African reggae singer.

With his 11 albums and worldwide tours, Alpha Blondy has brought an African flavor to the Jamaican-born musical genre of reggae. Although critics admit that Blondy has not yet fulfilled his early goal of becoming the next Bob Marley (probably the best-known reggae artist), they do hail the Côte d'Ivoire singer's passionate lyrics and charismatic performances.

The man born Seydou Kone was renamed Blondy, a variation on the Dioula word for bandit, by his grandmother, who raised him. Though little is known of his childhood, Blondy says he chose his new first name, Alpha, himself, and that he learned French from reading the Bible (though his grandmother also introduced him to the Muslim holy book, the Koran). He was expelled from school, reportedly for forming his first reggae band, the Atomic Vibrations. Eventually Blondy moved to New York City, where he studied and worked and continued to learn about reggae, often performing Bob Marley songs at Harlem nightclubs.

When he returned to the Côte d'Ivoire, Blondy began to make a name for himself as one of the boldest contemporary singers, dealing with such controversial subjects as police brutality and race relations. His first album, *Jah Glory* (1983), was a hit throughout West Africa. Blondy also sings in French, English, and Dioula, and with later releases he has extended his popularity worldwide. With his insistence on positive, loving images (he says his songs "are all really love songs") and his commitment to social justice, Blondy is among the world's most popular reggae performers and one of Africa's biggest recording stars.

Kate Tuttle

See Also

Christianity, African: An Overview; Harlem, New York; New York, New York; Jamaica.

Latin America and the Caribbean

Bluefields, city and region on the Caribbean coast of Nicaragua, home to the majority of Garifuna.

See Also

Garifuna.

Blues musician and folk artist James "Son" Thomas sits by one of his works, a sculpture of a woman in a coffin. *CORBIS/Philip Gould*

North America

Blues, The, an African American music originating in the late nineteenth century that connoted both an emotional state and a musical format. During the twentieth century the blues became the most familiar musical form in the world through its role in RHYTHM AND BLUES (R&B) and early rock 'n' roll.

The blues is a uniquely African American music and reflects the particular history and culture of black America. It emerged during the troubled times of the post-RECONSTRUCTION South, when Southern blacks experienced political disfranchisement, economic subordination, and systematic physical violence. During the twentieth century the blues moved from South to North, accompanying THE GREAT MIGRATION. The music itself shifted from simple rural blues to rhythmic and rollicking urban blues; it also became an important influence in JAZZ.

As African Americans rose to prominence in popular culture, the blues reshaped the vernacular music of the United States and the entire world. During the late 1940s the blues became an important element in the black popular music known as rhythm and blues (R&B). In the following decades it provided the musical structure – though not the emotional depth or state of mind – for much rock 'n' roll. In addition, bop, hard bop, and free jazz musicians introduced new musical complexities to the blues. Today the blues can be heard all over the world – in Norway and England, Japan and Taiwan, Brazil and Africa. But America is its true home.

The Origin of the Blues

The blues grew out of and reflected the social realities of the American South from the 1880s to the 1910s, the nadir of American race relations since Emancipation. During this time, most blacks lived in the South, where they faced increasing social, political, and economic subordination. There were few safe outlets for their hopes, dreams, and pride, the most important being the Black Church. But the main secular response was the blues.

There is no way to determine when the blues first appeared. It emerged from two earlier forms, field hollers and ballads. Field hollers were work songs, generally extemporized and unaccompanied, that evolved out of the call-and-response work songs that had set the pace for gang labor on antebellum slave plantations. African American ballads were narrative in form and were not meant to set or mesh with work rhythms. Some ballads employed the 4- or 8-line structure typical of white balladry, but another common lyrical form used a couplet and refrain line in a 12-bar form, similar to the 12-bar blues – as in the well-known "Stack O'Lee" or "Stagger Lee."

Musical Characteristics of the Blues

The blues is, above all, a vocalized music. Blues singers and instrumentalists employ a wide range of musical timbres and inflections that are modeled on the nuances of the human voice. Blues notes are the most distinctive of these musical effects. They are slightly flattened or played lower than their true pitch. The keening, moody dissonance of blue notes gives the blues a quality of loneliness, longing, or sadness. Blues notes also lift the blues from resignation to dissatisfaction and discontent.

The principal blue notes are the third and seventh notes of the scale, although the fifth note is sometimes played as a blue note, especially in the music of the bop era of the 1940s. More recently, free jazz musicians such as alto saxophonist ORNETTE COLEMAN and trumpeter Lester Bowie (b. 1941), who play with a strong blues sensibility but without traditional blues harmony, have shown that any note can be made a blue note.

The most common form of the blues is the 12-bar blues – standardized in particular through such W. C. Handy compositions as "Memphis Blues" (1912) and "St. Louis Blues" (1914). The 12-bar blues uses a single repeated stanza made up of three phrases, each 4 measures in length. There are also 8-, 16-, and 24-bar blues, and early recordings reveal that country bluesmen – generally singers who accompanied themselves on the guitar – commonly employed stanzas of odd and uneven lengths.

The blues encompasses a wide range of chord progressions. Early rural or country blues was rudimentary, using only three chords. On the other hand, bop musicians of the 1940s and 1950s often relied on harmonically advanced blues progressions. For example, "Blues for Alice" (1951) by alto saxophonist Charlie Parker makes use of numerous altered, substitute, and passing chords. But even the most complex blues progressions are direct extensions of the basic blues structure.

Blues Lyrics

The blues also features a simple lyrical structure. A standard 12-bar blues employs a 3-line stanza in which the first 2 lines are repeated and the final phrase responds to and generally rhymes with the first 2. Many blues lyrics convey sadness, as demonstrated in the following two excerpts, the first from "Crossroad Blues," by Robert Johnson (1936-1937), and the second from "Matchbox Blues," by Blind Lemon Jefferson (1927):

Well, the blues is a achin' old heart disease…
The blues is a low-down achin' heart disease,
Like consumption, killin' me by degrees.

I'm sittin' here wonderin' will a matchbox hold my clothes,
I'm sittin' here wonderin' will a matchbox hold my clothes,
I ain't got so many matches, but I got so far to go.

More than a music of sadness, the blues encompasses a wide range of emotions, including humor, sometimes salacious and sometimes ironic, as in "You Ain't Such a Much," by Dizzie Gillespie (1952):

I wouldn't give a blind sow an acorn, wouldn't give a crippled crab a crutch,
Say, I wouldn't give a blind sow an acorn, wouldn't give a crippled crab a crutch,
'Cause I just found out pretty mama that you ain't so such a much.

LEFT: With "Memphis Blues" (1912), arguably the first blues song to be published in sheet music form, composer William Christopher "W.C." Handy (1873-1958) began his long career as a popularizer of African American music. *CORBIS/Robert Dowling*
ABOVE: Bessie Smith (1894?-1937), famous for her renditions of "St. Louis Blues" and "Gimme a Pigfoot," was known as the Empress of the Blues. *Hulton Getty/Liaison Agency*

Although the blues addresses a broad range of subjects, most commonly its lyrics focus on matters of love and its discontents. Many topical blues memorialize significant events or hardships. Blind Lemon Jefferson's "Rising High Water Blues" described the destruction of a 1927 Mississippi River flood, and Charley Patton's "'34 Blues" addressed the hard times brought on by the GREAT DEPRESSION. Five days before the Japanese attack on Pearl Harbor, Big Bill Broonzy gave voice to black hopes of joining America's then-segregated air force in his "In the Army Now" (1941):

I got a letter this mornin' from a dear old uncle ["Uncle Sam"] of mine,
I got a letter this mornin' from a dear old uncle of mine,
Now, boys, I was walkin' today, but tomorrow I may be flyin'.

In effect, blues musicians were informal chroniclers of African American history, and the blues had an organic relationship to black life. Whether a specific blues spoke strictly in personal terms or broached larger social issues, the genre gave voice to black aspirations and experiences.

Early Regional Blues Styles

The blues emerged in three relatively isolated regions heavily populated by African Americans – the Mississippi Delta, the Piedmont, and East Texas. Guitarists Charley Patton, Robert Johnson, and SON HOUSE exemplified the Delta blues style. The Delta style featured slide guitar playing, in which the musician made use of a hard, smooth object such as a closed pocketknife or long glass bottleneck worn on a finger of the left (chord-playing) hand. By sliding the knife or bottleneck up and down the strings, the guitarist could bend notes and create distinctive, singing phrases.

In the Piedmont, the hilly upland extending from Virginia through the Carolinas all the way to Georgia, blues musicians such as Josh White (1908-1969) developed a sophisticated finger-picking technique that allowed them to play light and lyrical guitar accompaniments to blues vocals. East Texas blues, which also included parts of Louisiana, was rhythmic and driving, as seen in the playing of guitarists Leadbelly and Sam "Lightnin'" Hopkins. But New Orleans did not develop into an important blues center until much later, perhaps due to its tradition of marching bands, riverboat bands, and – among the Creole population – formal schooling in music.

The blues also exerted relatively little influence on early New Orleans jazz, which was more a product of RAGTIME, minstrel music, and circus and marching bands. Although some early jazz musicians – for example, cornetist Buddy Bolden – were well versed in the blues, they commonly looked down on the roughhewn rural bluesmen. In *Aspects of the Blues Tradition* (1968), Paul Oliver suggests that another source of the distance between early jazz and blues might lie in the incompatible keys favored by blues guitarists (E or A) and jazz horn players (B-flat).

There was also a strong piano tradition in the blues, emerging during the early twentieth century out of the pine-country timber camps of Georgia and the Carolinas; from countless jook joints scattered across Florida, Mississippi, and Texas; and from the rent parties and honky-tonks of Chicago. This style of playing, with its repetitive, rolling bass patterns, was popularized in the 1930s as boogie-woogie but its origins were considerably older.

ABOVE: **William Hudson Ledbetter (1885-1949), best known as Leadbelly, inspired a generation of black bluesmen and also helped bring the Blues to a white audience.** *CORBIS/Bettmann*
ABOVE RIGHT: **Romare Bearden's *Serenade*, completed in 1941, evokes the rural world in which the blues developed.** *© Romare Bearden Foundation/Licensed by VAGA, New York, NY*
RIGHT: **B. B. King and his guitar "Lucille" belt out some rhythm and blues.** *The Everett Collection*

Among the best-known boogie-woogie players are Pete Johnson (1904-1967), Albert Ammons (1907-1949), and Meade "Lux" Lewis – who occasionally performed piano trios together – and Jimmy Yancey (1894-1951), a legendary part-time musician who worked for decades as a groundskeeper at the Chicago White Sox's Comiskey Park. Boogie woogie shaped such subsequent R&B and rock 'n' roll pianists as Amos Milburn (1927-1980), LITTLE RICHARD, and Fats Domino. Memphis Slim, born Peter Chatman (1915-1988), was the most important of the postwar blues pianists who did not move into rock 'n' roll.

THE GREAT MIGRATION AND THE DISSEMINATION OF THE BLUES

Traveling bluesmen spread the blues throughout the black South, but for many years the blues remained little known to the rest of the nation. All that changed in the 1910s and 1920s with the rise of the recording industry and the start of the Great Migration, in which massive numbers of African Americans left the South for the cities of the North and the West Coast. Between the 1940s and the 1960s, the movement rose to a flood.

In making the move, African Americans carried the blues along, and generally speaking, the musical movement followed regional lines. Piedmont blues musicians generally headed up the eastern seaboard with many, like Josh White, ending up in Harlem. East Texas-style players moved west. The so-called blues shouters, JIMMY RUSHING and Big Joe Turner (1911-1985), helped create a distinctly blues-rooted jazz style in 1930s Kansas City. Other musicians, including electric guitarists Aaron "T-Bone" Walker and Clarence "Gatemouth" Brown (b. 1924), settled in Los Angeles, where they contributed to the city's emergence in the 1940s as a leading center of R&B. But the most important line of movement was from the Delta to Chicago, a route taken by such musicians as Broonzy and guitarist MUDDY WATERS.

During the 1920s the recording industry became an important mode of disseminating blues music. Recording companies established "race records" subsidiaries to produce music specifically for an African American audience, often including recordings of rural bluesmen. The recording industry also promoted a new musical tradition of what has been dubbed the classic blues singers.

Unlike their country blues counterparts, who were almost exclusively male, classic blues singers were generally women. A large number of these singers – including MAMIE SMITH and ALBERTA HUNTER – came out of vaudeville rather than the blues tradition. But Gertrude "Ma" Rainey and BESSIE SMITH, the most important classic blues singers, had performed the blues extensively throughout the South.

The classic blues era also featured larger ensembles. Rural blues generally involved individual guitarist-singers or very small groups, mainly using the guitar and the harmonica. Classic blues featured full ensembles and included such early jazz musicians as trumpeter Louis Armstrong and clarinetist and soprano saxophonist Sidney Bechet. Over the years, however, jazz gradually moved away from the blues. When big bands gained national popularity during the swing era of the 1930s, they mainly played dance music and pop tunes rather than the blues, although Count Basie's big band was a notable exception to this trend.

Since the 1940s jazz musicians have generally abandoned the raw directness and simplicity of early blues. Bop musicians such as Charlie Parker, trumpeter Dizzy Gillespie, and pianist Thelonious Monk often wrote and played blues, but their music – and the overall sound of jazz – was more complex and sophisticated than that of contemporaneous blues performers. Trumpeter Miles

Davis's album *Kind of Blue* (1959) and tenor saxophonist Oliver Nelson's *Blues and the Abstract Truth* (1961) radically extended the blues tradition. During the 1950s and 1960s Charles Mingus, Art Blakey and the Jazz Messengers, and Cannonball Adderley returned to an earthier form of musical expression, but they were influenced more by bluesy gospel music than by the blues itself.

The Blues Since World War II: Chicago Blues, the Blues Revival, and Its Decline

Within the blues tradition the most important development was the rise of Chicago blues. During the 1940s and 1950s Chicago blues musicians were largely transplants from Mississippi, but they modernized the Delta blues sound by exchanging their acoustic guitars for electrically amplified ones. In Chicago blues a small combo, consisting of one or two electric guitars, an electric bass, drums, and a piano or organ, replaced the solo performer. Sometimes the group included a small horn section – for example, a trumpet and one or more saxophones.

Postwar electric blues relied on the electric guitar's potential for angry and "dirty" playing, in sharp contrast to the pure, clean tone sought by contemporary jazz guitarists. Muddy Waters, with his jagged, edgy guitar lines and his band's driving backbeat, was the first musician to gain fame in the new style. Many others followed, including composer and bassist Willie Dixon; electric guitarists Elmore James (1918-1963), Luther "Guitar Jr." Johnson (b. 1934), and Luther Allison (1939-1997); harmonica players Sonny Boy Williamson, Howlin' Wolf, and Little Walter (1930-1968); and vocalist Koko Taylor.

Chicago blues was a key component of rhythm and blues, particularly as recorded and popularized by both Chess and Vee Jay Records. Through the playing of Chuck Berry and Bo Diddley, Chicago blues had a shaping influence on 1950s rock 'n' roll. Numerous other blues-based performers had a powerful impact on the larger pattern of American popular music, including New Orleans pianists Little Richard and Fats Domino; T-Bone Walker; and B. B. King, the most influential blues guitarist of the post-World War II era.

During the 1960s white rock musicians inspired a blues revival. The Rolling Stones, Eric Clapton, the Allman Brothers, and others recorded versions of earlier electric blues tunes and toured and recorded with Howlin' Wolf, Muddy Waters, guitarist Albert Collins (1932-1993), and other bluesmen. By the 1980s, however, King, Collins, and other African American blues musicians had discovered that their audiences were overwhelmingly white rather than black. As blues writer Paul Oliver noted, the blues had been "absorbed by popular music throughout the world with consequent damage to its identity"; in particular, by drawing upon "the modes of expression of the Church," the blues was transformed (and diluted) into gospel and soul music.

Perhaps even more tellingly, economic and social changes in African American life made the blues less relevant to black culture. During the 1970s the music most popular among inner-city black youth was the rhythmic and danceable music known as funk. In the 1980s rap became the music of choice among young blacks. Some younger blues musicians have continued to bring vitality to the genre. Electric blues guitarist Robert Cray (b. 1953) won a Grammy Award for his hit album *Strong Persuader* (1986), and the acoustic country blues stylist Keb' Mo' (b. 1951) has enjoyed considerable visibility.

But contemporary blues music has atrophied. Chicago bluesman Willie Dixon was sufficiently concerned over this state of affairs that in 1991 he founded the Blues Heaven Foundation, intended, among its various activities, to underwrite programs in blues education. The blues continues to flourish in backcountry jook joints of the Mississippi Delta, South Side Chicago blues bars, and other places. But throughout much of the United States, it stands in danger of becoming a musical pressed flower, well preserved in numerous blues festivals and urban nightclubs, but cut off from its living roots.

James Clyde Sellman

See Also

Chess Records; Adderley, Julian Edwin ("Cannonball"); Armstrong, Louis ("Satchmo"); Basie, William James ("Count"); Bechet, Sidney Joseph; Berry, Charles Edward Anderson (Chuck); Bolden, Charles Joseph ("Buddy"); Boogie Woogie; Broonzy, William Lee Conley ("Big Bill"); Chicago, Illinois; Chicago, Illinois; Creoles; Davis, Miles Dewey, III; Domino, Antoine ("Fats"), Jr.; Gillespie, John Birks ("Dizzy"); Handy, William Christopher (W.C.); Harlem, New York; Hopkins, ("Lightnin' ") Sam; Jefferson, ("Blind") Lemon; Johnson, Robert Leroy; Kansas City, Missouri; King, Riley B. ("B. B."); Ledbetter, Hudson William ("Leadbelly"); Lewis, Meade ("Lux"); Los Angeles, California; Mingus, Charles, Jr.; Minstrelsy; Monk, Thelonious Sphere; New Orleans, Louisiana; Parker, Charles Christopher ("Bird"); Patton, Charley; Rainey, Gertrude Pridgett ("Ma"); Walker, Aaron ("T-Bone"); Williamson, Johnny Lee ("Sonny Boy").

North America

Bluford, Guion Stewart (Guy), Jr. (b. November 22, 1942, Philadelphia, Pa.), American astronaut; first African American in space.

The eighth launching of the *Challenger* by the National Aeronautics and Space Administration (NASA) was a momentous occasion for the African American community. NASA brought more than 250 famous black educators and professionals to Houston, Texas, to witness Guy Bluford's historic venture into space. The launch, which took place at 2 AM on August 30, 1983, illuminated the dark skies for miles around, temporarily turning night into day. Bluford recalled how the blastoff was like riding in a high-speed elevator through a great bonfire.

Once in space, Bluford, a "mission specialist" who spent 15 months preparing for the trip, help launch a $45 million satellite that would provide communications and weather information to India and helped conduct experiments on the electrical separation of biological fluids in space. On the second day, President Ronald Reagan called the *Challenger* crew and said to Bluford, "You are paving the way for many others and making it plain that we are in an era of brotherhood here in our land." Bluford told the president that he was only part of a team and that he was pleased to be a participant.

Guy Bluford grew up in an educated, middle-class household in Philadelphia, Pennsylvania. His mother was a teacher and his father an inventor and mechanical engineer. The Blufords provided their three sons with a compelling example of personal drive, goal fulfillment, and a strong work ethic. Bluford's interest in space and aviation began in his early childhood, when he constructed model airplanes. He studied math and science in junior high school and set his career sights on aerospace engineering.

Bluford assembled an impressive résumé before entering NASA's astronaut program in 1978. He graduated from Pennsylvania State University in 1964 with a degree in aerospace engineering. Enrolled in the Air Force's Reserve Officers' Training Corps (ROTC) during college, he then trained to be a pilot at Williams Air Force Base in Arizona. After receiving his pilot wings in 1965, he went to Vietnam during the war, where as a member of the 557th Squadron he flew 144 combat missions.

Bluford worked as a flight instructor at Sheppard Air Force Base in Texas for five years before entering the Air Force Institute of Technology's graduate program in 1972. In 1974 he received an M.S. in aerospace engineering, and in 1978, following the completion of his dissertation, he earned a Ph.D. in the field. That same year, Bluford became one of 35 people accepted from more than 10,000 applicants to NASA's astronaut program. While an astronaut, he continued his studies at the University of Houston, receiving an M.B.A. in 1987. Following his retirement from NASA in 1993, he served as vice president and general manager of a computer software firm in Maryland.

Guy Bluford broke the color line in space exploration. Five months after his historic flight, another African American, Ronald E. McNair, traveled into outer space. Bluford himself would fly once more aboard the *Challenger*, in October 1985, and twice aboard the orbiter *Discovery*, in April 1991 and

December 1992. The Air Force, NASA, and numerous African American organizations have recognized Bluford's accomplishments with various awards. "From a black perspective," he has commented, "my flight on the shuttle represented another step forward. Opportunities do exist for black youngsters if they work hard and strive to take advantage of those opportunities."

Aaron Myers

See Also
Vietnam War.

North America

Blyden, Edward Wilmot

(b. August 3, 1832, St. Thomas, United States Virgin Islands; d. February 7, 1912, Freetown, Sierra Leone), Liberian nationalist and diplomat and early Pan-Africanist thinker.

Edward Blyden is considered a pioneer in Pan-Africanist thought, although the term *Pan-Africanism* was not coined until the end of Blyden's long life and career. Throughout his career as a diplomat, statesman, educator, and one of Liberia's most prominent champions, Blyden encouraged people of African descent around the world to embrace their history and culture and to return to Africa, their ancestral homeland. His call for "Africa for Africans" represented a vision that was truly ahead of its time, that of a proud, rich, black civilization spread throughout the African continent. Blyden's writings and speeches influenced leaders and philosophers such as Cheik Anta Diop, Kwame Nkrumah, Marcus Garvey, and C. L. R. James.

Blyden was born in 1832 into a middle-class free black family in Charlotte Amalie, St. Thomas, in the U.S. Virgin Islands. Although he was brought up in relative privilege, he quickly realized that his situation was unusual for most people of African descent. Blyden attended primary schools in Charlotte Amalie and Porto Bello, Venezuela, where his family lived briefly, before being apprenticed to a St. Thomas tailor at age 12. By then, he had already developed talents in languages, literature, and oratory that brought him to the attention of white minister John Knox, who encouraged him to become a minister.

In May 1850 Blyden traveled to the United States to attempt to enroll in Rutgers Theological College, Knox's alma mater. Rutgers and two other schools refused to admit him because he was black; thus Blyden received his first exposure to American racism. His predicament grew much worse with the passage of the Fugitive Slave Law that September, which left Blyden – and all other free African Americans – in danger of being mistaken for escaped slaves, captured, and sold into slavery. Members of the American Colonization Society (ACS) approached Blyden, and he was immediately attracted to the idea of their new colony in Liberia, a state in Africa made up of free people of African descent. With the ACS's encouragement and financial support, Blyden sailed for Monrovia, Liberia, in December 1850.

He enrolled at Monrovia's Alexander High School in October 1851; by 1858 he had become the school's principal. In between, he was also ordained as a Presbyterian minister, served as editor of the *Liberia Herald*, and published the first of his numerous pamphlets and essays. In *A Vindication of the Negro Race* (1857), Blyden rebutted contemporary theories of black inferiority, a theme to which he would return again and again. Many of his other early writings championed Liberia, and in 1861 Blyden made the first of seven return trips to the United States to attempt to recruit more colonists for his adopted country.

His recruitment efforts were difficult because the Civil War and the abolition of slavery in the United States left many African Americans optimistic that they would finally be accepted by American society. Blyden, however, argued that these small gains in legal status were irrelevant. He believed that whites' racist views of their own supremacy were so ingrained that blacks could never be more than second-class citizens unless they lived in an all-African country, a view many other black thinkers eventually shared. For his time, however, this was one of his frequent controversial stances.

Blyden's prominent positions in Liberia included professor of classics and later president of Liberia College; secretary of state of Liberia; Liberian commissioner to Great Britain and the United States; Liberian ambassador to the Court of St. James (Great Britain); and minister of the interior. He was publicly critical of Liberia's mixed-race ruling class. He boasted that he came from pure African heritage and argued that mulattos should not be included in the Africa for Africans movement. Not surprisingly, this stance proved unpopular in some circles. After an unsuccessful run for the presidency of Liberia in 1885, he immigrated to neighboring Sierra Leone, and he traveled back and forth between Sierra Leone and Liberia for the next 30 years.

Blyden became the center of a new controversy when he resigned from the Presbyterian Church in 1886 to become a Minister of Truth, and the next year published *Christianity, Islam, and the Negro Race*, which argued that Islam had been much better than Christianity for people of African descent. When Blyden first immigrated to Liberia, he had been enthusiastic about the idea of that country as an educated, Christian beacon for the rest of the African continent. But the more time he spent in Africa, the more he became convinced that Christianity and European education would not add anything to the cultural and intellectual wealth that already existed in Africa.

Blyden's renunciation of Presbyterianism allowed him to resolve an important aspect of his personal life. In 1856 he had married Sarah Yates, the niece of a prominent Liberian businessman. But since 1877 he had had a second relationship with Anna Erskine, a former schoolteacher from Louisiana, who was the mother of five of his eight children. When Blyden began publicly championing polygamy as an important African tradition, many critics believed that he was simply rationalizing his personal conduct.

For Blyden, however, polygamy was an integral piece of the respect for the African cultural legacies he had first developed during his travels through Africa as Liberian secretary of state. The same travels also inspired the vision of West African unity that governed the latter half of his intellectual career. In addition to his time in Sierra Leone, Blyden visited Lagos, Nigeria, in 1890 and 1894, then served as agent of native affairs there from 1896 to 1897. His time in these other countries helped shape his belief that Africans in general, and West Africans in particular, should come together as a community to celebrate their shared heritage and to fight against European racism and ethnocentrism.

By the time of Blyden's death in 1912 at age 79, his ideas were already starting to take root. The first Pan-African Conference was held in London in 1900. Although Blyden did not attend (possibly because he believed it should have been held in Africa and should not have been dominated by "mulattos" such as W. E. B. Du Bois), the conference rested on many of his ideas. In the decades following his death, Blyden's writings have been celebrated by successive generations of black nationalists – including his own grandson, Edward Wilmot Blyden III, whose Sierra Leone Independence Movement helped liberate that country from Great Britain. A new study of Blyden appeared at the height of the Black Power Movement in the 1960s, and his views on black identity, often radical in his own time, remain provocative and relevant today.

Lisa Clayton Robinson

See Also
Freetown, Sierra Leone; Nigeria; Pan-Africanism; Abolitionism in the United States; Civil War, American; Du Bois, William Edward Burghardt (W. E. B.); Free Blacks in the United States, 1619 to 1863; Fugitive Slave Laws; Garvey, Marcus Mosiah; James, Cyril Lionel Richard; Virgin Islands (United States and British); Islam and Tradition: An Interpretation.

Europe

Boateng, Paul (b. June 14, 1951, London, England), one of the first blacks elected to the British Parliament and the first black British cabinet minister.

Although he was considered a radical in the 1970s and 1980s, observers have described Paul Boateng as a "traditional" moderate since he took his seat in the British Parliament in 1987.

Boateng was born in Hackney, London, in 1951 to a Ghanaian father and a Scottish mother. When he was two, his family moved to the newly independent GHANA, where his father served as a cabinet minister. Boateng grew up in Ghana and attended the prestigious Accra Academy. When a 1966 coup placed his father in jail, he, his sister, and his mother fled to GREAT BRITAIN. They settled in Hemel Hempstead, where Boateng was the only black to attend his secondary school. His peers quickly accepted him, and he became captain of the debating team. He went on to study law at Bristol University.

At a time when the British Parliament had no members of African descent, Boateng embarked on an ambitious political career within the established power structure. At age 19 he began working for Ben Bimberg, a well-known radical civil rights lawyer. He later joined the Greater London Council (GLC), London's left-leaning metropolitan government, which Margaret Thatcher dissolved in 1986. From 1977 to 1981 he worked as legal adviser for the GLC's campaign to prevent excessive "stop and search" police procedures, which were damaging the relationship between the police and black communities. In the GLC, he acted as chair of the Police Committee and as vice chair of the Ethnic Minorities Committee. During the 1980s he also produced several radio and television shows about the history of peoples of African descent.

A member of the Labour Party, Boateng unsuccessfully sought election as a member of Parliament, or MP, in a Hertfordshire district in 1983. He finally won election in 1987 as MP for Brent South, a London suburb with a strong Labour leaning. In Parliament Boateng quickly distanced himself from the radical politics of the two other black MPs elected that year, BERNIE GRANT and DIANE ABBOTT. Boateng boycotted a meeting to discuss the creation of a "parliamentary black caucus," an effort he saw as divisive. Since his election, he has insisted that he is simply a politician who is black, not a politician who represents all blacks.

Witty, intelligent, and sharp on legal details, in Parliament Boateng has proved loyal to the Labour Party. Within two years, he won a seat on the high-ranking front bench of the House of Commons as part of Labour's treasury team. In 1992 he became the party's spokesperson on legal affairs and has worked to make legal services and procedures more efficient.

Soon after Labour's 1997 victory, Boateng became the first black to hold a cabinet position in Great Britain. As health minister, he has presented an aggressive agenda on issues ranging from the abuse of the elderly in nursing homes to restrictions on child labor. He has ordered reviews of social service providers, prompting local journalists to call him "a scourge of poor practice in social care, an enforcer of proper standards." He has also presented a government-funded plan to make headway against the increase in divorces by sponsoring counseling, advice, and assistance for troubled couples.

In his political career, Boateng has championed "family values," a priority he also maintains in his personal life. He has been a practicing Christian for his entire life and is now a Methodist lay minister. He spends much of his free time with his wife, Janet Alleyne, a social worker, and their five children.

Leyla Keough

SEE ALSO
Accra, Ghana.

Africa

Bobo, ethnic group of at least 800,000 people living predominantly in southern BURKINA FASO.

The Bobo were among the earliest settlers of the semi-arid savanna region of southwestern Burkina Faso (formerly Upper Volta). Similarities between the Bobo language and MANDE languages spoken in southern MALI provide linguistic support for the Bobo's oral traditions, which claim that their ancestors migrated from "Mande country," probably between the twelfth and fourteenth centuries C.E. These ancestors are believed to have first founded a village called Tinima, on the plateau east of the Houet River. Other early migrants to the area settled alongside the river, on the site now occupied by the city of Bobo-Dioulasso. Their descendants established settlements to the north, east, and west of this site.

In the past the Bobo referred to themselves as the *san-san*, or "the cultivating people." Merchant caravans traveled through Bobo country from at least the sixteenth century onward, but the Bobo themselves participated in the long-distance commerce only peripherally, primarily as suppliers of food for the caravans. The Bobo rejected as well the merchants' Islamic teachings, and instead organized their rituals of ancestor worship around village shrines.

The precolonial political organization of the Bobo was also largely village-based. Village elders presided over matters of marriage and inheritance, both of which were (and to a certain extent still are) shaped by the Bobo's "dual descent" kinship system. Rights to land, in other words, were traditionally passed patrilineally (from father to son) while movable forms of property, such as cattle or cooking pots, were passed matrilineally (from maternal uncle to son, or mother to daughter).

The lack of a centralized state made the Bobo vulnerable to slave raids and conquest in the eighteenth century, especially after the rise of the Dioula KONG empire in the northern part of modern-day CÔTE D'IVOIRE. Many Bobo communities defended themselves by moving closer together; the large size, dense settlement, and fortified housing characteristic of many older Bobo villages is an architectural legacy of the slave trade era.

When the French began their conquest of the southern Volta region in the late nineteenth century, they assumed that the Bobo peasants were the subjects of the resident Dioula traders. During the early years of COLONIAL RULE, however, unrest in Bobo country demonstrated the peasants' lack of respect for the Dioula "chiefs" appointed to collect taxes and recruit labor. This period also saw rapid cultural changes: the Catholic mission in Bobo-Dioulasso found many converts in Bobo villages just outside the city, while members of the Zara clan, who had already distinguished themselves by their participation in trade and warfare, converted to Islam. After forced labor was abolished in 1946, many Bobo villagers applied their farming skills to commercial crops such as cotton, maize, and vegetables.

Today most rural Bobo continue to earn their livelihoods from farming, often combined with seasonal migrant labor, small-scale trade or, in the case of women, millet beer brewing. Many Bobo villages are themselves home to MOSSI migrants from drought-prone provinces to the north. Like most other ethnic groups in Burkina Faso, the Bobo are not an organized force in national politics, but they do play an important role in the municipal government, business, and church communities of Bobo-Dioulasso.

Susanne Freidberg

SEE ALSO
Bobo-Dioulasso, Burkina Faso; Christianity: Missionaries in Africa; Islam and Tradition: An Interpretation; Slavery in Africa.

Africa

Bobo-Dioulasso, Burkina Faso, the second largest city in BURKINA FASO (formerly Upper Volta).

The city of Bobo-Dioulasso is located in one of the greener areas of Burkina Faso and has long benefited from the fertility of the surrounding countryside. According to the legends of the BOBO people, their ancestors migrated from present-day MALI sometime between the twelfth and fourteenth centuries C.E. and became the first inhabitants of what Bobo folk songs call "the plateau of abundance" in the southern Volta region. Over the following centuries long-distance traders settled among the Bobo peasants on this plateau and established a community known as Sya on the banks of the Houet River. Sitting at the crossroads of trans-Saharan and east-west trade routes, Sya was a lively market town by the time European colonization began in the late nineteenth century. French troops, facing fierce resistance from Sya's Zara warriors, conquered the town in 1895. They renamed it Bobo-Dioulasso (in Dioula, "house of the Bobo and the Dioula") and proceeded to build an administrative post and military camp.

In 1934 the completion of a rail line to the port city of Abidjan in Côte d'Ivoire attracted French trading firms to Bobo-Dioulasso and spurred increased exports of cotton and food crops, requisitioned from the city's hinterland. Thousands of West African recruits passed through the Bobo-Dioulasso military camp during World War II; in the postwar period, many veterans returned to the city to invest their pensions in trade or agriculture. A palatial central market, built in 1951, testified to the region's booming commerce; wide shady streets radiating from the city center delineated distinctive neighborhoods, ranging from the labyrinthine old town of Koko to the modern working-class quarter of Accartville. In the years leading up to independence, Bobo-Dioulasso became a stronghold for the Rassemblement Démocratique Africain (RDA), an anticolonial movement initially backed by the French Communist Party.

Ouagadougou became the national capital of Upper Volta at independence in 1960. As industry and trade as well as government services increasingly concentrated in the capital, Bobo-Dioulasso's economy and infrastructure gradually deteriorated. In the early 1990s structural adjustment austerity measures brought factory closures and layoffs, forcing more and more Bobolais into small-scale trade. Yet despite widespread economic hardship, Bobo-Dioulasso's multiethnic population (numbering around 400,000) supports thriving nightclub, cinema, and drumming scenes. Ringed by gardens and orchards that provision the city's renowned produce markets, Bobo-Dioulasso is a popular vacation destination for West Africans and Europeans alike.

Susanne Freidberg

See Also

Abidjan, Côte d'Ivoire; Ouagadougou, Burkina Faso.

Africa

Boganda, Barthélemy

(b. April 4, 1910, Bobangui, French Equatorial Africa; d. March 29, 1959, near Bangui, Oubangui-Chari [present-day Central African Republic]), nationalist leader and hero of the Central African Republic.

Born to a family of subsistence farmers, Barthélemy Boganda attended Catholic mission schools and seminaries in Brazzaville and Yaoundé. In 1938 he became the first Oubanguian Catholic priest. Sponsored by Catholic missionaries, Boganda was elected to the French National Assembly in 1946. Soon realizing the limits of his influence in France, he left the priesthood and returned to Oubangui-Chari to organize a grassroots movement of small African producers to oppose French colonialism. In 1949 he founded the Movement for the Social Evolution of Black Africa, a quasi-religious political party.

After his arrest for "endangering the peace" and detention for intervening in a local market dispute in 1951, Boganda became a messianic folk hero and Oubangui-Chari's leading nationalist. The French realized that opposing Boganda would be dangerous and sought to accommodate him. In 1956 Boganda agreed to European representation on election lists in exchange for the financial support of French business leaders. In 1958, with the rush toward independence in much of Francophone Africa, Boganda cautioned that independence for landlocked Oubangui-Chari lacked economic viability. Instead, he called for the federation of Oubangui-Chari with an independent United States of Latin Africa, including all of French Equatorial Africa as well as adjacent Belgian and Portuguese possessions. Such a federation proved unrealistic, however, and Boganda later accepted a constitution covering only Oubangui-Chari as the Central African Republic. Once called the "most capable of equatorial political men," Boganda was poised to become the first president of the independent CAR when he was killed in a mysterious plane crash in 1959, just prior to legislative elections. He was succeeded by his close confidant David Dacko.

Eric Young

See Also

Bangui, Central African Republic; Brazzaville, Republic of the Congo; Nationalism in Africa; Yaoundé, Cameroon.

Latin America and the Caribbean

Bogle, Paul

(b. 1822?, Stony Gut, Jamaica; d. October 24, 1865, Morant Bay, Jamaica), black political and religious leader who organized the 1865 Morant Bay Rebellion in Jamaica.

Paul Bogle is a beloved figure in Jamaica. Although his legal status at the time of his birth is unclear, most scholars believe that he was born free in Stony Gut, Jamaica, in 1822. He operated a small independent farm there and became a lay preacher in the Native Baptist Church. His affiliation with this antislavery branch of the Baptist Church brought him into contact with British and Jamaican abolitionists, including activist George Gordon. Methodist and Baptist leaders, as well as leaders of other religious denominations, were active participants in the antislavery struggle. As a result, members of local black congregations like Bogle's were often exposed to antislavery debates, pamphlets, and sermons.

When slavery was abolished in 1834, blacks in Jamaica were promised freedom at the end of what turned out to be a four-year period known as apprenticeship. The apprenticeship policy forced slaves to enter into labor contracts with their former owners. Although the period of apprenticeship was determined by the type of work and the plantation involved, the underlying rationale behind the policy was to help white planters make the difficult transition from chattel slavery to a system of wage labor.

The apprenticeship period gave white plantation owners time to adjust to the radical economic changes stemming from abolition. Many of them exploited this opportunity when they imposed strict labor contracts on black workers. The conditions set out in these contracts reduced the ability of workers to pursue alternative employment, keeping many beholden to jobs meted out by plantation owners. Apprenticeship was immediately challenged by abolitionists, many of whom called it another form of slavery. Bogle added his voice to the chorus, courageously criticizing the policies of colonial officials, including their failure to place limits on the power of Jamaica's white sugar planters. He translated these criticisms into political action during the 1840s when he became one of the few registered nonwhite voters in St. Thomas Parish.

Although Bogle's educational background is unclear, his leadership in the Native Baptist Church, his ability to meet the steep property requirements for nonwhite voters, and his friendship with George Gordon made him a respected leader in St. Thomas's predominantly black peasant community. Bogle's leadership in the black community and his willingness to challenge colonial officials was called upon during the economic crisis that hit the island in the 1860s.

The removal, years earlier, of protective duties on Jamaican sugar exports had placed a severe strain on many of the island's smaller sugar plantations. White landowners faced mounting economic challenges as the prices of sugar, rum, and molasses – all major Jamaican exports – fell around the world. They attempted to recoup their economic losses by overtaxing, overregulating, and exploiting the colony's black workers. These policies were met with militant resistance.

As the grievances of black peasants increased, an organized movement emerged, and Bogle was chosen as its leader. The peasants demanded reductions on taxes, restrictions on the rights of white employers to fire black workers at will, and higher wages. Bogle attempted to present these demands to the colony's governor but was refused a meeting. Colonial officials had little interest in the demands of peasants and were unwilling to entertain any notions of reform.

Bogle responded by organizing small, armed peasant militias that trained in the hills above Morant Bay. Although the peasants would have preferred a peaceful resolution, Bogle prepared them for armed resistance. On October 7, Bogle and a group of more than 100 men went to the courthouse of Morant Bay to support a man charged with trespassing on a plantation. An altercation erupted between the crowd and the police.

The police dispersed the crowd, and Bogle and his followers returned to Stony Gut. When the police arrived three days later to arrest Bogle, a large crowd gathered to protect him. The police withdrew, but an even more defiant Bogle led a march to the St. Thomas Vestry, the local governing body. When the police attacked the demonstrators, a riot engulfed the city. Twenty-eight people were killed, including the custos, who was the highest administrative official in the parish. When calm was finally restored, colonial officials whipped more than 500 blacks, burned down nearly 1000 cottages and huts, and executed over 500 protesters, including Bogle and Gordon.

It was in death that Paul Bogle had the greatest impact on the black resistance movement in Jamaica. His legacy is revered by political activists and laborers throughout the Caribbean and was recalled during the turbulent labor strikes of the 1930s. His face appears on the national currency and on stamps, and his statue stands on the site where he was executed by British colonial officials in 1865. Cuban president Fidel Castro even laid a wreath at Bogle's grave when he visited the country. Jamaicans of all races celebrate Bogle's role in the emergence of black nationalism and workers' rights, and he was named a National Hero in 1965.

Alonford James Robinson, Jr.

See Also

Great Britain; Sugar; Apprenticeship in the British Caribbean; Abolition and Emancipation in Latin America and the Caribbean.

Latin America and the Caribbean

Boissiere, Rafael de,

Afro-Trinidadian writer. His best-known collections of short stories and novels include *Crown Jewel* (1952), *Rum & Coca-Cola* (1956), and *No Saddles for Kangaroos* (1964) (*see* Literature, English Language, Caribbean).

Africa

Bokassa, Jean-Bédel

(b. February 22, 1921, Bobangui, Oubangui-Chari, French Equatorial Africa [present-day Central African Republic]; d. November 3, 1996, Bangui, Central African Republic), the self-proclaimed marshal, emperor, and "apostle" of the Central African Empire, "president-for-life" from 1966 to 1979, and reputed cannibal.

A career soldier who had endured a tragic childhood, Jean-Bédel Bokassa ruled the impoverished Central African Republic with brutal repression, used its revenues for his personal enrichment, and crowned himself emperor. He committed barbarities that caused an international outcry and led to his removal from power.

When Bokassa was six years old, his father, a village chief of the Mbaka people, was murdered. Bokassa became an orphan a week later when his mother committed suicide. Missionaries raised him until, at the outbreak of World War II, when he was 18 years old, he joined the French colonial army. He participated in the 1944 landings in Provence and later served in Indochina and Algeria, attaining the rank of captain and earning the Legion d'Honneur and the Croix de Guerre. In 1960, after Oubangui-Chari became the independent Central African Republic, Bokassa helped create its army and, in 1964, was given the rank of colonel by President David Dacko, a cousin, who made him the army chief of staff.

In a coup d'état in 1965, Bokassa seized power from Dacko. Over the next 11 years Bokassa governed the republic autocratically with a series of arbitrary decrees and periodic cabinet shuffles, all of which increased his power. He received military support from France, on which the Central African Republic remained economically dependent. In 1972 Bokassa proclaimed himself president-for-life with the rank of marshal. He ordered the torture and execution of political opponents. Meanwhile, in order to support his lavish lifestyle, he plundered the national economy, which was sustained by diamond and uranium exports.

In 1976 Bokassa proclaimed himself Emperor Bokassa I and renamed the country the Central African Empire. The coronation during the following year, complete with a diamond-studded crown, reportedly cost $200 million, which was largely underwritten by France. He used the occasion to crown his wife empress and to ennoble family members. Bokassa's reign was brief. In 1979 regulations forcing students to purchase school uniforms from a factory owned by the emperor's wife sparked violent demonstrations in the capital and Bokassa's car was stoned. He reacted brutally. Over 100 imprisoned children, aged 8 to 16, were massacred. Courts later concluded that Bokassa was personally involved in the killings. Other reports contended that the emperor did not participate directly but that he later ate some of the children. He claimed innocence, contending that he was a Christian and had a large family himself (55 children reared by 17 wives). However, it was the International Year of the Child, and foreign governments responded with sanctions. In September 1979 French troops reinstalled Dacko as president while Bokassa was abroad.

After seven years in exile in Côte d'Ivoire and France, during which time he was condemned to death in absentia, in 1986 Bokassa returned to the Central African Republic. Promptly arrested, he was sentenced again to death on charges of murder, although he was acquitted of charges of cannibalism. President André Kolingba later pardoned the aging Bokassa and released him from prison in 1993. He died in 1996 at age 75. He received a state funeral, and the state radio described him as "illustrious."

Eric Young

See Also

Bangui, Central African Republic; World War II and African Americans.

Africa

Bokyi

(also known as Boki and Nki), ethnic group of West Africa.

The Bokyi primarily inhabit Cross River State, Nigeria, and western Cameroon. They speak a Niger-Congo language and belong to the Ibibio cultural and linguistic cluster. Approximately 200,000 people consider themselves Bokyi.

See Also

Languages, African: An Overview.

Latin America and the Caribbean

Bola de Nieve

(b. September 11, 1911, Guanabacoa, Cuba; d. October 2, 1971, Mexico City, Mexico), Afro-Cuban pianist, singer, and composer, and a principal figure of *Afrocubanismo*, the cultural and political movement sought to affirm black culture.

Ignacio Villa, known by his stage name, Bola de Nieve, grew up in a poor neighborhood in Guanabacoa, Cuba. His parents introduced him to Afro-Cuban music when he was a child, and he was exposed to European classical music in his formal studies. His classical training began when he studied privately with Gerado Guanche. Later Villa enrolled in the Conservatorio de José Mateu, where he studied mandolin and flute as well as piano (*see* MUSIC, CLASSICAL, IN LATIN AMERICA AND THE CARIBBEAN).

At home he absorbed many elements of traditional Afro-Cuban music through his contact with RUMBA and other rhythms and dances. It has been suggested that his parents participated in African-based religions and that as a boy he had been educated in the music and practices of Afro-Cuban religion as well (*see* AFRO-CARIBBEAN RELIGIOUS MUSIC).

While still a boy, he helped support his family by performing in-house for neighborhood audiences. His professional career began in the 1920s with stints in silent movie theaters; he continued to study classical piano on the side. By the time he was in his mid-20s he had established a reputation as a skilled accompanist. In the early 1930s the Cuban singer Rita Montaner contracted him for a tour of Mexico. By now using the name Bola de Nieve, he remained in Mexico when Montaner returned to Cuba in 1933. In Mexico, he first established a career as an accompanist and later as a solo artist. His musical playfulness and powerful voice soon earned him a reputation there and in other Latin American countries. His rendition of famous boleros, *sones* (two genres of Cuban music) and other popular songs, such as Moisés Simmons's classic *El manisero* (The Peanut Vendor), are still widely cherished; together with some recent releases, they contributed to earning him a public in the United States.

Shortly after returning to his homeland, Bola de Nieve embarked on a prolific recording career. Often the sessions were grueling all-night affairs. One such stint was his 1950s recording for Radio Progresso titled *FM-62*, which many consider to be his greatest effort. He frequently performed and sang his own compositions as well as those of other *Afrocubanismo* composers, including Emile Grenet, ERNESTO LECUONA, and the poet NICOLÁS GUILLÉN.

Bola de Nieve enjoyed international fame, touring South America, Europe, and the United States. After the Cuban Revolution (*see* CUBA), he traveled to the former Soviet Union and to China and CANADA, and performed many times in Mexico, where he died in 1971.

Today Bola de Nieve holds a unique and controversial place in Cuban history. Some scholars, characterizing his work as a minstrel-like parody of black Cuban culture, point out that much of his repertoire comes from white composers and artists who used Afro-Caribbean culture to propagate stereotypes of blacks. Most critics, however, recognize the necessity of viewing Bola de Nieve within his own historical context. Like the Mexican singer Toña la Negra, Bola de Nieve soon realized that opportunities were scarce for black performers during the 1920s and that he could interpret only a very limited repertoire of Afro-Cuban themes. Ironically these early pioneers opened the door for later explorers of Afro-Caribbean tradition, such as MERCEDITAS VALDÉS, Chucho Valdés, and CELIA CRUZ.

Gordon Root

SEE ALSO
Russia and the Former Soviet Union; Bolero; Cuba; Son; Valdés, Jesús (Chucho); Music, Afro-Caribbean Secular; Religions, African, in Latin America and the Caribbean; Dance in Latin America and the Caribbean.

Latin America and the Caribbean

Bola Sete (b. July 16, 1923, Rio de Janeiro, BRAZIL; d. February 14, 1987, Greenbrae, California), Brazilian guitarist and composer.

Djalma Andrade received the stage name Bola Sete while playing guitar in a small jazz band in which he was the only black member (*see* JAZZ, AFRO-LATIN). Bola Sete means "ball number 7," the only black ball in Brazilian billiards.

Bola Sete began his formal music education at the Conservatory of Rio de Janeiro, where he studied classical guitar. His early influences, including Andrés Segovia, Django Reinhardt, and Charlie Christian, reveal the young artist's interest in both classical music and jazz (*see* MUSIC, CLASSICAL, IN LATIN AMERICA AND THE CARIBBEAN). His passion for these two genres remained constant throughout his career. As a young man he also played in various SAMBA and *choro* groups (two Brazilian musical genres with roots in the nineteenth century), composing numerous pieces, including one of his best-known early compositions, "Cosminho no Choro." As a result of his exposure to jazz, classical, and Brazilian popular music, he became familiar with a variety of styles, laying the foundations for the versatile and unique musical language that was to become his trademark in later years.

In 1952 Bola Sete embarked on his professional career and moved to Italy, where he played in various clubs and hotels. He returned to his homeland four years later, just in time for the initial stirrings of the bossa nova movement. It did not take long for him to absorb the new style and adapt it to his own variegated mix.

Shortly after returning to Brazil, he began a tour of South America. It was during these appearances that the manager of Sheraton Hotels noticed the talented guitarist and invited him to perform at the New York Sheraton. Later Bola Sete transferred to the Sheraton Palace in San Francisco, where he eventually met and began performing with American jazz legend Dizzy Gillespie. From that period on, Bola Sete made his home in the United States until his death in 1987.

By the end of his career, Bola Sete had recorded some 13 albums of both solo and ensemble music. Today the guitarist is remembered and revered by many for his seemingly boundless versatility. His discography runs the gamut of classical and popular music and includes works by composers as disparate as Bach, Villa Lobos, Jobim, Joni Mitchell, and the Beatles. In addition, he recorded many of his own compositions. Perhaps his best-known album is *Autentico*, which features two of his most popular pieces, "Soul Samba" and "Baion Blues."

Gordon Root

SEE ALSO
Gillespie, John Birks ("Dizzy"); Rio de Janeiro, Brazil.

North America

Bolden, Charles Joseph ("Buddy") (b. September 7, 1877, New Orleans, La.; d. November 4, 1931, Jackson, La.), African American coronet player and bandleader whose improvisational style is said to embody the first true New Orleans jazz.

Charles "Buddy" Bolden was a pioneering and creative force in the development of pre- and early JAZZ in turn-of-the-century New Orleans. He began playing coronet in a professional band in his teens and quickly established a reputation for a clear, powerful tone. Soon Bolden was leading his own band, earning the title "King" from an appreciative African American public. His influence came at a time when New Orleans was alive with bands of black musicians performing for marches, dances, and saloons.

As a soloist, Bolden had a keen ear and memory, which augmented skills in improvisation and embellishment. He is reportedly the first to "rag the blues" for dancing and thus to have essentially created jazz. Popular folklore has it that his coronet tone was so strong and his music so great that people could hear him from across the river. Jazz historians believe that Bolden's playing influenced contemporary and subsequent cornet and trumpet players such as "King" Oliver, "Bunk" Johnson, and Louis Armstrong.

Bolden was committed to a mental institution in 1906, probably as a result of alcoholism. Thus ended his musical career decades before his death in 1931. Tragically, he was never recorded.

David Kim

See Also
Armstrong, Louis ("Satchmo"); New Orleans, Louisiana; Oliver, Joseph ("King").

Latin America and the Caribbean

Bolero, a style of romantic ballad music with guitar accompaniment that originated in Spain; with rhythmic modifications, it flourished as a folk music in late nineteenth-century Cuba, its popularity spreading throughout Latin America during the 1920s and 1930s.

The bolero evolved in Cuba during the early twentieth century as a popular slow-tempo dance music. It was the product of an urban folk tradition, a vernacular form that developed before the era of audio recording. The first boleros were created by Cuba's itinerant *trovadores*, or street musicians. The bolero is romantic music and its lyrics are highly sentimental, sometimes maudlin, paying tribute to the glories of eternal love or celebrating the bittersweet pain of a love unrequited. By the early 1920s its popularity had spread not only throughout Cuba and Mexico but across Latin America.

In Cuba boleros were originally performed by solo voice and accompanied by guitar, but eventually they came to be most often performed by two voices. In Mexico groups such as Trío Calaveras introduced the practice of singing the bolero in tight three-part harmony. This trio style then spread to Cuba and elsewhere. Although it is danceable music, the bolero makes only limited use of African-derived Cuban percussion rhythms. This generally subdued quality sets the bolero apart from other Cuban dance music – including the rumba, son, or mambo, which are distinguished by driving percussion and a syncopated *clave* beat. The bolero is played four beats to the measure and features a distinctly nonsyncopated pattern in the bass, a half note followed by two quarter notes.

Boleros began as intimate music played by solo singer-guitarists or small voice-and-guitar ensembles. But during the mid-twentieth century the form was lifted from the realm of folk music and incorporated into Latin American popular music. In Cuba the bolero was adapted and arranged for larger ensembles – trumpet-led *septetos* and *conjuntos* and American-style big bands. During the 1950s bandleader Beny Moré, one of Cuba's greatest popular singers, was particularly effective in singing boleros in a big band setting. Although Moré performed many up-tempo mambos and rumbas, the slow bolero provided him with a natural showcase for his expressive voice and gift for lyric interpretation. As the careers of such singers as Moré, Bola de Nieve, and Toña La Negra reveal, the bolero has also provided a means for black Latin Americans to become celebrities.

James Clyde Sellman

North America

Bolin, Jane Mathilda

(b. April 11, 1908, Poughkeepsie, N.Y.), American judge; first African American woman to graduate from Yale Law School and to be admitted to the New York City Association of the Bar.

The daughter of Gaius C. and Matilda Bolin, Jane Bolin attended Wellesley College and was the first black American woman to graduate from Yale Law School. She was also the first black woman admitted to the New York City Association of the Bar. Bolin was appointed a United States judge in 1939.

Bolin battled racial discrimination in schools, and retired in 1978 after effecting many changes in the family court system of New York. She received honorary degrees from institutions such as Williams College and Tuskegee Institute.

Amelia Weir

See Also
New York, New York; Tuskegee University.

Latin America and the Caribbean

Bolivia, landlocked country in central South America; bordered on the north and east by Brazil, on the south by Argentina, and on the west by Chile and Peru.

To those who think of the Andes region and conjure up images of indigenous populations such as Aymara- and Quechua-speaking peoples, it is surprising to realize that black people also live in Bolivia. Even within the country itself there are citizens who are unaware of this fact. Many Bolivians, not aware of their country's historic involvement in the transatlantic slave trade, think that blacks are migrants from Brazil or other nearby countries. The scarcity of Afro-Bolivians in the country (about 2 percent of the population) may partially explain the superstition held by some citizens that pinching someone when they see a black person will bring good luck. Whatever the origin of this belief may be, the objectification of black people that it represents illustrates the subtle forms of racism that Afro-Bolivians find offensive.

Reputed to be the most Indian of the American republics because of its large Aymara- and Quechua-speaking population, Bolivia accords little if any recognition to other ethnic groups that reside within its territory. Afro-Bolivians are one such ignored group. It is currently impossible to know the number of blacks in Bolivia because the national census classifies populations only by language, not by race or ethnicity. Unlike indigenous people, blacks are not officially considered a separate ethnic group, since they speak Spanish and do not exhibit marked cultural traits that would distinguish them from the rest of Bolivia's populations. In mainstream society, Afro-Bolivians are pejoratively referred to as *negritos* (little black people) and are seen as part of Bolivia's history, not its present.

Currently, at a time when ethnic groups are receiving recognition and support from governmental and international sources, Afro-Bolivians are moving into the spotlight by showcasing their culture to demonstrate their contribution to Bolivian society. Hoping to distinguish themselves as a unique ethnic group, Afro-Bolivians attempt to rectify the marginalization caused by slavery and its aftermath. The reconstruction of dance, song, and music that were on the verge of extinction is part of this effort. An Afro-Bolivian movement has been established with the goal of effecting social change and promoting cultural awareness.

Standard History of Bolivia
In the middle of the fifteenth century, Inca armies from the region that is now Peru invaded the Bolivian highlands and defeated the indigenous peoples there. The Aymara, the predominant regional group, essentially maintained their way of life under Inca rule. The Inca extracted tribute labor from them but allowed the Aymara to keep their traditional leaders. In 1532 Spanish conquistadors entered the region and took advantage of political strife within the Inca Empire. The Spaniards subdued the indigenous populations and utilized the Inca system of tribute labor called *mita*. Under this Spanish-controlled system, Indians were drafted into periods of forced labor to establish the new society. When silver deposits were discovered in the southern town that is now Potosí, mining projects increased the need for laborers and the Spaniards began to import African slaves. More than half the silver in the New World came from the mines in Potosí between 1570 and 1650, thus making it highly profitable and the most densely populated area of South America.

Bolivia, known as Upper Peru throughout the colonial era, fell under the jurisdiction of the viceroyalty of Peru at Lima, and, after 1776, of the viceroyalty of La Plata, in Buenos Aires. As the last Spanish-American continental territory to be freed, Bolivia gained its independence in 1825 and was named for Simón Bolívar, the revolutionary figure who symbolized liberty. Since its liberation, Bolivia has been fraught with political, social, and economic instability. Misguided leadership drew the country into two wars that greatly diminished its territory. The entire Pacific coastal region was lost to Chile in the War of the Pacific (1879-1884), while sea access and oil were forfeited to Paraguay in the Chaco War (1932-1935). The unrest that gripped the country in the years following these wars culminated in the pivotal 1952 Bolivian National Revolution, led by tin miners. Universal suffrage, nationalization of

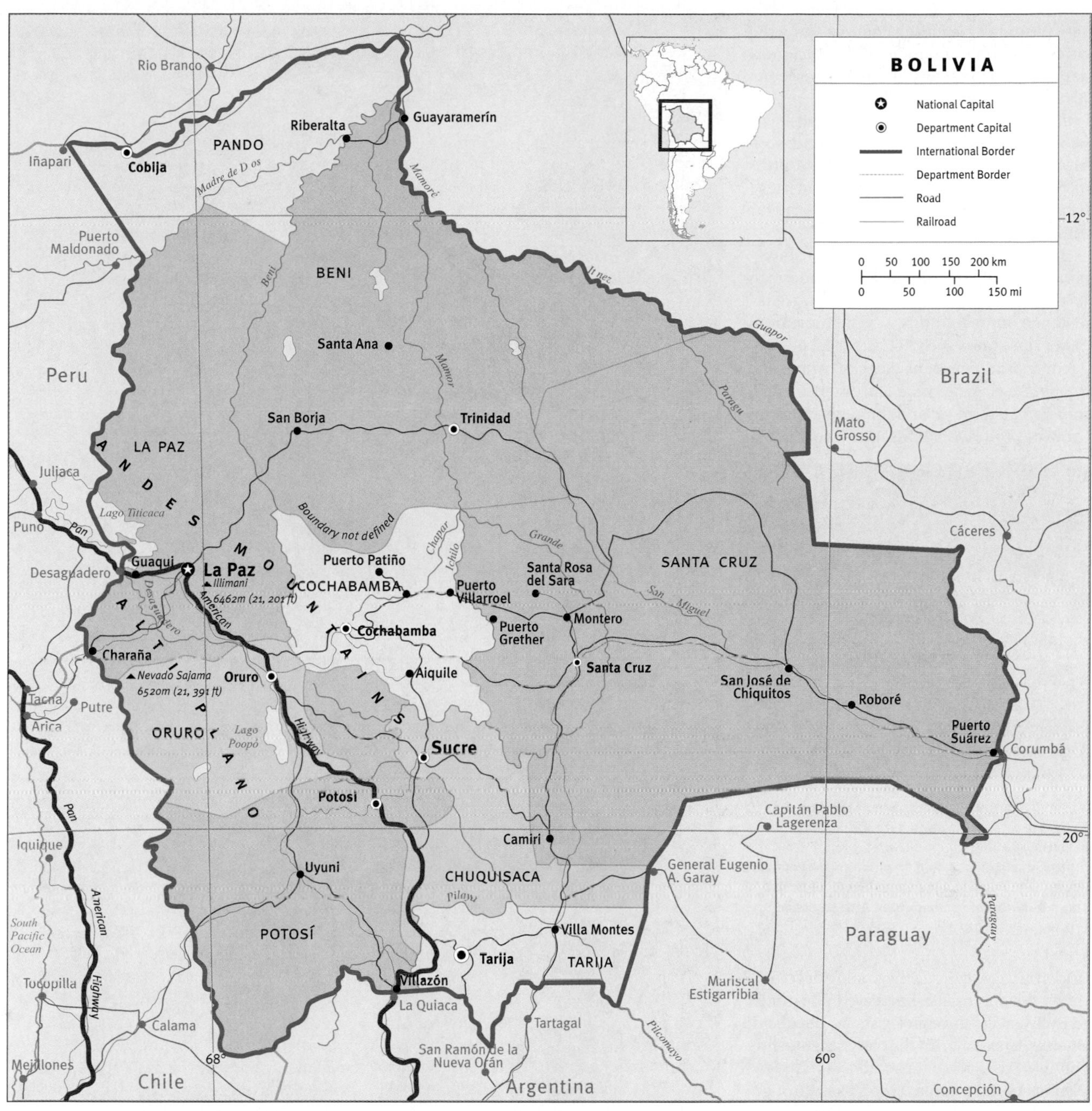

the tin mines, agrarian reform, and diversification of the economy were the results of the revolution that continue to affect Bolivia. Rising foreign debt and declining tin production plagued the military-controlled administration that lasted for 20 years into the 1980s. In 1982 the military returned governmental power to Congress and democratic elections began anew. Bolivia has since been tackling issues of coca eradication and the drug trade, strained relations with bordering countries, hyperinflation, and popular unrest.

Slavery

Bolivia's introduction to the slave trade began as early as 1535 with the expedition of Diego de Almagro, who brought the first African slaves into the region from Peru. Slaves were used to supplement the labor of the indigenous population in Potosí, whose numbers were rapidly declining due to poor working conditions and exposure to European diseases. Most scholars believe that the enslaved Africans were brought from Ríos de Guinea, a section of the West African coast that lies between the Senegal River and the Niger River. Others believe that Angola supplied most of the slaves to this region. The ambiguity is unlikely to be resolved for two reasons. First, Spain did not establish trading centers in West Africa, so captives were brought from diverse areas rather than one predominant region. Second, there was no standard form of classification for captured Africans. A slave's assumed origin would depend upon the labels given by the captors and the port of exit from which a slave sailed, neither of which was a reliable source of information.

Adverse conditions, including the high altitude and harsh labor conditions, caused a rapid decline in the African slave population, and Spanish authorities removed the remaining blacks from the Potosí mines in 1554. Under a system of forced tribute labor, indigenous populations replaced slaves as silver miners and blacks were moved into other positions (*see* Latin America, Blacks and Indians in: An Interpretation). Some slaves became domestic servants or even artisan apprentices in Potosí and Sucre. Others lived and worked in the Royal Mint, locked in the building to prevent escape. Most were transported to rural areas like the Cochabamba Valley and the Yungas (hot lands) region of La Paz to cultivate agricultural crops for the country's growing cities. The main products of the haciendas (large, agrarian estates) in the Yungas were sugar cane, citrus fruit, coffee, and coca. Coca leaf was the principal crop because it was needed as a stimulant and an appetite suppressant to maintain the efficiency of silver miners. Bolivia's coca-leaf cultivation met local demands and also supplied Peruvian mining towns.

Bolivia had the smallest African slave population of any colonial South American territory. The main reason was the great distance of the mining town of Potosí from major slave ports such as Cartegena, on the Pacific coast of present-day Colombia, and Buenos Aires, Argentina. The distance slave traders had to travel and the rugged terrain they had to traverse raised the cost of importing slaves. In the beginning of colonial times, the only established slave trade routes to Bolivia were through Paraguay, Brazil, and Buenos Aires. Later, in the early seventeenth century, Spanish administrators required that Pacific coastal colonies ship slaves through Panama. Although primarily used to support the lucrative mining operations, slaves were also valued as status symbols among members of the upper class. To own a slave for domestic services signified extreme wealth.

Above: Local school children in Chicaloma, La Paz, Bolivia display their project for a school fair, a cake they baked. *Photo by Rob Garrison*
Right: Music, dance, and traditional costumes are important in maintaining the heritage of Bolivia's small but vibrant community of African descent. *Photo by Rob Garrison*

The number of African slaves living in Bolivia during colonial times has been a subject of scholarly debate. Philip Curtin, in *The African Slave Trade: A Census*, estimates that 100,000 slaves were imported to Bolivia and the rest of the La Plata region (which included present-day Argentina, Uruguay, and Paraguay) throughout the entire trading period. Once in Bolivia, the black population grew and mixed with other ethnic groups. Calculating the number of blacks, therefore, is difficult because of racial mixture and the categories in which Spanish administrators placed blacks. Mixed-descent populations like mulattos (of African and European descent) and *zambos* (of African and Indian descent) were sometimes classified separately from the all-inclusive category of "black," while other records made no distinction. For example, records for the city of Potosí in 1611 indicate the presence of approximately 6000 free and enslaved blacks and mulattos, differentiating between the two groups with no mention of zambos. In the mid-1600s sources count the black population at 30,000 of a total 850,000 residents, but no subdivisions were made.

Independence

Most sources do not mention that Afro-Bolivians took part in the fight for independence when Bolívar's forces finally arrived in the country. Black Bolivians did participate in the war, but their numbers were so few that they did not constitute a significant contribution. Rebel forces achieved independence in 1825, and emancipation was legislated one year later in the constitution but was not upheld. As in most Latin American countries, Bolivia's constitution in 1831 contained a Free-Womb Law, which stated that no one born in Bolivia after independence was a slave but that those enslaved before 1825 were not liberated. Slavery continued uninterrupted, but the number of slaves decreased to about 1390 by the year 1846 because of legislation. Only in 1851 was total abolition decreed and the liberation of slaves completed (*see* Abolition and Emancipation in Latin America and the Caribbean). Information on the black population after abolition is sparse. The first national census in 1900 reported the number of Afro-Bolivians as 3945 under the category *raza negra* (black race), which included zambos and most likely mulattos.

Between 1900 and 1950 no complete census was compiled, so anything close to an exact figure for the Afro-Bolivian population during this period is unavailable. In a study he conducted in 1930, Gilberto Loyo, a Mexican geographic scholar, reported that there were 59,740 blacks in Bolivia. How Loyo arrived at this figure, or how he defined "black" as a category, is unknown. Considering the national census figure of nearly 4000 blacks in the year 1900, such dramatic growth in 30 years seems improbable. Information on the size of the Afro-Bolivian population after the 1900 census is based on scholarly estimates, since the census records after 1950 include no data on race.

After abolition, Afro-Bolivians were relegated to the background, beginning with a denied request to meet with the president in 1851. Some Afro-Bolivians said that they wanted to thank the president in person for their freedom from slavery, but at that time black and indigenous peoples were not allowed to enter the government palace. It would not be until the late 1990s that an audience with a governmental dignitary would be granted to an Afro-Bolivian group. Racial discrimination is the main reason for rejection of Afro-Bolivians by a society that sees slavery as black people's most significant contribution. Another reason for the lack of interest in the black population is that Afro-Bolivians have not been viewed as a distinct ethnic group by the government, unlike indigenous people. Through centuries of cohabitation with the Aymara-speaking people, blacks have assimilated much of this indigenous group's culture. Many Afro-Bolivian women wear *polleras* (indigenous dress) and have their hair braided into two plaits, like Aymara women. Rural Afro-Bolivians and indigenous people have much else in common. They have benefited equally from the 1952 Agrarian Reform, which made many of them landowners instead of tenant farmers. Blacks now work the same land as their ancestors and the ancestors of the Aymara. Like many indigenous communities, the towns in which rural Afro-Bolivian communities live often have no electricity, no potable water system, and no adequate sanitation facilities (i.e., household latrines). The main distinction between these two communities is government acknowledgement of indigenous ethnicity and the economic support received as a result, none of which has been granted to black Bolivians.

Settlement patterns also seem to determine differences between Afro-Bolivian and indigenous communities. In the communities of the Nor Yungas, where the incidence of interracial marriage and interethnic group socialization is lower, the differences between Afro-Bolivians and Aymara are more apparent. In contrast, black communities of the Sud Yungas have a less distinct presence owing to higher rates of interracial marriage and more pervasive acculturation. In the cities, Blacks live interspersed with indigenous and *mestizo* (of Indian and European descent) populations in the poorest neighborhoods. They compete for jobs as shop clerks, professional drivers, and domestic servants while settling in housing that may have insufficient electricity and inadequate sanitation.

Contemporary Times

Most of the limited written information on blacks in Bolivia focuses on slavery and colonial times. History texts rarely mention two of the important figures in Afro-Bolivian folklore and history. One of them, El Rey Negro Bonifaz (Black King Bonifaz), was enslaved with other Africans and brought to Bolivia to work on a hacienda in the Yungas. The slave owners of the Mururata hacienda gave him special privileges to keep the other slaves content. El Rey Negro was even given a crown, a scepter, and a cape to replace the valuable originals that were supposedly sent from Africa by his family. During festivals such as Easter, he was carried around in a litter and would dance the *zemba*, a royal dance that only he would perform. The Black King remained a figurehead in this section of the Yungas, and the tradition was continued with each successive generation. The last traditional Black King was El Rey Bonifacio Piñedo, who died in the 1960s but was succeeded by his grandson in 1982, allegedly as part of a cultural revival.

Another figure disregarded in Bolivian historical literature is Pedro Andavares, one of the few black soldiers who fought in the Chaco War in the 1930s. Andavares went to war for his country and had to fight not only the Paraguayan forces, but also racism within the Bolivian army. He returned to Bolivia a hero, and a monument was erected in his honor in Chicaloma, a small town in Sud Yungas. As one of the few blacks ever acknowledged for their contributions in Bolivia, Andavares still evokes pride among many Afro-Bolivians.

Although Afro-Bolivians have not historically been involved in national politics, they have worked in peasant syndicates in the Yungas region. Believing that the traditional syndicates were controlled by indigenous groups and that black representation was lacking, Afro-Bolivians in the Yungas tried to form their own syndicate, but this effort divided worker support and proved counterproductive. More concentrated organization has been achieved with the creation of *juntas*, which are permanent men's work groups and which no other ethnic group has. Large-scale organization for Afro-Bolivian communities is a challenge, since the concerns of one group are not always shared by the rest. Rural Afro-Bolivians have an interest in social justice, but their immediate concerns center on such local issues as declining crop value and the need for improved sanitation and potable water systems. Urban Afro-Bolivians, conversely, often are concerned with the African diaspora and the issues that affect all people of African descent in the world. Merging the interests of both groups into one social movement is difficult but not impossible.

Afro-Bolivian cultural movements were born of a local effort to cultivate the traditional dance and music forms of the black population. In 1982 a group of students from Coroico, Nor Yungas, formed a dance troupe to perform *la Saya*, an original Afro-Bolivian dance from the Yungas region. To ensure the authenticity of the compositions, the troupe collected and recreated traditional music, lyrics, costumes, and instruments. Having gained local support, they began to explore other dances in danger of disappearing, such as *la Cueca Negra* (a variation of an Andean dance), *el Baile de la Tierra* (traditional wedding music), *la Zemba* (a dance formerly associated with the Afro-Bolivian monarchy), and *el Mauchi* (funeral music). The troupe's initiative and its pride in Afro-Bolivian culture inspired the creation of similar groups throughout the black communities of the Yungas.

Naming themselves Grupo Afroboliviano, the troupe carried its performances to other parts of the country. In 1991 it released its first musical recording, *Saya*. This recording, along with performances at religious and folklore festivals, reintroduced many Bolivians to the unique Afro-Bolivian culture. In turn, this cultural revitalization evolved into a social movement whose aim is to gain recognition for Afro-Bolivians as a distinct ethnic group, help unite them as a community, and improve conditions in rural black communities.

The new movement began as two separate efforts, one in the Yungas valleys and the other in the city of La Paz. Rural blacks of the valleys were concerned with reviving a purer form of Afro-Bolivian dance and music. To this end, these communities held conferences between 1992 and 1994 to discuss and demonstrate a variety of dance and music forms. Animosity arose as each rural town claimed to have a more authentically African dance form (*see* Dance in Sub-Saharan Africa). While the people of the Yungas valleys argued over aesthetics, the residents of the city of La Paz worked at establishing connections with black cultural movements in other parts of the world (*see* Pan-Africanism and Afro-Latin Americans). The two factions met in 1994, called together in La Paz for a conference with the theme "Consolidando Nuestra Identidad" (Strengthening Our Identity). The meeting helped resolve tensions based on class differences between the two populations, and raised awareness of the black presence and its culture among the rest of Bolivian society.

The name Movimiento Cultural Saya Afroboliviano (Saya Afro-Bolivian Cultural Movement) was chosen to honor the dance that is used as a medium for cultural expression and a connection to the African past.

Another goal of the conference was achieved when an Afro-Bolivian contingent met with Vice President Victor Hugo Cárdenas to demand official governmental recognition of the Afro-Bolivian population as a distinct ethnic group. Cárdenas agreed to place relevant government offices in charge of assisting Afro-Bolivian populations. The results of this historic meeting are yet to unfold.

Today Afro-Bolivians are achieving far more recognition than in the past both politically and culturally. Grassroots leaders of the Saya Afro-Bolivian Cultural Movement have traveled to other countries to participate in conferences. Awareness of the movement, as well as support for its efforts, has increased. Agencies like the Washington, D.C.-based Organization of Africans in the Americas are now coordinating efforts with Afro-Latin populations to present the issues of these communities to Latin American government officials. With such steps, Afro-Bolivian communities hope to eliminate the racial discrimination that deeply affects their progress in Bolivian society.

Rob Garrison

See Also
Cartagena de Indias, Colombia.

Latin America and the Caribbean

Bonaire, an island in the Netherlands Antilles.

Africa

Bondei, ethnic group of Tanzania.

The Bondei primarily inhabit northeastern Tanzania between the Usambara Mountains and the coast. They speak a Bantu language and are closely related to the Shambaa people. Approximately 100,000 people consider themselves Bondei.

See Also
Bantu: Dispersion and Settlement.

North America

Bond, Horace Mann

(b. November 8, 1904, Nashville, Tenn.; d. December 21, 1972, Atlanta, Ga.), African American educator and university administrator who directed the historical research in support of *Brown* v. *Board of Education of Topeka, Kansas.*

Horace Mann Bond was born to Jane Bond and James Bond, an educator and Methodist minister. Bond was a precocious child, beginning high school at age nine and Lincoln University, an African American liberal arts college in Pennsylvania, at age 14. After graduating from Lincoln in 1923 Bond attended the University of Chicago, earning a Ph.D. in education in 1936.

A number of publications in the early 1930s helped Bond establish his scholarly reputation. These included *The Education of the Negro in the American Social Order* (1934), in which he linked poor education among blacks to their inferior social and economic status, and his dissertation, "Negro Education in Alabama: A Study of Cotton and Steel" (1939), in which he argued that Reconstruction represented a positive step for blacks. The latter work directly contradicted the scholarship of the day.

Bond drew the attention of the Julius Rosenwald Fund, which provided him with financial support throughout most of his career. The fund extended grants for his independent research and to universities with which he was affiliated. In 1934 Bond and his wife, Julia, traveled to Louisiana to document the progress of public schools in Washington parish's Star Creek District, keeping a journal that was published in 1997. Titled the *Star Creek Papers*, the journal contains a portrait of Washington county, genealogical charts, and a record of the lynching of Jerome Wilson; it is considered to offer one of the finest depictions of the Depression-era South.

Bond spent many years as an administrator at various black universities. From 1936 to 1939 he served as dean of Dillard University in New Orleans. In 1939 he became president of Fort Valley State Teachers College, leaving in 1945 to assume the presidency of his alma mater, Lincoln University. While at Lincoln he directed research for historical documentation in support of *Brown* v. *Board of Education of Topeka, Kansas*, in which school segregation was outlawed. Leaving Lincoln in 1957, Bond then became president of Atlanta University, serving there until his retirement in 1971.

During his educational career Bond became interested in Africa and supported the movements for African independence. He is the father of Julian Bond, the noted civil rights activist who became chairman of National Association for the Advancement of Colored People in 1998. Horace Mann Bond died in 1972.

William E. Ward

See Also
Brown v. *Board of Education*; Lincoln University (Pennsylvania); New Orleans, Louisiana.

North America

Bond, Julian

(b. January 14, 1940, Nashville, Tenn.), African American civil rights leader, politician, and educator.

Born in the Southern United States, Julian Bond grew up in the North, where his father, Horace Mann Bond, was president of Lincoln University in Pennsylvania. He began attending Morehouse College in Atlanta in 1957, where he cofounded the Committee on Appeal for Human Rights (COAHR) and organized sit-ins at the Atlanta City Hall cafeteria in 1960. That year he left direct campaigns to engage in communications work for COAHR when it joined several other groups to form the Student Nonviolent Coordinating Committee (SNCC).

In 1965 Bond won a seat in the Georgia House of Representatives in a newly created black district in Atlanta. However, his statements against the war in Vietnam led the House to bar him from his seat. In December 1966 the Supreme Court ruled in his favor and he was seated in 1967. In 1968 he led a separate delegation to the Democratic National Convention in Chicago to protest the exclusionary practices of the Georgia delegation. He brokered a deal to receive a partial vote and became the first African American placed in nomination for the vice presidency.

After leaving Georgia's House of Representatives in 1975, Bond was a Georgia state senator from 1975 to 1986, when he ran unsuccessfully for the United States House of Representatives. Since then he has served as regional president of the National Association for the Advancement of Colored People (NAACP), and as president of the Southern Poverty Law Center. He has taught at several universities, including American University in Washington, D.C., and the University of Virginia. In February 1998, Bond was elected chairman of the NAACP.

See Also
Lincoln University (Pennsylvania); Vietnam War.

Africa

Bongo (also known as Dor), ethnic group of East Africa.

The Bongo primarily inhabit northwestern Uganda and southern Sudan on the eastern shores of the Albert Nile. They speak a Nilo-Saharan language and belong to the Madi cultural and linguistic group. Approximately 300,000 people consider themselves Bongo.

See Also
Nile River.

Africa

Bongo, Omar (b. December 30, 1935, Lewaï, Gabon), president of Gabon (1967-).

Born in the village of Lewaï in southeastern Gabon, Albert Bernard Bongo was educated in Brazzaville, Republic of the Congo, and served in the French air force from 1958 to

1960, the year Gabon became independent of French colonial rule. He joined the Gabon ministry of foreign affairs in 1960, and in 1962 he was named assistant director of President Léon M'Ba's cabinet, then subsequently his chief of staff and his defense minister. In 1966 M'Ba, who was terminally ill, created the office of vice president to ensure Bongo's succession. Bongo took office as vice president in 1967. When M'Ba died that same year, Bongo assumed the presidency.

Bongo declared Gabon a single-party state in 1968, assuming the post of secretary-general of the newly created Gabonese Democratic Party. The sole candidate, Bongo swept the 1973 and 1979 presidential elections. In 1975 he announced his conversion to Islam (*see* Islam and Tradition: An Interpretation), taking the first name Omar. Though he was relatively permissive of dissent within the party, he was less tolerant of outside agitators, as evidenced by his 1982 decision to impose harsh sentences on members of a nonviolent opposition protest group.

Bongo encouraged foreign investment, and the stability of the government, combined with Gabon's mineral wealth (primarily petroleum and uranium), succeeded in bringing in a fair amount of foreign, particularly French, assistance and investment. Bongo has been accused of financial extravagance, including driving the country into debt in preparation for the 1977 Organization of African Unity (OAU) conference held in Gabon; constructing the massive Trans-Gabon rail system; and building a presidential palace at an estimated cost of $30 million.

In response to a coup plot discovered among the presidential guard in 1989, Bongo agreed to enact sweeping reforms, including the creation of a national senate, decentralization of the budgetary process, and freedom of assembly and press. He legalized opposition parties in 1991 and created a transitional government, the Gabonese Social Democratic Grouping. This government oversaw the introduction of a new constitution and the implementation of elections in 1993, in which Bongo won reelection with 51 percent of the vote.

Eric Young

See Also
Brazzaville, Republic of the Congo; Organization of African Unity; Mba, Léon.

North America

Bonner, Marita

(b. June 16, 1899, Brookline, Mass.; d. December 6, 1971, Chicago, Ill.), author whose autobiographical essay depicted the situation of African American women in 1925.

One of four children of Mary Noel and Joseph Bonner, Marita Odette Bonner was educated at Brookline High School and Radcliffe College, graduating with a B.A. in English and comparative literature in 1922. After teaching for two years at Bluefield Colored Institute in Bluefield, West Virginia, she moved to Washington, D.C., where she taught high school until 1930.

As a member of the literary "S" salon in Washington, Bonner met such members of the Harlem Renaissance as Langston Hughes, Georgia Douglas Johnson, and Jean Toomer and published her first story, "The Hands," in *Opportunity* (1925). She wrote the autobiographical essay for which she is best known, "On Being Young – A Woman – and Colored," in the same year. Although as a member of Washington's Krigwa Players she wrote three experimental plays – *The Pot Maker* (1927), *The Purple Flower* (1928), and *Exit: An Illusion* (1929) – her real focus, until she stopped publishing in 1941, was the short story.

Bonner married William Almy Occomy, an accountant, in 1930, and they moved to Chicago. She taught high school there, brought up her three children, and wrote interconnected short stories about the fictional Frye Street. Her literary preoccupations were intergenerational and interracial, depicting class conflict and the corruptive nature of the urban environment. She also won prizes from the magazines in which her stories most frequently appeared – *Opportunity* (supported by the National Urban League) and *Crisis* (a publication of the National Association for the Advancement of Colored People).

See Also
Chicago, Illinois; *Crisis, The*; *Opportunity: Journal of Negro Life.*

North America

Bontemps, Arna

(b. October 13, 1902, Alexandria, La.; d. June 4, 1973, Nashville, Tenn.), American poet, novelist, historian, playwright, editor, and anthologist of the Harlem Renaissance.

Arna Bontemps was born to parents of Creole descent who eventually converted to the Seventh Day Adventist faith. While Bontemps was young, his family moved to Los Angeles, California. Bontemps was affected deeply by the childhood loss of his mother and by his upbringing by a stern, pragmatic father who hoped, mistakenly, that his son would make the family trade of masonry his life's work. Educated at Seventh Day Adventist institutions, Bontemps graduated from Pacific Union College in 1923. In 1924 he took a teaching job at the Harlem Academy in New York City.

Literary success came early to Bontemps. His creativity and social conscience were stirred by the cultural vitality he found in 1920s New York. By 1926 his poetry had appeared in two of the most important journals of the period, *Crisis*, published by the National Association for the Advancement of Colored People, and *Opportunity*, published by the National Urban League. In fact, Bontemps was honored with the *Crisis*'s poetry prize in 1926 for "A Black Man Talks of Reaping" and with *Opportunity*'s 1926 and 1927 Alexander Pushkin poetry prizes for the poems "Golgotha Is a Mountain" and "The Return." This recognition placed him in the company of other poets seminal to the development of African American poetry, such as Langston Hughes, Countee Cullen, and Claude McKay.

Bontemps left Harlem for Alabama and a teaching position at a junior college in 1931, the same year his first novel, *God Sends Sunday*, was published. The story of Little Augie, the prodigal, fun-loving black jockey of 1890s St. Louis became the basis for his first effort as a playwright, *St. Louis Woman*. Written in 1937 with Countee Cullen, the play had a successful run on Broadway in 1946.

While in Alabama, Bontemps turned his literary prowess in two other directions. Hoping to provide black children with positive role models, he wrote his first children's book, *Popo and Fifina, Children of Haiti* (1932) in collaboration with Langston Hughes. Spurred on by the book's success, Bontemps wrote 15 other books for children and young adults, among them *Frederick Douglass: Slave, Fighter, Freeman* (1959) and *Young Booker: Booker T. Washington's Early Days* (1972). He also wrote the acclaimed historical novel *Black Thunder* (1936). Like much of his poetry, *Black Thunder* gives a lyrical yet realistic description of a passionate struggle for freedom. The children's and young adult books and the historical novel were innovative in their exploration of new genres for the growing canon of African American literature.

In 1943, after earning an M.L.S. degree, Bontemps became a librarian at Fisk University, where he took advantage of his position to preserve the papers of Hughes, Jean Toomer, James Weldon Johnson, and Cullen. During his time at Fisk, Bontemps edited some of the most important mid-century collections of African American literature. With Hughes, he brought out *The Book of Negro Folklore* (1958) and *American Negro Poetry* (1963). *Great Slave Narratives* (1969) and *The Harlem Renaissance Remembered* (1972) appeared under his own editorship.

After retiring from Fisk in 1966, Bontemps spent the remaining years of his life as a professor at the University of Illinois, Chicago Circle, and Yale University and as a writer-in-residence at Fisk.

See Also
Creoles; *Crisis, The*; Harlem, New York; *Opportunity: Journal of Negro Life.*

Cross Cultural

Boogaloo a style of music developed in the Latino community of New York City in the late 1960s and early 1970s; it merged rhythm and blues with Afro-Cuban music and attained a sizable following in the African American Community (*see* SALSA MUSIC).

North America

Boogie Woogie, an African American folk style of piano that emerged from the American Southwest in the first decade of the twentieth century and persisted into the 1930s and 1940s, when it profoundly influenced the development of jazz music and RHYTHM AND BLUES.

The origin of boogie woogie is lost in the unwritten history of black Southern bars and bordellos, though its birthplace is often cited as the logging camps of Louisiana and Texas. Musicians such as "Bunk" Johnson, "Jelly Roll" Morton, and Leadbelly (Huddie Ledbetter) claimed to have heard boogie woogie in Texas around the turn of the century, roughly at the same time that bluesman W. C. Handy reported its appearance in MEMPHIS, TENNESSEE. Native Texas bluesman Aaron "T-Bone" Walker, born in 1913, claims to have heard it in church as a child.

Boogie-woogie piano involves strong rhythmic bass notes played not unlike the left-hand part in RAGTIME. Peculiar to boogie woogie, however, is its rhythm's rolling feel, which includes 8 beats a measure instead of the more common 4. Some jazz historians hypothesize that this rhythm adapts for the piano the bass figures in guitar and banjo playing. Early boogie woogie adhered to the conventions of blues, following a 12-bar pattern and drawing melodic (right-hand) lines from blues songs. Boogie woogie sometimes incorporated Latin American styles, influenced by the tangos, rumbas, and sambas that entered the United States through New Orleans.

For the first three decades of the twentieth century boogie woogie developed as a vernacular music. It appeared in the repertoires of pianists in jook joints and on the "honky-tonk trains" that transported African American factory workers and their families north and south during THE GREAT MIGRATION that followed World War I. Indeed, for some listeners the constant, crowded rhythm of boogie woogie evokes the clicking and clacking of a train.

Jimmy Yancey, a groundskeeper for the White Sox at Comiskey Park in Chicago, is considered the father of the genre. Yancey performed expert variations at small Chicago clubs such as the bar of fellow pianist Cripple Clarence Lofton. Yancey did not record his music, however, until 1939, ten years after his followers had begun to release their own boogie woogie singles. One of Yancey's most talented disciples, Meade "Lux" Lewis, celebrated Yancey and his music in the 1938 composition, "Yancey's Special."

The term *boogie woogie* first entered popular usage with the release of "Pine Top's Boogie Woogie" by Clarence "Pine Top" Smith in 1928. The cut appeared with others songs by Smith on Vocalion Records in Chicago. Although Smith died the following year, his and Yancey's success made Chicago the surrogate home of the Southern genre. Boogie woogie emerged as the music of choice during Chicago's rent parties of the GREAT DEPRESSION era, when apartment residents raised money by featuring musicians in their homes.

Boogie woogie entered the jazz mainstream after two Spirituals to Swing concerts at Carnegie Hall in the late 1930s. It became a thread woven into more sophisticated jazz compositions by Count Basie, the Will Bradley Orchestra, and others. Boogie woogie was also a primary influence on the development of the Kansas City big band sound, as well as the rhythm and blues (R&B) style that, in the 1950s, developed into rock 'n' roll.

Since the 1950s boogie woogie has continued to evolve as a corollary to jazz. Notable recordings of this period include the work of Rocket 88 in the 1970s as well as German Axel Zwingenberger together with Lionel Hampton and Big Joe Turner in the 1980s.

Eric Bennett

SEE ALSO

World War I and African Americans; Basie, William James ("Count"); Blues, The; Chicago, Illinois; Hampton, Lionel Leo; Handy, William Christopher (W.C.); Jazz; Ledbetter, Hudson William ("Leadbelly"); Morton, Ferdinand Joseph ("Jelly Roll"); New Orleans, Louisiana; Smith, Clarence ("Pine Top"); Walker, Aaron ("T-Bone").

Africa

Boran (also known as the Borana), ethnic group of East Africa and the Horn.

The Boran primarily inhabit southern ETHIOPIA, northern KENYA, and neighboring southwestern SOMALIA. They speak an Afro-Asiatic language and are one of the OROMO peoples. Approximately 200,000 people consider themselves Boran.

SEE ALSO

Languages, African: An Overview.

North America

Borders, William Holmes (b. February 24, 1905, Macon, Ga.; d. November 23, 1993), minister and civil rights worker.

William Borders was the third generation of preachers in his family. He earned a B.A. from MOREHOUSE COLLEGE in Atlanta, Georgia in 1929; a B.D. from Garrett Theological Seminary in 1932; an M.A. from the University of Chicago in 1936; and an L.H.D. from WILBERFORCE UNIVERSITY in 1962. From 1937 to 1988 he served as pastor of the Wheat Street Baptist Church in Atlanta, where he was a leader in the fight for civil rights.

In 1939 Borders helped integrate Atlanta's police department, and in 1945 he directed a campaign to obtain jobs as bus drivers for African Americans. In the early 1960s he chaired the Adult-Student Liaison Committee, which worked to desegregate Atlanta's hotels, lunch counters, and restaurants.

Robert Fay

SEE ALSO

Civil Rights Movement.

Africa

Bororo (also known as the Wodaabe), ethnic group of West Central Africa.

The Bororo primarily inhabit the CENTRAL AFRICAN REPUBLIC, CAMEROON, NIGER, NIGERIA, and CHAD. They speak FULANI, a Niger-Congo language, and are a subgroup of the Fulani people. Approximately 200,000 people consider themselves Bororo.

SEE ALSO

Languages, African: An Overview.

Latin America and the Caribbean

Bossa Nova, an influential Brazilian musical style that developed in the 1950s. Led by composer Antonio Carlos Jobim, singer and guitarist João Gilberto, and lyricist Vinícius de Moraes, bossa nova developed in so-called samba sessions (an adaptation of jam sessions) held in Rio de Janeiro's wealthier neighborhoods (*see* JAZZ, AFRO-LATIN).

SEE ALSO

Rio de Janeiro, Brazil.

Boston Guardian. Please see GUARDIAN, THE

North America

Boston, Massachusetts, a city in the northeastern United States that, despite its long history of rejecting official racial discrimination, has nevertheless experienced great racial tension and distrust.

Boston has the contradictory nature of being racially progressive while at the same time being racially oppressive. It was a noted center of abolitionist activity during the antebellum period, yet white Bostonians also permitted segregation and other acts of exclusion of blacks. During the 1970s, when a judge ordered busing of students to integrate Boston's schools, racial tensions rose to the fore again.

Blacks first came to Boston in bondage in 1638, on the slave ship *Desiré*. Boston became a prominent port in the slave trade, although slavery never came close to reaching the proportions in Boston that it did in the American South. By 1700 an antislavery movement had begun in Boston, and in 1701 Boston's board of selectmen unsuccessfully attempted to create a bill to end slavery by hiring white servants in their place. Many slaves were allowed to purchase their own freedom, or were otherwise freed by their owners, especially when antislavery activist Samuel Sewall published *The Selling of Joseph* (1712), which was followed by numerous manumissions.

By 1752 blacks numbered 1500, or 10 percent of the population, and a free black community was beginning to form in Boston's North End, then known as New Guinea. Some slaves had already achieved prominence, including poets Phillis Wheatley and Lucy Terry Prince and artist Scipio Moorhead.

The events surrounding the Revolutionary War created a wave of antislavery sentiment, and blacks made efforts to secure their own freedom. On March 5, 1770, Crispus Attucks, an escaped slave, was the first of five people killed by British soldiers in a protest that became known as the Boston Massacre. In 1773 Caesar Hendricks, a slave, sued his owner for "detaining him in slavery." An all-white jury sided with Hendricks and awarded him damages. Also in 1773, Boston's blacks unsuccessfully petitioned the Massachusetts legislature to abolish slavery. Finally, in 1783 Massachusetts abolished slavery and granted voting rights to blacks and Native Americans. Blacks, free and slave, fought in the Revolutionary War (*see* Military, Blacks in the American).

But the ending of slavery did not necessarily signify that blacks were accorded social equality. Many whites were determined to maintain the structures of racial segregation. As a result, Boston's blacks engaged in self-help activities to promote their own well-being. Prince Hall's creation of the African Masonic Lodge in 1787 was one of the most notable institutions to arise. Forty-four of Boston's blacks founded the African Society, a mutual benefit society, in 1796. In 1805 Rev. Thomas Paul helped to found the African Baptist Church, the first black church in the Northern states. Shortly after that, the African Meeting House was constructed. Completed in 1806, it was the only black-owned property in the city, and it quickly became the focal point of black social life.

During the 1830s Boston became the center of abolitionist activities in the United States through such publications as William Lloyd Garrison's influential The Liberator. In 1832 Boston's abolitionist organization, the Massachusetts General Colored Association, reorganized and became the New England Anti-Slavery Society. Even as a small segment of the white population agitated to improve blacks' social conditions, blacks still faced regular indignities, such as public insults and segregated facilities. Frederick Douglass, for example, was forced to sit in a Jim Crow car on a train that he boarded in his hometown of Lynn, Massachusetts. William C. Nell was forcibly removed from the Howard Theater in downtown Boston for refusing to sit in the Jim Crow section. And, although public schools were provided for black children, they were poorly funded, scholastically inferior, and often inconveniently located for blacks.

In the 1840s Benjamin Roberts, a black printer whose daughter Sarah walked past five white schools on the way to the "colored" school she attended, requested that Sarah be admitted to the school closest to her home. The Primary School Committee's refusal to admit Sarah to the whites-only school led Roberts to sue for admission. The Roberts' legal counsel was Charles Sumner, an abolitionist and future United States senator who argued that racially segregated schools were necessarily inferior and that racial segregation in education was unconstitutional and damaging. Though his arguments did not persuade Massachusetts's Chief Justice Lemuel Shaw, the arguments closely paralleled those of Thurgood Marshall in *Brown* v. *Board of Education of Topeka* more than 100 years later.

A wave of Irish immigration began during the 1840s, threatening the precarious economic position that blacks had occupied in Boston. Many of the Irish immigrants came with few skills, putting them in direct competition with blacks who had historically occupied unskilled labor positions. Blacks also felt pressure with regard to housing.

Blacks became increasingly militant, best exemplified by the reaction to the Fugitive Slave Act of 1850, which mandated that citizens aid federal agents who were attempting to capture runaway slaves. Abolitionist activity in the city was refueled. During the Civil War, abolitionist activity led to the enlistment of blacks and the creation of the Massachusetts Fifty-fourth Colored Infantry, which formed in Boston.

In the postwar years, blacks from the upper South migrated to Boston, recruited by factory owners or by relatives. The city's black population doubled within a decade, giving blacks greater political clout. In the latter half of the nineteenth century black Bostonians in the city's "old" Ward 9 elected 20 black candidates to public office, including the city council, the state legislature, and the school committee. In addition, by the end of the nineteenth century, Boston boasted several successful black-owned businesses, including the Eureka Cooperative Bank.

Despite these advances, Boston's blacks still suffered from racial discrimination. Most blacks worked in menial jobs for near-subsistence wages. Banks refused to extend loans to black applicants. Paradoxically, Boston took great pride in its abolitionist past, as evidenced in the erection of the Massachusetts Fifty-fourth Colored Infantry monument on the Boston Common in 1893.

Seventy percent of African Americans held employment in menial jobs in 1910. The settlement houses and social services organizations prevalent in urban America during this era came to Boston in the form of the South End House and the Robert Gould Shaw House. Boston experienced a new wave of immigration of blacks from the Caribbean and the African nation of Cape Verde; during the 1920s the city's black population grew sixfold. In large part, however, the Great Migration missed Boston, and blacks still faced housing and job discrimination despite protests from civil rights groups. World War II brought Southern and Midwestern black migrants in search of work in the war industries, continuing into the 1950s. Although blacks were becoming a considerable demographic presence, greater political power eluded them because of the imposition of at-large city council seats.

In the 1960s Civil Rights Movement leaders sought to evoke change in Boston by exposing the city's de facto school segregation and other inequalities. The Student Nonviolent Coordinating Committee (SNCC) and the Congress of Racial Equality established offices in the city to fight housing discrimination. In 1961 the Boston branch of the National Association for the Advancement of Colored People successfully sued the Boston Housing Authority, charging racial discrimination. This essentially signaled the end of segregated housing.

The move to desegregate Boston's public schools provides perhaps the most famous example of the reforming impulse of activist blacks and progressive whites in conflict with the white community's resistance to such change. During the 1960s Boston's blacks sought to integrate Boston's schools and were the driving force behind the Massachusetts Racial Imbalance Act of 1965, which was intended to end de facto segregation in Massachusetts. The issue played out over a protracted period of time.

Proponents of integration developed plans for what are now called magnet schools, in addition to proposing "metropolitanization," a kind of merger between school districts in the city proper and in outlying areas. Resistance to these and other progressive plans finally led judge W. Arthur Garrity to order the busing of black students from Boston's Roxbury neighborhood to predominantly white schools in South Boston in 1974. This plan, which was known as Phase I, was to be temporary until Garrity could devise a better one. The school board complied with the judge's orders, but the plan was flawed and, predictably, many of South Boston's white residents resisted. Their anger took the form of throwing stones, rotten eggs, and rotten tomatoes at buses and shouting at black students. Resistance continued throughout the year, but schools were finally integrated.

Blacks seemed to be making political headway in Boston. Black politician Mel King ran unsuccessfully for mayor in 1979 and 1983, but he was supported in both elections by blacks and whites, with increasingly strong showings. Other prominent black politicians in Boston included State Representative Byron Rushing and State Senator Dianne Wilkerson. Still, political power lay in the hands of the white majority. Boston experienced an immigration of African Americans and other nonwhites so that, by the 1990s, the nonwhite population reached approximately 40 percent. This numerical strength has not translated to political power, however, as such age-old political maneuvers as gerry-mandering have diluted nonwhite political power. In addition, many of the modern immigrant population have no political power because they have not acquired United States citizenship.

African Americans are leaders in all areas of life in Boston – and include such figures as Rev. Eugene Rivers; *Boston Globe* journalist Wil Haygood; Fletcher Wiley, former president of the Boston Chamber of Commerce; Charles Stith, ambassador to Tanzania; leading civil rights lawyer Margaret Burnham; Kenneth Guscott of Long Bay Management; and Bob Moses, founder of the Algebra Project.

Robert Fay

See Also

Cape Verde; Transatlantic Slave Trade; World War II and African Americans; Abolitionism in the United States; American Revolution; *Brown* v. *Board of Education*; Civil War, American; Fifty-fourth Regiment of Massachusetts Volunteer Infantry; Fugitive Slave Laws; Great Migration, The; Mutual Benefit Societies; Student Nonviolent Coordinating Committee (SNCC).

Africa

Botha, Pieter Willem

(b. 1916, Eastern Cape, South Africa), Afrikaner nationalist and later prime minister (1978-1984) and president (1984-1989) of South Africa who devoted much of his career to upholding apartheid.

Pieter Willem Botha was raised in a militantly nationalistic Afrikaner family in the Eastern Cape. His mother's first husband was killed in the Boer War (1899-1902), in which his father also fought for the Boers. At an early age Botha himself became an Afrikaner nationalist, dropping out of the University of Orange Free State Law School in 1935 to help found the National Party. A year later he became public information officer for the party and served on the Sauer Commission, the agency that helped to formulate the National Party's racial program.

In 1948 Botha proved instrumental in helping D. F. Malan and the National Party come to power. That year he won a seat in Parliament, representing the Eastern Cape district of George. As a reward for party loyalty, he was appointed to a series of cabinet positions in the apartheid-era governments of Hendrik Verwoerd and B. J. Vorster, including deputy minister of the interior, minister of coloured affairs, and minister of public works and housing. In these positions Botha maintained allegiance to the government's policies of racial segregation.

In 1966 P. W. Botha, as he had become known, was appointed defense minister, and he used this position to build one of the most formidable military machines in southern Africa. Under Botha the South African Defense Forces (SADF) were an imposing threat to those African neighbors who dared challenge the country's apartheid policies. His power was consolidated in 1978 when he was chosen as the country's prime minister.

The initial goals of the Botha regime were to destroy perceived security threats in neighboring countries, incorporate English-speaking whites into the National Party, and exploit class and racial divisions within the antiapartheid movement. Reform and repression went hand in hand during Botha's tenure. For example, while he legalized black labor unions in 1973, at the same time Parliament made it a crime for any white to employ an African who was not registered to work in that city.

By 1983 the growing antiapartheid movement, both at home and abroad, forced Botha to make further reforms. He led the passage of a new constitution granting Indians and Coloureds political representation under a new tricameral legislature. Widely viewed as an attempt to weaken the antiapartheid coalition, the move did nothing to stop the massive protests led by the African National Congress (ANC).

In 1986 Botha convinced Parliament to repeal the ban on multiracial parties, the ban on interracial marriages, and the pass laws. But even while he appeared to be dismantling apartheid, he was also using the SADF and the South African Police to suppress resistance brutally. In 1984 alone, more than 200,000 Africans were arrested for violating pass laws. It is estimated that between 1980 and 1989 military raids by the SADF on neighboring African countries – including Zambia, Botswana, and Zimbabwe – took the lives of more than 1 million Africans, left nearly 3 million homeless, and caused more than $35 billion worth of damage.

Botha suffered a stroke in 1989 and resigned as party leader shortly thereafter. In August 1989 he lost his post as president after a rebellion in his cabinet. He maintained a relatively low profile for a number of years, but his refusal to testify before the country's Truth and Reconciliation Commission brought him back into the public eye in 1997. On the subject of human rights violations, he argued that he had made his peace before God and felt no need to appear before what he called a "circus." He was subsequently charged with contempt of court, and in early 1998 faced possible imprisonment. But there was no guarantee that at 82 years old and in poor health, Botha would be held accountable for his role in one of the most brutal political systems of the twentieth century.

Alonford James Robinson, Jr.

See Also

Verwoerd, Hendrik Frensch; Vorster, Balthazar Johannes; Labor Unions in the United States.

Africa

Botswana,

a landlocked country in southern Africa bordered by Namibia to the north and west, Zambia and Zimbabwe to the northeast, and South Africa to the southeast.

A woman cuts facets in diamonds mined in Botswana. *Jason Lauré*

In many ways, Botswana challenges stereotypical notions about African nations. Since 1970 this former British protectorate has boasted one of the fastest growing economies in the world. Spurred by the discovery of vast diamond deposits in the late 1960s, Botswana has swiftly transformed itself from an agrarian society, whose chief export was beef, into an efficiently managed, mineral-based economy. Botswana's economic success has been instrumental in ensuring its equally remarkable political stability; since independence in 1966, the Botswana Democratic Party (BDP) has kept its majority in the National Assembly, the country's chief legislative body, despite an open electoral process and the presence of numerous opposition parties.

In recent years, however, economic disparities have sparked growing popular discontent. Bostwana's mining and cattle economy has produced an ever-widening gap between a wealthy class of ruling Tswana

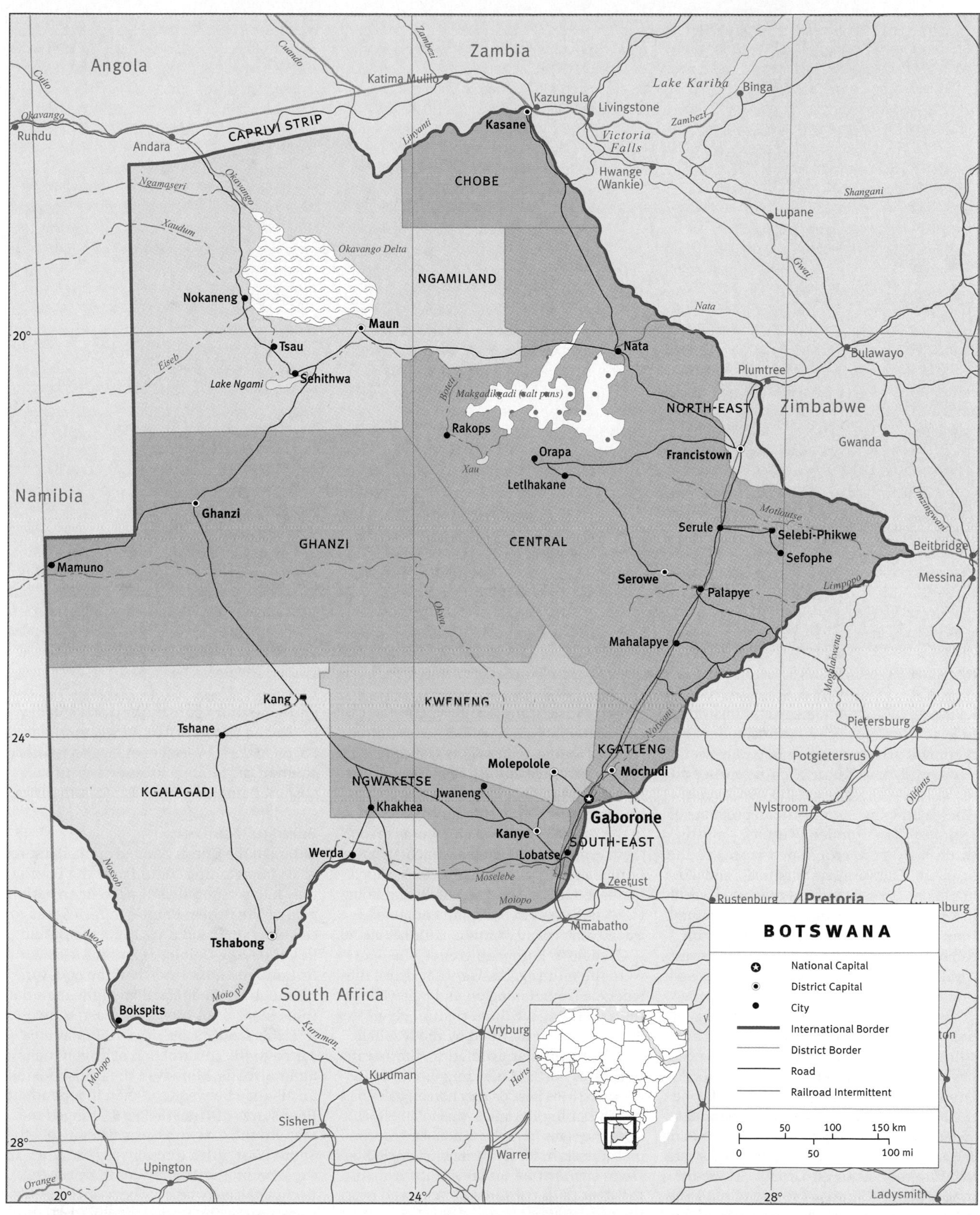

families and urban elites and a poor, ethnically diverse, and mostly rural population. For the present, however, Botswana appears poised to continue along its path of rapid economic development and political stability.

Early History

Archaeological finds show a human presence in the region known today as Botswana dating back many thousands of years. The earliest inhabitants were most likely the ancestors of the San (also known as Bushmen), hunter-gatherers who today inhabit the semi-arid steppes of southwestern Botswana, and the Khoikhoi, who probably originated in the north. Scholars believe that by the first century B.C.E., the Khoikhoi had adopted cattle herding and gradually spread southward across the eastern savanna. Bantu speakers probably arrived in the region by the first century C.E. They raised cattle, cultivated crops such as sorghum, and had the ability to forge iron tools. By the eighth century C.E. the Bantu-speaking ancestors of the present-day

This acacia tree, also known as an umbrella tree, spreads its limbs at the edge of the Mirami Reserve in Botswana. *CORBIS/Nevada Weir*

Kgalagadi had settled in eastern Botswana.

The ancestors of the Tswana, today the dominant ethnic group of Botswana, settled in the eleventh or twelfth century on the rolling plains around the Vaal River in what is now the South African province of Transvaal. They tended livestock – mostly cattle – and grew crops such as MILLET and sorghum. They were seminomadic and did not privately own land but measured wealth in terms of cattle. Clan chiefs maintained their wealth and authority by collecting tribute, and in turn loaned parts of their vast royal herds to peasant farmers for milk and breeding purposes.

Tswana territory extended into parts of present-day eastern Botswana by 1800 but still lay mostly to the south. That changed in the 1820s, during the time of warfare known as the MFECANE (or *difaqane*), when the NDEBELE, fleeing ZULU aggression, invaded the Transvaal region and began raiding Tswana and SOTHO settlements. Many Tswana fled into the KALAHARI DESERT, where the inhospitable climate of sparse rainfall and extreme temperature changes deterred the Ndebele from pursuing them further. By the mid-1830s the Ndebele had themselves continued northward into what is now Zimbabwe, and the refugee Tswana clans had resettled in the more arable lands near the Limpopo, one of the region's only perennial rivers.

Following the mfecane, Tswana culture coalesced around the eight most powerful clans, whose ruling families continue to dominate Botswana politics today. Bitter rivalries among many of the clans prevented them from forming a kingdom, as was the case for many other ethnic groups in southern Africa during this time. The division of the Tswana into rival chiefdoms made them especially vulnerable to incursions by European troops and missionaries, which increased in scale as the British and Boers (*see* AFRIKANER) to the south competed to extend their colonial territories further inland.

Of the two European groups, the Boers were the more aggressive. They drove the Ndebele from the region and believed that their victory gave them rightful claim to all lands formerly ruled by the Ndebele, including, in their estimation, the Tswana territories north of the Limpopo River. By the mid-1840s Boer commando brigades had begun raiding Tswana towns in an effort to drive the clans from the region. Despite formal appeals by local missionaries, including DAVID LIVINGSTONE, for British intervention, the Boer raids continued unchecked over the next 40 years.

In 1876 two paramount chiefs, Setshele of the Kwena clan and Khama of the Ngwato, began requesting British protection from the Boers, and in 1885 they finally received it. Although Setshele and Khama had no authority over other Tswana clans and ethnic groups in the region, the British used their request as a justification for claiming the entire territory constituting present-day Botswana as the British Protectorate of Bechuanaland. A section of Tswana territory south of the Molopo River was eventually absorbed into the Republic of South Africa.

BRITISH BECHUANALAND

Although the British claimed humanitarian goals for asserting control over the Tswana, they had territorial aims as well. An early goal of the British Empire in Africa was to establish an inland trade route that would link the Cape Colony of South Africa with Britain's territories north of the equator. Although Bechuanaland had little material value in terms of known natural resources or arable land, its flat, dry terrain was ideally suited to the construction of wagon roads and railroads. Moreover, the British feared an alliance between the then independent Boer states of Transvaal and Orange Free State to the east and German-controlled South West Africa (present-day Namibia) to the west on the Atlantic coast. By seizing Bechuanaland, which lay between these two rival groups, the British secured their expansion into the interior.

Economic development of Bechuanaland during the colonial period was, therefore, almost entirely limited to transportation. In 1897 workers completed a railroad across eastern Bechuanaland linking mining sites in the interior of what is now Zimbabwe to ports along the southern coast. The director of both the mining and railway projects was Cecil John Rhodes, whose British South Africa Company briefly held broad administrative powers over much of the Bechuanaland Protectorate. As South Africa's mining industry expanded, migrant workers from Bechuanaland traveled to South African gold and diamond mines, where they lived in guarded, segregated dormitories and earned a fraction of their white counterparts' wages. Cattle-owning Tswana took advantage of the new rail link to ship cattle for slaughter in the growing cities of South Africa, or even for export to Great Britain.

In 1910 Great Britain unified all its colonies in southern Africa in the Union of South Africa. A proviso in the union charter called for eventual incorporation of all British protectorates, including Bechuanaland. Tswana leaders, who had been allowed to keep many of their political powers in a British system of colonial administration known as indirect rule, successfully prevented this from taking place. However, they could not prevent the British from establishing economic conditions that guaranteed Botswana's dependency on South Africa well into the postcolonial period. The British never installed an infrastructure linking the region to seaports in any country but South Africa. Botswana thus remained heavily dependent on South Africa both for its imports and for what was then its sole export, beef. Economic

TOP: These fishermen, members of the Yei ethnic group, navigate their dugout canoe along the Chobe River in Botswana. *CORBIS/Peter Johnson*
LEFT: This elderly woman is a member of the San ethnic group, known for their traditionally nomadic lifestyle and elegant rock paintings.
CORBIS/David Reed
ABOVE: Gwi children sing and clap to a playful song in the Ghanzi district of Botswana.
CORBIS/Peter Johnson

underdevelopment further guaranteed that as drought and soil erosion prevented residents from maintaining even subsistence levels of agriculture, Botswana's adult male population would continue to provide a pool of inexpensive labor for South Africa's mines.

Despite these developments, relations between Bechuanaland and the British remained cordial. Many clans, particularly the Ngwato, adopted Christianity, and it was not unusual for clan chiefs and other elites to travel to Great Britain to attend university. One such attendee, the Ngwato heir-apparent Seretse Khama, created a furor in 1948 by marrying a white Englishwoman, Ruth Williams. That same year South Africa officially instituted its doctrine of apartheid, and the combination of events threatened to totally disrupt relations between the two countries. To appease South African whites, the British barred Khama from returning home to Bechuanaland. Only after he promised to renounce the Ngwato chieftancy did they allow him to return in 1956.

Khama considered the loss of the chieftancy a small price to pay. One of the things he had learned from his European schooling was that traditional Tswana political structures were doomed to extinction. Instead, Khama and his allies formed a European-style political party, the Bechauanaland (later Botswana) Democratic Party, or BDP, and campaigned on a nationalist platform to replace the British colonial government with an indigenous one set up along similar lines as a first step toward independence. Self-government came at first in 1961 in the form of a legislative council equally divided between black and white members, despite blacks outnumbering whites in Bechuanaland by a factor of 100. A more egalitarian system of universal adult suffrage swept the BDP into power in 1965, with Khama the prime minister of Bechuanaland. When the country achieved independence on September 30, 1966, Khama became president of the newly formed Republic of Botswana.

Independent Botswana

At the time of independence, Botswana was one of the poorest countries on earth. Its prospects appeared limited and its dependency on neighboring South Africa assured, with cattle grazing and subsistence farming as its only economic activities and over four-fifths of its area covered by the wastelands of the Kalahari Desert and, farther north, by the vast, economically useless Makgadikgadi Salt Pans and Okavango Swamp.

Botswana's economic salvation came just one year later, in a spectacular form: the discovery of diamonds in the Makgadikgadi Salt Pans near the town of Orapa. De Beers Consolidated Mines of South Africa had been exploring the interior of Botswana for deposits since 1955, but the Orapa site provided the first evidence that such mineral resources existed. By 1971 the Orapa mine was in production, with the Botswanan government receiving 70 percent of the revenues, and efforts had begun in earnest, fueled by international investment, to uncover further diamond sites. The largest of these, at Jwaneng in the Kalahari, opened in 1982. Botswana became the world's largest source of gem-quality diamonds.

The search for diamonds also led to the discovery of other mineral resources in Botswana. Chief among these turned out to be copper-nickel matte, coal, and soda ash. All told, the mining industry in Botswana accounts for more than half the country's GDP and 89 percent of its export revenues. Price fluctuations in the minerals market have not threatened Botswana's phenomenal economic growth, which has averaged 11 percent annually since independence and has not fallen below 4 percent since 1970. This stability derives largely from a series of National Development Plans put forth by the Botswana Democratic Party to cap excessive growth and preserve a substantial foreign exchange reserve.

Despite Botswana's economic prosperity, it remained dependent on South Africa for many of its imports and its overseas exports, nearly all of which still passed through South African ports. Khama and his successor, Dr. Quett Masire, therefore maintained a position of diplomatic neutrality toward the apartheid regime and other unstable, white minority-ruled states in the region, such as Rhodesia (later Zimbabwe) and South West Africa. Instead, Botswana helped organize the Southern African Development Community (SADC) to coordinate economic cooperation among the "frontline" states – the majority-ruled states of southern Africa bordering states under white minority domination. A 1979 conference of the frontline states in Botswana's capital, Gaborone, initiated a framework for cooperation that formed the basis for the Lusaka Declaration of 1980 on economic cooperation. A 1992 treaty formalized the structures of the SADC.

From independence until the late 1990s, the BDP remained Botswana's ruling political party; the numerous opposition parties, most notably the Marxist Botswana National Front, had little impact on its dominance. This was due partly to continued economic prosperity and partly to demography; the Ngwato, the largest of the Tswana clans, accounting for roughly a third of Botswana's population, dominated the BDP. Various indirect political restrictions in an otherwise democratic society, however, also helped to maintain the BDP's hold on power. For example, the BDP controlled Botswana's only daily newspaper, and its authority to grant mining and cattle-grazing rights gave party leaders and their allies near-total control of Botswana's economy.

The BDP was strongest in rural areas, where much of the population was dependent on the chiefly classes and the wealthy cattle owners who dominated the party. Opposition to the BDP government centered mainly in the rapidly growing cities, where the educated middle class sought to break the BDP elite's monopoly of power, and where large numbers of impoverished migrants from the countryside faced persistent unemployment. However, the retirement of President Masire and the orderly succession of his vice president, Festus Mogae, to the presidency in 1998 appeared to extend the BDP's firm grip on power.

Despite the continued existence of severe economic inequality and high unemployment (recorded at 21 percent in 1997), Botswana remained one of postcolonial Africa's few models for multiparty democracy and sustained economic growth during the late 1990s. Recent shifts toward privatization of Botswana's industrial and mining sectors have shown few signs of endangering the country's economic climate. Indeed, South Africa's transition to majority rule has created new economic opportunities for Botswana. South Africa's admission to the SADC in 1994 opened up the possibility of expanded trade and economic cooperation with Botswana's economically powerful southern neighbor.

Andrew Hermann

See Also

Bantu: Dispersion and Settlement; Colonial Rule; Gold Trade; Masire, Quett Ketumile Joni; Nationalism in Africa; Rhodes, Cecil; Christianity: Missionaries in Africa; Gaborone, Botswana.

Africa

Botswana (Ready Reference)

Official Name: Republic of Botswana
Former Name: Bechuanaland
Area: 600,372 sq km (231,805 sq mi)
Location: Southern Africa, north of South Africa
Capital: Gaborone (population 133,791 [1991 estimate])
Other Major Cities: Francistown (population 65,026), Selebi-Pikwe (39,769), Molepolole (36,928), Kanye (31,341), Serowe (30,706 [1991 estimate])
Population: 1,478,454 (1998 estimate)
Population Density: 2 persons per sq km (about 6 persons per sq mi)
Population Below Age 15: 42 percent (male 317,254; female 309,617)
Population Growth Rate: 1.11 percent (1998 estimate)
Total Fertility Rate: 4.03 children born per woman (1998 estimate)
Life Expectancy at Birth: Total population: 40.09 years (male 39.46 years; female 40.75 years [1998 estimate])
Infant Mortality Rate: 59.29 deaths per 1000 live births (1998 estimate)
Literacy Rate (age 15 and over who can read and write): Total population: 69.8 percent (male 80.5 percent; female 59.9 percent [1995 estimate])

Education: Most primary schools are supervised by district councils and township authorities, and are financed from local government revenues assisted by grants-in-aid from the central government. In the mid-1990s Botswana's primary schools had an annual enrollment of about 301,400, and secondary schools about 99,600; about 4500 students were enrolled in the University of Botswana in Gaborone.
Languages: English is the official language, but most people speak Setswana, a Bantu language.
Ethnic Groups: The Tswana are the largest ethnic group in Botswana. There are also significant populations of Kalanga and San.
Religions: About half the population practices indigenous beliefs; the remainder are Christians.
Climate: The climate of Botswana is semi-arid and subtropical, with warm winters and hot summers. The average annual rainfall varies from about 640 mm (about 25 in) in the north to less than 230 mm (less than 9 in) in the Kalahari Desert.
Land, Plants, and Animals: Most of Botswana is a flat to gently rolling tableland; the Kalahari Desert lies in the southwest. Savanna vegetation predominates in most parts of the country. Principal species include acacia, bloodwood, and Rhodesian teak. Wildlife is abundant and includes lions, giraffes, leopards, antelope, elephants, crocodiles, and ostriches.
Natural Resources: Diamonds, copper, nickel, salt, soda ash, potash, asbestos, coal, iron ore, silver
Currency: The pula
Gross Domestic Product (GDP): $7 billion (1997 estimate)
GDP per Capita: $3300 (1997 estimate)
GDP Real Growth Rate: 6 percent (1997 estimate)
Primary Economic Activities: The economy has historically been based on cattle raising and crops. Agriculture today provides a livelihood for more than 80 percent of the population but supplies only about 50 percent of food needs and accounts for only 5 percent of GDP. Subsistence farming and cattle raising predominate. Erratic rainfall and poor soils plague the sector. The driving force behind the rapid economic growth of the 1970s and 1980s has been the mining industry. This sector, mostly on the strength of diamonds, has gone from generating 25 percent of GDP in 1980 to 39 percent in 1994.
Primary Crops: Sorghum, maize, millet, pulses, groundnuts (peanuts), beans, cowpeas, sunflower seeds
Industries: Diamonds, copper, nickel, coal, salt, soda ash, potash; livestock processing
Primary Exports: Diamonds, copper, nickel, meat
Primary Imports: Foodstuffs, vehicles and transport equipment, textiles, petroleum products.
Primary Trade Partners: Switzerland, Southern African Customs Union (SACU), United Kingdom, United States
Government: Botswana is a parliamentary republic. Universal suffrage begins at age 21. The president is elected for a five-year term by the National Assembly, one of the two houses of Botswana's legislature. The president appoints a 10-member cabinet. Botswana's legislative branch consists of the 44-member National Assembly and the 15-member House of Chiefs. The House of Chiefs is a largely advisory body made up of the chiefs of the 8 principal tribes, 4 elected subchiefs, and 3 members selected by the other 12. Major political parties in Botswana include the Botswana Democratic Party (BDP), Botswana National Front (BNF), Botswana People's Party (BPP), and Botswana Independence Party (BIP).

Alonford James Robinson, Jr.

Africa

Bouabré, Frédéric-Bruly

(b. 1923, Zéprégéhé, Côte d'Ivoire), an Ivoirian visual artist and mystic.

Not much is known about Frédéric-Bruly Bouabré's early life. He was raised in the Daloa department of western Côte d'Ivoire, and the local Kru culture and community were an important part of his childhood. In 1948, when he was 24, the as yet undistinguished young man had a celestial vision in Dakar: the heavens opened themselves to him and he understood that he was to use his artistic talent to maintain and share the culture of his people, which is rooted in nature and folklore. After his vision Bouabré considered himself reborn as Cheik Nadro, or "he who does not forget," and he has devoted his life to his drawing and other creative projects.

Bouabré's drawings often form a series. They are generally small and rectangular and have a border of narrative text around them. In this regard, many of his drawings strongly resemble traditional African ideograms. The highly representative drawings in a series tell parts of a story and function much like a universal, visual language of symbols. Many of the drawings look childlike and simplistic. They are generally done in colored pencil on paper. The artist believes that through the use of simple, familiar materials and a direct, visual language of icons and symbols, his drawings are accessible to a wide audience. In this way, Bouabré has sought to promote the beauty and commonality of nature and of human experience. Whether they illustrate a traditional Kru folktale, reveal contemporary life in Côte d'Ivoire, or comment on international politics, Bouabré's drawings are meant to express the similarities among people of the global community.

Bouabré achieved considerable international success in the 1980s and 1990s. His first major international show was the "Magiciens de la Terre." This 1989 show gained for him and for other contemporary African artists worldwide attention when his works were exhibited at the Pompidou Centre in Paris. Subsequently, his works were shown across Europe as well as in Japan, Mexico, and the United States. Through these international exhibitions, Bouabré has brought his message of global commonality to a truly global audience. In 1998 he turned 75 years old and was living and working in Abidjan.

Christopher Tiné

See Also
Abidjan, Côte d'Ivoire; Dakar, Senegal.

Latin America and the Caribbean

Boukman

(b. ?, Jamaica; d. November 7, 1791, Fond Bleu, Haiti), one of the principal instigators and leaders of the Haitian Revolution.

The man known as Boukman was born a slave in Jamaica, at that time a British colony in the Caribbean. No one knows for certain whether Boukman was his real name. He apparently learned to read and write, and always carried a book with him. Thus he acquired the nickname "Boukman," meaning "the man with a book," or "the one who knows." It is thought that this man of knowledge for his epoch was a *n'gan* (in Haitian Creole a *hougan*), that is, a priest of Haiti's African-derived Vodou religion. Giant in stature, with a Herculean vigor, he was sold to a certain Turpin, the owner of a plantation in French-controlled Saint-Domingue (later to become Haiti). Appreciating Boukman's strength, his master gave him authority over his fellow slaves as a field commander. Boukman was also appointed a *cocher* ("coachman") to drive his master about in his fancy coach.

Boukman took advantage of these relatively important positions to gain great influence over the slaves of the plantation as well as other slaves in the nearby area. When the fruit was ripe, he gave the agreed-upon signal to begin a slave insurrection. On the night of August 14, 1791, he gathered all his partisans in a clearing of the nearby Bois Caiman (Caiman Forest) at Morne Rouge, in the northern part of Haiti. The ceremony was fortuitously timed, as the French Revolution had already created severe divisions within the society of colonial Saint-Domingue.

A substantial mythology and oral literature surround this event. According to many versions, during the culmination of the ceremony, held on a stormy night, an old priestess (or mambo) ritually sacrificed a pig. Those assembled were required to drink from the foaming blood of the slaughtered animal. They swore to revolt against their white masters, kill them, destroy their possessions, follow Boukman's orders, and fight for freedom or die for it.

The ceremony at Bois Caiman is a cornerstone in Haitian history and a central symbol of Haitian nationalism. Most important, it probably laid the groundwork for the organized rebellion that was soon to come. About a week later, on August 22, 1971, a slave revolt broke out at the same time in every corner of the Plaine du Nord, the richest and most opulent region of all Saint-Domingue. In a few hours, much of northern Saint-Domingue was ablaze. All the rich plantations, the industries of sugar production, the mills, the fields, the factories, the rich colonial mansions, went up in smoke. It is said that the flames of Saint-Domingue could be seen as far away as the BAHAMAS. The slaves killed their white masters and their wives and children. Boukman was reputed to be everywhere, encouraging his troops to burn, kill, and plunder. The rebellious slaves marched on the city of Le Cap, where 40,000 rebels laid siege to the town, in which whites and mulattos from the surrounding area had taken refuge. The carnage and sacking continued for weeks.

The rebellion attracted the attention of other colonial powers. The British, fearful of similar revolts in their colonies, initially sent help to the whites, while the Spanish, seizing upon an opportunity to challenge their French colonial rivals, supported the rebels. What had begun as a slave uprising spiraled into more widespread and complex conflict between the French authorities, Haiti's white elite, the free mulatto class, and slaves eventually united under the leadership of the former slave and skilled military leader Toussaint L'Ouverture.

Eventually the French authorities, under the command of Léger Félicité Sonthonax, managed to regain control of large parts of the island. But the damage caused by the slave revolt was irreparable. In an attempt to appease the rebels, Sonthonax declared the abolition of slavery on August 29, 1793. At this time the Spanish forces had already launched an invasion, joined by Toussaint L'Ouverture and his black regiments. With the declaration of abolition, Toussaint and his forces switched their allegiance, and by 1801 Toussaint had taken effective control of the entire island.

Toussaint wanted to restore order and discipline to Saint-Domingue and set its people back to work, but Saint-Domingue would never regain its former prosperity. Along with its economic system, the nation's social and racial structures had been irrevocably altered. The rebellion triggered by Boukman deeply altered the demographic situation in Haiti, as many of the island's white elite were killed or driven off the island; brought to light deep divisions among white plantation owners, freed mulattos, and black slaves; and forever destroyed the slave-based plantation system.

Boukman himself had always said he was invincible, claiming that he could become invisible and vanish into thin air. But on November 7, 1791, he died at the head of his troops in combat at Fond Bleu, near l'Acul in the north. As most of Boukman's slave partisans were convinced that their leader was immortal, he was beheaded on the spot and his head was planted on a pole at the city's gate, with the inscription "This is the head of Boukman, chief of the rebels."

Boukman had ignited a revolt that lasted 13 long years, ending only on January 1, 1804, when a convention at Gonaïves, controlled by JEAN-JACQUES DESSALINES, one of Toussaint's commanders, declared the country independent and renamed it Haiti. Boukman and his followers had not died in vain.

Paulette Poujol-Oriol

SEE ALSO
Toussaint L'Ouverture, François Dominique.

Latin America and the Caribbean

Boukman Eksperyans, Haitian roots-music movement (or *misik raisin*) pop group, exponents of Haitian *rara* music and traditional Vodou culture.

Since their formation in 1978, members of Boukman Eksperyans have been considered the founding figures of the MISIK RAISIN (roots-music) movement in HAITI. For 30 years prior to that period, COMPAS had remained the island's most popular music. During the 1970s, however, a new generation of Haitians found that they could no longer identify with the largely apolitical message of traditional compas. To them, the older style represented the Duvalier dictatorship and an epoch in which the Haitian people had become estranged from their own culture and traditional VODOU religion.

For Boukman Eksperyans, the solution to this problem lay in the acceptance and espousal of their Haitian roots. In their search for a more "authentically Haitian" music, the group began to incorporate instruments and dress from Vodou, and to speak out against the political oppression and ban of Vodou practices in Haiti. A member of Boukman Eksperyans has compared this environment to the physical oppression of slavery: "Mental slavery is much more serious than the physical. That's why we always say that Dessalines [a leader of the HAITIAN REVOLUTION] took away the physical slavery, but the slavery inside has not left us. We are slaves still."

The group takes its name from BOUKMAN, the Jamaican-born slave and reputed Vodou priest who initiated Haiti's independence uprising during the late eighteenth century. In a country torn apart by military unrest and government oppression, Boukman Eksperyans's outspokenness has not often been tolerated by the conservative governments. Accordingly, the group's 1990 song "*Kem pa sote*" was banned from Haitian airwaves. Two years later, its 1992 entry for Carnival was also banned.

Despite such setbacks, the group has remained firm in its decision to embrace the roots of its Vodou religion, and on its *Vodou Adaje* album Boukman Eksperyans urges its compatriots to do the same:

Haitians prefer to speak French
It's better if they speak Creole!
We're people of the Kongo, don't be
ashamed of it
Children of the Kongo, don't fear it
Born in Kongo, Guinee, Nago
People of the Petro way, Dahomey, Kongo
We're Creole
We'll never be ashamed of it...
Where have you come from? Africa!
Where are you going?
Who is your mother? Africa!

Gordon Root

SEE ALSO
Duvalier, François; Dessalines, Jean-Jacques.

Africa

Boumedienne, Houari (b. August 23, 1927, Clauzel, Algeria; d. December 27, 1978, Algiers, Algeria), second president of ALGERIA and leader in the struggle for Algerian independence.

In 1955 Houari Boumedienne joined the National Liberation Front (Front de Libération Nationale, or FLN) to fight for Algerian independence from French COLONIAL RULE. He rose rapidly as guerrilla commander, becoming the youngest colonel in the FLN two years after he enlisted. In exile by 1960, Boumedienne led the external Algerian armies in TUNISIA and MOROCCO.

After independence in 1962, Boumedienne backed exiled leader AHMED BEN BELLA during the conflict between internal and exiled leaders of the FLN over leadership of the new nation. He accompanied Ben Bella to Algeria, fighting battles with former allies to secure Ben Bella's position as Algeria's first prime minister and president, and his own position as vice president and defense minister. Several years later, in June 1965, Boumedienne engineered a bloodless coup that deposed Ben Bella and secured his own power as the country's leader.

As president, Boumedienne maintained the socialist vision of his predecessors. Remembered mostly for the bold reforms of his Four Year Plans, Boumedienne initiated an Agrarian Revolution and a Cultural Revolution. He nationalized both agricultural and industrial enterprises, including French hydrocarbon companies. In 1976 Boumedienne oversaw the creation of a National Charter, which defined a Third World socialist path for the country and a new constitution.

Despite the increased productivity of the Algerian economy, Boumedienne's government faced opposition from student groups as well as from other revolutionary leaders such as Ferhat Abbas, who saw the constitution and charter as the president's means of consolidating his own power.

Eleven years after his coup, Boumedienne was elected president in an unopposed contest. He died two years later of a rare blood disease.

Marian Aguiar

See Also

Front de Libération Nationale.

Africa

Bourguiba, Habib ibn Ali

(b. August 3, 1903, al-Munastir, Tunisia), nationalist leader and first president of Tunisia.

For over 30 years Habib Bourguiba guided the nation of Tunisia through its transformation from French protectorate into independent republic, and then through a period of intense social and political reform. Known as an outspoken, bold man with a wry wit, he is also thought of as a gradualist and a negotiator who used slow-moving tactics to achieve radical ends.

Bourguiba was born in a small village but studied in Tunis, Tunisia, before he traveled to Paris to study law and political science at the Sorbonne. He returned to Tunis in 1927, where he became increasingly active in the growing independence movement. He was the cofounder of the newspaper *L'Action Tunisienne,* which become a forum for opposition to the French protectorate. In 1934, dissatisfied with the conservatism of the Destour Party, at that time the leading Tunisian rights group, Bourguiba helped found the Neo-Destour Party.

The new organization took center stage in the nationalist struggle by demanding full independence. Under Bourguiba, it garnered broad-based popular support. It is estimated that by 1937 the Neo-Destour party had 28,000 activists and 49,000 supporters working out of 400 branches. Bourguiba built the group's infrastructure with branches in villages and provisions for replacing leadership in case of emergency. The party waged an intensive campaign using civil disobedience, including a strike in solidarity with nationalist movements in other North African countries.

In 1938 the French outlawed the Neo-Destour Party and shortly after imprisoned Bourguiba in Vichy, France. He was released four years later when the Germans invaded France. Despite his refusal to promise Tunisian support for the Axis powers, he was allowed to return to Tunisia.

Bourguiba fled to Egypt after the French resumed power following the war. Traveling throughout the Middle East, East Asia, Europe, and the United States for four years, he promoted the cause of Tunisian revolutionaries, who were waging an increasingly violent struggle for independence. He was invited back to Tunisia in 1949, where he engaged intermittently in negotiations with the French. After a period of civil unrest, Bourguiba was arrested once more in 1952 and kept under surveillance, both in and out of prison, for the next two years.

As France prepared to negotiate Tunisian independence, Bourguiba was released to lead the Tunisian delegation. Tunisia won independence in 1955 as a constitutional monarchy. Two years later, the *bey,* or king, was deposed and Bourguiba was elected president of the new republic. Although relations with the former colonial government were strained at first, particularly after a brief armed conflict over French military presence in Bizerte, for the most part Bourguiba maintained Tunisia's position of neutrality between the powers of Europe, the United States, and the Arab world.

As president, Bourguiba immediately initiated modernist reforms that curtailed the impact of traditional Islamic practices in civil society. He promoted women's rights (*see* Feminism in Islamic Africa), abolished polygamy, and brought education under state control. In one of his more controversial gestures, he advocated breaking the Ramadan fast in order to increase worker productivity. Following a path of moderate socialism, he allocated much of the national budget to education, agriculture, and health while limiting military spending.

Despite Bourguiba's general popularity, his moves to concentrate power raised concerns among some party members. For example, he turned on his minister of planning for initiating an unsuccessful plan to nationalize agricultural production and had the former protégé convicted for treason. During the early 1970s Bourguiba expelled most of his opponents from what came to be called the Destour Socialist Party. In 1975, he was appointed president-for-life by the Tunisian National Assembly.

Although Bourguiba allowed a considerable amount of freedom for opposition parties in the early years of his tenure, he became much less tolerant by the 1980s. Following the civil unrest that began in 1984, his administration used mass arrests to target both leftist organizations dissatisfied with some of the free market reforms of his late administration, and Islamic organizations opposed to his early social reforms. As Tunisians observed the erratic leadership of Bourguiba, by this time well into his eighties, rumors abounded about his deteriorating mental state. In 1987 Prime Minister Zine el-Abidine Ben Ali engineered a bloodless coup to depose him.

Since 1987 Bourguiba has been kept in close confinement by the government of Tunisia, held up as the symbolic father of Tunisia but kept out of sight. His disgust with this arrangement is no secret, and on at least one occasion, he has taken the opportunity of a live broadcast to disparage his "protectors." As one journalist put it, "rumor has it that it is his fury with his controlled residence that keeps him alive."

Marian Aguiar

See Also

African Socialism; Nationalism in Africa; France; Tunis, Tunisia; World War II and African Americans.

North America

Bourne, Saint Claire Cecil

(b. February 16, 1943, Brooklyn, N.Y.), African American writer, activist, and filmmaker dedicated to documenting African American culture.

St. Clair Bourne was the son of St. Clair Bourne Sr., who was an editor of the *Amsterdam News* and a reporter for the *People's Voice* in the 1930s. Although Bourne began his education at Georgetown University in 1961, he was expelled for student activism. In 1967 he received a B.A. from Syracuse University after working with the Peace Corps. Bourne began a degree in filmmaking at Columbia University in 1968 but was again asked to leave on account of his political activities.

From 1968 until 1970 Bourne was a producer, writer, and director for "Black Journal" (NET). He established his own company, Chamba Productions, and produced such African-American documentary films as *Something To Build On* (1971) and *Let the Church Say Amen!* (1973). In 1974 he received the Bronze Award from the New York International Film-TV Festival. In 1976 he acted as film coordinator for the World Black and African Festival of the Arts in Lagos, Nigeria.

Commissioned by the British Broadcasting Corporation (BBC), *The Black and the Green* (1982) documented Bourne's commitment to civil rights activism. He examined literary subjects in films such as *In Motion: Amiri Baraka* (1982) and *Langston Hughes: Keeper of the Dream* (1987). In 1989 the popular *Making "Do the Right Thing"* examined the work of a younger filmmaker, Spike Lee. In 1997 Bourne teamed up with Charles Fuller on a film about Oliver Law, an African American officer in the Spanish Civil War.

See Also

Lagos, Nigeria; Lee, Shelton Jackson ("Spike").

Africa

Boutros-Ghali, Boutros

(b. November 14, 1922, Cairo, Egypt), lawyer, professor, journalist, and diplomat; the first Arab and first African to serve as secretary-general of the United Nations.

Boutros Boutros-Ghali was born to a prominent Coptic Christian family in Egypt. His grandfather, Boutros Pasha Boutros-Ghali, served as prime minister of Egypt under the British protectorate from 1908 until his assassination in 1910. The younger Boutros graduated from the University of Cairo in 1946 with a bachelor's degree and went on to earn a doctorate in international law in 1949 from the Sorbonne in Paris. He pursued postdoctoral work at Columbia University in New York City, then assumed a post as professor of international law and international affairs at the University of Cairo. He worked as a journalist, writing for the daily *Al Ahram*. He also held teaching posts at Princeton University in the United States and at universities in India, Poland, and Tanzania.

In October 1977 Boutros-Ghali left his teaching post to serve in the government of Egyptian president Anwar al-Sadat as a minister of state for foreign affairs. The following month, after Egypt's foreign minister resigned to protest Sadat's intention to hold peace talks with Israel, Boutros-Ghali served as interim foreign minister. He accompanied Sadat on a visit to Jerusalem and later headed the negotiating team that crafted the Camp David Accords with Israel. Boutros-Ghali never became foreign minister, however, because it was a position traditionally reserved for Muslims.

Boutros-Ghali went on to build a career as an international statesman. An expert on development issues, he authored studies and articles on the disparity in wealth between rich and poor countries. He also negotiated agreements in several African conflicts, and his efforts helped win the prison release of South African leader Nelson Mandela. Boutros-Ghali was elected to the position of secretary-general of the United Nations (UN) in November 1991, based on many qualifications: his reputation as a negotiator; his first-name relationship with government officials in the East and the West; his fluency in Arabic, French, and English; and UN members' strong desire for an African in that position.

Boutros-Ghali faced a difficult tenure as head of the UN. His term in office began in 1992, when the world was reorganizing politically in the wake of the cold war. Boutros-Ghali attempted to negotiate several post-cold war conflicts with limited success. He supported sending UN peacekeeping troops to trouble spots around the globe, including the former Yugoslavia, Somalia, and Rwanda. He was outspoken and independent, and these traits did not sit well with some member countries, most importantly the United States. Although most of member nations supported Boutros-Ghali for reelection to a second five-year term in 1996, the United States, which was dissatisfied with his performance, forced his ouster.

Robert Fay

See Also

Mandela, Nelson Rolihlahla; Great Britain; South Africa; Sadat, Anwar al-.

North America

Boxing,

a sport in which each of two opponents, fighting with fists, attempts to knock out or land more punches than the other. Boxing is the only major American sport that has always been open to both blacks and whites.

Although fighting as sport has existed in one form or another for centuries, it was not until the eighteenth century, in England, that bare-knuckle fighting – sparring without gloves – became standardized. The sport quickly traveled to the American colonies, where many of its prime practitioners were African American slaves and ex-slaves. Bouts in the eighteenth and nineteenth centuries varied considerably. Often two men or boys were pitted against each other until one contestant could no longer stand. Such fights sometimes lasted as long as 100 rounds.

There were also more humiliating matches, known as battles royal, in which half a dozen blindfolded slaves were placed in a ring to flail at one another until one prevailed. In a few instances, slave fighters such as Tom Molineaux and Bill Richmond earned their freedom through boxing, or escaped most of the travails of slavery by touring abroad on boxing exhibitions. These sorts of manumissions, however, were rare.

Heavyweight John Arthur "Jack" Johnson was the first African American champion to capture national attention. Johnson began his boxing career as a child in battles royal during the 1880s and 1890s. Later, as a professional in glove-fisted fighting, Johnson scored dozens of victories. Because of his race, he was at first not allowed to challenge the white champion. Eventually, however, white sportswriters pressured boxing promoters into pitting Johnson against reigning champion Tommy Burns. They fought in December 1908 and Johnson won.

Following his victory, Johnson became a hero among blacks. Whites, however, were enraged as Johnson flaunted his victories and was seen in public with white women. In the hope of returning the title to white America, promoters prodded former champion Jim Jeffries out of retirement in 1910. Johnson's easy defeat of Jeffries sparked race riots in several cities. Johnson held the heavyweight title until 1915, when he was defeated by Jess Willard, a white Kansan.

For several years after Johnson's reign, white promoters kept African Americans from competing in championship fights. Keenly aware of this opposition, the handlers for up-and-coming fighter Joe Louis cautioned him against appearing arrogant and being seen with white women. In the 1930s Louis enjoyed a stunningly successful amateur and professional career and wide praise from whites for his dignified, restrained personality. Allowed to fight for the championship in 1937, he soundly defeated James Braddock and became an icon for blacks.

In 1936 Louis lost to the German boxer Max Schmeling in a match that had been billed as a fight between American democracy and Nazi totalitarianism. When Louis, in a rematch two years later, knocked out Schmeling in the first round, he became a hero to whites as well as blacks (this, at a time when African Americans were barred from competing in professional baseball and other "white" sports). Louis defended his title 25 times during the 1930s and 1940s. Despite financial ruin, a failed comeback, a cocaine addiction, and a mental breakdown, he remained one of America's most-loved sports idols.

Muhammad Ali, born Cassius Clay Jr., was the next great fighter to capture the American imagination. Widely admired by white and black America for his gold medal in the 1960 Olympic Games, Ali was known for his brash, colorful self-aggrandizement and spontaneous verse. In 1964 he won the heavyweight title against Charles "Sonny" Liston. Soon after, he converted to Islam and changed his name, angering many whites. When in 1967, as a member of the Nation of Islam, he refused to take part in the Vietnam-era draft, he was tried and convicted for his resistance, stripped of his title, and banned from boxing.

The United States Supreme Court overturned his conviction, and in the early 1970s he was back in the ring. In 1974 he recaptured the heavyweight title in the "Rumble in the Jungle," a widely publicized match in Zaire (now the Democratic Republic of the Congo) against George Edward Foreman. Ali also fought in several widely publicized matches against Joe Frazier, including the fierce, riveting "Thrilla' in Manila." Ali retired in the early 1980s, one of the world's most popular athletes.

In 1986, 20-year-old Mike Tyson's brutal efficiency made him the youngest heavyweight champion in history. Tyson also became the richest fighter in the history of the sport. In 1992 he achieved even greater notoriety when he was convicted of raping an 18-year-old woman. He served three years of a ten-year sentence, was released, regained the championship, then lost it to Evander Holyfield in 1996. In a 1997 rematch, Tyson was disqualified for twice biting Holyfield's ears, one time taking off part of his right ear.

TOP: Mike Tyson swings at Evander Holyfield in a 1997 title fight. Later in this Las Vegas match, Tyson bit Holyfield's ears, severing part of one, an action that prompted Nevada to suspend Tyson's license to box. *CORBIS/Michael Brennan*

LEFT: Boxer Tom Molineaux, America's first heavyweight champion, and an early African American sports champion, appears in an 1818 painting made at the time of his defeat to British champion Tom Cribb. *CORBIS*

ABOVE: In this 1978 title bout against Leon Spinks, Muhammed Ali regained the championship he had lost to Spinks just seven months earlier, becoming the first boxer ever to win the heavyweight boxing crown three times. *CORBIS/Bettmann*

Other prominent blacks in boxing include SUGAR RAY ROBINSON, who dominated the middleweight class in the 1940s and 1950s and who is widely regarded as the greatest fighter, pound for pound, in modern boxing. In the 1950s and 1960s FLOYD PATTERSON controlled the middleweight and then heavyweight classes; he was the first man to lose and then regain the heavyweight championship. In the 1970s and 1980s charismatic African Americans like Sugar Ray Leonard and "Marvelous" Marvin Hagler reigned in the lighter weight divisions. Heavyweights LEON SPINKS and LARRY HOLMES also enjoyed periods of supremacy in the 1970s and 1980s.

SEE ALSO

Baseball in the United States; Frazier, Joseph William (Joe); Free Blacks in the United States, 1619 to 1863; Hagler, Marvelous Marvin; Johnson, John Arthur (Jack); Liston, Charles ("Sonny"); Tyson, Mike; Vietnam War.

Latin America and the Caribbean

Boyer, Jean-Pierre

(b. Port-au-Prince, Haiti, 1776; d. Paris, France, July 9, 1850), president of southern and western Haiti from 1818 to 1820, and of all of Haiti from 1820 to 1843, Boyer united the country in the early years of its newly achieved independence.

A fair-skinned mulatto, Jean-Pierre Boyer was born free in 1776, in what was then the French colony of Saint-Domingue (now Haiti). Following independence in 1804, Haiti remained divided into southern and northern regions. In 1818 Boyer succeeded ALEXANDRE PÉTION, who had ruled southern and western Haiti since 1806. Rivals and conspiracies notwithstanding, Boyer managed to unite the country and governed for 25 years. During his presidency he achieved diplomatic recognition for the new republic in controversial negotiations with France, and attempted to institute far-reaching economic and legal reforms (*see* HAITI).

As a young adult Boyer had served with the French army. When the HAITIAN REVOLUTION broke out, splitting the country apart, he initially sided with the forces of André Rigaud, which tried to establish a mulatto-controlled republic in the south. With Rigaud's defeat by Toussaint L'Ouverture, the military commander of Haiti's black rebels, Boyer fled to France. In 1802 he returned to Saint-Domingue with the French army, which had been sent by Napoleon to restore French control over the incipient republic. Boyer subsequently deserted the French and fought under JEAN-JACQUES DESSALINES, L'Ouverture's commander. In 1804 Dessalines led the forces that finally defeated the French and declared Saint-Domingue's independence, renaming the nation Haiti. Dessalines declared himself the leader – and eventually the emperor – of Haiti. He was killed on October 17, 1806, as he attempted to put down an insurrection by mulatto generals, and the island split apart. Mulatto forces under Alexandre Pétion ruled a southern republic; in the north, HENRI CHRISTOPHE, who had been one of Toussaint's main commanders, established a separate kingdom.

Boyer served under Pétion and gained his support. Pétion made Boyer his private secretary and trusted counselor, and Boyer rose to supreme magistrate of the state in 1818. In March of that year when Pétion died, Boyer succeeded him as president of the south and west. When Christophe committed suicide in 1820, Boyer was able to thwart the northern secessionists and reunite the country. He then convinced the eastern Spanish-ruled part of the island of Hispaniola (now the Dominican Republic) to declare its independence from Spain and voluntarily join the Haitian Republic in 1821. In February 1822 he sent his troops into the former Spanish colony, finalizing its annexation and ruling over the entire island.

Boyer secured recognition of Haiti's independence by its former colonial ruler, France, but only by consenting to "buy" it with an indemnity of 150 million francs, which would serve as compensation for the lost properties of Saint-Domingue's colonists. These drastic conditions took a heavy toll on young Haiti's economic development, and Haiti was obliged to borrow from France the money to repay the first installment. In 1838 Boyer managed to renegotiate the treaty, obtaining a reduction of the indemnity from 150 to 60 million francs. In this new treaty, France fully recognized Haiti's independence, with no restrictive monetary clause. But Boyer never regained favor with the people of Haiti, who felt that he had "bought off" an independence achieved by blood and arms.

In addition to his international activities, Boyer attempted to restore prosperity and stability to Haiti. However, his government grew increasingly static and inefficient, and during his rule divisions between the mulatto elite and the large mass of rural black farmers widened. Among the new laws Boyer enacted were a new civil code (1825), a code of civil procedure (1826), a commerce code (1826), and a rural code (1826). During the early years of his rule, in a continuation of Pétion's policies, Boyer tried to gain peasant support by encouraging small landholdings. However, in the rural code of 1826, he reversed this policy and sought to implement a large plantation-based, export-oriented system, resurrecting land policies that had been initiated by Christophe and implemented by Toussaint. Severely criticized for its resemblance to the more drastic codes of former slavery, the new code sought to force peasants to work on large estates and restricted their movement. But Boyer's policies largely failed, and Haiti shifted from a plantation-based economy to one characterized predominantly by small landholders and subsistence production.

Boyer's administration was a gerontocracy, with the old civil and military servants from the times of Dessalines and Pétion maintaining their power. Boyer met with strong opposition from the parliament. More than once he ousted regularly elected congressmen, but gradually the opposition took momentum and the country escaped his grip.

Boyer's opponents declared their dissatisfaction with his rule in the famous Manifest de Praslin, and in 1843 a revolt broke out against him in the southern peninsula. The rebellion gained support in the whole south, then the west, and Boyer was forced to resign in April 1843. He fled the country, first to Jamaica and then to France, where he died seven years later at the age of 74, in a state of poverty.

Paulette Poujol-Oriol

See Also
Dominican Republic; Toussaint L'Ouverture, François Dominique.

Africa

Boza (also known as Bozo), ethnic group of West Africa.

The Boza mostly inhabit the shores of the Niger and Bani rivers in Mali and Niger. They speak a Mande language. Approximately 300,000 people consider themselves Boza.

See Also
Languages, African: An Overview; Niger River.

North America

Bradford, Alex (b. 1926?, Bessemer, Ala.; d. 1978?), African American gospel singer and composer known as "The Singing Rage of the Gospel Age."

Alex Bradford was born in Bessemer, Alabama where he grew up listening to the country blues, gospel quartets, and music in the Holiness Church. He moved to Chicago after serving in the United States Army in World War II and honed his singing and composing skills under the tutelage of gospel singers Mahalia Jackson and Roberta Martin. He composed "Since I Met Jesus" and "Let God Abide" for Martin. In 1954, Bradford created the Bradford Specials, an all-male gospel group. The Specials were famous for their colorful robes, soaring falsettos, and dramatic body gestures. Their biggest hit was Bradford's "Too Close to Heaven," which sold over 1 million records. By 1960 Bradford had moved to New York, where he began to experiment with gospel theater. Langston Hughes wrote the play *Black Nativity* for Bradford and Marion Williams in 1961. Bradford continued to participate in gospel theater, collaborating with Vinette Carroll and Micki Grant on *Don't Bother Me, I Can't Cope* in 1972 and *Your Arm's Too Short to Box With God* in 1976. In the 1970s Bradford formed the Creative Movement Repertory Company. He directed the Greater Abyssinian Baptist Choir of Newark, New Jersey, and served as minister in three churches. His impressive range and powerful voice garnered him the epithet the Singing Rage of the Gospel Age.

See Also
World War II and African Americans; Blues, The; Chicago, Illinois; Gospel Music; New York, New York.

North America

Bradley, David Henry, Jr. (b. September 7, 1950, Bedford, Pa.), African American novelist, essayist, and professor who focuses on the links between history and community.

Author of the award-winning novel *The Chaneysville Incident* (1981), writer David Bradley is profoundly concerned with personal and community history. Born and raised in a rural, coal-mining town, he is the son of a preacher, the late Rev. D. H. Bradley Sr., and Harriet M. Jackson Bradley, a local historian. A National Achievement Scholar in high school and a summa cum laude graduate of the University of Pennsylvania, Bradley began a serious study of nineteenth-century American history while doing post-graduate work in London in 1974.

Having come from a rural background, Bradley was alienated from urban blacks while a student in Philadelphia. He based his first novel, *South Street* (1975), on his own experience as an outsider in the city. The novel centers on the observations and interactions of a young black poet with the local hustlers, prostitutes, and bar patrons. Although *South Street* is now overshadowed by *The Chaneysville Incident*, it nevertheless exhibits Bradley's singular ability to depict convincing characters in the drama of life.

The Chaneysville Incident, Bradley's second novel, was inspired by a local legend verified by the detective work of Bradley's mother. While doing research for Bedford's bicentennial celebrations, she found the unmarked graves of 13 slaves. In danger of capture while traveling the Underground Railroad, the slaves had chosen suicide over reenslavement. Winner of many awards, among them the prestigious PEN/Faulkner Award in 1982, the novel narrates the journey of a history professor as he struggles to understand his natural father's suicide. Aided by his own father's journals and manuscripts, his surrogate father's stories from the past, and the support of his girlfriend, a white psychologist, the young professor connects his own history to that of his community.

Stints as an editor and English professor led Bradley to a position as professor of English and creative writing at Temple University, from which he resigned in 1996. He is a frequent contributor of essays and book reviews for national magazines and newspapers.

North America

Bradley, Edward R. (b. June 22, 1941, Philadelphia, Pa.), award-winning American television journalist and long-time correspondent for CBS's *60 Minutes*.

The son of Gladys and Edward R. Bradley, Ed Bradley earned a bachelor's degree in education in 1964 from Cheyney State College in Pennsylvania. He began a career in broadcast journalism in Philadelphia in 1963, where he reported for radio station WDAS. In 1967, Bradley moved to WCBS radio in New York, and joined CBS television news as a reporter in September 1971. From his post in Paris he was transferred to Saigon, Vietnam, where he covered the Vietnam War until 1974, when he began reporting from Washington, D.C. In addition to being CBS's White House correspondent, Bradley in 1978 became a principal correspondent on the news program *CBS Reports*. He anchored the CBS *Sunday Night News* from November 1976 until May 1981.

Bradley is best known for his investigative reporting and interviewing on CBS's Sunday night news show *60 Minutes*, which he joined in 1981 and for which he has won many journalism awards. Bradley won Emmys in 1983, one for "Lena," an interview with singer Lena Horne, and the other for "In the Belly of the Beast," an interview with convicted murderer and author John Henry Abbott. In 1991 Bradley received the Alfred I. duPont-Columbia University Silver Baton and another Emmy for "Made in China," an investigative piece about Chinese forced labor camps. Five years later in 1996, the Robert F. Kennedy Journalism Award grand prize went to Bradley for *CBS Reports'* "In the Killing Fields of America," a three-hour documentary on violence in the U.S.

Robert Fay

See Also
New York, New York; Philadelphia, Pennsylvania; Television and African Americans.

North America

Bradley, Thomas (Tom)

(b. December 29, 1917, Calvert, Tex.; d. September 29, 1998, Los Angeles, Calif.), five-term African American mayor of Los Angeles, California.

The first black mayor of Los Angeles, California, Tom Bradley served for 20 years, longer than any previous mayor of that city. Bradley's quiet, self-effacing manner attracted less national attention than other African American big-city mayors such as New York's David Dinkins or Washington's Marion Barry. Yet his national reputation was so strong that in 1988 he was on Democratic presidential nominee Walter Mondale's shortlist for vice-presidential candidates. The late Ron Brown, then chairman of the Democratic National Committee, praised Bradley for his ability "to hold a very complex and diverse city together."

One of seven children born to sharecropper parents on a cotton plantation in Texas, Bradley moved with his family to Los Angeles when he was seven. In high school he excelled both academically and athletically, winning a track scholarship to the University of California at Los Angeles (UCLA), which he entered in 1937. In 1940, after completing his junior year of college, Bradley left UCLA for a job with the Los Angeles Police Department (LAPD). While on the force Bradley studied law at night, earning a law degree from Southwestern University in 1956. When he retired in 1961 after 20 years with the LAPD, he had risen to lieutenant, at that time the highest rank achieved by an African American in Los Angeles.

Bradley entered politics almost immediately after leaving the police department and in 1963 became the first African American elected to the Los Angeles city council. He first ran for mayor in 1969, opposing conservative incumbent Sam Yorty, who labeled the moderate Bradley a front for "black militants and left-wing radicals." Yorty won, but Bradley challenged him again in 1973, this time beating Yorty with the support of a solid black vote and nearly half the white electorate.

At that time Los Angeles was still recovering from the 1965 Watts Riots. As mayor, Bradley focused on improving economic growth and reducing racial tensions. He was instrumental in bringing the Olympic Games to Los Angeles in the summer of 1984, which led to new jobs and increased tourism. He received the Spingarn Medal in 1985 from the National Association for the Advancement of Colored People.

Bradley's attention to the downtown business community often drew criticism from African Americans and others who felt that he was ignoring working-class and poor neighborhoods. In addition, though the city charter gave Bradley little control over the police department, many believed that he failed to address growing concerns about the LAPD's reputation for racist brutality. When in 1992 an all-white jury acquitted four white LAPD officers who had been videotaped beating African American driver Rodney King, the streets of Los Angeles again exploded in violence. The subsequent Los Angeles Riot left 58 people dead and caused billions of dollars in property damage. One year after the riot, which Bradley called "the most painful experience of my life," he announced that he would not seek reelection to a sixth term.

Kate Tuttle

See Also
Barry, Marion Shepilov, Jr.; Brown, Ronald H.; Dinkins, David Norman; Los Angeles Riot of 1992, Los Angeles Watts Riot of 1965, Los Angeles, California.

Latin America and the Caribbean

Bradshaw, Robert Llewellyn

(1916-1978), political leader from St. Kitts and Nevis.

Robert Llewellyn Bradshaw began his political career in the labor movement of St. Kitts and Nevis in the 1930s and 1940s. In 1945 he became president of the newly created St. Kitts-Nevis-Anguilla Labor Party. In 1966 he was elected chief minister of St. Kitts-Nevis-Anguilla. After the country was granted the status of associated statehood by Great Britain the following year, Bradshaw assumed the post of premier, a position he held until his death in 1978. During his term he sought full independence for the colony, though this did not come about until 1983.

North America

Braithwaite, William Stanley Beaumont

(b. December 6, 1878, Boston, Mass.; d. June 8, 1962, New York, N.Y.), African American poet, anthologist, critic, and editor who championed work by both black and white authors.

Although he praised and supported many African American writers, poet and critic W. S. Braithwaite always held the belief that the best writing was never racially or culturally specific, but spoke to universal themes. Braithwaite was born into a genteel Boston family, but after his father's death in 1884, he was eventually forced to leave school and take a job with a publisher to help support his family. He later said that it was while typesetting John Keats's poem "Ode on a Grecian Urn" that he realized he wanted to write poetry. His first pieces appeared in the *Atlantic Monthly* and *Scribner's*, and he published his first book, *Lyrics of Life and Love*, in 1904.

In 1906 Braithwaite began writing a regular column for the Boston *Transcript* in which he reviewed other contemporary poets, and in the same year he edited his first anthology, *The Book of Elizabethan Verse*. These accomplishments established him as a respected literary critic in addition to being a writer. After editing two more anthologies of older poetry, in 1913 he began publishing an annual collection of new poetry, the *Anthology of Magazine Verse and Yearbook*. Inclusion in Braithwaite's anthologies soon became an honor for young writers. He showcased black writers such as Langston Hughes, Countee Cullen, Claude McKay, and James Weldon Johnson and exposed them to a larger audience by including them with white writers such as Robert Frost, Edwin Arlington Robinson, and Amy Lowell. Cullen dedicated his famous Harlem Renaissance anthology, *Caroling Dusk*, to Braithwaite.

In 1918 Braithwaite received the Spingarn Medal, the highest honor of the National Association for the Advancement of Colored People, in recognition of his contributions to literature. He continued to work full-time as an editor and publisher until 1935, when he received an appointment as a professor of creative writing at Atlanta University. Six years later he published his autobiography, *The House Under Arcturus*. After his retirement in 1945, Braithwaite moved to Harlem, New York, where he published his *Selected Poems*, a novel, and a biography of the Brontë sisters before his death in 1962.

Lisa Clayton Robinson

See Also
Literature, African American.

Latin America and the Caribbean

Brand, Dionne

(b. 1953), Trinidadian poet and short story writer. Dionne Brand's writing reflects the racial and gender discrimination faced by black women and features resiliant female characters. Some of her more important works include *Primitive Offensive* (1980), *Chronicles of a Hostile Sun* (1984), and *San Souci and Other Stories* (1988) (*see* Literature, English Language, Caribbean).

Brand, Dollar. Please see IBRAHIM, ABDULLAH

Latin America and the Caribbean

Brathwaite, Edward Kamau, (b. May 11, 1930, Bridgetown, Barbados), Barbadian poet, critic, historian, and editor.

Many critics in the English-speaking Caribbean consider Edward Kamau Brathwaite the most important West Indian poet. Although Brathwaite is also a scholar and educator, he is best known for his poetry, which makes use of West Indian dialect and poses questions about roots and inheritance, matters of concern to Africans across the diaspora. (As Brathwaite puts it in one well-known line, "Where is the nigger's home?") Ghanaian author Kofi Awoonor has called Brathwaite "a poet of the total African consciousness."

Brathwaite was born Lawson Edward Brathwaite in Barbados in May 1930. He attended Harrison College, where he published his earliest work in the school paper that he and several friends cofounded. In 1949 he won the prestigious Barbados Island Scholarship to Cambridge University in England, where he received a B.A. in history in 1953 and a certificate in education in 1955.

While at Cambridge, Brathwaite published several poems in local journals and sent many pieces home to appear in *Bim*, the influential West Indian literary magazine that had been founded in Barbados in 1942. Through the *Caribbean Voices* program of the British Broadcasting Corporation, Brathwaite had the opportunity to broadcast many of his poems aloud in the 1950s, and his oral performances of his work came to be considered a key component of his poetry's power. He made companion recordings to several of his later books and was frequently celebrated for his use of authentic Caribbean speech patterns – the folk dialect Brathwaite calls "nancy forms," after the Anancy folktales. Anglo-American author T. S. Eliot was another influence on Brathwaite's work; Brathwaite was most interested by Eliot's use of African American JAZZ rhythms as a literary form.

From 1955 to 1962 Brathwaite was an officer in the ministry of education in GHANA, an experience that allowed him to see firsthand the African roots that have such profound importance for people of African descent in the Americas. After his return to the Caribbean, between teaching at the University of the West Indies in ST. LUCIA and JAMAICA and working on his doctorate in history at the University of Sussex, Brathwaite published three related collections of poetry that encapsulated his experience in Africa.

Rights of Passage (1967) poses the question, where do black people belong? *Masks* (1968) suggests Africa, but explores the ways in which that answer is still not adequate. *Islands* (1969) hypothesizes that the true answer might be "where he is" – in the unique cultures that blacks have created for themselves across the New World. These books were published together as the trilogy *The Arrivants* in 1973, and solidified Brathwaite's international reputation. He was awarded a Guggenheim Fellowship in 1971 and later won a Fulbright Fellowship.

Brathwaite received his Ph.D. from the University of Sussex in 1968, and throughout the 1970s, 1980s, and 1990s he was celebrated both as an academic and as a poet. In 1966 he had cofounded the Caribbean Artists' Movement, and from 1970 on he served as an editor of *Savacou*, its literary magazine, as well as an editor of *Bim*. Brathwaite added the name Kamau, which he had been given in Ghana, to his signature in 1976. His later books of poetry include *Other Exiles* (1975), *Mother Poem*, *Sun Poem* (1982), and *X/Self* (1987), which together form a second trilogy that traces a mythical narrative of West Indian history, and *Middle Passages* (1992). Brathwaite's 1986 nonfiction work *Roots*, a history of Caribbean literature and culture, won the prestigious Cuban-based Casa de las Americas prize for literary criticism.

Brathwaite remained on the faculty of the University of the West Indies in Jamaica for two decades but in 1991 joined the faculty of New York University, where he is reportedly at work on a third trilogy. In 1994 he received the $40,000 Neustadt International Prize for Literature, sponsored by *World Literature Today* and the University of Oklahoma, in recognition of his contribution to world literature.

Lisa Clayton Robinson

SEE ALSO
Anancy Story.

Latin America and the Caribbean

Brazil, largest country of South America, with a total area of 8,511,965 sq km (3,286,488 sq mi). It shares a border to the north with FRENCH GUIANA, SURINAME, GUYANA, and VENEZUELA; to the west, with COLOMBIA and PERU; and to the southwest, with BOLIVIA, PARAGUAY, ARGENTINA, and URUGUAY. Its Atlantic coastline stretches 7491 km (4655 mi).

Many people associate Brazil with the seductive rhythms of SAMBA, the annual Carnival celebration, soccer, and beautiful beaches. Few realize that Brazil's population includes the largest number of people of African descent in the Western Hemisphere. Only NIGERIA, with some 115 million people, claims a larger black population. The contribution of Africa to the population and development of Brazil has been prodigious and pervasive, and few, if any, aspects of Brazilian society and civilization have remained untouched by its influence.

The strong show of Afro-Brazilian culture during Carnival brings together Brazilians of all colors, helping to create the impression that Brazil is a racial democracy where people of diverse heritages live together happily and share in equal opportunities (*see* MYTH OF RACIAL DEMOCRACY IN LATIN AMERICA AND THE CARIBBEAN: AN INTERPRETATION). While white Brazilians tend to embrace this notion, black leaders say it is a myth. Despite the prestige they enjoy during the four days of Carnival, Afro-Brazilians as a group lack political and economic power. Even the firmest believers in racial democracy cannot deny that Afro-Brazilians lag in education, employment, health, housing, and a host of other social indicators. In Brazil, where slavery lasted longer than in any other country in the New World, the Afro-Brazilian struggle for complete freedom, initiated by rebel slaves such as ZUMBI, continues today.

STANDARD HISTORY OF BRAZIL

Official histories of Brazil usually begin with the arrival on April 22, 1500, of a Portuguese fleet commanded by Pedro Álvares Cabral in what is now Pôrto Seguro, BAHIA. In fact, several hundred indigenous groups, who had their own distinct languages and cultures, already populated the region. These included the Arawak and Carib groups in the north, the Tupi-Guaraní (the first to establish contact with the Portuguese settlers) on the east coast and in the Amazon River valley, the Gê of eastern and southern Brazil, and the Pano in the west. These groups were usually seminomadic and subsisted by hunting and gathering and by agriculture.

At the time of the Portuguese arrival, an estimated 2 to 5 million Indians were living in the territory that is now Brazil. At first, Indians along the coast traded and intermarried with the Portuguese settlers. After the colonizers began to take their best land, however, and enslave them, the Indians fought back, winning several battles. But the growing Portuguese presence after 1530 and the subsequent effects of disease and slave raiding decimated the coastal Indian populations and forced them into the interior.

Around 1530, Portuguese colonizers arrived and settled along the vast coastline, where they began to cultivate SUGAR. Over the course of the sixteenth century, a transition from native Indian to imported African labor occurred. Between 1580 and 1640, when the Portuguese Crown fell under the control of the Spanish Crown, men called *bandeirantes* conducted military missions to capture Indian slaves who had fled into the interior, initiating western expansion. The Jesuits also evangelized the native American Indian populations, consolidating scattered groups into towns and attempting to protect the Indians from slavery. From 1630 to 1654 the Dutch occupied northeastern Brazil.

The decline of the sugar industry in the late seventeenth century led some colonizers to journey further inland, where they dis-

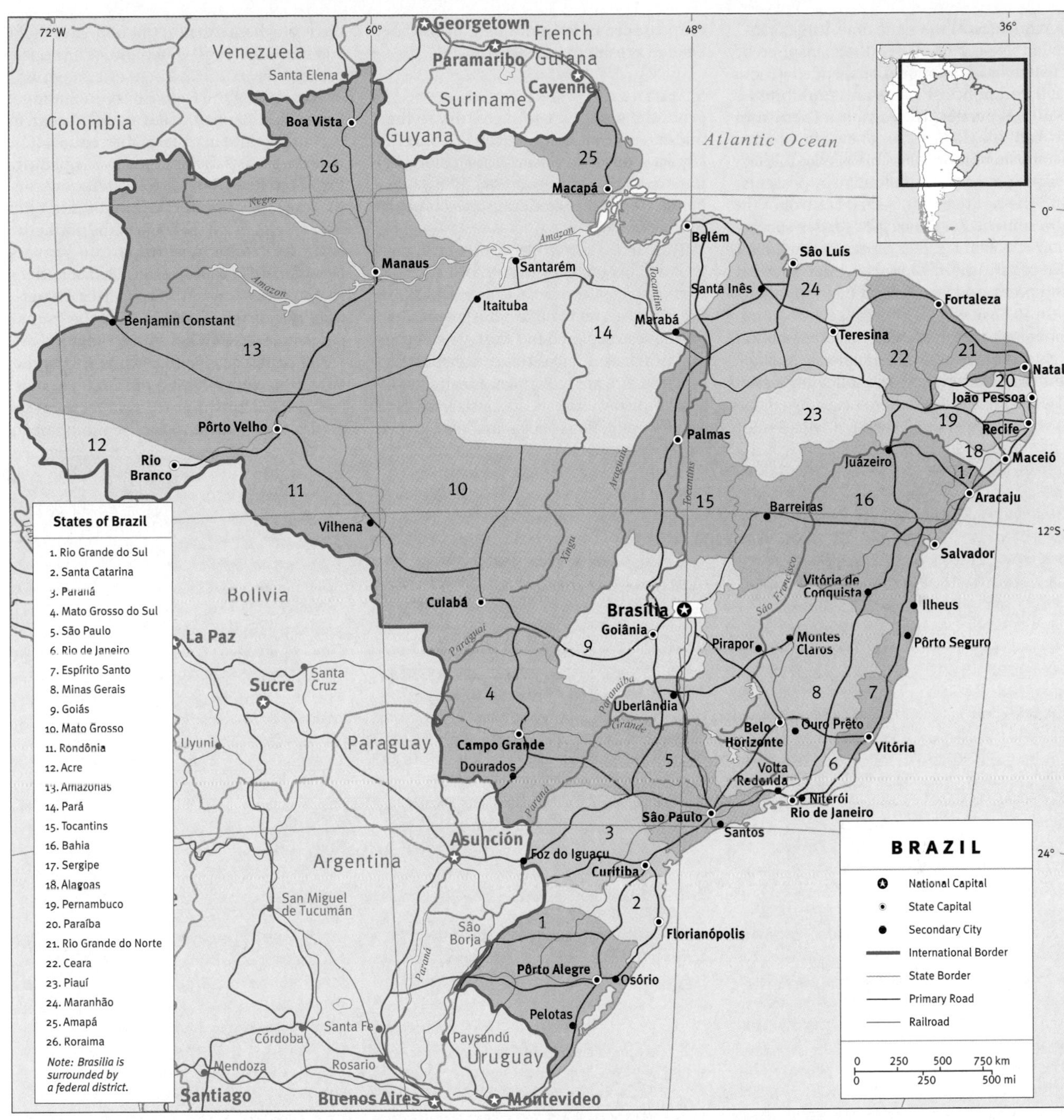

covered gold and diamond deposits in the area that is now the state of MINAS GERAIS. The precious metals and gems extracted in the eighteenth century, like the sugar grown since the sixteenth century, went from Brazil to Europe. Portuguese traders used the revenue to purchase slaves in Africa and ship them to Brazil (*see* TRANSATLANTIC SLAVE TRADE). This triangular trade continued well into the nineteenth century, when coffee became Brazil's most lucrative export. At this time, Europeans were encouraged to immigrate to Brazil to live and work on coffee *fazendas* (plantations) in the south, where growing conditions were ideal.

In 1808, following the invasion of Portugal by Napoleon and his troops, King João VI transferred the Portuguese court to Rio de Janeiro, which in 1763 had replaced Salvador as the capital of Brazil. He returned to Portugal in 1821, but his son Pedro I chose to remain. On September 7 of the following year, Pedro I declared Brazil an independent nation and himself king. Unique among Latin American countries, Brazil made the transition to independence through peaceful negotiation with Portugal, and as an independent country preserved a monarchical form of government. In 1831 Pedro I abdicated the throne to his son Pedro II, who ruled Brazil from 1840 to 1889. That year a military rebellion transformed Brazil's government from a monarchy to a republic, and Pedro II was forced into exile. During the reign of Pedro II, Brazil, along with ARGENTINA and URUGUAY, took part in the Paraguayan War (1865-1870). On May 13, 1888, Princess Isabel, acting as regent while her father was in Europe, emancipated all slaves by signing the Lei Áurea (Golden Law).

Founders of the republic transformed the former empire's provinces into states and replaced the parliamentary system with a presidential system, including a bicameral Congress and an independent supreme court. The next major political transition came in 1930, when a military coup brought the populist leader Getúlio Vargas to power. During his two terms (1930-1945, during which he ruled as dictator, and 1951-1954, as elected president) Vargas improved and expanded industrialization, public health services, and education, and attempted to centralize the government's sprawling bureaucracy. At the same time, Vargas's so-called "New State" (1937-1945), inspired by the Italian fascist model, suspended various civil and political rights and prohibited political parties. During a brief return to civilian rule (1945-1964), a new capital was established in Brasília. In 1964 the military, reacting mainly to mobilization by peasants and the political left, seized control of the government. For the next 21 years, a succession of military leaders repeatedly amended the constitution, suppressed free speech and press, and imprisoned their opponents.

In 1979, in what is known as the *abertura* (opening), the government restored political rights to the people and initiated a gradual return to democracy. The following period saw a significant growth in social movements as well as Brazil's civil society. Civilian rule was reestablished in 1985, when long-time opposition leader Tancredo Neves was elected by an electoral college, making him the first civilian president since 1964. However, Neves died unexpectedly before assuming the presidency, which fell to his vice president, José Sarney. In 1988 an elected assembly drafted and approved a new constitution, Brazil's eighth. In 1989, in the first presidential election by popular vote since 1960, Fernando Collor de Mello became president. He was impeached on charges of corruption in 1992 and replaced by his vice president, Itamar Franco. Fernando Henrique Cardoso was elected president in 1994.

Slave Trade

From the early sixteenth century to the mid-nineteenth century, Brazil imported the largest number of slaves of any colony in the Americas, absorbing more than 3.5 million of the 10 to 15 million slaves brought to the New World.

The earliest known arrival of African slaves in Brazil occurred in 1538 (*see* Slavery in Latin America and the Caribbean). During the hundred years before this event, the Portuguese explored the West African coast and purchased slaves there, transporting enslaved Africans to Portugal as early as 1433. The Portuguese had already enslaved Africans for the production of sugar in their colonies in Africa – Madeira and São Tomé – before bringing slaves to Brazil for the same purpose. With the colonization and development of Brazil, the Portuguese extended and intensified their slave-trading activities. When not operating directly between Africa and Brazil, the slave trade took a triangular form in which European goods went to Africa, Africans slaves went to Brazil, and sugar went from Brazil to Europe.

Portuguese settlers imported slaves from various parts of Africa. Initially, the principal suppliers of slaves to Brazil were the Portuguese *assentos* (monopolies) in the Sudanic Empires of western Africa, especially present-day Guinea. Then, after a period of trade along the Gold Coast, including Ghana and Benin, the Portuguese began to exploit the slave markets in the central and southwestern parts of Africa, principally in the Republic of the Congo and Angola. In the later stages of the slave trade, after the British suppressed the trade in the northern Atlantic, Brazil's most important sources for slaves were southwestern Africa and the Indian Ocean coast of East Africa, in particular Mozambique. Much of the human cargo entered Brazil through the ports of Salvador, Rio de Janeiro, and Santos. By the late 1800s, the abolition of the slave trade and the decline of northeastern sugar plantations had led to the formation of an intranational slave market in which coffee planters in the southern provinces purchased slaves from the northern provinces.

Members of the sisterhood *Irmandade da Boa Morte* light candles in preparation for a procession in Cachoeira, Bahia. *Michael Ende/Aurora*

The wide-reaching nature of the Portuguese slave trade made for an eclectic slave population. Africans sold into slavery and shipped to Brazil came from various segments of society. Many were war captives. Some were criminals or debtors. Others had been slaves in the African communities from which they came (*see* Slavery in Africa). Overall, the number of male slaves brought to Brazil was double that of female slaves, and adults were favored over children. Unlike the United States, Brazil preferred to purchase new African slaves rather than reproduce the slave population domestically.

The importation of African slaves to Brazil increased dramatically in the 1580s, when the sugar industry flourished. Demand for slave labor remained high during the following centuries with the mining of gold and diamonds and, much later, with the development of the coffee industry. Because they were imported at such a high rate, slaves often constituted a majority of the population in rural sugar-producing and mining regions. An estimated 100,000 slaves entered Brazil in the sixteenth century, 600,000 in the seventeenth century, 1.3 million in the eighteenth century, and 1.6 million from 1800 until the trade was effectively ended in 1850. These estimates do not take into account the number of slaves – sometimes as many as half of those on a slave ship – who perished during the so-called Middle Passage.

Slave importation was most intense during the first half of the nineteenth century, as it became evident that the slave trade would soon end. The British, who had outlawed their own slave trade in 1807 and slavery itself in 1833, campaigned to end the international slave trade, which gave Brazil a competitive advantage over Great Britain in the world sugar markets. Brazil deferred to the British by passing legislation that freed all slaves entering the country from November 7, 1831, onward. This law went virtually unenforced after 1837, when the proslavery Conservatives won control of the Brazilian government and a large-scale, illegal slave trade ensued. The arrival of British ships on the Brazilian coast in 1850, however, forced the government to draft the Queirós Law of September 4, 1850, which instituted severe penalties for slave traders. By 1852 Brazilian authorities had largely succeeded in suppressing the transatlantic slave trade.

Slavery

The Portuguese initially tried to enslave Brazil's indigenous population. But the Indians' susceptibility to European diseases and their general unwillingness to do plantation work led the Portuguese to rely more heavily on African labor. The switch from Indian to African labor occurred between the 1580s and the 1630s, as the sugar industry became central to the Portuguese economy.

Slaves brought to Brazil their knowledge of metallurgy, mining, cattle farming, and crop production. They modified and expanded their technical knowledge in Brazil, learning carpentry, jewelry making, and tailoring, among other trades. A small percentage of slaves worked in the master's house, performing domestic chores and caring for children. The vast majority worked outside the household. During the sixteenth and seventeenth centuries, most worked in the sugar fazendas or in the *engenhos* (mills) of the northeast; during the eighteenth century, most worked in the mines of Minas Gerais, Goiás, and Mato Grosso; and in the nineteenth century, the coffee plantations of Rio de Janeiro and São Paulo were the centers of slave labor. Slaves generally had a life expectancy of only another 7 to 15 years after the start of their captivity. The Portuguese forced them to work 15 to 18 hours a day, neglected their clothing and nutritional needs, and often punished them physically. The once-prevalent idea that Brazilian slavery was more benign than SLAVERY IN THE UNITED STATES has been largely discredited.

Unlike slaves in the United States, however, slaves in Brazil had the right to purchase their own freedom and, having numerous

Nelson Pereira dos Santos is one of Brazil's most important and innovative filmmakers. Especially well known are his films *Rio 40 Degrees* (1955) and *Memories of Prison* (1984). *Vantoen Pereira, Jr./Contexto*

Catholic holidays off throughout the year, were able to work for themselves and save money for that purpose. Some slaves, known as *negros de ganho* hired out their services and were sometimes allowed to live on their own, with the condition that they return a percentage of their profits to their owner. Other slaves were granted their freedom as a reward for long, faithful service. Records indicate that women were freed twice as often as men, and that enslaved *crioulos* (Brazilian-born, of African parentage) and *mulatos* (Brazilian-born, of mixed African and European parentage), though less numerous than African-born slaves, were favored over Africans as manumission candidates.

Free blacks and mulattos did not enjoy many privileges over their enslaved brethren. They were subject to laws that rarely distinguished between them and slaves. Like slaves, they were not allowed to carry weapons, dress extravagantly, or, with a few exceptions, hold public office. The employment opportunities of free blacks and mulattos were also severely circumscribed. Many free black and mulatto men endeavored to make a living as overseers on cattle ranches, in mines, or in boiling houses on sugar plantations. Less frequently they worked as artisans and barbers. Free black and mulatta females often sold goods on the street and at the markets, or worked as midwives. Although the extent to which a free black or mulatto was accepted by whites varied over time and from region to region, persons with lighter skin and a degree of wealth generally had a better chance of integrating into colonial society. Those least likely to gain entrance into the world of whites were enslaved blacks born in Africa who later acquired their freedom.

Africans, free and enslaved, were instrumental in the conquest and defense of the Portuguese colony. In the early stages of colonization, they helped push back coastal Indian populations and protect the settling population from Indian attacks. Black and mulatto regiments under black leaders such as HENRIQUE DIAS fought, along with native Indian soldiers, against the Dutch during the seventeenth century. In the early eighteenth century, some 6000 Afro-Brazilian soldiers from Minas Gerais helped recapture Rio de Janeiro from French invaders. A black regiment of similar size battled in the Paraguayan War. For their services, many black soldiers won freedom as well as eligibility for promotion. The army continued to be an important institution for Afro-Brazilians after the abolition of slavery, training emancipated slaves and thereby preparing them for integration into the larger society.

Religious brotherhoods – organizations affiliated with the Catholic Church that date to the seventeenth century – also facilitated the integration of black and mulatto slaves and freedpeople into Brazilian society. Brotherhoods were organized around the worship of particular saints, with black saints such as the Virgin of the Rosary, Saint Benedict, and Saint Iphigenia particularly popular among black and mulatto brotherhoods. These brotherhoods were also often racially divided. Some were all black and required that members be born in Africa or claim membership in a particular ethnic group, while others were exclusively white or mulatto. The fundamental purpose of the brotherhoods was to provide members and their families with Christian burials and social aid in times of debt and sickness. For these services all members – male, female, free, and slave – paid dues. Occasionally, brotherhoods helped slaves (and sometimes their own members) acquire their freedom, and offered freedpeople protection against exploitation.

Because they were the only legally permitted form of communal life for slaves in the colonial period, the brotherhoods were extremely significant social institutions, allowing their members to share their experiences collectively and seek solutions to their problems. They were thus crucial to the development and preservation of a distinctive Afro-Brazilian culture. Particularly important were the festivals held for the feast days of patron saints. These celebrations included dances called *congadas*, in which each brotherhood would honor its elected king, queen, and royal staff. Anthropologist Roger Bastide claimed that these festivities were "strictly African in inspiration" and that they revealed the symbolic continuation of African monarchical rule on Brazilian soil. Perhaps the most famous of Brazil's black brotherhoods is Our Lady of the Rosary, founded in 1865 in Salvador, Bahia, and still active today. Free and enslaved black women also joined brotherhoods, playing an important role in the administration of social aid. In addition, they formed their own sisterhoods, most notably Our Lady of the Good Death, founded in 1823.

Partly as a result of an intensified importation of African slaves (many of the same ethnic background) and the increasing demands made of slave labor, the first half of the nineteenth century saw a high incidence of slave revolts in the plantation areas of the northeast. Salvador, Bahia, experienced the greatest number – more than 20 between 1809 and 1835 – as well as the most severe revolts, the best known of which was the Malê (Muslim African) Uprising of 1835. Other major revolts of this era included the Sastre Rebellion (1798, in Bahia), the Black Nâgos revolts (1826-1835, in Bahia), the Jehad revolt (1835, in Bahia), the Sabinada revolt (1837, in Bahia), and the Balaiada movement (1838-1841, in Maranhão). The coffee-growing regions of São Paulo also witnessed numerous slave uprisings in the late nineteenth century, during the years leading up to abolition.

The most common and most widespread form of resistance by slaves was to escape from plantations and establish the independent black communities known in Brazil as *quilombos*. Often located in inaccessible areas, quilombos were typically small in size (less than 100 members) and sustained by a combination of subsistence agriculture, plantation raiding, and trade. Although they were predominantly black, some quilombos also included Native Indians and *mestiços* (of indigenous and European descent). Planters hired *capitães de mato* (bush captains), often free blacks, to hunt down fugitive slaves and destroy their communities. Although most quilombos were short-lived, a few fugitives would usually avoid recapture and form a new community. With thousands of members and a lifetime of almost a century, Palmares was the largest and most enduring quilombo.

The exact numbers and origins of the slaves who entered Brazil are uncertain, partly because in 1891 the statesman Rui Barbosa destroyed many of the records documenting slavery in Brazil. Information has also been clouded by the fact that a significant amount of mixing took place among slave populations, as did miscegenation among slaves, Indians, and white settlers (largely as a result of forced sexual relationships). Despite this, anthropologists studying African traditions in Brazil have been able to identify three primary Afro-Brazilian groups: the Yoruba and Fon (from present-day Nigeria and Benin, respectively), the Muslim Hausa (from present-day Nigeria and Niger), and the Bantu (today scattered across Africa).

The African impact on Brazil was extensive. African slaves introduced new foods into the colonial diet, including red peppers, black beans, and okra. They also created new dishes, such as *acarajé*, a fried bean fritter stuffed with a kind of shrimp particular to the northeast, and *feijoada*, a spicy black bean and pork stew that is the national cuisine. Hailing from an array of linguistic groups, African slaves incorporated a number of words into Portuguese and altered its pronunciation. They transplanted a rich music and dance tradition that led to the creation of samba and Capoeira. African slaves also influenced the colony's religious development by syncretizing African religions with Catholicism, resulting in the creation of religions such as Candomblé in Bahia, Xangó in Pernambuco, and Macumba in Rio de Janeiro. Although these Afro-Brazilian cultural forms were suppressed by the Brazilian government during the nineteenth century and most of the twentieth century, they have since been embraced by the dominant society as unique national traditions. Some Afro-Brazilian traditions, such as capoeira, have taken root in other countries in Latin America as well as in North America and Europe.

ABOVE: Thousands of children live on the streets of Brazil. The majority are male and of African descent. These youths frequently are harrassed by police who see the street children as future thieves. *CORBIS/Delmi Alvarez*
RIGHT: Music enlivens this 1987 demonstration for farm reform in Marabá, Brazil. *CORBIS/Stephanie Maze*
OPPOSITE: Public punishment of slaves was a common occurrence in nineteenth-century Brazil. Artist Johann Moritz Rugendas recorded a flogging at the Praça de Sant'Anna in Rio de Janeiro and published it in his *Voyage pittoresque dans le Brésil* (1835). *Oronoz*

Abolition Movement and Emancipation
Because Brazil had for centuries relied upon African labor, abolition was a gradual, difficult process in which legislation was often inconsistent with practice. For example, one early legal step toward abolition was the declaration that all slaves entering Brazil from 1831 onward were free – an edict that was not fully enforced until 1850. Foreign pressure from Great Britain led the Brazilian government to pass a series of laws to facilitate abolition. An 1869 law prohibited the breaking up of slave families; an 1871 law allowed a

slave to purchase himself at market value; also in 1871, the Free-Womb Law declared free all children born to slave mothers.

The political climate of the 1870s, in addition to the decline of the northeastern sugar economy, fostered the growth of a small but vocal abolition movement. After losing to the Conservatives in 1868, Liberals united and devised an extensive reform program that included abolition. Upon returning to power in 1878, they pressed the slavery question on the nation.

In March 1879, Deputy Jeronymo Sodré made a speech before Congress in which he criticized steps such as the Free-Womb Law and called for a complete and immediate end to slavery. Many historians regard this event as the beginning of the abolition movement in Brazil. At that time, largely in response to the end of the slave trade, Brazil had for more than ten years been making a concerted effort to attract European labor to work on the multiplying coffee plantations. In order to encourage planters to employ European immigrant workers, government officials drafted anti-slave trade laws and imposed interprovincial slave taxes. But up to the very eve of abolition, planters continued to use slaves and, even at exorbitant prices, to purchase more from the northern provinces.

One of the most prominent and eloquent spokesmen for the cause of abolition was Joaquim Nabuco (1849-1910), a lawyer, diplomat, and statesman from Pernambuco who authored *O Abolicionismo* (Abolitionism, 1883) and acted as president of the Sociedade Brasileira contra a Escravidão (Brazilian Anti-Slavery Society [established in Rio in 1880]). Numerous Afro-Brazilians assumed leading roles in the abolitionist movement. José Carlos do Patrocínio (1854-1905) wrote tirelessly for the cause of abolition in the *Gazeta de Tarde,* the most popular anti-slavery journal, and headed the Associação Central Emancipadora (Central Emancipation Association) in Rio. André Rebouças (1838-1898) advocated abolition through his writings and by organizing several abolitionist clubs. Luís Gonzaga de Pinto Gama (1830-1882), a former slave, became a prominent lawyer and defender of slaves in the courts. Another notable figure was the writer Antônio de Castro Alves (1847-1871), known as the Poet of the Slaves. Other important Brazilian abolitionists included Antônio Bento and Ferreria de Menezes. Abolitionism was

A Slave House **by Johann Moritz Rugendas appeared in his book, *Voyage Pittoresque dans le Brésil*, published in Paris in 1835.** *Courtesy of Houghton Library, Harvard University*

largely an elite movement; few free blacks were involved.

Beginning in 1884, several states freed their slave populations – Ceará, Amazonas, and then Rio Grande de Sul – inspiring the creation of emancipation clubs in urban centers across the nation. These events fueled abolitionism and led to the passing of the Saraiva-Cotegipe Law in 1885, which liberated all slaves once they reached the age of 60, and legislation issued in 1886 that declared public corporal punishment of slaves illegal. With the threat of whipping removed, many slaves abandoned the coffee plantations where they had been laboring. Overwhelmed, the military asked to be relieved of their duty to track down escaped slaves. Planters began to liberate their slaves, and major political leaders started to adopt abolitionist views and make plans to officially transform the labor system.

On May 13, 1888, when Princess Isabel signed the Lei Áurea, Brazil became the last country in the Western Hemisphere to abolish slavery. The simple document consisted of two articles: (1) "With effect from the date of the present law, slavery is declared to be abolished in Brazil"; and (2) "All provisions to the contrary are hereby repealed." Although emancipation contained no measure to compensate owners for their slaves, a new agricultural bank was established to extend credit to planters who were adjusting to a wage labor system. Former slaves, however, deprived of the land they had worked (emancipation contained no provision for the redistribution of land to freedpeople and their families) and largely squeezed out of the labor market by waves of immigrants, were forced into low-paying occupations and unemployment. The lack of major structural changes in the agricultural system made the abolition of slavery in Brazil a peaceful process that, some argue, did little to alter the poverty of the Afro-Brazilian population.

Freedom

In the years following abolition, the spread of pseudo-scientific theories about the inferiority of blacks led the Brazilian elite to launch a national program known as *branqueamento* ("whitening"), which sought to literally lighten the complexion of the country. Through European immigration, restrictions on non-European immigrants, and miscegenation, Brazilian officials hoped to resolve what they perceived as the negative influence of blacks and anticipated the gradual disappearance of Afro-Brazilians.

Inherent in branqueamento was the idea that the presence of European blood could make a person white – a concept very different from the "one-drop" rule in the United States, which asserts that even the smallest amount of African blood makes a person black. Perhaps this is why Brazil did not institute segregation following emancipation, as the United States did with the Jim Crow laws. The first challenge to these ideas came in 1933, when Brazilian sociologist Gilberto Freyre published *Casa Grande e Senzala* (The Masters and the Slaves). In addition to celebrating Brazil's mixed-race heritage, he argued that miscegenation had created a racial democracy in which racism did not exist. The political activism of Afro-Brazilians in the postabolitionist era, however, seriously challenged Freyre's claims.

The early twentieth century witnessed the founding of several Afro-Brazilian publications that fostered a sense of Black Consciousness and social awareness among the Afro-Brazilian population. As a result, numerous Afro-Brazilian organizations emerged to combat the racial discrimination and poverty stemming from branqueamento. The earliest were Centro Cívico Palmares (established in São Paulo in 1926) and Frente Negra Brasileira (FNB, established in São Paulo in 1931), both of which aimed to educate Afro-Brazilians and fight racial discrimination against them. After women gained the right to vote in 1932, a group of FNB women worked to end sexual discrimination and exploitation in the workplace. More recently, organizations such as the Geledés Instituto da Mulher Negra (founded in São Paulo in 1988) have continued the fight against gender oppression and discrimination.

Afro-Brazilian cultural forms have historically been an important means of expressing black resistance and articulating black aspirations. In 1944 Abdias do Nascimento, an Afro-Brazilian intellectual and senator, launched a black renaissance in the arts by founding the Teatro Experimental do Negro (TEN). Until it folded in 1968, this organization sought to promote black pride and consciousness through performances by and about Afro-Brazilians. Female members of TEN addressed gender issues through their performances and in a column titled "Fala Mulher" (Women Speak) in the organization's journal, *Quilombo*.

Afro-Brazilians have also challenged racism and oppression through literature, music, and Carnival. Afro-Brazilian issues have long been the focus of the groups Olodum and Ilé Aiyê, based in Salvador, Bahia, as well as the work of musician Gilberto Gil and of Quilombhoje, a coalition of Afro-Brazilian writers. Blocos Afros, Carnival organizations that focus on Afro-Brazilian themes, emerged in Salvador during the 1970s to creatively highlight the historical contributions of blacks to the development of Brazil.

The Civil Rights and Black Power Movements in the United States, as well as liberation movements in Africa and the Caribbean, inspired a new wave of black activism in Brazil during the 1970s. In 1978, with the organization of the politically active Movimento Negro Unificado Contra Discriminação Racial (MNU, Unified Negro Movement Against Racial Discrimination) in São Paulo, a black national movement was set into motion. Other black organizations followed, and on May 13, 1988 – the hundredth anniversary of the abolition of slavery in Brazil – they staged several marches and protests in an effort to draw attention to the racial inequality and discrimination Afro-Brazilians continue to experience.

Nevertheless, statistical information reflects the persistence of discrimination behind a facade of racial equality and harmony. Forty percent of black and mulatto Brazilians are illiterate, as compared to 25 percent of white Brazilians. Most of the residents in the city's favelas – slums where health and housing conditions are among the poorest found anywhere in the nation – are of African descent, as are most of the homeless people in Brazil's urban centers. Afro-Brazilians make up more than 80 percent of Brazil's prison inmates. Today, the average black Brazilian man earns $163 a month, or 41 percent of his white counterpart's average earnings. A recent study estimated that in Brazil a white male worker earns, on the average, 2.5 times more than a black worker and 4 times more than a black female worker.

Other manifestations of racism include the use of the phrase "person of good appearance" in job advertisements to mean "light-skinned," and the existence of two elevators in apartment buildings – one labeled "service" for maids and employees, the other labeled "social" for white residents. The harassment of Afro-Brazilians by the police is frequent and takes many forms, from outright violence to requiring blacks to present identification when in upper-class residential districts. These practices can be attributed to the common perception of blacks as poor or criminal or both.

There is also the problem of homeless street children, a predominantly black group of some 7 to 12 million who often survive through petty crime. Local businesses in the big cities often hire death squads composed of off-duty or retired policemen to kill them, reasoning that it is better to rid society of a black street child now than to deal with an adult black criminal in the future. In a widely publicized 1993 incident, eight street children between the ages of 11 and 19 were massacred in front of the Candelaria Church in the center of Rio de Janeiro. The Centro de Articulação de Populações Marginalizadas (CEAP, Center for the Mobilization of Marginalized Populations [established in Rio in 1989]) is one of many organizations that have taken responsibility for helping and protecting street children.

The efforts of earlier Afro-Brazilian organizations helped pave the way for the passing of the Afonso Arinos Law of 1951, which made racial and color discrimination a crime but has proved difficult to enforce. They also helped facilitate Afro-Brazilian participation in politics. Benedita Souza da Silva, for example, became the first black Brazilian member of Congress in 1987 and the first black woman senator in 1994. A handful of Afro-Brazilian cultural figures have also won political office: Abdias do Nascimento, retired soccer star Pelé (Edson Arantes do Nascimento), and musician Gilberto Gil. But much remains to be accomplished. Brazil has never had a black president. There are no black generals, no black supreme court members, and only a handful of blacks among the more than 500 members of Congress. Until 1980, the year in which Edivaldo Brito took office, the predominantly black city of Salvador, Bahia, had never had a black mayor. Abdias do Nascimento asserts that "It will take a long time to bring some Black Brazilians to the point of realizing [that] electing Black politicians is the only way to end our social and economic subordination."

The Afro-Brazilian movement has found it difficult to mobilize the majority of Afro-Brazilians because, as one activist pointed out, Afro-Brazilians tend to identify more with class concerns than racial ones. Census figures indicate that Afro-Brazilians do not exhibit a strong sense of black consciousness – only 5 percent categorize themselves as black, while the rest use any of more than 100 other terms that emphasize white or mixed rather than African ancestry. Despite the fact that downplaying one's African heritage has often been a key to personal social advancement in Brazil, a growing segment of the Afro-Brazilian population is discovering the richness of Afro-Brazilian history and the power of organizing as blacks to overcome persistent discrimination. With such mobilization comes the potential to open to Afro-Brazilians avenues for social advancement other than those in the realms of sports (especially soccer) and entertainment (especially samba) and to bring Brazil one step closer to being the racial democracy that it has pretended to be for so many years.

Aaron Myers

See Also

Bantu: Dispersion and Settlement; Congo, Republic of the; Middle Passage, The; Transatlantic Slave Trade; Palmares: An African State in Brazil; Maroonage in the Americas; São Tomé and Príncipe; Civil Rights Movement; Creoles; Afoxés/Blocos Afros; Gama, Luís Gonzaga Pinto da; Ilê Aiyê; Rio de Janeiro, Brazil; Silva, Benedita da; Abolition and Emancipation in Latin America and the Caribbean; Religions, African, in Brazil; Carnivals in Latin America and the Caribbean; Catholic Church in Latin America and the Caribbean; Education in Latin America and the Caribbean; Slave Rebellions in Latin America and the Caribbean; Soccer in Latin America and the Caribbean; Whitening; Black Consciousness in Brazil.

Latin America and the Caribbean

Brazil, Blacks and Politics in: An Interpretation

With official figures indicating that almost 50 percent of its 150 million inhabitants are of African descent, Brazil is both home to the largest black population outside Africa and the country where blacks are worst off vis-à-vis their white compatriots. Brazil is different from other multiracial nations, such as the United States and South Africa, where racist policies of apartheid fostered unity within oppressed groups that faced visible enemies, and where the very contradictions of segregationist policies opened paths for the social ascension of some members of these groups. In contrast, Afro-Brazilians are virtually excluded from the labor market and the world of business and are practically invisible in the mass media.

How can one explain the apparent paradox of such a large part of the population submitting to racial domination in the absence of the huge investments in repression by physical force that eroded racist systems in other countries? How can one explain the minimal political representation attained by Afro-Brazilians in the absence of any apparent legal or political obstacles to mobility; or the fact that movements demanding fair treatment for this large population have been unable to mobilize significant numbers within their ranks?

These seemingly inexplicable contradictions constitute the very fabric of Brazilian society. One of the keys to this riddle is found in history: the colonial system implanted by the Portuguese and their relations with indigenous groups, whom they massacred, and with enslaved Africans, long an oppressed majority of the population. The other key is found in ideology: the myth of "racial democracy," which depicted Brazilian society as virtually free of racial tensions due to the "natural" propensity for miscegenation of the Iberian peoples, particularly the Portuguese.

The main spokesman for the myth of racial democracy was the sociologist Gilberto Freyre. His work, particularly *The Masters and the Slaves* and *The Mansions and the Shanties,* described and defended Brazil's unique racial harmony. Racism and discrimination in this context were ascribed to isolated incidents that in no way constituted a permanent barrier to the social ascent of blacks and *mestizos* (people of mixed racial background). Through miscegenation, blacks would tend to disappear, and the Brazilian of the future would be *moreno:* an individual with slightly dark skin; of European features and culture; but incorporating some aspects of his or her African heritage, particularly a propensity for music, dance, and sensuality.

The myth of racial democracy has similarly assimilationist counterparts throughout Latin America, such as the "cosmic race" of Mexico or *café con leche* ("coffee and milk") in Venezuela. All reflect an effort originating in the mid-nineteenth century to maintain white European supremacy in countries with a significant presence of Native Americans or descendants of Africans, or both. This was a powerfully seductive myth, as it allowed some to dominate without guilt and others more easily to accept a domination that, portrayed as one based on class rather than race, could thus be overcome through social advancement. The success of the myth in reducing racial tension can be measured by the relatively low levels of ethnic rebellion in Latin America, particularly given the high degree of inequity that separates ethnicities in the region.

This does not, however, imply the absence of black resistance in Brazil, which, in fact, dates back to the early sixteenth century, when the first slaves were brought to work on the sugar cane plantations along the coastal plains. The Republic of Palmares is the most notable example of the many *quilombos* founded by escaped slaves as poles of resistance to the slave regime. Located in the heart of the Brazilian northeast, Palmares, under the leadership of the great ZUMBI, resisted incursions for a century, constituting the first free state of the Americas (*see* Rethinking Maroon Communities in Brazil). Nor should one overlook the Malê Uprisings, in which Muslim Africans and Afro-Brazilians shook BAHIA from the late seventeenth to the mid-eighteenth centuries. Although it was defeated, this resistance significantly contributed – along with the Industrial Revolution and consequent geopolitical shifts – to the final collapse of the slave regime on May 13, 1888.

Presented officially as the generous, humanitarian act of a white princess, the abolition of slavery signified the sudden insertion of millions into a labor market that reserved the best positions for European immigrants. These immigrants were generously subsidized by both sending countries and Brazil, which, as documents of the period candidly state, was determined to "whiten" its population.

It is at this point that the first postslavery Afro-Brazilian organizations emerged. Principal among these was the Black Brazilian Front, established in São Paulo in 1931. The Front marked the high point of Afro-Brazilian mobilization in that city, which had begun in the mid-1910s. Becoming a political party in 1936 only to be shut down along with other associations the following year by the newly installed Estado Novo (the fascist New State), the Front was unable to realize its stated goals of "creating a New Black Man" and achieving a "Second Abolition." Without doubt, however, it left an example followed by subsequent generations.

It is precisely at this time that the Brazilian state extensively employed the myth of racial democracy as a means of demobilizing black protest. This explains why, with the so-called redemocratization of 1945, the Black Brazilian Front did not reenter the political arena. Its place was filled by other organizations, among them the Black Experimental Theater (TEN), which I founded in Rio de Janeiro in 1944. The purpose of the TEN was not simply to promote theater, but rather to raise the consciousness of Brazilians in general and Afro-Brazilians in particular regarding the racial problems in our society. It did not preach the integration of Afro-Brazilians into European culture, as previous black organizations had done, but defended their right to cultivate their own ethnic and cultural values in a society that should be both egalitarian and pluralist. The TEN, beyond training black actors and actresses and opening a market for them, played an important role in forwarding Afro-Brazilian demands, by organizing meetings and seminars to discuss questions of interest. At one such meeting, the first proposal for antidiscrimination legislation in Brazil was born; later it was transformed into law – and duly neutralized – by the proposal of a white, conservative politician.

The struggles in the 1950s, 1960s, and 1970s of Africans and their descendants against imperialism, colonialism, and racism, which unfolded principally in Africa and the United States, served as inspiration for a new phase of Afro-Brazilian struggle in the 1970s: the Unified Black Movement. Drawing a following from the small population of black university students, the movement spread to all of Brazil's important cities. Its agenda included eliminating discrimination in the labor market and eradicating racism in schools and in the media, as well as recognizing famous black figures of Brazilian history. Its victories included official recognition of Zumbi dos Palmares as a national hero and the com-memoration of November 20, the date of his death in 1695, as the National Day of Black Consciousness.

We have seen some important changes in Brazilian society, which are without doubt attributable to black activism. While insufficient to accomplish the radical changes that are necessary, these victories nonetheless lay the groundwork for the future viability of such changes. Fundamental among these has been the acceptance by some opinion makers – meaning the political, economic, cultural, and media elite – that racism exists in Brazil and that it is important to adopt measures guaranteeing equal opportunities for Afro-Brazilians. The racial question has been redefined as a national question, giving rise to agencies at the federal, state, and municipal levels designed to confront it. This process has intensified with the election of black politicians identifying with the Afro-Brazilian cause, albeit still a tiny minority, far from proportional to the Afro-Brazilian population. At the same time, advertisers and the media have discovered a surprisingly large "black consumer market" and have consequently developed products and campaigns to reach it. While the motivations are in this instance commercial, the consequence has been a valorization of black images and a break with the prior invisibility of Afro-Brazilians in the media. All of these factors lead one to believe that at the dawn of the third millennium, Brazil may abandon the mask behind which it has always hidden its racism and seek to become a democracy without adjectives (*see* ABDIAS DO NASCIMENTO).

Abdias do Nascimento

SEE ALSO

Palmares: An African State in Brazil; Frente Negra Brasileira; Movimento Negro Unificado; Teatro Experimental do Negro; Myth of Racial Democracy in Latin America and the Caribbean: An Interpretation.

Latin America and the Caribbean

Brazil's Relationship with Africa: An Interpretation

The connection between Africa and BRAZIL dates back to the sixteenth century, when the Portuguese first brought slaves from Africa to work on the great plantations of their new colony (*see* SLAVERY IN LATIN AMERICA AND THE CARIBBEAN). The traffic in slaves lasted until 1888, some 66 years after Brazil had won its independence from Portugal, and involved close to 4 million persons from various parts of the African continent. The duration of the slave trade, coupled with the constant replenishment of its human stock, has meant that Africa's religious, cultural, and demographic presence in Brazil has been unusually strong. Indeed, Brazil is believed to be home to the world's second largest group of people of African descent, after the Republic of NIGERIA.

The religious and cultural traditions brought to Brazil by African slaves met with considerable disapproval among the dominant classes, who, in their mission to put a civilizing European gloss on the society, sought actively to rescue the country from the presumed danger and barbarity of the slaves' worship and practices. Traditional religions as practiced in Brazil came to absorb elements of Roman Catholicism, a blending of worships from which emerged a distinctly Afro-Brazilian tradition (*see* RELIGIONS, AFRICAN, IN BRAZIL). The sheer variety of cultural and religious practices found among the slaves meant that no monolithic Afro-Brazilian tradition or community would ever come into being, despite attempts by some observers to designate specific groups as torchbearers of African culture in Brazil.

The "return" to Africa of former Afro-Brazilians during the nineteenth and early twentieth centuries is an important phase in the history of Brazil-Africa relations. The returnees established vibrant Afro-Brazilian communities in Dahomey (present-day BENIN), GHANA, Nigeria, and TOGO and maintained active ties with Brazil through trade and cultural exchanges.

The emergence of independent African states, beginning in the late 1950s, marks the opening of modern-day relations between Brazil and Africa. In 1961 Brazil's newly elected president, Jânio Quadros, inaugurated what was at the time a groundbreaking and ultimately short-lived policy in Brazil's foreign relations: Brazil would rely less on its traditional alliance with the United States and "move closer" to Africa and Asia. To this end, Brazil established diplomatic relations with newly independent Ghana, CÔTE D'IVOIRE, Nigeria, and SENEGAL. Breaking with tradition yet again, Quadros appointed an Afro-Brazilian journalist to serve as ambassador to Ghana, the first time in living memory that an Afro-Brazilian has been so honored.

African heads of state have made highly publicized visits to Brazil: Emperor Haile Selassie of ETHIOPIA in 1960; Léopold Senghor, president of Senegal, in 1964; and Nelson Mandela, president of SOUTH AFRICA, in 1998. Africa has hosted visits from João Batista Figuereido, the last soldier-president of Brazil's period of military rule, and in 1996 from President Fernando Henrique Cardoso.

Brazil has sent official delegations on a variety of missions in Africa, occasionally with unexpected repercussions. The Afro-Brazilian delegation at the First Festival of Black Arts and Cultures held in Dakar, Senegal, in 1966, came under attack for excluding from its ranks the Black Experimental Theater, a pioneering group dedicated to challenging common ideas about black life in Brazil. (The clash between rival views of Afro-Brazil would be replayed a decade later at the Second Festival of Black Arts and Culture.) During a tour of seven African countries in late 1972, Brazil's foreign minister, Mario Gibson Barbosa, was repeatedly asked to explain Brazil's neutrality on the issue of Portuguese colonialism and the wars of liberation being waged by freedom fighters in ANGOLA, GUINEA and CAPE VERDE, and MOZAMBIQUE. In 1975 Brazil took the extraordinary step of recognizing the party of AGOSTINHO NETO as the sole and legitimate government of Angola, well before the ORGANIZATION OF AFRICAN UNITY could come to agreement on the matter.

Business and trade have featured prominently in present-day Brazil-Africa relations. Brazil exports consumer goods to Nigeria and Ghana and purchases oil from GABON and Nigeria. Brazil and its African competitors have entered agreements on production and on the exchange of such primary goods as cocoa and coffee. Trade delegations from Africa and from Brazil have crisscrossed the Atlantic with increasing regularity, most notably in the middle 1970s to the early 1980s.

Afro-Brazilians themselves have contributed to the special relationship with Africa. The Afro-Brazilian Chamber of Commerce and other cultural and solidarity groups have a strong interest in issues related to continental Africa and the ways in which they impact Afro-Brazilian life.

Events in South Africa following the release of Nelson Mandela and his subsequent visit to Brazil in August 1991 have fueled comparisons between the race relations of Brazil and South Africa, a development that provides a new twist to Africa-Brazil relations. Ever increasing numbers of Africans are taking up temporary residence in Brazil as students and businesspeople, and there are the occasional tourists. All have to deal with the racism faced daily by Afro-Brazilians. So, to the cultural, historical, and commercial molds in which Africa-Brazil relations have been traditionally cast we must add an additional factor: the domestic and international dimensions of race relations. The virtual absence of Afro-Brazilians from delegations sent to Africa or from leading sectors of Brazilian society can only baffle African observers who hear official Brazil's oft-repeated professions of an affinity with Africa rooted in history and culture. Whatever its internal contradictions, Brazil has been the prime initiator in its relations with African countries. As contacts of all sorts increase between Brazil and Africa, greater familiarity will do much to change this imbalance in the present relationship.

Anani Dzidzienyo

SEE ALSO
Mandela, Nelson Rolihlahla; Transatlantic Slave Trade; Teatro Experimental do Negro; Religions, African, in Brazil; Catholic Church in Latin America and the Caribbean.

Africa

Brazza, Pierre Savorgnan de

(b. January 25, 1852, Rome, ITALY; d. September 14, 1905, Dakar, SENEGAL), French-Italian explorer and general commissioner of the Moyen-Congo (present-day REPUBLIC OF THE CONGO).

After schooling and naval service in FRANCE, the Italian-born Pierre Savorgnan de Brazza became a naturalized French citizen in 1874. In the following year he led his first official trip to Africa to explore GABON. From 1875 to 1878 he traveled along the Gabon coast and up the Ogooué River to its source, also reaching the Alima River, a tributary of the CONGO RIVER.

In 1880, in competition with the American journalist and explorer Henry Stanley, Brazza traveled into the Congo River basin interior. There he signed a treaty with leaders of the TÉKÉ people, clearing the way for French control of the northern bank of the Congo River, an area that would be known as the Moyen-Congo. He served as general commissioner of the Moyen-Congo from 1884 to 1898, establishing the town that became Brazzaville and building the colonial administration. As commissioner, Brazza became disenchanted with the exploitive and brutal practices of concessionary companies, and in 1905 was appointed by the French government to investigate them. He died in Dakar, SENEGAL, on his return from the mission.

Eric Young

SEE ALSO
Brazzaville, Republic of the Congo; Dakar, Senegal; Stanley, Sir Henry Morton.

Africa

Brazzaville, Republic of the Congo,

capital of the Republic of the Congo and the country's largest city.

Fighting in 1993 and 1997 between rival Congolese militias twice reduced this picturesque city of wide boulevards and street cafés on the banks of the CONGO RIVER to rubble, destroying many of the buildings that housed its population of more than 900,000. Particularly hard hit were residential neighborhoods such as Bacongo, dominated by the Lari ethnic group, and the MBOCHI- and TÉKÉ-dominated Poto-Poto neighborhood, known for its cathedral, school of art, and writers' community. The city's other districts include the administrative center on the plateau, the Plain commercial district, and the M'Pila industrial zone.

Brazzaville was originally a small Téké settlement known as Nkuma. In 1880 the Téké's paramount chief ceded Nkuma to the French, who desired access to the interior of the Congo basin via the river and named it in honor of the explorer PIERRE SAVORGNAN DE BRAZZA. Although Brazzaville became the capital of French Equatorial Africa in 1903, it was not until the 1930s, when a railway was built from the city to the coast, that the city's population and commercial importance grew. In World War II, when Brazzaville was named the capital of Free France in sub-Saharan Africa, the city's population and infrastructure expanded further. After the war, Brazzaville became the center of the nationalist movement (*see* NATIONALISM IN AFRICA), and in 1960 it became the capital of independent Congo. After independence, rural migration to the city continued, seriously straining the public services. Urban unemployment reached 50 percent in the 1980s, and strikes, protests, and black-marketeering became common. Even after the 1997 civil war, Brazzaville remains Congo's commercial center and an important port, linked by ferry service to Kinshasa, which is directly across the 15-mile-wide river.

Eric Young

SEE ALSO
Congo, Democratic Republic of the; Kinshasa, Democratic Republic of the Congo.

North America

Breakdancing,

a form of African American dance that emerged from the hip hop culture of the South Bronx, New York, during the mid-1970s.

Breakdancing developed out of the Bronx, New York, disco scene. When disco DJs changed records, dancers would fill the resulting musical breaks, or "breakbeats," with movements that emphasized the rupture in rhythmic continuity. These highly acrobatic interludes developed into a new genre that mixed Afrodiasporic dance styles, reflecting the influence of the lindy hop, the Charleston, the cakewalk, and the jitterbug as well as the Afro-Brazilian martial-arts dance CAPOEIRA and the antics of Kung Fu movies.

From its birth in the Bronx in the 1970s breakdancing became a national phenomenon in the 1980s, when breakdancers often performed at various events, such as this 1984 competition. *CORBIS/Bettmann*

Breakdancing included "breaking" (flipping, spinning, pivoting on the head and hands), "up-rock" (a mock-combat style, often directed against an opponent), and "webbo" (fast footwork between other dance moves). When breakdancing spread to Los Angeles, California, dancers added the "electric boogie," automaton-like dance moves that incorporated pantomime. In the beginning, breakdancers adopted a confrontational attitude, as "crews" met each other in fake rumbles that often turned into real fights. Even peaceful displays resembled the competitive toasting of Bronx musicians in concurrently developing rap music.

Like other facets of the hip hop movement, breakdancing met with commercial success and public notoriety in the early 1980s. Paralleling Soho's embrace of Bronx graffiti art, Manhattan dance clubs welcomed breakdancers to their floors. And like rap, breakdancing appeared in a number of popular films, including *Wild Style* (1982), *Breakin'* (1984), and *Beat Street* (1984), which featured the Rock Steady Crew, breakdancing's most renowned posse. This publicity, which deemphasized breakdancing's confrontational aspect, turned the dance into a national sensation among white as well as black youths; suburban schoolchildren donned hip hop fashions, and some white teenagers signed up for breakdancing lessons.

Widespread media attention diminished breakdancing's power as a unique voice of self-affirmation for inner-city youth. Its influence, however, set the trajectory of subsequent dance trends. Black performers such as Michael Jackson, MC Hammer, and Missy Elliot draw from breakdance styles that never stop evolving. Even such breakdancing originals as Richard "Crazy Legs" Colón of the Rock Steady Crew continue to innovate and perform.

Eric Bennett

See Also

Cakewalk, The; Graffiti Art; Hip Hop in the United States; Jackson, Michael, and the Jackson Family; New York, New York.

Brent, Linda. Please see Jacobs, Harriet Ann

Europe

Bridgetower, George Frederick Polgreen

(b. February 29, 1780, Baila, Poland; d. February 29, 1860, London, England), Afro-British violinist of considerable talent who performed in concerts with Ludwig van Beethoven.

Called the Abyssinian Prince by an admiring public, George Polgreen Bridgetower gained renown throughout nineteenth-century Europe as a violinist of exceptional talent. As a youth, he became the prized violinist of the Prince of Wales, and he is said to have studied with Joseph Haydn. In 1803 he gave the first performance of Beethoven's *Kreutzer* Sonata for violin – written expressly for him – with the great German composer accompanying him at the piano.

Bridgetower grew up in London, England, the son of an African father and a European mother. At the age of ten, he debuted publicly as a violinist in Paris and soon after gave his first London performance, at the Drury Lane Theatre. His violin playing so impressed the Prince of Wales (later King George IV) that he was taken into the royal retinue. He also received extensive musical instruction from such noted violinists as Giovanni Mane Giornovichi and François-Hippolyte Barthélemon. By the late eighteenth century, Bridgetower had established himself as one of England's leading instrumental virtuosos, and in 1802 he began touring Europe.

Bridgetower's musical virtuosity gained him entry into Vienna's highest musical circles, and he soon met Beethoven. In 1803 the two musicians debuted the *Kreutzer* Sonata in a concert together at the Augarten Theatre. "As usual, Beethoven was late in finishing the sonata," wrote musicologist Gabriel Banat, "and the violinist had to read the first two movements from Beethoven's hardly legible manuscript, while the composer played his unfinished part mostly from memory." Beethoven held Bridgetower in high regard, both as a soloist and as a chamber group player. Wielding his influence among Vienna's leading aristocrats, he promoted Bridgetower in letters as "a master of his instrument, a very skillful virtuoso worthy of recommendation." Yet the two men later grew distant from one another – reputedly because of a quarrel over a woman.

After spending several years in Austria, Bridgetower returned to England, where he married and had one daughter. He received a bachelor of music degree from Cambridge University in 1811, taught music, and performed with the London Philharmonic Society Orchestra. During his later life he lived in Paris and Rome for many years before returning to England. He died in London at the age of 80.

Roanne Edwards

See Also

Great Britain.

North America

Briggs, Cyril Valentine

(b. May 28, 1888, Nevis, Leeward Islands; d. October 18, 1966, Los Angeles, Calif.), African American newspaper editor and writer; a radical presence in Harlem's New Negro Movement.

Among the individuals who contributed to the political and cultural foment of Harlem's New Negro Movement in the first decades of the twentieth century, Cyril Briggs was one of its most radical. Born in Nevis, Briggs immigrated to New York in 1905 and within a few years had worked for the African American newspapers the *Colored American Review* and the *Amsterdam News*. In 1919 he was forced to resign from the *News* after an editorial he wrote that described the League of Nations as the "League of Thieves" spurred an investigation by the United States Postal Service.

After leaving the *Amsterdam News*, Briggs committed his time to publication of his journal, the *Crusader*. Founded in 1918, the *Crusader*'s early editorials advocated black self-government and African independence and lent support to Marcus Garvey's nascent Universal Negro Improvement Association (UNIA). But within a year, the *Crusader* repudiated Garvey and the UNIA. In response to the violence of the Red Summer of 1918, in 1919 Briggs founded the African Blood Brotherhood (ABB), a semisecret organization that advocated black armed self-defense and aligned itself with the Communist Party USA (CPUSA). Briggs's embrace of Bolshevik principles alienated him from the vociferously anticommunist Garvey, and he became one of Garvey's strongest critics. "Is Mr. Garvey really in earnest when he talks about the liberation of Africa?" Briggs wrote in a *Crusader* editorial. "Or is he too busy resurrecting mediaeval systems and titles and making the glorious U.N.I.A. movement a tinsel show and a laughing stock to give time to real efforts in the liberation struggle." Briggs eventually supplied the U.S. government with information leading to Garvey's imprisonment on charges of postal fraud.

Briggs's involvement with the CPUSA increased during the 1920s and 1930s. He helped organize its black subsidiaries such as the American Negro Labor Congress (ANLC) – becoming the editor of its paper, the *Harlem Liberator,* in 1929 – and the League of Struggle for Negro Rights. In 1938, however, his continued advocacy of Black Nationalism led to his expulsion from the party.

Peter Hudson

See Also

African Blood Brotherhood; Garvey, Marcus Mosiah; Harlem, New York; New York, New York; Universal Negro Improvement Association; St. Kitts and Nevis; Communist Party USA, African Americans and the.

North America

Brimmer, Andrew F.

(b. September 13, 1926, Newellton, La.), economist and the first African American governor of the United States Federal Reserve Board.

An economist deeply involved in public policy and administration, Andrew Brimmer in 1966 was appointed a governor of the U.S. Federal Reserve Board, where he served until 1974. He worked to alleviate unemployment, the national deficit, and racial discrimination. In 1969, when small businesses were suffering, he urged African Americans to forsake "black capitalist" ventures and pursue work in large mainstream companies instead. He proposed an income-tax reduction plan to President Gerald L. Ford in 1974; in the following year, it became the basis of congressional legislation. In 1984, when black unemployment was double that of whites, Brimmer supported strategies that combined AFFIRMATIVE ACTION with self-help.

After high school, Brimmer joined the army, where he became a staff sergeant. He received a B.A. and M.A. in economics from the University of Washington, studied in India on a Fulbright fellowship, and subsequently earned a Ph.D. in economics from Harvard University. From 1958 to 1961 he taught economics at Michigan State University, where he wrote *Life Insurance Companies in the Capital Markets.* He also taught at the University of Pennsylvania and at Harvard University and managed his own consulting firm. From 1995 to 1998 he served as chair of the Financial Control Board in Washington, D.C., appointed by President Bill Clinton to deal with the District of Columbia's financial problems.

Latin America and the Caribbean

Brindis de Salas, Claudio

(b. August 4, 1852, Havana, Cuba; d. June 2, 1911, Buenos Aires, Argentina), Afro-Cuban violinist virtuoso and composer; sometimes referred to as the Black Paganini.

Born in the bustling city of Havana, a cultural center for the development of classical music in Latin America and the Caribbean, Claudio Brindis de Salas was already a concert violinist at the age of ten. His father, Claudio Sr., was a well-known musician, teacher, and orchestra leader. Brindis de Salas studied with a Belgian teacher in Havana and later with Danclas, David, Sivori, and others at the Paris Conservatory. He won awards and began traveling widely, earning many accolades in cities like Milan, Florence, Berlin, St. Petersburg, and London. As a violin virtuoso he earned the nicknames "the Black Paganini" and "the King of the Octaves." He toured with great success in Latin America, and in Buenos Aires, Argentina, his admirers gave him an authentic Stradivarius violin.

Brindis de Salas lived for a time in Berlin, married a German woman, and even became a German citizen. Kaiser Wilhelm II awarded him the title of Baron of Salas as well as the Black Eagle Cross and named him chamber violinist to the emperor. He was also made a knight of the Legion of Honor. His repertoire, geared to show off his technical brilliance, included the works of Sarasate, Paganini, Bach, and Handel. However, by 1900, forgotten by the court in Berlin, Brindis de Salas saw his career begin to decline.

After his last tour in CUBA, which was a financial disaster, he moved to Buenos Aires. There he suffered from tuberculosis, and died from the disease, in a state of poverty, on June 2, 1911. His corpse was unidentifiable until his passport was found. In 1917 a Buenos Aires newspaper tried to have his remains transferred to Cuba, his homeland, but it was not until 1930 that this final tribute was paid.

Alan West

See Also

Germany; Music, Classical, in Latin America and the Caribbean; Argentina; Havana, Cuba.

Latin America and the Caribbean

Brindis de Salas, Virginia

(b. 1908, Montevideo, Uruguay; d. 1958, Montevideo, Uruguay), Afro-Uruguayan poet, contributor to *Nuestra Raza* (the important black Uruguayan journal), and the first black South American woman to publish in book form and widely distribute her two volumes of poetry (*see* LITERATURE, BLACK, IN SPANISH AMERICA).

Poet Gabriela Mistral, the 1945 Chilean Nobel Laureate, praised the poetry of Virginia Brindis de Salas in a letter, claiming that as far away as Los Angeles, her poems were establishing important pan-American links among black people (*see* PAN-AFRICANISM AND AFRO-LATIN AMERICANS). Despite Mistral's assessment, as literary critic Carroll Young states, there is but one other indication that the work of Brindis de Salas was available outside of Uruguay: a 1954 German translation of her poem "Tango número tres."

Little is known about her life. She claimed to have been the niece of CLAUDIO BRINDIS DE SALAS, the famous Cuban violinist who had settled in Buenos Aires. Active in the small but thriving black Uruguayan community, she published a number of poems in *Nuestra Raza* before her first book appeared in 1946, *Pregón de Marimorena* (The Call of Mary Morena). Her second volume of poetry, *Cien cárceles de amor* (One Hundred Prisons of Love), followed shortly after in 1949. In the prologue to this volume she mentioned a third book, *Cantos de lejanía* (Songs from Faraway). This book never materialized, perhaps because the author lacked funds as a result of the economic crisis in URUGUAY between 1948 and 1960.

Most of her poetry addresses the social reality of black Uruguayans. Carroll Young notes that the themes of Brindis de Salas's poetry depart significantly from those of her contemporary white female poets, Delmira Agustini, Alfonsina Storni, Juana Ibarbourou, and Gabriela Mistral, who preferred to explore romantic and maternal love or women's roles in Uruguay, ARGENTINA, and CHILE. Infused with black consciousness, the verse of Brindis de Salas insists on exposing racial discrimination and the socioeconomic disadvantages of Afro-Uruguayans.

This radical bent put her at odds with colleagues like PILAR BARRIOS (1889-1974), who avoided confrontation, hoping to "impress upon the dominant culture the intellectual genius of the black Uruguayan community." If indeed Brindis de Salas's unflinching sketches of black Uruguayan life alienated her somewhat from leaders like Barrios, it might also help to explain in part why so many of her biographical details remain a mystery and possibly why her third book was never published.

The structure of *Pregón de Marimorena* is of particular interest, as Brindis de Salas did not simply write thematically about black pride but employed oral forms and traditional dances to structure her free verse. The book is divided into four sections, each one pointing to a different kind of African-derived music: "Ballads," "Calls," "Tangos," and "Songs." *Pregones*, or calls, date back to colonial times when blacks would announce their wares in the streets through distinguishable songs, a custom still observed in Brindis de Salas's day. Tango, the region's most popular dance form, was, however, often identified with white Argentine and Uruguayan culture. Thus, in an attempt to reappropriate the tango for Afro-Uruguayans, Brindis de Salas called it the "*Danza que bailaron los esclavos parche y ritmo en su elemental rueda de gallo*" (Dance that the slaves danced drum and rhythm in their rudimentary chicken ring) in her "Tango número dos" (Tango Number Two).

Thus, although little is known about her life, her poetry has survived. By the late 1990s her work had been anthologized and she was deservedly receiving more critical attention as Afro-Latin American writers were gaining greater recognition.

Joy Elizondo

See Also
Los Angeles, California; Tango; Dance in Latin America and the Caribbean.

Africa

Brink, André Philippus

(b. May 29, 1935, Vrede, South Africa), Afrikaner novelist whose books criticizing apartheid were banned by the South African government.

The son of an Afrikaner magistrate, André Brink grew up moving from village to village in rural South Africa, each characterized, he says, by "conservative Protestantism... generosity and narrow-mindedness." After receiving master's degrees in English and Afrikaans from Potchefstroom University, he went to Paris in 1959 to study at the Sorbonne. By his own assessment, the 1960 Sharpeville massacre in South Africa (in which the police killed at least 69 innocent protesters) sparked in him a new political awareness and prompted him to return home in 1961.

Brink began to write fiction while lecturing at Rhodes University. Two novels published in the early 1960s were largely apolitical, but his views on writing changed after he spent 1968 in Paris, where he witnessed student uprisings. Brink came to believe that "in a closed society, the writer has a specific social and moral role to fill." In its story of a mixed-race actor convicted of killing his white lover, his next novel, *Looking into Darkness* (1973), dealt directly with apartheid. It was the first Afrikaans novel banned by the South African government. Brink wrote his subsequent novels in both Afrikaans and English.

During the 1970s and 1980s, while enduring constant monitoring and harassment by the authorities, Brink published seven more novels: *An Instant in the Wind* (1976), *Rumours of Rain* (1978), *A Dry White Season* (1979), *A Chain of Voices* (1981), *Mapmakers* (1983), *The Wall of the Plague* (1984), and *States of Emergency* (1988). His novels have been translated into more than 20 languages. *A Dry White Season* won both the Martin Luther King Memorial Prize and the French Prix Medicis Etranger in 1980 and was made into a movie in 1989.

Brink has also written and directed plays, served as president of the Afrikaans Writers' Guild and as a member of South African PEN, and translated Shakespeare, Henry James, Albert Camus, and other authors into Afrikaans. His later books include *An Act of Terror* (1991), *The First Life of Admastor* (1993), *On the Contrary* (1993), *Imaginings of Sand* (1996), *Reinventing a Continent* (1996), and *The Novel: Language and Narrative from Cervantes to Calvino* (1998).

Kate Tuttle

See Also
Sharpeville, South Africa; King, Martin Luther, Jr.

Africa

British Central Africa. **Former name of Malawi.**

Latin America and the Caribbean

British Honduras. **Former name of Belize.**

Africa

British Somaliland. **Former name of the northern part of Somalia.**

Latin America and the Caribbean

Brito, Edivaldo **(b. 1937), elected in 1978 as the first black mayor of Salvador, Bahia, in Brazil (see Bahia).**

Europe

Brixton Riots of 1981, **the most publicized of the London 1980-1981 race riots, which showed the extent of social injustice and racial tension in Great Britain.**

The riots in London's Brixton district during the weekend of April 10, 1981, were the first large-scale racial confrontations between black British youth and white British police officers. Aggressive and likely racist behavior by the white officers contributed to these and subsequent disturbances. Violence between blacks and whites had erupted in Bristol in 1980 when the police raided a local café patronized mostly by blacks. Similar circumstances led to rioting in Liverpool and London; most notorious of the London disturbances were the Brixton Riots of 1981.

Since World War II the area of Brixton had been in a decline characterized by a falling population, homelessness, and high unemployment. Though several redevelopment plans had been proposed for this area in London since the 1960s, none was implemented. At the time of the 1981 riots less than half of Brixton's population were people of color. Most of these people of color were of West Indian descent, but some were of African, East Indian, or other cultural backgrounds. Nonwhites made up approximately 4 percent of the total population of Great Britain; almost half of these nonwhites were born in Great Britain. According to experts, many of these people faced educational and employment discrimination that fostered a sense of frustration and deprivation.

In 1981 in Brixton, police had begun stopping and searching suspects randomly to root out those who had committed minor offenses. Youths objected to these searches, which they claimed were used as a means of humiliation. Blacks, the most frequent target of the searches, complained of racism. At one point, police carried out 1000 such searches within nine days. This infuriated the local population and created tensions between white police officers and youths – mostly black.

On Friday, April 10, 1981, two policemen were trying to help a wounded young black man to a hospital. But while they waited for an ambulance, a local crowd assumed that the police had injured him and were preventing him from getting swift medical attention. Members of the crowd took the young man from the police and drove him to a hospital. In the meantime, blacks who remained on the scene began throwing bricks and rocks at the police. The police pursued the youths.

This began a three-day streak of violent looting and rioting against the police in Brixton by both black and white youths. The worst violence, on Saturday, April 11, lasted for over eight hours and covered a large geographical area. On Sunday over 1000 police were deployed to quell the riots, but by this time the disorders were not as violent; by Monday the violence had subsided. About 150 shops suffered losses, 28 properties were burned down, and other buildings were structurally damaged or entirely demolished. Only two people – both policemen – were injured and hospitalized. The police arrested a total of 282 people, most of whom were black.

Lord Leslie George Scarman, a former senior judge who had been appointed by the British government to report on the disorders, stated that "racial disadvantage is a fact of current British life" and that "urgent action is needed if [racism] is not to become an endemic, ineradicable disease threatening the very survival of our society." The Scarman report admitted that the police shared responsibility with blacks for the violence and advocated for more people of color on the police force, the swift dismissal of racist officers, and a review of policing methods in inner cities. The conservative government of Margaret Thatcher neglected the report's findings and emphasized the maintenance of "public order." Racial incidents continued to occur on a smaller scale after 1981, until the Riots of 1985 exploded in Brixton and Tottenham in London and in the Handsworth district of Birmingham.

Leyla Keough

See Also
Riots in Great Britain, 1985.

Latin America and the Caribbean

Brodber, Erna (b. April 20, 1940, Woodside, St. Mary, Jamaica), Jamaican novelist and sociologist.

Writer Erna Brodber was raised in rural St. Mary, Jamaica, by parents who were both social activists in their small community. After graduating from high school in Kingston, she worked as a civil servant and teacher in Montego Bay before entering the University of the West Indies (UWI), where she received a B.A. in history in 1963. She then taught at a private girls' school in Trinidad for one year before continuing her education. She earned an M.Sc. in sociology from UWI in 1968 and received a scholarship to study at McGill University in Canada and the University of Washington.

While in the United States, Brodber was greatly influenced by the Black Power Movement and women's movements of the late 1960s. After returning to Jamaica she became a lecturer in sociology at UWI and became well known for her research, serving as a visiting scholar at the University of Michigan and the University of Sussex. As a sociologist, however, Brodber was disturbed by the lack of case studies featuring Caribbean individuals and culture. Her first novel began as a fictional case study that she intended to use in her classes.

Jane and Louisa Will Soon Come Home (1981) recounts the story of a Jamaican woman's need to reconnect with her history and community. It was immediately hailed as a masterpiece within the canon of Caribbean fiction. Brodber's next two novels, *Myal* (1988) and *Louisiana* (1994), focus on similar themes and have received similar acclaim. Her novels often feature women protagonists who must come to terms with the complicated relationships between gender roles and color/cultural divisions within Caribbean society. Brodber received a Ph.D. in history from UWI in 1984 and continues to work as both a writer and a researcher.

Lisa Clayton Robinson

See Also
Kingston, Jamaica; Trinidad and Tobago.

North America

Brooke, Edward W., III (b. October 26, 1919, Washington, D.C.), first African American elected to the United States Senate since Reconstruction.

The only son of Helen Seldon and Edward W. Brooke, a lawyer, Edward Brooke attended Washington's Dunbar High School and graduated from Howard University with a chemistry degree in 1941. A U.S. Army captain, he fought in Italy in World War II and received the Bronze Star and combat infantryman's badge. After the war he earned a degree from Boston University's School of Law, where he was editor of the *Law Review*.

Brooke's political career began in 1950 when he left his private law practice to run unsuccessfully for the Massachusetts House of Representatives. In 1961 the newly elected Republican governor, John Volpe, appointed Brooke chairman of the Boston Finance Commission. Brooke resigned in 1963 when he was sworn in as Massachusetts attorney general, after winning the Republican nomination and election in 1962.

Known for his role as a crimebuster and an aggressive prosecutor of political corruption, Brooke was elected to the U.S. Senate on January 10, 1967. In the Senate he was appointed to the Banking and Currency Committee and to the Aeronautical and Space Sciences Committee. He held his Republican seat for two terms, until his defeat in 1978.

Brooke published *The Challenge of Change* (1966) and was the 1967 recipient of the Spingarn Medal from the National Association for the Advancement of Colored People.

See Also
World War II and African Americans.

North America

Brooks, Gwendolyn Elizabeth (b. June 17, 1917, Topeka, Kans.), American poet and novelist, a leading poet of the post-World War II era, and an important figure in the Black Arts Movement of the 1960s and 1970s.

As an infant, Gwendolyn Brooks moved with her parents, David and Keziah Wims Brooks, to Chicago's South Side, where she has resided ever since. Brooks was educated at Chicago public schools and Wilson Junior College. The major early influence on her literary career was her mother, who had Brooks giving dramatic recitals at the age of four. Largely through her mother's urging, the teenage Brooks met the leading black writers James Weldon Johnson and Langston Hughes, who encouraged her to write poetry. By age 16, Brooks had already published poetry in the Chicago Defender, the leading African American newspaper of that time.

Brooks's writing further developed as she participated in the vibrant literary scene of the South Side during the late 1930s and early 1940s, which included such important black writers as Richard Wright, Margaret Walker, Theodore Ward, Margaret Danner, Arna Bontemps, and Frank Marshall Davis. Inez Cunningham Stark's poetry workshop at the South Side Community Art Center in the early 1940s was particularly important in the development of Brooks's writing skills. Her poems began to appear in such leading journals and anthologies of the time as *Negro Story* and Edward Seaver's *Cross Section* series. During this period, Brooks also won many prizes and fellowships, including two Guggenheim Fellowships. Brooks's first collection of poetry, *A Street in Bronzeville*, appeared in 1945. A second book of poetry, *Annie Allen*, was published in 1949, earning her the Pulitzer Prize for poetry in 1950, the first time an African American had won the award.

Brooks's early collections are exciting mixtures of modernist treatments of traditional literary forms, such as the sonnet and ballad (heavily influenced by T. S. Eliot) and more popular African American forms after the manner of Langston Hughes. Despite these and other influences, Brooks created a unique poetic voice that grappled with issues of art, identity, race, gender, and the relationship between literature and popular culture more powerfully than that of any other poet in the immediate post-World War II era. Brooks further investigated these concerns in her single novel, *Maud Martha* (1953), a series of loosely connected sketches about a young African American woman from the South Side.

With the upsurge of the Civil Rights Movement in the late 1950s, Brooks's work became increasingly engaged with the events of the African American struggle for freedom. Her 1960 collection of poems, *The Bean Eaters*, contains poems about the 1955 murder of 14-year-old Emmett Till in Mississippi, lynching, and the integration of schools in Little Rock, Arkansas. While retaining much in common with her early style, Brooks's poetry became much more direct during this period. This directness and more overt focus on the immediate conditions and events of the African American community became even more pronounced after Brooks attended a black writer's conference at Fisk University in 1967. There she encountered leading Black Arts Movement writers, such as Amiri Baraka, who greatly influenced her. After the conference, Brooks became the black writer of the earlier generation most prominently identified with the Black Arts Movement. This affiliation was seen almost immediately in the 1968 collection *In the Mecca* ("the Mecca" referring to a South Side apartment building), which included poems to Malcolm X, slain civil rights leader Medgar Evers, and the Blackstone Rangers, a politicized Chicago street gang that became part of the Black Power Movement.

Brooks has retained this political engagement in her work to the present, an engagement seen not only in her poetry, but also in her decision to use African American-run publishing houses rather than larger commercial publishers. In addition to her poetry and her novel, Brooks has written two autobiographical works, *Report from Part One* (1972) and *Report from Part Two* (1997).

James Smethurst

See Also

World War II and African Americans; *Chicago Defender*; Chicago, Illinois; Evers, Medgar Wylie; Till, Emmett Louis.

North America

Broonzy, William Lee Conley ("Big Bill") **(b. June 26, 1893, Scott, Mississippi; d. August 15, 1958, Chicago, Illinois), prolific country bluesman who played a major role in the introduction of rural Southern music to Chicago.**

Big Bill Broonzy was born to sharecropper parents in Mississippi, and in his childhood he moved with his family between Mississippi and Arkansas, farming in both states. He first played music on homemade fiddles and guitars, and was performing at special occasions by the age of 15. Between the ages of 15 and 20 he developed his dexterous hollering vocal style, as well as his characteristically facile guitar technique. Music, however, remained but an avocation until he resettled in Chicago after serving in the army during World War I.

In the 1920s Broonzy embarked on a struggle to subsist as a professional musician, a struggle that continued until the last few years of his life. Throughout the decade he made numerous live appearances in Chicago nightclubs, yet he failed to garner much interest from record companies. In the 1930s, however, his luck changed with the explosion of Chicago's race record industry. Broonzy recorded on the Champion, Vocalion, Melotone, and Oriole labels, as well as Bluebird, where he helped develop the sound known as the Bluebird Beat Chicago Blues.

Broonzy had begun as a solo performer, but by the 1930s he was playing with small ensembles. These groups often included a piano, trumpet, and saxophone, as well as a rhythm section. At this time Broonzy worked with bluesmen such as Georgia Tom (Thomas A. Dorsey), Little Walter Jacobs, and Tampa Red (Hudson Whittaker). Dorsey was one among a number of Chicago bluesmen who appealed to emigrants from the South with songs that combined rural blues sounds with lyrics of an urban perspective.

After World War II, black audiences turned from the blues toward other kinds of popular music. Broonzy discerned the change in fashion and began marketing himself to the white fans who constituted the postwar folk revival. Although he had played at Carnegie Hall in the "From Spirituals to Swing" concert in the late 1930s, his popularity among white audiences was enhanced when he appeared with Sonny Terry, Brownie McGhee, and Pete Seeger. Broonzy's performances increasingly included protest and folk material as well as anecdotal flourishes, and he began touring extensively. He played at the London Jazz Club in 1951, gave performances with gospel superstar Mahalia Jackson, and appeared in Africa, South America, and Southeast Asia.

While working as a janitor at Iowa State University in the early 1950s, Broonzy learned to write from students there. In 1953 he finally made enough money from music to retire from other kinds of work. In 1955 his letters were published as an autobiography. He died of cancer in 1958.

Eric Bennett

See Also

World War I and African Americans; Chicago, Illinois; Dorsey, Thomas Andrew; Gospel Music.

North America

Brotherhood of Sleeping Car Porters, **the first successful African American trade union.**

Founded in 1925 by A. Philip Randolph, the Brotherhood of Sleeping Car Porters (BSCP) was instrumental in securing better wages and hours for the porters of the Pullman Company, but its significance goes beyond such accomplishments. The BSCP became an integral part of the fight for fair employment practices in other industries and helped bring black workers into the realm of organized labor. Under Randolph's leadership, the BSCP was also a voice for civil rights, providing the philosophical seed that bore fruit in the 1963 March on Washington.

The Pullman Palace Car Company was established in 1867 to provide luxurious service to train passengers. By the 1920s the company was the largest employer of African Americans. According to historians, Pullman favored black men as porters not only because they could be paid less than white men, but because white customers enjoyed being waited upon by African Americans. Working for Pullman also provided the porters some degree of status, at least within their communities. Wearing immaculate uniforms rather than field denims, and traveling to distant cities, they were seen as sophisticated professionals.

Yet the porters, many of whom were college-educated men, faced demeaning conditions at work. Placed in a servile relationship to white customers, porters were also exploited by their employers. Pullman paid black workers less than whites and restricted the men to jobs as porters. (Black women worked for Pullman as maids and launderers, but were for the most part not represented by the BSCP, which according to historian Melinda Chateauvert was more concerned with black manhood than with gender equity.) That such work was considered desirable is evidence of how few opportunities were open to educated black men at the time. One Pullman porter killed in a 1923 train crash was ultimately identified by his Phi Beta Kappa key; it is unlikely that any of his white Dartmouth classmates shined shoes for a living.

The first step toward fighting inadequate pay and inhumane working conditions (which included being allowed to sleep only in three-hour stints in the smoking room off the men's bathroom) came in 1920 with the formation of the Pullman Porters and Maids Protective Association (PPMPA). In addition, an industry-wide black union, the Railway Men's Association, tried to attract porters to its cause. Pullman attempted to defuse labor organizing by creating the Employee Representation Plan (ERP, a company union), and offering modest wage increases. Although porter dissatisfaction simmered, efforts to organize were stalled until A. Philip Randolph, editor of the *Messenger* and a strong voice for economic equality, addressed a meeting of porters in 1925. Randolph urged porters to reject the ERP and form their own union, and several of the porters agreed – if Randolph would lead them.

Starting in 1925, with only about 1900 members out of the nearly 10,000 porters, the union faced intimidation by the company as well as resistance by some workers who were satisfied with the ERP. In addition, Randolph and his organizers had to battle the black community's long-standing ambivalence toward labor unions. Historically excluded from white unions and the secure jobs they represented, many African Americans believed that they owed their allegiance to their employers, not to unions. Randolph's eloquence on behalf of the BSCP helped change attitudes, as did the support of the National Association for the Advancement of Colored People (NAACP). While Randolph led the public fight, lobbying federal courts and agencies, Chicago porter Milton Webster ran the daily administration of the union, which achieved its largest membership (4623) in 1928. After a series of setbacks, the 1934 passage of the Railway Labor Act finally forced Pullman to recognize the Brotherhood.

African American railway porters such as these men, pictured in 1910, were favored by railroad companies both because they could be paid less than whites and because many white customers enjoyed being waited on by blacks. Given the dismal job opportunities for African Americans at the time, being a porter was considered a good job.
CORBIS/Minnesota Historical Society

After negotiating its first contract with Pullman in 1937, the BSCP continued to represent the porters for more than 40 years, merging with the Brotherhood of Railway and Airline Clerks in 1978. The Pullman era had long since passed, but the union's contributions extended beyond the railroad industry. As one member of the powerful BSCP Ladies Auxiliary (made up mostly of porters' wives) later said, the union "laid the foundation for the CIVIL RIGHTS MOVEMENT in this country. It inspired black people by proving that they could organize and get results."

Randolph's national leadership led to an executive order banning discrimination in the defense industries (an order not strongly enforced), the establishment of the FAIR EMPLOYMENT PRACTICES COMMITTEE, and the desegregation of the United States armed forces. When Rosa Parks was arrested for refusing to give up her bus seat to a white man in 1955, it was BSCP member E. D. Nixon who helped organize the MONTGOMERY BUS BOYCOTT in protest. In 1963 A. Philip Randolph's 1941 call for a March on Washington was finally realized; the event brought the civil rights message to a worldwide audience.

Kate Tuttle

SEE ALSO

Labor Unions in the United States; Nixon, Edgar Daniel; Parks, Rosa Louise McCauley; Randolph, Asa Philip; March on Washington, 1941.

North America

Brown, Anne Wiggins (b. 1915, Baltimore, Md.), African American concert singer who originated the role of Bess in Gershwin's *Porgy and Bess.*

Anne Wiggins Brown attended Morgan College, Teachers College of Columbia University, and the Juilliard School of Music. At Juilliard she was the first African American to receive the prestigious Margaret McGill Scholarship.

In 1935 Brown starred in the original production of George Gershwin's *Porgy and Bess.* Gershwin was so impressed with her voice that he changed the name of his folk OPERA *Porgy and Bess* from the original title *Porgy* so that she would receive equal billing with baritone Todd Duncan. He also rewrote the role of Bess to include "Summertime" among her songs.

Brown returned to Broadway for the 1942 production of *Porgy and Bess.* She toured the United States and Europe as a soloist for several years, and eventually settled in Norway. When asthma ended her singing career, Brown became a voice teacher.

Lisa Clayton Robinson

Latin America and the Caribbean

Brown, Carlinhos (Antonio Carlos Santos de Freitas) (b. 1963, Salvador, Bahia, BRAZIL), one of the most acclaimed Afro-Brazilian musicians and cultural agitators in Salvador, BAHIA, in the 1990s, who has played a central role in defining the new Bahian sound as composer, performer, and director of several percussion troupes.

Carlinhos Brown grew up in the Candeal neighborhood of Salvador and received early training from a local percussionist known as Pintado de Bongô. Inspired by African American SOUL MUSIC of the 1970s, he adopted a stage name after one of his heroes, JAMES BROWN. In the 1980s he played percussion for Bahian pop celebrities such as Luiz Caldas, Moraes Moreira, and Caetano Veloso, whose recording of Brown's tune "Meia-lua inteira" achieved mass popularity. In the 1990s he collaborated with Bill Laswell, Herbie Hancock, and Wayne Shorter on *Bahia Black: Ritual Beating System;* Sérgio Mendes on his Grammy Award-winning *Brasileiro;* Brazilian vocalist Marisa Monte on *Rose and Charcoal* and *A Great Noise;* and Brazilian heavy metal band Sepultura on *Roots.*

In the early 1990s Brown founded Timbalada, the percussion-based pop group propelled by a legion of muscular young black men decorated with white body paint pounding out staccato phrases on lightweight, high-volume drums called *timbaus.* Unlike the more politicized and Afrocentric *blocos Afros,* the music of Carlinhos Brown and Timbalada largely avoids racial politics and social critique. Since 1993 the group has released an album nearly every year. In 1996 Brown recorded his first CD, *Alfagamabetizado,* an aesthetically and technically superb fusion of Afro-Bahian percussion, northeastern folk, and international pop.

Christopher Dunn

SEE ALSO

Hancock, Herbert Jeffrey (Herbie); Afoxés/Blocos Afros.

North America

Brown, Charlotte Hawkins (b. June 11, 1883, Henderson, N.C.; d. 1961), American civic leader and educator who founded the Palmer Institute (a prep school for African Americans) and argued against lynching and in favor of interracial cooperation.

Charlotte Hawkins Brown was born Lottie Hawkins on June 11, 1883, in Henderson, North Carolina, to Caroline Frances Hawkins and Edmund H. Hight. In 1888, Caroline and her new husband, Nelson Willis, moved the family to Cambridge, Massachusetts, where they operated a boarding house for Harvard students and a laundry. Around the time she graduated from Cambridge English High School, Lottie changed her name to the more serious sounding Charlotte Eugenia. She attracted the interest and support of Alice Freeman Palmer, who financed her education at the State Normal School in Salem, Massachusetts.

In 1902 Hawkins founded the Alice Freeman Palmer Institute in Sedalia, North Carolina, in honor of her mentor. In 1911 Hawkins married Edmund S. Brown, who then taught at the Palmer Institute. The couple divorced in 1915. The Palmer Institute began as a vocational school, but its curriculum evolved until it was a strictly academic institution, considered one of the finest preparatory schools for African Americans in the United States.

In addition to running the Palmer Institute, Brown fought tirelessly for African American civil rights, lecturing in opposition to LYNCHING and in favor of interracial cooperation. She helped to found the NATIONAL COUNCIL OF NEGRO WOMEN, the North Carolina State Federation of Negro Women's Clubs, and the North Carolina Teachers Association. She was also on the national board of the Young Women's Christian Association.

Brown served as the president of the Palmer Institute for 50 years before retiring in 1952. Even in retirement, however, she continued to act as the school's financial director and was deeply involved on its board of directors until her death in 1961. Though financial problems forced the Palmer Institute to close in 1971, Brown's tremendous contribution to African American education did not go unheralded. In 1983 the Charlotte Hawkins Brown Historical Foundation was incorporated and established on the Palmer Institute's campus, North Carolina's first historic site honoring either an African American or a woman.

Robert Fay

North America

Brown, Claude

(b. February 23, 1927, New York, N.Y.), writer best known for his autobiography, *Manchild in the Promised Land.*

Claude Brown, the son of Ossie Brock Brown, a domestic worker, and Henry Lee, a railroad worker, began *Manchild in the Promised Land* in 1963. Published in 1965, the book told of his troubled childhood in Harlem, a period during which he ran with a gang and was in and out of reform schools.

Brown abandoned street life, resumed his education, and was awarded a grant to study government at HOWARD UNIVERSITY, graduating in 1965. He studied law at Stanford University and then at Rutgers University, which he left in 1968 without a degree. In 1976 he published *The Children of Ham,* about struggling young blacks in Harlem.

SEE ALSO
Harlem, New York.

North America

Brown, Corrine

(b. November 11, 1946, Jacksonville, Fla.), Democratic member of the United States House of Representatives from Florida (1993-).

Corrine Brown was born in Jacksonville, Florida. She received a bachelor's degree in 1969 and a master's degree in 1971 from Florida A&M University. She also received an education specialist degree from the University of Florida in 1974 and an honorary doctorate in law from Edward Waters College. Brown was a college professor, a guidance counselor, and the owner of a travel agency before entering politics. In 1982 she was elected to the Florida State House, where she served for ten years. In 1992 she was elected to the United States House of Representatives from Florida's Third Congressional District, a curved band connecting Gainesville, Jacksonville, and Orlando, drawn specifically to create a district with a black majority. The district's three naval air facilities are major employers, as is Disney World in Orlando. Most of the district's population resides in Jacksonville.

In the 105th Congress (1997-1999), Brown sat on the Veterans' Affairs Committee as well as the Transportation and Infrastructure Committee. She is also a member of the CONGRESSIONAL BLACK CAUCUS.

Latin America and the Caribbean

Brown, Everald

(b. 1917), Jamaican painter and sculptor famous for his artwork inspired by Rastafarian and Ethiopian religions (*see* ART IN LATIN AMERICA AND THE CARIBBEAN).

North America

Brown Fellowship Society,

elite African American social club in Charleston, South Carolina.

In 1790 a group of five free African Americans organized a social club in Charleston, South Carolina, called the Brown Fellowship Society. With color restrictions and a $50 membership fee, the organization appealed to an elite group of mostly light-skinned, biracial men who wished to establish a social position similar to that of the white aristocracy. The strength of this identification was such that, in the words of one nineteenth-century member, "If [the white elite] stood for slavery, so did our fathers to a certain extent."

The Brown Fellowship Society provided services for its members, including education, medical care, and support for widows and orphans of the deceased. Renamed the Century Fellowship Society in 1890, it lasted into the twentieth century, generating a woman's auxiliary in 1907.

Marian Aguiar

SEE ALSO
Slavery in the United States; Free Blacks in the United States, 1619 to 1863.

North America

Brown, Hallie Quinn

(b. March 10, 1845, Pittsburgh, Pa.; d. September 16, 1949, Wilberforce, Ohio), educator, elocutionist, and leader in the American movement for women's rights.

Hallie Brown, born to former slaves Thomas Arthur Brown and Frances Jane Scroggins Brown, graduated from WILBERFORCE UNIVERSITY in 1873 and became a prominent educator and activist for civil and women's rights. She held several positions in institutions of higher learning, including professor of elocution at Wilberforce (1893) and Lady Principal (1892-1893) at Tuskegee Institute. Brown served as president of the Ohio State Federation of Women's Clubs from 1905 to 1912 and of the NATIONAL ASSOCIATION OF COLORED WOMEN from 1920 to 1924.

Alonford James Robinson, Jr.

SEE ALSO
Tuskegee University.

North America

Brown, Henry ("Box")

(b. 1815, Richmond, Va.; d. ?), American slave and abolitionist; escaped from slavery packaged in a wooden box.

Henry Brown was born a slave and labored first on a plantation and later at a tobacco factory in Richmond under a master who was regarded as relatively benevolent. Though he later described his life in enslavement as tolerable, Brown decided to escape in 1848 when his wife, Nancy, and their three children were sold away from him. To ensure his escape, Brown launched an ingenious plan that he said was divinely inspired.

In March 1849, Brown had a white abolitionist friend, Samuel A. Smith, package him in a wooden box and ship him by Adams Express to antislavery headquarters in PHILADELPHIA, PENNSYLVANIA. During the 27-hour journey, he spent much of the time on his head, as he was transferred back and forth from wagons, trains, and steamboats. An astonished group of abolitionists "received" him once he arrived in Philadelphia.

Antislavery groups helped Brown relocate, first to BOSTON, MASSACHUSETTS, and later to New Bedford, Massachusetts, where he became a regular speaker on the abolitionist lecture circuit. He toured the country with his box and his story. In an effort to boost his influence as an abolitionist, Brown commissioned the painting of a mural entitled *Mirror of Slavery.* Artists from Boston painted pictures depicting slavery in the South together with Brown's heroic escape. The mural covered several thousand square feet of canvas. Fearing he would be captured, Brown left America for England after Congress passed the Fugitive Slave Law in 1850.

Once in England, Brown toured the country, giving lectures on the horrors of slavery. After four years he disappeared and was not heard from again.

Alonford James Robinson, Jr.

See Also

Slavery in the United States; Abolitionism in the United States; Fugitive Slave Laws; Richmond, Virginia.

North America

Brown, Hubert G. ("H. Rap")

(b. October 4, 1943, Baton Rouge, La.), American writer and activist also known as Jamil al-Amin; outspoken advocate of Black Power, elected national chairman of the Student Nonviolent Coordinating Committee in 1967.

Hubert "H. Rap" Brown was born October 4, 1943 in Baton Rouge, Louisiana. In 1962 he dropped out of Southern University to join the Nonviolent Action Group (NAG) at Howard University. In 1965 he became chairman of the NAG. Labeled an "extremist" by the media for his nationalist views, he was an outspoken advocate of Black Power. In May 1967, when Stokely Carmichael stepped down, he was elected national chairman of the Student Nonviolent Coordinating Committee (SNCC).

That same year, Brown was charged by the states of Maryland and Ohio with inciting violence. He was harassed by the police and targeted by the Counterintelligence Program of the Federal Bureau of Investigation (FBI). While under indictment, he was arrested for transporting weapons across state lines. He resigned as SNCC chairman in 1968 and later that year was sentenced to five years in prison on federal weapons charges.

Fearing for his life, Brown refused to appear at his trial in Maryland, and in 1970 was placed on the FBI's Ten Most Wanted List. He was captured in 1972 and spent the next four years in prison. While incarcerated, Brown converted to Islam, taking the name Jamil ("servant of Allah") al-Amin ("the trustworthy"). After his release, Brown moved to Atlanta, Georgia, where he is in charge of the Community Grocery Store and serves as imam (spiritual leader) to Muslim families in and around Atlanta.

Alonford James Robinson, Jr.

North America

Brown, James

(b. May 3, 1933, Augusta, Ga.), American soul and funk singer, known as the Godfather of Soul, Soul Brother Number One, Mr. Dynamite, and the Hardest Working Man in Show Business.

James Brown grew up in Augusta, Georgia, where he did a little of everything: picked cotton, shined shoes, danced, and served time for armed robbery. Brown boxed and played pro baseball before an injury made him turn to music. After dabbling in gospel, he renamed his group, from the Swanees to the Famous Flames. The group's local popularity attracted the attention of Federal Records, which signed them to a contract in 1956. Their first record, "Please Please Please," did well, and "Try Me" topped the rhythm-and-blues charts in 1958.

As his band's fame spread beyond Georgia, Brown became ambitious. He staged elaborate dances, formed the James Brown Revue, and created a Carnival atmosphere at his live shows. An emcee worked the crowd into a frenzy before the singer came onstage, and Brown allegedly lost seven pounds each night through dancing. Soon he had a backup band (the J.B.s) in addition to the Flames, who were largely a vocal group. Although Brown wanted to record with the J.B.s, Federal Records refused. In response, Brown recorded the hit instrumental "Mashed Potatoes" under a pseudonym. This ruse attracted the attention of Federal Record's parent company, King Records, who allowed Brown and the J.B.s to record together. With King this group began a long and fruitful relationship. In 1962 the album *Live at the Apollo, Volume 2*, sold 1 million copies.

Seen here in a 1984 concert at the age of 50, James Brown brought funk music into national prominence in the 1960s and 1970s and helped pave the way for disco and hip hop. *CORBIS/Bettmann*

In 1965 Brown achieved artistic control of his records, and the result was unprecedented in popular music. Under Brown's tight direction, he recorded one hit after another. The music was notable for irresistible grooves, precision timing, and Brown's impassioned vocals. Brown specialized in an insistent dance music that was deeply charged with sexual electricity. In many ways, he pioneered the sound that evolved into funk and disco. Starting with "Papa's Got a Brand New Bag," Brown's string of hits continued through the 1960s with such songs as "I Got You," "Cold Sweat," and "Say It Loud, I'm Black and I'm Proud."

Through the late 1960s and into the 1970s, Brown became a spokesman among African American youth, and he targeted more of his songs toward disaffected ghetto youth. Not only did he preach responsibility in songs like "King Heroin," "Funky President," and "Don't Be a Drop-Out," he also invested in black businesses, bought several radio stations, and inspired kids with his tough but uplifting message. Other activities included traveling to Africa and writing music for several films.

Brown's success has been accompanied by personal difficulties. He faced legal trouble for failing to pay taxes and for allegedly assaulting his wife. Despite reorganizing his bands many times, Brown has had relatively few hits since the mid-1970s. Nevertheless, as he nears his fifth decade in music, Brown remains an inspirational performer who has influenced countless younger musicians. Hip hop bands have extensively appropriated funky grooves from his 1970s records in the sampling practices of the 1980s and 1990s.

See Also

Soul Music; Baseball in the United States; Boxing; Gospel Music; Hip Hop in the United States.

North America

Brown, Jim

(b. February 17, 1936, Simmons Island, Ga.), football player for Syracuse University and the Cleveland Browns, actor, and youth mentor.

By the time Jim Brown retired in 1965 after nine seasons in the National Football League (NFL), many sports writers described him as the best fullback ever to carry a football. Born in Georgia, he moved with his mother to Long Island, New York, at the age of seven. An all-state athlete in high school in football, basketball, and track, he became a four-sport star in college, adding lacrosse to his arsenal while at Syracuse University.

After graduating in 1957, Brown received job offers from professional baseball and basketball teams as well as invitations to become a boxer, but he chose to sign with the NFL's Cleveland Browns. The NFL named Brown Rookie of the Year in 1957 and chose him as its Most Valuable Player three times in his brief career. He played in the Pro Bowl nine times and set records for total yardage (12,312) and yards per carry (5.2). Brown retired in 1965 at the age of 29 at the height of his athletic powers. In 1971 he was inducted into the Football Hall of Fame. He is also enshrined in the Halls of Fame of College Football and Lacrosse.

In Brown's second career, as a movie and television actor, he has made more than 20 films, including Westerns such as *Rio Concho* and *The Dirty Dozen*. He has written two autobiographies, *Off My Chest* (1964) and *Out of Bounds* (1989), the second of which describes romantic affairs with many of his costars. In addition to acting, Brown has been instrumental in creating programs to help gang members and former prisoners complete their education and find work.

Kate Tuttle

North America

Brown, John (b. May 9, 1800, Torrington, Conn.; d. December 2, 1859, Charles Town, Va. [now West Virginia]), white American radical abolitionist, famous for his participation in antislavery warfare in the Kansas territory and for his 1859 raid on the federal armory in Harpers Ferry, Virginia.

The Last Moments of John Brown (c. 1884), by Thomas Hovenden, shows an idealized Brown kissing a black baby as he leaves the Charles Town jail to be hanged. The image is based upon a poem by John Greenleaf Whittier, who transformed what was a reporter's apocryphal story into an enduring myth. *Fine Arts Museums of San Francisco, Gift of Mr. and Mrs. John D. Rockefeller 3rd, 1979.7.60*

A hero to many, a madman to others, John Brown was one of the most controversial figures in pre-Civil War America. Like all abolitionists, his goal was the end of slavery in the United States. But unlike other antislavery activists, Brown was neither an idealistic pacifist nor a man willing to work through political and legal channels. Brown worked peacefully guiding fugitive slaves to freedom via the Underground Railroad, yet he was also involved in the killing of proslavery militants in the Kansas territories. He later led the Harpers Ferry raid, which he believed would inspire a massive slave revolt, and subsequently turned his trial for treason into a national pulpit to denounce slavery.

Brown was deeply influenced by his father, a devout Congregationalist who opposed slavery. Like many of his generation, Brown completed only a few years of formal schooling before apprenticing with his father, a tanner. In 1816 he entered divinity school in Massachusetts, but his plans to become a minister were thwarted by a lack of money, and he dropped out the following year. He married in 1820 and fathered 7 children. His first wife died in 1832; he remarried the following year, and with his second wife had 13 more children. To support his family, Brown worked as a farmer, a tanner, a surveyor, and a businessman, all without success. Chronically in debt, the Browns moved often, from Ohio to New York and throughout New England.

Throughout the 1840s and 1850s Brown was an active abolitionist. He worked with the Underground Railroad and in 1851 helped found the League of Gileadites, a racially mixed group that helped fugitive slaves after they escaped. In 1855 Brown followed several of his grown sons to the Kansas territory, which was then embroiled in a bloody civil war over whether it would enter the union as a slave state or a free state. In 1856 a band of proslavery extremists burned the free-state town of Lawrence, killing dozens, and Brown led a group of free-state partisans in exacting revenge. First, they killed five suspected proslavery settlers camped along the Pottawatomie River; then they launched a series of raids that culminated in a violent skirmish at the tiny village of Osawatomie.

Now known nationwide as Osawatomie Brown, the zealous abolitionist began gathering support for his next battle. In addition to seeking help from prominent black abolitionist friends such as FREDERICK DOUGLASS and Harriet Tubman, Brown drew support from noted white abolitionists, in particular a group of wealthy, intellectual New Englanders that came to be known as the Secret Six. Although these six men had previously advocated peaceful, nonviolent action, Brown's determination – as well as the turn of national events – changed their minds. The Secret Six gave Brown money and helped him plan a violent insurrectionary attack that they hoped would overthrow the institution of slavery.

Brown chose as his target the federal arsenal and armory in Harpers Ferry, Virginia. In July 1859, he arrived there with some of his men and rented a farm across the Potomac River, in Maryland. Throughout the summer, his army – comprising 22 men, 17 white and 5 black, including Brown – gathered and hid. As commander, Brown hoped that the strike on the armory would rouse the local slaves to rise up and claim their freedom; in anticipation of this, he had gathered some 1000 steel pikes for the slaves to use as weapons.

On the evening of October 16, the men struck. Seizing control of the armory, Brown sent small groups to take some prominent local citizens hostage. However, Brown then seemed paralyzed by indecision. Because he allowed the local trains to continue running, news of the raid quickly reached WASHINGTON, D.C., where the secretary of war authorized the dispatch of a batallion of marines led by Colonel Robert E. Lee. Meanwhile, local militias also converged on Harpers Ferry. Brown and his men were soon trapped – just as Frederick Douglass, who had opposed the plan for its impracticality, had predicted – and the anticipated slave uprising did not occur. About 36 hours after it had begun, the raid ended in the capture of Brown and the four other men who had survived the siege. Of the rest of Brown's party, ten were killed and seven escaped.

Brown was tried in Charles Town, Virginia, for treason, inciting slave rebellion, and murder – five townspeople and militia members had been killed. His trial sparked debate, particularly among white abolitionists, about whether he was insane. Some abolitionists wished to distance themselves from Brown's embrace of violence; others hoped that the insanity claim would spare him from execution. Brown's lawyers argued that he should not be tried as a common criminal, given that in 1858 his supporters, gathering in Canada, had named him commander in chief of a provisional antislavery government, and thus, in Brown's opinion, this was war. The judge disagreed and sentenced him to be hanged.

During the trial and before his execution, Brown continued to urge abolitionists to take action, even risk sacrifice, for their cause. As he had said after Kansas, "I have only a short time to live – only one death to die; and I will die fighting for this cause." He also predicted that much more blood would be shed before the slavery issue was finally settled. He was the object of nationwide attention before his death, and his words in his final days inspired many to call him a hero, a saint, a martyr. On December 2, 1859, Brown was hanged at Charles Town. Just over a year later, in December 1860, South Carolina became the first state to secede from the United States, beginning a series of events that would lead to the outbreak of the Civil War in April 1861.

In the years since his death, differing views of Brown have emerged. During the Civil War, Union soldiers marched to the song "John Brown's Body," and many Northern whites, most white abolitionists, and the vast majority of African Americans came to revere him as a martyr for liberty. To white Southerners, however, Brown was a madman, a monster. For years, white establishment historians regarded Brown with ambivalence, as a man whose cause was just but whose actions were insane acts of terrorism. Today, many scholars argue that Brown was a radical democrat, a sane but zealous man whose actions should be judged by the standards of wartime, and whose understanding that slavery in the United States would end only by bloodshed was prophetic.

Kate Tuttle

See Also

Slavery in the United States; Abolitionism in the United States; Civil War, American; Tubman, Harriet Ross; Underground Railroad.

North America

Brown, Ronald H.

(b. August 1, 1941, Washington, D.C.; d. April 3, 1996, nr. Dubrovnik, Croatia), American business-man and politician who was the first African American to serve as chairman of a national political party; the first black student to pledge a fraternity at Middlebury College; the first black chief counsel of a United States Senate standing committee; the first black law partner at Patton, Boggs, and Blow; and the first black United States secretary of commerce.

Ron Brown grew up in Harlem, graduated from Middlebury College in 1962, and enlisted in the U.S. Army. After his service, he worked for the National Urban League in New York while earning his law degree at night from St. John's University, where he graduated in 1970. He held several positions at the Urban League from 1968 to 1979, including general counsel, chief Washington spokesperson, deputy executive director, and vice president of Washington operations.

In Washington, D.C., Brown became active in the Democratic Party, and in 1979 served as deputy manager of Sen. Edward Kennedy's presidential campaign. A year later Kennedy appointed him the chief counsel to the Senate Judiciary Committee. In 1982 Brown resigned from the Senate Committee to become deputy chairman of the Democratic National Committee (DNC). He left the DNC and politics in 1986 to become a partner in the Washington law firm of Patton, Boggs, and Blow.

In 1988 Brown returned to politics as the convention manager for Jesse Jackson's presidential campaign. He was elected chairman of the DNC in 1989, the first African American in either political party to serve in that capacity. In 1993 President Bill Clinton appointed him secretary of commerce, and he is widely credited with revitalizing the department. Brown and 34 others were on a three-day economic tour of the Balkans for the United States Department of Commerce when their plane crashed during stormy weather. He is survived by his wife, Alma, and their two children.

Alonford James Robinson, Jr.

See Also

Harlem, New York; Jackson, Jesse Louis; New York, New York.

North America

Brown, Ruth

(b. December 30, 1928, Portsmouth, Va.), African American blues and musical theater singer, one of the pioneers of rhythm and blues (R&B).

Celebrated as Miss Rhythm, Ruth Brown has long been revered for her earthy, innuendo-laden rhythm and blues (R&B) singing. According to music critic Ron Wynn, "Nobody male or female sang with more spirit, sass, and vigor than Brown during the 1950s." She is also noted for her "yelp," which, says *New York Times* writer Ann Powers, "is one of the defining sounds of rock-and-roll, as primary as Little Richard's 'wooo!' or Jerry Lee Lewis's growl." Brown has recorded prolifically and is credited with having laid the foundation for Atlantic Records with such 1950s hits as "Mama, He Treats Your Daughter Mean," "5-10-15 Hours," and "Teardrops from My Eyes." An active performer still, in 1994 she was inducted into the Rock and Roll Hall of Fame.

"All of my childhood was spent singing spirituals," Brown once wrote. The daughter of Leonard Weston, a dockhand, and Martha (Alston) Weston, Brown grew up in a predominantly black community in Portsmouth, Virginia. She received musical training at a local Methodist church, where she sang in the choir her father directed. In the early 1940s she won first prize at the Apollo Theater's Amateur Night in New York City and went on to perform in local nightclubs. She also toured with United Service Organization performers throughout the South and in 1948 sang with the Lucky Millinder Band.

Describing her singing style of the times, Brown wrote, "I was more of a pop torch singer. I preferred the ballads." She soon began to sing R&B, and by the late 1950s had recorded more than 80 songs for Atlanta Records. In 1966, after her third divorce, she scaled back her career to care for her two children. "Until then," she said, "my sons had been like backstage babies, living in a drawer... while I performed in and out of train stations." Having received almost no royalties from her recordings, she worked intermittently as a bus driver, housekeeper, and teacher's aide while continuing to record.

In 1989 Brown enjoyed a dramatic comeback. In that year she won a Tony Award for her performance in the Broadway musical *Black and Blue* and recorded *Blues on Broadway*, for which she received a Grammy Award in 1990. In 1991 she began hosting the weekly music program *BluesStage* on National Public Radio. She has recorded more than a dozen albums, including her most recent, *The Songs of My Life* (1993) and *Live in London* (1994).

Roanne Edwards

See Also

Apollo Theater; Rhythm and Blues.

North America

Brown, Sterling Allen

(b. May 1, 1901, Washington, D.C.; d. January 13, 1989, Takoma Park, Md.); African American academic, poet, critic, and anthologist known for his research on black folklore and his poetry written in African American dialect.

Through his long career as a writer anthologist, critic, scholar, and educator, Sterling Brown became one of the most influential individuals in the field of African American literary studies. He was born into WASHINGTON, D.C.'s educated black middle class. His father, an ex-slave, was a prominent pastor and professor of religion at HOWARD UNIVERSITY, and his mother had been valedictorian of her class at FISK UNIVERSITY. Brown attended the well-known Dunbar High School, where Jessie Fauset and Angelina Weld Grimké were among his teachers, and graduated with honors in 1918. He then accepted a scholarship to Williams College in Williamstown, Massachusetts. There he was elected to Phi Beta Kappa, earned the distinction of being the only student awarded final honors in English, and graduated with a bachelor's degree cum laude in 1922. From there, he went to Harvard University to pursue a master's degree in English, which he received in 1923.

During his studies, Brown was drawn to younger American poets such as Edwin Arlington Robinson, Robert Frost, and Carl Sandburg, whose work convinced him that a well-crafted celebration of dialect and of everyday culture – "the extraordinary in ordinary life" – was possible in American poetry. But Brown would later acknowledge that his best teachers were always "the poor black folk of the South," because it was from them that he came to appreciate the black folklore and language that would form the basis of most of his own work. Brown's first exposure to this rich culture came just after his graduation from Harvard, when he took a teaching post at the Virginia Seminary in Lynchburg, Virginia, for three years.

In Virginia he began paying careful attention to the work songs, blues, and spirituals he heard, calling his visits to jook joints, barbershops, and rural farms "folklore-collecting trips." He also married Daisy Turnbull, his wife of more than 50 years, in Lynchburg in 1927. After leaving the Virginia Seminary, Brown taught at Lincoln University in Jefferson City, Missouri, and at Fisk University in Nashville, Tennessee, before accepting a post as professor of English at HOWARD UNIVERSITY in 1929, a position he would hold for the next 40 years. During 1931 and 1932 he returned to Harvard briefly to do doctoral work, and in 1932 he published his first collection of poetry, *Southern Road.*

Brown's first published poem, "When de Saints Go Ma'ching Home," had appeared five years earlier in the National Urban League's journal, *Opportunity.* Between 1927 and 1932 several more of his poems appeared in journals and were included in the HARLEM RENAISSANCE anthology *Caroling Dusk* (1927), edited by COUNTEE CULLEN, and *The Book of American Negro Poetry* (1931), edited by JAMES WELDON JOHNSON. The poetry in *Southern Road,* like these earlier pieces, brought to life the ballads and work songs Brown had collected. Many of his poems were written in African American dialect, imitated folk songs' verse and rhyme patterns, and used black folk heroes as protagonists. Unlike some earlier DIALECT POETRY by black and white writers that had been accused of caricature, Brown's work was praised for realistically portraying black speech and culture.

Southern Road received good reviews, but when Brown could not find a publisher for his second book of poetry, he returned to his scholarly work. In the next decade he published two critical books, *The Negro in American Fiction* (1937) and *Negro Poetry and Drama* (1937), and coedited an anthology, *The Negro Caravan,* which remains one of the most important collections of AFRICAN AMERICAN LITERATURE. Between 1936 and 1940 he was also national editor of *Negro Affairs* for the FEDERAL WRITERS' PROJECT, a federally funded program that hired writers to collect American folklore.

In the decades that followed, Brown turned much of his attention to teaching, spending semesters at Vassar College, Atlanta University, and New York University in addition to his post at Howard. He earned a reputation as a much-beloved instructor and was especially celebrated for his willingness to serve as a mentor; his students included STOKELY CARMICHAEL, KWAME NKRUMAH, OSSIE DAVIS, and AMIRI BARAKA. After he finally retired from teaching in 1969, Brown enjoyed a revival in his career as a poet.

In 1975 Brown published his second book of poetry, *The Last Ride of Wild Bill and Eleven Narratives. Southern Road* was reprinted in the same year. In 1979 he was asked to contribute an autobiographical memoir to the collection *Chant of Saints: A Gathering of Afro-American Literature, Art, and Scholarship,* and in 1980 poet Michael S. Harper edited *The Collected Poems of Sterling A. Brown,* which included the unpublished poems from the volume that had been rejected in the 1930s and which was awarded that year's Lenore Marshall Prize for an outstanding volume of poetry published in the United States.

During the 1970s and 1980s Brown received honorary doctorates from such institutions as Williams and Vassar colleges and Howard, Harvard, and Brown universities; was elected to the Academy of American Poets; and was named poet laureate of the District of Columbia. By the time of his death from leukemia in 1989, Sterling Brown had been confirmed as a key figure in the African American literary tradition.

Lisa Clayton Robinson

SEE ALSO

Blues, The; Fauset, Jessie Redmon; Grimké, Angelina Weld; Harper, Michael Steven; Lincoln University (Missouri); National Urban League; *Opportunity: Journal of Negro Life*; Spirituals, African American.

North America

Brown, Tony (b. April 11, 1933, Charleston, W. Va.), African American television talk-show host, educator, and writer, an active campaigner for black economic empowerment.

Best known for his weekly PBS television show *Tony Brown's Journal,* Tony Brown has become a controversial figure on the landscape of American race relations. Although once active in the CIVIL RIGHTS MOVEMENT, he has criticized present-day black activists for prioritizing civil rights at the expense of black business initiatives and education programs in computer technologies. He advocates black economic self-sufficiency and has consistently opposed welfare as well as AFFIRMATIVE ACTION policies that he believes mainly benefit middle-class blacks. "If America were capitalist," said Brown in an interview with Matthew Robinson of *Business Daily,* "it could not be racist. Racism is flourishing because we are awash in socialistic controls."

Tony Brown was reared by two domestic workers, Elizabeth Sanford and Mabel Holmes, who informally adopted him at the age of two months after his father deserted the family and left his mother destitute. His foster parents instilled in him a religiously based work ethic and an awareness of racial injustice. Although eventually reunited with his mother and three siblings, Brown credits Sanford and Holmes as well as nurturing schoolteachers for his "overachieving nature." A graduate of Wayne State University in Detroit, where he received a bachelor's degree in sociology (1959) and a master's degree in psychiatric social work (1961), Brown landed a job at Detroit's PBS station and soon after produced his own television show, *Colored People's Times* (C.P.T.).

In 1963 he helped coordinate the local "March to Freedom" with Martin Luther King Jr. – a watershed for Brown. Confronting a policeman who had severely harassed him, he understood for the first time why such militant blacks as Louis Farrakhan had so many followers: "Their very souls ache with the pain of insult and rejection," he would later write; "Only another black can know this." In later years, commentators would accuse Brown of promoting a Black Nationalist agenda.

In 1970 Brown became executive producer of *Black Journal* – a show renamed *Tony Brown's Journal* in 1977, currently broadcast on PBS – and in 1971 he founded and became the first dean of the School of Communications at HOWARD UNIVERSITY, a post he held until 1974. He has since continued to espouse his views through a variety of media, including his radio talk show *Tony Brown,* launched in 1995, and the Internet website *Tony Brown Online,* founded in 1996, an initiative aimed at strengthening black communities by providing online access to black businesses and an online dating service.

Roanne Edwards

See Also

Farrakhan, Louis Abdul; King, Martin Luther, Jr.; Television and African Americans.

North America

Brown v. Board of Education,

the 1954 United States Supreme Court decision that overturned the "separate but equal" doctrine that, since 1896, had made racial segregation legal in public facilities.

On May 17, 1954, in the case of *Brown* v. *the Board of Education of Topeka*, the U.S. Supreme Court ended federally sanctioned racial segregation in the public schools by ruling unanimously that "separate educational facilities are inherently unequal." A groundbreaking case, *Brown* not only overturned the precedent of Plessy v. Ferguson (1896), which had declared "separate but equal facilities" constitutional, but also provided the legal foundation of the Civil Rights Movement of the 1960s. Although widely perceived as a revolutionary decision, *Brown* was in fact the culmination of changes both in the Court and in the strategies of integration's most powerful legal champion, the National Association for the Advancement of Colored People (NAACP).

The Supreme Court had become more liberal in the years since it decided *Plessy*, largely due to appointments by Democratic presidents Franklin D. Roosevelt and Harry S. Truman. Though still all-white, the Court had issued decisions in the 1930s and 1940s that rendered racial separation illegal in certain situations. In *Smith* v. *Allright* (1944), it declared segregated political primaries unconstitutional. Four years later, in *Shelly* v. *Kraemer* (1948), the Court ruled that states could not enforce racially restrictive real-estate covenants. Over the next few years, often in response to cases brought by the NAACP's Legal Defense and Educational Fund, the Court further chipped away at the legal basis for state-sanctioned segregation.

Pushing the Court to this point had taken the NAACP more than 40 years. Since its founding in 1909, the organization had legally challenged racial inequality. Although for many years NAACP lawyers did not attack segregation itself, they found fertile ground in the rampant inequity it had spawned. This was particularly true in education. In 1929, for instance, the state of Alabama spent $36 per white student and only $10 per black student in its public schools. Such imbalance was widespread in the Southern states, where black schoolchildren endured overcrowded classrooms, insufficient libraries, undertrained teachers, and a lack of indoor plumbing. The NAACP's strategy throughout the 1930s demanded only that local governments provide African American children with facilities equal to those enjoyed by white children. Basing its lawsuits on individual states' or counties' failures to conform to *Plessy*'s formula of "separate but equal" in public accommodations, the NAACP won nearly every case.

On the national level, though, the NAACP, led by its first full-time legal counsel, Charles H. Houston, chose to focus on graduate and professional rather than elementary education. By demanding equal facilities on the graduate level, Houston hoped to force states into a difficult decision: either build prohibitively expensive new black professional schools or allow qualified African Americans to enroll in previously all-white law, medical, and other graduate schools. In 1936 Houston won a significant victory when Maryland's Supreme Court ordered the segregated University of Maryland Law School to admit Donald Murray, an African American student, rather than send him out of state for his legal education. A similar case went to the U.S. Supreme Court in 1938: in *Missouri ex rel Gaines* v. *Canada*, a 6-2 majority found that the University of Missouri, by denying a black student admission to its law school – though it did create a separate black law school in a building that also housed a movie theatre and a hotel – had created an unfair "privilege... for white law students" that it did not extend to similarly qualified African Americans.

Along with Houston, another black lawyer began to shape the NAACP's legal policy in the late 1930s. Thurgood Marshall, who later became the first African American U.S. Supreme Court justice, worked with Houston on *Murray* and by 1939 had succeeded Houston as NAACP chief counsel. Marshall also set up the NAACP Legal Defense and Educational Fund. Over the following decade, Marshall brought to the Court two graduate education cases that set the stage for *Brown*. In *McLaurin* v. *Oklahoma*, the state's segregated graduate school of education had admitted a black student, 68-year-old George McLaurin, but had segregated him within the school, roping off a separate seating area and scheduling his lunch hour at a different time from that of his white classmates. Sweatt v. Painter, a Texas case, concerned the state's offer of a separate law school for black students. Unlike *Gaines*, this school would come close to parity with the white school, including access to its library and faculty. In both cases, Marshall argued that segregation itself was inherently unequal and that it denied African Americans their rights to equal protection under the Fourteenth Amendment to the Constitution.

The Supreme Court decided both cases in 1950, the year in which Charles Houston died. In these rulings, the Court stopped just short of overturning *Plessy*. Meanwhile, the NAACP was considering a new challenge to the nation's segregated elementary schools. Within the organization, this was controversial. The 1948 NAACP conference stated a clear policy against joining lawsuits that recognized "the validity of segregation statutes" – as all the earlier "equalization" cases had done. Tackling local cases involving unequal elementary schools seemed to many to be a step backward. But when five groups of plaintiffs approached the NAACP beginning in 1949, Marshall and his colleagues agreed to help.

The cases came from Kansas, South Carolina, Virginia, and Delaware, with a related case from the District of Columbia. Each was a class-action lawsuit involving state-imposed school segregation. In the Virginia case, a group of African American high school students had initiated the action themselves. Along with the South Carolina plaintiffs, they faced obvious and extreme inequity; even South Carolina's governor had promised to improve black schools. In the Kansas case, the black and white schools were roughly comparable, and the lawsuit provoked local black opposition, as some African American teachers feared losing their jobs. But with inequality conceded in the Southern cases and not at issue in Kansas, the NAACP could at last directly challenge the constitutionality of segregation.

NAACP lawyers presented each case before federal tribunals in their respective districts. Among the evidence they presented was that of academic experts like social psychologist Kenneth B. Clark, known as the "doll man," whose work with children demonstrated the damaging psychological effects of segregation. As expected, the tribunals relied on Supreme Court precedent – *Plessy* – and ruled with the defendants. But the opinions gave Marshall hope. Delaware chancellor Collins Seitz wrote, "I believe the 'separate but equal' doctrine in education should be rejected, but I also believe its rejection must come from [the Supreme] Court."

Now consolidated under the name *Brown* v. *Board of Education*, the five cases came before the Supreme Court in December 1952. The NAACP followed the same strategy that had brought success in *Sweatt* and *McLaurin*. Marshall and his colleagues wrote that states had no valid reason to impose segregation, that racial separation – no matter how equal the facilities – caused psychological damage to black children, and that "restrictions or distinctions based upon race or color" violated the equal protection clause of the Fourteenth Amendment. Lawyers for the states argued that *Plessy* was correct: as long as accommodations were "equal," segregation itself hurt no one. They predicted dire consequences for integrated education, particularly in a South accustomed to segregation.

Though a majority of the justices already favored the NAACP's clients, some feared issuing a ruling that might have to be implemented by force. They decided to have the cases reargued the following term. In the intervening time, Chief Justice Fred Vinson died and President Eisenhower replaced him with California governor Earl Warren, who used his political skills to negotiate a unanimous Court verdict for desegregation.

The opinion, written by Warren and read on May 17, 1954, was short and straightforward. It echoed Marshall's expert witnesses, stating that for African American schoolchildren, segregation "generates a feeling of inferiority as to their status in the community that may affect their hearts and minds in a way unlikely to ever be undone." Critics decried such emphasis on psychological and sociological evidence, but Chief Justice Warren later argued for the importance of contradicting *Plessy*, which had stated that African Americans themselves had imagined any "badge of inferiority" conferred by segregation. The decision went on to say that segregation had no valid purpose, was imposed to give blacks lower status, and was therefore unconstitutional based on the Fourteenth Amendment.

Despite victory in the nation's highest court, desegregation was not immediate, easy, or complete. A separate decision, known as *Brown II* (1955), set guidelines for dismantling segregation. But without deadlines – the opinion contained the infamous phrase "with all deliberate speed" – desegregation came slowly. Throughout the South, whites reacted violently to school integration. Crowds threw rocks at black grade-schoolers in Little Rock, Arkansas, in 1957, and in 1962 Alabama governor George Wallace blocked the door when the first African American students attempted to enter the state university. Throughout the 1960s and 1970s urban schools increasingly experienced de facto segregation as middle-class whites fled to the suburbs. New strategies to achieve integration, like busing, sparked renewed frustration, anger, and resentment on all sides. At present, many urban American schools are nearly all-black while many suburban schools are all-white; in some cases, these schools are as unequal as those before *Brown*. Despite such setbacks, however, the case, considered by many legal scholars the most significant of the twentieth century, brought racial integration to thousands of American schools and inspired the Civil Rights Movement of the 1960s.

Kate Tuttle

TOP: Nettie Hunt hugs her daughter, Nikie, 3, on the steps of the Supreme Court building after the court announced its decision in *Brown* v. *Board of Education*. *CORBIS/Bettmann*

RIGHT: Attorneys George C. Hayes, Thurgood Marshall, and James Nabrit Jr., *left to right*, smile together in front of the Supreme Court building after successfully arguing their case against segregation in *Brown* v. *Board of Education*. *CORBIS/Bettmann*

See Also
Clark, Kenneth Bancroft; Fourteenth Amendment to the United States Constitution; Houston, Charles Hamilton; NAACP Legal Defense and Educational Fund; National Association for the Advancement of Colored People.

North America

Brown, Willa (b. January 2, 1906, Glasgow, Ky; d. July 18, 1992, Chicago, Ill.), American aviator, activist, and educator, the first African American officer in the Civil Air Patrol, and the only woman in 1943 to have both a mechanic's and a commercial license in aviation.

Willa Brown was born to the Reverend Eric and Hallie Mae Carpenter Brown. She lived briefly in Indianapolis, Indiana, but spent most of her childhood in Terre Haute, Indiana, where she graduated in 1920 from Sarah Scott Junior High School and Wiley High School in 1923.

In 1927 Brown received her bachelor of science degree in business from Indiana State Teachers College. After graduating, she taught public school in both Gary, Indiana, and Chicago, Illinois, where she developed an interest in aviation.

In 1935 Brown received a master mechanic's certificate from the Aeronautical University in Chicago, and three years later received a private pilot's license by passing her exam with a nearly flawless score of 96 percent. In addition, she earned a master's in business administration (MBA) from Northwestern University in Evanston, Illinois, in 1937, and a Civil Aeronautics Administration ground school instructor's rating in 1940.

After divorcing her first husband, Wilbur Hardaway, Brown married Cornelius Coffey, and the two formed the Coffey School of Aeronautics to train African American pilots in Chicago. In 1955 Brown was married a third time to the Reverend J. H. Chappell. She was the first African American officer in the Civil Air Patrol, the only woman in 1943 to have both a mechanic's and a commercial license in aviation, and president of the Pioneer Branch of the National Airmen's Association in Chicago. Brown retired in 1971 as a schoolteacher and died of a stroke in 1992.

Alonford James Robinson, Jr.

North America

Brown, William Wells (b. 1814, near Lexington, Ky.; d. November 6, 1884, Chelsea, Mass.), African American antislavery lecturer and groundbreaking novelist, playwright, and historian.

Scholars have called William Wells Brown the first African American to achieve distinction in writing *belles lettres,* or "fine letters." Brown's literary career is made up of "firsts": he is considered the first African American to publish works in several literary genres. But Brown was also known for his political activism, particularly in the antislavery movement, and political themes underscored his writing throughout his career.

Brown was born on a plantation outside Lexington, Kentucky, to a white father and a slave mother. He spent most of his childhood and young adulthood as a slave in St. Louis, Missouri, working at a variety of trades, and even traveling to New Orleans three times as a handyman to a slave trader. Brown became free on New Year's Day, 1834, when he was while it was docked in Cincinnati, Ohio, a free state.

Brown's middle and last names honored a white Quaker family, Mr. and Mrs. Wells Brown, who helped him escape. He settled in Cleveland, where he married Elizabeth Schooner. Next, Brown moved to Buffalo, New York, and spent nine years there working simultaneously as a steamboatman on Lake Erie and as a conductor for the Underground Railroad, the secret network of individuals who helped fugitive slaves escape to freedom in the Northern states or Canada.

In 1843 Brown began lecturing on his experiences in slavery for the Western New York Anti-Slavery Society, one of many American abolitionist groups. He eventually became a lecturer on behalf of women's rights and temperance, but it was as a fugitive slave speaking on the evils of slavery that he was best known. This provided the basis for the beginning of his career as a writer. In the wake of Frederick Douglass's successful autobiographical slave narrative in 1845, there was an increased demand for similar narratives. Two years later, Brown wrote his own, and the *Narrative of William W. Brown, a Fugitive Slave, Written by Himself* went through four American and five British editions in its first three years after publication.

Following his autobiography's international success, in 1849 Brown traveled to Europe. The combination of European demand for his antislavery speeches and the passage of the American Fugitive Slave Law in 1850 – which put him in danger of being returned to slavery if he were apprehended anywhere on American soil – led Brown to stay in England for the next five years. Between 1849 and 1854 he gave more than a thousand speeches and wrote two books that were important firsts for African American literature. In 1852 Brown published *Three Years in Europe; or, Places I Have Seen and People I Have Met,* the first travel book written by an African American; and in 1853 he published *Clotel, or, the President's Daughter: A Narrative of Slave Life in the United States,* thought by some to be the first novel written by an African American.

The plot of *Clotel,* although fictional, is based on the widespread belief that American president Thomas Jefferson had fathered several slave children. The title character, his beautiful mulatto daughter, is separated from her mother and sister when all three are sold at auction after Jefferson's death. Her new owner falls in love with her and, after fathering her child, promises to marry her but ultimately betrays his promise and sells her to a dealer. Clotel escapes from the dealer and attempts to free her child, but when she realizes she has been discovered, she drowns herself to avoid being returned to slavery.

In later years, *Clotel* has been criticized for its stereotypical portrayal of a "tragic mulatto" and its melodramatic plot and style. At the time of its publication, however, the novel was praised by antislavery groups for its skill in exposing slavery's horrors, and was compared favorably to Harriet Beecher Stowe's antislavery novel Uncle Tom's Cabin, which had been a runaway bestseller just a year earlier. *Clotel* was revised and reprinted three times in the United States during Brown's lifetime. It is still honored as one of the landmark texts in the African American literary tradition and is still available in contemporary editions.

In 1854 some of Brown's friends raised enough money to purchase his freedom, allowing him to return to the United States. Once home, Brown continued writing on the same themes in a different genre. In 1858 his play *The Escape; or, a Leap for Freedom* became the first drama published by an African American. Over the next two decades, he focused his efforts on yet another genre: historical works. These included two histories of the black race, another history on blacks and whites in the American South, and a rare military history of African Americans in the American Civil War. Brown's career as an orator slowed down after slavery ended, and he eventually settled in Boston and practiced medicine there until his death from cancer in 1884. But as a pioneering black writer, Brown left a lasting legacy to the generations of African American novelists, dramatists, and historians who would follow him (*see* Literature, African American).

Lisa Clayton Robinson

See Also
Abolitionism in the United States; Douglass, Frederick; Fugitive Slave Laws; New Orleans, Louisiana; Slave Narratives.

North America

Brown, Willie Lewis, Jr. (b. March 20, 1934, Mineola, Tex.), mayor of San Francisco, California, and former Speaker of the California Assembly.

After serving 31 years in the California State Assembly – the last 15 as Speaker, the second-most powerful position in the state – Democrat Willie Brown announced in 1995 that he would run for mayor of San Francisco. The 1990 passage of state term limits had effectively ended his tenure as Speaker. But the law, which some believed was specially designed to end Brown's long political career, merely forced him to seek new challenges. Following his victory as mayor over incumbent Frank Jordan, Brown gave the citizens of his adopted hometown an inaugural celebration that symbolized the qualities for which both the city and its mayor are famous: style, exuberance, and inclusiveness.

A native of Texas, Brown came to San Francisco in 1951 to attend San Francisco State University (then College), from which he graduated in 1955. He went on to earn a law degree from California's Hastings College of Law in 1958. Unable to find work with the city's white law firms, Brown went into private practice, at the same time joining the National Association for the Advancement of Colored People (NAACP), the Young Democrats, and the National Urban League. His political career began in 1962 with an unsuccessful run for the State Assembly; two years later he won the seat. From the start, Brown impressed his fellow legislators with his drive, intelligence, and irrepressible love of the game of politics – a game he says he plays "with great glee." Both as chairman of the assembly's Ways and Means Committee, which examined every bill involving state funds, and later as Speaker, Brown's grasp of legislative details and talent for deal-making were legendary.

Despite his reputation for brilliance, Brown faced criticism from many quarters. His expensive wardrobe and habit of dating much younger women (Brown and his wife, who have three grown children, have been separated for many years) attracted unfavorable public attention. In addition, the state bar of California and the FBI have both investigated his private law practice and investments for possible conflicts of interest with his legislative role. Neither group, however, has found any improprieties.

As San Francisco's first black mayor, Brown says he hopes to build on the city's relatively harmonious race relations and attack its problems – homelessness, acquired immune deficiency syndrome (AIDS), drugs, crime – in such a way as to be "a pilot project for... urban America." It is likely that his importance as a national black leader will increase with his new role. Jesse Jackson, for whom Brown raised $11 million as chair of Jackson's 1988 presidential campaign, says, "When Willie speaks, he will be heard from San Francisco to Miami." Brown has strong ties with Washington – President Bill Clinton's congratulatory phone call was a prominent part of the inaugural party. For his part, Brown promises to bring "strong, vibrant, risk-taking leadership" to the mayor's office.

Kate Tuttle

See Also

AIDS in the United States; Jackson, Jesse Louis; San Francisco and Oakland, California.

North America

Bruce, Blanche Kelso

(b. March 1, 1841, Farmville, Va.; d. March 17, 1898, Washington, D.C.), the first African American elected to a full six-year term in the United States Senate.

Blanche K. Bruce's professional career followed the arc of Reconstruction history. Having escaped from slavery during the Civil War, he moved south after the war to capitalize on the opportunities for economic and political advancement that were newly available there to African Americans. His political fortunes waned, however, after the late 1870s, when Southern Democrats regained control of politics and blacks were again relegated to second-class status socially and politically.

Bruce was born a slave in rural Virginia, but his childhood differed from that of most other slave children. He was regarded by his owner, Pettus Perkinson, more like a son than a slave. A favored playmate of Perkinson's son, Bruce was educated by the Perkinson tutor and rarely worked in the fields. He lived in Missouri at the outbreak of the Civil War and then escaped to Lawrence, Kansas, where he unsuccessfully attempted to enlist in the Union army. He then founded two schools for free blacks, one in Lawrence, the other in Missouri. In 1866 he entered Oberlin College in Ohio.

In 1869 Bruce settled in Bolivar County in the Mississippi delta. He believed that Reconstruction policies had created an advantageous climate for enterprising blacks, especially in areas – such as the delta – that lacked established black leadership. He quickly began buying land, first individual lots, then a 640-acre plot on which he established a cotton plantation using black labor; thus he became part of the planter class. He also entered local Republican politics, gaining the attention of white Republicans as a public speaker during the 1869 elections. Beginning at this time Bruce held a series of local appointive offices, including voter registrar for Tallahatchie County and tax assessor for Bolivar County. In 1871 Bruce H. T. Florey, Bolivar County's political boss, appointed Bruce sheriff of Bolivar County.

Bruce owed his rise in politics more to the patronage of powerful whites than to his black constituency, although he was popular with both. He had more in common with Southern white aristocrats, however, than with the poor blacks he represented. Cautious and conservative, Bruce endorsed a self-help philosophy that closely matched that of the political powers in the state, and his 1871 appointment as Bolivar County superintendent of education marked another political triumph. By the time he resigned the post in 1872, Bruce had established 21 schools that, although segregated, served both blacks and whites, and did so without raising taxes.

Bruce was considered the dominant political figure in Bolivar County by 1874, when the Mississippi legislature elected him to the U.S. Senate. Thanks largely to his association with New York senator Roscoe Conkling, Bruce was appointed to three committees: pensions, manufactures, and education and labor. Bruce did much to distinguish himself in the Senate. Despite his generally moderate political philosophy, he openly criticized the Republican Party and President Ulysses S. Grant for not supporting the Mississippi party during the elections of 1875. He also unsuccessfully urged his colleagues to seat P. B. S. Pinchback, an African American from Louisiana whose seat was contested.

Bruce believed that the best hope for black progress lay in participation in the larger American society. Therefore, he opposed proponents of emigration, such as the Back to Africa Movement, and the Exodusters – blacks who left the South for Kansas. Still, he lobbied for relief programs for the poorest of the Exodusters, reminding the Senate that such migration was the result of increased hostility and obstruction from Southern whites. In addition, Bruce argued against the Chinese Exclusion Act and for more humane treatment of Native Americans. Bruce's most visible position was as chairman of the Select Committee to Investigate the Freedmen's Savings and Trust Company, in which many ex-slaves lost money. Even though the Select Committee's report exposed corruption and incompetence on the part of its white directors, Bruce could not arrange for blacks to be reimbursed.

By January 1880 the Democratic Party largely controlled politics in Mississippi, and the state legislature replaced Bruce. Out of office and living in a city that was rapidly becoming segregated, he remained active in Republican Party affairs and continued to receive many political appointments, even as his social stature declined. He was named for the vice presidential nomination at the Republican National Conventions in 1880 and 1888, and was twice appointed registrar of the Treasury (serving from 1881 to 1885 and 1897 to 1898). He was also a successful lecturer and a member of the boards of the Washington, D.C., public schools and Howard University. But increasingly he was rebuffed by the whites with whom he and his wife had previously socialized. Thus, Bruce cultivated his relationships with other wealthy blacks in Washington, where he and his wife formed part of that era's black aristocracy. He died of complications from diabetes in 1898.

Robert Fay

See Also

Slavery in the United States; Civil War, American; Free Blacks in the United States, 1619 to 1863; Pinchback, Pinckney Benton Stewart.

Latin America and the Caribbean

Brunswijk, Ronnie

(b. 1961?), rebel leader in Suriname.

In 1986, Ronnie Brunswijk, a former presidential bodyguard, created the Surinamese Liberation Army (SLA) in response to policies adopted by military ruler Desi Bouterse that threatened the autonomy of Bush Negro communities. *Bush Negroes*, a term used by outsiders to refer to six maroon communities (descendants of runaway slaves), form about 10 percent of the country's population.

Brunswijk himself is a Ndjuka maroon and the SLA was composed largely of Ndjuka and Saramaka maroons. Following democratic elections in 1991, the SLA reached a truce with the government and signed a peace treaty the following year.

See Also

Maroonage in the Americas.

Africa

Brutus, Dennis

(b. ?, Salisbury, Southern Rhodesia [now Harare, Zimbabwe]), South African poet, teacher, and political activist whose lyric poetry is structured around a finely wrought tension between the personal and the political.

Dennis Vincent Brutus grew up in South Africa and received his B.A. degree there in 1947 from the University of Fort Hare, in Alice. He taught English and Afrikaans for 14 years in South African high schools before going on to study law at the University of Witwatersrand. He was a leader in the struggle against racism in sports, and his activity protesting apartheid, South Africa's policy of racial segregation, led to his arrest in 1963. Shot while trying to escape, he was then sentenced to 18 months' imprisonment on Robben Island, a high-security facility known for holding antiapartheid political prisoners.

Sirens, Knuckles, Boots, Brutus's first collection of poetry, was published the year he was imprisoned and established him as a gifted poet of tightly crafted political lyrics. While in prison he secretly wrote of his experiences in a series of poems to his wife, later published as *Letters to Martha* (1968). The poems offer powerful descriptions of appallingly brutal conditions and reflect a compassion that avoids any sense of self-pity.

In 1966, with his works banned in South Africa, Brutus left for England on an exit permit that did not allow him to return. He traveled to the United States, where he was hired as a professor of African literature at Northwestern University. He later held positions at the University of Texas, Swarthmore College, and the University of Pittsburgh.

Brutus brings diverse experiences to his poetry, unifying them through his attention to social injustice. There is great passion, even anger, in some of his lines, but the verse is always restrained and controlled. One sees a clear progression from a somewhat lush, even romantic tone in his early poems to an increasingly austere precision after the prison experience. Brutus's other collections include *Poems from Algiers* (1970), *A Simple Lust* (1973), *China Poems* (1975), *Salutes and Censures* (1984), and *Airs and Tributes* (1989).

Africa

Bubi, ethnic group residing on Equatorial Guinea's Bioko Island.

Although they were among the first inhabitants of Bioko Island, Equatorial Guinea, the Bubi have only recently become active in national politics. Archaeologists and linguists believe that ancestors of the Bubi were among the first groups to break from western Bantu, arriving in present-day coastal Cameroon and Gabon around 1500-1000 B.C.E., though, unlike many Bantu-speaking groups, they did not produce iron. Oral historians date their arrival much later. The Bubi migrated to Fernando Pó, also known as Bioko Island, in four waves beginning around the seventh century C.E. Settling mostly the island's northern coast, they developed four distinct dialects.

The Bubi grew palms and yams on the island's rich volcanic soils, fished, and made pottery and tools. They used small, round pieces of shell as currency. Their monogamous, matrilineal society drew distinctions primarily between occupational groups, such as hunters, fishers, and farmers, rather than between economic classes. The religion was monotheistic, and based on the worship of fire and other elements.

Several Bubi chiefdoms rose and fell over time. Political authority was generally diffused, and a chief's power was dependent on the approval of village elders. This changed in the nineteenth century when European merchants, who for years had largely avoided Bioko's rough coastline, began coming ashore, trading European goods for fresh fruits and other foods to sustain the crews while at sea. As the Bubi chiefdoms competed for trade with the Europeans, small chiefdoms were subsumed by larger ones. Ultimately, a supreme chief emerged among the previously disparate chiefdoms. Trading relations with Europeans were not always peaceful. King Moka, the Bubi supreme chief during the late nineteenth century, refused to meet with the Spanish after they colonized the island. In 1907 the Bubi rejected forced-labor laws imposed by the Spanish to increase the productivity of cocoa plantations, and this led to the so-called Bubi War, which was brought under control by Spanish colonial officials three years later. Foreign diseases such as smallpox and syphilis decimated the Bubi, cutting the population to around 12,000 in 1912.

After World War II the Bubi population recovered and became increasingly integrated with Nigerian workers, who were brought to the island as plantation laborers. Because of their self-imposed isolation, the Bubi played a relatively negligible role in the colonial state and the nationalist movement. Just prior to decolonization, the Bubi sought separation from the mainland of Equatorial Guinea (known as Mbini, or Rio Muni) but were unsuccessful. A Bubi served briefly as vice president after independence was granted in 1968, but mainland Fang soon marginalized and suppressed prominent Bubi politicians. Only recently have some Bubi groups become more visible opponents of Equatorial Guinea's dictatorial regime, having made several armed attacks on government military outposts in the late 1990s.

Eric Young

See Also

Bantu: Dispersion and Settlement; Nigeria.

North America

Buck and Bubbles, American piano and tap dance team of Ford Lee "Buck" Washington (b. 1906; d. 1955) and John William "Bubbles" Sublett (b. February 19, 1902, Louisville, Ky.; d. May 18, 1986, New York, N.Y.), who together revolutionized tap dancing and were the first African Americans to perform at Radio City Music Hall.

Buck and Bubbles teamed up in 1912 in Indianapolis. Bubbles, then ten, sang and danced, and Buck, aged six, accompanied on piano. After winning several amateur contests, they played professional engagements in Louisville, Kentucky (often in blackface), Detroit, Michigan, and New York City.

Bubbles developed a style of tap called "jazz tap." Before this, dancers danced on their toes and emphasized flash steps, which were athletic steps with extended leg and body movements. Bubbles changed this style by tapping with his heels and toes and developing complicated moves, such as double over-the-tops (a rough figure-eight that simulates tripping). His new style led tap into the bebop and "cool" jazz eras, and he became known as the "father of rhythm tap."

Audiences delighted in the duo's singing, dancing, and comedy routine, with Buck's variations in tempo that forced Bubbles to quickly adapt. By 1922 they were performing at New York's Palace Theatre, the nation's top vaudeville venue. They broke color barriers by headlining the white vaudeville circuit across the United States, and were featured in several Broadway revues in the 1920s and 1930s. During the 1930s the duo took their vaudeville act to the London Palladium. Their stage success resulted in roles in such movies as *Varsity Show*

Ford Lee "Buck" Washington and John William "Bubbles" Sublett delighted audiences with their singing, tap dancing, and comedy.
The Everett Collection

(1937), *Cabin in the Sky* (1943), *Atlantic City* (1944), and *A Song Is Born* (1948).

Buck and Bubbles performed together until shortly before Buck's death in 1955. Despite suffering a stroke in 1967 that left him partially paralyzed, Bubbles continued to perform. His last performance was in 1980 in the revue *Black Broadway*. John Sublett died May 18, 1986.

Robert Fay

See Also
New York, New York; Tap Dance.

Africa

Budjga (also known as Budga, Budya, and Budja), ethnic group of Zimbabwe.

The Budjga primarily inhabit northeastern Zimbabwe. They speak a Bantu language and are one of the Shona peoples. Approximately 300,000 people consider themselves Budjga.

See Also
Bantu: Dispersion and Settlement.

Africa

Budu (also known as the Babudu), ethnic group of the Democratic Republic of the Congo.

The Budu primarily inhabit the Haute-Zaire region of northeastern Congo-Kinshasa, on the western edge of the Ituri Forest. They speak a Bantu language. Approximately 200,000 people consider themselves Budu.

See Also
Bantu: Dispersion and Settlement.

North America

Buffalo Soldiers, African American cavalry and infantrymen who fought on the American Western frontier.

Black soldiers served in the United States Army during the Civil War, although they were not allowed to enlist until the conflict's closing years. By the time the war ended, 12 African American soldiers had won the military's highest decoration, the Medal of Honor. For the next 40 years, black soldiers would play a crucial role in the violent, chaotic history of the frontier West.

In the years following the Civil War, the federal government turned its energies toward an often bloody campaign to relocate Native Americans. Most of the white settlers embraced the theory of Manifest Destiny, and thus believed that they had the right to all of the Indian territory. Despite a series of promises to compensate the Indian communities, the U.S. government broke several treaties and forced hundreds of thousands from their homelands. Not surprisingly, many Native Americans reacted to these invasions violently, and soon there was an all-out war. Adding to this near-constant armed conflict was a growing presence of cattlemen, cattle rustlers, and hardened criminals.

Among the troops on the Indian Wars' front lines were two all-black regiments – the Ninth and Tenth U.S. Cavalry – and four infantry divisions. The units, authorized by an 1866 act of Congress, filled up quickly with volunteers for whom the $13-a-month salary, with free room and board, represented a significant improvement over civilian life. Many were former slaves, and were being offered their first chance at education through the bill's stipulation that the army teach the soldiers to read and write.

The two black cavalry units represented 20 percent of the U.S. Cavalry at the time, and their military duties took them from the Mississippi River to the Rockies, from the Canadian border to the Rio Grande. White soldiers called them "brunettes" (when they didn't use racist slurs), but the Indians they had come to fight nicknamed them Buffalo Soldiers, presumably referring to the black men's curly hair. Knowing that Native Americans respected and even worshiped the buffalo, the black units adopted the name for themselves. In time, the Tenth Cavalry's official insignia would contain a buffalo.

The Buffalo Soldiers often found themselves in conflict with the white settlers they were supposedly there to protect. In 1878 white cowboys and black cavalrymen fought in the streets of San Angelo, Texas, after the murder of a Buffalo Soldier by a white cowhand in a local bar. Less violent tensions were also common. Henry O. Flipper, the first black graduate of West Point and a lieutenant in the Tenth Cavalry, was court-martialed on trumped-up charges after white officers saw him riding with a white woman. As the historian William L. Katz notes, "It is ironic that these brave black soldiers served so well in the final and successful effort to crush American Indians, the first victims of white racism in this continent. But serve they did." Indeed, many did so with distinction. Twenty-three Buffalo Soldiers received the Medal of Honor for their heroism during the Indian Wars and the Spanish-Cuban-American War.

Kate Tuttle

See Also
American Indians; Civil War, American.

Africa

Buganda, Early Kingdom of, an East African kingdom, founded by the Baganda people, that reached the height of its power during the nineteenth century.

According to legend, the creator of Buganda was Kintu, the "First Man" and "First King," whose wife Nambi created bananas and cattle. Located on the northern shores of Lake Victoria, the Buganda kingdom was initially a tributary of the larger Bunyoro-Kitara state. Between the thirteenth and sixteenth centuries, Bantu-speakers settled in the region, as did Nilotic-speaking pastoralists migrating from the north. Together these groups became known as the Ganda-speaking Baganda.

Located in swamplands, Buganda was unattractive to rulers of the more powerful Bunyoro-Kitara kingdom and thus served as a refuge for political dissidents. Oral tradition names Kintu, the leader of a group of Bantu-speaking immigrants who arrived in the late fourteenth century, as the first *kabaka,* or king. Other sources claim that a political dissident, Prince Kimera, became the first real king in the fifteenth century.

Buganda monarchs presided over a well-organized hierarchy of patrilineal clan leaders, regional chiefs, and village headmen. Buganda villagers cultivated a variety of crops, but bananas were especially important both as a staple food and for beer. The villagers also kept cattle, a symbol of prosperity. For the monarchy itself, wealth was acquired through raids and the extortion of tribute from weaker neighbors, and was used to reward loyal subordinates. Buganda priests and mediums were also important members of society, responsible for guiding the worship of ancestors.

During the seventeenth century, under the reign of Kabaka Katerega (1636-1663), the Buganda kingdom began to expand rapidly, incorporating the Mawokota, Gomba, Butambala, and Singo peoples. At the same time the Bunyoro-Kitara kingdom was beginning to lose control over its expansive territory. By the late eighteenth century the power of the Bunyoro-Kitara kingdom had been dwarfed by the imperialistic Buganda.

The political organization of the Baganda marked a radical departure from the hereditary kings of the other kingdoms. While Ganda society was partrilineal, kings were selected matrilineally, effectively preventing fathers from passing power along to their children. Consequently, successions were marked by political upheaval and violence.

Early in the reign of Kabaka Mutesa I (1856-1884), Arab traders visited Buganda in search of slaves and ivory, for which they traded guns and gunpowder. Shortly thereafter, in 1862, the British explorer Cap. John Hanning Speke was given an audience with Mutesa while searching for the source of the Nile. In 1875 Henry Morton Stanley, another British explorer, arranged for the arrival of the Church Missionary Society (CMS). Stanley had noted that Mutesa had the ability to organize some 125,000 troops on a military campaign to the east and believed that Buganda might prove fertile ground for the British missionaries. Mutesa permitted them to occupy his court primarily because he hoped their presence would prevent an invasion by EGYPT. Mutesa himself practiced Islam and strictly limited the missionaries' evangelical activities. French Catholic White Fathers also proselytized in Buganda. Ultimately, the religious divisions that became established festered into civil unrest, leading to a religious-based civil war.

When Egypt fell under British control in 1882, the political winds radically changed for Buganda, which had previously used the British as a counterforce against the Egyptians. In 1894 the British began exerting control over Buganda through a combination of military force and diplomacy, establishing it as a protectorate. Although most Buganda chiefs were willing to collaborate, the kabaka Mwanga, who ruled from 1884 until 1899, refused to comply with the demands of the colonists. The British subsequently deposed the unruly king, then enthroned his infant son and appointed regents to rule in his place. The 1900 Uganda Agreement established ultimate British sovereignty over all of Uganda while guaranteeing the preservation of the Buganda monarchy. The Buganda kingdom lay at the center of the Uganda Protectorate, with the kabaka's throne located in Kampala, the capital. The Baganda were afforded special status under British rule; for example, they were granted land rights throughout Uganda at the expense of other ethnic groups.

In 1960 Buganda declared independence, but the British refused to recognize the monarchy's legitimacy. When UGANDA became an independent federation in 1963, however, Buganda retained its regional autonomy, and Kabaka Mutesa II became president of the federation. His rule ended three years later, when Milton Obote, more powerfully positioned as prime minister, ordered the abolition of the monarchy and an attack on the palace. Mutesa II fled to London, where he remained until his death.

In an attempt to foster Baganda political support, in 1993 the Buganda monarchy was restored by Ugandan president YOWERI MUSEVENI. Ronald Muwenda Mutebbi II took the throne, but the kabaka no longer rules over a constitutional monarchy; his role is only religious and ceremonial.

Numbering more than a million people, the Baganda remain the single largest ethnic group in Uganda, comprising some 50 distinct clans. Most Baganda are farmers, and bananas and yams are the mainstay of their diet. Although most Buganda identify themselves as Christian, indigenous religious practices remain important, particularly in rural areas.

Ari Nave

SEE ALSO
Kampala, Uganda; Mutesa I; Nile River; Pastoralism; Stanley, Sir Henry Morton; Christianity: Missionaries in Africa.

Africa

Builsa (also known as Builse, Bulse, and Kanjaga), ethnic group of West Africa.

The Builsa primarily inhabit the Upper Region of GHANA and southern BURKINA FASO. They speak a Niger-Congo language and belong to the GRUSI cultural and linguistic group. Approximately 200,000 people consider themselves Builsa.

SEE ALSO
Languages, African: An Overview.

Africa

Bujumbura, Burundi, capital of BURUNDI.

Originally a small fishing village known as Usumbura, Bujumbura has become a dangerous battleground. European traders and missionaries settled the area in 1899, when Ruanda-Urundi was a German colony. Located on the northern tip of LAKE TANGANYIKA, it served as the seat of German and later Belgian colonial administrations. Many colonial buildings remain along its wide, palm-tree-lined boulevards.

In 1962 Bujumbura became the capital and economic hub of independent Burundi after a short, nonviolent nationalist struggle led by political parties. It is one of the lake's major ports; food processing, the national brewery, light industry, and the coffee trade dominate the formal economy. Bujumbura is Burundi's largest city, with a population of approximately 250,000 and an annual growth rate of 5 percent. Population estimates are difficult, however, because waves of refugees have periodically flooded Bujumbura over the past several years, fleeing violence in the countryside and in neighboring RWANDA. In 1996 the capital itself became a site of violence between Hutu militia and the Tutsi-dominated Burundian army, particularly in the Kamenge suburb.

Symbolic of the hierarchy of social stratification between ethnic groups, clans, and families that exists throughout Burundi, the national university and the country's elite reside in the eastern hills of Bujumbura. Meanwhile, the crowded lowland suburbs, where public services are few, house most of the city's poor.

Eric Young

SEE ALSO
Hutu and Tutsi; Nationalism in Africa; Germany.

Africa

Bulawayo, Zimbabwe, second largest city in ZIMBABWE.

In the early nineteenth century, the NDEBELE king Lobengula established his homestead 5 km (3 mi) south of present-day Bulawayo, on the savanna near the Matsheumlope River. It was first named Gubuluwayo, or place of killing, after Lobengula's army destroyed the army of a nearby chief who refused to submit to his rule. In 1893 Lobengula burned down the town in order to prevent its takeover by European settlers. During the following year the settlers established a new town, Bulawayo, to the north. After the completion of a rail line to SOUTH AFRICA, Bulawayo grew quickly, becoming Rhodesia's principal city, until it was gradually eclipsed in the 1930s by Salisbury (present-day Harare). In the late 1990s Bulawayo's population was estimated at 700,000.

Bulawayo is laid out on a grid pattern, retaining many of the buildings and wide streets of the colonial era. It has a range of light and heavy industries. Bulawayo is the commercial and transportation hub of southern and western Zimbabwe, with road and rail links to South Africa, BOTSWANA, and ZAMBIA (via VICTORIA FALLS). The cultural and political center of the Ndebele people, Bulawayo's attractions also include a railway museum, a natural history museum, the Rhodes Matopos National Park, and the Khami Ruins. The city hosts the annual Zimbabwe International Trade Fair.

Recent drought conditions in Bulawayo have diminished water supplies, which has put a strain on public services. Plans are underway to build a water pipeline from the ZAMBEZI RIVER.

Eric Young

SEE ALSO
Harare, Zimbabwe.

North America

Bullins, Edward (Ed)

(b. July 2, 1935, Philadelphia, Pa.), American playwright whose plays reflect the realities of urban life experienced by ordinary African Americans.

Born Edward Artie, Ed Bullins grew up in a tough neighborhood in Philadelphia, where he participated in the violent street life and was nearly fatally stabbed. He dropped out of high school in 1952 to join the United States Navy, returning to Philadelphia in 1955 to complete his secondary education. Philadelphia was still violent, so he moved to Los Angeles in 1958. In 1961 he began attending Los Angeles City College and started writing. Curious about the lives of other African Americans, Bullins traveled throughout the United States. In 1964 he settled in San Francisco, where he began writing plays. He earned a B.A. from Antioch University in San Francisco in 1989.

His early plays draw on the experiences of his youth. Mainstream critics considered Bullins's these plays obscene, and Bullins was unable to find producers for them. This forced him to stage his plays himself where he could, including coffeehouses and pubs. The lack of commercial outlet for his work tempted Bullins to quit writing for the theater, but the work of other playwrights, especially *Dutchman* and *The Slave*, by LeRoi Jones (later Amiri Baraka), inspired him to continue.

In the mid-1960s Bullins became the cultural director of Black House, an African American theater group in Oakland, California, with a militant political and cultural outlook. Its members included Huey Newton, Bobby Seale, and Eldridge Cleaver, founders of the Black Panther Party. Through his association with Black House, Bullins was briefly the Black Panther minister of culture. Black House became divided, however, between members who viewed theater as a spur to political action and those who viewed it mainly as an art form. Committed to artistic vision rather than the political ideology of Black House's revolutionary wing, Bullins left Black House in 1967.

Bullins then became playwright-in-residence at New Lafayette Theatre in New York and eventually its associate director until 1972, when it folded. Although none of the plays he wrote while at New Lafayette was commercially successful, he received critical praise for his work, including the 1971 Obie Award for *The Fabulous Miss Marie* and *New England Winter* and the Drama Critics Circle Award for *The Taking of Miss Janie* as best American play of 1974-1975.

Bullins's plays focus on the lives of African Americans who live in ghettos. They contrast the ideal of the American dream with the brutal reality many African Americans face and with their battle to transcend that reality. His plays often reveal his distaste for political rhetoric as a substitute for action. Their unconventional structure allows the audience to interact verbally with the stage characters. To date, his most ambitious undertaking is the Twentieth-Century Cycle, a proposed collection of 20 plays that chart the African American experience and, to a lesser extent, race relations in the twentieth-century United States.

In 1978, after the death of his son, Bullins returned to the West Coast, founding the Bullins Memorial Theatre in California and, with fellow playwright Jonal Woodward, the Bullins/Woodward Theatre Workshop in San Francisco. In 1995 Bullins accepted a teaching position at Northeastern University in Boston, Massachusetts.

Robert Fay

See Also
Cleaver, Eldridge Leroy; Newton, Huey P.

Africa

Bulu, ethnic group of Cameroon.

The Bulu primarily inhabit southern Cameroon. They speak a Bantu language and belong to the larger Beti cultural and linguistic group. Approximately 200,000 people consider themselves Bulu.

See Also
Bantu: Dispersion and Settlement.

North America

Bunche, Ralph Johnson

(b. August 7, 1904, Detroit, Mich.; d. December 9, 1971, New York, N.Y.), American diplomat and political scientist who won the Nobel Peace Prize in 1950, the first black American so honored.

Ralph Bunche spent his early years with his parents in Detroit, Michigan, and Albuquerque, New Mexico. He attributed his achievements to the influence of his maternal grandmother, with whom he lived in Los Angeles, California, after he was orphaned at age 13. Lucy Johnson not only insisted that her grandson be self-reliant and proud of his race, but that he, a high school valedictorian, go to college.

Bunche enrolled at the University of California at Los Angeles and graduated summa cum laude in 1927. He went on to graduate school at Harvard University, where he became the first black American to earn a Ph.D. in political science from an American university and where he also won the prize for outstanding doctoral thesis in the social sciences in 1934. He conducted his postdoctoral research on African colonialism at Northwestern University, the London School of Economics, and the University of Cape Town, where he defied the South African government's objections to hosting a black scholar.

While still a graduate student, Bunche established himself as a professor and an activist for civil rights. In 1928 he joined the faculty of Howard University in Washington, D.C., where he founded and chaired the political science department. Bunche expressed his commitment to racial integration and to economic improvement for workers during his years at Howard by participating in civil rights protests and in the establishment of the National Negro Congress in 1936. From 1938 to 1940, Bunche collaborated with Swedish sociologist Gunnar Myrdal on the research for Myrdal's massive study of American race relations, *An American Dilemma: The Negro Problem and Modern Democracy* (1944).

After years as a scholar of international politics, Bunche assumed a more active role during World War II. In 1941 he left Howard and joined the Office of Strategic Services (the predecessor of the Central Intelligence Agency), where he specialized in African affairs. He moved to the State Department in 1944, and, as the first African American to run a departmental division of the federal government, continued to work on Africa and on colonial issues.

Bunche's association with the United Nations (UN) also began in 1944, when he participated in the Dumbarton Oaks Conference, which laid the groundwork for the UN Charter signed in San Francisco a year later. In 1946 Bunche went to work full-time for the UN at the request of the organization's first secretary-general, Trygve Lie. From 1947 to 1954 he served as the principal director of the Department of Trusteeship and Information from Non-Self-Governing Territories, a post that allowed him to assist with the process of decolonization.

Bunche first made his name as a peacemaker in 1949, when, defying all expectations, he negotiated the truce that ended the first Arab-Israeli War. Originally sent to Jerusalem in 1948 as the assistant to UN mediator Count Folke Bernadotte, Bunche stepped in when Bernadotte was assassinated and worked almost single-handedly to bring Israel and the Arab states to an agreement. For his efforts Bunche was awarded the Nobel Prize for Peace in 1950.

In 1955 Bunche was appointed UN undersecretary for special political affairs. In that capacity he oversaw UN peacekeeping operations in some of the most heated conflicts around the world. As director of UN activities in the Middle East during and after the Suez Crisis of 1956, he broadened the organization's peacekeeping role by creating the United Nations Emergency Force. He represented the UN during crises in the Republic of the Congo, Cyprus, India, Pakistan, and Yemen. His successor, Sir Brian Urquhart, described Bunche as "the original principal architect" of the concept of international peacekeeping.

Despite the demands of an international career that lasted until just before his death,

TOP: American diplomat Ralph Bunche was the first African American to win the Nobel Peace Prize in 1950. *Archive Photos*
ABOVE: Ralph Bunche, acting United Nations mediator for Palestine, attends a conference in Palestine in 1948. *Culver Pictures*

Bunche fulfilled extensive academic and civil rights commitments at home. His contributions as a scholar were recognized in 1953, when Bunche was elected the first black president of the American Political Science Association. A long-time member of the board of the NATIONAL ASSOCIATION FOR THE ADVANCEMENT OF COLORED PEOPLE (NAACP), he was awarded the organization's Spingarn Medal in 1950. He acted as an unofficial adviser to several civil rights organizations and joined Martin Luther King Jr. in the 1965 Selma-to-Montgomery Voting Rights March. In 1963 President John F. Kennedy awarded Bunche the nation's highest civilian honor, the Medal of Freedom. Bunche died in New York City a year after his 1970 retirement from the UN.

Lawrie Balfour

SEE ALSO
Cape Town, South Africa; Colonial Rule; Congo, Democratic Republic of the; Decolonization in Africa: An Interpretation; World War II and African Americans; *An American Dilemma: The Negro Problem and Modern Democracy*; King, Martin Luther, Jr.; Suez Canal.

Africa

Bunu (also known as the Kabba), ethnic group of NIGERIA.

The Bunu primarily inhabit central Nigeria, where the Niger and Benue rivers meet. They speak YORUBA, a Niger-Congo language, and are closely related to other Yoruba peoples. Approximately 200,000 people consider themselves Bunu.

SEE ALSO
Languages, African: An Overview; Niger River.

Africa

Bura (also known as Pabir and Babur), ethnic group of NIGERIA.

The Bura primarily inhabit the Borno State of northeastern Nigeria. They speak an Afro-Asiatic language belonging to the Chadic group. Approximately 300,000 people consider themselves Bura.

SEE ALSO
Languages, African: An Overview.

North America

Bureau of Refugees, Freedmen and Abandoned Lands, the first federal welfare agency, which was established to provide relief for free blacks and poor whites during the Civil War era.

On January 1, 1863, President Abraham Lincoln signed the Emancipation Proclamation, freeing nearly 4 million American slaves. But as black historian Lerone Bennett Jr. points out: "The freedpeople... were free – free to the wind and to the rain, free to the wrath and hostility of their former slave-masters. They had no tools, they had no shelter, they had no cooking utensils; and they were surrounded by hostile men who were determined to prove that the whole thing was a monstrous mistake." In March 1865 the federal government created the Bureau of Refugees, Freedmen and Abandoned Lands, or the Freedmen's Bureau, as a temporary solution to these problems.

A few days after Lincoln had signed the Emancipation Proclamation, the *Chicago Tribune* ran a story about the oncoming wave of Southern blacks. "In farm wagons, in coaches, on horseback, afoot and in buggies... this second movement from Egypt to the promised land fills the highways and the woods. The freed slaves come straight to our lines." According to Bennett, "Witnesses said the roads of the South were clogged in 1865 with black men and women searching for long-lost wives, husbands, children, brothers and sisters." By 1864 private agencies, such as the Quakers and the Freedmen's Aid Society, were stretched beyond capacity. Mutual aid societies run by free blacks, including the FREE AFRICAN SOCIETY, attempted unsuccessfully to pick up the slack. In December 1864 the American Freedmen's Inquiry Commission urged Congress and the president to create a government agency, and on March 3, 1865, the Freedmen's Bureau was established.

The bureau was scheduled to exist for no longer than one year after the end of the war. Its stated purpose was "the supervision and management of all abandoned lands, and the control of all subjects relating to refugees and freedpeople." More specifically, Lincoln authorized the bureau to provide food, clothing, and fuel for the relief of destitute refugees and freed slaves. But the bureau is best remembered for its early desire to relocate freedpeople and refugees to abandoned and confiscated lands, promising "40 acres and a mule." Unfortunately, most freedpeople saw no land, and those who did were forced to pay for it. In fact, renting tracts of land to freedpeople and refugees for three-year periods was the bureau's primary source of income.

On May 12, 1865, Lincoln appointed Gen. Oliver Otis Howard as commissioner of the bureau. Howard's first task was to expand its operations. During his time as a Union military officer, Howard, a humanitarian, became known as the "Christian general." He immediately used his military training and contacts to strengthen the bureau's infrastructure, creating local affiliates and hiring several assistant commissioners.

But by the latter half of 1865, the challenges of caring for the growing numbers of Southern free blacks had increased. Hungry and homeless former slaves were stranded in Wilmington, North Carolina, and rumors were spreading that thousands were pouring into Missouri from Arkansas and Texas. Although the bureau received little money from the federal government, Howard turned to the commissary general of the army for donations of food and clothing considered unfit for troops. The army provided rations of beef, pork, bread, and occasionally beans and coffee. By the end of 1865 the bureau was feeding nearly 50,000 people and operating 42 hospitals.

Howard's vision for the bureau went beyond providing food and clothing. He worked closely with existing private aid societies to build and support schools for former slaves. The bureau founded several black colleges and universities, including FISK UNIVERSITY, and it inspired the creation of others, such as HOWARD UNIVERSITY. It fought for fair and equal treatment of free blacks in civil courts, arguing that whites and blacks should be tried and punished without distinction as to race, and that blacks should be allowed to testify as witnesses.

Howard and his Freedmen's Bureau challenged entrenched Southern traditions. But championing justice and equality for all of the nation's people would be too much, too soon, for most white Americans. Just a few months after Howard was appointed commissioner, the bureau suffered a major setback as President Andrew Johnson granted amnesty to former Confederates. Johnson ordered the bureau to return all confiscated land to its original owners, which called for the removal of freedpeople from those tracts.

During this time Howard launched what became one of the bureau's most controversial projects. In 1866 the bureau turned its attention to preventing white businessmen from exploiting the labor of freedpeople. Howard instructed bureau agents to urge white employees and black laborers to enter into contracts specifying all details of the working relationship, including the type

This contemporary woodcut shows Northerners teaching former slaves how to read in the Reconstruction South. *CORBIS/Bettmann*

and duration of employment. Between 1865 and 1866, tens of thousands of labor contracts were signed.

But these contracts often came at the expense of black bargaining power, as many freedpeople found themselves underpaid and overworked. Often, the contracts sanctioned working conditions not much different from those that prevailed during slavery. Bureau agents often approved the use of gang labor, policies forcing women and children to work, and restrictions on the mobility of ex-slaves. Many freedpeople refused to sign labor contracts. In response, the bureau tried to force some freedpeople to sign contracts in exchange for rations and further aid. In some cases, bureau agents threatened to remove those who continued to refuse, including their wives and children, from freedperson camps.

Although many African Americans were mistreated by bureau agents, most remained loyal to the agency and its mission. In 1866 over 800 blacks packed a Wilmington, North Carolina church to express their support for Howard and the bureau. But black support was not enough. Angry whites, primarily ex-Confederates, consistently tried to undermine the bureau. RECONSTRUCTION dealt the final blow. As Reconstruction gained momentum, and Congress passed constitutional amendments that were intended to guarantee the rights of freedpeople, the Freeman's Bureau and its mission seemed obsolete, and the bureau was closed on June 30, 1872.

In 1874, two years after the bureau was closed, a congressional report called the agency a "complete success… with God on its side, the Freedmen's Bureau has triumphed; civilization has received a new impulse, and the friends of humanity may well rejoice." But later historians more often agree with the 1935 assessment of black scholar W. E. B. Du Bois: "The Freedmen's Bureau did an extraordinary piece of work, but it was a small and imperfect part of what it might have done."

Despite its shortcomings, the bureau did provide aid to hundreds of thousands of former slaves at a time when no other organization was able to do so. As Harriet Tubman said years before Lincoln signed the Emancipation Proclamation: "I was free, but there was no one to welcome me to the land of freedom. I was a stranger in a strange land." In many ways, the Freedmen's Bureau was created precisely to welcome the 4 million former slaves to freedom.

During its seven-year existence, the Freedmen's Bureau distributed an estimated 21 million rations to poor whites and free blacks, provided medical services to another million, and attempted to help ease the transition from slavery to freedom. But the bureau was crippled by Southern hostility, inadequate funding, and an inability to convince most of America's white citizens that helping black people was the nation's responsibility. As a result, thousands of poor whites and free blacks died from hunger and disease.

Alonford James Robinson, Jr.

SEE ALSO

Slavery in the United States; Bennett, Lerone, Jr.; Civil War, American; Du Bois, William Edward Burghardt (W. E. B.); Forty Acres and a Mule; Free Blacks in the United States, 1619 to 1863; Mutual Benefit Societies; Thirteenth Amendment of the United States Constitution and the Emancipation Proclamation; Tubman, Harriet Ross.

Latin America and the Caribbean

Burgos, Julia de

(b. February 17, 1914, Carolina, Puerto Rico; d. July, 1953, East Harlem, N.Y.), one of Puerto Rico's most celebrated poets of the twentieth century and a political activist within the movement for Puerto Rican independence.

Born in Carolina, a municipality in the northeastern region of the island of Puerto Rico, Julia de Burgos was the first of 13 children, only 7 of whom would survive. Her parents' modest rural home bordered a tributary of the Río Grande de Loíza. She later dedicated an important poem to this river and its region, Loíza, a predominantly black area of Puerto Rico.

In 1919 her parents moved to the nearby town of Río Grande, but Burgos soon returned to the rural life she loved in Carolina and, with financial help from friends and family, continued her studies. The family would move once more in 1928 so that she could attend the Universidad de Puerto Rico, where she received a bachelor's degree in education in 1933. It was here that her literary talents began to emerge and that she became deeply involved in nationalist political organizations. In 1935 she began teaching in the rural neighborhood of Cedro Arriba, Naranjito.

The 1930s witnessed the rise of Puerto Rican nationalist leader PEDRO ALBIZU CAMPOS and the heyday of the pro-independence movement (*see* PUERTO RICO). If Burgos's poetry draws from a historic Spanish pastoral tradition, it must also be read in the context of these times, which helped to forge her political convictions. For just as she dedicated many of her poems to nature, so too did the political climate on the island inform her work. "Domingo de Ramos" (Palm Sunday), for example, addresses the 1937 Ponce Massacre, in which a number of people were killed or wounded in a clash with police during a march sponsored by the Nationalist Party.

After the end of her brief marriage to Rubén Rodríguez, in 1937, she began to work for a public education radio program, which she soon gave up for political reasons. That same year she published *Poemas exactos a mí misma* (Poems Exactly Like Myself), followed in 1938 by *Poema en veinte surcos* (Poems in Twenty Furrows). In 1939 the Institute of Puerto Rican Literature awarded her its poetry prize for her third book, *Canción de la verdad sencilla* (Song of the Simple Truth). With few work opportunities available to her in Puerto Rico, Burgos emigrated to New York in 1940. She soon became an active member of that city's vibrant Puerto Rican community, and continued writing poetry (*see* Afro-Latino Cultures in the United States).

In 1942 she was forced into a series of odd jobs, including work as a seamstress and lab technician and occasionally as a reporter at the weekly *Pueblos hispanos*, founded by Juan Antonio Corretjer, a fellow Puerto Rican poet. During the ensuing years she struggled with alcoholism, among other health problems, and spent a significant amount of time in New York hospitals.

In her writings Burgos voiced the often difficult experiences, including economic hardship and discrimination, of many Puerto Ricans who emigrated to the United States during the 1940s and 1950s. During her stay at the Goldwater Memorial Hospital, she expressed her personal frustration in a letter to her sister: "Tengo hambre de libertad. Si me muero, no quiero que este trágico país se trague mis huesos. Necesitan el calor de Borinquen, por lo menos para fortalecer los gusanos de allá y no los de acá." (I am hungry for liberty. If I die, I don't want this tragic country to swallow my bones. They need the warmth of Borinquen [an endearing name for Puerto Rico] so at least they can fortify worms from there and not here.)

In 1953 she was found unconscious on a street in East Harlem. Shortly thereafter, she died in a hospital as a Jane Doe. Her remains were repatriated by her family. In 1960 the Puerto Rican intellectual elite dedicated to her memory the Second Congress of Puerto Rican Poetry, held in Carolina and Loíza. The volume *El mar y tú* (The Sea and You) was published in 1954. Since her death she has become one of the most renowned poets not only in Puerto Rico but throughout Latin America. In 1997 her poems were translated into English by Jack Agueros under the title *Song of the Simple Truth: The Complete Poems.*

Joy Elizondo

See Also

Harlem, New York; New York, New York.

North America

Burke, Yvonne Brathwaite

(b. October 5, 1932, Los Angeles, Calif.), African American politician and lawyer, the first black woman from California to serve in the United States House of Representatives.

"I visualize a time within the next ten years when we should have 50 black congressmen.... It's just a matter of time until we have a black governor and yes, a black president." In this 1974 *Ebony* magazine interview, Congresswoman Yvonne Brathwaite Burke outlined her hopes for the political future of African Americans – a future her own career has helped bring closer to reality. Born Yvonne Watson in South Central Los Angeles, Burke attended the University of California at Berkeley and the University of California at Los Angeles (UCLA). After graduating from the University of Southern California Law School in 1956, she began a private law practice and was appointed to the 1965 commission that investigated the Los Angeles Watts riots.

A year later, Burke was elected to the first of three terms in the California assembly, becoming the state's first black assemblywoman. In the state assembly she began to fight for the issues – such as women's and children's rights – that would characterize her career. She reached national prominence as vice chair of the 1972 Democratic National Convention, and later that year became the first black woman from California to serve in the House of Representatives. She had married her second husband, William Burke, in the middle of her campaign, and in 1973 became the first congresswoman to give birth in office when her daughter Autumn was born. In 1974 *Time* magazine named her as one of 200 future leaders.

During her six years in office Burke served on the Appropriations Committee and as chair of the Congressional Black Caucus. When she resigned abruptly in 1978, many supporters felt disappointment that her promising national political career had been prematurely cut short. Burke lost a 1978 election for attorney general of California, and after a temporary 1979 appointment to the Los Angeles County Board of Supervisors she returned to private practice until 1992, when she became the first African American to be elected to the county board. Her career has been called bittersweet because, in the words of one observer, "she was unable to build upon her extraordinary early accomplishments to make a lasting impact on national politics." Nevertheless, her achievements paved new ground for the black women leaders who have followed.

Lisa Clayton Robinson

See Also

Ebony; Los Angeles Watts Riot of 1965; Los Angeles, California.

Africa

Burkina Faso, landlocked West African country bordered by Côte d'Ivoire, Mali, Niger, Benin, Togo, and Ghana.

In 1984 the leaders of Upper Volta changed the name of this former French colony to Burkina Faso, a name that combines two of the country's many languages and means "land of upright people." As one of the world's poorest nations, Burkina Faso counts people among its most important resources; remittances from migrant laborers working in the more affluent Côte d'Ivoire sustain the households of many of the approximately 10 million citizens in Burkina Faso, over 80 percent of whom live in rural areas. The tradition of southward migration became firmly established during the colonial era, when France incorporated the Volta region into its West African empire precisely in order to turn the drought-prone but relatively populous Mossi plateau into a labor reserve. As the French colonial administration invested little in developing Upper Volta itself, de jure independence in 1960 heralded a new era of de facto dependence on foreign donors, especially France. But steady infusions of aid failed to prevent either the onset of two famines or the overthrow of six governments. In 1983 flight commander Thomas Sankara came to power promising an end to both neocolonialism and rural suffering. Although the Burkinabè revolution was cut short by Sankara's assassination in 1987, it did initiate improvements in rural literacy, health, and food security as well as women's rights. The current regime of President Blaise Compaoré has deregulated the economy, mended relations with the West, and pledged a commitment (viewed skeptically by many Burkinabè) to democracy. Burkina Faso is still extremely poor but enjoys a reputation for religious and ethnic tolerance as well as for its rich performing arts traditions.

Early History

Apart from Stone Age axes found in northern Burkina Faso, archaeology provides few clues about the region's first human inhabitants. The ancestors of the Lobi and Bobo peoples were among the earliest agriculturists, settling the savanna west of the Mouhoun (or Black Volta) River perhaps around 1100 c.e. While these lineage-based societies never developed centralized polities, migrants from the Dagomba region (in present-day Ghana) founded the Mossi dynasties on the more arid plateau to the north. The most powerful Mossi kingdom, Ouagadougou, was founded in the late fifteenth century. Nineteen smaller but fairly autonomous Mossi states ruled over territories to the north, west, and east and eventually assimilated many of the neighboring peoples into Mossi society. Both the Mossi and the southern peoples lived primarily from rainy-season agriculture, supplemented during the long dry season by hunting, foraging, and in some places fishing. Millet and sorghum were staples throughout the savanna; wetter conditions in the far south supported the production of root crops and, later, rice. In the far north, seasonal rainfall also shaped the migration patterns of Peul (or Fulani) pastoralists.

Situated between forest and Sahelian ecozones, the Volta region was traversed by caravan traders who dealt in COLA, gold, and slaves from the forest regions, salt from the Sahara, and luxury goods from North Africa. The traders brought weapons and horses to the court of Ouagadougou but found the most lively markets in southern towns such as Sya (now Bobo-Dioulasso), where MANDE-speaking Zara merchants had settled among the Bobo.

In the sixteenth century the Mossi expanded northward into the Sahel, where they were rebuffed by the armies of the SONGHAI EMPIRE, led by SUNNI ALI. But neither Ali nor his successor, ASKIA MUHAMMAD, was able to convince the Ouagadougou king, the *mogho naaba*, to convert to Islam. Although many Mossi traders eventually did convert, the Volta region has remained less Islamized than the rest of the Sahel.

In the eighteenth and nineteenth centuries, slavery became a common practice in the Volta region. Some Mossi kingdoms captured local peoples or bought slaves from other kingdoms to work as agricultural or domestic laborers. These slaves were often allowed to engage in wage-earning activities for themselves, such as cultivating food and raising cattle. At the same time, southern peoples were subjected to slave raids from the KONG empire (northern Côte d'Ivoire). With no armies and few weapons, peoples such as the Bobo lived in large, densely settled villages for protection.

COLONIAL CONQUEST

By the late nineteenth century, Great Britain and France were racing against each other to establish spheres of influence in the West African interior (*see* SCRAMBLE FOR AFRICA). In 1887 the French explorer Louis Binger visited Ouagadougou during his trip across West Africa. He was unimpressed by the Mossi Kingdom, noting that the Mossi cultivated only what they needed in order to subsist, "so that even if there are no paupers in their country, there are virtually no rich men either." Yet the Mossi region was densely populated, and Binger suggested that it would make a suitable "labor reserve" for French ventures elsewhere in West Africa. In particular, labor was needed for irrigated cotton production in the fertile but sparsely populated NIGER RIVER basin, which French engineers believed had the potential to become a "new Egypt."

The mogho naaba Wogbo refused Binger's invitation to make his kingdom a French protectorate. The explorer did, however, manage to secure a protectorate agreement from the Ouattara leader of Kong, whose empire by then included much of the southern Volta region. Over the next several years the French conquered regions to the east, west, and north of the Mossi Kingdom, and in 1895 French troops occupied Bobo-Dioulasso, overcoming resistance from the town's Zara warriors. The following year the French defeated Ouagadougou's Mossi army and burned down much of the city. Wogbo escaped and later sought British protection.

COLONIAL RULE

In 1898 France and Great Britain reached an accord, granting France dominion over Upper Volta. The territory was initially designated a military zone, but in 1904 it became part of the colony Haut-Sénégal-Niger, administered from Bamako. After their earlier experience with the recalcitrant Wogbo, the French were determined to undermine the authority of the Mossi kingship. When Wogbo's successor, Sighiri, died in 1905, the French replaced him with a 16-year-old naaba, who posed little threat to the colonial regime. They also replaced lower-level Mossi chiefs, where necessary, with more compliant appointees and imposed the *indigénat*, a legal system that effectively placed all judicial power in the hands of French administrators.

Led by a young boy, this man suffers from onchocerciasis, or river blindness, a devastatingly common parasitic disease in Burkina Faso. *CORBIS/David Reed*

The French could not afford to dismantle the Mossi Kingdom or other preexisting authority structures entirely. Although French officials were posted to each of the colony's administrative districts (known as *cercles*), they needed chiefs to collect taxes and recruit labor, and thus appointed them to these duties even in regions with no prior tradition of centralized authority. This was the case, for example, in the Bobo-Dioulasso cercle, where appointed Ouattara chiefs were usually unpopular and ineffective and were known for embezzling taxes.

The first quarter of the twentieth century was a period of extreme hardship for the peoples of Upper Volta. Although the French officially ended slavery in 1901, tens of thousands of Voltaics were forced each year to labor in cotton fields and construction sites, while others were conscripted into the military. Such policies, coupled with a punitive system of taxation, provoked popular revolts throughout the colony, ranging from a 2000-person anti-tax march in Ouagadougou in 1908 to a series of village revolts west of Bobo-Dioulasso in 1915-1916. Thousands also fled south to the British colony of Gold Coast, where labor laws were less coercive.

In 1919 the French made Upper Volta a separate colony in order to better control its people and develop its economy. As in the previous decades, thousands of laborers were forcibly recruited to build an administrative post in the new capital, Ouagadougou, as well as roads and rail lines intended to facilitate the export of cotton, a crop that peasants in many cercles were forced to cultivate. But the French invested little in irrigation, fertilizer, or other agricultural improvements in Upper Volta, since it was still considered primarily a labor reserve for neighboring colonies' projects. Consequently, cotton farming in more arid areas led quickly to soil degradation. This was especially the case because many rural households, having lost their most able-bodied members to compulsory labor projects, were too short-handed to tend their land properly. Forced cash-crop cultivation also took time and land away from grain farming, leaving rural areas dangerously vulnerable to food shortages.

This vulnerability became tragically obvious in the late 1920s, when a series of droughts coincided with plunging world prices for cotton and commodities after 1929. Famines in 1926 and 1930 led one French colonial official to warn of demographic collapse. By 1931 Upper Volta was not only famine-stricken but also bankrupt, and in September 1932 the country was dismantled and divided up among neighboring French colonies. Most of the territory went to Côte d'Ivoire, where Voltaic labor was needed for coffee and cocoa plantations as well as for the Abidjan-Ouagadougou railway.

The rail line reached Bobo-Dioulasso in 1934, and several European trade firms soon followed. Besides a handful of French administrators and soldiers, most of the town's

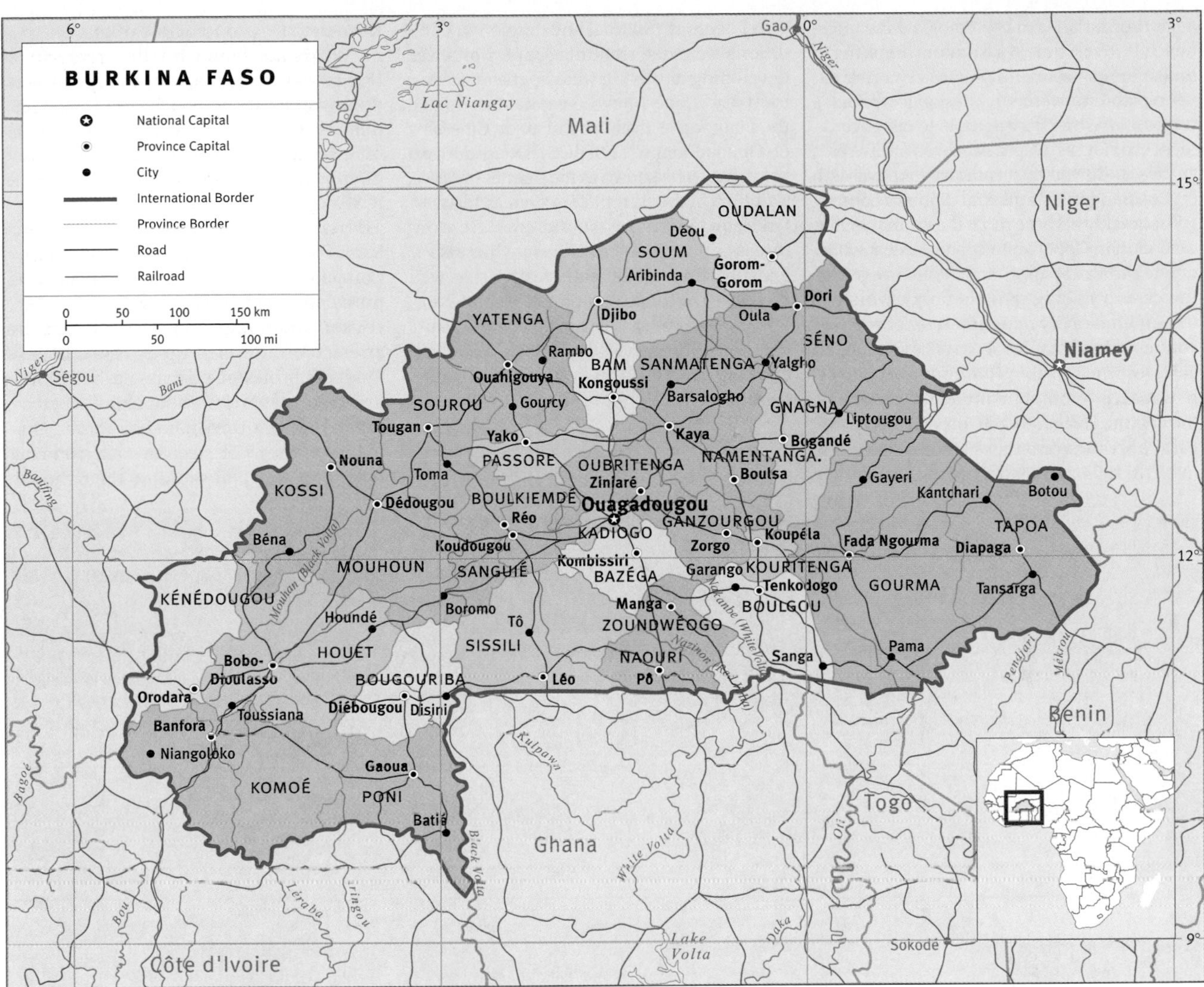

other European residents were Roman Catholic missionaries known as *Pères Blancs* (White Fathers). As elsewhere in the Volta region, the Bobo mission was hurrying to win converts during a time of rapid Islamization. The Pères Blancs targeted village youth, in particular; they offered catechism classes, staged festivities at the mission, and spoke out openly against forced labor.

When World War II began, over 10,000 Mossi volunteered for active military service. Some served in Europe or North Africa, but many remained in the Bobo-Dioulasso military camp or were used for forced labor. Soon after the war ended, the French government agreed to grant its colonies representation in the French National Assembly. Côte d'Ivoire received three seats, and in November 1946 Ivoirian Félix Houphouët-Boigny and two Voltaics, Daniel Ouézzin Coulibaly and Philippe Kaboré – all members of the radical Rassemblement Démocratique Africain (RDA) – were elected its deputies. In that same year, Mossi chiefs asked France to restore Upper Volta as a separate colony. They were primarily interested in reinstating their own political influence, but France agreed to their request; mainly, France sought to cut the region off from the anticolonial politics of Houphouët-Boigny and the RDA. The charismatic Ivoirian was already extremely popular around Bobo-Dioulasso, especially after he convinced the French National Assembly in April 1946 to abolish forced labor.

On September 4, 1947, Upper Volta was reconstituted on. The RDA remained popular in the southwest but lost support in the north to Mossi-dominated political parties, such as the conservative Union Voltaique (UV). Over the next decade, growing nationalist movements throughout Africa made decolonization inevitable. In Upper Volta, this was a time of relative prosperity; many World War II veterans invested their pensions in commercial agriculture, trade, and transport companies, and both Bobo-Dioulasso and Ouagadougou grew rapidly. Still, political factionalism during the 1950s, combined with the fact that Upper Volta was still landlocked and resource-poor, boded ill for independence.

In 1958, two years after universal suffrage was granted throughout French West Africa, France's African colonies took part in a referendum on whether to become semi-autonomous members of the French Community. Upper Volta, like all its neighbors save Guinea, voted yes. That same year saw the rise to power of Maurice Yaméogo, a Mossi member of the newly formed Parti de Regroupement Africain. After he was elected president of Upper Volta's Council of Ministers, Yaméogo moved to align himself with the now politically moderate RDA and its founder, Houphouët-Boigny, who would soon be president of Côte d'Ivoire. A 1959 treaty of economic cooperation between the two leaders indicated that Upper Volta, long the labor reserve of its wealthier neighbor, would continue to depend on Côte d'Ivoire for employment and port access.

Unlike many emerging African leaders, Yaméogo argued that his people were not ready for total independence; as he told one French official in 1959, "We cannot even build matchboxes." By then, however, France was committed to pulling out of all its West African colonies. Upper Volta became independent on August 5, 1960, and Yaméogo became its first president.

Independence

The next two decades fulfilled the political omens of the late colonial period. Yaméogo, an authoritarian leader even before independence, moved quickly to undermine the multiparty system and rein in the country's young labor movement. This tactic worked until 1966, when his attempts to cut government employees' wages provoked a wave of strikes, followed by a military takeover led by Col. Sangoulé Lamizana. Military coups subsequently became more the norm than the exception in Upper Volta's politics. Meanwhile, one regime after another failed to invigorate the country's stagnant economy, which remained heavily dependent on exports of cotton and migrant labor as well as on foreign aid. Despite a sizable community of international development and relief workers in the capital, Ouagadougou, drought-stricken rural northern provinces suffered famines in 1973-1974 and 1984-1985.

Yet even as political and economic conditions were deteriorating, Upper Volta was developing a thriving state-sponsored film industry. Since 1969 the capital has hosted the biennial Festival Panafrican du Cinéma de Ouagadougou (FESPACO). Ouagadougou has come to be known as the Cannes of Africa, and Burkinabè filmmakers such as Idrissa Ouédraego and Gaston Kaboré have won international renown. The state has also actively supported theater festivals, as well as Bobo-Dioulasso's biennial Bobo Fête, a week-long event featuring contests and cultural performances of all kinds (including cooking and hairdressing), drawn from traditions throughout the country.

Revolution and Rectification

In 1983 it was drama on the streets of Ouagadougou, not the cinema screens, that drew world attention. In the previous year, military officials had overthrown the regime of Saye Zerbo and established the 120-member ruling Conseil de Salut du Peuple (CSP). A left-wing faction within the CSP, led by the young flight commander Thomas Sankara and his long-time friend Blaise Compaoré, had gotten Sankara appointed as prime minister in January 1983. In May the conservative wing of the CSP had Sankara arrested on trumped-up treason charges. Students protested en masse in the capital, and troops led by Compaoré launched a rebellion from the Ghanaian border. On August 4, they marched into Ouagadougou, freed Sankara, and captured the national

radio, from where Sankara announced that the Conseil National de la Révolution (CNR) had taken over the country.

Upper Volta had seen many military rulers, but Sankara at age 33 was by far the youngest and most revolutionary. He initiated the renaming of the country Burkina Faso, and he himself was considered by many, both at home and abroad, to be a morally upright leader, though not always a pragmatic one. Once in power, he cut the wages of top civil servants (including himself) and donated all the government's luxury cars to the national lottery, using the proceeds for public spending. He was also an outspoken proponent of women's liberation. He appointed five women to ministerial posts, launched a campaign against female circumcision, and initiated changes in family law. The Sankara government's investments in rural schools, clinics, and agricultural extension services brought modest improvements in living standards and quite dramatic increases in food production. Sankara's foreign policy, meanwhile, aligned his country squarely with left-wing regimes such as those of Cuba, Libya, and North Korea. He rejected World Bank loan conditions and promised to "fight against the forces of neo-colonialism and imperialist domination."

Not surprisingly, such rhetoric discouraged foreign investment, just as Sankara's public references to the "big, fat, and gross" bourgeoisie led many Burkinabè merchants and entrepreneurs to take their businesses across the border. Even more serious, Sankara's heavy-handedness alienated nearly all the country's traditionally powerful constituencies. Mossi chiefs did not welcome his pledge to destroy rural "feudalism" and "patriarchy," and his harsh treatment of critics and striking workers eventually turned even the labor unions against him. Ultimately, however, it was Sankara's own peers – soldiers loyal to his best friend and fellow CNR member Blaise Compaoré – who assassinated him on October 15, 1987. Although Compaoré denied involvement in the murder, he did not hesitate to take power afterward.

Compaoré has ruled Burkina Faso since Sankara's death. He took office pledging to "rectify" the Sankara revolution and moved immediately to mend rifts with Mossi authorities, the army, the business community, and Western donor nations. His appointed government, the Front Populaire, announced the formation of a new umbrella party, the Organisation pour la Démocratie Populaire/Mouvement du Travail (ODP/MT) in 1989. A year later it drafted a new constitution that allowed for multiparty elections. But repression of political dissidents (including many university students) continued, and government control over preelection campaigning and media led opposition parties to boycott the December 1991 presidential elections. Compaoré won easily, but less than a quarter of the population voted. Since then, political parties in Burkina Faso have proliferated, but the ODP/MT has consistently dominated national elections.

On the economic front, "rectification" brought an end to Marxist-Leninism as an official government ideology. Faced with falling world cotton prices and growing debt, Compaoré agreed to a World Bank structural adjustment program in 1991. The accompanying austerity measures – including thousands of layoffs at state-owned factories and fee increases for education and other government services – provoked strikes by students and trade unions. The 1994 devaluation of the West African franc (the CFA) brought further price increases, especially for imported fuel, foodstuffs, and manufactured goods. Economic growth in recent years has been somewhat uneven, but the government's adherence to World Bank reforms has put Burkina Faso near the top of the list of poor nations targeted for debt relief by international donors.

The country is also counting on revenue from gold, which, since the Sankara government's reopening of the long-dormant Poura gold mine in 1984, has become Burkina Faso's second-largest source of foreign exchange, after cotton. Foreign mining firms and artisanal gold panners are now working at several sites around the country, but gold reserves are small and will not last much beyond the year 2000. The Burkina Faso government is also attempting to diversify its agricultural exports; the country is already Africa's second largest exporter of French green beans (after Kenya), and recent aid programs have secured European markets for sun-dried Burkinabè tomatoes and mangoes.

Despite its status as one of the world's poorest countries, Burkina Faso has in many ways fared better than its wealthier neighbors. It has experienced no debilitating civil wars, and is considered by many to be an oasis of ethnic and religious tolerance. Its economy has been competently managed, and rural areas – where approximately 80 percent of the population still live – have begun to reap the benefits of soil conservation programs dating from the 1980s. In 1998 Burkina Faso hosted the African Cup of Nations soccer tournament, Africa's biggest sporting event. Even though the home team lost in the

LEFT: People of the Bobo ethnic group live in this rural village of thatched houses. *CORBIS/Charles & Josette Lenars*

ABOVE: This young gold miner was photographed in Buda, Burkina Faso. *CORBIS/Caroline Penn*

OPPOSITE: Home to this large adobe mosque, Bobo-Dioulasso is Burkina Faso's second-largest city and is a center of Islamic study. *CORBIS/Charles & Josette Lenars*

Ablassey Nana shoots for the home team during the 1998 African Nations Cup. The tournament, in which Burkina Faso prevailed until losing in the semifinals, is widely considered Africa's largest and most important sporting event. *CORBIS/TempSport*

quarterfinals, positive international media coverage of the games' host suggested that the Burkinabè had, at the least, scored a public relations victory.

Roanne Edwards & Susanne Freidberg

See Also

Bamako, Mali; Bobo-Dioulasso, Burkina Faso; Compaoré, Blaise; Decolonization in Africa: An Interpretation; Explorers in Africa Since 1800; Gold Trade; Ouédraogo, Idrissa; Nationalism in Africa; Ouagadougou, Burkina Faso; Pastoralism; Sahara Desert; Sahel; Salt Trade; Structural Adjustment in Africa; Togo; Christianity: Missionaries in Africa; Female Circumcision in Africa; Islam and Tradition: An Interpretation; Slavery in Africa.

Africa

Burkina Faso (Ready Reference)

Official Name: Burkina Faso
Former Name: Upper Volta
Area: 274,200 sq km (about 105, 869 sq mi)
Location: Inland West Africa, bordered by Mali, Niger, Benin, Togo, Ghana, and Côte d'Ivoire
Capital: Ouagadougou, population 500,000 [1990 estimate])
Other Major Cities: Bobo-Dioulasso, population 250,000, Koudougou, population 70,000 (1990 estimate)
Population: 11,266,393 (July 1998 estimate)
Population Density: 38 persons per sq km (about 98 persons per sq mi)
Population Below Age 15: 44.9 percent
Population Growth Rate: 2.72 percent (1998 estimate)
Total Fertility Rate: 6.64 children born per woman (1998 estimate)
Life Expectancy at Birth: Total population: 46.1 years (male 45.38 years; female 46.85 years [1998 estimate])
Infant Mortality Rate: 109.15 deaths per 1000 live births (1998 estimate)
Literacy Rate (age 15 and over who can read and write): Total population: 19 percent (male 29.5 percent; female 9.2 percent [1995 estimate])
Education: Officially compulsory for children aged 7 to 13, but less than one-third of all children aged 6 to 11 attended school in the early 1990s, and only 7 percent of those aged 12 to 17. Far fewer girls than boys attend school. In the mid-1990s Burkina Faso's primary schools had an annual enrollment of about 650,195, secondary schools about 116,033, and vocational schools about 8808; about 9452 students were enrolled at the university level.
Languages: French is the official language but is not widely spoken outside of cities. More than half the population speaks Moore; the remainder speak a variety of Mande languages.
Ethnic Groups: Most people belong to two major West African cultural groups, the Voltaic and the Mande. The Voltaic are the most numerous and include the Mossi, who constitute about 60 percent of the population. Other principal ethnic groups are the Fulani, Lobi, Bobo, Sénufo, Gourounsi, Bissa, and Gourmantche.
Religions: About 65 percent of the population adhere to indigenous beliefs. About 25 percent are Muslim and 10 percent Christian (mainly Roman Catholic).
Climate: Semi-arid; the weather is cool and dry from November through March, hot and dry from April through May, and warm and rainy from June through October. Average annual rainfall ranges from 1000 mm (more than 40 in) in the southwest to less than 250 mm (less than 10 in) in the north. Average temperatures in Ouagadougou vary from 24° C (76° F) in January to 28° C (83° F) in July.
Land, Plants, and Animals: Burkina Faso is located on a plateau sloping generally to the south and situated from about 200 to 700 m (about 650 to 2300 ft) in elevation. The plateau is drained to the south by the Black Volta (Mouhoun), Red Volta (Nazinon), and White Volta (Nakanbe) rivers and to the east by small rivers connecting with the Niger; none are navigable. Most of the country is covered with savanna grasses and small trees. Animals include elephants, hippopotamuses, buffalo, antelope, and crocodiles.
Natural Resources: Mineral resources include manganese and gold as well as small deposits of copper, nickel, bauxite, lead, silver, iron ore, cassiterite (tin ore), and phosphates. Except in the southwest of the country, water is scarce and most of the soils are relatively poor.
Currency: The CFA franc
Gross Domestic Product (GDP): $10.3 billion (1997 estimate)
GDP per Capita: $950 (1997 estimate)
GDP Real Growth Rate: 6 percent (1997 estimate)
Primary Economic Activities: Agriculture (32 percent of GDP, 80 percent of employment), livestock, small-scale commerce, gold mining, and migrant labor (approximately 20 percent of the male labor force migrates annually to neighboring countries).
Primary Crops: Millet, sorghum, corn, rice, peanuts, shea nuts, sesame, cotton, and livestock
Industries: Cotton lint, beverages, agricultural processing, soap, cigarettes, and textiles
Primary Exports: Cotton, livestock products, and gold.
Primary Imports: Foodstuffs, petroleum, textiles, iron, steel, metal products, vehicles, electrical equipment, and machinery.
Primary Trade Partners: European Union (especially France), Côte d'Ivoire, Taiwan, and Thailand.
Government: Parliamentary; nominally a constitutional multiparty democracy. The executive branch is led by President Blaise Compaoré and an appointed 29-member cabinet, which includes Prime Minister Roche Kabore. The legislative branch is the elected 107-member National Assembly, currently dominated by President Compaoré's party, the Organization for Popular Democracy-Labor Movement (ODP-MT).

See Also

Ouagadougou, Burkina Faso; Senufo.

North America

Burleigh, Henry Thacker (Harry) (b. December 2, 1866, Erie, Pa.; d. September 12, 1949), American singer, composer, and arranger who arranged Negro spirituals for soloists.

Harry Burleigh became interested in music at an early age. Although poverty kept him from formal study, he sang at local churches and synagogues. With a scholarship he began studying in 1892 at the National Conservatory of Music in New York with the conservatory's director, Antonín Dvorák. In 1894 he was selected as the baritone soloist for St. George's Episcopal Church in New York, a position he held until 1946, and was also the soloist for New York's Temple Emanu-El from 1900 to 1925.

Until Burleigh published his arrangements, *Jubilee Songs of the United States of America,* in 1916, spirituals had been performed only in choral arrangements. By putting the spirituals into the form of art songs, they became available to soloists. The best known of his arrangements, "Deep River," was said to be the most performed song in concert in 1916. Though some criticized him for eliminating the spirituals' improvisational nature, Burleigh helped to popularize and preserve them. He also wrote and arranged many popular art songs, and from 1911 until his death in 1949, Burleigh was an editor for the music publisher Ricordi.

Robert Fay

Latin America and the Caribbean

Burnham, Linden Forbes Sampson (b. February 20, 1923, Kitty, British Guyana; d. August 6, 1985, Georgetown, Guyana), an Afro-Guyanese politician who served as independent Guyana's first prime minister and as head of state for 19 years (1966-1985).

Linden Forbes Sampson Burnham was born in 1923 to James Ethelbert Burnham and Rachel Abigail Sampson. James Burnham was headmaster of the Methodist Primary School in Kitty, a suburb of the capital city Georgetown. He instilled in his five children an appreciation for education, and Linden, the youngest male of the family, ambitiously pursued academic excellence.

After graduating from Central High School, Burnham attended the prestigious, all-male Queen's College. While there he won a British Guyana scholarship to study at the University of London in England. However, World War II forced him to remain in British Guyana, where he earned his bachelor's degree in correspondence and accepted an administrative position at Queen's College.

After the war Burnham traveled to England to complete his law degree, which he received in 1947 from London University. While in London, he became the first Guyanese student to be elected president (1947-1948) of the West Indies Student Union. In 1949 Burnham returned to British Guyana and opened a private law practice. In 1950 he helped Indo-Guyanese politician Cheddi Jagan form the People's Progressive Party (PPP), the first political party in Guyana. The PPP advocated for Guyana's independence from Great Britain and the establishment of a socialist society.

In the 1950s Burnham played a central role in the organized labor movement. A year after his marriage in 1951 to Sheila Bernice Lataste, an optometrist from Trinidad, he was elected president of the British Guyana Labor Union. He was so popular among organized labor groups that he was elected to the Georgetown City Council the next year.

In 1953 British Guyana held its first general elections with universal adult suffrage. The PPP was victorious; Burnham won a seat in the House of Assembly appointed as minister of education, while Jagan became the head of government. However, after only five months of this limited form of self-rule, the PPP was removed from power after a split developed between Burnham and Jagan. The more radical Jagan emerged with more support in the House of Assembly. The British government, led at that time by Winston Churchill, feared that Guyana might become a communist state and suspended its constitution, reverting the country to nonelected rule and sending troops to Guyana. Though several members of the PPP were arrested and detained, Burnham abided by British restrictions placed on nationalist politicians and was not jailed. An interim government ran the country (1953-1957), and Burnham left the PPP because of ideological and personal differences with Jagan.

In 1957 Burnham formed a rival political party, the People's National Congress (PNC). Two years later he was elected mayor of Georgetown, a position he held for seven years. In 1964, after a hard-fought general election, Burnham and the PNC were thrust into national power when they defeated Jagan and the PPP.

In 1966 Guyana received its independence from Great Britain, and Burnham became the country's first prime minister. Ruling Guyana for 19 years, he transformed the country and its governmental agencies into extensions of his party. During his tenure, Burnham nationalized several foreign-controlled bauxite and sugar companies, declared all governmental agencies to be organs of the state, and transformed Guyana into a cooperative (socialist) republic.

Although his administration was bitterly contested by many within Guyana, including Afro-Guyanese activist Walter Rodney, Burnham is a hero to many in the Afro-Guyanese community. He died unexpectedly on August 6, 1985.

Alonford James Robinson, Jr.

See Also
Trinidad and Tobago.

North America

Burns, Anthony, runaway slave whose reenslavement under the terms of the Fugitive Slave Act of 1850 served as a rallying cry for American abolitionists in the late 1850s.

The debate over slavery in America was already filled with acrimony and violence when Anthony Burns, a black fugitive slave, was arrested in Boston, Massachusetts, for violating the Fugitive Slave Act of 1850. Just four years after the controversial law was passed, the Burns case, as it is known, sparked outrage among abolitionists (*see* Abolitionism in the United States) throughout New England.

After being arrested in May 1854 Burns was placed in leg irons, as authorities prepared to return him to servitude in Richmond, Virginia. His arrest galvanized New England abolitionists already opposed to the Fugitive Slave Act. Two days after Burns was imprisoned, abolitionists stormed the courthouse in an unsuccessful attempt to rescue the former slave forcibly, and a deputy was killed.

Fearing more violence, federal officials sent armed military troops to defend the courthouse while Burns was ordered returned to his owner in Virginia. When the day came to send Burns back he was escorted to the Boston wharf by a heavily armed posse complete with cannons, shotguns, and pistols.

Although the arrest and deportation of Anthony Burns left abolitionists in the area angry and frustrated, they used his story to recruit more members and to convince the Massachusetts State Legislature to pass legislation the following year nullifying the Fugitive Slave Act.

Less than a year after his return to slavery Burns was emancipated when abolitionists from Boston collected enough money to purchase his freedom. He returned to the free states in the North, enrolled in Oberlin College (Ohio), and then proceeded to the Fairmount Theological Seminary in Cincinnati, Ohio.

Alonford James Robinson, Jr.

See Also
Slavery in the United States; Fugitive Slave Laws.

North America

Burroughs, Nannie Helen (b. May 2, 1879, Orange, Va.; d. May 20, 1961, Washington, D.C.), American educator, civil rights activist, feminist, religious leader, and founder of the Women's Convention and of the National Training School for Women and Girls, an auxiliary to the National Baptist Association.

Nannie Burroughs was born May 2, 1879 in Orange, Virginia, to John and Jennie Poindexter Burroughs. She later moved with her mother and sister to Washington, D.C., where she graduated from the Colored High School in 1896 and took a job at the Philadelphia office of the *Christian Banner.* Burroughs then moved to Louisville, Kentucky, and worked as a bookkeeper and editorial secretary of the Foreign Mission Board of the National Baptist Convention (NBC). She also organized the Women's Industrial Club there.

In 1900, at the NBC annual meeting, Burroughs gave an impassioned speech entitled "How the Sisters Are Hindered from Helping." She went on to found the Women's Convention, an auxiliary to the NBC, and served as its secretary for 48 years (1900-1948), and as president for 13 (1948-1961). In 1907 Burroughs claimed the Women's Convention represented nearly 1.5 million Baptist women. She was instrumental in the creation of the National Training School for Women and Girls, which was founded in 1909 and still operates today, renamed the Nannie Helen Burroughs School.

She published several books, including *What to Do and How to Do It* (1907) and *Slabtown District Convention* (1908). She was an active member of many clubs, such as the National Association of Colored Women, the National League of Republican Colored Women (president, 1924), and Daughters of the Round Table. She died of natural causes in Washington, D.C., on May 20, 1961.

Alonford James Robinson, Jr.

Africa

Burton, Sir Richard

(b. March 19, 1821, Torquay, England; d. Oct. 20, 1890, Trieste, Austria-Hungary [present-day Italy]), European adventurer, polyglot, ethnographer, and prolific writer who explored Africa, the Middle East, and Muslim Central Asia extensively.

Sir Richard Burton spoke 25 languages and multiple dialects, including Greek, Latin, English, French, Italian, Marathi, Punjab, Arabic, and Hindi. During his travels he observed an enormous range of cultural practices, which he documented in 43 manuscripts. He also wrote 2 books of poetry and 4 volumes of folklore.

Born to English parents, Burton was raised primarily in France. He briefly attended Trinity College, Oxford, but was expelled in 1842 for insubordination. He then joined the Bombay army and served in India (in present-day Pakistan) until 1850. Working as an intelligence officer, he learned to impersonate Muslim merchants. His reputation was called into question and his military career cut short when a rival officer spread word that Burton had been investigating homosexual bathhouses in Karachi, failing to divulge that Burton had done so under orders from a senior officer.

After returning to France and writing four books about India, Burton departed in 1853 for Cairo, disguised as an Afghanistani Muslim. From Cairo he traveled to Medina and then on to Mecca, a city forbidden to all non-Muslims. He sketched and described in great detail the mosque and the Ka'bah, the great Muslim holy site, and later documented the journey in *Pilgrimage to El-Medinah and Mecca* (1855).

Immediately afterward Burton traveled to Harar, in the Ch'erch'er Mountains of Somaliland (present-day Somalia), a center of Muslim missionary activity and slave trading. He described this risky journey in *First Footsteps in East Africa* (1856).

Later in 1855 Burton set off on an expedition to find the source of the White Nile with John Hanning Speke. The party was attacked en route and Speke was badly hurt. Burton himself was wounded by a javelin that pierced through his cheeks, forcing him to return to England. During the next year the two men resumed their search and this time faced debilitating illnesses. Burton, weak from malaria, had to remain in Tabora, while the somewhat healthier Speke continued alone to Lake Victoria, which he declared to be the source of the White Nile. Burton was skeptical of Speke's claim, which was based on hearsay rather than firsthand knowledge. Resentful that Speke's "discovery" was celebrated and unable to procure funds for resuming his own exploration, Burton became increasingly antagonistic toward his old friend.

Burton next traveled to Salt Lake City, Utah, where he conducted research on Mormonism for his book *City of the Saints* (1861). Back in London, he married his long-time love, Isabel Arundell, in 1861 – secretly, owing to her Roman Catholic affiliation.

From 1861 until 1864 Burton served as British consul to Fernando Po, a Spanish-ruled island off the coast of present-day Cameroon (but a part of Equatorial Guinea). During his stay, he visited several West African regions, including Dahomey (now Benin). His observations provided material for five more ethnographies. After returning to England, he was invited to debate Speke's claims at a meeting of the British Association for the Advancement of Science. While awaiting Speke's arrival, he was informed that Speke had shot himself while hunting and had died. Burton suspected suicide.

Burton spent four years at his next British consular post in Santos, Brazil. Unhappy and in poor health, he was helped by his wife, who traveled to England in order to use her influence to secure him a post in Damascus. He was dismissed from this post in 1871, ostensibly after he tried to protect members of a Muslim sect who wished to convert to Christianity. During the following year he became the consul to Trieste, Italy, where he lived with his wife until his death in 1890.

While in Trieste he published numerous books attacking Victorian values and exploring taboo subjects, from homosexuality to erotica. His translation of the *Kama Sutra of Vatsyayana* and his daring, unconventional essays notwithstanding, he was knighted in 1886. After Burton's death, his wife, fearing that her husband would be depicted as perverted and corrupt, burned virtually his entire collection of journals. Regardless of this historical loss, Burton's remarkable career and his contributions to African ethnography continue to be celebrated.

Ari Nave

See Also
Cairo, Egypt.

Africa

Burundi, a small country located between East and Central Africa, bordered by Rwanda, the Democratic Republic of the Congo, and Tanzania.

Nineteenth-century European travelers described the kingdom of Burundi as "a land of almost ideal beauty." Today, the national borders of Burundi, one of Africa's most densely populated countries, remain virtually unchanged, but political turmoil has disfigured its idyllic landscape. Formerly ruled by traditional monarchies, Burundi was colonized by Germany in the late nineteenth century and was under German and then Belgian administration until its independence in 1962. Just ten years after independence, an abortive coup d'état in 1972 provoked brutal massacres, claiming the lives of more than 100,000 people. Tens of thousands more have since died, particularly in 1988 and 1993, in what is usually referred to as "ethnic conflict" between the country's Hutu majority, composing approximately 85 percent of its 6 million inhabitants, and the 15 percent Tutsi minority. But this explanation for Burundi's violence overlooks the long history of cohabitation and intermarriage between these two groups. More fundamentally, it does not do justice to the extraordinarily complex social, economic, and political meanings of ethnic identity in Burundi.

Early Burundi Society

There are diverging theories on the origin of the hunter-gatherer Twa "pygmies," the first known inhabitants of present-day Burundi. Archaeological evidence indicates that the Twa occupied the area beginning around 70,000 B.C.E., whereas linguistic evidence suggests that they migrated to the region from West Africa around 5000 years ago. Further linguistic evidence reveals that Bantu-speaking cultivators from the lowlands of Central Africa migrated to the

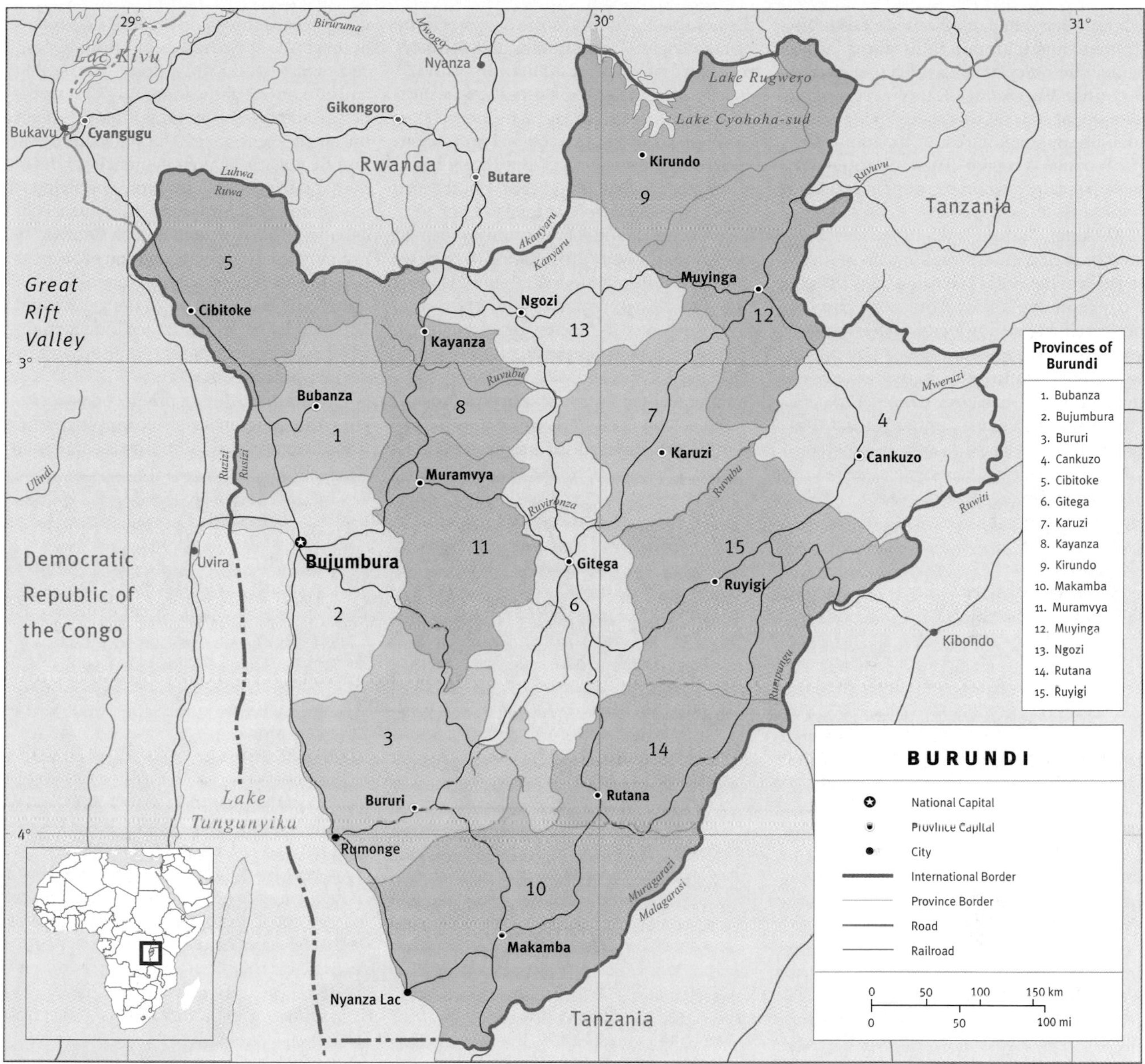

mountainous region between Lakes Kivu, Tanganyika, and Victoria sometime during the eleventh century (*see* Bantu: Dispersion and Settlement). These people took the name baHutu, or Hutu. Pastoralist Hima people, probably from present-day southern Ethiopia, though their exact origins are disputed, succeeded the Hutu in the mid-sixteenth century, becoming known as the baTutsi, or Tutsi. They established small hillside chiefdoms based on cattle-clientship, wherein the Tutsi would give the Hutu cattle as payment for their agricultural labor or surplus crops. Elsewhere the two groups established commercial relationships, again exchanging livestock for food crops. The Tutsi adopted the Hutu language as well as many of their customs, including practices of worshiping ancestors and the belief in the existence of a spiritual life in all living things.

Unlike most other parts of Africa, the kingdom of Burundi developed a national character well before European colonial intervention. In the mid-seventeenth century a Tutsi chief, Ntare, began building this kingdom through conquest. It eventually took the form of several provinces, each ruled by a distinct royal clan, the Batare, Bezi, Batanga, and Bambutsa. Because of succession disputes, by the end of the eighteenth century the king, or *mwami,* Gisabo claimed control over only half the kingdom, which by then covered the approximate area of present-day Burundi. But the system of succession was not clear. In the 1860s the princes, who with their immediate descendants comprised the *ganwa* monarchy, rebelled against the current king, Ntare II.

Barundi society was feudal in character, and its hierarchies extraordinarily complex. The ganwa monarchy formed the landholding aristocracy, whose "ethnic" identity as Tutsi was based primarily on their royal status. Socially subordinate to the ganwa were the Banyaruguru Tutsi, literally, the "people from above," and below them the Hima Tutsi. As in many other parts of Central and East Africa, the pastoralists, in this case the Tutsi, came to dominate the cultivators, the Hutu, through their control of cattle, the primary measure of wealth, as well as through their tradition of warfare. In fact, in the common Kirundi language, Hutu has two meanings, one cultural and the other social, defined as "social subordinate" or "social son." But these identities depended on social context: a Tutsi poor in cattle, for example, would be considered a client and a "Hutu" to a wealthier Tutsi patron.

The social stratification was complicated by a patrilineal kinship system that divided families between "very good," "good," "rather good," "neither good nor bad," and "bad." Inequality was a source of social cohesion; the poor and weak depended on protection and patronage from the rich and powerful, who in turn relied on clientage ties to legitimate and maintain their status. At the same time, precolonial Barundi society was exceptionally homogenous culturally, and allowed for considerable social and economic mobility. By acquiring cattle, for example, a Hutu could "become" Tutsi. Intermarriage between cultural ethnic groups, sometimes for status, was common.

Although Barundi society was vertically stratified, the Tutsi were not the political masters of the Hutu. The two groups shared a conception of the *mwami* as an absolute monarch whose authority was primarily spiritual, not political. It was the ganwa who ruled the provinces in the name of the mwami. Meanwhile, the *abanyarurimbi*, or "those who can judge," either Hutu or Tutsi but not ganwa, controlled the court system. Local disputes were arbitrated by the *abashingantache*, or "those of the small stick," posts open to anyone but typically held by elder Hutu men.

Boys in Bujumbura, Burundi, play checkers with bottle caps. *Betty Press*

Colonialism in the Heart of Africa

In the mid-1800s European explorers and missionaries, including John Hanning Speke, Richard Francis Burton, David Livingstone, and Henry Morton Stanley, all likely traveled through the Burundi kingdom. In the late-nineteenth-century rush to colonize the continent, known as the Scramble for Africa, Belgium, Great Britain, and Germany contested possession of Ruandi-Urundi, present-day Rwanda and Burundi, respectively, because the territory lay at the intersection between their respective colonial possessions and at the headwaters of the Nile River. Although the 1884-1885 Berlin Conference ceded control of Ruandi-Urundi to Germany, the exact boundaries of the colony remained in dispute until the 1910 Kivu-Mfumbiro Conference, attended by Belgium, Great Britain, and Germany. At the time, Germany was represented in the area by 40 soldiers, a handful of merchants and civil servants, and over 100 missionaries.

Colonization destroyed Burundi's fragile social cohesion and emerging national identity, largely because European colonial administrators, with help from missionaries, interpreted existing social stratification in terms of rigid ethnic categories, then allocated political power and material resources accordingly. Upon the defeat of Germany in World War I, the League of Nations transferred control of Ruanda-Urundi to Belgium as a mandate territory. Initially, the Belgian regime concentrated on developing export crop production, achieved through compulsory labor service and crop cultivation. But in 1929 it began to intervene in Burundian political structures, instituting a system of indirect rule by "ganwa-izing" the colonial civil service (*see* Colonial Rule). The Belgians considered the ganwa not only the "traditional" and thereby most appropriate rulers, but also a "higher race." This pitted the Batare and Bezi clans against each other while marginalizing southern Tutsi. The Belgians also promoted the mwami Mwambutsa IV as a modernizing ruler, and Roman Catholicism as a moral and religious extension of colonial rule. The colonial education system centered on training the children of the ganwa and Tutsi chiefs, although it also subsidized mission-run schools that focused on universal primary education.

The northern Tutsi's privileged access to education and civil service employment translated into economic advancement, at a time when colonial labor policies and taxation were subjecting most other Barundi to severe hardship. As social differentiation hardened into class stratification, tensions between the ganwa and other groups – both southern Tutsi and Hutu – increased. At the same time, generations-old rivalries between the Batare and the Bezi were aggravated by the Belgians' strategy of switching their support from one to the other, depending upon which clan or individual appeared the most reliable and malleable ally. In the 1950s, as the Barundi elite began pushing for self-rule and ultimately for independence, the Belgians settled on supporting Batare chief Baranyanka and his minor and Batare-dominated nationalist Parti Démocrate Chrétien, or PDC, over the more popular and radical Bezi-dominated Union Pour le Progrès National, or UPRONA. As the last Belgian resident, or governor, explains: "There was a certain connivance and even a direct complicity between our Authority and the PDC.... The PDC quickly became the bulwark we hoped to use in order to stop the cancerous metastasis of UPRONA's progress." Not surprisingly, Belgian support for the PDC only further strengthened UPRONA, which was led by the eldest son of Mwami Mwambutsa, the popular Prince Louis Rwagasore, who identified with the Bezi.

solidified ethnic identities in Burundi. Many Barundi Tutsi feared a similar nightmare, while the Hutu considered it a defining moment in their political aspirations. Adding to the heightened tensions, in October 1961 Prime Minister-Designate Prince Rwagasore was assassinated in a plot approved by the Batare leadership, who feared that the prince and UPRONA would favor the interests of the rival Bezi clan. The simmering discord in Burundi did not prevent the Belgians from implementing a rapid withdrawal from the territory.

Cycles of Violence in Burundi

On July 1, 1962, Burundi, as part of a short-lived economic federation with Rwanda, became an independent constitutional monarchy. Over the next few years, the new prevailed in the National Assembly. Then in January 1965 a Tutsi refugee assassinated the Hutu prime minister. In October, Hutu candidates won 70 percent of the new parliamentary seats, but the mwami appointed a Tutsi prime minister. Although the Hutu had not previously protested the Tutsi's overall political domination, they interpreted this move as an unacceptable shift in the balance of power. It sparked an unsuccessful coup attempt by the few Hutu officers in the Tutsi-dominated army. The army in turn purged all its Hutu and executed approximately 2000 Hutu politicians and intellectuals. Meanwhile the mwami fled, and in November 1966 the military officially abolished the monarchy and proclaimed a republic. Army captain Michel Micombero, a Hima Tutsi from the southern Buriri province, became president.

A teacher at a peace education class in Burundi instructs Hutu and Tutsi students in principles for working together, including working with love, peace, and joy. *CORBIS/Howard Davies*

Despite the social tensions fostered by colonialism, the nationalist movement had begun to forge a sense of Burundian unity by the late 1950s. This was shattered, however, by the 1959 Rwandan revolution, in which the majority Hutu peasantry overthrew the Belgian-backed Tutsi aristocracy and took firm control of the nationalist movement, killing many Tutsi in the process. Although the societies in the two Belgian colonies differed significantly, the Rwandan revolution nation's primary political divisions shifted rapidly from the long-standing rivalries between Tutsi clans to unprecedented hostilities between Tutsi and Hutu. Although many observers have blamed colonialism for creating these hostilities, political events of the 1960s were even more directly responsible. Between 1962 and 1965 Mwami Mwambutsa IV appointed a succession of ineffective prime ministers and dispute-torn cabinets, while relative parity between Hutu and Tutsi

President Micombero filled his government with southern Tutsi clan members, thereby undermining the power of the ganwa. Many of these supporters were ethnic "hard-liners" who vilified the Hutu masses in speeches and in the media. In response, Hutu soldiers organized a series of unsuccessful coup attempts, culminating in a 1972 uprising among Hutu groups ranging from refugees and Democratic Republic of the Congo-based guerrillas to schoolteachers, students, and civil servants. As many as 20,000 Tutsi were killed. Micombero retaliated not only by executing the instigators, but also by sending the military and youth groups into the countryside to kill all Hutu "intellectuals," meaning anyone with more than a grade-school education. More than 100,000 Hutu died between April and September 1972, and probably as many fled into neighboring countries. The international community, preoccupied with Vietnam and IDI AMIN's reign of terror in nearby UGANDA, did not respond. The year of *ikiza*, or catastrophe, congealed Hutu's collective identity as martyrs, historically oppressed and impoverished by an unscrupulous Tutsi elite.

In November 1976 Col. JEAN-BAPTISTE BAGAZA, also a Hima Tutsi from Buriri, overthrew Micombero in a palace coup. Bagaza's dictatorial government, composed almost exclusively of his fellow clan members, solidified Tutsi hegemony. Bagaza maintained tight control over the military, the single party (UPRONA), and the press, and Hutu representation in all branches of the government declined precipitously. Over time, Bagaza's dictatorial rule alienated the military as well as many Tutsi elite, leading to a bloodless coup in 1987 and the installation of Maj. PIERRE BUYOYA as president. Buyoya, also a Hima Tutsi from Buriri, came from a younger generation than his predecessor, and promised "profound change, in the sense of expanded social justice and of real democracy." But the pro-Hutu Party for the Liberation of the Hutu People (PALIPEHUTU) continued to urge Hutu to rise up against the Tutsi, and in August 1988 Burundi again descended into chaos. A local conflict in the north escalated and the government responded violently, with the death toll reaching approximately 20,000.

THE SIMMERING CONFLICT

Poverty and stiff competition for scarce resources have inevitably both contributed to and been aggravated by the ongoing violence. Burundi is one of the most densely populated countries in Africa, and dependence of the vast majority of its people on agriculture for their livelihood has resulted in severe deforestation and land degradation. Income from the only significant export crop, coffee, fluctuates greatly with global market prices, but many farmers are afraid even to cultivate their fields. Sporadic famines have become common. Successive governments, preoccupied with maintaining control through funding the military, have neglected agricultural and infrastructural development projects. Burundi's dilapidated industries, suffering from parts shortages, power outages, and high transportation costs, offer few employment opportunities to residents of Bujumbura, the national capital and only major city.

In the wake of the 1988 killings, President Buyoya, motivated by personal convictions as well as pressure from the international community, inaugurated a transition to democracy and national reconciliation. By the end of 1990 he had appointed Tutsi and Hutu in roughly equal numbers to UPRONA's Central Committee. His government had a Hutu prime minister and a constitution guaranteeing basic human rights and multiparty democracy. The Hutu leaders subsequently founded the Front Démocratique du Burundi (FRODEBU), which called for economic justice for the Hutu as well as Hutu political representation proportional to their population majority. In 1993 elections, FRODEBU and its leader, Melchoir Ndadaye, won convincingly and appointed a cabinet that included two-thirds Hutu and one-third Tutsi. Ndadaye also appointed former banker and political moderate Sylvie Kinigie as prime minister, one of the first women to hold that post in Africa. But in October of that year, members of the still Tutsi-led army overtook the presidential mansion and killed Ndadaye, putting a bloody end to the reconciliation process. Probably 20,000 Tutsi and 30,000 Hutu lost their lives in the violence that followed in the north of the country.

International condemnation convinced the army to return to their barracks; the coup leaders fled the country. In January 1994 a moderate Hutu FRODEBU member, Cyprien Ntaryamira, was sworn in as president. In April, Ntaryamira and his Rwandan counterpart, Juvénal Habyarimana, were en route from United Nations peace negotiations when their plane was shot down by still-unknown forces, an event that precipitated the Rwandan genocide. Although Burundi itself remained calm, thousands of Burundi Hutu, fearing Tutsi attacks, fled to Tanzania, and Burundi's political parties began to develop militias, in order both to protect their leaders and advance their interests. Ethnic-based parties, in other words, were further nurturing the conditions for civil war.

In September 1994 the moderate parties came to a power-sharing agreement, but extremists on both sides refused to recognize it. Sporadic fighting and atrocities continued throughout the countryside, and, increasingly, in the suburbs of Bujumbura. The Hutu hardliners' National Council for the Defense of Democracy (CNDD) has since waged a terror campaign against the government. In July 1996 Pierre Buyoya overthrew the elected but ineffective president, as the politicians maneuvered for power in the capital. An economic embargo imposed by Burundi's neighbors has put pressure on the government and CNDD to negotiate, but the talks have often stalled. Violence continued in parts of the country during the late 1990s, taking as many 1000 lives per month, according to some estimates. Yet while the recent years of democratization have by no means brought peace, the Catholic Church, human rights organizations, and independent media have become more vocal in their opposition to the violence, fear, and hatred perpetuated by the military and militias (*see* HUMAN RIGHTS IN AFRICA).

Eric Young

SEE ALSO

Bujumbura, Burundi; Ethnicity and Identity in Africa: An Interpretation; Hutu and Tutsi; Victoria, Lake; Pygmy; Tanganyika, Lake; Kinigi, Sylvie; Berlin Conference of 1884-1885.

Africa

Burundi (Ready Reference)

Official Name: Burundi
Area: 27,834 sq km (10,750 sq mi)
Location: Central Africa, bordered by RWANDA, TANZANIA, the DEMOCRATIC REPUBLIC OF THE CONGO (formerly Zaire), and Lake Tanganyika.
Capital: Bujumbura (population 300,000 [1993 estimate])
Other Major City: Gitega (population 95,000 [1987 estimate])
Population: 5,537,387 (July 1998 estimate)
Population Density: 228 persons per sq km (about 590 persons per sq mi)
Population Below Age 14: 47 percent
Population Growth Rate: 3.51 percent (1998 estimate)
Total Fertility Rate: 6.4 children born per woman (1998 estimate)
Life Expectancy at Birth: Total population: 45.56 years (male 43.79 years; female 47.38 years [1998 estimate])
Infant Mortality Rate: 101.19 deaths per 1000 live births (1998 estimate)
Literacy Rates (age 15 and over who can read and write): Total population: 35 percent (male: 49.3 percent; female: 22.5 percent [1995 estimate])
Education: Schooling is free and officially compulsory for children aged 7 through 12. In the early 1990s about 631,039 students annually attended primary schools and about 46,500 attended secondary schools. The University of Burundi (founded in 1960), located in Bujumbura, is the leading institution of higher education; it had an enrollment of about 3800 in the early 1990s.
Languages: Kirundi and French are the official languages. Swahili is spoken along Lake Tanganyika and in the Bujumbura area.
Ethnic Groups: The chief ethnic groups are the Hutu, a Bantu-speaking people making up about 85 percent of the population, and the Tutsi, a Nilotic-speaking people forming about 14 percent of the total. Since October 1993, hundreds of thousands of refugees have fled Burundi and crossed into Rwanda, Tanzania, and the Democratic Republic of the Congo because of ethnic violence between Hutu and Tutsi factions.
Religions: About 67 percent are Christian (62 percent are Catholic, 5 percent are Protestant), 32 percent practice indigenous beliefs, and Muslims constitute 1 percent of the population.

Climate: Tropical, moderated in most places by altitude. The average annual temperature is 20° C (68° F) on the plateau and 23° C (73° F) in the Great Rift Valley. Dry seasons are from May to August and from January to February.
Land, Plants, and Animals: Burundi is mostly a hilly plateau region, with an elevation ranging between 1400 and 1800 m (between 4600 and 5900 ft). Elevations decrease gradually to the east and southeast. The narrow western margin of the country, bordering the Rusizi River and Lake Tanganyika, lies in the trough of the Great Rift Valley. The main rivers are the Rusizi, the Malagarasi, and the Ruvuvu. Savanna vegetation, a grassland interspersed with trees, predominates in most of the country. Eucalyptus, acacia, and oil palm are the most common trees. Wildlife is diverse: the elephant, hippopotamus, crocodile, wild boar, leopard, antelope, and flying lemur are common, as are the guinea hen, partridge, duck, goose, quail, and snipe.
Natural Resources: Mineral resources include nickel, uranium, rare earth oxides, peat, cobalt, copper, platinum (which has not yet been exploited), and vanadium. Current environmental issues facing Burundi include soil erosion because of overgrazing and the expansion of agriculture into marginal lands; deforestation (little forested land remains because of uncontrolled cutting of trees for fuel); and loss of habitat, which threatens wildlife populations.
Currency: The Burundi franc
Gross Domestic Product (GDP): $4 billion (1997 estimate)
GDP per Capita : $660 (1997 estimate)
GDP Real Growth Rate: 4.4 percent (1997 estimate)
Primary Economic Activities: subsistence agriculture (54.1 percent of GDP, 93 percent of employment); industry (mining) (16.8 percent of GDP, 1.5 percent of employment); service industries (29.1 percent of GDP, 4 percent of employment)
Primary Crops: Coffee, cotton, tea, corn, sorghum, sweet potatoes, bananas, manioc, meat, milk, and hides
Industries: Assembly of light consumer goods such as blankets, shoes, and soap
Primary Exports: Coffee, cotton, hides, tea
Primary Imports: Textiles, motor vehicles, flour, and petroleum products
Primary Trade Partners: European Union, United States, and Asia
Government: Republic; a constitutional multiparty democracy. The executive branch is led by president Pierre Buyoya since September 27, 1996. The government is headed by Prime Minister Pascal-Firmin Ndimira (since July 31, 1996) and the Council of Ministers, who are appointed by the prime minister. The Assemblée Nationale (National Assembly) is a unicameral legislative branch, most of which (71 percent) is represented by the Burundi Democratic Front (FRODEBU), with most of the remaining seats (21 percent) filled by representatives of the Unity for National Progress (UPRONA) party.

Robert Fay

Africa

Busa (also known as the Busagwe and the Busanse), ethnic group of Nigeria.

The Busa primarily inhabit northwestern Nigeria, although some Busa live in northeastern Benin. They speak a Niger-Congo language and are one of the Bariba peoples. Approximately 200,000 people consider themselves Busa.

See Also
Languages, African: An Overview.

Africa

Busansi (also known as Bisa, Bissa, Boussansé, Busanga, and Bousanou), ethnic group of West Africa.

The Busansi primarily inhabit southern Burkina Faso, northern Ghana, and northern Togo. They speak a Mande southern language. Approximately 150,000 people consider themselves Busansi.

See Also
Languages, African: An Overview.

North America

Bush, Anita (b. 1883, New York, N.Y.; d. February 1974), African American actress and the founder of the Lafayette Players, the first major professional, black, nonmusical theater ensemble.

Born in New York City, Anita Bush was introduced to the world of theater by her father, a tailor whose clients included many New York actors and performers. At the age of 16 she joined the Williams and Walker Company as a dancer.

In 1915, determined that blacks should perform serious dramatic works, she formed the Anita Bush Players of Harlem, which later became the Lafayette Players. The company survived until January 1932, and was responsible for training over 300 black performers and introducing serious theater to many cities across the country. Bush left the group in 1920 and went on to costar in *The Crimson Skull* (1921), the first all-black Western movie.

See Also
Harlem, New York; New York, New York; Film, Blacks in American.

Africa

Bushmen, a term, often considered derogatory, used to describe Khoisan-speaking hunter-gatherers who live in the Kalahari Desert; these groups are also known as the San.

The first European encounter with the so-called Bushmen of southern Africa came shortly after Dutch colonists established a settlement on the Cape of Good Hope in 1652. The region's Nama herders told them about primitive, foraging peoples known as the Sonqua, or San. In 1660 the Dutch soldier Carl Riebeeck led an army mission into the mountainous regions of the Cape, where he reportedly came upon communities of foragers, whom the Europeans later called Bosjiemen, or Bushmen.

For nearly two centuries the Bushmen were vilified by Europeans, who viewed them as "wild creatures" who refused to be civilized. The Dutch *Bosjieman* is in fact derived from the term for bandit or outlaw. European accounts of the time frequently described Bushmen as mischievous bandits lurking on the peripheries of human settlement. During the seventeenth and eighteenth centuries, these perceptions were used to justify Afrikaner efforts to exterminate the people they called the "lowest race on earth." Between 1785 and 1795 alone, Afrikaner settlers are reported to have killed at least 2500 San and taken captive at least another 700. European missionaries were unconcerned with the mass killings because Bushmen were seen as "dogs" whose existence threatened human civilization.

By the mid-nineteenth century, however, European views of Bushmen had changed. Now the Bushman was cast as the "noble savage and hunter," eternally childlike and attuned to nature. Europeans marveled at Bushmen's "timeless existence," and scientists claimed that Bushmen represented the missing link to primitive society. Archaeological research on rock paintings of hunting scenes in South Africa's mountain ranges provided evidence for the theory that the Bushmen had not changed in thousands of years.

In the twentieth century the image of the primitive Bushman has been reinforced by photographs, films, and written works. In 1925 the Denver African Expedition catered to American audiences hungry for Tarzan-type images by bribing San people to pose for shots that emphasized their "exotic primitiveness." Later, ethnographic films such as John Marshall's *The Hunter* and written ethnographies such as Marjorie Shostak's *Nisa* supported these ideas by lending a pseudoscientific authority to popular images of the Bushmen.

In the late twentieth century Western images of the Bushmen, while as far removed as ever from the reality of San life, have become even more commercially valuable.

In 1978 Afrikaner film director Jamie Uys struck gold with *The Gods Must Be Crazy*, a popular film that reinforced notions of the happy but primitive Bushmen. In BOTSWANA, the government deliberately propagates the Bushmen myth. In the Central Kalahari Game Reserve, the biggest tourist attraction is the Bushmen themselves. As recently as 1996, however, the government of Botswana threatened to remove those Bushmen who did not conform to "traditional" Bushmen hunting and gathering techniques and who had acquired cattle herds and other un-Bushmenlike assets.

Elizabeth Heath

SEE ALSO
Christianity: Missionaries in Africa.

Latin America and the Caribbean

Bush Negroes, a term used for the six communities of self-liberated black people living in the interior of SURINAME.

Africa

Busia, Kofi Abrefa (b. July 11, 1913, Wenchi, Gold Coast [present-day Ghana]; d. August 28, 1978, Oxford, England), teacher, author, and former prime minister of GHANA.

Born a member of the royal family of Wenchi, Kofi Abrefa Busia attended the Kumasi Methodist and Mfantsipim secondary schools and Wesley College. He received a B.A. in politics, philosophy, and economics and then an M.A. in social anthropology from the University of Oxford. Busia wrote his doctoral thesis, titled "The Position of the Chief in the Modern Political System of Ashanti," in 1951. He held teaching positions at the Ghana University College at Legon in the African studies and sociology departments.

Busia left the university to devote himself to politics in 1956. In the fall of 1957, he formed the United Party, comprising various parties in opposition to President KWAME NKRUMAH. He was an outspoken opponent of Nkrumah's government. Busia fled to England in fear of the increasingly repressive government. In exile, he maintained his opposition to the Nkrumah regime and continued to teach and write, publishing *Urban Churches in Britain* (1956) and *Africa in Search of Democracy* (1967). Returning to Ghana after Nkrumah was removed, Busia participated in the writing of a new constitution. He was elected prime minister in 1969.

Facing very poor economic conditions, Busia expelled foreign workers and imposed new taxes, but his policies failed to stem rising unemployment and inflation. At the end of 1971, Busia devalued the cedi. The resulting massive inflation sparked resistance among the people and the military, leading directly to the end of his government. A month later, while out of the country, he was ousted by a coup d'état. He died of a heart attack on August 28, 1978, after living his last years in England.

Martha King

Latin America and the Caribbean

Bussa, an African-born slave in Barbados who was the leader of the 1816 Easter Rebellion, considered the first large-scale slave insurrection in the British Caribbean (*see* BARBADOS).

Latin America and the Caribbean

Bustamante, Sir Alexander (b. February 24, 1884, Blenheim, Jamaica; d. August 6, 1977, Kingston, Jamaica), charismatic leader and fierce orator who led the Jamaican Labour Party (1943-1977) and was the first prime minister of JAMAICA (1962-1967).

Born William Alexander Clarke, of an Irish immigrant father and a Jamaican mother of indigenous and African descent, Bustamante grew up in Blenheim, Jamaica, but ventured out into the world at the age of 21. As a young man he served in the Spanish army, then worked in various capacities in CUBA, PANAMA, and New York City. He returned to Jamaica in 1932 as a wealthy entrepreneur. Although shrewd investments had made him rich, Bustamante's concern for Jamaican sugar plantation workers led him to participate in protest marches, organize strikes, and become the treasurer of the Jamaican Workers and Tradesmen's Union (JWTU), which he helped found in 1937. His political activism continued alongside the social upheaval occurring in the 1930s throughout the WEST INDIES. After he was jailed and released in May 1938, he became a symbolic leader of the workers' movement. In that same year he formed the Bustamante Industrial Trade Union (BITU), and served as its president for the remainder of his life.

Bustamante was jailed by the British colonial government for his union and political activities from September 1940 to February 1942. In 1943 he formed the Jamaican Labour Party (JLP). His Conservative Party overwhelmingly won the island's first parliamentary election in 1944 in opposition to the socialist People's National Party (PNP), founded by his cousin and political rival Norman Manley (1893-1969). Bustamante later served as mayor of Kingston (1947-1948) and as chief minister of Jamaica (1953-1955). The JLP lost elections in 1955 and 1959. However, in 1961, Bustamante's opposition leadership against Jamaica's inclusion in the transitional West Indies Federation helped win the referendum, which was to pave the way for independence from Great Britain. Knighted in 1955, Sir Alexander Bustamante became Jamaica's first prime minister when the country gained independence in 1962. He fell ill in 1964, retired from politics in 1967, and died in 1977 at the age of 94.

SEE ALSO
Great Britain; New York, New York; Manley, Norman Washington.

Africa

Buthelezi, Mangosutho Gatsha (b. 1928, present-day KwaZulu-Natal), South African politician, chief minister of the former bantustan (or black homeland) KwaZulu (1976-1994), and founder of the Inkatha Freedom Party.

Born in what is now the province of KwaZulu-Natal, Mangosutho Gatsha Buthelezi is related to the Zulu royal family through his mother, Princess Magogo. He is descended from CETSHWAYO, a Zulu king who ruled in the late 1800s. Buthelezi's father, who was chief of the Buthelezi tribe, died when Buthelezi was 14 years old. Buthelezi's uncle, Maliyamakhanda, was appointed regent to govern the tribe until Buthelezi was ready to assume the role of chief.

Buthelezi received his early education at Christian mission schools (*see* CHRISTIANITY: MISSIONARIES IN AFRICA). He then attended South African Native College (now the University of Fort Hare) in Alice. During college Buthelezi joined the AFRICAN NATIONAL CONGRESS (ANC) Youth League. He was subsequently expelled from college because of his political activities, but in 1951 he received his degree in history and Bantu administration (a discipline designed to train black South Africans for certain government positions) from the University of Natal in Durban. In 1953 Buthelezi returned home and was appointed chief of the Buthelezi tribe.

During the 1950s the white South African government divided the black majority population according to ethnic groups and assigned them to separate territories that the government considered to be ethnic homelands. These territories, called bantustans (or black homelands), were part of the government's policy of apartheid, or separation of the races. Parts of Zululand became the bantustan of KwaZulu, designated for the Zulu people.

At first Buthelezi opposed this system but then decided to work within it. In 1976 he became the first chief minister of KwaZulu. Also in 1976, he founded the Black Unity Front to promote unity and federation of the bantustans. Buthelezi rejected the idea of full independence for the bantustans, arguing that apartheid could best be fought if the territories remained part of South Africa.

Around this time, Buthelezi reinvigorated a movement called Inkatha. The movement was originally founded as a Zulu cultural organization, but Buthelezi turned it into the political party called the Inkatha Freedom Party. The party grew rapidly, and it eventually became the dominant party of KwaZulu. Buthelezi attempted to forge the South African Black Alliance in 1978 with other political parties. His political power base remained confined to the Zulu, however, and only a portion of them were his firm supporters.

Tensions mounted between Inkatha and the ANC in the 1980s, after the ANC accused Buthelezi of cooperating with the South African government. Sporadic fighting between supporters of the two parties, carried out mainly in the black townships on the borders of South African cities, began in 1985 and continued in the 1990s, despite a peace agreement signed between the party leaders in September 1991. In 1991 the South African government was forced to admit that it had been supporting Inkatha financially. A 1994 inquiry further revealed that the government's security forces had been providing weapons for Inkatha to use in the township fighting. The government's support for Inkatha was intended to increase political divisions within the black population and to undermine popular support for the ANC.

Buthelezi initially refused to participate in South Africa's first free elections in April 1994, demanding that KwaZulu be granted a certain amount of autonomy and that the Zulu king occupy an official position in the KwaZulu government. KwaZulu, along with the other bantustans, was dissolved at the time of the 1994 elections. Buthelezi finally took part in the elections, after reaching an agreement that recognized the traditional authority of the Zulu king and postponed until after the elections further negotiations about regional autonomy. Inkatha won 10.5 percent of the vote in the national elections, gaining 43 seats out of 400 in the National Assembly, and Buthelezi was appointed minister of home affairs in the cabinet of President Nelson Mandela.

See Also

Bantu: Dispersion and Settlement; Mandela, Nelson Rolihlahla; Inkatha Freedom Party; South Africa.

North America

Butler, Octavia Estelle

(b. June 22, 1947, Pasadena, Calif.), American science fiction writer whose work examines representations of race, gender, and systems of enslavement.

Highly regarded for her science fiction novels and short stories, Octavia Butler was born in Pasadena, California, on June 22, 1947. A shy and dyslexic child, she was raised in Pasadena and attended John Muir High School. She then studied for two years at Pasadena City College before completing additional coursework at California State College and the University of California at Los Angeles (UCLA).

Butler read avidly as a youth and began writing short works of fiction at the age of ten. Her first novel, *Patternmaster*, was published in 1976 as part of a series that includes *Mind of My Mind* (1977), *Survivor* (1978), *Wild Seed* (1980), and *Clay's Ark* (1984). Though best known for her novels, Butler has won awards for her short stories, including a Hugo for "Speech Sounds" (1983) and both a Hugo and a Nebula for "Blood-Child" (1984).

Butler's work often displays her interest in racial themes, particularly the issue of slavery. Set in times ranging from precolonial Africa to a distant grim future, many of Butler's stories feature characters who deal with different forms of enslavement and struggle to free themselves from systems of bondage. Butler is also one of the first writers to introduce the black woman's experience in science fiction, as she features many African American and African female protagonists. Her work is celebrated outside science fiction circles for its character development and treatment of human relations and social causes.

Latin America and the Caribbean

Butler, Tubal Uriah (b. 1897, Grenada; d. February 20, 1997, Fyzabad, Trinidad), union leader and politician.

Though born in Grenada, Uriah Butler would eventually develop his career as a labor organizer and politician in Trinidad. In Grenada, he was affiliated with the Grenada Representative Government Movement, and served as a volunteer in the first contingent of the West Indies during World War I. In 1921 he migrated to Trinidad, where he settled in Fyzabad, a southern industrial town populated by workers from the dominant petroleum industry. He held a variety of positions in the oilfields – pipe fitter, rig man, and pump man – until 1929, when he was seriously injured.

Butler was a charismatic speaker, and he quickly became influential in the Trinidad Labour Party (TLP), an organization committed to expanding the voting franchise and to lobbying for constitutional change. His ascent was matched by his growing disillusionment with the TLP and its leader, Capt. Arthur Andrew Cipriani. Butler believed that the TLP was both insufficiently attentive to the needs of the rank and file and unduly placatory in its dealings with the colonial government.

In July 1936 Butler left the TLP and formed the British Empire Workers and Citizens Home Rule Party (BEW). He began to call increasingly for improvements in the living conditions of the oilfield workers. In May 1937 he was charged with sedition while addressing a workers' meeting. His supporters refused to let him be arrested. While Butler was in hiding, industrial unrest escalated, culminating in riots lasting from June 19 to July 7 of that year. The Oilfield Riots, also known as the Butler Riots, would mark the beginning of a formal labor movement in the colony, triggering the formation of the Forster Commission, with its mandate to investigate working conditions in Trinidad. After a three-month flight, Butler surrendered, was tried, and found guilty. He was sentenced to prison for two years. He served much of his sentence, although an appeal to the London-based Privy Council would later result in a ruling that overturned the original verdict. The ruling was made public in May 1939, six days after his release from prison.

Following his release, Butler was appointed general organizer in the Oilfield Workers Trade Union (OWTU), which was formed during the strikes. His affiliation with the union would be brief; he was expelled in August because of internal dissent and infighting. Butler's militant, confrontational style was increasingly at odds with the other leaders of the union, who were more interested in negotiated agreements with the government. In November 1939, after the outbreak of World War II, Butler was identified as a security risk because of his refusal to countenance bargaining strategies, and was imprisoned until the end of the war. The government was convinced that a repeat of the 1937 riots would be inevitable if Butler remained free.

Freed from prison in 1945, Butler continued to agitate for improved working conditions, and formally entered the political arena, seeking electoral office in 1946 in the colony's first election held under universal adult suffrage. The political climate was solidly pro-worker; the end of the war and subsequent economic decline had contributed to widespread industrial unrest. However, Butler ran for a seat in an unfamiliar urban milieu, Port-of-Spain, and lost. In 1950 he formed the Butler Party, a more formal incarnation of the BEW but with a political platform that called explicitly for the improvement of the political, social, and economic conditions of the entire working class. He ran in Fyzabad, where his natural constituency resided, winning office as his district's representative that year and in the subsequent 1956 election.

In November 1961 Butler was a member of the official delegation that traveled to England to discuss constitutional reform with the British government. The 1961 general election, in which Butler was defeated, marked the beginning of a national shift from an explicitly activist politics to a more pragmatic engagement with colonial authorities in the quest for independence. In 1975 he was awarded Trinidad's highest honor, the Trinity Cross.

Lorraine Anastasia Lezama

See Also

Great Britain; Trinidad and Tobago.

North America

Butts, Calvin O., III

(b. July 22, 1949, New York, N.Y.), community organizer, civic leader, and pastor of New York City's Abyssinian Baptist Church.

After graduating from high school in 1967, Calvin Butts earned a bachelor's degree from Morehouse College in 1971, a master's of divinity from Union Theological Seminary in 1975, and a doctorate of ministry from Drew Theological School in 1982.

After 17 years as an assistant and executive minister at the legendary Abyssinian Baptist Church in Harlem, New York, Butts was named pastor of the 5000-member congregation in 1989. His sermons and activities there command national attention. He has spoken out publicly against police brutality, so-called gangsta rap music, and the targeting of African American consumers by cigarette and alcohol manufacturers. In the 1980s Butts was criticized by both blacks and whites for refusing to denounce what some believe to be anti-Semitic preaching by Nation of Islam leader Louis Farrakhan.

The Reverend Butts has continued to challenge policies he perceives to be detrimental to the African American community. He was a vocal critic of the Democratic and Republican parties during the 1992 national elections, choosing instead to endorse independent candidate Ross Perot. Butts remains active in New York politics, prompting some to predict that he may follow in the political footsteps of former Abyssinian pastor, Sen. Adam Clayton Powell Jr.

Alonford James Robinson, Jr.

See Also

Farrakhan, Louis Abdul; Powell, Adam Clayton, Jr.

Africa

Buyoya, Pierre

(b. November, 24, 1949, Rutovu, Urundi [present-day Burundi]), army major and two-time president of Burundi.

Never content to be just a soldier, Pierre Buyoya has twice seized political power, pledging both times to bring peace and democracy to Burundi. Born into a modest Hima Tutsi family in the southern Bururi province, he received his primary education locally. He then went to Belgium for secondary school, university, and, later, military training. After returning briefly to Burundi in 1975 to command an armored squadron, he received further military training in France, and then joined Burundi's ruling UPRONA party. He was elected to its central committee in 1979. In the mid-1980s he began openly criticizing President Jean-Baptiste Bagaza, a former soldier and fellow Tutsi from Bururi, for his hostility toward the Catholic Church. In September 1987 Buyoya led a coup against Bagaza, charging him with corruption, failed economic policy, and constitutional violations.

Upon assuming the presidency, Buyoya suspended the constitution, released political prisoners, and lifted restrictions on the Catholic Church. He committed his government to healing Burundi's ethnic wounds, but a local conflict escalated and in August 1988 several northern provinces descended into violence, leading to the death of around 20,000 Barundi. Afterward, Buyoya appointed a Hutu prime minister, increased the number of Hutu in the cabinet, and established the Commission on National Unity to investigate the massacres and write a charter on national unity. Under pressure from international donors, he also set Burundi on a five-year path toward democratization. In 1993 elections Melchior Ndadaye defeated Buyoya in the national elections. The successive civilian governments proved weak and ineffective, and were under constant threat from both Hutu and Tutsi militants. Persistent political instability and conflict drew Buyoya back into the political fray. In July 1996 he again led a coup against the elected government, and has since continued to promote negotiations and reconciliation.

Eric Young

See Also

Hutu and Tutsi; Bagaza, Jean-Baptiste.

Africa

Bwiti, a religious cult based in Cameroon, Equatorial Guinea, and Gabon.

The religious cult of Bwiti is both syncretistic (fusing different belief systems) and multiethnic, and seeks to give its followers privileged knowledge of the world. Bwiti operates as a secret society, but unlike many African secret societies, its core members include both men and women. Anthropologists believe that the original religious practices revolved around the *byer*, or ancestral skulls, that were revered by the Fang ethnic group. When European missionaries saw the skulls, they became convinced that the Fang were cannibals, a myth that the Ndowe, the region's middleman merchants, perpetuated to discourage Europeans from venturing inland for trade. European religions and culture eroded Bwiti rituals and myths until the cult reemerged in the region of Cameroon, Equatorial Guinea, and Gabon during the late nineteenth century as a reaction to the destruction of African culture.

Although the Bwiti cult once recognized many gods, today, influenced by Christianity, it recognizes few. One of these is the creator god, known as Mebege or Mwanga, depending on the ethnic group. Although some practices and beliefs vary regionally, Bwiti seeks to create "one heartness" among its followers in order to counteract foreign influences. A carved pillar built over a prominent individual's grave signifies a place of worship, and dance plays an important part in many Bwiti ceremonies. Although forbidden by colonial officials and frowned upon by postindependence governments, Bwiti survives through adaptation and secrecy.

Eric Young

See Also

Dance in Sub-Saharan Africa.

C

Africa

Cabral, Amílcar

(b. September 12, 1924, Bafatá, Portuguese Guinea [now GUINEA-BISSAU]; d. January 20, 1973, Conakry, Guinea), nationalist leader and political philosopher from Guinea-Bissau.

Amílcar Lopes Cabral was born in Portuguese Guinea but automatically received Portuguese citizenship because both of his parents were from the CAPE VERDE Islands. After earning high marks in elementary school, he attended secondary school in the Cape Verde Islands and then, at the age of 21, entered the University of Lisbon in Portugal. He graduated with honors, and in 1950 entered the Portuguese colonial agriculture service and became increasingly active in revolutionary intellectual circles.

Between 1952 and 1954 Cabral conducted the first agricultural survey of Portuguese Guinea. As he gained an extensive knowledge of the land and of popular grievances, he helped increase political awareness among his friends, who were mainly of Cape Verdean descent. Increasingly involved in anti-Portuguese activities, he helped establish a "recreation association" and other quickly banned organizations before his return to Portugal. In Lisbon, and later in ANGOLA, he met revolutionary leaders from Angola and MOZAMBIQUE, including AGOSTINHO NETO, and secretly became involved in their activities while working as an agronomist.

In 1956 Cabral helped found the Partido Africano da Independencia da Guine e Cabo Verde (PAIGC), which organized labor unions to pressure the Portuguese government to provide a timetable for independence. After Portuguese police killed 50 striking dockworkers in Bissau in 1959, Cabral pushed the PAIGC to launch a protracted armed struggle for independence starting in 1963.

Combining Marxism-Leninism, social democracy, republicanism, and a disciplined approach to the study of material production, Cabral's revolutionary thought rested on two basic tenets: (1) those who accept a moral obligation to resist must actively participate; and (2) these personal convictions must grow into a broader conception of moral and social renewal. He advocated a "revolutionary democracy" in which the party would lead the uneducated African peasantry to power through violent struggle. The peasantry, in turn, would elect representative bodies. Cabral's writings also celebrated African culture, a stance that helped him become one of the continent's most renowned nationalist thinkers (*see* NATIONALISM IN AFRICA).

For the ten years between 1963 and 1973, Cabral directed the liberation struggle, serving as secretary general of the PAIGC, a role in which he was increasingly resented for his authoritarian practices. In addition, people of Cape Verdean descent dominated the movement, while members of mainland ethnic groups were largely excluded from power. In 1973 political opponents within the PAIGC assassinated Cabral in Conakry, GUINEA. His half-brother, LUÍS CABRAL, became president of independent Guinea-Bissau in 1974.

Eric Young

SEE ALSO
Conakry, Guinea.

Africa

Cabral, Luís

(b. 1931, Bissau, Portuguese Guinea [now GUINEA-BISSAU]), first president of Guinea-Bissau.

The younger brother of Amílcar Lopes Cabral, Luís de Almeida Cabral was born to Cape Verdean Creole parents in Bissau. After a local education and training as an accountant, Cabral worked for a Portuguese firm before joining with his brother to fight and overthrow Portuguese COLONIAL RULE.

In 1956 Luís and Amílcar Cabral helped found the Partido Africano da Independencia da Guine e Cabo Verde (PAIGC). In 1959 Portuguese colonial authorities killed 50 people in a dock strike that Cabral had helped organize. This led the PAIGC to cancel its policy of nonviolence and forced Cabral's flight to GUINEA. Upon his return in 1961, he helped create and became the secretary-general of the National Union of Guinean Workers (UNTG), which backed the PAIGC. With the advent of warfare later that year, Cabral joined guerrilla forces on the borders of the country and assumed increasing responsibility within the PAIGC over the years. By 1965 Cabral was a member of the PAIGC war council, and, in 1970 he became an executive committee member.

Amílcar Cabral, the leader of the PAIGC, was assassinated in 1973, and Luís assumed the leadership in his brother's place. On September 10, 1974 Guinea-Bissau gained independence and Luís Cabral assumed the presidency. He introduced a state-led socialist development policy and initially espoused democratic principles. His rule became increasingly repressive over time, however, as economic crises, disagreements among members of the PAIGC, corruption, and inefficiency generated unrest. After a 1980 coup successfully ousted Cabral, JOÃO BERNARDO VIEIRA assumed power and placed him under house arrest. Investigators uncovered evidence of mass graves containing the bodies of 500 of Cabral's political opponents. A court sentenced Cabral to death, but international pressure led to his release in 1981. Cabral went into exile in Cuba and later settled in Lisbon.

Eric Young

SEE ALSO
Bissau, Guinea-Bissau; Cabral, Amílcar; Cape Verde.

Latin America and the Caribbean

Cabral, Manuel del

(b. March 7, 1907, Santiago, DOMINICAN REPUBLIC), the most internationally recognized Dominican writer.

For much of his professional life, Manuel del Cabral served as a diplomat under the dictator RAFAEL TRUJILLO, but at the same time produced an extensive list of works published between 1931 and 1987: 28 books of poetry, 6 collections of short stories and prose-poems, 2 novels, a play, and an autobiographical essay, none of which has been translated into English.

The major themes of his work are political and social issues, Dominican national character, metaphysical problems, and erotic love. His political and social poetry has been compared to that of other great Latin American writers such as Pablo Neruda, César Vallejo, and Vicente Huidobro.

Cabral wrote a number of poems about Afro-Caribbean peoples, collected in *Doce poemas negros* (1935) and *Trópico negro* (1942). From the 1920s through the 1940s, artists around the world were taking an interest in things African. During this time Hispanic Caribbean writers like Cabral, Luis Palés Matos in Puerto Rico, and Emilio Ballagas, Ramón Güirao, and Nicolás Guillén in Cuba produced what is called Afro-Antillean, or Negrista, poetry. Much of this poetry employs images of African and Afro-Caribbean culture as well as "African-sounding" words and nontraditional poetic rhythms; it evokes an atmosphere both of sensuality and of ritual. Part of Cabral's poetry about blacks conforms to these aesthetic traits, but some of it uses other literary techniques to denounce the poverty, exploitation, and oppression of Afro-Caribbean peoples. He returned to the black theme in his 1973 novel *El presidente negro*, which imagines world reaction to an African American president of the United States.

Marveta Ryan

See Also
Negrista Poets.

Latin America and the Caribbean

Cabrera, Lydia (b. May 20, 1900, Havana, Cuba; d. September 19, 1991, Miami, Fla.), Cuban writer and cultural anthropologist who played a central role in documenting and promoting an appreciation of Afro-Cuban culture.

Lydia Cabrera is widely considered one of the two most important twentieth-century researchers and writers on Afro-Cuban culture; the other is Fernando Ortíz. Cabrera wrote more than a dozen volumes of investigative work on the subject, including her pioneering *El monte* (1954), subtitled "Notes on the Religion, the Magic, the Superstitions and the Folklore of Creole Negroes and the Cuban People," and *Reglas de congo* (1980), a book on Bantu (known as *congo* in Cuba) rituals. According to Ana María Simo, author of *Lydia Cabrera: An Intimate Portrait*, Cabrera's "is the most important and complete body of work on Afro-Cuban religions" of its time. Cabrera also wrote four volumes of short stories inspired by Afro-Cuban legends and beliefs. Her fiction is rich in metaphor and symbolism and has been compared stylistically with the writings of Spanish poet and playwright Federico García Lorca.

Cabrera was the youngest daughter of Elisa Bilbao Marcaida and Raimundo Cabrera, a noted lawyer, publisher, and social activist. She was raised in an upper-class household in Havana, surrounded by black nursemaids, cooks, and seamstresses. As a child, she was enchanted by the Afro-Cuban tales of her caretakers, a fascination that later influenced her writings and choice of profession. When she was 14, her first stories appeared in her father's well-known literary and political magazine, *Cuba y América*. Yet Cabrera felt stifled by her privileged upbringing, and in 1927 she moved to Paris. During the following decade, she traveled back and forth between Europe and Cuba, where she spent much of her time in the poor, predominantly black neighborhood of Pogolotti. There she made lifelong friendships among the black population, from whom she collected legends and materials later used in her fictional and scholarly writings.

In 1940 Cabrera published *Cuentos negros de Cuba*, 22 fictional stories that explore the beliefs, customs, psychology, and language of Afro-Cubans. Fernando Ortíz described the stories as "a collaboration between Negro folklore and its white translator." The book had already been published to wide acclaim in Paris in 1936, where a fascination with black culture had influenced the works of numerous writers and painters. In Havana the stories met with less success. Although the Afrocubanismo movement of the late 1920s and the 1930s had popularized Afro-Cuban cultural forms in Cuba, some members of the artistic elite believed that Cuban art, literature, and music should remain essentially white and middle-class. They instead found inspiration in European and *guajiro* (Hispanic peasant) culture, which, as Cuban composer Argeliers León notes, served "as a refuge for whites who sought a genre that was at once distinctively Cuban and yet devoid of African-derived elements." Cuba's avant-garde, on the other hand, had begun to minimize the folkloric aspect of Cuban culture in favor of social and aesthetic concerns; the poet Nicolás Guillén, for example, sought to underscore the social problems faced by Cuba's black underclass.

Some literary scholars have compared Cabrera's early fiction with that of the Negrista writers, in particular those who had a tendency to exoticize black culture and perpetuate ethnic stereotypes. Indeed, one eminent critic, Guy Pérez Cisnero, likened her stories to "vulgar snapshots taken in a tourist spot" that fail to capture the depth and complexity of real people. Such assertions, however, remain open to debate. Simo argues that Cabrera's stories reflect "a quiet, dignified familiarity" with Afro-Cuban life, while Seymour Menton, author of *Prose Fiction of the Cuban Revolution*, affirms that Cabrera's *Cuentos negros de Cuba*, as well as her second volume of stories, *Por qué: cuentos negros de Cuba* (1948), "constitute, along with Nicolás Guillén's poetry, the finest examples of Afro-Cuban literature." Cabrera herself described her fiction as "a reencounter with the world of fantasy of my early childhood."

Aware of the increasing likelihood of war in Europe, Cabrera returned to Cuba in 1938. Throughout the next four decades, she focused primarily on her anthropological research, a pursuit that took her into the black communities of the western provinces of Havana and Matanzas. In 1954 she established herself as a major intellectual figure with the publication of her book *El monte*, a meticulously researched study of Afro-Cuban religious beliefs, practices, deities, and folk medicine. In the following year, she became a consultant to Cuba's Insituto Nacional de Cultura (National Institute of Culture). During her tenure there she published three important works on Afro-Cuban culture: *Refranes de negros viejos* (1955), a book of Afro-Cuban proverbs; *Anagó: vocabulario Lucumí* (1957), a vocabulary of the Yoruba language spoken in Cuba; and *La sociedad secreta Abakuá* (1958), a collection of legends and tales told in the secret all-male society Abakuá.

Following the Cuban Revolution of 1959, Cabrera sought exile in Miami, Florida. Shortly thereafter, her house in Cuba burned to the ground under mysterious circumstances. Deprived of her books and research, she earned a living painting Afro-Cuban motifs on stones until 1970, the year in which she reestablished her writing career with the publication of *Otan Iyebiye: Las Piedras Preciosas*, a study of the ritual significance of precious stones. In 1977 her work was the focus of the Congress of Afro-American Literature, organized by Florida International University. Between 1970 and her death in 1991, she produced nine additional anthropological works as well as three collections of short stories, including *Ayapá – cuentos de Jicotea* (1971), considered by Simo to be "perhaps the most 'African' of her books."

Cabrera's books are still widely referenced by scholars today. According to the authors of *Cuban Consciousness in Literature: 1923-1974*, "few authors have had the influence that [Cabrera] has had on the [representation] of the Negro's identity and his incorporation into Cuban culture as an important and integral part of it."

Roanne Edwards

See Also
Ortiz, Fernando; Cuba; Abakuás.

Africa

Cacheu, Guinea-Bissau, the historic commercial center of present-day Guinea-Bissau.

Shortly after the Portuguese first reached the Cacheu River in 1446, *lançados* – Portuguese outcasts often married to African women – settled 20 km (12 mi) upriver on the south bank, in the Cacanda region inhabited by Papei, Manjaco, and other peoples. In the sixteenth and seventeenth centuries Cacheu became a center for the trade in slaves from Kaabu and other areas, but relations among the Portuguese, lançados, and Africans were often difficult. Eventually the Portuguese fortified the settlement, but it remained weak, underfunded, manned by undisciplined soldiers, and subject to frequent raids from nearby African groups. Foreign residents in segregated areas paid tribute to the Cacanda king for the right to stay, and ships anchoring at Cacheu paid him duties.

In the late 1600s European Portuguese sought to control Cacheu and dominate the slave trade, but both lançados and local Africans resisted. Shortly thereafter Cacheu's importance diminished when the slave trade shifted south and the Portuguese shifted their focus to Bissau. Cacheu's economy declined further beginning in the 1880s, when a series of punitive colonial "pacification" campaigns and counterattacks by Africans drove foreign traders away. In 1914 the Portuguese finally crushed all resistance, though by this time the town had become a sleepy backwater. Cacheu's prospects have improved with the recent discovery of phosphate deposits in the area.

Eric Young

See Also

Bissau, Guinea-Bissau; Transatlantic Slave Trade; Kaabu, Early Kingdom of.

Latin America and the Caribbean

Cacos, peasant rebels from northern Haiti who emerged in the 1860s and later led a revolt against United States occupation of the island (1915-1934).

After the downfall of Haitian president Jean-Pierre Boyer in 1843, the peasants of the south revolted and were named "piquets," because they carried a wooden pole, called a "pick," as a weapon. Peasants in the north followed their example in the 1860s. They became known as the Cacos movement. It is said that the term *Cacos* comes from the name of a small bird of prey. Others trace it to the name of a species of Haitian red ants that have a bad sting.

The Cacos movement appeared for the first time during the civil war of 1868. The rebellious peasants fought against President Sylvain Salnave in 1870. The Cacos proved themselves formidable fighters and instrumental to Salnave's overthrow. The movement was based in the northern part of the republic in an area comprising the towns of Vallieres, Capotilles, and Mont-Organise.

After Salnave's overthrow, the movement intermittently emerged as a political force. The Cacos played a role in the civil war of 1888-1889, which put the northerner Florvil Hyppolite into power and established the political supremacy of the northerners for some 30 years. For a time, then, the movement was dormant.

President Pierre Nord-Alexis (1902-1908) feared that its reactivation by politicians would lead to total chaos and the loss of Haitian independence to foreign military intervention. However, the Haitian statesman Cincinnatus Leconte decided to rally the Cacos to oust President Antoine Simon in 1911. Subsequently the Cacos remained central to Haitian political life and were involved in the ouster of four Haitian presidents between January 1914 and July 1915.

Following the United States occupation of the island on July 28, 1915, the Cacos fought against the Americans for a couple of weeks but were defeated. At the Quartier Morin they signed a cease-fire agreement. Their potential, however, was not destroyed, and in 1918 Charlemagne Péralte led their insurrection to drive out the American forces and their Haitian surrogates. Péralte tapped a nationalist sentiment enflamed by a number of policies implemented under the U.S. occupation. Among the most egregious was the reinstitution of the corvée, a system of forced labor into which thousands of Haitian men were drafted.

The insurrection gained a substantial popular following. Péralte formed a peasant army numbering several thousand. After a bloody war of two years, led by Péralte until his assassination in 1919, then by Benoît Batraville, the U.S. forces defeated the uprising.

The Americans had used all means to crush the Cacos, including aviation, bombing, heavy weaponry, and indiscriminate killings of the civilian populations. The key device the U.S. forces used to exterminate the Cacos was the establishment of the internment camp at Chabert in the Cacos zone. Operated under American management and under an American flag, it was officially a "labor camp." An estimated 5000 Cacos were "terminated" in Chabert. After their defeat by U.S. forces, the Cacos disappeared from the Haitian political scene forever (*see* Haiti).

Georges Michel

See Also

Péralte, Charlemagne Masséna.

Latin America and the Caribbean

Cafundó, a village in southeastern Brazil where the African language of former slaves has survived since the nineteenth century. The continued existence of Cafundó, which is also the name for the language spoken by Cafundistas, is significant because it was only "discovered" in 1978 and because it provides evidence of Brazil's African roots.

Cafundó is a rural community outside the heavily urbanized São Paulo metropolitan area, about 20 km (12 mi) from the city of Sorocaba. During the 1980s and 1990s only about 70 people lived in the hamlet of ten or so mud-and-straw houses. The people of Cafundó mostly cultivate rice, beans, and corn, which they supplement through hunting or working as agricultural laborers on nearby large farms.

According to the oral history of Cafundó, the people moved onto land in the area in the mid-1860s, when a local slave owner willed to two of his African slaves, Antonia and Ifigênia, their freedom as well as several hectares of land. Although all of Cafundó's present-day inhabitants claim descent from Antonia and Ifigênia, the inhabitants are split into two groups bearing little resemblance to one another. One group is distinctly Afro-Brazilian, while the other appears to be *caboclo*, a term used to describe the mixture of Europeans and natives.

Scholars have determined that the Cafundó language is indisputably of African origin, though its exact source has yet to be located. Most likely it is a member of the Bantu language family, with whom it shares syntactical and lexical similarities. Bantu languages have been spoken from equatorial to southern Africa for centuries; the Bantu region was raided and eventually colonized by Portugal for extraction of slaves and other resources. Nevertheless, Cafundó's extremely compact vocabulary – its lexicon contains approximately 200 words, primarily nouns of Bantu origin and 15 verbs – makes it difficult to pinpoint the language's origin.

It is not clear how the language survived intact in Brazil, where other African languages are no longer used in daily life (with the significant exception of Yoruba, called Nagô in Brazil, which is used as a sacred and specialized language of the Candomblé religion). Cafundó oral tradition attributes the language's survival to an ancestor named Tio Alexandre, who preserved the language for years while enslaved by the owner of Antonia and Ifigênia. Apparently the language was the slaves' special means of communication with one another on the plantation, and they found it useful to continue using it secretly long after they were freed. Today, as then, the inhabitants of Cafundó are also fluent in Portuguese, the official language of Brazil.

Apart from its distinctly African language, most Cafundó culture blends African and Brazilian roots. As one researcher has noted, "Despite the attention brought to it for being an African relic, Cafundó is properly speaking a black *caipira* (or peasant) culture, that is, one made up of various syncretic elements common to rural communities throughout the São Paulo region." For example, the Cafundó religion melds Roman Catholic and Afro-Brazilian rites, and the housing is like that of many other communities in rural Brazil.

Cafundó's continuing existence has also raised several questions about the nature of modernization and development in Brazil. Shortly after the community's "discovery," its inhabitants were involved in a violent land dispute with a local large landowner, who claimed part of the community's land. In addition, the community's location near a major metropolitan area has led some to speculate as to whether the community might be, in fact, partially the product of modernization and social change in southeastern Brazil. Instead of being the result of a "benevolent" donation of land by a former master to two of his slaves, the community's formation might have been part of a larger process in which ex-slaves were forced to become economically dependent peasants, indebted to their former owners. In this sense, Cafundó can be seen not as a folkloristic "living museum," but as a community deeply shaped, and still responsive to, Brazil's continuing economic and social transformation. Cafundó thus is significant not only as a rich source for the reevaluation of Brazil's African heritage, but also as an example of the social and economic challenges still confronting Brazil's black population.

See Also
Bantu: Dispersion and Settlement; Complexities of Ethnic and Racial Terminology in Latin America and the Caribbean.

Africa

Caillié, René-Auguste

(b. November 19, 1799, Mauzé, France; d. 1838, La Badeire, France), the first European explorer to visit Tombouctou (Timbuktu) and survive.

In 1825 the Paris Société de Géographie offered a prize of 10,000 francs to the first person to visit the legendary city of Tombouctou (Timbuktu) and return with a description of it; with this challenge they made official an undeclared competition among European explorers that had already claimed the lives of more than 20 men. Since 1788 explorers had been trying to reach the Sahelian market town, rumored to be the richest in Africa but also one of the most heavily guarded. Only one European, the Scottish explorer Maj. Alexander Gordon Laing, had yet entered the fabled city, but he was murdered only days after leaving. In 1827, however, French explorer René-Auguste Caillié embarked on a journey to Tombouctou that would at last win the prize.

Inspired by the adventures of Daniel Defoe's *Robinson Crusoe*, Caillié had already made two voyages to West Africa and the Caribbean before embarking for Tombouctou. In 1824 he sailed from France to the Senegambia region, where he lived for three years among local people, learning Arabic and Islamic traditions. Disguised as an Arab, Caillié left alone for Tombouctou in April 1827. He was beset with difficulties and sickness, and it took him almost a year to reach the city, but he was then admitted without a problem. What he saw, however, proved extremely disappointing; expecting a metropolis as prosperous and majestic as Djenné, he found Tombouctou to be nothing more than "a mass of ill-looking houses, built of earth." He left after two weeks and joined a trans-Saharan caravan traveling to Tangier, Morocco. From there Caillié departed for France, where after some dispute, he claimed the prize in 1829. He published an account of his trip a year later.

Elizabeth Heath

See Also
Djenné-Djeno, Mali; Sahara Desert; Tombouctou, Mali.

Africa

Cairo, Egypt, the capital of Egypt and one of the largest cities in Africa.

Cairo is the industrial, commercial, cultural, and administrative center of Egypt and the Arab League headquarters. Home to a number of universities and many Arabic-language publishing houses, Cairo is considered by many people to be the cultural capital of the Arabic-speaking world. It occupies approximately 453 sq km (about 175 sq mi) on both banks of the Nile River, and includes several of the river's islands. Its architecture, a mixture of the ancient and the modern, reflects its long and rich history.

Although Cairo proper was founded in 969 C.E., the area has been a center of civilization for roughly 5000 years. The ancient Egyptian capital of Memphis was founded in the fourth millennium B.C.E., approximately 25 km (about 14 mi) south of modern Cairo. Around 2500 B.C.E., construction began on a new Egyptian capital, which later was named Heliopolis by the Greeks, a short distance to the north, although this city declined in importance over the centuries. The Romans established a military stronghold and commercial center known as Babylon-in-Egypt in what is now Cairo's Misr al-Qadimah quarter.

The invasion of Egypt by Islamic Arabs in 641 C.E. sparked the foundation of the city that has become Cairo. The Arab city, known as al-Fustat (roughly, "tent city"), grew from the collection of tents pitched by the Arab army that was besieging Babylon-in-Egypt. Until the Arab invasion, Alexandria had served as Egypt's capital, but the Arabs established their capital at al-Fustat. In 969 the Fatimids, an Islamic dynasty from modern Tunisia, founded a new capital, al-Qahirah (Cairo). Cairo existed alongside al-Fustat until 1168, when the Fatimids attempted to repel an attack by Christian crusaders by burning al-Fustat. The crusaders were eventually defeated by a Syrian army led by Saladin, who later took control and founded the Ayyubid Dynasty in Cairo.

Meanwhile, Cairo had become the center of Egyptian economic, political, and cultural life. In the thirteenth century, the city became the capital of the Mamluks. During their rule the city achieved its greatest prosperity. Indeed, Cairo's grandeur exceeded that of any other city in Africa, Europe, or western Asia. The city became the center of the lucrative East-West spice trade, and was the home of the renowned al-Azhar University. The city began to decline after the bubonic plague devastated its population in 1348. Its central economic role disappeared when Portuguese explorer Vasco da Gama opened the route from Europe to the Indian Ocean ending Cairo's spice trade monopoly.

The Turks of the Ottoman empire seized the weakened Cairo in 1517 and made the city a provincial capital in its vast empire. Ottoman rule lasted until Napoleon briefly took the city for France in 1798. The Turks returned three years later and in 1805 appointed Muhammad Ali as the pasha. Muhammad Ali founded a dynasty that ruled Egypt, albeit under increasing British colonial domination. The British occupied Egypt beginning in the 1880s and declared it a protectorate in 1919. Ali's descendants ruled as puppets under British occupation until 1952, when a coup led by Gamal Abdel Nasser established the Egyptian republic, with Cairo as its capital.

Today Cairo remains the commercial and industrial center of Egypt. The city has numerous historical and cultural sites to which tourists have been drawn for centuries, including the Blue Mosque, the Museum of Islamic Arts, the Egyptian Museum (including the Tutankhamen collection), the Coptic Museum, the Al Gawhara Palace Museum, and – at nearby Giza – the Great Pyramids and Sphinx. The Citadel, begun by emperor Saladin in 1176, lies in east Cairo, also the site of the Muhammad Ali Mosque.

Cairo continues to grow rapidly, with an estimated population approaching 14 million (the official figure is closer to 7 million). Unemployment, pollution, and a shortage of decent housing pose numerous problems. Many of Cairo's citizens are rural migrants; they have few job skills and little prospect of regular employment. Their growing numbers strain the city's overburdened infrastructure. In recent years leaking sewer lines have caused the water table to rise in the city. The waterlogged ground has brought down historical buildings that had been constructed of dried mud bricks. Thus Cairo today presents contradictory images of both squalor and grandeur.

Robert Fay

See Also
Portugal; Tourism in Africa; Mamluk State; Alexandria, Egypt.

North America

Cakewalk, The, an African American dance that was appropriated by the white cultural mainstream it lampooned.

As a product of black folk culture, the cakewalk remains obscure in origin. Perhaps with African roots, it developed on plantations sometime before the Civil War, as slaves imitated the Grand March that concluded the cotillions and fancy balls given by whites. Although plantation owners often mistook the dance for childlike play, the cakewalk in fact had a satirical purpose. Promenading in pairs, dancers crossed their arms, arched their backs, threw back their heads, and strutted with exaggerated kicks. The cakewalk took its name from the cake that was awarded – by the judgment of a boisterous audience – to the couple with the most flair.

In the 1880s and 1890s white black-faced minstrels often ended stage shows with the cakewalk, or "peregrination for the pastry." Thus whites imitated blacks imitating whites, a cultural curiosity that only grew more complex when African Americans began imitating white MINSTRELSY.

With the advent of RAGTIME in the 1890s, the cakewalk became a national craze among both blacks and whites. The high-stepping exuberance of the cakewalk meshed perfectly with the march-based yet heavily syncopated new music. Cakewalking contests soon offered prizes bigger than cake, and ragtime pianists, as well as nimble dancers, vied for recognition. Although the cakewalk waned in popularity by the 1920s, its influence was felt in many subsequent dance trends.

Eric Bennett

See Also

Civil War, American.

At the height of its popularity between 1910 and 1920, the cakewalk was a high-strutting dance that African Americans created to mock the final promenade of whites' fancy balls. *Photographs and Prints Division, Schomburg Center for Research in Black Culture, The New York Public Library, Astor, Lenox and Tilden Foundation*

Latin America and the Caribbean

Caldas Barbosa, Domingos

(b. 1740, Rio de Janeiro, Brazil; d. 1800, Portugal), Afro-Brazilian poet and composer who served at the royal court of Dona Maria I in Portugal.

Domingos Caldas Barbosa was born in Rio de Janeiro to a white father, Antonio de Caldas Barbosa, and a black mother whose identity remains unknown. From an early age Caldas received a Jesuit education. He showed a talent for poetry and musical composition.

While still a young man, Caldas was drafted into the military and sent to serve in the Portuguese colony of Sacramento on the Rio de la Plata. Subsequently he obtained his discharge, returned home to Brazil, then boarded a ship bound for Portugal. He arrived in Lisbon in 1763 and shortly thereafter enrolled at the University of Coimbra.

It is unclear at what point Caldas's university studies were discontinued, but author Jane M. Malinoff asserts that the young poet took leave shortly after learning of his father's death. Unable to independently support the cost of his education, Caldas recalled his early ambitions and began searching for a position as a court poet.

The young poet's efforts came to fruition in 1783 when José de Vasconcelos e Sousa, the count of Pombiero, agreed to sponsor him. Caldas soon went to live in the count's household at the palace of Bemposta. From 1790 to 1795 Caldas was president of the Nova Arcádia, a literary group that met weekly at Count Sousa's residence.

The second important stage in Caldas's literary career came in 1798, when he published the first volume of *Viola de Lereno*, a collection of love songs that he completed in 1826. His eventual celebrity status was due largely to the popular musical performances of these compositions as *modinhas* or *lundús* (African-based musical forms) to the accompaniment of his viola. Later, in the hands of early-twentieth-century *choro* musicians, Caldas's songs are thought to have inspired the development of SAMBA.

Scholars Oneyda Alvarenga and Mozart de Araujo have argued that Caldas may have been the originator of the mondinha genre. Whether or not that is true, it is certain that he was instrumental in its popularization. Modernist poet Manuel Bandeira maintains that Caldas was the first Brazilian poet to employ a uniquely Brazilian voice. Malinoff traces this feature of Caldas's work to his frequent use of colloquial Brazilian Portuguese and his experimentation with Afro-Brazilian speech patterns and rhythms.

After a long and distinguished career as a poet and composer in Lisbon's aristocratic society, Caldas died in Portugal in 1800. In addition to the songs for which he became famous, he wrote numerous odes, several long poems, an opera libretto, and one epithalamium (nuptial song).

Joy Elizondo

See Also

Rio de Janeiro, Brazil.

North America

Calloway, Cabell (Cab)

(b. December 25, 1907, Rochester, N.Y.; d. November 18, 1994, Hosckessin, Del.), African American singer and bandleader famed for his showmanship and skill at jive.

Cab Calloway was the son of a lawyer who had expected his son to follow in his footsteps. But when Calloway was in his teens he left Baltimore – where his family had moved when he was six – to join an older sister in Chicago. She arranged his first job as a performer, in a vocal harmony quartet. In 1925, the year that Calloway cited as the start of his career, he became the drummer in the Sunset Orchestra; two years later he organized his own band, giving up the drums to focus on singing.

Around 1927 Calloway brought his band, the Alabamians, to New York City for a gig at Harlem's famed SAVOY BALLROOM, but he found little success and soon disbanded the group. After winning a role in *Connie's Hot Chocolates*, an all-black Broadway revue, Calloway gained acclaim for his rendition of Fats Waller's "Ain't Misbehavin'." On the strength of that performance, Irving Mills – Duke Ellington's manager – urged Calloway to return to bandleading, and in 1929 he took over a band, originally from St. Louis, known as the Missourians. In 1930 Calloway's group replaced Ellington's at New York's legendary COTTON CLUB.

It was at the Cotton Club that Calloway wrote and introduced "Minnie the Moocher" (1931), a song that would be forever linked to him. The song combined scat-singing with nonsense syllables and lyrics freighted with the argot of drug use, recounting how Minnie and her cocaine-using lover, Smokey Joe, went to Chinatown, where "he showed her how to kick the gong around" – slang for opium smoking. Calloway became known as a master of jive, the term then applied to African American slang (particularly that used by blacks in the entertainment industry). He wrote *The Hepster's Dictionary* (1938), which sold 2 million copies and became the New York Public Library's standard reference work on the subject.

While at the Cotton Club, Calloway perfected his showmanship, which extended beyond singing to include dancing and comedy. He was the first singer after Louis Armstrong to emphasize scat singing. "Minnie the Moocher," for example, featured the memorable call-and-response scat chorus – "Hi de hi de hi de ho." Like Armstrong, he first began using nonsense syllables after forgetting a song's lyrics. Calloway's comic routines, jive patter, and novelty songs often distracted attention from his vocal talents, though his astonishing range encompassed bass, baritone, and tenor; musicologist Gunther Schuller called Calloway the "most unusually and broadly gifted male singer of the thirties."

Calloway maintained the highest standard of musicianship and fronted one of the greatest of the big bands of the 1930s, featuring trumpeters Dizzy Gillespie, Doc Cheatham, and Jonah Jones; saxophonist Chu Berry; drummer Cozy Cole; and bass player Milt Hinton. Musicians recognized, as Gillespie recalled in his autobiography, that playing with Calloway "was the best job that you could possibly have." Nevertheless, Gillespie noted that Calloway "wasn't interested in developing... musicians," and Hinton complained of the complacency that he found in the Calloway band. On the other hand, despite his success – and unlike Louis Armstrong, his only counterpart as a black entertainer – Calloway consistently featured his supporting musicians. Although three-minute, 78-rpm records restricted the length of instrumental solos in his recordings, in live performances Calloway shared the spotlight generously.

During the 1940s Calloway appeared in several Hollywood films, most memorably *Stormy Weather* (1943), in which he was featured, resplendent in a white zoot suit, with his band. In the 1950s he had roles in several Broadway productions and won acclaim for his portrayal of Sportin' Life in *Porgy and Bess*, a role that George Gershwin reportedly created with Calloway in mind. In 1980 Calloway's performance in *The Blues Brothers* gained him a worldwide audience and renewed prominence, but from the 1920s to the 1990s he kept up a steady performing schedule. Interviewed for a 1991 article in *Contemporary Musicians*, Calloway scoffed at the notion that he might have musical heroes. "My heroes are the notes, man. The music itself," he declared. "You understand what I'm saying? I love the music. The music is my hero."

James Clyde Sellman

See Also
Armstrong, Louis ("Satchmo"); Berry, Leon Brown ("Chu"); Black Vernacular English; Chicago, Illinois; Gillespie, John Birks ("Dizzy"); Harlem, New York; Ellington, Edward Kennedy ("Duke"); New York, New York; Waller, Thomas Wright ("Fats"); Film, Blacks in American.

North America

Calloway, Nathaniel Oglesby

(b. October 10, 1907, Tuskegee, Ala.; d. December 3, 1979, Madison, Wis.), African American doctor, chemist, and civic leader.

Nathaniel Calloway was a man of many talents. He started his career as a chemist, graduating from Iowa State University (then College) in 1930 and earning his Ph.D. in 1933. After publishing influential research and teaching at both Tuskegee Institute and Fisk University, Calloway decided to enter medical school. In 1940 he enrolled at the University of Chicago, but, denied the opportunity to treat white patients, he transferred to the University of Illinois, from which he received his M.D. in 1943.

After World War II – during which he conducted research on recuperation theories – Calloway worked at Provident Hospital in Chicago, Illinois, ultimately becoming its director. In 1949 he founded an all-black group practice, and throughout the next 15 years he combined his medical work with civil rights activism. From 1955 to 1960 he served as president of the Chicago branch of the National Urban League. When his work took him to Wisconsin (where he headed a Veterans' Administration Hospital and served as a lecturer at the University of Wisconsin), he became president of the Madison branch of the National Association for the Advancement of Colored People.

Calloway was also a successful farmer. His purchase in 1955 of a 480-acre ranch in southern Wisconsin was the culmination, he said, of a childhood dream. Over the following two decades, Calloway and his family turned the land into a wildlife preserve and nature park, raising and tending buffalo, elk, and rare species of deer. Survived by his wife and seven children, Calloway died in 1979.

Kate Tuttle

Latin America and the Caribbean

Calypso, **the Carnival music of Trinidad that first appeared in the early twentieth century; characterized by simple melodies, infectious rhythms, and topical lyrics and often played by Trinidad's distinctive steel-drum bands.**

Most calypso music is created for Trinidad's extended Carnival. Carnival season commences soon after Christmas and reaches its climax on Carnival Tuesday, the day before Ash Wednesday and the beginning of Lent. During the nineteenth century, calypso music evolved out of earlier musical forms that reflect the island's complex cultural heritage.

Nineteenth-century Carnival music featured a variety of song types; particularly prominent were *belairs*, or traditional songs with lyrics in French Creole, and *kalindas*, which apparently originated in Angola or the Democratic Republic of the Congo. Certain districts of the Port of Spain made extensive use of African religious music, including songs and rhythms from Yoruba Shango and Dahomean *rada*. These African musical traditions in turn influenced Trinidadian street and Carnival music. For example, Shango rhythms can be heard in the music of steel drum bands in contemporary Trinidad and Tobago.

During the late nineteenth century, Trinidad's middle class took an increased interest in Carnival. Their involvement brought various changes, the most important of which, in musical terms, was to substitute English for French Creole. During the 1920s singing contests were held in "calypso tents"; these contests eventually became national competitions to crown a calypso monarch. Carnival ensembles varied widely in the early twentieth century. During the 1920s Venezuelan-style string bands came into fashion among the well-to-do. In the following decade American jazz band instrumentation – with trumpets, saxophones, and trombones – became popular. In 1934 two major calypsonians, Atilla the Hun (Raymond Quevedo) and the Roaring Lion (Hubert Charles, now known as Raphael do Leon), journeyed to New York City to record for the American record labels Decca and American Recording Company. These and subsequent recordings before World War II inspired a Depression-era calypso boom in the United States.

Carnival was banned on the island during World War II, but peacetime brought its welcome return. A new instrument was added to Carnival music in the mid-1940s – the steel drum, known in Trinidad as a pan and fabricated out of the oil-rich island's abundant 55-gallon oil drums. In 1950-1951 steel orchestras made their first recordings, and TASPO (Trinidad All Star Percussion Orchestra) completed an influential tour of England and France. Singer Harry Belafonte's best-selling album *Calypso* (1956) also brought the music worldwide recognition. By the late twentieth century, calypso music and steel orchestras were, for most non-Trinidadians, virtually one and the same.

Over the years Trinidad's calypso music has varied widely, in lyrics as well as instrumentation. Carnival music lyrics shifted from French Creole to British English to a Trinidadian Creole. Calypso songs often emphasize the enjoyment of Carnival, drinking, and sensuality, but calypso music also encompasses many topical songs, sometimes parodying national figures or political developments.

Calypso musicians often perform under colorful stage names, such as Lord Executor (Philip Garcia); Mighty Sparrow (Francisco Slinger); Lord Kitchener (Aldwin Roberts); Chalkdust (Hollis Liverpool), who is a schoolteacher; and the six-foot-four-inch Lord Shorty (Garfield Blackman).

In the 1970s Lord Shorty was responsible for the development of SOCA, which transformed calypso into modern dance music through the use of new rhythms and electronic instruments. Soca deemphasizes the role of lyrics, and though this is a development that many established calypsonians deplore, it has attracted a young audience that had displayed little interest in traditional calypso music.

James Clyde Sellman

SEE ALSO
Belafonte, Harold George (Harry); Great Depression.

North America

Cambridge, Godfrey MacArthur (b. February 26, 1933, New York, N.Y.; d. November 29, 1976, Hollywood, Calif.), comedian and award-winning stage and screen actor.

Born in HARLEM, NEW YORK, to Sarah and Alexander Cambridge, Godfrey Cambridge had an active career in theater, film, and stand-up comedy. He won an Obie award for his role in the off-Broadway play *The Blacks* (1961), and he was nominated for a Tony for his performance in *Purlie Victorious* (1962).

Cambridge's success on stage led to several television appearances and then to leading roles in films, including *Watermelon Man* (1970) and *Cotton Comes to Harlem* (1970). He was active in the CIVIL RIGHTS MOVEMENT, performing at rallies and organizing blacks in the entertainment industry. His compulsive eating problem was a factor in his death.

SEE ALSO
Film, Blacks in American.

Africa

Camel, a domesticated animal uniquely suited for desert transport.

The species of camel found in Africa is the single-humped Middle Eastern, or dromedary, camel, classified as *Camelus dromedarius*. Called Ships of the Desert, dromedary camels stand approximately 2 m (about 6.5 ft) tall at the shoulder and weigh approximately 700 kgs (about 1545 lb). Humans domesticated the intelligent and docile dromedary camel before 3000 B.C.E., but it was not until at least the seventh century that they were used widely in Egypt. For the next several centuries, camels were vital to trade between North Africa and the ancient savanna empires of GHANA, MALI, and Songhai because wheeled carts could not cross the SAHARA DESERT. The dromedary camel remains important to the nomads of the Sahara Desert, who use them both for transportation and as pack animals, and also for their milk, meat, hide, hair (for wool), and dried manure (for fuel).

Specially adapted to desert conditions, camels have small, hairy ears, two rows of eyelashes, and closing nostrils to keep out sand and dust. They have two coats: a hairy outer coat and a dense undercoat, which insulates them against desert heat during the day and cold during the night and in winter. Camels store fat in their humps, and in times of scarcity, can use this fat for sustenance or to produce water through oxidization. Camels can go several days without eating or drinking. They can lose as much as 25 percent of their body weight without ill effects because they can replace this lost weight by drinking up to 100 liters (about 25 gallons) of water in minutes. In addition, their mouths are specially adapted to eating nutrient-poor foods that other animals cannot eat, such as the thorns from acacia trees.

Robert Fay

SEE ALSO
Pastoralism; Songhai Empire.

Africa

Cameroon, African country on the Gulf of Guinea, bordered by NIGERIA, CHAD, Central African Republic, REPUBLIC OF THE CONGO, GABON, and Equatorial Guinea.

Cameroon, the country where Central and West Africa meet, is in many ways a microcosm of the continent. Resource-rich and ecologically diverse, the mountainous country is home to more than 250 ethnic groups. For centuries, the peoples of Cameroon experienced particularly *regional* histories, shaped in the south by the TRANSATLANTIC SLAVE TRADE and the Christian missionary presence, and in the north by the trans-Saharan slave trade, Islam, and neighboring savanna empires. During most of the colonial period, two different European powers controlled the country's east and west. Yet unlike much of the rest of postcolonial Africa, Cameroon has forged a strong sense of nationhood while maintaining relative economic and political stability. Still, Cameroon's state remains far from democratic, and its future stability is far from certain.

EARLY HISTORY

The first inhabitants of what is now Cameroon were various hunter-gatherer "pygmies" such as the Baka, who lived in the area in small, nomadic communities as much as 50,000 years ago. Evidence suggests that Bantu-speakers originated in present-day eastern Nigeria and western Cameroon well before the Early Iron Age, and eventually dispersed across Central, East, and southern Africa, taking with them agriculture, iron working, and unique pottery styles (*see* BANTU: DISPERSION AND SETTLEMENT). The Nok people, who lived near the Benue River from around 200 B.C.E. to the fourth century C.E., left rich archaeological evidence of their crafts.

Early farmers found fertile soil on the slopes of the volcanic mountain range that runs north from the coast, and the many rivers of the region supplied fish. The southern forested area, where agrarian peoples lived in small, patrilineal villages that were typically governed locally by chiefs and councils of elders, saw the gradual emergence of many ethnic groups, including the Bakweri, Duala, and FANG. In the grasslands and plateaus to the north and west, mostly dynasties developed, such as Tikar, Bamenda, Bamum, and BAMILÉKÉ. Cultivating yams and bananas, they developed extensive trade networks and practiced metal working, particularly in bronze.

Historians believe that the first foreigner to visit the area was a Carthaginian explorer named Hanno, who recorded sighting the volcanic MOUNT CAMEROON around 500 B.C.E. In the centuries after his arrival, trade caravans carried gold, salt, and especially slaves from northern Cameroon across the SAHARA DESERT to North Africa. Scholars estimate that as many as 10,000 slaves crossed the desert annually, many of them coming from present-day Cameroon. The trans-Saharan slave trade made some societies wealthy; between the tenth and fifteenth centuries, for example, the Sao kingdom flourished in the northern Chari delta, producing works of pottery, bronze, and copper.

IMPERIALISM AND THE TRANSATLANTIC SLAVE TRADE

Although commerce brought Islamic and Arab influences to northern Cameroon as early as the tenth century, the sixteenth-century invasion of the Massa people and the subsequent rise of the Kotoko kingdom broadened the Islamic presence. So too did the immigration of the FULANI people, whose slave-raiding practices caused northerners such as the Bali to flee south into the central highlands. In the 1800s groups from the center, such as the Fang and Beti, fled toward the coast, where they increasingly came into contact with Europeans.

In 1472 the Portuguese sailor Fernando Pó landed on the nearby island of Mbini, from which he presumably sighted the mainland, but not until some years later did Portuguese explorers sail into the estuaries. There they found swarms of prawns, and accordingly named the area Rio dos Camarões, or River of Prawns, which the British later Anglicized to Cameroons.

By the sixteenth century Cameroon had become a major source of slaves for the New World. African middlemen, many of them from the Bimbia and Duala ethnic

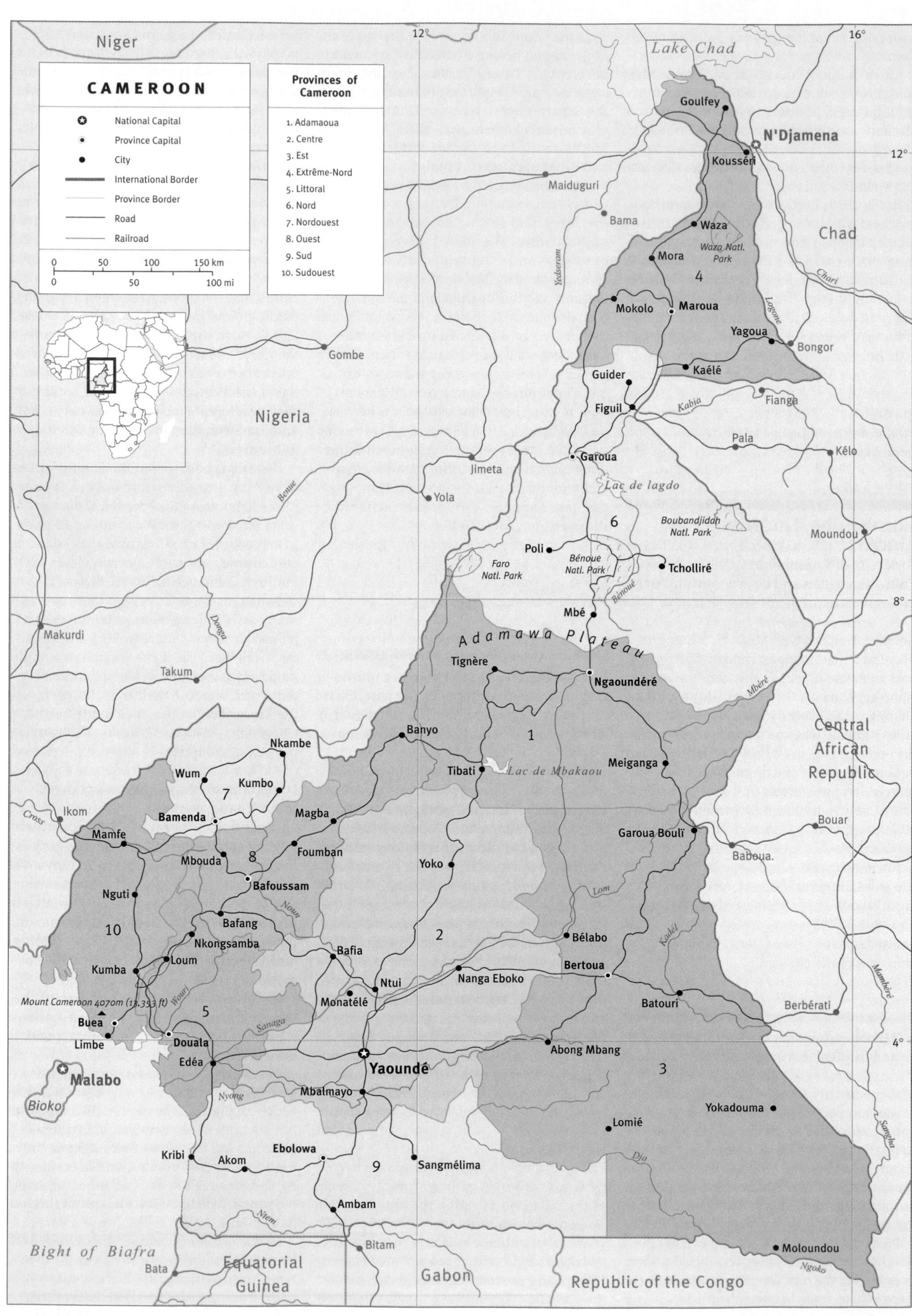
CAMEROON
National Capital
Province Capital
City
International Border
Province Border
Road
Railroad
0 50 100 150 km
0 50 100 mi
Provinces of Cameroon
1. Adamaoua
2. Centre
3. Est
4. Extrême-Nord
5. Littoral
6. Nord
7. Nordouest
8. Ouest
9. Sud
10. Sudouest
Niger
Nigeria
Chad
Central African Republic
Equatorial Guinea
Gabon
Republic of the Congo
Lake Chad
N'Djamena
Goulfey
Kousséri
Maiduguri
Bama
Waza
Waza Natl. Park
Mora
Mokolo
Maroua
Yagoua
Bongor
Kaélé
Guider
Figuil
Fianga
Pala
Kélo
Garoua
Jimeta
Yola
Gombe
Lac de lagdo
Boubandjidah Natl. Park
Moundou
Poli
Bénoue Natl. Park
Faro Natl. Park
Tcholliré
Mbé
Adamawa Plateau
Tignère
Ngaoundéré
Makurdi
Takum
Banyo
Tibati
Lac de Mbakaou
Meiganga
Nkambe
Wum
Kumbo
Ikom
Bamenda
Mamfe
Magba
Mbouda
Foumban
Bafoussam
Garoua Boulï
Bouar
Baboua.
Yoko
Nguti
Bafang
Nkongsamba
Loum
Kumba
Bafia
Bélabo
Bertoua
Nanga Eboko
Ntui
Monatélé
Batouri
Berbérati
Mount Cameroon 4070m (13,353 ft)
Buea
Limbe
Douala
Edéa
Yaoundé
Abong Mbang
Malabo
Bioko
Mbalmayo
Yokadouma
Lomié
Kribi
Akom
Ebolowa
Sangmélima
Ambam
Bitam
Bight of Biafra
Bata
Moloundou
Benue
Donga
Cross
Noun
Wouri
Sanaga
Nyong
Ntem
Lom
Kadeï
Mbéré
Logone
Chari
Kabia
Yedseram
Bénoué
Dja
Ngoko
Sangha
Mambéré
12°
16°
8°
4°

groups, transported slaves captured in the interior to the coast, where they were shipped to Calabar, the closest European settlement and slave-trading center. In exchange, these middlemen received cloth, liquor, firearms, and other manufactured goods. Supremacy in the trade shifted over time among the Portuguese, Dutch, British, French, and finally the Americans. Trans-Saharan trade declined during this period, though the rise of the Fulani empire, known as the SOKOTO CALIPHATE, in the early nineteenth century brought a resurgence of slave raiding in the north. An empire in the LAKE CHAD region established by RABIH, a slave trader originally from the Nile basin, also revitalized Islam in the area, and pushed more groups south into the Cameroon forests.

The abolition of the transatlantic slave trade in the early 1800s forced African traders to develop commerce in alternative commodities such as ivory, rubber, and cash crops. Exports of palm oil and kernels increased significantly as African farmers expanded production to meet demand in newly industrializing Europe. As cash and credit relations gradually replaced barter, many African merchants and chiefs became indebted to European trading firms.

Missionaries, especially from Anglophone countries, were also establishing a presence in Cameroon by the mid-nineteenth century. In 1844 a Jamaican Baptist named Joseph Merrick founded a mission at Bimbia. Other Christian denominations, many of whose missionaries were African American, settled in what became the town of Victoria (today known as Limbe). African converts educated in the early mission schools eventually formed a small Anglophone elite. By 1880 the Anglophone missionary presence, combined with British domination of regional trade, made it seem likely that Great Britain would formally colonize the area. In fact, Germany became Cameroon's first colonizer.

GERMAN, FRENCH, AND BRITISH COLONIALISM

In July 1884, as the European powers at the Berlin Conference agreed to the rules of the division of the African continent, the German explorer and diplomat Gustav Nachtigal signed a treaty with two DUALA chiefs. Germany sought to occupy territory before the British and French – who were extensively preoccupied in Nigeria and Gabon, respectively – and to break the Duala's monopoly over interior trade. German Kamerun became an exporter of agricultural products such as cocoa, palm, rubber, tea, and tobacco, grown on large German- or African-owned estates on the fertile slopes of Mount Cameroon. Africans were recruited, often by force, to work on the plantations, as well as on railway and road construction projects. Thousands died as a result of the harsh working conditions and the spread of disease. Political and economic conditions were somewhat different in the north, where the Germans governed indirectly through Fulani emirs but also weakened the Fulani's control over regional trade. Hausa traders from northern Nigeria gained influence over commerce during this period.

The movement of traders and laborers, the spread of pidgin English, and widespread resistance to colonial rule all fostered the creation of a new collective identity in German Kamerun. Resentful of threats to their trading monopoly, the Duala initially led the resistance to German rule and were soon joined by the Bafut, Kpe, Bulu, and others. The Germans relied on superior firepower and divide-and-rule tactics to quell a series of uprisings, but many parts of the interior remained outside effective German control until 1910. In 1914 the colonial government executed two of the most prominent resistors, MARTIN-PAUL SAMBA and Chief Rudolph Douala Manga Bell. Yet even as those living within the newly defined borders of Kamerun began to forge a common identity around the resistance movement, missionaries and the colonial government introduced other, more divisive identities. As well as creating an educated elite, Christian missionaries emphasized distinctions between Christian denominations, traditional (or indigenous) religions, and Muslims. The German colonizers particularly denounced the Muslim Hausas' trade with British Nigeria and their continued use of slave labor.

During World War I Belgian, British, and French colonial armies, including many African troops, invaded German Kamerun. After the war the League of Nations divided the colony roughly along the axis of the mountains, giving Great Britain control over an eastern slice of the territory (British Cameroons) and granting France the rest (French Cameroun), an area nearly ten times larger. Linguistic and economic differences soon developed between the French and British mandates (renegotiated as Trusteeship Territories after World War II), though both territories' economies depended on agricultural exports such as coffee. British Cameroons ended the use of forced labor in 1918 and left most cash-crop production to small-scale African farmers. In contrast, the French maintained forced-labor laws until the end of World War II in order to supply labor for large state-owned agricultural estates. Vast differences also existed between the British and French territories in infrastructure, education, and health care. Great Britain invested little in Cameroons and instead made it a marginal province of the colony of Nigeria, run largely by Nigerian civil servants, but France considered Cameroun one of its model colonies. Both the British and French territories, however, concentrated economic development in the fertile south rather than the remote and arid north.

Despite these differences, some sense of common identity still linked British Cameroons and French Cameroun. This was fostered by extensive trade and migration between the two territories – especially after the development of new rail and road links – and the growth of multiethnic urban centers such as Douala and Yaoundé. Resentment toward the large numbers of Nigerians recruited to work in labor-scarce regions also helped forge unity among inhabitants of the British and French territories.

THE NATIONALIST ERA

As elsewhere in Africa after World War II, nationalism blossomed in Cameroon. Nigerian nationalist leaders spoke of uniting southern British Cameroons with Nigeria, but this idea won little support among Cameroonians, who feared Nigerian domination. Meanwhile, for French Cameroun the primary question was the nature of its post-independence relationship with France. The 1944 Brazzaville Conference envisioned France maintaining close relations with Africa, but African agitation for independence had increased over time. In 1945 a newly created labor union called for strikes in Douala; three years later nationalists formed the socialist Union des Populations du Cameroun (UPC), which called for complete independence as well as reunification of the two Cameroons. Supported primarily by urban workers, students, and the southern-based Bassa and Bamiléké ethnic groups, the UPC responded to French efforts to suppress its organizing with a clandestine sabotage campaign, killing policemen, civil servants, and soldiers and bombing symbols of colonial rule.

In 1956 France, realizing the inevitability of decolonization, passed the *loi cadre*, which expanded the powers of African assemblies and enlarged the electorate in preparation for independence. Largely in exile or underground, the UPC leadership boycotted the assembly elections, which were instead dominated by the southern and central Démocrates, led by André-Marie Mbida, and the northern Union Camerounaise (UC), led by Ahmadou Ahidjo. France supported these more moderate parties, hoping for close relations with an independent Cameroon. Mbida proved to be a cautious nationalist, and his transitional government collapsed as Ahidjo and the UC broke from Mbida's governing coalition. In 1958 Ahidjo formed a new government, calling for immediate independence while reassuring France that close economic, cultural, political, and military ties would be maintained. Those ties proved immediately useful to Ahidjo, who depended on the French military to suppress the guerrilla campaign of the UPC, a conflict that killed an estimated 600 insurgents, 1500 government officials and police, and 15,000 civilians between 1955 and 1962.

INDEPENDENCE: STABILITY AND CONTINUITY

On the first day of 1960, the former French colony of Cameroun became the independent Republic of the Cameroon, with Ahidjo as its president. After more than a year in limbo, in February 1961 the people of British Cam-

eroons voted in a United Nations-sponsored referendum on the issue of unification with Nigeria or Cameroon. The north, historically more closely tied to its western neighbor, voted in favor of Nigeria, and the south voted in favor of Cameroon. In October 1961 southern British Cameroons joined the republic.

President Ahidjo ruled Cameroon for the next 22 years. Fearing the divisive potential of ethnic, regional, religious, and linguistic identities, he concentrated on building national unity. This he did in part through his broad popular appeal as the "father" of the nation, and in part through his eventual authoritarian control over a single-party state. Ahidjo centralized most decision-making and incorporated previously independent associations representing women, youth, and labor into the sole legal party, the Cameroon National Union (CNU). The police and military suppressed any vestiges of thc political opposition, including the moribund UPC, and censored the media. Infrastructure development projects, while intended to foster economic growth and national unity, also helped the government centralize control in the capital city, Yaoundé. In 1972 Ahidjo replaced the federation with a republic.

Ahidjo further solidified his rule by carefully balancing ethnic representation in the cabinet and National Assembly, and by dispensing patronage to supporters at all levels of the government bureaucracy, the military, and the business community. He was able to pursue such tactics through his control over the economy and his relations with France, which remained the primary destination for Cameroon's agricultural exports. French businesses, encouraged by a liberal investment code, also invested heavily in the country, particularly in oil exploration, mining, energy, and forestry. Despite poorly planned development projects, Cameroon's economy grew, especially in the late 1970s following the discovery of offshore oil reserves. Meanwhile, the national soccer team, the CAMEROON LIONS, emerged as one of Africa's dominant teams, a position they held into the late 1980s.

In November 1982 Ahidjo handed over power to Paul Biya, the prime minister and his chosen successor. Ahidjo, still head of the CNU, found Biya resistant to his efforts to run the country from behind the scenes. Conflicts between the two men led Ahidjo Loyalists in the Republican Guard to mount a bloody uprising, which Biya eventually suppressed. After initial progress toward democratization, Biya reverted to his predecessor's authoritarian style, and came to rely upon Ahidjo's political machinery of patronage to maintain loyalty. Ultimately, Biya built his

TOP: A woman cleans fish at Rey Bouba, Cameroon. *CORBIS/Michael & Patricia Fogden*
MIDDLE: Cameroon barbers ply their trade in an outdoor market. *© F. Varin/Explorer*
LEFT: The Kapsiki Mountains of northern Cameroon are among the driest parts of the country. *Wendy Waitriss*

own political machine by replacing the CNU with the Cameroon People's Democratic Movement and advocating "communal liberalism." Biya claimed that communal liberalism would ultimately include freedom and democracy but that single-party rule was necessary in the meantime to prevent regional, ethnic, and religious divisions. Widely recognized as corrupt, the Biya regime remained heavily dependent on France, which operated a military base in Cameroon and consistently vetoed other foreign powers' efforts to pressure Biya for reform.

By 1987, however, Cameroon's oil boom had ended, and government bureaucracy and debt had strained the national budget. Unable to buy political support, Biya faced growing civil unrest. In 1990 the National Assembly legalized opposition parties, but Biya's refusal to allow for a new constitution provoked a massive strike throughout the south. Although elections were finally held in 1992, Biya resorted to widespread fraud to defeat the opposition candidate, the Anglophone John Ndi of the Social Democratic Front. The government easily put down subsequent riots and the opposition faded. Even after a currency devaluation throughout the West African franc zone in 1994 sparked sharp price increases as well as protests in several countries, Cameroon experienced relatively little unrest.

Although a new constitution passed in 1996 provided for local and regional elections, it also gave the executive branch of government broad powers. In elections the following year, no opposition candidate dared challenge Biya's bid for another seven-year term, though recently he has suffered health problems. The economy continued to grow steadily in the late 1990s, with an increase in oil, timber, and coffee exports. Relative economic prosperity and strong-arm tactics against opponents have enabled Biya to withstand both international and domestic opposition, and to carry on his predecessor's plan to forge a sense of national unity among Cameroon's ethnic groups, regions, and linguistic blocs.

Eric Young

See Also

Ahidjo, El Hajj Ahmadou; Chad; Decolonization in Africa: An Interpretation; Equatorial Guinea; Ethnicity and Identity in Africa: An Interpretation; Nationalism in Africa; Pygmy; Yaoundé, Cameroon; Douala, Cameroon; Jamaica; Carthage; Islam and Tradition: An Interpretation; Trans-Saharan and Red Sea Slave Trade.

Africa

Cameroon (Ready Reference)

Former Name: French Cameroun and British Cameroon
Area: 475,440 sq km (183,568 sq mi)
Location: Coastal West Africa, bordered by Nigeria, Chad, Central African Republic, Republic of the Congo, Gabon, and Equatorial Guinea
Capital: Yaoundé (population 800,000 [1992 estimate])
Other Major Cities: Douala (population 1,200,000), Garoua (population 160,000), Maroua (population 140,000 [1992 estimate])
Population: 15,029,433 (1998 estimate)
Population Density: 28 persons per sq km (about 72 per sq mi)
Population Below Age 15: 46 percent (male 3,295,924; female 3,266,429 [1997 estimate])
Population Growth Rate: 2.9 percent (1996 estimate)
Total Fertility Rate: 5.9 children born per woman (1996 estimate)
Life Expectancy at Birth: Total population: 52.6 years (male 51.55 years; female 53.68 years [1996 estimate])
Infant Mortality Rate: 78.7 deaths per 1000 live births (1996 estimate)
Literacy Rate (age 15 and over who can read and write): Total population: 63.4 percent (male 75 percent; female 52.1 percent [1995 estimate])
Education: High rate of school attendance; about 2.1 million children attended primary and preprimary schools in the early 1990s; in secondary schools, about 410,000. The University of Yaoundé, established in 1962, has faculties of law, arts, and science. More than 64,500 students are enrolled in institutions of higher education.
Languages: French and English are both official languages, but French is more widely used; 24 major African languages are represented in Cameroon.
Ethnic Groups: Nearly one-third of the population are Cameroon Highlanders (31 percent), one-fifth are Equatorial Bantu (19 percent); some 200 ethnic groups are represented in the population, of which 11 percent are Kirdi, 10 percent Fulani, 8 percent Northwestern Bantu, 7 percent Eastern Nigritic, and less than 1 percent non-African. The remaining 13 percent are from other African ethnic groups.
Religions: About half the population adheres to indigenous beliefs (51 percent), about one-third are Christian (33 percent), and the remainder are Muslim (16 percent).
Climate: Tropical near the coast, dry inland. Average annual rainfall is about 4060 mm (about 160 in) along the coast; precipitation in the western mountains is year round, as much as 10,160 mm (400 in) annually; in the north, which has a dry season from October to April, yearly rainfall averages 380 mm (about 15 in). Average temperature along the coast is 25° C (77° F), on the central plateau 21° C (70° F), and in the dry north 32° C (90° F).
Land, Plants, and Animals: Cameroon has a dense rain forest along its coastal plain, with mountains in the west, including an active volcano, Mount Cameroon (4095 m/ 14,435 ft), the highest peak in western Africa. In the center is the Adamawa Plateau, becoming savanna plains in the north. Rivers flowing through Cameroon include the Nyong, Sanaga, Mbéré, Logone, and the Benue, linking up with the Niger River system.

Animals include elephants, lions, monkeys, chimpanzees, gorillas, and antelope.
Natural Resources: Timber, petroleum, bauxite, and iron ore
Currency: The CFA franc
Gross Domestic Product (GDP): $30.9 billion (1997 estimate)
GDP per Capita: $2100 (1997 estimate)
GDP Real Growth Rate: 5 percent (1997 estimate)
Primary Economic Activities: Agriculture (29 percent of GDP, 74.4 percent of employment), industry, transport, and other services
Primary Crops: Cacao, coffee, tobacco, cotton, bananas, rubber, palm products, sugar cane, plantains, sweet potatoes, cassava, millet, and corn. Livestock raised in the Adamawa Plateau region include cattle, goats, sheep, and pigs.
Industries: Lumber, petroleum production and refining, textiles, food processing, and light consumer goods
Primary Exports: Petroleum, coffee, cocoa, lumber, aluminum, and cotton.
Primary Imports: Machines and electrical equipment, food, and consumer goods, transport equipment, and petroleum products.
Primary Trade Partners: European Union (France and Germany), African countries (especially Nigeria), Japan, and the United States
Government: Cameroon is a unitary republic, under a constitution established in 1972. It has a multiparty regime currently dominated by the government-controlled Cameroon People's Democratic Movement (CPDM). The executive branch is led by President Paul Biya, who appoints the head of government (currently Prime Minister Simon Aachid Achu), a cabinet of federal ministers, and the governors of ten provinces. The legislative branch is the elected unicameral National Assembly.

Barbara Worley

See Also

Chimpanzee; Elephant; Gorilla; Lion; Yaoundé, Cameroon; Douala, Cameroon.

Africa

Cameroon Lions, the national soccer team of Cameroon and traditionally one of Africa's premier teams.

The Indomitable Lions have been a dominant force on the African soccer scene since the 1970s. In 1982 the green, red, and yellow Indomitable Lions reached soccer's World Cup for the first time. The team went on to win the Africa Cup of Nations in 1984 and 1988. The Indomitable Lions' reign peaked in 1990 when they reached the World Cup quarter-finals with passionate play and impressive individual skills. (They were eliminated by one of Cameroon's former colonial powers,

Great Britain.) In the early 1990s the national team was weakened by infighting among players, poor planning and administration, and a lack of funds. It was eliminated quickly in the 1994 World Cup and 1996 Africa Cup of Nations. Many observers concluded that the Indomitable Lions were a spent force, but in 1998 they returned to top form, qualifying for the World Cup with an unbeaten record in their group.

Cameroonian soccer stars have included goalkeeper Thomas Nkono and the legendary Roger Milla, who dazzled fans with his deft ball handling in the 1990 World Cup and who, at age 42, went on to be the oldest scorer in World Cup history. Many of the Cameroonian players compete on Asian, South American, and European teams.

German colonizers first introduced soccer, known in Africa as football, to Cameroon around 1880, and the game quickly became popular. Over time Cameroon developed a strong network of professional teams, especially in Yaoundé and Douala. Many of these teams have won the African Champions Cup, the continental professional league football championships.

Eric Young

See Also
Colonial Rule; African Cup of Nations.

North America

Campanella, Roy

(b. November 19, 1921, Philadelphia, Pa.; d. June 26, 1993, Los Angeles, Calif.), one of the first African American stars in major league baseball.

The son of John Campanella, an Italian fruit-stand dealer, and Ida Campanella, an African American woman, Roy Campanella began playing semiprofessional baseball with Philadelphia's Bacharach Giants when he was 16 years old. After playing briefly with the Giants, Campanella joined the Baltimore Elites of the Negro National League (NNL). He starred in the NNL until 1946, when he signed a minor league contract with the Brooklyn Dodgers. Campanella played for Dodgers farm clubs until 1948 – the year after Jackie Robinson broke baseball's color barrier – when he became the Dodgers' starting catcher.

An excellent all-around player, "Campy" starred from 1948 to 1957, helping the Dodgers capture five National League (NL) Pennants. He won the NL most valuable player (MVP) award three times, in 1951, 1953, and 1955. In 1951 Campanella hit .325 with 33 home runs and 108 runs batted in (RBI). His best season was in 1953, when he hit 41 home runs and 142 RBI, both major league records for a catcher. He also set a defensive record that year with 807 putouts. Campanella had a career average of .276, 242 home runs, and 856 RBI, totals that would have been greater had the major leagues not prohibited African American players until 1947. He was inducted into the Baseball Hall of Fame in 1969.

In January 1958 Campanella's baseball career was cut short by an automobile accident that left him a quadriplegic. He remained a Dodger, however, serving as a minor-league instructor and a community-relations officer. He published his autobiography, *It's Good to Be Alive*, in 1959.

Robert Fay

See Also
Baseball in the United States; Negro Leagues.

North America

Campbell, Luther

(b. 1961, Miami, Fla.), raunchy rapper and First Amendment icon.

Luther Campbell began his career in music in 1979 with Miami's Ghetto Style DJs, but found success with a West Coast group he established called 2 Live Crew. With Campbell at the helm, 2 Live Crew helped create a genre of rap variously known as Bass Music, Booty Music, and Miami Bass. Bass Music features quick beats, exaggerated low-end frequencies, and highly sexualized lyrics reminiscent of black comedians like Richard Pryor, Redd Foxx, and Rudy Ray Moore. Their debut album, *The 2 Live Crew Is What We Are* (1986), featured "Throw the 'D'" and "We Want Some Pussy," underground classics that reinvigorated hip hop.

The group's graphic if goofy lyrics and outrageous stage show did not go unnoticed. In June 1990, in the wake of intensive anti-Crew lobbying efforts by Florida governor Bob Martinez and the American Family Association, a Broward County judge ruled obscene the group's third album, *As Nasty As They Wanna Be*. When a record store owner was incarcerated for selling the disc and Campbell himself was arrested for performing at a Florida club, the stage was set for a First Amendment battle that made headlines across the country. The rapper was eventually cleared of all charges, and the publicity of the trial pushed sales of the album past 3 million.

Since the trial, Campbell has continued to perform and produce Bass Music in Florida, earning regional success. He is also the host of *Luke's Peep Show*, a sexually explicit pay-per-view cable television program.

Andrew Du Bois

See Also
Hip Hop in the United States; Pryor, Richard Franklin Lenox Thomas.

Europe

Campbell, Naomi

(b. May 22, 1970, London, England), the first black model to have appeared on the cover of every major fashion magazine, and one of the most highly paid models in the world.

Fashion critics praise Naomi Campbell as "the Josephine Baker of the 1990s." Her graceful beauty, natural modeling ability, and magnetism on the catwalk have earned her up to $1 million a year.

Campbell was born in England to Jamaican immigrants and raised by her mother in South London. Slender and stunning, her charm includes an Asian accent, attributed to the influence of her Chinese grandmother. When Campbell was 15 years old, a local modeling agent took one look at her and implored her to sign a modeling contract. At the time, Campbell was attending the prestigious London Academy of Performing Arts. After completing the school year, as her mother insisted, Campbell had her first photo shoot and signed with the Elite Model Management Agency in 1987. In 1989 she became the first black model to appear on the cover of the French *Vogue* magazine and the widely read September issue of the American *Vogue*. She has stayed with Elite except for a two-year hiatus in the mid-1990s.

Campbell has expanded her creative repertoire. She has sung and appeared in music videos. She has acted in movies, most recently in *Ready to Wear* (1994) and *Miami Rhapsody* (1995), and on television shows in the United States and Great Britain. She intends to pursue acting as her primary profession in the future. Campbell published her autobiography, *Naomi*, in 1996.

Leyla Keough

See Also
Jamaica.

Africa

Campbell, Roy

(b. October 2, 1901, Durban, South Africa; d. April 23, 1957, near Setubal, Portugal), South African poet of European descent.

Born into a prominent Scottish family in the Natal region of South Africa, Roy Campbell brought to the world of English letters a passionate love for the Africa of his childhood. After attending school in Durban, he left South Africa for Oxford College in England in 1918. He was already a writer; his youthful verses show the influences of Yeats, Shelley and Wordsworth, while featuring rich descriptions of African landscape, wildlife, and indigenous folkways.

Disappointed by Oxford, he drifted through the London arts scene. He had married in 1922, and moved with his wife to a remote cabin in Wales. It was there that he wrote

The Flaming Terrapin (1924), an epic poem hailed by critics for its energy and exuberance. According to biographer Peter Alexander, Campbell sought to combine "the intellect of Europe [with] the riotous life of Africa."

Campbell cultivated the image of the rude colonial while in Europe, and his poetry can, to modern eyes, appear to exoticize indigenous peoples. Yet he was a fluent speaker of the ZULU language and an advocate of African voting rights as early as 1925. Throughout his life Campbell returned often to South Africa, but never settled there permanently. In all, he published more than 20 volumes of poetry, prose, and translations before his death in a car crash.

Kate Tuttle

SEE ALSO
Durban, South Africa; South Africa.

Latin America and the Caribbean

Campeche, José **(b. 1751, San Juan, Puerto Rico; d. 1809, Puerto Rico), mulatto Puerto Rican painter; largely self-taught, Campeche developed a delicate style with a miniaturist's attention to detail, comparable to eighteenth-century European Rococo.**

José Campeche was the son of a free black and a Spanish-born mother. Influenced by his father, who was an artisan, he started drawing at an early age. He later had contact with the Spanish painter Luis Paret, who was exiled for three years (1775-1778) in Puerto Rico. Paret, a more experienced and formally trained painter, greatly influenced the style of the gifted Campeche.

He is best known for his paintings of religious images and political figures. Among his works are some of the first artistic representations of blacks in colonial slave society: the *Exvoto de la Sagrada Familia* (around 1800, Institute of Puerto Rican Culture Collection) and the street scene in *Gobernador Ustariz* (1789-1792, Institute of Puerto Rican Culture Collection). Another example is the artist's lost *Self-portrait* that survives in two copies done by Ramón Atiles and Francisco Oller. Although these images of blacks constituted only a small part of Campeche's oeuvre, they inaugurated the depiction of African subjects in Puerto Rican visual art.

Campeche became a respected member of the colonial society and an artist exemplar for subsequent generations of artists. He was well known throughout the Spanish Caribbean and in Spain, and was offered attractive commissions abroad as well as an invitation from the Spanish Crown to become a painter in the Royal Chamber. However, Campeche did not accept any of these offers. He never left his beloved island, and died of tuberculosis at the age of 57.

Carlos Dalmau

Latin America and the Caribbean

Campos-Pons, María Magdalena **(b. 1959, Matanzas, Cuba), Afro-Cuban multimedia artist and professor of painting whose works explore the relationship between personal memory and her African heritage.**

The multipanel photographs, installations, and performances of María Magdalena Campos-Pons often portray a mythic or ironic view of the self-portrait, using her own body as a canvas. Onto this canvas she inscribes symbolic messages that define her individual self in terms of domestic rituals and her national identity in relation to mythic origins.

Born to parents who labored in and about the sugar industry, Campos-Pons enjoyed the benefits of a universally free education instituted in Cuba by the 1959 Cuban revolution, headed by Fidel Castro. She received her artistic training at the National School of Art (1980) and the Higher Institute of Art (1985), both in Havana. In 1988 she attended the Massachusetts College of Art in Boston. Subsequently, she married Neil Leonard, an American, and established residency in the United States. Her works have been exhibited throughout Europe and the Americas.

Her art in Cuba prior to 1990 links the visual representation of Caribbean sexuality as flowers and fruits to burlesque popular refrains (*Sabor a Cuba* [A Taste of Cuba], 1988). Her monumental installations give popular conceptions of sexuality a mythic quality that challenges sexist assumptions about female sexuality (*Jardín erótico o algunas notas sobre la hipocresía* [Erotic Garden or Some Notes on Hypocrisy], 1988).

In the period since she left Cuba, her multimedia installations have focused on issues of border crossings and the historical and current condition of black people in the African diaspora ("*Tra...*" [Transfer/ Transgression/ Trouble/ Tragedy], 1991; and *The Seven Powers Came by the Sea*, 1993). They also explore the conception of a personal history as tied to childhood events grounded in specific sites of her hometown (*A Town Portrait*, 1994) and the formulation of a feminine identity (*Spoken Softly with Mama*, 1998).

Spoken Softly with Mama shows the strength of a mature artist at work, pulling together all the themes and media Campos-Pons has been refining through the years. This installation pays homage to women's work, washing, ironing, embroidering. Simple materials such as iron, linen, and thread are transformed into transparent glass, organza and silk, and the activity of folding and carrying ironed sheets is ritualized and given transcendental meaning. The artist projects her video self-portrait onto altarlike ironing boards that record the young woman's coming of age (disintegrating pomegranates) and that blend her artistic life with that of her female kin. Campos-Pons thus creates an exquisite mix of material and image, of musical, linguistic, and visual languages, to reconstitute classic and Afro-Cuban myths, the collective and the individual, the traditional and the contemporary.

Flora González

SEE ALSO
Afrocubanismo; Matanzas, Cuba.

Africa

Camus, Albert **(b. November 7, 1913, Mondovi, Algeria; d. January 4, 1960, near Sens, France), French-Algerian writer and philosopher and winner of the Nobel Prize for Literature in 1957.**

Albert Camus was one of France's most renowned twentieth-century writers. His impoverished boyhood in colonial North Africa led him into left-wing politics as a youth. Later, however, he became known for his belief in existentialism, a philosophy that argues that human beings are alone in a godless universe and must find meaning without the comfort of religion.

Camus was born in a small town in eastern Algeria. He was only a year old when his father, a farm laborer from France, died in battle in World War I. His mother moved the family to a working-class neighborhood in Algiers, where Camus excelled in the local elementary and high schools. As a teenager Camus contracted tuberculosis, a disease that robbed him of his first love, playing soccer, and plagued him his entire life. As a student at the University of Algiers, he studied philosophy, briefly joined the Algerian Communist Party, and acted in a theater troupe that staged plays for working-class audiences.

Camus wrote his thesis on the philosophers Plotinus and SAINT AUGUSTINE, but his first two published collections of essays, *The Wrong Side and the Right Side* (*L'Envers et l'endroit*, 1937) and *Nuptials* (*Noces*, 1938), featured personal meditations on his own family and homeland. In the late 1930s, while remaining active in the theater, he worked as a journalist for the *Alger-Républicain*. He reviewed books by Jean-Paul Sartre and other existentialist writers and wrote articles on a variety of social issues, such as the poverty faced by Muslims in Algeria's Kabylia region.

In 1940 Camus moved to Paris. There he wrote for *Combat*, a left-wing newspaper, and finished his first novel, *The Stranger* (*L'Etranger*), and a philosophical treatise, *The Myth of Sisyphus* (*Le mythe de Sisyphe*), both published in 1942. Both works attracted international attention for their stark yet sympathetic look at the alienation of modern life. In Mersault, the protagonist of *The Stranger*, Camus created a character so completely exiled from both social convention and his own emotional life that he kills seemingly without reason or remorse – a symbol, critics have noted, for the average person's passive complicity in the face of the social upheaval of the mid-twentieth century.

In his second novel, *The Plague* (*La peste*, 1947), Camus portrayed a town's reaction to a deadly epidemic. In examining human responses to random evil, he began to construct an existentialist argument for human solidarity in the face of an indifferent universe. This strain of moral, rather than ideological, judgment is also evident in his essay *The Rebel* (*L'Homme révolté*, 1951). Its critique of Soviet prisons angered some fellow existentialists, such as Sartre, who were sympathetic to Soviet Marxism. In his last novel, *The Fall* (*La chute*, 1956), Camus similarly dealt with estrangement and the hope for redemption in community.

When he died at 44 in a car accident, Camus left behind his second wife (an early marriage had ended in 1936) and two children. An unfinished novel was published in 1994 as *The First Man*. He had also published two plays and several collections of short stories and essays. While accepting the Nobel Prize in 1957, Camus said of writers "Whatever our personal frailties may be the nobility of our calling will always be rooted in two commitments difficult to observe: refusal to lie about what we know and resistance to oppression."

Kate Tuttle

See Also

Algeria; Algiers, Algeria; Theater, African; Islam and Tradition: An Interpretation.

North America

Canada

Black people have lived in Canada since the beginnings of transatlantic settlement. A few came as explorers, more came as slaves in the seventeenth and eighteenth centuries, still more as former American slaves fleeing to Canada between 1783 and 1865, and since as free immigrants from the United States, the West Indies, and Africa. Until the 1980s very few came directly from their ancestral continent, yet the label African Canadian is being used increasingly to include all Canadians of African descent, wherever they were born. In the 1996 census African Canadians composed approximately 2 percent of the total Canadian population.

Slavery in Canada

Africans participated in many of the earliest voyages to the territory now known as Canada. A legend persists that one of Jacques Cartier's crew members came originally from Africa, though the first name on record is that of Mathieu de Coste (or da Costa), who served the governor of Acadia in 1608 as an interpreter to the Micmac Nation. The first slave transported directly from Africa to Canada was a child brought to Quebec in 1628 by the English invader David Kirke and sold to a local resident upon Kirke's departure in 1629. The child was baptized in May 1633 as Olivier Le Jeune and died in 1654 while still a young man. Between 1628 and the British conquest in 1759, 1132 African slaves were brought to New France. Governor Denonville sought permission to establish a trade in African slaves in 1688, but Royal permission was denied and so there was never any direct importation from Africa. Most of the Africans came from the British colonies in North America or from the French West Indies. About 60 percent of the imported slaves were male and 40 percent female, and almost all of them were located in urban centers as domestic servants. Usually they were owned singly or in small numbers, and most served the same family throughout their lives.

Black slaves lived in the British regions of Canada in the seventeenth and eighteenth centuries – 104 were listed in a 1767 census of Nova Scotia – but their numbers were small until the Loyalist influx after 1783. As white Loyalists fled the new American republic, they took with them about 2000 black slaves: 1200 to the Maritimes (Nova Scotia, New Brunswick, and Prince Edward Island), 300 to Lower Canada (Quebec), and 500 to Upper Canada (Ontario). As in New France, Loyalist slaves were held in small numbers and were employed as domestic servants, farm hands, and skilled artisans. The system of gang labor, and its consequent institutions of brutality and control, did not develop in Canada. Because they did not appear to pose a threat to their masters, slaves were permitted to learn to read and write, Christian conversion was encouraged, and their marriages were recognized by law. In 1793 Upper Canada became the first territory in the British Empire to legislate the gradual abolition of slavery. By 1800 the other provinces of British North America had effectively limited slavery through court decisions requiring the strictest proof of ownership, which was rarely available. Slavery remained legal, however, until the British Parliament emancipated slaves throughout the empire effective August 1, 1834.

Free Black Settlement in the Maritimes

Numerically and historically more significant than the Loyalist-owned slaves were about 3500 free black Loyalists who migrated to Canada after the American Revolution. These were American-owned slaves who were promised freedom and equality by the British in exchange for their loyalty to the Crown. The British motive was to acquire the military and labor contribution of the runaway slaves and to deprive the American colonists of a valuable asset. But the terms of the proclamations inviting them to join the British led the blacks to believe that the British were genuinely opposed to slavery, and that a Loyalist victory would result in freedom for all slaves in the American colonies. This impression was reinforced by the fact that the earliest black Loyalists were sent into battle carrying a banner announcing "Liberty to Slaves." Their participation can therefore legitimately be understood as a war for independence.

The American victory required the evacuation of those who had remained loyal to Britain; among them were the approximately 3500 black Loyalists who settled chiefly in Nova Scotia and New Brunswick. They were located by government officials in half a dozen segregated communities on the outskirts of white towns. The largest was at Birchtown, near Shelburne, Nova Scotia. A census held in 1784 showed 649 men, 485 women, and 387 children living there, a total of 1521, making it the largest community of free black people anywhere in North America at the time. Despite the promise of equality, the black Loyalists did not in general receive grants of land sufficient to provide for themselves on their own farms. Disappointed, almost 1200 free blacks, or about a third of the total population, migrated to the British colony of Sierra Leone in 1792, where they founded the capital city of Freetown. Their descendants still identify themselves as Nova Scotian more than two centuries later.

In 1796 a band of almost 600 Jamaican maroons was transported to Nova Scotia. These were runaway slaves who had established independent communities in the interior of Jamaica and who posed a threat to neighboring slave plantations. After a military operation in 1795-1796, the Jamaican legislature exiled the captive maroons to Halifax. Although they were making a contribution by laboring on fortifications during the war with France, the British government decided in 1800 to ship the maroons to Sierra Leone in West Africa. Their arrival in Freetown coincided with a rebellion of the black Loyalists against their British governors. By siding with the colonial authorities, the maroons ensured the failure of the rebellion.

The reputation acquired by the British as champions of black freedom and equality encouraged a renewed flight from American owners during the War of 1812. In April 1814, recognizing a fait accompli, the British commander issued a proclamation offering to send runaway American slaves as "free settlers" to British colonies. By the end of the war, about 2000 black refugees had been settled in the Maritimes, more than 1500 in Nova Scotia, and the rest in New Brunswick. Like the black Loyalists, they were located in segregated settlements, mostly in the neighborhood of Halifax, and were given small land grants of about 10 acres per family.

Black Fugitives in Ontario

The black Loyalists, maroons, and black refugees had initially freed themselves, but they were brought as groups into Canada under government auspices and located in deliberately separated settlements. A small number of individual runaway American slaves also migrated to Canada beginning in the 1790s. Most of them headed for Ontario, where the 1793 Act guaranteed the freedom of any former slave entering the province. That same year Congress passed the first Fugitive Slave Law, making a flight to British territory more attractive. By 1830, when the term UNDERGROUND RAILROAD was coined, hundreds of slaves and freedpeople were crossing the border each year. Known collectively as the "black fugitives," they too tended to create voluntary settlements or concentrated urban districts, for self-defense against American slave catchers, for mutual economic assistance, and for support in the face of white Canadian prejudice. Most of the fugitive locations were near the American border, around Windsor, Chatham, London, St. Catharines, and Hamilton. Toronto had a growing black population, and there were smaller communities living in many parts of the province. Numbers increased, particularly after the Fugitive Slave Act of 1850 made a move across the border imperative for many American fugitives. By the time of the American Civil War, it is estimated that about 30,000 fugitives had found their way to Canada. This included more than 800 free African Americans who migrated from California to Vancouver Island in 1858, seeking to escape the racial discrimination that was imposed by law in their home state.

BLACK IMMIGRATION SINCE 1865

With the end of American slavery, thousands of African Canadians returned to the United States, but because of American legal inequalities, small groups of African Americans continued to migrate into Canada. The most significant movement came from Oklahoma between 1909 and 1911, when about 1500 black farmers settled in Saskatchewan, Manitoba, and especially Alberta, creating several distinct black communities across the prairies. The Oklahoma example prompted other blacks to migrate also, particularly western farmers as well as some from Chicago and other cities.

The black population in Canada did not increase substantially, however, until the 1960s, when immigration restrictions based on color and origin were removed. As a result, large numbers of qualified West Indians and Africans began to enter Canada. Between 1960 and 1995 there were about 300,000 immigrants from the West Indies and more than 150,000 from Africa, though since Canadian immigration statistics only register country of origin black immigrants cannot be distinguished from those of Arab, Asian, or European descent. According to the 1996 census, more than half of all African Canadians live in Toronto, and there are large concentrations in Montreal, Ottawa, and several other Canadian cities. This major influx has greatly outnumbered the original black population in every Canadian region except the Maritimes.

ECONOMIC LIFE

As in other parts of the Americas, slavery had a lasting impact on African Canadian economic life, both as a direct legacy upon the descendants of slaves and, even more significant, as a mentality produced in the dominant society. Accustomed to regard all blacks as slaves, colonial authorities imposed numerous obstacles on the black Loyalists and refugees as they tried to establish themselves as free settlers in the Maritimes. They did not receive the extent of land originally promised, and the small farms they were granted could not permit self-sufficiency through agriculture. As a result, the black pioneers were forced to seek employment as laborers in neighboring white towns, where their desperate condition made them vulnerable to exploitation and discrimination in employment and wages. In 1784 Canada's first race riot occurred in Shelburne, Nova Scotia, when white laborers attacked blacks, tore down their houses, and drove them out of town, on the grounds that by accepting lower wages the blacks were depressing the price of labor. Lack of property deprived blacks of the vote and other civil rights, preventing them from participating in the decisions of state. An economic depression after the War of 1812, and the postwar arrival of large numbers of working-class whites from Great Britain, blunted opportunities for upward mobility. Poverty and marginalization were thus constituted as basic components in the early black experience, and have been perpetuated over subsequent generations within an environment that continued to discriminate in terms of "race." Since they constituted a large proportion of the labor pool, blacks were essential to the foundation of colonial Nova Scotia and New Brunswick – it was they who cleared the fields, laid the roads, and constructed the public buildings – but they have never shared in the benefits of their own labor.

The fugitives who arrived in Ontario fleeing American slavery typically arrived destitute, and since there was no provision of government land grants they usually became laborers on the lands of others. An expanding frontier economy offered employment opportunities in road, canal, and railroad construction, and the proceeds were frequently used to purchase farms or establish small businesses. Competition from Irish immigrants escaping the famine of the 1840s, and then the increasing black population after 1850, meant a reduction in those opportunities. Many individual fugitives arrived with specialized skills, and some, especially those who had lived free in the Northern United States, brought capital to invest. On the West Coast, the California migrants entered a gold-rush economy in which their savings and skills produced considerable entrepreneurial success. Still, most black families across Canada remained dependent on the white-dominated economy for their subsistence. As so-called "scientific" racism became the common sense of the later nineteenth century among the majority population, employers regarded Africans as suitable primarily for service and unskilled labor. With few exceptions, the relative economic status of black families tended to drift even lower at the approach of the new century, and the children of small shopkeepers and artisans often found employment only in the lowest-paid categories of the labor market.

Throughout their history in Canada, black women had to seek paid employment, since black men rarely earned sufficient wages to maintain a wife at home. Experience in slavery, and indeed the heritage of Africa, disposed African Canadian women to participate economically to a much greater degree than was common in the English Canadian community. Women could find poorly paid work in the textile industry, though the most typical female employment was domestic service. A Montreal survey in 1928 revealed that almost 100 percent of employed black women were domestics; it was still 80 percent in 1941. Clerical and sales positions were denied to black women unless there was some family connection. Black women could be elevator operators and black men could stock the shelves, but neither could serve the public in shops and department stores. Small businesses such as hairdresser and barber shops continued, with a largely black clientele, but the grocery stores, tobacconists, and butcher shops of an earlier era, depending on nonblack customers to be viable, largely disappeared. Even with education or training, black people could not find work for which they were qualified.

The epitome of African Canadian male employment ambition in the first half of the twentieth century was the position of railway porter. As in the United States, black men were associated with personal service of the kind expected from a sleeping car porter. In the 1928 Montreal survey mentioned previously, 90 percent of employed black men worked for the railroad as porters, redcaps, shoeshiners, elevator operators, cooks, and waiters. During the 1920s and increasingly during the Depression of the 1930s, whites replaced blacks as cooks and waiters, and only the sleeping car porter remained a black enclave. It was only after World War II that blacks gained the right to promotion to sleeping car conductor and other senior positions, a symptom of a broader movement to remove restrictions in employment and other areas in Canadian life. The successful campaign for Fair Employment Practices laws, in which African Canadians featured prominently, eliminated overt discrimination in the 1950s, though the legacies of generations of disadvantage are still apparent, particularly in the Maritimes. Black immigrants are bringing every kind of skill to and are entering every corner of the Canadian economy, but the 1996 census figures indicate that employed blacks, whether immigrants or Canadian-born, have an average income that is 15 percent lower than that of their white neighbors.

ABOVE: John Ware, shown here with his wife and children, was a successful rancher and famous horse rider and bronco buster. *Glenbow Archives, Calgary, Alberta (NA-263-1)*
ABOVE RIGHT: The family of Thomas Mapp, who migrated to Amber Valley, Alberta, from Oklahoma around 1910, and became a successful farmer in Canada. *Glenbow Archives, Calgary, Alberta (NA-316-1)*

Community and Family

African Canadians have a wide variety of origins and histories, but they have shared a common tradition with the nonblack majority, the pioneering values of mutual reliance and the cooperative advancement of community rights. From pioneer times, African Canadians learned that they were vulnerable as individuals and therefore developed a tradition of communal response and mutual support. This has been a prevailing theme in African Canadian community life. There are recorded examples of black Loyalists selling their hard-won property in order to keep a community member out of debt, for indebtedness often led to indentured servitude and, for blacks, a return to slavery. The refugees engaged in communal land clearing and home building, and declined to dismember their communities in the 1830s when offered larger land grants on an individual basis. Their leaders replied to the government that as individuals they could not survive, and unless they could be relocated as community groups they would rather stay where they were. The Ontario fugitives demonstrated similar concerns in their vigilance committees against marauding kidnappers and in the voluntary establishment of organized communal settlements.

Black Loyalists and refugees most often arrived in family units. Among later fugitives, it was often the male partner who arrived first; he would then try to assist family members in escaping. Income from both partners was always necessary to sustain family life, and because of gender as well as racial divisions in the marketplace, there were sometimes more employment opportunities for black women than for men. Black women therefore played an important economic role in family life and experienced considerable independence as a result. Collaboration was required with other community members, particularly for child-care. Raised in a communal fashion, black children developed familylike relationships throughout the local community. A strong sense of group identity and mutual reliance produced an intimate community life and a refuge against white discrimination. As a result of these conditions, family and community have blended throughout much of African Canadian history.

The cement binding the black community has historically been the church. Church membership offered opportunities to participate in community affairs and produced networks for cooperative endeavor. Inevitably, the churches assumed the major social and political role in community life, and the clergy became the natural community leaders. The host of fraternal organizations, temperance societies, mutual-assistance bands, and antislavery associations formed by African Canadians were almost always associated with the churches. The churches also led the movement for greater educational and employment opportunities and for civil rights, especially in the era immediately after World War II.

The postwar decade also saw the emergence of regional and provincial secular organizations, such as the Nova Scotia Association for the Advancement of Colored People, established in Halifax in 1945, and the Canadian Negro Women's Association, founded in Toronto in 1951. Urbanization and increasing secularization in the last half-century have changed the role of the church and the local community. Governments now supply services that churches and charities once provided, and the clergy no longer play an intermediary role with the institutions of the white majority. Above all, the waves of new black immigrants are producing social conditions never before experienced by African Canadians, with significant implications for family and community structures. Even when they arrive in family groups, black

TOP RIGHT: Samuel Ringgold Ward founded the *Provincial Freeman*, a newspaper for the black Canadian community, in 1853. *Metropolitan Toronto Reference Library*

RIGHT: Jeff Edwards, an African American who migrated from Oklahoma to western Canada around 1910, owned this farm until his retirement, when he turned the property over to his son, Booker T. Edwards. The Edwards family was one of a group of black Oklahomans who settled in Amber Valley, Alberta. *Glenbow Archives, Calgary, Alberta (NA-704-1)*

immigrants are disconnected from the extended kinship networks and communities of their Caribbean or African homelands. Post-immigration stress can produce marital breakdown and generational conflict. In 1991 more than 13 percent of black families had a single parent, compared to just over 4 percent of other Canadian families, and over 90 percent of the single black parents were female. New demands are therefore being made upon existing community structures, which developed historically to suit different conditions. In response, a wide variety of more specialized organizations has recently arisen, such as business and professional associations, black labor caucuses, athletic clubs, organizations for black artists and social workers, and black-specific family services. There is no longer a single African Canadian community tradition, though the Canadian traditions of mutual support and cooperative promotion of community rights still prevails.

Church and School

The church was the first institution established in the various black communities scattered across Canada, and its influence pervaded every aspect of African Canadian life. In the Loyalist era, Anglican, Methodist, Baptist, and Huntingdonian chapels were founded in the Maritime black settlements. The black refugees were mostly Baptist or Methodist, and they established churches in their communities after 1815. Since most black settlements were physically separate, their churches too were separate from outside supervision. This nourished the development of distinct styles of worship and interpretation of the Scriptures. Even when they were members of mainstream congregations, the early black Christians were usually compelled to worship separately. In the 1830s, under the stewardship of the Reverend Richard Preston, the Baptist faith embraced almost the entire black population of Nova Scotia. Preston's crusade culminated in 1854, when he created the African Baptist Association of Nova Scotia as an autonomous black denomination.

Similarly, fugitives arriving in Ontario established churches in their settlements. The first Baptist churches in the province were founded by black preachers and were originally mixed, but by the 1830s white congregants had separated to form their own churches. In 1841 black Baptist representatives created the Amherstburg Baptist Association as a deliberately black denomination. The earliest black Methodists affiliated with the African Methodist Episcopal Church (AME) in the United States. In 1856, to demonstrate their loyalty to their new home, they created the all-Canadian British Methodist Episcopal Church (BME). Some AME congregations, however, voted to remain with their original affiliation, so both the AME and the BME have continued to operate in Ontario.

By the middle of the nineteenth century, in the Maritimes and Ontario, black Christians attended black churches, with black pastors who interpreted the Gospel and ministered to their congregations according to their needs. As head of what was often the only local black institution, the preacher tended to be the community's leader and chief negotiator with outside institutions.

There was one other institution, the school, which arose in the early black settlements and which was most often associated with the church. British charitable organizations sponsored schools in most of the Maritime black communities beginning in the 1780s, and the earliest teachers were the same men and women who served as preachers. Later, the Reverend Richard Preston encouraged the Baptists to use their church halls as schools. Special votes from the provincial legislature provided funds for the black community schools, but the support was never entirely satisfactory. In Ontario, until the end of the Civil War drew funds to the American freedpeople, British and American missionary societies established schools for fugitive children, as did some black congregations. In addition, the governments of both Nova Scotia and Ontario created legally segregated public schools, supported by local taxation and counterpart grants from the province. Almost every black child therefore had an opportunity to attend school, and very often the teacher was a black person and a member of the community. Funding, however, was chronically inadequate, and the quality of education tended to be inferior.

Combined with residential isolation and economic deprivation, poor schooling helped to perpetuate a situation of limited opportunity and restricted mobility. Several court cases in Ontario were brought by parents to challenge the exclusion of their children from the regular schools. Although the courts upheld the legality of segregated education, they did insist that every child must have access to an education and that therefore if no black school existed, black children must be admitted to the regular school. Over time, using such tactics as tax strikes and boycotts, parents were able to close the black schools and gain admission for their children to nonsegregated state schools. In Nova Scotia a similar legal solution developed in the late nineteenth century, but because the black communities tended to be more isolated, there were not the same opportunities to force integration. This changed in the 1950s and 1960s with urbanization and with the development of consolidated school districts incorporating the black settlements. Legislative reforms in the same period made segregation illegal across Canada.

Besides the societal trend toward urbanization and secularization, Caribbean and African immigration has had an immense impact, bringing new denominations and entirely new religions into the African Canadian culture. Immigration has also brought a very high proportion of well-educated and professional black people to Canada, with an average standard of achievement higher than Canadian-born blacks or whites. A situation of disadvantage remains in some of the historic communities, so special programs have been launched, such as the Transition Year Program at Dalhousie University for black and Micmac students, to correct the longstanding heritage of educational deprivation.

Formed in 1860, the Victoria Rifle Corps was an all-black unit that came to be known as "The African Rifles." *British Columbia Archives*

Participation in Mainstream Affairs

African Canadians have consistently sought to contribute to the affairs of their nation and to gain full rights as Canadian citizens, though not always with complete success. Much effort and organization have gone into campaigns to overcome racist restrictions in education, employment, accommodations, and civil rights. With some major exceptions Canadian law tended to be egalitarian, but private discrimination was legally permitted. The period since World War II has witnessed an intensification of the effort to eliminate racist restrictions, as made manifest in the passage of Fair Practices and Human Rights legislation in the 1950s and 1960s. The Charter of Rights and Freedoms (1982), the Employment Equity Act (1986), and the Multiculturalism Act (1988) promised greater and more systemic changes. The opportunities were still being realized a decade later.

Blacks demonstrated their loyalty to Great Britain and Canada in every war since the American Revolution. During World War I (1914-1918) their participation was initially rejected, but in 1916 they were admitted into a segregated unit, the Nova Scotia No. 2 Construction Battalion (Colored). There was no separate unit in World War II (1939-1945), but there remained restrictions on black participation in the air force and navy until 1943 and 1944, respectively. Overt discrimination in the military has been overcome in the general movement for racial equality since the war.

By the 1830s their right to vote was recognized, and in many parts of the country blacks ran for elected office. There have been black municipal councilors and school trustees since the middle of the nineteenth century, most notably William Hubbard, who served as councilor, controller, and acting mayor of Toronto between 1894 and 1907. Leonard Braithwaite was the first African Canadian in a provincial legislature when he was elected in Ontario in 1963, and Lincoln Alexander, from Hamilton, became the first black federal member in 1968. In 1985 Alexander was appointed lieutenant-governor of Ontario, the vice-regal post in the Canadian system representing the constitutional monarch. In 1993 Wayne Adams became the first black member of the Nova Scotian cabinet. Blacks have sat in the federal and provincial legislatures as Liberals, Conservatives, and New Democrats.

Through their own struggle against injustice and their insistence upon equality in the law, black Canadians have bequeathed an impressive structure of constitutional rights from which all Canadians benefit today.

Culture and Identity

African Canadians represent a cultural mosaic as diverse as any in the world, with substantial African, Caribbean, and African American contributions. Yet it is possible to recognize a Canadian trajectory in black cultural evolution. In their concentrated settlements, the early blacks had the opportunity to retain cultural characteristics carried from Africa and from American slavery, and to develop new adaptations in response to Canadian conditions. Their churches lent institutional support to the preservation and transmission of black culture, so that music, dance, folklore, even daily speech, became imbued with religious motifs. The original pioneers possessed the energy of those who had crossed a continent for their freedom, and an abiding faith that English Canadian institutions would fulfill the promise of equality. This often contradictory combination has reverberated through the development of black Canadian culture.

The earliest records of the black Canadian experience are autobiographical narratives. Three of the most influential black Loyalist preachers, Huntingdonian John Marrant, Methodist Boston King, and Baptist David George, left accounts of their lives in the eighteenth century. Autobiography was also the typical literary form for the nineteenth-century fugitives. Leaders of three Ontario black settlements, Josiah Henson of Dawn, Austin Steward of Wilberforce, and Henry Bibb of the Refugee Home, participated in the popular genre of the fugitive slave narrative. All are redolent with struggle against injustice tempered by a confidence in the good will of white society, and with liberal use of biblical quotation revealing the implicit amalgamation of religious and political principle.

The first black newspaper was the *Voice of the Fugitive*, edited by Henry Bibb and his schoolteacher wife, Mary, from 1851 to 1854. In its final year Bibb's paper was challenged by the *Provincial Freeman*, edited at least until 1859 by Mary Ann Shadd, the first female editor in Canada and the first black female editor anywhere in North America. Like the autobiographies, the two Ontario newspapers reflected their community's commitment to land ownership, self-reliance through mutual assistance, education, British loyalty, and Christian values, though Shadd disagreed with Bibb's support for the establishment of separate black communities. During World War I, J. R. B. Whitney edited the *Canadian Observer* in Toronto, and in 1923 James F. Jenkins founded the *Dawn of Tomorrow* in London; both extolled the same community ambitions as their predecessors. When Carrie Best founded the *Clarion* in New Glasgow, Nova Scotia, in 1946, she gave it the masthead motto "For Church and Community."

Black music tended to celebrate religious themes, and the church-based mass choir was its most typical expression both within the community and before Canadian society at large. In the twentieth century, African Canadians have contributed to ragtime, JAZZ, and blues, often gaining a reputation in the United States. Among them, Nathaniel Dett, Shelton Brooks, and Oscar Peterson all took their early training in a black church. More recently, Caribbean musical fashions have been introduced, including CALYPSO and REGGAE, and RAP music has come from the United States, but the black Canadian choir tradition has been maintained by Montreal's Jubilation Gospel Choir and the Nova Scotia Mass Choir, among others.

Beginning in the 1970s black Nova Scotia experienced a cultural renaissance, utilizing historic themes, personalities and styles of expression. This rebirth has been defined by poets – for example, George Elliott Clarke, Maxine Tynes, George Borden, and David Woods – but has been expressed as well in plays, novels, and films. Nova Scotia did not receive a numerically significant immigration from Africa and the Caribbean, but elsewhere in Canada it is primarily immigrants such as Austin Clarke and Dionne Brand who are resurrecting the black literary tradition and weaving into it a Caribbean memory and the migratory experience.

Since 1783 African Canadians have identified with Canada and with the Canadian dream, and although it has often been exposed as an illusion, black people have never lost their commitment to that ideal. Their usual tactic of quiet diplomacy has represented not satisfaction with the status quo, but rather a Canadian commitment to constitutionalism and, a recognition that success depends upon cooperation rather than confrontation with a majority population that is still 98 percent nonblack. Although an exciting new black culture is emerging as a result of immigration, common experience in Canada is encouraging a sense of shared destiny, and the traditional black community in Canada is being explored in literature and the arts in a search for the sustaining characteristics of this historic people. While there is no single community, identity, or culture among African Canadians, it is surely significant that in recent census questionnaires, when Canadians have been invited to designate their own ethnicity in a variety of fashions (including continent, region, or country of origin), the largest number, and a majority of the younger people, have chosen to identify as "black Canadian."

James W. St. G. Walker

See Also

Freetown, Sierra Leone; Clarke, Austin C.; Blues, The; Maroonage in the Americas; Brotherhood of Sleeping Car Porters; Cary, Mary Ann Shadd; Civil War, American; Fugitive Slave Laws; Peterson, Oscar Emmanuel; Slave Narratives.

Latin America and the Caribbean

Candomblé, an Afro-Brazilian religion developed primarily by West African Yoruban slaves and their descendants in northeastern Brazil.

Scholars distinguish three major types of Candomblés in Brazil, each of which is associated with different *nações* (literally, "nations," which refer to the African ethnic group origins of the Candomblé): the Gêgê-Nagô Candomblés, the Angola-Congo Candomblés, and the Candomblés de Caboclo. The first type is based on Yoruban and Fon religious traditions and languages, while the others are based on diverse Bantu and Brazilian sources. There is a great deal of variation between and within the three types of Candomblé, but all are strongly influenced by Yoruban beliefs and rituals. This article attempts to discuss the elements common to all three variants (*see* Religions, African, in Brazil).

Large numbers of Yoruban slaves from Nigeria and Benin were brought to Brazil during the eighteenth and early nineteenth centuries (*see* African Ethnic Groups in Latin America and the Caribbean). They believed in one Supreme Being, known as

Olorun, or Olodumaré, and numerous intermediary spiritual beings, known as orixás, which were in broad terms similar to the Christian God and Catholic saints of the Portuguese colonizers. Slaves recognized that some of the saints shared symbols and characteristics with their orixás and began to identify some of their orixás with the saints. For example, they identified Omolú, or Obaluaiyé, the orixá of smallpox and epidemic diseases, with Saint Lazarus the leper. This syncretism actually blended African and Catholic religious traditions in some Candomblés while it was only superficial in others. In either case, it allowed slaves to worship secretly their African deities behind the façade of the saints, and it contributed to the formation of the religion known as Candomblé, whose closest counterpart in the New World is Santería.

Top: The guardians and leaders of the Afro-Brazilian religious tradition of Candomblé are usually black women known as *mães de santo*. *Sergio de Souza/Contexto*

Above: In Salvador, Brazil, women prepare for a Candomblé ceremony, practicing a faith that blends Catholic and Yoruban elements. *CORBIS/Stephanie Maze*

Right: Possession by the *orixás* (deities) is an important part of Candomblé ceremonies. An orixá has temporarily taken control of this Candomblé devotee's body in Recife, Pernambuco. *Sue Cunningham/SCP*

In Candomblé, a devotee "belongs to" multiple orixás, who control the devotee's destiny and act as his or her protectors. The orixás are intermediaries between humans and Olodumaré, the creator of the universe. As the children and servants of Olodumaré, the orixás are all related by a common mythology, which is used to explain the social relations between people who worship different orixás. People's actions are understood individually in terms of their personal orixás. What a devotee does, eats, and wears on a daily basis is often influenced by his or her orixás, which are associated with specific days of the week, foods, animals, and colors. In addition to respecting the preferences of their orixás, devotees usually exhibit personal qualities akin to those of their orixás. For example, a devotee of Xangó, the orixá of thunder and lightning, will tend to be proud, aggressive, and stubborn, all of which are characteristic traits of this orixá. In this way, orixás often determine their devotees' behavior and daily decisions.

A spiritual force referred to as *axé* sustains Candomblés. Devotees increase their axé by carrying out daily devotional rites and through possession ceremonies. During these ceremonies drummers play a sequence of rhythms, each corresponding to the orixá being summoned, while devotees sing songs and execute dance steps associated with their personal orixás. The songs and dances collectively reenact the mythology of the orixás and individually reflect the human activity and aspect of nature that an orixá oversees. For example, the choreography of Oxóssi, who presides over hunting and the forest, involves the hunting and capturing of game. During these ceremonies, the orixás often descend into the bodies of their devotees, inducing an animated state of possession in which the devotees dance.

Centers of worship for Candomblé are called *terreiros* (grounds), and they encompass a sacred indoor and outdoor space with sanctuaries for the orixás, saints, and/or Indian-like spirits called Caboclos. The head of the terreiro is either a priest, sometimes referred to as a *babalorixá* or a *pai de santo* (father of the orixá), or a priestess, called an *ialorixá* or a *mãe de santo* (mother of the orixá). The priestess is traditionally a black woman who, in addition to being responsible for the spiritual well-being of the Candomblé members and the terreiro's material needs, uses divination to communicate with the orixás. To ascertain an individual's personal orixá or to help find a solution to a devotee's personal problem, the mãe de santo will toss 16 cowry shells, whose resulting patterns reveal the will of the orixás.

Some Candomblé members only visit the terreiro for such consultations, while others go through an elaborate initiation process that lasts several months and eventually allows them to be possessed by an orixá. During this induction period, initiates are kept in a secluded room, where they learn the songs, dances, and mythology of their orixás. In addition, their bodies are ritually prepared with herbal baths and drinks to receive the orixás. Initiation culminates in a ceremony marking the spiritual rebirth of the initiate, who becomes what is sometimes referred to in Portuguese as a *filho* or *filha de santo* (son or daughter of the orixá). In Yoruba, initiates are called *iaôs*. The initiation process creates a family of devotees related by spiritual rather than genetic ties.

In Brazil, Bahia continues to be the cradle of Candomblé. Although the religion is openly practiced today, historically its practice has been covert because of repression by church and state officials. Beginning in the nineteenth century, police raided Candomblé houses of worship, confiscating their possessions and arresting their members. The repression of some Candomblés lessened in the 1930s, when participants in two Afro-Brazilian congresses advocated the preservation of Candomblé as part of Brazil's African heritage. In addition, some terreiros deliberately recruited prominent figures in Bahian society as their *ogans*, or lay protectors, which lessened persecution against them to a certain extent. But it was not until Brazil officially declared its commitment to fostering religious freedom in the 1970s that Candomblé devotees began to practice their religion openly.

Following a 1983 conference on the orixá tradition and culture in Salvador, Bahia, some Candomblé priests and priestesses proposed doing away with the Catholic elements in Candomblé, principally the imagery of the saints, which they regard as no longer necessary for the worship of their African deities. Today, whether or not to desyncretize Candomblé continues to be a hotly debated issue.

Aaron Myers

See Also
Bantu: Dispersion and Settlement; Yoruba; Orishas; Xangô.

Latin America and the Caribbean

Capécia, Mayotte (b. 1916, Carbet, Martinique; d. 1955, Paris, France), a writer from Martinique best known for her two novels, *Je suis martiniquaise* (1948) and *La négresse blanche* (1950).

Lucette Céranus adopted the pen name Mayotte Capécia and later gained notoriety when Frantz Fanon denounced her as an example of black women's complicity in the victimization of colonized black males by white colonialists. Others, such as Clarisse Zimra, have refuted Fanon's reading. They present a more complex view of the relationships between Capécia's protagonists with Martinican men and with metropolitan white men, and the choice made by these protagonists to leave Martinique for France. Capécia is often studied in conjunction with the two Guadeloupean writers, Michèle Lacrosil and Jacqueline Manicom, because of her portrayal of the way in which West Indian women view themselves and their place in the colonial order. Capécia died of cancer in France in 1955.

Joelle Vitiello

Africa

Cape Colony, Dutch and later British colony in southern Africa; now part of South Africa.

Africa

Cape Coloured (also called Coloured), a term commonly applied to people of mixed ancestry who live in Cape Province of South Africa.

Like the Cape Malay and the Griqua, the Cape Coloured people are part of a larger South African group of mixed African, European, and Asian descent. Their ancestors include slaves brought to the Cape Colony from the Far East, Madagascar, and West Africa. The Cape Coloured people are the largest of these groups; they number almost 3 million and account for nearly 85 percent of the Cape Province population.

Although the term *Cape Coloured* was not used before the nineteenth century, the processes of intermarriage and assimilation that produced the Coloured social category began in the seventeenth century. Dutch settlers established the Cape Colony in 1652, and they met their need for meat and other foodstuffs by trading with local African populations, such as the pastoral Khoikhoi. They met their need for labor, however, by importing slaves. Assimilated local Africans and former slaves as well as the offspring of mixed marriages came to be known as Coloured. Most people who fell into this category spoke Afrikaans – a variation of Dutch infused with words from African languages – and became members of the Dutch Reformed Church. Many worked as laborers on the farms of Dutch settlers, who came to be known as Afrikaners, or Boers. In 1806 the British assumed control of Cape Colony, and in 1834 they abolished slavery.

Emancipated slaves swelled the colony's Coloured population, and many settled and found work in cities such as Cape Town and Port Elizabeth. This urban, Afrikaner-speaking population came to be known as the Cape Coloured, a group distinct from black Africans. The Cape Coloureds used this distinction to claim superiority over other African groups and to secure better-paying jobs.

Franchise restrictions began to undermine the political rights of the Cape Coloured population in the late nineteenth century. After British and Afrikaner colonies joined to form the Union of South Africa in 1910, laws such as the Civilized Labour Policy gave whites privileged access to jobs, and segregation policies confounded Cape Coloured aspirations of assimilation.

The rights of Coloureds – like those of all other "nonwhites" – were further undermined after the National Party (NP) came to power in 1948 and imposed the system of apartheid. Although their fluency in Afrikaans gave them an advantage over black Africans on the job market, they still suffered under apartheid policies. The 1949 ban on interracial marriages, for example, tore apart hundreds of families. In 1950 the Group Areas Act mandated the relocation of both black and Coloured urban populations. Tens of thousands of Cape Coloureds were forcibly removed from their homes in Cape Town and other cities, and were relocated to overcrowded townships outside the city limits.

Today, the Cape Coloured people have reasserted their unique position in South African society. Even after the injustices of the apartheid era, many Cape Coloured people support the NP. In general, Cape Coloureds have shown little enthusiasm for the African National Congress (ANC), despite Nelson Mandela's efforts to win their support; some have even accused the ANC of appointing only black South Africans to important political positions.

Elizabeth Heath

See Also
Afrikaner; Cape Town, South Africa; Mandela, Nelson Rolihlahla; South Africa; National Party; Slavery in Africa; African National Congress.

Africa

Cape Town, South Africa, major city in South Africa.

The present legislative capital of SOUTH AFRICA, Cape Town was also one of the first European colonial settlements in Africa. Located on the Western Cape some 48 km (30 mi) north of the Cape of Good Hope, modern Cape Town radiates outward from its harbor at Table Bay. With its seacoast nearly abutting the picturesque Table Mountain, Cape Town is widely considered one of the most beautiful cities in the world.

When European ships first landed on the Cape in the mid-seventeenth century, KHOISAN-speaking San hunter-gatherers and Khoikhoi pastoralists had already been living in the region for centuries. Portuguese explorers arrived first, but it was an official of the Dutch East India trading company, JAN VAN RIEBEECK, who established the settlement that he called De Kaap (the Cape). The company intended to use the site to provision ships traveling between the Netherlands and the Indies and brought Dutch settlers to build a town and farm the land. By the 1660s the Cape settlement was importing slaves from India (*see* INDIAN OCEAN SLAVE TRADE), Malaya, and MADAGASCAR to work the farms.

The early Dutch settlers depended on trade with Khoikhoi pastoralists to supplement their own scarce meat supply, but their efforts to expand onto Khoikhoi grazing lands met with opposition. A combination of European military force and imported diseases (especially the 1713 smallpox epidemic) nearly wiped out the Khoikhoi population. Over the next century, intermarriage between Khoisan speakers, Europeans, and imported slaves created a sizable mixed-race population, whose descendants came to be known as the Cape Coloured people. At the same time, descendants of the early Dutch settlers came to identify themselves as Afrikaners, or Boers. Today, about half the population of Cape Town is racially mixed.

By the late eighteenth century, European powers were vying for control over the strategic Cape region. To prevent an English takeover in 1781, the Dutch enlisted French help in building a fort outside their town, which by then had a population of approximately 14,000. Cape Town today shows the influence of both Dutch and French architecture and city planning, but in 1806 the town and the surrounding region were taken over by the British.

The nineteenth century saw the incorporation of Cape Town and several of its suburbs, the northward extension of its rail lines, and, in 1834, the emancipation of its slaves. But the opening of the SUEZ CANAL in 1869 elimnated much of the shipping traffic that had long passed through Cape Town's harbor, and soon after the discovery of gold and diamonds in the Afrikaner-held Transvaal region, Johannesburg had eclipsed Cape Town in size and wealth. Still, the port city remained an important way station for European and Indian migrants to the Transvaal.

When British and Afrikaner territories joined to become the Union of South Africa in 1910, Cape Town became its capital. The mining industries spurred industrialization and urbanization throughout South Africa, and during World War II the rapid growth of Cape Town led to the reclamation of 358 acres of formerly submerged land. It was known as the most racially tolerant of South African cities, with less residential segregation than Johannesburg or Durban and no racial restrictions on voting in local elections. But in the 1960s and 1970s the NATIONAL PARTY'S APARTHEID regime restricted participation in Cape Town elections to whites. It also enforced segregation by bulldozing old neighborhoods and forcibly relocating some 50,000 blacks, Indians, and "coloured" people into newly formed townships.

Cape Town's local government unsuccessfully protested the moves, and the city became an important center of the ANTIAPARTHEID MOVEMENT. Since the dismantling of apartheid in the early 1990s, Cape Town's residential segregation is no longer legally enforced but, as in the rest of the country, it has far from disappeared. Cape Town is now one of South Africa's most popular tourist destinations. The city's beaches, mountains, and nearby wine country attract visitors from around the world.

Kate Tuttle

SEE ALSO

Afrikaner; Cape Coloured; Explorers in Africa, 1500 to 1800; Gold Trade; Johannesburg, South Africa; Durban, South Africa; Tourism in Africa.

Africa

Cape Verde, a small West African country comprising ten volcanic islands and five islets off the coast of SENEGAL.

For more than 400 years, PORTUGAL claimed the rocky, arid islands of Cape Verde. This long history of COLONIAL RULE permanently affected Cape Verdean culture, making the small country seem distinct from other African nations – "more European." But such a view ignores the shared ancestries and political struggles that link the islands to the mainland. Cape Verde is home to a population descended from free people and West African slaves as well as a diverse mix of peoples: Fula, WOLOF, Papeis, Balanta, Bijago, Jalofa, Fulupe, Mandingo, Manjaco, Portuguese, Moroccan, Sephardic Jewish, Lebanese, Dutch, Genoese, Chinese, French, English, American, and Brazilian. The children of these settlers and passers-by forged a hybrid culture and language known as Crioulo (Portuguese for Creole), drawing upon the legacies brought to the islands by slavery and colonialism.

PORTUGUESE COLONIZATION AND SLAVE TRADE

It is possible that the Cape Verde Islands were visited by Phoenician traders in the fifth or fourth century B.C.E., and even more likely that North African sailors in the SALT TRADE passed through during the tenth and eleventh centuries C.E. Fishers from the region of present-day Senegal later landed in the area during their expeditions, but the islands were not permanently occupied until the Portuguese took possession of them in the fifteenth century. Exploration and slave trading had brought Portuguese ships past the southern islands for several years before the Genoan Antonio de Noli and the Portuguese Diogo Afonso claimed them for Portugal in 1455. Although the islands themselves offered limited natural resources, they were strategically located on what were soon to be busy transatlantic trade routes. Having recently settled the Madeira Islands, Portugal next moved to settle Cape Verde, intending to use the islands both as an entrepôt for its merchant ships and a site for producing tropical-climate crops, such as SUGAR and cotton.

The expansion of the slave trade across the Atlantic Ocean in the sixteenth century soon brought business and settlement to Cape Verde. Portugal made the islands its headquarters for its holdings on the Upper Guinea Coast, and by the sixteenth century was also using the region as a penal colony for convicts and political exiles. The islands were originally governed by the *companhia* system, a sort of feudal system in which the church or individuals oversaw small plantations where slaves, brought from mainland West Africa, cultivated cotton, sugar cane, and food crops. Early Cape Verdean society enjoyed considerable autonomy from the Portuguese monarchy, making it an attractive base for generations of traders and smugglers.

Despite efforts to develop plantation agriculture, little besides the population grew on the drought-prone islands, and the economy relied heavily on the commerce provided by passing ships, first those traveling to and from West Africa, and later, those crossing the Atlantic. Portugal's merchant ships exchanged rum, cloth, and other commodities for slaves acquired at ports all along the Upper Guinea Coast, and many of the goods and slaves passed at least briefly through Cape Verde. As a result, the islands' ports became targets for plunder by pirate ships sailing under the flags of FRANCE, Holland, and England. In 1656 Portugal sent a governor-general to oversee more directly the protection and governance of Cape Verde and the Portuguese-controlled Guinea Coast and to crack down on the smuggling that was eroding Portuguese control over the region's lucrative trades. But with the many free agents operating along the West African coasts – including both "official" European traders and independent smugglers – Portugal had little success in controlling trade of slaves or other articles of commerce.

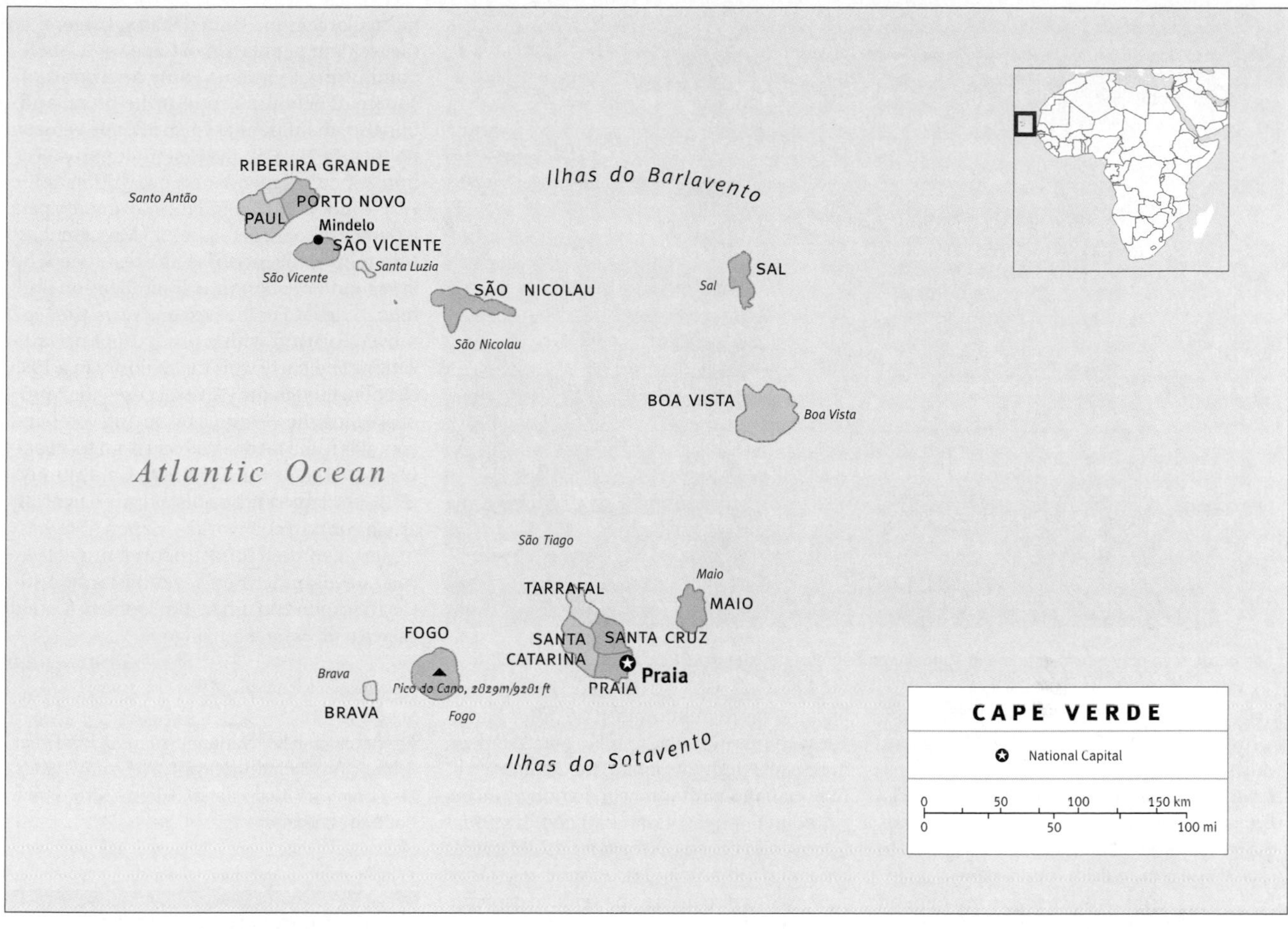

In 1750 the prime minister of Portugal, the marquis of Pombal, declared a trade monopoly for slaves and certain other commodities between Cape Verde, Guinea, and Brazil. Portugal's goal was to increase and streamline the export of slaves from West Africa to its American colony via Cape Verde, using the 41 ships of the royal *Campanhia Geral*, which the marquis controlled. Some of the slaves routed through the islands were also sold in Britain's North American colonies. Even after the fall of the marquis, Cape Verde remained a favored entrepôt among slave traders. It was closer to the Americas and considered safer than the ports of call on the Africa mainland, which were often controlled by powerful and well-armed African kings and merchants.

Not all African slaves brought to the islands went on to the Americas. Besides working on the cotton, sugar, and coffee plantations, slaves worked as domestic servants, as laborers in the islands' small salt-production enterprises, and as gatherers of plants used for dyes, including orchil and urzella. These dyes were in turn used by slave Wolof spinners and weavers to produce the colorful *pano* clothes that served as one of the main currencies in the slave trade. In addition, some freed or runaway slaves cultivated land in the hills of the interior.

Over the years, a heterogeneous Creole population developed, comprising convicts, exiles, Portuguese merchants, social outcasts, and Catholic clerics as well as slaves and migrants from the Upper Guinea Coast. Cape Verdean society made distinctions among the races and the classes, as well as between slaves who lived on the islands and those who simply passed through. At the same time, however, interracial unions between white masters and slave women, who made up more than half of the slave population, created a sizable *mestiço* (of indigenous and European descent) population. Over time, this mixed population came to include the children of mixed marriages between renegade traders (*lacondos*) and their African wives. Some of these traders were Jews fleeing the Spanish Inquisition from the late sixteenth to the mid-seventeenth century, when Portugal was under the rule of the Spanish Crown. Crioulo, a hybrid of Portuguese and various African languages, became the lingua franca of the mestiços. Crioulo was also spoken on the Guinea Coast, an indication of the ongoing multiethnic migration and trade between the islands and mainland.

Peasant Farming and Maritime Trade
Britain's 1807 edict banning slave trading spelled the end of an era for the local and regional economies which had developed around this commerce. Portugal officially abolished its own trade in 1836, though slavers continued to smuggle captives through Cape Verde for decades afterward. Meanwhile, the colony had become an entrepôt for other kinds of commodities from the mainland, including hides, ivory, wax, and dyewoods. With the invention of steam-powered boats, the islands also served as a refueling stop on the transatlantic passage.

The islands supported a growing Creole free peasantry, including manumitted slaves. Farmers cultivated grains, tended banana orchards, and raised livestock, especially goats, but the poor land made subsistence difficult, and a single season of drought often led quickly to famine. Many Cape Verdean farmers sought to bolster their economic security by seeking additional, if low-paid, work as sharecroppers or manual day-laborers, but many others signed onto American whaling ships and joined growing expatriate communities in New England.

In the late nineteenth century, even as Europeans were beginning to colonize most of Africa, opposition to Portugese Crown rule was growing in both Cape Verde and Guinea-Bissau. In 1886 the Portuguese monarchy sent troops to quell unrest; after 1910 the Portuguese republican government used similarly strong-armed tactics. A Fascist government took control of Portugal in 1926 and wrote colonial policy into the constitution with the Colonial Act of 1933. The government cracked down on communist groups in Portugal who were, among other things, assisting the budding nationalist movements of Lusophone

Cape Verde men play music at home in Mindelo, on São Vicente island. *CORBIS/Robert van der Hilst*

Africa. Dissidents from Guinea-Bissau and Portugal were sent to Cape Verdean prisons, which were known for their brutal conditions. Nevertheless, anticolonialist and anti-Fascist revolts continued to rock Guinea-Bissau and, to a lesser extent, the Cape Verde islands. In Cape Verde nationalism found expression in the literary-cultural *Claridade* movement. Using the literary journal *Claridade*, founded in 1936, Cape Verdean intellectuals both on the islands and abroad gave voice to Cape Verdean Crioulo culture. They also wrote critically about the social and economic oppression of Portuguese colonialism.

Anticolonial Resistance

Many Cape Verdeans opposed the new Fascist government as well as the strong-armed Portuguese tactics that had characterized relations with Cape Verde since the late nineteenth century. The colonial government believed it unnecessary to invest in land management and water conservation, and cheap labor made Cape Verde a profitable colony at little expense. Meanwhile, the people of the islands had suffered a series of droughts and bad harvests through the turn of the century. As people died daily from hunger while Portuguese troops landed on the island, Cape Verdeans prepared to revolt.

Fearing a growing nationalist sentiment, Portugal granted Cape Verde the status of overseas province. It also increased police powers in the colonies. Convicts and dissidents were sent to a notorious work camp on the Cape Verde island of São Tiago, where police used torture to quash resistance. Nationalists responded by rallying behind the Partido Africano da Independencia da Guine e Cabo Verde (PAIGC), a party founded in 1956 by Amílcar Cabral, and by staging a series of general strikes. The organization grew and became more militant in 1959, after Portuguese troops massacred striking dockworkers in Bissau. Four years later PAIGC launched a full-out nationalist war, with fighting concentrated in Guinea-Bissau and clandestine operations based on the islands. Portugal, receiving military and economic assistance from NATO, also used Cape Verde to garrison its troops.

Independence

Following the assassination of Cabral in 1973, the PAIGC intensified attacks against an increasingly weakened Portuguese military, and a year later Guinea-Bissau achieved independence. But the struggle continued with massive protests in Cape Verde. Although Portugal had wished to maintain the islands as an overseas territory, Cape Verde ultimately won independence on July 5, 1975, with PAIGC carrying the popular election. PAIGC leaders in both Cape Verde and Guinea-Bissau at first anticipated the unification of their two countries, but disagreements over socialist strategies as well as resentment about the perceived dominance of Cape Verdeans left the party divided. In 1980 the arrest of Guinea-Bissau president Luís Cabral split the ranks of the PAIGC, and shortly thereafter Pedro Pires, Cape Verde's prime minister and a prominent nationalist, helped found the Partido Africano da Independencia da Cabo Verde (PAICV). Pires moved quickly to silence any potential political opponents, thus ensuring a long term in office though with little popular support.

Under Pires the country followed a socialist path, with programs of nationalization and agrarian reform. Through the 1980s Cape Verde's close relationship with countries such as the Soviet Union, Cuba, and Libya generated opposition from diasporic communities, particularly in the United States. Larger than the resident population of Cape Verde, these communities were not only an important source of economic aid for the homeland, but also an influential voice in Cape Verdean politics. In 1991, in the first multiparty elections since independence, opposition to the PAICV mobilized behind the Movimento para a Democracia (MpD). Antonio Mascarenhas Monteiro replaced Pires as president, with an agenda of economic liberalization and human rights. For the next few years, the MpD moved forward with a program of privatization. The party won the majority in a 1995 election, though the PAICV accused the MpD of skewing the elections by buying votes and controlling the media. With aid from the World Bank as well as the European Community (EC) – the largest per capita aid given to nearly any nation in the world – Cape Verde has undertaken such infrastructural projects as road development on several islands and electrification and urban development around the city of Praia, São Tiago.

Marian Aguiar

See Also

African Socialism; Nationalism in Africa; Great Britain; Transatlantic Slave Trade; Netherlands, The; Creoles; Miscegenation; Pires, Pedro Verona Rodrigues; Bijagó.

Africa

Cape Verde (Ready Reference)

Official Name: Republic of Cape Verde
Area: 4033 sq km (1557 sq mi)
Location: Cape Verde is an archipelago, consisting of ten islands and five islets, in the Atlantic Ocean, due west of the westernmost point of Africa, near Mauritania and Senegal. The windward, or Barlavento, group of islands on the north includes Santo Antão, São Vicente, São Nicolau, Santa Luzia, Sal, and Boa Vista; the leeward, or Sotavento, group on the south includes São Tiago, Brava, Fogo, and Maio.
Capital: Praia, São Tiago (population 61,644 [1990 estimate])
Other Major Cities: Mindelo, São Vicente (47,109 [1990 estimate])
Population: 399,857 (1998 estimate)
Population Density: 111 people per sq km (about 288 per sq mi)
Population Below Age 15: 46 percent (male 91,409; female 89,810 [1997 estimate])
Population Growth Rate: 2.9 percent (1996 estimate)
Total Fertility Rate: 5.2 children born per woman (1997 estimate)
Life Expectancy at Birth: Total population 63.4 years (male 61.5 years; female 65.4 years [1996 estimate])
Infant Mortality Rate: 54.3 deaths per 1000 live births (1996 estimate)
Literacy Rate (age 15 and over who can read and write): 71.6 percent (male 81.4

percent; female 63.8 percent [1995 estimate])
Education: Six years of primary school are compulsory.
Languages: Portuguese is the official language; the national language, however, is *Crioulo*, a Creole based on archaic Portuguese incorporating many African elements.
Ethnic Groups: More than two-thirds of the people of Cape Verde are either mulatto (of mixed African and European descent) and are known as CREOLES, or *mestiços* (of indigenous and European descent). Nearly all of the remainder are of African ancestry.
Religions: Roman Catholicism is the dominant religion, but is often fused with indigenous beliefs.
Climate: Tropical and dry, showing little variation throughout the year. The average temperature in Praia, the capital, ranges from 20° to 25° C (68° to 77° F) in January and 24° to 28° C (75° to 83° F) in July. Winds are frequent, occasionally carrying clouds of sand from the Sahara in Africa to the east. Precipitation is slight and irregular, and the islands are subject to drought. Average precipitation in Praia is 260 mm (10 in), nearly all of which falls from August through September.
Land, Plants, and Animals: The islands are volcanic in origin, and all but three – Sal, Boa Vista, and Maio – are mountainous. The highest point, Pico do Cano (2829 m/9281 ft) on Fogo, is also the group's only active volcano. Vegetation is sparse and consists of various shrubs, aloes, and other drought-resistant species. Wildlife is limited and includes lizards, monkeys, wild goats, and a variety of birdlife.
Natural Resources: Cape Verde is located in the midst of rich fishing grounds, although the industry has yet to develop to its potential. Mineral resources are meager and primarily include pozzolana (a volcanic rock used in making cement) and salt. Salt is mined on Sal, Boa Vista, and Maio, with annual production of about 7000 metric tons.
Currency: The Cape Verdean escudo
Gross Domestic Product (GDP): $538 million (1997 estimate)
GDP per Capita: $1370 (1997 estimate)
GDP Real Growth Rate: 4.5 percent (1997 estimate)
Primary Economic Activities: 60 percent of the GDP comes from service-oriented industries, including commerce, transport, and public services. Despite scarce arable land and regular drought, 70 percent of the population lives in rural areas, and agriculture is the nation's principal economic activity. Fish-processing facilities have been constructed in Mindelo, and the government has initiated programs to modernize the fishing fleet. Cape Verde is attempting to capitalize on its strategic location at the crossroads of mid-Atlantic air and sea lanes by expanding airports and port facilities.
Primary Crops: Staple crops are maize and beans, sweet potatoes, coconuts, potatoes, cassava, and dates. Some bananas are grown for export, and sugar cane is raised for the making of rum. Fishing yields yellowfin tuna, skipjack, wahoo (a type of large mackerel), and lobsters.
Industries: Fish processing, salt mining, garments, ship repair, food, and beverages
Primary Exports: Fish and bananas
Primary Imports: Foodstuffs, consumer goods, industrial products, and transport equipment
Primary Trade Partners: Portugal, Spain, Netherlands, Brazil, the United States, and Japan
Government: A new constitution declared in 1992 affirmed Cape Verde as a multiparty democracy, expanding on reforms begun in 1990 that introduced free and popular elections for president and parliament. Legislative power is held by the 79-member National Assembly; members are elected by the voters to five-year terms. The head of state is the president, currently Antonio Mascarenhas Monteiro, also elected to a five-year term. A prime minister, currently Carlos Alberto Wahnon de Carvalho Veiga, is nominated by the assembly and appointed by the president.

Marian Aguiar

SEE ALSO
Sahara Desert.

Cape Verde Islands. Please see CAPE VERDE

Latin America and the Caribbean

Cap-Haïtien, Haiti, also Le Cap, city and seaport of northern HAITI; capital of Nord Department, on the Manzanillo Bay, an inlet of the Atlantic Ocean.

Cap-Haïtien has a spacious harbor and is an export center for coffee, cocoa, hides, honey, and logwood. In the seventeenth century the Spaniards built on the site of Cap-Haïtien a settlement that became a French possession in 1697. Under the French, who made it the capital of their colony of Saint-Domingue, it was a flourishing town, referred to as Little Paris. From 1811 to 1820 Cap-Haïtien was the capital of northern Haiti under HENRI CHRISTOPHE, who declared himself king of Haiti. Christophe was responsible for building several monumental structures in the town, including the Sans Souci palace and the Citadelle Laferrière fortress. The town was almost destroyed by an earthquake in 1842. According to a 1994 estimate, the population of Cap-Haïtien is 68,000.

Europe

Capitein, Jacobus Elisa

(b. February 21, 1718?, Elmina, Gold Coast [present-day Ghana]; d. 1747, Elmina, Gold Coast), the first African ordained as minister in an established Protestant church.

Jacobus Elisa Joannes Capitein was one of the few educated Africans in eighteenth-century EUROPE. He became a Protestant minister at a time when many Europeans doubted that Africans had a soul and questioned whether they could be converted to Christianity.

Capitein was born in West Africa, perhaps in Elmina on the Gold Coast (present-day GHANA), where he was sold into slavery at the age of eight. The man who bought him presented him to a Dutch captain and trader, Jacobus van Goch, at Elmina. Van Goch named him Jacobus Capitein and took him to the Netherlands in 1728.

They settled in the Hague, where Capitein learned Dutch. Van Goch acquiesced when Capitein expressed interest in a theological education. Capitein learned Latin, Hebrew, Greek, and biblical Aramaic and in 1735 he was baptized. In 1737 he won a scholarship to study theology at the University of Leiden.

Capitein explained that he was interested in theology because he wanted "to be able to show his countrymen the way from idolatry to the true worship of God." In his thesis paper he argued that Africans are equal to whites but condoned slavery as a means to convert "heathens." The thesis was published and became popular among slaveholders and plantation owners because it justified the slave trade. While attending university, Capitein wrote poems and essays and gave sermons, many of which were published and received significant attention in the Netherlands. Two portraits of him sold widely, and he was upheld as an example of Christianity's universality.

Capitein was ordained upon his graduation in 1742 and was appointed chaplain to the European community in Elmina. He attempted to apply his vision for successful missionary work – the use of African languages in teaching, the provision of a separate place of worship for the Africans, daily contact with the Africans, and the training of locals for missionary work. However, his efforts brought few conversions. His work among the Europeans was also unsuccessful; few of the resident Dutch soldiers and slave traders cared to attend church.

Capitein's mission was not only a failure professionally but also personally. His employer, the West India Company, would not permit him to marry an African woman and instead in 1745 sent a white Dutch woman, Antonia Grinderdos, to be his wife. Capitein's financial difficulties further strained this arranged marriage. The company paid him poorly and expected him to supplement his income with private enterprise. His trading initiatives were fruitless. Gradually, Capitein declined physically, emotionally, and financially. He died suddenly in 1747. His tragic career provided racists with another reason to believe that blacks should not be members of the Church. However, his mastery of European languages and his erudition proved to many Europeans that Africans were their equals.

Leyla Keough

See Also

Netherlands, The.

Latin America and the Caribbean

Capoeira, an Afro-Brazilian ritual developed by African slaves in Brazil; simultaneously a fight and a dance.

The Game

Capoeira combines various elements, including dance, combat, music, and song. It is performed to live music, with two capoeiristas taking turns at the center of a *roda*, or circle, formed by the players, musicians, and spectators. At the head of the roda is an ensemble of percussion instruments called the *bateria*. The bateria usually includes three *berimbaus* (bow-shaped instruments), an *atabaque* (a long, cylindrical drum), one or two *pandeiros* (tambourine-like instruments), an *agogô* (a double-headed bell), and a *reco-reco* (a small instrument with a corrugated surface). The bateria's rhythm and pace dictate the style and speed of the play in the circle, and the songs sung by the musicians often comment upon, criticize, or encourage the physical play.

The roda begins with a slow rhythm played on the berimbaus. One by one, the other instruments join in, and one of the more experienced players, usually the *mestre* (master, the leader of the group), begins to sing a solo called a *ladainha* (litany). The ladainha leads into the *louvação*, in which the players repeat after the singer phrases praising God and the singer's own mestre, among other things. Following the louvação is the *corrido*, a traditional call-and-response song. For the remainder of the roda, different members of the bateria take turns leading the players in the singing of various corridos.

At the beginning of the roda, two players squat in front of the berimbaus. Following the transition from the louvação to the corrido, the two players shake hands and enter the roda, often with a cartwheel-like move called an *aú*. Once in the roda, the two players mirror one another in a rocking, side-to-side step called the *ginga*, the most important and fundamental step in capoeira. In training sessions, the players learn how to execute various *golpes* (strikes) and *defesas* (defenses) while doing the ginga. In the roda, the two players spontaneously combine golpes and defesas, creating an interlocking series of movements. Players also use an array of acrobatic movements to move away from or around their partner. Actual physical contact between the two is rarely made. Instead, the game is a series of feints and counterfeints, with each player trying to anticipate the movement of the other, though occasionally the players will try to sweep each other off their feet or otherwise knock each other off balance.

The *jogo* (game) between two players may go on for several minutes. It ends at the discretion of one of the players or of the mestre, who stops the game by lowering a berimbau into the roda and playing a monotone note. The two players then return to the foot of the berimbaus, shake hands, and exit. Two new players replace them and another game begins. There is no explicit winner or loser in a game, and the physical conversation between the players may take several forms, depending on the music, spirit of play, or personal relationship between the players. The game can be playful, eloquent, and cooperative; mocking and teasing; or, occasionally, combative. Much of capoeira's beauty stems from its dynamism. Throughout the play, the stylish display of surprise and trickery is highly valued.

Celebrated capoeira Mestre João Pequeno, *left*, plays capoeira with one of his students at his academy in Bahia's oldest fort, Santo Antônio da Barra. *CORBIS/Stephanie Maze*

The Origins of Capoeira

Several scholars have documented capoeira's connection to central and southwestern Africa, especially Angola. During Brazil's colonial era, Angola, also a Portuguese colony, was one one of Brazil's principal sources of slave labor. Bantu words such as *Aruandé* (referring to the slave port of Luanda, Angola) frequently appear in capoeira songs. Anthropologists have identified the *n'golo*, or zebra dance, of southern Angola as the African prototype for what became capoeira in Brazil. They have also documented a variety of musical bows in central and southwestern Africa that are related to, or were perhaps transformed into, the berimbau.

Historians have not clearly documented how capoeira evolved in Brazil into its current form. Some capoeiristas argue that capoeira was brought intact to Brazil by African slaves, while others claim that it was forged in Brazil. Those arguing that capoeira had its genesis in Brazil are divided as to whether it developed in the *senzalas* (slave quarters on the plantations) or in *quilombos* (communities of escaped slaves) (*see* Maroonage in the Americas). One of the most enduring myths links capoeira to Zumbi, the king of the seventeenth-century quilombo of Palmares, who has become a symbol for contemporary Afro-Brazilian social movements. Despite their conflicting theories, many capoeiristas agree that slaves developed capoeira as a form of self-defense and that they preserved it under slavery by disguising it as playful dance.

Capoeira's Early History

The latter part of the eighteenth century was an important time in capoeira's development, as black neighborhoods emerged in Brazil's urban centers. At this time, capoeiristas began forming neighborhood-based gangs, which fought one another and terrorized the cities' inhabitants. They earned a criminal reputation and were often imprisoned for playing capoeira. However, they were sometimes sought by colonial officials for their fighting skills.

Capoeira is first mentioned in a series of newspaper articles in Rio de Janeiro around 1770. At that time a Portuguese lieutenant known as Amontiado, the bodyguard of Viceroy Marquis de Lavradio, often used capoeira to protect the viceroy. By the early nineteenth

Many capoeiristas agree that African slaves in Brazil developed capoeira as a form of self defense, but preserved it by disguising it as a playful dance.
Robb Kendrick/Aurora

century, capoeira was officially classified as a crime. In 1810 Maj. Nunes Vidigal, the first commander of the Royal Guard police force in Rio de Janeiro and reportedly an adept capoeirista, began to crack down on its practitioners. Shortly thereafter, in 1828, the Brazilian government employed a band of capoeiristas armed with razors who successfully quelled a group of rioting German and Irish soldiers in Rio de Janeiro. Capoeiristas also reportedly helped lead several attacks during the Paraguayan War (1865-1870). After the abolition of slavery in 1888, politicians sometimes hired capoeiristas to force people to vote a certain way or to disrupt the political gatherings of their opponents. Despite these collaborative efforts, the government persecuted capoeiristas for much of the nineteenth century and in 1890 enacted a federal statute outlawing capoeira. The stigmatization and repression of capoeira endured into the twentieth century.

In the 1930s, during the administration of Getúlio Vargas, a shift in the perception of capoeira began. Vargas relaxed restrictions on cultural festivities such as Carnival, which he brought under government sponsorship in 1932. Soon after, he began allowing the practice of capoeira, though it was initially limited to closed areas registered with the police. As a result, many capoeira academies began to open, first in Salvador, Bahia, then in other urban centers, and eventually throughout Brazil.

Mestre Bimba (Manuel dos Reis Machado, 1900-1974) opened the first capoeira academy in Salvador, Bahia, in 1932. He taught a hybrid form of capoeira known as *capoeira regional* that incorporated elements of *batuque*, a fighting technique that he had learned from his father. Bimba presented capoeira regional before the governor of Bahia in the late 1930s, and in 1955 he was congratulated by President Getúlio Vargas for turning capoeira into a "national fight."

As capoeira regional grew in popularity, Mestre Pastinha (Vicente Ferreira Pastinha, 1889-1982) opened his own academy in 1941 and worked to preserve the traditional form of capoeira, which he termed *capoeira Angola*. Mestre Pastinha presented capoeira Angola in 1966 at the Premier Festival International des Arts Negres de Dakar in Senegal. Today, Mestre Bimba and Mestre Pastinha are the two most celebrated figures in capoeira.

Capoeira Today

In 1975 Brazilian capoeira mestres Jelon Viera and Loremil Machado introduced capoeira in New York City. At about the same time, breakdancing was emerging in New York City, and many scholars have speculated that some breakdancing moves were inspired by capoeira. Mestres Viera and Machado paved the way for several other Brazilian capoeira mestres to set up academies throughout the United States and in Europe.

In the past capoeira has been a predominantly male activity. There are few known examples of female capoeiristas before the 1940s and 1950s; one was a woman called Maria Doze Homens. Today, some estimate that nearly half of capoeira's practitioners are female, some of whom have achieved the status of mestre. Historically, most capoeiristas have been lower-class Brazilian blacks and mulattos (of African and European descent). Since Mestre Bimba opened his academy, however, capoeira has been attracting an increasing number of upper- and middle-class Brazilians of European descent. With the spread of capoeira beyond Brazil, it is now practiced by people of all classes, races, and nationalities.

A consequence of capoeira's popularity has been its commercialization. It is a major tourist attraction in Brazil, especially in Bahia, and in the United States it has been marketed through Hollywood movies and video games. To ensure that capoeira does not lose its identity, mestres of both capoeira regional and capoeira Angola have formed national and international associations to help preserve the values and traditions of their respective forms. As a result of these efforts, capoeira regional and capoeira Angola continue to thrive both in Brazil and abroad.

Aaron Myers

See Also

Bantu: Dispersion and Settlement; Luanda, Angola; Palmares: An African State in Brazil; New York, New York; Rio de Janeiro, Brazil; Abolition and

Emancipation in Latin America and the Caribbean; Carnivals in Latin America and the Caribbean.

Latin America and the Caribbean

Carbonell, Walterio (b. 1925), Cuban historian who has written extensively on the history of Afro-Cubans; author of *Cómo surgió la cultura nacional* (1961, Birth of a National Culture) (*see* Cuba).

Europe

Cardiff, Great Britain, the capital and largest city of Wales, with perhaps the oldest multiethnic community in the United Kingdom (see Great Britain).

Cardiff was the world's leading exporter of coal and a major industrial center during the late nineteenth and early twentieth centuries. The rough seas of the Bristol Channel outside the city's port earned the district the name Tiger Bay. Cardiff attracted sailors from all over the world, including low-paid black seamen from Africa and the West Indies, along with others from the Middle East, India, and Southeast Asia.

By the 1890s sailors frequented seedy bars and houses of prostitution in the area around the Cardiff docks known as Butetown. As a result, Cardiff gained a reputation as a place of vice and corruption. In 1914, as whites left to fight in World War I, black immigrants came to fill the positions left behind. Up to 3000 people from British colonies in Asia, Africa, and the West Indies settled in Cardiff. Many of the blacks married local white women and decided to raise their families in Butetown.

After the war ended in 1918, whites returned to demand their jobs back. Unemployment was particularly high in Cardiff because the wartime production boom had ended. The industrial and seamen's unions demanded that employers hire whites before blacks. Racist whites further resented blacks because of the city's high rate of intermarriage between black men and white women.

These tensions exploded into violent riots over four days in the summer of 1919. Mobs of white people attacked blacks – mainly African immigrants – and destroyed their homes. Many blacks fought back with gunfire. After the second day the police and firefighters finally intervened and escorted some 1000 blacks out of town. Blacks who remained faced two more days of violence. In total, 14 men were hospitalized and 1 died. The police, some of whom were accused of assisting the rioting whites, arrested 15 blacks but only 4 whites.

The government responded to the employment disputes and riots by calling for the repatriation of blacks to their homelands. Unions then pressured the government to institute the Aliens Order Act of 1925, which required all blacks to prove their birth or continuous residence in Great Britain. Because many blacks did not keep such documentation, they were registered as aliens and subject to random deportation.

In Cardiff, authorities used the act as a tool for harassment and registered the entire black community as aliens. Although few blacks were actually deported as a result, many suffered layoffs and employment discrimination. The Shipping Act of 1935 contained a clause that allowed the government to subsidize only those companies that hired British nationals, a category that now excluded Cardiff's blacks. This final assault on their livelihood prompted blacks to establish the Coloured Seamen's Union to represent their concerns to the government. The union, with the assistance of the League of Coloured Peoples, helped many blacks to restore their status as residents or their British nationality and thus regain eligibility for work in the shipping industries.

Since the 1940s racial discrimination, unemployment, and poverty have racked the multicultural community of Cardiff. Even so, as writer Neil M. C. Sinclair stated in *The Tiger Bay Story* (1993), the Butetown in which he grew up during the 1950s was a happy and secure community. He took pride in what he called the "racially heterogeneous community representative of an advanced form of social existence," where "you can see the world in one square mile."

Beginning in the 1960s, as coal exports declined and industrial jobs disappeared, planners implemented a series of urban redevelopment projects in an effort to revive Cardiff's economy. The Cardiff Development Corporation began a project, probably the largest of its kind in Europe, in 1987, which was still active as of the late 1990s. Their plans included redesigning Butetown into a fashionable residential and commercial district. These changes aimed to draw young professionals, new companies, and tourists to the area. Cardiff hosted the 1998 summit of the European Union and planned to host the Rugby World Cup in 1999 in a new stadium.

The developers intended for the project to provide new housing and job opportunities to the local Butetown residents. But as of 1998 few could afford the luxurious residences being built, and most found it difficult to secure employment in the new companies. Thus, the redevelopment caused hardship for many black and low-income residents of Butetown. Many felt that it would destroy their already dwindling community.

Leyla Keough

North America

Cardozo, Francis Louis (b. February 1, 1837, Charleston, S.C.; d. 1903, Washington, D.C.), American minister, educator, and politician; first African American South Carolinian to hold a government office.

Francis Louis Cardozo was born free on February 1, 1837, in Charleston, South Carolina to a prominent Jewish businessman and economist, Isaac N. Cardozo, and a free African American woman whose name is unknown.

Cardozo was trained as a carpenter but at age 21 began to study for the ministry at the University of Glasgow in Scotland and at seminaries in Edinburgh and London. He won awards for his mastery of Greek and Latin. He returned to the United States as minister of Temple Street Congregational Church in New Haven, Connecticut. During Reconstruction (1865-1877), as a member of the American Missionary Association, he became principal of the Saxton School. In 1866 he helped establish and became superintendent of the Avery Normal Institute in Charleston to train African American teachers.

In 1868 Cardozo became involved in politics, acting as a delegate to the 1868 South Carolina state constitutional convention. As South Carolina's secretary of state (1868-1872), he became its first African American to hold a government office. He was state treasurer for five years until 1878, when he was appointed to the United States Treasury Department in Washington, D.C.

Considered a moderate by his peers, Cardozo found a home among the African American elite in Washington. He accepted a job there as principal of the Colored High School, administering the school from 1884 to 1896. He died in 1903 in Washington, D.C.

Alonford James Robinson, Jr.

Latin America and the Caribbean

Carew, Jan (b. September 24, 1920?, Agricola, Guyana), Guyanese writer and educator.

One profile of Jan Carew calls him "a prolific and versatile writer who has lived in South and North America, the Caribbean, Africa, and Europe and whose work includes novels, poetry, plays for theater, television, and radio, screenplays, essays, and books for children and young adults." This is a fitting summary of his diverse career.

Carew was born in a small village in British Guiana (now Guyana), in 1920 (some sources say 1925), the son of a planter. After graduating from the prestigious Berbice High School, he briefly taught there and then worked from 1940 to 1943 for the British Colonial Civil Service in British Guiana. From 1943 to 1944 he worked for the government of Trinidad

AND TOBAGO, before leaving the Caribbean to continue his education.

Carew went first to the United States, where he attended HOWARD UNIVERSITY and Western Reserve University (now Case Western Reserve University), and then to Europe, where he attended Charles University in Prague and the Sorbonne in Paris. He eventually received an M.Sc. from the Sorbonne, but his travels between schools were just the beginning of what he has called a lifetime of "endless journeying." After living in Paris, he lived briefly in Holland and toured as an actor with the Laurence Olivier Company before moving to London. There he worked at the University of London as a lecturer on race relations, and then as a broadcaster, writer, and editor with the British Broadcasting Corporation.

Despite these travels, Carew's first two novels, *Black Midas* and *The Wild Coast,* both published in 1958, have very vivid Guyanese settings. Later books would reflect the range of his experiences, such as *The Last Barbarian* (1960), set in Harlem; *Moscow Is Not My Mecca* (1964), set in the former Soviet Union; and *Save the Last Dance for Me* (1976), set in England. But even when Carew's books are not set in the Caribbean, they still often focus on Caribbean characters and on the struggle of colonized West Indians to define their own identity, whether at home or in exile. His nonfiction focuses on similar themes and has included such works as a study of Indian and African presence in the Americas and a history of GRENADA.

Carew's travels continued into the 1960s as he spent time in JAMAICA (with his second wife, Jamaican novelist Sylvia Winter), Spain, GHANA, and Canada. His positions during these years included director of culture in British Guiana and adviser to the prime minister there; Latin American correspondent for the *London Observer;* and adviser to the publicity secretariat of the government of Ghana. Carew's fiction and work for television gained wide notice during this period and he won several awards, including the Canada Arts Council Fellowship and the London *Daily Mirror*'s award for Best Play of 1964, for *The Big Pride*.

In 1969 Carew became a lecturer in Third World literature and creative writing at Princeton University. Since then he has had a second distinguished career as a university professor, most notably at Northwestern University in Evanston, Illinois, where he was professor of African American and Third World Studies from 1973 to 1987; he has been professor emeritus there since 1987. Carew has also served as a visiting professor at several universities, but his teaching has never disrupted his prodigious writing pace. His many honors and awards include the Casa de las Americas Award for poetry, the WALTER RODNEY Award from the Association of Caribbean Studies, and the London Hansib Publication Award.

Lisa Clayton Robinson

Latin America and the Caribbean

Carew, Rod (b. October 1, 1945, Gatun, Panama), Hall of Fame baseball player who played 19 major league seasons and became one of the most successful hitters of baseball's modern era.

Rod Carew started playing baseball at an early age in PANAMA. At age 17 he moved with his mother to New York City, where he played ball in sandlots. Signed by the Minnesota Twins organization when he was in high school, he played from 1964 to 1967 for minor league teams in Melbourne and Orlando, Florida. In his major league debut in 1967, he played second base for the Twins, hitting .292 in 137 games and winning the American League Rookie of the Year Award. In 1976 he was moved to first base, in part because of a serious knee injury suffered in 1970. In 1979, after announcing that he would become a free agent, Carew was traded to the California Angels. He hit .305 or better in each of the next five seasons before dropping below .300 for the first time since 1968. His playing career ended in the spring of 1986. He later became the batting coach for the Angels.

Carew, who threw right-handed and batted left-handed, won seven batting titles (1969, 1972-1975, 1977-1978) and had a lifetime batting average of .328. In 1969 he stole home seven times, setting a league record. In 1977 he won the American League's Most Valuable Player award after hitting .388, a career best, with 239 hits and 128 runs scored. In the 1985 season he became the 16th player in major league history to reach 3000 hits. He was inducted into the Baseball Hall of Fame in Cooperstown, New York, in 1991.

Throughout his career in the United States, Carew retained his citizenship and ties to PANAMA, where he is now a national hero. He endured a widely publicized struggle to help his daughter Michelle survive leukemia, with which she was stricken in 1995; she died in April 1996.

Kurt Mullen

SEE ALSO
New York, New York.

Latin America and the Caribbean

Caribbean Community (CARICOM), the Caribbean Community and Common Market, an economic and political association of predominantly Anglophone Caribbean nations created by treaty on July 4, 1973.

Despite its severe difficulties in the 1980s, the Caribbean Community and Common Market (CARICOM) is considered by many observers to be one of the most successful regional economic arrangements outside the European Community (EC). CARICOM grew out of CARIFTA, the Caribbean Free Trade Association, formed in 1968 by the English-speaking Caribbean countries to encourage development and economic independence in the region. In 1973 the larger CARIFTA countries – JAMAICA, TRINIDAD AND TOBAGO, GUYANA, and BARBADOS – formed CARICOM. By 1974 the eight other members of CARIFTA had joined: ANTIGUA AND BARBUDA, British Honduras (now BELIZE), DOMINICA, GRENADA, MONTSERRAT, ST. KITTS AND NEVIS, ST. LUCIA, and ST. VINCENT AND THE GRENADINES. The BAHAMAS joined CARICOM in 1983, although remaining outside the Common Market, and SURINAME joined in 1995. The British Virgin Islands and the Turks and Caicos became associate members of CARICOM in 1991.

CARICOM has a triple mandate: economic integration, the maintenance of joint institutions, and foreign policy coordination. Its highest decision-making body is the annual Heads of Government Conference, whose decisions are implemented by the Caribbean Community Secretariat based in Georgetown, Guyana. CARICOM has a common external tariff and common fiscal incentives for industry. Joint institutions include the University of the West Indies, the Caribbean Development Bank, and the Caribbean Investment Corporation, whose mandate is to assist the less developed countries of the region.

Tensions arose within CARICOM in the late 1970s due to an economic downturn. The 1979 revolution in Grenada and the arrival in power of socialist leader MAURICE BISHOP threw the region into crisis. Conservative leaders in Barbados, Dominica, and Jamaica, who opposed Bishop and supported the 1983 United States intervention, clashed with pro-Bishop leaders in Guyana, Trinidad and Tobago, the Bahamas, and Belize. CARICOM summits were canceled and postponed, and policy coordination broke down. Meanwhile, the United States, a major contributor to the Caribbean Development Bank, tried unsuccessfully to force a violation of CARICOM's constitution in 1981 by making U.S. grants to the bank conditional upon the bank's denial of educational loans to Grenada.

The economic crisis that hit the Caribbean during the early to mid-1980s caused additional damage to CARICOM. Guyana, Jamaica, and Trinidad and Tobago depleted their foreign currency reserves and had to submit to strict International Monetary Fund (IMF) conditions. Guyana began defaulting on intra-CARICOM loans, and Jamaica adopted a three-tier currency that weakened regional trade. Barbados and Trinidad placed taxes and other restrictions on CARICOM goods. The net result of these actions was a dramatic decline in CARICOM trade by 1986 to less than half of its 1981 level.

A revival of CARICOM began in 1987 at the eighth Heads of Government Conference, which called for the removal of all intraregional trade restrictions, although actual free trade remained an elusive goal. In addition, Guyana and Barbados advocated more cooperation in social policy, and proposed sharing representation at the United Nations and other intergovernmental organizations.

Since the early 1990s the greatest impetus for integration has come from the Organization of Eastern Caribbean States (OECS), a subregional body within CARICOM created in 1981 by Antigua and Barbuda, Dominica, Grenada, Montserrat, St. Lucia, St. Kitts and Nevis, and St. Vincent and the Grenadines. The OECS has for a while been seriously discussing a political union among these seven countries.

Jonathan Edwards

See Also
Turks and Caicos Islands; Virgin Islands (United States and British).

North America

Carmichael, Stokely

(b. July 29, 1941, Port-of-Spain, Trinidad; d. November 15, 1998, Conakry, Guinea), activist and writer who inaugurated the Black Power Movement of the 1960s.

Stokely Carmichael was not the first to use the phrase "Black Power," but he made it famous. Critical of Martin Luther King Jr's. peaceful approach, Carmichael advanced a militant stand on civil rights as chairperson of the Student Nonviolent Coordinating Committee (SNCC) in the 1960s.

A native of Trinidad, Carmichael moved with his family to a mostly white neighborhood in the Bronx, New York, when he was 11. He graduated from Bronx High School of Science in 1960 and, four years later, from Howard University in Washington, D.C., with a bachelor's degree in philosophy.

Carmichael became involved in civil rights protests during his years at Howard. He participated in demonstrations staged by the Congress of Racial Equality, the Nonviolent Action Committee, and SNCC. He was arrested as a Freedom Rider in 1961 and served seven weeks in Parchman Penitentiary for violating Mississippi's segregation laws. Carmichael returned to the South after college and devoted himself to the organization of SNCC's black voter registration project in Lowndes County, Alabama. There, he also founded an independent political party called the Lowndes County Freedom Organization, which used the black panther as its symbol.

Carmichael became chairman of SNCC in 1966. He catapulted into the national spotlight in August of that year, when he ended a speech with a call for Black Power. Black Power became a rallying cry for black protests during the 1960s and 1970s, and it created a wedge between SNCC and more moderate civil rights groups. Although it is defined in many ways, Black Power emphasizes independent political and economic development by blacks as a necessary element of social change. Carmichael and political scientist Charles Hamilton elaborate on the concept in their book, *Black Power* (1967).

A 1967 world tour to publicize the black struggle in the United States brought Carmichael more controversy in Washington, D.C. His passport was revoked for visiting Cuba and, when he returned to the United States, he faced indictment for sedition; however, he was never prosecuted. The following year, he became prime minister of the Black Panther Party.

In 1969 Carmichael began to focus his political activity on Africa. Having left the Black Panthers, he went to work for the All-African People's Revolutionary Party in Ghana. In that same year, he and his wife, the South African singer Miriam Makeba, went to live in the African nation of Guinea. In 1978 Carmichael took the first name of his mentor, Kwame Nkrumah of Ghana and the last name of Ahmed Sékou Touré of Guinea to become Kwame Turé. He continued to travel and to lecture on U.S. imperialism, Pan-Africanism, and socialism until his death from cancer in November 1998. His second book, a collection of speeches and essays titled *Stokely Speaks*, appeared in 1971.

Lawrie Balfour

See Also
Makeba, Miriam Zenzi; Touré, Sékou; King, Martin Luther, Jr.; Trinidad and Tobago.

Latin America and the Caribbean

Carneiro, Edison, **Brazilian anthropologist known for his research on Afro-Brazilian religions.**

Edison Carneiro was born and lived in Brazil's northeastern state of Bahia. Unlike many *mestiços* (people of indigenous and European descent) from his generation who denied their African origins, Carneiro dedicated his studies to the customs and traditions of the descendants of Africans in Brazil, particularly to the influence of African religion in Brazil. His work was pioneering in Brazil in the 1930s, when African religions were still repressed by the government. Carneiro is considered to be the first person systematically to record the practices, beliefs, and history of the Afro-Brazilian people. Among the rituals developed by Afro-Brazilians, Carneiro identified the Nagô rituals as the only authentic variant of the Afro-Brazilian religion of Candomblé, as opposed to the Bantu rituals. In his search for the pure African religion, he considered the Bantu sect to be a degenerated form of African religion.

Carneiro combined his studies with a strong political activism. He participated in the first Congresso Afro-Brasileiro in 1934 and organized the second Congresso Afro-Brasileiro in 1937, which took place in Bahia. For the first congress, he wrote an article titled "Xangô." At the second congress he presented two essays: "A Vision of Afro-Brazilian Religious Ethnography" and "The Physician of the Poor." These congresses united scholars as well as nonacademics to discuss Afro-Brazilian culture and contributions. In 1937 Carneiro helped to found the União das Seitas Afro-Brasileiras (Union of Afro-Brazilian Religions), an organization that struggled for the religious freedom of Afro-Brazilians.

Along with Brazilian intellectuals such as Arthur Ramos, Juliano Moreira, and others, Carneiro attacked the theory of the racial inferiority of the Brazilian population. Carneiro was also a contemporary of Roger Bastide, Valdemar Valente, and René Ribeiro, who represented a new generation that revived academic discussions about Afro-Brazilian religion in the 1940s. Carneiro's publications include *Religiões Negras* (1936), *Negros Bantú* (1937), *Quilombo dos Palmares* (1947), *Candomblés da Bahia* (1948), and many others. The Museum of Folklore in Rio de Janeiro is named after him.

Michelle Gueraldi

See Also
Brazil; Religions, African, in Brazil.

Latin America and the Caribbean

Carnivals in Latin America and the Caribbean, **celebrations of European origin that have been profoundly transformed by diverse New World African expressive cultures throughout the Americas.**

Although Carnival is celebrated in many Latin American and Caribbean cities, this description will focus on four different Carnivals: in Rio de Janeiro and Salvador, Bahia, in Brazil; Port of Spain, Trinidad; and New Orleans.

Carnival symbolism often references the Dionysian celebrations of Ancient Greece and the Bacchanalia, Saturnalia, and Lupercalia of Ancient Rome, but the festival tradition itself derives from Christian celebrations before Lent, the 40 days of fasting leading up to Easter. Carnival is historically associated with unrestrained, lewd, and even grotesque behavior among popular classes. One critical tradition, associated with the work of Russian literary critic Mikhail Bakhtin, maintains that Carnivals symbolically challenged established authority, inverted social hierarchies, and ridiculed elite culture. In different historical contexts, Carnivalesque laughter, parody, and satire relativized the legitimacy and supremacy of official culture sanctioned by the church, the royal court, the nobility, and/or the bourgeoisie. Of course, social order was always restored on Ash Wednesday, initiating the period of Lent. For this reason, other critics argue that Carnival helps to maintain the social order because it functions as a kind of pressure valve for popular discontent that otherwise could lead to a more sustained challenge to the dominant order.

A Carnival queen in fancy dress expresses the joy and release of Carnival in Port of Spain, Trinidad and Tobago. *John Nunley*

Similar ambiguities exist in the history of Carnival in the Americas, which was usually established by Roman Catholics from France, Spain, and Portugal. Although New World Carnivals were generally founded by white elites for their own amusement, slaves and free workers were, to varying degrees, allowed to celebrate. The ruling slaveholding elite of plantation societies regarded Carnival as useful for diffusing tensions inherent in the master-slave relationship, but also as potentially threatening because it provided the oppressed classes with the opportunity to congregate in groups and reaffirm their own cultural identities. While elites held masked balls, inspired by the famous Carnivals of Nice and Venice, the rest celebrated outside on the streets.

Carnival in Brazil

Brazil has the most widespread and dynamic Carnival tradition in the world. Dozens of Brazilian cities celebrate Carnival, but Rio de Janeiro is the most famous for its dazzling visual and musical extravagance. Carnival was brought to Rio in the early nineteenth century by Portuguese immigrants who celebrated the *entrudo,* in which popular revellers would spray each other with mud and sewage while the upper classes amused themselves with perfume sprays. The first masked ball was held at the Hotel Itália in 1840. Eight years later, a Portuguese immigrant initiated the Zé Pereira, a ragtag drum parade for the lower classes. In the 1850s the middle and upper classes developed their own parades featuring competing groups called *sociedades,* which sponsored allegorical floats. The city's black population generally participated in the *cordões,* which featured Afro-Brazilian percussion. By the 1870s family-oriented groups called *ranchos* emerged in the working-class neighborhoods and were noted for introducing annual Carnival themes.

In the late 1920s a new type of Carnival organization, the *escolas de samba* (SAMBA SCHOOLS), emerged as an alternative to the ranchos. Samba schools began as community-based groups in the predominantly black working-class neighborhoods and shantytowns, or FAVELAS, of Rio de Janeiro. They steadily expanded throughout the century into complex organizations with thousands of members. The first samba school, Deixa

TOP: Rio de Janeiro, Brazil, hosts the largest and most famous Carnival celebration in the world. The men in this picture are spinning musical instruments called *pandeiros* on their fingertips.
Craig Duncan/D. Donne Bryant Stock Photo
MIDDLE: While Rio de Janeiro boasts the most extravagant Carnival in Brazil, the celebration takes place throughout the country. These masqueraders in Olinda, Pernambuco, dance in the street.
Alex Braga/Contexto
LEFT: Carnival is an enormous event in Trinidad, and thousands of elaborately dressed people turn out to dance to the rhythms of soca and calypso. These revelers in are performing in Port of Spain.
Craig Duncan/D. Donne Bryant Stock Photo

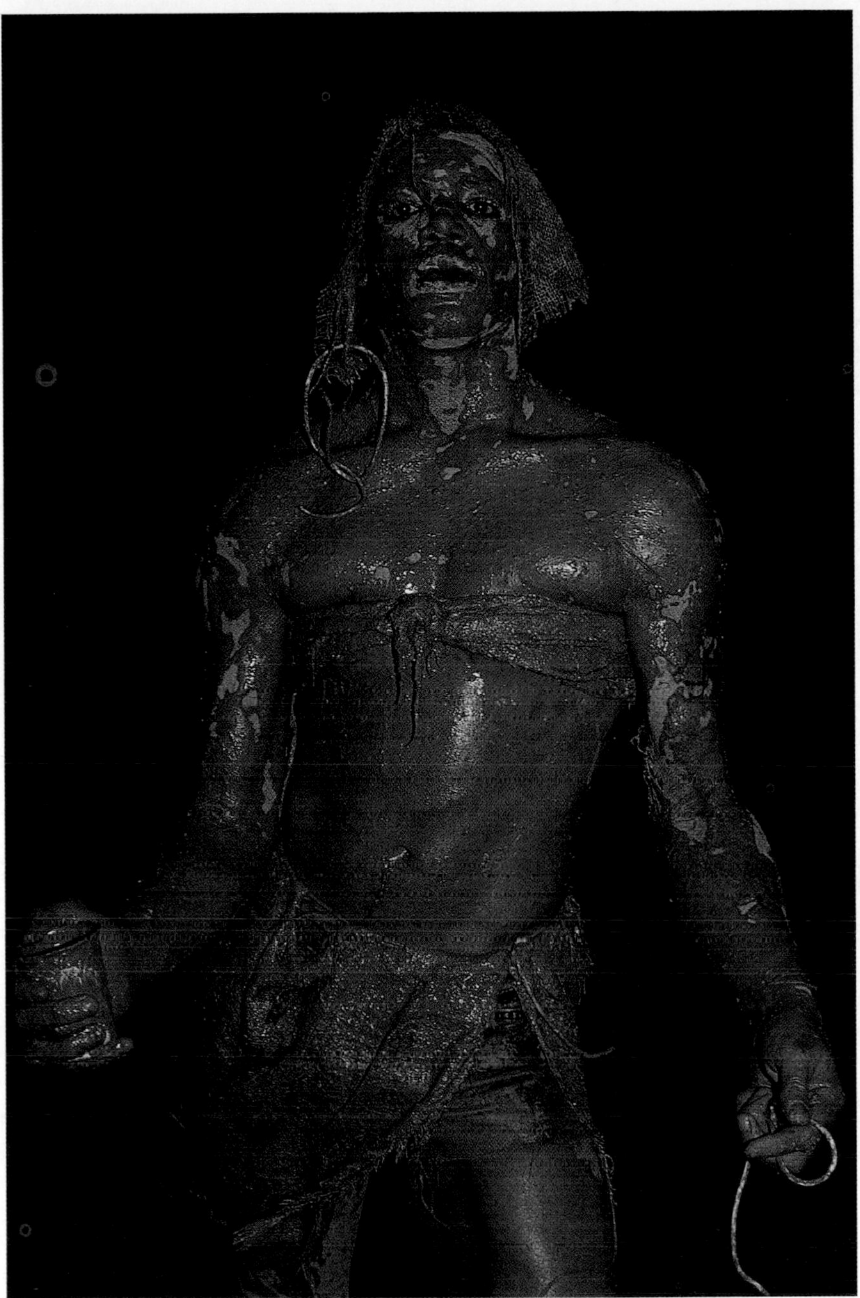

Coated with mud and ochre, a man enters the spirit of Jouvay, the early morning opening of Carnival in Port of Spain, Trinidad and Tobago. The soot and oil with which dancers cover their bodies symbolizes the suspension of ordinary life in Carnival. *Alex Castro*

Falar, was founded in 1928 by a group of musicians from Estácio, a neighborhood next to Praça Onze, the square near downtown Rio described at the time as a "miniature Africa." During the following year, residents of a local favela founded the Estação Primeira da Mangueira, which would become the oldest surviving samba school. It has remained among the top samba schools along with groups like Portela, Unidos da Tijuca, Império Serrano, Salguiero, Vila Isabel, Mocidade Independente, and Beija-Flor.

Since 1984 the top samba schools have paraded down the Passarela do Samba (the Samba Runway), popularly known as the Sambódromo, an official Carnival stadium that seats 90,000 paying spectators. Each samba school must have a Brazil-related theme, which is musically dramatized in the *samba-enredo* (theme samba) and represented visually by a series of massive *carros alegóricos* (floats). Several *alas* (wings) of revellers, including the *passistas* (master dancers) led by the *porta-estandarte* (flag bearer) and the *mestre-sala* (master of ceremonies), dance down the runway and sing the theme song while the large *bateria* (percussion ensemble) brings up the rear. Rich, famous, and/or beautiful *destaques* (famous personalities, or highlights) ride on top of the floats. On Ash Wednesday, the official jury announces the winner of the annual samba school contest, an event that generates millions of dollars in ticket sales and broadcast rights.

In the 1990s the Carnival of Salvador, Bahia, began to challenge the hegemony of Rio's Carnival in terms of national and international acclaim. The Bahian Carnival also began in the nineteenth century with annual pre-Lenten masked balls for the elite and the rowdy entrudo for the masses. By the late nineteenth century, Afro-Bahians had begun to develop distinct traditions. Within a few years after the abolition of slavery in Brazil (1888), Salvador saw the emergence of black Carnival clubs such as the Embaixada Africana (African Embassy) and the Pandegas D'Africa (African Merrymakers), which exalted African culture and its legacy in Bahia. Within a decade, these organizations were banned from the Bahian Carnival by elite white authorities who feared the Africanization of local culture.

The heirs to these Afro-Bahian Carnival clubs were the afoxés, neighborhood-based percussion groups that played *ijexá* and other sacred rhythms of CANDOMBLÉ, the most traditional Afro-Brazilian rhythms. The most famous afoxé, the FILHOS DE GANDHI (Sons of Gandhi), was founded in 1949 by a group of black stevedores inspired by the Indian anti-colonial leader. The all-male group wears white tunics and turbans in honor of OXALÁ, the Yoruba deity of peace in Candomblé. In the same year, two young innovators named Dodô and Osmar hit the streets during Carnival playing homemade electric guitars on the top of a Ford truck with rudimentary amplifiers called the *trio elétrico*. In the following decades, the trios elétricos developed into massive moving stages with sophisticated sound systems custom built onto large trucks. Originally used only by electric pop bands, these trucks are now also used by the percussion-based blocos as a moving stage for their singers.

In 1974, during the most repressive phase of military rule in Brazil, a group of young black petroleum workers from the neighborhood of Liberdade founded the first bloco Afro, called ILÊ AIYÊ, a Yoruba term meaning "house of life." They were inspired by the BLACK POWER and soul countercultures of the United States and the liberation of former Portuguese colonies in Africa. Unlike the afoxés, Ilê Aiyê used the Bahian Carnival as a stage for publicly denouncing racial inequality and celebrating the achievements of Africa and the diaspora. Within five years, other blocos Afros, like OLODUM, Muzenza, Araketu, and Malê Debalê, had emerged. The blocos Afros formed a movement that challenged the hegemony of electric pop bands with a more rootsy and militant sound inspired in part by Jamaican REGGAE. Local pop bands started producing electric covers of the annual bloco Afro Carnival hits. In the early 1990s some blocos, like Araketu and Olodum, began to produce less politicized and more orchestrated pop music in order to compete in local and national music markets. After much-publicized collaborations with Paul Simon

Dancers in the Spanish Town Road Jonkonnu Band of Kingston, Jamaica, wear traditional wire screen masks and elaborate costumes. *J. Bettelheim*

and Michael Jackson, Olodum enjoyed success in the international market for "world music." In the meantime, another wave of percussion-based groups, like Timbalada, Bolacha Maria, and Bragadá, introduced new visual styles and sounds to the Bahian Carnival.

Carnival in Trinidad

Like Brazil, Trinidad has a highly developed and competitive festival that revolves around the annual production of new Carnival songs. However, these songs are less beholden to specific themes and are generally more humorous and satirical. The Trinidadian Carnival was established in the early nineteenth century by the French Catholic planter class that colonized the island during the early period of Spanish rule. The English adopted many of these customs after gaining control of the island in 1802. While the elite attended masquerade balls, slaves and free people of color developed their own Carnival traditions like the Canboulay, which featured violent stick fights between rival groups. After a series of riots in the 1880s and the prohibition of the Canboulay, an emergent urban middle class established the Fancy Masquerade and its spinoff, the Calypso Tent, featuring competing singers called chantwells. Formal competitions began in the 1920s and eventually developed into a national contest, held during Carnival. In 1939 the Growling Tiger became the first Calypso King, which in the 1970s was renamed Calypso Monarch in deference to emerging female calypsonians.

Calypso music and the tent tradition gradually began to develop separately from the masquerade. In the late 1920s calypso entered a golden age that would last through World War II. Some calypsonians began to travel to New York to perform and record. This was the era of Houdini, Lord Executor, Lord Invader, Roaring Lion, and Attila the Hun, who helped to popularize the genre throughout the Caribbean, the United States, Europe, and Africa. Calypso was one of the first popular music and dance cultures of the African diaspora to have international appeal. Calypso also served as a powerful grassroots medium for expressing social and political protest in Trinidad, especially against British colonial rule (*see* Colonial Latin America and the Caribbean), which ended in 1962. Calypsonians continue to ridicule the foibles of local politicians and criticize social and economic conditions on the islands.

During the calypso era, a separate Carnival tradition emerged around informal groups playing bamboo instruments and biscuit tins. By the 1940s players began to pound out rudimentary notes on the tops of their tins to produce simple melodies. After the war, departing GIs left behind empty oil drums that were used to create larger and more complex instruments called steel drums, or "pans." Large steel bands were formed, and the new genre spread throughout the Caribbean and beyond. Each year during Carnival, steel bands from throughout Trinidad and Tobago compete in a contest called the Panorama.

In the 1970s calypso went through another period of transformation under the influence of African American dance music. New performers such as Lord Shorty, Arrow, Chalkdust, David Rudder, and Black Stalin innovated a new style called soca, a fusion of soul and calypso. Most soca is party music for dancing, yet some composers have renovated the critical oral tradition of the original calypsonians. In the 1980s and 1990s, Indo-Trinidadians (descendants of immigrants from India) created a distinct new hybrid called Chutney Soca.

Starting in early January each year, calypso and soca performers begin to compete in several "tents" (which are now halls and auditoriums) around Port of Spain, including Calypso Spektakula, Calypso Revue, Kaiso House, and Calypso Showcase. The national finals for the title of Calypso Monarch are held on Thursday of Carnival at the Queens Park Savannah. The parade competitions begin on the following Monday, called *J'ouvert,* the official opening day of Carnival. Early that morning roaming bands of revellers dressed in rags and smeared in colored mud and powders take over the streets, dancing behind moving sound systems blasting out Carnival hits. The gyrating dance is called "jump and wine." During the next two days, more than 40 groups of 200 to 400 masqueraders participate in the Parade of Bands, or *mas,* which passes by the Grandstand of Queen's Park Savannah. Top bands include Barbarossa, Harts Limited, Poison, and the Callaloo Company. This competition also determines the winner of the Road March title for the most popular song played during the Parade of Bands.

Mardi Gras in New Orleans

In many ways, the Mardi Gras of New Orleans is the most conservative Carnival tradition in the New World. While Carnival institutions in Brazil and Trinidad went through remarkable transformations throughout the twentieth century, the New Orleans Mardi Gras has maintained many of its old traditions, rooted in mid-nineteenth-century New Orleans. The New Orleans Mardi Gras also lacks any institutional framework, such as song competitions, which would encourage the annual production of timely flash-in-the-pan hits so typical of Latin American and Caribbean Carnivals. Instead, the street parades mostly feature marching bands from Louisiana high schools and amateur pickup bands on flatbed trucks, performing perennial classics like "Mardi Gras Mambo."

Carnival balls and street processions were documented in New Orleans as early as the late 1700s, but formal parades began only in the late 1830s. In 1856 a group of white Protestant men from Mobile, Alabama, chartered the first formal Carnival organization of New Orleans, the Mystick Krewe of Comus. After the Civil War, the Krewe of Rex was founded in honor of the Russian grand duke Alexis Romanoff, who visited New Orleans during Carnival in 1872. The parade of Rex continues to be the main public event of Mardi Gras (Fat Tuesday). The Krewe of Momus was established in 1872, and the Krewe of Proteus was founded a decade later. In addition to their annual parades, these four "old line krewes" hold formal balls in honor of their annually selected kings and debutante queens. Membership in traditional krewes is exclusively reserved for socially prominent and wealthy white males from old New Orleanian families. In 1991 an African American councilwoman, Dorothy Mae Taylor, successfully waged a campaign to deny parade permits to krewes that discriminated on the basis of race or gender. Of the four old line krewes, only Rex complied with the ordinance, while Comus, Momus, and Proteus ceased to parade and retreated to their exclusive balls.

Throughout the twentieth century, new krewes with less exclusive membership policies emerged, yet most are still overwhelmingly white. There are now over 60 registered Carnival krewes in New Orleans. Krewe parades generally feature allegorical floats interspersed with local marching bands, equestrians, and members of civic clubs in miniature dune buggies. Night parades often include a procession of gas torches called *flambeaux,* generally carried by black men, who receive tips from the crowd. Masked members pay hundreds or thousands of dollars to ride on the floats and throw plastic beads, cups, and doubloon coins to revellers down on the street. Observers have long noted that the distribution of trinkets symbolically reinforces social hierarchies, yet others defend it as safe family entertainment that is particularly well suited for children.

Parallel Carnival organizations of the African American community, like the Original Illinois Club (1894) and the famous Zulu Social Aid and Pleasure Club (1909), emerged at the turn of the century. The Zulu parade is traditionally held on the morning of Fat Tuesday, just before the Rex parade. Members dress in stereotypical African-style garb, put on blackface and Afro wigs, and distribute beads, cups, toy spears, and coveted hand-painted coconuts. In recent years, the Zulu parade has sparked controversy and dissent within the African American community. Critics argue that the Zulu masquerade humiliates the black community by reproducing false and demeaning representations of "African savages." Defenders claim that the Zulu parade is a shrewd parody of the pompous Krewe of Rex and that it ironically subverts negative stereotypes of black people. The 1990s saw the emergence of African American krewes like Ashanti-Vesta and Oshun, which feature more dignified, or less ironic, representations of Africa and the diaspora.

The most spectacular costuming and parading tradition belongs to the Mardi Gras Indians. The Carnivals of Brazil and Trinidad also have Indian masquerades, but none matches the rich and complex tradition in New Orleans. The historical memory of alliances between escaped slaves and indigenous peoples during the period of French and Spanish colonial rule may have provided early inspiration for these groups, which first emerged in the 1880s. Buffalo Bill's Wild West Show, which visited the city during the World Centennial Cotton Exposition of 1884, was also a likely influence. Indeed, the first Mardi Gras Indian gang was called the Creole Wild West Tribe, founded by Becate Batiste, the great-uncle of the legendary Allison "Tootie" Montana, who was big chief of the Yellow Pocahontas tribe for nearly 50 years before retiring in 1997. Another wave of tribes formed after World War II, including the Golden Eagles, Black Eagles, Wild Magnolias, Wild Apaches, Wild Tchoupitoulas, and Carrollton Hunters, which were formed in working-class black neighborhoods.

Mardi Gras Indian tribes have a complex hierarchy that usually includes a big chief, a second chief, a medicine man, and a retinue of spy boys and flag boys. A group of friends always follows behind, pounding out funky rhythms on tambourines and bass drums. Rival Indian tribes used to engage in violent street fights similar to the Canboulays of Trinidad, but in recent decades competition has been based on the elegance and beauty of their ornate feathered and sequined costumes. Each year, participants invest a great deal of time and money to create new costumes, which are outlandish stylizations of Native American dress. The highly original artistic and performative traditions of the Mardi Gras Indians take place separately from the official Carnival on the main avenues.

Creative Contribution

Carnival began as a festival of Christian Europe and was brought to the New World by white elites. During the past two centuries, it has been profoundly transformed by the creative energies of Africans and their descendants. Most of the dominant Carnival institutions and practices of today have emerged from marginalized black communities. Even in New Orleans, where Eurocentric institutions still occupy center stage during Mardi Gras, the Carnival organizations of the black community continue to thrive.

Christopher Dunn

See Also

Soul Music; Slavery in Latin America and the Caribbean; Jackson, Michael, and the Jackson Family; New Orleans, Louisiana; Afoxés/Blocos Afros; Bahia; Rio de Janeiro, Brazil; Trinidad and Tobago; East Indian Communities in the Caribbean; Abolition and Emancipation in Latin America and the Caribbean; Orishas; World Music, World Beat, and the Re-Africanization of Latin American Popular Music.

Latin America and the Caribbean

Carpentier, Alejo (b. 1904, Havana, Cuba; d. 1980, Paris, France), Cuban writer and novelist, one of the most important Latin American writers of the twentieth century.

The son of a French architect and a highly cultured Russian mother, Alejo Carpentier learned French at home and was exposed as a child to literature and other artistic forms, especially architecture and music, that would influence and shape most of his later work.

After interrupting his architecture studies at the University of Havana, Carpentier worked as a journalist from 1921 to 1924. During this period, he participated in some of the avant-garde movements that were gaining prominence in all of Latin America. In Cuba, avant-garde artists were rediscovering the Afro-Caribbean elements of their own culture and incorporating them in their work. In 1927 Carpentier wrote *El milagro de Anaquillé*, a "choreographic Afro-Cuban mystery in one act," inspired by initiation ceremonies.

After being imprisoned in 1927 for his opposition to the regime of Gerardo Machado, Carpentier left for France, where he earned a living as a journalist and studied musical theory. In 1933 he published his first novel, *¡Écue-Yamba-Ó!* ("the Lord be praised" in Afro-Cuban ñañigo dialect). This novel, later rejected by Carpentier as an immature experiment, combines French surrealist literary techniques with a sharp criticism of social injustices against poor Cuban blacks in a rural environment typically portrayed in the Spanish-American *novela de la tierra* (regionalist novel) of those years. The novel also shows the influence of Fernando Ortíz, as its original edition includes ethnographic descriptions of various ñañigo rituals, drawings of ceremonial symbols, and photographs.

In 1946, at the request of the Mexican publishing house Fondo de Cultura Económica,

Carpentier wrote his essay *La música en Cuba.* In it, he attempts to do justice to the important African contributions to the development of Cuban music.

Carpentier's next important novel, *El reino de este mundo* (1949), is a significant contribution to Afro-Caribbean literature. It follows Ti-Noel, a black slave, from the last years of the French colonial regime in HAITI through the violent period of the revolution to the rebellion against the emperor HENRI CHRISTOPHE. In the prologue, Carpentier introduces his concept of *lo real maravilloso* (approximately "the marvelous in the real"). This concept refers to the coexistence in Latin America, according to Carpentier, of the real and the marvelous within everyday life. (Haitian VODOU beliefs and ceremonies are an example of this in the novel.) This presence of the marvelous in everyday life is different from the "marvelous worlds" that surrealists and other experimental writers were trying to explore in Europe, which Carpentier saw as futile attempts to escape an everyday world with which they were already disenchanted.

Some critics consider his next major novel, *Los pasos perdidos* (1953), his masterpiece. At once a revision and a subversion of the Latin American novela de la tierra, it denounces the dehumanizing effects of twentieth-century urban life. A mythical voyage to the historical roots of Latin America, *Los pasos perdidos* reveals Carpentier's mature style: baroque, carefully crafted in its precise and long descriptions of details, and overwhelming in the range of its erudition.

El siglo de las luces (1962) encompasses the Caribbean, Europe, and the rest of Latin America within its scope of action. It takes place between 1789 and 1808, dates associated with the fall of the Bastille and the uprising of the Spanish populace against Napoleon's forces occupying Madrid. Shifting between the Old and New Worlds, it explores the ironic outcome of the cult of reason during the Age of Enlightenment, namely, that it ended in some of the bloodiest periods of terror in Western history. It also presents the crystallization of Creole consciousness that would very soon lead to the wars for independence in America.

In 1974 Carpentier published two novels, *El recurso del método* and *Concierto barroco.* The first takes place in a fictional Latin American country and portrays a fictional dictator who, although possessing many traits of the Cuban Gerardo Machado, also incorporates traits of other dictators and therefore stands as an emblematic figure for Latin America's long succession of dictators.

Concierto barroco narrates the fantastic journey in space and time of a wealthy Mexican traveler and his black Cuban slave. The novel is an exploration of the multiple elements that contributed to form a Latin American identity; once again, the important participation of the black slave Filomeno shows Carpentier's interest in doing justice to the African heritage in Latin America in general and in the Caribbean in particular.

La consagración de la primavera (1978), which centers on the life of a couple during the turbulent years of the Cuban Revolution, received mixed reviews because some critics felt that Carpentier was sacrificing literary complexity for the sake of political commentary and a celebration of the revolution.

Carpentier's last novel, *El arpa y la sombra* (1979), is a fictional rewriting of Christopher Columbus's diary, in which he denounces the violence that foreign interests have foisted on Latin America. Here the author continues to explore the historical and cultural elements that helped shape the New World.

Carpentier received many honors and awards, among them the Cervantes Prize in 1978.

Victor Figueroa

SEE ALSO

Colonial Rule; Literature, English Language, Caribbean; France; Mexico; Creoles; Haitian Revolution; Music, Afro-Caribbean Secular; Languages, Creole, in the Caribbean.

North America

Carr, Wynona (b. August 23, 1924, Cleveland, Ohio; d. May 12, 1976), gospel singer.

Wynona Carr's first records were *Each Day* and *Lord Jesus* (both 1949), made after she had formed the Carr Singers, a gospel quintet, in 1945. She is best known for "The Ball Game" (1952), one of a series of songs that parallel religious and secular themes. Others are "Dragnet for Jesus," "Fifteen Rounds for Jesus," and "Operator, Operator." Although she never enjoyed substantial commercial success, even when she tried to switch from sacred to secular songs, she left two impressive recordings: "Our Father" (1954) – which probably had an effect on Aretha Franklin – and the rhythm and blues hit "Should I Ever Love Again" (1957).

SEE ALSO

Franklin, Aretha Louise.

North America

Carrington, Walter C. (b. July 24, 1930, New York, N.Y.), African American public official, United States ambassador to SENEGAL in 1980 and to NIGERIA in 1993.

Walter C. Carrington was the eldest child of Walter R. and Marjorie Hayes Carrington. He graduated from Harvard College in 1952 and Harvard Law School in 1955 and was the first student elected to the National Board of the National Association for the Advancement of Colored People (NAACP). After serving in the United States Army, he was appointed to the Massachusetts Commission Against Discrimination, becoming, at age 27, the youngest person ever appointed to the commission in that state.

In 1961 Carrington joined the Peace Corps, serving for ten years in SIERRA LEONE, SENEGAL, and TUNISIA. He eventually became regional director of the Peace Corps in Africa. In 1971 he became vice president of the African-American Institute (AAI), an organization dedicated to developing human resources in Africa and to fostering dialogue between Africans and Americans.

In 1980 Carrington accepted an invitation from President Jimmy Carter to serve as U.S. ambassador to Senegal. After only one year, he went to HOWARD UNIVERSITY as director of the Department of International Affairs. He eventually spent time at Washington University, the Massachusetts Institute of Technology, and Marquette University.

Carrington was a consultant on international affairs for the Joint Center for Political and Economic Studies when he met California representative Mervyn Dymally of Los Angeles. He served as Dymally's chief of staff for 11 years. In 1993 President Bill Clinton appointed Carrington ambassador to Nigeria.

Alonford James Robinson, Jr.

SEE ALSO

National Association for the Advancement of Colored People.

North America

Carroll, Diahann (b. July 17, 1935, New York, N.Y.), African American singer and actor who starred in the first television series with a black woman as its main character.

Diahann Carroll grew up in a comfortable middle-class home in New York City and began singing in a church choir at age six. She won a music scholarship sponsored by the Metropolitan OPERA when she was ten. Encouraged by her mother, who took her to Broadway musicals and other performances, she applied to New York's High School of Music and Art and was accepted.

Born Carol Diahann Johnson, she took her professional name at age 16 when she appeared on Arthur Godfrey's Talent Search, a television showcase for aspiring performers. Despite her parents' wish that she attend HOWARD UNIVERSITY – she had earned money for college by modeling for *Ebony* magazine – she stayed in New York. She left college after one semester at New York University to accept a long-term nightclub engagement. Soon after she went on the road, singing at resorts in the Catskill Mountains and elsewhere, honing her demure, elegant image, a persona that caused one critic to describe her as "Doris Day in blackface."

At age 19 she won her first film role, costarring with Dorothy Dandridge, Harry Belafonte, and Pearl Bailey in *Carmen Jones* (1954), an all-black version of Bizet's opera. Returning to New York, Carroll next appeared in Truman Capote's *House of Flowers* on Broadway, a part that brought her a Tony Award nomination. In 1956 she married Monte Kay, a white casting director. On the set of her next movie, *Porgy and Bess* (1959), she met and fell in love with costar Sidney Poitier; their affair lasted nine years. During a brief reconciliation in 1961, Carroll and Kay had a daughter, Suzanne. Later that year, Carroll appeared again with Poitier in the film *Paris Blues* (1961).

Over the next decade Carroll had a series of successful roles, although she never escaped the racial discrimination that pervaded the entertainment industry. On the day after winning another Tony nomination for *No Strings* (1962), she learned that her role would be played in the movie version by a Eurasian actress. Between acting roles she continued to sing, appearing often in Las Vegas. Starring in *Julia*, a television series launched in 1968, Carroll played a widow who was raising her child alone. Despite the show's success, Carroll was stung by criticism of both the character's single motherhood and her unrealistically affluent lifestyle. In addition, the white press seemed to expect Carroll to act as a spokesperson for black America, an impossible task in a politically fractured era. Carroll quit the show in 1971.

Turning down offers for similar television roles, Carroll could not find anything in film to interest her until *Claudine* (1975), a realistic, gritty survivor's story in which she costarred with James Earl Jones. A series of love affairs (including two more marriages) left her financially and emotionally devastated. It was not until 1982 that she had another significant acting role, this time on Broadway in *Agnes of God*. Carroll then returned to the small screen to play "television's first black bitch" on the hit series *Dynasty*. She has also appeared on *A Different World*, a comedy about students at a historically black university.

Kate Tuttle

See Also

Belafonte, Harold George (Harry); *Ebony*; New York, New York; Television and African Americans; Film, Blacks in American.

North America

Carson, Julia (b. July 8, 1938, Louisville, Ky.), Democratic member of the United States House of Representatives from Indiana, first elected in 1997.

Born in Kentucky, Julia Carson was raised in Indianapolis, Indiana. In 1965, while working as a secretary for the United Auto Workers union, she was hired by Indiana congressman Andrew Jacobs Jr. Carson worked on his staff for eight years. In 1972 she was elected to the Indiana House of Representatives and in 1976 to the Indiana Senate, where she served on the Finance and Health Committees. In 1990 she was elected trustee of Center Township and directed an agency that provided assistance to the needy. When Congressman Jacobs retired in 1996, Carson ran for his position. She won 52 percent of the vote and became the first African American to represent Indianapolis in the United States House of Representatives.

Carson's constituency is Indiana's Tenth Congressional District, located in the city of Indianapolis. It includes a mix of African American and white neighborhoods.

In 1997 Carson was assigned seats on the Banking and Financial Services Committee and the Veterans' Affairs Committee. She is also a member of the Congressional Black Caucus.

Latin America and the Caribbean

Cartagena de Indias, Colombia, situated in a bay of the Caribbean Sea, was one of the principal slave ports of colonial Spanish America and a province of the new viceroyalty of Granada (present-day Colombia, Venezuela, and Panama); today, a trade port and tourist destination in northern Colombia, Cartagena conserves the most extensive and complete colonial military architecture of the Americas and was designated a United Nations World Heritage City in 1984 because of its "outstanding universal value."

Spanish Conquest

Spanish colonizers first encountered the bay of Cartagena in 1502, though it was not until 1533 that a permanent settlement was established. Pedro de Heredia, the city's founder, named the site and bay after Cartagena in Spain, adding "de Indias" (of the Indies) for its location in the Americas. Heredia and his men soon found gold and wrote back to King Carlos I of Spain requesting permission to import African slaves to the area to aid in searching for and extracting the precious metal (*see* Slavery in Latin America and the Caribbean). By 1545 Cartagena de Indias was developing into a prosperous port town, populated mainly by Spaniards who had been attracted by reports of gold. From 1580 to 1630 gold mines were exploited in the inland towns of Zaragoza, Cáceres, and Remedios, which were accessible from Cartagena by river. The mines extended the city's area of influence, determining much of its sociocultural and economic development. As Indian labor was decimated by disease and overwork, demand for black slaves increased. A 1600 census calculated that 300 Spaniards and some 3000 black slaves were living in the city and surrounding areas.

Maroons and Pirates

The city's location as a gateway to South America, its connection with the Caribbean, and the wealth produced from gold mining, trade, and the slave market prompted two important and ongoing events that marked its history from the onset. First, maroonage became a common practice, from the time of the early slaves brought by Heredia until the abolition of slavery. Escaped slaves, or *cimarrones*, as reflected in legends surrounding maroon leader Benkos Biohó, constantly had to defend their *palenques* (maroon settlements; *see* Palenque de San Basilio) from the military expeditions that were sent with orders to recapture or kill them. When caught, *palenqueros* were severely punished, often with death. They retaliated, however, by attacking the city's inhabitants and surrounding haciendas as well as the trade ships that traveled up the neighboring Magdalena River. The war against the palenques intensified dramatically during the eighteenth century. Though many palenques were destroyed, or their inhabitants eventually mixed in with the rest of the population, San Basilio remains today a symbol of resistance and freedom.

Second, Cartagena's inhabitants also lived under constant fear of foreign attacks, which began early on. French and British buccaneers ravaged the city in 1544, 1549, and 1568. The success of the European attacks was due in part to the Europeans' use of local cimarrones and free blacks who served as guides. Most notoriously, Sir Francis Drake plundered the city in 1585 with his troops of maroons from neighboring Panama. Though the Spaniards freed some slaves in order to help defend the city, many escaped and joined Drake's forces in the looting and fighting and then left with the English troops. Therefore, the fear that cimarrones would join pirate or other maroon rebels to take over the city carried into the seventeenth century. In 1741, England, determined to weaken Spain's dominion over the region, sent Adm. Edward Vernon to capture Cartagena. Vernon led 29,000 men recruited among British soldiers, settlers of Virginia and Maryland, indentured servants from Pennsylvania, and slaves and free blacks from Jamaica. The British troops lost the battle against the also racially mixed army of Cartageneros.

In sum, maroonage and attacks from the French and English powers looking to dominate the Caribbean determined the defensive character of the city. Between 1560 and 1780, military forts and thick stone fortification walls (still standing) were built with slave labor to surround and protect the city. In addition, Cartagena de Indias had to create and maintain a system of military defense from its early years. Blacks, slave and free, as well as members of the castes (formally instituted racial categories for people of mixed descent) gradually became incorporated into the troops. In 1619 an all-black artillery company was formed for the defense of the

The 16th- and 17th-century Spanish architecture shown here makes a stark contrast between the modern residential and the tourist sectors of Cartegena de Indias. *Liliana Obregon*

city, and by the mid-eighteenth century there were several color-segregated platoons. By the time Adm. Vernon attacked Cartagena in 1741, the city had an army of 3000 men; four of the companies were composed of mulattos and Indians, two of blacks, and one of quadroons (persons with allegedly one-quarter African blood).

Colonial Life

By the seventeenth century Cartagena de Indias had become one of the most important commercial holdings in Spanish America, second only to Mexico City (*see* Mexico). Merchants from elsewhere in the region, (Panama, Peru, Trinidad, Jamaica, Havana, Santo Domingo, Veracruz, and Honduras, as well as other cities in New Granada,) traveled to Cartagena to buy wine, oil, clothes, steel, books, fabrics, and other locally produced or imported goods as well as slaves.

This fluctuation of merchants, sailors, European immigrants, and African slaves into Cartagena accelerated the process of *mestizaje* (miscegenation among Europeans, Creoles, Africans, and indigenous people). Intense intermixing produced a complex system of social stratification based on color and lineage. The elite class comprised Europeans and Creoles (native-born whites) who were merchants, *encomenderos* (owners of lands and Indians; *see* Colonial Latin America and the Caribbean), cattle ranchers, priests, or part of the colonial bureaucracy. They lived or carried out their business inside the fortress walls of the city and in the nearby haciendas. Poor white Creoles usually worked as artisans and lived outside the walled city in the neighborhood of Getsemaní. Members of the castas worked as writers, teachers, small merchants, doctors, and barbers and lived in the less wealthy sector of the walled city or in Getsemaní.

Slaves and free blacks were at the lowest and most disadvantaged position in the social pyramid. When African slaves initially arrived, they were placed in one of 24 holding stations in the city and were cured, classified, baptized, and sold for local or foreign use. Domestic slaves, male and female, lived and worked in the mansions of the rich in the walled city doing a variety of tasks and were a symbol of prestige for their masters. Some female slaves were also put to work as street vendors or in prostitution, providing a stipend for their masters. Some more privileged female slaves and free black women were able to run small stands where they would sell bread and sweets, or were able to administer *pulperías* (small stores that sold liquor and staples). Most male slaves worked outside the city in agriculture, cattle ranching, sugar production, mining, and the reparation of ships. Many male slaves were also leased out by their owners on a temporary basis to work in the building of the fortress and walls, hospitals, jails, convents, and mansions.

The Roman Catholic Church

In unpredictable ways, the Roman Catholic Church either helped preserve or destroy the heritage of African culture that slaves brought with them to Cartagena. While carrying out the evangelization mission that was one of the first steps to acculturation in the New World, the Jesuit priest Alonso de Sandoval (1576-1652) devised a complex system of classification and description of Africans arriving in the port city, which he applied and documented for more than 40 years. Through trained slave translators, he was able to identify many nations and languages. He also annotated the physical characteristics, skin coloring, and tribal scar markings of each individual he baptized. In this manner, though Sandoval was part of the colonizing mission, he indirectly became the first ethnologist of Africans in the Americas and left a unique and interesting document that provides insights into the nascent history of blacks in Cartagena and the New World (*see* Colonial Critics of Slavery).

The Church unknowingly helped to provide a sanctuary for African culture through the creation and promotion of *cabildos* (also known as *cofradías*; *see* Cultural and Political Organizations in Latin America), which blacks were encouraged to join. Cabildos were established as mutual aid societies created in the hope of furthering control and preventing maroonage and rebellion. In the cabildos, slaves were allowed to meet among themselves, use their native languages, and perform their music, dance, and religious celebrations. Several cabildos in Cartagena identified with their African origins and thus took names such as Arará, Angola, Mandinks, Mina, and Carabalí, among others. In many cases drum beats would convoke members, and cabildos would compete among themselves for the most alluring rhythms. As Peter Wade's research points out, the cabildos were allowed to participate in the street celebrations of Cartagena's Virgin of la Candelaria and perform dances still existing today and identified as *bundes, mapalés, currulaos, gaita, bullerengue,* and *porros* (*see* Cumbia).

Not surprisingly, cabildo members often used meetings as a way to instigate rebellion and plan escapes. When Church officials began to understand the link between music and religious resistance, instruments were confiscated and performers punished. Even the priest Pedro Claver, remembered as the foremost protector of slaves, was a notable persecutor of drums and would confiscate whatever instrument he could find when public dances took place. In the 1730s the bishop of Cartagena prohibited the "sinful" street celebrations.

One of the most feared institutions of the Roman Catholic Church was the Spanish Inquisition. This tribunal was in charge of trying heretics of the Catholic faith, and in so doing it also persecuted African-derived forms of cultural and religious expression. Established in Cartagena in 1610, the Inquisition had jurisdiction over the New Kingdom of Granada as well as Puerto Rico, Venezuela, and Cuba. Documents from the trials of the Inquisition show that black women were often identified as subversive *brujas* (witches). These women were believed to be part of *juntas (*clandestine groups) that exchanged ethnobotanical, medicinal, and magical-religious knowledge among themselves. Their abilities as healers and witches became well known and were appreciated by Cartagena's aristocracy and even the inquisitors, who often called upon them for medical cures and ailments. As scholar Michael Taussig has pointed out, belief in witchcraft was a militant form of denying Christian faith and a way of resisting the oppressors' religion and culture. When they were publicly denounced, the Inquisition tried presumed sorcerers and witches as worshipers of the devil and a threat to Roman Catholic beliefs, and often severely punished them.

Cartagena Today

Cartagena is now a bustling tourist spot and hosts a major petrochemical complex. It continues to be an important port for Colombia and has preserved its majestic colonial architecture. However, as scholar Joel Streicker has observed, the social divisions of this city of 1 million are characterized by marked racial connotations even though 90 percent of the population is to some extent of African descent. *Blancos* (whites) – understood to mean people of the dominant, wealthy class though not necessarily light-skinned – have left the walled city for the modern high-rise buildings of the nearby Bocagrande Peninsula, where much of middle- and upper-class Colombian and foreign tourism also concentrates. *Negros* (blacks) are understood to be people of the lowest class, considered by the better off as having little or no "culture" (understood as manners) and as being lazy, rowdy, and potentially dangerous. They generally live in the slums and shantytowns around the city and work in the factories or service sector. At the bottom of the pyramid stand the *palenqueros,* direct descendants of runaway slaves, who continue to live in their communities in poverty and neglect as they have for almost 500 years. The palenqueros often live off the tourist sector in Cartagena, where they serve as "exotic" fruit vendors, coachmen, maids, and musicians. The complexities of the African heritage and the city's class and social structure are explored by the poetry of Jorge Artel, one of Cartagena's renowned poets.

Nevertheless, in recent decades Cartagena has enjoyed a reencounter with its African roots. Deborah Pacini-Hernández has studied the identity that poor black Cartageneros have created around what they call *música africana* (African music) or dance music from the diaspora (*see* World Music, World Beat, and the Re-Africanization of Latin American Popular Music). To attract foreign visitors, the city's tourist industry has taken advantage of this musical phenomenon by establishing the Caribbean Music Festival, which has been celebrated every year since 1983. Returning to its Afro-Caribbean identity has helped Cartagena distance itself from the image of the violent Andean Colombia. Interest in the African roots of Cartagena and surrounding mining and palenque areas has also been spurred by a growing number of anthropological studies, most notably those of Jaime Arocha, Nina S. de Friedemann, and Peter Wade.

Liliana Obregón

See Also

Great Britain; France; Maroonage in the Americas; Creoles; Central America; Jamaica; Trinidad and Tobago; African Ethnic Groups in Latin America and the Caribbean; Colonial Latin America and the Caribbean; Mandinka; Catholic Church in Latin America and the Caribbean; Punishment of Slaves in Colonial Latin America and the Caribbean; Havana, Cuba.

Latin America and the Caribbean

Cartagena Portalatín, Aída

(b. 1918, Moca, Dominican Republic; d. 1994, Santo Domingo, Dominican Republic), Afro-Dominican writer, educator, and editor.

Aída Cartagena Portalatín was part of a literary group called *La poesía sorprendida* (Surprised Poetry) in the 1940s. This group developed universal themes in a style that made comprehension difficult, in part because the group opposed the intellectually and politically repressive dictatorship of Rafael Trujillo. Although the group's literary journal ceased publication in 1947, this did not hinder Cartagena. With two books of poetry to her credit, she continued her artistic career, defying some traditional female roles.

Cartagena earned a degree from the Autonomous University of Santo Domingo (UASD) and a diploma from the School of Plastic Arts in Paris. She returned to the Dominican Republic and taught art history. In the late 1950s and the 1960s she founded the literary series "La isla necesaria" and directed other serial publications.

Much of her early poetic work reflects on inner life, love, dreams, and womanhood. When the dictatorship finally ended in 1961, she was able to address social and political issues more freely, using less hermetic language than she did in "poesía sorprendida." She comments on racial problems in the Dominican Republic and the United States in a few of her poems, including "Otoño negro" (Black Autumn, 1967) and "Memorias negras" (Black Memories, 1984). Cartagena treated black artistic and political movements in the 1986 essay "Culturas africanas: rebeldes con causa" (African Cultures: Rebels with a Cause).

Her published works span 40 years and include nine collections of poetry, two book-length essays, two novels, and a collection of short stories. Some of her poems were translated into English for a bilingual anthology entitled *Del desconsuelo al compromiso, or From Desolation to Compromise* (1988); it was edited by Daisy Cocco de Filippis.

Marveta Ryan

See Also

Dominican Republic.

North America

Carter, Bennett Lester (Benny)

(b. August 8, 1907, New York, N.Y.), African American multi-instrumentalist, one of the two great alto saxophonists of the swing era, and a groundbreaking composer and arranger for big bands, films, and television.

Benny Carter, who in his nineties is still performing, stands unrivaled among jazz musicians for the length of his career and the scope of his contributions. There have been other nonagenarians in jazz: pianist and composer Eubie Blake (1883-1983) performed publicly until he was 98; trumpeter Doc Cheatham (1905-1997) played the Blues Alley in Washington, D.C. the weekend before his death at 91; and in his late nineties, Benny Waters (1902-1998) was still playing energetic, jump-style alto saxophone. But none of these musicians can match Carter's more than 70-year musical career. Not only has Carter been continuously active, he has strongly influenced fellow musicians through his improvisations, arrangements, and overall musicianship and professionalism.

Best known – along with Johnny Hodges – as one of the two great alto saxophonists of the swing era, Carter is an exceptionally versatile musician. He is a superb soloist on trumpet, which he occasionally still plays on gigs and recording sessions. He has recorded on tenor, soprano, and C melody saxophones and on clarinet, piano, and trombone. He is also one of the foremost jazz arrangers: as jazz writer Gary Giddins has observed, Carter "is universally celebrated as the leading orchestrator of saxes." In the 1940s Carter was one of the first African American musicians to break Hollywood's color barrier. During the next quarter century, he focused more and more energy on composing and arranging for films and television. In the 1970s, however, he returned with undiminished energy to full-time jazz performance.

Carter grew up in San Juan Hill, a section of Manhattan, then one of the city's toughest neighborhoods and now the site of Lincoln Center for the Performing Arts. Trumpeter Bubber Miley lived in the neighborhood and became one of Carter's early musical idols. Carter began playing C melody saxophone in Harlem's smaller clubs while in his teens. During the mid-1920s, he started playing in larger bands, including those of Earl Hines and Fletcher Henderson. In 1927 Carter began a stint as alto saxophonist and arranger with Charlie Johnson's Paradise Ten, an important but underrated group that included Benny Waters as a sax player and arranger.

By 1930 Carter and Johnny Hodges had laid the foundations of jazz alto saxophone playing, and they reigned unchallenged until the appearance of Charlie Parker and bebop, or modern jazz in the mid-1940s. As a saxophone player, Carter is noted for his pure, rounded tone, harmonic sophistication, and virtuosity. Rather than building his solos out of repeated short phrases, known to jazz musicians as riffs, or by vertical elaboration of the song's underlying chord structure – as was typical of many jazz players during the 1930s – Carter's improvisations featured long melodic lines that prefigured the elliptical playing that characterized bebop.

In 1932 Carter organized his own band, in which Doc Cheatham played lead trumpet. Though a first-rate musician, Carter was not successful in his repeated attempts to form a lasting big band, perhaps because he lacked the requisite flamboyance and showmanship, or because the band's recordings failed to capture the public fancy. "I could never support [a big band]," he explained in 1987, "nor could it support me. I always had to be doing some outside arranging to... pay members of the orchestra." During the 1930s Carter also wrote a number of significant jazz compositions, including "Waltzing the Blues," one of the earliest jazz waltzes, and the jazz standard "Blues in My Heart."

During the GREAT DEPRESSION, Carter disbanded his own group and joined showman Willie Bryant's orchestra. Soon Carter left the United States and began an extended sojourn in Europe (1935-1938). Initially finding work as featured sax player and arranger for the house band of Chez Florence in Paris, he later led bands and recorded in Denmark, Holland, and England. While in London, he served as staff arranger for the British Broadcasting Corporation dance orchestra (1936-1938). In 1937 he took part in a celebrated recording session in Paris with tenor saxophonist and fellow American expatriate Coleman Hawkins and jazz guitarist Django Reinhardt. Carter's classic, swinging arrangements of "Crazy Rhythm" and "Honeysuckle Rose" were written for this session.

After his return to the United States, Carter led small groups and again tried to organize a big band. Both his big band and his small combos were important incubators of bebop. In 1941 trumpeter Dizzy Gillespie – soon to emerge alongside Charlie Parker as a co-creator of bebop – was added to Carter's combo for an extended nightclub appearance in New York City. Looking back on the experience in a 1976 interview, Gillespie said, "Playing with him was my best experience next to playing with Charlie Parker.... [I]t'll be a long time before people... realize what he contributed to our music." During the mid-1940s Carter's big band featured other bebop pioneers such as trumpeter Miles Davis, drummer Max Roach, and trombonist J. J. Johnson.

In the 1940s Carter settled in Los Angeles, the city that would be his home for several decades. The event that precipitated his Hollywood career was the abrupt departure of composer WILLIAM GRANT STILL from the set of *Stormy Weather* (1943), an all-black film starring Bill "Bojangles" Robinson and LENA HORNE and featuring a wide range of African American performers, including Cab Calloway and his orchestra, pianist Thomas "Fats" Waller, and the KATHERINE DUNHAM Dancers. Carter stepped in as an instrumentalist and arranger, and his contributions included the scores for Lena Horne's renditions of "Stormy Weather" and "Good for Nothin' Joe." Although he received no screen credit, he did gain further film work.

Between 1943 and 1957 Carter played on numerous soundtracks and contributed arrangements for two dozen films, including *Portrait of Jennie* (1948), *Panic in the Streets* (1950), *An American in Paris* (1951), and *The Sun Also Rises* (1957). He also composed for television, beginning in 1958 with the police drama *M Squad*. During the 1960s he aided a number of other jazz musicians who sought work in Hollywood, including J. J. Johnson, tenor saxophonist Oliver Nelson, and Argentinean pianist Lalo Schifrin.

One of the last recordings Carter made before becoming immersed in Hollywood was the jazz classic *Further Definitions* (1961). The album featured Coleman Hawkins in a saxophone ensemble that revisited Carter's arrangements for their renowned 1937 Paris session and included new music as well. Then, after years of curtailed performances and recordings, Carter emerged from Hollywood to record his first small-group album in a decade, *The King* (1976), which marked his active return to jazz.

In recent years Carter has recorded many notable albums. For *Central City Sketches* (1987), he joined the American Jazz Orchestra in playing a number of his arrangements and compositions, including the premiere recording of his six-part "Central City Suite." *My Man Benny, My Man Phil* (1989), with alto saxophonist Phil Woods, highlighted Carter's trumpet playing on two songs. *Harlem Renaissance* (1992) featured Carter, a big band, and the Rutgers University Orchestra, with a full string section, performing two recent Carter suites, "Tales of the Rising Sun" and "Harlem Renaissance."

James Clyde Sellman

SEE ALSO

Blake, James Hubert ("Eubie"); Calloway, Cabell (Cab); Davis, Miles Dewey, III; Gillespie, John Birks ("Dizzy"); Hawkins, Coleman Randolph; Henderson, Fletcher Hamilton, Jr.; Hines, Earl Kenneth ("Fatha"); Miley, James Wesley ("Bubber"); Parker, Charles Christopher ("Bird"); Roach, Maxwell Lemuel (Max); Robinson, Bill ("Bojangles"); Waller, Thomas Wright ("Fats").

North America

Carter, Betty (b. May 16, 1930, Flint, Mich.; d. September 26, 1998, New York, N.Y.), African American JAZZ singer credited with integrating bebop into swing jazz style.

Betty Carter, born Lillie Mae Jones, began working as a singer in Detroit clubs when she was in high school. In 1948 she began touring with Lionel Hampton, who gave her the nickname Betty Bebop. She settled in New York City in 1951, where she sang at the APOLLO THEATER, the Village Vanguard, and the Blue Note. She toured with Miles Davis (1958-1959) and Sonny Rollins (1963, Japan) and formed her own record company, Bet-Car Productions, in 1971. Carter's work includes *Baby It's Cold Outside* (1966, with RAY CHARLES) and *Look What I Got* (1988), for which she received a Grammy Award. In 1997 *Newsday* described her as the "best jazz singer alive"; the same year, she was awarded the National Medal of Arts by President Bill Clinton.

SEE ALSO

Davis, Miles Dewey, III; Hampton, Lionel Leo; Rollins, Theodore ("Sonny").

Latin America and the Caribbean

Carter, Martin (b. June 7, 1927, Georgetown, Guyana), Guyanese poet, activist, and politician.

"Politics... is a part of life and poets are interested in life... if politics is a part of life, we shall become involved in politics." In this quote from a 1978 interview, Martin Carter expressed his views on poets' political and social responsibilities, beliefs that have shaped his entire career.

Carter was born in Georgetown, British Guiana (now GUYANA). After graduating from Queens College, he took a job with the British Civil Service in Guiana. But he soon became involved with the political struggle to free his country from British colonial rule.

In 1953 Carter was jailed for supporting Guyanese activist CHEDDI JAGAN. While he had already self-published several books of poetry before his imprisonment, it was his book from that period, *Poems of Resistance from British Guiana* (1954), that gained him the greatest renown. His militant, idealistic portrayal of his country's political struggles became a model for many other Caribbean poets. After his release from prison, he worked as a schoolteacher and in private industry, all the while continuing his political activism. After Guyana finally became an independent nation, he served as the country's minister of information from 1967 to 1971. He returned to academia, lecturing at Leeds University in England in 1975-1976 and joining the faculty at the University of Guyana in 1977.

Carter continues to publish poetry. While books such as *Poems of Succession* (1977) and *Poems of Affinity* (1980) were thematically linked to *Poems of Resistance*, events such as the 1980 murder of Guyanese politician WALTER RODNEY appear to have shaken his optimistic faith in Guyana's post-independence future. Carter's *Selected Poems* was published in 1989.

Lisa Clayton Robinson

Africa

Carthage, ancient city of North Africa founded around 800 B.C.E. as a Phoenician colony on the Gulf of Tunis in present-day TUNISIA.

For three centuries, from about 500 to 200 B.C.E., Carthage was the capital of a commercial empire that dominated trade in the western Mediterranean. Beginning around 250 B.C.E., however, the Carthaginians found themselves increasingly in conflict with the expanding Roman Republic. After three ruthless wars of attrition, the Romans destroyed the city and scattered its inhabitants. Reestablished by the Romans in later years as a commercial outpost, Carthage languished for centuries after the fall of the empire. Today it is a pleasant suburb of Tunis. This article deals primarily with the ancient history of the city and its role, despite its ultimate defeat, in the growth of Roman Africa.

PHOENICIA

The Phoenicians were an ancient people who probably emerged from the Arabian Peninsula approximately 5000 years ago. After subduing the indigenous peoples of Syria and Palestine, they established a maritime trading empire at the eastern end of the Mediterranean. Ethnically and culturally a Semitic people, the Phoenicians worshiped a paramount god, Baal, and other minor divinities. They were intelligent and inventive; among other things, they invented the alphabet. They were also skillful mariners, willing and able to sail where no one else dared. Thus, for example, they did not fear, as the Greeks did, to sail beyond the Straits of Gibraltar. They probably circumnavigated Africa in the sixth century B.C.E. and sailed as far north as Britain, where many Carthaginian coins have been found.

Beginning as early as 1500 B.C.E., inhabitants of the Phoenician homeland (modern Lebanon and neighboring parts of Israel and Syria) came under pressure from other peoples of the Near East. Slowly but steadily over the next 1000 years, as their power in their homeland diminished, their "western empire" expanded. Tyre and Sidon, ancient Phoenician city-states, fell to various enemies, and Greeks challenged their domination of the Mediterranean and its shores. Ever innovative, the Phoenicians shifted their focus from old Phoenicia to Carthage, the "new" city that they had founded around 800 B.C.E. on the North African coast.

The founding date is questionable, as are many other Carthaginian dates. Carthaginians were not a literate or artistic people. They used the alphabet to improve business, whereas the Greeks, adopting it in the eighth century B.C.E., used the precious invention not only for business but also to write poetry, history, and philosophy. The Carthaginians left few records of their achievements and way of life. Intensely patriotic and fanatic believers in their religion, they were not proselytizers; for the most part they did not try to impose their beliefs or practices on others. Essentially, they wanted to be left alone to do business with the rest of the world.

This Carthaginian limestone bust, which represents a wealthy woman wearing an elaborate headdress, heavy earrings, and an ornate necklace, was found in Eleche, Spain. Carthage controlled southeast Spain when this sculpture was created in the late fifth-early fourth century B.C.E. *Nimatallah/Art Resource, NY*

CARTHAGE

Carthage exemplified everything Phoenicians held dear. The city on the bay, it was well situated for a maritime nation and offered anchorage for many ships. Its Mediterranean location was as close to Europe (at least to Sicily) as any other place on the African coast east of MOROCCO. The distance from Carthage to its colonies in western Sicily was less than 160 km (100 mi) by sea, a distance that the swift Carthaginian vessels could sail in a day. This narrow opening between the eastern and western Mediterranean could be patrolled and, if necessary, closed by a line of warships. The only way around was to pass through the perilous Straits of Messina (that is, to sail between Scylla and Charybdis). In addition to dominating both sides of this narrow gateway, Carthage also exerted control over Malta and other islands in the sea-lanes.

The high point of the Carthaginian hegemony may have occurred around 400 B.C.E. Carthage founded settlements, which the Greeks called *emporia*, along the entire coast from the Gulf of Sidra in present-day LIBYA through present-day Tunisia and ALGERIA to the Atlantic coast of Morocco, as well as on all the islands of the western Mediterranean, including the Balearics. Invading ships were sunk when captured, and a large army of Libyan and Nubian mercenaries could march either way from Carthage to counter invasions or put down revolts. The Carthaginian trade flourished not only by sea but also across the Sahara; routes terminating near modern

Tripoli opened much of sub-Saharan Africa to trade and commerce, especially in gold and precious jewels, for which the Carthaginians exchanged cloth and manufactured articles. At its height the city may have had as many as 500,000 inhabitants, and it was reputed to be the wealthiest city in the Mediterranean world.

The Punic Wars

The beginning of the end for Carthage came in 264 B.C.E., with the onset of the first Punic War. ("Punic" is derived from a Roman word for Phoenicia.) By that year Rome had acquired control of the entire Italian Peninsula and had begun to look both east, toward Greece, and west, toward Carthage. The Romans' first task was to capture the western half of Sicily, which Carthage had used as a fulcrum of its empire. Carthage could not permit the loss of Sicily, and so the war began. It lasted for 25 years and was a disaster for Carthage; not only was Sicily lost but also Sardinia, Corsica, Malta, and other islands, together with the monopoly of trade west of Italy.

Carthage did not despair; Phoenicians had moved west once before, from Tyre and Sidon to the coast of Africa; now they could move west again, to present-day Spain. A new empire was rapidly established, based on the wealth of Spanish silver mines and trade with the Iberian and Celtic peoples of the region. Again Rome was concerned and sought any excuse for another armed conflict. The Second Punic War began in 218 B.C.E. and ended in 201. Rome won and Carthage lost. Indeed, Rome's victory laid the foundation for the Roman Empire. But it was a near thing, and victory could have gone the other way. One man made the difference.

Hannibal (247-183 B.C.E.)

Hannibal, son of Hamilcar Barca, leader of the Spanish Empire, inherited command of the army after his father died and his brother was assassinated. Unlike his predecessors, he believed that Rome could be defeated only in its homeland, and he therefore determined to invade Italy. The Romans knew he was coming and moved into Gaul to stop his army of some 40,000 infantry, 10,000 cavalry, and 50 elephants. For the first of many times, Hannibal outwitted his opponents and headed for the Alps instead of following the coastal route, as Rome had expected. His passage through the rugged mountains is one of the great feats of military history. The army was harassed by Celtic tribes, who rolled rocks down on it from the heights. Snow falling on narrow icy paths created perilously slippery conditions. The elephants often fell to their death. Provisions ran short and hundreds starved, while thousands more deserted or were hurt or killed.

Reduced to 20,000 men, 6000 cavalry, and only a few of the war elephants, the army descended into the Po River valley after a journey of five months from Cartagena. A lesser man might have given up and gone home. Instead, Hannibal met one Roman army on the Ticino and defeated it, then overwhelmed a larger force in Lombardy a month later (December 218 B.C.E.). Italians began to join the army, which was augmented by Celtic recruits. Hannibal had hoped that an invasion of Italy might dismember the Roman state, and it seemed as if his hopes might be realized.

Hannibal's hopes rose even further in the following spring (April 217 B.C.E.), when he led his troops south to the Arno and then to (present-day) Arezzo and Perugia. In so doing, he trapped a large Roman army on the narrow shore of Lake Trasimeno. Descending from prepared positions in the hills, the invaders pushed the Romans back, killing thousands and forcing thousands more into the lake, where, encumbered by their armor, they drowned. The site of this famous battle, one of the worst defeats the Romans ever suffered, is near a small town now called Ossaia ("bony"). More than 2000 years later, plows in nearby fields still turn up bone fragments from the ancient encounter.

After its defeat at Ossaia, the Roman army was temporarily helpless. The Carthaginians had the chance to enter Rome, little more than 160 km (100 mi) away, but the troops were exhausted and could not take advantage of the opportunity. Meanwhile another Roman army was raised and, unwilling to test Hannibal in another battle, they watched as he wearily followed the river valleys south to Apulia and Campania, where he plundered the country, distributed large amounts of booty, and underwent treatment for wounds he had sustained.

Well rested after the winter, Hannibal again outwitted his foes. In the early summer of 216 B.C.E., in a swift maneuver, he seized the army supply depot at Cannae, on the Adriatic coast, and then prepared a trap. The Gauls and the Iberian infantry were drawn up in a line across the plain of Cannae, between the mountains and the sea. On either side were wings of cavalry, not easily visible from the plain. The Roman army, also rested and numerically much superior, attacked the center, which gave way little by little but did not break. Suddenly, without warning, the Libyan and Nubian cavalry circled and attacked from the rear, again annihilating the Romans at Cannae, one of the most famous battles in European history.

This great victory had the desired effect, and many Italian regions began to defect from Roman domination. But Hannibal, for reasons that are not clear, did not march on defenseless Rome; instead, perhaps hoping the peoples of Italy would do his work for him, he spent the winter of 216-215 B.C.E. in Capua. Disappointed, his new allies began to drift away. Fabius, the Roman general, adopted a strategy of never fighting but always threatening, and Hannibal found himself on the defensive for the first time. What is more, he had begun to lose support at home, where a new government of oligarchs, shocked by the expense of the campaign, charged him with misconduct of the war.

The rest of the story, after the ambiguous triumph at Cannae, involves a long, slow descent into loss and death, not only for Hannibal but also for his country. The final blow was delivered when still another Roman army, under Scipio Africanus, sailed across the sea and attacked Carthage itself. Hannibal abandoned Italy and rushed to defend his city. He met the Romans at Zama. The losses were terrible – 20,000 men and horses and all the elephants, supplies, and provisions. Though he himself escaped, the end had come. Harried from country to country by his enemies, Hannibal lived another 20 years; finally trapped in a small village near the Black Sea, he took poison. The year was 183 B.C.E.

"Delenda Est Carthago"

Carthage survived even this defeat; a treaty with Rome was signed, and although the treaty's provisions were severe, the city slowly began to prosper again. By 150 B.C.E. it was once more rich and, consequently, influential in African affairs. Cato the Elder, the fierce old conservative who hated all things not Roman, took it as his private crusade to see that Carthage was destroyed once and for all. He repeated the famous phrase "Delenda est Carthago," or "Carthage must be destroyed," on every possible occasion; and he had his way. In 146 B.C.E. the city was besieged, taken, and plundered; its inhabitants exiled or enslaved; its wall demolished; and its houses and public buildings burned to the ground. The site was dedicated to the infernal gods and, to ensure that it would never again be inhabited, its smoking ruins were sown with salt.

It seemed, however, that Carthage could not die. Only 25 years later a Roman colony was established on the site of the prior city. In due course New Carthage became the capital of the Roman province of Africa (incorporating present-day Tunisia and eastern Algeria) and a favorite vacation spot of the emperors.

Charles Van Doren

See Also

Tunis, Tunisia.

Latin America and the Caribbean

Cartola (Angenor de Oliveira)

(b. October 11, 1908, Rio de Janeiro, Brazil; d. 1980, Rio de Janeiro, Brazil), Afro-Brazilian musician who was one of the great samba composers of the twentieth century.

Cartola ("top hat") gained his nickname in the early 1920s because he always wore a fine hat, even while working as a mason. In 1929 he founded the second *escola de samba* (samba school), Estação Primeira da Mangueira, together with his partner, Carlos Cachaça. In the Carnival of that year, Mangueira paraded

An Afro-Brazilian musician, Cartola (his nickname meant "top hat") was one of the great samba composers of the twentieth century. *Roberto Garcia/Contexto*

to Cartola's composition "Chega de Demanda," which he would not record until 1974. Mangueira soon emerged as the preeminent samba school and continues to rank among the top Carnival organizations in Rio de Janeiro.

Throughout the 1930s famous Brazilian stars like Carmen Miranda, Francisco Alves, Mário Reis, and Araci de Almeida achieved success with interpretations of Cartola's songs. In 1940 Cartola participated in two albums titled *Native Brazilian Music* with PIXINGUINHA, DONGA, and João da Baiana, produced by Leopoldo Stokowski for the North American market. After performing with several samba ensembles throughout the 1940s, he left the Mangueira school and dropped out of the local music scene.

Cartola reemerged in the early 1960s as the bossa nova artists of the upscale south zone were searching for a more rootsy sound. In 1964 he and his wife, Zica, opened the Zicartola restaurant, which became a fashionable meeting place for artists and intellectuals. During this period, acclaimed artists such as Elisete Cardoso, Paulinho da Viola, Gal Costa, and Beth Carvalho recorded his songs. Cartola was 66 before he recorded his first album.

Christopher Dunn

SEE ALSO
Samba Schools; Rio de Janeiro, Brazil; Carnivals in Latin America and the Caribbean.

North America

Carver, George Washington

(b. 1864, Diamond, Mo.; d. January 4, 1943, Tuskegee, Ala.), African American agriculturist, inventor, and educator known for the development of peanut products.

In 1896 George Washington Carver, a recent graduate of Iowa State College of Agriculture and Mechanical Arts (now Iowa State University), accepted an invitation from Booker T. Washington to head the agricultural department at Tuskegee Normal and Industrial Institute for Negroes (now TUSKEGEE UNIVERSITY). During a tenure of nearly 50 years, Carver elevated the scientific study of farming, improved the health and agricultural output of Southern farmers, and developed hundreds of uses for their crops.

As word of Carver's work at Tuskegee spread across the world, he received many invitations to work or teach at better-equipped, higher-paying institutions. Yet he decided to remain at Tuskegee, where he could be of greatest service to his fellow African Americans in the South. Carver epitomized Booker T. Washington's philosophy of black solidarity and self-reliance. He worked hard among his own people, lived modestly, and avoided confronting racial issues. For these reasons he became, like Booker T. Washington, an icon for white Americans.

Carver's interest in plants began at an early age. Growing up in postemancipation Missouri under the care of his parents' former owners, he collected a variety of wild plants and flowers from the surrounding forests and fields and planted them in a garden. At the age of ten, he left home of his own volition to attend a colored school in the nearby community of Neosho, where he did chores for a black family in exchange for food and a place to sleep. He maintained his interest in plants while putting himself through high school in Minneapolis, Kansas, and during his first and only year at Simpson College in Iowa. During this period, he made many sketches of plants and flowers.

Carver made the study of plants his focus in 1891, the year he enrolled at Iowa State College. After graduating in 1894 with a B.S. in botany and agriculture, he spent two more years at Iowa State to complete a master's degree in the same fields. During this time, he taught botany to undergraduate students and conducted extensive experiments on plants while managing the university's greenhouse. These experiences served him well during his first few years at Tuskegee.

When Carver arrived in Tuskegee in 1896, he faced a host of challenges. There was a lack of facilities and funds for the agricultural department, which consisted only of a barn, a cow, and a few chickens. Carver's first task was to create a laboratory. A resourceful individual, he assembled a small group of students to collect materials that could be used to construct laboratory equipment – pots, pans, tubes, wire, and so on – and made the tools and devices necessary to conduct agriculture-related experiments.

There was also a lack of interest in the study of agriculture, which many of the students at Tuskegee associated with sharecropping and poverty. They tended to be more interested in learning an industrial skill or trade that would allow them to make a living beyond the farm. Carver dignified farming by infusing the discipline with science: botany, chemistry, and soil study. Over the course of a few years, Carver's department, renamed Scientific Agriculture, attracted an increasing number of students.

Carver used scientific means to tackle the third challenge he faced at Tuskegee: widespread poverty and malnutrition among local black farmers. Year after year, farmers had planted cotton on the same plots of land and thereby exhausted the topsoil's nutrients. By testing the soil, Carver discovered that a lack of nitrogen in particular accounted for consistently low harvests. While at Iowa State, Carver had learned that certain plants in the pea family extracted nitrogen from the air and deposited it in the soil. To maintain the topsoil's balance of nutrients, he advised farmers to alternate planting cotton and peanuts. This farming method proved effective, and within a few years, farmers saw a dramatic increase in their crop production. Carver then created an outreach program in which he traveled once a month to rural parts of Alabama to give hands-on instruction to farmers in this method and in other innovative farming techniques.

Because of Carver's emphasis on the cultivation of the peanut, peanuts flooded the market and their prices dropped. This predicament presented Carver with another challenge: how to prevent farmers from resorting to the exclusive cultivation of cotton, which had a higher market value. Carver began to explore alternative uses for the peanut that would increase its market value. He developed over 300 peanut products that included cheese, flour, and stains. Then, in 1921, he helped the United Peanuts Growers Association persuade Congress to pass a bill calling for a protective tariff on imported peanuts.

The development of the peanut also helped Carver resolve the problem of malnutrition in the rural South. He stressed that the peanut was a valuable source of protein that could enrich farmers' diets and improve their health. As part of his extension program, Carver taught farmers' wives how to preserve food and prepare tasty, well-balanced meals. For many black Southerners who had never given thought to eating tomatoes, which were once widely believed to be poisonous, Carver explained their nutritional value and demonstrated several recipes in which they could be used. He was also innovative with respect to the sweet potato and the pecan, introducing approximately 100 uses for each of those two foods.

Carver patented only 3 of his 500 agriculture-based inventions, reasoning "God gave them to me; how can I sell them to someone else?" He lived frugally, accepting only a small portion of his salary, and donated his life savings to a fund in his name that would encourage research in agricultural sciences. In 1916 he was appointed to the Royal Society of Arts in London, England, and in 1923 was awarded the prestigious Spingarn Medal of the NATIONAL ASSOCIATION FOR THE ADVANCEMENT OF COLORED PEOPLE (NAACP) for his contributions to agriculture. His ingenuity and resourcefulness can be seen today in the hundreds of scientific and artistic items of his invention which are on display at the Carver Memorial Museum on the campus of TUSKEGEE UNIVERSITY.

Aaron Myers

SEE ALSO

Washington, Booker Taliaferro.

North America

Cary, Mary Ann Shadd (b. 1823, Wilmington, Del.; d. 1893, Washington, D.C.), American editor and journalist; first African American woman to attend Howard Law School.

Mary Ann Shadd Cary was born to free blacks who were active abolitionists. Influenced by her parents' antislavery activities, the Quaker-educated Cary began a school for blacks in Delaware and taught in neighboring states. At the same time she began writing for Frederick Douglass's *North Star* and published "Hints to the Colored people of the North," a pamphlet on black self-reliance. During a trip to Toronto in 1851, at a lecture on the recently implemented Fugitive Slave Act, she met Henry Bibb, publisher of the abolitionist paper *Voice of the Fugitive*. Bibb convinced her of the need for teachers to educate fugitive slaves in Canada West (Ontario). Cary moved to Windsor, where she was hired as an instructor by black families and later received a small grant from the American Missionary Association.

Political differences soured Cary's relationship with Bibb. Owner of the only printing press in the area, he refused to print her pamphlet "Notes of Canada West" because he was opposed to her strong views against segregation and her belief that blacks should settle in Canada rather than hoping for an eventual return to the United States. The regular attacks on Cary in *Voice of the Fugitive* prompted the American Missionary Association to rescind its funding. Cary struggled to keep the school open until 1853, when the first issue of the *Provincial Freeman* was published. She began the *Provincial Freeman* to provide an alternative to Bibb's editorial policy. In so doing she enlisted the help of abolitionist Samuel Ringgold Ward. Lack of funding prompted Cary to suspend publication soon after the first edition and she left Windsor for the United States to find subscribers so that she could resume publication. She later set up offices in Toronto but the financial crisis of the *Provincial Freeman* continued. Cary published the paper sporadically until 1859.

In 1863, at the suggestion of Martin Delany, Cary accepted a commission from the governor of Indiana to act as recruitment officer for black volunteers in the Civil War. After the war she settled in WASHINGTON, D.C., where she worked as a teacher and principal through HOWARD UNIVERSITY. At 41, she was the first woman to attend Howard University Law School. She finished her law studies in 1871, but, believing that a woman's graduation would attract negative publicity, the university did not grant her the degree until 1881. Cary spent her last years working with the women's suffrage movement. She died of stomach cancer in Washington, D.C., in 1893.

Peter Hudson

SEE ALSO

Abolitionism in the United States; Bibb, Henry Walton; Civil War, American; Delany, Martin Robison; Douglass, Frederick; Fugitive Slave Laws.

Africa

Casablanca, Morocco, Moroccan port city; the nation's most important industrial and commercial center.

Some sources claim that the coastal city of Casablanca dates back in its origins to the seventh century, but the settlement left few historical traces until it developed as a BERBER town called Anfa in the thirteenth century. In 1468 the Portuguese attacked Anfa, which by then had become the base for a thriving piracy industry. The Portuguese remained a presence in the town they called *casa blanca*, or "white house," until an earthquake leveled it in 1755. A series of Moroccan rulers followed, building ramparts that encircled the white-washed houses and maze of streets. Now called Dar el Beida by the residents, the town became the commercial hub for the regions of Chaouia, Rehamnas, and Tadla, all of which exported goods such as cereals, wool, hides, beeswax, and oil to Europe. During this time Berbers from the HâHâ region south of Essaouira began moving to what was then still a small town.

Casablanca's mercantile population grew over the next 200 years. Spanish grain merchants paved the way for other Europeans traders, who arrived in large numbers after the reigning sultan opened the port to international commerce. By 1907, when the French military occupied MOROCCO, French merchants outnumbered all other Europeans. As Morocco's most active international trade center, Casablanca became the French Protectorate's chief port. The French built a modern port and a new city radiating from the Moorish section they called the Old Medina.

Casablanca played a critical role for the Allied forces during World War II. The city was one of three points of the North African invasion. It was host to the 1943 Casablanca Conference, during which Winston Churchill, Franklin D. Roosevelt, and Charles de Gaulle vowed to fight the Axis for unconditional surrender.

After the withdrawal of the French in 1956, the city suffered an economic lull, but as an industrializing, strategically located seaport, it soon regained its standing, becoming the commercial capital of Morocco. Casablanca's industries account for more than half of the total industrial production of Morocco and include textiles, electronics, sawmilling, furniture, construction materials, glass, and tobacco products as well as fishing. Exports include cereals, leather, wool, and phosphates. The city, made famous in the West by the film *Casablanca* (1942), attracts large numbers of tourists, who explore the juxtaposition of old and new quarters.

Casablanca has grown in population to more than 3 million inhabitants. With an urban area that includes some of Morocco's most elite neighborhoods, largest slums, and sprawling suburbs, Casablanca is currently Morocco's largest city.

Marian Aguiar

SEE ALSO

Portugal; World War II and African Americans.

Africa

Casely-Hayford, Joseph Ephraim (b. September 28, 1866, Cape Coast, Gold Coast [now Ghana]; d. August 11, 1930, Accra, Gold Coast), educator, journalist, lawyer, and politician, the most prominent African nationalist leader of the 1920s.

Joseph Ephraim Casely-Hayford spent his life working for the advancement of Africans in British West Africa. Born into the coastal elite of the Gold Coast (present-day GHANA), he studied at the Wesleyan Boys High School at Cape Coast and then at Fourah Bay College in Sierra Leone. During his early career he was principal of Wesleyan High School in Accra and later of Wesleyan High School at Cape Coast. In 1885 he turned to journalism and wrote for the *Western Echo*, the *Gold Coast Echo*, and the *Gold Coast Chronicle*. Although his career would focus on bringing political change to West Africa, he continued to write for the *Gold Coast Leader* from 1902 to 1930. In addition, he wrote the nonfiction work *Gold Coast Native Institutions* (1903) and the novel *Ethiopia Unbound* (1911).

As a politician and activist Casely-Hayford earned renown. His accomplishments are too many to list fully here. Called to the bar in 1896 after studying in London, he returned to the Gold Coast to represent the Aborigines' Rights Protection Society in its fight against a British legal initiative that threatened the land tenure system.

From 1916 to 1925 Casely-Hayford served as an appointed member of the Gold Coast's Legislative Council. From 1927 until his death in 1930, he was an elected member. He drew inspiration and ideas from a wide range of world leaders, including Mahatma Gandhi, W. E. B. Du Bois, and Marcus Garvey. Perhaps his greatest achievement was his instrumental role in founding the National Congress of British West Africa (NCBWA) in 1920. An early example of Pan-Africanism, this organization brought together nationalists from the British colonies of THE GAMBIA, NIGERIA, the Gold Coast, and Sierra Leone. The NCBWA worked unsuccessfully to gain self-rule for these colonies but set the trend for future political development.

Robert Fay

SEE ALSO

Accra, Ghana; Garvey, Marcus Mosiah; Du Bois, William Edward Burghardt (W. E. B.).

Latin America and the Caribbean

Castera, Georges (b. 1936, Port-au-Prince, Haiti), Haitian poet and painter.

Georges Castera became interested in literature first in HAITI, then in high school in Montpellier, France, where he discovered the surrealists and the Négritude poets (*see* NEGRISTA POETS and NÉGRITUDE). It was during his stay in France that he began to draw. Upon returning to Haiti, encouraged by Paul Laraque, he began to write in Creole (*see* LANGUAGES, CREOLE, IN THE CARIBBEAN). He has spent more than 20 years outside Haiti, mostly in Spain and the United States. He has always remained firmly connected to a popular imagination, both Haitian and international.

One of the best-known Haitian poets, he does not see himself as part of the artistic establishment despite his strong influence on the younger generation of poets. Poetry is for him a fundamentally revolutionary act; writing in Creole implies an engagement in social and political issues as well as a reflection on the creative process. Some of his poems parody the speeches of military leaders and comment on censorship and political violence.

Castera has always been an active member of the Haitian intellectual and literary community. He was a founding member, in 1989, of the cultural Haitian-Caribbean review *Chemins critiques*. His collections of poems, some in Creole and others in French, include *Le retour à l'arbre* (1974), *Konbèlann* (1976), *Biswit leta* (1978), *Zèb atè* (1980), *Rature d'un miroir* and *Quasi parlando* (1992), *A Wòdpòte* (1993), *Voix de tête* (1996), and *Alarive lèzanfan: Poèm krèyol* (1998). His highly stylized drawings have been exhibited in Haiti, and have been included as illustrations in issues of *Chemins critiques* and in Farah-Martine L'Hérisson's collection of poetry *Itinéraire zéro* (1995).

Joelle Vitiello

Latin America and the Caribbean

Catholic Church in Latin America and the Caribbean

For five centuries, throughout Latin America and the Caribbean, the relationship between the Catholic Church and people of African ancestry has been fraught with contradiction. The Church's complicity in slavery, its Eurocentric cosmology, and its bouts of inquisitorial zeal have rendered it an uninviting space for Afro-Latin identity. Yet the Church's need to attract converts, its overall tolerance of heterodoxy, and its public recognition of black saints have over time made major contributions to Afro-Latin cultures. To this day this contradiction, far from being resolved, has inner potentialities that are yet to be fully realized.

It is a major irony of world history that Christianity, which teaches the fundamental equality of all souls before God, condoned for 1800 years the most unequal of all institutions. The early Church fathers declared that slavery was a punishment for original sin. Medieval theologians accepted enslavement of prisoners in what they classified as "just" wars. In the fifteenth century the pope denounced the enslavement of Christians while explicitly offering up "pagans" as fair game. And, as Europeans began to drag Africans across the Atlantic as slaves, the Church pronounced this system justified as long as it was accompanied by the evangelization of the enslaved.

Thus began a monumental chapter in the history of hypocrisy. The Church bore witness to the slave trade by congratulating itself for bringing heathen souls into the light of Christian day. The Spanish, Portuguese, and French clergy in the colonies knew, however, that only a very limited number of Africans ever received instruction in the faith. The vast majority of slaves and their descendants rarely learned the Creed, let alone anything of the Bible. Generally, they remained indifferent to Catholicism, interpreted it according to their own views, or syncretized it with their own cosmologies.

From the start, European slave owners showed contempt for Africans' ability or need to understand their masters' religion. The holy water sprayed on enslaved Africans waiting to be packed into ships was little more than a tariff on export. If they survived the Middle Passage, enslaved Africans were sold to masters who by law were to see to their religious instruction but who rarely raised a finger to do so. Such things might interfere with production and make slaves rebellious. Many plantation owners refused even to let their slaves hear Mass; others told their slaves that baptism was evil magic. And the rural clergy were in no position to argue with the people who paid their salaries.

The situation was slightly different on estates run by religious orders. The Jesuits, for example, inculcated orthodoxy in their slaves, even taught them to read the Bible. They made sure, however, that they would draw no subversive conclusions. Passing over Paul's insistence that Christ knows man as "neither slave nor free," they emphasized instead the virtues of patience and resignation. "Know, my brothers," a Jesuit preached to slaves in PERU, "the Lord will send comfort for your hearts; he will reward you with that gift of the crown of Heaven, better than all the gold."

Enslaved men and women exposed to this message in the Catholic countries of the hemisphere rarely accepted it. Instead, they regarded the religion of their masters as a source of power and healing to be tapped here and now. Africans were already familiar with the healing powers of water. In Saint-Domingue (HAITI), for example, many slaves sought baptism repeatedly as a healing rite, to treat sickness and affliction. Others regarded the saints as the magical source of power that had enabled Europeans to found vast empires. It should come as no surprise that Catholic figurines were worshiped in runaway slave communities, such as the great seventeenth-century Brazilian *quilombo* of Palmares. Here, the runaways turned to Catholic saints not only because they served as a common denominator across ethnic African divides; they also obviously possessed great protective power.

Although in the countryside of the New World Catholic societies, slaves received little encouragement to participate in the Church, the situation was different in urban areas such as Lima, Salvador, and Havana. There, slaves worked as artisans, peddlers, and domestics, and the urban context offered them more time, mobility, and literacy than did the plantation. These were energies that could, from the point of view of white society, become volatile unless channeled quickly toward socially desirable ends. This was why Catholic whites in cities throughout the hemisphere urged people of color to become involved in the Church.

Many did, by entering a Catholic brotherhood (*irmandade* in Brazil, *cofradia* or *cabildo* in Spanish America). Confraternities were dedicated to particular saints, for whom they organized processions. The brotherhoods functioned as mutual aid societies, through which members gained access to credit, health care, and a decent burial. The latter was of special interest to Africans, for whom death without proper burial left the spirit dissatisfied and wandering. By the eighteenth century, hundreds of black brotherhoods had been founded and were busy building chapels.

The brotherhoods (which often included "sisters") embodied the Church's contradictory relationship to Africans. On the one hand, they were an assimilating force, drawing Afro-Latins into the values of respectability, status, and invidious distinction that served white society. Many black brotherhoods existed at the pleasure of white benefactors, who made donations to ensure that the "savages" would become civilized. Black confraternities were also notorious for reinforcing the distinctions from which the ruling class benefited. In BRAZIL, for example, only Dahomean blacks could belong to the brotherhood of Good Jesus of Redemption, and only Yorubas could enter the brotherhood of Our Lady of the Good Death. Other brotherhoods required that members be born in Angola or in Brazil; that they be slaves or freedpeople; that they be "pure" blacks or mulattos, and so on.

Despite these factors, the brotherhoods were often places where blacks were able to keep alive their own values, attitudes, and ideas. For example, they nourished a number of cults to revere black saints, including Benedict, Anthony of Categerona and Ephigenia. Costa Rican slaves revered a dark-skinned Virgin Mary who had appeared to a slave woman. Further, the brotherhoods instituted annual royal processionals, coinciding with the Feast of the Magi, for which they elected representative kings and queens. The dances and music played for these processionals were known as "congadas" in Brazil and CUBA, and kept alive the high value placed by West Africans on royalty.

The brotherhoods made another more underground contribution to Afro-Latin culture: the pairing of Catholic saints with African deities. The Church's evocative chromolithographs of suffering and triumphant saints forged powerful links between Catholicism and African gods. As long as members kept up appearances, the Church looked the other way. In Brazil, the Yoruba god of smallpox, Omolú, was identified with sore-covered Saint Sebastian. Oxóssi, goddess of the hunt, was linked to the warrior Saint George. And the Beji, the divine twins, were associated with Cosmos and Damian. In Haiti, meanwhile, Ezili, the Dahomean water goddess of love, became paired with the Virgin Mary; Benin's python god Damballah was associated with Saint Patrick, because of his triumph over snakes; and Legba, guardian of destiny who holds keys to the underworld, became Saint Peter. Similar correspondences developed elsewhere in the hemisphere.

One should not forget, as well, the role the black brotherhoods played in gaining freedom for slaves. A key function of the confraternity was to accumulate funds through donations, dues, and testamentary bequests, and to use them to buy certificates of freedom. Thousands of slaves throughout the hemisphere gained their freedom in this manner. And when the movements to end slavery reached a fever pitch in Brazil and Cuba in the late nineteenth century, black Catholic brotherhoods were key actors agitating for total abolition.

ABOVE: A man kneels in prayer along with other worshipers in a Cuban church. *José Azel/Aurora*
LEFT: This is a late 17th-century, polychromed wood statue of Saint Benedict of Palermo, the patron saint of Negroes in North America. *Oronoz*

Under slavery the Church had expended little effort to root out unorthodox practices in the black brotherhoods. This was largely due to the independence of colonial clergy from the dictates of Rome. Under the colonial system of the *patronato*, clerics answered to the secular, not religious, authorities, who were not greatly concerned with religious heterodoxy. By the start of the twentieth century, however, Rome had reestablished its authority in the Western Hemisphere; its top agenda was to eliminate impurities it still saw in the black brotherhoods. Between the 1890s and 1920s, practices such as the congadas were expelled from the Church and thrown onto the street, while religious syncretism was denounced and punished. People who held such practices dear were obliged to continue them elsewhere. In Brazil, the congada became the dance of kings and queens at Carnival time. Members of brotherhoods whose cosmovision included strong pairs of saints and gods carried these into the sacred precincts of other religions, such as Candomblé, Santería, Shango, and Batuque. For the next 60 years the Catholic Church in Latin America and the Caribbean maintained a distinction between doctrinal orthodoxy and the syncretisms of these other religions.

Since the 1980s, however, the pendulum has begun to swing in the opposite direction. As a result of the worldwide explosion of Protestant conversion, the Catholic Church has begun to experiment with accepting culturally diverse innovations of the High Mass. Throughout Latin America, for example, the Church has endorsed initiatives on the part of black clergy to perform "Afro Masses," which incorporate elements of Afro-derived dances, music, instruments, cosmologies, dress and food, and seek to keep alive the memory of slavery. In Brazil the Afro Mass is the result of a sizable black Catholic antiracist movement, led by black seminarians and clergy, which seeks to pressure the Church to include a call for racial justice in its social agenda.

A similar process is at work in Haiti. There the Church has started to acknowledge the value of the Afro religion on the island. Now the Church publicly praises Vodou artists and even employs them. In Haiti's new Catholic iconography, Christ, the saints, and apostles are often represented as black, and sometimes as officiating in Vodou temples. The same drums that are played during Vodou ceremonies are now permitted in some parish churches. And curates have been known to pour libations of water at the four cardinal points before the celebration of the Eucharist, echoing the gesture of the Vodou ritual leader who pours rum at the four corners of the Vodou cult center.

Traditional Catholic religiosity, especially saint worship, is also capable of nurturing racial identity and of generating reflection on racial inequality. For example, in Brazil there exists an enormously popular Catholic devotion to a semimythical nineteenth-century enslaved woman named Anastacia, believed to have been tortured to death when she refused to submit to the master's lust. In practice, Anastacia has inspired many people to struggle against racism. One black woman, a devotee of Anastacia's, was moved to found a hair salon dedicated to valorizing Afro-Brazilian women's beauty. Another founded the Slave Anastacia Women's Group, a small neighborhood-based group dedicated to educating local black women about their culture, their bodies, and their health. Still another woman, also stimulated by her love of Anastacia,

ABOVE RIGHT: An 1830s portrayal of the Fiesta de St. Rosalie, patron of blacks. *Oronoz*
RIGHT: Jean-Baptiste Debret's lithograph (1831) depicts Afro-Brazilian women entering a church to be baptized. *By permission of the Houghton Library, Harvard University*

started a small literacy program for poor black children in her neighborhood and honored Anastacia by naming the project after her.

The implication should be clear. Throughout the hemisphere Catholicism and its parent, the Catholic Church, are held in fairly low regard by black movement activists committed to building a strong sense of Afro-Latin identity and antiracist sentiment. It may, however, be too early to dismiss the potential contribution the Catholic Church can make to this struggle. While the contradictions of the Church's stance toward Afro-Latins have yet to be resolved, they continue to include promising syntheses of the Catholic world-view, black identity, and antiracism. It is, in the end, up to leaders of the hemisphere's black movements to decide whether they wish to follow these leads or create alternative ones.

John Burdick

See Also

Middle Passage, The; Transatlantic Slave Trade; Palmares: An African State in Brazil; Maroonage in the Americas; Abolitionism in the United States; Carnivals in Latin America and the Caribbean; Orishas; Religions, African, in Latin America and the Caribbean; Protestant Church in Latin America and the Caribbean.

Latin America and the Caribbean

Catimbó, a religion practiced in rural northeastern Brazil that combines Amerindian practices with European and African influences (*see* Religions, African, in Brazil).

North America

Catlett, Elizabeth (b. April 15, 1919, Washington, D.C.), African American sculptor and graphic artist whose art combines African and Mexican stylistic elements and who explores the themes of struggle and maternity.

While a student at Howard University in the 1930s, Elizabeth Catlett first encountered African sculptural art and the contemporary work of the Mexican muralists. These two art traditions inform most of Catlett's oeuvre. Her sculpted figures have the same voluminous, rounded forms of the people portrayed in the murals of such Mexican artists as Diego Rivera. At the same time, the faces of Catlett's sculpted figures have an owl-like, lunar quality that seems to be derived from African mask design. This stylized facial quality can also be observed in some of Catlett's graphic work, especially in her lithographs. In her linocuts, on the other hand, the faces and bodies of figures are rendered in a more realistic manner; these linocuts are stylistically related to the work of printmakers at the Taller de Gráfica Popular in Mexico City, where Catlett studied in 1946-1947. She combined what she learned in Mexico with what she observed in African art to create a unique idiom for representing the daily struggles of Mexicans and African Americans.

After graduating from Howard University's School of Art with honors in 1937, she pursued an M.F.A. at the University of Iowa, where she changed her concentration from painting to sculpture. Her thesis project, a sculpture entitled *Mother and Child,* was the first of Catlett's many works exploring the theme of maternity. It won the first-place award for sculpture at the 1941 American Negro Exposition in Chicago. This recognition led to a teaching appointment at Dillard University in New Orleans. After two years at Dillard, Catlett married artist Charles White, and the two of them taught briefly at Hampton University in Virginia before settling in New York City. There, Catlett taught art at the George Washington Carver School and studied lithography at the Art Students' League.

In 1946 Catlett was awarded a Rosenwald Fellowship to go to Mexico to execute a series on African American women. During her first year in Mexico, Catlett's marriage to Charles White fell apart. They divorced, and she married Mexican painter Francisco Mora in 1947. Catlett remained in Mexico and continued working at the Taller de Gráfica Popular. Of the Taller she said, "It was a great social experience because I learned how to use art for the service of people, struggling people, to whom only realism is meaningful." Through studies at local art schools, Catlett improved her ability to sculpt in wood, ceramics, and stone. In 1959 she became the first female teacher at the School of Fine Arts at the National Autonomous University of Mexico, serving as the head of the sculpture department. In 1962 she became a Mexican citizen. After her retirement from teaching in 1976, Catlett and her husband moved to Cuernavaca, where they have continued to work in adjacent studios.

Catlett's sculpture and works on paper have won acclaim in Mexico and the United States and can be found in major collections in both countries. She has frequently traveled back and forth between Mexico and the United States to exhibit and speak about her artwork. On April 1, 1961, she delivered a speech titled "The Negro People and American Art at Mid-Century" at the National Conference of Negro Artists (*see* Art, African American). On this occasion, she encouraged artists to look to black people for inspiration and to exhibit in black community spaces. "I have always wanted my art to service my people," she said, "to reflect us, to relate to us, to stimulate us, to make us aware of our potential.... We have to create an art for liberation and for life."

Aaron Myers

See Also

Art and Architecture, African; Chicago, Illinois; New Orleans, Louisiana; New York, New York; Washington, D.C.

Latin America and the Caribbean

Caturla, Alejandro García (b. March 7, 1906, Remedios, Cuba; d. November 12, 1940, Remedios, Cuba), Cuban composer of classical music and one of Cuba's leading representatives of a national musical style based on Afro-Cuban folklore.

Alejandro García Caturla, along with Amadeo Roldán, was Cuba's leading musical exponent of Afrocubanismo, an artistic and literary movement that looked to Cuba's urban black culture, folklore, and music for new art and literary forms. He employed the prevailing European compositional techniques but sought innovative ways to incorporate Afro-Cuban rhythms and melodic fragments into European instruments, on which he achieved folk timbres.

According to Cuban composer Argeliers León, Caturla "showed himself from his earliest years to be opposed to the virulent racism clearly reflected in the shining floors of the colonial mansions, which were always polished by black servants." Although born to a prominent family of Spanish descent, Caturla felt most at home within Cuba's urban black culture. He married a black woman and played in Afro-Cuban folk bands, an experience that led him, during his early career, to compose *danzones,* Afro-Cuban dance pieces. Caturla studied with composer Pedro Sanjuán in Havana (1926) and pianist Nadia Boulanger in Paris (1928) but primarily learned music on his own. He also pursued a legal career to support himself, eventually becoming a municipal judge in Remedios.

During the 1930s Caturla was influenced by two eminent Cubans: the Afro-Cuban poet Nicolás Guillén and the ethnomusicologist Fernando Ortiz. Guillén had developed a poetic language based on the Son, a popular Afro-Cuban musical form. His innovation inspired Caturla to further develop African-derived musical language in such compositions as *La rumba* (1933-1934) and *Berceuse campesina* (1939). The work of Ortiz led Caturla to employ the highly varied rhythmic patterns of African music.

Both Caturla and Roldán, writes music scholar Gerard Béhague, "raised the level of musical professionalism in Cuba and opened the way to international music circles for the following generation of Cuban composers." In 1940 Caturla was assassinated by a gunman allegedly hired by defendants on trial in his court.

Roanne Edwards

See Also

Afrocubanismo; Ortiz, Fernando.

Latin America and the Caribbean

Cayman Islands, a dependent territory of Great Britain consisting of three islands in the Caribbean Sea, 300 km (180 mi) northwest of Jamaica and 333 km (200 mi) south of Cuba.

When the Spanish explorer Christopher Columbus first saw the Cayman Islands during his fourth visit to the Caribbean in 1503, he named them Las Tortugas, Spanish for "the turtles," after the large number of turtles that inhabited the island. By 1530, however, other Europeans were calling the islands Caymanas, the Carib Amerindian name for crocodile, this time probably to describe the iguanas who shared the islands with the turtles. The islands were not inhabited by people when Columbus saw them, and though he claimed them for the Spanish Crown, Spain made no attempt to settle them. Instead, they were a popular stop for sailors from other European countries, who stayed just long enough to stock up on fresh water and turtle meat before continuing to other European islands.

By 1655 some Europeans had gradually begun to settle the island, although the earliest inhabitants were a motley mix of pirates, army deserters, shipwrecked sailors, and debtors. The Caymans became a British possession in 1670 as part of the Treaty of Madrid, and in 1734 the British established their first permanent settlement, made up of planters relocated from the larger colony at Jamaica. Because of these ties, the Caymans were considered a dependency of Jamaica, an arrangement that lasted until 1962. Most of the first colonists established themselves on Grand Cayman, the largest of the three islands in the group. Eventually a few spread out to Cayman Brac (Gaelic for "bluff," so named for the dramatic bluff that crosses the island) and a handful to Little Cayman.

It was these British settlers who brought African slaves to the Cayman Islands. Because the islands are not well suited for agriculture, they were never considered a good site for establishing plantation slavery. Instead, the slaves in the Caymans were employed primarily in turtle fishing, subsistence farming, and domestic tasks. The small numbers of both slaves and whites, and the close proximity in which the two groups lived in the absence of the plantation system, led to a considerable amount of intermarriage. As a result, nearly half of contemporary Cayman Islanders are of mixed European and African descent. The abolition of slavery in all British colonies in 1834 freed the slaves, but otherwise life in the islands remained unchanged through the nineteenth and much of the twentieth century.

When change eventually did come, the first wave was political. Jamaicans were among the first of the British colonies to push for independence from the British Crown, and they were granted that status in 1962. At that point the Cayman Islands could no longer be considered a dependency of Jamaica, so instead they became direct colonies of Britain. The new arrangement was accompanied by a new constitution that gave the islanders more power over their internal government, but otherwise very little changed; Cayman Islanders were for the most part content with their continued colonial status. But two developments in the second half of the century shook the status quo more noticeably and brought the Caymans increased prominence and prosperity: the rise of tourism and offshore banking.

The development of the islands' tourist industry was part of an increased emphasis on tourism throughout the Caribbean. The Cayman Islands established a tourist board in 1966, and since then have been extremely successful in attracting visitors to the territory. Their emphasis has been on the luxury North American market, and in 1994 over 1 million tourists visited the islands, 70 percent of them from the United States.

Banking provided the islands' second boon. The Cayman Islands have enjoyed tax-free status for over 200 years, and legend has it that King George III first granted the status to Cayman Islanders after several of them helped rescue members of the royal family from a dramatic shipwreck in 1788. But in the mid-1960s, legislators passed new laws to take advantage of that status by encouraging offshore banking, trust-company formation, and company registration in their islands. As a result, over 500 banks and thousands of companies are now registered in the islands, bringing revenue into the country. Also, 27 percent of the resident population are now foreign nationals who are often wealthy individuals taking advantage of the tax haven, and they add yet more money to the islands' strong economy.

Not all of these developments have been positive for Cayman Islanders. One notable effect has been the dramatic increase in the cost of living and the cost of land, to such an extent that young Cayman Islanders often have trouble affording homes. Another negative effect has been the large volume of drug trafficking that followed the islands' relaxed financial status. In the 1980s the United States requested and received permission from Britain to make more stringent checks on individuals and companies that the United States suspected of drug involvement. But in general, Cayman Islanders enjoy one of the highest per capita incomes and one of the highest standards of living in the world, obvious benefits from the financial activity in their country.

These benefits have led Cayman Islanders to be complacent about their own government. There are no organized political parties on the islands. Instead, candidates for the legislature's 15 elected seats have traditionally run on loose coalitions called teams. A brief effort in 1992 to create the new position of chief minister and encourage a party system is still under consideration but has met with little enthusiasm from most Cayman Islanders. Similarly, there is still no concerted drive for independence on the island. Instead, many Cayman Islanders remain content with the comparatively high status their present arrangement has brought them in the contemporary Caribbean.

Lisa Clayton Robinson

See Also
Abolition and Emancipation in Latin America and the Caribbean.

Latin America and the Caribbean

Caymmi, Dorival (b. April 4, 1914, Salvador, Brazil), a self-taught singer, guitarist, and songwriter who composed many classics of the modern Brazilian songbook, the most acclaimed of which portray the Afro-Brazilian cultural life of Bahia, his home state on Brazil's northeast coast.

More than the work of any other Brazilian singer-songwriter, Caymmi's music encouraged the popular recognition and acceptance of the cosmology and beliefs of the Afro-Brazilian religion of Candomblé. Several compositions, such as "É doce morrer no mar," "Rainha do mar," and "Promessa de Pescador," portray the life of local fishermen and their relationship to Yemanjá, the African deity of the sea. In other compositions, like "Você já foi a Bahia?," "O que é que a baiana tem?," and "Saudade da Bahia," Caymmi sings praises for the *baianas*, the local Afro-Brazilian women who sell *acarajé* (fried bean cakes) and *cocada* (coconut sweets) on street corners. In "Acontece que sou baiano" the singer calls on a *pai-de-santo* (Candomblé priest) to help him win the affections of a young woman. In 1972 Caymmi recorded "Oração da Mãe Menininha" in honor of Brazil's most celebrated Candomblé priestess, Mãe Menininha do Gantois. A popular songbook of his compositions was first published in 1947 and has since been reprinted several times. In 1953 the city of Salvador inaugurated the Dorival Caymmi Square in the oceanside neighborhood of Itapoã, home to a large fishing community. In the late 1950s the leading innovator of bossa nova, João Gilberto, popularized several other compositions such as "Rosa Morena" and "Doralice." In 1976 the Bahian vocalist Gal Costa dedicated an entire album to Caymmi's compositions on her album *Gal canta Caymmi*.

Christopher Dunn

See Also
Orishas.

North America

Cayton, Horace Roscoe, Jr.

(b. April 12, 1903, Seattle, Wash.; d. January 22, 1970), African American sociologist and educator, and author of the award-winning *Black Metropolis*, a social study of Chicago, Illinois.

Horace Cayton was born April 12, 1903, in SEATTLE, WASHINGTON to activist and publisher Horace R. Cayton Sr. and Susie Revels Cayton, daughter of former United States Senator Hiram Revels. Cayton dropped out of high school and joined the military, traveling to California, Mexico, and Hawaii before returning to Seattle in 1923. He finished high school and graduated from the University of Washington with a degree in sociology.

In 1934 Cayton served as assistant to the U.S. secretary of the interior, completing a study of African American workers in Birmingham, Alabama. In 1935 he was named an instructor of economics and labor at FISK UNIVERSITY in Nashville, Tennessee. By 1936 he had returned to Chicago to direct a Works Progress Administration (WPA) study that focused on inner-city life.

Cayton worked as a columnist for the *Pittsburgh Courier* and coauthored a book with George S. Mitchell titled *Black Workers and the New Unions* (1939). He was named director of Chicago's Parkway Community House, an African American settlement and study center in 1940. During World War II he refused to serve in the U.S. Army because it was segregated, enlisting instead in the Merchant Marines.

Cayton is best known for a social study of Chicago titled *Black Metropolis*, which he coauthored with ST. CLAIR DRAKE in 1945. The book received many awards, including the Anisfield-Wolf Award and the Outstanding Book on Race Relations from the New York Public Library. Cayton continued to write until his death in 1970.

Alonford James Robinson, Jr.

SEE ALSO

World War II and African Americans; Chicago, Illinois; *Pittsburgh Courier*; Revels, Hiram Rhoades; Works Progress Administration.

CBC. Please see CONGRESSIONAL BLACK CAUCUS

Africa

Central African Republic, a

country in the center of Africa bordered by the SUDAN, the DEMOCRATIC REPUBLIC OF THE CONGO, the REPUBLIC OF THE CONGO, CAMEROON, and CHAD.

Located in the middle of the continent, the Central African Republic (CAR) has the potential to be one of Africa's richest countries; during the colonial era, it was known as the Cinderella of the French Empire. The soil is highly fertile and the country possesses vast mineral wealth, valuable forests, and an abundance of wildlife for tourism. Although it has a diverse population, the CAR has experienced little ethnic or religious strife. Yet a tragic history has kept the country from fulfilling its potential. The slave trade and French colonialism devastated its population. Since independence, it has suffered a series of repressive and sometimes brutal regimes, and has remained economically and militarily dependent on France. And in recent years, despite efforts toward democratic reform, a number of attempted coups and rebellions have shaken the country. This ongoing violence and unrest make it unlikely that the CAR will soon realize the promise of its natural riches.

GEOGRAPHY AND EARLY HISTORY

A high plateau divides present-day CAR from east to west. The Ubangui River feeds the Congo, the CHARI River runs into the Chad Basin, and other minor tributaries feed the Nile. In the dry north, mountains reach 1400 m (4592 ft), and in the far southwest, forests experience a perpetual rainy season. The waterways that crisscross the region have created fertile land along fluvial basins.

Archaeological evidence (in the form of polished flint and quartz tools) shows that the migratory Aka "pygmies," known also as Babinga or Tvides, have fished, hunted, and gathered foodstuffs in the area of the present-day CAR for at least 8000 years. Around 2500 years ago, agricultural peoples settled in the region and cleared the thick brush of the present-day savanna belt to grow millet and sorghum. Arrangements of hundreds of megaliths, many of them several tons in weight, signify the development of a sophisticated agricultural society.

Linguistic evidence indicates that by the first millennium, speakers of Nilo-Saharan languages had entered the region from the east. At around the same time, speakers of Niger-Congo languages entered the region from the west and opened the forested southern areas to agriculture; gradually, they spread into the central and southeastern savanna areas. One or both of these groups introduced the technology of iron production to the region. Most of the savanna people lived in extended family compounds, with political and social order determined by kinship. As agriculturists, they were dependent on favorable weather, and droughts created scarcity.

The first evidence of kingdoms in the area that is now the CAR dates to the sixteenth century. By then, three Islamic kingdoms – DARFUR, Wadai, and Bagirmi – had emerged to the north, and over time extended their rule southward. These kingdoms, particularly Wadai and Bagirmi, carried out raids to capture slaves for the trans-Saharan trade, and people of the northern savanna fled south into the forests. Meanwhile, in the eastern part of the present-day CAR, an aristocratic caste with origins to the northeast had established kingdoms among the AZANDE people. Newly introduced crops, particularly maize and cassava, produced agricultural surpluses that supported these states and aristocracies.

THE SLAVE TRADE IN CENTRAL AFRICA

From the seventeenth to the nineteenth century, the trans-Saharan and transatlantic slave trades shaped the history of Central Africa. Indeed, there is evidence that slave raiders led captives from the eastern part of the region to the Indian Ocean for sale in coastal slave markets. In the mid-seventeenth century, the trans-Saharan slave trade expanded dramatically, with a few thousand or more enslaved people taken annually from the north of the region. At the same time, traders began to send additional slaves to the Atlantic coast and on to the New World. The number of Central Africans involved in the transatlantic route was small until the late eighteenth century, by which time other areas had become depopulated and demand for slaves had increased. Riverine communities, collectively called the Bobangi or Ubangians, formed extensive commercial networks, trading slaves and ivory for manufactured European goods with the TÉKÉ people on the lower CONGO RIVER. Canoes capable of holding at least 50 people plied the rivers, capturing unsuspecting individuals and taking undesirable inhabitants from villages. These slave raiders progressed southward, returning with cloth, jewelry, and guns. As the demand for slaves increased, animosity and violence grew between interior peoples and the raiding riverine traders.

As the transatlantic slave trade declined in the early 1800s, the trans-Saharan and internal African slave trades flourished in the north. Each of the northern kingdoms, including Wadai, Darfur, Bagirmi, and Kanem-Bornu, informally had its own raiding preserve in the region and conducted several raids during the dry season. Fulani slavers from Adamawa in present-day Cameroon conducted raids in the west. As with the transatlantic trade, it is not possible to determine the number of people taken from the area, but the social impact was clearly extensive. Historical enmities, decentralized social structures, and periodic migrations to evade slave raiders made it difficult for the peoples of the region to unify in opposition to the slave traders. Meanwhile, traders depopulated the area, particularly the central and eastern regions. They also brought goods such as salt, sugar, cloth, and tea; created trading posts; and promoted an indigenous merchant class; they also took ivory and destroyed the large elephant herds that once roamed the savanna. In addition, northerners, particularly the FULANI from Adamawa and the SOKOTO CALIPHATE, introduced Islam during slave raids and *jihads*, holy wars against the GBAYA and Mbun in the northwest.

The slave trade has marked the history of

each of the eight major ethnic groups of the present-day CAR. The Banda, Gbaya, Mandija, Mbun, and Sara all fell victim to slave raiders. The Mandija and Sara may in fact have entered the region fleeing slave raiders to the north and west. Azande chiefdoms formed alliances with different slave-raiding kingdoms, while the Hausa and Fulani first entered the region during the eighteenth and nineteenth centuries to obtain slaves for agricultural estates in Adamawa and Sokoto.

The scale of the trans-Saharan slave trade expanded in the second half of the nineteenth century. In 1879 Rabih, a military commander and slave trader from the Sudan, settled in the northeast of the present-day CAR. Over the next fifteen years he created an empire by raiding the area for slaves. This empire absorbed the kingdoms of Darfur, Bagirmi, and Kanem-Bornu, as well as most of the Azande chiefdoms, and exported slaves to North Africa and the Middle East. In 1894 Rabih moved his headquarters to the northwest and left Sultan al-Sanusi in charge of much of his territory in the present-day CAR. Al-Sanusi's domain, based at Ndélé, grew steadily until 1900, when French forces defeated Rabih and moved to incorporate the entire region into their colonial empire.

In 1880, as Rabih and al-Sanusi reigned in the east and north, many Gbaya and Mbun united to resist Fulani dominance in the northwest. A decade later they brought an end to Fulani control over the trade routes from the area. But this was exceptional. For the most part, the slave trade depopulated the region and created animosities among its peoples. Colonialists would soon exploit this discord to their own advantage.

French Colonialism

Located in the remote heart of Africa, the area that is now the CAR saw a relatively late arrival of Europeans and colonialism. At the Berlin Conference of 1884-1885, the European powers had determined the rules of the game for the Scramble for Africa. A few years later, in 1889, French expeditionary forces established a post on the Oubangui River in the present-day CAR. Paul Crampel's expedition of 1891 and others that followed secured treaties with African chiefs who were hoping to gain protection and advantage over their enemies. In 1894 France declared the area of Oubangui-Chari (the present-day CAR) a colony. French control of the area was at first tenuous. But in 1898, after the Franco-British confrontation at Fashoda on the Nile River, France sought to occupy Oubangui-Chari militarily in order to control the Chad Basin and unite French Central, West, and North African possessions. In 1900 French-led Algerian, Senegalese, and local troops completed their mission by killing Rabih and defeating his troops near Lake Chad.

Even before they had fully occupied the region, the French had set up concessionary companies to exploit its wealth of wild rubber and timber. Holding legal rights over the territories under their concession, 17 companies controlled more than half the land and subjected their populations to military conscription, taxation, and forced labor. These practices (as well as company abuses) led to international protests and incited local rebellions, particularly among the Gbaya and Mandija people, between 1909 and 1911. Local resistance forced the French to conquer the area piecemeal. The result was that the governor-general of French Equatorial Africa in Brazzaville held administrative responsibility for Oubangui-Chari, while poorly trained local administrators, headquartered at Bangui, exercised authoritarian rule.

Between the 1890s and 1930s French military aggression and forced labor requirements spread disease throughout the population. Meanwhile, French demands for cash crops and tax payments further undermined the people's ability to feed themselves. Scholars

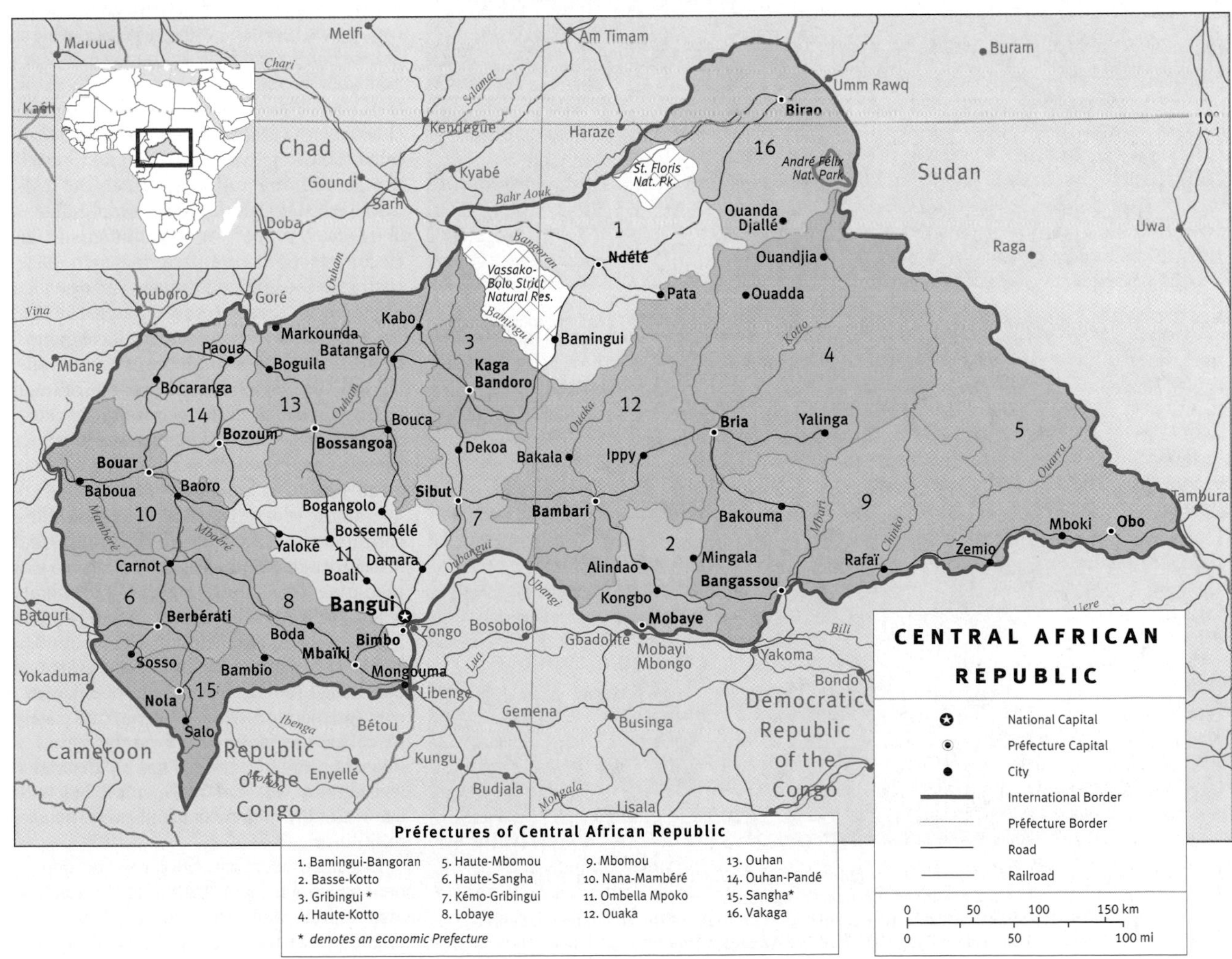

estimate that the region's population dropped by one-third to one-half due to malnutrition and disease during these decades. Between 1928 and 1930 much of the population once again rebelled in the so-called Kongo Wara War, a series of local revolts against forced labor and taxation. In the 1930s, facing widespread economic stagnation in French Equatorial Africa, colonial officials forced the population to grow cotton and coffee for the global market. Alarmed at the decline in the available labor force, the French developed a primary health care system in an effort to control the spread of sleeping sickness. The educational system, however, remained impoverished, and the companies were still controlled by Europeans.

During World War II, as prices rose for cotton, coffee, diamond, and rubber exports, Oubangui-Chari enjoyed economic prosperity. As a result, the French built new roads to facilitate trade. This boom began to open the economy to Africans, who entered into commerce, transport, timber, and commercial farming. After the war, French citizenship was extended to all Africans in French colonies, and a 1956 law granted Africans equal voting rights in colonial elections. These events encouraged a proliferation of nationalist political parties in Oubangui-Chari. Most prominent were the Union Oubanguienne and the quasi-religious Movement for the Social Evolution of Black Africa, led by BARTHÉLEMY BOGANDA, the first Oubangui Catholic priest and representative to the French National Assembly.

Boganda, recognizing the limits of his influence in France, returned to Oubangui-Chari to organize a grassroots movement of small African producers to oppose French colonialism. After his arrest and detention by the French, Boganda became a folk hero and, though no longer a priest, was considered a messianic figure and the leading nationalist. Still, the relatively conservative Boganda remained sympathetic to French interests and did not advocate for immediate independence. With the rush toward independence in much of Francophone Africa, however, in 1958 Boganda called for independence for Oubangui-Chari. He envisioned Oubangui-Chari not as an independent country, but as part of a larger, more economically viable United States of Latin Africa that would include the present-day states of ANGOLA, CAMEROON, both Congos, Chad, Gabon, RWANDA, and BURUNDI. But differences among the nationalist leadership in the various colonies soon made such a federation impossible, and later that year Boganda accepted a constitution covering only Oubangui-Chari, renamed the Central African Republic. Poised to become president of the independent CAR, Boganda was killed in a mysterious airplane crash in 1959, just before legislative elections. The 29-year-old DAVID DACKO, a family member and close confidant of the popular Boganda, succeeded him.

TOP: The distribution of seeds, as seen in this photo taken in the Central African Republic, is typical of many agricultural projects on the continent of Africa. *© G. Boutin/Explorer*
ABOVE: A bicycle wheel becomes festive headgear during celebrations of the coronation of Central African Republic emperor Bokassa I in 1977. *CORBIS/Yann Aarthus-Bertrand*

NEOCOLONIAL INDEPENDENCE

In August 1960, the Central African Republic became independent, with Dacko as president. France continued to be intimately involved politically, economically, and militarily in the CAR. The 1958 constitution, which preserved close ties with France, remained in effect, and initially a de facto dual French and Central African administration governed the CAR. Dacko relied heavily on French administrative and military support for his authoritarian rule. He introduced a single-party system in 1962, circumscribed legislative powers, and extended presidential terms to seven years. He was partially successful in securing local control of the economy through limited nationalization, but French corporations continued to control much of the economy. Dacko's greatest success was probably in education; the number of children attending school doubled during his presidency.

With the economy failing due to declining commodity prices, growing corruption, and ill-planned development projects, Dacko was preparing to relinquish power to his military chief of staff when his cousin, Col. JEAN-BÉDEL BOKASSA, overthrew him on December 31, 1965. Most Central Africans initially welcomed the change. But the next 13 years of Bokassa's corrupt, dictatorial, wasteful, and ultimately macabre rule nearly destroyed the country. Bokassa ruled by personal fiat. He dismissed legislators at will, had opponents killed, and allowed only a handful of people to participate in politics.

Like his predecessors, Bokassa was dependent on French support. Although he paid his own military well, after a rumored coup plot in 1967 he requested and received French military protection. In 1972 he named himself president-for-life and asserted authority over state-owned enterprises. French corporations retained control of most of the country's diamond exports, agricultural estates, timber concessions, and import-export trade. Bokassa, meanwhile, diverted income from these firms for his own enrichment. In the 1970s exports to and imports from France accounted for over 60 percent of the country's trade, and almost 90 percent of the CAR's aid came from France. But the country's development came to a standstill as Bokassa pocketed much of the aid or used it for unnecessary and unsuccessful projects.

After evading several coup attempts, in 1977 the president-for-life crowned himself Emperor Bokassa in an elaborate coronation ceremony modeled after Napoleon's, complete with a diamond-studded crown. The ceremony reportedly cost one-third of the government's annual revenue, though France underwrote much of the expense. Bokassa also enthroned several relatives, including his wife as empress, and created an imperial court near his hometown.

The renamed Central African Empire had a short life. A fiscal crisis in mid-1979 forced the government to reduce school loans and withhold payment of government salaries, and student protests and violent demonstrations became common in the streets of Bangui. In September of that year, students protested the requirement that they purchase uniforms from a factory owned by Bokassa's wife. In response, troops massacred more than 100 schoolchildren; according to many accounts, Bokassa himself participated in the slaughter. International outcry ensued, and the French, concluding that Bokassa had outlived his usefulness, sent troops to oust him. They reinstated Dacko as president and backed him financially, though he also remained dependent on the elites who had provided support for Bokassa as well as his own first presidency.

Dacko left the rebuilding of the country to France and concentrated his efforts on consolidating his power. But student protests, strikes, and occasional attacks on government officials continued, and opposition parties organized. In 1981, under both French and internal pressure, Dacko passed a multiparty constitution and held presidential elections that were clearly fraudulent. After winning, he moved to repress opposition militarily. Giscard d'Estaing's 1981 defeat in France, however, left Dacko without external support. When internal opposition reached new heights, army chief of staff André Kolingba forced Dacko to resign and declared himself president.

After a brief political honeymoon, a coup attempt surfaced and Kolingba clamped down on opponents of his military regime, especially the popular politician Ange Patassé. Kolingba increasingly relied on his ethnic kin from the Mbaka region, as well as a select group of corrupt officers within his military committee. To provide a veneer of legitimacy, Kolingba created a new party, the Central African Democratic Assembly, and held single-party elections in 1986. But his repressive rule and his enforcement of the economic austerity measures required by foreign lenders sparked strikes and riots in the capital. Facing growing internal unrest and international pressure, in 1993 Kolingba agreed to hold open presidential and legislative elections. Both Kolingba and Dacko ran; however, opposition candidate Patassé and his party, the Movement for the Liberation of the Central African People, won the elections on a platform promising to pay the back salaries of soldiers and civil servants.

The CAR's disastrous finances, however, made full repayment impossible. Anticipating a loss of influence under civilian government, the military mutinied in May 1996, and Patassé called on the French to suppress the revolt. Opposition politicians subsequently demanded elections. Unrest continued and many foreign aid workers left the country. In early 1998, the United Nations sent an all-African peacekeeping force to the CAR to enforce the so-called Bangui Accords of 1997, which called for an armistice and new elections. Thus the calamitous history of the Cinderella of Africa has continued to unfold.

Eric Young

See Also

Algeria; Bangui, Central African Republic; Chad, Lake; Brazzaville, Republic of the Congo; Nile River; Transatlantic Slave Trade; United Nations in Africa; France; Patassé, Ange-Félix; Pygmy; Senegal; Wildlife Management in Africa; Indian Ocean Slave Trade; Trans-Saharan and Red Sea Slave Trade.

Africa

Central African Republic (Ready Reference)

Former Name: Central African Empire
Area: 622,436 sq km (about 240,323 sq mi)
Location: Central Africa, north of Democratic Republic of the Congo (formerly Zaire), bordered by Cameroon, Chad, Republic of the Congo, and Sudan, and the Democratic Republic of the Congo
Capital: Bangui (population 451,690 [1988 estimate])
Population: 3,375,771 (1998 estimate)
Population Below Age 15: 44 percent (male 738,623; female 731,163 [1997 estimate])
Population Growth Rate: 2.1 percent (1996 estimate)
Total Fertility Rate: 5.4 children born per woman (1996 estimate)
Life Expectancy at Birth: Total population: 45.24 years (male 44.4 years; female 46.1 years [1997 estimate])
Infant Mortality Rate: 111.7 deaths per 1000 live births (1996 estimate)
Literacy Rate (age 15 and over who can read and write): Total population: 60 percent (male 68.5 percent; female 52.4 percent [1995 estimate])
Education: Officially compulsory; however, only about half of the eligible children of the Central African Republic receive primary education. Secondary and higher education facilities are limited. In the early 1990s about 308,400 pupils annually attended primary schools, and about 47,200 students were enrolled in secondary and technical institutions.
Languages: French is the official language, but Sango, an African language, is the most commonly spoken. Many other African languages are also spoken.
Ethnic Groups: The main ethnic groups of the Central African Republic are the Baya, Banda, Sara, Mandjia, Mboum, and M'Baka.
Religions: Approximately 24 percent of the total population follow African religions, 25 percent are Protestant, 25 percent are Roman Catholic, 11 percent are other, and 5 percent are Muslim.
Climate: Hot and humid; the average annual temperature is about 26° C (about 79° F). Annual rainfall varies from about 1800 mm (about 70 in) in the Ubangi River valley to about 200 mm (about 8 in) in the semi-arid north.
Land, Plants, and Animals: The Central African Republic is situated on the northern edge of the Zaire (Congo) River Basin. Most of the land is a plateau that ranges in elevation from about 610 to 790 m (about 2000 to 2600 ft). Savanna vegetation covers most of the country except for a dense rain forest in the southwest. Open grassland is found in the extreme north, and a dense rain forest covers a major part of the southwestern area. The country is drained by several major rivers, the Bamingui and Ouham rivers in the north, and the Ubangi, a tributary of the Zaire, in the south. Commercially valuable trees include the sapele mahogany and the obeche. Many species of wildlife are found in the country.
Natural Resources: Although relatively undeveloped, mineral resources include diamonds, uranium, iron ore, gold, lime, zinc, copper, and tin.
Currency: 1 Communauté Financière Africaine franc
Gross Domestic Product (GDP): $3.3 billion (1997 estimate)
GDP per Capita: $1000 (1997 estimate)
GDP Real Growth Rate: 4.1 percent (1995 estimate)
Primary Economic Activities: Agriculture (50 percent of GDP, 85 percent of employment), forestry, and mining
Primary Crops: Cotton, coffee, tobacco, manioc (tapioca), yams, millet, corn, bananas, and timber
Industries: Diamond mining, sawmills, breweries, textiles, footwear, assembly of bicycles and motorcycles

Primary Exports: Diamonds, timber, cotton, coffee, and tobacco
Primary Imports: Food, textiles, petroleum products, machinery, electrical equipment, motor vehicles, chemicals, pharmaceuticals, and consumer goods
Primary Trade Partners: European Union, Japan, Algeria, Cameroon, Namibia, United States, and Iran
Government: The Central African Republic is a multiparty republic. The executive branch is headed by a president (Ange Patassé since October 22, 1993) and the Council of Ministers, which the president directs. The president is popularly elected to a six-year term. Legislative authority is held by the National Assembly, made up of 85 members who are popularly elected to five-year terms. The Central African Democratic Rally is the leading political party. The president's party is The Movement for the Liberation of the Central African People.

Robert Fay

See Also
Congo River; Gold Trade.

Latin America and the Caribbean

Central America,

isthmus connecting North and South America, comprising the countries of Belize, Costa Rica, El Salvador, Guatemala, Honduras, Nicaragua, and Panama. The region is home to a small number of Afro-Central Americans, descended either from slaves shipped to Central America from Africa or the Caribbean (sixteenth to nineteenth century) or from West Indian workers of the United Fruit Company (late nineteenth to early twentieth century).

In the decades after 1513, when the Spanish explorer Vasco Núñez de Balboa crossed Panama and claimed the Pacific Ocean for Spain, slaves from Africa began to trickle into Central America. Spanish settlements were fewer in Central America than in other regions of the New World, in large part because few of the mines in the region yielded large loads and most agriculture was on a small scale. Lacking these economic engines, there was neither need nor money to pay for numerous slaves, especially since large Amerindian populations continued to be available in what are now Guatemala and Honduras (*see* Latin America, Blacks and Indians in: An Interpretation).

The importance of slaves increased slightly as the Amerindian population declined. In many areas, Amerindians died from exposure to European diseases; in other areas, notably El Salvador and Costa Rica, so many Amerindians were shipped to South America and Mexico to work mines and farms that large tracts of land were nearly depopulated. To fill the periodic labor shortages, the Spanish colonists imported African slaves, either from nearby colonies or directly from Africa. Two prominent slaving sites thus founded were the ranches and gold mines of Guanacaste and Punta Arenas in present-day Costa Rica. Slaves were also imported for specific undertakings that required large supplies of labor – as in the mid-1700s construction of Fort Omoa on the Atlantic coast of Honduras.

Historians portray slaves in Central America as generally receiving less abusive treatment and holding more privileged positions than their counterparts elsewhere in the New World. They argue that this condition owed more to the fact that Spaniards far outnumbered their African slaves than to progressive legislation or leadership. By 1824, after the Central American Federation (now Costa Rica, El Salvador, Guatemala, Honduras, and Nicaragua) became an independent territory from the colonial government of Spain, the small dependency on slaves for free labor made abolition a relatively uncontroversial act, without the opposition by landowners found in other countries in Latin America (*see* Abolition and Emancipation in Latin America and the Caribbean).

In many parts of Central America, especially El Salvador, the number of slaves was so minimal that by the early 1800s, through miscegenation and acculturation, people of African heritage were not identified, and did not identify themselves, as such; indeed, they had become virtually indistinguishable from the *mestizo* (of indigenous and European descent) population. Additionally, few slaves made for lax record-keeping (an anomaly in the Spanish colonies); thus less is known about the condition of black bondage in Central America than elsewhere (*see* Slavery in Latin America and the Caribbean).

The black population of Central America was bolstered over time by several waves of immigrants from the Caribbean. Blacks from the West Indies typically arrived by one of two routes: either they were brought by their masters as slaves or, having escaped, they arrived on their own. Central America's topography, chiseled by mountains and shrouded in forests, made escape an attractive and viable alternative for many slaves. After emancipation, in the 1800s and 1900s, still more free blacks followed, lured by the construction of railroads, plantations, and other enterprises. Many such immigrants from the West Indies found prosperity in the growing export economies, and some even joined the ranks of the economic and political elite.

Most such gains proved temporary. As railroads were completed, world markets for exports like bananas declined, and the racism of the mestizo majority grew, many people of African descent lost their jobs and were forced into low-paying and subsistence labor. In the 1990s blacks were estimated to make up about 1 percent of the Central American population. African culture nonetheless survives in such forms as the mixed Afro-Roman Catholic birth and funeral rituals of the Garifuna of Nicaragua and the extended families of Afro-Costa Ricans, many of whom still believe, as did their African ancestors, that children belong to the community rather than solely to the family.

What follows is a discussion of Afro-Central Americans by country, with the exception of Panama and Belize, which have independent entries, and El Salvador, where the black population is negligible.

Costa Rica

Though what is now Costa Rica has often declared itself a "white nation," the first census to report people of African descent in 1801 stated that blacks, *zambos* (of African and Indian descent), and mulattos (of African and European descent) made up as much as 17 percent of the total population. In the late 1700s Spanish colonists began importing African slaves from northern Africa and neighboring colonies to replace Amerindians who had been deported to other Spanish colonies or who had died as a result of contracting European diseases. Such imports, however, were small, restricted for the most part to a few cacao plantations and gold mines. As in neighboring Panama, the largest numbers of blacks arrived in Costa Rica not as slaves but as free laborers from the West Indies, particularly Jamaica.

Most of the immigrants came in the late 1800s to build the railroad that would haul coffee from the country's interior to the port of Limón, on the Atlantic coast. After the railways were completed, many of the workers stayed and took jobs on plantations, particularly the Atlantic coast banana fields of the ubiquitous United Fruit Company. West Indians continued to speak English, so they were particularly attractive to their employers at United Fruit, based in the United States. Many English-speaking blacks achieved management positions at United Fruit, and new ventures typically fueled labor from new West Indian immigrants. In many respects, West Indians were better off than the average Costa Rican. Additionally, being British citizens, and speaking the language of their patrons, West Indians tended to feel privileged compared to native-born Spanish-speaking Costa Ricans.

However, West Indians were dealt two major blows in the early twentieth century. In the 1920s and 1930s, when the banana plantations of eastern Costa Rica suffered a reversal of fortune, United Fruit began shifting its operations to western Costa Rica. West Indians rarely ventured there, since it was far from their communities, which were concentrated largely on the Atlantic coast. By the Great Depression years of the 1930s, the Costa Rican economy had plummeted along with the rest of the world's. The slight economic superiority enjoyed by West Indians during the Depression prompted mestizos to denounce it as preferential treatment for blacks. Since West Indian immigrants did not have full citizenship, a law was enacted in

1936 to give hiring preferences to Costa Rican nationals, leaving many blacks unemployed. At the same time, the government forbade blacks to seek employment in the country's mostly white interior – thus preventing them from following the banana jobs as they shifted from the Atlantic to the Pacific coast. Although West Indians had lived in agricultural rather than urban areas, these changes prompted many blacks to move to the cities, where they were forced to assimilate into Costa Rican culture for the first time. Among the West Indians remaining in the countryside, a few succeeded in establishing their own farms.

In Costa Rica's 1948 civil war, many West Indian immigrants and their descendants gave support to José Figueres, an exiled opposition leader. When Figueres won, he returned the favor by granting full citizenship to black immigrants. With citizenship came the price of further assimilation: West Indians were required to send their children to Spanish-language schools, and mastering the language became the only path to social mobility and cultural acceptance. Nonetheless, since a nationwide conference in 1977 to promote awareness of West Indian culture, English has enjoyed a revival among the black community, particularly in Limón, where the black population – a third of the city in the 1990s – remains largely separate.

Few Afro-Costa Ricans achieved national political power. However, black leaders such as Quince Duncan and Eulalia Bernard, inspired by the Universal Negro Improvement Association and by Marcus Garvey's visits to Costa Rica, continued to agitate for black rights at mid-century and established several community groups that furthered political activism. Despite a small West Indian educated elite, throughout Costa Rica most blacks remain poor, working as wage laborers or subsistence farmers still largely affected by racism and social discrimination. In 1992 the population of Afro-Costa Ricans was estimated at 64,000, or 2 percent of Costa Rica's 3.2 million people.

Guatemala

If Costa Rica likes to portray itself as white, Guatemala has characterized itself as an "indigenous country." As early as 1537, the town of Tianguey banned the unauthorized entry of blacks, zambos, or mulattos so they would not mix with the Indian population. Guatemala was one of the few areas of Spanish America where Amerindians remained a majority of the population both during and after the colonial era. As a result, few African slaves were imported to the area. This preference continued well into the twentieth century. In a 1936 law and the 1945 constitution the government officially prohibited "immigration of individuals of the black race."

By virtue of its shared borders with Belize and Honduras, however, Guatemala's slender Atlantic coast harbors a small population of Garifuna, the descendants of African and Carib Indian miscegenation who arrived at the end of the eighteenth century. The Garifuna of Guatemala were estimated to have numbered about 5000 in 1992. Most work as subsistence fishers and wage laborers in the forestry and shipping industries. Because they lack economic opportunities in Guatemala, many of the Garifuna have migrated to Belize and the United States. Still, traces of African culture can be found in Guatemala today; for example, the marimba, a popular dance with African syncopation, has survived from music brought to Central America by black slaves.

Honduras

Spanish colonizers brought the first Africans to what is now Honduras at least by 1540, when 165 slaves arrived. By 1545, with an increasing number of diseased and displaced Indians, some 5000 black slaves had been shackled and shipped to Honduras to perform domestic work and to labor on small farms, most of which grew a variety of vegetables and fruits for use within the colonies. As elsewhere in Central America, the number of slaves never

TOP: Schoolgirls ride in a pickup truck in San Miguel, El Salvador, capital of the region and an important trade center. *Francis/Hutchison*
ABOVE: ***Hegemonia cultural*** (Cultural Hegemony), 1992, Limon, Honduras. *Tony Gleaton*

exploded, owing to lack of large-scale mines or plantations. Most Afro-Hondurans arrived after independence, by way of the British West Indies. For the most part these were Garifuna, the descendants of African and Carib Indian miscegenation. In 1797 Great Britain forced between 3000 and 5000 Garifuna to relocate from St. Vincent to the Honduran island of Roatán, in the Bay Islands off Honduras's Atlantic coast. Most of the Garifuna were further relocated to mainland Honduras.

A small but important number of blacks also came from the British Cayman Islands. In the 1830s, as Great Britain considered abolishing slavery throughout its colonies, many white settlers in the Caymans feared what would befall them if their slaves, who vastly outnumbered them, were freed. In the early 1830s a small number of whites moved from the Caymans to the Honduran Bay Islands, which were then under partial British control. Some of these whites brought their slaves with them. After apprenticeship even more blacks arrived, apparently following the example of whites and hoping for economic gain. By the mid-1850s an estimated 700 black Cayman Islanders had moved to the Bay Islands, particularly the island of Utila, where by this time they once again outnumbered the whites.

The Cayman Islanders, now Afro-Hondurans, farmed small subsistence plots and relied heavily on fish and sea turtles for their living. When investors from the United States established fruit plantations in eastern Honduras, many of the former Cayman Islanders, as well as the Garifuna, went to work for them. As the plantations grew, the companies encouraged other West Indian blacks to immigrate, partly because they spoke English and partly because the Americans believed that West Indians were better suited to work in the coastal lowland climate of Honduras than the Amerindians of the Honduran highlands would have been. The immigration of West Indians, however, created tensions with nonblack Hondurans. The blacks had better salaries spoke English, and practiced Protestantism, all of which distanced them from the mestizo working class. Tensions between native-born and West Indian immigrants led to enactment of a law in 1903 that restricted the entrance of West Indian blacks. In 1929 Honduras banned such immigration completely. Many blacks (West Indian and not) lost their jobs, which were gradually filled by Amerindian and mestizo Hondurans as well as immigrant Salvadorans, who were generally preferred by the government.

Estimates of people of African descent in Honduras vary widely, from 100,000 to 320,000 (1.8 to 5.8 percent) of the country's 5.8 million people in 1994. The majority of Afro-Hondurans live in small communities and port towns on the northern Caribbean coast and in major metropolitan areas like San Pedro Sula.

Nicaragua

As in other parts of Central America, Spanish colonists brought a small number of African slaves to what is now Nicaragua; the economy could not support larger numbers. In the early 1600s British raiders and colonists settled on Nicaragua's isolated Atlantic coast, known as the Mosquito Coast. By the mid-seventeenth century many of these settlers had begun importing African slaves to work the coastal timber lands and agricultural plantations, and to help in the cross-country trade that the British had established with the Spanish, who lived across the forests and mountains in western Nicaragua. In 1687 the Mosquito Coast became a British protectorate, and African slaves were imported in earnest, mostly to speed timber extraction.

A century later, in 1787, Britain was forced to abandon its protectorate. Many of the slaves who had rebelled against or fled from the British, or who were simply abandoned by their departing masters, remained on the coast and formed black Creole villages like Bluefields and Pearl Lagoon. Since eastern

Nicaragua was remote from the capital, Managua, in the west, the growth of Creole power went largely unchecked by Spanish rule. Black Creoles assumed the economic and political positions once held by their masters, and the Mosquito Coast became something of a haven for free blacks and escaped slaves throughout Central America and the western Caribbean. When slaves were emancipated in the English Caribbean in the early 1830s, many resettled among Nicaragua's black Creoles.

In the early 1880s banana, mining, and timber companies from the United States began to penetrate the Atlantic coast. The Mosquito Coast's black Creoles, with their English language, Caribbean views of work, family and religion, and Caribbean foods, prospered under the american sphere of influence, which extended to the mid-twentieth century. Many of them migrated to cities like Managua to work as waiters, janitors, and drivers and in the secondary industries that developed from the growth of banana, mining, and timber companies. Others, capitalizing on their years of plantation work, became independent growers. In government, however, black Creoles were not so fortunate. In 1894 the national government in Managua sent a military force to eastern Nicaragua with the intent of gaining a firmer grip on the Mosquito Coast. Black Creoles in the coastal government were replaced almost entirely with mestizos, who were more beholden to the central government in Managua.

Tensions between mestizos and black Creoles have endured into and throughout the twentieth century. During the 1920s many black Creoles responded by becoming active in the Universal Negro Improvement Association of Marcus Garvey. Still others called for the secession of the Mosquitia region from Nicaragua. With the Great Depression, United States companies pulled out of the Mosquito Coast, forcing many black Creoles to seek work in western cities like Managua. As a result, black Creoles became more integrated with the rest of the country.

A small number of Garifuna, most of whom entered Nicaragua from Honduras in the 1830s, also live along the Atlantic coast. In 1994 Nicaragua's black Creoles numbered perhaps 36,000 (.9 percent) and Nicaragua's Garifuna perhaps 3000 (.08 percent) of the Nicaraguan 4 million people.

See Also

Cocoa; Transatlantic Slave Trade; Garvey, Marcus Mosiah; Garifuna; St. Vincent and the Grenadines; Cayman Islands.

Latin America and the Caribbean

Césaire, Aimé (b. June 26, 1913, Basse-Pointe, Martinique), Martinican poetic innovator and political leader; a father of the Négritude movement and one of the most important black authors writing in French in the twentieth century.

The second of six children in a family of relatively modest means, Aimé Césaire grew up with a strong appreciation for French culture. While most young Martinicans heard their bedtime stories in Creole, Césaire's father would read his son French poems by Victor Hugo, a fact that explains in part why Césaire never considered writing in Creole. When Césaire was 12 the family moved to Fort-de-France, where he enrolled at the Lycée Schoelcher and met Léon-Gontran Damas of French Guiana. Césaire's exceptional work there led to his obtaining a scholarship to finish his secondary studies in Paris, France, at the prestigious Lycée Louis-le-Grand. There he met the Senegalese Léopold Sédar Senghor, a man whose literary and political itinerary would closely follow his.

Césaire enrolled at the École Normale Supérieure in 1931 and began participating in the vibrant black student life of 1930s Paris. Through his work during these years at *L'Etudiant noir*, a newspaper formed by Senghor and Damas, Césaire met Suzanne Roussy, whom he married in 1937 and who would be one of his principal collaborators at the journal Tropiques. It was during his years in Paris that Césaire, along with Senghor and Damas, developed the philosophy of Négritude. This ardent defense of black identity and culture would serve as the guiding principle for Césaire's poetry, plays, and essays.

In 1939 Césaire permanently returned to Martinique and, after several years of teaching, turned his attention to politics. His commitment to Marxism was tenuous even then, but he presented himself in 1945 as a candidate for Martinique's *député* to France under the Communist Party banner and, in a surprising upset, won. Although Césaire has continued to serve as both député and as mayor of Fort-de-France since that time, in 1956 he left the Communist Party to form the socialist Parti Progressiste Martiniquais (PPM) for reasons that he specifies in the *Lettre à Maurice Thorez* (1956) – namely, that the Communists did not sufficiently address black concerns. It was several years later that Césaire wrote his *Discours sur le colonialisme* (1962, Discourse on Colonialism), an essay excoriating liberal French thinkers, among them Roger Caillois and Octave Mannoni, for their complicity with colonialism.

Césaire's ability to fuse race consciousness with politics while avoiding the pitfalls of many of his African and Caribbean counterparts has earned him the respect of his contemporaries. The Haitian poet René Depestre characterizes Césaire's brand of politics: "If there is one principal reason to praise Césaire... it is that he managed to limit the scope of Négritude to ethics and aesthetics and avoided building it up into a State ideology or political operation of messianic character. His wisdom allowed all those who recognized themselves in his words to avert the horrors of Papa Doc Duvalier's black totalitarianism." Nonetheless, a younger generation led by Raphaël Confiant has attacked what they consider to be Césaire's moderate position vis-à-vis political independence for Martinique and his rejection of the use of Creole.

It was during his years in Paris in the 1930s that Césaire began composing what is still considered his most important poetic work, if not the most important work of Francophone literature to date, the *Cahier d'un retour au pays natal* (Notebook of a Return to my Native Land). In 1939, the same year he returned to Martinique, Césaire quietly published the first version of this revolutionary poem in a small but respected Parisian journal, *Volontés*. But it was through a detour of sorts that the poem reached a wider audience. Césaire's writings in *Tropiques*, in which he blended the notion of Négritude with European surrealism, attracted the attention of André Breton, who came across the journal and its creators in 1941 while in Martinique on his way from occupied France to the United States.

Several years later, Breton contributed a preface to the 1947 edition of the *Cahier* that finally propelled the poem, and Césaire, into the literary spotlight. The *Cahier*, with its neologisms, historical references, and epic length (1055 lines), bears the imprint of the nineteenth-century French poet Lautréamont. The poem begins with a bleak portrait of the geography and psychology of Martinique and passes to an enumeration of the indignities suffered by blacks throughout their history. However, the poem ends on an optimistic note, representing the poet's awakening as well as the triumphant awakening of the black race. Césaire's first poems written after the *Cahier, Les armes miraculeuses* (1946, The Miraculous Weapons), contain mythological references and a more restricted range of images (sun, volcano, blood, water, death) that are meant to create meaning through association, though the poems still contain traces of surrealism's stream of consciousness, or "automatic," writing.

Césaire's next collection of poetry, *Soleil cou coupé* (1948, Solar Throat Slashed), begins to move away from the influence of surrealism to engage in more purely political concerns. The tension between these two tendencies reaches a crisis point in *Corps perdu* (1950, Lost Body). In these poems, Césaire seems torn between a self-contained poetry and the poetry of Négritude, which dictates that the poem address the injustices suffered by the black race. This crisis is resolved in the direction of Négritude poetry in the collection of poems *Ferrements* (1960), published on the eve of decolonization. Césaire's poetic output has decreased since the early 1960s, but in 1982 he published a collection entitled *moi, laminaire...* that the critic A. James Arnold has called "some of Césaire's most moving and mature poetry."

During the interval between *Ferrements* and *moi, laminaire...* , Césaire developed a reputation as a talented playwright. He continued his work of raising black consciousness in *La Tragédie du roi Christophe* (1964, The Tragedy of King Christophe), which presents a model for Caribbean independence in pre-Duvalier Haiti. Two other plays from the same period, *Une saison au Congo* (1967, A Season in Congo) and *Une tempête* (1969, A Tempest, an adaptation of Shakespeare's *The Tempest*), pursue Césaire's concerns with colonialism, decolonization, and the dangers of political power.

His preeminence in the French-speaking black world is largely the result of Césaire's ability to link race consciousness with his brilliant poetry and his shrewd politics without descending into the racial determinism of which his lifelong friend Senghor has been accused. The most striking monument to this ability remains the *Cahier*, a poem that breaks the barriers of race at the same time that it breaks the barriers of poetry.

Richard Watts

See Also

Duvalier, Jean-Claude; Haiti; Languages, Creole, in the Caribbean.

Africa

Cetshwayo (b. 1826?, Eshowe, Zululand [now in South Africa]; d. Feb. 8, 1884, Eshowe) the last independent Zulu king (1872-1879).

Cetshwayo was the son of Mpande, who was king of the Zulu from 1840 to 1872, and the nephew of Shaka, who ruled from 1816 until 1828 and greatly expanded the Zulu kingdom. Cetshwayo was raised in the northern part of the Zulu kingdom near present-day Nongoma, South Africa. In 1856 he defeated and killed his half-brother Mbulazi, whom Mpande had favored as the successor to the throne. After the British colonial forces in the nearby colony of Natal mediated between father and son, Cetshwayo publicly declared his loyalty to Mpande and was ceremonially proclaimed king in 1873.

For a time the British backed Cetshwayo in a land dispute between the Zulu and neighboring Afrikaners, or white settlers of Dutch origin. The British began to withdraw their support, however, after they had annexed the Afrikaner territory of the Transvaal in 1877 and no longer had a need for Zulu allies against the Afrikaners. Beginning in the late 1860s, Cetshwayo had worked to procure arms for his people. He was also determined to preserve the Zulu regimental system, which separated young men from their community at puberty and had them fight as one regiment until they reached marrying age. The regiments proved a highly effective way of controlling the fighting power in the kingdom. Local representatives of the British Empire used Cetshwayo's positions on arms and the regiment system, along with other minor incidents, to justify issuing an ultimatum on December 11, 1878, demanding that Cetshwayo disband his army.

Cetshwayo declared that he would not attack the British, but he refused to agree to the terms of the ultimatum. War between the British and the Zulu began in January 1879, with the Zulu forces achieving one significant victory at the Battle of Isandhlwana. The British defeated the Zulu in other battles, the last being the Battle of Ulundi. Cetshwayo was captured and sent into exile in Cape Town, while the British divided his kingdom into 13 parts.

Cetshwayo went to England in 1882 to plead successfully for his restoration as king. After he returned to Zululand in 1883, a civil war began between his supporters and those of his main rival, Zibhebhu, who controlled a large part of northern Zululand. Cetshwayo died in 1884. His son, Dinuzulu, succeeded him after a struggle with Zibhebhu.

See Also

Afrikaner; Cape Town, South Africa.

Africa

Chad, a landlocked country bordered by Libya, Sudan, Central African Republic, Cameroon, Nigeria, and Niger.

Chad's contemporary poverty and ethnic discord have deep historical roots. Beginning in the late first millennium, powerful kingdoms and empires arose in the central Sahel region. Their power derived in part from their control over the trans-Saharan trade carried by the Toubou and Arab pastoralists of the northern desert. The peoples of both the desert and Sahel regions adopted Islam during the Middle Ages. Until the late nineteenth century, the Sahel kingdoms carried out slave raids on the peoples of the south, who lacked states and complex social hierarchies and who maintained traditional religious practices.

French colonialism reversed the traditional dominance of the Islamic northern and central regions. The French concentrated development in southern Chad because of its greater agricultural capacity, while they disrupted the trans-Saharan trade that had made the northern and central regions powerful and wealthy. As a consequence, southerners, especially the Sara people, rose through the colonial civil service and dominated Chad's government after independence. Their indifference or hostility toward the peoples of the central and northern regions sparked resentment and, eventually, more than two decades of intermittent civil war. During the 1990s relative peace has slowly returned to Chad, as democratic elections have taken place and the country's war-torn economy has gradually recovered. However, the country remains one of the poorest in the world, and low-level ethnic conflicts continue, particularly in the south.

Geography and Early History

Chad's three distinct ecological zones have supported different ethnic groups pursuing a range of livelihoods. The northern portion is a desert whose inhabitants have traditionally practiced either pastoral nomadism or oasis agriculture. The seasonal grasslands of the middle region, the Sahel, have historically supported livestock herding. The southern section, known as the Sudanese zone, receives a higher rainfall that sustains a savanna environment of grasses, shrubs, and scattered trees. Large-scale agriculture has been possible only in this southern region.

People have inhabited the region of contemporary Chad for thousands of years. Although the arid Sahara occupies much of northern Chad today, this region once enjoyed a moister environment. Rock art discovered at Ennedi Plateau, today one of the driest regions of northern Chad, provides the earliest clues about the region's inhabitants. 9000 years ago in Ennedi, artists left remarkable depictions of local big-game hunting and harpoon fishing. Until perhaps 7000 years ago a much larger Lake Chad, known as Mega-Chad, covered 336,700 sq km (130,000 sq m) and stood 55 m (180 ft) above its current level. Over time, however, the region became drier, large numbers of people congregated around the receding shores of Mega-Chad, and by the second millennium B.C.E. local people were farming cereal crops such as millet. Oral histories suggest that an ancient lakeside people, the Sao, the ancestors of present-day Kotoko-speakers along the Chari and Logone Rivers, once dominated much of the region around the lake. Archaeological finds reveal that by the tenth century C.E. the Sao lived in walled cities and engaged in complex artistic practices, including iron and bronze casting using the lost-wax technique. Under the Kanem-Bornu empire, however, the Kanembu seem to have displaced and absorbed the Sao, until the Sao disappeared as a distinct ethnic group by the seventeenth century.

The Empires of the Sahel

By the fifth century B.C.E., the development of iron-smelting technology accompanied an increase in agricultural production in the southern savanna zone. By the fifth century C.E., desert peoples first acquired camels from either North Africa or the Nile Valley. These animals facilitated a trans-Saharan trade. Commodities such as salt, horses, firearms, and glass beads traveled south, while traders carried ivory and especially slaves north. The appropriation of surplus agricultural goods and the control over this trade gave rise to

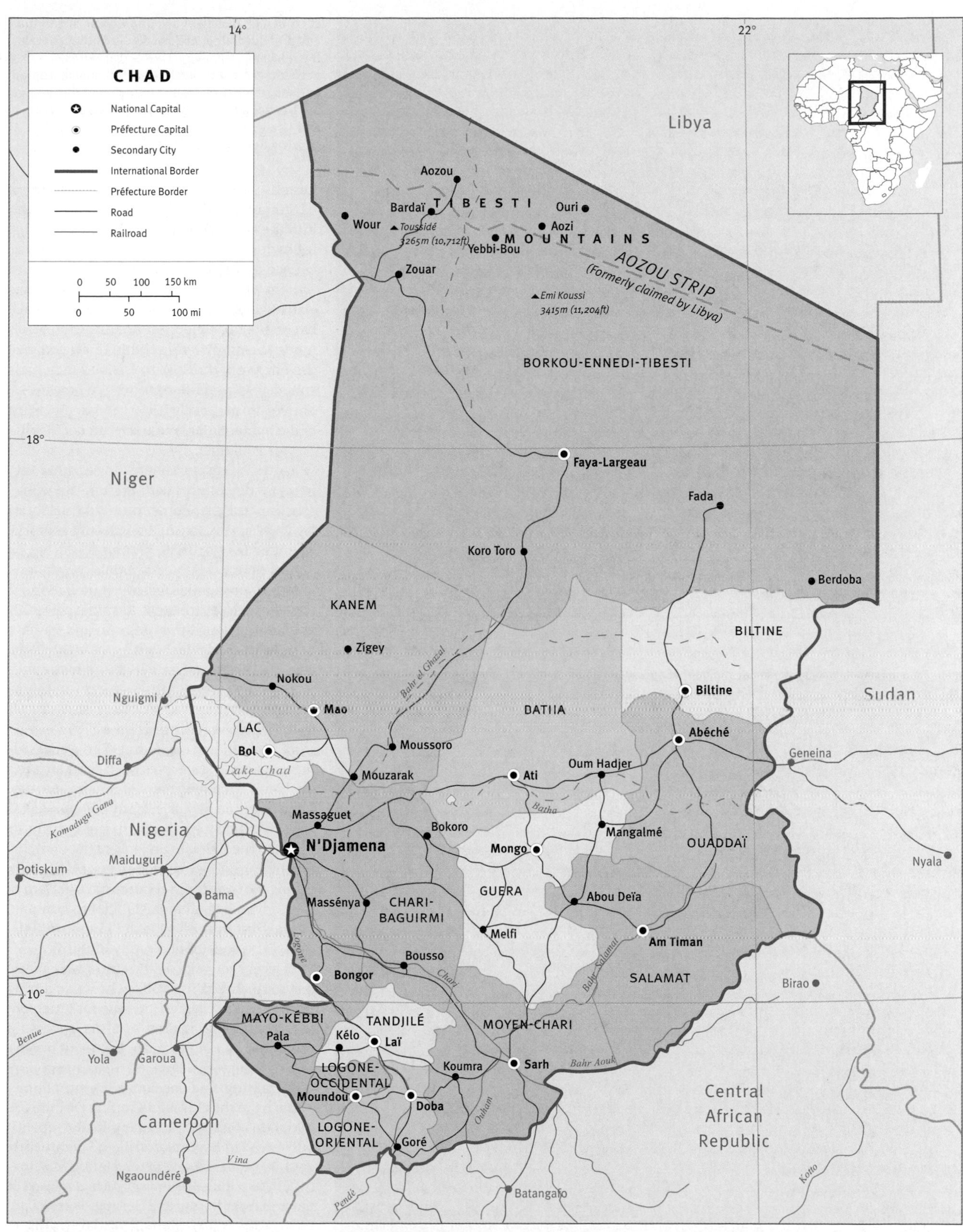

stratified societies, including the three historic kingdoms of Bagirmi, Kanem-Bornu, and Wadai.

In the ninth century the Zaghawa, pastoralists of the Ennedi Massif, established a centralized state around Kanem on the northeast shores of Lake Chad. The Kanem empire grew to encompass other groups, including the Toubou (Tubu), of the Tibesti Massif. From the mid-eleventh until the nineteenth century, the Sefuwa, a Kanembu lineage claiming descent from the Zaghawa, ruled the Kanem empire. Trans-Saharan traders brought Islam to Kanem, where it became widespread by the eleventh century.

During the fourteenth century, internal divisions in Kanem allowed Bulala Arabs to oust the Sefuwa from power. The Sefuwa fled to the region of Bornu in present-day Nigeria, where they regrouped and rapidly established a new powerful kingdom. (After intermarrying

LEFT: In a Chad market a young woman sits in the midst of decorated, hollowed gourds that contain the milk she is selling. *CORBIS/Paul Amasy*
BELOW LEFT: On the outskirts of N'Djamena, capital of Chad, the houses and entry pylon of this village are built of adobe. Adobe, made of mud or dung and straw baked in the sun, is widely used for construction in West Africa. *CORBIS/Paul Amasy*

with the Sao of Bornu, the Kanembu became known as the KANURI.) The Sefuwa recaptured Kanem in the sixteenth century. However, the Sefuwa rulers remained in Bornu and allowed the Bulula to continue ruling Kanem as tributaries. At its peak in the fifteenth century, Kanem-Bornu extended west to the borders of Songhai, in the Niger Basin, and north into the Fezzan, in present-day Libya. In the following century, however, TUAREG raids caused an increasingly famine-weakened Kanem-Bornu to lose control over the vital trans-Saharan trade routes through Fezzan. Excessive tax collection and internal strife made the empire vulnerable to attacks by the FULANI of the SOKOTO CALIPHATE, which conquered Kanem-Bornu's western provinces. Kanem-Bornu finally fell in 1893 to the army of the infamous Sudanese slave raider, Rabih Zubair Fadlallah.

Far to the east of Kanem-Bornu, near the present-day border with Sudan, the non-Muslim TUNJUR people founded the Wadai (or Ouadai) kingdom in the sixteenth century. In either 1611 or 1635, Maba people, led by Abd-el-Kerim, mounted a popular revolt and installed an Islamic Dynasty. Initially, Wadai was forced to pay tribute to the more powerful neighboring kingdoms of Bornu and DARFUR (in present-day Sudan). But by the eighteenth century Wadai had gained enough strength to assert its sovereignty and carry out raids on Kanem-Bornu. Wadai's wealth derived from its trade in slaves and the tribute it demanded from surrounding chiefdoms. The Wadai sultans organized slave raids over a vast area to the south, including parts of the present-day Central African Republic. Many of these slaves were marched from Wadai through Darfur to the Nile. The kingdom underwent frequent turbulent transitions between rulers, particularly during the nineteenth century. In 1835 Darfur took advantage of the instability to conquer Wadai, but in the 1890s the kingdom fell under the control of a proxy of Rabih.

Bagirmi, centered on the city of Massénya just southeast of Bornu, likewise arose during the sixteenth century. However, for much of their history the kingdom's Barma leadership remained subject to more powerful neighboring kingdoms. Bagirmi also engaged in slave raiding, and specialized in supplying eunuchs to the Ottoman Empire. Despite the adoption of Islam by its rulers, Wadai repeatedly invaded Bagirmi during the eighteenth century on the pretext of reinstating Muslim rule. In fact, the rulers of Bagirmi had refused to pay tribute to Bornu, and Bornu asked Wadai to invade on their behalf. Wadai captured thousands of Barma and other peoples and sold them into slavery. In 1892 Rabih captured Massénya. When the rulers of Bagirmi solicited protection from France, Rabih had Massénya burnt to the ground.

At the end of the nineteenth century Rabih embarked on a campaign to create a personally ruled empire spanning Central Africa. During the 1880s and 1890s he defeated Wadai and conquered Bagirmi, Adamawa (in present-day Cameroon), Bornu, and much of the present-day Central African Republic. He set up a capital at Dikwa, south of Lake Chad. The British gave some consideration to recognizing Rabih's sovereignty, but in 1900 they chose instead to partition his territory with France.

Fishermen working landlocked Lake Chad carry their nets. *Thoret/Explorer*

European Conquest and Colonization

The French faced fierce resistance from Rabih. After several small skirmishes, Rabih's army faced a large French force in 1900 at the Battle of Kousseri. Rabih was killed and his forces were defeated; the French slowly consolidated their control over the region. In 1910 Chad became a part of French Equatorial Africa. A decade later France instituted a civilian administration for southern Chad. However, due to Chad's isolation and political, economic and strategic unimportance, nearly half of all civil service positions were empty at any given time. Indeed, French officials were often assigned to Chad as a punishment.

For several years, the French failed to subdue the Muslim theocracy, the Sanusiya, who had ruled northern Chad and parts of Libya since the late nineteenth century. By 1919, however, the last of the sporadic fighting ceased, and the French exercised hegemony over the region. The northern areas of Chad remained fairly independent of French influence as long as their inhabitants complied with the slavery ban and did not interfere with French forces. This sparsely populated region, which the French designated the Borkou-Ennedi-Tibesti (BET) Prefecture, remained under the direct jurisdiction, if not the control, of the governor-general in Brazzaville until 1946. In reality, the Sanusiya order continued to have great influence in the north. Thus, Chad was the last territory in Africa that France fully colonized.

The French depended heavily upon soldiers from Chad to combat uprisings in its equatorial holdings. Village chiefs were required to fill quotas for conscripts. France also relied on forced labor to support its colonial effort. When people fled their villages to avoid forced labor or porterage, local collaborators would commonly kidnap women and children or confiscate movable property to coerce the men to work. Alternatively, French forces burned houses and crops to enforce demands for labor. Since the Muslim-dominated north resisted forced labor, the French concentrated their efforts on the south. Tens of thousands of Chadians labored on the construction of a railroad from Pointe-Noire to Brazzaville, in the present-day Republic of Congo, between 1921 and 1936. Sources estimate that perhaps half of the workers died as a direct result of inhuman working conditions.

French colonialism dramatically altered the economy of Chad. The French undermined the centuries-old trans-Saharan trade by regulating and taxing caravan routes, and by building motorable roads that diverted trade to the Atlantic coast. The disruption of the trans-Saharan trade served to impoverish the people of northern Chad.

France also instituted a head tax throughout its colonies after 1901. The French justified the tax as a means to make the colonies "self-sufficient." Of course, before the French arrived these regions were self-sufficient. In fact, the tax served to pay for the salaries of French officials and for the construction of transportation infrastructure primarily benefiting French entrepreneurs. Probably more important, the tax forced the peasantry to participate in the cash economy, either by growing cash crops or by working for a wage in French-owned enterprises. Farmers in the fertile south were forced to cultivate cotton to pay their tax. Colonial administrators required them to sell their crop to the French monopoly, Cotonfran, which paid below market value for their crops. Those unfortunates who could not pay often faced severe corporal punishment or imprisonment. The forced adoption of cotton made Chad vulnerable to famine and dependent on global market prices for the cash crop that continues to dominate its economy. It also undermined traditional society by replacing communal institutions with individual market relations.

French colonialism exacerbated the regional disparities. French authorities virtually ignored the arid Muslim north, including the areas of the former Sahel kingdoms that once dominated the region. Meanwhile, inhabitants of the south enjoyed the few advantages of colonial occupation. The most important of these was access to a western education and to low- and mid-level positions in the colonial bureaucracy. By the end of the colonial era, southerners, reversing the historical pattern, dominated the country's economy and politics.

Following World War II, Chad, along with other African colonies, gained limited autonomy as an overseas territory with representation in the French national assembly. The inhabitants were granted citizenship and political parties were legalized. A large number of political parties representing a broad range of interests had formed by the late 1950s. Conservative forces, such as the Union Démocratique Tchadienne (UDT), representing French commercial interests and traditional Muslim leaders, advocated the continuation of strong ties with France and respect for traditional authority. In contrast, progressive parties, including the Parti Progressiste Tchadien (PPT), organized by civil servants and labor activists, sought complete independence with social and economic reforms. The PPT received its greatest support from the Sara, an ethnic group that dominated the more modern and developed south, while Muslim merchants from the Sahel supported the UDT. After the introduction of universal suffrage in 1956, the PPT gained the lion's share of popular support.

Independence

In a 1958 referendum, Chad's voters chose to form a republic within the French community. PPT leader François Tombalbaye won election as prime minister in 1959. Chad declared independence in August 1960 with Tombalbaye as president. In 1962 the autocratic Tombalbaye banned all political parties except the PPT, and Chad became an increasingly corrupt one-party state dominated by the Sara. After demonstrations in the capital, N'Djamena, in 1963, Tombalbaye declared a state of emergency and dissolved the National Assembly. When French troops evacuated the BET in 1965, Sara administrators took over and proceeded to alienate the local population with their inefficiency and often insensitive and sometimes humiliating demands.

Discontent and alienation festered, particularly in the Muslim north, until in 1965, civil disobedience broke out. The resistance effort coalesced in 1966 into the Front de la libération nationale du Tchad (FROLINAT), operating from a base in Libya. Tombalbaye relied on French assistance to contain the insurgence, which, however, persisted. In the south Tombalbaye also lost support after instituting unpopular economic programs, banning Christian names in an *authenticité* program modeled after Mobutu Sese Seko's Zaire (present-day Democratic Republic of the Congo), and making harsh Sara initiation rituals mandatory for non-Muslim Chadians. Meanwhile, during the early 1970s, an increasingly severe drought ravaged Chad. The drought damaged the country's economically vital cotton crop and caused special hardship in the arid, livestock-dependent north.

In 1975 soldiers from the south assassinated Tombalbaye in a coup d'état. A military council, headed by Gen. Félix Malloum, took control of the government. Malloum called for reconciliation with FROLINAT. While one segment of FROLINAT, led by Hissène Habré, joined the Malloum government in 1978, the main body of the rebel force, led by Oueddei Goukouni, continued to combat government forces. When conflicts between Malloum and Habré deteriorated into armed conflict in 1979, Habré's forces occupied much of N'Djamena and forced Malloum into exile. Meanwhile, FROLINAT forces led by Goukouni also entered the capital and established a fragile accommodation with Habré. A brutal wave of ethnic killings swept both the north and the south. Remnants of the national army retreated to the south, where southerners established a separate provisional government. With the country in complete disarray, Nigeria, fearful of a compromised border, pressured the Organization of African Unity (OAU) to broker a peace agreement between the warring factions.

The result was the establishment in 1979 of a Gouvernement de l'union nationale de transition (GUNT). The GUNT coalition quickly broke down, however, and violence once again shook N'Djamena. Habré fled to the eastern town of Biltine and later to Sudan. Goukouni seized control and immediately looked to Libya for support. In 1980 Libya's head of state, Muammar al-Qaddafi, deployed 15,000 troops into Chad. In 1981 the two leaders called for a political unification of Chad with Libya. France reacted with alarm and maneuvered to force a Libyan withdrawal. Meanwhile, both the United States and France provided covert backing to Habré.

Habré's Forces armées du nord (FAN) seized N'Djamena, and Habré formed a new government in 1982. Goukouni, who had fled the country, soon returned to the north and regained control of the BET, again with Libyan support. Libya aimed to enforce its claim to the "Aozou strip," a swath of territory in northern Chad. France sent troops in 1983 to prevent Goukouni and the Libyans from moving south of an "interdiction line" between northern and central Chad, and the fighting briefly ceased. However, unresolved political and ethnic resentments sparked rebellion in the south. The fighting drove some 25,000 refugees to flee to the Central African Republic. By 1986 the fighting between the troops of Habré, supported by United States arms and French troops, and Goukouni, supported by Libyan forces, once again resumed. Habré reclaimed most of the north from Goukouni and the Libyans in 1987. In 1988 Chad and Libya resumed diplomatic relations and agreed to submit their territorial dispute to international mediation. In 1994 Libya accepted the judgment of the International Court of Justice, which rejected Libya's claims to the disputed territory.

Meanwhile, in 1989 a government minister and two senior military officers, including Idriss Déby, led an unsuccessful coup attempt. Déby fled to Sudan. Habré responded by trying to consolidate his power. A 1989 popular referendum approved a new constitution that established a single-party state and awarded Habré another seven-year term as president. However, in 1990 Déby returned from Sudan with 2000 troops, and Habré fled to Cameroon.

Despite promises to institute democratic reforms, Déby initially followed the familiar pattern of ethnic nepotism, patronage, and autocratic rule. However, in 1991 Déby declared his commitment to eventual democratic rule and permitted the registration of opposition political parties. During the early 1990s Déby's government faced civilian protests against austerity measures, including tax increases, layoffs, and salary reductions for civil servants and members of the military. At the same time, the government deflected a number of attempted coups and armed rebellions, particularly in the south. International human rights organizations criticized the regime for its response to the unrest. A transitional government drafted a constitution in 1994 for a multiparty democracy, and Déby declared an amnesty for political prisoners. A popular referendum approved the draft constitution in 1996, and Déby won the presidency in a multiparty election. After several postponements, Déby's party dominated legislative elections in 1997. Though Déby's defeated opponents claimed electoral fraud, international observers declared the elections free and fair.

Three decades of continual warfare have left Chad one of the poorest countries in the world. Though the economy has shown recent signs of improvement, a poor transport infrastructure and continued reliance on cotton and other crops vulnerable to drought have limited the country's potential for prosperity. Ethnic and religious divisions continue to run deep. The government continues to face armed resistance from rebels in the south demanding regional autonomy, and in 1998 Amnesty International charged the government with arbitrarily killing civilians from the south.

Ari Nave

See Also

Brazzaville, Republic of the Congo; Camel; Congo, Republic of the; Ivory Trade; Iron in Africa; Salt Trade; N'Djamena, Chad; Nile River; Pastoralism; Qaddafi, Muammar al-; Sahara Desert; Songhai Empire; Structural Adjustment in Africa; Rabih; Human Rights in Africa; Islam and Tradition: An Interpretation; Slavery in Africa; Trans-Saharan and Red Sea Slave Trade.

Africa

Chad (Ready Reference)

Area: 1,284,000 sq km (495,753 sq mi)
Location: Central Africa, south of Libya
Capital: N'Djamena (population 500,000 [1992 estimate])
Other Major Cities: Sarh (population 113,400), Moundou (102,000) (1988 estimate)
Population: 7,359,512 (1998 estimate)
Population Density: 5 persons per sq km (about 14 per sq mi)
Population Below Age 15: 44 percent (male 1,586,873; female 1,579,086 [1997 estimate])
Population Growth Rate: 2.7 percent (1996 estimate)
Total Fertility Rate: 5.8 children born per woman (1996 estimate)
Life Expectancy at Birth: Total population: 47.6 years (male 45.2 years; female 50 years [1996 estimate])
Infant Mortality Rate: 120.4 deaths per 1000 live births (1996 estimate)
Literacy Rate (age 15 and over who can read and write in French or Arabic): Total population: 48.1 percent (male 62.1 percent; female 34.7 percent [1995 estimate])
Education: In the 1990s there were 591,417 primary and 72,641 secondary students, attending approximately 2500 schools. In the late 1980s there were 3000 students enrolled at institutions of higher education, including the University of Chad.
Languages: French and Arabic are the official languages. Hausa is spoken in the Lake Chad region; Sara and Sango are spoken in the south. More than 100 different languages and dialects are spoken in all.
Ethnic Groups: The north is inhabited mainly by Muslim peoples, including Arabs, Toubou, Hadjerai, Fulbé, Kotoko, Kanembou, Baguirmi, Boulala, Zaghawa, and Maba. Mostly non-Muslims live in the south: Sara, Ngambaye, Mbaye, Goulaye, Moundang, Moussei, Massa; of the 150,000 nonindigenous inhabitants, 1000 are French.
Religions: Half the population is Muslim, one-fourth is Christian, and one-fourth of the people adhere to traditional beliefs.
Climate: The Saharan north is hot, dusty,

and dry throughout the year. South of the desert there is a hot, dry season from March to July; a rainy season from July to October, with average rainfall 250 to 750 mm (about 10 to 30 in); and a cool, dry season during the remaining months. Rainfall is higher in the south, averaging 1145 mm (about 45 in).
Land, Plants, and Animals: Chad's land-locked terrain is dominated by the low-lying Chad Basin (elevation about 250 m/820 ft), which rises gradually to mountains and plateaus on the north, east, and south. The greatest elevations are reached in the Tibesti massif in the north, with a maximum height of 3415 m (11,204 ft) at Emi Koussi. The northern half of the republic lies in the Sahara. The only important rivers, the Logone and Chari (Shari), are located in the southwest and flow into Lake Chad. The lake doubles in size during the rainy season.
Natural Resources: Petroleum (currently being developed), uranium, natron, kaolin, and fish
Currency: The CFAF (Communauté Financière Africaine franc)
Gross Domestic Product (GDP): $4.3 billion (1997 estimate)
GDP per Capita: $600 (1997 estimate)
GDP Real Growth Rate: 5.5 percent (1997 estimate)
Primary Economic Activities: agriculture (49 percent of GDP; 85 percent of employment), industry, and services
Primary Crops: Cotton, sorghum, millet, peanuts, rice, potatoes, and manioc (tapioca); cattle, sheep, goats, and camels
Industries: Cotton textiles, meat packing, beer brewing, natron (sodium carbonate), soap, cigarettes, and construction materials
Primary Exports: Cotton, cattle, textiles, and fish
Primary Imports: Machinery and transportation equipment, industrial goods, petroleum products, foodstuffs; textiles, and military equipment
Primary Trade Partners: United States, France, Nigeria, Cameroon, Italy, and Germany
Government: Chad is nominally a republic. It is a constitutional multiparty democracy, led by President Lt. Gen. Idriss Deby and Prime Minister Djimasta Koibla. Under the constitution passed in 1996, the legislature consists of the 125-member unicameral National Assembly, first elected in 1997.

Barbara Worley

See Also
Hausa Language; Sahara Desert.

Africa

Chad, Lake, **lake in Central Africa at the junction of Chad, Cameroon, Nigeria, and Niger, about 250 m (about 820 ft) above sea level.**

Lake Chad is fed principally by the Chari (Shari) and Logone rivers. Although the lake has no visible outlet, it is steadily decreasing in size from evaporation and underground seepage. In the rainy season the area of the lake is as great as 25,900 sq km (10,000 sq mi), but in the dry season it shrinks to as little as 10,360 sq km (4000 sq mi). In open water the depth of the lake varies from about 1m (about 3 ft) in the northwest to more than 6 m (20 ft) in the south. The numerous islands lying along its eastern shore are inhabited. The first Europeans to visit Lake Chad were a party of British explorers in 1823.

Chaga. Please see Chagga

Africa

Chagga, **an ethnic group of northeastern Tanzania and Kenya.**

The third largest ethnic group in Tanzania, the Chagga live on the fertile slopes of Mount Kilimanjaro, now one of Tanzania's most prosperous farming regions. The precolonial Chagga created an innovative irrigation system that enabled them to transport water 182.9m (600 ft) above river level, which later made it possible for them to grow such lucrative crops as bananas and coffee.

During the nineteenth century the Chagga, who lived in scattered villages governed by local chiefs, participated little in the increasingly active East African caravan trades. But under British colonial rule they became one of the colony's most vocal farming groups. In 1925 the Chagga organized the Kilimanjaro Native Planters Association (later called the Kilimanjaro Native Cooperative Union), a marketing organization that became the region's largest seller of coffee during British colonialism. After independence, the Chagga continued to prosper and their cooperative farms were later seen as a model for Tanzanian president Julius K. Nyerere's *ujamaa* villages. Although they are no longer the largest coffee producers in Tanzania, the Chagga continue to be one of the most prosperous groups and have played an influential role in Tanzanian politics.

Elizabeth Heath

See Also
Kilimanjaro; Nyerere, Julius Kambarage.

Africa

Chamba **(also known as Chamba-Daka, Daka, Samba, Tchamba, and Tsamba), ethnic group of West Africa.**

The Chamba primarily inhabit east-central Nigeria and neighboring Cameroon. They speak a Niger-Congo language. Approximately 300,000 people consider themselves Chamba.

See Also
Languages, African: An Overview.

North America

Chamberlain, Wilton Norman (Wilt) **(b. August 21, 1936, Philadelphia, Pa.), African American basketball player who won seven consecutive National Basketball Association (NBA) scoring titles from 1960 to 1966 and who is the NBA's second all-time leading scorer after Kareem Abdul-Jabbar.**

Wilt Chamberlain revolutionized the game of basketball, inspiring rule changes and creating a premium role for the big scoring and rebounding center. Over 14 seasons in the National Basketball Association, "Wilt the Stilt" – or, as he preferred to be called, "the Big Dipper" – averaged 30.1 points a game, second only to Michael Jordan. In the 1961-1962 season, playing for the Philadelphia Warriors, Chamberlain averaged 50.4 points a game. He scored 100 points in a single game against the New York Knickerbockers, played on March 2, 1963, in Hershey, Pennsylvania.

He was born Wilton Norman Chamberlain, the son of William Chamberlain, a custodian, and Olivia Chamberlain, a domestic and laundress. Heralded as the best prep player in the nation, Chamberlain led his Overbrook High School team to a 58-3 record and two city championships. The Philadelphia Warriors claimed future draft rights to Chamberlain upon his high school graduation.

Scoring 52 points in his 1956 college debut for the University of Kansas, Chamberlain led the Jayhawks to a 24-3 record and the national finals. Having quickly become known as the predominant college player of his era, Chamberlain won All-America honors his sophomore and junior years, which were his first two playing for Kansas. Though he was known for his surpassing height (7 ft, 1 in or approx. 2.13 m), it was his all-around athletic skills that made him a premier performer (he lettered in track and field at Kansas, setting a school record in the high jump, and was courted by managers hoping to convert his interests to boxing or football). Increasingly frustrated by opposing teams' stalling tactics and other schemes to limit his effectiveness, Chamberlain passed up his senior year to play a season for the Harlem Globetrotters.

From 1959 to 1961 Chamberlain played for the NBA's Philadelphia Warriors, the

Golden State Warriors from 1962 to 1965, the Philadelphia 76ers from 1965 to 1968, and the Los Angeles Lakers from 1968 to 1973. He won the league's Most Valuable Player award in 1960, 1966, 1967, and 1968, and was an All-Star every year of his career except 1970. In addition to his prolific scoring (31,419 points for his career, the first player to pass 30,000), he is also the leading rebounder in NBA history (23,924 total, 22.9 a game). He led the league in that category for 11 seasons and set the single game mark with 55.

Chamberlain won championships with the 76ers in 1967 and the Lakers in 1972. Though his archrival, Bill Russell, won more championships with the Boston Celtics, Chamberlain bested Russell in terms of individual statistics. In 142 head-to-head games, Chamberlain out-rebounded Russell 95 times and averaged 28.8 points a game to Russell's 14.5.

Responding to the charge that he played selfishly, Chamberlain retooled his game late in his career, placing greater emphasis on passing and defense. He led the NBA in assists in 1967-1968 and was named to the league All-Defensive team in 1972 and 1973. The only part of the game at which Chamberlain did not excel was foul shooting, in which he averaged a lowly 54 percent for his career.

Chamberlain was elected to the Naismith Hall of Fame in 1978. He helped found the International Volleyball Association and has sponsored several Southern California track teams. He has remained in the public eye since retiring from basketball, appearing in television commercials and movies and writing a 1991 memoir, *A View from Above*, that described the colorful bachelor life he leads in his self-designed house in Bel Air, California.

John Gennari

SEE ALSO
Track and Field in the United States; Football, Collegiate; Jordan, Michael Jeffrey; Russell, William Fenton (Bill).

Latin America and the Caribbean

Chamoiseau, Patrick (b. 1953, Fort-de-France, Martinique), one of the best known and most successful Martinican writers, whose novels and essays place particular emphasis on the affirmation of the sociopolitical and cultural status of the French Creole language.

In novels such as *Chronique des sept misères* (1986) and *Solibo magnifique* (1988), Patrick Chamoiseau explores the tensions and conflicts that race, class, and questions of language give rise to in MARTINIQUE. In his attempt to incorporate elements from oral Creole into his French prose, he has developed a complex rhythmic and lyrical style often filled with ironic humor.

Chamoiseau collaborated with Caribbean writers RAPHAËL CONFIANT and Jean Bernabé on the essay *Eloge de la creolité* (1989), one of the most influential theoretical pieces produced in the region in recent times. This essay is an affirmation of a Creole identity influenced by, but also different from the ideas of, Martinican writer and cultural theorist EDOUARD GLISSANT. The essay, which is also a manifesto, proclaims the heterogeneous character of the Caribbean and rejects all aspirations to a pure identity. Here, not only the racist inheritance of French colonialism is rejected, but also the nostalgia for pure African roots that these and other Creolité writers associate with AIMÉ CÉSAIRE and his NÉGRITUDE Movement.

Chamoiseau's novel *Texaco* (1992) won the prestigious Prix Goncourt, France's most important literary prize, and received wide critical acclaim when it was translated into English in 1997. It tells the story of Marie-Sophie Laborieux, a working-class woman who lives in Texaco, a community outside Fort-de-France named after the neighboring oil tanks. The novel traces her family roots back 150 years, exploring the legacy of slavery, colonialism, and memory as interpreted through oral history.

Chamoiseau has also written autobiographical narratives, *Antan d'enfance* (1990) and *Chemin-d'école* (1994), and coauthored, again with Raphaël Confiant, *Lettres créoles: Traces antillaises et continentales de la littérature, 1635-1975* (1991).

He remains one of the most innovative voices in contemporary Caribbean writing.

Victor Figueroa

SEE ALSO
France; Créolité; Literature, French Language, in Caribbean; Languages, Creole, in the Caribbean.

North America

Chaney, James Earl (b. May 30, 1943, Meridian, Miss.; d. June 21, 1964, Miss.), African American civil rights activist who participated in and was killed during the massive voter registration and desegregation campaign in Mississippi called FREEDOM SUMMER.

James Earl Chaney was born May 30, 1943 in Meridian, Mississippi, to Ben and Fannie Lee Chaney. In 1963 he joined the Congress of Racial Equality (CORE). A year later CORE united with the National Association for the Advancement of Colored People (NAACP) and the STUDENT NONVIOLENT COORDINATING COMMITTEE (SNCC) to form the Council of Federated Organizations (COFO). In 1964 COFO led a massive voter registration and desegregation campaign in Mississippi called Freedom Summer. As part of the Freedom Summer activities, Chaney was riding with two white activists in Mississippi when they were attacked and killed by the Ku Klux Klan on June 21, 1964.

Alonford James Robinson, Jr.

SEE ALSO
Congress of Racial Equality; National Association for the Advancement of Colored People.

North America

Chapman, Tracy (b. March 20, 1964, Cleveland, Ohio), African American singer and songwriter.

When Tracy Chapman's self-titled debut album was released in 1988, its success – more than 10 million records sold and 3 Grammy nominations – was unprecedented for an artist who had just months before performed only in local coffeehouses and on street corners in the BOSTON, MASSACHUSETTS, area. Her hit singles "Talkin' Bout a Revolution" and "Fast Car," and appearances at such newsworthy concerts as the tribute to AFRICAN NATIONAL CONGRESS leader Nelson Mandela on his 70th birthday, helped seal her reputation as the originator of a new wave in politically aware folk music.

Raised by a single mother, often in near poverty, Chapman says she understood "social conditions and political situations" from an early age. When she was in sixth grade she got her first guitar and immediately began writing songs of her own. On scholarship, she attended the Wooster School, a private boarding school in Connecticut, before enrolling in Tufts University in Medford, Massachusetts.

While at Tufts, Chapman became a popular local street musician. After seeing her at a SOUTH AFRICA protest rally, a classmate helped her secure a contract with an agent, who landed her an audition with Elektra Records. Despite what Chapman herself thought was probably an unmarketable style – direct, unadorned, and personal – her first album was an astonishing commercial and critical success. Her subsequent records, *Crossroads* (1989), *Matters of the Heart* (1992), and *New Beginning* (1995), have fared less well but have confirmed her reputation as a perceptive, intelligent, and complex songwriter.

Kate Tuttle

SEE ALSO
Mandela, Nelson Rolihlahla.

Africa

Chari, river in CHAD and the CENTRAL AFRICAN REPUBLIC.

The Chari River, nearly 900 km (600 mi) long, drains a 650,000 sq km (250,000 sq mi) basin in CHAD and the CENTRAL AFRICAN REPUBLIC before it flows into LAKE CHAD, a drainage basin with no outlet to the sea. The Bamingui River is its true headwater, though the Ouham River provides it with the most water, and a number of other tributaries feed the Chari. At N'Djamena it divides into several branches that flow to Lake Chad.

For hundreds of years the Chari was used

as a commercial waterway, especially by slave raiders from the north. In 1823 British explorers became the first Europeans to find the river, and in the early twentieth century it became a major transport route for French colonizers. Today, Sara and BANDA people live along its banks. River sediments provide fertile soil for foodstuffs as well as cotton, the main export crop, and river fishing supplements local diets. During the summer rainy season, large steam-driven barges navigate the lower 800 km (500 mi) of the Chari to transport trade goods between N'Djamena, Sarh, and other towns.

Eric Young

SEE ALSO
N'Djamena, Chad; Great Britain; France; Slavery in Africa.

Latin America and the Caribbean

Charlemagne, Manno (b. 1948, Port-au-Prince, Haiti), Haitian protest singer and politician, exiled as a result of his outspoken opposition to the Duvalier dictatorship and later for his involvement with leftist leaders during the military coup of 1991.

Manno Charlemagne was raised by his aunt in the working-class neighborhoods of Port-au-Prince and Carrefour. He was surrounded by the desperate violence and destitution of these poverty-stricken districts. According to Charlemagne, some of his earliest boyhood memories include images of people fleeing bullets or making homemade bombs. The extreme poverty that he encountered from such an early age helped to cultivate his acute sensitivity to political injustice. Later, as an *angaje* (politically engaged) musician, this awareness became his trademark and his ticket to success both in music and in politics.

Charlemagne began singing and playing guitar at the age of 16. In 1968 he formed his first band, a MINI-JAZZ group called Les Remarquables. His second group, Les Trovères, provided the artist with his first involvement in *twoubadou* music. It is in this environment that he first began to address the social issues that characterize his later career. He started to write songs that expressed a deep anguish for the poverty he witnessed.

In the 1970s Charlemagne teamed up with singer Marco Jeanty and they began to compose angaje songs together. In May 1978 the duo began their professional career, commencing a series of radio appearances. Their politically charged message attracted attention in university circles, and they soon developed a strong following. Later that year the duo released their first record, *Marco and Manno,* on New York-based Marc Records. Charlemagne's lyrics during this period reveal much about the condition of Haiti's poor and their unbalanced relation to the powerful:

Why doesn't life separate things equally,
fifty fifty?
Why does the shark bring such destruction,
Large tooth marks on the back of the little fish?

While the composer's social perception won the attention of the lower classes and intellectuals, it also attracted the suspicion of Haiti's totalitarian government (see HAITI).

When Ronald Reagan defeated Jimmy Carter in the 1980 United States presidential campaign, JEAN-CLAUDE DUVALIER, the son and heir of the infamous dictator FRANÇOIS DUVALIER, aptly perceived that human rights would no longer be a central issue in America's foreign policy. As a result, they were free to deal with internal affairs as they wished. No time was wasted in extinguishing state dissidents. Among the first to witness his show of strength were Haiti's angaje musicians. The records of Manno Charlemagne and numerous others were removed from stores, and many artists were arrested or forced into exile. Anticipating his eventual arrest, Charlemagne fled to the United States. He ended up in Boston, where he released several albums during the 1980s, including *Konviksyon* (1984) and *Fini les colonies* (1985).

After Duvalier resigned and went into exile in 1986, Charlemagne returned to his homeland. He promptly organized several percussionists and singers and started a group called Konbit Kalfou. Charlemagne remained firm in his political message, urging Haiti's poor to unite and create a government for the people. For six years, Haiti's most popular songwriter enjoyed a string of highly successful concerts and hit albums, before embarking on his political career as an ally of JEAN-BERTRAND ARISTIDE. In 1991 he was appointed adviser to the minister of interior and defense.

After a return to music for a few years during the ensuing military coup, Charlemagne resumed his political career in 1995 becoming mayor of Port-au-Prince. This was no small feat, considering that he was challenged by a U.S.-funded opponent and that his name did not even appear on the ballot. It remains a testament to his immense popularity in Haiti.

In April 1997 Mayor Charlemagne gave the Fugees, a Haitian-American hip hop group, the key to his city.

Gordon Root

SEE ALSO
Hip Hop in the United States; Port-au-Prince, Haiti.

Latin America and the Caribbean

Charles, Mary Eugenia (b. 1919), former prime minister of Dominica.

Also known as the Iron Lady of the Caribbean, Mary Eugenia Charles was the first female prime minister in the Caribbean and one of only a few black women to serve as a head of state. After practicing law for almost two decades, she became an outspoken critic against the government of Edward Oliver Le Blanc, and more specifically against the Seditious and Undesirable Publications Act, passed by his government. In 1968 Charles founded the Dominica Freedom Party. In 1980 she became prime minister of Dominica, a position she held until 1995. In 1983 she was elected chairperson of the Organization of Eastern Caribbean States. In that same year, she strongly supported the United States invasion of Grenada (*see* DOMINICA).

North America

Charles, Ray (Ray Charles Robinson) (b. September 23, 1930, Albany, Ga.), African American RHYTHM AND BLUES (R&B) pianist and singer, known as the father of Soul.

During the 1950s and 1960s Ray Charles was a key figure in the development of rhythm and blues, an African American style that transformed American popular music. Charles and other black R&B musicians gave popular music a broader expressive range and a powerful rhythmic drive, laying the groundwork for rock 'n' roll. In particular, Charles was a leader in incorporating the GOSPEL MUSIC of the black church into secular music, investing his compositions with propulsive energy and emotional power.

Born Ray Charles Robinson, he grew up in Greenville, Florida, where his parents, Aretha and Baily Robinson, moved when he was an infant. The United States was experiencing the worst years of the GREAT DEPRESSION, and Charles recalled, "Even compared to other blacks... we were on the bottom.... Nothing below us except the ground." At the age of four Charles developed glaucoma, and before he turned seven, he lost his sight. His mother secured his admission to the School for the Deaf and Blind in St. Augustine, Florida, where he spent the next eight years, during which time he learned to play the clarinet, piano, and alto saxophone. He also studied composition and learned to arrange music in Braille.

In 1945, following the death of his mother, Charles left the school. He formed a musical combo and played in jook joints. Finding Florida a difficult place to survive as a musician, he asked guitarist Gosady McGee what city in the continental United States was farthest from Florida. McGee's answer – SEATTLE, WASHINGTON – gave the two musicians a destination.

Charles quickly established himself in the small Seattle-area musical community and befriended a young musician named Quincy Jones. With bass player Milt Jarrett, who was also from Seattle, Charles and McGee formed a trio whose style and instrumentation mirrored those of the popular Nat King Cole Trio. Aside from Cole, Charles's early piano style and singing reflected that of blues balladeer Leroy Carr and pianist Charles Brown. In 1949 he traveled to Los Angeles and made

Seated at the piano, Ray Charles leads his band and singing group, the Raylettes, in a concert performance.
The Everett Collection

his first recordings for the small Swingtime label. "Baby Let Me Hold Your Hand" (1950) earned him a following in the black community, and he began touring with bluesman Lowell Fulson. During these years, Charles became addicted to heroin. Although never serving an extended jail sentence, he was arrested for narcotics possession in 1955, 1961, and 1965. After his third arrest, he stopped performing for a year, taking time off to kick his 17-year-old habit.

In 1952 Atlantic Records bought Charles's contract from Swingtime. Charles recorded for Atlantic from 1952 to 1959 and quickly emerged as one of its biggest stars. His recording of "I Got a Woman" (1954) spent 19 weeks on the R&B charts and marked the first appearance of his classic style. The song draws on black sacred music – it is based on a gospel song popularized by Alex Bradford – but when Charles sang, "She saves her lovin', early in the mornin', just for me," there was no doubt that his meaning was secular, not sacred. The musical arrangement and delivery reinforce the sexual undertone. Charles begins with a drawn-out, unaccompanied "well," and then the horn section joins in, pushing the beat and acting as an "amen" chorus. He heightens the intensity with intricate vocal ornamentation known as melisma, which conveys a sense of emotional intensity by bending and altering the pitches of notes, and at times his voice soars into a transcendent falsetto.

Charles collaborated with Quincy Jones on two important albums, *The Genius* (1959) for Atlantic and *Genius+Soul=Jazz* (1961) for Impulse! Records, a subsidiary of ABC-Paramount Records. In 1960 he signed with ABC-Paramount and recorded his best-loved hit, a version of Hoagy Carmichael's "Georgia On My Mind" (1960) that in 1979 became the official song of the state of Georgia.

During the 1960s Charles branched out into other musical styles, including country and western, such as "Your Cheatin' Heart" (1962), and middle-of-the-road pop music, such as "You Are My Sunshine" (1962); he even released a rendition of the Beatles' "Eleanor Rigby" (1968). He won a following that crossed racial lines, but his long-time fans lamented that some of this later work lacked the inspiration and edge of his Atlantic recordings. In 1961 he organized a successful big band that included such blues-grounded jazz players as David "Fathead" Newman.

During the 1980s Charles achieved the status of popular-culture icon. In 1986 he was one of the first inductees in the Rock and Roll Hall of Fame. Two years later, he provided the voice-over for a television commercial for the California Raisin Advisory Board, and in 1990 he appeared in a series of Diet Coke commercials that won accolades from the advertising industry and an enthusiastic response from the American public. Charles currently records for Quincy Jones's Qwest Records.

James Clyde Sellman

See Also

Soul Music; Blues, The; Cole, Nat ("King"); Jones, Quincy Delight, Jr.; Los Angeles, California.

Charlie Parker. Please see Parker, Charles Christopher ("Bird")

North America

Chase-Riboud, Barbara Dewayne **(b. June 26, 1939, Philadelphia, Pa.), African American writer and sculptor whose work reflects Asian and African influences.**

The daughter of Vivian and Charles Chase, Barbara Chase-Riboud won her first art prize at age 8. At 15 she won a *Seventeen* magazine award, and her prize-winning print was purchased by the Museum of Modern Art in New York. She received a B.F.A. from Temple University in 1957, and spent the next year in Rome and Egypt on a John Hay Whitney Foundation Fellowship. She received an M.F.A. from Yale University in 1960.

In 1961 Chase-Riboud married a French photojournalist, and she traveled with him throughout Europe, Asia, and Africa. Her drawings and sculpture began to include significant African and Asian influences. She was also influenced by struggles for civil rights and freedom in the United States and Africa. By the late 1960s her sculpture had been exhibited across the world.

Chase-Riboud's honors include a National Endowment for the Humanities fellowship in 1973, the Academic of Italy award in 1978, and an honorary doctorate from Temple in 1981. In 1974 she published her first book of poetry. Subsequently, she published several more volumes of poetry and novels, and as a writer is best known for her 1979 novel *Sally Hemings*, a historical romance about Thomas Jefferson and his slave mistress. *Sally Hemings* won the Janet Heidinger Kafka Prize for the best novel written by an American woman. In the mid-1990s Chase-Riboud relocated to Paris and Rome.

Lisa Clayton Robinson

Latin America and the Caribbean

Chauvet, Marie **(b. September 16, 1916, Port-au-Prince, Haiti; d. June 19, 1973, New York, N.Y.), a writer and playwright whose novel *Amour, colère et folie* places her alongside Jacques Roumain and Jacques Stéphen Alexis as one of Haiti's most eminent novelists.**

Born to a mother from St. Thomas (*see* Virgin Islands) and a Haitian father, Chauvet studied at l'Annexe de l'Ecole d'Institutrices in the 1930s before beginning to write. Her first play, *La légende des fleurs*, was performed in 1946. A production of *Samba* followed in 1947. *La légende des fleurs* was published in 1949 under the pseudonym Colibri. Between 1954 and 1970, Chauvet published four novels. *Fille d'Haiti*, published in 1954, won the Prix de l'Alliance Française. *La danse sur le volcan* followed in 1957, and *Fonds des Nègres*, which received the Prix France Antilles, was published in 1960. *Amour, colère et folie* was published in 1968. Her last complete novel, *Les rapaces,* was published posthumously in 1986. Chauvet was writing a novel titled *Fils d'Ogoun* at the time of her death.

Her best-known work, *Amour, colère et folie,* consists of three self-reflective stories originally conceived of as separate novels. With Haiti's Duvalier regime of the 1950s and 1960s as a backdrop, the novel depicts a world in which politics, eroticism, and violence merge. The first fictional account of the Duvalier regime, it is also one of the first Haitian novels to be written in the first-person narrative style. The critic Marie-Denise Shelton writes that "this work constitutes in the context of Haitian literature a turning point. In it, Chauvet defines a new aesthetic space, [a kind of writing] which blends realism, oneirism, and the fantastic" (*see* LITERATURE, FRENCH LANGUAGE, IN CARIBBEAN).

She was affiliated with Haiti Littéraire, a group of writers in Haiti that emerged in the early 1960s. Haiti Littéraire distanced itself from NÉGRITUDE and from a literature of protest to consider the problem of literary creation in more individualistic and psychological terms in response to what some members saw as the Duvalier regime's cooptation of the ideas contained within Négritude. Despite its remoteness from more radical politics of opposition, the movement was quickly stifled in the repression of the Duvalier regime; many of its members went into exile or were effectively silenced.

Chauvet's work has sometimes been criticized for reflecting a middle-class sensibility; for containing female characters who do not conform to Haitian mores; and for denouncing the Duvalier government. This last criticism led to Chauvet's exile and to the banning of *Amour, colère et folie* for a number of years in Haiti. Chauvet spent some time in Paris (*see* FRANCE) before settling in New York City, where she continued writing until she died of a cerebral hemorrhage in 1973. Her novels have been classified in a variety of ways: as sentimental, historical, nationalistic, or psychological. They have recently become the subject of growing critical attention.

Danielle Georges

SEE ALSO

Duvalier, François; New York, New York; Port-au-Prince, Haiti.

North America

Chavis, Benjamin Franklin, Jr.

(Chavis Muhammad) (b. January 22, 1948, Oxford, N.C.), Nation of Islam minister who helped organize the MILLION MAN MARCH; former executive director of the NATIONAL ASSOCIATION FOR THE ADVANCEMENT OF COLORED PEOPLE (NAACP); and long-time civil rights organizer.

Civil rights activist and former NAACP director Benjamin Chavis has said that "the struggle for freedom, the struggle for justice, was a part of my family roots even before I was born." Chavis, who grew up in North Carolina, became an NAACP member at age 12. At age 14 he joined the Southern Christian Leadership Conference (SCLC), and while in college at the University of North Carolina at Charlotte, he became the North Carolina SCLC coordinator. After his 1969 graduation he continued his civil rights work at the Washington office of the Commission for Racial Justice, an organization sponsored by the United Church of Christ, in which Chavis became an ordained minister.

In 1971 Chavis went to Wilmington, North Carolina, to help a student group protest discrimination. The action culminated in a week-long riot in which a black church was fired upon and a white grocery store burned down. Along with nine others, Chavis was convicted of arson and conspiracy in 1972. Although groups such as Amnesty International called the Wilmington Ten political prisoners, Chavis eventually served four years before his conviction was overturned by a federal court in 1980.

While in prison, Chavis began advanced theological study, and after his release, he was able to complete a doctorate at HOWARD UNIVERSITY. In 1986 he became executive director of the Commission for Racial Justice, where he worked to publicize what he called "environmental racism" – the practice of locating hazardous dumps near minority neighborhoods. He held the position until leaving for the NAACP.

Chavis served as executive director of the NAACP from April 1993 to August 1994 in a tenure that was as controversial as it was brief. In an effort to expand membership, Chavis reached out to NATION OF ISLAM leader Louis Farrakhan – for whom he went to work soon after leaving the NAACP – thus inspiring fear and worry among some NAACP members that the venerable institution would abandon its integrationist tradition in favor of a more militant, separatist identity. Chavis also attracted criticism for some of his other actions, such as hosting a "gang summit" in an effort to end black-on-black youth violence. Chavis was forced to resign after it was revealed that he had used NAACP funds to pay an out-of-court settlement in a sexual harassment case.

Chavis remained close to Farrakhan and other Nation of Islam leaders, and helped organize the 1995 Million Man March. Three years after his resignation from the NAACP Chavis joined the Nation of Islam, adopted the name Chavis Muhammad, and began a new career as a Muslim minister.

Kate Tuttle

SEE ALSO

Farrakhan, Louis Abdul; Southern Christian Leadership Conference.

North America

Chavis, John

(b. 1763, Granville, N.C.; d. June 13, 1838, N.C.), African American educator and minister who made great strides in the education of both black and white students in the South during the early nineteenth century.

Though most blacks in North Carolina were enslaved at the time, the Chavis family was legally free. Because he was free, John Chavis was able to pursue an education, helping him overcome the social and political oppression that thwarted most blacks of his time.

Chavis attended Washington and Lee University in Lexington, Virginia, graduating with high honors in 1801. His academic performance at Washington and Lee attracted much public attention because it contradicted the widespread belief that blacks were intellectually inferior to whites.

When he returned to North Carolina in 1808, Chavis founded a school for the children of white slave owners. The school proved extremely successful, and many of the students became highly influential citizens. In addition to teaching white students, Chavis taught the children of both enslaved and free blacks at night. His commitment to educating blacks greatly improved the social condition of the black community long before the abolition of slavery in 1865. A dedicated opponent of slavery, Chavis was an influential civil rights leader in the South. The circumstances surrounding his death remain unclear, although many suspect that he was murdered because of his work to better the lives of blacks.

SEE ALSO

Slavery in the United States; Free Blacks in the United States, 1619 to 1863.

North America

Checker, Chubby

(b. October 3, 1941, South Carolina), singer best known for his hit song "The Twist."

Born Ernest Evans, Chubby Checker grew up in PHILADELPHIA, PENNSYLVANIA, and worked plucking chickens in a poultry market. He first gained attention singing with the Quantrells on street corners in the evenings. His supervisor at work was impressed with his voice and introduced him to producers at the Cameo-Parkway label, where he was signed in 1959. One of his first songs, "The Class," reached the Top 40 later that year and led to an appearance on the Philadelphia dance show American Bandstand, hosted by Dick Clark. Clark's wife suggested that Evans change his name to Chubby Checker to model Fats Domino, a popular blues singer.

Renamed, Checker got a break when Hank Ballard failed to appear for the American Bandstand session and Checker played Ballard's song "The Twist." The song quickly reached number one on the pop charts, and sold over 3 million records. This television appearance started a nationwide dance craze. Checker went on to record 20 Top 40 hits by 1964, including "Pony Time," "Slow Twisting," and "Limbo Rock." His song "Let's Twist Again" was also a hit in Great Britain and sold even more copies there than the original.

Although he was never able to achieve that level of success again, Checker broadened his music to include RHYTHM AND BLUES, disco, and RAP. He also made several appearances on television and in movies demonstrating the twist. He continues to perform with his band, the Wildcats.

Africa

Cheetah, the fastest ground animal on earth, able to attain speeds of up to about 110 km per hour (about 68 mph).

Cheetah is the common name for a large cat belonging to the family Felidae, and classified as *Acinonyx jubatus*. The cheetah lives mainly in Africa, but small populations exist in Iran and northwestern Afghanistan. It weighs about the same as the leopard (50 to 60 kg/110 to 130 lb) but has a longer body, much longer legs, and a smaller head. The head and body, without the tail, are about 1.1 to 1.5 m (about 3.6 to 4.9 ft) long. The cheetah's short claws lack the sheath that covers retracted claws in other cat species, and its coat is yellowish-brown with black spots.

Female cheetahs are solitary animals except when raising their cubs. Mature males generally travel alone or in associations of two to three males, often siblings, joining females only to mate. A cheetah hunts by running rather than by leaping from ambush, as with the leopard. It hunts by day and by sight rather than by smell, concentrating on smaller game, such as Thomson's gazelle.

Formerly trained and used for hunting in Asia, LIBYA, and India, the cheetah is now extinct or endangered in much of its range. Even in Africa, where it still roams over a wide range of habitats, including open plains, woodlands, and mountainous regions, the cheetah is an endangered species. Scientists estimate that between 9000 and 12,000 still exist in the wild. One of the main threats to cheetah survival is habitat loss, but many cheetahs are also killed each year to protect livestock, or for sport. In addition, other carnivores, lions and hyenas particularly, prey on cheetah cubs, further lowering their numbers.

Because of extensive inbreeding in the wild, the cheetah is one of the least genetically diverse mammals. Genetic variation between cheetahs is so low that a given animal will not recognize the difference when a tissue graft from another cheetah surgically replaces its own tissue. These low levels of diversity make the cheetah species extremely vulnerable to disease and threaten its ultimate survival. Scientists hope to use modern captive breeding programs to increase genetic diversity in the species.

Robert Fay

SEE ALSO
Hyena; Lion.

Cross Cultural

Chemistry

From traditional African medicines to black participation in today's cutting-edge research, Africans and African Americans have a long history of innovation and discovery in chemistry, but only recently have their achievements been recognized.

Understanding the properties of substances and how to make practical use of them is the essence of chemistry, whether or not the study takes place in a formal laboratory. Today, mainstream scientists are finally acknowledging the efficacy of so-called folk medicines and other formulations devised and used for centuries by traditional practitioners throughout the world, including Africans and African Americans. From these folk practices in early African cultures to the "kitchen physick" of American slaves to achievements in the modern fields of physical, organic, nuclear, and analytical chemistry, Africans and African Americans have a long history of innovation and discovery in chemistry.

The development of plant medicine in Africa indicates a strong understanding of natural chemistry. Many African cultures used natural versions of aspirin, kaolin (an effective cure for diarrhea), and herbal treatments for skin infections. Even before they were exposed to Western science and medicine, African doctors had discovered effective herbal remedies for several diseases; the Zulus alone had found medicinal application for over 700 plants.

Africans brought their scientific knowledge with them to America, and during the slavery period, several emerged as experts in healing and medicine. In 1729 Lieutenant-Governor William Gooch of Virginia described a slave who "performed many wonderful cures of diseases [with]... a concoction of roots and bark.... " These folk remedies were similar to the kitchen physick, or household medicine, widely practiced by whites in colonial America.

Following the abolition of slavery, African Americans began to earn mainstream respect for their work in the laboratories of modern science. In the late nineteenth century, GEORGE WASHINGTON CARVER, the son of slaves, emerged as a pioneer in agricultural research. While working at Booker T. Washington's Tuskegee Institute, Carver found dozens of uses for chemicals he extracted from peanuts and potatoes; his research led to the development of hundreds of products, including shampoo, ink, and peanut butter. Carver later became a vocal advocate of growing peanuts as a source of protein.

During the twentieth century, several African American chemists achieved renown for their contributions. Lloyd A. Hall, former director, chief chemist, and president of the Griffith Chemical Company, discovered important food preservatives. Percy L. Julian, professor of organic chemistry at HOWARD UNIVERSITY and DePauw University, developed an inexpensive way to remove and prepare soybean protein for use in such products as cortisone, a drug used to treat arthritis, and physostigmine, an extract used in the treatment of glaucoma. Julian registered more than 130 chemical patents during the course of his career.

Other African American contributors to twentieth century chemistry include Warren Henry, a physical chemist who performed important research on superconductivity, magnetism, and small temperature changes in metal. Another leading chemist is Jane Wright, former director of the Cancer Research Foundation, who formulated several drugs and methods used in fighting cancer, including mithramycin, a drug that has proved promising in lab tests. William A. Lester Jr. gained renown as a theoretical chemist whose research focused on the problems of high-velocity molecular collisions and who later was chosen to manage the National Resource for Computation in Chemistry. James A. Harris helped to discover two chemical elements, rutherfordium (element 104) and hahnium (element 105).

Since 1916, when St. Elmo Brady became the first African American to earn a Ph.D. in chemistry, blacks have played an increasingly important role in American chemistry laboratories and lecture halls, although there are still disproportionately fewer African Americans in chemistry than in other academic disciplines. The number of black chemists is slowly increasing, however; data indicate that African Americans comprise nearly 4 percent of Ph.D. students in chemistry.

SEE ALSO
Slavery in the United States; Zulu; Abolitionism in the United States; Folk Medicine; Julian, Percy Lavon; Tuskegee University; Washington, Booker Taliaferro.

North America

Chesnutt, Charles Waddell (b. June 20, 1858, Cleveland, Ohio; d. November 15, 1932, Cleveland, Ohio), pioneering African American writer known especially for his short stories, which realistically depicted black life.

Charles W. Chesnutt was one of the first African American writers to become a mainstream success by portraying realistically the complexities of African American experience. In the process, he was unusually honest about the problems inherent in that experience, and his stories remain valuable for their descriptions of nineteenth-century black culture and attitudes.

Chesnutt's parents were mixed-race free blacks who had emigrated to Ohio but moved back south to Fayetteville, North Carolina, shortly after his birth. Chesnutt grew up during RECONSTRUCTION in relative privilege for an African American, and although he had a reputation for being largely self-taught, he attended a school founded by the Freedmen's Bureau. After working as a schoolteacher and then a principal in Southern schools during his late teens and early twenties, Chesnutt decided that he was too stifled by Southern racism and returned to the North to expand his opportunities.

In 1884 he settled back in Cleveland and began studying law, ultimately passing the bar exam and beginning a career as a legal stenographer. But Chesnutt had already begun writing short fiction, which was published in several local magazines and newspapers. In 1887 his first major story, "The Goophered Grapevine," was published in the *Atlantic Monthly*. It featured Uncle Julius McAdoo, a North Carolina ex-slave, telling stories about plantation life, and was rich in the descriptions of African American folk culture and "voudou" beliefs that came to characterize many of Chesnutt's works. "The Goophered Grapevine" was praised by both black and white critics and brought the author to a national audience.

Chesnutt continued to publish individual stories, and in the late 1890s the mainstream Boston publisher Houghton Mifflin decided to collect his works in two volumes. *The Conjure Woman* appeared in March 1899, followed that fall by *The Wife of His Youth and Other Stories of the Color Line*. The stories in these books continue the exploration of hoodoo and magic begun in "The Goophered Grapevine," but they also deal with some of the phenomena peculiar to American race relations, especially the tangled family lines that were a result of slavery and MISCEGENATION. Chesnutt's tales attacked white prejudice and racism in their varied forms. But they also explored the "color line" drawn not only between whites and blacks, but also within the black race. His stories include serious considerations of skin color prejudice and the impulse to "pass," unusual subjects in the literature of the time. Both books were successful, and they made Chesnutt the best-known African American fiction writer of his time.

Encouraged by this success, Chesnutt began writing full-time, which gave him the opportunity to write longer works. His biography of FREDERICK DOUGLASS (1899) was well received, but he then began writing novels, which never found the widespread audience that his stories had. Three novels published between 1900 and 1905 sold poorly, and eventually Chesnutt resumed his full-time career as a stenographer. But his black audience did not forget his influence on AFRICAN AMERICAN LITERATURE. In 1928 the NATIONAL ASSOCIATION FOR THE ADVANCEMENT OF COLORED PEOPLE gave him the Spingarn Medal, its highest honor, for his "pioneer work as a literary artist depicting the life and struggles of Americans of Negro descent." Chesnutt's work remains in print, and *The Norton Anthology of African American Literature* calls him "the first writer to make the broad range of African American experience his artistic province and to consider practically every issue and problem endemic to the American color line worthy of literary attention."

Lisa Clayton Robinson

SEE ALSO

Slavery in the United States; Vodou; Bureau of Refugees, Freedmen and Abandoned Lands; Free Blacks in the United States, 1619 to 1863.

North America

Chess Records, an influential record company that recorded African American RHYTHM AND BLUES (R&B) and Chicago blues.

Chess Records had a profound impact on American popular culture, popularizing the Chicago blues of MUDDY WATERS and Howlin' Wolf, and – through the infectious music of Chuck Berry – providing a major catalyst for the rise of rock 'n' roll. Phillip and Leonard Chess were Polish Jews who settled in CHICAGO, ILLINOIS, and became involved in recording as an adjunct to their Macomba Lounge, a nightclub on Chicago's south side, the heart of the city's black community. They founded Chess in 1949-1950 as a successor to Aristocrat Records (1946-1949), which released the first recordings of Muddy Waters as a leader. For Chess, Waters produced several R&B hits, including "I'm Your Hoochie Coochie Man" (1953) and "I'm Ready" (1954). He also recommended a young Chuck Berry to the Chess brothers, and Berry's first release, "Maybelline" (1955), helped make rock 'n' roll the new youth music.

The Chess offices were in a street-level storefront. Music writer Arnold Shaw noted that the unassuming quarters made it easier for black musicians simply to walk in, as Bo DIDDLEY, Sonny Boy Williamson, and Willie Mabon did. Chess recordings, notorious for their muffled, boxy sound, were produced in the back room of the office. To add echo, the Chess brothers hung a microphone in the bathroom. The poor sound quality of Chess recordings – and the prospect of a stronger national distribution – led the Flamingos, a successful vocal harmony group, to leave Chess in 1956 for Decca.

Besides Chicago blues and rock 'n' roll, Chess released hit recordings by vocal groups, such as the Moonglows' "Sincerely" (1954) and the Flamingos' "I'll Be Home" (1956), and, between 1960 and 1963, a string of ten Top 10 R&B singles by ETTA JAMES. In 1969, when Leonard Chess died, his brother sold Chess Records. By the 1990s the massive Music Corporation of America (MCA) owned the label and its catalogue.

James Clyde Sellman

SEE ALSO

Berry, Charles Edward Anderson (Chuck); Blues, The; Howlin' Wolf; Williamson, Johnny Lee ("Sonny Boy").

Africa

Chewa, an ethnic group of 2 million who live predominantly in MALAWI.

The Chewa are the single largest ethnic group in Malawi, constituting about a quarter of the population. Many also live in eastern ZAMBIA and northwestern ZIMBABWE. Their ancestors were a splinter group of the Maravi, Bantu-speakers who originally migrated to the region from Katanga (in the present-day DEMOCRATIC REPUBLIC OF THE CONGO), perhaps in the thirteenth century.

The Chewa broke away from the Maravi Confederacy in the eighteenth century and settled to the west along the Bua, Luangwa, and Dwangwa rivers. Those Maravi who moved into the interior became the Chipeta ("savanna dwellers"). The remaining Maravi came to be called the Nyanja ("lakeside people"), a large group whose population in Malawi is second in size only to the Chewa. The Chewa language, Chichewa (or Chinyanja), is one of Malawi's two national languages, and is spoken by approximately 6 million people.

In the nineteenth century NGONI groups emigrated north into Chewa territory, fleeing ZULU expansion into their lands. YAO and Swahili slave traders also arrived. These more recent immigrants adopted the Chichewa language and gained control over Chewa and Nyanja settlements. Politically decentralized, their communities proved vulnerable to slave raiders, and during the height of the INDIAN OCEAN SLAVE TRADE in the late eighteenth and early nineteenth centuries, large numbers of Chewa were captured and sold. But slaves also figured significantly within Chewa society (*see* SLAVERY IN AFRICA).

Most rural Chewa grow sorghum and maize as staple food crops, relying on cash crops such as tobacco for income. Hunting and fishing are also important activities. Chewa society has traditionally been relatively egalitarian, and its matrilineal villages are governed by chiefs who rule as much by consensus as through decree. Clan exogamy is the rule; members of the Banda clan, for example, marry Phiri or Mwale. Although maternal uncles traditionally arranged marriages, young men and women today actively court one another. A newlywed man is expected to engage in bride-service, gardening for his in-laws for two years before receiving a plot of his own.

The Chewa's masked Nyau dances and secret societies, both subjects of considerable ethnographic study, remain vital parts of contemporary Chewa culture. Boys undergo rites of passage in early adolescence to initiate them into the all-male Nyau society. When missionaries arrived in the region in the late nineteenth century, they identified the Nyau dances as pagan rituals that needed to be eliminated. But the dances persisted as a means of expressing not only general discontent with the colonial regime, but also more specific resistance to European cultural incursion and Christian proselytizing. In contemporary Chewa society, Nyau beliefs and Christianity are seen as two distinct world-views, the former associated with customary rural life, the latter linked to urban lifestyles and the West.

Ari Nave

See Also

Dance in Sub-Saharan Africa; Languages, African: An Overview; Swahili People; Christianity: Missionaries in Africa.

North America

Chicago Defender, the largest black-owned daily newspaper in the United States and a catalyst for the Great Migration.

Chicago Defender founder Robert Sengstacke Abbott took from his father the notion that "... a good newspaper was one of the best instruments of service and one of the strongest weapons ever to be used in defense of a race which was deprived of its citizenship rights." In fact, Abbott named the paper the *Defender* because he intended to use its pages to fight discrimination, segregation, and disfranchisement.

Abbott, who graduated from Hampton Institute in Virginia, earned a law degree from Chicago's Kent College of Law in 1898. Unable to practice law because of racial discrimination, he turned to the trade he had learned at Hampton – printing – and with an initial investment of only $25, he wrote, printed, and sold his four-page weekly newspaper door-to-door.

The *Chicago Defender* differed from other black publications of the time; Abbott courted a popular audience rather than only the well-educated black readership. The newspaper combined muckraking and political reporting with sensational stories involving scandals, prostitution and gambling rings, and murder. But the *Chicago Defender* had its biggest influence in its role as African Americans' advocate and adviser in the South.

The paper's Northern location meant that it could safely report stories that Southern black papers, for fear of white retribution, could not. The *Chicago Defender* exposed the daily horrors that characterized the racist South, including police brutality, lynchings, and white economic exploitation of the disfranchised black population. In response to the lynching of blacks by white mobs, the *Defender* once advised: "When the Mob Comes and You Must Die Take at Least One With You."

Such defiant statements earned the paper intense loyalty among African Americans and antipathy among white Southerners who sought to prohibit its sale and distribution throughout the South. By 1916 the *Chicago Defender* had become the best-selling black newspaper in the United States, and had begun urging African Americans to leave the South for the prospects of economic advancement and relative freedom that the wartime economy made possible in the North.

African Americans responded. In large part because of the newspaper's encouragement, hundreds of thousands of blacks migrated North – substantially increasing Chicago's population and changing the character of the city – in a population shift that became known as the Great Migration. Many blacks turned to the *Chicago Defender* for assistance in making the trip North and then adjusting to urban life. The paper reacted by organizing clubs that provided lower cost rail fares for migrants and directed new arrivals to jobs, housing, and social service agencies.

By 1918 the paper's circulation had reached 125,000. Many of the gains in readership were lost during the Great Depression, however, and by 1935 circulation had fallen to 73,000. In 1939, the year before he died, Abbott appointed his nephew, John Sengstacke, publisher. Sengstacke saw circulation numbers rise to 160,000 by 1945. In the following decades the paper lost readership because of the emerging electronic media, and because mainstream publications began to cover black issues. Sengstacke largely followed the editorial course of his uncle, arguing for social and economic equality for African Americans. The paper criticized the Civil Rights Act of 1964, for example, because it did not address discrimination and inequality in the North. The paper reverted to being a local Chicago publication (by 1980 the *Chicago Defender*'s circulation was approximately 20,000), although it continued to cover both local and national news and to advocate for fair housing, employment, and educational policies.

Sengstacke died on May 28, 1997, leaving the future of the *Chicago Defender* uncertain. In January 1998 the executors of his estate put the paper up for sale. Media observers speculated that the *Chicago Defender* could be sold to white investors. Many in the black community expressed disapproval and disappointment at that prospect, fearing the loss of what they saw as an authentic and unique African American voice.

Robert Fay

See Also

Press, Black, in the United States; Great Migration, The; Hampton University; Lynching.

North America

Chicago, Illinois

According to Pottawattomie Indians in the early nineteenth century, "The first white man to settle at Chickagou was a Negro." Jean Baptiste Pointe du Sable, an Afro-French trader, began the settlement of Chicago in approximately 1790.

In only 50 years, as Chicago became an important center of commerce for the grain and livestock trades, a vital African American community developed along the banks of the Chicago River. Composed of fugitive slaves fleeing the South and a small number of free blacks, the community acted in defiance of the Illinois Black Code, which required all African Americans to carry a certificate of freedom and post a $1000 bond. Together with white abolitionists, the black community vigorously protested against slavery, resettled more fugitive slaves from the South, and established important links on the Underground Railroad. By the outbreak of the Civil War, approximately 1000 blacks were living in Chicago.

Between 1875 and 1893, as Chicago industrialized, the black population increased from 5000 to 15,000, and the African American community organized into its own neighborhood and institutions in the "Black Belt," a 3-by-15-block area on the south side of the city. Unless they were used as strikebreakers, most African Americans were restricted from industrial and skilled labor jobs. Nonetheless, a middle class and a small, well-educated elite class emerged as the African American community established businesses, churches, women's social clubs, gambling houses, and dance halls. In 1871 John Jones was elected county commissioner, the first black public official. In 1876 J. W. E. Thomas became the first black state representative from Chicago. The first African American newspaper, the *Conservator*, was founded in 1878. By the end of the century, the African American elite had begun to speak out forcefully against racial injustice. Ida Wells-Barnett, the most outspoken member of the Afro-American Council, strongly attacked lynching as well as Booker T. Washington's conciliatory policies toward racial inequality.

Chicago's African American population increased dramatically between 1890 and 1920, when many African Americans moved north to find better jobs and to flee widespread racial violence. By 1910 the black population in Chicago had reached 40,000 among 2 million inhabitants; by 1920 it was 80,000, and a second, smaller black neighborhood had developed on the West Side. The community developed its own institutions, including a hospital, a training school for nurses, lodges, a bank, a YMCA settlement house, and branches of the National Negro Business League, the NAACP, and the Federated Women's Clubs. In 1905 Robert Abbott founded the *Chicago Defender* newspaper. Passionate in its call for racial justice and equal rights, the newspaper nonetheless honored Booker T. Washington. In 1915 Oscar De Priest became Chicago's first black alderman.

Labor shortages during World War I finally brought black workers into the industrial workforce, especially in the meatpacking houses, railway car companies, and steel mills. As the community expanded in size and wealth, white neighborhoods around the Black Belt tried to contain it through legal restrictions. In the workplace, many unions maintained segregated locals. During an economic crisis in the summer of 1919, a race riot broke out, characterized by mobs of young white men indiscriminately attacking African Americans in the Black Belt. Thirty-eight people died, 537 were injured, and 1000 persons were left homeless, the overwhelming majority of them black.

The prosperity of the 1920s produced a political and cultural rebirth comparable to that in Harlem. Black politicians were elected to citywide offices and the state legislature. In 1928 Republican Oscar De Priest became the first black elected to the United States House of Representatives since RECONSTRUCTION. In art, the painter Archibald Motley was nationally recognized for his portrayals of city life. Richmond Barthé became well known for his sculpture and paintings of life in Haiti. OSCAR MICHEAUX formed the Micheaux Film Corporation and produced pioneering "race movies."

The community also nurtured a prolific jazz scene that included New Orleans expatriate Ferdinand "Jelly Roll" Morton in the immediate postwar years. In 1921 cornetist Joseph "King" Oliver also arrived from New Orleans, where his band fused a polyphonic style with the melodic traditions of Chicago's cabarets and dance halls. Louis Armstrong developed his solo, improvisational style with Oliver and with his own Hot Five Band, as did pianist Earl "Fatha" Hines with Jimmy Noone's orchestra. They were often accompanied by vocalists ALBERTA HUNTER and ETHEL WATERS.

In the Depression, African Americans suffered more severely from joblessness and poverty than any other group in Chicago. Grassroots activism sparked support of black businesses and boycotts of those employers who did not hire black workers. But the overall political strength of the community lost out to a rising Democratic party machine. The New Deal, unionization, and World War II eventually sparked a recovery that placed African Americans in union jobs and led to the founding of the NEGRO AMERICAN LABOR COUNCIL. While not legal, segregation remained a fact of life.

A new generation of writers and musicians developed between the Depression and the 1950s. RICHARD WRIGHT, Gwendolyn Brooks, Willard Motley and MARGARET WALKER represented, in stark and eloquent terms, their views of urban black life and of an unrepentant racism in America. Beginning with Hudson "Tampa Red" Whitaker in 1928, Chicago developed a blues tradition rooted in the acoustical style of the Mississippi Delta musicians; in the 1930s and 1940s, Chicago blues evolved under Big Bill Broonzy into the amplified, hard-driving electric style identified with HOWLIN' WOLF, Arthur "Big Boy" Crudup, and MUDDY WATERS.

In the 1940s and 1950s, blacks had once again migrated in enormous numbers from the South. The South Side community tried to expand but met with both legal and violent opposition. The Chicago Housing Authority responded by abandoning neighborhood and racial integration in favor of high-rise housing projects amid the black community, earning Chicago a reputation as the most residentially segregated city in the United States. By 1962 civil rights groups had formed the Coordinating Council of Community Organizations (CCCO) to integrate housing and schools. In 1966 Martin Luther King Jr. and CCCO launched the Chicago Freedom Movement to push for open housing. Its demonstrations and marches produced only minimal results, but it was one of the first attempts to integrate Northern cities during the civil rights era. Jesse Jackson's OPERATION BREADBASKET, aimed at improving employment in the black community, had more success, but the modest improvement from both efforts led to despair and ultimately to devastating riots in 1966 and 1968.

The Black Nationalist Movement was one response to that devastation. Founded in 1967, the Organization of Black American Culture (OBAC) became an important institution in the BLACK ARTS MOVEMENT. More militant, political elements of the black community, however, were forcefully crushed. Chicago police raided the offices of the Black Panthers chapter on December 4, 1969, and shot to death chapter president Fred Hampton and Mark Clark. An independent commission called the dawn raid an act of "official violence," and the episode came to symbolize for many the intense opposition to black political power.

In 1983 a coalition succeeded in electing HAROLD WASHINGTON the first black mayor of Chicago. Often undermined by a hostile city council, Washington began to improve conditions and unite the African American community but died unexpectedly in 1988. His coalition soon dissolved into its constituent parts.

Today, deteriorating housing projects, an impoverished and overwhelmed public school system, high unemployment, and crime ravage the African American community on the South and West Sides it has occupied for generations. Some middle- to upper-class African American neighborhoods, however, have developed into influential constituencies of Chicago's African American and larger urban community.

Jim Mendelsohn

POPULATION OF CHICAGO 1840-1990

Year	Total Population	Black Population	% Black
1840	4,470	53	1.19
1850	29,963	323	1.08
1860	109,260	955	0.87
1870	298,977	3,562	1.19
1880	503,185	6,480	1.29
1890	1,099,850	14,271	1.30
1900	1,698,575	30,150	1.78
1910	2,185,283	44,103	2.02
1920	2,701,705	109,458	4.05
1930	3,376,438	233,903	6.93
1940	3,396,808	277,731	8.18
1950	3,620,962	492,265	13.59
1960	3,550,404	812,637	22.89
1970	3,366,957	1,102,620	32.75
1980	3,005,072	1,197,174	39.84
1990	2,783,726	1,087,711	39.07

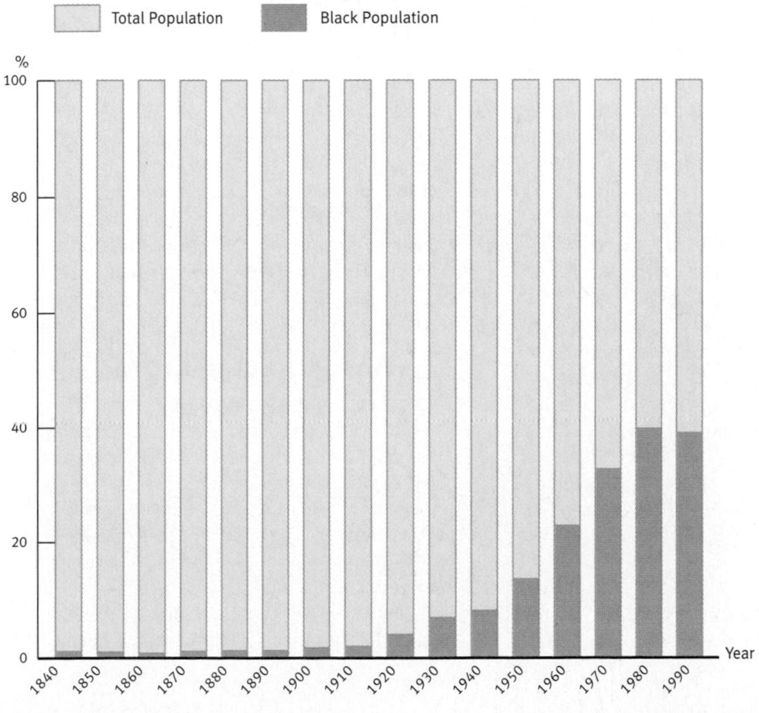

See Also

Armstrong, Louis ("Satchmo"); Barthé, Richmond; Black Panther Party; Brooks, Gwendolyn Elizabeth; Broonzy, William Lee Conley ("Big Bill"); *Chicago Defender*; DePriest, Oscar Stanton; Harlem, New York; Great Depression; Jackson, Jesse Louis; Hines, Earl Kenneth ("Fatha"); King, Martin Luther, Jr.; Morton, Ferdinand Joseph ("Jelly Roll"); Oliver, Joseph ("King"); Abbott, Robert Sengstacke; Washington, Booker Taliaferro; Wells-Barnett, Ida Bell.

North America

Chicago Riots of 1919, one of the largest American race riots during the Red Summer of 1919, inflamed by segregation and police discrimination.

In July 1919, Chicago, Illinois, erupted in a race riot that left 23 blacks and 15 whites dead, 537 people injured, and over a million dollars of property damage. One of 25 race riots that swept through the country during the Red Summer of 1919, the conflict in Chicago was galvanized, as historian William M. Tuttle Jr. has pointed out, by "gut-level animosities" between the city's white and black residents, for whom competition for residential housing and good union jobs had inflamed racial tensions.

Between 1910 and 1920 the population of the "Black Belt" on the south side of Chicago had almost tripled, while the perimeter of the neighborhood had remained relatively the same. Under the pressure of the Great Migration north, the conditions and quality of inner-city living declined drastically, with the black newcomers facing a mortality rate twice that of whites. Meanwhile, middle-class African Americans were making their way into previously all-white neighborhoods. For many, leaving squalid, overcrowded ghettos and seeking better jobs was an expression of the pride and self-respect forged in the crucible of World War I. These upwardly mobile families were often targeted by community-organized white violence directed at keeping the lines of segregation intact. Between 1917 and 1919, 26 bombs exploded at black residences in Chicago's white neighborhoods.

Adding to the racial antipathy that led to the riots were historic conflicts over labor. For decades the mostly white unions representing workers in Chicago's stockyards had excluded black workers; denied membership, blacks had often allowed themselves to be

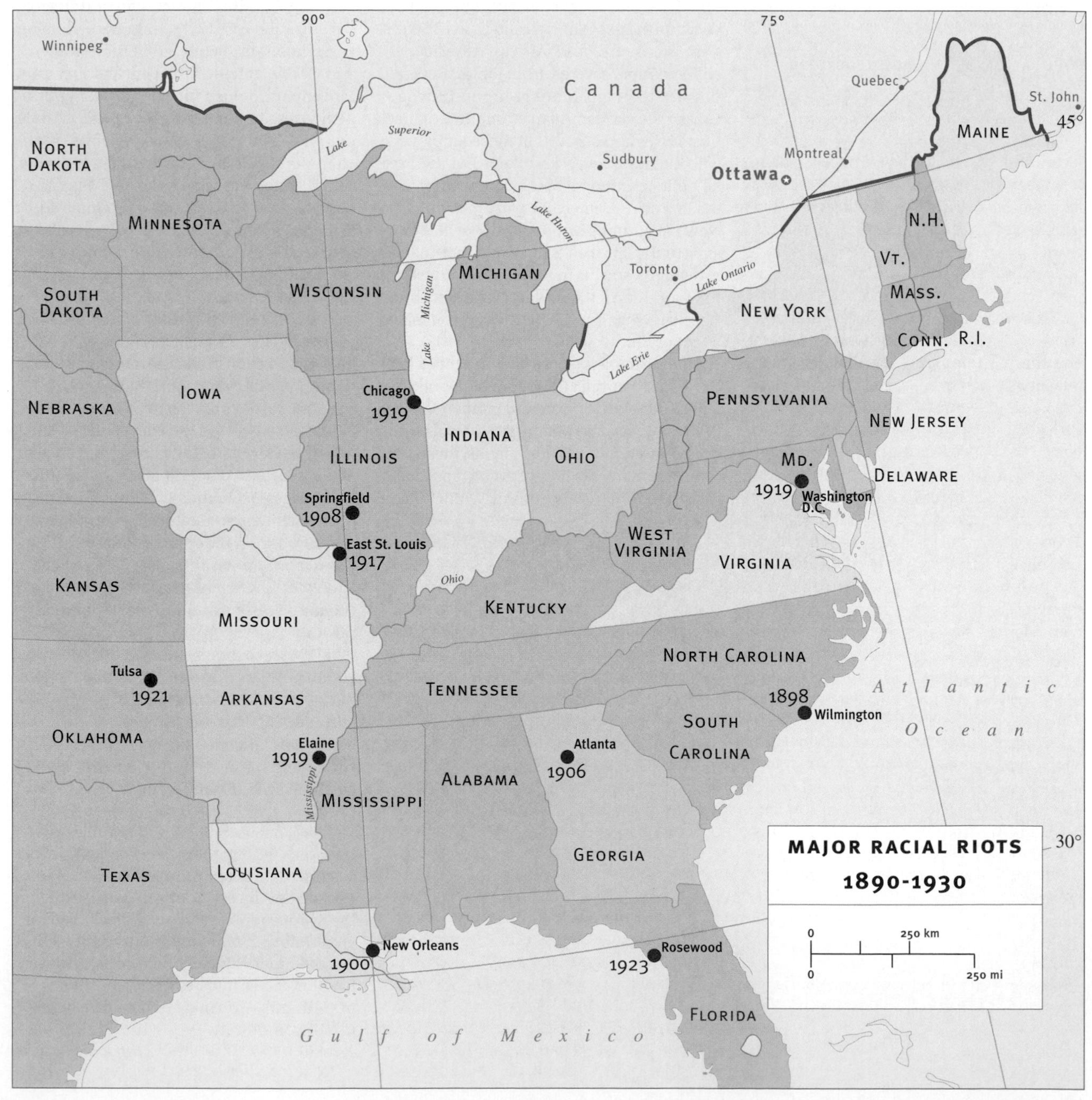

used as replacement labor during strikes. Despite some positive movement toward integration of labor unions, by the summer of 1919, most white workers were unionized and most black workers were not, and attitudes of resentment and mistrust had hardened on both sides.

The spark that finally ignited this overheated atmosphere came on July 27, 1919, when a 17-year-old African American, Eugene Williams, swam over the invisible line of racial segregation at the 29th Street Beach. An angry mob of whites stoned him as he swam in, and Williams drowned. When the police were called in, they refused to arrest any of the whites who had been seen throwing stones, and instead arrested one African American. A fight broke out between a growing crowd of blacks on one side and the police and whites on the other. Soon the riot overflowed from the beach, sweeping out into the rest of the city.

Over the next week, violence raged through Chicago. White workingmen attacked their black counterparts as they entered the stockyards. On both sides of the color line, gangs of youth attacked those who crossed the lines of segregated neighborhoods. The damage to property was extensive, especially in black sections, with thousands of African Americans left homeless. In addition, in a summer already marked by an unprecedented number of strikes, many workers stayed home as the rioting continued, bringing some industries and services to a near standstill.

As the violence continued, Chicago mayor William H. Thompson asked Illinois governor Frank O. Lowden to mobilize the state militia, but for reasons that are still unclear did not deploy the 3500 troops until July 30, when there had already been dozens of deaths and hundreds of casualties. Before then the Chicago police, overburdened and often racist themselves – seven black men had been shot by the police, but no whites – had been solely responsible for containing the violence. The killing was over by August 8, the day the militia were recalled. But despite calls for calm by African American organizations, including the NATIONAL URBAN LEAGUE, the NATIONAL ASSOCIATION FOR THE ADVANCEMENT OF COLORED PEOPLE (NAACP), and the Negro YMCA, tensions – especially on the stockyard floor – remained.

In the wake of the rioting, Governor Lowden appointed the Chicago Commission on Race Relations. Its groundbreaking 1922 report, *The Negro in Chicago*, warned that segregation and discrimination in labor and housing would continue to prove fertile grounds for violence.

Marian Aguiar

SEE ALSO

World War I and African Americans; Chicago, Illinois; Great Migration, The; Jim Crow.

Mounted police lead away an African American man during the Chicago riots of 1919. Labor and housing tensions were major causes of the violence. *CORBIS*

Latin America and the Caribbean

Chico Rei

(b. 1717, Quibango, kingdom of Congo [near present-day Kinshasa, DEMOCRATIC REPUBLIC OF THE CONGO]; d. 1774, Ouro Preto, MINAS GERAIS, BRAZIL), an African king sold into slavery in Brazil during the eighteenth century who worked to buy his own freedom and then the freedom of all his tribe.

In the late seventeenth century, gold was discovered in the area that is now the Brazilian state of Minas Gerais, triggering an inundation of gold prospectors from the surrounding provinces and Portugal. They brought large numbers of African slaves with them to extract the precious metal and began importing slaves from Africa's Gold Coast (present-day GHANA and the surrounding countries), a region known for its advanced mining activities. By 1720 the city of Ouro Preto had become the center of gold mining in Minas Gerais. This was the destination of the African king Chico Rei and many members of his tribe.

Chico Rei was originally named Galanga. He was the king of a small Congolese tribe of some 200 people in present-day Democratic Republic of the Congo. Around 1740 he and his tribe were taken prisoner by Portuguese slave traders and sold into slavery in Minas Gerais. Before leaving Africa, a Portuguese Catholic priest baptized the captives and gave them new names: Maria for the women, Francisco for the men. While en route to Brazil, the Portuguese slave traders noticed that many of the slaves looked to King Galanga for leadership. As a result, his name became Chico Rei – *Chico* being a shortened version of Francisco, and *Rei* being Portuguese for "king."

Many members of Chico Rei's tribe, including his wife and some of his children, died during the Middle Passage. Upon the ship's arrival in Brazil, barely more than a hundred members of the tribe were still alive. They were sold to the owner of the Encardadeira mine near Ouro Preto, in Minas Gerais.

During the eighteenth century in Minas Gerais, slaves often smuggled small amounts of gold out of the mines by hiding it in their hair, between their toes, in their ears, or in their mouth. They also took advantage of off-days, which included Sundays and a number of Catholic holidays, to work for themselves and save toward buying their *cartas de alforria* (manumission documents). In this way, over the course of five or six years, members of Chico Rei's tribe accumulated enough gold to purchase their king's freedom. Maintaining their tribal bonds, they then continued to pool their profits from autonomous work and smuggling and were eventually able to purchase the freedom of the prince, his wife, and then the princess.

At the same time, Chico Rei was working to free the remaining enslaved members of his tribe. After seeking assistance from the black brotherhood Nossa Senhora do Rosário, he became owner of a mine. His master sold the Encardadeira mine to him when its production decreased, and little by little, Chico Rei and the liberated members of his tribe collected enough gold to buy the freedom of all of those still enslaved.

While working to free all of his tribe, Chico

Rei was also making plans to construct a church for Ouro Preto's black population. Even those slaves who had been converted to Catholicism were generally not allowed to attend worship services at white churches. With the gold that had been extracted from his mine and with smuggled contributions from local slaves, Chico Rei built up a fund for the church's construction, which began after he secured the approval of colonial officials. The building of the Igreja Nossa Senhora Santa Efigênia no Alto Cruz (Our Lady of Saint Efigênia of the High Cross, one of the patron saints of the slaves) lasted some 30 years and involved the artistic collaboration of the famous mulatto sculptor Antônio Francisco ("Aleijadinho") Lisboa.

Chico Rei's legacy goes beyond the Church of Saint Efigênia. Some trace the beginnings of the coronation festival known as the Reisado do Rosário to Chico Rei. During the eighteenth century, this occasion drew large numbers of free and enslaved blacks and featured regal processions, African music and dance, and, most important, the crowning of a black king and queen. Originally held on January 6, the Reisado do Rosário spread throughout Brazil and eventually evolved into the modern-day congada celebration.

Chico Rei achieved legendary status among the slaves and earned the respect of the Portuguese slaveholders. Unlike the many slaves who took freedom into their own hands by escaping and joining fugitive slave colonies known as *quilombos*, Chico Rei pursued freedom within the legal constraints by paying for the liberty of each one of his former tribe members, who formed a colony of free blacks. Yet, despite his contributions and uniqueness as a freedom fighter, Chico Rei remains relatively unknown among Afro-Brazilian heroes.

Aaron Myers

See Also

Middle Passage, The; Catholic Church in Latin America and the Caribbean; Maroonage in the Americas; Religious Brotherhoods in Latin America.

North America

Children's Literature, African American, **literature by African American authors intended for children and young adults.**

In 1919 the African American intellectual W. E. B. Du Bois announced his plans to coedit a new magazine, *The Brownies' Book*, intended especially for black children. In his announcement, Du Bois outlined three main purposes for the new publication: "(a) To make colored children realize that being colored is a normal, beautiful thing. (b) To make them familiar with the history and achievements of the Negro race. (c) To make them know that other colored children have grown into beautiful, useful and famous persons."

Du Bois understood that black children needed literature of their own that would offer these lessons, which could not be found in mainstream children's literature. *The Brownies' Book* was unusual for its time, but in the decades that followed more and more black authors – including some of the best-known writers of African American literature – wrote books that teach the same three messages to black children and young adult readers.

There had been a few earlier attempts at publishing books and magazines specifically for black children. In 1887 the black writer Amelia Etta Johnson briefly edited the magazine *Joy*. Eight years later Paul Laurence Dunbar, the most famous black poet of his time, published *Little Brown Baby*, a volume of children's verse. Several other books followed, including Silas X. Floyd's *Floyd's Flowers, or Duty and Beauty for Colored Children* (1905) and the anthology *The Upward Path* (1920). But the success of the 1928 white-authored *Little Black Sambo* showed just how pervasive stereotypical racist images of blacks remained in mainstream children's literature, and how much work was left for the black authors who hoped to counter those portrayals.

Langston Hughes and Arna Bontemps were the next well-known authors to write books expressly for black children. In 1932 they cowrote the novel *Popo and Fifina*, and Hughes published *The Dream Keepers*, a collection of poetry. Bontemps went on to write several more children's stories and publish the poetry anthology *Golden Slippers*. Hughes and Bontemps also wrote nonfiction books for children documenting black achievements, and the noted historian Carter J. Woodson wrote several history books for children.

By the 1940s several other prominent black authors were writing fiction and poetry for children and young adults. Jesse Jackson's novel *Call Me Charley* (1945) and Lorenz Graham's *South Town-North Town* series (1958-1976) dealt with racial problems. Gwendolyn Brooks's poetry collection *Bronzeville Boys and Girls* (1956) featured black children living in urban settings. More white authors in the 1950s and 1960s also began writing books that portrayed African Americans more positively – and a few, such as Ezra Jack Keats, featured black characters almost exclusively. But the number of children's books with black characters, by either black or white authors, remained very small until the Civil Rights and Black Power movements, when a new group of authors appeared who were ready to communicate the message to their children that black was beautiful.

In fiction, Walter Dean Myers, Rosa Guy Louise Meriwether, and June Jordan, were among the many authors who began writing young adult novels set against a contemporary urban background. A different approach was taken by several other celebrated young adult novelists, such as Mildred Taylor, whose award-winning series that begins with *Roll of Thunder, Hear My Cry* is set in a 1930s rural Mississippi community; Julius Lester, who retold slave narratives and folktales in his novels; and Virginia Hamilton, who has used black folktales, nineteenth-century history, and futuristic science fiction throughout her imaginative career.

Nikki Giovanni, one of the most successful writers to emerge from the Black Arts Movement, has written several books of children's poetry. Other well-known contemporary children's poets include Eloise Greenfield and Lucille Clifton. Tom Feelings, Jerry Pinkney, John Steptoe, and Ashley Bryan are among the successful black illustrators of contemporary children's books. In the 1980s, when mainstream publishers' interest in black children's books declined, independent African American publishers such as Black Butterfly Press, Just Us Books, and the Third World Press stepped in to bridge the gap. But in the 1990s an increased interest in multiculturalism in American classrooms led to a renewed demand for these books – this time, to be read by children of all races. Novelist Alice Walker, poet Maya Angelou, and activist Rosa Parks have joined the ranks of children's book authors in the last decade.

In 1969 the Coretta Scott King Book Award was established to honor African American authors and illustrators for outstanding contributions to children's literature. These awards offer long-overdue recognition to the black writers and artists who have worked for decades to ensure that African American children and young adults will find positive, realistic depictions of themselves, their families, and their histories in the books that they read.

Lisa Clayton Robinson

See Also

Brooks, Gwendolyn Elizabeth; Woodson, Carter Godwin; Civil Rights Movement; Du Bois, William Edward Burghardt (W. E. B.); Giovanni, Yolande Cornelia ("Nikki"); Guy, Rosa Cuthbert; Parks, Rosa Louise McCauley.

North America

Childress, Alice **(b. October 12, 1920, Charleston, S.C.; d. August 14, 1994, Long Island, N.Y.), African American playwright and novelist and the first black woman to win an Obie.**

Alice Childress was the award-winning author of over a dozen plays and novels focusing on the plight of the poor, the role of community, and the struggle of blacks against racism, sexism, and classism. Born in South Carolina, she was raised in Harlem by her grandmother, Eliza Campbell, who inspired her early love of art and concern for the poor. Childress attended Public School 81, Julia Ward Howe Elementary School, and Wadleigh High School, which she left after three years.

Her playwriting career began in 1943 with the start of her 11-year association with the

American Negro Theatre, where she was instrumental in the organization's development. Her plays include *Florence* (1949), *Wine in The Wilderness* (1966), and *Moms* (1987). She was the first black woman to win an Obie Award, which she received for *Trouble in Mind* (1955). Although best known for her plays, she also produced a number of novels and children's books, including *Short Walk* (1979) and *Those Other People* (1990). Her numerous awards included a Rockefeller Grant, Writer-in-Residence at the MacDowell Colony, and a Harvard University appointment at the Bunting Institute. On July 17, 1957, she married Nathan Woodward, an artist and musician, with whom she lived until her death on Long Island, New York, in 1994.

See Also

Harlem, New York.

Latin America and the Caribbean

Chile, country of South America bordered on the west by the Pacific Ocean, on the north by Peru, on the northeast by Bolivia, and on the east by Argentina.

Chilean society prides itself on its racially mixed past, as expressed in the mythic belief in *la raza chilena*, a special race produced by noble Spaniards and the original inhabitants of the land, the Araucanian indigenous people. What this myth omits is the contribution that Africans brought to the racial mix. Not only are blacks ignored in the standard contemporary vision of Chilean society, but their role in the country's history is generally overlooked as well. While a fleeting look at the population of modern Chile might reveal a marginal presence of people of African descent, the Afro-Chilean contribution becomes clear upon closer examination. Blacks made their greatest impact in colonial Chile as exploited slave labor and honored soldiers, helping to forge a nation on the frontier. Once the new republic was established in 1818, Afro-Chileans seem to have all but vanished. There may be various reasons for their alleged disappearance, but the most likely explanation seems to be insufficient national research, reflecting a disinterest in this group by Chilean society as a whole.

Standard History

Before the Spanish conquest of Chile, the region was home to various indigenous populations, including the Diaguita, Pehunche, Cunco, and Araucanian. The Araucanian comprised the Picunche in the north, the Mapuche in the middle valleys, and the Huilliche in the south. Spanish invaders overwhelmed the Picunche and the Huilliche and assimilated these groups into their own peasant population. Only the Mapuche were able to resist domination by the conquistadors as Pedro de Valdivia's forces trekked southward after founding the city of Santiago de Chile in 1541. Between 1553 and 1558 the Mapuche organized an uprising that marked the beginning of ongoing intermittent warfare, which continued into the nineteenth century. The resistance of the Mapuche, combined with the death of most of the remaining indigenous forced laborers, led the Spaniards to import African slaves as a means of strengthening the labor supply.

Originally part of the viceroyalty of Peru, Chile gained greater governmental autonomy in the late 1700s. In 1810 it declared its independence from Spain and joined the rest of Spanish America in the war against royalist troops. With the establishment of the new republic (1818) came periods of instability, as conservatives and liberals vied for power. Boundary disputes with Bolivia and Peru culminated in the War of the Pacific (1879-1883). Chile won territory from both Bolivia and Peru, in the process incurring strained relations that continued throughout the twentieth century. Between the 1970s and 1989 Chile endured great social, economic, and political turmoil, first under the rule of Salvador Allende, then under the dictatorship of Augusto Pinochet, who adopted extreme measures to stabilize the economy and repress opposition to his rule. Democratic government was reinstated in December 1989, with the first Chilean presidential election in 19 years. Since then, Chile's economy and political system have significantly improved, with the help of governmental reforms.

Slavery

An undetermined number of blacks first entered Chile as both slaves and soldiers with the Spaniard explorer Diego de Almagro in 1536. Among them was Juan Valiente, a slave from Mexico who was allowed to join Almagro's expeditionary forces as a soldier and went on to distinguish himself as captain of the infantry. Blacks brought as slaves to Chile were used primarily to supplement the labor of the region's limited indigenous population, many of whom succumbed to the harshness of the work. Spanish administrators, who were working to establish and maintain the new colony, used slave labor in agriculture, limited gold mining, and construction. As a poor and remote colony, Chile could not afford to import large numbers of African slaves. Without significant exploitable resources, requests for additional slave labor were sometimes denied by the Crown.

Most of the African slaves brought to Chile and the Rio de la Plata region were of Angolan origin, taken from the Upper Guinea and Congo River stations. Slaves were initially imported to Chile through overland passages from Buenos Aires (*see* Argentina) and Montevideo (*see* Uruguay). When the Buenos Aires port was temporarily closed to traffic in the early seventeenth century, all legal goods for the southern region of South America were rerouted to Cartegena, Colombia. The alternate Pacific route, by which slaves were transported from Colombia to Panama City (*see* Panama), shipped to Callao, Peru, and finally walked overland into Chile, increased the cost of Chilean slaves and gave rise to an illegal trade. As in other Latin American countries, Chilean records of slave importation are incomplete because an unknown number of slaves were smuggled into the country. Scholars have estimated that approximately .01 percent of the entire Transatlantic Slave Trade was Chilean.

The Afro-Chilean population grew from about 7000 in 1570 among a total population of 624,000 to 20,000 just 20 years later among a total population of 586,000. Both free and enslaved blacks found a niche in urban as well as rural settings. Slaves worked as cowboys, sheepherders, and miners in rural areas and as domestic servants in the cities. Free laborers worked as saddle makers, coachmen, and reportedly even as executioners. On occasion Afro-Chileans became apprentices by exchanging labor for training in carpentry, shoemaking, and blacksmithing. Blacks in the cities were essential to the local economy and held positions in the mechanical trades alongside Spaniards, while Indians and *mestizos* (of indigenous and European descent) worked in agriculture (*see* Colonial Latin America and the Caribbean).

The status of Afro-Chilean slaves in colonial society was unique, since they gained notice as both subjugated laborers and valued soldiers. Legally all blacks held the lowest positions in the Spanish colonial hierarchy, yet Chilean administrators made exceptions that went against colonial law. Most likely it was Chile's great distance from the viceroyal seat of power in Lima, Peru, that enabled local authorities to ignore decrees of the Spanish Crown. Decisions to award some Afro-Chilean slaves supervisory positions over Indian labor gangs were legally disallowed but socially acceptable. A few blacks reportedly gained enough prestige as soldiers to receive *encomiendas* (land grants) with Indian tribute laborers. Juan Valiente was one such soldier who in the year 1550, according to historian Leslie Rout, became the first known black in the Americas to receive an encomienda. A few other blacks, including Juan Beltrán, Leonor Galiano, Gomez de Leon, and Cristóbal Varela, were honored with land grants, but these infrequent awards left the legal and social status of Afro-Chileans fundamentally unchanged. They were still considered slaves regardless of their awards.

Afro-Chileans' dual status as overseers and allies of the Indians affected relations between them. Colonial administrators in Spanish America, aware of this duality, constantly feared the exploitation of indigenous populations by blacks as well as alliances between the two groups. Their fears were justified. As early as the 1550s, escaped slaves had formed fugitive communities that raided towns and Indian villages. At the same time, *cimarrones*, as escaped slaves were called,

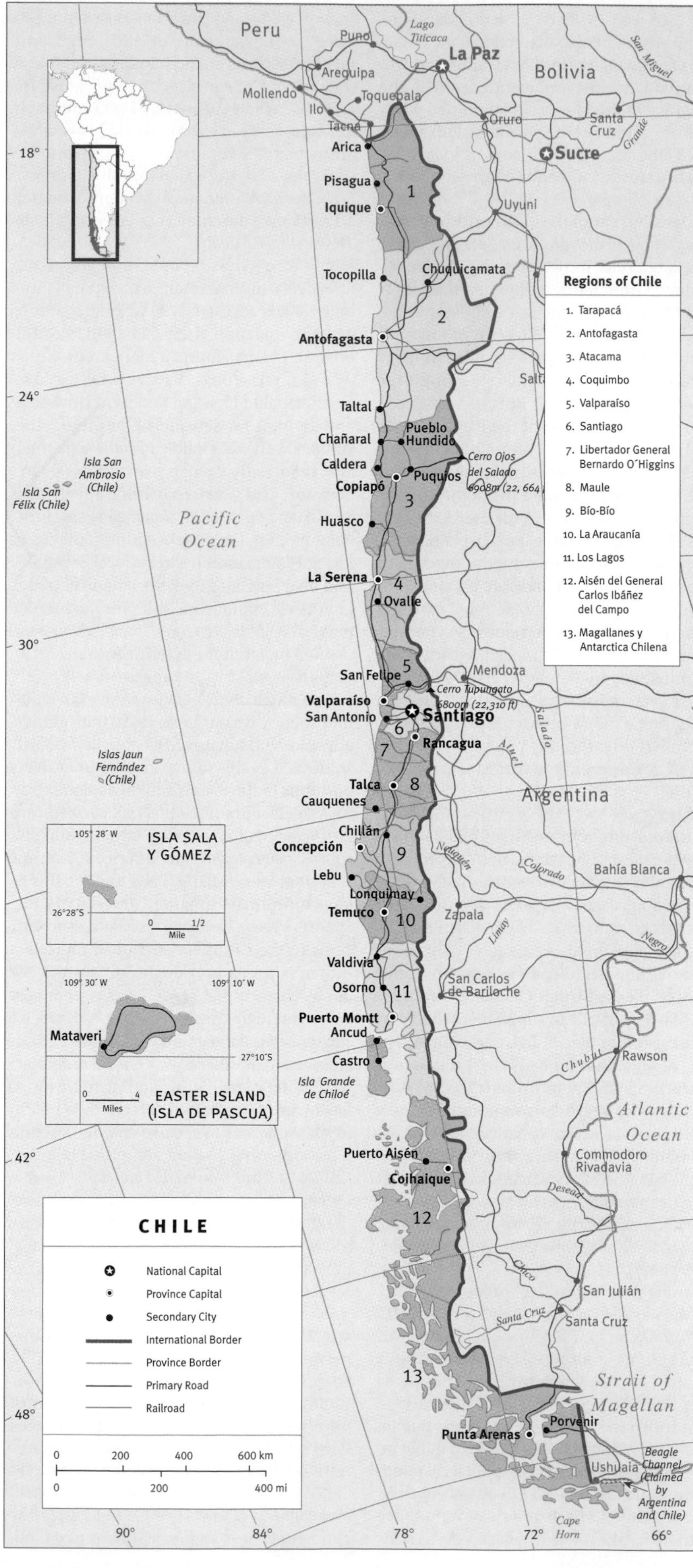

did not act alone. Indian groups joined in raids on Spanish settlements; in 1631 Indian hostility erupted in a large-scale attack on Santiago. Certain *cimarrón* groups were even reputed to have mulattos (of African and European descent) and Spaniards, in addition to Indians, among their members (*see* MAROONAGE IN THE AMERICAS).

Measures to avert a combined Indian-black revolt ranged from laws to separate the two groups to executions to curfews. Following an earthquake that devastated Santiago in 1647, and fearing an Indian-black uprising at the height of the city's vulnerability, Spanish officials executed an Afro-Chilean slave who had rallied support among approximately 400 slaves. When fugitive raids continued mainly undiminished in the face of such punishment, the Santiago municipal council passed laws prohibiting blacks, Indians, and mulattos from being out at night.

INDEPENDENCE

The first well-known proposal to abolish slavery in Chile coincided with the declaration of Chilean independence in 1810. In October 1811 philanthropist-economist Manuel de Salas proposed a law that would not only ban the slave trade in Chile, but would also improve conditions for those already enslaved and would free their children (*see* ABOLITION AND EMANCIPATION IN LATIN AMERICA AND THE CARIBBEAN). Salas further proposed that any slaves transported through Chile who stayed for more than six months would be declared free. The Salas proposal became law, and though it met with continued opposition from the country's conservatives, it remained in effect throughout the war of independence.

In August 1814 the rebel government, in need of soldiers, promised freedom to slaves in return for their joining the newly created all-black and mulatto military unit (although new recruits were required to compensate their former masters from their own salaries). Within a month the rebel government had discovered that owners were preventing their slaves from joining the military. Enlistment became obligatory, and punishment for slaves' failure to enlist was meted out to both owner and slave: a two-year exile and loss of half his estate for the former, and 100 lashes and a sentence of perpetual slavery for the latter. Although Chile won its independence in 1818, the promise of freedom was not immediately fulfilled. In 1823 an estimated 4000 Chilean slaves were freed, and Chile became the first Spanish American republic to enact total abolition (*see* RACIAL QUESTION DURING STRUGGLES OF INDEPENDENCE IN LATIN AMERICA).

CONTEMPORARY TIMES

As with other Latin American countries, such as Argentina and Uruguay, Chile's black population appears to have vanished from history records after emancipation in 1823. Unlike other African-descended populations in Latin America, Afro-Chileans have not resurfaced as a political force or as leaders in a cultural movement. In 1940 there were 1000 blacks and 3000 mulattos in Chile, according to the country census for that year. This was the most recent census to report a national count of Afro-Chileans. Historian Leslie Rout cites a personal source that placed Afro-Chileans at .017 percent of the total Chilean population of 9,786,000 in 1971.

Some Chilean scholars, such as Francisco Encina, claim that blacks died out on account of alcoholism, disease, and climate, yet these factors had no significant effect on other populations within Chile. The only explanation is that miscegenation has thoroughly blended the country's racial groups, making Afro-Chileans highly indistinct physically and culturally. Rout and other scholars suggest that the government-supported influx of white Eurpean immigrants during the mid-1800s, combined with an unofficial policy of discrimination against black immigration, contributed to the decline of the Afro-Chilean population. Without significantly observable physical or cultural traits suggesting African descent, the Afro-Chilean population is no longer clearly visible. Closer examination of Chilean culture may reveal African-influenced elements, but such scholarship has not yet emerged.

Rob Garrison

See Also

Angola; Cartagena de Indias, Colombia; Slavery in Latin America and the Caribbean.

Africa

Chiluba, Frederick (b. 1943, the Kitwe, Northern Rhodesia [present-day Zambia]), president of Zambia (1991-).

The son of Bemba-speaking miners, Frederick Chiluba was too poor to finish school, and he traveled to Tanganyika (present-day Tanzania) and worked on a plantation. When he returned in 1966, he became involved in the labor movement. While working as a credit officer in an engineering firm, he was elected president of the Building and General Workers' Union in 1971 and president of the Zambian Congress of Trade Unions in 1975.

An outspoken critic of Zambian president Kenneth Kaunda, in 1990 Chiluba cofounded the Movement for Multiparty Democracy (MMD), a coalition of opposition forces. All opposition parties were illegal at the time, and Chiluba was briefly detained for his role in the MMD. After growing popular unrest convinced the government to register opposition parties, multiparty presidential elections were held in 1991, and Chiluba defeated Kaunda by a wide margin. One of Chiluba's first official acts as president was to lift Kaunda's permanent state of emergency.

Chiluba faced numerous struggles in office, including accusations of corruption within his cabinet, popular resistance to the privatization of the state-run economy, fragmentation of the MMD, and criticism of his handling of ethnic tensions. Kaunda's party, the United National Independence Party (UNIP), regained popularity. In March 1993 Chiluba declared a state of emergency when he discovered what was called the Zero Option conspiracy, engineered by UNIP radicals to instigate public discontent and render the country ungovernable. Chiluba revoked the state of emergency two months later, however, after protests from Zambia's Western donor nations.

In May 1996 Chiluba's government passed an amendment to the constitution in an effort to obstruct the political comeback of Kaunda. The amendment limited presidents to two terms in office and required all presidential candidates to be from families who had lived in Zambia for at least two generations. Kaunda, born of Malawian immigrants, was disqualified on both counts. Kaunda's UNIP boycotted the 1996 elections, and Chiluba was elected for a second term. In October 1997 Chiluba survived a coup attempt waged by a small contingent of junior officers and soldiers.

Alonford James Robinson, Jr.

Africa

Chimpanzee, or chimp, anthropoid of equatorial Africa that, physically and genetically, is the animal most closely related to humans. There are two forms: the common chimp ranges from Sierra Leone and Guinea on the Atlantic Ocean to lakes Tanganyika and Victoria; the pygmy chimp is found only in the eastern Zaire (Congo) River Basin.

Characteristics

The male common chimp is up to 1.7 m (up to 5.5 ft) high when upright and weighs as much as 70 kg (up to 150 lb); the female is somewhat smaller. The chimp's long arms, when extended, have a span half again as long as the body height. The feet are better suited for walking than those of orangutans; the soles are broader and the toes shorter. The coat is dark, and the face, palms, and soles are bare. The ears, lips, and brow ridges protrude, and there is no tail. The brain of a chimpanzee is about half the size of the human brain.

Chimpanzees are diurnal and omnivorous, eating about 200 kinds of leaves and fruit; termites, ants, honey, and birds' eggs; and birds and small mammals. They spend their time in or near trees, avoiding direct sunlight, and the adults build sleeping nests each night in a tree. The female has a 35-day menstrual cycle, is receptive for 6.5 days of each cycle, and can breed at any time of the year. The gestation period is more than seven months long. A mother gives birth to a single offspring, or on rare occasions, to twins. Immediately after birth the helpless young clutches its mother's hair, riding on the mother's back when she travels. The young chimp is weaned at about four years but may continue to travel with the mother until the age of ten. Offspring sometimes maintain a bond with the mother throughout life, which may last up to 60 years in the wild.

Social Behavior

Chimpanzees form loosely organized bands of up to 80 individuals on fairly large home ranges, where the animals remain for years. Within a band, smaller groups may form, break up, and reform; sometimes a female migrates to another band. Males never migrate. Except between mother and young, little permanency exists in individual relationships. The female may mate with different partners. Members of a band cooperate in hunting and sharing of food. On finding a food source, they hoot, scream, and slap logs to attract others. A constant interplay occurs between adults, and all members of the group groom one another.

Communication and Intelligence

Chimpanzees communicate through vocalizations, facial expressions, posture, touch, and movement. A young chimp is able to make at least 32 different sounds, and the facial musculature can express a wide range of emotions. The animals show great intelligence in problem solving and the use of simple tools, such as a stripped twig to draw termites from their nest. Experiments suggest that chimps can learn to use language in a symbolic sense, but these results are disputed.

Chimpanzees belong to the family Pongidae in the order Primates. They make up the genus *Pan.* The common chimpanzee is classified as *Pan troglodytes.* The bonobo is classified as *Pan paniscus.*

See Also

Congo River; Victoria, Lake; Tanganyika, Lake.

Africa

Chimurenga Music, contemporary genre of Zimbabwean protest songs.

During the early 1970s singer-composer Thomas Mapfumo began to fuse elements of traditional Shona drumming and *mbira* (thumb piano) playing with Afro-rock styles to produce chimurenga music. "Chimurenga" is the Shona word for war or struggle. Historically, Shona resistance has had a musical component. For example, during the colonial period Chimurenga protest songs welded the call-and-response modality of traditional Shona music to the harmonies and melodies of Christian hymns, imported by missionaries. In the 1970s Mapfumo continued the tradition of infusing music with political content when he used Shona proverbs to incorporate anti-colonial lyrics into the new brand of music that he called chimurenga.

Chimurenga's subversive messages rallied Zimbabweans to throw off the yoke of colonial oppression, take pride in their culture, and ultimately declare political independence. *Shungu Dzinondibaya*, Mapfumo's first recording, which makes fun of a wealthy man who suddenly loses his fortune, marks an early stage in the development of chimurenga. However, it was his 1977 single "Pamuromo Chete" that deeply stirred the disfranchised people of Zimbabwe and brought them full-fledged chimurenga. Colonial authorities subsequently banned his LP *Hokoya* (Watch Out). Mapfumo's lyrics following independence in 1980, addressed the difficulties of nation building and economic development.

Chimurenga music draws on traditional Shona instruments and Shona musical structures. Chimurenga musicians dampen the strings of the electric guitar to mimic the sounds of the mbira, while the hi-hat and bass drums evoke the sounds of the hosho and the gourd rattle. The music follows both traditional rhythm patterns (*kitsinhira*) and traditional lead melody lines (*kushaura*). The result is a uniquely Zimbabwean form of music, steeped in tradition and transformed by contemporary instrumentation. In 1983 the Earthworks label introduced Europe to chimurenga music with the release of *Chimurenga Singles*, featuring Mapfumo.

Ari Nave

See Also

Zimbabwe; Christianity: Missionaries in Africa.

North America

Chisholm, Shirley

(b. November 20, 1924, Brooklyn, N.Y.), the first African American woman elected to the United States Congress and the first to campaign for the presidency, known for her incisive debating style and uncompromising integrity.

Shirley Chisholm is widely considered one of the foremost female orators in the United States. With a character that she has described as "unbought and unbossed," Chisholm became known as a politician who refused to allow fellow politicians, including the male-dominated Congressional Black Caucus, to deter her from her goals. In 1969 her first statement as a congressperson before the United States House of Representatives reflected her commitment to prioritizing the needs of the disadvantaged, especially children: she proclaimed her intent to "vote no on every money bill that comes to the floor of this House that provides any funds for the Department of Defense." While Chisholm advocated for black civil rights, she regularly took up issues that concerned other people of color, such as Spanish-speaking migrants and Native Americans. She also delivered important speeches on the economic and political rights of women and fearlessly criticized the Nixon administration during the Vietnam War.

Shirley Anita St. Hill Chisholm was the oldest of four girls born to parents who had immigrated from the West Indies, and who barely subsisted on their wages from factory work and housecleaning. When Chisholm was three, her parents, who wanted a better life for their daughters, sent Shirley and her sisters to Barbados to be reared by their maternal grandmother. For Chisholm island life seemed like a paradise, and she received an excellent education in Barbados's British school system. At the age of ten she returned to Brooklyn, where she was an outstanding student. Later, at Brooklyn College, she majored in sociology and joined the debating society, an experience that would help shape her cut-and-thrust oratory style. She also served as a volunteer in the Brooklyn chapter of the National Urban League and in the National Association for the Advancement of Colored People, where she debated minority rights.

In 1949, after graduating from college, Chisholm attended evening classes at Columbia University, earning a master's degree in child education. Meanwhile, she taught at a Harlem nursery school, and later acted as supervisor of the largest nursery school network in New York. It was through administering to hundreds of children, most of them African American and Puerto Rican, that Chisholm learned the executive skills that served her so well in the political arena. In 1953, as a key member of the Seventeenth Assembly District Democratic Club, she waged a successful political campaign to elect an eminent black lawyer to the municipal court.

Chisholm's political career took off in 1964, when she won by a landslide her campaign for the New York State Assembly. As an assemblyperson (1965-1968), she authored legislation that instituted SEEK (Search for Education, Elevation, and Knowledge), a program that provided college funding to disadvantaged youths, and introduced the bill that secured unemployment insurance for domestics and daycare providers. In 1968 Chisholm won a seat in the United States House of Representatives, where she served on a number of committees, including Education and Labor, and campaigned for a higher minimum wage and federal funding for daycare facilities. She also secured federal grants for a number of Brooklyn-based enterprises that benefited disadvantaged communities. In 1972 she became the first African American woman to campaign for the presidency, running as "a candidate of the people." In doing so she paved the way for others like herself who, as she said in her autobiography, *The Good Fight*, "will feel themselves as capable of running for high political office as any wealthy, good-looking white male."

Since her retirement from Congress in 1982, Chisholm has remained active as a political figure, an educator, and a spokesperson for women's rights. She has held several university teaching positions. During the 1980s she was a critical asset to Jesse Jackson's campaigns for the presidency. She also created and currently chairs the increasingly powerful National Political Congress of Black Women, and has served on the Advisory Council of the National Organization for Women.

Roanne Edwards

See Also

Harlem, New York.

Africa

Chissano, Joaquim

(b. October 22, 1939, Malehice, Portuguese East Africa [Mozambique]), president of Mozambique.

Joaquim Chissano enjoyed a privileged education as a youth but went on to become a leading member of the emerging Mozambican nationalist movement. He was one of the first black Mozambicans to attend the central high school in Lourenço Marques (present-day Maputo). He soon joined the Nucleus of African Secondary Students of Mozambique (NESAM), a nationalist organization of the young elite, and in 1959 became its president. The following year Chissano went to Portugal to study medicine but was soon forced to leave because of his political activities. He moved to Paris, where he helped to establish a nationalist student movement among the Mozambican exiles.

In 1962 Chissano went to Tanzania to take part in organizing the Frente da Libertação de Moçambique (Front for the Liberation of Mozambique or FRELIMO) and became the special assistant to FRELIMO president Eduardo Mondlane. Chissano fought in the war for independence but was primarily involved as a trainer in FRELIMO camps in Tanzania and as the movement's chief representative in Dar es Salaam. Following the negotiated end to the war in 1974, Chissano headed the transitional government until Mozambique won its full independence on June 25, 1975. Samora Machel then became president and Chissano became minister of foreign affairs, a position he held until 1986.

Although Chissano was not a highly visible member of the party, he played a vital role in securing international support for the beleaguered government and, while observers agree that Chissano was uncomfortable with FRELIMO's staunch Marxist-Leninism, he did maintain close relations with the Soviet Union and other socialist countries. But Chissano also improved ties with the West, securing humanitarian assistance and economic aid from Great Britain and the United States. He was also the architect of the 1984 Nkomati Accords with South Africa, in which South Africa agreed to stop supporting the insurgent group Mozambican National Resistance (RENAMO), and the Mozambican government agreed to cease its support for the African National Congress.

After Machel died in an airplane crash in

1986, Chissano became president and head of FRELIMO. He soon proved a far more pragmatic leader than his predecessor. He lifted restrictions on religious freedom, encouraged private enterprise, and showed greater tolerance for traditional chieftains and spiritual beliefs. Initially he maintained Machel's hard-line stance against RENAMO, but in 1988 he began secretly encouraging third-party negotiations. The efforts succeeded and after reaching a peace agreement with RENAMO, Chissano was reelected president in 1994 with 53 percent of the popular vote in national elections, besting RENAMO leader Afonso Dhlakama. Since his reelection, President Chissano continues to be seen both domestically and internationally as a consummate diplomat and pragmatist.

Eric Young

See Also
Dar es Salaam, Tanzania; Machel, Samora Moises; Maputo, Mozambique.

Africa

Chokossi (also known as Chakossi, Anoufou, Anufo, and Kyokosi), ethnic group of West Africa.

The Chokossi primarily inhabit northern Togo and neighboring northeastern Ghana. They speak a Niger-Congo language and belong to the Akan cultural and linguistic group. Approximately 100,000 people consider themselves Chokossi.

See Also
Languages, African: An Overview.

Africa

Chokwe, ethnic group of the Democratic Republic of the Congo, Angola, and Zambia; one of the richest trading groups in the Congo basin prior to Belgian colonialism.

Originally seminomadic hunters in the savanna of northeast Angola, the Chokwe migrated to the Congo basin in the early nineteenth century. There, they settled in villages and began participating in regional commerce with the neighboring Lunda. Dealing in ivory and wax, the Chokwe initially exercised little power in the Congo basin, where slave trading brought far higher returns; but they traded enough to build up a small armory of flintlock muskets, which would later prove highly valuable.

When the slave trade went into decline in the 1840s, the Chokwe's control over the wax and ivory trades made them one of the richest trading groups in the region. Over the next ten years the demand for wax, which they produced themselves by collecting beeswax from hives in the forest, increased 30 percent in the trading centers of Benguela and Luanda. Faced with an equally strong international demand for ivory, the Chokwe used their muskets to hunt elephants, eventually helping to decimate the local population. When ivory supplies grew scarce, the Chokwe turned to rubber tapping.

During the second half of the nineteenth century, the Chokwe population increased rapidly. Many migrated north in search of farmland and forests for rubber tapping. As they expanded, they took control of new trade routes and absorbed many smaller ethnic groups in the area between the Kwango River and the Kubango and Kunene rivers. In 1890, however, the military forces of King Leopold II's Congo Free State took control of the region and put an abrupt halt to Chokwe expansion. Today many Chokwe still live in what is now known as the Katanga (or Shaba) region, farming and working in the mining industries, although they are politically overshadowed by the Lunda ethnic group.

Elizabeth Heath

See Also
Colonial Rule; Congo River; Elephant; Ivory Trade; Leopold II.

North America

Christiana Revolt of 1851 (September 11, 1851), the first open defiance of the Fugitive Slave Act to end in bloodshed.

The violence on September 11, 1851, near the Quaker village of Christiana in southeastern Pennsylvania constituted one of the major rebellions against the Fugitive Slave Act of 1850, which deprived fugitive slaves of the right to a trial by jury, withheld their testimony, and nearly always assumed the guilt of the presumed runaway.

On the morning of September 11, slaveholder Edward Gorsuch and a team of United States marshals bearing federal warrants surrounded the home of William Parker, a local black leader and an escaped slave. Gorsuch believed that two of four runaway slaves who had escaped two years previously from his farm in the neighboring state of Maryland were hiding in Parker's home, and he demanded their immediate surrender. Parker, however, refused to release any slaves. Instead, his wife, Eliza Ann, sounded a dinner horn, a prearranged signal that alerted local blacks to the Parker home. In the meantime, gunfire erupted between the two opposing sides. About 100 blacks and 2 whites arrived shortly thereafter. Armed with guns, clubs, and farm tools, the assembled crowd attacked the posse of slave catchers, leaving Gorsuch dead and three members of his party, including his son, wounded.

President Millard Fillmore immediately sent a 45-man company of U.S. Marines to accompany a 40-man civil posse of Philadelphia policemen to the scene of the shooting. Arriving in Christiana on around September 13, this contingent promptly began arresting suspects. Thirty-eight people were accused, 35 of them blacks. Parker and the Gorsuch slaves fled to Ontario, Canada, where Canadian officials refused to respond to federal demands for extradition. Those arrested were charged with resisting the Fugitive Slave Act and with treason, and were imprisoned until their trial before the U.S. circuit court.

African Americans throughout the country raised funds to help provide legal counsel during their pretrial imprisonment and to assist their families. Supporters in Philadelphia created a Special Vigilance Committee on behalf of the Christiana Sufferers. After a three-month incarceration of the defendants, the prosecution tried a local white involved in the riot, Castner Hanway, as a test case upon which the fates of the remaining approximately 25 defendants would be decided. When Hanway was acquitted on lack of evidence, the remaining defendants were released and the remaining indictments dropped.

Southerners were furious with the verdict, while blacks became more willing to resist the Fugitive Slave Act. Simultaneously, abolitionists received increased support and sympathy. The Christiana Revolt further heightened the growing tension between the North and the South, which culminated in the Civil War.

See Also
Civil War, American; Fugitive Slave Laws; Fugitive Slaves.

North America

Christian-Green, Donna (b. September 19, 1945, Teaneck, N.J.), Democratic member of the United States House of Representatives from the Virgin Islands (1996-).

Donna Christian-Green comes from a family of public servants. Her father, Almeric L. Christian, was a Virgin Islands chief district court judge and her paternal grandmother, Elena L. Christian, was an educator in the Virgin Islands. Christian-Green graduated with a bachelor's degree from St. Mary's College in Indiana and earned a medical degree at George Washington University in Washington, D.C. After a medical career of more than 20 years, she entered politics as vice chairperson of the U.S. Virgin Islands Democratic Territorial Committee in 1980. She subsequently served on the U.S. Virgin Islands Board of Education and the U.S. Virgin Islands Status Commission. In 1996 she became the first woman elected to the U.S. House of Representatives from the U.S. Virgin Islands. During the 105th Congress, she served on the House Resources Committee.

See Also
Virgin Islands (United States and British).

Africa

Christianity, African: An Overview of the development of Christianity in Africa.

There has been a Christian presence on the African continent for nearly as long as people have considered themselves followers of Jesus Christ. Missionaries and traders have been credited for bringing Christianity to Egypt and North Africa (*see* ROMAN AFRICA: AN INTERPRETATION) in the very early days of the Christian movement. Because North Africa was part of the Roman Empire, the politics of Rome had an important bearing on the development of Christianity in Egypt and the Maghreb (comprising present-day LIBYA, TUNISIA, ALGERIA, and MOROCCO). The cosmopolitan city of ALEXANDRIA, EGYPT, became one of the most important centers of North African Christianity (*see* ALEXANDRIA AND GRECIAN AFRICA: AN INTERPRETATION).

The scholarship and teachings of theologians based in urban North Africa, such as Origen, Athanasius, Tertullian, and Augustine, shaped Christian thought and practice. Alexandria was also a center of Gnostic Christianity, nonorthodox sects dedicated to cultivating secret knowledge of the divine. The initial Egyptian converts to both Gnostic and orthodox sects were residents of cities, and many of them were Jews, Greeks, and Africans; these people were excluded from the Roman ruling elite. Until the early 300s C.E., Christians were occasionally persecuted for their beliefs by the Roman government. However, in 331 the emperor made Christianity the religion of the Roman Empire.

At the Bulawayo Cyrere Mission in Zimbabwe, where about one-quarter of the population is Christian, a wall painting depicts Simon of Cyrene carrying the cross to Golgotha. *G. Sioen/Rapho*

From the third century onward, Christianity gradually spread out of the cities to the countryside of Egypt and the Maghreb. As the religion became more popular, it developed practices and attributes that made it distinctive to the region and that influenced Christianity more generally. People worshiped in their own languages, such as Coptic in Egypt, instead of Greek or Latin, the languages of the empire. In Egypt the monastic and hermitic traditions developed and flourished. Through monasteries, Christianity spread to remote rural areas. The Egyptian Anthony became a celebrated exemplar of the Christian solitary life and asceticism.

In addition to religious practices, several theological disputes in North Africa divided the Church and reinforced the distinctiveness of African Christianity. Egyptian theologians believed that Christ had a single, divine nature. This Monophysite theology deviated from the orthodox (or Dyophysite) belief that Christ had both a divine and a human nature. The orthodox, or Catholic, church eventually declared the Monophysite interpretation a heresy, although it remained an important aspect of Egyptian and other mainly African and Asian traditions of Christianity. During the fourth and fifth centuries, the church in the Maghreb was bitterly divided between the Donatists and orthodox Christians. The Donatist movement venerated the martyrs of early Christianity, and advocated a hard-line interpretation concerning who could be included in the Christian community. Beyond their theological positions, the Donatists viewed themselves as champions of the poor and discouraged obedience to the state. The Donatists were considered heretics by the orthodox. The most able defender of catholic tradition against the Donatists was Augustine, bishop of Hippo. Although the Monophysite and Donatist disputes may appear abstract, they were important factors in shaping the local character of African Christianity.

Nubia (in present-day SUDAN) and ETHIOPIA became the other strongholds of Christianity in Africa. Unlike Egypt and the Maghreb, these areas had not been part of the Roman Empire, and thus its imperial politics had little influence on the course of Christianity in these regions. Christianity arrived in Nubia with monks and traders in the fourth or fifth century. Nubian Christians supported a full hierarchy of bishops, priests, and monasteries; a Monophysite form of Christianity became the religion of the kingdoms of Nubia. In the region of present-day Ethiopia, the leaders of the kingdom of AKSUM converted in the fourth century and likewise adopted Monophysite Christianity (*see* ETHIOPIAN ORTHODOX CHURCH). In addition to the activities of missionaries, traders and other travelers probably introduced Christianity into the region. The Aksumite kingdom laid the foundation for the future strong relationship between the church and state in Ethiopia.

In the 640s C.E., Arab invaders conquered EGYPT with little resistance. These new rulers were Muslim; the arrival of Islam brought about profound, though gradual, changes in the religious environment of the region. Until the tenth century C.E., most Egyptians were Christians. Even after Islam became the religion of the majority, Coptic Christian communities have remained in existence until the present day. In the Maghreb, the relationship between Christianity and the new social and religious order was somewhat different. The Arabs were only able to gain control of this region in the 690s after a series of lengthy sieges. The people of the Maghreb appear to have adopted Islam readily, and the Christian communities were reduced to tiny outposts. In Nubia the Christian states maintained peaceful relations with their Muslim neighbors from the 650s; for the next several centuries Nubia remained predominantly Christian. However, due to the conversion of rulers to Islam, the disappearance of state support for the church, and the lack of clergy, Christianity had disappeared from the Nubian states by the sixteenth century.

In the region of Ethiopia, Christianity was firmly embedded in the structures of the state and society. After the older kingdom of Aksum declined, successor states emerged in the Ethiopian highlands. In these states the distinctive features and symbols of Ethiopian Christianity emerged. For example, the Ethiopian Church emphasized its Old Testament genealogy and identified itself with Zion; Marian devotion was an important aspect of worship. Religious communities of monks and nuns played crucial roles in linking the populace to the church. Monasteries were sites of education and scholarship. Monks featured in the expansion of the Ethiopian culture and state. As the state expanded, the monks established churches in the wake of (or occasionally even ahead of) the conquering armies. Christianity also featured in the diplomacy of the empire; the emperors of the state forged links with the Holy Land. From the early 1400s Ethiopia made contact with European states. During this time the Ethiopian state was engaged in constant skirmishes with the neighboring Muslim states. By the 1500s these conflicts had escalated; the Ethiopian state barely managed to prevail, in part with the aid of Portuguese arms. In the following centuries Ethiopia and its church progressively turned its focus inward.

From the fifteenth century Europeans intensified their exploration, trading, and colonizing activities in the Americas, Asia, and Africa. Europeans often assumed that as part of their claims on other parts of the world, they had the responsibility to convert "the heathen" to Christianity. The Portuguese took the initiative in proselytizing as they established trading posts and settlements along the coasts of West, Central, and southern Africa. Initially, missionaries were interested in converting the leaders of the society, a process that had mixed results. Some leaders tolerated the activities of missionaries, while others forbade the missionaries from operating in their polities. In regions of European-African settlement, such as MOZAMBIQUE, Cape Verde, and coastal regions of Senegambia (*see* THE GAMBIA AND SENEGAL), Christianity was the religion of the community.

The kingdom of KONGO was exceptional in the extent to which it adopted Christianity as the religion of the state. Missionaries and lay confraternities, organizations for prayer and social activities, helped popularize Christianity beyond the ruling elite. In the early eighteenth century a young woman named Kimpa Vita (baptized Beatrice) led a popular prophetic movement, called the Antonine movement, which called for the end of endemic warfare and restoration of the monarchy. In different ways, lay confraternities and the Antonine movement illustrated the extent to which Christianity had been integrated into the religious and social life of Kongo.

Between 1500 and 1850 a great deal of the European activity in Africa focused on the TRANSATLANTIC SLAVE TRADE. Religious-based opposition to slavery and the slave trade was only intermittent; most Europeans considered slavery compatible with Christianity until well into the nineteenth century. In the midst of the slave trade, Christianity emerged as a unifying factor among people of African descent. In Europe and the Americas, people of African descent used the language of Christianity to protest the abuses of slavery. From the 1700s a handful of West African men, such as Philip Quaque and Jacobus Capitein, trained as Christian clergymen in Europe and returned to Africa, where they ministered to Africans and Europeans in coastal settlements.

An upsurge of interest in mission Christianity in North America and Europe brought a new wave of Protestant missionaries to Africa in the late eighteenth and early nineteenth centuries. Many of these missionaries were inspired by abolitionist ideals. Some missionaries, such as Johannes van der Kemp in South Africa, extended these principles to the advocacy of Africans' human rights. The settlements of SIERRA LEONE and LIBERIA were founded largely out of abolitionist activism; both regions were important sites of African Christianity. From these settlements, former slaves and people rescued from slave traders (such as Samuel Crowther) eventually evangelized across West Africa to the Niger Delta (in present-day NIGERIA). Additionally, people of African descent from JAMAICA, the United States, and other parts of the Americas, inspired by the prospect of returning to their ancestral homeland, became missionaries in Africa.

The ways in which Africans responded to Christianity depended on the religious and political environment in which they lived. Although missionaries were important in spreading the religion, many people first heard of Christianity from African catechists and preachers. Sometimes Christianity was mixed with indigenous beliefs, and gained currency even among those people who would not have defined themselves as Christians. African Christians did not always intend to renounce all of their previous alliances and traditions. By contrast, missionaries tended to associate Christian conversion with some degree of "civilization," ranging from monogamy to Western-style clothes. The extent to which Christianity required cultural change remained a matter of contention between converts and missionaries. Converts changed the focus of mission Christianity by integrating their own perspectives into the religion. African Christians often emphasized themes deriving from African systems of thought, such as fertility, healing, and the persistence of evil.

In the late nineteenth century, European powers formally colonized much of the continent (*see* SCRAMBLE FOR AFRICA). The exceptions were Liberia and Ethiopia, which, in the 1890s, had successfully repelled an Italian invasion. Many Western missionaries were favorably disposed toward colonialism. The number of missionaries increased during this time and the scope of their activities widened. In addition to evangelizing, Roman Catholic and Protestant mission societies often provided social services and resources for Africans, such as schools and hospitals, which the colonial state often did not provide. A small but significant group of Africans used the educational and work opportunities associated with missions as a way to adapt to the new social order. A mission-educated elite, comprising teachers, nurses, journalists, lawyers, and doctors, exercised an influence far beyond their numbers. Members of this group included some of the most articulate critics of colonialism.

Although many Africans would continue to be associated with mainline Protestant or Roman Catholic missions, in the late nineteenth century and early twentieth century the face of Christianity became much more diverse. New denominations, such as the Jehovah's Witnesses and the Seventh Day Adventists, gained adherents. There were also many African-initiated innovations in Christianity. In West and southern Africa during the 1890s, Christians who were dissatisfied with the racial discrimination in the mission churches broke away to form independent or "Ethiopianist" churches. Some independent churches emerged out of political disputes; during the 1920s and 1930s, thousands of Christians in Kenya abandoned the mainline Protestant churches and joined independent churches due to conflicts over education and female circumcision. Many independent churches arose from spiritual "calls." In the early 1900s William Wade Harris, a Methodist from Liberia, was inspired to preach by visions he had experienced. He told his listeners that they should be baptized, accept the Bible, reject traditional religion, and attend their nearest church. His South African contemporary Isaiah Shembe, a healer and a prophet, established the Church of the Nazarites. Independent churches, in all of their diversity, remain important features of African Christianity. In their hymns, ritual, and liturgy, many independent churches expressly draw upon African traditions and concerns.

These concerns were not limited to independent churches. During the twentieth century many Christians in Protestant and Roman Catholic churches attempted to integrate African culture into Christianity. Some missionaries began to rethink their churches' previous enthusiasm for Westernization, and emphasized the need to "Africanize" Christianity. For example, in the mid-twentieth century the Roman Catholic priest Placide Tempels and members of his church in Central Africa developed the lay organization Jamaa. This popular movement emphasized prayer, spirituality, and the African family and was modeled after indigenous models of social organization. Other lay groups, such as the Legion of Mary and women's prayer societies, not only provided a great deal of vitality within the church, but also were sites in which Africans made the religion their own.

The Christian presence in Africa continues to grow; by many estimates, in the year 2000 one out of every five Christians will be African. In the years since independence, the leadership of mainline Protestant denominations and the Roman Catholic Church in Africa has gradually become African. There continues, however, to be a considerable foreign missionary presence in Africa. African theologians have participated in worldwide debates about the Christian response to injustice in society, such as the arguments framed by liberation theologians in Latin America. In southern Africa, Christians opposed to APARTHEID formulated influential theological critiques of racial discrimination (*see* DESMOND MPILO TUTU). Many Christians have developed theological and practical responses to pressing political and social issues confronting modern Africa, such as poverty; acquired immune deficiency syndrome (AIDS); and politicized ethnicity. Other Christians have been deliberately apolitical and have focused on material security or on the afterlife. African Christians have attempted to forge communities that provide meaning for their members. The tension between a universal Christianity and local conditions remains a central concern facing the African Church.

Modupe Labode

SEE ALSO

Beatrice, Dona; Cape Verde; Crowther, Samuel Ajayi; Explorers in Africa, 1500 to 1800; Augustine, Saint; Egypt, Ancient Kingdom of; Nubian; AIDS in Africa: An Interpretation; Capitein, Jacobus Elisa; South Africa; Abolitionism in the United States; Christianity: Missionaries in Africa; Female Circumcision in Africa; Islam and Tradition: An Interpretation.

Africa

Christianity: Independent and Charismatic Churches in Africa

In 1704 a gravely ill Kongolese woman named DONA BEATRICE had a miraculous vision. Saint Anthony appeared to her, calling for the restoration of the kingdom of KONGO, which had been destroyed through years of internal wars, Portuguese interference, and the slave trade. Beatrice was formerly *nganga marimba*, or medium, and her claim to have died and arisen when Saint Anthony "entered her head" was in keeping with patterns of Kongo spirit possession and mediumship. However, the revelations received by Beatrice and her followers came from the Christian saints alone, and the vision her "Antonine" movement spoke of was decidedly nationalist in scope. The Antonians set up their headquarters among the ruins of the old capital of São Salvador, next to the abandoned cathedral. They called for the repopulation of the city, the reunification of the Kongo people, and the return of a divinely sanctioned ruler to head a new theocratic Kongo. She rejected the Capuchin version of church history, insisting that many Catholic saints, including Saint Anthony and Saint Francis, were in fact Kongolese. Moreover, she maintained that Jesus had been born in São Salvador and baptized in the CONGO RIVER, and that the Virgin Mary came from the northern province of Nsundi. While Beatrice did not openly denounce the missionaries or repudiate the authority of the pope, she revised Catholic prayers to emphasize intention over sacraments. She attempted to transform some of her leading followers (known as Little Anthonys) into an indigenous order of priests (whom she dubbed Angels) and crowned each one with a cloth headdress made from black *nsanda* bark, which symbolized the dark-skinned peoples of Africa. She also insisted that traditional sacred objects (*minkisi*), as well as crucifixes, be destroyed and replaced with small metal figurines of Saint Anthony. In 1706 she went so far as to claim that she had conceived a son by the Holy Spirit. Capuchin missionaries convinced the king, Pedro IV, that because the prophetess was supported by one of his rivals, she posed a serious threat, not only to the church but to Pedro's reign as well. She was burned at the stake for heresy in July of that year.

Antonianism is reputedly the earliest documented example of independent Christianity in sub-Saharan Africa. Generally, scholars have applied the label "independent" to autonomous, African-led denominations and congregations that were established in the nineteenth and twentieth centuries following the partition of Africa and the widespread colonization of the continent by European powers. Yet the Antonian movement, which developed in one of the most heavily evangelized regions of sub-Saharan Africa prior to modern times, manifests many of the same features that characterize later indigenous Christian movements. These features include (1) a charismatic, visionary founder or founders who disclose God's special dispensation for Africans; (2) insistence on the need for African clergy; (3) the reinterpretation of the Gospel according to indigenous beliefs, values, and religiocultural practices; (4) an emphasis on direct communication with God and/or the saints through revelation, prophesy, possession, and dreams; and (5) women's active involvement and leadership. The discussion that follows brings to light each of these features. It will become clear that African independent churches are not exclusively contemporary phenomena, but part of a centuries-old process of interpretation, adaptation, and indigenization of the gospel (*see* CHRISTIANITY, AFRICAN: AN OVERVIEW).

ETHIOPIAN AND ZIONIST CHURCHES

African independent churches (AICs) numbered more than 7000 in the 1980s, claiming nearly 15 percent of the Christian population of sub-Saharan Africa, or approximately 32 million members. In an attempt to impose some order on this dynamic and diverse collection of rapidly growing groups, scholars proposed various typologies. While most of these typologies proved artificial and distorting, there is one basic distinction that many outsiders continue to find useful: the distinction between the so-called Ethiopian or separatist churches and the Zionist or spirit churches.

Ethiopian churches (not to be confused with the ETHIOPIAN ORTHODOX CHURCH) insist upon black leadership and autonomy but do not reject Western liturgies, theologies, or doctrine. Missionary scholar Bengt Sundkler dubbed them Ethiopian after the Ethiopian Church founded in Johannesburg in 1892 by ex-Methodists, who, inspired by the black American AFRICAN METHODIST EPISCOPAL CHURCH (AME), rejected mission support and control, invoking Psalm 68:31: "Ethiopia shall soon stretch her hands unto God." Another example of these nineteenth-century separatist movements was largely the result of Bishop Samuel Ajayi Crowther's Niger Mission (1841-1891). A freed YORUBA slave and the first African bishop in the Anglican church, Crowther worked all his life for greater self-determination of Africans in Anglican mission churches, and was responsible for converting many people along the NIGER RIVER. The activism of men like Crowther and Lagos Baptist pastor D. B. Vincent Mojola Agbebi affected public sentiment such that, as historian Elizabeth Isichei puts it, "independency was in the air. In 1886 a layman wrote to the *Lagos Observer* exclaiming, "... A revolution must occur in the Episcopalian church.... We cry aloud complainingly... and a voice in reply comes to us ringing the word in our ears SECESSION! SECESSION! SECESSION!"

Agbebi joined other leading Baptists in 1888 in seceding from the American mission to form the Native Baptist Church. Shortly thereafter, the Christian Missionary Society orchestrated the disintegration of Crowther's episcopate by firing most of his African clergy and staff, and replaced the bishop with an Englishman after the former's death in 1891. In anger and protest, the Lagos churches separated from the Anglican Church establishing the United Native African Church, while Crowther's congregations in the Niger Delta came together to form a self-supporting African Anglican pastorate.

Like the Ethiopian churches, so-called Zionist or spirit churches insist on African leadership, but they also reject many of the teachings and theologies of the mainline, mission-seeded churches. They call for a thorough indigenization of the Gospel in terms of African religious realities and cultural forms (see African Religions: An Interpretation). Many churches of this type were founded after the turn of the century by charismatic African prophets, hence they are also known as prophetic churches. Messianic founders such as Isaiah Shembe in the Natal region of South Africa articulated the Old Testament ideal of a Promised Land or Holy City, a Zion that was spiritually ever-present but was also identified with sacred places in Africa. Shembe was an uneducated, itinerant Zulu preacher who gained a reputation as a faith healer and visionary. In 1911 he founded the Nazareth Baptist Church, which integrated features of charismatic Christianity such as baptism in the Spirit and casting out demons, with Zulu dance, music, and ritual, as well as adherence to certain Old Testament laws such as the Saturday sabbath, pork avoidance, and the practice of circumcision and polygyny (the latter two coincide with Zulu custom). Acting on an order from God, Shembe established Ekuphakameni, or Elevated Place, on a mountainside north of Durban, a religious center that has become perhaps the most famous in the African Zion movement. Nazarites see Ekuphakameni as the realization of God's kingdom on earth, and Shembe as a Christlike messiah who brought the promise of God's salvation to the Zulu. Present-day Nazarites continue to gather at Ekuphakameni to sing the more than 200 hymns composed by Shembe and to visit his tomb, where angels and ancestors of the church are also said to reside.

Grace Tshabalala, a leader in another Zionist community in KwaMashu Township, South Africa, once articulated the existential quality of living in Zion. For her, the concept of Zion hinged on her belief in being saved as a Christian, in the here and now. Amid the oppression and poverty of apartheid in the 1970s, Tshabalala asserted a realized eschatology: "I have Zion and Zion is my home," Tshabalala stated in an interview with the British Broadcasting Corporation, "Whenever I am sick, I have Zion; whenever I am happy, I have Zion.... Dead or alive, I am a Zionist." While preaching, Tshabalala felt as if someone were "pumping [her] blood," filling her with "power."

Throughout sub-Saharan Africa, Zionist or spirit congregations can be visually distinguished from mainline and Ethiopian churches by their distinctive style of dress: long gowns of solid colors, especially white, representing purity. Denominational insignia are often sewn across the breast or appliquéd on kerchiefs, turbans, or caps, and colored bars and patches are added to designate rank or religious office. Through appropriating garb originally reserved for the missionary priest or bishop, lay and ordained Africans alike assert their spiritual legitimacy and authority. In some instances, liturgical robes are considered essential to the reception of the Holy Spirit and the exercise of spiritual gifts. A

Missionaries baptize converts by immersion in the sea at Durban, South Africa. *CORBIS/Hans Georg Roth*

catechist in a Roho (spirit) church in western KENYA, for example, referred to his gown as his "working tool." Without it, he could not effectively proselytize.

Lively preaching, hymns, and prayers are essential to worship in African spirit churches. The lengthy services generally begin in a formal manner as the pastor leads the congregation through the standard components of the Christian liturgy such as invocation, recitation of the creed, collective confession, and Scripture lessons. The officiating pastor may deliver the initial sermon, but in many independent churches, laypeople are welcome to offer personal testimony and comment on Scripture. Preaching and singing complement each other. In many congregations, individuals freely interrupt the preacher to initiate songs whose lyrics highlight the sermon's theme. Hymns may be accompanied by bells, drums, and rattles; some churches condone only vocal music, which is characteristically spontaneous and responsive. Often, as worship progresses, singers increase the tempo, encouraging people to sway or dance. Through song and movement, members create an atmosphere conducive to ecstatic trance and, in some cases, speaking in tongues. Music can therefore open a channel for communication between God and/or the Holy Spirit and the congregation, facilitating the infusion of divine power into the community. Prayer, particularly when led by a charismatic preacher, can have the same effect.

Politics Parading as Religion?

The European administrative officials in African colonies in the late nineteenth and early twentieth centuries were frequently alarmed by the emergence of indigenous Christian movements. They saw African religious leaders as potential threats, subversive schemers who spread discontent and fueled opposition to European authorities, missionaries, and civil administrators alike. One such leader was SIMON KIMBANGU, a Baptist catechist who led a healing revival in 1921 in the Belgian Congo. Like Dona Beatrice 200 years earlier, Kimbangu was popularly perceived as a powerful nganga who had risen from the dead. Clutching his prophet's staff, Kimbangu would tremble and shake with the power of the Holy Spirit as he laid hands on those who came to him for healing. Thousands flocked to his village, N'Kamba, which soon became the Holy Jerusalem of the revival. Despite the fact that Kimbangu's movement was primarily religious and therapeutic, Belgian authorities were alarmed by the crowds he attracted. Kimbangu did not openly support separation from the mission churches, nor resistance to the government. However, many other *bangunza*, or prophets, some of whom preached in Kimbangu's name, traveled throughout Lower Zaire advocating nonpayment of taxes and foretelling the imminent demise of white rule. In June 1921, after European settlers complained that workers were leaving their estates in droves to join Kimbangu, the local administration sent soldiers to sack N'Kamba-Jerusalem and had many Baptist deacons and laypeople arrested. Kimbangu was seized but escaped, only to be recaptured in September and condemned to death. His sentence was commuted to life imprisonment; he died in 1951 after serving much of his term in solitary confinement.

Today Kimbanguism is among the largest and most successful examples of African independent Christianity, boasting over 4 million adherents in the Democratic Republic of the Congo alone. Officially instituted in 1959 as the Church of Jesus Christ on Earth through the Prophet Simon Kimbangu (EJCSK), Kimbanguism gradually made the transition from an underground protest movement to an established church recognized by the international Christian community (the EJCSK was admitted into the World Council of Churches in 1970). Today's Kimbanguists do not encourage spiritual ecstasy or faith healing; they emphatically reject traditional religion and advocate obedience to civil authority. However, they continue to celebrate their martyred founder as the black messiah, who proclaimed God's truth to Africans just as Christ proclaimed salvation to Israel.

Like other African independent churches with roots in the colonial period, Kimbanguism articulated resistance through religious symbolism, and expressed its religious vision in a political idiom; temporal justice and divine truth were intertwined. Some scholars have been inclined, as were Kimbangu's critics, to see independent Christianity as actual or symbolic political protest "pretending to be religious." However, the advent of national independence throughout most of Africa in the early 1960s did not herald the end of indigenous Christian movements. On the contrary, from 1970 to 1980, the growth rate of independent Christianity far exceeded that of the mainline churches. It soon became clear that monocausal explanations simply could not account for the diversity, richness, and persistence of indigenous Christian movements. AICs speak compellingly to a variety of people, especially the urban poor, creating a sense of community and family that counteracts the alienation resulting from social dislocation and massive migration to the cities. Charismatic and Pentecostal independent churches, with their lively hymns and dance, also provide an opportunity for free expression, emotional release, and a respite from hardship and daily drudgery. Above all, AICs provide access to healing power and spiritual renewal.

The Holy Spirit in African Form

African Zionist churches share much in common with charismatic and Pentecostal congregations around the world. They offer, as scholar Rosalind Hackett has observed, a "pragmatic spirituality" centering on "health, spiritual protection, fertility, material well-being and recognition of dualistic theories of sickness and misfortune." It is frequently said that whites brought the Bible but blacks received the Holy Spirit, and African indigenous congregations are proud of being "strong in the Spirit." The techniques AICs use to cultivate the spirit and the manner in which members articulate their faith have been profoundly shaped by older African religious institutions, practices, and ritual. Founders like Beatrice, Shembe, and Kimbangu, as we have seen, employed traditional methods of mediumship (dreams, trembling and trance, out-of-body journeys to celestial regions) in their ministries and were popularly perceived as diviner-healers. The Aladura (prayer) churches in West Africa integrate aspects of traditional Yoruba domestic shrine design in constructing their worship space to maximize communication with divine forces. Zionists in Natal use staffs to ward off malevolent forces, just as traditional Zulu "heavenheards" used theirs to chase lightning away. In the Lumpa church in MALAWI, central tenets and aspects of spirituality were expressed primarily through symbols and catechetical methods derived from traditional BEMBA initiation rites. By reinvigorating certain aspects of tradition while emphatically rejecting others, members of AICs create a spirituality that is at once profoundly African and an alternative to past ways.

The ability of independent churches to synthesize the old and the new is particularly apparent when one considers the extent to which women have assumed leadership. Forbidden to hold office, preach, or perform sacraments in most mission churches, women figured prominently in the founding of hundreds of AICs. Well-known examples include Christianah Abiodun, who cofounded the highly successful Nigerian Cherubim and Seraphim movement in 1955 with Moses Orimolade; Grace Tani, who established the Church of the Twelve Apostles in GHANA; Marie Lalou, who started the Deima (Holy Water) movement in CÔTE D'IVOIRE; Mai (Mother) Chaza, whose church in ZIMBABWE is named for her; Alice Lenshina, who started the popular Lumpa (Supreme) Church in Northern Rhodesia in 1954 whose members were exiled by the new Zambian government in 1970; and Gaudencia Aoko, cofounder of the Legio Maria, a Kenyan independent church with Catholic roots. The legacy of women's predominance in spirit-possession religion in many regions of precolonial Africa partly explains why women have been so readily accepted as leading mediums and healers in AICs. In the emergence of the Luo Roho movement in western Kenya, for example, a corps of armed female *askeche* (soldiers) protected their congregations, incorporating precedents from local cults in which women became possessed by the violent ghosts of slain warriors.

Most of the AICs founded by women are today headed by men; with increased institutionalization, women have, over time, been relegated to largely ceremonial, therapeutic, and supportive roles. There are exceptions to this trend, such as the Communion Church in Kenya, which promotes women priests. Moreover, the existence of parallel men's and women's hierarchies in many AICs, such as the Aladura, ensures women some degree of autonomy and control over their own affairs. Although the picture with regard to gender is complex and varied, it can be asserted that AICs continue to provide both men and women the opportunity to renegotiate traditional religious roles, identities, and experience in creative ways as they strive to be agents for God's spirit in the world.

Cynthia Hoehler-Fatton

See Also

Crowther, Samuel Ajayi; Johannesburg, South Africa; Nigeria; Transatlantic Slave Trade; Durban, South Africa; Zambia; Christianity: Missionaries in Africa.

Africa

Christianity: Missionaries in Africa, important factor in religious, cultural, and political change within African societies.

Christianity is an evangelizing religion and, as such, missionaries have been essential to the enterprise from its beginnings. As important as missions and missionaries are to African Christianity, one should not confuse the history of mission Christianity, or the history of missionaries, with the history of Christianity on the African continent. An active Christian community existed in Egypt from the earliest days of the religion. By the third century B.C.E., Christian communities had spread throughout North Africa. From these communities, Christianity gradually spread to Nubia and Ethiopia. Monks and priests proselytized to non-Christians; converts evangelized to their friends and families.

In the fifteenth century European trade and conquest brought a new form of missionary activity to Africa. Portuguese, Dutch, and other European traders established small settlements along the coast of Africa to trade in commodities and people, who were sold into the transatlantic slave trade. European governments and trading companies often supported missionary activity by maintaining that part of their reason for being in Africa was to convert the non-Christian. The case of the Portuguese exemplifies the close relationship between Crown and Church. In the Treaty of Tordesillas (1494), the pope recognized Portuguese claims to Africa. The Crown was also responsible for attempting to convert the indigenous people to Christianity. Much of the missionary effort over the next two and a half centuries was conducted under Portuguese authority. The vast majority of missionaries at this time were Roman Catholic priests; many of them belonged to religious orders such as the Jesuits, Capuchins, and Franciscans.

Missionaries often attempted to convert the ruling elite on the assumption that if the rulers were converted, the rest of the society would follow. These attempts met with varying degrees of success. Missionaries often alienated potential Christians by their criticism of African customs and their support of the slave trade. It was left to African Christians to generate religious-based critiques of slavery and the slave trade. Rulers were often reluctant to convert to Christianity because conversion often required them to renounce the traditional religions and practices that were the source of their power and authority. In Ethiopia, the emperor and royalty considered themselves to be in little need of mission activity, because they were already Christians; they saw the Jesuits as a conduit for building alliances with Europeans. In West Africa, Portuguese clergy attempted to proselytize in the Benin kingdom and the Warri state, in the Niger Delta. In the Mutapa state (in present-day Zimbabwe), the missionaries met with modest success. Missionaries also worked in Portuguese-African communities in Sierra Leone, Cape Verde, and Angola. Although some Africans became priests, missionary efforts were often hampered by the short supply of clergy, whether European or African.

One of the states that adopted Christianity was the kingdom of the Kongo (present-day Angola, Congo, and the Democratic Republic of the Congo). After encountering the Portuguese in the 1480s, the Kongo king converted to Christianity in 1491, and for the next few centuries the rulers of Kongo were Christian. Christianity initially served as a bridge between Kongo and Portugal, but by the end of the sixteenth century the relationship had deteriorated and the states were enemies. Part of the conflict arose from the effects of the slave trade in the region. Further, the Kongo state resented the ways in which the Portuguese controlled the supply of clergy and bishops to the region, and the Kongo tried to obtain clergy elsewhere. A Christian presence remained in the region into the nineteenth century, long after the state had dissolved. In Kongo, as in all areas in which Africans accepted Christianity, the local histories, politics, and religion set the framework in which people gave meaning to the new religion and integrated it into their society.

The Roman Catholic dominance of mission work lasted until the mid-1700s. With few exceptions, Protestants showed little interest in foreign mission work until the late eighteenth century, when a series of revivals helped spark interest in foreign missions among Protestants in Great Britain, northern Europe and the United States. Church people formed new societies for the promotion of mission work. Clergymen and laymen from all levels of society volunteered to become missionaries. In general, women could go to the mission field only as the wives or other relatives of the male missionary. The number of Roman Catholic priests and nuns increased during the nineteenth century as orders were founded specifically for mission work.

Many of the missionaries during this time were inspired by humanitarian concerns; they linked the abolition of slavery with their cause. Some missionaries protested against slavery and other abuses to which African people were subjected. Many missionaries saw "civilizing" Africans and converting them to Christianity as an extension of humanitarianism. They saw African cultures as degraded and uncivilized, and many missionaries thought that Africans had no religion. Thus it was part of the missionaries' Christian duty to share the benefits of Western civilization and Christianity with Africans. This perspective meant that missionaries often were dismissive of African cultures and beliefs. In their view, Christianity was linked with Western cultural patterns. Missionaries therefore encouraged converts to adopt Western gender roles and family structure, clothing, literacy, and housing. Christianity was commonly linked with Western patterns of work, agriculture, and consumption. David Livingstone, the Scottish missionary who traveled widely in southern and Central Africa in the mid-nineteenth century, summarized this sentiment when he declared in 1857 that Africa needed "Christianity and Commerce."

Like their predecessors, many missionaries attempted to convert African societies through the rulers, and thus change the entire society. Although relatively few African rulers converted to Christianity in the nineteenth century, several leaders invited missionaries to work within their polities. Moshoeshoe of the Sotho people used missionaries and mission stations as part of his strategy of state building. He used missionaries to negotiate with white settlers in southern Africa, and he also sent his sons to mission schools. In the kingdom of Buganda (in present-day Uganda), the rulers used Protestant and Roman Catholic Christianity, along with Islam and traditional religions, as factors within the complex politics of the state. Although rulers rarely converted to Christianity, other groups of people within society became associated with Christianity. Many of the early converts were somewhat marginal to the established order: young people, refugees, slaves, women. Not all converts were marginal, however. Ntsikana, a councilor to a Xhosa chief, was influential in bringing people to Christianity in early-nineteenth-century South Africa. He argued that Christianity did not require one to adopt Western culture, and his hymns became important expressions of African Christianity.

Sierra Leone and Liberia were important centers of missionary activity. These West African colonies were established to provide homes for former slaves and captives; as was the case in other colonies, thriving indigenous communities lived there well before the settlers arrived. A group of British abolitionists, including former slaves, established Sierra Leone in 1792. Liberia was established by the United States-based AMERICAN COLONIZATION SOCIETY in the 1820s and became an independent state in 1847. Sierra Leone's development illustrates the complex ways in which Christianity became part of the region's religious landscape. The colony's settlers included people of African descent from GREAT BRITAIN, CANADA, and JAMAICA. "Recaptives," Africans who had been captured into slavery but released by the British navy into Sierra Leone, were an important segment of the population. Many settlers were already Christian and they established Christian communities that became a base for further evangelization. Moreover, some settlers and recaptives became missionaries to other parts of Africa. The most famous of these missionaries was Samuel Crowther. Crowther had been captured into slavery as an adolescent and released into Sierra Leone. He converted and became an Anglican minister. He then led a mission of Africans to the Niger Delta in 1857. He was ordained a bishop of the Church of England in 1864 – the first African Anglican bishop.

Some of the most active promoters of Christian missions were people of African descent from the Americas and Europe. These missionaries thought that Christianity was important to bring to Africa; they often expressed a sense of responsibility to their homeland. From the 1700s through the twentieth century, people of African descent from the Caribbean (*see* PROTESTANT CHURCH IN LATIN AMERICA AND THE CARIBBEAN), the United States, Canada, and Europe worked as missionaries in Africa. Many of these missionaries were associated with predominantly black churches that originated in the United States, such as the AFRICAN METHODIST EPISCOPAL CHURCH and the National Baptist Convention. Other African American missionaries were associated with predominantly white churches.

In the last quarter of the nineteenth century, European powers undertook the rapid partitioning and colonization of Africa, a process often referred to as the SCRAMBLE FOR AFRICA. By 1902 Liberia and Ethiopia were the only independent states on the continent. Western missionaries' reaction to imperialism varied greatly. A few missionaries actively helped European governments defeat African states. Other missionaries protested against abuses associated with colonial governments but did not question these governments' authority to colonize Africa. Many missionaries had grown frustrated with the strength of African polities and were convinced that Christianity could advance only when the authority of African states had been destroyed. It appeared that most missionaries accepted colonialism and worked within the system. Some colonial governments attempted to forge close links with missionaries; both the Portuguese and Belgian governments privileged missionaries from their nations who were working in the colonies. Most missionaries and colonial governments worked closely together, although they did not have the same goals and were occasionally in conflict.

Colonial rule opened new opportunities for missionaries. The number of missionaries and mission societies working in Africa increased. Further, from the mid-1800s most mission societies opened their ranks to single women, and work among African women thus became a higher priority. In addition to the previously established societies, new groups such as the Salvation Army, Seventh Day Adventists, and Jehovah's Witnesses began work in Africa. In addition to evangelizing, many of these missionaries established schools, hospitals, and other institutions.

The number of adherents to Christianity increased steadily during this time. Some people were brought into contact with Christianity through work in the colonial economy, service in the military, or study at mission schools. Many people learned of Christianity from African catechists, preachers, friends, or family members. African Christians from areas as diverse as the SUDAN and South Africa acted as missionaries to other African groups. Africans who had been educated in mission schools formed the core of an elite who began some of the earliest challenges to colonialism. The vibrant African Christian community discussed and debated Western missionaries' attitudes toward colonialism, African culture, and "civilization." African Christianity developed distinctive features, such as prayer groups, that missionaries could rarely control. African Christians often emphasized aspects of the religion that had special meaning for their situation, such as healing and prophecy.

Missionaries often emphasized the essential

Although motivated by humanitarian impulses, Christian missionaries in Africa often discredited traditional local customs in favor of Western values and habits. *Courtesy of Church Mission Society, London*

equality of all people and claimed that their goal was to establish "self-standing" indigenous churches. Many missionaries saw the West as the model for a Christian community, however, and were reluctant to cede authority to Africans. This reluctance arose from a mix of bigotry, racism, and doubt concerning the leadership capacity of Africans. Western missionaries were often paternalistic in their relationship with African Christians. In practice this meant that very few Africans were in positions of authority until well into the twentieth century. Those few Africans who had been in leadership positions were often deposed. The fate of the Niger Delta Mission illustrates this tendency. In the 1890s white British missionaries took over the leadership of the station that had been established and run by Africans for over three decades.

In some areas, such as South Africa and coastal West Africa, Christians who were distressed with the attitude of missionaries broke away and formed "Ethiopian" churches. These churches were called Ethiopian in reference to Psalm 68:31: "Princes shall come from Egypt; Ethiopia shall stretch out her hands to God." While the theologies and practices of these Ethiopian churches were often comparable to those of mission churches, Africans were in charge. Often Christians who remained in mission churches were as frustrated with the paternalism of missionaries as were those who formed their own congregations. During this time Africans formed other, prophetic, independent churches, which have often been called Zionist. These independent churches are an important aspect of Christianity but were not always directly related to missions.

Soon after World War II, the European powers recognized that their colonies would eventually become independent. Missionaries in turn acknowledged that the end of colonialism would have an impact on their work. These missionaries began to emphasize developing African leadership in the church hierarchy. This process was somewhat slow; for example, Africans were in the minority among Roman Catholic bishops until the late 1960s. In many cases the number of Western missionaries working in Africa continued to increase. Many mission societies also acknowledged that their work in Africa would have to change, and that the emphasis should be on building a distinctive African church, instead of modeling the church on a Western form. In 1961 the International Missionary Council merged with the World Council of Churches; this controversial move indicated the extent to which mission churches should be considered an essential part of Christianity and not subordinate to the West. The Second Vatican Council (1962-1965) gave impetus toward creating a church that was more responsive to local needs and concerns.

As African colonies won independence, many missionaries were able to maintain good relations with new governments. The relationship between government and church within independent Africa is a related, but quite distinct, question. In states where the transition to independence was accompanied by violence or civil wars, missionaries tended to keep a low profile. In the southern African states of Zimbabwe, NAMIBIA, and South Africa, where racial discrimination against the African majority by the white minority was government policy, a few foreign missionaries, such as Michael Scott and Trevor Huddleston, spoke out against these practices.

Independence of African states has not meant the end of mission work. In the 1970s there were some calls by African Christians for a moratorium on foreign missions so that Africans could gain control of the church. There continues, however, to be a substantial foreign mission presence on the continent. The composition of this group of missionaries has shifted. In a trend dating from the mid-twentieth century, the number of missionaries from North America has increased; most of these missionaries are associated with conservative or fundamentalist evangelical agencies. Generally, the work of missions in post-independence Africa has broadened to include economic and social development, in addition to education and evangelizing.

Modupe Labode

SEE ALSO

Buganda, Early Kingdom of; Christianity, African: An Overview; Colonial Rule; Crowther, Samuel Ajayi; Egypt, Ancient Kingdom of; Niger River; Abolitionism in the United States; Christianity: Independent and Charismatic Churches in Africa; Islam and Tradition: An Interpretation; Slavery in Africa; Protestant Church in Latin America and the Caribbean.

Latin America and the Caribbean

Christophe, Henri

(b. October 6, 1767, Grenada?; d. October 8, 1820, Sans Souci Palace, Haiti), a hero of the HAITIAN REVOLUTION; Christophe was president of HAITI (1806-1811) and king of northern Haiti (1811-1820).

Many of the details about Henri Christophe's early life are unclear, but it is thought that he was born a slave on the British-ruled island of GRENADA. At a young age he ran away, eventually becoming the property of a French naval officer and then of a planter on what was then the French-ruled island of Saint-Domingue (now HAITI). In 1779 he was part of an armed group sent by the French to assist Americans in defending Savannah, Georgia, against the British. Christophe, at that time a slave orderly, may have fought in a battalion led by the Marquis du Rouvrary, and was wounded in a conflict in Savannah in October 1779. He then returned to Saint-Domingue, and some time during this period he purchased his freedom. By 1790 Christophe was part of a French militia force that overcame two Haitian rebel forces led by Vincent Ogé and Jean-Baptiste Chavannes. Christophe's prowess in battle led to his promotion to the rank of captain of the French colonial armed forces in June 1793.

In 1794, with the HAITIAN REVOLUTION already in progress, Christophe joined the forces led by the black rebel general Toussaint L'Ouverture. Though Toussaint had initially rebelled against the French, by this time he had sided with the French forces in response to the 1793 decree outlawing slavery. Christophe quickly distinguished himself as an excellent soldier, and Toussaint soon promoted him to the rank of brigadier general. Christophe's military leadership proved to be crucial to Toussaint when conflict erupted between his own forces and the mulatto forces led by André Rigaud. Christophe led the forces that besieged the port of Jacmel and commanded the garrison at Cap-Français. Christophe managed to keep things under control in the northern regions of Haiti in 1801 by crushing several insurrections, while JEAN-JACQUES DESSALINES, another of Toussaint's principal commanders, attacked the mulatto forces in the south. Christophe implemented a system of forced agricultural labor, known as *fermage*, in the areas under his control. His skill again impressed Toussaint, who went on to use the scheme throughout Saint-Domingue.

In January 1802 the Haitian Revolution took another turn when Napoleon sent a French fleet under the command of his brother-in-law, Gen. Charles Leclerc, to Saint-Domingue to defeat the black military leaders and restore slavery and colonialism. Toussaint, Christophe, and Dessalines were quickly pushed out of the main ports but went on to wage a guerrilla war in the interior. Christophe strategically set Cap-Français and other towns on fire, impeding and frustrating the French advance. But in April 1802, Christophe, running low on food and supplies, surrendered to the French forces. Toussaint and Dessalines also soon reached agreements with Leclerc; Toussaint was imprisoned (he eventually died in prison in 1803).

Disease had begun to decimate the French forces. Weakened, they then attempted to disarm the black population, and rumors spread that this was a prelude to the reimposition of slavery. Resistance grew and widespread fighting began anew. By October 1802 Christophe, along with Dessalines and the mulatto leader ALEXANDRE PÉTION, deserted the French and joined forces with the remaining rebels. With the mulatto and black forces united under the leadership of Dessalines, the French were routed, and Saint-Domingue – with the new name of Haiti – was declared independent on January 1, 1804.

After independence the country was divided into four districts, and Dessalines put Christophe in charge of the north. After Dessalines's death in 1806, Haiti split apart. Christophe was selected as the president by the Haitian Assembly, but he felt the election was more ceremonial than substantive, as the mulatto-controlled assembly retained most of the power. Indeed, Christophe was soon challenged by mulattos who supported Pétion. In response Christophe marched on Port-au-Prince but was forced to retreat by Pétion. This encounter forced Haiti's division into two states. Christophe retreated to the north, which he declared a separate state, while Pétion remained in control of the south. Haiti would remain divided for 13 years.

In the north Christophe set up a rigid system of discipline similar to that demanded of his soldiers. Christophe attempted to build a republic in the north, creating a Haitian currency, the gourde, and recruiting prominent Europeans, such as a royal physician from Edinburgh (Duncan Stewart) and a London mathematician (M. J. Moor), as advisers. He wanted northern Haiti to be an example of what black leadership and black people could accomplish. Christophe also implemented agricultural programs similar to those established under Toussaint, which largely maintained the plantation system, though without slavery. This system proved to be financially successful but created a highly divided society, with a small black elite controlling most of the land and wealth (though some historians argue that later in his life he broke up some of these large estates). Christophe also pursued educational reforms and attempted widespread social reforms, seeking both through coercion and paternalistic charisma to instill in the people of the north values of honesty, personal cleanliness, and obedience.

On March 28, 1811, Christophe declared himself king of the Kingdom of North Haiti and took the name Henry I. He built monuments and palaces, the most impressive being the Citadelle Laferrière fortress near Cap-Haïtien and the Sans Souci Palace. After suffering a stroke in August 1820, Christophe was paralyzed from the waist down. Rebellion among his soldiers grew and Christophe became despondent. He shot himself with a silver bullet in October 1820.

Gregory Freeland

See Also

Toussaint L'Ouverture, François Dominique.

Africa

Chuabo (also known as the Chwabo and the Maganja), ethnic group of Mozambique.

The Chuabo primarily inhabit the Zambezi River Valley in Mozambique. They speak a Bantu language and belong to the larger Maravi cultural and linguistic group. There are approximately 650,000 people who consider themselves Chuabo.

See Also

Bantu: Dispersion and Settlement.

North America

Church of God in Christ, the largest African American Pentecostal denomination.

Rev. Charles Harrison Mason and Rev. Charles Price Jones founded the Church of God in Christ (COGIC) in 1895 in Lexington, Mississippi, in an abandoned cotton gin building. Mason named the church in 1897, claiming that God revealed the name to him as he was walking the streets of Little Rock, Arkansas, via the Bible verse 1 Thessalonians 2:14: "For ye brethren became followers of the churches of God which in Judea are in Christ Jesus." In 1897 the church was chartered, with Jones at its head, in Memphis, Tennessee.

Mason and Jones were former Baptist ministers who were dismissed for being too closely aligned to the Holiness movement. Churches in the Holiness tradition are characterized by charismatic leadership, a simple lifestyle, enthusiastic worship that is rich in music, lay participation, and the priority accorded to the experience of baptism in the Holy Ghost. The term "sanctified" means that these churches consider themselves "congregations of saints."

In March 1907 Mason, along with ministers D. J. Young and J. A. Jeter, traveled to Los Angeles to experience William Seymour's Azusa Street Revival, where impassioned services and glossolalia (ecstatic speaking in tongues) attracted thousands of people. These gatherings are today considered the birth of modern-day Pentecostalism. There Mason received the "gift of the Spirit," as manifested by glossolalia. Mason and Seymour spent time together and became friends. Jones and Jeter split with Mason over the issue of glossolalia, since they felt, unlike Mason, that speaking in tongues was not necessary to validate one's baptism in the Holy Ghost. The split was complicated by legal disputes regarding the ownership of church properties. After these were resolved, Mason controlled the Church of God in Christ and Jones and his supporters founded the Church of Christ (Holiness) U.S.A. in Selma, Alabama. Mason soon afterward became COGIC's senior bishop.

Like the Azusa Street Revival, Mason's church was multiracial. These multiracial revivals and churches were regarded as a symbol of eminent eschaton, according to the New Testament verse, "when all nations shall come to Christ." Mason ordained many white ministers, and from 1909 to 1914 the number of white and black Churches of God in Christ was roughly equivalent. Many white members split off, however, to form independent churches or to join Assembly of God churches, a white Pentecostal organization founded in Hot Springs, Arkansas, in 1914.

Many Church of God in Christ cognate organizations were founded, such as the church's youth organization founded by Ozro Thruston Jones Sr. in 1914. This growth was accelerated in 1917 when Mason traveled with Seymour to Washington, D.C., to hold a revival. The church founded a foreign mission board in 1926. It also founded a newspaper, the *Whole Truth*, edited by D. J. Young. Mason's wife, Elise Washington Mason, whom he married in 1943, later became the paper's editor-in-chief as well as secretary of the home and foreign mission boards. To establish a church hierarchy, Mason consecrated five people to the office of bishop through the laying on of hands in 1933, one of the new bishops being Ozro Thurston Jones Sr.

Understanding the importance of women in his church, Mason established a national supervisor of women for the denomination. The first was Mother Lizzie Roberson, who was succeeded by Mother Lilliam Coffey and then Mother Annie L. Bailey.

By 1933 the Church of God in Christ had spread to all 48 American states. Part of its meteoric success can be attributed to the appeal of the passion and intensity of its worship services. As a sign of its dynamism and lay involvement, some attribute to COGIC the popularizing of congregation members shouting, "Yes, Lord!" or "Hallelujah!" during a worship service. Mason himself calls the exclamation "Yes, Lord!" "the Church of God in Christ national anthem." He describes a typical service by writing that "as the enthusiasm [of a service] grows, more and more people shout 'Yes' and 'Yes, Lord' as they feel moved" and that worshipers often come "out into the aisle to spin about with back bent, feet pumping in place, and hands raised high, fingers spread."

In 1945 the church constructed a headquarters called Mason Temple in Memphis, Tennessee. At the time it was the largest building in the country owned by African Americans. The street in front of the building was renamed Mason Street in honor of Bishop Mason. It was at this church that Dr. Martin Luther King Jr. made his last speech, in support of a sanitation worker's strike, on the evening before his assassination in 1968. The building is now a national historic landmark.

Upon the death of Bishop Mason in 1961, Ozro Thurston Jones Sr. became the church's senior bishop. Aside from being an early youth organizer in the church, he was a pastor in Philadelphia, Pennsylvania. Bishop Jones, with J. E. Bryant, helped codify the official doctrines of the church by writing *The Official Manual of the Church of God in Christ.*

Bishop J. O. Patterson Sr. (1912-1989), who was Mason's son-in-law, succeeded Jones. Patterson founded the C. H. Mason Theological Seminary in Atlanta in 1970. He changed the tradition of ministers wearing only suits and ties during worship services, replacing them with more formal ecclesiastical vestments. In 1984 he also helped established the World Fellowship of Black Pentecostal Churches. Bishop Louis Henry Ford succeeded him in December 1989.

The Church of God in Christ is today the

largest African American Pentecostal denomination and one of the influential branches of the international Pentecostal movement sparked by the Azusa Street Revival. COGIC has over 30,000 churches in America, with more than 5.5 million members. Another 2 million members live outside the United States.

See Also

Baptists; King, Martin Luther, Jr.; Pentecostalism; Seymour, William Joseph.

Church of Jesus Christ on Earth. Please see Kimbangu, Simon

North America

Church, Robert Reed, Jr.

(b. October 26, 1885, Memphis, Tenn.; d. April 17, 1952), American businessman and civic leader who was among the most influential African Americans in Southern politics during the 1920s.

Robert Reed Church Jr., born to Robert Church Sr. and Anna Wright Church, was the youngest son of the wealthy businessman. After graduating from Oberlin College in 1904, he took a job with a Wall Street bank in New York City. Three years later, he returned to Memphis, Tennessee, to work as a cashier for his father's Solvent Savings Bank and Trust, where he was named president in 1909. After his father's death in 1912, Church resigned as president, choosing instead to monitor his father's extensive property holdings throughout Memphis.

Turning to politics, Church founded the Lincoln League in 1916. He became a major contributor and director of the Tennessee Republican Party. He was a delegate to eight Republican National Conventions, an official on the National Advisory Committee for Negroes, a leader in voter registration, and a civil rights activist. Church was among the most influential African Americans in Southern politics during the 1920s.

When the Republican Party lost power during the 1930s, Church lost a powerful platform. He continued to champion fiscal conservatism, opposing President Franklin D. Roosevelt's New Deal. While many African Americans were beginning to join the Democratic Party, Church remained a loyal Republican. He was involved in a long-standing feud with his rival, the white Memphis politician "Boss" Edwin Crump. Crump systematically attacked the Church fortune, forcing Church to move to Chicago, where he unsuccessfully attempted to control Memphis Republican politics. Church died on April 17, 1952, while campaigning for Dwight D. Eisenhower.

Alonford James Robinson, Jr.

See Also

Church, Robert Reed, Sr.; New York, New York.

North America

Church, Robert Reed, Sr.

(b. June 18, 1839, Miss.; d. August 12, 1912, Memphis, Tenn.), American businessman widely considered to be the first African American millionaire.

Robert Reed was born a slave on June 18, 1839, in Mississippi. His mother, an African American slave, died in 1851, and Reed joined his father, a white riverboat owner, as a steward. After the Civil War, Reed moved to Memphis and began investing in saloons and pool halls. He soon acquired a collection of saloons and other businesses in the African American waterfront section of Memphis known as Beale Street. He so diligently monitored the progress of his investments, often visiting each one, that he was nicknamed the "Boss of Beale Street." In 1879 an epidemic of yellow fever hit Memphis, killing residents and driving down the price of real estate. Church capitalized on the opportunity to purchase a significant amount of property throughout Memphis. It is widely believed that Church was the first African American millionaire.

Although he was a wealthy and influential African American, Church was not active in political and civil rights issues. He attended the 1900 Republican National Convention as a delegate but remained committed to his career as a businessman. Despite his own relative silence on civil rights, Church did encourage his children, Mary Church Terrell and Robert Church Jr., to fight for political and social equality.

Church did become actively involved in civic affairs, providing land for a park in his name, financing the construction of a large auditorium and concert hall, and establishing the Solvent Savings Bank and Trust. He died on August 12, 1912, in Memphis from a sudden illness.

Alonford James Robinson, Jr.

See Also

Civil War, American; Terrell, Mary Eliza Church.

North America

Cincinnati, Ohio

In the early nineteenth century, Cincinnati alternated between tolerating antislavery forces and violently opposing an increase of African American presence or power in the city. By 1810, 80 free African Americans were living in the Bucktown section of Cincinnati, and they constructed a church that was reportedly a station of the Underground Railroad between 1812 and 1815. Fourteen years later, African Americans constituted nearly 10 percent of the population. In 1829 whites tried to force their emigration to Africa, then attacked and killed those who could not pay $500 bonds required of all free blacks. This prompted an exodus of more than 1000 blacks to Canada, where they established the Wilberforce settlement.

Yet Cincinnati also had a vigorous antislavery movement. Among the better-known white abolitionists were the Lane Seminary disciples of Lyman Beecher, James G. Birney, publisher of the *Philanthropist* newspaper, and Levi Coffin, the "national president" of the Underground Railroad. After 1841 African American abolitionists published their own newspaper, the *Disfranchised American*.

In the 1840s most African Americans in Cincinnati lived in Bucktown or, if wealthier, on McAllister Street. Most worked as riverfront laborers and domestics, but they included the celebrated landscape painter Robert Duncanson and the daguerrotypist James P. Ball. Denied public education until 1852, blacks established their own institutions of learning, notably Cincinnati High School.

By 1870 the African American population in Cincinnati had grown to approximately 5900 persons of a total 216,000 citizens. The black community expanded from Bucktown into Walnut Hills, but over the next 30 years industrialization forced the majority into the West End.

In 1879 historian George Washington Williams, author of *The History of the Negro Race in America*, became the first African American in the Ohio State Assembly. Ohio's Black Laws, which restricted the social and political rights of African Americans, were abolished in 1887, but segregation and profound inequities persisted. Wendell Phillips Dabney responded by organizing the reform-minded Douglass League in 1893 and by establishing the *Union* newspaper in 1907. In 1915 he headed Cincinnati's chapter of the National Association for the Advancement of Colored People. Many Cincinnati blacks considered emigration to Africa, however. After World War I (*see* World War I and African Americans), 8000 became members of the Cincinnati branch of Marcus Garvey's Universal Negro Improvement Association, led by William Ware.

From 1890 through 1930, many African Americans migrated to Cincinnati for industrial jobs. In 1920 the African American population in the city reached 30,000, most living in the West End. New Deal-era federal housing projects led to still more migration to the West End. By 1940 blacks were 12.2 percent of Cincinnati's population. Jessie D. Locker – later ambassador to Liberia under President Eisenhower – was elected city councilor in 1941 and Theodore M. Berry in 1942. Labor demand during World War II (*see* World War II and African Americans) and a postwar economic boom attracted more African Americans; the black community was one-fourth of the Cincinnati population by 1973. As in other Northern urban areas, frustrations over poverty, unemployment, and de facto segregation erupted into race riots in 1967.

By 1990 African Americans constituted one-third of Cincinnati's population. While increased numbers led to greater political representation, it did not prevent wholesale community displacement. Although Cincinnati elected three black mayors between 1972 and 1991 – Theodore Berry, J. Kenneth Blackwell, and Dwight Tillery – by 1973 blacks had been effectively forced out of the West End to make way for industry and the Mill Creek expressway. That displacement prompted some African Americans to move to the suburbs, but most moved to the Over-the-Rhine and Mount Auburn neighborhoods.

Jim Mendelsohn

See Also

Free Blacks in the United States, 1619 to 1863; Garvey, Marcus Mosiah; Williams, George Washington.

Africa

Cinema, African, generally defined as cinema made by and about Africans.

According to popular legend, cinema was first introduced to Africa in 1896, after a stolen bioscope mysteriously made its way to Cape Town, South Africa. For the next several decades colonial governments effectively delayed the development of an African film industry, but since independence African film directors have struggled to create a viable cinema of their own. Despite ongoing production and distribution problems, they have largely succeeded; African cinema is now internationally recognized, and African filmmakers now aspire to reach broader audiences in Africa itself.

Colonial-Era Cinema

Although Europeans and Americans started to make films in Africa soon after the medium was invented in the 1890s, Africa's colonial regimes restricted Africans' exposure to film and film production until the late 1950s. In British colonies as well as the Belgian Congo (present-day Democratic Republic of the Congo), for example, Africans were forbidden to watch European and American movies. French and Belgian colonial governments controlled the content of all of the films produced within their borders, and Africans were frequently forbidden to work on film productions. These restrictions reflected the colonial powers' concern about the influence of the cinematic medium on the African population. They assumed that Africans were incapable of distinguishing fact from fiction and would therefore take too seriously films that depicted Europeans and Americans unfavorably. They also feared the possible dissemination of subversive or anticolonial messages through film.

Despite these restrictions, some Africans still managed to learn about film and filmmaking. Primarily, they took advantage of colonial efforts to use film as an educational tool. In Tanganyika (present-day Tanzania), for example, the Bantu Educational Cinema Experiment (BECE) was devoted to producing films on hygiene, improved farming methods, and African folktales. Launched in 1935 and sponsored by the colonial office of the British Film Institute, the BECE's films were made in a variety of East African languages and shown to African audiences. The BECE periodically employed Africans to perform menial tasks, and its supervisor L. A. Notcutt urged that similar cinema projects, also employing Africans, be established throughout British Africa. The subsequent establishments of colonial film units throughout the British colonies provided Africans with one way to acquire filmmaking skills.

In the Belgian Congo a similar opportunity emerged for Africans interested in film. In the 1940s the colonial government's Film and Photo Bureau made educational and propaganda films specifically for the African population. In order to reduce costs the bureau employed African workers who were taught the basics of film production. In addition, Africans could acquire cinematic skills at the Congolese Center for Catholic Action Cinema (CCCAC) in Léopoldville (present-day Kinshasa) or Africa Films in Kivu, both of which were run by Catholic priests. The two companies' films – such as the CCCAC's series *Les Palabres de Mboloko*, starring an animated antelope – aimed to teach African audiences religious virtues. Both companies offered Africans an opportunity to learn cinematic techniques, but, as in the other colonial experiments, the content and format of the films produced by these groups were severely restricted by the colonial administration.

In the French colonies, France's goal of assimilating colonial subjects into French culture provided some aspiring African film directors opportunities to attend film school abroad. One of the first was the Senegalese Paulin Vieyra, who graduated from l'Institut des Hautes Etudes Cinématographiques in Paris in 1955. Vieyra later became a well-known film critic and historian. But he and other early Francophone African filmmakers were not permitted to return to Africa to make films. France's 1934 Laval Decree placed strict controls on any filmmaking in its colonies and denied African directors filming permits altogether.

By the late 1950s a number of Africans had acquired filmmaking skills, but they still had little autonomy. Instead, African directors were forced to comply with the paternalistic restrictions established by the colonies' production centers, which typically allowed them to make only "educational" films. Not until decolonization could African film directors begin building a film industry of their own.

Francophone Film Production and the FEPACI

After independence, film directors in the former French colonies took the lead in African cinema for a number of reasons. Francophone Africa had the largest number of film directors, many of whom had acquired sophisticated techniques from their studies abroad. Consequently, they were the best equipped to produce films capable of competing with American and European films for the attention of African audiences. In addition, France offered its former colonies financial and technical support for film production through institutions such as the Consortium audiovisuel international (CAI) and the Bureau du cinéma. The first to take advantage of such assistance was the Senegalese filmmaker Ousmane Sembène, whose 1963 *Borom Sarret* is now considered by many historians to be the first African film.

During the early years of independence Francophone film directors such as Ousmane Sembène, Timité Bassori (Côte d'Ivoire), Moustapha Alassane (Niger), Gaston Kaboré (Burkina Faso), and Med Hondo (Mauritania), not only produced films but also became advocates for African cinema. They identified and denounced the barriers to African film production, such as the European and American distributors' monopoly over African movie theaters (which enabled them to flood the market with foreign films); the lack of production facilities in Africa; and censorship by African governments. Francophone directors, in 1969, initiated the founding of the Fédération Panafricaine des Cinéastes (FEPACI), an organization that fought for the political, cultural, and economic liberation of African film.

The FEPACI's call for cultural liberation has indeed been heard. During the 1970s and 1980s many African filmmakers, with FEPACI encouragement, rejected sensationalistic Hollywood-style filmmaking in favor of productions about African daily life, politics, and social problems. The FEPACI has also helped to promote African film both in Africa and abroad and is a supporter of the Festival Panafricain du Cinéma de Ouagadougou (FESPACO), a biennial film festival held in the capital of Burkina Faso.

Africa's newest generation of Francophone filmmakers, however, has criticized FEPACI's failure to make African cinema more commercially viable in Africa itself. Filmmakers such as Souleymane Cissé (Mali) and Idrissa Ouédraogo (Burkina Faso) have asserted that the FEPACI tends to promote heavy-handed political films that lack technical sophistication. In order to win broader audiences, they argue, African filmmakers need to improve their techniques and choose plots that are accessible to rural African audiences.

Film Production Outside Francophone Africa

Non-Francophone African film production is relatively limited, except in South Africa. Among the other former British colonies, only Nigeria has built a sizable film industry. The growth of cinema in this country was due largely to the efforts of Nigerian film director Ola Balogun. Originally trained in theater, Balogun adapted a number of YORUBA plays for cinema and, between 1972 and 1982, produced nearly a film a year. Since then Balogun has largely abandoned film for television, which has a wider audience in Nigeria. Other former British colonies with smaller film industries include GHANA (whose industry includes directors Kwaw Ansah and King Ampaw), Tanzania (director Flora M'mbugu Schelling), and ZIMBABWE (directors Ingrid Sinclair and Tsitsi Dangarembgra).

In Lusophone Africa, liberation struggles have been a central theme in films produced since the 1960s. In the early 1970s, for example, French-Guadeloupean film director SARAH MALDOROR and Yugoslavian director Dragutin Popovic collaborated with members of three liberation movements – Partido Africano Pela Independencia de Guinè e Cabo Verde (PAIGC) in GUINEA-BISSAU and CAPE VERDE, Frente de Libertação de Mocambique (FRELIMO) in Mozambique, and the Movimento Popular de Libertação de Angola (MPLA) in ANGOLA – to pioneer a form of "guerrilla" cinema. Maldoror's *Sambizanga* (1972) was the best known of her several films on political struggles in Lusophone Africa.

Mozambique has been known as an innovator in film production since its National Film Institute opened in 1976 and French film directors Jean-Luc Godard and JEAN ROUCHE were invited to teach Africans low-cost film techniques. Years of civil war, however, made filming in this country difficult, and some of its filmmakers now live abroad. Rui Guerra, for example, lives in BRAZIL, where he is part of the Cinema Novo movement. Elsewhere in Lusophone Africa, Guinea-Bissau's first director, Flora Gomes, released *Mortu Nega* in 1989; Leao Lopes in Cape Verde followed soon afterward with the 1993 release of *Ilheu de Contenda*. In Angola, Zeze Gamboa and Ruy Duarte de Carvalho released several films in the late 1980s and early 1990s.

NORTH AND SOUTH AFRICA

The most prolific film industries in Africa today are located in North Africa – particularly in EGYPT, ALGERIA, and TUNISIA – and in SOUTH AFRICA. Nevertheless, both industries have historically been ignored by scholars of African cinema.

North African cinema, which is frequently classified with Arab cinema, has generally been disregarded because of the long-standing predominance of commercial interests in the Egyptian film industry, which is one of the oldest on the continent. Egypt produces several hundred films a year, most of them B-grade romances and musicals. Egyptian directors such as Salah Abou Seif, Mohamed Khan, and Youssef Chahine do produce serious films, however, on issues such as Arab identity and the threat of Islamic fundamentalism. Algeria and Tunisia also developed early film industries. Like many other Francophone African countries, they took part in the initial meetings of the FEPACI; in fact they hosted the organization's first two meetings. But by the mid-1970s their participation in FEPACI had waned, and their industries became increasingly dominated by mass-market filmmakers. Still, a number of Tunisian filmmakers have won international recognition, including Moufida Tlati, Karim Dridi, and Nadia Fares. Algerian director Mohamed Lakhdar-Hamina won a Cannes film festival Palme d'Or prize for his *Chronicle of the Years of Embers* (1976), which is about an Algerian peasant family that fights in the anticolonial war against France.

The South African film industry was long ostracized within the world of African cinema because it was dominated by white filmmakers who frequently used film to reinforce racial divisions and perpetuate negative stereotypes about Africans. A few exceptions included directors Donald Swanson, who opposed APARTHEID in *Jim comes to Jo'burg* (1949) and *Magic Garden* (1961); Zoltan Korda, who adapted the Alan Paton novel *Cry the Beloved Country* for film in 1951; and Lindi Wilson, whose *Last Supper at Hortsely Street* (1982) documented the forced removals of "nonwhite" residents in Cape Town's District Six.

South Africa's first black director, Gibson Kente, released the antiapartheid film *How Long* in 1976, but until the early 1990s few blacks were able to make films in South Africa. While in exile, South African film directors such as Nana Mahomo, Lionel N'Gakane, and Chris Austen produced a number of movies that have only recently been released in South Africa. Since the end of apartheid several talented film directors have emerged, including Thomas Mogotlane, Brian Tilly, and Oliver Schmitz. Their work has helped break down the former stigma against South African film at international festivals such as FESPACO.

In less than 40 years African cinema has moved beyond its origins in paternalistic colonial propaganda projects to sophisticated, internationally acclaimed filmmaking. But it has yet to win over the audience African directors wish most to reach – Africans. African filmmakers still face intense competition from European, American, and now Indian film industries, as well as difficulties breaking into the continent's film distribution networks, which are still largely foreign-controlled. Funds are tight for most African film directors, and the political climate in many countries has often precluded free expression. On the other hand, urbanization and the growing number of cinemas in Africa are helping to bring Africans into contact with the medium. International interest in African films, moreover, remains strong. In this light Africa's current filmmaking generation has reasons for optimism.

Elizabeth Heath

SEE ALSO

Cape Town, South Africa; Decolonization in Africa: An Interpretation; Front for the Liberation of Mozambique; Hondo, Abid Mohamed Medoun (Med); Ouédraogo, Idrissa; Kinshasa, Democratic Republic of the Congo; Mozambique; Paton, Alan Stewart; Ouagadougou, Burkina Faso; Senegal; Urbanism and Urbanization in Africa; Popular Movement for the Liberation of Angola; Islamic Fundamentalism: An Interpretation.

Latin America and the Caribbean

Cinema Novo

Like many of the other post-World War II national film movements, Brazil's Cinema Novo developed cinematic and discursive strategies that radically broke with the dominant cinema that preceded it. Driven by moral and political imperatives, Nelson Pereira dos Santos, Glauber Rocha, Carlos Diegues, and other directors provocatively probed issues of cultural identity. In BRAZIL, this meant coming to grips with the question of race. As Ismail Xavier noted, while many other Third World countries could fight a colonialist mindset by returning to "genuine" preimperialist practices, the only true "natives" in Brazil – the Indians – suffered a serious demographic decline after conquest, and currently constituted only a tiny minority of Brazil's population. Black culture, which had embedded within it a history of oppression, therefore frequently substituted as the locus of an oppositional aesthetics and as a site of national authenticity.

Through the analysis of a few selected films, this article examines the cinematic landscape that Cinema Novo directors surveyed and responded to, and the ways in which it influenced their portrayal of black culture. The shifts in ideology and the variety of perspectives operating within the movement are also illustrated.

By no means were Cinema Novo's films the first to portray Afro-Brazilian music, dance, and religion. The popular musical form known as *chanchada*, tied to Rio's SAMBA-filled Carnival, flourished in the 1940s and 1950s. These movies often negotiated a rich, complex, and tricky dialectic between "high" and "low" culture, shifting smoothly – even within a single scene – from Americanized entertainment to the more Africanized rhythms and movements of samba. Within many of these very entertaining films were sly critiques of pomposity and racism. At the start of the highly reflexive *Carnaval Atlantida* (1953), for instance, a movie executive intends to produce a film based on Greek mythology, which he sees as beautiful. By the end, he has scrapped this plan in favor of a far more popular, rhythmic, and Brazilian fare. One might justifiably say that dismissing these films – which were low cost, adored by audiences, and playfully deconstructive of the powers-that-be – was one of Cinema Novo's biggest mistakes.

Foreign directors seized on the black culture of the FAVELAS (or squatter settlements) too: Marcel Camus's *Black Orpheus* (1959) transposed the ancient Greek myth of Orpheus to Rio through a seductive blend of music, dance, actual Carnival footage, and Afro-Brazilian religion. Another potentially more interesting and progressive film was Orson Welles's unfinished opus *It's All True*, which sought to tell the history of samba. But his emphasis on black actors, and his criticism of the Brazilian government's destruction of Rio's famous Praça Onze, held by many to be the birthplace of samba, caused his RKO studio to panic, and they cut the film's funding.

One of the first Cinema Novo films to focus on Afro-Brazilian culture charted similar territory as the film Welles tried to make and starred the same performer he wanted to use, the much-loved *chanchada* actor Grande Otelo. Nelson Pereira dos Santos's short work, *Rio Zona Norte* (1957), Rio Northern Zone, centered on a poor composer from the favelas who is anxious to get his samba recorded. Lacking formal musical training, he is forced to rely on others to transcribe and sell his song. Naturally their promises of payment prove worthless: the tune seems almost to float out of the hands of its powerless and innocent creator and through the city, where it gets appropriated by those who are richer, whiter, better connected, and infinitely more corrupt. Only when he hears his music on the radio does the character discern the true situation. The work's documentary-like shooting style strengthens the sense of "reality" behind this tale of thievery – one unfortunately quite familiar to many black Brazilian musicians.

During its early period, Cinema Novo focused on the northeast, setting many of its stories in the very Africanized state of BAHIA as well as in the rural backlands. This move away from the overtly "modern" terrain of the city either explicitly or implicitly carried historical connotations. Carlos Diegues's *Ganga Zumba* (1936) (and his *Quilombo*, 1984) dramatized the struggle for freedom during the time of slavery, lionizing the figures who established and led the famous quilombo, or runaway slave community, of Palmares. In contrast to earlier, more sentimental Brazilian epics – and much like contemporary Cuban cinema, such as *El otro Francisco* (1974, The Other Francisco) and Tomás Gutierrez Aléa's *La ultima cena* (1976, The Last Supper) – *Ganga Zumba* depicted brutal slave owners and violent resistance; successful revolutionary strategies; and a cohesive, organized insurgent movement. It has been faulted by some, though, for its depiction of women; their defiance, as in Diegues's *Xica* (1976), mostly depended on their sexuality.

To trace Brazilian cinema's changing portrayal of black culture, it is worth contrasting three films set in Salvador, Bahia, Brazil's first capital city and the place where many slaves first set foot in the New World. The first, *O Pagador das Promessas* (1962, The Given Word), by Anselmo Duarte, precedes Cinema Novo; the second, Glauber Rocha's first feature, *Barravento* (1962, The Turning Wind), portrays the ambivalent attitude toward Afro-Brazilian religion that film critic Robert Stam finds common in early Cinema Novo; and the third, Nelson Pereira dos Santos's *Tenda dos Milagres* (1977, Tent of Miracles), uncritically embraces popular religion and culture.

Duarte's *O Pagador das Promessas* tells the story of a northeastern peasant named Zé who, to fulfill a promise he made to Saint Barbara for curing his donkey, carries a large cross on his back from his small town to a church in Salvador. He intends to bring the cross to an altar inside; but because Zé made his pledge to Iansã, an *orixá* (god) often symbolized by Saint Barbara in the Afro-Brazilian religion of CANDOMBLÉ, the priests refuse him entrance. Defiantly, Zé waits, joined by hundreds of supporters, who stage a virtual Carnival outside. But throughout, the film emphasizes the difference between the lighter-skinned Zé and many of the others: for Zé, Christianity is the principal religion, not Candomblé. While the others play CAPOEIRA, the Afro-Brazilian martial art, Zé remains motionless and culturally distinct. Cinematically, too, the style hews to classic Hollywood standards of shooting and editing, setting up Zé as a very individual hero who stands out against the backdrop of the crowd.

In contrast, *Barravento* fairly pulses with Bahian music, dance, and religious ceremonies. Avoiding what Maria Rita Galvão calls "exoticism and folklore," Rocha integrates these cultural practices into a highly critical examination of the world. Set in a community of extremely poor black and mulatto fishermen, the film depicts the ideological struggle of two men for the hearts and minds of the group. Firmino, who has just returned from a long stay in the city, is determined to revolutionize the villagers; Aruan is a fisherman "protected" by Iemanjá, the Candomblé orixá of the sea. Religion lies at the center of the battle: the fishermen put their faith in Iemanjá, sure she will keep them fed, while Firmino prefers that they fight for their food in more earthly, political ways.

The trajectory of *Barravento* leads to the dethroning and radicalizing of Aruan, Iemanjá's special son. From this emerges a contradictory portrait of Afro-Brazilian religion: on the one hand it appears as "the opiate of the people," chaining them to the past. On the other hand, Firmino must in effect *use* Candomblé to discredit it, as he sets about trying to get the religion's priests and priestesses to put a spell on Aruan that will sever his connection to the goddess. In this, as in other points throughout the film, the film perversely reasserts the power and effectiveness of Candomblé.

Rocha additionally serves up a loving documentation of the dances at the *terreiro*, or Candomblé temple. An overhead shot reveals the women spinning in intricate circular patterns, while close-ups show the detailed hand movements associated with each orixá. Candomblé is a trance religion, and the film's rapid editing creates a hypnotic, enveloping sensation in sympathy with the mediums being "mounted" by their gods. And all over the Bahian landscape, the sound of drumming and the songs of the orixás resound. While Rocha seems unsure of the effect Candomblé has on its practitioners, as a cultural tradition maintained with difficulty, particularly during slavery, it cannot be easily shunted aside.

Additionally, Rocha incorporates two other dance and music forms with strong African roots, both of which were prohibited by authorities at various points in Brazilian history: the *samba de roda*, a flat-footed, shuffling, sexy samba in which the dancers one by one (or occasionally in couples) come to the center of a circle and try to outdo each other with tricky acrobatic steps; and capoeira, the dance/martial art through which Firmino and Aruan stage their final standoff.

In Rocha's dialectical, often aggressive style of filmmaking, Afro-Brazilian culture stood in stark contrast to the forms favored by the white upper-class elite. Even *Terra em Transe* (1967, Land in Anguish), centering on populist politics and featuring no black leads, switches disjunctively from opera to samba to signal characters' loyalties, while *Antonio das Mortes (o dragão da maldade contra o santo guerreiro)* (1969, Antonio das Mortes: The Dragon of Evil Against the Warrior Saint) plays equally with a clashing mixture of modernist music and songs to the orixás Oxóssi and Ogum.

Dos Santos's *Tent of Miracles*, based on Jorge Amado's popular novel, takes the question of what makes Brazilian society unique as its subject. The film covers the world of music, dance, Carnival, and religion while unfolding a social history of oppression and racism that Brazil has still not wholly transcended. Using the device of a film within a film as a starting point, and a Hollywood-like shooting style, the story relates the life of a legendary black Bahian named Pedro Archanjo, whose keen intelligence and irrepressible energy allowed him to break down racial barriers. The tale focuses on the hoopla surrounding a week dedicated to exploring and celebrating the achievements of this man. In Amado's novel a policeman describes him as "mulatto, indigent, native of Bahia, always the know-it-all, wise guy, and life of the party." Academic panels, theatrical spectacles, a documentary film, and other special events will all display some aspect of Archanjo's life and work during the week of celebration. Its troubled preparations – including a capoeira fight over a play in Archanjo's honor – reveal the struggle to control history as well as Archanjo's image. Scenes from the past alternate with present-day sequences, juxtaposing the multiple (and not always honorable) motivations of the event's organizers with bygone injustices: we go back in time to see the black musical groups known as *afoxés* getting banned from Carnival (Archanjo leads them through the streets, shocking the white elite); the police breaking into terreiros, terrorizing Candomblé practitioners; and Archanjo writing a cookbook with Bahian recipes to show how much

Brazilian cuisine owes to blacks.

The catch is Amado's celebration of miscegenation, an ideology that also permeates dos Santos's film. *Tent of Miracles* attempts to locate the specifically Brazilian in its mulatto culture, finding in Ana Mercedes, a mulatta, and in Archanjo, symbols of the best that Brazil can produce. One black character in the film suggests that mixing destroys the black population rather than providing a source of strength. Given Brazil's complex racial system, with dozens of classifications based on various shades of color, Brazilian blacks have rarely shared Amado and dos Santo's unquestioned optimism. Rather, the exaltation of mulatto culture is often a source of bitter controversy, debate, and resentment.

The use of black popular culture as a source of inspiration for Cinema Novo continued to grow even as the movement began to split apart as a result of political pressures from the military dictatorship (Rocha went into exile and made films in Spain and Africa) and the different ideologies and ideas of cinema subscribed to by each director.

Karen Backstein

See Also
Palmares: An African State in Brazil; Rio de Janeiro, Brazil; Religions, African, in Brazil; Carnivals in Latin America and the Caribbean; Orishas.

Africa

Cinque, Joseph (b. 1813, Sierra Leone; d. 1879, Sierra Leone), an African man abducted into slavery who led a rebellion aboard the Spanish slave ship *Amistad*.

Although Sengbe – pronounced "Sin'gway," and later Anglicized as Joseph Cinque – lived for approximately 66 years, he is best known for his role in a drama that lasted a little more than three years. Scholars believe that Cinque, who belonged to the Mende ethnic group, was a married father before his abduction. When he was about about 26, slave raiders kidnapped him and sold him to Portuguese slave traders, who took him to Havana, Cuba. There Cinque and other abductees, were resold and put aboard the *Amistad*.

Shortly after the ship left Havana harbor, in June 1839, Cinque led a group of 53 slaves who freed themselves and killed all but two crew members. The rebels ordered these two to help them sail back to Africa, but the crew members tricked them into sailing north. About two months later the ship reached Long Island, New York, where United States naval officers arrested the Africans for murder and piracy.

Their case made a national celebrity of Cinque. He attracted both praise and condemnation. The proslavery *New Orleans Times Picayune* called Cinque a "black piractical murderer," while abolitionists considered him a heroic figure and called him "the Osceola of his race" and a "Hannibal or Othello." John W. Barber in *A History of the Amistad Captives* (1840) appealed for the captives' release: "These men deserve sympathy – they ought to have protection. Let me ask in their behalf, means to carry on their defense; let me ask the prayers of those who care for them and the perishing millions of Africa, that God will so order events as to deliver them from the bloody grasp of the executioner...." Former president John Quincy Adams defended Cinque and the others in court, and the U.S. Supreme Court eventually ruled in favor of the Africans and freed them to return to Africa.

In November 1841, the 35 surviving Africans sailed for Sierra Leone, where they landed in January 1842, more than three years after they had been abducted. Little is known of what Cinque did after his return. Some reports state that he became a slave trader himself, but there is no known documentation of this claim.

In 1997 American filmmaker Steven Spielberg recreated the dramatic but little-known events that Cinque and his fellow rebels survived in a film titled *Amistad*.

Robert Fay

See Also
Spain; Abolitionism in the United States; Amistad Mutiny.

Africa

Cissé, Souleymane (b. April 21, 1940, Bamako, Mali), Malian filmmaker; one of the most popular filmmakers in Africa.

Souleymane Cissé became a film devotee as a young child, when his brothers took him to the open air cinemas of Bamako. By the time he graduated from secondary school he had already organized a student film group and mastered the skills of a projectionist. After seeing a film on Patrice Lumumba, former leader of the Democratic Republic of the Congo, in 1962, Cissé decided to become a filmmaker and won a scholarship to the State Institute of Cinema in Moscow in 1963.

After graduating in 1969, Cissé returned to Mali, where he was hired to make newsreels and documentaries for the Ministry of Information. Three years later he completed his first fiction film, *Cinq jours d'une vie* (1972). This, like all of his subsequent feature films – *Den muso* (1975), *Baara* (1978), *Finyé* (1982), and *Yeleen* (1987) – won acclaim at international film festivals. Although Cissé's style has been influenced by Italian neorealism and by Soviet social realism, his working conditions have been shaped by the socioeconomic realities familiar to most African filmmakers. "To make a film belongs to the realm of miracle," he has explained. "I have to do everything. I am in turn producer, cameraman and technician. I lend a hand in every area." Despite these constraints Cissé's productions are lauded for their technical sophistication.

His feature films, which portray the conflicts between modernity and tradition through the stories of people who have moved from the rural countryside to urban centers, have proven extraordinarily popular in both Africa and France. *Baara* and *Finyé* have been two of the most commercially successful African movies to be seen on both continents.

In addition to working on his own films, Cissé has been an active member of the Fédération Panafricaine des Cinéastes (FEPACI) and has been leading the effort to increase African film distribution and help new African filmmakers overcome the technical and economic obstacles to their work.

Elizabeth Heath

See Also
Cinema, African; Bamako, Mali.

North America

Citizenship Schools, community-based adult educational programs that promoted literacy and voter registration and taught leadership skills to African Americans in the United States South during the 1960s.

Citizenship schools were initially a program of the Highlander Folk School in Monteagle, Tennessee, a center that promoted interracial cooperation and literacy training to help African Americans gain full citizenship. Consulted about the program's aims, Septima Clark, the African American activist and teacher from Johns Island, South Carolina, and the schools' first education director, successfully argued to expand the scope of the program. In addition to literacy training, she suggested informing people about their right to participate in and change the political system, as well as training community activists.

The first citizenship school opened in 1957 on Johns Island with no funds for buildings or staff. The original class met in a cooperative building, and their teacher, Bernice Robinson, was a volunteer. However, students learned both practical skills (Bible reading, signing their names, completing money orders and voter registration forms) and the critical skills needed to analyze and challenge oppression. By 1961 African American voter registration on Johns Island had increased by 300 percent, and 82 teachers were conducting schools in Alabama, South Carolina, Georgia, and Tennessee.

In February 1961 Highlander Folk School experienced funding difficulties and transferred the management of the citizenship schools to the Southern Christian Leadership Conference (SCLC). Septima Clark joined the SCLC in July 1961 as director of workshops. Though the Citizens Education Program, as it was renamed, was successful (by 1970 it had registered over 100,000 voters through 800 citizenship schools), it was discontinued owing to insufficient funding from an SCLC leadership that favored direct protest along with the Voting Rights Act of 1965.

Robert Fay

See Also
Clark, Septima Poinsette.

North America

Civil Rights Congress, American civil rights organization dedicated to protecting the civil rights and liberties of African Americans and suspected communists.

The Civil Rights Congress (CRC) was established in 1946 after three organizations closely associated with the Communist Party of America – the National Negro Congress, the International Labor Defense, and the National Federation for Constitutional Liberties – decided to merge. During its relatively brief existence, the CRC fought for the protection of civil rights and liberties of African Americans and suspected communists primarily through litigation, political agitation, and the mobilization of public sentiment. Communist leader and lawyer William Patterson served as executive secretary of the organization for the duration of its existence. At its peak the CRC had 10,000 members.

Like the National Association for the Advancement of Colored People (NAACP), the CRC pursued legal cases that challenged racism and political persecution, establishing a number of civil liberties rulings that expanded the rights of all Americans. It sought to repeal legislation designed to restrict dissent and silence left-wing opposition, such as the Smith Act (1940) and the McCarran Act (1950). In one of its first cases, the CRC defended Rosa Lee Ingram, a black tenant farmer who, together with two of her sons, was convicted and sentenced to death in 1947 for the murder of John Stratford, a white tenant farmer. As a result of the CRC's efforts, Ingram and her two sons were freed. In May 1951 the CRC provided legal representation and waged a public relations campaign to defend 11 Communist leaders convicted under the Smith Act.

At the height of the McCarthy period, in the mid-1950s, the CRC was itself investigated by various government entities, notably the House Committee on Un-American Activities and the Internal Revenue Service. In 1956 the Subversive Activities Control Board declared the CRC to be a "communist front," substantially controlled by the Communist Party of America. In that same year, the CRC was forced to close down because of the increased legal cost of the investigations and a decline in contributions.

Zebulon Miletsky

See Also
Communist Party USA, African Americans and the.

OPPOSITE PAGE: Black activists give the Black Power salute at a rally for the Black Panther Party. The Black Power Movement, which emerged in the mid-1960s, encouraged black solidarity and self-reliance.
CORBIS/Flip Schulke

North America

Civil Rights Movement

Patricia Sullivan

ORIGINS

The Reconstruction Era, 1865 to 1890s

The Civil Rights Movement had its roots in the constitutional amendments enacted during the Reconstruction era. The Thirteenth Amendment abolished slavery, the Fourteenth Amendment expanded the guarantees of federally protected citizenship rights, and the Fifteenth Amendment barred voting restrictions based on race. The Reconstruction amendments were, as civil rights lawyer Oliver Hill observed, "a second Bill of Rights" for black Americans.

Reconstruction radically altered social, political, and economic relationships in the South and in the nation. Former slaves participated in civic and political life throughout the South. Black elected officials served at all levels of government, from local offices to state legislatures and the United States Congress. During the early days of Reconstruction, state governments drew up new constitutions that implemented sweeping democratic reforms, including, for the first time in the South, a system of universal free public education.

Yet the meaning of freedom was vigorously contested in private and public life to the end of the nineteenth century. Newly enfranchised blacks understood citizenship to embody constitutionally protected rights, realized through political participation and ultimately secured by the federal government. They acted upon an expansive view of the democratic process through their participation in Republican Party politics and by exploring alliances with independent groups and, in some cases, the Democratic Party as well.

This vision competed with the Democratic Party's politics of "redemption," which promised the restoration of white hegemony and "home rule" for Southern states. As Democrats regained control of state governments throughout the South, the Ku Klux Klan and other vigilante groups sought to drive blacks from political life through a relentless campaign of fraud and violence. Black men continued to vote in large numbers, often going to the polls in groups, accompanied by family members.

By the late nineteenth century, however, reconciliation between the North and the South was nearly complete, and popular "scientific" theories about race favored white supremacist views. State governments controlled by Democrats drew up new constitutions and enacted a variety of laws that dramatically restricted suffrage in the South, virtually barring blacks from voting and vastly reducing the scope of government. A combination of municipal ordinances and local and state laws mandating racial segregation ultimately permeated all spheres of public life. The Supreme Court, in rulings such as Plessy v. Ferguson (1896), upheld the South's "new order," which essentially nullified the constitutional amendments enacted during Reconstruction.

Black Protest During the Age of Jim Crow, 1900 to 1930s

By the dawn of the new century, government and politics had become, as one historian noted, "inaccessible and unaccountable to Americans who happened to be black." While the rudiments of citizenship expired, black protest against new laws segregating streetcars spontaneously erupted in locally organized boycotts in at least 25 Southern cities from 1900 to 1906. Some boycotts lasted as long as two years, but these protests failed to stem the tide of segregation. Meanwhile, LYNCHING and other forms of antiblack violence and terrorism reinforced legal structures of white domination.

Black leaders and intellectuals continued to debate a broad range of political strategies. There was, for example, the accommodationism and self-help advanced by Booker T. Washington and others, the civil rights protests advocated by Ida B. Wells and W. E. B. Du Bois, and the nationalist and emigration movements promoted by leaders such as HENRY MCNEAL TURNER. These overlapping and sometimes contradictory approaches revealed the tensions and challenges inherent in what often was a daunting effort: how to build and sustain black communities amid the crushing environment of white racism while envisioning a way forward.

Yet traditions of freedom and citizenship, born in the crucible of Reconstruction, nurtured communities of resistance. African Americans continued to create strategies for social and political development through a separate public sphere. Black community life was dominated in large part by the church and shaped by other institutions such as fraternal organizations, schools, and newspapers. The black church focused the mobilization of community resources to provide educational and welfare services, leadership training, and organizational networks and served as a site of mass gatherings and meetings – a place, as Evelyn Brooks Higginbotham has written, "to critique and contest America's racial domination."

THE NAACP, WORLD WAR I, AND THE "NEW NEGRO"

In 1905 W. E. B. Du Bois, William Monroe Trotter (1872-1934), and other black militants founded the NIAGARA MOVEMENT, an organization committed to securing full citizenship rights for African Americans. The Niagara Movement was short-lived but its goals were adopted by the NATIONAL ASSOCIATION FOR THE ADVANCEMENT OF COLORED PEOPLE (NAACP), founded in New York in 1909 by an interracial group of reformers and civil rights activists. White progressives dominated the early leadership of the NAACP. But the NAACP provided the primary organizational and institutional foundation from which the black struggle for civil rights was mounted over the next half century.

World War I and the Great Migration altered the political and social landscape of black America. Beginning in 1914, wartime industrial opportunities in the North sparked a massive movement of nearly 1.5 million black Southerners to Northern urban centers, a migration that continued through the 1920s. While racial discrimination and segregation restricted black opportunities in the North, black community life flourished in Northern cities, where African Americans enjoyed free access to the ballot. As their numbers increased, the black vote in the urban North gradually became a factor of national consequence.

The participation of African Americans in World War I, the war that promised to "make the world safe for democracy," stirred the aspirations of a new generation determined to "make democracy safe for the Negro." Returning veterans formed organizations such as the League for Democracy, which advocated political activism and self-defense, and joined in establishing new branches of the NAACP throughout the South. Others, like CHARLES HAMILTON HOUSTON, enrolled in law school, determined to fight racial injustice through the courts.

Whites responded with a campaign of antiblack violence that erupted in a series of lynchings and more than 25 race riots throughout the country during the summer of 1919. The worst riot was in Chicago (*see* CHICAGO RIOTS OF 1919). In many instances blacks fought back, in the spirit of Claude McKay's defiant poem "If We Must Die." Yet state repression, supported by federal surveillance, effectively quashed the incipient democratic political initiatives spawned by the war.

During the 1920s the New Negro movement stretched the parameters of racial consciousness and expression. Urban communities nurtured the outpouring of black cultural, literary, and musical creativity that flowered in the HARLEM RENAISSANCE. Beyond the literary salons and art galleries, Marcus Garvey and his UNIVERSAL NEGRO IMPROVEMENT ASSOCIATION represented the largest mass black organization in the United States, one that promoted black economic development and celebrated Africa and racial pride. While W. E. B. Du Bois and some others dismissed Garvey as little more than a fool, Charles Houston contended that Garvey surpassed most race leaders of his time, for he had "made a permanent contribution in teaching the simple dignity of being black."

Despite cultural and economic changes ushered in by migration and urbanization, the status of African Americans remained largely unchanged. Some 80 percent of African Americans still lived in the Southern United States in 1930, where they were racially segregated, politically disfranchised, and economically marginalized. The fate of nine young black men in the SCOTTSBORO CASE of 1931 focused national and international attention on the fact that blacks in the South were completely beyond the protection of the law.

CHARLES HOUSTON AND THE LEGAL CAMPAIGN FOR CIVIL RIGHTS

With the normal channels of political participation closed to the vast majority of black Americans, Charles Houston envisioned a unique role for black lawyers as "social engineers," prepared to "anticipate, guide, and interpret his group's advancement." Houston, a graduate of Harvard Law School, joined the faculty of HOWARD UNIVERSITY Law School in 1924. He transformed Howard into a laboratory for the development of civil rights law and trained a generation of black lawyers to lead the assault on JIM CROW.

When Houston became chief legal counsel of the NAACP in the early 1930s, he and former student THURGOOD MARSHALL began laying the groundwork for a protracted campaign against racial discrimination in education. For Houston and Marshall, litigation was a slow and deliberate process, tied to the development of community support and participation. Houston and Marshall traveled as much as 16,667 km (10,000 mi) a year through the South, where they met with small and large groups, explaining the mechanics of the legal fight and its relationship to broader community concerns. An associate recalled that Houston's efforts in the South were fueled by his confidence in the capacity "within the black community and the Negro race to bring about change." During the 1930s Houston and Marshall implemented a major reorientation of the NAACP's program, focusing staff efforts on the expansion of black membership and the cultivation of local leadership and branches, especially in the South. In 1934 Houston wrote Walter White, then executive secretary of the NAACP: "The work of the next decade will have to be concentrated in the South."

THE NEW DEAL AND THE WORLD WAR II ERA

While the South was the primary arena of the black freedom struggle, the nationalizing trends of the NEW DEAL and World War II enhanced the possibilities for a broad legal and political challenge to the segregation system and made civil rights an issue of consequence throughout the country.

BLACKS AND THE ROOSEVELT ADMINISTRATION

The 1932 presidential election of Franklin D. Roosevelt in the depths of the GREAT DEPRESSION precipitated a sea change in American politics. New Deal programs and legislation expanded the scope of federal power and redefined the role of government and politics in American life. Government relief and job programs, along with the legalization of labor unions, stirred the expectations of groups long on the margins of national politics – industrial workers, sharecroppers, and African Americans of all classes.

When Roosevelt was inaugurated in 1933, racial segregation reigned in the city of Washington and in the corridors of government. The Republican Party offered no more than token representation to black Americans, and white Southerners dominated the Democratic Party. During the 1920s the NAACP had carved out a presence in the nation's capital through its efforts to gain support for antilynching legislation (*see* ANTILYNCHING MOVEMENT); in 1930 an NAACP lobbying campaign had helped defeat the nomination of John J. Parker, a white Southern conservative, to the Supreme Court. But there were no secure avenues through which African Americans could influence or shape government policy.

The implementation of a national recovery program, however, promised to have immediate and long-term consequences for black Americans. As more established black leaders deliberated about how to respond to the flurry of New Deal legislation, Robert C. Weaver, a doctoral student at Harvard, and John P. Davis (1905-1973), a new graduate of Harvard Law School, acted to ensure that black interests were represented. In the summer of 1933 the two men returned to their hometown of Washington and established an office on Capitol Hill, where they fought successfully against the racial wage differential in the first recovery program. Their efforts led to the establishment of the Joint Committee on Economic Recovery, a group of more than a dozen black organizations that included the NAACP and the NATIONAL URBAN LEAGUE (NUL). The committee lobbied for fair inclusion of African Americans in government-sponsored programs and publicized incidents and patterns of racial discrimination.

The NAACP and the black press, along with the Rosenwald Fund, successfully pressed for the appointment of black government officials to represent black interests from within the Roosevelt administration. Robert Weaver and William Hastie were among the first African Americans hired. Shortly after joining the Department of the Interior they integrated the lunchroom, sparking the reversal of the segregationist policies enacted by Woodrow Wilson. By 1935 black advisers were serving in many cabinet offices and NEW DEAL agencies and had created an informal network commonly known as the BLACK CABINET.

SOUTHERN BLACKS AND THE NEW DEAL

The Democratic rhetoric of the New Deal, along with federal programs, dovetailed with the NAACP's expanded activity in the South, the growth of industrial unionism in the region (*see* LABOR UNIONS IN THE UNITED STATES), and pockets of student and Communist Party activism. Together, these developments revived the expansive view of citizenship and politics that had informed black and biracial politics in the Reconstruction era.

Despite their conservative nature, early New Deal programs stirred the stagnant economic relationships that had persisted in the South since the 1890s. Federal work relief and credit, along with federal legislation securing the rights of labor to unionize, implicitly threatened the culture of dependency that shaped race and class relations in the South. New Deal initiatives combined with the organizing efforts of a revitalized NAACP and radical labor groups – such as the International Labor Defense – to support a renewed interest in politics on the part of the South's disfranchised.

Early in 1934 a South Carolina peach grower complained that black women would not work in the fields while their husbands had jobs with the federal Civil Works Administration. In Arkansas black and white sharecroppers organized the Southern Tenant Farmers Union to demand federal enforcement of guarantees provided by the New Deal's Agricultural Adjustment Administration. Organized groups of black citizens in Georgia and South Carolina attempted to vote in the Democratic primary that barred blacks in 1934, seeking entry into Roosevelt's party. Peter Epps, an administrator for the WORKS PROGRESS ADMINISTRATION in South Carolina, told an interviewer that blacks "talked more politics since Mister Roosevelt's been in than ever before."

Contemplating the impact of recent federal programs on black political consciousness, W. E. B. Du Bois noted that the government was attending to economic matters and furnishing jobs and food in the provincial South. The question bound to arise was, "How can this political instrument which is the federal government be used more widely and efficiently for the well-being of the mass of people?"

NEW DEAL POLITICAL COALITIONS: BLACKS, LABOR AND THE DEMOCRATIC PARTY

THE 1936 ELECTION

While blacks were essentially barred from voting in the South, black voters in the North emerged as a pivotal group in the 1936 presidential campaign. Following a steady stream of migrations from the South during the 1920s, blacks in the North came to cast significant numbers of votes in key industrial states. They had been drifting away from the party of Lincoln, establishing a tentative allegiance to the Roosevelt administration. Yet Roosevelt's party was also the party of Southern segregationists.

While the Roosevelt administration had failed to endorse racially sensitive legislation, such as an antilynching bill, it made other gestures that appealed to black voters. Roosevelt presided over a Democratic National Convention that, for the first time, opened its doors to the equal participation of black reporters and the handful of black delegates in attendance, drawing a howl of protest from Southern delegates. MARY MCLEOD

BETHUNE and other members of the Black Cabinet took part in a sophisticated campaign aimed at black voters. It included an extravagant multi-city celebration of the 73rd anniversary of the Emancipation Proclamation. Such actions reinforced the bonds woven by New Deal relief and jobs, ensuring Roosevelt's sweep of the black vote. "The amazing switch of this great group of voters is the real political sensation of the time," wrote a national political analyst.

The basis of Roosevelt's landslide victory in 1936 was a broad, class-based appeal, one that pledged an activist federal government committed to the "establishment of a democracy of opportunity for all people." African Americans, urban ethnic groups, industrial workers, and farmers responded, creating a new Democratic coalition that eclipsed the singular dominance of old-line Southern Democrats. For the next three decades the Democratic Party was a major site of the struggle waged to define a national policy on civil rights.

Race and the Politics of New Deal Reform

The late 1930s and the early 1940s witnessed the emergence of new organizations that were dedicated to expanding economic and political democracy in the South and were prepared to challenge Jim Crow laws. In 1937 a group of black students established the SOUTHERN NEGRO YOUTH CONGRESS (SNYC) in RICHMOND, VIRGINIA, dedicated to organizing black industrial workers in the South. During the next decade, SNYC grew into a regional organization based in Birmingham; in addition to supporting the work of organized labor, SNYC activists sponsored voter education and registration efforts and leadership training, often through community-based cultural activities.

In 1938 Roosevelt issued the *Report on the Economic Conditions of the South,* which identified the region as "the Nation's number one economic problem." In response to that report several thousand black and white Southerners met in Birmingham, Alabama, in

November 1938 and established the Southern Conference for Human Welfare (SCHW). At the founding of the SCHW, Birmingham police commissioner Eugene "Bull" Connor enforced segregated seating in the group's meeting hall. First Lady Eleanor Roosevelt responded by placing her chair on top of the hastily established line separating the two races. With the endorsement of the Roosevelt administration and the strong support of the Congress of Industrial Organizations (CIO), the SCHW launched a decade-long effort to expand political participation in the South.

Just weeks after Eleanor Roosevelt's dramatic gesture in Birmingham, the Supreme Court ruled that Lloyd L. Gaines be admitted to the University of Missouri Law School, giving the NAACP its first major victory in the campaign for equal education. Pauli Murray, whose application to the University of North Carolina had been rejected solely on the grounds of race, observed that *Gaines* was the "first major breach in the solid wall of segregated education since *Plessy*." It was, she wrote, "the beginning of the end."

World War II

By the late 1930s the crusading spirit of the New Deal had been obscured by mobilization for war and the increasing power of conservatives in Washington. Still, the war experience broadened the possibilities for civil rights struggles. On the eve of America's entry into the war, Osceola McKaine, a South Carolina NAACP organizer, observed: "We are living in the midst of perhaps the greatest revolution within human experience. Nothing, no nation, will be as it was when the peace comes.... There is no such thing as the status quo."

The demographic, economic, and political changes unleashed by the war had far-reaching consequences for African Americans. As scholar Henry Louis Gates Jr. has written, World War II "did more to recement black American culture, which migration had fragmented, than did any single event or experience." For the nearly 1 million African Americans serving in the armed forces, the army became "a great cauldron, mixing the New Negro culture, which had developed since the migration of the twenties and thirties, and the Old Negro culture, the remnants of traditional rural black culture in the South." The massive movement of black Southerners to centers of defense production in the North marked one of the largest internal migrations in American history.

Black civil rights activism accelerated under the banner of the Double V campaign, a movement first promoted by the *Pittsburgh Courier*. Double V advocates combined the fight against fascism abroad with the struggle for racial equality and full democracy at home. When the president failed to respond to black demands for equal inclusion in the war effort, labor leader A. Philip Randolph promised to lead 10,000 black Americans in a march on Washington to compel federal action. At the eleventh hour Roosevelt issued Executive Order 8802, which prohibited discrimination in defense industries and federal agencies and created the president's Fair Employment Practices Committee (FEPC) to implement the law. It was the first federal agency since Reconstruction devoted to dealing with racial discrimination.

The NAACP and the Southern Movement

During the war years, NAACP membership soared to nearly 400,000 nationally, and the rate of growth in the South surpassed that in all other regions. Having reported 18,000 members in the late 1930s, the NAACP claimed 156,000 members in the South by the war's end. Ella J. Baker, Southern field secretary for the NAACP, reported that the growth in membership brought a "new surge of identity" among black communities around the South. Through the organization of local branches and state conferences of the NAACP, Southern blacks created an infrastructure for sustained political struggle.

In the spring of 1944, the U.S. Supreme Court ruled in *Smith* v. *Allwright* that the all-white Democratic primary was unconstitutional. This ruling was the culmination of the NAACP's 20-year-long legal battle against the South's most effective legal means of barring blacks from political participation. "Once the Supreme Court opened the door in 1944," civil rights activist Palmer Weber recalled, "the NAACP charged into the whole registration and voting area very hard."

From 1944 to 1948 the NAACP, along with SNYC, the SCHW, and the CIO Political Action Committee (CIO-PAC), joined with other local and state groups to promote voter registration. When South Carolina Democrats continued to bar blacks from the party, black newspaperman John McCray and NAACP activist Osceola McKaine organized the South Carolina Progressive Democratic Party (PDP). The PDP sent a delegation to the 1944 Democratic National Convention in an unsuccessful effort to challenge old-guard Democrats for failing to open the state party to blacks. That fall the PDP ran its own slate of candidates. Black veterans, like Medgar Evers and Charles Evers in Mississippi, often took leading roles in voter registration efforts. In Birmingham black veterans marched in uniforms to the Jefferson County Court House to register to vote.

Henry Lee Moon, a journalist and a Southern field organizer for the CIO-PAC, reported: "Negro groups, sometimes in collaboration with labor and progressive groups, sometimes alone, are setting up schools to instruct new voters in the intricacies of registration, marking the ballot, and manipulating the voting machine." By the late 1940s the total number of registered black voters in the South approached 1 million; it had been estimated at 200,000 in 1940. The increases were most striking in South Carolina, where the number of black voters climbed from 3500 to 50,000, and in Georgia, where the number rose from 20,000 to 118,000.

Southern whites met growing black political participation with terror and fraud. There were countless individual acts of violence against blacks who voted, as well as public campaigns on the part of candidates like Eugene Talmadge in Georgia and Theodore Bilbo in Mississippi, inviting whites to do what was necessary to keep blacks from the polls. In several cases black veterans were gunned down after voting. Publicly staged acts of violence against blacks increased during the 1946 primary season and included the execution-style murders of two black couples in Walton County, Georgia. There is evidence that Talmadge stole his gubernatorial win in 1946 and that the Justice Department had enough information to indict him. But the department chose not to pursue the matter.

Postwar America: The Emergence of Civil Rights as a National Issue

Wartime experience and the growing power of the Northern black vote elevated the importance of civil rights in national politics. At the war's end, decolonization movements in Africa and Asia and the beginnings of the cold war between the United States and the Soviet Union heightened the rhetoric of freedom, democracy, and self-determination. In 1947, W. E. B. Du Bois sought unsuccessfully to enlist the United Nations in an international investigation of racial discrimination in the United States.

President Harry S. Truman responded to the call for civil rights reform by commissioning a review of racial discrimination, which resulted in a report that called for sweeping federal action against Jim Crow. Truman was reluctant to act in the face of strong Southern opposition. But a close 1948 presidential race in which victory in key Northern states hinged on the black vote compelled him to endorse a strong civil rights plank at the Democratic National Convention. Southerners left the convention in protest and ran their own candidate for president in 1948 on the States Rights Party ticket. Shortly after the convention, Truman issued an executive order desegregating the armed forces (*see* BLACKS IN THE AMERICAN MILITARY).

The confident Democratic initiatives of the 1930s and 1940s, however, were overwhelmed by two postwar political factors: (1) the cold war and the Truman administration's domestic loyalty-security program, which limited civil liberties; and (2) the acceleration of white Southern repression of any challenge to the Jim Crow system. Groups like SNYC and the SCHW became targets of government investigations. The Federal Bureau of Investigation (FBI) sought out suspected communists and fellow travelers, while a revived Ku Klux Klan terrorized blacks attempting to vote in the South and Southern civic leaders presided over fraudulent elections. Indeed, Charles Houston wondered why the loudly proclaimed crusade to "lead the world to democracy" did not extend to the Southern United States. Why were free and fair elections in Eastern Europe of greater import to the U.S. government than open elections in Alabama and Mississippi?

THE CIVIL RIGHTS STRUGGLE IN THE 1950S

During the 1950s the struggle against Jim Crow in the South remained distant from national issues and concerns. After 1948 the Democratic Party placated its rebellious Southern wing while its civil rights agenda floundered. Meanwhile, whites responded to the steady migration of Southern blacks to Northern cities by extending patterns of racial segregation and black exclusion in housing, employment, and education.

The foundation of the Civil Rights Movement remained anchored in the cumulative gains of the NAACP legal campaign and its extensive network of branches. Southern NAACP leaders, however, faced an emboldened defense of the racial status quo. In 1951 the Christmas Day assassination of Harry T. Moore, a leading NAACP organizer in Florida, and his wife inaugurated a decade of white terrorism and state-sponsored repression that heightened in the aftermath of the *Brown* decision.

BROWN V. BOARD OF EDUCATION

On May 17, 1954, the U.S. Supreme Court unanimously ruled in BROWN V. BOARD OF EDUCATION that the doctrine of separate but equal as applied to public education was unconstitutional. *Brown* marked the culmination of the NAACP's long legal battle; the Court had effectively reversed its 1896 decision in *Plessy* v. *Ferguson*, the cornerstone of the segregation system. By implication, state-mandated racial segregation in all areas of public life violated the Constitution.

However, the Court issued a separate ruling one year later concerning the enforcement of this momentous decision. Sympathetic to warnings of Southern white defiance, the Court allowed for a policy of gradual implementation that would, the opinion explained, be responsive to local conditions and problems. While calling for compliance "with all deliberate speed," the Court reflected the ambivalence of the justices, executive and congressional leadership, and the vast majority of Americans about dismantling racial segregation in the South. For most white Southerners, *Brown II* was a license to resist. During the next ten years, less than 1 percent of black children in the South attended "white" schools.

Brown was a major turning point in the struggle for civil rights, and it marked the beginning of the most celebrated chapter of the Civil Rights Movement. The decade that followed saw a heightening interplay between Southern blacks striving to realize the promise of *Brown* in the face of "massive resistance" by Southern whites and the equivocal response of the federal government, unfolding on an increasingly national and international stage.

EMMETT TILL, MONTGOMERY, AND THE EMERGENCE OF MARTIN LUTHER KING JR.

In August 1955, just three months after the court ruled in *Brown II*, 14-year-old Emmett Till was murdered in Money, Mississippi, for allegedly whistling at a white woman. Mamie Bradley, Till's mother, brought her son's body home to Chicago and insisted on an open casket so that all could see "what they did to my boy." *Jet* magazine's photograph of Till's badly mutilated body offered gruesome evidence of the terror that reigned in Mississippi, and it informed the consciousness of a new generation of young black people. The widely publicized trial and acquittal of Till's murderers confirmed what most already knew about the Southern system of racial injustice.

That December, Rosa Parks, a local NAACP leader in Montgomery, Alabama, refused to surrender her seat on a city bus to a white man. This action, and the mobilizing work of the Women's Political Council, sparked a boycott of Montgomery buses that lasted for 381 days. Local black leaders elected Martin Luther King Jr., the new 26-year-old minister of the Dexter Avenue Baptist Church, as head of the Montgomery Improvement Association (MIA), the organization that led the boycott and sued to end segregation on the buses. Hundreds of African Americans, mostly women, walked several miles to and from work each day; as one woman commented, "My feet is tired, but my soul is rested." This dignified protest contrasted with the city's efforts to intimidate the MIA leadership through indictments, injunction, and the bombing of King's house, and it attracted the attention of the national and international media.

By the time the Supreme Court struck down segregation on the buses in December 1956, King had become a seasoned leader of and eloquent spokesman for the emerging nonviolent movement. Early in 1957, King joined with other activist ministers and civil rights leaders like BAYARD RUSTIN and Ella Baker to establish the Southern Christian Leadership Conference (SCLC); King was elected its president, and Baker became the first executive director. The SCLC served as an umbrella organization, linking church-based affiliates throughout the South in the nonviolent struggle for racial justice and to "redeem the soul of America."

The NAACP, Little Rock, and School Desegregation

The fight for school integration had few supporters outside the black community. The NAACP aided parents who petitioned school boards to admit their children to the all-white schools, in compliance with the *Brown* decision, but the organization became the target of an extensive effort across the South to shut it down. In 1956 Alabama passed a state law effectively barring the NAACP from operating in that state; South Carolina barred NAACP members from state employment. Five other states enacted laws requiring the NAACP to register and to provide lists of members and contributors. While such state action was often unconstitutional, the burden was on local NAACP branches to spend scarce resources in fighting to overturn these laws. In the meantime, the White Citizens Council (WCC), founded in Sunflower County, Mississippi, in 1956, organized local businessmen and civic leaders throughout the South. WCC chapters used economic reprisals and manipulation of the law in an effort to intimidate and undermine civil rights activists and supporters.

Southern obstructionists met their first major setback in Little Rock, Arkansas. In 1957 a group of local parents, working with NAACP leader Daisy Bates, succeeded in winning a court order mandating the admission of black students to Central High School. Governor Orval Faubus employed the National Guard to block the admission of the nine young men and women selected to attend Central High. The governor's bold defiance of the federal courts compelled President Eisenhower, who was no supporter of school integration, to send in army troops and federalize the Arkansas National Guard in order to ensure peaceful compliance with the court order. After the school year ended, the governor closed the public schools to avoid further integration.

From 1957 to 1959 public schools in Virginia, Georgia, and Alabama closed rather than obey desegregation orders. In New Orleans, when public schools admitted four young black girls to the first grade, whites in the city rioted.

THE RIGHT TO VOTE

The Civil Rights Act of 1957 and Macon County, Alabama

While federal officials and the U.S. Congress sought to avoid the issue of racial integration, the Eisenhower administration – recognizing the possibility of wooing back Northern black voters to the Republican Party – was sympathetic to extending protection of black voting rights in the South. In 1957 Attorney General Herbert Brownell introduced legislation that sought to provide federal protection of basic citizenship rights. The final bill, the first civil rights bill enacted since 1875, was trimmed to meet the opposition of Southern Democrats and lacked strong enforcement provisions. But the Civil Rights Act of 1957 did create a Civil Rights Division in the Justice Department, authorized to prosecute registrars who obstructed the right of blacks to vote. The bill also established the U.S. Civil Rights Commission as an independent agency charged with gathering facts about voting rights violations and other civil rights infringements.

In the fall of 1958, the new Civil Rights Commission sent investigators to Alabama to gather information on voter discrimination. The Tuskegee Civic Association (TCA), a black organization established in the early 1940s to encourage voter registration, shared its extensive records documenting voter discrimination. As a result, the commission held nationally televised hearings in Montgomery, and a parade of black witnesses – farmers, hospital technicians, and Tuskegee professors – described the deceptive and often bizarre devices used by registrars in Macon County to keep blacks from registering to vote.

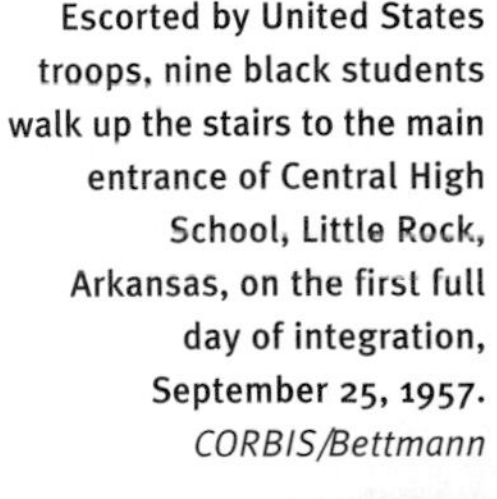

Escorted by United States troops, nine black students walk up the stairs to the main entrance of Central High School, Little Rock, Arkansas, on the first full day of integration, September 25, 1957. *CORBIS/Bettmann*

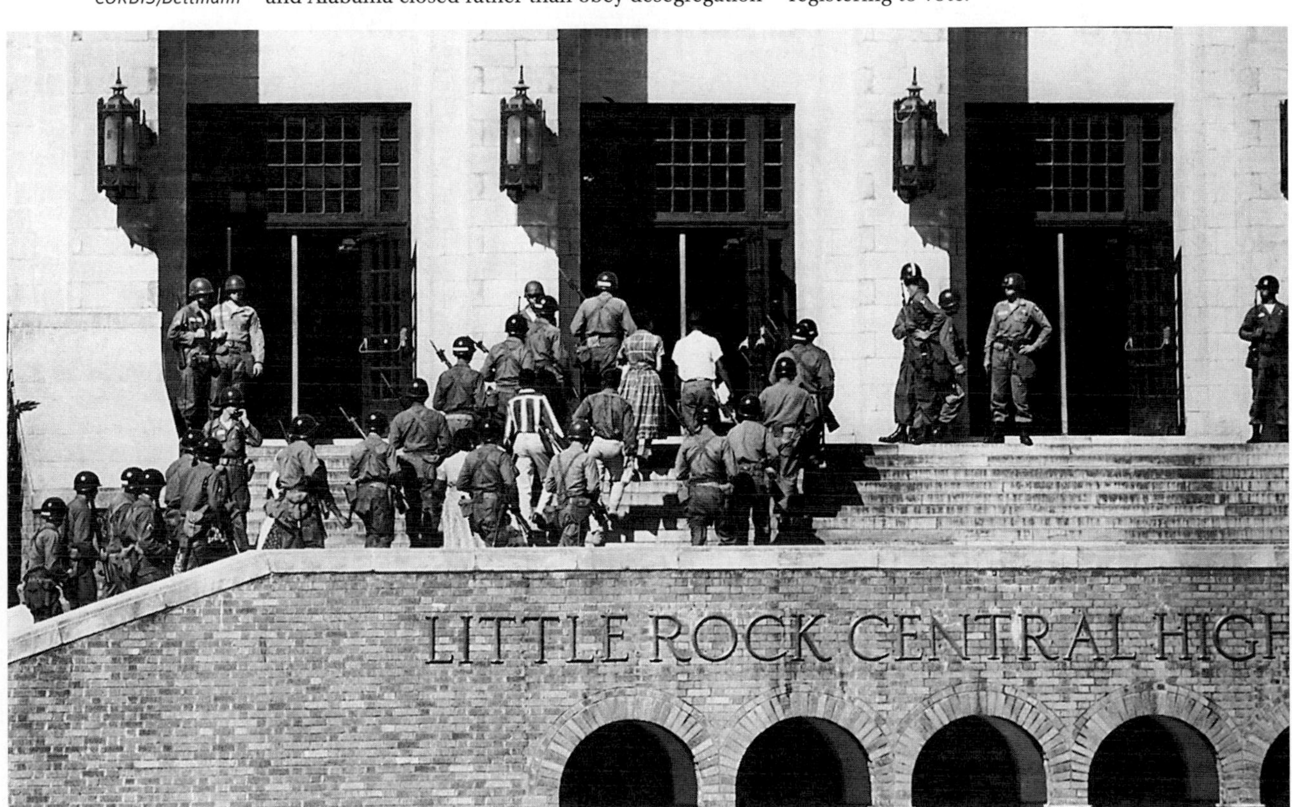

While presenting the case before the Civil Rights Commission and the American public, TCA founder Charles Gomillion and several associates were also preparing their suit against the city of Tuskegee for redrawing the political boundaries of the town so that black voters would be excluded. In 1960 the Supreme Court ruled unanimously in favor of the TCA in *Gomillion* v. *Lightfoot,* a case that marked a major step in broadening federal review of state voting practices.

Citizenship Schools and Black Voter Registration After Brown

Voter registration and education accelerated in communities around the South after the *Brown* decision. In 1957 Septima Clark (1898-1987), Bernice Robinson, and Esau Jenkins organized the Citizenship Schools program on South Carolina's Sea Islands, with the support of Highlander Folk School, one of the few politically active interracial organizations in the South. Over the next four years, the number of registered black voters on Johns Island tripled. The program was adapted in communities in Tennessee, Georgia, and Alabama.

In the mid-1950s in Mississippi, NAACP chapters and the Regional Council of Negro Leadership began a concerted effort to increase black voter registration. In 1954 just 4 percent of the state's eligible black voting-age population were registered. White reprisals were swift. Those attempting to vote risked losing their job and suffered other forms of economic intimidation. Leaders were often targets of physical violence. In 1955 George W. Lee, president of the NAACP branch in Belonzi, was gunned down by a mob of whites. That same year Lamar Smith, a political activist in Lincoln County, was assassinated in front of the courthouse in broad daylight. Several other leaders fled the state. Despite the efforts of a handful of organizers, including Amzie Moore, an NAACP leader in Cleveland, and

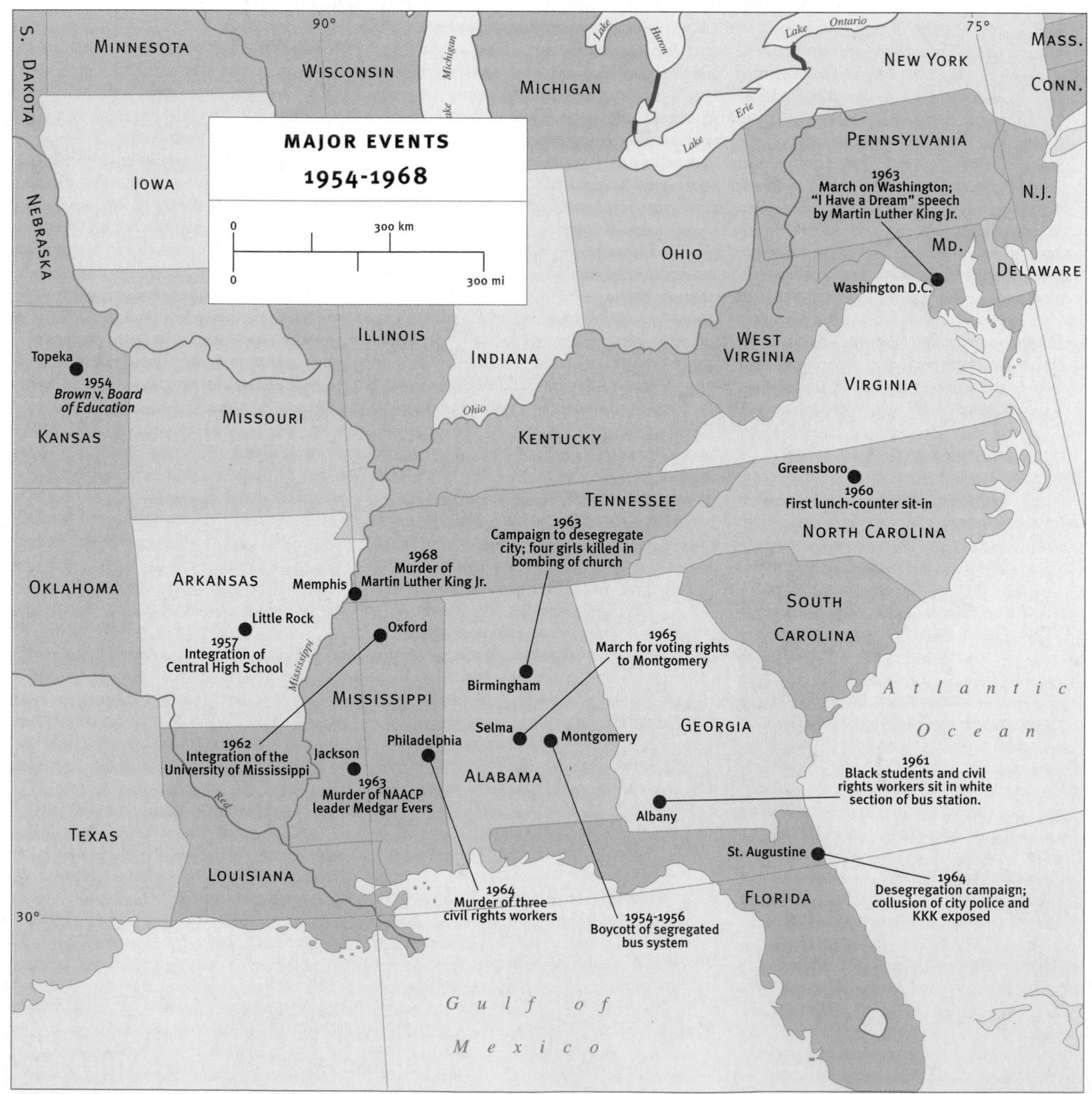

BELOW: A black student sits at a lunch counter in Nashville, Tennessee, in 1960. The "sit-in" movement began in February 1960 after four black college students in Greensboro, North Carolina, sat at a whites-only lunch counter to protest racial segregation in restaurants and other public acommodations. *CORBIS/Bettmann* **BOTTOM:** SNCC field secretaries, *left to right,* Frank Smith, Bob Moses, and Willie Peacock in the Greenwood, Mississippi, office one day before it was firebombed in March, 1963. *Magnum Photos/Danny Lyon*

Medgar Evers, political activity came to a standstill or was driven completely underground.

By the end of the decade the momentum for the kind of change that had seemed possible in the aftermath of *Brown* and the Montgomery bus boycott seemed remote in the face of hardening white resistance and the persistence of unchecked violence. Virginia Durr, a white civil rights activist in Montgomery, wrote plaintively to a friend in the North: "We have such a feeling here that we have been abandoned by the rest of the country and by the government and left to the tender mercies of the Ku Klux Klan and the White Citizens Council."

DIRECT-ACTION PROTESTS OF THE 1960s

On February 1, 1960, in Greensboro, North Carolina, 4 freshmen at Greensboro Agricultural and Technical College (A&T) sat at the "white" lunch counter in Woolworth's and asked to be served (*see* SIT-INS). The waitress refused; the young men waited, and left at the end of the day. The next day they were joined by 20 more students from A&T. Some white students from a local women's college "sat in" with black students on the third day. By the end of the week the "sit-ins" had spread to several other towns in the state, and students began targeting a broad range of public accommodations. By the end of February, sit-ins had been staged in towns and cities throughout the South.

The sit-ins inaugurated a direct-action mass protest movement that defied the racial and political boundaries of cold war America. In April 1960 young people who had participated in the sit-ins established the STUDENT NONVIOLENT COORDINATING COMMITTEE (SNCC) at a meeting convened by veteran activist Ella Baker. Working with rural Southern blacks, SNCC quickly became engaged in a movement for more fundamental social change – change that looked beyond the legalistic and legislative goals of the national NAACP and its white liberal allies. In particular, SNCC sought to empower black people at the local level.

Escalating black protest, along with fierce white resistance, invited more extensive coverage by the national press and tested the resolve of the president to enforce federal law. In the spring of 1961, the CONGRESS OF RACIAL EQUALITY (CORE) initiated a "freedom ride" from Washington to the Deep South. The interracial group of freedom riders challenged the newly elected John F. Kennedy and his administration to enforce a 1960 Supreme Court ruling (*Boynton* v. *Virginia*) that banned segregation on interstate transportation. One bus was firebombed outside Birmingham; another rode into a savage mob assault at the bus station in Montgomery. In Jackson, riders were arrested, as one historian has noted, "on charges of traveling 'for the avowed purpose of inflaming public opinion.'" SNCC and CORE sent a steady flow of reinforcements, who filled the local and county jails to overflow. Attorney General Robert Kennedy finally directed the Interstate Commerce Commission to enforce regulations barring segregation in interstate terminals.

MISSISSIPPI

During the early 1960s different groups and leaders experimented with a variety of tactics and strategies. SNCC and CORE organizers carved out a critical base as they fanned out across the South and established community-based projects to help support and sustain local organizing efforts around voting and mass protests against segregation.

In the summer of 1960 Robert P. Moses, a 26-year-old high school teacher from New York, traveled through Mississippi to recruit people for a SNCC conference to be held that fall. On the advice of Ella Baker, Moses sought out Amzie Moore, who told Moses about how white terrorism had crippled voter registration efforts in Mississippi. With Moore's encouragement, Moses and a team of SNCC workers returned the following summer prepared to live and organize in what was the poorest and arguably the most violently racist state in the nation.

The SNCC organizers joined with other civil rights activists in the state, including members of CORE, SCLC, and the NAACP, and created the Congress of Federated Organizations (COFO) to unify the efforts of all civil rights groups operating in Mississippi. Late in 1961 COFO's efforts won financial support from the newly established Voter Education Project, a foundation-based organization that Attorney General Robert Kennedy helped to establish. However, while the Kennedy administration, like the Eisenhower administration before it, was supportive of voter registration, it was not prepared to offer federal protection to those who sought to register – often in the face of violence, economic harassment, and, in some cases, death. The murder of Herbert Lee in 1961 and the beating and jailing of other voting rights activists had the desired effect. During 1962 and 1963, less than 4000 black voters were added to the rolls, while 394,000 black adults in Mississippi remained unregistered.

The NAACP in Mississippi, under field director Medgar Evers, supported several desegregation efforts during this period. In 1962 NAACP lawyers secured a federal court order to gain the admission of the first African American to the University of Mississippi. Riots engulfed the campus on the eve of James Meredith's enrollment, claiming two lives and injuring hundreds of others. The Kennedy administration sent federal troops to restore order, and federal marshals remained on campus to protect Meredith.

The desegregation of Ole Miss encouraged Evers to revive the campaign against segregation in Jackson. SNCC workers offered training sessions for sit-ins. In the spring of 1963, students sat in at Woolworth's, attempted to gain admission to the public library and "whites-only" public parks, and organized protest marches in downtown Jackson. The demonstrators were beaten by police and arrested. On June 12, 1963, as he returned from a strategy meeting, Medgar Evers was gunned down in the driveway of his house.

Martin Luther King Jr.: Emergence as a National Leader

Martin Luther King Jr., with his brilliant ability to articulate the ideals of the Southern movement to the nation at large, emerged as a national spokesman of the movement. King's eloquence was joined by his ability to bring media attention to flash points of peaceful black protesters and white racists. On occasion, the SCLC played a role in orchestrating these confrontations. Such tactics caused resentment on the part of young organizers laboring in communities over extended periods of time, beyond the glare of national attention. Indeed, the intervention of King and SCLC in Albany, Georgia, in 1962, the site of a major SNCC project, failed to achieve any concessions and probably undermined some of the organizing work that had been done. But Albany was a critical training ground for Birmingham, Alabama, which became a pivotal battleground in the Civil Rights Movement.

Birmingham

In 1963 Birmingham was arguably the most segregated city in the nation and the most racially violent. During the previous six years, there had been 18 unsolved bombings in black communities, winning it the nickname "Bombingham." Police Commissioner Bull Connor was prepared to maintain the city's color line at all costs.

On the invitation of Fred Shuttlesworth, the leading civil rights activist in the city, King and the SCLC launched Project C (for "Confrontation") in Birmingham early in the spring of 1963. A boycott of downtown stores was launched at the peak of the Easter shopping season, protesting the stores' refusal to hire black clerks, and demonstrators protested the city's segregation laws in mass marches to City Hall. Bull Connor secured a federal court order barring the demonstrations, leading to the arrest of scores of protesters and of King and several other SCLC leaders. From his cell King penned his famous "Letter from a Birmingham Jail," in response to a group of liberal white clergy who criticized the protests as ill-timed and charged King and his associates with stirring up tensions between the races.

In his letter King distinguished the "type of constructive nonviolent tension that is necessary for growth... the type of tension in society that will help men rise from the dark depths of prejudice and racism to the majestic heights of understanding and brotherhood." With regard to the timing of the demonstrations, King acknowledged that he had "yet to engage in a direct-action campaign that was 'well-timed' in view of those who have not suffered unduly from the disease of segregation. For years now, I have heard the word 'Wait!' ring in the ear of every Negro with piercing familiarity. This 'Wait' has almost always meant 'Never.'"

Yet local black business leaders and some clergy were beginning to question the value of the demonstrations. With the jails full, spirits flagging, and bail money spent, they began pressuring King to call off the protests. At this juncture James Bevel, a veteran of the Nashville sit-in movement, suggested a strategy for reviving the protests: invite children to march. Bevel reasoned that children had fewer constraints than their parents did. Moreover, in King's words, exposing young people to the wrath of Connor's police force would "subpoena the conscience of the nation."

On May 2 children and young adults from age 6 to 18 gathered at the Sixteenth Street Baptist Church, the movement headquarters, and marched to downtown Birmingham. The police arrested more than 900 and carried them off to jail in paddy wagons and school buses. On the second day, more than 1000 young people stayed out of school and assembled at the church to march. In an effort to abort the march, the police turned dogs and fire hoses on the demonstrators as they left the church. The pressure of the hoses, which was strong enough to strip the bark off trees, slammed children to the ground and sent others sailing over parked cars. As outrage spread through the black community, SCLC organizers struggled to keep blacks from retaliating.

With more than 2000 people in jail, the marches were still growing larger. The next major confrontation with the police occurred several days later in downtown Birmingham. Once again the police turned attack dogs and fire hoses on the demonstrators. Television coverage of the brutal police assault on children shocked the nation, while photos and news reports quickly spread around the world.

With Birmingham on the brink of a full-scale race riot, city businesses began negotiating with King through a Kennedy administration intermediary. A tentative agreement to desegregate downtown stores and employ black clerks sparked a spate of bombings. With federal troops stationed on alert outside the city, Mayor Albert Boutwell finally ratified the agreement and repealed the city's segregation laws.

In the aftermath of Birmingham, mass demonstrations spread throughout the South, involving more than 100,000 people. With Birmingham, the Civil Rights Movement had irrevocably commanded the attention of the nation and the world, opening the possibility for decisive legislative action.

The Kennedy Administration and Civil Rights

Birmingham marked a turning point for the Kennedy administration and its relationship to the Civil Rights Movement. Nearly three years earlier, the election of John F. Kennedy had raised the hopes of African Americans and their allies. The youthful Kennedy had actively courted black voters and brought vitality and a new vision to the presidency after eight years of Dwight Eisenhower. Yet the new administration faced the legislative reality of a Southern bloc that dominated key congressional committees whose support was critical to the success of the president's agenda.

The Justice Department, under Attorney General Robert Kennedy, pursued a more vigorous effort to enforce voting rights and school desegregation orders than the previous administration; but the jurisdiction of the Justice Department was limited. In any event, civil rights was not a priority issue for the Kennedy administration during its early years, a time when the cold war loomed large in presidential deliberations. If anything, Kennedy was most inclined to placate and appease powerful Southern Democrats. He bowed to the wishes of Sen. James Eastland of Mississippi and other like-minded Southern senators when making appointments to the federal bench in the South, and appointed a number of arch segregationists. They stood in contrast to moderate Republican judges like Frank Johnson and Elbert Tuttle, Eisenhower appointees who actively

A Birmingham policeman turns a fire hose on civil rights protesters taking part in a 1963 demonstration. *CORBIS*

Leaders of the March on Washington for Jobs and Freedom link arms as they head down Constitution Avenue on August 28, 1963. *CORBIS*

enforced civil rights law.

By June 1963 Kennedy was prepared to align himself and his presidency with the struggle for civil rights. On June 12, the day that Governor George Wallace attempted, unsuccessfully, to block the entrance of two black students to the University of Alabama, Kennedy addressed the nation. In a televised speech he told Americans that they could no longer ask black citizens to "be content with the counsels of patience and delay." He pledged that he would urge Congress to act on "the proposition that race has no place in American life and law." Seven days later he requested legislation from Congress that would ban segregation in public facilities, broaden the powers of the Justice Department to enforce school integration, and extend federal protection of voting rights.

The March on Washington

In response to the momentous events of the spring, veteran civil rights leader A. Philip Randolph broadened the agenda of a planned march on the nation's capital for jobs and equal opportunity. Other civil rights leaders joined with Randolph to orchestrate a mass gathering in Washington calling for passage of civil rights legislation, immediate integration of public schools in the South, and economic opportunity.

On August 28 an estimated quarter of a million people, black and white, from all parts of the nation assembled in front of the Lincoln Memorial in what was, at that time, the largest peacetime gathering in American history (*see* MARCH ON WASHINGTON, 1963). The day culminated with Martin Luther King Jr.'s speech "I Have a Dream," in which he looked toward an America of racial harmony and justice. Writer JAMES BALDWIN remembered the feeling: "For a moment it almost seemed that we stood on a height and could see our inheritance.... " MALCOLM X, who observed the march, commented to Bayard Rustin, "You know, this dream of King's is going to be a nightmare before it's over."

Less than a month after the March on Washington, the sense of foreboding articulated by Malcolm X overshadowed the euphoria of that extraordinary late summer day. On September 15 white terrorists dynamited the basement of Birmingham's Sixteenth Street Baptist Church during Sunday School, killing four young girls: Denise McNair and Cynthia Wesley, both 11 years old, and Carole Robertson and Addie Mae Collins, both 14. Dreading that the families would blame him for exposing the children to risk, King returned to Birmingham and presided over the funeral of the movement's youngest victims.

THE MOVEMENT AT HIGH TIDE: 1964-1965

During 1964 and 1965, the accelerated momentum of the Civil Rights Movement was fueled by the escalation of organized protest activity in the South, particularly in Mississippi and Alabama, and by the commitment of President Lyndon Johnson to enact strong civil rights legislation.

CIVIL RIGHTS ACT OF 1964

The heightened expectations tied to the leadership of John F. Kennedy had been brutally aborted on November 22, 1963, when the president was assassinated in Dallas, Texas. Within days of assuming the office of the presidency, Lyndon Baines Johnson, in an address to a joint session of Congress, promised that Kennedy's commitment to civil rights would be carried forward and translated into action. As a Southerner, Johnson did not underestimate the opposition a strong civil rights bill would meet. But none knew the workings of the Congress better than this former majority leader of the U.S. Senate, and as a legislative strategist Johnson had no equal. Roy Wilkins, executive secretary of the NAACP, was struck by the contrast between Kennedy and Johnson. While Kennedy talked "about the art of the possible," Wilkins explained, "he didn't really know what was possible and what wasn't on Capitol Hill." Johnson, in comparison, "knew exactly what was possible, and how to get it."

Johnson orchestrated a "no holds barred" campaign for a civil rights bill, untainted by compromise. He enlisted the help of NAACP lobbyist Clarence Mitchell and the formative Leadership Conference on Civil Rights (LCCR), a broad coalition of veteran lobbyists representing labor, church, and liberal groups. He held press conferences, directly enlisting the public in this great effort, and brought the full weight of his power and persuasive abilities to secure the votes of doubtful congressmen and senators. The civil rights bill passed the House on February 10, 1964, and, after much arm-twisting and ego stroking, it won Senate approval late in June. On July 2, 1964, Johnson signed the bill into law.

The Civil Rights Act of 1964 outlawed discrimination in public facilities and employment; authorized the attorney general to initiate suits to enforce school integration; and allowed for the withholding of federal funds to non-complying schools. While the legislation was directed specifically at removing the barriers to equal access and opportunity that affected African Americans, it vastly expanded the scope of federal protection of the rights of women and other minority groups who experienced discrimination. However, fearful that the issue of voting rights would sink the legislation, the president and his allies in Congress postponed action in that arena.

RIGHT TOP: A federal voter registrar fills out forms for prospective black voters in Canton, Mississippi, under the Voting Rights Act of 1965. *CORBIS*

RIGHT BELOW: In 1963 Alabama governor George Wallace holds up his hand as he "stands in the schoolhouse door" and attempts to prevent two African American students from entering the University of Alabama. *CORBIS/Bettmann*

Freedom Summer

In Mississippi, while efforts to register black voters stalled, the Congress of Federated Organizations launched Freedom Vote in the fall of 1963. More than 80,000 blacks participated in this mock election campaign and voted for unofficial Freedom Party candidates. The Freedom Vote enabled many black Mississippians who had never before voted to have the experience of casting a ballot, while demonstrating that despite white claims to the contrary, blacks were interested in voting. But it was clear that more aggressive action was needed. Bob Moses recalled that by the end of 1963, COFO organizers "were exhausted.... They were butting up against a stone wall, [with] no breakthroughs."

In an effort to revive a flagging movement, COFO launched the Summer Project in 1964, which brought hundreds of student volunteers, mostly white, into Mississippi to participate in a massive voter registration drive, with the expectation that the media would follow. White Mississippi prepared as if they were expecting an invasion. Freedom Summer, as it became known, was punctuated with violence and terrorism as well as the dramatic growth of black political participation – from the abduction and murder of three civil rights workers in June to the establishment of a new party, the Mississippi Freedom Democratic Party (MFDP). The MFDP sent a full delegation to the 1964 Democratic National Convention, challenging the seating of the delegation representing Mississippi's all-white party. The failure of the MFDP to win its challenge, and the way in which the president and key liberal Democrats attempted to undermine the challenge, left many disillusioned with the national Democratic Party. But the MFDP prepared the way for the expansion of black political enfranchisement in Mississippi and led to major revisions in the Democratic Party convention rules.

Selma and the Voting Rights Act of 1965

After Lyndon Johnson's landslide win over Barry Goldwater in the 1964 presidential election, the Justice Department began preparing to develop legislation around voting rights. However, the Southern movement ensured that the issue moved to the top of the president's agenda; the final battleground was Selma, Alabama. SNCC organizers had been working with the Dallas County Voters League in Selma for nearly two years when Martin Luther King Jr. and the SCLC arrived in Selma in January 1965. King began a series of marches geared at bringing media attention to the violence and discrimination that barred blacks from the polls. After several police attacks on marchers and the murder of Jimmy Lee Jackson by a police officer, King planned to lead a march to Montgomery, the state capital, and petition Governor George Wallace directly. On March 7, as the marchers attempted to cross the Edmund Pettis Bridge, they were clubbed by police on horseback and driven back across the bridge. The scene flashed across the country on the nightly news. Bloody Sunday, as it was named, mobilized public opinion in support of federal legislation, and Johnson acted almost immediately.

The president introduced a comprehensive voting rights bill to Congress on March 15 with a speech that was televised across the nation. "Their cause must be our cause, too," Johnson said. "Because it's not just Negroes, but it's really all of us who must overcome the crippling legacy of bigotry and injustice." Borrowing the words of the movement's anthem, he concluded, "And, we shall overcome." Five days later, with federal troops and marshals standing by, King led marchers

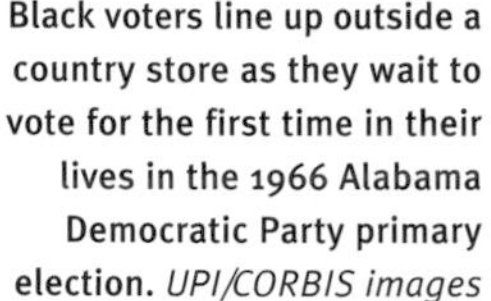

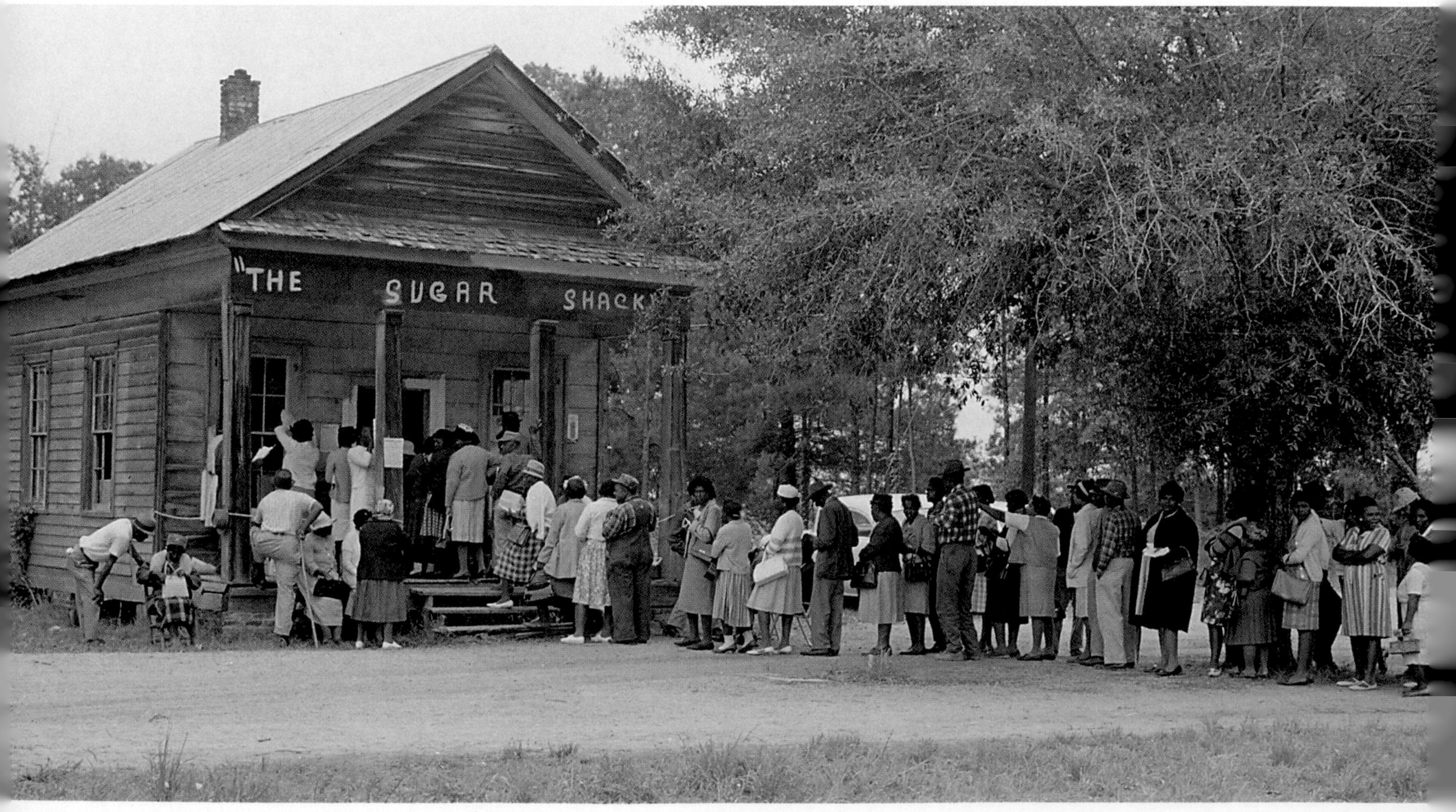

Black voters line up outside a country store as they wait to vote for the first time in their lives in the 1966 Alabama Democratic Party primary election. *UPI/CORBIS images*

on the four-day-long march to Montgomery; 25,000 had joined by the time they reached the capital. On August 6, President Johnson signed the Voting Rights Act, which provided federal supervision of voter registration practices, effectively opening up the polls to African Americans throughout the South for the first time since the end of Reconstruction.

Aftermath

The enactment of the Civil Rights Act of 1964 and the Voting Rights Act of 1965 reinforced the guarantees of full citizenship provided for in the Reconstruction amendments nearly a century earlier, and marked the end of the Jim Crow system in the South. The desegregation of public facilities was swiftly implemented, and the rapid increase in black voting had far-reaching consequences for politics in the South and the nation (*see* American Electoral Politics, Blacks in). With the enforcement powers of the federal government greatly enhanced, the desegregation of public schools proceeded steadily, though "white flight" and the proliferation of private schools often made integration an elusive goal.

The fall of Jim Crow in the South removed the most extreme manifestation of racial discrimination and inequality, only to reveal deeply entrenched patterns of racial discrimination woven deep into the fabric of national life. For African Americans segregated in Northern cities and locked into poverty, the gains of the Southern movement had little direct relevance. Five days after President Johnson signed the Voting Rights Act, black frustration erupted into nearly a week of rioting in the Watts section of Los Angeles; urban disturbances and rebellions followed in other cities over the next three years. In 1968 the National Committee on Civil Disorders (also known as the Kerner Commission), appointed by the president, described "a nation moving towards two societies – one black, one white, separate and unequal."

The Civil Rights Movement vastly expanded the parameters of American democracy and the guarantees of citizenship, while also raising new challenges in an ongoing struggle to advance racial and economic justice. Martin Luther King Jr. carried his efforts forward in very different settings: supporting challenges to residential discrimination in Chicago; protesting America's involvement in Vietnam; aiding striking garbage workers in Memphis; and developing plans for a Poor People's March on Washington, which went forward after his assassination in 1968. At the same time, the call for Black Power eclipsed the integrationist thrust of the early 1960s, focusing renewed attention on black political and economic empowerment, while heightened black consciousness and racial pride found expression in the cultural renaissance of the Black Arts Movement of the late 1960s and the 1970s.

See Also

Decolonization in Africa: An Interpretation; World War I and African Americans; World War II and African Americans; Bates, Daisy Lee Gatson; Chicago, Illinois; Du Bois, William Edward Burghardt (W. E. B.); Evers, James Charles; Evers, Medgar Wylie; Fifteenth Amendment to the United States Constitution; Fourteenth Amendment to the United States Constitution; Garvey, Marcus Mosiah; Great Migration, The; Hastie, William Henry; *Jet*; Voting Rights Act of 1965; King, Martin Luther, Jr.; Leadership Conference on Civil Rights; McKay, Claude; Meredith, James H.; Mitchell, Clarence Maurice, Jr.; Montgomery Bus Boycott; Moore, Harry Tyson; New Orleans, Louisiana; New York, New York; Parks, Rosa Louise McCauley; Randolph, Asa Philip; Shuttlesworth, Fred L.; Southern Christian Leadership Conference; White, Walter Francis; Thirteenth Amendment of the United States Constitution and the Emancipation Proclamation; Till, Emmett Louis; Washington, Booker Taliaferro; Washington, D.C.; Weaver, Robert Clifton; Wells-Barnett, Ida Bell; Wilkins, Roy Ottoway; Communist Party USA, African Americans and the; Black Church, The; Little Rock Crisis, 1957.

North America

Civil War, American

(April 12, 1861-May 26, 1865), devastating military conflict between the United States of America and 11 of its former states that had seceded and formed the Confederate States of America. The war took more than 600,000 lives but brought freedom to 4 million African American slaves.

The immediate and primary cause of the Civil War was the South's support for and the North's increasing opposition to slavery; however, several other economic and political factors conspired to make the issue of slavery potent.

Economic Causes

Since its settlement, the southern United States had received most of its income from farming, which depended heavily on slave labor. By 1860 cotton – King Cotton, as it became known – was the chief crop of the South and totaled 57 percent of all United States exports. Largely because of the dominance of cotton, the South resisted the industrialization that swept the North in the nineteenth century. Thus the South manufactured little, and most manufactured goods had to be bought from the North or imported from overseas. Meanwhile, the North by the eve of the Civil War had become an established industrial society. For economic and moral reasons the North did not use slave labor, instead relying on its own workers and European immigrants to power its factories, build its railroads, and settle the West.

Northerners demanded high tariffs on imports to protect their goods from cheap foreign competition. The South, however, wanted just the opposite: low tariffs on the many goods it imported. The persistent conflict over the tariff was crucial because, at the time, the federal government had few other sources of revenue – neither personal nor corporate income taxes existed. Thus the tariffs funded the turnpikes, railroads, and canals that were so important to Northern industrialization and Western expansion. The South preferred to do without these improvements in return for lower tariffs. This conflict was never fully resolved until after the Civil War.

Compromise over Slavery

In 1819 Alabama was admitted to the Union, balancing the number of free states and slave states. As long as the balance held, Congress would be forced to compromise on questions involving slavery; however, both free and slave states were loath to find out what would happen if the other side gained the upper hand. The balance was threatened almost as soon as it was achieved. In 1803 the United States had completed the Louisiana Purchase, and by about 1820 many of the settlers in the Purchase, and particularly in the area now known as Missouri, were petitioning for statehood. Under the U.S. Constitution, the federal government could not interfere with slavery inside a state; however, the government was free to refuse to admit a state whose constitution allowed slavery. A two-year struggle ensued in Congress over Missouri, as Northerners tried to ban slavery in the territory while Southerners argued that the territory should decide for itself whether to allow slavery. The result was the Missouri Compromise, which passed Congress in 1820. Under the compromise, Missouri was admitted to the Union as a slave state and, to maintain the balance, Maine was admitted as a free state. In the rest of the Purchase, slavery was prohibited north of Missouri's southern boundary (with the exception of Missouri) and allowed

Taylor, drummer with the Seventy-Eighth Regiment, United States Infantry, poses with his drum.
CORBIS

south of the boundary.

The Missouri Compromise held until the United States acquired vast new western lands in the Mexican-American War (1846-1848) and, shortly thereafter, gold was discovered in the new territory. California in particular received a large number of settlers, who were petitioning for statehood. Again Northerners wanted slavery banned while Southerners pressed for their share of slave states. Because tensions over slavery had been mounting since the Missouri Compromise, secession or civil war, or both, seemed a possible outcome of the conflict. Instead, the outcome was the Compromise of 1850. Under the new compromise, Congress admitted California to the Union as a free state, and decreed that other territories could decide the question of slavery for themselves. A harsh new Fugitive Slave Law, also part of the compromise, required Northerners to return escaped slaves to the South.

The Compromise of 1850 did little to ease tensions. Many Northerners called openly for people to disobey the Fugitive Slave Law, and the harshness of the law itself played a large role in making abolitionism – then considered an extreme position – respectable. Abolitionists such as Frederick Douglass and William Lloyd Garrison gained more influence in the North. In the South, many people believed that Northerners would go to any lengths, including subversion of the Constitution, to undermine slavery.

Two black Union soldiers are on picket duty in a Civil War photograph by Mathew Brady. *Archive Photos*

From Compromise to Confrontation

In the following year, the country was further stirred by the serial publication of Harriet Beecher Stowe's Uncle Tom's Cabin. Published as a book in 1852, the antislavery novel was widely read in the North, West, and South: many Northern and Western readers became more accepting of abolitionism, while Southerners angrily denounced the book.

In 1854 U.S. Senator Stephen A. Douglas, Democrat of Illinois, introduced and Congress passed the Kansas-Nebraska Act. The act repealed the Missouri Compromise, allowing territories to decide the issue of slavery for themselves. Many Northerners were outraged, and both Northerners and Southerners responded by sending settlers into the territories to oppose or promote slavery. Tensions escalated and a series of conflicts known as the Border War broke out. Combined with the Compromise of 1850 and the publication of *Uncle Tom's Cabin*, the dispute over Kansas and Nebraska triggered a massive political shift in American politics that allowed antislavery groups to found the Republican Party. By 1856 the party had enough support to run a candidate for president, and by 1860 the party had supplanted the once-popular Whig Party.

In 1857 the U.S. Supreme Court ruled in Dred Scott v. Sanford that Congress had no power to exclude slavery from the territories. The Court's ill-constructed reasoning and the polemical nature of its opinion further galvanized abolitionists. The following year Republican Abraham Lincoln challenged Douglas for his seat in the U.S. Senate. In a series of debates, Lincoln argued eloquently against extending slavery to the territories, swaying many Northerners and provoking fears in many Southerners. Although the Illinois legislature reelected Douglas, the Republican Party swept the state and gained considerable influence nationally. In 1859 John Brown conducted his ill-fated raid on a federal outpost at Harpers Ferry, Virginia, from which he intended to march an army of liberation to free slaves in the South. Captured, convicted, and executed, Brown became a martyr for Northern abolitionists and a reminder to the South that abolitionists were increasingly willing to fight to end slavery.

The final blow to national unity was the presidential election of 1860, which focused almost exclusively on slavery. Southern Democrats at the nominating convention in April, refused to support Northerner Stephen Douglas because of his moderate position on slavery. The Southerners walked out of the convention and nominated their own presidential candidate, John C. Breckinridge of Kentucky. Northern Democrats rallied behind Douglas. The Republicans nominated Lincoln, who won easily in November against the divided Democrats. Several leading Southerners had cautioned that if the Republicans won the election, the South might secede. On December 20, 1860, South Carolina made good on the promise. In January and February, Mississippi, Florida, Alabama, Louisiana, Georgia, and Texas also seceded. Shortly after Lincoln took office in March, he called on states to send militias to suppress the rebellion. The remaining Southern states – Virginia, Arkansas, North Carolina, and Tennessee – refused to send troops and seceded between April and June. Lincoln apparently hoped that the states would rejoin the Union without coercion, but this hope vanished on April 12,

1861, when Confederate forces attacked federal troops at Fort Sumter near Charleston, South Carolina.

African Americans Volunteer to Fight

Led by Frederick Douglass and other prominent abolitionists, most African Americans in the North viewed the Civil War as a fight to overthrow slavery. By the thousands, blacks volunteered for service in the Union army, only to be refused by President Lincoln. He argued repeatedly that the war was not being fought to end slavery but rather to restore the Union. Hoping that the war would be short-lived and that the Union would be quickly restored, he did not want to unnecessarily antagonize the South by enlisting black troops to fight against Confederate soldiers – a sure sign that Lincoln accorded African Americans equality with white Americans. Lincoln was also concerned about maintaining the support of two other groups: the slave-owning border states – Missouri, Kentucky, Maryland, and Delaware – that remained loyal to the Union; and the large number of proslavery, or at least nonabolitionist, Northern Democrats. A few Northern states, notably Massachusetts, disagreed with Lincoln's policy and pressured him to allow blacks to serve; however, many other states enacted laws banning blacks from state militias.

Many African Americans reacted to Lincoln's opposition by declaring that the blood of blacks was not worth spilling for a racist United States. Others, however, argued that African Americans had an obligation to demand equal treatment for themselves and to put an end to slavery for their Southern brothers and sisters. In the end, this voice won out and many Northern blacks supported the war effort in nonmilitary roles, such as working in munitions factories and hospitals. Still others enlisted in the Union navy, which had always allowed blacks to serve. By the end of the war, roughly 9000 blacks fought as sailors, but sailors were necessarily a small part of the 2.2 million men in uniform.

Blacks in Union Camps

Despite of federal policy, as Union regiments pressed into the South, they encountered slaves who regarded them as liberators and who fled to their protection. Union commanders had differing reactions to self-emancipated blacks. Abolitionists like Gen. Benjamin Butler, who fought initially in Virginia, declared escaped slaves contraband of war (the South, after all, maintained that slaves were only property), sheltered them in his camps, and put them to work, for example, as cooks. Furthermore, Butler argued that because the Confederacy had declared itself a separate nation, the Fugitive Slave Law did not apply to freed-people. Later Butler, fighting in the Mississippi Valley, and Gen. James Lane, fighting in Kansas, went so far as to use escaped slaves as scouts and soldiers. Many other generals, however, regarded the contrabands with indifference or, in accordance with Lincoln's policy, returned them to their masters. The earliest unit made entirely of African American enlisted men was probably the First South Carolina Volunteer Regiment. Formed by Gen. David Hunter in May 1862, the First South Carolina was Hunter's solution to his desperate need for combat-ready soldiers in the South Carolina Sea Islands. Lincoln's War Department reprimanded Hunter, disbanded the regiment, and reiterated that slaves should be returned to their owners.

This policy could not hold. As the war widened, thousands of slaves sought freedom behind Northern lines, and the logistics of reenslaving them was staggering. Increasingly, their owners had fled the Northern advance so that even slaves who remained on plantations were essentially free. The newly freed slaves presented problems to the Union army regarding shelter, food, and health; they also choked roads in their exodus, severely hampering the movement of Union troops. At the same time, it was becoming clear to Lincoln and his advisers that the war would not be brief and that the North would need more manpower than was initially anticipated.

Blacks Behind Confederate Lines

Of the 9 million people living in the South at the time of secession, more than 3.5 million were African American slaves. Although slaves did not fight for the South – the Confederacy even forbade a group of free black Louisianans from volunteering for service – every slave who contributed to the Confederate economy made it possible for a white Southerner to leave the plantation or the factory for the battlefront. While hundreds of thousands of slaves continued the plantation work they had always done, thousands more were forced into other roles. They built forts and bridges, assembled munitions, drove horse teams to transport troops and supplies, cooked meals, nursed the wounded and ill, and served as blacksmiths and laundresses. Because of black labor, an estimated 80 percent of military-age Southern men were able to serve in uniform. Throughout the war, Southerners feared slave revolts and increased patrols of rural areas accordingly; however, their fears were never fulfilled.

Slaves suffered from many of the wartime conditions that afflicted all Southerners, though more acutely. Food was scarce, and malnutrition and sickness grew with the war. Manufactured Northern clothes and tools also dwindled with time and were replaced with less reliable homemade articles. As slaveholders faced increasing financial burdens, slaves were sold more frequently, causing the separation of families; however, as more slaves were sold, their prices fell. Though many thousands of slaves fled to the protection of Union troops when the opportunity arose, many thousands more were herded by their owners farther into the Southern interior. Other slaves stayed with their owners out of simple affection, while still others felt too dependent on their owners or too frightened of the consequences to leave. For large numbers of slaves, these dislocations provided them with their first glance at the world beyond the plantation where they had lived their entire lives.

Momentum for Abolitionism

The arguments of Northern abolitionists gained ground as the war continued, in part because of the value of slaves to the South but also because Northerners were stunned at the lengths to which Southerners would go to fight for slavery. The North was also interested in denying the South imports and other aid from foreign countries, especially from Great Britain. One way to do this was to declare that the purpose of the war was to end slavery; Britain, having abolished slavery decades earlier, would have a difficult time helping a nation that was fighting to preserve slavery. For these and other reasons, Frederick Douglass's vocal campaign to change the war to a fight against slavery was increasingly supported by prominent white Northerners.

In the summer of 1862 Congress finally authorized Union troops to confiscate Southern property, including slaves, who could then be used in military-support roles. Freed slaves still could not fight, but Congress hoped that the act would give them an incentive to flee toward advancing Union troops. No longer hopeful of luring the South back into the Union, Congress also put an end to slavery in Washington, D.C., and banned slavery in the territories. In September 1862 Lincoln issued a preliminary Emancipation Proclamation freeing slaves in the South (though not in Northern border states, where slavery was still protected by the Constitution). The Emancipation Proclamation also finally permitted Southern freedpeople and Northern blacks to enter the armed services. Not everyone was pleased with the proclamation. Many whites still believed the war should be fought only to restore the Union, not to free slaves. Combined with Lincoln's controversial suspension of the writ of habeas corpus (by which accused criminals are brought before a court to determine whether their detention is lawful), with mounting losses on the battlefield, and with an unpopular military draft (beginning in 1863), the Emancipation Proclamation helped to bring about minor and major rebellions in the North.

Official Black Troops

For Northern blacks, however, the Emancipation Proclamation represented an enormous victory, and many urged their sons to enlist. In Massachusetts, abolitionist governor John A. Andrew immediately mustered a regiment of African Americans – the Fifty-fourth Regiment of Massachusetts – and other governors, tentatively at first, followed. At the time there was widespread skepticism among whites about whether blacks would fight and, even

SLAVE AND FREE STATES
AFTER THE COMPROMISE OF 1850
Free States and Territories
Slave States
Decision Left to Territory
0
300 km
0
300 mi
Canada
Mexico
Pacific Ocean
Atlantic Ocean
Bahamas
Cuba
45°
30°
Lake Winnipeg
Lake Superior
Lake Michigan
Lake Huron
Lake Ontario
Lake Erie
Columbia
Missouri
Snake
Colorado
Rio Grande
Ohio
Mississippi
Oregon Territory 1848
California 1850
Utah Territory 1850
New Mexico Territory 1850
Indian Country
Indian Country
Minnesota Territory 1849
Minnesota
Iowa
Indian Territory
Slaveholding Area of Five Civilized Tribes
Missouri
Arkansas
Louisiana
Wisconsin
Michigan
Michigan
Illinois
Indiana
Ohio
Kentucky
Tennessee
Mississippi
Alabama
Georgia
Florida
South Carolina
North Carolina
Virginia
Md.
Delaware
Pennsylvania
New Jersey
New York
Conn.
R.I.
Mass.
N.H.
Vt.
Maine

LEFT: A black family crosses Union lines in search of freedom during the Civil War. Slaves who took this route to freedom were called "intelligent contrabands" for they had, in effect, smuggled themselves out of bondage. *CORBIS*

LEFT MIDDLE: African American sailors aboard the USS *Vermont*. The United States Navy employed thousands of freed slaves during the Civil War. *CORBIS*

LEFT LOWER: This contemporary lithograph shows the African American troops of the 54th Massachusetts regiment leading the assault on Fort Wagner, South Carolina, on July 18, 1863, and the death of its commander, Col. Robert Gould Shaw, a white abolitionist. *CORBIS/Bettmann*

if they did, about whether they would fight capably. Although the few African Americans who had fought thus far in the Civil War had often done so with distinction, their service was little publicized. Initially, then, most of the newly recruited black regiments were confined to support roles. Only after the Fifty-fourth Massachusetts made a heroic and widely publicized assault in July 1863 on Fort Wagner, South Carolina, were blacks given a wider role in fighting. Even then blacks were almost never allowed to become officers. Black soldiers were also paid lower wages than whites until a protest by the Fifty-fourth Massachusetts prompted Congress in 1864 to equalize salaries and issue back pay – not, however, before William Walker of the Third South Carolina Volunteers was court-martialed, convicted of mutiny, and executed; he had led black soldiers in refusing to fight until pay was equalized.

In all, African Americans fought in roughly 40 major and 400 minor battles. These included Port Hudson, Louisiana (May 1863), where blacks made several bold assaults against devastating Confederate fire; Milliken's Bend, Mississippi (June 1863), where blacks fended off Confederates in hand-to-hand fighting; Fort Wagner (July 1863); Petersburg, Virginia (1864), where blacks endured terrible casualties as part of the siege of that city; and Richmond, Virginia (1865), the Confederate capital, which blacks were among the first troops to occupy.

The Confederacy treated all black soldiers, whether freedpeople by birth or by emancipation, as slaves subject to reenslavement and punishment. In several instances, Confederate troops simply murdered surrendering blacks, the most notorious example being Tennessee's FORT PILLOW MASSACRE. On April 12, 1864, three years to the day after the start of the Civil War, Union troops at Fort Pillow were surprised by an overwhelming Confederate force. As African Americans surrendered, Confederates shot men, women, and children indiscriminately. They also burned wounded black soldiers in their tents and nailed several African American sergeants to logs before setting them aflame. In all, about 200 African Americans were killed. After a government inquiry, Lincoln ordered a retaliation, but no action was taken.

By the end of the war almost 179,000 African Americans had served in the Union army and navy. Almost 3000 died from battle wounds, while 33,000 more died of disease. Among the important achievements for black soldiers was the promotion of MARTIN ROBISON DELANY, a doctor and writer, to the rank of major, the first African American to become a field officer. Black women, too, played important roles for the army; for example, Harriet Tubman served as a guide and scout and Elizabeth Bowser, a slave in the Confederate White House in Richmond, doubled as a Union spy.

End of the War: The North

Toward the end of the war Republican abolitionists were concerned that the Emancipation Proclamation would be viewed as a war act and thus unconstitutional once fighting ended. They were also increasingly anxious to secure the freedom of all African Americans, not just those freed by the Emancipation Proclamation. Thus pressed, Lincoln staked a large part of his 1864 presidential campaign on an amendment to the constitution that would abolish slavery throughout the United States. The president's campaign was bolstered by separate votes in both Maryland and Missouri to abolish slavery in their states. Winning reelection in November, Lincoln pressed the lame-duck Congress to amend the Constitution immediately rather than wait for the incoming Congress to act in April. On January 31, 1865, Congress approved the Thirteenth Amendment banning slavery in all U.S. states and territories. The amendment was ratified by the states in December.

In the last years of the war, the enactment of the Emancipation Proclamation, the service of blacks in the army, and the movement for the Thirteenth Amendment created an environment that allowed African Americans to demand broader equality. In Philadelphia, where streetcars were segregated before the war, African Americans secured a desegregation law from the state legislature. In Illinois, statutes preventing testimony from blacks in state courts were overturned. After protests by African Americans, segregated schools in Detroit and Rhode Island were desegregated. In several states, laws requiring blacks to own property before they could vote were seriously challenged for the first time. Many such activities would continue during Reconstruction.

End of the War: The South

The Confederacy, near the war's end, debated whether to enlist slaves as soldiers and, if so, whether slave-soldiers should be granted their freedom. In early 1865 the Confederate Congress passed a law that allowed a limited number of black soldiers to be conscripted. States were left to decide whether slaves who fought would be freed. Confederate president Jefferson Davis, however, allowed only slaves whose owners had volunteered them to serve in the Confederate army. By the end of the war, a few hundred were enlisted, but very few saw any significant action.

After the Confederacy was defeated, Southern blacks were confronted with freedom and the challenge of securing food and shelter. Some continued, out of necessity or choice, to work the land they had worked as slaves. Occasionally such African Americans worked out agreements with their former masters for wages or other forms of compensation like food and shelter; however, only in a few cases were their conditions much improved over slavery. Other former slaves migrated to towns and cities, hoping for work, education, or relief distributed by Northern freedpeople's aid societies and Union troops. Still others traveled more broadly, testing their freedom and seeking relatives from whom they had been separated by war or slavery. In the postwar Reconstruction years the United States would be forced to confront these and many other issues arising from the legacy of slavery.

See Also

Abolitionism in the United States; Fifty-fourth Regiment of Massachusetts Volunteer Infantry; Fugitive Slave Laws; Tubman, Harriet Ross; Thirteenth Amendment of the United States Constitution and the Emancipation Proclamation.

Latin America and the Caribbean

Clarke, Austin C. (b. July 26, 1934, St. James, Barbados), Barbadian novelist best known for chronicling the lives of West Indian immigrants in Canada in the 1960s and 1970s.

Austin Clarke's reputation as a writer rests primarily on the publication of what has come to be known as the Toronto Trilogy, which consists of the novels *The Meeting Point* (1967), *Storm of Fortune* (1973), and *The Bigger Light* (1975). He depicts the West Indian immigrants in Canada as deeply alienated from their adopted country as they struggle to overcome bone-chilling winters, sterile industrial cities, and racial discrimination.

Clarke graduated from the prestigious Harrison College in Barbados and received an Oxford and Cambridge Higher Certificate before immigrating to Canada in 1955 to study economics and political science at the University of Toronto. After working for a couple of years as a freelance journalist in Toronto and in rural Ontario, he turned to fiction writing. His first published novels, *The Survivors of the Crossing* (1964) and *Amongst Thistles and Thorns* (1965), were set in the Barbados of his youth. Reviewers of his early work saw a promising talent, especially in his ability to recreate Caribbean dialect.

Many of Clarke's characters come from the upper reaches of Barbadian society and must face the transition to drab working-class life in Canada. They live with the daily disappointments and frustrations of being, in one critic's words, "defrocked gentry, anxious to assume classy places in Canada's ruling class."

Clarke's displeasure with his native land comes across in his 1977 novel *The Prime Minister*, a scathing indictment of corruption in the Barbadian government that provoked many (unsuccessful) calls from officials on the island for its banning.

A Passage Back Home (1994) continues memoirs he began with *Growing Up Stupid Under the Union Jack* (1980). His most recent work, *The Origin of Waves* (1997), is his eighth novel.

Peter Hudson

North America

Clarke, John Henrik (b. January 1, 1915, Union Springs, Ala.; d. July 16, 1998, New York, N.Y.), African American writer, educator, and Pan-African nationalist.

John Henrik Clarke was a central figure in late-twentieth-century vernacular American Black Nationalism. As a teacher, writer, and popular public speaker, he emphasized black pride, African heritage – especially communalism – and black solidarity. From the rural South he rode a freight train to New York, where he actively participated in the literary and political life of Harlem in the 1930s. Arthur Schomburg, the black bibliophile, was a major intellectual influence. Largely self-educated, Clarke became professor of Africana and Puerto Rican Studies at New York's Hunter College and president of Sankofa University, an on-line Internet school.

Born to sharecropping parents, Clarke grew up in Columbus, Georgia, and aspired to be a writer. He produced poetry, short stories (notably "The Boy Who Painted Christ Black"), and books on African history (*The Lives of Great African Chiefs*) and on Africans in the diaspora (*Harlem U.S.A.*). An original member of the Harlem Writers Guild and a founding editor of *Freedomways* magazine, he is perhaps best known as the editor of William Styron's *Nat Turner: Ten Black Writers Respond* (1970), a critique of Styron's fictionalized version of Turner and the Southampton slave revolt.

Clarke served in the United States Air Force and attended New York University and the New School for Social Research. Beginning in 1964 he headed a federal antipoverty program. An active supporter of Pan-African political movements, he was on a first-name basis with many African leaders, and his Harlem home was a way station for visiting Africans. Clarke joined the faculty of Hunter College in 1969 and established the black studies program there and at Cornell. He was professor emeritus at Hunter and a highly sought-after speaker until his death at age 83. The following statement perhaps best summarizes his philosophy: "Wherever we are on the face of the earth, we are an African people."

See Also

Pan-Africanism; Harlem, New York; Schomburg, Arthur Alfonso; Black Nationalism in the United States.

Africa

Clark, John Pepper (also known as J. P. Clark-Bekederemo), (b. April 6, 1935, Kiagbodo, Nigeria), Nigerian poet, dramatist, journalist, and editor.

John Pepper Clark was raised in the Ijaw homeland of southern Nigeria by his maternal grandmother following his mother's death when he was a baby. When he was six, his father enrolled him in a school in the town of Okrika. After studying at Warri Government College from 1948 to 1954, he studied English at University College, Ibadan, where he founded the literary magazine the *Horn*.

Clark graduated with honors in 1960. After a year as a government information officer, he became an editorial and features writer for the Lagos *Daily Express*. His first play, *Song of a Goat*, a tragedy that drew on Ijaw dramatic traditions, was published in 1961. *Poems*, his first collection of poetry, came out in 1962, the same year he accepted a scholarship to study at Princeton University in New Jersey. Bitterly unhappy in the United States, Clark left school prematurely and chronicled his experience in the memoir *America, Their America* (1964).

Back in Nigeria, Clark translated Ijaw epic drama into English and in 1964 joined the English faculty of Lagos University, where he eventually became full professor. That same year saw the publication of both *A Selection of Poems* and *Three Plays: Song of a Goat, The Raft, The Masquerade*. Like *Song of a Goat*, Clark's next two plays were lyrical tragedies, written in verse. Another play, *The Ozidi of Atazi* (1966), grew out of Clark's Ijaw research, as did *The Ozidi Saga* (1975).

In 1970 Clark published *Casualties*, a collection of poems written during the Nigerian civil war (1967-1970). Unlike earlier poems that recalled childhood memories in rhythmic, sensual detail, the verse in *Casualties* was simple and somber. "Show me a house," one poem begins, "where nobody has died/Death is what you cannot undo." Coeditor of the literary magazine *Black Orpheus* in the late 1960s, Clark has also written such scholarly works as *The Example of Shakespeare* (1970) and *The Hero as Villain* (1978), as well as *A Decade of Tongues: Selected Poems 1958-1968* (1981), *Mandela and Other Poems* (1988), and *The Bikoroa Plays: Boats, The Return Home, Full Circle* (1985).

Kate Tuttle

See Also
Ibadan, Nigeria; Lagos, Nigeria.

North America

Clark, Kenneth Bancroft (b. July 24, 1914, Panama Canal Zone), African American psychologist, educator, and social activist whose research, in particular the "doll study," was crucial to the desegregation of public schools in the United States.

Kenneth Clark grew up with his mother in Harlem, where his childhood heroes included the poet Countee Cullen, who taught at his junior high school, and book collector Arthur Schomburg, who served as a curator at the 135th Street Branch of the New York Public Library. After attending integrated elementary and junior high schools, he graduated from New York's George Washington High School in 1931.

Clark distinguished himself as an undergraduate at Howard University, where he led demonstrations against segregation in Washington, D.C. While at Howard he met Mamie Phipps, who became his wife and closest intellectual collaborator. The Clarks then went to Columbia University to study psychology, and in 1940 Clark became the first black to receive a Ph.D. in psychology from Columbia. He joined the faculty of City College in New York City in 1942, becoming that college's first black permanent professor. He remained at City College until his retirement in 1975, but also served as a visiting professor at Columbia, the University of California, Berkeley, and Harvard.

Throughout his career Clark was committed to finding ways to use his expertise in the social sciences for the cause of racial justice. In the early 1950s he frequently served as an expert witness for the National Association for the Advancement of Colored People (NAACP) in its legal struggles against segregation. The work that earned him his greatest fame, however, was his research on the self-image of black children. Clark studied the responses of more than 200 black children who were given a choice of white or brown dolls. From his findings that the children showed a preference for the white dolls from as early as three years old, Clark concluded that segregation was psychologically damaging. This conclusion played a pivotal role in Brown v. Board of Education, the Supreme Court case that outlawed segregated education.

Although Clark fought for racial integration, his book *Dark Ghetto: Dilemmas of Social Power* (1965) was popular among Black Nationalists because it compared the situation of black citizens to that of colonized people. Clark's other writings include *Prejudice and Your Child* (1953), *Crisis in Urban Education* (1971), and *The Negro American* (1966), which he coedited with Talcott Parsons. His televised interviews with James Baldwin, Malcolm X, and Martin Luther King Jr. were published in a book titled *The Negro Protest* in 1963.

In addition to his activities as a scholar,

Throughout his career psychologist Kenneth Clark used his knowledge of social science in the cause of racial justice. *CORBIS/Robert Maass*

Clark was involved with a variety of community development programs and served as an adviser to local and national policymakers. In 1946 he and his wife founded the Northside Child Development Center in Harlem to serve the needs of emotionally disturbed children. He also played a key role in the establishment in 1962 of Harlem Youth Opportunities Unlimited, a program that influenced President Lyndon Johnson's War on Poverty program. And as the sole black member of the New York Board of Regents, he continued his fight against segregated education.

Clark's work for civil rights earned him the NAACP's Spingarn Medal in 1961. For his contributions to psychology, he was elected president of the American Psychological Association and received its Gold Medal award. After his retirement from City College as a professor emeritus, Clark organized a consulting firm that specializes in issues of racial policy.

Lawrie Balfour

See Also
Harlem, New York; King, Martin Luther, Jr.; Schomburg, Arthur Alfonso; Black Nationalism in the United States.

North America

Clark, Septima Poinsette (b. May 3, 1898, Charleston, S.C.; d. December 15, 1987, Charleston, S.C.), African American educator and civil rights activist.

Septima Poinsette Clark's parents, Peter and Victoria Poinsette, instilled a sense of social responsibility in Clark that she demonstrated throughout her professional life. Between the years 1916 and 1954, in addition to her teaching career, she helped provide adult literacy training; improve living conditions for African Americans on Johns Island, South Carolina;

change a law in Charleston that prohibited African American teachers from working in its segregated schools; and make African American teachers' salaries equal to those of white teachers. She earned a B.A. from Benedict College and an M.A. from Hampton Institute (now University).

Clark believed that literacy was an important component in gaining equality for African Americans, and at HIGHLANDER FOLK SCHOOL, a biracial training center for community activists in Tennessee, she developed CITIZENSHIP SCHOOLS, which taught adult literacy and basic life skills such as checkbook balancing and writing checks, and encouraged voter registration. In 1961 the program was transferred to the SOUTHERN CHRISTIAN LEADERSHIP CONFERENCE. By 1970 the project boasted over 800 schools and over 100,000 graduates, who formed the grassroots of the CIVIL RIGHTS MOVEMENT.

Clark retired in 1971 because she believed that long-term commitment to citizenship schools had waned. In 1979 President Jimmy Carter presented her with the Living Legacy award. In 1987 her second autobiography, *Ready from Within: Septima Clark and the Civil Rights Movement,* won the National Book Award.

Robert Fay

SEE ALSO
Hampton University.

Latin America and the Caribbean

Claver, Pedro. See COLONIAL CRITICS OF SLAVERY.

North America

Clayton, Eva (b. September 16, 1934, Savannah, Ga.), Democratic member of the United States House of Representatives from North Carolina since 1993, and the first African American woman elected to Congress from North Carolina.

Eva Clayton was born in Savannah, Georgia. She received a bachelor's degree from Johnson C. Smith University in 1955 and a master's degree from North Carolina Central University in 1962. She worked as director of a civil rights organization called the Soul City Foundation before she began a four-year tenure as assistant secretary for community development in the North Carolina Department of Natural Resources and Community Development in 1976. She started a management and consulting firm in 1981. In 1982 she also joined the Warren County Board of Commissioners, which she chaired for eight years.

When long-time U.S. representative Walter Jones died in September 1992, Clayton won a close primary contest against his son, Walter Jones Jr., for the Democratic nomination to fill the seat in North Carolina's First Congressional District. Clayton easily defeated her Republican opponent in the general elections of 1992, 1994, and 1996.

The irregularly shaped First District is a primarily rural, "black-majority" district created in a 1992 reapportionment of North Carolina's voting districts. Rocky Mount, Fayetteville, and Wilson are the largest cities in the district. Fort Bragg and Pope Air Force Base are located in Cumberland County. Paper manufacturers and government agencies are important employers in the district.

Just after her term in Congress began, Clayton was elected head of the 1993 freshman Democratic class. She earned seats on both the Agriculture Committee and the Small Business Committee. In the 105th Congress (1997-1999), she was ranking member of the Department of Operations, Nutrition, and Foreign Agriculture Subcommittee of the Agriculture Committee as well as the Budget Committee. She is also a member of the CONGRESSIONAL BLACK CAUCUS.

North America

Clay, William Lacy (b. April 30, 1931, St. Louis, Mo.), Democratic member of the United States House of Representatives from Missouri (1969-).

William Clay earned a bachelor's degree from St. Louis University in 1953, before serving in the United States Army (1953-1955). During military training at Fort McClellan in Alabama, he displayed an interest in civil rights activism, leading an effort to give blacks equal access to the swimming pool, the barbershop, and the noncommissioned officers club.

Returning to St. Louis in 1955, Clay became active in the CIVIL RIGHTS MOVEMENT. He participated in both the CONGRESS OF RACIAL EQUALITY and the NATIONAL ASSOCIATION FOR THE ADVANCEMENT OF COLORED PEOPLE. In 1959 he was elected to the St. Louis Board of Aldermen. He remained an alderman until 1964, when he became an official in the local Democratic Party.

In 1967 Missouri's voting districts were reorganized, and most of St. Louis's blacks were located in Missouri's First Congressional District. Clay won the First District congressional seat in 1968 with 64 percent of the vote, becoming the first black representative in Missouri's history. He was returned to office in subsequent elections.

Clay was a member of the Education and Labor Committee before the Republican takeover of the House in 1994. Between 1990 and 1994 he chaired the Post Office and Civil Service Committee. In the 105th Congress (1997-1999), Clay was the ranking Democrat on the Education and Workforce Committee.

North America

Cleaver, Eldridge Leroy (b. August 31, 1935, Wabbaseka, Ark.; d. May 1, 1998, Pomona, Calif.), African American writer, political activist, and former minister of information for the BLACK PANTHER PARTY.

After growing up in Wabbaseka, Arkansas, and Los Angeles, California, Eldridge Cleaver spent much of his young adulthood in the California state penitentiary system. Convicted on drug and rape charges in 1953 and 1958, he used his prison time to broaden his education. During this time, Cleaver studied the teachings of the NATION OF ISLAM and became a devoted supporter of MALCOLM X. With the assassination of Malcolm X in 1965, Cleaver broke his ties to the Nation of Islam and sought to carry on the mission of Malcolm X's Organization of Afro-American Unity.

Paroled in 1966, Cleaver went to work as an editor and writer for *Ramparts* magazine. Soon after his introduction to Huey Newton and BOBBY SEALE, cofounders of the Black Panther Party, in Oakland, California, Cleaver joined the Panthers and became the party's minister of information. In this role, he called on black men to "pick up the gun" against the United States government.

The year 1968 was one of turning points for Cleaver. He established himself as a gifted essayist and cultural critic with the publication of *Soul on Ice,* a collection of prison writings that earned him the Martin Luther King Memorial Prize in 1970. Also in 1968, Cleaver was selected as the presidential candidate of the Peace and Freedom Party. After a shoot-out in Oakland that left Cleaver and a police officer wounded and 17-year-old Bobby Hutton dead, Cleaver was charged with assault and attempted murder. His parole was revoked. Believing his life was in danger, Cleaver fled the country in November 1968.

He spent the next seven years in CUBA, France, and ALGERIA with his wife, Kathleen Neal Cleaver. Still actively involved with the Panthers, Cleaver published essays in *Black Scholar, Ramparts,* and the *Black Panther*, and served as the head of the International Section of the Black Panther Party in Algeria. After visits to North Korea, North Vietnam, and the People's Republic of China, however, Cleaver became increasingly critical of Marxist governments. A deal with the FBI allowed him to return to the United States in 1975 with a sentence of more than one thousand hours of community service.

After returning to the United States, his commitments shifted toward conservative politics and fundamentalist Christianity. He describes this transformation in *Soul on Fire,* which appeared in 1978. Cleaver lectured on religion and politics in the 1980s and ran as an independent candidate for Ronald Dellums's seat in the House of Representatives in 1984. After dropping out of the congressional race, Cleaver ran for a seat on the Berkeley, California, City Council. His ongoing struggle with drugs became public in 1994, when Cleaver was arrested in Berkeley.

A varied and prolific writer, Cleaver authored numerous political pamphlets, short stories, and poetry. His books *Eldridge Cleaver: Post-Prison Writings and Speeches* and *Eldridge Cleaver's Black Papers* both appeared in 1969. *The Black Panther Leaders Speak: Huey P. Newton, Bobby Seale, Eldridge Cleaver, and Company Speak Out Through the Black Panther Party's Official Newspaper* was published seven years later.

Lawrie Balfour

See Also

Dellums, Ronald V. (Ron); Newton, Huey P.; San Francisco and Oakland, California.

Latin America and the Caribbean

Clemente, Roberto

(b. August 18, 1934, Carolina, Puerto Rico; d. December 31, 1972, Puerto Rico), Puerto Rican baseball player and the first Latin American to be inducted into the Hall of Fame in 1973.

The son of a sugar-mill worker, as a youth Roberto Clemente achieved such skill at Puerto Rico's favorite sport that at age 14 he played in exhibition games against major league and Negro League players. After debuting with a local Puerto Rican team in 1952, he was signed by the Brooklyn Dodgers for a $10,000 bonus. In 1955 Clemente joined the Pittsburgh Pirates.

Clemente stayed with the Pirates for the rest of his career, for a total of 18 seasons. He won National League batting titles in 1961, 1964, 1965, and 1967, the National League Most Valuable Player award in 1966, and the Babe Ruth Award for his memorable performance in the 1971 World Series. He left the game with a batting average of .317 and 4000 hits. He also won 12 consecutive Gold Gloves and is considered by many experts the best defensive right fielder in the history of the game.

While Clemente was a key figure in the Pirates' 1960 World Series championship, it was his performance in their world championship run in 1971 that secured his place in baseball annals. Roger Angell's piece on the 1971 World Series in the *New Yorker* described "the shared experience, already fixed in memory, of Roberto Clemente playing the kind of baseball that none of us had ever seen before – throwing and running and hitting something close to the level of absolute perfection, playing to win but also playing the game almost as if it were a form of punishment for everyone else on the field."

Clemente is also remembered for his humanitarianism. He died in a plane crash on December 31, 1972, while en route from Puerto Rico to Nicaragua on a relief mission to help victims of an earthquake. During his professional career he protested the discrimination that Latino and black players encountered in the United States. The building of a Sport City, Clemente's project to help underprivileged Puerto Rican children in San Juan, was completed after his death, aided by contributions from his fans in Pittsburgh.

In 1973 the Baseball Hall of Fame inducted Roberto Clemente, waiving the customary five-year waiting period. In 1984 he became the second baseball player to be honored on a U.S. postage stamp.

Carlos Dalmau

See Also

Baseball in the United States; Negro Leagues; Puerto Rico; Baseball in the Latin America and the Caribbean.

North America

Clement, Rufus Early

(b. June 6, 1900, Salisbury, N.C.; d. November 7, 1967, New York, N.Y.), first African American elected to office in the South since Reconstruction.

Rufus Clement was the son of George Clinton Clement, a bishop of the African Methodist Episcopal Church (AME). After graduating as valedictorian of Livingstone College in 1922, he taught there, eventually becoming a professor and dean. He earned a degree at Garrett Theological Seminary and a Ph.D. from Northwestern University.

In 1931 Clement became the first dean of the all-black branch of the University of Louisville. Six years later he was appointed president of Atlanta University. His history-making election to the Atlanta school board occurred in 1954. Through his participation in the Civil Rights Movement, Clement helped integrate public schools, fought for voting rights, and helped end segregation in downtown Atlanta.

Eric Brosch

Africa

Cleopatra

(b. 69 B.C.E., Alexandria, Egypt; d. August 30, 30 B.C.E., Alexandria, Egypt), Egyptian queen and last ruler of the Macedonian dynasty of the Ptolemies.

Cleopatra VII was the second daughter of Ptolemy XII Auletes, king of Egypt. Although born in Egypt, she was a member of the dynasty of the Ptolemies. Ptolemy Soter, the dynasty's founder, had come from the Greek-speaking region of Macedonia with Alexander the Great and established a kingdom in Alexandria after Alexander's death in 323 B.C.E. (*see* Alexandria and Grecian Africa: An Interpretation). Upon her father's death, Cleopatra became queen in 51 B.C.E. at age 18, ruling with her 15-year-old brother, Ptolemy XIII. Fluent in Egyptian, unlike previous Ptolemy rulers, Cleopatra sought to strengthen her support among Egyptians by claiming that she was the daughter of Ra, the Egyptian sun god.

Ptolemy XIII, encouraged by his advisers, exiled Cleopatra and claimed the throne as his own. Cleopatra assembled an army from Syria, but could not assert her claim to the throne until the Roman ruler Julius Caesar arrived. Cleopatra intended to restore the Ptolemaic Empire, which had once stretched as far as Syria. Realizing Caesar's importance to her struggle, she enlisted his help. The two triumphed in 47 B.C.E. They executed Ptolemy XIII and restored Cleopatra to joint rule with her younger brother, Ptolemy XIV.

During the conflict Caesar and Cleopatra became lovers, either out of love or political ambition. When Caesar returned to Rome in 46 B.C.E., Cleopatra went with him. In Rome, Cleopatra gave birth to a son, Caesarion, reputedly Caesar's. She was still in Rome when Caesar was assassinated in 44 B.C.E. Cleopatra then allegedly poisoned her brother, Ptolemy XIV, and returned with little Caesarion to Egypt, where she named him coregent.

Caesar's apparent successor, Mark Antony, met with Cleopatra in 41 B.C.E. The two fell in love and Antony went with Cleopatra to Egypt, where he treated her as the ruler of an independent nation. In 40 B.C.E., Antony returned to Rome to marry Octavia, the sister of Octavian (later Caesar Augustus), who was Antony's rival in Rome. In the same year, Cleopatra gave birth to twins.

Antony began a campaign against the Parthians in present-day Iran in 36 B.C.E. and Cleopatra joined him at Antioch, where they married. Antony earned the enmity of Rome for this betrayal of Octavia. After his victory against the Parthians, Antony returned to Alexandria, where he and Cleopatra plotted the conquest of Rome and the creation of a shared empire, with their shared offspring as heirs. Octavian declared war on Antony and Cleopatra. At the Battle of Actium in 31 B.C.E., Octavian's fleet fought the combined forces of Antony and Cleopatra. In the middle of the battle, however, Cleopatra recalled her fleet, and she and Antony sailed for Alexandria. Having received a false report of Cleopatra's death, Antony killed himself. When Cleopatra failed to broker a deal with Octavian and realized that he intended to parade her in Rome as a spoil of war, she killed herself, either by taking poison or by inducing a poisonous asp to bite her. Shortly afterward Octavian ordered Caesarion killed, and the Ptolemaic Dynasty, which Cleopatra had worked so hard to maintain, ended.

The historical record of Cleopatra's life and death is scant, but she continues to capture the imagination of scholars and dramatists.

Robert Fay

See Also

Egypt; Alexandria, Egypt.

North America

Cleveland, James Edward

(b. December 3, 1931, Chicago, Ill.; d. February 9, 1991, Los Angeles, Calif.), African American gospel singer and composer known as the Crown Prince of Gospel.

A child prodigy, James Edward Cleveland began playing the piano when he was five years old. His family was too poor to afford a piano, so Cleveland practiced on the windowsill, painting the ledge with black and white keys. Growing up in Chicago, he was surrounded by the legends of the first generation of GOSPEL MUSIC. At the age of eight, he sang as a soloist for the Junior Gospel Choir at Pilgrim Baptist Church directed by the father of gospel music, Thomas A. Dorsey. Cleveland was also influenced by the Roberta Martin Singers, particularly Roberta Martin's piano playing.

By the time he was 15, Cleveland had joined the Thorne Crusaders, with whom he sang around Chicago until 1954. During this time he began composing, and wrote "Grace Is Sufficient" for his idols, the Roberta Martin Singers, when he was 16. The song has now become a gospel standard. In 1950 he joined Norsalus McKissick and Bessie Folk, two former Roberta Martin Singers, to form the trio the Gospelaires. After he left the Thorne Crusaders, Cleveland played piano and arranged for Albertina Walker's Caravans. His work with the Caravans solidified his reputation as an emerging star among the second generation of gospel performers.

During the latter half of the 1950s he composed, arranged, and performed with several groups, including the Meditations in DETROIT, MICHIGAN, the Gospel All-Stars in Brooklyn, and the Gospel Chimes in Chicago. Cleveland recorded with the Voices of Tabernacle Choir of Detroit in 1960. Together they performed the Soul Stirrers' song "The Love of God," which became a popular hit. According to scholar Tony Heilbut, with this recording "Cleveland simultaneously ushered in the decade and the modern gospel sound."

Capitalizing on this recent success, he signed a contract with Savoy Records to make several recordings with the Angelic Choir of Nutley, New Jersey. Their first recording, "Peace Be Still," sold over 800,000 copies and set the standard for modern gospel choir recordings. Cleveland's style moved between singing and preaching, alternating his gruff shouting with sweet falsetto. He used the choir as a response to his call and always recorded with a live congregation, a technique that combined the traditions of the Baptist and Holiness churches. Cleveland often claimed to be "part Baptist, part Sanctified."

During the 1950s and 1960s, his most prolific decades, Cleveland composed over 500 songs. His most popular included "Oh, Lord, Stand By Me," "He's Using Me," and "Walk On by Faith." Cleveland wrote in a colloquial style about everyday trials of the poor. Lyrics such as "One day I woke up, I had no food on the table/ But the God I serve, I know he's able," earned him the moniker "Knife and Fork King."

In 1968 Cleveland founded the Gospel Music Workshop of America to serve as an alternative for young performers to Dorsey's National Convention of Gospel Choirs and Choruses. By the mid-1980s the Workshop boasted several hundred thousand members. Cleveland trained and inspired many performers, most notably Aretha Franklin. In 1970 he founded the Cornerstone Institutional Baptist Church in Los Angeles, which held 7000 charter members at his death in 1991.

See Also

Chicago, Illinois; Dorsey, Thomas Andrew; Franklin, Aretha Louise; Soul Stirrers.

Latin America and the Caribbean

Cliff, Jimmy

(b. James Chambers) (b. April 1, 1948, Somerton, Jamaica), Jamaican musician whose film career introduced many Americans and Europeans to REGGAE.

Like many Jamaicans, Jimmy Cliff migrated from the countryside to Kingston, the country's capital, during the political upheaval that accompanied Jamaica's independence in 1962. At the time of the move, Cliff was 14 and already had been singing and playing music for years. He sought opportunity and adventure in Kingston, finding both when his improvised rendition of "Dearest Beverley" inspired a partnership between himself and a Chinese storeowner, Leslie Kong, who agreed to record and produce his music. By the age of 15 Cliff had become a Kingston celebrity. In the early 1960s he toured with a SKA band, appeared in the promotional video *This Is Ska*, and recorded early hits such as "Hurricane Hattie," "King of Kings," and "Miss Jamaica."

In 1964 Cliff appeared at the New York World's Fair and soon after moved to England to record for Island Records. He achieved widespread popularity in the Caribbean and Europe by 1965 but did not win a significant American following until "Wonderful World, Beautiful People" became a hit in 1970. Also popular were his protest song "Vietnam" (lauded by Bob Dylan) and his cover of Cat Stevens's "Wild World."

Cliff appeared in a semiautobiographical film, *The Harder They Come* in 1970. Released in the United States in 1973, the movie introduced many Americans to Jamaica's new music. *The Harder They Come* tells the story of a gun-slinging pop star who has risen from rural origins to achieve urban notoriety. Despite the success of the film's soundtrack, which featured Cliff's hit "Many Rivers to Cross," the film propelled his own career less than he had expected. Instead, it primed American audiences for the music of BOB MARLEY, the first global superstar of reggae. Ironically, Cliff himself introduced Marley to Kong, aiding a career that would eventually eclipse his own.

Although conditions were ripe for Cliff to follow Marley's lead, he opted instead to explore new directions with his music, releasing *Another Cycle* (1980), an album of soul and RHYTHM AND BLUES songs recorded in the United States. In the records that followed, Cliff moved toward a pop music sound that never won him popularity. Indeed, since *The Harder They Come*, Cliff's career has been characterized by sporadic and limited success. He released albums throughout the 1980s and 1990s, appeared in the 1986 movie *Club Paradise* alongside Robin Williams, and continues to tour. His crowning accomplishment, however, remains his hep personification of the reggae scene in *The Harder They Come*.

Eric Bennett

See Also

Soul Music; New York, New York; Jamaica; Kingston, Jamaica.

Latin America and the Caribbean

Cliff, Michelle

(b. November 2, 1946, Kingston, Jamaica) Jamaican-American novelist, short story writer, poet, and critic.

Michelle Cliff has described herself as a writer of "Afro-Caribbean (Indian, African, and white) experience and heritage and Western experience and education." Cliff was born in JAMAICA, but spent much of her childhood in New York and became a naturalized American citizen. After receiving her B.A. in European history from Wagner College in 1969, she worked briefly at the New York publishing house W.W. Norton before moving to London. In 1974 she received a M.Phil from Warburg Institute in languages and comparative historical studies of the Italian Renaissance.

Cliff then returned to New York and a career in teaching and publishing, which included co-editing a feminist journal with poet Adrienne Rich. In the late 1970s she also began publishing her own essays and poetry, and she published her first novel, *Abeng*, in 1984. *Abeng's* main character, Clare Savage, is a light-skinned, middle-class Jamaican girl, and Cliff has said that Clare's struggle to accept her mixed heritage and the privileges it has brought her was largely autobiographical. Much of her other work deals with similar legacies of colonialism on the contemporary Caribbean. Cliff's work is also celebrated for its explorations of lesbian sexuality, and she has become internationally known for her essays on racism and feminism.

Her second novel, *No Telephone to Heaven* (1988), followed Clare Savage to adulthood in Jamaica and the United States, and her third, *Free Enterprise* (1993), is a portrayal of nineteenth-century women revolutionaries. Cliff has also published collections of poetry and prose, and short stories and edited the works of Lillian Smith, and she has taught at many institutions, including Stanford University and Trinity College.

Lisa Clayton Robinson

See Also
New York, New York.

Africa

Climate of Africa

The precipitation and wind conditions of Africa are shaped by topography, latitudinal position, global wind patterns, and the moderating influence of oceans. Africa's climate, therefore, varies both regionally and over time.

Topography

Compared to other continents, Africa is flat. Yet since air temperature decreases with elevation by as much as 6.4° C (44° F) per 1000 m (3688 ft), the continent's mountainous regions, even those along the equator, can be quite cold. The plateaus and mountains south and east of the Congo Basin, which average between 1000 and 3000 m (3688 and 9864 ft) in elevation, exemplify the moderating influence that elevation has on direct solar angle.

Africa's landscape also differs from other continents in its lack of a major chain of mountains, such as the Rocky Mountains in North America and the Alps in southern Europe, which define distinct climatic regions by fully dividing masses of land. In Africa the discontinuity of mountain ranges and the large "unobstructed" stretches of land give wind patterns an especially important role in the determination of regional climate.

Winds

Blowing in patterns shaped by the earth's rotation around its axis and its alignment with the sun, winds tend to converge at the equator in a narrow strip called the Intertropical Convergence Zone (ITCZ). Due to high equatorial temperatures, air in the ITCZ heats and rises, creating the humid, rainy, low-pressure system that typifies equatorial climates. Rising air circulates away from the equator and moves toward the poles, forming a higher, oppositely oriented layer above the ITCZ winds. This higher stratum descends around the Tropics of Cancer and Capricorn, causing high-pressure systems that are dry and windy. The "friction" caused by these two patterns of air – one atop the other – explains much of the weather between the equator and the Tropics: humidity at one end, dryness at the other, with thunderstorms and variable weather between.

The ITCZ moves seasonally as the hemispheres shift in their relative distance from the sun. In the summer of the Northern Hemisphere, the ITCZ moves northward, bringing with it increased rains. In the winter, it dips below the equator while winds sweep the north. Because oceans and mountains affect the motion of the ITCZ, it moves across different regions (even of the same latitude) at different times; likewise, its speed varies from region to region. The ITCZ's passage over East Africa, for example, produces a very short rainy season. Other regions experience bimodal – or twice annual – rains: the first as the ITCZ moves poleward, the second as it returns.

The dry winds that originate in the tropical high-pressure systems blow toward the equator and in some places have a great influence on animal life, including that of humans. In the Northern Hemisphere these northeasterly winds originate in Asia, bring little water and much dust, and are called the Harmattan. Although the phenomenon is mirrored in the south, southeasterly winds – which hail from the oceans instead of a dry land-mass like Asia – are milder.

Latitude

Because Africa straddles the equator symmetrically, meteorological patterns in the Northern Hemisphere roughly mirror those in the Southern Hemisphere. The perennially warm and humid weather in the equator supports rainforests that thin to savannas outside the narrow band of ITCZ humidity. As high-pressure systems arise at the Tropics, savannas dwindle into desert. The Sahara Desert in the north has its analogue in the Kalahari and Namib deserts in the south. (For information on patterns of African vegetation, *see* biogeography of Africa.)

Africa is the most "tropical" continent, as most of its area falls between the Tropic of Cancer and the Tropic of Capricorn. About one third of Africa experiences temperatures above 38° C (100° F), and very few regions, for very short periods of time, experience daytime temperatures that approach freezing. In many other regions the high average temperature leads to high rates of evaporation and can severely limit agriculture.

Oceans

In addition to tempering the force of southwesterly winds in the Southern Hemisphere, the oceans moderate temperature in much of coastal Africa. Because it takes more heat to raise the temperature of water than it does to raise the temperature of land, the oceans take much longer to change temperature than does land. Furthermore the natural dissipation of heat energy causes warm currents to flow toward the poles and polar currents to flow toward the equator. Coastal temperatures, therefore, tend to be more moderate than temperatures inland, even where other variables, such as latitude and elevation, are equivalent. The moderating effect of water appears in a less dramatic form along the shores of Africa's larger lakes, such as Lake Victoria and Lake Tanganyika.

Climatic Zones

Roughly speaking, Africa's climatic zones fall into three broad catagories: humid equatorial, dry, and humid temperate. Within these zones, altitude and other localized variables produce distinctive regional climates.

Humid equatorial climate conditions prevail in West and Central Africa around the equator itself; along the Guinea Coast, in Gabon, Cameroon, Democratic Republic of the Congo, northeastern Republic of the Congo and surrounding countries; and in East Africa about 5° south of the equator in Tanzania, Mozambique, and Madagascar. The average monthly temperatures remain around 25° C (77° F). The regions nearest the equator receive year-round rainfall (the foothills of Mount Cameroon sometimes receive more than 10,000 mm (396 in) annually), while those north and south of it experience short dry winters and a lower average annual precipitation. Away from the equator the dry season lengthens, though the climate may remain mostly humid.

Where the dry seasons are long enough, equatorial regions give way to dry or semi-arid regions. In the north the Sahel stretches from east to west through Mali, Niger, Chad, and Sudan and borders the Sahara. In the south, a similar region surrounds the Kalahari and fills the interior. Annual rainfall seldom exceeds 500 mm (19 in) even as temperatures exceed those at the equator, sometimes reaching 45° C (113° F). In the deserts themselves, rainfall is even more scarce and temperatures more extreme. Although the daytime temperatures in the desert are high, due to the lack of vegetation and humidity, nights can be extremely cold. In fact, daily temperature fluctuation in arid regions often far exceeds variation in average monthly temperatures.

The northern coast and southern tip of Africa diverge from the pattern outlined above, where rainfall diminishes in relation to the region's distance from the equator. Because of oceanic and latitudinal moderation, these regions experience temperate or weather, including dry summers and wet winters.

Finally, climate in some parts of Africa is strongly affected by localized topographic or wind conditions. These include the cooler mountainous regions as well as the semi-arid regions in East and southeast Africa. The latter is explained by the short rainy seasons and the presence of Madagascar, which blocks oceanic winds.

Variability: Past, Present, and Future

The climate of Africa varies cyclically over periods of decades, centuries, and millennia as well as from year to year. For Africans annual variations both in the timing and duration of the rainy seasons are the most important, because they affect the availability of water for agriculture and livestock.

The precise relationships between deforestation, desertification, and drought are debated, but it is clear that recent climate change in Africa reflects human as well as nonhuman causes. Indeed, meteorological records over the last 150 years indicate a cooling and drying trend that can only partially be explained by the impact of humans.

Over the long term, Africa's climates have changed dramatically. Since the breakup of Gondwanaland (*see* Geomorphology, African), the earth has formed icecaps and Africa has cooled and dried considerably. For example, as recently as 6000 years ago, the region that is now the Sahara Desert abounded with life: Nile crocodiles can still be found in oases separated from the river by hundreds of kilometers of inhospitable clime.

Eric Bennett

See Also
Drought and Desertification; Kalahari Desert; Namib Desert; Nile River.

North America

Clinton, George (b. July 22, 1940, Kannapolis, N.C.), African American musician, pioneer of funk style.

George Clinton grew up in Plainfield, New Jersey, where he worked in a barbershop straightening hair and formed a musical group, the Parliaments. After moving to Detroit, Clinton and the Parliaments had a minor hit, "(I Just Wanna) Testify," in 1967.

Following a lawsuit over the band's name, Clinton formed not one but two new groups, with many overlapping players: the legendary Parliament and Funkadelic (known collectively as P-Funk). Parliament was more commercial; Funkadelic was outlandish, with musicians wearing diapers, Clinton emerging from a coffin, and plenty of references to sex and drugs. The bands merged in the 1970s, and their concerts, featuring such spectacles as giant spaceships landing onstage, became a major attraction.

For all his eccentricity, Clinton was an influential spokesman for African Americans; his song "Chocolate City" expresses, in terms both witty and poignant, the dream of an all-black government. Clinton and his many sidemen have swayed post-1970 musical styles. With Bootsy Collins playing bass and Bernie Worrell playing keyboards, P-Funk helped define funk, then helped push this genre into unpredictable new territory. Although Clinton has had little commercial success, he has vitally influenced both African American and white audiences.

Africa

Clitoridectomy. See Female Circumcision in Africa.

Africa

Clothing in Africa, as elsewhere, has long served more than one purpose. In addition to satisfying human needs for covering and adornment, textiles and clothing provide media for artistic expression for weavers, dyers, tailors, and clothing designers. For centuries, textiles and garments have been produced both domestically – for household and village community members – and commercially, for bartering or sale. Although the earliest cloth was made primarily of local natural fibers, today's African textiles and clothing incorporate a wide variety of materials and styles.

The precise origins of cloth production in Africa are lost in time, but archaeological findings indicate some of the earliest sites. Drawings of looms can be seen in the tombs of ancient Egypt, dating back to at least 2000 B.C.E. Archaeologists have found linen remnants in ancient Egypt, as well as fifth-century cotton cloth remnants in Meroe, in northern Sudan. In West Africa, woven fiber pieces dating back to the ninth century C.E. have been found in Nigeria, and woven cotton cloth dating to the eleventh century has been recovered in Mali. Evidence of loom use in Mauritania dates back to the eleventh century.

Traditions of Cloth Production and Design

Bark cloth, or cloth made from tree bark, predates the development of woven textiles in most parts of Africa. Today it is rarely used for day-to-day clothing, but some societies use it for ceremonial costumes. The Ganda of Uganda, for example, make fabric from the inner bark of fig trees, which is worn during ceremonial dances and other occasions when ancestors are being honored. Early clothing in Africa was also made from treated animal hides, furs, and feathers.

Many African societies weave cloth from locally grown cotton. In North Africa and the Sahel, women also spin and weave camel and sheep wool. Other sources of fiber include the raffia palm in Central and West Africa, jute and flax in West Africa and Madagascar, and silk in Nigeria, Madagascar, and East Africa. All these fibers can be dyed using vegetable and mineral dyes.

The two main kinds of textile looms in Africa are the double-heddle loom, used for narrow strips of cloth, and the single-heddle loom, used for wider pieces. The narrow strips are typically sewn together, then cut into patterns for clothing. The double-heddle loom is generally used only by male weavers, who use it to weave in colored threads and create richly textured fabrics. Weavers in North Africa and in Ethiopia also use ground looms, while looms similar to those used in Southeast Asia are found in Madagascar.

Although Africa's weavers produce a wide variety of patterned, colored fabric, they also weave plain cloth. This cloth can either be used "as is" for daily wear around the home or it can be decorated. Common fabric-decorating techniques include embroidery with brightly colored threads; appliqué designs, sewn on in contrasting fabrics; and dyeing.

Two of the most popular dyeing techniques in Africa are tie and dye, and resist dye. In tie and dye, designs are first tied or stitched into the cloth, using cotton or raffia threads. In resist dye, dyers draw on the cloth using an impermeable substance, such as candle wax or paste made from cassava, a tuber. They then dip the fabrics into solutions typically made from vegetable dyes, which color all but the covered areas. Indigo plants are used for deep blue dyes, while reddish brown dyes are extracted from cola nuts, the camwood tree, and the redwood tree. Greens, yellows, and blacks are prepared from other sources.

Most designs and motifs used to decorate fabric have names. Many designs are associated with particular plants, animals, events, or proverbs, and are often used in other crafts, such as house painting, carving, and pottery. Others incorporate Roman letters and numerals, Arabic script, or line drawings of contemporary objects, such as bicycles and cars. "Traditional" cloth production, in other words, is not only highly varied from place to place but is also influenced by societal and technological change.

In many African societies, women and men are responsible for different stages of cloth production. This division of labor, however, varies widely by region, and in many places has changed over time. For example, in Mali, women used to dye *bogolanfini* mud-cloth, but today young unemployed men in urban areas have taken up this craft. They typically produce lower-quality cloth, which is sold to tourists or exported. Indigo dyeing is women's work among the Yoruba and the Soninké of West Africa, but among the Hausa, dying of fabric is traditionally a men's craft.

Commercial textile and clothing production has a long history in some parts of Africa. In Tunisia, weavers and dyers as early as the tenth century C.E. organized guilds in order to protect their business. By the fifteenth century, the dyeing pits of Kano in northern Nigeria were renowned as far north as the Mediterranean coast. They are still in operation today. In Kano, as in many other precolonial centers of commercial textile production, the city's political elite were among the weavers' and dyers' most important clientele. Royal patronage fostered the development of special luxury cloths. The court of King Njoya of Baumun in present-day Cameroon, for example, produced especially fine examples of raffia-stitched tie and dye. The Asante court in Kumasi (in present-day Ghana) supervised the production of silk *kente* cloth.

Clothing Traditions Across the Continent

In North Africa, nomadic pastoralists in mountainous regions weave animal wool into thick cloth for tents, blankets, rugs, and cushions. The *mouchtiya* is a capelike shawl worn by married women, and like other clothing materials is woven on vertical looms. Across North Africa, both Arab and Berber influences are apparent in textile designs and clothing styles.

In the highlands of Ethiopia and Eritrea, Amharic and Tigrean women wear *kemis*, cotton dresses with fitted bodices, long sleeves, and full skirts. The *shamma*, a light shawl, is thrown over the head and shoulders. A border of woven or embroidered geometric designs highlights the otherwise white cloth. The designs include variations of the cross motif, which is central to the Ethiopian Orthodox Church. Men also wear the shamma, as well as shirts and baggy knee-length pants made of the same white cloth. In colder weather, people of this region have traditionally wrapped themselves in a heavy woven blanket (*kutta)* or cape (*bornos)*. When it rains they don a *wollo*, a cape made from finely woven grass. Farther east in the Horn of Africa, the pleated skirts and tight embroidered trousers and veils worn by Islamic Somali, Harari Oromo, and Argobba women reflect influences from the Indian subcontinent, cultivated over centuries of trade across the Indian Ocean.

Pastoral societies in the lowlands of the Horn of Africa, such as the Boran, make some of their own clothing out of goatskin. The women wear leather or cotton skirts trimmed with beads, metal rings, cowrie shells, and ostrich eggshell beads, and sometimes painted with cow blood. The cotton woven here is multicolored and striped, not unlike the *kikoi* cloth found along the Swahili coast of East Africa.

In the Sahara and Sahelian regions of West Africa, Tuareg men wrap their heads in a distinctive blue veil. The indigo-dyed wrap is put on during the initiation ceremonies marking the end of boyhood, and thereafter is rarely removed. The indigo from the veil and accompanying robes rubs off onto the skin, hence the Tuareg's nickname the "blue men." The Tuareg have traditionally purchased their indigo cloth from Hausa traders in markets along the Sahara's southern edge.

Elsewhere in West Africa, men in many societies weave cotton cloth in long narrow strips that are then stitched into large pieces. Among the Asante, the men wrap the long piece of cloth around the waist and then loop it over the shoulder, toga-style. Baggy pants that are tight around the lower leg are popular, as are elaborately embroidered, full-length robes. Women across West Africa

TOP: An Asante villager prepares Adimkra cloth. *M & E Bernheim*

LEFT: A woman dyes cloth in pots of indigo in Nigeria. *Betty Press*

commonly tie a long wrap around the waist, accompanied by a wide sash, a matching blouse, and a head wrap.

The Yoruba of Nigeria prepare an indigo-dyed cotton called *adire eleso*. The artists sew finely detailed patterns onto the cloth using raffia or cotton thread, then take the cloth to a dyer, known as an *aloro*, who, it is said, works under the protection of the Yoruba spirit Iya Mapo. Similar techniques are also used farther west, among the WOLOF, the Soninke, and the Mandinka, and as far south as the Kasai region in the DEMOCRATIC REPUBLIC OF THE CONGO.

Yoruba women cloth makers, known as *aladire*, use resist dye methods to make adire eleso. They use cassava paste to paint or stencil repeated abstractions of animals and plants onto the cloth. After dyeing the cloth indigo blue, they beat it with a wooden stick until it attains a bright glossy sheen. In Mali BAMBARA women also use the resist technique to produce a speckled blue fabric, while Soninké women coat cloth in paste and then run a comb through it to create a wavelike design after dyeing.

The colors and designs of the adobe architecture found in Tombouctou (Timbuktu) and other older cities in Mali are reflected in the Bambara's famous ochre-colored bokolanfini, or mud-cloth fabrics. Women first dye the cloth yellow with a vegetable extract, then carefully paint the cloth with specially prepared mud. After the mud is washed off, the designs appear in yellow against a dark brown background. Finally, dyers apply bleach to the yellow parts to change them back to the original color.

In GHANA, cloths sewn from narrow cotton strips are either kept white or dyed reddish brown with a dye obtained from the bark of the kuntunkuni tree. The artist then divides the cloth into blocks, and uses stamps made of calabash shells to decorate the fabric with designs, many of which are associated with proverbs. The finished cloth is worn toga-style by AKAN and EWE men.

Perhaps the most famous fabric produced in Ghana is kente, which was traditionally made by tailors of the Asante court, using European silk acquired first through trans-Saharan trade and later coastal trade. Richly colored and textured fabric, kente was once worn only by Asante royalty, but it has now become an international symbol for Africa. It is worn throughout the African diaspora as an acknowledgment of one's roots on the continent. Outside Ghana, it is still difficult to find large pieces of high-quality hand-woven kente. But cheap, mass-produced copies of kente designs – often printed rather than woven – are now sold worldwide.

One of the most distinctive textiles produced in Central Africa is raffia cloth. Men weave fibers from the leaves of raffia palm trees into squares that vary in size according to the length of the fibers. Tie and dyeing, weaving, cut-pile embroidery, and appliqué are all used to decorate the fabric with geometric designs. The squares are sewn edge to edge into larger pieces, which can be used for dance skirts and for burial cloths. Raffia cloth production has largely died out in more heavily populated areas along the coast, but the KUBA of the Kasai region continue to weave and decorate raffia cloth for use during funerals.

FOREIGN INFLUENCES

African societies have long incorporated imported materials, textiles, and styles into their own clothing traditions. For centuries, trans-Saharan trade caravans carried cloth back and forth between the city-states of the West African savanna and North Africa. After Europeans began plying Atlantic trade routes around the continent, they too participated in the textile trade. Certain kinds of cloth, in fact, served as currency in West Africa, to be exchanged for slaves or gold. In East Africa, foreign textiles arrived on ships that worked the monsoon trade routes between the Gulf of Arabia, India, and East Asia.

Beginning in the sixteenth century, Portuguese traders frequented the southern African port of Lourenço Marque (now Maputo, the capital of MOZAMBIQUE), bringing glass beads to exchange for ivory and gold. The NDEBELE people used the beads to decorate leather skirts and cloaks, as well as to make thick hoop necklaces, bracelets, and anklets.

In the late nineteenth century, a new cloth became popular on ZANZIBAR, an island city-state with a long history of transoceanic trade. During the 1870s enterprising Swahili women began to sew brightly colored imported handkerchiefs known as *lesos* into larger pieces of fabric, which were called *kangas*. Six lesos were cheaper than one piece of imported fabric of the same size. The textile industries in Manchester, England, and Holland soon caught on to this new market and began manufacturing similarly sized single cotton pieces that were intended to be sold in pairs. The kangas were worn mainly by women eager to establish their emancipated identity after the abolition of slavery on Zanzibar. They wrapped one kanga around the waist, another around the upper body, and a third around the head and thrown over the shoulder, covering the body in the Muslim fashion. The most popular kangas had proverbs and other sayings printed at the bottom. Kangas are now widely worn in East Africa; most are either produced by domestic industries in Kenya or Tanzania or imported directly from South or East Asia. Just as at the turn of the century, customers are always in search of new designs and new printed proverbs.

Nineteenth-century European traders found large markets for factory-produced wax-printed cloth in West Africa. The designs of this cloth imitated hand-dyed batik textiles, which the Dutch East India Company began importing from Java in the seventeenth century. West African women wore "dutch wax" wraps (or *pagnes*, in Francophone countries) in much the same way as women in East Africa wore kangas.

Today, most independent West African countries' domestic textile industries manufacture cloth decorated with "dutch wax" prints as well as other designs. These factories commonly produce special runs on request, to commemorate holidays or events. Genuine dutch wax cloths are still imported from Europe and are both prestigious and costly. Despite their foreign origin they are widely recognized as "African" fabrics. A large proportion of both the urban and international trades in dutch wax cloths is controlled by women traders based in West African cities such as Lomé, Lagos, and Abidjan. The most successful of these traders are known as Mama Benzis, a reference to their Mercedes Benz cars and other symbols of wealth.

British and Dutch merchants were not the only Europeans who encouraged Africans to adopt new clothing styles during the colonial era. Christian missionaries expected converts to wear modest European-style clothing. During World War I and World War II, pamphlets used during recruitment campaigns in the colonies featured pictures of soldiers smartly dressed in khaki shorts and shirts. Most colonial-era schools (like many today) required students to wear uniforms, similar to the blouse and skirt (for girls) or shorts (for boys) ensembles worn by European schoolchildren.

CONTEMPORARY TRENDS

Given the association of Western-style dress with the colonial powers, it is hardly surprising that many African anticolonial movements of the 1940s and 1950s made elements of traditional clothing symbolic of their campaign for independence. JOMO KENYATTA of Kenya wore a beaded *ogut tigo* hat and a beaded leather belt, while Ghana's KWAME NKRUMAH encouraged educated nationalists to wear the *fugu*, a waist-length tunic worn by the common man. At independence, many new republics designed a national dress, intended to unite the diverse peoples within their borders. In the former DEMOCRATIC REPUBLIC OF THE CONGO, MOBUTU SESE SEKO's *authenticité* campaign urged Zairieans to return to "authentic" African clothing styles.

Contemporary African governments and political leaders still exercise important influences over popular clothing styles. Kangas and *kitenges* have become wearable billboards, with special-edition designs promoting national health campaigns such as family planning, or celebrating presidential birthdays and national holidays. After THOMAS SANKARA came to power in BURKINA FASO in 1983, he declared locally woven cotton the national fabric and required civil servants to wear it. In southern Africa, men's "Kaunda suits" are named after KENNETH KAUNDA, the former president of ZAMBIA. In SOUTH AFRICA, Gatsha Buthelezi, head of the ZULU-dominated

Inkatha Freedom Party, encourages supporters to wear the skins and headdresses of Zulu warriors at public events. Former South African president Nelson Mandela's taste in brightly colored shirts has made them newly fashionable.

Economic conditions and changing technologies are also influencing African clothing styles. Currency devaluations carried out under structural adjustment economic reform programs have made imported materials and clothing more expensive, but markets for used clothing ("fripperie" in Francophone countries) remain consistently strong. A large proportion of the used Western clothing sold in Africa was originally donated to charities in the United States and Europe.

Whether new or secondhand, Western clothing is considered fashionable in contemporary Africa. So too are "new traditional" clothes, which mix traditional fabrics and styles with synthetic materials and Western designs. For example, Yoruba weavers of the traditional *aso oke* fabric now incorporate lurex and rayon threads into their fabric. In Mali, tailors use bogolanfini mud-cloth to make European-cut blazers, vests, and caps. Often tailors' customers, especially women, commission outfits using locally bought cloth but based on imported patterns or designs copied from fashion magazines.

Growing appreciation for handmade African fabrics, both as pieces of art and as materials appropriate for "high-fashion" clothing, bodes well for the survival of traditional skills. Contemporary artists such as Senabu Oloyede, Kekekomo Oladepo and Nike Davis, of Nigeria use indigo-dyed *adire* cloth in tapestries that explore modern themes. In Mali, Pama Sinatoa in Djenné and Ismael Diabaté, the Groupe Bogolan Kasobane, and the Atelier Jamana in Bamako have won renown for their bogolanfini clothes, while Chris Seydou used bogolanfini-inspired textiles in his contemporary clothing styles. In Nairobi, Kenya, the African Heritage Gallery commissions clothing and jewelry that draws on traditional styles from all over Africa.

Muhonjia Khaminwa

See Also

Abidjan, Côte d'Ivoire; Amhara; Kano, Nigeria; Kumasi, Ghana; Lagos, Nigeria; Egypt, Ancient Kingdom of; Lomé, Togo; Mandela, Nelson Rolihlahla; Maputo, Mozambique; Nationalism in Africa; Pastoralism; Sahara Desert; Soninké; Structural Adjustment in Africa; Swahili People; Tigre; Buthelezi, Mangosutho Gatsha; Djenné, Mali; Christianity: Missionaries in Africa; Slavery in Africa; Ancient African Civilizations; Mandinka.

North America

Clyburn, James

(b. July 21, 1940, Sumter, S.C.), Democratic member of the United States House of Representatives from South Carolina since 1993; a civil rights activist since his youth.

James Enos Clyburn was born in Sumter, South Carolina, and received a bachelor's degree from South Carolina State College in 1962. Over the next decade, he worked as a teacher, ran a neighborhood youth organization, and headed the South Carolina Commission for Farm Workers. In 1974 he took over as the state's human affairs commissioner, a position he held until 1992. After two unsuccessful attempts while commissioner to win the statewide Democratic nomination for secretary of state, Clyburn ran for South Carolina's redrawn Sixth Congressional District in 1992. Defending the strangely shaped Sixth District as a way of correcting past political discrimination against blacks, he won handily after the white Democratic incumbent, fearing a racially divisive campaign in the new black majority district, backed out of the election. This victory made Clyburn the first black since 1897 to represent South Carolina in the U.S. Congress.

The Sixth District, as created in 1992, was the poorest in the state, with nearly a fourth of its families living in poverty. The district's major crops include peanuts, tomatoes, and tobacco. Florence County, the most populous county in the district, is an important regional medical center and home to a major pharmaceutical research and development facility, as well as numerous manufacturing interests. Many district residents work outside the district in nearby military facilities.

In Congress, Clyburn served on the Transportation and Infrastructure Committee and the Veterans' Affairs Committee. He is also a member of the Congressional Black Caucus.

North America

Cobb, Jewell Plummer

(b. January 17, 1924, Chicago, Ill.), African American biologist, professor, and university administrator.

By her sophomore year in high school, Jewell Plummer Cobb had begun to work toward her goal of becoming a biologist. She received a bachelor's degree in biology from Talladega College in 1944, and master's and doctor's degrees from New York University in 1947 and 1950, both in cell physiology.

Cobb continued her research at several universities and eventually became involved in university administration. She was president of California State University at Fullerton and dean at Sarah Lawrence College, Connecticut College, and Douglass College. Cobb became Trustee Professor at California State College in Los Angeles in 1990.

Lisa Clayton Robinson

North America

Cobb, William Montague

(b. October 12, 1904, Washington, D.C.; d. 1990), African American physician, anthropologist, and civil rights worker who was awarded Howard University's first distinguished professorship.

William Montague Cobb was the son of William Elmer and Alexzine Montague Cobb. After earning an A.B. from Amherst College in 1925, Cobb entered Howard University Medical School, graduating in 1929. He then earned a Ph.D. in anatomy and physical anthropology from Western Reserve University in 1932. He taught at Howard University from 1932 to 1973, chairing the Department of Anatomy from 1947 to 1969. He was awarded Howard's first distinguished professorship in 1969.

Cobb was an authority on physical anthropology and published over 600 related articles in professional journals. He contributed to E. V. Cowdry's *Problems of Aging: Biological and Medical Aspects,* Cunningham's *Manual of Practical Anatomy,* Gray's *Anatomy,* and Henry's *Anatomy.* He dispelled myths about African American biological inferiority in the *American Journal of Physical Anthropology.* In 1949 he was elected president of the Anthropological Society of Washington and in 1958 of the American Association of Physical Anthropologists, rare posts for African Americans at that time.

Cobb is also noted for his civil rights work. In the 1940s he represented the National Association for the Advancement of Colored People (NAACP) in support of a national health insurance bill. His *Medical Care and the Plight of the Negro* and *Progress and Portents for the Negro in Medicine,* published in 1947 and 1948, respectively, helped inform the American public about the detrimental effects discriminatory practices had on African American access to health care and jobs in the profession. Cobb helped desegregate Gallinger Hospital (now D.C. General), and in 1952 he worked to end the exclusion of African Americans in the all-white Medical Society of the District of Columbia. He served as NAACP president from 1976 to 1982.

Robert Fay

Africa

Cobra

common name for certain members of a family of venomous snakes known for their intimidating behavior and deadly bite. Cobras are recognized by the hoods that they flare when angry or disturbed; the hoods are created by the elongate ribs that extend the loose skin of the neck behind the cobras' heads.

Many species of cobras are natives of Africa, although these reptiles are found throughout

Africa, the Philippines, and southern Asia. Among them is the spitting, or black-necked, cobra, found from southern Egypt to northern South Africa. This snake can spray its venom from a distance of about 2.4 m (8 ft) into the eyes of its victims, causing temporary blindness and great pain. Varieties of the spitting cobra range in color from dull black to pink, the paler-colored ones marked by a black band around the neck. The ringhals, a different type of spitting cobra confined to southern Africa, is one of the smallest of the cobras, reaching only about 1.2 m (4 ft) in length. It is dark brown or black with ridged, or keeled, scales and pale rings on the neck. The asp, or Egyptian cobra, is found along the northern coast of Africa.

The venom of cobras often contains a powerful neurotoxin and acts on the nervous system. With effective serum more available, however, the high death rate from cobra bites in some areas of Asia has decreased. Cobra venom has been used for many years in medical research because it contains an enzyme, lecithinase, that dissolves cell walls as well as membranes surrounding viruses.

Scientific classification: Cobras belong to the family Elapidae. The spitting cobra is classified as *Naja nigricollis,* the rhingals as *Hemachatus haemachatus,* and the asp as *Naja haje*.

Africa

Cocoa, **common name for a powder derived from the fruit seeds of the cacao tree; a leading export of coastal West Africa.**

Cocoa is produced through the processing of cacao seeds, or cocoa beans. The beans are harvested and then cured or fermented in a pulpy state for three to nine days. During this time, the heat kills the seeds and turns them brown. The enzymes activated by fermentation impart the substances that will give the beans their characteristic chocolate flavor later during roasting. The beans are then dried in the sun, cleaned in special machines, and roasted. After roasting, they are shelled and ground into chocolate. Cocoa has a high food value, containing as much as 20 percent protein, 40 percent carbohydrate, and 40 percent fat. It is also mildly stimulating because of the presence of theobromine, an alkaloid that is closely related to caffeine.

Until the end of the nineteenth century, Latin America was responsible for nearly 80 percent of the world's cocoa production. Although the Spanish and Portuguese introduced cocoa to the islands off West Africa, São Tomé and Príncipe, around 1800, they did not introduce the tree to the African mainland until 1879. Soon after its introduction, however, West Africa dominated cocoa production and by 1909-1910 nearly 75 million tons, or 30 percent of the world's cocoa, was produced in Africa. By the beginning of World War I, West Africa had far surpassed all other regions of the world in cocoa production, and it had become the region's leading export.

In colonial West Africa four countries in particular excelled at cocoa production – GHANA, CAMEROON, CÔTE D'IVOIRE, and NIGERIA. All of these countries continued to produce cocoa after independence and still rely on the crop for a substantial amount of their export revenue. Ghana, the world's largest cocoa producer and exporter, earns two-fifths of its total export revenue from cocoa despite a recent decline in harvests due to aging trees and crop infestations. Cameroon, Côte d'Ivoire, and Nigeria produce less cocoa than Ghana, but still rely on it for a significant amount of their revenue. In Côte d'Ivoire, cocoa alone accounts for a quarter for total agricultural land use and nearly 30 percent of the agricultural crops produced by farmers. In both Cameroon and Nigeria, cocoa is the major export crop.

Elizabeth Heath

SEE ALSO
São Tomé and Príncipe.

Codau. Please see DOGON

Latin America and the Caribbean

Code Noir. **See BLACK CODES IN LATIN AMERICA.**

Africa

Coetzee, John Maxwell
(b. February 9, 1940, Cape Town, South Africa), South African writer.

"In South Africa there is now too much truth for art to hold," writer J. M. Coetzee said of his home country in 1987, "truth by the bucketful, truth that overwhelms and swamps every act of the imagination." These words were prescient of the coming decade in South Africa, when APARTHEID collapsed and the nation struggled with the truth about its past (*see* TRUTH AND RECONCILIATION COMMISSION). Coetzee's remark also provides insight into his own writing, which for more than 20 years has depicted the brutality of apartheid and its psychological effects.

Coetzee was born in Cape Town, South Africa, into a middle-class family with roots that stretched back to the original Dutch settlers and more recent English immigrants. He received undergraduate degrees in both English and mathematics as well as a master's degree in English from the University of Cape Town. In 1965 he entered the University of Texas at Austin, where he completed a doctorate in linguistics.

Living in the United States during the Vietnam War provided Coetzee with material for his first novel, *Dusklands*, published in 1974. The work comprises two novellas, "The Vietnam Project" and "The Narrative of Jacobus Coetzee," which together portray the imperialism of both the United States and South Africa. Coetzee followed three years later with the experimental *In the Heart of the Country* (1977). Written as a series of numbered paragraphs narrated in the first person, present tense, the novel draws the reader inside the mind of the narrator, a young white woman who, driven mad by her desolate life in rural South Africa, describes killing her father not once, but twice.

Coetzee published his most celebrated novel, *Waiting for the Barbarians,* in 1980. In the words of critic David Attwell, this work focused on "that moment of suspension when an empire imagines itself besieged and plots a final reckoning with its enemies." Coetzee probed the psychology of the well-meaning but ultimately complicit rural magistrate and the chilling torturer in dark glasses who has been sent to suppress alleged "barbarian" unrest. *Waiting for the Barbarians* was published during a time when such figures were all too true to life: the antiapartheid activist Steve Biko had died at the hands of his prison torturers three years earlier.

Coetzee's next novel, *Life and Times of Michael K* (1983), is considered his most political, portraying the brutality of civil war in South Africa through the story of a man named Michael K. Rather than creating a hero, Coetzee created an ambiguous character, a gardener of uncertain race whose life is swept up in the war taking place around him. *Foe* (1986), a retelling of the story of Robinson Crusoe, developed the metaphor of inarticulation. A character that critic Gayatri Spivak has called the "wholly other," Coetzee's Friday is a black man who has had his tongue cut out. Here Coetzee points toward that which is unsaid and unspeakable – a metaphor for the disempowered voices outside the dominant story of history. Such a theme was particularly relevant in South Africa, where the apartheid government not only controlled the history taught in schools, but censored all other voices of dissent.

The question of authorized voice continues in the *Age of Iron* (1990). As a woman dies of cancer, she speaks from what Coetzee called "a private death" about the public world of South Africa's townships. Coetzee's next work, *The Master of Petersburg* (1994), is set in nineteenth-century Russia and retells, with some liberties, the life of Russian novelist Fyodor Dostoyevsky. In addition to numerous essays and interviews, Coetzee has recently published a memoir, *Boyhood: Scenes from Provincial Life* (1997).

Marian Aguiar

SEE ALSO
Biko, Stephen; Cape Town, South Africa; South Africa.

Latin America and the Caribbean

Coicou, Massillon

(b. October 7, 1867, Port-au-Prince, Haiti; d. March 15, 1908, Port-au-Prince, Haiti), Haitian poet and writer.

Massillon Coicou is considered one of the greatest poets in Haitian literature. His works include intimate love poems (*Passions*) as well as poems with nationalist themes (*Poésies nationales*). His poem *Impressions* reflects the metaphysical preoccupations of the author. His two theatrical plays, *Féfé candidat* and *Féfé ministre*, offer a caustic tableau of Haitian politics, in which Coicou revealed his lack of consideration for political puppets. Other works include *Oracle* (1893), *Liberté* (1894), *The Son of Toussaint L'Ouverture* (1895), and *Emperor Dessalines* (1906).

Coicou studied at the religious institution of the Frères de l'Instruction Chrétienne (in St. Louis de Gonzague) and then at the Lycée National. After serving in the army, he worked as a public servant and as a teacher.

President Tiresias Simon Sam, who was on friendly terms with Coicou's family, appointed Coicou chief of his cabinet. Coicou was later appointed first secretary with the Haitian legation in Paris. While in Paris, he frequented French literary circles, and some of his plays were performed on the French stage. His first historical play, *Liberté*, was presented in Paris at the Cluny Theater (1894). After returning to Haiti, Coicou taught philosophy at the Lycée Pétion while devoting his spare time to writing plays and poetry. An ardent partisan of his friend Anténor Firmin, Coicou supported his electoral campaign of 1902. Firmin's defeat and the summary executions of political prisoners under President Nord Alexis deeply affected Coicou, who took part in a plot to oust the old tyrant. The poet's involvement led to his arrest and execution in March 1908.

Paulette Poujol-Oriol

Africa

Cola, **or cola nut, a type of nut indigenous to West Africa, where for centuries it has been an important trade commodity and valued for its stimulant properties.**

The cola nut, the fruit of the cola tree, has long been chewed in West Africa to offset hunger, thirst, and fatigue; to treat ailments such as dysentery, headaches, ulcers, and impotence; and to celebrate social and religious occasions. Elsewhere it is popularly known as an ingredient in cola soft drinks, though today most companies have replaced the nut with synthetic chemicals. Both the effects and the enduring appeal of the bitter nut have been attributed to its pharmacology – a combination of two addictive stimulants, caffeine and theobromine, plus colatin, a heart stimulant. The effect of one cola nut is comparable to approximately three cups of strong coffee.

Native to West African forests, the cola tree is now also commercially cultivated in the West Indies and other tropical areas. While approximately 125 species of cola tree exist, most of the trees cultivated for their nuts belong to one of two species, *Kola nitida* or *Kola acuminata*. These evergreens grow to around 18.3 m (about 60 ft), have clusters of yellow flowers, and produce long brown pods twice a year. The pods must be hand picked, then soaked in water for several hours so that the nuts can be removed. Each pod yields from 3 to 12 chestnut-like nuts that range from red to white in color. The nuts are sun dried, carefully stored in moistened bundles, and regularly inspected to protect against spoilage and insects.

The care needed to procure and store cola nuts has historically made them a luxury item, to be served to guests and offered as gifts. Because Islam does not forbid the use of cola nuts as it does other stimulants, Muslims in West Africa often serve them at ceremonial and social functions.

The cola nut, like certain other luxury goods such as gold, has been traded throughout West Africa for at least 700 years. Trade between the forest and savanna regions was particularly important. Cola nuts were traded for many goods, such as salt, livestock, and iron products. Although sources differ on exactly how long cola trees have been commercially cultivated (they also grow wild), some evidence dates commercial production as far back as the fourteenth or fifteenth century. This evidence suggests that by the late sixteenth century, thousands of tons of cola nuts were being traded annually. The commercial cultivation of *Kola nitida*, which made up most of the cola trade, probably began west of the Bandama River, in modern-day CÔTE D'IVOIRE. Later the AKAN forests, in modern-day GHANA, became an important production zone. The cola nut was a standard commodity traded by DYULA and later Hausa long-distance merchants.

In addition to overland trading, by the mid-1600s Portuguese and Afro-Portuguese traders were transporting an estimated 225 metric tons of nuts per year along the Upper Guinea Coast. By the middle of the nineteenth century, trade extended to Europe and the United States, where cola nuts were used in pharmaceuticals and, later, in soft drinks. It is estimated that by 1910, Africa alone exported nearly 1000 tons of cola nuts annually. By then it was also cultivated as an export crop in the West Indies. By 1966 worldwide estimates of cola nut production reached 175,000 tons.

Robert Fay

SEE ALSO
Salt Trade.

North America

Coleman, Bessie **(b. January 26, 1892, Atlanta, Tex.; d. April 30, 1926, Jacksonville, Fla.), American aviator and stunt-flyer, the first African American woman aviator.**

Elizabeth Coleman, later known as Bessie, was born January 26, 1892, in Atlanta, Texas. Her mother, Susan Coleman, was African American, and her father, George Coleman, was one-quarter African American and three-quarters Choctaw Indian. While Coleman was still an infant her family moved to Waxahachie, Texas, but a few years later her father returned to an Indian reservation in the Oklahoma Territory. Coleman's mother was left to care for the large family by picking cotton and doing domestic work. Susan Coleman enlisted Bessie's help in these jobs; in return, Bessie was allowed to save the wages she earned to help finance her college education.

Coleman finished high school, but the money she had saved was only enough to pay for one semester at the Colored Agricultural Normal University in Langston, Oklahoma (later Langston University). She left the university for Chicago, where two of her brothers lived. There she took a course in manicuring and obtained a position in the White Sox barbershop. Through talking with her army veteran brother and reading about World War I, Coleman became interested in the new field of aviation. Resolved to become a pilot, she quit her job and applied to various aeronautics schools in the United States.

Because of racist and sexist policies, she was repeatedly rejected. With the encouragement of ROBERT SENGSTACKE ABBOTT, founder and editor of the *Chicago Defender*, and with financial assistance from Jesse Binga, founder and president of the Binga State Bank, Coleman took French language lessons and went to France to obtain her pilot's license. She graduated in June 1921 with a specialization in parachuting and stunt flying from the Federation Aeronautique Internationale. Coleman was the first African American woman aviator.

Coleman returned to the United States and became an accomplished stunt-flyer. Her barnstorming, as it was then called, won acclaim from all who saw her flying exhibitions; and for her daring stunts she became known as Brave Bessie. Initially she performed for white audiences, but after she established her reputation, she concentrated her shows in the South primarily for African Americans and insisted on desegregated audiences.

Through lectures she gave at schools and churches, Coleman inspired other African American men and women to pursue careers in aviation. Using funds she received from lecturing and performing, she dreamed of opening an aviation training school for African Americans. This goal was not met because of her untimely death at the age of 30. On

April 30, 1926, during a rehearsal for her show in Jacksonville, Florida, her plane had mechanical failures and somersaulted, sending Coleman 2000 feet to her death.

Coleman was memorialized throughout the 1930s in Bessie Coleman Aero Clubs and in the clubs' periodical, *Bessie Coleman Aero News*. In 1975 a group of black women in Chicago interested in aviation and aerospace founded the Bessie Coleman Aviators organization. She is also honored every Memorial Day by African American pilots who fly in formation above the Chicago Lincoln Cemetery and drop wreaths on her grave. For her pioneering efforts in opening the field of aviation to African Americans, Coleman was commemorated on a U.S. postal stamp in 1995.

Leyla Keough

See Also

World War I and African Americans; American Indians; *Chicago Defender*.

North America

Coleman, Ornette

(b. March 9, 1930, Fort Worth, Tex.), African American alto saxophonist, composer, and free jazz innovator.

Nearly 40 years after he appeared on the JAZZ scene, Ornette Coleman remains a controversial and innovative musician. Along with John Coltrane, Eric Dolphy, and Cecil Taylor, he is one of the major figures of the 1960s jazz avant-garde. Indeed, only Coltrane has had a greater influence on the recent development of jazz. During the 1960s Coleman was central to the rise of free jazz, which represented the first significant break with the conventions of bebop or modern jazz that crystallized in the 1940s. In the mid-1970s he formed the group Prime Time, which combined free jazz improvisation and heavy FUNK-based rhythms to create a new subgenre of "free funk."

A largely self-taught musician, Coleman began playing alto saxophone at 14 years of age and tenor two years later. No recordings document his early musical growth, but he was apparently influenced by alto saxophonist Charlie Parker, although he soon adopted a rough-edged, honking rhythm and blues (R&B) tenor sound inspired by Illinois Jacquet and Big Jay McNeely. In his playing, Coleman faced difficulties almost from the start. His high school band director forced him out for improvising during a performance of John Philip Sousa's "Washington Post March."

While playing professionally with Texas R&B bands, including Pee Wee Crayton's, Coleman encountered resistance from audiences and fellow musicians alike. Crayton, he recalled, "didn't understand what I was trying to do, and it got so he was paying me not to play." In 1950, shortly after the band arrived in Los Angeles, Crayton fired the young musician. Nor did Coleman find favor among Los Angeles's jazz musicians. He was forced to take work as an elevator operator. Gradually, he became acquainted with several like-minded players, including trumpeter Don Cherry, drummers Ed Blackwell and Billy Higgins, and bass player Charlie Haden. Tenor saxophonist Dewey Redman would be a key later addition to this core of allies.

In the late 1950s Coleman had two important breaks. In 1958 and 1959, record producer Lester Koenig recorded his first two albums, *Something Else: The Music of Ornette Coleman* and *Tomorrow Is the Question*. And later in 1959, through the efforts of pianist John Lewis, Coleman and trumpeter Cherry were able to attend the influential Lenox School of Jazz, which featured on its faculty such major musicians as Max Roach, Milt Jackson, Lewis himself, and Gunther Schuller. Shortly into the summer session, Coleman attracted more attention than the program's illustrious teachers. "Ornette Coleman," Lewis stated, "is doing the only really new thing in jazz since the innovations of Dizzy Gillespie and Charlie Parker in the forties and since Thelonious Monk." Coleman and Cherry's stint at Lenox also resulted in an important appearance at the Five Spot, one of New York City's premiere jazz clubs.

Coleman called his unique musical approach "harmolodics," an intertwining of harmony and melody beyond traditional notions of key or tonality. "Harmony, melody, rhythm," he explained, " – they can all become melody." Jazz historian James Lincoln Collier, noting Coleman's limited ability to read or write standard musical notation and evident lack of familiarity with traditional music theory, likened him to a "primitive artist." Between 1959 and 1961 Coleman recorded several albums for Atlantic Records that exemplified what came to be known as free jazz. Most significant among these was *Free Jazz: A Collective Improvisation*, which involved the interplay between eight musicians acting as a double quartet. *Free Jazz* is a probing musical conversation and the most important example of collective improvisation since the 1920s and the New Orleans jazz of Jelly Roll Morton and King Oliver. "We were expressing our minds and emotions," Coleman remarked, "as much as could be captured by electronics."

Many musicians and critics and the vast majority of jazz listeners rejected Coleman's new jazz as formless and abstract. But even critics of his playing recognized his importance as a composer. Critics have praised Coleman's many striking compositions, including "Peace," "Lonely Woman," and "Beauty Is a Rare Thing." In 1967 Coleman won a Guggenheim Fellowship, the first granted to a jazz musician. He has composed and performed film scores, including *Chappaqua* (1965), *Box Office* (1981), and *Naked Lunch* (1991). And in 1997 the New York Philharmonic performed his *Skies of America*, a large-scale work that was first recorded by the London Symphony Orchestra in 1972.

In the mid-1970s Coleman challenged listeners and critics anew by embracing electronic instruments and the rhythms of funk in his new band Prime Time, which featured two electric basses and two electric guitars. Prime Time demonstrated Coleman's continuing allegiance to his R&B roots, but musically it was no regression. His new band was the first to play collectively improvised funk. Once again he became a focal point of controversy. To many, his new music was unbearably loud, but it also for the first time gained Coleman a significant following of younger fans.

James Clyde Sellman

See Also

Coltrane, John William; Los Angeles, California; Gillespie, John Birks ("Dizzy"); Monk, Thelonious Sphere; Morton, Ferdinand Joseph ("Jelly Roll"); New York, New York; Oliver, Joseph ("King"); Parker, Charles Christopher ("Bird"); Rhythm and Blues; Roach, Maxwell Lemuel (Max).

North America

Cole, Nat ("King")

(b. March 17, 1919, Montgomery, Ala., as Nathaniel Adams Cole; d. February 15, 1965, Santa Monica, Calif.), African American pianist and singer; one of the most stylistically advanced jazz pianists of the 1940s and a leading popular singer of the 1950s and 1960s.

With a preaching father and musical brothers, Nat King Cole grew up amid performance and music. As a child he lived in Chicago, playing the organ in his father's church and performing in his brother Eddie's ensemble, the Solid Swingers. Cole began his career as a pianist in 1936 when he joined Eubie Blake's traveling revue *Shuffle Along*.

In 1937 Cole settled in Los Angeles and formed a trio with guitarist Oscar Moore and bassist Wesley Prince. In the early recordings of the combo, Cole displayed harmonic and melodic innovation that only his finest contemporaries – ART TATUM and Duke Ellington – could rival. Despite the extraordinary talents of both Moore and Cole, the combo met with limited success, due largely to the era's nearly exclusive demand for the music of big bands. The group achieved its first major success in 1944 with "Straighten Up and Fly Right," which featured a stellar three-part vocal arrangement.

In 1946 his version of Mel Torme's "The Christmas Song" became Cole's first mainstream hit. In this and many subsequent recordings, Cole showcased his sultry voice, singing highly orchestrated pop ballads. In 1948 he sold a million records with "Nature Boy"; other hits included "Route 66" (1946), "Unforgettable" (1950), and "Mona Lisa" (1950). Although Cole continued to record jazz, he shifted his focus from piano to voice, and his pop ballads soon wooed white as well as black audiences. In the late 1940s Cole's combo became the first black group to have its own radio program. In 1956 Cole landed a weekly television show, which was canceled, however, when producers failed to attract companies that would sponsor a black artist.

Although he achieved great popularity as a singer, Cole received little recognition for his innovations as a pianist, and many fans had no knowledge of his early career. Yet by the age of 21 Cole had established advanced chord voicings and harmonic substitutions that bebop innovators such as Charlie Parker were just beginning to discover. Cole's melodic style can be seen as an important link between swing and bebop.

Cole died of lung cancer in 1965, just as his financial and popular success seemed to be peaking. In 1991, however, he experienced an uncanny flourish of posthumous success when his daughter, Natalie Cole, released an album of technologically contrived duets in which she sang atop her father's original recordings.

Eric Bennett

See Also
Blake, James Hubert ("Eubie"); Chicago, Illinois; Parker, Charles Christopher ("Bird"); Ellington, Edward Kennedy ("Duke").

Europe

Coleridge-Taylor, Samuel

(b. August 15, 1875, Holborn, England; d. September 1, 1912, Croydon, England), Afro-English composer and conductor, one of the most important late nineteenth century composers of African descent.

In the late 1890s Samuel Coleridge-Taylor gained worldwide recognition as a composer and conductor who successfully brought West African and black American influences into the realm of classical music. He was a leading exponent of Pan-Africanism, which emphasized the importance of a shared African heritage as the touchstone of black cultural identity. According to music scholar Jewel Taylor Thompson, Coleridge-Taylor endeavored to produce "compositions which would do for Negro music what Brahms, Dvorák, and Grieg had done respectively with folk music of Hungary, Bohemia, and Norway."

Coleridge-Taylor grew up in Holborn, England, the son of an Englishwoman and an African physician from Sierra Leone. He began violin study at age seven with a local orchestral conductor who tutored him for seven years. In 1890 he entered London's Royal College of Music, where he soon revealed his talent for composition and conducted his works in college concerts. In the mid-1890s he began to incorporate African American idioms into his music – an innovation inspired by his friendship with the black American poet Paul Laurence Dunbar and London performances of the Fisk Jubilee Singers. He composed *African Romances*, seven vocal pieces set to Dunbar's poems, and performed with the poet in a joint recital in London. In 1898 he collaborated with Dunbar on the operetta *Dream Lovers* and composed *Danse nègre*, his first large-scale orchestral work to embrace black American folk themes.

The year 1898 proved critical for Coleridge-Taylor's career as a composer: thanks to the recommendation of British composer Sir Edward Elgar, he was commissioned to write an orchestral piece – his *Ballade in A-Minor* – for England's Three Choirs Festival. Two months later he premiered his widely popular *Hiawatha's Wedding Feast*, the first part of a trilogy based on Longfellow's *The Song of Hiawatha*. Both works received rave reviews in the London papers, and the *Hiawatha* piece, whose overture theme was drawn from the African American spiritual "Nobody Knows the Trouble I've Seen," secured his fame in England and abroad.

During the following decade Coleridge-Taylor composed several works with African and black American-derived rhythms and melodies, such as *Twenty-Four Negro Melodies Transcribed for the Piano* (1905), *Symphonic Variations on an African Air* (1906), and the orchestral rhapsody *Bamboula* (1910), named after a West Indian dance. He toured the United States three times, conducting concerts of his music and performing with such musicians as Harry T. Burleigh and Will Marion Cook.

In August 1912, at the age of 37, Coleridge-Taylor died of acute pneumonia. His music and Pan-Africanist ideas continued to exert considerable influence on African American composers, several of whom became leading figures of New York City's Harlem Renaissance. According to musicologist Samuel A. Floyd Jr., "Societies bearing [Coleridge-Taylor's] name sprang up in cities across the United States in the early years of the twentieth century…, [and he] probably served as a model for composers such as Robert Nathaniel Dett, William Grant Still, and Florence Price."

Roanne Edwards

See Also
Great Britain; Burleigh, Henry Thacker (Harry); Price, Florence Beatrice Smith; Spirituals, African American.

North America

Colescott, Robert H.

(b. August 26, 1925, Oakland, Calif.), African American painter whose raucous, colorful works deal with racial themes.

Robert H. Colescott parodies traditional paintings of historical events with an ironic wit and a lushly expressive style. Since the 1970s he has painted reinterpretations of many of the most famous paintings of Western art, substituting African Americans for white figures in these well-known works. In *George Washington Carver Crossing the Delaware: Page from an American History Textbook* (1975, Robert H. Orchard Collection, Cincinnati, Ohio), Colescott recast the characters from a well-known work by the American painter Emanuel Leutze, *Washington Crossing the Delaware* (1851, Metropolitan Museum of Art, New York City), as caricatures of early twentieth-century black minstrels. Colescott's borrowings honor great paintings even as they criticize them. *Les Demoiselles d'Alabama (Des Nudas)* (1985, Greenville County Museum of Art, South Carolina), for example, is a tribute to the Spanish artist Pablo Picasso's *Demoiselles d'Avignon* (1907, Museum of Modern Art, New York City); at the same time, Colescott ironically alludes to Picasso's use of art forms then considered primitive, such as African masks. More recently Colescott's paintings have addressed current racial issues such as urban violence (*Emergency Room*, 1989, Museum of Modern Art, New York City), the subjugation of black women, and the complexities of racial mixing.

Colescott earned both his B.A. (1949) and his M.A. (1952) from the University of California at Berkeley. He studied in Paris in 1949 and 1950 with the French artist Fernand Léger, who urged him to avoid abstraction, a form of art that Léger considered too remote from the interests of most people. Nevertheless, in his early career Colescott explored both abstract and representational painting and was strongly influenced by the figurative paintings of artists of the San Francisco Bay Area, such as Richard Diebenkorn and Joan Brown.

Latin America and the Caribbean

Collares, Alceu

(b. September 7, 1927, Bagé, Rio Grande do Sul, Brazil), a prominent Afro-Brazilian politician; former mayor of the city of Porto Alegre (1985-1989) and governor of the state of Rio Grande do Sul (1990-1994).

Alceu de Deus Collares was born to João de Deus Collares and Severina T. Collares in 1927. He hails from the state of Rio Grande do Sul, in the extreme southern portion of Brazil. The population of the state comprises mainly European immigrants. Recognizing his minority status and the overall racial prejudice against blacks in his state, Collares dubbed himself "the black from Rio Grande do Sul." He started to work at an early age as a fruit and vegetable vendor, a telegram messenger, a luggage carrier, and a telegraph operator. After graduating in 1960 from the Federal University of Rio Grande do Sul, he worked as an attorney specializing in tax law.

His first political position was as city representative of Porto Alegre, the capital of Rio Grande do Sul, in 1964. In 1970, when Brazil was under military dictatorship, Collares was elected to the federal Congress as a member of the Movimento Democrático Brasileiro (Brazilian Democratic Movement), which at the time was the only officially sanctioned opposition party. He was reelected in 1974 and again in 1978. His performance in the Congress led him to be chosen by the local press as the state's "best federal representative." From 1985 to 1989 Collares was mayor of Porto Alegre, and from 1990 to 1994 he was the state's governor. He was one of the founders of Leonel Brizola's Partido Democrático Trabalhador (Democratic Labor Party [PDT]) and also a leader of the Partido Trabalhista Brasileiro (Brazilian Labor Party).

Currently Collares is a member of the PDT's political council, which is the highest authority within the party and advises the party's national directorate. Besides Collares, the PDT's political council includes such distinguished Afro-Brazilian politicians as ALBUINO AZEREDO and ABDIAS DO NASCIMENTO. Collares is one of the PDT's secretaries for extraordinary issues. In 1998 he was a candidate for the federal Congress.

Latin America and the Caribbean

Colombia

Black people in Colombia do not form an easily defined category. Mixing among Native Americans, Africans, and Europeans, has occurred for centuries and with greater frequency than in North America. Also, social categorization does not divide people into "black" and "white"; instead, "black," "white," and "Indian" are polar points of reference within which many categories of racial mixture are recognized. In addition, there are the native inhabitants of the islands of San Andrés, Providencia, and Santa Catalina, islands off Nicaragua's Caribbean coast. These people belong historically and culturally to a West Indian cultural complex formed under British colonial influence, but since the 1950s they have been subject to formal incorporation within the Colombian nation. This essay will make only passing reference to them.

The terms used to refer to black people in Colombia are varied and politically charged. The term *negro*, "black," although quite common, can be used disparagingly; some people,

Untitled photograph of a boy with a boat in Quibdó, Chocó, Colombia, 1994. *Tony Gleaton*

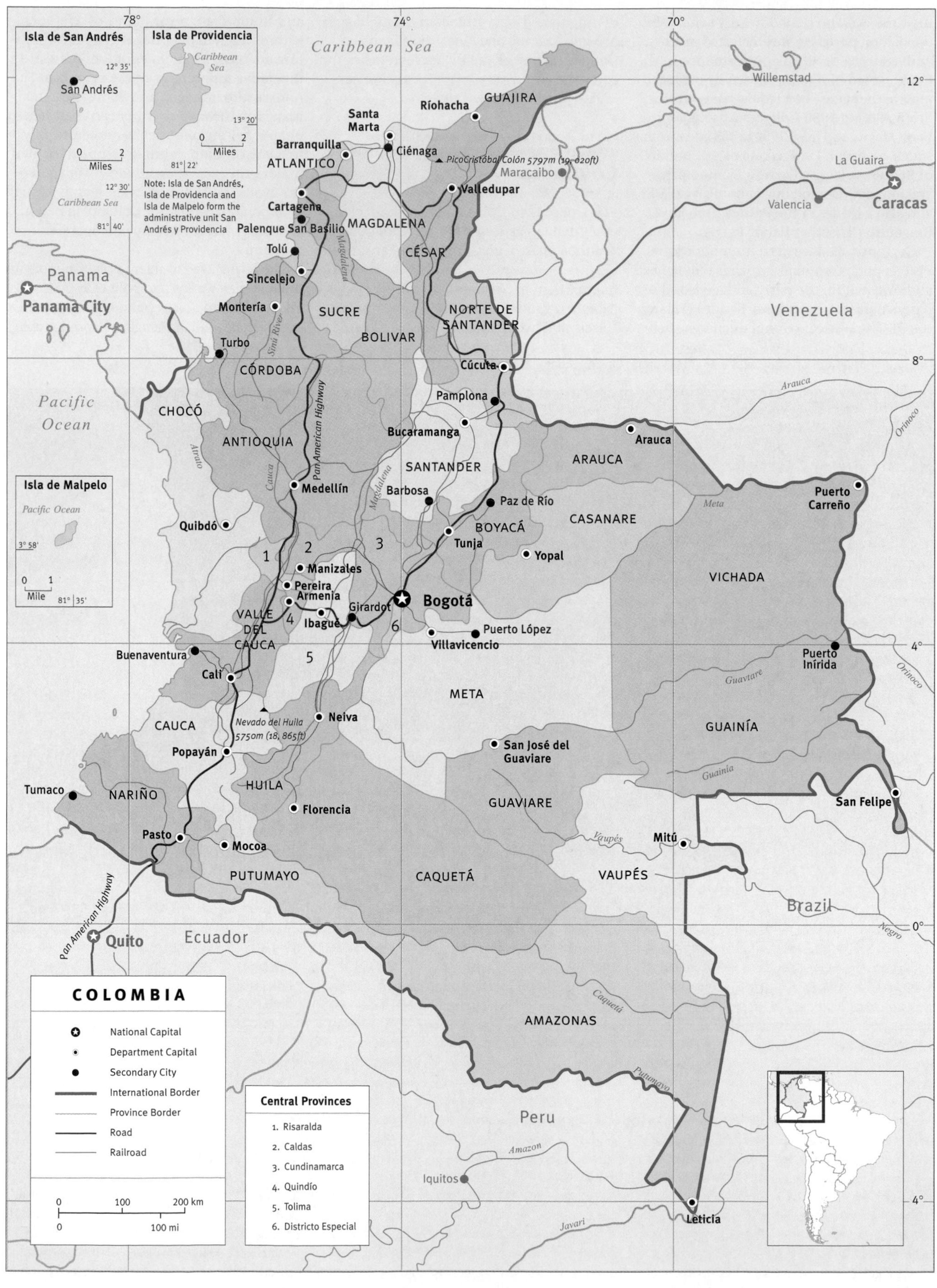
Isla de San Andrés
San Andrés
Caribbean Sea
Isla de Providencia
Caribbean Sea
Note: Isla de San Andrés, Isla de Providencia and Isla de Malpelo form the administrative unit San Andrés y Providencia
Isla de Malpelo
Pacific Ocean
Caribbean Sea
Pacific Ocean
Panama
Panama City
Venezuela
Caracas
La Guaira
Valencia
Maracaibo
Willemstad
Ecuador
Quito
Peru
Iquitos
Brazil
Pico Cristóbal Colón 5797m (19,020ft)
Nevado del Huila 5750m (18,865ft)
Pan American Highway
GUAJIRA
ATLANTICO
MAGDALENA
CÉSAR
SUCRE
BOLIVAR
NORTE DE SANTANDER
CÓRDOBA
CHOCÓ
ANTIOQUIA
SANTANDER
ARAUCA
CASANARE
BOYACÁ
VICHADA
VALLE DEL CAUCA
CAUCA
NARIÑO
HUILA
META
GUAINÍA
GUAVIARE
VAUPÉS
PUTUMAYO
CAQUETÁ
AMAZONAS
Ríohacha
Santa Marta
Barranquilla
Ciénaga
Valledupar
Cartagena
Palenque San Basilio
Tolú
Sincelejo
Montería
Turbo
Cúcuta
Pamplona
Bucaramanga
Arauca
Medellín
Barbosa
Paz de Río
Quibdó
Tunja
Yopal
Puerto Carreño
Manizales
Pereira
Armenia
Girardot
Bogotá
Ibagué
Puerto López
Villavicencio
Buenaventura
Cali
Puerto Inírida
Neiva
Popayán
San José del Guaviare
Tumaco
Florencia
San Felipe
Pasto
Mocoa
Mitú
Leticia
COLOMBIA
National Capital
Department Capital
Secondary City
International Border
Province Border
Road
Railroad
0 100 200 km
0 100 mi
Central Provinces
1. Risaralda
2. Caldas
3. Cundinamarca
4. Quindío
5. Tolima
6. Districto Especial

Afro-Colombians or not, avoid it. Some people use the euphemistic *moreno,* "brown," or the general *gente de color,* "colored people," to identify themselves and others. In the rural Pacific region, black people often refer to themselves as *libres,* "free people," a usage dating back to colonial times, although there is little collective memory of slavery or African origins. The term *costeño,* "coastal dweller," is often used to imply blackness, since many Afro-Colombians live in coastal regions. Since the late 1980s, with increasing black politicization, the term *negro* has been vindicated, especially in black activist and academic circles. The term *afrocolombiano,* Afro-Colombian, has also become popular in these circles. Reference to *las comunidades negras,* "black communities," has been institutionalized to some extent by a 1993 law that mentions them. The same law refers to the native blacks of Providencia and San Andrés as *raizales,* literally, "rooted ones."

Africans were imported from the 1520s into settlements along the northern coast of colonial New Granada, which included what later became Colombia. Cartagena, on the Caribbean coast, became the main slave port for the region and Africans were used in agriculture and personal service in this region and elsewhere from early on. The main occupation for Africans, however, was gold mining. From about 1560, colonial settlements in the gold-rich Cauca Valley and northern Antioquia increased the demand for slaves to compensate for the fast-declining supply of Indian labor. The Pacific coastal region was colonized effectively from the late seventeenth century, and the gold-mining economy there became a major location for the use of slave labor.

As in much of Latin America, although most slaves had limited opportunities to mine, farm, or sell on their own behalf, some were able to save money and buy their freedom. Freedom might also be granted by a master. Whites had children by black slave women and freed blacks also mixed with whites, *mestizos* (of indigenous and European descent), and Indians. By the 1770s, "free people of color" represented about 60 percent of the New Granadian population. They included everyone who was not classified as a white, Indian, or slave: mestizos, mulattos, free blacks, *zambos* (the term used for a person of Indian-black descent), and so forth. Free people of color lived in both rural and urban areas and were central to the economy as laborers, service providers, and producers of food and gold dust. Meanwhile, slaves took flight and escaped into uncontrolled areas, where they sometimes formed fortified villages, *palenques,* for their defense against the Spanish. It is partly this history of race mixture, manumission, and rebellion that makes the category "black" such a complex one in modern Colombia.

Colombia became independent in 1819, and slavery was abolished in 1851. By then, slavery was still important only in the Pacific and the Cauca regions. Ex-slaves became workers on the mines and farms of their former masters, or they became independent gold panners and farmers. In the Pacific region, mining patterns collapsed and freed slaves became independent miners and farmers.

TOP: Workers unload bananas for sale at the Quibdó River market in Chocó, Colombia. *Horner/Hutchison*
ABOVE: People line up at a sidewalk kiosk in the city of Cartagena de Indias on Colombia's Caribbean coast. *Horner/Hutchison*

The development of Afro-Colombian culture was not as overtly African-influenced as Afro-Cuban or Afro-Brazilian culture. New Granada was not a full-blown plantation society. The importation of slaves ended earlier, and slavery was already a rather weak institution in most areas by the mid-nineteenth century. Nevertheless, as in other regions of Latin America, there were associations of slaves and free blacks, *cabildos,* or councils, located mostly in cities such as Cartagena de Indias. These were organizations, sometimes similar to lay church brotherhoods with links to the church, that were allowed to hold their own dances and celebrations, often centered on drumming. In these, and in the palenques and communities of free blacks (for example, in the Pacific coastal region), Afro-Colombian culture developed.

In the twentieth century, blacks are concentrated in three main areas. The first is the Pacific coastal region, a very humid, heavily forested zone, crisscrossed with myriad rivers. It is very poor and infrastructurally underdeveloped and the population is estimated to be 80 to 90 percent black, with smaller populations of indigenous peoples, and whites and mestizos (mostly immigrants from outside the region). The second is the Caribbean coastal region, especially along the coastal belt itself and along the banks of some of the major rivers, the Magdalena, the Cauca, and the lower Sinú. This is mostly a flat, fairly dry region, more infrastructurally developed and urbanized, with large cattle-raising and agricultural enterprises. The third main area is the upper central Cauca Valley (especially in the northeast Cauca province and the southwest Valle del Cauca province). Much of this is sugar cane territory, with huge capitalist plantations. Black people work on these or as small peasants on land sandwiched between them or in the towns and cities of the region, especially Cali. Black people have also migrated in increasing numbers to other major cities, such as Medellín and Bogotá.

In the Pacific region, the economic activities of local blacks are varied, including agriculture (principally cultivation of plantains and corn), pig raising, fishing, hunting, and, in suitable areas, mining. Logging has been of growing importance since the 1960s. Independent black cutters can cut wood and sell their produce to intermediaries on whom they depend for credit, but most lumber is cut by large national and transnational companies, with a devastating impact on the local ecology. Since the 1970s artisanal mining has become increasingly mechanized, with small gas-driven pumps and mini-dredgers available on credit. Again, multinationals have used large-scale and very destructive dredging techniques in particular zones since the 1900s. In the southern Pacific region, intensive capitalist shrimp farming and the cultivation of African palms have also made inroads during the 1980s, causing yet more environmental degradation of one of the world's most biodiverse areas.

In the Cauca region, the growth of the SUGAR cane industry since the 1930s has meant intense pressure on peasant landholding, which is by legal title. Black peasants also work in the sugar cane industry for cash wages, and increasing pressure on land has intensified this and migration to the cities. In Cali, Medellín, and Bogotá, they join many black migrants from the Pacific region working chiefly as domestic servants (women migrants outnumber men), in the construction industry, and in informal occupations, although there are small numbers of black students and professionals.

In the Caribbean region, land-extensive cattle ranches have dominated since colonial times (although in the twentieth century some banana plantations also appeared) and have employed blacks and mestizos as sharecroppers and laborers. For maritime black settlements, fishing is an important source of subsistence and cash income. In certain areas, tourism also generates income, although most lucrative opportunities are controlled by nonblacks. In San Andrés and Providencia, tourism is also a major money earner, but again much of the business is controlled by nonblack immigrants from the Colombian mainland.

In all areas, blacks often suffer from racism, which is generally dissimulated and hard to pinpoint. Blacks in the Pacific region have, for example, lower life expectancy, higher infant mortality, and lower literacy rates than national averages. Rather than the simple result of direct racial discrimination, this phenomenon is due to the historically underdeveloped position of the region, a status that is itself linked to complex patterns of racism. Direct discrimination also exists, for example in urban labor and housing markets.

Culturally, blacks are often similar to local nonblacks who are at an equivalent class level. Family organization shows a higher incidence of matrifocality and serial unions (often common-law) than the national average and, in general, family organization shows a great flexibility and adaptability. Such patterns are not confined to blacks. Blacks practice variants of popular Catholicism similar to those practiced by many nonblacks. However, in the Pacific region, for example, these have a specific form, focusing on the worship of saints and on funerary rites in which the clergy often plays little part and singing is an important component. In PALENQUE DE SAN BASILIO, a former runaway slave community near Cartagena, language (a unique Creole) and ritual observance have a particular form that is traceably African.

In the 1960s a small educated minority of urban blacks, spurred mainly by the United States Black Power Movement, tried to create organizations that encouraged "black identity"; with the exception of Cimarrón, these had a marginal existence. In the late 1980s several self-help black peasant organizations, often sponsored by the church, began to emerge in rural areas of the Pacific region. In the early 1990s both types of organizations strengthened when national constitutional reform allowed issues of ethnic identity and multiculturalism to be voiced, mainly by more established indigenous organizations. The constitution of 1991 included a clause promising collective land rights for rural black communities in the Pacific region.

After two years of negotiation between representatives of black organizations and the state, Law 70 of 1993 was passed, which enshrined these rights. It also contained measures designed to improve education, training, access to credit, and material conditions for black communities nationwide. Black community participation in these spheres was ensured through the proposed inclusion of black representatives on the National Planning Council, regional planning corporations, and a consultative commission created to follow the progress of the law; the Ministry of Government created a division for black community affairs. Discrimination against black communities was outlawed and education had to reflect their cultural specificity. Finally, the law established a special constituency to elect two representatives to Congress from the black communities. Black organization thus reached a new stage of intensity, identifiable as a social movement. Conditions of life in the Pacific region and the general question of blacks' status in national society and culture became more public than ever before. However, as of 1998, land titling had been very limited and ineffective in the Pacific region, as the penetration of the area by capitalists had increased dramatically. The whole Pacific region had become subject to violence from guerrillas, paramilitaries, and the armed forces. Ethnoeducation had also not advanced far in terms of school curricula and, in 1997-1998, the special black electoral constituency was subjected to legal challenge as unconstitutional.

Black Colombians have made an important contribution to the nation's cultural life. Notable writers include MANUEL ZAPATA OLIVELLA (also a black history and folklore scholar and current ambassador to TRINIDAD AND TOBAGO), Carlos Truque, and ARNOLDO PALACIOS; influential poets include CANDELARIO OBESO and JORGE ARTEL. The lawyer and scholar DIEGO LUIS CÓRDOBA was an important politician and champion of black rights. Popular music in Colombia has been strongly influenced by blacks, and the dance music that became popular in the twentieth century (*porro*, CUMBIA, VALLENATO) originated in the Caribbean coastal region, where black cultural influence has been strong and musicians such as ALEJO DURÁN and TOTÓ LA MOMPOSINA have become nationally popular.

Peter Wade

SEE ALSO

Complexities of Ethnic and Racial Terminology in Latin America and the Caribbean; Maroonage in the Americas; Slavery in Latin America and the Caribbean; Cartagena de Indias, Colombia; Pacific Coast of Colombia; Cuba; Palenque de San Basilio; Brazil; Abolition and Emancipation in Latin America and the Caribbean; Catholic Church in Latin America and the Caribbean; Racial Question during Struggles of Independence in Latin America; Languages, Creole, in the Caribbean; Black Power; Religious Brotherhoods in Latin America.

Latin America and the Caribbean

Colonial Critics of Slavery,

religious men who wrote and preached against some aspect of the Spanish and Portuguese slave trade in the Americas during the sixteenth and seventeenth centuries.

African slavery was a generally accepted institution when the Spanish and Portuguese colonization of America began, while forced Indian servitude was questioned from the onset. The famous debate of Spanish theologians Juan Ginés de Sepúlveda and BARTOLOMÉ DE LAS CASAS over the legitimacy of Indian slavery took place in 1550. Meanwhile, the enslavement of Africans did not pose many moral questions to theologians; it was even looked upon benevolently by members of religious orders who often owned slaves themselves. There were, however, a handful of religious figures who questioned some aspects of black slavery and who left written testimony of their moral dilemma. Some priests accepted African slavery but were concerned about the bad treatment given to slaves; others were full-fledged abolitionists, who were excommunicated and deported for their advocacy on behalf of African slaves.

Tomás de Mercado

Tomás de Mercado (b. 1500-1530?, Seville, Spain; d. 1575, Spain) was a Dominican priest whose work influenced many moral theologians of the sixteenth and early seventeenth centuries. He is briefly but frequently cited by several authors who discuss the early debates on slavery because de Mercado was one of the first to question the participation of Spain in the international trade of black Africans (*see* Transatlantic Slave Trade). In the chapter entitled "Del trato de los negros de Cabo Verde" (On the Trade of Blacks from Cape Verde) of his book *Summa de tratos y contratos* (Of Trade and Contracts; Seville, 1569 edition) de Mercado argues that challenging the king of Portugal's jurisdiction over Cape Verde to capture Africans, "or the laws and uses established and issued for buying and selling [blacks]," was too complex and difficult an issue for him to resolve. Following the teachings of the Greek philosopher Aristotle, de Mercado reminded his readers of the three generally accepted "just causes" that in theory could justify "the capture or sale of blacks or any other peoples": in war, when the winners enslave the losers; in criminal law, when people commit certain offenses and are punished by losing their freedom; and in situations of extreme necessity such as hunger, "when a father has to sell his child."

Despite the specific causes proposed for legitimate enslavement, de Mercado doubted any of them applied to the slave market in the Americas (*see* Slavery in Latin America and the Caribbean). The priest wrote how "it was known by fame and public voice, that in capturing and bringing blacks from their lands to the Indies there were two thousand lies, and a thousand crimes and abuses were committed." In addition to a lack of a just cause, de Mercado believed slave merchants sinned further when hundreds of unjustly captured Africans died during a transatlantic voyage (*see* Middle Passage, The) or had no possibility of being freed once they reached the Americas. Taking into account the factual information on the slave trade, de Mercado opposed the use of the "just cause doctrine" to argue the further enslavement of Africans and advised those who participated in such a "beastly and brutal business" to avoid committing further sins, since the trade was suspect from its beginning.

Bartolomé de Albornoz

A few years later, after having read de Mercado's *Summa*, Bartolomé de Albornoz, a Dominican priest and a law professor at the University of Mexico, wrote in his *Arte de los Contratos* (Art of Contracts; Valencia, Spain, 1573) that certain "sales not prohibited by law, were for the conscience as much or more dangerous, such as the contracts concerning blacks." De Albornoz reasoned that if the king of Portugal permitted the slave trade, and priests bought and owned Africans, then it "must be good, because those who should give us example approve it." He then went on to recommend that anyone who wanted to justify the enslavement of people could refer to those causes cited in Tomás de Mercado's work. However, de Albornoz, apparently frustrated with these arguments, declared although the justifications "must be good," he "still did not understand them... because not even [de Mercado] shows much satisfaction with them." He wrote further that the "losers in war" cause as cited in Aristotle is wrongly interpreted, and "not even Jesus Christ" would have justified such a reason for enslavement.

Most important, de Albornoz claimed all humans were presumed free and consequently, it would be difficult to prove the just cause for which one person was enslaved. He also argued that natural law commands men to favor those who suffer, therefore the enslavement of "women, children, and those sold for causes of hunger" should not be condoned. De Albornoz argued against the commonly held belief that slavery was beneficial to the Africans because it was a way of spreading the Gospel among them. Christianizing of blacks, he wrote, could not be argued as a just cause because Jesus would not have advocated that to obtain "the freedom of the soul one should pay with the servitude of the body." Thus, de Albornoz recommended that merchants employ their strength in other areas and not in "such a bloody trade." This critique was so troubling that the tribunal of the Spanish Inquisition prohibited the further distribution and reading of his book (*see* Colonial Latin America and the Caribbean).

Luis de Molina

Two decades after de Albornoz wrote his treaty, Jesuit priest Luis de Molina (b. 1535, Cuenca, Spain; d. 1600, Madrid, Spain) authored a five-volume work titled *De Justitia et Jure* (On Justice and Law; 1594, full work published in 1614). In his book, de Molina discusses slavery among other moral issues. Like his predecessors, he follows the philosophy of Aristotle in order to argue that slavery was morally acceptable under certain limited conditions. He also listed the three just causes for enslavement, and went into further details of circumstances where such causes were plausible. However, with respect to the Portuguese slave trade, de Molina did not venture to give a final judgment on the just cause of the particular enslavement and trade of Africans by the Portuguese. Like de Mercado, he suggested that the dilemma be resolved by a group of distinguished theologians. Despite his cautious distancing from the primordial moral issue, de Molina spent many years studying and teaching in Portugal, which gave him firsthand information on how the trade was carried out. De Molina's conversations with slave traders in Portugal allowed him to question the methods in which African slaves were obtained and the abusive treatment that they had to endure during and after their voyage to the Americas. He concluded that there were strong arguments that would condemn the commerce of Africans as unjust and immoral, and that all of those who engaged in the trade, both sellers and buyers, would most likely be found "in a state of eternal damnation." On the other hand, he exempted those masters who bought African slaves in good faith and had no proof that they were captured unjustly.

Alonso de Sandoval

The observations of the Jesuit priest Alonso de Sandoval (b. 1576, Seville, Spain; d. 1652, Cartagena de Indias, Colombia) came from his personal experience as a missionary in Cartagena de Indias. Over a period of four decades de Sandoval carefully documented the arrival of slaves in Cartagena, the main gateway for their South American distribution. His book *Tractatus de Instauranda Aethiopum Salute* (Treaty on Ethiopian Slavery; Seville, 1627) presented a vast amount of information. This included observations he had gathered in his attempt to explain the diversity of Africans by describing their customs, religious attitudes, languages, ethnic scarification, diseases, and physical traits. He justified his project by stating that a broader and more sophisticated understanding of Africans was necessary for an effective mission of evangelization. He applied his theory to practice. De Sandoval trained slave interpreters who, according to him, could identify close to 70 languages. These multilingual slaves would accompany him when the new shiploads of slaves arrived from Africa. On board, de Sandoval sought to baptize each African in his own language, while he also tended to the sick and dying. In his book de Sandoval condemned the bad treatment of slaves and argued that they were human, created equal by God, and capable of many of the same actions as Spaniards. His ministry with suffering slaves went on for more than half a century, and was continued by his assistant, Pedro Claver.

Pedro Claver

Pedro Claver (b. 1581, Verdú, Spain; d. 1654, Cartagena de Indias, Colombia) was canonized in 1888 for his compassionate and devoted work with African slaves. In 1602 he entered the Society of Jesus . While he was studying philosophy in Majorca, Spain, his friend and mentor, Alfonso Rodríguez (also declared a saint in 1888), inspired him to evangelize in the Americas. He sailed to New Granada in 1610 and was ordained a priest in Cartagena in 1616. Under the initial guidance of Alonso de Sandoval, Claver devoted more than 40 years of his life to caring for thousands of sick and dying Africans.

Though Claver never directly questioned the institution of slavery, he was appalled at the condition in which the Africans arrived. Claver was especially devoted to caring for those slaves who were dying or in terrible states of pain and infection. He seemed unrepelled by the smells and infected scars that even de Sandoval had a hard time facing, as he explained in his book. Because of his healing mission, Claver became known as the Apostle of the Blacks. In his final vows he claimed to be "Pedro Claver, slave of the blacks forever."

Antônio Vieira

Among the Portuguese colonizers, there was also a notable religious figure who stood out for his criticism of the enslavement of Africans. Antônio Vieira (b. 1608, Lisbon, Brazil; d. 1697, Salvador, Bahia, Brazil) was a Jesuit priest and prominent Portuguese writer and thinker. He is sometimes referred to as the Bartolomé de Las Casas of Portuguese America because he fought for the freedom of Indians, but promoted the enslavement of Africans as an alternative. He accepted black slavery as a reality and an economic necessity, but he preached against the cruel punishment and abuse of African slaves that were common in seventeenth-century Brazil. In one of his sermons Vieira questioned, "But are not these men sons and daughters of the same Adam and the same Eve? Were not these souls rescued with the same blood of Christ? Are not these bodies born and do not they die like ours? Do they not breathe the same air? Does not the same sky cover them? Does not the same sun warm them? Which star is it that rules them; so sad, such an enemy, so cruel."

Francisco José de Jaca and Epifanio de Moirans

Despite questioning the treatment of slaves and the morality of the slave trade, none of the religious men mentioned above clearly advocated abolition. Today we know of only two priests of the colonial era who wrote treatises that openly condemned the trade and vocally proposed abolition in their sermons. Francisco José de Jaca (b. 1645?, Aragón, Spain; d. 1688?, Spain) and Epifanio de Moirans (b. 1644, Moirans, France; d. 1689, Tours, France) were Capuchin fathers and full-fledged abolitionists. Both men worked in lands that are known today as Venezuela and Cuba. Though little research has been done on their lives and works, it is apparent from the documents of their trial that de Jaca and de Moirans publicly proclaimed freedom for all bonded Africans and proposed that slave owners financially compensate blacks for the time spent in enforced labor. The priests refused to receive confession from the slave owners who did not promise to free and compensate their slaves. For this reason, the Roman Catholic Church received many complaints from white parishioners, and both men were consequently sanctioned and taken to trial. Each was divested of his authority to hear private confessions and his privilege to preach. In 1681, De Jaca and de Moirans were confined to a monastery in Havana, Cuba, while they awaited trial.

During their seclusion both priests wrote extensive arguments in their own defense. De Jaca authored a treatise titled *Resolución sobre la libertad de los negros y su originario en el estado de paganos y después ya cristianos* (On the Freedom of Blacks and Their Original Pagan State and after They Were Christians; 1681). De Moirans wrote *Servi liberi seu naturalis mancipiorum libertatis iusta defensio* (Free Slaves, or the Just Defense of the Natural Freedom of Slaves; 1682).

The de Moirans treatise is more sophisticated and organized, but his outline seems to have been based on the earlier work by de Jaca. Both priests defended three main convictions: all men are born free in nature, and blacks are free in their own right as humans; the slave trade is illegal and unjust; slave owners must free their slaves and compensate them financially for the moral and physical offenses professed on them, and for each day that the slave had to work in bondage. They criticized the arguments of theologians who justified slavery or who made only weak condemnations. The works of de Moirans and de Jaca also include extensive testimonials of the severe punishments and bad treatment of slaves they had personally observed in their travels through Caribbean America. In 1682 the priests were condemned to excommunication and later deported to Europe. Both died in their native countries imprisoned in convents.

Although their writings have remained obscure for more than three centuries, de Jaca and de Moirans are significant as the authors of the first abolitionist texts in the Americas and as the first European priests to have argued openly against the justifications for the slave trade in Africans. As such, they anticipated the freedom movement by more than a century.

Liliana Obregón

See Also

Slavery in Latin America and the Caribbean; Abolition and Emancipation in Latin America and the Caribbean; Catholic Church in Latin America and the Caribbean; Punishment of Slaves in Colonial Latin America and the Caribbean.

Latin America and the Caribbean

Colonial Latin America and the Caribbean, the period of Spanish and Portuguese occupation and governance of territory in the Americas beginning with Christopher Columbus's first landing in 1492 and ending with the war for Cuban independence in 1898. (For information on the colonial French, English, and Dutch Caribbean *see* Haiti, Martinique, Guadeloupe, French Guiana, Netherlands Antilles, and West Indies.)

The European conquest and colonization of the American continent was done with very little knowledge of the new territory's inhabitants or its lands. Partly as a consequence of this and partly due to their roles as colonizers, Europeans imposed their ideas and institutions on the indigenous peoples and the slaves brought from Africa (*see* Latin America, Blacks and Indians in: An Interpretation). The colonizers recreated their cultural, legal, and political orders without necessarily taking into account the diversity of the population that came together as a consequence of the colonial process.

Indigenous Peoples and Africans in the New World

There is disagreement among contemporary historians regarding the total population of the Americas before 1492: estimates range between 50 and 120 million. Since the combined population of Spain and Portugal was not greater than 8 million, the conquerors and settlers were vastly outnumbered in colonial territory. However, their deadly weapons, military strategies, and surprise attacks were formidable forces against societies that often welcomed white men or regarded them as godly creatures. Furthermore, infectious diseases brought by the colonizers decimated many of the native populations, including the great Aztec, Maya, and Inca civilizations of Mexico, Central America, and the Andes of South America. Many Native Americans were also weakened through forced acculturation, relocation, payment of tribute, and hard labor. Others submitted to the colonizers because fierce rivalries between indigenous groups made political alliances with the new strongmen seem beneficial.

Before 1492 western Europeans identified Africans as both slaves and as trading partners. Christianized African slaves who lived in Spain or Portugal and had adopted the language and culture of their masters were known as ladinos. Some ladinos even accompanied European explorers on their first missions to the Americas (*see* Garrido, Juan: A Black Conquistador in Mexico). Africa as a whole, however, was perceived in terms of its infidel population, which Christians felt gave them the right to wage wars against the continent. Enslavement of Africans and other pagan peoples through "just" (properly declared) wars was common, and acceptance of this practice was solidified with the knowledge that Africans enslaved and sold their own people (*see* Slavery in Africa). Soon the enslavement of Africans became one of the pillars on which seventeenth- and eighteenth-century European military enterprises and economies rested (*see* Slavery in Latin America and the Caribbean). The morality of the economy-sustaining institution was only questioned in a few generally disregarded critiques (*see* Colonial Critics of Slavery).

When colonized indigenous peoples were enslaved, however, there was a serious question as to the morality of their bondage (*see* Bartolomé de Las Casas). Unlike Africans, who were perceived as inhabitants of infidel and enemy territories subject to slavery, Native Americans had been conquered and made to submit to the laws and rules of Spain or Portugal. As a consequence, these peoples were understood as subjects of the European powers. The difference perceived by Europe between native inhabitants and black slaves led to the creation of separate laws and institutional provisions for the two groups (*see* Slave Laws in Colonial Spanish America).

Between 1517 and 1542 the Spaniards expanded their dominion from the Caribbean (Cuba, Hispaniola, and Puerto Rico) to include Central America, Mexico, Peru, and northern Chile, irrevocably changing the lives of indigenous peoples they found there and the Africans they brought with them. By the end of the sixteenth century the Spanish occupied large areas of the Caribbean and Central and South America. The Portuguese settled on the coast of Brazil. Some historians estimate the native population of the continent at roughly 8 million at the end of the seventeenth century; this figure represents about 10 percent of the total population before 1492.

Colonial Institutions

The European colonial enterprise in the Americas necessitated the creation of both commercial and political institutions of control. In order to regulate the Spanish colonies' trade, the Casa de Contratación (House of Trade) was established in 1507 in both Seville and Cádiz. The agency was responsible for administering the riches coming from the Americas, issuing sailing and slave licenses, and controlling emigrants, as well as defining the laws of navigation, commerce, and trade. In addition, the Council of Indies, established in 1524, was to oversee the management of the colonies. The council had legislative and fiscal powers and enjoyed exclusive jurisdiction over the colonies. It supervised the implementation of laws, made appointments to posts in the colonial government, acted as the highest appeal court, and determined geographical boundaries. A similar institution, Casa do Brasil (House of Brazil), was established in Lisbon for the administration of the Portuguese colony in the Americas. Fiscal matters in Brazil were controlled by a Portuguese treasurer general who oversaw Portugal's investments and issued licenses to extract and exploit different commodities in Brazil.

The Spanish king appointed "vice kings," or viceroys, to head the largest organizational units of the colonies in the Americas: the Viceroyalties of New Spain (established in 1535), Peru (1544), New Granada (1717), and La Plata (1776). Royal *audiencias* were powerful regional tribunals that not only had legislative and judicial functions but also performed executive duties. They had initial jurisdiction in fiscal matters, served as courts of appeal in criminal cases, advised colonial fiscal and administrative officials with the force of law, governed in the absence of royal Spanish authority, and enforced royal laws. In this capacity the audiencias became the backbone of the Spanish colonial administration and facilitated its continuous expansion throughout the continent. The audiencias were generally composed of a *regente* (leading officer), judges (criminal and civil), and *fiscales* (prosecutors). The most important posts in the audiencias were held by Spanish officials, but around one-quarter of the positions were held by white Creoles (persons of European descent born in the Americas). Blacks, Indians, and members of the castas (a socially intermediate category of people of racially mixed descent) were not allowed to occupy government positions. By 1650 the viceroyalty of New Spain included the audiencias of Santo Domingo, Guadalajara, Guatemala, and Mexico, and the viceroyalty of Peru included the audiencias of Panama, Santa Fé (Colombia), Quito (Ecuador), Lima (Peru), Charcas (Bolivia), and Chile.

Brazil initially also appointed viceroys who worked in a similar capacity to their counterparts in colonial Spanish America. However, Portugal eventually oversaw the administration of Brazil through its division into 12 hereditary *capitanias* (captaincies or large territorial divisions) assigned to 12 *donatários* (captaincy administrators). Each powerful donatário could in turn make land allocations and was in charge of the protection and evangelization of the indigenous peoples the Portuguese encountered in those territories. As administrative units, the captaincies also had jurisdictional functions and could hear criminal and civil cases. The original 12 captaincies underwent many divisions and reorganizations over 300 years of population increase and changing economic and political demands. By 1800 there were 10 main and 7 subordinate captaincies.

Town councils (cabildos in Spanish America and senados da câmara in Brazil) represented another important administrative layer of colonial government. The councils provided the colonizers' stronghold at a local level; they distributed land, supervised municipal officials, oversaw public works, regulated holidays, and maintained public order. Town councils excluded persons of African and Indian descent and formed their own interest groups as councilors obtained wealth and family prestige.

In sum, colonial officials were in charge of many aspects of daily life in the Americas and had considerable autonomy. They were capable of issuing legislation and making local decisions that did not always follow the orders and policies of Madrid and Lisbon. Because of the impossibility of direct supervision from the European centers, the officials were able to garner a great deal of power and wealth; such benefits were denied to people of African or indigenous descent, however, since they were not allowed to hold government posts.

Black and Indian Bondage

Before the arrival of the first shipments of African slaves, Spanish and Portuguese colonizers forced many indigenous people into servitude. Both the *encomienda* system of colonial rule over indigenous populations and the enslavement of Indians as prisoners of war enabled this exploitation soon after the arrival of the colonizers.

The encomienda system was introduced by Nicolás de Ovando during his term as governor of Hispaniola (present-day Haiti and the Dominican Republic) from 1501 to 1509. With the encomienda, the Spanish Crown granted colonizers the right to force Indians to work the land as well as pay tribute to the colonizers in exchange for their overseeing the community's Christian education and welfare. Land grants could include anywhere from a few indigenous people to thousands. In the initial decades of the conquest the Indians were forced to work in mines, cultivate crops, build houses, take care of animals, and deliver goods.

The encomienda system thus became the economic structure of the Spanish conquest. As the *encomenderos* (grantees) grew wealthier and acquired political power, the Indian population decreased as a result of disease and the hard labor conditions. The Spanish Crown tried to restrict the power of the encomenderos after hearing complaints from the colonies – notably from Bartolomé de Las Casas – regarding their excessive displays of power and abuse of the Indians. Restrictions and even the abolition of Indian forced labor were planned in such legislation as the Laws of Burgos of 1512 and the New Laws for the Good Treatment and Preservation of the Indians of 1542. However, limitations on the use of Indian labor caused a general uproar, as the encomienda system was perceived as essential to the survival and wealth of the colonies. The Council of Indies had to partially retract its legislative edicts in 1545. The Encomiendas were allowed to continue for at least another generation after the death of the first beneficiary.

Another form of colonial bondage, most common in Brazil, involved the acquisition of slaves through "just" (properly declared) wars. A law issued by the Portuguese Crown

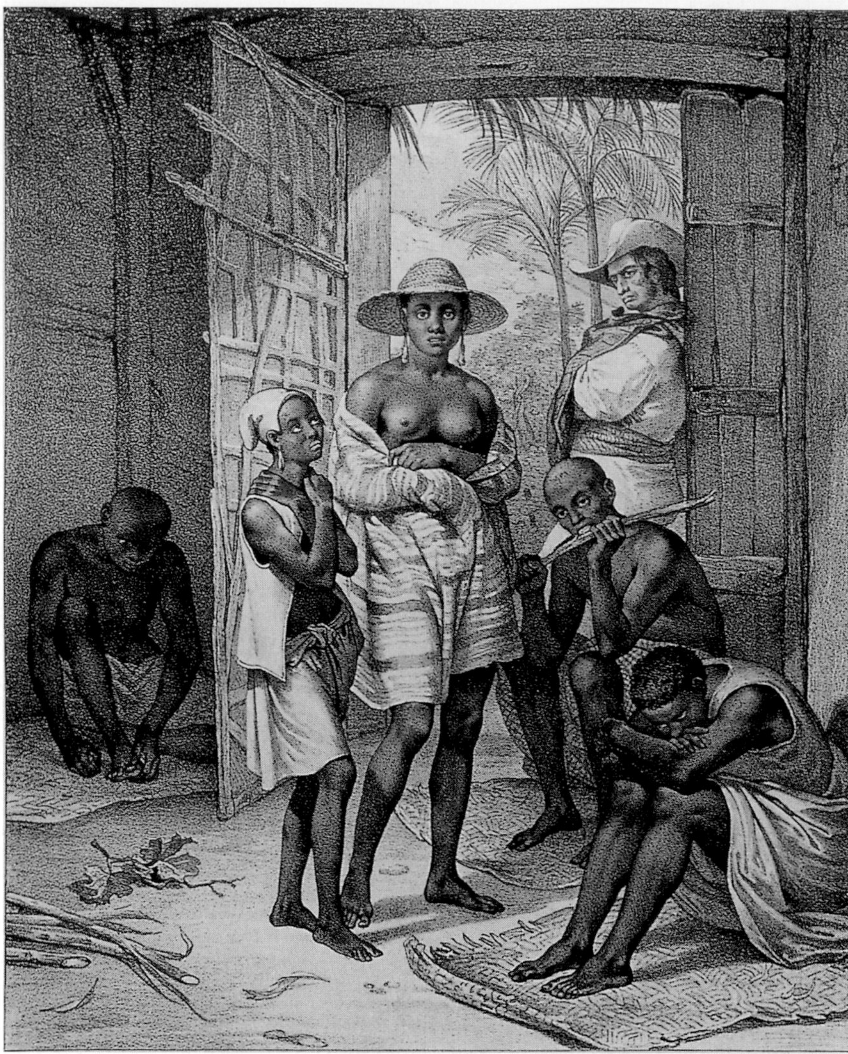

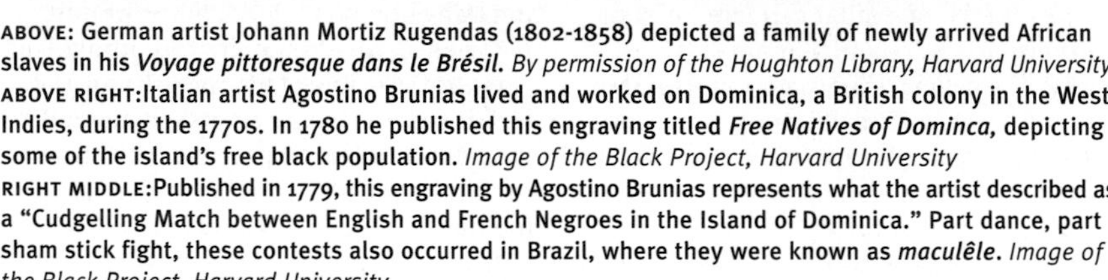

ABOVE: German artist Johann Mortiz Rugendas (1802-1858) depicted a family of newly arrived African slaves in his ***Voyage pittoresque dans le Brésil.*** *By permission of the Houghton Library, Harvard University*
ABOVE RIGHT: Italian artist Agostino Brunias lived and worked on Dominica, a British colony in the West Indies, during the 1770s. In 1780 he published this engraving titled ***Free Natives of Dominca,*** depicting some of the island's free black population. *Image of the Black Project, Harvard University*
RIGHT MIDDLE: Published in 1779, this engraving by Agostino Brunias represents what the artist described as a "Cudgelling Match between English and French Negroes in the Island of Dominica." Part dance, part sham stick fight, these contests also occurred in Brazil, where they were known as ***maculêle.*** *Image of the Black Project, Harvard University*
RIGHT: African slaves carried out most of the hard labor of mining gold and diamonds in the Minas Gerais region of Brazil. In 1835 Johann Moritz Rugendas published in his ***Voyage pittoresque dans le Brésil*** this lithograph illustrating a heavily guarded convoy transporting diamonds out of the interior to the coast. *Image of the Black Project, Harvard University*

in 1520 allowed for the legal capture of Indian slaves during war with a tribe that refused Christianity or was presumed to practice cannibalism. Indian slaves continued to provide a significant source of free labor in the colony of São Paulo and the northern state of Maranhão even after Africans replaced them on the SUGAR plantations. During the seventeenth century colonists in Brazil carried out slaving expeditions, focusing on the Guaraní Indians of São Paulo and the indigenous groups along the Amazon River valley. They rationalized that Indians were not technically slaves but *forros* (freedpeople). Because the forros were thought to have been brought to civilization at the colonists' expense – through the provision of clothing and a Christian education – the native inhabitants were indebted to their captors. All forms of Indian bondage were proscribed in Brazil by 1755, slightly later than similar emancipation was declared in Spanish America. However, an 1808 Brazilian law allowed for prisoners of war to be enslaved once more. Native bondage in Brazil was again prohibited in 1831.

As a result of an increased demand for labor, the scarcity of Indians who survived the conquest, and the moral questioning by theologians of involuntary Indian labor, a great number of Africans were imported to the Americas from the early sixteenth century to the late nineteenth century. In the first decades after the conquest male and female Africans were used as domestic slaves performing work in the kitchen, cleaning, and completing a variety of personal tasks for their masters. As economic opportunities for European exploitation increased, the slave trade grew and black males were forced to perform all sorts of hard labor: farming, cattle ranching, and meat processing in Brazil; silver mining in Mexico; working in the gold mines of Honduras, Colombia, Venezuela, Peru, and Chile; planting and tending cacao crops in Venezuela; cultivating grapes and olives in Peru; growing wheat in Chile; and harvesting sugar cane in Mexico, Colombia, Peru, and the Antilles. In Brazil many slaves excelled as highly skilled artisans, painters, musicians, and barber-surgeons. In Mexico some became teamsters and in Argentina and

Uruguay others served as gauchos (cowboys). Some slaves were even used as personal bodyguards. Slaves were also used in the indigo dye-processing plants in Central America and for pearl diving in Colombia and Venezuela. In almost all countries female slaves were dedicated to domestic service or used as public prostitutes, for the purpose of procreating slave children, or as objects of sexual gratification for their masters. In the Spanish Caribbean, where blacks outnumbered whites, female slaves were often allowed to tend small shops or sell goods in a marketplace.

The Caste System

African slavery and Indian servitude forced the Spanish royal government to create institutions and a bureaucracy that would place people of color both socially and conceptually in the new colonial societies. As scholar Peter Wade points out, ideally the Spanish would have liked to maintain a phenotypical administrative order organized around the structure of three distinctive groups: Europeans, blacks, and Indians. However, from the earliest days in the colonies the process of mestizaje (racial MISCEGENATION) began the irreversible diversification of the population. Due to the initial acceptance of black slave manumission through marriage, the scarcity of European women, and the disruption of traditional indigenous communities, racial mixing became a common occurrence.

People of mixed race were classified as members of a middle social category – below that of whites and above that of blacks and Indians – called the *castas*. The castas comprised mulattos (persons of European and African descent), *mestizos* (persons of European and Indian descent), *zambos* (persons of Indian and African descent), and many other persons whose ancestry was mixed. Above the castas was the ruling social class reserved exclusively for whites, and this was divided between the Peninsulars (European born) and the Creoles (American born). This modified caste system developed into a complex scheme based on ideas of racial categorization. The assumptions and rules of the system would seem irrational, inconsistent, and impossible to apply today. Racial nomenclature was initially the same throughout the Spanish and Portuguese colonies, but as miscegenation increased each viceroyalty identified different types of racial mixtures.

Members of the castas were afforded certain rights and privileges based on their ranking within that group. In principle, even if a member of the castas were partially of European descent, he could not hold positions of power or obtain social distinction. However, there were levels of hierarchy within the castas, and one's classification could be affected by a number of factors: being born in wedlock, being the child of a wealthy or noble parent, and identifying with the culture of the white colonizer all constituted marks in one's favor. The act of marrying someone with lighter skin would also improve one's ranking. In general, however, a person in the colonies was classified in society according to the amount of European blood he or she was perceived to have (or lack). The more "white" blood a person had, the more likely it was that he or she could obtain a higher socioeconomic status.

With the ongoing mixing, the castas came to constitute the majority of the population during colonial times. When authorities realized the extent of miscegenation and the growing economic and political threat that the mixed-race citizens presented to Spanish rule, legislation was implemented to control the natural diversity of the population. For example, some interracial marriages were prohibited by *cédulas* (legislation issued by the Spanish king), and others required the approval of the viceroy or local audiencia.

The most disadvantaged in the colonial system were those ranked below the castas: Indians, free blacks, and – last of all – black slaves. Members of these social groups had little chance of improving their situation. The caste system affected free people of African descent severely. Blacks, mulattos, and zambos could not enter primary school or obtain a university education (exceptions were sometimes made in this area if, upon the request for a certificate of *pureza de sangre* [purity of blood], the candidate exerted political influence or employed a white patron or money to bypass the requirement). In some cases public servants were also required to

An eighteenth-century print by Juan de Latginz shows a well-to-do family of mixed race in the Antilles. *CORBIS/Gianni Dagli Orti*

Between the seventeenth and nineteenth centuries in the Spanish viceroyalties of Mexico and Peru, artists produced several series of so-called castas paintings. As in this mid-eighteenth century example, these works illustrated the mixing of Native American, African, and European peoples in Central and South America. *Christie's Images*

certify their "cleanliness of blood, life and customs." Free women of African descent were prohibited from wearing gold jewelry, silk, and Spanish shawls, even if they were married to men of European descent. Official apartheid was also practiced in colonial Latin America: free blacks and members of the castas could only settle in certain designated residential areas and were prohibited from entering others. In Santo Domingo (present-day Dominican Republic) free blacks were prohibited from buying lands in 1768, and in Buenos Aires (present-day Argentina and Uruguay) in 1746 blacks were barred from practicing African dances. Free blacks in the colonies were excluded from certain jobs but were allowed to be carpenters, cobblers, brick masons, blacksmiths, tailors, and weavers.

Cooperation Between Free Blacks and Slaves

Just as blacks and Indians seldom formed political and military alliances against the Spanish in colonial Latin America, free blacks generally did not openly ally themselves with slave revolts or identify with the suffering of the enslaved. Many treasured their slightly superior status and could only concern themselves with their personal survival, freedom, and advancement in the colonial society. The distinguished historian Peter Voelz has shown that it was not uncommon for free blacks to own slaves, participate in armed efforts to capture runaway slaves, or raid Indian tribes to enslave their members. Black police and soldiers were often used to fight maroons (fugitive slaves) and hunt runaways (*see* Maroonage in the Americas). The policy that placed free blacks in such positions has been identified as part of a "divide-and-rule" strategy: potential alliances among subjects are weakened or made difficult when members of the same race are placed in opposing or confrontational situations. Individual interests and the survival instinct tend to overshadow any ideas of rebellion organized around an idea of racial consciousness.

The Roman Catholic Church in Colonial Latin America

Conquest and colonization in Latin America and the Caribbean were facilitated by the policies and activities of the Roman Catholic Church. The Church converted and thus controlled the indigenous population, cooperated with and strengthened the force of Spanish and Portuguese authority, and upheld the colonial system of racial categorization. Additionally, the Spanish Inquisition was orchestrated by the Church in order to try heretics as well as to enforce the system of racial classification.

The strength of the Church relied heavily on its alliance with the state. The close relationship between the two institutions was made official in 1508 with the *patronato real* (royal patronage) order given by Pope Julius II. This mandate recognized the secular clergy (priests and clerics in charge of parish administration) as another organ of the Spanish state. Through this arrangement, the Spanish king's decisions could control Catholic policies in the New World. The secular clergy participated in the initial spiritual conquest of the indigenous peoples with mandates from both the pope and the Crown. During the colonization period, the church set up an administrative and bureaucratic system in the colonies that mirrored the political interests of the Spanish Crown (*see* Catholic Church in Latin America and the Caribbean).

The Catholic Church's role in and influence on the life of colonial Latin American blacks was ambiguous and often contradictory. On the one hand, the Church often recognized that blacks were made equal by God and that they had certain rights. The Church sponsored religious brotherhoods known as *cofradías* or *cabildos* in which blacks could socialize and participate in community activities (*see* Cultural and Political Organizations in Latin America). On the other hand, as one of the largest landholders in the colonies, the Catholic Church had many slaves throughout Latin America and a vested interest in preserving the system of social exclusion and racial categorization. Church officials recorded the racial subcategories to which a couple or a newborn belonged and often denied interracial marriages. Roles within the church also were assigned according to the racial categorization of the colonial government. Peninsulars tended to occupy the upper echelons of the institution and white Creoles the lower, and this division led to much friction within the church. Royal cédulas allowed mestizos to become clerics but prohibited the entry of Africans into the priesthood. Given the scarcity of white Creoles, an exception for light-skinned mulattos was made in 1707 in Santo Domingo.

One of the most feared institutions of the Catholic Church in the Americas was the Spanish Inquisition. The Inquisition was composed of special tribunals established to try and punish heretics. There never was a separate Inquisition court in Brazil, but officials from the Inquisition office in Portugal made investigative visits to the colony, especially in the early eighteenth century. At first, the Inquisition had been directed against those suspected of practicing the Jewish faith in Spain, Portugal, or the colonies. However, as time went on the Inquisition became a political instrument through which the social and cultural traditions of African and indigenous people (their religious beliefs, sexuality, dances, etc.), which were often considered deviant and abhorrent, could be controlled and/or punished.

Legacies of the Colonial Era

As a result of nineteenth-century movements for independence in Latin America, caste classifications ceased to have formal consequences, tributes were no longer collected from indigenous peoples, and slavery was abolished (*see* Abolition and Emancipation in Latin America and the Caribbean). However, the independence movements did not necessarily improve the situation of nonwhites in Latin America. The privileged status of Europeans in the Americas ended and many were expelled from the continent after independence, but their jobs were taken over by white Creoles. As a consequence, members of what was previously known as the castas called for reforms or alternative political programs in their own interest. In some areas, such as Yucatán, Mexico, and Venezuela, pressures from the castas led to civil war (*see* Racial Question during Struggles of Independence in Latin America). However, although the institutionalized racial hierarchies and legal discrimination of the colonial era gradually disappeared, more than 300 years of complex racial and class discrimination took a toll on Latin American society. The social identifications, ideologies, and practices, of many Latin Americans at the end of the twentieth century continue to reflect the complicated racial categorization of their society in the past (*see* Complexities of Ethnic and Racial Terminology in Latin America and the Caribbean and Human Rights in Latin America and the Caribbean).

Liliana Obregón

See Also

Bolivia; Ecuador; Colombia; Peru; Education in Latin America and the Caribbean; Women, Black, in Colonial Hispanic Caribbean; Spanish-Cuban-American War; Transculturation, Mestizaje, and the Cosmic Race: An Interpretation; Religious Brotherhoods in Latin America.

Africa

Colonial Rule

Colonial rule is defined as the official occupation of a territory by a foreign power. In Africa, European powers ruled most of the continent from the late nineteenth century until the 1960s. This essay discusses the policies, problems, and legacies of European colonial rule in Africa.

European colonization of Africa followed a long history of contact between the two continents. Ancient Egyptian trade in the Mediterranean predates recorded history, and contact between Europe and other parts of North Africa dates back to the Greco-Roman period (*see* Carthage). Not until the fifteenth century, however, did the Portuguese establish trading posts on the sub-Saharan African shoreline. Although some early ports, such as Cape Town, became permanent settlements, most served as little more than entrepôts for the exchange of African and European goods. Over the next 400 years Europeans acquired slaves, gold, ivory, and later agricultural commodities from coastal traders and rulers, but, with the exception of South Africa and a handful of Portuguese holdings, made few attempts to settle or otherwise control the interior. By the second half of the nineteenth century, however, the rapidly industrializing European economies required reliable access to natural resources, new markets for their manufactured goods, and new sites for the investment of finance capital. The vast, mineral-rich African continent had the potential to offer all three.

Earlier European conquests of Asia and the New World had demonstrated the risks and costs of colonial occupation, leaving most late-nineteenth century European rulers initially reluctant to attempt the same in Africa. It would certainly have been easier and cheaper to maintain established trade relations with the African merchants and rulers who, since the abolition of the transatlantic slave trade in 1807, had been transporting vast quantities of agricultural commodities – cocoa, peanuts, and palm oil – to coastal towns such as Porto-Novo and Dakar. But African middlemen (and women) were not always amenable to the Europeans' terms of trade, and African rulers were in many cases preoccupied by internal power struggles and wars with neighboring states. European powers viewed the quickening pace of their own neighbors' trade and exploratory expeditions in Africa – such as Richard Burton's voyages through East Africa, French expeditions up the river Niger, and Heinrich Barth's travels throughout central and northern Africa – as an indication that preemptive action was necessary before a rival power established claims to valuable territory.

Thus, during the late nineteenth-century scramble for Africa, even leaders with little prior interest in colonization, such as German Chancellor Otto von Bismarck, staked claims to the continent. Meanwhile, Christian missionaries' calls for European intervention to end African slavery and "barbaric" practices (such as human sacrifice in the kingdom of Dahomey) provided a moral rationale for European political and economic ambitions. These ambitions were officially legitimated and negotiated at the Berlin Conference of 1884-1885, when European leaders agreed to partition the African continent into neatly bordered "spheres of influence." Rapid conquest and treaty making followed. By 1900 fewer than 30 years after the scramble had started, almost 90 percent of Africa was under European control.

Just as quickly, European powers were confronted with the basic problem of colonial occupation: how to rule effectively and cheaply over a foreign subject population. Although metropolitan governments had to invest in the initial occupation, it was anticipated that colonial administrations would become self-sufficient. In other words, they were expected to establish a system of rule that would generate revenue but not revolt. European colonial powers struggled to find this ideal system for the next half century.

Concessionary Companies

One of the earliest approaches to colonial rule in Africa was to delegate the task to one or more "concessionary companies." In German East Africa (present-day mainland Tanzania), French Equatorial Africa, and the Belgian king Leopold's Congo (later the Belgian Congo, present-day Democratic Republic of the Congo), for example, the metropolitan powers granted private companies large concessions of territory for economic activities such as mining, rubber tapping, plantation agriculture, and railroad construction. The companies were typically allowed to set up their own systems of taxation and labor recruitment. Although the concessionary system allowed European governments to occupy and exploit vast regions with a minimum of state financing and personnel, it proved untenable as a long-term solution. Especially in Central Africa, companies' use of forced labor and brutal discipline decimated regional populations, provoked public outrage in Europe, and often generated none of the anticipated profits. By the early twentieth century, most European governments were limiting the powers of the concessionary companies and establishing their own administrations.

Direct Rule

Most discussions of colonial rule distinguish between "direct" and "indirect" rule. Although the defining principles of the two forms of rule differed considerably, in practice direct rule administrations – most of which were in French colonies – incorporated elements of indirect rule, especially during the later colonial era.

Under direct rule, colonies were divided into districts administered by European appointees. In French West Africa, the chief district administrator, the *commandant de cercle,* was responsible for regional tax collection, labor and military recruitment, public works, education, local court cases, and the execution of dictates handed down from the colony's governor. Although Africans staffed the lower levels of the commandant's bureaucracy, most of the top officials were European. The commandant was expected to maintain public order and discourage offensive, or "backward," local customs. Thus direct rule was seen as a means of "civilizing" as well as controlling African populations.

Frequently, regional administrative borders cut through preexisting African polities and ethnic communities (*see* ETHNICITY AND IDENTITY IN AFRICA: AN INTERPRETATION). In parts of French West Africa, these borders marked a deliberate policy to divide and weaken militarily powerful groups such as the BAULE and the FON, who for years had resisted foreign occupation. Another part of this policy, at least in the years during and after conquest, was a campaign to dethrone the "great chiefs" of these and other African kingdoms and replace them with more malleable appointees. Generally, these traditional authorities were viewed not only as political threats but as obstacles to the "civilizing mission" of direct rule.

Direct rule encountered at least three practical problems. First, European governments lacked the personnel required to administer their African colonies effectively. Although schools of colonial administration were well established in Europe by the early twentieth century, debilitating diseases and harsh climates discouraged officers from seeking posts in Africa. European colonies often had fewer than one colonial officer for every 22,000 Africans, as was the case in KENYA in 1921. The Belgian Congo had a mere 2384 officials for an African population of 9.4 million; French West Africa, with an African population of 15 million, employed only 3660 French personnel.

Second, the administrators were responsible not only for large subject populations, but for vast territories. Travel over long distances was slow and arduous, and communication difficult. As a result, colonial governors had little contact with remote areas, where district administrators often proved incapable of or uninterested in carrying out the dictates of their superiors.

Finally, the officials' limited knowledge of local languages and customs, combined with their often total lack of legitimacy, undermined their ability to recruit labor, collect taxes, or carry out other administrative duties effectively. In the end, both the great chiefs and local village chiefs – both of which had greater legitimacy and more local contacts – proved indispensable to the project of colonial administration. For all these reasons, most European powers started modifying their approach to colonial rule in the early twentieth century.

The French appointed "traditional chiefs" to serve as adminstrators of the eight countries that comprised the colony of French West Africa. Photographed about 1943, these leaders pose in front of a French flag emblazoned with a patriarchal cross. *CORBIS/Hulton-Deutsch Collection*

INDIRECT RULE

The alternative method, first adopted by the British, was to rule indirectly through "traditional" African authorities. The logic of indirect rule was first articulated by F. J. D. Lugard, the high commissioner of the British protectorate of Northern NIGERIA. Based on his observations of the SOKOTO CALIPHATE and the kingdom of Buganda, Lugard recommended that colonial powers take advantage of existing African authority structures. In his book *The Dual Mandate in British Tropical Africa*, he argued that Africans were better off ruled through their own "traditional systems" and in accordance with the "customary laws" of their own "tribe." Under indirect rule, "tribal" authorities rather than European personnel would be given responsibility for regional administration and justice. Assumed to represent the highest of Africans' abilities, these kings and chiefs were expected to draw on customary laws to maintain obedience and public order, while encouraging their subjects to appreciate modern European values.

Lugard emphasized the moral qualities of indirect rule, but it also offered – at least in theory – a number of practical advantages. Foremost, it promised to be cheap: African chiefs could raise the money for their own salaries from their own subjects. Indirect rule also appeared safer and more effective: by coopting the chiefs' inherited legitimacy, the colonial powers hoped both to improve their ability to carry out routine functions, such as tax collection and labor recruitment, and to avoid large-scale revolts.

Above all, indirect rule assumed the sanctity of the tribe. In much of French West Africa, colonial administrations that had spent years trying to break down tribal authority structures ultimately sought to rehabilitate them. Besides locating and strengthening traditional authorities, colonial administrations endeavored to identify and delineate each tribe's homeland and customs. Often, they called on missionaries and anthropologists for help.

Indirect rule worked best in the regions where strong and highly organized states were already in place, like northern Nigeria, and where the recognized authorities, like the Sokoto caliph, welcomed European collaboration. On the whole, however, erroneous assumptions about the nature of "tribal" identity, authority, and customary law undermined the effectiveness and ultimately the sustainability of indirect rule.

Fundamental to the logic of indirect rule, for example, was the belief that Africa comprised hundreds of mutually exclusive, geographically distinct, and centrally ruled "tribes." In reality, African cultural identities were complex and dynamic. African polities also varied enormously in size and structure, from the hierarchical, multiethnic kingdoms of Kongo, Buganda, and Dahomey and the Sokoto Caliphate to the loosely federated chieftaincies of the Haya people to the village-based chiefdoms and councils of "stateless" peoples such as the Igbo of Nigeria, the Baule in the Côte d'Ivoire, and the Nyamwezi of Tanzania. Nomadic groups, such as the Berbers and Tuaregs of West Africa, also confounded European efforts to assign Africans to "tribal homelands."

European colonial officials handled the ambiguities by imposing their own categories and by inventing tribal authority structures where none existed. In 1930 the British administration of Tanganyika (present-day Tanzania) issued the *Native Administration Memorandum on Native Courts*, which defined tribes as "cultural units possessing a common language, a single social system, and an established customary law." Assuming that German colonialism must have destroyed Tanganyika's tribal kingdoms, the British administration grouped disparate communities of Sukuma people under a centralized chief. In Libya the Italian administration randomly divided the Bedouins in 1929 and appointed them to tribes and subtribes. In Ruanda-Burundi the Belgian government assigned Africans passes labeling them as either Hutu or Tutsi, thus creating a rigid distinction between previously contextual identities.

Identifying "authentic" tribal authorities proved no less complicated. Where there was no obvious tribal ruler, colonial administrations summarily appointed one – typically

This chain gang of women was photographed about 1927 in Tanganyika, which was controlled by Great Britain through indirect rule. The British used local "native authorities" to recruit forced labor for such tasks as building roads. *CORBIS*

a cooperative village "big man." Some nonhierarchical peoples, such as the Sagara of present-day Tanzania, were placed under the authority of a neighboring kingdom – in their case, the Zaramo – and expected to adopt its language and customs. In Kenya MAASAI religious leaders were appointed as chiefs, even though they had not previously held administrative responsibilities. In SENEGAL the French, despite concerns about the potential for mass Islamic resistance movements, reinforced the power of the *marabouts* (or holy men) of the Mourides brotherhood, because of their capacity to mobilize large numbers of disciples for peanut farming.

Even where European colonial powers had no trouble identifying chiefs and kings, they were not always satisfied with them. In Dahomey, the French replaced three "independent-minded" rulers within the first ten years of colonial rule. In Rhodesia (present-day ZIMBABWE) in 1927, the British abolished hereditary rights of succession and assumed the power to appoint chiefs, thereby minimizing the chances of chiefly disobedience. Elsewhere, chiefs considered unsuitable were replaced with others deemed more authentic. In southern Upper Volta (present-day BURKINA FASO), for example, the French replaced the KONG Jula they had originally appointed as canton chiefs with members of a local Zara clan (neither, in fact, had a long history of political domination in the region). Colonial administrators' ongoing efforts to find compliant local authorities meant that kings and chiefs enjoyed little job security.

However tenuous their employment, many African rulers were granted unprecedented powers by colonial administrations, often at the expense of preexisting judicial and advisory bodies. In precolonial SWAZILAND, for example, the king's power was checked by the queen mother and a council composed of royal family members, village headmen, and commoners. Under British rule, women and commoners were excluded from the council, and the king's decisions were subject to approval only by the British administration. In many parts of Africa, chiefs were expected to allocate land and adjudicate local disputes, both responsibilities that had previously often belonged to lineage heads or village councils. Backing up chiefs' new powers was the implicit threat of military force, provided by colonial armies and police.

TOP: Coffee plantation in German South-West Africa (present-day Namibia) in 1918. *CORBIS/Bettmann*
MIDDLE: European colonizers often used forced labor in Africa to tap rubber trees. Companies in the Belgian Congo were especially notorious for their brutal treatment of such laborers. Photographed in French Equatorial Africa, these workers stand for inspection of the buckets of rubber they have collected. *CORBIS/Hulton-Deutsch Collection*
LEFT: Under the evaluating eye of a colonial adminstrator in Togo about 1914, barefoot and armed Africans formed the colony's police troops. *CORBIS/Hulton-Deutsch Collection*

It soon became clear that this arrangement was susceptible to abuse. As George Padmore, the Caribbean Pan-Africanist, observed in 1936, "The chief is the law, subject to only one higher authority, the white official stationed in his state as adviser.... No oriental despot ever had greater power than these black tyrants, thanks to the support which they receive from the white officials who quietly keep in the background." Some chiefs took advantage of their powers to collect additional taxes, recruit extra labor for their own plantations, and extract exorbitant tributes and services from their subjects. One German official in Tanganyika, for example, estimated that many chiefs were collecting seven times the required tax and keeping the surplus. In the 1920s the British and French attempted to prevent chiefs from taking excessive cuts from local revenue by giving them fixed salaries. In general, however, chiefs known to be corrupt who were otherwise cooperative were usually allowed to remain in office.

Not all chiefs abused their powers, of course, but most found their legitimacy tested by the duties of their office. Collecting taxes, requisitioning crops, recruiting youths for compulsory labor service and military service – only the most gifted leaders managed to carry out these tasks without provoking resentment, rebellion, or flight. In colonial Upper Volta, for example, tens of thousands of Mossi youths responded to their chiefs' efforts to recruit them for road and agricultural projects by fleeing south to the Gold Coast (present-day Ghana).

Finally, colonial administrations' efforts to impose indirect rule were confounded by the ambiguities of so-called customary law. Lugard and other administrators assumed that each "tribe" possessed a set of stable, universally understood laws. In fact, many African societies' laws were contested and often changing, and the era defined by Europeans as "traditional Africa" – the nineteenth century – was a period of extraordinary upheaval. Shaka Zulu's conquests in southern Africa, the formation of the Sokoto Caliphate in West Africa, the rise of the trading empires of Msiri and Tippu Tip in East and Central Africa, and the holy wars of North Africa all had altered the political landscapes as well as belief systems across the African continent.

Whether or not "customary" laws were actually very old, most were not written down. As a result, colonial administrators consulted with chiefs, elders, missionaries, and anthropologists, all of whom described customs according to their own views and interests. Chiefs had an interest in strengthening their own authority to tax and fine subjects, while elders typically benefited from laws that allowed them control over youths and women. Missionaries often argued for the preservation for certain customs (as did anthropologists) but emphasized the injustices of those that interfered with their own evangelical objectives, such as arranged marriages.

Faced with a hodge-podge of often contradictory accounts, European officials codified those customary laws that seemed most likely to assure their own political, economic, and social objectives. Others they rejected entirely. In Rhodesia, for example, British commissioners were scandalized to learn that Ndebele women were allowed to marry whom they pleased. Assuming that the group's traditional laws must have been "forgotten or swept away," the colonial commissioner brought in a copy of the Natal Native Code of 1891 (first applied in the Natal colony of present-day South Africa) to teach them how to behave like traditional Ndebele. Colonial administrations outlawed other customs that offended European sensibilities, such as slavery (*see* Slavery in Africa), but were often unable to enforce, or were uninterested in enforcing, their own prohibitions.

Although the institution of customary law helped colonial officials win the cooperation of customary authorities, it did not prevent ongoing challenges to those authorities, especially at the local level. As the expansion of transportation systems and the market economy provided new opportunities for individual mobility and employment, formerly dependent members of rural communities – women and young men, in particular – often contested or simply disregarded the customary laws that dictated whom they owed labor or who they could marry. Village chiefs and elders found it increasingly difficult to exert control over their own kin members. Especially after World War II, high rates of urban migration placed more and more Africans outside the jurisdiction of customary law and into social settings and workplaces where they started to participate in growing nationalist movements. The stability that customary law was supposed to provide was fleeting at best.

Legacies

By the late 1940s it was clear that colonial rule in Africa could be sustained only at an unduly high cost. As European powers prepared for decolonization, Africans across much of the continent gained voting rights and increased representation in colonial legislatures in the 1950s. Faced with a new generation of African politicians, many of them schooled in socialist thought, chiefs and kings struggled to ensure themselves a role in the postcolonial power structure. Some, such as the kings of Swaziland and Morocco, did maintain real authority; but in more radical independent states, government leaders made a concerted effort to limit the powers of chiefs and other customary authorities.

Although scholars debate the extent to which contemporary Africa's political and economic woes can be "blamed" on colonial rule, it is clear that rigid ethnic categories created during the colonial era have become one of the greatest obstacles to nation building and regional stability in much of Africa. The fact that the postcolonial state has for many years been one of the only reliable channels of upward mobility in Africa has also undermined the stability and effectiveness of many governments. In addition, postcolonial African states have inherited their predecessors' ambivalence toward customary authorities. Modern African politicians look to village chiefs, spiritual leaders, clan heads, and other such authorities to support their development programs as well as their political campaigns, but cannot always depend on their loyalties. Finally, customary law remains a source of fierce debate, as African states continue to grapple with the problems of defining and legislating modern civil society.

Elizabeth Heath

See Also

African Socialism; Berber; Buganda, Early Kingdom of; Cape Town, South Africa; Dahomey, Early Kingdom of; Dakar, Senegal; Egypt; Gold Trade; Hutu and Tutsi; Ivory Trade; Law in Africa: Colonial and Contemporary; Leopold II; Lugard, Frederick John Dealtry; Nationalism in Africa; Niger River; Transatlantic Slave Trade; Porto-Novo, Benin; Rwanda; Shaka; Tuareg; Pan-Africanism; Marabout; Burton, Sir Richard; Bedouin; Anthropology in Africa; Christianity: Missionaries in Africa.

Latin America and the Caribbean

Colón, Jesús (b. January 20, 1901, Cayey, Puerto Rico; d. 1974, New York, N.Y.), Afro-Puerto Rican activist and writer.

Jesús Colón was born in Cayey, a rural town near San Juan. In a 1917 editorial, which would characterize much of his professional life, he wrote about the capacity of words to transform society. A few months later he arrived in New York City, where he spent the rest of his life. There he held many menial jobs, such as waiting tables and washing dishes. In 1918 he became a founding member of the Puerto Rican Committee of the Socialist Party; in the following decades he became a relentless organizer of other political and cultural groups. One year after his 1922 graduation from Boys High Evening School, he started writing for *Justicia*, the newspaper of the Puerto Rican Free Federation of Workers. Regular columns in publications such as *Gráfico* and the *Daily Worker* followed.

Colón's essays are among the first works of Hispanic literature to depict the experiences of immigrants in the United States, and his narrative voice blends Anglo and Hispanic cultures. In the anthologies *Puerto Rican in New York and Other Sketches* (1961) and *The Way It Was and Other Writings* (1993), his sketches are often anecdotal and humorous, but even funny remarks about linguistic confusions and castor oil veil a moving social critique. In an essay about the Statue of Liberty, Colón commented on the disparity between the principles it represents and the reality that immigrants face.

In the 1950s and 1960s Colón plunged into electoral politics. In the mid-1950s he ran unsuccessfully for the New York City Council and the New York State Assembly on the ticket of the American Labor Party. In 1969 he made his final attempt at electoral politics, running for New York City Controller for the Communist Party, also unsuccessfully. Because of his political activities, his energetic involvement in socialist labor organizations, his support of Puerto Rican independence and his prose, he was forced to testify before the House Committee on Un-American Activities in 1959. Colón continued to couple words and action until his death in New York City in 1974. Sidney Finkelstein, the American author and music critic, has said that Colón spoke not only to working people and Puerto Ricans but to the American people as a whole.

Alexandra Vega-Merino

See Also

New York, New York; Puerto Rico; Communist Party USA, African Americans and the.

Latin America and the Caribbean

Colón, Willie

(b. April 28, 1950, the Bronx, N.Y.), one of salsa music's pioneers, who started his recording career at age 16.

Willie Colón's first album, *El malo* (The Bad Guy, 1967), gave him the image by which he was known for the first decade of his career. This image made fun of the negative stereotype of violence attributed to Puerto Rican communities in New York City, especially those perpetuated by Hollywood movies. With some of his lyrics, this Mafia-style image helped develop the identification of the Puerto Rican community in New York with *salsa* music.

Some of Colón's lyrics are urban chronicles that narrate the life of the Puerto Rican *barrio* (or neighborhood) in New York, while other songs emphasize the African heritage of Puerto Rican culture (*see* Puerto Rico). Colón and his band's lead singer, Héctor Lavoe, introduced the *jíbaro* sound into salsa. Jíbaro music comes from the Spanish heritage of Puerto Rico, while salsa is based on Afro-Cuban rhythms. These rhythms are one of the main elements that intensified the connection between salsa music and Puerto Rican culture in New York City, and later in Puerto Rico itself. Colón is also one of the most continuously experimental composers and musical arrangers, and his compositions and musical arrangements differentiated salsa from traditional Cuban music (*see* son and rumba).

Colón has recorded and produced more than 30 records and has been nominated for five Grammy Awards in Latin music. He started his career as a trombone player and later also became the lead singer on his recordings. His recordings with Rubén Blades, *Metiendo mano* and *Siembra*, are among the best-selling records in salsa history. He also has recorded with Celia Cruz, Fania All Stars, Mon Rivera, and Ismael Miranda, among other great salsa singers and groups. His most outstanding records include *Cosa nuestra* (Our Thing, 1971), *El juicio* (The Trial, 1972), *Asalto navideño* (Christmas Assault, 1971), *El Baquiné de angelitos negros* (The Wake of the Little Black Angels, 1976), and *Solo* (1980).

Juan Otero-Garabis

See Also

New York, New York; Salsa Music.

North America

Coltrane, John William

(b. September 23, 1926, Hamlet, N.C.; d. July 17, 1967, Long Island, N.Y.), African American jazz saxophonist, composer, band leader, and stylistic and compositional innovator, widely recognized as the leader of the New Thing or Free Jazz avant-garde movement of the 1960s.

Shortly after John Coltrane was born, his family moved to a lower-middle-class neighborhood in High Point, North Carolina. The Coltranes lived within an extended family headed by Rev. William Blair, John's maternal grandfather, and they followed him to High Point when he accepted a pastorate there. John's father was a tailor and an amateur musician who sang and played the ukulele for his own enjoyment. His mother, Alice Coltrane (not to be confused with Coltrane's second wife of the same name), was a seamstress who sang and played piano in her father's gospel choir, and at one point wanted to be a concert pianist. Also included in Rev. Blair's household were his daughter, Betty; her husband, Goler; and their daughter, Mary. Cousin Mary (who was immortalized by a song with the same title on Coltrane's first album as a leader) was an only child like John, and the two of them grew up as siblings. While not well-to-do by black middle-class standards of today, Coltrane was protected from the poverty that many of his jazz colleagues experienced and seems to have had a reasonably happy childhood. Though shy, he did well in school, had a few close friends, and participated in social activities such as the Boy Scouts of America and neighborhood bands. In grade school he was an honor student, but his studies suffered in high school as his life grew more singularly focused on music.

Adolescence brought events that disturbed the stability of Coltrane's emotional life. Within the space of a few years, all three adult males in the household died, starting with the death of his father in 1939, when John was 13 years old. His grandfather died a few months later, and within three years both his aunt and uncle died. During this period of intense change Coltrane began his lifelong study of music. Playing in a community band first on alto horn, then on clarinet, he eventually switched to alto saxophone, the instrument that he would play throughout most of his apprenticeship as a musician. No one knows for sure how much of Coltrane's absorption into music was therapeutic, but almost from the beginning he practiced for many hours daily (at times till 3:00 or 4:00 in the morning), a habit that would prove legendary after he became a professional musician.

Education

After graduating from William Penn High School in 1943, Coltrane moved to Philadelphia, Pennsylvania. There he was soon joined by his mother, Cousin Mary, and his aunt, all of whom moved from New Jersey, where they had gone to profit from the lucrative work in Northern wartime plants. He enrolled briefly in the Granoff studios and later the Ornstein Conservatory, where he studied saxophone technique and music theory for eight years. At Ornstein, Coltrane excelled as a student and was known for his eagerness to absorb his lessons, especially the advanced theoretical concepts taught by Dennis Sandole. His studies were interrupted by a stint in the navy.

Coltrane played in various navy bands, mostly as a clarinetist, while stationed in Hawaii. With other navy musicians, he moonlighted as an alto saxophonist in a dance band. Coltrane was not yet the competent professional he would soon become on his return to Philadelphia, but was good enough to warrant special mention in a local newspaper article lamenting the imminent breakup of the band.

The discovery and commercial production of a rehearsal tape from this period has introduced this phase of Coltrane's artistry into the literature and constitutes the first of five periods into which Coltrane's career can be divided. The tape reveals that the 18-year-old Coltrane was an acolyte of Charlie Parker, with whom Coltrane would eventually play. According to Coltrane, Parker came to him in a dream, encouraging the younger musician in his harmonic studies during his "sheets of sound" period when many critics were denouncing Coltrane's music as being "anti-jazz" and full of tasteless displays of virtuosity.

Upon returning to Philadelphia, Coltrane resumed his studies at the Ornstein Conservatory. He also studied and practiced music with the local jazz brotherhood, which included many future jazz luminaries, such as Jimmy Oliver, Benny Golson, Howard McGhee, "Philly" Jo Jones, Lee Morgan, Jimmy Heath, Bill Barron, and Cal Massey.

Apprenticeship

By the late 1940s Coltrane had developed into a first-class rhythm and blues saxophonist. He switched from alto to tenor saxophone while working with Earl Bostic, who played the alto. On the alto Coltrane was heavily influenced by the playing style of Charlie Parker. On the tenor Coltrane had more varied influences from the start, as he was listening especially attentively to Dexter Gordon, Edward "Sonny" Stitt, Theodore "Sonny" Rollins, and Stan Getz. Though still relatively unknown to the public, Coltrane was admired by musicians and by the early 1950s he had served apprenticeship with many big name R&B and jazz artists, including King Kolax, Big Maybelle, Bull Moose Jackson, Dasie Mae and the Hep Cats, Earl Bostic, Eddie "Cleanhead" Vinson, Jimmy Smith, JOHNNY HODGES (his earliest model on the alto), and Dizzy Gillespie.

Despite the wealth of experience that he was gaining, this was a troubled time for Coltrane. He was underemployed as a musician and survived largely due to the support of his mother. He often took jobs that were as much theatrical as musical, jobs that he found demeaning and unsuitable for a serious musician. One of these required that he "walk the bar" – walking atop the bar while honking and screaming through his horn to delight the patrons. While living in Philadelphia, Coltrane also developed a heroin habit that was serious enough to affect his health and interfere with his professional life. As is often the case with heroin addicts, Coltrane abused alcohol in attempts to wean himself from heroin. Further, he had a chronic battle with weight and spent his adult life alternating between binging and dieting, eventually necessitating two wardrobes. He had a sweet tooth, especially for sweet potato pie, and eventually lost his upper front teeth (teeth that are important for forming the saxophone embouchure), medicating the pain with alcohol rather than visits to a dentist.

MASTERY

The year 1955 was a momentous one for Coltrane both personally and professionally: he married Juanita Grubbs (Naima) and joined the Miles Davis quintet. Coltrane's tenure with Davis lasted off and on through 1960, when he left Davis to form his own quartet. During these years, Coltrane's playing became more personal. He introduced a hard tone that struck some listeners as "hauntingly beautiful" and others as "harsh." Coltrane became a favorite among recording musicians; with Sonny Rollins he was now one of the leading hard bop voices on tenor saxophone.

Jazz saxophonist, bandleader, and composer John Coltrane emerged in the late 1950s as a leading innovator in jazz music, recording both with his own groups and as a soloist with trumpet player Miles Davis. Widely imitated and admired, he helped revolutionize the role of the saxophone in jazz. *Charles Stewart*

In Davis's band, Coltrane's playing reached the limelight through club and concert appearances throughout the country, a few television appearances, and commercial recordings. Coltrane began to attract critical attention through such recordings as *'Round About Midnight* (on the Columbia label), *Steamin', Relaxin', Cookin',* and *Workin'* (all on the Prestige label). In 1957 he was fired from Davis's band and traded places with Sonny Rollins, who left Thelonious Monk's quartet. Monk hired Coltrane for his famous Five Spot Café engagement, which lasted for several months. This engagement is legendary in jazz history for three reasons: first, it launched the Five Spot as the premiere club in New York for experimental jazz (other artists who similarly served the Five Spot were Cecil Taylor and ORNETTE COLEMAN); second, it marked the "rediscovery" of Thelonious Monk, who had been barred from playing in New York clubs through alleged police harassment; and third, during this engagement Coltrane came into maturity as a musician. In this band, he combined his astonishing technique with a set of innovative harmonic devices, developing what critic Ira Gitler famously termed "sheets of sound." Coltrane regarded Monk as a master teacher who was "a musical architect of the highest order."

Coltrane then returned to Davis's band, which became the most influential jazz combo of the late 1950s with recordings like *Kind of Blue* and *Milestones* (both on Columbia). This period marked a turning point in Coltrane's spiritual life. In 1957 he experienced a spiritual awakening that led him to tell his mother and his friend Eric Dolphy that he had seen God. Dedicating his life, and especially his music, to God, he found the strength to quit his heroin and alcohol addictions. A third phase of Coltrane's artistry emerged as he recorded under his own name and featured his original compositions. His study of Eastern religions and the music of India and Africa led him to pursue lengthy improvisations utilizing a set of pitches, or modes, rather than functional harmony as in bebop. At the same time he devised a set of harmonic formulas known today as "Coltrane substitutions." Coltrane also introduced the soprano saxophone as a viable jazz instrument, the first man to do so since Sidney Bechet over four decades earlier. Coltrane's music of this period can be heard on recordings such as *Giant Steps* (Atlantic), *Blue Train* (Blue Note), and his first "hit record," *My Favorite Things* (Atlantic).

Coltrane's fourth phase began in 1961 when he formed what became known as his classic quartet, featuring himself on tenor and soprano saxophones, McCoy Tyner on piano, either Jimmy Garrison or Reggie Workman on bass, and Elvin Jones on drums. Eric Dolphy also performed with the group periodically until his death in 1964. Coltrane had always divided jazz fans and critics into two camps, one praising and the other denouncing his music. During this stage, as his artistry developed, the distance between these two camps widened, with the fringes of each group shading toward excess. His extreme followers progressed from the adulation of fans to the reverence of devotees, while his extreme detractors not only disparaged his musical vision, but questioned his basic competence. The attacks were brutal enough for Coltrane and Dolphy to write an article with Don Demichael in *Down Beat* titled "Coltrane and Dolphy Answer the Jazz Critics." *Down Beat* solved its problem in an innovative fashion by assigning two reviewers for Coltrane records, one favorable and the other condemnatory.

The music made with his classic quartet is widely considered the high point of Coltrane's oeuvre. The quartet toured throughout the United States and Europe. Starting in 1961 Coltrane won the *Down Beat* Poll in at least one category every year. He was inducted in the *Down Beat* Hall of Fame in 1965 as Jazz Man of the Year when his landmark recording, *A Love Supreme*, was declared Record of the Year. Coltrane's work with the quartet was daringly innovative and has made him, after Charlie Parker, the most imitated saxophonist in jazz history. Also widely influential was the ensemble playing of the quartet. Coltrane was admired not only for being a musical innovator, but for the spiritual qualities of his music and persona. The music of the quartet can be heard on such recordings as *Africa Brass, Live at the Village Vanguard, Crescent, A Love Supreme, First Meditations,* and *Sun Ship* (all on Impulse).

The fifth and final stage of Coltrane's career is sometimes labeled as his avant-garde period. It began in 1966, after Tyner and Jones had both left the band, and were replaced with his wife Alice Coltrane (née Alice McCleod) on piano and Rashied Ali on drums. Pharoah Sanders (née Farrell Sanders) also joined the band on tenor and soprano saxophones. With this group Coltrane continued his explorations of sound, texture, and group improvisation, stretching the parameters of Western music. Due to Coltrane's untreated illness this band canceled its European tours, but did tour Japan in 1966. Recordings of this period include *Live at the Village Vanguard, Again, Interstellar Space, Live in Japan, Expression,* and *Stellar Regions* (all on Impulse).

Tapes found at his widow's house suggest that Coltrane was entering yet another phase of artistic development that was cut short by his death from liver cancer. The National Academy of Recording Arts and Sciences awarded him a Grammy Award for Lifetime Achievement posthumously in 1991 .

Salim Washington

See Also

Bechet, Sidney Joseph; Davis, Miles Dewey, III; Gillespie, John Birks ("Dizzy"); Gordon, Dexter Keith; Monk, Thelonious Sphere; Parker, Charles Christopher ("Bird"); Rollins, Theodore ("Sonny").

North America

Combs, Sean ("Puffy") (b. 1970, Harlem, New York), African American entrepreneur and rap impresario responsible for a string of hit records in the 1990s.

Born in Harlem and raised in Mount Vernon, New York, Combs attended Howard University and started working in the music industry as an intern at Andre Harrell's Uptown Records. He moved quickly through the ranks, producing hits for Uptown artists such as Jodeci and Mary J. Blige. At the age of 22 he was made a company vice president.

In 1993 Combs left Uptown to found Bad Boy Entertainment, where he began to assemble a crew of hip hop and R&B talent. Combs served as executive producer for both albums by Bad Boy's biggest star, Notorious B.I.G. After the 1997 shooting death of Notorious B.I.G., Combs (who raps as Puff Daddy) recorded a tribute song titled "I'll Be Missing You." The single was a smash hit, and it sent Puff Daddy's solo debut album, *No Way Out*, to the top of the charts. *No Way Out* picked up two Grammy Awards, including Best Rap Album, and Combs was named Soul Train's entertainer of the year.

Sean "Puffy" Combs's undistinguished, monotonous rapping style has come under fire in some hip hop circles, but his remarkable success as a producer is incontrovertible. His instantly recognizable rewrites of hit songs (culled from artists as diverse as David Bowie, The Temptations, and Led Zeppelin) have made multi-platinum stars out of rappers such as Lil' Kim and Mase, as well as Notorious B.I.G. and Combs himself. Indeed, as producer and performer, Sean "Puffy" Combs held the Number-One spot on the *Billboard* singles chart for an astonishing 22 weeks in 1997.

Andrew Du Bois

See Also

Harlem, New York; Hip Hop in the United States; Notorious B.I.G. ("Biggie Smalls"); Rhythm and Blues; Soul Train.

North America

Communist Party USA, African Americans and the

When the Communist Party of the United States (CPUSA) was officially founded in 1921, few people realized the critical role it would play in African American politics and culture. The product of several splinter groups emerging out of the Socialist Party's left wing in 1919, its founding members (like the Socialists before them) viewed the plight of African Americans as inseparable from the class struggle. The party's 1921 program asserted that "the interests of the Negro worker are identical with those of the white." Two years later Communist leadership recognized that black people in the United States constituted an "oppressed race" but considered Black Nationalism "a weapon of reaction for the defeat and further enslavement of both [blacks] and their white brother workers." However, pressure from the Communist International (Comintern), primarily V. I. Lenin and Indian Communist M. N. Roy, and popular support for Black Nationalist Movements within African American working-class communities, compelled the CPUSA to reconsider seriously its approach to the "Negro Question."

The Fourth Congress of the Comintern in 1922 adopted a set of theses describing blacks as a nationality oppressed by imperialism. Because black workers' struggles were now considered inherently anti-imperialist, American Communists were obliged to view Garveyism and other notable nationalist movements anew. During the 1924 Universal Negro Improvement Association (UNIA) Convention, the *Daily Worker* covered the proceedings and praised the organization for its militancy. At the Fourth National Conference of the Communist Party in 1925, conference members recognized that the Garvey movement was "an almost universal phenomenon among American Negro workers."

Thus it should not be surprising that many early black Communist recruits, at least in the urban North, were former Garveyites and black nationalists of various stripes. However, the most visible black radicals who rose to leadership positions in the Communist Party came out of an independent postwar black Left that had been deeply touched by the Bolshevik revolution as well as by workers' uprisings and racial violence in American cities during and after World War I. While these events did not propel large numbers of African American radicals into the Communist Party, it did reinforce their belief that socialist revolution was possible within the context of "race politics" and working-class unity.

Perhaps the most enigmatic group among the postwar black Left was the African Blood Brotherhood (ABB), a secret, underground organization of radical black nationalists with a large West Indian following; its leaders included Cyril Briggs, W. A. Domingo, Richard B. Moore, Bertha DeBasco, Gertrude Hall, and a radical Harlem schoolteacher named Grace Campbell. Founded in 1918 by Briggs, the ABB advocated armed defense against lynching, the right to vote in the South, the right to organize, equal rights for blacks, and the abolition of Jim Crow laws. In the pages of their publication, the *Crusader*, Briggs attacked Woodrow Wilson for not applying the concept of self-determination to Africa, and during the Red Summer of 1919, he demanded "government of the Negro, by the Negro and for the Negro." A unique experiment in black Marxist organization, the ABB was short-lived, killed off by its own internal logic; by the early 1920s its Marxist leadership decided that an interracial proletarian party would be a more effective form of organization and therefore opted to join the CPUSA.

The CPUSA's newfound respect for Garveyism and Black Nationalism more generally came a bit too late, however, since the UNIA was already on the verge of collapse. The party responded by forming the American Negro Labor Congress (ANLC) in 1925, an organization led chiefly by former ABB leaders determined to build interracial unity in the labor movement. Chapters were to be established throughout the United States, particularly in the South, but because of poor leadership and ill-conceived planning, the ANLC never gained popular support. In the end, although the Communists failed to redirect Garveyism, they did attract a handful of ex-Garveyites into their ranks.

The Communists' failure to mobilize significant black support in the early 1920s can be attributed partially to the Communist International's vision of internationalism, which extended beyond PAN-AFRICANISM or racial solidarity, or both. While Comintern officials recognized differences between anticolonial and European working-class movements, peasants, and proletarians, they still insisted that these struggles be united under the same banner. Even their conferences emphasized an international unity that few Americans, black or white, could ever imagine. In 1927, for example, African American delegates were invited to attend a conference in Brussels, held under the auspices of the League Against Colonial Oppression. Organized in 1926 by the German Communist Party (KDP) to combat procolonial sentiments emerging in Germany, the league was an important step toward coordinating various struggles for national liberation in the colonies and "semi-colonies," and it served as an intermediary between the Communist International and the anticolonial movement. It was at this conference that former ABB leader Richard B. Moore witnessed Europeans, Asians, and Africans pass a general resolution that proclaimed: "Africa for the Africans, and their full freedom and equality with other races and the right to govern Africa." It was indeed a remarkable sight for anyone who believed that the struggle for African freedom was only an African struggle.

The Communist movement's internationalism not only appropriated the familiar idioms of Pan-Africanism, but in many respects it cleared the way for a vision of black anti-imperialism that could transcend without negating a completely racialized world-view. Moreover, internationalism became a vehicle for African American radicals to cross cultural boundaries, to escape and challenge essentialist presumptions common among some segments of the CP about how the "authentic" Negro proletariat looked and talked. Lovett Fort-Whiteman, an early recruit who rose quickly within the Chicago CP's ranks, was emblematic of this sort of cultural internationalism. Soon after his return from the Soviet Union, the Texas-born Communist became a popular spectacle on the South Side of Chicago for strolling the streets draped in a Russian *rabochka*. Yet, this same internationalist vision sometimes hindered the party's work in the African American community. For example, black delegates from the Workers (Communist) Party and the ABB attending the first All-Race Conference in 1924 were treated with suspicion when they attached to their proposal for armed self-defense and working-class organization a statement endorsing the "Internationale" as the "anthem of Negro Freedom."

A major turning point for the party's racial politics occurred in 1928. That year, the Sixth World Congress of the Comintern, with input from Harry Haywood and South African Communist James La Guma, passed a resolution asserting that African Americans in the Southern black belt counties constituted an oppressed nation and therefore possessed an inherent right of self-determination. Not surprisingly, the resolution met fierce opposition from white, and some black, party leaders. But for many black Communists, particularly those in the urban North, the resolution on black self-determination confirmed what they had long believed: African Americans had their own unique revolutionary tradition. Once adopted, the Communist Party established institutions that could carry out the new slogan. They replaced the dying ANLC with a new organization called the League of Struggle for Negro Rights (LSNR), and its members subsequently chose poet LANGSTON HUGHES to serve as president. The LSNR proved to be somewhat more successful due to the popularity of its newspaper, the *Liberator*. Under the editorship of Cyril Briggs it became a journal of black news tailor-made for the African American community and a forum for radical black creative writers.

The self-determination slogan might have inspired a few black intellectuals already in the CP, but it was not the key to building black working-class support during the 1930s. The party's fight for the concrete economic needs of the unemployed and working poor, its role in organizing sharecroppers in Alabama, its militant opposition to racism, and its vigorous courtroom battles on behalf of African Americans through the International Labor Defense (ILD) attracted a considerable section of America's black working class and intelligentsia. In particular, the ILD's defense of nine young black men falsely accused of raping two white women in Alabama, known as the SCOTTSBORO CASE, crystallized black support for the CPUSA in the 1930s.

While it never occurred to most leading Communists that there could be a "Negro Woman Question" distinct from either the "Negro Question" or the "Woman Question," the way the party conceived of the class struggle opened up at least a few free spaces in which African American working-class women could pursue their own agenda and find their own autonomous voices. Although the party's early forays into labor organizing ignored the majority of African American women, because they were concentrated in domestic work and agriculture, black women joined the Communist-led Unemployed Councils, neighborhood relief committees, and a variety of housewife organizations and auxiliaries. In cities such as Chicago, Detroit, Birmingham, Los Angeles, and especially Harlem, black working women participated in relief demonstrations, resisted eviction efforts, confronted condescending social workers, and fought utilities shutoffs. Working through a variety of Communist-led mass organizations, from the International Labor Defense and the Housewives League to the Hands Off Ethiopia Campaign, the Harlem Communist Party produced a significant group of black women leaders, including Claudia Jones, Audrey Moore, Louise Thompson Patterson, and Bonita Williams. African American women also participated in Communist-led strikes, the most famous of which was the St. Louis nutpickers' strike of 1933, which involved at least 1200 black women.

For committed black women in the CPUSA, the Marxist education they received nurtured an incipient, albeit muted, feminist consciousness. The Communists not only encouraged working-class women's participation as activists but they also offered black women an empowering language with which to define and critique gender oppression. On both a personal and collective level, black women activists appropriated from the party's tabloid, *Working Woman*, such phrases as "the woman question" and "male chauvinism" as weapons with which to negotiate relationships, the sexual division of labor, and their participation in the movement. It was out of such discussions and actions that black working-class women developed an incipient class-conscious black feminist or, more appropriately, "womanist" perspective.

In 1935, in accordance with the Comintern's Seventh World Congress, the CPUSA called for a Popular Front against fascism, deemphasized its Marxist ideology, and eventually supported Roosevelt's NEW DEAL coalition. Communists not only joined mainstream black civil rights organizations in greater numbers but they became the primary force behind black coalition efforts like the National Negro Congress (1935-1946) and the SOUTHERN NEGRO YOUTH CONGRESS (1937-1948), both of which represented hundreds of black organizations. During the Popular Front black Communist labor organizers played a critical role in the formation of the Congress of Industrial Organizations (CIO), particularly in the mining, steel, marine transport, and meat-packing industries.

During this period the party also attracted a large number of black artists, including PAUL

Robeson and Langston Hughes. Communist cultural critics collected African American music, began to write jazz criticism, and insisted that black culture was the clearest expression of "American culture." And as black artists began working for the federally funded Works Progress Administration (WPA) in the late 1930s, Louise Thompson became a critical liaison linking black popular culture and Harlem's literati with Communist Popular Front politics. In 1938, for example, she and Langston Hughes organized the Harlem Suitcase Theatre, sponsored by the International Workers Order, which performed a number of works by black playwrights. This newfound appreciation of black culture opened up potential space for creative expression within CP circles. Communist papers published poems and short stories by black writers and carried articles and cartoons on black history, and CP auxiliaries sponsored plays by black playwrights, art exhibits, benefit jazz concerts, and dances.

The party gained a larger black following in such places as Harlem and Chicago because of its opposition to Italy's invasion of Ethiopia in 1935. And when African American radicals were unable to join Haile Selassie's army, many closed ranks with the Left and fought in the Spanish Civil War. Altogether over 80 black men and one black woman (a Harlem nurse named Salaria Kee) risked life, limb, and their own U.S. citizenship to defend a legally elected government from a fascist takeover and to get back at Mussolini for the invasion of Ethiopia. Hence African Americans who responded to the call regarded the Spanish Civil War as an extension of the Italo-Ethiopian conflict. At the same time, black volunteers did not forget racism and poverty in America; for them Spain had become the battlefield to revenge the rape of Ethiopia and part of a larger fight for justice and equality that would inevitably take place on U.S. soil. Indeed, a number of black intellectuals and artists adopted the Spanish cause as their own. Black newspapers, most notably the *Pittsburgh Courier*, the *Baltimore Afro-American*, the *Atlanta Daily World*, and the *Chicago Defender*, unequivocally sided with the Spanish Republic and occasionally carried feature articles about black participants in the Lincoln Brigade. Several black medical personnel from the United Aid for Ethiopia (UAE) offered medical supplies and raised money in the community; Harlem churches and professional organizations sponsored rallies on behalf of the Spanish Republic; black relief workers and doctors raised enough money to purchase a fully equipped ambulance for use in Spain; and some of Harlem's greatest musicians, including Cab Calloway, Fats Waller, Count Basie, W. C. Handy, Jimmy Lunceford, Noble Sissle, and Eubie Blake, gave benefit concerts sponsored by the Harlem Musicians' Committee for Spanish Democracy and the Spanish Children's Milk Fund. Spain meant so much to Paul Robeson that, according to his most recent biographer, it marked a critical turning point in his shift toward radical politics. So touched by the Lincoln Brigade was Robeson that he had hoped to make a film about black war hero Oliver Law. Poet Langston Hughes had planned to publish a book of essays titled *Negroes in Spain*, which would include a concluding section called "World Meaning of Spanish Struggle."

In the end, the Republicans lost the war and Franco ruled Spain for the next four decades. Only about half of the volunteers survived the war and few returning vets escaped injury. More significant, the defeat of the International Brigades in Spain can be attributed to the refusal of Western "democracies," the United States in particular, to come to the aid of the republic while the Nazis and Italian fascists used the Iberian Peninsula as a testing ground for modern weapons. (Indeed, rather than applaud these men and women for risking their lives in a battle America would officially join in 1941, Lincoln Brigade veterans were hounded by the FBI and a variety of "un-American activities" committees, and were labeled "premature antifascists.")

In the South, Communists worked with Southern liberals to found the Southern Conference for Human Welfare (1938) and related organizations committed to economic justice and equality. Young black Communists, in particular, formed the Southern Negro Youth Congress (SNYC). Founded in 1937, SNYC attracted a number of energetic activists, many of whom were young middle-class intellectuals who came of age in the South during the New Deal era. Although SNYC chapters were located throughout the South, its organizational centers were located in Atlanta, Richmond, New Orleans, and Birmingham, the latter serving as SNYC's national headquarters from 1939 until its demise in 1948. From its inception, SNYC's Communist and non-Communist leadership adopted a program that proved more radical than most other civil rights organizations of the period. Despite its rather traditional slogan of "Freedom, Equality and Opportunity," SNYC's program emphasized the right to vote, job security, the right of black workers to organize, and general improvement in the education, health, and welfare of black citizens. The Youth Congress also opposed regional wage differentials, police brutality, and segregation in public spaces. Although socialism was rarely mentioned in SNYC literature, it remained a point of discussion within Youth Congress circles throughout its 11-year history.

Protesters pass by the White House on their way to deliver a petition to the president urging the release of the Scottsboro Nine, a group of black men falsely accused of rape. *CORBIS/Underwood & Underwood*

Whereas the Nazi-Soviet Pact of 1939, the CP's sudden shift to an extreme antiwar position, the Dies Committee's investigation into "un-American" activities, and the rising anticommunism among CIO leaders weakened the party's base of support on the eve of World War II, its relationship to black workers and artists remained fairly strong, especially in Harlem. Between 1939 and 1940, for instance, black Communists led a boycott of *Gone With the Wind;* initiated a campaign to "End Jim Crow in Sports" and collected 10,000 signatures to demand the integration of blacks in major league baseball; organized numerous plays and jazz concerts; and persuaded blues composer W. C. Handy to lecture at the Workers School.

When Communists shifted to a prowar position after Germany invaded Russia in 1941, African American leadership, for the most part, adopted an uncompromising stance vis-à-vis the war effort, insisting on a "double victory" against racism at home and fascism abroad. While the CP essentially opposed the Double V campaign, arguing that too much black militancy could undermine the war effort, rank-and-file Communists and liberals close to the party continued to fight on the civil rights front throughout the war, demanding, among other things, the full integration of the armed forces and implementation of the FAIR EMPLOYMENT PRACTICES COMMITTEE. In spite of these measures, the party's opposition to the Double V slogan left many blacks feeling that the party had abandoned them for the sake of the war.

In 1944 General Secretary Earl Browder made the shocking decision to dissolve the Communist Party USA and form loosely structured Communist political associations. With membership at an all-time high, he believed that the party was now in a position to become a mass organization that could attract large numbers of ordinary Americans. However, the associations came to an abrupt end in 1945 when French Communist Jacques Duclos published an article sharply criticizing Browder's strategy. The subsequent expulsion of Browder and ascension of William Z. Foster to power in 1946 generated an internal crisis in the party, resulting in a wave of expulsions prompted by charges of Trotskyism, Browderism, and Negro Nationalism. As the country moved right and the McCarthy era got under way, the party under Foster moved further left and further into isolation, although Popular Front-style coalition politics lingered through the 1948 Progressive Party campaign. Communists and suspected Communists were jailed for violating the Smith Act (including black leaders such as Henry Winston, Ben Davis Jr., Claudia Jones, and Pettis Perry). By 1956 the CPUSA had become a shadow of its former self, never to achieve the status it once enjoyed in the 1930s and 1940s.

Despite the internal crisis, the party continued to defend black rights in the courts and streets through the Civil Rights Congress (CRC), a left-wing legal defense organization founded in 1946. Led by Communist William L. Patterson, the CRC gained notoriety for its militant defense of African Americans falsely accused of crimes and Communists accused of un-American activities, and for its historic petition to the United Nations charging the U.S. government with genocide against African Americans. One of CRC's better-known campaigns centered on Rosa Lee Ingram, a black Georgia tenant farmer and widowed mother of 12, who, along with 2 of her sons, was convicted and sentenced to death for the murder of a neighboring white tenant farmer, John Stratford. Stratford, who initiated the altercation on Ingram's property in November 1947, assaulted Rosa Lee with the butt of a rifle and, by some accounts, sexually harassed her. Her son intervened, wrested the gun from Stratford, and struck a blow to his head that proved to be fatal. Throughout the country, African Americans, white liberals, and radicals rallied in defense of Rosa Lee Ingram and her sons, angered especially by the speedy and unconstitutional trial that resulted in their conviction, the racist application of the death sentence in a clear cut case of self-defense, and the conviction of all three defendants, when the responsibility for Stratford's death lay with one of Rosa Lee's sons. The case spurred the creation of a number of radical women's organizations linked to the CRC campaign, founded primarily by black women who had some association with the Communist Party. Perhaps the most important organization was the Sojourners for Truth and Justice initiated by Charlotta Bass, SHIRLEY GRAHAM DU BOIS, Rosalie McGee, Louise Thompson Patterson, and Alice Childress.

During the next three decades, black Communists and ex-Communists such as Jack O'Dell, Mae Mallory, Abner Berry, HOSEA HUDSON, to name but a few, participated in various civil rights organizations, antiwar movements, labor unions, and black nationalist struggles. As an organization, however, the CP maintained a significant black constituency only in New York, Detroit, and California, the latter being regarded as a renegade state by the CPUSA Central Committee. While national CP leadership attacked Black Nationalism during the height of the BLACK POWER Movement, the California cadre, under the guidance of leaders such as Charlene Mitchell and Dorothy Healey, not only gave support to various nationalist movements but established an all-black youth unit called the Che-Lumumba Club in defiance of Central Committee directives. The movement to free Angela Davis, the last nationally renowned black Communist of the twentieth century, further strengthened the CP's black support in California.

After the collapse of the Soviet Union in 1989, the CPUSA practically fell apart. Internal debates flourished and the longtime general secretary, Gus Hall, was accused of stifling democracy and abandoning antiracism and the black liberation movement. At the 1991 party convention, a split occurred, prompting virtually every leading African American cadre, including Angela Davis, James Jackson, and Charlene Mitchell, to quit the party altogether, with the hope of reconstituting a new democratic left-wing movement. The vast majority of those who left the CPUSA founded the Committees of Correspondence.

Robin Kelley

SEE ALSO

Russia and the Former Soviet Union; Haile Selassie I; World War I and African Americans; Basie, William James ("Count"); Bass, Charlotta Spears; Blake, James Hubert ("Eubie"); Briggs, Cyril Valentine; Calloway, Cabell (Cab); *Chicago Defender*; Chicago, Illinois; Childress, Alice; Civil Rights Congress; Davis, Angela Yvonne; Detroit, Michigan; Garvey, Marcus Mosiah; Handy, William Christopher (W.C.); Harlem, New York; Socialism; Los Angeles, California; Lunceford, James Melvin (Jimmie); Moore, Richard Benjamin; Patterson, William; *Pittsburgh Courier*; Waller, Thomas Wright ("Fats"); Black Nationalism in the United States.

Africa

Comorians (also known as the Ngazija), ethnic group of the COMOROS.

The Comorians are people of mixed Bantu, MALAGASY, and Arab descent. They speak Comorian (or Ngazija), a Bantu language related to Swahili. Approximately 500,000 people consider themselves Comorians.

SEE ALSO

Bantu: Dispersion and Settlement; Swahili Language.

Africa

Comoros, an Indian Ocean island nation off southeast Africa.

The Comoro Islands is an archipelago country known for its perfumed crops – vanilla, ylang-ylang, and cloves – and a celebrated past awash in legends of early Jewish settlers and famous buccaneers. More recently, Comoros has earned a degree of notoriety as a home for mercenaries. On the four Comoro Islands – Njazidja, Nzwani, Mwali (formerly known as Grande Comore, Anjouan, Mohéli, respectively), and Mayotte – Islam is the predominant religion, but the influences of Arabic, African, MALAGASY, and European cultures are apparent both in the language and in daily life. Although the islands are a popular destination for European and South African tourists, they continue to struggle with problems they have faced since independence: low economic growth, scarce land and other resources, and chronic political instability.

EARLY HISTORY

The earliest visitors to the Comoro Islands may have been the Melano-Polynesian immigrants, who later settled nearby MADAGASCAR. Some scholars have suggested an early Jewish presence on the islands, based on the fact that many Comorians observe dietary restrictions and behavioral taboos associated with the Saturday Sabbath. The earliest archaeological evidence of widespread occupation dates to the tenth century C.E. East Africans, Persians, and Arabs are thought to have arrived around the thirteenth century, as the trade in gold, ivory, cloth, and other precious items increased between East Africa, Arabia, and India. As Arab traders stopped over on the islands while journeying between Madagascar and East African market towns such as Kilwa and Mombasa, the Comoros developed into an entrepôt where goods from Madagascar, including palm cloth, rice, and carved stone vessels, were exchanged for products from the mainland.

Some scholars, however, believe that it was not until after the Portuguese attacked Kilwa in 1506 that large numbers of Persians and Arabs settled permanently in the Comoros, where they developed independent urban centers, ruled by sultans, along the coasts. The Persians of the Comoros maintained close ties through marriage and trading with the SHIRAZI families of Kilwa and ZANZIBAR, who had themselves originally migrated from Shiraz, in Persia, during the first millennium. Other sources suggest that the Shirazi migrated from Persia to the Comorian island of Nzwani (or Anjouan), only later to disperse to East Africa. Whether the Shirazi were in fact Arab or Persian is debated. Today, they remain one of the country's largest ethnic groups.

When Portuguese and, later, other European merchant ships began to call at the Comoros in the sixteenth century, they found the islands controlled by multiple rival chiefdoms, such as Chingoni and Qualey on the island of Mayotte. Strife existed between these coastal sultanates and between the sultanates and communities living in the interior. Although the European powers did not at this point establish control over the islands, Dutch, French, and English ships later used them as a staging ground in their struggle against Portuguese domination in the southwest Indian Ocean. They traded iron for fresh supplies of water and food.

As European navies competed for control over Indian Ocean trade routes, the commerce in luxury goods stimulated the rise of piracy, which reached its height during the seventeenth and eighteenth centuries. The Comoro Islands offered pirates such as Davy Jones and Captain Kidd fresh water, a safe haven, and a strategic base for plundering European ships that passed through the Mozambique Channel while traveling to and from India. The islands' towns also provided markets for the pirates' stolen property. During the eighteenth century, however, European powers increased their military presence in the region. With the French navy established on Ile de France (present-day MAURITIUS) and English forces based on Anjouan, piracy became more risky.

During the eighteenth and nineteenth centuries, slaves became an increasingly important commodity in the Indian Ocean (*see* INDIAN OCEAN SLAVE TRADE). French plantations in the colonies of Ile de France, RÉUNION, and the SEYCHELLES created a tremendous demand for slave labor, much of which came from Madagascar. Arab merchants on the Comoros also sold slaves who had been captured in raids on village communities in the islands' interiors. Although many of the slaves were exported to neighboring islands, Comorian sultans also used slaves on SUGAR, clove, and sisal plantations.

As demand for slaves rose in the late eighteenth century, conflicts increased between the Comorian sultanates and chiefdoms, as well as between Comorian and Malagasy rulers. In the mid-1790s a sultan on the island of Anjouan asked his Betsimisaraka allies of northeastern Madagascar to raid his rivals in the nearby town of Mutsamundu. They went on to attack other Comorian communities, taking slaves as booty. Comorian sultans' desperate appeals to European powers for protection against Malagasy raids were ignored until 1816, when the British government intervened. That year, agents of Robert Farquare, the British governor of Mauritius, successfully pressured the Merina Empire of Madagascar to sign a treaty ending the slave trade. In the 1820s the Merina Empire overthrew the chief Malagasy raiders – the coastal SAKALAVA – and slave raids on the Comoros and elsewhere ended.

But the Merina-Sakalava rivalry had further implications for the Comoros. In 1828 the sultan of Anjouan, Abdallah, invited the Merina general Ramanataka to settle in the sultan's domain and help defeat his own enemies. Ultimately, Ramanataka established a Merina chiefdom on Anjouan. Not long afterward, the Sakalava leader Andriansouli joined relatives on Mayotte, and soon became one of the island's most powerful figures. Meanwhile, rulers on the island of Grande Comore (or Njazidja) maintained ties to the sultanate of Zanzibar and continued to resist alignment with European powers.

EUROPEAN INTERVENTION AND THE COLONIAL ERA

European colonization of the Comoro Islands came as a result of Anglo-French rivalry in the Indian Ocean. The process was gradual and occurred somewhat differently on each island. After the British won the Napoleonic Wars and established control of Mauritius in 1810, France looked to the Comoros as a base for preserving its regional influence. On Mayotte, they found a willing collaborator in Andriansouli, who signed a treaty in 1841 that established the island as a French protectorate. Great Britain responded by opening a consulate in Anjouan, ostensibly to monitor French adherence to antislavery treaties, but also to maintain intelligence of French activity in the region more generally.

Mayotte's local rulers provided French export firms with land to build plantations for the cultivation of sugar, vanilla, coffee, cacao, sisal, and other crops. Because Mayotte had been heavily depopulated by years of slave raids, the French looked to MOZAMBIQUE to supply contract labor. Although sugar production initially dominated Mayotte's economy, many plantations went bankrupt after world market prices fell in the 1890s.

The island of Mohéli (or Mwali) fell from the control of the Merina ruler Ramanataka when his heir married a Zanzibarian prince. Zanzibar controlled the island during the 1850s, until Merina nobles assumed command. The famous French entrepreneur Joseph François Lambert arrived on Mohéli in 1860 armed with a declaration by the Merina queen of Madagascar that granted Lambert complete ownership of the island. Lambert intended to share profits from plantation production with the queen. But the local population resisted, plundering Lambert's house in his absence. The French, meanwhile, sent the navy to reassert Lambert's claims. In 1886 the island became a neglected French protectorate; its local population remained poor and disfranchised in the following decades.

Grande Comore remained largely independent of European influence during the nineteenth century, though in 1843 the French secured the right to fell timber and recruit contract laborers from several sultans. The island's two dominant sultanates spent much of the century engaged in an extended conflict. In 1875 the French lent support to the powerful sultan of Bambao, Said Ali. Ali showed his appreciation by providing the French naturalist Léon Humblot concessions to as much land as he desired for plantations, as well as contract laborers. In return, Ali received 10 percent of all Humblot's profits. Angry sultans accused Ali of handing out land he did not own. One sultan acquired a German flag, which he had hoisted at Fumboni. In response, in 1883 the French declared the island a protectorate. Despite the occasional presence of the French military, popular uprisings forced Ali to flee the island twice; after the second time, he remained in Réunion until his death. Humblot became ruler of the island in 1892, but his reputation for tyranny and cruelty – children worked as forced laborers on his plantations – led to his removal by the French government four years later.

On the island of Anjouan, the sultan Abdallah established diplomatic ties with the British in 1844, hoping to legitimate his own authority and ward off French imperialism. British entrepreneurs, coming mostly from Mauritius, invested in plantations. They built a primary labor force of Arab-owned slaves, who were hired out as wage laborers, but whose owners confiscated most of their earnings. Abdallah's agreement to bring an end to slavery in 1882 alienated him from his Arab constituents. Unwilling to enact the unpopular law, and indebted to Mauritian

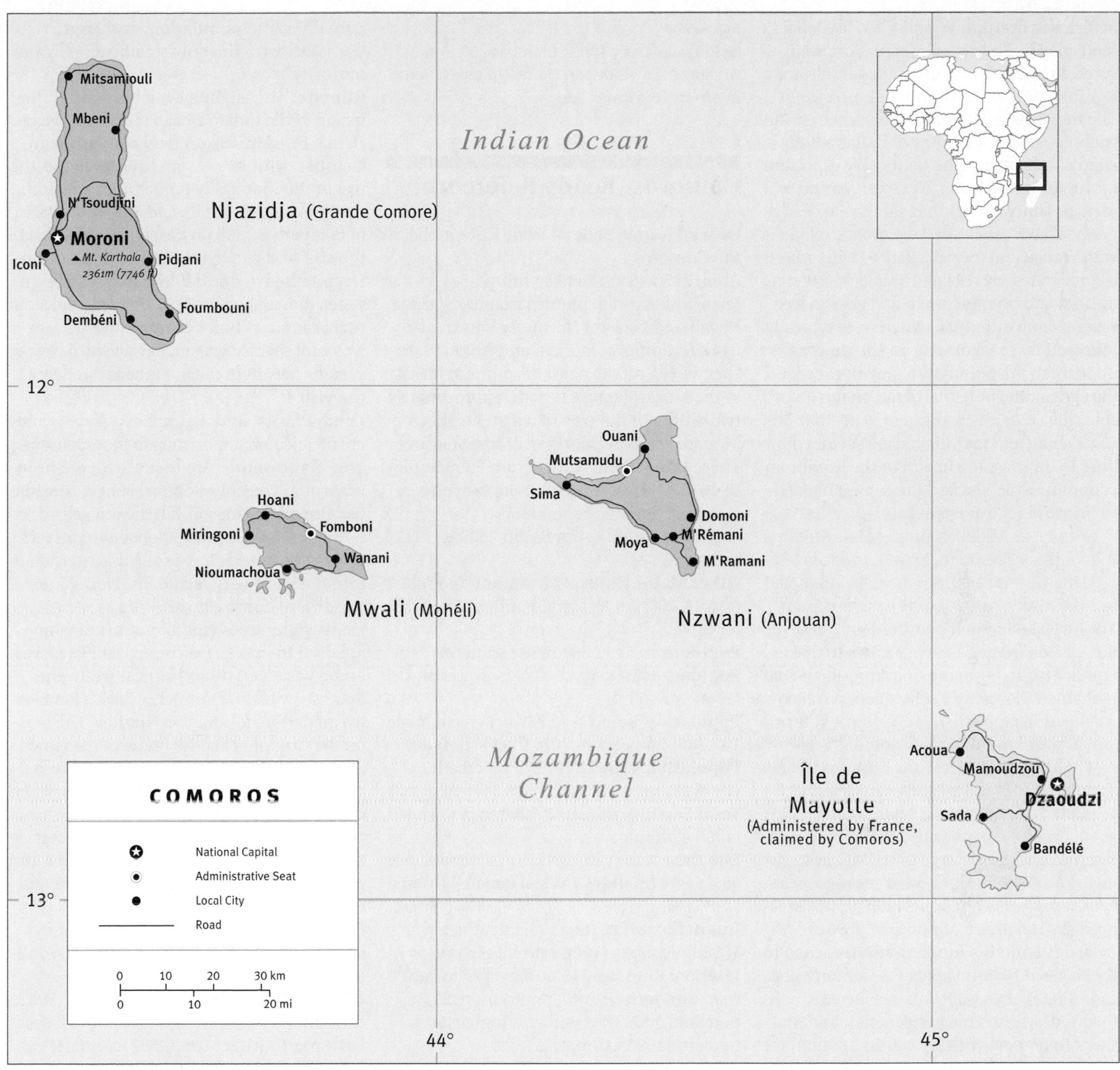

bankers, Abdallah initiated political ties with France. The French were quick to use deceit and the threat of force to gain control of Anjouan. By 1887 Abdallah had been stripped of most of his authority, and the French had forced him to abolish slavery. His land was parceled out to French colonists for plantation cultivation.

By 1909 all the islands were French protectorates. Three years later, they became part of the colony of Madagascar, and once resistant sultans were forced to abdicate to French authority. France invested little in the islands; until World War II, they ranked among the backwaters of the French Empire and were ruled from neighboring Madagascar. French companies dictated policy much as the sultans had previously, except that profits from cash-crop sales were diverted to France. During the 1920s and 1930s, many Comorians emigrated to Madagascar in search of employment. With only one secondary school for all of the Comoros, the islands offered few opportunities for advancement. Nor did they produce any significant indigenous political movements during this period.

Independence

During World War II, the British seized the Comoro Islands from Vichy France and handed them over to the Free French government, which later granted the colony greater autonomy as well as representation in the French parliament. In a 1958 popular referendum held within all French possessions, Comorians voted to remain a French territory, though with their own internal administration. Continued economic stagnation and French neglect, along with the death in 1970 of the moderate politician Said Mohammed Cheik, sparked calls for independence. In a 1974 vote the population reversed its initial decision in favor of full independence, with the exception of the inhabitants of Mayotte. As the center of French colonial administration, Mayotte had developed closer ties with Paris while distinguishing itself both linguistically and racially from the Arab-dominated rulers of the other islands of the Comoros. France thus retained control over Mayotte while granting independence to the other islands.

But this plan was unacceptable to the Comorian government. Led by President Ahmed Abdallah, in July 1975 the government unilaterally declared the independence of all the islands, including Mayotte. The United Nations recognized Comorian independence, but France refused to relinquish control over Mayotte. Relations between the two nations quickly worsened: France withdrew all support, and the Comorian government nationalized all French possessions. After only one month in office Abdallah was deposed in a coup led by Ali Soilih, with help from the French mercenary Bob Denard. Soilih's socialist government lasted until May 1978, when he in turn was overthrown and killed by Denard's mercenaries. Shortly afterward, Comorians voted to make the country a federal Islamic republic and elected Abdallah president. The mercenaries' continued presence on the islands – many served as Abdallah's bodyguards – resulted in the temporary expulsion of the Comoros from the Organization of African Unity (OAU) that same year.

Abdallah reestablished diplomatic relations with France and forged alliances with other Islamic states. He declared a single-party state in 1979, and over the next few years survived several coup attempts, which were typically followed by crackdowns on the political opposition. As population growth exceeded the agricultural potential of the islands' poor soils, the economy continued to decline. The tiny fishing and manufacturing sectors did little to improve the health of the Comorian economy, which lacked the capital needed to improve its infrastructure.

In 1989, as Abdallah prepared to run for a third term as president, he was assassinated by Denard's mercenaries, who then attempted to take direct control of the government. The arrival of French paratroopers, however, forced Denard and his colleagues to flee to SOUTH AFRICA. Supreme Court president Said Mohamed Djohar won subsequent presidential elections, promising economic reforms and a return to multiparty politics. But unrest continued. In 1991 the Supreme Court attempted to dismiss him for negligence; a year later, Djohar faced a failed coup attempt as well as strikers protesting World Bank and International Monetary Fund (IMF) austerity measures. The corrupt Djohar regime repeatedly outmaneuvered opposition groups seeking a greater share of political power.

Denard and his merceneries returned to the scene in 1995, invading the Comoros and capturing Djohar. Nine hundred French troops followed, arrested the mercenaries, and sent them to France. With Djohar in Réunion for medical treatment, Prime Minister Mohamed Caabi El Yachroutu stepped in as president. After the 1996 presidential elections, he was replaced by opposition leader Mohamed Taki Abdulkarim, and the country adopted a new constitution that embraced Islamic principles. Despite this change in government, the economy has remained weak and popular unrest continues.

In 1997 the islands of Anjouan and Mohéli announced their intention to secede: in light of the relatively high standard of living enjoyed by Mayotte, they wished to return to French administration. Initially, the French government affirmed its willingness to reincorporate the islands. Later, in a more cautious stance, it urged the OAU to find a peaceful settlement to the conflict. Troops from the capital of Moroni unsuccessfully tried to recapture Anjouan by force. As of the fall of 1998, no resolution to the political impasse had been reached.

Ari Nave

SEE ALSO

Gold Trade; Ivory Trade; Mombasa, Kenya; Organization of African Unity; United Nations in Africa; Tourism in Africa.

Africa

Comoros (Ready Reference)

Official Name: Federal Islamic Republic of the Comoros

Area: 2170 sq km (838 sq mi)

Location: A group of three islands, Njazidja, Mwali and Nzwani (formerly known as Grande Comore, Mohéli, and Anjouan, respectively), off the coast of southern Africa in the Mozambique Channel, approximately two-thirds of the way between northern MADAGASCAR and northern MOZAMBIQUE. These three islands broke from French rule in 1975, while a fourth island, Mayotte, remained a French dependency.

Capital: Moroni (population 25,600 [1993 estimate])

Other Major Cities: Mutsamudu (population 14,700) on Nzwani, Fomboni (8200) on Mwali

Population: 545,528 (1998 estimate)

Population Density: 500 persons per sq km (1300 per sq mi)

Population Below Age 15: 48 percent (male 137,235; female 136,207 [1996 estimate])

Population Growth Rate: 3.6 percent (1996 estimate)

Total Fertility Rate: 6.7 children per women (1996 estimate)

Life Expectancy at Birth: Total population: 58.7 years (male 56.4 years; female 61 years [1996 estimate])

Infant Mortality Rate: 75.3 deaths per 1000 live births (1996 estimate)

Literacy Rate (age 15 and over who can read and write): Total population: 57.3 percent (male 64.2 percent; female 50.4 percent [1995 estimate])

Education: Many children attend Islamic schools and state education is officially compulsory from age 7 to 16. Although 75 percent of the school-age group attend primary school, only 17 percent (20 percent of males, 15 percent of females) complete secondary schooling.

Languages: French and Arabic are the official languages, but most people use one of the island dialects, collectively called Shimasiwa. Shimasiwa dialects are related to Swahili.

Ethnic Groups: The population formed by successive settlements over at least 1000 years, including migrations from Madagascar. Residents trace lineage back to Kilwa, ZANZIBAR, islands off the coast of TANZANIA, and even Arabia and the Persian Gulf region. Some citizens descended from slaves from Mozambique. Today no strong ethnic conflicts divide the population; rivalries between the islands are more important than ethnic differences.

Religions: Sunni Muslims compose 86 percent of the population, and Roman Catholics form the only significant religious minority.

Climate: The islands, which lie within the region of the Indian Ocean monsoons, experience the dry season between April and October, with heavy rains and cyclones the rest of the year. Daily temperatures seldom rise above 30° C (85° F), and 5080 mm (200 in) of rain per year fall on the slopes of Karthala, the site of the heaviest rainfall in Comoros. Despite heavy rainfall, Njazdja retains no water, due to the porous nature of its volcanic rock. Islanders build cisterns to store rainwater for the dry season. In Nzwani, however, streams flow from the mountains throughout the year.

Land, Plants, and Animals: All three islands are of volcanic origin and are mountainous. The island shores are rocky, with offshore islets and a steeply sloping seabed. Njazidja has virtually no topsoil, but the volcanic rocks nevertheless support a dense rain forest. The other islands have soils that are rich in minerals and very fertile, providing ideal conditions for the growth of sugar cane, ylang-ylang trees (the blossoms of which are used to make a perfume), vanilla, cloves, and a wide variety of tropical fruits and flowers. A variety of flycatcher called Humblot's flycatcher breeds only on Njazidja. The seas off the Comoros are the home of the famous coelacanth, a fish that was thought to be extinct for millions of years until 1938, when one was caught live.

Natural Resources: Flowers and spices constitute the basic commercial crops and grow readily in the fertile soil of Mwali and Nzwani.

Currency: The Comorian franc

Gross Domestic Product (GDP): $400 million (1997 estimate)

GDP Real Growth Rate: 3.5 percent (1997 estimate)

GDP per Capita: $685 (1997 estimate)

Primary Economic Activities: Agriculture, horticulture, fishing, hunting, forestry, and tourism

Primary Crops: Vanilla, ylang-ylang, cloves, perfume oil, copra, and cassava (tapioca)

Industries: Tourism, perfume distillation, textiles, furniture, jewelry, construction materials, and soft drinks

Primary Exports: Vanilla, ylang-ylang, cloves, perfume oil, and copra

Primary Imports: Rice and other foodstuffs, petroleum products, cement, and consumer goods

Primary Trade Partners: France, SOUTH AFRICA, KENYA, and Japan

Government: After gaining independence from France in 1975, Comorans suffered a tumultuous 21 years of nationalist regimes, mercenary coups, and French intervention. In March 1996 Mohamed Taki Abdulkarim was elected president, in the first democratic elections of Comoros. The latest constitution was established in 1992. The president is elected for five years and can serve only two terms of office. The federal constitution allows each island to have autonomy in internal matters and to elect its own governor. The legislative branch of government comprises two multiparty houses, a federal assembly and a senate.

In 1997 Nzwani and Mwali attempted to secede from the Comorian government, possibly with the help of mercenaries. Citing corruption in the local government, secessionists sought to reunite with France. Although the revolt was put down and the French claimed no part in the affair, the future of Nzwani and Mwali is unclear.

Eric Bennett

SEE ALSO
Swahili Language.

Africa

Compaoré, Blaise (b. 1950, Ziniaré, Burkina Faso), president of BURKINA FASO (1987-).

Blaise Compaoré was born in Ziniaré. He joined the army, completed officers' training school in CAMEROON, and received a commission as second lieutenant in 1975. He met THOMAS SANKARA in 1978 in a paratroop commando class in MOROCCO, where they became close friends. When Sankara seized power in 1982 he named Compaoré minister of state to the presidency.

Soon afterward Compaoré and Sankara developed political and personal differences. Compaoré, fearing that he might be dismissed, led a violent coup in which Sankara and 13 government officers were executed in October 1987. Declaring himself president, Compaoré disarmed local militias and instituted a program of "rectification," ostensibly designed to resuscitate the nation's socialist revolution. In fact, he began moving Burkina Faso toward a market economy by privatizing state industries and implementing austerity measures. He also sought to improve relations with Western donors, especially France.

Compaoré formed the Organization for Popular Democracy-Labor Movement (French acronym, ODP-MT) as the new ruling party in April 1989 and pronounced a general amnesty for all political prisoners. In response to public unrest, he resigned his military commission in June 1991 and announced that he would run in multiparty elections as the civilian candidate of the ODP-MT, which would no longer endorse Marxist economic policies but rather free enterprise. Failed negotiations between the government and opposition groups about the democratic transition process erupted into violent clashes in October 1991, prompting the opposition to withdraw candidates and call for an election boycott. Compaoré, unopposed, won the election with only 22 percent of the electorate participating and was inaugurated in December 1991 for a seven-year term. Since then he has continued to liberalize the Burkina Faso economy as part of a World Bank structural adjustment plan. Although his role in the assassination of Sankara has not been forgotten at home, abroad he has sought to build a reputation as a regional peacemaker, by hosting and participating in talks aimed at resolving conflicts in neighboring countries.

SEE ALSO
Structural Adjustment in Africa.

Latin America and the Caribbean

Compas, Haiti's national dance music, which evolved from 1950s merengue and remained the dominant musical form well into the 1980s.

In HAITI in the 1940s, the pioneering sound of popular music was that of merengue and *voodoo-jazz*. There is a long history of heated debate between Dominicans and Haitians about which group originated the merengue. The primary difference between the two country's merengue forms is that the Haitian version favors a slower tempo and the guitar rather than accordion. Voodoo-jazz, which was born during the period of United States occupation (1915-1934), flavored the Afro-Haitian rhythms of VODOU ritual music with American swing JAZZ. Bandleader and saxophonist Jean-Baptiste Nemours unveiled a new dance in 1955 that would revolutionize Haitian music. Based on merengue, his adaptations slowed the dance's tempo and simplified its melodies. His guitarist termed the music *compas direct* (also spelled *kompa-dirék*), meaning "straight-ahead beat." Bass drums and hi-hat snares, cowbells, and guitars gave compas a distinct feel from merengue.

As Nemours rose in popularity, his house orchestra's fame challenged that of Haiti's reigning orchestra, Les Jazz des Jeunes. The danceability of compas was zealously embraced by audiences who lacked the special training to perform dances accompanying the voodoo-jazz of Les Jazz des Jeunes. Nemours soon emerged triumphant. By 1957 compas had established itself as the dominant musical form in Haiti.

The next decade came to be known as the *epòk polemik Nemou ak Siko* because of the rivalry between Nemours and his former band mate, saxophonist Wéber Sicot. Sicot's compas ensemble performed a Cuban-tinged variant of compas that he termed *cadence rampa*. Meaning "rampart cadence," the term heralded Scott's challenge to Nemours "from the ramparts." Imitation, appropriation, boasting, and outright mockery were the tools of choice for the feuding saxophonists. Fans loved the "polemic" between the Super Ensemble Compas Direct de Jean-Baptiste Nemours and Super Ensemble Cadence Rampa de Wéber Sicot, and the overall popularity of compas was heightened.

Haiti's dictator FRANÇOIS DUVALIER sought association with compas to enhance his political and social appeal. Scott, Nemours, and other favorites were regularly forced to perform at private political functions. When diversions from tyrannical dictatorship were needed, Duvalier would fund a *koudjay* party and feature compas music. These open street parties proffered free food, drink, and dancing to their lower-class participants. The fearsome secret police known as the TONTON MACOUTES would coerce their favorite compas bands into a koudjay performance, demand pro-governmental lyrics, and forbid the singing of any questionable tunes. In this repressive political climate compas bands were quite literally forced to sing romantic songs and songs of musical boasting.

Music protesting Duvalier's rule first appeared in the Haitian diaspora – out of reach of the Tonton Macoutes. Since Duvalier's rule, enormous numbers of upper- and middle-class Haitians have fled the nation, along with artists, activists, politicians, and musicians fearing governmental oppression. The largest diasporic Haitian communities are in New York and Miami.

Troubadour-style singer MANNO CHARLEMAGNE was the groundbreaking force in protest music performed inside Haiti. From 1978 onward Charlemagne has braved death threats, jail, and exile to produce music committed to the struggles of working-class Haitians. Charlemagne's poetic lyrics contain trenchant political commentary, and his body of work is highly influential.

Jace Clayton

SEE ALSO
Merengue: Music, Race and Nation in the Dominican Republic; Nemours, Jean Baptiste and Sicot, Wéber; New York, New York.

Latin America and the Caribbean

Complexities of Ethnic and Racial Terminology in Latin America and the Caribbean

An ethnonym is an ethnic or racial name or phrase that identifies a group of human beings in a social framework according to traits of geography, nation, parlance, phenotype, and other oblique cultural references. Ethnonyms can evoke disgust, derision, jocularity, facetiousness, irony, humor,and other emotional responses through caricature, irony, sarcasm, and other figures of speech. These labels not only characterize a group of people but also reveal the myriad historical, social, and migrational circumstances of their corresponding geographic areas. The many different types of contact among Europeans, Native American groups, and Africans in the Americas brought about fascinating new terms and word combinations for groups that existed at that time, as well as new ethnonyms for multiracial people resulting from miscegenation (*see* Race in Latin America).

Ethnonyms that Latin Americans and Latin Caribbeans – that is, speakers of Spanish, Portuguese, and French or French-influenced Creoles in the Americas – apply to each other run the gamut from names for black people, white people, indigenous peoples (also called Indians or American Indians), Asians, and multiracials. With regard to the terms most often applied to people of African descent, Latin Americans and Latin Caribbeans show a great propensity toward disparagement, pejoration, irony for comic effect, and caricature. For example, the Brazilian Portuguese words *tição*, meaning a piece of lit or partially burnt firewood, and *tição apagado,* meaning a piece of burnt-out wood or charcoal, connote, respectively, a black person and a black person dressed all in black. The image constructed by nonblacks who use these labels – that of an object not easily detectable in the dark – imposes inanimate status and "comical" qualities on black persons as they choose a mode of dress, even if it might be appropriate for the social occasion.

These two labels are not the only ones used as caricatured nicknames for black people in Brazil (*see* Race and Class in Brazil: An Interpretation). One of the other, more revealing caricatural ethnonyms is not a single word either but rather a phrase, specifically *pessoa que tem um pé na África,* or a person who has a foot in Africa, that is, someone who is part black. The notion of the foot in Africa synthesizes Brazilian attitudes toward blacks, in that disparagement is often implicit but not overtly stated. Brazilians can use this phrase to reflect one of the society's basic preconceptions: *things* from Africa that have been incorporated into Brazilian culture (food, religion, language, and so on) are to be extolled, but *people* of African descent are to be despised, no matter how partial that descent may be. Similar to the phrase *preto de alma branca,* or black person with a white soul, *pessoa que tem um pé na África* belittles by representing the person as not-white. These constructs reflect Brazilian social conditions that still perceive blacks as inferior to whites and that give things European sway over things African with regard to culture, language, and ethnicity.

Another distinguishing example of the Latin American penchant for caricature and derogation is seen in the use of animal labels for humans. The *urubu* is a type of black buzzard found all over Brazil. The label "urubu" has come to designate both a black person, because of the black color, and an Indian group found in the northeastern Brazilian state of Maranhão. *Babún* (baboon) connotes a black person or mulatto in twentieth-century Cuba. The implication is that people of African descent are more apelike than are non-Africans, an age-old comparison that has not lost its comedic edge for some. A similar usage can be found in the Southern American English phrases *yard ape* and *porch monkey,* highly derogatory epithets used for blacks by some whites. *Black buzzard* also exists in Southern American English as a white racist riposte to a black person perceived as bad or unfit. Since the buzzard is a scavenger, despised as one of the lowest forms of carnivore, calling a human a "buzzard" bolsters the injurious effect.

The Cuban expression *fósforo apagado,* or burnt-out match, connoting a black person dressed all in white, and the infamous *negro catedrático,* or "professor blacky," implying an uppity black – a parody common in both colonial and postcolonial Spanish American society – conjure visual and cultural images of blacks. The negro catedrático stands out as one of the most stereotypically negative ethnonyms for "black person" in Spanish America. Generally used in the Hispanic Antilles in the lampooning of a male of African descent, this term designates in a derogatory fashion a black person who feigns education or misuses language in a vain attempt to show that he is educated. The black person who speaks and acts with affected intelligence and polish is so designated on the basis of a certain theatrical type of black developed in nineteenth-century Cuban literature. This black theatrical character may represent the continuation of a medieval theatrical mockery of a black or Moorish character who spoke the European language in some bastardized form, usually one with Creole-like features. We know, for example, that Sabir, or Mediterranean Lingua Franca, was the language of commerce and the Crusades. Molière's use of this jargon in *Le bourgeois gentilhomme* to characterize the speech patterns of non-French also comes to mind in this instance. Such stereotypical features also figure in the history of Iberian letters as well, especially when the author is writing dialogue that features Africans or Muslims, or persons rudely labeled "blackamoors."

The question of what effects African influences have had on the languages of the Americas has often been asked. Although African terms are less numerous than words brought from Europe, Africans have inscribed their mark on Latin American and Caribbean ethnonymy. In Brazil, for example, one can find relatively numerous terms, most of which refer to Africans, originating in the Niger-Congo family of languages. This collection of terms includes *aça, candando, mganga, mumbanda, zumbi* from the kiMbundu language; *babá, jagunço, quêto* from Yoruba; *angolo* from Umbundu; *cabinda* from kiKongo; *banguela* from Banguela; *mbembo* from Lingala; and *quilombola* from a Bantu variety. The expatriation of African slaves from the West African coast underlies the derivation of these terms from the Niger-Congo family.

It is not surprising that some ethnonyms of African or possible African origin or those used by Africans in Brazil have the meaning "white person": *candango, carcamano, chena, gazula, mazombo, mbembo, mganga, mundele, sinhá, sinhô,* and *tango-mau,* among others. One might expect that all these labels meaning "white person" would carry pejorative connotations, but, on the contrary, most were of a respectful nature.

Caricatures employing physical characteristics generally focus on a prominent part of the body. Many point to the reputed large buttocks of those of African ancestry; thus, the Dominican Spanish word *culón,* or *culona,* meaning a person with a big bottom, refers to any person, but especially a black person, who has a large derrière. This allusion is common in other parts of the Caribbean, but especially in Jamaica, where the younger generations refer to a woman with a large bottom as a *chair,* because you can ostensibly sit on her rear. The Dominican and Jamaican words are at the same time derogatory, jocular, and sexist, depending on the conversation in which they are used, since both conjure up stigmatized images of large-bottomed black women. Similarly, Afro-Uruguayans call certain other blacks *negros de canilla fina,* or blacks with thin legs, in an attempt to be jocular.

The use of irony for comic or derogatory effect in Spanish America also prevails with regard to physical traits caricatured. The examples of *rubio,* or blond, and *capirro,* or red-headed, with reference to black people are a case in point. Consider the effect that NBA star Dennis Rodman's bleached blond hair had on crowds and the media; during the 1993-1994 basketball season Rodman, an African American, was the focus of many TV outtakes. These "opposites," actually bolster negative "images," and cause exaggerated, and thus comedic, reactions by overstating the unexpected.

Materials or substances with a dark or black color, including *tizón* (smudge, smut, or burnt piece of wood); *chapapote* (asphalt, pitch); *azabache* (jet); *negro azul* (blue black); *tinterillo* (ink user); and *coca cola* (see below) are used as ethnonyms for black people in American Spanish. Both *chapapote* and *negro como el chapapote* refer to the very dark skin color of blacks, and like *negro como el azabache* (black as jet), have a cousin in the Southern American English phrase *dark* or *black as pitch,* used in regard both to people and to things that are dark. Words such as *carbón* (coal), *teléfono* (telephone), *betún* (shoe polish), *chorizo* (sausage), *chocolate* (chocolate), and *charol* (patent leather) constitute segments of other phrases that caricature blacks in Spanish America, usually to complete a phrase like "*negro como un/el* ___" ("black as a ___"). Other such phrases include *negro como boca de lobo* (black as a wolf's mouth); *negro como el aura tiñosa* (black as a hurricane wind); *negro como el totí* (black as the totí, a very black bird native to Cuba); and *negro como mi alma* (black as my soul), all of which are used among Cubans and Cuban-Americans. Although not restricted to Cubans, these types of expressions, when placed in sequence with other selected terms, depict the black person in negative terms.

The combination of another ethnonym with *coca cola* (the product Coca-Cola®) creates an engaging dilemma: the person so described may not be black but rather just dark-skinned. The ethnonyms *mulato coca cola, prieto coca cola,* and *pardo coca cola* all indicate dark skin color, no matter the race of person, but the phrase *blanco coca cola* could leave listeners confused if they did not understand that skin color in Spanish American parlance does not always correspond to race.

In contrast, Haitians tend to speak of persons of African descent in terms of physical traits, but not just skin color, with hair texture acquiring high priority. For example, Haitian Creole *poivre,* also *pouav* or *pwav* (pepper), refers to a person with kinky hair texture, while *têt grèn* connotes a person with very kinky, short, tightly curled hair texture. *Têt gridap, grèn pouav,* and *pouav portori* imply a person with the most kinky short-hair texture. *Têt kròt,* literally meaning dung head, connotes a person with the most kinky hair texture, so short that it must be cut into small tresses for women. *Têt papou,* or Papuan head, refers to a person with the hair texture of an African, and *têt soua,* or silky head, refers to a person with silky hair.

Haiti's racial and ethnic realities are analogous to those of Spanish-speaking America. In her 1907 studies of racionomics in Haiti, Micheline Labelle identified two opposing racial classes: *noir* and *mulâtre.* These racial classes have been in conflict at the sociopolitical and economic levels since the colonial period. Cultural and racial struggles, according to Labelle, continue between the dominant classes, usually, if not always, constituted of mulattos (of African and European descent), and the lower classes, usually, if not always, formed of blacks. The aspiration to the dominant class is seen in the lexical manifestations and gradations Haitians employ to describe each other. Since the lower classes wish to improve their socioeconomic position, their quest is directed toward the social strata of mulattos. In the process, people of both classes endure the vagaries of racial designation as they renegotiate their social identities and have their racial identities renegotiated for them.

Regarding avoidance, Frederic G. Cassidy has cited increased miscegenation, abolition of the slave trade and slavery, and more universal rights as reasons that racial terms fall into disuse. His Jamaican English examples – *sambo,* or dark-skinned person; *middle-a-white,* or mulatto, among blacks; the insulting *red-Eboe* – reflect manners in which speakers may refer to themselves or others, as the social situation warrants. American English also provides examples, although in restricted use, of "in between" racial categories such as *high yellow;* these terms reflect the Anglo-American preoccupation with distinctions by color and ancestry with little regard to social factors. In the Anglo-American context, therefore, one is either white or not, that is, white or "other." In Brazil and Spanish America the concept of *limpeza de sangue* or *limpieza de sangre* (purebloodedness) fomented the process of "passing," or attempting to pass from a perceived lower race to a higher one (*see* WHITENING).

Terms referring generally to an English mulatto, or a person having one black and one white parent, abound in Spanish America, Brazil, and the French-influenced Americas. The sociohistorical and linguistic implications of such multilayered phrases progress from the simple lexeme (Spanish *mulato*) to the more complex derivation (Spanish *mulato pardo, mulato oscuro*) to the use of other terms for mulatto (Spanish *chino, mestizo, persona de color*). These and other terms may clarify the implications of the racial and ethnic caste systems of Spanish American societies. Euphemisms for blacks and people of mixed race from the colonial period included *pardo* (brown); *que se tenga por español* (taken for a white Spaniard); *recibido por español* (received as a white Spaniard); and *moreno* (brown, brunette). Such euphemisms attest to the fact that most Spanish officials, when confronted with the necessity of identifying a person's race, used the label *españoles,* or Spaniards, to designate those who were not definitely Indian or dark-skinned. Distinctions were then made between *españoles europeos,* or European Spaniards (that is, white), and *españoles americanos,* or American Spaniards (that is, maybe not totally white).

If there is a single term with a "global" presence, it has to be "mulatto"; labels that include or imply it are found in all African-influenced societies in the Americas. In Spanish America the labels which have been coined mainly in the twentieth century to refer to mulattos, include *abejón colorado* (red-haired mulatto) in the Dominican Republic; *blanquito de Santiago* (little white from Santiago) in Cuba; *grifo* in various parts of Spanish America; *mulato de tez cremosa* (creamy-skinned mulatto) in VENEZUELA; *zambo* in PERU; and *muzuruto* in ARGENTINA. No fixed pattern exists that will predict what term or terms emerge in a given location; most of those that do appear are usually restricted in use by country or region.

In the French-influenced Americas (Haiti, Canada, Louisiana in the United States, and Martinique), such terms as *mulâtre, milat, griffe,* and *gens de couleur* are used for "mulatto." Just as in Spanish America, French and French Creoles are rife with ethnonyms for the black-white racial cross, including *gens de couleur* (people of color), *milate,* and *café au lait* (coffee-and-milk-colored). French and French Creole speakers, like Spanish-speaking Americans, attempt to clarify their racial system by modifying the standard *mulâtre,* as in the oxymoron *mulâtre sang pur* (pureblooded mulatto).

In Brazilian Portuguese, designations for "mulatto" are ample, as in the examples *araçuaba, curiboca, moreno, mulato, mulato bem claro,* and *mulato caboclo.* Others consist of *moreno* in Paraná state; *branco da Bahia* (white from Bahia) in Bahia state and other areas; *sarará crioulo* (native-born mulatto); and *pessoa de cor* (person of color). Throughout the Americas the configuration of terms is bounded by place of use and defies any logical explanation for their existence or use.

The intersection of languages and cultures in Latin America and the Latin Caribbean took its cues from the Europeanization of the Americas after 1492. The ethnonyms found in the Americas transcend national boundaries and are ingrained in the very fabric of their societies. In essence, racial and ethnic terminology is an early example of the globalizing effect of cross-cultural contacts in the Americas.

Thomas Stephens

See Also

Nyerere, Julius Kambarage; Transatlantic Slave Trade; Uruguay; Crusades; Dominican Republic; Haiti; Abolition and Emancipation in Latin America and the Caribbean.

Africa

Conakry, Guinea, capital of GUINEA.

Conakry is on Guinea's Atlantic coast and is the nation's largest deep-water port. It originally comprised only Tombo Island, but today includes the Los Islands and the tip of Kaloum Peninsula, to which Tombo is connected by a causeway. The climate is tropical; much of the surrounding area is swampland.

The city's name comes from the language spoken by the Susa ethnic group that has dominated coastal Guinea since the seventeenth century. Conakry was originally a Susa fishing village. The French chose the site for a town in 1880. The town became the capital of French Guinea when the French declared Guinea a colony in 1891.

When the country gained independence under Ahmad Sekou Touré in 1958, Conakry remained its capital and became increasingly important as a processing and trading center for the iron ore and bauxite mined in the surrounding regions. Today, Conakry is Guinea's main deep-sea port and the site of the country's principal international airport. Conakry is also the country's political, cultural, and financial center.

Once the jewel of French colonialism, Conakry suffered immense poverty after independence. Four decades later, hunger remains common. Neglect of Guinea's rural economy has driven thousands of Guineans to leave the countryside and seek work in the city. Refugees from wars in neighboring SIERRA LEONE and LIBERIA have also swelled the city's population in recent years. As a result, the city has expanded rapidly. Its population in 1970 was estimated at 200,000; today it is believed to be over a million.

Kate Tuttle

See Also
Iron in Africa; Touré, Sékou; Soso.

Latin America and the Caribbean

Condé, Maryse (b. February 11, 1937, Pointe-à-Pitre, Guadeloupe), novelist, playwright, essayist, and teacher whose innovative, lyrical works explore the vicissitudes of self-imposed exile from one's home and one's people.

It would not be inappropriate to refer to Maryse Condé as a "restless soul." Born the last of eight children, she was raised in Guadeloupe and was sent to boarding school in Paris, partly because of her extreme boredom in local schools, at age 16. At the Lycée Fénelon in Paris, Condé developed a love of literature that was dormant during her years in Guadeloupe. In Paris she became acquainted with Marxist anticolonial circles, joining the Communist Youth movement in the mid-1950s.

While attending the Jean Genet play *Les Nègres* at the end of the decade, she met and fell in love with one of the actors, a Guinean named Mamadou Condé. (She would later say of the man she married in August 1959 that she fell in love with the character he played in *Les Nègres*.) They left for Africa in 1960; Condé's husband returned directly to his homeland and Condé herself initially spent some time in Côte d'Ivoire as a teacher. She was indifferent about this first contact with Africa, but was profoundly disillusioned by Ahmad Sekou Touré's Guinea, where she joined her husband later that year. After an initial period of exuberance in this newly independent country, she came to see Touré as more of an opportunist than a socialist (*see* African Socialism). Furthermore, she was treated as a complete outsider in her new home (the Guineans referred to her as "white," a cultural rather than racial insult given that both her parents were black).

In 1964, as the political situation in Guinea (and her marriage) broke down, Condé moved with her children to Ghana. Ghana's post-independence president, Kwame Nkrumah, was for Condé the embodiment of the just and charismatic socialist leader. Once again, though, Condé was forced to move, leaving in 1966 for London following Nkrumah's forced exile to Guinea. After three years of work for the British Broadcasting Corporation, she and her children uprooted themselves once more and returned to Africa, settling in Senegal, where she resumed teaching. There she met her second husband, Richard Philcox, a white Briton. Their relationship did and continues to elicit accusations that Condé betrayed her race by marrying a white, further complicating her connection to race consciousness movements (*see* Blackness in Latin America and the Caribbean: An Interpretation).

At about this time Condé grew frustrated with Africa and decided to return to France to finish her degree. While in Paris, she also worked as an editor at *Présence Africaine* (*see* Alioune Diop) and hosted a program on Francophone literature on Radio France Internationale. After completing her doctoral thesis, Condé began teaching at the university level, first in France and then in the United States, where her works were more positively received than in Europe or Africa. From 1978, when she had her first United States teaching post in the black studies department at the University of California at Santa Barbara, until the present, Condé has split her time between teaching appointments in the United States and summers in her native Guadeloupe. She currently teaches at Columbia University in New York City.

Condé's nomadic existence has had a profound impact on her works. Her first work, a play titled *Dieu nous l'a donné* (1972), centers on a Guadeloupean doctor trained in Paris who returns to his native village, and the conflict that ensues between traditional and modern medicine. Condé's first novel, *Hérémakhonon* (1976), is written in a style that has been compared to the "nouveau roman" (literally "new novel" or antinovel). This literary movement, which was spearheaded by the French novelist Robbe-Grillet during the 1950s, promoted the idea of a purely objective fiction. *Hérémakhonon* recounts the story of a young woman who travels from the Caribbean to Africa to find her place in the world. Becoming disillusioned, she eventually returns home.

Une saison à Rihata (1981, A Season in Rihata), her second novel, also describes the incursion of a foreign woman in the African context, this time into a love triangle that has a fictionalized Zaire as its background. Her breakthrough works are the two volumes of historical fiction *Ségou* (1984, Segu and The Children of Segu), which tell the story of an African family over the course of four generations from the time of the Bambara kingdom (Mali) to the era of French colonialism. Condé explores both the greatness and the decline of an African people through the life of one family. Her next work, a collection of stories titled *Pays mêlé* (1985), evokes the Caribbean. These stories represent a shift in orientation from Africa to the Americas that would be confirmed by her first work written in (and about) the United States: *Moi, Tituba, sorcière: Noire de Salem* (1986, I, Tituba, Black Witch of Salem). This work relates the true story of a black slave who is put on trial in Salem but is set free after admitting to practicing the witchcraft she had learned as a young woman in Barbados. The Caribbean is the setting for *La vie scélérate* (1987; Tree of Life), an exploration of class conflict in Guadeloupe, and in *Traversée de la Mangrove* (1989; Crossing the Mangrove), which returns to the theme of the outsider in Guadeloupe. Her most recent novels are *Les derniers rois mages* (1992), *La colonie du nouveau monde* (1993), and *Desirada* (1997).

Condé's novels and plays are as concerned with aesthetic innovation as with political demystification. Although her remarkable style has been roundly praised, her puncturing of African and Caribbean myths has raised the ire of many critics. This constant challenging of prevalent myths about the Caribbean is largely the result of an itinerant existence that renders impossible the belief in fixed cultural norms. Condé herself explains it this way: "What interests me is the intersection of cultures and the conflicts and changes that result from it."

Richard Watts

See Also
Touré, Sékou; New York, New York; Literature, French Language, in Caribbean; London, Blacks in: An Interpretation.

North America

Cone, James Hal (b. August 5, 1938, Fordyce, Ark.), African American theologian who articulates a black theology of liberation.

In 1969, a year after the assassination of Martin Luther King Jr., James H. Cone published *Black Theology and Black Power*, a treatise that called liberation the center of the Christian Gospel, and the blackness expressed in black consciousness the only tool of liberation. This formulation of a uniquely black theology saw Jesus and the Bible as identified with the poor and exploited, and Black Power as divinely inspired resistance against racial oppression.

Cone's thesis drew upon his own deep involvement in the African Methodist Episcopal Church; the strength of the black Arkansas community in which he was nurtured; and the influence of Malcolm X's cultural critique of mainstream Christianity. The son of Lucille Cone, a homemaker, and Charlie Cone, a woodcutter, James Cone attended Philander Smith College, Garrett Theological Seminary, and Northwestern University. He taught at Adrian College, Philander Smith College, and, after the publication of *Black Theology and Black Power*, joined the faculty of Union Theological Seminary in New York. He was promoted to full professor in 1973, and was named Charles A. Briggs Professor of Systematic Theology in 1977.

Although he grew up in the tradition of Martin Luther King Jr., Cone continues to be strongly influenced by Malcolm X, who said, "I believe in a religion that believes in freedom." In *Malcolm and Martin in America* (1991), Cone argues that the two leaders were in fact moving closer to each other, as King became more radical and Malcolm more moderate.

Cone's other publications include *A Black Theology of Liberation* (1970), *The Spirituals and the Blues* (1972), *The God of the Oppressed* (1975), and *For My People: Black Theology and the Black Church* (1984).

Richard Newman

See Also
King, Martin Luther, Jr.

Latin America and the Caribbean

Confiant, Raphaël (b. 1951, Le Lorrain, Martinique), novelist, essayist, and leading figure, together with Patrick Chamoiseau, of the Créolité movement.

Like many people on Martinique, Raphaël Confiant was raised to speak two languages: Creole at home and French in school or at work (*see* Languages, Creole, in the Caribbean). He developed an attachment to Creole, the oft-maligned spoken language of his island, and the underclass culture associated with it. With an eye toward gaining acceptance for Creole as a literary language, Confiant wrote his first five novels in this idiom. Influenced by authors such as the Haitian Franck Etienne (*Dézafi*, 1975) and the Martinican Gilbert Gratiant (*Fab' Compè Zicaque*, 1958), who were among the first to write in Creole, these works present the diversity of Creole culture in Martinique. Their lack of popular success, resulting in part from a limited Creole-reading audience, convinced Confiant that his subsequent novels should be published in French. But Confiant did not give up on Creole. His more widely read and appreciated novels, such as *Le nègre et l'Emiral* (1988), *Eau de café* (1991), *Commandeur du sucre* (1994), and *Le bassin de Joséphine* (1997), are written in a type of French that is heavily inflected by Creole. Instead of pushing the spoken language of Creole toward a written form, he has endeavored to make written French more "oral" and therefore more representative of Martinican popular culture.

Confiant's attempts to rehabilitate the Creole language and culture place him in opposition to the most important Martinican writer of the previous generation, Aimé Césaire. As Confiant asserts in *Eloge de la créolité* (1989; In Praise of Creoleness, translated in 1993), cowritten with Patrick Chamoiseau and Jean Bernabé, and in *Aimé Césaire: Une traversée paradoxale du siècle* (1993), Césaire and the Négritude movement were excessively invested in the struggle between black and white. As a result they overlooked the other peoples that create Martinique's unique cultural identity: the Chinese, Lebanese, East Indian, and other immigrants who have come to the island in the last 150 years as well as the Amerindians who populated the island before the arrival of Christopher Columbus.

Confiant's novels reflect the many voices that are obliged to interact in Martinique because of the historical forces that have put them there. Many of the novels' characters are products of the racial and cultural intermingling that has occurred in Martinique since slaves first arrived in 1640. The author himself is of Chinese and African descent, a mixture referred to in Martinique as *chabin*. Confiant's preoccupation with racial and cultural diversity in Martinique has been called a form of neo-exoticism by the Guadeloupean critic Willy Alante-Lima, but most critics see Confiant's fiction as indicating a path for moving beyond the black-white opposition that concerned most Martinican writers at the middle of this century.

Richard Watts

See Also
East Indian Communities in the Caribbean; Literature, French Language, in Caribbean.

Congo. Please see Kongo

Africa

Congo, Belgian. Former name of the Democratic Republic of the Congo.

Congo-Brazzaville. Please see Congo, Republic of the

Africa

Congo, Democratic Republic of the, the largest country in Central Africa, bordering nine other countries and the Atlantic Ocean.

One of the largest and most ethnically diverse African countries, the Democratic Republic of the Congo (henceforth Congo) is extremely rich in natural resources, including diamonds, copper, and gold, as well as the enormous hydroelectric potential of the Congo River. Historically, however, these resources have benefited only the political and commercial elite. Subject to one of the most oppressive regimes in all of colonial Africa, then to the 32-year rule of Mobutu Sese Seko, Congo is now impoverished and unstable. In 1996 rebel leader Laurent-Désiré Kabila rode to power on promises to revitalize and democratize the country. As Kabila settles into the presidency, the Congolese population and the international community wait to determine whether he can, in fact, govern this vast, diverse nation.

Precolonial History

Although relatively little is known about the early history of the Congo, it is believed that the first inhabitants were Pygmies who lived as hunter-gatherers in the rain forests of the northwest. During the first millennium B.C.E. Bantu-speaking peoples migrated from the north and settled throughout the Congo basin. They established agricultural communities and, after contacts with non-Bantu-speaking people, herded cattle. Some of these communities were eventually incorporated into relatively centralized states such as the fourteenth-century Kongo at the mouth of the Congo River, and the fifteenth-century Luba and Lunda kingdoms to the west of Lake Tanganyika. Other smaller states in the Congo basin area included the Teke, the Kuba, and the Chokwe.

The first documented contact with Europeans occurred in 1483, when a Portuguese explorer, Diogo Cão, sailed into the mouth of the Zaire River and encountered Kongo villages. Two years later, he took a group of Kongo emissaries back to Portugal. The group returned to Africa in 1491 with priests, soldiers, and European goods. The emissaries and Portuguese baptized the Kongo king, Nzinga a Nkuwu, and built a Catholic church in the capital. Although Nzinga a Nkuwu later abandoned Catholicism, his son, Nzinga Mbembe (later Afonso), became a devoted Christian. Upon his accession he made Catholicism the state religion.

Subsequent relations between the Kongo and the Portuguese were based on missionary pursuits and trade. Afonso encouraged missionaries to Christianize the Kongo. He also traded slaves and ivory to the Portuguese in exchange for European luxury goods to increase his prestige and authority. The slave trade, however, eventually resulted in the demise of the Kongo kingdom. Kongolese slave raids on neighboring peoples, including the Teke and Kuba, led to retaliation and wars, such as the Jaga War in 1569, that eventually destroyed the Kongo kingdom. Neighboring states such as the Luba and Lunda continued selling slaves and ivory to the Europeans through the late nineteenth century.

The Congo Free State

In 1874 the Anglo American journalist Henry Morton Stanley was commissioned by the *New York Herald* and the *Daily Telegraph* to complete the explorations of David Livingstone, a Scottish missionary who had spent several years mapping the Congo basin. For three years, Stanley explored the Zaire River. In 1877 he returned to Europe, where his reports of the region's untapped natural wealth caught the attention of King Leopold II of Belgium, who was keen to extend his personal domain. Leopold hired Stanley to return to the Congo basin to secure treaties with local chiefs and establish the contracts required to form a commercial monopoly, which would be called the African International Association. Stanley also put hundreds of men, both European and African, to work building a road along the Congo River. Leopold's actions spurred the Scramble for Africa, in which other European powers quickly staked claims to other parts of the continent and then met to formalize their claims at the Berlin West Africa Conference (1884-1885). There, Leopold was recognized as the legitimate authority in the region. In return, he promised to provide European traders and missionaries free access to the territory, which he named the Congo Free State.

Leopold subsequently declared all land not actively occupied or cultivated to be "vacant land" belonging to him and the Free State government. He also appropriated land that was not vacant, which led to violent conflicts between the Free State military, the Force Publique, and the region's powerful traders, Tippu Tip and Msiri. Keeping a significant portion of the territory for his own enterprises, Leopold granted vast concessions of land to various companies for mining, rubber tapping, and railroad construction. Free State companies, including Leopold's, regularly used threats of torture and execution to force Africans to tap rubber or work in the mines. Reporting on the conditions in the rubber-tapping regions, Rev. J. B. Murphy wrote that the system of compulsory labor had "reduced people to states of utter despair. Each town in the district is forced to bring a certain quantity of rubber to the headquarters of the commissaire every Sunday. If they will not they are shot down, and their left hands cut off and taken as trophies to the commissaire." Under the Congo Free State, the Congolese population dropped between one-third and one-half due to famine, epidemics, and state-sponsored violence. By 1900 the brutality of the Congo Free State was notorious. International groups pressed for reform, which the Free State haphazardly instituted in 1906. By 1908, however, it was clear that the reforms had been unsuccessful and Leopold, anxious to relieve himself of a burgeoning debt, handed the colony over to the Belgian government, which renamed it the Belgian Congo.

Belgian Congo

Although the new colonial government promised to abolish Leopold's abusive practices, it was also keenly aware that the colony must remain a profitable venture. As a result, the African population saw few real improvements. For example, the government prohibited slave labor but imposed high taxes, which effectively forced adult males to continue working for the rubber and mining companies. In addition, the government required Congolese villagers to spend at least 60 days each year cultivating export crops for the government. It also conscripted thousands to work on large infrastructure projects, such as the building of railroads, and to serve in the Allied forces during World War I and World War II.

Compared to some of the British and French colonial regimes, Belgian colonialism allowed Africans few opportunities in civil service or private trade. It did, however, encourage missionary work in order to "civilize and Christianize" the African peoples. Missionaries did actively convert Africans to Christianity and also built schools that became the primary source of education for Africans, especially at the secondary and higher levels. Many of the missionary-school graduates subsequently became teachers or employees at other mission-run enterprises. They formed an elite class of Africans known as the evolués, many of whom lived in major cities such as Elizabethville and Léopoldville.

In the early 1950s the evolués began petitioning the colonial government for reform, demanding the rights to own land, participate in elections, and serve in public office. The colonial government conceded these demands and permitted Africans to run in local municipal elections in 1957. These changes did not appease growing anticolonial sentiments in the Congo, however, and when the general population broke into riots in 1959 the evolués were the first to demand immediate independence.

The Belgian colonial government was caught off guard by the demands for independence. Although France and Britain had been discussing decolonization since the early 1950s, the Belgian government did not even consider the possibility until 1956, when Belgian law professor A. A. J. Van Bilsen published *A Thirty Year Plan for the Political Emancipation of Belgian Africa*. The riots of 1959, however, forced the government to realize that it had neither the force nor the authority to maintain control. As a result, when it met with African delegates at the Brussels Round Table Conference in 1960, it offered to grant independence within six months, an extraordinarily short time frame. The government encouraged the *evolués* to form political parties and hold elections, and proposed that Belgian nationals would help smooth the transition by staying in their government and military positions.

In May 1960 the first national elections were held in the Belgian Congo. Nearly 40 parties fielded candidates and, after much controversy, a coalition was finally formed between Patrice Lumumba's Congolese National Movement and Joseph Kasavubu's Bakango Alliance; Kasavubu was named president and Lumumba was named prime minister. On June 30, 1960, King Baudouin I of Belgium declared the Republic of the Congo independent.

Early Independence in the Republic of the Congo

Within a week of independence, however, large-scale chaos erupted. The Force Publique mutinied and violent conflicts broke out between Belgians and Congolese as well as between Congolese ethnic groups fighting over animosities fostered during colonialism. In addition, secessionist movements threatened to break up the republic. On July 11, 1960, Moise Tshombe, supported clandestinely by Belgium and the Union Minière mining company, declared Katanga province (Shaba) an independent state, and in August, Albert Kalonji declared the independence of South Kasai.

Belgium deployed troops to the Republic of the Congo to protect Belgian citizens, a move quickly interpreted as an attempt to restore Belgian authority. In the face of continuing riots, Lumumba asked the United Nations (UN) for assistance and the UN Security Council authorized a military force, made up mainly of African troops, to restore order in the Republic of the Congo and oversee the withdrawal of the Belgian troops. The UN troops arrived on July 15, 1960, but when they proved unable to move out the Belgian troops quickly, Lumumba accused the UN of supporting Western imperialists and asked the former Union of Soviet Socialist Republics (U.S.S.R.) for assistance. Dag Hammerskjold, secretary general of the UN, attempted to ameliorate the situation, but died in an airplane crash on his way to negotiate talks in the Republic of the Congo.

Lumumba's action angered President Kasavubu, who fired Lumumba and replaced him with Joseph Ileo. Before Ileo could take office, Col. Joseph Mobutu (later Mobutu Sese Seko) seized power through a military coup. Claiming that Lumumba had incited army mutiny, Mobutu ordered the prime minister's arrest. Lumumba was killed in January 1961, allegedly after being tortured by Mobutu's troops. In February 1961 Mobutu returned power to Kasavubu and Ileo.

For the next three years, UN forces and the Congolese military tried to reunite the fragmented Republic of the Congo. In 1963 Tshombe finally surrendered the Katanga province, and, ironically, was named prime minister in July 1964. A month later the Kasavubu and Tshombe government adopted a new constitution and renamed the country the Democratic Republic of the Congo. Their coalition, however, was short-lived. Taking advantage of widespread civil conflict, Mobutu again seized power in a military coup d'état and on November 25, 1965, named himself president.

The Mobutu Era

Immensely popular in the early years of his rule, Mobutu centralized and consolidated his power by crushing burgeoning rebellions in outlying provinces and executing dissident politicians. In 1970 he held presidential elections and was elected to a seven-year term. During this term, Mobutu implemented the ideology he called *authenticité* ("authenticity"; also called Mobutuism), which he used to justify his dictatorial power as well as his economic and social policies. He changed the name of the Democratic Republic of the Congo to Republic of Zaire and required citizens to Africanize all Christian names and adopt African-style dress. In addition, in an economic policy called Zaireanization, he nationalized foreign businesses, reclaiming the copper and diamond mines in the Shaba region (formerly Katanga), which would become the mainstay of the Zairean economy.

From 1970 until the late 1980s Mobutu built a cult of personality around his presi-

dency, calling himself citizen-president-founder and father of the nation. Comparing his role to the patriarchal authority of traditional chiefs, he claimed he had the authentic right to exercise absolute power over his "children," the Zairean people. He used the army, the police, and the Centre national de documentation, an internal spy agency, to enforce his dictates and quell dissent. He also destroyed political opposition by replacing political parties with one official state party, the Mouvement Populaire de la Revolution (MPR), and making every Zairean a member.

Mobutu's policies of authenticité and Zaireanization primarily benefited Mobutu and his friends, but they also fostered a rich musical scene. Because authenticité forbade certain kinds of foreign music, Zaireans coped with the harshness of daily life by creating their own genres, such as a vibrant music called *sekous* that combines modern music with traditional instruments. Kinshasa, which many consider the music capital of Central Africa, became home to musicians such as Franco (François Luambo Makiadi), who was known as the king of Zairean music; Papa Wemba; and Abeti Masiniki; and bands such as Docteur Nico et l'Orchestre African Fiesta and O. K. Jazz. Mobutu acted as a patron to some Zairean musicians and occasionally invited them to play at his palaces.

By the early 1980s Mobutu's government was notorious as a kleptocracy, in which public funds were used for private gain, especially for the gain of the president himself, who diverted vast sums of revenue into his personal bank accounts. Meanwhile, the Zairean economy and infrastructure deteriorated. Mobutu managed to maintain his authority over an increasingly disenchanted populace partly because he portrayed himself as a staunch anticommunist and therefore received generous financial and military support from France and the United States. Although the Western powers hoped their support would not only deter Soviet influence but also stabilize the mineral-rich region of Central Africa, Mobutu in fact aided insurgent movements in neighboring countries such as ANGOLA, CHAD, and SUDAN.

At the end of the cold war, Mobutu's power

immediately declared himself head of the Democratic Republic of the Congo.

Democratic Republic of the Congo
After taking power, Kabila pledged to revitalize the country, halt corruption, and rebuild the infrastructure, including the mines, which needed an estimated $8 billion to be restored to operation. Denying offices to any politicians or civil servants associated with Mobutu, including the extremely popular Etienne Tshisekedi, Kabila established his government and pledged not to hold elections for at least four years, or however long it took to build the necessary political and social institutions. Kabila's Banyamulenge supporters occupied several prominent positions in his new government.

Originally welcomed as a liberator, Kabila

Above: A Congolese woman watches two United Nations soldiers as they patrol in Leopoldville in 1960. *CORBIS/BETTMANN-UPI*

Top right: Maj. Gen. Joseph Mobutu (later Mobutu Sese Seko), commander in chief of the Congolese armed forces, talks with President John F. Kennedy during a 1963 visit to the White House in Washington, D.C. *CORBIS/Hulton-Deutsch Collection*

Right: Laurent-Désiré Kabila declared himself president of the Democratic Republic of the Congo on May 17, 1997. Here Kabila holds the country's new flag as he is sworn in. *Reuters/Peter Andrews/Archive Photos*

began to slip. Economic depression – due to falling copper prices and unrest among civil servants and the military, many of whom had been unpaid for years – forced Mobutu to make concessions to the political opposition. In 1990 he announced the creation of a multiparty democratic system. Although elections were never held, Mobutu agreed to a coalition government with Etienne Tshisekedi. In less than a month Tshisekedi was fired but was reinstated in 1992 and served until 1994, when Kengo wa Dondo was appointed prime minister.

Mobutu maintained a low profile in the early 1990s but again became the voice of power in 1994, when he allowed millions of people fleeing civil conflict in Rwanda to take refuge in Zaire, and the UN and France urged him to play a role in helping resolve the crisis. This renewed authority, however, was only temporary. Sick with prostate cancer, Mobutu was caught off guard by an insurrection movement that began in October 1996. During the next six months the Alliance of Democratic Forces for the Liberation of the Congo, a Zairean militia backed by Rwanda, Uganda, and Angola and led by Laurent-Désiré Kabila, rapidly advanced on the capital of Kinshasa. Kabila's forces consisted largely of soldiers from eastern Zaire's small Banyamulenge minority, often known as Tutsi because of their close ethnic ties to the Tutsi of neighboring Rwanda (*see* Ethnicity in Rwanda, An Interpretation). These forces attacked not only the remnants of Mobutu's army, but also the Hutu refugees whose presence on the border of Rwanda threatened that country's predominantly Tutsi government. Kabila's army was supported by villagers throughout the countryside and faced little resistance from Zairean army troops, who were unwilling to risk their lives for a government that had not paid them for several months. Western powers refused to intervene of behalf of Mobutu. On May 16, 1997, with Kabila's army ready to take control of Kinshasa, the ailing dictator stepped down from power and flew with his family to Morocco. Kabila lost some of his popularity soon after taking office. The Congolese were upset by the continued presence of foreign troops, as well as by some of his policies, such as banning pants and short skirts on women. In addition, Kabila has faced criticism from the international community, who suspect that his troops were responsible for the disappearance and assumed massacre of thousands of Hutu refugees. Although Kabila has not denied the allegations, during 1997 and 1998 he prevented UN officials from investigating the disappearances.

Meanwhile, Kabila ousted many of his Banyamulenge (or Tutsi) supporters from office and replaced them with members of other Congolese ethnic groups, mainly from Kabila's own home region, Shaba. This shift in ethnic allegiances accompanied a gradual deterioration in relations with Kabila's former allies, Uganda and Tutsi-ruled Rwanda, who accused him of harboring armed rebels opposed to the Rwandan and Ugandan governments in the forested borderlands of the

In the Democratic Republic of the Congo, as in much of Africa, dance has both important religious and secular functions. *© B. Gerard/Explorer*

eastern Congo. In mid-1998, Kabila's ousted Banyamulenge supporters, including former foreign minister Bizima Karaba, joined by former supporters of Mobutu and opposition figures such as Arthur Z'Ahidi Ngoma, mounted an armed rebellion against him. The rebels accused Kabila of ethnic discrimination and autocratic misrule. The rebel forces, known as the Congolese Movement for Democracy, quickly took control of parts of the eastern Congo with the assistance of troops from Uganda and Rwanda. Troops from a number of African countries, including Angola, NAMIBIA, and Zimbabwe, came to the aid of Kabila and defeated a rebel offensive on Congo's capital, Kinshasa. The warfare ruined Congo's chances of recovering from decades of economic and political deterioration. More ominously, the participation of other African nations in the conflict threatened to spark a broader regional conflict extending beyond the country's borders.

Elizabeth Heath

SEE ALSO

Bantu: Dispersion and Settlement; Explorers in Africa Before 1500; Hutu and Tutsi; Ivory Trade; Kinshasa, Democratic Republic of the Congo; Transatlantic Slave Trade; United Nations in Africa; Pygmy; Stanley, Sir Henry Morton; Tshombe, Moise-Kapenda; Christianity: Missionaries in Africa; Ethnicity in Rwanda: An Interpretation; Berlin Conference of 1884-1885; Afonso I.

Africa

Congo, Democratic Republic of the (Ready Reference)

Former Name: Republic of Zaire
Area: 2,344,885 sq km (905,365 sq mi)
Location: Central Africa, bordered by SUDAN, ANGOLA, BURUNDI, CENTRAL AFRICAN REPUBLIC, REPUBLIC OF THE CONGO, RWANDA, UGANDA, and ZAMBIA
Capital: Kinshasa (population 3,804,000 [1991 estimate])
Other Major Cities: Lubumbashi (formerly Elisabethville; population 739,082), Kisangani (formerly Stanleyville; population 373,397 [1995 estimates])
Population: 49,000,511 (1998 estimate)
Population Density: 19 persons per sq km (about 48 per sq mi [1995 estimate])
Population Below Age 15: 43 percent (male 5,201,585; female 5,003,503 [1997 estimate])
Population Growth Rate: 1.7 percent (1996 estimate)
Total Fertility Rate: 6.6 children born per woman (1996 estimate)
Life Expectancy at Birth: Total population: 46.7 years (1996 estimate)
Infant Mortality Rate: 108 deaths per 1000 live births (1996 estimate)
Literacy (age 15 and over who can read and write in French, Lingala, Kingwana, or Tshiluba): Total population: 77.3 percent (male 86.6 percent; female 67.7 percent [1995 estimate])
Education: About 60 percent of Congolese children between the ages of 6 and 11 attend primary school; attendance at secondary school has risen rapidly since the early 1960s. In the late 1980s about 4.4 million pupils annually attended primary schools; about 508,000 attended secondary schools; and about 558,000 attended vocational and teacher-training schools.
Languages: Although over 200 languages are spoken, French is the official language and the principal business and social language. Four African languages are also widely spoken: Swahili in the east, Kikongo in the area between Kinshasa and the coast, Tshiluba in the south, and Lingala along the Zaire River.
Ethnic Groups: More than 200 ethnic groups live in the Democratic Republic of the Congo, about 80 percent of which are Bantu-speaking peoples. Sudanese peoples live in the north, and small numbers of Nilotic, PYGMY, and other peoples are present in various areas. The largest single groups are the KUBA, Bakongo (KONGO), and Mongo (all Bantu), and the Mangbetu-Azande (Hamitic). A small number of Europeans live in the Democratic Republic of the Congo.
Religions: About 50 percent of the people of the Democratic Republic of the Congo are Roman Catholic, while 20 percent are Protestant and 10 percent are Muslim. Most of the rest adhere to traditional animist beliefs, although Syncretic sects, such as Kimbanguism, which combines Christian and traditional elements, likewise have a significant number of followers.
Climate: Extremely hot and humid except in the upland regions. The average annual temperature is about 27° C (about 80° F) in the low central area, with extremes considerably higher in February, the hottest month. In areas with altitudes above about 1500 m (about 5000 ft), the average annual temperature is about 19° C (about 66° F). Average annual rainfall is about 1520 mm (about 60 in) in the north and 1270 mm (50 in) in the south.
Land, Plants, and Animals: The dominant physical feature of the country is the Zaire (Congo) River basin. This region, constituting the entire central area, is a vast depression that slopes upward on all sides into plateaus and mountain ranges. The highest mountain group in this area is the Mitumba Range, on the country's eastern border. The Ubangi River, chief northern tributary of the Zaire (Congo), rises on the northwestern slopes of this range. In the southeast the basin is fringed by rugged mountain country, sometimes called the Katanga, or Shaba, Plateau. This region, about 1220 m (about 4000 ft) above sea level, contains rich copper fields, uranium, and other mineral deposits.

In the southwest of the Democratic Republic of the Congo the mountain chains are collectively designated the Kwango-Kwilu Plateau. Virtually impenetrable equatorial forests occupy the eastern and northeastern portions of the country. The largest, known variously as the Ituri, Great Congo, Pygmy, and Stanley Forest, extends east from the confluence of the Aruwimi and Zaire (Congo) rivers nearly to Lake Albert, covering some 65,000 sq km (some 25,000 sq mi). In this area, on the Ugandan border, is the Ruwenzori Range, containing the country's highest point, Margherita Peak (5109 m/16,762 ft). Large regions of the Congo Basin consist of savanna land.

Vegetation consists of rubber trees of various species, oil palms, coffee and cotton, banana, coconut palm, and plantain, teak, ebony, African cedar, mahogany, iroko, and redwood trees. Animals include the ELEPHANT,

LION, leopard, CHIMPANZEE, GORILLA, GIRAFFE, HIPPOPOTAMUS, okapi, ZEBRA, wolf, buffalo, mamba, python, CROCODILE, parrot, pelican, flamingo, cuckoo, sunbird, heron, and spur-winged plover. Insects include ants, termites, and mosquitoes, including the *Anopheles* mosquito, host of the malaria parasite. Another disease-bearing insect, prevalent in the lowlands, is the South African TSETSE FLY, disseminator of sleeping sickness.
Natural Resources: cobalt, copper, gold, cadmium, petroleum, industrial and gem diamonds, silver, zinc, manganese, tin, germanium, uranium, radium, bauxite, iron ore, coal, and hydropower potential
Currency: The zaire
Gross Domestic Product (GDP): $18 billion (1996 estimate)
GDP per Capita: $400 (1996 estimate)
GDP Real Growth Rate: 1.5 percent (1996 estimate)
Primary Economic Activities: Agriculture accounts for 65 percent of the labor force, while 16 percent are employed in industry; services account for another 19 percent of the labor force (1991 estimate).
Primary Crops: Coffee, sugar, palm oil, rubber, tea, quinine, cassava (tapioca), palm oil, bananas, root crops, corn, and fruits; wood products
Industries: Mining, mineral processing, consumer products (including textiles, footwear, cigarettes, processed foods, and beverages), cement, and diamonds
Primary Exports: Copper, coffee, diamonds, cobalt, and crude oil
Primary Imports: Consumer goods, foodstuffs, mining and other machinery, transport equipment, and fuels
Primary Trade Partners: United States, Belgium, France, Germany, Italy, United Kingdom, Japan, and South Africa
Government: Since the takeover of the government by rebel leader LAURENT-DÉSIRÉ KABILA in May 1997, the government has been in a state of flux. On May 28, 1997, Kabila, who assumed the presidency, issued a 15-point proclamation, which nominally established three branches of government. True power resides with Kabila, however. In addition to his role as commander-in-chief, Kabila can also rule by decree and hire and fire government employees at will. The democratic presidential and legislative elections that Kabila promised for April 1999 did not take place.

Robert Fay

SEE ALSO
Congo River; Gold Trade; Kimbangu, Simon; Kinshasa, Democratic Republic of the Congo; Swahili Language.

Africa

Congo Free State. **Former name of the Democratic Republic of the Congo.**

Congo-Kinshasa. Please see CONGO, DEMOCRATIC REPUBLIC OF THE

Africa

Congo, Republic of the, **a highly urbanized, oil-rich country in Central Africa, bordered by the DEMOCRATIC REPUBLIC OF THE CONGO, the CENTRAL AFRICAN REPUBLIC, CAMEROON, GABON, and the Atlantic Ocean.**

In the Republic of the Congo (henceforth Congo), regional shifts in population and power have long shaped the country's history. In precolonial times migrations, state formation, and slave trading concentrated population along the coastline and in the river valleys of the south, leaving northern peoples relatively isolated. French colonialism widened regional differences by pouring resources into urbanization and infrastructural development in the south while drawing military recruits from the less-developed north. In the early years of Congo's independence, Communist rhetoric flourished in the south's burgeoning cities – home to vocal intellectuals, students, and workers – but power was held by a military elite from the north. Some of the country's leaders have since attempted to address the uneven development between north and south, city and countryside. However, progress has been slowed by economic crises and by the highly militarized nature of national politics. Short-lived political liberalization in the 1990s was brought to an abrupt halt in 1997 by civil war, fought on the streets of the capital, Brazzaville.

EARLY CONGOLESE HISTORY AND IMPERIALISM

The earliest inhabitants of present-day Congo were small communities of forest-dwelling hunter-gatherer Pygmies known as the Binga. Historians believe that Bantu-speaking people migrated to the region from the northeast, around the Lake CHAD basin, in the early fifteenth century. Their arrival inaugurated an era of centralized state formation, beginning with the emergence of the Kongo kingdom in present-day ANGOLA, just south of the CONGO RIVER. The Vili split from the Kongo and moved north toward the coast, where they founded the Loango kingdom. It became a major slave-trading center, with Dutch, French, Portuguese, and British ships calling at the port, and caravan routes reaching far inland. On the central plateau the TÉKÉ, who are believed to have migrated there during the fifteenth century, established a kingdom known as Tio and controlled much of the commerce on the Congo River. The TRANSATLANTIC SLAVE TRADE would ultimately take some 13 million people from the Congo River basin before its abolition in the early nineteenth century.

Although participation in the slave trade made some of the region's kingdoms extraordinarily rich, the raids, warfare, and political rivalries engendered by the trade also contributed to their instability. In the late seventeenth century the once-mighty Kongo kingdom collapsed and many of the Kongo migrated north, forcing the Téké farther north. At the end of the eighteenth century the Mbochi migrated south from the western bank of the Congo River and became fishers, boat builders, hunters, and traders in the areas around the Sangha, Likouala, and Ubangi rivers. Over the long term, these patterns of migration, and the Arab slave trade in the north, led to much denser population settlement in the south of present-day Congo than in the north. They also formed the three main ethnic groups that inhabit present-day Congo: the Kongo, including the Vili and Lari subgroups (53 percent of the total population), the Téké (13 percent), and the MBOCHI (12 percent).

FRENCH CONCESSIONS, COLONIALISM, AND CONGOLESE NATIONALISM

By the 1780s FRANCE had become the major European influence in the region, having established more than 70 trading companies north of the Congo. French missionaries soon followed, though extensive European exploration did not come until 1875, when France dispatched PIERRE SAVORGNAN DE BRAZZA to fortify French claims. Aware that King LEOPOLD II of Belgium already had designs on the Congo River basin, de Brazza negotiated a treaty with the Téké and established a trading post. Competition between France and Belgium in the Congo basin led to the BERLIN CONFERENCE OF 1884-1885, which gave the northern bank to France. France appointed de Brazza commissioner of the Congo – then called Moyen-Congo – and subsequent negotiations between France, Belgium, and PORTUGAL delineated the present-day borders.

France exploited Moyen-Congo's resources through a concessionary system, which granted private companies, chartered by the French government, 30-year monopolies over vast tracts of land. The concession companies' forced labor regimes not only depleted the region's rubber and ivory supplies but decimated the population. Thousands of Africans died, and many others fled to the interior. By 1920 international outrage had brought an end to the system, which had, in fact, generated more bankruptcies than profits.

In the early 1930s the French built the Congo-Océan railway from Brazzaville to the deep-water port at Point-Noire, at a cost of 15,000 to 20,000 African lives. Many of the laborers, most of them northerners, eventually settled in the two cities. With the only major railway or port in French Equatorial Africa, which included Gabon, Chad, and Oubangui-Chari (the present-day Central African Republic), Moyen-Congo became the commercial and administrative center of the four territories. The French administration built the most extensive infrastructure as well as the greatest number of schools, courts, and hospitals in Moyen-Congo, particularly in Brazzaville, the capital. Although the colonial government remained strongly centralized – the governor-general ruled by decree – educated Africans were employed in the lower levels of the civil service.

During World War II Brazzaville became sub-Saharan Africa's capital of Free France, and Congo became an important source of troops (thousands of Congolese fought in Europe). The expansion of government bureaucracies and urban services during and after the war provoked a second wave of urban migration. Many urban occupations became associated with specific ethnic groups – entrepreneurs and religious leaders, for example, often came from the Lari and Sundi Kongo groups. The French colonial administration contributed to the growing economic and social differentiation between ethnic groups by recruiting northerners, considered more "backward" than southerners, into the military.

At the 1944 Brazzaville Conference, France promised limited self-rule and abolished forced labor. Not surprisingly, nationalism in Moyen-Congo began in the cities. Urban intellectuals and workers together built a strong trade union movement, influenced by French socialists and communists. Members of these groups also founded the Vili-supported Congolese Progressive Party, which sought a gradual progression to self-rule, and the maintenance of strong ties to France and to the Mbochi-dominated African Socialist Movement. The best-known nationalist hero, however, was the evangelical cult leader André Matsoua, who, despite his death in the late 1930s, was elected in absentia to the French National Assembly in 1945 and 1951.

By the mid-1950s nationalist movements throughout Africa had made colonialism excessively costly for France and the other European powers. In preparation for decolonization in the Congo, France expanded voting rights in 1956, under the *loi cadre*, and in 1957 held territorial elections. Fulbert Youlou, a defrocked Lari priest and founder of the Lari-dominated Democratic Union for the Defense of African Interests, or UDDIA, was elected vice president of the Moyen-Congo's government council. While Youlou was considered pro-French, he enjoyed strong support from fellow Lari as well as from the many Congolese who saw him as Matsoua's political and religious successor. In the 1958 elections, UDDIA victories made Youlou prime minister. When the Congo achieved independence on August 15, 1960, he became president.

The Political Economy of Independence

Youlou's government, making no secret of its close military and economic ties to France – or of its distaste for radical politics – quickly lost support among Congo's students and workers. As unemployment rates increased and evidence of government corruption accumulated, popular discontent mounted, culminating in widespread demonstrations in August 1963. Youlou was forced to resign, and the military replaced him with the southern Kongolese Alphonse Massemba-Debat.

A former schoolteacher, Massemba-Debat's first priority was to secure his authority over the country's politically influential urban workers, youth, and intelligentsia. He established a single-party state, marginalized conservative opposition, and handed out jobs in the expanding state bureaucracy. He also checked the power of the northern, French-trained military by boosting the role of both the party's National Youth Movement of the Revolution, or JMNR, and the militia Civil Defense Corps, composed primarily of southerners and trained by North Korea and Cuba. His nominally socialist economic policies established state-run enterprises and won significant financial support from the Eastern Bloc, but left private industry largely intact. Western investment in the country continued, especially in oil exploration.

Although Massemba-Debat's policies did not bring economic prosperity or much political support, they did set a precedent for the military regimes that followed his unremarkable term in office. Unpopular among Congolese radicals, conservative business interests, and army officers, he resigned in 1968. After a brief struggle with the JMNR, army captain Marien Ngouabi came to power in August of that year. He established the "vanguard" Congolese Worker's Party, or PCT, proclaimed a "people's republic," and officially adopted scientific socialism. The charismatic Ngouabi incorporated the police and gendarmerie into the military and brought them all under the control of the party. The greatest political implication of the 1968 coup, however, was the power shift to the north. Both Presidents Youlou and Massemba-Debat were Bakongo from the south, but Ngouabi and his successors have been fully or partially Mbochi from the north, where support for socialist policies was typically stronger. Ngouabi catered to the new power base by implementing reforms more radical than those undertaken by Massemba-Debat, such as nationalizing the main oil company, though many of his policies were more show than substance.

The discovery of oil offshore in 1969 and phosphate deposits in 1973 led to a brief development boom, outlined in the euphoric three-year (1975-1977) plan, but also to mounting contradictions. International banks loaned generously to the newly oil-rich Congo, allowing the government to pour money into infrastructure projects and social services (especially education), but also to accumulate a national debt of $4 billion. The nation's leaders, known for their taste for French couture, became even less convincing proponents of socialism than before, and left intact Italian and French corporate control over oil extraction. Except for the main urban centers, the country remained poor and underdeveloped; it was not until the early 1980s that paved roads reach the Congo's northern regions.

After a 1972 coup attempt, Ngouabi employed the military and security apparatus to crush the youth movement and any other opposition, while at the same time trying to broaden the government's populist appeal. He reestablished the national assembly and the post of prime minister, both of which he had abolished upon coming to power, and promised development projects to the rural population. But moves to cooperate with southern leaders and increase party control over the military alienated many hard-line northern military officers, some of whom were suspected of involvement in Ngouabi's assassination in 1977. Ngouabi was replaced by Brig. Gen. J. Yhombi-Opango. Known more for his opulent lifestyle than for his ideologies or policies, Yhombi-Opango accomplished little during his two-year term, which ended with a bloodless coup led by Col. Denis Sassou-Nguesso.

Sassou-Nguesso became president with the support of the PCT, the military, the National Assembly, and the sole legal trade union. To satisfy radicals and consolidate his rule, Sassou-Nguesso limited the powers of the PCT, expanded the paramilitary forces, promoted more northern Mbochis, and propounded Marxist-Leninist ideologies. He also renewed ties with the East, sending more military personnel to the Soviet Union, Eastern Europe, and Cuba for training, and allowing Cuba to use the Congo to ferry military troops and equipment to the Angolan government, which was engaged in civil war. Like his predecessors, Sassou-Nguesso came to rely on periodic purges of the top political leadership in which he attempted to eliminate opponents while maintaining at least the façade of an ethnic and regional balance within the government. Yet opposition groups, whether operating underground or from abroad, continued their calls for democracy and an end to "pseudo-socialism."

During a brief economic upturn in the early 1980s, Sassou-Nguesso sought to spread some of the wealth to the countryside, and in so doing both slowed urban migration and broadened his rural political base. He initiated rural infrastructural projects and restructured the National Assembly to include particular interest groups. But these measures did little to revive an agricultural sector stifled by years of state control. Moreover, generous government spending in both rural and urban areas waned in the mid-1980s, when declining oil revenues forced Sassou-Nguesso to undertake austerity measures as part of a World Bank-International Monetary Fund structural adjustment program. By then, the civil service employed 73,000 people – one-quarter of the labor force – and students had come to expect government jobs upon graduation. Not surprisingly, cuts in wages and

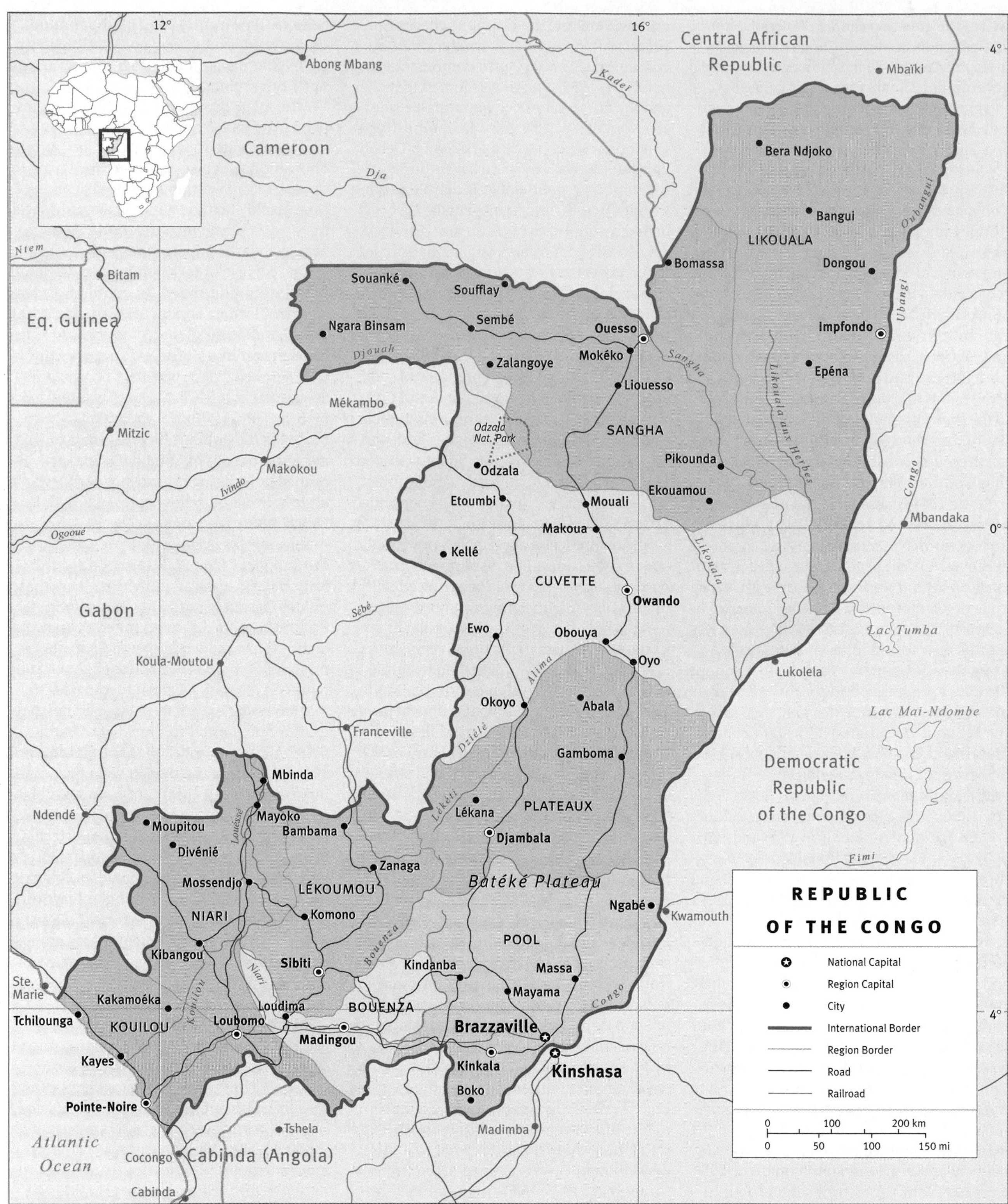

in education spending sparked strikes and riots in 1985-1986.

In the late 1980s the Congo government privatized, semiprivatized, or closed 76 of its 100 state-run industries. It also terminated state monopolies and liberalized investment codes, encouraging investment in mining (copper, gold, lead, potassium, tin, and zinc), secondary industries such as food processing and textiles, and timber. Congo's hardwood forests have since been rapidly logged. But an economy still strapped by low oil prices took its toll on the already tenuous legitimacy of the Sassou-Nguesso regime.

Economic liberalization, the loss of support from the disintegrating Eastern Bloc, and pressures from international donor agencies forced quick political liberalization in the Congo. In mid-1990 the PCT, which had a hand in governing as the sole legal party for the past 22 years, abandoned Marxist-Leninism and initiated a transition to multiparty rule. In early 1991 Sassou-Nguesso convened a national conference that, over the next 18 months, wrote a new constitution, established an interim government, and scheduled elections. In August 1992 the southerner Pascal Lissouba was elected president and his party won a plurality. Lissouba's party, the Pan-African Union for Social Democracy, or

UPADS, joined in a coalition with the PCT, and in an attempt at national reconciliation, appointed the northerner Yhombi-Opango prime minister. The PCT-UPADS coalition soon fell apart and in 1993 Lissouba called for new elections, which the UPADS won convincingly, over the Lari Bernard Kolélas and distant third-place Sassou-Nguesso.

Disagreements over legislative elections between Lissouba and Kolélas, who became mayor of Brazzaville, led to open warfare in 1993 between each man's private militias, forces popularly known as the Zulu and the Ninjas, respectively. In May 1997, shortly before scheduled presidential elections, Lissouba's forces tried to disarm members of Sassou-Nguesso's militia (known as the Cobras), claiming that they might disrupt campaigning. Clashes between the two forces exploded into civil war in the streets of Brazzaville, killing between 6000 and 10,000 people and largely destroying the city. In October 1997, with considerable Angolan assistance, Sassou-Nguesso and his Cobras took control of the capital. Sassou-Nguesso has promised national reconciliation, a return to civilian rule, and a professional military. To revive the war-torn economy and rebuild the capital, the president has liberalized the country's tax codes, and continues to encourage foreign investment and diversification of the export sector.

Eric Young

See Also
Brazzaville, Republic of the Congo; Decolonization in Africa: An Interpretation; Bantu: Dispersion and Settlement; Kongo; Pygmy; Structural Adjustment in Africa; Urbanism and Urbanization in Africa; Christianity: Missionaries in Africa; Trans-Saharan and Red Sea Slave Trade.

Africa

Congo, Republic of the (Ready Reference)

Area: 342,002 sq km (132,047 sq mi)
Location: Western Africa, bordering the South Atlantic Ocean, Gabon, Cameroon, Central African Republic, and the Democratic Republic of the Congo (formerly Zaire)
Capital: Brazzaville (population 760,300 [1990 estimate])
Other Major Cities: Pointe-Noire (population 387,774 [1990 estimate])
Population: 2,658,123 (1998 estimate)
Population Density: 8 persons per sq km (about 20 per sq mi) (1995 estimate)
Population Below Age 15: 43 percent (male 557,996; female 552,022 [1997 estimate])
Population Growth Rate: 2.2 percent (1996 estimate)
Total Fertility Rate: 5.15 children born per woman (1996 estimate)
Life Expectancy at Birth: Total population: 45.8 years (male 44.2; female 47.3 [1996 estimate])
Infant Mortality Rate: 108.1 deaths per 1000 live births (1996 estimate)
Literacy (age 15 and over who can read and write): Total population: 74.9 percent (male 83.1 percent; female 67.2 percent [1995 estimate])
Education: Free and compulsory for children ages 6 to 16. In the early 1990s about 502,900 pupils annually attended primary schools, and more than 183,000 attended secondary schools, including technical and teacher-training schools.
Languages: French is the official language; Lingala and Kikingo are the most widely spoken African languages.
Ethnic Groups: There are four major ethnic groups: the Bakongo (the major group, accounting for about 50 percent of the total population), the Mboshi, the Sanga, and the Téké, who live in the central region. There are 75 subgroups of these four major groups. About 12,000 Pygmies live in the Republic of the Congo, as do 8500 Europeans.
Religions: About half the population follows traditional religious beliefs. Most of the remainder are Christian, primarily members of the Catholic Church. Fewer than 1 percent are Muslim.
Climate: Tropical, with mostly high heat and humidity. While the Mayumbe Mountains experience a long dry season, parts of the Congo Basin receive more than 2500 mm (more than 100 in) of rainfall annually. Average temperatures in Brazzaville are 26° C (78° F) in January and 23° C (73° F) in July, with an annual rainfall of about 1500 mm (about 60 in). Temperatures along the coast are slightly cooler.
Land, Plants, and Animals: Along the Atlantic coast is a low, treeless plain, which rises inland to the Mayumbe Mountains, an almost completely forested region with an average elevation of about 550 m (about 1800 ft). In the south central region is the fertile valley of the Niari River. To the north lies the central highlands region, the Batéké Plateau. The plateau is cut by numerous tributaries of the Zaire (Congo) and Ubangi rivers. Dense tropical rain forests cover approximately half of the country and constitute a major natural resource. The principal commercial species are *okoumé* (a mahogany) and *limba* (a hardwood). Savanna vegetation is found in the northeast and the higher plateau areas. Wildlife is diverse and abundant, including antelope, giraffe, cheetah, crocodile, and numerous birds and snakes.
Natural Resources: Offshore petroleum potash, gold, iron ore, lead, and copper
Currency: 1 Communauté Financière Africaine (CFA) franc
Gross Domestic Product (GDP): $5.25 billion (1996 estimate)
GDP per Capita: $2000 (1996 estimate)
GDP Real Growth Rate: 4 percent (1996 estimate)
Primary Economic Activities: Agriculture, handicrafts, oil production, and forestry
Primary Crops: Cassava, sugar, rice, corn, peanuts, vegetables, coffee, cocoa, and forest products
Industries: Petroleum extraction, cement kilning, lumbering, brewing, sugar milling, palm oil, soap, and cigarette making
Primary Exports: Crude oil (90 percent of export revenue), lumber, plywood, sugar, cocoa, coffee, and diamonds
Primary Imports: Intermediate manufactures, capital equipment, construction materials, foodstuffs, and petroleum products
Primary Trading Partners: European Union, United States, Taiwan, Japan, and Thailand
Government: A multiparty republican system with a directly elected president (Pascal Lissouba since August 1992) who is elected to a five-year term. The president appoints the Council of Ministers, including the prime minister (Jacques Joachim Yhombi-Opango since 1993) and a bicameral legislature, the 125-seat National Assembly, and the 60-seat Senate. Presidential elections scheduled for July 1997 were postponed because of a civil conflict between President Lissouba's forces and militiamen employed by the former head of state, Gen. Denis Sassou-Nguesso.

Robert Fay

See Also
Pygmy.

Africa

Congo River, the second longest river in Africa.

The Congo River is about 4375 km (about 2720 mi) long, and its drainage basin is about 3,457,000 sq km (about 1,335,000 sq mi), covering almost all of the Democratic Republic of the Congo, the Republic of the Congo, the Central African Republic, eastern Zambia, northern Angola, and parts of Cameroon and Tanzania. From its headwaters at the junction of the Lualaba and Luvua rivers, it flows generally north until Boyoma (Stanley) Falls, where it begins to flow generally northeast, then west, and south to its outlet to the Atlantic Ocean at Banana, Republic of the Congo. It receives an average of 1500 mm of rain (about 60 in) per year, of which more than 25 percent discharges into the Atlantic Ocean.

The river can be divided into three main regions: the upper Congo, the middle Congo, and the lower Congo. The upper Congo has many tributaries, lakes, waterfalls, and rapids. The middle Congo has seven cataracts known collectively as Boyoma (Stanley) Falls, below which the river becomes navigable. The lower Congo begins where the river divides in two and forms the vast Malebo (Stanley) Pool. The capitals of the Republic of the Congo and the Democratic Republic of the Congo, Brazzaville and Kinshasa, respectively, face each other on opposite sides of Malebo (Stanley) Pool.

The Congo River has many tributaries, and its total of approximately 16,000 km (about 10,000 mi) of waterways make it one of the main transportation routes in Central Africa. Especially because the region's road systems have deteriorated during the past three decades, the river has become a vital trade artery, supporting a busy traffic in barges as well as smaller boats. It has great hydro-electric potential, although this has not been widely exploited, and it is home to numerous fish species and crocodiles.

In 1482, when the Portuguese navigator Diogo Cam became the first European to sail up the mouth of the Congo River, he met the rulers of the Kingdom of Kongo, marking the beginning of centuries of European slave trading and later colonialism in the region. In the late nineteenth century, Europeans began extensive exploration of the Congo River. The Scottish explorer and missionary DAVID LIVINGSTONE reached the Lualaba River, the Congo's largest tributary, in 1871. In 1876 and 1877, the American Henry M. Stanley traveled from the confluence of the Lualaba and the Congo, descending to the mouth of the Congo, a journey of about 2575 km (about 1600 mi). Not long afterward, Joseph Conrad published his novel *Heart of Darkness*, loosely based on his observations of the region then under the rule of Belgium's king LEOPOLD II.

More recently, the Congo River has witnessed the fall of governments. In May 1997 supporters of former dictator MOBUTU SESE SEKO crossed the river from Kinshasa to Brazzaville, fleeing the army of LAURENT-DÉSIRÉ KABILA. In September 1997, when troops of Gen. DENIS SASSOU-NGUESSO ousted Pascal Lissouba, then-president of the Republic of Congo, thousands boarded boats and fled from Brazzaville to Kinshasa.

Robert Fay

SEE ALSO

Brazzaville, Republic of the Congo; Crocodile; Explorers in Africa Before 1500; Kinshasa, Democratic Republic of the Congo; Kongo; Portugal; Stanley, Sir Henry Morton.

North America

Congress, African Americans in

Of the more than 11,000 representatives who have served in the United States Congress since 1789, fewer than 100 have been African Americans, and most of these members entered the institution in two distinct waves. The first wave occurred in the Forty-first Congress (1869-1871), when three black members were elected. The number of black members of Congress grew rapidly but peaked early in the Forty-fourth Congress (1875). After 1875 the presence of blacks in Congress was sporadic and dwindling. No blacks served during the Fiftieth Congress (1887-1889), three served during the Fifty-first (1889-1891), and between the Fifty-second and Fifty-sixth Congresses (1891-1901) there was only one black member per session. No blacks served in Congress between 1901 and 1929. The second wave of African American representation began in the late 1960s, and by 1970 nine blacks held congressional seats. In 1993 the number of blacks in Congress reached 40. As of 1998 that number had not been surpassed.

THE FIRST WAVE OF BLACK REPRESENTATIVES

Black representatives first entered Congress after the end of the Civil War and the emancipation of the slaves. All of the newly elected representatives came from states with high black populations – the former slave states of the South. From 1870 to 1897 South Carolina (which is 59 percent black) elected eight blacks to the House. Mississippi (54 percent black) and Louisiana (50 percent black) each elected one black to the House. Mississippi also sent two blacks to the Senate. Five other states with sizable black populations – Alabama, Florida, Georgia, North Carolina, and Virginia – elected 20 black representatives among them. However, far fewer blacks served in Congress than one might expect considering the size of the total black population in the Southern states. For instance, four former slave states – Arkansas, Tennessee, Texas, and West Virginia – never elected any black representatives during the RECONSTRUCTION era despite very sizable black populations. What was true for congressional elections also applied to politics at the state level.

Most of the 22 blacks in Congress served on at least one committee. Six served on the Education and Labor Committee, four served on the Agriculture Committee, and four served on the Public Expenditures Committee. Blacks were also represented on the District of Columbia, Library of Congress, Manufactures, Mining, Militia, Pensions, and War Claims committees. However, there was only one black committee chairman, Sen. Blanche Bruce, who served on the minor Levees and Dikes of the Mississippi River Committee.

The first wave of black representatives sought both to advance national policies affecting their states and districts – policies related to public education and protective tariffs for local products, for example – and to deal with more specifically black issues such as the provision of relief for depositors of the failed Freedmen's Savings and Trust Company. They also worked for the interests of Native Americans. Their successes, however, were confined to procuring easily obtained political patronage appointments such as postmaster, customs inspector, and internal revenue agent for some of their constituents. According to Eric Foner's *Reconstruction, 1863-1877*, black representatives had few legislative accomplishments: most of their bills languished in committee.

A number of events and forces brought an end to Reconstruction and black representation in Congress: the Hayes-Tilden Compromise of 1877; late nineteenth-century Supreme Court decisions that negated the effect of the Fourteenth Amendment and the Civil Rights Act of 1875; intimidation of black voters by the Ku Klux Klan; and all the other concomitants of the return to power of the former Confederates and their allies. By the turn of the century black representation seemed about to end, even at the descriptive level. Only one black member remained in Congress in 1900: George White of North Carolina, who voluntarily left Congress the following year.

THE SECOND WAVE OF BLACK REPRESENTATIVES

The second wave of black electoral activity in the twentieth century began in 1928 with the election of Republican Oscar DePriest from an inner-city Chicago district. Like almost all the Reconstruction-era blacks before him, DePriest was elected from a district with a majority of black voters. After serving in the Seventy-third and Seventy-fourth Congresses (1929-1934), he was defeated in 1934 by Arthur Mitchell, the first black Democrat elected to Congress. More than five decades passed before another black Republican was elected to the House. In 1942, after eight years of service, Mitchell resigned, and William Dawson, another black Democrat, succeeded him. Two years later Adam Clayton Powell Jr. was elected congressman in HARLEM, NEW YORK, and this meant that for the first time since 1891 there was more than one black representative in the House. In 1950 there was another breakthrough for black representation when Dawson gained enough seniority to become the first black to chair a standing committee, the Government Operations Committee. In 1960 Powell became chairman of the more important Education and Labor Committee. (Seven years later Powell was stripped of both his seniority and chairmanship after having been charged with an ethics violation.) Still another breakthrough came in 1966 when Edward W. Brooke was elected as a Republican senator from Massachusetts, a state whose population was less than 3 percent black. Brooke served until his defeat in 1978.

African American women were relative latecomers to Congress. The first woman to serve was Jeannette Rankin, elected to the House in 1916. Fifty-two years later SHIRLEY CHISHOLM (D-N.Y.) became the first black woman to serve in the House. In 1992 CAROL MOSELEY-BRAUN (D-Ill.) became the first black Democrat to serve in the Senate; she was also the first black woman senator and the fourth black senator. Unlike white women, who often followed their deceased husbands into office, black women did not use widowhood as a primary mode of entry into political life. All but one of the black women who served in Congress were highly educated, experienced politicians before they arrived on Capitol Hill. Rep. Shirley Chisholm had a master's degree from Columbia University and had served in the state assembly. Similarly, Rep. Barbara Jordan (D-Tex.) and Rep. Yvonne Burke (D-Calif.), both elected in 1972, had law degrees and had previously served in their state legislatures. In 1973 Cardiss Collins (D-Ill.), elected to replace her deceased husband, became the only black woman to have entered Congress through widowhood.

Regardless of their race or gender, black members of Congress are better educated and often come from higher-status jobs and backgrounds than most of their constituents. In the 105th Congress (1997-1999), for example, only 2 of 38 black members did not have at least a four-year degree. Fifteen held law degrees and had worked in the legal field; eleven held master's degrees; and one had a Ph.D. This level of educational attainment contrasts strikingly with that of the black population in general: in 1995 only about 14 percent of blacks aged 25 and older had received a bachelor's degree. Thus, twentieth-century blacks in Congress were similar in one respect to black representatives in the Reconstruction era – neither group reflected the typical makeup of the African American population at large. Many twentieth-century congressional blacks had already held political office, most often in state legislatures and city councils. Others had served as teachers or professors or had been business executives. However, such a disparity between representatives and the population they represent is not a major problem; few people would argue that politicians should personify their "average" constituent.

The Creation of a Congressional Black Caucus

In 1971 the nine current black representatives established the Congressional Black Caucus (CBC). After much consideration the representatives decided that their effectiveness hinged on the creation of a formal organization with its own rules, by-laws, and chair. Caucus founders viewed the organization as a vehicle that would allow individual black representatives to coordinate their efforts on behalf of downtrodden Americans, particularly African Americans. The organization adopted as its official motto the statement that "Black People have no permanent friends, no permanent enemies, just permanent interests."

From the start the CBC challenged the distribution of power in the House. Caucus members would eventually win a number of key leadership positions and prestigious committee assignments. The group would also establish its own foundation for raising money, its own research group, and an important political action committee.

In 1992 the CBC's membership reached its highest level, comprising 38 representatives, one delegate, and one senator. Full membership in the group has always been restricted to African Americans, but in the mid-1980s the organization voted to allow white representatives who had acceptable voting records to join as associate members.

Because of its increased size and heightened media attention, the CBC became a major political player during the first term of the Clinton administration. The group had a major role in shaping and passing some of the legislation supported by the president. CBC members were heading key committees, and they held other leadership posts as well: nine were assistant whips, three served on the Democratic Steering and Policy Committee, and one was a deputy whip. The Clinton administration came to consult the CBC on all major political decisions in recognition of its increased stature. During this time the organization was more visible than it had ever been in its history and was a key factor in many of the important political debates that took place in Washington. It had become a powerful force on Capitol Hill, a development brought about largely by the personal influence of some of its individual members and by its ability to deliver a substantial bloc of votes.

As fate would have it, though, just when the organization appeared to be making a substantial difference in Congress, the Democrats lost both the House and the Senate. The 1994 elections profoundly changed the political environment in which the CBC had to operate, as the group's members were forced to negotiate with unsympathetic Republicans. Despite the CBC's assertion that "black people have no permanent friends," the caucus had never functioned as more than an extension of the Democratic Party. As an interest group within the minority party, the CBC was destined to become more marginalized than ever. Though it had four times as many members in 1994 as it did at its birth in 1971, in the wake of the Democrats' defeat the caucus exerted little power or influence. Many of the highest-ranking black Democrats resigned from Congress, giving up years of seniority that took decades to attain. When the Democrats regain control of the institution, black Democrats will not have the seniority to claim many of the key chairmanships. Greater institutional power for blacks in Congress will take decades to achieve.

Carol Swain

See Also

American Indians; Brooke, Edward W., III; Bruce, Blanche Kelso; Civil War, American; Dawson, William Levi; Fourteenth Amendment to the United States Constitution; Jordan, Barbara Charline; Powell, Adam Clayton, Jr.

North America

Congressional Black Caucus,

the coalition of black members of the United States Congress committed to promoting and protecting policies favorable to the African American community.

The South African human rights activist Bishop Desmond Tutu once said, "Politics is the art of the possible." But for most of America's first 251 years, politics and political participation were reserved for whites only. African Americans were prohibited from voting and from holding political office and, since most were enslaved before 1865, were punished for participating in public protest. It was not until Reconstruction (1865-1877) and in 1870 the passage of the Fifteenth Amendment to the United States Constitution, giving black men the right to vote, that political participation by blacks became legal. Even then, it was weakened by officially sanctioned racial discrimination.

During Reconstruction 16 African Americans were elected to Congress and over 600 to state legislatures. But by 1877 many of the newly granted political rights were being rescinded by state officials. In the words of historian Eric Foner, "In illiteracy, malnutrition, inadequate housing, and a host of other burdens, blacks paid the highest price for the end of Reconstruction." It took 92 years for blacks to attain a measure of political representation in the U.S. Congress that was even close to nineteenth-century levels.

In 1969 the nine blacks then in Congress were isolated and powerless, unable to prevent passage of legislation detrimental to African Americans and other minorities. That year, Rep. Charles Diggs, a black Democrat from Michigan, formed the Democratic Select Committee, in the belief that a unified black voice could exert a measure of political influence in Congress. The committee investigated the murders of several Black Panther Party members in Chicago, Illinois, and defeated the nomination of conservative judge Clement Haynesworth to the Supreme Court. The potential strength of a collective black voice was immediately evident, and on June 18, 1971, at its first annual dinner, the Democratic Select Committee was reorganized as the Congressional Black Caucus (CBC), with Representative Diggs as its first chairperson.

Reactions to the CBC were immediate, as disapproval and opposition came from both blacks and whites. Black conservatives challenged the caucus's presumption in representing the entire black community. White liberals discounted the caucus's political effectiveness, and white conservatives labeled caucus members radicals and militants. During a trip to Africa, Vice President Spiro Agnew derogated the caucus by advising its members to take notice of the behavior of their African brethren, adding that they could "learn much" from them.

Despite the opposition, the CBC gained national attention in 1971 when its members presented President Richard Nixon with a list of 60 recommendations concerning foreign and domestic issues. In 1972 the caucus was one of the sponsors of the National Black Political Convention held in Gary, Indiana. That year, at the Democratic Party's national convention, the caucus drafted the Black Declaration of Independence, which urged the Democratic Party to commit itself to effecting complete racial equality. It also drafted the Black Bill of Rights, demanding, among other things, full employment and an end to subversive American military activity in Africa.

The caucus established the Congressional Black Caucus Foundation, a "nonprofit public policy, research, and educational institute," in 1976. Later that year, it formed the Congressional Black Caucus Graduate Intern Program to increase the number of African American professionals working for congressional committees. One year later, the caucus formed TransAfrica, an organization that lobbied on behalf of African interests. The caucus and TransAfrica, under the leadership of Randall Robinson, worked actively to secure economic sanctions against the apartheid regime in South Africa, to help build political stability in Haiti, and to establish a national holiday in honor of Martin Luther King Jr.

During its existence the Congressional Black Caucus was chaired by Reps. Charles Diggs (D-Mich.), Louis Stokes (D-Ohio), Ron Dellums (D-Calif.), Charles Rangel (D-N.Y.), and Kweisi Mfume (D-Md.). As its membership grew, the caucus developed broad support among black state legislators, black businesses, and black academics. This support contributed to the unprecedented 1992 election of 40 African Americans to Congress. In 1993 Carol Moseley-Braun (D-Ill.) became the fourth African American, and the first African American woman, to be elected to the U.S. Senate.

Although the CBC was divided on issues like the 1993 North American Free Trade Agreement (NAFTA) and the organization's relationship with the Nation of Islam, it consistently provided a clear and unified African American voice on issues like crime, welfare, and housing. It stood at the forefront of African American leadership in the U.S. Congress for 24 years before it was stripped of federal funding in 1994. At its pinnacle, the caucus wielded considerable political influence over many of the most important issues affecting the black community, the nation, and the world. Although the CBC is no longer officially sponsored by Congress, its impact continues to be felt as its members remain actively involved in the formation of the nation's laws and policies.

Alonford James Robinson, Jr.

See Also
Tutu, Desmond Mpilo; Dellums, Ronald V. (Ron); King, Martin Luther, Jr.; Rangel, Charles Bernard.

North America

Congress of Racial Equality,

American civil rights organization that pioneered the strategy of nonviolent direct action, especially the tactics of sit-ins, jail-ins, and freedom rides.

The Congress of Racial Equality (CORE) was founded in 1942 as the Committee of Racial Equality by an interracial group of students in Chicago. Many of these students were members of the Chicago branch of the Fellowship of Reconciliation (FOR), a pacifist organization seeking to change racist attitudes. The founders of CORE were deeply influenced by Mahatma Gandhi's teachings of nonviolent resistance.

CORE started as a nonhierarchical, decentralized organization funded entirely by the voluntary contributions of its members. The organization was initially co-led by white University of Chicago student George Houser and black student James Farmer. In 1942 CORE began protests against segregation in public accommodations by organizing sit-ins. It was also in 1942 that CORE expanded nationally. James Farmer traveled the country with Bayard Rustin, a field secretary with FOR, and recruited activists at FOR meetings. CORE's early growth consisted almost entirely of white middle-class college students from the Midwest.

From the beginning of its expansion, CORE experienced tension between local control and national leadership. The earliest affiliated chapters retained control of their own activities and funds. With a nonhierarchical system as the model of leadership, a national leadership over local chapters seemed contradictory to CORE's principles. Some early chapters were dominated by pacifists and focused on educational activities. Other chapters emphasized direct action protests, such as sit-ins. This tension has persisted throughout CORE's existence. Through sit-ins and picket lines, the group had some success in integrating Northern public facilities in the 1940s. With these successes it was decided that to have a national impact, it was necessary to strengthen the national organization. James Farmer became the first national director of CORE in 1943.

In April 1947 CORE sent eight white and eight black men into the upper South to test a Supreme Court ruling that declared segregation in interstate travel unconstitutional. CORE gained national attention for this Journey of Reconciliation when four of the riders were arrested in Chapel Hill, North Carolina, and three, including Bayard Rustin, were forced to work on a chain gang. In the aftermath of the 1954 Brown v. Board of Education decision, CORE was revived from several years of stagnation and decline. CORE provided the 1955 Montgomery Bus Boycott with its philosophical commitment to nonviolent direct action. As the Civil Rights Movement took hold, CORE focused its energy in the South.

CORE's move into the South forced the leadership to address the question of the organization's place within the black community. While whites remained prominent, black leaders were selected for high-profile positions. CORE remained committed to interracialism but no longer required that new chapters have an interracial membership, largely expecting little white support in the South. While middle-class college students predominated in the early years of the organization, increasingly the membership was made up of poorer and less educated blacks.

CORE provided guidance for action in the aftermath of the 1960 sit-in of four college students (who were not CORE members) at a Greensboro, North Carolina, lunch counter and subsequently became a nationally recognized civil rights organization. As a pioneer of the sit-in tactic, the organization offered support in Greensboro and organized sit-ins throughout the South. CORE members then developed the strategy of the jail-in, serving out their sentences for sit-ins rather than paying bail. In May 1961 CORE organized the Freedom Rides, modeled after their earlier Journey of Reconciliation. Near Birmingham, Alabama, a bus was firebombed and riders were beaten by a white mob. After this event CORE ended the rides; however, the Student Nonviolent Coordinating Committee (SNCC) resumed the rides in Mississippi. Some CORE officials resented SNCC for taking credit for the Freedom Rides, but CORE continued to locate field secretaries in key areas of the South to provide support for the riders.

By the end of 1961 CORE had 53 affiliated chapters, and they remained active in Southern civil rights activities for the next several years. CORE participated heavily in President John F. Kennedy's Voter Education Project (VEP) and also co-sponsored the 1963 March on Washington. In 1964 CORE participated in the Mississippi Freedom Summer project; two of the three activists killed that summer in an infamous case, James Chaney and Michael Schwerner, were members of CORE.

By 1963 CORE had already shifted attention to segregation in the North and West, where two-thirds of the organization's chapters were located. In an effort to build CORE's credibility as a black-protest organization, leadership in these Northern chapters had become almost entirely black. CORE's ideology and strategies increasingly were challenged by its changing membership. Many new members advocated militancy and believed that nonviolent methods of protest should be used only if they proved successful.

As the tactics were being questioned, so was the role of white members. In 1966 CORE endorsed the term Black Power, and by 1967 the word "multiracial" was no longer in the CORE constitution. Finally, in 1968, ROY INNIS replaced Farmer as the national director, and Innis soon denied whites active membership in CORE and advocated Black Separatism.

Under Innis's leadership CORE took a conservative turn, lending its support to black capitalism and nationalism. In the 1970s Innis joined Southern whites in promoting separate schools rather than desegregation. James Farmer cut his ties to CORE in 1976, returning in the 1980s in a bid to remake CORE into a multiracial organization. Innis, however, remained firmly in leadership. In the 1990s CORE chapters engaged in little direct organization, but Innis remains one of the most prominent black conservatives in the United States.

SEE ALSO
Chaney, James Earl; Chicago, Illinois; March on Washington, 1963.

Latin America and the Caribbean

Conspiración de la Escalera,

(November 1843-March 1844), an antislavery and anticolonial revolt involving slaves and free blacks in MATANZAS, CUBA, that provoked massive repression against Afro-Cubans when it was discovered by colonial authorities.

In November 1843, slaves on the sugar plantations of Matanzas Province began a rebellion that spread to neighboring plantations. As the revolt widened, slaves destroyed property, killed some whites, and freed fellow slaves. In 1844 colonial authorities investigating the uprising claimed to have uncovered a conspiracy in Matanzas to overthrow the Spanish colonial government. Eventually they alleged that vast networks existed that linked black slaves in rural areas to free blacks and mulattos in the cities. The Spanish forces, under the authority of Capt. Gen. Leopoldo O'Donnell, arrested, tortured, and killed hundreds in their efforts to suppress the rebellion. Investigation into subversive activities spread across the country, assuming the dimensions of a witch hunt. La Conspiración de la Escalera (Conspiracy of the Ladder) was named for the ladders to which accused black and mulatto conspirators were tied in order to be whipped. The year 1844 has gone down in Cuban history as the Year of the Lash.

Many Cubans were arrested merely for expressing abolitionist or anticolonial views. In particular, free black leaders were targets of the government roundup. Among those arrested and executed, for example, was the mulatto poet Gabriel de la Concepción Valdés (1809-1844), better known as Plácido. Historians suggest that he was probably arrested because the content of some of his verses was deemed subversive by the colonial government. Also implicated and tried in absentia was David Turnbull, the former British consul in Havana. Turnbull, who favored abolition, was accused of being the prime mover behind the conspiracy. Historians disagree as to what parts of these allegations were based in fact. Some see the charges as largely a product of colonialist fears; others see the aborted conspiracy as a critical example of Afro-Cuban political mobilization and an early manifestation of antislavery and anticolonial sentiment.

The colonial reaction clearly reflected white fears of the *peligro negro* (black menace), fears that had grown dramatically since the HAITIAN REVOLUTION (1791-1804). This revolution on the neighboring island of Hispaniola precipitated dramatic economic and social changes in CUBA. Before the nineteenth century Cuba had been a minor colony of settlers that produced relatively little for the world market and had a relatively small number of slaves. When Haiti's SUGAR plantations were disbanded after the revolution, Cuban sugar planters saw an opportunity to seize a larger portion of the world market. Cuban sugar production grew at a rapid pace, as did the importation of African slaves. As the ratio of slaves to free whites increased, so did the whites' dread of slave uprisings. The fear was intensified by stories Haitian planters brought with them when they migrated to Cuba after the revolution.

The potential for slave uprisings was not imagined. In the first decades of the century, slaves made scattered attempts to secure their liberty, aided by free black sympathizers. In 1812, for instance, JOSÉ ANTONIO APONTE, a free black carpenter, planned an unsuccessful slave revolt that broke out in several cities. In March 1843, the year in which the alleged conspiracy began, several revolts occurred in sugar mills in Matanzas Province.

After 1844 Cuban planters experimented with measures to reduce their reliance on black labor, importing Chinese and Indians from Yucatan to work as indentured servants. In addition, annexationist aspirations intensified among some Cuban landowners, who hoped to find security as citizens of a slave state within the United States. The crackdown on alleged conspirators reduced the ranks of prominent free black leaders and abolitionists. The harsh repression that was directed against both slaves and free blacks had the unintended effect of fostering stronger unity among Afro-Cubans in their commitment to independence and abolition (*see* MYTH OF RACIAL DEMOCRACY IN LATIN AMERICA AND THE CARIBBEAN: AN INTERPRETATION). Afro-Cubans would play a prominent role in later struggles for Cuban independence (*see* TEN YEARS' WAR and SPANISH-CUBAN-AMERICAN WAR).

Jalane Schmidt

SEE ALSO
Valdés, Gabriel de la Concepción ("Plácido"); Abolition and Emancipation in Latin America and the Caribbean.

Europe

Constantine, Learie Nicholas

(b. September 21, 1901, Diego Martin, Trinidad; d. July 1, 1971, London, England), accomplished Trinidadian cricket player and politician, and the first person of African descent to have been awarded a life peerage in Great Britain.

Sports critics and fans hailed Constantine as one of the best fieldsmen, hardest batsmen, and greatest bowlers in the history of cricket. This popularity assisted his later political career. He secured a position as a civil servant, and later as a peer, in GREAT BRITAIN. He also served in Trinidad as a legislator, minister, and ambassador.

Constantine was born in Trinidad to Anaise Pascal and Lebrun Constantine, a plantation foreman and famous cricketer who played for the West Indian team in England in 1900 and 1906. Learie Constantine played cricket as a boy, but upon his father's advice did not pursue a professional sports career until he had first completed his education at age 15 and then gained some experience working in legal services. Finally, he joined the West Indian team and played in England in 1923 and 1928.

In 1929 Constantine joined the Nelson team in the Lancashire Cricket League in England and helped them win eight league titles. He acquired a reputation for agility and fast bowling. During that time, he also freelanced, playing with the West Indian team. He led the West Indians to their first victory in a test match in 1929-1930 and assisted their win in the series against England in 1934-1935. After leaving the Nelson league in 1939, he continued to play cricket and coach teams. He also became an announcer and commentator for the British Broadcasting Corporation (BBC) and wrote several books on cricket.

When World War II began, Constantine remained in England and worked as a welfare officer for the labor ministry. He was responsible for the successful employment and integration of West Indian immigrants into British society. Here, he witnessed the problems of racism and discrimination in Great Britain. He, too, had experienced the unofficial color bar when he was refused lodging at a British hotel in 1943. In a highly publicized trial, he had won compensation for this indignity. His views are presented in a book titled *Colour Bar* (1954), which he wrote with the assistance of his close friend C. L. R. James.

Constantine continued to study law in his spare time and gained entrance to the English bar in 1954. He returned to Trinidad, where his popularity had soared. He entered local politics and won election as a legislator in 1956. From 1956 to 1960 he served as the chair, then the minister of community works and utilities, for Trinidad's first political party, the People's National Movement, which was led by chief minister ERIC WILLIAMS. When

Trinidad gained independence in 1962, Constantine left for Great Britain to serve as Trinidad and Tobago's first high commissioner to London.

Finding this diplomatic position confining, Constantine was happy to resign in 1964. He chose to remain in Great Britain, becoming involved again in sports broadcasting and political commentary. At a time when few blacks held positions of power, he was asked to serve several respected institutions: as a governor of the BBC, rector of St. Andrew's University, and member of the Race Relations Board and the Sports Council. He was knighted in 1962. In 1969 he became the first person of African descent to gain life peerage. He died of lung failure in 1971. Trinidad posthumously awarded him the country's highest decoration, the Trinity Cross.

Leyla Keough

See Also

James, Cyril Lionel Richard; Trinidad and Tobago.

Africa

Conté, Lansana (b. 1934, Dubréka, Guinea), president of Guinea (1984-).

Having assumed power in a nonviolent coup in 1984, Lansana Conté succeeded Ahmad Sékou Touré, Guinea's first president and the man who had led the country's independence movement. While Conté has been criticized for delaying free elections for nearly ten years, he is also credited with reversing some of Touré's most glaring excesses.

Little is known of Conté's childhood. He obtained a military education abroad and then returned to Guinea in 1958, just after the independence vote and Touré's installment as president. Having served three years in the French military, Conté joined the Guinean army and by 1975 had become a general. In 1984, a month after Touré's death, Conté and fellow military leader Diarra Traoré staged a bloodless takeover and installed the Military Committee for National Reparation (CMRN). One of Conté's first acts as president was to free some 97 political prisoners; another was to suspend Guinea's constitution.

A year later Conté weathered an unsuccessful coup attempt by Traoré, then prime minister. Conté responded by imprisoning at least 200 alleged coup plotters. By 1989 Guinea still had not held free elections, but the country showed signs of recovering from years of economic decline under the autocratic Touré. In particular, Conté's adherence to a World Bank structural adjustment program won approval from Western lenders such as France, who began to provide aid to Guinea. In 1990 Conté oversaw the writing of a new constitution, and in 1993 he won Guinea's first multiparty election, which outside observers claimed was rigged. Conté remained in power as of 1998.

Kate Tuttle

See Also

Structural Adjustment in Africa; Touré, Sékou.

Latin America and the Caribbean

Contemporary Afro-Brazilian Music, nearly as complex and heterogeneous as its country of origin; like African American music, it embraces an immense range of musical styles and subcultures.

Some observers would argue that it is inappropriate to distinguish Afro-Brazilian from Brazilian music, since black expressive cultures have contributed so profoundly to what is understood to be national culture. Perhaps no other artistic field in Brazil has been so deeply influenced by black cultures as popular music. Nevertheless, it is useful and necessary to identify distinct styles and movements in Brazilian popular music that are associated particularly with black urban communities. The past 20 years have witnessed the proliferation of Afro-Brazilian social, political, and cultural movements that explicitly reject the traditional belief in a unitary "national culture" (*see* Black Consciousness in Brazil). Yet, for the most part, contemporary Afro-Brazilian musical countercultures continue to be racially inclusive. An increasingly globalized world economy has intensified the influx of African and diasporic musical cultures, particularly from the United States and Jamaica, to major Brazilian cities. These forms of music and their attendant cultural styles, modes of dress, and dance steps have been widely appropriated and transformed by young urban Brazilians. Several broad currents in contemporary Afro-Brazilian music may be identified: contemporary samba, soul/funk/hip hop, reggae, *axé* music, and *mangue beat.*

Samba

Samba emerged in the twentieth century as the preeminent national music of Brazil. Modern urban samba was developed in the predominantly black favelas (shantytowns) on the *morros* (hills) of Rio de Janeiro. In addition to Carnival sambas presented each year by dozens of *escolas de samba*, or samba schools, there has been a thriving market for stylized pop samba since the first recordings of Carmen Miranda and Francisco Alves in the late 1920s. Since the 1960s several composer-performers like Zé Keti, Paulinho da Viola, Martinho da Vila, and Candeia have consciously reclaimed the roots of samba in the morros.

Contemporary samba grew out of the *pagode* movement of Rio during the early 1980s. Frustrated with the overcommercialization of pop samba, musicians from the working-class North Zone of Rio began to congregate informally on weekends to play samba and share rounds of beers. They developed a stripped-down, rootsy sound with lyrics about everyday life in Rio de Janeiro. With the aid of consecrated samba star Beth Carvalho, key participants in this budding movement founded the Grupo Fundo de Quintal (Backyard Group) and released their first album in 1980. This paved the way for other pagode composers and performers like Zeca Pagodinho and Jovelina Perola Negra. Another key figure in the Rio samba scene is Bezerra da Silva, an outspoken critic of police violence, racism, poverty, and government corruption. Using the latest slang of the morros, his songs tend to glorify *malandros*, streetwise hustlers who live on the margins of society. The 1990s saw an explosion of pop samba from São Paulo, led by groups like Raça Negra and Négritude Junior, which play a soulful fusion called *sambalanço*. In Bahia, groups like Companhia do Pagode, Gera Samba, and its spinoff, É o Tchan, have modernized the *samba-de-roda* (a traditional style from the Recôncavo, the region surrounding Salvador and All Saints Bay) while foregrounding sexual play in their lyrics and dance moves.

Soul, Funk, Hip Hop

Brazilians have experimented with African American music styles at least since the 1920s, when samba innovators like Pixinguinha absorbed influences from early jazz bands. In the early 1960s Jorge Ben introduced seamless and soulful fusions of pop samba and rhythm and blues. Toward the end of the Tropicália movement in 1968, Gilberto Gil also began experimenting with soul music after hearing Jimi Hendrix and James Brown. Milton Nascimento later recorded a pair of acclaimed albums with top American jazz musicians.

In the early 1970s, despite a repressive atmosphere under military rule, black urban youth began taking political, cultural, and aesthetic cues from the Black Power and soul movements of the United States. By the mid-1970s something of a countercultural movement called Black Soul had developed in Rio and quickly spread to São Paulo and beyond. Black Soul enthusiasts mounted dance parties around the city that attracted thousands of young Afro-Brazilians in platform shoes and Afro hairstyles. The first important sound system, Soul Grand Prix, put on multimedia slide shows that celebrated black political and cultural affirmation. Leaders of an emerging black political movement, the Movimento Negro Unificado (MNU), distributed flyers at the events. White critics charged that Black Soul was an inappropriate importation of African American cultural and political strategies that were irrelevant in Brazil's much touted "racial democracy."

The musical culture of Black Soul revolved primarily around recordings of pre-disco funk from the United States, yet local funk-samba fusion bands, like Banda Black Rio, also produced innovative records. Brazilian pop soul/funk singers like Tim Maia, Tony Tornado, and Cassiano also began to score hits during this period. Their heirs from the 1980s and 1990s include Ed Motta, Sandrá Sá, Skowa and the Mafia, Fernanda Abreu, and Daúde.

In the early 1980s the Black Soul movement faded, but the massive dance parties called *bailes funk* continued to proliferate in the working-class North Zone and urban periphery. Today, an estimated 150 sound systems produce 500 funk and hip hop dance parties every week in the metropolitan area of Rio. The bailes funk have provided contexts for predominantly black working-class teenagers, called *funkeiros*, to congregate, have fun, and construct social identities. Exaggerated reports of gang violence at the dances and highly publicized incidents of petty theft involving organized gang "sweeps" (*arrastões*) across middle- and upper-class beaches of the South Zone led to the repression and stigmatization of funkeiros in the early 1990s. More sympathetic observers have argued that most bailes are relatively free of violence, and most funkeiros have no association with gangs.

As in the United States and elsewhere, RAP has become a powerful vehicle for voicing the concerns of the black urban underclass. Brazilian rappers, most notably in São Paulo, have become increasingly engaged in defending hip hop culture and denouncing racial discrimination and social exclusion directed at the black population. They have also vigorously protested recurring police violence, including the notorious murder of 111 prisoners during an uprising in the Carandiru Prison of São Paulo and the unprovoked massacre of eight street children in front of the Candelária Cathedral in downtown Rio. In recent years, state and civic organizations have begun to support the rap movement as a viable source of leisure and self-affirmation for millions of urban youth. The leading rap groups are from São Paulo and include Thaïde and DJ Hum, Sampa Crew, Cultura de Rua, Codigo 13, Racionais MC, and Pavilhão 9, named after the prison pavilion that was site of the Carandiru massacre.

REGGAE

In 1969, when popular composer-musicians Caetano Veloso and Gilberto Gil were exiled to London by military authorities, ROCKSTEADY musicians from KINGSTON, JAMAICA, were just beginning to develop a new sound called reggae. With a large and growing Jamaican immigrant community in London, these innovations crossed the Atlantic with little lag time. In 1972 Veloso became the first Brazilian artist to reference the new style in the song "Nine out of Ten," in which he sang, "I walk down Portobello Road to the sound of reggae. I'm alive." Later in the decade, Gil became the leading Brazilian ambassador of reggae and its message of Third World liberation. In 1979 his recording "Não Chore Mais," a Portuguese version of BOB MARLEY's "No Woman, No Cry," became the anthem of the incipient redemocratization movement. In 1984 he recorded a pop reggae hit, "Vamos Fugir," with Marley's band, the Wailers. By that time, reggae had put down roots in Salvador, Bahia, the predominantly black city on the northeast coast where Gil had grown up.

Early Bahian reggae artists like Edson Gomes and Lazzo Matumbi began cutting records in the roots reggae style of Bob Marley, PETER TOSH, JIMMY CLIFF, and others. Reggae soon spread to other cities, notably to São Luis do Maranhão on the northern coast of Brazil. Afro-Brazilian reggae fans began to grow dreadlocks and congregate at reggae bars, while groups dedicated to the Rastafarian religion coalesced in the major urban centers. A certain Christian/Rastafarian fundamentalism still permeates the Bahian reggae scene, currently dominated by Sine Calmon and his group Morrão Fumegante (Smoking Weed).

Brazilian reggae artists and fans remained remarkably indifferent, even resistant, to the emergence of the up-tempo, rap-inflected DANCEHALL style reggae, which eclipsed the international popularity of roots reggae in the early 1980s. The reggae movement in Brazil accompanied the development of black political and cultural activism. The dancehall style, with its emphasis on sexual innuendo, male bravado, and material success, did not resonate with cultural and political aspirations of the Afro-Brazilian reggae community, which, for the most part, adhered to the Bob Marley legacy and roots reggae of the 1970s.

Roots/Rasta orthodoxy is less pronounced in reggae from Rio de Janeiro. The Rio-based group Cidade Negra (Black City) became one of the top Brazilian reggae bands of the 1990s, with a potent mixture of roots, dancehall, funk, and hip hop. The group has recorded with Jamaican dancehall star Shabba Ranks and with white Brazilian rapper Gabriel o Pensador (Gabriel the Thinker). It combines socially aware and romantic lyrics with a radio-friendly pop sensibility. Another Rio-based group, O Rappa, has produced a fusion of reggae, rap, and rock behind a radical critique of Brazilian society from the perspective of the urban slums. Together with the nongovernmental organization Afro-Reggae, they have conducted educational programs with the youth of Vigário Geral, a poor neighborhood that has suffered violent assaults by the police in recent years.

Reggae was introduced to Bahia during a time when community-based percussion ensembles, called blocos Afros, were revolutionizing the Carnival of Salvador. In 1974 a group of youth petroleum workers from Curuzu/Liberdade, the largest black neighborhood in Salvador, founded ILÊ AIYÊ, the first explicitly Afrocentric Carnival organization in Bahia. Within five years, several other blocos Afros were founded, including OLODUM, Malê Debalê, Araketu, and Muzenza. To a varying degree, all of the blocos Afros pursued social and political agendas within their communities and in the city. Each organization had particular interests: Muzenza celebrated Jamaica and roots reggae, while Araketu's early recordings evidence a profound connection with the Afro-Brazilian religion CANDOMBLÉ. All of the blocos Afros in some way expressed pride in African and diasporic cultures while protesting racial discrimination and inequality in Brazil.

AXÉ, MANGUE BEAT

In the mid-1980s the director of the Olodum's drum ensemble, Mestre Neguinho do Samba, invented a new hybrid rhythm, samba-reggae, which was soon emulated by other blocos Afros and electric pop bands like Banda Mel, Banda Reflexus, and Chiclete com Banana. By the late 1980s, the Carnival music of the blocos Afros had inspired a new Bahian pop sound called *axé* music (after the Yoruba term for divine power), pioneered by performers Margareth Menezes and Daniela Mercury. Meanwhile, several blocos Afros, like Araketu and Olodum, formed stripped-down electric bands for recording and touring, which allowed them to compete better in the local and national music markets. The most important innovations in Bahian pop music during the past decade have come from CARLINHOS BROWN, a brilliant composer, musician, and cultural agent who leads the percussion-based pop group Timbalada.

Farther up the coast in Recife, the industrial hub of the Brazilian northeast, a smaller musical movement called *mangue beat* came together in the early 1990s. Led by composer-singer Chico Science and his band, Nação Zumbi, the mangue beat movement proposed to renovate the cultural scene of Recife by fusing local styles like *maracatú* and *embolada* with funk, rap, and heavy metal. Other groups like Mundo Livre S/A and Mestre Ambrósio have continued the mangue beat movement following Chico Science's tragic death in an automobile accident in 1997. Although not identified with mangue beat, another northeastern luminary, Chico César, has also renovated regional folk styles to produce a light and joyful pop sound that has received critical acclaim.

Several other artists not associated directly with movements or currents in Brazilian popular music deserve mention. In 1975 two young Afro-Brazilian musicians, Luiz Melodia and DJAVAN, received first and second prizes, respectively, at the Abertura Music Festival, sponsored by TV Globo. With a jazzy feel and a penchant for sweet pop hooks, Djavan went on to achieve enormous success at home and abroad. Luiz Melodia remained somewhat of a countercultural cult figure, playing a soulful mix of samba, blues, funk, and reggae with poignant lyrics that often referenced his neighborhood in Rio de Janeiro, Estácio, home of the first samba school. In many ways, Melodia's soulmate from São Paulo is Itamar Assumpção, one of the most inventive Brazilian composer-musicians of the past 20 years. A key figure in São Paulo's alternative music scene, Assumpção has forged a unique fusion of samba, funk, and reggae noted for sophisticated and complex vocal arrangements. His lyrics document in detail the urban underground of metropolitan São Paulo.

The history of musical traditions and marketing categories in Brazil is not as racially coded as it is in the United States. There was never any Brazilian analogue to so-called "race music" of the 1940s and 1950s in the United States. Nor are there identifiable "crossover artists," because Afro-Brazilian artists have appealed to multiracial audiences almost since the beginning of the music industry. Most of the contemporary Afro-Brazilian artists discussed above continue to appeal to multiracial audiences, yet have initiated and developed trends that highlight the concerns of the black urban poor.

Christopher Dunn

See Also
Hip Hop in the United States; Afoxés/Blocos Afros; Benjor, Jorge; Brazil; Rio de Janeiro, Brazil; Rastafarians; Carnivals in Latin America and the Caribbean; Myth of Racial Democracy in Latin America and the Caribbean: An Interpretation; Salvador, Brazil.

North America

Conwell, Kathleen

(b. March 18, 1942, N.J.; d. September 1988), African American playwright and screenwriter whose films have been shown on the Learning Channel and the Public Broadcasting Service.

Kathleen Conwell was born and raised in New Jersey. After receiving a B.A. in philosophy and religion from Skidmore College, she became a member of the Student Nonviolent Coordinating Committee (SNCC). In 1966 she graduated from the Sorbonne in Paris with an M.A. in film. She started her writing career working for radio station WNET in New York City. She began teaching film history and screenwriting at the City University of New York in 1974.

Conwell wrote her first screenplay, an adaptation of a Henry Roth short story, in 1980. That same year she produced and directed *The Cruz Brothers and Mrs. Malloy*, which won first prize in the Sinking Creek Film Festival. She wrote and directed *Losing Ground* (1982), which won first prize at the Figueroa da Foz International Film Festival in Portugal, as well as *Madame Flor* (1987) and *Conversations with Julie* (1988). Her films have been shown on the Learning Channel and the Public Broadcasting Station.

Conwell has written several plays, including *In the Midnight Hour* (1981) and *The Reading* (1984). Theatre Communications Group named Conwell's play *The Brothers* one of 12 outstanding plays of the 1982 season. In addition to *Begin the Beguine* (1985) and *Only the Sky Is Free* (1985), a play about Bessie Coleman, she wrote *While Older Men Speak* (1986) and *Looking for Jane*. In 1988 she wrote a novel, *Lollie: A Suburban Tale;* in September of that year she died of cancer.

Leyla Keough

See Also
New York, New York; Film, Blacks in American.

North America

Conyers, John F., Jr.

(b. May 16, 1929, Detroit, Mich.), Democratic member of the United States House of Representatives from Michigan since 1965.

John Conyers Jr. earned a bachelor's degree in 1957 and a law degree in 1958 from Wayne State University. He was a member of the Michigan National Guard from 1948 to 1952. In 1952 he joined the U.S. Army and fought in the Korean War. He was an assistant to U.S. Representative John Dingell from 1958 to 1961, and from 1961 to 1963 he worked for the Michigan Workmen's Compensation Department. In the 1964 Democratic primary for the newly created black-majority Fourteenth Congressional District in Michigan, Conyers won by only 108 votes on a platform of Jobs, Equality and Peace. He was one of only six black representatives in Congress. He ran for mayor of Detroit in 1989 and 1993 but lost decisively both times.

The Fourteenth District lies north of downtown Detroit. More than 500,000 district residents live in the city. The district takes in an economically depressed area with a high crime rate. Once a thriving community built around the auto industry, the district lost thousands of auto manufacturing jobs, and many residents who could afford to move left for the suburbs.

Conyers was the first black to chair the House Judiciary Committee, which is responsible for all crime and civil rights legislation. When the Republicans gained control of the House in the 104th Congress (1995-1997), he became the ranking Democrat on the committee, a position he retained during the 105th Congress, which began in 1997.

See Also
Detroit, Michigan.

North America

Cooke, Samuel (Sam)

(b. January 22, 1931, Clarksdale, Miss., as Sam Cook; d. December 11, 1964, Los Angeles, Calif.), soul music pioneer, among the first African Americans to achieve pop stardom through gospel roots.

As a child, Sam Cooke performed in gospel ensembles in churches in Chicago, where his father was a minister. In his teenage years he joined the Highway QC's, a local group that emulated the renowned Soul Stirrers. Cooke's natural talent and magnetic personality soon drew the attention of singer and manager J. W. Alexander, who landed him a job as lead singer for the Soul Stirrers. Cooke began recording gospel classics with the quintet while honing his smooth vocals and writing music of his own.

In the mid-1950s Alexander, who had noted the success of gospel-gone-rhythm and blues acts such as Ray Charles, convinced Cooke to switch to secular pop music. Alexander's vision of Cooke as a pop sensation among young African American women came true in 1957 when he scored a number one hit on both pop and R&B charts with "You Send Me." Cooke recorded with Keen records until 1960, when he signed a deal with RCA, launching the most prolific leg of his career. During his RCA years he sent numerous songs up the charts, including "Chain Gang" and "Twistin' the Night Away."

Meanwhile Cooke entered into a business partnership with Alexander, who had begun his own music publishing company – a rare enterprise for an African American in the early 1960s. Cooke began producing performers on the Star label and took an interest in developing new talent. He also served as a role model in the black music world, inspiring singers such as Aretha Franklin to move from gospel to pop. Many consider Cooke a founding father of the hybrid soul, which blended gospel and R&B. Cooke's influence resounds in the works of such artists as Al Green, Wilson Pickett, Smokey Robinson, Marvin Gaye, and Otis Redding.

In 1964 a Los Angeles motel manager shot Cooke dead, allegedly in self-defense. Although some gospel devotees and religious fans – who felt betrayed by Cooke's break with the church – considered his death providential, musicians across genre and race took it as a tremendous loss. A crowd of 200,000 attended his funeral.

Eric Bennett

See Also
Soul Music; Chicago, Illinois; Franklin, Aretha Louise; Gospel Music; Robinson, William ("Smokey").

North America

Cooper, Anna Julia Hayward

(b. August 10, 1858, Raleigh, N.C.; d. February 27, 1964, Washington, D.C.), African American educator, writer, and activist known especially for her support of women's rights.

"Only the Black Woman can say 'when and where I enter, in the quiet, undisputed dignity of my womanhood, without violence and without special patronage, then and there the whole *Negro race enters with me*.'" In this passage from Anna Julia Cooper's speech "Womanhood a Vital Element in the Regeneration and Progress of a Race," published in her 1892 work *A Voice from the South: By a Black Woman of the South,* she expresses one of her most important beliefs. In her writings and speeches, Cooper often argued that the status of the entire black race was dependent on the status of the women who run the homes and raise the children, and that one of the best ways to elevate black women's status was to increase their educational opportunities. As an activist and educator, she spent most of her life simultaneously promoting these ideas and putting them into practice.

Cooper was born in Raleigh, North Carolina, in 1858, the daughter of a black slave woman and her white master. She decided that she wanted to be a teacher when she "was not far from... kindergarten age." In 1868 she enrolled at the newly opened Saint Augustine's Normal School and Collegiate Institute in Raleigh. After she completed her studies she was invited to join the faculty. In 1877 she married her fellow teacher George Cooper; but his death in 1879 left her a widow at the age of 21, and she decided to return to school and continue her education.

In 1881 Cooper enrolled at Oberlin College in Ohio, one of the few colleges that accepted black women. When she and two black female classmates graduated in 1884, they became only the second, third, and fourth African American women to receive bachelor's degrees. Cooper taught at WILBERFORCE UNIVERSITY for one year, and then returned to Saint Augustine's to teach German, Latin, and mathematics. In 1887 she was recruited to Washington, D.C.'s M Street High School, then the most prestigious African American high school in the country. It was at M Street that Cooper rose to prominence as a speaker and author. The 1890s have been called the "women's era" in African American history because of the rise of the BLACK WOMEN'S CLUB MOVEMENT and related activism, and Cooper was one of the women in the limelight.

In Washington, Cooper quickly became a leader in the circles of educated, middle-class African American women who were advocating for women's rights in general and black women's rights in particular, and she was soon in demand as a speaker across the country. Cooper was one of three black women to address the 1893 International Women's Congress in Chicago. She also addressed such groups as the American Conference of Educators (1890), the National Conference of Colored Women (1895), and the National Federation of Afro-American Women (1896), as well as the first Pan-African Conference, held in London in 1900. She was also the only woman elected to the prestigious AMERICAN NEGRO ACADEMY, whose other members included ALEXANDER CRUMMELL, Carter G. Woodson, and W. E. B. Du Bois. *A Voice from the South,* which she published in 1892, contained speeches and essays that represented many of her political opinions.

As the decade came to a close, Cooper's professional career returned to the forefront. In 1902 she became principal of her school, a rare achievement for a black woman, but she was demoted four years later when she criticized plans to institute a less demanding curriculum. She taught at Lincoln University in Missouri for four years before returning to M Street as a regular teacher. Cooper had earned a master's degree from Oberlin in 1877, and in 1911 she began to pursue her doctorate through summer courses in Paris and at Columbia University. She received her doctorate from the Sorbonne in 1925 at the age of 66, becoming the fourth African American woman to receive a Ph.D.

By that time Cooper, who never remarried, had raised two foster children as well as five great-nieces and great-nephews, whom she adopted in 1915. Still an active educator, in 1930 she became president of Frelinghuysen University in Washington, D.C., a school geared toward the needs of working African American adults. After Frelinghuysen lost its charter in 1937 and her favorite great-niece died in 1939, Cooper's public career and health began to decline, but she lived to the age of 105, passing away in her sleep in February 1964. Her extraordinary achievements and legacy are still celebrated, and in 1998 a new collection of her writings and speeches made her works accessible to a contemporary audience.

Lisa Clayton Robinson

SEE ALSO
Pan-Africanism; Du Bois, William Edward Burghardt (W. E. B.); Lincoln University (Missouri); Woodson, Carter Godwin.

North America

Coppin, Frances (Fanny) Jackson

(b. 1837, Washington, D.C.; d. January 21, 1913, Philadelphia, Pa.), African American school principal and church and civic leader, and one of the leading black women educators of the nineteenth century.

"I never rose to recite in my classes at Oberlin but I felt that I had the honor of the whole African race upon my shoulders. I felt that, should I fail, it would be ascribed to the fact that I was colored." In this memory of her college experience, Frances "Fanny" Jackson Coppin described a burden that many blacks still carry 150 years later – the suspicion that for their white peers, they somehow represent the entire race. Despite this pressure, however, Coppin shone at Oberlin College and went on to shine as a teacher, school principal, and activist throughout the next 50 years.

Coppin was born a slave in WASHINGTON, D.C., in 1837, the daughter of a slave mother and a white father. An aunt purchased her freedom when she was 12 years old and sent her to live with another aunt in New Bedford, Massachusetts. They moved to Newport, Rhode Island, where Coppin became a domestic servant and used her salary to hire a private tutor three hours a week. After briefly attending the segregated Newport public schools and Rhode Island State Normal School, she moved to Ohio to attend Oberlin College in 1860.

Coppin was the first black woman student in Oberlin's collegiate department, and her peers elected her class poet and a member of the prestigious Young Ladies Literary Society. In 1863, while still a student, she founded a night school for newly freed slaves who were migrating to Ohio during the Civil War. Her reputation as an educator spread, and when she graduated from Oberlin in 1865, she was hired as president of the girls' division of the Institute for Colored Youth in Philadelphia (later Cheney State College). Four years later, she became principal of the school, making her one of the only female principals at that time to head a coeducational school and a staff that included male teachers. As teacher and principal, she received widespread praise for her innovative educational methods and established an industrial department that became the first trade school for African Americans in Philadelphia.

Coppin also reached out to the larger community. She wrote a regular column on women's issues for the *Christian Recorder,* the national newspaper of the African Methodist Episcopal (AME) Church. She was president of the local Women's Mite Missionary Society, national president of the Women's Home and Foreign Missionary Society of the AME Church, and a vice president of the NATIONAL ASSOCIATION OF COLORED WOMEN. She was a vocal supporter of women's rights, especially the right to vote, and in her speeches encouraged women to strive for the same educational and employment rights that men had.

In 1881 she married the Reverend Levi Jackson, who became pastor of Philadelphia's famous Mother Bethel AME Church in 1896. When poor health finally led Coppin to retire as principal of her school in 1902, she accompanied her husband to his post as bishop of the AME Church in CAPE TOWN, SOUTH AFRICA. The Coppins returned to the United States in 1904 and settled in Philadelphia. Coppin had almost completed her autobiography when she died at her Philadelphia home on January 21, 1913. Her funeral was attended by thousands of people, and memorial services were held for her in Philadelphia, Baltimore, and Washington, D.C.

Lisa Clayton Robinson

SEE ALSO
African Methodist Episcopal Church; Civil War, American; Philadelphia, Pennsylvania.

Latin America and the Caribbean

Cordero, Rafael

(b. 1790, San Juan, Puerto Rico; d. 1868, San Juan, Puerto Rico), black Puerto Rican educator who spent most of his life teaching black and underprivileged children in PUERTO RICO at a time when education was not available to them.

Rafael Cordero was born into a humble family in San Juan. He was educated by his parents because, as a black, he could not enroll in any school. At the time, slavery was still legal in Puerto Rico, and blacks, whether free or not, were socially marginalized. Under these circumstances, Cordero decided to pursue what would become his life's vocation: teaching black children. In 1810 he opened his first school in San German and later moved it to San Juan. He eventually taught not only black but also poor white and mulatto children. Cordero did not earn a salary; he had to sustain his family by manufacturing cigars.

In his 58 years of teaching, Maestro Rafael, as he was called by his students and later by all Puerto Ricans, imparted primary instruction to several generations of children. His reputation grew, and even well-off families sent their children to his school. He would accept anyone who wanted to learn. Among his students were outstanding figures of Puerto Rican history, including the abolitionists José Julián Acosta and Román Baldorioty de Castro, the author Alejandro Tapia, and the journalist Sotero Figuero.

After many years of unselfish civic service Cordero was given a monetary award by the Economic Society of Friends of the Country. He used the prize money to buy clothes and books for his poorest students. The painter FRANCISCO OLLER paid tribute to Cordero's contribution to racial equality in Puerto Rico in *Escuela del Maestro Rafael* (Maestro Rafael's School) (*see* EDUCATION IN LATIN AMERICA AND THE CARIBBEAN).

Carlos Dalmau

SEE ALSO
San Juan, Puerto Rico.

Latin America and the Caribbean

Cordero, Roque

(b. August 16, 1917, Panama City, Panama), Afro-Panamanian composer, conductor, and teacher, and an internationally known composer of contemporary classical music.

During the 1960s Roque Cordero gained international recognition as an innovative composer of contemporary classical music. He has received numerous awards for his compositions, including the Koussevitzky International Recording Award in 1974 for his Violin Concerto (1962). Although he employs modern compositional techniques, he strongly identifies with his Panamanian heritage and has sought to create music with both Afro-indigenous character and universal appeal.

Cordero grew up in Panama City. As a teenager, he revealed a talent for musical composition and won several local prizes. In 1939 he wrote his first notable work for orchestra, the *Capricho Interiorano*. Impressed by the bold experimentalism of the Viennese composer Arnold Schönberg, he aspired to a Western musical education and in 1943 enrolled on a scholarship at the University of Minnesota in the United States. After extensive musical study with composer Ernst Krenek and conductor Dimitri Mitropoulos, in 1953 Cordero returned to Panama, where he became director of the National Institute of Music. In 1964 he was appointed conductor of the National Orchestra of Panama.

Musical nationalism prevailed in Latin America during the 1940s, and Panamanian popular music considerably influenced Cordero's compositions: the *Sonatina Ritmica* (1943), *Ocho Miniaturas* (1948), and *Rapsodia Campesina* (1953) all contain rhythmic elements taken from the *mejorana* or *tamborito*–popular Panamanian dances. Although he adopted an atonal musical language during the 1950s, he continued to use Panamanian dance rhythms and melodic figures. Sections of his Second Symphony (1956), for example, have a rhythm based on the CUMBIA, an Afro-Panamanian and Afro-Colombian dance.

In 1966 Cordero returned to the United States to teach composition and direct the Latin American Music Center at Indiana University. In 1972 he joined the music faculty at Illinois State University. Although he developed a distinctive style early in his career, it was his atonal compositions of the 1950s and beyond that won him international accolades. Such works strongly reflect twentieth-century classical styles but retain a Latin American accent.

Cordero's works have been performed at such contemporary music venues as the Museum of Modern Art's Summergarden series in New York City. In 1997 the *New York Times* hailed Cordero's *Dodecaconcerto* as "pungent and vital..., with its driving energy and slinky writing for saxophone."

Roanne Edwards

Latin America and the Caribbean

Córdoba, Diego Luis

(b. 1907, Quibdó, Chocó Province, Colombia; d. 1964), Afro-Colombian politician and an important figure in promoting black participation in electoral politics in COLOMBIA.

Diego Luis Córdoba was born near Quibdó, Chocó Province, and studied in Quibdó, later moving to Medellín and Bogotá to study law. He was politically ambitious during a time when Chocó's 90 percent black population was ruled by a small white elite. Córdoba was one of a growing number of educated blacks who were dissatisfied with this situation. He achieved national status as a radical student leader and stood as a Liberal candidate for the position of representative to Congress in 1933 but was not nominated.

Córdoba then started his own party, Acción Democrática (AD), later labeled *Cordobismo*, which gained the support of many local blacks. AD candidates were elected to the city council and found favor with some of the white elite. Córdoba was elected to Congress as an independent representative and AD gained local power. Córdoba declared himself a socialist, but his concern was also firmly with the blacks and the Chocó.

While Córdoba was a member of Congress, Quibdó's educational system was improved and democratized, encouraging the development of a strong local black middle class. The white elite began to leave Quibdó for other cities. In 1947, against many obstacles, Córdoba, by then a senator, pulled off a political coup by pushing through legislation making Chocó, until then an intendancy, into a full *departamento* (province). This move expanded the local bureaucracy greatly and gave more room to the growing educated black community. During his life, Córdoba was appointed judge in several jurisdictions, served as ambassador to VENEZUELA, and held a post as a university professor.

Peter Wade

SEE ALSO
Pacific Coast of Colombia.

North America

Cortez, Jayne

(b. May 10, 1936, Fort Huachuca, Ariz.), African American poet and performance artist who incorporates the rhythms and traditions of jazz into her writing.

Born on her father's army base, Jayne Cortez grew up in Watts, the black section of Los Angeles. She married saxophonist ORNETTE COLEMAN in 1954 and gave birth to a son. After their divorce in 1960, Cortez began studying drama and writing poetry. She spent the summers of 1963 and 1964 in Mississippi, where she helped register voters as part of the STUDENT NONVIOLENT COORDINATING COMMITTEE (SNCC) campaign.

Upon her return to Los Angeles, Cortez cofounded the Watts Repertory Theater. She served as its artistic director between 1964 and 1970. She published her first collection of poetry, *Pisstained Stairs and the Monkey Man's Wares*, in 1969, followed by *Festivals and Funerals* in 1971. After moving to New York City, Cortez formed Bola Press in 1972. Three years later she married artist MELVIN EDWARDS. From 1977 to 1983 she served as writer-in-residence at Rutgers University. Another collection, *Coagulations: New and Selected Poems*, was published in 1984.

Cortez has read her poetry, lectured, and

performed on four continents, and her work has been translated into 28 languages. JAZZ and blues rhythms and traditions permeate her work, as do African themes, forms, and language. In 1996 her fifth book of poems, *Somewhere in Advance of Nowhere*, was published.

Cortez often performs and occasionally records with jazz musicians. Among her eight recordings of poetry with music are *There It Is* (1982); *Maintain Control* (1986); and *Taking the Blues Back Home: Poetry & Music* (with the Firespitters, 1996). She currently lives in New York City.

SEE ALSO
Blues, The; Los Angeles, California; New York, New York.

Latin America and the Caribbean

Cortijo, Rafael

(b. 1928, PUERTO RICO; d. October 3, 1982, Puerto Rico), Afro-Puerto Rican musician who, along with Ismael Rivera, founded the musical group Cortijo y su combo in 1954.

Rafael Cortijo's music became an essential part of Puerto Rican culture through the musical group Cortijo y su combo. The group had a profound influence on Puerto Rican popular music of the 1950s because it promoted the African vernacular rhythms of PLENA AND BOMBA. It was the first black group that played in the Condado Hotel, one of the most exclusive hotels of the time in SAN JUAN, PUERTO RICO. The band's innovative style incorporated a spontaneous and strong sound. Cortijo y su combo clearly distinguished itself from other Puerto Rican bands, which appealed mainly to the tastes of white audiences. Songs such as "El bombón de Elena," "Quítate de la vía Perico," and "El satélite" brought popular stories to life.

Mayda Grano de Oro

North America

Cosby, Bill

(b. July 12, 1937, Germantown, Pa.), African American comedian whose multifarious talent, friendliness, and commitment to positive values led him to become a preeminent television celebrity in the 1980s and a performer admired by both whites and blacks.

Born in a poor section of PHILADELPHIA, PENNSYLVANIA, Bill Cosby left home for a stint in the United States Navy that lasted from 1956 to 1960. He studied at Temple University but dropped out to devote his time to standup comedy. After establishing his name on the night-club circuit in 1963, he auditioned successfully to fill a guest spot on Johnny Carson's *Tonight Show*. An instant success, Cosby became the first African American to host the program regularly. In 1965 he became the first black person to have a starring role on a predominantly white television drama, appearing with Robert Culp on the program *I Spy*. Because of his Emmy Award-winning success on *I Spy*, many fans considered Cosby "the JACKIE ROBINSON of television."

As a rising television celebrity, Cosby starred in his own program, *The Bill Cosby Show* (1969-1971), in which he played a high school basketball coach, Chet Kincaid. The Kincaid character neither pandered to white stereotypes nor expressed a black militant doctrine. In the mid-1970s Cosby returned to school, earning a doctorate in education at the University of Massachusetts in Amherst. Meanwhile he continued his television career with *The New Bill Cosby Show* (1972-1973), a comedy and variety program, and *Cos* (1976). An animated Saturday morning feature, *Fat Albert and the Cosby Kids* (1972-1977), delivered messages of rectitude and personal responsibility. Both *Fat Albert* and Cosby's frequent cameos on *The Electric Company*, a presentation of the Public Broadcasting Service (PBS), reflected his interest in children and education.

In the 1980s Cosby combined his paternal interests with the sophisticated humor of his prime-time career on the hit program *The Cosby Show* (1984-1992). *The Cosby Show* ranked third in Nielsen ratings its first season and held the number-one slot for three years. It created a glowing embodiment of the American middle-class dream and drew the attention of 38 million people. Cosby's vision of Dr. Cliff Huxtable, his beautiful lawyer wife, and their five handsome, successful children included jokes and conflicts that transcended race. While some critics claimed that *The Cosby Show* failed to address the reality of black America – or, worse, depicted successful blacks as assimilated blacks – others lauded its positive presentation of family values.

While *The Cosby Show* debunked racial stereotypes on screen, Cosby fought discrimination within the television industry. He took advantage of the show's tremendous success, demanding a large role in its production. He hired black writers and directors and invited black celebrities, such as Dizzy Gillespie and JUDITH JAMISON, to make guest appearances; he contracted Professor Alvin Poussaint, an African American professor of psychiatry from Harvard University, as an adviser; and he hung the artwork of black artist Varnette Honeywood on the walls of the set.

The Cosby Show marked the apex of Cosby's public celebrity and financial success, but his accomplishments extend beyond it. In addition to his numerous television ventures, Cosby has continued to perform live and has released more than two dozen comedy albums, many of which have won him Grammy Awards. He also has written a number of books, including the best-selling *Fatherhood* (1986) and *Love and Marriage* (1989), and several children's books in the Little Bill series for early readers. Throughout his career Cosby has endorsed the products of Fortune 500 companies such as Coca-Cola, Eastman Kodak, E. F. Hutton, and Jell-O.

Cosby's commitment to education has been persistent. In the 1980s he and his wife made frequent donations to African American colleges. In 1989 they gave their biggest gift, of $20 million, to SPELMAN COLLEGE. Cosby's philanthropy has benefited many other African American organizations, including the NATIONAL ASSOCIATION FOR THE ADVANCEMENT OF COLORED PEOPLE, the UNITED NEGRO COLLEGE FUND, the National Sickle-Cell Foundation, and the NATIONAL COUNCIL OF NEGRO WOMEN.

Eric Bennett

SEE ALSO
Gillespie, John Birks ("Dizzy"); Poussaint, Alvin Francis; Racial Stereotypes; Television and African Americans.

Latin America and the Caribbean

Costa Rica,

republic in southern Central America, bounded on the north by Nicaragua, on the east by the Caribbean Sea, on the southeast by Panama, and on the southwest and west by the Pacific Ocean. The uninhabited and densely wooded tropical Cocos Island, about 480 km (about 300 mi) to the southwest in the Pacific Ocean, is under Costa Rican sovereignty. The total area of Costa Rica is 51,060 sq km (19,714 sq mi). The country's capital is San José (*see* CENTRAL AMERICA).

Africa

Côte d'Ivoire,

a country in West Africa bordered by LIBERIA, GUINEA, MALI, BURKINA FASO, GHANA, and the Atlantic Ocean.

The recent history of Côte d'Ivoire is rife with contradictions. The country that offered some of the most sustained resistance to French colonialism has in the postcolonial era become one of France's most loyal clients. Economic growth and prosperity for elites and foreign investors have come at the price of poverty for large segments of the population. Finally, though many have praised Côte d'Ivoire as a model of political stability, its autocratic regime has maintained power by repressing democratic opposition. Côte d'Ivoire has had only two leaders since 1960: FÉLIX HOUPHOUËT-BOIGNY, who led the country from colonial rule through three decades of independence, and his successor, HENRI-KONAN BÉDIÉ. Both helped build a nation of political stability and limited economic prosperity known as the Ivoirian Miracle. At the same time, both have maintained a neocolonial dependence on France and

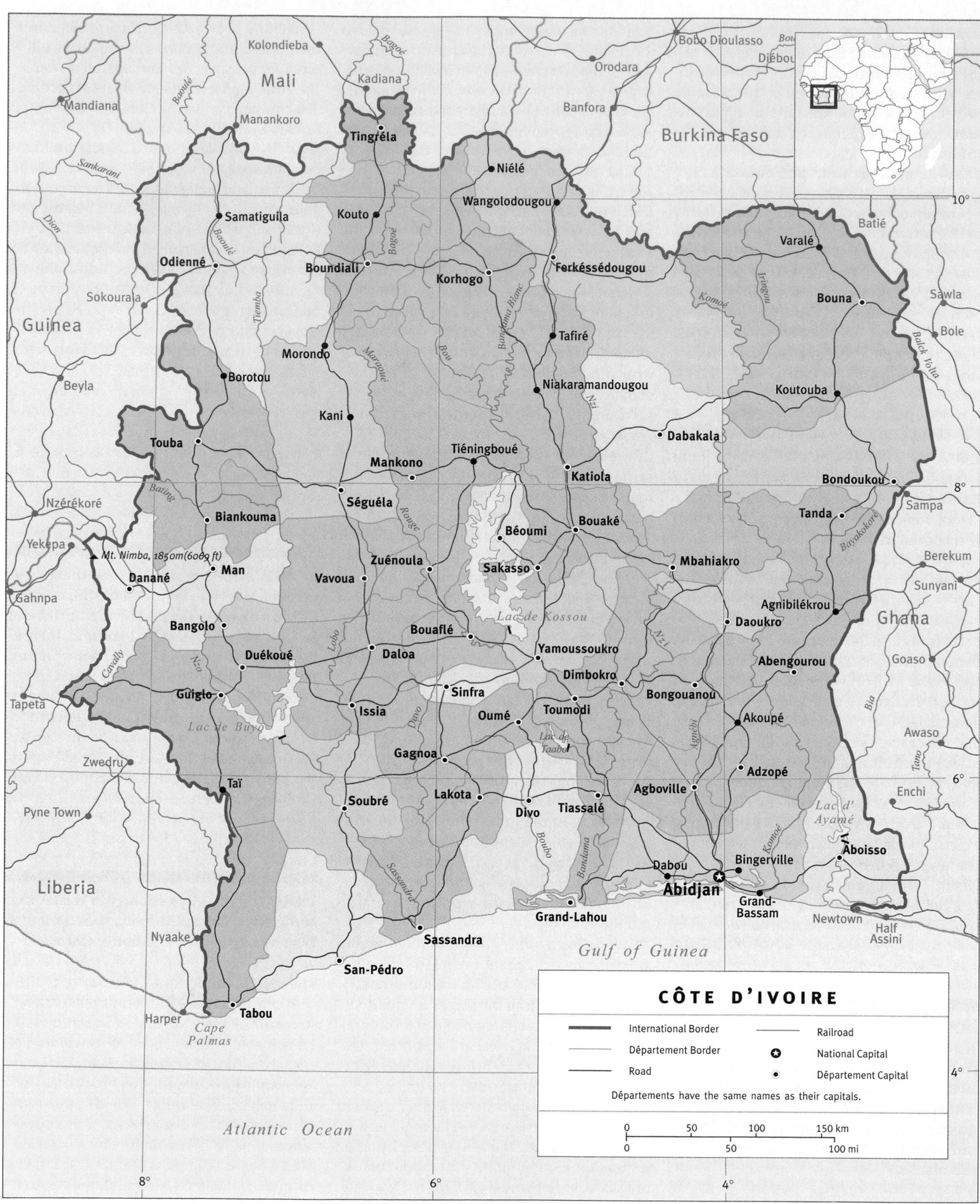

have blocked effective democratic reforms.

Precolonial History

Unlike many West African countries, little is known about the early history of Côte d'Ivoire. Historians believe that agriculture reached the region before Mande, Kru, and Akan groups assimilated much of its population. Fleeing states such as ancient Mali and Asante and searching for gold and cola nuts for the trans-Saharan trade, these groups began migrating to the area by the sixteenth century. By the mid-eighteenth century they had established five major kingdoms in the northern, central, and eastern regions: the Kong Kingdom, founded by the Jula and the Senufo; and the Abron Kingdom, the Baul Kingdom, and the Anyi Kingdoms of Indénié and Sanwi, all established by different Akan groups. Relying primarily on subsistence agriculture, these kingdoms brought the Saharan trade to the edges of the densely forested south. Nevertheless, the inhabitants of the largely autonomous forest villages remained essentially isolated from outside influences.

Dense woods in the south and a treacherous coastline protected Côte d'Ivoire from inroads by early European explorers, who made only halting contacts before the nineteenth century. The Portuguese briefly landed on the coast during the fifteenth century, and the French founded their first short-lived trading settlement at Assinie during the seventeenth century to trade guns and other European goods for gold and ivory. But inhospitable conditions prevented the establishment of permanent settlements, and thus Côte d'Ivoire largely escaped the horrors of the slave trade.

In the 1840s, however, the French, while patrolling the Gulf of Guinea to block the now illegal slave trade, decided to reestablish a foothold in the region of Côte d'Ivoire. In 1842, under orders from the Naval Ministry, Captain Bouët-Willaumez signed treaties with a number of coastal groups. For an annual tribute payment, the French obtained two strategic tracts of land – present-day Assinie and Grand-Bassam – where they built forts and trading posts. As GREAT BRITAIN acquired large possessions nearby, FRANCE attempted to expand in the region. During the next 25 years France concluded treaties with almost all the major coastal villages. Despite escalating European rivalry in the area, however, defeat in the Franco-Prussian War (1871) forced France to turn its attention away from Africa and back to European affairs. But, hoping to maintain control over the region, France named a merchant, Arthur Verdier, the first resident of Côte d'Ivoire in 1878 and gave him temporary control of Grand-Bassam and other nearby ports.

Verdier's main interests were commercial ventures along the coast; he built new ports and started a coffee plantation. He also sought to promote France's interests, and in 1887 hired Marcel Treich-Leplène to explore the NIGER RIVER basin and obtain treaties from its inhabitants. At the same time the French government sent Lt. Louis-Gustave Binger into the interior of Côte d'Ivoire. Treich-Leplène and Binger secured treaties with nine major groups, including the Abron and Kong, and when they met up in 1889 they declared the southern region a French protectorate. France solidified its claim in subsequent expeditions, and, in negotiations with Great Britain and Liberia, further clarified the boundaries of the French protectorate. (The French repeatedly redefined the northern border until 1947, when they determined its present shape.) In 1893 France declared Côte d'Ivoire a colony.

FRENCH COLONIZATION

France did not secure control of the entire Côte d'Ivoire until 1918. At first, Lt. Binger believed that existing treaties and economic incentives would provide all of the leverage necessary to secure French colonial rule, but within months he was proved wrong. Although African leaders had signed treaties giving the French control of their land, poor communication and intentional deception by the French meant that few fully understood the treaties. As a result, French attempts to establish new military and trading posts met with hostile resistance and attacks by groups such as the BAULE, DAN, BÉTÉ, and Dida. The French military spent years fighting many of these resistance movements. The most famous of these was Mandinka warrior Samory Touré's long struggle to resist French conquest. Touré, whose empire the French had previously destroyed, rebuilt at Dabakala and began extending his new empire into the northern part of Côte d'Ivoire. But the French again attacked Touré, ultimately defeating him in 1898.

Although the French had fought Touré in order to protect the prosperous Baule, the Baule not only obstructed the campaign against Touré but went on to resist French colonization for nearly another 20 years. As the French military moved through Baule territory on their way to attack Touré, they had conscripted Baule slaves as porters. This action had provoked armed attacks by the Baule and had forced the French to retreat and search out another path to Touré. Defeated and distracted by other campaigns, the French made minimal efforts to subdue the empire, but largely ignored the Baule problem.

By 1908, however, the continued resistance of the Baule and other groups underlined the failure of the French colonial government, which had no control over vast parts of the territory and could not even raise the obligatory "head tax" from the African population. Under pressure from the French government, the newly appointed governor, Gabriel Angoulvant, launched a brutal military campaign he called "pacification" and ordered troops to "seek and destroy" all rebels, their crops, and their homes. For the next seven years, the French colonial army combed the interior of Côte d'Ivoire, killed suspected resistors, and forced local rulers to accept French colonial authority. The results were devastating – the army killed thousands of Africans and subsequent famine caused the death of many more.

This ruthless campaign finally secured the entire region for France. In an effort to quell future resistance, the French filled civil service and administrative positions with either African commoners or precolonial rulers who had proved their loyalty to the French. These civil servants received the best the colonial system had to offer Africans – education, political and land rights, and economic security. In contrast, most of the African population felt only the burdens of French colonization.

Because France had decided that its African colonies must be self-sufficient, the colonial government devised two strategies to generate revenue. First, the government offered to sell land concessions to planters for private plantations. Although most of these concessions were sold to white Europeans, some Africans, mainly civil servants in the French colonial administration, also purchased land, and the wealthiest of these planters created a new class of local elites who were vocal in their demands for improved transport and shipping facilities. Second, the government established state mines, lumber, and infrastructure construction projects as well as huge state plantations that cultivated export crops, such as COCOA, coffee, and MILLET. These endeavors suffered from a shortage of labor. Consequently, the colonial government required each adult Ivoirian male to "volunteer" ten days of labor a year for state projects. Many Africans were in fact forced to work more to meet the vast labor requirements of the various projects. Still, a labor shortage persisted, and the government began recruiting workers from Upper Volta (present-day Burkina Faso), especially from the MOSSI ethnic group. This labor supply ultimately proved so valuable that Côte d'Ivoire annexed the southern part of Upper Volta in order to increase the colony's labor pool.

While the labor policy satisfied the needs of the colonial administration, it fostered antagonism and resentment among the African population. These feelings intensified during World War II, when the Nazi-supported Vichy government took over the colonies and not only doubled the forced labor requirement but conscripted laborers for the military. To the detriment of the local populations, the Vichy government also forced Ivoirian farmers to donate large portions of their crops to the military. Ivoirian intellectuals, civil servants, and communists soon joined together in protest and announced their support for Charles de Gaulle's exiled Free French government. A Baule planter and local administrator named Félix Houphouët-Boigny organized a coalition of African planters, called the Syndicat agricole africain (SAA), to protest the Vichy government's policies toward African planters. Although these organizations had little effect on the Vichy government, they did influence de Gaulle, who, in 1944, convened his exiled government and colonial administrators in Brazzaville to reassess France's relationship with its African colonies. During the conference, the group created a progressive list of postwar colonial reforms, few of which were enacted. Nevertheless, the Brazzaville Conference did plant the seeds for decolonization after World War II.

DECOLONIZATION

After the defeat of Germany in 1945, de Gaulle offered France's West African colonies greater political representation and allowed each to elect two delegates to the French Constituent Assembly, one representing the African majority and the other the European minority. Campaigning to end forced labor, Houphouët-Boigny won the African seat from Côte d'Ivoire. When the assembly convened in early 1946, Houphouët-Boigny secured passage of legislation ending the forced labor system, a major victory for the Ivoirian population. This success guaranteed him wide popular support throughout the colony. Upon his return he organized his supporters, including members of the SAA, into a new party, the Parti Démocratique de la Côte d'Ivoire, or PDCI. In October 1946 he tried to further increase his political leverage by joining the PDCI with the new multicolony party, the Rassemblement Démocratique Africain (RDA).

Led by Houphouët-Boigny and other prominent French West African leaders and supported by the French Communist Party, the RDA lobbied for parity between African and French citizens. Although the RDA supported widespread reforms, it did not press for decolonization. By 1948, however, the Communist Party had lost its place in the governing coalition, and France faced armed independence movements in North Africa and Indochina. Consequently, the French government began to view the RDA, and by extension Houphouët-Boigny and his PDCI, as a threat. For the next year Houphouët-Boigny and his party members faced harassment and persecution, including arrests. To regain French favor, Houphouët-Boigny decided to break with the Communist Party. By early 1956 he had won French support and had become the strongest African advocate of de Gaulle's vision of a French Union (later named the French Community), a federation of internally self-ruled countries under the executive control of the French president. But because the African population demanded complete independence, Houphouët-Boigny abandoned this plan for limited self-rule. As decolonization became inevitable, Houphouët-Boigny solidified his political power, and in November 1960, only two months after France declared Côte d'Ivoire independent, he was elected president by a landslide.

Côte d'Ivoire Under Houphouët-Boigny

During his first three years as president, Houphouët-Boigny built a centralized and highly personalized regime that successfully quelled dissent and political competition. At the same time, armed with French aid and a civil service full of French technocrats, Houphouët-Boigny engineered an economic boom, often called the Ivoirian Miracle, that helped build his popularity not only in the international financial community but among the Ivoirian population.

Meanwhile, rumors of a coup d'état prompted Houphouët-Boigny to further consolidate his power in a "benevolent," authoritarian one-party state. In 1962 an adviser warned him that PDCI members were plotting a coup. Houphouët-Boigny ordered the arrest of more than 125 people, 45 of whom were convicted and imprisoned. The supposed discovery of another plot in 1963 led him to purge the PDCI of more than 200 dissenters and limit the power of his closest advisers (and potential rivals). At the same time, he began crafting an intricate power system that maintained power by both silencing and coopting dissenters and by creating a group of loyal politicians who were personally indebted to the president for their positions, prestige, and wealth.

During the next two decades, Houphouët-Boigny used this system to monopolize political power. He controlled access to all government positions, including those in the military, civil service, and local government. At the same time, he maintained popular support and the guise of free speech by holding public forums that offered the populace a chance to speak to him in person. Advertised as an opportunity for constructive dialogue with a receptive and concerned president, the forums were nothing more than an opportunity to diffuse popular discontent. Houphouët-Boigny subsequently maintained the appearance of accountability by lavishing inordinate amounts of money and attention

These women and children are among the almost 3 million residents of Abidjan, the de facto capital of Côte d'Ivoire. *© Ph. Roy/Explorer*

on problems he chose to address and by scapegoating inadequate government officials, whom he promptly fired and replaced.

A strong economy supported this autocratic system. In 1960 Houphouët-Boigny had inherited one of the most developed economies in West Africa (only Ghana was more developed). But the Ivoirian economy remained heavily dependent on the export of crops, particularly coffee, cocoa, pineapples, and bananas. Although pre-independence completion of the Vridi Canal and the Abidjan port, one of the largest in West Africa, had helped bolster the economy and raised new revenues, few efforts had been made to promote sustainable economic growth. After independence, Houphouët-Boigny took up this challenge. Having maintained close ties with France since the colonial period, he asked the French government to encourage investment. Foreign investment, coupled with efforts to divert revenues from export crops into other economic sectors, such as manufacturing, helped boost economic growth to an annual rate of 10 to 12 percent during the 1960s. The discovery of oil further stimulated foreign investment, and by the early 1970s agriculture accounted for only 25 percent of the gross domestic product. It seemed that Côte d'Ivoire had sustainable prosperity.

But the worldwide recession of the late 1970s and early 1980s undermined the economic progress of Côte d'Ivoire and caused severe problems in Abidjan. The city, until then a focus of investment, had experienced a huge influx of rural villagers seeking stable wages. The sudden economic slowdown caused rampant unemployment and exacerbated tensions between Abidjan's rich and poor that soon erupted in protests. Protestors attacked Houphouët-Boigny's failure to "ivoirianize" the public sector, much of which was still run by French expatriates.

At the same time the recession depressed the price of Côte d'Ivoire's two main exports, cocoa and coffee. The price drop hurt rural farmers and plantation workers, many of them unskilled laborers whose migration from other African countries had been encouraged by Houphouët-Boigny's government. As a result, tensions between Ivoirian and migrant farmers escalated into violence throughout the late 1970s and early 1980s. Meanwhile, decades of exploitation had reduced the southern forest reserves and curtailed profits from another valuable export, hardwood. Exploration proved that the once-celebrated oil reserves would yield nothing more than a short-lived boom. Rampant inflation and increasingly severe droughts between 1973 and 1985 further exacerbated these problems.

Houphouët-Boigny succeeded for a while in deflecting public unrest and criticism onto other government officials. As the situation worsened in the early 1980s, however, he responded to critics by "ivoirianizing" the public sector and decentralizing municipal governments. Nevertheless, the government remained a target of widespread protests, organized by teacher and student unions and opposition groups such as the Ivoirian Popular Front, led by the exiled Laurent Gbagbo. As these continued, Houphouët-Boigny returned to his former policy and dissolved the unions, closed the universities, and arrested the protesters. Facing few serious threats, he had little incentive to change the system that maintained his power and enriched him and his family.

A dirt track winds through forested hills in northwestern Côte d'Ivoire. *CORBIS/Les Pickett; Papilio*

External pressures, however, forced the president to introduce the reforms that internal protests had failed to secure. In the late 1980s the International Monetary Fund and the World Bank pushed Houphouët-Boigny to implement austerity measures (*see* Structural Adjustment in Africa) that would further tax the already impoverished nation and inevitably bring new protests. At the same time foreign supporters, concerned about the health of the elderly leader and the future of Côte d'Ivoire, began pressing Houphouët-Boigny to open the system to potential successors. In April 1990 Houphouët-Boigny announced the first multiparty elections in Ivoirian history. The short notice and cumbersome bureaucratic restrictions put the opposition at a disadvantage, but it nevertheless nominated a candidate, Gbagbo, who ran in the presidential election. The election was won by Houphouët-Boigny with an 81 percent majority, but Gbagbo won a seat in the National Assembly in elections that took place a month later. Still, electoral reforms failed to bring substantive change to the Houphouët-Boigny system, and the president again sought to quell opposition and dissent.

The need to identify a successor soon overshadowed the repressive actions of the Ivoirian government. Already in weak health, in June 1993 Houphouët-Boigny was diagnosed with prostate cancer. He ruled the country from the hospital until his death six months later. Despite expectations of a long and violent power struggle, Henri-Konan Bédié succeeded Houphouët-Boigny smoothly. Since taking power, Bédié has continued many of the policies of his predecessor. His government refused to implement electoral reforms in the 1995 presidential election, and an opposition boycott tarnished Bédié's victory. Like Houphouët-Boigny, Bédié has taken measures to silence dissent and criticism. At the same time, he has benefited from a healthy economy and has made strategic economic concessions to key groups, such as civil servants and rural farmers, in an effort to strengthen the position of the PDCI. With support from France and other foreign donors, the PDCI's system of "one-party democracy" seems unlikely to falter in the near future.

Elizabeth Heath

See Also

Abidjan, Côte d'Ivoire; Decolonization in Africa: An Interpretation; Baule; Brazzaville, Republic of the Congo; Colonial Rule; Explorers in Africa Since 1800; Gold Trade; Ivory Trade; Sahara Desert; Samory Touré; Rassemblement Démocratique Africain; Mali Empire.

Africa

Côte d'Ivoire (Ready Reference)

Official Name: Republic of Côte d'Ivoire
Former Name: Ivory Coast
Area: 322,462 sq km (122,503 sq mi)
Location: Western Africa; borders the North Atlantic Ocean, Ghana, Burkina Faso, Mali, Guinea, and Liberia
Capital: Yamoussoukro (population 106,786 [1988 estimate]) has been the official capital since 1983; however, Abidjan (population 2,700,000 [1990 estimate]) is the de facto capital and contains the administrative center. It is also where most foreign governments maintain their official presence.
Other Major Cities: Bouaké (population 329,850), Daloa (121,842 [1988 estimate]), Gagnoa (population 59,500 [1986 estimate])
Population: 15,446,231 (1998 estimate, including at least 3 million immigrant workers and their families)
Population Density: 45 persons per sq km (about 116 persons per sq mi)
Population Below Age 15: 47 percent (male 3,537,190; female 3,496,749 [1997 estimate])
Population Growth Rate: 2.9 percent (1996 estimate)
Total Fertility Rate: 6.2 children born per woman (1996 estimate)
Life Expectancy at Birth: Total population: 44.8 years (male 43.6 years; female 46 years [1997 estimate])
Infant Mortality Rate: 82.4 deaths per 1000 live births (1996 estimate)
Literacy Rate (age 15 and over who can read and write): Total population: 40.1 percent (male 49.9 percent; female 30 percent [1995 estimate])
Education: Education is free, and primary education is compulsory. A vast television education program was established in the early 1970s that has helped to improve literacy rates. In the early 1990s about 1.5 million students annually attended primary schools and about 423,000 attended secondary and vocational schools.
Languages: French is the official language and a large percentage of the population uses it, especially for written communication. There are, however, over 60 other languages spoken in Côte d'Ivoire; of these, Dioula is the most widely used.
Ethnic Groups: The population of Côte d'Ivoire contains over 60 ethnic groups. The largest groups are Baule, 23 percent; Bété, 18 percent; and Senufo, 15 percent. Other groups include Malinke, Agni, Kru, Voltaic, and Mande peoples. There is a significant Lebanese community. A large number of immigrants come from Liberia, Burkina Faso, and Mali.
Religions: About 60 percent of the population adhere to indigenous beliefs. About 20 percent are Christians (mostly Roman Catholic) and 20 percent are Muslims.
Climate: Tropical along the coast, semi-arid in the far north, and varying at the center between forest and savanna. In the southern region temperatures vary between 22° C (72° F) and 32° C (90° F) and there are two rainy seasons, April to July and October to November. In the central part of the country, the temperatures are more extreme, ranging from 12° C (54° F) and 40° C (104° F). Annual rainfall average is 2100 mm (83 in) in coastal Abidjan and 1200 mm (about 48 in) in Bouaké, on the central plain.
Land, Plants, and Animals: Côte d'Ivoire is flat with some undulating plains, except for mountains in the northwest region. The north central region has savanna. From the coast to the southern central region there is dense forest containing obeche, mahogany, and iroko. Animals include the jackal, hyena, panther, elephant, chimpanzee, crocodile, and various lizards and venomous snakes.
Natural Resources: Rich, arable soil and forests containing commercially valuable hardwoods. Côte d'Ivoire has mineral deposits of gold, iron ore, manganese ore, diamonds, and petroleum. Hydroelectric plants on the Bia and Bandama rivers provide a significant amount of electricity.
Currency: The Communauté Financière Africaine (CFA) franc
Gross Domestic Product (GDP): $25.8 billion (1997 estimate)
GDP per Capita: $1700 (1997 estimate)
GDP Real Growth Rate: 6.5 percent (1997 estimate)
Primary Economic Activities: Agriculture (85 percent of population), industry, and commerce
Primary Crops: Coffee, cocoa, bananas, corn, rice, manioc, sweet potatoes, sugar, cotton, rubber, and timber
Industries: Foodstuffs, beverages, wood products, oil refining, automobile assembly, textiles, fertilizer, construction materials, and electricity
Primary Exports: Cocoa, coffee, tropical woods, petroleum, cotton, bananas, palm oil, pineapples, cotton, and fish
Primary Imports: Food, capital goods, consumer goods, and fuel
Primary Trade Partners: France, Nigeria, Japan, Netherlands, United States, and Italy
Government: Côte d'Ivoire is a constitutional republic with a multiparty presidential regime. The executive branch is led by President Henri-Konan Bédié and Prime Minister Daniel Kablan Duncan, who was appointed by the president. The legislative branch is the elected 175-member National Assembly, which is currently dominated by President Bédié's party, the Democratic Party of the Côte d'Ivoire.

Elizabeth Heath

See Also

Abidjan, Côte d'Ivoire; Yamoussoukro, Côte d'Ivoire.

Africa

Cotonou, Benin, largest city and main port of the People's Republic of Benin; it is also the country's de facto capital.

The commercial and administrative center of Benin, Cotonou is located on the Nokwe Lagoon on the Gulf of Guinea, about 35 km (22 mi) from Porto-Novo, the country's official capital. Originally called Kotuno (Fon for "estuary of death") by the kingdom of Dahomey, the malaria-ridden area was largely uninhabited until the late nineteenth century. In 1878, however, Dahomey king Ghezo offered it to the French, who were anxious to secure land holdings in West Africa. Soon afterward France asked permission to improve the shallow port but was denied by Ghezo's successor, Glele. This denial prompted occupation and, eventually, the Franco-Dahomean wars that led to French colonization in 1894. Under French COLONIAL RULE, Cotonou became the colony's main port.

After the completion of the Benin-Niger railroad in the early 1900s, Cotonou became the shipping hub for both Dahomey and NIGER. In 1963 the independent Beninese government used development grants to modernize the port. Since then the city has grown rapidly, attracting both international firms and rural migrants. Today, Cotonou is Benin's business headquarters and home to the main government buildings – the Supreme Court, National Assembly, and Presidential Palace. The population of Cotonou is approximately 430,000.

Since the colonial era, Cotonou's economy has been supported by the shipping business provided by the port and railroad. It is also home to a number of textile, food-processing, and light manufacturing plants. Many of Cotonou's residents earn their livelihood as traders or artisans, or as laborers on the growing city's numerous construction projects. The promise made by former president MATHIEU KÉRÉKOU – a government job for every college graduate – became clearly unrealistic during a time of nationwide austerity measures. Although the city has prospered in recent years, unemployment remains high.

Elizabeth Heath

SEE ALSO

Benin; Dahomey, Early Kingdom of; France; Porto-Novo, Benin.

North America

Cotton Club, a prestigious white-owned Harlem nightclub of the 1920s and 1930s that featured prominent African American musicians, singers, and dancers performing for a white clientele.

The Cotton Club was one of Harlem's premier nightclubs, renowned for its superb JAZZ music and the exotic routines of its female dancers. The club was also a constant reminder of the reality of segregation in the North as well as the South. Although its performers and waiters were all black and it was located for many years in the heart of Harlem in New York City, the Cotton Club had a whites-only policy, and it only hired female dancers who were light-skinned and who emulated white standards of beauty.

The Cotton Club had its beginnings in 1920, when the controversial African American boxing champion Jack Johnson opened the Club Deluxe on Lenox Avenue and 142nd Street in Harlem. Johnson sold the club to white gangster Owney Madden, who reopened it in the fall of 1923 as the Cotton Club. Under Madden, the Cotton Club's floor shows and decoration highlighted black primitivism and sensuality. Decorated inside and out in the style of a log cabin and featuring pseudo-jungle décor, the club's appearance starkly revealed prevailing white stereotypes of African Americans (*see* RACIAL STEREOTYPES).

Madden's timing was fortuitous, for during the 1920s New York City's elite displayed a sudden interest in black life and culture. In 1924 white bandleader Paul Whiteman premiered George Gershwin's jazz-influenced composition *Rhapsody in Blue* at New York City's Aeolian Hall, featuring the composer on piano. During the 1920s white author Carl Van Vechten published *Nigger Heaven* (1926), a popular novel about black life in Harlem, and hosted intimate soirées that featured such African American guests as blues singer BESSIE SMITH. The smart set considered it fashionable to journey into Harlem to visit the Cotton Club. "Join the crowds after theater," a 1929 advertisement declared. "All Broadway comes to Harlem."

The club's entertainment was certainly first-rate. Perhaps the most significant musician connected with the Cotton Club was Duke Ellington, whose orchestra played there from 1927 to 1931. Singer Cab Calloway first performed at the club in 1930, and in the following year his orchestra took over from Ellington's as the club's house band. During Ellington's tenure, the club was wired for radio broadcasts, which helped Ellington build a national audience for his music. Among the club's featured entertainers were singers ETHEL WATERS and BILLIE HOLIDAY and dancers Bill "Bojangles" Robinson and Earl "Snake Hips" Tucker; in the chorus line was a young LENA HORNE.

The 1929 stock market crash and the onset of the GREAT DEPRESSION put a damper on the Cotton Club's freewheeling entertainment, but the club did not shut down. The Harlem Riot of 1935 had a more serious impact. In the aftermath of the riots, Madden moved the club out of Harlem, reopening in 1936 in a supposedly safer downtown location on Broadway and 48th Street. The club continued in operation until 1940.

Aaron Myers

SEE ALSO

Calloway, Cabell (Cab); Harlem Riots of 1935; Harlem, New York; Johnson, John Arthur (Jack); New York, New York; Robinson, Bill ("Bojangles"); Ellington, Edward Kennedy ("Duke"); Segregation in the United States.

North America

Cotton Production in the United States, the South's most important agricultural product, following Eli Whitney's 1793 invention of the cotton gin, which permitted commercial use of American short-staple cotton; closely bound up with SLAVERY IN THE UNITED STATES and with late nineteenth-century sharecropping. During the early twentieth century African American scientist GEORGE WASHINGTON CARVER concentrated his agricultural research on improving cotton harvests. Since the 1930s, however, the number of African Americans engaged in cotton production has dropped greatly as a result of the impact of the boll weevil and the mechanization of cotton farming, both of which helped accelerate a massive twentieth-century black migration out of the South.

North America

Council on African Affairs, Pan-Africanist organization of the mid-century dedicated to increasing American awareness of colonialism and economic exploitation in Africa.

A group led by actor PAUL ROBESON and Max Yergan, former secretary of the Young Men's Christian Association (YMCA), founded the Council on African Affairs on January 28, 1937. Initially called the International Committee on African Affairs, the organization provided news and information about the brutalities of European colonialism in Africa. It remained the only such organization for many years.

The 70-member board of the council included United States Representative Adam Clayton Powell Jr., writer Alain Locke, and educator MARY MCLEOD BETHUNE. The scholar W. E. B. Du Bois became an active participant in 1948. Although this period was marked by strong anticommunist sentiment, the council did not reject members who were sympathetic to communism. In fact, the organization received most of its funding from a procommunist white radical, Frederick V. Field, owner of the Chicago-based department store chain Marshall Field & Co.

After moving to New York City in 1942, the council published a two-page newsletter, *News of Africa*, and a monthly journal, *New Africa* (later renamed *Spotlight on Africa*). By 1946 the council began picketing the South African embassy in WASHINGTON, D.C., and from 1945 to 1950, published the *African Bibliography*, which documented the atrocities of APARTHEID.

By April 1947 the U.S. attorney general had classified the council as a subversive organization, and in 1953, under the McCarran Act, it was required to register as such. Internal disputes and anticommunism weakened the organization. As the council splintered, funding dried up. After 19 years the organization was forced to close its doors in 1956.

Alonford James Robinson, Jr.

SEE ALSO

Pan-Africanism; Du Bois, William Edward Burghardt (W. E. B.); Locke, Alain Leroy; New York, New York; Powell, Adam Clayton, Jr.

North America

Craft, Ellen and William (Ellen: b. 1826, Clinton, Ga.; d. 1891, Ways Station, Ga.; William: b. 1824, Macon, Ga.; d. 1900, Charleston, S.C.), African American abolitionists known for William's autobiographical slave narrative that described the couple's dramatic escape from slavery.

William and Ellen Craft's self-liberation is one of the most remarkable escapes ever recorded in an African American slave narrative. This is in part due to the brazenness of their plan: the Crafts traveled by public transportation all the way from their home in Georgia to freedom in Philadelphia, even staying in hotels along the way. But their boldness was made possible by the brilliance of their disguise – which employed race, gender, and class passing to conceal Ellen, a black slave woman, as a white slaveholding man.

Ellen was born in Clinton, Georgia, to a biracial slave woman and her master, and was so light-skinned that she was often mistaken for a member of her father's white family. This infuriated her mistress and, as a result, at age 11 Ellen was given as a wedding gift to a daughter who lived in Macon. There she met William, whom she married in 1846. Two years later, the Crafts began to devise their escape plan, in which Ellen was to pose as a white male slaveholder traveling with "his" slave, William.

The plan required several levels of deception. Ellen had to pretend to be not just white, but a white man, because a white woman would not travel alone with a male slave. She cut her hair, changed her walk, and wrapped her jaw in bandages to disguise her lack of a beard. To hide her illiteracy, she wrapped her right arm in a sling to have a ready excuse for being unable to sign papers; and she explained all of the bandages by claiming to be an invalid traveling north to receive medical care. In this manner, the Crafts traveled from Georgia to Pennsylvania by train, steamer, and ferry without being discovered. They arrived in Philadelphia on Christmas Day, 1848.

In Philadelphia, they were befriended by abolitionists William Wells Brown and William Lloyd Garrison, who recognized the power of their story as an antislavery tool. The Crafts moved to Boston and began traveling as antislavery lecturers. But the passage of the Fugitive Slave Law in 1850, which mandated that fugitive slaves living anywhere in the United States must be returned to their owners, put their freedom in danger. Because of their celebrity, the Crafts were singled out by slavecatchers as targets. In November 1850, they fled to England, where they had five children, attended an agricultural training school, and continued to work as antislavery activists. William's autobiography, *Running a Thousand Miles for Freedom*, was published in London in 1860.

In 1868, following the Civil War, the Crafts returned to the United States with two of their children and settled in Ways Station, Georgia, near Savannah. There they farmed a cotton and rice plantation and attempted to start a school, although financial debts from the plantation and hostility from white neighbors ultimately led to the school's demise. Ellen Craft died in 1891. As she had requested, she was buried under her favorite tree on their land. William Craft eventually moved to Charleston, South Carolina, where he died in 1900. *Running a Thousand Miles for Freedom* was reprinted in Arna Bontemps's 1969 collection *Great Slave Narratives*. The Crafts' story remains a testimonial to the intelligence, cunning, and courage many African American slaves brought to their determination to be free.

Lisa Clayton Robinson

See Also

Abolitionism in the United States; American Anti-Slavery Society; Boston, Massachusetts; Civil War, American; Fugitive Slave Laws; Philadelphia, Pennsylvania; Slave Narratives.

North America

Creole Affair, an 1841 slave revolt in which blacks overthrew the crew of the United States ship *Creole* and sailed to freedom in the Bahamas.

On October 27, 1841, the brig *Creole* left Hampton Roads, Virginia, for New Orleans with 135 slaves on board. In early November off the coast of Florida about 20 slaves, led by Madison Washington, commandeered the ship, killing one white crew member. One slave was also killed during the revolt.

The likeliest destination for the fugitives was the free settlement of Liberia, in Africa, but since the *Creole* was unlikely to withstand such a journey, Washington ordered the crew to sail for the British port of Nassau in the Bahamas. On arrival, the slaves asked for asylum from Great Britain, which in 1807 had banned the trade of slaves and in 1833 had outlawed slavery altogether. Except for several men detained for mutiny and murder, the slaves of the *Creole* were granted their freedom.

Relations between the United States and Great Britain had been tense for several years before the *Creole* docked at Nassau. Although the United States had banned the slave trade in 1808, it had done little to cooperate with Great Britain to stop the continuing illegal slave trade. In particular, the United States refused to let Great Britain search its ships for slaves smuggled from Africa – a right Great Britain had negotiated with most other countries.

Consequently, many slave traders flew the U.S. flag to protect their contraband, prompting Great Britain to stop and search U.S.-flagged ships it suspected of harboring slaves. Proslavery Americans were outraged by these repeated breaches of sovereignty, and many Americans interpreted Great Britain's harboring of the *Creole*'s slaves as yet another breach.

When word of the *Creole* uprising reached the mainland, Secretary of State Daniel Webster demanded the immediate return of the slaves, who were, he argued, mutineers, murderers, and the property of U.S. citizens. Great Britain refused to comply. The stalemate made negotiation of the Webster-Ashburton Treaty (1842), which was intended to resolve border disputes between Great Britain and the United States, much more difficult. The treaty was ultimately signed, with Great Britain making concessions on its extradition policy and the United States agreeing to help suppress the international slave trade.

Domestically, the *Creole* affair was a predictable irritant to relations between the North and South. Joshua Reed Giddings, a Whig member of Congress from Ohio, introduced several resolutions in March 1842 stating that the slaves of the *Creole*, in resuming their natural rights to liberty, had violated no U.S. law. He further argued that because slavery was an institution of the separate states, not of the federal government, slavery did not exist in the province of the federal government – for example, on the high seas. The House, led by Southerners, censured Giddings and he resigned his seat; however, a few weeks later in a special election to fill the vacancy, he was reelected.

The *Creole* affair was put to rest when an Anglo-American commission ruled in 1853 that Great Britain had violated international law. In 1855 the slave owners received $110,330 in compensation, but the freedpeople of the *Creole* were not returned.

See Also

New Orleans, Louisiana; Slave Rebellions in Latin America and the Caribbean.

North America

Creoles, a name adopted by or applied to a number of ethnic groups in the New World who were descended from European colonists or African slaves, or both. "Creole" can also refer to the language of such groups.

Linguists generally refer to dialect with the lowercase "creole," while historians refer to Creole peoples with the upper-case spelling of the term. Historically, the word carries political as much as racial meaning, having denoted, at various times, people of both African and European descent, as well as their racially mixed offspring.

The word "Creole" derives from the Spanish *criollo*, meaning "native to the locality." In the sixteenth, seventeenth, and eighteenth centuries, it referred to American-born children of Spanish parents. With the settling of North America and the onset of the slave trade, *créole,* a French cognate, became in many places a name for all nonindigenous but locally reared inhabitants – including the descendants of both European colonialists and African slaves, and even, in some cases, new breeds of plants and livestock.

In most Caribbean communities, where ethnicity shaped social relations, "Creole" also became a loaded and divisive term. The history of the Creole people of the Louisiana territory offers the most famous example of the designation's politically charged usage, as well as of its confusing history.

In eighteenth-century Louisiana – where French and then Spanish colonists had children with members of each new wave of African slaves who worked their farms – "Creole" was used widely to refer to those of mixed descent. Its meaning narrowed after 1803, however, when the United States, having purchased Louisiana from France, banned slave-trading in the territory. At this time Anglo-American immigrants began arriving en masse, sometimes to the dismay of the European-descended colonists. In order to emphasize their sense of aristocratic superiority, the latter, through legislation, restricted the use of the title "Creole" to refer only to themselves. This restriction even excluded free blacks, including those who were part of the established aristocratic Creole culture. Thus for half a century, "Creole" connoted a predominantly white segment of New Orleans society.

After the Civil War, many upper-class blacks in New Orleans who had been free before the war reappropriated the appellation to distinguish themselves from former slaves, whom they considered unrefined. But although Louisiana's small black aristocracy successfully reclaimed the Creole title, they were never legally distinguished from freed slaves. In the twentieth century "Creole" applied increasingly to French-influenced African American people in New Orleans – including descendants of both the upper class and the slaves. Today the term connotes such people almost exclusively, as well as the music and cuisine that they helped to create.

Eric Bennett

See Also

Transatlantic Slave Trade; Spain; Free Blacks in the United States, 1619 to 1863; Civil War, American; New Orleans, Louisiana.

Latin America and the Caribbean

Créolité (Creoleness), literary and cultural movement launched in the early 1980s that promotes the mixed or hybrid nature of former French outposts in the Caribbean.

Focused primarily on Martinique and Guadeloupe, Créolité came about in response to the Négritude Movement (most influential from the 1930s to the 1960s) that posited African culture as the single alternative to the European culture that French colonization had imposed on the islands. Although Créolité acknowledges the important first step away from French culture taken by Négritude, it also has not hesitated to point to Négritude's omissions. In the century and a half since slavery was abolished in the French colonies (1848), indentured servants from China and India (*see* East Indian Communities in the Caribbean) and immigrants from Syria and Lebanon, as well as the children of mixed-race unions, have rendered the black-white dichotomy meaningless on the islands. For the Créolité movement, literature and politics in the French Caribbean must reflect these cultural changes.

Créolité came into official existence with the publication of its manifesto, *Eloge de la Créolité* (1989; In Praise of Creoleness, 1993), written by two Martinican authors, Patrick Chamoiseau and Raphaël Confiant, and a Martinican linguist, Jean Bernabé. Inspired by Edouard Glissant's notion of *antillanité* (Caribbeanness), Chamoiseau and his colleagues attacked both Négritude and French colonialism for attempting to locate Caribbean culture outside the islands. (The authors separate themselves from Glissant in the affinities they claim with non-Caribbean islands, such as Réunion Island, a French overseas territory off the east coast of Africa, and in their exclusion from their model of certain Caribbean islands dominated by one ethnic group.)

For the authors of *Eloge*, Caribbean or Creole identity resides precisely in the mixing or creolization of the numerous ethnic groups that has taken place *on* the islands. As early as the seventeenth century, different ethnic groups and their forms of expression were put into contact with each other on the plantations – albeit against their will – and this process has continued to the present. The Créolité writers readily admit that the phenomenon of mixing has occurred elsewhere in the world but assert that it has taken place so often in the Caribbean that no single identity has emerged as the dominant one, in spite of France's efforts to assimilate this region culturally. For the authors, it is precisely this unstable identity that must be cultivated.

Since two of its authors are novelists, *Eloge* – and, it should be noted, the Créolité movement as a whole – is principally concerned with how to transmit this sensibility in literature. The route chosen by Raphaël Confiant in his early works (such as *Jik deye do Bondye* [1978] and *Bitako-A* [1985]) was to write in French Creole, the language spoken and only recently written in this region of the Caribbean (*see* Languages, Creole, in the Caribbean). Creole is itself a reflection of the multiple influences in the islands and a symbol of resistance to French culture. However, for practical reasons (namely, the lack of a Creole-reading audience), French is the dominant language of literary expression for the Créolité writers. But this is a French inflected by the rhythms of Creole. Works such as Chamoiseau's epic novel *Texaco* (1992; winner of France's prestigious Prix Goncourt), Confiant's *Eau de café* (1991), and Gisèle Pineau's *L'Exil selon Julia* (1996) effectively blend French with Creole words and to create a new form of expression sometimes referred to as *fréole*. Créolité also manifests itself on a thematic level. Créolité writers – Confiant most of all – represent the vast array of ethnicities on the islands and the complicated interactions their cultural differences create.

Although the Créolité movement is widely praised, it has its critics. Maryse Condé, one of the most influential writers in the Caribbean today, has been careful to distance herself from a movement she considers to be excessively invested in Caribbean particularity and not sufficiently open to questions that affect all of humanity. The Guadeloupean critic Willy Alante-Lima has condemned the Créolité writers for their tendency to romanticize the Caribbean past, specifically in the person of the maroon, or runaway slave (*see* Maroonage in the Americas). Finally, the academic A. James Arnold has attacked the Créolité movement for constituting an exclusively male club. This last objection is less relevant as a result of the recent adherence of the very talented woman writer, Gisèle Pineau, to the Créolité movement. Furthermore, the vast majority of writers from the French Caribbean today, and even some from the Négritude generation (such as René Ménil), claim an affiliation with the movement, validating Créolité's aesthetic and political project.

Richard Watts

See Also

France; Réunion; Literature, French Language, in Caribbean.

Latin America and the Caribbean

Creolized Musical Instruments of the Caribbean, musical instruments, primarily of European origin, adopted by people of African descent for use in Afro-Caribbean music.

Afro-Caribbean music reflects the region's intertwining of African and European cultures together with less clearly visible Native American contributions. It not only makes use of a wide range of African-derived percussion instruments, but also incorporates many European instruments and adapts them to distinctly Afro-Caribbean musical ends. Anthropologists term this process of cultural adaptation *creolization*.

Perhaps the most important class of such instruments is the Spanish-derived guitar and its close relatives the *tres*, a six-stringed instrument with three sets of doubled strings, the *laúd*, and the *quatro*. During the nineteenth century, itinerant Cuban *soneros* most commonly played the guitar, tres, or laúd (*see* SON). In the twentieth century two popular Cuban ensembles, *septetos* and *conjuntos*, employed the tres along with percussion, trumpet, bass, and sometimes piano.

Early Caribbean musicians also adopted the violin, as seen in its use by Cuban *charanga* bands and by Haitian *menwat* groups, which perform VODOU music in the southern region of HAITI. During the first two decades of the twentieth century, pianist and composer Lionel Belasco, the most prominent Trinidadian bandleader in New York City, recorded early examples of CALYPSO music played by string bands. These recordings often included Belasco's cousin Cyril Monrose on violin and Gerald Clark on guitar or quatro.

The cello and double-bass are other members of the violin family that came into use in Afro-Caribbean music. During the 1930s, for example, Cuban cellist Orestes López and his brother Israel "Cachao" López, a double-bassist, played a significant role in creating and popularizing the MAMBO rhythm.

Caribbean musicians also took up a wide range of European wind instruments, including the trumpet, flute, saxophone, clarinet, and trombone. Flutes and violins were the melody instruments in Cuban charanga bands. Trumpets played the melody line in septetos and conjuntos. The Afro-Latin big bands of BENY MORÉ and Pérez Prado made use of trumpet, trombone, and saxophone sections (*see* AFRO-LATIN JAZZ). During the 1960s trombonist WILLIE COLÓN replaced the conjunto's trumpets with trombones and provided a distinctive ensemble sound for the emerging genre of SALSA MUSIC.

The piano was a key part of the conjunto and many other Caribbean ensembles. During the twentieth century, a number of accomplished pianists – including Bebo Valdés (b. 1918), RUBÉN GONZÁLEZ, Chucho Valdés, and Gonzalo Rubalcaba (b. 1963) – developed an Afro-Cuban jazz piano style. The Panamanian Danilo Pérez (b. 1966) has also emerged as an up-and-coming jazz musician. During the 1920s Cuban composers such as ALEJANDRO GARCIA CATURLA incorporated Afro-Cuban elements into classical piano music (*see* MUSIC, CLASSICAL, IN LATIN AMERICA AND THE CARIBBEAN).

More recently, the growing influence of rock 'n' roll has encouraged Caribbean bands such as Cuba's IRAKERE to adopt a number of electric instruments, including the electric guitar, electric bass, and electric piano. Afro-Caribbean musicians have played the synthesizer as well as the piano, and a number of Trinidadian SOCA performers have made use of drum synthesizers.

James Clyde Sellman

SEE ALSO

New York, New York; Cuba; López, Israel ("Cachao"); Panama; Pérez Prado, Dámaso; Valdés, Jesús (Chucho); Trinidad and Tobago.

North America

Crisis, The, official publication of the NATIONAL ASSOCIATION FOR THE ADVANCEMENT OF COLORED PEOPLE (NAACP).

The Crisis has been the official publication of the NAACP since 1910, and for its first quarter-century it also served as a public forum for the ideas of its first editor, noted black intellectual and civil rights activist W. E. B. Du Bois. The NAACP, founded in 1909, is an interracial organization that supports the struggles of people of color. Most of its original board members were white, and Du Bois's position as the editor of the *Crisis* made him the most powerful African American in the organization at that time. In turn, he established the *Crisis* as the most influential publication for African Americans during his tenure as editor.

Du Bois was first hired by the NAACP in June 1910 as its director of publicity and research. By September he had submitted a proposal to produce a monthly magazine that would document "very important happenings and movement in the world which bears on the great problem of interracial relations and especially those which affect the Negro-American." Du Bois intended the magazine's title, the *Crisis: A Record of the Darker Races,* to signify the current "critical time in the history of the advancement of men." The NAACP approved the proposal, a one-year line of credit, and hired Du Bois as editor. The first issue appeared in November 1910, 16 pages that sold for ten cents.

The magazine's standard departments included "Along the Color Line," which reported on politics, education, science, and art; "Along the Battle Line," which covered NAACP activities; "What to Read," which recommended recent books and articles; "Talks About Women," "Men of the Month," and features such as "Colored High Schools" and "American Negroes in College," which promoted race pride. The *Crisis* also became known for its inclusion of new literature by African Americans, including such landmarks as LANGSTON HUGHES's first published poem. In 1920 the *Crisis* was even briefly able to add a second publication, the *Brownies' Book,* intended for black children.

The inaugural issue of *Crisis* sold 1000 copies; within just over a year that figure had risen to 16,000, and the next year the paid circulation was at 30,000. Of those numbers, about 75 percent were sold to blacks, which showed that the *Crisis* reached a larger black audience in addition to the NAACP members who received the magazine as part of their membership.

Du Bois wrote many of the *Crisis*'s articles himself, but it was the editorial section where he – and by extension, the magazine – had the strongest impact. Du Bois used the editorial section to promote his ideas on whatever interested him, and in some cases, such as his famous 1919 essay protesting the racism black World War I veterans faced back home, they received national attention.

Predictably, Du Bois's strong opinions caused him problems throughout his tenure as editor. Du Bois's support of "social equality," including interracial marriage, was radical for his time, even for some of the progressive whites who supported the NAACP. Du Bois also openly criticized several African American institutions, including the black church, the black press, and black colleges whose governing bodies were predominantly white. These opinions caused controversy among some African American readers. Whenever Du Bois came under criticism from the NAACP's board of directors, he would claim censorship. Because he was the most prominent African American in the organization, he felt even more strongly that he should be allowed to state his views freely. His struggles with the board, combined with declining circulation, finally led to his resignation in 1934.

Without Du Bois the *Crisis* lost the singular voice that had brought it such recognition. But the magazine continued to serve as the NAACP's official publication and continued its focus on racism worldwide and the progress of efforts to fight it. Roy Wilkins succeeded Du Bois as editor, and Wilkins was followed in 1949 by James Ivy, who directed the magazine's coverage of the CIVIL RIGHTS MOVEMENT over the next 20 years. Circulation had fallen from a high of 100,000 in 1918 to 10,000 when Du Bois left, but by the late 1980s it had risen again to 350,000. Even these numbers were not enough to keep the *Crisis* from suffering a financial setback in the winter of 1996, which forced it to cease publication for six months. But with its July 1997 issue the *New Crisis* reasserted its position as the "premier, crusading voice for civil rights," and "an honest forum for the politics, art and literature of human liberation."

Lisa Clayton Robinson

SEE ALSO

World War I and African Americans; Literature, African American; Press, Black, in the United States; Du Bois, William Edward Burghardt (W. E. B.); Miscegenation; Wilkins, Roy Ottoway; Black Church, The.

North America

Crite, Allan Rohan

(b. March 20, 1910, Plainfield, N.J.), African American painter and printmaker known for his scenes of Boston's black community in the 1930s and 1940s, as well as for his drawings and paintings of religious subjects.

Oscar and Annamae Palmer Crite, Allan Rohan Crite's parents, moved to Boston before he was a year old. Crite attended Boston's School of the Museum of Fine Arts from 1929 to 1936, while also painting in the federal government's WORKS PROGRESS ADMINISTRATION (WPA) program. He graduated from

Harvard University's Extension School in 1968, where he also worked as a librarian for 20 years. In nearly seven decades of work, Crite has participated in numerous solo and group exhibitions.

Crite's early paintings are full of action and brilliant color, and filled with light. They depict the rich connections within a small urban black community. *Parade on Hammond Street* (1935) and *School's Out* (1936) are outstanding examples of what Crite calls his "reporting" of African American city life. A quieter double portrait, *Harriet and Leon* (1941), shows a dignified couple on a snowy street with a background of buildings, a truck, and children at play.

Crite does not distinguish between his realistic visual images of Boston's black community and his religious art; the secular and the spiritual are intertwined, he believes, and he states, "You only live one life." His painting *Madonna of the Subway* (1946) exemplifies this view, as does his *Self-portrait* (1938), in which he includes one of his religious paintings on one-quarter of the picture plane.

Crite used pen-and-ink drawings to create several books interpreting African American spirituals: *Were You There When They Crucified My Lord?* (1944); *All Glory* (1947); *Is It Nothing to You?* (1948); and *Three Spirituals from Earth to Heaven* (1948). An active Episcopalian, he has painted murals and altarpieces for churches in the United States and Mexico. Christ Church in Bronxville, New York, dedicated a stained glass window in his honor in 1994.

Crite's work is held in the collections of the Museum of the National Center of Afro-American Art, in Roxbury, Massachusetts; the Art Institute of Chicago; the Corcoran Gallery and the National Museum of American Art, both in Washington, D.C.; and the Schomburg Center for Research in Black Culture in New York. The Boston Athenaeum holds more than 30 oils, watercolors, and works on paper, which were the gift of the artist in 1971. He received the Harvard University Medal in 1986. Crite married Jackie Cox, an art consultant, in 1994. They are establishing the Allan Rohan Crite House Museum to preserve and exhibit the artist's work.

Betty Gubert

See Also
Boston, Massachusetts; New York, New York; Schomburg Library.

North America

Crittenden Compromise, **an attempt to appease Southerners on the eve of the American Civil War by guaranteeing their right to hold slaves.**

During the American presidential campaign of 1860, leading Southerners, such as Gov. William Henry Gist of South Carolina, made clear that they would urge the South to secede if Abraham Lincoln and his antislavery Republican Party won the election. The secessionists were abetted by outgoing president James Buchanan, who, fearful of a civil war, stated that the federal government had no right to force a state to remain in the Union. Almost immediately after Lincoln won in November, several Southern legislatures began discussing secession.

In December 1860, Sen. John J. Crittenden of Kentucky proposed four resolutions and six amendments to the Constitution that, in effect, would have resurrected and expanded the Missouri Compromise of 1820. That compromise, which Congress had repealed in 1854, protected slavery in newly created states south of the 36°30' parallel and banned slavery north of it. The Crittenden Compromise would have revived the 36°30' border and extended it to the vast territories in the West acquired after the Mexican-American War (1846-1848). Territories south of the line would be able to enter the Union as slave or free states, according to their desire; north of the line, slavery would be banned.

In other provisions, slavery in the District of Columbia was to be protected, and only individual states – not the federal government – could abolish slavery. The fugitive slave acts were also to be amended. Northern states could no longer refuse to enforce the acts, and the federal government would compensate slave owners if slaves escaped with the help of outsiders. Though not inaugurated, Lincoln made known his disapproval of the Crittenden Compromise, and in 1861 it was narrowly rejected by the House and Senate.

See Also
Fugitive Slave Laws.

Africa

Crocodile, **animal that was revered by some ancient Egyptian sects; one of the largest and most advanced reptiles.**

The Nile crocodile usually can be recognized by its long triangular snout, intermediate between the long, narrow snout of gavials and the short, oval snout of alligators and caimans. The Nile crocodile of Africa was revered by certain ancient Egyptian sects, and mummies of crocodiles have been discovered in Egyptian tombs. In modern times this species has been hunted so extensively that few remain in the lower Nile, but they are still abundant in the upper Nile and southward in Africa to the Cape of Good Hope. Crocodile eggs are used for food in some parts of the world. The skin is highly valued for leather, and the extract from the musk glands is used in the manufacture of perfumes. Because of overhunting, the Nile crocodile is considered an endangered species.

The Nile crocodile is a member of the *crocodilian* order. Crocodilians are well-adapted as predators, with few natural enemies. Bony plates, called osteoderms, form a kind of armor in their thick skin. Their teeth, about 30 to 40 in each jaw, are set into sockets in the jawbones and interlock when the mouth is closed. In crocodiles, the fourth tooth on each side of the lower jaw protrudes when the mouth is closed. The jaws of crocodilians are powerful enough in closing to crush the bones of small animals, but so weak in opening that they can be held together by hand. As the crocodilian floats almost completely submerged, its protruding nostrils and eyes and a portion of its back are the only parts visible as it stalks its prey. Crocodilians are the most vocal reptiles, producing sounds from quiet hisses to fearsome roars and bellows, usually during the mating season. On land crocodilians move quickly in a belly crawl but can also gallop and walk mammal-like on all four legs.

Crocodiles are physiologically the most advanced reptiles; their internal anatomy resembles that of birds. They have a four-chambered heart and well-developed senses. Cold-blooded like all reptiles – their body temperature depends on the environment – crocodilians bury themselves in mud to estivate or hibernate. In warm regions they are dormant during droughts; in colder regions, during winter.

Crocodilians are egg-laying, or *oviparous*, reptiles, reaching reproductive maturity at about the age of ten. The eggs, 20 to 90 in number and about the size of goose eggs, are buried in sand, mud, or vegetable debris, where they are left to hatch by the heat of the sun or of vegetable decomposition.

The Nile crocodile is classified as *Crocodylus niloticus*.

Robert Fay

See Also
Nile River.

North America

Crosswaith, Frank Rudolph **(b. July 16, 1892, Frederiksted, St. Croix, Virgin Islands; d. 1965), African American labor organizer, political activist, and journalist who helped found the Harlem Labor Committee and the Negro Labor Committee.**

Frank Crosswaith was born on St. Croix in the Danish West Indies (now the United States Virgin Islands) to William I. and Anne Eliza Crosswaith. He was educated at the University Preparatory School in Frederiksted and the Rand School of Social Science in New York. After graduating, he began his career in African American labor relations, becoming known as the Negro Debs because of his similarity to labor leader Eugene V. Debs.

A socialist, Crosswaith sought to ally African American workers with white workers under the banner of class. Thus, he opposed African American leaders who believed in racial alliance alone. In 1934 he helped found and then chaired the Harlem Labor Committee (HLC). He attempted to align the HLC with the American Federation of Labor (AF of L), which was then seeking African American members. This enabled African Americans to integrate unions that were previously closed to them.

In 1935 Crosswaith also helped found the integrated Negro Labor Committee, whose goals were to organize African American labor and highlight the common problems facing African American and white laborers. His zeal for equal employment opportunity was still evident at the March on Washington for Jobs and Freedom in 1963, at which he spoke.

Crosswaith's work in politics began in 1924 when he was vice chair of the American Labor Party during Robert LaFollette's presidential campaign. He lectured for the League for Industrial Democracy and the Socialist Party. He also edited the *Negro Labor News* for 12 years and cowrote *True Freedom for Negro and White Workers* and *Discrimination Incorporated*.

Robert Fay

See Also

American Federation of Labor and Congress of Industrial Organizations; Labor Unions in the United States; Socialism; March on Washington, 1963.

Africa

Crowther, Samuel Ajayi (b. 1806, Oshogun, Yorubaland [present-day Nigeria]; d. December 31, 1891, Lagos, Nigeria), the first African Anglican bishop.

Samuel Ajayi Crowther was born into a Yoruba family in western Nigeria. Until his mid-teens he was raised in traditional Yoruba society. In 1821, however, slave traders raided his home village, kidnapped him, his mother, and sisters, and separated them. Traders then sold Crowther to Portuguese slavers, who in 1822 loaded him onto a slave ship bound for Brazil. Luckily, a British antislavery warship intercepted his captors; they rescued Crowther and took him to Freetown, in Sierra Leone. There the Christian Missionary Society (CMS) took Crowther in, and he began attending mission schools.

Gifted linguistically, within six months of his arrival Crowther could read and write English. He went by his birth name of Ajayi until 1825, when he was baptized an Anglican and took the name Samuel Crowther after a CMS missionary of the same name. Crowther traveled to England in 1826 to study at a CMS school in London. The following year, he became the first African to graduate from the Fourbah Bay Institution (now College) in Sierra Leone. He then began to teach at missionary and government schools in and around Freetown.

In 1841 Crowther was selected to accompany the Niger expedition of the Society for the Extinction of the Slave Trade and the Civilisation of Africa, whose intent was to evangelize up the Niger River. Crowther distinguished himself, and an Anglican priest recommended him for the priesthood. He returned to England to study and was ordained a priest in 1843.

The CMS posted Crowther to its Yoruba mission, first at Badagry and later to his native area of Abeokuta, where he renewed contact with his mother and sister, who had also escaped slavery. Henry Venn, a progressive in the CMS administration, envisioned an indigenous African church, which he hoped Crowther might help build. Crowther, who had written a Yoruba dictionary and produced a Yoruba translation of the New Testament and the Book of Common Prayer, was a successful evangelist. He preached in Yoruba and won many African converts to Christianity. In 1857 the CMS chose him to head the Niger Mission, and he established missions in Akassa, Onitsha, Lokaja, and Idah.

In 1864, consecrated in a ceremony at Canterbury Cathedral as "Bishop of Western Equatorial African beyond the Queen's Dominions," Crowther became the first African to hold the title of bishop in the Anglican Church. Despite numerous obstacles, after a few years under Crowther's leadership the Niger Mission boasted 600 converts, 10 priests, and 14 catechists.

Despite these successes, Crowther faced opposition, especially among the younger generation of white CMS missionaries, who adhered to the Social Darwinist and racist theories of the day that justified colonialism, and who believed that they were better suited to run the mission than an African such as Crowther. These views doomed Venn's plan for an independent African church. Thus, the CMS forced Crowther to accept a white associate to administer the Niger Mission's finances, and Crowther faced accusations of incompetence. As a final insult, and in violation of established church procedures, the mission's finance committee suspended all of the African priests whom Crowther had ordained. Crowther resigned in protest in 1890. In the following year, he was making plans in Lagos to establish an independent African church when he suffered a stroke.

Robert Fay

See Also

Abeokuta, Nigeria; Freetown, Sierra Leone; Lagos, Nigeria.

North America

Crummell, Alexander (b. 1819, New York, N.Y.; d. September 10, 1898, Red Bank, N.J.), African American clergyman and missionary who encouraged African Americans and Africans to recognize their common experiences, he played a major role in shaping African American intellectual thought.

Alexander Crummell was the son of Boston Crummell, a self-emancipated black born in Africa, and Charity Hicks, an African American whose family had lived free in the United States for several generations. He received his early education at New York's African Free School and at Canal Street High School, both operated by African American clergymen. In 1835 Crummell and several other teenagers enrolled in a new academy for black students in Canaan, New Hampshire, but angry whites destroyed the school soon after it opened. He completed his secondary education at the Oneida Institute in Whitesboro, New York. Run by black and white abolitionists, Oneida combined studies of the classics with manual labor – a simultaneously intellectual and practical approach to life that Crummell would employ the rest of his years.

Graduating from Oneida in 1839, Crummell applied to the General Theological Seminary in New York City with the hope of becoming an Episcopal priest. He was rejected, almost certainly because he was black. He studied theology on his own and with ministers throughout New England, and worked with black parishioners in Massachusetts and Rhode Island. At several regional and national conventions for African Americans, he advocated for blacks to help themselves, for the abolition of slavery, and for the establishment of colleges for African Americans – and for the achievement of these goals within the framework of Christian morality. In 1844 Crummell was ordained an Episcopal priest, and he was soon ministering to a congregation of poor blacks in New York. Unable to raise the money to build a church, he left for Great Britain in 1848 with the hope of raising funds.

Relatively free from the effects of racial prejudice and enjoying a sympathetic audience of liberals, Crummell later referred to his time in Great Britain as one of the high points of his life. He first spent three years traveling the country and raising money for his church; during this time he also prepared with a tutor to enter Cambridge University. In 1851 he was admitted to Queen's College, Cambridge, from which he graduated with a bachelor's degree in 1853.

When he left England shortly after graduating, it was not for the United States but for the African nation of Liberia, which had achieved independence in 1847. In Liberia Crummell lectured broadly on the importance of black leaders and black institutions. He initially was little interested in the native population but ultimately founded churches throughout the country and became headmaster of a school in Cape Palmas. He hoped the school would train the future leaders of the nation, and throughout the rest of his life he espoused that one of the higher duties of American and African blacks was the "redemption," both religious and intellectual, of their African brothers.

Crummell took Liberian citizenship and subsequently made several trips to the United States to encourage emigration to Liberia and to raise money for Liberian causes. In this he was closely allied with the back-to-Africa philosophy of the AMERICAN COLONIZATION SOCIETY. In 1861 he published *The Relations and Duties of Free Colored Men in America to Africa* and in 1862 *The Future of Africa*. In these works he argued that blacks around the world shared a common experience of racial discrimination. In 1861 Crummell accepted a post at Monrovia's Liberia College, though a falling-out with the school prompted his firing five years later.

In the late 1860s Liberia entered a time of upheaval, as President James Royce was assassinated and struggle erupted between native Africans and emigrants, mulattos (of African and European descent) and blacks. Fearing for his life, Crummell returned to the United States in 1872. He settled in WASHINGTON, D.C., where he founded a church ministering to a black congregation.

In 1882 he published a collection of sermons called *The Greatness of Christ*, in which he argued that Christians could not find salvation merely by accepting Christ but that they must also work constantly for the good of humankind. In the following year Crummell called a conference to protest the lack of black bishops in the Episcopal Church. During the next several years he exhorted educated blacks to serve as a vanguard for the betterment of the race. Simultaneously he urged vocational training for most blacks. In this duality he anticipated the great debate in the next century between Booker T. Washington and W. E. B. Du Bois, for whom Crummell was a role model and mentor. In 1891 Crummell published another volume on the relationship between Africa and the United States, *Africa and America*.

Starting in 1895 Crummell taught theology at HOWARD UNIVERSITY, where he expanded his views on the importance of liberal arts and vocational education. In 1897 he co-founded the AMERICAN NEGRO ACADEMY in an effort to give shape to black intellectualism and to counter the rising discrimination and segregation of the late nineteenth century. He died in the following year.

SEE ALSO

Du Bois, William Edward Burghardt (W. E. B.); Episcopal Church; Free Blacks in the United States, 1619 to 1863; New York, New York; Washington, Booker Taliaferro.

Africa

Crusades, armed Christian pilgrimages between 1096 and 1291 C.E.; a joint effort by the Roman Church and various western European rulers to control the Holy Lands.

From the eleventh to the thirteenth century, successive popes summoned Christians on crusades to seize Jerusalem and the Church of the Holy Sepulcher and defend these lands from "infidels" (non-Christians). Thousands of Christians took vows to join what they believed was a just and holy war, though arguably their leaders had more interest in controlling the rich markets and trade routes of the east than in converting nonbelievers. Many scholars see the Crusades as a precursor to the European wars of conquest in the Americas and in parts of Africa two centuries later, wars also justified on religious grounds.

Though the Crusades transformed the history and consciousness of western Europe, Islamic rulers at the time were more concerned with Mongol attacks from the east and the Turkish threat to the north than with this localized conflict in Syria and Palestine. The establishment of the Crusader States in otherwise Islamic lands did unite Muslims. The Crusades increased Muslim consciousness of the importance of these lands to Islamic peoples. Muhammad is said to have ascended to heaven in Jerusalem and the Dome of the Rock mosque was built there in his honor. This collaborative opposition to the Franks, as Muslims called the Europeans, helped the Mamluks to rally Muslims behind their Islamic state incorporating EGYPT, Arabia, Syria, and Palestine.

The Crusades primarily aimed to capture Jerusalem, but a large number of them also targeted Egypt, the center of the Islamic empires of the Ayyubids (1169-1250) and the Mamluks (1260-1517), both of which controlled Syria and Palestine. Because Egypt had been a Roman province from 30 B.C.E. to 395 C.E. and a center of early Christianity, the Europeans felt justified in trying to regain it. Perhaps more important, Egypt controlled the rich Indian Ocean trade routes leading to Asia. During this period, Europeans began using religion to justify wars of conquest against Muslim lands more generally, including southern SPAIN, PORTUGAL, and North Africa.

Pope Urban II initiated the First Crusade in 1096. Selcuk Turks had conquered Syria and Palestine in 1077 and thus gained control of Jerusalem. The pope called for a crusade to liberate the Orthodox Christians of the Holy Lands from their Islamic "oppressors." Many scholars have asserted, however, that Muslims treated this Christian population with respect, and that there is no evidence that the Selcuks ushered in an era of Christian persecution. Some historians believe that the Roman Church instigated the Crusades in an effort to absorb the Orthodox Church. Others believe that, more often than not, the Crusades were a looting venture.

The First Crusade (1096-1099) was the only successful one: Europeans captured Antioch, Jerusalem, Edessa, and Tripoli. The next few Crusades sought mainly to defend these Crusader States. However, Nuradin, the Muslim ruler of Aleppo, defeated the Second Crusade at Damascus in 1148. Encouraged by this success, Nuradin's lieutenant, Saladin, moved on to conquer Fatimid Egypt. When Saladin captured Jerusalem at the Battle of Hattin in 1187, Europe responded with the Third Crusade, which failed to regain Jerusalem but captured Acre in 1191. This episode ended when the English king Richard the Lionheart signed a five-year truce with Saladin in 1192, giving Christians access to, though not control of, Jerusalem.

The Fourth and Fifth Crusades primarily targeted Egypt. Although they briefly captured Damietta, at the mouth of the Nile, in 1221, their main effect was to send the Byzantine Empire into a terminal decline and establish Venetian dominance in the Mediterranean. The Holy Roman Emperor Frederick II of GERMANY led the Sixth Crusade. Noted for his sympathy toward Muslims (his entourage included many Moors), Frederick's mission was more diplomatic than military. In 1229 he made a truce with the Egyptians, which left Jerusalem in Christian hands except for the area of the Dome of the Rock. Louis IX (known as Saint Louis) of France instigated the Seventh and Eighth Crusades. He occupied Damietta in 1249, only to lose it immediately thereafter. In 1291 the Mamluk sultan Baybars conquered Palestine and the last of the Crusader States, Antioch. This European defeat essentially ended the Crusades.

Various European powers tried unsuccessfully to revive the Crusades throughout the fourteenth and fifteenth centuries. Although they briefly captured Alexandria in 1365, the fight against the Muslims had shifted to Eastern Europe, where the Ottomans were gaining control, and the Iberian Peninsula, which Spanish and Portuguese forces gradually took back from the Moors before they embarked on their overseas conquests in the fifteenth century.

Leyla Keough

SEE ALSO

Roman Africa: An Interpretation; Nile River; Mamluk State; Tripoli, Libya; Alexandria, Egypt.

North America

Cruse, Harold Wright

(b. March 18, 1916, Petersburg, Va.), African American author of *The Crisis of the Negro Intellectual*, which provided a theoretical basis for black separation.

After his parents' separation, Harold Cruse moved with his father to New York City, where he completed high school. After serving in the quartermaster division of the United States Army from 1941 to 1945, he enrolled at City College of New York on the G.I. Bill, although he dropped out in his first year. During the 1950s and early 1960s, Cruse worked at various part-time jobs and became an active participant in left-wing politics in Harlem. It was during this period that he joined the Communist Party, which he later rejected. He also wrote two plays and a musical during this period, and, with AMIRI BARAKA (LeRoi Jones), established the Black Arts Repertory Theater and School in 1965.

In 1967 the *New York Times* hailed *The Crisis of the Negro Intellectual: A Historical Analysis of the Failure of Black Leadership* as "a mind-blowing experience". Cruse's influential book, which remains a controversial critique of racial integration, attacked black leaders for failing to develop a nationalist program for the political, economic, and cultural autonomy of black Americans. Cruse followed *Crisis* in 1968 with a collection of essays titled *Rebellion or Revolution?*

In 1968 he also joined the faculty of the University of Michigan as a visiting professor. At Michigan Cruse helped establish the Center for Afro-American and African Studies and, in 1977, became the first black professor without a college degree to be appointed full professor at an American university. His book *Plural but Equal* was published in 1982. In 1987 he became professor emeritus at Michigan.

Lawrie Balfour

SEE ALSO

Black Arts Movement; Harlem, New York; New York, New York; Communist Party USA, African Americans and the.

Latin America and the Caribbean

Cruz, Celia

(b. October 21, c. 1929, Havana, CUBA), Cuban-born, African American vocalist, one of the most recognizable singers of the popular Latin dance music known as salsa.

Nicknamed the Queen of Salsa, Celia Cruz has recorded more than 50 albums, collaborating with many of the leading figures of Latin popular music. During a career that has spanned more than four decades, Cruz has gained a reputation for her tireless work, warm personality, and emotive style of singing. In performance she is known for her skillful improvisation of lyrics. She is one of a few successful female vocalists in a genre dominated by men.

Born in a poor section of Havana, Cruz demonstrated her singing talents at a very young age, but she studied to be an elementary school teacher because her father did not consider singing to be a suitable career for a woman. Encouraged by her mother and a teacher, however, she nevertheless pursued a singing career.

Cruz began her musical career performing for prizes in contests held on the radio or at local venues. In 1950 she became lead vocalist for Sonora Matancera, one of the most popular *conjuntos* (ensembles) in Cuba. Although the group was criticized for hiring a black singer, Cruz's hard work and talent eventually won her popular acclaim. In 1960, following the Cuban Revolution, Cruz left Cuba for MEXICO. In 1961 she moved to the United States and a year later married Pedro Knight, a trumpeter for Sonora Matancera, who subsequently became her manager.

In the United States Cruz made a series of recordings for popular bandleader Ernesto "Tito" Puente from 1966 through 1972. Bandleader JOHNNY PACHECO and FANIA RECORDS owner Jerry Masucci took an interest in her, leading to her portrayal of Gracia Divina in the concert production and musical recording of *Hommy, A Latin Opera* (1973). *Hommy* gave further impetus to Cruz's career by bringing her a new generation of fans. In the mid- and late 1970s she collaborated with many of the best-known salsa performers, including Pacheco, Ray Barretto, WILLIE COLÓN, Bobby Valentín, and the Fania All Stars.

Cruz continued to perform actively through the 1980s and appeared in several celebrated reunion concerts with Sonora Matancera. In 1990 she shared a Grammy Award with Ray Barretto for their 1988 recording *Ritmo en el Corazón*. She was also recognized with an honorary doctorate from Yale University and, in 1994, with a National Medal of the Arts from President Bill Clinton. Cruz has appeared in several motion pictures, most notably the 1992 film *The Mambo Kings*.

SEE ALSO

Puente, Ernesto Antonio (Tito); Salsa Music.

Latin America and the Caribbean

Cruz e Sousa, João da

(b. November 24, 1861, Desterro [present-day Florianópolis], Santa Catarina, Brazil; d. November 19, 1898, Sítio, Minas Gerais, Brazil), Afro-Brazilian poet and writer, considered one of the most important poets of the nineteenth century in the Americas.

Since his mother had been freed by the time of his birth, João da Cruz, named after a Spanish mystic saint, was born free. His father would be granted his freedom ten years later, when Marshal Guilherme Xavier de Sousa participated in the war against Paraguay (1864-1870). Father and son incorporated the marshal's name – Sousa – into their own.

Guilherme de Sousa sponsored João's early education, and his wife, Clarinda, took it upon herself to educate the young boy from the age of seven. The marshal died in 1870 and left a house and some money to the Cruz e Sousa family. João attended public school beginning in 1869 and a provincial school from 1871 onward, continuously excelling in languages and the recitation of poetry. In 1877, barely 16 years old, Cruz e Sousa began to teach privately to supplement his family's income while publishing poetry in various newspapers in Santa Catarina. He founded a literary magazine in 1881 and published poems praising the Brazilian abolitionist Castro Alves.

Tired of the racism he encountered in Santa Catarina, a southern town with a strong European influence, Cruz e Sousa joined a theater group and traveled with it throughout the country, delivering abolitionist speeches that soon became famous (*see* ABOLITION AND EMANCIPATION IN LATIN AMERICA AND THE CARIBBEAN). Although he was honored in various cities by abolitionist organizations for his speeches and articles from this period, he never published his orations. This fact may have contributed to subsequent accusations that he was oblivious to the abolitionist movement (*see* WHITE ABOLITIONISTS IN BRAZIL).

In 1883 a new provincial governor named Cruz e Sousa public prosecutor, but the appointment was rejected by local politicians. Cruz e Sousa nonetheless returned to Santa Catarina in 1885 and there published his first book, *Tropos e fantasias* (Tropes and Fantasies; 1885), a collection of prose that included both sentimental texts and antislavery manifestos. At this time he read European literature extensively, particularly works by the French authors Baudelaire, Zola, and Flaubert.

The abolition of slavery in 1888 and the end of the Brazilian empire in 1889 did not increase opportunities for blacks as much as Cruz e Sousa had hoped (*see* BRAZIL). When he moved to Rio de Janeiro, then the capital of Brazil, he was able to obtain modest employment only after much insistence. While there, however, he contributed to the newspaper *Folha popular*, and became acquainted with Bernardino Lopes, Oscar Rosas, and the first group of Brazilian poets associated with the movement that came to be known as Symbolism. This literary style arose in part as a reaction to the rationalism of the Second Industrial Revolution, and embodied belief in the possibility of reaching Beauty and Truth through emotion. The first Symbolist manifestos published in Brazil date from this period, and they were signed by Cruz e Sousa and a few others.

Having obtained a job at a railway station in 1893, Cruz e Sousa married a young black woman, Gavita Rosa Gonçalves, with whom he would have four children. In that same year he published two books, *Missal*, a collection of prose pieces, and *Broquéis* (Shields), a book of poetry. The year 1893 is considered to mark the beginning of Brazilian Symbolism, largely because of the publication of these two books. Cruz e Sousa's work was increasingly admired in literary circles throughout Brazil.

Stricken with tuberculosis and in search of a mild climate, in 1897 Cruz e Sousa moved to the small town of Sítio in the state of MINAS GERAIS. He died the following year at the age of 37. His body was carried to Rio de Janeiro in a wagon designated for animals and left at the station's platform. It was claimed later by his companions.

Cruz e Sousa produced his best work, classics in the genre of Portuguese-language literature, from 1893 to 1897. During this time he wrote the poetry that would appear in the posthumous publications titled *Evocações* (1898, Evocations), *Faróis* (1900, Beacons), and *Últimos sonetos* (1905, Last Sonnets), books that were said to have renewed poetic expression in the Portuguese language. The literary critic Sílvio Romero maintained that 400 years of poetic production in Brazil culminated in Cruz e Sousa's work. Yet, in a move common to much of the criticism addressing the poet's work, Romero proclaimed the exceptional nature of Cruz e Sousa's achievement within his race; he declared Cruz e Sousa a singular example of a Brazilian black man who had achieved superior cultural development.

Cruz e Sousa, who would become known as the Black Poet or the Black Swan (also the nickname of Panamanian poet GASPAR OCTAVIO HERNÁNDEZ), came to focus his later poetry on aesthetic concerns, addressing his historical context in less obvious ways than he did in his early abolitionist works. This led to the accusation that he avoided the issue of blacks in Brazil. Biographical information and careful readings of his writings, however, indicate that Cruz e Sousa witnessed and experienced a great deal of suffering and humiliation as a member of the black community. Poems such as *Violões que choram* (Weeping of Guitars) and *Canção negra* (Black Song) offer passionate portraits of blacks in late-nineteenth-century Brazil. The poem *Pandemonium*, about Cruz e Sousa's mother's suffering as a slave, contains some of the most agonizing lines ever written about slavery in Brazil. A few texts published long after Cruz e Sousa's death – in particular *A consciencia tranqila* (The Tranquil Consciousness) and *Crianças negras* (Black Children) – have to a certain extent undone the reputation of Cruz e Sousa as a writer disconnected from the concerns of Brazilian blacks.

Marcos Natalí

SEE ALSO
Rio de Janeiro, Brazil.

Latin America and the Caribbean

Cuba, an archipelago comprising the island of Cuba, the Isle of Youth, and a number of smaller keys and islets. It is located at the entrance to the Gulf of Mexico, with the Atlantic Ocean to the north and the Caribbean Sea to the south. It lies south of the Florida Straits and east of the Yucatan Peninsula. It is the largest island of the Greater Antilles.

Many associate Cuba's history before the 1959 revolution with the resorts and casinos of the 1940s and 1950s that made it a favorite stopping point for American tourists; and after the revolution with cold war tensions and the singular figure of Fidel Castro. Less is known about Afro-Cuban participation and leadership in the struggle for independence from Spain in the nineteenth century or Afro-Cuban activism in the twentieth century.

SPANISH COLONY: 1492-1898

Relatively little is documented about the region we know as the Caribbean before the arrival of Christopher Columbus in 1492. Contemporary chronicles, along with more recent archaeological and anthropological accounts, have contributed to our knowledge of indigenous peoples of the region. Columbus reached Cuba on his first voyage without realizing it was an island, and discovered Ciboney, Guanahuatabey, and Taíno Arawak Indians. On other islands he found the Carib Indians, from whom the region takes its name.

Sebastián de Ocampo, in 1508, was the first European to sail around the coast, but it was Diego Velázquez who disembarked with 300 men in 1511 to conquer the island for Spain. Velázquez founded several towns, called *villas*, from the eastern Baracoa to the western San Cristobal de La Habana, later to become the capital.

As throughout the Americas, the struggle for freedom dates back to the clash between two peoples and cultures, the European and the Indian, the latter ill equipped to match the economic and military strength of the former. Nonetheless, the Spaniards encountered strong resistance from the Taínos of eastern Cuba, led by an Indian chief who had been driven from the neighboring island of Hispaniola (comprising present-day HAITI and the DOMINICAN REPUBLIC) and who was burned at the stake in 1512. More resistance was encountered in the 1522-1523 rebellion led by Cacique Guama, of Baracoa. Settlements established by runaways, called *palenques*, were refuge first to Indians fleeing their lands seized by the Spaniards and later to runaway slaves (*see* MAROONAGE IN THE AMERICAS). The indigenous population was soon decimated. In 1526 the first shipment of African slaves was brought to Cuba, to labor primarily on the SUGAR and coffee plantations. The first slave uprising took place just four years later, and in 1533 there was a slave strike in the mines.

The early black presence is reflected in the first major literary work in seventeenth-century Cuba, a poem titled *El espejo de paciencia* (The Mirror of Patience), by Silvestre de Balboa de Troya y Quesada. It describes the kidnapping of Bishop Fray Juan de las Cabezas Altamirano by the French pirate Gilberto Girón. A bold and brave black man, Salvador Galomón, kills the kidnapper and saves the eastern town of Holguín from danger. This early literary representation of the black juxtaposes the injustice of enslavement and the heroism of the black protagonist.

These two themes were to be repeated through history. The Indian and slave rebellions of the early colonization period might be regarded as forerunners to the rebellions that accompanied the huge influx of African slaves in the nineteenth century. The rebellions similarly had parallels with the abolitionist and independence movements of the late nineteenth century.

The slave trade experienced an economic boom following the demise of sugar in Saint-Domingue (present-day Haiti) after the HAITIAN REVOLUTION (1791-1804) and after Spain permitted Cuba, as of 1818, to trade with the world. The slave trade from Africa to Cuba had already increased during the 1762-1763 British occupation of Havana, which opened the island to trade and mercantilism. Over the next half century it grew rapidly, with an estimated 1 million African slaves in Cuba by the early years of the nineteenth century. Eighty-six percent of these slaves were imported after 1790, and more than 70 percent after 1817, the year Spain signed a treaty with Great Britain to end the slave trade, which Spain later ignored. With over half the population in Cuba of African origin or descent by the late nineteenth century, race and race mixing took on entirely new dimensions. With the decimation of the Indian population through war, disease, and displacement, the Hispanic and the African would form the two major roots of the nascent Cuban nation (*see* SLAVERY IN LATIN AMERICA AND THE CARIBBEAN).

Their relations, however, were turbulent. In 1812 a conspiracy planned by JOSÉ ANTONIO APONTE, a free black carpenter in Havana, in which whites also participated, sought to overthrow slavery and colonial rule. In 1826 the first armed uprising for independence took place in Puerto Príncipe (Camagüey Province), led by Francisco de Agüero and Andrés Manuel Sánchez. Agüero (white) and Sánchez (*mulato*, of mixed African and European ancestry) were executed, becoming the first martyrs of Cuban independence.

Throughout the nineteenth century, Africans in Cuba were allowed to form their own *cabildos* (councils), initially based on a specific grouping or "nation" of Africa but later Pan-African (encompassing several such groupings) and also African-Creole (including Africans and native-born Afro-Cubans). By the turn of the century, these evolved into the cultural, political, and mutual aid societies and clubs that would characterize twentieth-century black organizations.

From the time of its consolidation as a federal republic, the United States had coveted Cuba. Before the Civil War, desires to annex the island as a slave state were expressed by anti-abolitionists in the United States. President Franklin Pierce offered to buy the island in 1852. Pro-expansionist and anti-abolitionist, Pierce had been advised that Cuba was fast becoming Africanized and a second Saint-Domingue. Between 1857 and 1861 President James Buchanan tried to interest the United States Congress in buying Cuba, but Congress was divided over the issue of slavery. This expansionist ambition was mirrored on the island. Cuban slaveholders saw the possibility of annexation as protection for their economic interests. Other Cubans simply admired the modern nation to the north. These annexationist currents reined in the more revolutionary

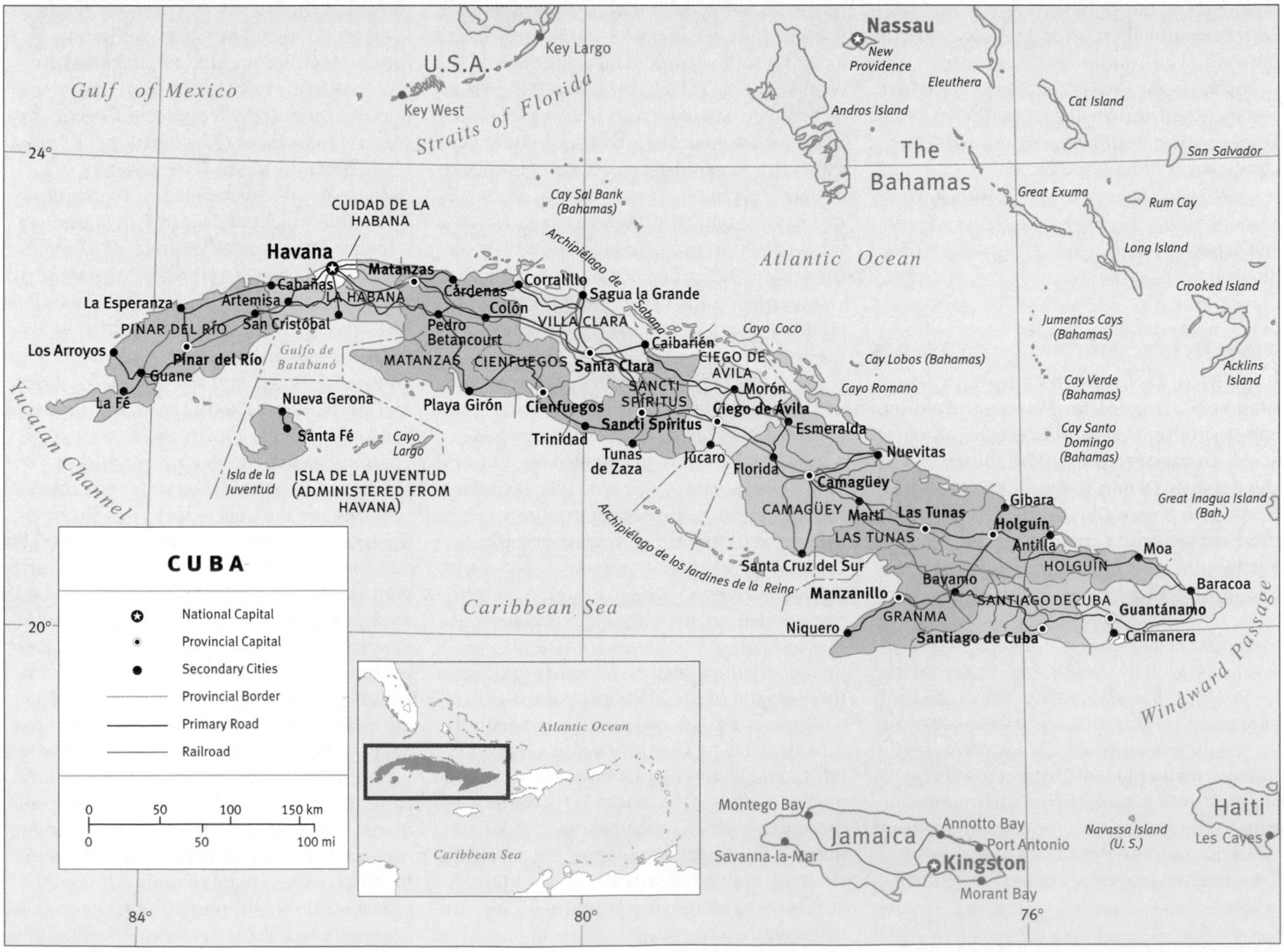

CUBA
National Capital
Provincial Capital
Secondary Cities
Provincial Border
Primary Road
Railroad
0 50 100 150 km
0 50 100 mi
Gulf of Mexico
U.S.A.
Key Largo
Key West
Straits of Florida
Nassau
New Providence
Eleuthera
Andros Island
Cat Island
The Bahamas
San Salvador
Great Exuma
Rum Cay
Long Island
Crooked Island
Acklins Island
Cay Sal Bank (Bahamas)
Jumentos Cays (Bahamas)
Cay Verde (Bahamas)
Cay Santo Domingo (Bahamas)
Great Inagua Island (Bah.)
Atlantic Ocean
Archipiélago de Sabana
CUIDAD DE LA HABANA
Havana
Matanzas
Cabañas
Cárdenas
Corralillo
Sagua la Grande
La Esperanza
Artemisa
LA HABANA
Colón
PINAR DEL RÍO
San Cristóbal
Pedro Betancourt
VILLA CLARA
Caibarién
Cayo Coco
Los Arroyos
Pinar del Río
Gulfo de Batabanó
MATANZAS
CIENFUEGOS
Santa Clara
CIEGO DE ÁVILA
Cayo Lobos (Bahamas)
Guane
La Fé
Nueva Gerona
Playa Girón
Cienfuegos
SANCTI SPÍRITUS
Morón
Cayo Romano
Ciego de Ávila
Santa Fé
Cayo Largo
Trinidad
Sancti Spíritus
Esmeralda
Nuevitas
Isla de la Juventud
ISLA DE LA JUVENTUD (ADMINISTERED FROM HAVANA)
Tunas de Zaza
Júcaro
Florida
Camagüey
Yucatan Channel
CAMAGÜEY
Martí
Las Tunas
Gibara
Holguín
LAS TUNAS
Antilla
Archipiélago de los Jardines de la Reina
Santa Cruz del Sur
HOLGUÍN
Moa
Baracoa
Manzanillo
Bayamo
SANTIAGO DE CUBA
Caribbean Sea
GRANMA
Guantánamo
Niquero
Santiago de Cuba
Caimanera
Windward Passage
Atlantic Ocean
Caribbean Sea
Montego Bay
Jamaica
Annotto Bay
Port Antonio
Savanna-la-Mar
Kingston
Morant Bay
Navassa Island (U. S.)
Haiti
Les Cayes
24°
20°
84°
80°
76°

aspirations of some in the independence struggle who sought full independence as well as abolition. In 1851, however, at the height of annexationist sentiments in the country, Joaquín de Agüero led an uprising against Spain. The uprising was accompanied by the first formal declaration of independence by men at arms against the Spanish colonial government.

A major stumbling block to the independence movement and the economic and social mobility of Afro-Cubans, however, was the unjust perception of the social and political role of the black, known popularly as *miedo al negro* ("fear of the black"). The phobia can be traced to the Haitian Revolution in the late eighteenth century. Before this time, the fear of slaves in Cuba was weaker in part because they were fewer and were outnumbered by the whites. After 1791 the "black fear" would grow with each new shipload of African slaves. While wars of independence erupted throughout the South American continent in 1808, Cuba did not follow suit, remaining Spain's "ever faithful Isle." The main reason for this political immobility by a class that had shouldered years of accumulated grievances against colonial rule was its fear of blacks. This explains its phobia concerning the 1844 CONSPIRACIÓN DE LA ESCALERA (Ladder Conspiracy), which was savagely repressed by the Spanish colonial authorities, who were supported by the planter class. Thousands were massacred, including the poet Gabriel de la Concepción Valdés, known as Plácido. (Throughout the nineteenth century literature played a significant role in exposing the horrors of slavery abroad, in the works of Plácido, those of the slave poet Franciso Manzano, and in Cirilo Villaverde's classic novel *Cecilia Valdés*.)

Cuba's wars of independence did not begin until much later in the century. The first one, the TEN YEARS' WAR, broke out on October 10, 1868. On this day the planter Carlos Manuel de Céspedes freed his slaves at La Demajagua sugar mill and called for an end to Spanish rule.

The crucible of Cuban nationhood was forged in struggle in which Afro-Cubans were an integral political element. The rebels' 1869 Constitution of Guáimaro proclaimed that "all inhabitants of the Republic at Arms are completely free," and their Central Assembly of Representatives, meeting in Camagüey, proclaimed the abolition of slavery.

Fear of blacks, however, played a central role in the war. Spain used it to sow doubt among conservative factions of the revolutionary forces as to the intentions of black officers who rose in the ranks, especially Generals José and Antonio Maceo. These tactics built on already existing divisions among the forces, comprising erstwhile slaveholders and slaves, the former in officer capacity and often ambivalent over the issue of abolition, and many of the latter in more subordinate, if not menial, roles. These divisions would prove the downfall of the Mambí (Liberation) Army in the first war. The motto of the elite was "Cuba, better Spanish than African."

The Treaty of Zanjón ended the Ten Years' War in 1878, but it recognized the freedom only of those slaves who had fought in the revolutionary ranks. It was opposed by the Maceos, among other black generals, for attaining neither independence nor abolition. When these veterans tried to resuscitate the independence movement in the so-called Little War of 1879-1880, the colonial press conducted a virulent campaign portraying it as a race uprising. Playing on the fact that the pillars of revolution in Oriente Province – Antonio and José Maceo, Quintín Banderas,

ABOVE: While women look on, men play a board game in the central Cuban city of Cienfuegos. *José Azel/Aurora*
FACING PAGE, TOP: Sugar was the foundation of Cuba's economy during much of the nineteenth century and continues to be an important crop today. Here, sugar cane cutters in Cuba's Guantanamo Province head out to the fields in the early morning. *José Azel/Aurora*

Guillermón Moncada, and Mariano Torres – were black, the Spanish press spread rumors of a black republic in the making. Gen. Antonio Maceo was seen as the black *caudillo* from the east and was accused of having designs on the presidency.

Though the slave trade to Cuba was officially outlawed in 1865, both slavery and the trade continued. It was only during the Ten Years' War, in 1873, that the last known slave shipment landed in Cuba. (In addition to African slaves, an estimated 150,000 to 250,000 Chinese contract laborers were taken to Cuba from 1847 to 1887, when Spain and China signed a treaty that ended the flow.) In 1880 (the year in which sugar production topped 700,000 tons, almost 600,000 of which was exported to the United States), the colonial authorities decreed the abolition of slavery but introduced a system akin to apprenticeship, known as *patronato*, whereby former masters would remain owners over an eight-year period. The patronato was rendered inoperative and ended earlier than originally planned, in 1886 (*see* ABOLITION AND EMANCIPATION IN LATIN AMERICA AND THE CARIBBEAN).

The initial declaration of the Ten Years' War, known as the Declaration of Yara, was made at a sugar mill and invoked freedom for the slaves as well as independence from Spain, reflecting the extent to which issues of abolition and independence were intertwined. However, neither the war of 1868-1878 nor that of 1879-1880 coalesced as a popular uprising. Such an uprising occurred only after the abolition of slavery in 1886, with the second war of independence from 1895 to 1898 (*see* SPANISH-CUBAN-AMERICAN WAR). Many of the rank and file of that war and its officers were black. They joined forces with white Cubans under the progressive call to forge a republic "with all and for the good of all." These were the words of JOSÉ MARTÍ, a Cuban of Hispanic origin, who in 1892, while living in exile in the United States, formed the Cuban Revolutionary Party. A great thinker, Martí had a genius for mobilizing men and women across classes and races with a vision of social justice in an independent Cuba. After returning to the island to fight for its independence, Martí died in battle in 1895.

Martí outlived by only two years a woman he much admired, Mariana Grajales Coello, mother of the Maceos and a tireless fighter in her own right, who reflects the active presence of women in the struggle against slavery and for national liberation. She also demonstrates the transnational links that existed at the time: she was born into the free mulatto class in Santiago de Cuba in 1808, of parents from Santo Domingo. She married

ABOVE LEFT: **A worker rolls a cigar by hand in Havana, Cuba. The country's tobacco products are prized worldwide.** *Hughes/Hutchison*

LEFT: **A young woman dances in the street on José Martí Day in Havana, Cuba. Martí is regarded as the father of Cuban independence.** *Wolfgang Kunz/Aurora*

Venezuelan-born Marcos Maceo and died in Kingston, Jamaica, in 1893. She lost her husband and 9 of her 13 children to the struggle, including the most famous of all, Gen. Antonio Maceo, who died in battle in 1896.

In 1898, with the Spaniards close to defeat, the United States, in collusion with Martí's U.S.-based successor in the Cuban Revolutionary Party, Tomás Estrada Palma, entered what unjustly became known as the Spanish-American War (because the name excluded Cuba). The aspirations of those seeking a Cuba "by all and for the good of all" were thus frustrated in the independence negotiated by the United States and Spain, without including Cuba. Insurgent forces on the island were to lose out, again with a marked racial dimension.

Republic: 1902-1959

In 1898 the U.S. battleship *Maine* exploded in Havana Harbor, killing 260 officers and crew. As a result, President William McKinley asked the U.S. Congress for the authority to intervene militarily against Spain. Santiago de Cuba capitulated to Theodore Roosevelt's Rough Riders in 1898. The United States militarily occupied Cuba from 1898 to1902 and again from 1906 to1908, paving the way for a lasting U.S. presence and huge U.S. investments. Perhaps most frustrating of all to those who fought for independence was the Platt Amendment to the Cuban Constitution of 1901. The amendment was included in the constitution only after prolonged debate and as a precondition for the withdrawal of U.S. troops. It gave the United States the right to intervene in Cuba militarily should circumstances be deemed to warrant such action. The Cuban government, moreover, was proscribed from entering into agreements with other countries without the consent of Washington. Military governor Leonard Wood supervised what the United States termed democratic elections, but the franchise excluded women, illiterates, and those with less than $250, effectively excluding most Afro-Cuban males as well. Conservative Tomás Estrada Palma was elected president. In 1903 the United States signed the Reciprocal Trade Treaty (which benefited the United States much more than it did Cuba) and built the Guantánamo Naval Base, which remains to this day. In the years 1904 to 1905 President Roosevelt formulated a corollary to the Monroe Doctrine: since the U.S. did not allow European nations to intervene in Latin America, the U.S. had the responsibility for preserving order and protecting life and property in those countries.

The U.S. presence bolstered conservative sectors of Cuban society, the early twentieth-century ruling class. This class pursued policies that actively sought a "WHITENING" (*blanqueamiento*) of the nation by attracting Spanish immigrants. More than 780,000 Spaniards are estimated to have entered the island between 1902 and 1931, though the number of permanent settlers is not thought to have been more than 250,000. By the 1920s whitening had failed. Nonetheless, in the early twentieth century, Cuba was one of the more Spanish of the Latin American republics, and the whitening policies had further marginalized blacks and mulattos economically and socially, sowing the seeds of great disillusion.

Diverse currents of thought developed regarding the "black problem." The first movement was led by Juan Gualberto Gómez, a leader in the struggle for independence who had been representative in Cuba of Martí's Cuban Revolutionary Party while the latter was in exile. Gómez was the black leader with the greatest prestige after the death of Antonio Maceo. Along with Gen. Bartolomé Masó, he was also the leading opponent of the Platt Amendment. He believed that equality between black and white could be realized when Afro-Cubans achieved educational levels on a par with those of the white population. This had been his primary aim in encouraging the establishment of black educational, recreational, and mutual aid societies and brotherhoods and bringing them together at the turn of the century under the rubric of the Central Directorate of the Colored Race. The directorate's central aims were to foment a "fraternal spirit," establish a "community of interests," avoid "collisions and antagonisms," and proceed in "cordial reciprocity" as a patriotic grouping integral to the new nation. To that end he worked tirelessly across the island. His dictum was "Educate yourselves so that nobody can throw in your face that you come from a 'savage' people."

A second movement was led by Martín Morúa Delgado, who had been pro-autonomy (whereby Cuba would be accorded certain powers of its own) up until 1896, then pro-independence (whereby Cuba would break away from Spain as a nation in its own right). He believed that racially exclusive groupings – even when they were founded for cultural and social betterment or mutual aid – harmed rather than benefited the sector they sought to help. Like Gómez, however, he believed that black people should be directly involved in working for their own betterment. The most influential black people were grouped in one of these two currents.

A third movement comprised those unable to find a voice in the mainstream political parties. Leaders who formed the Committee of Veterans of Color in the early years of the republic broke with the Liberal Party to found the Independent Party of Color in 1908 and fight for their own demands. Their continued aspiration was unity, but they saw the myth of racial democracy as working in favor of whites by silencing and deracializing Cubans. The party was outlawed in 1910 in an amendment authored by Martín Morúa, then a senator. A protest against this proscription in 1912 was harshly repressed by government forces. The leaders of this movement, Evaristo Estenoz and Pedro Ivonet, together with other veterans of the War of Independence, were killed in what has gone down in history as the Race War of 1912. One hundred years after the Aponte uprising of 1812, more than 3000 blacks and mulattos were killed, according to official records, and black people were terrorized throughout the island. Of these three movements, it might be said that Morúa Delgado appealed to elite sectors, Estenoz and Ivonet had a support base among more popular sectors, and Gómez was able to reach out to a broad range of sectors.

The Mexican Revolution of 1910 and the Russian Revolution of 1917 were to make their mark on the island, especially as an economic crisis in the 1920s derailed an earlier economic boom. Two key founders of the Communist Party of Cuba in 1925 were Julio Antonio Mella (mulatto) and Rubén Martinez Villena (white). The party was to gain strength in the labor movement by drawing on the working class, estimated to be some 80 percent black and mulatto, and including black immigrant workers from other Caribbean islands. Early communists proposed a "black belt" in Oriente Province (as had U.S. communists in the U.S. South). An attempt in this direction was led by black leader León Álvarez with the creation of soviets, worker- and peasant-led communities styled on those of the Russian Revolution. The soviets were set up in many of the Cuban sugar mills in the 1934 revolution but were short-lived, due to repression after the revolution. The Universal Negro Improvement Association, headed by Marcus Garvey, had a following among West Indian sugar workers in Camagüey and Oriente provinces.

The period 1912-1940 also witnessed the emergence of an Afro-Cuban middle class, which criticized Cuban racism, emphasized self-improvement in the black community and the importance of personal example, promoted African diasporic links, and called for political and cultural space. Gustavo Urrutia expressed this perspective in his column *Ideales de una raza* (A Race's Ideals) in the conservative newspaper *Diario de la Marina.* Marking this period of cultural renewal, AFROCUBANISMO, or *negrismo* (NÉGRITUDE), affirmed Cuba's African roots and celebrated its *mestizo* (mixed) heritage while seeking to redefine a national identity. The movement would give rise to the magical realism of ALEJO CARPENTIER (white) and the radical Afrocentric poetry of NICOLÁS GUILLÉN (mulatto).

President Gerardo Machado (1925-1933) was overthrown by a coalition of forces that included noncommissioned army officers under Sgt. FULGENCIO BATISTA. The 1933-1934 short-lived, populist, first presidency of Ramón Grau San Martín – who in 1934 abrogated the 1903 trade treaty with the United States and the Platt Amendment – was unpalatable to the United States, and Grau was deposed by strongman Batista. In what has been called the failed revolution of 1933,

Batista, from behind the scenes, ruthlessly quelled opposition. Out of this period, however, strong black communist leaders emerged in a solidly cross-racial labor movement. Three of the best known were Lázaro Peña, leader of the tobacco workers; Aracelio Iglesias, who led the dockworkers; and Jesús Menéndez, leader of the sugar workers In 1938 the Communist Party was legalized, and its name was soon changed to the Popular Socialist Party (PSP). Under the "united front" of World War II, when Communist parties worldwide adopted a conciliatory approach to ruling bourgeois regimes, Cuba's constituent assembly, which had a number of PSP members, promulgated one of the most progressive constitutions in Latin America in 1940. From 1944 to 1952 the Auténtico (Authentic) Party was in power, led by Presidents Ramón Grau San Martín (1944-1948) and Carlos Prío Socarrás (1948-1952). The intensification of the cold war set the stage for the assassinations of Jesús Menéndez and Aracelio Iglesias. Lázaro Peña, then head of the General Confederation of Labor, survived, but his leadership was challenged and the confederation split. The rupture persisted after Batista's next military coup in 1952, which led to his reinstatement as president.

Racial discrimination was disallowed under the 1940 constitution, and racial segregation did not exist as such. However, in the 1940s and 1950s people of color were relegated to the public and service sectors. There were no blacks in major U.S.-owned, white-collar companies (in the telephone and electricity companies, for instance) or in banks. In the U.S. chain Woolworth, known as Tencen (Ten Cents), no persons of color were employed. The same held for the first U.S.-style supermarkets, upper- and middle-market stores, hotels, and the service sector in general. People of color were overwhelmingly manual workers in the industrial manufacturing sector. Private schools, religious and lay, accepted very few blacks. Entire neighborhoods in cities and towns throughout the island, as well as entertainment and recreation facilities, were segregated. President Batista himself, a mulatto, was not admitted into certain elite social venues.

Of the many groups opposing Batista in the 1950s, the PSP was explicitly committed to ending racial discrimination, while the commitment was left implicit in the more general demands for social justice of other multiclass and multiracial movements. Societies of color proliferated in the first half of the century, following the ideal promulgated by Juan Gualberto Gómez that black Cubans should have their own organizations. These societies did not, however, transcend class barriers. Blacks in the professions and the world of art and culture, for example, had the Club Atenas (Athens Club), which opened its doors in 1917 in Havana. Santa Clara, notorious for its visible segregationism, had El Gran Maceo (the Great Maceo) for mulattos and certain well-placed blacks, and the Sociedad Bella Unión (Fine Union Society) for men and women of the black working class. The pattern was repeated throughout the island. A minority black middle-class voice, best personified by René Betancourt, continued to articulate a more conservative race-based African nationalist position. In his two books *Doctrina negra* (1950, Black Doctrine) and *El negro, ciudadano del futuro* (1959, The Negro, Citizen of the Future), Betancourt argued for economic liberation of blacks through a form of black capitalism, by creating black industrial and trade cooperatives. He distinguished between the social and the national, the latter encompassing all Cubans, black and non-black. For him, only Aponte and Estenoz could be considered "black leaders" in Cuba's history, as they were principally interested in the plight of Afro-Cubans – not Maceo, Gómez, or communist labor leaders, whose political goals addressed the Cuban nation as a whole.

Revolutionary Cuba

A young lawyer by the name of Fidel Castro, of Spanish (Galician) descent, was running in the elections that were preempted by the 1952 coup on behalf of the Ortodoxo (Orthodox) Party. (The Ortodoxos had split from the Auténtico Party, disillusioned by corruption under the Auténtico administrations.) A year later Castro led an attack on the Moncada Garrison in Santiago de Cuba, in which many

An elderly Cuban couple sit in front of a picture of Fidel Castro, the country's leader since the revolution of 1959. *Jeanette Ortiz Osorio*

of the attackers lost their lives or were jailed. Castro was jailed but was granted amnesty and in 1955 was deported to Mexico. He led a return expedition to Cuba in 1956 to form the Rebel Army in the eastern Sierra Maestra mountains. The armed struggle had its civilian counterpart in the 26th of July Movement and, combined with the activities of other civilian groups, developed into a popular struggle for social justice that triumphed on January 1, 1959.

With overwhelming mass support, the revolutionary government curtailed class privilege on a platform of agrarian reform and nationalization of industry, coupled with extensive education and health programs. The early exodus of Cubans to the United States, in particular Miami, was mainly wealthy and white. On the island, black Cubans regained dignity as the bases for institutionalized racism were dismantled. Propelled in no small measure by the hostile response of the U.S. government, ranging from an embargo on trade to counterespionage, the Cuban government entered the Eastern European socialist fold. In 1961, after the failed invasion of U.S.-supported Cuban exiles at the Bay of Pigs, Castro declared the socialist nature of the revolution. In 1962 Cuba was catapulted to the center of world attention with the missile crisis, averted by Soviet withdrawal of its missiles in return, among other things, for a U.S. commitment not to invade Cuba. In 1965 the revolutionary forces were regrouped under the new Communist Party of Cuba (Partido Comunista de Cuba, PCC).

The Cuban government sought to establish a socialist, state-run economy and society. In keeping with the Marxist emphasis on class, it gave a higher priority to disparities of class than those of race, in the belief that addressing the former would correct the latter. This belief was shaken by the 1980 exodus of 125,000 Cubans through the port of Mariel. In comparison with previous migrations, this one included poorer classes and about 25,000 Afro-Cubans. Although he had made declarations on race when he assumed the presidency, it was not until the 1986 PCC Congress that Castro raised the issue again. The congress was charged with symbolic significance, as 1986 marked the centennial of the abolition of slavery in Cuba. In a speech that was televised live but never published, Castro criticized the persistence of RACIAL STEREOTYPES and prejudice in Cuban society, lambasting political organizations for the under-representation of blacks, women, and youth in leadership positions. He spoke of continuing forms of discrimination and called for an affirmative action program, starting with the Communist Party itself. However, the leadership of the PCC continued to be predominantly white. The Fifth Party Congress in 1997 doubled the number of blacks in the Politburo to 6 of the 24 members: Juan Carlos Robinson Agramonte, Pedro Sáez Montejo, Misael Enamorado Dager, Juan Almeida Bosque, Esteban Lazo Hernández, and Pedro Ross Leal.

Cuba's foreign policy focused on Third World liberation and decolonization. Many black Cubans were proud of Cuba's involvement in Africa in the early 1960s (REPUBLIC OF THE CONGO) and in the mid-1970s, when President Castro responded to the call for help issued by President AGOSTINHO NETO of ANGOLA, newly independent from PORTUGAL, against invading South African forces. Castro defined Cubans as not only a Latin American people but also a Latin African people. "The blood of Africa runs deep in our veins," he declared, a sentiment strengthened when Cuba became chair of the Movement of Non-Aligned Nations and developed its own bilateral programs with African countries.

Cuba's growing contact with and knowledge of Africa was mirrored closer to home through links with radical black movements in the United States and in the Caribbean. When Castro visited JAMAICA, BARBADOS, and GRENADA in the summer of 1998, he articulated the links between those countries and Cuba: their historic past of European colonialism, the sugar plantation economy, and African slavery. Relations between Cuba and the independent Anglophone Caribbean date back to 1972, when diplomatic relations were established with TRINIDAD AND TOBAGO, Barbados, GUYANA, and Jamaica. Castro was in Jamaica in October 1977 at the invitation of then president MICHAEL MANLEY; 20 years later, in 1997, he was there for Manley's funeral; and in May 1998, Jamaican prime minister Percival Patterson was in Cuba to sign a joint investment agreement. In Grenada, Cuban construction workers helping to build an international airport faced the U.S. invasion forces in November 1983, which ended the socialist Grenadian Revolution of 1979-1983. Fifteen years later, in 1998, Grenadian prime minister Keith Mitchell thanked the Cuban people and their leader for what they had done for Grenada. In the 1990s Caribbean nations have been outspoken in condemning the U.S. trade embargo on Cuba. In 1997 the Caribbean Common Market (CARICOM), for instance, condemned an attempt by the U.S. Congress to sanction CARICOM for establishing closer trade relations with the island. It also recognized Cuba as a Caribbean nation eligible for consideration if it applied for membership.

Castro maintained close contacts with African American political activists as well. The Cuban Revolution triumphed in 1959, at the height of the U.S. CIVIL RIGHTS MOVEMENT and the cold war. In 1960 Castro was in New York for the United Nations General Assembly. When he was made less than welcome at the midtown Shelbourne Hotel, he moved his delegation to the more modest Hotel Theresa, in the heart of Harlem. Received there by cheering crowds, he met, among others, MALCOLM X, LANGSTON HUGHES, and President KWAME NKRUMAH of GHANA (who, at the United Nations, had condemned U.S. intervention in the Republic of the Congo). Soon afterward, between 1961 and 1969, Robert Williams – the former NAACP activist from Monroe, North Carolina, who was expelled for his militancy – lived in exile in Cuba, where he directed Radio Free Dixie. The station broadcast on a frequency that extended to U.S. Southern states, mixing jazz, blues, and gospel with news and commentary that attacked racism and supported civil rights. Williams espoused a Maoist political philosophy, however, and when his views conflicted with Cuba's rapprochement with the Soviet camp, he left Cuba for China and from there returned to the United States. In 1996 President Castro returned to the United Nations. He was rebuffed by New York mayor Rudolph Giuliani. Among the many invitations Castro received was one to meet with black religious leaders at Harlem's Abyssinian Baptist Church, where he spoke before 1500 people about Cuba and its role in Angola and the overthrow of APARTHEID in SOUTH AFRICA. In his introduction to Castro's speech, Rev. Calvin Butts said: "People ask me, 'Why are you inviting Castro to your church?' and I say to them, 'Because it is in our tradition to invite visionaries who fight for the freedom of all peoples.'"

In the 1990s the political and race divide between Cubans on the island (mainly black and mulatto) and Cubans in Miami (overwhelmingly white) was apparent in the receptions they gave South Africa's Nelson Mandela: in Cuba he was welcomed as a hero, while for many Miami Cubans he was most unwelcome. In June 1990, four Cuban American mayors of the cities in the Miami area signed a letter declaring Nelson Mandela persona non grata, shortly before a planned visit to Florida as part of his U.S. tour. Any sign of support for Cuba was to be denounced, and on the many occasions Mandela had expressed appreciation for Cuba's solidarity in ending apartheid. The African American community declared a boycott of Miami that was ineffective, and demanded an apology from the Cuban Americans that was never forthcoming. The conflict was a sign of growing Cuban American divisions, as those of Afro-Cuban descent distanced themselves from those of Hispanic descent.

In the 1990s Cuba experienced a broad range of political and economic changes. The 1989 collapse of Soviet-bloc socialism and the tightening of the U.S. embargo, in the form of the 1992 Torricelli-Graham Act and the 1996 Helms-Burton Act, precipitated an economic collapse that has disproportionately affected the black population. By 1993, the low point of the crisis, the economy had plummeted by about 50 percent. In the summer of 1994 there was rioting in Havana, the first demonstration of its kind since the 1959 revolution, and some 30,000 rafters took to the seas in desperation, many of them from poorer and blacker sectors of society. Strategies of joint state and international venture capital created an export and tourist industry, dollarized economic enclaves in which blacks played a lesser and more menial role. In addition, fewer blacks had family abroad to send dollar remittances to an economy in which the dollar became king. Consequently, more blacks were driven by necessity into the underground economy.

One of the most marked changes of the 1990s concerned religion, an arena of early conflict with the revolutionary state and party (declared atheist). The change was particularly notable regarding Afro-Cuban religions. Cuba was visited by two African leaders: in 1987, by the asantahene of Ghana, traditional king of the ASANTE people, and, in 1991, by the oni (king) of IFE, the sacred capital of the YORUBA. At its Fourth Congress in 1991, the PCC declared itself a lay party open to believers of all religions, paving the way for the 1998 visit of Pope John Paul II. This opening to religion, and especially those of African origin, however, was not without problems. Commercialization and vulgarization of Afro-Cuban "folklore" was accompanied by the growth of tourism, for example, inviting criticism of what some describe as Ocha- or Orisha-Tour – referring to packaged visits related to the Afro-Cuban religions Palo Monte and SANTERÍA.

"Cuba is a Baraguá," Castro declared in 1990, catapulting Afro-Cuban heritage to the forefront of national politics. The small eastern town of Baraguá was where Maceo refused to sign the peace treaty with Spain in 1878. Reference to Baraguá is double-edged. The 1868-1878 war was lost, the independence forces weakened and divided. However, Cuba would never be the same. Blacks, mulattos, and whites had fought the war together, albeit on unequal terms. Black Cubans liken Cuba today to a modern-day palenque. White Cubans talk about the Haitianization of Cuba. In the early nineteenth century, reprisals were taken by European colonial powers against the newly declared, independent black state of Haiti, the first of its kind in the Caribbean. The country turned in on itself, was ground down, and is today the poorest in the region. Fears are that 200 years later, Cuba could be driven along a similar road.

Jean Stubbs and Pedro Pérez-Sarduy

SEE ALSO

Mandela, Nelson Rolihlahla; Manzano, Juan Francisco; South Africa; Butts, Calvin O., III; Civil War, American; Garvey, Marcus Mosiah; National Association for the Advancement of Colored People; Harlem, New York; Williams, Robert Franklin; Maceo y Grajales, Antonio; Regla de Palo; Valdés, Gabriel de la Concepción ("Plácido"); Caribbean Community (CARICOM).

Latin America and the Caribbean

Cudjoe (birth and death dates unknown), escaped African slave in JAMAICA and leader of the eighteenth-century Clarendon maroon (fugitive slave) community.

The life and death of the Jamaican maroon Cudjoe has become a symbol of black resistance in Jamaica. Cudjoe's story as the eighteenth-century leader of the Clarendon maroons has also been a contested part of Jamaican history. Early European descriptions painted a caricatured portrait of him, while black recollections portrayed him as a fearless soldier.

Cudjoe was among more than 500 African slaves in the Jamaican parish of St. Clarendon who escaped after a violent insurrection in 1690. He emerged as leader of a loose confederation of runaway slaves who lived in the Clarendon hills. The Clarendon maroons, led by Cudjoe, organized themselves into small gangs that secretly wandered into white towns to steal food and weapons.

Although the Clarendon maroons were not unified, they became skilled soldiers and expert marksmen. Under Cudjoe's leadership they defended their freedom in a series of small skirmishes with colonial militias. They acquired additional guns and ammunition from the bodies of slain white soldiers. They also acquired weapons from those select slaves who were members of black militias formed by colonial officials to protect the island's shores from European pirates. Armed and battle-ready, Cudjoe's Clarendon maroons engaged in frequent battles with European militias for nearly 30 years after their initial escape in 1690.

In 1730 colonial militias waged a full-scale war on the maroons. Four years later colonial militias succeeded in destroying Nanny Town, the stronghold of the eastern (Windward) maroons. The survivors fled back into the mountains and joined Cudjoe's forces. His leadership and organizational skills thrust him to the forefront of what was then a sparse confederation of maroon gangs. By 1735 Cudjoe's military command and leadership had made him one of the most renowned maroon leaders in Jamaica. He unified rival maroon gangs and amassed a formidable army.

Cudjoe and his newly fortified army avoided British soldiers by moving constantly throughout the Jamaican hillside. They often lived in deep depressions in the hills called cockpits. Cudjoe's headquarters were located in a cockpit on the northwest section of the island called Petty River Bottom. The territory extended more than seven acres and was only accessible by a single, narrow passage. It was thus easily defensible, allowing him to turn his attention toward widening his military power.

In response to frequent colonial attacks on weaker maroon forces, Cudjoe placed a small group of his own soldiers under the command of his brother, Accompong, and sent them into the parish of St. Elizabeth to establish a military camp. Cudjoe set up camps in other parishes as well, including Hanover, Westmoreland, and St. James. These camps raided neighboring white towns, stealing food and weapons, and assisted other maroons in their battles with colonial militias. Cudjoe's fame grew with each successful stand, and his stronghold in Petty River Bottom made his capture all but impossible.

In the late 1730s his exploits convinced colonial legislatures to make Cudjoe's capture and execution their primary objective. In 1738 the legislature recruited a diverse blend of people to help destroy Cudjoe and his community of maroons. This new colonial militia included white colonists, Indian laborers, and freed slaves who were loyal to their former owners. But after more than a year of violent warfare, the war against Cudjoe stalled.

In response to fears that Cudjoe's reach would extend into other parishes, colonial officials signed a peace treaty with him in 1739, ending nearly 50 years of warfare (1690-1739). Under the terms of the peace treaty Cudjoe and his maroons were granted full freedom. They were given more than 1500 acres of land in the Clarendon area and allowed to cultivate coffee, tobacco, cotton, and COCOA there. They were allowed to sell their goods anywhere they wished, but they were required to obtain a license in order to sell products in town.

One of the most controversial terms of the 1739 agreement required the maroons to help the colonists suppress all future slave rebellions. In exchange for his cooperation in this area Cudjoe was named a lifetime chief of his community and given the power to punish his so-called subjects as he saw fit. Critics of the treaty argued that Cudjoe chose his freedom over the future freedom of others. Cudjoe and his peace treaty represented a schism that would widen between Jamaica's maroon and slave communities, yet his legacy as a freedom fighter remains strong.

Alonford James Robinson, Jr.

SEE ALSO

Maroonage in the Americas; Mooretown, Jamaica (Nanny Town).

North America

Cuffe, Paul (b. January 17, 1759, Cuttyhunk Island, Mass.; d. September 9, 1817, Westport, Mass.), philanthropist, merchant, and sea captain who advocated the mass emigration of blacks to Africa and who is considered by some to be the father of Black Nationalism in the United States.

In 1817, close to the time of his death, Paul Cuffe had a rich life upon which to reflect.

In 1811 the free-born Massachusetts merchant Paul Cuffe sailed to Sierra Leone to investigate repatriating African Americans there, a journey commemorated by this engraved silhouette. Four years later Cuffe transported 38 African Americans to Sierra Leone, which England had designated for repatriation of its African slaves. *National Portrait Gallery, Smithsonian Institution/Art Resource, NY*

He and his wife, Alice, had seven children. His family-run businesses had earned assets worth an estimated $20,000, making him the wealthiest man in his hometown of Westport, Massachusetts, and the wealthiest black man in the United States.

News of his death reached the other side of the Atlantic, illustrating how far his fame and influence had spread. Yet his life of accomplishment had not eliminated the racial discrimination that was built into American society. Ironically, following his funeral at the Westport South Friends Meeting House, which his financial support had helped to build, Cuffe was buried in a remote cemetery corner, far away from the white Quakers. He had not attained the one goal that had come to dominate his life and to which he had devoted so much time and money: the mass emigration of American blacks to Africa as an escape from that discrimination.

Much of Cuffe's life, and the life of his family, is the stuff of adventure novels. His ASANTE father, Cuffe (an Anglicization of "Kofi," which means "born on Friday") Slocum, a former slave who had purchased his freedom, died in 1772. The next year, at the age of 14, Paul Cuffe began working on whaling ships. He returned to Massachusetts in 1776, and, convinced that "commerce furnished to industry more ample rewards than agriculture," he taught himself mathematics and navigation and began sailing his own vessels. During the Revolutionary War, he made his living as a blockade runner, smuggling goods in and out of American harbors past British patrol ships. He later turned to whaling and trading, both domestically and internationally, which ultimately provided the core of his wealth. His ships were staffed exclusively by blacks, by which he hoped to demonstrate their equality to all observers.

Cuffe owned part or all of ten ships throughout his life, building or supervising in the construction of seven of them at his shipyard. In addition to his investments in whaling and sea commerce, he had interests in farming and fishing businesses. Cuffe engaged in business ventures with prominent Quakers, including William Rotch Jr. By 1806 Cuffe had acquired assets totaling approximately $10,000. In 1808 he was admitted into the Society of Friends, or Quakers, which had eluded his parents because of their race.

Even when pursuing his own fortune, Cuffe worked to benefit others, especially in opposition to racial discrimination. Members of his extended family often served as his crew or operated his businesses. He donated large sums of money for a Quaker meeting house and an interracial Quaker schoolhouse. In 1780 he and his brother refused to pay taxes, in protest against the Massachusetts state constitution, which excluded blacks and Indians from voting (Cuffe's mother was an Indian). In their complaint, the two brothers alluded to taxation without representation – an argument that, while not gaining them the vote, did reduce the family's taxes.

His religious ties brought him into contact with abolitionists, both in the United States and in England. He received an invitation from England's Royal African Institution to visit the colony of SIERRA LEONE, which had been reserved as a point of repatriation for Great Britain's freed slaves. Americans such as Benjamin Rush, James Pemberton, and James Brian of the Pennsylvania and Delaware Abolition Societies began corresponding with William Wilberforce, Thomas Clarkson, and Zachary Macauley, abolitionist members of Great Britain's parliament, about Cuffe's intention to repatriate American blacks there as well.

Cuffe's first voyage to Sierra Leone began when he and his crew of nine blacks sailed his brig, the *Traveler,* out of Westport on January 1, 1811. After this initial visit, Cuffe speculated on the possibilities of trade among blacks in the United States, England, and Sierra Leone. He also began to think about bringing skilled black immigrants to Sierra Leone. The War of 1812 postponed any hope of trade between the two nations, even though Cuffe requested that both nations allow him to continue with his plan. Many of America's black elite, including James Forten, ABSALOM JONES, and RICHARD ALLEN, supported Cuffe's plan.

After the war Cuffe and nine families (a total of 38 people) sailed for Sierra Leone on December 12, 1815. The families resettled there. After his return to the United States, Cuffe became even more certain of the need for black emigration; instances of racial discrimination demonstrated to him that blacks would never be considered equal by white Americans. In addition, Cuffe doubted whether slavery would ever be abolished. He began to support the AMERICAN COLONIZATION

Society (ACS), a group headed by white Southerners, whose goal was to remove manumitted slaves from the United States and ship them to Africa. Many abolitionists believed that the ACS was using Cuffe, and Cuffe believed it as well. He reasoned, however, that outside support for his repatriation plan was important, whatever the source or motivation, and so he continued his alliance with the white Southerners.

Although Cuffe died before he could put his plan into effect, his legacy to America is unquestionable. Historian Eric Foner writes that Cuffe's voyage to Africa "with emigrants from America and his financial success anticipated ideals later associated with black nationalists from Henry Highland Garnet to Marcus Garvey."

Robert Fay

See Also
Great Britain; American Revolution; Garvey, Marcus Mosiah; Manumission Societies; Black Nationalism in the United States.

Europe

Cugoano, Ottobah (b. 1757, Adjumako, Ghana; d. ?), African abolitionist in Great Britain who published an autobiographical book arguing against British racism and participation in the transatlantic slave trade.

Horrified by the atrocities he experienced on the Middle Passage voyage after being abducted by slave traders in West Africa in 1770, Ottobah Cugoano exclaimed, "Death was more preferable than life, and a plan was concerted amongst us, that we might burn and blow up the ship, and to perish all together in the flames." Though the plan was thwarted, the radicalism that marked the effort remained a theme in Cugoano's life.

Cugoano was bought by a white man in the West Indies and in 1772 was taken to England, where he learned to read and write and was baptized. His whereabouts were unknown until 1786, when he and another black man informed the abolitionist lawyer Granville Sharp of the unjust treatment of a slave tied to a mast by his owner. At the time, Cugoano worked for the court painter of the Prince of Wales, a connection he used to plead for abolition in a letter to the prince.

Cugoano expressed his abolitionist beliefs in his 1787 book, *Thoughts and Sentiments on the Evil and Wicked Traffic of the Slavery and Commerce of the Human Species*. Though many scholars assert that Cugoano did not write all of the text, according to literary critics Paul Edwards and David Dabydeen the book exhibits "an aggressive and often bitter urgency of tone" that suits what they call Cugoano's "overt and assertive black radicalism."

In *Thoughts and Sentiments*, Cugoano used rational and objective methods to advance radical arguments for abolition. He believed that although many slave traders worked in the name of Christianity, they sought only personal profit. He cited Protestants as "the most barbarous slaveholders" and likened explorers, slave traders, and their governments to the Antichrist. He equated slaveholders with robbers and believed slave revolts to be a moral duty. Though he did not advocate anarchy, he admonished British law, the monarchy, and Parliament for supporting the interests of the elite involved in the trade, and he prophesied divine retribution. In addition, Cugoano refuted secular and Christian claims of African inferiority as well as the assumption that ancient slave practices within Africa justified trade in Africans.

Cugoano proposed the abolition of the slave trade and the emancipation of slaves, recommending that the British fleet enforce the ban on the coast of Africa. Holding that every British person was responsible for the cruelties of slavery, "unless he speedily riseth up with abhorrence of it in his own judgement, and, to avert evil, declare himself against it," he suggested a day of atonement and fasting for all Britons.

However, Cugoano did not believe that the British would soon abolish slavery. In the meantime, he proposed pragmatic improvements such as the education of slaves in trades and Christianity, humane treatment, and freedom after seven years.

Cugoano married an Englishwoman and continued letter-writing campaigns as a member of the Sons of Africa, a black British abolitionist organization. Little is known of his later life, though reputedly in 1791 he was working to find skilled laborers among black Loyalists in Canada to journey to Sierra Leone.

Leyla Keough

See Also
Middle Passage, The; Abolitionism in the United States; Slavery in Africa.

Cuisine. Please see Food in African American Culture

North America

Cullen, Countee (b. March 30, 1903, Louisville, Ky.; d. January 9, 1946, New York, N.Y.), African American poet, novelist, and playwright; the best-known black writer of the Harlem Renaissance.

Yet do I marvel at this curious thing:
To make a poet black, and bid him sing!

In these last two lines of his poem "Yet Do I Marvel," Countee Cullen sums up the irony that he saw not only for himself but for all African American writers – the question of what happens when God makes a poet black in a world that discourages black creativity yet still bids him sing. Cullen was part of the generation of authors who emerged during the Harlem Renaissance and answered that question with their own writing.

Cullen's early history remained a mystery for decades, by his own choice. He was adopted as a teenager, and from that point on was always reticent about his birthplace and former family. But recent scholarship indicates that he was born to Elizabeth Lucas in Louisville, Kentucky, in 1903, and raised in New York by Elizabeth Porter, who may have been his maternal grandmother. His original surname was Porter, but sometime around Elizabeth Porter's death in 1918 he was taken in by the Reverend Frederick Cullen, pastor of Harlem's prominent Salem Methodist Episcopal Church, and his wife, Carolyn. Countee Cullen considered them to be his parents, and he readily absorbed their conservative values.

The Cullens sent their son to the predominantly white DeWitt Clinton High School. He was an excellent student and was editor of the school newspaper and literary magazine. He won a citywide poetry contest while still in high school, and wrote much of the material for his first two volumes of poetry as an undergraduate at New York University. His poetry received prizes in three national contests while he was still in college. In 1925 he graduated Phi Beta Kappa and published his first book, *Color*. He went on to receive a master's degree in English and French from Harvard University. In the meantime, poems from *Color* had received prizes from *Crisis*, *Opportunity*, and *Poetry* magazines.

At Harvard, Cullen studied poetry under Robert Hillyard, who emphasized composing in conventional poetic forms. Cullen graduated from Harvard in 1927 and returned to New York, where he became an assistant editor at *Opportunity*. In that same year he published his next two volumes of poetry, *Copper Sun* and *The Ballad of the Brown Girl: An Old Ballad Retold*, and edited *Caroling Dusk: An Anthology of Verse by Negro Poets*, one of the most important collections to emerge from the Harlem Renaissance.

Cullen was better educated in classical literary forms than many of the black writers who were his peers. His poetry was characterized by a use of traditional European verse patterns. He explained that he chose forms and ideas that he believed transcended race because he wanted to be regarded simply as a poet, not a black poet. In his allegiance to ballads, sonnets, and standard English poetic language, Cullen stood apart from other Harlem Renaissance poets who were experimenting with new literary forms based on jazz and blues. As a result, Cullen enjoyed more crossover success than other African American poets at the time, because white scholars and audiences recognized and applauded his technical skills.

Black audiences also praised his work, and

his best-known and most powerful poems were often ones with racial themes. For example, in the sonnet "From the Dark Tower," Cullen prophesies an eventual redemption for a race that has learned

to hide the heart that bleeds,
And wait, and tend our agonizing seeds
We shall not always plant while others reap...
We were not made eternally to weep.

In "Heritage," a longer poem, Cullen expresses longing for Africa along with doubt about what meaning it could hold for a twentieth-century African American:

One three centuries removed
From the scenes his father loved.
Spicy grove, cinnamon tree,
What is Africa to me?

Later in the same poem, Cullen reflects on what African Americans lost in terms of traditional beliefs and customs:

Quaint, outlandish heathen gods
Black men fashion out of rods,
Clay, and brittle bits of stone,
In a likeness of their own,
My conversion came high-priced;
I belong to Jesus Christ,
Preacher of humility;
Heathen gods are naught to me.

"Heritage" ends with a confession, of sorts:

Lord, I fashion dark gods, too,
Daring even to give You
Dark despairing features where,
Crowned with dark rebellious hair,
Patience wavers just so much as
Mortal grief compels, while touches
Quick and hot, of anger, rise
To smitten cheek and weary eyes.
Lord, forgive me if my need
Sometimes shapes a human creed.

By the late 1920s Cullen had become the most popular black poet in the United States, and had won more major literary prizes – from both black and white sources – than any other black writer.

Cullen's celebrity was reinforced when, on April 9, 1928, he married Yolande Du Bois, the only child of the black intellectual and activist W. E. B. Du Bois. Their lavish wedding, at the Reverend Cullen's church, was attended by 1000 guests and was one of the major social events of the Harlem Renaissance. It also appeared literally to place Cullen, and his generation of African American intellectuals, in the position of being heir to Du Bois. But Cullen had been involved for years with Harlem schoolteacher Harold Jackman. When Cullen and Jackman sailed for Paris two months after the wedding, leaving Cullen's wife behind, it became clear the marriage was not meant to be. Cullen and Du Bois were divorced in 1930.

Cullen's career took a turn at about the same time. In 1929 he had published *The Black Christ and Other Poems.* He had worked on the title poem for two years and considered it his masterpiece, but the book was not well received. He took a position as a French teacher at Frederick Douglass Junior High (where James Baldwin was among his students), and while he continued writing poetry, he began to experiment with other forms as well. These included *One Way to Heaven* (1934), his only novel, and *The Lost Zoo* (1940) and *My Lives and How I Lost Them* (1942), books of children's verse. In 1936, with his translation of *Medea,* Cullen also became the first twentieth-century African American writer to publish a major translation of a classical work.

Just before his death, Cullen collaborated with the black writer Arna Bontemps on a dramatization of Bontemps's novel *God Sends Sunday* as a musical, *St. Louis Blues.* The production had been criticized by some African American for its portrayal of lower-class black life, but it opened on Broadway two months after Cullen's sudden death from high blood pressure and uremic poisoning on January 9, 1946.

Cullen had remarried in 1940, and his second wife, Ida, survived him. After Cullen's death, Langston Hughes eclipsed him as the best-known poet of the Harlem Renaissance. The extraordinary degree of fame and recognition that Cullen enjoyed during his lifetime has been forgotten, but a contemporary scholar describes his achievements in this way: "Some of his poems are utterly unforgettable, so capable was he of setting down in precise language the subtle feelings that made him one of the most intriguing writers in African American literature."

Lisa Clayton Robinson

See Also

Blues, The; *Crisis, The*; Du Bois, William Edward Burghardt (W. E. B.); Harlem, New York; New York, New York; *Opportunity: Journal of Negro Life.*

Latin America and the Caribbean

Cultural and Political Organizations in Latin America

The 500-year history of black cultural and political organization in Latin America is immensely rich. It begins in the 1500s and 1600s with communities formed by runaway slaves who, after escaping from their masters, sought shelter in the forests and mountains of the region (*see* Maroonage in the Americas). These communities were known as *quilombos* or *mocambos* in Brazil, and *palenques* or *cumbes* in Spanish America (*see* Palenque de San Basilio). Most of them were small, mobile encampments that lasted a few years at most before being attacked and dispersed by colonial forces. As soon as one encampment was broken up, however, others would form; and occasionally they took permanent root, evolving into fortified villages and small towns built in African styles and governed by military commanders and priests.

The largest such settlement was Palmares, a federation of villages in the northeastern Brazilian state of Alagoas. Palmares lasted almost 90 years (c. 1610-1695) before being defeated by the Portuguese. At its height, it housed between 10,000 and 20,000 people. In the inland Brazilian state of Minas Gerais, royal officials documented the existence of 160 quilombos during the 1700s, some containing a thousand inhabitants or more. In 1720 officials in Venezuela estimated that 20,000 runaways were at liberty in the forests and plains of the colony, most of them organized into palenques.

Most slaves, however, remained in the power of their owners and therefore had to develop forms of community organization acceptable to masters and colonial officials. The form of organization most favored by those authorities were Catholic religious brotherhoods (*cofradías*). The brotherhoods had originated in Europe as a means for devout Catholics to take part in the financial support and administration of their parish churches (*see* Catholic Church in Latin America and the Caribbean). As Spaniards and Portuguese migrated to Latin America, they brought the brotherhoods with them; and by the early 1600s priests and colonial officials were promoting the creation of racially segregated brotherhoods for slaves and free blacks.

Cofradía activities were overseen by parish priests, who imposed an additional layer of surveillance and control on the black population. Despite this drawback, slaves and free blacks seized on the brotherhoods as one of the few available means for gathering as a community. Numerous black brotherhoods (and a few sisterhoods) were created in Latin America during the 1600s and 1700s: 21 in the Brazilian state of Minas Gerais; 11 in the Brazilian city of Salvador; 10 or more in the Cuban city of Havana; and others elsewhere.

Relations between the brotherhoods and the Church were not always easy. While accepting and indeed embracing Catholicism, Africans and Afro-Creoles strove at the same time to retain elements of African religion that priests found highly objectionable. Afro-Catholic religious celebrations invariably included African dancing, drumming, and singing; and many slaves and free blacks continued to venerate African gods while worshiping Jesus and the Virgin Mary.

Tension between the Church and the brotherhoods intensified during the late 1700s and early 1800s, when more Africans arrived in Latin America than ever before. Between 1800 and 1850, Brazil received 1.7 million Africans, about the same number as during the entire 1700s. Between 1800 and 1870, Cuba received more than 700,000, far more than during the previous three centuries combined (1500-1800). This increased African immigration, and the refusal of the Church to accommodate African practices within the brotherhoods, led to the creation of new cultural organizations that were openly African in orientation.

Some of these organizations, such as the "African nations" of Buenos Aires, or the "nation councils" (*cabildos de nación*) of Cuba, were state-chartered membership organizations based on African ethnic identities. Thus in Buenos Aires there were Cabinda, Hausa, Asanti, Republic of the Congo, Angola, Mozambique, and some 40 other national organizations; and in Havana, an even greater number and variety. The "nations" provided mutual aid benefits to members, and counseled and represented them in their dealings with Argentine and Cuban slavemasters, officials, police, courts, and so on. They also sponsored weekly dances on Sundays and large public celebrations on major religious and national holidays.

Outside ARGENTINA and Cuba, African national organizations were not formally recognized by the state and do not seem to have owned property or to have had fixed headquarters. Nevertheless, in Montevideo, Rio de Janeiro, Salvador, Cartagena, and other cities, members of African ethnic groups met regularly to hold public dances and celebrations, presided over by dance masters and "monarchs" elected for the day. Freed of the restraints imposed on the cofradías by the Church, the music and dances performed at these gatherings were now explicitly African. In turn, this music formed the basis for the development, later in the 1800s and 1900s, of musical forms that are now core elements of national cultural identity. Candombe in URUGUAY; SAMBA in BRAZIL; RUMBA, MAMBO, and SON in CUBA; TANGO in ARGENTINA; CUMBIA and VALLENATO in COLOMBIA; and other forms elsewhere are examples (*see* CONTEMPORARY AFRO-BRAZILIAN MUSIC).

In most African cultures of the 1700s and 1800s, music and dance were never far removed from religious observance; and the re-Africanization of Afro-Latin American culture that took place at this time extended to religion as well. Besides providing mutual aid and political and legal representation to their members, the Cuban cabildos served as the cradle for the development of that nation's three major African-derived religions: Palo Monte was based on Congolese religious traditions; SANTERÍA was based on YORUBA religious traditions; and Abakuá was a New World transplant of the Leopard societies of the Calabar coast.

During this period African-derived religions were also taking form in Brazil. Most African-based religious observance was clandestine. In 1796, however, a Dahomean congregation, Casa das Minas, was founded in the northeastern city of São Luis. In 1830, citing the freedom of religious expression guaranteed by the recent constitution of 1824, three free African women founded the oldest surviving CANDOMBLÉ (a Yoruba-derived religion) in Salvador, Ilê Iyá Nassô (also known as Casa Branca and Engenho Velho). Both congregations survive to the present, along with thousands of more recently established temples (mainly during the 1900s) devoted to Candomblé Macumba, UMBANDA, the Xangô cult, and other African-based sects (*see* RELIGIONS, AFRICAN, IN LATIN AMERICA AND THE CARIBBEAN).

African-derived music, dance, and religion today form core elements of the national cultures of Latin America. This was not the case in the 1800s and early 1900s, when African culture was rejected as barbarous and uncivilized by regional elites and by many native-born blacks and mulattos (of African and European descent). Most Afro-Latin Americans with aspirations of moving up in their national societies turned their back on African culture and instead joined the major political and social movements of the day, which, unlike such movements in the United States, were generally racially integrated. Throughout Spanish America, black soldiers and officers distinguished themselves in the armies and political movements that won independence from Spain in the first two decades of the nineteenth century (or in Cuba in the 1890s). Following independence, blacks and mulattos in Colombia, Cuba, ECUADOR, MEXICO, PERU, and VENEZUELA participated actively in the Liberal Party, which they viewed as more reformist and egalitarian than its Conservative opposition.

Even the most successful Afro-Latin Americans, however, found that racism and discrimination continued to bar their full participation in national social and political life. Middle- and upper-class social clubs and civic organizations refused to admit blacks and all but a few mulattos. In response, members of the black middle class created their own clubs and civic groups. These organizations were particularly numerous and active in Cuba, where 13 Havana-based institutions joined in 1887 to create the Directorio Central de las Sociedades de Color. At the first national convention of the Directorio, in 1892, 70 "colored societies" from all over the island took part. During the final decade of Spanish rule (1888-1898), the Directorio led a civil rights campaign that led to the final overturning of the colonial racial laws dating from the 1600s and 1700s and to Spain's declaration of full racial equality for blacks and mulattos.

Another middle-class Afro-Latin American response to racial exclusion was the formation in the early 1900s of all-black political parties, none of which survived for more than a few years. In 1908 the Partido Independiente de Color was founded by Afro-Cuban independence war veterans. Outlawed by an act of the Cuban Congress in 1910, it was brutally repressed by government forces in the Race War of 1912, in which 5000 to 6000 Afro-Cuban civilians were killed. The FRENTE NEGRA BRASILEIRA and the Partido Autóctono Negro, founded during the 1930s in Brazil and Uruguay, respectively, did not suffer the same repression but failed to attract a significant black vote.

Meanwhile black and mulatto workers were throwing their support not to black political parties, but to the labor movement that formed in much of the region during the early 1900s. Initially repressed by national governments, unions in Cuba, Venezuela, Colombia, Brazil, and other countries had helped by the 1930s and 1940s to bring labor-based populist regimes to power. These governments all adopted social and economic policies favoring the interests of organized labor, and declared themselves to be "racial democracies" in which whites, blacks, racially mixed "browns" (*pardos*), and indeed all racial groups would participate on terms of complete equality (*see* MYTH OF RACIAL DEMOCRACY IN LATIN AMERICA AND THE CARIBBEAN: AN INTERPRETATION).

These officially egalitarian ideologies, along with significant black economic progress during the 1940s, 1950s, and 1960s, tended to quiet racial protest during those years. During the 1970s and 1980s, however, inspired in part by the example of the Civil Rights and BLACK POWER movements in the United States, black activists in Brazil, Peru, Colombia, Central America, and Uruguay began to protest persisting racial inequalities in their countries. Numerous organizations were formed during those years to combat discrimination and prejudice, including the MOVIMENTO NEGRO UNIFICADO in Brazil, Cimarrón in Colombia, Movimiento Congo in Peru, Acción Reivindicadora del Negro Panameño in PANAMA, and many others.

Particularly in Brazil and Colombia, these organizations had some political impact, provoking national debate on the question of racial inequality as well as the enactment of new laws prohibiting discrimination (in the Brazilian Constitution of 1988) and protecting communally held Afro-Colombian lands (in the Colombian Constitution of 1991). But for the most part, black political movements in the region have drawn only limited popular support, and that mainly from the very small black middle class. Black workers and peasants have channeled their organizational energies in other directions: the labor unions and labor-based political parties that continue to play a major role in the region's politics; neighborhood and community associations; and, interestingly enough, the present-day African-based cultural organizations that are the lineal descendants of those created during the 1700s and 1800s, such as the Santería and Candomblé temples and the *blocos Afros* (Afro blocs), SAMBA SCHOOLS, and marching bands that celebrate Carnival and other major occasions in Brazil, Uruguay, Colombia, and other countries. Thus the historic past of Afro-Latin American cultural and political organizations remains alive in the present.

George Reid Andrews

See Also
Palmares: An African State in Brazil; Civil Rights Movement; Abakuás; Cartagena de Indias, Colombia; Afoxés/Blocos Afros; Rio de Janeiro, Brazil; Religious Brotherhoods in Latin America; Salvador, Brazil.

Latin America and the Caribbean

Cumbia, couple dance in the Caribbean regions of Colombia and Panama, influenced by the presence of African slaves in these areas dating back to the era of Spanish colonialization.

The term *cumbia* is of Bantu origin and likely derives from *nkumbi,* which in the KiKongo language indicates a type of drum used to accompany a ritual performed at the tomb of a great hunter. Other possible origins include the Mandingo place name *cumba* and the Kumba near Calabar in Nigeria. Cumba was also a kingdom in the Republic of the Congo. Among the Congolese, the word means "clamorous shouting, rejoicing" (*see* Languages, African: An Overview).

The origins of cumbia reach back to colonial times and to slave dances that took place at a bonfire. The dances were accompanied by drums and were later held around a tree believed to be sacred. As time went on, slave workers began to participate in Spanish religious festivals, and their dancing around groups of drummers replaced the sacred dimensions of these rites, with secular overtones. In the cumbia, the woman dances in short steps, never lifting her heels from the floor, sliding only forward, and flexes her knees slightly while moving her hips; she appears disdainful and proud. The man dances freely. Using his body, smile, and graceful charm, he plays at amorous conquest.

Nineteenth-century chronicles describing the festival of Candelaria, celebrated on February 2 in Cartagena, record the details of this dance, performed to the beat of the African drum, in which men and women circle each other, paired off but freely moving, never touching hands. The men pirouette and leap, showing off their skills at the caper; the women's heads are adorned with flowers, their hair made brilliant by tallow, their bodies perfumed with the essence of orange blossom. It is not known when the slaves' bonfire was replaced first by tinder and torches and later by a bundle (or *mazo*) of tallow candles – presented by the man to the woman he pursues. The mazo, bound in a kerchief or scarf, burns in such a way that when in the woman's hands its flame and curling smoke rise like a barricade against his advances.

In one of its variations, the dance moves in a spiral. The men form a ring that rotates in the opposite direction of the women, until the moment when each man faces his chosen partner and begins to circle her, intensifying his display of amorous attention until the two join to form a pair.

The important Afro-Colombian writer of black poetry, Jorge Artel, expresses his native affection for the dance in his poem *La cumbia:*

Cumbia! Black dance, dance of my land!
The dance itself cries out
in every electric gesture
in the crooked whirl
of epileptic thighs.
To beckon ancestors, this: Cumbia!
This sensuous music
to which my grandparents danced.
Aged wanderers,
family of blacks. Troublemakers' terror
and the terror of cumbiamberos
in fresh and far off cumbias
on the other sides of the sea.

The cumbia's traditional instrumentation includes two *tambores troncónicos* (drums in the shape of a tree trunk), a *tambora* (a traditional drum roughly analogous to a tom-tom) or *bombo* (bass drum), and a *guache* (an instrument of African origin composed of a cylinder containing holes and filled with seeds, which, like the maraca, is shaken to produce its sound). Often, the instrumentation includes maracas, of Caribbean origin, and a *caña de millo* (a pipe made of cornstalk) of indigenous origin. In certain areas, cumbia music is played on the accordion, accompanied by two drums and a *guacharaca* (a slotted board, played with a metal rod, akin to a washboard).

Though originally the cumbia was not vocal music, cumbias with lyrics can be heard, most often in Ciénaga, Mompox, Sampué, San Jacinto, El Banco, Soledad, Sincelejo, and other Caribbean regions of Colombia, each laying claim to the dance's particular indigenous and African roots. In the case of El Banco, a settlement on the Magdalena River, where an annual cumbia festival takes place, the use of the cornstalk flute (*flauta de millo*) has led some to attribute an indigenous origin to cumbia. It is true that in Cartagena de Indias, Native American Indians took part in festivities where, according to chroniclers, they danced to the rhythm of their *gaitas,* "a variety of flute resembling a pan-pipe.... Men and women held hands in a ring, with the *gaita* players in the center... beating out time on the ground with their feet... without leaps or capers." Descriptions such as this do not, however, confirm that cumbia comes from a specifically indigenous origin. Rather, they point to a process of evolution in which traces of African influence (including rhythm and drumming) combine with indigenous elements (the flute or pipe) and Spanish elements (the dancers' dress, for example) to form a confluence among three disparate worlds. In Colombia, cumbia is for this reason considered a national emblem (*see* World Music, World Beat, and the Re-Africanization of Latin American Popular Music).

Historical records since the seventeenth century show that black slaves seized the opportunity to come together and dance to African drumbeats on the hot sand during Catholic religious ceremonies in Cartagena de Indias and while Carnival masquerade balls swayed to the European rhythms of mazurka, *danzón,* and polka. These impromptu dance floors, exposed to the elements, became known as *salones burreros,* or mule-driver salons, since the dancers arrived from great distances astride their mules, which they left hitched to posts while they danced. Such humble diversions, and the locales in which black slaves found them, later became known as *cumbiambas,* and the performers as *cumbiamberos.* In Barranquilla, for instance, workers met in traders' neighborhoods such as Rebolo before the beginning of the nineteenth century, and before these occasions were officially incorporated into the festive Carnival celebrations in Barranquilla in 1875. The cumbiamberos who participate in the Carnival parade in Barranquilla have become a massive spectacle of street theater, with each group of dancers numbering up to 400. These groups emulate the samba schools in Rio de Janeiro's Carnival, preparing their choreographies, costumes, drumbeats, and flute riffs throughout the year (*see* Carnivals in Latin America and the Caribbean).

Nina Friedemann

See Also
Bantu: Dispersion and Settlement; Slavery in Latin America and the Caribbean; Cartagena de Indias, Colombia; Samba Schools; Rio de Janeiro, Brazil; Carnivals in Latin America and the Caribbean; Catholic Church in Latin America and the Caribbean; Colonial Latin America and the Caribbean; Dance in Latin America and the Caribbean.

North America

Cummings, Elijah (b. 1951-), Baltimore, Md. Democratic member of the United States House of Representatives from Maryland (1996-).

Elijah Eugene Cummings was born in Baltimore, Maryland. He became a member of Phi Beta Kappa and earned a bachelor's degree from Howard University in 1973. He graduated from the University of Maryland Law School in 1976. In 1982 he was elected as a delegate to the Maryland General Assembly. In 1984, at age 33, he became the youngest person ever to chair the Maryland Legislative Black Caucus. In January 1995 he was elected to serve as speaker pro tem of the Maryland House of Delegates.

When Representative Kweisi Mfume announced in December 1995 that he would retire from the United States House to lead the National Association for the Advancement of Colored People (NAACP), Cummings, along with 26 other Democratic candidates, prepared for the March 1996 special primary election. Cummings won the primary with 37 percent of the vote, an impressive margin considering the number of candidates, and went on to win the April 1996 general election over Republican Kenneth Kondner.

Cummings represents Maryland's Seventh District, which covers the inner city of Baltimore and includes some of the suburbs west of the city. More than 70 percent of the district population is black, and the Democratic Party has a huge edge over the Republican Party in the number of registered voters. Johns Hopkins University, the Baltimore Museum of Art, and the NAACP headquarters are located in the Seventh District.

In the 105th Congress (1997-1999), he was the ranking Democrat on the Civil Service Subcommittee of the Government Reform and Oversight Committee. He also served on the Transportation and Infrastructure Committee and is a member of the CONGRESSIONAL BLACK CAUCUS.

North America

Cuney, Norris Wright (b. 1846, Waller County, Tex.; d. 1950), African American politician and Texas Republican Party activist.

Norris Cuney was born in Waller County, Texas. He was in his mid-twenties when the FOURTEENTH AMENDMENT TO THE UNITED STATES CONSTITUTION was passed, guaranteeing citizenship to all African Americans. Cuney became actively involved in political affairs especially as a member of the Republican Party in Texas. He encouraged African Americans to abandon the Populist Movement and vote Republican. He made two attempts (1876, 1882) to be elected to the Texas state legislature but was defeated both times. He was successful at becoming sergeant-at-arms of the Seventeenth Legislature and remained active in the Republican Party.

Alonford James Robinson, Jr.

Cuogana, Ottobah. Please see CUGOANO, OTTOBAH

Latin America and the Caribbean

Curaçao, an island in the NETHERLANDS ANTILLES.

d

Africa

Dacko, David (b. March 24, 1930, Bouchia, Oubangui-Chari [present-day Central African Republic]), twice president of the Central African Republic (1960-1965, 1979-1981).

During his first presidency of the Central African Republic (CAR), David Dacko relied on the support of a narrow elite backed by French troops; he repeated this pattern during his brief return to power 14 years later. The son of a night watchman, Dacko attended local primary and secondary schools and went on to attend classes in neighboring Moyen-Congo, present-day Republic of the Congo. After his graduation he taught school until he was named a school director in 1955. He became friends with the Central African politician Barthélemy Boganda and was elected to the territorial assembly. In the self-governing period before independence, Boganda named Dacko minister of agriculture and, later, minister of interior and administrative affairs. When Boganda was killed in an airplane crash, Dacko succeeded him by claiming kin ties to him, despite the constitutional claim of Goumba, the vice president, to succession.

When the CAR became independent in August 1960, Dacko became president. For the next six years he governed the republic as a one-party state. He organized notables from various ethnic groups to support his government in the ruling party, the Movement for the Social Evolution of Black Africa. He maintained close economic and security relations with France, and relied upon French assistance to suppress dissent and opposition movements. French companies dominated the economy in a neocolonialist style, though some small African-owned industries were established in the country. School attendance doubled under Dacko, but most of the teachers were French.

As events unfolded in the neighboring Democratic Republic of the Congo (then Zaire) in 1964, Dacko feared that he would be overthrown by young radicals in the party, and he distanced himself from French neocolonialism in order to avoid this. He began a pseudo-nationalization of the economy, in which he established industrial enterprises, controlled the diamond industry, and reorganized agricultural production. Such moves angered the French, especially the dominant import-export companies, and Dacko moved to resign from power. Before he could resign, however, his army chief of staff, Jean-Bédel Bokassa, overthrew him on New Year's Eve of 1965.

Dacko spent a decade imprisoned and under house arrest, but in 1976 Emperor Bokassa released him and named Dacko his private counsel. In 1979 Dacko arrived at the presidential palace with French troops, overthrew Bokassa, and announced the end of Bokassa's empire and the restoration of the republic, with himself as president. In 1980 he created the Central African Democratic Union and held elections. Dacko won the elections, but the opposition and public contested them as fraudulent. In governing, Dacko relied on the same small group of notables who had supported him during his previous rule (and who had remained in power under Bokassa), and he relied on the French military for personal protection and for maintaining order.

Dacko faced growing popular unrest in the capital, Bangui, and withering French support with Giscard d'Estaing's departure from office, so he outlawed the two main opposition parties in an attempt to consolidate his power. But under pressure and with little apparent desire to retain the presidency, he yielded power to his chief of staff, André Kolingba, in September 1981.

Eric Young

See Also

Bangui, Central African Republic; France.

North America

Da Costa, Mathieu (b. ?; d. 1606?, Montreal, Quebec), first known person of African descent to visit Canada.

The history of black people in Canada can be dated back to the early seventeenth-century New World expeditions of the French explorer Pierre du Gua, Sieur de Monts. With du Gua was an African man, Mathieu de Costa, who worked as an interpreter between the French and the indigenous Mic Mac Indians. Little is known of de Costa, or of how he gained his surprising fluency in the language of the Mic Macs. Historians speculate that he may have visited Canada earlier as a crew member of a Portuguese vessel, fishing off the coast of Newfoundland.

Peter Hudson

Africa

Daddah, Moktar Ould (b. 1924, Boutilimit, Mauritania), first president of Mauritania (1961-1978).

Born in western Mauritania into a prominent Berber family of *marabouts* (Islamic religious scholars), Moktar Ould Daddah attended an Islamic school at Boutilimit, then the elite Sons of Chiefs' School in Senegal. At that time both Mauritania and Senegal were part of the French colony of French West Africa. Daddah graduated in 1940 and worked as an interpreter for the French colonial administration, then resumed his education in Paris, completing courses in law and Arabic studies.

Mauritania became a French overseas territory in 1946. In 1957, while practicing law in Dakar, Senegal, Daddah was elected to the territorial legislature and appointed to the executive council. In 1958 he was elected secretary-general of the Parti du Regroupement Mauritanien (PRM). In the following year he was elected president of Mauritania's first National Assembly. He served as head of state following full independence in August 1960 and was elected Mauritania's first president in 1961.

Daddah was reelected to three more five-year terms and oversaw Mauritania's transition to a one-party state in 1964, integrating all political parties as part of the PRM. He spearheaded Mauritania's move toward a North African and Arab alliance by severing relations with the United States during the 1967 Arab-Israeli war; securing Mauritania's membership in the Arab League in October 1973; and declaring Arabic the official language of instruction and commerce. These moves were met with resistance by the nation's black African minority. In 1973 Daddah also replaced the French franc with the Mauritanian ouguiya as the official currency.

In 1976 Daddah tried to annex the southern portion of neighboring WESTERN SAHARA. A nationalist group in Western Sahara known as Polisario Front resisted the occupation of their land and steadily fought back the Mauritanian army. The war, unpopular with Mauritanians of both Arab and African descent, drained the national budget and eventually led to the bloodless military coup that deposed Daddah in July 1978. Detained and later exiled to France, he was granted amnesty in December 1984, returned to Mauritania, and has remained active in opposition politics.

SEE ALSO

Colonial Rule; Nationalism in Africa; France; Polisario.

Africa

Dafi (also known as the Dafing and the Southern Marka), ethnic group of West Africa.

The Dafi primarily inhabit MALI and BURKINA FASO. They speak a MANDE language. Approximately 200,000 people consider themselves Dafi.

SEE ALSO

Languages, African: An Overview.

Africa

Dagari (also known as Dagara, Dagaba, and Dagati), ethnic group of West Africa.

The Dagari primarily inhabit northeastern GHANA and southern BURKINA FASO. They speak a Niger-Congo language and belong to the Molé-Dagbane cultural and linguistic group. Approximately 500,000 people consider themselves Dagari.

SEE ALSO

Languages, African: An Overview.

Africa

Dagomba (also known as Dagbamba), an ethnic group of northeastern GHANA and adjacent parts of TOGO.

The Dagomba speak Dagbane, a language belonging to the Gur subgroup of the Niger-Congo languages. Anthropologists believe that the Dagomba people arose when migrant horsemen, who arrived from the northeast, conquered indigenous Gur speakers around the fourteenth century C.E. These indigenous people farmed grains such as MILLET, raised cattle, and smelted iron. They acknowledged the authority of *tindamba*, or earth priests. The conquerors adopted the language of their subjects and ruled as an aristocratic caste.

Oral accounts state that a noble warrior, Nyagse, forged the Dagomba into a nation by conquering villages and massacring their priests. Nyagse created a hierarchical state in which power was won by competition but no man could rise higher than his father; therefore, only the sons of the *Ya-Na*, or paramount chief, could succeed him. A hierarchy of chiefs, all subjects of the Ya-Na, ruled the Dagomba chiefdom, known as Dagbon, but the indigenous tindamba allocated land, played a role in approving the appointment of chiefs, and maintained their spiritual powers.

The expansion of the neighboring GONJA kingdom during the sixteenth century drove the Dagomba from the western part of their homeland. The Dagomba conquered the KONKOMBA people to the east and built a new capital, Yendi, in the conquered territory. In this region, the Dagomba ruled the Konkomba as overlords. Dagbon prospered by taxing the lucrative trade passing through its territory. Hausa traders carried cola nuts, gold, and, later, slaves through from the forest region to the south. They returned with goods such as salt from the Sahara and cloth manufactured in the Hausa states. These traders also brought Islam to the Dagomba. The Dagomba aristocracy has largely adopted Islam, but much of the population continued to practice traditional beliefs at the end of the twentieth century.

Around 1745 ASANTE conquered Dagbon, which had been weakened by a war of succession. Asante required Dagbon to pay tribute in slaves until 1874, when the British defeated Asante. Dagbon declared its independence from the weakened Asante kingdom. In 1896, however, a German force of about 100 destroyed Yendi and defeated a 7000-man, poorly equipped Dagomba army. In 1899 the British and the Germans split Dagbon between German Togoland and the British Gold Coast. After World War I the British took control of western Togoland and reunified Dagbon under British administration. The British implemented indirect rule, in which Dagomba chiefs administered local government. This policy perpetuated Dagomba dominance over the Konkomba. The British largely neglected the economic development of Dagbon. To pay the head tax the British imposed, Dagomba had to migrate to the southern Gold Coast to work in mines and on cocoa plantations.

Today the more than 500,000 Dagomba are the largest ethnic group in the Northern Region of Ghana and are the dominant group in the Northern Region's capital, Tamale. Since independence, Dagbon has become known as the "granary of Ghana." Dagomba farmers produce much of the country's millet, maize, yams, and peanuts.

Unfortunately, over the past century, the Dagomba have faced repeated conflict. Following the death of Ya-Na Mahama II in 1954, a succession dispute erupted into violence. The federal government sent troops to Yendi and intervened to decide the succession. Ethnic tension has also plagued northern Ghana. Violence flared between the Dagomba and their KONKOMBA subjects over land use and ownership in 1914, 1917, the 1940s, and the 1980s. During the 1990s ethnic violence once again racked the region. Twelve people were killed in Tamale in 1994 when police fired on a group of Dagomba who had attacked some Konkomba.

David P. Johnson, Jr.

SEE ALSO

Colonial Rule; Gold Trade; Languages, African: An Overview; Iron in Africa; Salt Trade; Cola.

Africa

Dahomey, Early Kingdom of, precolonial West African kingdom located in what is now southern BENIN.

Dahomey reached the height of its power and prestige during the heyday of the Atlantic slave trade in the eighteenth and nineteenth centuries. Abomey, future capital of Dahomey, was founded around 1620 by Dogbari, who had fled Allada after a power struggle among his brothers for control of that kingdom. Under Dogbari's grandson, Wegbaja (c. 1645-1685), Abomey was expanded through military conquest and consolidated into a powerful state. Wegbaja's grandson, Agaja, conquered both Allada and Whydah in the 1720s, founding the kingdom of Dahomey with its capital at Abomey. Its government was an absolute monarchy with a well-established centralized state and bureaucracy. Dahomey became heavily involved in the European slave trade, which had begun in earnest a century previous with the arrival of the Dutch.

The rule of Gezu (1818-1858), who overthrew King Adandozan, marked the pinnacle of Dahomey's power and influence. Military victories enabled Dahomey to stop paying its annual tribute to the Oyo Empire of what is now NIGERIA. Still, the end of the slave trade in the mid-nineteenth century greatly affected the economic fortunes of Dahomey, forcing it to provide primary products for newly important colonial markets. Palm oil, its main export, was never able to generate the same kinds of revenues that the slave trade had yielded. After the French gained control of Porto-Novo, commerce declined. Under the leadership of Glele (1858-1889), Dahomean troops resisted the French occupation; in 1889 the entire French merchant community on the coast was forced to flee into British territory.

Benhazin (1889-1894), Glele's successor, was willing to trade with the French, but only if they agreed to grant Dahomey unconditional independence. In 1892 the French launched a full-scale offensive against Dahomey.

Benhazin surrendered in 1894 and was exiled to MARTINIQUE, and the kingdom became the French colony of Dahomey.

SEE ALSO
Transatlantic Slave Trade; Oyo, Early Kingdom of; Porto-Novo, Benin.

Africa

Dakar, Senegal, a major West African port and the capital and largest city of SENEGAL.

Cosmopolitan, hedonistic Dakar has been called the Paris of West Africa. Once the capital of French West Africa, Dakar no longer dominates West Africa economically or politically, but it remains an important cultural center. It lies on Cape Verde, near the westernmost point in Africa. Scholars have suggested two origins for the name Dakar. Fugitives from the tyrannical precolonial states of the interior called the Cape Verde Peninsula *Deuk Raw* ("land of refuge"), which might have evolved into Dakar. The name could also derive from the WOLOF word for tamarind tree, *Dakhar.*

Portuguese mariners first arrived along the Cape Verde coast during the mid-fifteenth century. They established a trading post on nearby Gorée Island, which exported slaves over the next 350 years. By the eighteenth century the French had taken control of Gorée. However, Gorée Island lacked a reliable supply of water, and its inhabitants sought a source of water on the nearby mainland. In the early 1700s the Lebu people occupied the small fishing and farming village of Ndakaru, on the Cape Verde Peninsula, on which Dakar is now built. The French constructed a trading post on the site around 1750.

To protect the merchants who settled there, in 1857 the French established a fort in Dakar. France was extending its control over Senegal, and the colonial administration needed a port close to the peanut-growing regions in the interior. In 1862 the French built a breakwater to protect Dakar's port and constructed a modern town on the site. The completion of West Africa's first rail line in 1885, which ran to Saint-Louis through Senegal's main peanut-growing regions, increased the city's economic importance and caused its population to grow. In 1878 its population was 1556, which grew to 18,447 by 1904. In 1887 Dakar was named one of the Four Communes of Senegal, and in 1890 the African residents of the communes, including Dakar, received partial French citizenship rights. Then in 1902 Dakar became the capital of the vast domain of FRENCH WEST AFRICA. With the completion of a rail line to Bamako, far to the east on the NIGER RIVER, Dakar became not only the political center, but also the economic center of much of West Africa.

Dakar was never rigidly segregated, and its residents' status as citizens gave them access to a French education and to French civil service jobs. In time, a French-speaking urban African elite arose, with a strong French outlook and often French ancestry as well.

After Senegal's independence in 1960, Dakar became the nation's capital. In addition to government offices, Dakar contains a sizable modern business district, where many international banks, multinational corporations, and international agencies maintain regional headquarters. It also has an international airport with good connections to Europe, North and South America, and many African cities. Further, it is the major port for Senegal and neighboring countries, and has a large agricultural processing industry. Dakar boasts a sizable middle class. Although its living conditions are generally better than those of Senegal's interior, Dakar nevertheless has sprawling shantytowns, often filled with unemployed migrants from the interior. High unemployment, chronic water shortages, and pollution also plague the city, which had a population of nearly 2 million in 1998.

Its beauty, relatively mild climate, and nearby beaches have made Dakar a popular tourist destination. Major sites include Gorée Island, which is now a museum. Other attractions include one of the oldest African art museums on the continent and a thriving nightlife. The French Cultural Center and various nightclubs offer venues for Dakar's lively music scene, which features some of the top African artists, while a number of cinemas offer the latest in Senegalese film. Several markets, including the large Marché Sandaga, offer local crafts and clothing.

David P. Johnson, Jr.

SEE ALSO
Bamako, Mali; Gorée Island, Senegal; France.

Latin America and the Caribbean

Damas, Léon-Gontran

(b. March 28, 1912, Cayenne, French Guiana; d. January 22, 1978, WASHINGTON, D.C.), the least known of the three principal founders and proponents of the NÉGRITUDE movement, and the first to illustrate it through poetry.

Léon-Gontran Damas was born into the mulatto bourgeoisie of Cayenne, the capital of FRENCH GUIANA, a territory vilified in Damas's day as a penal colony. The area contained significant Native American and *nègres bosh* (descended from fugitive African slaves) populations. Damas lost his mother in early childhood and received a bourgeois upbringing from his aunt; he would later reject the values of his youth, together with all forms of political and cultural assimilation. As an adolescent he attended the Victor Schoelcher High School in Martinique, where he first became friends with AIMÉ CÉSAIRE. After graduating he moved to Paris, where he studied literature, Asian languages, and law. He also collaborated in the production of the now-famous black publications *La revue du monde noir, Légitime Défense,* and *L'Etudiant noir.*

With the support of French anthropologist Paul Rivet, Damas returned to French Guiana in 1934 to investigate African cultural crossover among the nègres bosh. His account of the trip appeared in the form of *Retour de Guyane* (Return from Guiana), published less than a year after his book of poems *Pigments* (1937) appeared. Both works denounce the assimilationist policies of the colonial administration, and both were censured by the French colonial government. Police seized the remaining copies of *Pigments* in 1939, after poems from the collection that had been translated into Baule (*see* LANGUAGES, AFRICAN: AN OVERVIEW) incited Africans in CÔTE D'IVOIRE to resist conscription into the French army. The French also quietly attempted to buy up the print run of *Retour de Guyane.*

After World War II Damas traveled to the United States and began to solidify the connections he had made earlier in Paris among the American black intelligentsia: COUNTEE CULLEN, CLAUDE MCKAY, and especially Mercer Cook and LANGSTON HUGHES. He returned to his country and in 1948 was elected to the French Parliament to represent the new department of French Guiana (whose creation he had opposed). Until his electoral defeat in 1951 Damas proposed commonsense reforms and improvements in the colony; after leaving Parliament he broadened his activities and became a sort of roving ambassador of black consciousness. He began to travel extensively in Africa, giving lectures and recruiting and training African radio journalists in the context of his work as consultant and broadcaster for the French overseas radio service. He was eventually fired from that position.

Damas also served as editor of an early French series of the works of African writers; his role was comparable to that of Nigerian CHINUA ACHEBE in the Heinemann African Writers series. Damas later traveled to virtually all the countries of the diaspora for the United Nations Educational, Scientific, and Cultural Organization (UNESCO), returning more and more often to speak on campuses in the United States. He finally settled there in 1970, after the publication of two other volumes of poems: *Black-Label* (1956) and *Névralgies* (1966). By this time his contacts in the literary and political worlds of Africa, Europe, and the Americas made him uniquely able to serve as a bridge between the continents and language groups of the diaspora. In the United States he taught at Federal City College (now the University of the District of Columbia) and at HOWARD UNIVERSITY, where he held a position at the time of his death in 1978.

Damas's literary output was rather limited, and his work remained difficult to find until the definitive edition of *Pigments* was published by the Paris publishing house Présence Africaine in 1962. At several points in his career Damas had the misfortune of publishing at the same time that seminal works by Césaire and LÉOPOLD SÉDAR SENGHOR appeared. Césaire's *Cahier d'un retour au pays natal* (Return to My Native Land) was released in 1939, and Senghor's *Anthologie de la nouvelle poésie africaine et malgache de langue française* (Anthology of the New Black and Malagasy Poetry in the French Language) came to the attention of the public in 1948; these coincided, respectively, with Damas's *Pigments* and *Poètes noirs d'expression française* (Black Poets in the French Language). Although Césaire's *Cahier* and Senghor's *Anthologie* quickly overshadowed the works of Damas, the publication dates reveal the anticipatory quality of his literary products.

Both Senghor and Césaire have credited Damas with exerting a formative influence on their literary output. Although Damas was less prominent a politician and less prolific a publisher than either of his literary successors, he may have been more effective than either in coupling political activity with literary production and in representing the rising international black consciousness after World War II. Senghor felt that Damas was "the most nègre of us all," and the first to find the rhythm of the true *poésie nègre*. Most of the conclusions drawn by Senghor and Césaire reflect characteristics of Damas's work in *Pigments* and the long single poem *Black-Label*. Their insights focus on the incantatory repetitions of Damas's verse and the ideology of African revalorization for which Damas's rhythms provided a vehicle. For most of his critics, Damas became the poet of black anger's direct expression. His poem *Pour Sûr* illustrates the raw quality of the poet's sentiment:

Sure enough I'll get
fed up
and not even wait
for things
to reach
the state
of a ripe camembert

Then I'll put my foot in it
or else simply put
my hand around the neck
of everything that pisses me off in capital letters
colonization
civilization
assimilation
and all the rest
Until then
you will often hear me
slam the door

Damas and the other members of the Négritude movement were acutely aware of the rise of European fascism and the concurrent decline of colonial regimes. Some of Damas's lapidary pronouncements, however, were not popular with the critics of Négritude's essentialism, who began to accuse the author of making racist diatribes. Gerald Moore's introduction to *Seven African Writers* (1962) cites Damas's work as an example of Négritude "degenerating into a racialism as intolerant and arrogant as any other." To rescue Damas from such attacks, critics during the 1970s and 1980s tended to emphasize less political aspects of his writing. While such defenses recall and extol the very personal poems of *Névralgies*, Damas's most vigorous, satisfying, and freshest works are still his most politically and historically engaged: *Pigments* and *Black-Label*, as well as *Retour de Guyane*.

The poems in these collections do considerably more than act as a manifesto for a version of Négritude quickly dominated by Senghor's political and racialist ideology. In "Nuit Blanche," Damas shows an acute awareness of the historical and situational alienation of which Négritude was both an the expression and the cure:

My friends I've waltzed
waltzed like my ancestors
the Gauls never did
until my blood turned to viennese cream [. . .]

My friends I've waltzed
waltzed
waltzed crazily
often
I thought I was holding the waist of Uncle Gobineau
or of Cousin Hitler
or of some good Aryan chewing over his old age
on some park bench

Despite, or perhaps because of, his experience of cultural alienation, the poet succeeds in rewriting histories; with Damas writing the calypso, we have no doubt who will come off better in his dance with Uncle Gobineau (referring to Joseph-Arthur, Compte de Gobineau, a nineteenth-century French ethnologist who developed a theory of scientific racism, arguing the superiority of the white race) or Cousin Hitler. Perhaps even more than his fellow Caribbean Négritude poet Césaire, Damas feels at home anywhere in the history of the diaspora. Bridging the Anglophone and Francophone Atlantic worlds, and with an enormous personal experience on four continents, Damas was in a unique position to personify the new black historical consciousness of his day. In dancing the Viennese waltz, as he might a Caribbean mazurka, he proves himself, in scholar Mercer Cook's words, "the man of the diaspora par *excellence*."

Africa

Dan, ethnic group of West Africa who live in northwest CÔTE D'IVOIRE and northeast LIBERIA.

The Dan language belongs to the Southern (or Peripheral) MANDE branch of the Niger-Congo linguistic family (*see* LANGUAGES, AFRICAN: AN OVERVIEW) and is closely related to neighboring Kweni (or Gouro). Some scholars believe that the Dan originated in northwestern present-day Côte d'Ivoire. According to this view, MANDINKA expansion drove them to their present homeland in the seventeenth and eighteenth centuries. The Dan comprise two groups. The Damènou, or northern Dan, live in the mountains and cultivate rice. The southern Dan, or Boutyouleumènou, who share a number of cultural features with the neighboring KRU people, hunt collectively and cultivate tubers.

The government of Côte d'Ivoire calls the Dan the Yacouba (or Yakouba). The traditional Dan homeland spans the departments of Man, Biankouma, and Danané in Côte d'Ivoire, as well as Nimba County in neighboring Liberia. It is a region of grassy savanna and forested mountains, including the highest point in West Africa, Mount Nimba, with a height of 1752 m (over 6700 ft).

In Liberia the Dan, one of the country's 18 main ethnic groups, are often called Gio, a pejorative term that carries the meaning "slave people" in the Bassa language. The Dan resisted the authority of Westernized states based along the coast. The Nimba County town of Tapiple, also called Tapeta, is named for the Dan chief Tapi, who allied with the Liberian government troops that finally subjugated the region in the 1920s. In Côte d'Ivoire French governor Gabriel Angoulvant suppressed Dan resistance in a series of battles that ended in 1908.

The Dan also resisted the Islam of their northern neighbors and maintained vibrant religious and cultural traditions. They believe in the existence of two gods, one good and the other evil; they also believe that ancestral spirits influence the living. The Dan include male circumcision and female excision in initiation ceremonies (*see* FEMALE CIRCUMCISION IN AFRICA). Secret societies remain important. The most powerful of these, the Gor, gives initiates the right to become symbolic leopards and thus impart justice unnoticed. By thrusting a baton between combatants, the Gor have the right to stop war. When one of the brotherhood commits a serious offense, he may be poisoned with crocodile bile.

The Dan excel at dance dramas, with dialogue sung, spoken, or pantomimed. Dance societies often require secret initiations for children as young as two years old. Young girls perform the Gueu-Gblin and the Menton, while young boys dance the Gouah. The Dan also love spectacular acrobatics, which have become tourist attractions, in which men juggle small boys in the air above the point of a knife. Dan music, which features an all-wood drum, is not heavily influenced by European styles and retains much of its spiritual significance. African art collectors prize Dan masks and wall hangings.

In the late 1990s most Dan made a living by growing rice, manioc, coffee, COCOA, and COLA nuts. Men also migrated to work on the coast in the logging, palm-oil, and tourist industries. In 1998 the Dan numbered around 500,000, with more than 300,000 in Côte d'Ivoire and the remainder across the border in Liberia.

David P. Johnson, Jr.

SEE ALSO

Dance in Sub-Saharan Africa; Tourism in Africa; Islam and Tradition: An Interpretation.

Latin America and the Caribbean

Dancehall, **currently the most popular form of REGGAE in JAMAICA, featuring DJs toasting over raw rhythms with sparse melodic accompaniment.**

Dancehall grew out of the roots reggae scene of the mid-1970s. Beginning in the 1980s reggae tracks grew increasingly stripped down. Insistent percussion and sparse melodies took a back seat to the vocal acrobatics of DJs, vocalists who would chat, rhyme, and "toast" over the instrumental tracks. Starting with Count Machuki in the 1950s, there emerged a long tradition of talk-over DJs, but the form didn't become widely popular until the 1980s. DJs such as Yellowman started releasing albums recorded live in the Jamaican dance halls, and within a few years "dancehall" denoted this raw new form of reggae.

In 1980 Edward Seaga's conservative Jamaican Labour Party government rose to power amid a violent election, signaling a series of changes, such as decreased health coverage, which negatively impacted the urban poor (*see* JAMAICA). Dancehall reggae lyrics and attitude toughened up to reflect a hard-edged ghetto realism. The black consciousness of roots reggae singers was abandoned in favor of gun talk, sexual boasting (or "slackness"), and the pleasures of escape found in the dance hall itself.

Toying around with a newly purchased Casio electronic keyboard, dancehall producer Prince Jammy slowed down a rock rhythm, included reggae drums, and subsequently revolutionized Jamaican music with his all-electronic hit single "Under Mi Sleng Teng," sung by Wayne Smith. In the following months over 400 versions of Jammy's track appeared. Crowds loved the new "computah" sound, and producers were quick to embrace the cost-effective digital production.

While many Jamaican reggae fans and critics declared the new "ragga" dancehall to be a degenerate form, its popularity has grown steadily since 1985's "Sleng Teng" revolution. The economic constraints that made producers eager to replace expensive session bands with digital instruments encouraged greater experimentation because mistakes would be less costly. Although dancehall's detractors claim that the music is a robotic and simple regression from "superior" roots reggae, dancehall actually has more in common with early Afro-Jamaican forms than the roots reggae that proved so successful in international markets.

Dancehall DJs toast predominantly in Jamaican *patois*, a Creole language not readily understood by English speakers (*see* LANGUAGES, CREOLE, IN THE CARIBBEAN). The instrumental arrangements minimize European and North American harmonic and melodic elements in favor of strong rhythms and verbal wordplay that stem from early Jamaican and Afro-Jamaican sources. Remixes of ROCKSTEADY rhythms from the 1960s provide much of dancehall's rhythmic base. Leading bass-and-drums dancehall producers Sly Dunbar and Robbie Shakespeare scored a massive hit in 1991 by reworking the Maytals' 1966 hit "Bam Bam." Dub poet LINTON KWESI JOHNSON summarized the situation: "With the discovery of digital recording, an extreme minimalism has emerged.... On the one hand, this music is totally technological; on the other the rhythms are far more Jamaican: they're drawn from Etu, Pocomania, Kumina – African-based religious cults.... [T]he music is becoming even rootsier, with a resonance even for quite old listeners, because it evokes back to what they first heard in rural Jamaica."

Current dancehall features an occasional hip hop collaboration due to strong West Indian communities in the New York City neighborhoods of Brooklyn and the Bronx, where hip hop first developed. More recently, opera and country music are appearing in dancehall songs. Bounty Killer has recorded a stirring version of *Figaro* and an album entitled *HipHopera;* top DJ Beenie Man is one of many who have incorporated country and western into dancehall on best-selling albums.

Today dancehall's popularity continues unabated and the genre remains an aggressively populist form. About 5000 dancehall records are released in Jamaica each year, many of which never leave its shores. A loose attitude toward copyright and authorship, always a staple in Jamaican music, is evidenced most strongly in dancehall. DJs often use musical quotations, singing their own lyrics in the melodies of American hits or lifting lines from hip hop, pop, rock, or any number of foreign musical forms. The best-selling dancehall hits are immediately "versioned" as dozens of DJs take on the same rhythm track, using their voices to give each version a different rhythmic accent and feel while trying to outdo one another with impressive lyrics.

Dancehall is primarily heard in Jamaica and foreign cities with sizable West Indian populations. Racially mixed working-class communities in London developed British dancehall culture into various cross-cultural fusions (*see* LONDON, BLACKS IN: AN INTERPRETATION). In the early 1990s black London DJs incorporated dancehall toasting, dub reggae bass lines, and sped-up hip hop breakbeats to form a new musical form known as jungle. Early jungle sounds like a frenzied dancehall song, complete with simulated gunfire, elemental bass, and a DJ improvising crowd-moving lyrics. Dancehall toasters such as General Levy and Super Cat have scored hit singles in both genres. Around the same time, London's Southeast Asian community looked to West Indian dancehall for inspiration. The resulting synthesis was termed *bhangramuffin*, and combined equal elements of Indian *bhangra* and Jamaican raggamuffin (or dancehall) rhythms. British-Indian vocalist Apache Indian sings in Punjabi, English, and Jamaican *patois*, highlighting the multicultural nature of dancehall in Great Britain.

Jace Clayton

SEE ALSO

Jungle (Drum and Bass); Dub Poetry; Hip Hop in the United States.

Latin America and the Caribbean

Dance in Latin America and the Caribbean, **a vital means of expressing the aesthetic, spiritual, and even political solidarity of people of African descent which has strongly influenced the culture at large in this part of the world (*see* DANCE IN SUB-SAHARAN AFRICA).**

Because it is nonverbal, dance has often been perceived by Western observers as a relatively insignificant cultural medium, capable of communicating only abstract thought or emotion. In the African diaspora, however, bodily movement can be a form of prayer, or of protest. Sometimes it is both. In some cases, the brutal repression of verbal expressions of religious or political beliefs has necessitated this other, more discreet means of communication. Meaningful motion is an important and continuous aspect of diasporic culture, which assumes no necessary division between the mind and the body.

The worship of African deities in the Caribbean and Latin America (*see* RELIGIONS, AFRICAN, IN LATIN AMERICA AND THE CARIBBEAN) continues to be performed through dance, and the choreographies of these religious ceremonies bear an uncanny resemblance to those of West African ceremonies. VODOU in HAITI, SANTERÍA in CUBA, and CANDOMBLÉ in BRAZIL are all African diasporic religions in which dance is used to invoke and communicate with divine entities. All of these religions are syncretic – that is, they merge elements of one or more distinct African belief systems (largely Dahomean, YORUBA, or Kongo) with elements of Catholicism and, in some cases, Native American belief. But the danced invocation of gods (called *lwa* in Haiti, ORISHAS in Cuba, and *orixás* in Brazil) distinctly reflects African diasporic practice, even if these gods are sometimes referred to by the names of Catholic saints.

In all of these religions, worshipers perform ritual dance movements in a counterclockwise circle. These dances usually make subtle reference to the divine qualities of a specific god. Ogun, for example, a warrior god also associated with metalwork, draws his arms back and then thrusts them against each other, as though they were two blades striking. Ochun, a goddess of water and seduction, moves languorously while appearing to stare at herself in a mirror. As the ceremony progresses, the divinities, summoned through dance, begin themselves to animate the bodies in motion. This is what outside observers commonly refer to as "spirit possession," and it is usually marked by more virtuosic, inspired dancing. In such a ceremony, the dance itself exceeds the usual capacities of the individual body, as it becomes an instrument for worship by the entire community (*see* Music, Afro-Caribbean Religious).

Religious dances are usually distinguished from secular dances – those performed, ostensibly, for mere entertainment. In Latin America and the Caribbean, some of these forms are popularly understood to be African traditions, even as they achieve the status of "national dances." Rumba in Cuba, Bomba in Puerto Rico, and samba in Brazil all have names of Kongo origin and are commonly acknowledged as symbolic of each culture's African heritage. Other popular dances, such as merengue in the Dominican Republic or the contredanse in Haiti, are African stylizations of European folk and court dances. While none of these dances is explicitly religious or political, it would be reductive to understand them merely as enjoyable pastimes. Secular dances are occasionally performed within religious ceremonies; even in nonreligious contexts, dancers in these popular forms may insert subtle gestures from the religious dances, infusing their motion with a higher degree of significance. In addition, all of these dances, by virtue of their explicit performance of African cultural continuity, can be viewed as politically meaningful acts (*see* Music, Afro-Caribbean Secular).

One of the most powerful diasporic dance forms – powerful both as a bodily practice and as a politically symbolic activity – is Capoeira, an Afro-Brazilian martial art, dance, and game performed to music. Capoeira was derived from Kongo-Angolan kicking games, and there are related forms in the Caribbean. Historians surmise that the musical and dance dimensions of capoeira were developed by enslaved Africans in Brazil so they could practice fighting techniques under the guise of dance. In capoeira, dance becomes an effective defense technique: just as it historically allowed practitioners to pursue the art of self-defense, it allows players in the game to lure their opponents into vulnerable positions.

Virtually all of these dance forms have undergone periods of repression, or at least public censure. Capoeira was officially outlawed in 1890, and for years practitioners were subject to corporal punishment and exile. Vodou, Santería, and Candomblé have all been outlawed at different periods of Haitian, Cuban, and Brazilian history. Even

ABOVE LEFT: Photographed in Dangogo in 1968, men of the Saramaka tribe of Suriname maroons dance the *tjêke*, which is popular for funerals. *Richard Price*
ABOVE RIGHT: The Cuban National Folklore Dance Ensemble performs in Havana, Cuba. *José Azel/Aurora*
RIGHT: In his *Voyage pittoresque dans le Brésil*, German artist Johann Moritz Rugendas (1802-1858) depicts Afro-Brazilians dancing the batuca. *By permission of the Houghton Library, Harvard University*

LEFT: In the painting *Afro-Cuban Dance* of 1944, by Mario Carreño (b. 1913), a participant in a Yoruba-based religious ritual dances in a trance. *Courtesy Art Museum of the Americas of the Organization of American States, photograph by Oscar Monsalve*
BELOW: The rumba, here danced in the streets of Havana, originated in the predominantly black province of Matanzas, Cuba, at the turn of the century. *© D. Donne Bryant*

when national law has not prohibited the danced worship of African divinities, participants in these religions have suffered violent repression and censure both within their countries and abroad. Horrific misrepresentations of "voodoo" in Hollywood films have done much to propagate ignorance and discrimination. The popular, secular dance forms have also been perceived as overly sensual, even dangerous, by uninformed outsiders. Typical depictions of African diasporic music and dance forms as "infectious" or "contagious" may seem to incorporate innocent metaphors, but in fact such depictions have historically been used in attempts to control and contain legitimate cultural expressions.

Early in this century the antiracist Franz Boas, German-American anthropologist and ethnologist, argued that an important element in demonstrating the resilience and significance of African diasporic culture would be the study of dance. In the 1940s the anthropologist Melville Herskovits reiterated the plea for a serious consideration of diasporic dance forms. Unfortunately, the study of the history of these dances offers as many obstacles as it does possibilities. Historical documentation of dance is difficult to amass. Many of the written accounts suffer from the same misapprehensions that led to legal restrictions of the forms. Tracing the origin and development of various dance forms is difficult because improvisation and innovation are actually important components of the dance tradition: there is no *perfect* rendition of the rumba. Still, despite the challenges, diasporic dance continues to thrive and to inspire increasingly rich understandings of its importance to the vitality of a culture.

Barbara Browning

See Also

Angola; Benin; Merengue: Music, Race and Nation in the Dominican Republic; Plena and Bomba; Catholic Church in Latin America and the Caribbean; Religions, African, in Latin America and the Caribbean; Ogum; Oxum.

Africa

Dance in Sub-Saharan Africa,

an overview of traditional and contemporary dance in sub-Saharan Africa.

Traditional African Dance Forms

African dances are as varied and changing as the communities that create them. Although many types of African dance incorporate spirited, vigorous movement, there are others that are more reserved or stylized. African dances vary widely by region and ethnic community. In addition, there are numerous dances within a given community.

African communities traditionally use dance for a variety of social purposes. Dances play a role in religious rituals; they mark rites of passage, including initiations to adulthood and weddings; they form a part of communal ceremonies, including harvest celebrations, funerals, and coronations; and they offer entertainment and recreation in the forms of masquerades, acrobatic dances, and social club dances.

European explorers of Africa hardly understood either the aesthetics or the meanings of dances in the cultures they sought to scrutinize and conquer (*see* Explorers in Africa since 1800). Writers such as Joseph Conrad depicted African dance as an expression of both "savagery" and aggressiveness. European observers often focused on certain types of African dance that reinforced their stereotypes of blacks as sexualized, warlike peoples. Abandoning these stereotypes, a careful survey reveals extraordinary variety in both the social meanings and aesthetic styles of African dance forms.

Traditionally, dance in Africa occurs collectively in a community setting. It expresses the life of the community more than the mood of an individual or a couple. Dances mark key elements of communal life. For example, dances at agricultural festivals mark the passage of seasons, the successful completion of projects, and the hope for prosperity. In an annual festival of the Irigwe in Nigeria, men perform leaps symbolizing the growth of the crops.

Dance does not merely form a part of community life; it represents and reinforces the community itself. Its structures reproduce the organization and the values of the community. For example, dances are often segregated by sex, reinforcing gender identities to children from a young age. Dance often expresses the categories that structure the community, including not only gender but also kinship, age, status, and, especially in modern cities, ethnicity. For example, in the *igbin* dance of the Yoruba of Nigeria the order of the performers in the dance reflects their social standing and age, from the king down to the youngest at the gathering. Among the Asante of Ghana the king reinforces his authority through a special royal dance, and traditionally he might be judged by his dancing skill. Dance can provide a forum for popular opinion and even satire within political structures: the Ubakala and Bambara use dance as a form of criticism and commentary. Spiritual leaders also use dance to symbolize their connection with the world beyond.

Dances provide community recognition for the major events in people's lives. The dances of initiation, or rites of passage, are pervasive throughout Africa and function as moments of definition in an individual's life or sometimes as key opportunities to observe potential marriage partners. Highly energetic dances show off boys' stamina and are considered a means of judging physical health. The learning of the dance often plays an important part in the ritual of the occasion. For example, the girls among the Lunda of Zambia stay in seclusion practicing their steps before the coming-of-age ritual. Throughout Africa dance is also an integral part of the marking of birth and death. At burial ceremonies the Owo Yoruba perform the *igogo*, in which young men dance over the grave and pack the earth with stomping movements.

Dance plays a central role in therapy and healing in many parts of Africa. In the West African religious practice of *bori*, or *ajun*, women suffering from mental illness are brought to a shrine where they learn a ceremony involving song and dance for three months. This process of learning is as important for the women's therapy as the ceremony itself. The Tiv of Nigeria have a dance that expresses the vital life force in the world that combats disease and death. The !Kung San of Botswana perform a healing dance that includes both sexes and all ages, the healthy as well as the sick. Possession dance is another form of therapeutic ritual movement. Among the Shona in Zimbabwe the *mhondoro* spirit occupies the bodies of dancers, who move to a rhythm as the ancestors communicate wisdom.

Dance traditionally prepared people for the roles they played in the community. For example, some war dances prepared young men physically and psychologically for war by teaching them discipline and control while getting them into the spirit of battle. Some dances are a form of martial art themselves, such as Nigerian *korokoro* dances or the Angolan dances from which Brazilian capoeira is derived (*see* Brazil's Relationship with Africa: An Interpretation).

Dances often tell stories that are part of the oral history of a community. For example, the *bamaya* dance of Ghana narrates the legend of a man who was hungry and entered the

The one unifying aesthetic of African dance is an emphasis upon rhythm, which may be expressed by many different parts of the body or extended outside the body to rattles or costumes. African dances may combine movements of any parts of the body, from the eyes to the toes, and the focus on a certain part of the body may have a particular social significance. The Nigerian Urhobo women perform a dance during which they push their arms back and forth and contract the torso in synchronization with an accelerating rhythm beat by a drum. In Côte D'Ivoire a puberty dance creates a rhythmic percussion through the movement of a body covered in cowrie shells.

Africans often judge the mastery of a dancer by the dancer's skill in representing rhythm. More skillful dancers might express

TOP: Dancers celebrate the opening of a United Nations-sponsored well in Vahun, Liberia. *CORBIS/Liba Taylor*
ABOVE LEFT: Dance plays an important role in civic and religious life in Africa. Here, a Madagascan shaman dances in a healing ceremony. *CORBIS/John Garrett*
ABOVE RIGHT: Men possessed by Xangó, the Yoruba god of thunder, dance during a ceremony in Benin. *Fundação Pierre Verger*
OPPOSITE: Yoruba women dance, possessed by Xangó, the god of thunder. *Fundação Pierre Verger*

market dressed as a woman in order to steal a chicken. During the dance men play the role of the women in the market, imitating women's hip movements as women call out. Such stories often lie at the heart of a community's identity. The Ewe people of Togo and surrounding countries have created a dance to narrate a tale of the origin and migration of the community. Imitating the movements of a bird with the arms, dancers relate the story of the Ewe who followed the path of a bird when the group migrated from Benin to the west.

several different rhythms at the same time, for example by maintaining a separate rhythmic movement with each of several different parts of the body. Rhythm frequently forms a dialogue between dancers, musicians, and audience (*see* African Music). Typically, the rhythmic dialogue occurs between the dancers and the drums in West Africa and between the dancers and the chorus in East Africa. The call-and-response dynamic found in African traditions all over the world characterizes the rhythmic dialogue among dancers, music, and audience. Unlike many

Western forms of "art" dance, in which musicians and audience maintain a distance from the dance performance, African dance incorporates a call-and-response relationship that creates an interaction between those dancing and those surrounding them. The integration of performance and audience, as well as spatial environment, is one of the most noted aesthetic features of African dance.

Observers describe many of the dances as "earth centered," unlike many floating or soaring European ballet forms. Gravity provides an earthward orientation even in those forms in which dancers leap into the air, such as the dances of the KIKUYU of KENYA and the Tutsi of RWANDA.

One of the most remarkable aspects of African dance is its use of the movements of daily life. By raising ordinary gestures to the level of art, these dances show the grace and rhythm of daily activities, from walking to pounding grain to chewing. In the Côte d'Ivoire dance known as *ziglibit*, stamping feet reproduce the rhythm of the pounding of corn into meal. During the *thie bou bien* dance of SENEGAL, dancers move their right arms as if they were eating the food that gives the dance its name. The NUPE fishermen of Nigeria perform a dance choreographed to coincide with the motions of throwing a fishing net.

According to the beliefs of many communities, traditional African dancers not only represent a spirit, but embody that spirit during the dance. This is particularly true of the sacred dances involving masquerade. Dancers use a range of masks and costumes to represent spirits, gods, and sacred animals. These masks can be as much as 4 m (12 ft) high; sometimes they cover the entire body, sometimes just the face. At funerals and an annual festival, members of the Yoruba Egungun ancestral society perform in elaborate costumes representing anything from village chiefs to animals and spirits as they mediate between the ancestors and the living.

Masquerades take a number of different forms. Some masquerades are representative. For example, many of the pastoralist groups of Sudan, Kenya, and UGANDA perform dances portraying the cattle upon which their livelihood depends. During one such dance the KARIMOJON imitate the movements of cattle, shaking their heads like bulls or cavorting like young cows. In stilt dances, another variety of masquerade, stilts extend the dancers' bodies by as much as 3 m (10 ft). In the *gue gblin* dance of Côte d'Ivoire, dancers perform an amazing acrobatic stilt dance traditionally understood as a mediation between the ancestors and the living.

Acrobatic dances, such as those performed on stilts, are increasingly popular outside of their original sacred contexts. The SHOPE, the Shangana TONGA, and the SWAZI of southern Africa perform complex dances in which dancers manipulate a long shield and spear with great finesse as they move through a series of athletic kicks. The FULANI acrobats of Senegal, THE GAMBIA, and GUINEA perform movements similar to those of American break dancing, such as backspins and head- and handstands.

MODERN AFRICAN DANCE FORMS

Colonialism and nationhood have transformed African society, and new African dance forms have developed in new social contexts. Colonial rule shifted borders, and the cash economy prompted labor migrations. These migrations, often to multiethnic towns, undermined the tight-knit communities so basic to traditional dance, though the art form has survived in rural areas and in connection with traditional ceremonies. At the same time, urban living has given rise to an abundance of new dance forms. Thus modernization in Africa has allowed for some continuity, but it has also encouraged much innovation.

Christian missionaries initially forbade or limited traditional dance among Christian converts for fear of the dance's connection to indigenous religions (*see* CHRISTIANITY: MISSIONARIES IN AFRICA). In parts of West Africa colonial administrators banned dancing, which they felt might keep workers out too late at night or, worse, stir anticolonial sentiment.

Meanwhile, traditional dance shifted along with its social context. As people traveled during the colonial period, their dances went with them. As a consequence of labor migrations, people from a given ethnic group found themselves next to neighbors with very different dance styles. As rural migrants gathered in cities, for example in SOUTH AFRICA, dance forms gained new significance as markers of ethnic origin and identity. Since the 1940s at the Witwatersrand gold mines, "mine dancers" have competed in teams organized around ethnic origins.

New dance forms expressed nationalism and resistance. One dance of the ZULU in South Africa used rhythmic stomping and slapping of leather boots to express both the meter of work and a march against the oppression of APARTHEID. As a stirring cultural expression, dance could both evoke tradition and forge a new national identity. During the nationalist period (*see* NATIONALISM IN AFRICA), nationalist movements and later governments used dance as a way of expressing a country's identity. With schools such as Mudra-Afrique, founded in 1977 in Dakar, and events such as the All-Nigeria Festival of Arts, national governments used dance to transcend ethnic identity. Some dance companies, such as Les Ballets Africains in GUINEA, the National Dance Company of SENEGAL, and the National Dance Company of ZIMBABWE, gained international renown and represented their new nations abroad.

In recent years modern artistic productions have increasingly drawn on traditional dances. Dance troupes performing on stage have integrated traditional forms with new, improvised themes and forms. The dance theater of the Ori Olokun Company of Ife, Nigeria, for example, created a performance called *Alatangana* that depicts a traditional myth of the KONO people in Guinea. Dance has influenced several of WOLE SOYINKA's plays, including *The Lion and the Jewel* (1963), *A Dance of the Forests* (1963), and *Death and the King's Horsemen* (1975).

After World War II hybrid forms of dance emerged that integrated European and American dance influences. Highlife was the most famous of these forms, synthesizing the European ballroom dance techniques learned by soldiers abroad with traditional dance rhythms and forms. The highlife music and dance rose to popularity in the cities of West Africa during the 1960s, cutting across ethnic boundaries to express a common regional identity derived from the experience of colonialism and urbanization. In southern Africa people danced in discos to the modern African beat of *kwela*, and in Central and East Africa "Congo beat" music gained popularity.

The modern transformation of Africa has thus fostered remarkable creativity and diversity in dance forms. An essential element in everything from improvised traditional performance to ritual coming-of-age ceremonies to the nightlife of dancehalls and discos, dance remains a vibrant and changing part of African life.

Marian Aguiar

SEE ALSO

Angola; Dakar, Senegal; Hutu and Tutsi; Breakdancing; Brazil.

North America

Dance in the United States

Movement is a fundamental component of African American culture. It manifests itself firstly in dance, but also in a broad range of characteristics, which can be termed stylization, in the sense of an identifiable cultural institution, but also as stylishness in the sense of fashion. Black movement is not merely random, but, according to critic Albert Murray, African Americans "refine all movement in the direction of dance-beat elegance. Their work movements become dance movements and so do their play movements: and so, indeed, do all the movements they use every day, including the way they walk, stand, turn, wave, shake hands, reach, or make any gesture at all." This is a phenomenon that has characterized the African American community from the beginning, and its origin is clearly African. "We are almost a nation of dancers, musicians, and poets," OLAUDAH EQUIANO, the slave autobiographer, wrote in the eighteenth century, and the anthropologist Melville Herskovits in the

TOP LEFT: Chubby Checker introduces the twist at the Crescendo, a fashionable nightclub on the Sunset Strip in Hollywood, California, in 1961. *CORBIS/Bettmann*
TOP RIGHT: Accompanied by his shadow, Bill "Bojangles" Robinson tap dances up a flight of stairs in the Paramount movie ***The Big Broadcast of 1936.*** *CORBIS/Bettmann*
ABOVE: Young women dance in a park in Milwaukee, Wisconsin, in the 1980s. *CORBIS/Richard Hamilton Smith*

twentieth century said, "The dance itself has in characteristic form carried over into the New World to a greater degree than almost any other trait of African culture."

The result is that dance is probably the greatest African American contribution to world culture. While this is a distinction usually reserved for music, black music historically has never been designed for performance as such, but, rather to provide the medium for dancing. Dance is, in Alain Locke's phrase, "the cradle of Negro music." African American dance has hardly been studied at all, probably because Euro-Americans have seen vernacular black dance as primitive and sexual, merely an unfortunate residue of African "savagery." The pervasive role of dance in African life is well known, and the fact that slaves brought dance as part of their expressive culture to the New World is undisputed. But little is actually known about the early period of adaptions, borrowings, transformations, and survivals.

The first slave dance of which we have some knowledge is the Ring Shout, along with its relatives, other religious and non-religious circle dances. The Ring Shout is a clear transition between traditional West African dancing and the Afro-Protestant folk church that emerged as slaves came under the influence of the Evangelical Protestantism of the American South. The Shout survived under unlikely circumstances: the church forbade dancing as sinful, and the colonial governments banned the drum as a potential signal for revolt. The Ring Shout, however, used the human heel, hand clapping, and slapping parts of the body for rhythm, and its practitioners insisted it was not dancing since the feet barely left the floor and the legs were never crossed. The Shout was described in the *Nation* magazine of May 30, 1867, as a "jerking, hitching motion," a slide-together-slide movement involving the whole body. The word *Shout* does not mean ecstatic outbursts, but is probably derived from the Arabic term *saut*. Saut refers to the counterclockwise circumambulation of the Kaaba, the sacred stone of Mecca, by devout Muslim pilgrims.

THE CAKEWALK, a probable spin-off from the Ring Shout, became the first of a long line of black dances to cross over to white popular culture. Originating as a folk dance in which slaves covertly satirized the grand march of formal white-European cotillions, the Cakewalk's steps were improvised, but the forward movement was characterized by exaggerated prancing. The critic Carl Van Vechten described George Walker, the best of the black male Cakewalk dancers, as "throwing his chest and bottom out in opposite directions until he resembled a pouter pigeon more than a human being." On theater stages throughout the nineteenth century, however, the Cakewalk was performed by white people in blackface acting in the nation's most popular entertainment, MINSTRELSY. The Cakewalk constituted the Walk-around, or the minstrel show's grand finale, consisting ironically of white people imitating black people imitating white people.

African Americans began to recapture their traditions and present authentic black entertainment only in the closing years of the nineteenth century. Dora Dean and her husband Charles E. Johnson did the Cakewalk in Sam T. Jack's traveling Creole Show in the early 1890s, probably the first black dancers to bring the dance to the American stage. The Creole Show was the creation of Sam Lucas, an early black vaudeville performer, who persuaded Jack, a white man, to produce a show that would break away from the racist caricatures of minstrelsy. The Creole Show turned other tables as well by shattering gender stereotypes: there was a minstrellike half-circle of performers, but they were black women instead of white men, and the interlocutor was a black woman in drag. Clearly, a radical change was beginning to take place: African Americans had started the struggle to free the presentation of black bodies, movement, and images from white preemption and to take control of their own cultural lives.

With the Cakewalk, African Americans succeeded not only in recovering genuine black style, but they introduced it to a nation hungry for a new popular culture, one more consistent with the new urbanized, faster-paced society which had outgrown the Victorian restraint and sentimentality of the nineteenth century. In short, when BERT WILLIAMS, George Walker, and AIDA OVERTON WALKER combined the high-stepping Cakewalk with the irresistible rhythm of a new black music called RAGTIME, they were doing nothing less than introducing modern times. In a series of "ragtime musicals" beginning in 1897, Williams and Walker began a Cakewalk fad that spread throughout white society and enlivened white social life at all levels. Criticized by the respectable of both races as too uncontrolled, the Cakewalk nevertheless sparked the revolution in American social dancing that began around 1910 and guaranteed that future American dance, as well as its supporting music, would be profoundly black.

Following the decline of the Cakewalk along with the all-black musicals of the first decade of the twentieth century, there was no real African American presence on the national stage until NOBLE SISSLE and Eubie Blake's *Shuffle Along* of 1921. The show electrified New York and introduced a new kind of black dancing to white America. The speed, precision, and controlled abandon of the chorus line was breathtaking. *Shuffle Along* featured FLORENCE MILLS, the great jazz dancer of the decade, and was the training ground for those performers, including JOSEPHINE BAKER, who created the Roaring Twenties, the HARLEM RENAISSANCE, and the JAZZ Age as a decade marked by frenzied dancing. The success of *Shuffle Along* gave birth to so many imitative black shows that a popular song of the day was titled "Broadway's Getting Darker Every Year." Just as in the 1890s, the country was again ready to break out from convention and constriction, and it discovered, and expropriated for the second time, the fast-paced tempo of black movement to set the rhythm for a new time.

The apogee, and symbol, of the 1920s was the Charleston, which may have started as a black children's street dance and may have originated in Charleston, South Carolina. It was first danced on stage by Maude Russell, "the Slim Princess," a light complected woman from Texas. She opened the second act of Irvin C. Miller's 1922 *Liza*, the first black show to play on Broadway during the real, that is, winter, season. The Charleston did not make a serious impression, however, until the next year, when Elizabeth Welch performed it in Flournoy Miller and Aubrey Lyles's *Running Wild*. This time it was danced to the music by which it has been known ever since, an ideally appropriate and contagious tune by James P. Johnson, the Harlem stride pianist. The pattern was set for veracular black dances to define the decades, from the Lindy Hop, through the Twist and BREAKDANCING, to Hip Hop.

As black culture becomes American popular culture, and as American culture becomes world culture, it is clear that the apparently inexhaustible vitality of black dance and its music will fuel the ongoing revolution. Mary Arnold Twining reports from the African American community of the Sea Islands where, she finds, the inability to dance is considered impossible. There is a long and lively tradition of performers: William Henry "Juba" Lane, "King" Rastus Brown, Honi Coles, Ada Forsyne, GREGORY HINES, Bill "Bojangles" Robinson, Michael Jackson, Earl "Snake Hips" Tucker, ALVIN AILEY, CHOLLY ATKINS, CHUBBY CHECKER, the NICHOLAS BROTHERS, BILL T. JONES. And new steps continue to subvert the system by bubbling up from below: the Shimmy, Mashed Potato, Philly Dog, Black Bottom, Funky Chicken. In terms of the future, LANGSTON HUGHES writes: "And the Negro dancers who will dance like flame and the singers who will continue to carry our songs to all who will listen – they will be with us in even greater numbers tomorrow."

Richard Newman

SEE ALSO

Blake, James Hubert ("Eubie"); Hip Hop in the United States; Locke, Alain Leroy; Racial Stereotypes; Robinson, Bill ("Bojangles").

North America

Dance Theater of Harlem,

multiracial American dance troupe that was the world's first professional all-black classical ballet company.

Established just months after the assassination of Dr. Martin Luther King Jr., the Dance Theater of Harlem (DTH) has evolved into one of the world's most respected dance companies and a treasured artistic resource in the black community. As its founder and long-time director Arthur Mitchell has said, the group's goal is not only to present dynamic classical dance performances but also "to ignite some sort of passion in young people." To that end, in addition to its professional troupe of more than 30 dancers, the DTH sponsors a dance school in its New York home as well as Dancing Through Barriers, a program designed to nurture young artists in several other cities, including DETROIT, MICHIGAN, and WASHINGTON, D.C.

After its creation in 1969 the DTH grew quickly, its original 30 students burgeoning to 400 within months. DTH was originally conceived as a dance school, but Mitchell and his partner, the white teacher Karel Shook, expanded the school to include a dance troupe, which debuted at New York's Guggenheim Museum in 1971. A year later, the group moved from its original Greenwich Village headquarters to West 152nd Street in Harlem. The DTH has toured in England, Russia, and SOUTH AFRICA. During the 1992 South Africa visit, Mitchell encouraged his dancers to learn from as well as teach the dancers there. This was a typical gesture from a man renowned for pushing his students to visit libraries and museums, both to widen their artistic horizons and to teach them to act as role models.

Another aspect of the DTH's mission is to disprove the once-popular notion that black people are anatomically unable to dance ballet. (No longer exclusively African American, the DTH retains its commitment to dancers of all skin tones by dyeing costumes and shoes in varying shades of brown and beige.) When he joined the New York City Ballet in 1955, Mitchell himself was the first African American man to dance for a major company. In the works he pioneered with the DTH, Mitchell continued to build on the artistic legacy of his mentor, George Balanchine, while drawing from cultures not usually represented in classical dance. Some of the DTH's best-known ballets include *Dougla*, a work based on Afro-Caribbean history and art, and *Giselle*, a reworking that sets the classic ballet in the Creole community of New Orleans.

Lisa Clayton Robinson

See Also

Harlem, New York; King, Martin Luther, Jr.; New Orleans, Louisiana; New York, New York.

North America

Dandridge, Dorothy

(b. November 9, 1922, Cleveland, Ohio; d. September 8, 1965, Hollywood, Calif.), actress who was the first African American woman to receive an Academy Award nomination.

The daughter of a minister and an aspiring actress, Dorothy Dandridge began her career as a singer in 1951, performing at the Cotton Club in New York with the Dandridge Sisters (1951) and as a soloist with the Desi Arnaz Band.

As a child, Dandridge appeared in bit parts in several films. She moved quickly from playing small roles in films such as *Flamingo* (1947) to lead roles in a number of low-budget films, including *Tarzan's Perils* (1951), *The Harlem Globe-Trotters* (1951), and *Jungle Queen* (1951). Her breakthrough role was *Carmen Jones* (1954), for which she became the first black woman to receive an Academy Award nomination for Best Actress. Her next film, *Island in the Sun* (1957), which was the first mainstream film to portray an interracial romance, was not received as well. In 1959 she regained critical recognition for her role as Bess in *Porgy and Bess* (1959).

Despite her appearance on the cover of *Life* magazine after *Carmen Jones*, Dandridge still had difficulty finding suitable lead roles. There were few opportunities for an African American woman attempting to break into the glamorous roles dominated by white actresses, and Dandridge rejected the stock character roles available to black actresses. With fewer singing engagements, her career as a performer began to decline. Dandridge's professional crises were coupled with personal ones. After her divorce, she declared bankruptcy and lost her home. A short time later, she died of an overdose of antidepressants.

See Also

New York, New York; Film, Blacks in American.

Africa

Danquah, Joseph Kwame Kyeretwi Boakye

(b. December 21, 1895, Bepong, Kwahu, Gold Coast [present-day Ghana]; d. February 4, 1965, Nsawam Prison, Ghana), Ghanaian scholar, lawyer, and nationalist, the principal political rival of Kwame Nkrumah.

J. B. Danquah was one of the founders of the modern state of Ghana. He cofounded the country's first nationalist party in 1947. Danquah led the opposition to Kwame Nkrumah after Nkrumah became the country's leading nationalist figure. To silence Danquah, Nkrumah had him confined to prison, where he died under miserable conditions.

By birth, Danquah belonged to the royal family of Akyem Abuakwa, a province of Asante. He attended Basel Mission Schools in Akyem Abuakwa. Subsequently, he studied in London, England, where he received a law degree and a Ph.D. in ethics in 1927. He returned to the then British colony of the Gold Coast (now Ghana), where he practiced law privately. In 1931 he founded the *Times of West Africa*, which became a leading newspaper.

Danquah's editorial writing led him into politics in opposition to British colonial repression and exploitation. During the 1930s he also conducted research on which he based a controversial claim that the Akan people (of present-day Ghana) were descendants of the ancient kingdom of Ghana (in present-day Mali and Mauritania). On the basis of his work, the Gold Coast was renamed Ghana when it achieved independence in 1957. In 1937 he founded the Gold Coast Youth Congress, through which he intended to unite the Gold Coast African elite. In 1947 he cofounded the United Gold Coast Convention (UGCC), whose leadership invited Nkrumah, then in Great Britain, to serve as general secretary.

Political differences between the two leaders quickly emerged. While Danquah preferred working with the existing elite to find a gradual path to self-governance, Nkrumah appealed to the masses to support immediate independence. After the British appointed Danquah, but not Nkrumah, to a constitutional convention, Nkrumah left the UGCC to form the Convention People's Party (CPP), demanding immediate independence. Nkrumah's philosophy resonated with most Ghanaians, and in 1951, when Nkrumah won election as prime minister, Danquah assumed his role as leader of the opposition.

In 1960 Danquah ran for the presidency against Nkrumah and gained just 10 percent of the vote. Nkrumah's rule became increasingly totalitarian, and Danquah voiced his opposition to this trend. In 1961 Nkrumah had Danquah arrested and detained under the Preventive Detention Act but released him the following year. Danquah's continued attacks on Nkrumah and his policies drew Nkrumah's ire anew. Jailed again in 1964, Danquah was subjected this time to brutal conditions. He was chained to the floor and denied meals as well as medical treatment. He died of a heart attack while detained in prison as an enemy of the state, but received a hero's funeral in his hometown.

Robert Fay

See Also

Ghana, Early Kingdom of; Great Britain.

Latin America and the Caribbean

Danticat, Edwidge

(b. January 19, 1969, Port-au-Prince, Haiti), premier Haitian American writer in the United States.

Edwidge Danticat's three major publications, *Breath, Eyes, Memory* (1994), *Krik?Krak!* (1995), and *The Farming of Bones* (1998), extend the Haitian literary border to encompass the English language and United States geography as central elements in Haiti's unfolding narrative at the start of the twenty-first century. For her the United States becomes the site of abrupt and unavoidable change, and of struggles for cultural continuity; the sea becomes yet another "passage of death for modern-day Haitians." Haiti in Danticat's work is a complex place full of love, violence, pride, and pain.

When Danticat was four years old, her parents left Haiti for the United States to escape the Duvalier regime; Danticat and her brother, Eliab, stayed behind with family. This separation, of parents from their children, mirrors the experience of many Haitians who were forced to leave for different shores. It would take nine years for Danticat to reunite with her parents and meet her two youngest siblings, Karl and Kelly.

Danticat joined her family in the East Flatbush section of Brooklyn. She came to the States speaking no English. Her mother worked in a factory and her father was a cab driver. Danticat attended Brooklyn's Intermediate School 320 and then Clara Barton High School, where she wrote for the school newspaper on being Haitian and about adaptation, themes that would predominate in her first novel. She obtained a degree in French literature from Barnard College in 1990 and a master's in fine arts from Brown University in 1993. Her master's thesis for Brown evolved into the groundbreaking first novel, *Breath, Eyes, Memory*, in which she writes: "I come from a place where breath, eyes, and memory are one, a place in which you carry your past like the hair on your head. Where women return to their children as butterflies or as tears in the eyes of statues that their daughters pray to."

Danticat's work fuses two cultural experiences and captures with startling intensity the Haiti she remembers from her childhood, when her aunts, grandmother, and cousins regaled her with folklore about the country of her birth. She writes poignantly about women "being as strong as mountains." The young heroine of *Breath, Eyes, Memory* straddles two cultures and the subcultures within each when, in migrating to the United States, she tries to understand what she must hold on to and what she must leave behind. Her short story collection, *Krik?Krak!,* was nominated for the 1995 National Book Award. Employing the traditional form of Haitian call and response in which a person says *krik?* and the storyteller replies by offering a story, Danticat again blends the unexpected with the mundane, in prose that evokes and recreates the haunting terror and lushness of the Haitian cultural landscape. One of the stories in this collection, "1937," is the focus of her second novel, *The Farming of Bones,* about the massacre of Haitians by Dominican president Trujillo (see Dominican-Haitian Relations). The novelistic challenge of this book may be the greatest of her three major works to date, because of the silence surrounding the massacre.

Thus far, Edwidge Danticat continues to shape and define the emerging genre of Haitian American literature. In the epilogue to *Krik?Krak!* she says: "When you write, it is like braiding hair. Taking a handful of coarse unruly strands and attempting to bring them unity. Your fingers have still not perfected the task." Her work calls to mind other women writers like Paule Marshall, Zora Neale Hurston, Maryse Condé, and Sandra Cisneros. All of them write about young women coming of age; generational bonds that remain unbroken by time, geography, and violence; and the emergence of an assertive female sexual identity.

Sophia Cantave

See Also
Duvalier, François; Trujillo, Rafael.

Africa

Dar es Salaam, Tanzania,

the capital and largest port and city of Tanzania.

The administrative, commercial, and manufacturing center of Tanzania, Dar es Salaam is located on the East Africa coast southwest of Zanzibar. Originally a small farming and fishing village named Mzizima, it began changing rapidly during the late eighteenth century when the sultan of Zanzibar, Majid ibn Said, made the town his summer residence. Attracted by the safe harbor of the neighboring lagoon, the sultan renamed the town Dar es Salaam (Arabic for "haven of peace"), constructed a port, and made plans to move his capital from Zanzibar to the town. But Majid died before his plans were completed, and his successor, Barghash, attempted to control the city from Zanzibar through alliances with the local Swahili chiefs, or *jumbes.*

Although successful for several years, Barghash's absentee rule collapsed when the German East Africa Company took possession of the city in 1887. The company made Dar es Salaam the capital of the German East Africa Company in 1891 and soon afterward constructed a railroad to carry export crops from the interior to the port city. Dar es Salaam subsequently became the economic center of the colony and remained the capital when the British took over in 1916. Since independence, Dar es Salaam has remained the capital of Tanzania despite a 1972 proposal by President Julius K. Nyerere to move the capital to the more geographically central town of Dodoma. That plan was eventually dropped for lack of funds. Today, Dar es Salaam is the largest and most diverse city in Tanzania. It has a population of nearly 2 million people, including Africans, Europeans, Asians (particularly Indians), and Arabs.

Since colonial times, Dar es Salaam's economy has been supported by the trading and shipping business brought in by the international port and trans-African railroads. It is also home to an oil refinery and numerous factories that manufacture domestic and export goods such as textiles, clothing, and footwear. In recent years, Dar es Salaam has suffered from inadequate housing and drinking water as well as pollution and crime, all problems exacerbated by the city's rapid population growth and by a sluggish national economy. Municipal officials hope that plans to privatize city services, improve port facilities, and attract foreign investment will improve living conditions and stimulate the economy. The city has also begun to implement environmental cleanup and recycling programs.

An August 1998 bombing of the United States embassy in Dar es Salaam left 9 people dead and some 70 people injured. Previously, East Africa had been considered safe from terrorist attacks, but the bombing threatened to deter tourists – a vital source of foreign exchange – from visiting Tanzania.

Elizabeth Heath

See Also
Barghash ibn Said; Nyerere, Julius Kambarage; Swahili People.

Africa

Darfur, **a former independent sultanate in western Sudan.**

In prehistoric times, the peoples of what is now Darfur were related to those of the Nile Valley (including Egypt), whose caravans probably reached the region by 2500 B.C.E. According to tradition, the region's first rulers were the Daju. By around 900 C.E., Christianity had spread to the area; by the thirteenth century, however, the region had fallen under the domination of the powerful Islamic empire of Kanem-Bornu to the west, and the Tunjur replaced the Daju as the ruling elite of the region.

The sultanate of Darfur first entered the historical record during the seventeenth century, under Sulayman. Sulayman belonged to the Keira dynasty, which claimed Arab descent and which removed the Tunjur from power. Except for an interval during the nineteenth century, this dynasty ruled Darfur until 1916. Gradually the Keira merged with the Fur, the agricultural people over whom they ruled. (The state's name, Dar Fur, means "house of the Fur" in Arabic.)

The slave trade figured prominently in both the formation and expansion of the Darfur sultanate. Parties from Darfur obtained slaves and ivory by either raiding or trading with the stateless societies that lay to its south and southwest. Not only did Darfur's rulers export slaves to North Africa and along the "forty days' road," which crossed the desert from Darfur to Egypt, but slaves also served the sultan as soldiers, laborers, and bureaucrats. Sulayman's successors expanded the state. In 1786 Sultan Muhammad Tayrab conquered the province of Kordofan from the Funj sultanate of Sennar to the east.

In 1821, however, Egyptian forces conquered the Funj sultanate and wrested Kordofan from Darfur. Traders from Khartoum then began to compete in the slave trade with those in Darfur. Turkish-Egyptian forces under Rahma al-Zubayr conquered Darfur in 1874 and overthrew the Keira sultan. In 1885 a Sudanese rebellion under a religious leader called the Mahdi overthrew the Egyptian state, which had come under increasing British influence. In 1898 British forces defeated the Mahdist state and placed it under Anglo-Egyptian administration. Under their policy of indirect rule (*see* Colonial Rule), the British restored the Darfur sultanate under Ali Dinar Zakariyya. Ali Dinar played a significant role in an Islamic, anti-Western alliance that formed during World War I. The Anglo-Egyptian government subsequently invaded Darfur, killed Ali Dinar, ended the sultanate, and incorporated Darfur into Sudan. After Sudan attained independence in 1956, Darfur remained under Sudanese rule.

Robert Fay

See Also
Colonial Rule; Ivory Trade; Khartoum, Sudan; Nile River; Trans-Saharan and Red Sea Slave Trade.

North America

Dash, Julie (b. October 22, 1952, Long Island City, N.Y.), American filmmaker best known for *Daughters of the Dust*, the first full-length general release film by an African American woman.

Born and raised in the Queensbridge Housing Projects in Long Island City, Julie Dash stumbled into filmmaking at age 17, enrolling with a friend in a workshop at the Studio Museum in Harlem. By 19 she had made her first film, shot with a Super 8 camera using pictures from *Jet* magazine attached to pipe cleaners. Dash majored in psychology at the City College of New York but graduated in film production. In 1973 she wrote and produced a documentary, *Working Models of Success*.

Dash moved to Los Angeles after graduation, gaining experience working on many film crews. In Los Angeles, she became the youngest fellow ever at the Center for Advanced Film Studies. During her two-year fellowship, Dash adapted an Alice Walker short story, *Diary of an African Nun* (1977). An experimental dance film that she conceived and directed, *Four Women*, won the Gold Medal for Women in Film at the 1978 Miami International Film Festival. While working for the Motion Picture Association of America in Los Angeles in 1980, she attended the Cannes International Film Festival in France and cosponsored a session on several short films by black Americans.

In 1981 Dash won a grant from the National Endowment for the Humanities (NEH), which was awarded again in 1983 and 1985, and began making her most acclaimed films. *Illusions* (1983), shot in 10 days for under $30,000, explores the roles of black women in film. Set in 1942 Hollywood, the 34-minute film portrays two women, one a studio executive who passes for white, another a singer who dubs the voices of white starlets, who are both made invisible and voiceless as black women by the film industry and society at large. *Illusions* won the 1989 Jury Prize for Best Film of the Decade by the Black Filmmakers Foundation and the 1985 Black Cinema Society Award, among other honors.

Dash moved to Atlanta, Georgia, in 1986, where she formed Geechee Girl Productions, Inc., her own film company. She directed two projects for the National Black Women's Health Project in 1987, *Breaking the Silence: On Reproductive Rights* and *Preventing Cancer*. Two television productions followed: *Relatives* (1990) and *Praise House* (1991).

In 1981 Dash received a Guggenheim grant to study the Gullah culture of the South Carolina coast, which resulted in *Daughters of the Dust* (1992), making her the first African American woman to create a full-length general release film. The film is set during 1902 in the South Carolina Sea Islands, where a family meets for the last time before migrating to the North to seek better opportunities, a migration that puts at risk their African communal values. *Daughters* won first prize in cinematography at the 1991 Sundance Film Festival in Utah, where it premiered, and was televised nationally in 1992 on PBS's *American Playhouse*.

In the mid-1990s, Dash filmed two music videos (1992 and 1994), as well as a documentary about the life of Zora Neale Hurston. She received a Fulbright fellowship to work in London on a screenplay about the black British film collective Sankofa. She lives in Atlanta with her daughter, N'Zinga.

See Also
Harlem, New York; *Jet*; Film, Blacks in American.

Africa

Date Palm, common name for several related trees found in tropical regions.

The common date palm is native to northern Africa, southwest Asia, and India and is cultivated extensively in hot, dry regions throughout the world. The trunk is straight and rough and grows to a height of up to 18 m (up to 60 ft). It bears a head of waxy green, barbed leaves, about 3 m (about 9 ft) long and a number of branching spikes that, on the female tree, bear 200 to 1000 dates each. A cluster of dates weighs up to 12 kg (up to 25 lb), and the annual yield of a single tree may reach 270 kg (600 lb). The tree begins to bear about the eighth year, reaches maturity at 30 years, and begins to decline at about 100 years. From earliest times, fertilization has been aided by cutting off the male flower cluster just before the stamens ripen and suspending it among the flowers of the female tree.

In many parts of northern Africa, Iran, and Arabia, date palms are the main wealth of the people, and dates are the chief article of food. The fleshy part of the fruit contains about 58 percent sugar and 2 percent each of fat, protein, and minerals. Leaf stalks are used for basketry and wickerwork, leaves are woven into bags and mats, and fiber from both is made into cordage.

Another species, the sugar date palm, or toddy palm, is cultivated in India for its sap. The sap may be boiled down to form jaggery, or gur, a crude sugar; or it may be used as a fresh beverage or to make palm wine, from which arrack, a rumlike liquor, may be distilled.

Date palms are often cultivated in the southern United States for ornamental effect in regions too cool for the fruit to ripen. The blue date palm grows in clumps and has silvery blue foliage. The pygmy date palm is a dwarf species that is also popular in the northern United States as a greenhouse plant or houseplant.

Date palms belong to the family Palmae. The common date palm is classified as *Phoenix dactylifera,* the sugar date palm as *Phoenix sylvestris,* the blue date palm as *Phoenix zeylanica,* and the pygmy date palm as *Phoenix roebelenii.*

North America

Davenport, Willie D. (b. 1943, Troy, Ala.), African American track-and-field athlete who won the Gold Medal in the 110-meter high hurdles event at the 1968 Olympic Games in Mexico City.

Willie D. Davenport was educated at Southern University. His specialty was the indoor 60-yard high hurdles race, which is not an Olympic event. In the 60-yard hurdles, he won the United States national title five times (1966, 1967, 1969-1971).

Davenport also attained success in the outdoor high hurdles event, which in the United States at that time was either 110 m or 120 yards, depending on the year. At the 1964 U.S. Olympic trials, Davenport, then a U.S. Army private, was the unexpected winner in the 110-meter hurdles race. Hampered by a thigh injury, he failed to qualify for the finals at the 1964 Olympic Games in Tokyo, Japan. He won the 120-yard hurdles event at the U.S. national track-and-field championships for the next three years (1965-1967), and he earned a Gold Medal in the 110-meter hurdles at the 1968 Olympic Games. In 1969 he won the U.S. 120-yard national title again. He placed fourth in the 110-meter hurdles at the 1972 Olympic Games in Munich, West Germany, and third in the event at the 1976 Olympic Games in Montréal, Québec, Canada.

At the 1980 Winter Olympic Games, Davenport became one of the few athletes to appear in both the summer and winter Olympic Games, competing as a member of the U.S. four-man bobsledding team. He was inducted into the National Track and Field Hall of Fame in 1982 and into the U.S. Olympic Hall of Fame in 1991.

See Also
Track and Field in the United States.

North America

Davidson, Olivia America (b. June 11, 1854, Virginia (?); d. May 9, 1889, Boston, Mass.), African American educator.

The daughter of an ex-slave father and a free mother, Olivia Davidson was educated in Albany, New York, and began teaching school at age 16. In Albany, Davidson interacted with many Oberlin College liberals and black activists, and she carried this exposure to black self-sufficiency, education, and dynamism with her into her teaching engagements in Ohio, Mississippi, and Tennessee. In

1878 she returned to school at the Hampton Institute, where she met Booker T. Washington. Davidson joined him at Tuskegee Institute, where she served as a teacher, principal, and fundraiser for the new school. Davidson and Washington were married on August 11, 1886, after the death of his first wife. After the birth of two sons, Davidson's failing health kept her from the activities which had occupied her to that point.

Lisa Clayton Robinson

SEE ALSO
Tuskegee University; Washington, Booker Taliaferro.

Latin America and the Caribbean

Dávila, Angela María (b. 1944),

Afro-Puerto Rican poet, journalist, and political activist; together with ANA LYDIA VEGA and JULIA DE BURGOS, Dávila is one of the most widely recognized female voices to emerge from Puerto Rico.

Angela María Dávila, also known as Malavé, began her literary career as a contributor for the politically progressive journal *Guajana.* She became acquainted with its founders while attending university in Puerto Rico during the 1960s. She also published in several other sources at that time, including *Bayoan, Prometeo,* and *Surco.* Consequently, her work began to attract attention in literary circles, and by the mid-1960s she was considered one of Puerto Rico's most important writers. She was the only female writer included in *The Anthology of Young Poets* published by the Puerto Rican Cultural Institute in 1965.

Partly because of her marginalized status as one of Puerto Rico's few female poets, Dávila's work has often been compared to that of her compatriot, Julia de Burgos. The younger Dávila has acknowledged her indebtedness to the earlier Puerto Rican poet, and dedicated "Animal fiero y tierno" (1997, Fierce and Tender Animal) and several poems to Burgos. In the poem "Homenaje" (Homage), Dávila speaks of the solidarity between herself and Burgos: "From our pain there is much silent muted space of continuous borders there are many shadows and many broken songs there is much history." Here, Dávila plays with the theme of a running dialogue between Burgos's poetry and her own.

The literary critic Ivette Lopez was the first to recognize that while Dávila's work seems traditional in her usage of lyric motifs of nature (such as light, stars, and shadows), she breaks away from literary convention by combining avant-garde poetic devices, such as the dislocation of grammatical categories, the use of diminutives and augmentatives in unexpected places, colloquial discourse, and a proselike style.

Dávila's work was published widely in the 1960s and 1970s, when she made some of her most important contributions to Puerto Rican poetry, including "Animal fiero y tierno" and "Homenaje al ombligo" (1967, Homage to the Navel) (*see* LITERATURE, BLACK, IN SPANISH AMERICA).

Joy Elizondo

North America

Davis, Angela Yvonne

(b. Jan. 26, 1944, Birmingham, Ala.), African American political activist, philosopher, and educator whose imprisonment for murder generated worldwide protest.

Angela Davis was, in several ways, born into the heart of the civil rights struggle. Her family lived in the middle-class section of Birmingham, Alabama, that came to be known as Dynamite Hill because there were so many Ku Klux Klan bombings. Davis attended segregated schools where children were taught black history but at the same time were denied adequate school supplies and facilities. Her mother and grandmother encouraged Davis to fight for civil rights while she was still in elementary school. As a high school student, Davis helped organize interracial study groups that were broken up by the police.

When she was 15, Davis left Birmingham to attend the Elizabeth Irwin School in New York City. Teachers at the politically progressive school introduced Davis to the socialist ideas that informed her later activism. From 1961 to 1965 Davis attended Brandeis University in Waltham, Massachusetts, and graduated with honors. She spent her junior year in Paris, where her contact with Algerian students provided her with a global perspective on the struggle against colonialism and oppression. Her political commitments intensified in 1963, when four girls whom Davis had known were killed in the 16th Street Baptist Church bombing in Birmingham.

Davis began her doctoral studies in philosophy at the Johann Wolfgang von Goethe University in Frankfurt, Germany, but returned to the United States in 1967 when she decided that she could no longer stay away from the growing American racial conflict. She enrolled at the University of California at San Diego, where she continued to work with her undergraduate adviser, philosopher Herbert Marcuse. She earned her master's degree in philosophy in 1969, and within a year completed the requirements for the Ph.D., except for the dissertation.

While in graduate school Davis became increasingly politically active. At a workshop sponsored by the STUDENT NONVIOLENT COORDINATING COMMITTEE (SNCC), Davis met Frank and Kendra Alexander, both active members of SNCC, the Black Panthers, and the Communist party. Davis moved to Los Angeles to join the Alexanders in their work and in 1968 joined the Communist Party.

Davis was hired by the University of California at Los Angeles to teach philosophy in 1969. Despite the popularity of her courses and the positive recommendations of the faculty, she was fired by the state board of regents at the behest of Governor Ronald Reagan once her Communist affiliation became known. A court overturned the dismissal, but the regents refused to renew Davis's contract at the end of the 1969-1970 academic year.

Davis's political activities earned her international attention in 1970. Through the Black Panthers, Davis became an advocate for black political prisoners and spoke out in defense of the inmates known as the Soledad Brothers. After the killing of inmate George Jackson by guards at Soledad Prison, his younger brother, Jonathan, attempted to free another prisoner from a Marin County, California, courthouse by taking hostages.

An FBI poster lists Angela Davis among its ten most wanted fugitives after she went underground in 1970 to escape prosecution. Davis was eventually acquitted of all charges. *CORBIS/Bettmann*

Four people were killed in the shoot-out that followed. The guns Jackson used belonged to Davis. Even though she was not at all near the courthouse at the time, she was charged with kidnapping, conspiracy, and murder. When Davis defied the arrest warrant and went into hiding, she was placed on the FBI's ten-most-wanted list. Her capture in a New York motel room and subsequent imprisonment inspired "Free Angela" rallies around the world. Davis spent 16 months in jail before being released on bail in 1972; she was later acquitted of all charges.

From the "Free Angela" movement, Davis and others established the National Alliance Against Racism and Political Repression. She ran for office in 1980 and 1984 as the Communist Party candidate for vice president, and she continues to lecture widely about social justice issues. Currently, Davis is a professor of the history of consciousness at the University of California at Santa Cruz. She is the author of several books, including *If They Come in the Morning* (1971), *Angela Davis: An Autobiography* (1974), *Women, Race, and Class* (1983), and *Women, Culture, and Politics* (1989).

Lawrie Balfour

See Also
Algeria; Colonial Rule; Black Panther Party; Civil Rights Movement; Jackson, George Lester; New York, New York; Sixteenth Street Baptist Church (Birmingham, Ala.); Socialism; Communist Party USA, African Americans and the.

North America

Davis, Anthony (b. Paterson, N.J., February 20, 1951), African American composer and pianist whose innovations in modern classical music conflate jazz styles and global rhythms.

The son of the first African American professor at Princeton University, Anthony Davis studied classical music as a child in New York, and as an undergraduate at Yale University he played free-jazz with Anthony Braxton. After earning his B.A. at Yale in 1975, Davis moved to New York City, where he supported himself as a jazz pianist. As he developed musically, his compositions deviated from traditional jazz. He often abandoned improvisation and drew elements from Western classical music and African and South Asian rhythms. His recordings from this period include *Hidden Voices* (1979) and *Lady of the Mirrors* (1981). In 1981 he formed an eight-piece ensemble, Episteme, whose repertoire included a combination of improvised and scored music, blurring the distinction between jazz and classical music.

In the 1980s Davis began focusing much of his work on historical subjects. *Middle Passage* (1984) examined the degradation and despair of the slave ships (*see* Middle Passage, The) and was performed both by pianist Ursula Oppens and Davis himself. From 1981 to 1985 Davis collaborated with his brother Christopher and cousin Thulani Davis on an opera about black nationalist leader Malcolm X. *X: The Life and Times of Malcolm X* premiered in Philadelphia in 1985 and was performed by the New York City Opera in 1986. Davis's second opera, *Under the Double Moon* (1989), included a science fiction libretto written by Deborah Atherton, his ex-wife. Two subsequent operas, *Tania* (1992) and *Amistad* (1997), dramatized historical events (see Amistad Mutiny).

Davis has taught at Yale and Columbia Universities, composed scores for numerous dance companies, and written music for several films. His symphonic works have been performed by the New York Philharmonic, the Brooklyn Philharmonic, and the San Francisco Symphony. He won a Pulitzer Prize for his piano concerto Wayang no. 5 (1984).

Eric Bennett

See Also
New York, New York; Black Nationalism in the United States.

North America

Davis, Benjamin O., Jr.

(b. December 18, 1912, Washington, D.C.), first African American general of the United States Air Force.

Benjamin Oliver Davis Jr. was the son of Elnora and Benjamin Oliver Davis Sr., the first black general of the U.S. Army. After living on a number of military bases during his childhood, Davis entered a predominantly white high school in Cleveland, Ohio. He was elected president of his class and went on to attend Cleveland's Western Reserve University. He transferred to the University of Chicago but hoped to enroll in the U.S. Military Academy at West Point. At the time, the academy actively discouraged blacks from applying. With the help of black Chicago congressman Oscar DePriest, however, Davis took the entrance examinations and entered the academy in 1932.

At West Point, because he was black, Davis was subjected to four years of a campaign called silencing: no one ate with him, roomed with him, answered his questions, or spoke to him unless issuing an order. He nonetheless graduated in the top 15 percent of his class and became West Point's first African American graduate since Reconstruction. Because of his high class ranking, he should have been allowed to choose which branch of service to enter; however, when he requested the air corps (then a branch of the army), he was told that there were no black squadrons and that the government had no intention of assigning a black lieutenant to a white squadron. Instead he and his new bride, Agatha Scott, were sent to Fort Benning, Georgia. They found base facilities both there and in future postings racially segregated, and Davis was assigned several insignificant duties.

In the early 1940s President Franklin D. Roosevelt, seeking wider support among African Americans, approved several changes that gave blacks greater roles in the armed services. One such change was the promotion of Benjamin Davis Sr. as the first black general. Another was allowing African Americans into the air corps on an experimental basis. A training program for black pilots was established at the historically black Tuskegee Institute and Benjamin Davis Jr. was ordered to command the first class (*see* Tuskegee Airmen). Completing the training in 1942, Davis was given charge of the Ninety-ninth Pursuit Squadron, the first black air unit, and was sent the following year to North Africa to serve in World War II. Davis and his pilots were given little of the introductory training that young white pilots received from veterans at the front. Most of the Ninety-ninth's missions in North Africa were routine and combat-free, allowing Davis's superior officers to report to Washington that black pilots were not as capable as whites.

Late in 1943 Davis was placed in command of the 332nd Fighter Group, a larger black unit. Now a lieutenant colonel, Davis lobbied the Pentagon for combat assignments, and by early 1944 the 332nd received them. The group proved highly effective in the skies above Italy, and by mid-year a closely guarded report concluded that the 332nd was the equal of any unit fighting above southern Europe. Among Davis's awards from this period was the Distinguished Flying Cross.

After the war Davis argued for an end to segregation in the armed services, which Harry S. Truman promulgated in 1948. Davis then helped the air force, which had separated from the army, design plans for desegregating its bases. During the Korean War, he commanded a racially integrated flying unit and was afterward promoted to brigadier general, the first black to reach that rank in the air force. In 1965 he became the first African American in any military branch to reach the rank of lieutenant general. In 1970, after commanding the Thirteenth Air Force in the Vietnam War, he retired.

Beginning in mid-1970 Davis served as an assistant secretary at the Department of Transportation under President Richard M. Nixon. Overseeing the development of airport security and highway safety, Davis was one of the chief proponents of the 55-mile-per-hour speed limit to save gas and lives. He retired from the Department of Transportation in 1975 and in 1978 served on the American Battle Monuments Commission, on which his father had served decades before. In 1991 he published his autobiography.

See Also
World War II and African Americans; Davis, Benjamin O., Sr.; DePriest, Oscar Stanton; Tuskegee University.

North America

Davis, Benjamin O., Sr.

(b. May 28, 1880, Washington, D.C.; d. November 26, 1970, Chicago, Ill.), first African American general of the United States Army.

Benjamin Oliver Davis was the youngest of three children of Henrietta, a nurse, and Louis, a messenger for the federal government. Shortly after completing high school in Washington, D.C., he volunteered to serve in the army, which was then fighting the Spanish-Cuban-American War (1898-1899). He was given a temporary posting as a second lieutenant and after the war decided to continue his military career, enlisting as a private in the Ninth Cavalry. Sent to the Philippines, he became a sergeant-major, the highest enlisted rank in the army. Although blacks who tried to reach higher ranks were routinely thwarted by racism, in 1901 he took and passed examinations to become an officer. As a second lieutenant, he served at Fort Washakie in Wyoming.

In 1902 Davis married Elnora Dickerson, his high school girlfriend. The Davises were the only black couple at Washakie and were essentially shunned by the white officers and their families. In 1905 Davis received a transfer to WILBERFORCE UNIVERSITY, an all-black college in Ohio, where he taught military science. He was reportedly frustrated by a lack of discipline among the students and the low esteem with which administrators regarded military science. After four years of teaching, Davis served in LIBERIA as a military adviser. Finding Liberia's troops poorly trained and in disarray, he hoped to oversee a sweeping reform; however, the U.S. government was not yet ready to become so involved in the military affairs of other countries.

Davis's next posting was along the Mexican-American border, where he became a captain, though by 1915 he was again teaching at Wilberforce. Elnora died there while giving birth to a daughter, also named Elnora. Their two previous children were Olive and Benjamin O. Davis Jr., who became the first black general in the U.S. Air Force. In 1917 Davis returned to the Philippines, where he spent most of World War I overseeing supply operations. He married Sadie Overton and in 1920 was transferred to another teaching position, this time at Alabama's historically black Tuskegee Institute. Davis by now clearly understood that discrimination was responsible for several of his less significant postings. After he was transferred to another teaching position in Ohio, then promoted to lieutenant colonel in 1930 and returned to Tuskegee, black journalists began to ask why a high-ranking officer with more than three decades of service was in a classroom. Not until 1937 did Davis get his command, taking charge of the 369th Cavalry of the New York National Guard, a regiment of black troops. At Davis's prodding, the army redesignated the regiment from noncombat to combat status.

During the election year of 1940 President Franklin D. Roosevelt sought to shore up his wavering support among African Americans by promoting Davis to the rank of brigadier general, the first black to reach that position. To do so, Roosevelt overrode the army's ban against promoting officers over the age of 58. During World War II the army recruited more than 100,000 black troops; only a few years before, fewer than 5000 blacks were serving. Davis was appointed to oversee race relations among troops. He traveled the United States receiving complaints from black troops and calling attention to such things as discrimination in assignments and the racial segregation of donated blood. Davis also helped produce an educational film about black soldiers that received wide distribution and was followed by a postwar sequel on the role that black soldiers played in the war.

He spent much of 1942, 1944, and 1945 in Great Britain, where he discovered that despite a shortage of troops at the front, most black soldiers were not sent into combat positions. Davis recommended not only that Gen. Dwight D. Eisenhower use more black troops in combat but that he allow blacks to fill the ranks of fallen whites, which would have meant allowing blacks to serve shoulder-to-shoulder with whites. Eisenhower agreed to give blacks more combat positions but insisted that segregation continue, at least at the platoon level. Black platoons, however, were thereafter common in previously all-white battalions. Davis retired in 1948, later serving on the American Battle Monuments Commission.

SEE ALSO

World War I and African Americans; World War II and African Americans; Press, Black, in the United States; Davis, Benjamin O., Jr.; Tuskegee University.

North America

Davis, Danny K. (b. 1941, Parkdale, Ark.), Democratic member of the United States House of Representatives from Illinois (1997-).

Danny K. Davis received a bachelor's degree from Arkansas A.M.&N. College (now the University of Arkansas) in Pine Bluff in 1961, and a master's degree from Chicago State University in CHICAGO, ILLINOIS, in 1968. In 1977 he received a Ph.D. from Union Institute in Cincinnati, Ohio. His political career began in 1979 when he was elected to the Chicago City Council, a position he held for 11 years. In 1984 and 1986 Davis unsuccessfully sought the Democratic nomination for representative of the First Congressional District in Illinois. He was named to the Cook County Board of Commissioners in 1990 and held the position until 1997. In 1991 he made an unsuccessful bid for mayor of Chicago. Davis was elected to the U.S. House from Illinois's First Congressional District in November 1996.

The First District includes Chicago's downtown business district and the residential area on the city's west side. The Sears Tower and the Magnificent Mile – the home of high-end department stores and businesses – are downtown attractions, while the district's northern and western sections include the Cabrini-Green and Robert Taylor Homes housing projects.

In 1997 Davis served on the Government Reform and Oversight Committee and the Small Business Committee. He is also a member of CONGRESSIONAL BLACK CAUCUS.

North America

Davis, John Henry

(b. January 12, 1921, Smithtown, N.Y.; d. July, 1984, New York City, N.Y.), African American weightlifter who won the Gold Medal in the heavyweight class (now called super heavyweight) at the Olympic Games in 1948 and 1952.

John Henry Davis won his first world title in 1938 at age 17, competing in the light heavyweight class. In the years when Davis was competing, there were three individual lifts in weightlifting competition: the *press*, the *snatch*, and the *clean and jerk*. (The press was eliminated from international competition after the 1972 Olympic Games in Munich, West Germany.) The three were then compiled together to determine the overall lift. At the 1948 Olympic Games in London, Davis won the Gold Medal in the heavyweight class, setting world (and Olympic) records in the clean and jerk and the snatch and establishing Olympic records in the press and the three-lift total. Davis, who was trimmer and more fit than many of his competitors, became a hero in Europe after his performance and was known in France as L'Hercule Noir (the Black Hercules).

Davis triumphed again at the 1952 Olympic Games in Helsinki, Finland, breaking his own Olympic marks in the press, the snatch, and the three-lift total. He dominated heavyweight weightlifting during his career, capturing 10 United States national titles (1941-1943, 1946-1948, 1950-1953), five world titles (1946, 1947, 1949-1951), and the Pan American Games title in 1951 in Buenos Aires, Argentina.

After leg injuries ended his hopes of competing in the 1956 Olympic Games in Melbourne, Australia, Davis worked for the New York City Department of Corrections. In his job he established weightlifting programs for juvenile delinquents. He was posthumously inducted into the U.S. Olympic Hall of Fame in 1989.

North America

Davis, Miles Dewey, III

(b. May 25, 1926, Alton, Ill.; d. September 25, 1991, Santa Monica, Calif.), African American trumpet player and band leader who contributed significantly to bebop, cool jazz, modal jazz, and fusion or jazz-rock.

The role of Miles Davis is unparalleled in the history of JAZZ. Many great jazz musicians – including Louis Armstrong, Coleman Hawkins, Charlie Parker, and Dizzy Gillespie – gained renown for their technical mastery and their distinctive approaches to improvisation. Others, such as Duke Ellington, Count Basie, Thelonious Monk, Charles Mingus, and ORNETTE COLEMAN, achieved greatness less through instrumental prowess than through compositions and performances in a distinctive style. Davis is unique in having made his mark through neither technical mastery nor a single identifiable style, but rather through his constant evolution and stylistic innovation. Jazz scholar Joachim Berendt has observed that Davis three times altered the history of jazz, by introducing cool jazz, modal jazz, and fusion. Since his death, his influence has continued to be greater than that of any other jazz musician, including tenor saxophonist John Coltrane.

The son of a prosperous dentist who once ran for the state legislature, Davis grew up in a middle-class home in East St. Louis, Illinois. His mother, Cleota Henry Davis, was a classically trained musician who could, Davis recalled, "play a mean blues on the piano." He received his first trumpet at age 13 and by his mid-teens was playing in the St. Louis area, in the process befriending St. Louis jazz trumpeter Clark Terry. Shortly after graduating from high school in 1944, Davis substituted for a sick third trumpet player in Billy Eckstine's orchestra during its two-week gig in St. Louis.

The Eckstine band was then the most innovative group in jazz. It featured a number of the young lions of bebop, most notably Dizzy Gillespie on trumpet and Charlie Parker – Bird – on alto sax, but also tenor players Gene Ammons and Lucky Thompson, drummer Art Blakey, and vocalists Eckstine and Sarah Vaughan. "B's band changed my life," Davis recalled. "I decided right then and there that I had to leave St. Louis and live in New York City where all these bad musicians were." He was accepted by the Juilliard School of Music, which provided Davis with a pretext for moving that his parents would enthusiastically support.

Davis did attend Juilliard but never graduated; he gained far more of his musical education in the jazz clubs of 52nd Street. He quickly established himself in the jazz community, playing with tenor saxophonist Coleman Hawkins, pianist and composer Tadd Dameron, and pianists Bud Powell and Thelonious Monk. During 1946 and 1947 he became a regular member of the Eckstine band.

Davis had his first encounter with cocaine during his stint with Eckstine, and tenor player Gene Ammons introduced him to heroin. At the time, heroin use was rampant among younger jazz musicians. Davis recalled that "the idea was going around that to use heroin might make you play as great as Bird," who was known to be an addict. "A lot of musicians did it for that. I guess I might have been just waiting for his genius to hit me."

Davis soon had the chance to work with his musical idol on a steady basis. In 1947 he joined Parker's great quintet – which also featured Duke Jordan (piano), Tommy Potter (bass), and Max Roach (drums). During his stint with Parker, Davis perfected his bebop style. By 1949, however, he had acquired a heroin addiction that increasingly hindered his ability to play. In 1953 Davis returned to Illinois and, alone on a farm owned by his father, kicked his habit by sheer force of will. In part, that steely resolve reflected Davis's lifelong struggle to control a tightly coiled rage. Davis was never one to refuse a challenge, whether it was overcoming addiction or meeting a personal insult. He had a number of unpleasant encounters with white authorities, including a notorious police beating in 1959 outside Birdland, the New York City jazz club.

Over the course of 45 years, Davis's playing fell into five distinct, sometimes overlapping phases: bebop (1945-1948), cool jazz (1948-1958), hard bop (1952-1963), modal (1959, 1964-1968), and electric or fusion (1969-1991). After journeyman beginnings in bebop, Davis led the way for all of jazz music. His pathbreaking *Birth of the Cool* recordings of 1949-1950 established the conventions of cool jazz. A series of recordings in the early 1950s with trombonist J. J. Johnson, alto player Jackie McLean, and pianist Horace Silver heralded the hard bop movement, which simplified the musical universe of bebop and gave it harder rhythmic underpinnings.

In the mid-1950s Davis organized the first of his two classic quintets, featuring John Coltrane (tenor sax), Red Garland (piano), Paul Chambers (bass), and Philly Joe Jones (drums). This group alternately played blazing up-tempo hard bop numbers and ballads that featured Davis's pensive trumpet. In his ballad playing, Davis often used a harmon mute to achieve a distinctly poignant sound. During these years, he simplified his playing. On ballads, in particular, he made deliberate use of space, increasing the emotional depth of his solos by the silences that he left between notes and phrases.

Davis's quintet also inaugurated the next major phase of jazz with its increasingly modal playing. Modal jazz replaces standard diatonic scales and chords with other note sequences played in more open, harmonically indeterminate settings. In 1959, with white pianist Bill Evans replacing Garland and with the addition of alto player Cannonball Adderley, Davis's band recorded *Kind of Blue,* one of the most influential and most popular recordings in jazz history. The album, the first significant example of modal jazz, continues to exert a profound influence on young jazz musicians.

Further exploring the cool side of jazz, Davis collaborated with composer and arranger Gil Evans – who had first worked with the trumpeter on the *Birth of the Cool* sessions – on a series of memorable recordings that epitomize modern orchestral jazz, including *Miles Ahead* (1957), *Porgy and Bess* (1958), and most notably *Sketches of Spain* (1959-1960). During the same period, Davis's small group continued to play hard bop with blazing intensity. In 1964 Davis formed the second of his great quintets, this one featuring Wayne Shorter (tenor), Herbie Hancock (piano), Ron Carter (bass), and Tony Williams (drums).

The creative achievements of Davis's 1960s quintet quickly placed it at the musical forefront. The group's probing modal music drew jazz ever further in the direction of harmonic, melodic, and rhythmic freedom. On the other hand, Davis resisted what he saw as the anarchy of free jazz. "Look," he said, "you don't need to think to play weird. That ain't no freedom. You need controlled freedom." From 1964 to the end of his life, the trumpet player continually, if not always successfully, pursued his ideal of "controlled freedom." In the late 1960s he began experimenting with electric instruments and rock-based rhythms, as foreshadowed on his albums *Filles de Kilimanjaro* (1968) and *In a Silent Way* (1969).

Davis shook the jazz world with his subsequent album, *Bitches Brew* (1969), which introduced fusion or jazz-rock, a style that layered jazz improvisation over rock rhythms. Davis's new direction – and the playing of such sidemen as drummers Jack DeJohnette and Billy Cobham, electric keyboard players Chick Corea and Keith Jarrett, and electric guitarist John McLaughlin – alienated many of his old fans but attracted a large following among younger listeners. In the late 1970s Davis ceased performing, mainly because he was debilitated by a cocaine dependency. Yet in the early 1980s he again overcame drug problems and resumed his musical career.

In his autobiography, which appeared two years before his death, Davis declared, "I have to always be on the cutting edge of things because that's just the way I am and always have been." But in his final years Davis twice returned to his past style of playing. In 1990 he appeared as a sideman and featured soloist – playing once again in his 1950s harmon-muted ballad style – on the title song of singer pianist Shirley Horn's *You Won't Forget Me*. A year later, and only a few weeks before his death, Davis revisited his classic orchestral collaborations with Gil Evans at a Montreux Jazz Festival concert organized and conducted by Quincy Jones.

Of the many posthumous tributes to Davis, none was more astute than an editorial that appeared in the *Boston Globe.* "There were better players," it declared, "[and] certainly better people, but only Miles had that aura: a compound of danger, beauty, and arrogance. With the grace of a dancer, and [the] menace of a gun, Miles exuded a princely hauteur."

James Clyde Sellman

See Also

Adderley, Julian Edwin ("Cannonball"); Armstrong, Louis ("Satchmo"); Basie, William James ("Count"); Coltrane, John William; Eckstine, William Clarence (Billy); Gillespie, John Birks ("Dizzy"); Hancock, Herbert Jeffrey (Herbie); Hawkins, Coleman Randolph; Jones, Quincy Delight, Jr.; Mingus, Charles, Jr.; Monk, Thelonious Sphere; Parker, Charles Christopher ("Bird"); Powell, Earl ("Bud"); Roach, Maxwell Lemuel (Max); Ellington, Edward Kennedy ("Duke").

North America

Davis, Ossie (b. December 18, 1917, Cogdell, Ga.), widely acclaimed African American actor, playwright, producer, and director who has long been an activist and leader within the black community.

The son of a railway engineer, Ossie Davis grew up in Waycross, Georgia. The harassment of his parents by the Ku Klux Klan impelled him early on to become a writer so that he could "truthfully portray the black man's experience." At HOWARD UNIVERSITY, under the tutelage of drama critic Alain Locke, Davis developed his theatrical talent, performing in a 1941 production of *Joy Exceeding Glory* with Harlem's ROSE MCCLENDON Players. Following his theater debut, however, he received few job offers and for nearly a year found himself living on the street.

Davis never lost his sense of purpose. After serving in the United States Army during World War II, he returned to New York, where he won the title role in Robert Ardrey's play *Jeb* (1946). In 1948 he married fellow performer RUBY DEE, who became his lifelong collaborator on stage, on screen, and as a political activist. During the 1950s Davis and Dee were blacklisted for taking a radical stance in their work against the hard-line anticommunists of the McCarthy era. In an attempt to elude government agents assigned to tail them, Davis and Dee once hid for hours in a costume hamper following a performance of Chekhov's *The Cherry Orchard*. They also organized fundraisers within the theater to pay for the legal defense of black victims of racially based assaults. When in the 1960s Davis had attained celebrity status as an actor, he lent his artistic stature to advance the cause of civil rights by eulogizing both MALCOLM X and Martin Luther King Jr. at their funerals. In 1972 he chaired the Angela Davis Defense Fund.

Davis is best known for his roles in LORRAINE HANSBERRY's award-winning Broadway play *A Raisin in the Sun* (1959) and its 1961 film version, as well as for his own satirical play *Purlie Victorious* (1961), in which a black preacher outwits the local landowner to secure an inheritance and finance the building of a church. The play was well received by critics, who praised its mockery of RACIAL STEREOTYPES by blowing them out of proportion. He has since written and directed numerous films, including *Cotton Comes to Harlem* (1970) and *Countdown at Kusini* (coproduced with Dee, 1976), the first American feature film to be shot entirely in Africa by black professionals. Davis has also starred in numerous films that address issues critical to African Americans, such as Spike Lee's *Do The Right Thing* (1989), *Jungle Fever* (1991), and *Malcolm X* (1994).

Among the many awards Davis has received are the Hall of Fame Award for outstanding artistic achievement in 1989 and the U.S. National Medal for the Arts in 1995.

Roanne Edwards

SEE ALSO

World War II and African Americans; Civil Rights Movement; Davis, Angela Yvonne; Harlem, New York; King, Martin Luther, Jr.; Lee, Shelton Jackson ("Spike"); Locke, Alain Leroy; New York, New York; Film, Blacks in American.

North America

Davis, Sammy, Jr. (b. December 8, 1925, New York, N.Y.; d. May 16, 1990, Los Angeles, Calif.), African American singer, dancer, and actor who starred on the vaudeville stage, Broadway, television, and in motion pictures.

Sammy Davis Jr., the son of vaudeville performers Elvera Sanchez Davis and Sammy Davis Sr., began a life-long career of entertaining at the age of three, appearing in the vaudeville group in which his parents danced, Will Mastin's Holiday in Dixieland. Two years later, after his parents' divorce, he stayed with his father and officially joined the group. Davis made his movie debut with ETHEL WATERS in *Rufus Jones for President* (1933), and then filmed *Seasons Greetings*. Throughout the 1930s he toured with the Will Mastin Trio, becoming the central figure in the group, singing, dancing, and playing several instruments.

Sammy Davis Jr. talks with President Richard M. Nixon at the 1972 Republican National Convention. *CORBIS/Bettmann*

In 1943 Davis joined the army. He served for two years directing shows and touring military installations. After leaving the army he returned to the Will Mastin Trio, which became an established part of the club circuit playing bills with European-American entertainers Jack Benny, Bob Hope, and Frank Sinatra.

Davis's recording career began to take off in 1946, when he signed with Capitol Records. The song "The Way You Look Tonight" was selected by *Metronome* as record of the year and Davis was chosen as Most Outstanding New Personality. Decca Records signed him in 1954 and released *Starring Sammy Davis Jr.*, which reached number one on the charts. Later that year, Davis was in a near fatal car accident, lost his left eye and spent several months in the hospital. It was there that he converted to Judaism.

In 1956 he made his Broadway debut, starring in *Mr. Wonderful*, which included his father and adopted uncle from the Will Mastin Trio. He moved back to film with *The Benny Goodman Story* (1956), *Anna Lucasta* (1958), and *Porgy and Bess* (1959). In 1959 he married dancer Loray White, but soon left her for Swedish actress Mai Britt, whom he married in 1960. They had one child, and he adopted her two children.

In the 1960s Davis socialized and made films with the Rat Pack, a Hollywood group led by Frank Sinatra and Dean Martin. These films included *Oceans Eleven* (1960), *Sergeants Three* (1962), and *Robin and the Seven Hoods* (1964). Also during the 1960s Davis starred on Broadway in *Golden Boy*, which ran for 568 performances. His 1965 autobiography, *Yes I Can*, earned him the Spingarn Medal from the NATIONAL ASSOCIATION FOR THE ADVANCEMENT OF COLORED PEOPLE.

In 1970 Davis married Altovise Gore, while continuing with his recording career. He was criticized in 1972 for supporting Republican president Richard Nixon and for being photographed with him at the Republican National Convention. He abandoned his support of Nixon after the Watergate scandal of 1972. In 1974 Davis was hospitalized for liver and kidney problems resulting from alcoholism, a product of his days with the Rat Pack. He was back on stage later that year singing in *Sammy on Broadway*, and from 1975 to 1977 he starred in the television show *Sammy and Company*.

In the 1980s Davis published two more autobiographies, entertained U.S. troops in Lebanon (1983), and toured with Sinatra and Liza Minelli in 1988. In 1989 he filmed *Tap*, a tribute to the great tap dancers, with GREGORY HINES. Davis died of throat cancer the following year.

SEE ALSO

Tap Dance; Film, Blacks in American.

North America

Dawson, William Levi (b. April 26, 1886, Albany, Ga.; d. November 9, 1970, Chicago, Ill.), the second African American Democrat elected to the United States Congress from Chicago, and the first African American to chair a regular House of Representatives committee.

William Levi Dawson became one of Chicago's most influential politicians, serving as an elected representative and a political power broker in that city, both rarities for African

Americans of his generation. In this way he parallels the rising significance of African Americans in Democratic politics of the twentieth century.

In 1912, three years after he graduated magna cum laude from Fisk University in Tennessee, Dawson moved to Chicago to study law at Northwestern University. He interrupted his legal studies to serve in World War I, rising to the rank of captain after twice sustaining injuries, once in a mustard gas attack. Returning to Chicago, Dawson completed his law degree at Northwestern and entered into local politics. In 1942, after serving as alderman on the Chicago City Council, he successfully ran for Congress, holding his seat until retiring in 1970.

Dawson's quiet, unassuming demeanor was often contrasted with that of his contemporary, the flamboyant Harlemite Adam Clayton Powell Jr. One writer characterized them by labeling Dawson Mr. Inside and Powell Mr. Outside. Critics charged that Dawson was too accommodationist in his politics – too moderate and too conciliatory. Nevertheless, Dawson spoke out about the poll tax, and his impassioned speech to House colleagues was credited with defeating the Winstead Amendment, which would have allowed military personnel to choose whether or not they would serve in integrated units. In 1949 Dawson became chair of the House Committee on Expenditures in Executive Departments (later renamed the Committee on Government Operations), making him the first African American to chair a regular congressional committee. In addition, he served as assistant chairman of the Democratic National Committee, beginning in 1944, and later become its first African American vice chairman.

In Chicago, where his constituents knew him as simply "the Man," Dawson developed a considerable power base by awarding political appointments to his allies. His support of Richard Daley proved instrumental. In Daley's 1963 reelection campaign, 115,000 of his winning margin of 139,000 votes came from Dawson's wards. Similarly, President John F. Kennedy acknowledged Dawson's work in the 1960 campaign by offering him the position of postmaster general. Had Dawson accepted, he would have become the first black cabinet member, but he decided to remain in the House, where he felt he could do the most good. For all of the power he amassed, Dawson remained connected to his constituency. He returned to his district often and spent part of each day in his district office, visiting with constituents and working to solve their problems.

Robert Fay

See Also
World War I and African Americans; Chicago, Illinois; Harlem, New York; Powell, Adam Clayton, Jr.

North America

Deacons for Defense and Justice, **a black organization established to protect civil rights workers against the Ku Klux Klan.**

The Deacons for Defense and Justice, a group of African American men who were mostly veterans of World War II and the Korean War, organized in Jonesboro, Louisiana, on July 10, 1964. Their goal was to combat Ku Klux Klan violence against Congress of Racial Equality (CORE) volunteers who were participating in voter registration activities. Disciplined and secretive, the Deacons generally limited their activities to patrolling black neighborhoods and protecting mass meetings, CORE headquarters, and civil rights workers who were entering and leaving town. The Deacons accompanied marchers from Memphis, Tennessee, to Jackson, Mississippi, in the summer of 1966, during which Student Nonviolent Coordinating Committee (SNCC) leader Stokely Carmichael popularized the phrase Black Power.

The Deacons often inflated their membership numbers in order to appear more menacing to white extremists, and they once claimed to have 50 chapters throughout the South. The resulting picture painted by the national news media – thousands of armed and angry blacks involved in secret organizations that were spreading through the South – shocked many whites into speculating that the United States was heading for a race war. The membership claims of the Deacons attracted the notice of J. Edgar Hoover, director of the Federal Bureau of Investigation (FBI). During the investigation that Hoover ordered, and in which the organization cooperated, it came to light that the total membership was in the dozens, with only three chapters, all in Louisiana.

Ironically, as nonviolent civil rights activities were eclipsed in the later 1960s by the Black Power Movement, with its militant rhetoric and insinuations of racial violence, the Deacons' presence declined. By 1968 the Deacons for Defense and Justice had all but disappeared.

Robert Fay

See Also
World War II and African Americans.

North America

Deadwood Dick **(b. June, 1854, Davidson County, Tenn.; d. 1921?, Los Angeles, Calif.), African American cowboy.**

Deadwood Dick was born Nat Love, a slave in a log cabin, the youngest of three children. A lucky raffle ticket brought him the money to seek greater opportunities, so he started on foot for the West in 1869. On his arrival in Dodge City, Kansas, he found work as a cowboy. He immediately earned admiration for his ability to ride a bucking bronco that his new companions had furnished him for his initiation. Because of this feat, the "tenderfoot" was accepted by the Duval outfit at $30 a month.

At a Fourth of July celebration in 1876, after a cattle drive to Deadwood, South Dakota, he found himself in competition with the best cowboys in the West. He won the contest to rope, throw, tie, bridle, saddle, and mount an untamed bronco, a feat he accomplished in 9 minutes, a record, and won the shooting contests with a rifle at 100 and 250 yards and with the Colt 45 at 150 yards. Entering and finishing these matches with the confidence of a man who declared that "if a man can hit a running buffalo at 200 yards, he can hit pretty much of anything he shoots at," he was given the name Deadwood Dick by his admiring fans.

Later that year he was captured by American Indians and was adopted by the tribe against his will. He escaped after an amazing ride of 167 km (100 mi) in 12 hours of darkness, carrying with him two new bullet holes, part of the total of "the masks of fourteen bullet wounds on different parts of my body."

In 1890, with the passing of the great era of the cowboy, Deadwood Dick became a Pullman porter. Despite the slavery-era statutes that outlawed black literacy, he had learned to read and write at his father's knee, and in 1907 he wrote an autobiography titled *The Life and Adventures of Nat Love: Better Known in the Cattle Country as "Deadwood Dick."*

See Also
Black Cowboys.

Latin America and the Caribbean

Décima, **traditional Spanish poetic form, literally, a stanza of ten octosyllabic lines, with a particular rhyme scheme. This popular form is often improvised and performed with musical accompaniment (guitar). It is sometimes used in duels in which two poets play off each other's improvisations and in musical forms such as the Cuban son.**

In their Afro-Esmeraldian variant, décima oral poems generally are composed and recited by older black men, *decimeros* (*see* Nicomedes Santa Cruz), of the northwestern Ecuadorian province of Esmeraldas – one of the two "traditional" black regions of the country. In contrast to the traditional ten-verse décima, Afro-Esmeraldian décima is composed of 44 verses divided into five stanzas: one of four verses followed by four of ten. These oral poems have as their origin a written poetry that was popular during the Renaissance in Spain and in Europe called "the gloss" (*la glosa*). The link between the two poetic genres is obvious when their formal structures are compared. In both the Spanish gloss and the Afro-Esmeraldian décima the first verse of the quatrain ends the first ten-line stanza, the second verse of the quatrain ends the second ten-line stanza, and so on until the fourth verse of the quatrain that ends the fourth ten-line stanza.

Despite their formal similarities, the Spanish gloss and the Afro-Esmeraldian décima differ significantly in their language styles and provincialisms, issues addressed, sociocultural contexts, strikingly different positions of the poets within the colonial racial order, and so on. These fundamental differences require that we conceive the gloss and the décima as distinct poetic traditions.

During the colonial period Spanish glosses with biblical themes were used by Catholic missionaries as a tool for the evangelization of the slaves. Since then, the décima has been adopted by Afro-Esmeraldian popular poets as one of the preferred oral forms in Ecuador.

The tradition of the Afro-Esmeraldian décimas is fading away because the rural youths migrate en masse to the cities of Esmeraldas and Guayaquil and do not become apprenticed to a decimero. The décimas are looked at by urban blacks, whites, *mestizos* (people of mixed Indian and European ancestry), and mulattos alike as a characteristic institution of Afro-Esmeraldian culture. They are considered to be the relics of a cultural past, representing a naive world-view held by rural and uneducated blacks. Today, décimas are associated mostly with the northern sector of the province, where many blacks still live in relatively isolated small villages scattered in the dense rain forest.

Jean Muteba Rahier

See Also

Ecuador.

North America

Declaration of Independence,

American document of July 4, 1776, declaring the separation of 13 British colonies in North America from Great Britain; although the final document held that "all men are created equal," the Continental Congress deleted earlier passages that condemned slavery.

In an early version of the Declaration of Independence, Thomas Jefferson, the document's main author, denounced Great Britain for its role in the slave trade. He wrote of King George III: "He has waged cruel war against human nature itself, violating its most sacred rights of life and liberty in the person of a distant people who never offended him; captivating and carrying them into slavery in another hemisphere, or to incur miserable death in their transportation thither. This piratical warfare, the opprobrium of infidel powers, is the warfare of the Christian king of Great Britain. Determined to keep open a market where men should be bought and sold, he has prostituted his negative for suppressing every legislative attempt to prohibit or restrain this execrable commerce."

Both present-day historians and contemporaries of Jefferson have disagreed about whether this passage was a condemnation of slavery. Many Northern colonists interpreted it as such, but Southern slaveholders tended to distinguish Jefferson's condemnation of the slave *trade* from a condemnation of slave *ownership* – a position not as paradoxical as it may seem.

Some Enlightenment thinkers in America believed that while the brutal capture and transatlantic shipping of slaves was inhumane, the "management" of slaves who were already in America was not. Jefferson, who owned more than 100 slaves, may have held such views. Moreover, while slave ownership benefited many Southerners, the slave trade was still controversial because imported slaves lowered the value of slaves already in America. Many Southerners were also frightened by an increasing black population, which already outnumbered the white population in many areas.

Regardless of the passage's meaning, delegations from Georgia and South Carolina, both of which wanted slave trade and ownership to continue, encouraged the Continental Congress to delete any reference to slavery. Northern colonies, many of which had profited from the trafficking of slaves, were inclined to acquiesce. Further, several delegates in each region argued that it was simply untrue that George III had forced the slave trade on the colonies. Most historians agree that Jefferson's claims in this area were exaggerated. The passage was deleted with little protest.

In a separate passage, Jefferson condemned George III for allowing his governors to offer freedom to slaves if they would fight with the British against the colonists. This charge, too, was deleted, though the Declaration does condemn the king for waging war "with Cruelty and Perfidy" and for having "excited domestic insurrections against us" – probable references to the enlistment of slaves.

With slavery removed from the Declaration yet remaining pervasive in American life, the meaning of the Declaration's much-quoted preamble is unclear: "We hold these truths to be self-evident, that all men are created equal, that they are endowed by their Creator with certain unalienable Rights, that among these are Life, Liberty, and the pursuit of Happiness."

Some historians argue that Jefferson intended "all men" to mean both white and black men. Others, however, argue that in 1776 Jefferson did not have to say "all white men" because "white" was implicit. Nonetheless, a few Northern colonies included the clause "all men are created equal" in their state constitutions as a way of prohibiting slavery. Later abolitionists also invoked the preamble in their arguments against slavery.

See Also

Slavery in the United States; Transatlantic Slave Trade; Abolitionism in the United States.

Africa

Decolonization in Africa: An Interpretation

Frederick Cooper

The most difficult problem in writing the history of decolonization is the temptation to write it backwards. We know that almost all African colonies eventually became independent states, hence a tendency to relate the triumph of nationalism, of an African conquest of the colonial state. We know now that the fruits of independence have often turned bitter, hence a temptation to write the history of disappointment, of the continued subordination of Africa to Western powers. Neither the triumphalist history nor the story of frustrated aspirations is sufficient.

If instead of writing history from the present to the past, we watch it run forward, the history of Africa from the 1940s onward opens up to a much wider range of actions, aspirations, and possibilities. We see political movements directed not just at taking over the nation-state, but at revitalizing local belief systems or forging connections among people of African descent all around the world. We see African workers organizing to demand wages equal to those of whites, merchants seeking access to markets alongside European firms, peasants trying to restore harmony to the land. People act together as members of an Islamic brotherhood or as migrants from a particular rural area. Such collectivities are important not simply as they contributed to anticolonial or nationalist movements – even though many of them did – but because they helped reshape people's lives.

A number of scholars would dispense with the concept of decolonization altogether, for some because it never really happened – because Africa remains subordinated

Kenyan prime minister Jomo Kenyatta, *right*, waves to a crowd of supporters as he enters the East African Heads of Government Conference in Nairobi, Kenya, in 1964. With Kenyatta are, *left*, Julius Nyerere of Tanzania and, *center*, Milton Obote of Uganda. *CORBIS/Bettmann*

HEADS OF STATE – LISTED BY COUNTRY

Country	Head Of State		First Year In Office / Years In Power	
Algeria	*President*	Liamine Zeroual	1994	5
Angola	*President*	Jose Eduardo dos Santos	1979	20
Benin	*President*	Mathieu Kérékou	1996	3
Botswana	*President*	Festus Mogae	1998	1
Burkina Faso	*President*	Blaise Compaoré (Capt.)	1987	12
Burundi	*President*	Pierre Buyoya	1996	3
Cameroon	*President*	Paul Biya	1982	17
Cape Verde	*President*	Antonio Mascarenhas	1991	8
Central African Republic	*President*	Ange Patasse	1993	6
Chad	*President*	Idriss Deby (Lt. Gen.)	1990	9
Comoros	*President*	Mohamed Taki Abdulkarim	1996	3
Congo, Democratic Republic of the (formerly Zaire)	*President*	Laurent-Désiré Kabila	1997	2
Congo, Republic of the	*President*	Denis Sassou-Nguesso	1997	2
Côte d'Ivoire	*President*	Henri Konan Bédié	1993	6
Djibouti	*President*	Ismail Omar Guelleh	1999	
Egypt	*President*	Mohammed Hosni Mubarak	1981	18
Equatorial Guinea	*President*	Teodoro Obiang Nguema Mbasogo	1979	20
Eritrea	*President*	Isaias Afwerki	1993	6
Ethiopia	*President*	Negasso Gidada	1995	4
Gabon	*President*	El Hadj Omar Bongo	1967	32
Gambia, The	*President*	Yahya A. J. J. Jammeh	1996	3
Ghana	*President*	Jerry John Rawlings	1993	6
Guinea	*President*	Lansana Conté	1993	6
Guinea-Bissau	*President*	Malan Bacai Sanha	1999	
Kenya	*President*	Daniel Toroitich arap Moi	1978	21
Lesotho	*King*	Letsie III	1996	3
Liberia	*President*	Charles Ghankay Taylor	1997	2
Libya	*Revolutionary Leader*	Muammar al-Qaddafi (Col.)	1970	29
Madagascar	*President*	Didier Ratsiraka	1997	2
Malawi	*President*	Bakili Muluzi	1994	5
Mali	*President*	Alpha Oumar Konaré	1992	7
Mauritania	*President*	Maaouya Ould Sid Ahmed Taya (Col.)	1984	15
Mauritius	*President*	Cassam Uteem	1992	7
Morocco	*King*	Mohammed VI	1999	
Mozambique	*President*	Joaquim Alberto Chissano	1986	13
Namibia	*President*	Sam Nujoma	1990	9
Niger	*President*	Daounde Malam Wanke (Maj.)	1999	
Nigeria	*President*	Olusegun Obasanjo (Gen.)	1999	
Réunion	*President*	of France Jacques Chirac	1995	4
Rwanda	*President*	Pasteur Bizimungu	1994	5
São Tomé and Príncipe	*President*	Miguel Trovoada	1991	8
Senegal	*President*	Abdou Diouf	1981	18
Seychelles	*President*	France Albert René	1977	22
Sierra Leone	*President*	Ahmad Tejan Kabbah	1996	3
Somalia	*No Functioning Government at this time*			
South Africa	*President*	Thabo Mbeki	1999	
Sudan	*President*	Umar Hasan Ahmad al-Bashir (Lt. Gen.)	1993	6
Swaziland	*King*	Mswati III	1986	13
Tanzania	*President*	Benjamin William Mkapa	1995	4
Togo	*President*	Gnassingbé Eyadéma (Gen.)	1967	32
Tunisia	*President*	Zine El Abidine Ben Ali	1987	12
Uganda	*President*	Yoweri Kaguta Museveni (Lt. Gen.)	1986	13
Western Sahara	*Disputed Territory*			
Zambia	*President*	Frederick Chiluba	1991	8
Zimbabwe	*President*	Robert Gabriel Mugabe	1987	12

Source: CIA Data

Kwame Francis Nkrumah was inaugurated president of Ghana in July 1960. Sir Arko Gorshun, *left,* chief justice of Ghana, administers the oath of office to Nkrumah, *center.* The robed attendant holds the sword of state. *AP/Wide World Photos*

to Europe – for others because the term suggests that COLONIAL RULE marched along to its own end, rather than being overthrown by people striving to liberate themselves. The term is still useful, as long as one does not read more into it than it deserves. Colonialism may be distinguished from other systems in which a few people ruled over many by the institutions colonial regimes created that explicitly reproduced social difference and inequality. Colonial states drew and redrew distinctions among people under its rule, defining some as "natives" (in turn divided into "tribes") and others as "citizens" or "Europeans," with different rights and obligations, administered through different agencies. Although states often used similar techniques at home and overseas to command obedience, the ruling fiction in the colonies was difference, while the ruling fiction at home in Europe, at least since the nineteenth century, was the legal and political equivalence of citizens. Colonial rulers passed laws against intermarriage and tried to prevent whites from "going native," or "educated natives" from thinking too highly of themselves.

These distinctions became increasingly difficult – and then impossible – to sustain in the period after World War II. Decolonization entailed the transition from empires in which distinction was emphasized to a global system of states in which all states were formally equivalent and in which each regarded its own citizens as *formally* equivalent to one another.

The word "formal" is crucial. The world and its individual states have always been and remain riven by distinctions. Sovereignty allowed African leaders to make certain kinds of claims on world resources, and many became adept at appealing, using a vocabulary of "nation-building" and "development," to rich

Léopold Sédar Senghor walks through a crowd of officials and military officers in Dakar, Senegal. Senghor was the first president of Senegal, serving from 1960 to 1980. *CORBIS/Bernard and Catherine Desjeux*

states' interests in having a world order of states participating in global institutions and markets. Internally, sovereignty also had its uses: sovereign power could be used to reward friends and punish enemies, to forge symbols of national solidarity. The politics of running a state, in short, are not the politics of running a colony.

The Crisis of Colonialism

In 1945 the idea that most of Africa would be divided into independent states within 20 years would have struck most Europeans – and possibly most Africans – as unimaginable. By 1965 it was a fact. Part of understanding this transition is figuring out how the transfer of power became imaginable – in Paris, in Accra, in villages in rural Tanganyika (present-day Tanzania).

Another of the temptations the historian faces is that of making colonialism into more than it was – a solid and unchanging edifice of power. Colonists wanted to believe this, as did anticolonial movements, for it defined their own heroism. Colonialism, in fact, came apart at its cracks, even as colonial regimes tried to remake themselves.

What conquering powers could do best was concentrate forces – to smash African political units one by one, to punish rebellion brutally, and to round up labor or seize resources at certain moments. What they could do least well, try as they did, was to insinuate themselves into the routine exercise of power. In South Africa, Algeria, Southern Rhodesia (present-day Zimbabwe), and parts of other colonies, white settlers both forced indigenous people off their land and provided a surveillance and control over agricultural and mineral production that was impossible elsewhere. When two decades into the colonial period British rulers proclaimed themselves advocates of "indirect rule," they were accepting their incapacity either to make Africans into replicas of Europeans or else to turn Africans into the servants of European will. They insisted that keeping African societies in their allegedly timeless integrity had been British policy all along. Actually, this "ethnicization" of Africa – French Africa as well as British – came at a time shortly after World War I when educated Africans were building associations and political organizations and acting disturbingly like "citizens."

At the very time, in the 1920s, when European powers were pretending that Africans were living within tribal cages, many were deeply involved in boundary-crossing activities: as farmers, opening up new territories; as merchants, exchanging goods from different ecological zones; and as workers, seeking as best they could to obtain cash wages without losing access to land and community. Religious movements were shaping affinities that crossed or expanded lines of language and culture. African intellectuals forged connections throughout the African diaspora and with intellectuals from other colonized regions (*see* PAN-AFRICANISM), while working-class Africans entered into diasporic relations when black sailors and dockworkers from Africa and the Americas met on ships or in ports, and eventually contributed to the rise of the Garvey movement.

The colonialism that collapsed in the 1950s was not the stagnant colonialism of the 1920s or 1930s, but colonialism at its most arrogantly interventionist, its most self-consciously reformist. In the 1920s and 1930s France and Great Britain rejected efforts from within the colonial establishment for a more vigorous "development" of African resources. A crisis came with recovery from the 1930s depression, as African workers returned to employers slow to raise wages recently cut, to cities with virtually no social services. The result was a wave of strikes beginning in the British Copperbelt (in present-day ZAMBIA) in 1935, where it spread beyond the mines to engulf entire towns, extending to railroads in the Gold Coast and ports in KENYA, Tanganyika, and elsewhere. The wave struck the British West Indies as well. In London this was seen as an empire wide threat. More important, it revealed that pretending to keep colonized people in their tribal cages was a failure. The British government decided it had to reclaim the initiative with the Colonial Development and Welfare Act of 1940. This recognized that resources would have to be put into colonies – not just extracted from them – if social peace and colonial initiative were to be restored.

Then came the war – to which Africans contributed their bodies and their labor, and for which they received little. Another strike wave hit British Africa, and this time officials focused specifically on the labor question, partially giving in to wage demands and at last acknowledging the "worker" as something more than the "detribalized African." In French Africa, parallel developments occurred after the war – in the shadow of major strikes and urban conflicts between 1945 and 1948 – and also resulted in a new development initiative.

DEVELOPMENT IN THE SERVICE OF EMPIRE

The international situation had also changed. On the one hand, Europe needed African minerals and crops more than ever. On the other hand, empire became more vulnerable politically. Hitler gave racist ideologies a bad name, and imperial leaders were at pains to explain why "self-determination" was a useful cry against Nazi conquests but not against imperial domination. Would Africa simply become a zone of heightened extraction, or could imperial powers reconcile expanding production with containing protest and relegitimizing empire internationally? For France and Great Britain, the development idea seemed for a time to offer an answer: their capital and knowledge would both increase output and raise the standard of living of Africans. Development would be the salvation of empire.

In Portuguese Africa production was expanded within a highly authoritarian system of rule and a highly coercive system of labor recruitment. In Belgian Africa, development meant more power for the already powerful mining companies, which provided services to "stabilize" workers in their employment. Belgium boasted of health and other services, but it did little to train an elite and less to allow expression, suppressing numerous peasant uprisings, religious movements, strikes, and mutinies.

Modernizing colonialism sharply raised the stakes: the old empire on the cheap was becoming economically and politically impossible, while the expensive empire of the postwar era had yet to prove itself. In fact, the development drive did more to foster demands and disorder than to contain them. And meanwhile, the attempt to legitimize the colonial order was opening cracks in the structure of power, which African political movements quickly pried wider open.

POLITICAL MOBILIZATION IN AFRICA

If one can sense the vulnerability of European powers, one needs to understand the multiple ways in which Africans mobilized, and the diverse objectives that they sought. It is too easy to project backwards the struggle for the nation-state, but important to note the way in which African political parties brokered quite diverse movements and aspirations – well enough to create plausible political organizations, not well enough to deepen those connections into a sense of common purpose.

There were struggles to group together chiefdoms into larger units with more influence in the colonial capital, attempts to install younger or more "progressive" chiefs in place of reactionary ones, efforts of urban migrants to strengthen and expand their communities of origin, and attempts to combat spiritual threats to the health of local communities. These movements used local languages and religious beliefs, and they often involved people literate in English or French who might enhance oral tradition by compiling it in written form. There were Muslim brotherhoods with networks of Koranic schools and leadership hierarchies across West and North Africa as well as Christian communities and breakaway, sometimes millennial, religious organizations – all bringing people together in other ways. Pan-Africanism in its various forms confronted imperialism on a world scale, insisting that the oppression of people of color demanded a global liberation. South Africans had organized effective labor and strike movements from the 1920s, while Algerian workers – more of whom had jobs in France than in Algerian cities – built a powerful organization of North African workers in France, linked to currents of proletarian internationalism in Europe. It would soon catalyze radical nationalism in Algeria itself.

What was really new after World War II was the possibility of articulating these concepts not simply among people of African descent literate in French and English, but between the elites and wider groupings of people within their respective territories.

Before the war, political parties and other political organizations existed within a number of colonial

AFRICAN INDEPENDENCE
Chronology of African Independence

State	Date of Independence	Colonial Power	Notes
Ethiopia	Ancient		Italian occupation 1936-1941.
Liberia	July 26, 1847		Private colony 1822-1847. Home for freed American slaves.
South Africa	May 31, 1910	Britain	(Suid Afrika) Union of four colonies, Cape Colony, Natal, Orange River Colony (Oranje Vrij Staat) and Transvaal (Zuid Afrikaansche Republiek), the last two of which had been independent Boer republics to May 31,1902. The Union became republic outside British Commonwealth May 31, 1961. White minority rule. Unrecognized 'independent' homelands: Transkei October 26, 1976 Bophuthatswana December 6, 1977 Venda September 13, 1979 Ciskei December 4, 1981
Egypt	February 28, 1922	Britain	Joined with Syria as United Arab Republic (UAR) from February 1, 1958 to September 28, 1961. Federated with Kingdom of (North) Yemen from March 8, 1958 to December 26, 1961. Name UAR retained by Egypt to September 2, 1961.
Libya	December 24, 1951	Italy	British (Tripolitania and Cyrenaica) and French (Fezzan) administration 1943-1951.
Ethiopia (Ogaden)	February 28, 1955		Italian occupation 1936-1941. British administration 1941-1955.
Sudan	January 1, 1956	Britain & Egypt	Anglo-Egyptian condominium.
Morocco	March 2, 1956	France	(Marcoc)
Tunisia	March 20, 1956	France	(Tunisie)
Morocco (part)	October 29, 1956		International zone (Tangiers).
Ghana	March 6, 1957	Britain	(Gold Coast) including British Togoland (UN Trust), part of former German colony of Togo.
Morocco (part)	April 27, 1958	Spain	(Marruecos) Spanish southern zone.
Guinea	October 2, 1958	France	(Guinée Française)
Cameroon	January 1, 1960	France	(Cameroun) UN Trust. Larger part of former German colony of Kamerun.
Togo	April 27, 1960	France	UN Trust. Larger part of former German colony of Togo.
Senegal	June 20, 1960 (August 20, 1960)	France	First independent as 'Federation of Mali' with Mali (former French Soudan). Federation dissolved after two months. Joined Gambia in Confederation of Senegambia, January 1, 1982 to October 6, 1989.
Mali	June 20, 1960 (September 22, 1960)	France	(Soudan Française) Independent initially as 'Federation of Mali' with Senegal. Federation dissolved after two months.
Madagascar	June 26, 1960	France	(Malagasy, Republique Malagache)
Zaire	June 30, 1960	Belgium	Congo Free State (Etat Indépendent du Congo) May 2, 1885 to November 11, 1908 when it became the Belgian Congo (Congo Belge, Belgisch Congo). Name changed from Congo October 27, 1974.
Somalia	July 1, 1960	Italy & Britain	UN Trust. Union of two colonies, Italian and British Somaliland. British Somaliland independent prior to union on June 26, 1960.
Benin	August 1, 1960	France	Name changed from Dahomey November 30, 1975.
Niger	August 3, 1960	France	
Burkina Faso	August 5, 1960	France	Name changed from Upper Volta (Haute Volta) August 4, 1984.
Ivory Coast	August 7, 1960	France	(Côte d'Ivoire)
Chad	August 11, 1960	France	(Tchad)
Central African Republic (CAR)	August 13, 1960	France	(Oubangui-Chari, Republique Centrafricaine) Central African Empire from December 4, 1976 to September 20, 1979.
Congo (Brazzaville)	August 15, 1960	France	(Moyen Congo)
Gabon	August 17, 1960	France	
Nigeria	October 1, 1960	Britain	

AFRICAN INDEPENDENCE

Chronology of African Independence

State	Date of Independence	Colonial Power	Notes
Mauritania	November 28, 1960	France	(Mauritanie)
Sierra Leone	April 24, 1961	Britain	
Nigeria (British North Cameroon)	June 1, 1961	Britain	UN Trust. Part of former German colony of Kamerun. Plebiscite February 11-12, 1961.
Cameroon (British South Cameroon)	October 1, 1961	Britain	UN Trust. Part of former German colony of Kamerun. Plebiscite February 11-12, 1961. Union with Cameroon as United Republic of Cameroon.
Tanzania	December 9, 1961	Britain	(Tanganyika) UN Trust. Greater part of former German colony of Deutsche Ostafrika. Name changed to Tanzania following union with Zanzibar April 27, 1964.
Burundi	July 1, 1962	Belgium	UN Trust. Ruanda-Urundi, divided at independence, was smaller part of former German. colony of Deutsche Ostafrika.
Rwanda	July 1, 1962	Belgium	UN Trust. Ruanda-Urundi, divided at independence, was smaller part of former German. colony of Deutsche Ostafrika.
Algeria	July 3, 1962	France	(Algérie)
Uganda	October 9, 1962	Britain	
Tanzania (Zanzibar)	December 10, 1963	Britain	Union with Tanganyika as Tanzania April 27, 1964.
Kenya	December 12, 1963	Britain	
Malawi	July 6, 1974	Britain	(Nyasaland) Federated with Rhodesia October 1, 1953 to December 31, 1963.
Zambia	October 25, 1964	Britain	(Northern Rhodesia) Federated with Nyasaland and Southern Rhodesia October 1, 1953 to December 31, 1963.
Gambia	February 18, 1965	Britain	Joined with Senegal as Confederation of Senegambia, January 1, 1982 to October 6, 1989.
Botswana	September 30, 1966	Britain	(Bechuanaland)
Lesotho	October 4, 1966	Britain	(Basutoland)
Mauritius	March 12, 1968	Britain	
Swaziland	September 6, 1968	Britain	
Equatorial Guinea	October 12, 1968	Spain	Comprises Rio Muni and Macias Nguema Biyogo (Fernando Poo)
Morocco (Ifni)	June 30, 1969	Spain	(Territorio de Ifni)
Guinea-Bissau	September 10, 1974	Portugal	Guine-Bissau formerly Guine-Portuguesa.
Mozambique	June 25, 1975	Portugal	(Mocambique)
Cape Verde	July 5, 1975	Portugal	(Cabo Verde)
Comoros	July 6, 1975	France	Archipel des Comores. Excluding island of Mayotte which remains a French Overseas Territory (Territoire d'Outre-Mer).
São Tomé and Príncipe	July 12, 1975	Portugal	(St. Thomas and Prince Islands)
Angola	November 11, 1975	Portugal	Includes detached enclave of Cabinda.
Western Sahara	February 28, 1976	Spain	(Rio de Oro and Sequit el Hamra) On Spanish withdrawal seized by Morocco. Occupation disrupted POLISARIO, formed May 10, 1973.
Seychelles	June 26, 1976	Britain	
Djibouti	June 27, 1977	France	(Territoire Française des Afars et des Issas formerly Côte Française des Somalis)
Zimbabwe	April 18, 1980	Britain	(Rhodesia, formerly Southern Rhodesia) Unilateral Declaration of Independence (UDI) in effect from November 11, 1965 to December 12, 1979. Federated with Northern Rhodesia and Nyasaland October 1, 1953 to December 31, 1963.
Namibia	March 21, 1990	South Africa	(South West Africa) UN Trust. Former German colony of Deutsche Sudwestafrika.
Eritrea	May 24, 1993	Italy Ethiopia	British administration 1941-1952. Federated with Ethiopia September 11, 1952. Union with Ethiopia November 14, 1962.

AFRICAN INDEPENDENCE
Chronology of African Independence

African Territories and Islands Not Independent

State	Colonial Power	Notes
Spanish North Africa	Spain	Plazas de Soberania: Ceuta, Islas Chafarinas Melilla, Penon de Velez de la Gomera, Penon de Alhucemas. Small enclaves and islands on the north coast of Morocco.
Madeira	Portugal	(Arquipelago da Madeira)
Canary Islands	Spain	(Islas Canarias)
St Helena with Ascension and Tristan da Cunha	Britain	British Crown Colony.
Socotra	Yemen	
Mayotte	France	Island of Comoros Group. Territoire Française d'Outre-Mer.
Reunion	France	Ile de la Réunion, Département d'Outre-Mer (from 1946).
French Indian Ocean Islands	France	Ile Europa, Ille Juan de Nova, Bassas da India, Iles Glorieuses, Tromelin (all near Madagascar).

Source: I. Griffiths, *The Atlas of African Affairs* (1994).

territories, but most importantly across them – the National Congress of British West Africa and later the West African Students Union notable among these. In North Africa, where European colonization had never eclipsed the merchant or administrative elites of the previous Ottoman Empire, elite movements such as the Young Algerians or Young Tunisians (*see* TUNISIA) claimed meaningful forms of citizenship. In EGYPT a relatively brief period of formal British rule gave way in 1922 to a restored Egyptian monarchy, besieged by students, commercial elite, and other "modernizers," and increasingly by mobilization among workers and peasants, all demanding that the state be truly independent, be truly national, and respond to their needs. Throughout North Africa, Islamic reform movements sought to purify social life and link the region to a broader Islamic world. In the 1940s these movements focused more clearly on demands for political autonomy, but with considerable disagreement over whether this should take place in relation to France or Great Britain, under a monarchy poised between traditionalist and modernizing political movements, or in an explicitly national form.

In South Africa from 1912, the AFRICAN NATIONAL CONGRESS (ANC) drew on Anglo-American traditions of peaceful petition and protest to insist that democracy made sense in Africa too. By World War II, young educated elite throughout Africa were adding a new militancy, linkages to labor movements, and connections to radical anti-imperialists in European and colonial capitals. In French Africa, the Rassemblement Démocratique Africain organized a wide political movement in 1946, and territorial political parties came under its umbrella.

Social action was necessarily political, and political action invariably had social implications. Yet a labor union was, first of all, a labor union, struggling for better wages and working conditions. In the 1945-1950 strike wave, unions in French Africa turned the government's idea of a single, transoceanic "France" into demands that all workers within that unit receive the same pay and benefits. Although political leaders saw workers as a constituency, and unions saw political action as useful to their cause, a tension between the idea of solidarity among workers and unity among Africans grew. Similarly, the wide variety of movements among peasants – against the intrusiveness of colonial agricultural projects, over land issues, against below-market prices paid to farmers by colonial crop marketing boards – must be seen in all their specificity, though every success any movement had contributed to a broader sense of empowerment.

It was the genius of men such as KWAME NKRUMAH and Léopold Senghor that they could bring together diverse movements and tendencies. They were machine politicians in the best sense of the word. They drew together the poor peasant hemmed in by colonial agricultural policies, the well-off merchant feeling the heavy hand of the European import-export houses, the railway worker facing barriers to advancement, the literate clerk trapped in the racial hierarchy of a bureaucracy, the lawyer espousing constitutional justice into what – for a time at least – was a coherent movement against the injustices of colonial states. Studies of politics in different territories stress that political parties both were constrained by regional and ethnic differences and cut across them, and in any case the affiliations that defined an "ethnic group" changed in the course of political mobilizations.

The institutions that colonial powers created failed to contain political mobilization, but they often channeled it in certain directions. After World War II, France and Great Britain – but not Portugal and Belgium – sought to open up electoral institutions that would co-opt elite Africans and justify the argument that colonial stewardship was preparing Africans for a democratic, modern future. Limited as these initially were, colonial political institutions defined a game with clear rules. Politics was encouraged when it took the form of electoral campaigns for the legislative body created for each colony, for the local councils, and in the French case the territorial units that elected representatives to the Paris legislature, where they would constitute a numerically small voice in the sovereign body. In NIGERIA or SENEGAL, businessmen, teachers, and trade unionists became the building blocks of early parties. However, in French Equatorial Africa – where a particularly brutal and exploitive form of colonization had been practiced – the electoral system created by the French after 1945 constituted its own political reality, in which politicians turned categories such as urban youth into political units and redrew the boundaries of ethnic affiliations to fit the constituencies they were organizing.

Meanwhile, other forms of political connection – from Pan-Africanism to Muslim brotherhoods – received no such representation, no such encouragement. Indeed, from Sétif (Algeria) in 1945 to MADAGASCAR in 1947 to Central Kenya in 1952 or CAMEROON in 1956 and most notoriously Algeria after 1954, colonial repression was brutal toward movements that strayed beyond quite unclear limits. Yet the interest of Great Britain and France in stopping "extremism" gave the "moderates" more room to maneuver. Nkrumah and later JOMO KENYATTA successfully combined enough mass support with enough demonstrated respect for existing economic and political institutions to shed the label of dangerous demagogue for that of responsible moderate. Whether "modern national mass movements" – as political scientists in the 1960s called them – were all that modern, all that national, or all that mass is a complicated question; the languages and networks of mobilization were indeed diverse and contradictory.

ABANDONING AN EMPIRE: THE FRENCH AND BRITISH CASES

For all their searching for the moderates with whom to negotiate the evolution of the colonial relationship, Great Britain and France soon became trapped in an expanding spiral of demands: for broadening the franchise, for giving more power to elected legislatures, for making good on promises of equivalent salaries for African workers and agricultural opportunities in rural areas. By insisting that European society and the European standard of living were models for the world, France and Great Britain in fact legitimated a wide range of claims on European budgets.

As early as 1951 or 1952, officials in France and Great Britain were complaining about the results of the development drive: that heavy public expenditure was failing to stimulate private investment, that the inadequate infrastructure was choking on the new

A street in Algiers shows damage from one of 117 bombs that exploded almost simultaneously on March 7, 1962, during the height of the battle for Algerian independence from France. *Express Newspapers/Archive Photos*

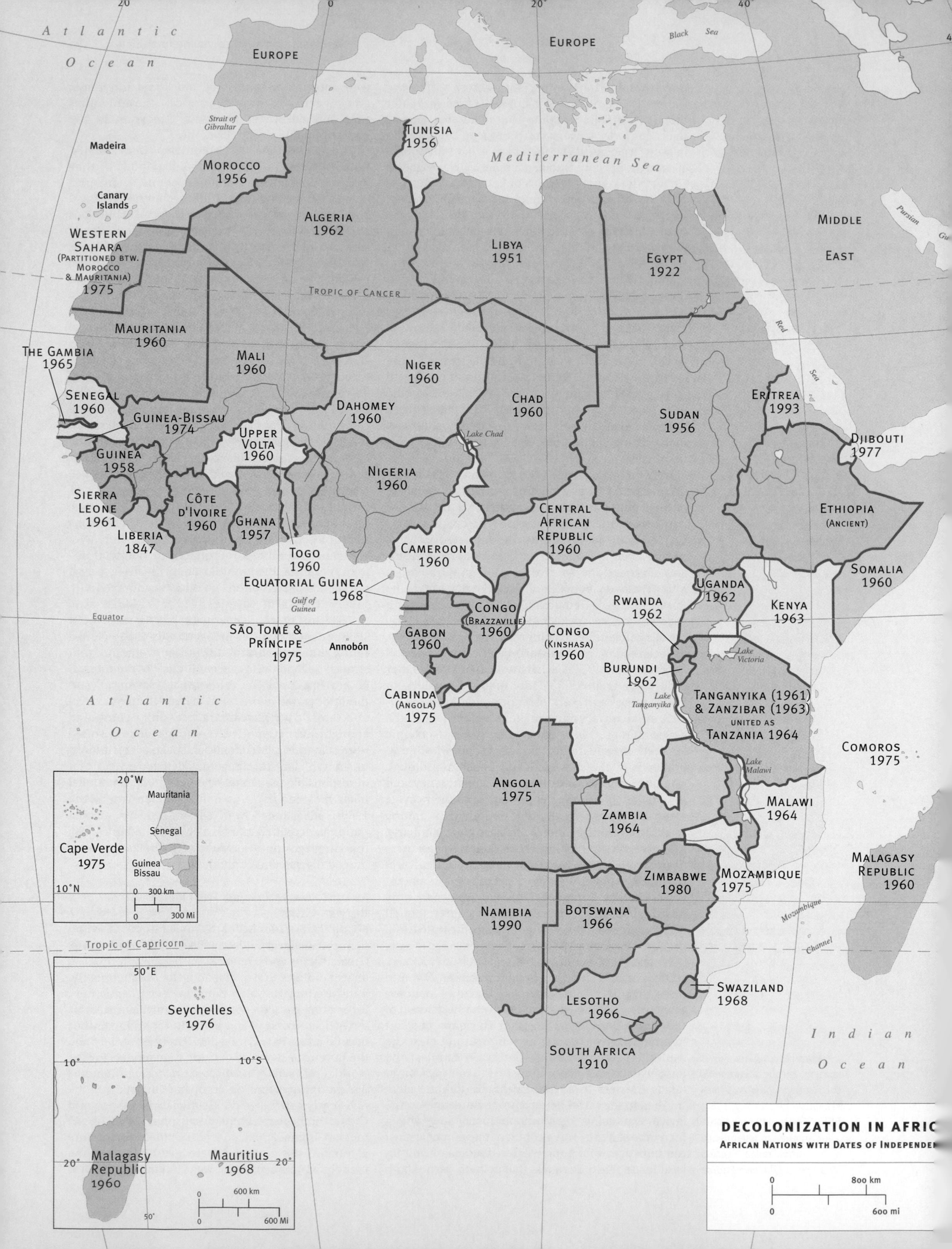
DECOLONIZATION IN AFRIC
AFRICAN NATIONS WITH DATES OF INDEPENDE
Atlantic Ocean
EUROPE
EUROPE
Black Sea
Mediterranean Sea
Strait of Gibraltar
Madeira
Canary Islands
MOROCCO 1956
TUNISIA 1956
ALGERIA 1962
LIBYA 1951
EGYPT 1922
MIDDLE EAST
Persian Gu
WESTERN SAHARA (PARTITIONED BTW. MOROCCO & MAURITANIA) 1975
TROPIC OF CANCER
MAURITANIA 1960
THE GAMBIA 1965
MALI 1960
NIGER 1960
CHAD 1960
SUDAN 1956
Red Sea
ERITREA 1993
SENEGAL 1960
GUINEA-BISSAU 1974
UPPER VOLTA 1960
DAHOMEY 1960
Lake Chad
DJIBOUTI 1977
GUINEA 1958
NIGERIA 1960
SIERRA LEONE 1961
CÔTE D'IVOIRE 1960
GHANA 1957
CENTRAL AFRICAN REPUBLIC 1960
ETHIOPIA (ANCIENT)
LIBERIA 1847
TOGO 1960
CAMEROON 1960
SOMALIA 1960
EQUATORIAL GUINEA 1968
UGANDA 1962
Gulf of Guinea
Equator
RWANDA 1962
KENYA 1963
SÃO TOMÉ & PRÍNCIPE 1975
Annobón
GABON 1960
CONGO (BRAZZAVILLE) 1960
CONGO (KINSHASA) 1960
Lake Victoria
BURUNDI 1962
Atlantic Ocean
CABINDA (ANGOLA) 1975
Lake Tanganyika
TANGANYIKA (1961) & ZANZIBAR (1963) UNITED AS TANZANIA 1964
COMOROS 1975
Lake Malawi
20°W
Mauritania
Senegal
Cape Verde 1975
Guinea Bissau
10°N
0 300 km
0 300 Mi
ANGOLA 1975
ZAMBIA 1964
MALAWI 1964
ZIMBABWE 1980
MOZAMBIQUE 1975
MALAGASY REPUBLIC 1960
NAMIBIA 1990
BOTSWANA 1966
Mozambique Channel
Tropic of Capricorn
50°E
Seychelles 1976
SWAZILAND 1968
LESOTHO 1966
SOUTH AFRICA 1910
Indian Ocean
10°
10°S
Malagasy Republic 1960
Mauritius 1968
20°
20°
0 600 km
0 600 Mi
50°
0 800 km
0 600 mi
20
0
20°
40°

Patrice Lumumba, leader of the movement for independence in the then Belgian Congo, is greeted by supporters as he arrives in Brussels for a conference in 1960. *CORBIS/Hulton-Deutsch Collection*

supplies coming in, that the lack of trained personnel (African and European) and the strength of African trade unions in ports, mines, and railways were driving up labor costs, and that African societies were stubbornly resisting colonial aspirations to change the way they produced and lived. Ironically, this was the great era of expansion of African exports – the most impressive of the colonial era – when exports of copper, COCOA, and coffee soared. But the act of imagination that had made "development" the watchword of colonialism created its own standards: officials began with an imagined end point – industrialization, European social relations, legislative institutions – rather than with the nature and dynamics of African societies themselves. Nor was the development project doing the political work expected of it: development efforts created more new points of conflict than they resolved (*see* DEVELOPMENT IN AFRICA: AN INTERPRETATION). More intensive agriculture by white or black farmers forced tenants off the land – a major cause of the rebellion in Kenya known as Mau Mau – and heavy-handed soil conservation or land consolidation projects led to peasant movements against this disruption of the harmony of relations with nature. Even the heroes of economic growth – prosperous cocoa farmers or owners of transportation fleets – often used their gains to challenge European-owned firms or support political activity that was critical of colonial rule.

By 1956 or 1957 British and French governments and part of the press were doing something they had not done before: coldly calculating the costs and benefits of empire. Old images that had once justified colonization now appeared in conservative arguments for letting go: Africa as vast, untamed space, inhabited by backward people, remote from the notions of "the citizen" or of "economic man" that the European elites associated with themselves. The two governments began to think about extricating themselves, a process that was as much an abdication of responsibility for the consequences of their own actions as the devolution of power.

Part of the postwar thinking about development and modernization eased the imaginative transition: development (unlike civilization) was a universal possibility, so that the European elites could expect that Africans would follow a foreordained path that would keep them in close relationship to Europe. But there was an element of cynicism too: an awareness growing out of the experiences of 1945-1955 of the conflict and uncertainty surrounding political and social change, and a desire that African governments, not European ones, be blamed for whatever went wrong.

African politicians had built their power bases within territories defined by the colonial powers. These boundaries and the institutions of state provided the basis for negotiated decolonization, marginalizing other kinds of affinities and aspirations. The recalculation was eased in GHANA by Nkrumah's espousal of his own variant of development, linking him economically to the very forces he criticized as neoimperialist; it was eased in MOROCCO and Tunisia by relatively coherent political movements willing to open the conservative elite to a measure of nationalism, but not too much. In Egypt, however, Gamal Nasser's coup of 1952 threw awry the neocolonial arrangements Great Britain had with the former regime and put in place a symbol of nationalism who influenced other decolonization struggles.

Great Britain and France had more trouble in colonies with white settlers, both because of the settlers' ability to play racial politics (and to threaten or effect a whites-only form of decolonization) and because of the intensity of social conflicts. It was most difficult of all for France to rethink its empire in Algeria. In this case, a divided French polity was caught between the Right's support of an "Algérie française" that denied Muslims full citizenship in their own country and the Left's attachment to "developing" Algeria, while Algerian nationalists themselves fought over strategies and objectives. A brutal colonial war from 1954 to 1962 called into question France's own republican principles. After 1962, newly liberated Algeria was torn by fighting and coups.

DECOLONIZATION IN PORTUGUESE AFRICA

The Portuguese Empire does not fit the timing outlined above. As a weak European power it lacked the confidence that its market power, capital, and technology could shape African evolution when it acted even slightly less "colonial." Moreover, Portugal itself was ruled by a dictatorship, and the legitimacy crisis that beset France and England after the war did not apply. Portugal set out to "develop" MOZAMBIQUE, ANGOLA, and GUINEA-BISSAU, but it was a thoroughly authoritarian version, entailing new waves of white emigration to Africa to take the leading roles in the "modern" sectors. But Portuguese Africa could not escape the ferment and opportunities around it – or the contradictions within. By the mid-1960s in Guinea-Bissau, Angola, and Mozambique, political movements, well aware of the liberation around them, had turned toward armed struggle, using bases in neighboring countries and a wide range of networks and affiliations, although the Portuguese limited their success by manipulating regional rivalries.

The Portuguese government had its own regional connections – with the white regimes of South Africa and, after 1965, Rhodesia (present-day Zimbabwe), which helped with military support as well as economic interaction. The region was caught up in cold war politics: Soviet support played an important role for nationalist movements such as the FRONT FOR THE LIBERATION OF MOZAMBIQUE (FRELIMO), POPULAR MOVEMENT FOR THE LIBERATION OF ANGOLA (MPLA), and PAIGC (as well as for the ANC in South Africa, and

ZANU and ZAPU in Rhodesia), and the United States quietly helped the South African and Portuguese militaries and some of the "anticommunist" guerrilla movements they sponsored, even while claiming to oppose racist governments. Portugal's entanglement with its African colonies and the effects of prolonged war came home to Portugal itself. A military coup d'état ended the dictatorship in 1974, and the decision of army and civilian moderates (some of whom knew African leaders from antigovernment networks) brought to an end over 400 years of colonization, in favor of an effort to "Europeanize" Portugal itself. As with the earlier decolonizations, this one involved an abdication of responsibility for the sins of colonial rule and for the viciousness of the final struggle itself, from the land mines and assassinations to the hasty pullout of Portuguese civil servants and professionals, seeking their European future.

White Rule in Southern Africa

The persistence of white rule in Rhodesia – to 1979 – and South Africa – to 1994 – has much to do with the ambiguity of the colonial situation there. For most Africans, these were the most colonial of colonial regimes, with a settled white population big enough to staff an effective military and bureaucracy, closely integrated into farms and industries that took control of African labor to ground (or below ground) level. But for many whites, particularly Afrikaans speakers (*see* Afrikaner), the sense of possessing the land in which they lived – and of having no "home" to go back to – was deep and the willingness to fight to stay strong. But their identification with Africa was not complete. Racial domination was also rooted in a sense of being "Western." And social life, especially as white society became relatively prosperous, implied belonging to a global bourgeoisie – of having access to the same commodities, sports events, and travel possibilities as Europeans and North Americans.

Here is where these regimes lost the battle of civilization, Christianity, progress, and democracy, a battle that had begun in the early twentieth century, when the first African national movements began to appropriate the vocabulary of democracy and rule of law. As much as liberation movements in Rhodesia and South Africa drew on affinities and a language of solidarity rooted in the daily lives of different African communities, they also built global networks via churches, labor unions, human rights and antiracist groups, and Pan-Africanist organizations – building on ideologies of self-determination and antiracism – to attack the legitimacy and sustainability of racist rule. In the end, the ruling regimes could not maintain unity and ideological coherence, even if for a time they could repress (but not eliminate) armed struggle. The last decolonization, 342 years after the original Dutch intrusion into South Africa, was, remarkably, a negotiated one.

The Consequences of Decolonization

What ended with the decolonizations of 1957-1965, of 1974, of 1979, and of 1994 were the very categories of empire and colony, of white rule. These had been considered normal for centuries; they ceased to be imaginable politically. Decolonization did not end social or political inequality, or the uneven power to determine what kinds of policies are discussible. The International Monetary Fund (IMF) is much better able to make the alleged mismanagement of exchange rates by an African government into an issue demanding correction than an African government is able to make the unavailability of clean water into a question requiring global action.

It would be a mistake either to see colonialism as a phenomenon that could be turned off like a television set – with all problems instantly turned into "African" problems – or to define a colonial "legacy" that determined what African polities could do, without considering the openings and closures that occurred during the process of struggle. The anxieties – and the brittle repressiveness – of new African rulers reflected as much their appreciation and fear of the diverse movements they had ridden to power as their inability to confront the divisions in society that colonial regimes had encouraged. Colonial regimes and their successors were gatekeeper states, facing great difficulty routinizing the exercise of power domestically outside of capital cities and commercial or mining centers, and best able to manipulate the interface between their country and the outside world. Their taxation power relied heavily on import-export controls, their patronage on insisting that outside resources pass through them. Their great fear was that social movements would draw on connections independent of the regime. Postcolonial gatekeeper states were more knowledgeable than colonial ones, better able to forge relations of clientelism within their boundaries, but without coercive power coming from without they were extremely vulnerable to any attempt to contest access to the gate itself. Hence the cycles of coups and military governments that beset Africa shortly after decolonization, and also the hostility of many governments to the political, intellectual, and cultural autonomy of their citizens.

Great Britain, France, and Belgium and later Portugal never learned how they could adapt state power to working with African societies as they actually were, not as they were imagined to be. In abdicating responsibility for the consequences of their own actions, the decolonizing powers assumed the easier task of judging how Africans carried out the tasks of "governance" that they themselves had been unable to perform. Such judgments need not be left unchallenged. The history of Africa from the 1940s reveals that many futures have been and can be imagined, that political mobilizations have taken place and can take place on a variety of lines, and that such mobilizations can turn what seemed impossible into an everyday fact. Such an observation applies as much to Africa's future as to its past.

See Also

Accra, Ghana; Mau Mau Rebellion; Nationalism in Africa; Senghor, Léopold Sédar; World War I and African Americans; Garvey, Marcus Mosiah; Nasser, Gamal Abdel.

North America

Dee, Ruby (b. October 27, 1924, Cleveland, Ohio) African American actress, writer, and social activist; the first black woman to play major parts in the American Shakespeare Festival at Stratford, Connecticut; and a major American film and television performer.

Ruby Dee, whose "frail sparrow figure,... bright, unsubdued eyes... [and] entire being, have a quality of wholeness that is rarely encountered in the theatre," was born Ruby Ann Wallace in Cleveland, Ohio. Her father, Marshall Edward Wallace, was a porter and waiter on the Pennsylvania Railroad; her mother, Emma Wallace, was a schoolteacher. They moved to Harlem while Ruby was a baby. Her education at Public School 119 was supplemented by classical literature and music at home. Although asked to leave Hunter College when her activities at the American Negro Theatre – a Harlem group that also included Hilda Simms, Harry Belafonte, and Sidney Poitier – took up too much of her energy and time, Dee graduated in 1945 with a B.A. in French and Spanish. She worked briefly as a translator for an import company, but her extracurricular activities soon became her career.

Dee's work has run the gamut of entertainment media; she has acted on stage and in film, television, and radio, and she has recorded poetry. Her Broadway debut, a walk-on part in *South Pacific* (a play about World War II that appeared before the Rogers and Hammerstein musical) came in 1943, while she was still at college. Only three years later, she appeared on Broadway in *Jeb* (1946), opposite her husband-to-be, Ossie Davis. They married in 1948, and have collaborated closely ever since. She achieved national recognition in the title role of *Anna Lucasta* (tour, 1946-1947) and went on to principal roles in *A Raisin in the Sun* (1959); *Purlie Victorious* (1961), subsequently filmed in 1963; and Athol Fugard's *Boesman and Lena* (1970), with James Earl Jones, for which she won an Obie in 1971. As Kate in *The Taming of the Shrew* (1965), and Cordelia in *King Lear*, she became the first black woman to play major parts in the American Shakespeare Festival. Most recently, she has appeared in *Two Hah Hahs and a Homeboy* (1995) with her husband and her son, Guy Davis.

Dee has appeared in over 20 films, most importantly as the baseball player's wife in *The Jackie Robinson Story* (1950), with Sidney Poitier in *Edge of the City* (1957), and in Spike Lee's *Do the Right Thing* (1989). Her television work is more extensive, including many guest appearances, the series *With Ossie and Ruby* (PBS, 1981), and dramas such as *Long Day's Journey into Night* (PBS, 1983). She has received numerous awards, including an Emmy for *Decoration Day* (NBC) in 1991, and a Literary Guild Award (1989) in recognition of her plays, poems and children's stories. She has been inducted into both the Black Filmmakers Hall of Fame (1975) and the Theater Hall of Fame (1988).

A well-known social activist and a member of the National Association for the Advancement of Colored People (NAACP) and the Southern Christian Leadership Conference, Dee speaks at many high-profile benefits. Having experienced firsthand the difficulties encountered by minorities in her profession, she established the Ruby Dee Scholarship in Dramatic Art for talented young black women.

See Also

World War II and African Americans; Belafonte, Harold George (Harry); Harlem, New York; Lee, Shelton Jackson ("Spike"); Television and African Americans; Film, Blacks in American.

Africa

Deforo, ethnic group of West Africa.

The Deforo primarily inhabit southern Mali and northern Burkina Faso. They speak a Niger-Congo language. Approximately 200,000 people consider themselves Deforo.

See Also

Languages, African: An Overview.

Africa

De Klerk, Frederik Willem (b. March 18, 1936, Johannesburg, South Africa), president of South Africa from 1989 to 1994 and co-winner of the 1993 Nobel Peace Prize.

F. W. De Klerk was born into an influential Afrikaner family with a long history of involvement in South African politics. His own political career began while he was still an adolescent, when he joined the youth section of the Afrikaner-dominated National Party.

In 1958 De Klerk received a law degree from Potchefstroom University. He practiced law in Veereniging from 1961 until 1972, all the while serving as chairman of the local chapter of the National Party. He then abandoned his law career and became a member of Parliament in South Africa. He rose quickly through the party's rank and file, with appointments to numerous cabinet posts. As a minister he had little patience for antiapartheid protests, but was known as a conciliator within the party.

After South African president Pieter Willem Botha had a heart attack in 1989, De Klerk became the leader of the National Party. Later that year the ailing Botha resigned and the Parliament elected De Klerk to replace him. Under Botha, the embattled government had already begun to relax certain apartheid restrictions, and De Klerk began his presidency by releasing several jailed senior leaders of the African National Congress (ANC), though not Nelson Mandela. In February 1990 De Klerk released Mandela, and the two began negotiations to end white minority rule. Within months, De Klerk had lifted the ban on African political parties. He also lobbied his own party to accept members of all races. In 1993 De Klerk and Mandela together won the Nobel Peace Prize.

In 1994 De Klerk ran as a National Party candidate in the first open elections in South Africa. Although he was returned to Parliament, the ANC had obtained the vast majority of seats, and Nelson Mandela ascended to the presidency. De Klerk joined Mandela's government as second deputy president.

Ari Nave

See Also

Antiapartheid Movement; Johannesburg, South Africa; Mandela, Nelson Rolihlahla; National Party.

North America

Delaney, Beauford (b. 1902, Knoxville, Tenn.; d. March 26, 1979, Paris, France), African American artist admired for his exquisite use of light and who painted portraits of many of the great figures of jazz.

Even as a young child growing up in Tennessee, Beauford Delaney was preoccupied with art, according to his younger brother, painter Joseph Delaney. Beauford Delaney received his first formal art training from Lloyd Branson, a white artist living in Knoxville. With Branson's encouragement, in 1924 Delaney went to Boston, where he studied painting at the Massachusetts Normal School, the South Boston School of Art, and the Copley Society.

In 1929 Delaney moved to New York City and held a variety of jobs while he established himself as a painter. Twelve of his portraits were displayed in a 1930 group show at the Whitney Studio Galleries (later the Whitney Museum of American Art). In exchange for working at the Whitney as a guard, telephone operator, and gallery attendant Delaney received studio space and a place to live. He had his first one-man exhibition in 1932 at the 135th Street Branch of the New York Public Library.

A music lover throughout his life, Delaney met and painted many of the great figures of jazz. W. C. Handy, Louis Armstrong, Duke Ellington, and Ethel Waters were among the musicians and singers who went to Delaney for their portraits. Additionally, he developed friendships with a wide range of writers and other artists in New York in the 1930s and 1940s. One of Delaney's closest friends was the novelist James Baldwin, who first visited Delaney's Greene Street studio (in the area now known as SoHo) when he was a teenager and always gave Delaney credit for showing him that a black American could make a

Artist Beauford Delaney poses next to several of his paintings. *Culver Pictures*

living as an artist. Other admirers included James Jones and Henry Miller, who published an essay titled "The Amazing and Invariable Beauford Delaney." Artist Georgia O'Keeffe painted a portrait of Delaney and composed a tribute to him for his 1973 one-man show in Paris.

Delaney is also remembered for his paintings of street scenes. Critics admired his use of color in these paintings and his efforts to convey the variations of light through more abstract paintings. "I learned about light from Beauford Delaney," Baldwin wrote in a 1965 issue of *Transition* magazine. In 1978 the Studio Museum in Harlem dedicated the first show of its Black Masters series to Delaney's work. His art was also exhibited in a one-man show at the Philippe Briet Gallery in 1991.

Delaney left New York for Paris in 1953 and remained there until his death. Because of his generosity to friends, Delaney struggled financially even after he became a successful artist. In 1961 he suffered a nervous breakdown. Although he continued to paint, he never fully recovered. He entered St. Anne's, a psychiatric hospital in Paris, in 1975, and died there four years later.

Lawrie Balfour

See Also
Armstrong, Louis ("Satchmo"); Boston, Massachusetts; Handy, William Christopher (W.C.); Harlem, New York; New York, New York; Ellington, Edward Kennedy ("Duke"); Art, African American.

North America

Delaney, Joseph

(b. September 13, 1904, Knoxville, Tenn.; d. November 20, 1991, Knoxville, Tenn.), African American artist known for his paintings of people, in individual portraits and in groups.

Joseph Delaney, the tenth child of Joseph and Delia Delaney, became a painter. His older brother, Beauford Delaney, was also a painter, but their styles differed greatly; Beauford painted abstract works, while Joseph painted representations of people, in portraits and in crowd scenes.

Joseph Delaney's canvases portray groups of people in everyday settings – as they go to church (*Harlem Sunday Morning*), participate in poignant events (*Penn Station in Wartime*, 1943), or join in comradeship (*Waldorf Cafeteria*, 1945, and *Easter Parade*, 1969). His expressionist works depict crowds; he shows them ice skating, riding the subway, or celebrating the end of a war. *Times Square, V-J Day* (1961) was painted 16 years after Delaney witnessed the joyous emotions of that day. Surreal elements, such as messages and crucifixions in the sky above, heighten the fervid scene.

Delaney began studying at the Art Students League in New York in 1930 with the artist and teacher Thomas Hart Benton, whose call for American scenes depicting people had a great influence on Delaney and his fellow students, including artists Jackson Pollock and George Bridgman. Delaney continued painting at the league until 1985. During the Great Depression he worked as a model, waiter, and window washer, but he also received some portrait commissions from society women. In that period he also taught drawing and participated in the creation of the *Index to American Design*.

Returning to Knoxville in 1985, Delaney became an artist-in-residence at the University of Tennessee, where he worked until the time of his death in 1991. His paintings are in private collections and in several public collections, including the Knoxville Art Museum, the National Museum of American Art, Clark-Atlanta University, and the University of Arizona Museum of Art.

Betty Gubert

See Also
Art, African American.

North America

Delany, Martin Robison

(b. May 6, 1812, Charles Town, Va. [present-day Charleston, W. Va.]; d. June 24, 1885, Wilberforce, Ohio), African American abolitionist, black nationalist, and author; the highest ranking African American officer during the Civil War.

During the nineteenth century Martin Robison Delany was a prominent African American leader, but his repeated political shifts undermined his standing and obscured his legacy. Recently, historian Sterling Stuckey has emphasized Delany's role in the development of black nationalist thought, concluding that his life and thought exerted an influence on W. E. B. Du Bois.

Delany was the son of a slave father and a free mother; her free status made her son free as well. As a child, he moved to Chambersburg, Pennsylvania. He attracted the attention of a prosperous mentor, John B. Vashon, who paid for his education. White abolitionist William Lloyd Garrison described him as "black as jet and a fine fellow of great energy and spirit," but Delany's separatist views alienated many potential allies.

In contrast to Frederick Douglass, whose outlook was integrationist, Delany stressed the importance of blacks' African heritage and the need for black self-reliance. African Methodist Episcopal Church (AME) bishop Daniel Payne wrote that Delany was "too intensely African to be popular.... Had his love for humanity been as great as his love for his race," Payne believed, his influence might have equaled that of Douglass.

Delany had a varied career. In 1843 he began practicing medicine and during 1850-1851 he attended Harvard Medical School. He wrote several books, including a novel, *Blake, or the Huts of America*, which was published serially in 1859 and in 1861-1862. Later in life, he dealt in real estate. But his true importance was as an advocate for African Americans. During the 1840s he published the *Mystery* (1843-1847), the first black-owned newspaper west of the Alleghenies. From 1847 to 1849 he joined Douglass as coeditor of the *Rochester North Star*. During the 1840s Delany wrote antislavery pamphlets, helped escaping slaves on their way to freedom, and staunchly opposed the efforts of the American Colonization Society to colonize blacks in Africa or assist them in emigrating elsewhere, which he viewed as a form of forced exile.

During the tumultuous 1850s, however, Delany changed his views. He began advocating emigration from the United States, for example, in *The Condition, Elevation, Emigration, and Destiny of the Colored People of the United States* (1852), the first book-length study of the status of African Americans. In 1856 he moved with his family to Chatham, Canada West (present-day Ontario). Delany was the only prominent black leader present at a gathering held in Chatham at which John Brown announced the formation of a rebel black state in exile and began planning for his 1859 raid on the federal armory at Harpers Ferry, Virginia.

During the 1850s Delany concentrated his prodigious energies on emigration and colonization ventures. He played a leading role in African American emigration conferences held in 1854, 1856, and 1858. Late in 1858 he set sail for West Africa. In 1859, after visiting Alexander Crummell in Liberia, Delany signed a treaty with Alake of Abeokuta, in present-day Nigeria, to allow African American settlement and the development of cotton production using free West African workers. But the coming of the Civil War disrupted those plans.

During the Civil War Delany served as a recruiting officer for the Commonwealth of Massachusetts, raising black troops for the Union army. In 1865 he was commissioned a major, making him the highest ranking black officer of the war. He was transferred to South Carolina and became the first African American to be given a field command. Following the war, he worked for the Freedmen's Bureau in South Carolina, which led to political office during the Reconstruction era.

During the 1870s Delany grew disenchanted with South Carolina's Reconstruction government and criticized fellow blacks and white carpetbaggers. In 1876 he announced his support for the Democratic candidate for governor, Wade Hampton III, who had been one of the richest slaveholders in the South. Hampton won and within two years had swept Delany and every other black official from state office. In his final years, Delany published *Principia of Ethnology: The Origin of Races with an Archaeological Compendium of Ethiopian and Egyptian Civilization* (1879) and was active in the ill-fated Liberian Exodus Joint-Stock Steamship Company.

James Clyde Sellman

See Also

Abeokuta, Nigeria; Abolitionism in the United States; Bureau of Refugees, Freedmen and Abandoned Lands; Civil War, American; Du Bois, William Edward Burghardt (W. E. B.); Payne, Daniel Alexander; Black Nationalism in the United States.

North America

Delany, Samuel R. (b. April 1, 1942, New York, N.Y.), African American science fiction writer, literary critic, and nonfiction author known as an important voice in African American literature and gay literature.

Samuel R. Delany's early work played a major role in the development of a more literary "new wave" in science fiction during the 1960s. In a genre known previously for its ideas rather than stylistic innovation, Delany's fist novels were heavily influenced by the formal experimentation of modernist and postmodernist writers such as James Joyce, Ralph Ellison, and Djuna Barnes, as well as the work of such leading science fiction writers as Isaac Asimov and Theodore Sturgeon.

Delany's writing was largely concerned with technology and the development of artistic and outlaw subcultures on the margins of society, anticipating the later "cyberpunk" trend in video, film, fiction, and graphic art. Delany's fiction may have been influenced by his being one of the very few African American science fiction writers of his generation, and by his open homosexuality (though he also had significant heterosexual relationships); from the beginning his work took up the issues of race and sexuality with a seriousness never before seen in mainstream science fiction. Since the 1970s his fiction and nonfiction work have increasingly been concerned with the investigation of race and sexuality, establishing him as one of the most powerful chroniclers of an African American gay sensibility.

Delany was born April 1, 1942, in New York City to Samuel R. Delany Sr., a successful funeral director, and Margaret Carey, a staff member of the New York Public Library. He grew up in Harlem, graduated from Bronx High School of Science, and attended the City College of New York. He married the poet Marilyn Hacker in 1961. They were divorced in 1980 and have one daughter.

Delany's first novel, *The Jewels of Aptor*, appeared in 1962. He won the first of his five Nebula Awards (the major award in science fiction) for his 1966 novel *Babel-17*. He has also won other major science fiction accolades such as the Hugo Award and the Pilgrim Award. The postmodern epic *Dhalgren* (1975) is considered by some critics to be Delany's most intriguing novel. Its protagonist is a bisexual African American named Kid who comes to a largely abandoned American city after an unnamed disaster. The novel describes Kid's experiences with the subcultures of the desperate, deviant, and/or voyeuristic people who remain in the city.

More recently Delany has focused on nonfiction writing. *The Motion of Life in Water* (1988), his autobiographical account of the intersection of the 1960s counterculture and the gay subculture of New York, has been widely acclaimed. His academic work as a teacher and literary critic has also become more prominent. He has been a member of the faculty of the University of Massachusetts at Amherst since 1988.

James Smethurst

See Also

Race: An Interpretation; Literature, African American; Harlem, New York; New York, New York.

North America

De La Soul, hip hop band from Long Island, New York.

De La Soul was formed in 1987 while its founders – Posdnous (Kelvin Mercer), Trugoy the Dove (David Joliceur), and Pasemaster Mase (Vincent Mason) – were still in high school. In 1989 the trio released its debut, *3 Feet High and Rising*. The highly acclaimed album was produced by Prince Paul of the rap group Stetsasonic, and it featured the smash hit "Me, Myself, and I," as well as offbeat tracks like "Plug Tunin'" and "Buddy." De La Soul sampled from a diverse group of sources, including the children's series "Schoolhouse Rock," a French language instruction manual, and the rock group the Turtles. The unauthorized use of this last sample resulted in a lawsuit with broader implications: the era of unrestricted sampling that had accompanied the rise of rap was over.

The success of *3 Feet High and Rising* made De La Soul the best-known representative of the Native Tongues posse – a hip hop clique that included the Jungle Brothers, Monie Love, A Tribe Called Quest, Queen Latifah, and Black Sheep. The Native Tongues sound was eclectic, but it was generally characterized by intelligent and idiosyncratic lyrics and laid-back beats.

De La Soul never fully capitalized on its sudden fame. While their debut had celebrated the D.A.I.S.Y. Age (often explained as Da Inner Sound, Y'all), *De La Soul Is Dead* (1991) was a playful and ambitious record that never quite found its audience. Its cover art – a wilted daisy – was intended to be symbolic of the band's artistic independence, but instead it came to represent their diminishing marketability. Nevertheless, the band continued to find critical acclaim in the face of industry indifference. Their third album, *Buhloone Mindstate* (1993), was by turns gritty, funky, and sublime; it opened with the trio chanting, "It might blow up but it won't go pop."

Three years later De La Soul released *Stakes Is High* (1996), which displayed a mature lyrical dexterity and an impressive array of subtle beats. If the group's recent career has been something of a commercial disappointment, they have nevertheless established themselves as one of the most original and important hip hop groups of the 1990s.

Andrew Du Bois

See Also
Hip Hop in the United States.

North America

DeLavallade, Carmen

(b. March 6, 1931, New Orleans, La.), African American dancer and choreographer long associated with Alvin Ailey.

Born to Creole parents, Carmen DeLavallade grew up in Los Angeles, where she was raised by an aunt. At age 16 she won a scholarship to study with modern dance pioneer Lester Horton, from whom she received broad training in ballet, modern, and ethnic dancing and in music, acting, set design, costuming, and lighting. She became a lead dancer in Horton's company in 1950, dancing Salome, a role he created for her, in *The Face of Violence*.

At this time, DeLavallade began her long association with Alvin Ailey. Between 1950 and 1954, she danced in four films, including *Carmen Jones* (1955). She later performed in several television productions, including Duke Ellington's *A Drum Is a Woman* (1957). DeLavallade moved to New York in 1954, where she danced in the Broadway musical *House of Flowers*. It was during this production that she met and married Geoffrey Holder, a fellow dancer and choreographer who created several dances for her, including her signature solo, *Come Sunday*. In 1956 she succeeded her cousin as prima ballerina at the Metropolitan Opera, dancing in *Aïda* and *Samson et Delila*. In the midst of her career, in 1957, DeLavallade gave birth to a son.

By the early 1960s DeLavallade had become an important guest artist in Ailey's company, accompanying it on its first European tour in 1962. She danced with Agnes deMille's American Ballet Theater in 1965, and in 1966 won a *Dance Magazine* award. DeLavallade taught for many years at the Yale School of Drama while continuing to dance. She appeared with the Bill T. Jones/Arnie Zane Dance Company at the Joyce Theater in New York in October 1993.

See Also
Creoles; Los Angeles, California; New York, New York; Television and African Americans; Ellington, Edward Kennedy ("Duke").

Latin America and the Caribbean

Delgrès, Louis

(b. 1772, Saint-Pierre, Martinique; d. May 28, 1802, Matouba, Guadeloupe), Guadeloupean heroic leader of the first major slave rebellion of Guadeloupe in 1802.

Little is known of the early life of this important figure, whose name appeared in Guadeloupean schoolbooks only recently. By all accounts he was of mixed race; it is widely assumed that his father was white and his mother black, though some sources claim the reverse. Louis Delgrès arrived in Guadeloupe as a member of the Antilles Battalion in 1795, during a complicated period in the history of the French Caribbean Islands. Slavery had been abolished in the colonies on February 4, 1794, by the revolutionary government in France. At the same time, the French were at war with the British over possession of several French islands, most notably Martinique, Sainte-Lucie, and Saint-Vincent.

To further complicate matters for the revolutionary administration in Guadeloupe in whose army Delgrès served, Toussaint L'Ouverture's plans to create an independent black republic in Saint-Domingue (present-day Haiti) started taking shape that same year. It was the aim of the Guadeloupean administration to ensure that the events taking place in Saint-Domingue would not take place on their island. As a result, many of the ostensibly free blacks were forced to remain on the plantations. But free mulattos were able to acquire a certain degree of power, as Delgrès did in two military campaigns on Sainte-Lucie and Saint-Vincent, during which he distinguished himself, earning the rank of battalion chief (commander) in 1799. But his real importance grew out of the events of 1801-1802.

Upon hearing that mulattos were assuming increasing power in Guadeloupe, Napoleon is said to have vowed that he would not "leave a pair of epaulets on the shoulders of a Negro." Napoleon's army of 3470 soldiers, led by Commander Richepanse, arrived in Pointe-à-Pitre, Guadeloupe, on May 6, 1802, to reimpose slavery. The mulatto governor of the island, Magloire Pélage, did not resist. But Delgrès, along with Captain Ignace, fled to the countryside, recruiting freed mulattos and blacks as they went, calling on them to "live in freedom or die." Heavy fighting ensued between the disorganized but determined troops of Delgrès, which included many women, and the army of Richepanse. During the several weeks of fighting, Delgrès inspired his soldiers with his devotion to the cause. He is known, for instance, to have played his violin while straddling a cannon aimed at Richepanse's troops.

After several stunning victories, the rebellion suffered a psychological blow on May 20, when Richepanse ordered black soldiers to fight with him against their own. The following day, Captain Ignace and about 800 of his rebel soldiers were massacred at Fort Baimbridge by Governor Pélage's troops. With the enemy closing in and the rebellion seemingly crushed, Delgrès and his troops prepared themselves for their final act. They gathered in a plantation house in the town of Matouba, placing a large stock of powderkegs around them. As Richepanse's soldiers attacked the rebels in great numbers at the entrance to the plantation, Delgrès set off the gunpowder, obliterating himself, his loyal troops, and a good part of Richepanse's army.

Following the tragic end to the rebellion, slavery was reimposed (it was finally abolished in 1848). Nearly all the blacks and mulattos who had professed loyalty to Delgrès were killed. The black soldiers who had fought with Governor Pélage were exiled, some of them sold as slaves in the United States. The mulatto officers, including Pélage, were arrested and deported to prison colonies in France, Senegal, and Madagascar. The ambiguity of the Delgrès figure in the historical imagination of Guadeloupeans is rendered in Daniel Maximin's novel *Lone Sun* (1989).

Richard Watts

See Also
Maximin, Daniel; Slavery in Latin America and the Caribbean; St. Lucia; St. Vincent and the Grenadines; Toussaint L'Ouverture, François Dominique; Abolition and Emancipation in Latin America and the Caribbean; Slave Rebellions in Latin America and the Caribbean.

North America

Dellums, Ronald V. (Ron)

(b. November 24, 1935, Oakland, Calif.), African American congressman who fought to limit military spending in favor of social welfare.

Ron Dellums earned an A.A. from Oakland City College, a B.A. from San Francisco State University, and an M.S.W. in psychiatric social work from the University of California at Berkeley. He was elected to the United States House of Representatives in 1970, after campaigning on his intention to end U.S. military involvement in Vietnam and his vow to fight for social justice in the United States and abroad.

Dellums was consistently a liberal voice in Congress. He fought to cut U.S. military spending, and sought a position on the House Armed Services Committee (which he chaired in 1993) to increase his knowledge of the military so that he could argue more effectively for military spending reductions. He worked to increase federal financial support for social programs, such as his national health care plan, which he first introduced in 1977.

Dellums sponsored bills to grant amnesty to resisters of the Vietnam War and to grant reparations to Japanese-Americans who were interned during World War II. He strongly supported the Equal Rights Amendment for women and worked to help create the Department of Education. In the area of foreign policy, he sponsored a bill for U.S. sanctions against South Africa for its apartheid policies for 15 years before it finally passed in 1986. In 1991 he opposed U.S. participation in the Persian Gulf War. He retired in February 1998 after 27 years in the House.

Robert Fay

See Also
World War II and African Americans; Vietnam War.

Africa

Dendi (also known as the Dandawa and the Dandi), ethnic group of West Africa.

The Dendi primarily inhabit BENIN, NIGER, and NIGERIA. They speak Songhai, a Nilo-Saharan language. Though they share cultural practices with other Songhai peoples, they have MANDE origins. Approximately 100,000 people consider themselves Dendi.

SEE ALSO
Languages, African: An Overview; Songhai People.

North America

Denmark Vesey Conspiracy, an extensively organized but thwarted plan to end slavery in South Carolina.

During the summer of 1822 an ex-slave named Denmark Vesey, who had purchased his freedom by winning a lottery 23 years earlier, gathered more than 9000 South Carolina slaves for an insurrection. The plan was to seize weapons and travel throughout the state to kill white slaveholders and liberate their slaves. Like past slave risings, the Denmark Vesey conspiracy was proof that slaves would go to great lengths to attain their freedom.

The word "conspiracy," which has acquired largely negative connotations, conveyed the unwillingness of most slaveholders to recognize the discontent among slaves condemned to an inhuman existence. The word also indicated the intense fear of slave uprisings that gripped the antebellum white South. Although the fear was common to most slaveholders, it was particularly strong in South Carolina. As far back as 1730 the whites there had found themselves outnumbered by their slaves, a distinction unique to the state. Most of the slaves worked in deplorable conditions, and those blacks who were free faced continuous hostility from whites. By 1822 conditions were ripe for a violent slave rebellion in the state, but the missing ingredient was a forceful leader. That leader was Denmark Vesey.

Around 1783 Vesey had arrived in Charleston as a young captive of a Bermuda slave trader named Joseph Vesey. A literate man and an avid reader of the Bible, Denmark could recite passages that condemned slavery. In 1799 his life changed dramatically: he won $1500 in the East Bay Street lottery and bought his freedom with $600 of his winnings. As a freedman, Vesey undertook carpentry as his trade, and had garnered $8000 by 1822, a fortune for an African American of that time.

Despite his personal prosperity, Vesey deplored the treatment of South Carolina blacks, both free and slave. Most of the state's 260,000 slaves worked in malaria-infested rice fields, and the more than 3000 free blacks were confined to Charleston, where they worked as longshoremen, shopkeepers, and house servants. With their conditions worsening, Denmark grew impatient and organized a massive disruption of the South Carolina slave empire.

Recruitment was based on the antiwhite sentiment of Charleston's slaves and the growing discontent of Charleston's free blacks. It took place at meetings held in local African churches and black carpentry shops. During the gatherings fiery speeches were read aloud, recalling the Virginia slave uprising led by Gabriel Prosser in 1800 and the revolution in Haiti. As Vesey and his aides perfected their appeals, the insurgents grew in number and diversity. Enslaved mechanics, sawyers, and lumberyard workers as well as blacks from different linguistic, religious, and ethnic backgrounds enlisted in the cause. Members of Vesey's inner circle even sent letters to HAITI, asking former slaves to join the attack in mid-July.

Despite the efforts at secrecy, the plan was betrayed on May 30. Denmark tried to push the insurrection forward to June 16, but to no avail. White officials offered black informants modest cash awards and immediately arrested the conspirators. On July 2, Vesey was captured. He refused to confess and was executed along with 34 other blacks. Thirty-seven men were deported to unknown locations.

Although the Denmark Vesey slave uprising was crushed by white officials, it left a mark on South Carolina society. The state legislature passed stringent laws restricting African American movement and requiring free black sailors docked in state ports to be jailed until their ship's departure. Denmark, after his death, was scorned by whites and revered by blacks. A recent proposal to erect a Vesey memorial in downtown Charleston sparked a firestorm of controversy.

Alonford James Robinson, Jr.

SEE ALSO
Free Blacks in the United States, 1619 to 1863; Gabriel Prosser Conspiracy; Haitian Revolution.

Cross Cultural

Dentistry, medical care and treatment of the teeth.

The earliest health remedies noted anywhere for care of the teeth are associated with North Africa. Dentistry was already practiced in Pharonic EGYPT by the time of priest Imhotep in about 2500 B.C.E. The name hieroglyphs of the world's first recorded dentist, Hesy-ra, and the title *ibhy* (dentist, a tusk-sign) appear on an inscription at Sakkara.

Although the Egyptians were superior surgeons and skilled at setting bones, operative dentistry was apparently not practiced in ancient Egypt. Thus there is no evidence in the dental remains of Egyptian mummies of teeth that were drilled and filled. The major dental problem of ancient desert-dwelling Egyptians was severely worn molars caused by airborne sand particles that mixed with bread dough being prepared for meals. As people chewed their bread, the sand ground away the cusps of their molars, sometimes eroding them to the gum line.

Most dental work in ancient North Africa involved prescribing herbal remedies, including mouthwashes, powders, and salves; soothing inflamed gums and loose and painful teeth; healing periodontal disease; and treating minor wounds in the oral cavity and on the lips. One very interesting archaeological find, however, appears to have been a set of ancient North African false teeth consisting of some natural teeth that were held together with gold wire, and attached in the wearer's mouth to the intact teeth.

MODERN DENTISTRY

Early United States dental practitioners were trained through apprenticeships, and by 1840, 125 African Americans had completed such instruction. Schools of dentistry did not exist until 1840 with the opening of Baltimore College of Dental Surgery. The first African American to be licensed as a practicing dentist, Robert Tanner Freeman, received the dentistry degree with the initial graduating class of the Harvard Dental School in 1869. A dental society was later named in his honor. The first black woman to receive a dental degree was Ida Gray Nelson Rollins, who graduated from the University of Michigan in 1890.

Dental departments were established at HOWARD UNIVERSITY in 1881 and at Meharry Medical College in 1886. Meharry was the first U.S. dental school to require a hospital-based four-year curriculum. Edward L. Turner, who became the School of Dentistry's supervisor in 1941, wrote in a 1939 edition of the college *Bulletin:* "I believe this school has an unique opportunity to develop an unusual type of dental teaching where medicine is stressed in teaching and dental aspects of diseases are amply stressed in medicine." Since then Meharry has attained renown as a school in which dentistry has been placed squarely in the context of general medicine. Thus dental school students study the whole person in assessing the condition of the teeth and mouth, and medical school students strive to explore the oral and dental effects of smoking, infant teething, and systemic illnesses like SICKLE CELL ANEMIA.

Of about 15,000 licensed dentists in the United States in 1885, only 25 were African Americans, a proportion that has remained low to this day. The National Medical Association, an organization that brought together and promoted the interests of black doctors, dentists, and pharmacists, emerged in 1895, and two years later black dentists had their own professional society, the National Dental Association.

Following World War I, the enrollment of blacks in the nation's dental schools increased dramatically. L. H. Jenkins, a 1924 graduate of Meharry School of Dentistry, recalled that before dawn on the first day of school, dozens of young African American men were lined up in front of the registrar's office. The 1930s Depression, however, led to a sharp decline in black enrollment, and the dental school at Meharry faced the possibility of closing. In 1945, with the end of World War II, enrollments again flourished, reaching 200 percent of Meharry's 1942 level. In 1945 the dental programs at both Howard and Meharry were granted full accreditation by the American Dental Association.

Meharry School of Dentistry took the lead in reaching out to the community and embracing black schoolchildren in its clinical program. In 1943 the school had four renovated clinics to serve the needs of the people. Cooperating with the Nashville school board, the dental students set up a public health field program in black primary and secondary schools to provide dental examinations and corrective work, as well as free toothbrushes packaged in test tubes for all the children. The traditional dental program involving local public school children has continued at Meharry ever since.

The number of practicing U.S. black dentists has remained disproportionately small. In 1990 only 2.6 percent of 148,800 dentists in the United States were African Americans.

Barbara Worley

See Also

World War I and African Americans; World War II and African Americans; Great Depression.

Latin America and the Caribbean

Depestre, René

(b. August 29, 1926, Jacmel, Haiti), poet, novelist, essayist, and left-wing activist whose politically committed yet evocative works bear the stamp of the Haiti he was forced to abandon at the age of 20.

Following the death of his father, René Depestre was raised in dire economic circumstances by his maternal grandmother. He later spent the last years of secondary school in Port-au-Prince.

It was in Haiti's capital city in 1942 that Depestre encountered one of his future exemplars, Alejo Carpentier. The Cuban novelist's conception of magical realism would have a profound effect on Depestre. Soon thereafter Depestre was thrust into the literary and political spotlight. His first collection of poems, *Etincelles* (1945), published when he was just 19, won him considerable praise.

But it was a journal founded by Depestre and Jacques Stéphen Alexis, *La Ruche*, that established Depestre's reputation as a political radical. Following the government's seizure of an issue of *La Ruche* devoted to André Breton in 1945, Depestre and Alexis helped organize a general strike that led to the eventual overthrow of President Elie Lescot in 1946. The government of Dumarsais Estimé that replaced Lescot's dictatorship was leery of Depestre's strong left-wing sympathies (his second book of poetry, *Gerbe de sang* [1946] was as violently political as *Etincelles*, 1945) and sent him to Paris on a government scholarship. He was expelled from France in 1951 following his involvement in anticolonial demonstrations, but not before he had published *Végétations de clartés*.

Following a short stay in Prague, Depestre accepted the invitation of Cuban poet Nicolás Guillén to come to Havana, but was almost immediately expelled by the government of Fulgencio Batista. After several years in South America, Depestre returned to Paris, where he worked with several activist journals, including *Présence Africaine*.

In 1959 Depestre returned to a Haiti controlled by François Duvalier and immediately began decrying the latter's "totalitarian Négritude." He was forced to leave Haiti that same year and arrived in a Cuba under the leadership of Fidel Castro. Although he was named adviser to the Cuban national publishing house by Che Guevara and received a teaching post at the University of Havana, Depestre was critical of the Castro regime. He left Cuba and the Communist Party in 1978. Two poetic works published during his time in Cuba, *Poésie cubaine* (1967) and *Poète à Cuba* (1976), nonetheless focus on the heroism of the Cuban Revolution and the dangers of American imperialism. From Cuba, Depestre went to Paris to work for UNESCO, where he remained until his retirement in 1986.

The creative work from his prolific second stay in France includes one book of poems, *En état de poésie* (1980); two novels, *Le mât de cocagne* (1979) and *Hadriana de tous mes rêves* (1988; Prix Renaudot); and two collections of short stories, *Alléluia pour une femme-jardin* (1981) and *Eros dans un train chinois* (1990). It is also during this time that he wrote one of his best-known works, *Bonjour et adieu à la négritude* (1980), an essay that suggests some of the shortcomings of the Négritude ideology.

Depestre has been called a "rooted nomad," for even though he has spent most of his life in exile, his work is firmly rooted in Haiti. For all their revolutionary ardor, Depestre's poems also manage to evoke the myths of Haitian Vodou. They are likewise replete with images of a sexuality that is divorced from guilt and sin. For most critics of Depestre, it is in *Un arc-en-ciel pour l'occident chrétien* (1967) that these three poetic elements – political commitment, eroticism, and Vodou – are most harmoniously expressed.

Richard Watts

See Also

Présence Africaine; Port-au-Prince, Haiti; Literature, French Language, in Caribbean; Havana, Cuba.

North America

DePriest, Oscar Stanton

(b. March 9, 1871, Florence, Ala.; d. May 12, 1951, Chicago, Ill.), first African American elected to the United States Congress since Reconstruction and first-ever African American congressman from the North.

Oscar Stanton DePriest was the son of former slaves. His father, a part-time farmer and hauler, and his mother, a laundress, fled Southern poverty and racism in 1878, settling in Kansas as part of the Exoduster migration. DePriest left home when he was 17. He lived first in Ohio and then in Chicago, where he worked as a painter and decorator. By 1905 he owned his own painting and decorating business and in another decade capitalized on the Great Migration that brought tens of thousands of blacks to South Chicago by opening a lucrative real estate practice.

DePriest became active in politics, delivering black votes to Chicago's powerful Republican Party. He was rewarded in 1904 when he was elected as a Cook County commissioner, a post he lost in 1908. In the following years he threw his support to both black and white candidates, Republicans and Democrats, and in 1915 became Chicago's first black alderman, as a Republican. Two years later DePriest was indicted for ties to organized crime. Although acquitted in 1918 (with the help of lawyer Clarence Darrow), he stepped down from the city council pending elections.

Throughout the 1920s DePriest continued selling real estate and practicing politics, eventually becoming the leading black broker of power for Republican mayor William ("Big Bill") Hale Thompson. When one of Chicago's incumbent Republican congressmen died during the 1928 election campaign, a Republican committee chose DePriest to replace him. Again indicted for underworld ties, DePriest nonetheless defeated his white Democratic opponent, largely on the strength of the black vote. In 1929 he became the first African American in Congress in 28 years. After the election, the indictment was dropped for lack of evidence.

In Congress, DePriest launched several unsuccessful measures related to race. One bill would have allowed a court defendant to move his trial if he feared an unfair hearing because of his race or religion. Another bill would have fined and jailed officials who allowed prisoners to fall into the hands of a mob; if a lynching occurred, the county would have had to pay the victim's relatives $10,000. DePriest also opened a rancorous debate by proposing that blacks be allowed to eat in the House restaurant. (As a congressman, the prohibition did not apply to him.)

Among DePriest's successes was a bill that prohibited the Civilian Conservation Corps, a New Deal work program, from discriminating in hiring. DePriest also increased Congress's appropriation to Howard University and sent black appointments to the U.S. Military Academy at West Point and the U.S. Naval Academy at Annapolis. Ignoring threats to his life, he spoke widely in the South, where he urged blacks to organize and vote. When a southern newspaper criticized DePriest for advocating equality, he reportedly responded, "They have Jim Crow theatre laws and Jim Crow streetcar laws, but what they need is Jim Crow bedroom laws."

DePriest's years in Congress saw the abandonment of the Republican Party by African Americans in favor of the Democratic Party. Although DePriest survived the sweeping Democratic elections of 1930 and 1932, he was vulnerable for his refusal to support aid to the poor and place taxes on the rich. In 1934 he was defeated by a black Democrat. He served again as a Chicago alderman from 1943 to 1947.

See Also

Chicago, Illinois; Exodusters; Great Migration, The.

Latin America and the Caribbean

Deschamps Chapeaux, Pedro

(b. 1913), Cuban historian who has written extensively on the history of Afro-Cubans. His works include *El negro en el periodismo cubano en el siglo XIX* (1963, The Black in Nineteenth-Century Cuban Journalism); *El negro en la economía habanera del siglo XIX* (1970, The Black in the Nineteenth Century Havana Economy); and *Batallones de Pardos y Morenos* (1976, Battalions of Free Coloreds and Blacks) (*see* Cuba).

Hector Hyppolite, one of Haiti's leading primitive painters, created this *Portrait of Jean-Jacques Dessalines*. *Christie's Images*

Latin America and the Caribbean

Dessalines, Jean-Jacques

(b. 1758, Grande-Rivière du Nord, Haiti; d. October 17, 1806, Pont-Rouge, Haiti), one of the leaders, with Toussaint L'Ouverture, of the Haitian Revolution; first emperor of Haiti.

Jean-Jacques Dessalines was born to Congolese parents on the Cormiers plantation in Saint-Domingue (as Haiti was known prior to independence). He was given the name of the plantation owner, Duclos, before assuming the name of the freed black landowner who purchased his services as a slave, Dessalines. Unlike his future comrade-in-arms, Toussaint L'Ouverture, Dessalines was treated harshly as a slave and joined the ranks of maroons (runaway slaves) at a young age. In 1792 he became a partisan of the slave uprising led by Boukman, a slave of Jamaican origin, and impressed his compatriots with his courage in fighting. Yet Dessalines committed acts of cruelty that frightened some in the rebellion. His capacity for violence would contribute in equal measure to his precipitous rise and fall.

Following the abolition of slavery in Saint-Domingue in 1793, Toussaint L'Ouverture allied himself with the French. Dessalines joined him, eventually becoming Toussaint's second in command. Dessalines was instrumental in keeping British and Spanish forces at bay and helped Toussaint consolidate control of the island by putting down the mulatto rebellion led by André Rigaud, reportedly killing between 5000 and 10,000 of Rigaud's supporters. In return, Toussaint promoted Dessalines to general and made him governor of the south of the island. When Toussaint promulgated a constitution in 1801 that effectively proclaimed Saint-Domingue's independence, Dessalines defended Toussaint from the troops led by the French general Charles Leclerc, whom Napoleon Bonaparte had sent to reclaim the island.

Although he was loyal to Toussaint until the latter's capture and deportation to France in 1802, Dessalines had learned enough from his mentor to realize that he had to return once again to the French fold or suffer the same fate as Toussaint. But this alliance would not last long. After spending only a short time on the island, the French troops were decimated by yellow fever. Leclerc himself succumbed to the disease on November 2, 1802. Shortly thereafter, Dessalines initiated a new rebellion that would conclude successfully on January 1, 1804, the day on which Dessalines declared Saint-Domingue independent from France. He renamed the country Haiti (an Arawak Indian word) and had himself appointed, as Toussaint had done in 1801, governor for life (*see* Haitian Revolution).

It was at this point that Haiti's ongoing cycle of violence and retribution began in earnest. Dessalines ordered the execution of most of the whites who remained on the island, as well as anyone who questioned his authority. In a sign of the new regime's growing instability, several of Dessalines's officers – including two future leaders of the country, Henri Christophe and Alexandre

PÉTION – did not carry out these orders. To give his authority more symbolic resonance, Dessalines proclaimed himself Emperor Jacques I of Haiti on September 2, 1804, following the lead of Bonaparte, who, a few months earlier, had pronounced himself Emperor Napoleon I of France. Dessalines did not bother creating a noble class, since, as he put it, only he was noble. Whereas the Haitian people revered Toussaint and his ability to govern, they simply feared Dessalines. Citizens of Haiti were divided into two categories of forced labor: agricultural and military. As public anger spread regarding these policies and others, some of Dessalines's lieutenants hatched a plot to wrest power from their tyrannical leader. They ambushed Dessalines on October 17, 1806, dismembering the body of the man many say served as an example for the brutal twentieth-century regime of FRANÇOIS DUVALIER.

Richard Watts

SEE ALSO

Maroonage in the Americas; Toussaint L'Ouverture, François Dominique; Abolition and Emancipation in Latin America and the Caribbean.

North America

Detroit, Michigan, former Underground Railroad stop, industrial hub, and Great Society success story that, until three days of rioting in 1967, symbolized affluence and freedom for many African Americans.

French slaveholders founded Detroit, but when Michigan joined the United States in 1837, the state legislature abolished slavery. The city soon earned a reputation as a major stop on the UNDERGROUND RAILROAD, and, by the Civil War, FUGITIVE SLAVES constituted the largest group of African Americans in Detroit. The black community founded a reading room, a Young Men's Debating Club, and even an African-American Philharmonic Association, and many abolitionists made Detroit their center of activity.

After the Civil War the black population in Detroit increased sevenfold as freedpeople, largely from Virginia and Kentucky, arrived in search of work. Empowered by growing numbers as well as the Fifteenth Amendment, which gave freedpeople the vote, African Americans began to seek and win local political offices.

African American auto workers pack car lids and roofs on the assembly line at a Chrysler plant in Detroit, Michigan. *CORBIS/Bettmann*

By the turn of the twentieth century Detroit's liberal reputation and worsening conditions in the South motivated sharecroppers to migrate en masse. The burgeoning automobile industry in Detroit at first refused to hire blacks, unlike secondary industries, such as glass and iron. In the second decade of the twentieth-century, however, in an effort to meet growing production demands, automobile manufacturer Henry Ford offered a five-dollar/eight-hour work day to all workers regardless of race. Ford sent recruitment fliers south, single-handedly initiating a demographic shift that redefined Detroit. Between 1910 and 1930 the African American community grew from 5000 to 120,000. Although Ford hired blacks for the most grueling industrial jobs, the quality and wage of factory work were preferable to the hardships of sharecropping and domestic service. With more money, time and independence, African American industrial workers in Detroit developed a middle class.

German and Irish Americans in Detroit saw black newcomers as rivals for housing and jobs, and by the 1920s, the Ku Klux Klan had become a powerful force in the city. When a black physician, Ossian Sweet, moved into a white neighborhood in 1925, a mob of angry residents besieged his house. Sweet defended himself and his family with a gun, shooting two members of the crowd, one of whom died. Represented by Clarence Darrow in a famous series of trials, Sweet was acquitted on grounds of self-defense. This victory stood out, however, amid routine racial injustices such as restrictive housing policies and unpunished police brutality.

Still, by the onset of World War II Detroit had become the home of many black politicians, religious leaders, and celebrities. W. D. Fard founded the NATION OF ISLAM in Detroit in 1930. In 1936 John Sengstacke founded the *Michigan Chronicle*, which became the city's leading black newspaper. Arriving in Detroit in 1938, Rev. James Francis Marion Jones (Prophet Jones), a popular radio evangelist, broadcast to large audiences. From 1935 to 1949 Detroit native JOE LOUIS held the title of world heavyweight boxing champion, having begun his career under the patronage of black Detroit businessman John Roxborough.

The wartime industrial boom encouraged further African American migration to Detroit, from Canada and rural Michigan as well as the American South. After converting their facilities to produce tanks and airplanes, Detroit auto industries drew as many as 50,000 blacks between 1942 and 1945. Again repercussions and racial conflict followed. White workers protested the presence of African Americans in their factories, and the DETROIT RIOT OF 1943 resulted when white auto workers moved into a new housing project nominally built for blacks.

POPULATION OF DETROIT 1810-1990

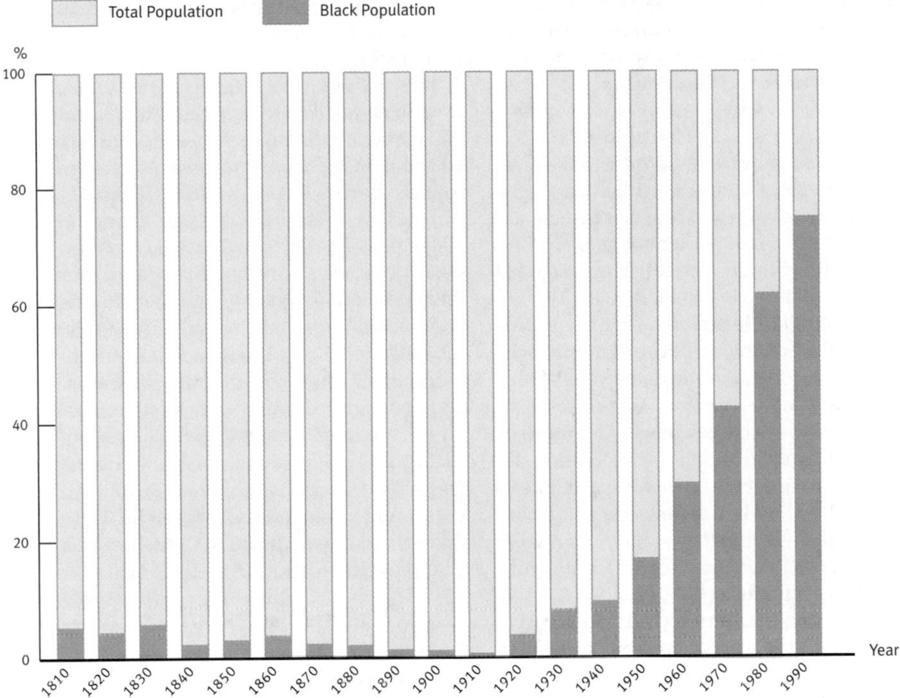

Year	Total Population	Black Population	% Black
1810	2,227	113	5.07
1820	1,422	67	4.71
1830	2,222	126	5.67
1840	9,102	193	2.12
1850	21,019	587	2.79
1860	45,619	1,403	3.08
1870	79,577	1,897	2.38
1880	116,340	2,821	2.42
1890	205,876	3,431	1.67
1900	285,704	4,111	1.44
1910	465,766	5,741	1.23
1920	993,678	40,838	4.11
1930	1,568,662	120,066	7.65
1940	1,623,452	149,119	9.19
1950	1,849,568	300,506	16.25
1960	1,670,144	482,223	28.87
1970	1,511,482	660,428	43.69
1980	1,203,339	758,939	63.07
1990	1,027,974	777,916	75.67

Despite dwindling job opportunities after the war, the black population continued to grow. Detroit successfully accommodated the newcomers until 1967, garnering praise as a model postwar city. Serious racial tension underscored the peace of the 1950s and 1960s, and a false sense of prosperity characterized much popular opinion, including that of many blacks. While poor African Americans suffered housing discrimination and police brutality, the black middle class made significant cultural and political gains. Detroit's chapter of the NATIONAL ASSOCIATION FOR THE ADVANCEMENT OF COLORED PEOPLE was the largest in the nation. In 1954 Charles Diggs Jr. was elected to the United States House of Representatives, and other blacks obtained high posts in the Democratic Party through their affiliation with the powerful, multiracial United Auto Workers (UAW).

In 1959 Berry Gordy founded Motown Records, which skyrocketed such performers as the Jackson Five and the Temptations to national stardom. Motown soon embodied the illusion of a harmonious and affluent Detroit. Its performers were glamorous, their songs nationally known, their city home to other successful blacks as well as liberal white politicians. Under the leadership of Mayor Jerome Cavanaugh, Detroit appeared to implement social reform programs successfully. Cavanaugh sought and won an estimated $230 million in federal funds,

Michigan National Guardsmen advance on rioters in Detroit's west side in 1967. *CORBIS/Bettmann*

much of which was earmarked for programs benefiting Detroit blacks. Cavanaugh welcomed the moderate factions of the Civil Rights Movement to Detroit: in 1963 he invited the Reverend Dr. Martin Luther King Jr., and cooperated with the Walk to Freedom, in which 125,000 people marched for civil rights.

Neither the social and political advances of the Civil Rights Movement, however, nor the social reform funding of the local government could stem Detroit's widespread racial discrimination, persistent police bigotry, and growing unemployment rates. These tensions exploded in the Detroit Riot of 1967, which gutted the city, scared whites to the suburbs, and left blacks in an economic wasteland. The riot tarnished the glamour of Motown and revealed the limits of federal solutions to local problems.

The movement of whites and industry out of the city and into the surrounding suburbs accelerated in the wake of the riots. In 1973 Coleman Young was elected the first black mayor of Detroit; he went on to serve for a record 20 years. Young inherited a city with a declining industrial base, deteriorating housing, and one of the highest crime rates in the nation. With the cooperation of the city's business and labor leaders, he pursued an ambitious effort to revive downtown Detroit, anchored around a new office-retail complex on the city's riverfront called the Renaissance Center. Although these efforts failed to stem the city's economic decline, Young inspired the confidence of the city's majority black population. Under Young, the city's police force was integrated and police brutality complaints fell from more than 2300 in 1975 to 825 in 1982.

In 1994 Dennis Archer succeeded Young. The city's second black mayor, Archer has been credited with creating new possibilities for economic growth through plans for a new sports stadium, the development of casinos along the city's riverfront, and other corporate ventures. Detroit has also benefited from the Clinton administration's support for urban development and a renewed commitment to fair and affordable housing.

Eric Bennett

See Also

World War II and African Americans; Abolitionism in the United States; Press, Black, in the United States; Civil War, American; Fard, Wallace D.; Fifteenth Amendment to the United States Constitution; Great Migration, The; Jackson, Michael, and the Jackson Family; King, Martin Luther, Jr.; Motown; Temptations, The; Young, Coleman Alexander.

North America

Detroit Riot of 1943, **the first modern, large-scale urban riot in which both African American and white mobs wreaked havoc on a major American city.**

Between 1910 and 1930 the African American population of Detroit had increased from 5700 to 120,000, and although de facto segregation in large measure kept blacks separated from whites, racial tensions were building. Competition for limited jobs, housing, and recreational facilities aggravated those tensions. Black residents were particularly angered when the Sojourner Truth Homes, which the federal government had built for blacks, were reassigned to whites.

Belle Isle, the city's segregated municipal beach, was a popular place for Detroit residents to escape the summer heat. On June 20, 1943, a fight broke out between groups of blacks and whites. News of the altercation spread throughout the city, and that night a full-scale riot erupted. Ill-equipped and unprepared, the Detroit police force was unable to stop the riot. Federal authorities were reluctant to intervene unless the situation was declared a state of emergency, but several government officials feared that such a declaration would be interpreted as a sign of weakness by America's wartime enemies.

Late on the night of July 21, military police restored order. Twenty-five African Americans and 9 whites lost their lives in the violence; 675 people were injured; and 1893 were arrested. City officials were quick to blame the riot on the African American community's growing militancy. However, one positive event emerged from the disturbances: the formation of Mayor Edward Jeffries' Interracial Committee, the first governmental organization in the nation given the authority to investigate and prosecute racial discrimination.

Alonford James Robinson, Jr.

See Also

Detroit, Michigan.

North America

Detroit Riot of 1967, **one of several racial disturbances in American cities during the summer of 1967.**

The summer of 1967 was a turbulent time in American history. Racial confrontations escalated into full-scale urban riots in Newark, New York City, Cleveland, Washington, D.C., Chicago, Atlanta, and Detroit. On the morning of July 23, 1967, Detroit police raided an illegal black drinking establishment on 12th Street, handcuffing its patrons and forcing them outside. Fearing for their safety, the police retreated after a crowd of black observers gathered at the scene. Initially, the crowd looted and burned white-owned stores, but as the riot moved into its second day, African American stores were destroyed as well. Before the National Guard brought the rioting to an end on July 25, 43 African Americans had been killed, 1189 injured, and 7231 arrested.

The Detroit Riot of 1967 became a symbol of African American despair and had lasting consequences. Detroit's liberal political coalition was destroyed; many whites moved to the suburbs, and by the 1970s, Detroit's African American majority faced economic stagnation. Yet Detroit fought back, just as it had 24 years earlier when the Detroit Riot of 1943 had left 34 people dead, including 25 African Americans. By the late 1960s federally sponsored antipoverty programs, aid to black churches and organizations, and municipal committees devoted to racial unity had earned Detroit a reputation as one of the most progressive cities in the country. Despite these efforts, significant problems continued to plague the city, including police brutality, inadequate housing, and economic inequality.

Alonford James Robinson, Jr.

See Also

Atlanta, Georgia; Chicago, Illinois; Detroit, Michigan; New York, New York; Newark, New Jersey.

Africa

Development, **the goal of higher living standards achieved through sustained economic growth, and the policies and programs intended to achieve that goal.**

Until the end of World War II, the term *development* generally referred to biological growth processes, and its economic significance was only metaphorical. But development acquired a new meaning when President Harry Truman's 1949 inaugural speech introduced a term that implied the antithesis: "We must embark on a bold new program for making the benefits of our scientific advances and industrial progress available for the improvement and growth of the underdeveloped areas. More than half of the people of the world are living in conditions approaching poverty.... Their poverty is a handicap and a threat to both them and to more prosperous areas.... "

Thus development was defined as a need and a goal as soon as certain areas, among them the entire African continent, were defined as "underdeveloped." Within several years development became an important field of study in economics, sociology, and other social sciences, and the design and implementation of development plans and projects became the defining purpose of national and international agencies, such as the United States Agency for International Development (USAID).

In postwar African colonies, emerging nationalist movements demanded not only political self-rule but also the freedom to achieve levels of material prosperity comparable to those enjoyed in the so-called developed world. After decolonization the leaders of Africa's new nations were highly conscious of popular demands for development, but the national development plans that were supposed to achieve this goal drew primarily on the theories and recommendations of European and North American economists. One notable exception was the Nobel Prize-winning West Indian economist Sir ARTHUR LEWIS, whose theories on economic growth in poor countries underlaid much development planning in the 1960s and 1970s.

Economists generally agreed that development required some degree of industrialization in order to provide jobs and goods for growing populations. Whether or not they said so explicitly, most also assumed that development involved not only economic growth but also social and cultural *modernization* – a presumably evolutionary process in which the values and practices of "traditional" societies gave way to the modern ideas of the West.

Clearly, the overwhelmingly agrarian economies of Africa, Latin America, and Asia – collectively referred to as the Third World – faced a much more competitive global economy than did early industrial Europe and North America. But development theorists argued that the Third World could "catch up," provided it drew on the experience and technological advances of the industrialized world. For many years the main debate centered on the question of exactly how poor nations should do this. Liberal theorists such as Lewis argued that they should focus on exporting goods that best exploited their "comparative advantages," such as abundant cheap labor, climates suitable for tropical crops, and in some cases mineral resources. Many theorists from the Third World (in particular from Latin America), on the other hand, argued that their countries should instead aim to reduce their dependency on global markets by establishing their own industries as quickly as possible.

Workers sort dried tobacco leaves at a factory in Zimbabwe. *CORBIS/Brendan Ryan; ABPL*

In practice, most newly independent African countries attempted some of both: they maintained agricultural and mining export sectors developed during the colonial era but also established "light" industrial sectors for processing agricultural products and manufacturing consumer goods such as textiles and bottled beverages. In general, states with close ties to the free market economies of the West, such as CÔTE D'IVOIRE and KENYA, leaned more toward export-led development, while socialist regimes in countries such as GUINEA, TANZANIA, and post-1974 ETHIOPIA were more committed, at least rhetorically, to self-sufficiency through industrialization.

Whatever their ideological orientation, most African countries in the 1960s and 1970s necessarily relied heavily not only on imported technology to build their industries, but also on loans from foreign banks and governments to finance all aspects of development. Some achieved "miracles" of economic growth – Côte d'Ivoire's economy for example, was described this way – while others, such as Tanzania, made impressive gains in social welfare through the improved provision of basic services such as education, health care, and clean water.

But in the early 1980s, worldwide recession, higher oil prices, and changes in the conditions of international lending plunged Africa's fragile economies into prolonged crisis. Many African countries still earned most of their foreign exchange from exports of a single crop or mineral, and prices for most of these primary commodities dropped

ABOVE: The Kariba dam (146 m [420 ft] high) creates a bridge between Zambia and Zimbabwe, controlling flooding and supplying hydroelectric power to both countries. *CORBIS/Michael Busselle*
RIGHT: The Birchenough Bridge spans the Sabi River in Zimbabwe. *CORBIS/Michael St. Maur Sheil*

during the recession. At the same time, bank interest rates rose sharply worldwide, leaving many heavily indebted Third World countries at risk of bankruptcy.

When BRAZIL and MEXICO – both countries with massive debts – threatened to default, the world's major banks and multilateral lending institutions closed ranks and agreed upon a radical change in the conditions for future lending. Henceforth, loans would be contingent on the borrowing nation's willingness to undertake economic liberalization through World Bank-designed structural adjustment programs (SAPs). These programs required countries to deregulate their economies by cutting price controls and subsidies; loosening regulations on trade and foreign investment; privatizing state-run industries; downsizing government social services and bureaucracies; and often devaluing their currencies.

In theory, countries that carried out these reforms would achieve not only greater solvency but also sustained economic growth and thus – according to the neoliberal premises of structural adjustment – development. But as more and more African nations undertook SAPs in the 1980s and early 1990s, it became clear that whether or not these programs brought higher export earnings and growth rates (the results have been mixed), they did lead to widespread hardship, especially among the urban poor, who were most affected by higher food prices and social-service cutbacks.

In many African countries several of the key indicators used by the United Nations to measure development, such as per capita income and infant mortality rates, actually worsened in the 1980s. The hardship caused by SAP liberalization was not the only reason:

unfavorable world markets, prolonged droughts, political instability, and the persistence of corrupt and undemocratic regimes also helped to make the 1980s into what became known as Africa's "lost decade."

Approaches to development in Africa shifted somewhat in the 1990s. In the West, the collapse of the Soviet Union was taken as a clear sign of the "failure" of socialist approaches. Yet as many in Africa observed, in most countries rapid economic liberalization had just as clearly failed to achieve development, by any definition. At the same time, scientists and environmental groups warned that resource depletion carried out in the name of Third World development – through the logging of tropical rainforests and the mining of fragile tropical soils, for example – would eventually threaten wealthy nations as well as poor nations (*see* Biogeography of Africa).

Governments and development agencies responded to these criticisms by embracing "sustainable development." This concept was rather ambiguously defined by the United Nations-sponsored World Commission on Environment and Development in 1987 as "development which meets the needs of the present without compromising the ability of future generations to meet their own needs." In Africa, sustainable development has come to refer to a wide range of projects and programs. In principle, this kind of development not only preserves natural resources but also employs technologies that can be easily maintained by the communities involved (unlike the tractors imported for many agricultural development projects in the 1960s and 1970s). Solar-powered food dryers, for example, are considered "appropriate technologies" for village income-generation projects in the sun-baked country of Burkina Faso. Sustainable development also aims to bring local people into the planning processes, both so they can identify what they most need and so they feel they have a stake in a project's success.

Due to the decentralized nature of sustainable development programs, it is easier to judge the success of a particular village project, in the eyes of the local population, than to determine whether the combined effects of many grassroots efforts are helping African countries achieve either economic growth or improved living standards. Skeptics point to African countries' low rating on the United Nations "development index" as evidence that the continent is economically further behind than ever and ill-equipped to face the challenges of economic globalization. On the other hand, around the time President Bill Clinton of the United States toured Africa in April 1998, the American media reported enthusiastically on what the president called the "African renaissance."

(For other articles related to development, *see* Development in Africa: An Interpretation; Human Rights in Africa; Human Rights in Latin America and the Caribbean; and Tourism in Africa.)

Susanne Freidberg

See Also
African Socialism; Decolonization in Africa: An Interpretation; Drought and Desertification; Education in Africa; Food in Africa; United Nations in Africa; Population Growth in Sub-Saharan Africa; Structural Adjustment in Africa; Urbanism and Urbanization in Africa.

Above: Water churns through the power generating station at the Aswan High Dam on the Nile River in Egypt. *CORBIS/The Purcell Team*
Left: An irrigation ditch runs through fields in Merti, Kenya. *CORBIS/Liba Taylor*

Africa

Development in Africa: An Interpretation

At the end of four decades of postwar development, the results are so varied that one is tempted to reject the common expression "Third World" when describing all the countries that have been the subject of development policies over these decades. Today, we justifiably oppose a newly industrialized competitive Third World to a marginalized Fourth World, to which Africa in its entirety belongs.

The Goals of Development

The primary objectives of development policies in Asia, Africa, and Latin America since World War II (or from 1960 for sub-Saharan Africa) were the same, despite the different ideological discourses that accompanied them. Development was a nationalist project, aimed at the rapid modernization and enrichment of society through industrialization. That this goal was so widely shared is easily understood if we simply recall that in 1945 most of Asia (excluding Japan), much of Latin America, and all of Africa (including South Africa) was rural, nonindustrialized, and governed by either archaic regimes (the landowning oligarchies of the Americas, the monarchies of the Middle East) or colonial ones (Africa, India, Southeast Asia). Beyond their great diversity, nationalist movements in all these regions sought liberation through political independence – a goal proclaimed at the Bandung

Conference in 1955 – and development through industrialization.

Liberation movements throughout Africa shared this modernist vision, which was by definition a capitalist, bourgeois vision. This does not imply that these movements were inspired, much less led, by a bourgeoisie, in the full sense of the term. An African bourgeoisie did not exist – or hardly existed – at the time of independence, and today, almost 40 years later, it exists only in an embryonic state. But the ideology of modernization really did exist, and it gave meaning to people's revolt against colonization. It also provided a rationale for "capitalism without capitalists."

Modernization, in other words, was expected to bring the economic and social institutions basic and specific to capitalism: the wage relationship, business management, urbanization, stratified education, a sense of national citizenship. This was expected to occur even though other characteristics of advanced capitalist societies, namely political democracy, were woefully lacking in newly independent African nations, a lack some argued was justified by the exigencies of "catching up" rapidly with the economic standards of the industrialized West.

In capitalism without capitalists – that is, without a middle-class business community – the state and its technocrats were to substitute. The radical wings of national liberation movements especially opposed the emergence of such a middle class, suspecting that it would pursue its own immediate interests at the expense of longer-term national goals. These radical wings looked instead to the ideologies and methods of the Soviet Union, where the state had already achieved a quite dynamic form of capitalism without capitalists, aimed above all at catching up with the Western world.

Even in countries where radical wings did not come to control the postcolonial government, Soviet-style state-run modernization was the rule rather than the exception. To understand why, it is worth reviewing briefly the historical relationship between the radical or "socialist" tendencies and the moderates between and within African liberation movements. In some movements the division was frank and clear; in others, it was kept hidden in the interest of presenting a unified front. Some divisions were rooted in class differences among movements' supporters – peasants, laborers, educated intellectuals – while others derived from different movements' sources of political and organizational training (European communist parties, for example, or trade unions or churches). In any case, the divide between radical and moderate tendencies grew wider as the two principal colonial powers, England and France, moved toward rapid decolonization.

Africa in 1960 was divided into two blocks: on one side the Casablanca group, rallying behind the banners of EGYPT'S GAMAL ABDEL NASSER, the Algerian FRONT DE LIBÉRATION NATIONALE, and GHANA'S KWAME NKRUMAH; on the other, the Monrovia group, made up first of the most loyal pupils of Gaullist France and liberal Great Britain (CÔTE D'IVOIRE and KENYA, among others). In the former Belgian Congo (now the DEMOCRATIC REPUBLIC OF THE CONGO), meanwhile, PATRICE LUMUMBA was attached to the first group, but major forces in his country sympathized more with the second. When Lumumba became prime minister, "moderate" forces, with support from Belgium as well as from South Africa, responded by declaring the secession of Katanga and Kasai. It was MOBUTU SESE SEKO who played the reconciliation card and reunited the country. The Congolese example set the stage for further attempts to bring together radical and moderate camps and eventually gradually edge out the former. Emperor Haile Selassie's genius lay in his understanding that by 1963 it was time to reconcile the Monrovia and Casablanca groups, which he achieved through the creation of the ORGANIZATION OF AFRICAN UNITY (OAU) in Addis Ababa.

The reconciliation created new conditions for pursuing the goals of the Bandung Conference in Africa. All African countries formally showed their support for these goals by becoming members of the Non-Aligned Movement, even if they remained in the lap of the Western powers – even in certain cases under their direct military protection. But by proclaiming their support for the radical nationalism espoused at Bandung, Africa's rulers acquired a certain ability to maneuver. The sanctity of the national development project explains why, despite imperialist pressures from abroad, the initiators of "African socialism" – Ghana, GUINEA, MALI – were followed by successive generations of radical regimes, such as those in Congo-Brazzaville, BENIN, and TANZANIA. It also helps explain the wide margins granted to the nationalist extravagances of dictators at the opposite end of the political spectrum, such as Mobutu.

Welder at the Bong iron ore mine north of Monrovia, Liberia. *CORBIS/Albrecht G. Schaefer*

THE RESULTS OF DEVELOPMENT

How we assess the results of development obviously depends on how we define "development" itself, which is an ideological and invariably vague concept.

If we adopt the criterion used by national liberation movements – that is, of "national construction" – the results are on the whole arguable. The reason is that whereas the development of capitalism in earlier times supported national integration, contemporary globalization instead breaks up societies on the periphery of the world economy. However, the ideology of the nationalist movements ignored this contradiction, having been enclosed in the bourgeois concept of "making up for a historic backwardness." This ideology assumed that "backwardness" would be overcome through participation in the international division of labor, not through "delinking" from that system. The disintegrating effect of capitalism was more or less dramatic, depending on the specific characters of the precolonial societies. In Africa, where artificial colonial demarcation did not respect the previous history of its peoples, the disintegration wrought by capitalist forces made it possible for "ethnicism" to survive, despite the efforts of postcolonial ruling classes to get rid of its manifestations. When economic crisis suddenly destroyed the ability of new states to finance transethnic policies, the ruling class itself broke up into fragments which, having lost their claims to legitimacy based on the achievements of development, then sought new claims, often associated with ethnic loyalties.

If instead we adopt socialism as a criterion of development, the results contrast greatly. Of course, it should be understood that "socialism" here means the kind defined by radical populist ideology. It was a progressive vision, emphasizing maximum social mobility, the reduction of income disparities, a sort of full employment in urban areas – in some ways, it envisioned a poor version of the welfare state. From this viewpoint, the achievements of a country like Tanzania offer a remarkable contrast with those of the former Zaire, Côte d'Ivoire, or Kenya, where the most extreme inequalities have persisted for 30 years, both in times of rapid economic growth and subsequently in times of slump.

But the criterion of development that conforms to the logic of capitalist expansion is very different; it is about the ability to be competitive in world markets. From this point of view the results are contrasted to the extreme. The contrast is especially brutal between Asia and Latin America, where many countries have become competitive industrial exporters, and all of Africa, which remains attached to the export of primary products. The former are the new Third World (or what I call the "periphery of tomorrow"), the latter what we now call the Fourth World, which is expected to be marginalized in the new stage of capitalist globalization.

Women draw water from a well, part of an irrigation project designed to improve women's lives and work in the Gambia. *Betty Press*

The Failure of Development

The explanation of the failure of development in Africa as a whole should bring into play all the complexity of the interactions between specific internal conditions and the logic of world capitalist expansion. Because these interactions are too often ignored, current explanations for Africa's failures – both those advanced by economists and by Third World nationalists – remain superficial.

Economists and many other analysts lay emphasis on phenomena that they isolate from the overall logic of the system, like the corruption of Africa's political class, the weakness of its economic base, the backwardness and very low productivity of agriculture, "tribal" fragmentation, and so forth. These explanations inevitably recommend as their solution greater insertion into the world capitalist economy. For this, Africa would need true "capitalist" businesspeople, it would need to break the self-reliance of the rural community by systematically promoting commercial agriculture, and so on. This reasoning is inadequate because it ignores the overall system in which the proposed reforms would operate. We already know, for example, that truly capitalist agriculture in rural Africa would produce a huge surplus labor population. Given the current state of Africa's economies, this labor could not be employed in industry as it was in nineteenth-century Europe. History does not repeat itself.

Third World nationalists stress other phenomena, no less real, like the fact that world prices for Africa's raw materials are steadily declining. They also cite, justifiably, the numerous political and even sometimes military interventions of Western powers, who are always hostile to the forces of progressive social change, and who always come to the rescue of reactionary and archaic forces. But these arguments are not structurally linked to the logic of internal conflicts, so they oppose the "external" to the "nation," whose contradictions are overlooked.

My analysis, by contrast, places responsibility for the failure of development in Africa on colonialism and on the neocolonial policies of independent Africa's ruling classes. It also considers the consequences of the geopolitical strategies pursued in Africa by the world's superpowers.

The international division of labor that has created such inequality between the industrialized centers and the nonindustrialized peripheries of the world economy dates back to the Industrial Revolution in early nineteenth-century Europe. The role of the nonindustrialized countries in this division of labor has been to participate in world trade by exporting products for which they have an advantage based on nature (such as minerals or tropical fruits) rather than on the productivity of labor. Africa was seen to fit this role, as were the other peripheries of Asia and Latin America, which, in terms of their participation in world markets, did not distinguish themselves from Africa until after World War II. One therefore understands why the European powers went on the attack in Africa and then partitioned it among themselves at the Berlin Conference of 1884-1885 (*see* Scramble for Africa). Colonization did not involve, as has too often been said, a "wrong" calculation, whose absurdity history would have subsequently demonstrated. Rather, the aim of colonization, for the powers that could afford it, was to acquire a preemptive right over the continent's natural resources.

Once Africa had been conquered, it was necessary to "develop" it. To understand how this was undertaken, we must consider both the logic of world capitalism – what natural resources did the various regions of the continent possess? – and the precolonial history of different African societies. For the purposes of this analysis, we can examine the three different types of colonial economies. The trading economy, first, incorporated the small-scale peasantry into the world tropical products market by subjecting it to the authority of market monopolies; this made it possible to keep the rewards for peasants' labor to a minimum. Second, southern Africa's mining economies depended on cheap labor from "tribal reserves." Laborers were forced to migrate from the inadequate conditions of these reserves, yet their wages, brought back to the reserves, helped sustain traditional subsistence farming and thus helped keep labor cheap. Finally, in regions where the local social conditions did not permit the establishment of a trade-based economy and the mineral resources did not justify the establishment of labor reserves, concessionary companies created economies of pillage, based on taxation and forced labor. The Congo River basin (split between the colonies of the Belgian Congo and the French Moyen-Congo) belonged to this third category.

Whatever the initial appearances, all the ways in which colonial Africa was incorporated into the world capitalist economy were later to prove catastrophic for Africans. Colonial development is indeed responsible for the major obstacles that continue to afflict the continent.

First, colonialism delayed by a century any beginnings of an agricultural revolution. In colonial Africa a surplus could be extracted from peasant labor and from the continent's natural wealth without any investments in modernization (which meant no machines or fertilizer), without genuinely paying for the labor (which was instead sustained by the produce of the peasant farm), and without even maintaining the natural conditions for producing wealth (which meant that soils were farmed to exhaustion and forests stripped). In the regions where the economy of pillage was practiced, colonial development resulted in particularly acute backwardness.

Simultaneously, colonial development in the context of an unequal international division of labor excluded the formation of any local middle class. On the contrary, each time a middle class started to form, the colonial authorities hastened to suppress it.

Therefore the weakness of Africa's national liberation movements and later its independent states was also a colonial legacy. It was not the product of a pristine but long-gone precolonial Africa (as the ideology of global capitalism would argue, drawing on its usual racist discourse). The critics who blame Africa's problems on its corrupt political middle classes, its lack of economic direction, and its tenacious rural community structures forget that these features of contemporary Africa were all forged between 1880 and 1960.

It is hardly surprising that these features have endured. Suffice it to say that the responsibility of the metropoles was great, because despite all the obstacles of colonial society, liberation movements did produce elites potentially capable of going further – capable, in other words, of exploiting opportunities for getting Africa out of its rut. But when this happened, all effort was made to destroy these opportunities.

To see how Africa's colonizers have ensured its failure, we need only look at the famous Lomé Agreements, which have linked – and continue to link – sub-Saharan Africa to the European Community (EC). These agreements have indeed perpetuated the old division of labor by relegating independent Africa to the production of raw materials even when, during the "Bandung period" between 1955 and 1975, other Third World regions were embarking on an industrial revolution. These agreements have made Africa lose about 30 years of potential progress during a decisive moment of historic change. Undoubtedly, African ruling classes were partly responsible for the continent's involution, particularly when they joined the neocolonial camp against the aspirations of their own people, whose weaknesses they exploited.

The collusion between the African ruling classes and the global strategies of imperialism is therefore, definitively, the ultimate cause of failure. These collusions were shaped by the geostrategic concerns of the postwar period (1945-1990). Consider the consequences of these geostrategic concerns in the southern part of former Zaire and southern Africa more generally. The entire region, including Katanga Province (now Shaba), Zambia, Zimbabwe, and South Africa, was to the American camp of the cold war a unique strategic zone, important for its mineral resources (including South Africa's rare minerals and gold) as well as its location, controlling communications between the South Atlantic and the Indian Ocean. The Soviet Union sought to destroy American influence in this zone by forming alliances with African national liberation movements, especially the most radical ones, in Angola, Mozambique, Zimbabwe, and South Africa. The Western powers responded by supporting, practically without conditions, the regimes of Mobutu in Zaire, Kamuzu Banda in Malawi, Jomo Kenyatta and Daniel Moi in Kenya – despite their notorious corruption and their extreme antidemocratic practices – just as they supported the "anticommunist" forces of Jonas Savimbi in Angola, Mozambican National Resistance (RENAMO) in Mozambique, and pressed for a federal compromise in South Africa, even if it was to the detriment of a genuine democratic solution.

Inversely, geostrategic considerations compelled the Western imperialists to support or at least to tolerate the initiatives of the middle classes of East Asia, which partly explains at least the "success" of this region in the period of postwar capitalist expansion.

But today a new leaf has been turned. Anti-Soviet geostrategic concerns are no longer justified. The Bandung era has ended, and new relationships of collusion are being forged between the global powers and countries on the periphery of the world economy. These countries' own economies, however, are now very different from one another, due to the unequal achievements of the Bandung project in Asia, Latin America, and Africa. We can now classify these countries into four groups, according to what they achieved – or failed to achieve – in their attempts to modernize.

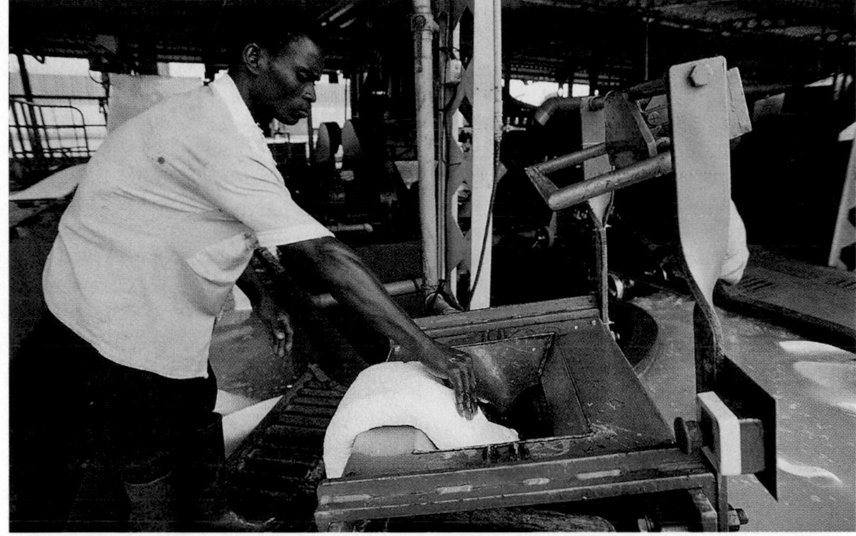

LEFT: A worker processes latex in a factory in Côte d'Ivoire. *Portali/Rapho*
BELOW LEFT: Workers construct a Lutheran mission school in Otjimbingwe, Namibia. *CORBIS/Peter Johnson*

Successful industrialization: countries that are competitive or potentially competitive on global markets fall into this category. This group includes the major industrialized countries of Latin America and East Asia, as well as potentially India, Russia, and certain Eastern European countries. Egypt and Algeria could also belong to this group.

Unsuccessful industrialization: these are countries that one cannot imagine being "competitive." Probably most countries of the Middle East and North Africa belong in this category, as do Nigeria and South Africa. In the future, they could face the destruction of their industrial base, in other words, deindustrialization.

Successful growth: these countries achieved growth, at least for a brief period, within the old international division of labor, that is, by exporting raw materials. This includes oil-exporting countries (Nigeria, Angola) and countries with copper or other mineral resources, such as Zambia and Congo. It also includes a few exporters of tropical agricultural commodities, such as Côte d'Ivoire, Kenya, and Malawi.

Unsuccessful growth: most countries of sub-Saharan Africa fall into this category, because they failed to achieve growth as raw material exporters. Their failures were not invariably due to bad policies, but rather in some cases to objective conditions. Ghana, for example, had achieved its potential as a cash crop exporter during the colonial era; independent Côte d'Ivoire's economic "miracle" was simply a matter of that country catching up with the colonial achievements elsewhere in West Africa.

The first group lies at the core of the periphery of tomorrow. Their economies will continue to run on what I call "outputting" industrialization, which in turn will continue to be controlled by the global economic superpowers. These superpowers will maintain control through monopolies in five key areas: high technology, the global financial system, global natural resource access, mass media (and thus public opinion worldwide), and weapons of mass destruction. The second, third, and fourth groups listed above – meaning all of Africa – belong to the next generation's "marginalized periphery." Here is the challenge.

NEW VISIONS AND NEW STRATEGIES

What can be done now? We must take both a medium- and long-term perspective, given the new global framework. Over the long term, Africa must industrialize and must become competitive. But this is still very far off, and to achieve this goal the global system must be reshaped. Third World countries must "delink" from the global economic superpowers in order to create large regional blocs, in the form of a "Pan-African" bloc, a "Pan-Arab" bloc, and so forth. Delink-ing does not mean autarky, even at the regional level. However, it should allow for regional industrial complementarity. Forming large regional blocs is the only way to mitigate the negative effects of the five aforementioned monopolies. It is the only way to establish negotiated, controlled, and pluriregional interdependency.

More immediately, individual nation-states must fight to achieve "popular" development – that is, growth for the benefit of the majority. This means building an industrial base capable of supporting an agricultural revolution. It also means transforming the overexploited "informal sector" into a "popular economy" that permits workers to negotiate collectively.

Nation-states must protect this popular development from the devastating effects of uncontrolled economic openness. Finally, they must allow for the creation of popular, autonomous political forces. This is the political precondition for popular development, and democratization must be understood in these terms. Third World nation-states must struggle, in other words, not only to build formal democratic systems (with multiparty elections and so forth), but they must also progressively democratize society.

This implies, among other things, a transformation of gender relations.

Samir Amin

See Also

African Socialism; Addis Ababa, Ethiopia; Algeria; Banda, Ngwazi Hastings Kamuzu; Congo, Republic of the; Decolonization in Africa: An Interpretation; Ethnicity and Identity in Africa: An Interpretation; Gold Trade; Moi, Daniel arap; Nationalism in Africa; Savimbi, Jonas Malheiro; Haile Selassie I.

Africa

Diagne, Blaise (b. 1872?, Gorée, Senegal; d. 1934), Senegalese statesman; the first African deputy to the French National Assembly (1914-1934).

Blaise Diagne was born on Gorée, an island off Dakar, the capital of Senegal. The son of a cook and a housemaid, he was adopted by a wealthy *métis* (Afro-French) family when he was very young. The family provided him an exceptional education; he attended a Roman Catholic primary school in Senegal and secondary school in France. He returned to Senegal to attend Saint-Louis University and graduated first in his class in 1890. He joined the French Customs Service in 1892 and served until 1914. During his career he was posted throughout the French colonial empire in Africa and South America. These relocations were often the result of his vocal criticism of oppression and racial discrimination in the colonial system, earning him the reputation of a troublemaker. He left the French Customs Service in 1912, after a short leave spent lecturing in France on French colonial problems.

Diagne returned to Senegal in 1913 and ran for a seat in the French Chamber of Deputies. During his campaign he promised to clarify Senegalese political rights, particularly the right to enlist in the French army, and called for the equalization of the French assimilation policy that benefited métis over Africans. He also campaigned to abolish the head tax, create pensions, and allow Africans the right to organize labor unions. Gathering support among African student groups, civil servants, and Muslims, particularly marabout from the interior, Diagne defeated a métis incumbent, a member of the Carpot family, in the 1914 elections and became the first black African to win a seat in the French parliament.

Diagne was seated in parliament only six weeks before the French entered into World War I. He immediately proposed a resolution to enlist Senegalese into the French army in exchange for the rights and privileges of full French citizenship. This proposal was made into law on October 19, 1915, and Diagne was asked by Prime Minister Georges Clemenceau to serve as governor-general for military recruitment in French West Africa. Diagne accepted the position and enlisted 60,000 Africans into the French Army.

In 1919 Diagne founded the Republican Socialist Party, the first Western-style sub-Saharan African political party, which soon dominated Senegalese politics. In addition to his own victory in the 1919 election, his party won complete control of the local governments in the four communes of Senegal. Beginning in 1923, however, Diagne's actions alienated many of his African supporters. First he abandoned his demands for the Africanization of the white-dominated Senegalese economy, in exchange for the support of métis and French merchants in Senegal. He was also accused of allowing the French to rig his 1928 reelection to guarantee his victory in return for representation on his councils and party. Finally, in 1930, he defended France's policy of forced labor before the International Labour Organization (ILO) in Geneva, shortly before accepting an appointment as French undersecretary of state for the colonies. During the Great Depression of the 1930s, Diagne negotiated France's first subsidies for African farmers. He died in 1934.

Elizabeth Heath

See Also

Dakar, Senegal; Gorée Island, Senegal.

North America

Dialect Poetry, the genre born in the mid-1890s that relies on Southern African American speech and that has had a strong influence on twentieth-century black cultural movements.

Dialect poetry, popularized by writers like Paul Laurence Dunbar in the 1890s, was seen as both reinforcing and criticizing stereotypes of African Americans. Such poetry, employing an approximation of Southern African American vernacular speech, often expressed a nostalgia for the pre-Emancipation South. Its purpose was to celebrate the singularity of black vernacular speech, and its primary audience was white readers.

The origins of the verse lie in the caricatures of blacks in nineteenth-century minstrel shows, the sentimental evocations of the Old South in plantation-tradition literature, and the dialect verse of white regional poets outside the South. The depictions of blacks as inferior, childlike people, speaking a substandard variant of English, pandered to white audiences, who cited it to justify their views of white superiority.

Black writers of dialect poetry appropriated not only the language of this tradition but also its stereotyping. Paul Laurence Dunbar (1872-1906), however, discarded the debasing tendencies and relied on authentic folk sources that subtly challenged the white stereotypes. The racially charged atmosphere of the day kept him from making his protests explicit, so some critics faulted his work as accommodationist, and whites still saw the stereotypes. Dunbar's "An Ante-Bellum Sermon" evinces these complexities, while his "We Wear the Mask" is often cited to show his bitter awareness of the dilemma inherent in the form.

Dialect poetry fell out of vogue after World War I but was revived in the 1920s by the writers of the Harlem Renaissance, who were ambivalent about the form; these authors predicted both the debates on its representation of blacks and the contradictory readings it later provoked. James Weldon Johnson, a close associate of Dunbar's, spurned his own early dialect work. Although he wanted, according to the American historian Richard Newman, "to represent the unique black sermonic language" in his poetry, he dismissed dialect poetry as merely "pathos and humor." Langston Hughes and Sterling A. Brown, however, defended it and composed in the style.

In the 1960s, members of the Black Arts Movement saw dialect poetry as an important progenitor of a distinctive African American cultural tradition. Though the rural and politically inconsistent dialect poetry was in many ways distant from the polemical urban poetry of the 1960s and 1970s, Black Arts writers reclaimed the genre and were influenced by its attempts to preserve the African American vernacular.

Peter Hudson

See Also

World War I and African Americans; Black Vernacular English; Brown, Sterling Allen; Minstrelsy; Racial Stereotypes; Accommodationism in the United States.

Latin America and the Caribbean

Dias, Henrique (b. c. 1600, Pernambuco; d. c. 1661, Recife, Pernambuco), soldier of African descent who from 1633 to 1654 led black and mulatto soldiers in various battles against the Dutch in colonial Brazil.

In the early seventeenth century, commercial interests carried Dutch explorers to Brazil, where they seized control over parts of the northeastern states of Bahia (1624-1625) and Pernambuco (1630-1654). By occupying a central part of the Portuguese colonial empire, the Dutch geographically divided Brazil and threatened its political stability. Thus in 1633, Henrique Dias, a native of Pernambuco, enlisted himself in the national effort to oust the Dutch from colonial Brazil. Dias soon became the captain of a black regiment consisting of both free and slave soldiers. He was thus known as the Governor of the Blacks, Creoles, and Mulattos. Beginning with only 20 men, the regiment grew to some 300 soldiers by the end of the war. They were instrumental in several victories leading to the expulsion of the Dutch from Brazil in 1654. Some sources claim that Dias also participated in efforts of the Portuguese Crown to vanquish runaway slave communities known as *quilombos*.

Dias was born to black parents in Pernambuco during the first years of the seventeenth century. His grandparents were members of the royalty in ANGOLA. It is not certain whether Dias was born free or a slave, but historians do know that he was a free man when he joined colonial forces in the early 1630s. If Dias was born a slave, he purchased his freedom, as slaves were allowed to do under Portuguese law, or he was set free by a master.

In his many clashes with Dutch forces, Dias battled with unyielding tenacity and suffered injury repeatedly. When his left hand was wounded in the 1637 campaign at Pôrto Calvo, he decided to have it cut off so that his return to the field would not be slowed by the healing process.

Because of his valiant service to the Portuguese Crown, Dias was named a *fidalgo*, making him perhaps the first European nobleman of African descent in the Americas, and a *mestre-de-campo*, the military's most prestigious title. These and other honors did not come easily. From 1656 to 1657 Dias traveled to Lisbon, Portugal, to appeal to the queen for the monetary and land awards hitherto granted to other war participants but denied to him and his black regiment. He succeeded in obtaining monetary compensation for his soldiers as well as freedom for those soldiers who were previously enslaved. He made sure that there would continue to be an active black regiment after the war, and he even secured land holdings for his four daughters.

During his service, Dias occasionally defied orders – for instance, refusing to fight in Angola in 1644 and taking a brief leave in 1645 to be with his ailing wife. He also wrote letters to colonial officials, including the king Dom Pedro II, protesting the way in which he and his regiment were often verbally abused by other members of the military. He spent the last years of his life in Pernambuco overseeing the activities of his black regiment and directing the church he began constructing on his estate in 1646. Henrique Dias is regarded by many as the hero of the restoration of Pernambuco.

Aaron Myers

SEE ALSO
Maroonage in the Americas.

Africa

Dib, Mohammed (b. July 21, 1920, Tlemcen, Algeria), Algerian poet and novelist.

In the following evocative passage from a short story, Mohammed Dib conveyed not only the brutal trauma of the 1954-1962 Algerian war for decolonization, but also the enduring hope for independent rule: "There are times when I should like to meet my death in one of the numerous outrages committed every day; this blood that splashes us, this stench as from a slaughter-house, makes me heave and fills me with horror. Then I suddenly feel such a hunger for life, such a thirst to know what it will be like after, that I am ready to face all the armies and police forces in the world."

Dib was born in Tlemcen (now Tilimsen), ALGERIA, to a family of modest means. His father sent him to a French school, a decision that shaped Dib's later choice to write in French. After serving as an interpreter for the Allied army, Dib became a man of many roles: he drew sketches for rug patterns, taught school, worked as a union organizer, and wrote for several newspapers. These jobs exposed him to a variety of Algerian characters – from the urban poor person to the well-intentioned colonial landholder – many of whom he would later represent in his fictional works.

Dib published his first long poem, "Vega," in 1947, and has always considered himself primarily a poet. His poetry, which includes five published collections, draws on Algerian oral poetic traditions as well as classical Arabic and modern French influences.

Yet Dib is probably best known for his trilogy about the Algerian struggle for self-rule. *La grande maison* (1952), *L'Incendie* (1954), and *Le métier à tisser* (1957) portray childhood and adolescence in the midst of urban poverty and the oppression of COLONIAL RULE. Critics have noted that the three novels grow progressively more radical in their political stance, mirroring an increasingly militant nationalist struggle (see FRONT DE LIBÉRATION NATIONALE). In 1959 Dib was deported for his nationalist leanings, and settled in FRANCE.

Like many exiles, Dib looked back to his home country in much of his subsequent work, creating from memory a tangible sense of the Algerian landscape and people. A poetry collection, *Ombre gardienne* (1961), was followed by the novels *Qui se souvient de la mer* (1962), *Cours sur la rive sauvage* (1964), and *La danse du roi* (1968), all of which broke from the realism of his trilogy to incorporate elements more fantastic and psychological.

In his short stories, poetry, and 14 novels to date, Dib has written on the lasting effects of the war on the fighters' psyches; the prominent role of women in the struggle for Algerian independence; debates about the future of the new nation; and the psychological experience of exile. In almost all of his work, he has explored the universal themes of love and death. As critic François Desplanques says, Dib has sought to portray the history of the conquered, the living dead who "have been crushed by the weight of destiny." Critics characterize his later works as more complicated, merging sections of poetry with poetic prose. But Dib has in fact always incorporated poetic elements into his work – "a progression of kaleidoscopic sensations" representing the sights, smells, and sounds of the war as it passed through the lives and thoughts of the individual.

Marian Aguiar

SEE ALSO
Literature, French Language, in Africa; Nationalism in Africa.

North America

Dickerson, Earl Burris (b. 1891, Canton, Miss.; d. September 3, 1986, Chicago, Ill.), lawyer, business executive, and first black Democratic alderman in the city of Chicago.

Born in Mississippi, as a teenager Earl Dickerson moved to Chicago, where he attended Evanston Academy, Northwestern University, and the University of Illinois, where he earned a B.A. He served in the United States Army as a low-ranking officer during World War I (1914-1918), then returned to Illinois and took a degree in law from the University of Chicago in 1920, becoming the law school's first African American graduate. In the following year he became counsel for a new black-owned insurance company, Liberty Life; he continued his association with the company, later called Supreme Life, for five decades.

Dickerson soon became active in the Democratic Party and was rewarded with an appointment in 1923 as an assistant corporation counsel for Chicago. By 1933 he was an assistant attorney general for Illinois, and in 1939 he became Chicago's first black Democratic alderman. On the city council he worked against racial discrimination in housing and public transit. He was unable to fulfill his ambitions of becoming a member of Congress or a federal judge, but in 1941 he was appointed to President Franklin Roosevelt's FAIR EMPLOYMENT PRACTICES COMMITTEE, one of two black members. Dickerson's strong opposition to job discrimination was probably the reason he was not reappointed to the committee in 1943. Throughout his life Dickerson played prominent roles in the NATIONAL ASSOCIATION FOR THE ADVANCEMENT OF COLORED PEOPLE (NAACP) and the NATIONAL URBAN LEAGUE.

SEE ALSO
World War I and African Americans.

Africa

Dida, ethnic group of Côte d'Ivoire.

The Dida primarily inhabit central coastal Côte d'Ivoire west of Abidjan. They speak a Niger-Congo language belonging to the Kru cluster. Approximately 200,000 people consider themselves Dida.

See Also

Abidjan, Côte d'Ivoire; Languages, African: An Overview.

North America

Diddley, Bo (b. December 30, 1928, McComb, Miss.), African American singer, guitarist, and songwriter; member of the Rock and Roll Hall of Fame.

Bo Diddley, born Otha Elias Bates, was sent as a baby by his family to live with cousins in Chicago, Illinois, where he took the name McDaniel. He learned to play the guitar in his teens. At 23, he took a regular job at the 708 Club in Chicago, playing blues and rhythm and blues. He toured the Midwest with rhythm and blues groups and as a solo artist.

As rock 'n' roll began its rise to popularity in the mid-1950s, he began to write songs in the new style. He came to the attention of Chess Records in Chicago and took the name Bo Diddley in his first recordings for the label. Sources differ on the name's origin. It may have been a childhood nickname for a mischievous boy, a slang term for a witty storyteller, or the name under which he had boxed in his youth.

He gave his first single the same name. The song "Bo Diddley" became a nationwide hit in 1955. Diddley produced more Top 10 singles during the next five years. He established himself as a major concert attraction, known for his distinctive cigar-box shaped guitar as well as his vital performances.

Diddley's music owed much to the blues. Songs like "I'm a Man" and "Who Do You Love" emphasized his persona of powerful independence and manhood. The distinctive stuttering rhythm of many of his compositions became a hallmark of early rock 'n' roll.

Diddley continued to tour and record in the four decades that followed his early fame. He was inducted into the Rock and Roll Hall of Fame in 1987.

See Also

Blues, The; Boxing.

Latin America and the Caribbean

Diegues, Carlos (b. May 19, 1940, Alagoas, Brazil), Brazilian filmmaker and one of the pioneers of Cinema Novo, a modern, socially committed cinema that arose in the late 1950s and 1960s in response to changing conceptions of Brazilian national identity.

Carlos Diegues is one of the most prolific and controversial film directors of the Cinema Novo generation. Like other filmmakers of New Brazilian cinema, he aimed "to study in depth the social relations of each city and region as a way of critically exposing, as if in miniature, the sociological structure of the country as a whole." Of particular interest to Diegues were the social and historical dimensions of Afro-Brazilian culture. While some critics have accused Diegues of perpetuating racial and sexual stereotypes, others contend that some of his films countered the notion – expounded by the sociologist Gilberto Freyre – that Brazil is a racial democracy and that slavery in Brazil was less brutal than in the United States.

During the early 1960s Cinema Novo filmmakers, influenced by the populist agenda of President João Goulart, focused their films on the country's impoverished rural communities. Diegues's first professional film, *Escola de Samba, Alegria de Viver* (1962, Samba School, Joy of Living), portrays the samba schools organized by black *favela* (or squatter settlement) dwellers as a part of the preparations for Carnival. Like many films of the time, it is flawed by a didactic approach to the country's poor communities. As film scholar Randal Johnson notes, *Escola de Samba* provides "a view from the outside looking in, and rejects popular culture in favor of a paternalistic... view of the people."

Rejecting his early didacticism, Diegues produced his first feature film, *Ganga Zumba* (1963), with a predominantly black cast. Based on João Felício dos Santos's novel *Ganga Zumba*, the film focuses on the lives of three fugitive slaves who eventually make their way to Palmares, the seventeenth-century maroon republic that survived nearly a century, despite repeated attacks by the Dutch and Portuguese. As film scholar Robert Stam confirms, "*Ganga Zumba* deserves praise for its uncompromising portrait of Brazilian slavery.... An ode to black liberation, [it] assumes a black perspective throughout, showing blacks not as mere victims but as active historical agents." Due to a lack of funds, Diegues was not able to reconstruct the second half of dos Santos's novel until 1984, with the film *Quilombo* – a representation of the history of Palmares that employs aspects of Afro-Brazilian popular culture, such as Carnival and Candomblé.

Although Diegues believed that Cinema Novo should be socially committed, he defended cinematic pluralism and the filmmaker's freedom of expression. "In this sense," as Johnson notes, Diegues "opposed authoritarianism of both the Right and the Left, and for this he has been harshly criticized by both sides." Diegues's intensely personal approach to filmmaking is exemplified in Xica da Silva (1976), the true story of an eighteenth-century black woman, who, through a 43-year liaison with a rich public official, becomes the "power behind the throne." Detractors found fault in the very conception of the film as a comedy about slavery; they also criticized the film's lack of historical accuracy and its portrayal of Xica's sexual power. Popular critics, on the other hand, received the film enthusiastically, as did the Brazilian public. Indeed, fellow Cinema Novo filmmaker Glauber Rocha praised *Xica da Silva* as an "Afro-feminist, pan-sexualist, libertarian, nationalist, radical and humanist... tropical baroque." In 1996 *Xica da Silva* became a popular television miniseries.

Roanne Edwards

See Also

Palmares: An African State in Brazil; Slavery in Latin America and the Caribbean; Racial Stereotypes; Favelas; Carnivals in Latin America and the Caribbean; Myth of Racial Democracy in Latin America and the Caribbean: An Interpretation.

Africa

Digo, ethnic group of East Africa.

The Digo primarily inhabit northeastern coastal Tanzania and neighboring Kenya. They speak a Bantu language and belong to the Mijikenda cultural and linguistic group. Approximately 300,000 people consider themselves Digo.

See Also

Bantu: Dispersion and Settlement.

North America

Dill, Augustus Granville (b. 1881, Portsmouth, Ohio; d. March 9, 1956, Louisville, Ky.), African American sociologist, coeditor of the Atlanta University studies of African American life, and business manager of the *Crisis* magazine.

The son of John Jackson and Elizabeth (Stratton) Dill, Augustus G. Dill received a B.A. in 1906 from Atlanta University, where he was a student of W. E. B. Du Bois. On Du Bois's advice, Dill earned a second B.A. at Harvard University in 1908.

Returning to Atlanta to assist Du Bois on his sociological project of documenting all dimensions of black life in American society, Augustus coedited four major studies from 1911 to 1915. In 1910 Dill replaced his mentor as associate professor of sociology when Du Bois left Atlanta University to found the *Crisis*, the journal of the National Asso-

CIATION FOR THE ADVANCEMENT OF COLORED PEOPLE. In 1913 Dill was hired by Du Bois as the *Crisis*'s business manager, a post he held until 1928. Arrested that year in New York City as a homosexual, Dill was fired by Du Bois. Unable to find work, Dill spent the rest of his life in obscurity.

SEE ALSO

Crisis, The; Du Bois, William Edward Burghardt (W. E. B.); New York, New York.

Dingaan. Please see DINGANE

Africa

Dingane (b. 1795?; d. 1840?), one of the great southern African ZULU chiefs (1828-1840).

Together with other members of his family, Dingane took part in the assassination of the increasingly despotic Zulu warrior chief SHAKA, his half-brother, on September 24, 1828. Dingane subsequently murdered his co-conspirators and became king of Zululand.

As king, Dingane tried to end the ten years of continual war, but to keep the kingdom from splintering he was forced to continue Shaka's repressive policies. In 1837 Dingane was asked for a grant of land by Pieter Retief, one of the leaders of the migration of Boers known as the Great Trek (1835-1843). Fearful of the encroaching Boers, Dingane hedged and asked Retief to show good faith by capturing some cattle that had been stolen by a Tlokwa chief. Retief retrieved the cattle and returned them to Dingane in February 1838. By then the Boer pioneers were already coming over the Drakensburg Mountains with their wagons and cattle, and news reached Dingane of the complete defeat of Mzilikazi, another Zulu chief, by separate Boer forces. Dingane took fright and on February 6, 1838, he invited Retief and his party to a feast of celebration in his *kraal* (circular compound), where his warriors murdered them. His *impis* (regiments) then attacked the immigrant camp and some 600 Boers were killed.

The death of Retief and his followers was avenged on December 16, 1838, at the Battle of Blood River when Andries Pretorius, another Great Trek leader, killed 3000 Zulus with a force of 500 men. After this defeat, some of Dingane's followers broke away and followed his brother Mpande, who collaborated with the Boers to defeat Dingane's forces in 1839. Dingane was overthrown by Mpande in January 1840; he fled to SWAZILAND, where he was murdered.

Africa

Dinka, the largest ethnic group in southern SUDAN, numbering over 2 million people.

The Dinka are divided into 25 subgroups, each with its own name. Each once occupied a distinct territory. Each group is further subdivided into a number of lineages based on patrilineal descent (descent through the father's line). The groups were led politically by a chief from a dominant lineage within the group, but his authority depended on general consensus and the cooperation of individuals. The religious authority of each group's spear master (chosen from a second prominent lineage) complemented the primarily secular power of the chiefs. The spear master represented the power of tradition and the authority of the ancestors. Like their NUER neighbors, the Dinka derived their livelihood mainly from cattle raising, though the cultivation of MILLET, fishing, and hunting were important supplemental activities.

During the eighteenth and nineteenth centuries the Dinka expanded their control over southern Sudan. The Dinka expansion displaced some Nuer, but the Nuer retreated into the Sudd, a swampy area along the White Nile and its tributaries. The actions of Sudanese and Egyptian slave raiders (*see* TRANS-SAHARAN AND RED SEA SLAVE TRADE) seriously weakened the various Dinka chieftaincies, but they nevertheless tenaciously resisted both Turco-Egyptian control in the nineteenth century and the British in the twentieth.

A mutiny of southern Sudanese troops in 1955 on the eve of Sudanese independence initiated the Sudanese Civil War. Since the beginning of this conflict, Dinka such as JOHN GARANG DE MABIOR have played a leading role in the civilian and military organizations pressing for greater autonomy or independence for the southern Sudan. The Sudanese Civil War has caused massive population relocations and much suffering among the Dinka, who have endured heavy casualties and famine and have had to seek refuge in the cities of northern Sudan.

Robert Baum

SEE ALSO

Nile River.

North America

Dinkins, David Norman

(b. July 10, 1927, Trenton, N.J.), first black mayor of New York City (1989-1993).

In his inaugural address on January 1, 1990, New York mayor David Dinkins invoked the theme of racial progress on which he had successfully campaigned. "I stand before you today," he said, "as the elected leader of the greatest city of a great nation, to which my ancestors were brought, chained and whipped in the hold of a slave ship. We have not finished the journey toward liberty and justice, but surely we have come a long way." When he defeated three-time mayor Edward Koch, Dinkins, a Democrat, became the city's first black mayor. A contrast to the outspoken and pugnacious Koch, Dinkins's dignified civility seemed likely to soothe a racially tense city.

Born in Trenton, New Jersey, Dinkins moved as a child to Harlem with his mother, who worked as a maid. After serving in the United States Marines during World War II, Dinkins entered HOWARD UNIVERSITY, from which he graduated in 1950. He earned a law degree from Brooklyn Law School in 1956. After launching his legal career – Dinkins did not give up his private law practice until 1975 – he embarked on a political career characterized by alternating defeat and victory. Under the tutelage of career politician J. Raymond Jones, known as "the Harlem fox," Dinkins won a seat on the New York State Assembly in 1965, which he lost in 1966 due to reapportionment.

Dinkins's career suffered another blow in 1973, when his nomination to be the city's first black deputy mayor was withdrawn following the revelation that he had failed to file income tax returns for the previous four years. A new job as city clerk, which he held from 1975 to 1985, helped Dinkins rebound, and after three tries he was elected Manhattan's borough president in 1985. In 1989 he topped popular incumbent mayor Edward Koch in the Democratic primary, and went on in the general election to defeat the Republican Rudolph Giuliani by the narrowest victory margin since 1905.

As mayor, Dinkins led a diverse city with a population of more than seven million. In trying to "be Mayor of all the people," as Dinkins had pledged, he attracted criticism for indecision, passivity, and an inept management style. Qualities of deliberation and civility that had served him well in previous jobs seemed to infuriate both blacks and whites. When African Americans and Orthodox Jews rioted in Crown Heights, Brooklyn, in 1991, many felt Dinkins was ineffective in his efforts to calm the violence.

After serving one term, in which he balanced the city's budget and presided over a dramatic decrease in the city's crime rate, Dinkins lost the 1993 election to former prosecutor Rudolph Giuliani. Despite this defeat, however, his tenure as mayor proved historic. As he told journalist Todd Purdum, "The value of being an African American mayor is not limited to things a mayor can do." Speaking before black schoolchildren, Dinkins always counseled that they could achieve anything, never failing to add, "You *know* that you can be mayor."

Kate Tuttle

SEE ALSO

World War II and African Americans; Harlem, New York; New York, New York.

Diola. Please see JOLA

Africa

Diop, Alioune (b. January 20, 1910, Saint-Louis, Senegal; d. May 2, 1980, Paris, France), Senegalese writer and editor who became a central figure in the Négritude movement.

Alioune Diop was born in Saint-Louis, Senegal, whose inhabitants enjoyed automatic French citizenship during the colonial period. He obtained his secondary education at the Lycée Faidherbe in Saint-Louis, then studied in Algeria and at the Sorbonne in Paris. He took a position as professor of classical literature in Paris and represented Senegal in the French senate after World War II. In 1947 Diop founded *Présence Africaine*, perhaps the most influential intellectual journal of its time on anticolonial and emancipatory culture and politics among Africans and peoples of African descent. With frequent contributions from his friend and associate Léopold Sédar Senghor, Diop's journal helped foster the Négritude movement, which aimed to promote an African cultural identity and the liberation of the people of Africa and the African diaspora. In 1949 Diop founded Présence Africaine Editions, a leading publishing house for African authors.

Diop's journal, though anticolonial in spirit, published the work of notable black politicians, poets, fiction writers, and essayists from Africa, the Caribbean, Europe, and the United States from a variety of ideological perspectives. Although the journal became increasingly political, Diop's own work often focused on the significance of the arts in African culture. A devout Catholic, he also wrote essays critical of the colonial tendencies of some church organizations.

The energetic Diop's contributions to the Négritude movement extended beyond his own publishing ventures. He founded the Société Africaine de Culture (1956) and helped organize several conferences for black writers and artists, including the first and second International Congress of Black Writers and Artists in Paris (1956) and Rome (1959); the first World Festival of Negro Arts in Dakar (1966); and the second Festival of Black and African Arts and Culture in Lagos (1977).

Diop left a cultural legacy that has continued since his death in 1980. Cultural ministers from the sub-Saharan states established a literary prize in his honor in 1982; the 50th anniversary celebration of *Présence Africaine* was held in Paris in 1997; and Présence Africaine Editions remains active under the direction of Yandé Christian Diop, his widow.

Robert Fay

See Also
Colonial Rule; *Présence Africaine*; Dakar, Senegal; Lagos, Nigeria.

Africa

Diori, Hamani, (b. 1916, Soudouré [French West Africa]; d. 1989, Morocco), first president of Niger (1960-1974).

Hamani Diori was the son of a Djerma public health official in the French colonial administration. Diori attended the distinguished William Ponty Teachers Training College in Dakar, Senegal. At that time, both Niger and Senegal were part of the French colonial territory of French West Africa. He worked as a teacher in Niger from 1936 to 1938 and then as a Hausa (*see* Hausa Language) and Djerma language instructor at the Institute of Overseas Studies in Paris.

In 1946, while working as the headmaster of a school in Niger's capital city of Niamey, Diori cofounded the Parti Progressiste Nigérien (PPN, or Progressive Party of Niger). It was a regional branch of the interterritorial Rassemblement Démocratique Africain (RDA, or African Democratic Rally), the party led by Félix Houphouët-Boigny of Côte d'Ivoire. During the same year, Diori was elected to the French National Assembly. He was defeated in his 1951 reelection bid by his cousin Djibo Bakary.

Diori worked as a headmaster until he was elected to the assembly again in 1956 and was chosen to be the deputy speaker. Organizing a powerful coalition of Hausa, Fulani, and Djerma leaders, including chiefs and traditionalists, in support of Niger's independence referendum, Diori gained French favor. In 1958 he was appointed prime minister. In November 1960, shortly after Niger gained independence, he was elected as Niger's first president and was reelected in 1965 and 1970.

Throughout his presidency Diori remained in the international spotlight, often serving as a spokesperson for African affairs and as a popular arbitrator in conflicts involving other African nations. Increasingly criticized at home for his negligence in domestic matters, Diori put down a coup in 1964 and narrowly escaped assassination in 1965. Finally, as a result of the corrupt mismanagement of drought-relief funds by members of his administration, Diori was overthrown in a 1974 military coup. He was imprisoned for six years and detained under house arrest for an additional seven years. After his release in 1987, Diori moved to Morocco, where he died.

Jessica Hochman

See Also
Niamey, Niger.

Africa

Diouf, Abdou (b. 1935, Louga, Senegal), Senegalese political leader and president of Senegal (1981-).

Abdou Diouf studied at schools in Senegal and France, receiving a degree in law and political science at the University of Paris in 1959 and a diploma at the French Overseas Civil Service School in 1960. Returning to Senegal, he served as director of international technical cooperation, deputy secretary-general to the government, and secretary-general of the defense ministry in his first two years with the civil service. Diouf joined the Union Progressiste Sénégalaise (UPS) in 1961, and quickly became known as the protégé of President Léopold Sédar Senghor. From 1961 to 1970 he received appointments to a number of positions, including minister of planning and industry (1968-1970).

In March 1970 Senghor named Diouf prime minister. In January 1981 Senghor stepped down, naming Diouf as his successor. Diouf was subsequently elected to three five-year terms in 1983, 1988, and 1993. Shortly after taking office, Diouf amended the constitution to accelerate the move toward a multiparty state, but carefully controlled the ability of opposition parties to form coalitions strong enough to challenge him. More recently, in the wake of postelection demonstrations and student and labor unrest aimed at economic reforms, he has allowed rival alliances and has appointed members of the opposition to ministerial posts.

In 1993 Diouf reached a negotiated settlement and cease-fire with the Mouvement des Forces Démocratiques de la Casamance (MFDC), the armed separatist movement in the isolated southern agricultural region of the country. However, the agreement collapsed and hostilities between MFDC guerrillas and government forces resumed in April 1995.

See Also
Senghor, Léopold Sédar.

Dioula. Please see Dyula

North America

Divine, Father (b. 1880?, Rockville, Md.; d. September 10, 1965, Philadelphia, Pa.), founder of the Peace Mission Movement.

Born George Baker, Father Divine was the son of George Baker, a day laborer, and Nancy Smith, a domestic worker. He moved to Baltimore at age 20, where he was active in the Baptist church and soon began an itinerant ministry throughout the South. In 1906 he was present at the birth of modern Pentecostalism, the Azusa Street Revival in Los Angeles.

Baker moved with a small group of followers to Harlem in 1915 and preached as Major J. Divine. It was here that his Peace Mission Movement evolved and that he became known as Father Divine. In 1919 he bought a home in a white Long Island neighborhood in Sayville, New York, and established it as a cooperative and communal dwelling known as Heavens.

His worship services in Sayville attracted thousands of people, but in 1931 Divine's white neighbors had him arrested on charges of disturbing the peace and being a public nuisance. He was found guilty of these charges and received the maximum fine and a one-year jail sentence. The judge, Lewis J. Smith, died of a heart attack four days after the trial. It is purported that Father Divine, in response to this event, commented, "I hated to do it." Although he probably did not make such a remark, the report of having done so established his celebrity as a religious leader. With his popularity increasing during the 1930s, Divine transferred his head-

The Peace Mission Movement, which combined Pentecostal theology with practical self-help efforts, was at the height of its popularity when this photo of Father Divine was taken in 1936. *CORBIS/Bettmann*

quarters to Harlem and expanded the operations of his Peace Mission Movement. In addition to conducting religious services, he ran an employment agency, and provided further aid to the poor during the Depression by opening businesses and administrating a national network of relief shelters.

The popularity of Divine derived in part from his theology, which was dependent on New Thought, a religious philosophy that asserted the unlimited power of the human mind and language. His movement tried to eliminate racism by removing the words "Negro," "colored," and "black"; rather, people were simply "light-complected" or "dark-complected." Divine himself claimed to have transcended race, and his movement was multiracial. Many followers believed that Father Divine was God, and that he could channel spiritual powers to give them health and good fortune as well as salvation. He symbolized his connection to supernatural powers by supplementing his worship services with abundant multicourse banquets. However, he enforced strict morality among his flock, requiring chastity and abstinence from alcohol. As evidence of their conversion to Divine's system, believers broke family ties and took new names.

The popularity of Divine's movement declined with the economic recovery of the 1940s. In 1946 he married a 21-year-old Canadian white woman who was one of his disciples. She was known as Sweet Angel, and upon marriage became Mother Divine. The group moved their headquarters from Harlem to Philadelphia in 1953, where Divine purchased the large Woodmont estate, which he renamed the Kingdom of Peace. In the manner of his previous missions, this center provided affordable food and lodging to his followers.

After Divine's death, Mother Divine acquired control of the movement. She claimed that her husband did not die but chose to live in a spiritual form. The movement survives today with a small number of followers.

See Also
Baltimore, Maryland; Great Depression; Harlem, New York; Los Angeles, California; Philadelphia, Pennsylvania.

Latin America and the Caribbean

Dixon, Graciela (b. 1956, Colón, Panama), Afro-Panamian lawyer, professor, human rights advocate, and political leader of the Panamanian Left.

Graciela Dixon was born in the city of Colón, Panama. She attended the Abel Bravo School and went on to study law at the University of Panama. As a young lawyer, Dixon founded her own law firm, Abogados Asociados, which she continues to direct. Her firm sought compensation from the United States for more than 600 Panamanians of African descent who lost family members, homes, and possessions or suffered physical and psychological damage as a result of the United States invasion of Panama in December 1989.

Dixon has also been a law professor, teaching courses in human rights, political science, and social security law. She is a nationally recognized advocate of the rights of women and children. She has served as the national consultant for the United Nations Children's Fund and participated in a program that promotes sustainable development for the poorest segments of the population.

Dixon has also been active in Panamanian politics identified with the Left. She was a leader of Panama's Revolutionary Workers Party (PRT) and ran as an independent candidate for Panama's legislature. In June 1997 she was the only female candidate in the race for Panama's first ombudsman. Until December 1997 Dixon acted as vice president of the board of directors of the Regional Interoceanic Authorities (ARI), an institution created by the Panamanian government in 1993 to administer and promote investment in the Panama Canal area in preparation for its reversion to Panama in the year 2000. Dixon resigned this position when she was appointed by President Ernesto Balladares (and confirmed by the Legislative Assembly) to serve on Panama's Supreme Court as a justice – a post seldom held by women in Panama or in any other Latin American country. Dixon has been a Supreme Court magistrate since January 1998.

Liliana Obregón

See Also
Human Rights in Latin America and the Caribbean.

North America

Dixon, Julian (b. August 8, 1934, Washington, D.C.), Democratic member of the United States House of Representatives from California (1979-).

Julian Carey Dixon was born and raised in a black, middle-class neighborhood in Washington, D.C., and served in the United States Army from 1957 to 1960. He received a bachelor's degree from California State University, Los Angeles, in 1962 and a law degree from Southwestern University in 1967. While in school he worked for six years as a legislative aide to California state senator Mervyn M. Dymally. Dixon practiced law from 1967 to 1973 and entered electoral politics in 1972, when he was elected to the California Assembly. Six years later he was elected to the U.S. House seat in California's Thirty-second Congressional District.

The Thirty-second District encompasses dozens of distinct ethnic neighborhoods in Los Angeles. Economically, the district ranges from wealthy neighborhoods in the north to extremely poor areas of south central Los Angeles in the east. Dixon proved to be extremely popular with his constituency, generally winning his reelection bids with 75 percent of the vote or better.

In the 105th Congress (1997-1999), Dixon served on the Appropriations Committee and the Select Intelligence Committee. He is also a member of the Congressional Black Caucus.

See Also
Los Angeles, California.

North America

Dixon, Willie (b. July 1, 1915, Vicksburg, Miss.; d. January 29, 1992, Burbank, Calif.), prolific African American blues musician who composed, produced, and recorded both his own and his contemporaries' music.

Willie Dixon performed in a gospel quartet as a youth and was greatly influenced by the blues piano of Little Brother Montgomery. Dixon initially decided, however, to capitalize on his massive frame and make his fortune as a heavyweight boxer. In the 1930s he moved from Mississippi to Chicago and in 1937 won the Illinois State Golden Gloves heavyweight championship. He switched to music later that year, after a dispute with his manager over money.

Dixon played bass for a number of groups in the 1940s but his career was interrupted by a jail sentence when he refused to honor the draft. In 1946 he joined Leonard Caston and Bernardo Dennis in the Big Three Trio, a group that played blues, pop, BOOGIE WOOGIE, and novelty music. The Big Three Trio toured the Midwest and recorded with Columbia Records until they disbanded in 1952. By that time Dixon had secured a part-time job with CHESS RECORDS, for which he worked until 1971.

Through Chess Records, Dixon collaborated with star after star. He was soon serving the company full-time, working as A&R (artist and repertory) man, composer, arranger, session musician, and talent scout. Bluesmen such as MUDDY WATERS, HOWLIN' WOLF, and Little Walter & His Jukes recorded Dixon originals; Dixon himself recorded with Waters, Chuck Berry, Bo DIDDLEY, and many more. During his two decades with Chess, Dixon helped pioneer the new Chicago Blues that transformed languid, rural, acoustic songs into hard-edged electric numbers. When Dixon temporarily left Chess for Cobra Records in 1957, he helped develop Chicago's West Side sound by producing the music of Buddy Guy, Otis Rush, and Magic Sam.

During the 1960s Dixon performed with Memphis Slim in American and European concerts that sparked widespread interest in blues and folk among young white listeners. British bands of the late 1960s such as Led Zeppelin and Cream reflected Dixon's influence, scoring smash hits with psychedelic versions of his old blues songs. Such bands covered – and in some cases stole – Dixon's compositions.

Dixon continued to record throughout the 1980s and 1990s. In his old age he became a blues activist, founding, in 1991, the Blues Heaven Foundation. The organization contributed funds to music education programs and helped old blues musicians win royalties for songs others had plagiarized. In 1989 he published his autobiography, boldly yet not inaccurately titled *I Am the Blues*. Dixon died in 1992 of heart failure. He was inducted into the Rock and Roll Hall of Fame in 1994.

Eric Bennett

SEE ALSO

Berry, Charles Edward Anderson, (Chuck); Blues, The; Gospel Quartets.

Latin America and the Caribbean

Djavan (Djavan Caetano Viana)

(b. 1949, Maceió, Alagoas, Brazil), contemporary Afro-Brazilian pop music composer and performer.

Djavan was born and raised in the northeastern state of Alagoas, BRAZIL, where he played guitar in various pop bands before moving to Rio de Janeiro in 1973 and beginning his professional career. In 1975, at the age of 27, he encountered his first national success, taking second place in the Abertura Festival for his composition "Fato Consumado." From that point on, his career has steadily expanded, and some 14 albums later, he is one of the most acclaimed artists of Brazilian pop music.

As a composer, Djavan draws his influences from such diverse sources as SAMBA, bossa nova, rock, JAZZ, FUNK, and RHYTHM AND BLUES. His unique fusion of these varied elements has brought him consistent international success ever since the release of his premiere album *A Voz* in 1979. Djavan's universal appeal has led artists as disparate as Caetano Veloso and the Manhattan Transfer to record his compositions. In addition, he has worked closely with other international artists, including STEVIE WONDER, Ernie Watts, and Quincy Jones.

Djavan has recorded many of his albums in the United States, and some of them, such as *Não e Azul Mas e Mar* (1996), have been supported with full-scale United States tours. He has also toured extensively throughout Japan and Europe. Djavan has aimed his music at Latino markets as well. In 1994 he released an album called *Esquinas* in which all his major hits were rerecorded in Spanish. The album was distributed in ARGENTINA, CHILE, Costa Rica, VENEZUELA, and SPAIN. When asked about the universal appeal of his music, Djavan simply replies, "My albums are created with a unique intention: the world is just a singular market."

Gordon Root

SEE ALSO

Jones, Quincy Delight, Jr.; Rio de Janeiro, Brazil.

Africa

Djebar, Assia

(b. August 4, 1936, Cherchell, ALGERIA), Algerian writer and motion picture director, known for her works about women in the Islamic societies of North Africa. She is one of a generation of female writers offering a view of history that gives women a central role. Central concerns in her work include voice, memory, and language.

Assia Djebar was born Fatima-Zohra Imalayen in Cherchell, a small coastal town west of Algiers, to a schoolteacher father and a mother who died while Djebar was a child. She finished her early studies in Algeria, then became the first Algerian student to be admitted to the prestigious L'Ecole Normale Supérieure de Sèvres in France. In 1957 she earned a degree in history from the Sorbonne in Paris. She went on to teach history at the University of Rabat in MOROCCO, and later studied history in TUNISIA and taught at the University of Algiers.

Djebar's first novel, *La soif* (1957; translated as *The Mischief*, 1958), received both critical and popular attention. It was followed by *Les impatients* (The Impatient Ones) a year later, which drew criticism for its eroticism and *bourgeois* (middle-class) values. Two more novels followed: *Les enfants du nouveau monde* (1962, The Children of the New World) and *Les alouettes naïves* (1962, The Innocent Larks). She also worked in theater, coproducing the play *Rouge l'aube* (1960, Red Dawn), and wrote poetry, collected in *Poemes pour l'Algérie heureuse* (1969, Poems for a Happy Algeria).

Djebar then stopped writing for several years, citing discomfort from writing about subjects too close to her own life – especially in a traditional society where women did not speak of the self (*see* FEMINISM IN ISLAMIC AFRICA). During this period she concentrated on filmmaking, creating *Walid Garn* (1977), which deals with women's responses to liberation struggles. She then made a controversial feminist film, *La nouba des femmes de Mont Chenoua* (1979, The Festival of the Women of Mount Chenoua), for Algerian state television. The film weaves together what Djebar called "a polyphony of women's voices." In her next film, *La Zerda et les chants de l'oubli* (1982, Zerda or the Songs of Forgetting), Djebar superimposed Algerian women's songs over French news reels of World War I (1914-1918) to document women's participation in the war.

Djebar resumed writing with a collection of stories and an essay, *Femmes d'Alger dans leur appartement* (1980; translated as *Women of Algiers in Their Apartment*, 1992). Her next novel, *L'amour, la fantasia* (1985; translated as *Fantasia: An Algerian Cavalcade*, 1985), alternates two women's voices as they explore historical boundaries. With this work, Djebar began challenging the assumption that women's private lives should never become public, and the symbolic act of unveiling becomes a recurring theme. *Ombre sultane* (1987; translated as *A Sister to Scheherazade, 1989*), the second work in a quartet that begins with *L'amour, la fantasia*, alternates narratives from two women, one emancipated and one traditional. *Loin de Medine: Filles d'Ismael* (1991, *Far From Medina*) addresses questions that Islam and the Koran pose for women. Her novel *Vaste est la prison* (Vast Is the Prison) was published in 1995. In 1996 she received the Neustadt International Prize for Literature.

SEE ALSO

Algiers, Algeria; Rabat, Morocco; Islam and Tradition: An Interpretation.

Africa

Djenné-Djeno, Mali (also known as Jenné-Jeno and ancient Djenné), an ancient city whose ruins lie in present-day Mali.

The ruins of a city now known as Djenné-Djeno lie in the central Niger Valley approximately 3 km (2 mi) from present-day Djenné. According to archaeological evidence, Djenné-Djeno was founded before the second century B.C.E. It developed into a major trading center before its decline after the eleventh century C.E. and its desertion in the fourteenth century C.E., when urban life and trade shifted to present-day Djenné. At its pinnacle, between 700 and 1000 C.E., the town had a population of at least 10,000 people; it encompassed an area of around 33 hectares (82 acres).

Djenné-Djeno's excavation, begun in 1977, challenged long-held theories about early history in the Sahel. Prior to the dig, historians believed that before contact with the Arab world around 1000 C.E. through trans-Saharan trade routes, the Sahel borderlands lacked long-distance trading systems, cities, and complex societies. These historians, relying on the ethnocentric chronicles of early Arab travelers, believed that Arabs first introduced complex social structures to the southern populations during the eleventh century. But archaeological evidence from Djenné-Djeno revealed a city that had emerged long before this date. Well before the eleventh century, the population of Djenné-Djeno, including numerous skilled artisans, engaged in considerable long-distance trade. The city, which lacks evidence of the dominant elite who ruled the cities of Europe and the Middle East, may have possessed a relatively egalitarian society governed by various overlapping groups.

The existence of a complex urban society at Djenné-Djeno as early as the fifth century C.E. proves conclusively that cities and complex societies evolved south of the Sahara independently of influences from North Africa. Recent archaeological finds from the ancient kingdom of Ghana substantiate the early development of sub-Saharan urbanism. The form of Djenné-Djeno and other recently excavated urban centers, organized loosely in clustered settlements, suggests the development of a unique kind of urbanism indigenous to the Sahel and surrounding regions.

Elizabeth Heath

See Also

Ghana, Early Kingdom of; Niger River; Sahara Desert; Djenné, Mali; Ancient African Civilizations.

Africa

Djenné, Mali, a city in Mali.

Located 400 km (about 250 mi) north-northeast of Bamako and 354 km (220 mi) south of Tombouctou, Djenné was once a major commercial and intellectual center. Djenné was originally a small fishing village inhabited by the Bozo people, located near the ancient trading center at Djenné-Jeno. In the early thirteenth century the Soninké founded a trading town at the site of present-day Djenné. It soon became a major market for trade between Tombouctou and the southern forest regions. Trade with Tombouctou followed the Bani and Niger rivers. Djenné provided the desert city with food and cotton as well as gold, ivory, slaves, cola nuts, and spices in exchange for salt and North African goods.

As a trading center, Djenné offered traders security against bandits: the city is completely encircled by the Bani and Niger rivers for nearly half of the year. However, the city's protected location did little to deter conquerors lured by the city's wealth. In the fourteenth century the city was absorbed by the Mali Empire. In 1491, after the fall of Mali, the Songhai ruler Sunni Ali built a naval fleet that allowed him to conquer the city. During the sixteenth century, Djenné fell briefly to Moroccan invaders. The Moroccan soldiers later abandoned the city to the Bambara kingdom of Ségu, which occupied it from 1670 to 1810. It was during this period that Djenné became a center of Islamic learning renowned for its distinctive mud-brick mosque. In the nineteenth century Djenné was conquered by both Cheikou Amadou (who ruined the city's great mosque during the attack) and the religious leader al-Hajj Umar Tal. In 1893 the French occupied the city; they rebuilt the mosque in 1905. Under French colonial rule Djenné lost its commercial importance to nearby Mopti. Today the town is a local trade center for fish, coffee, and cola nuts. It has an estimated population of 15,000.

Elizabeth Heath

See Also

Bamako, Mali; Gold Trade; Ivory Trade; Djenné-Djeno, Mali; Morocco; Niger River; Songhai Empire; Tombouctou, Mali; Cola; Trans-Saharan and Red Sea Slave Trade.

Djerba, Tunisia. Please see Jarbah, Tunisia

Africa

Djibouti, a small coastal country in the Horn of Africa bordering Eritrea, Ethiopia, and Somalia.

Djibouti's strategic location on the Strait of Mandeb, where the Red Sea meets the Indian Ocean, has shaped its history. For centuries, the region was a crossroads where the peoples of Africa and the Middle East mingled and traded. In modern times, Djibouti, devoid of significant natural resources, has depended economically on its role as an outlet to the European and Indian Ocean trade for landlocked Ethiopia. While Djibouti's arid countryside supports a population of nomadic pastoralists, the country produces only 3 percent of its required food. Most of the population lives in the capital of the virtual city-state, Djibouti City, whose rail connections and free port provide most of the country's income. Because of the economic and military vulnerability of the country, the population moved slowly to sever ties with France, and Djibouti was one of the last African colonies to declare independence. Though Djibouti has a strong commercial sector and one of Africa's best telecommunications infrastructures, much of the population remains impoverished. And while the country has avoided the warfare that has devastated its neighbors, long-standing ethnic antagonisms continue to divide its population.

Early History

Little is known about the early history of the region. For thousands of years, since the first human populations migrated out of Africa, the area of present-day Djibouti has provided a gateway to the Middle East, just 23 km (14 mi) across the Strait of Mandeb. In prehistoric times, the first speakers of Semitic languages (spoken today in both Ethiopia and the Middle East) passed through the region, as did cultural innovations such as nomadic pastoralism, which still provides a livelihood for many Djiboutians.

Before the rise of Islam, the ancient walled seaport city of Zeila developed just east of present-day Djibouti, in a region then dominated by the Christian kingdom of Abyssinia in the area presently known as Ethiopia. Arab and Persian traders inhabited the city, as did the Afar (Danakil) people, who also populated the countryside. The booming trade in slaves and silver supported the rise of the kingdom of Adal, centered on Zeila. Adal dominated present-day Djibouti and parts of the surrounding region. The earliest written record of its capital, Zeila, comes from the Arab geographer al-Ya'qubi, who noted the prominence of Arab traders when he described the port in 889 C.E.

Zeila was one of the principal points through which Islam came to the Horn of Africa. By the eighth or ninth century Islam had become firmly established in the coastal communities, although it only had an impact on the population at large after the tenth and eleventh centuries. With the widespread adoption of Islam and improved access to Arabian and Persian markets, Muslim kingdoms such as Adal succeeded in asserting their independence from Christian Abyssinia. During this time, large numbers of Somali Issas migrated into southern parts of the region, driving the Afars to the north. From the thirteenth until the sixteenth century, power struggles between the Muslim sultanates and the Christian Abyssinians shook the region, though the area of present-day Djibouti generally remained Muslim. In the late sixteenth century, invaders from the west defeated Adal; a number of independent Afar sultanates, including Tadjoura, Raheita, and Aussa, filled the power vacuum. These sultanates exist to this day, although the sultans have limited political power.

Thus, by the seventeenth century, the traditional cultures and political structures of present-day Djibouti had taken shape. Both the Afars and the Issas are Afroasiatic-speaking pastoralists who share many cultural traditions, social structures, values, and beliefs. The traditional political cultures of the two groups differ, however. The Afars belong to hierarchical chiefdoms divided into noble and common clans. The Issas, in contrast, consist of more egalitarian clans, although they recognize a religious leader, the Ogaz, who resides in Ethiopia. The territory of the Afars extends into neighboring Eritrea and Ethiopia, and that of the Issas extends into Ethiopia and Somalia.

Arabs dominated the trade in the Horn of Africa until the nineteenth century. They paid tribute to local Afar and Issa chiefs for passage of their caravans into the interior. By the sixteenth century Portuguese traders began to anchor at ports such as Tadjoura and Obock. These ports exported commodities such as slaves, coffee, and perfume in exchange for firearms, salt, and cloth, which were carried by caravans to inland markets in Ethiopia. The growing trade with Ethiopia attracted the attention of the French, who also sought control over Indian Ocean commerce. After several exploratory expeditions, the French gained a foothold at Obock in 1862 in exchange for a fee paid to the local sultan. With the opening of the Suez Canal in 1869, the coastal ports on the Strait of Mandeb took on great strategic importance. However, it was not until 1881 that France established a trading company in Obock and sent a small number of colonizers. In 1884 the French concluded a similar agreement with the sultan of Tadjoura.

Colonial Period

In 1888 France established the colony of French Somaliland. The French initially chose the port of Obock as its administrative center. When the French decided to develop the colony as a commercial gateway to Ethiopia, however, they abandoned Obock, since surrounding mountains made it too costly to construct a railroad into the hinterland. In its place they selected Djibouti City because of its easier access to the interior. Djibouti City was named the capital of French Somaliland in 1896. The French governor, Léonce Lagarde, established strong ties with Ethiopia and signed a treaty with Emperor Menilek in 1897 declaring French Somaliland as Ethiopia's trade outlet. In the same year, the French began construction of the rail line. It reached Addis Ababa in 1917 and greatly expanded the volume of trade passing through Djibouti City. During this period, many Somalis, including some belonging to non-Issa clans, migrated to French Somaliland for construction work on the railroad, and increasing numbers of Arab merchants settled in the city to take advantage of the growing trade.

French control of the region met with some resistance when Issa and Afar nomads refused to be disarmed or pay taxes. Instances of violence, however, were minimal. France was primarily concerned with the construction of the railroad and the development of Djibouti City and largely ignored the inhabitants of the interior. Under French rule, conflicts between the Afars and the Issas over pasture and cattle were recurrent, and Tadjoura continued to be a center of the illegal trade in Ethiopian slaves who were destined for Arabia and Persia.

In 1935 Italy invaded Ethiopia with an eye on French Somaliland. Unhappy with their dependence on the French rail line, the Italians invested heavily in the construction of a road to Assab, where they built up a port to compete with Djibouti City. When Italy declared war on France in 1940, Italy had some 40,000 troops in Ethiopia, whereas the Allies had only about 9000 troops in the region. However, France soon fell to Germany, and in 1940, the fascist Vichy government secured control of French Somaliland. Its actions included the summary execution of literate Somalis as "potential defectors." By 1942 British troops had forced the Italians in Ethiopia to surrender, and after a British blockade of Djibouti City's port, the Vichy French surrendered as well. The Free French, allied with Great Britain, assumed control.

In 1946 France instituted significant changes in the political structure of French Somaliland. It created a representative council that exercised some degree of self-government. The 20 council seats were allocated equally to French nationals and local people. French Somaliland also became an overseas territory, granting the inhabitants French nationality and representation in the French National Assembly. However, in granting equal numbers of seats to Afars, Arabs, and Somalis (including the Issas), the French exacerbated preexisting ethnic tensions, particularly since these groups' populations in the country were not equal. (The population is roughly 20 percent Afar, 35 percent Issa, 20 percent non-Issa Somali, 5 percent Arab, and 5 percent French; the remainder are other foreigners.) Armed conflicts broke out between the Gadaboursis and Issas in 1949. The French electoral system classified both of these groups as Somalis and thus permitted them to elect only one representative between them. The election of a Gadaboursi in 1949 left Issas feeling disenfranchised, which provoked an assault on the elected senator. The attack sparked a riot resulting in 38 deaths.

In 1958 France offered each overseas territory the opportunity to decide by popular referendum whether to remain part of the Republic of France or to become a completely autonomous state. Over three-quarters of the colony's electorate chose to remain within the French community as part of the Fifth Republic, in some measure out of fears of forcible

***Boutres*, Arab boats powered by a single sail, are moored along with more modern craft in Djibouti's main harbor.** *© Le Tourneur/Explorer*

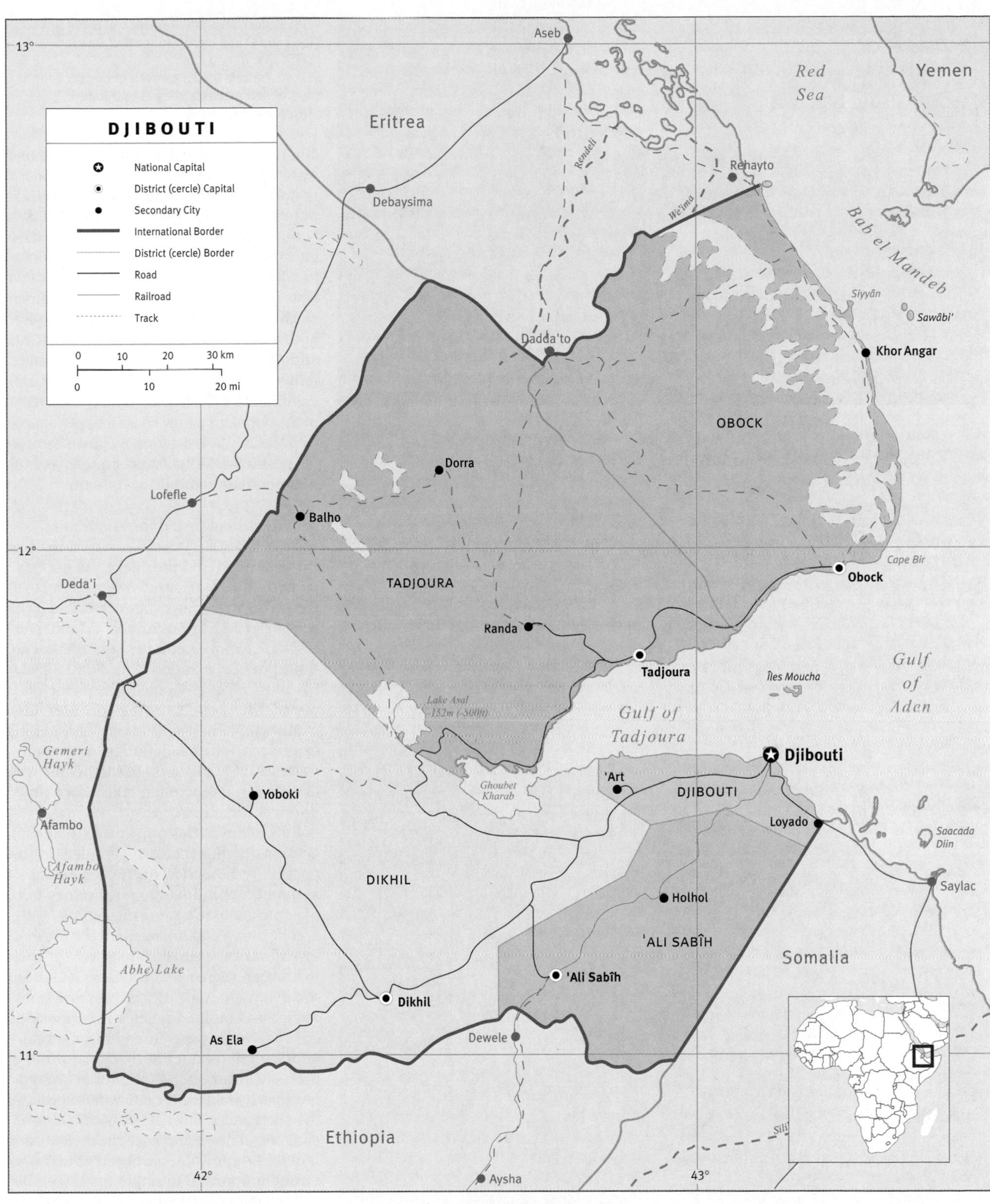

annexation after the unification of British and Italian Somaliland into an independent Somalia. Many also doubted the feasibility of independence for French Somaliland alone, given its lack of natural resources.

Many Issas and other Somalis supported independence and perhaps union with Somalia, while the Afar sought to maintain ties to France, largely in order to avoid Somali domination. Consequently the French strengthened their ties with the Afar community. After Charles de Gaulle's visit to Djibouti City sparked nationalist riots that left several people dead and many wounded, the government scheduled a second referendum on independence in 1967. However, just prior to the referendum, France expelled thousands of ethnic Somalis, labeled alien residents, from the territory. Thus, even though the Issas, the largest group in the territory, overwhelmingly supported independence, the Afars dominated the referendum, which endorsed continued association with France. That year, France signaled its alignment with the Afar minority and its opposition to Somali nationalism by renaming French Somaliland the French Territory of the Afars and the Issas.

However, the French gradually abandoned their commitment to an Afar-dominated

LEFT: Pedestrians cross an open plaza in Djibouti City, capital and important port of Djibouti. *CORBIS/Wolfgang Kaehler*
BELOW: Traders lead a caravan of camels bearing bags of salt across a plateau in Djibouti. *© Ribieras/Explorer*

colony. After 1967 Somali immigration had resulted in an increasingly nationalist Somali majority resentful of Afar dominance and potentially sympathetic to unification with Somalia. Meanwhile, the success of Marxist guerrillas in neighboring Ethiopia (home to a large Afar population) sparked French fears that Ethiopia's revolutionary government might absorb the territory. Pressured by both the Organization of African Unity (OAU) and other international agencies, France reluctantly agreed to hold yet another referendum in 1977, in which nearly 95 percent of the population now chose independence. On June 27, 1977, the former French Territory of the Afars and the Issas emerged as the independent Republic of Djibouti.

The Republic of Djibouti

Hassan Gouled Aptidon, an Issa, became the country's first president. He quickly leaned toward personal rule and in 1979 created a single-party state controlled by his supporters. The Afar formed a clandestine resistance movement, the Front démocratique pour la libération de Djibouti (FDLD). In 1981 and 1987 Gouled was reelected president; he had been the only permitted candidate in these elections. When a bomb exploded in the headquarters of Gouled's party in 1986, over a thousand people were arrested in a draconian crackdown on political dissidents.

Ethnic hostilities only intensified as Gouled's regime increasingly ruled out the possibility of political expression by Afars and others. A militant Afar resistance force of some 3000 troops organized after 1991 and began to capture much of the north of the country. French diplomats were unable to broker an agreement between Gouled and the insurgent Afars. Under pressure from France and numerous emerging opposition groups, Gouled was forced to schedule another referendum in 1992 to approve a draft constitution that permitted limited multiparty politics. Though voters approved the referendum, most Afars boycotted it and challenged its result. Since the constitution required opposition parties to obtain government approval to run in the December 1992 elections, Gouled was able to eliminate any serious challenge to his power. Not surprisingly, his party won every seat in the National Assembly, since most of the population had boycotted an election that they viewed as a hoax. Fighting continued. In July 1993 the government mounted a large and successful offensive against the Afar resistance movement.

The Afar insurgents, though greatly weakened, did not surrender. International human rights organizations attacked the Gouled regime for allegedly committing summary executions, detaining people with-out charge, and harassing the civilian population. Thousands of civilians fled toward the Ethiopian border. In the face of a military impasse, the Afar insurgency movement split, and one faction entered into negotiations with the Gouled government. The negotiations led to a comprehensive treaty in December 1994. The accord provided for a power-sharing agreement based upon ethnic quotas to ensure fair representation, and an amnesty for the Afar insurgents, many of whom ultimately joined Djibouti's armed forces.

Ongoing domestic unrest and heavy military spending damaged Djibouti's economy during the early 1990s. The country experienced increasing difficulty servicing its debt, and international lenders demanded that the government increase taxes and cut spending. In 1995 trade unions and teachers held strikes in response to these government austerity measures. Meanwhile, the aging Gouled had to leave the country from December 1995 until February 1996 to seek medical treatment in France. Because Gouled had monopolized power, a destabilizing struggle for succession ensued. Upon his return, he suspended the civil rights of prominent opposition leaders and restated his intention to remain in office until his term expires in 1999. While Gouled brought a certain degree of political continuity, a failing economy continues to plague Djibouti. High unemployment has generated social ills such as increased drug use and prostitution, as well as an impending acquired immune deficiency syndrome (AIDS) epidemic.

In elections held in April 1999 the ruling party candidate Ismail Omar Guelleh won 73 percent of the vote and defeated Moussa Ahmed Issis. However, the course of a post-Gouled Djibouti remains uncertain. Many analysts fear the reemergence of ethnic conflict between the Afars and the Issas. The Afars constitute one-fifth of the population; they are the second largest ethnic group and they dominate the north. One-third of Djiboutians, mainly in the south, identify themselves as Issas; they are the single largest ethnic group in the country. The presence of numerous refugees from Ethiopia and illegal aliens from Somalia poses another problem for Djibouti. Estimates vary, but tens of thousands of refugees now reside in Djibouti, where they strain the country's limited environmental and financial resources.

Ari Nave

SEE ALSO
Addis Ababa, Ethiopia; Languages, African: An Overview; Menilek II; Organization of African Unity; Pastoralism; Djibouti, Djibouti; Indian Ocean Slave Trade; Issa.

Africa

Djibouti (Ready Reference)

Official Name: Republic of Djibouti
Former Name: French Territory of the Afars and Issas; French Somaliland
Area: 22,000 sq km (13,675 sq mi)
Location: Eastern Africa; borders the Gulf of Aden, the Red Sea, ERITREA, and SOMALIA
Capital: Djibouti (population 348,000 [1993 estimate])
Other Major Cities: Roseau (population 20,755 [1991 estimate])
Population: 440,727 (1998 estimate); population swelled in 1992 due to the influx of 20,000 Somali refugees.
Population Density: 43.1 persons per sq km (69 persons per sq mi [1998 estimate])
Population Below Age 15: 43 percent (male 92,920; female 92,584 [1997 estimate])
Population Growth Rate: 1.5 percent (1998 estimate)
Total Fertility Rate: 6 children born per woman (1998 estimate)
Life Expectancy at Birth: Total population: 51 years (male 49.1 years; female: 53.1 years [1998 estimate])
Infant Mortality Rate: 102.4 deaths per 1000 live births (1998 estimate)
Literacy Rate (age 15 and over who can read and write): Total population 46.2 percent (male 60.3 percent; female 32.7 percent [1995 estimate])
Education: Primary and secondary schools are mostly taught in French, though Islamic teaching has recently been emphasized, due to Saudi Arabia's expressed willingness to subsidize such efforts. In 1995-1996, there were 591,784 primary school students; 10,008 secondary school students; 104 teacher-training school students; 1,748 vocational school students; and 130 students enrolled at institutions of higher education.
Languages: Arabic and French are the official languages; Somali and Afar are also widely spoken.
Ethnic Groups: About 20 percent of the population are Afar, 35 percent Issa, 20 percent non-Issa Somali, 5 percent Arab, 5 percent French; other foreigners make up the remaining 15 percent.
Religions: 94 percent of the population are Muslim, while the remaining 6 percent are Christian.
Climate: Torrid and dry, although humidity is high in the monsoon season from June to August. The average annual rainfall varies from 210 mm (about 8 in) in December to 400 mm (about 16 in) in June.
Land, Plants, and Animals: Djibouti's landscape is extremely varied, ranging from low desert plains in the west and south to mountains in the north. Most of the country is volcanic desert and still geologically active. As rainfall is infrequent, vegetation is minimal. Wildlife includes antelopes, gazelles, hyenas, jackals, and ostriches. Offshore in Djibouti's waters marine life includes tuna, barracuda, and grouper.
Natural Resources: Minerals (including gypsum, mica, amethyst, sulfur); geothermal energy, natural gas; livestock, fish
Currency: 1 Djiboutian franc
Gross Domestic Product (GDP): $520 million (1997 estimate)
GDP per Capita: $1200 (1997 estimate)
GDP Real Growth Rate: .5 percent (1997 estimate)
Primary Economic Activities: The economy is based on the services Djibouti, a strategic port, provides as both a transit port for the region and as an international trans-shipment and refueling center, and to a lesser extent on the railroad to Addis Ababa. As it has few natural resources and little industry, the country depends heavily on foreign aid, particularly from France. Due to scant rainfall, most food must be imported. During the last six years, due to recession, civil war, and a high population growth rate (including immigrants and refugees), economic growth has evaded Djibouti.
Primary Crops: Fruits, vegetables; goats, sheep, and camels
Industries: Small-scale dairy products and mineral-water bottling
Primary Exports: Hides and skins, coffee
Primary Imports: Foods, beverages, trans-port equipment, chemicals, petrole um products
Primary Trade Partners: SOMALIA, ETHIOPIA, Thailand, FRANCE, Yemen, and Saudi Arabia
Government: Djibouti became a constitutional republic with a multiparty system by referendum on September 4, 1992. Guerrilla warfare erupted in 1991 due to ethnic tensions between the Afars in the north and the Issa majority in the south. The president, currently Ismail Omar Guellah, is elected by popular vote to a six-year term. A Council of Ministers is responsible to the president. The head of government is currently Prime Minister Barkat Gourad Hamadou. Djibouti's legislative branch is a 65-seat unicameral Chamber of Deputies whose members are elected to serve five-year terms. The dominant political party is the president's party, the People's Progress Assembly (RPP). Other parties include the Democratic Renewal Party (PRD) and the Democratic National Party (PND).

Marian Aguiar

SEE ALSO
Djibouti, Djibouti.

Africa

Djibouti, Djibouti, capital city of the Republic of Djibouti.

The country of Djibouti can almost be considered a city-state. It is the most urbanized country of sub-Saharan Africa and it has only one urban center, Djibouti City. Between 65 and 75 percent of the entire country's population live in the city. Afars, Issas, and non-Issa Somalis, in addition to a sizable Yemeni Arab population, make Djibouti City their home. A significant number of French and other European expatriates also reside there.

Originally, the French chose the city of Obock, on the opposite side of the Gulf of Tadjoura, as the capital of their Somaliland colony. However, surrounding mountains made the construction of a railway from Obock to the Ethiopian interior too costly. Seeking to expand the volume of trade, the French signed a treaty in 1885 with Issa chiefs enabling the governor, Léonce Lagarde, to establish a new capital on coral reefs that extended from the southern shore of the Gulf of Tadjoura. There, in 1888, the French began to construct the city of Djibouti. In 1896 they designated it the capital of the Côte Française des Somalis (the French Somali Coast), as the territory was then known.

The construction of a railroad and a deep-water port beginning in 1897 created jobs that drew people to the nascent Djibouti City. By 1899 the population had grown to 10,000 people, of whom some 200 were Europeans, primarily on contract to construct the railroad to Addis Ababa. In 1900 the population was estimated at 15,000. The railroad tracks extended from Djibouti City to Dire Dawa by 1903, and reached Addis Ababa in 1917. With the completion of the rail line, Djibouti City became the chief outlet for Ethiopia's external trade. The volume of trade flowing through the port grew dramatically.

Djibouti City became a center for the arms trade in particular. European merchants would import outdated firearms from Belgium and sell them to Arab traffickers. These weapons were primarily destined for Ethiopia and Arabia. The port lost some significance after the 1930s when the harbor of Aseb (in present-day ERITREA), developed by Italy to reduce Ethiopia's dependence on the port at Djibouti, drew an increasing share of Ethiopia's trade.

Djibouti continues to serve as the main import-export point for products destined for Ethiopia. Its container port serves the only railroad reaching Ethiopia's interior. The modern Ambouli International Airport also handles air freight destined for other parts of Africa. With a stable, market-based currency and reliable satellite- and cable-based telecommunications, a significant banking industry has developed. In addition, the country hosts a French naval base and several thousand French troops.

Surrounded by an arid desert, the city provides some of the only employment opportunities in the country, attracting not only residents from the countryside but also immigrants from neighboring war-torn and impoverished countries. The population of the city almost tripled, from 124,000 in 1972 to 348,000 in 1993 – far outpacing the actual economic opportunities. The result has been widespread unemployment or underemployment, and the rise of large, squalid shantytowns on the city's outskirts.

This pervasive poverty has promoted a widespread, officially tolerated trade in the drug qat, an Ethiopian green-leaf narcotic, to which many Djiboutians are addicted. To supplement their meager incomes, many of Djibouti's women engage in prostitution, for which French soldiers and transient tradesmen provide a steady demand. Ethnic discord, both between Afars and Somalis and between the dominant Issas and other Somali groups, has also plagued the city, which is largely segregated along ethnic lines.

Ari Nave

SEE ALSO

Addis Ababa, Ethiopia; Djibouti; Ethiopia.

North America

Dobbs, Mattiwilda (b. 1925, Atlanta, Ga.), American OPERA singer; first black person to sing at La Scala in Milan, Italy, and second black woman to sing at the Metropolitan Opera House in New York City.

Mattiwilda Dobbs, a coloratura soprano, was born in Atlanta, Georgia, to Irene Thompson Dobbs and John Wesley Dobbs, a mail clerk who later organized the Georgia Voters League. Dobbs attended SPELMAN COLLEGE (1946) and Columbia University (1948). She studied with Lotte Leonard (1946-1950), a lieder and Wagner specialist, and won the MARIAN ANDERSON Award in 1947.

A John Hay Whitney Fellowship (1950-1952) allowed her to study in Paris under Pierre Bernac and Lola Rodriguez de Aragon. Her professional career began when she won first prize at the International Music Competition in Geneva in 1950. In 1953, at the request of Herbert von Karajan, she became the first black person to sing at La Scala in Milan. Success at Glyndebourne in the same year led to a command performance for Queen Elizabeth II and the king and queen of Sweden at Covent Garden; the latter awarded her the Order of the North Star, and she sang at Covent Garden from 1953 until 1958.

Following a positive critical reception at the New York Town Hall in 1954, Dobbs made her American opera debut at the San Francisco Opera House, in Rimsky-Korsakov's *Le Coq d'Or* (1955). In 1956 she became the second black woman to appear at the Metropolitan Opera House in New York City, as Gilda in Verdi's *Rigoletto*. She married a Swedish journalist, Bengt Jansen (1957), and although she has taught at HOWARD UNIVERSITY (1976-1991) and other U.S. establishments, her career has been centered in Europe. She was elected to the Metropolitan Opera Association National Board in 1989.

SEE ALSO

Atlanta, Georgia; New York, New York.

North America

Doby, Lawrence Eugene "Larry" (b. December 13, 1923, Camden, S.C.), American baseball player; second African American to play in the major leagues and the first in the American League.

Larry Doby's family moved from South Carolina to Paterson, New Jersey, in 1938. After graduating from Eastside High School in 1942, Doby attended Long Island University and Virginia Union University. In 1946 he signed with the Newark Eagles of the Negro National League (NNL), helping them win the NNL pennant and making the all-star team. In 139 NNL games, Doby achieved a .378 average with 25 home runs.

In 1947 the Cleveland Indians bought Doby's contract from the Eagles. He played his first game for the Indians on July 4, 1947, 11 weeks after Jackie Robinson broke the color barrier by playing for the Brooklyn Dodgers in the National League. Though Doby was the second African American to play in the major leagues, he was the first in the American League. He was subjected to the same racist treatment that Robinson received, but received little of the media attention that Robinson did. He played sparingly and hit a poor .156 in 1947, but in 1948 Doby hit .301 during the season and helped the Indians win the World Series by batting .318.

Doby retired in 1962 after a successful 13-year major league career with the Indians, the Chicago White Sox, and the Detroit Tigers. He was a seven-time all-star, led the league in home runs in 1952 and 1954, and drove in 100 or more runs in five seasons. In 1978 he became the second African American to manage a big league team after Frank Robinson, when he managed the White Sox for part of the season. Since 1995 he has been special assistant to American League president Gene Budig. In March 1998 Doby was inducted into the Baseball Hall of Fame.

Robert Fay

SEE ALSO

Baseball in the United States; Negro Leagues.

Africa

Doe, Samuel Kanyon (b. May 6, 1951, Tuzon, Liberia; d. September 9?, 1990, Monrovia, Liberia), leader of LIBERIA from 1980 to 1990.

Samuel K. Doe, the Liberian leader whose 1980 military coup ushered in 17 years of violence, corruption, and confusion, left office a casualty of assassination, the act that had brought him there ten years earlier. Doe's ten-year rule was significant not only for what it created but for what it ended: more than a century of single-party rule, and the political domination of Liberia by an Americo-Liberian elite.

A member of the Krahn ethnic group, Doe grew up in the Liberian interior. After elementary school he briefly attended a Baptist high school but soon dropped out. While a soldier, Doe graduated from high school, studied radio and communications, and became an expert sharpshooter. At the time he ascended to the rank of master sergeant in 1979, he had no known political affiliation. But his colleagues said that Doe, like many indigenous Liberians, resented the privileged position of Americo-Liberians.

On April 12, 1980, Doe and a band of dissident soldiers overthrew and assassinated the elected president, William Tubman. Doe, who named himself head of state and commander in chief, publicly shot Tubman's cabinet members after parading them naked through the capital city of Monrovia. Despite his reputation for brutality, Doe maintained Liberia's traditionally close ties to the United States, including a state visit in 1982. After future president Charles Taylor and other rebel leaders launched a civil war in 1989, Doe spent months trapped inside the presidential palace, and was ultimately killed by rebel forces.

Kate Tuttle

See Also

Americo-Liberians; Taylor, Charles Ghankay; Monrovia, Liberia; Tubman, William Vacanarat Shadrach.

Africa

Dogon, an ethnic group of south-central Mali.

According to oral tradition, the Dogon were originally members of the Keita, a Mande-speaking group from the headwaters of the Niger River who fled their homes sometime between the tenth and thirteenth centuries because they refused to convert to Islam. The oral tradition may show that the Dogon absorbed Mande-speaking refugees from the centralized Islamic kingdoms of the Niger basin. However, the Voltaic (or Gur) language of the Dogon suggests a more ancient presence in their present-day homeland. They inhabit the rugged and isolated Bandiagara escarpment and surrounding regions southwest of the Niger bend. The cliffs at the edge of the escarpment protected the group from outside invaders. Dogon settlements concentrate around isolated pockets of arable land, where they farm millet as a subsistence crop. Traditionally, the Dogon have shared this territory with the pastoral Fulani, who exchanged their dairy products for Dogon grain and produce.

The Dogon's rugged and isolated territory left them relatively unaffected by French colonialism and missionary work, though the French did introduce the cultivation of onions as a cash crop during the 1920s. By maintaining their precolonial cultural traditions, the Dogon have attracted the attention of numerous ethnographers, including the French anthropologist Marcel Griaule and the French ethnographic filmmaker Jean Rouche. In recent years, however, the Dogon have increased their participation in the cash economy. Some villages have specialized in traditional crafts and performances in order to attract commercial tourism. Some Dogon have even left their homeland in search of wage labor, particularly in Bamako and the mines of Côte d'Ivoire. Unfortunately, the Dogon have also recently faced animosity from their Fulani neighbors, with whom they compete for scarce mineral resources and mining jobs.

Traditionally, the extended patrilineal family forms the basic social unit of the Dogon, who lack strong centralized authorities. A *hogon*, or headman (traditionally the oldest man in the area), provides spiritual leadership and arbitrates disputes for one or more villages. The hogon performs rituals and safeguards the religious masks for which the Dogon are famous. The power of the hogon, however, is relatively weak; a council of elders holds decision-making power within each village. The Dogon fall into at least four smaller groups: the Dyon, Arou, Onon, and Domno. Like neighboring Mande groups, the Dogon maintain a kind of caste system based on occupation. Farmers rank at the top of the system, while blacksmiths and hunters, who perform "polluting" work, are lower on the caste scale.

Unlike their Muslim neighbors, most Dogon still practice a traditional religion with a complex mythology. This has received considerable anthropological attention. Dogon cosmology considers every being a combination of complementary opposites; elaborate rituals are necessary to maintain the balance. Ancestor worship is an important facet of Dogon religion. Members of the Society of Masks perform rituals to guarantee that a person's "life force" will flee from his or her corpse to a future relative of the same lineage. One of the most famous Dogon rituals is the Sigi – a series of rituals performed once every 60 years – recorded by filmmaker Jean Rouche. Islamic missionaries, however, have had some success among the Dogon, and approximately 35 percent of the Dogon population are now Muslim.

Elizabeth Heath

See Also

Bamako, Mali; Colonial Rule; Tourism in Africa; Islam and Tradition: An Interpretation.

Latin America and the Caribbean

Dominica, island country between the Caribbean Sea and the North Atlantic Ocean, about half the distance between Puerto Rico and Trinidad and Tobago.

Dominica is nicknamed the Caribbean's "nature island" because of the lush foliage, green mountains, and abundant farms that cover the country. These natural resources are now touted as a tourist attraction, but in the centuries following European colonization, they also provided a fortunate haven for many indigenous and enslaved Dominicans. The rugged terrain made it difficult for white colonists to establish permanent settlements on the island, and then difficult for them to cultivate large plantations there. The mountains and forests even made Dominica a refuge for slaves from other islands who knew its terrain could provide a safe hiding space. Even today, Dominica is one of the least overdeveloped islands in the Caribbean. Dominica is home to one of the last remaining indigenous communities in the Caribbean, and it is among the few islands where most of the land is owned and worked by individual farmers.

A young girl poses in a Dominican national dress, whose styles derive from West African models.
Hatt/Hutchison

Dominica's first permanent inhabitants were Arawak Indians, who migrated to several Caribbean islands from South America in about 1000 B.C.E. In approximately 900 C.E. the Dominican Arawaks were invaded by the more aggressive Caribs, who named the oval-shaped island Wai'tukubuli, which means "tall is her body." When Christopher Columbus first sighted the island on November 3, 1493, he named it Dominica after the Spanish word for Sunday, the day of his "discovery." He and his men were in the middle of their second voyage to claim the entire New World for Spain, and they planned to add Dominica to their list of possessions. But the island's terrain was so rugged, and the Carib resistance so fierce, that the Spanish were unable to establish a permanent settlement there.

Instead, over the next 100 years European ships were allowed to stop on Dominica only long enough for the sailors to gather wood and water and to trade their knives, glass, and tools for Carib plantains, fruit, and tobacco. But Spain, England, France, and Holland were each establishing successful colonies on other Caribbean islands, and Dominica's lush soil remained tempting. In the seventeenth century European countries tried again to claim Dominica – first England in 1627 and then France in 1632, although neither was successful. Dominican Caribs, meanwhile, not only continued to defend their own home but also joined Caribs from other islands to attack colonists in St. Lucia, Antigua, Montserrat, and Barbuda. By 1686 England and France were both frustrated enough with the situation that they signed a neutrality treaty pledging to allow Dominica to "be inhabited by the savages to who [sic] it has been left."

But by the same period, the Dominican Carib population had begun sharply declining as a result of the years of battle and the diseases carried by the colonists. As their numbers dropped, French lumber workers quietly began settling the island, and soon English, Spanish, and Portuguese families followed. It was the French, however, who were to have the most lasting impact on the colony, largely because they were the first to import African slaves to work the land. By 1750 half of the island's 3000 inhabitants were enslaved West Africans, and these first black Dominicans would quickly become the island's majority.

France and England continued fighting over the island. Despite a 1748 treaty that reaffirmed Dominica's neutrality, it was declared a British territory in 1763 and a French one in 1778, and was reclaimed by the British in 1783. After two unsuccessful French attacks in 1795 and 1805 – during which the main city, Roseau, was burned to the ground – Dominica ultimately remained a British colony until independence in 1978, although French patois and Roman Catholicism remain predominant even today. But slavery developed very differently in Dominica than in the French or English Caribbean colonies, mainly as a result of the differences in topography.

The densely forested, hilly land made it impractical to operate massive sugar plantations such as those found on neighboring islands. Instead, most slaves lived on smaller estates that grew cotton and tobacco and that set aside land for slaves to grow their own gardens and raise their own livestock. Many slaves then brought their extra produce to the island's Sunday markets, and some Dominican slaves were able to earn enough money from this extra labor to purchase their freedom. This led to a class of free blacks on the island called *affranchis,* who often went on to buy estates and slaves of their own.

Dominican society was also enriched by the presence of several other groups, most notably the surviving Dominican Caribs and runaway slaves from other islands. By the 1770s the Caribs had been pushed to a 232-acre "reserve" on the east coast, but they succeeded in reestablishing their communities there and coexisting with the white colonists who had taken over their home. Meanwhile, before the French and British had even begun to settle the island, slaves on nearby islands had been able to see that Dominica's trees and mountains made it an excellent place to hide. For decades some had braved the short water crossing to escape into the Dominican hills, and by 1785 there were 13 camps of "nègres maroons," or runaway slaves, established around Dominica's center. After several camps tried to recruit Dominican slaves, four chiefs were found and executed in 1786, but those who survived continued leading their free black colonies.

After the 1795 French attack, British slaveholders devised a new use for their black slaves – military recruits. By 1797 slaves from several estates had been drafted to serve in the army, where they were called the Black Rangers. Soon afterward the governor of the colony purchased 200 African slaves expressly to form an extra regiment, the Eighth West Indian. These slave-soldiers were treated so harshly that they revolted in 1802, and while many of them were able to escape to the maroons, 34 were court-martialed and hanged. The period of such blatantly cruel mistreatment of Dominican slaves was nearly over. In 1807 Great Britain abolished the slave trade, and it was clear that full abolition in its colonies would eventually follow.

In Dominica it was also clear that the large numbers of free black farmers were not content with a political system that did not allow them equal franchise. An appointed council and a popularly elected House of Assembly ruled the colony, and black Dominicans wanted to participate in the elections. By the 1830s the island's black majority experienced dramatic changes. In a historic advance, the 1831 Brown Privilege Bill gave property-holding free blacks the right to vote and seek political office. Three black Dominicans were elected to the House of Assembly the very next year, and by 1838 the assembly had a black majority, making it the only British Caribbean colony to have a black-controlled legislature in the nineteenth century. This new majority came about because on August 1, 1834, slavery was formally abolished in all British colonies, allowing 14,175 black Dominicans to join the country's free population. As more and more black families were able to acquire their own small farms and estates, more of them became eligible to vote in the colony's affairs.

The eighteenth-century artist Agostino Brunias painted African slaves performing the handkerchief dance on Dominica, as local mulattos and Europeans observe. *Simon Dickinson Ltd., London*

Several black political leaders emerged during this period. James Garraway became

president and senior Council member, making him the first person of African descent to achieve high office in the British colonial dependencies. Charles Gordon Falconer, the prominent editor of the colony's liberal newspaper, led fellow legislators to push for social welfare laws. But white Dominicans, already financially devastated by abolition, fought to regain control of the colony's government. In 1863 they succeeded in dissolving both the House of Assembly and the Council, replacing them with a single legislative assembly, which by 1865 was split in half between elected and appointed members. In 1898 Dominica became a British Crown colony governed by a legislative council with six nominated members, completely ending the island's first era of popularly elected government.

Even before that development, black Dominicans had sometimes found themselves at odds with the island's government. In 1844 riots broke out in several villages after rumors that a proposed government census was actually a precursor to the reinstitution of slavery. A decade later 130 Dominicans were imprisoned for defying the 1856 Road Act, which stipulated that all Dominicans were required either to pay taxes to support road maintenance or to work on the road crews without pay. And in 1893 four men were killed and two women injured in the village of La Plaine when soldiers attempted to evict a man who could not pay his land taxes.

Many of these conflicts arose because Dominican society remained dominated by small landowners whose farms and villages were essentially self-sufficient and who were unhappy with government-imposed taxes that rarely brought them any visible improvements. Few public schools or even paved roads had been established in Dominica by the turn of the twentieth century. With the establishment of the Crown colony government, however, Great Britain made new efforts to implement programs to modernize the island.

By the start of World War I more roads had been built; telephone and electric lines were installed on much of the island; water and sewage systems had been improved; and processing lime juice for export to Great Britain and the United States had become a profitable industry for many of Dominica's farmers. The Carib territory was also officially expanded, from 232 to 3700 acres. A 1916 hurricane and a string of root diseases in 1924 put an end to the island's reign as the world's leading lime producer, but Dominicans were able to recover by turning to new crops. Soon bananas and coconuts were thriving on the island's farms.

Dominicans also made strides toward increased self-government in the 1920s, with the 1925 return of four elected members to the country's legislature. In 1931 the Constitutional Reform Association emerged.

A teenager sells black consciousness T-shirts in a market in Roseau, the capital of Dominica. *Taylor/Hutchison*

The next year, Dominican politician C. E. A. Rawle chaired a conference at Roseau at which 17 Caribbean political leaders came together to argue for a West Indian federation that would end Crown colony rule and establish full adult franchise across the region. Britain responded by attempting to placate Dominica's citizens, giving the country a new constitution in 1936 that allowed for a majority of elected legislative members and a governor. But Dominicans continued to push for even stronger reforms.

In a trend that was being repeated across the Caribbean, the unions served as a key vehicle for political changes. In 1945 the Dominica Trade Union was formed, followed by the Dominica Workers' Association in 1946 and the Teachers' Union in 1949. Throughout the region, the islands' black majorities were pushing toward political independence from their colonizers, and, while this process was slow, it was ultimately successful. In Dominica, British authorities finally granted universal adult suffrage in 1951. Dominicans used their new right to vote to support the Dominica Labour Party (DLP), the country's first political party. In 1961 the DLP's Edward Oliver LeBlanc, a small farmer, led the party to victory and became the first person from outside the country's urban elite to lead the Dominican government.

LeBlanc's platform stated that "it was time for the little man to begin enjoying the fruits of his labour." Under his leadership Dominica was granted associated statehood in 1967, an arrangement under which Great Britain continued to control Dominica's foreign affairs, but the country's domestic affairs were entirely self-governed – just one step away from full independence. When LeBlanc stepped down as premier in 1974 he was succeeded by Patrick John, who oversaw the transition to full independence on November 3, 1978. Less than a year after the symbolic victory of independence, however, John was forced out of office after protests over his government's restrictions on the right to free speech and widespread charges of corruption.

In August 1979, while the interim government was still attempting to restore order, Dominica was devastated by Hurricane David, leaving the country in a state of chaos. But the July 1980 elections provided an opportunity for a fresh start. A new party came to power, the Dominica Freedom Party, and with it barrister and politician Mary Eugenia Charles, who became the first female to be elected head of state in the Caribbean, and one of the few black female heads of state in the world. After weathering two unsuccessful coup attempts during her first year of office (including one that ex-prime minister John was convicted for having organized), Charles went on to earn international respect for supporting the 1983 United States invasion of Grenada in her role as chair of the Organization of East Caribbean States. When Charles resigned in 1995, she was succeeded by Edison James.

Contemporary Dominica is still strongly influenced by its unique blend of Carib, French, British, and African cultures. Its 3000-member Carib community is the largest in the Caribbean. While cricket is considered the island's national game, and the judicial and educational systems are both based on British models, the common language is still a French-based patois, and the dominant religion is Roman Catholicism. The culture, meanwhile, has a decided Afro-Caribbean flair. As one travel guide points out, "African, West Indian and native Carib traditions all contribute to a Creole culture, resulting in a mix of language, food, art and customs.... Common sights include Carib dugout canoes, stilt houses, Rastafarian dreadlocks, and red, green and yellow African clothing." Caribbean music also reflects these roots, and REGGAE, CALYPSO, and ZOUK are the island's most popular rhythms.

Dominicans take pride in claiming that their island is the only one Columbus would still recognize if he were to arrive today, because so much of its mountainous landscape remains the same. The island's shortage of the wide sandy beaches that have become synonymous with Caribbean vacation spots has kept it from becoming a widely popular tourist destination. But in recent years Dominica has begun to advertise its considerable resources as ideal for hikers, naturalists, and those who simply enjoy visiting untouched green spaces. Its resources also remain ideal for Dominica's thousands of small farmers and estate owners.

Lisa Clayton Robinson

See Also

Maroonage in the Americas; Slavery in Latin America and the Caribbean; Antigua and Barbuda; Rastafarians; Abolition and Emancipation in Latin America and the Caribbean; Catholic Church in Latin America and the Caribbean.

Latin America and the Caribbean

Dominican-Haitian Relations

Few islands in the world have been divided between two states for any length of time, and perhaps no island has given rise to such distinct collective identities as has the relatively large Caribbean island of HISPANIOLA, shared by HAITI and the DOMINICAN REPUBLIC. The history of Dominican-Haitian relations has followed a shifting and stormy course over the past 300 years. Those relations have played a profound role in shaping the politics, economics, and racial and national identities of each country.

One can trace Dominican-Haitian relations back to the early seventeenth century, when predominantly French small farmers and hunters, along with pirates and adventurers, began occupying the unpopulated western third of Hispaniola, an island that had been claimed in its entirety by Spain. Intermittent clashes between French and Spanish colonists followed, even after the 1697 Treaty of Ryswick recognized the de facto occupations of FRANCE and SPAIN around the globe. Periodic confrontations also continued despite a 1731 agreement that partially defined a border between the two colonies along the Masacre and Pedernales rivers. In 1777 the Treaty of Aranjuez established a definitive border between what Spain called Santo Domingo and what the French named Saint-Domingue, thus ending 150 years of local conflicts and imperial ambitions to control the entire island.

The eighteenth century was more an era of collaboration than confrontation between the Spanish and French parts of the island. A booming plantation society in Saint-Domingue based on African slave labor required livestock from Santo Domingo to supply its food, drive its mills, transport merchandise, and provide hides for leather. To some extent this expanding trade between the two countries pulled Santo Domingo out of its subsistence economy and impelled a measure of commercial development, which had been absent since the decline of the sixteenth-century SUGAR industry. Saint-Domingue remained, though, the envy of Dominican elites for the wealth generated by its plantations, which were relatively unencumbered by colonial monopolies and taxes on the slave trade (*see* COLONIAL LATIN AMERICA AND THE CARIBBEAN).

Ironically, commercial backwardness provided certain advantages for the Afro-Dominican majority in Santo Domingo. Slaves were far less profitable in a predominantly subsistence and cattle-ranching economy. This rendered their manumission relatively frequent and their escape less constrained than in Saint-Domingue. Former slaves and their descendants mixed with poor Spanish colonists; exploited Santo Domingo's vast, untamed woods; and constituted a vital and enduring free peasantry essentially hidden from the cities and outside the reach of the colonial state.

The relatively limited racial distinctions among Santo Domingo's predominantly free and mulatto rural population contrasted sharply with the central role of slavery and the rigid racial segmentation in Saint-Domingue's plantation society. These conditions in the French colony, together with the HAITIAN REVOLUTION, led to a strong black identity in Haiti with no counterpart in the Dominican Republic.

The onset of the Haitian Revolution in 1791 initiated a turbulent period of war and shifting sovereignty that engulfed both sides of the island. In Spanish Santo Domingo, the revolution triggered elite emigration, curtailed local investment, destroyed the main market for cattle (Saint-Domingue), and led to a series of Haitian invasions and occupations. Intra-European wars further complicated the situation. In the midst of the Haitian Revolution, Spain ceded the Spanish part of Hispaniola to France in return for lands that had been conquered in Europe (as agreed to in the 1795 Treaty of Basle). This drew Santo Domingo deeply into the battles of the Haitian Revolution, as France sought to use its new acquisition as a base from which to quash the revolt.

In 1801 Haitian leader François Toussaint L'Ouverture sought to frustrate the French strategy by occupying Santo Domingo. Before the arrival of the French troops, his army marched east and expeditiously took over the former Spanish colony. When French forces landed the following year with the aim of seizing the entire island, they were unable to capture Saint-Domingue. They did succeed, however, in occupying Santo Domingo (minus a broad swath of the central frontier region occupied by Haitian troops since 1794). French forces in Santo Domingo threatened Haitian sovereignty, and the French governor of Santo Domingo further provoked Haiti by authorizing colonists to capture and enslave Haitians. In 1805 Haitian president JEAN-JACQUES DESSALINES responded with an unsuccessful invasion of Santo Domingo. His retreat is associated in the Dominican Republic with the wanton destruction of lives and property, including massacres in the towns of Santiago and Moca.

Dominicans ejected the French in 1808 and reincorporated themselves into the Spanish Empire. Various factors, however, continued to foster Haitian interests in controlling the entire island, including persistent fears of a French invasion as well as hostility to the slavery regime that remained in Santo Domingo. At the same time, certain Dominican groups advocated union with Haiti. The leaders of this movement included ranchers who sought free trade with Haiti. But popular backing for unification came from slaves – roughly 15 percent of the population – and much of the nonwhite majority in general, who anticipated that unification would lead to emancipation and greater equality. Commencing on November 15, 1821, leaders of several Dominican frontier towns adopted the Haitian flag. Propelled by this movement, other Dominican forces that opposed unification with Haiti declared independence on November 30. They quickly succeeded in ousting the Spanish governor and capturing the capital. These forces founded the Independent State of Spanish Haiti, which affirmed the continuation of slavery and thus precluded popular support for the new state.

In 1822 Haitian president JEAN-PIERRE BOYER ordered the occupation and annexation of Spanish Haiti. His troops met virtually no resistance. Slavery was immediately abolished and land was promised to the freed slaves (*see* ABOLITION AND EMANCIPATION IN LATIN AMERICA AND THE CARIBBEAN). This garnered much support for Haiti among Santo Domingo's nonwhite majority but deeply antagonized slave owners and elites in general. Abolition of slavery ensured that Santo Domingo could not develop into a wealthy plantation society by capturing the world sugar market once supplied by Haiti. In addition the Haitian state appropriated extensive properties belonging to the church and to exiled landowners. These were distributed not only to peasants but also to Haitian military leaders and clients.

Over time Haiti's "unification of the island" became increasingly vexing to the Dominican population overall. First, Haiti sought to repay an overwhelming debt owed to France for properties confiscated in the Haitian Revolution with taxes on Dominicans. Second, the Haitian state demanded that peasants engage in commercial agriculture and sought to eliminate collectively used property.

In 1844 the Dominican Republic gained independence from Haiti. The ease with which a small and weak Dominican military overthrew Haitian rule and withstood repeated Haitian invasions that continued until 1856 suggests a relatively high level of Dominican popular support for separation from Haiti. This cohesion reflected the movement's rejection of any possible return of slavery and its public affirmation of racial unity. Many of its leaders were mulatto and black, such as Francisco del Rosario Sánchez and JOSÉ JOAQUÍN PUELLO.

Proclamations of racial unity, though, may have alienated elite supporters of separation from Haiti, some of whom favored subsequent annexation to France. Many in this group would later support annexation to Spain and to the United States. Annexationism was motivated in part by fear of another Haitian occupation, despite Haitian president Fabré Geffrard's assurance to the Dominican government in 1860 that Haiti no longer had designs on its country. The movement toward annexation also stemmed from antagonism among the predominantly white

Dominican elite toward popular politics and culture and its increasing embrace of Western discourses of positivism and racialism. Dominican intellectuals posited that the country's predominantly "mixed" population could never "advance" on its own toward "progress" and "civilization." This ideology was also manifest in official proclamations favoring European migration as a recipe for social and economic progress. Such thinking followed the prevailing currents throughout Latin America, but it was more invidious – and ironic – in a society predominantly of African descent (*see* WHITENING).

In 1861 the Dominican Republic reincorporated itself within the Spanish Empire. The population, however, did not accept the return of Spanish rule: not its economic monopolies, its efforts at racial segregation, or its insistence on Spanish customs and forms of jurisprudence. After less than two years a peasant revolt exploded into the Dominican Republic's most bloody war, and the Spanish were defeated by 1865. Interestingly, Dominican victory was facilitated by Haiti. Despite formidable warnings from Spain against intervening, Haiti provided arms, money, and refuge for Dominican troops. The Haitian state certainly had its own interest in expelling from the island an imperial power that still condoned slavery. Nonetheless, this aid constituted a notable instance of Dominican-Haitian collaboration.

Despite the history of Haitian invasions and wars for Dominican independence, anti-Haitian sentiment generally did not attain a virulent and racist character in the nineteenth-century Dominican Republic. In part this stemmed from the greater wealth and education of the Haitian population. Many Dominican parents sent their children to school in Haiti. Furthermore, racism was tempered in an era when the Dominican presidency was primarily occupied by blacks or mulattos, despite the fact that these leaders were the targets of racist criticisms and accused of being "pro-Haitian."

On the other hand, new forms of racism and anti-Haitianism began to develop in the late-nineteenth-century Dominican Republic, though they appeared predominantly within the elite population. First, the location of the border between the two countries remained an unresolvable issue. Dominicans insisted that the 1777 Treaty of Aranjuez still applied despite a century of war, conquest, and shifting sovereignty, while Haitians demanded a border corresponding with the de facto occupations of the two states. The conflict revolved around a substantial portion of the central frontier region where no natural borders existed, as they did in the north and south. This border dispute broadened, moreover, at the end of the nineteenth century, as Haitians began steadily migrating to sparsely populated areas of the frontier under Dominican control. There, most immigrants began clearing and farming unoccupied lands. One Dominican objection to this migration was that it could serve as a pretext for Haitian claims to a border located still farther to the east.

A second objection among Dominican intellectuals to the immigration of Haitians was that this "pacific invasion" was steadily "Haitianizing" and "Africanizing" the Dominican frontier, rendering Dominican culture more "barbaric" and "backward," and injecting new and undesirable admixtures of "African blood" into the Dominican racial composition. Popular Haitian culture, and VODOU in particular, became demonized as a threat to the Dominican nation. Haitian influence was identified as an obstacle to the elite's aims to render the country "modern" and "civilized," notions associated with European culture and whiteness. Even the African dimensions of popular Dominican religion, music, and idiom were now deemed to be the products of "Haitianization" and considered to impede progress.

There is little evidence that anti-Haitianism among the Dominican elite found much resonance at first outside the elite. In the Dominican frontier Haitians and Dominicans mixed freely, creating a bilingual and bicultural population with only limited ethnic segmentation and conflict. What would begin piquing popular Dominican prejudices in other regions was the influx of migrant Haitian laborers. In the 1870s the burgeoning Dominican sugar industry in the eastern provinces relied on Dominican workers. But after an 1884 sugar crisis, wages dropped, Dominican laborers returned to subsistence farming, and the industry turned to migrant workers. At first laborers came primarily from the Anglophone Caribbean, but in the 1920s and 1930s Haitian cane cutters began to provide an even cheaper labor force for an industry that was again in crisis. Like immigrants throughout the world who work at the lowest rung of the labor market, Haitian sugar workers in the Dominican Republic became the target of popular hostility, competition, and prejudice.

The most tragic and seismic event in Dominican-Haitian relations occurred in October 1937. At the orders of the Dominican dictator RAFAEL TRUJILLO, 10,000 to 20,000 persons of Haitian descent living mostly in the northern frontier were slaughtered by machete over the course of six days at the hands of the Dominican military – without warning, provocation, or ostensible conflict. Those killed were mostly small farmers. Virtually no sugar workers were attacked. A few months later, a barrage of killings and repatriations of Haitians occurred in the southern frontier.

The Haitian massacre occurred without any clear motive. In fact, it followed a period of improved relations between the two countries. In 1936 the border dispute had finally been resolved. The Dominican press had continued its reporting, begun in 1934, on the increasing warmth of Dominican-Haitian collaboration and cultural exchange. Emblematic of these new relations, Haitian president Sténio Vincent had renamed the main street in Port-au-Prince Rue Trujillo, while Trujillo christened a route in the Dominican frontier Vincent Road. In the years preceding the massacre the Dominican state did not legislate against Haitian migration, nor did it carry out any general repatriations of Haitians.

Nonetheless, profound tensions were simmering between Haiti and the Dominican Republic in the pre-massacre years. The Trujillo regime had begun to "Dominicanize" the frontier by evicting a number of Haitians from agricultural colonies on the border that had been established in the pre-Trujillo years. The regime also built new schools and instituted special curricula in the frontier, emphasizing standardized Spanish and patriotic symbols and histories. At the same time the Dominican state reportedly opposed the immigration in 1937 of Haitians who had recently been expelled from CUBA when that country "nationalized" its sugar workers. Finally, many members of the Dominican elite, including top state officials such as acting secretary of state JOAQUÍN BALAGUER, were virulently anti-Haitian.

If the causes of this violence remain murky, the effects are more clear. In addition to the murder of thousands of Haitians, the massacre destroyed the frontier's vital bicultural and transnational community. After the massacre there was a flood of official anti-Haitian sentiment in the Dominican Republic to justify the genocidal act. The Dominican press and state officials denounced Haitians as a "backward," "African" race that had "invaded" the country with its pernicious "superstitions," culture, and "blood." The massacre was implicitly linked to a nationalist ideology of Trujillo as the "civilizer" and "modernizer" of the Dominican Republic, extolling the dictator's public works campaigns and transformation of the Dominican peasantry into "modern" agriculturalists underwriting the nation's exceptional self-sufficiency.

For a variety of reasons beyond the Trujillo regime's impressive capacity to circulate propaganda, anti-Haitian feeling increased during the second half of the twentieth century in regions and classes where it had not been salient before. This was largely due to the growing role of Haitians as cane cutters working under slavelike conditions, with which they became associated. Haitian laborers were not permitted to work outside the sugar plantations; thus their freedom of movement was impeded, along with their capacity to make demands. Another factor in the growth of anti-Haitianism during this period was that Haiti as a whole became poorer and militarily weaker than the Dominican Republic for the first time in the 1930s, exacerbating the country's negative image. Finally, the massacre itself gave force to anti-Haitianism because of a collective need to justify the killings with which Dominicans were associated, even though the violence had been carried out under a dictatorship.

Recently, growing numbers of Haitians have moved into areas of the Dominican economy beyond sugar production, largely in response to the demand for cheap labor following a Dominican agricultural crisis in the 1980s. Although many Haitians have been forcefully returned to sugar plantations by police and army dragnets during the sugar harvest, in general a diversification of Haitian roles in both urban and rural areas has taken place. On the one hand, the dispersion of Haitians and Dominicans of Haitian descent – currently making up some 5 percent of the population – has fed elite hostility and popular resentment. On the other hand, the more varied integration of Haitians into the Dominican economy could ultimately lead to a degree of social mobility and reduced anti-Haitianism.

Under the regime of François and Jean-Claude Duvalier, the Haitian state had garnered significant fees from the Dominican government for the laborers it contracted to work on Dominican sugar plantations. Since the fall of the dictatorship in 1986, however, this system has been discontinued. Instead, the "slave" conditions of Haitian cane cutters have occasioned official protests and become an important nationalist issue.

Although both Haiti and the Dominican Republic are nations predominantly of African descent, the history of Hispaniola has produced two polar and often clashing collective identities. In Haiti a strong, black identity emerged, and the term "white" has been a synonym for "foreign." No popular black identity ever formed in the Dominican Republic, and the terms "black" and "Haitian" have been inextricably linked. These contrasts in ideology stem from radically dissimilar colonial histories of slavery and struggles for independence as well as interaction and conflicts between the two countries themselves.

Richard Turits

See Also

Duvalier, François; Slavery in Latin America and the Caribbean; Port-au-Prince, Haiti; Toussaint L'Ouverture, François Dominique; Géffard, Nicolas Fabre.

Latin America and the Caribbean

Dominican Republic,

a country in the Caribbean that is located on the eastern two-thirds of the island of La Hispaniola, with Haiti occupying the western part of the island; bounded on the south by the Caribbean Sea, on the north by the Atlantic Ocean, on the east by the Mona Passage, which separates it from Puerto Rico, and on the west by Haiti.

In 1492 Christopher Columbus became the first European to arrive on the island of La Hispaniola. Spain fought with France for control of the island until 1697, when it was divided into two territories by the Peace of Ryswick: French Saint-Domingue, which occupied the westernmost third and became the Republic of Haiti in 1804; and Spanish Santo Domingo, which occupied the eastern two-thirds and became the Dominican Republic in 1844, after having been controlled by Haiti for 20 years. The population of the Dominican Republic, which fought for independence from Spain in 1865 and against the United States occupation in 1916, has always been composed mainly of blacks and mulattos.

The nation's African heritage is evident in every aspect of Dominican life: music and dance, cuisine, language, the Dominican Vodoun religion, and the Gagá cult. But this heritage has been marginalized by the widespread belief that Dominicans are mostly Hispanic, or even Taíno Indian, rather than black. Nevertheless, Dominicans generally recognize their African heritage as part of their ethnicity, though they do not necessarily see blackness as central to their identity. For Afro-Dominicans the process of defining racial identity has been complicated by the fact that the Dominican nation emerged from the black Republic of Haiti. The antiblack and anti-Haitian ideology of the Dominican Republic's dominant classes has existed alongside the awareness of the Dominicans' African heritage (*see* Dominican-Haitian Relations).

At the time of Columbus's arrival, around 400,000 Taíno Indians inhabited the island of Hispaniola. Europeans saw the Taínos as a natural resource to be exploited in the development of the colony. The number of Taínos dramatically diminished in the first years of Spanish colonization as a result of European disease and the *encomienda* system, in which the Taínos were distributed among the colonizers to perform forced labor in the mines and farms, with the requirement that they be taught the Catholic faith. The encomiendas became characteristic of the Spanish colonial system in the Americas. Many Taínos committed suicide, and many Taíno women aborted pregnancies so that their children would not be born into the conditions that they themselves endured. Census figures from 1508 indicated that only 60,000 Taínos remained. Between 1515 and 1517 the scarcity of Taíno labor prompted 800 European settlers to emigrate to Central and South America in the search for gold and better labor resources. In 1516 there were only around 715 Spaniards and free blacks in the island of La Hispaniola, which meant a total population of less than 4000 people, including enslaved Africans. The few remaining Taínos were distributed among the most powerful settlers. In 1519 a mere 3000 Taínos were extant. Within the first 40 years of Spanish occupation, the Taíno population had been almost completely destroyed.

Conquest and Colonization

The first enslaved African to reach Hispaniola arrived with Columbus. Santo Domingo is considered the "cradle of blackness in the Americas" because it was the port of entry for the first slaves traded to the New World. From 1492 until 1510 (the process was made official in 1500), the island saw a slow introduction of *ladinos* (Christianized blacks), and *bosales* (slaves imported directly from Africa). They came from what today are the countries of Guinea, Cape Verde, São Tomé, the Republic of the Congo, Mali, and Angola. In the process of the transatlantic slave trade, these people came to be grouped under ethnic labels such as the Arará, Manicongo, and Lucumí (or Yoruba), among others (*see* African Ethnic Groups in Latin America and the Caribbean). The price of an individual slave varied from 90 to 150 pesos, making slaves a costly investment. These slaves performed different kinds of work. They could be laborers in the sugar cane fields; in the early years, gold miners; *jornaleros*, or slaves who were hired out by their owners to a third party for a specific amount of time; or domestic servants.

When the island's gold was totally exhausted, agriculture seemed a more plausible means of acquiring wealth. In 1510 and after a period of trial and error, the settler Gonzalo de Vellosa established one of the first successful sugar cane mills, fomenting investments in Santo Domingo, where the transportation facilities were better and most of the elite lived. By 1516 he finally proved that the sugar business could be lucrative. The number of black slaves increased with the growth of the sugar industry and the multiplication of sugar refineries, which also used a remaining small number of Taínos as labor force. Many Europeans emigrated to the island in the hope of becoming wealthy traders. Nevertheless, from 1520 to 1540, after gold and laborers in Santo Domingo became scarce, many Europeans left the island for Mexico and Peru. Blacks on the island always outnumbered whites. In 1542 there were 30,000 blacks, 6000 whites, and only 200 Taínos. At the end of the sixteenth century, 61 percent of the population was black, 23 percent was white, and 15 percent was mulatto.

After 1581 ginger cultivation and cattle raising surpassed the production of sugar cane in economic importance, bringing changes to the slave system. Cattle raising required fewer slaves than sugar cane production. Slaves were permitted to bear arms. The years after 1568 were very difficult. The number of slaves decreased significantly due to diseases, sparking a labor crisis. In 1606 only 800 slaves were dedicated to the production of sugar, while 6742 worked

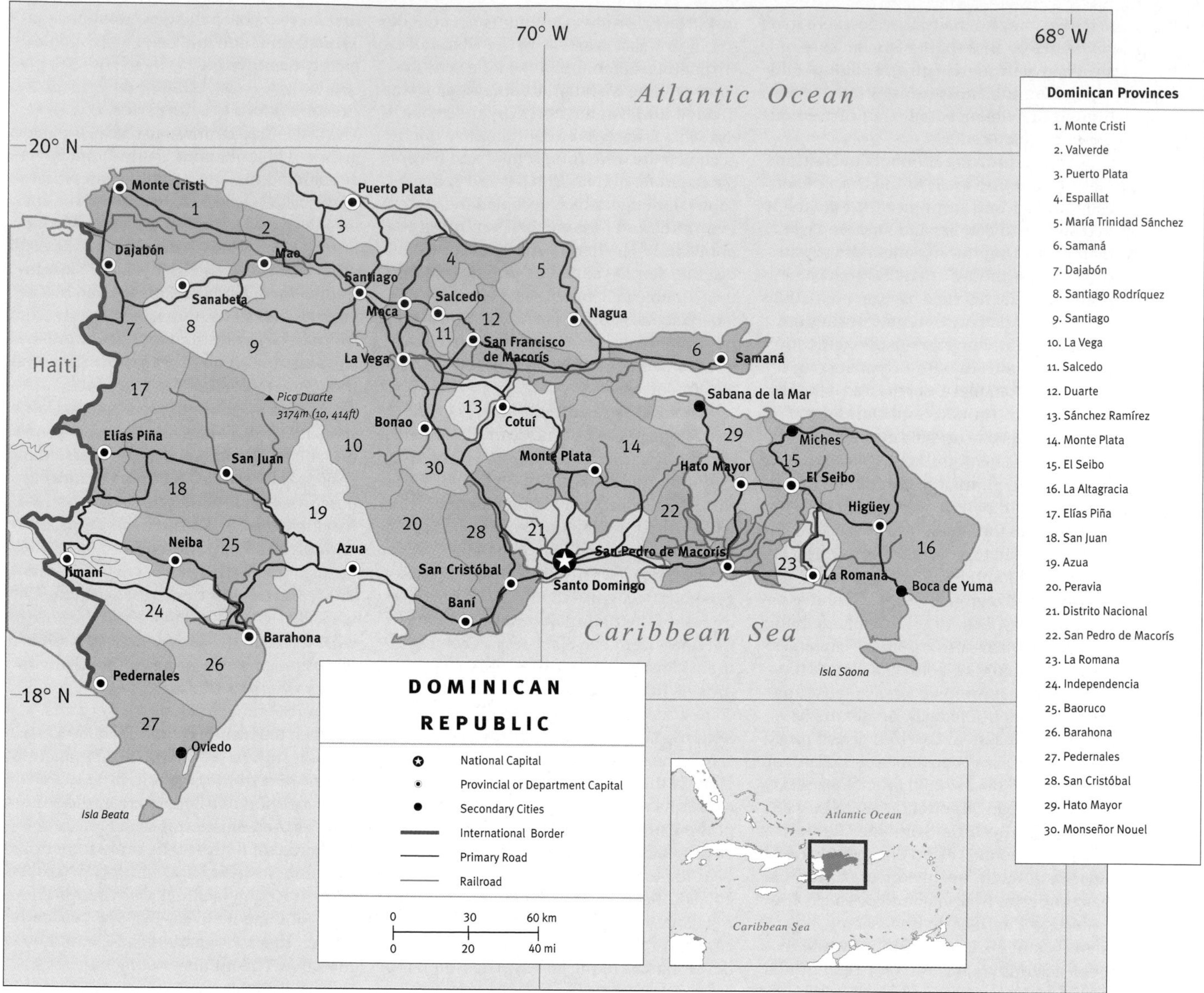

cultivating ginger, cassava, and corn and 88 worked as domestic servants.

Blacks and mulattos dominated Santo Domingo's population for many reasons. The number of slaves who were imported legally or introduced to the island as contraband increased as a result of slave marriages as well as interracial reproduction. With the downfall of the plantation economy, these people had no alternative but to stay on the island. A significant number of slaves crossed the border from French Saint-Domingue to escape brutal conditions, and formed maroon communities such as San Lorenzo de las Minas (established 1678) (*see* Maroonage in the Americas). In addition, many slaves, such as Pablo Alí and his Batallón de los Morenos, won their freedom by fighting for the Spanish monarchy during the Haitian Revolution, which resulted in the establishment of the Republic of Haiti in 1804. When the slaves in Santo Domingo were finally given their freedom by the Haitians in 1822, the island's population had a majority of free blacks.

Emancipation and Abolition

The Código Negro Carolino, written by the colonial elite out of fear and prejudice against blacks, was a system of laws that regulated every aspect of the lives of Santo Domingo's slaves, giving slaveholders the authority to decide what slaves ate, where they lived, and what they wore, and to exercise control over slaves' religious beliefs, activities, and other such considerations. Slaves were severely punished for their disobedience. The Código was established because Creoles lived in fear of slave revolts, which they tried to prevent by favoring the importation of black slaves directly from Africa who were therefore without the language of their new country. Still, the first registered black insurrection in Santo Domingo, which took place in the sugar refineries owned by Almirante Diego Colón and Melchor de Castro in 1522, was facilitated because it was led by an ethnic group called the *gelofes*, known for their strength and pride, who shared the same language. Another effort toward preventing revolts was the importation of African women who might create family bonds with male slaves and give birth to new slaves, thus also offering a solution to the problem of a diminishing labor force.

The slaves who escaped to the mountains were called *cimarrones*. They organized themselves into maroon settlements, called *manieles*, which had their own economic and social structures. The number of manieles grew as the slave population increased. Manieles existed outside the colonial settlements; at night, cimarrones came down from the mountains to burn the refineries and obtain food. Those who were caught faced harsh punishment.

In 1537 records noted that a group of cimarrones led by Juan Vaquero repeatedly assaulted Spanish settlers from Santo Domingo in the southern part of the island. Other known maroon leaders were Sebastián Lemba and Juan Criollo in Higuey, Diego de Ocampo in La Vega, and Diego de Guzmán in Barouco. San José de Ocoa, the best-known maroon settlement in Santo Domingo, was subjugated by the Spanish in 1666. Nevertheless, others, like the Neiba settlement (a section of what is now Barahona) integrated into colonial society after reaching an agreement with the Spanish in 1783. Other settlements existed in Cotui, Buenaventura, Samaná, Azua, and San Juan de la Maguana.

In 1801, during the Haitian Revolution, the former Haitian slave and military leader Toussaint L'Ouverture took possession of Spanish Santo Domingo for Republican France. He abolished slavery and won the love and respect of the vast majority of Dominicans. Nevertheless, in 1802 French soldiers invaded the island and restored slavery. Santo Domingo remained under French control until the 1809 War of Reconquest, in which Creoles, aided by the Spanish governor of Puerto Rico, took over the island to again bring it under Spanish jurisdiction. In 1812 blacks and mulattos, slave and free, attempted to return the island to Haiti, but the plot was discovered and its leaders were publicly executed.

In 1822 Haitian president JEAN-PIERRE BOYER took over Santo Domingo, bringing the whole island under his rule for 22 years. He abolished slavery, gaining the favor of the black community but not the approval of the Creole elite. In 1824 and 1825 Boyer invited 6000 free African Americans to the island. Many of them settled in the towns of Samaná and Puerto Plata and acclimated to the Creole way of life. To this day, the descendants of these people in Samaná maintain a culture that is distinct from the rest of the Dominicans.

In 1838 the white Creole Juan Pablo Duarte founded the Sociedad Secreta La Trinitaria, which promoted independence from Haiti with the goal of forming the Dominican Republic. Independence was achieved on February 27, 1844. Many Afro-Dominicans, such as Francisco del Rosario Sánchez and JOSÉ JOAQUÍN PUELLO, played key roles in the struggle for independence. Immediately afterward, the new government was challenged by an uprising in Monte Grande by Afro-Dominicans who had fought for independence with SANTIAGO BASORA as their leader. They feared annexation to Spain, which still enslaved blacks in CUBA and Puerto Rico. On July 17, 1844, it was proclaimed by law that any slave entering the Dominican Republic from that day forward be free upon arrival. After 1844, however, what could be considered enslaved labor was imported from the WEST INDIES. Known disparagingly as the *cocolo* community, these workers continued to arrive until the 1940s. In San Pedro de Macorís alone, the number of cocolos increased from 500 in 1884 to 7000 in 1918.

Independence was followed by 20 years of highly unstable governments, dominated by Pedro Santana and Buenaventura Báez, and other authoritarian leaders known as *caudillos*. They went in and out of power several times, but both had intentions of returning the republic to a colonial state under different European countries. In April 1860, Santana, who was the president at the time, backed by the Creole elite, negotiated the annexation of the republic to Spain, sparking the Restoration War (1863-1865), which resulted in Spain's final withdrawal from the Dominican Republic. Starting as a peasants' rebellion, the Restoration War evolved into a conflict in which Afro-Dominicans who feared the reinstitution of slavery played a central role. One such Afro-Dominican was the military leader GREGORIO LUPERÓN. The war marked the first time that Afro-Dominicans united to fight for their sovereignty and, in the process, served as political and military leaders. Dominican politics remained unstable until 1882, when the Afro-Dominican ULÍSES HEUREAUX initiated two decades of dictatorship. This era was characterized by a growing dependence on the United States, which oversaw the Dominican Republic's economy after the assassination of President Heureaux in July 1899.

Women meet to discuss community affairs and plan political action in Padre Las Casas, Dominican Republic. *Philip Wolmuth*

THE DOMINICAN REPUBLIC IN THE TWENTIETH CENTURY

The influence of the United States increased over the years, reaching its peak in 1916 when the United States invaded the Dominican Republic and instituted a military government that lasted until 1925. The United States justified this invasion as a national security strategy since U.S. participation in World War I was imminent, and many of the Dominican political leaders of the time expressed public support for Germany. The invasion was met with resistance by many Afro-Dominicans, among them RAMÓN NATERA, GREGORIO URBANO GILBERT, and Mateo Liborio. However, some economic and social conditions seemed to improve under U.S. rule. During this period, the Dominican Republic became the second largest exporter (after Cuba) of sugar cane. Many Haitians were brought to work as *braceros*, sugar cane cutters. They worked under the same inhumane conditions to which slaves had been subject previously, a situation tantamount to slavery. The sugar cane industry, which has been one of the primary sources of Dominican wealth, was possible because the Haitian braceros took these highly undesirable jobs due to their limited economic options.

The U.S. invasion brought resentment caused by the occupants' racist attitudes toward Dominicans. Furthermore, the departure of occupying forces was followed by growing racial hatred against Haitians, which found fertile ground in the regime of dictator Rafael Leonidas Trujillo. The former commander in chief of the Dominican National Guard, which was created and trained by the U.S. Marines during the occupation, Trujillo ruled from 1930 until his assassination in 1961. His regime was characterized by a savage campaign against Haitians. In 1937 he ordered the killing of at least 25,000 Haitians as part of an attempt to "whiten" the country. During his regime, participation in any kind of Vodou ceremonies was prohibited by a government campaign that sought to eradicate African spiritual expressions. In another example of repression and prejudice, on December 28, 1962, the year after Trujillo's death, the mainly Afro-Dominican peasant community of PALMA SOLA, which challenged the racial, political, and economic status quo of the country, was massacred by the Dominican military.

In 1963, two years after Trujillo's assassination, Juan Bosch won the elections for the opposition's Dominican Revolutionary Party, which had been founded in 1939 by anti-Trujilloist exiles with the support of the middle and lower classes. Dominican armed forces, directed by General Wessín y Wessín, staged a successful coup against Bosch's presidency in that same year. Bosch went into exile in Puerto Rico, and military powers ruled the republic, though a sham civilian government, presided over by a triumvirate, was established.

Dominicans who sought a civilian government revolted again in 1965. A battle broke out between Loyalists, who wanted to maintain the triumvirate and were led by General Wessín y Wessín, and Constitutionalists, who wanted Bosch to return. The specter of communism and the possible victory of the Constitutionalists was used to justify a second invasion by the United States on April 28, 1965. The conflict was formally ended on August 31, with the Act of Dominican Reconciliation. This act stated that a temporary government would preside until national elections were held in June 1966.

JOAQUÍN BALAGUER was elected president in the 1966 elections and reelected in 1970 and 1974; he lost the 1978 elections but returned to power in 1982. Balaguer perpetuated Trujillo's racial policies and hatred toward Haitians. In 1989 he wrote *La isla al revés: Haití y el destino dominicano* ("The Island Turned on its Head: Haiti and Dominican Destiny") in which, after stating that Dominicans are Hispanic, "white and Christian," he exposes his racist ideology by attributing to Haitians the responsibility for the "progressive ethnic decadence" of the Dominican nation.

In 1994 Balaguer ran against JOSÉ FRANCISCO PEÑA GÓMEZ for the presidency. Born of Haitian parents, Peña Gómez became the first Afro-Dominican of Haitian descent to be elected president with an overwhelming victory. Nevertheless, the victory occurred despite a massive campaign against him, with Balaguer claiming that Peña Gómez's "Haitianness" represented "real blackness," disqualifying him from representing the Dominican people, according to Balaguer's definition of national identity. Balaguer's opposition ultimately prevented Peña Gómez from assuming the presidency by alleging that the elections were fraudulent. After new elections, Leonel Fernández, playing by Balaguer's rules, became president and Peña Gómez was restricted to the position of major in the armed forces.

Many Afro-Dominicans have been essential figures in the development and history of the country. They have stood out in all areas, from politics to the arts. Personalities like Maximiliano Gómez, head of the left-wing party Movimiento Popular Dominicano, and FLORINDA MUÑOZ SORIANO, known as Mamá Tingó, who fought with the peasants from Hato Viejo for the right to own their land, have struggled for social justice and better living conditions. Afro-Dominican writers like BLAS JIMÉNEZ, MANUEL DEL CABRAL, NORBERTO JAMES, Ramón Aristy Marrero, and AÍDA CARTAGENA PORTALATÍN are recognized for their great talent. Some, like JOHNNY VENTURA, have crossed the national borders to become true cultural, as well as political, leaders.

The relationship between race and Dominican national identity has been a very important factor in the formation of the country. Ethnic and racial identification vary depending on who defines whom, with people stressing one of the Dominican Republic's three different roots, the Taíno, the Spanish, and the African. The Dominican Republic's African heritage is without doubt an essential part of that definition: this has been true even when racism and the definition of Dominicans as mainly Hispanic have been institutionalized; when many prefer to call themselves *indio* (Indian, the official racial designation) to avoid blackness, while knowing that the native Indians have been extinct for centuries; and even when, more often than not, the Dominican Republic's African roots are diminished or not recognized.

Mayda Grano de Oro

In Samaná, province of the Dominican Republic located in the northeastern region, Dominicans enjoy a Sunday dance in Las Terrenas. Around 1825 a large group of African Americans settled in this area, where many of their descendants still live. *Maggie Steber/Aurora*

See Also
Gómez Horacio, Maximiliano; São Tomé and Príncipe; Slavery in Latin America and the Caribbean; Marrero Aristy, Ramón; Mateo, Liborio; Trujillo, Rafael; Toussaint L'Ouverture, François Dominique; Abolition and Emancipation in Latin in Latin America and the Caribbean; Black Codes in Latin America; Hispaniola.

North America

Domino, Antoine ("Fats"), Jr.

(b. February 26, 1928, New Orleans, La.), African American singer, pianist, and songwriter whose songs topped both rhythm and blues and rock 'n' roll charts during the 1950s.

Fats Domino was one of the few black musicians of the 1950s to successfully span RHYTHM AND BLUES (R&B) and rock 'n' roll, appealing to young white audiences while maintaining his popularity with black audiences. His formula for success was a driving, boogie-woogie style of piano playing and a New Orleans Creole style of singing.

Domino was born and raised in New Orleans, where French Creole was his first language. He learned to play the piano by the age of nine and was performing at local music venues by the time he was a teenager. His musical career took off in the late 1940s after he teamed up with Dave Bartholomew, a former Duke Ellington trumpet player, and his band. After signing a contract with New Orleans-based Imperial Records, Domino collaborated with Bartholomew to record "The Fat Man" (1950), his first R&B hit. His "Goin' Home" reached the number one slot on the R&B charts in 1952.

Domino's songs began to storm *Billboard*'s rock 'n' roll charts in the mid-1950s. "Ain't That a Shame" (1955) marked the beginning of a string of hits in 1956 that included "I'm in Love Again," "My Blue Heaven," and "Blueberry Hill." Domino continued to record hits with Bartholomew, who served as his arranger, conductor, and producer, and even made some movie appearances before leaving Imperial Records in 1962.

Even though some of his songs were stolen and quickly marketed by such white artists as Pat Boone and Ricky Nelson, Domino put more than a dozen songs in the Top 10 and sold more than 65 million records between 1950 and 1962. With the exception of Elvis Presley, no other artist was more popular than Fats Domino during the 1950s. In 1986 he was inducted into the Rock and Roll Hall of Fame.

Aaron Myers

See Also
Boogie Woogie; Creoles; New Orleans, Louisiana; Ellington, Edward Kennedy ("Duke").

Latin America and the Caribbean

Donga

(Ernesto Joaquim Maria dos Santos) (b. April 5, 1889, Rio de Janeiro, Brazil; d. August 25, 1974, Rio de Janeiro, Brazil), Afro-Brazilian musician and composer and one of the principal innovators of SAMBA, a musical genre developed in the early twentieth century that later emerged as the national music and dance of BRAZIL.

Donga grew up in a social milieu with former slaves from the northeastern state of BAHIA who had migrated to Rio de Janeiro after abolition in 1888. His mother, known as Tia Amélia, was a Bahian woman who hosted many CANDOMBLÉ celebrations in their home in the neighborhood of Cidade Nova. Starting around 1910, a young group of musicians and composers, including Donga, PIXINGUINHA, João da Baiana, Sinhô, and Heitor dos Prazeres, frequented the famous parties of another *baiana* known as TIA CIATA. At her house they entertained guests with traditional Afro-Brazilian rhythms such as *lundu*, *maxixe*, and *marcha*, which they mixed with imported styles such as the *habanera*. In November 1916 Donga registered the song "Pelo telefone" (By Telephone) at the National Library, becoming the first composer officially to use the term *samba*. The song was recorded by the Banda Odeon in time to become a huge hit in the Carnival of 1917. Around this time, Donga began playing guitar in a seminal group led by the flutist Pixinguinha, Os Oito Batutas, which popularized the emerging genre. In 1922 the group performed in Paris, France, for six months, then in ARGENTINA. Although he was a pioneer of samba, Donga's only individual LP recording was released posthumously.

Christopher Dunn

See Also
France; Rio de Janeiro, Brazil; Carnivals in Latin America and the Caribbean.

North America

Dorsey, Thomas Andrew

(b. July 1, 1899, Villa Rica, Ga.; d. January 23, 1993, Chicago, Ill.), African American pianist, arranger, and composer, known as the "Father of Gospel Music."

Thomas A. Dorsey's name is synonymous with modern GOSPEL MUSIC. Dorsey composed over 1000 songs in his lifetime, half of which were published. With creative genius and business savvy, Dorsey popularized songs that combined the rhythm and tonality of blues with lyrics about personal spiritual salvation. Countless gospel performers achieved their first success singing Dorsey's music. His most famous song, "Precious Lord, Take My Hand," is one of the most popular gospel songs in America.

Dorsey was born to Etta and Thomas Madison Dorsey. Thomas Madison was an itinerant preacher, and Etta played the organ in church. As a child, Dorsey was regularly exposed to spirituals and Baptist hymns. Extended family members introduced Dorsey to rural blues and shaped-note singing. In 1908 the family moved to Atlanta, where Dorsey learned to play the piano by watching pianists at a vaudeville theater on Decatur Street. Dorsey also saw Ma Rainey and BESSIE SMITH perform at this theater. By age 12 Dorsey had become a proficient piano player, honing his improvisational skills at dances and rent-parties around Atlanta. After teaching himself to read music, Dorsey left Atlanta and traveled to Chicago in 1916.

In Chicago Dorsey continued his musical training and learned the skills of composing and arranging. He copyrighted his first blues composition, "If You Don't Believe I'm Leaving, You Can Count the Days I'm Gone," on October 9, 1920. During the 1921 National Baptist Convention, Dorsey heard W. M. Nix sing "I Do, Don't You" and became convinced that his mission in life was to evangelize through music. In 1922 Dorsey wrote his first two sacred songs, "If I Don't Get There" and "We Will Meet Him in the Sweet By and By." Dorsey's evangelical efforts did not last long, and he returned to secular music, joining Will Walker's "The Whispering Syncopators" a few months after being saved at the Convention. While playing with the "Syncopators" Dorsey began composing blues in the style of W. C. Handy for the Chicago record companies. Dorsey's first hit came when King Oliver's Creole Jazz Band recorded his composition "Riverside Blues" in December 1923. The success of Bessie Smith's recording of "Downhearted Blues" in 1923, however, soon made Dorsey's vaudevillian blues obsolete. Almost single-handedly, Smith swayed the blues recording industry to her "downhome" style. Fortunately for Dorsey, he was well versed in this style from his days playing in Atlanta.

In April 1924 Dorsey became piano player and director of Ma Rainey's Wild Cat Jazz Band. For the next two years Dorsey served as composer, arranger, and conductor for this touring band. (During that time, Ma Rainey's only rival among popular downhome blues singers was Bessie Smith.) After suffering from incapacitating depression starting in 1926, Dorsey underwent a second conversion in 1928. This conversion and the death of a close friend inspired Dorsey to compose his first gospel blues song "If You See My Savior, Tell Him That You Saw Me."

Again, however, the financial lure of commercial secular music convinced Dorsey to begin composing and playing the blues. This time his partner was guitar player Hudson Whitaker. Together they recorded over 60 songs as Georgia Tom and Tampa Red between 1928 and 1932. Dorsey and Whitaker are credited with creating the "hokum" blues style. "Hokum" consisted of guitar and piano instrumentation, up-tempo rhythms, strong bass, and usually included sexually suggestive lyrics. Popularizing this style with their seminal double entendre blues, "It's Tight Like That," Dorsey and Whitaker went on to write and record such songs as "Pat That Bread," "You Got That Stuff," "Where Did You Stay Last Night?" "It's All Worn Out," and "Somebody's Been Using That Thing."

At this point in his career Dorsey was straddling the fence between sacred and profane music. He continued recording blues with Whitaker as well as selling sheet music of his gospel songs and organizing a gospel choir at Ebenezer Baptist Church. After Dorsey's wife Nettie and their child died in August 1932, Dorsey forsook the blues. While in St. Louis to promote his gospel songs, Dorsey was called home to find that Nettie had fallen ill. When he returned Nettie had died and their child was on the verge of death. Stricken with grief, Dorsey sat at his piano to console himself and composed "Precious Lord, Take My Hand."

Dorsey met Sallie Martin, the "Mother of Gospel Music," in 1932, and they collaborated until 1939 organizing gospel choruses and publishing gospel songs. Together they founded the National Convention of Gospel Choirs and Choruses in August of 1933. The 1930s were Dorsey's most prolific years. Mahalia Jackson replaced Sallie Martin as Dorsey's singer in 1939, and they toured together until 1944. The Jackson-Dorsey combination ushered in the golden age of gospel music, during which many artists achieved their first success with a Dorsey song. Singers such as Sister Rosetta Tharpe ("Rock Me"), Marion Williams ("Standing Here Wondering Which Way To Go"), The Soul Stirrers ("Never Turn Back"), Dixie Hummingbirds ("When the Gates Swing Open"), and Bessie Griffin ("Shake My Mother's Hand") had popular hits with Dorsey's songs. Elvis Presley and Red Foley garnered gold records from singing Dorsey's song "Peace in the Valley." Dorsey continued promoting gospel music as the head of the National Convention of Gospel Choirs and Choruses until his death in 1993.

See Also

Atlanta, Georgia; Blues, The; Chicago, Illinois; Handy, William Christopher (W.C.); Oliver, Joseph ("King"); Rainey, Gertrude Pridgett ("Ma"); Soul Stirrers; Tharpe, "Sister" Rosetta; Spirituals, African American.

Africa

Dos Santos, José Eduardo

(b. 1942, Luanda, Angola), president of Angola (1979-) and head of the ruling Popular Movement for the Liberation of Angola Party (MPLA).

José Eduardo Dos Santos was born in Luanda. He joined the Marxist MPLA's youth organization as a boy and enlisted in its guerrilla army at age 19. He was sent to study in the Union of Soviet Socialist Republics (USSR) on an MPLA scholarship from 1963 to 1970. He graduated with degrees in petroleum engineering and radar telecommunications. Dos Santos served as MPLA representative in Yugoslavia and the People's Republic of the Congo (formerly Zaire, now the Democratic Republic of the Congo) before being elevated to the party's Central Committee in 1974. After Angola achieved independence from Portugal in 1975, he held important ministerial posts in the MPLA government. He was only 37 years old when he became president on September 21, 1979, succeeding Agostinho Antonio Neto, the first president of Angola.

Dos Santos moved swiftly to consolidate his power within the government. A political moderate and a pragmatic leader, he replaced those in his administration who wanted to govern strictly according to communist doctrine with competent administrators and technicians. However, his attempts to build on the economic and political work of his predecessor were unsuccessful because of the continuing civil war between the MPLA and the National Union for the Total Independence of Angola (UNITA). The civil war began following Angolan independence when the MPLA and UNITA each formed a government claiming to represent the new nation. Each side received aid from foreign powers that saw Angola, with its oil reserves, as strategically important.

Dos Santos's government had the support of the U.S.S.R., which contributed to the cost of as many as 50,000 troops from the Communist nation of Cuba. UNITA was aided by the United States. Angola was also important to South Africa, which ruled southwest Africa (now Namibia), where a black nationalist movement was waging a guerrilla war for independence. South African military intervention in Angola began in late 1975 in support of UNITA's bid to take control of the newly independent country. South Africa invaded again in support of UNITA in 1981, 1983, and 1987 to 1988. South African troops were finally withdrawn from Angola in 1989 as part of the international agreement leading to Namibian independence.

The South African invasions of Angola helped dos Santos strengthen his control within the MPLA, and he was able to make major economic, diplomatic, and political changes. In August 1987 he announced a major economic recovery plan. Blaming the nation's problems on the excessive centralization of socialist planning, corruption, and too much bureaucracy, he proposed privatization of some state enterprises, banking reforms, and measures to encourage foreign investment. In 1988 he introduced plans to further liberalize Angola's economy. Small businesses were opened to private enterprises, and joint ventures with international firms were allowed for the first time. Angola also affiliated with the International Monetary Fund (IMF) and the International Bank for Reconstruction and Development, known as the World Bank.

In foreign policy, dos Santos met with Mikhail Gorbachev, then leader of the USSR, in 1988 to discuss the removal of Cuban troops from Angola. At that time, South African troops still occupied a portion of southern Angola. Dos Santos signed the first of a series of agreements that resulted in the withdrawal of all foreign troops from Angola. South African troops withdrew across the southern border in 1989. Cuban troops left in a staged withdrawal that was completed by May 1991.

In the political arena, in 1990 the MPLA's Third Party Congress pledged to create a multiparty political system, to study the draft of a new constitution eliminating the central role of the party, and to transform its ideology from Marxism-Leninism to democratic socialism.

Dos Santos consistently supported the often frustrating peace process within Angola, which began in earnest in 1990 after Namibia became an independent nation and the cold war diminished. The May 1991 peace accord brokered by Portugal, the United States, and the USSR put an end to the fighting and led in the fall of 1992 to national elections, in which the MPLA and dos Santos ran against UNITA and its leader, Jonas Savimbi. Although the MPLA won the parliamentary elections and dos Santos appeared to have won a close victory in the presidential race, the election results became irrelevant when UNITA resumed fighting.

For the first few months of 1993, it appeared as if Savimbi's forces might achieve through war what they had not gained at the polls. The government, however, was able to mobilize international support from UNITA's former allies, the United States and South Africa. In May 1993 the United States government recognized Angola, began pressuring Savimbi to settle the war, and, for the first time, made U.S. aid available to the Angolan government. By late summer 1993, UNITA's offensive had stalled. The dos Santos government returned to peace negotiations, now brokered principally by the United Nations and African nations. A fragile peace was established by the Lusaka Protocol of November 20, 1994, signed in Lusaka, Zambia, in which dos Santos was confirmed as president and Savimbi was offered the vice presidency. In February 1995 the United Nations Security Council adopted a resolution establishing a strong international force of 7000 troops to monitor the cease-fire and oversee the implementation of the Lusaka agreement. The 1996 United Nations force was a much more adequate peace-keeping force than the one sent in 1992. Although implementation was slower than anticipated, particularly in the area of UNITA troop demobilization, there were grounds for optimism, since both sides now realized that they could not achieve a military victory and that economic recovery and the continuation of democracy depended upon the establishment of a lasting peace.

See Also

Luanda, Angola; Lusaka, Zambia; Neto, Agostinho; Russia and the Former Soviet Union; Savimbi, Jonas Malheiro; Popular Movement for the Liberation of Angola.

Douala. Please see Duala

Africa

Douala, Cameroon, the largest city and commercial hub of Cameroon.

The town of Douala first developed on the southeastern shore of the Wouri River estuary in the 1700s as a station for the transatlantic slave trade. Dutch merchants initially dominated the transatlantic trade, but the town was also frequented by ethnic Duala traders, many of whom acted as middlemen in the human traffic. British influence slowly usurped the Dutch until 1884, when Germany, after signing a treaty with two Duala chiefs, formally colonized Cameroon. With a good harbor, Douala quickly became the colony's largest trading center, attracting African migrants as well as German and, later, French and British colonists. During World War II, it briefly served as the colonial capital.

Although Yaoundé is now the capital of Cameroon, post-independence infrastructure projects have solidified Douala's role as a national and regional economic hub. Today Douala handles approximately 95 percent of the country's foreign trade as well as exports from other countries in Central Africa. Industries include light manufacturing, agricultural processing, and transportation, construction, and engineering services. Douala is also Cameroon's largest city, with a population of over 1 million, up from 450,000 in 1976. Social and economic problems have accompanied the city's rapid growth. The Bassa industrial zone, the New Bell commercial area, and the Bonapriso center of official activity have all grown dramatically, creating shortages in public services, especially health and sanitation. Douala has a large population of migrant laborers from the Cameroon interior and neighboring countries; ethnic Bamiléké run many of the city's businesses.

Eric Young

North America

Douglas, Aaron (b. May 26, 1899, Topeka, Kans.; d. February 2, 1979, Nashville, Tenn.), African American artist closely associated with the Harlem Renaissance; Douglas synthesized formal and symbolic elements of African art with a modern European aesthetic.

Aaron Douglas came to Harlem from Topeka, Kansas, in 1925, the year in which the cultural critic and philosopher Alain Locke launched the "New Negro" Movement. This movement expressed African Americans' new pride in their African heritage, which manifested itself in literature, song, dance, and, most significantly for Douglas, art.

Shortly after his arrival in Harlem, Douglas made the acquaintance of the German American portrait artist Winold Reiss, who illustrated the March 1925 New Negro issue of *Survey Graphic* for Locke. Both Reiss and Locke encouraged Douglas to develop his own American black aesthetic from design motifs in African art. Douglas followed their suggestions and sought examples of African art, which in the 1920s were beginning to be purchased by the collections of American museums and galleries. Locke recognized that the sculptural art of Africa had inspired the art of such leading modernists as Pablo Picasso and Constantin Brancusi and that it could lead to the creation of great art by African Americans.

Douglas developed a unique aesthetic that linked black Americans with their African past by using imagery derived from African sculptural and ancestral art to express aspects of the black experience in the United States. The two principal types of works he executed were drawings and murals. His drawings were characterized by bold, sharply delineated designs in black and white. On the other hand, softer outlines, superimposed forms, and a subdued color scheme in the red-green range characterized his murals. Douglas's murals focus on African American history and religious practices.

Though he had been instructed in the academic mode of painting at the University of Nebraska, Douglas rejected realism in favor of a geometric painting style that he developed while studying under Reiss during the late 1920s. Douglas reduced forms to their fundamental shapes, such as circles, triangles, and rectangles. He tended to represent both objects and black people as silhouettes. Most of these forms are hard-edged and angular, reminiscent of the Art Deco designs popular in the United States during the early twentieth century. Some figures, however, have a curvilinear character, apparently influenced by the contemporary Art Nouveau trend in France that endows them with a sense of movement. One critic compared the rhythmic quality and arrangement of Douglas's figures to those of Greek vase paintings.

Douglas began his artistic career as an illustrator, working in black and white with an occasional touch of gray. He burst onto the art scene in 1925 with a cover illustration for *Opportunity* magazine and a first-place award from the *Crisis* magazine for his drawing *The African Chieftain*. Douglas became a regular contributor to each of these publications. In that same year, he collaborated with Reiss to illustrate Locke's *The New Negro*, a landmark anthology of black writers.

Douglas's visual exploration of African motifs and his use of black subjects commanded the attention of the black intellectual and writer James Weldon Johnson, who commissioned Douglas to illustrate his *God's Trombones: Seven Negro Sermons in Verse* (1927). Douglas considered his work for this book to be his most important and most mature set of illustrations. *God's Trombones* attempts to capture the rhetoric of the black preacher, and in illustrating its pages, Douglas said, "I tried to keep my forms very stark and geometric with my main emphasis on the human body. I tried to portray everything not in a realistic, but in [an] abstract way – simplified and abstract as… in the spirituals."

In *God's Trombones*, Douglas offered an unconventional interpretation of traditional biblical themes. In *Go Down Death*, for example, death is depicted not as an evil force, but as a swift rescuer that many slaves welcomed as a means of deliverance from the hardships of bondage. In another illustration, *The Crucifixion*, Douglas challenges traditional representations of this event by focusing on the benevolence of Simon, the dark-skinned man who took up the cross for Christ on his way to Mount Calvary, rather than exclusively on the suffering of Christ. Throughout the series, Douglas depicts blacks as central to biblical history.

In the same year that Douglas completed the illustrations for *God's Trombones*, he executed for Club Ebony a mural series inspired by Harlem's nightlife. Like his illustrations, it was done in black and white. Art collector and historian Albert C. Barnes was impressed with the murals and remarked that Douglas should try doing them in color. He offered Douglas a year-long scholarship to study color at his art school outside Philadelphia, and Douglas, who had very little experience in mixing colors, accepted. As a result of this study, Douglas came to incorporate color in his murals.

The mural series for which Douglas is best known is *Aspects of Negro Life* (1934), now at the Countee Cullen Branch of the New York Public Library. It consists of four chronological compositions. The first, *The Negro in an African Setting*, highlights the African heritage of African Americans through representations of African dance and music. The second spans three stages of African American history: slavery, emancipation, and Reconstruction. *The Idyll of the Deep South*, the third composition, portrays the

Aaron Douglas portrayed the heroic contributions black workers have made to the building of the world's civilizations, from ancient Egypt to twentieth-century America. This 1944 painting is entitled *The Creation*. *Collection of Fisk University, Nashville, Tennessee*

problem of LYNCHING and how African Americans, in spite of this omnipresent threat, continued to work, sing, and dance. The final mural, *Song of the Towers,* charts three events: the mass migration of blacks to Northern industrial centers during the 1910s, the flowering of black artistic expression in 1920s New York City known as the Harlem Renaissance, and the onset of the GREAT DEPRESSION in the 1930s.

In *Aspects of Negro Life*, Douglas used a technique that became his signature mural style. First he arranged a series of concentric circles that expanded from a fixed point. Then he imposed figurative elements on this circular background. While layering the composition, Douglas maintained the continuity of the circular design by altering a person's or object's shade of color in the places where it intersected with a circle. As a result, a person or object would bear several diffused shades of the same color. This procedure lent to Douglas's murals a mystical, dreamlike quality. The chromatic complexity and sophisticated design of *Aspects of Negro Life* is unparalleled by other murals done during the Works Progress Administration's Federal Art Project (WPA/FAP), a NEW DEAL program that supported unemployed artists.

Douglas was not exclusively an illustrator and a muralist, although these two mediums occupied most of his career. Influenced by a year of independent study at the Académie Scandinave in Paris, he occasionally painted portraits and landscapes, which were more naturalistic than his other work. He was also a social activist who, as the first elected president of the Harlem Artists Guild (1935), worked to obtain WPA recognition and support for African American artists. Finally, Douglas was an educator. After graduating from the University of Nebraska, he taught art at Lincoln High School in Topeka, Kansas, from 1923 to 1925. Beginning in 1939, he occasionally taught drawing and painting at FISK UNIVERSITY in Nashville, Tennessee. After earning a master's degree in art education from Columbia University in 1944, he became a permanent member of the Fisk University faculty, serving as a professor in and as chair of the art department until his retirement in 1966. He continued to lecture and paint until his death in 1979. He was one of the first African American artists to affirm the value of the black experience, and his artistic vision was permeated by his refusal "to compromise and see blacks as anything other than a proud and majestic people."

Aaron Myers

SEE ALSO

Art and Architecture, African; Music, African; Dance in Sub-Saharan Africa; Slavery in the United States; *Crisis, The*; Great Migration, The; Harlem, New York; Locke, Alain Leroy; *Opportunity: Journal of Negro Life*; Works Progress Administration.

North America

Douglass, Frederick

(b. February 1818?, Talbot County, Md.; d. February 20, 1895, Washington, D.C.), the principal nineteenth-century African American spokesperson, abolitionist, reformer, author, and orator.

THE HISTORICAL SIGNIFICANCE OF FREDERICK DOUGLASS

Frederick Douglass was more than a great African American leader; he was, in the words of his biographer William S. McFeely, "one of the giants of nineteenth-century America." He was a man driven by his anger at injustice, McFeely observed, a man who "never ran away from anything," except the bondage of slavery. Even in that, he took flight not simply to escape but to engage: upon gaining his freedom, the former slave turned in his tracks and confronted the institution head on.

Douglass had a prominent role in nineteenth-century reform, not only through his abolitionism but also in his support for women's rights and black suffrage. Unlike many of his contemporaries, he stayed true to his principles, remaining steadfast in his commitment to integration and civil rights. Douglass was militant but never a separatist. He rejected the nationalist rhetoric and latter-day conservatism of black abolitionist Martin R. Delany as well as the accommodationism of Booker T. Washington.

Douglass was also a literary figure. Aside from drafting countless speeches and essays, he excelled at autobiography. His three memoirs – *The Narrative of the Life of Frederick Douglass* (1845), *My Bondage and My Freedom* (1855), and *Life and Times of Frederick Douglass* (1881, revised 1892) – represent his greatest literary achievement. Although born into slavery and self-educated, Douglass was a superb stylist who avoided the florid tendencies typical of his era.

His sense of cadence, flair for the dramatic, and taut narrative style give the best of his writing a lean, modern feel. His first autobiography is the archetype of that uniquely American genre of SLAVE NARRATIVES as well as a literary masterpiece. Beyond its inherent drama – the account of a young slave whose growing awareness of his bondage compels him to make a successful bid for freedom – the *Narrative* tells a story of self-discovery and of a character reinventing himself, perhaps the underlying theme of all American and AFRICAN AMERICAN LITERATURE.

EARLY YEARS AND EXPERIENCE OF SLAVERY

Douglass was probably born in February 1818. The son of a slave named Harriet Bailey and an unknown father rumored to be his master, Douglass was first known as Frederick Bailey. He later viewed the uncertainties surrounding his birth and parentage as the direct result – and particular crime – of slavery. He was raised by his grandparents, Betsy and Isaac Bailey, and at first had little direct contact with the institution of slavery. Isaac Bailey was a free black; Betsy was owned by Aaron Anthony, a slaveholder who also managed the plantation and slaves of the more wealthy Col. Edward Lloyd.

Betsy Bailey enjoyed unusual freedom, living far from the watchful eye of her master, apparently on the condition that she care for young slave children so that their mothers might continue working. As a result, Frederick scarcely knew his own mother. When she died, he heard the news "with much the same emotions I should have probably felt at the death of a stranger." Frederick had his first real encounter with the institution of slavery at age six, when he was taken from his grandmother and moved to the home of Aaron Anthony. There he heard the story of Denby, shot to death by one of Edward Lloyd's overseers. He also recalled hearing screams one morning and discovering Anthony whipping Douglass's young aunt Hester.

MOVING TO BALTIMORE AND LEARNING TO READ

When Frederick was eight years old, Anthony's daughter Lucretia Anthony Auld and her husband, Thomas, arranged for him to go to BALTIMORE, MARYLAND, to live with Thomas's brother Hugh Auld and his wife, Sophia. For Frederick, the move opened a new world and instilled a lifelong conviction that education was the path to self-betterment. Sophia Auld took the initiative in his education, reading to him from the Bible and teaching him biblical passages. But when her husband learned of the lessons, he ordered her to stop, declaring that Frederick "should know nothing but the will of his master and learn to obey it." His outburst confirmed the young slave's belief that education mattered, and he continued painstakingly teaching himself until at last he was able to read.

At age 12 Frederick mustered the courage to purchase his first book, a risky thing for a supposedly illiterate slave to do. The book, *The Columbian Orator,* reflected a patriotic conviction that oratory offered the best means to instill civic virtue and respect for liberty, and included among its perorations, "[T]here is... no post so honourable as his, who defends THE RIGHTS OF MAN." Hugh and Sophia Auld soon concluded that life in Baltimore was making Frederick too independent-minded, and they sent him back to Thomas Auld.

In his early teens Frederick was caught up in the evangelical fervor of antebellum American Protestantism. His overriding concern was with salvation. But when conversion failed to soften Thomas Auld's harshness, Frederick lost faith in religion. Indeed, the newly converted Auld hired Frederick out to Edward Covey, a man with a reputation as a "nigger-breaker." Covey's hardscrabble farm had a panoramic view of the Chesapeake, and the sailing vessels that plied those waters later gave Douglass one of his most moving images. "You are loosed from your moorings and are free," he recalled thinking as he watched the tall ships. "I am fast in my chains, and am a slave!... I will run away. I will not stand it. Get caught, or get clear, I'll try it."

With several of Covey's slaves, Frederick tried to escape, but the group was betrayed and jailed. As the leader, Frederick faced sale to the Deep South, notorious for the sometimes deadly harshness of its plantations. But Thomas Auld intervened, promising that if Frederick behaved himself he would be freed when he turned 25. Auld also allowed him to return to Baltimore, where he was apprenticed in the shipbuilding industry. Ironically, some of the ships that Frederick helped to build were slavers, engaged in the clandestine slave trade that continued long after United States law forbade it.

Escape from Slavery and Abolitionism

But Frederick could not bear to defer his freedom until he was 25. After returning to Baltimore, he had met and fallen in love with a free black woman named Anna Murray, and the two decided to leave the South. Posing as an unemployed seaman, Douglass made his way to freedom by himself in 1838 via that informal network of free blacks, Quakers, and antislavery activists known as the Underground Railroad. Upon reaching New York City, he abandoned his slave name of Bailey and became Frederick Johnson to avoid recognition and capture.

As soon as Anna Murray was able to join him, the two were married. They made their way to New England and lived for several years in New Bedford and Lynn, Massachusetts. In New Bedford Frederick discovered that his new name Johnson was widely shared, including by his free black hosts, Nathan and Mary Johnson. He decided to choose another name, and Nathan suggested that one might be found in Walter Scott's *Lady of the Lake.* Frederick chose Douglas, spelling it "Douglass," as prominent black families in Baltimore and Philadelphia did.

To support his growing family, Douglass found work on New Bedford's wharves. His first child, Rosetta, was born on June 24, 1839; she was joined during the next decade by Lewis Henry, Frederick Jr., Charles Redmond, and Annie. Douglass also began participating in local antislavery activities, and his reputation spread quickly. In 1839 he heard a speech by the renowned abolitionist William Lloyd Garrison, who inspired Douglass to become an orator. In his antislavery activism, Douglass began to draw more and more upon his own experience under slavery.

In 1841 William C. Coffin, a New Bedford Quaker, invited the young speaker to an antislavery gathering on Nantucket that included such prominent abolitionists as Garrison, Wendell Phillips, and Parker Pillsbury. Douglass attended, and in years to come it was his impassioned speech that listeners most remembered. At the close of the meeting, the Massachusetts Anti-Slavery Society offered to employ him as an antislavery speaker. It was in that role that Douglass walked onto the stage of history.

Douglass's career as an abolitionist made him a celebrity. But his militancy – and his travels through the racially segregated North – also exposed him to rough treatment. In Pendleton, Indiana, he was attacked by a mob wielding stones and rotten eggs and in the melee had his hand broken. His biographer William McFeely recounted that more than once Douglass was physically removed from railroad cars for sitting among whites. On one occasion he held the armrests with such an iron grip that when he was ejected from the train, "he still had his seat." Not surprisingly, Douglass began speaking out against Northern segregation and racial prejudice as forcefully as he did against slavery.

Other Antebellum Reform Activities

The publication of his *Narrative* and an extended speaking tour in Great Britain furthered Douglass's fame, and he was recognized as the nation's preeminent black leader. But his activism was not confined to African American issues. At the 1848 women's rights convention in Seneca Falls, New York, Douglass was the only male supporter of women's suffrage, and he remained active in the cause throughout his life. In 1847 he moved to Rochester, New York, and began a career as a reform journalist, which would include editing *North Star* (1847-1851), *Frederick Douglass' Paper* (1851-1860), *Douglass' Monthly* (1859-1863), and the *New National Era* (1870-1874). He remained in Rochester until moving to Washington, D.C., in 1872.

Douglass remained constant in advocating principles of freedom and equality, but gradually he lost his faith in moral persuasion. In 1851 he parted ways with Garrison and the Quaker pacifists. During 1859 Douglass met in secret with the white abolitionist John Brown to hear about his planned raid on the federal armory in Harpers Ferry, Virginia. For two days Brown fruitlessly tried to convince Douglass to join him. Douglass's objections were less matters of principle than of tactics. He warned Brown that he would be "going into a perfect steel trap, and that once in he would not get out alive." After Brown's raid, Douglass faced arrest for his involvement in the plot and was forced to flee the country for several months. When he returned, he was convinced that the problem of slavery would not be resolved short of war. Events soon bore him out.

Douglass During the Civil War and Reconstruction

When the Civil War began, Douglass struggled to broaden its aims. At the outset, President Abraham Lincoln proclaimed that the war was being fought simply to preserve the Union, and that slavery would not be affected. Douglass argued that the president could ennoble the conflict and enlist Northerners' idealism by making it a fight against slavery, and he urged the army to recruit black soldiers. He was successful on both counts. In 1863 Lincoln's Emancipation Proclamation (*see* Thirteenth Amendment of the United States Constitution and the Emancipation Proclamation) both committed the Union against slavery and called for black volunteers, although they would serve in segregated units under the command of white officers. Douglass rejected such segregation and the implication that only whites were fitted for command, but he was tireless in recruiting African American volunteers. He also insisted that the army should provide black volunteers with the same pay, supplies, and treatment given white soldiers.

During the Reconstruction era that followed the war, Douglass watched in frustration as the Republican Party, once a stronghold of reform, embraced the interests of American business and the status quo. In the 1870s, as the inadequate program of Reconstruction drew to an end, the party abandoned any commitment to improving the lot of African Americans in the South. Yet unlike many other black leaders, Douglass remained a loyal Republican as he continued fighting for the causes he believed in, particularly the Fifteenth Amendment, ratified in 1870, which granted black males the vote. In this effort, however, he found himself at odds with former allies in the women's movement who opposed extending suffrage to black men if women were not also included. The result was a long-standing breach between white feminists and black civil rights activists. Yet Douglass himself never ceased in his efforts on behalf of either group.

Douglass's Later Life

In 1882 Douglass's wife died, and 17 months later he married his white secretary, Helen Pitts. The union aroused hostility from whites and blacks alike, which Douglass genuinely could not comprehend. He wrote his friend Amy Post, "What business has the world with the color of my wife?" Douglass's all-inclusive humanism left him unprepared for the opposition, including that within his own family.

During his later years, Douglass held several low-level but symbolically important posts, including United States marshal for the District of Columbia (1877-1881); recorder of deeds for the District of Columbia (1881-1886); chargé d'affaires for Santo Domingo, capital of the Dominican Republic; and minister to Haiti (1889-1891). On the other hand, Douglass seemed to lose heart in the face of the nation's conservatism and deepening segregation. Rather than retire, however, he joined the battle one last time. Through the inspiration of African American journalist and political activist Ida B. Wells, Douglass joined in the emerging ANTILYNCHING MOVEMENT. In the 1890s, as the lynching of blacks reached an all-time high, Wells and Douglass struggled to rouse the nation from its complacency.

Douglass's "Lynch Law in the South" appeared in the *North American Review* in 1892 and blamed lynching less on lynch mobs themselves than on the underlying "sentiment created by wealth and respectability." Moreover, as commissioner for the Republic of Haiti's exhibit at the 1893 World's Columbian Exhibition in Chicago, Douglass provided Wells with a desk in the Haitian pavilion from which to distribute thousands of copies of her latest antilynching pamphlet. Douglass also remained active on other fronts, and on the day of his death attended a meeting of the National Council of Women.

Conclusion

More than any nineteenth-century politician or captain of industry, Frederick Douglass was truly a self-made man, down to his self-chosen surname. Denied a patrimony and uncertain even as to the date of his birth, he took destiny into his own hands and wrested greatness from the meanest of beginnings. In three autobiographies, he created the literary character of Frederick Douglass, but far more tellingly, he carved that character deep into the granite of American public life, as a social reformer, a Republican party activist, and the moral conscience of an often forgetful nation. In seeking to change the course of American social development, Douglass relied on a steady moral compass that resisted half-measures and ill-founded prejudice in favor of solid principle – above all, that the American people ought to be free, equal, and racially integrated.

James Clyde Sellman

See Also

Slavery in the United States; Transatlantic Slave Trade; Abolitionism in the United States; Baltimore, Maryland; Civil War, American; Delany, Martin Robison; Fifteenth Amendment to the U.S. Constitution; Free Blacks in the United States, 1619 to 1863; New York, New York; Washington, Booker Taliaferro; Wells-Barnett, Ida Bell; Philadelphia, Pennsylvania; Slave Narratives; Accommodationism in the United States.

North America

Douglass, Sarah Mapps

(b. September 9, 1806, Philadelphia, Pa.; d. September 8, 1882, Philadelphia, Pa.), African American educator, author, and abolitionist.

Sarah Mapps Douglass was born into a position of relative privilege for a nineteenth century black woman, and she used her advantages to help other African Americans. Her family were prominent free blacks in Philadelphia with a tradition of social activism. Through private tutoring Douglass received a better education than most women of her day, and in the 1820s she opened her own school for black children.

The school was supported in part by the Philadelphia Female Anti-Slavery Society, which her mother had cofounded. As an active member of that group and the Philadelphia Female Literary Society, Douglass spoke out against both Southern slavery and Northern racism. She participated in the Anti-Slavery Conventions of American Women in 1837, 1838, and 1839 and was a contributor to the antislavery newspaper the *Liberator.* Her closest friends in her abolitionist circles included the Forten sisters, from another prominent free black family, and the Grimké sisters, who were white. In May 1838 Douglass and several other black guests attended Angelina Grimké's wedding. Two days later a mob set fire to the headquarters of the Pennsylvania Anti-Slavery Society and an orphanage for black children in protest of the interracial social gathering.

In 1855 she married the Reverend William Douglass. Two years earlier, she had begun teaching at Philadelphia's Institute for Colored Youth (later Cheney State College), where she remained until her retirement in 1877, training students to become teachers at black public schools. After the Civil War she served as vice chairman of the Women's Pennsylvania Branch of the American Freedmen's Aid Commission. By the time she died in 1882, Douglass's work as an activist and educator had left a lasting mark on Philadelphia's African American community.

Lisa Clayton Robinson

See Also

Abolitionism in the United States; Civil War, American; Free Blacks in the United States, 1619 to 1863; Grimké, Charlotte L. Forten; *Liberator, The*; Philadelphia, Pennsylvania.

North America

Dove, Rita

(b. August 28, 1952, Akron, Ohio), African American poet and writer, who became the second African American woman to win the Pulitzer Prize for her collection of poetry *Thomas and Beulah* in 1987; served as United States Poet Laureate from 1993 to 1995.

Rita Dove was born August 28, 1952, in Akron, Ohio, to Ray and Elvira Hord Dove. After graduating with a B.A. summa cum laude from Miami University in Ohio in 1973, she received a Fulbright award to study at the University of Tübingen in West Germany. From there she went to the Iowa Writers Workshop, where she completed an M.F.A. in creative writing in 1977.

Dove joined the faculty of Arizona State University in 1981 and spent 1982 as writer-in-residence at the Tuskegee Institute. While at Arizona State she participated in several literary panels for the National Endowment for the Arts (1984-1986), served on the board of the Associate Writing Programs from 1985 to 1988, and was the organization's president in 1986-1987. In 1987 she became a member of the Commission for the Preservation of Black Culture of the Schomburg Center for Research in Black Culture. She also held several editorial positions on such journals as *Callaloo, Gettysburg Review* and *TriQuarterly.* She received a Guggenheim fellowship in 1983 and the Lavan Younger Poets Award from the Academy of American Poets in 1986. She then wrote *Thomas and Beulah* (1986), a collection of poems based on her grandparents' lives for which she won the Pulitzer Prize for Poetry in 1987. Dove was the first African American woman to achieve this award since Gwendolyn Brooks received it in 1950.

In addition to several chapbooks, including *Ten Poems* (1977) and *The Only Dark Spot in the Sky* (1980), Dove's early works of poetry include *The Yellow House on the Corner* (1980) and *Museum* (1983). These works "won praise from reviewers for their technical excellence and unusual breadth of subject matter." Her other poetry collections include *Grace Notes* (1989), *Selected Poems* (1993), *Mother Love* (1995), and most recently, *On the Bus with Rosa Parks* (1999). She also wrote a novel, *Through the Ivory Gate* (1992), a play titled *The Darker Face of the Earth* (1994), a book of short stories titled *Fifth Sunday* (1995), and a collection of essays, *The Poet's World* (1995). Critics praise her poetry, in which she "gathers the various facts of this life and presents them in ways that jar our lazy assumptions. She gives voice to many positions and many characters." Critic Emily Grosholz declares that, "Dove can turn her poetic sights on just about anything and make the language shimmer."

At age 40 Dove became the youngest person and first African American to be honored as U.S. Poet Laureate, a title she held from 1993 through 1995. In addition to honorary doctorates from numerous colleges and universities, including Dartmouth College and Columbia University, she has received, among other awards, the NAACP Great American Artist Award (1993), the Renaissance Forum Award for Leadership in the Literary Arts from the Folger Shakespeare Library (1994), the Chrales Frankel prizel National Medal in the Humanities (1996), and the Levinson Prize from *Poetry* magazine (1998). In 1993 she received an endowed chair at the University of Virginia as the Commonwealth Professor of English. She lives in Charlottesville with her husband, Fred

Viebahn, a German novelist, and their daughter, Aviva.

Leyla Keough

See Also
Brooks, Gwendolyn Elizabeth; Tuskegee University; Schomburg Library.

North America

Dozens, The, a black game of verbal insult and boasting.

The exact origins of the dozens is uncertain. But it resembles traditional African "joking relationships" in many ways and seems to draw heavily on the African oral tradition. Like preaching, signifying, rapping, and toasting, the dozens reinforces the high value placed on verbal skills in the African diaspora. Also called "playing the dozens," "joning," "sounding," and "woofing," the dozens is most popular among adolescent boys, who usually play the game in front of a neutral audience who egg on the participants. The contestants must develop the ability to remain poised and master the verbal dexterity to respond quickly and creatively to their opponent's insults without becoming angry or violent.

The style of the games can be "clean" or "dirty," the insults rhymed or unrhymed. Rhyming insults are more characteristic of contests between children, while teenagers and adults stress creativity and improvisation. The insults in the so-called clean dozens tend to attack intelligence, achievements, or appearance. For example, "Your sister is so ugly, she'd make a freight train take a dirt road." In the dirty dozens, participants often refer to an opponent's mother in derogatory sexual terms.

Social scientists have for years theorized that the dozens is a release for a racially oppressed group, or a way of helping African American males project a masculine identity in a matriarchal culture. In recent years, however, researchers have tended to emphasize the game's role in helping African Americans resolve conflicts nonviolently and deal with personal insults impassively – valuable lessons in a racially hostile society.

Robert Fay

North America

Drake, St. Clair (b. January 12, 1911, Suffolk, Va.; d. June 14, 1990, Palo Alto, Calif.), anthropologist and sociologist; coauthor of the classic study *Black Metropolis* and an early leader in the development of black studies programs.

The son of a Baptist minister from Barbados and a Virginia schoolteacher, John Gibbs St. Clair Drake grew up in Pittsburgh, Pennsylvania, and Staunton, Virginia. As a student at Hampton University in Virginia from 1927 to 1931, he majored in biology, but it was his studies of anthropology with Prof. W. Allison Davis that defined Drake's future career.

After graduating Hampton, Drake worked as a high school teacher in rural Virginia and continued his study of anthropology. His contributions to a social survey of life in a Mississippi town were published as part of Davis's study *The Deep South*. Drake also became involved in the peace movement, spending his summers with Quaker activists. Reflecting on the "peace caravan" that took him and other demonstrators through the South during the summer of 1931, Drake commented that he "just missed the lynching rope" on several occasions.

Drake won a Rosenwald Fellowship to continue his education and, in 1937, entered a graduate program in anthropology at the University of Chicago. For his dissertation on race relations in the British Isles, he completed a year of field research on the black inhabitants of Cardiff, Wales. He married Elizabeth Johns, a white sociologist, in 1942. For his World War II service, he joined the Merchant Marines so that he would not be part of any branch of the segregated services (*see* Military, Blacks in the American).

From 1946 to 1968 Drake taught at Roosevelt College (now Roosevelt University) in Chicago. While at Roosevelt, he coauthored his most famous book, *Black Metropolis* (1945), a comprehensive study of life on Chicago's South Side. With his colleague Horace Cayton, Drake recorded the segregation, discrimination, and poverty experienced by the residents of Bronzeville. The book remains a classic of urban studies.

Drake's intellectual interest in Africa led him to spend several years there. He was a close adviser to Kwame Nkrumah of Ghana, and taught sociology at the University of Ghana from 1958 to 1961. He also advised other African leaders, taught in Liberia, and created training programs for Peace Corps volunteers in Africa. Once he returned to the United States, Drake became a founder of the American Society for African Culture and of the American Negro Leadership Conference on Africa.

In 1969 Drake became the first permanent director of Stanford University's African and Afro-American Studies program. This was a time when students across the United States were demanding such programs, and Drake's response at Stanford served as a model for black studies departments elsewhere. During his tenure at Stanford, Drake also published the two-volume *Black Folk Here and There* (1987-1990). The recipient of many honorary degrees, Drake was a professor emeritus of sociology and anthropology at Stanford when he died in 1990 at his home near the campus.

Lawrie Balfour

See Also
World War II and African Americans; Baptists; Cayton, Horace Roscoe, Jr.; Chicago, Illinois.

North America

Dred Scott v. Sanford, 1857 case in which the United States Supreme Court ruled that U.S. territories could not prohibit slavery and that neither free nor enslaved blacks had constitutional rights.

Scott's Case

Dred Scott was born a slave in Virginia around 1795, His original name was Sam Blow. Peter Blow, his owner, moved him first to Alabama in 1818, then to St. Louis in 1830. After Blow died, his son sold Sam to John Emerson, a surgeon in the U.S. Army. In 1834 Emerson was transferred to Fort Armstrong, Illinois, where slavery was prohibited by the Northwest Ordinance of 1787. The ordinance had

Chief Justice Roger Taney crafted the Supreme Court's decision in the 1857 *Dred Scott* v. *Sanford* case.
CORBIS/Bettmann

allowed then territories in the West to become states with the condition that they forbid slavery. Like many other slave-owning army officers, Emerson did not believe that his postings in free states subjected him to antislavery laws, so he brought Sam with him.

Two years later Emerson was transferred to Fort Snelling in what is now Minnesota but was then part of the Wisconsin Territory. Slavery in the territory was banned by the Missouri Compromise of 1820, in which Congress decided that with the exception of Missouri, slavery would be prohibited in the territories north of latitude 36° 30'.

At Fort Snelling, Sam married Harriet, the slave of another army officer, and in 1838 the couple returned with Emerson to St. Louis. At some point in these moves, Sam took the name Dred Scott, which may have been a joke contrasting his tiny stature with that of the corpulent general Winfield "Great" Scott. In 1843 Emerson died and left his property – including slaves – in trust to his wife. In 1846, with the help of friends, Scott sued Mrs. Emerson in local court for his family's freedom. His lawyers argued that the Scotts' stay in free territory had emancipated them, citing several precedents in Missouri case law, the most important of which was *Rachael* v. *Walker* (1837). The Scotts lost the case, moved for the verdict to be set aside, and at a new trial in 1850 won their freedom.

Mrs. Emerson appealed to the Missouri Supreme Court, which issued a 2-to-1 decision in 1852 returning the Scotts to slavery. The court stated that earlier court precedents, including its own, were made under circumstances that were no longer valid. Noting the rise of abolitionism in the country, the court argued that the antislavery movement threatened the "overthrow and destruction of our government." Thus slave states could not be expected to uphold the law of free states, and a slave, whether on free soil or not, was still a slave. The case was a forceful rejection of the Missouri Compromise and probably would have been heard by the U.S. Supreme Court had Scott appealed directly. Instead, Scott's lawyers counseled another course.

In the Federal Courts

While the state court case was being processed, Mrs. Emerson's brother, John Sanford of New York, had taken over the affairs of her estate. In 1853 Scott filed suit against Sanford, this time in federal court. Scott argued that because he and Sanford lived in different states, their case required a federal trial. Sanford argued that Scott was still a slave and even if he were free, a black descendant of slaves was not entitled to bring suit. The federal court in St. Louis rejected Sanford's argument that free blacks could not bring suit, but concluded that Scott was still a slave. Scott appealed, and in 1856 the U.S. Supreme Court heard his case.

Not wanting to affect the presidential elections of 1856, the Court postponed its ruling in *Scott* v. *Sanford* until two days after President James Buchanan's inauguration. On March 6, 1857, a mostly Southern 7-to-2 majority found that Scott was still a slave. The Court therefore needed only to agree with the lower court, remand parts of the decision that needed clarification, and be done with the case. However, several recent events conspired to put pressure on the Court to make additional rulings that would settle the question of slavery.

Chief among these events was Congress's 1850 passage of the Fugitive Slave Act, which placed severe penalties on Northerners who helped runaway slaves. Northern states responded by enacting laws to obstruct Southerners trying to capture fugitives. In 1854 Congress passed the even more controversial Kansas-Nebraska Act. The act largely overturned the Missouri Compromise by letting territories choose or reject slavery instead of leaving that decision to the federal government. The territories' right to choose, known as popular sovereignty, prompted intense conflicts in the territories and earned Kansas the label Bleeding Kansas. Slavery opponents in the Democratic, Whig, and Free Soil parties responded to the tension by creating the Republican Party in 1854. When Republicans proclaimed their aim to abolish slavery in the territories, conservative Democrats countered by calling for a slave code in the territories.

Against this backdrop, Chief Justice Roger B. Taney decided to use *Scott* v. *Sanford* to address the constitutionality of slavery. Writing for the court, he gave an extremely narrow interpretation of the Constitution's view of blacks. Taney began by arguing that the Constitution did not allow Congress to regulate slavery – or anything else – in the territories. Rather, the Constitution's statements about regulating territories applied only to those territories in the states' possession in 1789, when the Constitution was ratified. Since the United States acquired the Louisiana Territory through the Louisiana Purchase in 1803, Congress had no power to regulate Purchase territories until they became states. The ruling effectively made the Missouri Compromise unconstitutional – only the second time that the Supreme Court had declared a statute of Congress unconstitutional. (The first was *Marbury* v. *Madison* in 1803.) Taney's ruling on the Missouri Compromise was especially unnecessary since the Kansas-Nebraska Act superseded it.

Taney also interpreted the Constitution's Fifth Amendment, which prohibits the taking of property without due process of law, to apply to slaves. He argued that since slaves were property, they could not be taken from their owners, regardless of whether they had crossed into a free state or territory. He further asserted the Constitution never intended blacks – even free blacks in free states – to be citizens. Therefore, even if Scott were free, he was not entitled to bring a suit in a federal court. Taney based this decision largely on a clause of the Constitution that he interpreted as denying blacks some of the rights and duties of citizenship, such as serving in militias. In perhaps the best-known sentence of his opinion, Taney characterized blacks as beings of an inferior order and altogether unfit to associate with the white race, either in social or political relations; and so far inferior, that they had no rights that the white man was bound to respect; and that the negro might justly and lawfully be reduced to slavery for his benefit.

Justices Benjamin R. Curtis and John McLean dissented. They cited accounts showing that many blacks were citizens both before and after the ratification of the Constitution, and they argued that the authors of the Constitution fully intended its protections to apply to them. Therefore, they said, Scott had the right to sue. They also argued that the Constitution intended Congress to regulate all U.S. territories at all times, not just territories controlled by the states in 1789. Finally, since a law banning slavery freed any slave who entered the law's jurisdiction, Scott and his family were freed by virtue of their stay on free soil and could not be returned to slavery after returning to a slave state.

Soon after the Supreme Court issued its decision, Dred Scott and his family were sold to a son of Peter Blow, Scott's original owner, who freed them instantly. Scott did not live long enough to see the many changes his case brought about. In September 1858 he died of tuberculosis in St. Louis.

Aftermath

The ruling, one of the most infamous in the Court's history, horrified overlapping groups of Northerners, abolitionists, and Republicans. Democrats hoped that by declaring free soil in the territories unconstitutional, *Scott* v. *Sanford* would kill the Republican Party. Instead, the ruling stimulated rapid growth in the party and made abolitionism, which had struggled for respectability, a more popular stance. Even Northerners who did not care about slavery in the territories worried that *Scott* v. *Sanford* could be used to legalize slavery in the North.

In the presidential election of 1860, Republican candidate Abraham Lincoln used such arguments repeatedly against Democratic candidate Senator Stephen A. Douglas. Douglas, a leading proponent of popular sovereignty, derided Lincoln's charges. In an argument that became known as the Freeport Doctrine, Douglas said that territories could nullify the Court's ruling simply by refusing to pass laws that would protect property in slaves. The Freeport Doctrine angered Southerners and provoked a split in the Democratic Party that guaranteed the presidency for Lincoln. Lincoln's victory was the first election in which a U.S. president was elected without a majority of votes. The Civil War was not long in coming.

During the war the Union government acted as though the Court had never ruled on *Scott* v. *Sanford*. Congress abolished slavery in all federal territories in June 1862, and later that year Lincoln's attorney general issued an opinion that free black men born in the United States were citizens. In 1865 the Thirteenth Amendment, which abolished slavery, was ratified. In 1868 the Fourteenth Amendment, which declared all persons born or naturalized in the United States to be citizens, was ratified; the amendment was intended as a direct refutation of *Scott* v. *Sanford*.

See Also

Slavery in the United States; Abolitionism in the United States; Civil War, American; Fourteenth Amendment to the United States Constitution; Free Blacks in the United States, 1619 to 1863; Fugitive Slave Laws; Thirteenth Amendment of the United States Constitution and the Emancipation Proclamation.

North America

Drew, Charles Richard (b. June 3, 1904, Washington, D.C.; d. April 1, 1950, Burlington, N.C.), African American surgeon and hematologist who made pioneering discoveries about blood plasma and set up blood banks in the 1930s and 1940s.

Charles Richard Drew became interested in studying blood as a student at McGill University in Montreal, CANADA, during the late 1920s and early 1930s. At that time, medical science had not yet determined how to preserve blood, a dilemma that became Drew's mission. Later, while interning at Presbyterian Hospital in New York City and pursuing a doctorate at Columbia University, Drew discovered that unlike whole blood, which deteriorates after a few days in storage, blood plasma – the liquid portion of the blood without cells – can be preserved for long periods of time and substituted for whole blood in transfusions.

In the late 1930s Drew set up an experimental blood bank at Presbyterian Hospital and wrote a thesis titled "Banked Blood: A Study in Blood Preservation," which earned him a doctor of science in medicine from Columbia University in 1940. His medical breakthrough helped save thousands of lives by making more blood available to the many people in need of transfusions.

Drew's discovery came at an opportune time. In 1939 World War II broke out in Europe and by 1940 the British, in desperate need of blood to save the lives of injured soldiers, turned to the United States for help. The Blood Transfusion Association chose Drew as the medical supervisor of the Blood for Britain program. Drew arranged for large amounts of plasma to be flown to England and set up several blood banks there.

After the success of his blood preservation and transfusion efforts in Europe, Drew was enlisted by the American Red Cross in 1941 to establish a blood bank program in the United States. In that same year, the United States War Department declared that "it is not advisable to collect and mix Caucasian and Negro blood indiscriminately for later administration to members of the military forces." Drew protested the segregation of blood and, as a result, was forced to resign his position as director of the Red Cross Blood Bank Program. He argued, "The blood of individual human beings may differ by blood groupings, but there is absolutely no scientific basis to indicate any differences according to race." Not until 1949 did the U.S. military end the segregation of banked blood.

Before becoming an internationally known hematologist, Drew established himself as a star athlete and a surgeon. His accomplishments in football, basketball, baseball, and track at Dunbar High School in Washington, D.C., earned him an athletic scholarship to Amherst College in Massachusetts. As in high school, Drew was voted the best all-around athlete at Amherst and, in 1926, he graduated with highest honors. Between 1926 and 1928 he coached football and served as athletic director at Morgan College in Baltimore while teaching biology and chemistry.

Drew embarked on his surgical studies in 1928 at McGill University Medical School, where he also dominated several sports. He was named to McGill's medical honorary society and was awarded a Julius Rosenwald Fellowship before receiving his M.D. and a master of surgery degree in 1933. In 1935, after interning for two years at Canadian hospitals, he accepted a teaching position at HOWARD UNIVERSITY in WASHINGTON, D.C. Three years later he won a fellowship from the Rockefeller Foundation that funded his famous studies on blood. In 1944 he was awarded the prestigious Spingarn Medal by the NATIONAL ASSOCIATION FOR THE ADVANCEMENT OF COLORED PEOPLE.

Surgeon and blood specialist Dr. Charles Richard Drew was the first director of the American Red Cross Blood Bank. *Photographs and Prints Division, Schomburg Center for Research in Black Culture, The New York Public Library, Astor, Lenox and Tilden Foundation*

Following his World War II service and work with the American Red Cross, Drew returned to Howard, where he taught and practiced surgery until his death in an automobile accident in 1950.

Aaron Myers

SEE ALSO

World War II and African Americans; New York, New York.

North America

Drifters, The, an African American RHYTHM AND BLUES band that scored hit after hit in the 1950s and 1960s.

The Drifters is a group name under which numerous musicians have performed. The group began in 1953 when Atlantic Records cofounder Ahmet Ertegun learned that tenor Clyde McPhatter had been fired from his position with Billy Ward & His Dominoes. That night, the story goes, Ertegun searched for McPhatter in Harlem and immediately got him to agree to form a new band. The two then recruited singers to back McPhatter's superb lead vocals, hiring Bill Pinkney and Andrew and Gerhart Thrasher. By the end of that year "Money Honey" had become the first of the group's many smash pop and R&B hits. But late in 1954 the Drifters were forced to reorganize when McPhatter was drafted by the United States Army.

The remaining members continued without him, adopting in turn David Baugh, Johnny Moore, and Bobby Hendricks as front men. When McPhatter returned from the service, he pursued a solo career instead of rejoining the group, and in 1958 manager George Treadwell fired the rest of the original members. In their place he hired the Crowns to assume the Drifters' name. Singer Ben E. King was the new leader, while the prolific white songwriting team of Jerry Leiber and Mike Stoller composed most of the group's material. The new Drifters rivaled the old in sending songs up the charts; their hits included "There Goes My Baby," which popularized the use of strings in traditional R&B arrangements.

Although King left the group in 1960 to record as a solo act, the Drifters, led by Rudy Lewis and later Johnny Moore, continued to release hit songs, including "Up on the Roof" (1963) and "Under the Boardwalk" (1964). By the end of the 1960s, however, their albums were receiving less play; in the 1970s their releases were successful only in Europe. In 1977 they represented the United States in Russia. In the late 1970s and the 1980s and 1990s, the Drifters persisted as a nostalgia act, its members gaining weight and losing fans. They appeared at the 1998 Sportours Superbowl Gala for Superbowl XXXII and were inducted into the Rock and Roll Hall of Fame in 1988.

Eric Bennett

North America

Driskell, David (b. June 7, 1931, Eatonton, Ga.), African American artist, teacher, and curator whose painting is characterized by frequent depictions of nature, vibrant colors, and African stylistic influences.

Born in Eatonton, Georgia, David Driskell grew up in North Carolina. After attending public high school, he studied art in 1953 at the Skowhegan School of Painting and Sculpture in Maine, and went on to receive a degree in art from HOWARD UNIVERSITY. He received a master's degree in art from Catholic University of America in 1962.

His teaching career began in 1955 at Talladega College in Alabama and continued when he was made professor of art at Howard in 1962. In 1966 he left Howard to become chairman of the department of art at Fisk University. He took leave to spend 1969-1970 as a visiting professor at the Institute of African Studies at the University of Ife, Ile-Ife, Nigeria. From 1978 to 1983 he fulfilled his last permanent appointment as chair of the art department at the University of Maryland, stepping down to return to research and painting.

In addition to Driskell's teaching career, he has curated several important exhibitions of African American art, including a touring exhibit titled *Hidden Heritage: Afro-American Art 1800-1950* and, in Tokyo, *The Art of Black America in Japan.* Driskell has written several books to accompany his exhibitions, among which are *Two Centuries of Black American Art* (1976) and *Hidden Heritage: Afro-American Art* (1985). His paintings have been shown throughout the United States.

Latin America and the Caribbean

D'Rivera, Paquito (b. June 4, 1948, Havana, Cuba), jazz saxophonist, clarinetist, and bandleader in the Afro-Cuban jazz tradition, and a founding member of Irakere, the leading Afro-Cuban jazz ensemble.

In 1960 Paquito D'Rivera entered the Havana Conservatory, where he studied woodwinds. Two years later he began playing professionally. During his mandatory military service, D'Rivera played in an army band. He then joined the Orquesta Cubana de Musica Moderna (OCMM) and in 1973 became a founding member – along with Chucho Valdés and Arturo Sandoval – of the Afro-Cuban jazz rock ensemble Irakere, Cuba's most popular jazz group. In 1980 D'Rivera defected to the United States, settling in New York City, where he worked with Dizzy Gillespie and pianist McCoy Tyner and started his own band. In 1989 he joined Dizzy Gillespie's last group, the United Nations Orchestra, made up in equal numbers of African American and Latin American jazz musicians, for a tour of Europe and the United States. Since Gillespie's death in 1993, D'Rivera has led the ensemble.

D'Rivera plays alto saxophone in a style that is grounded in bop but approaches the harmonic realm marked out by John Coltrane and Eric Dolphy. He is also a first-rate clarinetist, and has performed on soprano saxophone and flute as well. His music continues to evoke the history and traditions of Afro-Cuban jazz. His *40 Years of the Cuban Jam Session* (1993), for example, attempted to recapture the atmosphere of the *descarga,* or Cuban jam sessions that originated in the late 1950s and included such Cuban expatriates and descarga mainstays as Israel "Cachao" Lopez and Chocolate Armenteros.

James Clyde Sellman

See Also

Coltrane, John William; Gillespie, John Birks ("Dizzy"); Jazz, Afro-Latin; Armenteros, Alfredo "Chocolate; López, Israel ("Cachao"); Valdés, Jesús (Chucho).

Africa

Drought and Desertification, the degradation of arid, semi-arid, and subhumid land by a combination of human and nonhuman processes. Desertification endangers ecosystems across the globe and is of particular concern in countries where population growth and economic disadvantage tend to exacerbate ecological instability. Africa has many such countries, especially in the Sahel region bordering the southern Sahara Desert.

Hundreds of qualified people have tried to explain *desertification* (a term coined in 1949), but because the process invokes questions of sociology, biology, politics, and culture, no consensus exists. The history of African desertification has included recurring conflicts between and among peasants, pastoralists, European colonial regimes, intrusive local governments, and international environmental organizations. Often one party will brandish inconclusive scientific data against another, clouding conflicts that were already murky. The social and scientific complexity of desertification leaves more questions than answers. Are "natural" cycles or human abuses the greater culprit?

A careful look at the actual physical processes in arid, semi-arid, and subhumid environments helps to clarify the problem. Scientists have isolated three separate states of trauma in such ecosystems: drought, desiccation, and dry-land degradation. Only the third directly involves human-induced environmental distress, but dry-land degradation often arises from desiccation and drought.

Drought

Any dry period that seriously disturbs the normal conditions of an environment is called a drought. Especially in arid and semi-arid environments, however, "normal conditions" must be invoked gingerly, as droughts may be common occurrences. In fact, the peoples who inhabit arid and semi-arid regions of Africa have many different means of coping with drought, as do the flora and fauna.

A drought is a dry spell from which an environment can recover – that is, from which an environment incurs little irreversible damage. Although drought most often connotes a lack of rain, it can also occur when rain falls at the wrong time – out of sync with the growing season – or on degraded soil that limits transpiration by plants. Scientists sometimes distinguish between *meteorologic* drought (low rainfall), *hydrologic* drought (low stream flow), and *agricultural* drought (sporadic or ill-timed rains).

Desiccation

When a prolonged drought causes irreversible damage, the period of trauma is referred to as desiccation. Desiccation can both eradicate species of flora and fauna and force changes in human livelihoods. Although more destructive than drought, desiccation is just as natural, and decade-long cycles of dryness punctuate Africa's history. Unfortunately, desiccation presents graver challenges to human intervention, as it is hard to detect and even harder to ameliorate. Indeed, long-range solutions – if ill-conceived or poorly executed – can lead to dry-land degradation.

Dry-Land Degradation

When human abuses contribute to the trauma caused by drought and desiccation, the results can be serious and permanent. Geographer Michael Mortimore has suggested the following model. During a drought year animals die and crops fail. Farmers and pastoralists survive by selling off assets, including livestock, as well as firewood cut from nearby forests and scrub lands. The next year the rains may return, but if farmers lack manure, their yields are poor and they must cultivate more land, shortening regenerative fallow periods. This strategy can lead to soil exhaustion as well as to conflicts with nearby pastoralists, who typically rebuild their herds during post-drought years and may depend on the same land for grazing. Meanwhile economic, environmental, and social problems of dry-land degradation are further exacerbated by rapid population growth.

Some scientists postulate that the damage is even more profound. Land degradation can cause erosion, which, in turn, can cause dust storms. When wind draws dust into the atmosphere, the resulting cloud may inhibit rainfall. Furthermore, defoliated land reflects more solar energy than land with vegetation, and thus is often cooler; land that cools the air above it may also inhibit rainfall. In short, humans can make temporary trauma permanent by causing self-perpetuating processes of environmental change. These particular processes may contribute to desertification because they occur in the zones bordering deserts and can appear to extend the desert further. While the original picture (discussed below) was of an interminably advancing Sahara, more recent models describe pockets of degradation that expand until they join together.

The History of the Controversy

Concerns about the apparent advance of the desert date back to the 1920s and 1930s, a period of unusually low rainfall. The reports of British forester E. P. Stebbing were particularly influential. Compiling evidence from earlier French studies as well as from his expeditions through British and French colonies in Saharan West Africa, Stebbing blamed spreading sand and decreased vegetation on population growth and indigenous farming methods. Stebbing's work established the paradigm of blame that dominated discussions of dry-land degradation for decades. His most conspicuous yet pervasive mistake was to deny natural factors such as the cyclical variations in rainfall that occur over several years or even decades.

Along with his observations, Stebbing issued a request that an official investigation of the problem be made. In 1936-1937 the Anglo-French Forestry Commission complied with this request and collected data that in large part refuted Stebbing's claims. Nevertheless, debate about desertification continued until wetter conditions returned to the Sahel in the 1950s and colonial scientists turned their attention to other matters.

When drought struck the region in the 1970s, the debate was reborn in Stebbing's spirit. United Nations-sponsored quantitative research produced an abundance of alarming but not very accurate data. The Sahara, one study claimed, had advanced about 100 km (60 mi) in 17 years; soon scientists, legislators, and UN representatives spoke of the Sahara's annual 6 km (3.6 mi) expansion, a spurious claim.

Although data focused international attention and aid on arid-land environmental problems, they also provided justification for measures to control the populations blamed for desertification. In some countries, governments blamed nomadic herders for overgrazing the savannas. Often they attempted to restrict movement with sedentarization programs that led only to overgrazing and further abuses, exacerbating traditional problems with modern ills. In other cases farmers' practices were held responsible, which also led to wrong-headed correctives: in Guinea, those who burned brush to clear fields and fertilize soil were nominally subject to the death penalty.

In general these measures were based on very little understanding of the livelihoods of the peoples involved and overlooked the reasons why they were sometimes pushed into circumstances in which they may have had to overexploit local resources simply to survive. Consequently they often failed to reverse environmental degradation. Sedentarization programs had a particularly poor record.

In the 1980s new research incorporating remote sensing and historical data challenged earlier, highly simplified models of desertification. One particularly extensive study conducted by geographers from Lund University in Sweden concluded that "no major change in vegetation cover and crop productivity was identified, which could not be explained by varying rainfall characteristics." At the Earth Summit in Rio De Janeiro in 1992 and an international Convention to Combat Desertification in 1994, many authorities acknowledged the complexity of the issue and the importance of incorporating local needs and knowledge into antidesertification programs.

Current Solutions

In the Sahel some efforts to combat desertification at the local level have yielded promising results. In Burkina Faso, for example, village "land management programs" draw on village labor and expertise to carry out soil and water conservation projects such as tree planting, the construction of microdams, and the erection of terraces and soil mounds to limit water runoff and thus diminish soil erosion. Government and donor agencies help by providing funds, fertilizers, and technical assistance. Such programs have in some cases restored the fertility of once "desertified" land. Whether or not local successes alone can arrest further dry-land degradation, however, remains an open question.

Eric Bennett

Africa

Duala an ethnic group of southern Cameroon.

The Bantu-speaking Duala migrated to the coastal areas of what is now southern Cameroon from the Congo River basin during the sixteenth century, and were among the first Africans in the region to come into contact with the European merchants who arrived soon thereafter. The Duala became prominent middleman traders, transporting slaves, ivory, and wild rubber from the interior in exchange for cloth, liquor, and firearms. The Europeans welcomed their entrepreneurial and collaborative spirit.

In 1884 two Duala chiefs signed an annexation agreement with Germany that permitted the Germans to explore and occupy much of the area that is now southern Cameroon. Many Duala sold their land to European settlers, or to Bamilékés who had migrated south from the highlands to take advantage of the economic growth in and around the thriving port of Douala. European missionaries translated the Bible into Duala and used the language in church. Over time, however, German-Duala relations soured as colonial officials tried to break the Duala trading monopoly, and many Duala, among them Chief Rudolph Douala Manga Bell, helped launch the nationalist struggle against colonial rule. Today, the Duala music, called the *makossa*, and dance are important national symbols that have won international recognition, and the Duala language has become the region's commercial lingua franca.

Eric Young

See Also
Bamiléké; Bantu: Dispersion and Settlement; Ivory Trade; Nationalism in Africa; Transatlantic Slave Trade; Douala, Cameroon; Christianity: Missionaries in Africa.

Latin America and the Caribbean

Dub, a radical musical approach in which studio effects and the manipulation of prerecorded vocal and instrumental tracks were used to "version" reggae songs.

In the late 1960s Jamaican sound systems such as King Tubby's Hi-Fi would play instrumental versions of reggae songs at outdoor parties during which DJs would "talk over" the rhythms and entertain the crowd. As King Tubby (Osbourne Ruddock) gained popularity for his instrumental mixes and superior sound quality, producers Bunny Lee and Lee "Scratch" Perry urged him to utilize his electrical engineering skills and take the sound further.

Tubby began radically to rework prerecorded reggae tracks from his home studio in Kingston. With its emphasis on the bass guitar and heavy, slow-paced rhythms, roots reggae provided the ideal form for his sonic explorations. Using homemade and modified mixing equipment, Tubby started dropping in vocal snippets and infinitely echoing horns, adding ghostly layers of delay and reverb, soloing various instruments, inserting sudden silences, and employing a range of other studio effects. The overall sound has been described as "urban, rural, tropic, aquatic, lo-tech, mystical."

Audiences loved the soulful roots reggae mutated with futuristic effects, and by 1972 the dub craze hit Jamaica and Tubby was the undisputed king. Errol "ET" Thompson was another early dub engineer, although later in the decade his work was superseded by that of Tubby's apprentices, Prince Jammy and Scientist. Tubby's popularity had top producers hiring him to "dub" their songs. Economic demand for variety, coupled with a fickle audience, led Tubby to new creative heights. A song mixed in the afternoon could be cut on a "dub-plate special" (one-of-a-kind acetate record) and played on a sound system that night. The crowd's response provided instant feedback. The speed with which this all occurred meant that dub evolved at an astonishing rate. Popular demand birthed and developed an avant-garde format.

In 1973 several dub-only albums were released with enormous commercial success. Dub's largest buying audience was the urban poor. Middle- and upper-class Jamaicans looked down on the form as being rough and uncouth – and also as one of the reasons that their large clubs playing popular foreign music were not so well attended. Dub's lackadaisical approach to copyright laws (every dub pirates an "original" tune) led to its suppression on Jamaican radio. Despite all these opposing factors, the grassroots popularity of sound systems secured dub's success.

Dub's aggressive experimentation lacked

the marketability of popular reggae, and it did not reach an international audience until the 1980s, at roughly the same time as dub's heyday drew to a close in Jamaica. In the 1980s British dub arose with Mad Professor's prolific efforts and Adrian Sherwood's On-U Sound record label. These British dubs are characterized by a crisper, more digital approach than their Jamaican antecedents. In the United States the Brooklyn-based Wordsound record label keeps the lo-fi creativity of dub alive by fusing it with hip hop and Middle Eastern influences.

Dub laid the theoretical groundwork for much contemporary electronic music. For the first time, the sound engineer was viewed with equal or more importance than the actual musicians. The artistry shifted from live performers to behind-the-scenes technicians. Dub mixers would take a preexisting song and subtract, rather than add, to create new versions. The ethos of dub – that every song exists to be reinvented and "versioned" – has far-reaching implications, from dance music remixes to sample-based genres such as hip hop and jungle.

Jace Clayton

See Also
Jungle (Drum and Bass); Hip Hop in the United States; Jamaica; Kingston, Jamaica.

Africa

Dube, John Langalibalele

(b. 1871, Inanda, South Africa; d. 1946), South African minister, educator, journalist, and writer who campaigned for the rights of fellow blacks.

John Langalibalele Dube was born near Inanda, Natal (in what is now KwaZulu-Natal Province) in eastern South Africa. He studied at Oberlin College, in Oberlin, Ohio, and was ordained a minister before returning to Natal. In 1903 he was one of the founders and the editor of the first Zulu newspaper, *Ilanga lase Natal* (Sun of Natal). In 1909 he founded the Ohlange Institute for Boys and then a school for girls, both near Durban. In the same year Dube helped convene a South African Native Convention at Bloemfontein to oppose the "European descent" clause in the draft constitution for the Union (now Republic) of South Africa, intended to bar men of color from Parliament.

On January 8, 1912, Dube was elected the first president general of the South African Native National Congress (which later became the African National Congress). He led the opposition to the 1913 Natives Land Act, which began the process of partitioning land according to race. After heading an unsuccessful delegation to Prime Minister Louis Botha, Dube led a delegation to the British government in London, which was also unsuccessful. He described the 1917 Native Administration Bill, which hastened the partition of land, as a policy of extermination. By the 1920s, however, more radical black leaders were denouncing Dube as too conservative.

Although political involvement took up much of his life, Dube also published the first novel in the Zulu language, about the Zulu chief Shaka (1930), as well as several other books. In 1936 he received a doctoral degree from the University of South Africa. In 1937 he was elected to the Native Representative Council in Natal, where he served until his death.

North America

Du Bois, Shirley Graham

(b. November 11, 1896?, Indianapolis, Ind.; d. March 27, 1977, Beijing, China), African American author, musical director, composer, playwright, and political activist; second wife of the prominent black scholar and activist W. E. B. Du Bois.

The oldest of five children of Rev. David A. Graham and Etta (Bell) Graham, Shirley Graham Du Bois moved with her family to various locations throughout the United States. As a teenager in Colorado Springs, she first met W. E. B. Du Bois when he came to lecture at the local African Methodist Episcopal (AME) Church. Soon after high school, she married a local man, Shadrack T. McCanns; the marriage soon ended, leaving her to support two small children. "In quick succession I knew the glory of motherhood and the pain of deep sorrow," she wrote later. "For the years immediately following, everything I did… was motivated by my passionate desire to make a good life for my sons."

The nomadic quality of Graham's early life carried over into her educational experiences, just as it would in her later years. After attending classes at Howard University's School of Music, in 1930 she spent time in Paris, France, where she studied music and French at the Sorbonne. In that same year she entered Oberlin College in Ohio, earning a bachelor's degree in music (1934) and a master's degree in music history (1935), with an emphasis on Africa. In addition to her studies as a vocalist and composer, she wrote plays and in 1932 became the first African American woman to produce an all-black opera based on her one-act play *Tom-Tom,* a portrayal of black Americans and their music from the seventeenth century to the present.

During the late 1930s Du Bois worked for the Federal Theater Project designing sets and composing musical scores for all-black stage productions, including an adaptation of Eugene O'Neill's *The Hairy Ape* and Theodore Ward's *Big White Fog.* The recipient of a Julius Rosenwald grant in 1938, she attended the Yale School of Drama, where she focused on writing and directing plays, including the comedy *Elijah's Ravens* (1941) and the tragedy *Dust to Earth* (1941). Between 1944 and 1964 she turned her talent to writing critical biographies on noted African Americans, including Frederick Douglass, Phillis Wheatley, and Booker T. Washington.

Du Bois's artistic and scholarly endeavors were deeply motivated by a desire to convey the struggles and achievements of blacks. She actively protested racial injustice and in 1943 became the New York field secretary for the National Association for the Advancement of Colored People (NAACP), where she worked alongside W. E. B. Du Bois. In him she found a kindred soul, and in 1951 the two married. After spending several years with her new husband in Brooklyn, New York – where he was surveyed by government agents for his political radicalism – she took refuge with him in Ghana in 1961, returning briefly to the United States in 1971 and 1975. She died on March 27, 1977, in Beijing, China, where she was undergoing treatment for cancer.

Roanne Edwards

See Also
African Methodist Episcopal Church; Du Bois, William Edward Burghardt (W. E. B.); Howard University; Washington, Booker Taliaferro.

North America

Du Bois, William Edward Burghardt (W. E. B.)

(b. February 23, 1868, Great Barrington, Mass.; d. August 27, 1963, Accra, Ghana), writer, social scientist, critic, and public intellectual; cofounder of the Niagara Movement, the National Association for the Advancement of Colored People (NAACP), and the Pan-African Congress; editor of the NAACP magazine the *Crisis.*

Along with Frederick Douglass and Booker T. Washington, historians consider W. E. B. Du Bois one of the most influential African Americans before the Civil Rights Movement of the 1960s. Born only six years after emancipation, he was active well into his nineties. He died in 1963, on the eve of the March on Washington. Despite near-constant criticism for his often contradictory social and political opinions – he was accused, at various times, of elitism, communism, and black separatism – Du Bois remained throughout his long life black America's leading public intellectual.

Born in a small western Massachusetts town, Du Bois and his mother – his father had left the family when he was young – were among the few African American residents. Of his heritage, Du Bois wrote that it included "a flood of Negro blood, a strain of French, a bit of Dutch, but, Thank God! No 'Anglo-Saxon'…." After an integrated grammar-school education, Du Bois attended the historically black Fisk University in Nashville, Tennessee, then Harvard University, from which he received a bachelor's degree in 1890. That fall Du Bois began graduate work in history at Harvard under the legendary professors George

Santayana, William James, and Josiah Royce. Du Bois was especially influenced by Albert Bushnell Hart, one of the fathers of the new science of sociology. After two years at the University of Berlin (1892-1894), he received a Ph.D. from Harvard in 1895. His dissertation, "The Suppression of the African Slave-Trade to the United States of America, 1638-1870," was published in 1896 as the first volume in the *Harvard Historical Studies* series.

Despite exceptional credentials, discrimination left Du Bois with no options other than a job at Wilberforce College, a small black school in Ohio. Arriving in 1895, Du Bois left a year later with his wife, his former student Nina Gomer. They went to Philadelphia, where the University of Pennsylvania had invited Du Bois to conduct a sociological study of that city's black neighborhoods. The work led to *The Philadelphia Negro* (1899), which provided the model for a series of monographs he wrote while at Atlanta University, whose faculty he joined in 1897. As a young sociologist, he sought to "study [social problems] in the light of the best scientific research." But the persistence of segregation, discrimination, and LYNCHING led Du Bois to feel increasingly that "one could not be a calm, cool, and detached scientist while Negroes were lynched, murdered, and starved.... "

In 1903 Du Bois published his first collection of essays, *The Souls of Black Folk,* which many have called the most important book ever written by an African American. In it he identified "the color line" as the twentieth century's central problem, and dismissed the accommodationism advocated by Booker T. Washington. "[When] Mr. Washington apologizes for injustice," Du Bois wrote, "does not rightly value the privilege and duty of voting, belittles the emasculating effects of caste distinctions, and opposes the higher training and ambition of our brighter minds... we must unceasingly and firmly oppose [him]." In 1905 Du Bois joined with William Monroe Trotter, militant editor of the black newspaper the *Boston Guardian,* in forming the NIAGARA MOVEMENT, a short-lived effort to secure full civil and political rights for African Americans. In its wake, Du Bois helped found the most influential civil rights organization of the twentieth century: the NATIONAL ASSOCIATION FOR THE ADVANCEMENT OF COLORED PEOPLE (NAACP).

Unlike the Niagara Movement, the NAACP was an interracial organization from the start. Its leadership was largely white; as director of publications and research, Du Bois was the only African American among its early officers. In 1910 Du Bois left Atlanta for the NAACP's New York City headquarters, where he founded the *Crisis,* the association's magazine. As editor he published the work of LANGSTON HUGHES, COUNTEE CULLEN, and other HARLEM RENAISSANCE literary lights as well as his own wide-ranging and provocative opinions. From 1910 until his resignation as editor in 1934, Du Bois's editorials revealed the continuing evolution of his political thought. Early calls for integration and an end to lynching hewed the NAACP line, while his pleas for African American participation in World War I brought scorn from more radical black voices. His insistence on absolute equality for "the talented tenth" of black intellectual elites coexisted uneasily with arguments for self-segregation and technical training for the black masses. Such shifting opinions, along with his sometimes haughty self-assurance, meant that – as one biographer has noted – Du Bois would always have "influence, not power."

Increasingly, Du Bois looked beyond American race relations to international economics and politics. In 1915 he wrote *The Negro,* a sociological examination of the African diaspora. In 1919 he helped organize the second Pan-African Congress (*see* PAN-AFRICAN CONGRESS OF 1919). Visiting Africa in the 1920s, he wrote that his chief question was whether "Negroes are to lead in the rise of Africa or whether they must always and everywhere follow the guidance of white folk."

W. E. B. Du Bois, pictured here in about 1920, was the first black person to earn a doctoral degree from Harvard University. Throughout his long life Du Bois served as one of black America's leading intellectual voices. *Brown Brothers*

Along with anti-imperialism, Du Bois also expressed interest in SOCIALISM, possibly in response to the disproportionate effect that the GREAT DEPRESSION was having on African Americans, as well as his favorable impressions of a visit to the Soviet Union in 1926. Meanwhile, starting with a new essay collection, *Darkwater: Voices from Within the Veil* (1920), Du Bois's writing became more militant and controversial, and conflicts with NAACP secretary Walter F. White led to Du Bois's resignation as editor of the *Crisis* in 1934.

Returning to Atlanta University, Du Bois continued to write weekly opinion columns in black newspapers, as well as books such as *Black Reconstruction in America* (1934); *Black Folk: Then and Now* (1939); and *Dusk of Dawn: An Autobiography of a Concept of Race* (1940). In 1939 he founded *Phylon,* a journal devoted to race and cultural issues, whose radical nature may have contributed to his forced resignation from Atlanta University in 1944. Then in his mid-seventies, Du Bois did not retire but instead rejoined the NAACP staff (although he did not resume editorship of the *Crisis*). Declaring that he would spend "the remaining years of [his] active life" in the fight against imperialism, Du Bois helped reorganize the Pan-African Congress, which in 1945 elected him its international president. In that same year he published *Color and Democracy: Colonies and Peace,* and in 1947 produced *The World and Africa.* Du Bois's outspoken criticism of American foreign policy and his involvement with the 1948 presidential campaign of Progressive Party candidate Henry Wallace led to his dismissal from the NAACP in the fall of 1948.

During the 1950s Du Bois's continuing work with the international peace movement and open expressions of sympathy for the Soviet Union drew the censure of the United States government and further isolated Du Bois from the civil rights mainstream. In 1951, at the height of the cold war, he was indicted under the Foreign Agents Registration Act of 1938. While he was acquitted of that charge, the Department of State refused to issue him a passport in 1952, barring him from foreign travel until 1958. Once the passport ban was lifted, Du Bois and his wife, the writer SHIRLEY GRAHAM DU BOIS, traveled extensively, visiting England, France, Belgium, and Holland, as well as China and the Soviet Union, and much of the Eastern Bloc. On May 1, 1959, he was awarded the Lenin Peace Prize in Moscow. In 1960 Du Bois attended his friend KWAME NKRUMAH's inauguration as the first president of GHANA; in the following year the Du Boises accepted Nkrumah's invitation to move there and work on the *Encyclopaedia Africana,* a project that was never completed. Du Bois died at the age of 95, six months after becoming a Ghanaian citizen.

Kate Tuttle

SEE ALSO

Russia and the Former Soviet Union; Pan-Africanism; World War I and African Americans; Press, Black, in the United States; *Crisis, The*; Jim Crow; New York, New York; Philadelphia, Pennsylvania; Washington, Booker Taliaferro; White, Walter Francis; Wilberforce University; Communist Party USA, African Americans and the; March on Washington, 1963.

Cross Cultural

Dub Poetry, politically charged verse, usually employing patois and REGGAE rhythms, that became popular throughout the Caribbean diaspora in the early 1980s.

Dub poetry originated in the sound system culture of post-independence JAMAICA. Beginning in the late 1960s, sound systems – mobile discos – roamed the country, playing the latest reggae releases at parties and clubs. DJs "toasted" their audiences over instrumental or "dub" versions of various tracks. Providing a New World update to West African oral traditions, they improvised patois raps, exhorted their audiences to dance, and offered a running commentary on current political affairs. DJs such as Big Youth, U-Roy, and King Stitch gained popularity as much for their toasts and personas as for the music backing them.

These DJs set the stage for the development of both dub poetry and the bass-heavy DANCEHALL, or ragga, style that succeeded reggae as Jamaica's premier popular music in the late 1980s. Dancehall broke from the politically charged "conscious" lyrics of reggae and the early sound-system DJs and toasters. Its lyrics were instead filled with sexually explicit "slackness" or murder-obsessed, ultraviolent "gun talk." Dub poetry, on the other hand, followed reggae and developed with a political edge.

The sound systems were, to paraphrase PUBLIC ENEMY rapper Chuck D, Jamaica's CNN. In a region where literacy was low, the sound-system DJs acted as "chatting newspapers," in the words of Dutch dub poetry scholar Christian Habekost. Dub poetry followed suit to varying degrees, maintaining "conscious" lyrics and communicating "cultural vibes": it aligned itself with Black Nationalism, especially through the teachings of the Jamaican Pan-Africanist Marcus Garvey and the theology of Rastafarianism. In some cases, the "Babylon shitstem" – the Euro-American neocolonial empire – was examined through the lenses of native Marxism and feminism.

The dub poet's mantra of "Word, Sound and Power" refers both to this political sensibility and to the strong audience reaction elicited by performed verse. Roots of such "word, sound and power" can be found in the contemporary oral traditions forged by Jamaican poet, performer, and folklorist LOUISE BENNETT and Barbadian poet, historian, and literary critic EDWARD KAMAU BRATHWAITE. Dub poetry also draws heavily on "dread talk" – the unique vocabulary developed by RASTAFARIANS.

LINTON KWESI JOHNSON (LKJ), a Jamaican-born immigrant to England, was the first to use the term "dub poetry." In a 1976 article in the British journal *Race and Class*, he used it to describe the improvised raps of the sound-system DJs, not knowing that it would soon be used to describe his own style of reggae-influenced poetry. Since the mid-1970s LKJ had been publishing, recording, and performing a unique style of patois verse politicized by Rastafarianism and BLACK POWER and set to reggae rhythms. Meanwhile in Jamaica, community activist Oku Onuora was writing politically charged poetry while serving a 15-year sentence for armed robbery in a Kingston prison (he said he had been trying to obtain money to help ghetto youth). Unaware of LKJ's use of the term, Onuora also called his work dub poetry, stating that it was poetry not simply set to reggae, but with "a built-in reggae rhythm."

In Jamaica dub poetry was initially supported by the climate created by then Prime Minister MICHAEL MANLEY's experiments with democratic SOCIALISM in the 1970s. Manley and his People's National Party (PNP) placed a high value on the role of the arts in forging a national identity. Kingston's Cultural Training Centre, incorporating schools of fine arts, music, drama, and dance, was opened to nurture indigenous arts. The School of Drama became an integral part of the early dub poetry scene. Attending the school on a scholarship after his release from prison, Onuora was introduced to seminal poets Mikey Smith, Jean "Binta" Breeze, and the group Poets In Unity – all of whom were students. MUTABARUKA and the Panama-born Faybiene Miranda were the only major Jamaican dub poets not associated with the school. In England, where the Labour-controlled Greater London Council provided financial support to local cultural initiatives, LKJ, Benjamin Zephaniah, and other poets benefited from a similar environment.

With the release of major records by all of the prominent dub poets in the early 1980s, dub began receiving popular and critical acclaim. European critics, seeking the next generation of reggae innovators in the wake of BOB MARLEY's death, embraced the form. Dub poetry also began to be adopted by West Indian artists outside Jamaica and England. In Trinidad, Brother Resistance popularized rapso, a form similar to dub poetry. After meeting Onuora at Havana's Eleventh World Festival of Youth, Lillian Allen introduced dub poetry to CANADA. Toronto hosted the International Dub Poetry Festival in April 1993, and is home to Canadian poets such as Allen, Clifton Joseph, Devon Haugton, and Ahdri Zhina Mandiela. Under the name De Dub Poets, Allen, Joseph, and others combined poetry with community activism. They successfully challenged the League of Canadian Poets to acknowledge their radical departure from traditional poetics and to grant the group membership.

Dub poetry has not been without its critics. It has been said to rely too heavily on performance, causing the written form to suffer from a lack of energy, subtlety, and depth. Many have charged that the label "dub poetry" is a misnomer for what is, in effect, simply poetry. The explicit political content has been seen as myopic, and the reliance on reggae has become, in the words of Breeze, "as constraining in its rhythms as the iambic pentameter." Breeze's own work, as well as records like LKJ's *Things and Times* and Joseph's *Oral/Trans/Missions*, among others, reach for rhythms outside of reggae.

While the mid-1990s have seen the continued popularity of dub poetry, its audience is nowhere near the size of dancehall's, and a succeeding generation has not emerged to take over the tradition. But as Caribbean and black British reggae-rooted electronic music like DUB and Jungle are gaining popularity in the United States, many dub poets are finding new audiences as their verse is recorded by a younger generation of record producers.

Peter Hudson

SEE ALSO

Jungle (Drum and Bass); Pan-Africanism; Garvey, Marcus Mosiah; Barbados; Kingston, Jamaica; Rastafarians; Trinidad and Tobago; Languages, Creole, in the Caribbean.

Africa

Duiker, common name for several species of small to medium-sized ANTELOPE that live in shrub lands and forests of central and southern Africa.

The gray (or bush) duiker ranges into mountain plateaus. Duikers have short, straight, or slightly curved horns, often absent in females of the gray duiker. The largest duikers stand no higher than 87 cm (34 in) at the shoulder; the legs are short, the back arched, and the hooves pointed. The animals are numerous but shy and rarely seen; usually they travel alone or in pairs. They eat a wide range of vegetation and occasionally carrion or small birds, and they are hunted for their meat.

Scientific classification: Duikers belong to the family Bovidae. They are classified in the genera *Cephalophus* and *Sylvicapra*. The gray duiker is classified as *Sylvicapra grimmia*.

Europe

Dumas, Alexandre, Père

(b. July 24, 1802, Villers-Cotterêts, France; d. December 5, 1870, Puys, France), French novelist, dramatist, and essayist of African descent, a central figure in nineteenth-century French Romantic literature.

In 1893 the playwright George Bernard Shaw described Alexandre Dumas *père* (senior) as "a summit of art," comparing him to Mozart: "you get nothing above Dumas on his own mountain.... If you pass him you come down on the other side instead of getting higher." Dumas's literary work is striking in its breadth and originality, and is accessible to all lovers of adventure regardless of their social or educational background. In theater, Dumas created two new genres, the prose historical drama and the *drame moderne*, and, although dated today, his plays enjoyed unprecedented success in their time. His greatest novels, rich in passionate characters, lively dialogue, and gripping plots, have lasting appeal, and many, such as *Les trois mousquetaires* (The Three Musketeers), have become household names.

The story of how young Dumas – a provincial, light-skinned boy, whose tightly curled hair revealed his African ancestry – rose to become the supreme literary entertainer of his time is as intriguing as his novels. His father, Thomas-Alexandre Dumas Davy de la Pailleterie, was the son of the French Marquis Antoine-Alexandre Davy de la Pailleterie and a black slave woman named Marie-Cessette Dumas. Thomas-Alexandre was born in the French colony of Saint-Domingue (later HAITI), where he remained until he was brought to FRANCE at age 18. On enlisting in the French army, he dropped the name Davy de la Pailleterie, because his father disapproved of his enlistment, and took instead the name of his black mother. He rose to the rank of general but quarreled with Napoleon while on campaign with him in EGYPT. On his way back to France, he stopped in the kingdom of Naples, which, unbeknownst to him, had recently declared war on France. He was imprisoned for two years in wretched conditions that ruined his health. He returned to France in 1801 and died five years later, leaving his widow and children in relative poverty in the rural town of Villers-Cotterêts.

Were it not for a Swedish aristocrat, Adolphe de Leuven, who began vacationing at Villers-Cotterêts when Dumas was 16, Dumas would probably never have pursued a literary career. De Leuven convinced Dumas to collaborate with him on a number of light theatrical pieces, and also introduced Dumas to the historical romances of Sir Walter Scott. Dumas moved to Paris in 1823, continued to write vaudeville plays with de Leuven, and supported himself by working as a copyist for the duke of Orleans. There he found another mentor in the literary-minded assistant director, E. H. Lassagne, who guided him to the authors who would most aid the development of his literary gifts.

The next major step forward came in 1828, when a friend, Charles Nodier, invited Dumas to become a member of his literary salon, which included such leaders of the French Romantic movement as Victor Hugo, Alfred de Vigny, and Alphonse de Lamartine. In the following year, Dumas premiered to great success his historical drama *Henri III et sa cour* (Henry III and His Court) at the prestigious Comédie-Française theater. This triumph secured his financial position and reputation in Paris as a dramatist of verve and substance. From 1829 until 1851 he brought out a new play in Paris almost every year; in some years he premiered four or five. His most original and critically acclaimed plays, such as the psychological drama *Antony*, the melodrama *La tour de Nesle* (The Tower of Nesle), and his comedy *Mademoiselle de Belle-Isle*, date from the 1830s. Most of his plays were received with enthusiasm. In his plays and novels he wrote for the widest possible audience, and although some elite writers faulted his literary style, they envied his popularity.

Dumas's career as a novelist began between 1837 and 1843. During this period, after some disappointing reactions to some of his plays, he sought a new audience among the readers of *romans-feuilletons* (serial novels published in newspapers and journals). In 1838 he published four novels, including two romans-feuilletons, but it was not until the publication of *Le chevalier d'Harmental* in 1842 that he became established as a novelist. During the next 13 years, he produced a wealth of novels. His most important historically inspired works are the D'Artagnan trilogy, which includes his most famous work, *Les trois mousquetaires*; the Valois cycle, which includes *La reine Margot* (Marguerite de Valois) and draws on the bloody religious wars in France in the 1570s and 1580s; and the five Marie-Antoinette romances, which span the reign of Louis XVI and the French Revolution. His *Le comte de Monte-Cristo* (1846, The Count of Monte-Cristo), which enjoyed instantaneous and enduring success and which has a more contemporary setting, is described by literary scholar F. W. J. Hemmings as "an epic fantasy of vengeance."

The standard edition of Dumas's complete works runs to 301 volumes, and some scholars have raised doubts about the authenticity of some of his work. As French writer André Maurois observed in his biography of Dumas, "no one has read *all* of Dumas; that would be as impossible as for him to have written it all." It is true that Dumas collaborated with friends on some of his novels and plays. His most important collaborator was Auguste Maquet, who helped with many of his historical novels, sketching out plots and characters. However, as literary scholar Richard Stowe concludes, "while Dumas might not have been able to write certain of his novels without his collaborators, without him none of the best ones could have been written at all."

Dumas's nonfiction works – travel writings and a 3000-page memoir – present a portrait of an energetic and curious adventurer. Indeed, Dumas often found himself personally caught up in the political upheavals of mid-nineteenth-century Europe. In 1832, shortly after *La tour de Nesle* had begun its highly successful first run, he was present at a violent clash between French troops and republican insurrectionists in Paris. He took the revolutionaries to a nearby theater that was running one of his plays, *Napoléon Bonaparte*, broke down the door, and distributed the props from the play – a cache of weapons – to the delighted republicans. He then went home to rest. The next day he learned that the uprising had been crushed and all the revolutionaries massacred. He also read an account in a Paris newspaper of his own capture and execution by firing squad. The author of the account deplored the premature termination of such a promising literary career, and Dumas wrote to thank him for the kind obituary.

In 1860 Dumas became a close friend and collaborator of Giuseppe Garibaldi, the unifier of Italy, accompanying Garibaldi's "redshirts" during their invasion of Sicily. Dumas subsequently went to Naples to rouse opposition to the monarchy of Francis II, whose grandfather had been responsible for the imprisonment of Dumas's father. Dumas organized a team of tailors to sew and distribute red shirts, and set off fireworks to encourage Garibaldi's supporters in the city. After the king fled Naples and Garibaldi arrived and took control, he publicly embraced Dumas as a sign of gratitude.

Of Dumas's many trips through Europe, his longest and most eventful was a nine-month journey across the Russian Empire, beginning in June 1858. He was astonished to find people across the country who knew his books: monks in a remote monastery on Lake Ladoga in the north; administrators in Astrakhan on the Caspian Sea; and Persians in the Caucasus, who had retranslated his books from Russian into Persian. He also took many sea voyages in the Mediterranean – one of the few pursuits that gave him rest from a life of intense work and activity: "As soon as my sight is lost in immensity... there falls on my senses a delightful twilight, something that smokers of opium and eaters of hashish can alone understand – that voluptuous absence of the will."

Dumas had many mistresses throughout his life and fathered a number of children, including Alexandre Dumas *fils* (junior), who in later years became a conservative moralist and writer. Earlier, however, Dumas and his son went out dancing together, and they shared mistresses. As the young Alexandre once remarked to a disapproving middle-aged woman, "At least, if he doesn't set me a good example, he provides me with an excellent excuse." One of Dumas's last mistresses was Adah Menken, an actress, ballet dancer, and minor poet from New Orleans, who was widely believed to be an African American Creole, and who first performed in Paris in 1866. Known as the Naked Lady, she specialized in riding horses bareback across stage seminude. She described Dumas as "the King of Romance, the child of Gentleness and Love."

A few days before he died, Dumas recounted a dream to his son Alexandre. In the dream he had been standing on the peak of a mountain made up of all his books. Gradually, the ground beneath his feet had given way, leaving only a small heap of pumice stones and ashes. Deeply troubled, he asked his son if he believed that his work would survive after his death. To his son's reassurance, contemporary scholars and readers can add their own affirmation: the mountain of Dumas's life and work still towers.

Jonathan Edwards

SEE ALSO
New Orleans, Louisiana.

North America

Dunbar-Nelson, Alice

(b. July 19, 1875, New Orleans, La.; d. September 18, 1935, Philadelphia, Pa.), African American writer, journalist, and activist whose work focused on the multiracial experience, women's rights, and race relations.

Alice Dunbar-Nelson was born into a mixed Creole, African American, and Native American family. She graduated from the two-year teacher training program at Straight College (now Dillard University) in 1892, and taught school at various times throughout her life.

Dunbar-Nelson published her first book, a collection of poetry, short stories, essays, and reviews called *Violets and Other Tales,* in 1895. Paul Laurence Dunbar, the famous poet, began to correspond with her after admiring her poetry (as well as her picture) in a Boston magazine. They married on March 8, 1898.

The Dunbars moved to Washington, D.C., where they were lionized as a literary couple. Dunbar-Nelson's second collection of short fiction, *The Goodness of St. Rocque,* was published in 1899 as a companion to her husband's *Poems of Cabin and Field.* While Dunbar was known for his dialect poetry, Dunbar-Nelson's stories explored the Creole and multiracial experience. The couple separated after four years of marriage, and Paul Laurence Dunbar died four years later, in 1906. But Dunbar-Nelson continued to be honored for the rest of her life as the widow of the famous poet.

After her marriage had ended, Dunbar-Nelson moved to Wilmington, Delaware, where she taught school. Her mother, sister, and four nieces and nephews joined her there, and her extended family continued to live with her throughout most of her life. During this period Dunbar-Nelson continued her education with courses at Cornell University, Columbia University, and the University of Pennsylvania. She also edited such works as *Masterpieces of Negro Eloquence* (1914) and *The Dunbar Speaker and Entertainer* (1920). She was involved in several relationships with both men and women during this period, and in 1916 she married journalist Robert Nelson.

Together with Nelson, Dunbar-Nelson published the *Wilmington Advocate* newspaper from 1920 to 1922. She went on to write regular columns for several newspapers over the next decade. She also continued her work as a political and social activist. A few years earlier she had participated in World War I relief efforts and the fight for women's suffrage. During the 1920s she served on the Delaware Republican Committee, headed the Delaware Crusaders for the Dyer Antilynching Bill, and was executive secretary of the Inter-Racial Peace Committee.

Dunbar-Nelson remained active in the African American literary community, and her poems were included in Harlem Renaissance journals and anthologies. Her circle of friends included such renowned African Americans as Langston Hughes, W. E. B. Du Bois, Carter G. Woodson, and Mary McLeod Bethune. Dunbar-Nelson kept a diary in 1921 and from 1926 to 1931, which describes many of these friendships and mentions romantic relationships with several women during this period. In 1932 she and her husband moved to Philadelphia, where she became an influential member of African American social and literary circles. She died of heart disease three years later.

Lisa Clayton Robinson

See Also

World War I and African Americans; American Indians; Creoles; Du Bois, William Edward Burghardt (W. E. B.); Philadelphia, Pennsylvania; Woodson, Carter Godwin.

North America

Dunbar, Paul Laurence

(b. June 27, 1872, Dayton, Ohio; d. February 9, 1906, Dayton, Ohio), African American poet, often remembered for his Dialect Poetry.

Three years before his death in 1906 at the age of 34, Paul Laurence Dunbar wrote these lines in his poem, "The Poet":

He sang of life, serenely sweet,
With, now and then, a deeper note,
From some high peak, nigh yet remote,
He voiced the world's absorbing beat.
He sang of love when earth was young,
And Love, itself, was in his lays.
But ah, the world, it turned to praise
A jingle in a broken tongue.

Its words may express his own regrets about the direction of his literary career. Dunbar was the most famous African American poet and one of the most famous American poets of his time. His career brought him international fame and by any measure was a tremendous success. Although Dunbar felt his best work was his poetry in standard English, he was celebrated almost exclusively for his folk poetry about African Americans written in dialect – the "jingle in a broken tongue." This identification of Dunbar with dialect poetry disappointed him during his lifetime and alienated some later African American readers. But Dunbar's poetry has also been praised by readers from W. E. B. Du Bois to Nikki Giovanni, who recognized the challenges Dunbar faced as a turn-of-the-century black poet trying to sound the "deeper note."

Dunbar's parents had both been slaves on plantations in Kentucky. Although Dunbar was born in Ohio during Reconstruction, his parents' stories about slavery were the basis for some of his folk poetry. He attended Dayton public schools and was the only student of color at Dayton High School, where he was class president, editor of the school paper, president of the literary society, and class poet. After graduating in 1891 Dunbar tried to pursue a career in journalism; when he could not find a writing job because of his race, he became an elevator operator. He earned the nickname "the elevator boy poet," however, when he continued writing.

Dunbar took out a loan to publish his first book, *Oak and Ivy,* in 1893. Later that year, he read his poetry at the World's Columbian Exposition in Chicago, where he was praised by Frederick Douglass and other prominent African Americans. Dunbar became a crossover literary sensation in 1896, when his second book, *Majors and Minors,* was noticed by the well-known white critic and writer William Dean Howells. Howells arranged for an expanded version of the book, titled *Lyrics of Lowly Life,* to be published by the mainstream white firm of Dodd, Mead. The national publication, and the speaking tour that followed, made Dunbar famous among black and white audiences. His reputation soon spread overseas.

William Dean Howells was also among the first critics to reserve his praise for Dunbar's dialect poetry, and from that time, poems and short stories in dialect became the basis for most of Dunbar's popularity. Although there was a handful of other African Americans who had published works in dialect before Dunbar, most of his direct literary inspiration in that genre seemed to come from white authors in the sentimental "plantation tradition" of American literature. This literature, which was extremely popular in the decades following the Civil War, was often written by Southerners who romanticized black slaves and scenes of plantation life. Dunbar used dialect that resembled the words of these authors more closely than it resembled actual African American speech, and he also tended to portray the folk simplicity of slaves' lives rather than the injustice and oppression of slavery itself.

Dunbar's dialect poetry is often about courtship, folk traditions, and other benign aspects of the slave experience. Its neutral tone on slavery added to its popularity with white audiences but was often criticized by black readers. "When De C'on Pone's Hot," for example, is a nostalgic tribute to slave cooking, and its narrator clearly states that any troubles slaves had were instantly erased by the good feeling experienced when dinnertime came:

[G]loom tu'ns into gladness... joy drives out de doubt
When de oven do' is opened,
An' de smell comes po'in out.

In some of his dialect poetry, however, Dunbar does include an awareness and irony missing from white plantation literature. In "An Ante-Bellum Sermon," for example, he quotes a slave preacher's speech, a familiar topic for parody. But within this sermon, the preacher's message is about Moses delivering his people from slavery, and the wrath God then brought to bear on the slaveholders. And the preacher makes very plain that even though his text is ostensibly "judgin' Bible people by deir ac's," it has a special relevance to his audience:

So you see de Lawd's intention,
Evah sence de worl' began,
Was dat His almighty freedom
Should belong to evah man.

Dunbar's poetry in standard English takes his feelings on race even further. Poems such as "Douglass," "The Colored Soldiers," and "Black Sampson at Brandywine" are specific tributes to black individuals. And several of his best-known poems appear to speak powerfully about race without ever mentioning it as such. In "Sympathy," for example, Dunbar creates the powerful image of empathy with the caged bird who still sings – an image that poet Maya Angelou recalled in the title of her autobiography. And in "We Wear the Mask" – which begins with the line "We wear the mask that grins and lies" – he speaks of the necessity of presenting a contented face to the world to mask the deep pain and anger within. Many readers see this poem as Dunbar's explanation for the minstrel role he himself played by writing dialect poems that pandered to white audiences.

Dodd, Mead published four volumes of Dunbar's poetry during his lifetime. Although his audiences always favored his dialect poetry and short stories, Dunbar also wrote standard poetry, four novels, and several essays. In 1895 he began to correspond with another black poet whose work he admired, Alice Moore. The correspondence led to marriage in 1898, and although the marriage ended amicably just four years later, while it lasted Dunbar and Alice Dunbar-Nelson were a celebrated literary couple. Dunbar's literary fame, great as it was, came to a premature end. Near the beginning of his marriage, Dunbar contracted tuberculosis, and eventually developed a dependency on the alcohol prescribed as a painkiller. Within a few years, he was limited by both the disease and the alcoholism, and he died on February 9, 1906.

In the last several decades, scholars and readers have started to reconsider Dunbar's life and work. He remains a key figure in the African American literary tradition not only because he was one of the first black authors to create a sensation on the mainstream American literary scene, but also because his writing – even in dialect – contains powerful nuances that still move readers.

Lisa Clayton Robinson

See Also

Slavery in the United States; Literature, African American; Civil War, American; Douglass, Frederick; Du Bois, William Edward Burghardt (W. E. B.); Giovanni, Yolande Cornelia ("Nikki"); Minstrelsy.

Latin America and the Caribbean

Duncan, Quince

(b. December 5, 1940, San Jose, Costa Rica), Afro-Costa Rican writer of West Indian descent famous for his short stories and novels about blacks who migrated from the Antilles to the Atlantic coast of Central America in the late nineteenth and early twentieth centuries. Duncan's fiction illustrates the culture shock of this group as it adjusted to the Spanish-speaking society.

Quince Duncan was born in San Jose, Costa Rica at a time when black people were not welcome in the capital city. When he was two years old his parents took him to Limon, Costa Rica's most important port in the Caribbean and a center of black West Indian culture. There he was reared by his maternal grandparents. He spoke English at home but needed to learn Spanish for primary school. At age 15 he returned to San Jose and worked while struggling to continue his formal education and master Spanish.

Duncan's short narratives include *Los cuentos del Hermano Araña* (1975, Anansi Stories), traditional Caribbean folktales handed down by his Jamaican-born grandfather and various elders, as well as Afro-Costa Rican historical fiction. "Un regalo para la abuela" (A Gift for Grandma) is a delightful trickster tale from *Una canción en la madrugada* (1970, Dawn Song) about Cocobelo, a Jamaican immigrant who resists being drafted by the government or revolutionary forces during the Civil War of 1948. Cocobelo pretends to be the grandmother of his wife, Ruby; soldiers adore what they presume to be a charming old woman and regale her with silk stockings. Cocobelo's manhood is tested during this ordeal. His lifemanship (or the ability to survive in a hostile environment and still maintain a healthy self-concept with humor) is reminiscent of Langston Hughes's fictional character Simple, who became a representative for the black Everyman. The tragicomic blues theme of survival through humor ("laughin' to keep from cryin'") emerges from Duncan's narrative.

The title story from *La rebelión Pocomía y otros relatos* (1976, The Pocomia Rebellion and Other Stories) depicts the events surrounding the revolt of oppressed railroad workers. Up to that time there had been little or no documentation of the insurrection in Costa Rican history. *La rebelión Pocomía* illustrates Duncan's use of musical practices such as drumming, dancing, and chanting in African- derived religions as symbols of survival mechanisms throughout the diaspora. Also featured in this collection is "El partido" (Go-o-o-o-al!) – the all-too-familiar story of the hero athlete. Melico Pérez, the protagonist, claims $10,000 for winning a soccer match against the unbeaten Saprissa team, but he feels the disrespect of his coach and the public during the game. As Pérez's rookie team, Sonora, files onto the field, a rival Saprissa fan eggs one of its players, shouting, "Marvin, stomp that nigger." This remark intensifies Pérez's identity crisis: "To eat or not to eat. No more, no less. That's the real question. Because a long time ago, others defined my being: underdeveloped, Afro-Latin-indigene, black among whites, white Indian among blacks, white Negro among indigenous people, but in any case, underdeveloped, a bum." Pérez's soccer victory is meaningless in the face of his displacement.

Duncan's most representative novel is *Los cuatro espejos* (1973, The Four Mirrors), which, like Ralph Ellison's *Invisible Man* (1952), depicts the odyssey of the protagonist's search for his identity. Charles MacForbes wakes up blind one morning, unable to outline his features in the bathroom mirror. As he journeys from San Jose to Limon, he undergoes a psycho-emotional transformation that progressively enables him to see himself clearly. The themes of alienation, double consciousness, and invisibility are intertwined with those of self-acceptance from an Afrocentric perspective and pride in one's heritage (*see* Literature, Black, in Spanish America).

One of Duncan's more recent works is *Kimbo* (1990), a novel about an artist-singer who has achieved fame in his society. When the prominent citizen Señor Barrigón (Mr. Potbelly) is kidnapped, Kimbo is implicated and made to stand trial on circumstantial evidence for a crime he contends he did not commit. Ironically, the sensational ambiance of this thriller and untimely death of the hero metaphorically point toward the "death knell" given to O.J. Simpson's career as an important public figure during the so-called trial of the century, even though *Kimbo* was published five years before the trial took place.

Although Duncan has written literary criticism and published the play *El trepasolo* (1993), it is his fiction that best captures the trials and triumphs of people of African descent in Costa Rica. The author's focus has shifted from dealing exclusively with the interaction of blacks and nonblacks in Costa Rica to a broader approach that includes the shared history of African-descended people throughout the diaspora, an approach he calls Afro-realismo.

Dellita Martin-Ogunsola

North America

Dunham, Katherine

(b. June 22, 1909, Glen Ellyn, Ill.), African American dancer, choreographer, and anthropologist who incorporated African-based cultural forms into dance.

Born to Fanny June Taylor, a French Canadian and Native American, and Albert Dunham, Katherine Dunham attended school in Chicago and began to dance at a young age. After a short time at Joliet Junior College, she attended the University of Chicago, where she received a B.A., an M.A. and a Ph.D. in cultural anthropology. To help finance her education, she worked as a librarian and taught dance. Eventually, Dunham opened a dance school and established a black dance troupe later called the Chicago Negro School of Ballet.

In order to explore the cultural and social dimensions of African-based dance forms, Dunham obtained a Guggenheim Award from the Julius Rosenwald Foundation for travel to the Caribbean. In JAMAICA, she was accepted into a community of maroons, who allowed her to view their sacred war dance, the *Koromantee* (*see* MAROONAGE IN THE AMERICAS). Similarly, in HAITI, she was initiated into VODOU and subsequently permitted to participate in secret ritual dances. Throughout her life, Dunham has maintained a special relationship with Haiti through continued association with Haitian arts, politics, and society. The Haitian government awarded her several medals and citations, including honorary citizenship.

Dunham wrote several books, including *Journey to Accompong* (1946), *A Touch of Innocence* (1959), *Kasamance* (1967), and *Islands Possessed* (1969). She presented lectures and demonstrations at Yale University, Case Western Reserve, Southern Illinois University, and the University of Chicago. She also served as a committee member of the Illinois Project of the Federal Writers' Project from 1935 to 1940.

Dunham communicated her knowledge of cultures primarily through choreography and dance performance. In 1940 she formed the Katherine Dunham Dance Company, which toured the world performing dances she choreographed. These include *L'An'Ya* (1938), *Le Jazz Hot* (1939), *Tropics* (1939), *Bal Nègre* (1943), *Tropical Revue* (1943), and *Shango* (1945). Dunham choreographed and performed in several shows and films, such as the Broadway musical *Cabin in the Sky* (1940) and the motion picture *Star-Spangled Rhythm* (1942). In 1943 she established the Dunham School of Arts and Research in New York City, which offered classes in dance, theater, and world cultures. Dunham became the first black woman to choreograph an opera, *Aida*, for the New York City Metropolitan Opera, in its 1963-1964 season.

After her company's last appearance in 1965, Dunham went on to represent the United States in the Festival of Black Arts in SENEGAL. She also acted as cultural adviser for the Senegalese government and helped train the National Ballet of Senegal. In 1967 she relocated to St. Louis, and in affiliation with the Edwardsville campus of Southern Illinois University developed and directed the Performing Arts Training Center, a school for disadvantaged youth.

For her accomplishments, Dunham has received many honorary degrees and awards, including the *Dance Magazine* Award (1968), the University of Chicago Alumni Professional Achievement Award (1968), the Albert Schweitzer Music Award (1979), the Kennedy Center Award (1983), and the Distinguished Service Award of the American Anthropological Society (1986).

Leyla Keough

Latin America and the Caribbean

Dunkley, John (1891-1947), Jamaican artist known for his landscape paintings (*see* ART IN LATIN AMERICA AND THE CARIBBEAN).

Latin America and the Caribbean

Durán, Alejo (Gilberto Alejandro Durán Díaz)(b. 1919, El Paso, Colombia; d. 1989), Afro-Colombian accordion player in the genre of VALLENATO music from the Caribbean coastal region of COLOMBIA.

Alejo Durán was born in the village of El Paso, Cesar Province, where he eventually worked as an agricultural laborer. His father, uncle, and two brothers, Luis Felipe and Náfer, already played the accordion, and at 24 years of age Alejo began to learn, surrounded by other important figures in the vallenato tradition such as Abel Antonio Villa, Luis E. Martínez, and Guillermo Buitrago, who were already making recordings in Colombia's nascent music industry.

In 1949 Durán formed a four-piece group (accordion, drum, scraper, and guitar). The group toured locally, playing the simple picaresque and quasi-narrative songs of the genre, often with romantic themes. At this time Durán married and settled in Magangué, until the union broke up. He moved to Montería in 1957 and then to various other towns in the region. His first hit record was "El Cero treinta y nueve," in 1954, his own composition, as were most of his songs. Later he recorded with the Barranquilla firms Atlantic and Tropical. In 1968 he won first prize at the newly founded Festival of the Vallenato Legend.

At his death, Durán left behind many children and some 120 LPs, including such classic hits as "Fidelina," "Pedazo de acordeón," "Cachuca bacana," and Juancho Polo Valencia's "Alicia adorada." Durán was distinctive for his simple style and low gruff voice, very different from the more elaborate style of the vallenato that became popular nationally in the 1970s.

Peter Wade

Latin America and the Caribbean

Durand, Oswald (b. September 17, 1840, Cap-Haïtien, Haiti; d. April 22, 1906, Haiti), Haitian poet and politician.

In 1842 at age 2, Charles Alexis Oswald Durand became an orphan when an earthquake destroyed the city of Cap-Haïtien in northern HAITI, on the Atlantic Ocean. He then went with his grandmother to the frontier town of Ouanaminthe. Little is known of his first years of studies, but at age 16 he was already working for his living as a tinsmith. While making pots and pans in the tiny village of St.-Louis du Nord, he read and wrote his first verses. He was later offered a job as a primary school teacher.

Demesvar Delorme, already a renowned politician and writer, assisted Durand in publishing his first books of poetry. Durand was elected to the Chamber of Deputies in 1885, where he served several terms. He was elected president of Parliament in 1888.

In 1888 Durand was invited to France as a guest of honor of the famous Société des Gens de Lettres. His "godfather" in French literary circles was the celebrated poet and playwright François Coppée, the favorite author of Sarah Bernhardt, then the world's most renowned actress.

Durand's reputation as a poet grew, particularly after the publication of "Choucoune" in 1883, which recounts the seduction of the narrator's beautiful black mistress by a white foreigner. Much of his poetry calls up images of Haitian women and the Haitian landscape. Durand's love poems are widely known in Haiti, and he is considered by many to be Haiti's greatest poet. When he died suddenly on April 22, 1906, Haiti mourned for its national bard. Other works include *Quatre nouveaux poèmes* (1896) and *Rires et pleurs* (1899).

Paulette Poujol-Oriol

SEE ALSO

Cap-Haïtien, Haiti; Literature, French Language, in Caribbean.

Africa

Durban, South Africa, South African city, formerly Port Natal.

Situated on the eastern Cape of SOUTH AFRICA, Durban is the capital of the KwaZulu/Natal Province and the country's most active seaport. It is surrounded by the Drakensburg mountain range to the west, the Indian Ocean to the east, and the rolling hills of KwaZulu/Natal to the north and south. Although the area had been visited by European traders and explorers starting in the sixteenth century, its natural harbor was not fully utilized until the British arrived in 1824. They acquired land through treaties with the ZULU king SHAKA and named their settlement Port Natal. In 1835 the city's name was changed to Durban, after Sir Benjamin D'Urban, then governor of the Cape Colony.

By 1855 Durban's British colony had begun exploiting the harbor, which continues to export raw materials and manufactured goods from the entire Witwatersrand region. In addition to trade, Durban's economy depended on the SUGAR industry; beginning in 1860 large numbers of laborers were imported from India (*see* INDIAN COMMUNITIES IN AFRICA). By the 1950s Durban's population was about evenly divided among Europeans, Indians, and Africans, with a small number of mixed-race people officially designated as "coloured." As in the rest of South Africa, nonwhites were forcibly relocated to single-race townships during the following decades. In the early 1970s black workers in Durban protested their economic inequality and political oppression with a series of strikes, which led to the founding of several black trade unions.

Since the dismantling of APARTHEID, residential restrictions no longer apply, but the city is still far from integrated. Durban remains an important seaport and the center of the South African sugar industry; another important aspect of the local economy is the city's popularity as a tourist destination. In 1991 the population of the greater metropolitan area was over 1 million people.

Kate Tuttle

SEE ALSO

Cape Coloured; Explorers in Africa, 1500 to 1800; Tourism in Africa.

North America

Durham, North Carolina

In 1866, as Durham incorporated, African Americans arrived from the neighboring farmlands they had worked as slaves. Yet in that same year, even though the Civil War had ended the previous year, the state of North Carolina passed a black code. It later rejected the Fourteenth Amendment, which guaranteed full citizenship to African Americans. Racist vigilante groups repeatedly attacked African Americans in their first years of freedom. By 1867 hostility and resistance to the laws of the nation led to federal, military rule of the state for ten years – the beginning of RECONSTRUCTION.

Despite such difficulties, a black community developed as Durham became the center of tobacco processing in the United States. In 1868 Edian Markum organized a school and the Union Bethel Church, later St. Joseph's African Methodist Episcopal (AME) Church. By 1870, 698 African Americans were living in Durham.

Between 1870 and the turn of the century, black neighborhoods developed in the hollows and bottomlands of Durham. An uneasy peace existed between the distinctly separated black and white communities. Unlike most of their counterparts in the South, many white business owners in Durham relied on black workers in their factories.

By 1900 the black middle class had begun businesses that soon grew into successful corporations. In 1898 John Merrick and a group of investors formed the North Carolina Mutual and Provident Association, now the NORTH CAROLINA MUTUAL LIFE INSURANCE COMPANY. Its success, especially under Charles Clinton Spaulding, led to the creation of a real estate company, textile and hosiery mills, and, by 1906, the *Durham Negro Observer*. Black leaders helped to found a hospital for blacks and, in 1910, North Carolina Training College, which became North Carolina Central University. In 1908 the Mechanics and Farmers Bank was formed, and in the 1920s the Banker's Fire Insurance Company and the National Negro Finance Corporation were established.

These businesses became the financial and political foundation for a black elite who had the wealth and power to advance a civil rights agenda and to ensure good business conditions by maintaining the fragile peace that they had brokered between African Americans and whites in Durham. E. Franklin Frazier wrote in his famous quote that this capital of the black middle class "is not the place where men write and dream; but a place where black men calculate and work."

Nonetheless, racial hostility and poor living conditions tested any peace. JIM CROW laws were in force and the white supremacy movement was strong. Most African Americans faced open, sometimes violent, opposition in the labor force. In 1920 the mortality rate among blacks in Durham was three times higher than the white rate. As of 1926, 64 percent of all African Americans in Durham died before the age of 40, and 80 percent lived in substandard, badly ventilated housing. These conditions prompted many African Americans to move to Northern cities.

Business leaders attempted reform. Charles Spaulding organized the Durham branch of the Commission on Interracial Cooperation, which did not challenge segregation but called for an end to racial discrimination. In 1935 business leaders formed the Durham Committee on Negro Affairs (DCNA) to increase job opportunities for African Americans. Seven years later the DCNA and the Durham chapter of the NATIONAL ASSOCIATION FOR THE ADVANCEMENT OF COLORED PEOPLE (NAACP) organized a conference of Southern black leaders that resulted in the Durham Manifesto, a call for the total cessation of segregation.

The 1920s and 1930s also produced a distinct music and entertainment scene in Durham. Blind Boy Fuller (Fulton Allen), Blind Gary Davis, and Sonny Terry developed the Piedmont blues – a lively, acoustic-style blues that often included whoops, calls, and foot tapping. At warehouse dances in Durham, Duke Ellington and Eubie Blake played.

In 1954 the Supreme Court decision BROWN V. BOARD OF EDUCATION ushered in a new era of activism, and the more conservative DCNA gave way to the NAACP, the CONGRESS OF RACIAL EQUALITY (CORE), the STUDENT NONVIOLENT COORDINATING COMMITTEE (SNCC), and the SOUTHERN CHRISTIAN LEADERSHIP CONFERENCE (SCLC). In 1959 Anita Brame and Lucy Jones became the first black schoolchildren to integrate a white school in Durham, and within a year, student SIT-INS and boycotts had led to the integration of many restaurants and stores. In 1961 Duke University began to integrate, and civil rights lawyers, led by Floyd McKissick, sued to end segregation at Durham High School.

By the late 1960s activism was focusing on neighborhoods, where Operation Breakthrough led demands for better city services and facilities. Mass rallies in 1967 and economic boycotts in 1968 improved some conditions. But the slow rate of change and the assassination of Martin Luther King Jr. radicalized community leaders such as Howard Fuller, who formed the short-lived Malcolm X Liberation University in 1969.

In 1970 a court-ordered plan to integrate schools prompted white flight from Durham and the development of private, Christian academies. These demographic changes led to H. M. Michaux's election as the first black state representative from Durham in 1972; in 1992 Melvin J. Watt was elected the first black congressperson from Durham. According to the 1990 census, African Americans constituted 46 percent of the nearly 137,000 inhabitants of Durham.

Jim Mendelsohn

SEE ALSO

Slavery in the United States; African Methodist Episcopal Church; Black Codes in the United States; Blake, James Hubert ("Eubie"); Blues, The; Civil War, American; Fourteenth Amendment to the United States Constitution; Frazier, Edward Franklin; Great Migration, The; King, Martin Luther, Jr.; Spaulding, Charles Clinton; Ellington, Edward Kennedy ("Duke").

Africa

Duruma, ethnic group of East Africa.

The Duruma primarily inhabit coastal northeastern TANZANIA and adjacent parts of KENYA. They speak a Bantu language and belong to the larger MIJIKENDA (Nyika) cultural and linguistic group. Approximately 200,000 people consider themselves Duruma.

SEE ALSO

Bantu: Dispersion and Settlement.

North America

Du Sable, Jean Baptiste Pointe (b. 1750? St. Marc, Saint-Domingue [present-day HAITI]; d. August 28, 1818, St. Charles, Mo.), trader, trapper, and first permanent non-American Indian resident of the area now called CHICAGO, ILLINOIS.

Jean Baptiste Pointe Du Sable's biography combines conjecture and lore with a few established facts. He was probably born in

Saint-Domingue (present-day Haiti) around 1750 to a French mariner and an African-born slave. He may have been educated in Paris and employed as a sailor during his young adult life. Du Sable entered North America through either Louisiana or French Canada and first appeared in historical documents in 1779, when a British Officer in the Great Lakes region reported that the local trader "Baptist Point de Sable" was "much in the interest of the French."

The British detained Du Sable for suspected "intercourse with the enemy," but he soon impressed his captors as a well-educated and highly capable frontiersman. British governor Patrick Sinclair sent Du Sable to the St. Clair River region to manage trade and serve as a liaison between Native Americans and Britons.

In 1784 Du Sable returned to the southern shore of Lake Michigan, where apparently he had lived before his arrest. Du Sable added to whatever prior "Eschikagou" landholdings he had kept while away, building a cabin, a bake house, a dairy, a smokehouse, a barn, a horse-mill, a stable, a workshop, and a poultry house. Although Du Sable owned land elsewhere in the region, he settled for 16 years in the area that would come to be called Chicago. Du Sable traded, trapped, and served as the local cooper and miller. By 1790 his settlement had become a major link in the chain of frontier commerce.

In 1788 Du Sable married a Potawatomi Indian woman named Kittihawa, or Catherine, with whom he raised two children. Once married, Du Sable became increasingly involved in the life of Kittihawa's tribe. He sold 21 of his 23 pieces of European artwork, probably as a means to acculturate with Native American ways. His bid in 1800 for tribal chieftaincy failed, and soon after he sold his holdings and moved from the Chicago area.

Despite the enormous sum that he received for his property ($1200), Du Sable never regained the prosperity he had attained at his Chicago trading post. Real estate records suggest that he lived in St. Charles, Missouri, from 1805 to 1814 and that he probably died in poverty.

As the first permanent non-native resident of the region, Du Sable is credited as the founder of Chicago. In 1912 the city placed a plaque on the corner of Kinzie and Pine streets to commemorate his settlement. Du Sable appears in a frieze created for the Illinois Centennial Building in 1965 and was featured on a stamp in 1987. A Chicago public high school also honors him by bearing his name.

Eric Bennett

Africa

Dusé Mohammed Ali (b. 1866?, Alexandria?, Egypt; d. June 26, 1945, Lagos, Nigeria), an early and influential proponent of Pan-Africanism.

Although information about Dusé Mohammed Ali's origins is sparse and inexact, he claimed that he was born in Egypt to an Egyptian army officer and a Sudanese mother. In 1876 he was sent to England for an education. As a young man he took up acting and toured the United States and Canada before returning to England in 1898.

Dusé left acting in 1909 for a career as a journalist, publishing articles critical of British racism and imperialism in the *Islamic Review* and the *New Age*, a leading socialist literary journal. In 1911 he published *In the Land of the Pharaohs*, a short anti-imperialist history of Egypt, much of which he was accused of plagiarizing. Nevertheless, the book enjoyed an enthusiastic reception among black intellectuals of the day.

In 1911 Dusé began to publish *African Times and Orient Review*. While the publication failed to gain a large circulation, its wide geographical distribution (subscribers lived in England, West Africa, the United States, the West Indies, and even Japan) meant that Dusé's ideas had a wide influence. He helped shape the ideas of the West Indian Pan-Africanist Marcus Garvey, as well as those of Joseph Casely-Hayford, an activist in the Gold Coast (present-day Ghana).

In the *Review*, Dusé promoted the investment of capital in West African farming and commercial enterprises, unsuccessfully attempting to convince the British Colonial Office to provide loans. Following World War I, he proposed founding an African bank to help African traders erode the European trading monopoly. The Colonial Office declined to help finance the project, and Dusé could not raise the necessary $5 million himself.

In 1931 Dusé settled in Nigeria, where he became manager and editor of the *Comet*, a popular Lagos newspaper. By 1933 the paper's circulation had reached 4000, making it the top-selling weekly in Nigeria.

Robert Fay

See Also
Casely-Hayford, Joseph Ephraim; Lagos, Nigeria; Great Britain; Sudan; Garvey, Marcus Mosiah.

Latin America and the Caribbean

Dutch West India Company, trading company incorporated by the States-General of the Netherlands in 1621 to share world trade with the Dutch East India Company.

In return for subsidies to the state, the West India Company was granted a monopoly of trade in the Americas and Africa, with the right of colonizing and of maintaining armed forces (*see* Colonial Rule; Colonial Latin America and the Caribbean). The colonizing activities of the company were notable for the settlement of New Netherlands (later New York), Suriname, and Curaçao, an island in the Netherlands Antilles. In Brazil the company took Bahia in 1623 but later lost it to the Spanish and Portuguese; the company established itself at Pernambuco and elsewhere until 1661, when it resigned all rights in the country. Armed forces of the Netherlands were used to impose the sovereign rights of the company wherever possible and to plunder Spanish and Portuguese settlements worldwide.

The trading career of the Dutch West India Company was not as successful as that of its sister company, the Dutch East India Company. In 1674 the former was dissolved because of financial difficulties. A new company lasted until 1795, when it, too, collapsed in the course of the French invasion of the Netherlands. Another West India Company, formed in 1828, was completely unsuccessful.

Latin America and the Caribbean

Duvalier, François (b. April 14, 1907, Port-au-Prince, Haiti; d. April 21, 1971, Port-au-Prince, Haiti), president-for-life of Haiti from 1957 to 1971 and founder of the country's only hereditary regime, which ended with the overthrow of his son Jean-Claude Duvalier in 1986.

Born into a lower-middle-class Haitian family, François Duvalier attended local primary schools and later the Lycée Pétion, where he was taught by his political mentor, Dumarsais Estimé. Duvalier subsequently attended medical school at the national university, earning a degree in 1934. He then turned to civil service, working for the Haitian government for the next ten years. It was during this time that Duvalier became part of a collective known as the Griots, a group of intellectuals inspired by the Négritude movement who sought to glorify Haiti's African heritage.

In *Le problème des classes à travers l'histoire d'Haïti* (1946), a work that many deem a vulgarization of the Négritude ideology developed in Haiti by Jean Price-Mars, Duvalier and Lorimer Denis rejected a Marxist analysis of class and claimed that the historical supremacy of the mulatto elite was an ethnic rather than an economic phenomenon. This work became the basis of what has been characterized as Duvalier's black fascism. Duvalier joined the Worker-Peasant Movement (MOP) led by Daniel Fignolé in 1946, and quickly rose to the rank of secretary general. That same year, a military coup removed the mulatto president Elie Lescot from office and put Dumarsais Estimé, a black, in his place. Estimé promptly made Duvalier director general of public health.

Duvalier was forced to abandon his post in December 1950, following a coup led by the black commander of the presidential guard, Paul Eugène Magloire. Duvalier's allegiance to Estimé kept him in hiding until August 1956. Duvalier eventually reemerged and challenged Magloire for the presidency.

Under pressure from a number of political sources, Magloire was forced to leave the country. In a race with the wealthy mulatto businessman Louis Dejoie, Duvalier – with the support of the Griots and the military – won handily, his supporters taking 23 of 37 seats in the Chamber of Deputies and all the seats in the Senate.

Duvalier titled himself "Papa Doc," invoking the paternalism and authority that surround the Haitian presidency, and immediately began consolidating power, first removing all military personnel opposed to him and, in 1959, forming his own personal militia, the infamous TONTON MACOUTES, composed mainly of peasants from Haiti's rural regions. But even prior to the formation of the Tonton Macoutes, Duvalier had begun a reign of terror that lasted 14 years, claimed the lives of between 30,000 and 60,000 of his political opponents, and brutalized countless others, many of them mulattos. It was during this period that he attempted to manipulate the United States, which feared a turn toward Communism in the Caribbean following Fidel Castro's successful revolution in CUBA in 1959.

In a famous speech in June of 1960, Duvalier effectively blackmailed the United States by stating that if more aid were not forthcoming he would be forced to obtain it "elsewhere." The Kennedy Administration eventually shunned Duvalier. As the 1960s progressed, power became increasingly personalized in Haiti. Duvalier dissolved the parliament in 1961 and had himself declared president-for-life in 1964. VODOU, a religion previously dismissed by Haitian leaders as obscurantist, also came to play a role in Duvalier's campaign of terror. Duvalier, who claimed that Vodou was a part of African tradition that should be integrated into Haitian life, cultivated the image of the Vodou priest in an attempt to inspire fear in the masses.

Duvalier also strove to be viewed as a world leader, often comparing himself to JEAN-JACQUES DESSALINES, Charles de Gaulle, Mao Zedong, Vladimir Lenin, and – during episodes of extreme megalomania – Christ. These empty symbolic gestures were coupled with corruption on a grand scale. Setting the example for future kleptocrats like MOBUTU SESE SEKO of Zaire (now the DEMOCRATIC REPUBLIC OF THE CONGO), Duvalier transferred most of the country's wealth to himself and his allies during his reign. As his health worsened, Duvalier planned to pass his power and privilege on to his son, Jean-Claude. In a referendum just two months prior to his death, Papa Doc called on the Haitian people to ratify this transfer. With 2,391,916 voting in favor and none against, this referendum represented Duvalier's last act of corruption. Summing up Duvalier's tenure, a longtime opponent put it this way: "Duvalier has performed an economic miracle. He has taught us to live without money, to eat without food, to live without life."

Richard Watts

Latin America and the Caribbean

Duvalier, Jean-Claude (b. July 3, 1951), president of HAITI (1971-1986).

Born while his father, the tyrannical François "Papa Doc" Duvalier, was in political exile in the Haitian countryside, Jean-Claude Duvalier spent the first years of his life in hiding. When Papa Doc assumed the presidency in 1957, Jean-Claude – a mere six years old – began the process of being groomed as his successor. A dying François Duvalier announced on January 22, 1971, that his son, at the age of 19, would assume the role of president for life.

With the death of François Duvalier, Jean-Claude essentially became a figurehead for the regime while his mother, Simone Ovide Duvalier, ran the country. Over time, however, the younger Duvalier assumed more power, appointing members of Haiti's mulatto elite whom he had met in school to important posts in his government and inviting some of the departed elite to return, with the promise that there was no risk of persecution.

Duvalier's regime loosened the grip of the government censors, and political criticism began to appear in the press. Human rights abuses were curtailed in order to secure United States foreign aid, which, along with aid from Canada, France, and Israel, made possible several important agricultural development projects. Duvalier also initiated educational reform by hiring qualified foreigners as teachers and administrators. But the corruption and terror that had characterized his father's regime subsided only temporarily, and the gradual liberalization soon ended.

During the 1979 legislative elections, "Baby Doc" Duvalier resorted to bribery and force, which ensured victory for his political allies in all but one constituency. A political crack-down followed in November 1980, during which 200 of his political opponents were arrested, tried in courts that were under his direct control, and, in many cases, deported. In that same year, he moved even closer to the mulatto elite when he married Michele Bennett, the daughter of a bourgeois mulatto family.

These factors – combined with the fact that Haiti's already weak economy was crumbling under the weight of foreign debt – contributed to a precipitous decline in the popularity of Baby Doc's regime with his father's traditional power base, the black middle class. Those who felt shunned by the younger Duvalier's regime were, therefore, unwilling to intercede in 1986 when high school students began striking, first in the countryside and later in Port-au-Prince. These demonstrations were followed by a complete shutdown of the private sector. As it became clear that Duvalier could no longer effectively control the country, the U.S. government asked him to resign as president and arranged for his exile to FRANCE.

Richard Watts

SEE ALSO

Duvalier, François; Human Rights in Latin America and the Caribbean.

Africa

Dyula (also known as Jula, Diula, Wangara, and Kangah), an ethnic group of CÔTE D'IVOIRE, BURKINA FASO, MALI, GHANA, and GUINEA-BISSAU.

"Dyula" is a MANDE word meaning "itinerant trader"; it refers both to the ethnic group and to the occupation for which they are best known. Little is known about the Dyula before the thirteenth century, when they emerged as the main trading class of the ancient MALI EMPIRE. Their Mande language suggests that they originated in the empire's heartland along the upper NIGER RIVER. The Dyula traveled throughout West Africa and traded gold, COLA nuts (a natural stimulant), salt, and cloth. They played an important role in organizing the production of cloth and, according to some historians, spurred increased production of cloth and other trade goods during the sixteenth and seventeenth centuries. Along with trade goods, the Dyula helped disseminate the advanced culture of the western SAHEL, including Islam, the dominant religion of the Dyula, as well as Arabic and Sudanic architecture.

Over the centuries most Dyula settled in large market towns, where they had greater trade opportunities. Frequently, this required them to live among other ethnic groups, such as the SENUFO, the MOSSI, and the ABRON, and to accept a second-class "stranger" status among the larger group. Over time Dyula groups became a permanent addition to the surrounding communities, although Dyula traders retained a distinct sense of identity and history through trade connections with other Dyula. During the sixteenth century, however, one group of Dyula traders living among the Senufo along the border of present-day Côte d'Ivoire founded their own kingdom – KONG – which prospered until the late nineteenth century as a hub for trade routes radiating south into the forest and north into the Sahel.

Today most Dyula still work in commerce, and many still produce textiles for trade. In many regions they continued to dominate long-distance trade in the 1990s. Many of them practice some form of subsistence farming. The Dyula are also known as Islamic scholars. Among some related groups, such as the BAMBARA, it is common for Islamic converts to refer to themselves as Dyula. Most Dyula children attend Koranic schools, and Dyula often view state-sponsored secular education with distrust.

Elizabeth Heath

SEE ALSO

Gold Trade; Languages, African: An Overview; Salt Trade.

e

Early African American Women's Organizations. Please see Women's Organizations, Early African American

Latin America and the Caribbean

Early Rastafarian Leaders,

along with Joseph Hibbert, and Archibald Dunkley, Leonard P. Howell was one of the central architects and preachers of the early Rastafarian ideology in Jamaica.

Leonard P. Howell, Joseph Hibbert, and Archibald Dunkley were the first three Rastafarian leaders in Jamaica and, according to scholar Barry Chevannes, the "main architects of the Rastafari movement for the first twenty years." Their followers, notes Chevannes, invested them "with heroic, if not divine, abilities." Although they found ideological inspiration abroad and preached independently of one another in Jamaica, their doctrines were fundamentally the same. They subscribed to both the Back-to-Africa program of Marcus Garvey and Ethiopianism, a political and spiritual glorification of Ethiopia based on such biblical references as verse 31 of Psalm 68: "Princes shall come out of Egypt; Ethiopia shall soon stretch out her hands unto God." During the late 1920s Ethiopianism and Garvey's concept of a black national identity based on race became the ideological basis of Rastafarianism and a broad-based popular movement. This development was further fueled by the crowning in 1930 of Prince Tafari Makonnen as Haile Selassie, as emperor of Ethiopia.

Among the early leaders, Howell had the greatest impact on the early development of Rastafarian ideology in Jamaica. According to Robert A. Hill, a scholar of Rastafarianism, Howell performed "the role of catalytic agent in igniting the radical millenarian consciousness that based itself on the doctrine of the divine kingship of Ethiopia's Ras Tafari."

The oldest of ten children, Howell grew up in the Bull Head Mountain district of upper Clarendon. In 1896 he served in the Ashanti Wars and learned several African languages. In 1918 he joined the United States Army tranport service as a cook. After five years of military service, he was granted U.S. citizenship. He earned a living as a construction worker in New York City, where he encountered Garvey and the American Communist Party leader George Padmore, both of whom significantly influenced Howell's politics and philosophy.

Hibbert and Dunkley, both Jamaican workers, also spent considerable time abroad. At age 17, Hibbert migrated to Costa Rica, where he joined the Ancient Order of Ethiopia, a Masonic Lodge. Dunkley found employment as a seaman with the United Fruit Company. Howell, Hibbert, and Dunkley all returned to Jamaica between 1931 and 1932. At this time both Ethiopianism and religious revivalism – a syncretism between Christianity and the island's African religions – were in full swing among the lower classes. They came into contact with one another in the slums of Kingston, where they independently pursued their millenarian activities. Kingston thus became the center of the early Rastafarian movement, which eventually spread throughout the island.

In 1933 Howell established himself in the eastern parish of St. Thomas, where he proclaimed in public speeches that Ras Tafari was the true King and Lord of the black race. He negated the authority of Jamaica's colonial government and legal institutions, and told blacks not to pay taxes or rent on the land they cultivated. He also predicted that on August 1, 1934 – the 100-year anniversary of the abolition of British slavery in Jamaica – Jamaican blacks would repatriate to Africa. To this end, he encouraged male Rastafari to grow their beards, which, like the rod of Moses, would symbolically serve the purpose of parting the sea to allow them passage to Abyssinia. Howell's activities were closely monitored by the police; in December 1933 he was arrested, charged with sedition, and sentenced to two years' imprisonment. Soon after, Hibbert and Dunkley were arrested and imprisoned, and the movement was temporarily forced underground.

Following his release from prison, Howell published *The Promised Key* (1935). The book was based on two main sources: the Ethiopianist doctrines of *The Holy Piby* (known as the Black Man's Bible), by Robert Athlyi Rogers, published in 1924 in Newark, New Jersey; and Rev. Fitz Balintine Pettersburgh's *The Royal Parchment Scroll of Black Supremacy*, published in 1926 in Jamaica. Howell's book appeared under the name Gangunguru Maragh, meaning "teacher of famed wisdom" in Hindi. That he would have chosen a Hindi name reflects the wide variety of spiritual influences, including East Indian mysticism, present in Jamaica's religious practices of the time. Indeed, as Hill points out, "the popular belief in the power of the occult played a formative role in the early stages of Rastafari consciousness..., since in its early stage it possessed close and organic links with the belief and ritual systems of Jamaican folk religion." Around 1940 Howell established a commune called Pinnacle in the Hills of Saint Catherine, near Kingston. According to scholar Leonard E. Barrett Sr., "Life in the commune was strictly patterned after the Maroon communities of Jamaica. Howell served as chief (African style) and was reported to have taken thirteen wives for himself" (*see* Maroonage in the Americas). The commune – the home of more than 500 brethren – earned money by planting and selling crops, including marijuana.

In 1954 Pinnacle was destroyed and its members disbanded by the police. Claiming to be the Messiah himself, Howell lost most of his followers, and in 1960 he was reputedly committed to the Kingston psychiatric hospital. Nonetheless, the Pinnacle commune proved critical to the early development of the Rastafarian movement. As Barrett confirms, Pinnacle was "the wilderness experience which became the 'bridge-burning act,' solidifying the movement around certain rites and practices with which they [the Rastafarians] are now identified." Indeed, communal living and ganja smoking as a sacred rite have remained central to Rastafari culture.

Roanne Edwards

See Also

Haile Selassie I; Garvey, Marcus Mosiah; New York, New York; Kingston, Jamaica; Rastafarians; Communist Party USA, African Americans and the; Abolition and Emancipation in Latin America and the Caribbean; Black Nationalism in the United States.

Africa

East African Community, an East African regional organization later renamed the Commission for East African Cooperation.

Modeled in part on the European Economic Community (the predecessor of the European Union) the East African Community (EAC) was originally created by the Treaty for East African Cooperation of June 6, 1967. Now in its second incarnation, the community seeks to promote development through economic cooperation among its member states, KENYA, TANZANIA, and UGANDA. When the EAC was first formed, the member states' joint ownership of the East African Railways Corporation, the East African Airways Corporation, the East African Harbours Corporation, and the East African Ports and Telecommunications Corporation, represented the most comprehensive regional integration organization in Africa. Acrimony among its members, however, led to its disintegration in 1977, followed by a prolonged process of dividing the organization's assets and liabilities.

Economic problems in each country during the 1980s and 1990s led to renewed interest in regional cooperation. In March 1996 the East African Community was revived, under the name Commission for East African Cooperation (EAC). The new union intends to create a common market by the year 2000, and to promote open borders for the member countries' citizens. It also aims to establish regional cooperation in transport, communications (member nations have discussed investing $69 million for a digital telecommunications network), trade, industry, investment, customs, energy, tourism, and agriculture. An East African Business Council has been established to foster invesment among private businesses. In May 1998 the EAC proposed to bring the member states into a still closer union by adopting a single currency and by establishing a regional legislative assembly (consisting of three representatives from each country) and a court. A referendum on the proposal was slated for November 1998 and then postponed to July 1999.

Robert Fay

Latin America and the Caribbean

Easter Rebellion, a slave rebellion on Barbados, also known as Bussa's Insurrection, which took place on April 14, 1816. The rebellion was one of the largest slave insurrections in the British Caribbean (*see* BARBADOS).

Latin America and the Caribbean

East Indian Communities in the Caribbean, the history of forced and voluntary immigrants from India and their descendants in the Caribbean.

East Indians comprise 40 to 50 percent of the total population on the Caribbean nations of Trinidad, GUYANA, and SURINAME, and a smaller number in Caribbean countries such as JAMAICA and BELIZE. Within their Caribbean communities, East Indians maintain the Indian customs, languages, and religions their ancestors brought generations ago. But despite these traditions, the cultures and identities of East Indians in the Caribbean have been transformed by more than 150 years of shared history with Afro-Caribbeans.

In 1838, just four years after the abolition of slavery in British-held territories, the first boat of indentured laborers arrived in British Guiana (present-day Guyana). Planters on SUGAR estates formerly worked by African slaves sought a replacement for slave labor and looked to the model of MAURITIUS, where East Indian labor was used both for its cheapness and for the perceived docility of a work force far from home. The experiment in indentured labor was cut short, however, at least briefly, when anti-indenture groups in India and Great Britain successfully pressured to halt the import of indentured labor from 1838 to 1844. The promise of reform helped lift the ban and paved the way for an expansion of indentured labor after 1844. The treatment of women in particular had been a rallying cry for reformers. With the great disparity in numbers of men and women, a type of de facto prostitution, in which several men were "assigned" to a woman, had already begun. Recruiters began to seek widows and women of "moral character" to meet gender regulations (100 men to 40 women), and a colonial office oversaw indentures – at least officially.

Guyana, Trinidad, and later Suriname and JAMAICA became major destinations for ships bearing indentured labor from India. The workers were Hindu, Muslim, Sikh, and Christian, mostly from agricultural parts of the Indian regions of Uttar Pradesh, Bihar, and Madras. Many were younger sons without inheritance, or poor men and women from villages controlled by wealthy landowners.

In the Caribbean, where social and economic relations between a white minority and a black majority were fixed by a legacy of exploitation on the basis of skin color, East Indians soon occupied a position in the middle of the pyramid. They literally took the places of the former slaves, continuing the harvests in the sugar cane fields and living in the old slave quarters. The blacks freely. Historian Kusha Haraksingh suggests "in Trinidad in particular... far from withdrawing from plantation labour, freedpeople (especially women, children and those males past their prime) were being systematically pushed out by planters making way for contract workers." This created some tensions between the former slave and East Indian communities in British Guiana, Trinidad, and Suriname, particularly during a period of drought and economic depression in the 1850s. In nineteenth-century Jamaica, where resident labor was more secure, indentured laborers were viewed more positively as potential consumers for the produce of independent black farmers. On all of the islands, there was some intermarriage, and a small Indo-African population added to the mix of races and cultures in the Caribbean.

The recruiting company Gillanders, Arbuthnot and Co. assured planters that the Indians had "no religion, no education and in their present state, no wants beyond eating, drinking and sleeping." Planters who wished for more security than that had it: strict laws controlled the laborers' work and mobility. A laborer who did not work one day could face imprisonment for two to four days; a worker who left the estate without permission, even for court proceedings against his or her employer, faced similar reprisals. The history of such restrictions under slavery enabled planters to push through such measures. As Kusha Haraksingh points out, "throughout the indenture period, the assumptions and premises of slavery continued to inform management attitudes." Drawing on strategies already used under slavery, planters played on tensions within the heterogeneous East Indian community to ensure control. Lower-caste workers were placed as "drivers" over high-caste workers, and planters avoided hiring workers from the same region of India. Planters ensured that laborers remained in debt and on the estate by immediately providing rations at inflated cost.

By the mid-1870s Indians constituted 90 percent of the sugar-estate labor force in Trinidad and British Guiana. Unlike indentured laborers in Africa (see INDIAN COMMUNITIES IN AFRICA), many remained on the islands after finishing a five-year contract. Alcoholism and disease, particularly hookworm, ravaged their poverty-stricken settlements. The conditions in Suriname were particularly bad, with the terms of the five-year contracts violated and workers forced to remain under conditions of near slavery.

In the late nineteenth century the East Indian communities increasingly began to resist their exploitive conditions. East Indians sparked a series of revolts in the 1880s and 1890s, including strikes, arson, and even murder. Some simply left the estates or even the islands, settling on the Windward Island of GRENADA. These problems did not stem the flow of indentured labor. When indentured labor was finally halted in 1916, it was because of antirecruitment pressure back in India.

By this time there were some 143,000

Indians in Trinidad alone. Most remained living in rural areas and working on the sugar estates. The drop in sugar prices in the 1930s precipitated a crisis, as wages plummeted and the price of necessities soared. Competition for employment created tensions between blacks and East Indians, particularly in the urban areas of Jamaica where there was a series of interethnic riots in the 1930s, the largest in 1938. In Trinidad, however, a labor movement brought the black and East Indian communities together as nothing previously had. The East Indian communities in both the agricultural and industrial sectors initiated a series of labor strikes, involving 15,000 estate workers who protested unemployment, harsh work conditions, and low wages. Some turned to more violent forms of resistance, looting estate offices and stores.

As some East Indians moved off the estates to the cities in search of other work, they came in contact with the Afro-Caribbean community in large numbers for the first time. Integrated unions, such as the Trinidad Workingmen's Association (TWA), originally a predominantly black working-class organization, brought workers together in solidarity across race lines.

Other organizations were more communal, promoting either political rights, such as the East Indian National Association (1898) in Trinidad, or cultural preservation, such as the East Indian Association (1925) in Jamaica. These organizations also supported the anticolonial movement in India and laid the groundwork for a generation of East Indian nationalists in the Caribbean.

Cheddi Jagan took up the cause of nationalism in British Guiana, founding the People's Progressive Party – the country's first multiracial nationalist party – with Forbes Burnham. As premier of Guyana between 1957 and 1964, the Marxist-Leninist Jagan held the support of the East Indians, radicals, and Cuba's Fidel Castro. Faced with increasing opposition from Great Britain and the United States as well as race riots inside Guyana, Jagan lost the elections in 1964. In Trinidad, though political leadership continues to be dominated by people of African descent, East Indians have reached high positions in the government.

The 1960s saw the rise of Black Nationalism throughout the Caribbean and a widening gulf between blacks and East Indians. Many East Indians maintained solidarity with the cause, some even converting to the Rastafarian movement in Jamaica. Many others feared an African-dominated government, pointing to anti-Indian discrimination in President Burnham's government in Guyana from 1964 to 1985. East Indians, in turn, were accused of not integrating, and criticized for the perceived exclusiveness of Indian communities.

Today, the majority of East Indians in Trinidad, Guyana, and Jamaica continue to live in rural areas. The festivals, architecture, and food on these islands attest to the impact East Indians have had on these places. Such writers as V. S. Naipaul and Sam Selvon have used literature to articulate the complexity of Indo-Caribbean identity. These writers, along with the many Indo-Caribbean immigrants resettled in Great Britain, Canada, and the United States, have brought to the rest of the world a sense of the multiethnic milieu of the Caribbean.

Marian Aguiar

See Also
Burnham, Linden Forbes Sampson; Trinidad and Tobago.

North America

East St. Louis, Illinois, Riot of 1917, one of the worst racial riots in American history, stemming from the employment of African Americans in a white-owned factory.

In 1917 East St. Louis, located across the Mississippi River from St. Louis, was a town rife with racial tensions. On one side, there were demands by white unions that future black settlement in the town be prohibited; on the other, there were unproved rumors that white women and girls were being harassed by black men. The riot ignited on May 28, after word spread that a white store owner had accidentally been shot by a black man during a holdup.

A white mob of over 3000 ravaged African American stores, homes, and churches. Eyewitnesses reported that the police and National Guard stood by passively, choosing to search black homes for concealed weapons instead of disarming the white mobs in the street. Several days later, on July 1, a drive-by shooting by a carload of whites prompted black residents to arm themselves. When an unmarked police car drove through the next night, the residents opened fire, killing two white police detectives inside. The bullet-ridden car, displayed in front of police headquarters, prompted another mob of whites to take to the streets in revenge. On July 2 eyewitnesses reported that scores of African Americans were gunned down as they ran from their burning homes. One of the most tragic events was the shooting of a small black child who was then thrown into a burning building to die. It is estimated that more than 100 African Americans lost their lives in the riot.

Eighty-two whites and 23 blacks were indicted by the Illinois attorney general, but only 9 of the whites were sent to prison. Seven white police officers charged with murder were collectively fined $150. In contrast, all-white juries convicted 10 African Americans in the murders of the undercover detectives, sentencing them to 14 years in prison.

Alonford James Robinson, Jr.

See Also
Labor Unions in the United States.

Africa

Ebira (also known as Edbira, Egbura, and Igbira), ethnic group of Nigeria.

The Ebira primarily inhabit the Plateau, Bendel, and Kwara states of Nigeria. They speak a Niger-Congo language and belong to the Nupe cultural and linguistic group. Approximately 1 million people consider themselves Ebira.

See Also
Languages, African: An Overview.

Africa

Ebola, a rare viral disease found primarily in Central Africa and Sudan.

First discovered in 1976, Ebola was named after the Ebola River in the Democratic Republic of the Congo, where cases were first reported. Several strains of the virus have since been discovered, including Ebola Sudan, Ebola Zaire, Ebola Reston (which affects only monkeys), and possibly a fourth variant, Ebotai, found in Côte d'Ivoire. The disease is spread through direct contact with bodily fluids and through close personal contact or exposure to contaminated hypodermic needles. Ebola is a filovirus, meaning that it causes hemorrhagic fever.

The disease onset begins approximately 4 to 21 days after infection by the virus and is associated with muscular pain, headache, and sore throat. As the disease progresses, patients become weak and nauseated. Vomiting, diarrhea, and rashes develop within days, followed by severe kidney and liver dysfunction associated with massive internal hemorrhaging and blood clotting. Ebola Zaire has been fatal in 90 percent of diagnosed patients, while Ebola Sudan has a mortality rate of 60 percent. As the exact pathology of the virus remains unclear, to date there is no cure, only prevention through containment.

The life cycle of the Ebola virus remains unknown. The genetically stable virus must reside in a naturally occurring host between the occasionally occurring human outbreaks. While nonhuman primates are susceptible to the virus and can serve as vectors of the disease, Ebola does not persist in these populations because, as with humans, it quickly kills off most of the hosts. Nonhuman primates are therefore probably not the natural reservoir of the virus.

During the first two outbreaks in 1976 in Zaire and western Sudan, 550 people were infected; of these, 340 died. In 1979 in Sudan, 34 people were diagnosed with the virus, leading to 22 deaths. A number of other incidences have since been reported by the World Health Organization and the Centers for Disease Control in the United States, including an outbreak in 1995 in Kikwit, Zaire, where 244 of 315 people died, and a smaller outbreak in GABON during 1996.

Publicity surrounding recent outbreaks raised fears of a worldwide epidemic. However, it appears that Ebola is rapidly contained: outbreaks seem to be self-limiting, because its hosts die off before the virus has the opportunity to be transmitted. Therefore, the disease is not considered to pose a large-scale public health risk.

Ari Nave

Ebonics. Please see BLACK VERNACULAR ENGLISH

North America

Ebony, published by the Johnson Publishing Company, *Ebony* is the largest circulation African American magazine.

In 1945 John H. Johnson founded *Ebony* magazine. Already publisher of the successful *Negro Digest,* Johnson aimed to create a monthly magazine that told about black life and achievements in words and photographs, similar to *Life* magazine, the popular weekly. It was an instant success. The first press run of 25,000 copies sold out within hours. By 1950 circulation exceeded 300,000. While circulation grew rapidly, Johnson at first had a difficult time securing advertising from white firms. Johnson's persistence, along with *Ebony's* appeal as a dependable vehicle for tapping into a national market of black consumers finally attracted major advertising dollars, securing the magazine's great financial success.

Known as "the magazine by and for us," *Ebony* began by offering picture essays on sports heroes and entertainment figures, and highlighting black achievement in all areas of American life. Over the years the magazine has added sections on cooking and health. As editor in chief, noted black historian Lerone Bennett Jr. has included articles detailing the historical achievements of black Americans. In similar fashion the magazine's editorial staff also works hard to track and to feature prominent black civic leaders. Each year the magazine publishes a list of the 100 most influential blacks in America.

By the 1990s *Ebony's* circulation topped 2 million; roughly 12 percent of its readership is white. The magazine is distributed in 40 countries, many in Africa. In 1995 Johnson Publishing Company launched an African version of its popular American edition, calling it *Ebony South Africa.*

Alonford James Robinson, Jr.

SEE ALSO

Bennett, Lerone, Jr.

Latin America and the Caribbean

Eboué, Félix (b. December 26, 1884, Cayenne, Guyana; d. May 17, 1944, Cairo, EGYPT), the highest-ranking French colonial administrator of African descent of his time, close friend and ally of General de Gaulle's during World War II.

A very bright child with a nearly photographic memory, Félix Eboué was at the head of his primary school class. He received a French government scholarship to attend high school in Bordeaux, France, where he met René Maran, a Martinican-born NÉGRITUDE writer. His passion for learning translated into a passion for politics, as the young man aligned himself with the socialism of Jean Jaurès, publisher of the left-wing daily, *L'Humanité.* Eboué finished his secondary studies in 1905 and entered the French Colonial School in 1906 at a time when the colonial vocation was not considered incompatible with socialism.

Upon completing his studies in 1908, he turned down a coveted position as colonial administrator in MADAGASCAR to take a similar position in the REPUBLIC OF THE CONGO (Brazzaville) where he thought he could do more to help the people of his race. He immediately distinguished himself in his style of administration. In his duties of collecting taxes and recruiting porters for the rubber companies, Eboué preferred to negotiate and barter with local chiefs than use force to get them to comply, as many of his predecessors had.

He was also passionate about the economic development of Africa, believing that the material conditions of the colonial subjects would improve if they devoted more energy to agriculture and less to harvesting rubber. He introduced cotton in the Oubangui-Chari region in 1924, a crop that would become the cornerstone of the economy in French Equatorial Africa.

Eboué's successful development projects and ability to convince hostile indigenous groups to join the French empire by peaceful means allowed him to rise quickly through the ranks of the colonial administration. For his long and arduous work in Africa, he was named secretary general of MARTINIQUE in 1932. Eboué brought the same style of leadership to this post that he had employed in Africa and was able to win the support of the local population expeditiously. Just 30 months later, though, he was sent back to Africa, where it was deemed that he could be more effective.

Over the next several years, Eboué spent time in both the Caribbean and Africa in positions of increasing authority, ending up as governor of CHAD in 1939, on the eve of World War II. Following the armistice of June 1940 between the French government in Vichy and the Nazis, General de Gaulle's government in exile called on the governors of the colonies to lend their support to his movement, and Eboué was the first to do so. Other colonial governors followed Eboué's courageous lead. Because of his actions, Eboué was condemned to death in absentia by a Vichy court in 1941, a sentence that was never carried out.

Throughout the war, Eboué provided assistance to de Gaulle's movement at every turn. It was no surprise when at the end of the war, de Gaulle turned to Eboué to organize the 1944 Brazzaville conference that would redefine the relationship between colonizer and colonized, giving the colonies more autonomy and beginning the process that would eventually lead to their independence.

Exhausted by the war years in Africa and, in particular, by the complexities of the Brazzaville conference, Eboué requested three months' leave from the minister of the colonies, René Pléven, so that he could travel to the Middle East. After passing through the SUDAN, he arrived in CAIRO, EGYPT, where he intended to stay a short while before continuing on to Palestine, Syria, and Lebanon. However, he contracted pneumonia in Cairo, was admitted to the hospital on April 16, 1944, and died one month later. He was mourned by many, especially by de Gaulle, who, in a letter to Eboué's widow, wrote that "Félix Eboué was my friend and nothing can make me forget the man, the companion, the brother in arms that he was to me during the greatest struggle of our time."

Richard Watts

SEE ALSO

Brazzaville, Republic of the Congo; France; Guyana.

Latin America and the Caribbean

Echemendía, Ambrosio (b. 1843 Trinidad, Cuba; d. circa 1880s), Afro-Cuban poet born a slave in Trinidad, Cuba (a municipality near the city of Cienfuegos).

Ambrosio Echemendía was one of the remarkable cases of slaves in CUBA who wrote poetry to attain his manumission with the profits from his publications. An exceptional poet, he has not been as studied as other nineteenth-century black Cuban intellectual figures such as Plácido, Manzano, or Morúa Delgado.

After completing some elementary education in a school that accepted black children, his owner furthered his education by giving him individual instruction and encouraging him to write poetry. His only published book, *Murmuríos del Táyaba* (1865, Murmurs of the Táyaba), is a collection of poetry in which he used the pseudonym Máximo Hero de Neiba. Shortly thereafter, his master took him to the nearby city of Cienfuegos, east of Havana, where the proceeds from the sale of his book, along with a general collection taken among the city's elite, allowed him to purchase his freedom. Francisco Calcagno, the Cuban educator and writer, featured him prominently in his *Poetas de color* (1878) and in the *Diccionario biográfico cubano* (1886) (*see* LITERATURE, BLACK, IN SPANISH AMERICA).

The poems in *Murmuríos del Táyaba* center on two main themes: the campaign for Echemendía's freedom and a justification for writing poetry rather than improvising it. In several of his poems, Echemendía notes that his authorship was challenged because he felt uncomfortable giving oral improvisations, a practice common among poets at the time. Responding to the skeptical reader in a series of poems (such as "A un incrédulo de mis versos"), Echemendía explained his preference for the written word. He used his ability as a writer to move the reader and garner sympathy for his cause, strategies reminiscent in many ways of those used by Juan Francisco Manzano in his autobiography. An important defining characteristic of Echemendía's poetry is that it establishes a relationship between the author's condition and his literary production. The poem "Al Damují" (To the Damují) is widely considered to represent the best of his writing. This sonnet, which was published in a Cienfuegos newspaper before it appeared in *Murmuríos del Táyaba*, promises that if given the chance to become part of civil society, the author will prosper in the same way that the city has flourished. Only a free writer, the sonnet insists, can have an authentic poetic voice; otherwise, his poetry is just "a sigh," or, as the title of the collection suggests, murmurings.

Little is known of Echemendía's life after his manumission; few of his poems were published after 1865, and the date of his death is uncertain. However, the success of his publishing effort inspired other Afro-Cuban enslaved poets, such as Manuel Roblejo, Juan Antonio Frías, and Néstor Cepeda, to campaign for their freedom by writing and publishing poetry.

Sonia Labrador Rodrigués

SEE ALSO
Manzano, Juan Francisco; Slavery in Latin America and the Caribbean; Morúa Delgado, Martín; Valdés, Gabriel de la Concepción ("Plácido"); Trinidad and Tobago; Havana, Cuba.

North America

Eckstine, William Clarence (Billy) (b. July 8, 1914, Pittsburgh, Pa.; d. March 8, 1993, Pittsburgh, Pa.), African American JAZZ singer and bandleader.

Billy Eckstine became famous in the 1950s as the smooth-voiced baritone singer of such hits as "Fools Rush In" and "Skylark," but music critics and serious jazz fans know him as the man whose big band launched such renowned performers as Dizzy Gillespie, Miles Davis, Charlie Parker, Dexter Gordon, and SARAH VAUGHAN. Eckstine (born Eckstein) began his musical career on a piano his father had bought for his two sisters. A star athlete, Eckstine soon joined his WASHINGTON, D.C., high school choir and found himself more compelled by his musical talents. After attending HOWARD UNIVERSITY, he began singing with various groups, touring in the Midwest before settling in Chicago in 1939, where he joined the band led by Earl "Fatha" Hines.

It was with Hines that Eckstine had his first hit, the blues song "Jelly Jelly," which he wrote and sang. In 1944 he formed his own big band. Always a favorite with other musicians, the band helped pioneer the then-new bebop sound. Its avant-garde musicianship often overshadowed Eckstine's more traditional vocals, and the band suffered from being badly recorded. Though it left behind no notable recordings, music historians consider it one of the most influential big bands of its era.

Eckstine's solo career took off after the band dissolved in 1947. With his deep, romantic voice, elegant presence, and good looks, he became a popular performer. Often referred to as "Mr. B," he garnered several film roles in the following decades, and many have called him the first black sex symbol. He continued to perform until he suffered a stroke in 1992. Eckstine died in 1993.

Kate Tuttle

SEE ALSO
Chicago, Illinois; Davis, Miles Dewey, III; Gillespie, John Birks ("Dizzy"); Gordon, Dexter Keith; Hines, Earl Kenneth ("Fatha"); Parker, Charles Christopher ("Bird").

Africa

Economic Community of West African States, a West African regional organization.

Modeled after the European Economic Community (the predecessor of the European Union), the Economic Community of West African States (ECOWAS) seeks to promote regional development through economic and diplomatic cooperation among its member states. The ECOWAS was created when representatives of 15 countries – BENIN, BURKINA FASO, Côte d'Ivoire, THE GAMBIA, GHANA, GUINEA, GUINEA-BISSAU, LIBERIA, MALI, MAURITANIA, NIGER, NIGERIA, SENEGAL, SIERRA LEONE, and TOGO – signed the Treaty of Lagos on May 28, 1975. CAPE VERDE joined in 1978.

The member countries' leaders meet once a year; each country also sends two representatives to serve on the ECOWAS Council of Ministers. ECOWAS oversees a tribunal and five commissions: (1) Trade, Customs, Immigration, Monetary, and Payments; (2) Industry, Agriculture, and Natural Resources; (3) Transport, Communications, and Energy; (4) Social and Cultural Affairs; and (5) Administration and Finance. Commission goals include the elimination of tariffs and other regional trade barriers along with the promotion of open borders for all citizens of the member countries. Since 1981 the ECOWAS treaty has included both a protocol of non-aggression and a mutual defense clause.

The original goal of ECOWAS was to unite the small national markets of its members, and thus create a regional market large enough to attract additional investment. ECOWAS countries were to eliminate tariffs on members' unprocessed goods by 1990 and on industrial goods between 1996 and 2000. Progress toward these goals has been hampered, however, by persistent tensions between individual member states and between Anglophone and Francophone members. ECOWAS's international defense force, the Military Observer Group (ECOMOG), intervened in the civil wars of both Liberia and Sierra Leone in the 1990s. Dominated by Nigerian troops, ECOMOG was widely questioned as an effective military force, but it eventually helped to end fighting in both countries.

Robert Fay

SEE ALSO
Côte d'Ivoire.

Latin America and the Caribbean

Ecuador, country on the northwest coast of South America, bordered by Peru to the south and east, Colombia to the north, and the Pacific Ocean to the west.

Ecuador shares with COLOMBIA and PANAMA a region comprising the Pacific Lowlands Black Culture. This unique Afro-Hispanic culture stretches from Ecuador's ESMERALDAS Province through the San Juan River of the Valle del Cauca Department and the Chocó region of Colombia to Panama's Darién Province. It developed through Afro-Hispanic migration and intermixing beginning in the colonial period. Blacks in Ecuador settled in the three main geographic regions of the country (the highlands, the coast, and the tropical lowlands of the Amazon region in the east), often displacing or mixing with indigenous populations to create the ethnic diversity that exists today.

During colonial times, the Spanish minority imposed a social system of formally stratified ethnic castes that discriminated against the racially mixed majority. Remnants of that system persist in Ecuadorian society, reflected in a broader ideology of racial and cultural WHITENING *(blanqueamiento)*, held up as an ideal achievable through the process of *mestizaje* (racial and cultural mixing, generally implying assimilation into a dominant culture). The belief in racial and cultural blending toward whiteness is overwhelmingly strong in Ecuador, even among black communities. It is in part responsible for the socioeconomic rifts that deeply divide Ecuadorians.

The widespread acceptance of the ideology of whitening is evident in the use of *negro* (black), a term that can be offensive to Ecuadorians because it implies lower-class status and other negative stereotypes. Dissociation from this term and its connotations has led to the use of various labels to define Ecuadorian people of African descent. Most of these labels have political and historical implications, often reflecting class boundaries. *Negro fino* ("refined black"), for instance, is used to differentiate blacks with higher levels of education and white-collar jobs from the rest of the community. *Gente morena* (dark people), *moreno* (brown-skinned), *gente negra* (black people), and *zambo* (of African and Indian descent) all describe degrees of racial mixture and may carry pejorative connotations or implications about social status, depending on the context and the user.

Afro-Ecuadorians self-identify in various ways, making political unity difficult; despite their differences, they have mobilized to effect change. To this end, relatively small circles of intellectuals and political activists have adopted the terms *Afro-latinoamericano* and *Afro-ecuatoriano*, which emphasize the unity of all people of African descent.

Standard History

Ecuador was once a territory on the edge of the Inca Empire divided into several warring nations. The conquest of the area by the Incas in the late fifteenth century was a protracted and unstable process. The tenuous stability of Inca rule was further shaken by a civil war in the Inca Empire in the early sixteenth century. When the Spanish explorers Francisco Pizarro and Sebastián de Benalcázar entered Ecuador in the 1530s, therefore, some Indians welcomed them as liberators from the Incas rather than as conquerors. The Spaniards established colonies in the highlands and to a lesser extent on the coast, but few settled in tropical lowlands, mainly on account of Indian attacks.

In 1563 the Spanish Crown centralized its control of the region with the establishment of the Audiencia de Quito as an administrative center. From this point, the colonial economy of the highlands flourished, based largely on the exporting of textiles to other areas of the Spanish Empire. The coastal city of Guayaquil also attained a measure of importance as a port during the colonial period, a process gaining further impetus from the development of cacao exports in the late eighteenth century. The Audiencia fell under the jurisdiction of the viceroyalty of Peru. Between 1717 and 1723 it was transferred to the viceroyalty of New Granada, with Bogota as its administrative center; then reincorporated into the viceroyalty of Peru; and in 1739 finally incorporated into New Granada. The struggle for independence from Spain began in 1809, and was won in 1822 by the army of Antonio José de Sucre in the decisive Battle of Pichincha. Quito then came to form part of Gran Colombia, which also included the area of present-day Venezuela, Colombia, and Panama. Regional rivalries, however, created instability; in 1830 Ecuador withdrew under its present name.

Following its formation as a new republic, Ecuador was divided between Liberals, with a stronghold in the coastal city of Guayaquil, and Conservatives, centered in the highland city of Quito. The nineteenth century was marked by political instability, regional rivalry, civil wars, and dictatorial rule. The late nineteenth and early twentieth centuries saw a shift in political dominance from Conservatives to Liberals and from the highlands to the coast. This was in part due to the growing economic importance of the coastal region, based on the export of cacao.

Political instability continued into the twentieth century. Economically, the export of bananas in the 1940s and 1950s and of oil in the 1970s produced periods of relative prosperity. President José María Velasco Ibarra (1934-1935, 1944-1947, 1952-1956, 1960-1961, and 1968-1972) stands out as a dominant political figure. A Conservative who pressed for some populist measures, such as land reform, Velasco Ibarra was ousted in all but his third term in office. Ecuador's territory was reduced by about half in a border dispute with Peru in 1941, a conflict that has tarnished relations with this neighboring country ever since. The postwar years were also marked by two periods of military government (1963-1966, 1972-1979).

In 1978 a referendum was held on a new constitution, and a president was democratically elected the following year. The period of democratization that followed, however, was marked by economic crisis and continued political instability. President León Febres Cordero (1984-1988) faced numerous unsuccessful coups. Market reforms implemented in the 1990s worsened the lot for the nation's poor and were met by growing opposition within civil society, particularly from political groups organized by the nation's indigenous population. President Sixto Durán Ballén (1992-1996) thus faced massive opposition, as did his successor, Abdalá Bucaram (1996-1997), whom the Congress removed from office for "mental incapacity" following a general strike in February 1997 in which protesters called for his impeachment.

Slavery

African slaves were first imported to Ecuador by Spanish explorers in the early 1550s, principally to work as agricultural laborers in areas where the Indian population was scarce or rebellious. Slaves were also put to work in gold mining, domestic service, and cattle ranching. Don Juan de Salines Loyola traveled with African slaves when he went to conquer the Jívaro, an indigenous group in the tropical region of Loja, in the south. According to Norman E. Whitten and Diego Quiroga, blacks later joined with Indians of the region in the Jívaro uprising of 1579. Africans arrived in the present-day northwest coastal province of Esmeraldas when a slave ship traveling between Panama City and the viceroyalty of Peru crashed ashore in 1553. The 23 slaves on board escaped from the ship and established a community among the Indians in the area; the *zambo* (of mixed African and Indian descent) population that emerged was later to dominate the region.

The escaped slaves in Esmeraldas were led first by Anton and then by Sebastián Alonso de Illescas, a *ladino* slave (a Hispanicized slave who had lived in Spain) known for his skills as a political strategist. Establishing *palenques* (self-sufficient communities of runaway slaves and their descendants), the zambos frustrated the Spaniards, who for years attempted to destroy what historians have since termed the Zambo Republic in Esmeraldas. This pole of resistance attracted more runaway slaves. Finally, in 1599, an unconventional truce was reached when a contingent of zambo chieftains traveled to Quito from the Zambo Republic to recognize the sovereignty of Spain. Once the Spaniards had been appeased in this way, the local colonial government allowed zambo settlements to function with relative autonomy (*see* Maroonage in the Americas).

Most of the African slaves brought to Ecuador and those brought to other Andean countries were taken from West Africa in the Upper Senegal, Angola, Nigeria, and Gold Coast (present-day Ghana) regions of the continent. Usually they were transported to Ecuador through Cartegena, a city on the Pacific coast of the territory of present-day Colombia, then by overland routes to the Chocó region, and finally southward into Ecuador. Slave ships also sailed between Panama City and the viceroyalty of Peru, where traders would begin their way north.

Estimates of Ecuador's slave population indicate that it was small in comparison to neighboring Colombia's. No comprehensive figures are available, because of chronological gaps in the records and the fact that Ecuador was part of the viceroyalty of New Granada. Approximately 200,000 bondsmen were imported to the viceroyalty of New Granada during the entire slave trade. By the 1720s there were about 2000 African slaves in the region of Ecuador, increasing to more than 7000 by the census of 1782. More slaves were imported after many escaped to Esmeraldas in the west, the Amazon lowlands in the east, or large towns and small cities in the south. The free black population also began to grow in the early 1800s as gold mining died out and more people were able to buy their freedom. The Spanish system of ethnic castes and racist attitudes limited opportunities for free blacks more generally.

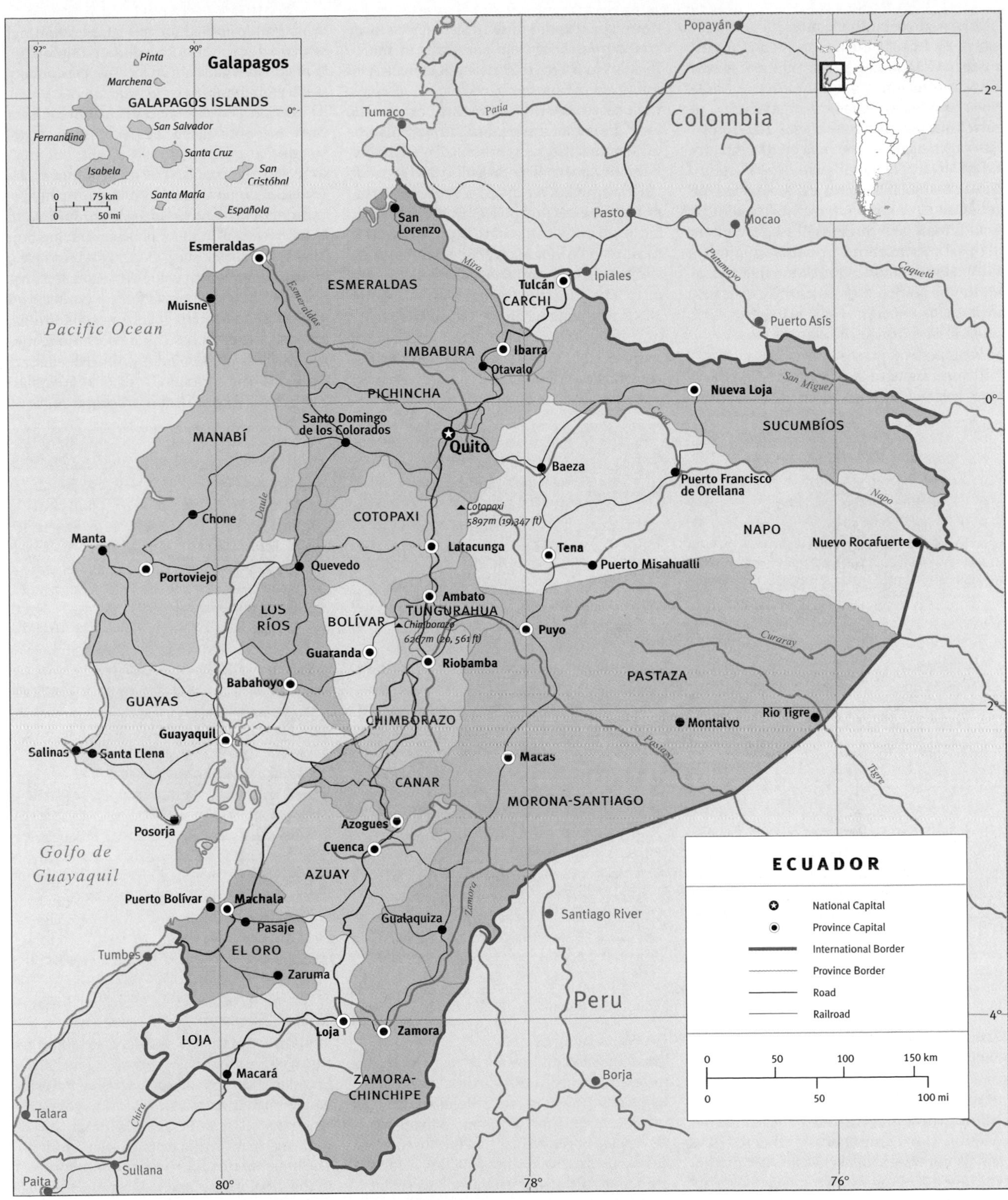

These free and newly freed populations survived largely through gold mining and subsistence agriculture.

Independence

The liberating armies of Simón Bolívar reached the interior of Ecuador in 1821 and enlisted or forcibly recruited an undetermined number of slaves into battle. Those who willingly joined the liberators were attracted by promises of emancipation and a better life without the Spanish aristocracy. Rebel forces sometimes threatened both free and enslaved Afro-Ecuadorians with a choice between perpetual slavery and enlistment. The decision was obvious for those who had a choice, while others had no power to choose. Members of the Ecuadorian slave-owning elite, not wishing to forfeit their property, controlled their slaves as tightly as they could (*see* Racial Question during Struggles of Independence in Latin America).

Ecuador won its independence from Spain in 1822 and became part of Gran Colombia until 1830. In 1821 a Free Womb Law was passed in Gran Colombia, declaring that children born of slave women were free, though a period of "apprenticeship" was required that effectively bound these free blacks to their mothers' masters until the age of 21. In 1825 the importation of slaves to Gran Colombia was also banned. Juntas de Manumisión (manumission committees) were established during this time to raise funds to purchase slaves' freedom. Slave owners often circumvented these laws, however, and Ecuador's withdrawal from Gran Colombia marked a step backward on the road to emancipation. Subsequent Ecuadorian governments passed laws that allowed special permission to be granted for the importation of slaves and that extended the period of apprenticeship. By the mid-1830s Ecuador was serving as a supplier and a port for the slave trade (*see* SLAVERY IN LATIN AMERICA AND THE CARIBBEAN).

Beginning with independence in 1822, slavery slowly decreased; there were about 8000 slaves in 1822 and approximately 6800 slaves three years later. Around this time, more than 75 percent of the slave population lived in the coastal provinces, where owners prevented the creation of manumission committees or rendered existing committees ineffective. In 1852 there were about 2000 slaves left in Ecuador. The decrease was due in large part to pressure from the British, who forced the signing of an antislave trade treaty for all of Spanish America. Total abolition in Ecuador was proclaimed in 1851 and was ratified a year later, once it was determined how much slave owners should be compensated for the release of their slaves (*see* ABOLITION AND EMANCIPATION IN LATIN AMERICA AND THE CARIBBEAN).

Despite strong British opposition to slavery, a form of involuntary bondage continued in Ecuador until 1894. Referred to as *concertaje*, the system permitted former masters to coerce their newly liberated slaves into signing labor contracts that continued their servitude. Thus, Afro-Ecuadorians who were already liberated returned to the same type of labor that they had performed in servitude.

In the late nineteenth century the Ecuadorian government advanced several measures to colonize the province of Esmeraldas, subletting sections of land to European and American companies. The region enjoyed some prosperity through harvesting tagua nuts. The construction of a railroad in the 1850s was planned, though the plans went unfulfilled. These projects spurred a large migration of Afro-Ecuadorians, Colombians, and Jamaicans, brought by British companies, to Esmeraldas Province.

Adriàn Sánchez Galquez painted this 1599 work titled *Mulatto Ambassadors to Province Esmeraldas*, showing Afro-Indian ambassadors from Esmeraldas (Ecuador). This is the earliest signed and dated painting from South America. *CORBIS/Archivo Iconografico, S.A.*

CONTEMPORARY TIMES

The first half of the twentieth century brought little advancement for Afro-Ecuadorians. Some large towns in the predominantly black province of Esmeraldas had no hospitals, electricity, or paved roads. In the absence of easy access to health-care facilities, recurring epidemics plagued the population, causing many deaths. Significant changes did not occur until the 1950s, when an agricultural boom brought about the construction of the long-since planned railroad connecting Esmeraldas Province to Quito. More jobs were created, resulting in a growth in income for the coastal town of San Lorenzo. Migrants from surrounding towns, the highlands, and Colombia came seeking business opportunities and began to settle. With this relative prosperity came the broad use of wage labor, which undermined the *minga*, a communal work system of Afro-Ecuadorians. Although individuals could gain an income, community ties in San Lorenzo were weakened.

In towns and cities across Ecuador, conflicts arose over increased socioeconomic stratification and competition for jobs. In San Lorenzo these conflicts had racial overtones and sometimes culminated in police brutality or murder. White and *mestizo* (of European and Indian descent) migrants began buying out small-town black shopkeepers and replacing mulatto middlemen who had negotiated business for the black population. Blacks believed that the Ecuadorian government ignored their requests for assistance because Esmeraldas was a predominantly Afro-Ecuadorian province. The community felt disempowered by the lack of political representation or support from the government. Reaction to these situations took the form of an Afro-Ecuadorian literary protest movement involving writers such as ADALBERTO ORTIZ and NELSON ESTUPIÑÁN BASS, whose work promoted pride in the African heritage of Afro-Ecuadorians. The hope was to undermine the growing belief in the ideologies of mestizaje and blanqueamiento (whitening), which devalued Afro-Ecuadorians and Indian ethnic groups. This literary protest had less effect than its participants envisioned. Blacks remained marginalized economically, while whites and mestizos held positions of power.

Economic and social marginalization has been part of black history since slaves were first brought to Ecuador, yet Afro-Ecuadorian cultural forms have become popular in the society. Literature such as the DÉCIMA, a genre of poetry from Esmeraldas, has gained international fame, as has the music of this ethnic group. *La bomba, arrullo,* and the rhythms of the *currulao* are but a few examples of the variety of Afro-Ecuadorian music forms. The music ceremonies that blacks perform revolve around themes from their history and cultural beliefs. The Afro-Esmeraldian festival *La tropa,* for example, reenacts the formation of a *palenque*. The social embrace of these cultural forms, however, has occurred in a context of continued discrimination against Afro-Ecuadorians.

To confront this continuing racism, Afro-Ecuadorians from various regions mobilized in 1988 to form the Asociación de Negros Ecuatorianos (ASONE), or Association of Black Ecuadorians. Representatives from around the country, including the cities of Guayaquil, Quito, and Ibarra and the regions of Loja and Chota-Mira, joined Esmeraldians in this movement to "rescue national dignity" by eliminating the racism that plagues Ecuadorian society. Described as both a Black Ethnic Movement and a Nation-State Nationalist Movement, ASONE sought modernization without significant disruption of traditional lifestyles. It also intended to minimize the elite control that has held blacks and indigenous peoples in the lower classes. Another principal goal was to unite Afro-Ecuadorians across economic, ecological, and sociopolitical barriers. Since much of Afro-Ecuadorian identity is region-based, relations among some groups have historically been tense. For instance, blacks from the highlands often have not associated with other Afro-Ecuadorians because highlanders tend to define themselves by community of origin rather than by their ancestral African roots. Unity through ASONE demonstrates the drive of Afro Ecuadorians to resolve their differences and work together to improve their marginalized status.

The Afro-Ecuadorian Cultural Week, which took place in Quito during October 1997, brought together various black communities. This festival featured traditional cooking, dances, native costume exhibits, and music in an effort to expose the rest of Ecuadorian society to myriad aspects of Afro-Ecuadorian culture. During this celebration of culture, Afro-Ecuadorians, in a collective effort, brought forth a proposal for legislation to protect their land and labor rights and to create a National Day of the Black Person. This proposal would bring much-needed attention to the issues of poverty and discrimination facing black communities in Ecuador. Organizers and supporters of the event believed that once these issues were politicized, the government would be compelled to acknowledge the problems faced by the black population and then facilitate change (*see* Cultural and Political Organizations in Latin America). It is unclear whether the Ecuadorian government has made a commitment to assist its black community.

Working with indigenous peoples, who historically have paved the way for the rights of ethnic groups in the country, has proved beneficial for Afro-Ecuadorians. A protest march from Puyo to Quito united blacks from Esmeraldas Province with indigenous peoples of the Oriente to fight for political rights and social justice. The march began a trend in which these two ethnic groups are continuing to work together to achieve mutual goals. In January 1998, the World Bank approved a loan of $25 million to assist with the development of indigenous and Afro-Ecuadorian communities by investing in community-based infrastructure, social infrastructure, micro-enterprises, and other areas. While the results of this project have yet to emerge, its existence suggests that the growing activism of Afro-Ecuadorians and their alliances with other groups have made them increasingly effective agents for change.

Rob Garrison

This 1783 painting, *Trajes y Frutos del Ecuador,* by Vincente Alban, represents an Ecuadoran lady with her African servant standing beside a basket of local fruits. *Oronoz*

See Also

Transatlantic Slave Trade; Cartagena de Indias, Colombia; Pacific Coast of Colombia; Transculturation, Mestizaje, and the Cosmic Race: An Interpretation.

North America

Edelman, Marian Wright

(b. June 6, 1939, Bennettsville, S.C.), founder and president of the Children's Defense Fund, America's leading advocacy group for children.

Marian Wright Edelman was the youngest of Arthur and Maggie Wright's five children. When blacks in her hometown of Bennettsville, South Carolina, were forbidden to enter city parks, her father, a Baptist minister, built a park for black children behind his church. Edelman would later credit him with instilling in her an obligation to right wrongs. She attended Spelman College in Atlanta and spent her junior year in France, Switzerland, and Eastern Europe. Returning to Spelman in 1959, she helped organize protests for the nascent Civil Rights Movement. She graduated valedictorian the following year, then took a law degree from Yale.

By 1964 she was working as a lawyer in Mississippi, where volunteers for the Civil Rights Movement were jailed and often beaten on fabricated charges. In the course of representing them for the National Association for the Advancement of Colored People (NAACP), she became the first black woman to pass the bar in Mississippi. She also became a nationally recognized advocate for Head Start, a pre-kindergarten education program. This work brought her to Peter Edelman, an attorney and member of Sen. Robert Kennedy's staff, whom she married in 1968 and with whom she would have three children, Joshua, Jonah, and Ezra.

Relocated to Washington, D.C., Edelman started the Washington Research Project (WRP), which sought to discover how existing and proposed laws affected the poor. Over the next several years, the project evolved into the Children's Defense Fund (CDF). Meanwhile, Edelman directed Harvard University's Center for Law and Education in Cambridge, Massachusetts, and became the first black woman to serve on the board of directors of Yale University. When the CDF was incorporated in 1973, Edelman became its president. She returned to Washington in 1979 to direct the day-to-day operations of this increasingly influential advocacy group.

Edelman was aware that with more than half of black children being born out of wedlock, many of them to teenagers, future generations of blacks were assured of living in poverty. She also realized that because teenage pregnancy affected both whites and blacks, a campaign against it could attract broad support. In the early 1980s the CDF sponsored thousands of television, radio, and billboard advertisements counseling teenagers about the risks and costs of pregnancy. Careful to sidestep the controversial issue of abortion and focus instead on pregnancy prevention, the campaign proved popular. Observers widely agreed that it raised the public's awareness about teen pregnancy; its effect on the incidence of teenage sex and pregnancy, however, was less clear.

Edelman pursued other parts of CDF's agenda in Congress. With the slogan, "One dollar up front saves many dollars down the road," CDF won an increase in Medicaid coverage for poor children (1984); financial aid, albeit limited, for child care (1990); and an increase in funding for Head Start (1992). By the late 1980s Edelman had gained a national reputation as "the children's crusader." The staff and budget of CDF grew correspondingly. Other CDF Efforts have met with little or no success, including the attempt to secure medical insurance for every child and pregnant mother and to change the welfare reform bill of 1996 – which the organization asserted would put millions of children into poverty.

Latin America and the Caribbean

Edgell, Zee (b. October 21, 1940, Belize City, Belize), Afro-Belizean writer who has focused on the Belizean independence movement, the country's various ethnic traditions, and the lives of women in Belize.

Zee Edgell was born Zelma Inez Tucker to Creole parents in Belize. Trained as a journalist in London, she worked as a newspaper reporter in Jamaica before returning to Belize. There she met and married Al Edgell, a North American who worked for humanitarian relief agencies such as CARE (Cooperative for Assistance and Relief Everywhere).

Their work took the couple to such places as Afghanistan, Bangladesh, Nigeria, and Somalia, and during that time Edgell wrote her first novel, *Beka Lamb* (1982). Set in 1951, it describes the birth of the Belizean independence movement, in what was then British Honduras, and calls particular attention to women's contributions of labor and money to the movement. *Beka Lamb*, one of the first novels published by a Belizean about Belize, was also one of the first novels by a Belizean to achieve international attention. It soon became a standard text in many Caribbean high schools.

Edgell's second novel, *In Times Like These* (1991), tells the story of Pavana Leslie, an unmarried Creole mother of twins who returns to her homeland of Belize in 1981, just before the country achieves independence from Great Britain.

In the 1980s and 1990s Egdell worked as an instructor of English language and literature in Belize City and the United States, and administered educational programs in Belize City.

See Also
Creoles.

Africa

Edo (also known as Bini, Oviedo, and Benim), ethnic group of Nigeria.

The Edo primarily inhabit Edo state in southern Nigeria. They comprise several subgroups who speak a Niger-Congo language (*see* Languages, African: An Overview). Between the fifteenth and nineteenth centuries, the Edo ruled the powerful kingdom of Benin. Today approximately 1 million people consider themselves Edo.

See Also
Benin, Early Kingdom of.

Africa

Education in Africa

Historical Origins of the Western School in Africa

The Western model of schooling in evidence throughout Africa was introduced by European missionaries during the colonial period. The Protestant and Catholic churches' agenda was evangelical and antislavery. Training in reading, writing, and scripture served the evangelical interest.

Under colonial rule, access to education in Africa was restricted, as were curricular offerings and the length of study. African children were prepared for the roles deemed appropriate by those in power. Sons of chiefs had privileged access to schooling, a practice that served both religious and political motives. Prior to independence, few African children attended school beyond the primary level. By 1960 only 25 percent of primary-school-age children were in school, compared to twice that level in Latin America and Asia.

Although Western-style education predominates in contemporary Africa, Islamic schools continue to operate throughout the continent. Also known as Madrassah, these schools teach followers lessons of the Koran. In some countries, such as Malawi, Western-modeled schools and the Koranic schools cooperate, while in other places Islamic schooling exists in lieu of Western schooling.

The Relationship Between Education and Development

Educational development in Africa is based on the widely held belief that formal education is a prerequisite to development. This faith in the ability of education to contribute to development has its roots in the postwar experience of Europe and parts of Asia and Latin America, where development was acccomplisheded through industrialization. The industrialization model of development assumes that the inculcation of a set of skills, attitudes, and values borrowed from the Western world is a necessary first step. Instruction in school is a useful, if not ideal, means for this transformation. But because schools have been promoted as meritocratic institutions, they have encouraged individual achievement rather than the structural changes needed to bring about development.

Nevertheless, the belief that education would bring economic and social benefits to newly independent African countries validated both African governments' and citizens' investments in schooling. Many people viewed education as the means to a better life – a perception supported by the rise of educated Africans to leadership positions at the time of independence. Education was viewed as a basic right of citizenship and the fruit of independence. Governments saw education as necessary not only for building modern, productive economies but also for building national unity. Campaigns to "Africanize" national civil services by replacing Europeans with newly educated citizens served both economic goals and popular demands.

Quite apart from the promised economic and political returns, education became internationally recognized as a "basic human right" along with food, shelter, and health (*see* Human Rights in Africa). As development strategies emphasizing "basic needs" gained to mass education to help fight poverty.

Western-modeled education has been strongly criticized in parts of Africa for assuming the centrality of "modern" Western values. It has been called elitist and neocolonial. Some countries have experimented with alternatives, such as Education for Self-Reliance in Tanzania, and the mass adult literacy programs in Mozambique. Still, there have been remarkably few efforts to radically restructure educational systems in Africa. Attention has centered on "reform" rather than restructuring, with the focus on particular elements of the system, such as curriculum, pedagogy, or teacher training.

Post-Independence Expansion

In independent Africa, ministries of education became responsible for the provision, management, inspection, and support of preprimary, primary, and secondary schools and of universities and colleges, including teacher training colleges as well as vocational, technical, and other training institutions. The education systems inherited from the

Young students are hard at work in a Kenyan classroom. *CORBIS/Liba Taylor*

colonial era were highly centralized, and African governments kept them centralized in order to develop a sense of national identity and to ensure control over resource allocation. In line with the centralized model, many governments made education compulsory. The duration of compulsory education varies across countries, from five years in MADAGASCAR to ten years in GABON. Between six and eight years is most common.

African educational systems expanded greatly in the first years of independence. Primary enrollment rose from 11.8 million in 1960 to 20.9 million in 1970 (not including SOUTH AFRICA and NAMIBIA). Secondary enrollment increased from 793,000 in 1960 to 2.5 million in 1970. This expansion was buoyed by popular demand for education and by governments' and international organizations' faith in education as a prerequisite to economic development. Yet while the expansion opened school doors to segments of the population that had no previous access to formal education, it was not egalitarian. Most national educational systems served only about 50 percent of the school-age population and, like colonial educational systems, they typically favored urban populations.

Overall, Africa's adult literacy rates have improved significantly: approximately 56 percent of all adults were considered literate in 1994, compared to only 27 percent in 1970. The 46 percent literacy rate for adult females covers a broad range, from 7 percent in NIGER to 72 percent in South Africa.

Function and structure in African countries' educational systems continue to reflect their colonial heritage. This is particularly true with respect to examination and certification systems, mediums of instruction, and school inspection systems. Generally, Francophone African countries have lower participation rates than Anglophone countries at both primary and secondary levels. While former British colonies approached universal entry to primary schooling in the 1980s, in former French colonies only 70 percent of children received at least one year of primary schooling. Differences in human resources are also evident. At the primary level, Anglophone African countries have fewer pupils per teacher (fewer than 40), compared to more than 48 pupils per teacher in Francophone Africa.

Research indicating that educated women had fewer children focused attention on improving female access to education in the 1970s and 1980s, when both male and female enrollments increased in Anglophone and Francophone African countries. However, even in 1980 there was still a 23 percent gender gap between male and female enrollment, only slightly better than the 24 percent gap in 1960. In 1980 school enrollment rates for females in African countries were the worst in the former Portuguese colonies and in Italy's former colonies in the Horn of Africa, where on average only 38 percent of school-age females were receiving an education.

The Sahelian countries (GUINEA-BISSAU, SENEGAL, THE GAMBIA, MAURITANIA, MALI, BURKINA FASO, NIGER, and CHAD), most of which are former French colonies, perform less well than the rest of the continent on many education indicators. These indicators include public expenditure on education as a percentage of either gross national product (GNP) or government expenditure, female gross enrollment rates, and male and female literacy rates.

EDUCATION REFORM UNDER FISCAL CRISIS: QUALITY AND QUANTITY CONCERNS

In the 1980s much of Africa was in economic crisis. Most countries suffered a decline in real per capita income, and living standards fell back to or below 1960 levels. The impact of the crisis continues to be felt in education, where many African governments have been unable to sustain previous levels of funding. Although they have continued to build schools to meet the demands of growing populations, inadequate resources have led to a decline in the quality of education offered.

African governments have turned to external funding to help finance the recurrent as well as the capital costs of education. Today it is taken for granted in most African countries that any type of education reform will require external support. Now that most countries have undertaken structural adjustment reform programs that limit government spending on social services such as education, the influence of foreign funding agencies has grown. Increased external control over the planning and running of Africa's education systems perpetuates the continent's dependence and poverty.

While per capita expenditure in education has declined seriously since the 1980s, relative government investment in education remains significant. African governments today allocate between 12 and 20 percent of the recurrent budget to education; Nigeria spends only 7 percent of its budget, while Namibia spends 27 percent. For sub-Saharan Africa as a whole, this equates to 5.5 percent of the GNP – comparable to public expenditures on education in industrialized countries. Most African governments in recent years have allocated an increasing proportion of their education budgets to primary and secondary education and a decreasing amount to tertiary education. Public expenditure figures for adult literacy are difficult to ascertain. In most African countries, between 80 and 90 percent of the recurrent education budget goes toward teachers' salaries, leaving very little for teaching and learning materials. The lack of materials has contributed to the declining quality of schooling in Africa today.

The World Conference on Education for All in 1990 resulted in an agreement to increase participation in quality primary schooling and adult literacy training. Among the African countries that drew up educational Plans of Action, most are unlikely to reach the Education for All goals by the year 2000. In fact, since 1980 there has been a decline in primary education participation rates. For boys of primary school age, 78 percent were in school in 1993 compared to 90 percent in 1980. Female participation declined less sharply, with 65 percent of primary-school-age girls in school, compared to 68 percent in 1980. High annual population growth rates (averaging 2.8 percent per year for sub-Saharan Africa) account for some of the drop.

Despite the decreased rate of participation and the decline in per capita expenditure on education, the gender gap at the primary school level in sub-Saharan Africa as a whole has been halved in the period since the economic crisis began, from 23 percent in

LITERACY RATES IN AFRICAN COUNTRIES

Country	% Literate (15 and over) Population
Algeria	61.6
Angola	42.0
Benin	37.0
Botswana	69.8
Burkina Faso	19.2
Burundi	35.3
Cameroon	63.4
Cape Verde	71.6
Central African Republic	60.0
Chad	48.1
Comoros	57.3
Congo, Democratic Republic of the	77.3
Congo, Republic of the	74.9
Côte d'Ivoire	40.1
Djibouti	46.2
Egypt	51.4
Equatorial Guinea	78.5
Eritrea	N/A
Ethiopia	35.5
Gabon	63.2
Gambia, The	38.6
Ghana	64.5
Guinea	35.9
Guinea-Bissau	53.9
Kenya	78.1
Lesotho	71.3
Liberia	38.3
Libya	76.2
Madagascar	80.0
Malawi	56.4
Mali	31.0
Mauritania	37.7
Mauritius	82.9
Morocco	43.7
Mozambique	40.1
Namibia	38.0
Niger	13.6
Nigeria	57.1
Réunion	79.0
Rwanda	60.5
São Tomé and Príncipe	73.0
Senegal	33.1
Seychelles	58.0
Sierra Leone	31.4
Somalia	24.0
South Africa	81.8
Sudan	46.1
Swaziland	76.7
Tanzania	67.8
Togo	51.7
Tunisia	66.7
Uganda	61.8
Western Sahara	N/A
Zambia	78.2
Zimbabwe	85.0

Source: *U.S. Central Intelligence Agency, World Factbook* 1998

1980 to 12 percent in 1993. At the secondary level, growth in enrollment rates has continued, especially for females. While in 1980 only 10 percent of the female age group were in secondary school, by 1993 the figure had risen to 22 percent. For males, the figures increased for the same period from 20 percent to 27 percent. The gender gap at the secondary level therefore was also halved from 10 percent to 5 percent.

The Evolution of Planning and Policy Formulation Approaches

Approaches to education planning have evolved since the early years of independence, when planning was in principle guided by an approach referred to as "social demand." This term became meaningless once governments made education compulsory, and thus created a legal demand for schooling. In the 1970s African governments experimented with "manpower planning," reflecting their view that the future was predictable and that an education system could be designed to fulfill labor market needs.

However, as development economists and agencies such as the World Bank and the International Monetary Fund have come to exercise greater influence over African governments' overall economic planning, investment analyses for education have gained saliency. In addition, educational policymaking in Africa draws increasingly on the findings of educational research. Yet since the economic crises of the 1980s, critics have noted that African education systems, while expanding quantitatively, have failed to bring about higher employment rates, more equitable societies, or more accountable governments. The narrowing of education reform agendas in Africa, and the tailoring of agendas to fit the neoliberal economic policies prescribed by foreign assistance agencies, has generated increasing dissatisfaction. The emphasis on efficiency, critics argue, comes at the expense of equity and accountability to internal constituencies – in other words, the citizens, including students.

This critique has in turn generated greater appreciation for the complexity of educational problems. Poor retention and low achievement in African education systems – as indicated by high repetition and school dropout rates – are no longer seen strictly as "internal efficiency" problems but as symptoms of deeper problems that must be better understood if education in Africa is to improve.

In recent years a number of African countries have made changes in their historically top-down, centralized education policy and planning processes. Some of these efforts have been stimulated by the introduction of multiparty democracy, as in Benin and Ghana, or by the transition to majority rule, as in Namibia and South Africa. In addition, with structural adjustment and education sector support programs placing more emphasis on "getting policy right," governments are assigning a higher priority to education policymaking.

There is a growing recognition of the need for a more participatory policy formulation process, involving a broad range of stakeholders. Under the old approaches, education planners tended to be divorced from school conditions. Indeed, it was considered desirable, for the sake of objectivity, to avoid close links between planners and the schools in which plans were implemented. Participatory planning, on the other hand, requires that planners play a more pragmatic role and keep in mind the reality of schooling processes when they formulate policy. This is proving challenging as Africa's government education planning units struggle to move from crisis management to long-term strategic planning. This process involves the setting and weighing of priorities and ongoing consultation with stakeholders.

As part of the search for alternative policy processes, relationships are changing between governments and local nongovernmental organizations (NGOs). In some situations, governments have solicited the assistance of NGOs in providing services once provided by the governments themselves, such as preschool education. In other cases, relations between governments and NGOs have been more contentious.

Opportunities

Exploration of the relationship between education and social-economic change in Africa is ongoing. This is good news, provided the exploration looks for answers to the questions "Education for whom?" and "Education for what?"

The growth of a number of African organizations focused on education is a promising development in this regard. These include regional research networks such as the Educational Research Network for Eastern and Southern Africa (ERNESA); the Southern African Comparative and History of Education Society (SACHES); the Forum for African Women Educationalists (FAWE); and the Association for the Development of Education in Africa (ADEA). FAWE has 30 national chapters throughout Africa and is focused on supporting girls' and women's education. ADEA is a partnership between African education ministers and international funding agencies, and aims to coordinate the agencies' assistance to education in Africa. It now strives to provide space for African-defined diagnoses and solutions and operates through 11 working groups.

Sue Grant Lewis

See Also

Development in Africa: An Interpretation; Population Growth in Sub-Saharan Africa; Structural Adjustment in Africa; Christianity: Missionaries in Africa.

Latin America and the Caribbean

Education in Latin America and the Caribbean, access and barriers to education for Afro-Latin Americans.

The history of formal education in Latin America and the Caribbean is also the history of the systematic exclusion of blacks from access to educational institutions, and the methodical denial of their social contribution to the making of the new societies in the postcolonial era. The participation of Afro-Latin Americans in the educational system can be divided into roughly three epochs: the colony (until the nineteenth century), post-abolition (from the 1830s onward in most countries), and the contemporary period (from the 1970s till the present).

The Colonial Period

For about 300 years, only a small white elite had access to schools and universities, and thus it is not surprising that at the dawn of the nineteenth century at least 90 percent of the population in Latin America and the Caribbean was illiterate. People of African descent, particularly slaves, were forbidden from entering most educational institutions. The few opportunities available to slaves were found with a master who, out of kindness or convenience, provided a rudimentary education, or with a member of the clergy who in the process of Christianization taught slaves how to read and write. Exception occurred in Portuguese America during the mandate of the marquis of Pombal in the mid-eighteenth century. Alarmed by the erosion of the Portuguese language in Brazil, given the growing influence of Tupi (the language of the Tupi Indians), the marquis ordered in 1758 the mandatory usage of the Portuguese language and the teaching of Portuguese to all recently arrived Africans. But even this decree was never translated into any formal or systematic instruction.

Despite formal restrictions against free blacks, their access to education was somewhat broader, except for black and mulatto women, who, like most white women, were strictly barred from educational facilities. By the end of the eighteenth century the number of free blacks had surpassed that of slaves in Spanish colonial America and a number of Caribbean colonies. With sheer numbers and economic independence, free blacks were able to found elementary schools. In Cuba, Doroteo Barba, a black schoolteacher, founded around 1795 the first school for black pupils in the island. Previously, the only school that admitted blacks was the Belén school in Havana. Just as in Cuba, other Spanish colonies (e.g., Peru and Colombia) saw the founding of primary schools that permitted the entrance of black males.

In a few cases, free blacks were even able to join the halls of higher education. Members of the Spanish elite with illegitimate mulatto children often made provisions to school their children, especially those who demonstrated academic talent. In the eighteenth century Julián Francisco Campo's father, a high Spanish official in Cuba, used his influence to ensure that his son, a mulatto, would gain admittance to the university in Havana to study law. Others found white patrons to assist them. Peruvian physician and poet José Manuel Valdés, the son of an Indian musician and a black laundrywoman, received his secondary education at the Augustinian school of San Ildefonso through the intercession of his white godparents. Valdés became a highly esteemed physician, a professor at the University of San Marcos in Lima, and a member of the Royal Medical Academy in Madrid. Jamaican scholar and poet Francis Williams, born of black parents probably at the beginning of the eighteenth century, won the patronage of the duke of Montague. The duke obtained him entrance to Cambridge University, where he distinguished himself in mathematics. Williams also published many songs and poems and opened his own school in England.

For other free blacks, social ascent and entrance to the university came when the Spanish Crown decided to sell *cédulas de gracias al sacar* (certificates of whiteness). The policy behind the cédulas was aimed at "improving" the status of mixed-blood people at the end of the eighteenth century. It was dictated by needs to increase political stability and to improve the fiscal condition of the Crown. In one instance, a former mulatto slave who held a cédula requested the backing of the Spanish Crown in his efforts to force admittance of his son to the university in Caracas. The Crown supported his petition over the protests of the institution.

Even after free blacks graduated from the university, not all professions were open to them, particularly those related to public office. However, money, skill, and connections were sufficient to erase skin color, and could open the avenue to some positions of modest status. In 1639 in Lima, José Nuñez de Prado, a mulatto notary, bought the post of *procurador* (solicitor). A protest ensued and the viceroy turned the case over to a law professor at the University of San Marcos. The latter advised the viceroy to confirm the sale because Nuñez, he said, was in fact a quadroon, not a mulatto; was a person of indisputable ability; and had paid twice as much for the post as any previous holder. The viceroy was swayed by the logic and advised the Crown to confirm the appointment.

Entering the clergy was another means of securing some education, even though the Church was more jealously guarded against free blacks than were the universities. Martín de Porres, born in Lima at the end of the sixteenth century, became the one of the few black saints in Spanish colonial America. But even Porres, the illegitimate son of a Spaniard and a Panamanian black slave, was never ordained as a priest, and had to content himself with being a lay brother in a Dominican monastery.

These examples serve to underscore the initial argument: blacks and mulattos who were able to obtain any form of education were extraordinary for their rarity. The great majority were prevented from receiving any form of education during the colonial era. Even after the wars of independence in Spanish America at the beginning of the nineteenth century, several decades would pass before the socioeconomic condition of blacks, including access to formal education, underwent even minimal improvement.

The Post-Abolition Period

The first region in Latin America to develop mass education was the British Caribbean after the abolition of slavery in Great Britain in the 1830s. (Slavery was officially abolished in 1834, but it continued until 1838 under a system of apprenticeship.) The establishment of primary schools was the indirect result of Haiti's struggle for independence(*see* Haitian Revolution). The British Crown wanted to avoid at all costs another bloody "Hayti" and believed that the provision of mass schooling would not only placate the former slaves' desire for revenge, but would also socialize them into remaining loyal subjects to the Crown. As early as 1835, the Reverend John Sterling wrote to the British Crown about the need for public schools in the West Indies. According to Sterling, if the Crown did not adopt measures to exert "power over the minds" of former slaves, society would certainly collapse. The imperial policy of extending education was successful in part because it coincided with the goals of the colonized people, who saw education as the primary means of improving their social mobility. As a result, elementary school enrollment, catering mainly to black children, so that by 1900 the Anglophone Caribbean had proportionately more children in primary schools than any Latin American country, and almost as many as the most advanced Western European nations.

Paradoxically, Haiti, the first country in Latin America to become independent, and whose efforts led in part to the spread of mass schooling in the British colonies, did little to provide education to the masses. Internal strife, lack of political will, and an enduring state of bankruptcy left education underdeveloped there. By 1900 less than 2 percent of the relevant age population were enrolled in primary education, and primary school enrollment only reached 50 percent of Haitian children until the mid-1980s.

In Spanish America, after the wars for independence, efforts for national consolidation focused on education as a key issue, and laws were passed to universalize free

TOP: Children eagerly raise their hands in a class at Carmen René Memorial School in Castries, St. Lucia. *Horner/Hutchison*
ABOVE: A teacher and her students walk hand in hand in Havana, Cuba. *Jeanette Ortiz Osorio*

elementary schooling. Several presidents, including Benito Juárez of Mexico, Domingo Faustino Sarmiento of Argentina, and José Pedro Varela of Uruguay, championed mass schooling in Latin America. Education, it was believed, was the sine qua non for achieving progress and unifying the nations. Colombian president Mariano Ospina Rodríguez, founder of the Conservative Party, expressed the prevailing sentiment when he said, "The art of civilizing men is called education."

The avowed enlightened views of these leaders notwithstanding, educational projects did not necessarily include nonwhites. Of all the political leaders of the time, Sarmiento was probably the staunchest supporter of mass education, a view spelled out in his *De la Educación Popular* (On Popular Education), published in 1849. Yet he specifically excluded blacks and Native Americans because, as he wrote, they "are incapable or inadequate for civilization." Toward the end of his life, Sarmiento published *Conflicto y armonías de las razas en América* (1883, Conflict and Harmonies of the Races in America), in which he stated that the backwardness of his continent was in large part due to the inferior genetic composition resulting from the mix between whites, blacks, and indigenous peoples. The pro-white nationalist discourse, which a few decades later was transformed into the blessings of a *mestizo* (mixed-race) society, albeit with a persistent bias toward whiteness, has permeated the curricula of the schools up until the present.

Even with the laws and the lofty speeches by politicians clamoring for free, universal public schools, a combination of factors – including protracted civil wars, meager financial resources, and a dearth of qualified personnel – contributed to the evaporation of such a grandiose dream. By the beginning of the twentieth century, the schools that had been built were founded almost exclusively in the larger cities. Since at least 80 percent of the population was located in the rural areas and small towns, literacy rates remained dismal. The few scholars who took it upon themselves to study the topic of blacks in the educational system in an effort to improve blacks' dignity – e.g., the Brazilian Bastos de Avila's *O Negro na Escola* (1934, Blacks in the School System;) – believed nevertheless in the scientific validity of Eugenics and the importance of Whitening society.

It was only after World War II, with the creation of multilateral organizations such as the United Nations and the World Bank, that concrete efforts to universalize primary education took place in Brazil and in Spanish-speaking countries. In the mid-1950s the first office of Educational Planning in Latin America was established in Colombia, and ministries of education throughout the hemisphere put in place rational and modern plans to educate most of the population. As a result, by the 1970s more than half the population in Latin America knew how to read and write. These comprehensive programs took important steps toward including groups, such as blacks and indigenous peoples, that had traditionally been excluded from primary schooling, although access to the secondary and tertiary levels of education remained a distant dream.

These programs were not without their critics. One powerful figure to challenge mainstream educational methods was the Brazilian educator Paulo Freire (1921-1997). He developed adult literacy programs that sought not only to teach individuals to read and write but also to foster a critical understanding through a process of "conscientization." Drawing upon people's own lived experiences as material for discussion, the method was designed to generate a greater awareness of the socioeconomic and political forces shaping their world, and of their own voice and agency as potential forces for resistance.

In the late 1940s and 1950s Freire developed these literacy programs in his home state of Pernambuco, in the Brazilian northeast. His success prompted Brazil's populist president João Goulart to appoint him to head a national literacy campaign in 1963. This project was cut short by the 1964 military coup that eventually sent Freire into exile. In the late 1960s Freire developed a national literacy campaign in CHILE that won an award from the United Nations Educational, Scientific, and Cultural Organization (UNESCO). He would later work with the World Council of Churches and a number of other entities in the area of education. His works, notably *Pedagogy of the Oppressed* (1970) and *Education for Critical Consciousness* (1973) have been central in the development of critical pedagogies. His method was incorporated by liberation theologians in the organization of Christian base communities. It has also been incorporated into programs addressing the issue of race, among GARIFUNA communities in BELIZE, Miskito Indians in Nicaragua, and black organizations in the Colombian Atlantic coast.

THE CONTEMPORARY PERIOD

As black cultural and civil rights groups began to emerge in different Latin American countries in the 1960s and 1970s, new intellectual spaces were opened in the field of sociology to study Afro-Latin Americans and their participation in, and depiction by, different social and political institutions. In the field of education research, the new texts left behind earlier and more questionable scholarship by the likes of Bastos de Avila, and waged an all-out battle to decry forms of racism that had permeated the schools since colonial times. One eloquent example of this new research was *As Belas Mentiras* (The Beautiful Lies), a book published in 1979 by the Brazilian researcher Maria de Lourdes Chagas Nosella.

In general, however, there has been a paucity of sociological research in Latin America and the Caribbean about race relations in the regions' educational systems and the distribution of educational opportunities among different ethnic groups. The problem is compounded because most national census bureaus do not collect socioeconomic data based on ethnicity. And even when they do, questions arise regarding the accuracy of the results. The category "ethnicity" is ultimately subjective, and responses to it vary, depending on whether they are self-reported or defined by a data collector. Thus, there is a dearth of statistical documentation in areas as basic as national literacy, attrition, and graduation rates.

The little research available has focused on two main issues: first, racism inside schools, particularly the presence of blacks in the curriculum and the relationship between the different educational actors. The second issue is blacks' educational access, graduation rates, and socioeconomic mobility. Regarding the first issue, one generalization that seems to hold true for Spanish-speaking Latin America and Brazil is that blacks have been methodically eliminated from any reference in school textbooks outside the slavery period. Social history classes have erased the presence of blacks even before the start of the republican era. Many noteworthy historical facts are never learned by the average high school student: the high percentage of blacks in the liberation armies of Simón Bolívar and José Francisco de San Martín; the great number of free and enslaved blacks forced to participate in the infamous Triple Alliance War (between ARGENTINA, Uruguay, and BRAZIL against PARAGUAY); and the development of Colombia's Chocó region, which has remained one of the world's most biologically diverse, thanks in part to the sustainable economic activities of a mostly black population.

Even when blacks have been included in discussions about the slavery period, they have been portrayed as passive recipients of a brutal reality. Although active resistance was far from the norm for obvious reasons, slaves throughout the Americas did revolt against their masters from the beginning of the sixteenth century all the way to the passage of abolition laws (*see* ABOLITION AND EMANCIPATION IN LATIN AMERICA AND THE CARIBBEAN). One dramatic manifestation of the culture of resistance was the creation of maroon communities throughout Latin America, which at times boasted tens of thousands of inhabitants (*see* MAROONAGE IN THE AMERICAS). Some of these strongholds, such as the PALENQUE DE SAN BASILIO near Cartagena, Colombia, persist today.

While black historic and social contributions are largely excluded from the curricula, students are confronted by a display of negative images of blacks. In a 1990 study of school textbooks and black-white representations, the Brazilian researcher Vera Moreira Figueira found that blacks were less often given names and that they were described as more sexually promiscuous and aggressive than whites and as intellectually inferior to them. Blacks' physical traits were often exaggerated to the point of caricature, with very thick lips, bulging eyes, and extremely salient buttocks. She also studied racial prejudice in poor, racially integrated schools in Rio de Janeiro, using the hypothesis that integrated schools would exhibit little stereotyping. Moreira Figueira found that among 309 students, ages 7-18, blacks were described as ugly (86 percent of respondents), thieving (84 percent), and dumb (83 percent). Whites were described as pretty (95 percent), studious (75 percent), and rich (94 percent). There was no variation between the responses of white and nonwhite students.

Another form of racial tension is experienced in the school systems of English- and French-speaking Caribbean nations. Historically, formal education has been delivered there in the country's official language, while the vernacular Creole has been relegated to a subordinate and inferior status. The imposition of the standard language, spoken by a lighter-skinned minority, over the vernacular Creole, spoken by a darker-skined majority, serves as a tool to retain the current social and economic stratification. According to the scholar Lawrence Carrington, research conducted by regional universities since the 1960s that has advocated the use of Creole as a viable and important linguistic code of instruction has not entered in any meaningful manner the region's educational systems or even displaced notions of the superiority of English, French, or Dutch.

Reform efforts in Caribbean countries have indeed taken place. For example, in Haiti in 1978, the ministry of education introduced Creole as a language of instruction and as a subject in the curriculum. But since these changes are often not mandatory, most schools and teachers simply disregard the new rulings. Even in those schools and offices that do use Creole as a language of communication, the dominant language still retains the higher status. Perhaps the only true dissenting voice to the denigration of the Creole language was heard in socialist GRENADA during the mass literacy campaigns of the early 1980s. Even though it was a short-lived experiment that ended with the 1983 United States invasion, a vernacular Creole was successfully validated and legitimated for the first time in Caribbean history.

With respect to the second issue, structural inequalities in education, the main difficulty is the lack of national statistics along racial lines. With the notable exceptions of Brazil and Cuba, Latin American countries tally literacy rates according to gender, age grouping, and urban-rural location, and neglect the element of ethnicity. However, the few studies that are available, and regional census data from countries that have compiled statistics, indicate that nonwhites have much lower literacy rates than whites; nonwhites obtain schooling levels inferior to those of whites who belong to the same socioeconomic group; and the return for schooling in terms of salary is proportionately lower for nonwhites than for whites.

In Brazil the 1987 census showed that the illiteracy rate for whites was 18 percent whereas for blacks and mulattos it was 36 percent. Given that nonwhites are found in disproportionate numbers in the lower socioeconomic strata, researchers Carlos Hasenbalg and Nelson do Valle Silva wanted to determine if class, not race, was the main reason for the discrepancy. They analyzed the data for poor families from the 1982 Brazilian census, and found that the rate of children from 11 to 14 years old who had never been to school was 10 percent for whites and 20 percent for nonwhites. As the salary per capita went up, the racial differential started to diminish, but even in the higher socioeconomic levels the racial differential still favored whites. Studies conducted in the state of São Paulo in 1986 revealed that nonwhite earnings were consistently lower than those of whites. In studies comparing illiterate nonwhite and white workers doing the same job, nonwhites earned 91.4 percent the wage of whites; with an elementary or a high school degree, the earning differential was much greater, with nonwhites earning 59.5 percent the wage of a white worker.

Cuba stands out as an exception to the rest of Latin America in the provision of educational access to nonwhites. There has been a drawn-out controversy to determine if the 1959 revolution has significantly reduced racism or not. Critics of the Cuban Revolution point out that prior to 1959 blacks had ample access to education, just as much as whites. Alejandro de la Fuente studied the issue of educational access before and after the revolution, and reached a different conclusion. His research revealed that although by Latin American standards Cuba did have high literacy rates across ethnic groups before the Cuban Revolution, after the revolution the racial differential was eliminated. In 1943, the last year before 1959 for which there are figures available, 25.5 percent of whites and 30.5 percent of nonwhites were illiterate. Students of Cuba believe that by 1959 the racial differential had probably increased, because during the 1940s and 1950s the educational system markedly deteriorated. By 1981, not only had illiteracy for all ethnic groups virtually disappeared (0.8 percent for whites, 1.2 percent for nonwhites), but throughout the educational system racial differences were minimal (of all whites, 4.7 percent were university students; of blacks, 3.9 percent; and of mulattos 3.3 percent). This is not to say that Cuba has eliminated racism altogether – manifestations are seen in the overrepresentation of blacks in Cuban prisons, the underrepresentation of blacks in high government posts, and a racist mentality in the society as a whole – but, important advances have been made.

Reducing Racism in Education

An important step has already been taken by several Latin American countries through the passage of progressive legislation. In Colombia the National Congress passed the General Law of Education (1994) which, among other things, defined specific plans to ensure that populations who have been traditionally excluded, such as indigenous groups and blacks, receive ample access to educational institutions. The law also mandated research into and the development and diffusion of the histories and contributions of all ethnic groups so that schools throughout the country can provide multicultural curricula in the social sciences. Finally, the law established ethnoeducation as an important developmental strategy to make sure that groups who possess a language and a culture of their own, different from the dominant linguistic code and traditions, receive bilingual and bicultural education. Nicaragua, Ecuador, and Honduras have passed similar legislation since the mid-1980s.

In order to accomplish the noble goals stated in the new laws, several aspects need to be considered. First, universities and ministries of education must engage in the difficult task of reconstructing and introducing in schools the histories of Africans and their descendants in Latin America. Significant gaps in the curricula – some of which are already well documented – include the disregard for cultural differences among African groups brought to the Americas; the omission of the culture of resistance and maroonage during slavery; and the silence surrounding the social and economic contributions of blacks in the consolidation of the new nation-states in the nineteenth and twentieth centuries.

Second, for bilingual countries in which the vernacular Creole is an essential part of the life of its inhabitants, children should be allowed to master the knowledge codes and linguistic skills of the dominant group while still learning to appreciate and retain their own language and traditions. Most scholars believe that both linguistic registers ought to have a space in the educational system, in a relationship not of substitution but of complementarity and equal status.

Third, universities and other institutions of higher learning should establish programs to ensure a greater diversity in their student bodies so that they more closely resemble the region's or country's ethnic composition. Universities should engage in aggressive recruitment campaigns, including the provision of financial aid packages, to guarantee that nontraditional students feel welcome in the academic institution.

Fourth, schools of education and normal schools must provide new and veteran teachers with pedagogical orientation on forms of oppression in society, such as sexism, classism, and racism. Particular attention should be given to the power of textbooks and the media, in order for teachers to learn to challenge constructions of race and ethnicity that reproduce racist ideologies.

Alberto Arenas

See Also

Uruguay; Cartagena de Indias, Colombia; Central America; Pacific Coast of Colombia; Porres, San Martín de; Languages, Creole, in the Caribbean; Havana, Cuba; Slave Rebellions in Latin America and the Caribbean.

Africa

Edward, Lake, also Edward Nyanza, lake in east Central Africa, in Democratic Republic of the Congo and Uganda.

Located 988 m (3240 ft) above sea level, Lake Edward has an area of about 2150 sq km (about 830 sq mi) and is connected on the northeast with Lake George (or Lake Dweru), in Uganda, by means of the Kazinga Channel. Lake Edward is fed by the Rutshuru River, a headstream of the White Nile. The lake has only one outlet, the Semliki River, which links it with Lake Albert to the north. High escarpments run along the western shore of the lake, and mountains rise on the northwestern shore. The water is brackish with mineral salts. Many fish and crocodiles live in the lake, and waterfowl abound on its shores. The Anglo-American explorer Sir Henry Morton Stanley discovered the lake in 1889. The lake was formerly called Albert Edward Nyanza.

See Also

Explorers in Africa Since 1800.

North America

Edwards, Melvin (b. May 4, 1937, Houston, Tex.), African American sculptor known for his works of welded steel and other metals.

Melvin Edwards was born in Houston, Texas. He studied painting at the University of Southern California (USC) and began sculpting in 1960. He received his B.F.A. from USC in 1965. He first gained critical attention with a series of sculptures titled *Lynch Fragments*, which by 1997 totaled more than 150 individual works constructed since 1963. The sculptures in this series are made using both forged and welded parts of knife sheaths, automotive gears, chains, ball bearings, horseshoes, and other metal. The works, which are each about the size of a human head and hang on a wall, explore themes of violence and incorporate both American and African symbolism.

In 1967 Edwards moved from California to New Jersey and his work shifted away from the manipulated, unpainted metal. A solo exhibition at the Walker Art Center in Minneapolis, Minnesota, in 1968 included geometric shapes painted in red, blue, and yellow. *Homage to My Father and the Spirit* (1969, Ithaca, New York), an outdoor sculpture at Cornell University, is a large-scale work that incorporates discs and triangles in painted steel. In a 1970 solo exhibition at the Whitney Museum of American Art in New York City, Edwards suspended barbed wire and chains from the ceiling to confront the viewer with the brutality of these materials.

Since the 1970s Edwards has spent time in several African countries studying their art and architecture. One result of his studies is a monumental sculpture at Morgan State University titled *Holiday at Soweto* (1976-1977, Baltimore, Maryland). The work is constructed out of steel and consists primarily of three circles, each 2.44 m (8 ft) in diameter. Cutouts in two of the circles are large enough for a person to walk through. According to Edwards, the piece was inspired by the incomparable singing of Billie Holiday, who grew up in Baltimore, and by a 1976 protest against the use of the Afrikaans language in black schools in Soweto, South Africa. Edwards wanted the work to express the great possibilities open to young black people living in Africa and the United States. A later piece, *Gate of Ogun* (1983, The Neuberger Museum, Purchase, New York), takes its name from the god of metalwork in Nigeria's YORUBA culture. It, too, combines African and American elements and allows the viewer to walk in and around it. Edwards has also created smaller wall-hung sculptures of brushed stainless steel, which are dedicated to Ogun.

SEE ALSO
Art and Architecture, African; Nigeria; Soweto, South Africa; Baltimore, Maryland; New York, New York.

Africa

Efik, ethnic group of West Africa.

The Efik primarily inhabit southeastern coastal NIGERIA and neighboring western CAMEROON. They speak a Niger-Congo language and are closely related to the IBIBIO people. Approximately 2 million people consider themselves Efik.

SEE ALSO
Languages, African: An Overview.

Africa

Efutu (also known as Afutu and Fetu), ethnic group of GHANA.

The Efutu primarily inhabit south-central Ghana. They speak a Niger-Congo language. They originally belonged to the Guan cultural and linguistic group but since the eighteenth century have assimilated with the surrounding FANTE people. Approximately 150,000 people consider themselves Efutu.

SEE ALSO
Languages, African: An Overview.

Africa

Egba, ethnic group of NIGERIA.

The Egba primarily inhabit southwestern Nigeria. They speak YORUBA, a Niger-Congo language, and are one of the Yoruba peoples. Approximately 2 million people consider themselves Egba.

SEE ALSO
Languages, African: An Overview.

Africa

Egypt, the nation in the northeastern corner of Africa, where a land bridge connects the continent with Asia; it borders the Mediterranean Sea to the north, Israel to the northeast, the Red Sea to the east, SUDAN to the south, and LIBYA to the west.

Since ancient times, Egypt's cultural and political significance has extended far beyond its borders. Ancient Egypt, whose pharaohs first came to power nearly 5000 years ago, pioneered one of the world's earliest advanced civilizations. Ancient Egypt served as a crossroads between the Middle East and sub-Saharan Africa, and its culture and people included elements from both neighboring regions. During the Twenty-fifth Dynasty (about 767-671 B.C.E.), black pharaohs from the neighboring kingdom of Kush ruled Egypt, and links of trade and migration have linked Egypt with East and Central Africa since prehistoric times. The ancient Egyptians' distinctive culture, which developed in the fertile Nile Valley and Delta, surrounded by hostile deserts, provided a model for surrounding peoples, including the Greeks. By the fourth century B.C.E. the tide had turned, and Greek-speaking Macedonian invaders conquered Egypt. Repeatedly over the centuries, Egypt has undergone foreign domination and exploitation only to reemerge as a powerful cultural and political center across wide areas of Africa and the MIDDLE EAST. After three centuries as the center of the powerful Ptolemaic Empire, Egypt was conquered by the Romans, who made it a province of their own empire and appropriated its agricultural surplus to feed Roman soldiers and citizens.

Conquered by Muslim Arab armies during the seventh century, Egypt became the center of the powerful MAMLUK STATE during the thirteenth. Subdued by the Ottoman Turks during the sixteenth century, Egypt went on to conquer large parts of present-day Sudan and the Arabian Peninsula under Muhammad Ali after 1805. Virtually a colony of Great Britain by 1900, Egypt emerged as a champion of Arab nationalism (*see* NATIONALISM IN AFRICA) under GAMAL ABDEL NASSER in 1952. Today Egypt's significance revolves around its cultural and political leadership in the Arab world and its important role in Middle Eastern geopolitics.

GREEK AND ROMAN DOMINANCE

In 332 B.C.E. Alexander the Great conquered Egypt. He ended the rule of the pharaohs, which had endured through 30 dynasties for nearly 2600 years before his conquest. Alexander's conquest initiated a period Hellenic dominance (*see* ALEXANDRIA AND GRECIAN AFRICA: AN INTERPRETATION) in Egypt that lasted nearly a millennium. In the struggle for power after Alexander's death, Egypt became a separate kingdom under the reign of Ptolemy, who had been one of Alexander's Macedonian guards. The Ptolemaic Dynasty continued for 300 years until the Romans conquered Egypt in 32 B.C.E. and dethroned CLEOPATRA, the last of the Ptolemies. Unlike the Ptolemies, the Romans ruled Egypt from afar, while a heavy Roman military presence enforced the export of Egypt's rich grain to nourish Rome's heartland in (present-day) Italy.

By the fourth century C.E. most Egyptians had converted to Christianity. The establishment of a new imperial capital at Constantinople marked the beginning of Egypt's Byzantine period (330-640 C.E.). During this time Egyptians adopted the Greek alphabet for writing the Egyptian language, which had until then still been written in demotic, a form of writing based on hieroglyphics. This final form of the Egyptian language is known as Coptic, the language of the Coptic Orthodox Church in Egypt today.

THE EMERGENCE OF ISLAMIC EGYPT

When the prophet Muhammad united the tribes of Arabia under his leadership in Mecca in about 630 C.E., his Muslim Arab warriors became a potent new force that quickly and easily destroyed the old world order. They forced the Byzantine Empire to retreat north into Anatolia (now part of Turkey), as the Arabs took control of Syria and Egypt, and later North Africa and the Iberian Peninsula. The Arab conqueror of Egypt, Amr ibn al-'As, defeated the Byzantine forces at Heliopolis in 640. In Egypt as elsewhere, non-Muslim subjects had to pay an extra tax. However, the Arabs allowed the overwhelmingly Coptic Christian Egyptians to live freely. Under Amr ibn al-'As, Egyptians enjoyed a period of relative prosperity, tolerance, and peace.

The Umayyad Dynasty (661-750), which ruled Egypt from Syria, began to incorporate Egyptians into Muslim society. Arabic became the official language rather than Coptic or Greek, and the empire promoted a new inclusive Muslim identity rather than an exclusive Arab identity. The empire also allowed the migration of Arabian tribes into Egypt to settle. The conversion of a majority of Egyptians to Islam and the replacement of spoken Egyptian by Arabic, however, took several more centuries to complete.

In the Abbasid period (750-945), power over affairs in Egypt vacillated between the centralized authority of the empire in the Abbasid capital of Baghdad (in present-day Iraq) and the local rulers of Egypt, who used Egypt's wealth to raise armies and challenge the authority of Baghdad. During both the Umayyad and the Abbasid eras, the empire used soldier-slaves – often Turkish or Circassian – as an alternative source of military power. They had been bought as young men outside Muslim lands, converted

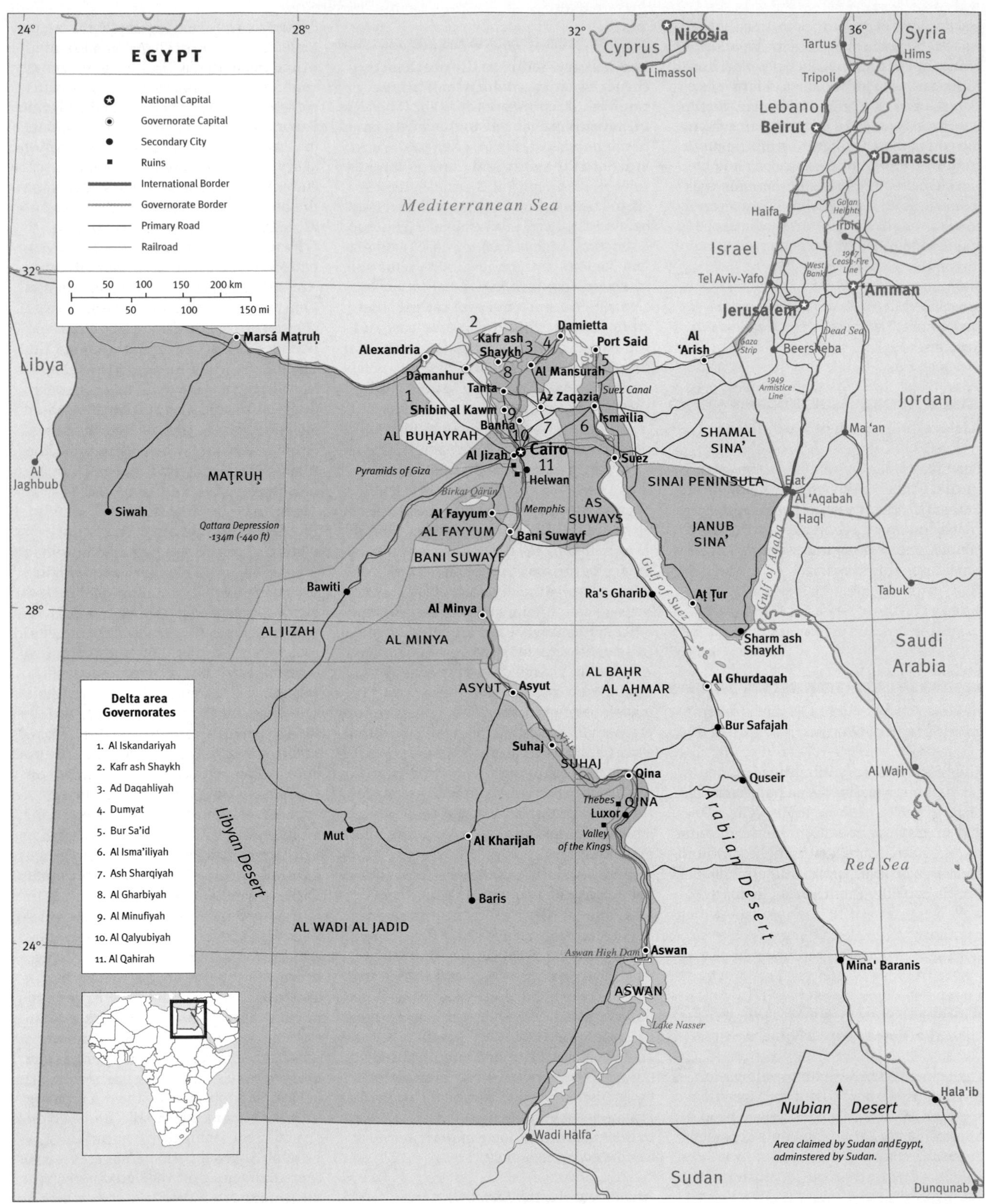

to Islam, trained in the arts of warfare and statecraft, and employed to maintain a loyal military force for the central ruler. These regiments of slaves, rewarded for their loyalty with various favors, became power brokers in Baghdad and often seized power themselves. In 834 Turkish soldier-slaves received the governorship of Egypt in exchange for their military support for the caliph (the Islamic ruler) in Baghdad, and several times Turkish governors became so powerful that they ruled Egypt autonomously. The most famous of these was Ahmad ibn Tulun, who ruled Egypt from 868 to 884.

The next ruling dynasty was the Fatimids, who belonged to a Shi'ite sect of Islam. They had established a state in present-day TUNISIA, and they set out to challenge the Sunni Muslim Abbasids for control of the Muslim world. Their empire eventually expanded west and east to cover all of North Africa, the Levant, and parts of the Arabian Peninsula. In 969 the Fatimids conquered Egypt and moved their capital there; Egypt became the center of an empire again, rather than a mere province and granary. The Fatimids founded al-Qahira, or modern Cairo, as their capital. After two centuries of rule, the Fatimid Empire began to crumble. In 1169 the Fatimid rulers in Egypt had to call on the forces of their former Sunni enemies in Syria to repulse the European Crusader invaders. The commander of these forces was Salah al-Din al-Ayyubi, known in Western history as Saladin, the leader who expelled the Crusaders from the Middle East. Salah al-Din not only successfully defended Egypt from the Crusaders, but also replaced the Fatimid ruler and founded a brief dynasty of his own, known today as the Ayyubids.

The Mamluks quickly succeeded the Ayyubids. The word Mamluk means "owned" in Arabic, and the Mamluks were originally the slave armies of the Ayyubid rulers. In 1250 the Mamluks took power from the ruling Ayyubids and formed their own dynasty, which was to last formally until 1517. The Mamluk era is divided into two periods, that of the Bahri and that of the Borji Mamluks. In the first period under the Bahri Mamluks, Egypt became the center of the Middle Eastern Islamic world. Controlling the lucrative trade routes connecting the Red Sea (by which ships brought the spices and silks of Asia) and the Mediterranean, the Bahri Mamluks grew rich. The dynasty supported the arts, and the Bahri era was generally one of great prosperity and cultural development. Under the Borji Mamluks after 1382, however, Egypt, racked by natural disasters and repeated outbreaks of the bubonic plague, entered a period of decline.

Competition among leading Mamluk families further devastated Egypt's ecology and social fabric. The crops the ruling families collected from peasants as tribute or taxes allowed the Mamluks to purchase more slaves (*see* Slavery in Africa) and expand their military power, which in turn enabled them to increase their demands on peasants for taxes. This practice often forced desperate peasants to abandon settled life and flee into the desert as nomads. In the long run, this overexploitation ruined Egypt's prosperity. Meanwhile, at the end of the fifteenth century, Egypt lost its vital monopoly over trade from the Indian Ocean to the Mediterranean and Europe when the Portuguese began using the sea route around the Cape of Good Hope. As the infighting among the Mamluk increased, their rule became more chaotic and decentralized, and they were unable to face the rising new power of the Middle East, the Ottomans.

The Ottomans were Turkish tribes originally from central Asia who had gradually conquered the Byzantine Empire. At the beginning of the sixteenth century the Ottoman Empire, under Selim the Magnificent, turned its attention to Persia, the Middle East, and North Africa. Ottoman forces arrived in Egypt in 1517. They successfully employed the new military technologies that were sweeping both Europe and the Middle East. The use of powerful firearms had changed the techniques, organization, and cost of warfare and contributed to the rise of larger, more centralized states in the western Atlantic and Mediterranean. The Ottomans exacted taxes and tribute to maximize the flow of wealth back to Istanbul, the new name given to the old Byzantine capital of Constantinople. Once again Egypt had become the granary of an empire in a distant land. However, as time progressed, the Ottoman state relied on the Mamluks to govern Egypt. By the end of direct Ottoman rule in Egypt at the close of the eighteenth century, the Mamluks had once again brought the country to the brink of complete ruin. By 1800 the population of Egypt had declined to between 3 and 5 million, whereas in the days of the pharaohs it was estimated at 30 million. In comparison, the population of Egypt was estimated at 57 million in 1996.

Muhammad Ali and the Emergence of Modern Egypt

Ottoman power reached its zenith around 1600. Over the next two centuries, rising European powers managed to turn back Ottoman expansion. Napoleon's invasion of Egypt in 1798, however, shook the Ottoman world. Napoleon attacked Egypt to establish French dominance there and preempt any similar move on the part of the British. His modern armies, supplied with the new weapons of the nascent industrial era in Europe, easily routed the Mamluk forces.

In a pattern that has been repeated to this day, Egypt became a theater of European geopolitical designs. The British aided the Ottoman rulers in ousting the French and reestablishing Ottoman control over Egypt. The British had decided that the Ottoman Empire should serve as a buffer state against Russian expansion. The vulnerable Ottoman Empire gained renewed vitality by virtue of its strategic location between two rival imperialist powers and on the major communications and trade routes with British India and the Far East.

However, local interests disrupted the best-laid imperialist plans. In Egypt Muhammad Ali, the Ottoman military commander sent by Istanbul in 1801 to evacuate the French, had designs of his own. Muhammad Ali recognized the importance of the industrial revolution happening in Europe. He worked to industrialize Egypt and, in particular, to industrialize its military. In order to finance imports of European factories and advisers, the government exported first food grains and later sugar and long-staple cotton. Egypt's resulting military strength allowed it to conquer parts of the Arabian Peninsula during the 1810s and much of present-day Sudan during the 1820s.

Muhammad Ali's regime sought economic as well as military power. It organized Egypt's farms into one large state enterprise run by state administrators. The state also monopolized trade. To maximize state revenues, Muhammad Ali banned Europeans from trade within Egypt. Egypt dealt directly with European traders only at the Mediterranean port of Alexandria. This trade monopoly angered British and French merchants, and neither London nor Paris looked favorably upon Muhammad Ali's military and economic ambitions. When the British prompted the Ottoman rulers to enforce special trading privileges for European merchants throughout the Ottoman Empire, they forced Muhammad Ali to relinquish his trade monopolies, withdraw his troops from Anatolia, Syria, and the Arabian Peninsula, and reduce the size of his army. In return, in 1841 he received the hereditary title Khedive of Egypt. While still nominally a part of the Ottoman Empire, Egypt became, in fact, a modern dynasty of Muhammad Ali and his descendants, which continued until 1952.

Muhammad Ali's son, Said, and his grandson, Ismail, continued their forebear's drive for modernization, but their relationship with the European powers differed significantly. Unlike Muhammad Ali, his son and grandson accepted foreign loans and granted concessions to European contractors. Their financial inexperience and the unscrupulousness of international lenders brought financial troubles and eventually the loss of political autonomy.

Said and Ismail vastly expanded the physical infrastructure of Egypt. They commissioned railroads, irrigation schemes, ports, and other communications and transport facilities, but their investments left the Egyptian government deeply indebted. The Suez Canal typified their predicament. The French engineer Ferdinand de Lesseps manipulated the Egyptians into providing the land and labor and borrowing most of the capital for the project. In return, the Egyptians received almost nothing. The canal was completed in 1869; by 1875 the British government under Prime Minister Benjamin Disraeli had bought the indebted Egyptian government's majority share of stock, and the Egyptians lost control over this vital communications and commercial link, built with Egyptian funds on Egyptian territory.

The increasing contact with Europe also brought new cultural trends. Said and Ismail founded schools to train Egyptian personnel capable of administering the rapidly modernizing economy. Religious thinkers who had always seen Islam as the highest achievement of humanity tried to understand the new precarious position of the Muslim world in relation to European domination. They championed a return to the scriptural roots of Islam. Their call for pan-Islamic resistance to European dominance sparked the first of the modern Islamist cultural movements. The movement spread among the urban elite of the emerging national community of

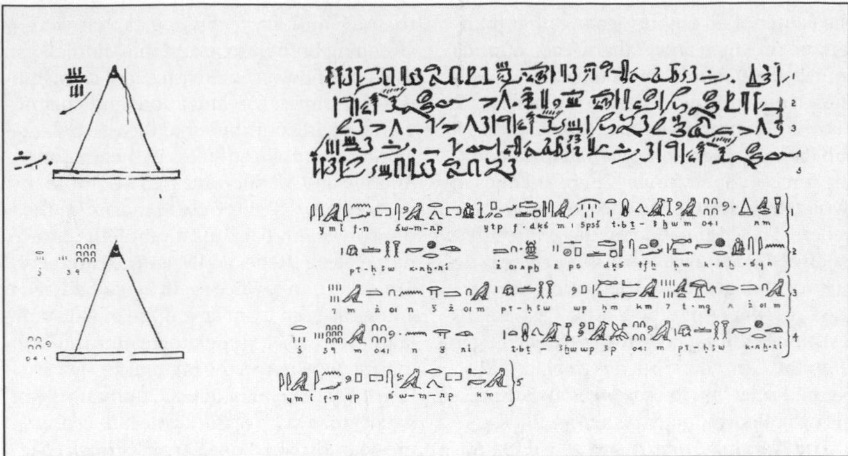

ABOVE: **This granite statue of Hatshepsut depicts the queen wearing a pharaoh's false beard and kneeling to make offerings to the gods. The sculpture comes from Hatshepsut's temple at Deir-el-Bahari.** *Giraudon/Art Resource, NY*

RIGHT: **The ancient Egyptian symbol for the number ten looked like an upside-down letter "U." This geometry problem is written in ancient Egyptian, *(below)*, and translated into Demotic, *(above)*.** *Roger-Viollet*

Egypt. At the same time, there were those who attempted to marginalize the influence of religion in daily life and to adopt the more secular attitudes of contemporary Europe.

Debt led to two significant developments: European control of the country and the advent of private property in agricultural land, previously owned by the state. When Egypt began to default on its loans to European bankers, a joint French-British agency intervened in 1876 to oversee government tax collection and the fulfillment of Egypt's financial obligations to European bankers. Private property came into being when the government attempted to raise domestic revenue by granting private property rights in exchange for current payment of future taxes. However, Ismail's modernization of the Egyptian military had created an Egyptian officer corps that increasingly resented European encroachment on Egyptian sovereignty. When one of these officers, Ahmad 'Urabi Pasha, led a revolt against the Europeans and their Egyptian allies, the British used the opportunity to begin a military occupation of the country in 1882 that was to last until 1954.

Egypt Under British Domination

The British exercised increasingly effective control over the affairs of the country, although they allowed the khedive to remain as the nominal ruler of Egypt and left most government offices in the hands of Egyptians. However, a British adviser oversaw each Egyptian government ministry. The British blocked efforts by the khedive who came to the throne in 1892, Abbas Khilmi, along with Egyptian nationalist intellectuals, to resist British rule. In 1898 Egyptian and British forces jointly reconquered Sudan, which had declared its independence in 1885. Meanwhile, the British administration streamlined the Egyptian economy into an efficient agricultural export machine. A new class of wealthy Egyptian landowners supported the British in the development of the cotton and sugar export economy. In 1907 these Egyptian landowners began to demand more control over the economy through the establishment of a national bank. This would become part of the institutional basis of modern Egyptian nationalism.

At the onset of World War I (1914-1918), when the Ottoman Empire sided with Germany, the British declared that Egypt no longer belonged to the Ottomans. The British declared Egypt a protectorate in 1914 and ruled through martial law during the war. Though the 1918 Versailles Treaty and the new League of Nations promoted the *concept* of individual nations' right to self-determination, the league actually helped perpetuate European COLONIAL RULE over Africa and Asia. The European victors at Versailles granted a mandate over Egypt to the British. Such paternalism deeply offended Egyptian nationalists, who formed a committee to travel to London and Paris to ask for a seat at the League of Nations and to claim their right to self-determination. In response, British authorities arrested the Egyptian leaders and deported them to the SEYCHELLES. This British act of repression provoked a mass outpouring of nationalist protest and unrest in Egypt. In turn, the British backed a 1922 declaration of "independence" that limited Egyptian sovereignty and preserved British control of the military, the Suez Canal, and the Sudan, which they then jointly ruled with Egypt. The British retained this control by exploiting internal political divisions in Egypt, particularly the competing claims of the royal family, who sought to retain a role in Egyptian politics, and the nationalists, who wished sovereignty to lie only with the Egyptian people. The British helped devise a constitution granting extensive powers to the new king (the former sultan), including the power to dismiss the nationalist-dominated Parliament. Thus during the 1920s and 1930s there were frequent dismissals of Parliament and ensuing protests.

Egyptian industrialization and urbanization accelerated during these decades; these processes gave rise to class divisions and mass politics. During the 1930s in particular, new mass organizations contrasted with the more elitist parties that had previously dominated the Parliament. The most significant of the new organizations was the Muslim Brotherhood. It was established in 1928 – not by a member of the religious establishment, but by a lay state schoolteacher – in order to spread institutions supporting Muslim morality. The Brotherhood built schools, student associations, and social organizations to aid the poor. Though not formally a political party, the Brotherhood was to become a powerful force in Egyptian society.

At the same time, the currents of Arab nationalism were developing throughout the Arab world. This movement sought first and foremost to overcome European imperialism, but it also held a larger humanist vision combining social equality, rationalist social planning, and cultural modernism. Arab nationalism promised economic progress for the wide segments of society excluded by the elitist economic and political structure of much of the Middle East until then, and it would inspire the coup that deposed Egypt's British client monarchy.

Arab Nationalism and Postcolonial Egypt

During World War II Egypt played an important role in the Allied war effort; after the war popular demands grew for true political independence from the British, and, more important, for social development. A few very wealthy landowners and industrialists monopolized political and economic power in Egypt. These elites engaged in petty strivings for personal power and ignored the economic and political concerns of the Egyptian people. With popular frustration mounting, the ineptness and defeat of the Egyptian army in the first Arab-Israeli war in 1948 finally triggered the collapse of the old order.

Two political currents were capable of challenging Egypt's entrenched elites: the Muslim Brotherhood and the Arab nationalists. Arab nationalist soldiers, led by Gamal Abdel Nasser, seized the moment in July 1952 and toppled the monarchy in a coup d'état. At first the Brotherhood and the nationalists maintained an uneasy alliance, for though many of their ideals and goals coincided, they had some fundamental philosophical disagreements, particularly around the issue of religion. By 1954 relations between the two groups had soured, and Nasser, who became prime minister in April 1954, began a campaign of repression against the Brotherhood.

Nasser's legitimacy depended on his ability to overcome the social, economic, and political problems that the former regime had been unable to resolve, one of which was the occupation of the Suez Canal zone by British troops. Nasser negotiated a British evacuation in 1954. In 1956 he nationalized the Suez Canal after the United States and the World Bank refused to help finance the ASWAN HIGH DAM. In response, the French, British, and Israelis mounted an attack on Egypt that the Egyptians could not repel. The attack, though successful, provoked a worldwide reaction against what was clearly an imperialist war. Both the United States and the Soviet Union demanded that the attacking forces withdraw. The result was a resounding political victory for Nasser and the Egyptians.

In retaliation for the attack, Nasser confis-

BELOW: A fisherman pulls in his net as he fishes the Damietta arm of the Nile River in Egypt. *CORBIS/Kevin Fleming*
RIGHT: Buyers and sellers bargain over camels at the Imbaba market in Cairo. *CORBIS/K.M. Westermann*
BOTTOM: The mausoleum of Barquq stands in the foreground of this view of Cairo. *CORBIS/K.M. Westermann*

cated the property of British and French firms operating in Egypt. These initial confiscations were clearly political in nature and not part of an overall economic strategy. However, as the cold war spurred the superpowers' involvement in the Arab world, Egypt increasingly turned to the Soviet Union, both as a patron and a model. By the early 1960s Egypt was building a state socialist economy (*see* African Socialism). The state undertook extensive industrial development, and, though markets still functioned, the state controlled prices for most products. In agriculture, the state confiscated the land of the very wealthy landowners and leased it to landless peasants; it set up cooperatives to raise agricultural productivity and channeled the surplus into urban industrial investment. The government introduced laws that protected peasants from eviction even when they could not pay rents, and made rental agreements hereditary on both private and state land. All of these measures aimed to improve the livelihoods of the middle and lower income classes on whose support Nasser relied.

However, Nasser's Arab nationalism suffered a humiliating setback. In 1967 growing tensions between Israel and the Arab nations of Egypt, Jordan, and Syria erupted in the Six-Day War. The Israeli army seized Egypt's Sinai Peninsula and other Arab territories. Following Nasser's death in 1970, his successor, Anwar al-Sadat, decided to reposition Egypt geopolitically by spurning Soviet aid and aligning with the United States. Sadat hoped that U.S. mediation could resolve the conflict with Israel and that U.S. aid would help Egypt to grow economically. As part of this realignment, Sadat traveled to Israel in 1977 at the invitation of Israeli prime minister Menachem Begin to begin peace negotiations. Sadat's perceived betrayal of the Palestinian and Arab nationalist cause sparked outrage in the Arab world, and Arab leaders expelled Egypt from the Arab League.

Sadat turned away from state-led industrialization and moved to liberalize the Egyptian economy. He removed controls that prohibited foreign multinationals from operating in Egypt; he also lessened restrictions on foreign commodities and opened Egyptian markets to multinational competition. Still, the government has been slow to abandon the state-owned industrial structure, and the agricultural laws protecting peasants from eviction were only effectively repealed in 1997. Because of Egypt's strategic importance, the United States has tolerated Egypt's hesitation to privatize and deregulate its economy; it has not forced Egypt to follow a strict structural adjustment program, even though Egypt receives the second-largest share of U.S. foreign aid.

Meanwhile, another force was rising in the Middle East: a reorganized Islam-based (or Islamist) political opposition. Most of the Arab nationalist regimes adopted secularism and socialism. Islamist ideology fundamentally opposed these secular tendencies and the reliance on Western, albeit socialist, visions of modern society. Saudi Arabia and its major Western ally, the United States, had supported and funded the Islamist political opposition during the 1960s and 1970s, and Saudi support for some groups continued into the 1980s and possibly later. The power of the Organization of Petroleum Exporting Countries' (OPEC) oil cartel and the incredible flow of wealth into the Arabian Peninsula after 1973 further shifted power within the Middle East away from the Arab nationalist regimes and toward U.S.-aligned Saudi Arabia and the Gulf States.

In Egypt, Sadat's political maneuvers also fostered the growth of Islamist political movements. Nasser's regime had imprisoned many Islamist political leaders in order to curtail opposition, but this repression, in fact, bred more strident opposition. Sadat attempted to use the Islamist opposition for his own political ambitions by abandoning socialist policies and releasing many of Nasser's political prisoners. Ironically, his attempt to court the Islamists proved deadly for him. The infusion of jail-hardened leadership strengthened many Islamist groups, and they began to mobilize against the Sadat regime after its accommodation with Israel and the United States and its failure to follow an Islamist program. Perceiving a threat to his regime, Sadat arrested 1300 opposition leaders in September 1981. Angered by the arrests and his rapprochement with Israel, radical Islamists assassinated Sadat the following month.

Egypt under Sadat's successor, President Hosni Mubarak, has faced increasing pressure from populist Islamist groups who often represent those dissatisfied with the absence of true democracy and the lack of substantial economic progress, particularly among the poor. The regime has faced military attacks by political Islamist groups throughout the nation, and Mubarak has relied primarily on the military to defend his regime. In 1992 a series of attacks in southern Egypt provoked a large-scale military crackdown. The military failed to suppress the militant opposition completely, and in 1995 attacks resumed, this time at popular tourist sites. Tourism represents one of three main sources of foreign exchange for Egypt, aside from foreign aid; the others are worker remittances and oil. Hence, the attacks on tourist sites aimed to destroy the economy and bring down the regime. The worst such attack, in Luxor in late 1997, showed that the military strategy has not been able to root out such groups.

A woman addresses a crowd on one of the principal streets of Cairo. This incident, which took place in 1919, marked the first time Egyptian women entered public political debate. *CORBIS/Bettmann*

Under Mubarak the Egyptian regime has undertaken partial democratization, though limited by the fear of religiously inspired opposition groups. Political parties are allowed to operate in Egypt, but only those few approved by the regime. Upon coming to power President Mubarak promised to accept the constitutional limit of two terms; however, during his second term he urged Parliament to amend the constitution so that he could legally remain in power. The largest Islamist political group is the Muslim Brotherhood, which is still legally prohibited from political work. The Brotherhood represents a moderate form of Islamist opposition, and it exerts its power through participation in other, legal political parties. During the 1990s Mubarak's continued reliance on the military and his ban on Islamist political opposition threatened his regime's stability, particularly when ordinary Egyptians continue to face economic hardship.

In the late 1990s Egypt remains the cultural center of the Arab world. Egyptian television, videos, and music are seen and heard throughout the Arab world, and intellectuals from throughout the Arabic-speaking world congregate in Egypt, especially in Cairo. Egypt plays a leading role in Arab regional politics as well as in international diplomacy. Egypt, or "the mother of the world" in local parlance, thus maintains its role as a vibrant political and cultural center in the modern world, a role it has played repeatedly since ancient times.

Charles Schmitz

See Also

Egypt, Ancient Kingdom of; Kush, Early Kingdom of; Nile River; Structural Adjustment in Africa; Sadat, Anwar al-; Alexandria, Egypt; Cairo, Egypt.

Africa

Egypt (Ready Reference)

Former Name: United Arab Republic (with Syria)
Official Name: Arab Republic of Egypt
Area: 1,001,450 sq km (about 386,662 sq mi)
Location: North Africa, on the Mediterranean Sea, bordered by the Gaza Strip, the Red Sea, Sudan, and Libya
Capital: Cairo (population 6,800,000 [1995 estimate])
Other Major Cities: Alexandria (population 2,917,300), Giza (3,700,100), Port Said (399,800), Suez (326,800) (1986 estimates)
Population: 66,050,004 (1998 estimate)
Population Density: 64 persons per sq km (164 per sq mi)
Population Below Age 15: Total population: 36 percent (male 12,173,882; female 11,637,239 [1998 estimate])
Population Growth Rate: 1.86 percent (1998 estimate)
Total Fertility Rate: 3.4 children born per woman (1998 estimate)
Life Expectancy at Birth: Total population: 62.07 years (male 60.09 years; female 64.14 years [1998 estimate])
Infant Mortality Rate: 69.23 deaths per 1000 live births (1998 estimate)
Literacy Rate (age 15 and over who can read and write): Total population: 51.4 percent (male 63.6 percent; female 38.8 percent [1995 estimate])
Education: Compulsory for children between the ages of 6 and 11; 89 percent of primary school-age children were enrolled in school in the mid-1990s. Secondary school enrollment was 65 percent, including vocational and teacher training schools. Seventeen percent of college-age Egyptians attended universities or other institutions of higher education during this time. Egypt has 13 state universities, as well as numerous technical colleges and institutes of art and music.
Languages: Arabic is the official language; English and French are also used by educated classes.
Ethnic Groups: Egyptians, Bedouins, and Berbers of Hamitic descent make up 99 percent of the population, while Greek, Nubian, Armenian, and other European groups (mostly Italian and French) make up the remaining 1 percent.
Religions: Muslim, 94 percent; Coptic Christian and other, 6 percent
Climate: Hot, dry, and dusty over most of the country; the hot season is from May to September and the cool season from November to March. In the coastal region, average annual temperatures range from a maximum of 37° C (99° F) to a minimum of 14° C (57° F). Wide variations of temperature occur in the deserts, ranging from a maximum of 46° C (114° F) during daylight hours to a minimum of 6° C (42° F) after sunset. During the winter season desert temperatures often drop to 0° C (32° F). The most humid area is along the Mediterranean coast, where the average annual rainfall is about 200 mm (8 in). Precipitation decreases rapidly to the south; Cairo receives on average only about 29 mm (1.1 in) of rain a year, and in many desert locations it may rain only once in several years.
Land, Plants, and Animals: Egypt is situated on a desert plateau bisected by the Nile River. Less than one-tenth of the country is settled or under cultivation, principally along the valley and delta of the Nile, in desert oases, and around the Suez Canal. Over 90 percent of the country is in the desert, including the Libyan Desert west of the Nile, the Arabian Desert in the east, and the Nubian Desert in the south. The Sinai Peninsula consists of sandy desert in the north and rugged mountains in the south. The vegetation of Egypt is confined largely to the Nile delta, the Nile Valley, and the oases. Wild animals include the gazelle, desert fox, hyena, jackal, wild ass, boar, jerboa, ichneumon, lizard, poisonous snakes, crocodile, hippopotamus, and numerous species of birds and insects.
Natural Resources: Petroleum, natural gas, iron ore, phosphates, manganese, limestone, gypsum, talc, asbestos, lead, and zinc
Currency: The Egyptian pound
Gross Domestic Product (GDP): $267.1 billion (1997 estimate)
GDP per Capita: $4400 (1997 estimate)
GDP Real Growth Rate: 5.2 percent (1997 estimate)
Primary Economic Activities: Agriculture (40 percent of employment), fishing, oil production, manufacturing, tourism, and other services
Primary Crops: Cotton, rice, corn, wheat, beans, fruits, vegetables; cattle, water buffalo, sheep, goats, and fish
Industries: Textiles, food processing, chemicals, petroleum, construction, cement, and metals
Primary Exports: Crude oil and petroleum products, cotton yarn, raw cotton, textiles, metal products, chemicals, fruits, and vegetables
Primary Imports: Machinery and equipment, food grains, fertilizers, wood products, durable consumer goods, and capital goods
Primary Trade Partners: United States, European Union, and Japan
Government: Constitutional republic. The executive branch is led by President Mohammed Hosni Mubarak, nominated by the 454-member People's Assembly (elected in late 1995) and validated by a national, popular referendum. The prime minister (currently Kamal Ahmed al-Ganzouri) and the Cabinet are appointed by the president. The legislature comprises the 454-seat People's Assembly, currently dominated by Mubarak's National Democratic Party, and the 264-seat Advisory Council, which plays only a consultative role.

Barbara Worley

See Also

Mubarak, Hosni; Nile River; Alexandria, Egypt; Cairo, Egypt.

Africa

Egypt, Ancient Kingdom of,

an ancient African civilization centered in the Nile delta and the lower Nile Valley.

The origins of ancient Egyptian civilization, which many regard as one of the principal sources of Western culture, cannot be established with certainty. Archaeological evidence suggests that early dwellers in the Nile Valley were influenced both by the cultures of the Middle East and by surrounding African cultures. Describing the development of Egyptian civilization, like attempts to identify its intellectual foundations, is largely a process of conjecture based on archaeological discoveries of enduring ruins, tombs, and monuments, many of which contain invaluable specimens of the ancient culture. Inscriptions in hieroglyphs, for instance, have provided priceless data.

The framework for the study of the dynastic period of Egyptian history, between the First Dynasty and the Ptolemaic Period, relies on the *Aegyptiaca* of Manetho, a Ptolemaic priest of the third century B.C.E., who organized the country's rulers into 30 dynasties, roughly corresponding to families. General agreement exists on the division of Egyptian history, up to the conquest of Alexander the Great, into Old, Middle, and New Kingdoms with intermediate periods, followed by the late and Ptolemaic periods. New evidence and increasingly sophisticated dating techniques, however, have allowed continual refinement of chronology and genealogy.

Prehistory

Some 60,000 years ago the Nile River began

its yearly inundation of the land along its banks, leaving behind rich alluvial soil. Areas close to the floodplain became attractive as a source of food and water. In time, climatic changes, including periods of aridity, further served to confine human habitation to the Nile Valley, although this was not always true. From the Chalcolithic Period (the Copper Age, beginning about 4000 B.C.E.) into the early part of the Old Kingdom, people apparently used an extended part of the land.

In the seventh millennium B.C.E., Egypt was environmentally hospitable, and evidence of settlements from that time has been found in the low desert areas of Upper (southern) EGYPT; remains of similar occupation have been discovered at NUBIAN sites in modern SUDAN (*see* KUSH, EARLY KINGDOM OF). Enough pottery has been found in Upper Egyptian tombs from the fourth millennium B.C.E. (in the Predynastic Period) to establish a relative dating sequence. The Predynastic Period, which ends with the unification of Egypt under one king, is generally subdivided into three parts, each of which refers to a site at which its archaeological materials were found: Badarian, Amratian (Naqada I), and Gerzean (Naqada II and III). Sites in Lower (northern) Egypt (from about 5500 B.C.E.) have yielded datable archaeological material of apparent cultural continuity but no long-term sequences such as those found in Upper Egypt.

Early Dynastic (or Archaic) Period

Archaeological sources indicate the emergence, by the late Gerzean period (about 3200 B.C.E.), of a dominant political force that was to become the consolidating element in the first united kingdom of ancient Egypt. The earliest known hieroglyphic writing dates from this period; soon the names of early rulers began to appear on monuments. This period began with a 0 Dynasty, which had as many as 13 rulers, ending with Narmer (about 3100 B.C.E.), followed by the First and Second Dynasties (about 3100-2755 B.C.E.), with at least 17 kings. Some of the earliest massive mortuary structures (predecessors of the pyramids) were built at Saqqarah, Abydos, and elsewhere during the First and Second dynasties.

The Old Kingdom

The Old Kingdom (about 2755-2255 B.C.E.) spanned five centuries of rule by the Third through the Sixth Dynasties. The capital was in the north, at Memphis, and the ruling monarchs held absolute power over a strongly unified government. Religion played an important role; in fact, the government had evolved into a theocracy, wherein the pharaohs, as the rulers were called, were both absolute monarchs and, possibly, gods on earth.

The Third Dynasty was the first of the houses that ruled from Memphis, and its second ruler, Zoser, or Djoser, who reigned about 2737-2717 B.C.E., emphasized national unity by balancing northern and southern motifs in his mortuary buildings at Saqqarah. His architect, Imhotep, used stone blocks instead of traditional mud bricks in the complex there, thus creating the first monumental structure of stone; its central element, the Step Pyramid, was Zoser's tomb. In order to deal with affairs of state and to administer construction projects, the king began to develop an effective bureaucracy. In general, the Third Dynasty marked the beginning of a golden age of cultural freshness and vigor.

The Fourth Dynasty began with King Snefru, whose building projects included the first true pyramid at Dahshor (south of Saqqarah). Snefru, the earliest warrior king for whom extensive documents remain, campaigned in NUBIA (or Kush) and LIBYA and was active in the Sinai. Promoting commerce and mining, he brought prosperity to the kingdom. Snefru was succeeded by his son Khufu (or Cheops), who built the Great Pyramid at Giza. Although little else is known of his reign, that monument not only attests to his power but also indicates the administrative skills the bureaucracy had gained. Khufu's son Redjedef, who reigned about 2613-2603 B.C.E., introduced the solar element (Ra, or Re) in the royal titulary and the religion. Khafre (or Chephren), another son of Khufu, succeeded his brother to the throne and built his mortuary complex at Giza. The remaining rulers of the dynasty included Menkaure, or Mycerinus, who reigned about 2578-2553 B.C.E.; he is known primarily for the smallest of the three large pyramids at Giza.

Under the Fourth Dynasty, Egyptian civilization reached a peak in its development, and this high level was generally maintained in the Fifth and Sixth Dynasties. The splendor of the engineering feats of the pyramids was approximated in every other field of endeavor, including architecture, sculpture, painting, navigation, the industrial arts and sciences, and astronomy; astronomers first created a solar calendar based on a year of 365 days. Old Kingdom physicians also displayed a remarkable knowledge of physiology, surgery, the circulatory system of the body, and antiseptics.

Although the Fifth Dynasty maintained prosperity, with extensive foreign trade and military incursions into Asia, signs of decreasing royal authority became apparent in the swelling of the bureaucracy and the enhanced power of nonroyal administrators. The last king of the dynasty, Unas, who reigned about 2428-2407 B.C.E., was buried at Saqqarah, with a body of religious spells, called Pyramid Texts, carved on the walls of his pyramid chamber. Such texts were also used in the royal tombs of the Sixth Dynasty. Several autobiographical inscriptions of officials under the Sixth Dynasty indicate the decreasing status of the monarchy; records even indicate a conspiracy against King Pepi I, who reigned about 2395-2360 B.C.E., in which the ruler's wife was involved. It is believed that during the later years of Pepi II, who reigned about 2350-2260 B.C.E., power may have been in the hands of his vizier (chief minister). Central authority over the economy was also diminished by decrees of exemption from taxes. The nomarchs – governors of nomes (districts) – were rapidly becoming individually powerful, as they began to remain in place rather than being periodically transferred to different nomes.

First Intermediate Period

The Seventh Dynasty marked the beginning of the First Intermediate Period. As a consequence of internal strife, the reigns of this and the succeeding Eighth Dynasty are rather obscure. It is clear, however, that both ruled from Memphis and lasted a total of only 25 years. By this time the powerful nomarchs were in effective control of their districts, and factions in the south and north vied for power. Under the Heracleopolitan Ninth and Tenth Dynasties, the nomarchs near Heracleopolis controlled their area and extended their power north to Memphis (and even into the delta) and south to Asyut (Lycopolis). The rival southern nomarchs at Thebes established the Eleventh Dynasty, controlling the area from Abydos to Elephantine, near Syene (present-day Aswan). The early part of this dynasty, the first of the Middle Kingdom, overlapped the last part of the Tenth.

The Middle Kingdom

Without one centralized government, the bureaucracy was no longer effective, and nomarchs openly championed regional concerns. Egyptian art became more provincial, and no massive mortuary complexes were built. The religion was also democratized, as commoners claimed prerogatives previously reserved for royalty alone. They could, for instance, use spells derived from the royal Pyramid Texts on the walls of their own coffins or tombs.

Although the Middle Kingdom (2134-1784 B.C.E.) is generally dated to include all of the Eleventh Dynasty, it properly begins with the reunification of the land by Mentuhotep II, who reigned 2061-2010 B.C.E. The early rulers of the dynasty attempted to extend their control from Thebes both northward and southward, but it was left to Mentuhotep to complete the reunification process, sometime after 2047 B.C.E. Mentuhotep ruled for more than 50 years, and despite occasional rebellions, he maintained stability and control over the whole kingdom. He replaced some nomarchs and limited their power, which was still considerable. Thebes was his capital, and his mortuary temple at Dayr al Bahri incorporated both traditional and regional elements; the tomb was separate from the temple, and there was no pyramid.

The reign of the first Twelfth Dynasty king, Amenemhet I, was peaceful. He established a capital near Memphis and, unlike Mentuhotep, deemphasized Theban ties in favor of national unity. Nevertheless, he gave the important Theban god Amon prominence over other deities. Amenemhet demanded loyalty from the nomarchs, rebuilt the bureaucracy, and educated a staff of scribes and administrators. The literature was predominantly propaganda designed to reinforce the image of the king as a "good shepherd" rather than as an inaccessible god. In the last ten years of his reign, Amenemhet ruled with his son as co-regent. *The Story of Sinuhe,* a literary work of the period, implies that the king was assassinated.

Amenemhet's successors continued his programs. His son, Sesostris I, who reigned 1962-1928 B.C.E., built fortresses throughout Nubia (or Kush) and established trade with foreign lands. He sent governors to Palestine and Syria and campaigned against the Libyans in the west. Sesostris II, who reigned 1895-1878 B.C.E., began land reclamation in Al Fayyum. His successor, Sesostris III, who reigned 1878-1843 B.C.E., had a canal dug at the first cataract of the Nile, formed a standing army (which he used in his campaign against the Nubians), and built new forts on the southern frontier. He divided the administration into three powerful geographic units, each controlled by an official under the vizier, and he no longer recognized provincial nobles. Amenemhet III continued the policies of his predecessors and extended the land reform.

A vigorous renaissance of culture took place under the Theban kings. The architecture, art, and jewelry of the period reveal an extraordinary delicacy of design, and the time was considered the golden age of Egyptian literature.

Second Intermediate Period

The rulers of the Thirteenth Dynasty – some 50 or more in about 120 years – were weaker than their predecessors, although they were still able to control Nubia and the administration of the central government. During the latter part of their rule, however, their power was challenged not only by the rival Fourteenth Dynasty, which won control over the delta, but also by the Hyksos, a little-known group of people who invaded from western Asia. By the Thirteenth Dynasty there was a large Hyksos population in northern Egypt. As the central government entered a period of decline, their presence made possible an influx of people from coastal Phoenicia (roughly, present-day Lebanon) and Palestine (present-day Israel, Gaza, and the West Bank) and the establishment of a Hyksos Dynasty. This marks the beginning of the Second Intermediate Period, a time of turmoil and disunity that lasted for some 214 years. The Hyksos of the Fifteenth Dynasty ruled from their capital at Avaris in the eastern delta, maintaining control over the middle and northern parts of the country. At the same time, the Sixteenth Dynasty also existed in the delta and Middle Egypt, but it may have been subservient to the Hyksos. More independence was exerted in the south by a third contemporaneous power, the Theban Seventeenth Dynasty, which ruled over the territory between Elephantine and Abydos. The Theban ruler Kamose, who reigned about 1576-1570 B.C.E., battled the Hyksos successfully, but it was his brother, Ahmose I, who finally subdued them, reuniting Egypt.

The New Kingdom

With the unification of Egypt and the founding of the Eighteenth Dynasty by Ahmose I, the New Kingdom (1570-1070 B.C.E.) began. Ahmose reestablished the borders, goals, and bureaucracy of the Middle Kingdom and revived its land-reclamation program. He maintained the balance of power between the nomarchs and himself with the support of the military, who were accordingly rewarded. The importance of women in the New Kingdom is illustrated by the high titles and position of the royal wives and mothers.

Once Amenhotep I, who reigned 1551-1524 B.C.E., had full control over his administration – he was co-regent for five years – he began to extend Egypt's boundaries in Nubia and Palestine. A major builder at Karnak, Amenhotep, unlike his predecessors, separated his tomb from his mortuary temple; he began the custom of hiding his final resting place. Thutmose I continued the advances of the new Imperial Age and emphasized the preeminence of the god Amon. His tomb was the first in the Valley of the Kings. Thutmose II, his son by a minor wife, succeeded him, marrying the royal princess Hatshepsut to strengthen his claim to the throne. When he died in 1504 B.C.E., his heir, Thutmose III, was still a child, and so Hatshepsut governed as a regent. Within a year, she had herself crowned pharaoh, and then mother and son ruled jointly. When Thutmose III achieved sole rule upon Hatshepsut's death in 1483 B.C.E., he reconquered Syria and Palestine, which had broken away under joint rule, and then continued to expand his empire. His annals in the temple at Karnak chronicle many of his campaigns. Nearly 20 years after Hatshepsut's death, he ordered the obliteration of her name and images. Amenhotep II, who reigned 1453-1419 B.C.E., and Thutmose IV tried to maintain the Asian conquests in the face of growing threats from the Mitanni and Hittite states of western Asia, but they found it necessary to use negotiations as well as force.

Amenhotep III ruled peacefully for nearly four decades, 1386-1349 B.C.E., and art and architecture flourished during his reign. He maintained the balance of power among Egypt's neighbors by diplomacy. His son and successor, Akhenaton (Amenhotep IV), was a religious reformer who fought the power of the Amon priesthood. Akhenaton abandoned Thebes for a new capital, Akhetaton, which was built in honor of Aton, the disk of the sun on which his monotheistic religion centered. The religious revolution was abandoned toward the end of his reign, however, and his son-in-law, Tutankhamen, returned the capital to Thebes. Tutankhamen is known today chiefly for his richly furnished tomb, which was found nearly intact in the Valley of the Kings by the British archaeologists Howard Carter and Lord Carnarvon in 1922. The Eighteenth Dynasty ended with Horemheb, who reigned 1321-1293 B.C.E.

The founder of the Nineteenth Dynasty, Ramses I, who reigned 1293-1291 B.C.E., had served his predecessor as vizier and commander of the army. Reigning only two years, he was succeeded by his son, Seti I, who reigned 1291-1279 B.C.E.; he led campaigns against Syria, Palestine, the Libyans, and the Hittites. Seti built a sanctuary at Abydos. Like his father, he favored the delta capital of Pi-Ramesse (now Qantir). One of his sons, Ramses II, succeeded him and reigned for nearly 67 years. He was responsible for much construction at Luxor and Karnak, and he built the Ramesseum (his funerary temple at Thebes), the rock-cut temples at Abu Simbel, and sanctuaries at Abydos and Memphis. After campaigns against the Hittites, Ramses made a treaty with them and married a Hittite princess. His son Merneptah, who reigned from 1212 to 1202 B.C.E., defeated the Sea Peoples, invaders from the Aegean who swept the Middle East in the thirteenth century B.C.E., and records tell of his desolating Israel. Later rulers had to contend with constant uprisings by subject peoples of the empire.

The second ruler of the Twentieth Dynasty, Ramses III, had his military victories depicted on the walls of his mortuary complex at Medinet Habu, near Thebes. After his death the New Kingdom declined, chiefly because of the rising power of the priesthood of Amon and the army. One high priest and military commander even had himself depicted in royal regalia.

Third Intermediate Period

The Twenty-first through the Twenty-fourth dynasties are known as the Third Intermediate Period. Kings ruling from Tanis, in the north, vied with a line of high priests, to whom they appear to have been related, from Thebes, in the south. The rulers of the Twenty-first Dynasty may have been partially Libyan in ancestry, and the Twenty-second Dynasty began with Libyan chieftains as kings. As the Libyans' rule deteriorated, several rivals rose to challenge them. In fact the next two dynasties, the Twenty-third and Twenty-fourth, were contemporaneous with part of the Twenty-second Dynasty, just as the Twenty-fifth (Kushite) Dynasty effectively controlled much of Egypt during the latter years of the Twenty-second and the Twenty-fourth dynasties.

Late Period

The Twenty-fifth through the Thirty-first dynasties ruled Egypt during the time that has come to be known as the Late Period. The Kushites ruled from about 767 B.C.E. until they were ousted by the Assyrians (from present-day Iraq) in 671 B.C.E. Egyptian independence was reestablished early in the Twenty-sixth Dynasty by Psamtik I. A resurgence of cultural achievement, reminiscent of earlier epochs, reached its height in the Twenty-sixth Dynasty. When the last Egyptian king was defeated by Cambyses II in 525 B.C.E., the country entered a period of Persian domination under the Twenty-seventh Dynasty. Egypt reasserted its independence under the Twenty-eighth and Twenty-ninth dynasties, but the Thirtieth Dynasty was the last one of Egyptian rulers. The Thirty-first Dynasty, which is not listed in Manetho's chronology, represented the second Persian domination.

The Hellenistic and Roman Periods

The occupation of Egypt by the forces of Alexander the Great in 332 B.C.E. brought an end to Persian rule. Alexander, who came from Macedonia in present-day Greece, appointed Cleomenes of Naucratis, a Greek resident in Egypt, and his Macedonian general, known later as Ptolemy I, to govern the country. Although two Egyptian governors were named as well, power was clearly in the hands of Ptolemy, who in a few years took absolute control of the country.

Rivalries with other generals, who carved out sections of Alexander's empire after his death in 323 B.C.E., occupied much of Ptolemy's time, but in 305 B.C.E. he assumed the royal title and founded the Ptolemaic Dynasty (*see* Alexandria and Grecian Africa: An Interpretation). Ptolemaic Egypt was one of the great powers of the Hellenistic world, and at various times it extended its rule over parts of Syria, Asia Minor (present-day Turkey), Cyprus, Libya, Phoenicia, and other lands.

Partly because indigenous Egyptian rulers had a reduced role in affairs of state during the Ptolemaic regime, they periodically demonstrated their dissatisfaction by open revolts, all of which were, however, quickly suppressed. In the reign of Ptolemy VI, Egypt became a protectorate under Antiochus IV of Syria, who successfully invaded the country in 169 B.C.E. The Romans, however, forced Antiochus to give up the country, which was then divided between Ptolemy VI and his younger brother, Ptolemy VIII; the latter took full control upon the death of his brother in 145 B.C.E. The succeeding Ptolemies preserved the wealth and status of Egypt while continually losing territory to the Romans (*see* Roman Africa: An Interpretation). Cleopatra was the last great ruler of the Ptolemaic line. In an attempt to maintain Egyptian power she aligned herself with Julius Caesar and, later, Mark Antony, but these moves only postponed the end. After her forces were defeated by Roman legions under Octavian (later Emperor Augustus), Cleopatra committed suicide in 30 B.C.E.

For nearly seven centuries after the death of Cleopatra, the Romans controlled Egypt (except for a short time in the third century C.E., when it came under the power of Queen Zenobia of Palmyra, in present-day Syria). The Romans treated Egypt as a valuable source of wealth and profit and were dependent on its supply of grain to feed their multitudes. Roman Egypt was governed by a prefect, whose duties as commander of the army and official judge were similar to those of the pharaohs of the past. The office, therefore, was one with which the native population was familiar. Because of the immense power of the prefects, however, their functions were eventually divided under Emperor Justinian, who in the sixth century C.E. put the army under a separate commander, directly responsible to him.

Egypt in the Roman period was relatively peaceful; its southern boundary at Aswan was only rarely attacked by the Ethiopians (*see* Ethiopia). Egypt's population had come under the influence of Greek culture under the Ptolemies, and it included large minorities of Greeks and Jews, as well as other peoples from Asia Minor. The mixture of the cultures did not lead to a homogeneous society, and civil strife was frequent. In 212 C.E., however, Emperor Caracalla granted the entire population citizenship in the Roman Empire.

Alexandria, the port city on the Mediterranean founded by Alexander the Great, remained the capital as it had been under the Ptolemies. One of the great metropolises of the Roman Empire, it was the center of a thriving commerce between India and Arabia and the Mediterranean countries. It was the home of the great Alexandrian library and museum and had a population of some 300,000 (excluding slaves).

Egypt became an economic mainstay of the Roman Empire not only because of its annual harvest of grain but also for its glass, metal, and other manufactured products. In addition, the Indian Ocean trade brought in spices, perfumes, precious stones, and rare metals from the Red Sea ports. Once part of the empire, Egypt was subject to a variety of taxes as well.

In order to control the people and placate the powerful priesthood, the Roman emperors protected the ancient religion, completed or embellished temples begun under the Ptolemies, and had their own names inscribed on them as pharaohs; the cartouches of several can be found at Isna, Kawn Umbu, Dandara, and Philae. The Egyptian cults of Isis and Serapis spread throughout the ancient world. Egypt was also an important center of early Christendom and the first one of Christian monasticism (*see* Christianity, African: An Overview). Its Coptic or Monophysite Church separated from mainstream Christianity in the fifth century.

During the seventh century the power of the Eastern Roman (Byzantine) Empire was challenged by the Sassanids of Persia, who invaded Egypt in 616. Byzantine forces expelled them again in 628, but soon after, in 641, the country fell to the Arabs, who brought with them a new religion, Islam (*see* Islam and Tradition: An Interpretation), and began a new chapter of Egyptian history (*see* Egypt).

See Also

Thebes, Egypt; Alexandria, Egypt.

Africa

Egyptian Mythology, specifically, the religion of ancient Egypt.

The religious beliefs of the ancient Egyptians were the dominating influence in the development of their culture, although a true religion, in the sense of a unified theological system, never existed among them. The Egyptian faith was based on an unorganized collection of ancient myths, nature worship, and innumerable deities. In the most influential and famous of these myths a divine hierarchy is developed and the creation of the earth is explained.

Creation

According to the Egyptian account of creation, only the ocean existed at first. Then Ra, the sun, came out of an egg (a flower, in some versions) that appeared on the surface of the water. Ra brought forth four children, the gods Shu and Geb and the goddesses Tefnut and Nut. Shu and Tefnut became the atmosphere. They stood on Geb, who became the earth, and raised up Nut, who became the sky. Ra ruled over all. Geb and Nut later had two sons, Set and Osiris, and two daughters, Isis and Nephthys. Osiris succeeded Ra as king of the earth, helped by Isis, his sister-wife. Set, however, hated his brother and killed him. Isis then embalmed her husband's body with the help of the god Anubis, who thus became the god of embalming. The powerful charms of Isis resurrected Osiris, who became king of the netherworld, the land of the dead. Horus, who was the son of Osiris and Isis, later defeated Set in a great battle and became king of the earth.

Local Gods

From this myth of creation came the conception of the ennead, a group of nine divinities, and the triad, consisting of a divine father, mother, and son. Every local temple in Egypt possessed its own ennead and triad. The greatest ennead was that of Ra and his children and grandchildren. This group was worshiped at Heliopolis, the center of sun worship. The origin of the local deities is obscure; some of them were taken over from foreign religions, and some were originally the animal gods of prehistoric Africa. Gradually, they were all fused into a complicated religious structure, although comparatively few local divinities became important throughout Egypt. In addition to those already named, the important divinities included the gods Amon, Thoth, Ptah, Khnemu, and Hapi, and the goddesses Hathor, Mut, Neit, and Sekhet. Their importance increased with the political ascendancy of the localities where they were worshiped. For example, the ennead of Memphis was headed by a triad composed of the father Ptah, the mother Sekhet, and the son Imhotep. Therefore, during the Memphite dynasties, Ptah became one of the greatest gods in Egypt. Similarly, when the Theban dynasties ruled Egypt, the ennead of Thebes was given the most importance, headed by the father Amon, the mother Mut, and the son Khonsu. As the religion became more involved, true deities were sometimes confused with human beings who had been glorified after death. Thus, Imhotep, who originally was the chief minister of the Third Dynasty ruler Zoser, was later regarded as a demigod. During the Fifth Dynasty the pharaohs began to claim divine ancestry and from that time on were worshiped as sons of Ra. Minor gods, some merely demons, were also given places in local divine hierarchies.

Iconography

The Egyptian gods were represented with human torsos and human or animal heads. Sometimes the animal or bird expressed the characteristics of the god. Ra, for example, had the head of a hawk, and the hawk was sacred to him because of its swift flight across the sky; Hathor, the goddess of love and laughter, was given the head of a cow, which was sacred to her; Anubis was given the head of a jackal because these animals ravaged the desert graves in ancient times; Mut was vulture-headed and Thoth was ibis-headed; and Ptah was given a human head, although he was occasionally represented as a bull, called Apis. Because of the gods to which they were attached, the sacred animals were venerated, but they were never worshiped until the decadent Twenty-sixth Dynasty. The gods were also represented by symbols, such as the sun disk and hawk wings that were worn on the headdress of the pharaoh.

Sun Worship

The only important god who was worshiped with consistency was Ra, chief of cosmic deities, from whom early Egyptian kings claimed descent. Beginning with the Middle Kingdom (2134-1668 B.C.E.), Ra worship acquired the status of a state religion, and the god was gradually fused with Amon during the Theban dynasties, becoming the supreme god Amon-Ra. During the Eighteenth Dynasty the pharaoh Amenhotep III renamed the sun god Aton, an ancient term for the physical solar force. Amenhotep's son and successor, Amenhotep IV, instituted a revolution in Egyptian religion by proclaiming Aton the true and only god. He changed his own name to Akhenaton, meaning "Aton is satisfied." This first great monotheist was so iconoclastic that he had the plural word *gods* deleted from monuments, and he relentlessly persecuted the priests of Amon. Akhenaton's sun religion failed to survive, although it exerted a great influence on the art and thinking of his time. Egypt returned to the ancient, labyrinthine religion of polytheism after Akhenaton's death.

Burial Ritual

Burying the dead was of religious concern in Egypt, and Egyptian funerary rituals and equipment eventually became the most elaborate the world has ever known. The Egyptians believed that the vital life force was composed of several psychical elements, of which the most important was the ka. The ka, a duplicate of the body, accompanied the body throughout life and, after death, departed from the body to take its place in the kingdom of the dead. The ka, however, could not exist without the body; every effort had to be made, therefore, to preserve the corpse. Bodies were embalmed and mummified according to a traditional method supposedly begun by Isis, who mummified her husband Osiris. In addition, wood or stone replicas of the body were put into the tomb in the event that the mummy was destroyed. The greater the number of statue-duplicates in his or her tomb, the more chances the dead person had of resurrection. As a final protection, exceedingly elaborate tombs were erected to protect the corpse and its equipment.

After leaving the tomb, the souls of the dead supposedly were beset by innumerable dangers, and the tombs were therefore furnished with a copy of the BOOK OF THE DEAD. Part of this book, a guide to the world of the dead, consists of charms designed to overcome these dangers. After arriving in the kingdom of the dead, the ka was judged by Osiris, the king of the dead, and 42 demon assistants. The Book of the Dead also contains instructions for proper conduct before these judges. If the judges decided the deceased had been a sinner, the ka was condemned to hunger and thirst or to be torn to pieces by horrible executioners. If the decision was favorable, the ka went to the heavenly realm of the fields of Yaru, where grain grew 3.7 m (12 ft) high and existence was a glorified version of life on earth. All the necessities for this paradisiacal existence, from furniture to reading matter, were, therefore, put into the tombs. As a payment for the afterlife and his benevolent protection, Osiris required the dead to perform tasks for him, such as working in the grain fields. Even this duty could, however, be obviated by placing small statuettes, called ushabtis, into the tomb to serve as substitutes for the deceased.

See Also
Thebes, Egypt.

Ejagham. Please see EKOI

Africa

Ekiti, ethnic group of NIGERIA.

The Ekiti primarily inhabit Ondo State and Kwara State in western Nigeria. They speak YORUBA, a Niger-Congo language, and are one of the Yoruba peoples. Approximately 1 million people consider themselves Ekiti.

See Also
Languages, African: An Overview.

Africa

Ekoi, ethnic group of western CAMEROON and eastern NIGERIA that is known for its unique written script.

Originally hunters and warriors who migrated from the north, today most Ekoi are either farmers, growing yams and palms, or urban workers, especially in Nigeria's Cross River State. Ekoi society has historically been politically decentralized, with councils of elders governing village affairs. The men's Leopard Society, the *Ngbe* or *Ekpe*, also plays a judicial role, while priestesses of the women's Numm Association oversee certain kinds of domestic relations.

Historians believe that the Ekoi invented *Nsibidi*, a complex writing system based on signs and pictograms, around the turn of the century. The term Nsibidi also referred to a secret society of executioners, and the Ngbe's use of the Nsibidi script reinforced the Leopard Society's judicial authority. The script and its symbolic power, along with Ekoi art and dance, all reached the Americas during the TRANSATLANTIC SLAVE TRADE. They appear in CUBA, and the Nsibidi scriptis believed to have influenced the writings of runaway slaves in GUYANA and SURINAME.

Eric Young

Africa

Ekonda, ethnic group of the DEMOCRATIC REPUBLIC OF THE CONGO.

The Ekonda primarily inhabit the Equateur Province of western Congo, also known as Congo-Kinshasa. They speak a Bantu language and belong to the Mongo cutural and linguistic group. Approximately 300,000 people consider themselves Ekonda.

See Also
Bantu: Dispersion and Settlement.

Africa

Ekwensi, Cyprian

(b. Sept. 26, 1921, Minna, Nigeria), Nigerian novelist, short-story writer, and children's author who has portrayed the moral and material problems besetting rural West Africans as they migrate to the city. A prolific and popular writer, he owes his great success to his ability to write realistically about current issues affecting ordinary people.

Born Cyprian Duaka Odiatu Ekwensi in Minna, Nigeria, he began his secondary education at Government College in Ibadan and completed it at Achimota College in present-day GHANA (then the Gold Coast) in 1943. In the early 1950s he studied pharmacy at the Chelsea School of Pharmacy in London, England. While working at various jobs – forestry official, teacher, journalist, and broadcasting executive – Ekwensi pursued his writing career.He got his start as a writer by reading his work on a West African radio proram. His first published success came with the novella *When Love Whispers* (1948). *People of the City* (1954), a collection of short stories tied together almost as a novel, chronicles the frantic pace of life in modern Lagos, Nigeria's commercial capital. The book introduced the critical view of urban existence that won Ekwensi national as well as international attention.

From 1957 to 1961 Ekwensi was head of features at the Nigerian Broadcasting Company, and from 1961 to 1967 he was federal director of Information Services. During this period he wrote his most successful novel, *Jagua Nana* (1961), the story of a vibrant middle-aged prostitute who moves between the corrupt, pleasure-seeking life of the city and the pastoral life of her rural origins. He continued exploring the contrast between the appeal of city life and its corruption in his collection *Lokotown and Other Stories* (1966). During the Nigerian Civil War (1967-1970) Ekwensi was director of the Broadcasting Corporation of Biafra, and in 1968 he won the Dag Hammarskjöld International Prize for Literary Merit.

After the war Ekwensi continued his career as a writer, reflecting on the war and its aftermath in the novels *Survive the Peace* (1976) and *Divided We Stand* (1980). In 1986 he published a sequel to *Jagua Nana* called *Jagua Nana's Daughter*. His children's books include *The Passport of Mallam Ilia* (1960), *The Drummer Boy* (1960), and *Juju Rock* (1966).

SEE ALSO

Ibadan, Nigeria; Lagos, Nigeria; Nigeria.

North America

Elaine, Arkansas, Race Riot of 1919,

a riot by white mobs that resulted in the deaths of 200 blacks and in the convictions of black union members. In a highly unusual step a federal court intervened against a racially biased Southern court and overturned the convictions.

In the summer of 1919 black sharecroppers and tenant farmers in Elaine, Arkansas, were angered by suspicions that they were being cheated by wealthy white landowners. Whites were accused of deliberately suppressing wages and undervaluing the price of cotton produced on black farms. A group of black farmers established the Progressive Farmers and Householders Union, and hired a white attorney to negotiate with white landowners for higher wages and better cotton prices.

On September 30 a group of white officials from the Missouri-Pacific Railroad set out to disrupt union activities by firing upon a group of blacks attending a union meeting. Union members returned fire, killing two whites. Word of the gunfight spread quickly, and soon hundreds of armed whites arrived in Elaine bent on revenge. The white mobs burned black homes and businesses. In response to the mayhem, federal troops targeted blacks who were trying to protect their possessions and defend their lives. Hundreds of blacks were arrested and many were forcibly held in the basements of the city's public schools.

Two hundred African Americans were killed in the riot and 67 African Americans were indicted for inciting violence. A white mob gathered outside the courthouse as 12 black union members were convicted and sentenced to die. In 1921 the NATIONAL ASSOCIATION FOR THE ADVANCEMENT OF COLORED PEOPLE (NAACP) persuaded the Arkansas Supreme Court to reverse six of those convictions. The NAACP appealed the six remaining convictions to the U.S. Supreme Court; in 1923 the Court ruled that the Arkansas convictions had violated federal due process law. In January 1925 the remaining black union members were released, marking one of the first times that a federal court had intervened to reverse a racially biased Southern court.

Alonford James Robinson, Jr.

SEE ALSO

Labor Unions in the United States.

Africa

Eland,

the world's largest ANTELOPE, found in small populations throughout woodland areas of sub-Saharan Africa.

Elands belong to the family Bovidae. Scientists have identified two eland species, the common eland, classified as *Taurotragus oryx*, and the derby eland, classified as *Taurotragus derbianus*. The common eland has a fawn-colored coat, and it develops a broad, deep-fringed dewlap, a flap of skin that hangs from the throat. The derby eland of southern Africa attains a height of about 1.8 m (about 6 feet) at the shoulder. Both species possess strong horns that spiral straight upward. They use their horns either in food gathering or in competition with other elands. Horns can grow to about 1.2 m (about 4 feet) in large males; in females the horns are shorter and more slender. Male and female elands generally live in separate, small herds, except during mating season, when they group in herds containing hundreds of each sex.

Elands can live for more than 20 years in captivity, although life expectancy in the wild is typically shorter. Elands are easily tamed and potentially valuable as domestic animals, because they produce milk and meat more inexpensively than cattle. In addition, the eland's grazing habits are less destructive to the environment than those of cattle. The Masaai people of East Africa, for example, have sustained Eland herds on the grasslands of the Serengeti for centuries, drawing their blood for food.

Wildlife specialists classify the common eland as "vulnerable" and the derby eland as "endangered." Both species are threatened by habitat loss and in some areas over-hunting. An estimated 12,000-15,000 derby eland remain in the wild.

Robert Fay

North America

Elaw, Zilphia

(b. 1790, Pa.; d. 1845, England), early independent itinerant preacher whose autobiography, *Memoirs*, is a crucial resource for studying women in African American Christianity.

Zilphia Elaw was born to a free family in Pennsylvania and was raised near Philadelphia. When her mother died in 1802, Elaw was forced to live with a Quaker family as a servant. She found the Quaker practice of silent worship too dry, and preferred more expressive devotion. In her *Memoirs*, the only extant source of information on her life, Elaw reports at age 14 having a vision of Jesus Christ that changed her life. She joined the METHODIST EPISCOPAL CHURCH in 1808.

Two years later she married Joseph Elaw and the couple moved to Burlington, New Jersey. Her husband had been expelled from the Methodist Church and disapproved of his wife's zeal, which nevertheless became more intense. In 1817 at a revival Elaw fell into a trance during which, she believed, God sanctified her soul. After her husband died in 1823, she dissociated herself from the Methodists and became an itinerant preacher, evangelizing through the northeastern and mid-Atlantic regions of the United States. In 1828, at great risk, she preached to blacks and whites in the slave states of Maryland and Virginia. In western Pennsylvania she worked with JARENA LEE, the early African American female evangelist.

Independent of a religous denomination, Elaw relied exclusively on her inner prophetic voice. Her sermons often denounced slavery and racism. In 1840 Elaw felt that God had commissioned her to preach in England, where she reportedly delivered over 1000 sermons.

See Also
Slavery in the United States; Black Church, The.

North America

Elder, Robert Lee **(b. July 14, 1934, Dallas, Tex.), a professional golfer who in 1967 became only the second African American to qualify and play on the Professional Golfers' Association (PGA) Tour.**

Born Robert Lee Elder, Lee – as he is known – spent his early years in Dallas, Texas. His father, Charles, was employed as a coal truck driver in Dallas before he was killed in combat during World War II. Elder's mother, Sadie, died shortly thereafter. Lee and his seven siblings moved between homes before they finally settled with a relative in Los Angeles, California.

Elder learned to play golf as a teenager while working as a caddy at clubs throughout San Bernadino, California. Between 1959 and 1961 he served in the United States Army, where he was named captain of the golf team at Fort Lewis, Washington. When he was discharged from the army he joined the African American United Golf Association (UGA) Tour. Elder dominated the UGA, winning titles in 1963, 1964, 1966, and 1967. While on tour he met and married Rose Harper, a professional golfer in the women's division of the UGA.

In 1967 Elder became the second African American (Charlie Sifford was the first) to qualify and play for the Professional Golfers' Association (PGA) Tour. He emerged as one of the most successful golfers of the 1970s and 1980s. Among his many accomplishments, he was the first African American to be invited and to play in the South African PGA Open (1971) and the first African American to qualify for the prestigious Ryder Cup Golf team (1979). In 1984 Elder joined the Seniors PGA Tour, where he brought his tournament winnings total to more than $1 million. A heart attack in 1987 slowed him down, but he has recovered fully and continues to play on the Seniors Tour.

See Also
South Africa; World War II and African Americans.

North America

Elders, M. Joycelyn Jones **(b. August 13, 1933, Schaal, Ark.), surgeon general of the United States (1993-1994) whose outspokenness led to her dismissal.**

Jocelyn Elders was born Minnie Joycelyn Jones in a poor, remote farming village of southwestern Arkansas. Her parents, Haller and Curtis Jones, were sharecroppers, and all eight of their children – Joycelyn was the oldest – worked with them in the cotton fields. The family shared a three-room cabin with no electricity, and the children walked several miles to attend an all-black school. At age 15, Elders received a scholarship to Little Rock's Philander Smith College, also entirely black. There she saw a doctor for the first time in her life and also met Edith Jones, the first black woman to attend the University of Arkansas Medical School (UAMS). Elders later credited these experiences with inspiring her to become a doctor.

Having received her bachelor's degree in 1952 at age 19, Elders spent the better part of the next two decades ascending the rungs of the medical profession: serving first in the United States Army, where she trained as a physical therapist and qualified for assistance for medical school tuition; attending UAMS as one of only three minority students; graduating with her M.D. in 1960 and marrying Oliver Elders the same year; supervising a staff of white men as chief pediatric resident at the University of Arkansas Medical Center in 1963; earning an M.S. in biochemisty from UAMS in 1967; and serving on the UAMS faculty from 1971. Elders specialized in the research and treatment of diabetic children, establishing a reputation through her publications and practice as the state's expert in the field.

In 1987 then-governor Bill Clinton appointed her director of the Arkansas Department of Health. The first black woman to hold the position, Elders set out to extend the state's health care network to poor communities and, in particular, to reduce teenage and unwanted pregnancies. In these attempts, she angered conservatives by advocating sex education, distribution of condoms to students, and in-school informational health clinics. In less controversial matters, Elders oversaw an increase in health screenings for young children from less than 5000 a year to nearly 50,000 a year; an increase in the immunization rate of two-year-olds from one-third of children to nearly two-thirds; and moderate increases in the number of women participating in prenatal and breast-cancer screenings.

In 1993 Clinton, as U.S. president, nominated Elders for the post of U.S. surgeon general. Her support for sex education, distribution of condoms, abortion rights, and the use of marijuana for medical purposes brought her predictable, if stern, opposition from conservatives in Congress and around the country. Elders did little to ease their fears. Shortly before her confirmation hearings in the Senate, she characterized her opponents thus: "Abortion foes are part of a celibate, male-dominated church, a male-dominated legislature, and a male-dominated medical profession." Elders was nonetheless confirmed in September.

During her brief tenure she tried to increase medical services in rural and poor communities by promoting the training of nurse practioners, physician assistants, and certified nurse midwives. She also proposed increasing taxes on tobacco (a policy Clinton supported) and on alcohol (a policy Clinton did not then support). She continued to raise controversy in her public pronouncements: her continued advocacy of sex education and condom distribution prompted some conservatives to refer to her as the Condom Queen; her statement that legalizing drugs should be studied for its potential to reduce crime prompted Clinton to clarify that he did not share this position. Liberals, meanwhile, regaled her as a hero. In December 1994 she was asked whether masturbation should be encouraged as a way to discourage minors from having sex. She responded that masturbation "is part of human sexuality and a part of something that perhaps should be taught." The next day President Clinton asked for and received her resignation. Soon thereafter, Elders returned to her teaching position at the University of Arkansas Medical Center.

Africa

Elephant, **the largest living land mammal; the elephant's existence has been threatened by its diminishing habitat and the demand for the ivory from its tusks.**

Elephants are grayish brown, with thin, rough body hair, an elongated trunk, and tusks. The African elephant ranges south of the Sahara. It reaches a height of 4 m (13 ft) at the shoulder, and can weigh as much as 7000 kg (15,400 lb). African elephants have distinctive, large ears, which may reach a length of 1.5 m (about 5 ft) from top to bottom.

The Trunk

The boneless, muscular trunk, the most distinctive feature of elephants, is actually a greatly elongated upper lip and nose used to convey grasses, leaves, and water to the mouth. Elephants consume as much as 225 kg (495 lb) of forage a day in this manner and drink as much as 190 liters (50 gals) of water, drawing it through their nostrils and squirting it into the mouth. An extremely versatile organ, the trunk is also used to trumpet calls, pull down trees, rip off foliage, and draw up dust for dust bathing. It is also a highly sensitive organ, which the animals raise into the air to detect wind-borne scents. By means of fingerlike lobes on the end of the trunk and by the sucking action of the two nostrils, elephants can pick up and examine small objects.

Walking Movements

Despite their great weight, elephants walk almost noiselessly and with exceptional grace. Their columnar legs keep their bulk moving forward in smooth, rhythmic strides. A thick cushion of resilient tissue grows on the base of the foot, absorbing the shock of their weight and enabling them to walk high on the foot's hooflike toes. Elephants normally walk about 6.4 km/h (about 4 mph). When migrating, they often trek single file. They can charge at up to 40 km/h (25 mph), and, although they cannot gallop or jump over ditches, they readily take to rivers and lakes, where the water supports them and enables them to swim for long distances without tiring. Elephants commonly feed in the morning, evening, and at night, and rest during the middle of the day.

Tusks and Teeth

The tusks, which are deeply embedded in the skull, are actually enormously enlarged incisors. Record tusks of the male African elephant have measured 3.5 m (10.5 ft) long. Elephants have only four molar or grinding teeth, one to each side of the upper and lower jaws; each is a massive plate about 30 centimeters (about 12 in) long and 10 cm (4 in) wide. When worn down by the coarse vegetation that elephants eat, these teeth are replaced by larger ones that shift forward from the rear of the jaws. At about 40 years of age, the animal's final and largest molars come into position and last for about 20 years. Elephants' longevity is comparable to that of humans.

Sensory Perception

The great ears of the African elephant are probably used for ventilation and visual communication as well as for hearing. The eyesight is poor, the eyes being comparatively small and fixed on the animal's large and relatively immobile head. Observers first noted in the 1980s that elephants produce rumbling sounds with their nasal passages that are below the range of human hearing. Because such sounds travel well and because elephant hearing is better at low frequencies, the animals very likely use these sounds to communicate with one another over long distances.

Social Structure

Elephants are gregarious and keenly sensitive to one another's calls and movements. They associate in herds of 15 to 30 or more usually related members led by an old female, called a matriarch. Herds are usually made up of females, immature elephants, and mature bulls. Bulls driven from herds live alone or in bachelor herds.

Reproduction

Cow elephants commonly mate by their 15th or 16th year, usually with a bull that is able to contend with other bulls in the herd. A mating pair often separates from the herd for several weeks. After a gestation period of 21 to 22 months, usually one calf is born and is able to follow the herd within a few days. Calves are vulnerable to leopards and tigers, which are among the few nonhuman predators of elephants. The calves suckle the female's teats, which are just behind the forelegs, for nearly five years before weaning. Cows give birth to from 5 to 12 calves in a lifetime.

Status in the Wild

Elephant populations have been severely reduced in recent decades because of hunting and the expansion of cattle-grazing lands. In southern Africa, however, populations have been growing so much that they have begun to overgraze the savanna as well as damage farmers' crops. Wildlife officials in South Africa and neighboring countries have carried out periodic culls to control herd size, and have also experimented with elephant contraception.

Elephants make up the family Elephantidae in the order Proboscidea. The Indian elephant is classified as *Elephas maximus* and the African elephant as *Loxodonta africana*.

Robert Fay

See Also

Ivory Trade; Sahara Desert; Wildlife Management in Africa.

North America

Ellington, Edward Kennedy ("Duke") (b. April 29, 1899, Washington, D.C.; d. May 24, 1974, New York, N.Y.), African American jazz pianist and bandleader, and the greatest composer in the history of jazz.

For nearly half a century Duke Ellington led the premier American big band, and through his compositions and performances he brought artistic credibility to African American jazz. Ellington played the piano, but his orchestra was his true instrument. In the late 1920s he perfected an exotic style that was later termed jungle music. During the 1930s Ellington developed a lush approach to orchestration that introduced new complexity to the simplistic conventions of swing-era jazz. Throughout the 1930s and 1940s he struggled against the limitations of the three-minute 78 rpm recording and the general adherence to 12- and 32-bar song forms, in the process vastly extending the scope of jazz. Personally and politically, he preferred to avoid direct confrontation; yet he was active as far back as the early 1940s in the cause of racial equality.

Ellington took what had begun as a vernacular dance music and created larger and more artistically challenging musical forms, exemplified in his three-movement composition *Black, Brown, and Beige* (1943). Due to his fame as a bandleader, Ellington-the-pianist is often overlooked. Yet particularly during the 1960s some of his most creative playing took place in small groups and demonstrated his willingness to engage such younger musicians as tenor saxophonist John Coltrane.

Ellington's Musical Beginnings and His Move to New York City

Ellington was born to a middle-class black family in Washington, D.C., at a time when Washington was the nation's preeminent black community. He began studying piano at age seven and quickly exhibited a gift for music. He began playing professionally as a teenager in a style derived from ragtime, which had a particularly strong influence in the vicinity of Baltimore and Washington. By 1919 he had emerged as a leader of small groups that played for local parties and dances. Although ragtime pianists led most of these bands, the other musicians were mainly reading musicians who played in a sweet style and did not improvise.

In 1922 Ellington moved to New York City, which was then emerging as the nation's jazz capital. He played with various theater orchestras and with jazz-oriented bands like the one led by Elmer Snowden (1900-1973). He also made his first foray into musical theater, writing the music for an ill-fated Broadway comedy, *Chocolate Kiddies of 1924*. In 1924 he took over the Snowden band, and that six-man group became the nucleus of the Ellington Orchestra. By 1926 the group had grown to 11 members; the most important additions were cornetist Bubber Miley and trombonist "Tricky Sam" Nanton (1904-1946). Through their influence the orchestra moved away from its sweet style and embraced a bluesy and improvisational jazz.

Like many jazz pianists of the day, Ellington came under the sway of the Harlem "stride" piano style, exemplified in the playing of James P. Johnson (1894-1955) and Willie "the Lion" Smith. The stride style essentially divides the piano keyboard into three ranges. The pianist's left hand covers the two lower ranges, alternating single bass notes at the bottom with chord clusters struck higher up. The style takes its name from the characteristic, bouncing "oom-pah, oom-pah" produced by the pianist's striding left hand. The pianist's left hand thus establishes a propulsive beat and outlines the tune's harmonic structure; the right hand plays melody, adds ornamentation, and improvises solo lines. Ellington evolved from this rather florid piano style, in part, by simplifying it and by adding harmonic complexities and dissonance that at times foreshadowed the playing of bop pioneer Thelonious Monk and free-jazz pianist Cecil Taylor (b. 1929).

Ellington at the Cotton Club, 1927-1931

In the fall of 1927 the Ellington Orchestra secured a long-term gig at the Cotton Club, New York City's most prestigious nightclub, which was wired to permit "live" remote radio broadcasts that gave Ellington nationwide recognition. The demanding stint at the Cotton Club also gave him a crash course in composing and arranging. Many of his early orchestrations involved little more than transposing note for note what he composed at the piano to the instruments of the band. While at the Cotton Club he became more adventuresome in his

American composer, bandleader, and pianist Duke Ellington poses in 1931 with members of his band Nuf Said. *CORBIS/Bettmann*

harmonies and voicings, and he began to experiment with changes in tempo and meter. By 1928 his orchestra had emerged as the nation's foremost jazz ensemble, surpassing the bands of Fletcher Henderson and King Oliver.

During 1927-1928 Ellington made a series of recordings that epitomized the orchestra's first classic style. They featured the growling, plunger-muted solos of Miley and Nanton, who virtually defined the orchestra's jungle style. Miley also composed or cowrote several key songs, including the masterpieces "East St. Louis Toodle-Oo" (1926) and "Black and Tan Fantasie" (1927). These songs and Ellington's lyrical "Black Beauty" (1928) were staples in the band's repertoire for years to come.

Moving Beyond the Boundaries of Dance Music

Ellington gained further exposure during the 1930s. The orchestra was featured in RKO's popular Amos 'n' Andy film *Check and Double Check* (1930). In 1931 Ellington wrote his first extended work, "Creole Rhapsody." The Victor version of the song, recorded in June 1931, filled two sides of a 12-inch 78 rmp record and was eight and a half minutes long. In the mid-1930s Ellington wrote the score for a nine-minute musical film, *Symphony in Black* (1935), which featured a young Billie Holiday and foreshadowed *Black, Brown, and Beige*.

Devastated by the death of his mother in 1935, Ellington wrote *Reminiscing in Tempo* (1935) as his tribute to her. His most ambitious work to date, it was a unified composition that filled four album sides. None of Ellington's contemporaries in jazz had attempted such large-scale works. Among his important shorter compositions of this period were "Mood Indigo" (1930), "It Don't Mean a Thing If It Ain't Got That Swing" (1932), "Sophisticated Lady" (1933), and the haunting ballad "In a Sentimental Mood" (1935).

During the mid-1930s new swing bands – under the leadership of Count Basie, Jimmie Lunceford, and such white bandleaders as Benny Goodman and Artie Shaw – threatened to eclipse the Ellington Orchestra. Although Ellington's "In a Sentimental Mood" never became a hit, Goodman's simplified 1936 rendition did. Moreover, the personnel of the Ellington Orchestra, normally quite stable, underwent considerable turnover during the mid-1930s.

Despite these difficulties, the Ellington Orchestra had many strengths, in particular its many talented soloists. Most swing big bands got by with two or three prominent soloists. During the mid-1930s Ellington's Orchestra featured nine significant solo talents: alto saxophonist Johnny Hodges; clarinetist Barney Bigard (1906-1980); baritone saxophonist Harry Carney (1910-1974); trumpeter Cootie Williams (1910-1985); cornetist Rex Stewart (1907-1967); trombonists Nanton and Lawrence Brown (1907-1988); vocalist Ivie Anderson (1905-1949); and Ellington himself on piano. Despite setbacks, the Ellington Orchestra toured constantly during the Great Depression and made successful visits to Europe in 1933 and 1939.

The Great Ellington Band: The Early 1940s

By 1940 Ellington and his orchestra had overcome the difficulties of the mid-1930s. In 1938 Billy Strayhorn began his nearly 30-year stint as Ellington's closest collaborator; he composed such memorable works as the orchestra's longtime theme, "Take the A Train" (1941). Ellington himself had a burst of creativity during which he produced some of his most enduring compositions. He benefited from an outstanding group of musicians, including two vital new additions – tenor saxophonist Ben Webster (1909-1973) and virtuoso bassist Jimmy Blanton (1918-1942). Among the orchestra's most important recordings of this period were "Ko-Ko" (1940), "Cotton Tail" (1940), and "I Got It Bad and That Ain't Good" (1941).

In 1943 Ellington appeared at New York City's prestigious Carnegie Hall. The first African American bandleader to be so honored, he responded with the 44-minute-long *Black, Brown, and Beige: A Tone Parallel to the History of the American Negro*, a pathbreaking work in twentieth-century American music. Unfortunately, the ambitious piece broke the conventions of both jazz and classical music, satisfying neither audience. The critical response deeply disappointed Ellington; following his Carnegie Hall appearance (and an earlier run-through in Boston), he never performed the work in its entirety again.

Later Large-Scale Works and Ellington's Social Activism

Neither Ellington nor Strayhorn was dissuaded from creating other large-scale jazz suites, including the *Liberian Suite* (1947); *Harlem* (1951); the *Festival Suite* (1956); *Such Sweet Thunder* (1957), a musical tribute to Shakespeare; *Suite Thursday* (1960), which paid tribute to author John Steinbeck; and the *Far East Suite* (1966). Ellington also composed film scores for *Anatomy of a Murder* (1959) and *Paris Blues* (1961).

In 1965 Ellington broke new ground with his first *Concert of Sacred Music*, commissioned by San Francisco's Grace Episcopal Church. In the concert the Ellington Orchestra was joined by the Grace Cathedral Choir; the Herman McCoy Choir; singers Jon Hendricks (b. 1921), Esther Marrow, and Jimmy McPhail; and tap dancer Bunny Briggs. "In the Beginning, God," Ellington's opening movement, won a 1966 Grammy Award for best original jazz composition. In 1968 Ellington composed a *Second Sacred Concert*. At the time of his death he was preparing a third.

From the early 1940s Ellington was active in the emergent Civil Rights Movement, although his role has largely been overlooked. In 1941 he wrote the score for the groundbreaking musical *Jump for Joy*, which challenged the demeaning stereotypes of African Americans in Hollywood films and throughout American popular culture. *Jump for Joy* had a buoyant sense of optimism that is suggested in such numbers as "Uncle Tom's Cabin Is a Drive-In Now."

Ellington's speaking voice, like his musical one, was eloquent and complex. He disliked head-on confrontation. As Ellington biographer John Edward Hasse has observed, *Music Is My Mistress*, the composer's 1973 autobiography, contains "hardly a negative word," passing in silence over various personal conflicts and his negative encounters with Jim Crow segregation. This indirection was equally evident in his political activism. During the Carnegie Hall premiere of *Black, Brown, and Beige*, Ellington looked out on the formally attired ranks of New York's elite and declared: "[W]e find ourselves today struggling for solidarity, but just as we are about to get our teeth into it, our country is at war, [so, of course], we... find the black, brown, and beige right in there for the red, white, and blue."

Though stressing African American patriotism, Ellington – in his distinctly oblique way – voiced black aspirations for racial equality and integration.

In 1951 Ellington premiered *Harlem*, which he regarded as his most successful extended work, at a benefit concert for the National Association for the Advancement of Colored People (NAACP). Two months before the concert he wrote to President Harry S. Truman, stating that concert proceeds would "help fight for your civil rights program – to stamp out segregation, discrimination, [and] bigotry." He suggested that Truman's daughter, Margaret Truman, serve as honorary chair for the event. Ellington biographer Hasse notes that Truman or someone on his staff wrote on the letter "an emphatic 'NO!' in inch-high letters, underlined twice."

Ellington's Later Career

During the 1950s and 1960s Ellington and his orchestra led a split existence. They debuted substantial extended works in concerts and recordings, but they also endured a grueling schedule of one-night stands in which the orchestra reprised old hits with what bordered on formulaic playing. An inspiring performance at the 1956 Newport Jazz Festival helped draw the orchestra out of a creative slump. Ellington also found inspiration in a series of small-group recordings, such as *Money Jungle* (1962), featuring bassist Charles Mingus and drummer Max Roach, and *Duke Ellington and John Coltrane* (1962), a classic collaboration between two of the seminal figures in jazz.

In these years Ellington faced the loss of several long-term orchestra members, including the irreplaceable Johnny Hodges, who died in 1970. But the greatest loss was that of Billy Strayhorn, who died of throat cancer in 1967. In *And His Mother Called Him Bill* (1967), Ellington paid tribute to his long-time collaborator with a set of Strayhorn compositions; the emotional recording sessions yielded one of the orchestra's last great albums. In 1969 President Richard Nixon presented Ellington with the Medal of Freedom at a gala 70th birthday party.

Ellington gave little sign of slowing down in the early 1970s, but in 1973 he learned that he had lung cancer. Even after he was hospitalized in the spring of 1974, he continued to work on new compositions. Following his death, some 65,000 people came to view his body, and more than 10,000 turned out for his funeral. In subsequent years Ellington's reputation has continued to grow. He is rightly acclaimed as one of America's greatest composers.

James Clyde Sellman

See Also

Amos 'n' Andy; Basie, William James ("Count"); Coltrane, John William; Henderson, Fletcher Hamilton, Jr.; Lunceford, James Melvin (Jimmie); Miley, James Wesley ("Bubber"); Mingus, Charles, Jr.; Monk, Thelonious Sphere; New York, New York; Oliver, Joseph ("King"); Racial Stereotypes; Roach, Maxwell Lemuel (Max); San Francisco and Oakland, California; Smith, Willie ("the Lion"); Film, Blacks in American.

North America

Ellison, Ralph (b. March 1, 1914, Oklahoma City, Okla.; d. April 16, 1994, New York, N.Y.), African American writer; author of *Invisible Man* (1952), one of the most famous twentieth-century American novels.

The great irony of the career of Ralph Ellison, one of the most acclaimed and influential of all American novelists, may be that when he died at the age of 80, he had only published one novel. His second, on which he had been working for almost 40 years, was still unfinished. But with that extraordinary first work, *Invisible Man*, Ellison changed the standards for the American novel. As the *Norton Anthology of African American Literature* says, with *Invisible Man* Ellison simultaneously "defined the historic moment of mid-twentieth century America" and "single-handedly re[wrote] the American novel as an *African American* adventure in fiction."

Ellison was born in 1914 in Oklahoma City. His parents had migrated to Oklahoma from the South because they hoped the West might offer better opportunities for African Americans. Ellison's father, an avid reader, named his son Ralph Waldo after the nineteenth-century white American writer Ralph Waldo Emerson. His father died when Ellison was only three, and his mother worked at a variety of jobs to raise Ralph and his brother. Ellison attended segregated public schools in Oklahoma City and excelled in music. When he graduated, local officials – afraid he would try to integrate a white Oklahoma college – gave him a scholarship to Tuskegee Institute in Alabama, and he arrived there by hitching a ride on a freight train in 1933.

Ellison had been encouraged to read widely since childhood, but a sophomore English class introduced him to a new variety of authors. He was especially captivated by the way he felt T. S. Eliot's poem "The Waste Land" captured the rhythms of jazz. Ellison later said that discovery of the potential connections between music and literature was what led him to consider writing instead of music as a career. In 1936, when his scholarship ran out, he took what he thought would be a short break in New York, planning to save enough money to return in the fall. Instead, Ellison met the great writers Langston Hughes and Arna Bontemps, who in turn introduced him to novelist Richard Wright. Once he had been exposed to the black New York literary scene, he essentially remained in it, and in New York, for the rest of his life.

Ellison took a series of odd jobs to support himself and studied writers Ernest Hemingway, James Joyce, and Fyodor Dostoyevsky. In 1938 he took a position with the Federal Writers' Project collecting black folklore and oral histories through interviews with older African Americans, which provided him with stories and insights that ultimately found their way into his later writings. Meanwhile, Wright, who was already known in New York as a writer and a Communist Party activist, became Ellison's mentor. Ellison's first published work was a 1937 book review in *New Challenge*, a radical journal that Wright edited. More reviews and essays in similar journals followed over the next few years. Ellison's first short stories, "Slick Gonna Learn" (1939) and "The Birthmark" (1940), explored the political and social constraints on black life in a narrative mode similar to the novel Wright was working on, *Native Son* (1940). When even Wright criticized Ellison's style for being too derivative of his own, their relationship deteriorated. Ellison gradually rejected Wright's aesthetics and his politics, and matured into a style that was indisputably his own.

In 1940 and 1941 Ellison published two essays that praised the use of African American folklore in African American fiction. Black folklore, language, and customs figured prominently in several of his subsequent stories, including "Flying Home" (1944), which most closely prefigured *Invisible Man.* "Flying Home" was initially meant to be part of a novel about a black American World War II pilot captured by the Nazis. But in 1945, while still at work on that project, Ellison wrote a single sentence on a piece of paper: "I am an invisible man." He later recalled that at the time, he had no idea what that line meant, but he became consumed by trying to imagine what kind of character would say such a thing. Over the next seven years the line turned into a story of its own, and became the opening sentence of *Invisible Man.*

Invisible Man follows its unnamed black protagonist from South to North, from youth to adulthood, and from innocence and naiveté to experience and awareness. At the novel's beginning, the protagonist is just about to graduate from high school with a scholarship to attend a prestigious Southern black college. He is ambitious and optimistic that the world will be full of promise for a smart black boy who works hard. But shortly before leaving home he has a dream in which his dead grandfather appears to him and, in a parody of a high school graduation, presents him an engraved plaque that reads "To Whom It May Concern: Keep This Nigger Boy Running."

The protagonist is kept running for the rest of the novel – by the patronizing white trustees and accommodationist black founder of his college; by the white men he hopes will hire him when he is forced to leave school and seek work in New York; by the boss at the paint factory where he does find a job; and by the leaders of the Brotherhood, an organization much like the Communist Party, who recruit and train him to be a leader but reject him when he becomes more powerful than they would like. At the novel's end, the protagonist finally realizes that he has suffered because he has allowed his identity to be defined by others who do not really know him, who see him as indistinguishable from other black people, who do not value his individuality. He has been defined by people to whom he is invisible.

Invisible Man was immediately celebrated not only as a key exploration of the contemporary African American psyche, but also for its very modern depiction of the fragmentation, invisibility, and lack of self-knowledge many people experienced in the larger American society. In 1965 a poll of 200 critics called *Invisible Man* "the most distinguished American novel written since World War II." Ellison followed the book with two successful collections of his essays, interviews, and speeches on the African American experience, *Shadow and Act* (1964) and *Going to the Territory* (1987). In the late 1950s he began work on his much-awaited second novel.

During the 1960s many black writers were critical of Ellison's belief that African Americans are fundamentally American, shaped by the United States more than by Africa. But within several years, public opinion had swayed to affirm Ellison's point of view, and readers once again held high hopes for the next novel, which Ellison hinted would be a multivolume magnum opus. He apparently kept going even after a fire at his summer home destroyed a year's worth of manuscript, but he died of cancer in 1994 without having completed it. Several of Ellison's unpublished short stories were posthumously collected along with his earlier stories in the 1996 volume *Flying Home.* In 1999 Random House published *Juneteenth*, a 400-page novel that Ellison's literary executor crafted from the thousands of pages Ellison left when he died.

In his creation of a new style that embraced black folk tradition and emphasized the importance of self-knowledge and self-awareness for African Americans, Ellison broke new ground for the generation of black authors who followed him. And his sharp observations on the problem of black "invisibility" in white culture gave new insights on the American racial scene to a generation of black and white readers.

Lisa Clayton Robinson

See Also

World War II and African Americans; Literature, African American; New York, New York; Tuskegee University; Communist Party USA, African Americans and the.

Africa

Eloyi (also known as the Elowi, Epe, Aho, Eloyi, Afu, and Afao), ethnic group of Nigeria.

The Eloyi inhabit the Benue, Plateau, and Kwara States of Nigeria. They speak a Niger-Congo language and are related to the larger Idoma cultural and linguistic group. Approximately 100,000 people identify themselves as Eloyi.

See Also

Languages, African: An Overview.

Latin America and the Caribbean

El Salvador, a country in Central America.

Africa

Embu, ethnic group of Kenya.

The Embu primarily inhabit the Eastern Province of Kenya. They speak a Bantu language and are closely related to the Kikuyu people. Approximately 300,000 people consider themselves Embu.

See Also

Bantu: Dispersion and Settlement.

Africa

Emecheta, Buchi (b. July 21, 1944, Yaba, Nigeria), Nigerian writer whose novels have focused on the lives of women.

Florence Onye Buchi Emecheta was born near the city of Lagos, Nigeria. At a young age, she lost both her mother and her father, who was killed while serving the British army in Burma. After completing a degree at the Methodist girls' high school in Lagos, she married Sylvester Onwordi at age 16. The couple moved to London, and during the next six years, Emecheta bore five children while supporting the family financially. She began to write during this time, but, as she later said in an interview, "The first book I wrote, my husband burnt, and then I found I couldn't write with him around."

Emecheta left her husband in 1966, supporting herself for the next few years by working at the library in the British Museum. She enrolled at the University of London, where she received a sociology degree in 1974. In her first literary works she represented her own experiences of poverty, racism, and motherhood, "the cumulative oppression resulting from being alien, black and female," as she described it. These reflective, semifictional accounts were first published in *New Statesman* and later collected into her first novel *In the Ditch* (1972). She followed this with *Second-Class Citizen* (1974), which drew on the earlier years of her life and her experience of immigration. Both *In the Ditch* and *Second-Class Citizen* dealt with the socioeconomic problems of Africans in both Africa and the diaspora, and particularly highlighted the multiple oppressions of women.

Emecheta's next novel, *The Bride Price* (1976), was set in Nigeria in the early 1950s. She told the story of a young Ibo woman who defies tradition by running away with a man descended from a slave caste. The novel portrays a woman constrained by Ibo social hierarchies and beliefs, including the belief that if the bride price is not paid, the bride will die in childbirth. The story ends without resolution: Emecheta leaves the reader to imagine whether the traditional prophecy is fulfilled. In *The Slave Girl* (1977), set in early twentieth-century Nigeria, a young girl is forced into domestic slavery by her brother, then bought from her master by a suitor.

Emecheta uses the narrative to illustrate a parallel between slavery and marriage.

Emecheta published her best-known work, *The Joys of Motherhood*, in 1979. This story, depicting the migrant rural Ibo community in Lagos, spans the time in Nigeria between the 1930s and independence in 1960. Emecheta focuses on the lives of women who can achieve status only through motherhood – specifically, their ability to bear sons.

Emecheta's early portrayals of oppressive gender relations created a great deal of controversy, especially among her African readership. Some critics accused her of portraying African men unfairly. Others, especially in the West, held her up as one of Africa's most eloquent feminists. Yet Emecheta herself has consistently rejected the title "feminist." In an interview, she clarified her position: "I do believe in the African kind of feminism. They call it WOMANISM, because, you see, you Europeans don't worry about water, you don't worry about schooling, you are so well off. Now, I buy land, and I say, 'OK, I can't build on it, I have no money, so I give it to some women to start planting.' That is my brand of feminism."

In her later novels, Emecheta addressed a range of sociopolitical issues. *Destination Biafra* (1982) was, in the words of Emecheta, a novel that "needed to be written" about the civil war that wracked Nigeria from 1967 to 1970. *Double Yoke* (1982) dealt with the moral deterioration of postcolonial Nigeria. The *Rape of Shavi* (1983), an experimental departure from Emecheta's realist style, was a slightly disguised tale of colonization. Emecheta returned to the theme of the immigrant experience with the novel *Gwendolen* (1989) (published in the United States as *The Family*), about a Caribbean immigrant girl who experiences rape and incest.

Throughout much of her writing career, Emecheta has taught at various universities. In addition, she founded the publishing company Ogwugwu Afor, which specializes in African literature. She has also published an autobiography, two children's books, and several books for young adults, amassing an impressive total of 16 works published in 14 years.

Marian Aguiar

SEE ALSO

Lagos, Nigeria; Women Writers in English-Speaking Africa.

Latin America and the Caribbean

Engenho Velho, **one of the oldest *terreiros*, or temples, of the Afro-Brazilian religion of CANDOMBLÉ. Located in the northeastern state of Bahia, it is thought to have been established by three freed African women in the 1830s and may have existed long before then.**

Africa

Environmental Movements in Africa, **Africa-based political and social movements that mobilize around environmental threats to health and livelihood.**

International conservation groups have focused worldwide attention on the threats to Africa's wildlife and forests. These issues, however, are not necessarily the primary concerns of most environmental movements in Africa itself. Rather, these movements have tended to mobilize around threats to those local or regional natural resources that are considered crucial to health and livelihood. In some regions wildlife is, in fact, considered a vital natural resource by local people, but elsewhere the more pressing issue is the protection of land and water supplies.

Environmental movements in Africa also do not necessarily share the environmental priorities of national governments. To accommodate donor nations and to encourage wildlife tourism, for example, some governments in the wildlife-rich regions of East and southern Africa have displaced farming and pastoral communities to create large tracts of land for wildlife reserves. In addition, governments across the continent have often proven willing to sacrifice environmental well-being to attract foreign investment, generate economic growth, and achieve the broader but more ambiguous goal of development. Africa's environmental movements have many different goals, but nearly all are demanding that citizens – particularly citizens whose voices have traditionally been marginalized – be granted greater control over the uses of national, regional, and local resources. In that sense, environmental movements in Africa are invariably political. These points are illustrated by the following three cases.

MOVEMENT FOR THE SURVIVAL OF THE OGONI PEOPLE

The Ogoni people's struggle against pollution and resource destruction by the oil industry in their homeland in southeastern NIGERIA shows how environmental concerns coincide with struggles for self-determination. In 1958, when Nigeria was still a British colony, Royal Dutch Shell Oil discovered large deposits of petroleum and natural gas in Ogoniland, resources that Shell and the British government – and later, the Nigerian government – sought to exploit. Oil exports have since become vital to the Nigerian economy; revenue from oil exports has brought in approximately $30 billion since 1958, and in recent years accounted for approximately 95 percent of Nigeria's export income.

But the oil industry has brought severe ecological problems to Ogoniland, an area of 650 sq km (about 403 sq mi) on the NIGER RIVER delta. Although densely populated, the area's rich land and waterways have traditionally supported the Ogonis' farming and fishing economy. More recently, however, Ogoniland has been nicknamed the Drilling Fields, and some environmental organizations estimate that between 1976 and 1991 the area was subjected to more than 3000 oil spills, averaging about 700 barrels each. In addition to spills, gas flares burn 24 hours a day, producing incessant noise and causing respiratory problems in nearby Ogoni villages. Acid rain has left farm lands barren; drinking water has become polluted; and fish have disappeared from nearby rivers.

Moreover, Ogoniland has received little of the wealth generated by the oil industry. For years the area had no paved roads, plumbing, or electricity, and schools and health facilities were inadequate. Both economic and environmental injustices, therefore, motivated the founding of the Movement for the Survival of the Ogoni People (MOSOP) in 1990. The group's leaders – among them writer and activist Ken Saro-Wiwa – tied Ogoniland environmental destruction directly to the Ogonis' lack of political voice in a country where they number only about half a million among more than 100 million, and where military regimes have historically done little to protect the rights of minority ethnic groups.

Soon after its founding, MOSOP published the Ogoni Bill of Rights, which demanded rights not only to environmental protection and "a fair proportion" of local resources, but also to religious freedom, the development of Ogoni culture, and above all the political autonomy of the Ogoni people, as "a separate and distinct ethnic nationality" within the Federal Republic of Nigeria. MOSOP's goals clearly went beyond environmental cleanup.

Some 300,000 Ogonis – 60 percent of their total population – gathered on January 4, 1993, in a massive peaceful demonstration protesting Shell's activities and the resulting degradation. Shell's complaints about the demonstration drew a decisive response from the Nigerian government, which called in the military three months later to break up a protest against construction of a new pipeline in Ogoniland. According to a 1997 MOSOP account, an estimated 2000 Ogoni men, women, and children were killed by the Nigerian military and many more were arrested. Ken Saro-Wiwa (along with eight other MOSOP activists) was charged with murder and convicted in what was widely viewed as a suspect procedure. His hanging in November 1995 provoked international condemnation, but the Nigerian government had never recognized the Ogoni claims as legitimate. Although Shell ceased its operations in Ogoniland in 1993 and sought to placate the Ogoni by building schools, hospitals, and roads in the region, it refused to assume responsibility for environmental cleanup (*see* ENVIRONMENTAL RACISM: AN INTERPRETATION).

THE GREEN BELT MOVEMENT

Like many environmental efforts in Africa, the Ogoni movement is simultaneously a struggle for minority rights. With a slightly different emphasis, Kenya's Green Belt Movement has used tree-planting campaigns to empower women and to draw connections between environmental and economic impoverishment (*see* FEMINISM IN AFRICA: AN INTERPRETATION). Kenyan biologist WANGARI MAATHAI founded the Green Belt Movement in 1977, at a time when deforestation was contributing to both soil erosion and rising fuel costs. As in many African countries, most Kenyan households use wood as their primary fuel source. The tree-planting campaign addressed a widespread problem whose effects are felt particularly by rural women, since it is they who most often walk long distances to collect firewood.

Since its formation the Green Belt Movement has employed more than 80,000 people, mostly women, and planted more than 15 million trees. The women are paid for each tree they plant that survives past three months; as the trees grow, the women can use the fruit, leaves, and branches. With offices now in 30 African countries, the movement promotes organic farming techniques and hosts seminars on environmental management and sustainable development. Founder Maathai emphasizes that the Green Belt Movement is not only providing material benefits to women but is helping them take control of their environment.

Maathai has not hesitated to speak out publicly on the links between environmental degradation and poverty, and to criticize her own government's environmental and development policies. The response from the Kenyan government has been harsh. For example, she was beaten and jailed after organizing a protest against a proposed office building in Uhuru Park, one of the few remaining green spaces in Kenya's capital city, Nairobi. Although the government canceled the project, President DANIEL ARAP MOI labeled Maathai "subversive" and evicted the Green Belt Movement from its offices in Nairobi.

LESOTHO HIGHLANDS WATER PROJECT: RURAL AND URBAN COALITIONS

In southern Africa, the completion of the first phase of the massive LESOTHO Highlands Water Project (LHWP) in early 1998 sparked a protest movement that brought together environmental, church, and civic groups from both Lesotho and SOUTH AFRICA. The LHWP supplies water from Lesotho's Orange River to South Africa's industrialized Gauteng Province, which includes Johannnesburg and outlying black townships such as Soweto and Alexandra. The protesting groups detailed the negative effects of the LHWP on the numerous poor communities in southern Africa affected by the project and pointed out that none of these communities had been consulted beforehand. Civic groups in Soweto and Alexandra noted that while black township residents, like other South African taxpayers, had helped pay for the $1.1 billion project, much of the water supply in Gauteng was directed into the swimming pools and gardens of wealthy, predominantly white neighborhoods, and nearly a fourth of the supply leaked out through poorly maintained pipes. Many needy areas, meanwhile, had no piped water at all. Protesters objected that upstream, further dam construction on the Orange River would flood thousands of hectares of farmlands and pastures – which are already scarce in Lesotho – and dislocate hundreds of rural households. They also objected that the project would divert Orange River water away from the rural regions of NAMIBIA and possibly damage the area's fisheries.

The protesters appealed to the governments of South Africa and Lesotho as well as the World Bank, requesting that the project be delayed until environmental impact studies had been conducted and until the people negatively affected by the dams had received just compensation. In June 1998 the World Bank approved a $45 million loan for construction of a second dam, claiming that the revenue Lesotho earned from the LHWP would provide it with enough revenue to resettle and compensate rural communities and would generate 40,000 jobs.

The endorsement of the World Bank made it appear unlikely that the groups opposed to the project would have all their demands met. But opposition had come from a broad-based, binational coalition of groups, both rural and urban, and this reflected the growing strength of environmental movements in southern Africa. Since the fall of APARTHEID in South Africa, especially, these movements have been expanding across national borders and embracing a far broader range of issues. While wildlife conservation dominated the environmental agenda in white-ruled South Africa, the greater southern Africa region's "environmental justice" movements, which call for protecting the environments of people as well as animals, grew rapidly in the 1990s.

Robert Fay

SEE ALSO

Kenya; Johannesburg, South Africa; Nairobi, Kenya; Soweto, South Africa; Pastoralism; Saro-Wiwa, Kenule Beeson; Tourism in Africa; Wildlife Management in Africa.

Cross Cultural

Environmental Racism: An Interpretation, **the expression of racist assumptions in thought, action, or patterns of inaction, either in the formulation of environmental policy or the enforcement of environmental laws.**

The phrase *environmental racism* emerged in public usage to describe the circumstances surrounding a specific historical incident. In 1982 in North Carolina a plan was devised to collect 32,000 cubic yards of soil contaminated with polychlorinated biphenyls (PCBs) from 14 different locations throughout the state and to store it in a toxic waste facility in Warren County. The land chosen for the site had been owned predominantly by blacks since the time of slavery. It appeared to local residents that this site had been chosen not for its environmental suitability but rather because it was located in a poor, predominantly black, and politically powerless community.

State officials had not counted on the outrage or effectiveness of local citizens. Residents organized and protested the siting of the toxic dump, and more than 500 people were arrested in a large public demonstration protesting the implicit racism behind the choice of the Warren County location. The choice was considered a blatant example of the way in which communities of color are often doubly victimized in environmental matters: they are subjected to a disproportionate share of toxic pollutants and are also systematically excluded from decision-making processes affecting their own health and safety. Both the pattern of toxic dumping itself and the process of excluding communities of color from discussions of environmental policy came to be known as forms of environmental racism.

The citizens' demonstration against the Warren County dumping empowered other communities to examine their own circumstances. As communities of color across the United States and around the world have spoken up about similar patterns of environmental victimization and exclusion in decision-making processes, environmental racism has come to be understood as a pervasive and endemic feature of modern industrial society. Perhaps most important, it has become apparent that while individuals may express environmental racism in their assumptions or behavior from time to time, it is more common for environmental racism to manifest itself as a form of institutionalized racism. *Institutional racism* is a pattern of collective thought, action, or inaction characteristic of institutions like municipalities, state governments, private corporations, or national or international regulatory and enforcement agencies. Thus, individuals in management or decision-making positions in these institutions may not personally be racist, yet by acting to execute the established priorities of their institutions they may unwillingly or unwittingly perpetuate and extend patterns of environmental inequity and injustice – in short, they may propagate environmental racism.

Numerous studies since the 1982 Warren County incident provide further examples of environmental racism. At the request of Congressman Walter Fauntroy, the United States General Accounting Office conducted a study in 1983 of eight Southern states to examine the relation between the location of hazardous waste landfills and the racial and economic status of the surrounding communities. The results revealed a clear bias in the placement of the landfills: three of every four landfills were located near communities populated predominantly by minorities. In 1987 the Commission on Racial Justice of the United Church of Christ published a study titled "Toxic Wastes and Race in the United States," which pointed to the fact that 60 percent of black and Hispanic Americans live in communities with uncontrolled toxic waste sites.

In both urban and rural settings around the United States, communities of color and minorities have experienced levels of risk far higher than the norm in the society as a whole. Sociologist Robert Bullard has summarized the problem: "A growing body of studies clearly show that communities of color bear a disproportionate burden of pollution problems in the United States. Communities of color are adversely affected by industrial toxins, dirty air and drinking water, and the location of municipal landfills, incinerators, and hazardous waste treatment, disposal, and storage facilities."

Environmental racism is not confined only to the United States. Indeed, some of the most egregious examples of this elitist planning come from areas of the world formerly under colonial domination or currently subject to patterns of corporate exploitation with little or no governmental oversight or control. A striking example of this kind involves the Shell Oil Company's treatment of the Ogoni people of southeastern NIGERIA. For more than a decade Shell's oil extraction practices polluted the Ogoni's land and water and damaged their health and welfare. In response, the Ogoni organized the Movement for the Survival of the Ogoni People (MOSOP), led by writer and activist Ken Saro-Wiwa. On November 10, 1995, Saro-Wiwa was executed by the Nigerian government on what many regarded as trumped-up charges despite the vocal objection of numerous social justice, environmental, and human rights organizations worldwide. In this instance both the Nigerian government and Shell Oil were considered responsible for the pattern of environmental racism in eastern Nigeria (*see* ENVIRONMENTAL MOVEMENTS IN AFRICA).

To combat specific cases of environmental racism as well as the institutional habits of thought, action, and inaction that work to perpetuate the problem, environmental justice, or "ecojustice," movements have emerged within the United States and around the world. In October 1991 the First National People of Color Environmental Leadership Summit, held in WASHINGTON, D.C., issued a formal declaration of the Principles of Environmental Justice, which clarified and publicly recognized the problem of environmental racism in America. Partially in response to this milestone declaration, in February 1994 President Bill Clinton issued Executive Order 12898 with a specific mandate for federal agencies: "... each Federal agency shall make achieving environmental justice part of its mission by identifying and addressing, as appropriate, disproportionately high and adverse human health or environmental effects of its programs, policies, and activities on minority populations and low-income populations in the United States.... "

Following the official governmental order, private environmental action groups and resource centers have begun to document instances of environmental injustice and help communities organize themselves to resist environmental racism. The Environmental Justice Resource Center (EJRC) of Clark Atlanta University, under the direction of Robert Bullard, has taken a leadership role in this respect, producing two editions of the important *People of Color Environmental Groups Directory.* In addition, the National Council of Churches has provided resources for its member groups to act on ecojustice issues, and the EcoJustice Network and the Working Group on Environmental Justice have created sites on the World Wide Web, providing public access to information about environmental justice and environmental racism.

Tim Weiskel

SEE ALSO
Colonial Rule; Slavery in the United States; Saro-Wiwa, Kenule Beeson; Human Rights in Africa.

North America

Episcopal Church, **Protestant denomination with a long history of upperclass tradition and missionary work that has fostered African American leadership.**

The Episcopal Church was first introduced to the slave populations of the British colonies in the New World during the 1620s. The largely Anglican planter class of the British colonies of Maryland, Virginia, and the Carolinas debated the value of baptizing the children of African slaves and providing them with religious instruction. The more pious among them did Christianize their slaves, though many planters refused to do so, fearing that it would lead to slaves losing their status as property on either moral or legal grounds. Through the English Society for the Propagation of the Gospel in Foreign Parts – an Anglican evangelical organization dedicated to bringing the Gospel to blacks and Native Americans – many slaves received a Christian education. The Church of England also founded the first schools for blacks and trained the first African American missionaries.

In 1787, following United States independence, Americans split from the Church of England and formed the Protestant Episcopal Church of America. With England's loss of the colonies, the Church lost its most effective conduit into the souls of African Americans: the Loyalist planters. Black missionaries from Northern Episcopal congregations, however, continued this evangelical work and also engaged in abolitionist and desegregationist activities.

After the Civil War the number of black Episcopalians dropped sharply. Because the church's upperclass tradition devalued dancing, singing, and shouting – the hallmarks of the African American rural church – poor rural blacks who felt alienated soon left. Only the black upper classes were drawn to it, finding its establishment nature an appropriate accessory to their social aspirations. Furthermore, many blacks were lured away by the evangelical efforts of black Methodist and Baptist churches, which promised autonomous congregations rooted in African American cultural practices.

Despite the church's integrationist tendencies, many of its leaders were inspired by early articulations of Black Nationalism and PAN-AFRICANISM. African American missionaries James Theodore Holly and Samuel Ferguson focused their work in HAITI and LIBERIA, respectively, believing that these countries held a stronger prospect for black self-determination than did the United States. ALEXANDER CRUMMELL, on the other hand, cofounder of the AMERICAN NEGRO ACADEMY and founder of St. Luke's parish in Washington, D.C., worked for black liberation and church reform in the United States.

In the 1880s white Southern Episcopalians, threatened by an increase of black middle class parishioners in the urban South, successfully pushed for diocesan segregation and removed the authority of black congregations and clergy by placing them under the jurisdiction of white missionary organizations. In response, Alexander Crummell founded the Conference of Church Workers Among Colored People, in 1883, and the Women's Auxiliary to the Conference, in 1894, to appeal this decision. His demands were ignored. The organizations, however, provided a forum for black Episcopalians to discuss their status within the church.

These problems vexed the church well into the twentieth century and stymied its growth. The 1960s witnessed a revitalization of the church as its ranks were bolstered by the recent immigration of Anglicans from the Caribbean. Responding to the climate created by the CIVIL RIGHTS MOVEMENT and BLACK POWER, the Union of Black Episcopalians was formed in 1968 to address the historically aggrieved role of African Americans within the church as well as questions of black self-determination. Members of the Episcopal clergy also spoke out against sexism, and the first female ordination of the Episcopal church was held within a black parish. In 1988 Barbara Harris, an African American woman, became the first female bishop in not only the Episcopal Church, but in all churches that claim apostolic succession.

Peter Hudson

SEE ALSO
Abolitionism in the United States; American Indians; Baptists; Civil War, American; Black Church, The; Washington, D.C.

Africa

Equatorial Guinea, a small country on the coast of Central Africa including both the Bioko Island, just south of NIGERIA, and the mainland province of Mbini, lying between CAMEROON and GABON.

Equatorial Guinea is an anomaly in Africa. Due to early migration patterns, a multiethnic society, dominated by the FANG, resides on the mainland, while a single ethnic group, the Bubi, live on Bioko Island. Early European imperialism and the TRANSATLANTIC SLAVE TRADE exaggerated the differences between the island and mainland. The only Spanish colony in sub-Saharan Africa, Equatorial Guinea was run by a dictatorial colonial regime, primarily devoted to exploiting the small territory's rich natural resources. The leadership since independence has proven equally undemocratic: for three decades two men from the same family have ruled Equatorial Guinea, making use of clan patronage and widespread repression to maintain their rule and their control over the country's wealth. Increasing oil exports in recent years have brought extraordinarily high rates of economic growth (67 percent in 1997). But most of the country's 350,000 citizens have seen little, if any, of the profits.

EARLY HISTORY AND EUROPEAN EXPLORATION

For hundreds of years vast differences existed between the two pieces of present-day Equatorial Guinea. The first inhabitants of the Mbini region (also known as Rio Muni) were the Bayele Pygmies, though little is known of these people's culture, as it was lost through mixing with other groups. In the second millennium B.C.E. the NDOWE people migrated to the coast of present-day Equatorial Guinea from present-day Cameroon, splitting off into several related ethnic groups. The Ndowe were followed by the Fang (*see* BANTU: DISPERSION AND SETTLEMENT), who are today the country's largest ethnic group, composing 80 percent of the population. Included among the Fang are several cultural subgroup "tribes," or *ayong*, and within these are several more important familial clans, or *ndebot*. Common culture and intermarriage united the groups, as Fang custom prohibited marriage within the clan of one's mother. The numerous clans lived in egalitarian villages with no central authority, practicing the shifting cultivation of yucca, peanuts, yams, and malanga on the rich tropical plateau. Leadership depended upon wealth – measured with a currency of spearheads – and charisma. Although conflict between and among the Ndowe and Fang was common, it was limited in scope.

The island of Bioko has a longer history of Bantu-speaking inhabitation, though interpretations differ with the evidence. Archaeologists and linguists believe that the Bioko language cluster was one of the first groups to break from western Bantu, arriving in present-day Gabon probably around 1500-1000 B.C.E., while oral historians date their arrival much later. From there the BUBI migrated to Bioko Island around the seventh century C.E., though unlike many Bantu-speaking groups, they did not produce iron. Several successive societies rose and fell over time, concentrated primarily on the northern coastline. They grew palms on the rich soils of the volcanic islands, fished, and engaged in pottery and tool making. Although little is known of the early political and social organization of the Bubi of Bioko, it appears that political authority was diffuse, with the chief's power dependent on the approval of village elders.

The island's and mainland's early relations with Europeans exaggerated their differences. In 1472 the Portuguese navigator Fernando Pó explored both regions, and named the island after himself. Portugal formally claimed the lands in the 1494 Treaty of Tordesillas with SPAIN. But attempts to establish SUGAR plantations on the island were abandoned due to the difficulty of cultivation and access, as natural ports were few. Furthermore, although some European vessels took individual captives, a regular slave trade never developed on Bioko.

By contrast, the Mbini mainland and the nearby islands of Annobón (or Pagalu) and Corisco became important sites for commercial agricultural production, as well as busy markets for slaves and other commodities. In the sixteenth and seventeenth centuries, the islands supplied slave ships bound for Portuguese East Africa with fresh fruit and cattle. Soon these islands' inhabitants, many of whom had migrated from the mainland and others from Portuguese East Africa (present day ANGOLA), developed distinctive Creole cultures and languages. On Bioko, meanwhile, the Creole culture would not develop until the nineteenth century, when West Africans and slaves returned from the Americas were brought to the island by the British. They settled among the Bubi, creating a people that became known as the Ferninandos.

EUROPEAN IMPERIALISM AND SPANISH COLONIALISM

European imperialism and Spanish colonialism exaggerated the economic and cultural differences between Mbini and Bioko, even while uniting the two territories politically. Spain, seeking a dependable base for its slaving operations, purchased Annobón from Portugal in 1777. A year later the Treaty of Pardo provided for Portugal to cede part of the mainland as well as Bioko and other islands in exchange for lands in BRAZIL. The Spanish presence remained negligible. Trading stations controlled by the British, Dutch, Portuguese, and Spanish on the islands continued to supply both slaves and provisions to passing merchant ships into the mid-1800s, then switched to provisioning the vessels sent to enforce the British ban on slave trading. British enterprises established and operated palm plantations on Bioko, though when they were unable to compete with other palm-exporting regions, they switched the focus of production to COCOA.

The influx of Europeans brought a host of diseases to the islands and mainland, decimating the indigenous populations. European trade also led to conflicts over access and to the emergence of centralized states. On the mainland, for example, Europeans pushed the Ndowe inland, bringing them into conflict with the Fang, who sought European goods. On Bioko, where the Bubi had long lived without central authorities, control over European trade enabled the Bubi chief Moka to establish a kingdom.

After decades of concentrating its efforts on CUBA and MOROCCO at the expense of Equatorial Guinea, Spain finally laid claim to all of present-day Equatorial Guinea in 1900, at the Treaty of Paris. Four years later, a decree established the colony as a "colony of exploitation," not one of settlement, and it delineated rules concerning land concessions. The colonial administration's top priority was the export of timber and agricultural products, namely cocoa, coffee, and palm oil. Finding labor to produce these crops, however, proved difficult. The administration had relatively few troops or other tools of coercion at its disposal, and local people actively resisted colonial occupation and labor policies. On Bioko, it took Spanish forces until 1910 to defeat the king Moko and subsequent Bubi leaders. Colonization proved even more difficult in the forested Mbini interior, where one Fang leader actually captured the governor-general. Not until an all-out pacification campaign in 1926-1927 did the colonial state destroy organized resistance and put in its place a system of indirect rule, in which administrative dictates were carried out by pliable chiefs. But even then the local labor supplies were insufficient. Instead, the colony turned to importing laborers, including Liberians, Angolans, Mozambicans, and Asians, to work on the cocoa and coffee plantations.

Apart from the plantations, Spain did little to develop the colony's economy or infrastructure. On the mainland, the major town, Bata, consisted of little more than a few shacks. The inhospitable forest made the construction of roads or railways difficult, hindering the forestry industry. Despite these conditions and a climate conducive to tropical disease, Equatorial Guinea attracted many fortune-seeking European settlers, making it a colony with one of the highest ratios of Europeans to Africans in Africa. Like neighboring Portuguese colonies, Equatorial Guinea distinguished "assimilated" (or *emancipado*) and "nonassimilated" Africans, depending on land ownership and education. But since the colony had few schools, only a small fraction of the African population was able to acquire this status. Even those who did were excluded from political representation.

Although Equatorial Guinea's educated elite were few in number, they were at the

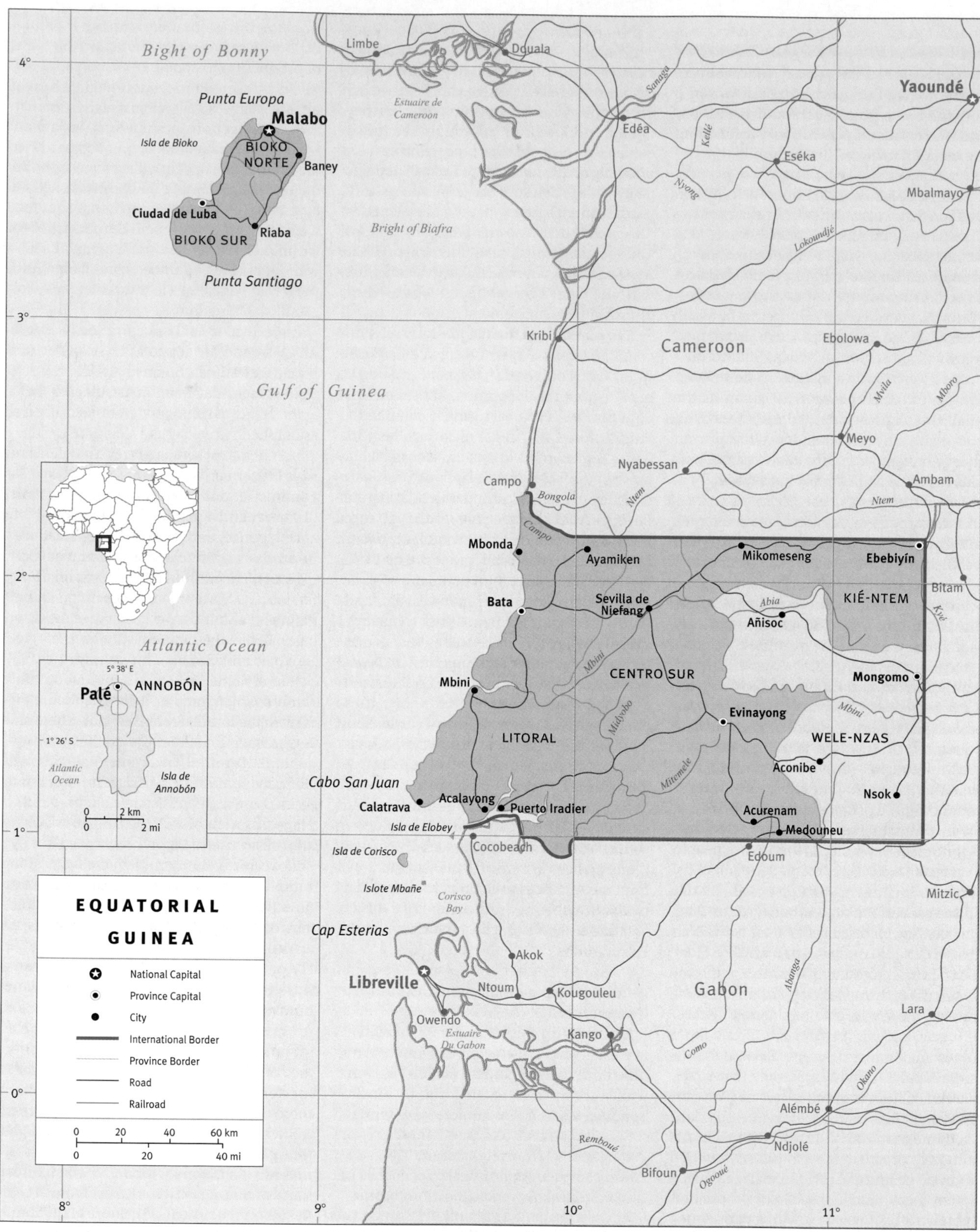

forefront of the nationalist movement, which began in the late 1950s under the leadership of Acacio Mañá, a Fang activist calling for African teachers' salaries to equal those of Europeans. Mañá was denounced by a priest and later executed by Spanish authorities; his martyrdom politicized Equatorial Guineans and led to the establishment of pro-independence parties, namely the National Movement for the Liberation of Equatorial Guinea and the Popular Idea of Equatorial Guinea. Violent repression on the part of colonial officials forced the parties into exile.

Spain, however, was bound to United Nations agreements to prepare Equatorial Guinea for self-rule. It held a referendum on self-determination in the colony in 1963, and municipal and legislative elections the following year. By the time a pre-independence constitutional conference was held in 1968, the nationalist movement had fragmented into parties representing Mbini, Bioko, or specific ethnic groups. The constitution created a very strong executive government, modeled after Franco's regime in Spain (and made Bioko and Mbini the two provinces of Equatorial Guinea, though the power soon shifted to Mbini, especially the Fang and its Esangui clan). In September 1968 FRANCISCO MACÍAS NGUEMA, the minister of public works and a Fang backed by Spanish and French commercial interests, was elected president.

FAMILIAL POLITICS AND UNDERDEVELOPMENT IN INDEPENDENT EQUATORIAL GUINEA

On October 12, 1968, Equatorial Guinea gained its independence. Almost immediately the new government faced the anger of 70,000 Nigerian migrant workers prohibited from sending their pay home, due to the ongoing Biafran war. To divert attention, President Macías Nguema began denouncing the Spanish who had remained in Equatorial Guinea, many of whom left. In March 1969 an alleged coup attempt – eyewitnesses claimed it was staged – was followed by a swift government crackdown on the political opposition.

For the next decade Macías Nguema, the self-proclaimed Unique Miracle, ruled Equatorial Guinea with an iron fist. He used the military youth organization the Youth in Step with Macías, as well as the presidential bodyguard, which included Cubans and North Koreans, to carry out repression and political killings. In terms of the numbers of deaths relative to the total population, Macías Nguema's regime was even more murderous than Idi Amin's in UGANDA. Fearing threats to his rule, Macías Nguema had thousands of political opponents killed. Over 130,000 – or one-fourth of the population – fled the country. Because he had no navy of his own, the president banned and destroyed all seagoing vessels (except the presidential "yacht") in order to prevent smuggling, an action that destroyed the fishing industry. During this period the economy collapsed; as foreign workers and the educated elite fled the country, the per capita gross national product (GNP) fell over 60 percent within the decade.

Macías Nguema went unchallenged until his own security forces turned on the military, killing five members of the National Guard in August 1979. Other Guard officers, military graduates, and relatives of the president gained control of Bioko and Bata. After overcoming intense resistance from presidential Loyalists in the interior, those leading the revolt captured, tried, convicted, and executed Macías Nguema for his role in torture, executions, and embezzlement. He was replaced by the nephew who had turned against him, army commander Teodoro Obiang Macías Nguema Mbasogo. On taking power, he announced that "for 11 years, politicians have made a mess of everything" and henceforth "the military will oversee everything... even if there are civilians in the government." The new leadership paid salary arrears to all troops and established a Supreme Military Council to run the country. Many members of the previous regime remained in the government.

Construction workers examine construction drawings for a public works project in Equatorial Guinea. *François Rojon/Rapho*

In the early 1980s the president brought more civilians into the government, though real power remained in the hands of the Fang-dominated military and president. Obiang's presidential guard, composed of Moroccans, Spaniards, and South Africans, thwarted numerous coup attempts, including an army mutiny in 1985. As opposition groups in exile alerted the international community to events in Equatorial Guinea, Obiang made limited political concessions. In 1987 he created the Democratic Party of Equatorial Guinea but made membership mandatory. In the next year he created a national assembly but declared himself the head of both the party and the assembly. Legislative elections in July 1988 were lackluster and limited to a few urban centers.

The appearance of political change lured international investment. Having adopted the West and Central Africa CFA franc in 1985, Equatorial Guinea began to develop closer economic ties with France, and soon adopted French as the second official language, after Spanish. French businesses entered the profitable timber, fuel, and fishing sectors. Timber grown on Mbini, especially the softwood *okoumé* used for making plywood, became the country's leading export, followed by cocoa. The fishing industry, especially in tuna and shellfish, made a slow recovery. Equatorial Guinea has also earned foreign exchange by *importing* waste, including New York City garbage and toxics from the South Africa-based Anglo-American Company. On Annobón, where the waste is dumped, the incidence of certain skin diseases is now among the highest in the world.

In the late 1990s foreign investors were showing the greatest interest in Equatorial Guinea's petroleum reserves. Oil was first discovered offshore in the early 1980s and has now replaced timber as the primary export, accounting for approximately 70 percent of the GNP. But many of the country's other resources – among them gold, iron, thorium, and manganese – remain untapped, and most of its citizens are impoverished. Since the country gained independence, much of the agricultural sector has been controlled by chiefs, elected by the people, who were responsible for maintaining timber harvests, and cocoa and coffee plantations though most of the revenues have gone to government officials and their companies. The leadership's handling of the economy has resulted in a deteriorating national infrastructure and a deficiency in public services. Equatorial Guinea today has only approximately 330 km (200 mi) of paved road. Transportation between the islands and mainland is by air only, because the country possesses only one boat, the presidential yacht.

Most of the wealth generated by the oil boom has gone directly into the hands of Obiang, his family members, and friends within the Esangui clan, leading many observers to question the effectiveness of the country's political reforms. Torture and arrests of opponents remain common, and few exiles have accepted the government's offer of amnesty. In 1993 Obiang legalized political parties, most of which were controlled by close associates and family members. Violence preceded legislative, municipal, and presidential elections in 1993, 1995, and 1996, the last of which gave Obiang 99 percent of the vote. The disparity in wealth between rich and poor has led to growing discontent, manifested in sometimes violent protests and attacks on Bioko and Annobón islands. Many believe that the growth of the oil industry, under the control of American and French companies, will hinder development and political change because the profits within Equatorial Guinea will continue to go mostly to Obiang and the Esangui clan, who have controlled Equatorial Guinea for the past few decades.

Eric Young

See Also
Colonial Rule; Colonial Rule; Explorers in Africa Before 1500; Nguema Mbasogo, Teodoro Obiang; United Nations in Africa; Portugal; Pygmy; South Africa; Afro-Atlantic Culture: On the Live Dialogue Between Africa and the Americas.

Africa

Equatorial Guinea (Ready Reference)

Official Name: Republic of Equatorial Guinea
Former Name: Spanish Guinea
Area: 28,051 sq km (about 10,831 sq mi)
Location: Western Africa, bordering the North Atlantic, between Gabon to the south and east and Cameroon to the north. Equatorial Guinea also includes islands off the coast, the largest of which is Bioko.
Capital: Malabo, on Bioko (population 38,000 [1989 estimate])
Population: 454,000 (1998 estimate); many thousands more are believed to be living abroad, due to the nation's tumultuous political climate.
Population Density: 14 people per sq km (37 per sq mi)
Population Below Age 15: 43 percent (male 97,993; female 97,470 [1998 estimate])
Population Growth Rate: 2.56 percent (1998 estimate)
Total Fertility Rate: 5.1 children born per woman (1998 estimate)
Life Expectancy at Birth: Total population: 53.93 years (male 51.61 years; female 56.31 years [1998 estimate])
Infant Mortality Rate: 93.45 deaths per 1000 live births (1998 estimate)
Literacy Rate (age 15 and over who can read and write): Total population: 78.5 percent (male 89.6 percent; female 68.1 percent [1995 estimate])
Education: Free and compulsory for children between the ages of 6 and 14. Still, an estimated 30 percent of school-age children do not attend primary school, and even fewer advance to secondary school. The Spanish National University of Distant Education operates centers for higher education at Malabo and Bata. Some Equatorial Guineans also go abroad (mostly to Spain and France) for a college education. In 1990 there were 578 college and university students.
Languages: Spanish is the official language, but Fang, a Bantu language, is most widely spoken.
Ethnic Groups: Ethnic lines correspond to geographic boundaries, with Bubi and Fernandinos populations on Bioko and a Fang population in Río Muni.
Religions: About 90 percent of the people are affiliated with the Roman Catholic church, although traditional beliefs are widely practiced.
Climate: Tropical; the average annual temperature in Malabo is about 25° C (77° F) and on average more than 2000 mm (80 in) of rain falls a year. The wettest season is December through February.
Land, Plants and Animals: On the mainland the terrain rolls gently and is heavily forested. The Mbini (formerly Benito) River drains about 60 percent of the land. Bioko has fertile volcanic soil watered by several large streams.
Natural Resources: The rich volcanic soil supports extensive agriculture.
Currency: The Communauté Financière Africaine franc
Gross Domestic Product (GDP): $660 million (1997 estimate)
GDP per Capita: $1500 (1997 estimate)
GDP Real Growth Rate: 10 percent (1995 estimate)
Primary Economic Activities: Agriculture and forestry
Primary Crops: Coffee, tropical hardwood timber, cassava, and sweet potatoes
Industries: Oil, soap, cocoa, yucca, coffee, and seafood processing
Primary Exports: Coffee, cocoa beans; timber
Primary Imports: Petroleum, food, beverages, clothing, machinery
Primary Trade Partners: Cameroon, France, Italy, Netherlands, Spain, and United States
Government: Under the 1982 constitution, Equatorial Guinea was a single-party state. This governmental party was named the Democratic Party of Equatorial Guinea in 1987. A new multiparty constitution was approved by public referendum in 1991. It established an 80-member House of Representatives to replace the existing 41-member legislature. Under the constitution, the voters elect a president to a seven-year term and legislators to five-year terms. Obiango Macías Nguema Mbasogo has been president since 1979 and was last re-elected in 1996.

Eric Bennett

See Also
Nguema Mbasogo, Teodoro Obiang; Malabo, Equatorial Guinea.

Africa

Equiano, Olaudah

(b. 1745, Nigeria; d. April 31, 1797, England), African ex-slave and abolitionist who wrote the first autobiographical slave narrative.

First published in Great Britain in 1789, *The Interesting Narrative of the Life of Olaudah Equiano, or Gustavus Vassa the African, written by himself,* became a bestseller within Olaudah Equiano's lifetime, with nine English editions and one American as well as translations in Dutch, German, and Russian. Though Ottobah Cugoano, an African abolitionist in England, had published an autobiographical account in 1787, it was probably heavily edited, and thus *The Interesting Narrative* is considered the first autobiography of an African slave written entirely by his own hand. This makes Equiano the founder of the slave narrative, a form central to African American literature.

Equiano describes his abduction in Africa, his enslavement in the West Indies, and his manumission in Britain, as well as the legal insecurity and terror faced by both enslaved and free West Indian blacks. His autobiography greatly influenced the rhetorical strategies, content, and presentation of later nineteenth-century slave narratives, such as Frederick Douglass's *The Life and Times of Frederick Douglass* (1845).

Equiano was born the son of an Ibo chief in present-day Nigeria. When he was 11 years old, he and his sister were captured by African traders and sold to Europeans. He was transported to the West Indies, where Michael Pascal, an Englishman, bought Equiano and named him after the Swedish hero Gustavus Vassa. Though Equiano at first detested the name, he later used it in most of his writings and became known by it. Equiano served as a seaman with Pascal in the Seven Years War (1756-1763) in Canada and the Mediterranean. In 1757 Pascal took Equiano to England, where his honesty and trustworthiness won him friendship and support from many English people. During this formative period, Equiano was educated and converted to Christianity.

To Equiano's dismay, in 1763 Pascal sold him to an American, Robert King. By this time, Equiano knew seamanship, hairdressing, wine making, and arithmetic and had become fully literate in the English language. He worked for King as a seaman and trader, once again coming in close contact with the atrocities of the transatlantic slave trade. Even after he bought his freedom in 1766, Equiano elected to remain at sea for several years. He voyaged to the Arctic as a surgeon's assistant and to the Mediterranean as a gentleman's valet, and for a time lived among the Moskito Indians of Nicaragua.

Equiano returned to England in 1777 and became active in the abolitionist movement. He brought the massacre of 130 slaves on the ship *Zong* to the attention of the white abolitionist lawyer Granville Sharp, thereby greatly influencing public support for abolition of the slave trade. He also wrote on behalf of abolition and interracial marriages. In 1792 he married Susannah Cullen, a white Englishwoman, with whom he had two daughters.

In 1787 Equiano was appointed Commissary for Stores to the Expedition for Freed Slaves, and settled in Sierra Leone (*see* London's Black Poor and the Sierra Leone Settlement Plan). Though at first he was "agreeably surprised that the benevolence of government had adopted the plan of some philanthropic individuals," he soon discovered fraudulence among the organizers. Equiano invited outsiders to view the negligent conditions under which the blacks lived on board the ship set to sail to Sierra Leone and described corrupt procedures to a friend in a letter that was later published. He was later dismissed from his post as a "troublemaker."

Though demoralized, Equiano returned to England and published his autobiography. He fought unceasingly for abolition as a member of the Sons of Africa and in his letter-writing and public-speaking campaigns until his death in 1797.

Leyla Keough

See Also
Igbo; Great Britain; Abolitionism in the United States; Miscegenation; Slave Narratives.

North America

Eric B. and Rakim (b. Eric Barrier and William Griffin) (New York, N.Y.), hip hop duo who revolutionized the art of rapping.

Eric B. and Rakim's debut album, *Paid in Full* (1987), amply displayed DJ Eric B.'s danceable beats and restrained turntable technique, but the real revelation was Rakim – generally regarded as one of the most skilled MCs in hip hop history. "To me, MC means move the crowd," he rapped, in a deadpan voice simultaneously inviting, threatening, and cool. Rakim's rhymes were peppered with witty analogies ("I draw a crowd like an architect") and distinguished by careful construction: on "My Melody," Rakim declaims, "I'm not a regular competitor / first rhyme editor / Melody arranger / poet etcetera."

The duo returned in 1988 with *Follow the Leader*, an innovative album that won similar acclaim. Eric B. created increasingly sophisticated beats, over which Rakim further shattered RAP's conventions of rhyme and meter. Rakim, an adherent of the gnostic NATION OF ISLAM, wove intricate allegories about rap itself, presenting an image of a man with a microphone defending his art. Tracks like "Follow the Leader" and "Lyrics of Fury" (later covered by the black British musician Tricky) never achieved huge crossover success, but the album's creative beats and rhymes sent the hip hop world running to catch up.

Let the Rhythm Hit 'Em (1990) was the duo's third and final gold record; they finally split up after *Don't Sweat the Technique* (1992). After four years of relative silence, Rakim received a hero's welcome – along with mild critical and commercial success – when he reemerged with his solo debut, *The 18th Letter*, in 1997.

Andrew Du Bois

See Also
Hip Hop in the United States.

Africa

Eritrea, nation in the Horn of Africa, bordering the Red Sea, SUDAN, ETHIOPIA, and DJIBOUTI.

Eritrea is one of the world's newest nations and one of its poorest. Small and drought-prone, it boasts few natural resources. But Eritrea's Red Sea location has a rich cultural history, produced over centuries of migrations and trade, as well as a long history of warfare, fueled largely by the strategic interests of its neighbors and other foreign powers. Compared to other African countries, Eritrea has some of the oldest traditions of Islam and Christianity and one of the shortest experiences of European colonialism: less than 50 years under Italian rule. The region's colonial borders, however, took on new significance as soon as ITALY was removed from power and Eritrea was handed over to Ethiopia.

In the face of Emperor HAILE SELASSIE I's despotism, Eritrean nationalism developed quickly and endured through roughly a 30-year war for independence, ending when Eritrea became Africa's newest nation in 1993. Since then, the country has enjoyed a remarkable political consensus, and most agree that it is a society where ethnic distinctions matter less than differences in religion and lifestyle between the Christian agricultural highlands and the Islamic pastoral lowlands. Although during the war Eritrean freedom fighters never received much outside support, independent Eritrea soon became the darling of the international aid community, lauded for its honest government and economic pragmatism. In mid-1998, however, renewed tensions with ETHIOPIA threw into doubt Eritrea's future recovery.

From Ancient Trade to Colonial Domination

The region now known as Eritrea has a long history of human habitation. Cave paintings in Akele Guzai and Sahel provinces date to 6000 B.C.E. Scholars believe that Nilotic-speaking peoples (*see* LANGUAGES, AFRICAN: AN OVERVIEW) from the forests of southern SUDAN were the earliest inhabitants. They were followed by Cushitic-speaking pastoralists from the desert of northern Sudan and later – probably between 3500 and 4000 years ago – Semitic-speaking agriculturalists from the southern Arabian Peninsula (now Yemen). Around 2500 years ago the arrival of the Semitic-speaking Sabeans, also from Arabia, linked the region to the Sabean's Red Sea and Indian Ocean trade networks. These early Semitic immigrants also brought Judaism to the Horn of Africa.

Trade with EGYPT, Meroe, and the Arabian Peninsula fostered the development of towns and centralized political authority. By the second century C.E., the kingdom of AKSUM dominated a stretch of territory reaching from its highland capital of the same name (now a town in Ethiopia) to the coast. The kingdom exported ivory, slaves, tortoise shell, and RHINOCEROS horn from the East African interior, and imported textiles, glass and metal goods, and wine. During the mid-fourth century C.E., the Aksum royalty adopted Christianity. Ethiopian Orthodox (or Coptic) Christianity eventually became the dominant religion in the highlands, where most of the population practiced sedentary agriculture.

The population in the lowlands was sparser, and the arid conditions favored nomadic pastoralism. By 702 C.E. Arab merchants had brought Islam to the Dahlak Islands, and from there it spread gradually along the coast and through the lowlands, establishing a cultural divide that still exists in Eritrea today. Culturally and spiritually, the coast increasingly looked toward the Arab world. Arabic was the language of scholarship and the window to the outside world. By the early nineteenth century, the TIGRE, the dominant coastal group, had become entirely Muslim. The highlands, however, remained Coptic, one of the oldest organized Christian churches, which spread from Egypt in the first centuries C.E. The mountain people, mostly Tigrinya, were largely settled agriculturalists.

By the sixteenth century foreign powers were jockeying for control over territory in the Horn of Africa. The Portuguese established the first trade posts, followed by the Ottoman Turks, who captured and fortified the port city of Massawa in 1557. For more than 300 years control over the territory now called Eritrea was caught up in the imperialistic ambitions of EGYPT, Portugal, and later Great Britain and Italy, as well as the neighboring Ethiopian Empire. As Europeans rushed to colonize Africa in the late nineteenth century (*see* SCRAMBLE FOR AFRICA), Italy, despite its previous lack of interest in establishing colonies on the continent, looked to the Horn. The Italian government sought to preempt other colonial powers from carving up all of Africa among them but also hoped to establish settler colonies for dispossessed Italian peasants and to find new markets for Italian goods.

In 1885 Italian troops occupied Massawa. Four years later they occupied Asmara, which had been ceded to them by the Ethiopian emperor Menilek in exchange for weapons. In 1890 Italy declared colonial control over "Eritrea" – a name taken from the Greek word for the Red Sea. It intended to take over the vast Ethiopian Empire as well, but its troops were soundly defeated by Emperor Menilek's army in 1896. Eritrea's borders, therefore, reflected not a preexisting political or cultural entity but only turn-of-the-century military realities.

Italian Colonial Rule

Although many Italians did not support their country's colonization campaign – which also included the occupation of SOMALIA and LIBYA – Mussolini would later call Eritrea "the heart

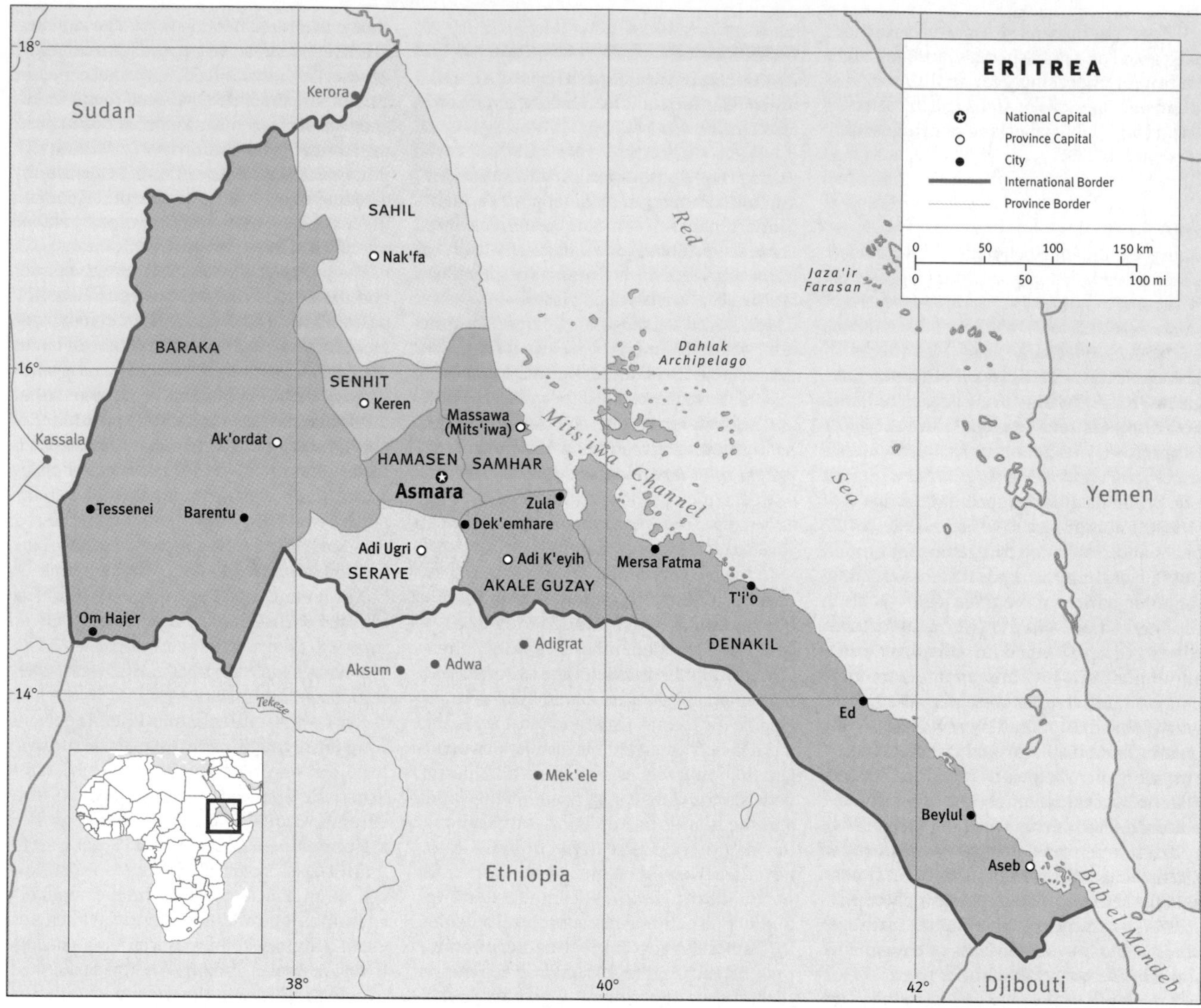

of the new Roman Empire." Establishing COLONIAL RULE over this part of the "empire" did not come easily. The colonial administration expropriated over one-fifth of Eritrea's arable land between 1893 and 1895, in anticipation of massive Italian immigration to the colony. But an armed uprising involving hundreds of Eritreans in late 1894 required two months and thousands of Italian troops to put down, and forced the administration to scale back its plans for Italian resettlement. In 1903 the administration halted land expropriation altogether and began leasing seized lands back to the Eritrean peasantry, in part due to threats of further rebellion.

The Italian immigrants settled mostly in the fertile countryside of the highlands, where they relied on the labor of dispossessed peasants to produce a wide variety of export crops, or in Asmara, Massawa, and the port of Aseb (also known as Assab), where they established trade and manufacturing firms. By the early 1920s coffee, much of it produced on Eritrean peasant farms, had become the colony's largest export. Other major exports included cotton, skins and hides, salt, tobacco, and fresh and canned foodstuffs. Eritrea also supplied Italy with wheat and other grains. Italy's search for gold in Eritrea proved largely fruitless, apart from small quantities mined near Asmara. Although reserves of iron ore, lead, and white mica were also found around the capital, these were left largely unexploited. By contrast, Italy invested generously in infrastructure. By 1911 the small colony was spanned by 119 km (approximately 74 mi) of railroads, including one line that twisted and tunneled through the mountainous region between Massawa and Asmara. While the railway as well as an extensive road system facilitated the transport of export crops, Italy never earned a profit from Eritrea, and in fact had to subsidize its colonial administration.

One of the Longest Wars in History

In 1935 Italy invaded Ethiopia. For the next six years Eritrea served as an Italian base for its East African military campaigns. Thousands of Italians took up residence in Asmara, and industrialization and infrastructure development accelerated. Thousands of conscripted Eritrean soldiers fought for the Italians. In 1941, however, the British demolished their East African defenses and occupied Eritrea. After the war the British allowed the formation of Eritrean trade unions, publications, and political parties, all of which fostered a growing sense of national identity. For several years Eritrea's political status lay in limbo, as first the Allies and later the United Nations (UN) debated its future.

At first most Eritrean Christians favored union with Ethiopia, and Orthodox priests often threatened to excommunicate anyone favoring independence. But Muslims, who feared domination by a Christian state, advocated independent statehood. The pro-independence Muslim League was formed in 1946. In the following year Woldeab Woldemariam, a labor activist and early advocate of Eritrean independence, helped launch the Christian-dominated Liberal Progressive Party. Muslims and Christians clashed repeatedly between 1946 and 1951.

After Haile Selassie heavily lobbied the United States and other leading UN members, the UN voted to federate Ethiopia and Eritrea in 1951. Over the next ten years Selassie's regime tightened its grip on Eritrea. Factories in Asmara were dismantled and brought to Addis Ababa, pushing what was once one of

the most industrialized colonies in Africa into poverty. Political dissent was suppressed as the Ethiopian government forced prominent Eritreans into exile, shut down newspapers, and banned trade unions and political parties. In 1958 the Eritrean flag was banned.

Ethiopian repression hit Eritrea's urban and highland populations especially hard, and they responded accordingly. In 1958 underground unions staged a general strike in Asmara and Massawa, and students joined workers in massive protests against the loss of local autonomy. The Ethiopian government reacted immediately. Troops fired on protesters, wounding or killing more than 500. Throughout Eritrea, support for the national government evaporated, and Christians began joining the independence movement.

In 1960 Selassie declared Amharic, the language of Addis Ababa and Ethiopia's largest ethnic group, the official language, and banned other languages from the schools. That same year, Eritrean leaders, including Edris Mohammed Adem, former president of the Eritrean Assembly, met secretly in Cairo to form the Eritrean Liberation Front (ELF), whose members represented a broad spectrum of society. In September 1961 Eritrean independence advocates battled with police on Mount Adal. Two months later an ELF military campaign in the west marked the beginning of a long and arduous war. Although at first they fought with antiquated Italian rifles, eventually the ELF troops developed into one of Africa's most disciplined military forces. In 1965 the ELF established four regional commands. In 1966 Eritrea's future president, Isaias Afwerki, dropped out of the University of Addis Ababa and joined the ELF, and a Christian-dominated fifth zone was created in the highlands.

Foreign powers soon chose sides in the Eritrean independence struggle. Arab states, sympathetic to appeals by fellow Muslims, were the first to back the ELF, while Israel backed Selassie. Other major powers viewed the conflict in the context of the cold war, which meant that Selassie, a reliable anti-communist, received backing from the United States and Europe. His army became one of the largest and best equipped in Africa. Although the Eastern bloc supported the ELF with rhetoric, it sent little material aid. Socialist countries did train small groups of ELF fighters, however. Afwerki and another leader, Ramadan M. Nur, went to China for training in 1967, and in the following year other groups went to Cuba.

As the war intensified, Eritrean refugees streamed into Sudan. The Ethiopian military's tactics of burning villages and killing their inhabitants, rather than intimidating the population into submission, only increased support for independence, even among Christian highlanders who had previously supported Addis Ababa. The ELF, meanwhile, focused on guerrilla tactics, such as blowing up bridges and hijacking airplanes.

Despite success in battle, the rebel movement faced serious internal divisions by the early 1970s. Afwerki and other highlanders eventually split from the Muslim-dominated ELF leadership and formed the Eritrean People's Liberation Front (EPLF). The two groups were soon fighting on different fronts and periodically fought with each other. Although the ELF was initially Christian-dominated, it defined itself as a secular organization. Both groups professed Marxist principles and stated they were fighting not just for political independence but also for revolutionary goals, such as the nationalization of private property.

During the war women received equality in areas controlled by the EPLF, and child marriage was outlawed in 1978. Political and military setbacks ultimately weakened the ELF, and the EPLF emerged as the main independence force. Over the next several years the Eritrean struggle survived in large part because of its success at mobilizing all possible resources, including popular support in the countryside. One-third of the fighters were women, for example, and they trained and

TOP LEFT: Stevedores load a cargo ship in the Eritrean port of Massawa. *Wolfgang Kaehler, 1999*
MIDDLE: A major port on the Red Sea, Massawa has a long history of trade and foreign occupation, which is reflected in its Arab, Turkish, and Italian architecture. *Wolfgang Kaehler, 1999*
ABOVE: A young Eritrean woman loads donkeys with casks of water. *CORBIS/Caroline Penn*

fought alongside men. The EPLF promoted equality between the sexes in areas under its control. It also assured Muslim civilians that freedom of religion would be protected. Perhaps most important, the EPLF managed to provide the basic rural services that neither the Italians nor Ethiopians had bothered with: it opened 165 schools during the war, educating some 27,000 students. The EPLF also improved rural public health standards by creating a corps of mobile health teams and Italian-trained doctors and establishing a network of pharmacies, laboratories, and village clinics. Many of the facilities were built underground to avoid Ethiopian bomb attacks.

A large proportion of the EPLF's budget for such programs came from abroad. Even before the war, large numbers of Eritreans had migrated to the Persian Gulf, Europe, and North America in search of employment, and now expatriate communities became a key source of monetary support for the rebel movement. Some observers estimate that Eritreans abroad sent back $20 million a month – up to 70 percent of their salaries, in some places – enabling the ELF and EPLF to sustain the war despite in-fighting, drought, military setbacks, and political isolation. The rebels also stole massive amounts of military supplies from the Ethiopian army.

The war's geopolitical alliances changed in 1974, when Haile Selassie was overthrown in a military coup led by Haile Mariam Mengistu. Like the Eritrean rebel groups, the new Ethiopian regime, known as the Derg, claimed to be Marxist, but it was soon clear that the Derg was concerned less with equality and social change than with maintaining a strong central state. Still, the Soviet Union, China, and Cuba threw their support behind the new Ethiopian Red Army, which launched a massive campaign in 1978 that pushed the rebels northward and out of all the major cities. The Eritrean refugee population in Sudan swelled to 500,000 by 1981. The Ethiopian army under Mengistu purposely targeted food supplies in rebel areas – they burned crops and granaries and slaughtered livestock – so Eritrea was already vulnerable to famine by the time drought struck in 1984. Massive food aid shipments from the West arrived in Addis Ababa, but very little relief reached Eritrea.

This woman fought for the Eritrean Popular Liberation Front during her country's struggle for independence from Ethiopia in 1978. *RBIS/Françoise de Mulder*

In the late 1980s the Eritreans began to regain lost ground and won a number of key battles against the large but poorly trained and increasingly demoralized Ethiopian army. As the Soviet bloc itself began to crumble, the EPLF moderated its Marxist tone and began to collaborate with the growing rebel movements within Ethiopia, such as the Ethiopian People's Revolutionary Democratic Front (EPRDF), led by Meles Zenawi.

The last major battle of the independence struggle took place on May 19, 1991. The Ethiopian army collapsed at Decamare, outside Asmara, and fled north toward Sudan in a disorganized rout. In the meantime, Ethiopian rebels were approaching Addis Ababa. With the Soviet Union in collapse, the Derg was doomed. On May 21 Mengistu fled into exile in Zimbabwe, and Zenawi took over as acting president. Recognizing that the EPRDF could not have triumphed without EPLF support, Zenawi agreed to Eritrean independence. Afwerki acted as Eritrea's de facto head of state until a UN-supervised referendum on independence was held in 1993. Ninety-eight percent of the electorate voted yes, and independence was declared on May 24, 1993. Afwerki was formally elected president soon afterward.

Independent Eritrea

With independence, Eritrea began to rebuild. The war had created a refugee population of at least 750,000, many of whom came streaming back from Sudan soon after the fighting ended. Seventy thousand veterans – many of whom had known no other life beyond the war – also had to be reincorporated into society. One of the government's long-term goals was to rebuild Eritrea's industrial base, but with drought a chronic threat and three-quarters of the country's 2.7 million people dependent on outside food aid, intensifying agricultural production was an immediate priority – as was removal of the land mines still littering the countryside.

During its first years of independence, Eritrea won accolades for its honest government and determination to achieve self-sufficiency. The country has refused loans and aid packages with strings attached and has resolved to rebuild the destroyed Massawa-Asmara railroad using only Eritrean labor. The government recruited 70-year-old former train engineers out of retirement to help restore steam engines from the 1930s. At the same time, Eritrea's once-Marxist leaders welcomed foreign investment in certain sectors, such as coastal tourism.

Some of the wartime objectives of the EPLF, now renamed People's Front for Democracy and Justice (PDJ), have become government objectives, such as education and legal equality for women, and rural primary health care. It has also pledged to protect religious freedom, though some smaller groups, notably the Jehovah's Witnesses, have complained of persecution. Overall, the sense of national unity forged during the long war has translated into widespread popular support for the government, which at least initially was largely composed of former fighters. Some outside observers, however, have criticized the PDJ's authoritarian tendencies. The constitution passed in 1997 gave considerable power to the central government but also called for multiparty elections.

Eritrea has had tense relations with its neighbors in recent years. It broke diplomatic relations with Sudan in 1994 over concerns that it was cultivating Islamic fundamentalism in border areas. This concern prompted the United States to supply both Eritrea and Ethiopia with military aid. For its part, Sudan has accused the Eritreans of supporting southern Sudanese rebels. In 1996 Eritrea skirmished briefly both with Djibouti over a contested border and with Yemen over ownership of a collection of small Red Sea Islands.

Perhaps most serious, armed conflict with Ethiopia erupted again in June 1998 and in March 1999. In both instances the immediate cause of the fighting was again a disputed border, but tensions over trade issues had been building for months. When Eritrea became independent, the two countries had agreed to share Ethiopia's currency (the birr) and Eritrea's port access, but these cooperative relations began to deteriorate in 1997, especially after Eritrea introduced its own currency, the nafka. Despite efforts by the United States, the Organization of African Unity (OAU), and neighboring African countries to resolve the conflict diplomatically, both sides continued to arm themselves, insisting that nothing less than national sovereignty was at stake.

David P. Johnson, Jr.

See Also

Addis Ababa, Ethiopia; Asmara, Eritrea; Christianity, African: An Overview; Ethiopian Jews; Ethiopian Orthodox Church; Ivory Trade; Massawa, Eritrea; Menilek II; Afwerki, Isaias; United Nations in Africa; Russia and the Former Soviet Union; Pastoralism; Tourism in Africa; Cairo, Egypt; Islam and Tradition: An Interpretation; Islamic Fundamentalism: An Interpretation; Trans-Saharan and Red Sea Slave Trade.

Africa

Eritrea (Ready Reference)

Official Name: State of Eritrea
Former Name: Eritrea Autonomous Region in Ethiopia
Area: 121,144 sq km (46,774 sq mi)
Location: Northeastern Africa; borders the Red Sea, Djibouti, Ethiopia, and the Sudan and includes the Dahlak Archipelago in the Red Sea
Capital: Asmara (population 400,000 [1993 estimate])
Population: 3,842,436 (1998 estimate)
Population Density: 28 per sq km (73 per sq mi); approximately 80 percent of Eritrea's population lives in rural areas.
Population Below Age 15: 43 percent (male 826,686; female 818,323 [1998 estimate])
Population Growth Rate: 3.39 percent (1998 estimate)
Total Fertility Rate: 5.9 children born per woman (1998 estimate)
Life Expectancy at Birth: 55.31 years (male 53.19 years; female 57.51 years [1998 estimate])
Infant Mortality Rate: 78.51 deaths per 1000 live births (1998 estimate)
Literacy Rate (age 15 and over who can read and write): Total population: 20 percent (1993 estimate)
Education: Few schools functioned during the war of independence that ended in 1993. Officially, seven years of primary education are now compulsory, with lower grades taught in African languages and higher grades in Arabic or English.
Languages: The main language groups are Tigrinya, Tigre, Kunama, Hedareb, Afar, Bilien, Saho, Nara and Rashaida. Arabic is also widely spoken, but English is used in secondary schools and universities.
Ethnic Groups: Ethnic Tigrinya, 50 percent; Tigre and Kunama, 40 percent; Afar, 4 percent; Saho (Red Sea coast dwellers), 3 percent; other, 3 percent
Religions: Muslim, Monophysite creed of the Ethiopian Orthodox church, Roman Catholic, and Protestant
Climate: The narrow coastal plain receives little rainfall and is extremely hot, with a mean annual temperature of 30° C (86° F). The mean annual temperature in Asmara, located in the plateau highlands, is 16° C (61° F). The plateau receives 400-500 mm (16-20 in) rainfall per year, while the hill country north and west of the core plateau generally receives less. The Denakil depression in the southeast has been the site of some of the highest temperatures recorded on earth, and receives practically no rain.
Land, Plants, and Animals: Eritrea's topography consists of four types of land surface. The Red Sea coastal plain widens to include the Denakil Desert in the south. The south central plateau highland is the most agriculturally fertile and densely populated part of the country. To the north of the highlands lie hill country, and to the west lie broad plains. These plains lie to the west of the Baraka River and north of the Setit River. The Mereb (or Gash), the Baraka, and the Anseba flow from the plateau west into Sudan, while the Falkat, Laba, and Alighede flow from the northern highlands to the Red Sea. Off the coast, more than a hundred small islands make up the Dahlak Archipelago.
Natural Resources: Eritrea's resources have supported a largely agricultural way of life. The nation possesses potentially valuable potash deposits and possibly gold, iron, and petroleum, but exploration and exploitation of its mineral resources were severely hindered by three decades of war. The Red Sea is rich in fish, but commercial fishing in Eritrea is also relatively underdeveloped.
Currency: The nafka
Gross Domestic Product (GDP): $2.2 billion (1996 estimate)
GDP per Capita: $600 (1996 estimate)
GDP Real Growth Rate: 6.8 percent (1996 estimate)
Primary Economic Activities: More than 80 percent of the population engage in agriculture that nonetheless produces only a quarter of the total gross domestic product. The country's small industrial sector is recovering from the war. Migrant labor is also an important source of income.
Primary Crops: Sorghum, lentils, vegetables, maize, cotton, tobacco, coffee, and sisal (for making rope); livestock includes goats; fish
Industries: Food processing, beverages, clothing, and textiles
Primary Exports: Livestock, sorghum, and textiles
Primary Imports: Processed goods, machinery, and petroleum products
Primary Trade Partners: Ethiopia, Italy, Saudi Arabia, United Kingdom, United States, and Yemen
Government: A May 1993 decree set up a National Assembly, a president, and a Council of Ministers. Isaias Afwerki was elected by the National Assembly and currently serves as president. The country's nine provinces are under the control of administrators appointed by the president. In addition to the People's Front for Democracy and Justice (formerly the Eritrean People's Liberation Front), other political organizations include the Democratic Movement for the Liberation of Eritrea and the Eritrean Liberation Front (ELF).

Marian Aguiar

See Also

Asmara, Eritrea.

North America

Erving, Julius ("Dr. J")

(b. February 22, 1950, Hempstead, N.Y.), professional African American basketball player popularly known as "Dr. J," innovator of the slam-dunk, and one of the most electrifying players in basketball history.

Julius Erving, born Julius Winfield Erving Jr., recalled, "My first [slam] dunk was at the Prospect Elementary School, where they had 8-foot baskets and 13-foot ceilings. By the time I was in ninth grade, I was dunking the regular baskets." In 1976, during the All Star game of the American Basketball Association (ABA), he astounded the basketball world with a soaring dunk from the free throw line. Another one of Erving's legendary shots was his suspenseful windmill reverse lay-up in a 1983 National Basketball Association (NBA) championship game.

Julius Erving grew up playing BASKETBALL on New York City playgrounds and then for Roosevelt High School. A six-foot-six, 200-pound forward, he attended the University of Massachusetts. During his sophomore and junior years (1969-1971), Erving led his team in scoring in 46 of 52 varsity games.

Erving bypassed his senior year and signed a contract with the ABA's Virginia Squires. He was named Rookie of the Year for the 1971-1972 season and led the Squires to the ABA 1973 playoffs. Late in 1973 he was traded to another ABA team, the New York Nets. During his three seasons with the Nets (1973-1976), Erving earned the ABA's Most Valuable Player (MVP) award three times and helped his team capture the 1974 and 1976 ABA championships. In five ABA seasons, Erving averaged 29 points and 12 rebounds per game, and made the ABA All-Star Team each year.

After the 1976 season, Erving left the ABA to play in the NBA. From 1976 until his retirement in 1987, he played for the Philadelphia 76ers, averaging 22 points and seven rebounds per contest. In addition to making the NBA All-Star Team for 11 consecutive years, Erving was declared the NBA's MVP in 1981 and helped the 76ers triumph over the Los Angeles Lakers for the 1983 NBA title.

With 30,026 points, Erving ranks third, after KAREEM ABDUL-JABBAR and Wilt Chamberlain, on the all-time ABA-NBA scoring list. Since his retirement, Erving has been engaged in child-centered civic activities, corporate business, and sports broadcasting. In 1993 he was inducted into the Basketball Hall of Fame.

Aaron Myers

SEE ALSO

Chamberlain, Wilton Norman (Wilt); New York, New York; Philadelphia, Pennsylvania.

Latin America and the Caribbean

Esmeraldas, province on the northern Ecuadorian coast with a large Afro-Ecuadorian population; site of an Afro-Ecuadorian maroon community.

The province of Esmeraldas, on the northern coast of ECUADOR, constitutes the southern extremity of a vast black cultural area called the Pacific Lowlands, which includes the Pacific coasts of COLOMBIA and of the province of Darién in PANAMA. Mangroves abound on the seashore and in the dense rain forest inland. Around 70 percent of the province's population is of African descent. The rest of the population is composed of Amerindians (the Cayapas or Chachis) and *mestizos* (persons with both European and Native American ancestry). The mestizos migrated principally from the Ecuadorian Andes, from the province of Manabí, and from southern Colombia. For the most part, they constitute the Esmeraldian elites.

Mestizaje and *blanqueamiento* are key terms in understanding Esmeraldians' attitudes and ideas about race. The popular expression *mejorar la raza* (to improve the race) denotes blanqueamiento by pointing to the publicly acknowledged ideal of darker-skinned people marrying lighter-skinned individuals to secure upward mobility. Esmeraldas has a phenotypic typology that ranges from the most negative category to the most positive one. The bottom category is the blue blacks *(negro azul),* the top is the whites, with a series of intermediate types such as, nonexhaustively: the *morados,* dark-skinned individuals with "fair" (non-kinky) black hair; the mulattos, brown-skinned with kinky hair; the *trigueños,* lighter-skinned than the mulattos with softer dark hair; the *zambos* or *colorados,* light-skinned persons with light and fair brown, red, or even blond nappy hair; and so on.

In the southernmost county, Muisne, the percentage of black population is small; the city of Esmeraldas – at the center of the province – is multiracial, while the northern counties of San Lorenzo and Eloy Alfaro are considered places of "pure" blackness and backwardness. It is in the villages of the north, principally in the ones more distant in the forest, that Afro-Esmeraldian traditions have survived the best. The most renowned Afro-Esmeraldian traditions include the music of the *marimba* (a sort of xylophone); the Afro-Esmeraldian *décimas* (oral poems of 44 verses); the festivities and celebrations of Easter and of the Roman Catholic Epiphany (Festival of the Kings); the *arrullos* (saint days); the *chigualos* and *alabados* (funerals); and the oral tales of Nephew Rabbit and Uncle Tiger.

Black immigration to the province of Esmeraldas began in the sixteenth century, with the commerce between Spain's Central American and Caribbean colonies and the Vice-Kingdom of Peru. In the sixteenth century the number of slaves transported was minimal. The merchants who traveled between Panama and Callao (PERU) were mostly transporting merchandise. Sometimes they carried one or two slaves, but rarely more.

It is in this context of commercial development that a famous shipwreck took place establishing the first black population in the province. The facts were immortalized in the chronicle of Miguel Cabello Balboa, a missionary who obtained the information in 1577 from one of the shipwreck survivors, the ex-slave SEBASTIÁN ALONSO DE ILLESCAS. Illescas had become the leader of what some historians called the Republic of Zambos. (A zambo is an individual who has black and Native American ancestry.) The ship in question had belonged to the Spaniard Sebastián Alonso de Illescas, whose name the slave had taken after his confirmation in Seville, Spain. The ship, en route to Callao, was carrying 23 slaves – 17 men and 6 women – a large number for the time. After 30 days of navigation, the ship stopped in front of the Esmeraldian coast. The Spanish crew debarked with the slaves to hunt game and replenish the stock of drinking water. Before they had the chance to return to the ship, a powerful thunderstorm wrecked it against the reefs. The slaves killed the Spanish crew and escaped into the forest. The maroons (*see* MAROONAGE IN THE AMERICAS) then subjugated groups of indigenous people. Subsequent shipwrecks provided more slaves. During the period of the zambo society, Esmeraldian blacks and zambos associated closely, intermarrying with various groups of Native Americans. (Although the Republic of Zambos marks the beginning of black immigration in Esmeraldas, the numerically more important movements of black immigration from present-day Colombia came about later.)

Spanish prospecting in the area began in the first decades of the eighteenth century and was focused on the Santiago River basin. Between 1820 and the beginning of the twentieth century, the prospectors were followed by successive penetrations of *señores de minas,* owners of concessions and slave gangs who disposed of significant capital and stimulated the creation of villages on the banks of the rivers. These enterprises were financed mainly by capitalists from the mining region of southern Colombia (Barbacoas and Popayán), who brought their slaves with them. The participation of capitalists from Quito, Ecuador's capital, was very limited. At the end of the nineteenth century and the beginning of the twentieth, a few Americans and Europeans invested in Esmeraldian mining concessions. In addition to the arrival of slaves from Colombia, a British company also organized the immigration of Jamaican blacks to work in its mines on the Santiago River.

Esmeraldas gained its independence from Spain in 1820. (Ecuadorian independence from Spain took place by province.) At the time, the few Esmeraldian mines, which never produced up to expectations, were in a state of abandonment, with a slave population of a few hundred. It is fair to say that the colonial mining in Esmeraldas resulted in failure and that this economic stagnation gave Esmeraldian blacks relatively more autonomy than slaves elsewhere in the Americas.

In Ecuador the abolition of slavery took decades. Beginning in 1821, it ended with the Urbina Decree, signed on July 25, 1851, and ratified by the Convention of Guayaquil on September 18, 1852.

For Ecuador's ruling Liberals (white and mestizo elite) in the mid-nineteenth century, modernization and the development of international commerce were seen as the principal means for growing the nation's economy. To this end, the national government took measures in each province. In 1846 a decree encouraged the colonization of Esmeraldas. Both the Espinel-Moncatta Convention of 1854 and the Icaza-Pritchett Contract of 1957 gave British creditors a greater presence in Esmeraldas Province, in part to repay Ecuadorian debt and in part to bring progress to the region. The Icaza-Pritchett Contract gave control to the British Ecuador Land Company over extensive tracts of land. Despite the hopes of the Ecuadorian government, the Ecuador Land Company invested little in the province. Instead it sublet sections of its lands to other foreign (British, German, and American) or national commercial companies. These companies dedicated themselves to the export of forest products, such as rubber, tobacco, and *tagua* nuts from the tagua tree that they bought from farmers and black gatherers who lived in the forest areas of Esmeraldas. Despite the lack of investment, the Esmeraldian concessions to the Ecuador Land Company gave an important boost to the province's commercial activities, thanks to what has been called the "tagua boom," the first period of economic prosperity in the history of Esmeraldas.

The tagua nut, also called "vegetable ivory," was used in Europe and North America to produce buttons and combs. Beginning in 1870, following the commercialization of the nuts of the tagua tree, the Esmeraldian economy experienced an important growth in exports. In 1887 the tagua produced more than 75 percent of the province's export revenue; and until around 1940, it was its principal export. Between 1850 and 1912 gold exports represented a vacillating proportion of the wealth exported from Esmeraldas, but they never became a stable source of revenue. The province also exported, in smaller quantities, gameskin, leather, exotic wood, cacao, and coffee. In the 1940s, with the development and production of plastic in industrialized countries, demand for tagua nuts decreased sharply.

During the boom, vast areas of tagua trees were maintained under strict company control, and several mechanisms were used to subordinate the local economies. The virtual monopoly over the extended regions suited for gathering forced many workers, mostly blacks, to enter into a relationship of dependence with the companies that dominated the areas or to colonize distant, unoccupied forest lands. In addition to the blacks and zambos who already inhabited the province, the labor required for gathering drew new immigrants from 1850 to 1920. They were mostly ex-slaves from the Colombian region of Barbacoas and, to a lesser extent, from the province of Imbabura in the Ecuadorian Andes.

After a depression in the 1940s, the province of Esmeraldas experienced another period of economic prosperity, the banana boom, beginning in about 1948. American companies that had invested in the Central American banana plantations suffered great losses following a series of cyclones and the proliferation of nematode threadworms (*sigatoka negra*). These companies decided that Ecuador presented the most favorable conditions for replacing the Central American plantations. It is therefore only since 1948 that, due to international market forces, Ecuador engaged in credit and incentive programs for banana production. This new economic juncture furthered the integration of Esmeraldas with the rest of the country.

The immigration of various ethnic groups continued with the banana boom, including blacks from the Colombian region of Barbacoas and mestizos from the Manabí Province. An asphalted road linking Esmeraldas and Quito was completed in the 1960s. During the 1980s and 1990s three factors led many residents from the northern part of Esmeraldas Province to migrate to the city of Esmeraldas and, importantly, to Guayaquil, Guayas Province, which is the urban center of the Ecuadorian coast and the most populous city of the country. These were (1) construction of the most important Ecuadorian oil refinery near the city of Esmeraldas; (2) a decrease in the province's banana production; and (3) a prolonged national economic depression. In their new places of residence, Afro-Esmeraldians are usually found at the bottom of the socioeconomic ladder and often endure racial discrimination.

Jean Muteba Rahier

See Also

Slavery in Latin America and the Caribbean; Décima; Jamaica; Transculturation, Mestizaje, and the Cosmic Race: An Interpretation; Abolition and Emancipation in Latin America and the Caribbean; Whitening.

North America

Essence, African American women's magazine, founded in 1970, focusing on health, self-improvement, beauty, fashion, fiction, and issues of interest to contemporary, upscale black women.

In 1970 Clarence Smith and Edward Lewis published 50,000 copies of *Essence*, the first issue of a monthly magazine aimed at black women in the post-civil rights era. It was designed to build self-esteem, encourage a more powerful self-concept, and provide a platform for African American women to express themselves during a time when the black middle class was expanding rapidly. *Essence* currently has a circulation of 1 million subscribers and a worldwide readership of 7.6 million.

Marcia Gillespie became editor in chief in 1971 and centered *Essence*'s content on the politics of black women's work. Gillespie was succeeded by Susan Taylor, formerly the health and beauty editor, who shifted the magazine's focus to black women's personal experiences. Under Taylor's leadership, *Essence* has become a highly respected and successful publication, the core of a $100 million communications empire.

Much of the magazine's success is attributable to *Essence*'s affirmative portrayal of black women, and to its carefully crafted artwork and photographs. Articles deal frankly with such issues as sexuality, human immunodeficiency virus (HIV) and acquired immune deficiency syndrome (AIDS), weight and physical fitness, political commentary, travel, and how to start a business or return to school. Taylor's own regular column, "In the Spirit," serves as an inspirational and motivational meditation. Taylor states that the mission of *Essence* is "to inspire and uplift black women, to help our sisters move their lives forward so that they can carry the word and uplift the race."

See Also

AIDS in the United States; Civil Rights Movement; Hair and Beauty Culture.

Latin America and the Caribbean

Estebanico (also known as Estevanico, Esteban, Estevanico the Moor, Esteban de Dorantes, Black Stephen) (b. 1503?, Azemmour, Morocco; d. 1539?, Hawikuh, N. Mex.), an Arab slave who became an explorer and guide in New Spain (Florida, Texas, and northern Mexico), he is allegedly the first black man to have set foot on the territory of the present-day United States.

Estebanico may have been captured by Portuguese slave traders in North Africa between 1513 and 1521, and later sold in Europe. He was bought by a Spanish explorer named Andrés de Dorantes, whom he accompanied on a 1528 expedition, led by conquistador Pánfilo de Narváez, to settle unknown territory in northern America. When they arrived in Florida, Narváez's group of some 300 men encountered many obstacles and were forced to split up in order to survive.

The legendary explorer Alvar Nuñez Cabeza de Vaca headed the group that included Estebanico. They traveled around the area now known as the Florida Panhandle and the Mississippi River, and harsh climatic conditions caused them to suffer shipwreck on what is now Galveston Island in Texas. Eventually, almost all of the expedition's members died from hunger, thirst, exhaustion, or disease, or in clashes with native tribes. In his account of the expedition, Cabeza de Vaca relates that there were only four survivors: himself, Alonso del Castillo Maldonado, Andrés de Dorantes, and Estebanico. The four were captured and enslaved by different tribes, and were only reunited after six years of separation.

Estebanico, along with other members of the reunited group, learned some shamanist practices and traditional healing from Cabeza de Vaca. Together, the foursome traveled from Galveston to Mexico City, allegedly performing cures on the Indians they encountered and earning a reputation as medicine men. Estebanico took charge of communicating with the local people in order to plan which routes to take. As a result of this close contact, he learned several native languages and began adorning himself with traditional amulets, feathers, and necklaces. Word of the group's healing powers spread far and wide. Indians of New Mexico later described them as "four great doctors, one of them black, the other three white, who gave blessings (and) healed the sick."

Around 1536 the group once again came in contact with Spanish colonizers. Some historians believe that when they reached Mexico City, Estebanico was sold to the viceroy, Antonio de Mendoza. Fascinated by Estebanico's stories, Mendoza sent his new slave to act as a guide and translator for Father Marcos de Niza, a Franciscan missionary who headed a new expedition in search of the legendary Seven Golden Cities of Cibola. Because he knew the territory, as well as the languages of several tribes, Estebanico journeyed ahead of de Niza to prepare the way for the Spanish colonizers. When he reached the Zuñi warriors, however, they captured and killed him, for reasons that remain a mystery.

Liliana Obregón

See Also
Portugal.

Latin America and the Caribbean

Estimé, Dumarsais

(b. April 21, 1900, Verrettes, Artibonite, Haiti; d. July 20, 1953, New York, N.Y.), Haitian president (1946-1950).

Before he became president of Haiti, Dumarsais Estimé was elected deputy to the National Assembly in 1930 and later served as minister of education in the cabinet of President Sténio Vincent. In his education post, he founded or raised teacher salaries; mandated vaccinations in primary schools; made sports obligatory in all schools, both public and private; and initiated interscholastic sports competitions.

In 1946 he was elected president by the National Assembly. He was supported by the black intelligentsia and represented the return to power of the black elite, after the ouster of mulatto president Elie Lescot. Not widely liked at the time he took office, Estimé went on to become one of Haiti's most popular leaders.

As president, Estimé launched populist and nationalist reforms in the areas of labor legislation, education, health care, and sanitation. He supported projects to attract tourism to the island, notably the Universal Exposition for the 200th anniversary of Port-au-Prince. He initiated construction programs to rebuild or clean some of the slums in the capital and construct or repair roads and bridges. He also reinstated the ban on foreign ownership of land which had been abrogated under United States occupation of the island from 1915 to 1934.

In 1950 Estimé's attempt to amend the constitution so that he could remain in power precipitated his ouster by the military. Though he died in exile three years later, in a New York hospital, he is remembered by many in Haiti as a progressive leader and a remarkable statesman.

Paulette Poujol-Oriol

See Also
Port-au-Prince, Haiti.

Latin America and the Caribbean

Estupiñán Bass, Nelson

(b. 1912, Esmeraldas, Ecuador), Afro-Ecuadorian poet and novelist; alongside Adalberto Ortiz and Antonio Preciado Bedoya, he is one of the prominent black writers of this South American country.

After graduating as a public accountant in 1932, Nelson Estupiñán Bass taught accounting for a few years in various high schools in the city of Esmeraldas. His first poems were published in 1934 in the socialist newspaper *La Tierra*, from Quito. He has been the director-founder of various Esmeraldian literary magazines: *Marimba*, *Helice*, and *Meridiano Negro*. In his early years Marxism had a great impact on his writing. He visited China and the Soviet Union and is an ex-president of the Ecuadorian Society of the Friends of the Democratic Republic of Germany. Several North American literary critics have translated some of his novels and studied various aspects of his work. Primarily a novelist, Estupiñán Bass also wrote, particularly at the beginning of his career, collections of poems, including *Audición para el negro* and *Canto negro por la luz*, as well as a few plays (*see* Literature, Black, in Spanish America).

Beyond his importance as a figure in Afro-Esmeraldian literature, Estupiñan Bass is garnering increasing recognition as a major Ecuadorian author. Among other national literary prizes, he has received the prestigious Premio Eugenio Espejo from the Casa de la Cultura Ecuatoriana in 1993.

His first novel, *Cuando los guayacanes florecían* (When the Guayacans Were in Bloom), is the best known of the nine novels he has written to date. First published in 1954, it has been translated into Russian, English, and French, and has been reedited in Spanish four times.

The narratives of his novels are characterized by a thematic tension between two different, and in some ways opposed, aims: on the one hand he strives to celebrate blackness, Afro-Esmeraldian identity, and the respectability of Afro-Esmeraldian cultural traditions in particular. On the other hand he downplays race, making it secondary to class; as a main character in one of his novels puts it: "The only choice we have is the union of all the poor people. This is the only solution. When we, the poor, will be united, there will be no injustice, no exploitation, no robbery; until we do that we will be the daily meal of the big people." The novel insists that all dominated people of Ecuador – black, indigenous, and *mestizo* (people of both European and Native American ancestry), small farmers and workers – and beyond Ecuador, all dominated people of the world, should unite against their oppressors: the capitalists and big plantation owners, and their allies in corrupt governments. The ultimate objective of his heroic characters is the installation of a socialist society in which race would be meaningless, and in which poor people would be able to remedy their slights by abandoning their old ways and by educating themselves in order to better participate in modernity.

In an interview with Millicent Bolden, Nelson Estupiñán Bass addressed the future of the black people of the world: "I think that what's going to happen is what is already happening in my province: race-mixing *[mestizaje]*. I am certain that racial crossing will have to happen because love does not know borders.... I think that perhaps, the destiny of the world is total hybridization.... This would also mean the disappearance of white people... and a new physical type, which will be just like what the writer José Vasconcelos had said, will emerge: the cosmic man *[el hombre cósmico]*" (*see* Transculturation, Mestizaje, and the Cosmic Race: An Interpretation).

Every novel of Estupiñán Bass has clearly shown his taste for experimentation with literary techniques, such as varying narrative structures. In *Cuando los guayacanes florecían*, abundant provincialisms require the non-Esmeraldian reader frequently to consult a glossary provided with the story. In *Las Puertas del Verano*, two juxtaposed narratives, one on the left page and the other on the right, meet only at the end of the book. A recent novel, *Al Norte de Dios*, tells the story of a "profane God" living on

Earth, with constant references to American show business.

Jean Muteba Rahier

Africa

Ethiopia, a country in the Horn of Africa bordering ERITREA, DJIBOUTI, KENYA, SOMALIA, and SUDAN.

More than 3000 years ago the Greek poet Homer sang of "the blessed Ethiopians." The Englishman of letters Samuel Johnson wrote a novel 200 years ago about an Ethiopian prince, in which the philosophers of the country contemplated the mysteries of the universe. In the twentieth century, Pan-Africanists such as W. E. B. Du Bois saw Ethiopia as the "all-mother of men," an ancient land of immense importance to human history, while the followers of Marcus Garvey dreamed that the children of slaves might return to Africa and live in Ethiopia, a nation that in the biblical Book of Psalms "stretched out her hands unto God." More recently, television and newspapers have depicted Ethiopia in harsh terms as a land of famine, war, and very little else, but the country possesses an extraordinary history, which remains little known outside its borders.

The land we now know as Ethiopia witnessed the birth of modern humanity more than 100,000 years ago, and it was home to some of Africa's most ancient and advanced civilizations. Indeed, Ethiopia is one of the oldest nations on earth. For centuries the people of Ethiopia's highlands have maintained a rich cultural legacy, including a literary tradition dating from more than 2000 years ago and a form of Christianity dating from the time of the Roman Empire. Over the centuries many of the country's people came to practice Islam, and by the twentieth century, Ethiopia incorporated one of the most ethnically and culturally diverse populations in Africa. From the 1960s to the early 1990s Ethiopia suffered a long economic decline, famine, and civil warfare, first under an autocratic emperor and later under a brutal socialist military government. In the late 1990s Ethiopia faced the challenge of overcoming ethnic strife and years of economic mismanagement to recover the prosperity and cultural richness it once enjoyed.

PREHISTORY

Ethiopia was home to some of our earliest human ancestors. Some of the oldest remains of *Homo sapiens*, dating back about 130,000 years, have been found in the far south, along the Kibish River in the Omo Valley region. Until 1994 the oldest known branch of the human family tree was represented by fossil remains found in 1974 at Hadar, 350 km (217 mi) northeast of the Ethiopian capital, Addis Ababa. The famous partial skeleton called Dinqinesh, or Lucy, a specimen of *Australopithecus afarensis* that dates from between 3 and 3.6 million years ago, is exhibited in the National Museum at Addis Ababa. Discoveries of even older hominid remains have now surpassed *Australopithecus afarensis*. The remains of 17 individuals, identified as members of a new species, *Australopithecus ramidus*, have been found at Aramis, on the north side of the Awash Valley, about 75 km (47 mi) south of the Hadar region. These new finds take the record in Ethiopia back 4.4 million years, and appear to confirm estimates that the hominid line diverged from that of modern apes between 4 and 6 million years ago.

About 8000 years ago inhabitants of present-day Ethiopia had begun to practice animal husbandry. The region's people, most likely speaking Cushitic languages (*see* LANGUAGES, AFRICAN: AN OVERVIEW), were practicing agriculture 2000 years ago at the latest. By about 1000 B.C.E. Semitic-speaking peoples had entered the northern highlands, perhaps from southern Arabia. There they probably intermarried with the existing population. These people were the ancestors of today's TIGRE, Tigray, and AMHARA (as well as other, smaller ethnic groups), who speak languages belonging to the Semitic family, which includes Arabic and Hebrew.

EARLY HISTORY

The early history of Ethiopia, whether legendary or confirmed by archaeology, is rich and fascinating. The country's northern borderlands may have been the location of the fabulous land of PUNT *(Pwene)*, known to the ancient Egyptians as a source of luxuries, especially incense, for the courts of the pharaohs. Aromatic resins are still collected in some areas of Tigray Province and Eritrea. The ancient Egyptians called this country the Land of God (*Ta-neter*).

Between about 800 and 300 B.C.E. a literate and highly developed civilization flourished in the Eritrean and Tigray highlands. Its rulers referred to themselves as the kings, or *mukarribs*, of Da'amat and Saba, and may have ruled over parts of south Arabia known as Saba (or Sheba). The title mukarrib indicated something like "federator," and in south Arabia (present-day Yemen) the title referred to the ruler of tribes that were linked by covenant. The people of Da'amat in Ethiopia wrote inscriptions in a language and a script very similar to those found on inscriptions in southern Arabia, and presumably the peoples on both sides of the Red Sea shared a common cultural background. Only a few traces of the civilization of Da'amat remain, but they are often spectacular. At Yeha the impressive temple of the god Ilmuqah still stands; it is the most ancient building in Ethiopia. Inscribed altars and some splendid stone sculptures from this period are now on display in the National Museum.

After this period the uplands became the seat of one of the greatest of all the ancient African civilizations; the empire was ruled from its capital city of AKSUM (*see* ANCIENT AFRICAN CIVILIZATIONS). South Arabian and Aksumite sources, written in the ancient Ethiopian language known as Ge'ez, refer to the so-called Habash people who inhabited the empire. The name of this people is the basis of the word "Abyssinia," by which Ethiopia has often been known. The name of Ethiopia is taken from a Greek expression meaning "burnt faces." The Greeks applied this term to the Kushite kingdom and black Africa in general. In the fourth century C.E. the kings of Aksum began to use the Greek term (*Aithiopia*) for their own country when they wrote in Greek. A trilingual inscription of Ezana, the king who converted to Christianity about 340 C.E., employs both names. This is the first known use of the word "Ethiopia" by one of its own rulers to describe part of the modern country. The land was usually called Aksum, after its capital.

According to early church historians such as Rufinus of Aquileia (345?-410 C.E.), a young Syrian named Frumentius brought Christianity to Ethiopia (*see* ETHIOPIAN ORTHODOX CHURCH). Around 330 C.E. he was made bishop of Aksum by Athanasius, patriarch of Alexandria. This established a custom that continued for over 16 centuries. Until 1959 the Alexandrian patriarch of the Coptic Church of Egypt appointed the bishops who headed the Ethiopian Church. They were always foreign, and usually Egyptian.

During the Aksumite period the northern regions of Ethiopia belonged to an international trade network linking the Nile, the Mediterranean, and the Indian Ocean. Aksum's control over this rich trade provided the basis for its prosperity and cultural achievements. In the sixth century C.E., King Kaleb of Aksum sent a military expedition across the Red Sea to depose the Jewish king Yusuf Asar of Himyar. Even though historical details about the period are relatively meager, objects recovered from excavations indicate a high level of material prosperity, with pottery, architecture, and coinage attesting unique Aksumite styles. By the Aksumite period, the AGAW and other peoples who spoke Cushitic languages had come under the dominance of a ruling class who spoke the Semitic language Ge'ez.

Over a period of seven centuries Aksum firmly left its mark on highland northern Ethiopia. The choice of Christianity, the style of architecture, and the form of kingship were retained even after the city itself ceased to be the political center. The empire first shaped the general cultural heritage of highland Ethiopia, including Christian religion and Semitic language. From every point of view, the Aksumite kingdom was a golden age in Ethiopian history. Its kings erected stone *stelae* (or pillars) whose height surpassed any other monolithic monuments in the ancient world, and they employed a gold coinage at a time when very few other societies were wealthy

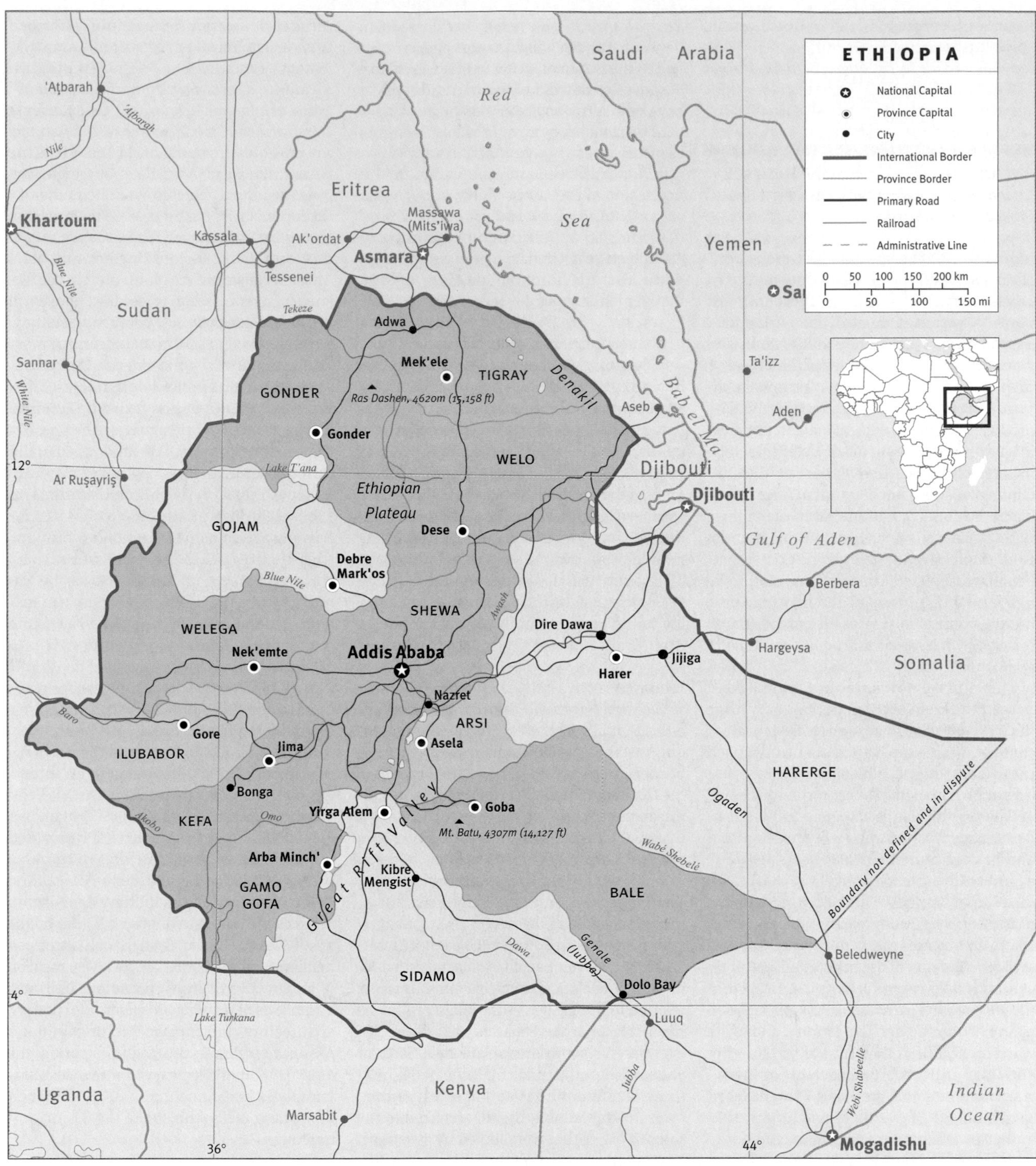

or sophisticated enough to do so.

The zenith of Aksum occurred in the sixth century. Soon after, the rise of Islamic power in the Red Sea deprived Aksum of control over the trade that had been its major source of wealth. Its kings were forced to curtail their overseas projects, abandon many of their trading links, and retreat to the highlands. Arab geographers describe an Ethiopian state ruled from a capital called Ku'bar. This Ethiopian Christian kingdom seems to have maintained itself for several centuries, though it was often threatened by expansionist Muslim states to the east and south. Almost nothing is known about it, aside from the occasional remarks in the reports of Arab geographers or in the chronicles of the patriarchs of Alexandria. These chronicles record a disaster that occurred late in the tenth century, when a foreign queen is said to have seized power, killing the reigning *negus,* or king. This incident has been preserved in Ethiopian legends that tell of a queen called Gudit, whom the chronicles blame for destroying Aksum.

In spite of such defeats, the highland kingdom seems to have been able to keep its Christian culture more or less intact. The Zagwe Dynasty, which ruled from about 1137 to 1270, figures in traditional Ethiopian sources as a break in the historical sequence, when a "usurping" dynasty of Agaw origin seized control of the throne. Royal chronicles and accounts of Ethiopian saints provide some information about this period of Ethiopian history. The capital city during this period was Adafa or Roha, which was later named after Lalibela himself, who is said to have commissioned the city's famous churches, cut from the living rock (*see* LALIBELA, ETHIOPIA). The Zagwe kings did not rule over a large area. The limits of Zagwe power seem to have encouraged the Muslims of the coast, who grew strong enough to establish states as far west as present-day Shewa.

The church hierarchy and remnants of the old elite resented Zagwe rule. With the support of the church, the Solomonic Dynasty ousted the Zagwe from power around 1270. Traditional church accounts describe the Solomonic Dynasty as descendants of the "legitimate" rulers, in contrast with the Zagwe "usurpers." In other words, church documents back the new dynasty's claims of descent from King Solomon of Israel and the QUEEN OF SHEBA through their son Menilek, the legendary first emperor of Ethiopia. In return for the church's support, the Solomonic rulers awarded the Ethiopian Church control over vast stretches of land, which gave the church a source of wealth and power that endured until the revolution of 1974. This dynasty continued into the nineteenth century, and was linked with the family of the last emperor, HAILE SELASSIE I. The dynasty's power was based in the Amhara regions (including Shewa). There seems to have been no real capital. The emperor and his court were perpetually on the move, establishing temporary administration as the need arose. During the dry season, when military campaigns were possible, the capital took the form of a vast but rigidly disciplined city of tents.

The founder of this new dynasty was Yekuno Amlak (r. 1270-1285), and some of his successors were remarkable rulers who consolidated and extended the kingdom or made significant contributions to religious and cultural life. During the early years of the dynasty, royal chronicles give some information about wars with Muslim states such as Ifat, which controlled the area around the Red Sea coast and even some of the highlands of Shewa. For the first time, the Christian kingdom was able to expand toward what are now the southern provinces of Ethiopia. Amda Seyon (r. 1314-1344) even absorbed some Muslim districts, although his empire extracted tribute from more or less autonomous regions instead of imposing direct control. Other emperors campaigned in the north, to gain access to the Red Sea, as well as in the south and the east. Zar'a Ya'qob (r. 1434-1468) controlled a substantial central Ethiopian state in relative tranquillity, which allowed the new growth of arts and literature. However, few churches, manuscripts, or paintings survive from this period. Much of the territory and the cultural heritage was soon to be lost, and any further territorial expansion was to remain modest until the late nineteenth century.

Ethiopian men wear traditional, richly woven textiles at the Feast of Timqat in Gonder. *Christian Sappa/Rapho*

INVASIONS AND DISORDER

In the sixteenth century the Portuguese search for a mythical Christian ruler named Prester John led to the Solomonic emperors of Ethiopia. A first envoy, Pero da Covilhão, was sent in 1487. He arrived six years later during the reign of Eskender, but was never permitted to leave. More envoys arrived in 1508, and in the following year a letter was sent to Portugal with an Ethiopian ambassador, Matthew the Armenian. He finally reached Portugal in 1514 and returned with a Portuguese embassy in 1520. The arrival of the Portuguese embassy enabled one of its members, Francisco Alvares, to write the first detailed description of the country, the only account we have of the medieval kingdom before Muslim incursions destroyed much of its Christian culture.

The great rivals of the Christian emperors were the Muslim rulers of Adal, the region lying east of the Awash River as far as the sea coast, and including Harer. In 1516 the emperor LEBNA DENGEL had defeated the emir Mahfuz of Adal. Perhaps because of this victory, he neglected to make a military alliance with the Portuguese, but a strong and determined leader soon arose among the Muslims. The imam Ahmad ibn Ibrahim of Harer, known as Grañ ("the left-handed"), won a great victory in 1529, and Muslim armies invaded most of Christian Ethiopia. Lebna Dengel, who had received the Portuguese embassy enthroned in his great pavilion hung with silks and brocades, became a fugitive until his death at Debra Damo in

1540. According to Arabic as well as Ethiopian sources, Muslim forces ransacked and burned churches, monasteries, and treasuries.

This might have been the end of the unique Christian civilization that had flourished in northern and central Ethiopia since Aksumite times, but the new emperor Galawdewos rescued the state with the aid of Portuguese troops under Cristovão, the son of Vasco da Gama. The decisive factor was the possession of firearms, which the Muslim troops had already acquired in large numbers across the Red Sea. Ahmad Grañ and Cristovão da Gama both lost their lives, but the tide had definitively turned in favor of the Christian state. Christian forces sacked Harer itself, although it survived as the greatest Muslim center in Ethiopia, a trading city in contact with the Red Sea coast and beyond.

After this episode the Solomonic emperors established Christian rule once again over the devastated central regions, but both the Muslim states and the Christian kingdom soon had to defend themselves against a new threat: the Cushitic Oromo peoples. During the sixteenth and seventeenth centuries, Oromo-speaking herdsmen began to migrate from the south, and rapidly became the chief enemies of the Christian state of the north and center. They occupied many parts of what is now Ethiopia, and marriages with Oromo chiefly families meant that some of the Solomonic emperors became part Oromo.

For about a century after their entry into Ethiopian affairs, the Portuguese remained active in the region. Jesuit missionaries attempted to convert the country to Roman Catholicism, with little lasting success. With the accession to the Ethiopian throne of Fasiladas, a firm adherent of the Ethiopian Orthodox Church, the Roman Catholic venture was finished. He expelled the Jesuits in 1632 and made an arrangement with the Turkish authorities at Massawa to execute any foreign priest who might attempt to enter the country.

After the expulsion of the Portuguese, Ethiopia was again isolated from European influence. During the following centuries, foreign travelers made occasional visits to the country, which was now ruled from the new capital built at Gonder, north of Lake T'ana. Like the Jesuits before them, these visitors recorded their observations of different peoples, plants and animals, political affairs, religious issues, opportunities for trade, and many other features of Ethiopian life. The earlier Gonder period included powerful emperors whose deeds are described in the royal chronicles. Gonder itself is a remarkable testimony to their efforts, the first capital after centuries during which the empire had been governed from tents. The turrets and battlements of its castles still stand, along with some of the 44 churches that once embellished the city.

In the eighteenth century, however, the power of the central monarchy began to decline. Gonder slowly fell into decay as great provincial lords, largely of Oromo origin, competed to enthrone rival puppet kings. The custom of exiling male members of the royal family to a remote mountain, to prevent them from plotting against the current emperor, actually provided a reservoir of princes with the required Solomonic blood that provincial lords could recruit in any new attempt to seize power. With the assassination of Iyasu I in 1704, the monarchy became increasingly unstable. After the emperor Iyo'as was murdered in 1769, the empire began to collapse, even though the theory of Solomonic rule remained intact. This chaotic period, known as the Era of the Princes, continued until the middle of the nineteenth century, with feeble emperors dwelling at Gonder completely at the mercy of the great provincial lords. Some of the emperors lived in such poverty amid the ruins of their palaces that scarcely enough money could be found to provide a decent burial. Only the magic of their Solomonic descent, or perhaps the need for the great chiefs to have someone to bestow the title of *ras* (supreme commander), kept the system alive.

Piecemeal Modernization and the Struggle Against Colonialism

In the middle of the nineteenth century an interloper named Kassa overthrew the power of the provincial lords as well as the old imperial tradition. He eliminated most of his rivals and restored a strong and united Ethiopia, even subduing Shewa, which had maintained a separate existence under rulers claiming descent from Lebna Dengel. Kassa was crowned in 1855 as Tewodros II, and

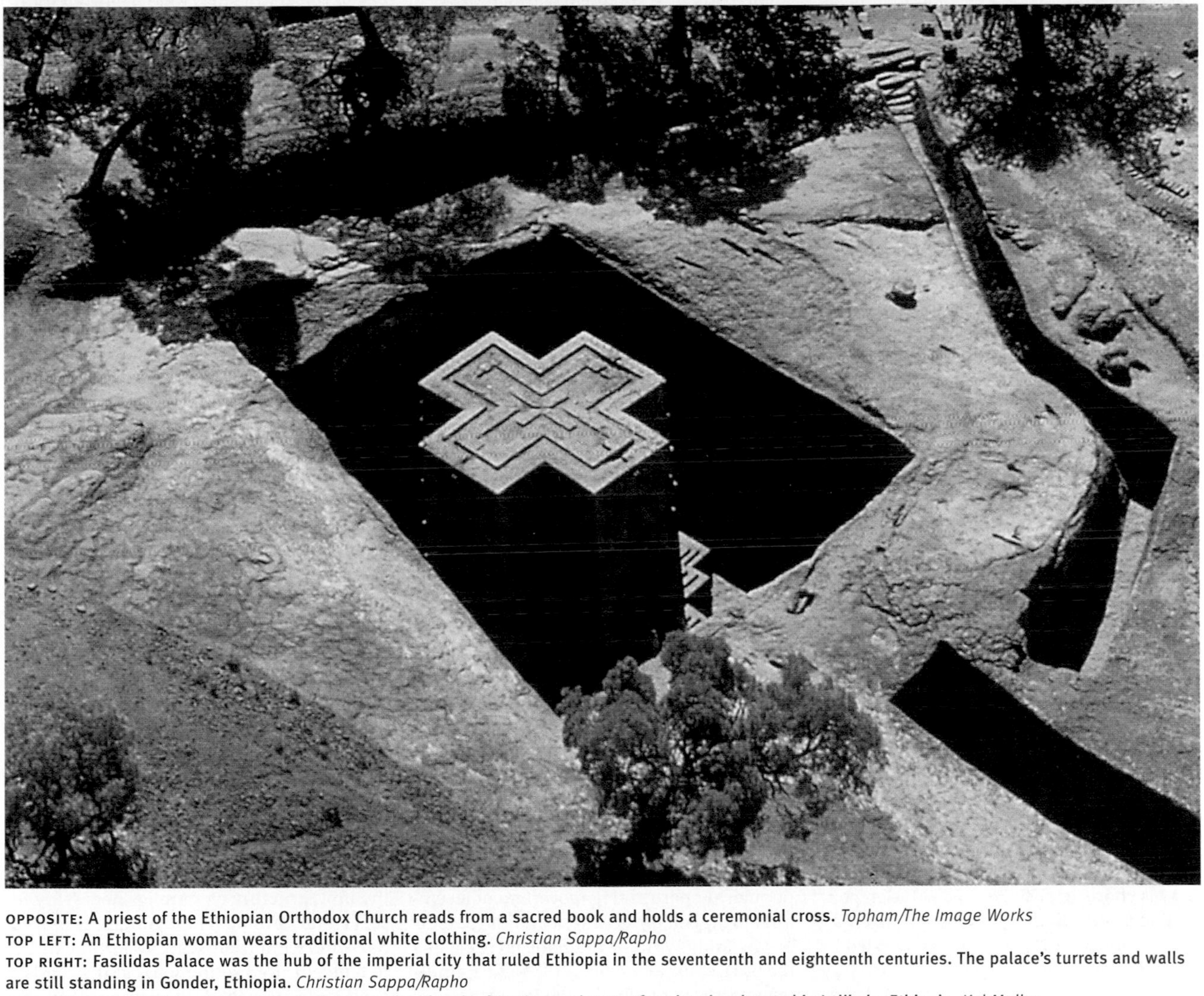

OPPOSITE: A priest of the Ethiopian Orthodox Church reads from a sacred book and holds a ceremonial cross. *Topham/The Image Works*
TOP LEFT: An Ethiopian woman wears traditional white clothing. *Christian Sappa/Rapho*
TOP RIGHT: Fasilidas Palace was the hub of the imperial city that ruled Ethiopia in the seventeenth and eighteenth centuries. The palace's turrets and walls are still standing in Gonder, Ethiopia. *Christian Sappa/Rapho*
ABOVE: Carved out of the living rock around 1200, the Church of St. George is one of 11 churches located in Lalibela, Ethiopia. *Kal Muller*

the genealogists duly found a Solomonic background for him. Recognizing the growing threat of European imperialism, Tewodros attempted to modernize Ethiopia's army and establish a strong central state. To fund this modernization program, he imposed higher taxes on peasants and seized church lands; these actions alienated both the overtaxed peasantry and the country's powerful clergy. Meanwhile, a diplomatic argument with Great Britain led to the Napier expedition in 1868. The British besieged Tewodros at his capital, Maqdala, where he committed suicide as British forces overran his defenses. However, even this disaster did not completely destroy the attempts he had made to strengthen and modernize his empire.

As the European world grew more aware of Ethiopia, Yohannes IV and MENILEK II, the two emperors who succeeded Tewodros, fought to retain their independence against

Sudanese expansionism and Italian colonialism. Yohannes had been the ruler of Tigray, and emerged victorious from the struggle to fill the vacuum left by the death of Tewodros and the British departure. He resisted a quest for power by his tributary, the king of Shewa. He failed to keep Italy from acquiring the Red Sea ports of Aseb (1869) and Massawa (1885), but resisted Italian incursions inland. Yohannes died fighting the Sudanese Mahdi (*see* Mahdist State), and was succeeded in 1889 by Menilek II of Shewa.

With the Ethiopian treasury drained by ongoing warfare, the new emperor needed peace to establish himself on his throne; this put him in a weak position as he faced the Italians. In 1890 Menilek agreed to the Treaty of Wichale granting Italy control of Eritrea, but the treaty's Italian translation awarded Italy a protectorate over the whole of Ethiopia. After replenishing his treasury, Menilek defeated the Italians at the Battle of Adwa in 1896. This was a unique achievement. Alone among African states, Ethiopia succeeded in retaining independent sovereignty in the face of European colonialism. Even though Menilek lost some territory in Eritrea, he made up for this by his own expansion to the south. Between 1896 and 1906 Ethiopia grew to its present size, as Menilek conquered areas previously ruled by the Oromo or other peoples. Menilek also succeeded in ejecting the last independent Muslim emir from Harer.

Determined to keep his country independent, Menilek used taxes collected from these conquered territories to fund a modernization program. He founded a new capital at Addis Ababa and commissioned Ethiopia's first modern schools and hospitals. He hired foreign advisors and concluded an agreement with a French firm to construct a railroad, completed in 1917, from Addis Ababa to the Indian Ocean port of Djibouti in French Somaliland. During the reign of Menilek, Ethiopia acquired its first modern bank, postage stamps, and a national currency. The first modern roads were constructed, the basis of a telephone and telegraph system installed, and a rudimentary cabinet established. The new transport infrastructure enabled Ethiopia's land-owning elite to export cash crops, primarily coffee, for sale on the global market.

Menilek's grandson Lij Iyasu reigned briefly (1913-1916) after his grandfather's death, but his efforts to give Ethiopia's Muslim population a voice in the government angered the country's Christian elite. A group led by an aristocratic official, Ras Tafari, ousted Lij Iyasu from office and named Menilek's daughter Zawditu as empress, with Ras Tafari as the new regent. Tafari continued attempts to modernize the empire. He abolished slavery and recruited graduates of the new schools to staff a modern civil service. Coffee exports provided revenues for the expansion of Ethiopia's modern infrastructure, and the country's market economy expanded. Tafari kept Europeans from gaining control of Ethiopia's economy, as they had elsewhere in Africa, by requiring at least partial local ownership of all enterprises.

In 1930, upon the death of Zawditu, Tafari was crowned Emperor Haile Selassie I. Coffee exports continued to bankroll his ambitious modernization program. However, his reign faced a crisis in 1935 when Italian troops invaded Ethiopia. The Italian forces won a quick victory, and Italy formally annexed the country the following year. Although there was great international sympathy for Ethiopia, no material assistance was offered, and the fascist occupation lasted for five years. The Italian colonial administration undertook a significant amount of road building and other construction work, and carried out a modern expansion of the capital at Addis Ababa. However, Ethiopian patriot resistance continued in the countryside. Fascist rule collapsed after Italy, under Benito Mussolini, entered World War II. A combined army of Ethiopian and British troops liberated Ethiopia in 1941. Haile Selassie was restored to the throne, and his country became a founding member of the United Nations.

As the cold war between the Soviet bloc and the West came to dominate global affairs, Haile Selassie aligned himself with the West. In return, the Western powers awarded Ethiopia the former Italian colony of Eritrea in 1952. With access to Western markets, Ethiopia earned healthy revenues from coffee exports during the 1950s. With Western and, especially, with United States assistance, new hospitals, schools, and roads were built, banking and currency were reorganized, and a national airline established. Addis Ababa was chosen as the headquarters for both the United Nations Economic Commission for Africa and the Organization of African Unity.

Although the emperor introduced a new constitution in 1955 granting limited rights to the Ethiopian people, the constitution left ultimate power in the emperor's hands. Meanwhile, the emperor failed to respond to calls for further democratization and land reform to end the concentration of the country's land in the hands of the church and aristocracy. Frustrated by the emperor's intransigence, students began to protest and the imperial bodyguard attempted a coup in 1960. Although the aging emperor crushed the opposition and retained his hold on power, his regime lost popular support, and his government faced ongoing rebellion in Eritrea and the Somali borderlands. With the dramatic increase in the price of imported oil in 1973 and a simultaneous drought and famine in northern Ethiopia, Ethiopia's economy collapsed. Strikes and demonstrations in Addis Ababa forced the resignation of government officials in early 1974. Soon thereafter, a military committee known as the *derg*, led by Haile Mariam Mengistu, seized control of the government and moved to dismantle the entrenched aristocratic power structure for which they blamed the country's ills. On September 12, 1974, the derg removed the emperor from his throne, and by the end of the year Mengistu's faction, which was committed to Soviet-style socialism, had driven moderates from the government.

The Revolution and its Aftermath

With the old establishment shattered, Mengistu installed a revolutionary socialist government (*see* African Socialism). Abandoning earlier contacts with the United States, he relied on support from the Soviet Union. Several groups challenged revolutionary policies on ideological or ethnic grounds, but Mengistu's regime brutally repressed internal opposition. In 1975 the Ethiopian government carried out a sweeping land reform that seized land from its previous owners and made it the property of the state. This land nationalization eliminated the power base of the land-owning aristocracy and church, which for centuries had relied on the collection of rents from the country's peasantry. Meanwhile, internal unrest, including an ongoing independence struggle in Eritrea, encouraged a Somali invasion in 1975, which the Ethiopian government defeated in 1978 with massive Soviet and Cuban aid. The government nationalized (placed under state ownership) factories, banks, and insurance companies and in 1984 established a ruling party, the Workers' Party of Ethiopia.

During the 1980s separatist movements in Eritrea and Tigray mounted increasingly successful military campaigns. Meanwhile, the Ethiopian government's land reform and agricultural policies ruined the country's fragile ecological balance, and harvests declined. Government exploitation of the peasantry further hampered both agricultural production and the distribution of food, and in 1984 a grueling famine gripped the country. News of famine brought Ethiopia to the attention of Western media. This publicity resulted in extensive international aid, which emphasized humanitarian relief rather than development. The country thus remained one of the poorest in the world. The Mengistu regime's radical responses to the problems of drought and famine – resettlement and "villagization" – made the situation worse. Resettlement programs involved the relocation of peasants, sometimes forcibly, to uncultivated lands where they often lacked the infrastructure or supplies necessary for successful farming. These programs moved peasants from their scattered homesteads to concentrated settlements along roads, supposedly to facilitate the delivery of aid and services, but also to facilitate government surveillance. Both programs further disrupted the country's agriculture and provoked accusations by Ethiopian and foreign observers that dissident groups were being starved deliberately.

In 1988 rebels in Eritrea and Tigre joined forces and successfully fought Ethiopian government troops. Rebels expanded their control over Eritrea and northern Ethiopia during 1989 and 1990. The rebels from Tigray formed alliances with other ethnically based opposition groups to form the Ethiopian People's Revolutionary Democratic Front (EPRDF). By April 1991 all of Eritrea was under the control of the Eritrean People's Liberation Front (EPLF), and the forces of the EPRDF advanced on Addis Ababa. Mengistu fled to exile in ZIMBABWE in May 1991, and his regime collapsed.

The EPRDF established a transitional government with MELES ZENAWI as president in Ethiopia, while the EPLF controlled Eritrea. In 1993 Eritrea declared its independence. The EPRDF announced the reorganization of the country as a federal state divided into regions along ethnic lines. The new government promoted this reorganization as a way to acknowledge the country's ethnic diversity, but the reorganization angered many Asmara (the ethnic group that had traditionally dominated Ethiopia), who felt that the plan jeopardized national unity. The EPRDF muzzled the opposition and in 1992 carried out parliamentary elections. The Ethiopian Parliament approved a new constitution in 1994, and Meles Zenawi won election as prime minister in 1995.

During 1992 and 1993 the transitional government had agreed to a structural adjustment plan intended to liberalize the economy. However, the government failed to return property seized by the Mengistu regime to private owners. The economy stagnated, and the government's heavy regulation of commerce discouraged agricultural production and food distribution. Once again, in 1994, famine threatened Ethiopia. International assistance saved many lives, and in 1995 the government finally established a process for returning nationalized land to private control. However, this process aroused opposition because it favored supporters of the EPRDF, who were allowed to claim larger allotments of land than families who had received titles to land under the regime of Emperor Haile Selassie or Lt. Col. Mengistu. The government also announced controversial plans to privatize its commercial and industrial holdings. The redistribution of land appeared to improve the country's agricultural fortunes: the country enjoyed good harvests in 1996 and 1997. Its overall economy seemed to be recovering from years of government mismanagement. However, ethnic strife and raids carried out by discharged soldiers continued to plague the Oromo and Somali regions. In 1998 a border dispute with Eritrea threatened to torpedo Ethiopia's peaceful recovery from years of warfare. Thus, it remained uncertain whether the country would be able to overcome recent misfortunes and reclaim its historical legacy as one of Africa's richest and most culturally advanced lands.

Roderick Grierson and Stuart Munro-Hay

SEE ALSO

Addis Ababa, Ethiopia; Explorers in Africa Before 1500; Explorers in Africa, 1500 to 1800; Ibn Battutah; Egypt, Ancient Kingdom of; Kush, Early Kingdom of; Massawa, Eritrea; Nile River; Pan-Africanism; Du Bois, William Edward Burghardt (W. E. B.); Garvey, Marcus Mosiah; Djibouti, Djibouti; Alexandria, Egypt; Christianity: Missionaries in Africa; Slavery in Africa; Gonder, Ethiopia; Ethiopic Script and Language.

Africa

Ethiopia (Ready Reference)

Official Name: Federal Democratic Republic of Ethiopia

Area: 1,130,000 sq km (436,300 sq mi)

Location: Eastern Africa; bounded by ERITREA, DJIBOUTI, SOMALIA, KENYA, and the SUDAN

Capital: Addis Ababa (population 2,200,186 [1993 estimate])

Population: 58,390,351 (1998 estimate)

Population Density: 51 persons per sq km (133 persons per sq mi)

Population Below Age 15: 46 percent (male 13,468,783; female 13,398,500 [1998 estimate])

Population Growth Rate: 2.2 percent (1998 estimate)

Total Fertility Rate: 6.88 children born per woman (1998 estimate)

Life Expectancy at Birth: Total population: 40.8 years (male 39.7 years; female 42 years [1998 estimate])

Infant Mortality Rate: 125.6 deaths per 1000 live births (1998 estimate)

Literacy Rate (age 15 and over who can read and write): Total population: 35.5 percent (male 45.5 percent; female 25.3 percent [1995 estimate])

Education: Free education exists from primary school through the college level, but regular school facilities are available to only about one-third of the children of school age. In the early 1990s about 2.8 million students attended primary and secondary schools run by the government and religious groups. Addis Ababa University (1950) has branches in several locations.

Languages: Amharic is the official language; Tigrinya, Orominga, Guaraginga, Somali, Arabic, and English are also spoken.

Ethnic Groups: The AMHARA, a highland people partly of Semitic origin, and the related Tigreans constitute about 32 percent of the total population. The OROMO people, living mainly in central and southwestern Ethiopia, constitute about 40 percent of the population. The Shangalla, a people found in the western part of the country from the border of Eritrea to Lake Turkana, constitute about 6 percent of the population. The SOMALI, who live in the east and southeast, notably in the Ogaden region, are approximately equal in number to the Shangalla. The Denakil inhabit the semidesert plains east of the highlands. The nonindigenous population includes Yemenis, Indians, Armenians, and Greeks.

Religions: About 40 percent of the people of Ethiopia are Christians, many from the Ethiopian Orthodox Union Church, an autonomous Christian sect headed by a patriarch and closely related to the Coptic church of Egypt. Christianity is predominant in the north; all the southern regions have Muslim majorities, who represent about 45 percent of the country's population. The south also contains large numbers of animists. The Falashas, who practice a type of Judaism that probably dates back to contact with early Arabian Jews, were airlifted to Israel in 1991 during Ethiopia's civil war.

Climate: The principal rainy season occurs between mid-June and September, followed by a dry season that may be interrupted in February or March by a short rainy season. The tropical zone has an average annual temperature of about 27° C (about 80° F) and receives less than about 510 mm (about 20 in) of rain annually. The subtropical zone, which includes most of the highland plateau, has an average temperature of about 22° C (about 72° F) with an annual rainfall ranging from about 510 to 1530 mm (about 20 to 60 in).

Land, Plants, and Animals: The Ethiopian Plateau, a high table land covering more than half the total area of the country, is split by the Great Rift Valley. In the north, the plateau is cut by many rivers and deep valleys, and capped by mountains in the region surrounding Lake T'ana (the lake in which the Blue Nile rises). The northeastern edges of the plateau are marked by steep escarpments, which drop to the sunbaked coastal plain and the Denakil Desert. Along the western fringe the plateau descends gradually to the desert of SUDAN. Along the southern and southwestern limits, the plateau lowers toward Lake Turkana (formerly called Lake Rudolf). The lower areas of the tropical zone have sparse vegetation, but in the valleys and ravines almost every form of African vegetation grows profusely. Afro-alpine vegetation is found on the highest slopes. The GIRAFFE, leopard, HIPPOPOTAMUS, LION, ELEPHANT, ANTELOPE, and RHINOCEROS are native to most parts of the country. The lynx, jackal, hyena, and various species of monkey are also common. Birds of prey include the eagle, hawk, and vulture. Heron, parrot, and such game birds as the snipe, partridge, teal, pigeon, and bustard are found in abundance. Among the many varieties of insects are the locust and TSETSE FLY.

Natural Resources: The resources of Ethiopia are primarily agricultural. The plateau area is fertile and largely undeveloped. The wide range of soils, climate, and elevations permits the production of a diversified range of agricultural commodities. A variety of mineral deposits exist; iron, copper, petroleum, salt, potash, gold, and platinum are the principal ones that have been commercially exploited.

Currency: The birr

Gross Domestic Product (GDP): $29 billion (1997 estimate)

GDP per Capita: $530 (1997 estimate)
GDP Real Growth Rate: 5 percent (1997 estimate)
Primary Economic Activities: The economy of Ethiopia remains heavily dependent on the earnings of the agricultural sector. Participation by most of the people in the monetary economy is limited; much trading is conducted by barter in local markets. Traditional agriculture, including livestock raising, is the most characteristic form of Ethiopian economic activity. Commercial estates, which are run by the government, supply coffee, cotton, sugar, fruit, and vegetables to the nation's processing industries and for export. Coffee is Ethiopia's most important commodity, engaging about one-fourth of the population.
Primary Crops: Coffee, cotton, sugar, fruit, vegetables, pulses (chickpeas, lentils, haricot beans), oilseeds, and cereal grains; livestock includes cattle, sheep, goats, poultry, and smaller numbers of horses, mules, donkeys, and camels.
Industries: Food processing, beverages, textiles, chemicals, metal processing, and cement
Primary Exports: Coffee, leather products, and gold
Primary Imports: Capital goods, consumer goods, and fuel
Primary Trade Partners: Germany, Japan, Saudi Arabia, France, Italy, and United States
Government: Ethiopia is a federal republic. According to the 1994 constitution, the head of state is the president, currently Negasso Gidada, who is nominated by the legislative body, the Council of People's Representatives. A president may not serve more than two six-year terms. The council also nominates a prime minister from among its members, a position currently held by MELES ZENAWI, who is the chief executive and heads a Council of Ministers made up of representatives from a coalition of parties constituting a majority in the legislature. The Council of People's Representatives consists of a maximum of 550 directly elected members; at least 20 of these representatives must be members of minority ethnic groups.

Marian Aguiar

SEE ALSO
Addis Ababa, Ethiopia; Ethiopian Jews; Rift Valleys.

Africa

Ethiopian Jews, an ethnic group of northwestern ETHIOPIA who practice a form of Judaism. Since the 1980s the vast majority of Ethiopian Jews have migrated to Israel.

Outsiders have often referred to the Ethiopian Jews as Falasha, meaning "moved" or "gone into exile" in the ancient Ge'ez language. Today the community considers the term derogatory and prefers instead Beta Israel, a Hebrew term for House of Israel.

Although the origins of Judaism in Ethiopia remain a mystery, it is likely that the community's roots extend back 2500 years. Some Beta Israel believe that they are descendants of Menilek – according to legend, the son of King Solomon and the QUEEN OF SHEBA. Others believe the Beta Israel to be the tribe of Dan, one of the ten lost tribes of Israel. Still others trace the group's history to the biblical parting of the Red Sea, holding that the Jews of Ethiopia were those who did not cross in time and thus escaped from EGYPT by heading south. Some scholars have suggested that the Beta Israel are the descendants of a group speaking Agaw (a Cushitic language), converted by Jews from southern Arabia (present-day Yemen) roughly 2000 years ago.

When the kingdom of AKSUM adopted Christianity as its official religion during the fourth century C.E., however, the Beta Israel were forced to relocate to the mountainous region around Lake Tana. Over the centuries the Beta Israel, numbering in the hundreds of thousands, ruled a powerful state in what is today Ethiopia. Beginning around 1400, however, the Solomonic Dynasty of Ethiopia gradually subdued this Jewish people. During the seventeenth century the Ethiopian emperor finally defeated the Jewish state and seized the people's lands. Most Beta Israel gradually gave up their Agaw language and adopted the TIGRINYA or AMHARA language of their neighbors.

A woman and her baby join some of the almost 30,000 Ethiopian Jews airlifted from Addis Ababa to Israel in 1991. *Reuters/Corbis-Bettmann*

The situation of the Beta Israel worsened toward the end of the nineteenth century. By 1900 only 60,000 to 70,000 remained; the rest had fallen victim to famine or disease or been forcibly converted to Christianity. In 1923 Dr. Jacques Faitlovitch, a Polish-born Jew, took up their cause. He put the Beta Israel in contact with Jewish communities around the world, opened a school in Addis Ababa for them, and sent several to Jewish schools in Europe. Although Faitlovitch's activity came to a halt during the Italian occupation of Ethiopia, for the first time in modern history the Beta Israel had some contact with other Jews. Since Ethiopia's liberation in 1941 the Jews in Ethiopia have theoretically had equal rights under the law. However, the community continued to face persecution and discrimination and, along with many other Ethiopian groups, suffered a great deal under the repressive regime of HAILE MARIAM MENGISTU.

Religiously, the Beta Israel have always identified themselves as exiles from the land of Israel and as believers in the faith of Moses. For almost 2000 years they were completely isolated from the rest of the Jewish world. They never learned of the Talmud, the codification of Judaism's oral law, or of any of the post-biblical traditions, such as the holiday of Hanukkah. So isolated were they from the rest of the Jewish world that many did not know that other Jews still existed, or that the majority of them were white.

The religious life of the Beta Israel is based on the Torah (the first five books of the Bible), its oral interpretations as passed down from generation to generation, and the community's own holy writings. Some Beta Israel customs are comparable to Jewish practices based on oral law and rabbinical literature; others resemble ancient customs practiced by Jews during the biblical and Talmudic periods. Beta Israel villages, usually set apart from neighboring Christian villages, were always situated near a body of water for ritual purposes of immersion and purification. Religious life revolved around the synagogue (*mesgid* or *beit makdas*).

The community has always kept strictly to the kosher diet and has observed the Saturday Sabbath as a day of rest. The Beta Israel celebrate all the festivals mentioned in the Torah in addition to those of their own tradition. The timing of holidays is determined by a religious lunar calendar exclusive to the Beta Israel. A traditional priesthood (the *Kohanim*) has led the community's religious life, and the priesthood has gained increasing importance during the upheavals of the twentieth century as the repository of the group's traditions. Because the Beta Israel have transmitted rituals orally, the expertise of the priests has been a critical element in maintaining the liturgical cycle.

Before 1977 all but a handful of Beta Israel lived in Ethiopia. In 1984 and 1991, however, the Israeli government arranged two dramatic airlifts (Operation Moses and Operation Solomon, respectively) to bring thousands of Ethiopian Jews to Israel. Today more than 60,000 Beta Israel live in the state of Israel, while only a few thousand remain in Ethiopia, concentrated in the capital of Addis Ababa.

The migration to Israel brought difficulties for the Ethiopian community. The abrupt move from the rural villages of Ethiopia to the very white, Westernized, and mostly urban society of Israel proved an extreme and disorienting transition for many. Before coming to Israel few Beta Israel knew any Hebrew. Even their Bible is written in Ge'ez, a precursor to the modern languages of north-central Ethiopia, Amharic and Tigrinya. While free from the religious persecution they faced in Ethiopia, the Beta Israel now face racism and a daily struggle for integration in Israel. This struggle was exacerbated in January 1997, when it was discovered that the Israeli government was automatically discarding blood donated by Ethiopian Jews out of a fear of acquired immune deficiency syndrome (AIDS). The discovery of this racist policy led to a protest of over 15,000 Ethiopian Jews in Jerusalem and drew widespread publicity.

Most Ethiopian Jews in Israel now live in very poor, segregated towns, with unemployment running well above the national average. More surprisingly, the Beta Israel have faced constant challenges to the authenticity of their Jewishness. On the more positive side, the community enjoys greater educational opportunities than ever before in its history, and several hundred Ethiopian Jews are enrolled in colleges and graduate programs in Israel.

Rachel Antell

SEE ALSO

Christianity, African: An Overview; Addis Ababa, Ethiopia; Ethiopic Script and Language.

Africa

Ethiopian Orthodox Church,

formerly the established Christian church of ETHIOPIA, which has played a central role in the culture of Ethiopia's AMHARA and TIGRE peoples.

Scholars are uncertain about the precise origins of the Ethiopian Orthodox Church. The traditional story states that two brothers from Tyre (in modern Lebanon) – Saint Frumentius (later Ethiopia's first bishop) and Aedesius – Christianized Ethiopia (*see* CHRISTIANITY, AFRICAN: AN OVERVIEW) in the fourth century C.E. by winning the support of King Ezana of AKSUM and evangelizing the king's subjects. According to other traditions, three followers of Jesus – Matthew, Bartholomew, and Andrew – traveled to Ethiopia. Some doubt the accuracy of these traditions; however, it seems plausible that through trade connections with the Middle East, Christianity may have reached Ethiopia during the first century C.E. The New Testament book Acts of the Apostles states that the apostle Philip converted an Ethiopian eunuch.

Ethiopia has an ancient tradition of contact with the Middle East, particularly ancient Israel. Amhara and Tigre, the main languages of the Ethiopian highlands, like Hebrew, are Semitic languages. Ethiopian traditions claim that the biblical King Solomon of Israel fathered a son with the Ethiopian queen Makidda (known in the Bible as Sheba). This son, Menilek, stole the Ark of the Covenant, the symbol of Israel's status as God's chosen people. Thereafter, according to the Ethiopian tradition, Judaism was the state religion until Ethiopians' conversion to Christianity confirmed their status as the chosen people of God. To this day, Ethiopian Christianity maintains an emphasis on Old Testament dietary laws and strict rules of circumcision, and, in addition to the Christian Sunday Sabbath, Ethiopian Christians observe the traditional Jewish Sabbath day of Saturday.

The Ethiopian Orthodox Church is one of the Oriental Orthodox churches, like the Coptic Orthodox Church of EGYPT, the Syrian Orthodox Church, the Armenian Orthodox Church, and the Indian Orthodox Church of Malabar (or Kerala). These churches rejected the conclusion of the Council of Chalcedon of 451 on the dual human and divine nature of Christ. Instead, the Oriental Orthodox churches insist that Christ has a single, unified nature that is at once human and divine. The disagreement led to the separation of these five churches from the Eastern Orthodox churches, the Catholic Church of Rome, and, by extension, the Protestant churches that later broke with the Roman Catholic Church.

The archbishop, or *abuna* ("our father" in Arabic), stands at the top of the church's hierarchy. Until 1951 the Patriarch of Alexandria appointed the abuna, following a tradition extending back to Saint Frumentius. According to church tradition, Frumentius went to Alexandria to request that a bishop be sent to Ethiopia; the Alexandrian Patriarch thereupon appointed Frumentius the first abuna of Ethiopia. Since 1951, theoretically at least, the Ethiopian clergy have selected the abuna. In fact, however, successive Ethiopian governments have influenced the selection process or imposed their own candidates. The clergy consists of priests and deacons, whose main functions include celebrating mass and serving as confessors to local families. *Debteras* are laymen who play music and dance at services; perform wizardry, fortune telling, and astrology; and serve as scribes for the nonliterate.

The practices of the Ethiopian Church can be quite severe. The church mandates circumcision for boys. In addition, it requires the controversial practice of female circumcision. Fasting, which consists of omitting breakfast and eating only vegetables, imposes an exacting demand on the faithful. A full fasting schedule, required only of the clergy, runs 250 days a year. The laity must fast 165 days per year: every Wednesday and Friday, and the two months during Lenten and the Easter seasons. Besides Sunday services, Ethiopian Christians must attend services on holy days, during which, as on the Sabbath, they must also refrain from manual labor. Except for fast days, services begin at six o'clock in the morning and last about three hours. Services for Easter begin Friday and end Sunday at midnight. None but the sick may sit during the services.

The church building centers on the *tabot*, a replica of the Ark of the Covenant that has been sanctified by a bishop. The church recognizes the sacraments of baptism, penance, Eucharist (or holy communion), marriage, anointing of the sick, and holy orders. Saints, who have been especially empowered by God to intercede on behalf of the faithful who pray to them, figure prominently in Ethiopian Christianity.

The Ethiopian Orthodox Church has a history of monasticism probably dating back to at least the fourth century. Many Ethiopian monasteries trace their origins to the so-called nine monks, who came from Syria in the fifth century. Believers contend that the monastic life is the highest stage of Christian life. Devout Ethiopian Christians hope to live their last years as monks or nuns, and many take monastic vows during old age. Two types of monasticism predominate in Ethiopia: anchoritism (solitary meditation and prayer) and cenobitism (communal life).

The Amhara and Tigre peoples of the northern and central highlands have traditionally been the strongest adherents of Ethiopian Christianity, and the beliefs and customs of the church form an essential part of traditional Amhara and Tigrean culture. The Aksumite monarchy designated the Ethiopian Orthodox Church the state church by the sixth century C.E, a position it held until 1974. Until then the state financed the church and awarded it extensive land grants. Until 1900 the church was the only source for education for Ethiopian children, and that education centered on religion. The vast land holdings of the country's cenobitic monasteries and their legal jurisdiction over the large areas they controlled gave them considerable power. The church lost much of this power in 1974 when the government of HAILE MARIAM MENGISTU nationalized their holdings, ended their legal powers, and disestablished the church, which then held equal status with other religions.

The church faced many challenges after 1974. It lost its main sources of revenue. It lacks modern theological seminaries, and with the establishment of modern secular colleges, the church lost its monopoly on education. With the church's loss of power and the declining prestige of a traditional religious education, church leaders fear that they will fail to attract enough young men to the priesthood. Church services are in the ancient language of Ge'ez, no longer spoken in Ethiopia, and many think that the services themselves are antiquated.

Even without government support the church retained great influence in the country in the mid-1990s. Thus the government required that clergymen appointed to important church offices meet its approval. Eritrean independence in 1991 highlighted the controversial nature of continued state control over the church. Eritrean leaders insisted on the creation of an Eritrean Orthodox Church separate and distinct from the Ethiopian Orthodox Church. This church later affiliated with the Coptic Church of Egypt. Bishops from Ethiopia sent protest letters to the Patriarch at Alexandria. The Ethiopian government, wishing to maintain good relations with Eritrea, removed the protesting bishops from their offices and appointed replacements it deemed more politically acceptable. In 1993 the government's appointment of an Egyptian abuna, Patriarch Paulos, sparked angry popular protest.

Robert Fay

SEE ALSO

Eritrea; Alexandria, Egypt; Female Circumcision in Africa.

Africa

Ethiopian Theater, **twentieth-century cultural form combining local vernacular expressive practices and Western performative traditions, shaped by shifting Ethiopian political culture.**

Theater, as understood in the West, is a fairly new phenomenon in ETHIOPIA. The first recorded Ethiopian play is a satirical adaptation and translation of the fables of La Fontaine, by Tekle-Hawaryat Tekle-Mariam. Titled *Yawrewoch Komediya* (Comedy of the Animals), it was performed before members of the royal court sometime between 1912 and 1916.

Because of political censorship, all dramatic activity following *Yawrewoch Komediya* was banned until the coronation of Emperor HAILE SELASSIE I in 1930. Between 1930 and 1935 theater studies began in schools, and the first stage was built at the Lycée Menilek II in 1934. Although there was no theater during the Italian military occupation (1935-1940), theatrical activity was renewed on the emperor's return from exile in 1941 by two politically opposed groups: the Hager Fikir (Patriots) Association, and the Municipality Theater Company. The latter produced the first genuinely popular play, Yoftahé Negussé's *Afajeshign* (You Got Me Caught), a piece that was critical of the emperor's methods of handling the war.

In 1955 Emperor Haile Selassie commissioned the 1400-seat Haile Selassie Theater (later the National Theater). In the early years, the theater was run by the Austrians Franz Zulveker and Richard Hager, who staged historical and religious dramas such as *David and Orion* (1956), by Prime Minister Mekonnen Endalkachew, and the tragedy *Tewodros* (1959), by Girmachew Tekle-Hawaryat. The influence of this early theater is felt to this day in the naturalism of the well-known director and playwright Melaku Ashagre's contemporary work.

With the return of two highly qualified theater professionals from abroad in 1960 – the playwright Tsegaye Gebre-Medhin (from the Royal Court Theater, London) and the actor Tesfaye Gessesse (trained at Northwestern University) – Ethiopian theater moved into its contemporary phase. Gebre-Medhin was chosen to run the Municipality Theater Company, and also started a short-lived theater school that produced some of Ethiopia's best actors, such as Wegayehu Negatu and Alem-tsehay Wedajo.

Wedajo is the best-known Ethiopian playwright both within and outside the country. He has written plays in English, such as the *Oda Oak Oracle*, published in London in 1965 and described by Albert Gérard in 1971 as "one of the finest plays to have been written in Africa." Further work in English drama includes his translations of Shakespeare. In Amharic, Wedajo has created highly wrought, erudite, poetic dramas that treat Ethiopian political and social history on a large scale. Wegayehu Negatu and Debebe Eshetu are particularly famous actors from this period, and for many, epitomize classic Ethiopian acting.

Theater after the Marxist revolution of 1974 was mainly characterized by agit-prop and protest productions, and became more popular than ever before. Many theater professionals were now trained in the former Soviet Union or other eastern European countries. When the University of Addis Ababa established a theater arts department in 1979, classes in performance, playwriting, directing, theater history, and stagecraft expanded the repertoire and the scope for experimentation. An example is Tsfaye Gessesse's *Teatre Sidada* (When Theater Begins to Crawl), which is a trio of related plays (Gessesse's *Teatre Sidada*, Albee's *Zoo Story*, and Strindberg's *The Stronger*) linked by two quasi-supernatural characters.

Efforts also have been made here to draw on more complex Ethiopian traditions – most importantly by Fisseha Belay, whose *Simegn Sintayehu* (I Saw So Much When I Wished) is based on the strategies of rural Ethiopian courtship and the Ethiopian fondness for verbal wit and improvisation. A tendency toward the fantastic, which is a strong element in traditional Ethiopian storytelling, is the hallmark of Manyegezawal Endeshaw, a young director trained in this department. Due to the presence of the Theater Arts Department Playhouse and the University Cultural Centre, Addis Ababa, the capital city, now has two major venues.

In the late 1970s and through the 1980s

HAILE MARIAM MENGISTU's Marxist government became progressively more repressive toward the arts. At this time youth involvement escalated in the form of variety shows and political plays closely controlled by the government. On the whole, however, rather than risk being included in the catalogue of banned plays and imprisonments, theater professionals fell back on history plays and translations such as *Hamlet, Othello,* and *Oedipus the King*. While this can be seen as a form of self-censorship, there is also a more subtle intention: the onus of making and interpreting social statements is placed on the audience's well-developed ability to understand the oblique political allegory. In fact, this unspoken contract has led to a remarkably interactive and vital audience-performer relationship.

Theater has blossomed since the fall of Mengistu's government, including many private theater companies, although most have been short-lived. Only the Kendil/Candle Theater Company (founded in 1995) has been able to fund its own venue. Fueled by a belief in theater as an overt tool for political and social criticism, this company has been particularly influenced by Brecht and Dario Fo. Recent developments also include the emergence of a diasporic theater community, largely in the United States (to which theater professionals have been forced to flee) but also in Great Britain, where, for example, Tsegay Gebre-Medhin's *Tewodros* was produced in 1987.

SEE ALSO
Addis Ababa, Ethiopia.

Africa

Ethiopic Script and Language,

the major written and spoken Semitic languages of historical and present-day ETHIOPIA.

The writing tradition of Ethiopia is one of the greatest cultural achievements in Africa. Known as *lessana ge'ez* (meaning "the language of the free"), or simply as Ge'ez, classical Ethiopic was used in the Aksumite royal inscriptions of the fourth century C.E., in translations made from Greek, Syriac, Arabic, and other languages, and for a vast body of original Ethiopian literature that includes stories of Christian saints and martyrs, poetry, historical chronicles, and treatises on magic, law, and medicine.

Although it ceased to be spoken by the twelfth or thirteenth century, Ge'ez remained the language of literature and religion. Like Hebrew and Arabic, it is a Semitic language. The modern Semitic languages of Ethiopia – such as TIGRINYA, TIGRE, Amharic (*see* AMHARA), Harari, and Gurage – developed from Ge'ez in a manner comparable to the emergence of Spanish, French, and the other Romance languages from Latin.

Ge'ez is written in a script developed from the South Arabian characters found in inscriptions on both sides of the Red Sea as far back as 3000 years ago. It consists of 26 consonants that can be modified to represent syllables containing any of 7 vowels. This produces 182 different characters. Another 4 characters represent labial consonants, and an additional 7 consonants were created for Amharic. With their vowel markings, these consonant signs raise the total to 251 characters. The script is beautiful, and scholars are studying the various styles of Ethiopic calligraphy to help classify and date manuscripts preserved in churches and monasteries.

Roderick Grierson

Africa

Ethnicity and Identity in Africa: An Interpretation

THE IDEA OF THE "TRIBE"

What is ethnicity in Africa? One thing is certain: it is very often misunderstood. Many people, including many contemporary Africans, suppose that in the precolonial period, all Africans lived in groups called "tribes." A "tribe" is thought of as a group of people who are descended from common ancestors and ruled by a hereditary "chief," who share a single culture (including, in particular, language and religion), and who live in a well-defined geographical region. Tribal identities are often assumed to be unchanging and ancient.

Many people also suppose that virtually all the contemporary ethnic groups in modern Africa are descended from these kinds of "tribes." While some precolonial African societies, such as some of the small AKAN states of southwestern GHANA and southeastern CÔTE D'IVOIRE, did come close to such a model, most did not. Even where they did approach this model, it was often a quite recent development. So it is usually misleading to speak of modern ethnic groups as "tribes." Nevertheless, many contemporary Africans use the word "tribe" to talk about their identities, and we cannot understand modern African social and political life unless we understand what they mean by this term.

PRECOLONIAL SOCIAL IDENTITIES

Tribal identities, understood in this way, were not the only nor even the most important of the identities recognized in precolonial Africa. People also belonged to clans or lineages, both groups defined by shared ancestry. (In Islamic North Africa, in fact, the word "tribe" has most often been used to refer to lineages.) The smallest subgroup of a lineage is a family. Households and extended families were also important sources of identity, as they continue to be today.

In many places people also belonged to age sets, groups of men or women who reached maturity within the same few years. Members of an age set operated together for many social purposes, and their social roles shifted as they passed through different stages of life. Finally, people of different lineages and ages belonged to village communities. Although they might have shared many of their daily life activities with their village neighbors, they often had political loyalties to rulers elsewhere, and connections through trade and secret societies to people in other villages and towns.

One reason that precolonial Africans' membership in such a variety of groups is often overlooked today is that many of these earlier forms of identity began to lose their power in the colonial period. Village identities became less important as rates of urbanization in Africa increased, especially after World War II. Secret societies were often deliberately targeted for destruction in the colonial period, because they involved rituals and religious beliefs inconsistent with Christianity or European norms of civilization. And age-set membership became less relevant once colonial rulers deprived age sets of their role in community political structures.

THE ORIGINS OF "TRIBAL" NAMES

If "tribes" were not the most important forms of identity in precolonial Africa, why do they seem so important now? We must recognize that the ethnic groups of contemporary Africa have a variety of origins. It is often helpful to focus not so much on the history of a group of people and their descendants but on the history of a particular ethnic name, or "ethnonym." Many contemporary African ethnonyms are products of the interaction between the ideas of European colonial officials and anthropologists, on the one hand, and preexisting ways of classifying people in Africa's many precolonial societies, on the other. Typically, ethnonyms fall into one of four categories.

1. PRECOLONIAL STATES

Probably the easiest modern ethnonyms to explain are those based on the names of precolonial African nations. A few examples include ASANTE in West Africa, Buganda in East Africa, and ZULU and SWAZI in southern Africa.

But, as with "tribes," certain standard modern assumptions about kingdoms do not apply. For example, while their kings were, indeed, hereditary, in the sense that they had to have a certain ancestry to become rulers, none of them had a guaranteed rule of succession by, say, an eldest son. In Asante, for example, the king's successor was chosen from the royal family by a group of king makers. If they did not agree, long periods of conflict could ensue, including civil wars.

Another common misassumption is that these nations would share a single language and culture. In each of these states and others like them there was, indeed, a single language of government, which was the language of a dominant ethnic group, and many cultural practices were widely shared. But at the moment of European colonization, many states were undergoing expansion. As a result the king often claimed authority over people who were culturally quite different, including people who spoke completely different languages. Some of these people would have recognized the king's claim to sovereignty over them; others would not. So the boundaries of the king's sway were not well defined: they shrank when a subject people resisted, and they expanded when the king responded by sending out armies to establish (or reestablish) control.

While these states existed before colonization, their development had often been shaped by other kinds of contact with outsiders. The Asante state, for example, acquired significant military technology through trade with the Danes, the Portuguese, and the British, and it taxed commerce between the coast and the Asante hinterland. Long-standing trans-Saharan trade patterns also linked the Asante state to the Islamic societies of North Africa.

Nor were these kingdoms stable, established political systems, where people lived according to unchanging customs: SHAKA formed the modern Zulu nation quite rapidly in the early nineteenth century, drawing on a powerful army and innovative military tactics. His conquest, known as the MFECANE, in turn led to the formation of several other southern African states, as skilled leaders such as Moshoeshoe, founder of the Basotho Kingdom, offered vulnerable communities protection in return for tribute and military service. In West Africa, meanwhile, the Asante nation underwent civil wars and various constitutional crises in the eighteenth and nineteenth centuries.

When European anthropologists and colonial officials arrived in Africa, they were convinced that people there lived in tribes. Some early European explorers referred to the rulers of precolonial states as "kings," the states as "kingdoms" or "countries," and the people as "the Asante," "the Baganda," or "the Zulu." But by the early twentieth century, when these peoples had all been incorporated into the British Empire, it became standard to refer to their rulers as chiefs and the citizens as tribesmen.

There are exceptions to this pattern. The kingdom of ETHIOPIA, where people spoke a number of languages and recognized a variety of religious and cultural traditions, was ruled by a Christian AMHARA monarchy. The kingdom's people were never assumed to belong to a single "tribal" group, partly because a Christian emperor fitted easily into existing European ideas about societies, partly because Ethiopians themselves recognized ethnic divisions within the kingdom.

2. CULTURAL GROUPS

A second group of modern ethnonyms refers to groups that have related languages and often share important cultural practices but were not necessarily ever members of a single political community. The broadest such term in Africa is "Bantu," which refers to hundreds of groups in East, Central, and southern Africa who speak related but typically not mutually intelligible languages (though in many of these languages the word for "people" is "bantu"). The common elements in these languages came from an earlier "proto-Bantu" language spoken by Central African peoples whose descendants, over centuries, migrated south and east. But there is no reason to think that all modern speakers of Bantu languages share descent from these earlier migrants (just as we would not assume that the reason most people in the United States speak English is that they are descendants of people from England).

In West Africa, the term *Akan* refers to a number of groups in Ghana and Côte d'Ivoire. Here the similarities are more substantial, since many of the Akan languages are mutually intelligible, and the majority of Akan people – in particular, the Asante, Fante, and Akwapim people – speak one of several main dialects of a language called "Twi." Most Akan people also share cultural traits other than language; for example, most are matrilineal, meaning they trace descent through their mothers rather than their fathers.

Another example of a culturally based identity is that of the Swahili people of coastal East Africa, which is defined partly by their Swahili language (a Bantu language much influenced by Arabic), partly by their residence in trading towns, and partly by their connection to Islam. However, many people who speak Kiswahili – which has been used as a trade language for centuries and is now the official government language in TANZANIA – would not claim to be Swahili (*see* SWAHILI COAST).

The bonds of language, Islam, and trade are also important elements in the identity of the widely dispersed HAUSA and DYULA peoples of West Africa. Over centuries, participation in long-distance trade led to the establishment of Hausa and Dyula communities in several different parts of West Africa. Leaders of some of these communities established precolonial states, such as the Hausa state of Kano in northern NIGERIA, and the Dyula KONG Empire in northern Côte d'Ivoire. Today, Hausa and Dyula are the region's two most common African trade languages, and many West African cities have distinct Hausa and Dyula neighborhoods.

3. CREATIONS OF THE COLONIAL PERIOD

Most ethnonyms are derived from African words. But some of these words came to be used in the colonial period to refer to peoples who lived in the same region but had not previously been politically united. Many people in the region of southeastern Nigeria now called Igboland, for example, lived in small towns governed by councils of senior men. Others lived in larger towns with more centralized political systems. These different communities spoke related languages, but they could not necessarily understand one another. They had religious leaders – priests responsible for overseeing rituals and handling problems such as ill health or failed harvests – but no sovereign political leaders whom British colonial officials could easily identify as chiefs. So instead the colonial administration either treated the priests as chiefs, requiring them to assume a new political role, or they appointed so-called warrant-chiefs to carry out the duties expected of colonial-era chiefs, such as tax collection. The British also began to consider all the people who spoke this region's related languages as speakers of different dialects of one language called "Igbo."

These impositions alone, however, did not create modern Igbo identity. As people from southeastern Nigeria traveled to other parts of the colony to work and trade, they came into contact with people who spoke languages more foreign than the languages spoken by their more immediate neighbors. They also encountered customs more foreign than those practiced by other societies in southeastern Nigeria. So many migrants of this region, based in towns in the north and west of Nigeria, came increasingly to think of themselves as members of a single Igbo "tribe." At the same time, other Nigerians came to regard them as a single "tribe" also. This new identity had tragic consequences later on, when Igbo people in these towns were violently attacked in the period leading up to the Nigerian civil war (1967-1970).

Similar processes occurred in many parts of Africa, as people moved from rural communities to newly expanding urban areas. Whether these were colonial administrative capitals such as Lagos and Nairobi or mining towns such as Johannesburg in SOUTH AFRICA, cities became places where people developed new practices and ways of organizing their collective life, based on interpretations of "traditional" customs in the rural areas from which they had come.

4. INVENTED IDENTITIES

Some ethnonyms lumped together people who had no shared social origins at all. The term *Coromanti*, for example, often referred in the seventeenth and eighteenth centuries to African slaves in the New World who had all been bought at slave markets in a particular region of the West African coast, in present-day Ghana. Since these and other slave markets typically sold people who came from many different regions of West Africa, this ethnonym imposed on people a completely fictional "tribal" identity. Because they had been brought together by captors whose language was Akan, these slaves did, however, speak an Akan language; as a result, in the New World, Akan-speaking "Coromanti" slaves did sometimes join together in slave revolts (as, for example, in a plot discovered in BARBADOS in 1675).

Similarly, the term *Bushman* was used to refer to a very wide range of people who lived over a vast area of South Africa, ANGOLA, BOTSWANA, and NAMIBIA, even though they certainly had no sense of a shared identity. While these people did mostly speak one of the many KHOISAN languages (which are descended from languages spoken in this region before the arrival of Bantu speakers), this did not mean that they would have understood one another if they had met. But the term has also been used to refer to the Basters in Namibia, who have both European and African ancestry and who speak Afrikaans. In fact, the ethnonym "Bushman" has been used to refer to almost anyone in southern Africa whose appearance is neither that of the typical dark-skinned Bantu speaker nor that of the typical light-skinned European. It has been used, in effect, as if it referred to a "race" that lived in this area before the arrival of Bantu-speaking settlers from the north, and many people have then gone on to assume that this "racial" group had shared culture and traditions.

MODERN ETHNICITY IN AFRICA

As we have seen, then, many African ethnonyms reflect misunderstandings of history. Historians have pointed out that this is true for most modern identities, not only those in Africa. Now-discredited ideas about race have played a central role, for example, in shaping national identities in Europe. The idea of an Anglo-Saxon race, for example, was important in the development of both modern British identity and white American identity in the United States. The fact that these identities are founded on mistaken beliefs does not deprive them of their power to shape people's attitudes and behavior. Many modern Africans identify themselves as Akan or Igbo or Swahili, or members of one of the hundreds of other modern African ethnic groups. Because national politics requires people to collaborate with one another to compete for resources, political leaders often mobilize these ethnic groups to create voting blocs or to organize "sides" in civil conflicts.

Once ethnic identities become politically significant, people who previously thought of themselves as belonging first and foremost to some small local group may decide to identify with a larger, more widely distributed group that seems successful at winning resources. Such considerations help explain why many coastal East African people adopted Swahili identity in the late nineteenth century, and why many people in contemporary Ghana and TOGO have assumed EWE identity. So the size and boundaries of ethnic groups may shift with shifting political fortunes.

Indeed, some anthropologists, such as the Norwegian Frederick Barth, have argued that the very idea of ethnicity exists only where there are boundaries between "us" and "them" within a shared social context. As a result, they say, we can really only speak of ethnicity in the context of many groups, defined by real or imagined shared ancestry, either living together within a single political system or, at least, in regular contact. If that is right, then the boundaries of African colonies and then nations – drawn around people with very different languages, cultures, religions, and traditions – have created an ideal context for the flourishing of ethnicity that we in fact see in modern Africa.

It is not surprising, in this context, that "tribalism" now appears to many people to be one of modern Africa's major problems. For by "tribalism" people usually mean the *illegitimate* appeal to ethnic loyalty. When people speak of "tribalism," they are really assuming that to act on the basis of ethnic loyalty is always wrong. This is because appeals to ethnic loyalty often occur in contexts of national-level competition between an "us" and a "them," and so ethnicity becomes divisive. But, of course, ethnic loyalty (in Africa as elsewhere) can also lead people to do good things for fellow members of their "tribe," even when this is not at the expense of others.

The significance of "tribalism" in Africa can also be exaggerated. Ethnicity is not the basis for political mobilization. Religion, for example, has been important in shaping political loyalties in Nigeria. Islam and Christianity and many other traditional religions are important to people's lives in Nigeria, as, of course, they are in many countries. Islam and Christianity have come to be identified, to some degree, with the political interests of the north and the south of Nigeria, respectively, even though many Christians live in the north and about a third of the YORUBA people in the southwest are Muslim. Politics are also shaped by religion in SUDAN where, again, Muslims are concentrated in the north and non-Islamic peoples in the south.

In a different way, professional interests – those of doctors or lawyers or civil servants – and class interests, which join together, say, industrial workers in trade unions, are also important bases of political mobilization. So are the shared interests of peasant farmers of many different ethnic groups, or the interests of the medley of ethnic groups that live together in a particular region of a country. And, increasingly, in the modern world, national interests have become important. Last but by no means least, gender shapes the concerns of Africans as it does of people everywhere, and women's organizations are an extremely important part of the contemporary social and political landscape of Africa. So like the generations before them, contemporary Africans, whether or not they consider themselves members of a "tribe," count many other identities as important.

Kwame Anthony Appiah

SEE ALSO

Afrikaner; Igbo; Bantu: Dispersion and Settlement; Buganda, Early Kingdom of; Bushmen; Christianity, African: An Overview; Colonial Rule; Ethiopian Orthodox Church; Explorers in Africa, 1500 to 1800; Johannesburg, South Africa; Kano, Nigeria; Lagos, Nigeria; Languages, African: An Overview; Swahili Language; Lesotho; Moshoeshoe; Nairobi, Kenya; Nationalism in Africa; Transatlantic Slave Trade; Slavery in Latin America and the Caribbean; Swahili People; Urbanism and Urbanization in Africa; African Religions: An Interpretation; Anthropology in Africa; Islam and Tradition: An Interpretation; Fante.

Cross Cultural

Ethnicity and Politics: An Interpretation

I center my remarks on an attempt to identify and characterize a significant shift that has been going on (and is still going on) in black cultural politics. This shift is not definitive, in the sense that there are two clearly discernible phases – one in the past which is now over and the new one which is beginning – which we can neatly counterpose to one another. Rather, they are two phases of the same movement, which constantly overlap and interweave. Both are framed by the same historical conjuncture and both are rooted in the politics of antiracism and the postwar black experience in Britain. Nevertheless I think we can identify two different "moments" and that the difference between them is significant.

It is difficult to characterize these precisely, but I would say that the first moment was grounded in a particular political and cultural analysis. Politically, this is the moment when the term "black" was coined as a way of referencing the common experience of racism and marginalization in Britain and came to provide the organizing category of a new politics of resistance, among groups and communities with, in fact, very different histories, traditions, and ethnic identities. In this moment, politically speaking, "the Black Experience," as a singular and unifying framework based on the building up of identity across ethnic and cultural difference between the different communities, became "hegemonic" over other ethnic/racial identities though the latter did not, of course, disappear. Culturally, this analysis formulated itself in terms of a critique of the way blacks were positioned as the unspoken and invisible "other" of predominantly white aesthetic and cultural discourses.

This analysis was predicated on the marginalization of the black experience in British culture; not fortuitously occurring at the margins, but placed, positioned at the margins, as the consequence of a set of quite specific political and cultural practices that regulated, governed, and "normalized" the representational and discursive spaces of English society. These formed the conditions of existence of a cultural politics designed to challenge, resist, and, where possible, transform the dominant regimes of representation – first in music and style, later in literary, visual, and cinematic forms. In these spaces blacks have typically been the objects, but rarely the subjects, of the practices of representation. The struggle to come into representation was predicated on a critique of the degree of fetishization, objectification, and negative figuration that are so much a feature of the representation of the black subject. There was a concern not simply with the absence or marginality of the black experience but with its simplification and its stereotypical character.

The cultural politics and strategies that developed around this critique had many facets, but its two principal objects were, first, the question of *access* to the rights to representation by black artists and black cultural workers themselves; second, the *contestation* of the marginality, the stereotypical quality, and the fetishized nature of images of blacks, by the counterposition of a "positive" black imagery. These strategies were principally addressed to changing what I would call the "relations of representation."

I have a distinct sense that in the recent period we are entering a new phase. But we need to be absolutely clear what we mean by a "new" phase because, as soon as you talk of a new phase, people instantly imagine that what is entailed is the *substitution* of one kind of politics for another. I am quite distinctly not talking about a shift in those terms. Politics does not necessarily proceed by way of a set of oppositions and reversals of this kind, though some groups and individuals are anxious to "stage" the question in this way. The original critique of the predominant relations of race and representation and the politics that developed around it have not disappeared and cannot possibly disappear while the conditions that gave rise to it – cultural racism in its Dewesbury form – not only persist but flourish. There is no sense in which a new phase in black cultural politics could replace the earlier one. Nevertheless it is true that as the struggle moves forward and assumes new forms, it does to some degree *displace*, reorganize, and reposition the different cultural strategies in relation to one another. If this can be conceived in terms of the "burden of representation," I would put the point in this form: that black artists and cultural workers now have to struggle, not on one, but on *two* fronts. The problem is how to characterize this shift – if indeed, we agree that such a shift has taken or is taking place – and if the language of binary oppositions and substitutions will no longer suffice. The characterization that I would offer is tentative, proposed mainly to try to clarify some of the issues involved, rather than to preempt them.

The shift is best thought of in terms of a change from a struggle over the relations of representation to a politics of representation itself. It would be useful to separate out such a "politics of representation" into its different elements. We all now use the word "representation," but, as we know, it is an extremely slippery customer. It can be used, on the one hand, simply as another way of talking about how one images a reality that exists "outside" the means by which things are represented: a conception grounded in a mimetic theory of representation. On the other hand, the term can also stand for a very radical displacement of that unproblematic notion of the concept of representation.

My own view is that events, relations, structures do have conditions of existence and real effects outside the sphere of the discursive; but only within the discursive, and subject to its specific conditions, limits, and modalities, do they have or can they be constructed within meaning. Thus, while not wanting to expand the territorial claims of the discursive infinitely, how things are represented and the "machineries" and regimes of representation in a culture do play a *constitutive,* and not merely a reflexive, after-the-event, role. This gives questions of culture and ideology and the scenarios of representation – subjectivity, identity, politics – a formative, not merely an expressive, place in the constitution of social and political life. I think it is the move toward this second sense of representation that is taking place and that is transforming the politics of representation in black culture.

This is a complex issue. First, it is the effect of a theoretical encounter between black cultural politics and the discourses of a Eurocentric, largely white, critical cultural theory which in recent years has focused so much analysis on the politics of representation. This is always an extremely difficult, if not dangerous, encounter. (I think particularly of black people encountering the discourses of poststructuralism, postmodernism, psychoanalysis, and feminism.) Second, it marks what I can only call "the end of innocence," or the end of the innocent notion of the essential black subject. Here again, the end of the essential black subject is something that people are increasingly debating, but they may not have fully reckoned with its political consequences.

What is at issue here is the recognition of the extraordinary diversity of subjective positions, social experiences, and cultural identities that compose the category "black"; that is, the recognition that "black" is essentially a politically and *culturally constructed* category, which cannot be grounded in a set of fixed transcultural or transcendental racial categories and which therefore has no guarantees in Nature. What this brings into play is the recognition of the immense diversity and differentiation of the historical and cultural experience of black subjects. This inevitably entails a weakening or fading of the notion that "race" or some composite notion of race around the term "black" will either guarantee the effectivity of any cultural practice or determine in any final sense its aesthetic value.

We should put this as plainly as possible. Films are not necessarily good because black people make them. They are not necessarily "right-on" by virtue of the fact that they deal with the black experience. Once you enter the politics of the end of the essential black subject you are plunged headlong into the maelstrom of a continuously contingent, unguaranteed, political argument and debate: a critical politics, a politics of criticism. You can no longer conduct black politics through the strategy of a simple set of reversals, putting in the place of the bad old essential white subject, the new essentially good black subject. Now, that formulation may seem to threaten the collapse of an entire political world. Alternatively, it may be greeted with extraordinary relief at the passing away of what at one time seemed to be a necessary fiction. Namely, either that all black people are good or indeed that all black people are *the same.* After all, it is one of the predicates of racism that "you can't tell the difference because they all look the same."

This does not make it any easier to conceive of how a politics can be constructed that works with and through difference, that is able to build those forms of solidarity and identification that make common struggle and resistance possible but without suppressing the real heterogeneity of interests and identities, and that can effectively draw the political boundary lines without which political contestation is impossible, without fixing those boundaries for eternity. It entails the movement in black politics from what Gramsci called the "war of maneuver" to the "war of position" – the struggle around positionalities. But the difficulty of conceptualizing such a politics (and the temptation to slip into a sort of endlessly sliding discursive liberal-pluralism) does not absolve us of the task of developing such a politics.

The end of the essential black subject also entails a recognition that the central issues of race always appear historically in articulation, in a formation, with other categories and divisions and are constantly crossed and recrossed by the categories of class, gender, and ethnicity. (I make a distinction here between race and ethnicity to which I shall return.) To me films like *Territories, Passion of Remembrance, My Beautiful Laundrette,* and *Sammy and Rosie Get Laid,* for example, make it perfectly clear that this shift has been engaged, and that the question of the black subject cannot be represented without reference to the dimensions of class, gender, sexuality, and ethnicity.

Difference and Contestation

A further consequence of this politics of representation is the slow recognition of the deep ambivalence of identification and desire. We think about identification usually as a simple process, structured around fixed "selves" that we either are or are not. The play of identity and difference that constructs racism is powered not only by the positioning of blacks as the inferior species but also, and at the same time, by an inexpressible envy and desire; and this is something the recognition of which fundamentally *displaces* many of our hitherto stable political categories, since it implies a process of identification and otherness that is more complex than we had hitherto imagined.

Racism, of course, operates by constructing impassable symbolic boundaries between racially constituted categories, and its typically binary system of representation constantly marks and attempts to fix and naturalize the difference between belongingness and otherness. Along this frontier there arises what Gayatri Spivak (1987) calls the "epistemic violence" of the discourses of the other – of imperialism, the colonized, orientalism, the exotic, the primitive, the anthropological, and the folkloric. Consequently the discourse of antiracism has often been founded on a strategy of reversal and inversion, turning the "Manichaean aesthetic" of colonial discourse upside down. However, as Frantz Fanon constantly reminded us, the epistemic violence is both outside and inside, and operates by a process of splitting on both sides of the division – in here as well as out there. That is why it is a question, not only of "black-skin, white-skin" but of *Black Skin, White Masks* – the internalization of the self-as-other. Just as masculinity always constructs femininity as double – simultaneously Madonna and Whore – so racism constructs the black subject: noble savage and violent avenger. And in the doubling, fear and desire double for one another and play across the structures of otherness, complicating its politics.

Recently I have read several articles about the photographic text of Robert Mapplethorpe – especially his inscription of the nude, black male – all written by black critics or cultural practitioners. These essays properly begin by identifying in Mapplethorpe's work the tropes of fetishization, the fragmentation of the black image, and its objectification, as the forms of their appropriation within the white, gay gaze. But as I read, I know that something else is going on as well in both the production and the reading of those texts. The continuous circling around Mapplethorpe's work is not exhausted by being able to place him as the white fetishistic gay photographer; this is because it is also marked by the surreptitious return of desire – that deep ambivalence of identification that makes the categories in which we have previously thought and argued about black cultural politics and the black cultural text extremely problematic.

This brings to the surface the unwelcome fact that a great deal of black politics, constructed, addressed, and developed directly in relation to questions of race and ethnicity, has been predicated on the assumption that the categories of gender and sexuality would stay the same and remain fixed and secured. What the new politics of representation does is to put that into question, crossing the questions of racism irrevocably with questions of sexuality. That is what is so disturbing, finally, to many of our settled political habits about *Passion of Remembrance*. This double fracturing entails a different kind of politics because, as we know, black radical politics has frequently been stabilized around particular conceptions of black masculinity, which are only now being put into question by black women and black gay men. At certain points, black politics has also been underpinned by a deep absence or more typically an evasive silence with reference to class. Another element inscribed in the new politics of representation has to do with the question of ethnicity. I am familiar with all the dangers of "ethnicity" as a concept and have written myself about the fact that ethnicity, in the form of a culturally constructed sense of Englishness and a particularly closed, exclusive, and regressive form of English national identity, is one of the core characteristics of British racism today. I am also well aware that the politics of antiracism has often constructed itself in terms of a contestation of "multiethnicity" or "multiculturalism." On the other hand, as the politics of representation around the black subject shifts, I think we will begin to see a renewed contestation over the meaning of the term "ethnicity" itself.

If the black subject and black experience are not stabilized by Nature or by some other essential guarantee, then it must be the case that they are constructed historically, culturally, politically – and the concept that refers to this is "ethnicity." The term "ethnicity" acknowledges the place of history, language, and culture in the construction of subjectivity and identity, as well as the fact that all discourse is placed, positioned, situated, and all knowledge is contextual. Representation is possible only because enunciation is always produced within codes that have a history, a position within the discursive formations of a particular space and time. The displacement of the "centered" discourses of the West entails putting in question its universalist character and its transcendental claims to speak for everyone, while being itself everywhere and nowhere. The fact that this grounding of ethnicity in difference was deployed, in the discourse of racism, as a means of disavowing the realities of racism and repression does not mean that we can permit the term to be permanently colonized. That appropriation will have to be contested, the term disarticulated from its position in the discourse of "multiculturalism," and transcoded, just as we previously had to recuperate the term "black" from its place in a system of negative equivalences. The new politics of representation therefore also sets in motion an ideological contestation around the term "ethnicity." But in order to pursue that movement further, we will have to retheorize the concept of "difference."

It seems to me that, in the various practices and discourses of black cultural production, we are beginning to see constructions of just such a new conception of ethnicity: a new cultural politics that engages rather than suppresses difference and that depends, in part, on the cultural construction of new ethnic identities. Difference, like representation, is also a slippery, and therefore contested, concept. There is the "difference" that makes a radical and unbridgeable separation; and there is a "difference" that is positional, conditional, and conjunctural, closer to Derrida's notion of *différence*, though if we are concerned to maintain a politics it cannot be defined exclusively in terms of an infinite sliding of the signifier. We still have a great deal of work to do to *decouple* ethnicity, as it functions in the dominant discourse, from its equivalence with nationalism, imperialism, racism, and the state, which are the points of attachment around which a distinctive British or, more accurately, English, ethnicity has been constructed. Nevertheless, I think such a project is not only possible but necessary. Indeed, this decoupling of ethnicity from the violence of the state is implicit in some of the new forms of cultural practice that are going on in films like *Passion* and *Handsworth Songs*. We are beginning to think about how to represent a noncoercive and a more diverse conception of ethnicity, to set against the embattled, hegemonic conception of "Englishness" that stabilizes so much of the dominant political and cultural discourses, and that, because it is hegemonic, does not represent itself as an ethnicity at all.

This marks a real shift in the point of contestation, since it is no longer only between antiracism and multiculturalism but *inside* the notion of ethnicity itself. What is involved is the splitting of the notion of ethnicity between, on the one hand, the dominant notion that connects it to nation and "race" and, on the other hand, what I think is the beginning of a positive conception of the ethnicity of the margins, of the periphery. That is to say, a recognition that we all speak from a particular place, out of a particular history, out of a particular experience, a particular culture, without being contained by that position as "ethnic artists" or filmmakers. We are all, in that sense, *ethnically* located and our ethnic identities are crucial to our subjective sense of who we are. But this is also a recognition that this is not an ethnicity that is doomed to survive, as Englishness was, only by marginalizing, dispossessing, displacing, and forgetting other ethnicities. This precisely is the politics of ethnicity predicated on difference and diversity.

The final point that I think is entailed in this new politics of representation has to do with an awareness of the black experience as a *diaspora* experience, and the consequences that this carries for the process of unsettling, recombination, hybridization, and "cut-and-mix" – in short, the process of cultural *diaspo-*

raization (to coin an ugly term) that it implies. In the case of the young black British films and filmmakers under discussion, the diaspora experience is certainly profoundly fed and nourished by, for example, the emergence of Third World cinema; by the African experience; the connection with Afro-Caribbean experience; and the deep inheritance of complex systems of representation and aesthetic traditions from Asian and African culture. But in spite of these rich cultural "roots," the new cultural politics is operating on new and quite distinct ground – specifically, contestation over what it means to be "British." The relation of this cultural politics to the past, to its different "roots," is profound but complex. It cannot be simple or unmediated. It is (as a film like *Dreaming Rivers* reminds us) complexly mediated and transformed by memory, fantasy, and desire. Or, as even an explicitly political film like *Handsworth Songs* clearly suggests, the relation is intertextual-mediated, through a variety of other "texts." There can, therefore, be no simple "return" or "recovery" of the ancestral past that is not reexperienced through the categories of the present: no base for creative enunciation in a simple reproduction of traditional forms that are not transformed by the technologies and the identities of the present. This is something that was signaled as early as a film like *Blacks Britannica* and as recently as Paul Gilroy's important book *There Ain't No Black in the Union Jack* ([1987] 1991). Fifteen years ago we did not care, or at least I did not care, whether there was any black in the Union Jack. Now not only do we care, we must.

This last point suggests that we are also approaching what I would call the end of a certain critical innocence in black cultural politics. And here it might be appropriate to refer, glancingly, to the debate between Salman Rushdie and myself in the *Guardian*. The debate was not about whether *Handsworth Songs* and *The Passion of Remembrance* were great films or not, because, in the light of what I have said, once you enter this particular problematic, the question of what good films are, which parts of them are good and why, is open to the politics of criticism. Once you abandon essential categories, there is no place to go apart from the politics of criticism, and to enter the politics of criticism in black culture is to grow up, to leave the age of critical innocence.

It was not Salman Rushdie's particular judgment that I was contesting, as much as the mode in which he addressed the films. He seemed to me to be addressing them as if from the stable, well-established critical criteria of a *Guardian* viewer. I was trying, perhaps unsuccessfully, to say that I thought this an inadequate basis for a political criticism and one that overlooked precisely the signs of innovation, and the constraints under which these filmmakers were operating. It is difficult to define what an alternative mode of address would be. I certainly did not want Salman Rushdie to say that he thought the films were good because they were black. But I also did not want him to say that he thought they were not good because "we creative artists all know what good films are," since I no longer believe we can resolve the questions of aesthetic value by the use of these transcendental, canonical cultural categories. I think there is another position, one that locates itself *inside* a continuous struggle and politics around black representation but that then is able to open up a continuous critical discourse about themes, the forms of representation, about the subjects of representation, above all, the regimes of representation. I thought it was important, at that point, to intervene to try to get that mode of critical address right, in relation to the new black filmmaking. It is extremely tricky, as I know, because as it happens, in intervening, I got the mode of address wrong too! I failed to communicate the fact that, in relation to his *Guardian* article, I thought Salman was hopelessly wrong about *Handsworth Songs*, which does not in any way diminish my judgment about the stature of *Midnight's Children*. I regret that I could not get it right, exactly, because the politics of criticism has to be able to get both things right.

Such a politics of criticism has to be able to say (just to give one example) that *My Beautiful Laundrette* is one of the most riveting and important films produced by a black writer in recent years and precisely for the reason that made it so controversial: its refusal to represent the black experience in Britain as monolithic, self-contained, sexually stabilized, and always "right-on" – in a word, always and only "positive," or what Hanif Kureishi has called "cheering fictions": "the writer public relations officer, as hired liar. If there is to be a serious attempt to understand Britain today, with its mix of races and colors, its hysteria and despair, then, writing about it has to be complex. It can't apologize or idealize. It can't sentimentalize and it can't represent only one group as having a monopoly on virtue." *Laundrette* is important particularly in terms of its control, knowing what it is doing, as the text crosses those frontiers between gender, race, ethnicity, sexuality, and class. *Sammy and Rosie* is also a bold and adventurous film, though in some ways less coherent, not so sure of where it is going, overdriven by an almost uncontrollable, cool anger. One needs to be able to offer that as a critical judgment and to argue it through, to have one's mind changed, without undermining one's essential commitment to the project of the politics of black representation.

Stuart Hall

Africa

Ethnicity in Burundi: An Interpretation

Contrary to an all too prevalent opinion, BURUNDI, not RWANDA, will go down in history as the site of the first ethnic genocide recorded in post-independence Africa. Between May and December 1972, 22 years before the Rwanda holocaust, an abortive Hutu uprising led to the massacre of anywhere from 100,000 to 200,000 of their kinsmen at the hands of an all-Tutsi army. Further outbursts of ethnic violence occurred in 1988 and 1990, albeit on a smaller scale, again primarily aimed at Hutu elements – a sinister prelude to the continuing killings triggered by the assassination of Prime Minister Melchior Ndadaye, on October 21, 1993, by Tutsi officers.

What gives ethnicity in Burundi its singularly savage edge is not the resurgence of age-old antagonisms between Hutu and Tutsi, but the way in which the concept has been manipulated by urban elite (and the media) to legitimize their claims to power. Hutu and Tutsi are not categories set in stone. As identity markers they have been constantly redefined to serve the purpose of ideologues and politicians. At least two other factors have contributed to invest ethnic divisions with an exceptional potential for violence. One is the relative size of the two principal communities: the Tutsi account for roughly 15 percent of a total population of some 6 million, and the Hutu 85 percent. As in Rwanda, the tension between minority rights and majority rule translates into irreconcilable ethnic claims and counterclaims. For most Tutsi, majority rule means the tyranny of the Hutu majority, and possibly their annihilation as a minority; for the Hutu, democracy means nothing if not the rule of the majority, irrespective of ethnic considerations. Further sharpening the edges of ethnic conflict is the vertical pattern of stratification that has come to characterize Hutu-Tutsi relations, with the Hutu, in most instances, at the bottom of the heap, socially, economically, and politically. If democracy means majority rule, the latter in turn is seen by many Hutu as the only route to social justice.

If much of the history of modern Burundi is a metaphor for ethnic polarization, this is not to suggest that COLONIAL RULE did not play a significant role in the reshaping of collective identities. To take the full measure of these transformations, something must be said of social relations in precolonial Burundi.

HUTU AND TUTSI: THE FALLACY OF PRIMORDIAL ANTAGONISMS

As identity markers, Hutu and Tutsi are not colonial inventions. These labels were part and parcel of the Burundi social landscape centuries before the advent of colonial rule. At no time, however, did they convey anything like the hatreds and inhumanities witnessed since independence. More often than not, occupational and ethnic identities tended to coincide, and because of the symbolic significance attached to cattle ownership, Tutsi pastoralists were held in somewhat greater esteem than the Hutu agriculturalists. Even so, not all Tutsi were on the same footing. To this day, the high-status Tutsi-Banyaruguru ("those who are closer to the Court") are clearly differentiated from the lowly Tutsi-Hima, heavily concentrated in the south. Although as of 1998 the Tutsi-Hima were in control of the army as well as much of the government, they were traditionally viewed with almost undisguised contempt by Hutu and Tutsi alike.

Ethnicity, in short, was by no means the sole determinant of social status; indeed, social rankings within each group – such as between different patrilineages (*imiryango*) – were far more significant in deciding individual life chances. Clientage relations also afforded opportunities for upward mobility. Patron-client ties ran from top to bottom of the social pyramid, like so many vertical chains of dependency, linking Hutu to Tutsi, Tutsi to Tutsi, Tutsi to princes (*ganwa*), and princes (as well as Hutu court officials) to king (*mwami*). It is at this level that the contrast between the complexity of the traditional social system and the present Hutu-Tutsi dichotomy is most apparent; not only did ethnic identities cut across patron-client statuses, but a Tutsi cast in the role of client vis-à-vis a more powerful patron would be referred to as a Hutu. The term *Hutu*, in other words, has both ethnic and social connotations. Anyone born of a Hutu father is a Hutu, irrespective of the mother's identity; and anyone in a subordinate position could be referred to by a superior as a Hutu, here meaning "social son." It would thus be perfectly conceivable for someone simultaneously to assume a double social identity as Hutu and Tutsi, a phenomenon known as *kwihutura*. Conferment of a Tutsi identity for services rendered to a Tutsi patron was a fairly frequent occurrence, thus providing yet another avenue of social mobility.

The real power holders were neither Hutu nor Tutsi but princes, or ganwa, and the fact that they were seen to constitute a distinctive socioethnic category contributed in no small way to defuse tension between Hutu and Tutsi, since neither group was directly involved in succession struggles. In fact, by appealing to both Hutu and Tutsi to strengthen their hand against their rivals, factional struggles among ganwa served to reinforce cross-ethnic solidarities. Thus, writing in 1931, a White Father missionary, Bernard Zuure, concluded that it would be idle to look for differences of attitude and behavior between Hutu and Tutsi, for these, he added, "have become so minimal that one can speak of a common culture."

From a society characterized by highly complex, vertically structured sociopolitical networks, Burundi has now become a greatly "simplified" – indeed rigidly polarized – social field, where Hutu and Tutsi are the only political relevant categories. To grasp fully the significance of this all-encompassing metamorphosis we need to look back to the fundamental changes brought about under the aegis of the colonial state in both Rwanda and Burundi, and in the years immediately following independence.

The Transformation of Ethnic Identities

Colonial rule has significantly reshaped the contours and meaning of ethnic identities, first by ignoring altogether the social rankings inherent in family and clan structures, second by removing from office a number of Hutu chiefs and subchiefs and replacing them with Tutsi elements, and third by investing the concept of ethnicity with normative meanings borrowed from the "Hamitic hypothesis," an idea propounded by many missionaries. The aim was to make Burundi society more "legible" – that is, easier to understand – and thus more amenable to administrative efficiency. And what better model of efficiency than Rwanda, where Tutsi-Hutu polarities seemed pleasantly unencumbered by the complexities of criss-crossing social hierarchies and regional subloyalties?

As if to bolster the legitimacy of kingship, the main recipients of Western education were overwhelmingly of Tutsi and princely origins. While the highly skewed pattern of access to schools clearly favored the Tutsi for positions in the colonial administration, the *corvée* labor, compulsory cultivation, and taxes demanded of the Hutu masses also widened the gap between Hutu and Tutsi.

The emergent restratification of Burundi society not only allowed for efficient economic production and colonial administration, but it was also entirely consistent with the preconceptions underlying the "Hamitic" view of Hutu-Tutsi relations. Widely perceived as the prototype of the Hamites – described by C. G. Seligman as "pastoral Europeans arriving wave after wave, better armed as well as quicker witted than the dark agricultural Negroes" – for some missionaries the Tutsi were ideally equipped by nature to act as the privileged intermediaries between the European colonizer and the "dark agricultural" Hutu masses.

But if the requirement of administrative legibility made Burundi society look increasingly like its neighbor to the north, Hutu-Tutsi tensions seemed almost nonexistent compared to those in Rwanda in the mid-1950s. When Burundi became independent in 1962, the country was as yet untouched by the demons of mobilized ethnicity; it was still a constitutional monarchy, and the main line of political cleavage was between rival princely families, each claiming the support of Hutu and Tutsi. By then, however, Rwanda had become a Hutu-dominated republic, and Burundi, like Uganda and the Democratic Republic of the Congo, was hosting tens of thousands of Rwanda's Tutsi refugees. The impact on Burundi has been little short of devastating.

The "democratic" ideals of the 1959 Hutu revolution in Rwanda eventually became a major pole of attraction for Hutu politicians in Burundi – and a source of permanent revulsion for the Tutsi minority. The projection of the Rwanda situation into Burundi thus lies at the root of the self-fulfilling prophecy. It led many Tutsi in Burundi to anticipate a fate similar to that of their Rwanda kinsmen, should power pass into Hutu hands, and it led not a few Hutu to look to Rwanda as the model polity.

The dominant trend since 1962 has been toward greater social polarization along Hutu-Tutsi lines, culminating with the 1972 carnage and the emergence of a radical, bitterly anti-Tutsi movement, the so-called Parti pour l'Emancipation du Peuple Hutu (PALIPEHUTU). That the PALIPEHUTU was born in the refugee camps of Tanzania is no coincidence. Since the late 1950s refugee flows between Rwanda and Burundi have played a critically important role in intensifying ethnic hatreds, and this is true of both Tutsi and Hutu refugees. Thus a crucial factor in the process of ethnic polarization that followed in the wake of the Rwanda revolution has been the massive exodus of Tutsi refugees into Burundi. Many became actively involved in Burundi politics, casting their lot with the more radical elements of the Tutsi populations. It is noteworthy that Burundi's first Hutu prime minister, Pierre Ngendadumwe, was assassinated in 1965 by a Tutsi refugee from Rwanda, and when the carnage of Hutu began in 1972, many Tutsi refugees volunteered for the predominantly Tutsi army.

The Genocide

The 1972 bloodbath must be understood in light of the more or less systematic exclusion, from 1965 onward, of Hutu elements from positions of responsibility in the government and the army. In spite of their landslide victory at the polls in 1965, Hutu deputies were denied the right to appoint a government of their choice, which in turn led to the abortive Hutu-instigated coup of October 19, 1965, followed by extensive purges of the army and the gendarmerie and the physical elimination of every Hutu leader of any standing. In the Muramvya province, home of the hard-core Hutu opposition, a brutal repression ensued, causing thousands of casualties among Hutu civilians.

A somewhat similar scenario unfolded seven years later, except this time the repression reached genocidal proportions. On April 19, 1972, a Hutu-led insurgency exploded in the normally peaceful lakeside towns of Nyanza-lac and Rumonge, in the southern tip of the country. Hundreds if not thousands of Tutsi civilians fell under the blows of the insurgents. The repression began almost instantly. Week after week, month after month, tens of thousands of Hutu men and youngsters – civil servants, teachers, university students, schoolchildren – were rounded up and killed by mixed teams of youth groups and soldiers. Their bodies were buried in mass graves throughout the country, while the carnage continued unabated until August. By then almost every educated Hutu was either dead or in exile. The aim, in short, was to eliminate for the foreseeable future any serious threat to Tutsi hegemony. For the next 20 years the Tutsi minority was able to exercise virtually unfettered control of the army, the government, the civil service, the provincial administration, the university, and the economy. Thus transformed, Burundi became the mirror image of Rwanda.

The impact of the 1972 butchery on ethnic relations was by no means limited to Burundi. In Rwanda a terrible backlash swept through many secondary schools as well as the University of Butare, causing the deaths of hundreds of Tutsi students. It was among exiled Hutu, however, that the genocide's effects on collective representations of ethnicity were most marked: suddenly, the massive inhumanities inflicted on Hutu civilians seemed entirely consistent with the view of Tutsi as Hamitic invaders, whose cunning is surpassed only by their innate cruelty.

History and Ethnic Memory

In Burundi as elsewhere, ethnic violence is the product of mobilized ethnicity. It is a recent, urban-based phenomenon. As such, it has little in common with the more fluid, diffuse, negotiable social identities that once characterized traditional societies. Nonetheless, any attempt to make sense of Burundi ethnicity must consider how "ethnic entrepreneurs" have tried to reconstruct the past in order to mobilize support and validate their claims to power.

Illustrative of this phenomenon are the "mythicohistories" elaborated by PALIPEHUTU leaders in the years immediately following the genocide. In an undated document penned by the late Remi Gahutu, the party's founder and president, the 1972 killings are seen as historically linked to the centuries-old domination of a "Hamitic" minority, a form of feudal oppression directly related to the "dehumanization of the Hutu serfs." That a small Hamitic minority could have succeeded in imposing its domination on the Hutu majority can only be explained by taking into account the former's consummate skills in the use of ruse and cruelty; the poisoned gift of cows and the "bait of beautiful women" were indeed key ingredients in the strategy employed by the Tutsi to reduce their unsuspecting Hutu hosts into bondage. Much the same story, and worse still, was told to anthropologist Liisa Malkki by Hutu refugees in Tanzania: "In order to get food, the Tutsi flatters a Hutu, a cultivator. He says, 'I give you my daughter, even two or three cows.' Like this. Then the Hutu accepts, seeing a beautiful woman with a long nose and very tall also in stature, elegant if you wish, and who squanders smiles.... Then this Hutu begins to despise the other Hutu because he is flattered and he boasts about his Tutsi wife."

What emerges from this and many other accounts is an image of the Tutsi as the archetype of the Hamitic "bad guy," whose presence in Burundi has been historically linked to the transformation of "Bantu" into "Hutu," from free people into slaves.

Seldom anywhere (with the exception of Rwanda) has the past been manipulated in more blatant violation of the historical record, and with more obvious political designs: to cast irreparable moral discredit on the Tutsi as a group. In Liisa Malkki's words, the discourse of the PALIPEHUTU, echoed in the stories told by refugees, is not "a description of the past, nor even an evaluation of the past, but a subversive recasting and reinterpreting of it in fundamentally moral terms."

In refutation of the Hamitic caricature projected by Hutu ideologues, Tutsi elite typically argue that ethnicity in Burundi is at best a figment of the Hutu imagination, at worse the despicable offspring of a "tribal ideology" introduced by the European colonizer. Ethnic differences, they argue, are simply not relevant to an understanding of the country's problems. According to a tract written by Tutsi intellectuals in 1988, the Tutsi have never oppressed the Hutu: "So deep are the strands of social solidarity woven (between Hutu and Tutsi)... that there are no grounds of objective antagonisms between the two groups."

In the wake of the genocide, two radically opposed forms of ethnic memory emerged: one seeking to project into the precolonial past a conflict situation of recent origins, the other projecting into the present the basic ethnic harmony of traditional Burundi. One version aims to falsify the past to explain recent ethnic killings, the other aims to embellish the past so as to deny altogether the existence of a fundamental Hutu-Tutsi problem, beyond what was issued from the perverse imagination of the European colonizer.

Violence and Ethnicity: The Infernal Dialectic

Contrary to what the foregoing might suggest, not everyone in Burundi succumbed to the siren song of ideological manipulation. Many Hutu saw through the Hamitic delusions of the PALIPEHUTU, and many Tutsi privately scoffed at the posture of ethnic amnesia adopted by some of their kinsmen. But in the sharply polarized arena of post-genocide Burundi, their voice carried little conviction. One of the most tragic consequences of recurrent ethnic violence has been to reduce sharply the political space available to moderates among both Hutu and Tutsi. Indeed, extremists at both ends of the ethnic spectrum – who include members of the army and the militias among Tutsi, and members of the PALIPEHUTU, the Front de Libéraion Nationale (FROLINAT), the Conseil National pour la Défense de la Démocratie (CNDD) among Hutu – have succeeded in wrecking every attempt at a viable constitutional compromise.

The most dramatic example occurred on October 21, 1993, when the all-Tutsi army undid in a matter of hours all the accomplishments of a carefully engineered four-year transition to democracy. With the assassination of President Melchior Ndadaye by a group of noncommissioned officers, Burundi began a seemingly endless descent into hell – from which it has yet to recover. In his dual capacity as Burundi's first Hutu president and leader of the Front des Démocrates du Burundi (FRODEBU) – a party dominated by Hutu moderates, but whose membership included a substantial number of Tutsi – Ndadaye was immensely popular among the Hutu. The news of his death hit the countryside with the force of an earthquake. A *grande peur* (great fear) seemed to seize the Hutu hillside communities; suddenly images of the 1972 bloodbath reappeared in their minds; Ndadaye's death was the harbinger of a replay of 1972.

In an uncontrolled outburst of collective rage, Hutu peasants turned against their Tutsi neighbors, killing tens of thousands; in one community after another, scores of men, women, and children were hacked to pieces, speared or clubbed to death, or doused with kerosene and burned alive. Equally terrifying was the repression unleashed by the army, causing as many deaths among Hutu as the Hutu had caused among Tutsi. As many as 100,000 people may have died in the course of a carnage in which Hutu and Tutsi finally reached equal status.

This is not the place to explore the causal connection between the events of October 1993 in Burundi and the Rwanda genocide, six months later, except to note that the assassination of Ndadaye greatly strengthened the conviction of Hutu extremists – and not a few moderates – in Rwanda that "the Tutsi simply cannot be trusted." What must be emphasized is the extent to which the Rwanda genocide, once projected back into the Burundi situation, was held up by Tutsi radicals in Burundi as "proof" of the genocidal intentions of the Hutu as a group. By then ethnicity and genocide became the two sides of the same conceptual coin, but not without some extraordinary adjustments of historical facts. The discourse of Tutsi extremists, for example, says nothing about the 1972 genocide of Hutu by Tutsi, as if the horrors of 1972 had been obliterated forever from their collective memory.

What is emerging in Burundi are two radically different memories, nurturing different ideologies and political cultures. New traditions are being invented by Hutu and Tutsi designed to strengthen their claims and justify their prejudices. Both as a concept and an empirical referent, ethnicity in Burundi is thus as far removed from its precolonial roots as the present ramshackle polity is from the old monarchical order. Whether a meaningful and mutually acceptable compromise can be found – a compromise that could lay the foundation for the reinvention of the state and the redefinition of citizenship in Burundi – remains to be seen.

René Lemarchand

See Also

Hutu and Tutsi; Pastoralism; Christianity: Missionaries in Africa.

Africa

Ethnicity in Rwanda: An Interpretation, an examination of the historical development of relations between the Hutu and Tutsi peoples of Rwanda.

Introduction

Who are the Hutu and the Tutsi? This is a question that came into every discussion I had during my visits to Rwanda. While the Hutu opposition had been a target of the 1994 massacre, this was a political matter; the Tutsi had faced true genocide – the attempt to eliminate them as a people. Given this single fact, which illuminates the tragedy of Rwanda for the world at large, I was nonplused to be told over and again by leading people in the Rwandan Patriotic Front (RPF – the Tutsi-dominated ruling party after 1994): "We speak the same language, have the same culture, and live on the same hills; we are the same people." But in casual conversation and out on the street, some of the same individuals would readily identify Hutu and Tutsi individuals. Sometimes they were identified by physical appearance, but in a place like Ntarama in the southern lowlands, where Tutsi made up as much as a third of the population, and where there had been many intermarriages – a third of the Tutsi daughters were married to Hutu, I was told – this was hardly a reliable method. During the killings, people were asked to produce their identity cards.

Not surprisingly, one of the issues hotly debated in the Rwandese Alliance for National Unity (RANU), formed by refugees in Uganda in 1979, was whether the difference between Hutu and Tutsi was one of class or ethnicity. I remembered what I had heard from a Nigerian colleague at a conference organized by the Dakar-based Council for Development of Social Research in Africa (CODESRIA) early in 1995. If he went to a discussion on Rwanda and Burundi, he could close his eyes and tell the identity of a speaker from these countries by the twist of their argument: if a person claimed that there were no differences between Hutu and Tutsi, or that the difference was one of class, the speaker was most likely a Tutsi, for a Hutu intellectual was most likely to argue otherwise, that the difference was one between distinct ethnic, or even racial, groups.

It is difficult to believe that the Hutu-Tutsi difference is based on class, for both groups are internally differentiated. One finds Hutu and Tutsi in the same class: the Tutsi pastoralists I saw in the southern lowlands were as poor and wretched as the Hutu peasants I met along the way. If the view that there is "no difference" – or only a class difference – tends to focus on socioeconomic processes, the preoccupation of the "ethnic difference" perspective is with the biological and the historico-cultural. If the "no difference" view tends to suffer from historical amnesia – specifically of how power was organized in the precolonial Rwandan state – that of "ethnic difference" tends to freeze the history of the Rwandan state at its colonial stage, turning a historical outcome into a primordial difference. If loss of historical memory leads to a tragic political innocence, historical fixation leads to a no less tragic pathology. One side overlooks the limits on politics, the other slights the possibility of political action. Neither is able to appreciate the political potential in a given situation.

A careful review of the history of the Rwandan state reveals that Hutu and Tutsi are bipolar identities reproduced by a form of the state that institutionalized them as such: there cannot be one without the other. In this relationship, first shaped by the precolonial Rwandan state but fully crystallized by the colonial state, Tutsi came to be identified with power and Hutu with subjecthood.

The Precolonial Rwandan State

When I returned from Kigali, I immersed myself in whatever literature I could find on Rwandan history. I realized that the further back one went, the mistier the historical background. Shrouded in a rich mythology is the question of the origin of the Tutsi. Caught up by the notion that differences and conflicts in human society are the result of racial differences, early European explorers and administrators came up with the "Hamitic hypothesis": that the Tutsi were a superior non-Bantu race who had come from the direction of Ethiopia and conquered indigenous agriculturalists (Hutu) and forest dwellers (Twa). This racist theory was discredited in the heyday of anti-imperial nationalism, but there is still no consensus among historians and anthropologists on the origin of the Tutsi. At least three accounts can be found in the literature.

The first is a dietary explanation of the difference most identified with Walter Rodney; strangely enough, it was standard reading for the RPF cadres in the late 1980s and early 1990s. In his influential work *How Europe Underdeveloped Africa*, Rodney argued that the Twa remained "pygmies" because "they wandered around in small bands, hunting and digging roots, thereby failing to assure themselves of plentiful or rich food." The Hutu "were more socially advanced than the Twa" because "they did not live entirely on the whims of nature." But in comparison to the Tutsi, the Hutu remained "short and stocky" because "the quality of their food fell short of the protein-rich Tutsi diet." And so the Tutsi pastoralists, "subsisting on a constantly accessible and rich diet of milk and meat," turned out to be "one of the tallest human groups in the world."

The second explanation accepts the migration theory, that the pastoralists came from outside Rwanda, but argues that their relations with the agriculturalists were peaceful and symbiotic: they exchanged dairy products for garden vegetables. Forcefully put forth by the late Samwiri Karugire, the noted Ugandan historian, it has since been embraced by various political protagonists, including the president of Uganda and many in the leadership of the RPF.

Neither the dietary hypothesis nor the theory of peaceful coexistence gets to the question that I think is the key to understanding the precolonial period: the nature of the political power organized as the Rwandan state. Walter Rodney accepts that "the system of social relations which emerged in Rwanda was more completely hierarchical... than in most parts of Africa." Similarly, Edward Steinhart, taking inspiration from Samwiri Karugire, concludes with reference to Ankore that "the system of pastoral domination, which had evolved from meagre beginnings in the fifteenth century, had by the early nineteenth century become one of the most rigid and authoritarian systems of political and social exploitation in the intralacustrine region." Scholars agree that if there was a system more hierarchical than that in Ankore, it was in Rwanda.

A third explanation has recently been put forth by Archie Mafeje in a book called *The Theory and Ethnography of African Social Formations*. While Mafeje dismisses the Hamitic hypothesis, his work is based on a critical summary of colonial anthropology. Mafeje's starting point is Bunyoro, where, "somewhere in the fifteenth century," there occurred the "first known processes of political centralization" in the intralacustrine region. In Bunyoro, "the introduction of pastoralism as an elite pursuit must be attributed to... invaders who, probably, migrated from south-eastern Ethiopia and southern Somalia with their long-horned cattle." But the Chwezi dynasty did not last long in Bunyoro. In "a few generations," the Chwezi "were chased out by [B]ito invaders" from the north, moving in a "south-westerly direction where ecological conditions are ideal for cattle-keeping" and "reappeared as conquering [H]ima herders in Ankore, Rwanda and Burundi." But if the Chwezi "disappeared" on the way from Bunyoro to Ankore, and "reappeared" as the Hima in Ankore, the Hima "disappeared" on the way to Rwanda, where they "reappeared" as the Tutsi.

Mafeje is at pains to point out that at the

outset Tutsi migration was largely peaceful: "land was plentiful in the areas of migration of the Bahima." Later, though, this seems to have led to forcible conquest and the creation of the Rwandan state: "as the population increased as more [T]utsi kept on entering the country and more land had to be tilled to feed them" and "as cattle were increasing," "the [H]utu had to move from the most fertile soil." But the very fact that our author has to speak of "disappearance" and "reappearance" suggests that what is involved here is a stringing together of facts that are otherwise separated by many a historical gap. The result is likely to be as much fiction as fact.

That much of what passed as historical fact in academic circles has to be considered as tentative – if not outright fictional – is becoming clear as postgenocidal sobriety compels a growing number of historians to take seriously the political uses to which their writings have been put, and their readers to question the certainty with which many a claim has been advanced. In the process, several claims that had come to be regarded as sacred cows no longer appear so self-evident. For example, David Newbury questions the long-held assumption that the Hutu were always agriculturalists and the Tutsi pastoralists. He argues that "the people who came to be known as '[H]utu' had cattle here long before those known as [T]utsi appeared on the scene." Certainly, if Hutu had in fact had a natural aversion to cattle rearing and had always been cultivators, it would have made little sense in the precolonial period to put restrictions on Hutu owning cattle. We must acknowledge that these identifications are less mere facts unrelated to power than historical artifacts created alongside the institutionalized power of the precolonial Rwandan state.

Constructing a State

This history is important, not because of where the Tutsi and the Hutu originally came from, but because in their coming together they created certain political institutions that outlived that history and shaped a tragic future. The key political institution forged through their contact was the precolonial Rwandan state. It established a double domination, of a pastoralist aristocracy over a subject peasantry, and of Tutsi over Hutu – and Twa. While the question of the historical origin of the Tutsi is shrouded in mystery, that of the nature of the state they built is not.

The parameters of the cultural complex called Kinyarwanda are much larger than the domain of the present-day state called Rwanda. The disparity between their size was even greater in the precolonial period than it is today. Kinyarwanda is said to have one of the largest groups of speakers of any African language, roughly 10 million. Long before the consolidation of the Nyiginya Dynasty as the state of Rwanda in what is known as the central court complex, people speaking variants of Kinyarwanda were widely settled in the region. Outside central Rwanda, where the precolonial Rwandan state was based, there are at least two zones that were culturally – but not politically – Kinyarwanda. The first of these is today divided between northern Rwanda and western Uganda, settled by a people known as the Kiga – "the people of the mountains" – who shared the same language but not the same social and political culture as those within the ambit of the Rwandan state. Not only did they have different settlement patterns, clan categories, and marriage forms, but their political life was highly decentralized and community-based, in sharp contrast to the centralized hierarchy of the state of Rwanda. Here there were no Tutsi and no Hutu, at least not until German colonialism integrated part of this area into the Rwandan polity. The cultural difference between what then became northern Rwanda and the rest of the country would later reappear – under the two Hutu republics – as the difference between northern and southern Hutu. The second major cultural zone that lay outside the precolonial state of Rwanda is today divided between western Rwanda and eastern Congo-Kinshasa. These speakers of Kinyarwanda live south and west of Lake Rweru (Edward), and north and south of Lake Kivu, in Congo-Kinshasa. Unlike the Kiga of the north, the Banyabwisha of the west had long accepted delegates from the central court: their social institutions closely resembled those in the central region.

All Banyarwanda spoke Kinyarwanda, the Bantu language originally spoken by the peasant population of Rwanda. Thus we come to the point that the people called Tutsi, and those who came to be called Hutu, spoke the same language, lived on the same hills, and had more or less the same culture, depending on the cultural zones in which they lived. But they had yet to become one people.

I will make my point by contrasting two states that were organized in the intralacustrine region – Rwanda and Buganda. Like Buganda, Rwanda was a highly centralized kingdom, with a standing army and an official bureaucracy. But unlike Buganda, the state in Rwanda defined rulers and subjects as belonging to two distinct social groups, pastoralist and agriculturalist, one noble, the other commoner. The kings, considered divine, were all Tutsi; army commanders were all Tutsi. While the entire population was affiliated to the army, there is – once again – no agreement among historians as to whether the warriors were exclusively Tutsi or whether this held true only for an earlier period. Nonetheless, most seem to agree that participation within the army was structured hierarchically. In this context, as Antoine Lema puts it, "the corpse of a Tutsi had more value than that of a Hutu or a Twa.... The Hutu were deprived [of] the right to [a] glorious, honourable, heroic death, since the Tutsi had also social monopoly on that." In the civil bureaucracy, the Mwami of Rwanda appointed and dismissed all chiefs, of which there were three types: *the chief of men*, who was in charge of recruiting soldiers; the *chief of pastures*, who ruled over grazing lands; and the *chief of landholding*, in charge of agricultural land and production. The chief of landholding was more likely to be a Hutu, for agriculture was said to be a Hutu calling. In the lower ranks of the administrative hierarchy, non-Tutsi functionaries were more common.

There was one institution in precolonial Rwanda that prevented the Tutsi-Hutu distinction from hardening into castelike difference, just as it prevented the formation of a Hutu counterelite that would in time challenge Tutsi domination. This was *kwihutura:* the rare Hutu who was able to accumulate cattle and rise through the socioeconomic hierarchy could *kwihutura* – "shed Hutuness" – and achieve the political status of a Tutsi. It is clear that we are talking of a political distinction, one that divided the subject from the nonsubject population, and not a socioeconomic distinction between exploiters and exploited or rich and poor.

This is why the ruling aristocracy in precolonial Rwanda needs to be understood as both pastoral and Tutsi. The Hutu made up the *subject* population, while the Tutsi – even when not part of the ruling group – had more of an identification with power and a more privileged relationship to the state. While socioeconomic processes led to class differentiation, particularly among the Tutsi, the political differences created by how the state was organized reflected more than just class differences. It seems to me that the Tutsi developed a political identity – they "formed a distinct social category, marked by marriage and ethnic taboos," says Mafeje – a self-consciousness of being distinguished from the subject population. Thus the mere fact of some physical difference – often the nose, less often the height – could become symbolic of a great political difference. The colonial state built on this political difference, making it the central political artifact around which was constructed the state's local apparatus. As a result, these otherwise incidental physical differences came to bear the weight of an entire history of state formation.

The Colonial State

While the Rwandan state clearly lost its independence with colonization, what was not so apparent was that its apparatus actually expanded during the colonial period. The territory it administered reached its widest span under German colonialism, since it was only with German military support – particularly the subjugation in 1912 of the northern districts – that Mwami Musinga was able to enlarge the state's boundaries. The Germans had but 5 civil and 24 military officers, on Rwandan soil in 1914. They could rule only through the institutional reach of the Tutsi-created state apparatus.

The Germans understood Africa through the optic of late-nineteenth century imperial Europe, which saw humanity as a conglomeration of races that required identification and hierarchical classification. Such was the inspiration behind the new discipline of physical anthropology, whose foot soldiers now began to classify the Tutsi and the Hutu as separate races, one "Hamitic" and superior, the other "Bantu" and inferior. But it was the Belgians who, from 1929 to 1933, turned this theory into the very basis of organizing the administrative apparatus of the colonial state. They classified the population into the Tutsi and the Hutu (and the Twa) and issued passes identifying all. Even the relative flexibility of the precolonial period – kwihutura – was removed, and the distinction was frozen into a rigid castelike structure. Indirect rule came to be rule through cooperative elements in the Tutsi oligarchy, those who managed the lowest rungs of the colonial administration that were also the highest rungs of the subordinate but semiautonomous district-level state apparatus.

The reorganization of the precolonial state was highly important. The key shift was in the redefinition of the powers of the state agents called chiefs. The previous trinity of chiefs was abolished and powers that had hitherto been separate and differentiated were fused in a single agent. To quote from René Lemarchand's study of colonial Rwanda, "the old balance of forces between cattle chiefs, land chiefs and army chiefs, which in previous times had served to protect the Hutu peasantry against undue exactions" was abolished. This "concentration of powers in the hands of a single chief, exercising unfettered control over his people, was bound to lead to abuses: not only did it deprive the Hutu of opportunities to play one chief off against another, but it also eliminated the channels of appeal offered by the previous arrangement." At the same time, most Hutu chiefs on the lower rungs of the colonial administration were dismissed and replaced by those classified as Tutsi. Such institutional change not only augmented state power but made it more despotic in character.

Belgian rule was harsh by any standards. Force was integral to the process of exploitation – particularly forced labor. And the indigenous mask of this brutal foreign domination was the hierarchy of Tutsi chiefs. So severe was Belgian rule, and with such impunity was it translated into practice by the Tutsi chiefs, that hundreds of thousands of Hutu peasants fled into Uganda in the decade after 1928 to take up jobs as migrant laborers in the coffee farms of Buganda. At first the Belgians found it convenient simply to pass on every demand – say, the upkeep of roads – to "customary" chiefs so that they used their "customary" prerogative to get the job done, without payment and with a minimum disruption of order. The chiefs also found it convenient to add their own demands to this list of "customary" exactions. The list grew as colonial law made *ubureetwa* services, a kind of forced labor, incumbent on all Hutu men. Catherine Newbury explains, "The services performed were usually of the most menial kind – collecting and drying firewood for the use of the hill chief's household, serving as night watchman, fetching water, cultivating the hill chief's fields.... Hutu were not only expected to perform such services without pay, but were often subjected to mistreatment as well." The smaller the chief, the more arbitrary could be the imposition: as one [Catholic] Church observer noted, a *petit* Tutsi chief and his wife "could take almost anything they please – bananas, yams, etc. – and the Hutu must comply lest he be expelled from his fields."

Money and Schooling

But not everything under this political system was hard. There were two broad processes under way – the expansion of a money economy and school-based Western education – that would erode Tutsi economic supremacy while, for a time, leaving intact their political supremacy. The money economy opened up opportunities for enrichment other than through the ownership of cattle, weakening the bonds of pastoral servitude that had been the colonial contract between patron and client. In this context, the expanding school system of the 1940s and 1950s provided the structural basis for the emergence of a Hutu counterelite. School education for children of Hutu families was a church initiative. Admission records of the Groupe Scolaire in Astrida (now Butare), a church institution that admitted students from the three Belgian colonies of Rwanda, Burundi, and the Congo, show that Hutu students were virtually excluded until after the Second World War, but the attitude of the European clergy went through a major shift in the mid-1950s. Postwar newcomers, according to Lemarchand, were likely to come from *"le petit clergé"* – of "relatively humble social origins," and with a "previous experience of social and political conditions in the French-speaking provinces of Wallonia," they were "more generally disposed to identify with the plight of the Hutu masses."

When the Hutu graduates of the Group Scolaire at Astrida entered the job market in the mid-1950s, they found there were few places for educated Hutus. Literally shut out of jobs in the civil service and the private sector, they turned to the church for opportunities, not just to make a living but also to articulate their major social grievance: the institutionalized exclusion of Hutu from what they saw as a Belgian-supported Tutsi monopoly over all avenues of advancement. With the support of a sympathetic clergy, they took control over church publications – the most important being the Kinyarwanda-language magazine *Kinyamateke* – and began to address those who would listen sympathetically, mainly the Hutu masses below and visiting United Nations commissions above.

Though administered by Belgium, Rwanda was a UN trust territory. Under UN tutelage, the process of decolonization unfolded as a series of electoral reforms. Elections set the context in which the Hutu counterelite forged their consciousness against the Tutsi elite. Such a consciousness emerged from the throes of a political contest. Tutsi identity, forged with the creation of the Rwandan state, long preceded Hutu identity. Tutsi consciousness was a consciousness of power, while Hutu consciousness would come to be one of lack of power, and of a struggle for power.

The development of a Hutu consciousness was a protracted affair, stretching over the entire span of the colonial period. As late as independence in 1962, the "Hutu" of the northwestern region insisted on being considered Kiga – like their neighbors in southwestern Uganda – not Hutu. Hutu consciousness developed in phases: before the Second World War, it was a consciousness of subjecthood that transcended all locally anchored identities; in the 1950s it became the consciousness of a people taking power. This shift took place only with the emergence of a Hutu counterelite which, propelled center stage by a series of electoral contests, put forth "Hutu power" as a program for overcoming their identity as a subject people. Branded with a subject identity – "Hutu" – the counterelite emerging from the ranks of the socially oppressed would hold it up as a badge of pride: Hutu Power! In turning a chain into a weapon, Spartacus-style, in trying to forge an identity for liberation from an emblem of servitude, it was neither the first nor would it be the last. One only need think of a related example: Black Power!

Hutu Power and Its Consequences

The backdrop to these electoral contests was a series of UN decolonization missions that were regularly dispatched to its trust territory after the Second World War. In 1953 elections were held to create advisory councils to state organs, in 1956 the first general election, another in 1959, and the last general elections in 1960 and 1961. This series of elections, and the anticipation of a transfer of power, triggered a chain of events leading, first, to a loosening of the hold of the Tutsi elite on the lower reaches of the state apparatus, and then, to extreme political polarization between the Tutsi and the Hutu – a prelude to an anti-Tutsi pogrom. The shift from indirect to direct elections showed that there was considerable likelihood of a Hutu victory at the polls. There was a clear victory in the 1956 elections of Hutu candidates at the subchief level, where the vote was direct, but not at higher levels, where the vote was indirect.

This was accompanied by an ideological polarization between Tutsi and Hutu, dramatized by two rival documents issued in anticipation of the 1957 UN trusteeship mission. First was *Mise au Point*, a call for an all-Rwandan emancipation issued by the

Mwami's High Council, advocating a transfer of power to ease racial tensions between black and white. Within a month followed the *Bahutu Manifesto*, written by Kayibanda and eight other Hutu leaders, all church-affiliated, and a Belgian priest. The difference between the two documents could not have been sharper: independence first, the view of the Tutsi elite, was the claim of the precolonial rulers for a restoration of their prerogatives; democracy before independence, the view of the Hutu counterelite, spelled out its demand for power. One highlighted the racial contradiction in the colony – between white and black – while the other underlined the social contradiction among the colonized.

On October 19, 1959, in anticipation of the next round of elections, and with the blessing of church authorities, a Hutu political party – the Parti du Mouvement de l'Émancipation Hutu (PARMEHUTU) – was created out of the old cultural association, Mouvement Social Muhutu. Almost immediately, there followed confrontations between PARMEHUTU militants and those of the pro-monarchy Tutsi party, the Union Nationale Rwandaise (UNAR), and Tutsi chiefs in charge of the local state apparatus. These came to a head in and around Gitarama the next month: when news spread that a group of young UNAR militants had attacked the PARMEHUTU leader Dominique Mbonyumutwa, pogroms spread from all over the country. The visiting UN mission of 1960 estimated the killings at 200 but added, "the number may be even higher since the people preferred to bury their dead silently." Some Tutsi chiefs were killed, others were forced to resign. A state of emergency was declared and the country put under the command of Col. Bem Guy Logiest.

It was in this context that Belgium carried out nothing less than a coup d'état. Arguing that the presence of Tutsi as subchiefs and chiefs "disturbed the public order," Bem Logiest began the replacement of Tutsi chiefs with Hutu, thus shepherding a "revolution" against what had hitherto been the colonial power's own authorities. Half the chiefs and subchiefs on the eve of the 1960 and 1961 general elections were Hutu – and the chiefs had control of the ballot boxes. Without this reconstitution of the local state hierarchy, it is difficult to explain the dramatically different outcome of subsequent elections. Two tendencies gelled around PARMEHUTU and UNAR. In the 1961 election, PARMEHUTU secured 77.4 percent of the popular vote, UNAR 16.8 percent. Independence followed on July 1, 1962. The new government was based on a power-sharing arrangement between PARMEHUTU and UNAR.

Unstable as it was, this power sharing came to an end with the attempt by the Tutsi refugees, who had fled in 1959 to Burundi, to return to power through an invasion called *Inyenzi* – cockroaches. The response was an organized countrywide killing of prominent Tutsi personalities, who had been previously arrested, and sectors of the Tutsi population: each of the country's ten prefectures was made an emergency zone under the command of a minister who organized "self-defense" groups among the Hutu population. It is difficult to know how many were killed. The UN guessed 1000 to 3000; the World Council of Churches estimated 10,000 to 14,000. Writing in *Le Monde* on February 6, 1964, Bertrand Russell termed it the most horrible systematic extermination of a people since the Nazi extermination of Jews. No African state except Burundi even raised a voice. The smashing of the counterrevolution, for that is how this pogrom was hailed, eroded any middle ground: the Tutsi who were killed were precisely those who had cut themselves off from the court and from the monarchists, and had hoped for a republican regime in which they could serve.

In the context of this historical account, we can draw the following conclusions:

1) The distinction between Tutsi and Hutu is a sociopolitical distinction. It is not just a colonial creation. Created in the precolonial period, the distinction was polarized by the colonial state, and would be inflamed and institutionalized by the postcolonial state.

2) The Tutsi identity crystallized at the time of the formation of the precolonial Rwandan state. It was a self-consciousness of being in or near power, or simply identifying with power. By contrast, the Hutu identity that gelled later was a self-consciousness of those subject to power. The Hutu identity – and its springboard, the 1959 revolution – cannot be dismissed as simply a sign of backwardness. This identity was limited to the framework of the colonial state, particularly the Tutsi hierarchy of chiefs. It is from this Hutu point of view that 1959 looks like a revolution, and 1994 must look like a counterrevolution.

3) Those who insist that the Hutu and the Tutsi are separate ethnic or cultural groups should ponder one fact: the identity Hutu-Tutsi is bipolar. Neither can exist in isolation. Rwanda's First Republic understood that so long as there is a sociopolitical identity called Tutsi, there will be another called Hutu. So it tried to entrench and keep alive both identities by reenacting the "revolution" as Hutu power through periodic pogroms, expulsions, and the redistribution of property to its militants in 1959, 1963, and so on. In time, the reenactments borrowed imagery from the French Revolution. Committees of Public Safety posted lists of "counterrevolutionaries": in 1972 these were Tutsi who were found in prominent positions in the educational system or the civil service. The pogrom of 1972 gathered in intensity as Hutu refugees were flushed into Rwanda, seeking shelter from a rampaging Tutsi-dominated army in neighboring Burundi. In this context the minister of defense, Jouvenal Habyarimana, staged a coup d'état, proclaiming that the "cultural revolution" of 1973 would but complete the "social revolution" of 1959.

4) The Second Republic tried to bring the "permanent revolution" that, in reality, was a permanent terror to an end by embedding the identities Hutu and Tutsi in institutions. Habyarimana institutionalized a hierarchical pluralism that he justified as a form of reverse discrimination (affirmative action) that would restore balance to Rwandan society through a system of quotas designed to redress the grievances of a hitherto oppressed majority. The Tutsi would be allowed a subordinate status in civil society, provided they accepted a subject status in political society. In this context Habyarimana made every attempt to ensure a symbolic Tutsi presence in the state apparatus: in late 1990 there was one Tutsi in a 19-member cabinet, one ambassador, two deputies in a 70-seat National Assembly, and two members in the 16-person central committee of the ruling party, the MRND. Did not the 1959 revolution turn the world that the Hutu knew upside down, but without changing it in other ways? If the corpse of a Tutsi had more value than that of a Hutu in an earlier era, did not the revolution arrive at a point where the corpse of a Tutsi had less dignity than a human corpse? If the upwardly mobile Hutu could shed his Hutuness (kwihutura) and enter the ranks of power, was not Habyarimana's nominal integration of Tutsi in the state hierarchy, right up to the cabinet, a sort of a *kwitutsira?*

The allocation of resources and positions within the state was said to reflect the actual numerical weight of the majority and the minority in society, so the demographic question became a hot political issue. The Second Republic maintained that the Tutsi constituted no more than 9 percent of the total population of Rwanda. This had the status of a state-sanctioned truth, and the figure remained unchanged over decades. Officialdom had little to say about intermarriages between Hutu and Tutsi and the official identity of children of these marriages. Despite centuries of intermarriage, the people of Rwanda were neatly divided into Hutu and Tutsi (or Twa); none was Hutsi.

5) Hutu and Tutsi in Rwanda are more political than cultural identities: when one is power, the other is subject. These bipolar identities are backed up by a form of the state that divides Rwandan society into a permanent majority (Hutu) and a permanent minority (Tutsi). How can Rwanda break out of this notion of the state as a representation of one of two permanently defined parts – one a majority, the other a minority? For any society to continue to exist, democratic competition – whether party-driven or not – presumes the existence of an order based on the consent, not of a majority, but of all. If political competition is not to be destructive of life, all those who participate in it – whether they win or lose – must accept the rules of the game. The creation of a consensus-based political community must precede the adoption of any

majority-driven political competition. Failure to learn this lesson will place Rwanda once again in a state of permanent tension. How to move from an order based on conquest to one based on consent is the challenge for Rwanda today.

Mahmood Mamdani

See Also
Bantu: Dispersion and Settlement; Buganda, Early Kingdom of; Colonial Rule; Hutu and Tutsi; Congo, Democratic Republic of the; Kigali, Rwanda; Law in Africa: Colonial and Contemporary; Nationalism in Africa; Pastoralism.

Latin America and the Caribbean

Etienne, Franck (Franketienne) **(b. April 12, 1936, Port-au-Prince, Haiti), poet, playwright, novelist, teacher, and politician whose strikingly original works in both Creole and French mark him as a key figure in contemporary Haitian literature.**

Born to a black mother and a white father, Franketienne (this is the Creolized spelling of his name that he adopted in 1972) grew up in one of Port-au-Prince's poorer neighborhoods. In a society stratified by race, he had the light skin color of the mulatto elite but lacked both the economic means and the family connections to have access to that world. At school, he was called *blanc manant* (white peasant), a derogatory nickname he later embraced.

Franketienne's work reflects his in-between status in Haitian society. He writes about the black bourgeoisie in the novel *Mur à crever* (1968), but also represents rural life in Haiti, as in *Dézafi* (1975), one of the first novels ever written in Creole. His poetry also bears the mark of his desire to exist in two worlds simultaneously. In his collections of poems, such as *Chevaux de l'avant-jour* (1967), he attempts to situate himself, as he puts it, "between those who see poetry as a 'pure art' and those who use it for purely political, purely militant ends."

In his writing as well as in his painting, inspired in part by the work of Hieronymus Bosch, images of putrefaction abound. One of the few Haitian writers who did not go into exile during the reign of the Duvaliers (*see* Duvalier, François; Duvalier, Jean-Claude), Franketienne expressed his horror at Haiti's self-destruction through the metaphorical description of the island as a body plagued by leprosy, wasting away in its own filth. This imagery appears most strikingly in the nightmarish *Fleurs d'insommnie* (1986), published just after Jean-Claude Duvalier's removal from office. Although he is considered a poetic innovator, Franketienne's importance lies perhaps more in his uncompromising resistance to the Duvaliers and in his willingness to be a voice of the Haitian people when they had none.

Richard Watts

See Also
Port-au-Prince, Haiti; Literature, French Language, in Caribbean; Languages, Creole, in the Caribbean.

Africa

Euba, Akin **(b. April 28, 1935, Lagos, Nigeria), Nigerian composer whose classical works combine elements of European and Yoruba music.**

In 1972 Akin Euba's *Dirges* was premiered at the Munich Olympic Games, a tribute to his achievement in synthesizing Western and African musical traditions. Throughout his career Euba has striven to create African classical music that is accessible to Africans and non-Africans alike. In his opinion, "The contemporary African composer… must create music for his own people and for all people at large and must act as an interpreter between the two."

Euba received an extensive musical education at Trinity College of Music in London, at the University of California at Los Angeles, and at the University of Ghana at Legon, where he received his Ph.D. in 1974. He has taught at Trinity College and at the University of Nigeria at Ife, and has published numerous academic articles on African music.

Most of Euba's earlier music fits into the Western classical or art music tradition. His first major work, a string quartet completed in 1957, is strongly influenced by Bela Bartók, and his 1967 symphonic study *Olurounbi* contains only peripheral references to the Yoruba folk tradition. Euba incorporated significantly more African material into his later works. His *Six Yoruba Songs* (1975) are transcribed for voice and piano with little modification of the original folk songs on which they are based. He also composed a setting of Léopold Senghor's poem *Chaka* – an important work that Nigerian literary scholar Abiola Irele believes "comes closest to an original conception of African art music… [as] the musical material, both in its structure and its instrumentation, is felt to proceed organically from the African musical tradition." Euba is currently Mellon Professor of African Music at the University of Pittsburgh, Pennsylvania.

Roanne Edwards

See Also
Music, African; Lagos, Nigeria; Senghor, Léopold Sédar.

Cross Cultural

Eugenics, **a scientific and social movement whose central tenet ascribes human behavior to genetic makeup and which supports social policies to maintain "racial hygiene."**

The philosophy behind the eugenics movement is that intelligence, health, and social behavior are determined solely by genetic makeup. Popular in the United States, England, and Germany from early in the twentieth century until World War II, eugenics dismisses the influence of social and economic factors on human behavior and advocates policies aimed at maintaining the "fitness" of a "superior" racial stock – that of white Anglo-Saxons.

British biologist Francis Galton coined the term *eugenics* in 1883 to describe his research on a trait he was convinced had been passed down through the generations of his own family – genius. Like other biologists of the time, Galton's interest in human heredity was piqued by the theories of species evolution outlined in Charles Darwin's classic treatise *On the Origin of the Species by Means of Natural Selection* (1859). Darwin's followers' application of his views to politics and economics, which has come to be known as social Darwinism, was the precursor to eugenics. Social Darwinists espoused a competitive model of species evolution summarized in the belief in "survival of the fittest." Because weaker, recessive genetic material would be naturally weeded out, the healthiness of a race would be ensured.

Social Darwinism's laissez faire attitude toward evolution distinguished it from the aggressive policies of the eugenics movement, which sought ways to intervene in human behavior to maintain "racial health." Eugenics aimed to institutionalize methods to ensure the continued "improvement" of the white race. Two branches of the field emerged to facilitate this, "positive" and "negative" eugenics. According to eugenicists, through positive eugenics, the stock of genetically healthy individuals would be improved and increased through selective breeding procedures. Negative eugenics was applied to unhealthy individuals. Through antimiscegenation laws, curtailing immigration from countries considered to harbor weaker genetic material, forced sterilization, and mercy killings, negative eugenics would restrain the reproduction of the genetically unfit.

Early in the twentieth century the eugenics movement quickly gained public support in the United States, Germany, and Britain. The United States' first sterilization law was passed in 1907 in Indiana. Three years later, Charles Davenport, the doyen of the American eugenics movement, opened the Eugenics Record Office in Cold Spring Harbor, New York. Through the office, Davenport, a strong promoter of forced sterilization, meticulously reported on what he believed to be the intellectual degeneracy of the poor, criminals, and a range of ethnic and racial communities.

Numerous states enacted antimiscegenation and sterilization laws between 1911 and 1930. The infamous *Buck* v. *Bell* Supreme Court case of 1927, in which Justice Oliver Wendell Holmes authorized the sterilization of a Virginia woman on the grounds that "three generations of imbeciles" was enough, led to thousands of forced sterilizations across the country. The crowning moment of the U.S. eugenics movement was the passage of the Immigration and Restriction Act of 1924. Supported by a coalition of eugenicists and corporate interests concerned with American standards of "racial hygiene," it effectively barred immigration from Eastern European and Mediterranean countries by instituting drastically reduced quotas.

Eugenics has been largely discredited since World War II. The atrocities committed by the Nazis during the Holocaust forced a rethinking of eugenics policies. Contemporary geneticists now view human behavior as determined by a complex interaction of biological, social, and economic factors. Beliefs in the innate power of race in influencing human behavior have been debunked. The central tenets of eugenics still persist, however. The publication in 1994 of Richard J. Herrnstein and Charles Murray's controversial *The Bell Curve: Intelligence and Class Structure in American Life,* demonstrates the continued appeal of biological explanations of human behavior.

Peter Hudson

See Also
Race: An Interpretation; National Socialist Sterilization Policies in Germany; World War II and African Americans.

Europe

Europe, a subcontinent lying directly across the Mediterranean Sea from Africa where Africans and people of African descent have had a presence since ancient times.

Although their populations did not approach those in the United States or Latin America, many blacks did land on the shores of Europe, particularly after the rise of the TRANSATLANTIC SLAVE TRADE in the sixteenth century. Though most blacks in Europe worked as slaves or paid servants during the early modern period, a few blacks and people of African descent achieved renown as artists and scholars. During the early twentieth century Europe was the site of a remarkable intellectual, political, and artistic ferment among Africans and people of African descent that prompted such movements as PAN-AFRICANISM and NÉGRITUDE. Since the 1950s a wave of black immigration has transformed many European nations and given rise to a new population of Afro-Europeans.

Early African Presence

There are some accounts of blacks and other Africans in Europe before the sixteenth century, especially in southern Europe, where small numbers of blacks arrived as early as Roman times. Roman armies captured African slaves in battle in 146 B.C.E. African writers and philosophers, such as SAINT AUGUSTINE (born in ALGERIA in 354 C.E.), traveled to the centers of scholarship in ancient ITALY. African soldiers joined the Roman army and went on campaigns to GERMANY in 58 B.C.E. and to GREAT BRITAIN in 200 C.E.

Muslim African armies conquered SPAIN and PORTUGAL beginning in the eighth century. The Christian Spanish and Portuguese fought the Moors – including both North and West Africans – and branded them "infidels" and "impure." Over the course of their centuries-long resistance to Muslim rule, the Spanish and Portuguese developed racist images of Africans, and these racist images traveled to northern Europe during the Middle Ages even before northern Europeans had much contact with Africans. There were occasional exceptions: the thirteenth-century Holy Roman (German) emperor Frederick II's army and entourage contained African soldiers and entertainers. By the fifteenth century, as Portuguese navigators began to explore the coast of West Africa, European art and literature had begun to depict Moors, or Africans – terms often used interchangeably at the time.

Slaves and Free Blacks in Early Modern Europe

It was not until the slave trade that a significant population of blacks existed in Europe. After the Muslims were driven from Spain and Portugal in the fifteenth century, the new Christian rulers funded large-scale seafaring voyages of discovery (*see* EXPLORERS IN AFRICA BEFORE 1500). The first African slaves were brought to Lisbon in 1444; soon slaving be-

OPPOSITE: The black king first appears in paintings of the Adoration of the Magi in the early fifteenth century. The three kings came to symbolize the three known continents: Africa, Asia, and Europe. The splendid African king in this triptych by German artist Hans Muelich was painted in 1572. *Image of the Black Project, Harvard University*

RIGHT: Three young African-French children stand before a wall in Paris. France's black population grew quickly in the 1980s and 1990s as immigrants from Africa and the West Indies joined hundreds of thousands of people of African descent who had lived there for generations. *CORBIS/Owen Franken*

BELOW RIGHT: A member of the court of Vienna in the eighteenth century, Mmadi-Make, also known as Angelo Solliman, is pictured here in an engraving after a portrait by painter Johann Nepomuk Steiner. *Erich Lessing/Art Resource, NY*

came common, justified by the Papal Bull of 1452, which condoned slave raiding as a crusade against "heathens." Slave labor on SUGAR plantations in the colonies produced considerable wealth for Europe. European nations competed for the right to trade slaves from Africa to the Spanish colonies. In the seventeenth century THE NETHERLANDS and then FRANCE and Great Britain took over the main responsibility for slave trading to the Americas.

Although heavily involved in the slave trade, most European nations, with the exception of Spain and Portugal, did not condone slavery on their own soil. The British, for instance, claimed that their soil was too pure to hold slaves. The Dutch freed the first slaves brought to the Netherlands. Despite these sentiments and laws, West Indian slave owners visiting or even residing in Europe brought their slaves with them.

During subsequent centuries black populations in Europe grew. Lisbon and Seville were the largest slave ports in Europe in the fifteenth and sixteenth centuries. Partly as a result, by 1600 roughly 10 percent of these cities' populations were black (14,000 blacks in Seville; 15,000 in Lisbon). By the late eighteenth century Great Britain had a black population of about 15,000. These blacks were mostly slaves used as domestic help. As in earlier centuries, wealthy Europeans made gifts of black slaves to royal courts, where they acted as entertainers or musicians or served as decoration. In the eighteenth century young black boys were fashionable as pages for wealthy ladies in Europe; their mistresses often discarded these boys when they reached adulthood.

Slaves faced considerable legal ambiguity in Europe. Believing that they would be freed by law in countries banning domestic slavery, or by baptism in countries banning the enslavement of Christians, many slaves tried to escape in Europe. Some were recaptured and brought before judges, who were inconsistent in their verdicts – some escapees were forced back into slavery, others were freed. In the James Somerset Case in England in 1772, the escaped slave James Somerset was freed from his West Indian master. The case allowed many to claim that slaves were free in

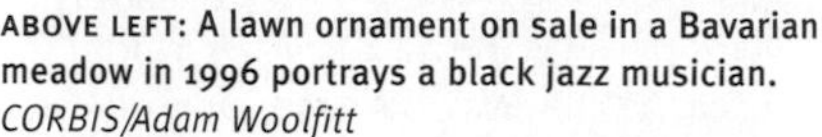

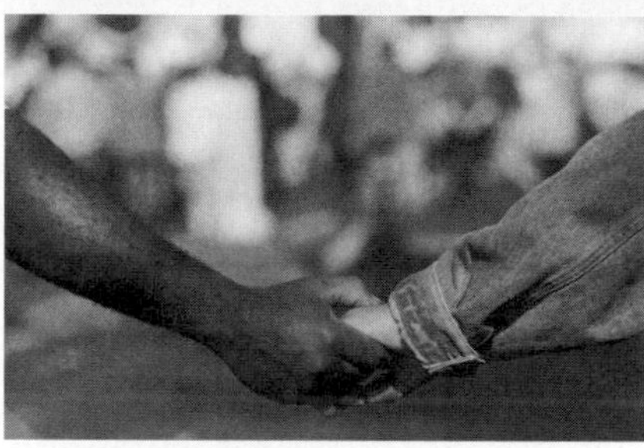

ABOVE LEFT: A lawn ornament on sale in a Bavarian meadow in 1996 portrays a black jazz musician. *CORBIS/Adam Woolfitt*
ABOVE RIGHT: At a ceremony held in 1965 in the Basilica of St. Peter in Rome, Pope Paul VI, assisted by African and European clergy, officiates at the beatification of new African saints. *CORBIS/David Lees*
RIGHT: Black and white demonstrators join hands at a rally held in Paris in 1995 to protest racism. *CORBIS/Owen Franken*

Great Britain. As a result, thousands of blacks sided with the British during the American Revolution. As in the colonies, the children of white masters and enslaved black women were often manumitted and schooled. This practice was more common in Spain and Portugal, where slavery was permitted and regulated. Some slaves were given a specified period of service in which to buy back their freedom, though, as part of the deal, these manumitted slaves were sometimes required to serve their former master for a lifetime. The benefit for manumitted slaves who agreed to continue to work for their masters was that their children would be born free.

Few freed slaves could find work except as servants, though some worked as sailors. Sailing was one of the few occupations open to blacks in Europe from a very early stage. A few blacks who had wealthy patrons managed to obtain an education and contributed greatly to their respective European societies. In 1707 the Dutch West India Company gave slave Anton Wilhelm Amo to the German dukes of Wolfenbüttel. Amo attended the university, obtained a doctorate, and became a noted scholar, eventually returning to Africa. In 1700 the black slave Abram Hannibal was presented to Tsar Peter the Great of Russia. The tsar sent Hannibal to Paris, where he learned engineering. After receiving his degree, Hannibal returned to Russia to design structures. Juan de Pareja was a noted painter in seventeenth-century Spain and Italy. During the eighteenth century Jacobus Capitein studied in the Netherlands, became the first African ordained as a Protestant minister, and returned to Africa. Olaudah Equiano, a slave who became literate in English, bought his freedom from his master and settled in London in the eighteenth century. Equiano joined the abolitionist movement and acted as an administrator for the Sierra Leone settlement plan. These men were, in some part, "Enlightenment experiments," upheld by their patrons and by abolitionists as examples of the humanity and potential of Africans.

Abolition and Black Workers, Students, and Soldiers in Europe

In the nineteenth century both whites and blacks campaigned for the abolition of slavery by spreading news of its atrocities as well as disseminating information on the economic disadvantages of the slave trade. Denmark was one of the first European states to abolish its slave trade in 1802. Great Britain followed soon after with the Abolition Act of 1808 and the emancipation of slaves in 1834. The Netherlands abolished the trade in 1814 and freed slaves in Dutch territories in 1863. France had outlawed slavery in 1794, but Napoleon Bonaparte revived it in 1804. Even with the revolutionary call for "liberty, equality, and fraternity," the French continued a legally ambiguous slave trade during the early nineteenth century; in 1848 they finally abolished slavery. Great Britain pressured Portugal to abolish its slave trade in 1831; Portugal emancipated slaves in 1877. Spain began gradual abolition with the 1870 Moret Law.

The emancipation of the slaves in France meant that blacks gained citizenship, voting, and election rights. Blacks represented French colonies in the country's Parliament during the nineteenth century. Other countries were slower to make such progress. In Great Britain blacks were not elected to Parliament until 1987. In fact, most blacks who remained in Europe during this era of postemancipation faced lives of poverty and exclusion in European cities.

Many free blacks assimilated into white European populations. Whereas in the United States a person need only have one black ancestor to be considered black, in Europe those with African ancestry did not necessarily consider themselves black. The nineteenth-century French novelist Alexandre Dumas père and the father of modern Russian literature, Aleksander Sergeyevich Pushkin, both had African ancestry, but neither identified himself as black; they thought of themselves as Europeans. Louis Alons, a black man in the Netherlands, married a white woman; in official registries their children and grandchildren were considered white. Of course, because of racism in Europe, in most cases it was not beneficial to announce one's African ancestry; if possible, people denied their African background. Intermarriage among free black men and white working-class women was not uncommon in Europe, especially since few black women lived there. For the most part, the English, Dutch, and French did not object to marriage between blacks and whites as long as they had the same class background. In the nineteenth century many blacks assimilated into European populations in this manner.

Within a few years of the abolition of the slave trade, European powers entered the "Scramble for Africa," dividing up the continent and instituting colonialism (*see* Colonial Rule). Great Britain, Portugal, Germany, France, Belgium, and, to a lesser extent, Spain and Italy were all involved in colonizing Africa. Africans, now as colonial subjects, traveled to Europe to obtain an education, and some gained positions of power in the colonial administrations. Many fought as servicemen for the colonial powers.

When World War I began, many blacks fought in European armies and many others took jobs in Europe left vacant by whites gone off to war. For the most part, Europeans appreciated the contributions of black troops. The French praised Africans and African Americans as their saviors in the war and treated them as such. In France, many African Americans for the first time experienced a society relatively free of racist customs and institutions. After World War I, France welcomed African American JAZZ musicians, artists, and writers, and a substantial expatriate community of blacks was formed in Paris. Blacks from the United States and Africans also received moral support after the war from the newly formed communist Soviet Union. The Soviets defined racism and colonialism as ways in which capitalists exploited the working class and therefore saw blacks as allies. In the 1930s the Soviets recruited black Americans to help them in an agricultural campaign in Uzbekistan and treated them as honored guests.

However, blacks were not always so welcome. In other parts of Europe the wartime influx of blacks alarmed whites returning from war. In Great Britain, in an atmosphere of widespread unemployment as soldiers were discharged and wartime production phased out, working-class whites accused blacks of taking their jobs. Many called for the forcible return of blacks to Africa or the West Indies. This anger culminated in rioting in Cardiff, Wales, in 1919. Some whites also resented postwar interracial marriages with blacks. Most Germans despised blacks in the French army sent to occupy the German Rhineland after the war, especially when these blacks married or had affairs with German women and gave rise to a small but very visible black German population. One of the many atrocities committed in World War II was the forced sterilization of close to 400 of these Afro-Germans.

During the first half of the twentieth century, dramatic intellectual, political, and cultural innovation and exchange took place among blacks gathered in Europe from many parts of the world. Consciousness of a shared African identity increased and Pan-Africanism flourished. The African American scholar and activist W. E. B. Du Bois led the first Pan-African Congress in Paris in 1919; later conferences were held in Great Britain. Many of the blacks who came to Europe during this period, including future African presidents JOMO KENYATTA and KWAME NKRUMAH, protested the injustice of colonialism and organized movements to end it. Léopold Sédar Senghor and Aimé Césaire drew on a common African heritage and on the experience of racism and colonization to forge a positive, modern African approach to cultural expression in the Négritude Movement. Meanwhile, artists and musicians such as JOSEPHINE BAKER, PAUL ROBESON, and Sidney Bechet, among others, dazzled Europe with their talents.

By and large, black intellectuals and artists in Europe had a different experience than in the United States. In Europe they were free of the discrimination and segregation that were enforced by JIM CROW laws, though racism did occur, for example, when blacks competed with whites for employment. With the coming of World War II, thousands of blacks joined the Allies in fighting fascism. Many Africans and African Americans felt that their service and sacrifice entitled them to demand an end to legal discrimination and colonialism. Within 20 years of the end of World War II, most African and West Indian nations did gain their independence (*see* NATIONALISM IN AFRICA), and African Americans achieved a number of civil rights victories (*see* CIVIL RIGHTS MOVEMENT); within Europe, however, racial prejudice seemed to worsen.

POSTWAR IMMIGRANTS AND "GUEST WORKERS"

In the 1950s and 1960s Europe experienced an economic boom. European countries recruited blacks to work in industry, and new black immigrant communities developed. Most of the West Indians and Africans (especially North Africans) who came to Europe during this period were guest workers looking for temporary employment or political refugees seeking asylum. Many planned to return to their homelands eventually. They came believing that they would be accepted as equals, particularly since, as a result of colonialism, they shared a language and often a culture with Europeans. Although they were initially welcomed as a needed work force, whites began to view African immigrants as threats to their employment as the European economy began to falter in the late 1960s. Even in France, acceptance of blacks wore thin and racism became more common.

European definitions of race and ethnicity differ from those in the United States. In several European countries the word for "black" can refer to people without any African ancestry. Many white Europeans have grouped people of African descent in Europe with people of Middle Eastern, South Asian, and even East Asian descent and have labeled them all black. Some Europeans of non-European ancestry have taken advantage of this label and fought collectively for their civil rights in Europe. This has not been easy. Many white Europeans assume that blacks are not European; they view blacks, even those born and raised in Europe, as immigrants or foreigners. Thus, many residents of Great Britain, Germany, the Netherlands, France, and other European countries do not recognize dark-skinned fellow citizens as their equals.

These assumptions have made life in Europe difficult for its permanent black population, who consist mostly of the children and grandchildren of 1960s immigrants. Discrimination is rampant in housing, education, and employment. In some countries, such as Germany, citizenship depends on ancestry rather than place of birth. In these countries, some blacks, even though born and raised in Europe, are not even eligible for citizenship. In other countries, such as Spain and France, anyone born in the country enjoys automatic citizenship. Especially since the 1980s, European governments have been formulating policies on legal and illegal immigration, citizenship, voting, and election rights for these populations. The Dutch lead Europe in offering citizenship, voting, and election rights to their black populations, both immigrant and native-born. Within the European Union (EU), border controls between member states have loosened since 1990, but EU states have also taken measures to tighten Europe's external borders and restrict immigration from the rest of the world.

CONTEMPORARY AFRO-EUROPEANS

As European nations attempt to deal with the legacies of their involvement in the slave trade and colonialism, an Afro-European identity has begun to take shape in the 1990s. Organizations of blacks have proliferated, both to provide a forum for blacks and to advocate for their rights. Blacks are increasingly being elected to European government offices. In many European nations, black culture – in music, art, fashion, and entertainment – enjoys great popularity. Even though people of African descent make up less than 1 percent of most European countries' populations (perhaps 2 percent in Great Britain), this minority is growing and increasingly visible.

Leyla Keough

SEE ALSO

London's Black Poor and the Sierra Leone Settlement Plan; Russia and the Former Soviet Union; Capitein, Jacobus Elisa; Cardiff, Great Britain; Césaire, Aimé; Senghor, Léopold Sédar; Dumas, Alexandre, Père; National Socialist Sterilization Policies in Germany; Pushkin, Alexander; Sharp, Granville; World War I and African Americans; World War II and African Americans; Pan-African Congress of 1919; Bechet, Sidney Joseph; Du Bois, William Edward Burghardt (W. E. B.); West Indies.

North America

Evans, Mari E. (b. July 16, 1923, Toledo, Ohio), African American poet and teacher.

Mari Evans lost her mother at age seven and was raised by her father, an upholsterer, whom she credits with nurturing her love of writing. She attended the University of Toledo. LANGSTON HUGHES's works influenced her considerably from an early age, and Hughes himself later became a friend and mentor.

A "blues philosopher" who believes that a poet must be politically engaged, Evans became a respected figure in the BLACK ARTS MOVEMENT. Her work focuses on such wide-ranging themes as black enslavement and poverty in the United States, the oppression blacks share with other Third World peoples, and failed relationships between black men and women. In addition, it celebrates blackness, Africa, and the struggles of the CIVIL RIGHTS MOVEMENT. Her work has been published in more than 200 anthologies, and among her best-known works are *I Am a Black Woman* (1970) and an edition of collected essays, *Black Women Writers (1950-1980): A Critical Evaluation* (1984). She has also authored several works for children.

From 1968 to 1973 Evans created and hosted a weekly television program, *The Black Experience*, in Indianapolis. She also adapted Zora Neale Hurston's *Their Eyes Were Watching God* as a musical, *Eyes* (1979). Evans has held numerous teaching posts at universities, including Purdue, Northwestern, Cornell, and Indiana. Among many honors and awards, she received an honorary doctorate in 1979 from Marian College and won a National Endowment for the Arts Creative Writing Award in 1981. Evans is divorced and has two sons, and lives in Indianapolis.

See Also
Slavery in the United States.

North America

Evans, Minnie Jones

(b. December 12, 1892, Long Creek, N.C.; d. December 6, 1987, Wilmington, N.C.), African American artist whose mixed-media work is a response to divine visions.

Minnie Evans was raised by her mother, grandmother, and great grandmother in Wilmington, North Carolina. She left school after the fifth grade and began working. At age 16, in Wrightsville Beach, North Carolina, she married Julius Caesar Evans, with whom she had three sons. She was perpetually employed in low-income jobs. Her artistic career began on Good Friday in 1935, when she began drawing in response to visions, voices, and dreams she claimed to have had since childhood, whose message, she said, was "Draw or die!"

Working with simple materials – crayon, graphite, ink, and oils on paper or board – Evans created thousands of mixed media drawings and collages inspired by her visions, in which stylized flowers and foliage, exotic birds, strange creatures, angels, and royal or divine figures are major motifs. Self-taught (hence an "outsider" rather than "folk" artist) and a devout Christian who knew much of the Bible by heart, Evans said she did not consciously plan her compositions but listened to "the angel that stands by me and directs me what to do."

Beginning in 1962, photographer Nina Howell Starr was instrumental in getting Evans's work exhibited and discussed in print. In 1983 a short film was made of her life, *The Angel That Stands By Me*. Evans's work has been exhibited at dozens of galleries and museums, including a 1975 solo show at the Whitney Museum of Art in New York, where her art is in the permanent collection.

See Also
Art, African American.

North America

Evers, James Charles

(b. September 11, 1922, Decatur, Miss.), American civil rights leader and politician; first African American mayor of a biracial Mississippi town since Reconstruction.

James Charles Evers is the oldest of two sons of James and Jessie Evers, impoverished Mississippi farmers. After serving in the United States Army in World War II, Evers attended Alcorn A&M College (later Alcorn State University). In 1963 a white supremacist, Byron de la Beckwith, shot and killed Evers's brother Medgar Evers, who was the Mississippi field secretary of the National Association for the Advancement of Colored People (NAACP). Evers returned to Mississippi from Chicago, replaced his brother as field secretary, and continued his struggle for social justice for African Americans. In his tenure as NAACP field secretary, Evers led several successful boycotts and voter registration drives. He became a leading civil rights figure, not only in Mississippi, but throughout the United States.

In 1969 Evers was elected mayor of the town of Fayette, Mississippi, most of whose residents were African Americans. His victory was symbolic of the progress that African Americans had made in overcoming the segregation and disfranchisement imposed by white Southerners. Evers served as mayor of Fayette from 1973 to 1981, and from 1985 to 1987.

In 1971 Evers was unanimously nominated by the Democrats to run for governor of Mississippi. Though he lost the election, he was the first African American in Mississippi to run for its highest office. Because many younger African Americans in Mississippi see him as symbolic of a bygone era, Evers's popularity has declined. However, his importance in gaining equal rights for African Americans in Mississippi cannot be denied.

Robert Fay

See Also
World War II and African Americans; Chicago, Illinois; Civil Rights Movement; Evers, Medgar Wylie; Jim Crow.

North America

Evers, Medgar Wylie

(b. July 2, 1925, Decatur, Miss.; d. June 12, 1963, Jackson, Miss.), African American civil rights leader whose assassination for his work as field secretary for the National Association for the Advancement of Colored People (NAACP) in Mississippi galvanized the Civil Rights Movement.

As a representative of the NAACP, Medgar Evers worked for the most established and in some ways most conservative African American membership organization. He was, by all accounts, a hardworking, thoughtful, and somewhat quiet man. Yet the work he did was groundbreaking, even radical, in that he risked and eventually lost his life bringing news of his state's violent white supremacy to nationwide attention. When Evers was assassinated in his front yard by Byron de la Beckwith, a white racist, he became a symbol of the brutality with which the old South resisted the Civil Rights Movement.

Raised in a small central Mississippi town, Evers absorbed his parents' work ethic and strong religious values early. Friends, including his brother, Charles, remember him as a serious child with an air of maturity about him. At age 17 he left school to serve in the army during World War II, where, according to writer Adam Nossiter, his experience fighting the supremely racist Nazis made a lasting impression on him. After the war Evers got his high school diploma and immediately entered Alcorn A&M College, where he played football, ran track, edited the campus newspaper, and sang in the choir.

Upon graduation Evers took a job with Magnolia Mutual Insurance, one of Mississippi's few black-owned businesses. Through his employer, he became involved with the NAACP, selling memberships at the same time that he was selling insurance policies. Despite its moderate, systematic approach, the NAACP was still considered a radical organization by many in Mississippi; it was a state in which, as Nossiter writes, the organization had essentially given up hope. Too likely to be victims of harassment, assault, or murder for any kind of political action, blacks in Mississippi's Delta region were often afraid even to talk about the NAACP.

In 1954, when the national organization decided to hire field secretaries in the Deep South, Evers moved to Jackson, the state capital, and went to work full-time for the NAACP. He had two main roles – to recruit and enroll new members, and to investigate and publicize the racist terrorism experienced by African Americans. It was a dangerous job. Evers was followed, mocked, threatened, and beaten while he traveled throughout Mississippi – the state that had seen more lynchings than any other in the country. Organizations like the White Citizens' Councils and the State Sovereignty Committee spied on him. In May 1963, a month before Evers was murdered, someone threw a bomb into his garage.

Not only did Evers continue the NAACP's long-standing research on lynching, he also worked on the legal front, filing petitions and organizing protests against the Jim Crow segregation that still made it impossible for African Americans to go to movie theaters, eat in restaurants, or make use of public libraries, parks, and pools. Throughout the spring of 1963 he was the leader of a series of boycotts, meetings, and public appearances that were designed to bring Mississippi out of its racist past.

Just before midnight on June 11, 1963, when Evers was arriving home, Beckwith shot him in the back; Evers died a few minutes later. In two separate trials in 1963 and 1964, all-white juries could not decide Beckwith's fate. Free for more than 30 years after committing murder, Beckwith was finally convicted and jailed for the crime in 1994.

Kate Tuttle

See Also

World War II and African Americans; Military, Blacks in the American; Lynching.

North America

Evers-Williams, Myrlie

(b. 1933, Vicksburg, Miss.), African American civil rights activist, first woman chairperson of the National Association for the Advancement of Colored People (NAACP).

Myrlie Evers-Williams was raised by her grandmother, McCain Beasley, and her aunt, Myrlie Beasley Polk. She married civil rights activist Medgar Evers in 1951, and together they worked for the NAACP to end discrimination and segregation in Mississippi. Medgar Evers was assassinated in 1963 by the white supremacist Byron de la Beckwith.

After her husband's death, Evers-Williams moved her family to California, where she continued to work for the NAACP by speaking publicly about her struggles for black equality. In 1987 she became the first black woman to serve as commissioner on the Los Angeles Board of Public Works. She was elected vice-chairperson of the NAACP in 1994, and in 1995 became the first woman chairperson. In 1998 Julian Bond succeeded Evers-Williams as chair of the NAACP. With William Peters, she coauthored *For Us, the Living* (1967).

See Also

Civil Rights Movement; Evers, Medgar Wylie.

Africa

Evora, Cesaria

(b. 1941, Mindelo, Cape Verde), internationally renowned Cape Verdean singer.

One of seven children, Cesaria Evora was born into a musical family, including not only her violinist father, who died when she was a child, but also her uncle Francisco Xavier da Cruz, a songwriter whose songs she has recorded. Evora herself was singing in bars in Mindelo by age 16.

Evora sings in Criuolo, a Creole derived from Portuguese and African languages. She is most famous for singing *morna*, which roughly translates to "songs of mourning." As with many other kinds of folk music, morna songs are handed down from generation to generation, and trace dominant themes in a people's history. Many morna songs, for example, lament Cape Verdeans' losses to the slave trade and emigration. Often accompanied by acoustic guitars, violins, accordions, and *cavaquinho*, a four-string guitar or ukulele, Evora's vocals have been described as a cross between Edith Piaf and American jazz singer Billie Holiday.

Evora's career grew after she made a recording for national radio at age 20. She received offers from bars and nightclubs throughout the ten Cape Verdean Islands, and soon became known as the "queen of morna." Although several tapes of her music traveled to Portugal and the Netherlands, she never performed outside Cape Verde. Evora once recalled, "I used to sing for tourists and for the ships when they would come here. That's why I always thought that maybe if I made it, people from different countries would love my music." By the 1970s, however, she quit recording and performing, claiming that she was not "making any money."

Evora emerged from retirement in 1985 to contribute two songs to an album of Cape Verdean women's music. Soon after, the Cape Verdean concert promoter Jose da Silva convinced her to come to France to record. There she became known as the "barefoot diva," because she regularly performs shoeless. Whether Evora's habit is a symbol of her empathy for Cape Verde's poor women and children (as has been claimed) or simply a personal preference, the nickname became the title of her first album, *La Diva aux Pieds Nus* (1988). After *Distino di Belita* (1990) and *Mar Azul* (1991), Evora made her first international hit at age 51 with *Miss Perfumado* (1992), which sold 200,000 copies.

Evora undertook a tour of the United States in 1995 in support of that year's release, *Cesaria Evora*, which was a gold record in France and reached number seven on Portugal's charts. Her popular success has been reinforced by critical and peer recognition. In 1996 *Cesaria Evora* was nominated for a Grammy Award in the United States as best world music album. In addition, at the 1997 KORA All Africa Music Awards, Evora received the Judges Merit Award, Best Artist from West Africa Award, and Best African Album. A regular performer at world music festivals, Evora has opened for such pop acts as Natalie Merchant and counts pop star Madonna as a fan.

Even after reaching global stardom, Evora has chosen to remain in Cape Verde with her mother and her children and grandchildren (thrice divorced, she has vowed never to marry again). "I wasn't astonished by Europe," she has said, "and I was never that impressed by the speed and grandeur of modern America. I only regret my success has taken so long to achieve."

Kate Tuttle

See Also

Cape Verde; Transatlantic Slave Trade; World Music, World Beat, and the Re-Africanization of Latin American Popular Music.

Africa

Ewe,

ethnic group of coastal West Africa whose approximately 4 million members inhabit southeastern Ghana, southern Togo, and adjacent parts of Benin.

The broad Ewe grouping comprises a number of "clans" or ethnic subgroups, all speaking languages of the Niger-Congo family (*see* Languages, African: An Overview) but each with its own history and specific customs. These subgroups include the Anlo of Ghana, and in Togo the Ouatchi, Mina, Adja, and so-called Brazilians, a group with diverse origins (including freed slaves) who settled on the coast as traders during the early nineteenth century. The Ewe are the largest ethnic group in Togo, and economically they dominate the country. The Ewe are closely related to the Fon of Benin, but are distinguished by their historical resistance to states such as the Fon-dominated kingdom of Dahomey.

The early history of the Ewe is little known. According to oral tradition, they began a gradual westward migration from Oyo, in the Yoruba region of modern Nigeria, in the thirteenth century c.e. However, archaeological evidence suggests a longer continuous presence in the Ewe heartland of southern Togo. One theory suggests that this tradition may have arisen during the eighteenth century, when Oyo dominated Dahomey and neighboring parts of present-day Togo. Another theory proposes that Yoruba migrants may have at one point achieved cultural hegemony over the indigenous population of the Ewe region.

Oral tradition tells of the Ewe's flight from a brutal seventeenth-century tyrant, King Agokoli of Notsé. This experience may have shaped Ewe groups' long-standing opposition to strong leaders, and hindered state formation. Although the precolonial Anlo Ewe of present-day Ghana formed a regional confederacy of kinship groups, all acknowledging the primacy of a chief priest, most Ewe remained in small local polities. In these polities the power of hereditary chiefs was tempered by the authority of lineage patriarchs, and by local assemblies of male and female elders. Lacking a centralized state, the precolonial Ewe also lacked a strong sense of group identity. Instead, Ewe territory provided a place of refuge from the neighboring kingdoms of Dahomey and Asante. Ga- and Fanti-speaking peoples such as the Mina settled among the Ewe as refugees from Asante hegemony, and gradually adopted Ewe language and customs. On the other hand, the Ewe's lack of a strong state structure left them prone to frequent slave raiding from the seventeenth to the nineteenth century.

In addition to sharing a language and certain historical experiences, precolonial Ewe communities were knit together by trade, as market women exchanged fish and imported European goods for the agricultural produce of interior groups. However, European colonial powers partitioned Ewe territory by the end of the nineteenth century between the British in the Gold Coast (today Ghana), the Germans in Togoland, who occupied the Ewe heartland, and the French in Dahomey (today Benin). Paradoxically, the disruption of trade caused by this partition may have sparked the formation of a common Ewe identity.

When British and French mandates further divided the Ewe heartland of southern Togoland, it was primarily the resulting trade disruption that gave rise to the Ewe unification movement after World War I. The movement for the unification of Togoland and all Ewe territories (including those in the Gold Coast) gained momentum after World War II, but the rival colonial powers, fearing a loss of influence in the region, held plebiscites in which non-Ewe Togolese, fearing Ewe domination of a unified Togoland, overwhelmingly opposed unification and outvoted the Ewe minority.

Living near the coast, the Ewe have historically benefited more than their northern neighbors from trade and economic development, and enjoy relatively high rates of literacy. Since the colonial period, they have prospered as owners of COCOA plantations and have played a disproportionately large role in the commerce and civil service of both Togo and Ghana. Especially in Togo, their economic power has earned the resentment of northern ethnic groups such as the KABRÉ, whose connection to the military regime of Gen. Gnassingbé Eyadéma has excluded the Ewe from political power in Togo since the days of independence. Today the Ewe lead the opposition to his regime.

Mark O'Malley

SEE ALSO
Dahomey, Early Kingdom of; Colonial Rule; Eyadéma, Gnassingbé; Transatlantic Slave Trade; Scramble for Africa.

North America

Ewing, Patrick (b. August 5, 1962, Kingston, Jamaica), African American professional basketball player who became a center for the New York Knicks in 1985 and who was a member of the United States men's basketball team that won a Gold Medal at the 1992 Summer Olympic Games.

Patrick Ewing played cricket and soccer as a youngster in JAMAICA before moving in 1975 to Cambridge, Massachusetts, where he first played BASKETBALL. His first organized games took place at the Achievement School, a remedial center for junior high students where Ewing worked on his language skills. At Rindge and Latin High School, where Ewing reached his full height of seven feet, he starred as the basketball team's center, leading the team to three consecutive state championships. By his senior year Ewing's basketball record had rendered him the most sought-after college recruit in the country. He chose to attend Georgetown University in part because of the notable reputation of its basketball coach, John Thompson.

In his freshman year Ewing led Georgetown to the 1982 National Collegiate Athletic Association (NCAA) championship game. In the 1983-1984 season the team won the NCAA championship for the first time, and Ewing was named the tournament's Most Valuable Player. That summer he played on the U.S. Olympic basketball team, which won the Gold Medal. The following year, when Georgetown again reached the NCAA finals, the National Association of Basketball Coaches named Ewing the college player of the year.

In the NBA draft of college players in 1985, Ewing was the first player chosen. He signed a contract with the New York Knicks for $1.7 million, at the time the highest salary ever paid to an NBA rookie. Although injuries forced Ewing to miss 51 games in his first two years with the Knicks, he was named rookie of the year in 1986 and led all first-year players in scoring and rebounding. In 1988-1989 the Knicks won the NBA's Atlantic Division for the first time in 18 years. In 1991-1992 Ewing was named to the second team of the NBA's All-League and All-Defensive Teams. In 1992 Ewing earned a Gold Medal at the Summer Olympic Games as a member of the first U.S. Olympic basketball team to allow NBA players.

Africa

Excision. *See* FEMALE CIRCUMCISION IN AFRICA.

North America

Exodusters, African Americans who fled the post-Reconstruction South for the promise of freedom in Kansas.

Throughout the spring of 1879, the banks of the Mississippi River were crowded with hundreds of black families awaiting the steamships that would take them north to St. Louis, Missouri. Many had seen posters promising free transportation to the farmland of Kansas, where they could escape the South's poverty and terrorism. The Exodusters – so-called for their participation in the Kansas Fever Exodus of 1879 – were refugees resolved to make a better life for themselves.

The South the Exodusters left behind was increasingly treacherous. Following Emancipation in 1865, the RECONSTRUCTION period had increased African Americans' political and economic power. But white Southerners fought back with a campaign they called "redemption," attempting to overturn the pro-black liberal Republican legislation of the Reconstruction era. Racist groups such as the White League and the Ku Klux Klan mounted a campaign of murder and terrorism designed to destroy black political activism. Democrats stole elections through blatant ballot stuffing and by intimidating or assaulting blacks who attempted to vote. Former slaveowners – who still controlled the land, tools, livestock, cotton gins, and markets – kept nearly all black tenant farmers in an unending state of severe poverty.

Faced with these conditions, many African Americans considered migration out of the South. For years, a steady stream of blacks from the border states of Tennessee, Kentucky, and Missouri had formed their own colonies in Kansas, attracted by the state's abundant land, fertile soil, and abolitionist history. By the time the 1879 Louisiana Constitutional Convention declared that the issue of suffrage should be one of "states' rights" – effectively denying blacks the vote – thousands of African Americans had had enough. Fearful of a return to slavery, some 6000 people gathered their belongings and fled in a matter of weeks.

At St. Louis, it became clear that the rumors of free passage to Kansas were false. The Exodusters were stranded. Though ridiculed for their credulity, the Exodusters resisted returning to the South. "I'd sooner starve here," one woman told a reporter. As historian Nell Painter points out, it was "terrorism and poverty," not swindlers and pipe dreams, that drove the Kansas Fever Exodus. Many Exodusters saw themselves as modern versions of the Israelites, leaving persecution behind as they headed for a promised land. Some called Kansas "the Negro Canaan."

They were aided in their migration by a group of clergymen from the black churches of St. Louis, along with various Eastern philanthropists, who had formed an organization called the Colored Relief Board soon after the refugees began arriving. With the Kansas Freedmen's Aid Society, the board helped more than 5000 Exodusters reach Kansas from St. Louis. Around 4000 arrived later from Texas. Altogether, nearly 15,000 African Americans came to Kansas throughout 1879 and 1880. Although most remained impoverished, they fared better economically than they would have in the South. About three-quarters of the families came to own their own homes. "All in all," Painter writes, "the Exodus to Kansas was a qualified but real success."

Kate Tuttle

SEE ALSO
Slavery in the United States; Abolitionism in the United States; Thirteenth Amendment of the United States Constitution and the Emancipation Proclamation.

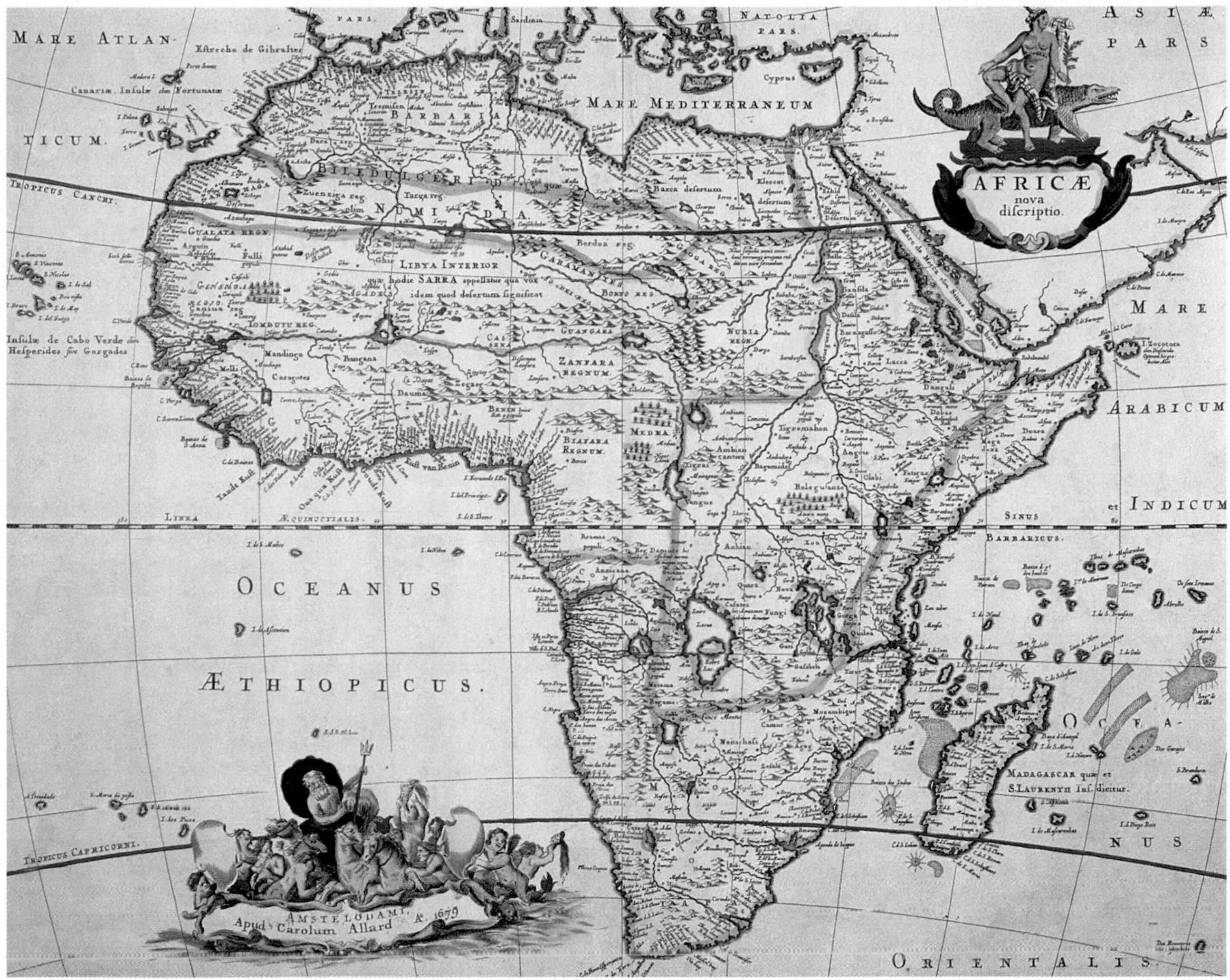

This European map of Africa was made in 1679. *CORBIS/Anthony Bannister; ABPL*

Africa

Explorers in Africa Before 1500, foreigners who traveled to sub-Saharan Africa before 1500 to investigate its geography and peoples.

Outsiders have remained in contact with the peoples of Africa since the first modern humans began trickling out of the continent. Desert nomads have crossed the Sahara and coastal traders have crossed the narrow Strait of Mandeb for thousands of years. From the beginnings of history, the Mediterranean Sea facilitated continuous contact between North Africa and the peoples of Europe and the Middle East. Certainly trade connections existed between Egypt and the peoples of sub-Saharan Africa by the second millennium B.C.E., and Carthaginians and Asian peoples may have been trading along the coasts of Africa more than 2000 years ago. However, none of these ancient traders or explorers left written accounts that survive today, so we know little about them and nothing of what they saw during their travels.

Our earliest surviving accounts of sub-Saharan Africa come from ancient Greek authors. Herodotus of Halicarnassus wrote extensively about Africa. It was during his travels to Egypt and LIBYA in the middle of the fifth century B.C.E. that Herodotus learned about Africa. He was highly knowledgeable about the Nile as far south as Gondokoro. Some of his work was based on the travels of the Egyptian pharaoh Necho II, who ruled from about 610 to 594 B.C.E.

Early European knowledge of East Africa came from two sources: the *Periplus of the Erythraean Sea*, written during the first century C.E. by an anonymous Greek trader who lived in Egypt, and Ptolemy's *Geography*, probably written in the second century C.E.

Between 1000 and 1500 C.E., Berber Ibadi traders of North Africa traveled south across the Sahara. Other Arabs and North Africans traveled south of the Sahara on a religious mission to convert sub-Saharan Africans to Islam. Traders from the Arabian Peninsula also made regular journeys to coastal East Africa. Many of these traders settled in coastal communities, where they contributed to the emerging Swahili culture.

In the fourteenth century, IBN BATTUTAH, a North African who explored out of curiosity, traveled extensively throughout North Africa, EGYPT, and East Africa, and crossed the Sahara to the West African kingdom of Mali, including the city of Tombouctou (Timbuktu). Descriptions of his journeys were published in the *Rihlah* (Travels), which greatly expanded knowledge of African geography in the Muslim and Western worlds.

Chinese explorers also traveled to Africa at an early date. Chinese writings include information on East Africa, mainly gathered from Muslim traders, as early as the eighth century C.E. Chinese rulers began sending trading expeditions across the Indian Ocean during the fifteenth century, and two of these expeditions reached the Horn of Africa, one in 1417-1419, the other in 1421-1422. Fei Hsin, an officer who participated in these voyages, wrote an account of his observations that survives today. By the middle of the fifteenth century, Chinese knowledge of Africa exceeded that of Europeans.

Beginning in the fifteenth century, PORTUGAL became the first European nation to undertake an extensive investigation of Africa. Prince Henry (later known as Prince Henry the Navigator) spearheaded the explorations. Shortly after 1419, Henry established a research institute to gather information about

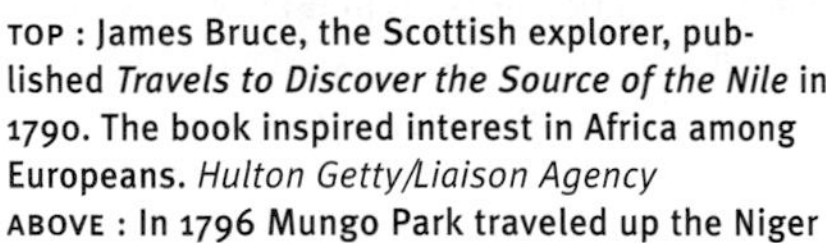

MUNGO PARK.

TOP : James Bruce, the Scottish explorer, published *Travels to Discover the Source of the Nile* in 1790. The book inspired interest in Africa among Europeans. *Hulton Getty/Liaison Agency*
ABOVE : In 1796 Mungo Park traveled up the Niger River and arrived at Ségou in present-day Mali. *Archive Photos*
ABOVE RIGHT: Scottish explorer and medical missionary David Livingstone reads the Bible to some of his African workers in an engraving dating from 1875. *CORBIS/Bettmann*
RIGHT: In an undated engraving, titled *Scene on the River Nile at Philae, Above Syene,* Dutch explorer Alexandrine Pieternella François Tinné and her party explore the Nile in 1862. *Archive Photos*

Africa. Besides his desire for increased trade and for exploration, he was motivated by a dream of forming a Christian union with the legendary Prester John of Africa. In addition, he intended to divert the Muslim-dominated overland GOLD TRADE by sending Portuguese ships to the west coast of Africa. By the 1480s Africa's west coast was well known to the Portuguese.

The Portuguese also sought a greater share of the spice trade, which reached Europe via the Indian Ocean and the Mediterranean Sea. Pedro da Covilhã explored the east coast of Africa during the late 1480s. The knowledge he gathered may have aided the voyage of VASCO DA GAMA, who in 1497-1498 became the first known European to sail around the Cape of Good Hope to the Indian Ocean. Though Portuguese government officials remained predominantly on the coast, Portuguese clergy, especially the Jesuits, traveled inland to seek converts to Catholicism. Portuguese missionaries reached as far as ANGOLA, the kingdom of Monomotapa (also known as Munhumutapa) in present-day ZIMBABWE, and ETHIOPIA.

These Portuguese explorers connected the African coast with Europe and the rest of the world. Their explorations changed the course of African history and paved the way for later explorers. They also paved the way for the continent's exploitation and the beginnings of the brutal slave trade.

Robert Fay

SEE ALSO

Explorers in Africa, 1500 to 1800; Egypt, Ancient Kingdom of; Nile River; Transatlantic Slave Trade; Sahara Desert; Swahili People; Swahili People; Tombouctou, Mali; Mali Empire.

Africa

Explorers in Africa, 1500 to 1800, foreigners who traveled to sub-Saharan Africa between 1500 and 1800 to investigate its geography and peoples.

Earlier explorers had essentially finished mapping the African coast by 1514. The interior posed a far more formidable obstacle, however. During the period between 1500 and 1800, Europeans accumulated knowledge intermittently and established few outposts beyond coastal areas.

One of the first Europeans to explore inland Africa was LEO AFRICANUS, who was born in Granada, SPAIN, and lived there until 1492, when Spain expelled all Muslims. He then traveled with his parents to MOROCCO. In about 1507 he began traveling around North and Central Africa, where he served as a diplomat. He visited Tombouctou (Timbuktu) twice. After his second visit there, he traveled to EGYPT via the Bornu Kingdom and LAKE CHAD. He also visited present-day SUDAN twice between 1509 and 1513, and his observations provided the basis for European knowledge of the region until well into the nineteenth century. After his African travels, Leo Africanus settled for a time in Rome, Italy, where he published *Navigationi et viaggi* (1550), subsequently translated into English as *A Geographic Historie of Africa* (1600).

The Portuguese exploration of Africa, which began in the fifteenth century, continued in the sixteenth. But their inland explorations remained modest in comparison to their earlier coastal discoveries. The Portuguese Antonio Fernandes explored present-day southern ZIMBABWE, where he visited the gold mines of Monomatapa (or Munhumutapa) between 1511 and 1514. In 1616 Gaspar Bocarro traveled as far as Tete on the ZAMBEZI RIVER. During the late eighteenth century, the Portuguese established bases on the Zambezi, first at Sena, then at Tete, hoping to control trade from these locations. In 1793 Alexandre da Silva Teixeira reached the Luvale people of present-day ZAMBIA. In 1798 Francisco José de Lacerda journeyed from Tete to the court of the Kazembe on Lake Mweru on the southeastern border of present-day Congo-Kinshasa.

The Portuguese also gained considerable knowledge about ETHIOPIA, a Christian empire that they initially believed to be the legacy of the legendary Prester John. Francisco Alvarez, a member of a Portuguese embassy to the court of Ethiopian emperor LEBNA DENGEL, provided descriptions of Ethiopia that greatly increased European knowledge of that country, as did Jesuits such as Pedro Páez (who also discovered the source of the Blue Nile) and António Fernandes. In addition, the Frenchman Charles Poncet visited the Ethiopian court at Gonder in about 1699.

The travels and discoveries of the Portuguese generated interest in other European nations, which began to send their own expeditions to Africa. Portuguese power gradually declined during the sixteenth and seventeenth centuries, and after 1600, British, Dutch, and French traders began to seize control of Portuguese trading coasts, particularly in West Africa. In 1652 the Dutch established the first permanent European post at the Cape of Good Hope in present-day SOUTH AFRICA. By the early 1700s Dutch colonists had begun to explore the region's interior. In West Africa, British traders had traveled as far as the Barracuda Falls by 1651, and by 1659 Cornelius Hoges had reached Bambuk in present-day eastern SENEGAL. During the seventeenth century, the French sailed up the SENEGAL RIVER as far as Malam. In 1700 the French established a fort in the region.

The British adventurer James Bruce published *Travels to Discover the Source of the Nile* (1790), which added insight to European knowledge of Africa and also sparked interest in Africa among Europeans, especially in London and Paris. This popularity led to the establishment in London in 1788 of the Association for Promoting the Discovery of the Interior Parts of Africa, also called the African Association. It was this organization that supported James Watt and Matthew Winterbottom in their travels to FOUTA DJALLON and the Rio Nunez in present-day GUINEA. In 1796 Mungo Park traveled up the NIGER RIVER and arrived at Ségou in present-day MALI.

In the final 25 years of the eighteenth century, travel books dealing with Africa attracted an enthusiastic audience. The nature of exploration would change, however, in the nineteenth century. Although many nineteenth-century explorers came as Christian missionaries, the information they gained on their travels contributed to the colonization of Africa.

Robert Fay

SEE ALSO

Congo, Democratic Republic of the; Explorers in Africa Before 1500; Explorers in Africa Since 1800; Kanuri; Tombouctou, Mali.

Africa

Explorers in Africa Since 1800, foreigners who traveled to sub-Saharan Africa after 1800 to investigate its geography and peoples.

Building on the work of earlier explorers, European explorers of Africa after 1800 provided information used by European powers to carry out their colonization of the continent. By crisscrossing the vast continent's interior, nineteenth-century explorers, many of them Christian missionaries, contributed far more to Western knowledge of Africa and its peoples than earlier explorers had. These Europeans discovered that beyond the African coast lay a continent much more hospitable than their legends and myths of the "dark continent" had suggested.

European exploration of Africa during the nineteenth century had three main goals: (1) the elimination of the slave trade, (2) the imposition of "legitimate" commerce, and (3) the spread of Christianity among Africans. This new phase of exploration began at the end of the eighteenth century. The Association for Promoting the Discovery of the Interior Parts of Africa – founded in 1788 by a small group of wealthy Englishmen and popularly called the African Association – first supported the exploration of North and West Africa. The association funded the efforts by Scotsman Mungo Park to travel to the upper NIGER RIVER during the 1790s. Park discovered that the river flowed eastward, not westward as LEO AFRICANUS had incorrectly asserted.

Some of the African Association's members convinced the British government that the exploration of Africa was an endeavor worthy of government support, and it was in the employ of the British that Park undertook another – but fatal – expedition in 1805 to chart the course of the Niger. The British government also funded famed explorers Maj. Dixon Denham and his two fellow travelers, Lieut. Hugh Clapperton and surgeon Walter Oudney, who crossed the Sahara after visiting Bornu and Hausaland from 1823 to 1825. The brothers John and Richard Lander, who charted the course of the lower Niger in 1830, were funded by the British, as was the German HEINRICH BARTH, who charted the central and western Sudan from 1850 to 1855.

The quintessential Christian missionary explorer was perhaps DAVID LIVINGSTONE, who in 1841 traveled to South Africa as a member of the London Missionary Society. In 1853 Livingstone traveled from the south to VICTORIA FALLS and from there west to Luanda. He then turned to the east and found the mouth of the ZAMBEZI RIVER. Livingstone's subsequent book, *Missionary Travels and Researches,* went through nine editions in England and transformed public opinion of the continent.

Britain's Royal Geographical Society formed in 1830 and took the place of the African

French explorer Pierre Savorgnan de Brazza founded the colony of Moyen-Congo, present-day Republic of Congo, in 1880. *CORBIS/Leonard de Selva*

Association. Unlike its predecessor, it received government funding. Its officers had access to high-placed government officials, and in 1858, it arranged for Livingstone to undertake an expedition up the Zambezi as British consul in charge. After his expedition stalled at the Quebrabasa Falls, Livingstone traveled up the Shire River, attempting to reach the African interior, again without success. He may have taken consolation in the discovery of LAKE MALAWI. Livingstone continued his exploration at his own expense (his travel books had made him a fortune), and he spent his final years, from 1867 to 1873, in the upper reaches of the Congo.

Early in the nineteenth century, France – which had been active in the slave trade and had sent explorers up the Senegal in the eighteenth century – contributed little to the exploration of Africa. The only journey of note was undertaken by René Caillié, who went from Rio Nunez to Tombouctou (Timbuktu) and across the Sahara to Tangier. In contrast to the French, Germans and German speakers contributed much to European knowledge of Africa, many working with British support.

German missionaries combed East Africa in their search for converts. Missionaries Johannes Rebmann, Johann Ludwig Krapf, and J. J. Erhardt were the first Europeans to see Mount Kilimanjaro and MOUNT KENYA. Gerhard Rohlfs traveled extensively in the Sahara. Gustav Nachtigal built on the work of Rohlfs. Between 1870 and 1874, Nachtigal explored present-day SUDAN and CHAD. During the SCRAMBLE FOR AFRICA, Nachtigal played a key role in establishing German colonies. Through threats and manipulation, he secured treaties in 1884 with Mlapa III, the chief of Togoville, TOGO, and with the DUALA people of CAMEROON, that provided the basis for German colonial claims to those regions. Later that year, Nachtigal signed a treaty establishing an additional colony in what is currently NAMIBIA.

As European colonial powers completed their conquest of most of the continent during the 1890s and the early twentieth century, their scouts and agents surveyed the territory to be subdued. Mary Kingsley, one the few European women to explore the continent, toured the interior of present-day Gabon during the 1890s. By about 1914 virtually the entire continent had been surveyed by the representatives of European governments.

It is also important to remember that most, if not all, European explorers relied on Africans as soldiers, guides, translators, porters, cooks, and personal servants. Given the possible hazards in Africa – such as hostile animals, Africans seeking to defend themselves against intruders, rough terrain, and disabling diseases – the success of a European explorer's journey depended on the ability and skill of his African employees. Although they faced the same difficulties as their famous employers, their names, sadly, are largely lost to us today.

Robert Fay

SEE ALSO

Hausa; Congo River; Explorers in Africa, 1500 to 1800; Kilimanjaro; Luanda, Angola; Transatlantic Slave Trade; Sahara Desert; Tombouctou, Mali; Caillié, René-Auguste.

Latin America and the Caribbean

Exú (known as Exú in BRAZIL, and as Elegbara or Eleggúa in CUBA and the United States), one of the major ORISHAS, or Yoruba deities.

Exú, or Eleggúa, is regarded differently in the Cuban tradition than he is in Brazil. The trickster deity of the crossroads, in Cuba, Eleggúa is regarded as temperamental, but helpfully benign if properly propitiated with candies, toys, and children's parties. In Brazil, Exú is regarded as extremely dangerous, and special propitiatory ceremonies are held several hours before major rituals to send him away so that he will not disrupt the ritual (*see* RELIGIONS, AFRICAN, IN BRAZIL; RELIGIONS, AFRICAN, IN LATIN AMERICA AND THE CARIBBEAN; SANTERÍA; and CANDOMBLÉ).

Eyadema, Etienne. Please see EYADÉMA, GNASSINGBÉ

Africa

Eyadéma, Gnassingbé (b. 1936, in Pya, Togo), president of TOGO (1967-).

In power for 32 years, General Eyadéma has outlasted all other African leaders. He owes his longevity both to a system of patronage that earned the support of important segments of Togolese society and to personal control over the country's military, which has consistently and often violently repressed political opposition.

According to official sources, Eyadéma was born on December 27, 1936, as Étienne Gnassingbé, to KABRÉ peasants. He completed six years of school before enlisting in the French army in 1953, like other poor young Kabré. He served in Dahomey, Indochina, ALGERIA, and NIGER. Upon his discharge in 1962 he returned to Togo, as did over 600 other mostly Kabré French veterans.

When Togo's then president, Sylvanus Olympio, refused to enlarge Togo's 150-man army to accommodate these veterans, a number of them, including Gnassingbé, staged West Africa's first military coup in January 1963, during which Olympio was killed. After the killing, Gnassingbé took Eyadéma, a Kabré word implying courage, as his surname. He claims that Olympio was firing a gun while seeking refuge at the gates of the U.S. embassy, but other accounts suggest that Eyadéma murdered a defenseless Olympio.

Under Nicolas Grunitzky, chosen by the coup's instigators as Olympio's successor, Eyadéma assumed leadership of an expanded military. When Olympio's political heirs threatened to unseat Grunitzky and bring Olympio's murderers to justice, a military junta seized power in early 1967. Later that year, Eyadéma dismissed the junta, named himself president, and had himself promoted to the rank of general.

Togo was just beginning large-scale phosphate exports when Eyadéma assumed power. Phosphate revenues funded a program of political patronage, infrastructural development, and free trade that earned Eyadéma support throughout Togo, and particularly among Lomé's powerful market women. Following the example of his idol, Zaire's president MOBUTU SESE SEKO, Eyadéma instutionalized his rule by establishing Togo as a one-party state. He built a personality cult around himself and had larger-than-life images of himself installed throughout the country. According to an official legend of invincibility, his survival of a mysterious plane crash and coup attempts imply divine intervention on his behalf.

However, the patronage gradually degenerated into fiscal irresponsibility and debilitating cronyism. When phosphate revenues declined in the late 1970s, a severe debt crisis brought on by an economically unviable industrialization program forced Eyadéma to cut spending and implement austerity measures mandated by the International Monetary Fund. An increasingly paranoid Eyadéma withdrew into a circle of sycophants and undermined or eliminated potential rivals. The military, overwhelmingly Kabré and led by recruits Eyadéma handpicked from his home village of Pya, has perpetuated Eyadéma's grip on power, subjecting his political opponents to repeated imprisonment, torture, and murder.

During the 1990s internal and international pressures have forced Eyadéma to allow a more open political process. However, he has retained a firm grip on power, and harassment of opposition leaders by the military on the eve of the 1998 election suggested that at age 62, Eyadéma intends to remain in power for many more years.

Mark O'Malley

SEE ALSO

Dahomey, Early Kingdom of; Lomé, Togo.

North America

Eyes on the Prize, award-winning PBS television series documenting the CIVIL RIGHTS MOVEMENT from 1954 to 1965.

Following its release in 1987, *Eyes on the Prize* became the most celebrated documentary series in the history of public television. Many reviewers hailed the documentary as the finest depiction to date of the civil rights era. Carolyn Fluehr-Lobban of *American Anthropologist* wrote that what distinguishes the series from its predecessors "is not only its comprehensive grasp of the civil rights period, but its fair and equal representation of all of the signal events and the heroes and heroines of the Civil Rights Movement." The series won more than 20 awards, including the Peabody Award and the DuPont-Columbia Award, and has become a standard reference source in American libraries and schools.

Produced by African American Henry Hampton of Blackside, Inc., *Eyes on the Prize* comprises six one-hour television programs. It covers the 11 years between the landmark 1954 Supreme Court ruling to desegregate schools and, in 1965, the march from Selma to Montgomery and passage of the Voting Rights Act. Narrated by civil rights activist JULIAN BOND, the series combines archival films, newsreels, photographs, and interviews with those involved in the events. To accompany the series, Viking/Penguin published two guides for instructional use: *Eyes on the Prize: America's Civil Rights Years* by Juan Williams and *A Reader and Guide: Eyes on the Prize* edited by Clayborne Carson.

In 1990 Hampton produced *Eyes on the Prize II*, which chronicles the continuing civil rights struggles of African Americans from 1965 to 1985.

Roanne Edwards

See Also
Brown v. Board of Education; Television and African Americans; Voting Rights Act of 1965.

Latin America and the Caribbean

Ezeiza, Gabino (b. February 3, 1858, Buenos Aires, Argentina; d. October 12, 1916, Buenos Aires, Argentina), Afro-Argentine poet, editor, journalist, and one of the most famous of the *payador* (dueling singers) of his time.

The son of an ex-slave, Gabino Ezeiza first picked up a guitar at age 15. Drawing from a rich oral tradition of earlier payadores, he gradually attracted an impressive following by taking his improvisational virtuosity on the road. The *payada*, a duel-like exchange in which singer-guitarists spontaneously compose formulaic refrains, is derived from both Spanish versification and African traditions of musical contests. In Argentina, it is considered "popular literature," inextricably tied to the most symbolic of national figures: the *gaucho* of the *pampas* (roughly equivalent to cowboys on the range). While still a teenager, Ezeiza began writing for *La Juventud*, a Buenos Aires newspaper for and by members of the black community. From 1876 to 1878, while still building a reputation as a payador, publishing poetry, and writing news, he became the editor of *La Juventud*.

Before the twentieth century and the disappearance of the Afro-Argentine (*see* Argentina) community, payadores, whether gauchos or not, were typically rural blacks who traveled the countryside performing at private ranches and *pulperías* (local bars). Ezeiza brought payadas into the spotlight, moving them from backwater milieus to circuses and theaters in the heart of Buenos Aires. He produced nearly 500 compositions, including *Salve* (Hail), *Libertador* (Liberator), *Heroica* (Heroic), *Paysandú*, and *El remate* (The Conclusion), many of which were known throughout the country. During his years as a payador he engaged the best of his opponents, including Higinio D. Cazón (1830-1914) and Luis García (1875-1961). One payada, with rival Pablo Vásquez, took place in Teatro Florida in 1891 and lasted for three nights straight.

In 1892 Ezeiza won a sizable amount in the lottery and purchased a circus called Pabellón Argentina. He continued performing, attracting fans of some notoriety, including president-to-be Hipolito Yrigoyen, whose middle-class party, the Radical Civic Union, Ezeiza actively supported. Though his lyrical themes shied away from politics or overt black consciousness, he deftly managed to one-up frustrated opponents who made race-based attacks.

Joy Elizondo

f

North America

Fair Employment Practices Committee (1941-1946), a short-lived United States federal agency charged with investigating and correcting discrimination in the defense and other industries, established in response to A. Philip Randolph's March on Washington Movement.

Since the United States entered World War I in 1917, African Americans had protested both the segregation of the U.S. military and the rampant job discrimination in the war-powered defense industries. A number of black leaders, among them A. Philip Randolph – president of the BROTHERHOOD OF SLEEPING CAR PORTERS (BSCP), the first African American labor union – saw such inequities as symptomatic of the dismal economic situation most African Americans faced. Black workers, often the last hired and first fired, had been disproportionately affected by the GREAT DEPRESSION of the 1930s, and for most work remained an important issue. As the country prepared to enter World War II, Randolph spearheaded a movement that sought economic justice for African Americans.

Along with Walter White, secretary of the NATIONAL ASSOCIATION FOR THE ADVANCEMENT OF COLORED PEOPLE (NAACP), and T. Arnold Hill, of the NATIONAL URBAN LEAGUE, Randolph asked President Franklin D. Roosevelt to end segregation in the armed forces and open wartime jobs to black workers. After a disappointing first meeting with Roosevelt in September 1940, Randolph began to plan what became known as the March on Washington Movement, issuing a call for a "March on Washington for jobs in national defense and equal integration in the fighting forces of the United States." Randolph wrote that the demonstration would "shake up official Washington," "gain respect for the Negro people," and build "self-respect among Negroes." With the help of BSCP members – who numbered around 10,000 – Randolph sought to mobilize at least that many to march on July 1, 1941.

To avoid the embarrassing attention such a large demonstration would attract, Roosevelt met again with Randolph and White on June 18. This time, with the threat of the march – its size now predicted at 100,000 by White – hanging over him, the president capitulated. On June 25 Roosevelt issued Executive Order 8802, which outlawed discrimination in "the employment of workers in defense industries or government" and provided for the creation of a Fair Employment Practices Committee (the FEPC, originally called the President's Committee on Fair Employment Practices). It did not, however, affect the position of blacks in the military, which was not desegregated until 1948.

The FEPC was responsible for enforcing the antidiscrimination law, and in so doing conducted investigations, gathered evidence, and reported abuses. It is not clear, however, exactly how effective the FEPC proved in curtailing government job discrimination, although the number of African Americans working for the federal government grew rapidly in the 1940s. Originally composed of two black and two white members, as the FEPC grew larger only white members were added. Milton Webster, vice president of the BSCP, and NAACP activists Clarence M. Mitchell Jr. and Charles H. Houston were among the African Americans who filled the perpetual two black slots on the FEPC.

The FEPC lost power throughout its brief existence, twice facing reorganization, and was disbanded in 1946. Despite its failure to become permanent – bills to establish a permanent FEPC failed to pass the U.S. Senate in 1946, 1950, and 1952 – the FEPC inspired a host of state agencies. The March on Washington Movement that was directly responsible for its creation continued, and found new expression in the CIVIL RIGHTS MOVEMENT of the 1960s, mostly notably in the landmark MARCH ON WASHINGTON of 1963.

Kate Tuttle

SEE ALSO

World War I and African Americans; World War II and African Americans; Military, Blacks in the American; Houston, Charles Hamilton; Labor Unions in the United States; Mitchell, Clarence Maurice, Jr.; Randolph, Asa Philip; White, Walter Francis; March on Washington, 1941.

Africa

Fang, an ethnic group of CAMEROON, GABON, and EQUATORIAL GUINEA.

The Fang, a Bantu-speaking people, occupy southern Cameroon, much of mainland Equatorial Guinea, and northern Gabon. They are a dominant group in the region, despite the fact that they are relatively recent migrants. The Fang are also referred to as the Pahouin or Fan. They can be divided into three linguistic groups: the Fang proper, the BULU, and the BETI. Each of these groups can be further divided into several ethnic subgroups.

Although scholars originally believed that the Fang came from the upper NILE RIVER, most now agree that they split from other Bantu-speaking groups and migrated to northern Cameroon around the seventh or eighth century. From there they migrated farther southwest to the coastal regions in the nineteenth century. Though the evidence of the exact causes is contested, pressures from other groups, such as the HAUSA, and attempts to flee the trans-Saharan slave trade played a part as did trade and the belief that the Europeans were rich spirits from the sea. Successful hunters and renowned warriors, the patrilineal Fang pushed such groups as the NDOWE farther to the coast and settled in the interior forests as farmers. The large patriarchal clans of polygamous families in the south had little centralized political authority, whereas their counterparts in the north had clan chiefs and were more centralized.

The transatlantic and trans-Saharan slave trades from the sixteenth to the nineteenth century took thousands of Fang from the region as others, such as the Ndowe, acted as middlemen. To secure control over trade in the interior, the Ndowe spread the rumor that the Fang were cannibals, something European missionaries were convinced of when they found skulls in Fang households. In fact, the Fang did not practice cannibalism, but ate parts of deceased persons in order to gain the deceased person's qualities. Spiritual beliefs, including ancestor worship, also influenced the methods and styles of Fang iron working and wood carving. These trades and crafts were largely destroyed by European influence.

Under Spanish and French COLONIAL RULE, some Fang participated in the IVORY TRADE, while others worked as laborers on COCOA plantations. Many Fang adopted Christianity, although syncretistic and more "traditional" religious sects such as the BWITI became popular. In French-ruled Cameroon and Gabon, the Fang often cooperated with the administration, came to dominate the military and civil service, and consequently received economic and educational benefits. In Spanish Guinea, colonial officials favored the BUBI and perpetuated the myth of Fang primitivism. However, many Fang joined the military, which they later used as a power base to control independent Equatorial Guinea. Some Fang resisted outright European intrusion and in 1926 formed the Elar-ayong Movement in Cameroon to create unity within the Fang nation. Most Fang elite were conservative nationalists, preferring a slow transfer of power. Fang politicians have dominated the governments of several countries since independence: Gabon, Equatorial Guinea, and, to a somewhat lesser degree, the more ethnically heterogeneous Cameroon.

Eric Young

SEE ALSO

Bantu: Dispersion and Settlement; Languages, African: An Overview; Iron in Africa; Transatlantic Slave Trade; Trans-Saharan and Red Sea Slave Trade.

Latin America and the Caribbean

Fania Records, the most important SALSA MUSIC record company.

Founded in 1964 by the Dominican band leader JOHNNY PACHECO and the Italian-American lawyer Jerry Massuci, Fania is responsible for spreading the term *salsa*, a label used to name the Afro-Cuban and Afro-Caribbean music that was produced in New York City. This company was responsible for a deep change in the Afro-Cuban music played in New York City in the 1950s and 1960s. Its main contribution was to match small groups and new interpreters with recognized musicians and band leaders, facilitating the introduction of a new New York-based sound into Afro-Cuban music. This musical style combined strong Afro-Cuban roots with other Afro-Caribbean rhythms, such as CALYPSO, CUMBIA, bomba, and plena, and with sounds and styles from African American musical forms, such as soul and rock 'n' roll. This gave the Afro-Caribbean rhythms the taste of New York City's life.

Fania popularized New York Latin music among the Latin communities in the United States and among Spanish-Caribbean countries with the recordings of its band, the Fania All Stars. Especially significant were the records *Fania All Stars Live at Cheeta* and *Fania All Stars Live at Yankee Stadium*, and the promotional movies *Our Latin Thing* and *Salsa*. Among the most important bands and musicians that recorded for Fania in the late 1960s and early 1970s were Pacheco, Ray Barretto, Larry Harlow, WILLIE COLÓN, Bobby Valentín, and Roberto Roena and his Apollo Sound. Later, Fania included other salsa big names like CELIA CRUZ, Eddie Palmieri, Ismael Rivera, and Rubén Blades. But because of the emphasis on commercial success, Fania, which started as the company that allowed the free combination of rhythms and musical sounds that developed into salsa, became part of the mainstream industry. It thus controlled this musical production, reducing experimentation and promoting a more homogeneous sound that facilitates its consumption.

Juan Otero-Garabis

SEE ALSO

Soul Music; New York, New York; Plena and Bomba.

Latin America and the Caribbean

Fanon, Frantz (b. July 20, 1925, Fort-de-France, Martinique; d. December 6, 1961, Washington, D.C.), political philosopher, essayist, psychologist, and revolutionary who, in his short but full life, developed and acted upon theories for the decolonization of Africa.

Born into a conventional, bourgeois family, Frantz Fanon grew up with assimilationist values that encouraged him to reject his African heritage. This influence was countered by one of Fanon's high school teachers, AIMÉ CÉSAIRE, who introduced Fanon to the philosophy of NÉGRITUDE and taught him to embrace the aspects of self that the colonizer had previously forced him to reject. The encounter with Césaire proved to be a turning point in Fanon's intellectual development.

In 1940, following France's capitulation to the Germans in World War II, the part of the French Navy that had declared its allegiance to the collaborationist Vichy regime began the occupation of MARTINIQUE. As a result, 5000 French soldiers commandeered the resources of the island, leaving the resident population to fend for itself. It was in this context that Fanon first experienced the full force of white racism. He experienced similar racial alienation after joining De Gaulle's Free French forces in 1943 and serving with them in ALGERIA. The experiences of the war left Fanon deeply cynical about France's commitment to humanist ideals when it came to its black population.

Upon his return to Martinique, Fanon became involved in politics, helping Césaire win a seat in the French parliament. In 1947, after the death of his father, he went to France to pursue an advanced degree, enrolling in medical school at Lyon University in 1948. While obtaining his degree (he specialized in psychiatry), Fanon continued to read the thinkers to whom Césaire had introduced him: Hegel, Marx, Lenin and, in particular, Sartre. He also formed a student journal, *Tam-Tam*, that attracted the attention of the editors of *Présence Africaine*. It was through his connection to this journal that he was able to meet Sartre, who remained Fanon's friend for life. It was also during this time that he began writing *Peau noire, masques blancs* (1952; translated as *Black Skin, White Masks*, 1967), a work that took its inspiration from Césaire's protest poetry but brought a psychiatrist's eye to the question of the intellectual and cultural alienation of blacks in a world dominated by whites and white values.

Peau noire, masques blancs describes the untenable position of the black bourgeoisie in Martinique who, disdainful of their own race, realize with regret that they cannot become white. Still, Fanon separates himself in this work from the philosophy of Négritude by rejecting the idea of an immutable black essence and by seeking a solution to the problems he describes in a nonracist humanism. In the same year as the publication of this book, Fanon married a white French woman, Josie Dublé. Fanon has been criticized for marrying a white woman by those who see that act as a betrayal of his own ideals. But as Emmanuel Hansen points out, Fanon's "writings about the Manichaean world are descriptive and not proscriptive. It is precisely this idea of the black man being sealed in his blackness and the white man being encased in his whiteness that he wanted to avoid."

In 1953 Fanon began the African chapter of his life. He assumed the post of chief of staff at the psychiatric hospital in Blida, ALGERIA, where he treated French soldiers who were suffering the effects of inflicting torture on the local population during the day, and surreptitiously treated the Algerian victims of that torture at night. Fanon came to the conclusion that there was no cure for his patients in such a barbaric context. He resigned from the hospital and, after participating in a strike of doctors sympathetic to the Front de Libération Nationale (FLN, the group waging war against the French colonizer), was expelled from Algeria.

Fanon left for TUNISIA in 1957 to work full time for the FLN, writing for its official organ, *El Moudjahid*. During his time there he published *L'An V de la révolution algérienne* (1959), a sociological study of the effects of revolutionary war on the Algerian population. Fanon also began to serve as a diplomat for the FLN and was appointed representative of the Algerian Provisional Government in Accra, GHANA, in March 1960. But Fanon's seemingly boundless enthusiasm for the cause of Algerian and, more generally, African liberation was tempered in late 1960 when he learned that he was suffering from leukemia. He was sent to the Soviet Union for treatment, but once there he was encouraged to go to a center for the treatment of leukemia at the National Institute of Health in Bethesda, Maryland. Fanon could not bring himself to travel to the "nation of lynchers," as he put it, and returned to Accra, where he immersed himself in the work of completing *Les damnés de la terre* (1961; translated as *The Wretched of the Earth*, 1967).

In this best known of his works, Fanon diagnoses the ills not only of a race – as in *Black Skin, White Masks* – but of a continent under colonial rule. The cure for the African continent was violence: it was only through violence, he believed, that colonized peoples could free themselves from both the material and the psychological oppression of colonialism. The society that would come on the heels of revolutionary decolonization would be one that would allow Africans and other formerly colonized peoples to acquire what Fanon called an "authentic existence." Shortly prior to his publication of this work (with a preface by Sartre), Fanon had a relapse of his leukemia and was forced to seek treatment in the United Sates. According to the American journalist Joseph Alsop, the Central Intelligence Agency (CIA) arranged for Fanon to be brought to WASHINGTON, D.C., where he was kept in a hotel room for eight days prior to being hospitalized. It is impossible to know what transpired during that time, but Fanon's wife has denied that he gave any information to the CIA. Fanon died in a Washington, D.C., hospital while reading the proofs of *The Wretched of the Earth*. A collection of essays by Fanon on the decolonization of Africa, *Pour la révolution africaine* (1964; *Toward the African Revolution*, 1969), was published posthumously.

Richard Watts

SEE ALSO
Présence Africaine; World War II and African Americans; Front de Libération Nationale.

Africa

Fante (also known as Fanti), ethnic group of GHANA.

The Fante primarily inhabit central coastal Ghana. They speak a Niger-Congo language and belong to the AKAN cultural and linguistic group. Over 1 million people consider themselves Fante.

SEE ALSO
Languages, African: An Overview.

Latin America and the Caribbean

Far I, Prince (Michael Williams) (b. 1944, Spanish Town, Jamaica; d. Septem-ber 15, 1983, Kingston, Jamaica), Jamaican vocalist, composer, and producer best known for vocal and instrumental recordings projecting a dramatically prophetic and apocalyptic vision inspired by Rastafarianism.

Prince Far I was born in Spanish Town and grew up in the Waterhouse area of Kingston, JAMAICA. His musical career began in 1970 when he convinced the REGGAE producer Coxsone Dodd (who employed him as a security guard at Studio One, Jamaica's most famous recording studio) to let him record when a scheduled musician failed to appear for a session. Dodd was so taken by Prince Far I's talent as a DJ (someone chanting or talking-singing spontaneously over prerecorded rhythm tracks) that he released several Prince Far I recordings under the name he created for the performer, King Cry-Cry. As he gained confidence and sought other producers for his recordings, Williams changed his name to Prince Far I. Distinguishing features of his recordings under the name King Cry-Cry or Prince Far I include a thunderously deep bass delivery of intensely personal lyrics laced with Rastafarian themes. His first album-length recording, *Psalms for I*, offered transfigured biblical psalms chanted to bass-heavy reggae rhythm tracks, delivered with a tone suggesting prophetic fervor enflamed by a sense of imminent apocalypse. His lyrics insist on the need for Jamaicans to maintain a spiritual awareness of African roots. His instrumental recordings include innovative experiments in DUB (a studio-created remixing of recordings heavily emphasizing atmospheric bass and drum lines). Best known are the *Cry Tuff Dub Encounter* albums. His career was cut short when he was tragically murdered one year short of his 40th birthday.

Norman Weinstein

SEE ALSO
Kingston, Jamaica; Rastafarians.

Africa

Farah, Nuruddin (b. 1945, Baidoa, Somalia), a contemporary Somali writer.

As the son of Aleeli Faduma, a woman considered a master of Somali oral poetry, Nuruddin Farah was born into an artistic tradition of language. Unlike his mother, however, he found his own expression in the foreign tongue of English, on the written page, and in a location far from his home country. With a nonlinear, complicated prose style influenced by Western modernist and contemporary Indian writing as well as by Somali oral tradition, Farah has developed a distinct voice in contemporary English-language African literature.

Farah's education brought him first to the capital city of Mogadishu, then to England, and finally to Punjab University in Chandigarh, India, where he received his B.A. in 1970. By this time he had already published the novella *Why Die So Soon?* (1965) and written his first novel, *From a Crooked Rib* (1970). Centering on the journey of a woman from her small village to Mogadishu, the novel depicts the different worlds that exist within the nation of Somalia. With his complex treatment of gender, particularly his perceptive representation of female characters, Farah initiated an exploration of female and male identities that would characterize his fictional work.

Meanwhile, events in Somalia prompted a shift in Farah's focus. In 1969 MUHAMMAD SIAD BARRE staged a coup d'état and established a military dictatorship. In Farah's next novel, *A Naked Needle* (1976), he grappled with the subject of revolution. Ultimately, the work was unsuccessful both in his own eyes (he prevented the reprinting of the book) and in the eyes of the censors, who halted its publication for several years. In 1972 Farah started a fictional series in the newly scripted Somali language, but censorship once again stood in his way.

By this time it was clear that Farah presented a threat to the Barre's regime. While traveling abroad, Farah learned that he would be in danger if he returned to Somalia. He began a life of exile, living at times in other parts of Africa, including NIGERIA, as well as in Europe and the United States. During this time he taught at several universities and worked as a playwright.

In 1979 Farah returned to the project of portraying dictatorship in a trilogy that he would dub *Variations on the Theme of an African Dictatorship. Sweet and Sour Milk* (1979) was followed by *Sardines* (1981) and *Close Sesame* (1983). In this work, Farah grappled with the nature of tyranny. Drawing connections between interpersonal dynamics and the political culture of the state, Farah's trilogy was as much a critique of patriarchy as it was of state totalitarianism.

In perhaps his best-known work, *Maps* (1986), Farah returned to the issue of national identity (*see* NATIONALISM IN AFRICA) as he traced a young man's path from his village to the city. A sophisticated work that experimented with shifting narrative voice, *Maps* sifted through layers of selfhood and identity. The second novel in a planned trilogy, *Gifts* (1992), considered the theme of dependency (*see* DEVELOPMENT IN AFRICA: AN INTERPRETATION), juxtaposing a love relationship with the politicized context of African economic dependency. In 1998 he won the Neustadt Prize for his novel *Secrets*, which explores life in Mogadishu in the period leading up to the recent civil war.

Marian Aguiar

SEE ALSO
Mogadishu, Somalia; Somalia.

North America

Fard, Wallace D. (b. ?; d. ?), primary founder of the NATION OF ISLAM.

Wallace D. Fard entered public life in Detroit, Michigan, in the summer of 1930. Hailing from obscure origins, perhaps Egyptian or

Hawaiian, he peddled "notions" – trinkets, silks, and raincoats – to residents of Paradise Valley, a predominantly African American neighborhood of Detroit. Fard claimed to have come from Africa, identified his goods as the wares of African peoples, and satisfied his customers – many of whom were uprooted Southerners – by providing them with a sense of cultural identity and stories of a common heritage. At first he moved from house to house, talking of his travels, but soon popular interest in his anecdotes encouraged him to move his storytelling to a hall.

Although Fard initially proscribed foods and moral codes, he began to address deeper theological concerns as his popularity grew. He cited the Bible, not to teach Christianity but to debunk it, espousing instead the Islamic faith. Fard called white people "blue-eyed devils," scorned their "tricknology" – which facilitated the exploitation of blacks – and taught that human culture began in Africa. He advocated an independent republic of African Americans in the United States and instituted the practice of dropping Western European surnames. By assuming, instead, the last name "X," followers of Fard rejected the names given to them in slavery.

What began as an impassioned travelogue grew into a multitiered organization, 8000 members strong. Under the auspices of the Lost Found Nation of Islam, Fard founded the University of Islam in Detroit (a school for elementary and high school students) and the Muslim Girls Training Corps, as well as the Fruit of Islam, a paramilitary organization that trained men in the use of firearms. Fard appointed and trained both a Minister of Islam and a retinue of underlings to preside over the Nation, enabling him to relinquish his duties and withdraw from the public eye. Elijah Poole, a former member of the Moorish Science Temple of America (*see* Noble Drew Ali), succeeded Fard, adopting the name Elijah Muhammad.

In 1934 Fard disappeared as mysteriously as he had arrived, and every speculation about his disappearance remains unsubstantiated. Elijah Muhammad capitalized on this mystery, transforming Fard's disappearance into a serviceable mythology upon which he based the Nation's religious authority. By 1942 the Nation had assigned Fard divine status as an embodiment of Allah; through the end of the twentieth century Fard provided the spiritual foundation of the Nation's life.

Eric Bennett

See Also
Slavery in the United States; Detroit, Michigan; Islam and Tradition: An Interpretation.

North America

Farmer, James (b. January 12, 1920, Marshall, Tex.; d. July 9, 1999, Fredericksburg, Va.), educator, administrator, and founder of the Congress of Racial Equality (CORE).

Raised in an environment that valued education and religious faith, James Farmer was an outstanding student. After skipping several grades in elementary school, at age 14 he entered Wiley College in Marshall, Texas (where his father, one of the few African American Ph.D.s in the South, had taught). Graduating in 1938, Farmer went on to Howard University's School of Religion. He graduated from Howard in 1941. Farmer opposed war in general, and more specifically objected to serving in the segregated armed forces. When the United States entered World War II later that year, he applied for conscientious objector status but found that he was deferred from the draft because he had a divinity degree.

Rather than become an ordained Methodist minister, Farmer, who told his father he would rather fight that church's policy of segregated congregations, chose to go to work for the Fellowship of Reconciliation (FOR). Farmer was FOR's secretary for race relations, helping the Quaker, pacifist organization craft its responses to such social ills as war, violence, bigotry, and poverty. It was a job that left Farmer, who was then living in Chicago, Illinois, enough time to begin forming his own approach to these issues – one based less on FOR's religious pacifism than on the principle of nonviolent resistance.

Founded in 1942, Farmer's new group, CORE, was at first called the Committee on Racial Equality; the name was later changed to the Congress of Racial Equality. Using pacifist techniques borrowed from the Indian nationalist leader Mohandas K. Gandhi, CORE members sought to end racial segregation and discrimination by putting their bodies on the line. Some of CORE's first actions included restaurant sit-ins, in which African American and mixed-race groups tried to be served at various Chicago restaurants, where, despite civil rights statutes on the books in Illinois, many of the establishments still refused to serve black customers. CORE's sit-ins were so successful that they greatly influenced student activists nearly 20 years later.

In addition to sit-ins, stand-ins, and boycotts, CORE pioneered the technique called Freedom Rides. Starting in the late 1940s and most famously used in 1961, Freedom Rides tested the legality of segregation on interstate transportation in the South. Always risking violent retaliation and often enduring jail for their efforts, CORE members were specially trained to maintain a peaceful, nonviolent demeanor. Their work led to the desegregation of more than 100 Southern bus terminals.

CORE also worked with other civil rights groups on issues such as school desegregation, voter registration, and job training (most notably during 1964, known as Freedom Summer, when CORE collaborated with the Student Nonviolent Coordinating Committee [SNCC]). By the late 1960s, however, Farmer, seeing CORE drift away from its Gandhian roots, left the organization he had founded and had led for more than 20 years. Always an active writer and speaker, he continued to lecture publicly on civil rights and eventually took a teaching position at Lincoln University in Pennsylvania. In 1968 Farmer ran for the United States Congress on the Liberal Party ticket and was defeated by Shirley Chisholm, an African American running as a Democrat. He went to work for Republican president Richard M. Nixon's administration as assistant secretary of health, education, and welfare shortly thereafter.

In the years since retiring from politics (1971), Farmer served on many organizational boards, including the Coalition of American Public Employees. He also continued to teach and lecture widely. In 1985 he published his autobiography, titled *Lay Bare the Heart*, and in 1998 President Bill Clinton awarded him the Congressional Medal of Freedom. Farmer died a year later.

Kate Tuttle

See Also
World War II and African Americans; Military, Blacks in the American; *Brown* v. *Board of Education*; Civil Rights Movement; Howard University; Lincoln University (Pennsylvania); Student Nonviolent Coordinating Committee.

North America

Farrakhan, Louis Abdul (Louis Eugene Walcott; b. May 17, 1933, Bronx, N.Y.), African American religious leader, head of the Nation of Islam, a black religious organization in the United States that combines some of the practices and beliefs of Islam with a philosophy of black separatism.

Louis Farrakhan preaches the virtues of personal responsibility, especially for black men, and advocates black self-sufficiency. His message has appealed primarily to urban blacks, and draws on a long history of black nationalists who have called for black self-reliance in the face of economic injustice and white racism. His more inflammatory remarks have caused critics to claim that he has appealed to black racism and anti-Semitism to promote his views.

Born Louis Eugene Walcott in New York City, Farrakhan grew up in Boston, Massachusetts. He attended Winston-Salem Teacher's College in North Carolina, and worked as a nightclub singer in the early 1950s. In 1955 Malcolm X, a minister for the Nation of Islam, convinced Walcott to join the organization. Walcott dropped his last name and became known as Minister Louis X. The practice of dropping surnames is common among black Muslims, who often view them as names that were imposed on slaves and handed down over the years by white society. He later adopted the name Abdul Haleem Farrakhan and came to be known as Louis Farrakhan.

Farrakhan's speaking and singing abilities helped him to rise to prominence within the Nation of Islam, and he led the group's mosque in BOSTON, MASSACHUSETTS. In 1963 a split developed between Malcolm X and ELIJAH MUHAMMAD, the leader of the Nation of Islam, and Malcolm X was suspended as a minister. Malcolm X had become increasingly dissatisfied with the group's failure to participate in the growing CIVIL RIGHTS MOVEMENT, and Muhammad seemed threatened by the growing popularity of Malcolm X. Farrakhan sided with Muhammad in this dispute. In 1964 Malcolm X left the Nation of Islam and formed a new group, the Organization of Afro-American Unity (OAAU). Farrakhan publicly criticized Malcolm X for his break with the Nation of Islam. In 1965 Malcolm X was assassinated while addressing an OAAU rally in New York City. Three black Muslims were eventually convicted and jailed for the killing. While Farrakhan denied any connection with the shooting and never faced any charges related to Malcolm X's death, he later conceded that he had helped to create an atmosphere that may have induced others to carry out the assassination.

After the death of Malcolm X, Farrakhan became the head of a large mosque in Harlem, a neighborhood in New York City, and was the principal spokesperson for Muhammad. Farrakhan held high office in the Nation of Islam until Muhammad died in 1975. Muhammad's son, Wallace Muhammad, succeeded his father and asked Farrakhan to move to Chicago to assume a new national position. Wallace Muhammad downplayed Black Nationalism, admitted nonblack members, and stressed strict Islamic beliefs and practices. Under Wallace Muhammad, the group's name changed to the World Community of Islam in the West, and later, to the American Muslim Mission.

In the late 1970s Farrakhan led a dissident faction within the organization that opposed any changes in the major beliefs and programs that had been instituted by Elijah Muhammad. In 1978 Farrakhan left Wallace Muhammad's organization and formed a new organization that assumed the original name, the Nation of Islam, and reasserted the principles of black separatism.

Farrakhan's public profile rose throughout the 1980s as he established new mosques, used radio appearances to increase his following in black communities, and was the featured speaker at events that often drew large crowds. His message of black self-reliance and mistrust of whites struck a responsive chord among young urban blacks, many of whom viewed Farrakhan as a courageous leader willing to confront a racist society. His followers praised his insistence that blacks assume moral and economic responsibility for themselves – that they avoid drugs and crime; that they provide for their children; that they stay in school and become involved in their communities.

Controversy surrounding the Nation of Islam also grew, primarily because Farrakhan attacked white society and voiced the anti-Semitism growing among some blacks in the inner cities. He was once quoted as calling Judaism a "gutter religion" and referred to German dictator Adolf Hitler, who was responsible for killing millions of Jews, as a great man. Farrakhan's controversial remarks on the radio and at press conferences were widely condemned by other black leaders.

In the 1990s Farrakhan continued his call for poor blacks to make stronger commitments to education and to their families. He also called on blacks to end black-on-black crime and to be less dependent on government welfare. In October 1995 Farrakhan organized the MILLION MAN MARCH in WASHINGTON, D.C. At the march, hundreds of thousands of black men vowed to renew their commitments to family, community, and personal responsibility. Although the march renewed criticism of Farrakhan's anti-Semitic statements and some black leaders refused to participate, it was widely regarded as a successful display of black solidarity. It helped Farrakhan move closer to the political mainstream, and some people also saw it as indicating the strength of his appeal to a significant segment of the black population.

In January 1996 Farrakhan made a 20-nation "world friendship tour" that included stops in Iran, LIBYA, and Iraq – all nations that the United States government regarded as pariah states run by dictators. On the tour Farrakhan repeatedly criticized the U.S. government, provoking condemnation by U.S. officials.

SEE ALSO
Harlem, New York; New York, New York; Black Nationalism in the United States.

North America

Fattah, Chaka

(b. 1956, Philadelphia, Penn.), Democratic member of the United States House of Representatives from Pennsylvania (1995-).

Chaka Fattah was born in PHILADELPHIA PENNSYLVANIA in 1956. He received a bachelor's degree in business and economics in 1978 from the University of Pennsylvania. In 1982, at age 25, he became the youngest person ever elected to the Pennsylvania House of Representatives, and he served as a state representative until 1989. He received a master's degree in government administration in 1986 from the University of Pennsylvania and completed the Senior Executive Program for State Officials in 1988 at the John F. Kennedy School of Government at Harvard University. He then served in the Pennsylvania Senate from 1989 to 1995.

In 1994 Fattah ran for a second time for the U.S. House of Representatives from Pennsylvania's Second Congressional District after losing in 1991, and this time he beat Lucien Blackwell in the Democratic primary with 58 percent of the vote. He went on to win the general election with 85 percent of the vote. He was reelected in 1996 with nearly 90 percent of the vote.

The Second District is located in the city of Philadelphia, including the racially diverse neighborhood of West Philadelphia. Drexel University, the University of Pennsylvania, and the United States Postal Service are major employers.

In Congress, Fattah was elected whip of the CONGRESSIONAL BLACK CAUCUS in December 1994. He was also appointed to the Democratic Policy Committee and the Democratic Congressional Campaign Committee. In the 105th Congress (1997-1999) Fattah sat on the Government Reform and Oversight Committee, and was ranking member of its subcommittee on the Postal Service. He also sat on the Education and the Workforce Committee.

North America

Fauset, Jessie Redmon

(b. April 27, 1882, Camden County, N.J.; d. April 30, 1961, Philadelphia, Pa.), Influential African American novelist and editor during the Harlem Renaissance.

Poet LANGSTON HUGHES referred to Jessie Fauset as one of "the three people who mid-wifed the so-called New Negro literature into being," a statement that reveals how influential Fauset was as an editor during the HARLEM RENAISSANCE of the 1920s and 1930s. But Fauset was also the era's most prolific black novelist, publishing four books between 1924 and 1933. In both capacities, Fauset helped shape one of the most important movements in AFRICAN AMERICAN LITERATURE.

Fauset was born in what is now Lawnside, New Jersey, and grew up in Philadelphia. She hoped to attend Bryn Mawr College, but instead of admitting a black student, Bryn Mawr arranged for Fauset to receive a scholarship to Cornell University. There, Fauset became the first black woman in the country to be elected to Phi Beta Kappa, the academic honorary society. She also began corresponding with the noted black intellectual W. E. B. Du Bois, whose work she admired, forming an association that would become the cornerstone of her literary career.

After graduation Fauset moved to WASHINGTON, D.C., where she taught at the prestigious all-black M Street (later Dunbar) High School from 1905 to 1919 while taking courses toward a master's degree in French from the University of Pennsylvania. But beginning in 1912,

Fauset was also a literary contributor to the *Crisis*, the journal of the NATIONAL ASSOCIATION FOR THE ADVANCEMENT OF COLORED PEOPLE (NAACP), which Du Bois edited. When the *Crisis* created the position of literary editor at its New York office in 1919, Du Bois offered it to Fauset, and she accepted.

It was at the *Crisis* that Fauset cultivated the talents of many younger Harlem Renaissance writers, including Langston Hughes, JEAN TOOMER, COUNTEE CULLEN, and CLAUDE MCKAY. Under her tenure, the *Crisis* became one of the major publishing outlets for black writers at the time. But Fauset also published short stories, essays, reviews, and poems of her own in both the *Crisis* and its short-lived children's magazine, *The Brownies' Book*. In 1924 she published her first novel, *There Is Confusion*. Many of her stories and all four of her novels feature light-skinned, middle-class black protagonists. Fauset stated that one of her goals was to present normally "the homelife of the colored American," without the melodrama or caricature that she often saw in white writers. But her fiction did explore the ways in which race and gender affect characters, even in their domestic lives.

Fauset left her position at the *Crisis* in 1926 – perhaps because of a falling out with Du Bois – and took another teaching job, this time in New York. Although *There Is Confusion* had been well received by black critics, she still had difficulty securing publishers for her later novels – perhaps because she was a novelist at a time when black poets were in vogue. But she continued to write, publishing *Plum Bun* in 1929, *The Chinaberry Tree* in 1931, and *Comedy: American Style* in 1933. In 1929 Fauset married insurance broker Herbert Harris, and in the early 1940s they moved to Montclair, New Jersey, signaling her formal retirement from the New York scene. After Harris's death in 1958, Fauset lived with her stepbrother in Philadelphia until her death on April 30, 1961. Jessie Fauset left a lasting impression on the African American literary tradition at a formative period through her profound influence on the authors she nurtured, and through the merits of her own work.

Lisa Clayton Robinson

SEE ALSO

Crisis, The; Du Bois, William Edward Burghardt (W. E. B.); New York, New York; Philadelphia, Pennsylvania.

Rio de Janeiro's *favelas* (squatter settlements) are the largest and most populous in Brazil. Favelas inhabitants are predominantly people of African descent. *CORBIS/Dave G. Houser*

Latin America and the Caribbean

Favelas, **squatter settlements or shantytowns that provide shelter to millions of Brazil's poor, among them a large percentage of Afro-Brazilians.**

Favelas represent the plight and promise of the urban poor in BRAZIL. Although they can be found throughout the country, favelas are most numerous in Rio de Janeiro, once the nation's federal district (1889-1960) and still its second largest city. Shantytowns such as Rocinha and Jacarezinho have become an indelible part of the landscape of the Cidade Maravilhosa (Marvelous City). Other Brazilian metropolises – São Paulo, Salvador, Recife – have their own favelas, with populations numbering in the hundreds of thousands, but these setttlements have not attained the political prominence or journalistic notoriety of the ones in Rio.

The favela is fundamentally different from inner-city slums and tenements, the types of poor people's housing prevalent in the developed world. The latter are usually rundown buildings owned by a landlord where the occupants pay rent. Squatter settlements, by contrast, are units of self-constructed housing built on terrain seized and occupied illegally, most often located in the urban periphery. Residences are built without license, usually on lands belonging to third parties. Inside the favela there is a near total absence of numbered streets, sanitation networks, electricity, telephones, or plumbing. This is not to say that the favela lacks organization. Popularly elected residents' councils maintain order; religious institutions, social clubs, and political parties forge bonds among *favelados* (squatters) and connect them to the outside world.

The physical environment of a favela daunts the imagination. The architecture of favela homes ranges from multiple-story brick and concrete structures to homes with dirt floors and walls made of baked clay. Zinc foils and strips from aluminum cans improvise a roof. The proximity of shacks to one another provides fertile ground for tetanus and other diseases deadly to children, and fires spreading from one shanty to the next can destroy a settlement overnight. Garbage strewn about undermines the rustic housing, and mudslides cause hundreds of deaths every year. Yet favela living is a rational choice for many of the poor. Shantytowns offer proximity to the workplace, saving the laborer costly transportation fare and hours of travel. There is a political advantage to favela residency as well; so long as they stay within city limits, squatters can claim the right to public services like education and health care.

History

Shantytowns have kept pace with the modernization of Rio de Janeiro. The belle époque of the 1890s, when the city sought to become the Paris of South America by opening new roads, demolishing old buildings, and eradicating life-threatening diseases, witnessed the birth of the first favela, located on Providência Hill overlooking downtown. It was founded in 1897 by Afro-Brazilian veterans of the military campaign against the messianic rebel Antônio Conselheiro. But not until the 1940s, following the mass exodus of rural laborers from the interior of Brazil to Rio de Janeiro in search of industrial jobs, did favelas overtake slums as the principal form of housing for the urban poor. Workers who had recently arrived in Rio could not afford to live in tenement slums. Cramped rooms made it impossible to raise a large family, and the municipal code gave the landlord extensive powers of eviction. The only alternative for many migrants was to erect their own houses in violation of the law. Lawmakers tacitly agreed to condone the shantytowns as a way of removing the poor from the inner city while still giving industry and the middle class access to cheap labor. The 1940s witnessed the construction of dozens of favelas on hills, beaches, swamps, abandoned construction projects, and garbage dumps all over the federal district. During the next 50 years their population doubled every decade and spilled over into the metropolitan suburbs; according to government estimates in 1990, Rio contained over 2 million squatters, making one out of every three *cariocas* (residents of Rio de Janeiro) a favela dweller.

The Favelas and Race in Rio de Janeiro

Although Brazil has never practiced legal segregation or housing discrimination, there is a distinct connection between race, employment, and the formation of the shantytowns. Blacks and mulattos are found in greater proportion in the favelas than in the rest of the city, while whites are underrepresented but hold crucial positions in economic and political life. The favelas have, however, rearranged patterns of residency in Rio de Janeiro, moving many people of color closer to the middle-class white population. Domestic service for women and construction work for men are the most common occupations for favelados, and new shacks tend to spring up where well-off whites buy their homes and manage their factories. Few shantytowns are found in predominantly black and mulatto neighborhoods. For this reason, favela residents are likely to see themselves as a community of the downtrodden, not a racial enclave, and favela politics is dominated by concerns of social class rather than race.

Afro-Brazilian Culture and the Shantytowns

Some foreign observers have claimed that the favelas represent an outpost of African civilization in Brazil, a transferal of that continent's architecture and community life to the New World, but this theory is dubious. The physical construction and political organization of Rio's shantytowns bear more resemblance to the squatter settlements in the rest of Latin America than to communities in Africa. Nevertheless, key elements of Afro-Brazilian social and cultural life find their fullest expression in the favelas. The famous SAMBA schools that display their dancers during Rio's pre-Lent Carnival originated there. Afro-Brazilian religions, some blending African beliefs with Roman Catholicism, have their largest following in the favelas, where churches may double as temples of Macumba, CANDOMBLÉ, and UMBANDA. As many favelados are the descendants of slaves, coparenthood, godparenthood, and other kinship practices that were found among the slaves imported to Brazil also continue to flourish in the shantytowns more than in the rest of the nation.

Julio Cesar Pino

See Also

Rio de Janeiro, Brazil; Religions, African, in Brazil; Carnivals in Latin America and the Caribbean.

Africa

Faye, Safi (b. 1943, near Dakar, Senegal), Senegalese film director, one of the few independent women filmmakers in Africa.

Safi Faye is not only one of the few independent African women film directors, but also one of the few making ethnographic films. The daughter of a village chief and businessman of SERER origin, Faye moved to Dakar at age 19 to become a teacher. While in Dakar she became interested in the educational and ethnographic uses of film and upon meeting Jean Rouch, the French filmmaker and ethnologist, she embarked on a film career.

Faye acted in Rouch's *Petit à petit ou Les Lettres persanes* (1968). She also learned about Rouch's style of cinéma-vérité, characterized by an unobtrusive camera and spontaneous nonprofessional acting, which would later influence her own film work. With Rouch's encouragement she moved to Paris in 1972 and enrolled in the Ecole Pratique des Hautes Etudes to study ethnology, and the Louis Lumière Film School to study film. She completed film school in 1974, and began using film as a way to publish her ongoing research on the Serer. By the time she received her Ph.D. she had produced three films – *Kaddu beykat* (1975); *Fad'jal* (1979); and *Goob na na* (1979).

Faye has since held a number of academic positions in Europe, while continuing to make ethnographic films. Although much of her work focuses on the Serer, she has also produced documentaries for the United Nations and German and French television stations, filmed in both Europe and Africa. In a 1970s interview she described her methods: "I go talk to the farmers in their village. We discuss their problems and I take notes. Even though I may write a script for my films, I basically leave the peasants free to express themselves in front of a camera and I listen. My films are collective works in which everybody takes an active part." Because the messages communicated by peasants through Faye's work are, as she intends, clearly political, government censorship in Africa has prevented most of them from being shown.

Elizabeth Heath

See Also

Cinema, African; Dakar, Senegal.

North America

Federal Writers' Project, a project funded by the United States government during the 1930s to collect American history through oral narratives, including the testimonies of ex-slaves.

Although their accuracy and usefulness have been debated, the SLAVE NARRATIVES collected through the Federal Writers' Project (FWP) represent a significant addition to the study of American slavery. The FWP began in 1935 as part of President Franklin D. Roosevelt's WORKS PROGRESS ADMINISTRATION, which created new jobs for Americans suffering during the GREAT DEPRESSION. The Writers' Project hired unemployed writers to collect folklore and histories from each state for a series of books called *Guide to America,* and President Roosevelt's BLACK CABINET – African American advisers John Davis, William Hastie, and Robert Weaver – persuaded the administration to include oral testimonies of former slaves and other African Americans as part of this program.

As a result thousands of African Americans were interviewed between 1935 and 1939 through the FWP's Office of Negro Affairs. The FWP produced more than a dozen collections of rural and urban black studies. Its largest contribution to black history and literature is the slave narrative collection. More than 2000 ex-slaves in 18 states, an estimated 2 percent of the surviving ex-slave population, were interviewed. The topics discussed in the conversations included the type of work the interviewees had done as slaves, what they ate and what they wore, and what their families and homes were like. Published collections of their narratives include Benjamin Botkins's anthology *Lay My Burden Down: A Folk History of Slavery* (1945) and George P. Rawlins's comprehensive 41-volume *The American Slave: A Composite Autobiography* (1972, 1977, 1979).

The FWP employed several prominent African American writers. Sterling A. Brown was the FWP Negro Affairs director, and ZORA NEALE HURSTON briefly directed the Florida office. RICHARD WRIGHT, ARNA BONTEMPS, and MARGARET WALKER worked in the office, and Wright, CLAUDE MCKAY, and RALPH ELLISON all worked in New York. The position gave many of these writers extra time for their own writing – Hurston, for example, finished three novels during her fieldwork, and Wright wrote *Twelve Million Black Voices* as part of the project and *Native Son* during his free time.

But while the FWP was an excellent opportunity for these black authors, the program failed to employ large numbers of African Americans – in 1937, only 106 out of the 4500 writers were black. Several state offices simply refused to hire black workers for the project. Many historians have argued that the racial inequality on the staff undermined the value of the endeavor, because black interviewees tended to censor themselves when they were responding to white questioners. This has become one of the major criticisms of the project.

There have been other criticisms of the narratives as well. Most of the writers had no standard training or background in conducting interviews. They did not use tape recorders, so it is difficult to tell how accurate their transcriptions were. Many writers either rephrased the subjects' answers in their own words, or exaggerated the African American dialects that they heard. There is also evidence that writers cut certain material altogether, including accounts of severe cruelty by whites. Two-thirds of the interviewees were over 80 years old at the time of the interviews, and they were trying to recall events that had taken place over 70 years earlier. Finally, because most of them had been slaves only as children and only during the last two decades of American slavery, their experiences may not have been representative of the broader African American slave experience.

Despite these limitations, the FWP narratives remain one of the most extensive sources of first-person information on African American slavery. They continue to be useful to scholars, historians, and general readers interested in learning more about the slave experience. A 1990s series of paperback selections titled *I Was a Slave* made the narratives available in an affordable new edition.

Lisa Clayton Robinson

SEE ALSO

Slavery in the United States; Brown, Sterling Allen; Hastie, William Henry; New York, New York; Weaver, Robert Clifton.

Latin America and the Caribbean

Fedon, Julien, a mixed-race landowner in Grenada who, inspired by the French Revolution, led a rebellion against British colonial rule that lasted from March 1795 to June 1796 (*see* GRENADA).

Latin America and the Caribbean

Feliciano, José "Cheo" (b. 1935), Afro-Puerto Rican singer of salsa and boleros. Born in Ponce, he moved to New York, where he launched his singing career. In the 1950s he sang on occasion with the Tito Rodriguez big band. Between 1957 and 1967, he attained considerable success singing with the Joe Cuba Sextette. In the 1970s he sang with the Fania All Stars.

SEE ALSO

Salsa Music.

Africa

Female Circumcision in Africa

Female circumcision is a term commonly used to refer to surgical operations performed in over 30 African, Middle Eastern, and southeast Asian countries, by immigrants from those countries living elsewhere, and by physicians in Europe and the United States between roughly 1850 and 1950. As this geographic and historical range suggests, these operations take place in a wide range of cultural and historical contexts and can have very different meanings and effects. All involve the surgical modification of female genitals in some way, though this may range from relatively minor marking for symbolic purposes to the most radical operation, infibulation.

Female circumcision varies widely even within Africa, where it is practiced across a band of the continent that includes parts of MAURITANIA, SENEGAL, THE GAMBIA, GUINEA-BISSAU, SIERRA LEONE, LIBERIA, MALI, BURKINA FASO, CÔTE D'IVOIRE, GHANA, TOGO, BENIN, NIGER, NIGERIA, CHAD, CAMEROON, CENTRAL AFRICAN REPUBLIC, DEMOCRATIC REPUBLIC OF THE CONGO (formerly Zaire), SUDAN, EGYPT, ERITREA, ETHIOPIA, DJIBOUTI, SOMALIA, KENYA, TANZANIA, and UGANDA. The percentage of women circumcised in each country varies considerably (e.g., from 5 to 10 percent in Uganda and 25 to 30 percent in Ghana to 80 percent in the Sudan), as does the kind of operation practiced, its cultural and personal significance, and its history. Female circumcision is not practiced at all by some communities within this broad area, but it is commonplace in others. Christians, Muslims, and followers of traditional religions all might practice forms of female circumcision. Communities have adopted, abandoned, and modified the practices over time, reflecting ongoing political and religious changes as well as interaction among cultures on the African continent.

The general term *female circumcision* includes at least three clinically distinct kinds of surgery. Clitoridectomy removes all or part of the clitoris and the hood, or prepuce, which covers it. This is sometimes called sunna circumcision, though sunna circumcision might also refer to preputial cutting alone. The name *sunna* relates the practice to Islamic traditions, though most Muslim scholars and theologians deny Koranic justification for female circumcision. The second type, excision, includes clitoridectomy but also removes some or all of the labia minora; all or part of the labia majora might also be cut. The amount of tissue removed in these two kinds of circumcision varies within these general definitions. The most extreme form of circumcision, infibulation, goes beyond excision. After removing the labia, the sides of the vulva are joined so that scar tissue forms over the vaginal opening, leaving a small gap for urination and menstruation. Infibulation is also called pharaonic circumcision, a name originating in beliefs that the practice was part of ancient Egyptian life. Infibulated women often require surgical opening to allow first intercourse and birthing; in many cases women are reinfibulated after each childbirth. In addition to these three well-recognized types of female circumcision, a fourth is sometimes included. The mildest form (sometimes called "mild sunna"), this involves a symbolic pricking or slight nicking of the clitoris or prepuce. Worldwide, excision and infibulation are the most widely practiced types of female circumcision. In Africa, infibulation is most common primarily in the Horn of Africa.

The health problems that can be associated with these operations are well known, but there has been little epidemiological research to determine how widespread they are in different areas. Immediate risks, all related to hygienic conditions and care during and after the operations, include infection, shock, excessive bleeding, and urinary retention. Public health education programs often aim first to improve these conditions or to provide hygienic training for midwives and traditional surgeons. Longer-term health problems are most common with infibulation but can be associated with excision as well. Most of these problems are consequences of heavy scarring and the covering over of vaginal and urinary openings after infibulation: keloid scars, vulvar cysts, retention of urine or menses, painful menstruation, difficulty urinating, and chronic pelvic infections. Heavily scarred women often require surgery before childbirth and may have prolonged labor.

Whether and how circumcision affects women's sexuality is much debated. It is important, however, to distinguish between sexual desire, sexual activity, and sexual pleasure. Sexual desire and sexual activity may not diminish with female genital operations. Evidence about sexual feeling and pleasure is variable, difficult to define or measure, and hard to find in the literature. Euro-American opponents of the practices assert that circumcised women feel no sexual pleasure, but a number of African women disagree with these assertions. Studies suggest that the effect varies widely depending on the type of operation performed, prior sexual experience, and other factors. Some African activists also suggest that the stress on sexual pleasure in anticircumcision campaigns derives from a recent and primarily Western concept of sexuality.

In many places where female circumcision is practiced, the physical operation is but one moment in an elaborate ceremony. For instance, for the Okiek people in Kenya, initiation into adulthood includes circumcision for boys and excision for girls, but the full initiation process continues for several months and involves moral instruction, family and community engagement, and the negotiation of new social relationships. While the operations are a central initiation trial and create a permanent physical mark of adulthood, initiation cannot be reduced to circumcision or excision alone. In many other societies, initiation does not involve circumcision at all.

In every case the purposes and meanings of female circumcision are related to specific cultural understandings of identity, personhood, morality, adulthood, gender, bodily aesthetics, and other important issues. In the Sudan, for instance, female circumcision is seen as enhancing a woman's purity, cleanliness, and beauty. For the Kikuyu people of Kenya, circumcision was the foundation of moral self-mastery for women and men alike, performed as part of initiation into adulthood. The age of those circumcised varies widely according to these cultural understandings. In much of Mali and the Sudan, for instance, girls are circumcised at six to eight years, while various communities in Kenya and Sierra Leone perform the operation in the early teens. For the Yoruba people of Nigeria, male circumcision and female excision are not related to adulthood initiation but rather to moral concepts of shame and fertility. They often circumcise their children at just a few days old, much like male circumcision in the United States and Europe. When female circumcision was performed on American and European women, it was done at a much later age than elsewhere in the world, and for quite different reasons. In Africa, for example, the operation is usually considered part of a person's social and moral development, and so is rarely performed after puberty. In Europe and the United States, however, doctors between roughly 1850 and 1950 regularly prescribed clitoridectomy for adult women as medical treatment for insomnia, sterility, and masturbation (which was defined as an ailment at that time).

Many societies practice male but not female circumcision, but the reverse is rare. Where both are practiced, they can only be understood fully in relation to each other. A single word refers to both operations in many African languages, and this correspondence is often central to the way their practitioners understand them. The English translation, "female circumcision," maintains this parallel between male and female genital operations, though anticircumcision activists have criticized the term for being misleading.

Both male and female genital operations have engendered long histories of debate and opposition, often centered around cross-cultural disagreements about the meaning and worth of the practices. The value of Jewish male circumcision, for instance, was debated in Rome during the first century C.E., and male circumcision has become a topic of heated opposition in the United States again today. Female circumcision practices have been the subject of international political controversies and abolition campaigns since at least the 1910s. Contemporary campaigns continue the tradition and rhetoric of colonial and missionary opposition and also build on decades of activism within Africa. Health considerations have consistently been part of the debate, particularly in relation to infibulation. The issues have also been defined at various times in terms of colonialism, neocolonialism, feminism, sexuality, and human rights.

In Kenya, for instance, debates about female circumcision began almost as soon as European missionaries arrived. Along with colonial administrators, they made judgments about which local customs violated Christian behavior and sought to discourage them. Campaigns to abolish female circumcision in central Kenya were among these efforts. When the Church of Scotland Mission and segments of the Church Missionary Society tried to prohibit the practice in the 1910s and 1920s, Kikuyu female circumcision became connected with the anticolonial movement and the defense of cultural tradition. Jomo Kenyatta, the future first president of Kenya, was a prominent opponent of colonial attempts to alter Kikuyu custom. Opposition to the colonial campaign to abolish female circumcision provided an impetus for starting independent schools and churches in central Kenya. The Kikuyu circumcision controversy was shaped by church interests and politics in England as well as by events in Kenya itself. It was also related to changing notions of the body and changes in Kikuyu social relations, such as marriage patterns, relations of authority between men and women and between women of different generations, and the waning of *ngweko* (sexual play between young people). Since 1979 the Kenyan government has conducted several anticircumcision campaigns that were tinged with Christian and colonial overtones. A 1982 ban had little effect. In 1996 a national organization proposed an alternative initiation ceremony as a substitute. Other countries have their own histories of circumcision debates and policies.

International efforts to have female circumcision addressed by the World Health Organization (WHO) in the late 1950s were not effective. In the 1970s a number of publicity campaigns and publications converged to galvanize international attention. These included articles in African publications, a press conference held in Switzerland before the WHO Assembly in 1977, and publications by Fran Hosken and Mary Daly in the United States. The Inter-African Committee on Traditional Practices affecting the Health of Women and Children was formed in Geneva in 1977. A 1979 WHO seminar in Khartoum helped to make female genital operations a regular topic at international conferences. Anticircumcision activity during this time was also buoyed by the declaration of the United Nations Decade of Women (1975-1985).

Since the early 1990s international debates about female circumcision have again become increasingly heated and highly politicized. Greater media coverage in the 1990s and publicity over legal cases concerning African immigrants in France and the United States brought the debates to a much wider audience. In the United States, involvement by such well-known figures as novelist Alice Walker also helped to publicize and polarize the debate. A number of African scholars and activists based in the United States (such as Seble Dawit, Salem Mekuria, and Micere Mugo) have been highly critical of the way Walker and others have represented female circumcision in Africa. They argue that Walker and others are engaged in neocolonial depictions that demonize African practitioners, distort the social meanings and contexts involved, portray African women only as victims, ignore decades of activism in Africa, and isolate female circumcision from other issues of women's health, economic status, and education.

The growing intensity of these debates became encapsulated in the very terms used between the 1970s and 1990s. In the 1970s anticircumcision activists increasingly criticized the term *female circumcision*, claiming that it condoned a brutal custom by creating false similarities between male and female circumcision. A more partisan alternative was coined and eventually popularized: *female genital mutilation*. The new term *mutilation* did not attempt impartial description, but instead judged and condemned the practices through a label that defined them all as intentional mistreatment and disfigurement. Promotion of the new term was part of an escalating anticircumcision campaign that used sensationalism and gory images. As this term became more common, it was shortened to an acronym, FGM. Others reject this term as misrepresenting the intentions of African families, criminalizing parents and relatives, and judging them through Euro-American cultural values. A number of alternative terms have come into use in the mid-1990s, seeking more neutral ground: *genital surgery, genital operations, genital modification,* and *body modification*. This last term acknowledges broad similarities among such practices as male and female genital surgery, genital/body piercing, and other cosmetic surgery. Attempting to find an appropriate phrase, *New York Times* reporter Celia Duggers used the term *genital cutting* in her late-1996 articles, a term she adopted from demographic and health surveys but that did not catch on in popular usage. Female circumcision and FGM remain the most common terminology in English.

Both female circumcision practices and the arenas of debate have shifted over the years as other circumstances have changed and different constituencies have become involved. Public health education about the potential risks of the operations has increased in most countries where they are practiced. Similarly, an increasing number of female circumcisions are performed in health clinics and hospitals, or by specialists who have received some hygienic training. As noted above, alternative rituals have also been proposed in some countries, though it is not clear whether they will be widely adopted. Intense debates continue among African activists about whether a medicalized, minor form of female genital modification should be promoted as an interim substitute for more severe operations. Because African immigrant communities often practice female circumcision, they have brought all these debates to the fore in Europe and the United States, where immigrant populations have grown in recent decades. Sweden, Switzerland, the United Kingdom, and several other European countries passed laws restricting the operations in the 1980s and early 1990s. The United States followed suit in 1997.

Contemporary controversies about female circumcision cross a number of social and legal arenas, from family and household relations to international tribunals. The debates involve three interacting arenas: (1) *home countries,* where circumcising practices have traditional standing in some communities; (2) the *United States and Europe,* which also have a little-remembered history of female genital operations but where female circumcision is now associated particularly with immigrant communities; and (3) *international campaigns* conducted by international bodies and action groups that seek to intervene in the first two arenas and redefine issues central to particular communities and nations. The social, cultural, and historical contexts of debates vary in each of these arenas and involve many different actors, issues, positions, and perspectives.

The debates cannot be characterized in simple terms; they are not, for example, merely contests of women versus men or Africans versus outsiders. Rather, they now involve national governments and politicians; nongovernmental organizations; churches and religious officials; national and international action groups; the World Health Organization and other international agencies; and journalists – not to mention diverse religious and ethnic communities with different circumcision practices and different histories of involvement in these debates. National, state, and municipal judiciaries and agencies that deal with immigrant communities (e.g., the Immigration and Naturalization Service and Health and Human Services in the United States) also participate in some debates.

Within each circumcising community, differences of gender, age, education, religion, and wealth also influence attitudes and positions. For example, in some African settings a Christian mother, her non-Christian husband, his educated brother, and their school-age daughter might disagree about whether the girl should participate with her friends in initiation ceremonies during a school holiday. American media coverage of the legal case of Fauziya Kasinga illustrated just such a range of positions within her own family and community in Togo; Kasinga was granted political asylum in the United States in 1996, citing fear of forced circumcision.

Conflicting values and interests are at the crux of the controversy. In the 1980s and 1990s, legal cases dealing with African immigrants in Europe and the United States have raised these issues in particularly clear and urgent ways. There is no single, simple answer to the questions and dilemmas raised by genital operations, because they are variable practices with different meanings and histories. Decisions about whether and how to maintain, alter, or abolish the operations and associated practices cannot be imposed or legislated overnight, as the long history of the controversy shows, but can only be effective when the many different people directly involved take part. Local support and involvement are essential for any changes in these practices to take place.

Corinne Kratz

See Also

Christianity, African: An Overview; Education in Africa; Khartoum, Sudan; United Nations in Africa; Feminism in Africa: An Interpretation; African Religions: An Interpretation; Christianity: Independent and Charismatic Churches in Africa; Christianity: Missionaries in Africa; Human Rights in Africa; Islam and Tradition: An Interpretation.

Africa

Feminism in Africa: An Interpretation

In contrast to earlier times in the twentieth century, today we can talk about "African feminism" because African women themselves do so, and because they have quite clear ideas about what they mean when they use the term. Albertina Sisulu, the respected senior woman in the African National Congress (ANC) of South Africa, and the wife of Walter Sisulu, symbolized this new wave of female activism when she joined the women's walkout at the ANC Party Conference in Durban in 1992.The walkout demanded that the ANC commit itself to 33 percent female representation in Parliament and other government positions in the new South Africa to come. This form of feminism in South Africa is but one of many feminisms in Africa. Feminism varies both among the various nations as well as among different cultural subgroups on the continent. Nevertheless, African women's recognition of something they call "feminism" marks a new political sophistication borne of their deep engagement with the difficulties and challenges now facing their societies. The emergence of African feminism signals women's desire to play a role in determining the direction of development.

Thus, African feminism is Janus-faced: it looks forward to women's new goals, as well as backward to statuses and roles that women leaders have played in the past. African women are beginning to voice their opinions about the failed elections, military coups, political upheavals, refugee movements, economic recessions, structural adjustment, and other crises that severely affected their lives during the 1980s and 1990s. They are beginning to affirm their own identities while transforming societal notions of gender and familial roles.

African feminism is highly political, and it is a response to African social and political developments rather than an outgrowth of Western feminism. African women know that women and children have borne the brunt of the recent crises, as measured in high child mortality rates, lowered female literacy rates, the continuing confinement of women to agricultural work, and their exclusion from modern, technical, and scientific fields. Many African women (and some African men as well) are committed to correcting these disparities and forging new relationships between state and society, even though Western powers and global institutions still exercise tremendous influence over the economic and political conditions of African states.

Since the United Nations Fourth World Conference on Women, in Beijing, China (September 1995), Western governments and development agencies have urged respect for women's human rights and initiatives for "women's empowerment" in African state policies. This Western pressure has provided some support for women's activism. On the other hand, many African politicians viewed Western efforts with suspicion and have questioned the autonomy and legitimacy of women's actions. This controversy has not deterred African women activists. They know this may be their best opportunity to create a place for themselves in national life. Therefore, they are determined that "we will not miss the boat this time around."

The Distinctive Features of African Feminism

African feminism differs from Western feminism because it has developed in a different cultural context. Today, African women are seeking to redefine their roles in ways that allow them a new, culturally attuned activism. This is not a totally novel challenge, since there is evidence of gender hierarchy, female subordination, and women's struggles to reshape their statuses and roles within traditional African cultures in earlier historical periods. Gender asymmetry and inequality, particularly the distinction between public (political) and private (household) spheres, certainly existed in indigenous African social life. Gender inequality solidified during and following the phases of Islamic expansion and as European conquerors attempted to subdue or ignore female leaders. However, in Africa, female subordination takes intricate forms grounded in traditional African cultures, particularly because it is partially shaped by the "corporate" and "dual-sex" patterns that Africans have maintained through their history. Since culture is not static, new forms of asymmetry and inequality have arisen. Politicians and laypersons alike sometimes present this inequality as customary, but this is a distortion of African history. Women's contemporary activism and their attempts to fashion an African feminist approach to public and private life have emerged in response to these inequities.

The forms of African feminism emerging in various parts of the continent do not grow out of individualism within the context of industrial societies, as did Western feminism. In the West, economic and social trends historically pushed women into more active roles in the economy, and Western feminism has focused on women's struggle for control over reproduction and sexuality. However, African women have had a different experience. African feminist debates do not focus on theoretical questions, the female body, or sexual identity. Rather, like many of its Third World counterparts, African feminism is distinctly heterosexual, supportive of motherhood, and focused on issues of "bread, butter, culture, and power." The average fertility rate in Africa has stayed near six children per woman, and this reality shapes African women's lives. The practical orientation of African feminism grows out of a cultural heritage of female integration within corporate, agrarian, and family-based societies, and a more recent history of political domination and economic exploitation by the West.

In contrast to Western feminism, which emphasizes individual female autonomy, African feminism emphasizes authentic public participation and decision making by women. The issue of African clitoridectomy (*see* Female Circumcision in Africa) is one that African women say they themselves should be and are working to resolve – not Western women. African women are now exploring ways to incorporate their own views of women's development into African development policies and the activities of nongovernmental organizations. During the 1990s women leaders both inside and outside of government criticized the effects of national policies on women. Political leaders and the military victimized some women for their criticism of social policies: women's demonstrations were disrupted, they were jailed, their markets were burned, and they were forced out of public positions. Nevertheless, African women's experiences of the hardship of economic restructuring and the growing democratization of their societies during the 1990s have pushed them toward greater boldness in voicing their grievances and focusing attention on women's status within their societies.

The Cultural Roots of African Feminism

Africans, perhaps more than the peoples of other regions, tend to fuse nature and culture in their traditional conceptions of women's roles. Scholar Ali Mazrui has said that African women have controlled earth, fire, and water – three of the four elements in traditional culture. They have thus held responsibility for preparing food, acquiring fuel for cooking, and tilling the soil, in addition to other productive and reproductive tasks. Although Western observers stereotypically equate women's roles with "nature" and the domestic sphere of family, reproduction, household, and marriage (the private realm), and associate men's roles with "culture" and human complexity in political and economic roles (the public realm), this dichotomy does not hold true in Africa. Most African women combine roles as mothers and as economic contributors. The African feminists of the 1990s are – equally – mothers of several children, community participants, and public persons. African women have always sought to take on politically and economically responsible roles.

Thus African feminism builds upon a solid tradition of female inclusion in a wide variety of social roles in African cultures. The prevalent Western myth of an African "matriarchy" has no validity here, since women typically do not seek to dominate. Although African women are frequently assertive and strong, the norms of their own societies have usually shaped their roles. These norms situate gender relations within the context of social groupings, such as extended families and secret societies, or encourage what is called dual-sex organization, in which women form their own associations separate from male associations to accomplish their tasks. In some areas, such as West Africa, women's ability to form dual-sex groups in their own interest is highly developed, creating a façade of egalitarianism, while the tradition of separate women's groups is weaker in East and southern Africa. Dual-sex organization was also more firmly rooted in matrilineal areas of West and Central Africa, where descent was traced through women, than in patrilineal areas of East, West, and southern Africa, where men form the core of the family.

Although men generally dominated traditional African societies, women led wars of resistance against foreign powers. The Berber prophetess Kahina held back the Arab invasion in the eighth century; and the female prophetess Nehanda of Zimbabwe led her people in resistance to the imperialism of Cecil Rhodes during the late nineteenth century. Queen Mother Yaa Asantewa fought against British colonial conquest in the Asante kingdom (present-day Ghana). Women who were organized as sisters, wives, market women, and artisans could alter decisions they considered harmful to other women. The early twentieth-century example of the Aba Riots, or "Women's War," among the Igbo of Nigeria demonstrated women's ability to use their associations to protest colonial or community decisions that clashed with women's interests. However, as centralization and statehood emerged, rulers attempted to limit women and control the political process. This type of state bias against women increased during the nineteenth and early twentieth centuries, when colonial regimes (*see* Colonial Rule) attempted to conquer and reshape African societies.

Women have enjoyed representation in social groupings, for example through dual-sex organization, throughout most of African cultural history. This has been advantageous for African women, since they have been able to assume positions allotted to their kin groups within the community. Women could rise to positions of political, religious, or economic prominence if they belonged to prestigious families. Perhaps more consistently than in any other region of the world, there have been high-status female leaders all across Africa, from ancient Egypt to South Africa, including queens, queen mothers, chiefs, and priestesses. In matrilineal societies, the queen mothers, women chiefs, and priestesses were not feminists, but simply leaders and decision makers. Nevertheless, their leadership did inspire some female activism. Likewise, the dual-sex model is widely scattered across the continent, and often power is balanced between male and female leaders. The dual-sex model assumes its ultimate form in the dual-monarchy of king and queen mother, which exists in many AKAN societies, as well as in SWAZILAND. Women helped to shape the political traditions, charters, and constitutions of traditional African societies that were enshrined in proverbs, oral traditions, and myths of state.

Islamicization, colonial conquest, Christianization, economic crisis, and other changes over time have resulted in renegotiation of the traditional social contract. Often this has given rise to gender-biased relations and an attempt to exclude women from political life. Queen NZINGA of ANGOLA opposed Portuguese conquest by mobilizing those who supported her right to rule against those who opposed the notion of female leadership. However, in nearly every part of the continent, even in Islamic areas, the preexisting base of female involvement and activism escaped complete destruction, and often unique forms of female resistance emerged. In many countries African women found ways of linking new practices with older principles of women's participation and activism.

CONTEMPORARY AFRICAN FEMINISM

The crises in African economic and political life have caused serious hardship for women in the 1980s and 1990s, but this has also generated a new burst of African feminism. Previously, African states were hesitant to discuss women's issues and grievances publicly. However, they were not hesitant to accuse women of subversion or a lack of patriotism when their organizations demonstrated against state policies or when they lobbied international organizations to im-prove conditions for women. Often, African leaders targeted women when they acted collectively to protest wage cuts or artificially high food prices. Sometimes governments victimized female merchants and entrepreneurs by charging that these women were hoarding commodities or illegally producing products, and states defamed female aristocrats who offered political opposition.

It is not surprising that the economic arena has generated many defiant responses from African women and feminist organizations. Women are responsible for much of the farm work in Africa, but colonial rule and the market economy have often isolated women from sources of finance and sometimes damaged their traditional rights to own land. A result has been the concentration of resources in male hands. Women have noted that increasingly, under the pressures of the market economy, their families and lineages have fragmented. Men have divorced or delayed marriages, and men have migrated across borders seeking work in response to resource scarcity at home. During the 1980s and 1990s the International Monetary Fund and World Bank pressured African countries to implement structural adjustment programs that required cuts in health care, social services, and education. These programs harmed women and children disproportionately. But now, African women are refusing to suffer "down on the farm." Much of women's feminist activism in the 1990s is designed to focus state and public attention on the welfare of women and children, and to create new economic policies that are beneficial to the entire populace.

Likewise, although African women played important roles in nationalist politics or liberation struggles that brought their countries to independence, very few were chosen as government ministers or diplomats, and most were excluded from leadership positions in political parties. Nevertheless, women in such countries as CÔTE D'IVOIRE and KENYA used their astute knowledge to build women's political organizations that could apply pressure on political parties and begin to hold state politicians accountable to the community. The experiences of women in Côte d'Ivoire, Ghana, Nigeria, Kenya, and South Africa provide us with examples of effective feminist action in the current period of democratization and the struggle against military rule.

Now, at the dawn of the twenty-first century, African women have taken a leadership role in setting new economic and political agendas. One of the legacies of the United Nations Fourth World Conference on Women, held in Beijing in 1995, is that African women are determined to shape the policies of their countries. They have pushed for additional support for girls' education, including training for careers in industrial fields, the sciences, agriculture, or the professions, and for greater gender sensitivity in government and private-sector hiring policies.

Increasingly, African women have led national dialogues about women's human rights. In West and East Africa, and also in Zimbabwe, NAMIBIA, and South Africa, women are stepping up their campaign against sexism and exploitation. African feminists have opposed such practices as early marriage, female genital mutilation, women's exposure to acquired immune deficiency syndrome (AIDS) through unsafe sex practices (*see* AIDS IN AFRICA: AN INTERPRETATION), and various forms of medical neglect. In northern Nigeria and Côte d'Ivoire, as well as in South Africa and Kenya, Muslim women have argued that they can be good Muslim wives and mothers even as they pursue professional training, a role in community and regional dialogues, or public office (*see* FEMINISM IN ISLAMIC AFRICA).

African feminists today have fostered a greater awareness of the connections between gender and the political economy of the state by openly discussing the links between the public and private experiences of African women. They have challenged the reluctance to talk about gender conflicts, and they have prompted women to address collectively political actions that affect their lives. African feminists have generated a new model of what feminism is about and new feminist views of civil society, the family, and the state. They have stepped forward to defend their views in international gatherings of policy makers and feminists in the conviction that their approaches will yield more positive results for African local, regional, and national development than will feminist approaches that are imported from Western societies.

Gwendolyn Mikell

SEE ALSO

Egypt, Ancient Kingdom of; Mazrui, Ali A.; Structural Adjustment in Africa.

Africa

Feminism in Islamic Africa

Approximately one-third of Africa's population is Islamic, and a number of African countries identify themselves as Islamic states. Many goals of the feminist movement in Islamic Africa are common to feminist movements throughout the world – access to education (*see* EDUCATION IN AFRICA) and the labor market, and power in the world of public decision-making. But in Islamic Africa, the movement has also responded to the particular problems women face in their own countries, problems shaped by cultural identity and class.

HISTORICAL CONTEXT

The feminist movement in Islamic Africa draws on a rich tradition of women's political participation. In nineteenth-century EGYPT, middle- and upper-class women formed organizations that promoted modernizing projects such as health-care reform and girls' education. Other women participated in male-dominated political movements, especially the anticolonial resistance of the mid-twentieth century. The contribution of these women to nationalist struggles brought dangers unique to their sex: in ALGERIA, fighters such as Djamila Boupasha, raped by French military police while in custody, suffered sexual brutality during the quest for an independent nation.

Some of the women now considered forerunners of contemporary feminism might not have called themselves feminists. Women's groups and publications frequently took a decidedly conservative stance on such issues as family and childrearing (as they often still do), but they also provided a forum for women to collectively understand their lives within an Islamic world. According to feminist historian Mervat Hatem, even the bulk of Algerian women's contributions to the liberation struggle, such as nursing, cooking, and hiding weapons, could be seen as an extension and reinvention of women's traditional duties.

After independence, women's organizations in numerous countries, including Algeria, Egypt, and TUNISIA, were often linked to postcolonial governments. Civic funding for women's programs provided contraception, literacy training, or classes on domestic budget management, thus serving political and economic agendas as well as feminist ones. Other women's programs, from the 1970s to 1990s, were sponsored by international organizations such as the United Nations, or operated as small autonomous collectives. In the last 40 years women throughout much of Islamic Africa have gained the right to work and to vote. In Algeria women have been elected to the National Assembly; in Egypt they have entered the civil service as well as several professional fields in significant numbers.

In recent years Islamic feminists have begun to consider *which* women have gained from these reforms. Increasingly, they have acknowledged the extent to which class and culture mediate the role of Islam in African women's lives. For example, poor women have always worked outside the home throughout Islamic Africa, especially in rural areas. In addition, Islamic norms that govern gender relations or women's roles in one location may be entirely foreign to women in another. The religious and social standards applied to urban North African women may be unknown to Muslim nomad women in East and West Africa – or to women in the Islamic communities of coastal West Africa, where Muslim women have historically played highly visible roles in urban and regional trade. The priorities of these women have not always been the same as those of Islamic feminist leaders.

Feminism and Islam

In recent years the rise of Islam as a means of asserting national and cultural identity has shaped the feminist discussion taking place within Islamic societies in Africa. Feminists have questioned whether Islamic theology and law are inherently oppressive to women, or whether sexism lies in the ways in which the Koran and other Islamic texts have traditionally been interpreted by male-dominated institutions ranging from national governments to rural brotherhoods. They have also debated, along with their critics, whether feminism is a Western concept, and at odds with an Islamic society.

Most feminists in and beyond Islamic Africa agree that some of the feminist victories of the 1960s through the early 1980s have been eroded since the rise of Islamic fundamentalism in the late 1980s. In Algeria, feminists fought against the Family Code legislation passed in 1984, which counteracted feminist gains concerning such issues as equal inheritance and equal divorce rights. Today women who stray outside the conservative norms dictating female dress and behavior risk anything from public censure to state persecution to vigilante violence, particularly in Algeria. In response, new feminist groups have sprung up in Egypt, Algeria, Morocco, and Tunisia, often working with human rights groups.

Some of these activists argue that Islamic law itself is inherently patriarchal: Islamic law recognizes only patrilineal succession, in which children inherit titles and property from their fathers, while before the advent of Islam, many sub-Saharan societies observed matrilineal succession, in which mothers and their families controlled the inheritance of titles and property. In addition, Islamic law allows fathers to have custody of their children, and allows polygamy and unilateral divorce for men only.

Other African feminists argue that Islam and feminism are potentially compatible if interpreted in a profeminist way. According to scholar Mervat Hatem, feminist activists such as Malak Hifni Nassif and Huda Shaarawi in Egypt and Bechira Mrad in Tunisia call for a "synthesis" in contemporary Islamic society. They propose a model that would maintain the structure of traditional family life while affirming the value of women's education and employment outside the home.

Still other feminists, such as the Egyptian Nawal el Saadawi, argue that such an ideal ignores the fact that a Muslim woman's public and private lives cannot be separated. In Islamic cultures, the responsibility of maintaining tradition often falls upon women. Through childrearing, as well as her dress and conduct, a woman is expected to uphold her society's traditional values, both at home and in public. Furthermore, in many nations the norms and values of the private sphere are, in fact, encoded in civic law. Feminists have organized around these so-called Personal Status Laws since the early twentieth century. These national codes, which regulate marriage, family, and spousal relations, effectively legislate the rights of women. For example, even if a woman has a legal right to work or run for office, she may be lawfully restricted from these activities if her husband objects to them. Tunisia is often cited as the most progressive Islamic country because of its relatively liberal Personal Status Laws.

As the rise of Islamic movements has coincided with the ongoing globalization of Western media and culture, debates within the feminist community (and elsewhere) about norms and practices affecting Islamic African women have become increasingly charged. At stake, often, are claims to cultural authenticity. Three of the most controversial issues are the veil, female circumcision, and polygamy.

Since the wearing of a veil in observance of Islamic codes of modesty is relatively rare south of the Sahara, the veil is a subject of debate primarily in North Africa. There, many Islamic women see the veil as a symbol of the oppression of women's bodies and sexuality. In Algeria, women who refuse to wear the veil have been subject to discrimination and, sometimes, violence. But others, including some feminists, value the veil as a form of cultural expression that also allows women to escape unwanted sexual attention.

Female circumcision, the cutting, removal, or closure of female genitalia practiced in numerous North and sub-Saharan African societies – including many non-Islamic ones – has in recent years generated debate well beyond Africa. When Egypt's Health Ministry banned the practice in 1996, conservative religious leaders challenged the ruling, arguing that Islamic law condoned female circumcision. When Egypt's highest court upheld the ban in late 1997, anticircumcision groups worldwide rejoiced. Although feminists within Islamic countries have criticized what they consider a mutilation of women's bodies, not all Muslim women want the practice ended. In Egypt as well as other African countries, the older women who typically perform the circumcision operation often depend on the income it provides, and many mothers continue to have their daughters circumcised in order to assure that they will be marriageable. The issue is a complicated one, in which feminists fight to change not only the laws, but social notions of femininity as well.

Polygamy has also been a subject of heated debate. Whether or not a government has banned this age-old practice is often viewed as a key measure of how it treats women generally. Yet African women have various attitudes toward polygamy, depending often on age, class, and culture. For example, one woman might welcome the extra help and companionship of a co-wife – in rural areas especially, co-wives often share cooking and farming duties – while another might view a new wife as a threat to her own economic security and marriage.

These and other issues have provided material for a wealth of feminist activism, scholarship, and creative work in Islamic Africa. Nawal el Saadawi's now classic text *The Hidden Face of Eve* was a groundbreaking study from Egypt, and writers such as the Moroccan Fatima Mernissi are continuing a tradition of feminist scholarship. The lives of women in Islamic Africa have been portrayed in the fiction of authors such as Mariama Bâ from Senegal and Assia Djebar and Leila Sebbar from Algeria.

Marian Aguiar

See Also

Nationalism in Africa; Female Circumcision in Africa; Islam and Tradition: An Interpretation.

North America

Feminism in the United States

"Shall it any longer be said of the daughters of Africa, they have no ambition, they have no force?" asked Maria W. Stewart in 1831. "By no means," she answered. "Let every female heart become united." Stewart's call for black women's unity, together with calls offered by other prominent nineteenth-century black feminists such as Sojourner Truth, Mary Ann Shadd Cary, Harriet Tubman, and Lucy C. Laney, marked the origins of black feminism in the United States. These nineteenth-century black women laid the intellectual and political cornerstone of black feminism, but African American women in the twentieth century brought black feminism as a political movement, and black feminist thought as its intellectual voice and vision, to full fruition.

What Is Black Feminism?

Black feminism originated in the lived experiences that enslaved African women brought with them to the United States in the eighteenth and early nineteenth centuries. African women were socialized to be independent, self-reliant, and resourceful. While this African feminism was modified by slavery, being enslaved also encouraged black women to maintain these key elements of their African self-definitions as women.

Black feminism is the process of self-conscious struggle that empowers women and men to realize a humanistic vision of community. African American women's experiences with work and family during slavery and after emancipation led them to develop a specific perspective on the relationships between multiple types of oppression. Black women experienced not just racism but sexism, classism, and other forms of oppression. This struggle fostered a broader, more humanistic view of community that encouraged each person to develop his or her own individual, unique human potential. Such a community is based on notions of fairness, equality, and justice for all human beings, not just African American women. Black feminism's fundamental goal of creating a humanistic vision of community is more comprehensive than that of other social action movements. For example, unlike the women's movement in the United States, black feminism has not striven solely to secure equal rights for women and men, because gaining rights equal to those of black men would not necessarily lead to liberation for African American women. Instead, black feminism encompasses a comprehensive, antisexist, antiracist, and anti-elitist perspective on social change. Black feminism is a means for human empowerment rather than an end in and of itself.

Core Themes in Black Feminism

Since its inception in the early 1800s black feminism has reflected a uniformity of theme and philosophical outlook. Despite differences of age, sexual orientation, ethnicity, and regional origin within the country, all black women share the universal experience of being African American women in a society that denigrates women of African descent. This commonality of experience suggests that certain characteristic themes will shape black women's thought and activism. Contemporary black feminist scholars' efforts to reclaim a long-standing yet suppressed black feminist intellectual tradition reveal black women's historical attention to four core themes: the legacy of struggle, the search for voice, the interdependence of thought and action, and the significance of empowerment in everyday life.

One core theme has been the legacy of struggle against racism, sexism, and social class exploitation. Despite heterogeneity within the community, this legacy has fostered a heightened consciousness among black women intellectuals about the importance of thinking inclusively about how race, class, and gender shape black women's lives. The legacy of struggle against racism, sexism, and classism is a common thread binding African American women regardless of historical era, age, social class, or sexual orientation.

This legacy of struggle and its resulting humanistic vision differentiate black feminism from historical expressions of white feminism in the United States. While middle-class white feminists condemn the restrictions of affluence, most black women struggle against the oppression of racism and poverty. As a result, black feminists' central concern has been the transformation of societal relations based on race, class, and gender.

The search for voice or the refusal of black women to remain silenced constitutes a second core theme of black feminism. In order to exploit black women, dominant groups have developed controlling images or stereotypes claiming that black women are inferior. Because they justify black women's oppression, four interrelated controlling images of black women – the mammy, the matriarch, the welfare mother, and the jezebel – reflect the dominant group's interest in maintaining black women's subordination. Challenging these stereotypes has been an essential part of the search for voice.

Black women's lives involve a series of negotiations aimed at reconciling the contradictions of their own internally defined images of self as black women with these controlling images. Much black feminist thought reflects this search for a self-defined voice that expresses a black feminist standpoint. Being labeled "black women" makes African American women especially visible and exposes them to the negative treatment afforded black women as a group. From their experiences black women have developed a unique vision and voice that many have used as a source of strength. The controlling images of black women are so negative that they require resistance if black women are to have any positive self-images. For African American women, the search for voice emerges from the struggle to reject controlling images and embrace knowledge that is essential to their survival.

Another core theme is the impossibility of separating intellectual inquiry from political activism. This theme of the interdependence of thought and action stresses the connections between black women's ideas and their actions. Historically, black feminism has merged the two forms of expression by espousing a both/and orientation that views thought and action as a part of the same process. This both/and orientation grows from black women's experiences living as both African Americans and women, and, in many cases, in poverty. It is this interrelationship between thought and action that allows black women to see the connections among concrete experiences with oppression, to develop a self-defined voice related to those experiences, and to enact the resistance that can follow.

The last core theme in black feminism is empowerment in the context of everyday life. Black feminism cannot challenge race, gender, and class oppression without empowering black women to take action in everyday life. Black feminist thought sees black women's oppression and their resistance to oppression as inextricably linked. Thus, oppression responds to human action. Black feminist thought views the world as a dynamic place where the goal is not merely to survive or fit in, but to experience ownership and accountability. The very existence of black feminism suggests that black women always have a choice and the power to act, no matter how bleak a situation may appear to be. It also shows that although the empowerment of individual black women is important, only collective action can effectively eradicate long-standing political, social, and economic inequalities.

Empowerment for African American women is achieved through a variety of methods. Empowerment occurs when a formerly silent black mother in the inner city complains to school officials about her child's treatment. Empowerment happens when black women take organized political action through churches, sororities, community advocacy groups, civil rights organizations, and unions. Black feminism can incorporate a variety of political strategies to bring about a more humanistic and just community. The program is not built into the philosophy itself. Instead, the adage "make a way out of no way" captures the range of strategies pursued by African American women to empower themselves and others.

Despite its overall consistency of thematic expression, black feminism has not been expressed in the same way across different historical periods. Black feminism in the twentieth century can be divided into three major periods: Laying the Foundation (1890-1920), when black women organized a national political movement and first articulated black feminist thought; Working for Change (1920-1960), when black women advanced the humanistic vision in black feminist thought primarily within African American communities; and Contemporary Black Feminism (1960-present), when black feminism as a political movement and black feminist thought as its intellectual voice emerge. Each period has its own specific set of historical issues, distinctive organizational and institutional locations, and a resulting unique expression of the core themes of black feminist thought.

Laying the Foundation: 1890–1920

During the period from 1890 to 1920 African Americans organized on the national level, aiming to "live as we climb." The growth of Jim Crow segregation in schools, employment, political life, and public accommodations heralded deteriorating conditions in the South and fostered a mass migration of blacks to cities of the North. This increasing urbanization created African American communities that could support a range of ideas and organizations.

Politically, women struggled for suffrage and African Americans demanded political and civil rights, an end to the terrorism of lynching, and adequate standards of living. Spurred on by these catalysts, middle-class black women began to organize on a local level to undertake educational, philanthropic, and welfare activities. Black women's clubs were founded in a number of cities. The growth of black urban communities and the urgent needs of the poor gave rise to a national black women's club movement.

The National Federation of Afro-American Women was founded in 1896 and elected Margaret Murray Washington as its president. The National League of Colored Women was founded in Washington, D.C., in 1892. Together these two organizations represented more than 100 local black women's clubs. After their merger into the National Association of Colored Women (NACW) in 1896, Mary Church Terrell was elected president. The NACW became a unifying force, an authoritative voice in defense of black womanhood.

The black women's club movement was both an activist and intellectual endeavor. The leadership of the national organization worked not only to eliminate black women's oppression but also to produce analyses of that oppression. The work of these black feminist intellectuals was influenced by the four core themes of black feminism, particularly the merger of action and theory. The activities of early-twentieth-century black women such as Ida B. Wells, Fannie Barrier Williams, Mary Terrell, Anna Julia Cooper, and others illustrate that theme. These women produced analyses of subjects as diverse as the struggle for education, sexual politics and violence, race pride, racial prejudice, the importance of black women collectively defining black womanhood, and inclusion in white women's organizations. Since the vast majority of African American women in the early twentieth century were burdened both by long hours in either agricultural or domestic work and by shouldering the responsibilities of caring for families, they had little time to engage in either theorizing or organizing. The activities of the club women on behalf of all African American women, not just those of the middle class, remain noteworthy.

African American women in the black women's club movement did not identify themselves as black feminists. The concept shared by Wells, Terrell, and Cooper was much closer to Sojourner Truth's perspective – "I suppose I am about the only colored woman that goes about to speak for the rights of the colored women" – than to that of today's black feminists. Yet these women did construct and shape black feminism as a political movement and black feminist thought as its intellectual voice and vision.

To lay the foundation for black feminism, black women leaders challenged black women to reject the negative images of black womanhood so prominent in their times. Cooper, a black woman born into slavery and the recipient of an M.A. from Oberlin College in 1884 and a Ph.D. in Latin from the Sorbonne in Paris, spent the bulk of her life as an educator. In her book *A Voice from the South*, she described black women's legacy of struggle against racism and sexism by protesting black women's vulnerability to sexual violence: "I would beg… to add my plea for the Colored Girls of the South: – that large, bright, promising, fatally beautiful class… so full of promise and possibilities, yet so sure of destruction; often without a father to whom they dare apply the loving term, often without a stronger brother to espouse their cause and defend their honor with his life's blood; in the midst of pitfalls and snares, waylaid by the lower classes of white men, with no shelter, no protection."

Refusing to be silenced, Fannie Barrier Williams, the first black woman admitted to the Women's Club of Chicago and organizer of the first training school for black women in Chicago, championed the power of self-definition at the turn of the century, a period of heightened racial repression. Williams viewed the black woman not as a defenseless victim but as a strong-willed resistor: "As meanly as she is thought of, hindered as she is in all directions, she is always doing something of merit and credit that is not expected of her." She saw the black woman as "irrepressible. She is insulted, but she holds up her head; she is scorned, but she proudly demands respect…. The most interesting girl of this country is the Colored girl."

In their writings and teachings, early twentieth-century black feminists urged black women to forge their own self-definitions and to be independent and self-reliant. Through their actions in building a powerful national black women's club movement, they championed the utility of black women's relationships with one another in providing a community for black women's activism and self-determination. They analyzed why black women had such hard lives, and they empowered black women to make changes in their daily lives. This fusion of theory and activism is characteristic of black feminism, becoming the foundation on which subsequent black women were able to work for change.

Working for Change: 1920–1960

The Great Depression, the New Deal, World War II, and the Civil Rights Movement all brought sweeping changes in African American community structures and corresponding shifts in the organizational bases for black feminism. Heightened de jure segregation in the South and de facto segregation in the North during this period meant that most African American women lived in highly segregated environments. Since the majority of black women worked in domestic service, their contact with white people, especially white women, afforded few opportunities for interracial interaction among equals. Until the resurgence of national organizing in the Civil Rights Movement of the 1960s, the decline of the black women's club movement in the 1920s left most black women with few options for participation in national political movements.

The period from 1920 to 1960 seemingly lacked a self-conscious black feminist movement that both identified itself as such and that explicitly advanced the core themes of black feminism. However, racism during the 1930s through the 1950s was so pervasive that black women advanced a black feminist agenda primarily through existing black organizations. High participation in the labor force coupled with substantial family responsibilities meant that most African American women during this period had little time or inclination to participate in organizations designed exclusively to address issues unique to black women. By far the largest number of African American women either worked within existing black organizations, such as churches or local self-help groups, or participated in black political movements to ensure that black women and men alike would be treated with dignity. Thus, while they lacked the overarching organizational structure of a strong, national black women's organization expressing a black women's position, black women undertook activism generally in the context of fostering local black community development.

Those women who engaged in political activities such as starting schools or organizations typically aimed at building black community institutions. While some organizations were designed to address issues unique to African American women, the majority aimed to serve both women and men. This choice does not make black women less feminist – instead, it represents the feminism inherent in black women's humanistic vision of community. Instead of just talking about inequality between women and men, these women built institutions based on black feminist principles. In keeping with the black feminist core theme of the fusion of theory and action, their feminism was embedded in their actions. By working on behalf of everyone, they were in effect working for black women.

Mary McLeod Bethune's work reflects the complexity of how black women of this period saw their special mission of working for black women. Elected president of NACW in 1924, Bethune continued efforts to acquire a federal antilynching bill, help rural women and those in industry, train clerks and typists, and support the rights of black women globally. Bethune's effort to build the Daytona School for Girls into the coeducational liberal arts school Bethune-Cookman College demonstrates her commitment to black community development and offers a glimpse of how many black women worked for change during this period. Still, Bethune's noteworthy influence on national politics foreshadowed the actions of black women in the contemporary period. Her life marks the transition from the foundation-laying activities of early twentieth-century black feminists to the broad-based activities characterizing contemporary black feminists.

Black women worked on behalf of the core themes of black feminist thought although they rarely described their work in these terms. Each core theme was woven through black women's political work and much of everyday life. For example, black women working in the Civil Rights Movement during the 1950s advanced the humanistic vision of community in black feminist thought. Women like Fannie Lou Hamer, Rosa Parks, Ella J. Baker, and Septima Clark were tireless workers for black community development. Since it came out of church groups, the movement was carried largely by women. Many rural black women showed extreme courage. "Dyin' is all right," said Mary Dora Jones, who was told that her house would be burned down if she continued to let civil rights workers stay there. "Ain't but one thing 'bout dyin'. That's make sho' you right, 'cause you gon' die anyway." A similar view was expressed by Hamer, the daughter of sharecroppers and a Mississippi civil rights activist: "The only thing they could do to me was kill me, and it seemed like they'd been trying to do that a little bit at a time ever since I could remember." Women like Jones and Hamer did not call themselves "black feminists" – this naming occurred in a later period – but they clearly lived the core themes of black feminism through their actions.

The search for voice and the refusal to be silenced pervade the words and actions of a range of women throughout this period. For example, Jones, Hamer, and numerous women in the civil rights struggle used their voices to challenge white racism. Other women fostered a black feminist agenda by refusing to be silenced, even within the context of black-controlled organizations. Black feminist activist Pauli Murray was president of the 1944 class at the Howard University School of Law. Since she was also the only woman, she did not receive the same privileges as her black male classmates. The discovery of this fact, remembers Murray, "aroused an incipient feminism in me long before I knew the meaning of the term 'feminism.'"

In other cases black women acquired wide-ranging influence within black organizations and used their status to advance women's issues. For example, in the 1920s Amy Jacques Garvey's women's page in the *Negro World*, the newspaper of the Universal Negro Improvement Association, took a strong women's rights position. As Paula Giddings notes, "while she held no specific office, it would have been hard to find anyone with greater influence in the UNIA, save for Marcus Garvey himself."

The refusal to be silenced was not confined to women in political movements. Zora Neale Hurston's work, especially her widely read 1937 novel, *Their Eyes Were Watching God*, aimed to give voice to black women's thought through fiction. By placing black women's issues in the center of their work, other black women writers of this period – including Ann Petry in *The Street* (1946), Gwendolyn Brooks in *Maud Martha* (1953), and Lorraine Hansberry in *A Raisin in the Sun* (1959) – explored a black woman's standpoint as something framed by both blackness and womanhood.

A black feminist emphasis on the importance of empowerment in the context of everyday life finds expression in multiple locations during this period. For example, Ella Baker, a major figure in the Civil Rights Movement who worked closely with students, believed that teaching people how to be self-reliant fosters more empowerment than teaching them how to follow. Baker recounts how she nurtured the empowerment of student civil rights workers: "I never intervened between the struggles if I could avoid it. Most of the youngsters had been trained to believe in or to follow adults if they could. I felt they ought to have a chance to learn to think things through and to make the decisions." Baker and Clark were particularly consistent in forwarding a humanistic vision of community through their leadership styles.

Contemporary Black Feminism: 1960–Present

The fundamental distinguishing feature of contemporary black feminism is the self-conscious voicing of black feminist perspectives. Though turn-of-the-century black women laid the organizational framework of institutions and ideas on which subsequent black women built, until recently African American women neither called themselves black feminists nor identified what they were doing as working on behalf of black feminism. They worked on behalf of black women and advanced a black feminist agenda, but they refused to be categorized as solely advancing the special interests of any one group. In contrast, the contemporary period is characterized by the emergence of a broad-based movement that encompasses both traditional humanistic approaches and issues unique to black women. Contemporary black feminism embraces the key contributions of the two prior periods: articulating a black women's agenda and building an organizational base to advance core themes of black feminism. Contemporary black feminism expresses and gives voice to this long-standing, preexisting intellectual and political movement.

Contemporary black feminism advances the same core themes as its predecessors but does so from very different institutional locations and with a very different voice. Two major trends of the last 30 years fostered these changes. First, increasing social-class stratification among black women made more women available to think about and work on behalf of black feminist concerns. Black women graduated from high schools and colleges in record numbers, and they were no longer placed exclusively in domestic service jobs. Instead, they occupied previously unavailable positions, especially in academic institutions. The emergence of a sizable group of literate, middle-class black women meant that black feminist thought as the intellectual component of black feminism could be more readily advanced. This does not mean that only middle-class black women embrace black feminism. Rather, differential access to resources shapes black women's abilities to bring black feminism to voice.

Second, black women's growing sense of disenchantment with the racism in the women's movement and the sexism in the Civil Rights and Black Nationalist Movements led to a growing focus on black women's concerns. Specifically, black women in male-controlled nationalist organizations became increasingly unwilling to trade their silence for an ill-defined unity. Similarly, the narrow scope of the early phase of the contemporary women's movement – expressing the concerns of white middle-class women – held little appeal. African American women perceived that neither black organizations nor white feminist groups spoke fully for them. Thus emerged the need to develop a distinctive black feminist agenda that built on the core themes long guiding black women's actions yet simultaneously spoke to issues specific to African American women.

Contemporary black feminism dates to the efforts of numerous trailblazing African American women in the 1970s who stated black women's concerns as women. While these far-reaching efforts did not constitute a black feminist agenda per se, they did contain the powerful precursors of one. Toni Cade Bambara's publication of *The Black Woman: An Anthology* in 1970 marked the beginnings of a black feminist agenda. The black women in her anthology raise many issues still being explored today. For example, Frances Beale's article "Double Jeopardy: To Be Black and Female" provides a summary of race, class, and gender as interconnected oppressions. Several works of fiction also served to articulate black feminist thought. Ntozake Shange's 1975 choreopoem *For Colored Girls Who Have Considered Suicide/When the Rainbow Is Enuf*, Toni Morrison's 1970 novel *The Bluest Eye*, and Alice Walker's 1976 novel *Meridian* all raise issues specific to black women that have significance beyond black women. Echoing *Tomorrow's Tomorrow* – Joyce Ladner's groundbreaking 1972 study of black adolescent girls – social science researchers like Bonnie Thornton Dill, LaFrances Rodgers-Rose, and Cheryl Townsend Gilkes centered their work on the lives of African American women. Historians, including Jeanne Noble, Sharon Harley, Rosalyn Terborg-Penn, Darlene Clark Hine, and Elsa Barkley Brown, showed a willingness to ground their research in the lives and experiences of African American women. Paula Giddings's *When and Where I Enter: The Impact of Black Women on Race and Sex in America* (1984) provided an especially important synthesis of African American women's history. Political figures were increasingly willing to discuss their politics in the race-, class-, and gender-specific black feminist framework. For example, SHIRLEY CHISHOLM'S 1970 autobiography, *Unbought and Unbossed*, resonates with the core themes of black feminist thought.

Many black writers and scholars took the ideas first expressed in these diverse sources during the 1970s and began to hone them into black feminist theory. During the 1980s African American women developed black feminist thought by emphasizing the unique concerns of African American women and explicitly exploring the core themes in black feminist thought. Noteworthy examples of important contemporary works include Angela Davis's 1981 book on African American women's political economy, *Women, Race and Class;* bell hooks's 1981 analysis of black women and feminism, *Ain't I a Woman;* the groundbreaking 1982 essay by the Combahee River Collective, "A Black Feminist Statement"; Alice Walker's 1983 *In Search of Our Mothers' Gardens;* Barbara Smith's 1983 anthology of black women's writings, *Home Girls: A Black Feminist Anthology*, dealing with the overlooked issue of black lesbianism; Audre Lorde's important 1984 collection of essays, *Sister Outsider;* the works of black feminist literary critics, like Barbara Christian's 1985 *Black Feminist Criticism, Perspectives on Black Women Writers* and Hazel Carby's 1987 *Reconstructing Womanhood;* June Jordan's collections of political essays, *Civil Wars* in 1981 and *On Call* in 1985; and Filomina Chioma Steady's 1987 essay "African Feminism: A Worldwide Perspective." These works spoke to black women inside and outside academia who were developing black feminist thought.

By the 1980s the many decades spent building black feminism as a political movement and expressing its vision through black feminist thought had grown into a broad-based black women's movement located in a variety of organizational settings and expressing various interpretations of black feminism. While they choose multiple strategies, African American women of all types typically ground their actions in the core themes of black feminism.

Contemporary black feminism finds a home in multiple organizational settings. First, many black women belong to and remain active in traditional black women's organizations such as churches, sororities, and black women's clubs and local organizations. Others remain active in organizations devoted to black community development such as the NATIONAL ASSOCIATION FOR THE ADVANCEMENT OF COLORED PEOPLE and the NATIONAL URBAN LEAGUE.

Second, this period marks the formation of new black women's organizations. Some are housed within professional associations, such as the Association of Black Women Historians. Others represent black women organized to focus on specific issues. For example, the National Black Feminist Organization, founded in 1973, explicitly addressed the concerns of black women. The National Coalition of 100 Black Women, founded in 1981, focuses on voter registration and mobilization.

Third, black feminist intellectuals in academia have used their writings and teachings as vehicles for the spread of black feminism. *All the Women Are White, All the Blacks Are Men, But Some of Us Are Brave*, a 1982 anthology edited by Gloria T. Hull, Patricia Bell Scott, and Barbara Smith, was devoted to legitimizing black women's studies as a serious area of intellectual inquiry, and it offered a road map for black women academicians laboring to develop black feminist thought. Other works devoted to developing black women's studies and black feminist thought include *Black Womanist Ethics*, by Katie Geneva Cannon (1988); *Talking Back: Thinking Feminist, Thinking Black*, by bell hooks (1989); *Women, Culture, and Politics*, by Angela Davis (1989); *Black Feminist Thought: Knowledge, Consciousness and the Politics of Empowerment*, by Patricia Hill Collins (1990); and *Invisibility Blues*, by Michele Wallace (1990).

Fourth, black feminists have become actively involved in the women's movement and have begun to influence its purpose and direction. National women's organizations such as the National Organization for Women and the National Women's Studies Association are increasing efforts to grapple with race and class in their push for gender equality.

Fifth, black women who have acquired recognition or leadership positions in organizations and institutions that do not appear to be dealing directly with black women's issues have often used their positions to advance black feminist agendas. For example, during her tenure as the national head of Planned Parenthood, FAYE WATTLETON typically did not identify herself as being a black feminist but did advance programs perceived by many to be highly beneficial for black women. Bernice Johnson Reagon's work in African and African American culture at the Smithsonian Institution attends to black women as creators of culture. Marian Wright Edelman's founding and astute stewardship of the Children's Defense Fund, one of the most respected advocacy organizations in Washington, D.C., offers a similar example. Wattleton, Reagon, and Edelman tap a legacy of struggle wherein challenging the interconnectedness of race, class, and gender is a central tenet. Black women musicians like the five vocalists and one sign language interpreter in SWEET HONEY IN THE ROCK, as well as emerging black female rappers like Sister Souljah and QUEEN LATIFAH, demonstrate a willingness to raise their voices in song about black feminism.

Moreover, many black women who have been successfully elected to public office, such as Shirley Chisholm and Cardiss Collins, or who hold other governmental positions, such as ELEANOR HOLMES NORTON, MARY FRANCES BERRY, and PATRICIA ROBERTS HARRIS, have used their positions to advance a black women's vision of a humanistic community.

To an extent that they have not in prior periods, black feminism as a political movement and black feminist thought as its intellectual voice and vision find multiple expression in diverse organizational settings in the contemporary era. As the community of African American women has grown more heterogeneous, so has the expression of black feminism. Thus the foundation laid by early black feminists has supported and nurtured the complex and growing movement of today.

Patricia Collins

SEE ALSO

Slavery in the United States; World War II and African Americans; Antilynching Movement; Bethune, Mary McLeod; Bambara, Toni Cade; Brooks, Gwendolyn Elizabeth; Clark, Septima Poinsette; Cooper, Anna Julia Hayward; Davis, Angela Yvonne; Edelman, Marian Wright; Garvey, Marcus Mosiah; Great Migration, The; hooks, bell; Hurston, Zora Neale; Jordan, June; Lorde, Audre Geraldine; Morrison, Toni; Parks, Rosa Louise McCauley; Petry, Ann Lane; Racial Stereotypes; Shange, Ntozake; Terrell, Mary Eliza Church; Tubman, Harriet Ross; Walker, Alice; Wells-Barnett, Ida Bell; Black Nationalism in the United States.

Africa

Fennec, common name for a small canine of the deserts of North Africa.

The fennec's body is about 35.7 to 40.7 cm (about 14.1 to 16.0 in) long; the bushy tail is about 17.8 to 30.5 cm (about 7.01 to 12.0 in) long. The fennec is pale brown to almost white and closely resembles its relative, the fox, except for the erect ears, each of which is as large as the face. The fennec can dig with great speed, and when pursued it seems almost to dive into the sand. Its burrow is lined with a collection of soft material, such as bits of fur and feathers. The fennec usually sleeps during the day, coming out at night to seek its prey. It feeds mainly on mice, small birds, lizards, and insects and sometimes supplements this diet with fruit. The fennec sometimes drinks at water holes, although studies suggest that it need not do so. The ability of fennecs to go without water for indefinite periods of time is an adaptation to their desert habitat.

Scientific classification: The fennec belongs to the family Canidae. It is classified as *Vulpes zerda.*

Latin America and the Caribbean

Fernandes, Florestan (b. 1920, São Paulo, Brazil), a Brazilian social scientist who had a powerful influence on the study of race relations in Brazil, documenting the importance of race in Brazilian society and the existence of racial discrimination.

Florestan Fernandes was one of a group of social scientists who challenged the Brazilian myth of racial democracy, which held that racism was not a significant factor in Brazilian society (*see* Race and Class in Brazil: An Interpretation). Fernandes criticized what he termed the Brazilian "prejudice of having no prejudice." Together with other Brazilian and foreign social scientists, partly inspired and funded by the Race Relations Project of the United Nations Educational, Scientific, and Cultural Organization (UNESCO), Fernandes revolutionized the study of race, though his conclusions would later be the subject of much debate. According to fellow social scientist Carlos Hasenbalg, Fernandes "substantiated the significance of racism and racial discrimination in industrial and capitalist Brazil, but saw them as an archaic survival from the seignorial, pre-capitalist and pre-industrial past."

Fernandes was born in the city of São Paulo, Brazil, in 1920. His family's income was so limited that he was forced to interrupt his studies while attending middle school at around 14 years of age. He later finished school at Ginásio Riachuelo and was then admitted to the School of Philosophy at the University of São Paulo, where he studied social sciences, graduating in 1941. In 1945 and 1946 Fernandes completed his postgraduate work in sociology and anthropology at the Escola Livre de Sociologia e Política de São Paulo. He obtained a master's degree in social sciences with a thesis titled "The Social Organization of the Tupinambás," which became a classic in the study of Brazil's indigenous societies. He concluded a doctorate at the University of São Paulo in 1951 with a thesis titled "The Social Function of War in Tupinambá Society."

Fernandes began teaching sociology in 1953 at the University of São Paulo's School of Philosophy, Social Sciences and Literature. By 1964 he was already a full professor after concluding his postdoctoral studies with the thesis "The Integration of the Negro in a Society Without Classes." His vast academic output includes 36 books and numerous articles that address the themes of race, folklore, Marxism, education, and revolution, among many others. Some of his best-known books are *The Negro in Brazilian Society* (1969), *Folklore em questão* (1978), *Natureza sociológica da sociologia* (1980), *Ditadura em questão* (1982), *Que tipo de república?* (1986), *Nova república* (1986), and *Desafio educacional* (1989).

Fernandes's teaching career in Brazil went into abeyance for about a decade beginning in 1969, when the country's military dictatorship removed him from his position at the university. He became a titular professor at the University of Toronto from 1969 to 1972, when he returned to Brazil. He had earlier taught at Columbia University in New York City, from 1965 to 1966, and was a visiting scholar at Yale University in 1977. In 1978 he taught in Brazil once again, at the Pontífica Universidade Católica, and returned to the University of São Paulo's School of Philosophy in 1986. Fernandes has been active in Brazil's democracy movement as an adviser to the leftist Partido dos Trabalhadores (the Workers Party). In 1986 he was elected to the National Congress as a member of the Partido dos Trabalhadores. Brazil had by then returned to a democratic system based on universal suffrage, after more than 20 years of military dictatorship. Fernandes was a distinguished participant in the 1988 National Assembly, which drafted Brazil's Federal Constitution.

Michelle Gueraldi

See Also

Myth of Racial Democracy in Latin America and the Caribbean: An Interpretation; UNESCO Race Relations Project.

Latin America and the Caribbean

Fernández Robaina, Tomás (b. 1941), Cuban librarian and bibliographer. His works include *Bibliografía de estudios afro-americanos* (1969, Bibliography of Afro-American Studies), *La prosa de Guillén en defensa del negro cubano* (1982, The Prose of Guillén in Defense of the Black Cuban), *Bibliografía de temas afrocubanos* (1986, Bibliography of Afro-Cuban Themes), and *Bibliografía de autores de raza de color* (1988, Bibliography of Authors of the Colored Race) (*see* Cuba).

Africa

Fès, Morocco, a city in northern Morocco.

According to legend, Fès was founded in 807 C.E. by the great sultan Mawlay Idris II as two cities on opposite sides of the river Fâs, one Berber and one Arab. These accounts draw upon the renown of Idris II as a Berber ruler who brought together the imperial Arab culture with that of the indigenous Berbers, and made Fès the capital of the first Moroccan empire. Other accounts hold that Idris I built one city in 789, carving its boundaries into the earth with a pick-ax of silver and gold, and that his son founded the twin city across the river nearly 20 years later. The fact remains that the ruling family chose to locate their capital on a commercial crossroads along a main route to the eastern Maghreb and a route to the savanna kingdoms south of the Sahara. Enriched by trade, early Fès also became a center of Islamic scholarship, especially after the opening in 859 of al Qarawîyîn University, based in what is now the oldest mosque in North Africa.

When Fès came under the rule of the Umayyads Dynasty (980-1012), an Islamic Spanish population settled the city on the right bank and a Tunisian population settled on the left. The Almoravid sultan united these cities in 1069, turning Fès into a major Islamic metropolis. Under the reign of the Marinids (1258-1549) the city flourished, attracting scholars from throughout the Islamic world. The Marinids built the royal palace adjacent to the mosque, importing elements of both the culture of Andalusia (southern Spain) and North African architecture. They also built *mellahs*, walled compounds, around the city's Jewish quarter, ostensibly to "protect" the Jews but in effect creating a ghetto.

After Fès fell to the Sa'dians in 1549, Marrakech and Meknès became the chief imperial cities and the political significance of Fès declined. But the city maintained its status as an important center for religious scholarship as well as for the production of handicrafts such as the fez, a brimless hat worn by many Muslims. By the nineteenth century, many of the citizens of Fès were doing business with European traders and investors. The treaty establishing the French protectorate was signed at Fès in 1812.

Shortly afterward the French built a modern district, including an industrial quarter, but left the old city essentially intact. Today, traditional guilds based in the Medina, or old city, continue to oversee the production of traditional handicrafts, including pottery, leatherwork, carpets, and richly embroidered cotton and silk textiles.

The Medina's workshops, bazaars, and mazelike alleys have become popular tourist attractions, and many locals earn a full-time living as guides. Others work in the industrial quarters in oil-processing plants, tanneries, soap factories, and textile and flour mills. Fès is also a marketplace for produce from the surrounding fertile countryside, including beans, olives, grapes, and livestock.

Marian Aguiar

See Also

Marrakech, Morocco; Sahara Desert; Almoravids.

North America

Festivals in the United States,

celebrations that express African American identity.

The three types of African American festivals – coronation, emancipation, and commemoration – took place primarily in the North during the antebellum era. They served as occasions for challenging past and present assumptions about African Americans as well as opportunities to build solidarity between peoples of African descent in the United States. On these occasions, people attended dances, fairs, parades, picnics, and religious services. Many African American festivals originating in colonial times have provided models for contemporary marches and demonstrations such as those of Marcus Garvey and the CIVIL RIGHTS MOVEMENT.

One of the earliest African American celebrations was the coronation festival, or "Negro election." It emerged in mid-eighteenth-century New England and was modeled after the white community's state elections. In the Negro elections, which were organized by slaves and financially supported by masters, blacks elected a leader, preferably African born and of known royal descent. Slaves of wealthy masters were also favorable candidates because of their potential access to a greater pool of material resources and because slaves referenced status in their own community by the status of their master. Slaves and masters usually regarded the elected leader as a dignified, authoritative official. His multiple roles included negotiating in the interest of the slave community and resolving tensions between the slaves and masters. By electing their own leaders, African American slaves performed roles they had always been denied, thereby preparing themselves for participation in public affairs. Negro elections continued through the mid-nineteenth century.

Another coronation festival in which slaves united around an elected black leader was Pinkster. It derived from a Dutch celebration called *pfingster*, which African Americans adopted in the mid-eighteenth century. Pinkster took place on top of a hill in Albany, New York, close to an all-black cemetery and the place where several African Americans had been executed in 1793 for attempting to set fire to the city. Although a dark symbolism loomed over the festivities, it was attended by Dutch, French, German, and Native American peoples, which presented a rare opportunity to entertain the utopian notion of a harmonious, multiethnic society. This festival was especially popular in the early 1800s.

Between the AMERICAN REVOLUTION and the Civil War, slaves established a tradition of emancipation festivals in which religious and secular black leaders, free and slave, publicly evaluated African Americans' progress toward liberation and their capacity for self-government. These were occasions for remembering the contributions of blacks to the development of the United States, and of fostering race pride and race memory. Emancipation festivals involved major associations such as churches and temperance societies and were hotly debated in the press. They were relatively sober events often accompanied by vehement protest. Over the years, the orations of black speakers became increasingly aggressive in demanding freedom and the redressing of past grievances.

Though it is an emancipation celebration for most white Americans, the Fourth of July became a date of rebellion for many African Americans. Black leaders who spoke at early Independence Day celebrations encouraged free and enslaved blacks to seek moral improvement in order to become more worthy citizens. As the abolitionist movement (*see* ABOLITIONISM IN THE UNITED STATES) grew, however, the Fourth of July became an opportune time for black leaders to remind the nation of how the concept on which it was founded, liberty, was contradicted by the existence of slavery. In his famous address of 1852, "What, to the American Slave, is your Fourth of July?" FREDERICK DOUGLASS said, "Your prayers and hymns, your sermons and thanksgivings with all your religious parade and solemnity, are to him mere bombast, fraud, deception, impiety and hypocrisy – a thin veil to cover up crimes which would disgrace a nation of savages." In several Northern cities, the Fifth of July became a black alternative to the Independence Day holiday and an opportunity to advance the antislavery argument.

For one short period of time between 1808, the date of the official end of the slave trade, and the 1830s, January 1 was to slaves what the Fourth of July was to white Americans. At these emancipation festivals black leaders stressed the common origins of enslaved and freed blacks in the New World, and debated the colonization of Africa. New Year celebrations were held mostly in New York and Philadelphia, the Northern cities with the largest number of blacks. Although January 1 acquired new significance after 1863, when American slaves were emancipated, it never became a black national holiday. Some African Americans, such as those living in Boston, held emancipation festivals on the date that slavery was abolished in their state, July 14, as opposed to national or international dates of emancipation.

Beginning in 1834, African Americans celebrated August 1, the date of the abolition of slavery in the West Indies. On that date the British Parliament emancipated approximately 670,000 slaves, renewing enslaved African Americans' hope for general emancipation. At this time England, which had set an example for the United States to follow, and CANADA, which accepted fugitive slaves and protected them from slave catchers, became important symbols of liberation for African Americans. August 1 was observed in 13 different states and, like many emancipation festivals, was characterized by the contradictory moods of hope and despair, praise and denunciation.

The concept of freedom is central to both emancipation and commemoration festivals. Yet unlike emancipation festivals, which are associated with dates of liberation, commemoration festivals are associated with individuals who worked to achieve liberation. In 1814 slaves in Wilmington, Delaware, created a commemoration celebration called the Big Quarterly, which continues to be observed. It is a celebration in honor of Peter Spencer, founder of the Union Church of Africa, and is both religious and musical in character. Before emancipation slaves had to secure passes from their masters in order to attend, since Delaware was heavily policed against UNDERGROUND RAILROAD activities. The Big Quarterly spread to other parts of the country and became a celebration in honor of all religious black leaders and their determination to found autonomous churches.

Another commemoration festival in honor of a particular individual is called Jerry Rescue Day. In 1851, the year following the enactment of the Fugitive Slave Law, slaves in Syracuse, New York, staged a protest to commemorate the rescue of a slave named Jerry who ran away, then was captured and imprisoned temporarily while arrangements were made to return him to his master. Abolitionists broke him out of prison and set him free in the North.

African Americans celebrated other individuals during the antebellum era. The African American community in Cleveland, Ohio, commemorated NAT TURNER's 1831 Rebellion, while those in BOSTON, MASSACHUSETTS, paid tribute to CRISPUS ATTUCKS through the 1850s. The Jon Konnu (John Canoe) festival is still celebrated today in North Carolina. In all of these commemoration festivals, black revolutionaries, rebels, and fugitives were exalted as exemplars of the relentless spirit that should characterize the African American fight for freedom.

Unlike these localized, predominantly black American festivals, Carnival is internationally celebrated and attracts a racially mixed crowd (*see* CARNIVALS IN LATIN AMERICA AND THE CARIBBEAN). In the Caribbean and South America, the European Carnival tradition of the colonizers mixed with African festival traditions of the slaves to create a vibrant Creole celebration. Carnival traditionally takes place during the week before Lent. On this occasion people from different racial and socioeconomic backgrounds come together to indulge in food, drink, music, and dance. Carnival, which was for many slaves the only opportunity for revelry, has been interpreted as a "safety valve" that allowed poor and oppressed peoples to vent their pent-up frustration.

Although the largest and most famous Carnivals are held in Trinidad and BRAZIL, New Orleans in Louisiana hosts an equally renowned Carnival celebration featuring the Mardi Gras and ZULU parades. In the Mardi

Gras parade, some African Americans dress up as Native Americans, a motif also popular in the Brazilian Carnival, to celebrate the indigenous population's fighting spirit and ancestral worship tradition. The Zulu Parade emerged in the mid- to late nineteenth century as a separate Carnival event, since blacks were not allowed to participate in Mardi Gras. Though it is intended as a parody of the white paraders' royal parade, the Zulu Parade's African and minstrel motifs, such as blackface painting, have been criticized by members of the African American community as too burlesque.

Caribbean traditions continue to have an impact on African American culture through celebrations such as the West Indian Festivals of Toronto, Canada, and Brooklyn, New York. As more and more Caribbean peoples immigrate to the United States, their festivals grow in scope and influence, fostering a Pan-West Indian consciousness among African Americans.

Aaron Myers

See Also

Great Britain; Boston, Massachusetts; Creoles; Civil War, American; Free Blacks in the United States, 1619 to 1863; Fugitive Slave Laws; Garvey, Marcus Mosiah; New Orleans, Louisiana; New York, New York; Philadelphia, Pennsylvania; Thirteenth Amendment of the United States Constitution and the Emancipation Proclamation; Trinidad and Tobago; Abolition and Emancipation in Latin America and the Caribbean; Carnivals in Latin America and the Caribbean.

North America

Fetchit, Stepin **(b. May 30, 1902, Key West, Fla.; d. November 19, 1985, Woodland Hills, Calif.), American actor known for his film portrayal of stereotypical African American minstrel characters.**

Born Lincoln Theodore Monroe Perry, "Stepin Fetchit" became an almost mythical figure in African American popular culture. After attending a Catholic boarding school until he was 12, Perry joined the vaudeville circuit accompanied by comic Ed Lee performing a minstrel act called "Step 'n' Fetchit: Two Dancing Fools from Dixie." In the early 1920s Perry went solo and retained Stepin Fetchit as his stage name. As Stepin Fetchit, he became quite popular on the Theater Owners Booking Association (TOBA) performance circuit. After moving to Hollywood, Perry appeared in more than 40 films between 1927 and 1976, including *In Old Kentucky* (1927), *Judge Priest* (1934), and *The Steamboat Round the Bend* (1935).

See Also

Minstrelsy; Racial Stereotypes; Film, Blacks in American.

Fez, Morocco. Please see Fès, Morocco

Africa

Fiction, English-Language, in Africa, **an overview of African literature written in English.**

Since the 1960s African literature in English has garnered increasing international attention and literary awards and has made its way into classrooms worldwide. The novels of writers such as Chinua Achebe, Wole Soyinka, Ama Ata Aidoo, Ngugi wa Thiong'o, and Nadine Gordimer have introduced readers to histories and cultures still poorly understood outside Africa. In contrast to the ethnographies and travelers' accounts that long shaped the West's images of Africa, literature by African writers portrays diverse, dynamic societies and the complex human relationships within them. It has also helped validate African cultural traditions: in the words of Chinua Achebe, it has shown "that African people did not hear of culture for the first time from Europeans; that their societies were not mindless but frequently had a philosophy of great depth and value and beauty, that they had poetry and, above all, they had dignity." This validation has been critical to African audiences as well, since colonialism had propagated a myth of cultural inferiority not just abroad but among Africans themselves. But Anglophone African writers have not simply recorded African history and promoted African intellectual and cultural achievements. They have also contributed to world literature many thought-provoking works that are, above all, art.

Any attempt to generalize about African literature, even only about that composed in English, is immediately problematic: Africa is an enormous continent, and its literary movements and individual writers are highly diverse. In addition, much of what is considered African literature has been written by Africans living in the United States or Europe. Author Buchi Emecheta of Nigeria, for example, wrote her early novels about a young African woman in England while she herself was living there. These and other works about experiences of exile and immigration could also be considered literature of the diaspora (*see* Literature, African American and Literature, Black, in Spanish America). Africa is not always the primary point of reference even for African writers who remain in their home countries; the works of these authors deal with themes central to literature worldwide, such as identity, alienation, political struggle, romantic love, gender relations, religion, and childhood.

The first Anglophone novel published in Africa by a black African author was *Guanya Pau* (1891), by the Liberian J. J. Walters. A graduate of Oberlin College in the United States, Walters was perhaps influenced by the eighteenth-century writings of Africans abroad, including Phillis Wheatley and Olaudah Equiano. Thus an early relationship was established between African writing in English and that of the African diaspora (*see* Literature in Eighteenth-Century Britain and the United States).

Given the important role missionaries played in the spread of English, it is not surprising that early Anglophone works grappled with issues of Christianity. Some of these books, such as *Ethiopia Unbound* (1911), by journalist E. Casely-Hayford of Ghana, explored the fraught relationship between African identity and Christianity, providing a model for later nationalist works (*see* Nationalism in Africa). Others portrayed Christianity more sympathetically. In his novella *An African Tragedy* (1928), R. R. R. Dhlomo represented urbanization in South Africa as a morally corrupting force.

South African writers in the first half of the twentieth century also used literature to protest racism and economic inequality. One of the earliest works of black South African literature, the *Mafeking Diary: A Black Man's View of a White Man's War* (1900), by Sol T. Plaatje, recounted events during the Boer War. Plaatje's *Native Life in South Africa* (1916) protested the Natives Land Act (1913), a precursor to later apartheid laws. In the 1940s literature by Peter Abrahams and Alan Paton depicted the effects of Westernization on traditional ways of life and the extreme poverty of the black urban population. During the Sophiatown Renaissance in the 1940s and 1950s, fiction by writers such as Can Themba gained national recognition in *Drum*, a literary magazine edited by, among others, South African author Es'kia Mphahlele. Ironically, despite the prolific nature of black South African protest literature, works by white authors such as Paton reached a far broader audience; white authors were consistently afforded more freedom and opportunities than their black counterparts.

African writers have produced vivid representations of the experience of colonialism. Influenced by the philosophy of Négritude, Anglophone writers gave voice to this historical moment in the company of Francophone authors such as Albert Memmi, Léopold Sédar Senghor, and Ousmane Sembène. Nigeria led the publishing explosion that occurred during and after decolonization with Chinua Achebe's novel *Things Fall Apart* (1958), which is still one of the most famous novels ever written by an African author. It related the history of European colonialism in Africa from the point of view of the colonized. Focusing on an Igbo man's contentious relations with encroaching British administrators and missionaries, Achebe described the social upheavals wrought by colonialism on Igbo village life. Other African novels of this era probed the individual, psychological experience of colonialism. *A Grain of Wheat* (1967), by Ngugi wa Thiong'o of Kenya, centered on events surrounding the Mau Mau uprising in the 1950s but drew in stories of individual lives and references to Kikuyu myth. Organizing the plot around individual choices and intimate friendships, Ngugi created a vivid picture of the dilemmas faced by Kenyans who were waging armed rebellion against the British.

Many African writers attended missionary schools and then European universities, and their writings reflect their own struggles to navigate through a minefield of modern and traditional values. They portray characters torn, for example, between romantic love and obligations to respect their family's marriage arrangements, between the norms learned at school and those learned at home, and between the freedom and opportunities of the city or foreign country and the familiarity and security of the village. Women writers such as AYI KWEI ARMAH, Buchi Emecheta, and Tsitsi Dangarembga gave voice to the challenges particular to women in postcolonial Africa (*see* WOMEN WRITERS IN ENGLISH-SPEAKING AFRICA). In her novel *Changes* (1991), for example, the Ghanaian Ama Ata Aidoo explored a woman's difficult decision to leave her polygamous marriage. The psychological narrative work of South African-born BESSIE HEAD in *A Question of Power* (1973) used the trauma of a mental breakdown to portray the life of a woman on the margins of society.

Anglophone writers in Africa have challenged postcolonial state power and social hierarchies, often at risk to their own lives. Many authors aimed their barbs at government corruption and violence. In the wake of Nigeria's civil war, for example, Wole Soyinka's play *Madmen and Specialists* (1971) portrayed a cannibalistic genocide. In *The Beautiful Ones Are Not Yet Born* (1968), the Ghanaian novelist Ayi Kwei Armah portrayed a society decaying under a corrupt neocolonial state. Like a number of politically engaged writers across Africa, SOMALI NURUDDIN FARAH wrote fiction that offended government authorities, and he was forced into exile by the military regime of MUHAMMAD SIAD BARRE. Undoubtedly inspired by the events in his home country, Farah published *Sweet and Sour Milk* (1979), the first in a trilogy he titled *Variations on the Theme of an African Dictatorship*. In Nigeria the novel *Sozaboy: A Novel in Rotten English* (1985), by Ken Saro-Wiwa, exposed the corruption of Nigeria's military government. Even authors concerned primarily with stylistic experimentation – such as Nigerian author BEN OKRI – have continuously engaged the contemporary social and political issues of Africa in their work.

South Africa's apartheid regime lasted long after most African colonial regimes had withdrawn, and it remained a central theme in a wide variety of South African writings. Short stories by ALEX LA GUMA, such as those in the noted collection *A Walk in the Night* (1962), highlighted economic inequalities through vivid portrayals of township poverty. *Muriel at Metropolitan*, a 1979 autobiographical novel by MIRIAM TLALI, told of a young black educated woman making her way in a divided country. *Waiting for the Barbarians* (1980), by J. M. Coetzee, was an unforgettable account of the psychology of domination written from the point of view of a rural magistrate who uncovers his own complicity in oppression. *Burger's Daughter*, a novel by the Nobel Prize winner Nadine Gordimer, portrayed a regime so oppressive that the novel's heroine – a young white woman whose parents have already been jailed for Communist Party ANTIAPARTHEID MOVEMENT activities – is eventually compelled to join the struggle herself.

As writers explored the social and psychological legacies of colonialism and apartheid, they also began to examine the ways in which their own writing related to this history. For some, writing in English became increasingly problematic. Ngugi wa Thiong'o eventually decided to write literature only in Kikuyu because, as he said, "Language carries culture, and culture carries, particularly through orature and literature, the entire body of values by which we perceive ourselves and our place in the world." Achebe, on the other hand, saw English as a necessary tool in building a body of African literature that would be accessible to readers throughout the continent as well as abroad.

Other African authors have experimented with writing styles in order to draw on their own diverse cultural and literary backgrounds. Most but not all the novels about colonialism and independence struggles were written as realist narratives, which made them easily accessible to Western audiences. Yet Africa's own traditions of song, poetry, myth, and allegory incorporate a rich variety of styles and metaphors. Many authors have drawn on elements from these traditions, for example by giving characters mythical names. Some writers, such as the Nigerian AMOS TUTUOLA, author of *The Palm-Wine Drunkard* (1952), have modeled their writing on oral storytelling traditions. Nigerian Nobel Prize winner Wole Soyinka's fictional works often weave YORUBA mythology into contemporary story lines. Booker Prize-winning Nigerian Ben Okri has developed a style many have compared to magical realism, incorporating both traditional mythic influences and influences of European modernism to explore issues such as urban poverty, bureaucratic corruption, and the exploitation of power by an elite minority.

It is important to realize that the African literature that reaches international audiences represents only a small portion of the literature produced in Africa. Literary critics, elite literary prize committees, and publishing companies together have shaped the canon as we see it. The internationally recognized canon of African literature in English has also been defined in part by historical circumstances. For example, Nigerian and South African writers tend to predominate in anthologies and academic coursework on African Anglophone literature. Their renown reflects the fact that they come from countries with large populations, relatively high literacy rates, and active literary movements and magazines, but their writing should not be assumed to represent the entirety of African Anglophone literature.

Marian Aguiar

SEE ALSO

Casely-Hayford, Joseph Ephraim; Christianity, African: An Overview; Decolonization in Africa: An Interpretation; Sophiatown, South Africa; Liberia; Mau Mau Rebellion; Paton, Alan Stewart; Senghor, Léopold Sédar; Plaatje, Solomon Tshekisho; Saro-Wiwa, Kenule Beeson; Ousmane Sembène; Urbanism and Urbanization in Africa; Coetzee, John Maxwell; Christianity: Missionaries in Africa.

North America

Fields, Mary (b. 1832?, Tenn.; d. 1914, Cascade, Mont.), African American stagecoach driver whose colorful life symbolized the freedom that some blacks found on the nineteenth-century American frontier.

Mary Fields was born a slave in Tennessee, but little else is known of her early life. Some historical accounts have placed her on the Mississippi River in the early 1870s, and at least one researcher claims that she was a passenger on the *Robert E. Lee* when it raced the steamer *Natchez* in June 1870. By 1884 Fields was living in Toledo, Ohio, working for an order of Ursuline nuns as a handywoman. She became attached to the mother superior of the convent, Mother Amadeus, who is variously reported as a close friend or the master in a master-servant relationship. Shortly after Fields arrived at the convent, Mother Amadeus left for Montana to open a school for Blackfeet Indian girls. When she fell ill in Helena, Fields came to her aid and decided to stay in Montana.

Fields assisted the Catholic mission, helping to build a new convent and to deliver food and cargo from depots to the mission. She was said to be 1.8 m (6 ft) tall, to weigh more than 91 kg (200 lb), and to be more than a match for the wild animals and anything else that might threaten her cargo. At the same time Fields gained a reputation at the mission and nearby towns for her terrible temper. She often fought with the hired men, one time going so far as to enter a gun duel. After the Catholic bishop in Helena received several complaints about Fields, she reluctantly moved away.

Apparently with the help of Mother Amadeus, Fields established a restaurant in Cascade, a village 100 km (60 mi) north of Helena. The restaurant failed, in part because Fields allowed customers who were short of money to run up credit. Her next job, in the 1890s, was as a stagecoach driver for the United States government, again a position that Mother Amadeus helped her obtain. Dressing in men's clothes, smoking cigars, and drinking in saloons, she carried freight and passengers between Helena and Cascade.

Many of her passengers were unaware that she was a woman in her sixties.

In 1903 Stagecoach Mary, as she had become known (she was also called Black Mary), retired and settled in Cascade. She was the only African American in town. She washed laundry to make money and, her temper tamed and her character by now legendary, became popular with the townspeople. The mayor of Cascade allowed her alone among women to drink and smoke in the saloons with men. When the owner of a local hotel leased it, he is said to have done so with the proviso that Fields continue to be fed there for free. Fields was also one of the most devoted fans of the Cascade baseball team, presenting them with flowers from her garden for a good play, and the team rewarded her by making her something of a mascot. Because her birthday was unknown, Cascade often celebrated it more than once a year, and when her laundry business burned down in 1912, many of the townspeople contributed to its reconstruction.

See Also

American Indians.

Latin America and the Caribbean

Fierro, Francisco "Pancho"

(1810-1879), self-taught mulatto artist who became one of Peru's most famous *costumbrista* painters (*see* Art in Latin America and the Caribbean).

North America

Fifteenth Amendment to the United States Constitution,

amendment ratified on March 30, 1870, that guaranteed African American men the right to vote.

The Fifteenth Amendment states that "the right of citizens of the United States to vote shall not be denied or abridged by the United States or by a State on account of race, color, or previous condition of servitude." The text also gives Congress the power to enforce the amendment. Although African Americans had been freed from slavery and made citizens after the Civil War by the Thirteenth and Fourteenth Amendments, Southern states used a variety of tactics, including violence, to keep blacks from voting, and even some Northern states had not given blacks the franchise. Radical Republicans in Congress proposed the Fifteenth Amendment to rectify this problem.

Most people, blacks and whites alike, believed that the franchise was the best assurance of progress and success for the freedpeople. Most whites felt that the right to participate in the political process was, in fact, all the nation owed the former slaves. But debate immediately arose over how strongly worded the amendment should be. Many Republicans feared that if the language was not strong, the South would keep blacks from voting through such indirect means as poll taxes and violence. Other Republicans, however, believed that all states – Northern and Southern – should have the right to keep illiterate citizens from voting. (Many Northerners feared the growing influence of foreign immigrants and wanted the literacy test to limit their power.) The resulting compromise was the Fourteenth Amendment, which was ratified with the

help of Reconstruction governments in the South, but which soon proved incapable of guaranteeing the franchise for blacks.

For a brief period during RECONSTRUCTION many African Americans voted, and some were elected to public office. In the late 1870s, however, enthusiasm for ensuring black equality waned in both the North and the Republican Party, and by 1877, when federal troops were withdrawn from the South, blacks were left to the power of whites committed to "redeeming" the South – that is, to restoring white supremacy. To quash the black vote, Southern states employed the poll tax, which poor blacks (and whites) were hard-pressed to pay; the literacy test, which uneducated blacks were ill-equipped to pass; confusing election procedures, which were not explained to blacks; and the grandfather clause, which allowed anyone whose father or grandfather had been registered to vote before the Fifteenth Amendment – in other words, almost any white man – to continue voting even if he could not pay the poll tax or pass the literacy test.

Where these methods failed, Southerners established whites-only voting in party primaries (which guaranteed election as the South became overwhelmingly Democratic) or gerrymandered electoral districts, thus diluting the strength of black voters. Most effective were intimidation and violence, including cross burnings, forced unemployment, imprisonment on trumped-up charges, house and church burnings, rape, beatings, and murder.

Not until the twentieth century would the Supreme Court invoke the Fifteenth Amendment in striking down state grandfather clauses and white primaries. But such changes had little effect on black voting: during World War II, only 5 percent of Southern blacks were registered to vote. Not until the VOTING RIGHTS ACT OF 1965 did discrimination in voting begin to end and did courts enforce the Fifteenth Amendment.

SEE ALSO

Slavery in the United States; World War II and African Americans; Civil War, American; Fourteenth Amendment to the United States Constitution; Thirteenth Amendment of the United States Constitution and the Emancipation Proclamation.

OPPOSITE: This 1870 lithograph celebrating the passage of the Fifteenth Amendment shows recently emancipated African Americans engaged in education, work, and political life. *CORBIS*

North America

Fifty-fourth Regiment of Massachusetts Volunteer Infantry, **one of the first black Union regiments of the AMERICAN CIVIL WAR (1861-1865), whose bravery in battle convinced many white Northerners that blacks not only were willing to fight but could do so with ability.**

At the beginning of the American Civil War, thousands of blacks throughout the North volunteered for service in the Union army but were declined. President Abraham Lincoln believed that the war would be short-lived and feared that enlisting black volunteers would unnecessarily antagonize the South. He was also afraid of losing the support of the four slave-owning border states that remained tenuously loyal to the Union, as well as alienating the North's large number of proslavery (or at least nonabolitionist) Democrats. Both the border states and Democrats, it was assumed, would have seen the enlistment of black troops as a sign that the North meant to abolish slavery, which was not an original aim of the war.

As the war widened, however, it became clear that the Union Army needed more manpower. Not only were Northern blacks not contributing, but freed Southern slaves in Union-occupied lands were either returned to their owners or used by the army, if at all, for labor. Moreover, slaves in the Confederacy contributed mightily to the wartime economy, freeing white Southerners to fight. In the summer of 1862 Congress authorized Union troops to confiscate Southern property, including slaves, who could then be used in military-support roles. Congress hoped the act would give slaves an incentive to flee toward advancing Union troops. In September Lincoln issued a preliminary Emancipation Proclamation freeing slaves and allowing the entry of both newly freed slaves and Northern blacks into the armed services.

John A. Andrew, the abolitionist governor of Massachusetts, authorized the formation in his state of a black regiment to be led by white officers. In early 1863 Col. Robert Gould Shaw, the 25-year-old son of a prominent Boston antislavery family, was given command of the Fifty-fourth Massachusetts Volunteer Infantry. Blacks, some from elite families (two sons of FREDERICK DOUGLASS were among the troops), came from throughout the North to serve in the regiment. The officers were drawn from New England's white elite, mostly from families with abolitionist views.

Although the Fifty-fourth Massachusetts was among the best known of the black regiments, it was not the first. In 1862 several Union commanders fighting in the lower Mississippi Valley, on the Kansas-Missouri border, and in the South Carolina Sea Islands had quietly organized black troops and sent them into combat. Although these early black soldiers fought with distinction, their actions were little publicized. Many Northerners remained dubious as to whether blacks would make good soldiers, and the new black troops were relegated largely to support roles.

The Fifty-fourth completed its training in May 1863 and in July was sent from Boston to the South Carolina Sea Islands, at the mouth of Charleston Harbor. Confederate troops were stationed on several of the harbor's protective islands, including a well-guarded garrison at Fort Wagner on Morris Island. Fort Wagner was buffered on one side by ocean and on the other by swamp, leaving only a narrow neck of thick-sanded beach for a land approach. On the evening of July 18, several Union regiments were ordered to attack the fort by land, and the Fifty-fourth, numbering about 650 men, was placed at the front of the charge.

The fort was believed to be weakened by earlier shelling from the Union Navy. But as the Fifty-fourth soon discovered, the Confederate base was largely untouched, allowing its occupants to rain shells and gunfire on the Union troops. Suffering devastating casualties, the Fifty-fourth nonetheless advanced to the fort's walls, breaching its defenses. Colonel Shaw was killed on the rampart. William H. Carney, the Fifty-fourth's standard bearer, was shot in both legs, the chest, and one arm but dragged himself to safety with the colors aloft. He became the first black recipient of the Congressional Medal of Honor. Finally overwhelmed, the Fifty-fourth and other Union regiments retreated; almost half of the Fifty-fourth's officers and enlisted men were killed or wounded.

A correspondent from the *New York Tribune* gave a vivid report of the battle for Northern readers, prompting widespread praise from politicians, writers, and abolitionists. Thereafter, the ability of the black soldier largely ceased to be an issue of debate, and the idea of freeing Southern slaves also became much more popular. These events helped Lincoln change the war from a fight exclusively to end a rebellion against the United States government to a moral fight to end slavery. The events also hastened the enlistment of black troops – 186,000 of whom were mustered in the next three years.

The Fifty-fourth Massachusetts also played an important role in gaining equal pay for black soldiers. In 1862 the federal government authorized payment to black soldiers but at a lower wage than to white soldiers. The Fifty-fourth refused to accept any pay until it was the same as whites'. Following the battle at Fort Wagner, the movement to equalize pay grew in strength, and in the summer of 1864, Lincoln's attorney general ruled that all soldiers were entitled to the same pay. Congress passed an act making it so, and in late 1864 the soldiers of the Fifty-fourth received their back wages.

With the death of Shaw, Col. Edward N. Hallowell, who was seriously wounded at

Wagner, took command of the regiment. Several months passed while the unit filled with new recruits. In early 1864 the replenished regiment was part of a force that occupied Jacksonville, Florida, without resistance. A wing of the Union forces, including the Fifty-fourth, continued inland from Jacksonville; at Olustee, they were met by a large and well-supplied Confederate force. Ill-supplied and poorly prepared, the forward Union regiments were routed until the Fifty-fourth Massachusetts and another black regiment reinforced them from the rear – saving them from complete devastation at the cost of heavy casualties to themselves.

Near the end of the war the Fifty-fourth fought in several campaigns in Georgia and South Carolina, and was among the first of Northern troops to occupy Charleston. Throughout their tour of duty, the Fifty-fourth and other black regiments fought with the knowledge that they might be enslaved or executed if taken prisoner. The Fifty-fourth Massachusetts was mustered out in August 1865. The movie *Glory* (1989), which told the story of the Fifty-fourth, created popular interest in the black regiments of the Civil War.

See Also
Slavery in the United States; Abolitionism in the United States; American Anti-Slavery Society; Military, Blacks in the American; Free Blacks in the United States, 1619 to 1863.

Latin America and the Caribbean

Filhos de Gandhi, the largest and most famous of the *afoxés*, or black Carnival organizations, in Salvador, Bahia, with processions that are closely associated with the Afro-Brazilian religion of Candomblé.

Members of Filhos de Gandhi, a well-known Afro-Brazilian *afoxé*, gather in the streets of Salvador, Bahia, to celebrate Carnival. *Vantoen Pereira, Jr./Contexto*

Filhos de Gandhi (Sons of Gandhi) is part of a long tradition of black socioreligious organizations called *afoxés* that began in the late nineteenth century. Pândegos da África (Revelers of Africa) was one of the first afoxés to parade in Salvador's Carnival, bringing the ceremonial songs and dances of the Candomblés to the street celebration. With the advent of the Getúlio Vargas dictatorship in 1930, the Brazilian government repressed afoxés and other manifestations of Afro-Brazilian religion. By the beginning of the 1970s the only remaining afoxé was Filhos de Gandhi, and it was almost defunct. The growth of black pride during that decade, however, breathed new life into Filhos de Gandhi and, following their example, several more afoxés began to appear at Salvador's Carnival.

Filhos de Gandhi was founded on February 18, 1949. It was named after India's famous independence leader Mahatma Gandhi, who had been assassinated a year earlier. The stevedores who founded this afoxé were inspired by the American film *Gunga Din* (1939) and by Gandhi's message of peace and nonviolent resistance. In accordance with Gandhi's decree that alcohol and women can disrupt an organization's internal peace, the group follows a male-only admission policy. In contrast to the frenzy of Carnival, the Filhos de Gandhi's procession is solemn. They carry banners picturing Gandhi and dress themselves in white turbans, sandals, white robes, blue socks, and blue-and-white sashes. For these reasons, their procession has been referred to as the White Blanket of Peace. In 1983 their theme was East Indian Originality, but they remained faithful to Candomblé traditions, wearing strings of beads representing different orixás and singing "Salutation to Oxulá." This song, whose chorus praises Gandhi as *Babá*, the Yoruban word for father/elder, reflects the syncretic character of Carnival.

Many have credited Brazilian musician Gilberto Gil with the revitalization of Filhos de Gandhi. Motivated by the heightened black consciousness of the 1970s, Gil sought out the afoxé that he remembered from his childhood. He said, "I found about 20 of them, with their drums on the ground, in a corner of the Praça da Sé [in the historic neighborhood of Pelourinho in Salvador]. They didn't have the resources, nor the will, to take part in Bahian Carnival." He joined the group, committing himself to their philosophy of spiritual discipline, and beginning in 1976 paraded with them for six consecutive Carnivals. He recorded the afoxé "Patuscada de Gandhi" (The Revelry of Gandhi) on his 1977 *Refavela* album. Gil's energy and prestige revitalized the afoxé, whose membership increased to 1000 members by 1980 and to more than 4000 by 1990. Filhos de Gandhi's rise to prominence has led to the creation of the first all-female afoxé, Filhas de Gandhi (Daughters of Gandhi [est. 1981]), and the first children's afoxé, Gandhi Erê.

Aaron Myers

SEE ALSO

Afoxés/Blocos Afros; Carnivals in Latin America and the Caribbean; Salvador, Brazil.

North America

Film, Blacks in American, a historical overview of black filmmaking and the portrayal of blacks in American film.

The thread of African American history is spun from two sources: the struggle to define a place in the wider American life and the effort to maintain an authentic black presence in the larger American culture. This duality has meaning in the realm of filmmaking because the tools of cinema – film and cameras – cost more than the paper and pencil tools of writers. It is the cost of doing business that affects, indeed, threatens the black presence on the screen.

The costly collaborative nature of filmmaking has blurred the definition of a "black" movie. Is it black if it is merely angled toward blacks, or must it be made by blacks, or both? Critics disagree, although a few traits of black films seem characteristic. They might be either pastoral, speaking nostalgically about a rural past, such as Spencer Williams's pious *The Blood of Jesus* (1940), or hip and urbane, in a current jive idiom, such as OSCAR MICHEAUX's *Swing* (1938) or BESSIE SMITH's *St. Louis Blues* (1929). Some black movies have provided a voice of advocacy, such as the Colored Players' *The Scar of Shame* (1927), in which an old lecher mourns the heroine whose passing reminds him that "our people have much to learn." Others have celebrated small victories, such as Michael Roemer's *Nothing but a Man* (1963), with a lead actor who will fix flat tires for a living but knows that he will never take on the stereotypical role of "picking other people's cotton." This theme is echoed in Ivan Dixon's *The Spook Who Sat by the Door* (1973), in which a cabal of black heroes joyously mounts an all-but-hopeless black insurrection.

Often a black movie provides an anatomy of black cultural life, a glossary of style, patois, and politics, such as Michael Shultz's *Car Wash* (1976). Sometimes a so-called crossover movie finds an audience on both sides of the racial divide by drawing on a black cultural trait that speaks to black *and* white audiences. King Vidor's *Hallelujah!* (1929), for example, used the metaphor of a railroad train going to hell much as Eloyse Gist, the black evangelist, had done in her own *Hell Bound Train*, each conveying the same sense of pious urgency entwined with an almost erotic sensibility. In much the same way, Spike Lee, in his *Do the Right Thing* (1989), drew a crossover audience into a dramatic debate over what, indeed, the right political thing *was*. Sometimes a black-angled movie succeeds as a crossover because it successfully mingles cultures. For example, Marcel Camus's *Orfeo Negro* (1959) retold the Greek myth of Orpheus and Eurydice, set in the annual Afro-Brazilian Carnival (*see* CARNIVALS IN LATIN AMERICA AND THE CARIBBEAN). In Trevor Rhone's *The Harder They Come* (1973), the REGGAE singer JIMMY CLIFF plays a victim of a sleazy recording-industry boss. Driven to a life of outlawry, Cliff adopts a fantasy life of revenge in the mode of an American cowboy (not unlike Travis Bickle in Martin Scorsese's *Taxi Driver*). And in almost any PAUL ROBESON or JOSEPHINE BAKER film of the 1930s, the theme involves a poignant outreach across racial cultures.

In any case, African American movies, whether so-called race movies made for black audiences or crossovers for a wider reach, arise from "the particular cultural conditions" (as the historian Gerald Mast wrote) of black life and history that surely "influence, if not dictate" the imagery and voice of black film. Therefore, the black critic James Snead has argued that a black cinema must "coin unconventional associations for black skin within the reigning film language" to replace well-known stereotypical images.

THE SILENT ERA

African American images first appeared on the screen in 1898, only months after the first theatrical projection of moving images. At first benign in their effect, the earliest films showed black soldiers embarking for the SPANISH-CUBAN-AMERICAN WAR and West Indians at their daily tasks. In 1903 a

1973's *Cleopatra Jones* starred Tamara Dobson, pictured here in a fight, in an action-packed spy thriller of the blaxploitation era. *CORBIS/Bettmann*

14-minute Uncle Tom's Cabin appeared. Thereafter, as editing for narrative effect improved, black figures fell more in line with the racial stereotypes of the day, appearing as chicken thieves, venal preachers, and the like. They only rarely turned up in marginally authentic roles in films such as *The Fights of Nations* (1907), which at least depicted black culture, albeit in a warped form. As thc 50th anniversary of the Civil War approached in 1910, collective nostalgia for the war inspired maudlin tales of fraternity. Black slaves, once the focus of the combat, were reduced to sentimental figures who often sided with their Southern masters against their Northern liberators. The most renowned and artistically the most compelling of the genre was D. W. Griffith's The Birth of a Nation (1915).

The first steps toward a specifically black cinema arose out of these rituals of white chauvinism. Bill Foster, an African American whose work has been lost, made such films as *The Railroad Porter*, probably a light comedy set in a particularly black milieu in 1912. *The Birth of a Race* (1918), two years in the making and perhaps three hours in length, began as a response to Griffith's film. But its succession of producers and backers, including Booker T. Washington's Tuskegee circle, Universal Pictures, and Julius Rosenwald of Sears, Roebuck, lost touch with the original concept. Nonetheless, it inspired George P. Johnson and his brother, Noble, to found the Lincoln Motion Picture Company to carry forward the quest for a black cinema, only to fail because of a nationwide influenza epidemic that shuttered theaters.

After World War I the American movie industry gradually moved to California – to Hollywood. The ensuing Jazz Age offered little new to African Americans. Few movies offered blacks parts with any authenticity. Such parts included the grizzled hobo in Jim Tully's tale of the lowly, *Beggars of Life* (1928); the seaman boldly played by the boxer George Godfrey in James Cruze's *Old Ironsides* (1926); the faithful renderings of blacks in *Showboat* (1927) and *Uncle Tom's Cabin* (1927); and those in early sound films such as Dudley Murphy's *St. Louis Blues* (1929). However, blacks generally played out conventional roles as chorus girls, convicts, racetrack grooms, boxing trainers, and flippant servants.

The sameness of the images surely led to the first boom of race movies that were made by black, and often white, producers specifically for black audiences. George and Noble Johnson made as many as four such films that were black versions of already defined Hollywood genres – success stories, adventures, and the like – all of them since lost. In Philadelphia the Colored Players crafted a canon, most of which survived in the late 1990s, that included a Paul Laurence Dunbar story, a black *Ten Nights in a Bar Room* (1926), and their masterpiece, *The Scar of Shame* (1927), a melodrama about caste and class in black circles.

Of all African American filmmakers of the era, Oscar Micheaux dominated his age. A sometime Pullman porter (*see* Brotherhood of Sleeping Car Porters), homesteader, and novelist who sold his books door to door, he was also a legendary entrepreneur who both broke with and built on Hollywood genres. More than any other known figure, Micheaux took up themes that Hollywood left untouched: lynching, black success myths, and color-based caste. For years there was scant access to his work: there was only *Body and Soul* (1924), starring the black athlete, singer, and activist Paul Robeson. But his recently rediscovered films of equal stature, among them *Within Our Gates* (1920) and *The Symbol of the Unconquered* (1921), have allowed fuller study.

Sound Film in the Jazz Age

The coming of sound film at the onset of the Great Depression momentarily daunted black filmmakers. On the one hand, Hollywood for the first time could exploit black musical traditions, while, on the other, makers of race movies lacked the capital to invest in sound filmmaking or wiring old ghetto theaters. Fortified by sound, white filmmakers acted with unaccustomed boldness. Al Jolson's "talkie" *The Jazz Singer* (1927) linked the oppression of blacks with that of white immigrants. Several short films attained equal social meaning, among them *The St. Louis Blues* (1929); Duke Ellington's *The Black and Tan Fantasy* (1930) and his allegorical *Symphony in Black* (1934); and Jimmy Mordecai's fable of the black migration from Southern farms to Northern cities, *Yamacraw*. MGM's *Hallelujah!* (1929) and Fox's *Hearts in Dixie* (1929) similarly focused on the tensions of this migration and devoted rare attention to the details of black life. Dudley Murphy's film version of Eugene O'Neill's *The Emperor Jones* was graced with a charming prologue by the black activist and poet James Weldon Johnson that would have eluded O'Neill. This film closed the brief era of socially engaged films by bringing Paul Robeson to the screen in the title role. Taken together, these films hinted at the "unconventional associations" for which James Snead had called.

However, corporate Hollywood returned to its profit-driven caution. Marc Connelly's Pulitzer Prize-winning musical drama of 1930, *The Green Pastures*, for example, took half a decade to reach the screen in truncated form. Thereafter, black Americans, as usual, waited for small favors, such as Robeson's "Joe" in a 1936 remake of *Showboat*, Clarence Muse's rebellious slave in *So Red the Rose* (1935), Clarence Brook's Haitian doctor in John Ford's *Arrowsmith* (1931), and ten years of Hattie McDaniel's flip servants in films ranging from *Alice Adams* (1933) to *Gone With the Wind* (1939). Other nods at the reality of black life included John M. Stahl's social drama based on Fannie Hurst's novel of the practice known as passing (for white), *Imitation of Life* (1934), and a sprinkling of black proletarians among the outcasts of Depression-ridden America.

Once again, black makers of race movies strained to fill the void, this time in competition with a cadre of white producers. Micheaux recovered from a bankruptcy, remade his autobiography as *The Exile* (1931), broke into talkies with *The Girl from Chicago* (1932) and *Swing* (1938), and survived the Depression. George Randol, a sometime Broadway actor, joined him, as did William Alexander, who would make black newsreels during World War II, and other blacks. A few interracial films swelled their ranks. In Texas, Alfred Sack and Spencer Williams turned out the evocative *The Blood of Jesus* (1940), while Muse joined with B-moviemaker Harry Fraser to make a film biography of the boxer Henry Armstrong (played poignantly by himself).

Perhaps because of these white newcomers, race movies achieved a synthesis of black and Hollywood styles in which gangster movies, westerns, and musicals promoted black concerns. At the height of this movement, from 1937 to 1940, gangster movies linked poverty with the incidence of crime and included celebrations of black aspiration. Ralph Cooper's *Am I Guilty* (1940), for example, obliged a black physician to choose between patching up a crook or ministering to the sick, a version of similar dilemmas in other films of the genre. Some, like Bert and Jack Goldberg's *Paradise in Harlem* (1940), focused on Harlem's communal spirit, in this case revealed in a jazz version of *Othello* mounted as a fundraiser to fight urban crime. Similar themes appeared in a 1939-1940 cycle of all-black westerns and a series of Louis Jordan musicals, including one, *Beware* (1946), in which he saves a black college from closure.

The War Years and Their Aftermath

With the onset of World War II, at a moment when American propaganda embraced brotherhood, tolerance, and equality as war aims, makers of race movies slipped from view – victims of short rations of raw film stock. Yet black activists and their government together pressed filmmakers to address wartime racial injustice. The black railway porter's union, led by A. Philip Randolph, threatened a march on Washington unless the government granted equality of opportunity in war industry; the National Association for the Advancement of Colored People (NAACP) held its annual convention in Los Angeles, partly to lobby Hollywood directly for better roles; and the black *Pittsburgh Courier* campaigned on its front pages for a Double V: a simultaneous victory over foreign fascism and domestic racism.

OPPOSITE: Hattie McDaniel, ***right,*** won an Academy Award for Best Supporting Actress for her portrayal of Mammy in David O. Selznick's 1939 blockbuster ***Gone With the Wind.*** At left is British actress Vivien Leigh, who played Scarlett O'Hara. *Culver Pictures*
BELOW LEFT: Morgan Freeman was nominated for an Academy Award as Best Actor in the 1994 film ***The Shawshank Redemption.*** *Archive Photos*
ABOVE: Comic Eddie Anderson poses in a publicity shot for the film ***Man About Town,*** in which he appeared with actors Jack Benny and Dorothy Lamour. *The Everett Collection*
RIGHT: American actor Ruby Dee in a scene from Spike Lee's film ***Do the Right Thing,*** released in 1989. *The Everett Collection*

In response, federal agencies made several movies of advocacy. First among them in quality and breadth of distribution to both army and civilian theaters was the United States War Department's *The Negro Soldier* (1944), written by Carlton Moss, who also starred in the film. Late in the war, the government commissioned or inspired short civilian films on the theme of equitable race relations, among them *Don't Be a Sucker, It Happened in Springfield,* and *The House I Live In* (which won an Oscar in 1947 as the best short film). The studios joined the ranks – partly at the urging of the U.S. Office of War Information – and racially integrated the military years before the armed forces themselves would do so. Among works with an integrated cast were MGM's *Bataan* (1943), Twentieth Century Fox's *Crash Dive* (1943), and Columbia's *Sahara* (1943). Movies set in civilian life, among them *Since You Went Away* (1944) and Alfred Hitchcock's *Lifeboat* (1943), made similar gestures.

Documentaries strove for a similar liberal voice. Gjon Mili's *Jammin' the Blues* (1944) (a *Life* magazine "movie of the week") so evoked the mood of a black jazz club that seasoned newspaper reporters thought it had been done with a hidden camera. Janice Loeb and Helen Levitt's *The Quiet One* (1947) caught the dedication that social workers gave to the plight of black juveniles. And the United Auto Workers sponsored an animated cartoon, *The Brotherhood of Man* (1947), that took up the fate of racism in postwar America.

In the spring of 1949 at least three movies addressed racial issues: MGM's movie version of William Faulkner's *Intruder in the Dust* made racism an issue of conscience rather than politics; Louis DeRochemont's *Lost Boundaries* came from a *Reader's Digest* report on passing for white in a Vermont village; and, boldly for the times, Darryl Zanuck asked Jane White, daughter of Walter White of the NAACP, to do an uncredited but sweeping job of script doctoring on *Pinky*, yet another story on passing.

AFRICAN AMERICAN WINNERS OF ACADEMY AWARDS

Year	Performer	Category	Performance
1939	Hattie McDaniel	Best Supporting Actress	*Gone with the Wind*
1947	James Baskett	Special Award	*Song of the South*
1963	Sidney Poitier	Best Actor	*Lilies of the Field*
1971	Isaac Hayes	Best Song (from film)	"Theme from Shaft" – *Shaft*
1978	Paul Jabara	Best Song (from film)	"Last Dance" – *Thank God It's Friday*
1982	Louis Gossett Jr.	Best Supporting Actor	*An Officer and a Gentleman*
1984	Stevie Wonder	Best Song (from film)	"I Just Called to Say I Love You" – *The Woman in Red*
1985	Lionel Richie	Best Song (from film)	"Say You, Say Me" – *White Nights*
1986	Herbie Hancock	Original Score	*Round Midnight*
1989	Denzel Washington	Best Supporting Actor	*Glory*
1990	Whoopi Goldberg	Best Supporting Actress	*Ghost*
1996	Cuba Gooding Jr.	Best Supporting Actor	*Jerry Maguire*

Thereafter, in the 20 years following Sidney Poitier's debut in Zanuck's *No Way Out* (1950) – an era that might well be dubbed "the age of Sidney Poitier" – scores of films emerged from Hollywood, each with an obligatory scene, sequence, or subplot involving a small, often painfully obvious victory over racism. Indeed, Poitier won an Oscar for his Christ-like savior of a group of nuns in *Lilies of the Field* (1963) and starred in the culmination of the genre, *Guess Who's Coming to Dinner* (1968). As if warning of the ominous price to pay for not following the liberal path to racial harmony, Harry Belafonte's *Odds Against Tomorrow* (1959) closed with a scene in which two prejudiced bank robbers, one black and one white, blow themselves to bits rather than team up to pull off a job. By the 1950s such movies played a sort of backbeat to the actual Civil Rights Movement.

Civil Rights and Blaxploitation

During the 1960s, with the full flowering of the Civil Rights Movement, such films began to take on a harsher, more politically demanding edge. At first from abroad, later from sources outside the major studios, they challenged the simplistic optimism of Poitier's heyday. Costa-Gavras's *The Battle of Algiers* (1966) seemed to some black militants a textbook for direct action, while Amiri Baraka spoke of the movie version of his short play *Dutchman* (1967) as a "revolutionary revelation." Even the Hollywood movies hardened: Robert Mulligan's film version of Harper Lee's novel *To Kill a Mockingbird* (1962) ended with the death of its black protagonist, and Sidney Lumet's *The Pawnbroker* (1965) is set in a harsh Harlem dominated by a coldly ominous drug dealer (played by Brock Peters). By way of contrast, more pastoral films such as Martin Ritt's *Sounder* (1972) and Gordon Park's autobiographical *The Learning Tree* (1969) seemed childlike in their remoteness from the coming wave of angry films.

Catalysts for this turn toward rage, the cities of the late 1960s burst into riots of despair at the assassination of Martin Luther King Jr. and the seeming exhaustion of his movement. Awaiting the arrival of this new wave of films were hundreds of derelict, cavernous downtown theaters, along with thousands of black youths upon whom the Civil Rights Movement had had scant impact. The prototype of the new genre, soon dubbed "blaxploitation" films by the trade paper *Variety*, was Melvin Van Peeble's *Sweet Sweetback's Baad Asssss Song* (1971). More than any other movie, *Sweetback* defined its era. Jangling in its lighting and music track, and heady with contempt for the white social order and its cops, the film's success all but invited Hollywood's major studios to rush forward in pursuit of the new audience. MGM's *Shaft* (1971), for example, played to the crowd by featuring a mouthy, streetwise hero who, in reality, was not an outlaw in Sweetback's mold but merely a plainclothes cop. From the outset, the Hollywood studio version of this black, urban, outlaw culture cynically followed a familiar pattern. *Cool Breeze* (1972) was remade from *The Asphalt Jungle*, *The Lost Man* (1969) from Canon Reed's *Odd Man Out*, and *Up Tight* (1968) from John Ford's film of an Irish rebellion, *The Informer*. The Hollywood studios even plundered genres like horror movies in films such as *Blacula* (1972) and *Blackenstein* (1972).

The New Black Cinema

Meanwhile, a younger generation of black filmmakers emerged from academic settings: the film schools of the University of California at Los Angeles (UCLA), the University of Southern California, New York University (NYU), and later from historically black schools such as Howard University. Variously they embraced Van Peebles, Micheaux, and African filmmakers such as Ousmane Sembène of Senegal as their cultural models. For the first time women joined black filmmakers' ranks.

Asserting that black expression could be appreciated on its own terms, this new black cinema aimed to preserve black culture both within the Hollywood system and apart from it. New distributors, including the Black Filmmakers Foundation, California Newsreel, and Women Make Movies, Inc., aimed at select audiences and academic circles rather than mass markets. Yet there were crossovers such as Warrington Hudlin, who made *Black at Yale* (1977) and *Street Corner Stories* for the new distributors, but who also penetrated Hollywood, together with his brother Reginald. St. Clair Bourne's *Let the Church Say Amen* (1972) revealed both a filmmaker and a movement journalist. Women's films ranged from Madeleine Anderson's documentary pieces, Kathleen Collin's *Cruz Brothers and Miss Malloy*, and Ayoka Chinzira's satiric *Hair Piece: A Film for Nappy Headed People* (1985) to Julie Dash's commercially distributed, nostalgic *Daughters of the Dust* (1991). Others who crossed the line between the avant-garde and the commercial were Charles Burnett with his *Killer of Sheep* (1977) and Haile Gerima (of Howard University) with, most successfully, his fable of a clash between African and American sensibilities, *Sankofa* (1993).

The best known of the new black filmmakers during the 1980s and 1990s was probably Spike Lee, an NYU alumnus. He managed to win large audiences for almost everything he produced – film school exercises, credit-card-financed early efforts such as *She's Gotta Have It* (1986), television commercials, and promotional pieces. He also directed a string of Hollywood successes, including one of the most politically challenging and commercially successful films of the new black cinema, *Do the Right Thing* (1989).

As black filmmakers became more prolific, black actors in Hollywood – Danny Glover, Halle Berry, Will Smith, Denzel Washington, and Jada Pinkett Smith, among others – got steady, rather than sporadic work. By the late 1990s the steadily expanding black presence in American film seemed to assure a solid future for the new black cinema.

Thomas Cripps

See Also

Ousmane Sembène; World War I and African Americans; World War II and African Americans; Belafonte, Harold George (Harry); Blaxploitation Films; Civil War, American; Great Migration, The; Harlem, New York; King, Martin Luther, Jr.; Lee, Shelton Jackson ("Spike"); Los Angeles, California; Parks, Gordon, Sr.; Philadelphia, Pennsylvania; *Pittsburgh Courier*; Racial Stereotypes; Randolph, Asa Philip; Van Peebles, Melvin; Washington, Booker Taliaferro; White, Walter Francis; Ellington, Edward Kennedy ("Duke"); March on Washington, 1941.

Africa

Fipa (also known as Wafipa), ethnic group of Tanzania and Zambia.

The Fipa primarily inhabit the region just east of southern Lake Tanganyika. They speak a Bantu language. Approximately 200,000 people consider themselves Fipa.

See Also

Bantu: Dispersion and Settlement.

Africa

First, Ruth (b. 1925, Johannesburg, South Africa; d. 1982, Mozambique), South African journalist and opponent of APARTHEID, the South African government's policy of racial segregation.

Ruth First's parents were immigrant Jews from Lithuania. Born in Johannesburg, First joined the SOUTH AFRICAN COMMUNIST PARTY (SACP) at an early age. As secretary of the Progressive Youth Council, a communist organization, she approached Nelson Mandela, one of the founders of the African National Congress (ANC) Youth League, to ask for affiliation with the group but her request was rejected. She studied social science at the University of the Witwatersrand, in Johannesburg, and was an active supporter of the black miners' strike of 1946. Beginning in 1947 she worked as a journalist. Three newspapers for which she wrote, the *Guardian, Clarion,* and *New Age,* were banned by the NATIONAL PARTY government because they were critical of government policies.

With activist Rev. Michael Scott, First visited South West Africa (present-day NAMIBIA) in 1947. As an investigative journalist, she helped reveal the appalling conditions under which blacks were obliged to work. In 1949 she married JOE SLOVO, the SACP leader, and they had three daughters. First was arrested in 1956 along with 156 others, including ANC members Mandela and ALBERT JOHN LUTHULI, on charges of being part of a nationwide conspiracy to commit treason. In the early 1960s she edited the political and literary monthly *Fighting Talk* and the Transvaal newspaper *New Age,* which supported the ANC.

Following the publication of her book *South West Africa* in 1963, First was subject to a banning order, which prohibited the publication in South Africa of anything she wrote. Later that year she was arrested and held in solitary confinement for 117 days under the law that permitted the government to hold people it suspected of dangerous antistate activities for 90 days without trial, then release and immediately rearrest them. First became a political exile in 1964 and went to Great Britain, where she lectured at Durham University and wrote extensively about South Africa. During that time, she wrote *117 Days* (1965) about her experience in solitary confinement. In 1978 she became research director at the Centre for African Studies in Maputo, MOZAMBIQUE. In 1982, while in Mozambique, she was killed by a letter bomb.

SEE ALSO

Johannesburg, South Africa; Mandela, Nelson Rolihlahla; Maputo, Mozambique; African National Congress.

First World War. Please see WORLD WAR I AND AFRICAN AMERICANS

North America

Fishburne, Laurence (b. July 30, 1961, Augusta, Ga.), African American stage and motion-picture actor whose consistently commanding performances have won widespread critical acclaim.

Laurence Fishburne III began his acting career as Larry Fishburne. Between the ages of 10 and 13 he performed on the television series "One Life to Live," making his film debut at age 12 in *Cornbread, Earl and Me* (1975). He won a role as a jittery young soldier in the motion picture *Apocalypse Now* (1979), an epic drama of the VIETNAM WAR by American director Francis Ford Coppola. He later delivered notable performances in Coppola's films *Rumble Fish* (1983) and *The Cotton Club* (1984).

Fishburne played in a number of strong supporting roles throughout the 1980s, appearing in the films *The Color Purple* (1984), *School Daze* (1988), and *King of New York* (1990) before establishing himself as a powerful leading actor in *Boyz N the Hood* (1991). His role in the film as a wise but embittered father signaled the beginning of a new era for Fishburne, symbolized by his return to using his full first name, Laurence. In 1993 he was nominated for an Academy Award as best actor for his riveting performance as American rhythm-and-blues singer Ike Turner in *What's Love Got to Do With It* (1993). His other films include *Searching for Bobby Fisher* (1993), *Higher Learning* (1994), *Othello* (1995), and *Hoodlum* (1997).

In addition to winning critical praise for his film performances, Fishburne has received acclaim for his work for television and the stage. His television performances include roles in "A Rumor of War" (1980), "Pee-Wee's Playhouse" (1986-1991), and "The TUSKEGEE AIRMEN" (1995). In 1992 he was named Best Actor at the Tony Awards for his performance in the world premiere of the stage play *Two Trains Running* (1990), by American playwright AUGUST WILSON. He also wrote, directed, and starred in a one-act play, *Riff Raff* (1995).

SEE ALSO

Lee, Shelton Jackson ("Spike"); Rhythm and Blues; Television and African Americans; Walker, Alice; Film, Blacks in American.

North America

Fisk Jubilee Singers, choral group from Fisk University that introduced African American spirituals to a worldwide audience in the 1870s and helped preserve the work songs of the slaves.

The Fisk Jubilee Singers was founded in 1867 by George L. White, the treasurer and vocal-music teacher at FISK UNIVERSITY in Nashville, Tennessee. The university had been established two years earlier to educate newly freed black slaves. Since few students could afford the tuition, the school needed other sources of revenue, and White came up with the idea of a performing choir as a way to raise money.

After several successful local appearances, the reputation of the 11-member choir began to spread, and in 1871 the Jubilee Singers embarked on a tour of the Northeast, performing mainly in churches before all-white audiences. Their repertoire included anthems, popular ballads, and operatic excerpts, but their most popular pieces proved to be AFRICAN AMERICAN SPIRITUALS and work songs, which many in their audiences were hearing for the first time. Highlights of the tour included a performance before 40,000 people at the World's Peace Jubilee in Boston in 1872 and a concert for President Ulysses S. Grant in WASHINGTON,

The Fisk Jubilee Singers brought African American spirituals and work songs to a wide public in North America and Europe. *The Everett Collection*

D.C. That first tour was a big hit and spurred widespreadinterest in plantation hymns and other Southern black music. The Jubilee Singers eventualy took their show to several European countries, including a performance for Queen Victoria in England.

With the money they raised, Fisk University was able to complete construction in 1875 of its first permanent building, called Jubilee Hall. Other black schools such as Hampton Institute, Tuskegee Institute, and Howard University soon followed with traveling choirs of their own. To many of the newly freed African American slaves, the spirituals and work songs represented an unwelcome reminder of slavery, and they were eager to discard them. But thanks to the work of the Fisk Jubilee Singers and other groups like them, these songs did not die, and are now celebrated as an indigenous American music.

Lisa Clayton Robinson

See Also

Boston, Massachusetts; Hampton University; Thirteenth Amendment of the United States Constitution and the Emancipation Proclamation; Tuskegee University.

North America

Fisk University, one of the first and most respected African American liberal arts institutions.

Like many other new schools for African Americans at the end of the Civil War, Fisk University was founded and largely supported by white benefactors. But it differed significantly from other black schools, such as Tuskegee and Hampton Institutes, in its emphasis on liberal arts education rather than vocational training. Its founders saw Fisk as a school that would measure itself by "the highest standards, not of Negro education, but of American education at its best."

Fisk was established in Nashville, Tennessee, in October 1865 by Erastus Milo Cravath and the Reverend Edward P. Smith, both members of the American Missionary Association, and John Ogden, superintendent of the Tennessee Freedmen's Bureau's Department of Education. It began as an elementary school to meet the basic educational needs of the newly freed slaves, and its first students ranged in age from 7 to 70. In 1867 Tennessee passed a new law that mandated free elementary schools for all races. Since this meant that many of its elementary students would be able to receive a public education, Fisk was able to focus on postgraduate and college courses. In August 1867 Fisk was incorporated as a private, coeducational university providing higher education for men and women of all races.

In 1873 Fisk's trustees purchased a 40-acre site for a campus with money that had been raised by the successful concert tour of the Fisk Jubilee Singers. The school quickly developed a reputation for academic excellence, and Fisk-trained teachers were highly sought after by the segregated Southern school system. By the 1930s the Association of American Universities rated Fisk not only as the best predominantly black institution, but also as one of the better small private universities in the country.

Like many other historically black colleges and universities, Fisk faced financial problems as a result of 1970s school desegregation, as predominantly white schools began to compete for black applicants and government funding was cut. Fisk's difficulties became a financial crisis in the early 1980s, but a major fundraising effort allowed the university to recover. During the 1990s Fisk's enrollment hovered around 900, and entering students were typically ranked in the top fifth of their high school classes. Fisk's art collection and its special library collections on African American and African diaspora history, including the papers of W. E. B. Du Bois, Amy and Marcus Garvey, and Langston Hughes, are recognized worldwide.

Over the years Fisk has had many distinguished graduates and faculty members. Du Bois, a noted intellectual and social critic, received a B.A. from Fisk in 1888. Booker T. Washington, Tuskegee's founder, served on Fisk's board of trustees, and his wife and children graduated from Fisk. In the twentieth century, historians John Hope Franklin and Charles H. Wesley and writers Nikki Giovanni and Frank Yerby were all Fisk graduates. Writers Arna Bontemps, Sterling Brown, Robert Hayden, and James Weldon Johnson and artist Aaron Douglas taught at Fisk, and pioneer sociologist Charles S. Johnson became Fisk's first black president in 1947. Thurgood Marshall, who later became the first African American Supreme Court justice, was an early participant in Johnson's Race Relations Institute. A survey found that in 1990 approximately one in six practicing African American physicians, dentists, and lawyers was a Fisk graduate.

Lisa Clayton Robinson

See Also

Brown, Sterling Allen; Bureau of Refugees, Freedmen and Abandoned Lands; Civil War, American; Du Bois, William Edward Burghardt (W. E. B.); Garvey, Marcus Mosiah; Giovanni, Yolande Cornelia ("Nikki"); Hampton University; Hayden, Robert Earl; Johnson, Charles Spurgeon; Tuskegee University; Washington, Booker Taliaferro; Wesley, Charles Harris.

North America

Fitzgerald, Ella (b. April 25, 1917, Newport News, Va.; d. June 15, 1996, Beverly Hills, Calif.), African American singer; one of the greatest jazz vocalists of all time, she was known as the First Lady of Song.

Jazz vocalist Ella Fitzgerald performs in the 1950s, a decade during which she made classic recordings in her mature style. *CORBIS/Hulton-Deutsch Collection*

Ella Fitzgerald was quite possibly the greatest vocalist in the history of jazz. Only Billie Holiday and Sarah Vaughan offer her any serious competition. Of the three, Holiday came first and profoundly influenced the entire course of jazz singing, but she had a small voice, limited range, and never really moved beyond the 1930s swing jazz style. Vaughan, who emerged in the mid-1940s, was the first to sing with a truly operatic range; she had nearly perfect pitch and superb technique. Both Vaughan and Fitzgerald were blessed with pure voices and exceptionally clear enunciation. But only Fitzgerald melded the headlong swing of the 1930s with the adventurous harmonies of modern jazz.

Fitzgerald was born into poverty in Newport News, Virginia. When she was three years old, her mother moved her to Yonkers, New York, as part of the Great Migration of African Americans out of the South. In 1932 her mother died, and Fitzgerald went to live with an aunt in Harlem. On a dare, she entered herself as a dancer in one of the Apollo Theater's weekly Amateur Night in Harlem contests. But at the last moment, on November 21, 1934, she decided to sing instead, performing "Judy" and "The Object of My Affection" in the style of her idol Connee Boswell of the Boswell Sisters. Fitzgerald won the competition and secured a job singing with Tiny Bradshaw's band.

After alto saxophonist Benny Carter brought her to the attention of drummer and band leader Chick Webb, Fitzgerald joined Webb's band, then appearing regularly at Harlem's Savoy Ballroom. Webb became Fitzgerald's mentor and legal guardian, and in 1935 she commenced a recording career that would ultimately span six decades. At first Fitzgerald's singing showed little in the way of jazz improvisation and was closer to a straight pop music sensibility, but she achieved national popularity in 1938 with the hit "A-Tisket, A-Tasket," a medium-tempo novelty number that she recorded with the Webb band. After Webb died in 1939, Fitzgerald fronted the group until mid-1942, when it broke up and she continued as a solo artist.

During the bebop or bop era of the mid-1940s and early 1950s, Fitzgerald honed her jazz abilities and emerged as one of the foremost exponents of scat singing, in which the singer's voice mimicked a soloing horn, using nonsense syllables in place of words or song lyrics. During 1946 she toured with Dizzy Gillespie's big band and in the late 1940s recorded exciting scat versions of "Oh, Lady Be Good" and "How High the Moon." In 1948 *Downbeat*, the jazz magazine, proclaimed her "as great a master of bop as she has been of swing." Fitzgerald later recalled, "I thought bebop was 'it,' and that all I had to do was go someplace and sing bop." But when many listeners rejected the complex harmonies and challenging angularity of modern jazz, she decided to modify her style.

What she achieved in the 1950s was a remarkable synthesis of accessibility and sophistication. A year after appearing in the film *Pete Kelly's Blues* (1955), Fitzgerald signed with Norman Granz's Verve Records and made some of the greatest recordings of her career. The range of Fitzgerald's mature style is exemplified by her hilarious 1960 rendition of "Mack the Knife," recorded during a concert in Berlin in which she forgot Bertolt Brecht's lyrics and spontaneously invented her own, as well as in a series of Verve *Songbooks*, each offering her classic interpretations of the music of a particular composer, notably Cole Porter (1956), Duke Ellington (1958), and George and Ira Gershwin (1959). "I never knew how good our songs were," Ira Gershwin remarked, "until I heard Ella Fitzgerald sing them."

Fitzgerald maintained a busy schedule into the 1980s, touring from 40 to 45 weeks a year, appearing at numerous jazz festivals, and recording prolifically. She also received countless awards and honors, including 13 Grammy Awards, a National Medal of the Arts, a 1979 Kennedy Center Award for lifetime achievement, and honorary degrees from Dartmouth College and Yale University. On receiving an honorary doctorate of music at Yale, she remarked with characteristic modesty, "Not bad for someone who only studied music to get that half credit in high school!"

Fitzgerald's voice began to fade by the mid-1970s, though her solid professionalism and unerring rhythmic sense allowed her to continue making creditable music. During the 1980s, however, diabetes, failing eyesight, and heart trouble increasingly restricted her concert appearances,and in 1991 she retired from active performance. Yet apart from Sarah Vaughan, Fitzgerald was without peer as a jazz vocalist for more than a generation, and her compelling sense of swing influenced all who followed her.

James Clyde Sellman

See Also

Carter, Bennett Lester (Benny); Gillespie, John Birks ("Dizzy"); Great Migration, The; Harlem, New York; Ellington, Edward Kennedy ("Duke").

North America

Flack, Roberta (b. February 10, 1940, Black Mountain, N.C.), African American singer known for a style that combines jazz, soul, blues, and pop.

Born to Laron and Irene Flack, who both played piano, Roberta Flack began playing by ear as a toddler. She began taking formal lessons at 9, and at 15, she received a scholarship to Howard University in Washington, D.C., where she majored in music education.

Flack taught music and English in North Carolina and Washington, D.C., for several years after her graduation in 1958. She began her singing career at clubs in the evenings. She initially sang opera, but she soon gained a following by singing popular music that incorporated elements of jazz, soul, blues, and pop. She released her first album, *First Take*, in 1969. Her second, *Chapter Two* (1970), sold over a million copies. She gained national recognition that year after appearing on many television shows, and *Downbeat* magazine named her 1970's Female Vocalist of the Year.

In 1971 her song "The First Time Ever I Saw Your Face" was included on the soundtrack of the movie *Play Misty for Me;* it became a number-one hit and won a Grammy Award for record of the year. She had more number-one songs with "Killing Me Softly with His Song" (1973) and "Feel Like Makin' Love" (1974). Her other hit songs include two duets, "The Closer I Get to You" (1978), with Donny Hathaway, and "Tonight I Celebrate My Love" (1983), with Peabo Bryson, and "Set the Night to Music" (1991).

Lisa Clayton Robinson

See Also

Soul Music; Blues, The.

FLN. Please see Front de Libération Nationale

Flo-Jo. Please see Griffith-Joyner, Florence Delorez

Latin America and the Caribbean

Flores, Pedro (b. 1894; d. 1979), Afro-Puerto Rican composer who wrote a number of classic boleros, a romantic musical style. These include "Obsesión" (Obsession) and "Amor Perdido" (Forbidden Love) (*see* Bolero).

North America

Folk Medicine, African American approaches to health and healing that dominated life during slavery and that have continued to influence some people's understanding of medical practice.

During times of slavery many African Americans maintained the spiritual view of health that had characterized their African ancestors. They believed that good health arose from harmony with nature and other people; poor health, from discord. Sickness could stem from the curses of others, deviance from religious rectitude, or conflict with the natural environment. In the Caribbean Latin America particularly, these beliefs combined with Roman Catholicism to produce syncretic religions such as Vodou, Shango, and Curanderismo, all of which emphasize the supernatural essence of healing (*see* Traditional Healing in Latin America and the Caribbean).

Slave culture regarded "root doctors" or "witch doctors" with high esteem and valued herbal cures, such as mullen leaves, camphor, sulphur, and multifarious roots. Although some of these cures had value in a Western scientific sense, many more reflected traditional beliefs. One lockjaw remedy, for example, involved withdrawing the nail, squeezing out the excess blood, and then wrapping the wound with bacon, tobacco leaves, and a penny. Most medicinal formulas probably combined elements of both science and faith.

The culture of folk medicine was, and is, often conducive to healing. Faith and trust are essential ingredients for recovery, whether in modern medicine or so-called magical cures. Root doctors provided the authority in which such faith and trust were grounded. Anthropologist Wilbur H. Watson writes: "By its reinforcement through collective suggestion that the cure should be maintained, the primary group induces a sense of obligation in the patient to avoid a relapse, and thereby avoid disappointment of the group, and the personal shame that tends to follow moral failure."

Slave owners, who usually scorned continuations of African culture, usually permitted slaves to practice traditional medicine. Folk cures absolved them of the responsibility to pay for a white physician and, given the quality of medical care in the antebellum American South, these cures were often just as effective. From times of slavery to the present, folk medicine has been primarily, but not exclusively, the domain of older women.

After the Civil War folk medicine suffered the double blow of malpractice lawsuits and the beginnings of modern medical knowledge. Traditional cures remained in currency, however, especially in isolated rural and economically depressed areas. Throughout the twentieth century a retaining of old ways paralleled the growth of scientific practice, and a traditional approach was often viewed as an acceptable supplement to modern medicine. A Sea Islander from the South Carolina coast, for example, might employ a modern cure for constipation while seeking recourse to magic for a fever.

Through the late twentieth century, many pharmacies in the South reflected this double-tiered system by stocking traditional herbal remedies. In addition to conventional drugs, these stores sold camphor, asafetida, flowers of sulphur, spirits of turpentine, and oil of cloves, as well as patent medicines such as Humphreys 11, Black Draught, John the Conquerer Root, and Lydia Pinkham's Vegetable Compound. The contemporary interest in natural and holistic healing and alternative medicine has brought back many African American-based root and herbal remedies formerly thought to be superstitious.

Eric Bennett

See Also
Slavery in the United States; Civil War, American.

Africa

Fon, also called the Agadja, an ethnic group of the Republic of Benin whose ancestors built the powerful precolonial kingdom of Dahomey.

Closely related to the Adja and Gun ethnic groups, the Fon were once a part of the Adja Kingdom in Tado (part of present-day Togo). In the late seventeenth century, however, the Fon broke from the Adja and migrated to Allada. According to Fon legend, the group was forced to leave after Agasu, the son of an Adja princess and a leopard, unsuccessfully attempted to usurp the Adja throne. Agasu and his followers fled to Allada and established their own kingdom, but a later succession struggle forced Agasu's son Dogbari to migrate to Abomey, where he and his Fon subjects established the kingdom of Dahomey around 1620.

Dahomey quickly evolved into a highly centralized monarchy, and its large, sophisticated army enabled the Fon to conquer neighboring kingdoms and expand their territory throughout most of southern Benin. On its conquests the army commonly took captives, who were used as slave labor on the king's plantations or as sacrificial offerings in the annual religious ceremonies held to honor royal ancestors. These ceremonies were also an opportunity for the Dahomey kings to assemble their provincial chiefs and confirm their loyalty.

The Dahomey kingdom expanded during the seventeenth century and the early eighteenth century, reaching its pinnacle during the reign of Agaja (1708-1740). By this time the kingdom stretched from the Abomey Plateau to the Atlantic Coast, and was well positioned to participate in European trade, particularly the booming transatlantic slave trade. Although some scholars believe that the Dahomey intended to end or at least curtail the slave trade, the kingdom became one of West Africa's biggest suppliers of slaves, and it grew heavily dependent on the trade for revenue.

But after 1807, when Great Britain formally prohibited slave trading, Dahomey's rulers were forced to pursue other commodities. They ordered their subjects to produce palm oil and used slaves on their state palm plantations. Despite high European demand for palm oil, however, the Dahomey kings found its production less lucrative than selling slaves, and attempted to increase revenue by levying heavy taxes and leasing ports, such as Cotonou and Whydah, to the French. By the late nineteenth century the French were claiming that they had been ceded the land, and when the Dahomey king Glele demanded that France relinquish control of the ports, France took the dispute as an opportunity for conquest. In 1892 the French launched an attack against Glele's successor, Behanzin; two years later they captured him and occupied the kingdom, which subsequently became part of the colony of Dahomey.

The French colonial administration preserved some of the centralized authority structures of the Dahomey Kingdom because it found them useful for enacting colonial dictates on the local level. Many of the kingdom's chiefs, almost all Fon, were appointed to the colonial civil service. As independence neared, the Fon were mobilized by Tometin Justin Ahomadegbe into a political party, the Bloc Populaire Africain. Today, as Benin's single largest ethnic group – numbering approximately 2 million – the Fon wield significant political power and were instrumental in the 1991 election of Nicéphore Soglo. The majority still live in the southern half of the country and are the principal producers of the country's staple crops, including maize and millet.

Elizabeth Heath

See Also
Dahomey, Early Kingdom of; France; Soglo, Nicéphore; Cotonou, Benin.

Latin America and the Caribbean

Fontes, Hermes (b. August 28, 1888, Buquim, Brazil; d. December 25, 1930, Rio de Janeiro, Brazil), mulatto Brazilian journalist, orator, poet, and prose writer.

Born in the state of Sergipe, a son of rural laborers, Hermes Fontes was orphaned at an early age. A highly precocious child, he studied in his hometown and in Aracaju and made such an impression upon the governor of Sergipe that he took Fontes to Rio de Janeiro and sponsored his education in the humanities.

As a student Fontes was involved in journalism and literary pursuits, publishing his poetry in journals by the age of 15, and his first book, *Apoteoses* (1908), at age 20. He continued to pursue journalism, working for the *Diário de Notícias*, became a civil servant, and took part in the antimilitary campaign of Rui Barbosa, earning acclaim for his oratorical skills.

Fontes was a greatly esteemed poet in his time. His work is representative of a phase of transition in Brazil from Parnasianism to symbolism. The exquisitely crafted and objective language of Parnasianism, which stressed emotional control, gradually gave way to symbolism, which tried to express emotions indirectly through poetic symbols. Despite being a pained pessimist, Fontes had an extraordinary imagination and considerable technical skill, able both to capture the essence of his era and translate his personal anguish into works of great clarity and form, such as those found in *A Lâmpada Velada* (1922) and later in *A Fonte da Mata* (1930). Fontes was also an accomplished prose writer.

Despite his literary success, a failed marriage, physical challenges, and other personal misfortunes drove him into morbid melancholy, which culminated in his suicide on Christmas Day, 1930.

Nicola Cooney

See Also
Brazil.

Africa

Food in Africa

Africa's regional diets and culinary patterns, or "foodways," vary on the basis of ecology, culture, class, and other factors. Climate and ecological conditions, for example, determine what food crops and livestock are practical to grow locally. Dietary patterns are also influenced by cultural and religious norms, and by a region's history of contact with foreign foodstuffs and cultures through trade, migration, and colonization. In the second half of the twentieth century, African foodways have been particularly transformed by urbanization and related changes in women's work and by foreign donations of "food aid." Now more than ever, diets vary across class, with the wealthy typically eating not only a greater quantity and variety of foods than the poor but also different foods. This essay discusses some of these variations in African foodways, as well as broad patterns and historical trends.

In Africa as in most of the world, most people structure their diets around a relatively small number of starchy or carbohydrate-rich foods. Grains such as millet, sorghum, rice, and maize (corn) and tubers such as yams and cassava (manioc), for example, form the central ingredient of the most common meals in Africa and provide the bulk of the daily caloric intake. These staple starches are traditionally accompanied by protein-rich legumes, such as peas, beans, or peanuts, and by smaller quantities of foods that add both flavor and nutrition, such as vegetables, oils, spices, and meat or fish. These latter foods are often referred to as relishes, condiments, or sauces. Anthropologist and food historian Sidney Mintz calls them "fringe" foods, to emphasize the centrality of the "core" starches. This "core-fringe-legume" pattern of food consumption predominates in Africa, except in pastoralist societies, where milk and meat play more central roles.

Core Foods

Africa's oldest staple starch crops vary across ecological zones (*see* Biogeography of Africa). The major cereal grains – millet, sorghum, and maize – are all common in semi-arid regions. Millet and sorghum, both indigenous to Africa, predominate in the drier regions of the Sahel and in eastern and southern Africa. Millet can grow in areas where rainfall averages 275 to 400 mm (11 to 20 inches) annually, while sorghum requires between 800 and 1000 mm (30 to 40 inches) of rain annually. Maize, a New World crop first introduced by the Portuguese beginning in the late fifteenth century, is now one of the most widely cultivated food crops in Africa. It can grow in a variety of conditions and be used in many ways, but it is less drought-resistant than either sorghum or millet.

Tubers such as cassava, yams, and sweet potatoes, and tree crops such as bananas and plantains (some tree crops are indigenous to Africa and some arrived centuries ago from Asia or the New World) are typically grown in the humid forest ecozones of Central Africa, the Great Lakes region of East Africa, and coastal West Africa. Cassava production in particular has increased in the twentieth century, because while in the field it requires little tending, and it can keep for months underground before harvest. But cassava is low in protein, and in raw form it is toxic.

Most rice in Africa is grown under either lowland (also known as paddy) or upland conditions. In the bend of the Niger River in West Africa, indigenous African lowland rice production dates back an estimated 3000 years. Both the rice species and the cultivation methods from this region later crossed the Atlantic with African slaves (*see* Agriculture, African, in the Americas: An Interpretation). Asian paddy rice varieties are also cultivated in areas suitable for irrigation. Upland rice depends on rainfall, not irrigation, and thus grows only in wetter regions. Many rural development projects in Africa since the 1960s have centered on rice production, in part because in comparison to other crops, demand for rice has increased enormously in Africa's cities.

Wheat, which favors a cooler and drier climate, grows in relatively few regions. Major areas of production include the highlands of Ethiopia and Kenya and certain parts of Sudan. Barley is a staple-food crop in Egypt but is not widely cultivated elsewhere. In Ethiopia and Eritrea, *teff*, an indigenous wheatlike grain, has been a staple food crop for centuries.

Common Preparations of Core Foods

Compared to the highly varied and often quite elaborate preparations typical of fringe foods, the preparations of core starches are fairly simple. One very common dish made of millet, maize, or sorghum is a stiff porridge known in different regions of sub-Saharan Africa as *to, putu, pap, nsima, bidia, oshifima,* or *ugali*. Once the grains have been ground into flour – a task women once did by hand but increasingly do in mills – they are mixed with cold water until a thin paste forms. Next the cook mixes in boiling water and stirs continuously until it thickens, then adds more flour until the consistency is so thick that the spoon stands straight up in the pot. This kind of porridge is often consumed communally and typically by hand, with each person scooping out bite-size portions to dip in sauce.

Couscous, made from steamed granules of sorghum flour, is a popular dish in North Africa. In Ethiopia and Eritrea, the traditional core of many meals is *njera*, large puffy pancakes made from teff flour. Like boiled grain dishes, njera and most other baked breads are relatively bland but their accompaniments are often quite spicy.

Tubers and starchy tree crops are most commonly boiled, roasted, or fried. Because cassava and some yam varieties contain toxic chemicals, they must be soaked in water for several hours or days before cooking. Once soaked and boiled, cassava and yams, like boiled plantains, are frequently pounded into a thick, heavy paste called *fufu* (or *futu*), a popular albeit labor-intensive West African dish. Like porridge dishes, fufu is often eaten communally and by hand and is always accompanied by a soup or stew. Dried, grated cassava, known as *gari*, is a popular "convenience" food in coastal West Africa, because it keeps well and can be easily reconstituted with boiling water.

Fringe Foods

Although fringe foods typically account for a smaller proportion of caloric intake than the core starches, they are by no means a peripheral part of the diet. Whether served as sauces, soups, spreads, or fillings, dishes made of vegetables, spices, and sometimes animal protein and fat add color, nutrition, and variety to the daily bowls of porridge or rice. These dishes vary both seasonally and regionally, depending in part on the ingredients available locally. For example, in Senegal sauces made with peanuts, one of the country's main crops, are served with rice and occasionally chicken. Farther south in Nigeria and Ghana, palm oil stew is a more common complement. In Kenya, boiled *sukuma wiki*, a green similar to spinach, accompanies maize or millet ugali, whereas in Central Africa the greens of potatoes and cassava plants are common sauce ingredients.

Many ingredients found in traditional African fringe dishes reflect foreign influences. The tomato, for example, was brought from the New World by the Portuguese in the sixteenth century and is now cultivated and consumed throughout much of Africa. In coastal East Africa, spices from Asia and the Middle East flavor the sauces served on rice and fish. Similarly, North African cuisines employ many of the ingredients found in other Mediterranean culinary traditions, such as saffron, cinnamon, mint, and chickpeas.

Colonial Influences

European influence on African food habits prior to colonialism was generally limited to the introduction of new crops such as maize and tomatoes. Colonization led to significant changes both in what foods Africans produced and what foods they had available to purchase. It is important to note that dietary patterns were transformed not only by the introduction of new crops and imported goods, but also by changes in households' use of land, labor, and income.

Colonial-era taxes, for example, often forced peasant households to shift at least some of their land away from food crops over to export crops, such as cotton, coffee, and cocoa, which were typically overseen by male household heads. Taxation and compulsory labor service also forced rural men and sometimes women to leave their farms for work on plantations, in mines, and on road and railway projects. In many areas women had to assume greater responsibility for food production, and often on more limited land. In one common adaptation to these constraints, women switched from labor-intensive crops such as millet to ones requiring less weeding and other upkeep, such as cassava. In general, as rural households devoted more of their resources to income-earning endeavors, they also began to purchase a larger proportion of their food supplies.

Compared to the efforts colonial administrations made to develop export crop production in Africa, most of the time they paid relatively little attention to staple food crop production. During the First and Second World Wars, however, some colonies made cultivation of certain crops compulsory in order to assure food supplies for the military bases. In the British colonies of East Africa, for example, peasants in some regions were forced to grow maize, and in the French colony of Upper Volta (now Burkina Faso), peasants near the military camp in Bobo-Dioulasso were forced to grow potatoes and peanuts.

Imported foods intended for European settlers also made their way into the African diet, as did "European" foods manufactured in Africa. Initially only a small minority of Africans, mostly the educated urban elite, partook of foreign and costly foods such as bread, pasta, margarine, and soft drinks. In some circles the ability to buy and serve European cuisine became a marker of status, like Western-style clothing. Certain foods, however,

eventually became a part of the working-class diet. Men who migrated to urban areas in search of wage labor were among the earliest regular consumers of goods like bread and tea, partly because they were convenient. Migrant laborers also helped introduce these foods to rural regions by bringing them back to their families.

Today, regional variations in some popular European foodstuffs reflect the influence of the colonial powers' own cuisines. In the cities of Francophone West Africa, for example, people eat baguettes and drink café au lait, while in the former Italian colonies they eat pasta, and in the former British colonies square bread loaves and tea predominate. Demand for Western-style processed foods is now partially met by domestic production. Bread in Africa is typically made in small or medium-size urban bakeries, while commodities such as instant coffee and margarine are produced in factories owned by multinational corporations. Although these foods are no longer consumed only by an elite few, during times of economic hardship they are too expensive for the vast majority of the population, urban or rural.

Food Aid

Since independence, food donated or sold on concessional terms by foreign countries – also known as food aid – has transformed both dietary and agricultural production patterns in Africa. Governments of many newly independent African countries willingly accepted food aid because it compensated for their own production shortfalls and ensured that cheap food supplies were available for politically important urban populations. For the United States and the European Union, food aid became a means for disposing of their own agricultural surpluses as well as for establishing African markets for their exports. The United States' Food for Peace Program, for example, granted African and other Third World countries low interest loans for the purchase of major U.S. agricultural commodities, such as wheat and soybean oil. The U.S. Congress approved the program in 1954 with the explicit aim of building new overseas markets. It succeeded: countries like Nigeria continued to purchase U.S. wheat even when the aid program was reduced, partly out of the concern to maintain political stability in the cities, where most wheat and other aid foods are consumed. Food aid from the European Union has also helped establish African markets for European goods, such as dried milk products. Although food aid programs were once justified on humanitarian grounds, they have been widely criticized for undermining markets for Africa's domestically produced foodstuffs and for fostering an overdependence on imported foods. The dangers of such dependency became apparent in many African countries in the 1980s, when austerity measures imposed under World Bank structural adjustment

OPPOSITE: **Women visit stalls of fruit sellers at an open-air market in Burkina Faso.** *© D. Riffet/Explorer*
LEFT: **Young Tuareg men share a bowl of millet, a grain that is one of the staple foods of Africa.** *M & E Bernheim*
BELOW LEFT: **People examine fruits and vegetables on sale at a monthly market in N'Goro N'Goro in Tanzania.** *© S. Cordier/Explorer*

programs drove up prices for import-based foods such as wheat, bread, and milk. The announcement of price rises set off "bread riots" in many African cities.

"STREET FOODS"

Finally, African food habits have changed along with the patterns and pressures of daily life, especially in the cities. As more and more people – especially women – commute across large cities to work and attend school, midday meals at home have become less practical. Instead, students, marketplace traders, and industrial and office workers rely on so-called street foods for one or more meals daily. Sold from kiosks and carts in cities throughout Africa, street-food fare is eclectic: offerings range from the traditional rice-and-sauce dishes popular among the cities' various African ethnic communities to African "fast foods" like fried plantains and bean fritters to Middle Eastern-style kebabs and European-style sandwiches. For many, street foods are not only more convenient but also more economical than home prepared meals. Some traditional African dishes require extensive preparation, so when the price of the ingredients and the cooking fuel are factored into the time spent shopping and cooking, it is often cheaper to buy these dishes from street vendors, who prepare them in large quantities.

The variety of snacks and meals sold on the streets of African cities reflects an enduring theme in African cuisines: despite the many changes prompted by colonialism, urbanization, aid, and trade, traditional dishes based on locally produced ingredients are still valued. Indeed, because such dishes are now sold in multiethnic cities and eaten by migrants and travelers, they have become familiar far beyond the regions where they were originally developed. Senegalese rice-and-peanut sauce can be found throughout West Africa, for example, and Ethiopian restaurants specializing in njera dishes are common in East African cities such as Nairobi. Restaurants founded by African immigrants in Europe and the Americas have also popularized these cuisines abroad.

Elizabeth Heath

SEE ALSO

Bobo-Dioulasso, Burkina Faso; Drought and Desertification; Eritrea; Nairobi, Kenya; Transatlantic Slave Trade; Pastoralism; Portugal; Structural Adjustment in Africa.

North America

Food in African American Culture, **African American cuisine predominant in the Southern United States and influenced by African styles of preparation and cooking.**

African American food, also known as "soul food," is closely related to the cuisines of both Africa and the American South. African slaves brought to the New World many of their native fruits and vegetables, including yams, watermelon, okra, and several varieties of beans, all of which were soon adopted into the diets of their owners. Slaves who were taken into the plantation owner's house as cooks and other servants learned to combine their own food with the food of their masters. African American cuisine also grew out of the slaves' resourcefulness in utilizing the cast-off ingredients of the master's meals. They developed methods to cook parts of the pig not eaten by their owner's family and feasted on the snout, ears, feet, tail, ribs, thighs (hocks), stomach (maw), and small intestines (which when boiled and fried are known as chitterlings, or "chitlins").

The West African diet featured starchy foods such as rice and yams, both of which became important parts of the early African American diet. Although African slaves did not introduce rice into the Americas, their experience with rice cultivation in Africa helped make possible large-scale rice production in the Carolinas and the Gulf Coast. Using both African and American cooking methods, African American slaves roasted, boiled, fried, and baked native yams and sweet potatoes. Sweet potato pie continues to be a popular Southern dessert.

Beans were a major component of the African diet and were brought to the Americas by slaves. As in Africa, these bean varieties, including black-eyed peas, lima beans, and kidney beans, were typically simmered and flavored with a piece of meat. Another popular African import, the okra plant, was usually fried or boiled and is a principal ingredient in gumbo, a spicy Cajun dish associated with Louisiana's Creole culture that has its roots in seventeenth-century Africa.

Chicken, fish, and goat constituted important sources of protein for West Africans. While Africans usually cooked these meats in stews or over flames, many slaves in America adopted the European practice of frying meat, which best prevented it from spoiling on road trips. Fried chicken was developed in the South during the nineteenth century and quickly became popular throughout the United States. In addition to chicken, pork, opossum, and raccoon were the meats most widely consumed by African American slaves.

In the eastern colonies the mingling of Native, European, and African cultures produced a hybrid cuisine that included, among other things, barbecue. Many of the Africans who came to colonial South Carolina arrived from the West Indies, where, as linguistic evidence suggests, barbecue originated (*barbacoa*). Thus, enslaved Africans may have learned some culinary techniques, including barbecue, from West Indians. When cooking over a fire, American slaves began to baste their meats with sauce instead of serving it on the side, as had been the practice in Africa. Because of regional differences in livestock, "barbecue" came to mean pork in the eastern United States and beef in the western United States.

The West African tradition of cooking all edible parts of plants and animals helped the slaves to survive in the United States. Although Europeans occasionally ate the leaves of plants, slaves often prepared these leaves, especially collards, by simmering them in oil, peppers, and spices. They also creatively processed and cooked corn, the food most often made available to them by their owners. From corn, slaves made corn bread, grits (bleached and hulled corn kernels), hoecakes (cornmeal cooked on the blade of a hoe over a flame), and hush puppies (deep-fried cornmeal with onions and spices).

In spite of emancipation, urbanization, and migration to the cities of the North, African Americans have preserved their foods and cooking methods. In the twentieth century, African American foods have been produced for the mass market and many celebrated soul food restaurants have opened, most notably Sylvia's in Harlem. Yet African American food and cooking methods had attracted attention early in United States history. The black-owned and black-operated restaurant Fraunce's Tavern in New York City was one of George Washington's favorite restaurants. Today, African American cuisine is heavily influenced by Caribbean and South American cooking.

Aaron Myers

See Also

Slavery in the United States; Great Migration, The; Harlem, New York; New York, New York; Thirteenth Amendment of the United States Constitution and the Emancipation Proclamation; Puerto Rico; Jamaica.

North America

Football, Collegiate, **team sport at American colleges at which African Americans have excelled, despite a history of exclusion from predominantly white colleges and universities.**

Historically black colleges and universities (HBCUs) were for many years the epicenter of black college football. African American football players were not welcome on white campuses until the late 1950s, and not until the late 1960s in the Deep South. Jim Crow segregation forced the development of separate teams and leagues for black players. The first black college football game took place in North Carolina in 1892, when Biddle College defeated Livingston College. Thereafter, black college football became a major social event on campus, bringing students and alumni together.

By the turn of the century several major school rivalries had developed, including Virginia Union-Virginia State, Tuskegee-Talladega, and Fisk-Meharry. The intensity and popularity of these rivalries persuaded several colleges to form a conference in 1912. That year Howard University (District of Columbia), Lincoln University (Pennsylvania), Hampton Institute (Virginia), and Shaw (North Carolina) formed the Colored Intercollegiate Athletic Association (CIAA). Within a few years several more black conferences were formed to showcase black college football, including the Southwest Athletic Conference (SWAC), the Southern Intercollegiate Athletic Conference (SIAC), and the Midwestern Athletic Conference (MWAC).

Premier Black College Programs

These regional conferences brought national exposure to several outstanding black college football programs. In the 1920s Tuskegee Institute had the most dominant black college program. Its teams won nine SIAC titles between 1924 and 1933, and featured one of the most exciting running backs of that era, Ben Stevenson. Although Tuskegee captured most of the attention during this time, another running back dazzled crowds with his athleticism. Franz "Jazz" Bird, who played at Lincoln in the early 1920s, was nicknamed the "black Red Grange" after the famous white football star Red Grange.

In the 1930s Morgan State succeeded Tuskegee as the nation's premier black college football program. Coached by Edward Hurt, Morgan State won seven CIAA championships between 1930 and 1941. The team was led by running backs Otis Troupe and Thomas "the Tank" Conrad. In the Midwest Athletic Conference, Kentucky State consistently fielded top teams throughout the 1930s, including tight ends William Reed and Robert Hardin, running back George "Big Bertha" Edwards, and quarterback Joseph "Tarzan" Kendall.

Despite dwindling resources, black colleges continued to attract many of the finest players after World War II. In the late 1940s Morris Brown College running back John "Big Train" Moody and Kentucky State guard Herbert "Lord" Trawick were named All Americans by members of the black press. In the 1950s Morgan State sent several players to the National Football League (NFL), including Roosevelt Brown, Leroy Kelly, and Willie Lanier. Florida A&M stars Willie Gallimore and wide receiver Bob Hayes also had successful professional careers.

Grambling State has produced more professional players than any other black college. Under the leadership of Eddie Robinson, Grambling sent more than 200 players to the NFL, including the league's first black player, running back Paul "Tank" Younger, and its

AFRICAN AMERICANS IN THE COLLEGE FOOTBALL HALL OF FAME

Year Inducted	Name	Position	Institution
1956	Kenneth Washington	HB	University of California Los Angeles
1968	Buddy Henry Young	HB	University of Illinois
1974	James Parker	G	Ohio State University
1976	Oliver Matson	FB	University of California San Francisco
1977	Gale Sayers	HB	University of Kansas
1983	O.J. Simpson	HB	University of Southern California
1984	Charles Taylor	G	Stanford University
1990	Earl Campbell	HB	University of Texas
1994	Tony Dorsett	HB	University of Pittsburgh
1995	Paul Robeson	End	Rutgers University
1995	Mike Singletary	LB	Baylor University
1997	Ricky Hunley	LB	University of Arizona
1997	Dave Robinson	DL	Pennsylvania State University
1997	Joe Delaney	RB	Northwestern State University of Louisiana
1997	Frank Hawkins	RB	University of Nevada
1997	Gary Johnson	DT	Grambling State University
1997	Bruce Taylor	DB	Boston University
1997	George Rogers	RB	University of South Carolina
1998	Bo Jackson	RB	Auburn University
1998	Mel Long	DT	University of Toledo
1998	Johnny Roland	RB	University of Missouri

first African American quarterback, James Harris. Grambling graduates also include halfback Sammy White; defensive backs Everson Walls, Roosevelt Taylor, and Willie Brown; defensive tackle Junious "Buck" Buchanan; defensive end Willie Davis; and the first black quarterback to play in a Super Bowl, Doug Williams. Coach Eddie Robinson is the grandfather of black college football and has paved the way for others, such as Ed Hurt (Morgan State), Earl Banks (Morgan State), and Jake Gaither (Florida A&M).

Of all the black college graduates who have played PROFESSIONAL FOOTBALL, Walter Payton, Jerry Rice, and Art Shell may be the most famous. Payton, a graduate of Jackson State, was one of the most gifted running backs in NFL history. He finished his career with the Chicago Bears as the league's career rushing leader and a member of the NFL Hall of Fame. Jerry Rice, a graduate of Mississippi Valley State, is arguably the best wide receiver ever to play the game. He joined the San Francisco 49ers in 1985 and continues to lead them in receptions. Rice holds the NFL record for most career touchdowns. Art Shell, a graduate of Maryland State, was an NFL Hall of Fame lineman before becoming only the second African American to be named a professional football head coach.

Stars at Predominantly White Schools

While historically black colleges and universities gave African American athletes a forum from which to showcase their athletic talents, small numbers of black football players were standouts at predominantly white schools. As early as 1889, William Henry Lewis and William Tecumseh Sherman Jackson were among the first blacks to play collegiate football at predominantly white schools. Both attended Amherst College in Massachusetts from 1889 to 1891. Lewis later graduated from Harvard Law School and in 1903 became the first African American to serve as U.S. assistant attorney general.

By the late 1890s a few predominantly white schools had begun recruiting black players, including George Jewett at the University of Michigan in 1890 and George Glippin at the University of Nebraska in 1892. Throughout the 1890s several blacks earned spots on predominantly white football teams. In 1890 William Arthur Johnson was a running back at the Massachusetts Institute of Technology (MIT). That year Howard Cook played at Cornell, Howard Lee at Harvard, George Chadwell at Williams, William Washington at Oberlin, and Alton Washington at Northwestern. By the turn of the century black players at predominantly white colleges were gaining national attention for their athleticism.

Among the first was Robert Marshall, a standout at the University of Minnesota between 1903 and 1906. In 1904 Marshall scored 72 points in one game. Walter Camp named him a Second Team All-American in 1905 and 1906. Several years later another African American earned national recognition: Frederick Douglass "Fritz" Pollard, enrolled at Brown University in Rhode Island in 1915. Pollard was an exceptional running back, defensive back, and kicker. He led Brown to the Rose Bowl in 1916 and was named an All-American the same year. The third black player to dominate at a predominantly white college during this time was PAUL ROBESON, a four-sport athlete at Rutgers University in New Jersey. At six-foot-three-inches tall, Robeson was an intimidating presence on the football field. He was a dominant lineman, was recognized as an All-American, and was a member of the Phi Beta Kappa academic honor society.

Throughout the 1920s black players excelled at schools throughout the Northeast, West, and Midwest. Fred "Duke" Slater was a star tackle at the University of Iowa from 1919 to 1921, and Charles West and Charles Drew were running backs at Washington and Jefferson in Pennsylvania. Drew later became a doctor and gained international recognition for his discovery of a technique to preserve blood plasma. At Duquesne Ray Kemp played tackle and at New York University (NYU) David Myers was a defensive end. During the 1930s, Iowa, Northwestern, and Ohio State included black players on their rosters, including Oze Simmons, Homer Harris, William Bell, and Bernard Jefferson. These players managed to succeed in environments that were often hostile to blacks.

During his career at Rutgers, Paul Robeson suffered numerous injuries, including a broken nose and a separated shoulder, all as a result of dirty play by opposing white players. In 1923 Jack Trice of Iowa State died from internal bleeding after an excessively rough game against the University of Minnesota. At most white schools, blacks were barred from living in white dormitories and discouraged from playing quarterback. They were excluded from Southern schools altogether. Between 1918 and 1937 no African American was named a First Team All-American, despite blacks' dominance at schools such as the University of Iowa, Ohio State, and the University of California at Los Angeles. The first black player after Paul Robeson to be named First Team All-American was Jerome Holland, a tight end at Cornell in 1937. That year Syracuse bowed to Southern tradition by benching quarterback Wilmeth Sadat-Singh when the team traveled to the University of Maryland. Boston College followed the example set by Syracuse when its team benched Louis Montgomery during the 1937 Cotton Bowl against Clemson.

Breaking Racial Barriers

Although racism continued to segregate blacks and whites in America throughout the 1940s and 1950s, several African American players managed to continue breaking racial barriers. In 1948 Denny Hoggard and Wally Triplet (Penn State) were the first African Americans to play in the Cotton Bowl. A year later Levi Jackson was the first black to be named captain of the Yale football team. In 1956 Jim Parker of Ohio State became the first black to win the Outland Trophy, an award recognizing the best lineman in the nation. By 1960 some of the most racist Southern universities found themselves on the losing side of battles with integrated teams, including the University of Alabama, whose head coach swore he would never let a black man play on his team.

Since 1970 African Americans have won a majority of the annual Heisman Trophies and several of the most recent Outland Trophies. In 1980 Dennis Green became the first African American head coach at a predominantly white school. He led Northwestern from 1981 to 1985 and Stanford University from 1989 to 1991, then became the head coach of the Minnesota Vikings of the National Football League. Black coaches such as Ronald Cooper, Ronald Dickerson, and Jim Caldwell have made strides at the Division I-A level as well. Today, most of the country's top programs, including those with long-standing histories of racial discrimination, such as the University of Alabama, the University of Georgia, and the University of Tennessee, have predominantly black football teams.

Alonford James Robinson, Jr.

See Also

World War II and African Americans; Drew, Charles Richard; Hampton University; Pollard, Frederick Douglass (Fritz); Tuskegee University; Shell, Arthur.

North America

Football, Professional, American team sport that originated in 1869 from a combination of two popular international games, rugby and soccer. During the early years of professional football, African Americans were banned from teams affiliated with the National Football League (NFL). Today, the NFL boasts that African Americans' presence in the sport has helped make professional football an international sensation.

The first known African American to play professional football was running back Charles Follis, who signed with the Shelby Athletic Club (Shelby, Ohio) in 1902. Despite the presence of Follis, professional football in the United States moved toward full racial integration in intermittent waves. In 1933, after 31 years of limited racial integration on the playing field, the country's premier football league – the National Football League – banned African American athletes from participating in league play. When the NFL was reintegrated in 1946, black players made an immediate impact upon the game, leading their teams in rushing, passing, and receiving. Their presence in professional football owes much to the courage and fortitude of several early black pioneers.

Early Black Stars

When Follis retired from professional football in 1906, he was replaced in the same year by Charles "Doc" Baker, the second African American professional football player. Baker played two years as a running back with the Akron Indians. In 1911 another African American, Henry McDonald, began a six-year career as running back with the Rochester Jeffersons. The year 1919 saw the founding of the sport's first governing body, the American Professional Football Association (APFA), which was replaced in 1922 by the NFL.

Both leagues signed African American players. Robert "Rube" Marshall starred as tight end for the Rock Island Independents from 1919 to 1921, and Frederick "Fritz" Pollard had a three-year stint with the Akron Pros. Pollard became the first African American head coach when he was signed by Akron in 1920. He went on to coach at Milwaukee (1922), Hammond (1923-1924), and again at Akron in 1925-1926. Other African Americans continued to enter professional football throughout the 1920s. Paul Robeson, Jay "Inky" Williams, John Shelbourne, James Turner, Edward "Sol" Butler, Dick Hudson, Harold Bradley, David Myers, and Duke Slater all starred for teams in the APFA and the NFL.

Racial Segregation

The spirit of racial integration ended in 1933 when NFL team owners banned African Americans from playing in their league. Even in that climate, several NFL owners stood out for their racist beliefs, including George Preston Marshall, whose Washington Redskins became the last professional football team to integrate when they signed Bobby Mitchell in 1962.

When the ban on black players was imposed in 1933, several black entrepreneurs tried unsuccessfully to establish black professional teams. In 1935 Hershel "Rip" Day founded the New York Brown Bombers in honor of black heavyweight boxer Joe Louis. In 1935 Fritz Pollard was hired by the Bombers, for whom he coached for two years. The team dissolved after Pollard's departure and folded completely within a few years. But African Americans seeking to play professional football were given another opportunity when the newly founded American Professional League and the Pacific Coast Professional League decided to integrate in 1944. Several college football stars went on to successful careers in these leagues, including Kenny Washington (San Francisco Clippers), Ezzrett Anderson (Los Angeles Mustangs), and Jackie Robinson, who played for the Los Angeles Bulldogs before becoming the first African American to integrate major league baseball.

Reintegration

The NFL reluctantly responded to the integration of its rivals. The Los Angeles Rams became the first NFL team to integrate when they hired black veterans Kenny Washington and Woody Strode in 1946. The New York Giants and the Detroit Lions were the only other NFL teams to welcome black players during the 1940s, when such players as Melvin Grooms, Bob Mann, Emlen Tunnell, and Roosevelt Brown endured hostility as they competed against all-white teams. Although the NFL integrated slowly, its principal competitor, the All-American Football Conference (AAFC), did so much more swiftly. In 1946, the same year in which the Rams integrated, the Cleveland Browns of the AAFC signed black college stars Marion Motley and Bill Willis, who went on to spectacular careers. By 1947 Buddy Young, Joe "Fletcher" Perry, Elmore Harris, Bert Piggott, Ezzrett Anderson, and Len Ford had joined Motley and Willis in the AAFC.

Fearing their dominance would be eclipsed, the NFL began recruiting black players in the 1950s. Given the opportunity to prove themselves, these African American players exceeded expectations. Those who stood out in the 1950s and 1960s include Jim Brown, Gale Sayers, Lenny Moore, and John Johnson, as well as wide receiver Charles Taylor, defensive end David "Deacon" Jones, all-purpose runner Leroy Kelly, and offensive linemen Roosevelt Brown and Jim Parker. By the 1970s African Americans were among the NFL's top stars. Orenthal James "O.J." Simpson, Tony Dorsett, Eric Dickerson, Walter Payton, Earl Campbell, and Franco Harris were the

Opposite: Shown evading a tackle, Randall Cunningham of the Minnesota Vikings was one of the first African American quarterbacks to achieve stardom in the National Football League. *CORBIS/AFP*
Above: James Haynes of the New Orleans Saints sits on the sidelines during the last minutes of a losing game. Nearly 70 percent of players in the National Football League are African American. *CORBIS/Bettmann*
Right: Considered by many the best fullback ever to carry a football, Hall-of-Famer Jim Brown rushes here in 1965. *CORBIS/Bettmann*

AFRICAN AMERICANS IN THE NATIONAL FOOTBALL LEAGUE HALL OF FAME

Year Inducted	Name	Position	Team Affiliation
1967	Elmen Tunnell	DB	New York Giants/Green Bay Packers
1968	Marion Motley	RB	Cleveland Browns/Pittsburgh Steelers
1969	Joe Perry	RB	San Francisco 49ers/Baltimore Colts
1971	Jim Brown	RB	Cleveland Browns
1972	Olie Matson	RB	Chicago Cardinals/Los Angeles Rams/Detroit Lions/Philadelphia Eagles
1973	Jim Parker	OL	Baltimore Colts
1974	Richard Lane	DB	Los Angeles Rams/Chicago Cardinals/Detroit Lions
1975	Roosevelt Brown	OL	New York Giants
1975	Lenny Moore	RB	Baltimore Colts
1976	Len Ford	DL	Los Angeles Dons/Cleveland Browns/ Green Bay Packers
1977	Gale Sayers	RB	Chicago Bears
1977	Bill Willis	MG	Cleveland Browns
1980	Herb Adderley	CB	Green Bay Packers
1980	David "Deacon" Jones	DL	Los Angeles Rams/San Diego Chargers/ Washington Redskins
1981	Willie Davis	DL	Cleveland Browns/Green Bay Packers
1983	Bobby Bell	DL	Kansas City Chiefs
1983	Bobby Mitchell	RB	Cleveland Browns/Washington Redskins
1983	Paul Warfield	WR	Cleveland Browns/Miami Dolphins
1984	Willie Brown	DB	Denver Broncos/Los Angeles Raiders
1984	Charley Taylor	WR	Washington Redskins
1985	O.J. Simpson	RB	Buffalo Bills/San Franciso 49ers
1986	Ken Houston	SS	Houston Oilers/ Washington Redskins
1986	Willie Lanier	LB	Kansas City Chiefs
1987	Joe Greene	DL	Pittsburgh Steelers
1987	John Johnson	FB	San Francisco 49ers/Detroit Lions/ Pittsburgh Steelers/Houston Oilers
1987	Eugene Upshaw	OL	Oakland Raiders
1988	Alan Page	DL	Minnesota Vikings/Chicago Bears
1989	Mel Blount	CB	Pittsburgh Steelers
1989	Art Shell	OL	Oakland/Los Angeles Raiders
1989	Willie Wood	DB	Green Bay Packers
1990	Franco Harris	RB	Pittsburgh Steelers/Seattle Seahawks
1990	Buck Buchanan	DL	Kansas City Chiefs
1991	Earl Campbell	RB	Houston Oilers/New Orleans Saints
1992	John Mackey	TE	Baltimore Colts/San Diego Chargers
1993	Larry Little	G	San Diego Chargers/Miami Dolphins
1993	Walter Payton	RB	Chicago Bears
1994	Tony Dorsett	RB	Dallas Cowboys/Denver Broncos
1994	Leroy Kelly	RB	Cleveland Browns
1995	Kellen Winslow	TE	San Diego Chargers
1996	Charlie Joiner	WR	Houston Oilers/Cincinnati Bengals/San Diego Chargers
1996	Mel Renfro	DE	Dallas Cowboys
1997	Michael Haynes	CB	New England Patriots/Los Angeles Raiders
1998	Mike Singletary	DL	Chicago Bears
1998	Dwight Stephenson	C	Miami Dolphins

league's leading rushers. In the late 1980s African American players made gains in positions from which they had been discouraged, particularly that of quarterback. Among the African Americans to play quarterback in the NFL are James Harris, the first black quarterback in the league; Warren Moon; Randall Cunningham; and Doug Williams, the only African American quarterback to lead his team in a Super Bowl.

Although African Americans have excelled on the football field, they have not been welcomed in management positions. Sixty-seven percent of all players in the NFL are black, yet there are no African American owners and few general managers. Art Shell became the first African American head coach in the NFL and the second in professional football history when he was hired by the Los Angeles Raiders in 1989. There are still only a handful of black coaches in the league, including Dennis Green (Minnesota), Tony Dungy (Tampa Bay), and Ray Rhodes (Philadelphia). Gene Upshaw remains one of the few blacks to lead the NFL Player's Association.

Alonford James Robinson, Jr.

See Also

Baseball in the United States; Football, Collegiate; Pollard, Frederick Douglass (Fritz); Simpson, O.J.; Shell, Arthur.

North America

Foote, Julia (b. 1823, Schenectady, N.Y.; d. 1901), evangelist and itinerant preacher who became the first ordained woman deacon and the second ordained woman elder in the African Methodist Episcopal Zion Church.

The daughter of former slaves, Julia Foote attended a segregated white Methodist church with her family during her childhood. When she was a teenager her family moved to Albany, New York, and joined the local African Methodist Episcopal (AME) Church. Foote had a conversion experience in that church in 1838.

The next year she married George Foote and moved with him to Boston. Before her conversion, Foote had agreed with the conventional opinion that women should not preach; but after her arrival in Boston, she felt the call to preach and pray in public. Despite the disapproval of her parents, husband, and minister, and the threat of excommunication from her church, Foote began a career as an evangelist. During the next four decades, she traveled and preached throughout New England and the mid-Atlantic states, and as far away as Detroit, San Francisco, and Canada, preaching the doctrine of sanctification, or of the possibility of the soul's liberation from sin. Crowds of both whites and African Americans came to hear her sermons, in which she also spoke out against racism and sexism.

Foote's autobiography, *A Brand Plucked from the Fire,* was published in 1879, and details many of her travels and speaking experiences. From 1884 until her death, she lived with Bishop Alexander Walters and his family, and assisted him at the same time that she continued her own ministry. In 1900 Bishop Walters ordained Foote in the African Methodist Episcopal Zion Church; she became only the second woman to be ordained into the ministry by any Methodist denomination.

Lisa Clayton Robinson

See Also

African Methodist Episcopal Church; Boston, Massachusetts.

North America

Ford, Harold Eugene (b. May 20, 1945, Memphis, Tenn.), Democratic member of the United States House of Representatives from Tennessee (1975-1997).

Harold E. Ford received a bachelor's degree from Tennessee State University in 1967, a degree in mortuary science from John Gupton College in 1969, and a master's degree from Howard University in 1982. He worked as a funeral director in his family's business. He was elected to the Tennessee state House of

Representatives in 1971 and became known for his fiery speeches and good organizing skills. In 1974 he defeated Republican incumbent Dan H. Kuykendall by fewer than 1000 votes to win Tennessee's Ninth Congressional District seat. The Ninth District, which consists of most of Memphis and a few suburbs, became a black-majority district in 1976, and Ford won all his reelection campaigns by comfortable margins.

Early in his House career, Ford was given a seat on the Ways and Means Committee and became chairperson of the Human Resources Subcommittee. However, when Republicans assumed control of the House in 1995, Ford became the ranking minority member.

In 1996, at the height of his career, Ford announced that he would not seek reelection: "I went with a new vision in 1974," he said, "and I think it is time for a new vision and a new generation to come." The following year, Harold E. Ford Jr. won his father's former seat and became, at 26 years old, the youngest member of the 105th Congress.

See Also
Memphis, Tennessee.

North America

Ford, Harold, Jr. (b. 1970, Memphis, Tenn.), Democratic member of the United States House of Representatives from Tennessee (1997-).

Harold Ford Jr. was born in Memphis, Tennessee. He received a bachelor's degree in American history from the University of Pennsylvania in Philadelphia in 1992 and a law degree from the University of Michigan in Ann Arbor in 1996. In 1992 he served as special assistant for justice and civil rights issues on President-elect Bill Clinton's transition team. He was also an assistant to Tennessee senator Jim Sasser on the Senate Budget Committee. In both 1992 and 1994 he managed the successful reelection campaigns of his father, Harold E. Ford Sr., who represented Tennessee's Ninth Congressional District. In 1993 he worked for U.S. secretary of commerce Ron Brown as a special assistant to the Economic Development Administration. Ford was elected to the U.S. House from Tennessee's Ninth Congressional District in November 1996. At 26 he was the youngest member of the 105th Congress. He was also the first African American in U.S. history to succeed his father in Congress. Harold E. Ford Sr. had served in Congress for 11 years.

The Ninth District covers the city of Memphis. The city is a major distribution center. Federal Express Corporation, a leading overnight delivery service, is based in Memphis, and one-third of the nation's cotton crop passes through the Memphis Cotton Exchange. Health care facilities such as St. Jude's Hospital, an important pediatric care center, are significant sources of employment.

In 1997 Ford served on the Education and Workforce Committee. He is also a member of the Congressional Black Caucus.

See Also
Ford, Harold Eugene.

North America

Ford, James W. (b. December 22, 1893, Pratt City, Ala.; d. 1957), African American Communist Party official; Ford became the first African American on a presidential ticket when he ran for vice president with William Z. Foster in 1932.

James W. Ford was born in Pratt City, Alabama, on December 22, 1893. In 1913 he entered Fisk University in Nashville, Tennessee, and graduated in 1920 after serving in the army during World War I. He then moved to Chicago, where he became a postal worker and joined the Chicago Postal Workers Union and the American Negro Labor Congress, both affiliates of the Communist Party USA.

Ford joined the Communist Party in 1926 and rose rapidly through its ranks. In 1928 he was a delegate to the party's executive committee meeting in Moscow. In 1931 he became vice president of the party's League of Struggle for Negro Rights. He was the first African American on a presidential ticket, running for vice president with William Z. Foster in 1932. They received 102,991 votes.

In 1933 Ford was selected to head the party's section in Harlem. It was decentralized and many of its members diverged from the party's platform by endorsing Black Nationalism, which the party believed would alienate white workers. Ford efficiently returned the organization to communist orthodoxy, and increased its membership from 560 to 1000.

In 1936 he was again selected as the Communist Party's vice presidential candidate, but he and running mate Earl Browder received fewer than 50,000 votes. During World War II Ford's power in the national party diminished, though he remained the head of the Harlem section. In the 1950s he was the executive director of the National Committee to Defend Negro Leadership, a group founded to aid African American party members who were convicted under federal antisubversion laws that arose because of cold war antipathy toward the Communist Party.

Robert Fay

See Also
World War I and African Americans; World War II and African Americans; Harlem, New York; Communist Party USA, African Americans and the; Black Nationalism in the United States.

North America

Foreman, George Edward (b. January 10, 1949, Marshall, Tex.), African American two-time heavyweight boxing champion whose long career has included evangelical preaching and sitcom acting.

George Foreman grew up in Houston, Texas, and led a rough early life, dropping out of high school, drinking heavily, and committing petty larcenies. In 1965 he turned his life around by joining the Job Corps, where he was introduced to boxing. Showing exceptional natural aptitude, Foreman won his first official amateur fight in 1967 with a first-round knockout. His talent developed quickly and by 1968 he had won a Gold Medal for the United States at the Summer Olympic Games in Mexico City.

In 1969 Foreman launched a record-breaking professional career. By 1973 he had knocked out 36 consecutive opponents and won the title of heavyweight champion from Joe Frazier. Foreman defended his title until 1974, when underdog Muhammad Ali knocked him out in Kinshasa, Zaire.

After a fight in Puerto Rico in 1977, Foreman experienced a religious epiphany that prompted him to retire from boxing and become a self-ordained evangelical Christian minister. Returning to Houston, he founded the George Foreman Youth and Community Center, to which he devoted most of his time. During the 1980s he became a television personality by promoting products, and in 1993 his amicability earned him his own situation comedy, *George*.

Ostensibly to raise funds for his social programs, Foreman returned to professional boxing in 1987. His comeback astonished the boxing world, especially as it culminated in his defeat of heavyweight champion Michael Moorer in 1994. Foreman regained his title at the unprecedented age of 45.

Eric Bennett

See Also
Kinshasa, Democratic Republic of the Congo; Frazier, Joseph William (Joe); Houston, Texas; Television and African Americans.

North America

Forman, James (b. October 4, 1928, Chicago, Ill.), civil rights activist who is credited with giving the Student Nonviolent Coordinating Committee (SNCC) a firm organizational base.

While reporting for the *Chicago Defender* in 1960, James Forman learned of black farmers in Tennessee who had been evicted by their white landlords for registering to vote. In support, Forman joined a program sponsored by the Congress of Racial Equality (CORE) that provided relief services to the displaced farmers. Later that year, he participated in

Freedom Rides, in which blacks rode in buses throughout the South testing court-ordered integration of public transportation. Forman then joined SNCC and began working for black civil rights full time.

Having served in the air force during the KOREAN WAR, Forman possessed more maturity and experience than most of the young members of SNCC. His organizational skills thrust him into a leadership role at the organizationally weak SNCC, where he directed fundraising and supervised staff. In 1964 he became SNCC's executive secretary, a post he held until 1966. In addition, Forman participated in many of SNCC's direct-action protests and helped organize voter registration drives in Alabama and Mississippi. Soon after the FREEDOM SUMMER of 1964, however, arguments over SNCC's direction, strategies, and tactics consumed the organization's leaders. Amid this debate in 1968 Forman left SNCC to seek economic development opportunities for black communities.

Forman published his memoir of the CIVIL RIGHTS MOVEMENT, *The Making of Black Revolutionaries: A Personal Account,* in 1972; a new edition was published in 1997. He earned a master's degree in African and African-American Studies at Cornell University in 1980 and a Ph.D. from the Union of Experimental Colleges and Universities (in cooperation with the Institute for Policy Studies) in WASHINGTON, D.C., in 1982. He crystallized his studies in his 1984 book, *Self Determination: An Examination of the Question and Its Application to the African-American People.* Forman has been active in the fight to gain statehood for the District of Columbia.

Robert Fay

SEE ALSO
Chicago Defender.

Latin America and the Caribbean

Forró, music and dance style from the Brazilian northeast. Forró is traditionally played by a trio consisting of accordion, triangle, and drum (*see* LUIZ GONZAGA).

Africa

Forros, the dominant Creole population of SÃO TOMÉ AND PRÍNCIPE, also known as *filhos da terra.*

Shortly after their discovery in the late fifteenth century, the islands of São Tomé and Príncipe, which lie off the coast of GABON in the Gulf of Guinea, were settled by Portuguese, mostly criminals expelled from their homeland, and African slaves brought there as laborers on the islands' SUGAR plantations. The first governor of the new colonies, now known as São Tomé and Príncipe, dictated that each Portuguese convict be given a slave woman as his wife. Their mixed-race children, known as *mestiços,* occupied a privileged position – some were sent abroad for an education – and were the ancestors of today's *forros.* Many prospered as traders and later, at the beginning of the coffee and COCOA boom in the nineteenth century, some took over the old sugar plantations to become successful farmers.

By the turn of the century, Portuguese landowners had foreclosed on these lucrative cocoa estates and driven the forros into a marginal position in the island's plantation economy. During the 1930s, faced with the loss of workers due to laws against conscripted African labor, the Portuguese, who controlled the colonial government, imposed taxes and other legal constraints aimed to force the forros into manual labor on the plantations, work they had historically disdained as beneath them.

It was the middle-class forros, frustrated by their lack of representation in the colonial government and angered at its policies, who initiated the Sãotoméan nationalist movement. Since Portugal granted São Tomé its independence in 1975, forros have dominated the islands. São Tomé's first president, Manuel Pinto da Costa, came from one of the islands' oldest forros families, as did its second president, Miguel Trovoada. Speaking a Portuguese Creole and preserving traditional West African music and dance, the forros are the descendants of the island's earliest inhabitants and consider themselves the only true Sãotoméans. Forros culture, in particular the *tchiloli,* a ritual theatrical dance, defines Sãotoméan national identity to this day.

Kate Tuttle

SEE ALSO
Nationalism in Africa; Transatlantic Slave Trade; Creoles.

North America

Fort Pillow Massacre, fort in east central Tennessee, on the east bank of the Mississippi River, north of Memphis, noted as the site of the so-called Massacre of Fort Pillow during the AMERICAN CIVIL WAR (1861-1865).

Fort Pillow was constructed by Confederate forces under the direction of Gen. Gideon Pillow in the spring of 1862, but was abandoned by them on June 4 of the same year. A small Union force occupied the fort on June 5, and it remained in their possession, lightly garrisoned, until April 12, 1864, when it was reinforced by about 500 men, most of them black. On that day, the fort was attacked and overpowered by a strong Confederate force under Nathan Bedford Forrest. The Confederates were later accused by the United States War Department of deliberately massacring more than 300 in the fort after their surrender (*see* MILITARY, BLACKS IN THE AMERICAN). Only about 160 white and 40 black prisoners were taken.

North America

Fortune, Amos (b. 1710?, Africa; d. November 17, 1801, Jaffrey, N.H.), African American slave who purchased his own freedom and was a founder of the public library in Jaffrey, New Hampshire.

Amos Fortune was born in Africa, but as a young man of about 15, he was captured into slavery (*see* SLAVERY IN THE UNITED STATES). Eventually sold to Ichabod Richardson of Woburn, Massachusetts, Fortune learned the tanning trade from his master, worked for him for 40 years, and was able to purchase his own freedom at age 60. He went into business for himself, paid his church and town taxes in Woburn, and at age 68 purchased Lydia Somerset, herself a slave, and married her. Somerset soon died and Fortune bought and married Violate Baldwin and moved to Jaffrey, New Hampshire, with her and her daughter Celyndia, whom he adopted.

Fortune became a successful tanner, bought land, and built a house. He aided local blacks by training apprentice tanners and by taking the indigent into his home. On January 28, 1796, Fortune participated in a meeting of local citizens who voted to establish a town library, and he took on the task of binding the library's books. Amos Fortune died in 1801 and left his estate to his wife. His will provided that upon the death of his wife the money would go to the local school and to the Congregational Church, where he had been obliged to sit in a segregated pew in the balcony. The church purchased a silver communion service, and the school continues to use income from his gift for prizes.

Fortune is buried next to his wife in the Jaffrey cemetery, under a tombstone inscription presumably of his own composition: "Sacred to the memory of/ Amos Fortune/ who was born free in Africa/ a slave in America/ he purchased liberty/ professed Christianity/ lived respectfully/ and died hopefully."

Margit Liander

North America

Forty Acres and a Mule, a phrase whose meaning has evolved since its Civil War beginnings. It is also currently the name of filmmaker Spike Lee's film company.

The phrase "40 acres and a mule" probably stems from a field order given in 1865 to former slaves in the Savannah area of Georgia. On January 16, 1865, Gen. William T. Sherman of the Union Army issued Special Field Order 15. This order reserved the Sea Islands and areas of coastal South Carolina, Florida, and Georgia for freedpeople to own. Each person or family was to receive a 40-acre plot of agriculturally fit land. With Sherman's permission, the army could also loan mules to former slaves. About 40,000 blacks settled 400,000 acres of land (called Sherman Land) within six months. In March 1865 Congress authorized the Freedmen's Bureau to rent 40-acre plots of confiscated and abandoned lands to freedpeople.

The land reform and redistribution remained crucial to the freedpeople's demands and very controversial in congressional debates during the RECONSTRUCTION period. Land became a widespread expectation of the ex-slaves, both because most thought the land belonged to them, as they had tilled it while enslaved, and because of pervasive rumors. On May 25, 1865, President Andrew Johnson ordered that the 40-acre plots be returned to the former slave owners. Radical land redistribution never took place. "Forty acres and a mule" became a symbol not only of the limitations of Reconstruction but of African Americans' unfulfilled reparations, expectations, and hopes.

Martha King

SEE ALSO

Bureau of Refugees, Freedmen and Abandoned Lands; Civil War, American; Lee, Shelton Jackson ("Spike").

North America

Fourteenth Amendment to the United States Constitution,

amendment ratified on July 28, 1868, that was intended to guarantee the civil rights of African Americans.

During the Civil War the Thirteenth Amendment freed Southern slaves, but after the war most blacks in the segregated South were able to realize little of their new freedom. President Andrew Johnson, who wanted to accommodate the defeated Confederate states, was reluctant to press the South for black equality. As a result, Radical Republicans in Congress drafted and secured passage of the Fourteenth Amendment. Their intent was partly to guarantee black freedom as granted by the Thirteenth Amendment and partly to limit the power of the reconstructed South.

The Fourteenth Amendment contains five sections, the heart of which is Section 1 (discussed below). Section 2 guarantees that if black men (or other male citizens) are denied the right to vote, their state's representation in Congress will be reduced proportionately. Section 2 was motivated by Republicans' fears that although blacks were now considered fully in the apportionment of representation to Congress (previously black men counted for only three-fifths of a person for congressional apportionment), because they were too intimidated to vote, the white South might gain *more* representation in Congress as a result of freeing the slaves. In fact, the North's fears proved correct, but Section 2 was never enforced. Section 3 forbids former Confederate soldiers to hold political office, but enforcement of this ban also turned out to be short-lived. Section 4 absolves the United States government of responsibility for the war debt of the Confederate states. Section 5 gives Congress the power to enforce the amendment.

Section 1, historically the most important of the sections, is divided into four main clauses. The first clause, known as the citizenship clause, grants state and federal citizenship to "all persons born or naturalized in the United States" with the exception of Native Americans. The citizenship clause was intended to undo Supreme Court rulings such as DRED SCOTT V. SANFORD (1857), in which the court held that neither slaves nor their descendants were citizens of the United States.

The second clause, known as the privileges and immunities clause, holds that no state shall "abridge the privileges or immunities" of citizens. This was an attempt to keep Southern states from passing racially discriminatory laws. The full potential of the clause was never realized, however, because the Supreme Court ruled in 1873 that only the rights of *federal* citizenship were protected by the clause. States, said the court, were free to restrict the rights of *state* citizenship as they saw fit. Because most matters of everyday life were governed by states, the practical effect of the ruling was that schooling, housing, employment, and other immediate concerns were ruled by discriminatory state laws; federal law protected mostly uncommon circumstances, such as life on the high seas.

The third clause of Section 1, the due process clause, holds that states shall not "deprive any person of life, liberty, or property without due process of the law." A restatement of a similar clause in the Fifth Amendment, it soon opened a debate among scholars and judges about whether the clause was meant to "incorporate" the Bill of Rights into the Fourteenth Amendment. In other words, was the clause an attempt to apply the protections of the Bill of Rights to the states instead of just to the federal government? (In *Barron v. Baltimore* [1833], the Supreme Court had ruled that the Bill of Rights did not apply to state laws.) The debate over the due process clause has never been resolved, but judges in the 1960s and 1970s used it to secure some rights for blacks and other minorities, including several rights related to desegregation.

A fourth and final clause, the equal protection clause, provided the framework for many antidiscrimination rulings. The clause holds that no state shall "deny to any person within its jurisdiction the equal protection of the laws." In the late nineteenth century the equal protection clause was routinely ignored by states and finally rendered useless by the Supreme Court in PLESSY V. FERGUSON (1896). In *Plessy* the court established its doctrine that facilities could be "separate but equal" – that segregation alone did not violate the equal protection clause. More than half a century later, however, the court relied on the equal protection clause to reverse *Plessy*. In BROWN V. BOARD OF EDUCATION (1954) the court argued that segregation was "inherently unequal" and therefore a violation of the Fourteenth Amendment. Thus rehabilitated, the equal protection clause provided the basis for desegregation of schools and housing as well as reapportionment of unfairly drawn congressional districts. The equal protection clause has also been used to guarantee the right to birth control devices and abortions.

SEE ALSO

American Indians; Civil War, American; Thirteenth Amendment of the United States Constitution and the Emancipation Proclamation.

North America

Four Tops, The,

African American vocal group that recorded during the MOTOWN label's golden age.

Originating in DETROIT, MICHIGAN, in 1953, the Four Tops were one of the most popular and successful of the soul-influenced pop acts that emerged in the 1960s. Motown signed the four singers – Levi Stubbs Jr., Renaldo Benson, Lawrence Payton, and Abdul Fakir – in 1963, and almost immediately they began producing hit after hit. Motown, a black-owned label, is largely credited with creating a highly commercial style that popularized black musical influences such as gospel and blues. The company also boasted the songwriting talents of Brian Holland, Lamont Dozier, and Eddie Holland, who not only penned most of the Four Tops' biggest hits – including "Baby, I Need Your Loving" (1964) and "Reach Out, I'll Be There" (1966) – but provided the raw material for other Motown hit machines, such as the Supremes and the Temptations.

Motown recording artists Levi Stubbs Jr., Renaldo Benson, Lawrence Payton, and Abdul Fakir – the Four Tops – topped the 1960s charts with their soul-influenced pop. *The Everett Collection*

Four years after Holland, Dozier, and Holland left Motown in 1967, the Four Tops left as well, recording with Dunhill Records a series of RHYTHM AND BLUES hits, including "Ain't No Woman (Like the One I Got)" (1973). During the 1980s and 1990s, the Four Tops toured extensively but recorded little new material.

Kate Tuttle

SEE ALSO
Soul Music; Blues, The; Gospel Music; Supremes, The; Temptations, The.

Africa

Fouta Djallon, a region of GUINEA that functioned as an autonomous Islamic state during the nineteenth century.

Now mainly a geographic term for the central Guinean highlands, the name Fouta Djallon also refers to an independent state that existed within the borders of present-day Guinea from the mid-1700s to the late 1800s. The region had been home to the YALUNKA (Jallonke) people since around the eleventh century. The Yalunka, who were mostly farmers, were part of the MANDINKA, or Malinke, ethnic group. They practiced a traditional religion. In the fifteenth century members of another ethnic group, the FULANI, began to enter the region peacefully. Starting in the seventeenth century, Fulani people (also known as Fulbe, or Peul) from the Futa Toro Empire in the area presently known as SENEGAL began entering the Fouta Djallon, bringing with them the Islamic faith.

The Muslim Fulani gradually conquered the entire Fouta Djallon and, despite their inferior numbers, became the dominant group, using both Yalunka and non-Muslim Fulani as slaves. The Muslim Fulani built a highly structured religious state, organizing a federation of seven provinces known as *diwals* under the ultimate control of a head of state known as the *alimami.* The position of alimami alternated between two leading families, the Alfyas and Soriyas, an arrangement that succeeded for more than 100 years.

Contact with European traders and colonialists began as early as the 1790s, when British expeditions, based in SIERRA LEONE, began to explore the interior. By the 1830s, historian Winston McGowan says, the French, based in Senegal, started trying to establish connections with Fouta Djallon. This interest was based in part on the area's abundant resources, which included gold, ivory, coffee, rice, and cattle. In addition, Fouta Djallon had a strategic location along the trade route connecting the Upper NIGER RIVER basin with the coastline.

By the 1880s competition between British and French authorities prompted each colonial power to seek an exclusive relationship with the ruling alimamis. In 1881 the alimamis signed an ambiguous treaty with the French. The French held that the document placed Fouta Djallon under French possession or protection, while the alimamis intended it merely as an acknowledgment of friendly relations. In 1893, bowing to pressure from Fouta Djallon, the French offered a new treaty conforming to the alimamis' interpretation.

Despite the diplomatic, administrative, and scholarly prowess of its people, the state of Fouta Djallon began to break down in the 1890s. Internal divisions, particularly between the two dynasties that had long shared power, played a part in this. The constant pressure of negotiations with colonial powers further weakened Fouta Djallon solidarity, as the Fulani disagreed among themselves how much to aid anticolonial efforts, including those of SAMORY TOURÉ, the Mandinka freedom fighter. Today the area is still known as the home of Guinea's Fulani people, who continue to practice Islam and raise cattle.

Kate Tuttle

SEE ALSO
Colonial Rule; Explorers in Africa, 1500 to 1800; Gold Trade; Ivory Trade; Great Britain; France; Islam and Tradition: An Interpretation; Slavery in Africa.

North America

Foxx, Redd (b. December 9, 1922, St. Louis, Mo.; d. October 11, 1991, Hollywood, Calif.), African American comedian and actor known for his television role on *Sanford and Son.*

Born John Elroy Sanford, Redd Foxx was the second son of Fred Sanford, an electrician, and Mary Alma Hughes Sanford, a minister. Called Redd because of his red hair and light complexion, he added the name Foxx after baseball player Jimmy Foxx. Redd Foxx dropped out of high school to play in a washtub band with friends. In 1939 they went to New York, calling themselves the Bon-Bons, but the group dissolved during World War II.

Rejected by the army, Foxx began to perform standup comedy in nightclubs. He teamed with Slappy White, and the two worked the African American nightclub circuit from 1951 to 1955. After the two broke up, Foxx moved to the West Coast to work. In 1956 he recorded the first of his 50 "party albums," comedy records featuring adult humor. The albums eventually sold over 20 million copies.

Although he had never acted, Foxx accepted a small role as a junkman in the popular movie *Cotton Comes to Harlem.* NBC executives liked the character so much that they developed it into a situation comedy character. In 1972 *Sanford and Son* first appeared on television, with Foxx in the starring role of Fred Sanford, a gruff junk dealer. The show lasted until the 1977 television season and with it, Foxx attained mainstream popularity. He appeared in several other films, including *Norman... Is That You?* in 1976 and *Harlem Nights* in 1989. Foxx suffered a fatal heart attack while on the set of a new situation comedy, *The Royal Family,* in 1991.

Robert Fay

SEE ALSO
World War II and African Americans; New York, New York; Television and African Americans.

Europe

France, a country in Western Europe where blacks have had a presence for centuries.

The French historian Henri Blet claimed: "Frenchmen have never adopted racial doctrines affirming the superiority of whites over men of color." It is true that the French Revolution, with its pioneering slogan of liberty, equality, and fraternity, inaugurated a still vigorous French intellectual tradition of rationalism, tolerance for difference, and resistance to authority. It is also true that many twentieth-century black musicians, writers, and artists have experienced France as a haven of racial tolerance. Yet France, like other European powers, was an active participant in the TRANSATLANTIC SLAVE TRADE and developed a colonial empire (*see* COLONIAL RULE) that systematically subordinated blacks to whites. France has also been a major contributor to European racist ideologies over the centuries, including late nineteenth-century "scientific" racism and the current views of the National Front. Moreover, while many more blacks live in France today than ever before, they are largely relegated to the least desirable positions in society.

BLACKS IN THE ANCIEN RÉGIME

Although blacks have lived in and visited France since Roman times, we know little about the sporadic contacts that took place prior to the late seventeenth century. Apparently, a black woman from SUDAN named Ismeria married Robert d'Eppes – a relative of the French king – and was enshrined as a black madonna after her death in the mid-thirteenth century. Records also mention an Anselme d'Ysalguier from Toulouse, who lived in the African town of Gao (capital of the SONGHAI EMPIRE) for eight years and returned home in 1413 with a black wife and daughter. Traders brought a number of Africans to France in the late sixteenth century and the seventeenth century as galley slaves to row warships. However, in 1571, when a ship owner attempted to sell some black slaves in Bordeaux, the city council ordered him to release them on the grounds that slavery did not exist in France.

Until the eighteenth century, the only sources of information on Africans that were available to literate Frenchmen were prejudiced and fantastical. Islamic travelers depicted Africans in a starkly negative light.

For example, the account of LEO AFRICANUS, a Muslim traveler who had visited Tombouctou (Timbuktu), declared, "The Negroes are brutes without reason. They live like animals, without rules or laws." Leo's account was published in France in 1556. Other accounts, such as Pierre Bergeron's *Voyages fameux de Vincent Le Blanc*, published in 1648, drew on the ancient Greek and Roman traditions of spicy traveler's tales. According to Bergeron, the peoples of interior Africa are "so dirty that they eat the intestines of animals full with manure without washing them."

With the establishment of colonies on GUADELOUPE and MARTINIQUE in 1635 and of the West India Company in 1670, France entered into plantation slavery and the transatlantic slave trade in earnest. From that time onward, French plantation owners, military commanders, and government officials frequently brought their slaves on trips to France as servants, status symbols, and curiosities. Slaves were also sent as gifts from African kings to French aristocrats and royalty. As French SUGAR plantations began to generate wealth, slave-trading ports such as Nantes and Bordeaux became boomtowns.

African princes, both genuine and phony, visited France. One of the most interesting impostors was Aniaba, who claimed to be heir to the throne of Assinie in CÔTE D'IVOIRE. He came to Paris in 1687 and received a royal welcome: Louis XIV became his godfather and the famous orator Bossuet presided at his baptism in Notre Dame in 1692. However, when the chief of Assinie died in 1700 and a French warship sent Aniaba back to claim his homeland, the indifferent reception given him by the local people revealed him as a phony. ABRAM HANNIBAL, a true Ethiopian prince, lived in Paris, where he studied military engineering and served in the French army from 1716 to 1723 before returning to his master, Peter the Great, in Russia.

Until 1716 no rules covered the blacks present in France, apart from the widely held belief that slavery did not exist in the country (the so-called Freedom Principle). The Edict of October 1716 set conditions whereby slave owners could bring their slaves to France, register them, and retain them while they were on French soil. The two approved purposes for bringing slaves to France were to give them religious instruction or to provide training in a trade such as carpentry; in practice, most slaves received neither. The Declaration of 1738 reiterated the provisions of the edict and set a three-year limit on the amount of time a slave could remain in France; it also forbade slaves from marrying in France, with or without their masters' consent; and it prohibited slave owners from freeing their slaves in France except in their wills. The government's intention was to ensure that French slaves were put to work as much as possible in the colonies, where they were of most economic value.

A legal loophole, however, arose from the fact that neither the 1716 edict nor the 1738 declaration was registered by the Parlement of Paris, which had jurisdiction over one-third of France, and maintained the opinion that, since slavery did not exist in France, it could not register any legislation containing the word "slave." In fact, many slaves successfully petitioned the Parlement for their freedom during the eighteenth century. One landmark case was that of Louis, a slave who was declared free in 1762. His master, Sir Jean Jacques Le Fevre, was ordered to pay Louis back wages, plus interest for the seven and a half years Louis had worked for him in France.

Around this time officials began to voice their fear of the presence of blacks in France. According to Guillaume Poncet de la Grave, the king's representative to the Admiralty Court, "The introduction of too great a quantity of Negroes into France... is a dangerous consequence.... We will soon see the French nation disfigured if such an abuse is tolerated. Moreover, the Negroes are, in general, dangerous men."

Many Algerians fleeing civil war lived in shantytowns like this one near Nanterre on the outskirts of Paris, France, in 1961. *CORBIS/Hulton-Deutsch collection*

In 1762 the government issued an ordinance requiring the registration of all black people living in France, whether slaves or free blacks. The presence of blacks in France was no longer an issue purely pertaining to the slave colonies: it had become an issue of race. Although Poncet de la Grave had complained of a "deluge" of blacks in France, only 159 blacks were registered in Paris after the 1762 ordinance; in comparison, the total population of Paris was between 500,000 and 600,000. Moreover, few blacks committed crimes. One notable exception was Jean Mor, a 20-year-old slave from Martinique who in 1764 was executed in the town of Brest by strangling and burning, a common punishment at that time, for having attempted to kill his master by lacing his gravy with an African poison.

In 1777, in a law known as the Police des Noirs, the French government suspended all lawsuits for freedom and prohibited further arrivals of blacks in France. As one of the drafters of the law wrote: "In the end, the race of Negroes will be extinguished in the kingdom as soon as the transport of them is forbidden." The government made sure that the Parlement would ratify the law by using the word "black" as opposed to "slave." However, the implementation of the law was hindered by bureaucratic infighting and by the fact that slave owners continued to bring slaves with them to France. Indeed, Thomas Jefferson's slave and mistress SALLY HEMINGS accompanied one of his daughters to Paris in 1785 and remained there for several years.

French Emperor Napoleon, here rallying his troops in Egypt before the Battle of the Pyramids in 1798, reinstated slavery in France in 1802. *Archive Photo*

1789-1914: New Freedom and Opportunities

Although the French revolutionary movement proclaimed the ideals of liberty, equality, and fraternity, in practice its leaders were unwilling to even discuss the abolition of slavery. Indeed, the economic prosperity of the French bourgeoisie (or propertied middle class), the primary beneficiaries of the 1789 revolution, stemmed partly from the wealth of colonial plantations and depended on the slave trade. Even the leading abolitionist movement, the SOCIÉTÉ DES AMIS DES NOIRS, promoted a gradual emancipation and compensation for slave owners. These factors made the French National Convention's decision in 1794 to abolish slavery in the French Empire all the more surprising.

In fact, the emancipation of the slaves came in response to the massive slave rebellion in Saint-Domingue (present-day HAITI), France's most prized Caribbean colony, between 1791 and 1793. The rebellion (*see* HAITIAN REVOLUTION) received arms from two forces opposed to revolutionary France: royalists who wanted to restore the French monarchy, and foreign powers – notably Great Britain and Spain – that hoped to take over Saint-Domingue. In 1793 the two civil commissioners of Saint-Domingue abolished slavery in the colony, with the belief that only this would end the rebellion. France learned of the abolition when the colony's three deputies, two of them black, arrived in Paris in January 1794 and announced the decision. The convention then had no choice but to abolish slavery in all French domains. Although much self-congratulatory rhetoric accompanied the passing of the decree, it was significant that the revolutionary leader Robespierre refrained from signing it.

The thinkers of the eighteenth-century French Enlightenment, known as the *philosophes*, were famous for their articulation of liberal ideals such as democracy and political freedom. What is less well known is that these writers – men such as Montesquieu, Diderot, and Voltaire – were also instrumental in the development of modern European racism. To begin with, the philosophes' knowledge of, and interest in, Africa was severely limited: out of the 3867 books in Voltaire's library, only four were about Africa. Most relied on the travelers' tales of the seventeenth and early eighteenth centuries for their knowledge of Africans. The philosophes then simply perpetuated preexisting stereotypes of Africans. Thus Voltaire said of blacks that their intelligence was "far inferior," that "they are incapable of great attention," and that they had only "a few more ideas than animals." In the *Encyclopédie* Diderot described the people of Côte d'Ivoire as debauched, without religion or belief in life after death.

Until the eighteenth century French scholars' view of blacks had been dominated by the long-standing equation between blackness and evil. The philosophes and their contemporaries sought to understand the differences between blacks and whites from a more "scientific" perspective. They attached great importance to environmental factors. Montesquieu believed that the heat made Africans lazy and immoral, and that they needed an authoritarian government in order for their societies to function. The leading French abolitionist of the late eighteenth century, Abbé Henri Grégoire, shared this view. The physical features of Africans attracted widespread speculation. The scientist Louis Daubenton asserted that Africans were born looking like Europeans: the Africans' dark skin, he believed, was a degenerative effect of the sun's heat, and their facial features a result of having had their noses squashed and lips pulled out by their parents. Constantin-François Volney argued that African facial features resulted from prolonged squinting at the sun. Such thinkers believed that all men were born equal, but that their experience of different environments resulted in a hierarchy, with Europeans at the top and Africans at the bottom. According to this logic, Africans removed from their negative environment could revert to the superior status of Europeans.

The philosophes demonstrated a marked ambivalence regarding the issue of slavery. Montesquieu declared that "slavery is against nature," and then added, "though in certain countries it is founded on natural reason." He also recognized its economic value: "Sugar would be too expensive if the cane were not harvested by slaves." Voltaire opposed slavery on political grounds, yet he believed that blacks were born to be slaves, and deserved to be. In his *Essai sur les moeurs* (An Essay on Universal History) he wrote: "As a result of a hierarchy of nations, Negroes are thus slaves of other men... a people that sells its own children is more condemnable than the buyer; this commerce demonstrates our superiority; he who gives himself a master was born to have one."

Gradually, during the course of the late eighteenth century and early nineteenth century, French intellectual thought underwent a crucial shift in its perception of blacks. The view that blacks were essentially degraded Europeans gave way to the belief that the black race was biologically separate from, and innately inferior to, the white race, and that this inferiority was inherited over time. Georges Cuvier, in his work *Tableau élémentaire de l'histoire naturelle des animaux* (1798, Elementary Survey of the Natural History of Animals), declared in a crystallization of the racist thought of his time: "The white race, with oval face, straight hair and nose, to which the civilized peoples of Europe belong and which appears to us the most beautiful of all, is also superior to others by its genius, courage, and activity... a cruel law... seems to have condemned to an eternal inferiority the races of depressed and compressed skulls."

During the nineteenth century French intellectuals, including those opposed to slavery, passionately adopted this biological determinism. Among its adherents were the positivist thinkers Auguste Comte and Henri de Saint-Simon. Joseph-Arthur de Gobineau's *Essai sur l'inégalité des races humaines* (Essay on the Inequality of Human Races), a seminal work in the development of so-called scientific racism, warned of the collapse of European civilization due to intermarriage with inferior races.

The enormously influential phrenologists believed that head shape and brain size were the core determinants of human nature. A physician named Virey, in a book published in 1801, wrote: "Among us [whites] the forehead is pushed forward, the mouth is pulled back as if we were destined to think rather than eat; the Negro has a shortened forehead and a mouth that is pushed forward as if he were made to eat instead of to think." Also, in its entry on blacks, the Larousse dictionary of 1866 stated that their lesser intelligence resulted from a smaller brain size. Such views, and the alleged savagery and animalism of Africans, pervaded the works of popular French writers, including Jules Verne, Honoré de Balzac, and Pierre Loti. By the 1880s the research methods of scientific racism had been discredited in France, and the accounts of French travelers to Africa were conveying a more realistic picture of blacks to French readers. However, the belief that blacks were innately inferior to whites remained powerful in the minds of many French people.

While white intellectuals remained mired in racist speculation, blacks made significant contributions to French society during the late eighteenth and the nineteenth centuries. A number of blacks fought on the French side in the French Revolutionary and Napoleonic Wars of 1792-1815. A group led by Julien Raimond, a free black man and pamphleteer from Saint-Domingue, formed the Black Legion in 1792 to defend Paris against the attacking Prussian and Austrian forces. Joseph de Boulogne, Chevalier de Saint-Georges, was made the commander of the legion, and Alexandre Dumas (the father of writer Alexandre Dumas Père) was appointed the second in command. The legion saw little service against the enemy: its main claim to notoriety was its role as a firing squad for executing aristocrats in 1794 during the revolutionary Reign of Terror. After a general draft was introduced in 1793, other blacks in France joined the army, fighting in black-only and mixed-race units. Joseph "Hercule" Damingue led a "Battalion of Black Pioneers," distinguished himself in Napoleon Bonaparte's campaigns in Italy and Egypt (as did Alexandre Dumas), and was honored for his service.

The 1794 emancipation had the desired effect in Saint-Domingue: Toussaint L'Ouverture's black army soon abandoned the Spanish cause and fought from then on for France. However, in 1802 Napoleon – firmly convinced of the inferiority of blacks, the evils of intermarriage, and the importance of maintaining the slave plantations – restored slavery and the Police des Noirs. Partly as a consequence, France lost Saint-Domingue in 1804. At the Congress of Vienna in 1815, France was forced to agree to the abolition of the international slave trade, although French slaving ships continued to ply the coast of Africa through the 1820s with the tacit acceptance of the French government. French slavery itself continued until 1848. The restoration of slavery seems to have had little harmful effect on blacks in France; there is no evidence that former slaves were returned to their owners. In fact, the regulations, by prohibiting the transport to France of slaves yet permitting free blacks to enter the country, actually encouraged slave owners to free their slaves before taking them as servants to France.

During the 1820s and 1830s a group of colonial mulatto activists living in Paris in exile, including Adzée Louisy, the poet Louis T. Houat, and Mondésir Richard, wrote a series of pamphlets opposing slavery and highlighting racial mistreatment in the colonies. The most prominent pamphleteer was Cyril Charles Auguste Bissette, who in 1834 founded the *Revue des colonies* – the first literary journal in France devoted to black culture – andwas awarded the Legion of Honor in 1851. The 1848 emancipation completed a gradual process in which black pamphleteers, such as Bissette, and white abolitionists, such as Alexis de Tocqueville and Victor Schoelcher, had campaigned steadily against slavery, plantation owners had freed many of their slaves, and France had come to derive much of its sugar from domestically grown sugar beet rather than slave-grown sugar cane. Under the terms of the 1848 act, all slaves received French citizenship, the right to vote (males only), and equal treatment under the law. The 1848 revolution established a 750-member National Assembly with deputies from France and all the French colonies. Several blacks, including Bissette and François-Auguste Perrinon, were elected to represent the Caribbean colonies (*see* Abolition and Emancipation in Latin America and the Caribbean).

Blacks began to come to France for their education in the early nineteenth century, and many stayed to pursue literary or artistic careers, inspired by the stunning successes of Alexandre Dumas *père* and his son Alexandre Dumas *fils*. Beginning in 1795 the French government granted scholarships to the sons of colonial black leaders for study in France. However, many blacks came independently. Guillaume Guillon was sent by his father, a baron in Guadeloupe, to study painting in Paris. He had a successful career, eventually becoming a professor at the Ecole des Beaux-Arts (College of Fine Arts); his painting *Mort de Virginie* was later hung in the Louvre. Auguste Lacaussade from Réunion was sent to Nantes in 1827 for his education and developed a successful career as a French poet, winning prizes from the Académie Française for his work. From the 1830s onward a steady stream of black and mixed-race intellectuals from New Orleans,

Proclamation de la liberté des noirs aux colonies (Proclamation of Freedom for Blacks in the Colonies) was painted by French artist Auguste-François Biard in 1849, following the abolition of slavery in France in 1848. *Lauros-Giraudon/Art Resource, NY*

including Victor Séjour, Pierre Dalcour, and Louis and Camille Thierry, came to France to study, and a number of them remained to pursue literary careers.

Prompted by Africa's fabled riches, the urge to compete with other European powers in the "SCRAMBLE FOR AFRICA," and notions of French cultural supremacy, France launched a massive acquisition of territory in Africa in the late nineteenth century. In 1822 a French geographer wrote: "We want... Africa, with the rest of the world, to pay its tribute to our industry, to send to our cities overfilled with men its treasures, products, precious metals... Africa must in its turn fall to modern civilization." France's leading intellectuals rallied to the imperialist cause, including the writer Victor Hugo, who declared in 1849: "France is composing a magnificent poem that has as its title: the colonization of Africa... she bears in her hand light and liberty; she knows that, for a savage people, to be occupied by France is to begin to be free; for a city of barbarians, to be burned by France is to begin to be enlightened." Some blacks even fought on the French side during the African conquests: Alfred Amédée Dodds, who was one of the few black French generals in the nineteenth century, led France's conquest of Dahomey in 1892-1893.

Blacks continued to come to France in the late nineteenth and the early twentieth century. As before, most worked as servants, although artists and intellectuals also settled in France or stayed for extended periods. Notable black residents in France during this period were Julien Girard, a scholar of Latin and Greek from Guadeloupe who later became a professor of philosophy at the prestigious Lycée Louis-le-Grand; the African American painter HENRY OSSAWA TANNER, who settled in Paris; and the African American sculptor META VAUX WARRICK FULLER. A number of prominent African Americans visited France at this time, and as honored visitors were well treated by the French – a fact that proved crucial for the later development among African Americans of the myth of a "color-blind" France. Prominent visitors included IRA ALDRIDGE in 1867; FREDERICK DOUGLASS in 1886; Mary Church Terrell, who repeatedly visited between 1888 and 1921; Booker T. Washington in 1899; JAMES WELDON JOHNSON in 1905; the Reverend HENRY HUGH PROCTOR, who toured the French battlefields in 1919; and W. E. B. Du Bois, who fell in love with France during visits in 1894, 1906, and in 1918, when he was sent by the NATIONAL ASSOCIATION FOR THE ADVANCEMENT OF COLORED PEOPLE to investigate antiblack prejudice in the American forces (*see* MILITARY, BLACKS IN THE AMERICAN) in France during World War I.

WORLD WAR I TO THE 1960S: A GOLDEN AGE FOR BLACKS IN FRANCE

World War I (1914-1918) marked a turning point in the black experience of France and, similarly, in France's perceptions of blacks. According to some estimates, 40 percent of the French soldiers in the Crimean War (1853-1856) were black, and many blacks fought for France in the Franco-Prussian War (1870-1871). However, it was in World War I that blacks distinguished themselves as the "saviors of France." African soldiers in the French army, whose numbers totaled 135,000 by the end of 1918, fought in most of the major battles of the war. Around 200,000 African American soldiers fought in France on the Allied side. The black troops, especially the so-called *tirailleurs sénégalais* (the Senegalese riflemen), were widely praised for their valor. Most important, at least for the African Americans, was the contrast between the discrimination, segregation, and lynchings in the United States at the time and the welcoming attitude of the French. Officials and the general public were grateful for blacks' assistance in the war effort, and villagers voiced few complaints against blacks being billeted in their houses. One African American soldier wrote to his mother: "These French people don't bother with no color line business. They treat us so good that the only time I ever know I'm colored is when I look in the glass." Many French reacted with surprise and indignation to the racist behavior of white Americans toward African Americans. The French government ordered the burning of an American document instructing the French that fraternizing with blacks was an affront to American national policy. Not surprisingly, many African Americans chose to remain in France after the end of the war. Those who returned gave their fellow blacks compelling yet flawed images of a racially harmonious society.

The African American GIs were the first to introduce France to JAZZ. The 369th Regiment included a sizable jazz band led by James Reese Europe, and during 1918 Europe's band played all over France to enthusiastic audiences, including French head of state Raymond Poincaré. With the renewal of nightlife in Paris after the end of the war, jazz clubs such as Zelli's, Chez Florence, and Le Grand Duc sprang up, and African American entertainers such as Louis Mitchell, Sidney Bechet, Eugene Bullard, Ada "Bricktop" Smith, and the legendary JOSEPHINE BAKER visited or settled in the city. Jazz became the most popular musical form in Parisian nightclubs and dance halls, and with the growing ownership of radios in the 1920s, it soon found its way into French homes.

The presence of African American entertainers in Paris had an important effect on French intellectuals. Blackness was highly fashionable at the time; many artists and writers saw Western culture as exhausted and decadent, and admired the spontaneity and (for them) the exoticism of African art and African American music. Picasso and the Cubists along with Matisse, Derain, and other Paris-based painters drew on African forms and colors in their work, and classical composers, such as Maurice Ravel, incorporated jazz elements into their music. Beginning in 1925 Josephine Baker, dancing in the Revue Nègre, gave many French people their introduction to the beauty of the black body in motion. An illustration of the French fascination with African Americans is provided by the white French drummer Alain Romans, who recalled that at that time it was difficult to get a job as a white musician. As the only white member of a black band, Romans played a number of gigs in blackface, including once when a little girl screamed after touching his face and getting black paint on her fingers. As historian Tyler Stovall has remarked, "Whereas in America blackface enabled theaters to present the black aesthetic without blacks, freezing them out of the white entertainment world, in Paris a white musician's use of blackface reflected the dominant position of blacks as jazz performers."

Although the GREAT DEPRESSION of the 1930s dimmed the vitality of Parisian nightlife and, correspondingly, the opportunities for jazz entertainers, by then jazz had carved out a permanent position in Parisian clubs. It had also gained a respect among French intellectuals, signaled by the publication in 1934 of Hugues Panassié's *Le Jazz Hot*, the first significant study of jazz written in France. Jazz performers such as Bill Coleman came to Paris for extended stays. Others, such as PAUL ROBESON, Duke Ellington, and Louis Armstrong, paid shorter visits. The 1930s also saw the success of Bal Nègre, a nightclub in the Montparnasse district that specialized in the *béguine*, a Caribbean dance form (*see* DANCE IN LATIN AMERICA AND THE CARIBBEAN), and that catered to a French West Indian clientele.

Still, racist perceptions frequently arose from beneath the French fascination with black entertainers. The eminent playwright Robert de Flers condemned the Revue Nègre, saying that the show "makes us revert to the ape in less time than it took us to descend from it." The novels of Paul Morand, such as *Magie Noire* and *Baton Rouge*, draw a parallel between black dancers such as Josephine Baker and primitive savagery: "This young witch pulverized the musical, sentimental, and political melodies of the whites, forcing them to return to the beginnings of the world, to the simplicity of the jungle... she imposed on them the old African totemic dances."

After World War II, during which the Nazi occupiers of Paris banned jazz, African American jazz musicians – many of them among the quarter of a million African Americans who fought in the liberation of France in 1944 – initiated a rapid revival of jazz in France, symbolized by Dizzy Gillespie's 1948 concert in Paris and the International Paris Jazz Festival the following year. During the 1950s the jazz drummer Kenny Clarke settled in France, and Miles Davis spent extended periods of time there. Since then jazz has retained a prominent place in French culture.

Many prominent African American writers lived in France between the world wars, including CLAUDE MCKAY, who spent part of the summer of 1923 posing nude as an artist's model on the Left Bank in Paris; COUNTEE CULLEN, who declared that "Paris is where I would love to build my castles in Spain"; LANGSTON HUGHES; Walter White; JEAN TOOMER; Gwendolyn Bennett; and Anna

The great French writer André Gide was a champion of civil rights for blacks. *CORBIS/Bettmann*

RIGHT: Lilian Thuram, born on Guadeloupe, joined the French national soccer team in 1996 and soon was considered one of the best defenders in international play. *CORBIS/Christian Liewig; TempSport*
BELOW RIGHT: Teenagers stand in line outside a Paris movie theatre. In 1998 more than 350,000 people of West African descent lived in France; an estimated 400,000 West Indians lived in Paris alone. *CORBIS/Owen Franken*
OPPOSITE: A Tunisian baker working in Roubaix, France. *CORBIS/Marc Garanger*

Julia Cooper, the first African American to receive a doctorate from the Sorbonne. During the 1930s Paris became the center of the literary movement known as NÉGRITUDE. With institutions such as the publication *Revue du monde noir* and social gatherings hosted by the Nardal sisters, the movement brought McKay and other African American writers together with leading French-speaking African and Caribbean writers – such as Léopold Senghor and AIMÉ CÉSAIRE – in a joint effort to define the meaning of blackness. At the same time, some French white intellectuals were propagating new, less stereotyped views of Africa. For example, in his book *The Negroes*, Maurice Delafosse pointed out the similarities between the medieval kingdoms of West Africa and those of Europe.

After the hiatus of World War II, the African American and French-speaking African and Caribbean literary communities reestablished themselves in Paris. In the eyes of French intellectuals, African Americans were no longer symbols of an exotic African primitivism: they were viewed instead as bearers, and critics, of a powerful American popular culture that both attracted and threatened the French. During the 1950s three prominent African American writers – RICHARD WRIGHT, JAMES BALDWIN, and CHESTER HIMES – settled in France. The French-language African literary journal *Présence Africaine* was started in 1947 by a group of writers directed by Alioune Diop of SENEGAL. RENÉ MARAN, a native of Martinique who won the prestigious Prix Goncourt in 1921 for his novel *Batouala*, is perhaps the best-known French black writer of the twentieth century. In 1950 a prize known as the Grand Prix de la Mer et de l'Outre-Mer was established in order to reward literary effort on the part of black writers in France and in the French colonies. Among black residents of France who have won the award are JOSEPH ZOBEL and Clement Richer. In 1956 Richard Wright, along with Léopold Senghor, Aimé Césaire, and the black French poet David Diop, organized the Congress of Negro Artists and Writers – the first official gathering of African American and French-speaking black intellectuals.

Black participation in French politics increased after World War I, and from that time until the late 1950s many French cabinets included a black member in recognition of the importance of the colonies. Prominent examples are FÉLIX HOUPHOUËT-BOIGNY from Côte d'Ivoire, Léopold Sédar Senghor from Senegal, who edited the text of the French

Constitution of 1946, and the Senegalese statesman Blaise Diagne. In an illustration of France's success in gaining the acquiescence of black leaders in colonialism, Diagne, in the opening speech of the 1919 Pan-African Congress in Paris organized by W. E. B. Du Bois, praised the civilizing mission of French imperial rule (*see* Pan-African Congress of 1919).

Although the black Frenchman Gratien Candace was elected in 1938 to the position of vice president of the Chamber of Deputies, the number of black representatives in the French legislature increased dramatically only during the Fourth Republic (1946-1958). During this period the president of the senate was a black man – Gaston Monnerville from Martinique – and more than 50 blacks sat as deputies or senators, but this figure declined significantly after 1958 as the African colonies opted for independence. In 1949 the black French Guianese Félix Éboué – who in 1940 as governor of Chad had defied the Nazi-affiliated Vichy government and sided with Charles de Gaulle's Free French – was buried in the Panthéon in Paris, the highest honor available to a French citizen.

The few blacks in France during the 1920s and 1930s rarely met with openly expressed racial discrimination, and interracial love affairs, such as that between the black pianist Henry Crowder and the English heiress Nancy Cunard, were well tolerated. The greatest problems, in fact, came from white American visitors, such as the woman who stormed out of her Paris hotel after learning that a black woman was staying there, shouting at the owner: "I could never think of using the same bath as her," to which she received the response: "What do you fear, madame, that the colored lady will stain the tub?" Some French establishments collaborated with the white American position, especially those with a large American clientele. For example, La Coupole café refused to admit Claude McKay because of his skin color.

In Paris, African Americans recreated an African American community in a more tolerant environment than that of the United States. Louis Mitchell and Margaret Brown, both African American, operated American restaurants in Montmartre, and African Americans also owned two clothing boutiques in the district. Leroy Haynes opened a soul food restaurant in Montmartre in 1949, but most African Americans after World War II congregated in the Latin Quarter and in Montparnasse.

The 1960s to the Present: The Glitter Wears Thin

The growing number of black and other immigrants since the 1960s has fundamentally altered the relationship of blacks to French society. Before that period blacks constituted a tiny minority of musicians, writers, and artists outside the mainstream of French society, and most French perceived them as exotic and unthreatening visitors. While many French may have thought them inferior, due to the racist intellectual legacy outlined above, in person they could treat blacks with esteem and affection and show an interest in and respect for their culture. Moreover, most blacks in France before the 1960s were willing to adapt to French culture, whether out of a desire to assimilate into an apparently tolerant society (in the case of African Americans) or due to their French cultural heritage (in the case of blacks from the long-established colonies of the French Caribbean).

A 1961 estimate placed the number of blacks living in France between 30,000 and 40,000. As early as the 1960s, opinion polls were revealing antiblack prejudice. A survey conducted by the Ministry of Cooperation in 1962 revealed that more than half the respondents believed in the superiority of whites over blacks, and another poll of the same year showed that one out of every five people believed that there were too many blacks in France.

It is true that since the 1960s the greatest targets of racial animosity in France have been North Africans and people of North African descent. French bigots may have focused on North Africans due to their large numbers (around 5 million, or nearly a tenth of the population); their adherence to Islam, which precludes an easy integration into French society; and the legacies of the brutal Algerian war. In 1961 the African American writer William Gardner Smith recorded a massacre in the center of Paris in which the French police shot or beat to death more than 200 Algerians taking part in a demonstration. However, racial attacks have also targeted blacks. Wilmot Alfred Fraser, a black American visiting Paris in the 1960s, described French racism as "but an attenuated form of what I have known in the USA." Since the 1960s the increase in openly expressed racism in France has contrasted with the greater freedoms brought about by the Civil Rights Movement in the United States.

By 1980 more than 200,000 blacks resided in France, most of them unskilled workers living in slum conditions and competing directly with whites for employment and housing. In 1972 a bill outlawing racial discrimination passed in the French legislature. In previous years, its passage had been blocked by deputies arguing that such a bill was not necessary since racism did not exist in France.

In the 1980s French racism became a militant political force in the form of the extreme-right National Front party led by Jean-Marie Le Pen, which showed a hatred for people of color reminiscent of nineteenth-century racist thinkers. In response to the rise of the National Front, in 1984 young Arabs, blacks, and Jews founded SOS-Racisme, an antiracist movement spanning racial and ethnic boundaries. Led by Harlem Désir, a French West Indian, the movement organized mass demonstrations, protested racial discrimination and police harassment, and distributed thousands of badges bearing the slogan *Touche pas à mon pote* (Leave my buddy alone).

The National Front and its supporters blame so-called immigrants for France's economic woes – in particular, unemployment – and call for the end of legal immigration and the forcible expulsion of all immigrants from the country. (French racists often use the term "immigrants" broadly to refer to "people of color." This usage ignores the fact that many people of color were born and raised in France.) Many political leaders have adopted aspects of the National Front's language. In a 1992 interview with the *New York Times*, French president Jacques Chirac lamented the situation of French workers living next to so-called immigrants "with a father, three or four wives, about 20 kids, earning $10,000 a month without working... If you add to that the noise and the smell, the French worker goes crazy." Indeed, the National Front has carefully harnessed the frustrations and resentments of the French working class and channeled them into racial animosity toward so-called immigrants, who become the scapegoats for the country's economic and social troubles.

By 1998 there were more than 350,000 blacks from West Africa living in France, and more than 400,000 French-speaking West Indians living in the Paris metropolitan area alone. The influx of blacks has led to a thriving African and Caribbean cultural life in large cities such as Paris, which boasts black radio stations (Tropique FM and Afrique FM), restaurants (Le Kaissa and La Savane), discotheques (Ruby's and Rex), publications (*Jeune Afrique*), districts (Barbès-Rochechouart), and rap groups such as Rootsneg, which give impoverished blacks a means of expressing their anger in a nonviolent fashion.

Conclusion

The experiences of blacks in France have included those of the downtrodden servants and slaves of the pre-emancipation era, the jazz stars of the years between the world wars, the intellectual elite of the mid-twentieth century, and the Afro-French working class of more recent years. Although informed by a legacy of racist thinking, many French have approached blacks with curiosity and benevolence so long as the blacks concerned are intellectuals or artists, small in number, outside the mainstream of French society, and unthreatening to the French way of life. As a more substantial black population has developed in France since 1960, the polished veneer of tolerance has often worn off to reveal fear and resentment. Yet something important has remained. In the 1989 Bastille Day parade celebrating the bicentennial of the French Revolution, officials chose African American singer Jessye Norman to perform the French national anthem "La Marseillaise." French scholar Michel Fabre noted "the will of the French government to make a national commemoration into an international celebration via a member of the 'colored' majority of the world, to give the principles *'liberté, égalité, fraternité'* ['freedom, equality, fraternity'] their fullest meaning." This was more than mere propaganda, for the ideals of the revolution have survived in France to provide a crucial counterbalance to racist undercurrents during the late twentieth century.

Roanne Edwards and Jonathan Edwards

See Also

Présence Africaine; Algeria; Dahomey, Early Kingdom of; Diop, Alioune; Ethiopia; Russia and the Former Soviet Union; Senghor, Léopold Sédar; Dumas, Alexandre, Père; Slavery in Latin America and the Caribbean; Tombouctou, Mali; World War I and African Americans; World War II and African Americans; Armstrong, Louis ("Satchmo"); Bechet, Sidney Joseph; Cooper, Anna Julia Hayward; Davis, Miles Dewey, III; Du Bois, William Edward Burghardt (W. E. B.); Gillespie, John Birks ("Dizzy"); New Orleans, Louisiana; Lynching; Smith, Ada "Bricktop"; Terrell, Mary Eliza Church; Washington, Booker Taliaferro; White, Walter Francis; Ellington, Edward Kennedy ("Duke"); Toussaint L'Ouverture, François Dominique; French Guiana.

North America

Franklin, Aretha Louise

(b. March 25, 1942, Memphis, Tenn.), the preeminent black female vocalist of the 1960s and 1970s, who earned, through her secular and gospel masterpieces, the title Queen of Soul.

As a daughter of the renowned Baptist preacher C. L. Franklin and his wife, Barbara Siggers Franklin – whose singing won the laurels of Mahalia Jackson – Aretha Franklin was born into gospel. As a child she began to sing in her father's New Bethel Baptist Church in Detroit, Michigan, which he had built up to a congregation of 4500. C. L. Franklin recognized his daughter's talent and had her performing in New Bethel's choir by the age of 8. She sang solos at age 12, and at age 14 made her first recordings, including a version of Thomas A. Dorsey's gospel classic "Precious Lord, Take My Hand." She also began touring with her father, singing wherever he served as an itinerant preacher.

From Franklin's earliest days, something more than pure vocal bravura ignited her performances. Profound emotion infused her singing. Music historian Peter Guralnick writes, "... her voice and phrasing worked on even the most familiar sentiments and material... as to suggest a whole other subtext of experience." For Franklin this subtext was real and tragic. Her mother had left the family when Franklin was 6 and died a few years later. Franklin's subsequent childhood years, characterized by shyness, despondency, and extreme dependence on her father, ended with a pregnancy at age 15. Jo King, who managed Franklin's early gospelcareer, said of her, "I realized I had a real woman here, one who knew more than I did when it came to men, alcohol and everything. She had tremendous depth."

Although childhood difficulties influenced Franklin's development, she also had positive role models. Mother figures included American gospel singers Mahalia Jackson, Marion Williams, and Clara Ward, whose rendition of "Peace in the Valley" at the funeral of Franklin's aunt apparently inspired her resolve to sing professionally. One of her father's parishioners, James Cleveland, moved in with the family and helped Franklin with her piano playing. Most important, Franklin's friendship with gospel-gone-soul singer Sam Cooke inspired her to leave the church for a professional career in music.

At age 18 Franklin went to New York, cut demos, took voice lessons, and signed a five-year recording contract with Columbia Records. Supervised by John Hammond – who had "discovered" such musicians as Count Basie, Charlie Christian, Lionel Hampton, and Billie Holiday – Franklin recorded pop standards, Broadway tunes, and jazz ballads. Due to overwrought, often saccharine arrangements, Franklin's recordings with Columbia met with limited success. Although some historians attribute her early mediocrity to Columbia's mismanagement, Franklin often chose such arrangements for herself.

By 1966 Columbia Records had incurred approximately $80,000 in debt from Franklin's nine-album stint. They terminated her contract, but Jerry Wexler of Atlantic Records swiftly signed her to his company. He encouraged Franklin to drop her Columbia sound, thereby initiating her career in soul. Wexler claims that he "urged Aretha to be Aretha" – and indeed her Atlantic recordings of the late 1960s pulsed with an authenticity that attracted millions of fans. Although Franklin was not known as an innovator, she expressed a level of sincerity unprecedented in pop music. A 1967 article in *Time* magazine stated, "She does not seem to be performing so much as bearing witness to a reality so simple and compelling that she could not possibly fake it."

Franklin's first release with Atlantic, "I Never Loved a Man (The Way I Love You)," sold a million copies and was followed by four other million-selling records that same year. Between 1967 and 1969 she won four Grammy Awards. In addition, Franklin became politically engaged, singing a soulful rendition of "The Star Spangled Banner" at the 1968 Democratic convention. Her cover of "Respect" by Otis Redding transformed the song into an anthem of black feminist pride. Franklin also became associated with the Civil Rights Movement by singing at the funeral of Martin Luther King Jr., a friend and colleague of her father.

During the 1970s Franklin won six more Grammy Awards, sending song after song up the R&B charts. Although she continued to release secular soul, Franklin returned to her gospel roots in 1972 with a double-album collection titled *Amazing Grace* that featured her former mentor, James Cleveland. In 1980 Franklin left Atlantic Records for Arista and that same year made her film debut in *The Blues Brothers*. Through the 1980s and 1990s she continued to release new work and began donating large sums of money to the UNITED NEGRO COLLEGE FUND, the NATIONAL ASSOCIATION FOR THE ADVANCEMENT OF COLORED PEOPLE, and SICKLE CELL ANEMIA research.

By the end of the century, Franklin had recorded almost 50 albums. Her popular recognition as the Queen of Soul extended to include the esteem of white politicians: in 1986 the state of Michigan declared her voice a natural resource, and in 1989 state senator Carl Levin honored Franklin for her financial support of the fight against drunk driving. Displaying her ongoing affiliation with the Democratic Party in 1997, she performed at President Clinton's second inaugural celebration.

Eric Bennett

SEE ALSO

Soul Music; Basie, William James ("Count"); Cleveland, James Edward; Cooke, Samuel (Sam); Dorsey, Thomas Andrew; Gospel Music; Hampton, Lionel Leo; King, Martin Luther, Jr.

North America

Franklin, John Hope

(b. January 2, 1915, Rentiesville, Okla.), historian and educator who helped to establish African American history as a respected academic discipline.

In June 1997, when President Clinton assembled a seven-member panel to advise him about racial strife in the United States, he chose John Hope Franklin as its chair. This was not the first time that the then 82-year-old historian had made history. As a college student, he had protested to President Franklin Roosevelt after a local black man was lynched. As a young scholar, he had provided historical research for THURGOOD MARSHALL's brief in BROWN V. BOARD OF EDUCATION. For Franklin, the task of correcting American history in the light of black experience had always been a crucial part of the fight for racial equality.

Born in the all-black Oklahoma frontier town of Rentiesville (*see* BLACK TOWNS), Franklin moved with his family to Tulsa in 1926. His father, Buck, was a lawyer who resisted segregation in the courtroom and spent every night reading and writing. His mother, Mollie, was a schoolteacher who, along with her children, was once expelled from a train because she would not obey segregated seating rules (*see* JIM CROW).

After graduating from the segregated Tulsa public school system, Franklin received a B.A. from FISK UNIVERSITY in Nashville, Tennessee, where he was graduated with honors in 1935. He earned a doctorate in history from Harvard University six years later and spent the early years of his career teaching at historically black colleges, including Fisk, North Carolina Central, and HOWARD UNIVERSITY.

Franklin made the front page of the *New York Times* in 1956 when he was hired as the chairman of the all-white history department at Brooklyn College. Brooklyn College president Harry Gideonse said of the appointment, "Maybe it will help the University of Alabama students see that color is not a bar to scholarship." Despite this recognition of his scholarly accomplishments, Franklin and his family were refused service by 135 real estate agents in New York. When they finally found a house on their own, no New York bank would loan them the money to buy it. In 1967 Franklin moved to the University of Chicago, where he again chaired the history department.

Although Franklin's books are wide-ranging in their subjects, their cumulative effect has been to continue the work begun by W. E. B. Du Bois and Carter G. Woodson in demonstrating that the study of the black experience is essential to American history. Of his many books, *From Slavery to Freedom: A History of American Negroes* is the most famous. Since its publication in 1947, *From Slavery to Freedom* has gone through seven editions (the most recent is subtitled *A History of African Americans*) and has introduced hundreds of thousands of students to black history. Franklin's other books include *The Free Negro in North Carolina, 1790-1860* (1943), *The Militant South* (1956), *Racial Equality in America* (1976), *George Washington Williams* (1985), and *The Color Line: Legacy for the 21st Century* (1993). The late 1990s saw Franklin at work on a study of runaway slaves titled *Dissidents on the Plantation*.

The recipient of more than 100 honorary degrees, Franklin is James B. Duke Professor of History Emeritus at Duke University. Among the many organizations that he has headed are the American Historical Association, the American Studies Association, and the United Chapters of Phi Beta Kappa. He has also served as a delegate to the 21st General Conference of the United Nations Educational, Scientific, and Cultural Organization (UNESCO) in 1980, been inducted into the Oklahoma Hall of Fame, and received the presidential Medal of Freedom.

Lawrie Balfour

SEE ALSO

Chicago, Illinois; Du Bois, William Edward Burghardt (W. E. B.); Fugitive Slaves; Lynching; New York, New York; Woodson, Carter Godwin.

North America

Fraternities and Sororities, Black, in the United States,

predominantly black social and service organizations whose members generally join in college and remain active throughout their lives.

Fraternities and sororities, also known as Greek-letter societies, have been an integral part of American higher education since 1776, when white students on the campus of William and Mary College founded Phi Beta Kappa, the first fraternity in America. Since then, fraternities (men only) and sororities (women only) have provided social and professional networks for students and alumni/ae on college campuses across the nation. But like most organizations founded during this period in American history, white fraternities and sororities were not open to blacks. The first African American Greek-letter society was founded in 1904, when six doctors in PHILADELPHIA, PENNSYLVANIA, formed Sigma Pi Phi fraternity. Today, there are an estimated 800,000 active members in the nine major black fraternities and sororities, with chapters around the world.

The National Pan-Hellenic Council serves as the "official coordinating agent" for the major black fraternities and sororities. The Notorious Nine, as they are called, are Alpha Phi Alpha fraternity (founded at Cornell University in 1906), Alpha Kappa Alpha sorority (HOWARD UNIVERSITY, 1908), Kappa Alpha Psi fraternity (Indiana University, 1911), Omega Psi Phi fraternity (Howard University, 1911), Delta Sigma Theta sorority (Howard University, 1913), Phi Beta Sigma fraternity (Howard University, 1914), Zeta Phi Beta sorority (Howard University, 1920), Sigma Gamma Rho sorority (Butler University, 1922), and Iota Phi Theta fraternity (Morgan State University, 1963). There are other black fraternities and sororities that are not associated with the National Pan-Hellenic Council, but these nine are the largest and most popular.

Members are selected by a rigorous process, called pledging, in which hopeful candidates are often required to memorize the organization's history and traditions and participate in several weeks of secret initiation rituals. As with mainstream white fraternities and sororities, some black Greek-letter societies have been criticized for specific rituals, called hazing, that have included emotional, verbal, and even physical abuse. But after several hazing-related deaths in the 1980s, the National Pan-Hellenic Council banned hazing in 1990, endorsing instead pledging activities that are designed to build community among potential candidates and welcome them into the organization.

The exclusiveness of black fraternities and sororities has led some to criticize them for perpetuating class elitism, but while members are college-educated by definition, most black fraternities and sororities emphasize a lifelong commitment to community service. On many college campuses members provide after-school tutoring, volunteer in homeless shelters, and raise scholarship money to give to promising black high school students. Fraternities and sororities provide an important social and professional network for their members following graduation. The members attend national conventions, participate in public service events, and mentor younger members. Martin Luther King Jr., Thurgood Marshall, Zora Neale Hurston, Shirley Chisholm, Adam Clayton Powell Jr., and Sarah Vaughan are just a few of the many well-known African Americans who have been members of fraternities and sororities.

Alonford James Robinson, Jr.

See Also
King, Martin Luther, Jr..

North America

Fraunces Tavern, a historic New York City landmark whose founder is thought by many to have been black.

Fraunces Tavern, located in lower Manhattan and still operating as a restaurant, was opened in 1762 by Samuel Fraunces (1722?-1795), a West Indian immigrant who built his business by catering to those with a taste for English cooking, especially elegant desserts. As well as being a successful entrepreneur and chef, Fraunces was deeply involved in the American Revolution and set up the tavern and its adjoining inn as a meeting place for the independence movement. Known by his contemporaries as "Black Sam," he was an avid supporter and close confidant of George Washington. His involvement in the revolution included giving aid to American prisoners of war, but the high point followed the war, when Washington bade farewell to his troops at a commemorative feast at Fraunces Tavern.

Samuel Fraunces's racial origins have long been a matter of debate. Recent research suggests that he may have been the son of white plantation owners, and he is listed as white in a 1790 census. There are those, however, who maintain that Fraunces's nickname and birthplace make it likely that he was black and perhaps passed for white. As of yet, there is no conclusive evidence about his race. On January 25, 1975, Fraunces Tavern made the political spotlight when it was bombed by members of the Fuerzas Armadas de Liberación Nacional (FALN), a Puerto Rican independence movement. Four people died in the explosion. It has never been clearly established why Fraunces Tavern was a chosen target; members of FALN later claimed that they set off the blast in retaliation for a "CIA-ordered" bombing in Puerto Rico 14 days earlier.

Suzanne Albulak

See Also
New York, New York.

North America

Frazier, Edward Franklin

(b. September 24, 1894, Baltimore, Md.; d. May 17, 1962, Washington, D.C.), sociologist and activist famed for his pioneering studies of black families and his critique of the black middle class.

Taught from an early age that education was the key to both personal success and social justice, E. Franklin Frazier used his learning as a weapon during his lifelong battle against racial inequality. In a tribute to Frazier, the *Journal of Negro Education* called him "a nonconfomist, a protester, a gadfly." He attacked the pretension of the black middle class, went to jail for picketing D. W. Griffith's film The Birth of a Nation, and publicly defended W. E. B. Du Bois and Paul Robeson although to do so meant that he risked being branded a communist.

Frazier grew up in Baltimore, Maryland, and attended Howard University on scholarship. Shortly after graduating from Howard with honors in 1916, he began his career as a professor. Despite teaching commitments throughout the 1920s and 1930s, he earned a master's degree from Clark University in 1920 and a Ph.D. in sociology from the University of Chicago in 1931. From 1929 until 1934 he taught at Fisk University in Nashville, Tennessee. In 1934 he was hired as the chair of the sociology department at Howard, where he remained until his retirement in 1959.

The Negro Family in the United States (1939), Frazier's first influential book, discredited the idea that problems such as illegitimacy, divorce, and desertion could be traced to biological or cultural defects. Instead, Frazier demonstrated that problems within black communities mirrored the shortcomings of American society as a whole. In 1949 he published *The Negro in the United States*, the first comprehensive textbook on black experiences.

Frazier's most controversial book, *Black Bourgeoisie*, appeared in 1957. This study concluded that the black middle class had earned "status without substance" and criticized affluent blacks for abandoning the cause of social equality in the hope of becoming part of the American elite. Despite charges of racial disloyalty, Frazier continued to write about class differences within black communities in an effort to provide a systematic account of American race relations. His other books include *The Free Negro Family* (1932), *Race and Culture Contacts in the Modern World* (1957), *The Negro Church in America* (1963), and *On Race Relations: Selected Writings* (1968). Frazier's research extended beyond the United States to include studies of race and culture in Brazil and the West Indies. Additionally, he was instrumental in the development of African studies in the United States.

Not content to restrict his activities to the university, Frazier was always a public intellectual. After a race riot in 1935, the mayor of New York City appointed him to conduct a survey for the Commission on Conditions in Harlem. In 1944 the United Nations Educational, Scientific, and Cultural Organization (UNESCO) named him an international authority on racial issues. He was elected the first black president of the American Sociological Association, served as president of the International Society for the Scientific Study of Race Relations, and was a founding member of the American Association for the Advancement of Science.

Lawrie Balfour

See Also
Chicago, Illinois; Du Bois, William Edward Burghardt (W. E. B.); Harlem Riots of 1935; Harlem, New York; New York, New York; Communist Party USA, African Americans and the.

North America

Frazier, Joseph William (Joe)

(b. January 12, 1944, Beaufort, S.C.), African American boxer, 1964 Olympic Gold Medalist, and world professional heavyweight champion whose bouts with Muhammad Ali were among the greatest in Boxing history.

At 1.8 m (5 ft 11 ½ in) and 97 kg (205 lb), young Joe Frazier seemed an inauspicious candidate for heavyweight champion of the world. He grew up in Philadelphia, Pennsylvania, where he trained with Yancy "Yank" Durham. Frazier won 38 of his 40 amateur bouts, culminating in his heavyweight triumph at the 1964 Olympic Games in Tokyo, Japan, and turned professional the following year.

Known as "Smokin' Joe" and "Joltin' Joe," Frazier launched his professional career with a string of knockouts. His first 11 opponents went down within six rounds. Frazier became the heavyweight champion on February 16, 1970, after knocking out Jimmy Ellis in five rounds. The following year, on March 8, Frazier clashed with Muhammad Ali in one of the most anticipated and most highly publicized contests in the history of the sport. The fight was Ali's first bout since 1967, the year he was stripped of his heavyweight title for refusing to fight in the Vietnam War. Frazier responded to Ali's prefight public banter by saying, "The arm is still mightier than the mouth." Frazier won the 15-round contest by a unanimous decision.

Frazier successfully defended his title twice after the Ali bout, bringing his victory count to 31. Then, in a January 22, 1973, title bout in Kingston, Jamaica, George Foreman knocked out Frazier in the second round. This loss signaled the demise of Frazier's boxing career. In a 12-round exhibition rematch in 1974, Ali defeated Frazier. In their third bout, the 1975 Thrilla in Manila (Philippines), Ali defeated Frazier in the fifteenth round. Frazier retired in 1976 after George Foreman knocked him out in the fifth round of their rematch. He attempted a comeback in 1981 but was defeated by Floyd Cummings. Frazier finished with a record of 32 wins (27 by knockout), four losses, and one draw. He was inducted into the *Ring*'s Boxing Hall of Fame in 1980 and into the International Boxing Hall of Fame in 1990. Since his retirement, Frazier has performed and recorded gospel and rock-inspired music with his ensemble, the Knockouts. Though the group has not been a critical success, Joe Frazier asserts, "I'm still smokin'."

Aaron Myers

See Also
Foreman, George Edward; Gospel Music.

Africa

Fredricks, Frankie

(b. October 2, 1967, Namibia), Namibian sprinter.

Although he was a talented athlete as a youth, Frank Fredricks never expected to be in the Olympic Games. His country, Namibia, was a colony until 1990 belonging to South Africa, which was banned from Olympic competition because of the South African policy of apartheid. Yet Fredricks, who has become one of the world's premiere sprinters, has brought four Olympic medals home to Namibia.

An only child, Fredricks was raised by his mother in Katutura township, just outside the Namibian capital, Windhoek. His mother worked several jobs to send him to private schools, where he excelled in both soccer and academics. In high school he started running track, specializing in sprinting. He won both the 100- and 200-meter races in the South African school championships his senior year. After graduating, he passed up several college scholarship offers to accept a management training position with the Rossing Uranium Mine Company, which sponsored his education at Brigham Young University in the United States, where he enrolled in 1987.

At Brigham Young, Fredricks not only earned degrees in computer science and business administration, but also became the national collegiate champion in his two sprint events in 1991. When Namibia gained its independence in 1990, the ban on its international competition was lifted, and Fredricks carried the flag for the Namibian team in the 1992 Olympic Games in Barcelona, Spain. He won silver medals in the 100- and 200-meter events.

In international competition leading up to the 1996 Olympic Games Fredricks not only ended Michael Johnson's two-year unbeaten streak with a personal best 19.82 seconds in the 200-meter, but he also came within one one-hundredth of a second of breaking the world record in the 100-meter. Fredricks added two more silver medals in the Atlanta games, coming in second behind Donovan Bailey in the 100-meter and Johnson in the 200-meter.

Kate Tuttle

See Also
Olympics, Africans and the; Namibia; Windhoek, Namibia.

North America

Free African Society, **established in the eighteenth century, one of the first African American religious organizations to provide blacks with a place of worship and a place to meet and organize politically.**

In 1787 the Free African Society was founded in Philadelphia by black Methodists Richard Allen and Absalom Jones in response to a decision by white members of St. George's Methodist Church to enforce racially segregated church services. The society's stated purpose was to enhance the quality of life for African Americans, but its immediate objective was the creation of a space for African Americans to worship and organize. During its five-year existence, the Society was run entirely by African Americans.

Although the society was nondenominational, it maintained ties to both the Quakers and the Methodist Church. The society supported the abolitionist movement, opposed proposals for black emigration and colonization, and worked to ameliorate tensions between blacks and whites. In 1792, during the American yellow fever epidemic, volunteers from the Free African Society worked as nurses and undertakers as a gesture of good will toward the white community.

As the society grew, it collected regular membership dues, and in Quaker tradition, formed a visiting committee to make sure that all members conformed to the society's strict code of conduct. The society became even more closely associated with Quaker practices when, in November 1789, members voted to begin meetings with 15 minutes of silent prayer.

This move angered Allen, who left the organization to found the Bethel African Methodist Episcopal Church, the "mother church" of the African Methodist Episcopal Church. In 1792, under the leadership of Absalom Jones, the society closed its doors, changing its name to the African Episcopal Church of St. Thomas.

Alonford James Robinson, Jr.

See Also
Abolitionism in the United States; American Colonization Society; Philadelphia, Pennsylvania.

North America

Free Blacks in the United States, 1619 to 1863, **those African Americans who were not enslaved.**

In 1966 black author James Baldwin wrote: "To be born in a free society and not be born free is to be born into a lie." A century after the Emancipation Proclamation, Baldwin's words conveyed the pain and the passion that characterized the lives of free blacks in America between 1619 and 1860. Many scholars suggest that during this period, free blacks in America were "more black than free." As historian Leonard Curry explains, "Their educational attainment was limited, their social development was thwarted, occupations were closed to them, housing was denied to them, personal safety eluded them, and basic human dignity was begrudged them." "Because they were black," Curry adds, "freedom was always and everywhere for them cruelly incomplete."

These free Negroes, as they were called at that time, were scattered throughout three distinct regions: the North, the Upper South, and the Lower South. Each region had its own flavor. Many of slavery's most vociferous critics lived in the Northern region, which comprised Pennsylvania, New York, New Jersey, and the states of New England. The Upper South featured large tobacco plantations and included Virginia, Maryland, North Carolina, Tennessee, Kentucky, and Washington, D.C. The Lower South, often referred to as the Deep South, supported rice and cotton plantations and comprised South Carolina, Florida, Georgia, Alabama, Mississippi, and Louisiana.

Free blacks in America were first documented in Northampton County, Virginia, in 1662. By 1776, 60,000 African Americans – approximately 8 percent of the national black population – were free. The free black population continued to rise steadily, which intimidated many proslavery whites. Between 1800 and 1810 the free black population nearly doubled, from 108,395 to 186,446. By 1810, 4 percent of all African Americans in the Deep South, 10 percent in the Upper South, and 75 percent in the North were free. Most free blacks in the North were concentrated in urban cities such as Boston, New York, and Philadelphia. Between 1800 and 1850 the free black population in the nation's 15 largest cities increased sixfold, compared to a threefold increase for the entire white population. By 1860 there were close to 500,000 free blacks in the United States, approximately 9 percent of the entire black population. It can be said with confidence that on the eve of the Civil War there were, at least, half a million stories of freedom.

Attaining Freedom

Freedom did not come easily. Thousands of runaway slaves were captured, returned to slavery, or executed by white posses. Thousands more refused even to entertain the notion of freedom, some out of fear, others out of apathy. Harriet Tubman, famed black conductor of the UNDERGROUND RAILROAD, said, "I freed thousands of slaves. I could have freed thousands more, if they had known they were slaves." Most slaves, however, were not apathetic about freedom.

The most common route to emancipation came through manumission, which entailed the formal release of a slave. A slave could be manumitted privately by an individual or officially by a state law. Vermont became the first state to guarantee immediate manumission when it outlawed slavery in its 1777 constitution. After the AMERICAN REVOLUTION, many states followed Vermont's lead and changed their own laws regarding manumission. Several other Northern states, including New York, New Jersey, and Pennsylvania, adopted a policy of gradual manumission, which meant that the children of all current slaves would automatically be free once they reached a certain age, generally 21 or 25. In the South no states changed their laws to require mandatory manumission, but several did make manumission easier, including Delaware, Maryland, and Virginia. In fact, in Delaware private manumission was so pervasive that 75 percent of all blacks in the state were free by 1810. But in most states private manumission was rare and restricted. Most slaveholders were encouraged to free their slaves only in their wills, if at all.

Not all free blacks were formally manumitted. Thousands "voted with their feet for freedom." It is estimated that between 1776 and 1860 close to 1000 slaves each year ran away. Many of those were forced to leave family members behind as they traveled cautiously along the Underground Railroad – a clandestine network comprising people (black and white) who guided runaway slaves to freedom in the North. Former slaves from the Caribbean also "voted with their feet" when thousands immigrated to America after the HAITIAN REVOLUTION.

Those who did not run away or immigrate from HAITI often purchased their freedom. In 1799 a South Carolina slave named Denmark Vesey won $1,500 in the East Bay Street lottery and bought his freedom for $600. A few slaves who could not afford to buy freedom devised clever escapes. In 1849 a North Carolina slave named Henry "Box" Brown had himself packaged in a wooden box and shipped by Adams Express to antislavery headquarters in Philadelphia. During the 27-hour journey, he spent much of the time on his head as he was transferred back and forth from wagons, trains, and steamboats.

REGIONAL VARIATIONS

Hardship did not end with freedom. There were distinct regional variations in both the status and treatment of free blacks during this period. Free blacks in the North were excluded from most public schools, prohibited from interstate travel, barred from voting in many states, and often harassed by hostile white mobs. Finding a decent job in the North was extremely difficult. Jobs open to free blacks were limited mostly to domestic service and subsistence farming. There were few free black skilled artisans. Furthermore, the jobs that were available to free blacks were found predominantly in urban cities such as Boston, Philadelphia, and New York. At a time when less than 20 percent of all Americans settled in urban areas, 60 percent of Northern free blacks lived in major urban cities.

In the Deep South less than 2 percent of the black population were classified as free in 1860. Often referred to as CREOLES or mulattos, a significant proportion of free blacks in the Deep South were wealthy, light-skinned aristocrats. Some Creoles looked down on dark-skinned free blacks, and many despised the negative stigma that was associated with being black. The free black elite in such cities as Mobile, Pensacola, and New Orleans prided themselves on their fine clothing and "respectable" air. Whites in the Deep South employed the few free blacks mainly as day laborers and domestic servants. Many more free blacks worked as carpenters, masons, mechanics, and tailors.

The large personal fortunes of a few free blacks in the Deep South permitted them to own slaves. By 1830, 13,000 black slaves were owned by nearly 4000 free blacks. Many bought slaves in an effort to protect family members, but others sought to expand personal fortunes. By 1860 free blacks in the Deep South owned an estimated $9 million worth of property, more than most Southern whites and nine times as much as free Northern blacks.

Life was much more difficult for the 10 percent of the black population classified as free in the Upper South. Free blacks in cities such as Baltimore and WASHINGTON, D.C., were poorer, more rural, and less educated than free blacks in the rest of the nation. Finding employment was not as difficult as it was in the North. Most free blacks in the Upper South worked with slaves as farmhands, casual laborers, and factory hands. Thousands more found work as blacksmiths, barbers, and shoemakers. Working closely with black slaves left free blacks in the Upper South geographically and psychologically connected with the enslaved. In fact, in 1800 free blacks supported a planned slave rebellion organized by Gabriel Prosser, a black slave in Virginia. This and similar planned uprisings, such as those organized by Denmark Vesey in South Carolina (1822) and NAT TURNER in Virginia (1831), terrified whites.

SEGREGATION AND DISCRIMINATION

Proslavery whites adamantly believed that the presence of free blacks anywhere was an immediate threat to slavery everywhere. As a result, free blacks in both the North and the South were systematically isolated and segregated. Says historian Leon F. Litwack, "Free blacks were often educated in segregated schools, punished in segregated prisons, nursed in segregated hospitals, and buried in segregated cemeteries." White supremacy gained momentum as the free black population encroached on white lifestyles. Poor whites in the North resented the growing competition from free black laborers. White mobs attacked and killed free blacks in Philadephia (1829, 1849), Boston (1843), Providence (1831), New York (1834), and Washington, D.C. (1835). White mobs also destroyed black churches, businesses, homes, schools, and meetinghouses.

White repression was not limited to violence. In 1850 the Fugitive Slave Act required that all known runaway slaves be forcibly returned to their white masters, even in the North, which led to increased harassment of blacks everywhere. In 1857 the United States Supreme Court's Dred Scott decision declared that no blacks, slave or free, were citizens of the United States. In addition to legal discrimination, white hostility led to the establishment of white segregationist organizations such as the AMERICAN COLONIZATION SOCIETY. The society's chief objective was to encourage free blacks (and, later, manumitted slaves) to emigrate to West Africa, and it is estimated that the organization sponsored the emigration of between 12,000 and 20,000 African Americans throughout the nineteenth century.

FREE BLACK COMMUNITIES AND INSTITUTIONS

Free blacks responded in a variety of ways to the violence and systematic discrimination waged by many whites. Free blacks often worked within their own communities to establish hundreds of independent black institutions, among which churches were the earliest and most important. By 1787 there were black Baptist, Methodist, Presbyterian, and Episcopalian congregations throughout the country. Most free black churches were located in the North. Two of the most prominent denominations included the African Methodist Episcopal and the African Methodist Episcopal Zion churches.

Schools for free blacks were equally important institutions. With the exception of Boston after 1855, most free blacks were prohibited from attending white public schools. In response, many free black communities established schools of their own. One of the most successful was the AFRICAN FREE SCHOOL in New York City. Opened in 1787 after several Northern states abolished slavery, the school became an essential vehicle for the primary education of African Americans in New York City for almost 50 years.

Similar schools were sponsored by free black churches and free black mutual aid societies, such as the FREE AFRICAN SOCIETY in Philadelphia, founded in 1778, and the BROWN FELLOWSHIP SOCIETY of Charleston, South Carolina, founded in 1790. In addition to churches, schools, and mutual aid societies, free blacks organized literary clubs, debating societies, and secret fraternal organizations, including the Freemasons and the Odd Fellows.

A significant number of free blacks reacted to white repression by becoming politically active. Many free blacks encouraged voluntary emigration to Africa. Others urged free blacks to join slaves in the violent overthrow of slavery. Most, however, worked diligently to improve the lives of other African Americans, both free and slave. FREDERICK DOUGLASS, WILLIAM WELLS BROWN, and William and Ellen Craft published influential SLAVE NARRATIVES depicting their turbulent paths to freedom. These narratives brought the cruelty of slavery to an international audience, and inspired antislavery activism in many parts of the country. Wealthy free blacks such as the Forten family in Philadelphia contributed time and money to the American Anti-Slavery Movement. Whatever the strategy, many free blacks worked tirelessly to improve the chance for freedom for the 4 million slaves who still labored on the eve of the Civil War.

The history of the free black population in America is rife with adversity, but it is a vivid reminder of the courage and perseverance that have characterized the African American experience. As Pulitzer-Prize winning author ALICE WALKER states, "In the end, freedom is a personal and lonely battle and one faces down fears of today so that those of tomorrow might be engaged."

Alonford James Robinson, Jr.

SEE ALSO

Slavery in the United States; Abolitionism in the United States; African Methodist Episcopal Church; African Methodist Episcopal Zion Church; American Anti-Slavery Society; Baltimore, Maryland; Baptists; Boston, Massachusetts; Brown, Henry ("Box"); Civil War, American; Craft, Ellen and William; Denmark Vesey Conspiracy; *Dred Scott* v. *Sanford*; Fugitive Slave Laws; Fugitive Slaves; Gabriel Prosser Conspiracy; Manumission Societies; New Orleans, Louisiana; New York, New York; Philadelphia, Pennsylvania; Tubman, Harriet Ross; Thirteenth Amendment of the United States Constitution and the Emancipation Proclamation.

North America

Freedman's Bank, **a financial institution established after the Civil War to aid economic development among African Americans; its unexpected bankruptcy, combined with the federal government's unwillingness to intervene, left thousands of African Americans and African American institutions penniless.**

The Freedman's Bank (officially called the Freedman's Savings and Trust Company) was chartered in 1865 as a nonprofit, philanthropic organization whose aim was to benefit the black community after the Civil War by encouraging thrift among African Americans. Although it was not affiliated with the Freedmen's Bureau (*see* BUREAU OF REFUGEES, FREEDMEN AND ABANDONED LANDS), both organizations were chartered at the same time, and directors at the Freedmen's Bureau also served on the board of directors at the Freedman's Bank. Blacks believed that the bank was government-backed, a notion that the predominantly white directors encouraged by using Abraham Lincoln's likeness in bank advertisements. To further inspire black confidence, the directors hired black politicians, ministers, and businessmen to serve as cashiers and advisory board members at local banks.

African Americans responded. In addition to individual deposits, African American organizations such as churches and benevolent societies invested in the Freedman's Bank. Most of the deposits were small, below $50. By 1874 more than 72,000 African Americans had deposited more than $3 million in the bank, which had established branches in all Southern states, as well as in Philadelphia, New York City, and Washington, D.C.

The bank's original charter stipulated a conservative approach, focusing on interest payments to its investors and stable investments such as government securities. Based on initial success, the directors, hoping to increase the return to investors, amended the bank's charter in 1870, allowing the bank to invest in speculative enterprises and to issue loans. Most of these investments centered on white businesses, however, and individual blacks were often unable to acquire loans, which led to black protest. In addition, many of the loans were large and unsecured. When these businesses began to fail in the early 1870s, the bank became insolvent. Most of the bank's white directors resigned during the Panic of 1873. The remaining directors attempted to keep the institution solvent, and named FREDERICK DOUGLASS bank president in 1874; however, the bank closed a few months later.

Bills introduced in Congress would have provided for the government to provide a full refund of the depositors' investments, but the legislation was never passed. The bank had to sell its assets to begin reimbursing its depositors, but only about half of the bank's investors received reimbursements – and then, only approximately 20 percent of their deposits. The federal government's unwillingness to assume any responsibility for reimbursing the freedpeople alienated many African Americans.

Robert Fay

SEE ALSO

Civil War, American; New York, New York; Philadelphia, Pennsylvania; Washington, D.C..

North America

Freedmen's Hospital, **established by the federal government during the Civil War to offer health services to former slaves, black soldiers, and the indigent; provided treatment and medical training for several generations of African Americans.**

Freedmen's Hospital was founded in 1862 to serve former slaves and Union soldiers in the Civil War. At that time – and, indeed, until the CIVIL RIGHTS MOVEMENT – many hospitals and medical colleges were segregated, leaving black patients with few health care options and aspiring black physicians and nurses with limited choice about where to study and practice medicine. The Freedmen's Hospital not only provided service to poor whites and blacks in WASHINGTON, D.C., but through its close association with Howard University's Medical College (the two joined in 1868 to form a teaching hospital), it came to offer medical training to African Americans.

Part of the hospital's mission was to provide medical care to the indigent despite inadequate federal funding; the hospital was prohibited from admitting paying patients until 1912. During its history, administrators worked amid a deteriorating physical plant and outdated equipment, and the hospital received more patients than it could afford. Yet through the 1950s Howard University/Freedmen's Hospital and another prominent African American teaching hospital, Meharry Medical College in Nashville, Tennessee, trained 85 percent of the black doctors in the United States. A number of distinguished African American doctors served as surgeons-in-chief of the hospital, including DANIEL HALE WILLIAMS, who performed the first open-heart surgery and founded the Freedmen's Hospital School of Nursing in 1894, and Charles Drew, who developed the first techniques for separating blood plasma, making possible widespread blood transfusions.

In the mid-1950s a government study recommended that a new hospital be built and that responsibility for its administration be given to Howard University, recommendations that President John F. Kennedy signed into legislation in 1961. A new Howard University Hospital opened in 1975.

Robert Fay

SEE ALSO

Civil War, American; Drew, Charles Richard; Howard University.

Africa

Freedom Charter, **the document written in 1955 by the African National Congress and other antiapartheid groups to express their goals for a free South Africa.**

After South Africa's NATIONAL PARTY won its second term in power in 1953, Z. K. Matthews, a regional leader of the African National Congress (ANC), proposed a symbolic act of opposition to the National Party's apartheid regime. Like many within the ANC, Matthews was uncomfortable with the more militant actions of the ANC's Congress Youth League and its founders, Nelson Mandela, Oliver Tambo, and others. With government harassment threatening to force the ANC underground, Matthews hoped to reprise the organization's role as the public, national voice opposing apartheid. He called for a national convention "representing all the people of this country irrespective of race or colour, to draw up a Freedom Charter for the democratic South Africa of the future."

On June 25, 1955, more than 3000 delegates, representing about 200 organizations, met at Kliptown, a multiracial village outside Johannesburg. The intervening two years had been spent planning for the Congress of the People, as it was called, by soliciting the ideas and opinions of average South Africans. Thousands of fliers asking "If you could make the laws, what would you do?" had been distributed. Armed with the people's wishes, the congress delegates – most of whom were members of the ANC, the South African Coloured People's Association, the South African Indian Congress, and a white antiapartheid group called the Congress of Democrats – drafted the Freedom Charter.

The charter affirmed in its preamble that "South Africa belongs to all who live in it, black and white," then set forth ten main propositions, including "The People Shall Govern," "All Shall Be Equal before the Law," and "There Shall Be Peace and Freedom." The charter also called for equality in education, freedom in land ownership, and equal access to jobs and housing. Although it was criticized by some for its apparent advocacy of socialist economic principles, the Freedom Charter was adopted as the ANC's official platform in 1956. Nearly 30 years later, Nelson Mandela hailed it as "a revolutionary document," one that represented "the people's demands to end the oppression."

Kate Tuttle

See Also

Johannesburg, South Africa; Mandela, Nelson Rolihlahla; South Africa.

North America

Freedom's Journal, the first African American newspaper in the United States.

Begun in 1827 as a rebuttal to often racist journalism in the mainstream white press, *Freedom's Journal* was the first in what would become a long line of African American newspapers. Its editors, Samuel Cornish and John Brown Russwurm, proposed in their first editorial that their paper, a weekly, would provide an opportunity for black people to speak for themselves rather than be represented by whites. As the first black-owned and edited newspaper in the country, *Freedom's Journal* was a strong proponent of the abolition of slavery, and Cornish and Russwurm often employed black abolitionists.

Despite the newspaper's wide popularity not only in its New York base but elsewhere – some subscribers were from as far away as Haiti – its publication history was brief. From the beginning there had been conflict between Cornish and Russwurm, mostly regarding whether African Americans ought to emigrate to Africa. Cornish, a staunch integrationist, resigned from *Freedom's Journal* in the fall of 1827, leaving Russwurm increasingly to use the paper as a pulpit for his views in favor of African recolonization by free blacks. By 1829 Russwurm had accepted a position as superintendent of education in Liberia, the African nation founded by the American Colonization Society for repatriated blacks, and soon thereafter *Freedom's Journal* ended publication.

Lisa Clayton Robinson

See Also

Slavery in the United States; Abolitionism in the United States; Press, Black, in the United States; New York, New York.

North America

Freedom Summer, a highly publicized campaign in the Deep South to register blacks to vote during the summer of 1964.

During the summer of 1964, thousands of civil rights activists, many of them white college students from the North, descended on Mississippi and other Southern states to try to end the long-time political disfranchisement of African Americans in the region. Although black men had won the right to vote in 1870, thanks to the Fifteenth Amendment, for the next 100 years many were unable to exercise that right. White local and state officials systematically kept blacks from voting through formal methods, such as poll taxes and literacy tests, and through cruder methods of fear and intimidation, which included beatings and lynchings. The inability to vote was only one of many problems blacks encountered in the racist society around them, but the civil rights officials who decided to zero in on voter registration understood its crucial significance as well as the white supremacists did. An African American voting bloc would be able to effect social and political change.

Freedom Summer marked the climax of intensive voter-registration activities in the South that had started in 1961. Organizers chose to focus their efforts on Mississippi because of the state's particularly dismal voting-rights record: in 1962 only 6.7 percent of African Americans in the state were registered to vote, the lowest percentage in the country. The Freedom Summer campaign was organized by a coalition called the Mississippi Council of Federated Organizations, which included the Congress of Racial Equality (CORE), the National Association for the Advancement of Colored People (NAACP), and the Student Nonviolent Coordinating Committee (SNCC). SNCC volunteers, led by Robert Moses, played the largest role, providing 90 to 95 percent of the funding and 95 percent of the headquarters staff. By mobilizing volunteer white college students from the North to join them, the coalition scored a major public relations coup as hundreds of reporters came to Mississippi from around the country to cover the voter-registration campaign.

The organization of the Mississippi Freedom Democratic Party (MFDP) was a major focus of the summer program. More than 80,000 Mississippians joined the new party, which elected a slate of 68 delegates to the national Democratic Party convention in Atlantic City. The MFDP delegation challenged the seating of the delegates representing Mississippi's all-white Democratic Party. While the effort failed, it drew national attention, particularly through the dramatic televised appeal of MFDP delegate Fannie Lou Hamer. The MFDP challenge also led to a ban on racially discriminatory delegations at future conventions.

Freedom Summer officials established 30 "Freedom Schools" in towns throughout Mississippi to address the racial inequalities in Mississippi's educational system. Mississippi's black schools were invariably poorly funded, and teachers had to use hand-me-down textbooks that offered a racist slant on American history. Many of the white college students were assigned to teach in these schools, whose curriculum included black history, the philosophy of the Civil Rights Movement, and leadership development in addition to remedial instruction in reading and arithmetic. The Freedom Schools had hoped to draw at least 1000 students that first summer and ended up with 3000. The schools became a model for future social programs like Head Start and for alternative educational institutions.

Freedom Summer activists faced threats and harassment throughout the campaign, not only from white supremacist groups, but from local residents and police. Freedom School buildings and the volunteers' homes were frequent targets; 37 black churches and 30 black homes and businesses were firebombed or burned during that summer, and the cases often went unsolved. More than 1000 black and white volunteers were arrested, and at least 80 were beaten by white mobs or racist police officers. But the summer's most infamous act of violence was the murder of three young civil rights workers, a black volunteer, James Chaney, and his white co-workers, Andrew Goodman and Michael Schwerner. On June 21, Chaney, Goodman, and Schwerner set out to investigate a church bombing near Philadelphia, Mississippi, but were arrested that afternoon and held for several hours on alleged traffic violations. Their release from jail was the last time they were seen alive before their badly decomposed bodies were discovered under a nearby dam six weeks later. Goodman and Schwerner had died from single gunshot wounds to the chest, and Chaney from a savage beating.

The murders made headlines all over the country and provoked an outpouring of national support for the Civil Rights Movement. But many black volunteers realized that because two of the victims were white, these murders were attracting much more attention than previous attacks in which the victims had all been black, and this added to the growing resentment they had already begun to feel toward the white volunteers. There was growing dissension within SNCC's ranks over charges of white paternalism and elitism. Black volunteers complained that the whites seemed to think they had a natural claim on leadership roles, and that they treated the rural blacks as though they were ignorant. There was also increasing hostility from both black and white workers over the interracial romances that developed during the summer. Meanwhile, women volunteers of both races were charging both the black and white men with sexist behavior. These conflicts led to lasting divisions within SNCC, especially over the role of white volunteers. Some African American officials, such as STOKELY CARMICHAEL, reacted by gravitating toward the all-black Black Power Movement, while many white volunteers returned to their college campuses and became involved in other forms of social activism, such as the antiwar and women's movements.

Despite the internal divisions, Freedom Summer left a positive legacy. The well-publicized voter registration drives brought national attention to the subject of black disfranchisement, and this eventually led to the 1965 Voting Rights Act, federal legislation that among other things outlawed the tactics that Southern states had used to prevent blacks from voting. Freedom Summer also instilled among African Americans a new consciousness and a new confidence in political action. As Fannie Lou Hamer later said, "Before the 1964 project there were people that wanted change, but they hadn't dared to come out. After 1964 people began moving. To me it's one of the greatest things that ever happened in Mississippi."

Lisa Clayton Robinson

SEE ALSO

Black History Month/Negro History Week; Chaney, James Earl; Civil Rights Movement; Fifteenth Amendment to the United States Constitution; Lynching; Moses, Robert Parris; Voting Rights Act of 1965; Black Power.

North America

Freeman, Morgan **(b. June 1, 1937, Memphis, Tenn.), African American stage, television, and motion-picture actor best known for his critically acclaimed character roles.**

Morgan Freeman began acting as a child, enlisted in the United States Air Force at 18, and later returned to acting while enrolled at Los Angeles City College. He then moved to New York City, where he perfected his craft in minor stage plays and appeared on the television soap opera *Another World.* He made his Broadway debut in 1968 in an all-black production of *Hello Dolly!* and went on to win a Tony Award nomination for his performance in *The Mighty Gents* (1978) and Obie Awards (given for off-Broadway work) for his roles in *Coriolanus* (1979), *Mother Courage and Her Children* (1980), and *The Gospel at Colonus* (1983).

Freeman's film debut, in the low-budget children's feature *Who Says I Can't Ride a Rainbow?* (1971), led to a recurring role on the educational television series *The Electric Company* broadcast by the Public Broadcasting Service from 1971 to 1977. In his first Hollywood movie, *Brubaker* (1980), a prison reform drama directed by Robert Redford, Freeman made a strong impression in a small but important part as a death-row inmate. His breakthrough came in 1987, when his chilling performance as a pimp in *Street Smart* earned Best Supporting Actor Awards from the New York Film Critics Circle, the Los Angeles Film Critics Association, and the National Society of Film Critics, in addition to an Academy Award nomination for Best Supporting Actor.

Freeman was nominated for Academy Awards as Best Actor for his performances as a long-suffering chauffeur in the sentimental drama *Driving Miss Daisy* (1989) and as a prison inmate in *The Shawshank Redemption* (1994). In 1993 he made his directing debut with *Bopha!*, a drama set in South Africa under the country's policy of strict racial segregation known as APARTHEID. His performance as a world-weary police detective in the 1995 thriller *Seven* won wide critical praise. Freeman's other films include *Clean and Sober* (1988), *Glory* (1989), *Unforgiven* (1992), *Kiss the Girls* (1997), and *Amistad* (1997).

SEE ALSO

New York, New York; Television and African Americans.

Africa

Freetown, Sierra Leone, **the capital of SIERRA LEONE.**

Freetown lies near the tip of a mountainous peninsula on the Atlantic coast of Sierra Leone. Home to about half a million people before the civil war started in 1991, it is the largest city in the country of Sierra Leone. Both African and European cultures have left their imprint from the earliest days in Freetown. The city is the cradle of the KRIO (or Creole) language and culture established by the descendants of freed slaves who intermarried with indigenous people. Freetown was the longest-lasting outpost of British COLONIAL RULE in West Africa. Fourah Bay College, established in 1816, has made Freetown a preeminent center of learning and intellectual life in West Africa for most of the last 200 years.

Freetown was established in 1787. British philanthropists chose the site as a place to send poor black people, mainly freed slaves from Great Britain (*see* LONDON'S BLACK POOR AND THE SIERRA LEONE SETTLEMENT PLAN), North America, and the Caribbean. In 1808 the town became the capital of the new British Crown colony of Sierra Leone. The town served as the administrative center for all of Great Britain's West African possessions until the 1870s, and as a headquarters for British naval forces engaged in intercepting the outlawed slave trade. Between 1808 and the 1860s thousands of people who were freed from slave ships settled there. By the 1840s the town was well established as a major center for trade, exporting palm oil, peanuts, gold, and hides. Freetown had excellent access to interior trade routes that were exploited by European, Krio, and other African traders. This trade attracted merchants and laborers from the surrounding area. Minerals – especially diamonds and bauxite – have surpassed agricultural products as the city's main exports since 1930.

During the 1990s civil war repeatedly devastated Sierra Leone and Freetown. The fighting undermined Sierra Leoneans' infrastructure, economy, and civil liberties. In 1997 a military coup ousted the democratically elected president Ahmad Tejan Kabbah, but on February 14, 1998, Nigerian troops liberated Freetown from control of the military junta, and Kabbah returned in March to initiate the difficult process of reconstruction.

SEE ALSO

Gold Trade.

Latin America and the Caribbean

Free Village System, **a collective response by displaced black workers who wanted independence from the rigidity of Jamaica's plantation economy.**

In Jamaica in the years immediately following abolition (1834) (*see* ABOLITION AND EMANCIPATION IN LATIN AMERICA AND THE CARIBBEAN), colonial officials prevented former slaves (*see* SLAVERY IN LATIN AMERICA AND THE CARIBBEAN) from purchasing land by restricting the amount of land available to blacks and by allowing white landowners to charge black tenants exorbitant rents. The plantation economy relied on a continuous supply of black labor, and white landowners, acting in collusion, kept wages low and rents high to prevent blacks from gaining a foothold in the colony.

The concept of the free village emerged in 1835 when a white missionary, Rev. James Phillippo, purchased a large plot of land in the town of Sligoville. Phillippo divided the land into small plots and sold them to black families at affordable prices. Soon, white missionaries and wealthy free blacks were purchasing large plots of land to create similar free villages.

The free village became the embodiment of black empowerment in the decades following emancipation. Villagers built schools and organized Saturday markets to sell and exchange goods. In the process they created self-sufficient free black communities. By 1840 free villages began appearing in provinces such as Clarendon, St. Thomas-in-the-Vale, St. Andrew, and St. James. Most were in remote loctions and required villagers to travel long distances to obtain fresh water and supplies. However, despite the difficulties inherent in forming self-sufficient free black communities, there were more than 2000 free villages by the 1860s.

Although colonial officials never supported the establishment of free villages, they were unable to prevent their growth. Free villages became thriving free black communities and contributed to the development of Jamaica's domestic economy by promoting small businesses and local markets.

Alonford James Robinson, Jr.

See Also
Jamaica.

Latin America and the Caribbean

Free Womb Laws, laws passed in a number of countries in Latin America and the Caribbean during the protracted progress toward the abolition of slavery. They stated that children born to slave women were free, though the measure was at times circumvented with provisions requiring a period of "apprenticeship," during which time formally free blacks were nonetheless legally tied to masters (*see* Abolition and Emancipation in Latin America and the Caribbean).

Latin America and the Caribbean

Freire, Paulo, influential Brazilian educator who challenged mainstream educational methods (*see* Education in Latin America and the Caribbean).

FRELIMO. Please see Front for the Liberation of Mozambique

Africa

French Dahomey. Former name of Benin.

Africa

French Equatorial Africa.

Former French colony incorporating the following present-day nations: Chad, the Central African Republic, the Republic of the Congo, and Gabon.

See Also
Congo, Republic of the.

Latin America and the Caribbean

French Guiana, a former French colony and present-day overseas department of France on the northeastern coast of South America, with the Atlantic Ocean to the north, Suriname to the west, and Brazil to the south and east.

French Guiana's original inhabitants were Indians known as Carib and Arawaks, whose numbers probably did not exceed 25,000. Their first contact with Europeans occurred when Christopher Columbus landed there in 1498 during the course of his third voyage to the New World. Columbus was moved by the region's beauty; in his travelogue he compared the Oyapock River to the river that flows out of the Garden of Eden, as described in the Bible. As a result of this account, subsequent explorers assumed that hidden in Guiana's interior was the legendary lost city of gold, Eldorado (referred to in Genesis 2:10 as lying at the end of a branch of the same river). The search for this city and its treasure was foremost in the minds of Spanish and Portuguese explorers from the sixteenth century. Their lack of success did not dissuade the French, who made their first appearance in Guiana in 1604, from undertaking the same quest. However, France's search for gold in Guiana was accompanied by colonial ambitions.

Although France did not officially possess Guiana until 1667 and only consolidated control of the territory in 1817, the French brought slaves from Africa to Guiana as early as 1652 (*see* Transatlantic Slave Trade). In contrast to the Caribbean Islands, the slave population in Guiana grew very slowly, mostly as a result of the small number of colonizers. Slave ships preferred to avoid this less lucrative trading spot, stopping there solely when circumstances forced them to do so. The slave population was only 5728 in 1765 and reached a high point of just 19,261 in 1830. Furthermore, many of these African slaves, like a number of their colonial masters, were felled by tropical diseases shortly after their arrival in Guiana. Other slaves fled to the interior of the country, reproducing in certain instances the hunter-gatherer existence they had known in Africa. As a result of these factors, and the sheer difficulty of engaging in agriculture in such a heavily wooded land, the plantation colonialism that was so successful for the French in Martinique and Guadeloupe was a failure in Guiana.

The French persisted in their efforts to develop Guiana. When the colony's principal industries, sugar and timber, collapsed following the abolition of slavery in 1848, France decided to transform Guiana into a penal

A French Guiana woman sorts stalks of sesame plants. *Egan/Hutchison*

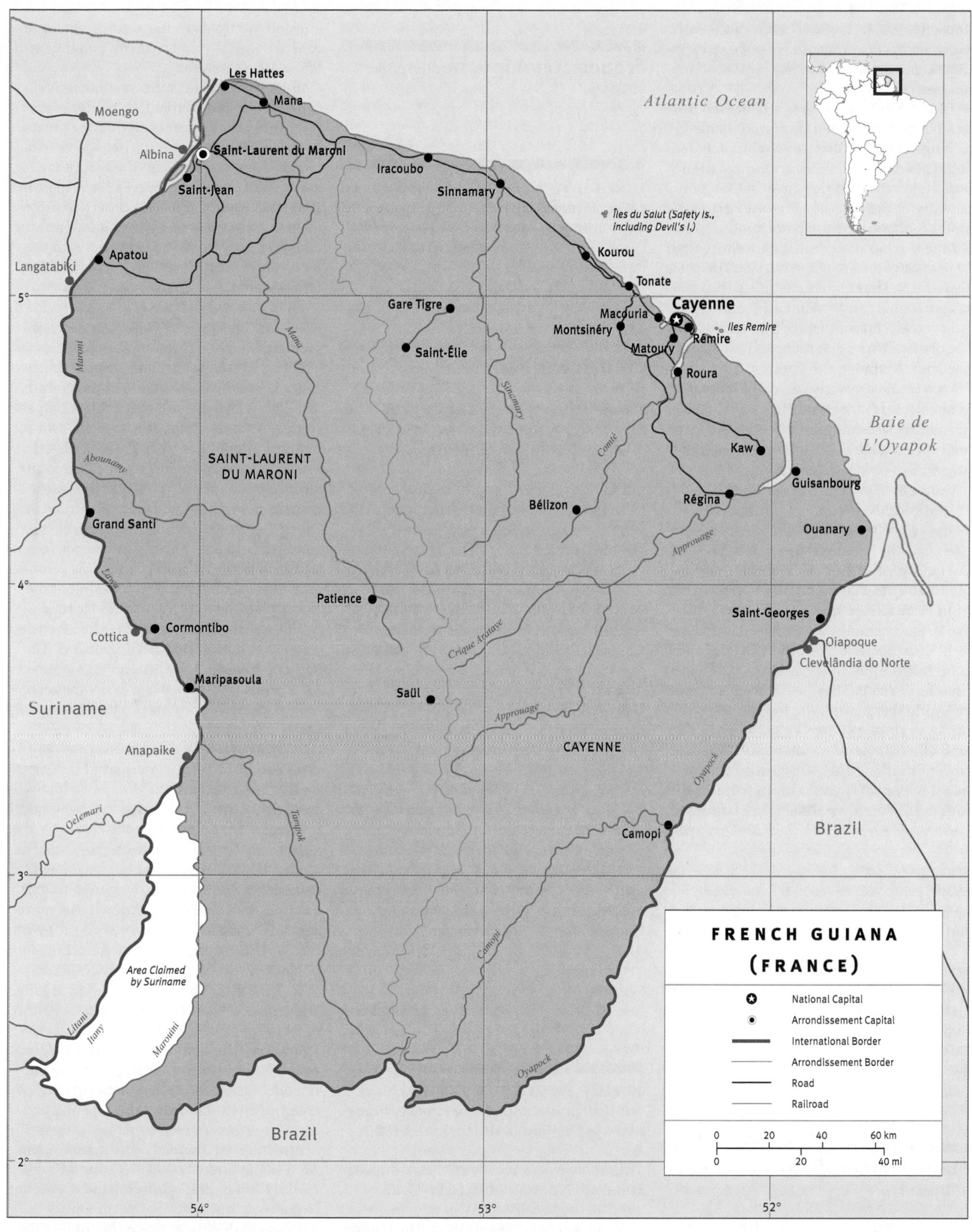

colony. The colonial administrators defended the idea in these terms: France would be rid of its worst element, and the prisoners – who, according to the system of *doublage* (doubling), had to remain in the colony following their initial sentence for an equal amount of time – would eventually form a stable colonizing population. Seventy thousand convicted criminals were sent to Guiana from 1852 to 1939, including Alfred Dreyfus and Henri Charrière, whose attempt to escape Devil's Island was celebrated in Charrière's novel *Papillon* (1969). However, 90 percent of these prisoners died of malaria or yellow fever, and those who survived rarely lived long after their release. The prisons were shut down in 1946, the same year in which Guiana became a French overseas department. A more successful venture for developing Guiana was the European Space Agency's establishment of a satellite launching pad in

Kourou in 1968. However, most of the jobs provided by this project have gone to expatriates, and the benefit to the local economy has been negligible.

Today, French Guiana is still perceived as a land of unfulfilled potential. Plans for developing the interior of Guiana have largely been abandoned, with most of the population living along the coast (50 percent live in the capital, Cayenne). Forestry and fishing are now the largest industries, with fish exports accounting for more than 60 percent of total revenue in 1992. There is also a small amount of agriculture (rice, cassava, bananas, and sugar cane) and logging activity, but not enough to sustain the population. Unemployment is quite high, particularly among the young, and many in French Guiana survive on unemployment benefits from France. For this reason, there is no independence movement to speak of. What political agitation exists in French Guiana is the result of border disputes with Suriname.

Culturally, French Guiana has not been able to compete with the French Caribbean Islands to its north. Few Guianese writers other than the NÉGRITUDE poet LÉON-GONTRAN DAMAS are known outside of their department. The most significant figure to emerge from French Guiana is Félix Eboué (1884-1944), a descendant of African slaves who went on to become a reformer of the French colonial administration and one of Gen. Charles de Gaulle's most trusted advisors during World War II. Still, the descendants of runaway slaves, known as maroons, along with other elements of the population, are currently attempting to forge a cultural renewal in French Guiana through their ties with the CRÉOLITÉ movement in Martinique.

Richard Watts

SEE ALSO
Éboué, Félix; Maroonage in the Americas; Abolition and Emancipation in Latin America and the Caribbean.

Africa

French Guinea. **Former name of the Republic of Guinea.**

SEE ALSO
Guinea.

Africa

French Somaliland. **Former name of DJIBOUTI.**

Africa

French Soudan. **Former name of the Republic of Mali.**

SEE ALSO
Mali.

Africa

French Togoland. **Former name of TOGO.**

Africa

French West Africa. **Former French colony incorporating the following present-day nations: MAURITANIA, SENEGAL, MALI, GUINEA, BURKINA FASO, CÔTE D'IVOIRE, BENIN, and NIGER.**

North America

French, William P.

(b. February 19, 1943, Great Barrington, Mass.; d. January 14, 1997, New York, N.Y.), American book dealer; expert on African American books and bibliography.

William Plummer French was born on February 19, 1943, in Great Barrington, Massachusetts, the son of Frank J. French, vice president of Allied Chemical Co., and Bettina Plummer French. He worked at University Place Book Shop in New York, owned by Walter Goldwater, and became fascinated with African American books and literature, a field the shop specialized in to serve two major collectors, Arthur Schomburg and Arthur Spingarn.

Self-taught by books in the store, French became probably the country's most knowledgeable expert on African American books and bibliography. He compiled two biographical pamphlets on black poetry, and in 1979 co-edited *Afro-American Poetry and Drama, 1760-1975*. Predeceased by his wife, the painter Garland Eliason, French died in New York of a stroke on January 14, 1997. He is survived by his son, Will. A book-collecting prize at the Department of Afro-American Studies at Harvard commemorates his memory.

Richard Newman

SEE ALSO
New York, New York; Schomburg, Arthur Alfonso.

Latin America and the Caribbean

Frente Negra Brasileira, **black political group and political party organized in São Paulo, Brazil, in the 1930s.**

The Frente Negra Brasileira (Black Brazilian Front, or FNB) was founded on October 12, 1931, in the Brazilian city of São Paulo as a political and civic organization. The founder of the organization, and one of its principal leaders, was Arlindo Veiga dos Santos. The "Front" was the most active black political organization in BRAZIL during the 1930s. The wave of public campaigns and protests conducted by black organizations such as the Centro Cívico Palmares during the 1920s had attested to Afro-Brazilians' readiness to organize politically and to claim equality with the white population.

In its early years, support for the FNB spread throughout Brazil. Its center of gravity seemed to rest on its clamor for greater Afro-Brazilian political participation – so much so that Arlindo Veiga dos Santos ran for city council elections in São Paulo in 1933. In 1936 the FNB became a political party. By that time, however, the organization's growing conservatism and identification with the authoritarian ruler Getúlio Vargas had fostered divisions within its ranks.

From its beginning the FNB was associated with the Getúlio Vargas government. By giving political support to Vargas, blacks expected to receive recognition of their importance in the political life of the country as well as satisfaction of their claims. Vargas represented the opposition to the Old Republic (República Velha), which excluded blacks from a more important role in the country's social and political life. After overthrowing the Old Republic in the so-called 1930 Revolution, Vargas established a centralized and populist government that lasted until 1945.

In 1937 he inaugurated a period of dictatorship known as the Estado Novo, and prohibited the formation of political parties and other opposition organizations. His authoritarianism notwithstanding, Vargas was acclaimed by black workers as the "father of the poor" because of his programs targeting native Brazilian workers, most of whom were black. For example, the Law of the Nationalization of Labor, promulgated in 1931, benefited the Brazilian-born work force to the detriment of the immigrants, who had previously been systematically favored in the labor market at the expense of Afro-Brazilians.

The FNB did achieve some success in its campaigns against racial discrimination. For example, Vargas directly ordered the enlistment of 200 blacks in response to the FNB's demand to remove barriers to the admission of blacks into the São Paulo Civil Guard.

By 1933 the FNB's anti-immigrant orientation had evolved into an extreme nationalism. Some of the leaders of the FNB, such as Veiga dos Santos and Pedro Paulo Barbosa, who was a partisan of fascism, started to remodel the organization's political mission, creating divisions within the organization. Soon, the more moderate and left-wing members of the FNB founded other organizations, such as the Clube Social da Cultura Negra (Social Club of Black Culture) and the Frente Negra Socialista (Black Socialist Front).

Accused of elitism since the mid-1930s, the FNB did not manage to build larger channels of communication with the mass of black workers, who did not identify with the organization. Conversely, the FNB often rejected manifestations of Afro-Brazilian culture. For instance, it condemned the Rua Direita gatherings, seeing them as manifestations of the moral degradation of Afro-Brazilians. Rua Direita was a gathered during the evenings and on Sunday afternoons to socialize from the 1930s through the 1940s, when these gatherings were repressed. The repression was due to racist complaints made by whites.

Vargas outlawed political parties in 1937. The FNB, weakened and divided, finally closed its doors in May 1938.

Michelle Gueraldi

Latin America and the Caribbean

Freyre, Gilberto (b. March 15, 1900, Recife, Pernambuco, Brazil; d. July 18, 1987, Recife, Pernambuco, Brazil), Brazilian author and social historian who espoused the idea of Brazil as a racial democracy.

Gilberto Freyre was born into an upper-class family in Brazil's northeastern state of Pernambuco. The son of a law professor, he was educated in his hometown, Recife, and studied social and political sciences at Baylor University in Texas and Columbia University in New York. At Columbia, Freyre was influenced by the pioneering anthropologist Franz Boas, who led the academic challenge against theories of racial determinism. After a brief imprisonment in 1930 on federal charges that he was "a leftist agitator," Freyre traveled to Portugal and then back to the United States, where he taught a course on the development of Brazilian society at Stanford University. This led to his most famous book, *Casa grande e senzala*, published in 1933 (translated as *The Masters and the Slaves*, 1946). In 1934 he helped organize the Primeiro Congresso Afro-Brasileiro (First Afro-Brazilian Congress) in Recife. A political conservative, Freyre served as a federal congressman from 1946 to 1951 and helped rewrite Brazil's constitution. In his lifetime he produced more than 100 literary works. Many of these, such as *Sobrados e Mucambos*, published in 1936 (translated as *The Mansions and the Shanties*, 1963), addressed slavery (*see* Slavery in Latin America and the Caribbean) and race relations in Brazil. *Casa grande e senzala*, which was published in six languages, won Freyre international acclaim and established him as one of Latin America's most influential thinkers.

The spread of pseudoscientific theories about the inferiority of blacks in Brazil during the 1920s and 1930s led to a strengthening of the ideal known as branqueamento, or the view that in order to progress, Brazil had to "whiten" its population. Immigration policies between 1890 and 1902 had encouraged European immigrants and restricted the immigration of Africans and Asians. The effort to lighten the country's complexion was also pursued by the Brazilian foreign minister Baron Rio Branco, who sought to appoint whites to diplomatic positions between 1902 and 1912. At this time, intellectuals such as Raimundo Nina Rodrigues put forth the so-called scientific thesis that the presence of Africans in Brazil, and the history of miscegenation (mixing of the races), placed the nation's progress in serious jeopardy.

Casa grande e senzala (subtitled *A Study in the Development of Brazilian Civilization*) was published at a time of uncertainty in Brazil with respect to national and racial identity and the nation's economic and social development. Freyre's thesis ran counter to arguments on race that many had made up to that point, and forever changed the way many Brazilians viewed themselves and their history. Calling his thesis Luso-Tropicalism, Freyre argued that Portuguese colonization had been uniquely adaptive, and that slavery in Brazil had been singularly lax and benign. Relations between the races in Brazil, therefore, had been marked by intimacy and flexibility. Perhaps the most important part of his analysis concerned his theory of miscegenation. The interbreeding of Portuguese, Indians, and Africans in Brazil, he said, had resulted in a complex racial heritage that should be celebrated as a positive force. Brazil's population was a distinctively "hybrid" New World creation, providing a nation with a new way to conceptualize its identity as it struggled to modernize.

Thus Freyre, at a single swipe, reversed theories of the supposed "negative" impact of Africans upon Brazilian culture. The new "meta-race," he argued, was marked by its *morenidade*, or "brownness," and by its harmonious, nonracist social relations: "The crossbreeding so widely practiced here corrected the social distance which otherwise would have remained enormous between the plantation mansion and the slave quarters. What the large-landholding, slave-owning monoculture produced in the way of aristocratization, dividing Brazilian society into classes of masters and slaves, with a piddling and insignificant middle section of freedpeople sandwiched between the two antagonistic extremes, was in great part neutralized by miscegenation's social effects."

In seeking to explain the uniqueness of Brazilian culture as he saw it, Freyre looked to the culture brought to the country by its Portuguese colonists and the structure of social relations under colonialism and slavery. The Portuguese had developed a sense of respect for people of color, he asserted, from their long history of relations with the dark-skinned Moors who had ruled Portugal for centuries. What emerged was not only a unique Portuguese intimacy with different races, but perhaps more important, a predisposition on the part of the early Portuguese colonists to be attracted to dark-skinned women. Freyre believed that the Portuguese even preferred dark-skinned women, suggesting that they had no compunctions about having sexual relations with Brazil's indigenous inhabitants and, at a later stage, with African slave women.

Freyre also advanced the theory of "Iberian exceptionalism," which held that Portuguese slavery was markedly different from, and more benign than, slavery practiced by other European powers. The Portuguese colonizers of Brazil, he asserted, followed the Arab rather than the European model of slavery, treating the slave as "part of the family of the owner." Brazilian slave owners ruled as they saw fit, exercising a power that was hierarchic and patriarchal, but also intimate and personal. Three factors accounted for this flexibility: (1) the supposed "laxity" of early Brazilian Roman Catholicism, (2) the shortage of Portuguese women during early colonization, and (3) the lack of a strong colonial rule. The paternalistic power of the Brazilian slave owner, combined with the high rate of miscegenation, meant that the offspring of white slave owners and their black female slaves were afforded a higher social status than other slaves. By comparison, slaves in the United States, Freyre suggested, were more often mistreated because Anglo-Saxon law did not recognize their human status (considered them "property"), nor were they allowed to purchase their freedom, unlike slaves in Brazil.

In this way, Freyre depicted Brazil as a racial democracy, where everyone shared in a mixed racial heritage and where relations between the races were harmonious, if hierarchical (*see* Myth of Racial Democracy in Latin America and the Caribbean: An Interpretation). He portrayed Brazilians as a unique mixed-race people who have inherited intellectual sophistication from their European ancestors and sensuality from their African ancestors. Freyre thus convinced Brazilians and many others that the country's racial potpourri, and the influence of Africans in the mix, was actually an asset and should be a source of national pride.

Freyre's theories on slavery in Brazil and the nature of race relations there have been the subject of many debates. In his day, his ideas were regarded as revolutionary. Viewed through a contemporary lens, they have been widely challenged and discredited. Critics dispute the idea that slavery under the Portuguese was more benign than under other European powers, that Portuguese colonization was more flexible and less racist, and that Brazil is free of racism and racial tensions. Freyre has also been criticized for applying a model based on Brazil's colonial northeast to the rest of the country. Some critics have suggested that Freyre's defense of the uniqueness of Portuguese colonization was unfairly used as an attempt to justify continuing Portuguese rule in Angola and Mozambique in the late 1960s.

Casa grande e senzala has also been criticized for failing to address the cruelty of slavery and for sentimentalizing the relationship between master and slave (though it documented, in detail, the cruelties and sadism of the Portuguese slave owners). Responding to this charge in a 1980 interview with the *New York Times*, Freyre said, "I knew some of the children of the slaves. That probably affected my view of it. I am accused of romanticizing slavery, but I had good reason to think that not all slaves were victims of cruel treatment. My main theme was that the average slave in agrarian, patriarchal Brazil was happier in lots of ways than the working men in the first period of the industrial society in Europe and in Brazil."

Despite the criticisms of his work, many have credited Freyre with challenging European racist theories, which asserted that racial differences were innate and that miscegenation led to degeneracy. While his thesis of Brazil's racial democracy is increasingly disputed, his studies challenged a view that saw Africans in Brazil as a single monolithic group whose impact on the nation could only be negative. Moreover, his work helped pave the way for the study of Afro-Brazilian history and culture.

Aaron Myers

SEE ALSO
Whitening.

Africa

Front de Libération Nationale, **Algerian national independence organization.**

"The struggle will be long, but the outcome is certain," the Algerian independence group National Liberation Front (FLN) declared in 1954. This proclamation marked the union of diverse nationalist groups – reformist, communist, and Islamicist – in a joint struggle for liberation from colonial rule. It also marked the beginning of one of the bloodiest wars of independence, one that turned international attention to Africa's struggle for decolonization.

Algerian resistance to French rule dated back to ABD AL-QADIR's revolt in 1837, and nationalist sentiment had been growing since the early twentieth century. The FLN broke from more reformist predecessors by declaring as its goal full "national independence through the restoration of the Algerian state, sovereign, democratic and social, within the framework of the principles of Islam." The organization was prepared for armed struggle to achieve these ends, and, with the Armée de Libération (ALN), launched a brutal military campaign in August 1955. The French retaliated against an FLN-planned massacre in the town of Constantinois with a carnage justified by "collective responsibility."

The severity of the French response only served to drive more Algerian groups into the fold of the FLN. Political exiles planned the struggle from MOROCCO and TUNISIA while military units trained in isolated Aurès Mountains sites. At the Soummam Congress in 1956, the FLN declared itself the sole representative of Algeria, and launched an urban guerrilla campaign. Women played a significant role in this campaign; young women passing as French, or older domestic workers dressed in concealing traditional garments, carried weapons and bombs into restricted French quarters. Soon French police began to view all city residents as suspect and used brutal methods to eliminate resistance.

The war of independence left hundreds of thousands of Algerians and thousands of French dead. The struggle was recorded for the world by FLN political theorist FRANTZ FANON, a psychiatrist from MARTINIQUE, and endorsed by such prominent intellectuals as Jean Paul Sartre. International pressure on France increased, and the colonial government finally began to move toward decolonization.

After negotiations in 1960, the FLN and France reached the Evian Accords, which granted Algeria political autonomy and settlers some rights. But the French settler vigilante force, the Organisation de l'Armée Secrète (OAS), continued searching out and killing suspected FLN supporters even without the official support of the French government. Finally, a referendum passed that granted full independence to Algeria in July 1962. The FLN leader AHMED BEN BELLA became the first prime minister.

Following independence, solidarity among nationalists broke down, both within the FLN and among rival nationalist parties. In the next year all other parties were banned, and the FLN remained the only legal party in Algeria until 1989.

Marian Aguiar

SEE ALSO
Algeria; Nationalism in Africa; France.

Africa

Front for the Liberation of Mozambique, **Mozambican revolutionary movement and political party.**

FRELIMO (Frente da Libertação de Moçambique) led the anticolonial movement in Portuguese-ruled MOZAMBIQUE and has in turn ruled the country since independence. The party formed in 1962 from a coalition of three nationalist organizations: the Mozambican National Democratic Union, the African Union of Independent Mozambique, and the Mozambican African National Union. As PORTUGAL steadfastly opposed the decolonization sweeping the rest of Africa, the party's leaders, including its president Eduardo Mondlane, concluded that national liberation was obtainable only through an armed struggle. FRELIMO initiated Mozambique's war for independence in September 1964, supported by China and Eastern bloc countries that provided military assistance and training. Throughout the decade-long war, the party espoused an ideology of national unity and remained the sole legitimate opposition group. Occasionally, however, it experienced internal fragmentation, primarily due to the dominance of southerners in the party.

In 1975 Mozambique became independent under the leadership of Samora Machel and the FRELIMO party. Always espousing nationalism and scientific socialism, in 1977 it officially became a Marxist-Leninist "vanguard party." As the ruling party, FRELIMO vacillated between highly centralized administrative policies and efforts to empower the masses through *grupos dinamizadores*, party groups that would move throughout the country explaining the political, legal, and social services system to the rural population. Most commentators agree that there was little, if any, difference between the party and the state. Like many Marxist parties in Africa, FRELIMO's membership remained small, confined primarily to employees of the state bureaucracy and state-run enterprises.

At its Fifth Congress in 1989, FRELIMO dropped Marxist-Leninism and has since espoused political liberalism and promoted a free market economy. Even after the introduction of multiparty electoral politics in 1992, FRELIMO retained its political dominance. In the 1994 elections to the newly formed Assembly of the Republic, it won 129 of 250 seats.

Eric Young

SEE ALSO
Decolonization in Africa: An Interpretation; Machel, Samora Moises.

Africa

Fugard, Athol **(b. June 11, 1932, near Middleburg, South Africa), South African playwright whose dramatic works deal with the personal wounds inflicted by apartheid.**

Best known for his plays *Blood Knot* and *Master Harold... and the Boys*, Athol Fugard has brought to a wide audience images of life in SOUTH AFRICA under APARTHEID. The child of an English father and AFRIKANER mother, Fugard grew up in Port Elizabeth, the Cape Province city where most of his plays are set. He studied philosophy and anthropology at the University of Cape Town, then left just before graduating and hitchhiked the length of the continent to Port Sudan, where he spent the next two years working on a steam ship.

Returning to South Africa in 1956, Fugard married Sheila Meiring, an actress whom he credits for developing his interest in theater. In 1958 he became a clerk for the Fordsburg Native Commissioner's Court. The court handled cases of people accused of violating the PASS LAWS, which were among the many laws restricting Africans' right to live and work where they pleased. Fugard called the job "the ugliest thing I have ever been part of," but it also inspired the intimate view of apartheid's cruelty that became an ever-present element in his work.

By 1959 Fugard had written and produced two plays, *No-Good Friday* and *Nongogo*, and he and his wife moved to London to gain theatrical experience. They stayed only a year, returning to South Africa after the Sharpeville massacre in 1960. Fugard's next play, *The Blood Knot*, opened in 1961 with Fugard and an African actor, Zakes Mokae, playing two mixed-race half-brothers confronting the psychic toll of institutionalized racism. At the same time Fugard began protesting the official segregation of theater audiences.

In 1967 the South African government seized Fugard's passport and placed him under surveillance. But the harassment did not stop Fugard from collaborating in 1972 with black actor-playwrights John Kani and Winston Ntshona on *Sizwe Banzi Is Dead* and *The Island*, each of which was nominated for three Tony Awards. His 1982 play *Master Harold... and the Boys* concerns the relationships between a privileged white boy and his family's black servants. Considered one of the best playwrights in the English-speaking world, Fugard continues to write and produce plays (*see* THEATER, AFRICAN).

Kate Tuttle

SEE ALSO
Cape Town, South Africa; Sharpeville, South Africa.

North America

Fugitive Slave Laws, laws passed by the United States Congress in 1793 and 1850 providing for the return of runaway slaves to their owners.

EARLY FUGITIVE LAWS

Before the American colonies won independence from Great Britain, several Southern legislatures passed laws providing for the return of runaway slaves. Under some of these laws, slaves who resisted arrest could be killed and their owners reimbursed by the government. Under others, penalties were levied against people who protected runaways and rewards given to those who caught them. The laws, however, had little effect outside the colonies that passed them, leaving Northerners free to harbor escaped slaves.

In 1787 the Confederated Congress passed the Northwest Ordinance, which banned slavery from the Northwest Territory but allowed slaves who fled to the territory to be caught and returned to their owners. The ordinance did not, however, require governments or settlers to cooperate in the capture and return of runaways. Two years later the U.S. Constitution took effect, with a clause in Article IV, Section 2, that said runaway slaves and indentured servants "shall be delivered" to their masters when requested. The Constitution did not specifically require governments to help in the return of fugitives.

FUGITIVE SLAVE ACT OF 1793

Congress intended the Fugitive Slave Act of 1793 to resolve these ambiguities. Slave catchers were permitted to capture a runaway slave in any state or territory and needed only to prove orally to a federal or state judge that the person was an escaped slave. The slave was not guaranteed a trial by jury, and the judge's decision was final. Anyone sheltering an escaped slave could be fined $500, a stiff penalty at the time.

The law met with opposition in many – though not all – Northern states, several of which responded by passing laws to protect free blacks and fugitive slaves. These laws, known as personal liberty laws, required a slave catcher to produce extra evidence that his quarry was a runaway and often gave the accused the rights to appeal and to trial by jury. In some states, the laws also made it easier to extradite a runaway slave once his or her slave status was proven. Generally the Fugitive Slave Act was unevenly enforced and contributed to further rancor between North and South.

In 1842 the U.S. Supreme Court held in *Prigg* v. *Pennsylvania* that the North's personal liberty laws unconstitutionally interfered with the Fugitive Slave Act. The Court said that while states did not have to enforce the federal law, neither could they interfere with it. *Prigg* prompted many Northern states to amend their statutes, directing judges and law enforcement officers simply to do nothing about fugitive slaves. The only recourse left to slave catchers was to abduct runaways themselves.

FUGITIVE SLAVE ACT OF 1850

Conflict between South and North peaked in 1850 over the issue of whether to allow slavery in newly acquired territories and newly admitted states. Congress addressed the conflict with a series of acts known collectively as the Compromise of 1850, part of which included the Fugitive Slave Act of 1850, a substantial reworking of the 1793 law. Under the new law, accused runaways were not allowed to testify at their trial and were specifically denied a trial by jury. To circumvent sabotage on the part of Northern states, federal commissioners would be appointed in every county to rule on fugitives. Commissioners received $10 when they ruled that an accused African American was a fugitive but only $5 when they ruled that he or she was a free black. Officers charged with arresting a fugitive could be fined $1,000 for refusing to help and could also be charged for the value of a slave who escaped while in their custody. Private citizens could be similarly fined and jailed for obstruction.

In the North the law prompted widespread calls for civil disobedience. Large disturbances broke out in Boston; Syracuse, New York; and Oberlin, Ohio. Coupled with the publication of Harriet Beecher Stowe's UNCLE TOM'S CABIN (1852), which dealt in part with a fugitive slave, the 1850 law made abolitionism and support for the UNDERGROUND RAILROAD respectable, where before they had seemed radical.

Many Northern states passed another round of personal liberty laws to protect free blacks and escaped slaves; others actively undermined it. This response proved to many Southerners that the North would go to any lengths – even subversion of the Constitution – to deprive the South of slavery. The South moved inexorably toward secession and the country toward civil war. In 1864 the Fugitive Slave Laws were overturned when President Abraham Lincoln issued the Emancipation Proclamation.

SEE ALSO
Slavery in the United States; Abolitionism in the United States; American Revolution; Free Blacks in the United States, 1619 to 1863; Thirteenth Amendment of the United States Constitution and the Emancipation Proclamation.

North America

Fugitive Slaves, antebellum African Americans who liberated themselves by running away from the slave South to freedom in the North, Canada, or Mexico.

American slavery was a lifelong institution from which the only respites were manumission, death, or running away (*see* SLAVERY IN THE UNITED STATES). Manumission was rare – most African Americans who were born slaves died as slaves – but a significant number "stole themselves," as they were legally the property of their owners, and escaped. The numbers are unknown, but perhaps as many as 100,000 black men, women, and children escaped during the nineteenth century.

While much self-liberation was the work of individuals, a secret network called the UNDERGROUND RAILROAD provided help through experienced guides, secure routes, and safe houses. Two of the best-known "conductors" were Harriet Tubman, who, at great personal danger, ventured into the South many times to bring out fugitives, and WILLIAM STILL, the Philadelphia abolitionist whose book *The Underground Railroad* (1872) was the only daily diary record of a Railroad leader. He emphasized that fugitives were brave people who risked their lives for freedom, not merely recipients of the kindness of white abolitionists.

Escape was a constant, if secret, theme in slave culture. Many spirituals, for example, included double meanings, with shoes and chariots as symbols of movement, and Canaan or the Promised Land as the image of

Africa or CANADA. Slaveholders' advertisements for runaways represent one of the best sources for physical descriptions of slaves; many bore the scars of the whip or of actual mutilations.

The issue of fugitive slaves became one of national significance when Congress approved the Fugitive Slave Law of 1850 (*see* FUGITIVE SLAVE LAWS), which required Northerners to cooperate in the capture of runaways. Opposition to the act led to civil disobedience and brought the Civil War closer. The war itself saw wholesale self-liberation as thousands of slaves fled the plantations for the freedom of Union Army lines.

Richard Newman

SEE ALSO

Maroonage in the Americas; Abolitionism in the United States; Civil War, American; Tubman, Harriet Ross; Spirituals, African American.

Africa

Fulani (also known as Peul, Fula, and Fellata), a pastoral people of West Africa widely dispersed through parts of SENEGAL, GUINEA, MALI, NIGER, NIGERIA, and CAMEROON, with smaller numbers in surrounding countries.

The Fulani inhabit a vast territory stretching from Senegal on the Atlantic coast to the CENTRAL AFRICAN REPUBLIC to the east. Throughout this region they live side by side with other peoples, and they do not form a majority in any of the countries they inhabit. The Fulani are the only cattle-raising people in West Africa.

The Fulani are the most thoroughly pastoral people of West Africa: more than half of them raise livestock, to varying degrees of exclusivity. Early explorers and researchers noted the cultural and physical differences between the Fulani and neighboring African groups. The Fulani themselves are keenly aware of their distinctive physical appearance: some have relatively fair skin, long hair, and aquiline features. The popular image of the Fulani is that they are the cattle keepers of West Africa. However, many Fulani today have adopted settled agricultural or urban livelihoods.

Traditionally, the pastoral Fulani have practiced varying degrees of nomadism. Some have migrated widely in search of water and pasture for their herds, while others have migrated seasonally between summer pasture and a more settled winter existence, which has often included crop cultivation. The Fulani have traditionally exchanged dairy products for cereals and vegetables produced by neighboring agricultural peoples. The Fulani reckon descent patrilineally; lineage groups form the basis for the social organization of the pastoral Fulani. Until the seventeenth century the highest level of political organization among the pastoral Fulani was the autonomous band with its headman. Although some pastoral Fulani maintain traditional animist beliefs, most have adopted Islam.

Scholars believe that the Fulani originated in the grasslands surrounding the valley of the SENEGAL RIVER, in the area known today as Senegal. This belief rests on both historical evidence and the similarities between the Fulani language, Fulfulde (also known as Pulaar, Fula, and Peul), and the languages of the SERER and the WOLOF of Senegal. These languages belong to the West Atlantic group of Niger-Congo languages (*see* LANGUAGES, AFRICAN: AN OVERVIEW).

Until the eleventh century, the Fulani practiced a traditional pastoral lifestyle on the western fringes of the ancient kingdom of Ghana. With the fall of Ghana in the eleventh century, a new Islamic state, known as Tekrur, arose in the Senegal valley, and some Fulani for the first time adopted a settled existence. They merged with the settled population to form a Fulfulde-speaking subgroup known as the TUKULOR. By the fourteenth century Fulani groups had begun a gradual migration southward and eastward from their original homeland. By the fifteenth century they had arrived in the FOUTA DJALLON region of present-day Guinea and in the Macina region of present-day Mali. A century later, pastoral Fulani had reached Hausaland and Bornu in northern present-day Nigeria. By the eighteenth century the Fulani had taken up herding on the northern grasslands of present-day Cameroon.

As the Fulani migrated throughout West Africa over the centuries, significant differences emerged among the different groups who considered themselves Fulani. Most Fulani, known as the *Fulani bororo*, or "cattle Fulani," maintained a traditional pastoral existence. Others, however, known as the *Fulani gida*, or "town Fulani," took up a settled existence in the towns of kingdoms such as Mali, Songhai, and especially the Hausa states.

Over the centuries Fulani groups increasingly adopted forms of Islam practiced by neighboring peoples. As they migrated eastward, the rulers of powerful states such as Songhai and the states of Hausaland exacted fees and taxes from both Fulani herdsmen and Fulani merchants living in towns. During the sixteenth century Fulani began to adopt radical, Sufi-influenced forms of Islam. These included the Qadiriyah and Tijaniyah orders that were carried across the Sahara by the Tuareg, who had come to dominate the region around Tombouctu (Timbuktu). These Islamic sects maintained the right of believers to rebel against unjust rulers in order to create a society based on Islamic principles.

Such groups inspired reform movements led by Fulani, often with support from neighboring peoples, who advocated *jihad*, or holy war, to replace rulers perceived as corrupt and greedy with an austere and devout Muslim theocracy. The first Fulani jihad replaced the MANDE rulers of Bondu, in present-day western Mali, with a Fulani theocracy in the late seventeenth century. During the eighteenth century the Fulani established similar theocracies in Fouta Djallon and the Futa Toro region of present-day Senegal. The most famous and powerful of the Fulani theocracies, however, was the SOKOTO CALIPHATE of present-day northern Nigeria. This vast empire arose as the result of a jihad led by a Fulani cleric, USMAN DAN FODIO, against the Hausa states during the early nineteenth century. Soon thereafter, a Fulani theocracy established control in the Macina region. During the mid-nineteenth century the religiously inspired Fulani and Tukulor led by AL-HAJJ UMAR TAL established a state that controlled most of present-day Mali.

In each of these states, Fulani gida occupied positions of religious and secular leadership. Fulani remain prominent throughout much of this region today. In northern Nigeria the Fulani gida have gradually merged with wealthy Hausa to form an ethnic group sometimes called Hausa-Fulani. This group remains the effective ruling class of northern Nigeria.

There are certain key features common to both Fulani bororo and Fulani gida. The first of these is Fulfulde, the language of the Fulani. Although the basic language is the same throughout West Africa, there are regional dialectal differences, and in all areas the Fulani borrow words from neighboring languages. A second feature common to the Fulani is a shared moral and ethical code known as *Pulaaku*. The Fulani's wide geographic dispersal makes it difficult to estimate their population. However, probably at least 15 million people in West Africa speak Fulfulde.

Yaa Pokua Afriyie Oppong

SEE ALSO

Ghana, Early Kingdom of; Pastoralism; Songhai Empire; Tombouctou, Mali; Tuareg; Mali Empire.

Fulbe. Please see FULANI

North America

Fuller, Meta Vaux Warrick (b. June 9, 1877, Philadelphia, Pa.; d. March 18, 1968, Framingham, Mass.), African American sculptor, one of the earliest studio artists to depict black themes.

"Art must be the quintessence of meaning. Creative art means you create for yourself. Inspirations can come from most anything. Tell the world how you feel... take the chance... try, try!" This statement by Meta Vaux Warrick Fuller reflects the spirit of a woman who created bold, dramatic work that took new chances in African American art. Fuller was born in Philadelphia in 1877, the daughter of two successful entrepreneurs.

Her father owned a catering business and a barber shop, and her mother was a hairdresser. She grew up in a privileged home, receiving lessons in art, music, dance, and horseback riding. When one of her high school projects at the J. Liberty Tadd Industrial Art School was selected to be part of Tadd's exhibit at the 1893 World's Columbian Exposition in Chicago, her public career as an artist began.

In 1894 Fuller received a three-year scholarship to the Pennsylvania School of Industrial Art, followed by a one-year post-graduate fellowship in 1897. As a student she received several awards and prizes for her sculpture. Her work had a signature bold, sensational style that her instructors felt would be especially successful overseas, so in September 1899, Fuller sailed for Paris. During the next four years she studied at the Académie Colarossi and the Ecole des Beaux-Arts and received private guidance from such prominent sculptors as Auguste Rodin and Augustus Saint-Gaudens. Rodin was an especially significant early supporter, and after he praised her 1901 sculpture *Secret Sorrow (Man Eating His Heart)*, her work was exhibited at several important galleries.

In Paris Fuller drew inspiration for her sculptures from Greek myths, French literature, and the Bible as well as various European traditions. Her works often portrayed dramatic and even grotesque figures – other titles included *Medusa, The Wretched*, and *Man Carrying a Dead Comrade* – and were praised for their force and power; the French press called Fuller "the delicate sculptor of horrors." But even as she was developing a reputation based on this genre of work, new influences began to present themselves.

One of her earliest friends in Paris was the African American painter Henry O. Tanner. In 1900, during a trip to Paris, W. E. B. Du Bois saw Fuller's work at the Paris Universal Exposition, and both Tanner and Du Bois began encouraging her to explore African American subjects. Fuller initially resisted these suggestions, content with the images that had made her a success in Paris. But when she decided to return to the United States in October 1902, she found the art world in her hometown unwilling to accept her. After the cold reception she received from mainstream Philadelphia critics and dealers, Fuller began constructing new pieces that appealed to the black Philadelphia audience. In the process, she became one of the first African American studio artists to depict African American faces and themes.

In 1907 Fuller became the first black woman artist to receive a federal commission for her work when she was asked to contribute a set of tableaux on African American history for the Jamestown Tercentennial Exposition. The finished work was awarded a gold medal and brought her national attention, but over the next few years, several events temporarily slowed Fuller's art. In 1909 she married Liberian neurologist Solomon Fuller and moved with him to Framingham, Massachusetts; within two years she had two infant sons (a third was born in 1916). In 1910 a fire in the Philadelphia warehouse where Fuller had stored her pieces destroyed 16 years' worth of work, including everything she had created in Paris. The fire devastated Fuller and caused her to stop sculpting altogether for three years. But in 1913 she accepted a commission from Du Bois to create a sculpture for New York's state celebration of the 50th anniversary of the Emancipation Proclamation, and the second phase of her career began.

Over the next few decades, Fuller bcame known for pieces that celebrated African and African American history, struggle, and heritage. These included the 1914 work *Ethiopia Awakening*, which portrayed an African woman removing mummy bandages from her eyes; the 1919 work *Mary Turner: A Silent Protest Against Mob Violence*, which commemorated the much-publicized 1917 LYNCHING of a pregnant woman; and the 1937 piece *The Talking Skull*, which dramatized an African fable. Fuller is sometimes remembered as a HARLEM RENAISSANCE artist because her work from this period coincided with the flowering of art by other black writers, musicians, and artists that began in New York in the 1920s.

In 1950 Fuller again temporarily retired from sculpting, this time to care for her ill husband and to recover from her own tuberculosis. But by the late 1950s she had returned to her art, creating a bust of educator CHARLOTTE HAWKINS BROWN in 1956 and a series of works depicting notable black women for the NATIONAL COUNCIL OF NEGRO WOMEN in 1957. In the 1960s Fuller sculpted works that reflected her support of the CIVIL RIGHTS MOVEMENT: *The Crucifixion*, which commemorated the four girls killed in the 1963 Sixteenth Street Baptist Church bombing in Birmingham, Alabama, and *The Good Shepherd*, which celebrated the clergymen who had marched to Selma, Alabama, with Martin Luther King Jr. By the time she passed away in 1968 at age 90, Fuller had spent more than 70 years creating art that "[took] a chance" and "[told] the world" how she felt, in the process becoming one of the most innovative black artists of the twentieth century.

Lisa Clayton Robinson

SEE ALSO

Du Bois, William Edward Burghardt (W. E. B.); King, Martin Luther, Jr.; Sixteenth Street Baptist Church (Birmingham, Ala.); Tanner, Henry Ossawa; Thirteenth Amendment of the United States Constitution and the Emancipation Proclamation; Philadelphia, Pennsylvania; Art, African American.

Africa

Fulse (also known as Foulse), ethnic group of West Africa.

The Fulse primarily inhabit west-central BURKINA FASO. They speak a Niger-Congo language and belong to the GRUSI cultural and linguistic group. Approximately 100,000 people consider themselves Fulse.

SEE ALSO

Languages, African: An Overview.

North America

Funk, a musical style pioneered by JAMES BROWN and SLY AND THE FAMILY STONE during the late 1960s and 1970s; funk evolved from SOUL MUSIC, deepening its rhythms and incorporating psychedelic elements inspired by late 1960s rock 'n' roll.

Funk evolved from soul music during the late 1960s, much as BLACK POWER grew out of the CIVIL RIGHTS MOVEMENT. During the 1960s RHYTHM AND BLUES (R&B) performers drew upon the harmonies and vocal style of GOSPEL MUSIC to create the distinctive style that became known as soul music. Soul music voiced the pride and optimism that many blacks shared during the Civil Rights Movement. By the late 1960s, the political climate had deteriorated. The VIETNAM WAR displaced President Lyndon Johnson's War on Poverty, and between 1965 and 1968 violence erupted in many black urban neighborhoods. The civil rights coalition was increasingly divided as the Black Power Movement brought a new militancy to African American politics.

Popular music could not help reflecting such influences, and for African Americans the result was funk. Funk was a heavily rhythmic, dance-oriented music with lyrics that mostly focused on sex, drugs, and partying. Surprisingly often, however, funk lyrics spoke to contemporary black pride and anger. In "Say It Loud (I'm Black and I'm Proud)" (1968), James Brown sang, "We'd rather die on our feet, than be livin' on our knees." Sly and the Family Stone recorded equally militant lyrics in such songs as "Don't Call Me Nigger, Whitey" (1969) and on the album *There's a Riot Going On* (1971). Parliament's "Chocolate City" (1975) envisioned the possibilities of an all-black American government.

Ultimately, funk music was not about political commentary; it was about the beat. Trombonist Fred Wesley – who in the 1970s worked with such leading funk performers as Brown, GEORGE CLINTON, and bassist Bootsy Collins – explained the essential elements of a funk song: "If you have a syncopated bass line, a strong, strong, heavy back beat from the drummer, a counter-line from the guitar, or the keyboard, and someone soul-singing on top of that in a gospel style, then you have funk."

Funk music deepened the heavy rhythms of soul music, and it followed the lead of guitarist JIMI HENDRIX in bringing the beat and performing style of psychedelic rock 'n' roll into African American popular music.

The key funk innovator was the "godfather of soul," James Brown. His bands featured tightly riffing horn sections coupled to an underlying rhythm that turned decades of black music topsy-turvy by putting the accent on one and three, rather than on the back beats (two and four). Brown's albums *Out of Sight* (1964) and *Papa's Got a Brand New Bag* (1965) predated the stylistic label funk, but they clearly foreshadowed the style.

Although Brown set the stage for funk, Sly Stone completed the funk synthesis. Stone formed Sly and the Family Stone in 1967 in San Francisco, a hotbed of counterculture activity that was home to the psychedelic rock bands Jefferson Airplane and the Grateful Dead. Sly and the Family Stone was the first interracial rock band, and it included women and men as well as blacks and whites.

The band had its greatest success between 1968 and 1971, including an appearance at the 1969 Woodstock Festival. Sly and the Family Stone's early hits, "Everyday People" (1968) and "Hot Fun in the Summertime" (1969), suggested a pop-music innocence, but in concert the group's punchy horn riffs and frenzied guitar solos merged a strong funk beat with intense, psychedelic rock-style guitar solos.

More than any other musician, George Clinton has kept funk music alive. Through the 1970s and 1980s Clinton and his related and overlapping groups Parliament and Funkadelic, which during the 1970s began performing together as P-Funk, kept the funk beat alive during an era dominated by disco and punk rock. Other popular funk bands included Earth, Wind, and Fire; the Ohio Players; the Commodores; and the Bar-Kays. In the 1980s, funk – especially the recordings of Clinton and Brown – provided the music for many early rappers (*see* Rap).

James Clyde Sellman

Africa

Fur (also known as Keira), ethnic group of Sudan.

The Fur primarily inhabit the Darfur region of Sudan; the region's name means House of the Fur. The Fur ruled the powerful kingdom of Darfur from the seventeenth to the late nineteenth century. The Fur speak a Nilo-Saharan language. Approximately 800,000 people consider themselves Fur.

See Also
Languages, African: An Overview.

Fur Trappers. Please see Mountain Men

Futa Jallon. Please see Fouta Djallon

g

Africa

Ga, ethnic group of southeastern GHANA.

The indigenous inhabitants of Ghana's coast, the Ga are the dominant ethnic group of Ghana and the founders of the capital city of Accra. They speak a language of the Kwa branch of the Niger-Congo language family and are closely related to the neighboring ADANGBE, who speak a similar language.

Legend states that the Ga people arrived from the east, in a series of land and sea migrations, before the fourteenth century; however, linguistic and archaeological evidence suggests that the ancestors of the Ga occupied their present homeland for more than a thousand years. In the Ga language, the name "Ga" refers both to the Ga people and to the city of Accra.

Before the arrival of Europeans, the Ga lived in villages along the coast, where they fished, and inland, where they cultivated root crops, oil palms, and plantains. Coastal Ga traded fish with inland Ga for agricultural products. Men fished and raised crops while women dominated trade. Villages were organized by kinship ties. Each village was divided into seven residences, or *akutsei*, which were in turn divided into smaller kinship units, called *we*. Each of the seven akutsei had a chief, who wielded limited power. Priests, called *wulomei*, exercised authority over the Ga. Wulomei maintain considerable influence today, even though the Ga are now largely Christian. Village elders also held significant influence.

As a patrilineal society, a Ga individual's social rank and condition usually depended on his or her father's position. However, girls could inherit property from their mother and married adults often continued to live with their parents, a pattern that persisted in the 1990s. Agricultural and fishing cycles, as well as the forces of nature, held prominent places in Ga worship. Boys underwent ritual circumcision. Funerals were the most elaborate rite of passage.

With the arrival of the Portuguese in the fifteenth century, the trade in gold from the AKAN homeland to the north shifted toward the coast. Subsequently, Akan peoples sought to extend control over the Ga as a means of securing direct access to trade opportunities. Probably in order to defend themselves, the Ga adopted centralized kingships modeled after those of the Akan. Like Akan kingships, the main Ga towns – Accra, Osu, Labadi, Teshi, Nungua, and Tema – each held stools, which symbolized unity and power. Okai Koi, who ruled from about 1610 to 1660, extended his rule over all Ga territory and fought the Akwamu, an Akan people. Okai Koi committed suicide in 1660 after suffering defeat by the Akwamu. By 1680 the Akwamu had incorporated the Ga as a vassal state.

With the construction of several forts in and around Accra beginning in 1650, the Europeans gradually came to dominate the coast. Accra quickly became a major gold and slave-trading center. Many inland Ga moved to the coast for economic opportunities.

As the city of Accra expanded during the colonial era and after independence, increasing numbers of Ga settled in the city and its environs. As a result, the Ga are today one of the most urbanized peoples of West Africa. In the 1990s Ga comprised roughly half the population of metropolitan Accra, and Ga was the main everyday language of the city. Many Ga work as laborers, traders, and government officials. With a population of around 3 million, the Ga are one of Ghana's largest ethnic groups.

David P. Johnson, Jr.

SEE ALSO

Accra, Ghana; Gold Trade; Languages, African: An Overview; Transatlantic Slave Trade.

Africa

Gabon, coastal country in Central Africa, bordered by EQUATORIAL GUINEA, CAMEROON, and REPUBLIC OF THE CONGO.

Densely forested and rich in natural resources, Gabon has one of Africa's strongest economies. Gabon suffered less from the slave trade than other areas along Africa's Atlantic coast. However, French settlers, commercial enterprises, and colonial administrators irreversibly transformed its economy and society in the nineteenth century. The French created a two-tiered society, with a small elite loyal to French political and commercial interests and a poor, disfranchised majority. The leaders of independent Gabon have preserved and maintained this division. At the head of Gabon's elite is President OMAR BONGO, who has maintained a firm monopoly on power since 1967. Although Bongo's government has made investments in transportation and social services, the country's large oil wealth has benefited primarily Bongo and his clients, and the vast majority of the population remains impoverished.

EARLY HISTORY

For thousands of years, the ancestors of the Babongo people, or "Pygmies," inhabited the tropical rain forest that today covers three-quarters of the area of present-day Gabon. The Babongo hunted chimpanzees, gorillas, and other forest animals and gathered vegetable foods for their livelihood. Most archaeologists believe that Bantu peoples first arrived in the region around 1300 B.C.E. and established small farming communities at the edge of the forest. The Bantu gradually expanded into the surrounding forest. By the seventh century C.E. they acquired iron-making skills and came to dominate the region. Besides hunting and fishing, the Bantu survived by growing YAMS, bananas, and oil palms.

Extended families and clans provided the foundation of the social structure; ethnic identities were fluid and secondary in importance. Male leaders, or "big men," gained prominence through hunting, war, trade, and rituals and distinguished themselves by the number of their dependents: wives, children, in-laws, servants, slaves, and Pygmy hunters. Women bore and raised children, made pottery, cultivated crops, danced, and performed religious rituals. Bantu peoples used iron for tools, weapons, and jewelry; woven raffia circulated as a form of currency. Over time, clans grouped into scattered villages of a few dozen to several hundred people, located along trade routes such as rivers or footpaths. Most villages held common beliefs in ancestral worship, sorcery, and witchcraft, although these beliefs were often clan-specific in their details; many villages

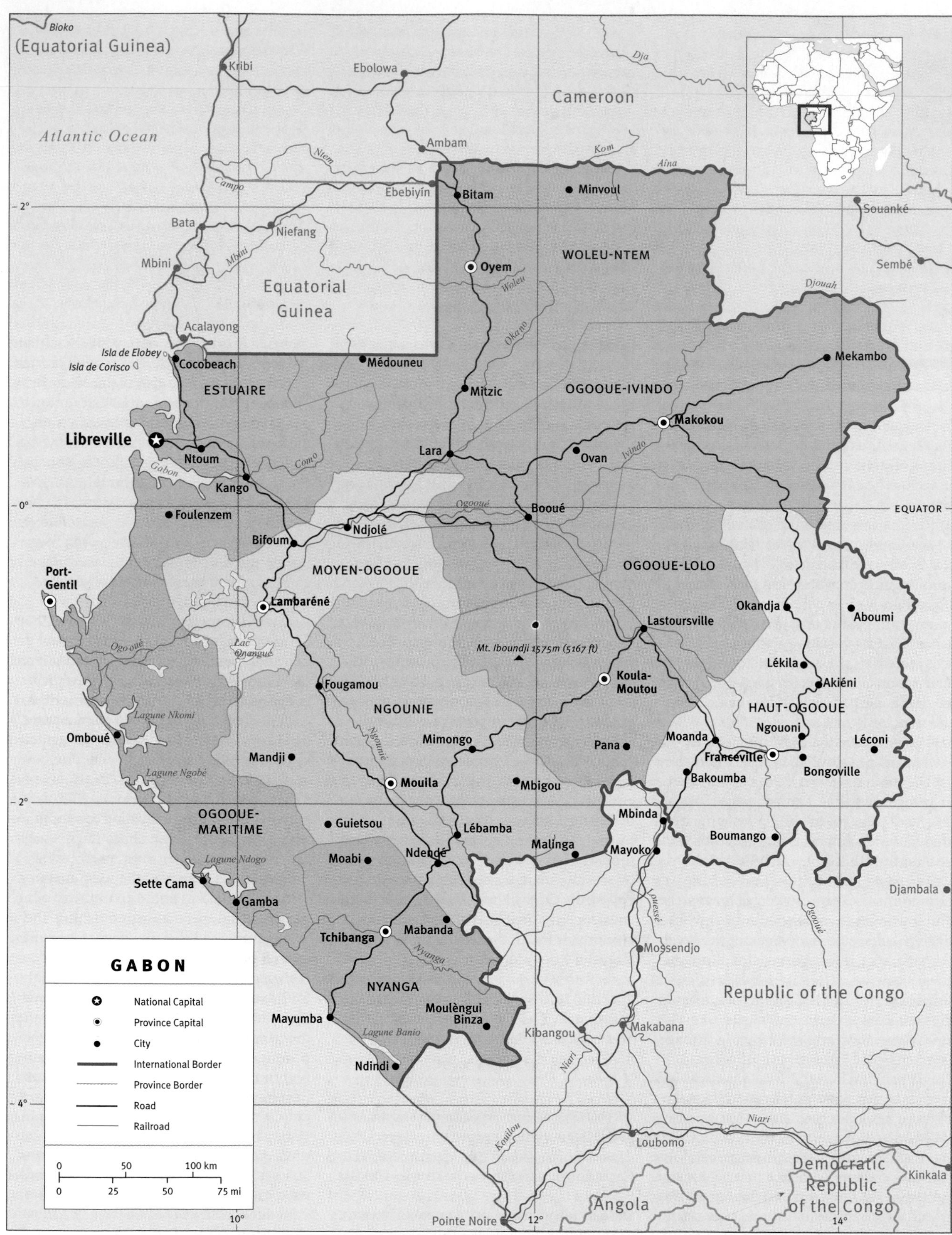

maintained secret societies. The peoples of early Gabon generally lacked state structures, though by the fourteenth century C.E., the kingdom of Loango had extended its rule northward from present-day Congo-Brazzaville along the Gabonese coast.

Imperialism and French Colonialism

Slavery, international trade, and French colonialism brought profound changes to Gabon. In 1472 the Portuguese first visited the Gabon Estuary, which they named the Gabão, or "hooded cloak," because of its shape. From the late sixteenth through the eighteenth century, French, Dutch, and British traders visited the coast and exchanged manufactured goods and salt for slaves and ivory. Local inhabitants rose in opposition to European mercantilism, most spectacularly in 1600 when a group of Ndiwa attacked the Dutch at Corisco Island.

Coastal trade reached its apex in Gabon in the late eighteenth and early nineteenth century with the height of the transatlantic slave trade. The coastal MPONGWE and Orungu apparently acted as slave brokers. Through trade they acquired the wealth to support an aristocratic elite and to maintain a privileged status in Gabon through the colonial period and down to the present day. However, Gabon never attracted large numbers of slave traders because it had a small population, mostly concentrated in the inaccessible interior. At their height between 1815 and 1830, slave shipments from Gabon did not exceed a few thousand slaves per year.

The French established a colonial presence in Gabon beginning in 1839 partly in an effort to halt the slave trade in West Africa and partly to provide naval protection along the coast for French trading companies. French mercantile vessels suffered regular attacks from the Mpongwe, Orungu, and other coastal peoples who had profited from the slave trade and were angry at France's attempts to abolish it. In 1839 the French admiral Edouard Bouët-Willaumez arrived in the Gabon Estuary on his ship, the *Malouine*, and within the next several years had signed treaties with most of the *oga*, or chiefs, of the estuary and coast. In the treaty of 1846, for example, France claimed "all the land that seemed appropriate for the creation of military and agricultural establishments," and also set aside land for Roman Catholic missionary activities.

The arrival of the French coincided with an important shift in the ethnic balance of Gabon. The fact that Bouët-Willaumez signed separate treaties with the various oga demonstrates the absence of a political structure uniting the Myènè-speaking clans of the estuary at that time. Meanwhile, the FANG people, who subsequently became the largest ethnic group in Gabon, had begun their migration into the region from the north. To many Fang, the coming of the French fulfilled an ancient Fang legend in which white warriors arrived from the sea.

During the 1840s French, British, and German firms traded along the estuary, where they competed for the ivory and rubber brought from the interior. The French established cotton and sugar cane plantations but faced a lack of manual labor. In an attempt to solve this problem, Bouët-Willaumez in 1849 settled 52 Loangan slaves, who had been taken from a Dutch slave ship, in a site on the Gabon Estuary. On arrival in this new village of Libreville (Freetown), the French granted the slaves their "freedom" and put them to work as wage laborers on the plantations.

The arrival of the Europeans and their values undermined the clan-based societies of the estuary. In the economic sphere, cash transactions replaced bartering, and status increasingly depended on material wealth. Christian missionaries aggressively promoted new ideologies that undermined established patterns of authority. Meanwhile, Europeans were beginning to penetrate the interior: in the 1840s French naval officers explored the hinterland of the estuary; in the 1850s the explorer Paul du Chaillu led expeditions into the northern and southern interior; and other explorers charted the interior over the following decades.

During the 1880s France's interest in Gabon intensified. By this time the "SCRAMBLE FOR AFRICA" among the European powers was fully underway. France saw the Gabon region as a source of raw materials, as well as an important gateway to the Congo basin. The trading and military posts France had established in Gabon allowed France to claim the area as part of its sphere of influence at the BERLIN CONFERENCE OF 1884-1885. The underfunded colonial administration divided the territory into parcels and sold development concessions to 40 private companies. The companies received trading monopolies granting them exclusive authority over their domains. Employing harsh forced-labor practices, they exploited the rubber and ivory resources aggressively. However, many such companies failed to produce long-term financial returns and went bankrupt.

The concessionary system devastated the Gabonese population. Many people had to abandon subsistence farming. French companies disrupted indigenous trade routes. The companies paid most Africans for their labor in goods or in a currency only used by the concessionary company, and made little effort to develop the infrastructure of the regions under their control. This social and economic dislocation resulted in famines and epidemics that killed many thousands of Gabonese. Some Africans resisted forced-labor policies, but company militias dealt swiftly and harshly with any resistance.

In 1910, after the concessionary system had failed to yield profits or to provide an effective basis for administering its African colonies, the French created the federation of French Equatorial Africa, with a capital in Brazzaville, composed of French Congo (present-day Republic of the Congo), Oubangui-Chari (present-day CENTRAL AFRICAN REPUBLIC), CHAD, and Gabon. The French colonial government created a two-tiered social system in Gabon. A small governing elite – mainly composed of wealthy Mpongwe traders and those of dual European and African descent – enjoyed citizenship status. The vast majority of the population were subject to the *indigénat*, an administrative system that imposed upon them an inferior legal and political status accompanied by onerous tax and labor obligations.

With Gabon's ivory and rubber stocks depleted, French colonial administrators neglected the country's development, although during the 1920s timber became an increasingly important export. The French also introduced COCOA and coffee as cash crops. Indigenous Gabonese were forced either to cultivate cash crops such as these or to work for a wage, harvesting timber, in order to pay required taxes.

Many Gabonese opposed French colonialism. In the early 1900s local rebellions were common. The most serious of these was the Fang rebellion in 1903 led by Emane Tole. Indeed, it was not until World War I that French colonial authority encompassed the interior. However, the nascent Gabonese anticolonialist movement in the estuary region was divided between the Mpongwe elite and Fang newcomers who threatened the Mpongwe's privileged status.

During and after World War II relations between France and its African colonies shifted dramatically. In 1944 Charles de Gaulle organized the Brazzaville Conference as a means to unite the French African possessions against Germany and to initiate greater democracy in the African colonies. The indigénat system was abolished in 1946, when Africans received the right to vote. In 1956 the French National Assembly passed a *loi cadre*, or enabling law, that created representative assemblies within the French colonies and spurred the creation of political parties in Gabon and elsewhere.

The most prominent political figures during this period were the Mpongwe leader Paul Gondjout and the Fang leaders LÉON MBA and Jean-Hilaire Aubame; the latter two had served in the French colonial administration. Mba and Gondjout formed an alliance, supported by the wealthy Mpongwe business community, the coastal Fang elite, and the French timber interests, and managed to outmaneuver Aubame and his northern Fang supporters. Few Gabonese pushed for complete independence; in the 1958 referendum the population voted overwhelmingly for continued association with France. However, by 1960 the federation of French Equatorial Africa had effectively disintegrated, and the French sought to grant independence to Gabon.

INDEPENDENT GABON

On August 17, 1960, Gabon became an independent parliamentary republic with Léon Mba serving as prime minister. Mba continued to rely heavily on French civil servants and technicians for administrative support and on the French military for security. In return, Mba assured the French a base for pursuing their interests, which included a steady supply of uranium from Gabonese mines for their nuclear program. Mba worked to consolidate his personal power by removing other leaders such as Gondjout and Aubame from positions of authority. With his encouragement, the National Assembly imposed strict limitations on freedom of speech and political assembly. In 1964 Mba attempted to create a one-party state by dissolving the National Assembly and calling new elections. In response, a group of young army officers overthrew the government

BELOW: Fishermen on the beach at Cape Lopez near Port-Gentil in Gabon repair their nets. *Magnum Photos/Bruno Barbey*
BOTTOM: A Gabonese father holds his infant daughter. *CORBIS/The Purcell Team*
BELOW RIGHT: This Kota figure is made of wood overlaid with copper and brass. The function of such sculptures was to keep watch over the bones of important ancestors. *CORBIS/Charles & Josette Lenars*

in a coup d'état, arrested Mba, and set up a provisional government led by Aubame. A swift military intervention by French paratroopers from Dakar and Brazzaville restored Mba to power. After 1964, opposition to Mba weakened in the face of a permanent French military presence in Libreville. Under Mba's rule, Gabon began extensive exploitation of its mineral resources. French firms provided much of the investment capital for this development, and along with a small Gabonese elite they have reaped most of the benefit. During the early 1960s Gabon began to export both manganese and uranium. Prospecting for petroleum began.

When Mba died in 1967, his handpicked successor, Albert-Bernard Bongo (now named Omar Bongo), assumed the presidency. Many Gabonese welcomed Bongo, a TÉKÉ from

the southeast. His accession appeared to end Fang-Mpongwe political dominance, and opponents of Mba welcomed Bongo's call for national renewal and his decision to grant amnesty to those who had participated in the 1964 coup. Indeed, Bongo carefully co-opted his political opponents by offering them positions in his government. He also consolidated his personal power: he established a single party in 1968 under his control, the Parti Démocratique Gabonais (PDG), and a single trade union within the party.

The rapid growth in oil exports gave Gabon one of the highest per-capita incomes in sub-Saharan Africa. The petroleum-based economy, highly dependent on French corporations and technical workers, became a cornerstone of Bongo's rule. Gabon's prosperity allowed the development of a patronage system, whereby Bongo provided a clique of loyal and dependent bureaucrats lucrative government positions, some paying over $200,000 per year. Economic prosperity also enabled the construction of the expensive

Transgabonais Railroad from 1974 to 1987. It linked the southeast, with its mineral wealth, to the port at Libreville and served as a potent symbol of national unity. The government also instituted a network of social services such as education and public health.

During the 1980s the Bongo regime faced several significant challenges. In 1981 an opposition group, the Mouvement de Redressement National (MORENA), formed and denounced government corruption, the single-party system, and the economic disparity between rich and poor. The government severely repressed MORENA; its leader, the priest Paul Mba-Abessole, fled to Paris.

Bongo's government faced an even graver challenge when declining oil prices and a weakening United States dollar initiated a prolonged economic crisis in 1986. Gabon had difficulty servicing its heavy debt burden, and in the late 1980s international lenders forced Gabon to implement an austerity program (*see* STRUCTURAL ADJUSTMENT IN AFRICA). This program had its harshest effects on the middle classes and the impoverished masses. Unemployment rose and state bureaucrats had their wages slashed. The patronage system that had propped up Bongo's rule collapsed. When the international press exposed the Bongo regime's corrupt and oligarchic nature, widespread popular discontent erupted in strikes and street protests. Meanwhile, Gabon's elite continued to live opulently: one source estimates that 2 percent of the population controlled 80 percent of the country's gross national product.

After the suspicious death of a leading opposition figure, serious riots in Libreville and Port-Gentil led the government to declare a state of emergency and to call upon French troops to intervene. In 1990 Bongo held a national Conference on Democracy of government and opposition political figures in an attempt to stem the unrest. Although the publicity leading up to the conference explicitly rejected any discussion of a multiparty system, the conference recommended open elections for a reconstituted National Assembly in September 1990. Bongo's PDG won these elections with a two-seat majority. However, he formed a government of national unity, with one-third of ministerial appointments held by opposition members.

Although significant, Bongo's moves toward more democratic rule proved short-lived. As the 1993 presidential elections approached, opposition candidates found themselves subject to police harassment and opposition media outlets were silenced. The election results, in which Bongo won 51 percent of the vote, were widely regarded as fraudulent, and rioting erupted in Libreville. In response, in 1994 the PDG and the opposition parties signed an accord that installed a transitional coalition government, revised the electoral code, and scheduled legislative elections for 1996. Divisions in the opposition enabled the PDG to secure a clear victory in these elections. In the presidential elections of December 1998 Bongo retained his office by winning 66 percent of the vote, but once again charges of widespread voting fraud marred the victory. As Bongo ages and is eventually replaced, the question is whether his authoritarian style will outlast him. Much will surely depend on the influence of Western powers such as France and the United States, who have favored Bongo for creating an apparently stable climate for investment despite the lack of economic and political equality under his regime.

Gabon's abundant natural resources, combined with its small population, have created a strong economy by African standards. Inflation has dropped in recent years due to the government's tight monetary and fiscal policies, while real Gross Domestic Product (GDP) has continued to grow. Yet Gabon remains heavily dependent on oil exports and the vagaries of the international oil market. The International Monetary Fund (IMF) deemed Gabon's recent performance "broadly satisfactory," but implemented a structural adjustment program in 1995 that required Gabon to diversify and privatize its economy and improve its social services, particularly to the urban poor and the rural population. As Gabon's GDP continues to rise, Gabon has recently taken to calling itself the "Kuwait of Africa." This is an apt comparison, since Gabon, like Kuwait and other Middle Eastern oil economies, is unhealthily dependent on oil, and is deeply divided between a small, wealthy elite and a poor majority. Around

A Gabonese musician plays for dancers at Akok.
© Blanc Pattin/Explorer

50 percent of the Gabonese population live in the cities of Libreville and Port-Gentil. Agriculture remains poorly developed. As a result, Gabon relies heavily on food imports; prices of staples such as plantains are three times higher in Libreville than in the neighboring country of Cameroon.

The environmental costs of Gabon's state-driven capitalist development have been considerable. Although Gabon still contains some of Africa's densest forests, with up to 80,000 species of plants, they are threatened by powerful and prosperous timber industries. Indeed, one of Gabon's leading exports has been wood and wood products; Gabon's forests have been logged faster than they can recover. Many researchers believe that deforestation sparked the 1995 Gabonese EBOLA outbreak that spread to Congo-Brazzaville. By stressing the forest ecosystem and increasing human exposure to forest animals, deforestation could lead not only to more Ebola outbreaks but also to other new infectious diseases.

Roanne Edwards

SEE ALSO

Chimpanzee; Colonial Rule; Bantu: Dispersion and Settlement; Explorers in Africa Since 1800; Gorilla; Ivory Trade; Iron in Africa; Transatlantic Slave Trade; Pygmy; Libreville, Gabon; Loango, Early Kingdom of; Christianity: Missionaries in Africa.

Africa

Gabon (Ready Reference)

Official Name: Gabonese Republic
Area: 267,667 sq km (103,347 sq mi)
Location: Bounded on the northwest by EQUATORIAL GUINEA, on the north by CAMEROON, on the east and south by the REPUBLIC OF THE CONGO, and on the west by the Atlantic Ocean
Capital: Libreville (population 365,650 [1993 estimate])
Other Major Cities: Port-Gentil (population 164,000), Franceville (75,000) (1988 estimate)
Population: 1,207,844 (1998 estimate)
Population Density: 5 persons per sq km (about 13 persons per sq mi); over half the population lives in cities, and much of the interior is uninhabited.
Population Below Age 15: 33 percent (male 202,364; female 202,249 [1998 estimate])
Population Growth Rate: 1.48 percent (1998 estimate)
Total Fertility Rate: 3.81 children born per woman (1998 estimate)
Life Expectancy at Birth: Total population: 56.51 years (male 53.55 years; female 59.56 years [1998 estimate])
Infant Mortality Rate: 85.43 deaths per 1000 live births (1998 estimate)
Literacy Rate (age 15 and over who can read and write): Total population 63.2 percent (male 73.7 percent; female 53.3 percent [1995 estimate])
Education: Schooling is compulsory in Gabon for all children between ages 6 and 16, though not all children in that age group actually attend school. In the early 1990s about 210,000 pupils were annually attending primary schools, and about 56,700 students were enrolled in secondary schools. The country has technical institutions and teachers colleges, as well as a university, the Université Omar Bongo (founded in 1970).
Languages: The official language is French, but many Gabonese speak Bantu languages.
Ethnic Groups: The ethnic makeup of the Gabonese is diverse. Of the country's approximately 40 ethnic groups, most belong to the FANG, Pounou, Nzeiby, or TÉKÉ groupings. Europeans, mostly French, form a small but prominent minority. Pygmies are believed to have been the original inhabitants of the country, but only a few thousand remain.
Religions: About 60 percent of the population is Christian, primarily Roman Catholic. Most of the remainder, except for a small Islamic community, follow traditional beliefs.
Climate: Gabon has a hot and humid climate. The temperature varies only slightly throughout the year, hovering around 27° C (80° F). The dry seasons stretch from February to April and October to November. In Libreville the annual rainfall often exceeds 2500 mm (100 in).
Land, Plants, and Animals: Coastal lowlands gird the western shores of Gabon. The interior contains a plateau zone that extends over the entire northern and eastern sections of Gabon and part of the south. The Cristal and Chaillu mountains cut across the interior, sending numerous rivers down to the Atlantic. Dense equatorial rain forest covers three-quarters of the country.
Natural Resources: Gabon is rich in mineral resources. Deposits of uranium, manganese, and petroleum dot the country, all of which are being exploited. Large deposits of iron ore, considered among the richest in the world, have also been discovered. Other Gabonese resources include lead and silver ore. Stands of okoume, mahogany, kevazing and ebony make the forests of Gabon valuable.
Currency: The Communauté Financière Africaine franc
Gross Domestic Product (GDP): $6 billion (1996 estimate)
GDP per Capita: $5000 (1996 estimate)
GDP Real Growth Rate: 3.0 percent (1996 estimate)
Primary Economic Activities: Agriculture, forestry, fishing, and mining
Primary Crops: Cassava, plantains, sugar cane, yams, and taro
Industries: Food and beverage, textile, lumbering and plywood, cement, petroleum extraction and refining, manganese, uranium, and gold mining
Primary Exports: Crude oil, timber, manganese, and uranium
Primary Imports: Foodstuffs, chemical products, petroleum products, construction materials, and machinery
Primary Trade Partners: France, African countries, United States, Japan, and the Netherlands
Government: Under a constitution adopted in 1991, the voting population elects the president directly for a term of five years, as well as a 120-member National Assembly. The current president is El Hadj Omar Bongo; Bongo has appointed Paulin Obame Macías Nguema as prime minister.

Eric Bennett

SEE ALSO

Bongo, Omar; Libreville, Gabon.

Africa

Gaborone, Botswana, formerly Gaberones, the capital and largest city of BOTSWANA.

Located in southeastern Botswana near the Notwani River, Gaborone was founded in 1890 by CECIL RHODES's British South Africa Company (BSAC). Originally the site was a fortified white settlement that protected railway and telegraph lines built by the BSAC linking the Cape Colony, later a part of SOUTH AFRICA, with the mines of present-day ZIMBABWE. At that time the administrative headquarters of the Bechaunaland Protectorate (present-day Botswana) was located at Mafeking (now Mafikeng), a small town actually located within the borders of the Cape Colony. As Bechaunaland neared independence in the 1960s, its leaders determined to establish a capital within the country's borders. They chose Gaborone as the site because of its proximity to both the country's main rail line and a water source, the Notwani River. Construction at the site, including a dam on the Notwani, began in 1963. In March 1965 the new city was declared the capital of Bechaunaland; one year later it became the capital of independent Botswana. In 1969 the city's name was changed from Gaberones to Gaborone.

Since it was built in the twentieth century to serve a specific purpose, Gaborone is a well-designed, modern capital. Its primary activity remains government administration. There is also a small manufacturing sector within Gaborone, and at the heart of the city is a pedestrian shopping district with hotels and a casino. Noteworthy institutions located in the capital include the Botswana National Museum and Art Gallery, the University of Botswana, and the Botswana Agricultural College. During the 1990s the city emerged as a stronghold of the Botswana National Front (BNF). The BNF opposed the Botswana Democratic Party, which has controlled Botswana's national government since its independence.

Andrew Hermann

North America

Gabriel Prosser Conspiracy,

one of the first attempted American slave rebellions.

The Gabriel Prosser Conspiracy of 1800 was one of the earliest and most extensively planned slave insurrections in American history. The plan, which was drawn up by a slave named Gabriel Prosser, called for slaves to seize weapons, kill their white masters, and free thousands of fellow slaves throughout Virginia. If a tumultuous thunderstorm and an act of betrayal had not undermined the plot, many historians believe the rebellion would have been successful.

The word "conspiracy," which has come to have almost exclusively negative connotations, was the description used by whites at that time. The word conveyed the unwillingness of most slaveholding whites to recognize the widespread discontent in the slave community. The word also suggests the fear of slave uprisings that gripped antebellum white Southerners. Virginia was no exception. Stories of the bloody HAITIAN REVOLUTION and the fiery congressional debates over slavery made their way throughout slave communities. In Virginia, as in many other slave states, the seeds of rebellion were in place, but no charismatic leader had emerged. That leadership finally came from the slave named Gabriel Prosser, an intelligent and well-respected young blacksmith on the Prosser plantation just outside Richmond.

Gabriel Prosser (who took the last name of his owner, Thomas Prosser) taught himself to read and write by studying the Bible. His tremendous physical strength made him one of the best blacksmiths in the Richmond area. Recognizing this, Thomas Prosser permitted him to work for whites around town in exchange for a disproportionate share of his income. This angered and humiliated Prosser, but he agreed to the arrangement in exchange for the limited freedom to travel it would bring.

Prosser's strong opposition to slavery and his sense of impending political crisis facing the nation persuaded him that the time for insurrection had come. He selected the night of August 30 for the revolt and, with the aid of his wife and brother, was able to spread word of the plot to slaves throughout the Richmond area. Prosser estimated that between 500 and 600 slaves stood poised that night to become the first in America to break the shackles of slavery.

But a severe thunderstorm hit Virginia that night, making both mobility and armed resistance all but impossible. Prosser attempted to postpone the insurrection until the next night, but two slaves had already betrayed the cause. By morning, hundreds of slaves were arrested. Prosser managed to escape by boarding a schooner headed for Norfolk, Virginia. Several days later, another slave, attempting to collect a $300 reward, betrayed Prosser by notifying the police of his whereabouts. He was arrested in Norfolk and sent to Richmond for trial.

Prosser and 26 other slaves were convicted of insurrection and executed. Many others faced long prison sentences. A crackdown immediately followed the foiled insurrection. Shaken by the rebellion, Virginia officials formed a state militia to monitor slave gatherings and prevent future uprisings. Throughout the South, laws restricting African American literacy were strengthened, and the freedom of slave artisans to contract out their labor was curtailed. Although Prosser's conspiracy failed, it inspired similar failed plots in North Carolina in 1802 and in South Carolina in 1822.

Alonford James Robinson, Jr.

SEE ALSO

Slavery in the United States; Richmond, Virginia.

Gadhafi, Moammar. Please see QADDAFI, MUAMMAR AL-

North America

Gaines, Ernest J.

(b. January 15, 1933, Oscar, La.), African American novelist and short story writer best known for his 1971 novel *The Autobiography of Miss Jane Pittman.*

Although Ernest Gaines has spent much of his adult life in the San Francisco Bay Area, all of his work returns to the setting of his southern Louisiana childhood, with its complicated intersections of African American, Creole, Cajun, and white culture. Gaines was born on the River Lake Plantation in Point Coupée Parish County, Louisiana, and raised largely by a disabled great-aunt who later provided the model for his powerful fictional character Miss Jane Pittman. The parish had no black high school, and when Gaines was 15 his mother and stepfather sent for him to join them in Vallejo, California, where he could continue his education. After graduating from high school, he attended a junior college and served in the military before receiving a bachelor's degree in English from San Francisco State College in 1957.

In college Gaines began to read voraciously and write his own stories. He was never exposed to black writers. His literary models were such white American writers as Ernest Hemingway and William Faulkner and European writers such as Russian novelist Leo Tolstoy. He decided early, however, to focus his own writing on what he knew – which meant portraying African American culture and language. Gaines published his first short stories in a college literary magazine, where they were noticed by the white literary agent Dorothea Oppenheimer. Oppenheimer helped Gaines obtain a fellowship to Stanford University to study creative writing and a contract with Dial Press that led to his first novel, *Catherine Carmier* (1964).

Catherine Carmier and Gaines's second novel, *Of Love and Dust* (1967), both use interracial relationships as a means of exploring the complexities of racial intolerance and injustice in Louisiana. He explored similar themes in the short story collection *Bloodline* (1968). Each of these books bolstered his literary reputation, but it was *The Autobiography of Miss Jane Pittman* (1971) that brought Gaines widespread recognition. In this novel the eponymous 108-year-old heroine tells her life story in her own words – a life story that follows Miss Jane and her community through slavery, RECONSTRUCTION, JIM CROW, and the CIVIL RIGHTS MOVEMENT. The compelling narrative that resulted – still considered Gaines's masterpiece – became a best-selling book and a successful made-for-television movie.

Gaines followed that novel with *In My Father's House* (1978), *A Gathering of Old Men* (1983), and *A Lesson Before Dying* (1993). Throughout his career one of Gaines's hallmarks has been his ability to capture authentic African American voices. Most of his novels and short stories are first-person narratives, and his skill in portraying black speech is felt in every line. Gaines is also applauded for his gift of evoking the Louisiana community he describes – a process he calls "knowing the place, knowing the people." By doing both successfully, he is able to write about them so convincingly that his readers feel as if they know the place and people too.

This talent proved especially important in *The Autobiography of Miss Jane Pittman*, which reached an audience of unprecedented breadth. Said one critic, "More than any other single book, this novel helped white Americans understand the personal emotions and the historical events that had produced the civil rights revolution." Gaines lives in California, but since 1983 has spent part of each year as a professor of English at the University of Southwestern Louisiana in Lafayette.

Lisa Clayton Robinson

SEE ALSO

Slavery in the United States.

Latin America and the Caribbean

Gairy, Eric

(b. 1922; d. 1997), former prime minister of Grenada. Gairy entered public life as a union leader in Grenada. In 1951 he founded the country's first political party, the pro-union, pro-independence Grenada United Labour Party (GULP). Gairy went on to become the country's first black elected leader. He led the assembly from 1951 to 1957, 1961 to 1962, and again from 1967 until 1974 when he became the country's first prime minister. Gairy was removed from power in a military coup in 1979 (*see* GRENADA).

Africa

Galago, common name for any of several small African primates of the loris family, sometimes called bush babies.

Galagos are nocturnal and arboreal in habit, eating fruit, insects, and tree gums. They build nests in trees. The largest species, found on the east coast of Africa, measures 27 to 46 cm (11 to 18 in), exclusive of the tail. The smallest species, Demidoff's galago, measures only 10 to 16 cm (4 to 6 in). Their tails are longer than their bodies; their hind legs are longer and stronger than their forelegs, with elongated ankle bones. Their strong digits, well adapted for grasping branches, are all nail-bearing except the second on the hind foot, which is clawed. Galagos are covered with a soft, fawn-gray or brown, woolly fur. They are distinguished from other primates by their dentition (dental features). They fold their large, hairless, thin ears lengthwise close to the head when at rest and while leaping through trees. The head is small and round like that of a cat. The immense eyes are a rich brown color, translucent, and marked with minute lines, with large, oval pupils contracting in daylight to vertical slits. Galagos usually have one to three young per litter. **Scientific classification:** Galagos belong to the family Lorisidae. The largest species is classified as *Otolemur crassicaudatus*. Demidoff's galago is classified as *Galagoides demidoff*.

Latin America and the Caribbean

Gama, José Basílio da

(b. July 22, 1740, São José do Rio das Mortes (later São José del Rei, now Tiradentes), Minas Gerais, Brazil; d. July 31, 1795, Lisbon, Portugal), mulatto poet and significant contributor to Brazil's school of Arcadian literature.

Born of noble ancestors, José Basílio da Gama was orphaned at an early age. With the help of a benefactor, he was sent to the Jesuit College in Rio de Janeiro. The Jesuits were considered too independent by the Church in Rome and were being expelled from Brazil and Portugal (*see* Catholic Church in Latin America and the Caribbean). Their expulsion in 1759 interrupted Gama's studies at the Jesuit College, but he continued at the São José Episcopal Seminary.

Gama next moved to Italy and Portugal, where he lived and studied from 1760 to 1767. In Rome, he was accepted in the Arcadia Romana, home of the Arcadian movement in neoclassical literature, whose writers were particularly interested in exploring pastoral settings. The Arcadia Romana, which had been founded in Rome in 1690, gave Gama protection from persecution, allowing him to write under the pseudonym Termindo Sipílio.

In 1767 he ventured back to Rio de Janeiro and in June 1768 he returned to Lisbon. Immediately upon his arrival he came under suspicion of being in favor of the Jesuit presence in Portugal. He was condemned to exile in Angola and imprisoned. While waiting to be deported, he composed a moving poem celebrating the marriage of Maria Amália, the daughter of the Marquês de Pombal. Touched by Gama's poetry, the Marquês pardoned him, bestowed him with titles of nobility, and made the poet an official secretary of the kingdom.

In order to thank Pombal and continue in his favor, Basílio da Gama wrote the poem *O Uraguai*. The original version, however, was openly pro-Jesuit, while the official version published in 1769 by Pombal's printer is harshly critical of Jesuit missions. Nevertheless, *O Uraguai* is considered Gama's most notable work. An epic poem in free blank verse, it relates the tale of the War of the Seven Reductions (1752-1756), which was waged jointly by the Spanish and Portuguese colonizers against the Jesuits and their Tupi-Guaraní Indian missions in Uruguay. The poem's idealistic Arcadian portrayal of the Indians and sympathy with their plight paved the way for future generations of Indianist writers.

Upon the death of Pombal, Gama left for Brazil. There, via Portugal, the Arcadian literary movement had caught on, and in 1780 Gama joined Escola Mineira, a group of Arcadian writers in Minas Gerais state.

Toward the end of his life he returned to Lisbon and was admitted in the Academy of Sciences. Gama's last major work, another epic poem, *Quitúbia* (1791), is a tale named for an Angolan hero and based on his life. Full of African rhythms, Bantu vocabulary, and references to African geography and culture, *Quitúbia* marks an important step in the representation of blacks in Brazilian colonial literature. Gama's work may thus be seen as an early articulation of an inherently Brazilian literary voice.

Nicola Cooney

See Also

Bantu: Dispersion and Settlement; Rio de Janeiro, Brazil.

Latin America and the Caribbean

Gama, Luís Gonzaga Pinto da

(b. June 21, 1830, Salvador, Bahia, Brazil; d. August 24, 1882, São Paulo, Brazil), a founding member of the abolitionist movement in Brazil; a mulatto journalist, poet, and legal activist who worked to free Africans who had been enslaved after the ban on the international slave trade.

The son of a wealthy Portuguese nobleman and an ex-slave from Ghana, Luís Gonzaga Pinto da Gama was born free. His mother, Luisa Mahin, sold fruits and vegetables in the streets of Salvador, Bahia, and played a leading role in the Malê revolts during the early nineteenth century. For her involvement in these slave rebellions, she was sent to Rio de Janeiro, from where she was reportedly deported to West Africa. A few years later, when Gama was about ten years old, his father sold him into slavery to pay off gambling debts. Because Gama had been born to a free mother and his father was not recognized in any legal documents, this sale of him was illegal.

After being shipped among several cities, Gama wound up in São Paulo, where he worked as a servant for eight years. Beginning in 1847 he developed a close friendship with a law student named Antonio Rodrigues do Prado, who resided in the home where he worked. Prado taught Gama to read and write, and cultivated his interest in law. The following year, after acquiring documents that proved he was born free, Gama ran away and enlisted in the army. During his free time he worked as a clerk for a private law practice headed by Angolan-born Francisco Maria de Sousa Furtado de Mendonça, who instructed him in the law.

After six years of military service Gama was discharged in 1854 for insubordination. For the next two years he worked as a copyist in several São Paulo police stations. He spent his free time writing poems, which were published in newspapers. In 1859, only 12 years after becoming literate, he published his first and only book, *Primeiras Trovas Burlescas* (First Comic Ballads), a collection of social satire poems. Some of the most popular poems criticized mulatto society for aspiring to European ideals and ignoring their black brethren in bondage. One reads:

If all the upstart nobles in these regions,
Whose ancestors to Guinea owed allegiance,
From pride of birth or other vice besetting
Their Negro race are hastily forgetting:
If each mulatto with his bleached complexion,
To some compelling madness in subjection,
Or in the hope of future status prizes,
His black-as-pitch great-grandpapa despises:
By novelties like these be not dismayed, sir,
Such rarities – Brazil's new stock-in-trade, sir.

His most widely read poem, "Quem Sou Eu?" (Who Am I?), extends to all Brazilians the derogatory term *bode* (goat), usually used to describe blacks, in order to underscore a shared humanity in the midst of their differences. Gama adds:

In supreme eternity,
Home of the Divinity,
Billy goats are canonized,
And by us are idolized.
In the choir of cherubs singing
Many kids are also bleating.

In the 1850s Gama dedicated himself to the abolition of slavery. He began by legally petitioning for the freedom of Africans who were enslaved in violation of the November 7, 1831, law that ended the international slave trade. This law had declared that all Africans who entered the country from that day forth were free; still, many were illegally enslaved afterward. He also began to make antislavery speeches and attempted to raise funds to free slaves on an individual basis. But Gama's efforts were largely ignored, as most of his contemporaries still relied heavily on slave labor.

In order to rally support for abolition, in the 1860s Gama joined the liberal political movement and helped found the Brazilian Republican Party, which favored replacing the Portuguese monarchy with a democratic form of government. Launching an attack on two fronts, he said, "I loathe bondage and all masters, particularly kings." Thus, Gama's fight against slavery encompassed the dissolution of the monarchy. Other abolitionists, such as JOAQUIM NABUCO, a white, aristocratic politician from Pernambuco, sought to preserve the monarchy while pursuing abolition. Also in contrast to Gama, Nabuco and many other white abolitionists believed that blacks should not participate directly in the abolition movement. This split within the movement became apparent in the early 1870s, after the enactment of the Lei do Ventre Livre (the 1871 Law of the FREE WOMB), which freed all children born to enslaved mothers. Gama left the Brazilian Republican Party in 1873 after its members drafted and approved a gradual emancipation plan rather than (as he had demanded) an immediate one.

While campaigning in the political arena, Gama also produced social and political satire in the form of poems and short articles. In 1864 he founded the antislavery journal *Diabo Coxo* (Lame Devil). Four years later, he obtained a position at one of Brazil's most important newspapers, *O Ipiranga*, and went on to publish numerous antislavery articles under the pseudonym Afro. In 1869 Gama joined the editorial staff of the newspaper *Radical Paulistano*, where he met other young abolitionists, such as RUI BARBOSA, Antonio de Castro Alves, and JOAQUIM NABUCO.

Gama's efforts to free slaves through litigation were as important and persistent as his abolitionist activities in politics and the press. Despite the fact that he had no formal education in law and no law degree, in courts of law he successfully won the freedom of hundreds of slaves and became known for his eloquence, sarcastic wit, and aggressive character. On one occasion, he declared to a jury that "Every slave who kills his master, whatever the circumstances, does so in self-defense."

In the late 1880s the abolition movement intensified, and some planters – especially those in the northeast, where the SUGAR industry was in decline – began to emancipate their slaves. This fact, combined with a late-blooming but increasingly vocal abolition movement and the prohibition of corporal punishment, led many slaves to simply abandon their former owners. During the 1880s Gama worked relentlessly: in 1881 he founded the Caixa Emancipadora Luís Gama (Luís Gama Emancipation Fund) to purchase the freedom of slaves, and in 1882 he established the Centro Abolicionista de São Paulo (Abolitionist Center of São Paulo). But Gama would not live to see the realization of the cause to which he had devoted his life. He died of complications from diabetes in 1882, at age 52. Nearly six years later, on May 13, 1888, Princess Isabel signed the Lei Áurea (Golden Law), which emancipated all of Brazil's slaves.

Aaron Myers

SEE ALSO
Transatlantic Slave Trade; Rio de Janeiro, Brazil; Abolition and Emancipation in Latin America and the Caribbean; Slave Rebellions in Latin America and the Caribbean.

Africa

Gama, Vasco da (b. 1469, Sines, Alemtejo; d. 1524, Cochin, India), Portuguese explorer who established the colony of Mozambique.

Vasco da Gama was en route to India when he became the second European to sail around the Cape of Good Hope in 1497. During the two-year voyage commissioned by King Manuel of PORTUGAL, da Gama stopped at various points along the East Africa coast, including present-day Mozambique, Mombasa, Malindi, and ZANZIBAR. It was during his stop in Malindi that da Gama met ibn Majid, the pilot who taught him the route and navigation skills necessary to complete his journey to Calicut. After an unsuccessful attempt to establish a trading post in India, da Gama returned to Portugal in 1499 with many stories of East Africa.

In 1502 da Gama was again commissioned by the king to round the Cape of Good Hope, this time to establish economic and political sovereignty over areas of East Africa. Da Gama founded the Portuguese colonies of Mozambique and Sofala (now part of Mozambique) and imposed Portuguese rule on the coastal islands of Zanzibar and Kilwa. The Portuguese maintained control of the coastal islands until 1729, when a group of Omani Arabs took over the islands. After founding the colonies, da Gama traveled to India to avenge the death of fellow explorer Pedro Cabral, and continued his commercial activities. Da Gama was appointed the Portuguese viceroy to India in 1524, but died three months after arriving in India to assume the position.

Elizabeth Heath

SEE ALSO
Mozambique; Mombasa, Kenya.

Africa

Gambia River, one of the longest navigable rivers in West Africa, flowing 1170 km (700 mi) from the highlands of FOUTA DJALLON in GUINEA, north into SENEGAL, and westward through the Gambia to the Atlantic Ocean.

The Gambia River is navigable for approximately 667 km (approximately 400 mi), through most of the country called the Gambia, which takes its name from the river. Strong tides and little change in elevation allow saltwater encroachment for more than 170 km (100 mi) upstream. Along this saline stretch the riverbanks are covered by mangrove swamps, which shelter a variety of fish and shellfish and attract a rich diversity of birds. Some mangrove swamps have been cleared and converted into rice paddies, which must be protected from saltwater encroachment by an elaborate system of dikes. Beyond the mangroves, rainy-season floodplains support an important area for swamp rice cultivation. The Gambia River valley was one of three areas (along with the NIGER and Casamance river valleys) where African varieties of rice (*oryza glaberrima*) were first domesticated more than 2000 years ago.

Historically, the Gambia River was an important conduit for MANDE expansion west toward the Atlantic Ocean. After the arrival of Europeans along the Atlantic coast, the river became a major trade route for the export of gold, as well as slaves from the western Sudan, Senegambia, and Casamance areas. With the partition of Senegambia into French and British spheres in 1889, the Gambia River was isolated from most of its natural trading hinterland and declined in importance as a West African commercial artery. In 1978 Senegal and Gambia created the Gambia River Development Organization, which had the primary objective of restoring the Gambia River's position as one of the two most important rivers of West Africa.

Robert Baum

SEE ALSO
Gambia, The; Gold Trade.

Africa

Gambia, The, a small country on the far west coast of Africa.

Only a small strip of Atlantic coastline keeps the Republic of the Gambia from being completely surrounded by its larger neighbor, SENEGAL. Never more than 50 km (30 mi) wide, the Gambia stretches for more than 500 km (300 mi), along both banks of the GAMBIA RIVER and into the center of Senegal. The Gambia owes its creation to British economic interests, first in the TRANSATLANTIC SLAVE TRADE, then in the coastal trade in agricultural and manufactured commodities. But the British zone of control ended where their boats encountered the Gambia River waterfalls, never reaching into the river basin's natural hinterland. This severely constrained the Gambia's economic growth and ultimately shaped its national character. Most ethnic groups of the Gambia are found in larger numbers within Senegal, and the small nation still struggles to forge a national identity, apart from a shared experience of British COLONIAL RULE. The Gambia's peculiar geography illustrates the irrationality of Africa's colonial boundaries, and the difficulty of using them as the basis for the creation of nation-states in the postcolonial era.

Precolonial History

Despite the Gambia's small size, it is a country of extraordinary diversity. Located at the frontier between the open savanna to the north and the Guinean forest and wooded savanna to the south, it also represents a cultural frontier between Sudanic cultures and those at the northern limits of the Guinean forest. The Sudanic cultures of the MANDINKA, WOLOF, and Fula were characterized by hereditary caste groupings that determined a member's occupation and potential marriage partners. The Mandinka and Wolof had strong traditions of kingship and centralized authority, and with the exception of the precolonial Wolof, they were markedly patriarchal. The Sudanic peoples' economies were based primarily on MILLET and sorghum production, artisanry, and long-distance trade. In contrast, the forest-dwelling JOLA, Bainounk, and Manjaco peoples had neither occupational castes nor kingly traditions, and were generally more open to women's participation in public life. These forest-dwelling communities practiced wet rice agriculture and limited their commerce to local markets. The Gambia was one of the areas where an African species of rice (*oryza glaberrima*) was first domesticated more than 2000 years ago (*see* AGRICULTURE, AFRICAN, IN THE AMERICAS: AN INTERPRETATION).

Little is known about the first inhabitants of the Gambia, but they probably included ancestors of populations that are today known as the Bainounk, Niominka, and Bassari. During the first millennium they built numerous clusters of stone circles that most likely had ritual significance in early Senegambian religion. Beginning in the thirteenth century, Mandinka warriors from the empire of Mali, led by Tiramaghan Keita, conquered much of the Gambia River valley. Many of its indigenous inhabitants embraced a Mandinka ethnic identity, swelling a fairly small group of Mandinka immigrants from MALI into the region's dominant population. Wolof, Serer, and Fula immigrants also entered the area during this period. As the empire of Mali weakened, new Mandinka states emerged along the Gambia River, including Barra, Kombo, Baddibu, and Niumi. The Mandinka empire of Gabou controlled most of the upper river. Although Islam had already been introduced to the area, most people adhered to indigenous forms of religion.

Portuguese travelers first entered the region in 1455. In the sixteenth century the Portuguese established trading factories along Bintang Creek, a tributary of the Gambia River, where they purchased beeswax, gold, ivory, and slaves from Mandinka and Bainounk merchants. The duke of Courland established a small trading post in 1661 on an island near the mouth of the river. Two years later the British expelled the Courlanders and established their own fort on the site, which they renamed James Island. In 1681 the French established a trade settlement at Albreda. While the French and British traders pushed the Portuguese out of the region, they tried to expand the area's involvement in the transatlantic slave trade. At its late eighteenth-century peak, approximately 8000 slaves were sold to European merchants in the Gambia each year; in addition, large numbers of people died in warfare or slave raids, or while being transported to slave-trading posts along the Gambia River.

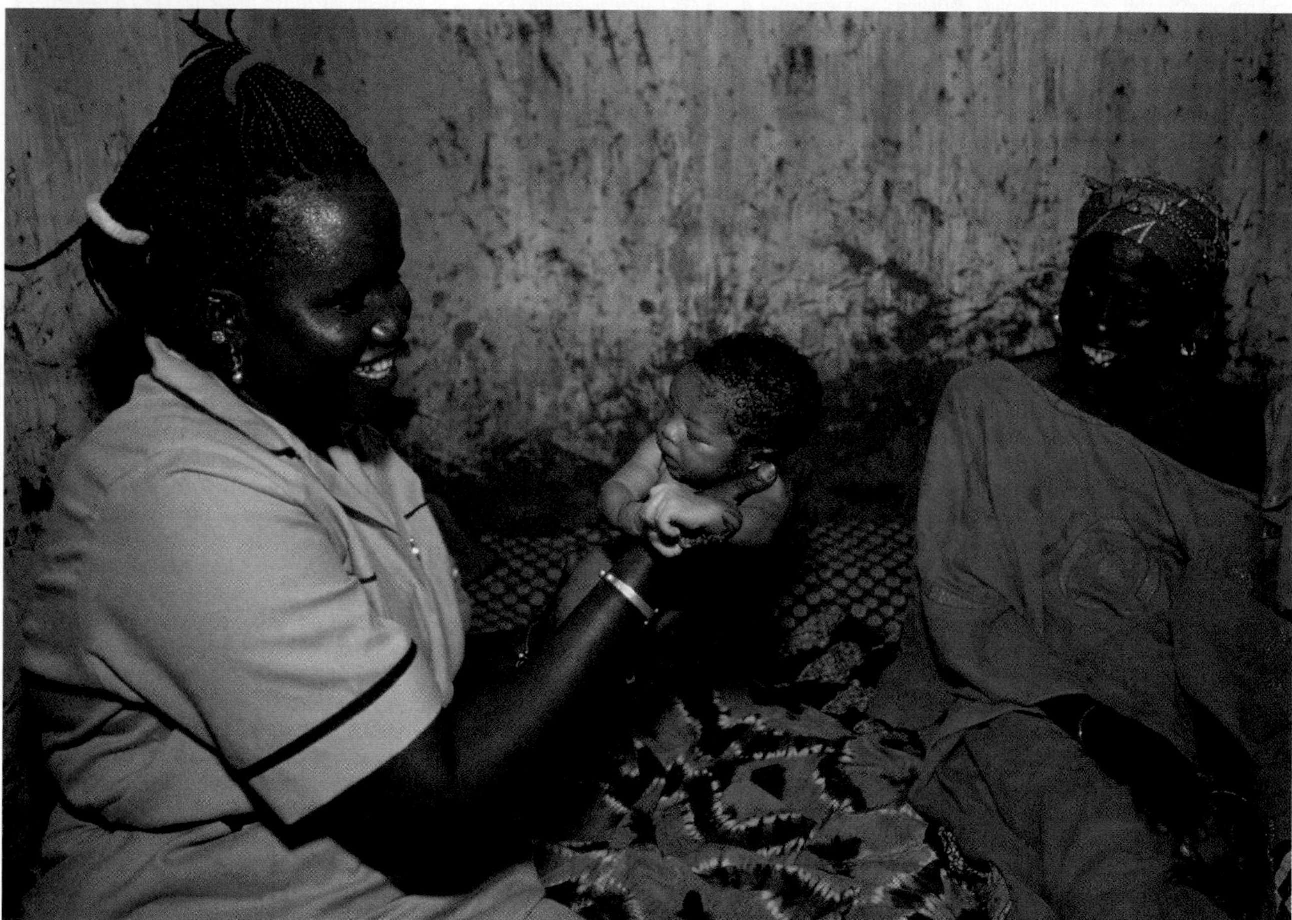

A district nurse holds a newborn baby in the Gambia. *CORBIS/Liba Taylor*

After the British abolition of the transatlantic slave trade in 1807, and with the end of the Napoleonic Wars, British interests shifted toward the suppression of the trade by other Europeans and Americans. To achieve that end, in 1816 the British established a

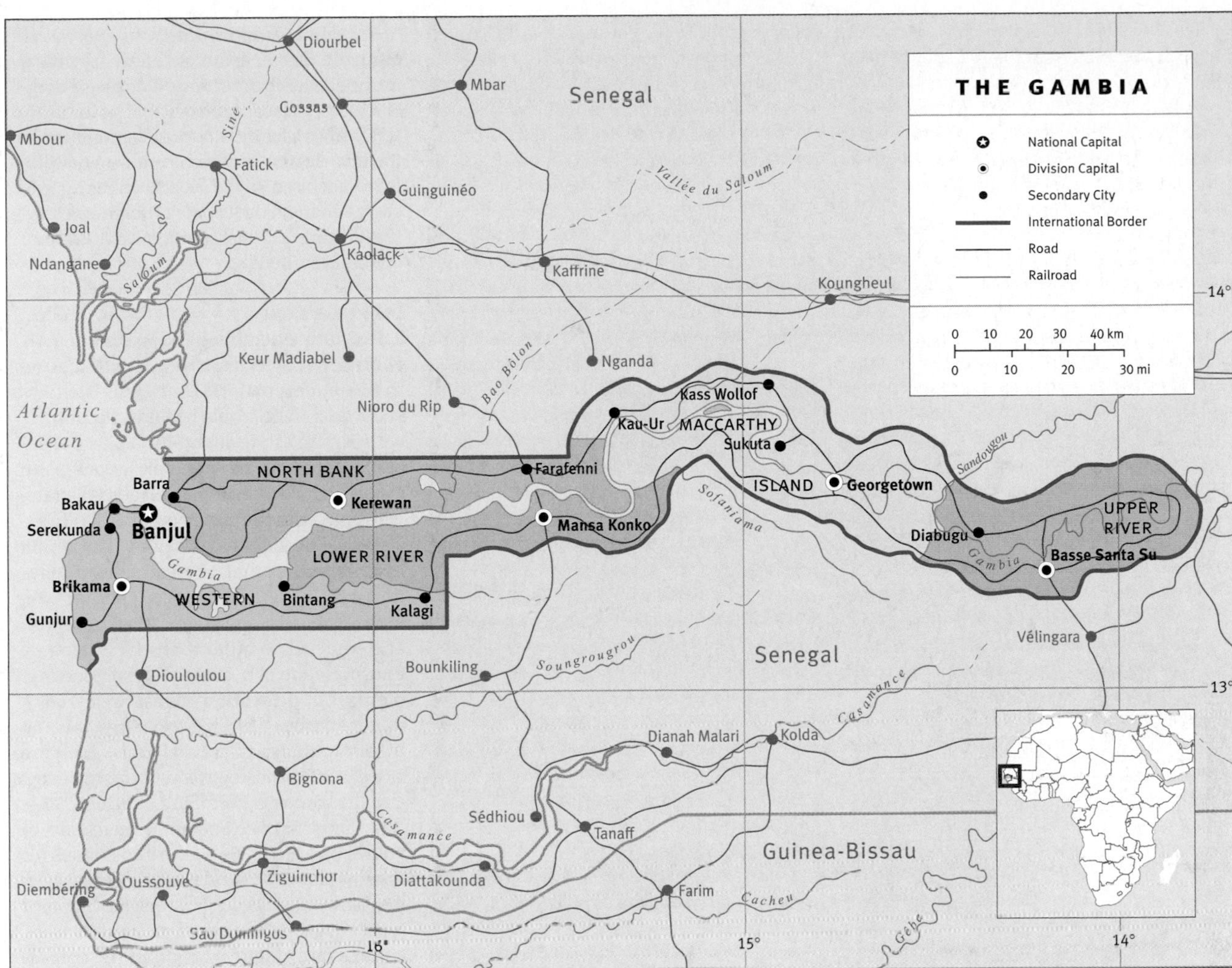

new naval base and settlement at the mouth of the Gambia River, on Banjul Island, and named the settlement Bathurst. Its small garrison was charged with curtailing the Gambian slave trade and encouraging British commerce along the Gambia River and in coastal Senegambia. The British, however, did little to secure the natural trading hinterland of the Gambia, while the French gradually extended control over most of the Senegambia region and its major cash crop, peanuts.

A reason for British reluctance to venture farther inland was the fear that any expansion of the colony would entangle them in the considerable political turmoil in the region, caused by the breakdown of the Mandinka-dominated state system in the early nineteenth century. Throughout the latter half of the century, the Soninke-Marabout Wars, fought between followers of Islamic political leaders known as Marabouts and followers of an older Mandinka form of leadership, who were called Soninke, had become increasingly violent. Eventually the British were drawn into these conflicts, but not before the French had occupied much of the surrounding territory and the power of the Soninke essentially had been destroyed. By the late nineteenth century the Gambia had become predominantly Muslim.

For much of the nineteenth century, the Gambia was not even considered a separate colony; from 1821 until 1888, it was administered as a district of Sierra Leone. For many years it seemed that it would be only a matter of time before the British ceded its few settlements to the French, who had periodically offered to take them in exchange for their own Gabon or Côte d'Ivoire. But the British consistently refused these offers, and after the Berlin Conference of 1884-1885 they were left with a colony in the Gambia that extended little more than 25 km (15 mi) in either direction from the riverbanks. In 1889 the French and British agreed on what are now the approximate boundaries of the Gambia, leaving the French colony of Senegal with control over many communities that had previously traded through the Gambia.

British Colonialism

In 1894 the British proclaimed a protectorate over the interior areas of the Gambia, distinguishing it from the colony, which consisted of the town of Bathurst and the Kombo area on the adjacent mainland. In the protectorate the British established a system of indirect rule, relying on government-appointed chiefs to exercise local authority. In the colony a limited form of direct rule was established. Because the Gambia was small in size, the British invested little in developing its economy. Most Gambians remained in rural areas, cultivating peanuts, millet, sorghum, and rice, though some went to work in the peanut-shelling and peanut-oil factories in Bathurst (now Banjul), or on the docks. Although employment opportunities were limited, the colony attracted migrants fleeing forced labor policies and conscription in French-ruled Senegal.

After World War I newspaper editor Edward Small and other early nationalists founded the Gambia's first labor unions and a Gambian branch of the National Congress of British West Africa, both of which pressed for Gambian economic and political empowerment. During World War II, Senegal was initially allied with the Vichy French, putting British control of the Gambia in jeopardy. But in 1943 French West African authorities shifted their allegiance back to the Allies, and the threat to the Gambia was removed.

After the war limited political participation in government was extended to the protectorate. The first political parties, the Democratic Party and the United Party, were formed in 1951, followed the next year by

the Muslim Congress Party. In 1959 David Jawara, a former colonial veterinary officer, founded the Protectorate People's Party. His party gained a plurality of votes in the 1960 election for the House of Representatives, the first election in which rural voters were fully franchised. In the 1962 elections Jawara's party, renamed the People's Progressive Party (PPP), won decisively, and Jawara became the chief minister.

Independence

The Gambia achieved independence on February 18, 1965, and Jawara was chosen to be the new nation's prime minister. Five years later the Gambia became a republic, with Jawara as president. It quickly became apparent that the new republic lacked many things, including experienced administrators who could run the government. Apart from a two-year college for teachers, the Gambia had no schools that offered higher education, and its only secondary schools were in the Bathurst-Kombo area. River transport and some all-weather roads facilitated the transportation of peanuts to the processing plants, but little other industry existed. A major source of foreign exchange was the trans-Gambia ferry at Farafenni, which provided a critical link between northern Senegal and the southern Casamance region. Long waits at the ferry helped many merchants on both shores attract Senegalese customers for the low-duty consumer goods available in the Gambia. Smuggling between the Gambia and Senegal (where tariffs on imports were considerably higher) began in the colonial era and remains a widespread practice.

In the late 1960s the Gambia began to promote its scenic beaches as winter vacation spots for European tourists. British and Scandinavian investors built elaborate hotel complexes in the coastal communities of Bakau and Fajara. By 1975 more than 25,000 tourists, mostly from Sweden and Denmark, visited the Gambia each year. Local artisans increased production of batiks, tie-dyes, and other crafts to meet the demand for souvenirs, and Gambian farmers found new markets for their fruits and vegetables in resort restaurants. But most of the tourist industry profits were repatriated to hotel and tour company operators back in Europe. Tourism also created social problems, as the overwhelmingly Muslim Gambians found their streets and beaches invaded by crowds of relatively affluent, scantily clad vacationers. Some young people, more men than women, went into prostitution, while others sought intimate relationships that would let them pursue greater opportunities in Europe. The incidence of rapes of tourists and premarital pregnancies among Gambian women also increased.

Aside from the development of a tourist industry, the Jawara government failed to

Women carry firewood on their heads as they walk along a street in Banjul, the capital and largest city of the Republic of the Gambia. *CORBIS/Nik Wheeler*

Gambian village women wear traditional dress. *CORBIS/Liba Taylor*

diversify the economy. Close to 85 percent of the population made a living primarily from agriculture, yet peanuts remained the only significant cash crop, and the country continued to be highly dependent on imports of rice and other staple grains. The Sahel drought of the 1970s and subsequent erratic rainfall further undermined rural productivity and economic security.

In 1981 Kukoi Samba Sanyang, a leader in the leftist Movement for Justice in Africa, attempted a coup d'état while President Jawara was away in England. With the aid of Senegalese troops, the coup was suppressed, but not before more than 1000 people had been killed. Part of the cost of this assistance was the creation of a confederation between the two countries, known as Senegambia, which was dominated by Senegal and received little support in the Gambia. In 1989 the confederation disbanded and the Gambia resumed its status as an independent state, still headed by President Jawara. In 1994 Jawara was overthrown by a group of young military officers led by YAHYA JAMMEH, who then became president of the republic. In 1996, in response to considerable outside pressures, Jammeh held national elections. He was elected president by a small margin, amid accusations that the military government had used intimidation to influence voters.

Since taking power, Jammeh has tried to restore international confidence in his government and to revive tourism. His well-publicized ban on skin lighteners and hair straighteners, however, was designed to discourage the tourism-related sex industry. Since he has been in office, Jammeh has emphasized the improvement of economic infrastructure by expanding Yundum Airport, paving roads, and building new schools and hospitals.

Robert Baum

SEE ALSO

Colonial Rule; Gold Trade; Ivory Trade; Jawara, Sir Dawda Kairaba; Tourism in Africa; Marabout; Mali Empire.

Africa

Gambia, The (Ready Reference)

Official Name: Republic of the Gambia
Area: 11,295 sq km (4,361 sq mi)
Location: Western Africa; borders the North Atlantic and SENEGAL
Capital: Banjul (formerly called Bathurst) (population 44,188 [1983 estimate])
Population: 1,291,858 (1998 estimate)
Population Density: 87 persons per sq km (about 225 persons per sq mi)
Population Below Age 15: Total population: 46 percent (male 296,108; female 295,136 [1998 estimate])
Population Growth Rate: 3.42 percent (1998 estimate)
Total Fertility Rate: 5.0 children born per woman (1998 estimate)
Life Expectancy at Birth: Total population: 53.9 years (male 51.5 years; female 56.3 years [1998 estimate])
Infant Mortality Rate: 77.1 deaths per 1000 live births (1998 estimate)
Literacy Rate (age 15 and over who can read and write): Total population: 38.6 percent (male 52.8 percent; female 24.9 percent [1995 estimate])
Education: Primary education in the Gambia is free but not compulsory. In the early 1990s nearly 52 percent of all eligible primary-school-aged children attended school, but only 15 percent of all children between the ages of 14 and 20 attended school.
Languages: English is the official language, but each ethnic group uses its own language. The most common languages are MANDINKA, WOLOF, and FULANI.
Ethnic Groups: The population comprises the Mandinka, accounting for 42 percent of the population; the Fulani, who predominate in the eastern part of the country and account for 18 percent of the population; the Wolof, who live mainly in Banjul and the western part of the country; the JOLA, who live in the western region; the Serahuli; and a small Aku community.
Religions: About 90 percent of the population is Muslim. About 9 percent is Christian, and 1 percent adheres to indigenous beliefs.
Climate: Subtropical with distinct hot and

cool seasons. The temperatures range from 16° C (about 60° F) in the cool season, which lasts from November to May, to 43° C (110° F) in the summer. The rainy season lasts from June to November and the average annual rainfall is about 1020 mm (about 40 in).
Land, Plants, and Animals: Almost all of Gambia borders on the Gambia River. The country's land varies between sand and swamp land. Mangroves, oil palm, rubber vine, cedars, and mahogany trees thrive in this environment. Animals include the leopard, wild boar, CROCODILE, HIPPOPOTAMUS, and several species of ANTELOPE. Some game birds, such as the GUINEA FOWL and the sand grouse, are also plentiful.
Natural Resources: Natural resources include the Gambia River, one of Africa's best navigable waterways; fish; and soil suited to growing peanuts.
Currency: The dalasi
Gross Domestic Product (GDP): $1.23 billion (1997 estimate)
GDP per Capita: $1000 (1997estimate)
GDP Real Growth Rate: 21 percent (1997 estimate)
Primary Economic Activities: Agriculture (75 percent of the population), tourism, commerce, and services
Primary Crops: peanuts, millet, sorghum, rice, corn, cassava (tapioca), palm kernels, and livestock
Industries: Peanut processing, fish and hides, beverages, agricultural machinery assembly, woodworking, metalworking, and clothing
Primary Exports: Peanuts and peanut products, fish, cotton lint, and palm kernels
Primary Imports: Foodstuffs, manufactures, raw materials, fuel, machinery, and transport equipment
Primary Trade Partners: Great Britain, China, France, Germany, Russia, and the United States
Government: The Gambia is a republic under multiparty democratic rule. Following a coup d'état in July 1994, YAHYA JAMMEH named himself chairman of the Armed Forces Provisional Ruling Council. Bowing to external and internal pressure, Jammeh held elections in September 1996, and was elected to a five-year term with 55.5% of the vote. The unicameral National Assembly has 49 seats, of which 45 are elected and 4 are presidential appointees.

Elizabeth Heath

SEE ALSO
Banjul, the Gambia.

Africa

Ganda (also known as the Baganda), ethnic group of UGANDA.

The Ganda were the founders and rulers of Buganda, a kingdom extending northwest from LAKE VICTORIA. Most Ganda continue to live in this region of southern Uganda. Some Ganda also inhabit neighboring KENYA and TANZANIA. They speak a Bantu language. The Ganda, who number approximately 4 million people, are the largest ethnic group of Uganda and play a prominent role in the political-economic life of the country.

SEE ALSO
Bantu: Dispersion and Settlement; Buganda, Early Kingdom of.

Latin America and the Caribbean

Ganga Zumba. African king who led the maroon settlement Quilombo dos Palmares, in Brazil. Ganga Zumba died in 1685. He was succeeded by Zumbi (*see* PALMARES: AN AFRICAN STATE IN BRAZIL).

Latin America and the Caribbean

Gantois, Mãe Menininha do (b. February 10, 1894, Salvador, Bahia, Brazil; d. August 13, 1986), one of the most famous and revered priestesses of BRAZIL's African-derived CANDOMBLÉ religion; also known as Maria Escolástica da Conceição Nazaré.

Mãe Menininha do Gantois was born to Afro-Brazilian parents of Nigerian descent. A resident of the city of Salvador in BAHIA, Mãe Menininha was one of the most respected Brazilian *mães-de-santo* or *ialorixás* (Candomblé priestesses) of her time. She was widely consulted and revered throughout Brazil. She was the head of the Terreiro do Gantois, a temple founded by her aunt and godmother Pulquéria da Conceição, also an ialorixá. Mãe Pulquéria nicknamed her goddaughter Menininha, which means "little girl" in Portuguese (*mãe* means mother, and is a title often given to Candomblé priestesses). Mãe Menininha was a devotee, or "daughter," of OXUM, one of the orixás (deities) of Candomblé's pantheon (*see* CANDOMBLÉ and RELIGIONS, AFRICAN, IN BRAZIL).

The temple that Mãe Menininha headed, the Terreiro do Gantois, is one of the oldest and most respected Candomblé temples in Bahia and is recognized as one of the more orthodox or traditionally African Candomblé centers. The Terreiro do Gantois was actually founded after Mãe Pulquéria diverged from an older temple, Engenho Velho, thought to be one of the oldest Candomblé temples in Bahia. ENGENHO VELHO was founded by three freed African women, and traces its history back at least to the 1830s and perhaps even a hundred years earlier. A dispute over leadership at Engenho Velho led to the founding of two new temples: the Terreiro do Gantois by Mãe Pulquéria and Ilé Axé Opô Afonjá by Mãe Aninha, another of the most revered ialorixás in Brazil. Mãe Menininha took over the leadership of the Terreiro do Gantois in 1922.

Mãe Menininha dedicated her life to Candomblé during a time when African religions were still repressed in Brazil. She suffered imprisonment and violent persecution by the police due to her involvement with Candomblé. Her resistance to these discriminatory governmental policies against Afro-Brazilian religious practices was essential for the survival of Candomblé as an important part of Brazilian culture. Along with other prominent Candomblé priestesses such as Stella do Oxóssi, Mãe Menininha also asserted the Africanness of Candomblé, emphasizing that the religion was not the same as Roman Catholicism.

When Mãe Menininha died at age 92, the governor of the state of Bahia declared three days of mourning, and tens of thousands of people watched as her coffin passed through the streets of Salvador. Celebrated and honored by the Brazilian masses and by the elite, Mãe Menininha advised and inspired artists, intellectuals, politicians, and others. Pierre Verger, one of the most prominent academic experts on Candomblé, stated: "She was the last of the old, very respected priestesses. With her a whole generation is gone." The Terreiro do Gantois, located in the neighborhood of Federação, was set aside as a national public historic landmark, to be preserved and protected.

Michelle Gueraldi

SEE ALSO
Verger, Pierre Fatumbi; Orishas; Salvador, Brazil.

North America

Gantt, Harvey Bernard (b. January 14, 1943, Charleston, S.C.), African American politician and architect; mayor of Charlotte, North Carolina; and two-time candidate for United States Senate.

The turbulent political life of Harvey Gantt made him the most visible symbol of race baiting in American politics in the 1990s. Following narrow losses to incumbent North Carolina senator Jesse Helms, a conservative Republican, in 1990 and 1996, Gantt, his supporters, and the media all cited Helms's use of racially inflammatory political advertising.

One Helms television ad, which implied that Gantt supported race-based hiring quotas, played on white voters' fears that AFFIRMATIVE ACTION could cost them their jobs. Other ads linked Gantt to out-of-state money – he did, in fact, financially benefit from support from national groups looking to defeat Helms – and attacked his liberal views on abortion and homosexuality. Needing 40 percent of the white vote to become the South's first black senator since RECONSTRUCTION, Gantt suffered from the inaccuracy of polling in multiracial elections: as one 1990 voter said, "[White] people will say one thing, but when they get into that voting booth, they'll have a hard time voting for a black man."

Mayor of Charlotte from 1981 until 1987, Gantt is also partner in a private architectural firm, Gantt Huberman, and has taught at both the University of North Carolina at Chapel Hill and his alma mater, Clemson University in South Carolina, where in 1963 he became the school's first African American student.

Kate Tuttle

Africa

Garang de Mabior, John (b. 1945, Sudan), rebel leader from southern Sudan.

Born in 1945, John Garang de Mabior grew up in a Dinka community in southern Sudan. In 1970 he joined the Anya-Nya, the military organization waging a war for an independent southern Sudan. After the Addis Ababa Agreement in 1972, which temporarily halted the Sudanese civil war, Garang became deputy director of the military research branch of the Sudanese army. In 1981 he earned a doctorate in agricultural economics from Iowa State University with a dissertation on the agricultural development of southern Sudan. His work with the Sudanese government ended abruptly in 1983 with President Gaafar Muhammad al-Nimeiri's declaration of Islamic law and his dissolution of the southern Sudanese regional assembly.

That same year Garang founded the Sudan People's Liberation Movement (SPLM) and adopted a broader strategy than his Anya-Nya predecessors. He emphasized the cultural diversity of the entire Sudan, not just the north and the south. He advocated a federal system of government to ensure regional autonomy for all cultural minorities. Simultaneously, as commander of the affiliated Sudan People's Liberation Army (SPLA), Garang advocated a military solution in the fight for autonomy and organized a highly effective military organization, primarily in the south. Since 1983 the SPLM and SPLA have successfully resisted the Islamic governments of Sudan, though at a considerable cost in military and civilian deaths. Two periods of devastating famine, intensified by the difficulty of delivering food supplies to a war zone, have caused a massive rural flight to urban areas of northern and southern Sudan. Garang has proven adept at generating support among northern Sudanese minorities and among conservative Christian organizations in the West. Both of these groups have reacted with concern to what Garang has presented as Muslim persecution of a southern Sudanese Christian minority. In fact, most southerners are neither Christian nor Muslim, but followers of religions that are indigenous to the region.

Robert Baum

Latin America and the Caribbean

Garcia, José Maurício Nunes (b. September 22, 1767, Rio de Janeiro, Brazil; d. April 18, 1830, Rio de Janeiro, Brazil), Afro-Brazilian composer and priest, the most distinguished Brazilian composer of his time.

Known as the father of Brazilian music, José Maurício Nunes Garcia gained recognition in the early nineteenth century as a composer of church music. He wrote hymns, masses, chants, antiphones, and Te Deums, and his Requiem Mass (1816) is considered by music scholars to be one of the most significant masses ever written in Latin America. Although he wrote mostly sacred music, he was influenced by secular styles, most notably by Italian opera and by the Viennese masters Haydn and Mozart. One of Haydn's former students, the Austrian musician Sigismund Ritter von Neukomm, considered Garcia "the greatest improviser in the world on the clavichord."

Garcia was the son of a Portuguese lieutenant, Apolinário Nunes Garcia, and a black woman, Vitória Maria da Cruz. He studied harpsichord, viola, and solfège at the academy of Salvador José de Almeida e Faria, also of African descent, and was soon singled out for his exceptional musical gifts. In 1784 Garcia participated in the founding of the Brotherhood of Saint Cecilia, one of the leading professional music fraternities of his time.

In 1791 Garcia entered the Brotherhood of São Pedro dos Clérigos and soon afterward was ordained a priest – the ideal profession for musicians with neither wealth nor aristocratic title. During the colonial period (early 1500s to 1820s), Brazil's musical life was centered in the Portuguese Catholic Church, and in 1798 Garcia was appointed chapel master of Rio de Janeiro Cathedral, the most important musical position in the city. It was an exceptional offer, as such musical positions rarely went to black composers. As chapel master, his responsibilities included conducting, composing, and teaching music as well as performing as an organist. He also offered music courses to the public free of charge, a practice he maintained for more than 25 years.

In 1808 the Portuguese royal family, having fled Portugal after Napoleon's invasion of the Iberian Peninsula, arrived in Rio de Janeiro – a development that led to increased opportunities for local artists. Dom João VI, the Portuguese king and a patron of music, recognized Garcia's talent and appointed him chapel master of the Royal Chapel. As the leading court musician, Garcia began to compose more secular works, such as *Ulissea, A Heroic Drama*, a cantata with arias as well as choral and orchestral parts. In 1809 Dom João awarded Garcia the habit of the Order of Christ.

But after the arrival in Brazil in 1811 of Marcos Portugal, the most famous Portuguese composer of the time, Garcia's standing as a court musician declined. As music scholar Claver Filho notes, Portugal "found José Maurício in the post of chapel master, but the latter did not face up to him, racial prejudice was against him, and Marcos treated him with sovereign disdain." Eventually forced to relinquish his Royal Chapel duties to Portugal, Garcia organized his musical activities around the city's brotherhoods, and in 1819 he conducted the Brazilian premiere of Mozart's *Requiem*.

Although Garcia was far more esteemed by the Rio de Janeiro public than was Portugal, his health suffered, adversely affecting his capacity to compose. Moreover, following Brazil's political independence from Portugal in 1822, artistic development languished from lack of funds, and Garcia, denied his pension, died in poverty.

Roanne Edwards

Latin America and the Caribbean

Garifuna, people of mixed Amerindian and African descent, whose unique culture originally developed in the eastern Caribbean islands; they later resettled along the coast of southern Central America, where they continue to live today.

The origins of the Garifuna are not entirely clear, but their Arawak-speaking Indian ancestors almost certainly hailed from tropical forests in South America. Between 5000 B.C.E. and 1400 C.E. these peoples migrated in successive waves to the islands of the Lesser Antilles, where European navigators later encountered them. Europeans identified all peoples in the Caribbean as either Caribs or Arawaks, creating a latter-day debate among modern ethnohistorians about whether these were in fact two separate ethnic groups. While some experts argue that Caribs and Arawaks indeed had distinctive traits, others believe that Europeans simply grouped native peoples by whether they were hostile or friendly. Thus the European colonizers used the term *Carib* (meaning "wild" or "fierce") to refer to any group that refused to be subdued. *Arawak* was used as a category for groups the Europeans saw as more easily managed and who typically lived in agricultural settlements. (Arawaks were also known as Taínos.) If Arawaks and Caribs were separate groups, it is highly probable that the ancestors of the Garifuna were a mixture of both.

By the sixteenth century England and Spain had enslaved most of these native peoples for work on Caribbean plantations or the natives had died as a result of disease or war (*see* Slavery in Latin America and the Caribbean). The few who retained their freedom sometimes retaliated by raiding

European plantations, often carrying off black slaves who had been imported from Africa. Other African slaves fled from their masters to the sanctuary of the free Indian islanders.

One particular center of Carib resistance to European rule were the islands of DOMINICA and St. Vincent. In 1635 two Spanish slave ships were shipwrecked off the coast of St. Vincent, and the Caribs welcomed the newly freed slaves into their communities. Over the decades the Africans and Amerindians intermarried, developing a hybrid culture, and in time became a single group now known as Garifuna or Garinagu. To Europeans, they were known as Black Caribs, to distinguish them from Yellow or Red Caribs. Though many state that the Garifuna are phenotypically black, culturally they retain many elements of their Carib heritage, such as their own Arawak language and native patterns of subsistence, political organization, and kinship. Men in Garifuna society commonly devoted themselves to warfare and trade, while women were responsible for subsistence and child rearing.

By the seventeenth century the Garifuna were reduced to their strongholds on Dominica and St. Vincent. On St. Vincent, especially after 1700, they prospered. Their communities were led by war chiefs, each of whom typically had several wives. Women farmed while men hunted, fished, and traveled to other islands to trade tobacco and other goods for European manufactures and weapons. The main subsistence crop was bitter manioc, a food source commonly utilized by many tropical South American Indian groups. Several French settlers also lived on St. Vincent, and the two communities apparently lived largely without conflict, perhaps bonded by their antipathy toward Great Britain.

Because of their partial descent from runaway African slaves, the Garifuna had often been seen as a challenge to the institution of slavery and the further colonization of the Caribbean. Toward the end of the eighteenth century, intermittent violence between Garifuna and English settlers in the Caribbean intensified. By 1795 Britain launched an extensive military campaign against the Garifuna on St. Vincent; on capturing a Garifuna village, the British burned canoes, houses, and crops to the ground. Reduced to near starvation, the Garifuna surrendered in late 1796 and early 1797. They probably numbered slightly fewer than 5000, but after being interned by the British on the island of Baliceau, about half of them died as a result of unsanitary conditions and disease.

ABOVE: Youngsters listen enthusiastically to an older fisherman on a boat to the Pearl Lagoon in Nicaragua. *Candace Freeland/D. Donne Bryant Stock Photo*
RIGHT: Garifuna woman poles her canoe for early morning fishing on the Pearl Lagoon located on the Atlantic coast of Nicaragua. *Candace Freeland/D. Donne Bryant Stock Photo*

In March 1797 the captives were shipped from Baliceau to the island of Roatán, in the Bay Islands just off the Honduran coast. (Roatán was home to other blacks whom Britain had earlier deemed unruly.) There the Garifuna were deposited, malnourished and ill, with a few food supplies, tools, and seeds. Spain, which occupied most of mainland Central America, had long since laid claim to the Bay Islands (a claim disputed by the British), and the Garifuna appealed to Spain to extend its protection to them. In May 1797 the Spanish took control of the island and brought the Garifuna to the Honduran port of Trujillo. There the men resumed their life of fishing and soldiering (this time for the Spaniards) and the women returned to farming. The Garifuna farms apparently prospered and supplied food for both the Garifuna and colonists.

Over the next decade the Garifuna migrated northwest along the Atlantic coast as far as present-day Dangriga, Belize, and southeast as far as the Patuca River in eastern Honduras. They were soon as disenchanted with their Spanish rulers as they had been with the British, and many became allied with British smugglers who prowled the coastline and relied on Garifuna labor for the profitable woodcutting industry.

During this time the Garifuna added European influences to their mixed Indian and African culture, and their always dynamic culture became even more complex. Spanish words were added to the Garifuna's largely Arawak language, and as interaction with the British increased, English words were introduced as well. The Garifuna also began a gradual conversion to Roman Catholicism, although many Garifuna maintained a belief that spirit helpers would help cure illness and find lost objects. (Today, the belief in spirit helpers survives, interwoven with beliefs in similar powers attributed to Catholic saints.)

Central America achieved independence from Spain in 1821. In 1832 most Garifuna supported the forces trying to overthrow Francisco Morazan, president of the Central American Federation. The rebellion failed, and the Garifuna were forced to flee their Honduran homes. Some returned to the relative sanctuary of the Bay Islands, while others dispersed north to British Honduras (now Belize) or south to the remote Miskito Coast of Honduras and Nicaragua. They continued their fishing and agricultural work and became skilled at sea transport. When large American fruit companies established outposts in Honduras, Belize, and Nicaragua in the nineteenth century, Garifuna were much in demand as growers and dockworkers.

During World War II both the United States and Great Britain experienced shortages of dockworkers and merchant mariners. With the banana industry crippled by plant disease and war, many Garifuna migrated to the United States and Great Britain to fill ship-related jobs. After the war, the well-traveled migrants returned home, sparking a further migration abroad. Large numbers of Garifuna eventually settled in New York, as well as London, Los Angeles, and New Orleans. Estimates have put their New York population at more than 50,000 by the late 1990s.

By the late 1970s the Garifuna population in Central America was estimated at about 80,000. Exact population estimates do not exist, as the Garifuna are not only geographically dispersed but are rarely counted as a separate ethnic group in the countries where they live. Nevertheless, it is clear that most of the Garifuna live in dozens of small communities along the shore of northern Honduras, where their numbers in the late 1990s were uncertain but almost definitely totaled more than 100,000. In Belize they numbered about 16,000, in Guatemala about 6000, and in Nicaragua about 3000. The Garifuna culture has been marked largely by Indian-derived elements such as language, subsistence techniques, and some religious beliefs, but also by the influence of their African ancestors, which has deeply marked their oral tradition, dance, drum styles, and agriculture. The unique Garifuna culture persists and continues to develop.

See Also

Transatlantic Slave Trade; Los Angeles, California; New Orleans, Louisiana; New York, New York.

North America

Garnet, Henry Highland

(b. 1815, New Market, Md.; d. February 12, 1882, Monrovia, Liberia), minister and abolitionist whose advocacy of an uprising to free the slaves made him one of the most controversial African American leaders of the nineteenth century.

Henry Highland Garnet was born a slave on a plantation in Kent County, Maryland, where his grandfather, a former chieftain in Africa, was a leader of the slave community. In 1824 Garnet's father escaped, taking the rest of his family with him to New York City. While the father became an active leader of the African Methodist Episcopal Church, Garnet was enrolled in the African Free School. He spent several years afterward as a sailor and a farmer's apprentice before returning to school, this time under the tutelage of abolitionists Theodore S. Wright and Peter Williams Jr., who ran the Canal Street School for African Americans.

After graduation from the Canal Street School, Garnet and several other young blacks, including abolitionist and nationalist Alexander Crummell, enrolled in a newly established academy in New Canaan, New Hampshire. Only weeks after the school opened, angry white neighbors destroyed it and threatened the boys' lives. Garnet and Crummell left for the Oneida Institute in Whitesboro, New York, where both studied theology. Garnet completed his studies by 1840.

Settling in Troy, New York, Garnet attached himself to a black congregation and transformed the area into an important center for abolitionism. His church soon became a stop on the Underground Railroad and he published several short-lived abolitionist periodicals. In 1842 he married Julia Williams. The following year he became an ordained Presbyterian minister and made his stormy debut in national politics with his speech at a Buffalo convention for African Americans. Titled "Address to the Slaves of the United States of America," Garnet's real audience was the assemblage of African American leaders, whom he urged to fulfill God's will by ending slavery. At the time, invoking Christianity to call for what was essentially a slave insurrection was quite radical. Garnet's remarks brought him into direct conflict with Frederick Douglass, who favored the more gradualist approach to abolition advocated by William Lloyd Garrison that involved appeals to morality. Douglass called on the conventioneers at Buffalo to defeat a resolution for distribution of Garnet's speech. A heated debate followed and Douglass's motion narrowly carried the day.

Garnet's address nonetheless gained him national notoriety, and at later conventions he introduced the speech again. Eventually the address was published, by which time even Douglass supported a slave uprising. In 1850 Garnet left for a tour of Europe, where he hoped to enlist support for his causes, which now included a boycott of cotton. Cotton, the chief product of the South, was as essential to slavery as slavery was to it. Ultimately, Garnet failed in his quest. He did, however, serve as a delegate to the World Peace Congress in Frankfurt, and in the next few years he favorably impressed English and Scottish congregations and antislavery societies to whom he spoke.

Presbyterians in Scotland raised funds for Garnet to minister to blacks in Jamaica, where he arrived in 1853. Illness forced him to return to the United States in 1856, whereupon he became pastor of Shiloh Presbyterian Church in New York City. He was soon elected president of the newly created African Civilization Society (ACS). ACS hoped to repatriate African Americans to Africa and to use them for the dual purposes of introducing Christianity to that benighted continent and creating an agrarian economy to compete with and undermine the slave-based economy of the American South. Again Douglass opposed Garnet's appeals, arguing that black colonialism was little better than white colonialism. Garnet, however, had powerful allies in his Pan-Africanist movement, including his old friend Alexander Crummell and Martin Robison Delany. The movement, however, never realized its goals.

When the Civil War broke out, Garnet joined with other African Americans in

Although his call for an uprising to end slavery was viewed as too radical, even by most other abolitionists, Presbyterian minister Henry Highland Garnet nonetheless became the first African American to address the United States Congress, which he did in 1864. *Photographs and Prints Division, Schomburg Center for Research in Black Culture, The New York Public Library, Astor, Lenox and Tilden Foundation*

pushing the reluctant Abraham Lincoln to use the opportunity the war provided to abolish slavery. He also urged Lincoln to allow blacks to serve in the Union Army, a request to which Lincoln eventually yielded. Garnet paid a price for his outspokenness. In the NEW YORK CITY DRAFT RIOT OF 1863, his life was endangered, his church badly damaged, and many blacks were killed. He nonetheless continued his advocacy and recruitment of black troops.

In 1864 he moved his ministry to Washington, D.C., where, on the anniversary of the ratification of the Thirteenth Amendment, he became the first African American to speak before Congress. During the postwar RECONSTRUCTION, he pressed for more government aid to the freed slaves, and he briefly served in the Freedmen's Bureau. Throughout the 1870s he became steadily angrier at the federal government for refusing to distribute land to the freedpeople, and he eventually settled into an uneasy retirement in New York. His wife, Julia, died in 1871, and several years later he married the feminist educator Sarah Thompson.

In 1881 the government asked Garnet to serve as minister to LIBERIA. He had been in poor health for some time, but having long entertained the dream of redeeming Africa, he accepted the offer. He left in 1881 and died the following February.

SEE ALSO

Pan-Africanism; Bureau of Refugees, Freedmen and Abandoned Lands; Civil War, American; Thirteenth Amendment of the United States Constitution and the Emancipation Proclamation; Williams, Peter, Jr.

Marcus Garvey, dressed in the uniform he adopted after the first UNIA convention elected him provisional president of Africa, rides in a parade. *CORBIS/Underwood & Underwood*

enterprise intended to provide a means for African Americans to return to Africa while also enabling black people around the Atlantic to exchange goods and services. The company's three ships (one called the SS *Frederick Douglass*) were owned and operated by black people and made travel and trade possible between their United States, Caribbean, Central American, and African stops. The economically independent Black Star Line was a symbol of pride for blacks and seemed to attract more members to the UNIA.

In August 1920, 25,000 people attended the first UNIA convention in New York's Madison Square Garden. There, Garvey was elected president-general of the organization, and the Declaration of Rights of the Negro Peoples of the World was written. Members of the convention outlined the formal organization and leadership, calling for a commissioner of each chapter area. The document demanded that black schoolchildren should be taught African history. The convention produced an anthem – the "Universal Ethiopian Anthem" – and red, black, and green became the colors of African peoples. Around this time, a UNIA leader was sent to LIBERIA to develop further Garvey's idea for a colony there.

As a result of large financial obligations and managerial errors, the Black Star Line failed in 1921 and ended operations. Constant criticism from the NATIONAL ASSOCIATION FOR THE ADVANCEMENT OF COLORED PEOPLE (NAACP) (most visibly from member W. E. B. Du Bois) and United States government opposition took its toll on the UNIA. Early in 1922 Garvey was indicted on mail fraud charges regarding the Black Star Line's stock sale. He was convicted and given a maximum prison sentence of five years by Judge Julian Mack, also an NAACP member. Garvey appealed and was defeated; he entered the Atlanta federal penitentiary.

Garvey's second wife, Amy Jacques Garvey, led a national campaign for Garvey's release. During this time, she also edited and published two volumes of his speeches and writings titled *Philosophy and Opinions of Marcus Garvey* (1923 and 1925). The petition drive succeeded in winning Garvey's release after he had served nearly three years of his sentence. He was immediately deported to Jamaica and barred from entering the United States again. In Jamaica, Garvey held two more UNIA conventions. He also started two publications: *Black Man,* a monthly magazine, and the *New Jamaican.* But controlling and leading the different international branches from Jamaica proved difficult. A core group in the United States continued to support Garvey; they published the *Negro World* into the 1930s. Garvey, however, turned to Jamaican politics. He lost a race for a colonial legislative council seat in 1930. He did, however, sit on the municipal council of Jamaica's capital.

Garvey moved to London in 1935. For the next few years he held annual conventions in Canada and continued to publish *Black Man.* After suffering a second stroke on June 10, 1940, Garvey died, having fathered two sons with Amy Jacques Garvey, Marcus Jr. and Julius. After his death, his leadership and significance continued to be influential and was recognized around the world. In the United States Garveyism was central to the development of the black consciousness and pride at the core of the twentieth-century freedom movement. The Jamaican Rastafarian movement and the United States NATION OF ISLAM both grew out of and have been influenced by the UNIA. Jamaica named Garvey its first national hero.

Martha King

SEE ALSO

Pan-Africanism; World War I and African Americans; Du Bois, William Edward Burghardt (W. E. B.); Great Migration, The; Harlem, New York; Tuskegee University; Washington, Booker Taliaferro; Kingston, Jamaica; Rastafarians.

Latin America and the Caribbean

Gay and Lesbian Movements in Latin America and the Caribbean

At the time of the European discovery and colonization of the New World, homosexuality – labeled "sodomy" – was considered by authorities to be "the most vile, filthy and dishonest of sins, inspiring God's ire and detestable even to the devil." Love between people of the same sex was treated as a serious crime, meriting the same punishment as regicide or treason. For three centuries the tribunals of the Inquisition and the royal courts of SPAIN and PORTUGAL tried, tortured, and severely punished hundreds of sodomites, many of whom were burned at the stake. Of the New World colonies, BRAZIL saw the harshest and most extensively documented repression against homosexuals. Ironically, today it is the country where they find strongest representation in the gay and lesbian movement, as reflected in the number of related organizations, in political victories in the struggle for full citizenship, and in the number of Afro-Brazilian gay groups.

Reliable evidence indicates that when the first Africans were transported to the New World, homosexuality existed and was widely practiced on three continents. In Europe, despite draconian civil and religious legislation against sodomites, homosexuality existed at all levels of the social ladder. In the Americas homosexuality and transvestism existed from north to south, in nomadic tribes as well as the great civilizations of PERU and MEXICO. Similarly, in Africa, the existence of homosexuality was noted among many ethnic groups in both the Bantu and Sudanese regions. These included the Ambo, AZANDE, Barea-Kumana, Cligente-Humbi, Des Amines, Hovas, Maconde, Manghabei, Mesagin, NAMA, NUPE, OVIMBUNDU, Sacalavas, Siwan, Tamala, Thonga, Unianvesi, and others.

Despite the myth that homoeroticism did not exist in precolonial Africa but was the product of European influence, historical documentation confirms the practice of homosexuality and male transvestism in at least two important areas of African diaspora: the kingdoms of Congo-Angola and Benin. In 1591, for instance, Francisco Manicongo, a slave in Salvador, BAHIA, was accused of sodomy. His accuser claimed to have traveled extensively in the Congo-Angola region, where "black sodomites who serve as patient women in the nefarious sin are called *'quimbanda'* and wear a cloth wrapped around them tied in the front." Manicongo wore such a cloth and refused to wear the men's clothing provided by his master. Two sixteenth-century authors who traveled in the lands of Queen Ginga also used the word "quimbanda" in reference to a large group of homosexual witch doctors, both feared and respected by their communities, who dressed as women. The existence of homosexuality on the African continent is thus documented as early as the first century of the diaspora.

In Portuguese America, of 85 men accused of sodomy between 1591 and 1769, 41 (48 percent) were of African descent, belonging to the Angola, Mixicongo, Guine, and Manicongo ethnic groups. Over a dozen Afro-Brazilian women were accused of lesbianism in Inquisition records. For instance, the domestic slave Francisca Luiz was denounced for maintaining a tumultuous relationship with a white woman. In Mexico in 1658, 123 men, including several of African descent, were accused of sodomy; 14 were burned at the stake.

Documented accounts of homosexual encounters involving blacks in the New World refer principally to interracial contacts. In CUBA, for instance, there are reports of homosexual black slaves, who "had a husband for whom they cooked and cleaned. They were good workers, taking care of their gardens, whose fruits they gave to their husbands, who sold them to peasants." References to relations between blacks are much fewer, possibly reflecting the clandestine nature of these encounters and the relative disinterest of the white elite. While there are some cases of homosexual masters sexually abusing their slaves, documentation suggests that sexual violence was much more prevalent in heterosexual encounters.

An interracial relation is precisely the topic of the first homosexual novel of the Americas, *O Bom Crioulo* (1985), by the Brazilian Adolfo Caminha, which reflects the passion between a black sailor and a young white seaman. Notable black homosexuals in Latin America included the Brazilian writer and translator João do Rio (1881-1921), naive painter Raimundo Oliveira (1930-1966), and the actor and dancer Mario Gusmão. A great number of priests of Afro-American religions in Latin America and the Caribbean (VODOU, SANTERÍA, CANDOMBLÉ) are homosexual, there being in the YORUBA pantheon several hermaphrodite and bisexual divinities, including Oxalá, Oxumaré, Logun-Ede, Iansã, and Osain.

The gay and lesbian movement in Latin America saw its inception in ARGENTINA in 1969. Mexico and Brazil followed suit, with the first groups forming in the 1970s. According to the international gay tourist guide *Spartacus,* there are social venues open to gays and lesbians in all countries of Latin America and the Caribbean. It is only in half, however, that there is intermittent news of any group's defending the rights of homosexuals. Despite the cultural diversity of these countries, Latin America as a whole is characterized by virulent machismo and homophobia. These factors, reinforced by the omnipresent control of the family and the difficulty that the young encounter in attaining economic independence, inhibit the process of coming out. This helps to explain the small size and short duration of activist gay and lesbian groups. Social ostracism, public humiliation, and police persecution are part of day-to-day life for gays and lesbians throughout Latin America and the Caribbean.

Despite the fact that the population and culture of a number of countries are strongly marked by their African heritage, Afro-American gays and lesbians have little national or international visibility. Homosexual groups in the region remain predominantly white. Some with greater Afro-American participation include the following: in PUERTO RICO, the Committee for the Rescue of Privacy, which organized in 1983 and held its first conference on homosexuality in 1987; in the DOMINICAN REPUBLIC, the Friends Always Friends Group and the Mitilene Group; in SURINAME, the Workgroup on Homosexuality, founded in 1981; and in Curaçao, the Antilles Homophile Group. Jamaica's Freedom Movement, led by Larry Chang, instituted a program for jail visits to gay prisoners, started a youth subgroup and a health clinic for the gay community, and published the *Jamaica Gayly News.*

It is in Brazil that black gay organizations have been more lasting. In 1980 the Grupo Gay da Bahia was organized in Salvador. Afro-Brazilian activists were among its founders and represent most of its members. In 1996 the group Dudu-Ade (from the Yoruba "dudu," meaning black, and "ade," meaning homosexual) was organized in São Paulo with the support of the Workers Party. That same year, Quimbanda-Dudu was founded in BAHIA. Today, it continues its struggle against racism and homophobia, working to prevent the spread of AIDS (acquired immune deficiency syndrome) among members of the Candomblé faith.

In general, while facing continuing difficulties, the gay and lesbian movements in Latin America have gained some strength over the past decade and attained some notable victories. In 1997 gay and lesbian groups successfully challenged the constitutionality of Ecuador's sodomy law. In Mexico Patria Jimenez was elected as the first openly gay national deputy in Latin America. A number of cities, including Buenos Aires, have passed antidiscrimination laws that protect sexual minorities, although many of these are routinely disregarded. While the participation of Afro-American gays and lesbians has been important in many of these struggles, most groups in the region are predominantly white; and movements organized around a homosexual black identity are rare.

Luis Mott

SEE ALSO

Bantu: Dispersion and Settlement; Benin, Early Kingdom of; Sudan; Homosexuality in Africa: An Interpretation; Jamaica; Religions, African, in Latin America and the Caribbean; Orishas; Salvador, Brazil.

North America

Gay and Lesbian Movements in the United States

THE HARLEM RENAISSANCE

In 1926, Bruce Nugent wrote a homoerotic essay for the premier issue of a controversial Harlem publication called *FIRE!!* Alongside articles by LANGSTON HUGHES and ZORA NEALE HURSTON, Nugent's piece – written under the pseudonym Richard Bruce – described a male homosexual relationship. Although the article and the publication provoked criticism from some blacks for the controversial topics it explored, it marked an important milestone for blacks in the gay movement.

Many leading figures of the HARLEM RENAISSANCE were known to be homosexual or bisexual. Historian Eric Garber has noted that "[h]omosexuality was clearly part of this world." It included well-known artists and writers such as BESSIE SMITH, Mabel Hampton, WALLACE THURMAN, Bruce Nugent, CLAUDE MCKAY, COUNTEE CULLEN, Alain Locke, and others.

Following the Harlem Renaissance, few black musicians in the pre-civil rights era were more distinguished than BILLY STRAYHORN, who joined the Duke Ellington Orchestra in 1939 as a pianist, arranger, and lyricist. As a black gay man, he worked in the shadow of Ellington, with whom he developed a close working relationship. Strayhorn created *Lush Life* (1938) and wrote *Take the A Train* (1941), the theme song of the Ellington band, and he is credited with nearly 200 solo and joint compositions.

THE CIVIL RIGHTS MOVEMENT

By the 1950s several black writers who had confronted the vexing issue of segregation in America began to address questions of sexual orientation as well. In 1956 JAMES BALDWIN, a black gay man, published the novel *Giovanni's Room*, his first homosexual love story. A year later the young playwright LORRAINE HANSBERRY, a black lesbian, wrote a letter to the *Ladder*, an early lesbian publication, where she suggested that "homosexual persecution and condemnation has at its roots not only social ignorance, but a philosophically active anti-feminist dogma." Hansberry would go on to achieve widespread acclaim when her play *A Raisin in the Sun* (1959) opened on Broadway to rave reviews.

During the 1950s and 1960s, a number of black lesbians and gay men participated in the CIVIL RIGHTS MOVEMENT in the South and the North, but none was so well known as BAYARD RUSTIN. In 1955 Rustin was a close associate of A. Philip Randolph, the cofounder of the LEADERSHIP CONFERENCE ON CIVIL RIGHTS. Dispatched to help Martin Luther King Jr. with the Montgomery bus boycott, Rustin soon became a close adviser to King as well. Their relationship was strained when King, under pressure from conservative elements in the SOUTHERN CHRISTIAN LEADERSHIP CONFERENCE, agreed to distance himself from the openly homosexual Rustin. His best-known achievement was as the principal organizer for the 1963 MARCH ON WASHINGTON for Jobs and Justice. But Rustin, as a known homosexual, had to fight for this role against the objection of NATIONAL ASSOCIATION FOR THE ADVANCEMENT OF COLORED PEOPLE (NAACP) executive secretary Roy Wilkins, and he was not allowed to hold the actual title as march director. The CIVIL RIGHTS MOVEMENT awakened America's consciousness to the unfulfilled promises of the nation and set the stage for other movements, including the gay liberation movement.

STONEWALL

On Friday, June 27, 1969, eight New York City police officers raided a gay bar at 57 Christopher Street in Greenwich Village. The manager of the Stonewall Inn was served with a warrant for selling liquor without a license, and police ordered patrons to leave the bar. As the patrons congregated outside, unlike at previous raids, they taunted the police with catcalls and openly defied them by throwing bricks and bottles. Led in part by black and Latino drag queens, a spontaneous rebellion erupted against the practice of police harassment of homosexuals. As word spread in the following days, hundreds of gays and lesbians, including African Americans, showed up in Sheridan Square to show their solidarity. The Stonewall Rebellion, as it has become known, marked a turning point for gays and lesbians, and it has since become the defining moment in American gay and lesbian history.

POST-STONEWALL

After Stonewall, increasing numbers of gay, lesbian, bisexual, and transgendered Americans began to emerge "out of the closet." African Americans have played a critical role in the gay movement's development during this time.

Activists in the 1970s began to make connections between the politics of race, class, gender, and sexual orientation. On August 15, 1970, HUEY P. NEWTON, supreme commander of the BLACK PANTHER PARTY, published a letter in the party newsletter stating, "the women's liberation front and gay liberation front are our friends." In April 1977 a group of black feminists called the Combahee River Collective issued a statement addressing the "interlocking" system of "racial, sexual, heterosexual, and class oppression." In October 1979, during the gay community's first national march on Washington, hundreds of participants gathered at Harambee House for a Third World conference on gays and lesbians of color, titled "When Will the Ignorance End?" In 1980 black gay activist Melvin Boozer helped push the Democratic Party when he addressed the convention and explained the similar pain of racism and homophobia.

From the late 1970s to the present, numerous organizations formed to represent the interests of black homosexual, bisexuals, and others. These include the National Coalition of Black Lesbians and Gays, the National Black Lesbian and Gay Leadership Forum, the Unity Fellowship Church Movement, and the National Body of the Black Men's and Women's Exchange. Some activists, such as veteran organizer Mandy Carter, played leading roles with both black gay organizations and mainstream gay organizations. As the acquired immune deficiency syndrome (AIDS) epidemic began to impact black gay men disproportionately in the late 1980s and 1990s, many black gays and lesbians created new community organizations to respond to the crisis.

Black gays and lesbians became more prominent in the 1980s and 1990s. On the screen the works of Marlon Riggs and Isaac Julien have created a new genre of black gay films. On the dance stage ALVIN AILEY and BILL T. JONES produced works that have been seen by audiences worldwide. In literature black gay writers Essex Hemphill, E. Lynn Harris, and James Earl Hardy have written books that explore the black gay experience. Black openly gay and bisexual writers such as Sapphire and Samuel Delany have written popular novels that focus on issues other than sexual orientation.

Black writers, intellectuals, and activists have left a profound impression on the gay rights movement. Linda Villarosa served as executive editor of Essence magazine and introduced hundreds of thousands of black women to black lesbians when she coauthored a "coming out" piece with her mother. Barbara Smith's groundbreaking anthology *Home Girls* presented dozens of perspectives of black feminism that integrated black lesbian viewpoints. Others such as Cheryl Clarke, Angela Davis, ALICE WALKER, and JUNE JORDAN have shared their experiences about bisexuality and lesbianism in their writings and public comments.

Black lesbian feminist writer Audre Lorde spoke at the 20th anniversary of the 1963 March on Washington, and activist Phill Wilson addressed the 30th anniversary march in 1993. Lorde produced literature so expressive and unique that she became a cultural icon in both the black community and the gay community. Wilson has articulated the interests of black gay men living with AIDS as he has played a leading role in the fight against the disease nationally and internationally.

Openly gay, lesbian, or bisexual entertainers such as Me'Shell N'degéOcello, LITTLE RICHARD, Nona Hendryx, Sylvester, and RUPAUL have changed and challenged the music industry. In sports Glenn Burke, a black openly gay member of the Los Angeles Dodgers, is credited with inventing the "high five" in 1977. In fashion black gay designers such as Patrick Kelley and Willi Smith have helped to shape the industry. In politics a new breed of black openly gay elected officials emerged, including Ken Reeves, the first black mayor of Cambridge, Massachusetts; Sabrina Sojourner, the shadow United States representative from the District of Columbia; Keith St. John, an alderman in Albany, New York; and Sherry Harris, a city council member in Seattle.

In April 1993 three black gays and lesbians participated in a White House meeting as part of the first group of gay and lesbian leaders to meet with an American president. In the same year, when the Clinton Administration discussed plans to allow homosexuals to serve openly in the military, black gay men and lesbians were involved and affected. One such soldier was Perry Watkins, who had been drafted into the army in 1968 during the height of the VIETNAM WAR. At the time he was drafted, Watkins acknowledged his homosexuality, but was nevertheless admitted into military service. He served openly gay until he was discharged in 1982 for homosexuality. Watkins fought the discharge for several years and finally won reinstatement when the United States Supreme Court refused to hear the U.S. Army's appeal case. He later retired with an "honorable discharge" and became the only openly gay person to retire with full honors from the military.

In 1995 hundreds of black lesbians, gay men, and bisexuals assembled in New York for a conference called "Black Nations/Queer Nations?" to explore the intersections of race and sexual orientation. By October of that year, when the NATION OF ISLAM organized the MILLION MAN MARCH in Washington, D.C., more than 200 people took part in a contingent that carried signs and placards identifying themselves as black gay men. In the 1990s leaders of the CONGRESSIONAL BLACK CAUCUS, the LEADERSHIP CONFERENCE ON CIVIL RIGHTS, the National Association for the Advancement of Colored People, the NATIONAL COUNCIL OF NEGRO WOMEN, and the Southern Christian Leadership Conference have joined in support of laws protecting gays and lesbians from discrimination.

Keith Boykin

SEE ALSO

Davis, Angela Yvonne; Delany, Samuel R.; *Essence*; King, Martin Luther, Jr.; Locke, Alain Leroy; Lorde, Audre Geraldine; Nugent, Richard Bruce; Randolph, Asa Philip; Riggs, Marlon Troy; Seattle, Washington; Washington, D.C.; Wilkins, Roy Ottoway; Ellington, Edward Kennedy ("Duke"); March on Washington, 1963.

North America

Gaye, Marvin **(b. April 2, 1939, Washington, D.C.; d. April 1, 1984, Los Angeles, Calif.), African American singer and songwriter, a recording artist for Motown Records, and one of the most popular and influential singers of rhythm and blues (R&B) music in the 1960s and 1970s, whose songs were notable for their brooding, introspective qualities.**

Marvin Gaye began singing in church as a child. The son of a poor Pentecostal minister, he grew up listening to the music of American blues singer RAY CHARLES, which became a major influence on his work. In 1958 Gaye joined an R&B vocal group called the Moonglows. Three years later he signed a recording contract with Tamla, one of the MOTOWN record companies, serving as a drummer for studio sessions and, later, as a singer. Influenced by American singers Frank Sinatra and Nat "King" Cole, Gaye had hoped to sing in the popular style known as crooning, but after his first album – a series of JAZZ standards – received little attention, Motown had him record up-tempo SOUL MUSIC material. The result was a series of songs that became classics, beginning with "Stubborn Kind of Fellow" (1963) and culminating in "I Heard It Through the Grapevine" (1968).

Gaye's other popular records from this 1960s Motown era include "Can I Get a Witness" (1963), a song with traits of GOSPEL MUSIC and a strong influence on British rock groups such as the Rolling Stones (the group recorded the song in 1964); "How Sweet It Is" (1964), a song with jazz influences; and "Ain't That Peculiar" and "I'll Be Doggone" (both 1965), pensive songs written and produced by American Motown artist Smokey Robinson. Later in the decade Gaye recorded a series of romantic duets with Motown singer Tammi Terrell, including "Ain't No Mountain High Enough" (1967), "If This World Were Mine" (1967), "You're All I Need to Get By" (1968), and "What You Gave Me" (1969).

Shortly after Terrell's death in 1970, Gaye established a new style of soul music with the album *What's Going On* (1971), a deeply personal and spiritual reflection on family and social issues and particularly on the VIETNAM WAR (1959-1975). A work that blended styles of soul, jazz, and rock music, the album marked one of the first times Motown had given an artist nearly complete creative control.

During the next ten years Gaye recorded and produced a series of brooding, erotic songs, including "Trouble Man" (1972), "Let's Get It On" (1973), and "I Want You" (1976). By the end of the 1970s his career was in decline and his personal problems were mounting. He retreated to Europe, where he recorded the hit song "Sexual Healing" (1982). He then returned to the United States and, after a disappointing musical tour, moved in with his parents. In 1984, in the midst of a heated quarrel, he was shot to death by his father.

In 1982 Gaye won two Grammy Awards for "Sexual Healing." In 1987 he was inducted into the Rock and Roll Hall of Fame.

SEE ALSO

Blues, The; Cole, Nat ("King"); Pentecostalism; Rhythm and Blues; Robinson, William ("Smokey").

Africa

Gbari **(also known as Agbari and Gwari), ethnic group of NIGERIA.**

The Gbari primarily inhabit the Niger State of western Nigeria. They speak a Niger-Congo language. Approximately 500,000 people consider themselves Gbari.

SEE ALSO

Languages, African: An Overview.

Africa

Gbaya, **an ethnic group of the western CENTRAL AFRICAN REPUBLIC, eastern CAMEROON, northern REPUBLIC OF THE CONGO, and northwestern DEMOCRATIC REPUBLIC OF THE CONGO.**

The Gbaya, who speak a Niger-Congo language, today number close to 1 million, mainly in the west of the Central African Republic. Fleeing FULANI slave raids and holy wars connected with the founding of the SOKOTO CALIPHATE, the ancestors of the animist Gbaya migrated to the region from present-day northern Cameroon and NIGERIA in the early 1800s. They incorporated many of the indigenous inhabitants, creating the six basic subgroups of the Gbaya. Fulani continued to raid the Gbaya region each year to capture slaves for sale, both in the Caliphate and to trans-Saharan caravans.

The traditional Gbaya political organization was decentralized, with village chiefs acting as symbolic leaders and judges rather than political rulers. Only in emergencies were war chiefs temporarily elected, as among the BANDA. In war, age sets ensured unity by cutting across clan identities. The clans managed trade with foreigners, marriage arrangements, and religious customs.

French colonizers disrupted these traditions by increasing the powers of village chiefs. They imposed brutal forced labor on many Gbaya, for example on the Congo-Ocean railway. In 1928 the Gbaya initiated the three-year Kongo Wara War against French rule. The French suppressed the rebellion in a "nightmare campaign" that decimated the Gbaya population. However, many Gbaya became nationalist leaders and later figured prominently in political circles.

Today most Gbaya remain rural farmers, growing cassava, corn, peanuts, tobacco, and yams and supplementing their diet by hunting and fishing. For cash, many Gbaya grow rice or coffee, prospect for diamonds, or work for mining companies.

Eric Young

SEE ALSO

Transatlantic Slave Trade.

Africa

Gebrselassie, Haile

(b. April 18, 1973, Arssi, Ethiopia), Ethiopian track and field star.

When Haile Gebrselassie was a child, he ran 25 km (15 mi) round trip to school each day – barefoot – good training for his future career as one of the world's elite runners. Like his brother before him, he began running competitively as a teenager. In 1992 he won both the 5000- and 10,000-meter races at the World Junior Championships. The next year, competing against adults for the first time, he won the 10,000-meter and finished second in the 5000-meter in the World Championships. In 1996 Gebrselassie not only won the 5000-meter event in the World Indoor Championships, he also set an indoor world record, the first Ethiopian to do so. He followed that feat by winning a Gold Medal in the 10,000-meter at the 1996 Olympic Games in ATLANTA, GEORGIA, setting a new Olympic record.

Treated to a victory parade in Addis Ababa that was attended by nearly a million people, Gebrselassie became a national hero. In 1997 he set three more world records: in the 5000-meter, 10,000-meter, and 2-mile races. In addition, he has won the 3000-meter event in worldwide competition, and reportedly plans to begin training for marathons. Gebrselassie splits his time between Addis Ababa, where he has a job with the police department, and THE NETHERLANDS, where he lives with one of his brothers and continues training.

Kate Tuttle

SEE ALSO

Addis Ababa, Ethiopia; Olympics, Africans and the; Ethiopia; Track and Field in the United States.

Africa

Gedi, East African coastal town founded in the thirteenth century, the ruins of which are now an important historic site in KENYA.

Located 16.7 km (10 mi) south of Malindi, Gedi is something of a mystery. Built on a coral spur, its outer wall encompassed 45 acres. The opulent town proper resided within an inner wall, containing a palace, three pillar tombs, and a great mosque as well as several smaller mosques and private houses. Lying 6.7 km (4 mi) inland and 3.3 km (2 mi) from a navigable creek, Gedi was undoubtedly influenced by Swahili culture but probably did not participate directly in the trade that linked towns along the SWAHILI COAST. Gedi was never mentioned by the Portuguese, who occupied Malindi from 1512 to 1593, nor in any other written record from around the time it was inhabited. Yet the ruins of Gedi show clear evidence of a highly developed and wealthy African civilization.

Archaeological excavations have determined that Gedi was founded in the thirteenth century and was probably rebuilt during the fifteenth century, the height of its prosperity. Gedi was abandoned in the sixteenth century, reoccupied for a short time, and then permanently abandoned in the early seventeenth century.

Many of the construction details indicate that builders considered the comfort and well-being of the city's occupants when constructing Gedi. The palace, for example, features sunken courts, the purpose of which was to create a longer shadow and therefore a cooler, more pleasant place to sit. Walls contained pegs for hanging carpets. In private residences, walls were thick and roofs were constructed of stamped red earth, also to create a cool living environment. All of the private residences and the palace included partitioned lavatories with washing bowls and bidets, as well as strong rooms off the owner's bedroom for storing valuables. These rooms contained no doorways; instead, one entered via a trapdoor reached by climbing a ladder. Sumps were located throughout the town to hold surface water that would otherwise have compromised the walls of structures.

A few hundred meters from the palace stood the great mosque, which was built around the middle of the fifteenth century. Constructed of stone, the roof was covered with coral tiles laid in lime concrete. A broad-bladed spear, a traditional Swahili symbol of kingship, was carved into its entranceway. Located at intervals around the inside walls were square niches in which lamps were placed for night prayers. Set in its north wall and framed with a herringbone border was an arched *qibla*, which showed the direction of Mecca, toward which Muslims are supposed to pray. On the east was a veranda and a court, which contained a well, cistern, and lavatory.

Archaeologists puzzle over why Gedi's residents abandoned it but can offer no definitive answers. Possible reasons for its downfall include a Portuguese or Galla attack, a decrease in water tables that eliminated the water supply, or some sort of epidemic. The ruins were declared a historic monument in 1927 and are open to the public.

Robert Fay

SEE ALSO

Swahili People.

Latin America and the Caribbean

Géffard, Nicolas Fabre (b. 1806; d. 1878), president of Haiti (1859-1867).

Nicolas Géffard had been a general in the Haitian army during the reign of FAUSTIN ELIE SOULOUQUE. He participated in Soulouque's unsuccessful effort to invade the DOMINICAN REPUBLIC in 1849. In 1859 Géffard led the insurrection that deposed Soulouque and subsequently assumed the presidency. In 1867 he himself was forced to flee to JAMAICA, where he lived until his death (*see* HAITI).

Africa

Geomorphology, African, the physical characteristics of the African continent.

Many of Africa's salient geomorphological features result from the continent's tectonic movement. The science of plate tectonics explores the motion of the earth's outer crust caused by convective currents in a molten substratum called the asthenosphere. Geophysicists believe that Africa once sat at the center of a massive continent, which Austrian scientist Eduard Suess named Gondwanaland. About 250 million years ago, Gondwanaland broke into the land masses of South America, Australia, Antarctica, India, Saudi Arabia, and Africa. Like puzzle pieces, their coastlines seem to line up. In addition, geologists have discovered a close correspondence in rock deposits on these continents, and paleontologists have found a similar concurrence in the fossil record.

Because the other continents drifted away from Africa, its tectonic history was less cataclysmic than that of other Gondwanaland fragments. Africa bears no fault-block mountains – that is, ranges that have arisen from the collision of tectonic plates. Instead, expansion and rifting characterize its geological history.

Although on average Africa sits 640 m (2100 ft) above sea level, higher than other continents, its continental shelf – a region of shallow shoreline water – drops off far more quickly than those of many other land masses. This limits the potential for offshore marine fishing, because shallow-water breeding grounds are small. In addition, the lack of natural harbors makes navigation difficult for large ships.

Geographers often divide the African continent in half, drawing a line from northern ANGOLA to northwestern ETHIOPIA to demarcate "high" and "low" regions. The lowland northern and western side of the continent average in height from about 300 to 460 m (about 985 to 1510 ft), while the highlands to the south and east average from 1220 to 1525 m (about 4000 to 5000 ft). Despite the division, all of sub-Saharan Africa shows a gradual downward slant from east to west.

On the "high" side, continental uplifting caused by the breakup of Gondwanaland has given rise to numerous mountain ranges and highland regions. These include the GREAT ESCARPMENT, which parallels Africa's southern coast from Angola to southern MOZAMBIQUE; the Cape Fold Mountains and the Drakensburg Mountains in SOUTH AFRICA; the Mitumba Mountains in the DEMOCRATIC REPUBLIC OF THE CONGO; and the highland regions of KENYA and ETHIOPIA. On the "low" side of the continent, highland regions in GUINEA, CAMEROON, and the SAHARA DESERT break up otherwise flat landscapes.

A system of RIFT VALLEYS adds to the dramatic topography of East Africa. The rift valleys formed as tectonic plates expanded, opening wide and steep chasms that stretch for nearly 7000 km (4350 mi), from Jordan through the Red Sea to central Mozambique. Vertical walls reach 900 m (about 2955 ft) in some places, and the valley width ranges from 32 to 80 km (20 to 50 mi). LAKE TANGANYIKA, LAKE MALAWI, and Lake Turkana all lie within these valleys. The tectonic forces

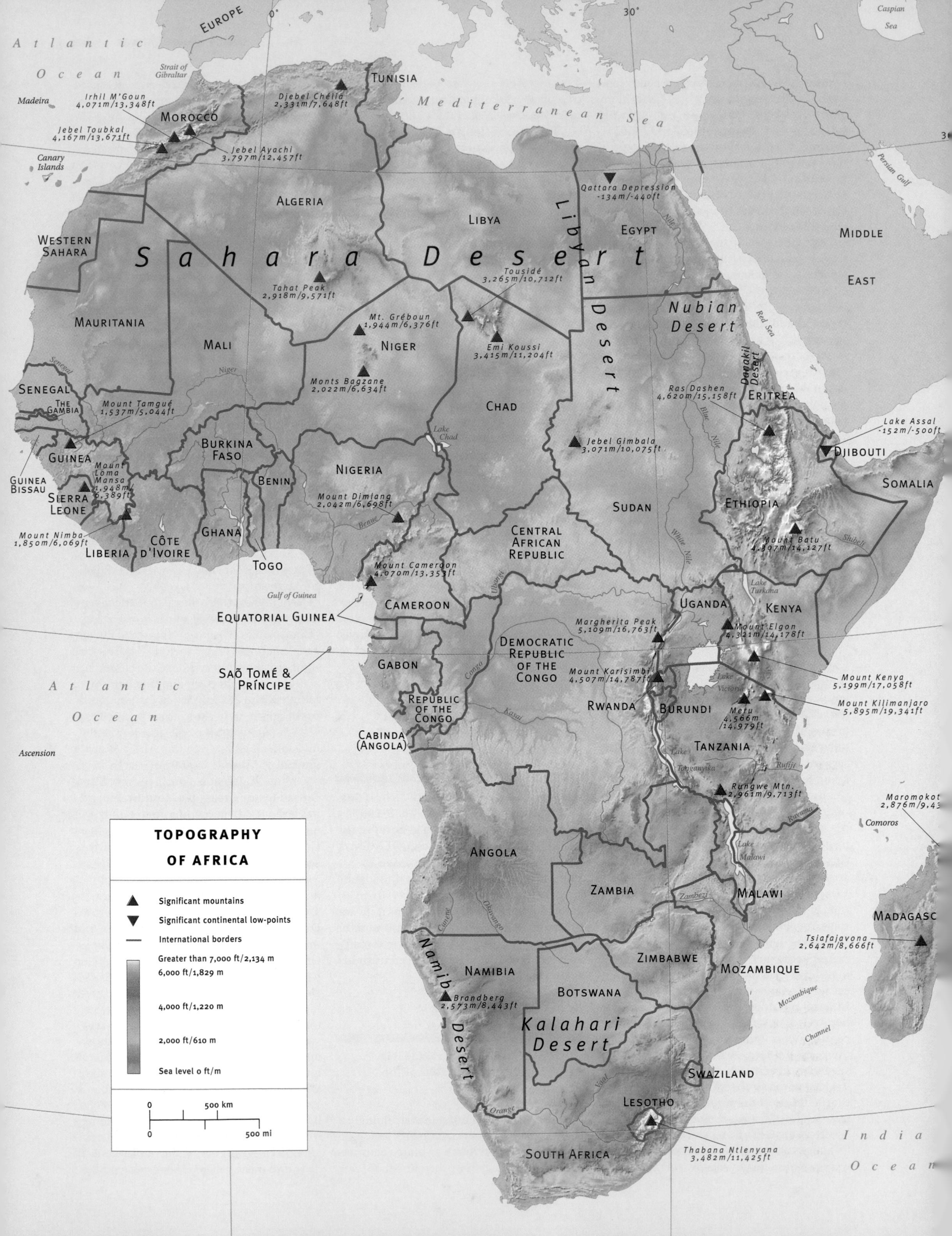

TOPOGRAPHY OF AFRICA
Significant mountains
Significant continental low-points
International borders
Greater than 7,000 ft/2,134 m
6,000 ft/1,829 m
4,000 ft/1,220 m
2,000 ft/610 m
Sea level 0 ft/m
0
500 km
0
500 mi
Europe
Atlantic Ocean
Strait of Gibraltar
Madeira
Canary Islands
Mediterranean Sea
Caspian Sea
Persian Gulf
Red Sea
Middle East
Morocco
Tunisia
Algeria
Libya
Egypt
Western Sahara
Mauritania
Mali
Niger
Chad
Sudan
Senegal
The Gambia
Guinea
Guinea Bissau
Sierra Leone
Liberia
Côte d'Ivoire
Burkina Faso
Ghana
Togo
Benin
Nigeria
Cameroon
Equatorial Guinea
São Tomé & Príncipe
Gabon
Republic of the Congo
Cabinda (Angola)
Central African Republic
Democratic Republic of the Congo
Eritrea
Djibouti
Ethiopia
Somalia
Kenya
Uganda
Rwanda
Burundi
Tanzania
Angola
Zambia
Malawi
Zimbabwe
Mozambique
Namibia
Botswana
Swaziland
Lesotho
South Africa
Sahara Desert
Libyan Desert
Nubian Desert
Danakil Desert
Namib Desert
Kalahari Desert
Gulf of Guinea
Ascension
Comoros
Mozambique Channel
India Ocean
Lake Chad
Lake Turkana
Lake Victoria
Lake Tanganyika
Lake Malawi
Niger
Senegal
Benue
Nile
Blue Nile
White Nile
Ubangi
Congo
Kasai
Rufiji
Ruvuma
Zambezi
Cunene
Okavango
Orange
Vaal
Shebeli
Irhil M'Goun 4,071m/13,348ft
Jebel Toubkal 4,167m/13,671ft
Jebel Ayachi 3,797m/12,457ft
Djebel Chélia 2,331m/7,648ft
Qattara Depression -134m/-440ft
Tahat Peak 2,918m/9,571ft
Tousidé 3,265m/10,712ft
Mt. Gréboun 1,944m/6,376ft
Emi Koussi 3,415m/11,204ft
Monts Bagzane 2,022m/6,634ft
Mount Tamgué 1,537m/5,044ft
Mount Loma Mansa 1,948m/6,389ft
Mount Nimba 1,850m/6,069ft
Mount Dimlang 2,042m/6,698ft
Mount Cameroon 4,070m/13,353ft
Jebel Gimbala 3,071m/10,075ft
Ras Dashen 4,620m/15,158ft
Lake Assal -152m/-500ft
Mount Batu 4,307m/14,127ft
Margherita Peak 5,109m/16,763ft
Mount Elgon 4,321m/14,178ft
Mount Karisimbi 4,507m/14,787ft
Mount Kenya 5,199m/17,058ft
Meru 4,566m/14,979ft
Mount Kilimanjaro 5,895m/19,341ft
Rungwe Mtn. 2,961m/9,713ft
Maromokot 2,876m/9,43
Madagasc
Tsiafajavona 2,642m/8,666ft
Brandberg 2,573m/8,443ft
Thabana Ntlenyana 3,482m/11,425ft

LARGEST LAKES IN AFRICA

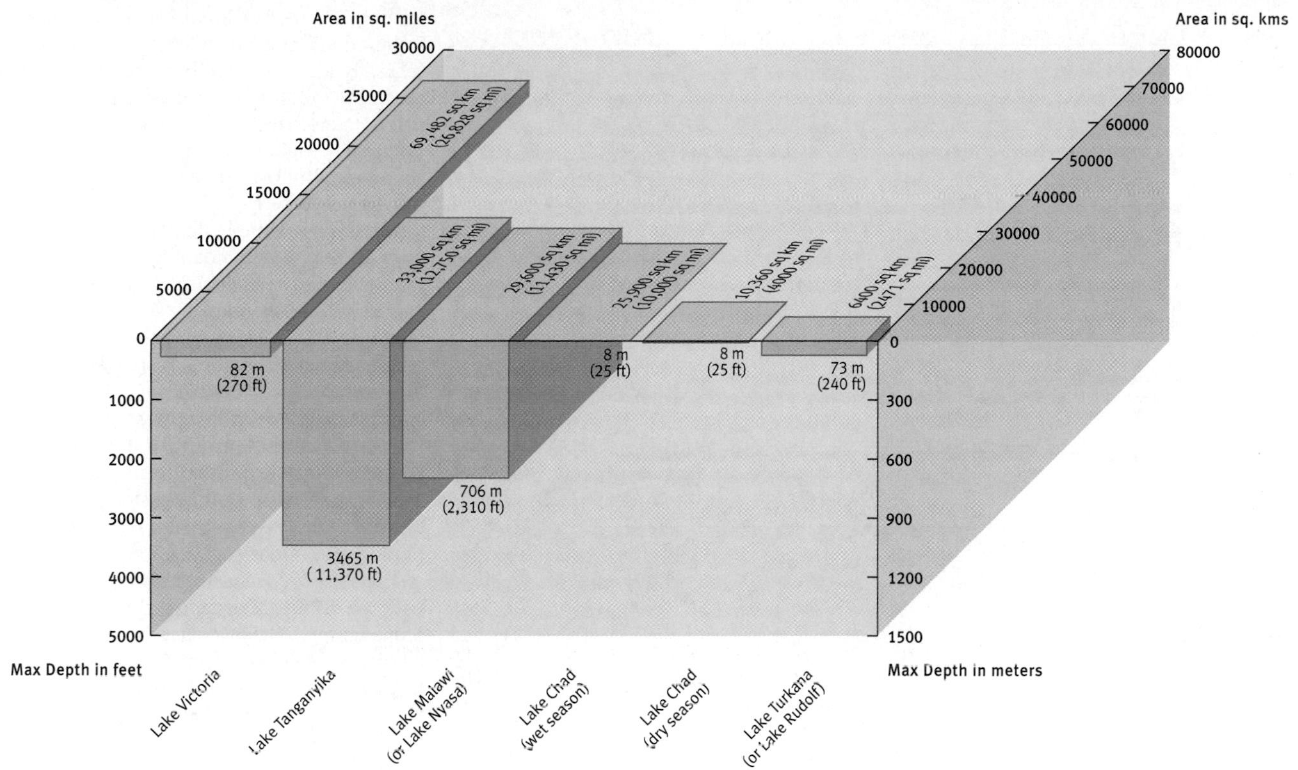

LARGEST DESERTS IN AFRICA

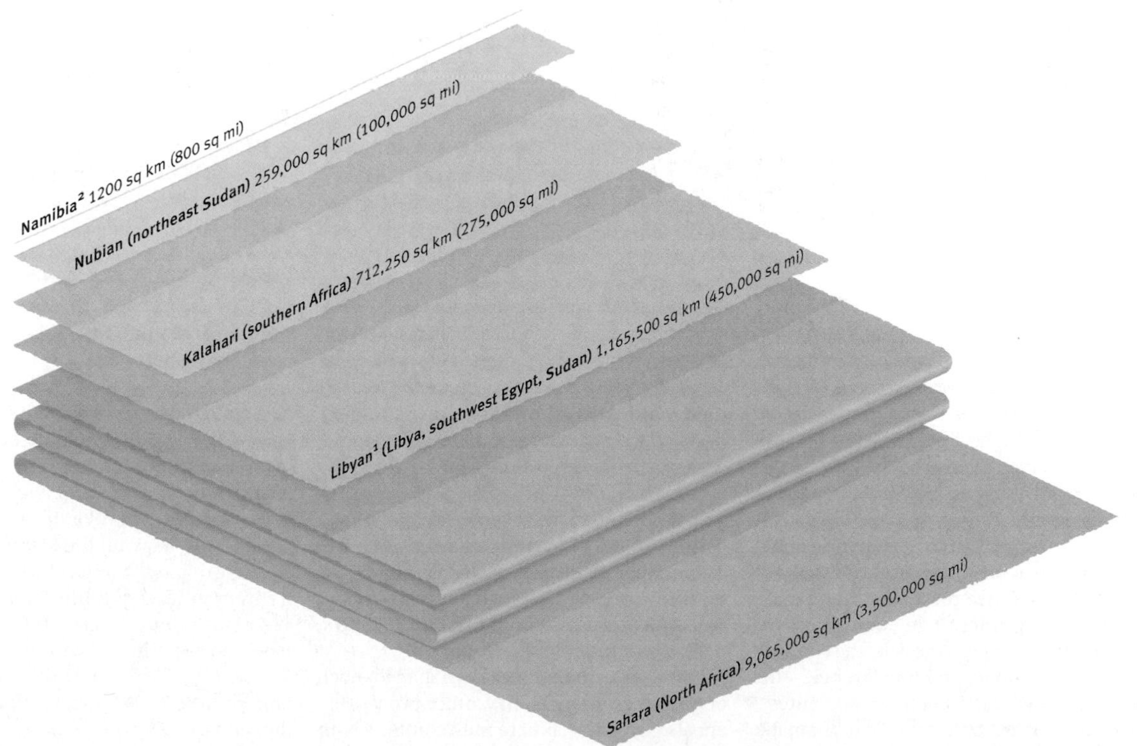

[1]Part of Sahara Desert
[2]Length; width varies from 48 to 160 km (30 to 100m)

LARGEST RIVERS IN AFRICA

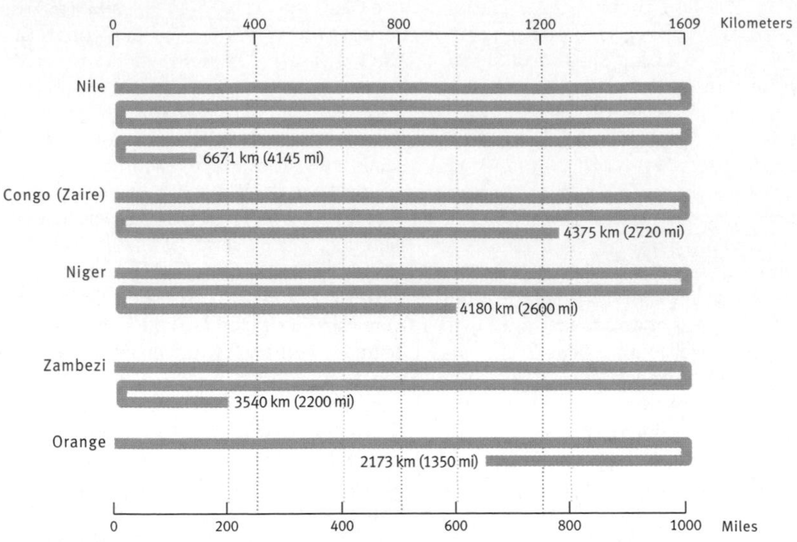

HIGHEST MOUNTAINS IN AFRICA

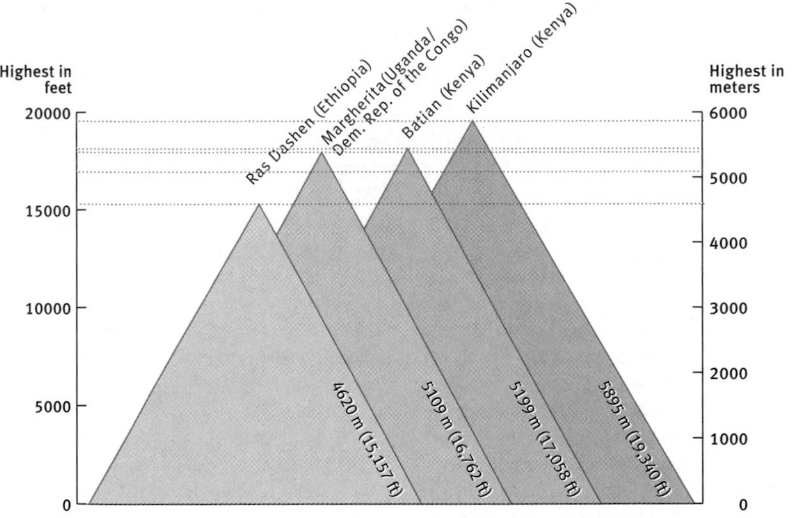

behind the rift have caused extreme displacements of geological strata, allowing paleontologists and anthropologists access to prehistoric fossil records. Volcanic activity also contributed to the rifting process and created Africa's highest peaks, MOUNT KENYA and Mount Kilimanjaro. Although the change is imperceptible in human time, it is rapid for geologic time – and soon, geologically, East Africa will break from the continent, much as MADAGASCAR "recently" did.

The rivers of Africa reveal another peculiarity of the continent's geological history. Of the five major rivers – the Nile, the Orange, the Niger, the Congo, and the Zambezi – the last three follow odd and circuitous routes before draining into an ocean. Their dramatic changes of direction over long distances suggest that in ages past they drained into landlocked basins rather than into the ocean. Geomorphologists suspect that only with subsequent uplift did these rivers find their way to the coast. The presence of such basins across the continent lends credence to the theory. Broad shallow basin formations in CHAD, SUDAN, and the KALAHARI DESERT serve as the sole repositories for waters from inland rivers.

Because the major rivers of Africa follow twisting routes, they prohibit extensive navigation. Some of the same waterfalls and rapids that prevent their use as transportation, however, hold great potential for hydroelectric power generation.

Although tectonic forces have shaped much of Africa's geomorphology, other processes are also at work. Climate may combine with chemistry to produce dramatic formations (*see* CLIMATE OF AFRICA). In Africa's Guinea Savanna regions, inselbergs – solitary, dome-like outcroppings of rock – arise when weather causes some minerals to deteriorate faster than others. Climate also influences soil production: when winds and rain erode rocks, they create the mineral particles that combine with organic material to become soil. Because the "parent material" from rocks contains the mineral component of soil, rock composition plays an important role in soil fertility.

The slopes of many highland regions, for example, support abundant flora and in some places intensive agriculture, because their volcanic, basaltic bedrock contains high amounts of iron-magnesium minerals. Soil erosion and a phenomenon called *leaching*, however, prohibit any simple correlation between bedrock and fertility: when moisture runs downhill or drains into the watertable, it often takes mineral content with it. For this reason, the soil on hilly slopes of rain forest is often less rich than the proliferation of plant life might suggest.

The soils of Africa correspond roughly with the biomes that define the continent's biogeography. Oxisols exist throughout 40 percent of the tropical rain forests and contain high amounts of iron and aluminum oxides. Ultisols predominate in subhumid or Guinea Savanna regions. They are often less weathered and thus more fertile than oxisols, even if they contain less biomass. Altisols, named for their high aluminum content, occur in savanna regions. When well maintained, they can support extensive agriculture. Vertisols abound in subhumid to arid regions. They are rich in minerals, but their high clay content makes them difficult to cultivate. The aridisols of the deserts and the SAHEL, finally, contain little organic material.

Eric Bennett

SEE ALSO

Biogeography of Africa; Congo River; Kilimanjaro; Niger River; Nile River; Zambezi River.

Africa

Gerima, Haile (b. March 4, 1946, Gondar, Ethiopia), Ethiopian film director, critic, and professor.

As a child, Haile Gerima acted in his father's troupe, performing across ETHIOPIA. In 1967 he moved to the United States and two years later enrolled in the University of California at Los Angeles (UCLA) drama school. There he became familiar with the ideas of MALCOLM X and wrote plays about slavery and black militancy. After reading the revolutionary theory of THIRD CINEMA, however, Gerima began to experiment with film.

Gerima returned to Ethiopia in 1974 to film *Harvest: 3,000 Years*, his first full-length film and the only one of his works to be shot in Africa. Although famine and the recent military overthrow of Emperor Haile Selassie placed severe restrictions on the film crew, the final result was a sophisticated examination, through the story of a village that finally overthrows its feudal landlord, of the centuries-old oppression of the Ethiopian peasantry. The film was well received on the international film circuit and won the 1976 Oscar Micheaux Award for Best Feature Film from the Black Filmmakers Hall of Fame.

Since *Harvest*, most of Gerima's film projects have examined problems facing African Americans. Although he is Ethiopia's best-known film director, he has spent most of his career in the United States. In 1976 he released *Bush Mama*, a black-and-white film about the political awakening of a black welfare mother. That same year, he joined the faculty of HOWARD UNIVERSITY. In 1977 he released a documentary on the case of the Wilmington 10, *Wilmington 10-USA 10,000*, which he made with the help of students at Howard University and volunteers from the local community. In 1982 he finished *Ashes and Embers*, a story about African American Vietnam veterans, and in 1985 released *After Winter: Sterling Brown*, a documentary about Sterling Brown, also made with student cooperation. His recent works include *Sankofa* (1994) and the forthcoming *The Death of Tarzan, Donald Duck and Shirley Temple* (working title), a documentary on the history of film in Africa, and *In the Eye of the Storm* (working title), about European colonialism in Africa.

Although Gerima has worked and lived in the United States since 1969, he maintains close ties with other African film directors. An active member of the Fédération Panafricaine des Cinéastes and the Comité Africain des Cinéastes, he has coordinated several colloquiums and meetings of African film directors in the United States. His own studio, Mypheduh Films, Inc., is one of the leading distributors of films by Africans and African Americans in the United States.

Elizabeth Heath

SEE ALSO

Cinema, African; Slavery in the United States; Haile Selassie I; Brown, Sterling Allen; Vietnam War.

Africa

German East Africa. Former name for the mainland of present-day TANZANIA.

Africa

German Southwest Africa. Former name of NAMIBIA.

Europe

Germany, a country of northern Europe where blacks have had a presence for centuries.

Although there is thought to have been a black presence in the area that would become Germany since the time of Julius Caesar (whose Italian troops conquered parts of the Rhineland, 58-50 B.C.E.), blacks first began to appear in larger numbers in the Middle Ages and the Renaissance. Contacts came, at first, through trade with Africa, and Africans began to appear in art (portraits of Africans living in Germany) and literature (the courtly epic *Parzival*, written in the twelfth and thirteenth centuries) early on. Germans also engaged in the slave trade. Traders brought Africans back in order to prove they had visited the continent and made "presents" of Africans to royal courts; *Hofmohren*, "court Moors," were not uncommon. Often, such court Moors were treated as servants or buffoons. An exception was ANTON WILHELM AMO (from the area known today as GHANA), who was given to the Dukes von Wolfenbüttel by the Dutch West India Company in 1707. Amo studied at the universities in Halle and Wittenberg and went on to become a leading German Enlightenment scholar.

Germany came late to its colonial empire, acquiring TOGO, CAMEROON, German East Africa (present-day TANZANIA), and German Southwest Africa (present-day NAMIBIA) by 1885 in the SCRAMBLE FOR AFRICA. The Berlin Conference, called in 1884 by German chancellor Otto von Bismarck, established African colonial boundaries (*see* COLONIAL RULE). This empire would last only 35 years, until the end of World War I (1914-1918). But the acquisition of African colonies, German emigration there, and German missionary activities increased encounters with blacks and led to a spate of travel literature that provided Germans with a largely stereotypical picture of Africa. German attitudes toward their colonial subjects were paternalistic and, of course, racist: Germans came more and more to see blacks as inferior and exotic – part "noble savage," part primitive barbarian.

German colonial policy was extremely brutal. A series of revolts in its colonies in the early part of the century, such as that of the HERERO in present-day Namibia, were put down with great cruelty and loss of life. Mixed-race children born in the colonies were not recognized as Germans. Germany, unlike FRANCE or England, did not grant citizenship to its colonial subjects, and to this day German citizenship depends on blood descent, a fact that continues to shape German attitudes toward race. Still, colonial Africans did develop bonds with Germany; even today, in fact, the Herero of Namibia wear German dress. Africans from the colonies came to Germany to study, and some remained.

After World War I Germany was stripped of its colonies. Equally important for the history of black Germans, the Versailles Treaty that ended the war provided for a 15-year occupation of the Rhineland region by the victorious powers. Among the French occupying forces, a large contingent – as many as 40,000 – hailed from France's African colonies. The Germans decried the "humiliation" of occupation by black troops, calling it "the black disgrace," and the public image of these soldiers, promulgated through the press, public statements, and political propaganda, was that of barbaric rapists. The accusation of rape was more fiction than reality, connected in part with myths of black sexuality; few incidents of rape were actually recorded. The presence of black troops did, however, result in the birth of a number of mixed-race children. In reality, Germans were most outraged that the French would degrade Germans by forcing upon them occupiers of what they considered an inferior race. There were those even in Germany who pointed out the hypocrisy of condemning French barbarity while ignoring that of German soldiers, both in the colonies and within Germany itself.

The French occupation left behind between 500 and 800 children of mixed race, popularly known as "Rhineland bastards." Even in the Weimar Republic of the 1920s, some Germans advocated sterilization of these children – an approach growing out of the eugenic movement popular throughout Europe and North America at the time. Theories of racial purity and the dangers of mixed blood were already in circulation. Under the National Socialists (also known as Nazis), they would become determinative.

When the Nazis took power in 1933, the propagation of the Aryan race became a priority; at the same time, steps were taken to ensure the elimination of what they considered degenerate influences on the race. At first Nazi policy toward the small number of blacks in Germany was cautious. Considerations of foreign policy and economics required that Africans from the colonies or elsewhere in Europe be treated respectfully, and this also affected the treatment of Afro-Germans.

This caution disappeared as German foreign policy became more aggressive after 1937. However, in contrast to their program with regard to the Jews, the Nazis did not aim to exterminate black Germans. Their main fear in regard to blacks was racial mixing, and their solution was sterilization (*see* NATIONAL SOCIALIST STERILIZATION POLICIES IN GERMANY). A law already existed mandating the forced sterilization of certain groups deemed "unfit," including the mentally ill. Though it shared the same ideological origins, the program to sterilize the black Germans took place separately, in great secrecy. Parental permission, though ostensibly required, was most likely coerced. Ultimately, it is thought that roughly 385 of the Rhineland children were sterilized.

Black Germans were also persecuted in other ways under the Nazis; often they were deprived of schooling or jobs, and some were deported to concentration camps. (The plight of blacks in Nazi Germany was portrayed in the character played by black German actress Karin Boyd in the 1981 German-Hungarian movie *Mephisto*, directed by Istvan Szabo.) Others survived by working as actors (a number of films with colonial themes were made during the period) or in circuses.

Following the war, victorious Allied soldiers once again occupied Germany, and again, in West Germany, many of these were black – specifically, black American – (*see* MILITARY, BLACKS IN THE AMERICAN). Once again, one legacy of occupation was several thousand mixed-race children, most of whom remained in West Germany with their white German mothers when their GI fathers returned to the United States. While racism against them was no longer institutionalized, the "occupation babies" still faced numerous hurdles. Ignorance and paternalism, as well as a sometimes unconscious racism, combined to make the situation of these children and their mothers difficult. Some West Germans even suggested sending these children abroad to solve what was seen as a "problem."

In the early 1950s, when many of the children entered school, they became the focus of scholarly and media attention. Cartoons and popular articles, as well as films such as *Toxi* (the story of the child of a black American soldier and German mother who is adopted by a German family), attempted to inform the public about these children and to create sympathy. Often, however, they also promoted traditional stereotypes or, like *Toxi*, painted an unrealistically positive picture.

As this generation of black Germans grew older, they shared the experience of stereotyping, discrimination, and being treated as different by a society that defined itself as white. At the same time, West Germany was their country; they were socialized as Germans and had internalized German attitudes and values. The lack of a cohesive Afro-German culture or community prevented the formation of a separate identity, or even an awareness of similar experiences.

This began to change in the 1980s. In 1984 African American poet Audre Lorde taught several courses at the Free University in West Berlin, where she met black German women. Her presence sparked a process of growing awareness that led to the 1986 book *Farbe Bekennen: Afro-deutsche Frauen auf den Spuren ihrer Geschichte* (Showing Our Colors: Afro-German Women Speak Out), by May Opitz, Katharina Oguntoye, and Dagmar Schultz. For the first time, a group of Afro-German women wrote about the history of blacks in Germany and interviewed black German women of different ages and backgrounds. The phrase "Afro-German" was coined by Lorde and the book's authors, replacing words like "mulatto" and *Mischling*, or "half-breed." In the same year, a group of Afro-Germans founded the Initiative Schwarze Deutsche (Black German Initiative, or ISD), a group dedicated to breaking through the isolation in which black Germans had been living, providing a supportive environment in which to explore their identity, and disseminating information about blacks in Germany. Around 1993 the group changed its name to Initiative of Black Germans and Blacks in Germany to include blacks from other backgrounds living in Germany. ISD now has chapters in most major German cities and sponsors a yearly Black History Month. Soon after ISD was formed, a group of black women founded the black women's organization ADEFRA, which publishes the magazine *Afrekete*.

Meanwhile, a parallel process had taken place in East Germany. Students from African countries such as Cameroon, Ghana, and NIGERIA began to be sent to study in East Germany in the 1950s and 1960s, followed in the 1970s and 1980s by students from ANGOLA, MOZAMBIQUE, and other socialist-ruled countries. Relationships with East German women resulted in the birth of mixed-race children there as well. Often the students were required to return to their home countries after completing their studies, so that, as in West Germany, the children frequently grew up without their black parent. They experienced the same isolation as black children in the West. Though racism was officially forbidden in East Germany, black Germans felt it nevertheless, but there was no opportunity for them to come together as a group.

With the fall of the Berlin Wall in 1989, Afro-Germans from the East made contact with the ISD, and some founded organizations of their own, such as I. G. Farbig in Leipzig. These East-West contacts were not immune to the frictions that affected all contacts between East and West Germans; Afro-Germans from the East, for example, rejected the West German preference for excluding whites from their groups. However, Afro-Germans in both parts of the country have been affected by, and have joined in resisting, the racism and xenophobia that grew exponentially following the fall of the Wall. Racist behavior and attacks on foreigners and anyone who looks "different" have risen in both eastern and western Germany, increasing the insecurity of the black German population.

The appearance of *Farbe Bekennen* and the founding of the ISD raised awareness of the existence of an Afro-German minority in Germany. However, united Germany's roughly 300,000 black residents (this includes Africans and Americans as well as Afro-Germans, though no precise figures are available) are still not a highly visible presence. In recent years the black television moderators Cherno Jobatey of Berlin and Arabella Kiesbauer of Austria have become popular personalities in Germany, and in the early 1990s a black German hip hop group called Advanced Chemistry, based in Heidelberg, produced several popular songs about racism. But they are among the few black Germans in visible positions. Police forces in some German cities have made highly publicized efforts to recruit members of minority groups, including black Germans.

The greatest difficulty for Afro-Germans continues to lie in German society's vision of itself. Despite the fact that it has become increasingly ethnically diverse over the years, Germans still generally do not consider themselves a multiracial society, and German is still synonymous with white in the popular mind, both within and outside Germany. Black Germans complain that white Germans view black Germans' problem as one of hostility to foreigners rather than racism. This view implicitly relegates nonwhite Germans to the status of outsiders, even when they were born and raised in Germany, holding German passports and citizenship. At the same time the prevailing German view refuses to recognize that race hatred, not foreignness, is the basis of the hostility that Afro-Germans face.

Afro-Germans have begun in recent years to reclaim their history and to develop an identity based, in part, on their shared experience of belonging to a culture that does not entirely accept them. In years to come, the question will be whether German society will come to expand its definition of "German" to encompass different origins, and thereby also embrace Germans of African heritage.

Belinda Cooper

SEE ALSO

Transatlantic Slave Trade; Initiative of Black Germans and Blacks in Germany; Great Britain; Italy; Netherlands, The; Eugenics; Hip Hop in the United States; Lorde, Audre Geraldine; Racial Stereotypes; Berlin Conference of 1884-1885.

Africa

Ghana, a coastal West African country that borders TOGO to the east, BURKINA FASO to the north, and CÔTE D'IVOIRE to the west.

Known as the Gold Coast until it achieved independence in 1957, the area that is now Ghana was one of the richest in Africa before its conquest by the British. By the early 1800s the wealthy and powerful ASANTE Empire controlled most of the country's modern territory. During the colonial period, Ghanaians led the struggle against British colonialism. As the first European colony south of the Sahara to gain independence, Ghana inspired nationalist movements throughout Africa and the world. Yet despite its wealth and proud traditions, Ghana, like other African countries, has struggled with persistent poverty, mounting debt, and political instability and repression. The AFRICAN SOCIALISM espoused by its independence leader, KWAME NKRUMAH, brought political and economic disaster. In recent years the country has seen economic recovery and democratization, but a dependence on foreign capital still keeps Ghana from reclaiming its former power and prosperity.

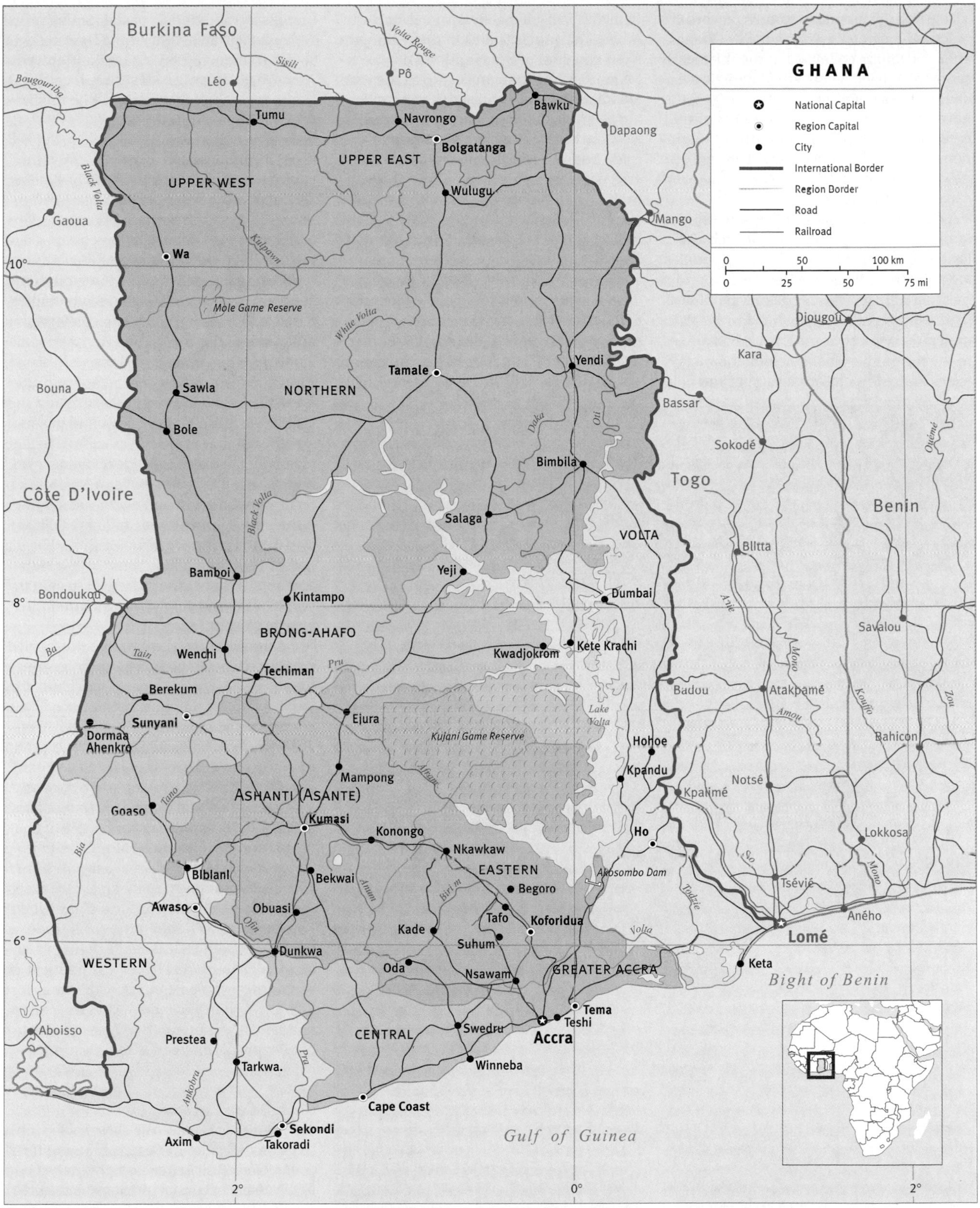

Early History

Archaeological evidence demonstrates a human presence in modern Ghana for at least the past 35,000 years. Agriculture reached the region by 2000 B.C.E., and iron production began by the first century C.E. A mix of PASTORALISM and cereal cultivation has predominated in the northern savanna region, while the cultivation of roots, tubers, and palm tree crops, supplemented by hunting and fishing, has prevailed in the southern forest zone.

Many Ghanaian ethnic groups have traditions of migration from outside the region before the arrival of Europeans. For example, the DAGOMBA supposedly came from the northeast, while both the GA and EWE have traditions that locate their origins to the east. The name Ghana refers to an ancient empire centered in present-day MALI and

MAURITANIA whose descendants, according to legend, migrated to present-day Ghana after the empire collapsed in the thirteenth century. Archaeological and linguistic evidence suggests, however, that existing groups have continuously inhabited the country for at least 2000 years. Traditions of migration may refer to relatively small groups of newcomers who achieved hegemony over existing populations.

Traditionally, lineages, or clans, have held land communally and commanded the loyalty of their members. The AKAN peoples are matrilineal, while the Ga, the Ewe, and most northern groups are basically patrilineal. By the fourteenth century Muslim MANDE traders (known also as the DYULA) had arrived in the region to exchange cloth and metal wares from the SAHEL for cola nuts and gold from the Akan, ultimately destined for North Africa. The earliest states in the region, the Akan kingdom of Bono and the northern Mamprusi kingdom, arose during the fourteenth century to control this rich trade.

The arrival of Europeans selling superior weaponry shifted the focus of the Akan gold trade from the Muslim north to the southern coast during the sixteenth century and probably stimulated an Akan expansion toward the coast. Portuguese explorers arrived in 1471 and established trading posts soon afterward. The Portuguese traded firearms and slaves from other parts of Africa for gold dust. Slaves labored to increase the wealth of the Akan states and firearms enabled the states to expand. By 1642 the Dutch had displaced the Portuguese from the region, and by 1670 Great Britain and Denmark had established additional coastal trading posts. Because the Dutch, British, and Danes sought slaves to meet a growing demand in the New World colonies, slaves replaced gold as the region's main export, while firearms remained the main import.

An Asante chief sits enthroned, clad in royal kente cloth and covered in gold regalia. *Leo de Wys, Inc./Richard Saunders*

The growth of the slave trade provoked wars of conquest. Firearms facilitated the capture of prisoners who could be sold as slaves for more firearms. By the late seventeenth century the powerful Akan kingdom of Akwamu had conquered the coastal Ga and Ewe, who subsequently adopted Akan state institutions. By the end of the eighteenth century, however, Asante, an Akan empire based in the interior, had conquered Akwamu and parts of the coast, though the coastal Fante (another Akan group) resisted Asante. Asante also conquered large areas of the north, including the kingdoms of Gonja and Dagomba. Conquered regions had to send slaves each year to Asante as tribute. Asante maintained trade connections not only with Europeans on the coast, but also with Muslim regions to the north and northeast. By the eighteenth century HAUSA traders had taken over the interior trade formerly carried by the Dyula. Their demand for slaves, cola nuts, and other Asante exports helped sustain the empire even after the British banned the coastal slave trade.

On the coast the slave trade transformed traditional social relations. An indigenous but increasingly westernized merchant class arose, including the "merchant princes" who controlled the slave trade. Merchants organized plantation agriculture and manufacture to provision the slave traders, and a working class developed to provide the necessary labor. An influential "mulatto" stratum arose through the intermarriage of European merchants and local women. Members of this group often had the advantage of a Western education and served as mediators between European merchants and local elites. When European states banned the slave trade, as did Denmark in 1802, Great Britain in 1807, and the Netherlands in 1814, a political economic crisis ensued. Coastal states lost their main source of income and weaponry and became vulnerable to Asante, whose gold exports financed a steady supply of firearms.

GOLD COAST COLONY

Attempting to replace the slave trade with "legitimate trade" in British-manufactured goods, Great Britain increasingly intervened in the affairs of coastal African states. In 1821 the British government assumed control of Gold Coast possessions from the private African Company of Merchants. Because Asante incursions in the coastal region threatened commercial interests, Great Britain initiated the First British-Asante

War (1822-1826). A peace treaty in 1831 ended Asante claims to the coast and brought an upswing in trade, missionary activity, and British power on the coast. In 1844 Fante rulers agreed to British legal jurisdiction; in 1850 Great Britain purchased the Danish coastal possessions and established an informal colonial government.

Great Britain's efforts to extend its power and gain control of the gold trade led to the Second British-Asante War (1863-1873). After Great Britain ceded its western coastal possessions in 1867 to the Dutch, who remained passive allies of Asante, Fante leaders formed the Fante Confederation, with a constitution based on European models, to resist the Dutch and Asante. When the Dutch abandoned their possessions in 1872, the confederation dissolved. In 1874 the British

ABOVE: Kwame Nkrumah, president of Ghana from 1960 to 1966, was a crusader against colonialism and for African solidarity. *CORBIS/Bettmann*
RIGHT: For centuries kente cloth has been made from strip textiles woven by Asante men and boys. Cloths called "Asasia" are made entirely of silk and may only be worn by royalty. *CORBIS/Seattle Art Museum*

burned the Asante capital of Kumasi, forced Asante to accept a humiliating treaty, and declared the Gold Coast (south of Asante) a Crown colony. British victory ended the power and prestige of the Asante state, which suffered a series of crippling succession struggles, while Asante's northern vassals, including Bono, Gonja, and Dagomba, broke away from the empire.

As the Germans and French seized interior regions to the east, north, and west of the Gold Coast in the SCRAMBLE FOR AFRICA, British merchants sought to extend COLONIAL RULE over the interior to protect markets for British goods and exploit the rich Asante gold fields. In 1896, after the Asante refused to accept a British protectorate, Great Britain sent an expedition to Kumasi to demand full payment of the reparations stipulated in the 1874 treaty. When the Asante king failed to meet this demand, the British sent him into exile. An Asante noblewoman, YAA ASANTEWA, organized a national struggle to resist British rule in the Third British-Asante War (1900). After heavy losses on both sides, Asante surrendered for the last time and the British exiled Asantewa, along with the entire Asante leadership. Between 1896 and 1910 Great Britain gradually conquered the peoples to the north of Asante, many of them former Asante tributaries. In 1902 the British annexed Asante and the Northern Territories. When Great Britain acquired the western third of German Togoland after World War I as a mandate, the colonial government at Accra ruled the entire territory of modern Ghana.

During the 1890s the British government attempted to claim uncultivated lineage land to lease to British lumber and mining firms. In response, the Aborigines' Rights Protection Society, composed of the coastal elite in alliance with interior chiefs, successfully defended lineage land rights. Thereafter, mining firms were required to secure leases from chiefs and lineage heads, whose wealth and power grew as a consequence. During the colonial period, British firms mined not only gold, but diamonds, manganese, and, beginning in the 1940s, bauxite. British firms also exploited the Gold Coast's forests for timber.

The coastal elite's resistance to land alienation formed part of a larger and less successful effort to resist economic displacement by better-financed European rivals. As foreign competition undermined their commercial strength, members of the coastal elite acquired a Western education in mission schools or Great Britain. Increasingly, they found employment as professionals and mid-level civil servants, since British appointees monopolized the top posts.

After European powers banned the slave trade, Gold Coasters sought other commodities to exchange for European manufactures. While Asante could rely on the export of gold until the British conquest, residents of the coastal region turned to the production of cash crops. Until the 1890s the most important of these was the oil palm, tended by indigenous cultivators. By the turn of the century peasants in Eweland (then largely part of German Togoland), Akwapim, and Asante were turning to the production of COCOA. By the 1920s the Gold Coast produced more than half of the world's cocoa.

The cultivation of cocoa further transformed social relations. In Asante and neighboring regions, cocoa production increased the income and power of the chiefs and lineage heads who controlled the land. In the southeast, among the Akwapim and Ewe, cocoa production sustained a rural middle class of small farmers, some of them wealthy enough to employ migrant wage laborers. Migrant laborers traveled to the cocoa-growing regions, mainly from the interior Northern Territories and northern Togo.

The Northern Territories remained largely undeveloped, mostly because its distance from ports made the transport of cash crops uneconomical. Its inhabitants relied primarily on subsistence farming, supplemented by migrant labor in the mines and cocoa groves of the south. British authorities viewed the north as a labor reserve and relied heavily on northern forced labor (until the 1920s) or coerced labor (for which chiefs received a per capita fee) for the operation of mines and the construction of transportation infrastructure. This export of labor probably perpetuated the north's underdevelopment.

Shoppers stroll past wares displayed at the market in Kumasi, Ghana's second largest city and the former capital of the Asante Empire. *Christian Sappa/Rapho*

The colonial transportation infrastructure facilitated the export of minerals and cash crops. The Gold Coast's first railway connected coastal Sekondi with interior gold-mining districts in 1898, and was extended to Kumasi in 1903. By the 1920s the network connected Accra with the interior, including cocoa-producing regions. In 1928 workers completed the Gold Coast's first deep-water harbor at Takoradi, and during the 1920s and 1930s the government commissioned new roads in cocoa-growing districts.

A nationalist opposition began to form during the 1920s, when Great Britain introduced indirect rule, delegating local administration to "traditional" authorities. In the Asante region and most of the Northern Territories, where chiefs retained political and economic power, this policy met with little opposition. On the coast, however, members of the powerful mercantile and professional class – who had long since displaced traditional chiefs as the regional elite – resented their continued exclusion from real power despite educational and professional qualifications that equaled or exceeded those of British officials. Members of this group, together with representatives from THE GAMBIA, SIERRA LEONE, and NIGERIA, founded the National Congress of British West Africa, demanding majority rule. In response to these demands, Great Britain agreed to limited minority representation for the local elite in the Gold Coast's Legislative Council.

During the 1940s the movement toward independence gained momentum. As the Gold Coast suffered economically to support the British war effort, and Gold Coast recruits fought alongside British soldiers in the name of "democracy" and "liberty" denied them at home, many perceived the moral bankruptcy of colonialism. Meanwhile, the successful independence struggles of Ireland, India, and Pakistan inspired Gold Coast nationalists. Joseph Danquah and other leading nationalists founded the United Gold Coast Convention (UGCC) in 1947 and invited Kwame Nkrumah to lead the group's campaign for representative self-government. When British

LEFT: Built by the Portuguese in the fifteenth century and later owned by the Dutch and English, Fort Elmina held Africans before shipment to the slave markets of the Americas. *Frank Fournier*
BELOW LEFT: A Ghanaian fisherwoman dries sardines on a rack. *CORBIS/Liba Taylor*

troops fired on demonstrators in 1948 and riots erupted, the British jailed Nkrumah, Danquah, and other leaders for "incitement."

The young Nkrumah's radical populism proved threatening to the coastal elite and Asante chiefs who dominated the UGCC, and when they ousted him in 1949, he founded the Convention People's Party (CPP). The CPP organized workers and farmers for the first time in a mass movement for independence and staged strikes and other actions. British authorities again imprisoned Nkrumah for "subversion" and "sedition." The British governor convened a committee of the elite, who drew up a new constitution in 1951 providing for internal self-rule and a legislative assembly that reserved large blocks of seats for chiefs and British officials. However, the CPP won an overwhelming majority of elected seats in 1951, and British authorities released Nkrumah from prison to serve as prime minister. In 1954 Nkrumah's government introduced a new constitution providing for direct election by universal suffrage. As prime minister during the mid-1950s, Nkrumah advocated a mixed economy, sought to attract foreign capital, and focused on the modernization of agriculture and rural development.

Nkrumah and the CPP faced increasing internal opposition. The National Liberation Movement (NLM), led by Kofi Busia and based in the Asante region, opposed Nkrumah's government in the 1954 elections. The NLM criticized the CPP for its perceived dominance by southerners, its slighting of the Asante region in legislative representation, and its limitations on the powers of chiefs. The NLM pushed for the establishment of a federal state with regional governments, while the CPP advocated a unitary state. Meanwhile, Ewe activists, concentrated in the southern part of the British Togoland Mandate, pushed for unification with the Ewe of French Togo.

In separate 1956 plebiscites, however, a majority of British Togoland residents voted for unification with an independent Gold Coast (though a majority in Ewe districts opposed this), and 70 percent of voters in the remainder of the Gold Coast territories voted for independence according to the CPP's unitary (nonfederalist) platform. In 1957 Great Britain granted independence within the British Commonwealth to the Gold Coast, now renamed Ghana.

Republic of Ghana

As the first African colony south of the Sahara to gain independence, Ghana became a model and an inspiration for movements throughout the continent seeking an end to colonial rule. Under Nkrumah, Ghana espoused nonalignment. Nkrumah advocated political unification of Africa under his own leadership and played an instrumental role in the creation of the Organization of African Unity (OAU) in 1963.

Domestically, Nkrumah espoused "African socialism." Strong export earnings during the late 1950s provided the basis for nationalization of private firms, the creation of a large parastatal sector, an attempt at industrialization, and infrastructural expansion. Projects completed under Nkrumah's leadership included the large modern port at Tema, expansion of the road and rail network, and Akosombo Dam, which created Lake Volta, the world's largest artificial lake. The dam supplies hydroelectric power to much of Ghana, as well as to neighboring Togo and Benin. Road construction in the north facilitated the production of food crops for sale in the more urbanized south. The government expanded health and social services, and Ghana became the first African nation south of the Sahara to provide free and compulsory primary education. By the early 1960s a drop in cocoa prices undermined the financial viability of these ambitious programs, while Nkrumah's use of development programs as patronage for often unqualified favorites escalated costs. By the mid-1960s Ghana's debt threatened its financial stability, and living standards declined.

After independence, Nkrumah moved to suppress opposition. Nkrumah and the CPP drew support mostly from farmers, workers, and market women in the southern coastal region, while the regional elite and their clients, both on the coast and in the interior, opposed the government. Shortly after independence, the Avoidance of Discrimination Act (1957) banned all regional parties. Consequently, the opposition merged to form the United Party, led by Kofi Busia. In 1958 the Emergency Powers Act and the Preventive Detention Act gave the government sweeping powers to detain dissidents without trial. Many suffered torture or even death in detention. Meanwhile, Nkrumah assumed increasingly autocratic powers. With the establishment of a republic in 1960, Nkrumah became head of both government and state. He assumed sole control of the CPP and banned all opposition within the party. In 1964 the government secured majority approval for a referendum that declared Ghana a one-party state under the CPP.

With opposition to Nkrumah's corrupt and increasingly unpopular government effectively outlawed, a joint military-police junta seized power in a 1966 coup that in Ghana was widely believed to have been backed by the Central Intelligence Agency (CIA) of the United States. This junta, known as the National Liberation Council (NLC), suspended Nkrumah's major development projects, released political detainees, investigated official corruption, and proclaimed a market economy. Trade liberalization and reductions in taxes won favor among small proprietors and market women, and chiefs enjoyed the restoration of many powers Nkrumah's government had removed. The NLC's austerity program won it financial assistance from the International Monetary Fund (IMF) and World Bank but caused widespread unemployment and hardship. As strikes escalated in 1968 and 1969, the junta created an assembly to draft a constitution for a return to civilian government.

In a 1969 election from which Nkrumah's supporters were banned, Kofi Busia became prime minister. Backed by a coalition of the southern elite and Akan chiefs, Busia's government continued the NLC's economic conservatism. When another drop in the price of cocoa precipitated a financial crisis in 1971, his government raised prices and interest rates, cut government spending, and devalued the currency. A wave of unrest culminated in Busia's removal from office in a 1972 coup staged by troops unhappy with cuts in military spending.

The new military government, known as the National Redemption Council (NRC) and led by Colonel Acheampong, excluded the leadership of the earlier NLC and reversed many of its policies. The NRC nationalized several private companies in 1972, including the largest gold-mining firm, and declared a moratorium on debt payments, which led the IMF to suspend its credit. The NRC suppressed opposition with a Subversion Decree and a Protective Detention Decree. In 1975 Acheampong transferred power to a new Supreme Military Council (SMC), which excluded his rivals in the NRC. Although the military government enjoyed brief popularity when rising cocoa prices revived the economy in 1972, ongoing economic mismanagement, corruption, rising oil prices, and a persistent drought only deepened Ghana's economic woes in the long run.

In the late 1970s professionals and students held a series of nationwide strikes to demand an end to military rule. In 1977 the SMC agreed to a transition plan for the establishment of an elected government. When the SMC rigged a referendum in 1978 approving continued military rule, another wave of strikes moved the SMC to replace Acheampong with General Akuffo, who appointed a constitutional assembly and scheduled elections for 1979. On the eve of the 1979 elections, a group of junior officers, led by Flight Lt. Jerry John Rawlings and backed by popular opinion, overthrew the SMC and formed the Armed Forces Revolutionary Council (AFRC). Elections took place as scheduled, while the AFRC purged state offices of corrupt SMC appointees and executed Acheampong and Akuffo. After three months, the AFRC yielded power to an elected government headed by Hilla Limann.

Limann's government inherited a ruined economy and failed to respond effectively when a drop in cocoa earnings led to rampant inflation and severe food shortages. Corrupt government officials made deals with black market profiteers. The government's popularity plummeted when it responded violently to strikes and demonstrations by workers. By 1981 Ghana was approaching famine and bankruptcy, and Rawlings again led a group of soldiers in a successful coup.

Rawlings, who enjoyed widespread support among workers and the poor, pledged to eliminate corruption and profiteering and to give the masses a voice in the government. Declaring that "bourgeois democracy fosters social inequality," he dissolved parliament, banned parties, established the Provisional National Defense Council (PNDC) in 1982, and appointed civilians, many of them radicals, to head government ministries. He encouraged Revolutionary Defense Committees (RDCs) to assume the powers of local government. By 1983 another drought and a wave of fires had deepened Ghana's economic crisis and again brought the country to the brink of famine. Rawlings became disenchanted with leftist ideology and dismissed his most radical ministers. By 1987, after several coup attempts against Rawlings, his PNDC had consolidated its control over the military and the RDCs.

During the mid-1980s Rawlings negotiated a structural adjustment plan with the IMF and began a program of austerity and economic reform, including privatization, a reduction in the size of the state sector, renewed investment in infrastructure, and incentives for cocoa producers. His government sought foreign investment in the country's mining sector. By the late 1980s Ghana's 15-year economic decline had been reversed, and both economic output and real income were rising.

But austerity measures provoked protests by workers and students, and Rawlings faced pressure from international donors to implement democratic reforms. In 1988 Ghana held nonpartisan elections for local government, and in 1989 Rawlings promised to restore parliamentary democracy. The government announced a timetable for multiparty elections in 1992, and voters approved a new constitution. Rawlings's National Democratic Congress (NDC), with widespread support in the south and parts of the far north, won a substantial victory over the opposition National Patriotic Party (NPP), which was based in Asante and neighboring regions. Despite alleged irregularities, outside observers judged the election "free and fair."

Democratization has brought new challenges. Critics have charged Rawlings with abandoning economic discipline and lavishing patronage on voters. Since the 1992 elections, increased government spending has produced budget deficits. A removal of import controls won the favor of market women but has led to a growing trade deficit. However, Rawlings and the NDC won a majority again in 1996 in elections accepted as fair by the NPP, and renewed economic reforms have since attracted increased foreign investment. An improved economic and political climate and the appointment of a Ghanaian, Kofi Annan, to head the United Nations in 1997 have been sources of pride for many Ghanaians. These developments, along with United States president Bill Clinton's historic 1998 visit to Ghana, have restored Ghana's prominence among African nations.

Mark O'Malley

See Also

Accra, Ghana; Busia, Kofi Abrefa; Danquah, Joseph Kwame Kyeretwi Boakye; Ghana, Early Kingdom of; Gold Trade; Kumasi, Ghana; Iron in Africa; Nationalism in Africa; Transatlantic Slave Trade; Great Britain; France; Germany; Netherlands, The; Portugal; Rawlings, Jerry; Structural Adjustment in Africa; Cola; Miscegenation; Slavery in Africa.

Africa

Ghana (Ready Reference)

Official Name: Republic of Ghana
Former Name: Gold Coast
Area: 238,537 sq km (92,099 sq mi)
Location: Western Africa; borders Togo, Burkina Faso, Côte d'Ivoire, and the Atlantic Ocean
Capital: Accra (population 953,500 [1990 estimate])
Other Major Cities: Kumasi (population 399,300), Sekondi (116,500) (1990 estimate)

Population: 18,497,206 (1998 estimate)
Population Density: 73 persons per sq km (about 190 per sq mi)
Population Below Age 15: 43 percent (male 3,985,219; female 3,947,640 [1998 estimate])
Population Growth Rate: 2.13 percent (1998 estimate)
Total Fertility Rate: 4.5 children born per woman (1996 estimate)
Life Expectancy at Birth: Total population: 56.82 years (male 54.77 years; female 58.92 years [1997 estimate])
Infant Mortality Rate: 77.5 deaths per 1000 live births (1998 estimate)
Literacy Rate (age 15 and over who can read and write): Total population: 64.5 percent (male: 75.9 percent; female: 53.5 percent [1995 estimate])
Education: Primary school and the first three years of secondary school are free and officially compulsory. In the late 1980s nearly 2.3 million children were enrolled in primary schools, and almost 770,000 were enrolled in secondary schools.
Languages: English is the official language of Ghana and is used in schools. There are at least nine other languages used in Ghana, including Akaupem-Twi, Asante-Twi, Dagbani, Dangbe, Ewe, Fanti, Ga, Kasem, and Nzima, which are also used in schools.
Ethnic Groups: There are at least seven major ethnic groups in Ghana, including the FANTE, ASANTE, NZIMA, AHANTA, GA, Moshi-Dagomba, and GONJA peoples.
Religions: About 62 percent of the population are Christian. About 22 percent adhere to indigenous beliefs and about 16 percent are Muslim.
Climate: The climate of Ghana is tropical, but temperatures vary with season and elevation. In most areas there are two rainy seasons, from April to July and September to November. In the north, however, one rainy season lasts from April to November. Annual rainfall is 1100 mm (43 in) in the southern areas and 2100 mm (83 in) in the north. The harmattan, a dry desert wind, is felt in the north from December to March and in the south in January. The average annual temperature is 26° C (79° F).
Land, Plants, and Animals: Ghana is mostly lowland with a small range of hills on the eastern border. Eastern Ghana also has one of the largest artificial lakes in the world, Lake Volta, which was created from the Volta River by the Akosombo Dam. The vegetation varies from savanna in the northern two-thirds of the country to a tropical forest zone in the south; much of the natural vegetation in central Ghana has been destroyed by land clearing for agriculture. The southern forests include the giant silk cotton, African mahogany, and cedar trees. Animals include the leopard, HYENA, buffalo, ELEPHANT, wildhog, ANTELOPE, and monkey. Ghana has many species of reptiles, including the cobra, python, puff adder, and horned adder.
Natural Resources: Mineral resources include gold, diamonds, manganese ore, and bauxite. Ghana has small deposits of petroleum and natural gas. Forests and access to the ocean are also valuable resources.
Currency: The Cedi
Gross Domestic Product (GDP): $36.2 billion (1997 estimate)
GDP per Capita: $2000 (1997 estimate)
GDP Real Growth Rate: 3 percent (1997 estimate)
Primary Economic Activities: Agriculture (55 percent of employment), manufacturing, and services
Primary Crops: Cocoa, rice, coffee, cassava (tapioca), peanuts, corn, shea nuts, bananas, and timber
Industries: Mining, lumbering, light manufacturing, aluminum, and food processing
Primary Exports: Cocoa, gold, timber, tuna, bauxite, aluminum, manganese ore, and diamonds
Primary Imports: Petroleum, consumer goods, foods, and capital equipment
Primary Trade Partners: United States, United Kingdom, Germany, Netherlands, and Japan
Government: Ghana is a Constitutional democracy. The executive branch is led by President Jerry John Rawlings. The legislative branch is the elected 200-seat National Assembly, currently dominated by the Every Ghanian Living Everywhere Party.

Elizabeth Heath

SEE ALSO

Accra, Ghana; Rawlings, Jerry.

Africa

Ghana, Early Kingdom of, great empire of the western Sudan.

Ancient Ghana was important in the ninth century C.E., when it controlled the Wangara area (between the upper NIGER and SENEGAL rivers), which produced great quantities of gold for trade across the Sahara. Slaves were also traded with the gold in return for salt from Teghaza in the desert and cloth from North Africa.

In the eleventh century the kingdom of Ghana was described by the Islamic historian al-Bakri (c. 1000). Raised in Muslim Spain, al-Bakri wrote historico-geographical surveys of West African kingdoms and empires in Arabic, albeit from a distance. He never traveled south of the Sahara, but instead contented himself with the reports of trans-Saharan traders and explorers. Nonetheless, Ghana was at the apex of its power during the years al-Bakri performed most of his investigations, and it was he who claimed that it was so rich in gold that dogs there had golden collars and the ruler of the empire was called "lord of the Gold."

Ghana included what is now western MALI and southeastern MAURITANIA, and its area was probably as large as modern NIGERIA. A strong central government presided in the capital city, which was divided into two parts – a town for the traditional rulers, who were pagans, and a town for the merchants, who were mostly Muslims. Historians believe that the town of Koumbi Saleh (in what is now Mauritania) was the capital of ancient Ghana in its later years.

The power of the empire declined because of competition from other states in the GOLD TRADE. In about 1076 the Almoravid rulers of the Maghreb attacked and destroyed Koumbi Saleh, but the invaders were forced to withdraw, and Ghana was able to recover. In about 1203, however, it was defeated by the army of Sumanguru, a leader of the people from the area of Takrur to the west. Sumanguru captured Koumbi Saleh, but soon after he, too, succumbed. He was defeated by an army of MANDE-speaking peoples, and by the end of the thirteenth century the remains of ancient Ghana became part of the empire of ancient Mali. KWAME NKRUMAH renamed the Gold Coast after this illustrious ancient kingdom when it became the first of the British colonies in sub-Saharan Africa to achieve independence in 1957.

For a detailed history of modern Ghana, *see* GHANA.

SEE ALSO

Gold Trade; Sahara Desert; Almoravids; Koumbi Saleh, Mauritania; Trans-Saharan and Red Sea Slave Trade.

Africa

Ghanaian Coffin Art, post-World War II GA tradition of building carved and brightly decorated coffins, shaped like animals or objects, that celebrate the deceased.

In the culture of the Ga, on the southern coast of GHANA, funerals have long had an element of entertainment, spectacle, and celebration. But the Ga tradition of building representational coffins dates only to the middle of the twentieth century: it was developed in the Ga village of Teshi, near the capital city Accra. The coffins, hand-carved from mahogany or lighter *wawa* wood and brightly painted, represent animals and other worldly objects that symbolize myth, success, or prestige. Akan proverbs suggest animals appropriate for these images, including the hen, the bull, the lion, the fish, and the shellfish. Other representations are related to the profession of the dead person, such as a canoe for a fisherman, a truck for a truck driver, or a saw for a carpenter. Still other coffins, shaped as jet planes or Mercedes-Benz cars, indicate the owner's prestige in the community.

The first coffin craftsman was Ata Owoo (1904-1976), a carpenter and wood carver in Teshi, where, since the end of World War II, the chief, or *mantse*, has on special occasions ridden in a palanquin, carried on the shoulders of the strongest men in the village. By the end of the 1940s Ata Owoo had the largest and most successful wood shop in Teshi and was commissioned to build a palanquin in the shape of an eagle. The chief of a neighboring village, a COCOA farmer, was so impressed by Ata Owoo's work that he asked the workshop to build him a similar palanquin in the shape of a cocoa pod. Ata Owoo began the project, but the chief died before he could finish, and the cocoa pod was used as his coffin instead.

Ata Owoo later encouraged local carpenter Kane Kwei (1922-1992) to pursue the art form. In discussing his work, Kane Kwei stressed that the forms were not traditional; rather, each piece was a wholly original creation inspired by and intended for the person it would eventually contain.

It was Kane Kwei's coffins that were first discovered by the international art world in 1973, when a Los Angeles, California, gallery owner visited his workshop in Teshi. She immediately ordered seven coffins for import and resale abroad. The workshop worked night and day to fill the order, with Kane Kwei's cousin and apprentice, Paa Joe (b. 1945), playing a particularly important role. Feeling underappreciated, Paa Joe decided to leave the workshop and, in 1977, opened his own. For many years the two workshops coexisted in Teshi, annually producing about 30 coffins each. In 1992 Kane Kwei died, and Paa Joe designed his coffin. Uncharacteristically plain, it was a simple wooden box with four small wood carvings on the corners – a saw, a hammer, a chisel, and a set square.

Today Paa Joe continues to build his distinctive coffins in Teshi, although at a somewhat slower pace of 10 to 15 pieces each year. The average price, depending on the amount of advance notice and the complexity of the piece, is US $400, roughly equal to the average yearly income of a person in Teshi.

Christopher Tiné

SEE ALSO

Accra, Ghana.

North America

Gibson, Althea

(b. August 25, 1927, Silver, S.C.), African American athlete, and first African American to win major tennis tournaments.

Althea Gibson, who moved with her family to Harlem at the age of three, was from an early age involved in many competitive sports. She began to play tennis in Police Athletic League paddle tennis games. In 1945 she won the girls' singles championship of the all-black American Tennis Association (ATA), and from 1947 to 1956 she held the title for the ATA women's singles. In 1946 she moved to North Carolina to live with Dr. Hubert Eaton, who, along with Dr. R. Walter Johnson, took an interest in her career. Under their tutelage, Gibson's game matured, and she developed her fast footwork and signature big serve.

In 1953 Gibson graduated from Florida Agricultural and Mechanical University. During the 1950s she began to challenge racial segregation in tennis by playing at tournaments sponsored by the United States Lawn Tennis Association (later renamed United States Tennis Association), which had previously been restricted to white players. In 1950 Gibson became the first black competitor at the National Championships (later renamed the U.S. Open) in Forest Hills, New York. She was invited to compete only after Alice Marble, a four-time singles winner at Forest Hills, expressed her disgust at the efforts to stop Gibson from playing because of her race. In 1951 Gibson was the first black person to play tennis at the Lawn Tennis Championships at the All-England Club in Wimbledon, England.

Gibson's game slowed down in the early 1950s, at which point she worked as a physical education teacher in Missouri for two years. However, her game was revitalized by a tennis tour of Southeast Asia organized by the United States State Department in 1955. In 1956 she won the women's singles championship at the French Open Tournament and then went on to win both the women's singles and doubles championships at Wimbledon and the U.S. National Championships at Forest Hills in 1957. In the same year, the Associated Press honored her with the Female Athlete of the Year Award. In 1958 she repeated her victories in the women's singles at both Wimbledon and Forest Hills.

Gibson retired from competitive tennis in 1959, turning her attention to other interests. During the 1960s she played professional golf, joining the U.S. Ladies Professional Golf Association in 1963, although she did not have the same success with golf that she had had with tennis. Gibson worked for the New Jersey state sports commission during the 1980s, and lectured and taught clinics on tennis. In 1971 she was elected to the International Tennis Hall of Fame.

During the 1990s Gibson attempted a golf comeback and continued to speak about tennis and physical fitness in general. She authored two books: *I Always Wanted to Be Somebody* (1958) and *So Much to Live For* (1968).

SEE ALSO

Harlem, New York.

North America

Gibson, Bob

(b. November 9, 1935, Omaha, Nebr.), African American baseball player, a hard-throwing right-handed pitcher known for his competitive intensity and respected for his fastball.

Bob Gibson's fastball helped him win 251 major league games over 17 seasons (1959-1975), all while playing for the St. Louis Cardinals. He played both baseball and BASKETBALL for Creighton University. He signed a contract with the Cardinals in 1957 and played in the minor leagues, where his raw pitching skills were refined. He toured briefly with the HARLEM GLOBETROTTERS basketball team in the winter of 1958 before pursuing baseball exclusively.

Gibson's best year was 1968, when he earned 22 victories, set the major league season record for lowest earned run average (1.12), and struck out what was then a league-record 268 batters. He was named the National League's most valuable player (MVP) for 1968 and also earned the first of his two Cy Young Awards (1968, 1970), given to the outstanding pitcher in each league. In three World Series appearances (1964, 1967, 1968), he started nine games, completed each of them, and had seven consecutive victories. Gibson set two World Series pitching records during the 1968 series. He had the most strikeouts in a single game (17) and the most strikeouts in a World Series (35), although the Cardinals lost the series to the Detroit Tigers. He was elected to the Baseball Hall of Fame in 1981.

SEE ALSO

Baseball in the United States.

North America

Gibson, Joshua

(b. December 21, 1911, Buena Vista, Ga.; d. January 20, 1947, Pittsburgh, Pa.), African American baseball player, widely regarded as the Negro Leagues' greatest hitter.

Walter Johnson, a pitcher for the Washington Senators, said in the 1930s, "There is a catcher that any big-league club would like to buy for $200,000. His name is Gibson.... He can do anything. He hits the ball a mile. And he catches so easy he might as well be in a rocking chair. Throws like a rifle.... Too bad Gibson is a colored fellow." During the late nineteenth and early twentieth centuries, black baseball players like Gibson were barred from major league competition and played in the segregated Negro Leagues.

Josh Gibson's professional career began in Pittsburgh, Pennsylvania, when, in a 1930 game between the Homestead Grays and the Kansas City Monarchs, he was called from the stands to replace the Gray's injured catcher. Still a teenager, Gibson proved himself a valuable contributor to the team, hitting 75 home runs in the following season. He played with the Grays from 1930 to 1931 and from 1937 to 1946, and played for the cross-town rivals, the Crawfords, between 1932 and 1936.

Gibson temporarily left the Grays in 1937 when he joined other Negro League stars to play in the DOMINICAN REPUBLIC, and from

1940 to 1941 when he played for Veracruz in the Mexican League. Between 1933 and 1945 Gibson spent the off-season playing in summer leagues in such countries as PUERTO RICO, CUBA, and VENEZUELA. In 1943 he was diagnosed as having a brain tumor and, refusing to have surgery, died four years later, just before the 1947 season.

The six-foot-one, 215-pound Gibson is best remembered for his graceful, long-distance batting. He is credited with the longest hit at New York's Yankee Stadium, Babe Ruth's home for 12 seasons. A lack of consistent records makes it difficult to determine accurately Gibson's career statistics. One historian, John Coates, estimates that he had 823 home runs and a batting average of .379, including his pro winter league figures. Gibson garnered numerous home run, batting, and Most Valuable Player titles. In 1972 he was inducted into the Baseball Hall of Fame.

Aaron Myers

SEE ALSO

Baseball in the United States; Negro Leagues; Pittsburgh, Pennsylvania.

Latin America and the Caribbean

Gil de Castro, José (b. 1785; d. 1841), Afro-Peruvian painter, also known as "El Mulato Gil," celebrated for his meticulous portaits of Peru's heroes who fought for independence from Spain (*see* ART IN LATIN AMERICA AND THE CARIBBEAN).

Latin America and the Caribbean

Gil, Gilberto (b. June 29, 1942, Salvador, Bahia, BRAZIL), a brilliant Afro-Brazilian musician-composer who combines local concerns with a cosmopolitan, global sensibility; since the mid-1960s, Gil has also intermittently engaged in struggles for social and racial equality, democratization, and environmental preservation.

Gilberto Gil was raised in a comfortable middle-class family in Ituaço, a small town in the dusty interior of BAHIA State. After moving to Salvador in 1951, he began to learn the accordion, but he switched to guitar after hearing João Gilberto's version of "Chega de Saudade," which inaugurated the bossa nova movement. In the early 1960s he studied business administration at the Federal University of Bahia and began to perform with other local artists like Caetano Veloso, Maria Bethânia, Gal Costa, and Tom Zé. In 1965 he moved to São Paulo and began working for a multinational company while continuing to pursue an artistic career. At that time he was active within the left-wing artistic milieu, which opposed the newly installed military regime.

Gil gained national recognition in 1967 at the Third Festival of Brazilian Popular Music aired by São Paulo's TV Record. He performed "Domingo no Parque," which fused Afro-Brazilian CAPOEIRA music with the sounds of a psychedelic rock band, Os Mutantes. His performance was an inaugural moment of TROPICÁLIA, a radical cultural movement that revitalized Brazilian arts. Although his partner, Caetano Veloso, is regarded as the primary intellectual author of Tropicália, Veloso himself has claimed that he was merely the apostle of Gil, the real prophet of the movement. In any case, the tropicalist movement radically transformed the conception, production, and consumption of popular music in Brazil. During the tropicalist period, Gil composed and recorded several key songs, such as "Geléia Geral" (lyrics by Torquato Neto), an ironic critique of Brazilian culture; and "Batmacumba," whose lyrics are visually structured as a concrete poem forming a bat in flight.

The music of Gilberto Gil expresses a strong sense of Afro-Brazilian pride and addresses problems of social and racial inequality. *Alex Cabral/Contexto*

In late 1968 Gil and Veloso were arrested by military authorities, who were suspicious of their subversive cultural activities; the musicians were eventually exiled to London. By that time, Gil had already begun to use elements of African American soul, which anticipated subsequent experiments with REGGAE, FUNK, RAP, and other musical forms of the African diaspora. In 1977, after performing at the Second International Black Arts Festival in NIGERIA, Gil recorded *Refavela*, his most self-consciously black-identified album, which featured songs by the Afro-Bahian Carnival groups FILHOS DE GANDHI and ILÊ AIYÊ. Two years later, he recorded his biggest hit ever, "Não Chore Mais," a Portuguese version of BOB MARLEY's "No Woman, No Cry," which became the anthem of the redemocratization movement.

During the 1980s Gil became increasingly involved in the civic and political life of Brazil. After an unsuccessful bid for the mayor's office in 1988, he was elected to the municipal council, where he focused on protecting the environment and promoting Afro-Brazilian culture. He retreated from party politics in the 1990s to focus on music and nongovernmental activism. He maintains an expansive web site that updates his activities as a musician and public intellectual.

Christopher Dunn

SEE ALSO

Soul Music; Salvador, Brazil.

North America

Gillespie, John Birks ("Dizzy") (b. October 21, 1917, Cheraw, S.C.; d. January 7, 1993, Englewood, N.J.), African American trumpet player, the co-creator with alto saxophonist Charlie Parker of bebop or modern jazz, and an Afro-Cuban jazz innovator.

John Birks "Dizzy" Gillespie may have been the greatest trumpeter in the history of JAZZ. His bravura trumpet playing featured a brilliant but sensitive tone, a wide range, and mind-boggling speed and articulation. To the wider public, Gillespie's name also conjured up images of his distinctive trumpet with its upswept bell, the way his cheeks bulged out when he played, and his penchant for clowning that included a seriocomic campaign for president in 1964. But Gillespie was extremely serious about his music and was a leader in two major developments in jazz. Beginning in the 1940s he played a key role in bringing Afro-Cuban music into American jazz. More significant, during the mid-1940s Gillespie was a primary force, along with alto saxophonist Charlie Parker, in the development of bebop or modern jazz.

Although Gillespie's role in this movement is well known, he has generally received less attention than Parker, in part because Gillespie did not fit the stereotype of the ill-fated and misunderstood musician. Jazz has a long tradition of mythologizing its troubled geniuses. Gillespie was in many respects closer to being the counterpart in modern jazz of Louis Armstrong in traditional jazz. As Armstrong had done in the 1920s, Gillespie redirected the course of jazz and expanded its improvisational possibilities. Both men played with a technical facility that astonished their peers. And like Armstrong, Gillespie had a winning personality and a gift for comedy.

John Birks Gillespie was born in Cheraw, South Carolina, the youngest of James and Lottie Gillespie's nine children. His father, a brickmason who led a band on the weekends, died not long before John's tenth birthday. During the GREAT DEPRESSION, the fatherless family survived by dint of hard work and struggle. Lottie Gillespie did laundry for white families, and John and his siblings picked cotton. Gillespie showed an early interest in music and took his first piano lessons from a neighbor. He was also influenced by the sanctified church. "I first learned the meaning of rhythm there," he recalled in his autobiography *To BE, or not... to BOP,* "and all about how music could transport people spiritually."

In 1929 Gillespie joined the school band, playing trombone and, later, trumpet. His first public performances were in accompaniment to amateur minstrels in school minstrel shows. Gillespie and several other members of the band formed a small group that played at local dances, white and black. In 1933 Gillespie received a scholarship to Laurinburg Technical Institute, a black high school in North Carolina, which he attended until his family moved to PHILADELPHIA, PENNSYLVANIA, in 1935. There Gillespie joined the big band of prominent local bandleader Frankie Fairfax, and members of the Fairfax band soon dubbed the antic young trumpeter "Dizzy."

After two years of playing in Philadelphia, Gillespie decided to move to New York City, the nation's jazz capital. He lived with older brother James P. Gillespie, played in jam sessions, and sat in with various groups, including Chick Webb's big band at the SAVOY BALLROOM. During these years Gillespie's major influence was the dynamic swing trumpeter Roy Eldridge. Gillespie played many of Eldridge's "licks" or characteristic phrases and memorized entire solos that his idol had recorded. Gillespie made his recording debut in 1937, soon after joining Teddy Hill's big band, and then joined the band on a European tour.

American jazz innovator Dizzy Gillespie, wearing a Nigerian robe, plays his trumpet with its characteristic upturned bell. *Philippe Renault/Gamma-Liaison*

After returning from Europe, Gillespie discovered that the regulations of New York City's musicians' union made it difficult for him to find work. The only regular gig he found was with Cass Carr, "a West Indian guy who played the musical saw." Gillespie said that Carr "played for all the ethnic things" and "for all the communist dances," including a gig at the Communist Party of the United States of America's Camp Unity. "White-black relationships were very close among the communists," Gillespie recounted. Gillespie himself became a "card-carrying communist," although he later downplayed the significance of this decision.

After resolving his problems with the musicians' union, Gillespie played with some of the most prominent big bands of the day, including those of Cab Calloway, ELLA FITZGERALD, Benny Carter, Lucky Millinder, Earl Hines, and Billy Eckstine. In 1937 Gillespie had met dancer Lorraine Willis, and three years later the two were married. During these years Gillespie began moving beyond Roy Eldridge's trumpet playing and the musical conventions of the swing era. Dissatisfied with the clichés and constraints of swing-era jazz, he began to explore new harmonic directions.

Gillespie faced considerable resistance from older jazz musicians. Bandleaders Les Hite and Lucky Millinder each fired the young trumpeter, and Cab Calloway disparagingly referred to Gillespie's trumpet solos as "Chinese music." Rather than tempering his style, Gillespie began to proselytize. When the Calloway band was playing its regular gig at the COTTON CLUB, Gillespie took bass player Milt Hinton up to the roof during band breaks to teach him bass parts that fit Gillespie's harmonically challenging solos.

After-hours jam sessions proved far more important than the musically regimented big bands in creating the bebop or bop revolution. The key gathering places for creative young musicians were two Harlem nightspots, Minton's Playhouse and Monroe's Uptown House. Gillespie explained: "What we were doing... was playing, seriously... blending our ideas into a new style of music.... We had some fundamental background training in European harmony and music theory superimposed on our own knowledge of Afro-American musical tradition.... Musically, we were changing the way that we spoke, to reflect the way that we felt."

The house band at Minton's was especially significant and included pianist Thelonious Monk and drummer Kenny Clarke. Guitar player Charlie Christian, a member of the Benny Goodman Sextet, kept a spare amplifier at Minton's so that he could sit in whenever he was in town.

During these years Gillespie met an alto player from Kansas City named Charlie Parker.

Parker had independently achieved harmonic breakthroughs comparable to those of Gillespie. Indeed, Parker alone had the technical mastery and creativity to make him Gillespie's musical peer. The two men became better acquainted during stints in two important incubators of modern jazz, the big bands of Earl Hines (1943) and Billy Eckstine (1944). Later in 1944, when Gillespie and bass player Oscar Pettiford formed the first true bop group – a quintet that debuted at the Onyx Club on 52nd Street – Parker was out of town, and tenor saxophonist Don Byas became the second frontline instrument. The Gillespie-Pettiford quintet marked the full emergence of modern jazz.

Shortly afterward, however, came the group that in Gillespie's opinion achieved the "height of the perfection of our music." This quintet included Parker and commenced a long stint at the New York nightclub the Three Deuces. During 1945 Gillespie and Parker also recorded a series of bebop classics, often taken at blistering tempos, including "Dizzy Atmosphere," "Salt Peanuts," and "Shaw Nuff." Playing some of the tightest unison lines in the history of jazz, the two seemed to breathe and think as one. In the late 1980s, more than 30 years after Parker's death, *New York Times* columnist Bob Herbert asked Gillespie how close he and Parker had been. "How close are those two coats of paint?" the trumpeter replied.

Gillespie, far more than Parker, retained an interest in big bands, and he led several during the late 1940s and mid- to late 1950s. In 1946 he recorded the blazing and apocalyptic "Things to Come," a classic example of big band bop. And in the following year, his big band introduced Afro-Cuban music to jazz audiences. When Gillespie played in Cab Calloway's orchestra, Cuban trumpet player Mario Bauza had introduced him to the rhythms and harmonies of Afro-Cuban music.

In 1947 Gillespie turned to his old friend Bauza for advice on hiring a percussionist who could bring a Latin flavor to his big band. Bauza recommended Cuban percussionist Luciano "Chano" Pozo, whom Gillespie featured prominently on several memorable Latin jazz recordings, including "Manteca" (1947) and "Guarachi Guaro" (1948). After economic difficulties forced him to break up his big band in 1950, Gillespie retained his interest in Afro-Cuban music. In 1951 he recorded what would become his best-known Latin composition, the moody "Tin Tin Deo."

At a party in 1953, Gillespie's trumpet was accidentally knocked over and its bell bent upward. When Gillespie tried to play it, he found that he actually preferred the bent shape because the upturned bell made it easier to play softly and improved his ability to hear his own playing. Soon after, he had the Martin Company build him a trumpet designed with an upswept bell, and he played similar instruments for the rest of his life. Also in 1953, at Toronto's Massey Hall, Gillespie played with Parker in one of their rare reunions. A recording of that performance made by bass player Charles Mingus reveals the continued brilliance of Parker and Gillespie's collaborations. Yet by the mid-1950s, when Parker died, the musical innovations of the two men were so thoroughly integrated into jazz that many listeners and critics had begun to take them for granted. Gillespie, however, continued to play vital and challenging music, mostly in small-group settings but occasionally in larger ensembles.

In 1956 Gillespie was invited by the United States State Department to organize a big band and act as a musical goodwill ambassador on a world tour. It was the first time the American government had recognized the most distinctly American art form – jazz. The new Gillespie band included the young trumpeter Quincy Jones and featured a number of Jones's compositions and arrangements. The tour was a resounding success, and the band continued to play together until 1958. Gillespie also performed a number of large-scale works, including pianist Lalo Schifrin's "Gillespiana" (1960) and "The New Continent" (1962); trombonist J. J. Johnson's "Perceptions" (1961); and, as the featured soloist with Machito and his orchestra, composer Arturo "Chico" O'Farrill's "Afro-Cuban Jazz Moods" (1975).

In 1971 Gillespie toured with an all-star group known as the Giants of Jazz that included Thelonious Monk, drummer Art Blakey, and saxophonist Sonny Stitt. The response of audiences and critics was overwhelmingly positive, and for the rest of his life Gillespie was regarded as one of the giants of jazz. He well understood his own musical influence, particularly on jazz trumpeters. "If he's younger than me and playing trumpet," Gillespie declared, "then he's following in my footsteps." Even in his mid-seventies, he kept up a grueling schedule of appearances at nightclubs and jazz festivals. During the 1980s Gillespie's embouchure weakened and his playing became more erratic, but his live performances remained dynamic and musically challenging. He continued to play actively until early 1992.

James Clyde Sellman

See Also

Armstrong, Louis ("Satchmo"); Calloway, Cabell (Cab); Carter, Bennett Lester (Benny); Eckstine, William Clarence (Billy); Harlem, New York; Hines, Earl Kenneth ("Fatha"); Jones, Quincy Delight, Jr.; Mingus, Charles, Jr.; Minstrelsy; Monk, Thelonious Sphere; New York, New York; Parker, Charles Christopher ("Bird"); Pozo y González, Luciano (Chano); Communist Party USA, African Americans and the.

North America

Gilpin, Charles Sidney

(b. November 20, 1878, Richmond, Va.; d. May 6, 1930), African American actor and singer, best known for his title role in Eugene O'Neill's Pulitzer Prize-winning Broadway play, *Emperor Jones*.

Charles Gilpin, the youngest of 14 children, was born in Richmond, Virginia, to Caroline Gilpin, a nurse, and Peter Gilpin, a laborer in a steel-rolling mill. Gilpin's first job, as a printer's assistant at the *Richmond Planet*, taught him skills that would later be useful between theatrical engagements, but by age 18 he had begun touring nationally with minstrel groups such as the Perkus and Davis Great Southern Minstrel Barn Storming Aggregation (1896) and the Smart Set (1905).

Gilpin's first dramatic appearances were at the Pekin Theater in Chicago (1907-1911) – the first legitimate Negro theater – and with various touring companies. In 1915 he joined the Anita Bush Players at the Lincoln Theater in New York; the group soon combined with the Lafayette Theater Company, also in Harlem. Here, Gilpin was both star performer and director.

Gilpin made his Broadway debut as William Custis in John Drinkwater's *Abraham Lincoln* (1919), a performance that impressed Eugene O'Neill so much that he cast Gilpin in the title role of his Pulitzer Prize-winning Broadway play, *Emperor Jones*. This was the pinnacle of Gilpin's career, and marked the first time a black actor had played a role of such magnitude. The National Association for the Advancement of Colored People awarded him the Spingarn Medal for his "notable performance" in 1921; the Drama League elected him one of the ten persons who had contributed the most to American theater, and President Warren G. Harding received him privately at the White House. Gilpin suffered a breakdown in 1929 and died in Eldridge Park, New Jersey, on May 6, 1930.

See Also

Chicago, Illinois; Harlem, New York; Lafayette Theatre; Minstrelsy; New York, New York; Richmond, Virginia.

North America

Giovanni, Yolande Cornelia ("Nikki")

(b. June 7, 1943, Knoxville, Tenn.), groundbreaking African American poet who began writing during the Black Arts Movement and who continues to celebrate black culture in her work.

Nikki Giovanni, one of the best-known contemporary black poets, rose to prominence in the 1960s as part of the generation of young black poets of the Black Arts and Black Power movements whose work reflected their radical political views. A typical poem of hers from that era, "My Poem," begins:

i am 25 years old
black female poet
wrote a poem asking
nigger can you kill
if they kill me
it won't stop
the revolution

While Giovanni's Black Arts Movement poetry is still often anthologized, her range has expanded over the decades to reflect other facets of the African American experience.

Giovanni, originally named Yolande Cornelia after her mother, was raised in Wyoming, Ohio, but spent summers and her junior and senior years of high school with her grandmother in Knoxville, Tennessee. Intelligent, bold, and outspoken since childhood, she entered FISK UNIVERSITY at age 17 but was asked to withdraw later that fall for "attitudes [which] did not fit those of a Fisk woman." Giovanni returned four years later and eventually graduated with an honors degree in history in 1967. As an undergraduate, she helped reinstate Fisk's chapter of the STUDENT NONVIOLENT COORDINATING COMMITTEE (SNCC) and was part of a writing workshop led by black author John O. Killens.

The year she graduated, Giovanni published her first poetry collection, *Black Feeling*. She followed it with *Black Talk* (1968) and *Black Judgment* (1970). These books secured her reputation as one of the most accessible of the young writers whose poems encouraged black solidarity and revolution, and she soon became the most prominent woman writer of the Black Arts Movement. Giovanni was also well-known for dynamic readings of her poetry, and she recorded several albums of her readings set to gospel and other black music, including *Truth Is on Its Way*, which became a bestseller in 1971. That same year she published a collection of autobiographical essays, *Gemini: An Extended Autobiographical Statement on My First Twenty-Five Years at Being a Black Poet*.

At about the same time, her poetry became less aggressively political and more reflectively personal. As Giovanni explained the transition, "I like to think I've grown and changed... How else can I ask people to read my work or listen to me?" In 1969 she gave birth to a son, and she has since written several books of poetry meant for black children. Giovanni's poetry for adults in collections such as *My House* (1972), *The Women and the Men* (1972), and *Cotton Candy on a Rainy Day* (1978) explored relationships between black men and black women, connections between families, and simple questions of identity and purpose for the African American women who found themselves, as she said:

black female and bright
in a white male mediocre world.

In the 1980s and 1990s Giovanni published two more books of essays, which address both personal and larger social issues. The recipient of numerous honorary degrees and awards, in 1989 she became professor of English at Virginia Polytechnic Institute and State University, and continues to write and lecture around the country. In 1996 she published *The Selected Poems of Nikki Giovanni*, a comprehensive volume that reflects her artistic and personal evolution during her first three decades as a writer. Above all, in her poetry, essays, and speeches she still celebrates black identity, which she sees as the defining characteristic of African American poets, who "see love and beauty in the blooming of the Black community; power in a people whose only power has been the truth."

Lisa Clayton Robinson

SEE ALSO
Literature, African American; Women Writers, Black, in the United States; Gospel Music.

Africa

Giraffe, tallest of all animals. Giraffes inhabit dry, tree-scattered terrain south of the Sahara. The male averages 5.3 m (17 ft) in height, and with its 40-cm (15-in) tongue is able to reach high into acacia trees, the leaves of which are one of its main foods.

The giraffe, like most mammals, has only seven neck vertebrae, which are greatly elongated to support its extremely long and muscular neck. Due to the great distance between the animal's heart and head, its vascular system is equipped with valves so that sufficient blood reaches the brain. Both sexes have two or four short, blunt, skin-covered horns. The long, flexible tongue and long, muscular upper lip are used to rip leaves from branches. Giraffes have chestnut brown blotches against a buff background, markings that blend with the dappled shadows of tree branches. As giraffes age, their color grows a darker brown. Each animal has a unique set of markings. A giraffe's life span is up to 26 years in the wild and up to 36 years in captivity.

Giraffes have a keen sense of smell and hearing and an outstanding sense of sight. They congregate in loosely organized herds of two to ten members, with individuals often joining and leaving again. Each herd is led by an adult bull and consists of cows, calves, and sexually immature males.

Giraffes gallop with the hind feet reaching in front of the fore feet and the neck swinging widely, giving the appearance of slow motion, although they can actually reach 56 km/h (35 mph). When walking they pace, moving the two feet of one side forward simultaneously. Due to their great weight, which averages 800 kg (1800 lb), they are unable to traverse boggy swamps or riverbeds. On dry, hard land, however, they range widely and are found hundreds of kilometers from water. Unlike many grass-eating herbivores of Africa, giraffes do not migrate during dry seasons because they get their food and most of their moisture from leaves. They can go for more than a month without drinking, and the few times they do drink, they must spread their long forelegs widely to reach the water. For this reason giraffes rarely graze grass. When giraffes vocalize, they emit moans or low notes. They usually sleep in standing positions. They protect themselves by kicking with their large, heavy hooves. Lions are their chief predators.

During mating season males vie for females by butting with their heavy necks and heads. After about 15 months the cow bears a single calf, 1.7 to 2 m (5.6 to 6 ft) high, which can stand as soon as 20 minutes after birth. Calves come to sexual maturity in about four years. Once heavily hunted for their thick, leathery skins, giraffes are now protected.
Scientific classification: The giraffe belongs to the family Giraffidae. It is classified as *Giraffa camelopardalis*.

SEE ALSO
Sahara Desert.

Latin America and the Caribbean

Giral, Sergio (b. 1937, Havana, CUBA), Cuban director and journalist who, like SARA GÓMEZ, belongs to the second generation of Cuban Film Institute (Instituto Cubano de Arte e Industria Cinematográficas, ICAIC) filmmakers who worked under the tutelage of Tomás Gutiérrez Alea, the best-known Cuban director. Giral has directed over 20 documentaries and several major films, many of which deal with issues of slavery, race, and his Afro-Cuban cultural heritage.

Born to a Cuban father and a North American mother, Sergio Giral has lived in Cuba and the United States. After finishing high school in Cuba, he spent two years studying painting at the Art Students League in New York. Following the triumph of the 1959 Cuban Revolution he returned to live in Havana. There he began engineering studies but then joined the Cuban Film Institute in 1961. His films include a slave trilogy – comprising *El otro Francisco* (1974, The Other Francisco), *El rancheador* (1976, The Slave Hunter), and *Maluala* (1979) – and a film on contemporary Cuban issues, *Techo de vidrio* (Glass Ceiling; 1982). In 1986 Giral directed *Plácido*, about the nineteenth-century black Cuban poet and patriot Plácido Valdés; in 1990 he directed *María Antonia*, dealing with the world of prostitution, gambling, and drugs in 1950s Havana. Since the 1990s Giral has resided in Miami, where he works as a freelance writer.

In Giral's two most important full-length films, *El otro Francisco* and *María Antonia*, the director seeks to give voice to Afro-Cuban culture. *El otro Francisco* is a response to the nineteenth-century Cuban antislavery novel *Francisco* by ANSELMO SUÁREZ Y ROMERO, which the film criticizes for its representation of the black slave from the white abolitionist's point of view. In a bold critique of the historical melodrama, the literary and cinematic genre in which subjective emotions play a greater role than historical forces, Giral's film reveals the social and historical contexts of the abolitionist movement in Cuba and of slavery between 1830 and 1868. The film thus alternates between scenes that depict the violence perpetrated on the black slaves by the SUGAR barons and salon discussions regarding the mechanization of sugar production and the profitability of abolishing slavery. In so doing, *El otro Francisco* exposes the economic and political forces behind Cuban slavery and portrays an emerging revolutionary movement propelled by a good number of slave rebellions throughout the island (*see* SLAVE REBELLIONS IN LATIN AMERICA AND THE CARIBBEAN). Ultimately, Giral depicts the black slave as an agent of history rather than as a docile, highly idealized individual.

With *María Antonia*, based on the 1967 play of the same name by Cuban playwright Eugenio Hernández (b. 1937), Giral explores the difficult position of the mulatta in 1950s Havana when faced with the sexist image of the black woman as perversely sexual and emotionally unstable. To counteract this image, Giral creates a racially and culturally mixed character who syncretizes the image of Oshún, the YORUBA goddess of love, with the Catholic Our Lady of Charity (*see* CATHOLIC CHURCH IN LATIN AMERICA AND THE CARIBBEAN). The narrative is structured in terms of a series of flashbacks with the female character in religious consultation with a *santero* (a priest in SANTERÍA, the Yoruba-based religion practiced in Cuba), who interprets her fate. Thus, the santero's prophesy coincides with the film's narrative plot, and the priest symbolically assumes the role of the director. Giral's work, then, may be seen as a performance in which Afro-Cuban myth and Cuban history interact through the medium of cinematic language.

Flora González

SEE ALSO
Slavery in Latin America and the Caribbean; New York, New York; Valdés, Gabriel de la Concepción ("Plácido"); Race in Latin America; Abolition and Emancipation in Latin America and the Caribbean; Image of the Mulatta in Latin America and the Caribbean; Oxum; Havana, Cuba.

Africa

Giriyama (also known as Giriama and Giryama), ethnic group of KENYA.

The Giriyama primarily inhabit coastal Kenya. They speak a Bantu language and belong to the Nyika cultural and linguistic group. Approximately 550,000 people consider themselves Giriyama.

SEE ALSO
Bantu: Dispersion and Settlement.

Africa

Gisu (also known as Bagisu, Gishu, Masaba, and Sokwia), ethnic group of UGANDA.

The Gisu primarily inhabit eastern Uganda. They speak a Bantu language. Approximately 800,000 people consider themselves Gisu.

SEE ALSO
Bantu: Dispersion and Settlement.

Africa

Gladiolus, genus of herbaceous flowering plants of the iris family with sword-shaped leaves and showy flowers, widely cultivated in gardens and used as cut flowers.

Some 180 species of gladiolus exist, mostly native to southern Africa. Modern cultivation dates from the early nineteenth century. Because of the ease with which gladiolus hybridize and the length of time they have been bred for color, flower size and shape, and other desirable features, it is now impossible to assign most *cultivars* (cultivated forms) to botanical species.

Gladiolus are generally not hardy in temperate zones and are grown as annuals from *corms* (swollen underground stems) or *cormels* (small, hard structures produced at the bases of corms) after the ground has warmed. The irregular funnel-shaped flowers are borne in vertical rows on long, unbranched flower stalks.

Scientific classification: Gladiolus belong to the family Iridaceae.

Latin America and the Caribbean

Glissant, Edouard

(b. September 21, 1928, Sainte-Marie, Martinique), Martinican novelist, poet, playwright, and essayist who seeks to move beyond NÉGRITUDE by expressing, in French, a specifically Caribbean identity.

Born into a modest family, Edouard Glissant gained a solid literary and philosophical foundation while distinguishing himself as a student at the Lycée Schoelcher in Fort-de-France. He entered Martinique's literary-political nexus at a young age, participating with schoolmate FRANTZ FANON in AIMÉ CÉSAIRE's successful election campaign of 1945. This would be, however, the last time that Glissant closely identified himself with Césaire, Martinique's leading exponent of Négritude. Glissant would subsequently move away from a politics based on race toward one based on identification with a place, the Caribbean, and its history.

Still, while a student of ethnography and philosophy in Paris in the late 1940s and early 1950s, Glissant became a visible figure in so-called Black African cultural circles, with ties to the journal *Présence Africaine*, the Société Africaine de la Culture, and, in a sign of things to come, a number of left-wing Caribbean political groups. It was during this time that Glissant first experimented, in a style that is always innovative and often difficult, with expressing his political convictions in poetry and fictional prose. In what proved for him to be a decade of creative ferment, he published three collections of poetry in the 1950s (*Un champ d'Iles*, 1953; *La terre inquiète*, 1954; *Les Indes*, 1956) and, more important, had his first literary success with the novel *La lézarde* (1958 winner of the Prix Renaudot).

But Glissant's role as codirector of the Front antillo-guyanais pour l'indépendance with the Guadeloupean writer PAUL NIGER put his literary project momentarily on hold, his second novel coming only in 1970. As a result of the group's call for the independence of the French Overseas Departments of Martinique, GUADELOUPE, and Guyane, Glissant was labeled an enemy of the French state and was forbidden to return to Martinique between 1959 and 1965. It was during this period that he visited Fidel Castro's CUBA, witnessing the aftermath of the Bay of Pigs invasion. This event strengthened Glissant's conviction concerning the need for inter-Caribbean solidarity.

Upon his return to Martinique in 1965, Glissant turned away from direct political action, channeling his energies instead into founding a private secondary school, the Institut Martiniquais d'Etudes (IME), which also served as a research center and the editorial base for the short-lived journal of Caribbean literature and politics, *Acoma* (1971-1973). In 1982 he assumed editorial control *Le courrier de l'UNESCO*, (published in 32 languages), the main journal of the United Nations Educational, Scientific, and Cultural Organization, but had left by 1988 for the post of director of the Center for French and Francophone Studies at Louisiana State University.

The intellectual project that Glissant develops in essays over the course of his career, many of which are collected in *Le Discours antillais* (1981; translated as *Caribbean discourse*, 1989), can be summed up with the word *antillanité* (Caribbean-ness). Glissant posits antillanité not as a refusal of Négritude but as a way of moving beyond its limitations. Whereas Négritude finds its inspiration in an immutable black essence, Caribbean identity, for Glissant, has its origins in an event; THE MIDDLE PASSAGE, the voyage made by his ancestors from Africa to the Americas in the hulls of slave ships. Antillanité is contingent, a function of the complex heritage of the Caribbean and its relation to its surroundings. "Relation" is, in fact, another word that is important in Glissant's lexicon. History, language, time, and space: it is the *relation* of these factors to each other that determines an always-shifting Caribbean identity. It can be said that Glissant's novels are *related* to each other in that the same characters or their relatives and descendants keep appearing and the same chain of historical events is continuously evoked. Glissant's body of work – with its complex mixture of French and Creole languages and realities, its evocation of Caribbean history, and its definition of a specifically Caribbean identity – has led PATRICK CHAMOISEAU to refer to Glissant as the spiritual father and leader of the new Creole literary movement. But Glissant himself has objected to the terms, preferring simply to be called an *initiator*.

Richard Watts

SEE ALSO

Présence Africaine; Transatlantic Slave Trade; Créolité; Martinique.

North America

Glover, Danny (b. July 22, 1947, San Francisco, Calif.), African American actor whose career has spanned television, theater, and film.

Danny Glover was born in San Francisco to politically active parents, and as a youth participated in the student activism of the Haight-Ashbury district, a center of 1960s counterculture activity. He studied economics at San Francisco State University and, after graduating, took a job as an economic planner for the city of San Francisco. While in his twenties he began participating in the American Conservatory Theater's Black Actors' Workshop but kept his job in the mayor's office until 1975. When he was nearly 30 years old, he began acting professionally, landing television roles on "Gimme A Break," "Chiefs," "Lou Grant," and "Palmerstown, USA," an Alex Haley production.

Glover distinguished himself as an actor of great promise in the early 1980s when he appeared in two plays by South African playwright ATHOL FUGARD in New York: with *The Blood Knot* (1980) Glover made his off-Broadway debut, and for his performance in *Master Harold... and the Boys* (1982) he garnered high acclaim. He also appeared in *The Island, Sizwe Banzi Is Dead, Macbeth,* and *Suicide in B Flat.*

Impressed by Glover's performance in *Master Harold,* Hollywood director Robert Benson cast him as a sharecropper in *Places in the Heart* (1984), Glover's first leading role in a big-budget production. Glover's watershed came in 1985, however, when he appeared in three of the year's most successful movies: *Silverado, Witness,* and *The Color Purple.* Thereafter, lead roles in numerous top-grossing films, including *Lethal Weapon* (1987), its two sequels, and other action films, indicated Glover's mainstream acceptance.

Glover continued to appear on television, most notably in *Mandela* (1987) and *Queen* (1993), another Alex Haley project. Although Glover has at times been attacked for role choices, especially his clichéd character in *Lethal Weapon 3,* he considers acting a political vocation. His serious dramatic work – such as *The Color Purple* and *Mandela* – and awards from the NATIONAL ASSOCIATION FOR THE ADVANCEMENT OF COLORED PEOPLE (NAACP) and the TransAfrica Forum, reflect his interest in race and politics.

Eric Bennett

SEE ALSO

Haley, Alexander Palmer (Alex).

Africa

Gnu, also WILDEBEEST, large African ANTELOPE.

The gnu, or wildebeest, has an oxlike head, horns, and shoulders; bristly facial hair and mane; and a horselike tail. Two species exist: the black wildebeest, which was once abundant in SOUTH AFRICA but has now been hunted back to about 10,000 individuals; and the blue wildebeest, herds of which are common on grassy plains from KENYA south to northern South Africa. Both sexes of both species have broad, smooth horns that curve downward, outward, and then upward.

Blue wildebeests, which vary from bluish-gray to brown, form resident nursery herds of females and young. Single males defend territories and court estrous females crossing their land. Males without territories form loose bachelor herds. In dry seasons some herds migrate in huge congregations.

Although the bristly faces and massive shoulders make gnus appear menacing, they go into antics when approached, dashing off and wheeling about to gaze at the intruders. Females bear single calves, which can run just a few minutes after birth. The young are frequently taken by hyenas, and the adults are a favorite prey of lions.

Scientific classification: Gnus belong to the family Bovidae. They make up the genus *Connochaetes.* The black wildebeest is classified as *Connochaetes gnou* and the blue wildebeest as *Connochaetes taurinus.*

Africa

Gogo, ethnic group of TANZANIA.

The Gogo primarily inhabit Tanzania's central highlands. While the Gogo speak a Bantu language, they have adapted many of the cultural traits of MAASAI pastoralists. Approximately 800,000 people consider themselves Gogo.

SEE ALSO

Bantu: Dispersion and Settlement; Pastoralism.

Africa

Gola, ethnic group of West Africa.

The Gola primarily inhabit western LIBERIA and neighboring SIERRA LEONE. They speak a Niger-Congo language belonging to the Western Atlantic group, although they have borrowed considerably from the neighboring MENDE people. Approximately 200,000 people consider themselves Gola.

SEE ALSO

Languages, African: An Overview.

North America

Goldberg, Whoopi (b. November 13, 1954, Chelsea, N.Y.), comedian, film star, and the first African American woman to win an Oscar (1990) since HATTIE MCDANIEL (1939).

Whoopi Goldberg was born in New York City, where she exhibited early talent as a performer. She struggled with her studies and was later diagnosed as dyslexic. Dropping out of high school, she spent her teen years amid the fashions, credos, and drugs of the hippie movement. She maintained involvement in theater through chorus roles in the Broadway productions *Hair, Jesus Christ Superstar,* and *Pippin.*

In 1974 Goldberg moved to California and worked a variety of jobs as she tried to launch her acting career. She helped found the San Diego Repertory Theater and began performing one-woman shows, including *Moms,* which showcased the life of black comedian Jackie "Moms" Mabley. Goldberg's satiric bite, as well as her talent for playing numerous character types, attracted the attention of producer Mike Nichols, who helped her stage an eponymous show of skits on Broadway.

Goldberg's success in New York caught the attention of Hollywood, and in 1985 Steven Spielberg cast her in his adaptation of Alice Walker's *The Color Purple.* After Goldberg received an Academy Award nomination for her portrayal of Celie, a poor young black woman who overcomes the limitations of her life in the segregated South, her status as a film actor was ensured. Since 1985 she has appeared in over two dozen movies, including *Sister Act* (1992), *The Lion King* (1994), *Boys on the Side* (1995), and *Ghost* (1990), for which she won an Oscar as Best Supporting Actor.

Goldberg also has appeared extensively on television, making regular cameos on *Star Trek: The Next Generation* and *Moonlighting.* In 1992 she cofounded *Comic Relief,* an annual fundraiser to help the homeless. In addition to her Oscar, Goldberg has won a

Grammy, a Golden Globe, and several Emmy nominations. She hosted the Oscar Award ceremonies in 1994, 1996, and 1999.

Eric Bennett

See Also

Mabley, Jackie ("Moms"); New York, New York; Television and African Americans; Walker, Alice.

Africa

Gold Coast. Former name of Ghana.

Africa

Gold Trade, the production, trade, and use of gold in Africa from precolonial to contemporary times.

The Precolonial Gold Trade

Gold was a major commodity in precolonial Africa. African rulers valued it as a prestige item in their own lands and exported it to overseas markets. The standard gold weights used during the Constantine era of the Roman Empire have been found in West Africa, indicating that gold crossed the Sahara as early as the fourth century. Around the mid-eighth century, the governor of Ifriqiya (present-day Tunis) proposed digging wells from southern Morocco to the West African savannas to facilitate the transport of gold and slaves.

Although Arab sources suggest that enormous amounts of gold crossed the Sahara before the tenth century, some scholars believe that camel caravans carried a total of only 2000 to 3000 kg (4400 to 6600 lb) across the desert during the first millennium C.E. Demand increased in the eleventh century, when the Fatimid caliphate of North Africa sought gold as a means of financing its battles against the Umayyads of Spain and the Abbasids of Baghdad. Other early markets for Africa's gold included the courts of India and the Far East.

Gold deposits in several different regions enriched Africa's precolonial cities and kingdoms. In West Africa, for example, trade in gold from Bure, on the headwaters of the Niger River, stimulated the rise of the Mali Empire in the thirteenth century. In the fourteenth and fifteenth centuries, the trade in gold in the Akan region (present-day Ghana) provided revenue for the Bono Kingdom. Much of the gold traded in the cities of Djenné and Tombouctou came from Bambuk, just south of the upper Senegal River. Gold deposits in Dafina and Lobi were exploited beginning, probably, in the mid-fourteenth century.

Gold was also important to commerce and precolonial state formation in East and Southern Africa. The Arab explorer al-Masudi noted significant gold exports from the Mozambique coast in the year 916. The city-state of Mapungubwe, located on the southern banks of the Limpopo River, rose during the tenth century after establishing control over the gold trade. With the demise of Mapungubwe, power shifted south to Great Zimbabwe. Scholars speculate that the founders of the Great Zimbabwe Kingdom owed their wealth to control of the twelfth-century trade in gold from the Save River valley. Skeletons have been discovered at the bottom of narrow, ancient mining shafts in the region. At the peak of the trade, an estimated 1000 kg (2204 lb) of gold passed through Great Zimbabwe annually. The port cities of Sofala and, later, Kilwa (in present-day Tanzania), where much of this gold was destined, flourished from the commerce. After Great Zimbabwe collapsed around 1450, a succession of gold-trading dynasties originated in the region of present-day Zimbabwe and Mozambique, beginning with Mutapa and Torwa in the fifteenth century, and followed by Rozwi in the seventeenth century.

The early years of gold trading and mining were best documented in West Africa. Mande merchants carried much of the gold from the forest regions to Tombouctou and other savanna towns; they hid gold dust in quills to avoid being robbed. They exchanged the gold for commodities such as salt, swords, iron, copper, cloth, silk, and horses. Arab, Berber, and Jewish traders then carried the gold north across the desert on dromedaries. Numerous dangers existed along the way, as a 1352 account by the Berber explorer Ibn Battutah testifies. Sandstorms could disorient navigators, and caravans that were heedless of vital watering holes could perish en route. One such unfortunate camel caravan, dating from the twelfth century, was recently discovered. Two thousand brass bars weighing a total of approximately 907 kg (1 ton) were found among the remains.

Merchants' need to measure accurately quantities of gold led to the use of standardized weights. Arab traders are believed to have brought the first scales and weights to West Africa, where a sophisticated artistic tradition of gold weights later developed, particularly among the Akan. Elsewhere, seeds were routinely used to measure quantities of gold under a standardized system that spread with the Arab trade in gold across the Sahara. In North Africa, mints for coining gold dinars were built in Kairouan (Tunisia) and Fustat (Egypt) during the eighth century, as gold replaced cowries and iron as the most important medium of exchange.

Little is known about early methods of gold mining. The peoples who actually mined or panned for gold typically did not reveal to traders the exact sources of the valuable mineral. The few existing records portray gold mining as an often arduous and dangerous task. In Bambuk, gold mining was a dry-season activity; men would quarry the ore, from which women would extract the gold. Slaves were often employed to work in the mineshafts, and accidents were probably common, as they have been in more contemporary mines.

After Portuguese sailing ships began to call on ports such as Shama and Elmina (both in present-day Ghana) during the fifteenth century, the West African gold trade gradually began to turn away from the Sahara. The Portuguese acquired some 42,185 kg (93,750 lb) of gold, mostly from Mande traders, during the fifteenth and sixteenth centuries. Much of this gold came from the interior Asante region. Other Europeans followed, including French pirates who preyed upon gold-laden ships from as early as 1492. English merchants became increasingly active after the mid-sixteenth century; they were followed by the Dutch. In the nineteenth century, when the British colonized the region that provided so much of the precious metal, they called it the Gold Coast.

Gold and Colonialism

Since the late nineteenth century, South Africa has become the continent's greatest producer of gold. It is estimated that half of the world's current gold reserves are located in South Africa. The 1886 discovery of gold in the Afrikaner-controlled Transvaal region attracted many independent miners as well as large European-owned companies, but only the latter had the heavy machinery needed to exploit deep deposits. After the Boer War (1889-1902), the Transvaal fell under British control. The gold mines there and in the Rand (an area near Johannesburg, which by the 1890s was producing one-fourth of the world's gold) required huge labor forces. Many of the workers migrated from rural areas in South Africa or neighboring colonies, seeking wages to pay colonial taxes. South Africa's gold mines were dangerous and paid whites much higher wages than blacks or coloureds received. But they also became sites of early labor organization and protest.

The Contemporary African Gold Industry

Gold remains an important commodity for South Africa, but its mining industry faces numerous problems. Because shallow reserves have been exhausted, costly deep mining is now required. The quality of gold ore has declined over time, narrowing profit margins. Furthermore, each year hundreds of miners are killed and thousands are injured in mining accidents.

Since the end of Apartheid, many of South Africa's largest mining companies, such as the Anglo-American Corporation, have begun to invest in gold exploration and mining in Ghana and other West African countries. For example, they recently spent more than US $300 million to develop the Sadiola mine in Mali. The Gold Fields company, founded by Cecil Rhodes, draws an increasing proportion of its revenue from Ghana's Tarkwa mine. The long-dormant gold industry of Burkina Faso has become that nation's second largest source of revenue, after cotton;

second largest source of revenue, after cotton; much of the initial investment capital came from the United States and Canada. Foreign firms are also exploring mining operations in East and Central Africa, in countries such as the REPUBLIC OF THE CONGO and Tanzania.

Ari Nave

SEE ALSO

Cape Coloured; Explorers in Africa Before 1500; Djenné-Djeno, Mali; Johannesburg, South Africa; Iron in Africa; Sahara Desert; Salt Trade; Tombouctou, Mali; Tunis, Tunisia; Trans-Saharan and Red Sea Slave Trade.

Latin America and the Caribbean

Gomes, Antônio Carlos

(b. July 11, 1836, Campinas, BRAZIL; d. September 16, 1896, Belém, Brazil), Brazilian composer of African descent, the most distinguished nineteenth-century Brazilian opera composer, who also achieved considerable success in Europe.

The reigning master of Brazilian OPERA, Antônio Carlos Gomes achieved world renown in 1870 when his opera *Il Guarany* premiered at La Scala in Milan, Italy. Although he adhered to the conventions of mid-nineteenth-century Italian opera, he looked to Afro-Brazilian themes for some of his operas and instrumental works. Music scholar Claver Filho considers Gomes's piano piece *A caiumba* (1857), a dance based on the African congada, "the first composition that ushered in Brazilian pre-nationalism."

Gomes was the second son of Fabiana Maria J. Cardoso and Manuel José Gomes, a composer and bandleader born to a black freedwoman and an unknown father. Manuel José also taught piano and violin in Campinas and introduced his two young sons to the rudiments of music. Antônio Carlos debuted publicly at age 11, playing the triangle in his father's orchestra in a ceremony honoring Emperor Pedro II. He studied clarinet, violin, and piano, for which he composed his first pieces. His brother, José Pedro de Santana Gomes, studied violin and viola and later became Brazil's most important late nineteenth-century violinist.

In 1859 Antônio Carlos Gomes enrolled in the Rio de Janeiro Conservatory of Music. He had already composed his first mass (1854) and was soon commissioned to write a cantata by the conservatory's director, Francisco Manuel da Silva. Following the premiere of his cantata *The Last Hour at Calvary* (1859), Gomes was appointed conductor at the Imperial Academy of Music and National Opera. In 1863 he won a government scholarship to study in Italy based on the success of his operas *A noite do castelo* (1861, Night in the Castle) and *Joana de Flandres* (1863), both performed in Portuguese.

Gomes spent a good part of his life in Italy, and his compositions were considerably influenced by the prevailing styles of Italian masters Rossini, Bellini, Donizetti, and Verdi. Nonetheless, he wrote two operas, *Il Guarany* (1870) and *Lo Schiavo* (1889), which drew on Brazilian subjects. *Il Guarany*, based on the novel of the same title by Brazilian author José de Alencar, took for its heroes the Guarany Indians. It also included indigenous dances, but its musical style was principally Italian. *Lo Schiavo*, on the other hand, was originally based on the liberation struggles of black slaves in Brazil. Yet Italian theater directors preferred an Indian theme, hoping to repeat the success of *Il Guarany*. In order to have his opera produced, Gomes had to replace the black subjects with Indians and to transfer the scenes from the eighteenth to the sixteenth century.

In 1893 Gomes toured the United States, where he conducted some of his works at Chicago's Columbia Universal Exhibition. Appointed to head the Conservatory of Music in Belém, he returned to Brazil in 1895 but died of cancer three months after assuming the directorship.

Roanne Edwards

SEE ALSO

Portugal; Slavery in Latin America and the Caribbean; Rio de Janeiro, Brazil; Music, Classical, in Latin America and the Caribbean.

Latin America and the Caribbean

Gómez Horacio, Maximiliano

(also known as "El Moreno") (b. May 5, 1943, San Pedro de Macorís, Dominican Republic; d. May 23, 1971, Brussels, Belgium), Afro-Dominican leader of the left-wing party Movimiento Popular Dominicano (Dominican Popular Movement) after 1962.

Maximiliano Gómez believed that the revolutionary movement in the DOMINICAN REPUBLIC should be based on the country's particular historical and sociocultural conditions, not on the European classics of socialist thought. Before beginning his political career, Gómez worked in the SUGAR cane refineries of his hometown. He participated in the armed revolt that ended with the United States invasion of April 24, 1965. After achieving the highest rank in his organization in 1967, Gómez struggled against JOAQUÍN BALAGUER's dictatorship in the Dominican Republic.

In 1970 he was incarcerated and then went into exile. He died under mysterious conditions in Brussels, Belgium, in 1971.

Mayda Grano de Oro

Latin America and the Caribbean

Gómez, Sara

(b. 1943, Cuba; d. 1974, Cuba), Afro-Cuban film director internationally known for her film *De cierta manera* (One Way or Another), which presents a feminist perspective on racial and gender tensions in revolutionary Cuban society.

Sara Gómez grew up in CUBA and initially worked as a journalist. In the 1960s she decided to change her profession and began studying film at the Instituto Cubano del Arte e Industria Cinematográficos, or ICAIC (Cuban Institute for the Arts and Film Industry). Since its establishment in 1959, the ICAIC had become an umbrella for the evolution of Cuban cinema under the guidelines of the political and ideological transformations of the 1960s. The films produced during this era became known as Imperfect Cinema because the directors used unconventional techniques to differentiate their films from the polished image of Hollywood productions. Gómez, together with other important Cuban filmmakers such as SERGIO GIRAL, worked in this environment as an assistant director to renowned filmmakers Jorge Fraga, Tomás Gutiérrez Alea, and Agnes Varda.

After gaining experience with such prominent directors, Gómez ventured out on her own. She directed a series of documentary shorts, including *I'll Go to Santiago* (1964), in which the city of Santiago de Cuba and its people are the central characters. In 1967 Gómez directed the 30-minute documentary *We've Got Rhythm*, where she presents the history of Cuban music through interviews with local elderly musicians.

Gómez is best known for her black-and-white film *De cierta manera* (1975), in which she examines the problems of being both black and female in post-revolution Cuba. The movie presents the lives of a mulatto factory worker and a white schoolteacher who are subjected to the gender, class, and racial prejudices that still linger in their society. Gómez used her experience in directing documentaries and her feminist views to present a critique of gender roles from within the Cuban Revolution. Her film is a collage that juxtaposes the African, European, and nationalist elements present in Cuban identity, showing how both gender and race relations need to be radically transformed in the post-revolution era.

"Sarita," as her friends called her, died of an asthma attack while *De cierta manera* was in post-production. Her film was completed posthumously by director Tomás Gutiérrez Alea. Since the death of Gómez, her work has become a landmark for film criticism and independent filmmaking in Latin America.

Liliana Obregón

Africa

Gonder, Ethiopia,

the capital of the kingdom of ETHIOPIA from the seventeenth through the nineteenth century.

The palaces at Gonder remain mysterious. We know when they were built, and we know do not know who the craftsmen were that created a style unknown elsewhere in the country. Ethiopian emperors liked to display their wealth and power by employing foreign experts. Perhaps the palaces incorporate the skills of Italian or Indian masons. Contacts with both countries had increased after the Portuguese had arrived in Ethiopia in the sixteenth century.

In 1632 the emperor Fasiladas built the first castle at Gonder, then a village near Lake T'ana. He may not have intended to create a new capital, but he hoped to find a better residence during the rainy season than the tents of the earlier nomadic court. During the following decades, however, Gonder did become the capital of the empire, and it remained so until the middle of the nineteenth century. It seems that each emperor built his own castle, ignoring those of his ancestors – a custom that may lie in the competitive nature of Amhara and Tigrinya society, where young men have traditionally proved their status by surpassing their elders as well as their rivals. The fact that their defensive walls would not have withstood the military technology of the day suggests that they were constructed largely for display.

Gonder declined during the chaotic Era of the Princes (1706-1853), when powerful local warlords dominated the emperors who lived among the crumbling palaces. The emperor Tewodros II, whose supremacy ended the anarchy of the princes, sacked Gonder twice during the 1860s, removing the treasures of its churches. The troops of the Mahdi (*see* Mahdist State), the Islamic reformer who founded a state in neighboring Sudan, also burned the city during the 1880s. Many of the most impressive castles and churches remain, however, along with a charming pavilion known as the Bath of Fasiladas, where the festival of Timqat is still celebrated every year to mark the baptism of Christ.

Today Gonder is an important regional economic and cultural center and the capital of Gonder province. It had a population of about 100,000 in 1990.

Africa

Gonja (also known as Gongya), ethnic group of West Africa.

The Gonja primarily inhabit northwestern Ghana and northeastern Côte d'Ivoire. They speak a Niger-Congo language and belong to the Guan linguistic group. They established a powerful kingdom during the seventeenth century that was conquered by the Asante kingdom during the following century. Today approximately 200,000 people consider themselves Gonja.

See Also

Côte d'Ivoire; Languages, African: An Overview.

Latin America and the Caribbean

Gonzaga, Chiquinha

(b. October 17, 1847, Rio de Janeiro, Brazil; d. February 28, 1935, Rio de Janeiro, Brazil), Brazilian composer, pianist, teacher, conductor, and theater director, best known for composing Brazil's first written song for Carnival, "Ô Abre alas" (roughly "Hey, Make Way"), still sung today.

Francisca Edwiges "Chiquinha" Neves Gonzaga was born to an unwed mother of mixed race. After being officially recognized by her father, she received all the trappings of an education befitting the daughter of a military man so that she might serve in the court of Pedro II. After a severe upbringing, she married a wealthy commander in Brazil's merchant marines when she was still a teenager. Yet, much to her family's chagrin, she swapped an oppressive home life for the bohemian music halls of Rio at age 18.

Though Gonzaga had performed her first song, "Canção de Pastores," at a family gathering on Christmas Eve in 1858, her first successful composition, a polka titled "Atraente," was not published until 1877. In the meantime, cut off by her family, she managed to build a reputation as a piano teacher and made a living playing in *choro* groups as well. Choro, an established Brazilian musical form by 1870, originated from foreign rhythms but transformed them into *choroso* (crying) tunes, eventually syncopating them with rhythmic "breaks" and thematically enacting a duel-like improvisation of a dispute. *Chorões*, or choro groups, serenading in city streets, like Mexican mariachis or Spanish *tunas*, consisted largely of performers from a growing middle class who, like Gonzaga, were increasingly intolerant of both an anachronistic monarch and the persistence of the institution of slavery.

In 1885 Gonzaga made her debut as a Teatro de revista composer with the operetta *A Corte na roça*. These one-act musical comedies with roots in Parisian vaudeville shows, much like Spanish *zarzuelas*, represented a performance space for the popular classes to satirize principal social and political events of the day. That same year, Gonzaga became the first woman in Brazil to direct her own musical theater piece, *A filha do Guedes*, presiding over a military band of police, no less. In addition to nearly 2000 popular songs, she produced 77 works of musical theater during her career and in 1899 created the first song written especially for Carnival, "Ô Abre alas."

Gonzaga was equally active in fighting for the social causes she supported, and donated a portion of the profits from the sale of her printed music to the Confederação Libertadora for the abolition of slavery. In 1893 she was jailed for writing *Aperto o botão*, because of its prorepublic stance. In 1917 she cofounded, along with Oscar Guanavarino and Viriato Corrêa Gastão Tojeiro, the Sociedade Brasileira de Autores Teatrais in order to establish and protect artistic copyrights, and was the society's first provisional director as well as its only female member.

Since Gonzaga's death in 1935, two plays and three books have been written about her life. She has been recognized by the Academia Brasileira de Teatro and by various national samba schools for her enormous contribution to Brazilian popular music. The Troféu Chiquinha Gonzaga is awarded each year in Brazil to the best new independent artists, and her music continues to be recorded.

Joy Elizondo

See Also

Abolition and Emancipation in Latin America and the Caribbean; Carnivals in Latin America and the Caribbean.

Latin America and the Caribbean

Gonzaga, Luiz (b. December 13, 1912, Exú, Brazil; d. August 2, 1989, Recife, Brazil), northeast Brazilian accordionist, singer, and composer who popularized the rural dance form *baião*.

Luiz Gonzaga do Nascimento grew up in the small village of Exú in the parched, semi-arid zones of the *sertão* (the backland region of northeast Brazil). His father, a farm worker by trade, played the *sanfona* (Brazilian accordionlike instrument), and his mother sang novenas (prayers of request) in the local church. While still a young boy, Gonzaga became enthralled with the sound of the sanfona and expressed a desire to learn to play. His mother, however, would not allow him to pursue his interest. Nevertheless, the eager Gonzaga managed to explore the instrument in secret, sneaking away to a festival or the marketplace and practicing on other musicians' sanfonas.

In a short time Gonzaga developed a reputation for his talent on the instrument, and the neighbors began to ask him to play. At first, Gonzaga had to do so secretly but eventually his mother consented.

At age 18 Gonzaga left his village and reported for military duty in Minas Gerais. While there, he gained important performing experience playing for the officers, and by the time he left the military in 1939, Gonzaga was ready to test his musical abilities in the bars and cafés of Rio de Janeiro. There he refined his skills and eventually began to perform live for Radio Tupi. The *cariocas* (residents of Rio de Janeiro) soon became intrigued with Gonzaga's distinctive northeastern style and as a result of his growing popularity, RCA soon offered him a record deal.

In 1945 Gonzaga met another northeastern musician, Humberto Teixeira. Together they further explored the music of their homeland, composing *baiãos* with rhythms that were little known in the southeast. These imports gained a broad audience, particularly among the poor and working class. This new dance form rapidly caught on in Brazil's large cities, and the Gonzaga-Teixeira team soon had many imitators, including Waldir Azevedo, whose baião "Delicado" became world famous. In 1953 they arranged the sertão folk song "Mulher Rendeira" for Lima Barreto's film *Os Cangaçeiros*, which was awarded the Golden Palm at the Cannes Film Festival. The song was subsequently heard all over the world.

The Gonzaga-Teixeira team scored another big hit with their baião "Asa Branca," which mourns the plight of a farmer who is forced to leave his drought-ridden land and seek a living elsewhere. The *sertanejo* (inhabitant of the sertão) assures his mourning wife that he will return when the rains come:

When the green of your eye
Is spread over the plantation
I swear to you
Don't cry
Then I will return again
My dear

This piece has been recorded by many contemporary Brazilian artists, including Caetano Veloso and Luiz Gonzaga Jr. Gonzaga's compositions drew on other northeastern musical styles: *calango, forró, xamego*, and others. He recorded many other popular songs during his successful career, including "Vira e Meixe," "Dezesette e Setecentos," and the baiãos "Paraiba," "Juazeiro," and "Assum Preto."

In August 1989 Luiz Gonzaga died in Recife, Brazil, and was buried in his hometown of Exú. Throughout his lifetime Gonzaga had remained strongly attached to his sertão roots, and had always dreamed of giving something back to his community of origin. The artist's dreams were fulfilled after his death when his son, Luiz Gonzaga Jr., also a famous musician, founded a cultural center for the local inhabitants of Exú. In addition, the younger Gonzaga helped to provide gas, water, and roads for the impoverished sertanejos and created a park around his father's birthplace.

Gordon Root

See Also
Rio de Janeiro, Brazil.

Latin America and the Caribbean

Gonzales, Lélia

(b. February 1, 1935; d. July 10, 1994), an Afro-Brazilian woman who was a pioneer in Brazilian political and academic circles and who was dedicated to the causes of women and blacks.

Lélia de Almeida Gonzales obtained several academic degrees, including a bachelor's degree in history and philosophy at the Rio de Janeiro State University, a master's degree in communications at the Federal University of Rio de Janeiro, and a doctorate in social anthropology at the University of São Paulo. She directed the Department of Sociology at Rio de Janeiro Catholic University.

Gonzales figured prominently in post-1950s intellectual life in Brazil. She was one of the first black women to teach at the Federal University of Rio de Janeiro, and in 1978 was one of the founders of the Movimento Negro Unificado (Unified Black Movement). In 1979 Gonzales was also one of the founders of the Working Group on Themes and Problems of the Black Population in Brazil at Cândido Mendes University in Rio de Janeiro. The group has produced various unique essays on Afro-Brazilian issues. A strong activist for women's rights in Brazil, Gonzales particularly focused on the importance of education for the advancement of Afro-Brazilian women. Gonzales's initiative to organize a course on African culture, for the first time in Brazil, in 1976, is an illustrative part of her successful career.

Gonzales published several books, including *Festas Populares no Brasil* (1987, Popular Festivals in Brazil) and *Lugar do Negro* (1982, The Place of the Black), and a variety of articles, including "The Unified Black Movement: A New Stage in Black Political Mobilization."

Michelle Gueraldi

See Also
Rio de Janeiro, Brazil.

Latin America and the Caribbean

González, José Luis

(b. March 8, 1926, Santo Domingo, Dominican Republic; d. December 8, 1996, San Juan, Puerto Rico), one of the most influential Afro-Puerto Rican authors of the second half of the century. In his novels, numerous essays, and short stories, González reexamined the African contribution to Puerto Rican culture and identity.

Born in Santo Domingo to a Dominican mother and a Puerto Rican father, José Luis González moved to Puerto Rico when he was four years old. He published his first book of short stories, *En la sombra*, in 1943, when he was just 17 years old, and in 1945 he was awarded the Premio Instituto de Literatura (San Juan) for another collection of short stories, *Cinco cuentos de sangre* (Five Stories of Blood). He obtained a degree in social sciences from the University of Puerto Rico in 1946 and later completed postgraduate studies at the New School for Social Research in New York and the Autonomous University in Mexico. González openly opposed United States colonialism and favored Puerto Rican independence. In 1955 he renounced his United States citizenship and became a Mexican citizen. He taught literature at the Autonomous University of Mexico and maintained his Mexican domicile until his death. Yet he is considered a Puerto Rican author because of his close personal ties with the island and because most of his work focused on the social, political, and racial problems that affected Puerto Rico and its people.

In 1979 González published *El país de los cuatro pisos* (The Four-Storied House), a controversial essay in which he challenged the traditionally accepted notion of a unitary nation, product of the *mestizaje* (the admixture of Spanish, Taíno, and African roots), by analyzing the relation among class struggle, ethnic groups, and culture. González believed that the traditional definition of the Puerto Rican as *jíbaro*, or white peasant, expressed by the influential white Puerto Rican poet Antonio Pedreira (1899-1939) in *Insularismo* (1934), grossly underestimated the African element. The jíbaro was glorified by the Creole elite in order to deny the African heritage and oppose the growing influence of Anglo-American culture dominant since the 1898 U.S. occupation of the island (*see* Spanish-Cuban-American War).

González characterized the evolution of Puerto Rican national culture in terms of ethnic "floors." The first and most important floor in the forging of Puerto Rico's national identity was African. The Taínos, the first inhabitants of the island, died as a consequence of the Spanish conquest during the sixteenth century. González claimed that although early Puerto Rican blacks did not have a clear national consciousness, they were the first to conceive of the island as their home. The jíbaros, constituting the second floor, settled in Puerto Rico in the second half of the eighteenth century, rather late compared to Afro-Puerto Ricans. Further, they adopted many of the life habits of the slave population, including their diet and dress code. The U.S. occupation of Puerto Rico after the Spanish-Cuban-American War in 1898 added a third floor to the house. The fourth floor was created in the 1940s with Operation Bootstrap, the accelerated process of modernization that industrialized the nation but undermined the sovereignty and autonomy of the island and promoted massive Puerto Rican immigration to the United States.

According to González, these ethnic floors are not static, but rather overlap and influence one another. Like nationhood itself, they are sociocultural, dynamic phenomena. Gonzalez's provocative account of the development of Puerto Rican cultural identity became an instant classic, and no serious discussion on Puerto Rican nationality can ignore it.

Though he was residing in Mexico, Gonzáles wrote for several newspapers and magazines in Puerto Rico, Cuba, Ecuador, and New York. In 1984 he published another collection of short stories, *Las caricias del tigre* (The Tiger's Caresses), which was awarded the Mexican Magda Donato Prize for literary creation. In 1990 the University of Puerto Rico named him Doctor Honoris Causa.

Carlos Dalmau

See Also
Dominican Republic; New York, New York; Transculturation, Mestizaje, and the Cosmic Race: An Interpretation.

Latin America and the Caribbean

González, Rubén (b. April, 1919, Santa Clara, Cuba), Afro-Cuban jazz pianist and a master of the full range of Cuban musical styles.

When pianist Rubén González recorded *Introducing… Rubén González* (1996), he was 79 years old. It was his first album under his own leadership. He had last recorded in the mid-1940s, as part of the legendary Afro-Cuban *tres* player Arsenio Rodríguez's *conjunto* (a 9- to-11-member ensemble combining a rhythm section, stringed instruments, and two trumpets playing the melody line). In a career spanning more than half a century, González mastered many divergent styles of Cuban music, including the *danzón*, the bolero, the *guaracha*, the Son, the mambo, and the *chachachá*. He encapsulated much of Cuba's twentieth-century musical history. But while renowned within Cuba, he was unknown to the wider world.

As a youth González studied at the Cienfuegos Conservatory, showing such devotion to his studies that he completed them by age 15. He did not, however, continue formal studies that would have led to a career as a concert pianist. He later explained, "I wanted to play Cuban *son;* that's what I always loved and still love." In 1941 he moved to Havana and played for such leading Cuban ensembles as La Orquesta Paulina, Los Hermanos, Conjunto Camayo, and the bands of Raúl Palans and Mongo Santamaria.

In 1943 González joined Rodríguez, who advised him, "Just play your own style, whatever it is, but don't imitate anyone." He developed a distinctive piano style that is both romantic and angular, characterized by strong lyricism and swirling arpeggios. His mature playing is by turns tender, bouyant, and percussive. Although González officially retired from music in 1991, his recent recording has for the first time brought him significant recognition outside Cuba.

James Clyde Sellman

See Also
Santamaría, Ramón ("Mongo").

Africa

Goodall, Jane (b. April 3, 1934, London, England), British primatologist whose work with wild chimpanzees in Tanzania greatly influenced primatological field methods as well as human understanding of primates.

Jane Goodall, the daughter of an engineer father and a novelist mother, received no college training in biology before her first trip to Africa, as a tourist, at age 23. She went to Kenya, where she met paleontologist and anthropologist Louis Leakey. Goodall was a passionate amateur natural historian, and Leakey hired her as his secretary. In 1960, with Leakey's help, Goodall established a camp in the Gombe Stream Game Reserve in Tanzania, from which she ventured out each day to observe chimpanzees.

During the early 1960s, with extreme patience and slow progress, Goodall became acquainted with a group of chimpanzees on the shores of Lake Tanganyika. By winning their trust, Goodall was able to sit among them, observing a hitherto undiscovered complexity of relationships. Goodall learned that chimpanzees maintain specific social hierarchies, eat animals as well as plants, and are capable of making and using simple tools. Her chimpanzee subjects inserted thin branches and stiff grass into ant-holes to harvest dinners of ants, and, when sick with diarrhea, wadded together leaves that they used like toilet paper. These discoveries refuted the prevalent notion that humans are distinguished from other animals by the ability to make tools.

In 1964 Goodall married a Dutch photographer who had been sent to document her work. Through his pictures, as well as coverage in *National Geographic* magazine (and later in a *National Geographic* television documentary), Goodall's methods and findings became famous. She continued her studies in Tanzania throughout the 1970s and 1980s, and published a number of books, including her first popular account, *In the Shadow of Man* (1971).

In the 1980s and 1990s Goodall devoted her attention and celebrity status to animal-rights issues, particularly the treatment of chimpanzees used for laboratory tests, and cofounded the Committee for the Conservation and Care of Chimpanzees. Her work continues under the auspices of the Jane Goodall Institute for Wildlife Research, Education, and Conservation.

Eric Bennett

See Also
Chimpanzee.

North America

Gooden, Dwight (b. November 16, 1964, Tampa, Fla.), African American professional baseball player who led the New York Mets to victory in the World Series in 1986.

Dwight Eugene Gooden's father, a semi-professional baseball coach, introduced him to the sport as a child, and by high school Gooden was a star pitcher. Upon graduating in 1982, he was drafted by the Mets, and in 1983 he pitched in the minor leagues and was selected as minor league Player of the Year.

Pitching for the Mets in 1984, Gooden led the major leagues with 276 strikeouts (a major league rookie record), posted a 17-9 win-loss record, and was voted National League (NL) rookie of the year. In 1985 he led the NL in complete games (16) and innings pitched (277) and led the major leagues in wins (24), earned run average (1.53), and strikeouts (268). He was unanimously voted the 1985 NL Cy Young Award recipient as the league's outstanding pitcher. The following year he became the first pitcher in major league history to strike out 200 batters in each of his first three seasons. In postseason play that year, he helped the Mets win the league championship and the World Series.

Over the next few years Gooden continued pitching well, although he underwent rehabilitation therapy for a substance-abuse problem in 1989. He won 19 games in the 1990 season, but after winning 13 games in 1991, he missed the season's last month due to shoulder surgery. He returned to play in 1992. In 1994 Gooden was suspended for 60 days for violating his substance-abuse program, and the suspension was subsequently extended to the entire 1995 season after he repeatedly tested positive for cocaine use. The New York Yankees signed Gooden to a contract after his suspension, but released him at the end of 1997 after injuries had hampered his pitching. Gooden joined the Cleveland Indians before the start of the 1998 season.

See Also
Baseball in the United States.

Africa

Gordimer, Nadine (b. November 20, 1923, Springs, South Africa), South African novelist and Nobel Prize winner who was a vocal opponent of the system of apartheid.

"I have come to the abstractions of politics through the flesh and blood of individual behavior. I didn't know what politics was about until I saw it all *happening to people*." In this 1965 interview, Nadine Gordimer assessed her political consciousness with a self-scrutiny that characterized much of her political writing. In her novels and short stories, she has captured the "flesh and blood of individual behavior" in minute and sentient detail, chronicling daily life in South Africa under apartheid and portraying the human face of resistance.

Gordimer grew up in a small gold-mining town near Johannesburg, the daughter of a Lithuanian Jewish father and an English mother. Although she read voraciously during her early years, she was taken out of school at age 10 because of a perceived heart ailment; she had little formal schooling. Trailing her mother to afternoon teas, the lively Gordimer spent her time observing and mimicking the people she would later portray so astutely – the "well-meaning" members of white South African society. By age 15, when her first story appeared in an adult journal in 1939, Gordimer was already a seasoned writer of children's stories.

A new world opened to Gordimer in 1949 when she began taking courses in Johannesburg at the University of Witwatersrand. There she mixed with musicians, journalists, and writers, crossing for the first time the color line that segregated blacks from whites. As she read the philosophies of Marxism, nationalism, and existentialism, she began to question the social structure of apartheid. She also became involved in the political and cultural movement of the Sophiatown renaissance, which produced the literary journal *Drum*.

During the same year in which she started classes in Johannesburg, Gordimer published her first book of short stories, *Face to Face*. Her first novel, *The Lying Days* (1953), was a loosely autobiographical coming-of-age story. She gained international recognition when her stories were published in the *New Yorker* magazine during the 1950s. A prominent critic of apartheid and an open supporter of the AFRICAN NATIONAL CONGRESS, she continued to live in South Africa under apartheid despite the repeated banning of her books. The remarkably prolific Gordimer has published 12 novels and 13 short story collections.

In the words of critic Stephen Clingman, her writing has represented "the rise to power of the NATIONAL PARTY in 1948; the life under apartheid; the political, social and cultural world of the 1950s; the sabotage and resistance of the 1960s, as well as their defeat by the state; the rise of the Black consciousness movement in the 1970s and the Soweto Revolt; the revolution which seemed to have begun by the 1980s." In her well-known novel *Burger's Daughter* (1979), Gordimer examines the political choices made necessary by the heroine Rosa Burger, the daughter of two communist revolutionaries, who finds herself ultimately unable to opt out of political commitment. Like two of her earlier books, *Burger's Daughter* was initially banned.

Without compromising her realistic portrayal of the political world, Gordimer also explores the realm of sexuality in works such as the *Late Bourgeois World* (1966), *July's People* (1981), and *Sport of Nature* (1987). Under a political system where the body – skin color, hair texture, facial features – defines identity, she has argued that the political and sexual are inextricable. Her narrative style, influenced by such Russian authors as Turgenev, links the social, political, and personal. Using the gestures, words, and thoughts of her characters, she portrays "a society whirling, stamping, swaying with the force of revolutionary change."

In numerous essays, collected into four volumes, Gordimer has commented on the politics of writing and the evolution of leftist political action. She has also written on aesthetics and literary criticism, and on her own travels around a rapidly changing continent. In her autobiographical essays she probes and scrutinizes the evolution of her own thinking – always with a self-critical gaze at her own position as a white woman.

A self-proclaimed political radical, Gordimer was one of the most visible opponents of apartheid for those outside South Africa. With a long-established readership abroad, her words have reached a broader audience than those of most black authors writing on similar issues. Her international reputation, particularly after she won the Nobel Prize for literature in 1991, has protected her from some of the reprisals that faced other South African radicals. After receiving the Nobel, Gordimer spoke about the responsibility that she felt attended such international prestige: "I have two roles in my life – one as a writer and another one, my commitment to the cause of freedom in South Africa and creating a new postapartheid culture in South Africa." In her most recent novel, *House of Gun* (1998), Gordimer highlights the interpersonal relationships that have always been a major part of her work, setting the story within the climate of violence that continues to mark postapartheid South Africa.

Marian Aguiar

SEE ALSO

Sophiatown, South Africa; Johannesburg, South Africa; Women Writers in English-Speaking Africa; Nationalism in Africa; Soweto, South Africa; Black Consciousness in Africa.

North America

Gordon, Dexter Keith

(b. February 27, 1923, Los Angeles, Calif.; d. April 25, 1990, Philadelphia, Pa.), African American JAZZ musician.

Dexter Gordon was one of the most influential tenor saxophone players of the 1940s movement known as bebop. He also played a major role in the development of saxophone styles after the big-band era of the 1930s and 1940s.

Gordon began playing the clarinet at age 13. By age 17 he had switched to tenor saxophone. An important early influence was tenor saxophonist Lester Young, whose smooth phrasing prefigured that of the bebop style. In 1940 Gordon left high school, began playing in a local band, and was invited to tour with the big band of vibraphonist Lionel Hampton. Gordon remained with Hampton for three years.

In 1943, after working briefly with bandleader Fletcher Henderson, Gordon recorded with a quintet that featured pianist Nat "King" Cole. The following year Gordon played with the big band of trumpeter Louis Armstrong before joining the orchestra of singer Billy Eckstine. In Eckstine's band, Gordon met up with trumpeters Dizzy Gillespie, Fats Navarro, and other musicians central to bebop, a style that featured elaborate improvised melodies over rapid chord progressions. During 1945, having relocated to New York City, Gordon recorded "Groovin' High" and "Blue 'n' Boogie" with Gillespie's quintet and played frequently with musicians Charlie Parker, Miles Davis, Bud Powell, and Max Roach. In 1946 Gordon returned to California, although he continued to perform on both the East and West Coasts for a number of years. Between 1947 and 1952 he made a series of highly popular recordings with tenor saxophonist Wardell Gray.

Tenor saxophonist Dexter Gordon played a prominent role in the 1940s bebop movement. *Christian Ducasse/Gamma-Liaison*

In 1960 Gordon acted in the play *The Connection* by Jack Gelber. Gordon also composed and performed music for the play. Following a successful tour of Europe in 1962, he moved to Copenhagen, Denmark. For the next 15 years he remained in Europe, where he appeared at major jazz festivals, taught music, and recorded frequently. He returned permanently to the United States in 1977.

Gordon has influenced numerous American jazz musicians, including tenor saxophonists Sonny Rollins and John Coltrane. He was named Musician of the Year by *Downbeat* magazine in 1978 and 1980, and was elected to the *Downbeat* Hall of Fame in 1980. In 1986 he acted in and performed music for the motion picture *Round Midnight,* earning an Academy Award nomination for best actor. Also in 1986 he received a Jazz Masters Award from the National Endowment for the Arts. Shortly before his death, he acted in the film *Awakenings* (1990).

SEE ALSO

Armstrong, Louis ("Satchmo"); Cole, Nat ("King"); Coltrane, John William; Young, Lester Willis ("Prez");

Davis, Miles Dewey, III; Eckstine, William Clarence (Billy); Gillespie, John Birks ("Dizzy"); Hampton, Lionel Leo; Henderson, Fletcher Hamilton, Jr.; Navarro, Theodore "Fats"; New York, New York; Parker, Charles Christopher ("Bird"); Powell, Earl ("Bud"); Roach, Maxwell Lemuel (Max); Rollins, Theodore ("Sonny").

Latin America and the Caribbean

Gordon, George (b. 1820?, Cherry Garden Estate, Kingston, Jamaica; d. October 23, 1865, Morant Bay, Jamaica), a nineteenth-century politician, activist, and minister of African descent who worked to improve conditions for Jamaica's working poor.

George Gordon was born in JAMAICA to a black slave and her wealthy white master. His father, Joseph, devoted more time to running his estate and furthering his political career than he did to his colored son (of mixed black and white ancestry). Like most wealthy whites in Jamaica during the 1820s, Joseph Gordon was both a member of Jamaica's exclusive House of Assembly and a *custos* in Saint Andrew's Parish, the highest administrative official in the local province.

As the illegitimate son of the slave master, George Gordon learned the importance of self-reliance at an early age, even teaching himself how to read and write. Much to his father's surprise, he showed signs of proficiency in accounting at an early age. By age ten he was a skilled bookkeeper, and around this time Joseph Gordon decided to free his son, sending him to live with his godfather, businessman James Daley, in Black River, Jamaica.

With freedom, Gordon developed his entrepreneurial skills. In 1836, probably while still a teenager, he began operating a produce store in Kingston, Jamaica. The business proved quite lucrative and Gordon soon began to purchase his own land. With his newfound wealth he sent his three sisters to study in Europe and opened his own accounting firm in Kingston. He also saved his father's troubled estate, paying off debts and rescuing his own birthplace, Cherry Garden Estate, from creditors.

As a wealthy businessman Gordon was well acquainted with Jamaica's economic and political realities. He became particularly concerned with the appalling conditions facing Jamaica's poor and sick, most of whom were black. Translating his concern into activism, he threw his hat into the political arena and in 1844 was elected to the House Assembly as the representative of Saint Andrew's Parish. Although he only served one term, he championed many of the issues most important to black and colored Jamaicans, including the excessive punishments meted out to poor peasants for petty crimes.

Gordon worked on behalf of Jamaica's working poor as a Baptist minister as well. Beginning in the early 1850s he traveled throughout Jamaica, delivering lectures and sermons to Baptist congregations. In 1860 he opened three independent Baptist churches at Bath, Springs Garden, and Kingston. Gordon used Scripture to challenge the institution of slavery. He spoke out against the overwhelming power held by Jamaica's white planter class. He criticized the government's oppressive political and economic systems, and demanded that the government repeal the 1842 Master and Servants' Act, which had placed absolute power over the mostly black labor force in the hands of wealthy white landowners. Similar laws denied land to needy black farmers and prevented many of them from either purchasing or occupying abandoned land.

Growing antigovernment sentiment reached a peak in the 1860s with the appointment in Great Britain of Edward John Eyre as governor of Jamaica. Eyre refused to cooperate with those who sought to bring balance to Jamaica's economy and polity. He also refused to meet with the organizers of a large mass protest, including black activist PAUL BOGLE, a friend of Gordon's who had been ordained by him years earlier as a deacon. Historians believe that Gordon was preoccupied with other matters at the time that Bogle began organizing a public demonstration against Eyre in October 1865. Though away from Morant Bay on the day of the protest, Gordon was deeply committed to the march and its organizers.

On October 11, 1865, marchers in Morant Bay clashed with police. Colonial officials declared martial law after a week of rioting. In a brutal crackdown more than 600 black protesters were arrested and tried for conspiracy. Gordon was in Kingstown at the time of the uprising, but he too was arrested and tried for conspiracy. He was convicted and hanged outside the Morant Bay courthouse on October 23, 1865. A century later, in 1969, George Gordon was named a National Hero – the highest distinction awarded by the Jamaican government.

Alonford James Robinson, Jr.

SEE ALSO

Slavery in Latin America and the Caribbean; Kingston, Jamaica.

Africa

Gorée Island, Senegal, island off the coast of SENEGAL, used as a slave port throughout the TRANSATLANTIC SLAVE TRADE.

Settled by southbound Portuguese explorers in the mid-fifteenth century, Gorée Island was first called Palma and served as a port of call for Portuguese ships sailing along the west coast of Africa. Though small, barren, and lacking fresh water, the island was of strategic importance to the Portuguese because it was sheltered by the tip of the CAPE VERDE Peninsula, had excellent anchorage for large ships, and lay only 4 km (2.4 mi) from the African mainland, at the intersection of several major Atlantic shipping routes. Explorers on their way to Asia around the southern tip of Africa, including Vasco da Gama and Fernando Po, frequently stopped on the island to pick up supplies and conduct repairs, and as contacts with the mainland developed, the island became a key European outpost to Africa.

Because of its strategic value, possession of the island was hotly disputed; in 1588 the Dutch seized it from the Portuguese, renamed it Goede Reede (later corrupted to Gorée), and built two defensive military forts on it. In the next three centuries Gorée changed hands 17 times, fought over by the Portuguese, the Dutch, the French, and, briefly, the British. The island became increasingly valuable because it offered whoever controlled it a monopoly on the trade in hides, gum, ostrich feathers, wax, gold and, most important, slaves.

Through Gorée, Senegambia became one of the most important outlets of the slave trade, supplying at least a third of the captives exported before 1600. By the sixteenth century Gorée had become a bustling port where slaves from the entire region were assembled, examined, and branded before being sent to the Americas. As one of the principal slave ports of the transatlantic slave trade, Gorée was the site of great cruelty, brutality, and violence for nearly three centuries. After the end of the slave trade in the mid-nineteenth century, economic activity shifted to the mainland and Gorée declined steadily. It is now a historic tourist attraction administered by the Senegalese government.

Africa

Gorilla, the largest, rarest, and most powerful anthropoid ape.

Gorillas inhabit the forests of equatorial Africa from the western lowlands near the CAMEROON coast to an altitude of about 3000 m (about 10,000 ft) in the central highlands of the DEMOCRATIC REPUBLIC OF THE CONGO and UGANDA. Three geographically distinct types are recognized: the western lowland gorilla, the eastern lowland gorilla, and the more densely coated mountain gorilla.

PHYSICAL CHARACTERISTICS

The male gorilla may attain a height of 1.6 m (5.5 ft) and a weight of 181 kg (400 lb) in its natural surroundings. It is several centimeters taller and much fatter in captivity. The female is about 30 cm (about 12 in) shorter and half the weight of the male. The skin of the gorilla is black, and the hair is coarse and near black, turning gray on the backs of old males (hence called silverbacks). The muzzle is short and hairless, with a flat nose, flaring nostrils, and strong jaws. The eyes and ears are small, and the brow ridge is prominent. The brain case and bulk are smaller than in humans. The skeletal structure of the gorilla is similar to that of humans, but the bones are thicker, the arms much longer, and the legs shorter. The spine lacks the curvatures for a sustained erect posture; thus, while the animal frequently stands upright and walks erect for short periods by grasping at tree branches or other support, it more often moves about in a stooped position, using the knuckles of the hands to bear part of its weight.

Behavior

Little was known about the life of gorillas in the wild until the publication of *The Mountain Gorilla: Ecology and Behavior* (1963), a pioneering study by the American zoologist George B. Schaller, who observed the animals for several years. His work was followed by that of another American zoologist, Dian Fossey, who studied and lived among the mountain gorillas from 1963 until her death in 1985 at the Karisoke Research Center, which she had established in Rwanda in 1967. Gorillas, contrary to legend, were found to be shy and amiable creatures, usually living in groups of 5 to 15. A typical band includes a silverback, 1 or 2 subdominant males, several mature females, and young. Most of the young males are driven out at maturity and may form all-male groups or loosely attach themselves to other bands. A silverback defeated by a male challenger thereafter leads a solitary life.

Gorillas build makeshift camps each night after a day of foraging for the succulent plants, berries, and leaves that constitute their diet. At times the females and young sleep in trees on platforms made of small branches and leaves, while the older males nest on drier grass at the base of the tree. A hooting sound is uttered as an alarm signal or to note any unusual event; when it is used by the male leader, the entire group is instantly attentive. Other calls include sharp grunts for invoking discipline and low growls for expressing pleasure. All gorillas beat their chests; in the male this behavior may serve as a display of power or intimidation. The gorilla has no natural enemies, but the male leader will charge all intruders while the females and young flee to a safe distance. Intruders who run away may be chased and killed; those who stand their ground are not harmed.

The sexual cycle in the gorilla is the same as in the human. The female menstruates about every 28 days and may mate in any season. Single or, occasionally, twin young are born after 9 months, are suckled for about a year, and mature at 11 to 12 years. The known life span is about 30 years.

Intelligence

The mental capacity of the gorilla is still being explored. Not as curious or excitable as its nearest relative, the chimpanzee, the gorilla shows more persistence and memory retention in solving a problem and is more likely to perform a task out of interest than to earn a reward. It also discriminates between geometrical shapes more effectively. After some success with chimpanzees, researchers in the mid-1970s turned their attention to communicating with gorillas by means of the American Sign Language, and one gorilla mastered more than 100 words.

Endangered Status

Gorillas are now considered to be in danger of extinction because of encroachment on their habitat and continued hunting. **Scientific classification:** gorillas belong to the family Pongidae. They are classified as *Gorilla gorilla.* The western lowland subspecies is classified as *Gorilla gorilla gorilla,* the eastern lowland subspecies as *Gorilla gorilla grauere,* and the mountain subspecies as *Gorilla gorilla beringei.*

North America

Gospel Music, a style of African American sacred music that arose in the twentieth century, incorporating improvisation, blues harmonies, and a strong feeling of swing; gospel music builds upon long-standing traditions of black religious expression and stands as one of the most significant African American musical creations.

Gospel music is one of the four most significant musical creations that emerged out of African American culture during the twentieth century. Yet it has received far less attention than have jazz, blues, or rap music, the other main black musical innovations. Jazz, blues, and rap attained greater recognition in part because they offer secular music in an increasingly secular age; they were also at various times perceived as controversial or subversive.

Gospel music has been less visible – to white society, in particular – because it conveys religious affirmation rather than an aura of social rebellion. Yet gospel music reflects the core of African American culture. Although there is a parallel tradition of white gospel music that arises out of the evangelical Protestantism of the Appalachian South, gospel music is at heart an African American phenomenon.

Gospel music mirrors the larger contours of twentieth-century black history. To give the music its due requires setting it in its proper context. That context is complex. First, gospel music is part of a larger transformation in black Christianity that took place during the late nineteenth and the twentieth centuries, above all, as a result of the Great Migration. Second, gospel music cannot fully be understood apart from African American worship practices and spirituality. Finally, any account of gospel music must assess the larger impact it has had on American popular culture.

Black Christianity in the North and South

Gospel music arose in Northern urban areas, above all, in Chicago, where pianist and composer Thomas A. Dorsey played a key role in formalizing the style. The emergence of gospel music represented a return to distinctly African American religious values after a period in which many Northern blacks aspired to a white middle-class religiosity. Gospel music evolved as a result of the changing balance between Northern-born and Southern-born blacks, whose religious experiences and cultural values diverged sharply.

In the South, African American religion took shape under conditions of forced secrecy and racial separation. It remained quite distinct, not only from white evangelical Protestantism, but also from the worship practices of Northern free blacks. In the antebellum years, Southern slaveholders restricted slaves' freedom to worship. For slaves, religion was bound up in the notions of "steal aways" (secret religious gatherings) and "hush harbors" (secluded spots where the slaves could gather in relative safety) (*see* Slave Religion).

During the antebellum years spirituals were the most characteristic form of black religious music. Spirituals gave collective voice to African American sufferings and aspirations. Their lyrics emphasized Old Testament stories of Daniel in the lions' den, David's victory over Goliath, and God's role in bringing his children out of bondage in Egypt. Spiritual singing was informal and participatory; it featured spontaneous and informal harmonies, an antiphonal or call-and-response structure, and a strong emphasis on rhythm.

During the post-Civil War years Jim Crow racial segregation reinforced the distance separating the white and black Christians of the South, ensuring that Southern black Christianity retained its distinctiveness. In the North, by contrast, the free black community took a different approach. Northern free blacks had taken the lead in the formal organization of black religious life, establishing the first black congregations late in the eighteenth century, and in 1816 founding the African Methodist Episcopal Church (AME) in Philadelphia.

Early AME services were emotional and extroverted gatherings that featured spontaneous prayer, shouting, and clapping of hands. But by the latter nineteenth century many Northern blacks opposed such practices as backward and unsophisticated. AME bishop Daniel Alexander Payne, for example, characterized spirituals as "'corn-field ditties' [that] produce the wildest excitement among the thoughtless masses."

Many Northern black congregations – Baptist as well as AME – emulated the religious music of middle-class white Protestantism. Large congregations hired choral directors, introduced formal choirs to replace congregational singing, and performed classical religious music, including Handel's *Messiah* and Mendelssohn's *Elijah*. Historian Michael W. Harris concluded that the apparent goal of these churches was "the virtual annihilation of as many vestiges of [distinctly] black worship customs as possible."

The Great Migration and African American Spirituality

The Great Migration, which brought massive numbers of Southern blacks to the urban North and West, posed an insurmountable obstacle to the assimilationist goals of the Northern black elite. During the first two decades of the twentieth century, hundreds of thousands of poor blacks left the rural South for Northern urban areas. Ultimately, Southern migrants came to outnumber the Northern-born. Migrants came in search of opportunities for economic betterment. What is less recognized is how the Great Migration affected black religious life.

The new Southern arrivals brought their spiritual values with them and in the process worked a profound transformation in the institutional form of black Christianity. Southern black spirituality was most evident in the beliefs and practices of the Pentecostal, Holiness, or Sanctified churches that began appearing across the South during the 1880s and 1890s. Some Southern migrants organized Pentecostal or Sanctified churches in Northern cities, but at the outset most migrants turned to the established AME or Baptist congregations.

These uprooted Southerners wanted to hear impassioned preaching; they wanted worship to be spontaneous and participatory, with interjections by the faithful, such as cries of "Praise Jesus!" They expected "moaning," the term for the wordless humming and vocalization; those who came out of the Pentecostal tradition also expected that the faithful might speak in tongues or be anointed by the Holy Spirit. In response, a new breed of black minister appeared in Northern pulpits, making powerfully emotional appeals, shouting and gesturing, and eliciting active responses from the faithful.

The First Gospel Music Composers

Gospel music was the musical counterpart of the profound changes in religious life that were catalyzed by the Great Migration. It built upon the revival songs of such late-nineteenth-century white evangelicals as Ira Sankey. The lyrics of these revival songs differed sharply from earlier black spirituals. Where the spirituals addressed collective hardships, revival songs were profoundly individualistic. They employed sentimental language and focused on individual salvation and on Jesus' role as a personal comforter. By the late nineteenth century white evangelicals began using the term *gospel songs* in referring to this nondenominational revival music.

Although African Americans embraced the lyrical conventions of the gospel songs, they made gospel music distinctly their own. Charles Albert Tindley was the first African American to compose and publish gospel songs. His 1916 collection, *New Songs of Paradise*, included 37 of his gospel compositions. In 1921 Tindley gained wider recognition when the National Baptist Convention selected several of his songs for inclusion in its songbook *Gospel Pearls*.

Tindley also inspired Thomas A. Dorsey, a prolific composer who is universally recognized as the "father of gospel music." The Georgia-born Dorsey was a blues pianist who did not come naturally to religious music. As a young man he moved to Chicago, where he found success during the mid-1920s as pianist and bandleader for blues singer Gertrude "Ma" Rainey.

Yet Dorsey retained an interest in religion. He regularly attended the annual gatherings of the National Baptist Convention and in 1921 composed his first sacred song, "If I Don't Get There." His early sacred works observed the musical conventions of the white revival song tradition, using simple melodies and basic, straightforward harmonies. During the late 1920s, however, it appeared unlikely that he would devote himself to sacred music. Recording under the name Georgia Tom, he released a series of highly popular songs that were larded with sexual double-entendre, evident in his hit "It's Tight Like That" (1928).

Nonetheless, a combination of opportunity and personal tragedy turned Dorsey from his lucrative popular music career. In 1932 Rev. Junius C. Austin, pastor of Chicago's Pilgrim Baptist Church, appointed him the director of the Pilgrim Baptist Church's newly formed gospel chorus, the second such group to be organized at an old-line church. The position gave Dorsey an opportunity to shape the direction of African American sacred music. His musical destiny was sealed later that year by a devastating personal loss. In August 1932, while he was attending a revival in St. Louis, his wife, Nettie Dorsey, died in childbirth, and his infant son died the following day.

Out of the depths of his grief, Dorsey created what is arguably the greatest of all gospel songs – a personal favorite of Rev. Martin Luther King Jr. and the song that singer Mahalia Jackson performed at King's funeral – "Take My Hand, Precious Lord" (1932):

Precious Lord, take my hand, lead me on, let me stand,
I am tired, I am weak, I am worn.
Through the storm, through the night, lead me on, to the light,
Take my hand, Precious Lord, lead me home.

That song resolved Dorsey's inner conflict between his career as a blues pianist and his calling to write sacred music. It was also the first wholly successful gospel blues song. By melding improvisational blues harmonies with religious themes, this song created modern gospel music.

From that time forward, Dorsey devoted his life to disseminating blues-flavored gospel music. Singer Sallie Martin became his vocalist and chief collaborator. The two demonstrated Dorsey's music and helped organize gospel choirs throughout the United States. In 1933, together with Willie Mae Ford Smith and a number of other gospel singers, they organized the National Convention of Gospel Choirs and Choruses. Martin continued to sing with Dorsey until 1935; then Mahalia Jackson, the greatest of all gospel soloists, succeeded her for a ten-year stint. Martin and especially Jackson were gifted singers and were instrumental in popularizing Dorsey compositions such as "There Will Be Peace in the Valley" (1939). Dorsey worked with many other performers who became prominent in gospel music, including Roberta Martin (1907-1969) and James Cleveland.

Apart from Dorsey, the most important early gospel music composers were Lucie E. Campbell (1885-1963) and Rev. William Herbert Brewster (1897-1987). Among Campbell's best known compositions are "In the Upper Room with My Lord" and "Just to Behold His Face" (1951). Likewise, Brewster's "Move On Up a Little Higher" (1946) and "Surely God Is Able" (1950) have become familiar gospel standards. But, as author and gospel singer Horace C. Boyer observed, a gospel composition only "begins to have real life when it enters the performance medium."

The African American Character of Gospel Music

Gospel music incorporates distinctly African American traditions of performance and worship, reflecting the character of African American spirituality. The essence of gospel performance is participation. Gospel singers employ a wide range of vocal techniques and colorings to make their music emotionally compelling and to draw their listeners in. As is true in jazz and blues, gospel musicians stress expressive range over tonal purity. They punctuate their singing with growls, dips, slides, blue notes, moans, and falsetto effects – techniques that would not seem musical to anyone schooled in the conventions of European classical music. As in jazz and blues, gospel music highlights individual expression through improvised, spontaneous creation.

Gospel musicians try to reach their listeners on an immediate, emotional level. The climax of any gospel song comes during what musicians refer to as the "drive section" or the "working section," in which the accompanists repeat a brief instrumental vamp or vocal phrase while the lead singer improvises variations on the lyrics and interpolates new lines. The repetitive patterns build tension and provide a perfect platform for lead singers to raise the emotional intensity, often to a fever pitch. This intensity serves a direct religious purpose, drawing listeners and performers together in an ecstatic spiritual communion and producing a sense of openness to God that encourages the salvation of sinners.

In a variety of other ways, gospel singers try to close the distance between performers and listeners. They regularly introduce songs with anecdotes, often in the form of personal confession – what Willie Mae Ford Smith called "sermonettes." Some move freely among their audiences, encouraging listeners to join in the singing and to take God into their hearts. On occasion, the musicians themselves are swept up in the ecstatic moment.

The Dixie Hummingbirds, popular during the 1950s, featured the gifted lead singing of baritone Ira Tucker (b. 1925). The group, which excelled at both sweet harmony singing and the more recently developed hard-gospel style, gained a new generation of fans after it sang on Paul Simon's recording "Loves Me Like a Rock" (1973). *Archive Photos/Frank Driggs Collection*

Gospel Performance: Itinerant Musicians, Quartets, and Choral Groups

Although Dorsey is acclaimed as the founder of gospel music, the gospel impulse was evident elsewhere in black culture. First, elements of gospel music can be seen in the playing of such itinerant musicians as Blind Willie Johnson. Johnson, a Texas-born guitarist who attended the Pentecostal Church of God in Christ as well as the Baptist Church, recorded on several occasions during 1927-1930, leaving some 30 titles of mainly religious music. Although his music is not strictly regarded as gospel, his songs incorporate similar elements, including blues harmonies, call-and-response structures, emotionally charged singing, and a highly rhythmic delivery.

Johnson's slide guitar playing was similar to that of blues musicians of East Texas and the Mississippi Delta, and his gravelly, impassioned delivery recalled the singing of Delta bluesman Charley Patton. But Johnson devoted such driving songs as "Church, I'm Fully Saved Today" (1930) to religious purposes. Other musicians who spread the word of God include Blind Joe Taggart and the blind Pentecostal pianist Arizona Dranes. By and large, however, such performers existed on the periphery of American culture, and their religious influence is hard to assess.

A second and more substantial influence on gospel music were the many black vocal harmony groups. Most of these groups were male quartets. Initially they performed a cappella, but by the 1920s and 1930s many had added a guitarist for instrumental accompaniment. Vocal quartets were popular in African American communities during the late nineteenth and early twentieth centuries. They drew inspiration from the quartet singing featured in minstrel shows and built upon the formal instruction in part-singing that Northern teachers and missionaries introduced throughout the South after the Civil War. Of his boyhood in Florida during the 1890s, author James Weldon Johnson reminisced: "Pick up any four coloured boys or young men anywhere and the chances are ninety out of a hundred that you have a quartet.... Indeed, it may be said that all male Negro youth of the United States is divided into quartets." These quartets performed a mixed repertory that included spirituals, ragtime-inspired pieces such as "Waiting for the Robert E. Lee," white revival songs, and the early black gospel songs of C. A. Tindley.

During the twentieth century a number of quartets began to perform full-time, marking the start of gospel music's commercialization. The earliest extant recording of a black religious quartet was made in 1902 by the Dinwiddie Colored Quartet. The group's singing was mannered and formal, incorporating few blue notes and little of the jubilant energy of gospel music. But a later generation of quartets embraced the gospel fervor. Many prominent gospel quartets were founded in the 1920s and 1930s, including the Fairfield Four in 1921, the Blue Jay Singers during 1925-1926, the Harmonizing Four in 1927, the Dixie Hummingbirds in 1928, the Soul Stirrers during 1931-1932, the Golden Gate Quartet in 1934, and the Swan Silvertones in 1938.

Prior to World War II the Golden Gate Quartet had the greatest early impact on quartet singing. Influenced by the Mills Brothers, the Golden Gate Quartet incorporated jazz-style improvisations in its early recordings, with the singers mimicking the sounds of trombones, trumpets, and other instruments. The group sang with a pronounced swing feeling and a percussive style of delivery that was widely imitated. Among the Golden Gate Quartet's early recordings is a striking rendition of Dorsey's "If You See My Savior" (1937).

Men predominated in quartet singing, but in gospel music as a whole, women played an equally central role. Female vocalists were important to the congregations and choirs of black Protestantism. The most prominent gospel soloists were women, including Sallie Martin and Mahalia Jackson. In 1938 Sister Rosetta Tharpe, a member of the Pentecostal Church of God in Christ, appeared with bandleader Cab Calloway at New York City's Cotton Club. That same year she was featured in John Hammond's "Spirituals to Swing" concert at New York's Carnegie Hall, as were the Golden Gate Quartet and Mitchell's

Christian Singers. A short time later, Tharpe signed a contract with Decca Records, becoming the first gospel singer to record for a major label.

During the 1930s and early 1940s several female gospel groups organized. In 1934 Gertrude Ward (1901-1981) established the Ward Singers, which featured the lead singing of her daughter Clara Ward (1924-1973). In 1940 Sallie Martin founded the Sallie Martin Singers, and the Original Gospel Harmonettes were organized three years later. Pianist, composer, and singer Roberta Martin founded the Roberta Martin Singers in 1933 as a male gospel ensemble but added female voices in the early 1940s.

The Golden Age of Gospel Music, 1945-1965

The period from the mid-1940s to the mid-1960s constituted the golden age of gospel music. Many leading gospel soloists established their reputations in the postwar years. The greatest of these was Mahalia Jackson, who combined a powerful voice with matchless control. Jackson was a sensitive interpreter of lyrics who could distill the emotion of a piece through her use of dynamics, vibrato, and a jazz-influenced rhythmic sense.

From 1947 to 1954 Jackson made influential recordings for the small Apollo Records label, including the first million-selling gospel recording, her 1947 rendition of Brewster's "Move On Up a Little Higher." In 1954 she signed with Columbia Records and gained even wider recognition, including a 1954 network CBS television series and appearances at the Newport Jazz Festival in 1956 and 1958. Although Jackson and such gospel singers as Marion Williams (1927-1994) and Dorothy Love Coates (b. 1930) are most often regarded strictly as gospel singers, they were gifted improvisers who rank among America's finest jazz vocalists.

In the late 1940s Williams won acclaim when she joined Clara Ward as a lead vocalist with the Ward Singers. Williams developed into one of gospel music's foremost lyric sopranos. She made particularly effective use of the upper part of her soprano range for improvised cries, a technique that influenced the singing style of rock 'n' roll innovator Little Richard. Coates, featured with the Original Gospel Harmonettes during 1951-1959 and 1961-1971, was a galvanic singer; her harsh timbre and intensely rhythmic delivery mimicked sanctified preaching. The Caravans, a small female choir established in 1952 by contralto Albertina Walker (b. 1929), introduced more prominent soloists than any other gospel group, including Bessie Griffin (1922-1989), Inez Andrews (b. 1935), Cassietta George (1929-1995), the dynamic soprano Shirley Caesar (b. 1938), and James Cleveland, who served as the group's accompanist and arranger during the mid-1950s.

LEFT: Clara Ward and Marion Williams sing as the Ward Family Singers, a long-running gospel group that was founded in 1931 by Gertrude Murphy Ward and her two daughters, Clara and Willa. *Lloyd Yearwood*

ABOVE: Thomas A. Dorsey composed both "Precious Lord, Take My Hand" and "Peace in the Valley" and is widely considered the father of gospel music. *Archive Photos/Frank Driggs Collection*

LEFT: Mahalia Jackson (1911-1972) is generally known as the world's greatest gospel music performer. *CORBIS/Bettmann*
BELOW LEFT: Beginning his career at the age of 8 when he served as a Baptist church soloist, American singer and composer James Cleveland was a towering figure in gospel music. *The Everett Collection*

There were also important male gospel singers. Arguably, the greatest of these was Brother Joe May (1912-1972). May, a student and protégé of Willie Mae Ford Smith, came to the attention of a talent scout for Specialty Records during the 1949 National Convention of Gospel Choirs and Choruses. The power and immediacy of May's huge tenor voice made his debut recording of Dorsey's "Search Me Lord" (1949) a gospel hit. Thereafter he toured widely, often together with such vocal groups as the Soul Stirrers or the Pilgrim Travelers, a gospel quartet formed in the early 1930s.

Like May, ALEX BRADFORD and James Cleveland were formidable male vocalists, but their reputations rest less on their singing than on their compositions, arrangements, and choir directing. Bradford made his first recordings in 1951 and for two decades directed the Greater Abyssinian Baptist Choir of NEWARK, NEW JERSEY. In 1961 he and Marion Williams were the leads in LANGSTON HUGHES's gospel musical *Black Nativity*, which had a two-year run on Broadway.

Cleveland's first important composition, "Grace Is Sufficient" (1947), quickly became a gospel-music standard. From 1954 to 1956 he accompanied the Caravans, and during the 1960s he made a series of gritty and spontaneous-sounding recordings with choirs, including the 300-voice Angelic Choir of Nutley, New Jersey. Cleveland's recordings helped make large choirs, rather than gospel quartets or small groups, the most popular format for gospel music during the 1960s.

Gospel quartets achieved their greatest popularity during the late 1940s and early 1950s. In the post-World War II years, some groups – including the Harmonizing Four and the Dixie Hummingbirds – continued the sweet harmonies of traditional quartet singing. Other quartets embraced a harder-edged, harsher style of singing known as hard gospel, which had been foreshadowed before the war by the Famous Blue Jay Singers. The Soul Stirrers – through the powerful singing of Robert H. Harris (b. 1916), the Soul Stirrers' lead vocalist from 1937 to 1950 – became the leading exponent of the hard gospel style.

During the 1930s the Soul Stirrers was the first quartet to employ "lead switching," in which two lead singers traded off in the middle of a song, generally with an element of competitiveness. Quartets that featured two leads commonly juxtaposed a mellow-voiced tenor with a tenor or baritone who had a harsher, raspier sound. This technique is evident, for example, in the Swan Silvertones' classic Vee Jay recordings of 1956-1966, notably on the traditional "Oh, Mary Don't

You Weep" (1959) and Dorsey's "How I Got Over" (1959).

The Impact of Gospel Music on American Popular Culture

Gospel music had its greatest impact on American popular music in the 1950s and 1960s. Some gospel quartets turned to performing secular music. During the late 1940s the Golden Gate Quartet added folk songs and topical music to its sacred repertory, and the Trumpeteers recorded secular songs under the name the Four Rockets. In the early 1950s several members of the Selah Jubilee Singers transformed themselves into the rhythm and blues (R&B) group the Larks. Likewise the Royal Sons Quintet of Winston-Salem, North Carolina, won far greater renown singing R&B as the Five Royales. During the 1960s the Staple Singers, a family-based group, shifted from gospel to folk music and, later, to soul music.

Gospel music also had a palpable impact on secular R&B groups. Vocal groups such as the Orioles and the Moonglows adopted the lead-switching techniques and the hard gospel sound that were pioneered by the Soul Stirrers. The singing styles of such R&B and soul music stars as Ray Charles and Otis Redding likewise reveal the profound impact of gospel music – and its ecstatic emotionalism – on American popular music.

R&B also had an influence on gospel groups. For example, the Mighty Clouds of Joy, organized in Los Angeles in the mid-1950s, became the first gospel quartet to use electric keyboards, electric bass, and drums – in place of the usual accompanying guitarist. The Mighty Clouds of Joy modeled its singing and carefully choreographed dance steps on the performance style of contemporary soul music groups, which accounted for its nickname, the "Temptations of Gospel." The electric instruments and obvious debt to R&B upset gospel purists, but appealed to many younger listeners.

In addition, many individual gospel singers shifted from sacred to secular music. One of the earliest to do so was Sam Cooke, who between 1950 and 1956 had taken R. H. Harris's place as lead singer for the Soul Stirrers. In 1956 Cooke made his first recordings of secular music and, in the following year, gained his first Top 10 hit with "You Send Me" (1957). Other gospel performers who turned to popular music included Wynona Carr (1924-1976), Aretha Franklin, Lou Rawls, and Johnny Taylor.

During the 1950s and 1960s gospel music had a powerful impact on American culture because it spoke directly to the hopes and aspirations of African Americans. It was intimately bound up with the Civil Rights Movement. "We Shall Overcome," the best-known civil rights song, was adapted from C. A. Tindley's gospel hymn "I'll Overcome Someday" (1901). The Civil Rights Movement made use of gospel songs and gospel-style spirituals, including "This Little Light of Mine" and "Guide My Feet." For a time during the late 1950s and early 1960s, singer Dorothy Love Coates shifted her energies wholly to civil rights activism, working closely with Martin Luther King Jr. The Student Nonviolent Coordinating Committee (SNCC) Freedom Singers and the Nashville Quartet similarly melded political activism and gospel intensity.

Gospel Music since the 1960s

In 1969 Edwin Hawkins (b. 1943) recorded a rendition of "Oh Happy Day" that became a major pop hit and marked out a new direction for gospel music. Hawkins's recording introduced a softer, smoother style, which the music industry has labeled Contemporary Gospel. Unlike the rough-edged, impassioned singing of such earlier gospel stars as James Cleveland and Dorothy Love Coates, Contemporary Gospel recordings utilize sophisticated production techniques and emphasize lighter pop-music textures. Among the most influential artists in the Contemporary Gospel tradition are Andrae Crouch (b. 1950) and Bebe and Cece Winans.

In vocal harmony music, Sweet Honey in the Rock and Take 6 have furthered the tradition of gospel quartets and small choral groups. In 1973 singer and civil rights activist Bernice Johnson Reagon formed the a cappella group Sweet Honey in the Rock, a female vocal ensemble that performs an eclectic mix of political music, folk songs, spirituals, and gospel. In the album *Feel Something Drawing Me On* (1989), the group focused on sacred music.

Take 6, a male ensemble of six devout Seventh Day Adventists, evolved from a quartet formed in the early 1980s by students at Oakwood College, a Seventh Day Adventist college in Alabama. The group's primarily a cappella music has updated the swinging style and instrumental mimicry of the Golden Gate Quartet. The album *Take 6* (1988) combined original songs and new arrangements of such gospel quartet classics as the Trumpeteers' "Milky White Way" (1947) and the Swan Silvertones' "Oh, Mary, Don't You Weep" (1959). Using complex jazz harmonies, witty lyrics, and an infectious, contemporary sound, Take 6 won Grammy Awards for its original song "Spread Love" (1988) and for the albums *Take 6* and *So Much 2 Say* (1991).

The influence of rap music began to be felt in gospel during the 1990s, although gospel musicians preferred to label their performances "street poetry" rather than rap. Large ensembles such as Sounds of Blackness have used the conventions of rap music to reinvent sacred songs, and some gospel quartets, such as the Williams Brothers, have employed synthesizers and percussion overdubs. The Williams Brothers included rap vocals on one selection of their album *Hand in Hand* (1992). Such innovations have inspired considerable controversy among those devoted to more traditional gospel styles.

Conclusion

Once little heard beyond African American places of worship, gospel music now reaches an audience of millions, white as well as black. It emerged from dowdy storefront churches and camp meeting revivals and went on to transform American popular music. Today it is recognized as a vital element in America's cultural heritage, as seen in such Smithsonian Institution projects as Bernice Johnson Reagon's *We'll Understand It Better By and By: Pioneering African American Gospel Composers* (1992) and the Smithsonian's gospel music collection *Wade in the Water* (1994).

Gospel lyrics reflect the influence of late nineteenth-century white evangelicalism, but blues-based harmonies, first popularized by Thomas A. Dorsey, distinguish traditional black gospel music. The gospel singing style – improvisational, impassioned, and jubilant – is an expression of African American culture no less profound than jazz or the blues. It is likewise particularly suited to spiritual uplift and religious transformation. By the 1930s gospel music was the dominant form of African American religious music, whether sung by self-accompanied solo musicians, smoothly harmonizing vocal quartets, energetic gospel choirs, or full congregations.

The two decades after World War II were gospel music's golden age. Gospel music was heard not only in black churches, but also in stylish supper clubs, major jazz festivals, and formal concert halls. It became an important part of the American music business, with major record companies seeking to record gospel performers. Prominent gospel singers – such as Mahalia Jackson, James Cleveland, the Swan Silvertones, and the Dixie Hummingbirds – gained unprecedented visibility in American popular culture, and several gospel performers crossed over and found pop-music success. Moreover, for African Americans involved in the Civil Rights Movement, gospel music helped catalyze political as well as religious transformation.

In the 1970s, however, many younger performers abandoned traditional gospel in favor of the lighter, pop-oriented sound of Contemporary Gospel. Contemporary Gospel ranges from the smooth, jazz-inspired harmonies of Take 6 to the smooth, pop-inspired stylings of Andrae Crouch. Several gospel writers have criticized this new genre of gospel music. Anthony Heilbut, for example, remarked that Contemporary Gospel was "an amalgam of 'temporary' and 'con.'" Gospel singer and scholar Horace C. Boyer regretted that Contemporary Gospel, which makes "few references to God, Christ, and heaven," found its greatest popularity among "music and dance loving people who cared nothing for the gospel background or significance" of the music. In any case, Contemporary Gospel music is far richer than the music-industry label.

Present-day gospel music encompasses a wide range of styles and ensembles, of which commercially recorded gospel music constitutes only a small fraction. Most gospel music continues to be sung at religious services or community functions in African American communities across the nation. In such settings it continues to be a music of active participation and spiritual uplift. As Rev. C. L. Franklin (1915-1984), father of Aretha Franklin, explained, gospel music "raises the bowed-down head and gives hope to the weary traveler." Gospel singers, whether amateurs or seasoned professionals, see themselves as witnesses for the Lord, spreading the word of God's saving grace, offering inspiration to the faithful and strength to the weak of heart.

James Clyde Sellman

See Also

World War II and African Americans; Baptists; Blues, The; Calloway, Cabell (Cab); Chicago, Illinois; Cleveland, James Edward; Cooke, Samuel (Sam); Dorsey, Thomas Andrew; Free Blacks in the United States, 1619 to 1863; Franklin, Aretha Louise; Great Migration, The; Johnson, "Blind" Willie; King, Martin Luther, Jr.; Minstrelsy; New York, New York; Pentecostalism; Philadelphia, Pennsylvania; Rainey, Gertrude Pridgett ("Ma"); Rawls, Louis Allen (Lou); Temptations, The; Tharpe, "Sister" Rosetta; Spirituals, African American.

North America

Gospel Quartets, **small African American vocal groups that contributed to the development of gospel music, often existing outside a religious setting by performing both sacred and secular music.**

The gospel-quartet style developed during Reconstruction when the musical traditions of jubilee singing, shape-note singing, and blackface minstrelsy conflated. Late nineteenth-century gospel quartets were primarily a casual, amateur phenomenon, frequently characterized by family groups performing at special events such as picnics, celebrations, and church services. Though repertoires often centered on spirituals and hymns, secular selections were not uncommon. Early quartets usually performed a cappella (without instrumental accompaniment) and often created original approaches to harmony and counterpoint.

By the turn of the century the form was popular and well established. Soon, hubs of expertise began to develop in the South, particularly around Norfolk, Virginia, and Birmingham, Alabama. The best groups gained regional renown, and in the 1920s and 1930s quartet singing assumed a commercial side, when groups such as the Famous Blue Jay Singers and the Golden Gate Quartet went professional. The former sang in the animated style of Pentecostal congregations. The latter favored upbeat hymns over downtempo spirituals and helped usher in the modern gospel music sound, doing for quartet singing what Thomas A. Dorsey had done for congregational song.

Like gospel music in general, the quartets experienced a major commercial boom after World War II. Some "quartets" added members, either singers or instrumentalists, gaining in richness what they lost in accuracy of title. Major record labels recorded the biggest names, and some groups landed weekly radio shows. Stars of the era included the Soul Stirrers, the Fairfield Four, the Swan Silvertones, the Dixie Hummingbirds, the Clara Ward Singers, and the Mighty Clouds of Joy. In the 1960s the quartet sound became rougher; groups such as the Five Blind Boys of Alabama and the Five Blind Boys of Mississippi incorporated the hoarse and emotive vocal styles that church gospel had popularized.

Following their postwar boom, the gospel quartets lost popularity due to changes in musical fashion, and were in some cases overshadowed by secular spinoffs. Their influence was apparent, however, in the songs of soul musicians and, later, the R&B superstars of Motown Records.

Eric Bennett

See Also

World War II and African Americans; Dorsey, Thomas Andrew; Motown; Pentecostalism; Spirituals, African American.

North America

Gossett, Louis, Jr. **(b. May 27, 1936, Brooklyn, N.Y.), African American film and stage actor known for his portrayal of compassionate authority figures.**

A stage actor from age 17, Louis Gossett Jr. gained national recognition for his Emmy Award-winning role as Fiddler in the popular television adaptation of Alex Haley's *Roots* (1977). In 1982 he became the third African American to win an Academy Award, as Best Supporting Actor for his role as Sergeant Emil Foley in *An Officer and a Gentleman.*

Gossett grew up in a predominantly Jewish neighborhood in Brooklyn, New York. He was the only child of Louis Gossett Sr., a porter, and Helen (Wray) Gossett, a domestic and community activist. Inspired by his mother's activism, he ran for and was elected president of his high school senior class. He was voted best all-around athlete and acted in a school play – a success that led Gustave Blum, a former Broadway director, to encourage him to audition for the Broadway play *Take a Giant Step* (1953). Gossett won the role of Spencer Scott, a black boy coming of age, and subsequently received the Donaldson Award as Best Newcomer of the Year.

Gossett went to New York University (NYU) on an athletic-drama scholarship and majored in dramatic arts while aspiring to become a professional basketball player. He also continued his acting career, appearing on television and in several Broadway and off-Broadway productions, including Kurt Weill's musical *Lost in the Stars* (1957). After graduating from NYU in 1959, he was drafted by the professional basketball team the New York Knickerbockers. Soon after, he won a role in Lorraine Hansberry's award-winning Broadway play, *A Raisin in the Sun* (1959), and decided to focus on acting.

During the 1960s and 1970s Gossett appeared in numerous stage performances, including the musical *Tambourines to Glory* (1963), based on Langston Hughes's novel, and Conor Cruise O'Brien's *Murderous Angels* (1971), in which he played the Congolese political leader Patrice Lumumba – a role for which he received the Los Angeles Drama Critics Circle Award. He also debuted in his first film, a screen adaptation of *A Raisin in the Sun* (1961), and in the mid-1960s created an acting school in New York's Lower East Side for disadvantaged black youth.

Despite Gossett's considerable talent, he received few substantive film offers after his appearance in *An Officer and a Gentleman* in 1982. For several years he struggled with depression and drug addiction while appearing in such films as *Enemy Mine* (1985) and *Iron Eagle* (1986), in which he starred as the tough-talking airforce colonel Chappy Sinclair. During this time, he adopted an abandoned boy whom he had seen on an ABC news segment about homeless children. "My life wasn't working for me," he told *People Weekly* writer Mark Goodman. "Let me help somebody else and get out of myself."

Gossett continues to pursue an active film and television career. In 1989 he starred as a crime-fighting professor in the short-lived television series *Gideon Oliver*, and in 1992 played the retired boxer Honey Palmer in *Diggstown* (1992). In addition to acting, Gossett has lent his voice to a variety of historical figures in documentaries, such as the BBC's critically acclaimed series *The Great War and the Shaping of the Twentieth Century* (1996).

Roanne Edwards

See Also

Haley, Alexander Palmer (Alex).

Africa

Gouin **(also known as the Guin and Kpen), ethnic group of West Africa.**

The Gouin primarily inhabit far northern Côte d'Ivoire and southwestern western Burkina Faso. They speak a Niger-Congo language and are closely related to the Senufo people. Approximately 100,000 people consider themselves Gouin.

See Also

Côte d'Ivoire; Languages, African: An Overview.

Africa

Gouled Aptidon, Hassan

(b. October 1916, near Djibouti), president of the Republic of Djibouti.

At age 14 Hassan Gouled Aptidon, born to an Issa family, left his home in the village of Garissa to live at a Roman Catholic mission. During his youth he earned a living as a local peddler and a construction worker.

Gouled began his political career as an activist in the Somali and Danakil Youth Club during the 1940s. He quickly rose to prominence. From 1952 to 1958 he represented French Somaliland (present-day Republic of Djibouti) in the French Senate. He successfully lobbied for continued association with France in a 1958 referendum, and represented the overseas territory in the French National Assembly from 1959 to 1967. During this period France increasingly favored the minority Afar ethnic group over the more numerous Issa people, fearing that Issa allegiance to Somalis would result in the territory being annexed by the newly independent Somaliland. Angered by French favoritism toward the Afar, Gouled, an Issa, unsuccessfully advocated independence in a second referendum in 1967. In 1972 Gouled became president of the nationalist Ligue Populaire Africaine pour l'Indépendance (LPAI).

The LPAI won broad-based support for independence, and a third referendum in May 1977 endorsed the formation of an independent Republic of Djibouti. In the elections that followed, Gouled became president and his LPAI was swept to power. Initially Gouled sought to create an ethnically representative government. However, within a few years the Afar minority began to feel alienated and underrepresented. In 1979 Gouled dismantled the LPAI and outlawed other parties. He created a single-party state and won reelection in 1981 and again in 1987 as the only candidate permitted on the ballot.

During the early 1990s Gouled faced growing popular discontent and an armed Afar rebellion. Attempting to defuse the opposition, he permitted multiparty elections in 1992. However, he chose which opposition groups could contest seats in the election, leading most Djiboutians to boycott the elections.

Organizations such as Amnesty International criticized Gouled's regime severely for terrorizing the civilian population, torturing prisoners, and denying due process, particularly during the Afar insurgency of the early 1990s. At the same time, he won praise for maintaining a stable government despite the conflicts that have torn the neighboring countries of Ethiopia and Somalia, where he even helped to broker peace agreements. In recent years Gouled sought to address Afar demands by increasing government representation for the minority group.

Ari Nave

See Also

Christianity: Missionaries in Africa.

Africa

Goun

(also known as Gun), ethnic group of West Africa.

The Goun primarily inhabit southeastern Benin. They speak a Niger-Congo language and belong to the Adja cultural and linguistic group. Approximately 300,000 people consider themselves Goun.

See Also

Languages, African: An Overview.

Africa

Gowon, Yakubu

(b. October 19, 1934, Plateau State, Nigeria), a soldier and statesman who headed the military government of Nigeria from 1966 to 1975.

Former Nigerian president Yakubu Gowon, the country's military ruler from 1966 to 1975, advocated unity for Nigeria and national reconciliation after the conclusion of the Biafran War. After his ouster in a bloodless coup, Gowon took the role of senior statesman and continued to work toward regional cooperation in West Africa.

A Christian missionary's son, Gowon was born into the Angas ethnic group in the northern region of Nigeria. He completed secondary school in Zaria, Nigeria, in 1953. He joined the Nigerian army and began his military training in Teshie, Ghana, in 1954. In 1955 he moved to Great Britain, where he completed his studies at the Royal Military Academy in Sandhurst in 1956.

Gowon served in Ibadan, at the Nigerian-Cameroon border, and in Congo-Kinshasa. He attained the rank of lieutenant colonel by 1963. At the beginning of 1966, he commanded the Second Battalion. As the senior northern officer who survived the January 1966 Igbo-led coup, Gowon was appointed army chief of staff. Northern officers chose him to head the new military government after the northerner-led countercoup of July 1966.

Once in power, Gowon desired a quick return to civilian rule, but Nigeria faced civil conflict. Massacres of Igbos in the north frightened and outraged Nigeria's Igbos, who dominated the Eastern Region. In 1967 Gowon declared a state of emergency and divided Nigeria's four regions into 12 states. This redrawing of internal boundaries effectively put most of Nigeria's lucrative oil fields just outside Igbo territory. Consequently, under Igbo leadership, the Eastern Region seceded in 1967 as the independent state of Biafra. After the Biafran War in 1970, Gowon sought reconciliation and declared that there would be "no victor and no vanquished." From 1970 to 1975 Gowon implemented policies aimed at reconstruction. He helped establish the National Youth Service Corps (NYSC) and the Economic Community of Western African States (ECOWAS). He issued a nine-point transition program by which power would be transferred to a civilian government in 1976.

In July 1975, however, the army overthrew Gowon while he attended an Organization of African Unity (OAU) meeting in Kampala, Uganda. Gowon fled to Great Britain, where he lived in exile and earned a doctorate in political science at Warwick University. He returned to Nigeria in 1991. He continued to advocate national reconciliation and, after the 1993 military coup, a peaceful return to democratic rule. During the 1990s he headed the committee to review the ECOWAS treaty, assumed the post of chairman of the National Oil and Chemicals Marketing Company, headed Nigeria Prays (a religious organization dedicated to social, political, and religious reconciliation in Nigeria), and continued to work with the NYSC.

Robert Fay

See Also

Congo, Democratic Republic of the; Ibadan, Nigeria; Kampala, Uganda; Economic Community of West African States.

Europe

Grace Allen Case,

1827 appeal of a legal decision in Antigua, in which it was decided that a slave, even if considered free in England, could be repatriated into West Indian slavery.

The case of Grace Allen proved that a slave's presence in England, as scholar Folarin Shyllon put it, "suspended but did not extinguish" the status of slavery. In 1772 Judge William Murray Mansfield had decided that it was illegal in England to hold the former slave, James Somerset, and sell him back into West Indian slavery; as a result, many believed that the Mansfield Decision had freed all slaves in England. However, as the *Liverpool Mercury* reported the day that the appeal for the Grace Allen Case in England was decided, the boast that English air was too pure, and its soil too free, for slavery to exist "proves to be most woefully unfounded."

Grace Allen lived in England with her mistress from 1822 to 1823 and afterward returned to Antigua with her. Two years later an English customs officer seized Grace from her mistress, claiming that Grace, having resided in England, was a free subject of the king and could not be placed back into slavery. He also charged that her mistress had transported Grace illegally without a contract for service outside the West Indies and without registering Grace with the proper authorities, stipulations that had recently been instituted in order to regulate the slave trade.

The attorney general of Antigua refused to argue Grace's case at length because he did not believe that Grace could be free. The notion that slaves were property was widespread in the West Indies; it was also supported by colonial law. Thus, on August 5, 1826, it was decreed "that the woman Grace be restored to the claimant with costs and damages for her detention."

The decision was appealed to the High Court of Admiralty in England on the assumption that she was a free subject of the king. In June 1827 it was presented to Judge Lord Stowell, who, reluctant to decide the issue, took three months to issue a judgment. He finally decided in favor of the mistress, who claimed that Grace was removed voluntarily, not forcibly, from England to the West Indies, and thus the Mansfield Decision did not apply. Stowell went on to explain: "For I think it demonstrable that she could derive no character of freedom... merely by having been in England, without manumission.... If she depends upon such a freedom, conveyed by a mere residence in England, she complains of a violation for a right which she possessed no longer than whilst she resided in England, but which had totally expired when that residence ceased and she was imported into Antigua."

The case was furiously debated in both English and West Indian presses. Slaveholders were relieved that the decision favored their economic interests, whereas abolitionists felt it was illogical that a black once free was not always free. But Stowell's decision was based on the current reality of the Empire, as he commented: "It has been said that the law of England discourages slavery, and so it certainly does within the limits of these islands [British Isles]; but the law uses a very different language and exerts a very different force when it looks to her colonies, for of this trade in those colonies it gives almost unbounded protection."

The decision in the Grace Allen Case proved that a slave, even if free while in England, could revert to being a slave upon departure. Unfortunately, other cases followed suit and, until the abolition of slavery in Great Britain in 1833 and the emancipation of slaves in 1834, the transport of slaves between England and the West Indies continued, virtually unencumbered by the legal decision in the James Somerset Case.

Leyla Keough

See Also

Great Britain; Slavery in Latin America and the Caribbean; Abolitionism in the United States.

North America

Grace, Charles Emmanuel ("Sweet Daddy") (b. 1882?, Cape Verde Islands; d. January 12, 1960, Los Angeles, Calif.), flamboyant African American evangelist who acquired substantial wealth and founded an unusual Christian religious group.

Charles Emmanuel "Sweet Daddy" Grace was of mixed African and Portuguese descent, born in the Cape Verde Islands around 1882, probably as Marceline Manoël de Graça. He was among the numerous Cape Verdean immigrants who arrived in the United States during the first decade of the twentieth century. In the Cape Verdean communities of New Bedford and Cape Cod, Massachusetts, he worked as a short-order cook, a cranberry picker, and a sewing machine and patent medicine salesman.

Grace founded his first church in West Waltham, Massachusetts, around 1919. By the mid-1920s he had moved south and was holding large, popular revivals and tent-meetings around Charlotte, North Carolina. In 1927, with an estimated 13,000 followers, Grace incorporated the United House of Prayer for All People of the Church on the Rock of the Apostolic Faith. The church grew rapidly and soon included branches all along the eastern seaboard, claiming some 500,000 people in 100 congregations in 67 cities.

Grace attracted followers through his extravagant showmanship. He baptized with fire hoses, sponsored bands and parades, and tossed candy to his followers (hence "Sweet Daddy"); he dazzled with his long hair, multicolored robes, and tricolored fingernails. His followers attributed to him the power to bless such ordinary items as soap, coffee, and eggs – which Grace happened to sell himself – and many believed that buttered toast from his plate had the power to heal. Although Grace did not claim the divinity that his followers imputed, neither did he deny it. "I never said I was God," he once clarified, "but you cannot prove to me I'm not."

Many people outside of Grace's church considered him a con man. During services that pulsed with erotic undercurrents, his parishioners would often pin dollar bills to his vestments. In addition to tithes, Grace accrued wealth from real estate, buying property from Prophet Jones in Detroit and Father Divine in Harlem. He spent a good portion of his income on his congregations, however, supplying apartments, pension funds, burial plans, and free food to the faithful.

Grace died very rich and left behind a fortune in disarray. Of his $25 million estate, it was unclear how much was his own personal wealth and how much belonged to the church. In addition, the IRS claimed millions of dollars in back taxes, initially demanding $6 million but ultimately settling for $2 million. After Grace's death in 1960, his church continued under Bishop Walter T. McCullogh, who legally won the title over rival churchman James Walton.

Eric Bennett

See Also

Cape Verde; Detroit, Michigan; Harlem, New York.

North America

Graffiti Art, a New York City folk-art phenomenon among African American and Hispanic urban youth, characterized by brilliant color and cryptic intricacy.

In the late 1960s a Greek American teenager from Washington Heights, New York, achieved notoriety by painting his nickname, or "tag," Taki 183, throughout New York City. Taki 183's fame sparked the envy and imagination of hundreds of black and Hispanic teens, who began leaving tags of their own. Graffiti soon became a competitive sport, as numerous artists vied to be the most prolific. As competition grew, stylistic prowess replaced sheer ubiquity as the coveted distinction, and enormous, three-dimensional murals superceded unembellished tags. Because graffiti artists wished to display their tags before as large an audience as possible, they selected subway cars – which traversed the entire city – as their canvas.

By the mid-1970s, the color and style of graffiti art had become part of the hip hop aesthetic. City officials, however, considered the murals to be signs of delinquency and disorder. Starting in 1977 the Transit Authority tightened security in train yards and began washing coaches with a solution of petroleum hydroxide. As artists braved razor wire, guard dogs, and this new toxic chemical, tagging became a sport of subterfuge as well as a display of skill.

The efforts of the Transit Authority were overwhelmingly successful, however, and many graffiti artists began photographing work they knew would be obliterated. Graffiti culture thus came to exist in photographs, videotapes, and fanzines as well as on the street. It spread to other cities, and, particularly in Los Angeles, often demarcated the territory of different gangs.

While New York officials tried to eradicate graffiti, the Manhattan art scene gobbled it up. In the late 1970s the artist Fab Five Freddy (later the host of the television program "Yo! MTV Raps") established a connection between the uptown graffiti artists and the downtown galleries. Soon numerous artists painted on real canvases and earned large sums of money for their work. Subject to art-world caprice, however, the trend was short-lived.

Although its daring practitioners have declined in numbers, graffiti persists as an art and an aesthetic. Hip hop periodicals chronicle the innovations of new graffiti artists, while T-shirts, music videos, and the fashions of famous RAP artists reflect their influence.

Eric Bennett

SEE ALSO
Hip Hop in the United States; New York, New York.

North America

Grandmaster Flash, Melle Mel, and the Furious Five,

an African American musical group that was important in the creation of RAP music.

Now regarded as one of the founding groups – along with Afrika Bambaataa and Kool Herc – of what hip hop and rap fans call "old school" rap, Grandmaster Flash and the Furious Five was formed in 1977. Flash, born Joseph Saddler, began acting as a disc jockey (DJ) at local parties in the early 1970s while still in high school in the Bronx. Like some other DJs of the time, he began making a kind of musical collage by playing two or more records at once and experimenting with scratching – manually moving the needle across the disc to create a new, rhythmic sound. Flash teamed up with fellow DJs Cowboy (Keith Wiggins), Melle Mel (Melvin Glover), Kid Creole (Nathaniel Glover, brother to Melle Mel), Mr. Ness (Eddie Morris), and Rahiem (Guy Williams) – the Furious Five.

The group became the most popular rap act in New York City, playing parties, balls, and nightclubs. Soon after the SUGARHILL GANG released the first rap hit single, "Rapper's Delight," in 1979, Grandmaster Flash and his band signed with Sugar Hill Records, the first company to market rap to a national audience. The group's 1982 hit single, "The Message," a starkly poetic look at the nightmares of urban poverty, is credited by critics with changing rap's focus from buoyant dance music to a forum for social commentary.

By 1984 the original band had split up, reforming into two separate groups – one led by Flash, the other by Melle Mel. In 1987 they reunited, and have since toured along with other old school rap artists.

Kate Tuttle

SEE ALSO
Hip Hop in the United States; New York, New York.

North America

Granger, Lester Blackwell

(b. September 16, 1896, Newport News, Va.; d. January 9, 1976, Alexandria, La.), African American civil rights leader and director of the NATIONAL URBAN LEAGUE (NUL).

The son of a doctor and a teacher, Lester Blackwell Granger grew up in NEWARK, NEW JERSEY, and earned a bachelor's degree from Dartmouth College in 1918. He served as an artillery lieutenant during World War I (1914-1918), after which he taught school in the South. In 1922 he took a post at Ironsides, the state vocational school for African Americans in Bordentown, New Jersey, where he taught for most of the next 12 years. He became involved with the National Urban League, first as an educational secretary, then as a labor leader. In the 1930s he was instrumental in the Urban League's efforts to create trade unions for blacks.

In 1941 Granger became the league's executive director. Although a gradualist in combating racial discrimination, he pressed the United States government during World War II (1939-1945) to desegregate the armed forces and the defense industry (*see* MILITARY, BLACKS IN THE AMERICAN). After the war he pressed the government to deny funding to racially discriminatory housing developments, and he helped black workers oppose discrimination in the labor movement. As the CIVIL RIGHTS MOVEMENT gathered momentum in the late 1950s, Granger's critics called on him to accelerate his desegregation and antidiscrimination efforts and to use more aggressive tactics. Granger argued for a more moderate approach based on education and persuasion, and within the Urban League his view largely prevailed. He resigned from the league in 1961 and in 1962 taught at Dillard University in New Orleans.

SEE ALSO
World War I and African Americans; World War II and African Americans; Labor Unions in the United States; New Orleans, Louisiana.

Europe

Grant, Bernie

(b. February 17, 1944, Georgetown, Guyana), radical grassroots organizer and politician who became one of the first black members of Parliament (MPs) in GREAT BRITAIN in 1987.

Bernie Grant has been a controversial parliamentarian, more at home with grassroots organization and black radicalism than with establishment politics in the House of Commons. Described as "a leader walking the rope between street heroism and government office," Grant has defended his black constituents and articulated their views.

Grant grew up in Georgetown, the capital of GUYANA, where he attended a Jesuit school. In 1963 he and his parents, Eric and Lily Grant, moved to Great Britain, where he attended Tottenham Technical College and then studied mining engineering at Heriot-Watt University in Edinburgh. He left the university because of racist policies that refused blacks' entrance to a program to study mining in SOUTH AFRICA. He worked as a railway clerk and a postal employee until he became a trade union official.

During the 1970s Grant led a campaign against the National Front, a white supremacist organization active in Britain. Though blacks celebrated him for his efforts, the white press depicted him as a dangerous and violent black extremist. This only made him more popular among blacks, and many urged him to seek election to the Haringey Borough Council. He won election in 1978, and in 1985 was elected leader of this council. He thus became the first black leader of a local political body in EUROPE.

Grant then received a nomination for the Tottenham seat in Parliament. It was unclear whether the Labour Party would support him. He had defied Labour in 1985 by refusing to condemn the killing of a police officer in the Tottenham riots. He sympathized with young blacks from the Broadwater Farm estate in Tottenham, saying that the police had gotten a "bloody good hiding." Nevertheless, he won election representing Tottenham in 1987 and joined two others, DIANE ABBOTT and PAUL BOATENG, in becoming the first black members of Parliament.

In Parliament Grant has remained an outspoken populist. He advocates for blacks and other oppressed groups – including women, youth, the Irish, the poor, and the elderly. He fights racism not only in England but in Europe, too, as chair of the Standing Conference on Race Equality in Europe (SCORE). Grant openly challenged the party line by supporting the creation of a black section within the Labour Party and a black parliamentary caucus.

In his most controversial initiative in Parliament, he suggested in 1995 that the British government financially support Africans and West Indians who want to return to their homelands as a reparation for the British involvement in slavery and colonialism. In the past, fascists and racists had proposed repatriation schemes as a means to rid Great Britain of its black population. Thus, some view Grant's proposal as damaging to race relations in Great Britain. Grant insists that this plan is not a substitute for fighting racism in Great Britain, but is about creating positive choices for black people. He is a member of the Committee of Eminent Persons on Reparations for Africa and chair of the African Reparations Movement in the United Kingdom.

Leyla Keough

SEE ALSO
Colonial Rule; Riots in Great Britain, 1985; Slavery in Latin America and the Caribbean.

Latin America and the Caribbean

Gratiant, Gilbert

(b. December 27, 1895, Saint-Pierre, Martinique; d. November 1985, Paris, France), poet, novelist, and critic; precursor of Négritude generation who was among the first to use Creole as a literary language.

Gilbert Gratiant, of mixed African and European descent, grew up in a literary household that, unlike most mixed-race families in MARTINIQUE, did not attempt to hide its African roots. This consciousness of his heritage was evident in his earliest literary project: in 1926 he helped found the short-lived journal *Lucioles*, the first forum to explore the Franco-Caribbean literary identity of Martinique. But the moderate tone of this journal would earn Gratiant the scorn of René Ménil and ETIENNE LÉRO, two of the young editors of the journal *Légitime Défense* (first and only issue in 1932), who accused Gratiant of catering to the taste of the elite mixed-race bourgeoisie of Martinique. This episode would profoundly mark the rest of Gratiant's literary career.

Following the end of World War II, Gratiant wrote his most important poem in French, *Credo des Sang-Mêlé* (1950), in which he renewed his call for a synthesis of European and African cultural influences in Martinique. In the same volume, he published all his collected poetry in Creole under the title *Fab' Compè Zicaque* (published as a separate volume in 1958 and reprinted in 1970). Although Gratiant was not the first to transcribe French fables into Creole, he pushed the use of the language into uncharted, more original areas.

After being rejected by at least part of his own generation, Gratiant's literary blending of the Creole and French languages and of French and African cultural influences has been embraced by a younger generation of Martinican writers. In their collective manifesto, *Eloge de la créolité* (1993, "In Praise of Creoleness"), Gratiant's stylistic heirs, Jean Bernabé, PATRICK CHAMOISEAU, and RAPHAËL CONFIANT, pay homage to this "visionary of Caribbean authenticity." Contributing to the renewal of interest in Gratiant's work is the recent publication of his *Fables créoles et autres récits* (1995), which contains texts in both French and Creole and a preface by AIMÉ CÉSAIRE.

Richard Watts

SEE ALSO

Languages, Creole, in the Caribbean; Négritude.

North America

Gray, William Herbert, III

(b. August 20, 1941, Baton Rouge, La.), African American congressman, minister, and foundation president; he held the highest ranking leadership position attained by an African American in the United States House of Representatives.

William H. Gray III was born to William H. Gray Jr., a Baptist minister and president of two Florida colleges, and Hazel Yates Gray, a high school teacher. In 1949 his father became pastor of the large and powerful Bright Hope Baptist Church in Philadelphia and moved his family north. In 1963 Gray graduated from Pennsylvania's Franklin and Marshall College and became an assistant pastor in Montclair, New Jersey. He earned a master of divinity degree from Drew Theological School in 1966, became senior minister at his church the same year, and earned a degree in theology from Princeton in 1970. As a minister Gray tried to help his poor parishioners by establishing housing projects. He also set an important precedent by suing (and prevailing against) a landlord who refused to rent an apartment to him because he was black.

In 1972, after his father died, Gray returned to Philadelphia and became pastor of Bright Hope. He continued to advocate for better housing and in 1976 made his first run for Congress, losing narrowly to Robert Nix, a black Democratic congressman for whom Gray had interned in college. Gray, also a Democrat, accused Nix of doing little as unemployment and poor housing ran rampant through his district. In 1978 Gray ran again and won.

Gray served on the House Foreign Affairs and Budget Committees, but after Republican Ronald Reagan became president in 1981 he resigned from the Budget Committee. In 1983 he returned to the committee, where he earned a reputation for integrity and compromise, and in 1985 became the committee's chair. He played a key role in ushering through Congress many of the large budget bills of the 1980s.

Gray was also active in foreign policy, especially United States policy toward Africa. He was largely responsible for winning U.S. sanctions against South Africa's APARTHEID regime over several Reagan vetoes. He also supported aid to many African nations, and he defended U.S. anticommunist measures in Africa, including covert action in ANGOLA and sanctions against the Communist government of ETHIOPIA.

In 1989 Gray, by then vice-chair of the CONGRESSIONAL BLACK CAUCUS, became the majority whip for the Democratic Party, the third highest rank in the House leadership. In the same year a CBS news report implicated him in a criminal investigation by the Justice Department. The department, then under the control of Republican president George Bush, was at first silent about whether Gray was a target of the investigation. Only after being pressed by Gray did the department acknowledge that he was not a target. The rumors nonetheless damaged Gray's political position.

In 1991 Gray surprised many observers by announcing his retirement from Congress to become president of the UNITED NEGRO COLLEGE FUND (UNCF). At UNCF he raised large sums of money and began projects to improve the curricula of historically black colleges and universities.

SEE ALSO

Philadelphia, Pennsylvania.

Europe

Great Britain, **an island nation off the northwestern coast of Europe where blacks have had a presence for centuries.**

Although it is commonly believed that blacks first entered Great Britain after World War II, a black presence there can be traced back to 200 C.E. As a result of British participation in the slave trade during the sixteenth century, a black community developed that by the eighteenth century numbered 15,000 in London alone. An irony that marked the African-British relationship is that although the British took pride in the freedom of their own land, they institutionalized slavery and colonialism abroad. Even after abolition, decolonization, and the influx of a large number of blacks after World War II, another contradiction remains: despite the fact that people of African descent have lived in Great Britain for centuries, many white British have refused to accept that their black neighbors, too, are British. But this is slowly changing, as blacks increasingly become involved in local and national politics and gain recognition for their contributions to British culture.

THE EARLY AFRICAN PRESENCE

Several accounts indicate that Africans served in Britain as soldiers in the Roman legions of Septimius Severus as early as 200 C.E. Some scholars claim that in 862, Africans captured in Viking raids on SPAIN and North Africa were brought to Ireland, where they were called "blue men." A small number of blacks were pages and entertainers in the courts of both King James IV of Scotland (r. 1488-1513) and Queen Elizabeth I of England (r. 1558-1603). In general, British contact with the people they called "Ethiopes" or "blackamoors" was mediated by Mediterranean EUROPE until 1554. That year, five West Africans sailed to England with the English captain John Lok for training as interpreters, to facilitate the emerging trade between Africa and England.

As Great Britain's involvement in the slave trade increased, its black population grew. Says historian Gretchen Gerzina, "The African became part of the everyday language of Englishmen. Even in the sixteenth century, when Shakespeare wrote *Othello* he was not, as past critics have argued, particularly 'confused' about racial identities... He too would have seen black people on the streets of London for most of his adult life and so would his audience." During the Elizabethan era, blacks began to appear as characters in literature, plays, and other entertainment. Although Shakespeare presented the Moor Othello as a sympathetic character, at this time blacks were more often depicted in art and literature as representations of filth, evil, sin, ugliness, and even the devil. Whiteness, meanwhile, began to be equated with purity, virtue, beneficence, beauty, and God. This literary development was accompanied by scientific speculation on race that perpetuated negative ideas about blacks as well as theories of black inferiority.

The Slave Trade

The discovery of a sea route around Africa's southern coast in 1488 by the Portuguese explorer Vasco da Gama and the subsequent development of a Portuguese seaborne empire helped open a new world for Europe, as did exploration of the Americas. In 1497, when John Cabot led the first royally sponsored transatlantic expedition, Great Britain began to participate in the "Age of Discovery;" within a century, Great Britain rivaled Spain and France for dominance in the West Indies. Between 1609 and 1632 the English gained control of St. Kitts, Nevis, Barbados, Antigua,

Made by Society for the Suppression of the Slave Trade founder Josiah Wedgwood in 1787, this medallion galvanized many in the English and American abolitionist movement. *By kind permission of the Trustees of the Wedgwood Museum, Barlaston, Staffordshire, England*

Belize, Montserrat, and Bermuda. But it was not until Jamaica was wrested from the Spanish in 1655 that sugar – and thus slaves – became a commodity for exchange.

In 1562 Queen Elizabeth I sent naval pioneer John Hawkins to the Atlantic coast of Africa to compete with Spain in the trans-atlantic slave trade. This involvement laid the foundations of a British overseas empire that depended on a monopoly on sugar production and the transport of slaves. This mercantilist system was implemented through restrictive trade practices, such as a series of Navigation Acts, passed by the government in the seventeenth and eighteenth centuries, which stipulated that only English ships could transport products to English ports.

English slaving expanded under James I (r. 1603-1625), but it was not until the 1660s that the transport of blacks from the British-controlled African ports of the Gambia and the Gold Coast to the Caribbean became a matter of English policy. In 1663 England chartered the Company of Royal Adventurers – renamed the Royal African Company in 1672 – which officially designated blacks commodities, or chattel, to be exchanged across the Middle Passage in the slave trade. This company held a monopoly on slaving, annually transporting some 70,000 slaves until 1698, when all Englishmen were granted the right to trade in slaves. During the 1730s a preference for traffic in gold dust and ivory drew profits away from slaving. But in the 1740s British, French, and Spanish competition in the Caribbean resumed, and in 1750 a new company, Merchants Trading to Africa, dealt in slaves through ports in London, Liverpool, and Bristol. Such European conflicts in the West Indies continued until the 1763 Treaty of Paris, which established Great Britain as the wealthiest colonial power, second in size only to Spain.

The Emergence of a Black Population in Great Britain

One result of John Hawkins's slave expedition and subsequent forays was an increase of the black population in England so significant that in 1596 Queen Elizabeth proclaimed "blackamoores... of which kinde of people there are allready hear too manie... should be sent forth of the land." The queen hired a merchant to take blacks from Great Britain to Spain and Portugal, and an official of the Privy Council directed all civil authorities to "aide and assist him to take up suche blackamoores as he shall finde within this realme" and "to be served by their owne countrymen [rather] than with those kinde of people." The growth of poverty during the Elizabethan era – combined with the fact that blacks could be paid less than the white working class – exacerbated xenophobia. But whites of all classes opposed a black presence, and their agreement on this issue facilitated the emerging image of English identity as distinctly white.

Little changed as a result of Elizabethan policy. By the 1670s blacks outnumbered whites in the West Indies, and many blacks continued to arrive in England. Some Africans were sent to England to be educated in Christianity for missionary service; some African princes, as well as the mixed-race children of West Indian planters, also arrived for secular training in the English language or other trade skills.

In 1791 Prince John Naimbanna of Sierra Leone was sent to England for schooling; upon his return to Africa, he fell ill and died. Tragic tales of royal lives struck a chord in the British upper classes, and the histories of these African princes were widely read. White Englishwoman Aphra Behn's novel *Oroonoko* (1688), a sympathetic story of an enslaved African prince, was adapted for the stage and gained wide popularity. Ukawsaw Gronniosaw, born an African prince, tells of his betrayal by a merchant who sold him into American slavery in *A Narrative of the Most Remarkable Particulars in the Life of James Albert Ukawsaw Gronniosaw, An African Prince, as Related by Himself* (1770). A similar story is told of William Ansah Sessarakoo in *The Royal African; Or, A Memoir of the Young Prince of Annamaboe.* Sessarakoo's life inspired poems and plays and roused British sympathy.

A 1731 law that prohibited blacks from learning trades made it difficult for them to live independently in Great Britain, and in fact most blacks at the time worked as household servants. A few were held as "pets" by bourgeois women who dressed them elaborately and treated them lavishly, such as the "favored African youth" of the duchess of Queensbury, Julius Soubise, who was educated in the social graces and equestrianism. Some were seen as a vital part of the household and treated with respect. Jack Beef was aide to magistrate John Baker; Francis Barber was treated as a son by writer Samuel Johnson, who schooled Barber and left him a generous inheritance. Ignatius Sancho lived an independent life after serving the duke of Montague until he made enough money to open his own grocery business. Poor blacks who did not find work as servants were often forced to beg, and black beggars became familiar sights on the sidewalks of London.

Yet some blacks in Great Britain in the eighteenth century won success and influence. A small number figured prominently in the arts and in sports – black entertainers such as concert violinist George Bridgetower won fame in England, as did boxers Tom Molineaux and, later, Bill Richmond. Others were politically active. Ottobah Cugoano (John Stuart) was a radical abolitionist, as was Olaudah Equiano, who served in many literary and official capacities and acted as an administrator of the Sierra Leone Settlement. These Africans, among others, frequented pubs, corresponded, and gathered together. By the eighteenth century London and other ports such as Liverpool and Bristol had acquired active, self-sufficient, and even prosperous black communities, the members of which soon organized for the abolition of slavery and the slave trade.

Slavery and British Law

The population of approximately 15,000 people of African origin or descent in eighteenth-century London posed a dilemma for the white English. As the scholar Edward Fiddes wrote in 1934, England "had landed herself in a hopeless illogical position. She justly prided herself on the personal liberty which Englishmen enjoyed under the Common Law," but "she sanctioned and even promoted a severe system of slavery in her colonies." As there was no parliamentary legislation on slavery in England, courts wavered in their decisions regarding slaves. In part because certain courts decided that Africans could be held as property because they were considered "heathens," it was popularly believed that baptism could confer freedom.

Some judges upheld Lord Chief Justice John Holt's 1706 comment in court that "as soon as a Negro comes into England, he becomes free: one may be a villain [serf] in England, but not a slave." Adherents to this opinion, which became known as the HOLT DECISION, asserted that a slave brought to England could not be forcibly returned to slavery in the West Indies. This precept had been upheld in the seventeenth century in the cases of Katherine Auker and Dinah Black, slaves brought by their masters from the West Indies to England, who sued for and won their freedom. But these cases, Gerzina claims, "did little more than keep the two women employed and off the streets while the English judicial system wavered over problems of property versus humanity."

Caribbean slaveholders continued to bring their slaves to England and other parts of Great Britain on travel for months or even years, and insisted that their slaves – whether or not free in England – return to the West Indies as their property. The Holt Decision was contradicted in 1729 by the YORKE AND TALBOT OPINION, in which Attorney General Philip Yorke and Solicitor General Charles Talbot supported West Indian slaveholders with the proclamation "that a slave, by coming from the West Indies, either with or without his master, to Great Britain or Ireland, does not become free; and that his master's property or right in him is not thereby determined or varied." They also asserted that "baptism did not confer freedom."

Although the Yorke and Talbot Opinion permitted slaveholders to maintain their slaves' subject status while traveling, freedom was sometimes granted on a case-by-case basis to those slaves who were able to go to court. In the Tom and Mary Hylas Case of 1768, Mary, a slave who had been promised her freedom upon her marriage to Tom Hylas, was kidnapped by her master and forced to return to the West Indies. With the legal advice of the white abolitionist GRANVILLE SHARP, Mary's husband sued successfully for damages and her return.

A highly religious Englishman, Granville Sharp had joined the abolitionist cause after his involvement in the Jonathan Strong Case of 1767. In this case Jonathan Strong, a black slave, was freed from his former master's attempt to sell him back into slavery. Throughout the trial, Sharp expressed outrage that British courts permitted the morally and legally reprehensible system of slavery to continue on English soil. It was not until the James Somerset Case of 1772 that Sharp was able to convince an influential judge – Lord Chief Justice William Murray Mansfield – that Yorke and Talbot were wrong. Mansfield declared that "there was no right in the master forcibly to take the slave and carry him abroad" from England.

But kidnappings and the forcible repatriation of slaves from England to the West Indies continued. In the 1822 GRACE ALLEN CASE, tried in the West Indies, it was concluded that a "slave's residence in England merely suspended the state of slavery which revived on return to the New World colonies." This case, among others, revealed that the Somerset Case was largely ineffective in prohibiting forced repatriation. Nor did the case outlaw slavery in England, as the Joseph Knight Case had outlawed it in Scotland in 1778. Nevertheless, it brought the horrors of slavery to the forefront of public discussion and helped instigate a public outcry for abolition.

An early nineteenth-century political cartoon by British caricaturist Isaac Cruikshank lampoons the gradual abolition of slavery, advocated by many in England. *© The British Museum*

THE BLACK POOR AND THE SIERRA LEONE SETTLEMENT

The Somerset Case gained a reputation, mostly because of false reports in the British and foreign press, of being a guarantee of freedom to all slaves in Great Britain. For American slaves, this reputation lent weight to the British promise that freedom would be their reward for supporting the British during the AMERICAN REVOLUTION. After the British were defeated in 1783, a number of African American soldiers went to Great Britain seeking freedom as well as the payment promised them for military service. Instead, they found a country that not only was unable to accommodate them economically, but forbade them to learn trades.

Forced to work as servants or beg, these blacks settled in major urban areas and seaports while the white English debated solutions to the growing number of black poor. The Committee for the Relief of the Black Poor was founded in 1786 by white abolitionists Jonas Hanway, William Wilberforce, and Granville Sharp, among others. The committee helped ease the burden of poor blacks by providing money and accommodations, but it soon became overextended. As they had been during the reign of Queen Elizabeth I, blacks in Great Britain were again blamed for unrest and unemployment, and a plan was made to resettle them elsewhere. Henry Smeathman, a white businessman who had recently returned from Africa, proposed to settle the black poor in Sierra Leone at a cost of £14 per person. Within one year, he claimed, they could create a self-sustaining community and even send profits home to Great Britain. The Sierra Leone Settlement Plan was supported by the government, the committee, and several prominent abolitionists, including Olaudah Equiano, who at one point administered the project.

But the plan was a fiasco from the beginning. Though Smeathman had claimed that there was "an anxious desire of getting on board the Ship [that was] appointed to carry them to the coast of Africa," fewer than 500 blacks enlisted for the 1787 voyage. Furthermore, Smeathman had misrepresented the hospitality of Sierra Leone's climate and political condition for settlement, and many of the blacks who sailed there died from starvation or disease; those who survived lived in constant fear of enslavement.

Sir Learie Constantine, former high commissioner for Trinidad and Tobago and a West Indian cricket player, takes his seat in the House of Lords in 1969. *Hulton Getty/Liaison Agency*

Abolition and Emancipation

The English public had little knowledge of the extent of the Sierra Leone debacle. In fact, the settlement scheme was presented to the public as a positive part of a wider government move toward abolition. Public sympathy for abolition had taken hold by the end of the eighteenth century. A particularly horrifying tragedy occurred in 1781, when, as a result of shortage of supplies to feed and aid slaves, and in order to collect insurance money, the captain of the English ship *Zong* threw 133 captive Africans overboard. As the event became known, public outrage over the horrors of slavery grew, and abolitionist arguments became more accepted.

In 1787, the same year that poor blacks sailed for Sierra Leone, members of the Committee for the Relief of the Black Poor joined with a pietistic religious group called the Clapham Sect to form the Committee for the Abolition of the Slave Trade, or the Abolition Committee. These abolitionists, along with white Quakers such as Samuel Hoare and Thomas Knowles, dedicated their time and energy to letter-writing and speaking campaigns against slavery. A similar effort was undertaken by Equiano, Cugoano, and other black abolitionists, who formed an abolitionist organization called the Sons of Africa.

Black radicals also contributed to the cause by supporting abolitionism in conjunction with broader working-class movements. William Cuffay sought radical political reform through the working-class Chartist movement for parliamentary reform, which protested social injustice in industrial Great Britain. William Davidson was part of a revolutionary plot to assassinate English cabinet members and overthrow the English government on charges that it was racially and economically unjust. Robert Wedderburn, as a follower of the underground movement of the radical millenarian Thomas Spence, demanded the equality of blacks and all the underclass within the context of a struggle for land reform.

White Englishmen and women joined the abolitionist cause by boycotting goods produced by the slave trade and wearing badges of the Wedgwood medallion, which portrayed a kneeling black man in shackles crying, "Am I not a man and a brother?" Meanwhile, however, in his parliamentary battle against the slave trade and slavery, the abolitionist and parliamentarian William Wilberforce, who was supported by Prime Minister William Pitt, sought to allay white fears that the abolition of slavery would result in England becoming crowded with West Indians. Caribbean slaveholders, afraid of losing their livelihoods, exploited these fears with accounts of violent slave uprisings and speculation about the miscegenation and black poverty that abolition would bring to England. But abolitionist arguments were bolstered by a glut in the sugar market, which prompted free trade supporters to propose limiting the slave supply in an effort to control sugar output. In addition, the English were tired of compensating Caribbean plantation owners for their losses, and with industrialization, a new trade strategy was developing that favored greater open market competition. The English were also increasingly looking to India and China for trade, and less to the West.

Thus, economic interests supported political and moral arguments, and the British slave trade with its colonies was outlawed by the 1807 Abolition Act. Because most abolitionists supported a gradualist plan for the end of slavery and the emancipation of slaves, however, Caribbean slavery was not abolished by the British Parliament until 1834, when a system of apprenticeship was put in place, and all slaves were not freed until 1838.

Blacks in Nineteenth-Century Great Britain

After abolition, black students, freed slaves, domestic servants, and sailors from the West Indies trickled into Great Britain, but for several reasons the black population was less visible during the nineteenth century than might have been expected. One factor was the increased dispersion of blacks throughout Great Britain. The explosion of trade and the development of steamships and new ports, as well as new railways to Manchester and other industrial towns, made it easier to travel throughout the nation. Black sailors, who had been readily accepted at English ports since the seventeenth century, continued to arrive, especially after their position was legitimized by an 1823 Act of Parliament that stated they were "as much British seamen as a white man would be." (Newer settlers of color, however, such as Indians, were not accorded this status.) But these sailors now landed not only in London or Cardiff, Wales, but in Liverpool, Bristol, and other seaports. In addition, the Customs Act of 1832, which sought to prevent participation in the slave trade by fining ship captains who brought Africans to England, may have limited the entrance of free Africans.

Many blacks were absorbed into the white lower class through interracial marriage. In particular, the high ratio of black men to black women encouraged the intermarriage of black men and white women. Olaudah Equiano and Francis Barber both married white women, and intermarriage became common within the working class, where blacks were often accepted as equals. The English objected more to marriage across class lines than marriage across racial barriers. For instance, a number of whites objected to the marriage of the royal-born Ukawsaw Gronniosaw to a white Dutch servant on the grounds of class, not race.

Local blacks continued to contribute to the cultural life of Great Britain. The composer Samuel Coleridge-Taylor attended the Royal College of Music and later composed *Hiawatha's Wedding Feast*, which gained wide popularity in Europe. The actor Ira Aldridge played Othello on the English stage. Individual blacks from various places also passed through Great Britain in the nineteenth century. African American abolitionists such as Frederick Douglass, Paul Cuffe, Nathaniel Paul, and Charles Lenox Remond went to England to lecture on slavery, temperance, and racial prejudice; during the 1890s Ida B. Wells-Barnett took her antilynching campaign to England and Scotland, exposing American racial atrocities to an international audience. African nationalist Edward W. Blyden served as the Liberian ambassador to England and in various official capacities for the British government in Sierra Leone. Mary Seacole, a former American slave, risked her life to nurse soldiers in the Crimean War and became a revered figure in England. These and many other blacks comprised a growing and recognized, if transient, population that contributed to the artistic, intellectual, and political life of nineteenth-century Great Britain.

Colonialism and Pan-Africanism

The end of the slave trade was followed by a new system of exploitation – colonialism. The Navigation Acts had been repealed in 1849 in favor of less restrictive trade policies, and industrialization had encouraged the British to seek actively raw materials as well as mass markets in which to sell products made from these materials. With these factors in mind, Great Britain, France, and Germany, and to a lesser extent the Netherlands, Italy, Portugal, and Spain, competed for African land and resources, sending explorers to scramble for Africa. Despite intense African resistance in many areas, the continent was divided up and administered by these powers for much of the twentieth century.

In Great Britain at the beginning of the twentieth century, many blacks faced poverty caused by unemployment and racial discrimination. With the onset of World War I, however, whites left for war, and blacks helped supply needed labor for industry. Although British law barred blacks from combat duty, some blacks in Great Britain and the colonies were hired as sailing crews in the British navy. Where blacks did serve, the British established segregated units.

This discrimination continued after the war, when blacks who had fought were excluded from victory celebrations. Although the English encouraged repatriation, the black community's numbers actually increased during these years. Those who stayed in Great Britain faced severe racism, stemming in part from white resentment of the employment shortage and interracial marriage; those who returned to the West Indies or Africa did so with resentment and anger over British prejudice. As a result of these tensions, in the summer of 1919 white-on-black violence escalated into riots in a number of British cities, including Liverpool, Manchester, Barry, Newton, and Hull. In the Cardiff Riots of 1919 in Wales, nearly 1000 blacks sought refuge at prisons and fire stations as police attempted to shield them from white violence. It was clear that much of the population of Great Britain did not consider blacks British nationals.

The government reinforced the feeling that blacks were unwelcome. The Aliens Order Act of 1925 obliged not just "aliens" but any "coloured" seamen to register with the authorities and prove their citizenship. Because many blacks in British Commonwealth nations lacked the official documentation required to prove citizenship, they were designated aliens and became subject to deportation. Facing this discrimination, the black community in England began to form advocacy organizations such as the League of Coloured Peoples (LCP), founded in 1931. Often compared to the United States' National Association for the Advancement of Colored People (NAACP), the LCP admitted whites as members and advocated a legal and diplomatic approach to improving the welfare of Great Britain's blacks. The organization's newsletter, the *Keys*, published the work of renowned black writers, including cultural historian and activist C. L. R. James.

In the early twentieth century London became a center of black intellectual activity and Pan-Africanism, a movement to unite people of African descent in a common struggle for independence. In 1912 Dusé Mohammed Ali, a Sudanese-Egyptian, established the outspoken newspaper *African Times and Orient Review*, the first political paper by and for blacks to survive past its initial publication (it lasted until 1920). The West African Student Union (WASU) was established in 1925 "to encourage sound and scientific study of African history, laws, customs, and institutions with a view to preserving the African identity" and served as a center for West African students promoting African nationalist movements until the 1950s. In 1921 the Second Pan-African Congress held several sessions in London, and in 1923, the Third Pan-African Congress was held entirely in London.

At this time, the presence of blacks in English politics also increased. In 1913 John Robert Archer was elected the first black mayor in England for the city of Battersea. He went on to become president of the African Progress Union, established in 1918, and led the British delegation to the Pan-African Congress in Paris in 1919. African American actors continued to flock to England, such as George William Walker, who at the turn of the century performed in *Dahomey* in London, and Florence Mills, who captivated London in the musical revue *Blackbirds of 1926*.

During the 1920s Africans Jomo Kenyatta and Kwame Nkrumah; West Indians Aimé Césaire, Eric Williams, C. L. R. James, and George Padmore; and Americans Paul

Black activist Bernie Grant became one of the first black members of the British Parliament.
CORBIS/Zen Icknow

Robeson and Marcus Garvey helped galvanize a powerful Pan-Africanist community in London. Some of these blacks formed the organization International African Friends of Abyssinia, to protest the 1936 Italian invasion of Ethiopia and welcome the exiled emperor of Ethiopia, Haile Selassie I, to London. Financed by Ras Tafari Makonnen of British Guiana (present-day Guyana), this organization was absorbed into the International African Service Bureau, which in 1944 became the Pan African Federation.

By the 1930s and 1940s a generation of blacks born in Great Britain had come of age. Much of this generation had grown up poor and suffered from racism, including that of Oswald Mosley's fascists. "Mosleyites" blamed black immigrants for the growing poverty of working-class whites, spread antiblack propaganda, and advocated for the repatriation of blacks to the West Indies. These blacks had seen Great Britain's racial policies progress somewhat, but had also witnessed the British tolerate and even accommodate American segregation and racism within the military during World War II. Moreover, an informal "color bar" existed in Great Britain. For instance, Learie Constantine, a Trinidadian cricketer hired by the British government, was refused a room at a London hotel because he was black. The court case that followed did much to expose the implicit racism of British policies. The Pan-African community was concerned with both the plight of blacks in Great Britain and the struggle for self-determination among peoples in Africa. For instance, the Fifth Pan-African Congress, held in Manchester in 1945, was devoted as much to planning strikes and boycotts against imperial rule in Africa as it was to fighting for racial equality in Great Britain.

World War II had brought another influx of colonial blacks – skilled labor to work in factories, and soldiers and sailors to fight the war. More than 4000 West Africans enrolled in the Royal Air Force, as did more than 6000 West Indians. These colonial subjects hoped that fighting for freedom in World War II would hasten the independence of the colonies from imperial rule. Their hopes were not ungrounded – at this time, as Great Britain faced a racist and fascist enemy, many blacks gained sympathy for their antiracist and anticolonialist efforts, and increased awareness had already elicited progessive actions from the government. The Colonial Development and Welfare Acts of 1940 and 1945 were an effort to distinguish Great Britain ethically from Nazi Germany. And in 1941 England had signed the Atlantic Charter, which affirmed the right of all peoples to self-determination.

After the war Great Britain began decolonization in many of its territories. Although officials envisioned a slow route for African self-government, riots in Accra, Ghana, soon proved that this would not be the case. Many African and West Indian nationalists followed suit, and by the 1960s most countries in Africa and the West Indies had gained independence.

Immigration and Race Relations

The postcolonial era has been characterized by an influx of formerly colonized peoples into urban centers such as London. This "colonization in reverse," as Jamaican poet Louise Bennett calls it, began when 492 Jamaicans arrived in England on the *Empire Windrush* in 1948. That year's Nationality Act offered colonial subjects British citizenship and the opportunity to stay in Great Britain as long as they wished. Following World War II, London Transport, the British Hotels and Restaurant Association, and the National Health Service recruited Jamaicans to work in Great Britain, greeting them with a "Welcome Home" sign upon their arrival. West Indians in fact preferred to migrate to the United States, where 65,000 British Commonwealth citizens were allowed entrance every year. But the United States' 1952 McCarran-Walter Act made an official distinction between British citizens and West Indian citizens, and permitted only 800 Caribbean individuals to immigrate to the United States each year – a virtual ban. This funneled immigration to Great Britain, where by 1958 the West Indian population had reached 125,000. The total number of blacks in Great Britain by the late 1950s was about 192,000, or less than .5 percent of the population.

Most West Indians migrated to England for purely economic reasons, intending to return to their homelands as soon as possible. While in England, however, they generated a distinct culture, a tendency reinforced by discrimination in employment and housing. The 1956 Suez crisis caused an economic recession, and racial tension mounted as a result. In London in 1958 these tensions resulted in white violence toward blacks, escalating into the NOTTINGHAM AND NOTTING HILL RIOTS, 1958.

The government responded by threatening to close its borders. However, a resultant race to "beat the ban" caused increased immigration, primarily of unskilled blacks, and the immigrant population soared to more than 300,000 by 1962. That year, the Commonwealth Immigrants Bill was enacted to restrict the entrance of colonial citizens with passports to those who also had employment vouchers; a clause permitted deportation if they were convicted of a crime within five years of their entrance.

This reaction to racial tensions – which essentially blamed the immigrants – was repeated in 1965, when the number of employment vouchers available to immigrants was restricted. Although earlier immigration laws had treated aliens and Commonwealth citizens differently, the Immigration Acts of 1968 and 1971 essentially lumped them together and stated that only those who could trace their heritage to grandparents born in Great Britain would be exempted from immigration controls. This meant that whites who had traveled to administer the British Empire could return freely to Great Britain and be secure in their citizenship, while nonwhites who had gained Commonwealth citizenship as a result of their countries' domination by the expanding British Empire did not have such security. A 1981 Nationality Act later imposed a system of tiered citizenship, wherein those who lived in and traced their ancestry to Great Britain gained primary citizenship rights and Commonwealth citizens were placed in second and third categories that offered limited rights to reside in Great Britain and gain citizenship.

Critics have argued that in the 1960s and 1970s, politicians in Great Britain often denied the political relevance of blacks by omitting the issue of race in their debates. In an effort to ease racial strife within the nation, restrictive immigration laws were accompanied by race-relations legislation; the 1966 Race Relations Act, for instance, was passed to prosecute those who incited racial violence or practiced racial discrimination. (Ironically, the first person to be convicted on this charge was black.) The 1976 Race Relations Act made racial discrimination unlawful in training, housing, education, and the provision of goods, facilities, and services, and created the Commission for Racial Equality (CRE). Some scholars claim that organizations such as the CRE have shielded politicians from addressing race directly.

In the 1980s a black presence was becoming more permanent in small cities such as Birmingham, Manchester, Leeds, and Bristol. In London, Trinidadians settled in Notting Hill, site of the famous Notting Hill Carnivals, and Jamaicans settled in Brixton, where a vibrant Rastafarian culture emerged. But the reactions of both the white British and the government to blacks made it clear that they were, as Walvin notes, "not overseas Brits, but blacks living in white society." As one West Indian leader in Great Britain at the time explained, "The Notting Hill riots taught us one bitter lesson: we were black first and British last."

Blacks organized for their rights in groups such as the West Indian Standing Conference, founded in 1959, and found themselves increasingly influenced by the American CIVIL RIGHTS MOVEMENT. Inspired by the 1964 visit of MALCOLM X to London, blacks formed the Racial Adjustment Action Society (RAAS) to advocate for "the human rights of coloured people," reexamine black identity, and protect blacks' "religious, social, and cultural heritage." In 1965, following an influential visit to England by Martin Luther King Jr., an organization called the Campaign Against Racial Discrimination (CARD) was formed to combat racial discrimination and oppose immigration bans on Commonwealth citizens.

Extreme conservatives such as Enoch Powell in the 1960s and the neofascist National Front in the 1970s objected not only to immigration, but to the use of

Born as a neighborhood party in 1966, the Notting Hill Carnival, now held every year in August, has grown into a massive celebration of Caribbean and West Indian culture. *CORBIS/David Cummings; Eye Ubiquitous*

English law to protect blacks in riots, claiming that this would in effect be a defense of hardened criminals. This stereotype was based partly on the higher crime rates in impoverished black neighborhoods, but mostly on xenophobic propaganda. The police force developed Special Patrol Group units to fight crime, but their presence in fact increased the possibility of violence. A massive police presence at the 1976 Notting Hill Carnival led to police confrontations with black youth. The Bristol Riots of 1980 were the result of a strong-arm anticrime swoop on a café where the majority of patrons were black. Riots followed in the summer of 1981 in such cities as Liverpool and Manchester; most notorious were the BRIXTON RIOTS OF 1981. After additional riots in Brixton and Birmingham in 1985, one black woman, tired of the severe police control, declared that blacks were "living in a concentration camp with fringe benefits."

The Commission for Racial Equality reported in 1987 that very high levels of racial discrimination still existed in employment, housing, and other social sectors, and that the government had proved unwilling to strengthen antidiscriminatory measures. In the late 1980s Prime Minister Margaret Thatcher's nationalism upheld a concern with English identity that furthered anti-immigrant sentiment. Thatcher claimed in 1978 that if immigration were not controlled, Great Britain would be swamped with more than 4 million outsiders. In the 1990s racially motivated violence against blacks continued to rise, with some 60,000 attacks every year.

CONTEMPORARY GREAT BRITAIN

Nevertheless, in the 1990s Africans and West Indians who were fleeing political troubles, or seeking a better life or temporary employment, continued to migrate to Great Britain. Unemployment was still rampant – up to 25 percent in some areas – but employment measures had successfully placed blacks in public sector jobs, creating a small black middle-class community. Though discrimination still existed, blacks were also beginning to rise in the ranks of British government and politics. In 1987 four blacks, including DIANE ABBOTT and BERNIE GRANT, were elected to British Parliament, and formed a parliamentary Black Caucus.

Since the 1980s an active black feminist community has been organized by various groups, including the Brixton Black Women's Group (BBWG) and the Organization of Women of Asian and African Descent (OWAAD) (recently disbanded). Black homosexuals and bisexuals in Great Britain have also organized on behalf of their rights in such organizations as the Black Lesbian and Gay Group. The Labour Party, derided by conservatives in the 1960s with the campaign slogan "If you want a nigger neighbour, vote Labour," was elected in May 1997 and proudly counted Trevor Phillips, who is of African descent, as Prime Minister Tony Blair's right-hand man. Blacks have also entered the monarchy: a black man whose father was a famous cricketer from Jamaica was dubbed Lord Taylor of Warwick. In addition, blacks of African and Caribbean descent were among the best athletes playing for British teams.

STUART HALL, a prominent figure in the growing field of black British cultural studies, claimed that British identity was increasingly contested, and was undergoing a constant process of redefinition during the 1990s. The term "black British," coined by Trinidadian novelist of South Asian descent Sam Selwyn, defined as black all people in Great Britain who were of non-European origin, including Africans and Asians. Widely used in the 1980s, this term has since lost popularity, in part because of a growing sense of distinction and an assertion of black African or West Indian identity.

At the end of the 1990s Great Britain was marked by a confluence of cultural traditions. Alongside the royal tradition into which Lord David Pitt of Hampstead was accepted, blacks were contributing to cultural life with Rastafarianism and other cultural traditions and musical styles derived from Africa and the Americas. Although blacks comprised less than 2 percent of Great Britain's population, black culture set the tone for urban fashions and youth culture (*see* LONDON, BLACKS IN: AN INTERPRETATION).

A vibrant black arts tradition has developed in Great Britain, beginning with the Caribbean Artists Movement, which was formed in 1966. Black arts have been significantly supported by the Greater London Council, a government organization that funded the arts until its dissolution in 1987. Although it was not until 1973 that the first book by a black person born in Great Britain was published there–*Black Britain*, by Chris Mullard–a notable black literary community, boasting of writers such as Caryl Phillips and poets such as LINTON KWESI JOHNSON, was blossoming. In the 1990s black-oriented magazines such as the *Voice*, *New Nation*, and *Arena* provided a forum for black British views and foster a sense of community.

Perhaps it was premature for William Davidson to assert in 1820 that blacks had finally "claimed their rights as Englishmen"; for, as he did then, many blacks still feel "a stranger in a strange land." But certainly it is fair to say that since decolonization, Britain has evolved into a multicultural "New Commonwealth" with a dynamic cultural life and a firm democratic tradition, in part due to the substantial contribution of its black population.

Leyla Keough

SEE ALSO
Colonial Rule; Dusé Mohammed Ali; Decolonization in Africa: An Interpretation; Explorers in Africa Since 1800; Gold Trade; Ivory Trade; Liberia; Middle Passage, The; Nationalism in Africa; Race: An Interpretation; Slavery in the United States; Transatlantic Slave Trade; London's Black Poor and the Sierra Leone Settlement Plan; Bridgetower, George Frederick Polgreen; Riots in Great Britain, 1985; Cardiff, Great Britain; Constantine, Learie Nicholas; Gronniosaw, James Albert Ukawsaw; Netherlands, The; Notting Hill Carnival; Pitt, David; Portugal; Antilynching Movement; Blyden, Edward Wilmot; Garvey, Marcus Mosiah; James, Cyril Lionel Richard; King, Martin Luther, Jr.; Miscegenation; Wells-Barnett, Ida Bell; Antigua and Barbuda; Rastafarians; St. Kitts and Nevis; Christianity: Missionaries in Africa.

North America

Great Depression, a massive economic collapse in the United States and throughout much of the world that had particularly serious consequences for African Americans.

The Great Depression was a time of economic hardship throughout the United States that fell with particular severity on African Americans. But it also brought important political and social developments that in the years ahead would transform African American life. For blacks the Depression started long before the October 1929 stock market crash. During the 1920s Southern black farmers suffered the devastating impact of the boll weevil on their cotton harvests. They also faced a collapse in farm prices that followed World War I as President Woodrow Wilson lifted agricultural price supports and the government canceled wartime orders.

In one of the largest internal migrations in American history, which came to be known as the Great Migration, many African Americans abandoned farming and moved to cities in the North as well as the South. However, the low-wage jobs that they found in urban areas forced them to live in cramped low-rent districts that became black ghettos. The Great Migration also sharpened racial hostilities, as revealed in the unprecedented support given the Ku Klux Klan in the North. The formal onset of the Depression only made matters worse, economically as well as in race relations.

By 1932 roughly half of the black workers in New York, Chicago, Philadelphia, and Detroit were without jobs, and nearly one out of three African American families was receiving some form of public assistance. Moreover, the black unemployment rate greatly exceeded the white rate. In Pittsburgh during 1933, for example, 48 percent of black workers were unemployed; the comparable figure for whites was 31 percent. The number of lynchings of African Americans also rose – from 7 in 1929 to 20 in 1930 to 24 in 1933, the worst year of the economic collapse.

Blacks responded to hard times and heightened racial hostility with increased militancy. The NATIONAL ASSOCIATION FOR THE ADVANCEMENT OF COLORED PEOPLE

As the Great Depression dragged on, poverty, despair, and idleness became endemic in many rural communities. *Archive Photos*

(NAACP) struggled to secure a federal antilynching law. The Communist Party of the United States of America (CPUSA) also played an active role in fighting for black rights, for example, in the 1931 SCOTTSBORO CASE and the 1932 case of Angelo Herndon, a black Communist who led a protest of unemployed workers in Atlanta, Georgia. It was the driving force in the National Negro Congress (1936-1946) and in the SOUTHERN NEGRO YOUTH CONGRESS (1937-1948). Other examples of Depression-era black radicalism include the Southern Tenant Farmers Union, founded in 1934, and the 1935 Harlem Riot.

On occasion white liberals actively supported black rights. The Congress of Industrial Organizations unionized thousands of black industrial workers in integrated unions such as the United Auto Workers and the United Steel Workers. In 1939 First Lady Eleanor Roosevelt helped arrange an Easter Sunday recital by famed black contralto MARIAN ANDERSON at Washington's Lincoln Memorial after the Daughters of the American Revolution refused her permission to appear at a concert hall owned by the organization. Moreover, President Franklin Roosevelt appointed an unprecedented number of black advisers, known collectively as the BLACK CABINET, including William Hastie, Robert C. Weaver, and MARY MCLEOD BETHUNE.

But African Americans found themselves shortchanged by Roosevelt's NEW DEAL. The National Recovery Administration permitted lower wages for blacks than for whites doing the same work. Racial discrimination was evident in the hiring and housing policies of the Tennessee Valley Authority (TVA) as well as in the segregated camps of the Civilian Conservation Corps. Many landowners, rather than share Agricultural Adjustment Administration subsidies with their black sharecroppers, had their tenants evicted and kept the entire payment for themselves.

Although a 1935 executive order banned discrimination in Works Progress Administration (WPA) projects, a subsequent cut in the WPA budget brought a sharp economic downturn, the so-called Roosevelt Recession, that jeopardized many black families. WPA policies were the subject of widespread protest, as seen in topical blues such as Casey Bill Weldon's "WPA Blues" (1936) and Porter Grainger's "Pink Slip Blues," sung by Ida Cox in 1939. Furthermore, Roosevelt refused to endorse two key black political goals – a federal antilynching law and abolition of the poll tax.

Nonetheless, in 1936 African Americans rallied around Roosevelt and the New Deal. This support represented an electoral shift of historic proportions – for the first time since Emancipation a majority of black voters cast their ballots for the Democratic Party. On the other hand, this political support was not unquestioning, as a number of Depression-era black protests make clear. Paradoxically, the key protest of these years never took place. In 1941, as increased defense spending rapidly lifted the country out of depression, blacks found themselves almost wholly excluded from the new defense jobs. For example, the head of North American Aviation, then greatly expanding its work force, announced that blacks would only be considered for jobs "as janitors and other similar capacities."

African Americans answered with the first March on Washington, more than two decades before the better-known 1963 protest led by Rev. Martin Luther King Jr. The strategy behind the march foreshadowed that of the future CIVIL RIGHTS MOVEMENT, particularly its use of large-scale direct-action protest in a powerfully symbolic setting, its focus on influencing the federal government, and its careful orchestration of national news coverage to multiply the impact of the planned demonstration.

The key forces behind the 1941 March on Washington were the BROTHERHOOD OF SLEEPING CAR PORTERS (a black labor union) and the Communist-led National Negro Congress. A. Philip Randolph, president of both organizations, proposed a gathering of at least 100,000 African Americans in the nation's capital to protest unfair defense industry hiring practices. Never had the capital faced such a massive demonstration, and a nervous Roosevelt wanted to prevent it altogether.

The result was a signal victory for Randolph. In June 1941 Roosevelt signed Executive Order 8802, prohibiting discrimination throughout the federal government as well as in defense work and establishing the Fair Employment Practices Committee to oversee the new policy. In response, Randolph called off the march, but he maintained his March on Washington organization to remind Roosevelt not to neglect black Americans.

James Clyde Sellman

SEE ALSO

World War I and African Americans; American Federation of Labor and Congress of Industrial Organizations; Antilynching Movement; Blues, The; Chicago, Illinois; Detroit, Michigan; Great Migration, The; Harlem Riots of 1935; Hastie, William Henry; King, Martin Luther, Jr.; Lynching; New York, New York; Philadelphia, Pennsylvania; Randolph, Asa Philip; Weaver, Robert Clifton; Works Progress Administration; Communist Party USA, African Americans and the; March on Washington, 1963; March on Washington, 1941.

Africa

Great Escarpment, **dividing range crossing ANGOLA, NAMIBIA, SOUTH AFRICA, LESOTHO, SWAZILAND, MOZAMBIQUE, and ZIMBABWE. This major geographic feature separates the high plateaus of the southern African interior, including the vast High Veld, from the coastal lowlands.**

The Great Escarpment appears U-shaped on a map, extending from east central Angola south to the boundary between South Africa's Western Cape and Northern Cape provinces, then east, and finally north, ending south of the Zambezi Valley in Zimbabwe. It runs parallel to the coast at varying distances, between 55 and 240 km (35 and 150 mi) inland in South Africa. The valley of the Limpopo River between South Africa and Zimbabwe is the only significant break along its 5000 km (3100 mi) length. The escarpment varies greatly in form, from a relatively subdued feature in parts of Angola and Namibia and in northeastern South Africa to a sheer 1300 to 2300 m (4300 to 7500 ft) cliff in the Drakensberg Mountains of Lesotho and KwaZulu-Natal Province, South Africa. The Great Escarpment incorporates numerous local ranges, among them the Serra da Chela in east central Angola; the Khomas Hochland and Tsarisberge in Namibia; the Roggeveldberge, Nuweveldberge, and Drakensberg in South Africa; and the Chimanimani Mountains along the Mozambique-Zimbabwe border. It is a major drainage divide, separating rivers that flow to the coast, often through deep gorges, from those that flow inland, usually joining the Limpopo or Orange River. Several rivers crossing or flowing off the escarpment have considerable, mostly undeveloped, potential for hydroelectric projects. The escarpment has been a major impediment to the development of rail and road linkages between the coast and the interior.

North America

Great Migration, The,

mass movement by black Americans in the early twentieth century from the predominantly rural, segregated South to the urban North and West, where they sought greater economic, social, and political freedom.

At the end of the Civil War (1861-1865) and the abolition of slavery, 91 percent of America's 5 million African Americans lived in the Southern states, roughly the same percentage as in 1790. Blacks made up 36 percent of the total Southern population (as compared with 3 percent of the total Northern population) and worked mostly as sharecroppers, tenant farmers, and domestic servants. Very few owned property. Most black farmers were heavily in debt and struggled to pay rents. Other forms of labor open to blacks were similarly low-paying and exploitative.

The RECONSTRUCTION era (1865-1877), which kept protective Union troops in the South and brought blacks the constitutional guarantee of full citizenship, raised hopes and expectations for better jobs and civil rights. A small but important minority of blacks found work in industries such as coal mining, timber, and railroads, and others received a limited education. As Reconstruction drew to a close, however, and with it the emergence of Northern dominance over Southern life, white legislatures in the South began to pass JIM CROW laws codifying state and local segregation and discrimination. Blacks, especially those attempting to exercise the franchise, were the victims of lynchings and other terrorism. Opportunities in school, work, and politics dwindled. Some blacks responded by migrating to Northern border states, especially Kansas (*see* EXODUSTERS). Their numbers, however, were limited to a few tens of thousands, and the migration was mostly to rural areas. In 1910, nearly 50 years after the war had ended slavery, 89 percent of all blacks remained in the South, and nearly 80 percent of those lived in rural areas.

Several events early in the second decade of the twentieth century coalesced to change black patterns of settlement. From 1913 to 1915 falling cotton prices brought on an economic depression that seriously hurt Southern farmers, both black and white. Just as they began to recover, they were struck by an overwhelming infestation of boll weevils, insects that destroyed much of the cotton crop between 1914 and 1917. In the Mississippi Valley, farmers suffered an additional plague: severe floods in 1915 ruined crops and homes, especially of blacks, who lived in disproportionate numbers in the valley's bottomlands. The few Southern blacks who had owned their own farms before 1910 were now largely reduced to sharecropping and tenant farming; most sharecroppers and tenant farmers, meanwhile, slid deeper into debt.

At the same time Northern industries were undergoing an economic boom, fueled in part by the start of World War I in Europe (1914-1918). The North and West were also experiencing a labor shortage: following several years of cheap labor from unlimited foreign immigration, Congress had now restricted the number of new immigrants. The labor shortage became even more acute as the United States entered the war in 1917. While wages in the South ranged from 50 cents to $2 a day, wages in the industrial North, expanded because of the war effort, ranged from $2 to $5 a day.

Southern blacks responded to these forces by filling Northern jobs by the hundreds

At the start of the Great Migration, most African Americans lived in the South and did agricultural work. Those who migrated north often found themselves working in industrial settings, such as this man, photographed at the Buckeye Steel Casting Company in the 1910s. *Ohio Historical Society*

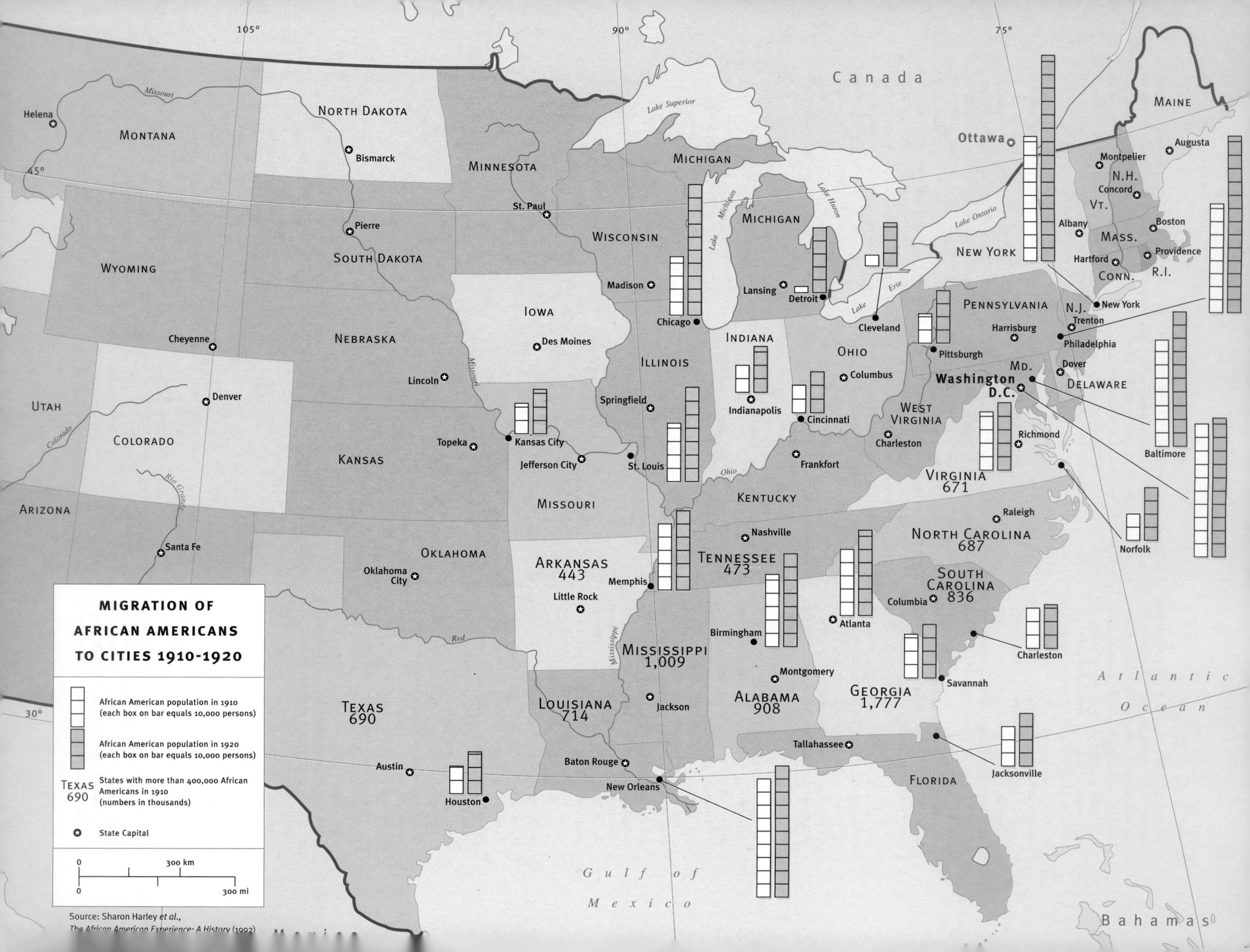
MIGRATION OF
AFRICAN AMERICANS
TO CITIES 1910-1920
African American population in 1910
(each box on bar equals 10,000 persons)
African American population in 1920
(each box on bar equals 10,000 persons)
TEXAS 690
States with more than 400,000 African Americans in 1910
(numbers in thousands)
State Capital
0
300 km
0
300 mi
Source: Sharon Harley et al.,
Canada
Gulf of Mexico
Atlantic Ocean
Bahamas
105°
90°
75°
45°
30°
Lake Superior
Lake Michigan
Lake Huron
Lake Ontario
Lake Erie
Missouri
Colorado
Rio Grande
Red
Mississippi
Ohio
MONTANA
NORTH DAKOTA
MINNESOTA
MICHIGAN
WYOMING
SOUTH DAKOTA
WISCONSIN
IOWA
NEBRASKA
ILLINOIS
INDIANA
OHIO
UTAH
COLORADO
KANSAS
MISSOURI
KENTUCKY
ARIZONA
OKLAHOMA
ARKANSAS
443
TENNESSEE
473
MISSISSIPPI
1,009
ALABAMA
908
GEORGIA
1,777
LOUISIANA
714
TEXAS
690
FLORIDA
SOUTH CAROLINA
836
NORTH CAROLINA
687
VIRGINIA
671
WEST VIRGINIA
PENNSYLVANIA
NEW YORK
MAINE
N.H.
VT.
MASS.
CONN.
R.I.
N.J.
MD.
DELAWARE
Washington D.C.
Ottawa
Helena
Bismarck
St. Paul
Pierre
Madison
Lansing
Detroit
Chicago
Cleveland
Pittsburgh
Harrisburg
Philadelphia
Trenton
New York
Albany
Hartford
Providence
Boston
Concord
Montpelier
Augusta
Dover
Baltimore
Richmond
Norfolk
Raleigh
Charleston
Columbia
Savannah
Atlanta
Jacksonville
Tallahassee
Montgomery
Birmingham
Nashville
Memphis
Little Rock
Jackson
Baton Rouge
New Orleans
Austin
Houston
Oklahoma City
Santa Fe
Denver
Cheyenne
Lincoln
Topeka
Kansas City
Jefferson City
St. Louis
Springfield
Des Moines
Indianapolis
Cincinnati
Columbus
Frankfort

of thousands. Between 1915 and 1920, from 500,000 to 1 million African Americans left the rural South for the urban North; several thousands more moved to the West. Others remained in the South but moved from the country to the city. On their arrival in the North, migrants found not just better wages but the freedom to vote, less exposure to white violence, and, sometimes, better schools for their children. Racism remained persistent, however. Discriminatory real estate practices forced blacks into ill-maintained and segregated housing, contributing to the rise of the urban black ghetto. Blacks were routinely excluded from labor unions, and many migrants were forced into menial jobs as butlers, waiters, and the like, or served as replacement workers ("scabs") during strikes by white unions.

The increased competition among blacks and whites for jobs and housing sparked race riots in dozens of Northern cities, including major white-on-black riots in East St. Louis in 1917 and Chicago in 1919. For blacks, the riots were an enduring reminder that white violence was not restricted to the states of Jim Crow. For the nation, the tensions caused by black migration made many people aware of what blacks had known for some time: the problems of race were an American, not only a Southern, phenomenon.

Despite the problems, migrants in the North wrote to family and friends in the South with stories of better living conditions, better jobs, and more freedom. Often they sent money and offered other help for the move. Prominent black newspapers such as the *Chicago Defender* and leading black aid societies such as the National Association of Colored Women proclaimed (often overzealously) the virtues of the Promised Land, and helped newly arrived blacks find jobs. Northern companies, including meat-packing, automobile, and steel businesses, even sent agents to recruit blacks from the South.

In addition to the tide of unskilled laborers flowing out of the South, many of the few black mechanics, apprenticed workers, musicians, and professionals also left. Together with Northern skilled laborers, they made up a small new Northern black middle class, which established its own unions, social and fraternal orders, churches, and welfare services. The growth of this middle class during the 1920s was not without conflict. As wealthier blacks moved into better housing left by whites, poor blacks were left concentrated in overcrowded ghetto neighborhoods.

Southern states, which relied heavily on black agricultural, domestic, and sometimes industrial labor, tried to stop the population flow. Several state legislatures and city councils passed laws fining and jailing "vagrant" or "landless" blacks – that is, blacks who were traveling. They also fined and jailed Northern labor recruiters and Southern blacks who encouraged other blacks to move. In several states, the *Chicago Defender* was banned.

TOP: A woman and a boy, their car packed with belongings, were part of the mass movement of blacks out of the South during the early part of the twentieth century. *Library of Congress*
ABOVE: Chicago, where this family has just arrived, was a major destination for migrating African Americans. The city's black population increased by 500 percent from 1910 to 1930. *Schomburg Center for Research in Black Culture*

Black people left in large numbers nonetheless. In addition to the hundreds of thousands who left before 1920, another 700,000 to 1,000,000 African Americans moved north and west in the 1920s.

The effect on Northern and western cities was dramatic. Detroit's black population, which was estimated at fewer than 6000 before World War I, grew to more than 120,000 at the end of the 1920s. Chicago's black population grew from about 40,000 in 1910 to about 240,000 in 1930. New York's grew from 100,000 to 330,000. Western states, previously home to few blacks, received a smaller but still significant influx. In Los Angeles the population of 8000 blacks in

1910 increased to almost 40,000 in 1930. By 1940, 23 percent of blacks in the United States were living in the North and West; black majorities in Louisiana, South Carolina, and Mississippi had come to an end. In the areas they left behind, several thousands of farm acres were reported idle, and many businesses in these areas were forced to close or slow down.

Widespread as the black exodus from the South was, black movement within the South was greater. The same forces of farm depression, industrialization, and wartime labor shortage that prompted many blacks to leave altogether prompted more blacks (as well as whites) to move from the Southern farm to the Southern city. Whereas blacks comprised at most 10 percent of some Northern cities in the 1920s, in the South they were routinely 25 to 50 percent of a city's population.

The Great Depression of the 1930s slowed the Great Migration, but the start of World War II (1939-1945) had similar effects on migration as the start of World War I. This time, a sagging farm economy, rapid economic growth, persistent Southern racism, and a national labor shortage were accompanied by mechanization of Southern farms and increasing gains in the Civil Rights Movement. However, as blacks again left en masse, they moved not just to the cities of the Northern Rust Belt, but increasingly to the cities of the West, especially Los Angeles, San Francisco, and San Diego. By 1960, at the end of the second wave of migration, 40 percent of the nation's blacks lived in the North and West, and nearly three-quarters of all American blacks lived in cities – the same percentage that had lived in rural areas at the start of the century.

For those who participated in it, and even for their children and grandchildren, the Great Migration continues to resonate as one of the most powerful stories of African American struggle and opportunity. Its impact can be seen in African American literature, music – particularly in the urban blues pioneered by such Southern transplants as John Lee Hooker – and visual arts, perhaps most notably in the paintings of Jacob Lawrence, whose *Migration* series explores the images and themes inspired by his parents' migration north.

See Also

Slavery in the United States; World War I and African Americans; World War II and African Americans; Press, Black, in the United States; *Chicago Defender*; Chicago Riots of 1919; Chicago, Illinois; Civil War, American; Detroit, Michigan; East St. Louis, Illinois, Riot of 1917; Labor Unions in the United States; Lawrence, Jacob Armstead; Los Angeles, California; Lynching; New York, New York; San Francisco and Oakland, California; Art, African American.

Africa

Great Zimbabwe, the most famous of a large group of stone-walled enclosures on the Zimbabwean plateau.

In the language of the Shona people of the eastern half of Zimbabwe, the word *zimbabwe* means "stone building." The highest point of the site is a fortress that has a commanding view of the surrounding grasslands and can only be approached through a series of narrow defiles. Although there is some controversy about its origin, most scholars think that the structure was erected by Shona people over the course of about 400 years, beginning in the early eleventh century. Great Zimbabwe served as a royal residence until the early fifteenth century, when the king moved elsewhere, perhaps because the adjacent soil was exhausted and thus could no longer support a royal court. It remained an important religious shrine until the nineteenth century. The modern Zimbabwe nation took its name from this major cultural monument.

Africa

Grebo, ethnic group of West Africa.

The Grebo primarily inhabit southwestern Côte d'Ivoire and southeastern Liberia. They speak a language belonging to the Kru group. Approximately 300,000 people consider themselves Grebo.

See Also

Languages, African: An Overview.

North America

Green, Al (b. April 13, 1946, Forrest City, Ark.), African American singer and minister, pioneer of 1960s soul music.

Al Green (originally spelled "Greene") was born into a large family of sharecroppers. At age nine he formed a gospel quartet with three of his brothers, the Green Brothers. Green always enjoyed nonreligious music, however, and at age 16 formed his first pop group in Michigan, where his family had moved. In 1967 he released "Back Up Train," which became a minor hit.

Green's career gained momentum in 1969 when he met producer Willie Mitchell, who signed him to Hi Records in Memphis, Tennessee. Their partnership resulted in an innovative new soul sound featuring spare instrumentation (simple horns and backbeats, muted guitar) accompanied by Green's quiet but insistent vocals pleading lyrically for the possibilities of love and often taking off into wild falsettos. Though quieter than the Stax sound, Green's music was nonetheless complex, and it was a popularly welcomed change from the heavily produced records of the late 1960s. A string of hits followed in the early 1970s, including "Let's Stay Together," "I'm Still in Love With You," "Here I Am (Come and Take Me)."

Despite popular success, Green was pulled by the tug of his gospel origins, especially after a girlfriend's suicide in 1974. In 1976 he became the pastor of the Full Gospel Tabernacle in Memphis. His musical output since then has been primarily gospel, but it remains as intensely personal as his songs about romantic love.

See Also

Gospel Music; Stax Records.

North America

Green Pastures, The, an all-black Broadway musical and Hollywood film that, despite its racial stereotyping, gained widespread appeal among blacks during the late 1930s.

First produced as a Broadway musical in 1930, *The Green Pastures* featured an all-black cast and starred Shakespearean actor Richard B. Harrison in the lead role of De Lawd. The show garnered a Pulitzer Prize for its white author Marc Connelly, who based his story on white writer Roark Bradford's book of tales, *Ole Man Adam and His Chillun*. African American poet Langston Hughes characterized the musical as "a naïve dialect play about a quaint funny heaven full of niggers."

In 1936 the film studio Warner Brothers, in collaboration with Connelly, turned the musical into a motion picture. The cast of the movie version of *The Green Pastures* was also all black, and included the popular Hall Johnson Choir – founded in 1925 by the African American violinist and choral conductor Hall Johnson – and such notable actors as Rex Ingram, Ossie Davis, and Eddie Anderson. African American film historian Thomas Cripps says that the film "rose above the common ruck, averted the worst taints of Southern metaphor, and brought black Southern folk religion to a wide and appreciative audience. Blacks, except for a few intellectuals, enjoyed it and lionized the players."

The Green Pastures was produced at a time when Hollywood film roles for African Americans were scarce, and often limited to portrayals of chauffeurs, butlers, and housemaids. Even independent black filmmakers depended largely on white capital and distributors and were thus compelled to accommodate the preferences of white audiences. That *The Green Pastures* had an appealing story and provided jobs for 95 black actors and singers suggested to many a hopeful future for blacks in the film industry.

Yet the film, like the original Broadway musical, also stereotyped rural blacks: in depicting a black folk version of the Bible's Book of Genesis, for example, it portrayed heaven as a grand fishfry with mammies for angels. Some critics claimed that *The Green Pastures* merely created an illusion of black success that diverted blacks from the principal goal of independent black cinema – to empower and affirm the black community through positive, realistic media representations.

The Green Pastures, like the earlier Hollywood black musical films *Hearts in Dixie* and *Hallelujah!* (both 1929), grossed far less income than Warner Brothers had anticipated. Consequently, major film studios became reluctant to take on all-black musical films, and black actors and film producers returned to musical shorts. More than a decade passed before the prospects of blacks in film began to change significantly.

Roanne Edwards

See Also

Anderson, Eddie ("Rochester"); Racial Stereotypes; Film, Blacks in American.

North America

Gregory, Frederick Drew

(b. January 7, 1941, Washington, D.C.), African American astronaut and research test pilot who in 1989 became the first black space commander.

Frederick Gregory made his first space flight in 1985, two years after Guion Bluford became the first African American in space. On this mission Gregory served as a pilot and, in collaboration with 16 other crew members, conducted various medical experiments. In November 1989 Gregory capitalized on Bluford's historic achievement by becoming the first black space commander. Two years later he commanded a second space shuttle mission. These missions successfully put satellites into orbit for the purposes of secret intelligence and national defense. During the second mission Gregory prevented the shuttle Atlantis from colliding with a huge Soviet rocket apparatus and, after a navigation device failed, safely returned Atlantis to earth three days early. He spent a total of 456 hours in space.

Frederick Gregory showed an early interest in flying. Gregory's father, an educator, and his mother's brother Dr. Charles Drew, who conducted pioneering blood plasma research in the late 1930s, inspired and encouraged him. After graduating from Anacostia High School in Washington, D.C., however, Gregory had difficulty securing the sponsorship of a congressperson that was required for admission to the United States Air Force Academy. Determined to help Gregory realize his dream, his father ultimately convinced New York congressperson Adam Clayton Powell Jr. to nominate him.

Gregory was an experienced and versatile research test pilot before becoming an astronaut. After receiving a B.S. in 1964 from the U.S. Air Force Academy, he spent a year training to be a helicopter pilot. In 1967 he served as a rescue pilot in the Vietnam War. Gregory returned to Vietnam in 1975 to rescue American refugees during the evacuation of Saigon, flying more than 550 missions. During the late 1960s he flew T-39 and F-4 Phantom jets while stationed at Air Force bases in Missouri and Arizona. In 1970 and 1971 he attended the U.S. Naval Test Pilot School in Maryland.

From 1971 to 1978 Gregory was a research and engineering test pilot at Wright-Patterson Air Force Base in Ohio (1971-1974) and at the National Aeronautics Space Administration's (NASA's) Langley Research Center in Virginia (1974-1978). He received an M.S. in information systems from George Washington University in 1977 and was accepted into NASA's astronaut program in 1978. During these formative years, he learned to fly more than 50 different types of aircraft – including gliders, helicopters, jets, and transports – and spent more than 6500 hours in the air.

Gregory prepared for his first space flight in 1985 by completing a year of astronaut training and working extensively in the Shuttle Avionics Integration Laboratory. Leading up to his first space command mission in 1989, he worked as a capcom (the person who communicates with astronauts during flights), chief of the Operation Safety Branch, and chief of astronaut training.

After his second command mission in 1991, Gregory was appointed associate administrator of the Office of Safety and Mission Quality at NASA Headquarters. He has spent a great deal of time speaking to students around the country, emphasizing the importance of obtaining an education from various sources: "An education that comes not just from the schools," he has observed, "but also from the churches, the home, the community... encourages a youngster to strive for something a little bit more."

Aaron Myers

See Also

Aviators, African American; Bluford, Guion Stewart (Guy), Jr.; Drew, Charles Richard; Powell, Adam Clayton, Jr.

North America

Gregory, Richard Claxton "Dick"

(b. October 12, 1932, St. Louis, Mo.), African American comedian and civil rights activist whose social satire changed the way white Americans perceived African American comedians.

Dick Gregory entered the national comedy scene in 1961 when Chicago's Playboy Club booked him as a replacement for white comedian "Professor" Irwin Corey. Until then Gregory had worked mostly at small clubs with predominantly black audiences (he met his wife, Lillian Smith, at one such club). Such clubs paid comedians an average of $5 dollars per night; thus Gregory also held a day job as a postal employee. His tenure as a replacement for Corey was so successful – at one performance he won over an audience that included Southern white convention goers – that the Playboy Club offered him a contract extension from several weeks to three years. By 1962 Gregory had become a nationally known headline performer, selling out nightclubs, making numerous national television appearances, and recording popular comedy albums.

Gregory began performing comedy in the mid-1950s while serving in the army (*see* Military, Blacks in the American). Drafted in 1954 while attending Southern Illinois University at Carbondale on a track scholarship, he briefly returned to the university after his discharge in 1956, but left without a degree because he felt that the university "didn't want me to study, they wanted me to run." In the hopes of performing comedy professionally, he moved to Chicago, where he became part of a new generation of black comedians that included Nipsey Russell, Bill Cosby, and Godfrey Cambridge. These comedians broke with the minstrel tradition, which presented stereotypical black characters. Gregory, whose style was detached, ironic, and satirical, came to be called the "Black Mort Sahl" after the popular white social satirist. He drew on current events, especially racial issues, for much of his material: "Segregation is not all bad. Have you ever heard of a collision where the people in the back of the bus got hurt?"

From an early age Gregory demonstrated a strong sense of social justice. While a student at Sumner High School in St. Louis he led a march protesting segregated schools. Later, inspired by the work of leaders such as Dr. Martin Luther King Jr. and organizations such as the Student Nonviolent Coordinating Committee (SNCC), Gregory took part in the Civil Rights Movement and used his celebrity status to draw attention to such issues as segregation and disfranchisement. When local Mississippi governments stopped distributing federal food surpluses to poor blacks in areas where SNCC was encouraging voter registration, Gregory chartered a plane to bring in seven tons of food. He participated in SNCC's voter registration drives and in sit-ins to protest segregation, most notably at a restaurant franchise in downtown Atlanta, Georgia. Only later did Gregory disclose that he held stock in the chain.

Through the 1960s Gregory spent more time on social issues and less time on performing. He participated in marches and parades to support a range of causes, including opposition to the Vietnam War, world hunger, and drug abuse. In addition he fasted in protest more than 60 times, once in Iran, where he fasted and prayed in an effort to urge the Ayatollah Khomeini to release

American embassy staff who had been taken hostage. The Iranian refusal to release the hostages did not decrease the depth of Gregory's commitment; he weighed only 44 kg (97 lbs) when he left Iran.

Gregory demonstrated his commitment to confronting the entrenched political powers by opposing Richard J. Daley in Chicago's 1966 mayoral election. He ran for president in 1968 as a write-in candidate for the Freedom and Peace Party, a splinter group of the Peace and Freedom Party, and received 1.5 million votes. Democratic candidate Hubert Humphrey lost the election to Republican Richard Nixon by 510,000 votes, and many believe Humphrey would have won had Gregory not run. After the assassinations of King, President John F. Kennedy, and Robert Kennedy, Gregory became increasingly convinced of the existence of political conspiracies. He wrote books such as *Code Name Zoro: The Murder of Martin Luther King Jr.* (1971) with Mark Lane, a conspiracy theorist whose ideas Gregory shared and espoused in numerous lectures.

Gregory's activism continued into the 1990s. In response to published allegations that the Central Intelligence Agency (CIA) had supplied cocaine to predominantly African American areas in Los Angeles, thus spurring the crack epidemic, Gregory protested at CIA headquarters and was arrested. In 1992 he began a program called Campaign for Human Dignity to fight crime in St. Louis neighborhoods.

In 1973, the year he released his comedy album *Caught in the Act*, Gregory moved with his family to Plymouth, Massachusetts, where he developed an interest in vegetarianism and became a nutritional consultant. In 1984 he founded Health Enterprises, Inc., a company that distributed weight loss products. In 1987 Gregory introduced the Slim-Safe Bahamian Diet, a powdered diet mix, which was immensely profitable. Economic losses caused in part by conflicts with his business partners led to his eviction from his home in 1992. Gregory remained active, however, and in 1996 returned to the stage in his critically acclaimed one-man show, *Dick Gregory Live!*

Robert Fay

See Also

Track and Field in the United States; Cambridge, Godfrey MacArthur; Chicago, Illinois; King, Martin Luther, Jr.; Los Angeles, California; Minstrelsy; Racial Stereotypes.

Latin America and the Caribbean

Grenada, country consisting of several islands in the Caribbean Sea north of Trinidad and Tobago and Venezuela; one of the largest islands of that area of the Caribbean.

Visitors to Grenada often consider it their favorite of the Caribbean island nations, and tourist guides boast of the country's friendly people, its beautiful landscape, and its status as the Spice Isle of the Caribbean. But Grenada is still often associated with its 1983 government coup and the subsequent United States-led takeover of the island. In October of that year, Grenadian leader Maurice Bishop – who had himself come to power through an earlier coup – was assassinated. In response, 1900 U.S. soldiers and 300 additional Caribbean troops from Barbados, Jamaica, Dominica, Antigua, St. Kitts and Nevis, St. Lucia, and St. Vincent invaded Grenada and took temporary control of the government. The factors that led both the U.S. and the Grenadian revolutionaries to that conflict are rooted in a long history of struggle for control of the beautiful country.

Grenada's first inhabitants were Arawak Amerindians, who probably migrated north from Venezuela via Trinidad and Tobago between 1 and 500 C.E. But between 700 and 1000 C.E. in the island's first takeover, the Arawaks were wiped out by the Carib Amerindians (Caribs). By the time Spanish explorer Christopher Columbus and his crew became the first Europeans to see Grenada in 1498, the island, whose Amerindian name was Camerhogne, was covered with well-established Carib settlements.

Columbus did not stop on the island, but he did rename it Concepción in his journals as he sailed by. Over the next few decades other passing Spanish sailors gave it the name Granada, recognizing the similarity of the country's landscape to the lush green hills of Granada, Spain. In later years the name was modified again – the French changed it to Grenade, and the British finally changed it to Grenada. The fact that the Spanish, French, and British all had a hand in naming the island gives some indication of the progression of European powers that struggled to control the island during the colonial period.

Grenadian Caribs successfully resisted European settlement efforts well into the seventeenth century. In 1650, after earlier British and French attempts had failed, 200 French colonists arrived from Martinique and settled at Port Louis, bringing cannons, rifles, and gunpowder. By 1654 the last surviving Carib families had retreated to a cliff at the north of the island. When the French finally attacked them there, the remaining Caribs committed suicide by jumping into the ocean rather than surrendering. The cliff – Le Morne de Sauteurs (Leapers' Hill) – is still visited today.

Once the French had established control of Grenada they began planting tobacco, indigo, cotton, coffee, and sugar. Each of these crops required a large, cheap labor force to be profitable, and European planters across the Caribbean began meeting their labor demands by importing African slaves. By 1753, after 100 years of French control, Grenada's population included 1262 whites, 179 free blacks, and 11,991 slaves.

The members of the small free black population were primarily the mixed-race offspring of white French planters and their black slaves, and the mixed allegiances of free blacks to both groups would prove important in one of Grenada's future political conflicts. In 1763 the British took over Grenada. They immediately alienated and angered both black and white Grenadians by outlawing Roman Catholicism and the French language, placing new restrictions on property owning and mobility for free blacks, and forcing the slaves to work longer hours in an attempt to make the island more profitable. The French were able to briefly recapture the island between 1779 and 1783, but once the British regained control their rule was even harsher. Eventually, several free black Grenadians joined forces with white French Grenadians to plan a rebellion.

The leader of the rebellion, Julien Fedon, was a wealthy mixed-race landowner. Fedon and his supporters were inspired by the recent French and Haitian revolutions, as well as revolts by the Caribs in St. Vincent and the Maroons in Jamaica (*see* Slave Rebellions in Latin America and the Caribbean). The Fedon Rebellion lasted from March 1795 to June 1796. During that period 24,000 slaves left their estates to join Fedon, other free blacks, and white Frenchmen in fighting for a common goal: Grenada's installation within the French Republic as a free state that did not allow slavery.

During the rebellion the slaves and their allies were able to take over the majority of the island, destroy many of its plantations, and capture and kill a number of British prisoners, including the British governor of the island. But when the British finally managed to bring in effective reinforcements, the rebels were captured and forced to surrender. Dozens of blacks were executed, many more were deported to slave estates on other islands, and Fedon himself apparently drowned in an attempt to escape at the end of the conflict. French hopes of recapturing Grenada ended with the rebellion, and the island remained a British colony for nearly 200 more years.

But even as the British fought to preserve slavery on Grenada, the combination of a changing economy and increased criticism of slavery by white abolitionists at home was gradually signaling an end to the system as a whole. In 1834 slavery was finally abolished in all British territories (*see* Abolition and Emancipation in Latin America and the Caribbean). For most of Grenada's black majority, however, life remained the same after emancipation in many ways. Throughout the nineteenth century many former slaves continued to be employed as agricultural laborers on white-owned estates. Some of these workers were bound to *metayage* (sharecropping) systems, which at their worst replicated the conditions of slavery.

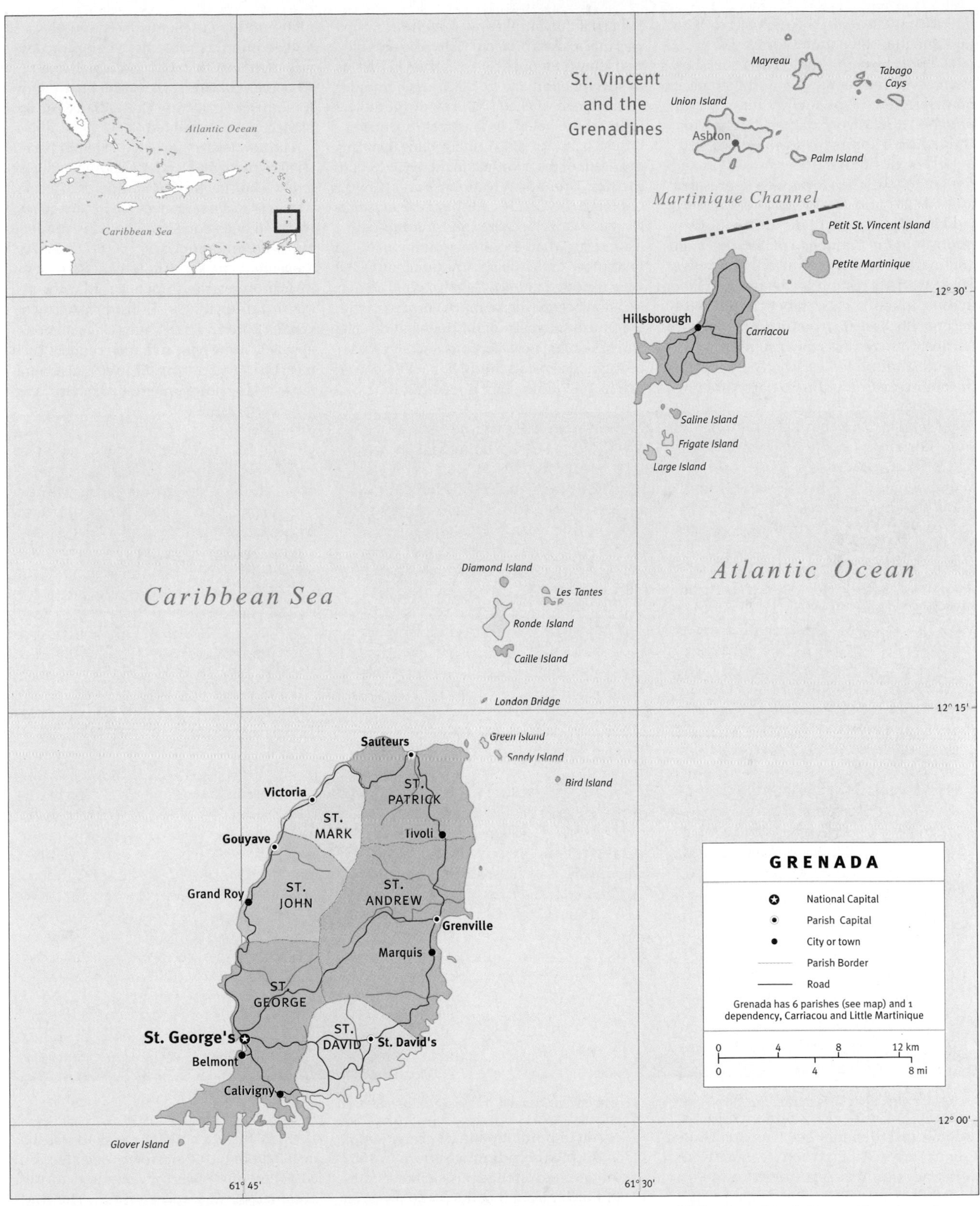

Gradually, however, more and more black Grenadians were able to buy or lease their own small pieces of land. Often, they formed small freehold villages at the edges of larger estates. By the turn of the twentieth century there were enough mixed-race and black Grenadian freeholders for a new black bourgeoisie – including teachers, doctors, lawyers, and civil servants – to develop. As black Grenadians gained more economic stability, their next step was to increase their political power.

Under British Crown colony rule the local Grenadian legislature was made up primarily of individuals appointed by the British government, which meant that the white minority still held complete political control. T. Albert Marryshow was one of the first middle-class black Grenadians to take a strong public stand against this inequality. From 1915 to 1935 Marryshow edited the newspaper the *West Indian*, which continually called for political autonomy for Grenada and the rest of the West Indies. In 1925 Britain responded by amending Grenada's constitution to allow 5 of the Legislative Council's 16 seats to be elected. Marryshow won one of those seats in the next election and remained on the council for 33 years.

The progress represented by Marryshow's election was not enough for most Grenadians, however. New crops such as nutmeg had provided a relatively stable economy for Grenadian laborers for several decades, but even within that economy wages had remained low. The worldwide depression of the 1920s and 1930s was a reminder to working-class Grenadians and workers throughout the Caribbean of how precarious and market-driven their livelihoods were. These workers responded by forming labor unions. In many cases labor unions have become the base for a country's first political parties; Grenada was no exception.

In 1951 union leader Eric Gairy founded the country's first political party, the pro-union, pro-independence Grenada United Labour Party (GULP). When elections were held under universal suffrage for the first time that October, GULP won easily and Gairy became the leader of the assembly. Gairy had risen from a poor childhood in rural Grenada to his new position as the first black leader of the country's government, and he was especially popular with rural and working-class black Grenadians. But many Grenadians, including many middle-class and upper-class blacks, disliked him intensely.

Part of the antipathy within these groups was due to class bias, but Gairy also became well known for publicly expressing his beliefs in such phenomena as UFOs, the Bermuda Triangle, and witchcraft, and many Grenadians found these beliefs embarrassing. Once in office Gairy was also criticized for ignoring the needs of the poor, and in the 1957 elections the new Grenadian National Party (GNP) defeated the GULP, and the more moderate Herbert Blaize became the country's new leader. But when economic conditions failed to improve under Blaize, Gairy and the GULP were reelected in 1961. Gairy's second administration began with so much corruption that the British colonial administration intervened and scheduled new elections for 1962; these brought Blaize and the GNP back to power. But in 1967 Gairy won once again.

Several important political changes took place during this administration. In 1967 Britain granted Grenada associated statehood, which meant that the island was given full control of its domestic affairs and was one step closer to independence. Grenada finally won full independence on February 7, 1974, after 200 years of British rule. But what should have been a triumphant occasion raised new concerns for many Grenadians. With independence, Gairy became the country's first prime minister, giving him even more power and prominence. Under his leadership the country faced serious social and economic problems. Unemployment was high, health care was dismal, and only 15 percent of Grenadian students went on to high school. Many Grenadians felt new leadership was needed.

The new leadership finally came with a new political party, the New Jewel Movement (NJM), led by Maurice Bishop. Bishop and his allies were part of a new generation of Grenadians who had been educated abroad in the 1960s and were influenced by the BLACK POWER Movement and such prominent African and African American thinkers as MALCOLM X, Martin Luther King Jr., KWAME NKRUMAH, and WALTER RODNEY. These young Grenadians were appalled by the poor conditions under which most black Grenadians still lived and committed to taking power in order to change them.

A woman swirls her skirts during the "Big Drum" dance ceremony in Grenada. *Till Leeser & H. J. Burkard/Aurora*

When the next national elections were held in 1976, the GULP narrowly defeated the NJM, but most observers felt the victory was obtained by widespread fraud. The NJM did gain 6 of the legislature's 15 seats, and Bishop became the opposition leader in the government. But the NJM's goal was complete control, and when Gairy left the country on March 12, 1979, for a visit to the United States, NJM forces attacked his army and overnight forcibly took control of the government. With this revolution Maurice Bishop became the new prime minister of what was named the People's Revolutionary Government (PRG).

The PRG's stated goals – to provide work, food, decent housing and health care, and better education – were widely supported by the public. The chant on the streets the next day was "Freedom come, Gairy go, Gairy gone with UFO." But the PRG's model and closest ally in the Caribbean was Fidel Castro's CUBA, and that alliance immediately alienated the new government from the United States, its most powerful neighbor. Cuba and the Soviet Union sent much-needed financial aid and other resources to Grenada. They also sent military supplies and personnel, which made the United States especially uneasy, and the United States accused a Cuban-sponsored airport project of being a cover-up for a Soviet air base.

Meanwhile, by 1983 the PRG government was in severe financial trouble. The grants from Cuba and the Soviet Union that sustained it at first were gone, and the Grenadian public, who had already gotten used to the initial benefits the PRG had brought them, was beginning to demand more. The financial crisis led to so much instability and disagreement within the PRG that in September 1983 a faction of the party contested Bishop's place as leader. When Bishop refused to share power, a group from within the PRG staged a coup, and on October 19 Bishop, two ministers, and over a dozen of his supporters were assassinated.

It was in the midst of this internal chaos that the United States decided to intervene; an invasion was ordered by President Ronald Reagan on October 25. Within one week the United States had taken control of the country, and over the next 12 months the United States worked with the British governor-general to restructure the country's political situation. The first postinvasion elections were held in December 1984, and ironically the two candidates to emerge with the most support were once again Eric Gairy and Herbert Blaize. Gairy led in the polls for most of the campaign, but after the United States strongly urged the opposition parties to form a last-minute coalition, Blaize was elected instead. While the transition was peaceful, the new government was split by factional fighting. No party won a decisive majority in the 1990 elections, and although Nicholas Brathwaite was able to lead a coalition government for several years, he voluntarily stepped down in February 1995. In June of that year, Keith Mitchell was elected as prime minister.

New economic troubles surfaced in the mid-1990s, after the banana crop failed and a mealybug infestation damaged the cocoa crop. Grenada has considered forming a federation with Dominica, St. Lucia, and St. Vincent and the Grenadines that would ease financial pressures in all four countries. Illiteracy also remains a problem. On the other hand, Grenada has seen many recent successes. The tourist industry is growing, and Grenada is considered a haven for snorkelers and sailors. The spice industry that gives Grenada its nickname also remains strong; more spices are grown per square mile on Grenada than anywhere else in the world. Even with so much political turmoil in recent memory, Grenada appears poised to enter the new century as a peaceful, stable nation.

Lisa Clayton Robinson

SEE ALSO

Transatlantic Slave Trade; Slavery in Latin America and the Caribbean; Haitian Revolution; King, Martin Luther, Jr.; Antigua and Barbuda; St. Vincent and the Grenadines.

North America

Griffith-Joyner, Florence Delorez

(b. December 21, 1959, Los Angeles, Calif.; d. September 21, 1998, Mission Viejo, Calif.), African American track athlete who won three Gold Medals and one Silver Medal at the 1988 Olympic Games.

Florence Griffith-Joyner came out of semi-retirement in track to dominate the 1988 Summer Olympic Games in Seoul, South Korea. After capturing a Silver Medal in the 200-meter dash at the 1984 Games, Griffith-Joyner worked as a customer service representative at a bank during the day and a hair stylist at night. In early 1987 she decided to return to competition and enlisted her former track coach at the University of California at Los Angeles, Bob Kersee, to help her train for the 1988 Olympic Games. Her husband, Al Joyner, winner of the 1984 Olympic Gold Medal in the triple jump and brother of heptathlon record-holder Jackie Joyner-Kersee, also coached Griffith-Joyner.

Griffith-Joyner's record-breaking performance at the 1988 Olympic Games was motivated in part by a second-place finish at the 1987 World Championship Games in Rome, Italy. Although she was a member of the Gold Medal-winning 1600-meter relay team, her Silver Medal finish in the 200-meter dash led her to say, "When you've been second best for so long, you can either accept it or try to become the best." At the 1988 Olympic Games, she won Gold Medals in the 100- and 200-meter dashes and in the 400-meter relay.

Griffith-Joyner set new world records, clocking 10.49 seconds in the 100-meter quarterfinal and 21.34 seconds in the 200-meter final. She also surpassed Wilma Rudolph's 1960 record of three Gold Medals after helping the 1600-meter relay team capture the Silver Medal. For these accomplishments in 1988, she received the Jesse Owens Award, given to the year's top track and field athlete, and the Sullivan Award, given to the year's most outstanding amateur athlete.

Griffith-Joyner earned the nickname "Flo-Jo" for her blazing speed. She also became known for her flashy one-legged uniforms and long, painted fingernails. She wore colorful combinations of bikini briefs over one-legged tights and low-cut tops in part because she found most standard uniforms uncomfortable. She retired from track in 1989 in order to devote more time to endorsement activities, modeling, writing, and coaching her husband. Along with former BASKETBALL player Tom McMillen, President Bill Clinton appointed Griffith-Joyner chairperson of the President's Council on Physical Fitness and Sports in 1993.

Griffith-Joyner died of an apparent heart seizure on September 21, 1998, just four days short of the tenth anniversary of her first Gold Medal at the 1988 Olympic Games. To many, Griffith-Joyner represented the embodiment of a new ideal for American women – a perfect combination of strength and beauty. She also had an exemplary record of community service, for which she won the 1989 Harvard Foundation Award for outstanding contributions to society. After learning of her death, President Bill Clinton said, "We were dazzled by her speed, humbled by her talent, and captivated by her style. Though she rose to the pinnacle of the world of sports, she never forgot where she came from."

Aaron Myers

SEE ALSO

Track and Field in the United States; Joyner-Kersee, Jacqueline; Owens, James Cleveland ("Jesse"); Rudolph, Wilma Glodean.

Grillo, Frank. Please see MACHITO

North America

Grimké, Angelina Weld

(b. February 27, 1880, Boston, Mass.; d. June 10, 1958, New York, N.Y.), African American poet, playwright, author of first staged play in the United States by an African American.

Angelina Weld Grimké was born to Archibald and Sarah Grimké. Her father, the son of a slave, was a lawyer and the executive director of the NATIONAL ASSOCIATION FOR THE ADVANCEMENT OF COLORED PEOPLE (NAACP). He was also the nephew of white abolitionists Sarah and Angelina Grimké and the brother-in-law of African American poet and essayist Charlotte Forten Grimké. Grimké's mother was white. Sarah Grimké left her husband when Angelina was 3, taking her daughter with her; she returned Angelina to her father when she was 7, and never visited her again.

Grimké attended several elite private schools and graduated from the Boston Normal School of Gymnastics in 1902. Most of her writing was done over the next 25 years, which she spent teaching English in WASHINGTON, D.C. Her best-known work, the play *Rachel*, was produced by the NAACP in March 1916. *Rachel* was the first play by an African American that was meant to be staged (in contrast to earlier costume dramas, such as WILLIAM WELLS BROWN's, which were simply read aloud). Both *Rachel* and Grimké's second play deal with themes of racial injustice.

Grimké's poetry was included in such works as Alain Locke's *The New Negro* (1925) and Countee Cullen's *Caroling Dusk* (1927). Her poetry dealt with more conventional romantic themes, often marked with frequent images of frustration and isolation. Recent scholarship has revealed Grimké's unpublished lesbian poems and letters; she did not feel free to live openly as a gay woman during her lifetime. She spent the end of her life living alone in New York City.

Lisa Clayton Robinson

SEE ALSO

Cullen, Countee; Grimké, Charlotte L. Forten; Locke, Alain Leroy; New York, New York.

North America

Grimké, Archibald Henry

(b. August 17, 1849, Charleston, S.C.; d. February 25, 1930, ?), lawyer, activist, and diplomat who was appointed United States consul to Santo Domingo and lobbied in Washington for civil rights progress.

Archibald Henry Grimké was born a slave to parents Henry Grimké, a European-American plantation owner, and Nancy Weston, an African American slave. Henry Grimké's sisters, Sarah and Angelina, were prominent abolitionists. After Emancipation, Archibald Grimké attended Lincoln University in Pennslyvania. With the help of his aunts Sarah and Angelina, he attended Harvard Law School. Graduating in 1874, he practiced law in BOSTON, MASSACHUSETTS, where he became editor of *Hub*, a Boston Republican newspaper in 1884, and also wrote for the *Boston Herald* and *Boston Traveler*. He left the Republican Party in 1886 because of its indifference to the plight of African Americans and quickly became one of the most powerful African American Democrats in Massachusetts.

As a scholar and writer, Grimké published major biographies of William Lloyd Garrison (1891) and Charles Sumner (1892). In 1894 he was appointed United States consul to Santo Domingo. When he returned to Washington, D.C., in 1898, he published extensively on black issues and dedicated himself to civil rights. From 1903 to 1919 he served as president of the AMERICAN NEGRO ACADEMY, an African American intellectual organization.

Grimké joined the NATIONAL ASSOCIATION FOR THE ADVANCEMENT OF COLORED PEOPLE (NAACP) as president of the District of Columbia branch in 1913. Serving as president until 1923, he lobbied Congress and the administration of President Woodrow Wilson to end racial segregation. In 1919 he received the Spingarn Medal, the most prestigious award given by the NAACP.

Matthew Goff

SEE ALSO

Slavery in the United States; Abolitionism in the United States; Grimké, Angelina Weld; Lincoln University (Pennsylvania); Dominican Republic.

North America

Grimké, Charlotte L. Forten

(b. August 17, 1837, Philadelphia, Pa.; d. July 22, 1914, Washington, D.C.), African American abolitionist and educator whose diaries are an important record of the Civil War era.

Charlotte Forten Grimké was born into a prosperous and educated Philadelphia family that had been free for several generations. Her grandfather was a sail maker, a family business continued by her father; both men were abolitionists. Because the schools in Philadelphia were segregated, as a teenager Forten moved to Salem, Massachusetts, and attended Higginson Grammar School. Her work as an abolitionist was galvanized by the 1854 case of a fugitive slave who was captured in Salem and returned to the South. After this event Grimké began to attend antislavery rallies and publish her poetry in the *Liberator* and the *National Anti-Slavery Standard*. WILLIAM WELLS BROWN, William Lloyd Garrison, and Wendell Phillips were among the abolitionists she met at this time.

Grimké began her career as a teacher while living in Salem. She combined her abolitionist convictions and teaching skills during the Civil War, when she was named the first black teacher of the PORT ROYAL EXPERIMENT. In November 1861 the Union Army had gained control of the Sea Islands off the coast of South Carolina, and white landowners fled the islands, leaving behind thousands of slaves. The United States government sent Northern teachers to train the abandoned slaves for citizenship, among them Grimké, who taught on St. Helena Island for nearly two years. Her essays about her experiences there appeared in the *Atlantic Monthly* in May and June 1864.

After the war Grimké continued her work with former slaves as secretary of the Freedmen's Relief Association in Boston. She held a variety of other jobs in the 1860s and 1870s, becoming a clerk at the Treasury Department in 1873. Five years later she married Francis J. Grimké, a Presbyterian minister and the brother of Archibald Grimké, a writer and activist who served as president of the Washington, D.C., branch of the NATIONAL ASSOCIATION FOR THE ADVANCEMENT OF COLORED PEOPLE (NAACP) between 1913 and 1923. The Grimkés spent most of their married life in WASHINGTON, D.C., where their home became a social and intellectual gathering place for African Americans. Prone to poor health from a young age, Grimké remained politically active in organizations such as the NATIONAL ASSOCIATION OF COLORED WOMEN until the last few years of her life.

Grimké's literary legacy consists largely of work published posthumously – five diaries kept between 1854 and 1892 that provide an intimate portrait of her own development as well as that of the nation. These diaries remain one of the most valuable records of the Civil War era. They offer a glimpse of the end of slavery from the perspective of a free black woman who had been present for President Abraham Lincoln's reading of the Emancipation Proclamation in 1863; who was moved by a meeting with Harriet Tubman; who served as a nurse to slaves and Union soldiers during the war; and who dedicated her life to opposing racial slavery and injustice.

Lawrie Balfour

SEE ALSO

Abolitionism in the United States; Literature, African American; Boston, Massachusetts; Civil War, American; Fugitive Slaves; Grimké, Archibald Henry; Philadelphia, Pennsylvania; Tubman, Harriet Ross; Thirteenth Amendment of the United States Constitution and the Emancipation Proclamation.

Europe

Gronniosaw, James Albert Ukawsaw

(b. 1710, Nigeria; d. 1775, Great Britain), African prince sold into slavery whose life story became an influential book.

Ukawsaw Gronniosaw's idyllic childhood as a prince in the area that is now NIGERIA came to an abrupt end when a merchant persuaded the teenaged Gronniosaw to travel to the Gold Coast (present-day GHANA) and then sold him into American slavery. Years later, in GREAT BRITAIN, Gronniosaw related his story to a Dutch woman, who wrote and published *A Narrative of the Remarkable Particulars in the Life of James Albert Ukawsaw Gronniosaw, An African Prince, as Related by Himself* (1770). Class-conscious British readers were sympathetic to the story of the victimized African prince; the book was widely read and later influenced the British SLAVE NARRATIVES of the authors and abolitionists OLAUDAH EQUIANO and OTTOBAH CUGOANO.

Gronniosaw was a slave to several Dutch families in colonial New England. His last owner was Theodorus Jacobus Frelinghuysen, a Dutch Reformed minister in New Jersey, who bought Gronniosaw in 1730, taught him Dutch, and presided over his conversion to Christianity. On his deathbed in 1748, Frelinghuysen granted freedom to Gronniosaw. Gronniosaw left to serve in the British Navy and then moved to London, where he became known as James Albert Ukawsaw Gronniosaw.

After spending the year of 1762 in Netherlands, Gronniosaw returned to London to marry a white weaver he had met previously. His minister and friends objected to the marriage not because of the difference in race, but, according to Gronniosaw, "because the person I had fixed on was poor."

The Gronniosaw family moved frequently, finding work where they could but suffering long periods of poverty and deprivation. Shortly after moving his family to Kidderminster, a town whose inhabitants were known for their religiosity, Gronniosaw narrated his life story to a young local woman. She published it in the hope that the sales would profit the Gronniosaws; little is known of their lives after this. The document, however, helped enable the abolitionist battle in England and remains one of the most compelling slave narratives.

Leyla Keough

See Also

Race: An Interpretation; Slavery in the United States; Netherlands, The; Abolitionism in the United States.

Africa

Groupe Africain du Cinéma, Le, a group of film students who produced the first film by black Africans and helped to end French colonial restrictions on African filmmaking.

In 1955 a young Senegalese film director living in Paris, Paulin Vieyra, created a film troupe with three other African friends – Manadou Saar, Robert Cristan, and Jacques Melo Keno. Calling themselves Le Groupe Africain du Cinéma, the three filmmakers attempted to direct and shoot the first film by Africans in Africa.

Vieyra and his friends petitioned the French government for the right to film an independent movie in Senegal. Their petition was rejected under the Laval Decree, a law that restricted the content of films shot in Africa and prohibited Africans from making films in Africa altogether. As a result, Le Groupe Africain du Cinéma remained in Paris, where it shot the first African film, *Afrique sur scène*, in late 1955.

At the same time the group was determined to overturn the Laval Decree as a first step toward building an autonomous African film industry. Gathering the support of prominent French film directors and filmmakers, they again petitioned the French government, but the latter did not overturn the Laval Decree until 1962. Even after 1962, France continued to exert its influence over the Francophone African film world, because few of its former colonies had the funds or the equipment to promote film production independently.

Elizabeth Heath

Latin America and the Caribbean

Grupo Gay da Bahia. An activist gay and lesbian organization formed in 1980 in Brazil (*see* Gay and Lesbian Movements in Latin America and the Caribbean).

Africa

Grusi (also known as Grunsi, Grunshi, Gourounsi, and Gurunsi), ethnic group of West Africa.

The Grusi primarily inhabit northern Ghana and southern Burkina Faso. Some Grusi live in Togo. They speak a Niger-Congo language. Approximately 600,000 people consider themselves Grusi. The term also refers to a cultural and linguistic grouping that includes the Grusi proper and several related groups, including the Builsa, the Dagari, the Kasena, the Lilse, and the Sasala.

See Also

Languages, African: An Overview.

Latin America and the Caribbean

Guadeloupe, a Caribbean island located at the northern end of the Windward Islands, which was colonized by France in the 1600s and has been a French overseas department (a *Département d'Outre Mer*) since 1946.

Guadeloupe, which was first colonized by the French in 1635, has produced sugar cane and its derivatives for France for nearly three centuries, thanks to the labor of African slaves and their descendants. Since the abolition of slavery in 1848, and the incorporation of the island and its dependencies into France in 1946, the predominantly black population of Guadeloupe has had to negotiate the double cultural inheritance at the root of its Creole civilization. At once African and French – with lesser proportions of Amerindian, East Indian, and Chinese cultures – Guadeloupe has striven for the economic, cultural, and psychological autonomy denied it by the structural dependencies instituted via the forces of French centralization, and, indeed, ongoing colonization.

In turn, this emphasis on Guadeloupe's ties with France has long led to a denial of an African heritage, whose recuperation and revindication began following the Martinican poet-statesman Aimé Césaire's elaboration of the concept of Négritude in the 1930s. The particular characteristics of this social and existential paradox are unique, among African diasporic communities, to the French overseas departments of Guadeloupe, Martinique, and French Guiana. This unresolved conflict, like the one that W. E. B. Du Bois identified among African Americans of the United States, has nonetheless proved highly productive. The tiny island of Guadeloupe (with a population of 390,000 in 1990) has produced a number of renowned writers, including Maryse Condé, Simone Schwarz-Bart, and Gisele Pineau.

Guadeloupe and its dependencies form a single, heterogeneous "department" in the French state. This department consists of the island of Guadeloupe, itself divided into the Basse-Terre and Grande-Terre halves, as well as the Saints archipelago, Marie-Galante, la Désirade, the Petites-Terre Islands, Saint-Barthélémy, and a portion of the island of Saint-Martin (the other half being controlled by the Dutch). Guadeloupe became known to European civilization during Columbus's second voyage, when he stopped there in November 1493. The island was then populated by the Caraibe people, originally from the Amazon. Their numbers were soon depleted by Spanish raids in search of slaves, and by 1660 those remaining had been forced to flee to the neighboring, uncolonized islands of Dominica and St. Vincent. The geopolitical centrality of Guadeloupe dates from Columbus's first voyages, when the island came to serve as the first New World destination on transatlantic crossings by Spanish galleons. Despite Guadeloupe's importance, the Spanish were more preoccupied with the Greater Antilles (the island of Hispaniola, now Haiti and the Dominican Republic, and Cuba) and the exploration of the North and South American continents. As a result, the French were free to colonize Guadeloupe in 1635.

France's decision to occupy Guadeloupe and Martinique was driven by the desire to exploit the benefits of piracy and the slave trade, following the example of Great Britain and the Netherlands. In 1502 a single boatload of Africans arrived at Guadeloupe, but it was only under the French king Louis XIV that the importation of slaves to the island became institutionalized, under finance minister Colbert, with the creation of the West Indies Company (1664) and the Company of Senegal (1672). The French Code Noir of 1685 defined the parameters of slavery within the French colonies, describing the juridical terms and limitations of the reduction of human beings to commodified objects of exchange and exploitation within the plantation system (*see* Black Codes in Latin America). The punishments administered under its jurisdiction ranged from flagellation, imprisonment, and irons to torture, dismemberment, and death by hanging.

This regime of terror invoked the active resistance of Guadeloupean slaves, who resorted to stealing, poisoning animals, burning buildings, and organizing revolts. Escaped slaves, particularly after 1730, formed maroon communities in the forests of both Basse-Terre and Grande-Terre, procuring arms, munitions, and food through wide-ranging networks throughout the islands. In 1736 one of these groups residing

Women attending the Cooks Festival in Guadeloupe sport colorful outfits made of madras cloth. *Suzanne Murphy/D. Donne Bryant Stock Photo*

in the hills above Pointe Noire attempted to instigate an islandwide revolt. The revolutionaries were betrayed and the revolt failed; its leaders were beaten or hanged, and the succeeding hunt for maroons greatly diminished their numbers for the next 40 years. The plantation system in Guadeloupe grew especially quickly during the British occupation of the island from 1759 to 1763, during which period the British brought in 40,000 slaves to work the sugar plantations. This influx nearly doubled the slave population: from 41,000 in 1750, it numbered 90,139 in 1790.

Unlike its counterpart in Haiti, the enslaved population of Guadeloupe reacted slowly to news of the French Revolution in 1789. No major revolt preceded the French republic's abolition of slavery on February 4, 1794, though a series of isolated revolts in the towns of Baillif, Trois-Rivières, and Ste. Anne contributed to the urgency of that decree. Two commissioners of the French Republican Convention, Victor Hugues and Pierre Chrétien, brought the decree to Guadeloupe, along with the instrument of the Committee of Public Safety's terror: the guillotine. Hugues successfully enlisted freed slaves to drive out the British, who had occupied the island in the midst of the French Revolution's power vacuum. Hugues subsequently executed or exiled many of the white landowners and merchants sympathetic to the British and the restoration of the French monarchy. This weakened the social and economic domination of the white *Béké* class on Guadeloupe in comparison with neighboring Martinique, though their actual numbers decreased by less than 10 percent between 1790 and 1813.

The rapid increase in the slave and freed colored population meant, nonetheless, that whites made up only one-tenth of the population after the British occupation, compared to more than one-third in 1735. With the weakening of the white landowning class, a class of colored merchants asserted itself in the 1790s, and blacks and mulattos were incorporated into the colonial military. In 1802 these soldiers, including the Martinicans Louis Delgrès and Magloire Pélage and the Guadeloupean Jean Ignace, revolted against the troops of Napoleon Bonaparte, who were sent to reinstitute slavery on the island of Guadeloupe. In contrast to former Haitian slaves such as Toussaint L'Ouverture and Jean-Jacques Dessalines, these mulatto leaders had never known the terrors of slavery and retained an identification with France that prevented them from adopting the guerrilla tactics so successful in Saint-Domingue (now Haiti). Their revolt was quickly suppressed, and on May 28, 1802, Louis Delgrès spectacularly blew up himself, his troops, and the attacking French in a heroic gesture of desperate refusal to submit to the reimposition of slavery. Antoine Richepanse, the leader of the French force of 1802, was then free to reinstitute slavery brutally, ensuring its continuation until the abolition of slavery on April 27, 1848 (*see* Abolition and Emancipation in Latin America and the Caribbean).

The abolition of slavery, following the February 1848 revolution in France, had been preceded by unsuccessful palliative measures attempting to stave off full abolition. After the island witnessed a final acceleration in the creation and prosperity of sugar plantations during the 1820s, Louis Philippe's July Monarchy gave full legal rights to free colored men, who by 1835 outnumbered whites in Guadeloupe 19,000 to 12,000. In 1834 Great Britain outlawed slavery in its colonies, following the abolitionist arguments of Wilberforce, and many Guadeloupean slaves risked their lives escaping to freedom in the neighboring British-controlled islands of Montserrat, Antigua, and Dominica. In 1845 the Mackau Law was adopted in an attempt to "humanize" the institution of slavery. For the first time, slaves were juridically recognized as human beings, allowed to own possessions and land, allowed to buy their freedom, and limited to nine and a half hours of work per day. Beyond the questionable logic of a "humanized" slavery, the law was completely ineffectual, since slave owners were free to interpret the law as they saw fit.

This situation was exacerbated by the first crisis of sugar production, brought on by the introduction of the inexpensively produced sugar beet in metropolitan France. In the ensuing economic depression, the government's main concern upon abolition was to maintain the economic functioning of the sugar plantations by converting former slaves into an agricultural proletariat. Associative contracts at first bound freed slaves to the plantations, specifying the division of profits among landowners, overseers, and workers to the detriment of the often uneducated workers. Later, workers were granted land to cultivate on their own, selling their crops to the landowners or to the new centralized sugar factories, or *grandes centrales*. Neither practice was sufficiently profitable for landowners in the now highly competitive global sugar market, and they imported 6000 African and 40,000 East Indian laborers between 1854 and 1889 to replace former slaves and their children who were unwilling to work for minimal wages.

Despite an economic rebound during the 1860s, in 1884 Guadeloupe once again entered into economic decline. In the decades following the French revolution of 1848, political power was dispersed among conservative landowners and Republican, mixed-race moderates. The crisis of the 1880s and 1890s and the reintroduction of universal male suffrage in the Third Republic allowed the appearance after 1892 of a new political force of black politicians such as Hégésippe Légitimus and Achille René-Boisneuf. These politicians asserted a political ideology of racial pride that successfully shifted the balance of political power away from the financially weakened and numerically inferior white landowners and mixed-race centralists.

An ornate statue stands in a public square in Basseterre, Guadeloupe. *Henderson/Hutchison*

Guadeloupe from this period on maintained a decidedly leftist bent on social issues, though the island has consistently voted to conserve whichever party happened to hold power in France.

Eleven thousand Guadeloupeans fought in World War I and 1470 died. The continuing crisis of sugar production was met with a series of largely ineffectual measures (promotion of rum production, conversion to banana farming in the 1930s), and the island came increasingly to depend on the importation of untaxed French goods. Beginning in the 1960s the French government promoted the implementation of a tourism-based infrastructure, to the detriment of local productive forces which were reduced to artisanry and the conditioning of prefabricated imported goods. Guadeloupe has maintained a trade deficit rising from roughly four to one in the 1970s to nearly ten to one in 1985 in the value of imported goods compared to that of exports.

Guadeloupe's dependency on France was confirmed with the March 19, 1946, law of departmentalization, defended by the representatives Gaston Monnerville of French Guiana and Aimé Césaire of Martinique. Departmentalization bestowed on Guadeloupe and its dependencies supposed legal equality with the mainland French departments. Adopted in a postwar French Assembly dominated by the Communist Party, its implementation was hindered with the succeeding return to political power of French conservative forces. The combination of an underdeveloped productive infrastructure and expensive labor due to newly acquired social benefits made it increasingly impossible for Guadeloupe to compete in global sugar and banana markets. Because of the numerical dominance of the descendants of slaves and their geographical separation from the white metropolitan French power structure, social movements in postwar Guadeloupe have tended to adopt the guise of political revindication, rather than the racially oriented struggles of the North American Civil Rights Movement. The writings of Martinique-born Frantz Fanon, the Algerian War (1954-1962), and the Cuban Revolution radicalized the desire for Guadeloupean independence and decolonization.

In the midst of economic instability and a rapidly increasing population, a series of postwar social movements and strikes culminated in the formation of the Group for the National Organization of Guadeloupe (GONG) in January 1963 and the Front for Guadeloupean Autonomy (FGA) in 1965. Both organizations strove openly – and at times violently – for Guadeloupean independence from France, despite the predominance of pro-Gaullist sentiment in the island. On March 20, 1967, a white merchant unleashed his dog upon an invalid cobbler in front of his store, and riots ensued throughout the island. Two months later, French troops opened fire on striking workers, killing between 7 and 49 Guadeloupeans.

Throughout the 1970s the movement for Guadeloupean independence continued, at times becoming violent. The drive for independence, always limited to a minority of the Guadeloupean population, gradually weakened throughout the 1980s. It received a decisive blow when in 1989 the effects of Hurricane Hugo reconfirmed the island's dependency on French support. The island's enormous trade deficit is supported by the infusion of social support funds by the French government (social security medical support, unemployment payments, support for families with children, pensions, and a 40 percent augmentation to functionaries' salaries), furthering the island's dependency on the mainland. This ongoing situation of dependency has brought on what EDOUARD GLISSANT has called "one of the rare 'successful' colonizations of modern history." Overcoming this "soft" subjugation in an era of increasing globalization will require Guadeloupeans to rethink the meaning of decolonization – in its political, economic, and psychological terms – as they struggle to realize their autonomy in this complex corner of the African diaspora.

Nick Nesbitt

SEE ALSO
Transatlantic Slave Trade; Maroonage in the Americas; Du Bois, William Edward Burghardt (W. E. B.); Haitian Revolution; Antigua and Barbuda; St. Vincent and the Grenadines; East Indian Communities in the Caribbean; Schwartz-Bart, Simone; Toussaint L'Ouverture, François Dominique; Slave Rebellions in Latin America and the Caribbean.

North America

Guardian, The, Boston-based, African American newspaper, edited by William Monroe Trotter, that challenged Booker T. Washington's philosophy of accommodation in the first half of the twentieth century.

The *Guardian* was founded in November 1901 by William Monroe Trotter, a Harvard-educated, African American businessman, and George Washington Forbes, an Amherst-educated, African American librarian. Trotter and Monroe founded the newspaper in part because racially discriminatory JIM CROW laws, which were prevalent in the South, were spreading to parts of the Northeast. Soon after its founding the *Guardian* targeted black leader Booker T. Washington as a chief obstacle to racial equality. Washington was immensely popular among whites and many blacks for his views that African Americans should set aside goals such as political equality, which he claimed were out of reach, and focus instead on modest economic gain through industrial education and hard work.

The *Guardian's* editorials sharply attacked Washington for ignoring the link between economic and political growth; for claiming that race relations were improving, when in fact they were worsening; for enjoying his political influence at the White House while urging other blacks to ignore politics; and for disregarding liberal arts education – and, indeed, all higher learning – while building his educational empire at the Tuskegee Institute on the strength of liberal-arts-educated *Guardian* had a circulation of more than 2500.

The conflict with Washington was not without cost. Forbes, facing a libel suit by Washington and vulnerable because of his employment at a city library, left the paper within a few years of its founding. Washington also wielded his influence with businessmen and other newspapers in an attempt to silence and condemn the *Guardian*. Although Trotter's was initially a lone voice, the *Guardian* gained prominence after Washington spoke in Boston in July 1903. A confrontation between the two men, later called the Boston Riot, led to a one-month jail term for Trotter and – when it became clear that Washington's lawyers were pursuing the case to its end – growing support for Trotter's cause. The *Guardian* played a significant role in energizing W. E. B. Du Bois, the NIAGARA MOVEMENT, and other anti-Washington forces.

When Trotter supplemented the *Guardian's* political reporting with news and gossip from cities across the country, its national readership grew markedly. After Forbes left, Trotter's wife, Geraldine Pindell Trotter, became instrumental in supporting and editing the newspaper, and Trotter's sister Maude Stewart and brother-in-law Charles Stewart provided financial and editorial help. In its later years the newspaper prominently protested the racist 1915 film *The Birth of a Nation* and succeeded in having it banned in Boston. The *Guardian* also protested the segregation of blacks in the armed forces during World War I and came to the defense of the Scottsboro defendants in the 1931 SCOTTSBORO CASE. After Geraldine's death in 1918 and William's death in 1934, Maude Stewart continued publication of the newspaper until she died in 1957. The *Guardian* ceased operations in 1960.

SEE ALSO
World War I and African Americans; *Birth of a Nation, The*; Military, Blacks in the American; Boston, Massachusetts; Du Bois, William Edward Burghardt (W. E. B.); Washington, Booker Taliaferro.

Latin America and the Caribbean

Guatemala, a republic in Central America with the largest population in the region, more than 11 million people. A rugged land of mountains and volcanoes, beautiful lakes, and lush vegetation, Guatemala is the third largest nation in Central America. Guatemala City is the capital and largest city (*see* CENTRAL AMERICA).

Africa

Gude (also known as Cheke, Mapuda, and Mubi, the Shede, and the Tchade), ethnic group of West Africa.

The Gude primarily inhabit eastern NIGERIA. They speak an Afro-Asiatic language in the Chadic group. Approximately 100,000 people consider themselves Gude.

SEE ALSO
Languages, African: An Overview.

Africa

Guéré (also known as Gewo, Krahn, Kran, and Wé), ethnic group of West Africa.

The Guéré primarily inhabit western CÔTE D'IVOIRE and neighboring eastern LIBERIA, where they are usually known as the Kran. They speak a Niger-Congo language in the KRU group and are closely related to the WOBÉ people. The Guéré number more than 200,000.

SEE ALSO
Languages, African: An Overview.

Latin America and the Caribbean

Guerrero, Vicente

(b. August 10, 1783?, Tixtla, New Spain [Mexico]; d. February 14, 1831, Oaxaca, Mexico), one of the leaders of the Mexican war of independence and a president of the young republic of MEXICO.

Vicente Guerrero was born in Tixtla, now a part of Guerrero, the state in Mexico named for him after his death. He was of mixed race, probably descended from Africans, Spaniards, and Native Americans. His dark complexion earned him the nickname "el Negro." For most of his early life he lived in the region where he was born and worked as a wage laborer and a teamster.

In 1810 Mexico's war of independence erupted. Guerrero sympathized with rebel demands, including an end to the restrictive caste system. In December 1810, when JOSÉ MARÍA MORELOS called for troops in south central New Spain (present-day Mexico) to join him in the revolt, Guerrero enlisted in the rebel forces. He soon was leading troops in the field and by 1812 had become a lieutenant colonel. During 1812 he attacked port towns on the Pacific coast and helped capture Oaxaca. The following year he concentrated on solidifying the rebels' gains in southern New Spain.

At the end of 1813 royalist forces (supporting continued Spanish colonial rule) dealt the rebels the first of what would be a long series of defeats. By 1814 Guerrero's forces had been whittled to a few hundred soldiers with only three rifles among them. He nonetheless routed a royalist detachment in southern Mexico with this meager force, using a surprise night raid and capturing several hundred guns. This exploit won him enduring fame.

By 1815 most of the insurgent leaders, including Morelos, had been captured or killed, and the rebel forces were reduced to hit-and-run assaults. Guerrero was the main strategist of many of these raids, and in March 1816 he was named general of the remaining rebels. Later in 1816 he had a new difficulty to confront: Juan Ruíz de Apodaca, the new viceroy of New Spain, used liberal pardons and amnesties to entice many rebel leaders to put down their arms. At the same time Ruíz began a massive campaign against those like Guerrero who continued to fight. In short order, forces under Ruíz were in control of most of the key areas of the colony, and on several occasions over the next four years Guerrero's bases were destroyed. Guerrero, however, eluded the royalist troops and continued his sporadic but destructive assaults on outlying parts of New Spain, achieving something of a stalemate.

When Spain itself underwent a liberal revolution in 1820, Mexicans entertained new hopes for independence. The following year royalists and conservatives in New Spain formed a new government. Gen. Agustín de Iturbide, a leading royalist general, put forward what became known as the Plan de Iguala, proposing an independent constitutional monarchy in Mexico that protected the Catholic Church, the upper class, and other conservatives. The plan promised equality for Spaniards and Creoles (those born in Mexico). In February 1821 Guerrero reluctantly joined with Iturbide to form a united force under Iturbide's command. On August 24, 1821, Viceroy Juan O'Donojú recognized Mexico's independence.

Iturbide assumed control of the independent state, but he quickly proved to be authoritarian. In early 1823 Guerrero led a revolt that eventually toppled him, but early in the revolt Guerrero was shot in the chest. The damage to his lungs hindered him throughout his life. After the revolt Guerrero was named part of an executive body established to govern the new republic. In 1824 Guerrero ran unsuccessfully for president, then briefly retired from public life. He was called back into military service in 1827 when a revolt by conservatives broke out against the government. By early 1828 he had quelled the revolt.

Later in 1828 Guerrero, by now the most revered populist leader in Mexico, made another run for the presidency. He lost narrowly to the conservative candidate of the upper class, Gen. Manuel Gómez Pedraza, but neither Guerrero nor his supporters accepted the election results as legitimate. Guerrero's supporters rebelled against Gómez Pedraza's government, and Guerrero soon joined the rebels. Gómez Pedraza acknowledged defeat and left the country, and on April 1, 1829, Guerrero became president.

As president, Guerrero quickly alienated the upper class with calls for a graduated income tax, property taxes, and protective tariffs to bolster the staggering economy. Under Guerrero, Afro-Mexican slavery (*see* SLAVERY IN LATIN AMERICA AND THE CARIBBEAN), which had declined sharply since its peak in the 1600s, was finally abolished. In July 1829, prompted by Mexican conservatives, Spain invaded Mexico, but Guerrero was prepared; his forces surrounded and easily defeated the Spaniards at Tampico, on the Caribbean coast. The situation in Mexico, however, continued to deteriorate, and in December 1829 Guerrero was forced from office. At first he pledged his support for the government of Anastasio Bustamante, but when Bustamante's repression increased and a rebellion against him spread, Guerrero decided to join the rebels. In January 1831 Guerrero was betrayed by one of his closest friends and handed over to Bustamante's troops. He was executed a few weeks later in Oaxaca.

SEE ALSO
Abolition and Emancipation in Latin America and the Caribbean.

Africa

Guèye, Lamine (b. 1891, Médine, French Sudan [now Mali]; d. June 10, 1968, Dakar, Senegal), influential anticolonialist Senegalese politician who organized the first modern political party in French-speaking Africa.

Born to Senegalese parents in present-day MALI, Lamine Guèye fought in France during World War I and remained to study law. He returned to Senegal in 1922. The first black lawyer in French-speaking Africa, he was elected mayor of Saint-Louis in 1925. From 1931 to 1934, he served as a magistrate on the island of RÉUNION in the Indian Ocean. In 1935, as an opponent of French colonialism, he assumed leadership of the Parti Socialiste Sénégalais (PSS). He focused on recruiting the educated elite and made the PSS into the first modern political party in French-speaking Africa. In 1936 he affiliated the PSS with the French Socialist Party (SFIO).

Guèye promoted Léopold Senghor's career, and both men won seats representing Senegal in the French Constituent Assembly in 1945 and 1946. As a member of the Assembly, Guèye helped secure eligibility for French citizenship for all colonial subjects. From 1946 to 1961 Guèye served as the mayor of Dakar. Rejecting what he saw as Guèye's narrow focus on elite support, Senghor broke with Guèye in 1948 to establish his own party, the Union Progressiste Sénégalaise. This party became Senegal's dominant party and later defeated Guèye and SFIO candidates.

Senghor and Guèye reunited in 1958 and sought unsuccessfully to combine French African colonies in an independent federation, losing to those who sought separate statehood for each colony. Upon Senegal's independence in 1959, Guèye was elected president of the Senegalese National Assembly – an office he held until his death in 1968.

SEE ALSO
Colonial Rule; Dakar, Senegal; Senghor, Léopold Sédar; Senegal.

Latin America and the Caribbean

Guillén, Nicolás (b. July 10, 1902, Camagüey, CUBA; d. July 16, 1989?, Havana, Cuba), Afro-Cuban poet, writer, journalist, and social activist, one of the Caribbean's foremost NÉGRITUDE poets, who placed the historical and social sufferings of blacks at the center of his poetic universe.

Nicolás Guillén is widely considered Cuba's preeminent poet, on a par with such Latin American literary masters as Jorge Luis Borges, Pablo Neruda, and César Vallejo. According to literary scholar Josaphat B. Kubayanda, "Guillén's poetry was the first successful development in Cuba of a vital and original aesthetic based upon the black and African elements on Caribbean soil." He was also a committed Communist, and his poems and journalism powerfully reflect his political and national concerns. Like the black American singer and antifascist activist PAUL ROBESON, Guillén devoted much of his life to the pursuit of peace, both in racially torn, prerevolutionary Cuba and abroad. He traveled extensively throughout the world and in 1954 received the Lenin International Peace Prize.

Guillén is equally a part of the community of black poets exemplified by HARLEM RENAISSANCE writers CLAUDE MCKAY, Sterling Brown, and LANGSTON HUGHES. In 1929, after Hughes told Guillén in an interview that it was his "greatest ambition to be the poet of the Blacks," Guillén noted, "Yes, I certainly understood; and I feel that the poem which opens this man's book of poetry springs from the depths of my own soul: 'I am a Negro / Black as the night is

Black / Black like the depths of my Africa.'" Indeed, it was Guillén's powerful core of black-inspired poetry that inaugurated a sophisticated AFROCUBANISMO in literature and effectively contributed to freeing Cuban letters from the hegemony of Spanish culture.

GUILLÉN'S EARLY POETIC DEVELOPMENT: THE MOTIVOS DE SON

In 1930 Guillén incited a national stir with the publication of *Motivos de son*, eight short poems inspired by the SON, a popular Afro-Cuban musical form, as well as by the daily living conditions of Cuban blacks. Composed in Afro-Cuban vernacular, the collection parted dramatically with the Spanish literary canon and served to establish black culture as a legitimate focus of Cuban literature. Cuban poet Angel Augier noted that "it is possible that neither before nor after has a collection of poems provoked a greater journalistic stir in Cuba." According to literary scholar Keith Ellis, "It is as if Guillén had touched on something... that the people collectively could recognize as having been on the tips of their tongues and that awaited the articulation Guillén gave to it."

Prior to the publication of *Motivos de son*, several of Guillén's contemporaries, such as the NEGRISTA POETS José Zacarías Tallet and Ramón Guirao, had already written on what they saw as the exotic and folkloric dimensions of black people. Their poetry often depicts blackness in both erotic and animalistic terms. A similar portrait of blacks could be found in much of the Western world during the 1920s, a time when blackness was in vogue, especially in art and literature. Yet, unlike the *negrista* poets, Guillén's writings focused on the social problems faced by Afro-Cubans. In prerevolutionary Cuban society, most blacks were relegated to the poorest living conditions and lowest educational levels. Guillén made it his life's work to confront and portray these realities – a stance that set him apart from most of his Cuban literary contemporaries. Defining his position as an artist, he wrote: "I deny the art that sees in the Negro only a colorful motif and not an intensely human theme. I believe that the true artist, who is always profoundly human, ought to dedicate himself to the definitive work, the one that is created with the blood and bones of men."

Like Langston Hughes in the United States, Guillén believed that black artists must be free to "express our individual dark-skinned selves without fear or shame." Although many blacks of the time thought that he had created caricatures of them, recent scholarship has emphasized that he used irony and sarcasm to shatter such stereotypes and to reconstruct positive images of blackness.

Guillén was the sixth child of Argelia Batista y Arrieta and Nicolás Guillén y Urra, both of mixed African and Spanish descent. Guillén's father, a liberal journalist and political activist, introduced him to Afro-Cuban music when he was a child. "I had found myself in the hands of a maestro in this art, whom everyone called Señor Pérez, and who never managed to get me to come down from the roof of my house where I used to wait for him flying kites," the poet recalled in a 1972 interview with *Cuba Internacional*. In 1917 Guillén's father was assassinated by government soldiers – an event that left Guillén, his five siblings, and his mother destitute. According to literary scholar Dennis Sardinha, Guillén's mother "managed to keep them in school and as they came out with their qualifications, they met with some of the most flagrant and disillusioning acts of racial discrimination that could be experienced." Like the United States prior to the mid-1960s, prerevolutionary Cuba had a system of legalized segregation. "This turned me into a rebel," said Guillén, "and from that rebellion sprang my nonconformity not only as regards racial prejudice, but also against all the others."

Considered Cuba's national poet, Nicolás Guillén was one of the most important Négritude poets in the Caribbean. Also a political activist, he was ideologically committed to the pursuit of world peace. *Photographs and Prints Division, Schomburg Center for Research in Black Culture, The New York Public Library, Astor, Lenox and Tilden Foundation*

Guillén began writing about the social problems faced by blacks in the late 1920s. His first poems appeared in *Camagüey gráfico* in 1920 and in 1922 his first collection of poems, *Cerebro y corazón* (Brain and Heart), was published. He also began legal studies at the University of Havana but soon dropped out of the program to pursue his literary interests. In 1926 he became a regular contributor to the Sunday literary supplement of Havana's *Diario de la Marina* and in 1929 published "El camino en Harlem," an article that condemned Cuba's racial structures. During the same year he interviewed Langston Hughes in Havana. Guillén deeply admired Hughes, who became a lifelong friend. He felt that Hughes, more than any other poet, had succeeded in bringing black popular music, such as blues and JAZZ, into American literature. Ian Isidore Smart, author of *Nicolás Guillén*, notes that "Langston Hughes had a most transcendental impact on Guillén; in fact he literally triggered Guillén's turning to the *son* as the vehicle for his most original poetic expression."

GUILLÉN AS AN IDEOLOGICALLY COMMITTED POET

During the early 1930s Cuba was rife with national tensions as a result of the GREAT DEPRESSION in the United States and a surge in political repression under the rule of Gerardo Machado (1924-1933). Moreover, the United States, in an attempt to protect its economic interests, had become increasingly involved in the Caribbean Basin. These factors led to the replacement of Machado in 1933 by the equally repressive FULGENCIO BATISTA (1933-1959). They also incited an upsurge in Cuban nationalism and the more public appearance of African-influenced cultural forms among the middle classes. As Robin Moore, author of *Nationalizing Blackness*, notes: "The arts of socially marginalized blacks, for centuries dismissed by Cuba's middle classes, took on new significance as symbols of nationality."

Guillén was deeply affected by Cuba's political and economic instability. His poetry collections *Sóngoro consongo* (1931) and *West Indies Ltd.* (1934) reflect his anti-imperialistic stance and the centrality of history – of both Cuba and the black diaspora – to his creativity. "Guillén's verses are splattered and spangled with the blood, chains, and tortures of the collective past," wrote Kubayanda. He also became increasingly committed to Marxism, and in 1937 joined the Cuban Communist Party. During the same year he published *Cantos para soldados y sones para turistas* (Songs for Soldiers and Sones for Tourists). The poems reflect his ideological commitment and convey images of affluence amid poverty, political unrest, and the excesses and tyranny of the Batista regime. Although the subjects of Guillén's poetry sometimes appear almost dehumanized, it is the harshness of their lives that Guillén compassionately sought to underscore.

Guillén was as much a political activist as a poet. In 1937 he traveled to SPAIN as a delegate to the Second International Congress of Writers for the Defense of Culture. In an address before the congress, he condemned fascism and reaffirmed his black roots: "I have come here, comrades, to bring the voice of one of the groups... which has suffered perhaps more than any other, from the injustice of men; which for centuries has had its muscles paralysed by slavery.... I come as a black man." In 1940 he ran as a candidate for mayor of Camagüey and in 1948 was a senatorial candidate for the Cuban Communist Party. Both campaigns were unsuccessful, and he continued his political activities abroad: in Europe, Latin America, the Caribbean, the United States, and the Soviet Union. Following his visit to CHILE in 1953, he was refused reentry into Cuba for his opposition to the Batista regime. During the next six years he lived in exile, first in Paris, FRANCE (1955-1958), then in Buenos Aires, ARGENTINA. His collected poems of the period, *La paloma de vuelo popular* (1958, The Dove of Popular Flight), poignantly convey the experience of exile – that of both the poet and others forced into refuge for their political activism.

Guillén deeply identified with the plight of blacks beyond his native Cuba – a concern particularly reflected in his *Elegías* (1958, Elegies). Written between 1948 and 1958, the elegies focus on the theme of social justice and forcefully reaffirm Guillén's problack consciousness. Included in the collection are elegies to the black Haitian poet JACQUES ROUMAIN; the black Cuban labor leader Jesús Menéndez, a friend of Guillén's who was murdered in 1948; and Emmett Till, the 14-year-old African American boy who was murdered by whites in 1955 and found mangled in the Tallahatchie River. In the elegy "El apellido," Guillén reflects on the loss of his ancestral ties to Africa and repeatedly questions his true identity. The poem conveys Guillén's sense of alienation from a heritage he does not know firsthand, and thus reveals the irrevocable loss inflicted by slavery.

THE IMPACT OF THE 1959 CUBAN REVOLUTION ON GUILLÉN'S LATER WORK

Upon his return to Cuba in January 1959, Guillén was hailed as a national hero for his lifelong support of revolutionary change in Cuba. Fidel Castro awarded him the task of designing a new cultural policy and setting up the Union of Writers and Artists of Cuba, of which Guillén became president in 1961. He also became a member of the National Council of Education and the Central Committee of Cuba's Communist Party. Like the poet Pablo Neruda in Chile, Guillén wrote poems that even the most uneducated Cubans could remember and recite and he soon became known as Cuba's national poet. In 1981 he was awarded the JOSÉ MARTÍ National Order, Cuba's highest honor.

During the next two decades Guillén wrote and published numerous collections of poetry, including *Tengo* (1964); *El gran zoo* (1967); *La rueda dentada* (1972); *El diario que a diario* (1972); and *Sol de domingo* (1982). According to Kubayanda, these later poems strongly reflect Guillén's political concerns at the expense of his "race and roots." She argues that "he devoted his attention almost exclusively to the Cuban Revolution." In the view of Clement A. White, however, Guillén remained passionately preoccupied with the future of black people – a future he believed hinged on the establishment of global Communism. "His poetry after 1959," affirms White, "dispels negative myths, protests against and condemns society's treatment of those of African descent; indeed his stinging indictment... is conveyed with great compactness and telling irony." Guillén died in Havana at age 87.

Roanne Edwards

SEE ALSO

Russia and the Former Soviet Union; Slavery in Latin America and the Caribbean; Blues, The; Brown, Sterling Allen; Till, Emmett Louis; Havana, Cuba; Havana, Cuba.

North America

Guillory, Ida Lewis ("Queen Ida") **(b. January 15, 1929, Lake Charles, La.), African American accordionist and leader of a popular ZYDECO band.**

Despite a musical childhood, the Grammy Award-winning accordionist Ida Lewis "Queen Ida" Guillory started her performing career relatively late in life. After growing up along the Louisiana and Texas Gulf Coast, she and her family moved to San Francisco, California. There Guillory married and raised three children while working part-time as a school bus driver. It was not until her children were nearly grown that she took up the accordion, an integral part of both cajun and zydeco music and an instrument that two of her uncles also played. Returning to zydeco, a rhythmic, dance-oriented music with both African and French influences (a style Guillory calls "earthy – simple, but happy"), she began playing at home and at parties and in 1975 made her debut at a San Francisco Mardi Gras party, where she was dubbed "Queen Ida."

Along with her Bon Temps Zydeco Band, Guillory has toured extensively throughout the United States and abroad, including a trip to Africa in 1989. Her energy, charisma, and talent have made her a popular performer at music festivals, and she has appeared on television (on *Saturday Night Live* and *Austin City Limits*) as well as in such films as the documentary *J'ai été au bal*. In 1983 she won a Grammy Award for her live album, *On Tour*. Guillory also coauthored a cookbook, *Cookin' with Queen Ida* (1990), which features Creole recipes. Of her late-blooming fame, Guillory says, "I believe it's never too late to expand your human potential."

Kate Tuttle

SEE ALSO

Creoles; San Francisco and Oakland, California.

Africa

Guinea, **a coastal West African country bordered by GUINEA-BISSAU, SENEGAL, MALI, CÔTE D'IVOIRE, LIBERIA, and SIERRA LEONE.**

Although today Guinea struggles with persistent poverty, the country possesses agricultural and mineral riches and an equally rich history. In precolonial days the area now known as Guinea was homeland to several distinct ethnic groups – principally the MANDINKA (or Malinke), FULANI, and Susa. The region was also the site one of Africa's longest lasting, autonomous Islamic theocracies, known as FOUTA DJALLON. Under French COLONIAL RULE, Guinea was one of the most productive of West African colonies. Its lucrative exports included rubber and bananas. However, French investors and merchants retained most of the wealth those exports produced.

Guinea achieved renown as the first of the French colonies to claim independence, and it served as an example to other African nations seeking autonomy. Guineans voted in 1958 to break ties with France. In the words of Guinea's first president, SÉKOU TOURÉ, Guinea chose "poverty in freedom to opulence in slavery." In fact, poverty has haunted Guinea since independence. Hunger and disease are widespread; literacy levels are low, even by African standards; and the infant mortality rate is among the highest in the world.

EARLY HISTORY

Archaeologists have found evidence of human occupation in present-day Guinea dating back 30,000 years. Artifacts show that inhabitants of the central Guinean savanna were farming cereals such as MILLET and sorghum by 1000 B.C.E. The people of the southeastern forest region were cultivating YAMS, oil palms, and vegetables by 100 B.C.E. By around 200 B.C.E. the region's inhabitants were smelting iron. Anthropologists believe that the earliest inhabitants of upper Guinea may have been the ancestors of modern MANDE speakers.

Upper Guinea (the northeastern savanna region) formed part of the heartland of the great Mande empires of Ghana and Mali (*see* ANCIENT AFRICAN CIVILIZATIONS). The first of these, ancient Ghana, also extended into present-day Mali and MAURITANIA. Ghana achieved its power by controlling trade – in particular, by exacting duties in gold for the transport of salt from northern mines – and it dominated the western savanna from the eighth to the eleventh century. Ghana was supplanted by the MALI EMPIRE, which arose around 1200 C.E. under the leadership of the Mandinka king SUNDIATA KEITA. Mali also exploited the rise of long-distance trade, including gold and slaves transported across the Sahara for markets in the north of Africa (*see* TRANS-SAHARAN AND RED SEA SLAVE TRADE). The upper Guinea city of Kankan became a center of Islamic scholarship under Mali's rule.

Ancestors of the BAGA, NALU, and Kissi peoples once occupied most of present-day Guinea west and south of the Mande upper Guinea region. However, migrations of Mande-speaking peoples starting in the tenth century drove the ancestors of the Baga and Nalu toward the coast and the ancestors

of the Kissi toward the forests of the southeast. Gradually, the Mande-speaking Susa people came to dominate the Fouta Djallon highlands of central Guinea, while the KPELLE and LOMA moved into the forest region.

Internal divisions caused the slow collapse of the Mali Empire beginning in the fourteenth century. Starting in the fifteenth century, a new migration brought Fulani herders to the Fouta Djallon highlands. Although the first Fulani migrants mostly followed traditional religious practices, subsequent waves included Islamic Fulani migrating from areas presently known as Senegal. Islamic Fulani founded Fouta Djallon, an Islamic theocratic state in the early eighteenth century. Fouta Djallon was a strictly hierarchical society with a ruling class (led by two families from which the *alimamies*, or leaders, were chosen), artisans, and slaves (mostly consisting of non-Muslim Fulani and non-Fulani inhabitants). To escape this forced servitude, the Susa people who had lived in the region began moving to coastal lower Guinea, where they dominated and gradually absorbed the existing Baga and Nalu population.

The Susa and other coastal peoples established trade relations with the Portuguese, who first arrived on the coast during the fifteenth century. European powers were attracted to the region's strategic location for trade to the NIGER RIVER Valley. By the eighteenth century the French and English came to dominate the coastal trade. The Europeans traded guns, alcohol, and other products for ivory, gold, and slaves (although the TRANSATLANTIC SLAVE TRADE remained relatively small scale in Guinea). By the early nineteenth century, they had begun to explore the hinterland. The first English expedition inland was in 1816; the French soon followed, with explorations in 1818 and 1827.

Meanwhile, the Fulani maintained a powerful theocratic state in the Fouta Djallon. Their culture of Islamic revival helped spark the rise of the TUKULOR Empire in the 1840s. Its leader, AL-HAJJ UMAR TAL, a Fulani-speaking Islamic scholar, ruled over a kingdom that included parts of upper Guinea and the area composed of present-day Senegal and Mali.

COLONIZATION

In the early nineteenth century the French established a trading settlement on the northwest coast as an outpost of their colony in Senegal. In 1849 they declared the coastal region a protectorate, administered from Senegal. They concluded treaties of mutual protection with indigenous leaders and began erecting an administrative structure that eventually included the entire area now known as Guinea. France established three military posts in the region by 1866. At first, the French promoted the cultivation of peanuts, but the humid coastal climate proved unsuitable for this cash crop. During the 1880s the French shifted their focus to the extraction of rubber. On the site of an old Susa fishing village known as Conakry, the French founded a town in 1880. In 1891 Conakry became the capital of the newly founded colony of French Guinea.

French colonization met heavy resistance. The Fulani of the Fouta Djallon continued to resist French control. Meanwhile, the Mandinka-dominated region produced one of Guinea's historic heroes: SAMORY TOURÉ. Touré built an empire covering much of present-day eastern Guinea, southern Mali, and northern Côte d'Ivoire during the 1880s. He fought colonization by the French for nearly 20 years until his defeat in 1898. Although the French defeated Fouta Djallon in 1896 and captured Touré in 1899 in a series of bloody campaigns, isolated resistance movements continued for another 20 years.

Under colonial rule, French commandants headed the colony's administrative districts. Each of these, in turn, oversaw several smaller districts, ruled by indigenous African leaders. The colonial government selected these "chiefs," often from a different ethnic group than the people of their districts, on the basis of their loyalty to the colonial government. As a result, local puppet-chiefs reinforced French rule in Guinea.

Colonial rule also transformed Guinea economically. French laws made former communally held land available for purchase, and France's colonial "head tax" on all Guineans increasingly forced people to supplement traditional subsistence farming with participation in the cash economy. The head tax compelled many Guineans to cultivate cash crops, especially rubber in the coastal and forest zones, and peanuts in upper Guinea. During the 1920s, after a collapse in the demand for Guinean rubber, French officials introduced coffee cultivation to the forested highlands. During the 1930s French investors established banana and pineapple plantations in the country, and the head tax compelled many Guineans to seek menial jobs on these plantations. Meanwhile, educated Guineans found employment in the lower levels of the civil service. For the French, Guinea became a fairly lucrative holding, as its economy shifted from traditional occupations like subsistence farming and craft production to large-scale farming of peanuts and tropical fruits for export.

THE INDEPENDENCE MOVEMENT

The French colonial system, increasingly under attack by both French Socialists and the educated elite of Africa, began to loosen after World War II (1939-1945). In 1945 new colonial laws permitted the formation of political parties and trade unions. The growth of unionism in Guinea received added impetus from European communist and socialist parties as well as religious organizations. The Guinean labor movement formed part of a larger Pan-African movement, promoted through regional meetings sponsored by the French Confédération Générale du Travail (CGT).

Fighting a system in which European workers earned three to four times more than indigenous Guineans on the same jobs, the country's communications workers were the first to organize. Sékou Touré, who would become independent Guinea's first president, got his start as the secretary-general of the postal workers' union in 1945. The rise of unions such as Touré's occurred alongside similar growth of political parties. In 1946 Touré was instrumental in the formation of the Rassemblement Démocratique Africain

Village children watch a bead game near Kurikori, Guinea. *M & E Bernheim*

(RDA). He also helped found its Guinean branch, the Parti Démocratique de Guinée (PDG). Labor unions functioned not only as effective mobilizers across ethnic group lines; they also served as a training ground for the country's future political leaders.

Strikes in 1950 and 1953 helped mobilize the entire population against the inequities of colonial rule. Even nonunionized workers, according to Touré's account, contributed food aid to striking workers. As historian Claude Rivière points out, such shared struggles contributed to a growing sense of nationalism among indigenous Guineans. Although they had retained more control over local issues than some other colonized people, Guineans increasingly sought more political autonomy along with more economic fairness. The man at the center of both movements was Touré.

Elected to the National Assembly in both 1951 and 1954, Touré was barred from his seat until 1956, when he won office as Conakry's mayor. By then the Mandinka from upper Guinea had gained a reputation as both a powerful speaker and a shrewd politician. By 1957 he was both vice president of the Executive Council of Guinea (the national governing body) and the founder of the Union Générale des Travailleurs d'Afrique Noire (UGTAN), a new labor union for Africans under French colonial rule. Immensely popular among the poor and dispossessed of Guinea, Touré effectively quashed rival political parties and by 1958 was the acknowledged leader of Guinean anticolonialism.

France's war with ALGERIA spurred a further liberalization of its colonial policy. French president Charles de Gaulle proposed that the colonies be allowed to choose, by referendum, whether to adopt internal self-rule as part of a Franco-African confederation or to claim complete independence. Led in large part by Touré's inspiring rhetoric – although the PDG conducted no campaign on the matter – Guinea, alone among the French colonies, chose full independence. The vote conducted on September 28, 1958, was 1,134,324 to 56,981.

Touré's Reign and Beyond

Instantly decried as part of a worldwide communist movement, Guinea's vote for independence sparked a harsh French reaction. De Gaulle recalled French administrators, technical workers, and the French machinery that was crucial to Guinea's modern infrastructure. In addition, France cut off all financial aid to its former colony and left Guinea's economy in danger of total collapse.

Touré assumed office as Guinea's first president shortly after the Republic of Guinea gained independence on October 2, 1958. Drawing from his experience both in building coalitions as a union leader and in neutralizing political opponents, Touré effectively co-opted rival parties into the PDG. His efforts at attracting foreign aid, according to historians, were masterful: Touré emphasized the "positive neutralism" of Guinea in relation to cold war allegiances and portrayed Guinea as being punished for personally challenging de Gaulle. Despite the influence of such political theorists as Karl Marx and Ghana's KWAME NKRUMAH, Touré's anticolonialist approach was also strategic and pragmatic. Although he reached out to both Eastern and Western powers, Touré's anticapitalist stance tended to attract the most aid from the Eastern bloc nations such as the Soviet Union, which helped develop Guinea's potential for the mining of bauxite (the raw material for aluminum production).

Within Guinea, Touré began to centralize authority under an increasingly dictatorial state. According to most historians, the combination of limited economic opportunity and growing political repression led as many as a million Guineans to seek refuge in neighboring states. As his long tenure continued – he would retain the presidency until his death in 1984 – Touré faced a series of assassination attempts and coup plots. According to analysts, it is difficult to distinguish between the real threats to Touré's power and those manufactured to justify the jailings and even executions of his political rivals. By the late 1960s Touré began outlawing opposition parties and labor unions. He had prominent Fulani and Mandinka leaders jailed or executed without trial, on the suspicion that these large ethnic groups could mobilize effective opposition.

By the late 1970s, after years of mismanagement by state-run monopolies and dwindling foreign aid, Guinea's economy had reached a standstill. The population began to demonstrate against Touré's policies. Faced with riots in 1977, Touré prudently launched a series of changes. He traveled widely and approached Western lenders – governmental and private – for help in building a more capitalist economy, and he opened the government monopolies to competition. In addition, he tried to improve relations with Guinea's West African neighbors.

In March 1984 Touré died of a heart attack in a Cleveland, Ohio, hospital. The Guinean government fell into turmoil. On April 3, 1984, the Comité Militaire de Redressement National, a military junta headed by Col. LANSANA CONTÉ, seized control. At first, Conté, who chose fellow soldier Diarra Traoré as his prime minister, seemed poised to reverse many of Touré's excesses. He freed some 97 political prisoners. At the same time, however, he suspended Guinea's constitution.

As president, Conté changed the country's name back to the Republic of Guinea. Since 1978, under Touré, the official name had been the People's Revolutionary Republic of Guinea. Conté promised a gradual evolution toward a multiparty democracy, with free elections to be held sometime in the future. It was not long before opposition to Conté arose. His own prime minister, Traoré, allegedly attempted to overthrow him in 1985. Conté jailed and executed several of the alleged plotters. In 1987, perhaps fearing that Traoré's supporters would attempt another coup, Conté held secret trials in Conakry and had 60 people sentenced to death for "crimes against the state." Since then, Conté's administration has responded to ongoing protests by imposing limits on free expression, public meetings, and opposition parties. In December 1993 Guinea held the first multiparty elections in the country's history. Conté won the presidency by a slim majority in what observers report was an election rife with fraud. In the second multiparty elections held in December 1998, Conté's four opponents accused him of manipulating voter registration in order to win another term in office.

Guinean President Sékou Touré speaks before the United Nations in 1962, protesting the lack of African representation on the security council. *CORBIS/Bettmann*

A violent revolt of at least 2000 soldiers demanding higher pay in 1996 forced President Conté into hiding. Reports suggest that as many as 50 people died during two days of rioting in Conakry. In an attempt to restore confidence in his ability to improve the financial lot of Guineans, Conté appointed an economist, Sidya Touré, to the office of prime minister in 1996.

Neither Conté nor his rivals have found an effective solution to the country's grinding poverty. Guinea remains one of the poorest countries in the world. This poverty persists even though Guinea is the world's second largest producer of bauxite. The country also has important reserves of iron ore, diamonds, and gold. A structural adjustment plan imposed by foreign lenders in the late 1980s has brought little economic improvement. Though structural adjustment measures have boosted exports of minerals and cash crops, they have also ensured that foreign investors will reap most of the benefits. Associated austerity measures have limited the ability of Guinea's government to invest export earnings in economic development that would benefit the country's population. Instead, Guinea is required to devote much of its export revenue to pay interest on its debt to foreign lenders. The influx of refugees from neighboring Sierra Leone and Liberia throughout the 1990s has further strained Guinea's weak economy.

Kate Tuttle

See Also

Conakry, Guinea; Decolonization in Africa: An Interpretation; Explorers in Africa Since 1800; Ghana; Ghana, Early Kingdom of; Gold Trade; Ivory Trade; Iron in Africa; Nationalism in Africa; Pan-Africanism; Sahara Desert; Salt Trade; Structural Adjustment in Africa; Rassemblement Démocratique Africain; Soso; Islam and Tradition: An Interpretation; Slavery in Africa.

Africa

Guinea (Ready Reference)

Official Name: Republic of Guinea
Former Name: French Guinea
Area: 245,857 sq km (94,925 sq mi)
Location: Guinea is bounded on the north by Guinea-Bissau, Senegal, and Mali, on the east and southeast by Côte d'Ivoire, on the south by Liberia and Sierra Leone, and on the west by the Atlantic Ocean.
Capital: Conakry (population 705,000 [1989 estimate])
Other Major Cities: Kankan (population 278,000 [1989 estimate])
Population: 7,477,110 (1998 estimate)
Population Density: 30 persons per sq km (78 people per sq mi)
Population Below Age 15: 44 percent (male 1,634,344; female 1,644,863 [1998 estimate])
Population Growth Rate: .83 percent (1998 estimate)
Total Fertility Rate: 5.59 children born per woman (1998 estimate)
Life Expectancy at Birth (total): Total population: 46.0 years (male 43.5 years; female 48.5 years [1998 estimate])
Infant Mortality Rate: 128.9 deaths per 1000 live births (1998 estimate)
Literacy Rate (age 15 and over who can read and write): Total population: 35.9 percent (male 49.9 percent; female 21.9 percent [1995 estimate])
Education: Education is free and officially compulsory for all children between the ages of 7 and 12, but in the early 1990s only about 37 percent of eligible children actually attended school. Private schools were nationalized by 1962. The universities at Conakry and Kankan, along with 21 other institutions, provide higher education.
Languages: While French is the official language, almost every Guinean speaks one of eight national languages: Malinke, Soso, Fulani, Kissi, Basari, Loma, Koniagi, or Kpelle.
Ethnic Groups: Fulani constitute 35 percent of the population, the largest group. Most other Guineans are from the Mande group, either Malinke, in northeastern Guinea, or Soso, in the coastal areas.
Religions: About 85 percent of the population practices Islam. Most of the remainder adhere to traditional beliefs. Christians form a small portion of the total population.
Climate: The dominant factor in the consideration of climatic variation is altitude. Rainfall varies most and temperature varies least in lower Guinea. Rainfall in Conakry averages 4300 mm (about 170 in) in a year, while temperature averages 27° C (81° F). In the mountainous plateau region, less rain falls and the mean temperature is 7° C (13° F) degrees lower. The climate in the highlands is equatorial, with no clearly distinguishable seasons. The rainy season in the remainder of the country occurs from April or May to October or November. In terms of heat, April is the cruelest month; July and August are the wettest.
Land, Plants, and Animals: Guinea divides into four major topographic regions. Lower Guinea, the coastal plain, extends in from the coastline. Beyond the plain is middle Guinea, the Fouta Djallon, a mountainous plateau region with an average elevation of 910 m (about 3000 ft). The savannas of Upper Guinea undulate gently, breaking occasionally into rocky outcroppings of some elevation. In the extreme southeast are forested highlands. The vegetation of Guinea includes dense mangrove forests along the coast, sedge in the Fouta Djallon, savanna woodland in upper Guinea, and rain forest in the highlands. Animal life abounds. Snakes and crocodiles are common, as are tropical birds, including parrots. Mammals include leopards, hippopotamuses, wild boars, antelopes, and civets.
Natural Resources: Bauxite ore, iron ore, diamonds, gold, petroleum, uranium, cobalt, nickel, and platinum
Currency: The Guinea franc
Gross Domestic Product (GDP): $8.3 billion (1997 estimate)
GDP per Capita: $1,100 (1997 estimate)
GDP Real Growth Rate: 4.8 percent (1997 estimate)
Primary Economic Activities: Agriculture and mining
Primary Crops: Rice, cassava, plantains, vegetables, and citrus fruits
Industries: Bauxite, gold, diamonds; alumina refining; light manufacturing; and agricultural processing industries
Primary Exports: Bauxite, alumina, diamonds, gold, coffee, pineapples, bananas, and palm kernels
Primary Imports: Petroleum products, metals, machinery, transport equipment, textiles, and grain
Primary Trade Partners: France, Côte d'Ivoire, China, and Germany
Government: Since 1990 Guinea has made a transition from a one-party, military regime to a multiparty, constitutional civilian system. The new system has a unicameral legislature of 114 seats and universal adult suffrage. Presidential elections were held late in 1993 and again in December 1998; Lansana Conté is the current president. Legislative elections took place in 1995 after being postponed several times.

Eric Bennett

See Also

Conakry, Guinea; Iron in Africa.

Africa

Guinea-Bissau, a small country on the West African coast that lies north of Guinea and south of Senegal.

Guinea-Bissau is one of the poorest countries in the world. Its poverty derives from a long history of slave trading, Portuguese colonial neglect, an 11-year war for independence, post-independence economic mismanagement, and a lack of natural resources. The small, lineage-based communities of Guinea-Bissau have resisted domination by a series of overlords, including the precolonial kingdom of Kaabu, European slave traders, European Fulani marauders, Portuguese colonialists, and finally the Cape Verdean elite of the nationalist movement. This strong tradition of resistance has been a unifying theme in Guinea-Bissau's history.

Early History

Archaeologists believe that small groups of hunters, gatherers, and fishing people occupied the region by 9000 B.C.E. A more pronounced migration toward the coast came around 900 C.E., when wars, poverty, and climatic shifts pushed new groups into the region from points farther east. They were primarily agriculturists and hunters, though some raised cattle on the eastern savanna. The low alluvial plains and mangrove swamps along the coast and rivers sustained salt extraction and tidal agriculture. Over time chiefdoms proliferated. Lineages held land communally and worshiped local gods in addition to their own ancestors.

The Mandinka were one of the last groups to arrive in the region. Their kingdom of Kaabu, the region's first real kingdom, emerged in present-day northeastern Guinea-Bissau around 1250, originally as a tributary of the Mali Empire. Kaabu remained powerful for the next six centuries, as it conquered small chiefdoms throughout the region and enslaved their inhabitants. Many groups fled south and west from Kaabu to the coastal lowlands. Others, such as the Balanta, literally "those who refuse," and the Bijagó of the islands, resisted Kaabu ascendancy and Mandinka dominance. Even when the Balanta were forced to pay tribute to the Mandinka, their adherence to traditional patrilineal succession limited the ability

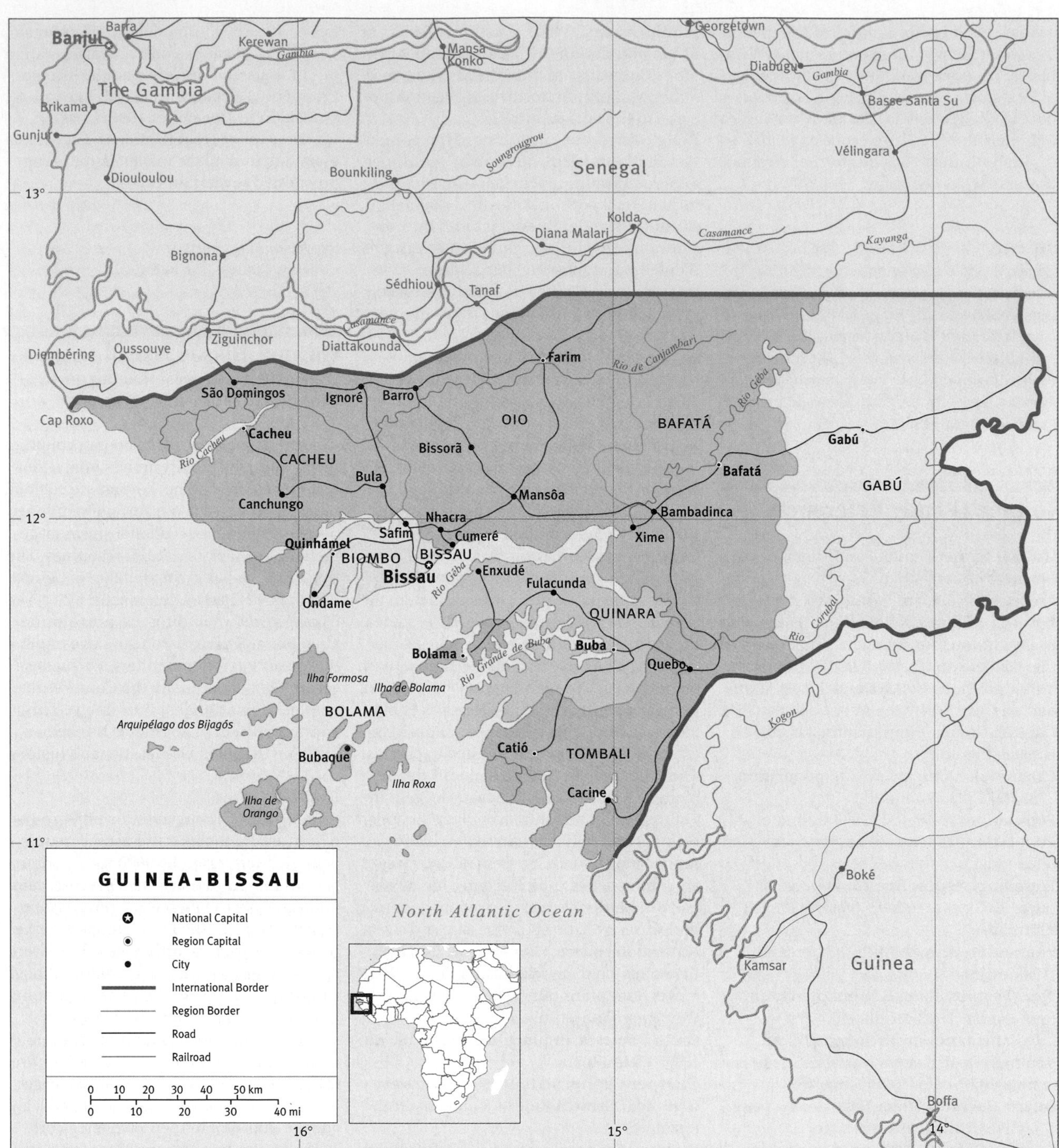

of the Mandinka Empire to incorporate them. Kaabu expanded during the late fifteenth and the sixteenth centuries, when Songhai assaults on the Mali Empire and trade with the Portuguese enabled Kaabu to exercise greater autonomy.

The Slave Trade and Foreign Domination

In 1446 the Portuguese explorer Nuño Tristão sailed into the Bijagós Archipelago and up some of the rivers, though he died on his return trip. It was not until ten years later that Diogo Gomes returned to Portugal to tell of the "Rivers of Guinea." The estuaries facilitated trade, and the coastal market town of Cacheu was the commercial center of the region from the late fifteenth to the nineteenth century. At first, the small Portuguese population remained confined to a few coastal settlements, where they paid tribute to local chiefs or kings for the right to stay.

Portuguese and *mestiços*, or those of indigenous and European descent, traded alcohol, horses, manufactured goods, textiles, and weapons for copra (coconut flesh, containing the oil), gold, ivory, palm oil, and, increasingly, slaves. Kaabu and other chiefdoms and kingdoms had long been involved in the Arab trans-Saharan slave trade, and they simply shifted some of this trade to the Portuguese on the coast. Some groups, such as the Balanta, Nalu, Felupe, Manjaco, and others, resisted these slave raiding parties. Nevertheless, scholars estimate that from the coming of the Portuguese to the end of the eighteenth century around 600,000 people were sent down the rivers of Guinea to the international slave market. The Portuguese sent slaves to their Cape Verde Island territory, where they were put to work on sugar plantations or shipped to the Americas.

As the transatlantic slave trade shifted farther south during the eighteenth century, Portuguese immigrants, mestiços, and Cape Verdeans began establishing larger agricultural estates, or *feitorias*, along the rivers, and growing peanuts, coffee, sugar cane, and cotton. In the interior, Kaabu, socially

LEFT: Young men from Guinea-Bissau engage in a traditional wrestling match. *© M. Koene/Explorer*
BELOW: These girls on the Bijagós Islands off Guinea-Bissau play traditional drums and wear a combination of mass-produced and handcrafted clothing. *CORBIS/Dave B. Houser*

stratified and intimately involved in the slave trade, had reached its height, with 44 provinces providing troops and tribute. When Portugal outlawed the slave trade in 1837, competition in the illicit slave trade increased. Kaabu provincial governors contended for power and control of the trade in intra-dynastic feuds.

The Islamic Fulani people, who had been subject to heavy Kaabu taxation for generations, eroded the power of the war-torn kingdom through religious conversion and jihads, or holy wars. Often supplied with firearms by the Portuguese, Fulani from the area presently known as Guinea began pushing north in the mid-1800s. The wars between the splintering Kaabu Kingdom and the Fulani culminated in 1867 when soldiers loyal to the Fulani *marabout* (religious leader) Timbo Adbul Khudus forced the surrender of Kaabu, though internal rivalries kept the Fulani from consolidating their rule. However, the fall of Kaabu enabled Portugal to divide the peoples of the region and to rule them through pliable chiefs. In the 1870s and 1880s, Fulani slaves, uncompensated by their Fulani masters for fighting against the Mandinka, revolted. The Portuguese granted the rebellious slaves sanctuary, and in return many of them assisted in Portugal's "pacification" campaigns to subdue the indigenous population.

Portuguese Colonialism and African Resistance

When Portugal declared Portuguese Guinea a province in 1879, the Portuguese presence in the region was limited and the Africans, although divided, increasingly resisted. Suffering from tropical diseases and laboring under a lack of funding from colonial authorities on the Cape Verde Islands, the military had thus far failed in its efforts to "pacify" the region. The change in colonial status enabled the Lisbon government to allocate military resources directly to Guinea, which it declared a military district in 1892.

Portuguese pacification campaigns from the 1880s to the 1910s generally remained unsuccessful. The Africans had firearms clandestinely supplied by traders. In addition to these weapons, the Africans used their intimate knowledge of the territories along the rivers to hold off the Portuguese military campaigns with ease. In 1908 nearly the whole Portuguese population was forced into the fort at Bissau. In the next decade the new republican government in Portugal placed a greater emphasis on crushing African resistance, and the colonial administration succeeded in conquering most of the land, through manipulation and force, and in gaining the support of the Fulani.

Under a fascist dictatorship from the 1920s until 1974, Portugal centralized administrative control over the territory and instituted a harsh system of forced labor and heavy taxation. The Portuguese controlled the administration, and mestiços and Cape Verdeans held more than 70 percent of the administrative posts. Appointed *regulos*, or chiefs, almost all of whom were Fulani, implemented forced labor on oil palm, rice, and peanut plantations. The lack of capital investment under the Portuguese limited the productivity of these ventures and created the basis for the country's persistent poverty. If they were not on forced-labor plantations, many Africans worked on state-run agricultural estates for wages to pay the high taxes demanded by the colonial state. Other Africans worked as subsistence farmers, producing enough surplus to pay taxes. Through education, employment, land ownership, or military service, Africans could attain the privilege of *assimilado* status, or Portuguese citizenship with full rights, but few did so. Discriminatory policies as well as attempts to separate ethnic groups and place them under the control of pliable regulos proved ineffective, because many Africans remained

outside the colonial state. For example, the Balanta and the Bijagó resisted colonial authority until 1936.

In 1956 Amílcar Cabral founded the Partido Africano da Independência de Guiné e Cabo Verde (PAIGC). Originally established to advocate peacefully for independence, the party led the nationalist struggle for the next 18 years. In 1962, three years after Portuguese soldiers killed 50 striking dockworkers in Bissau, the PAIGC launched a "people's war" for independence. The southern mangrove swamps and northern forests proved favorable ground for PAIGC guerrillas. Armed with military supplies from Eastern bloc countries, the party effectively controlled two-thirds of the country by 1968, far more than their counterparts the Front for the Liberation of Mozambique (FRELIMO) and the Popular Movement for the Liberation of Angola (MPLA) would ever control in Mozambique or Angola. Even with nearly 50,000 troops, Portugal's counterinsurgency efforts failed. The population, who hated the abuses of Portuguese colonial rule and perceived its weakness, supported the nationalists.

After Cabral's assassination in 1973 by a political opponent, the Cape Verdean Aristides Pereira took over the party's leadership. The PAIGC regrouped and was so successful that it made a unilateral declaration of independence in September 1973. One year later, after a coup d'état in Portugal, Lisbon recognized Guinea-Bissau's independence, and the PAIGC took control with Luís Cabral, Amílcar Cabral's half-brother, as president.

Independence

The PAIGC, the only legitimate nationalist organization during the independence struggle, was divided between the Cape Verdean-dominated senior ranks and the young soldiers of various ethnic groups from the mainland, especially the Balanta. The party also imposed harsh discipline on soldiers and peasants alike. When Cape Verde became independent in 1975, leaders of both countries anticipated unification, but mainland resentment of mestiço and Cape Verdean domination stood in the way. Meanwhile, the relocation of the party leadership to the capital in Bissau widened the gap between the rural population and party officials, who acquired urban lifestyles and relied on ex-colonial civil servants for technical know-how. As the sole legal party, the PAIGC kept a tight hold on power, and bureaucratic inefficiencies multiplied.

The government tried to revitalize the war-ruined economy through an expansion of state-run agricultural projects and state trading cartels, as it had attempted to do while fighting the independence war, but

ABOVE: Ancestor figurines carved by Bijagó sculptors. *Werner Forman/Art Resource, NY*
LEFT: A man in Guinea-Bissau harvests peanuts, one of the country's few cash crops. *CORBIS/Dave B. Houser*

this was unsuccessful. At the PAIGC's Third Congress in 1977, the state outlined its goal of agricultural and industrial development. The state allowed individuals to own land privately, but state-run trading monopolies would conduct the trade in their agricultural goods. Furthermore, the central government would control all taxation, large-scale fishing projects, mining, forestry, and industrial development. By 1983 the government realized that state-led development schemes were failing due to corruption, inadequate technical training, and a lack of necessary foreign capital. Guinea-Bissau's dependence on the export of a few cash crops (cashew nuts, peanuts, palm oil) compounded these difficulties, since prices for these crops fluctuated widely and tended to remain low. With the failure of the government's heavy-handed, state-centered approach to economic development, the informal economy flourished.

The simmering Cape Verdean-Guinean ethnic differences came to a boil after independence, when the government proved authoritarian and inefficient. In 1980 these differences and the marginalization of the mainlander-dominated military led the former vice president and respected guerrilla commander João "Nino" Vieira to overthrow Cabral. In the short term, the influence of Cape Verdeans and mestiços declined and the government abandoned its attempt to control the economy; but the government remained authoritarian, and the economic and ethnic problems persisted. In the early 1980s the government demoted prominent Cape Verdeans and mestiços as the Balanta in the military agitated for a greater political role. Historically the Balanta, the largest ethnic group, with about 32 percent of the population, were the primary cultivators of Guinea-Bissau's staple crop of rice, but their tradition of dispersed social organization hindered their incorporation into the central government. Balanta discontentment reached its peak in the mid-1980s in the form of a messianic cult and a coup attempt.

The PAIGC sought to consolidate its control through single-party elections in 1984 and 1989. It expanded executive powers so that Vieira could squelch the opposition. Corruption pervaded the government. A 1987 structural adjustment program, sponsored by the International Monetary Fund (IMF), moved the country away from its centrally planned economy and trade with Eastern bloc countries. Divisions over the program arose within the government, as ministries feared their reduction.

Illegal opposition political parties advocating for democratic reform – many of which were led by émigrés in Portugal or neighboring Guinea – never offered a viable alternative to the supremacy of Vieira and the PAIGC. It was only international pressure and the debate concerning the implementation of the structural adjustment program that led dissenting members of the political elite to convince Vieira in 1990 to move toward political liberalization. In 1991 the PAIGC abolished its political monopoly in Guinea-Bissau; political parties soon proliferated. Nevertheless, in the first multiparty election ever held in Guinea-Bissau, in 1994, Vieira narrowly won the presidency and the PAIGC won 62 of 92 seats in the National Assembly. After being re-elected in 1997, Vieira was overthrown by a military faction in May 1999. Head of Parliament Malan Bacai Sanha was appointed interim president, pending elections in November 1999.

Guinea-Bissau has remained economically stable but poor. In the late 1990s its inflation has stabilized at around 15 percent. It has strictly adhered to its structural adjustment program, including cuts in public spending, accelerated privatization, and a restrictive monetary policy, and it has begun negotiations to enter the West African monetary system and adopt the CFA franc. These steps aim to alleviate the severe poverty of Guinea-Bissau. Today, primary education is free and compulsory, but there are few secondary schools and no institutions of higher learning, and the illiteracy rate stands at 46 percent. Most of the country's 1.2 million people live in the countryside as subsistence farmers. The main economic activities are small-scale agriculture, forestry, and fishing, though over 50 percent of the country's export earnings come from cashew nuts.

Guinea-Bissau's unexploited reserves of oil have so far caused more problems than benefits. During the mid-1980s the country's relations with Guinea to the south over offshore oil reserves had to be resolved at the World Court. Beginning in 1989 relations between Guinea-Bissau and Senegal also became strained over fishing and oil rights. After Guinea-Bissau agreed to only 15 percent of the oil rights, this disagreement was settled in 1993. The country's bauxite and phosphate reserves offer better prospects for generating revenue.

Guinea-Bissau has served as a refuge for dissidents, refugees, and pilgrims from neighboring countries. Complicating the dispute between Guinea-Bissau and Senegal over offshore natural resources was the fact that Casamance separatists from Senegal had been using Guinea-Bissau as a sanctuary. In 1993 nearly 20,000 Senegalese fled to Guinea-Bissau to avoid the violence in the Casamance region. In 1998 some units of Guinea-Bissau's armed forces rebelled against the government after President Vieira dismissed army chief Gen. Ansumane Mane on corruption charges. Rebelling officers were accused of smuggling arms to the Casamance separatists. The Senegalese government sent troops to help Vieira end the insurrection.

Indigenous African religions remain prominent in Guinea-Bissau, and pilgrims from Muslim-dominated Senegal and Guinea visit the country's many oracles and shrines. Around two-thirds of the population retain indigenous African religions and one-third follow Islam; a negligible Christian population is growing slowly. Adherence to indigenous African religions is yet another form of the resistance that has characterized the history of Guinea-Bissau's people.

Eric Young

See Also

Cabral, Amílcar; Cape Verde; Colonial Rule; Colonial Rule; Gold Trade; Ivory Trade; Portugal; Songhai Empire; Structural Adjustment in Africa; Vieira, João Bernardo; Cacheu, Guinea-Bissau; Kaabu, Early Kingdom of; Slavery in Africa; Trans-Saharan and Red Sea Slave Trade.

Africa

Guinea-Bissau (Ready Reference)

Official Name: Republic of Guinea-Bissau
Former Name: Portuguese Guinea
Area: 36,120 sq km (about 13,945 sq mi)
Location: Western Africa; borders the North Atlantic Ocean, between Senegal and Guinea
Capital: Bissau (population 200,000 [1994 estimate])
Population: 1,206,311 (1998 estimate)
Population Density: 32 persons per sq km (about 83 persons per sq mi)
Population Below Age 15: 42 percent (male 256,315; female 255,208 [1998 estimate])
Population Growth Rate: 2.32 percent (1998 estimate)
Total Fertility Rate: 5.1 children born per woman (1998 estimate)
Life Expectancy at Birth: Total population: 49.1 years (male 47.4 years; female 50.8 years [1998 estimate])
Infant Mortality Rate: 111.6 deaths per 1000 live births (1998 estimate)
Literacy Rate (age 15 and over who can read and write): Total population: 53.9 percent (male 67.1 percent; female 40.7 percent [1996 estimate])
Education: In the late 1980s about 650 primary and secondary schools had a combined annual enrollment of more than 86,100 students. The country has several teacher training colleges. The government has undertaken a successful program to lower the high adult illiteracy rate, which stood at 81 percent in 1980.
Languages: The official language is Portuguese, but many people speak Crioulo, which combines Portuguese with African elements.
Ethnic Groups: The Balanta, Fulani, Malinke, Mandyako, and Pepel constitute the major ethnic groups, while Cape Verdeans form a small but significant minority.
Religions: A little over one half of the population follows traditional beliefs; 38 percent are Muslim and 8 percent are Christian.
Climate: The climate is tropical, with a mean annual temperature of 25° C (77° F). The rainy season lasts from June to November, bringing an average of 1950 mm

(about 77 in) of rainfall.
Land, Plants, and Animals: Vegetation consists of mangrove and rain forest on the coastal plain and a savanna woodland on the interior plateau.
Natural Resources: Tropical hardwoods, bauxite, phosphate, and petroleum
Currency: The Communauté Financière Africaine franc
Gross Domestic Product (GDP): $1.15 billion (1997 estimate)
GDP per Capita: $975 (1997 estimate)
GDP Real Growth Rate: 5 percent (1997 estimate)
Primary Economic Activities: Agriculture and fishing
Primary Crops: Cashew nuts, peanuts, rice, corn, beans, cassava (tapioca), and palm kernels
Industries: Agricultural processing and beverages
Primary Exports: Cashew nuts, palm kernels, peanuts, and fish
Primary Imports: Foodstuffs, machinery, petroleum products, and transport equipment
Primary Trade Partners: China, Germany, Netherlands, Portugal, and Senegal
Government: A constitution enacted in 1984 vests legislative power in the 150-member National People's Assembly, the members of which are chosen from directly elected regional councils. The legislature elects the five-member Council of State and its president, who heads the government. A political liberalization program approved in 1991 ended one-party dominance in Guinea-Bissau. By 1994, 12 political parties had been recognized and the first multiparty presidential and legislative elections were held. João Bernardo Vieira was re-elected president in 1997 only to face a crisis in June 1998 when a military faction revolted and accused him of corrution. When, according to a peace agreement reached in November 1998 in Abuja, Nigeria, the presidential guard refused to disarm, the military faction attacked on May 8, 1999, toppled Vieira's government, and appointed the head of Parliament, Malan Bacai Sanha, as interim president. Francisco Fadual was named interim prime minister. Elections are scheduled for November 28, 1999.

Eric Bennett

See Also
Vieira, João Bernardo.

Africa

Guinea Fowl, common name for six species of birds native to Africa; one species also occurs on Madagascar and other Indian Ocean islands.

Among guinea fowl, the sexes are alike in color: mostly black, dotted in all except two species of one genus with small, light-colored spots. The head and upper neck are bare, but two species of a second genus have a bushy tuft of feathers on the crown.

The helmeted guinea fowl is the most widely distributed species and has several subspecies distinguished by the size, shape, and color of the wattles at the corner of the mouth and by the size and shape of the bony "helmet" on the crown. The West African subspecies has long been domesticated, and introduced wild-type populations are found in Arabia and the West Indies.

Domestic guinea fowl are nervous and noisy birds, and are therefore not widely raised commercially. On small farms and in some large chicken farms they act as alarms, raising a clamor in the presence of predators.

The two guinea fowl with small, light-colored spots inhabit dense, primary forest in West Africa. The white-breasted guinea fowl, black with a broad white collar, is considered one of the most endangered species of Africa because of habitat destruction and hunting pressure. The black guinea fowl is rare but has a larger range.

The largest and most ornate species is the vulturine guinea fowl, of open scrubby country in East Africa. It has a cape of long hackle feathers extending from the lower neck to the breast. These feathers are white, edged with black and bright cobalt blue. This species may be readily seen in the nonbreeding season in flocks of up to 30 individuals.
Scientific classification: Guinea fowl belong to the family Phasianidae of the order Galliformes. They are sometimes placed in their own family, Numididae. The species with a bushy tuft of feathers on the crown are classified in the genus *Guttera.* The helmeted guinea fowl is classified as *Numida meleagris,* its West African subspecies as *Numida meleagris galeata,* and the white-breasted guinea fowl as *Agelastes meleagrides.* The black guinea fowl is classified as *Agelastes niger* (sometimes *Phasidus niger*) and the vulturine guinea fowl as *Acryllium vulturinum.*

North America

Guinier, Lani (b. April 19, 1950, New York, N.Y.), African American civil rights lawyer and a leading spokesperson on racial issues; in 1998 she became the first black woman to be appointed to a tenured professorship at Harvard Law School.

In June 1993 civil rights lawyer Lani Guinier became the focus of a heated national debate. President Bill Clinton, who had nominated her to head the United States Justice Department's Civil Rights Division, abruptly withdrew his nomination. He did this after media critics, mostly from the political right, contended that Guinier's legal writings on racial and electoral issues were antidemocratic. She was a "hard-hitting extremist," according to a *New York Post* editorial.

Guinier's writings criticize the single-member, winner-takes-all local electoral system, in which black candidates are seldom elected except in majority black districts. Many voting-rights lawyers have advocated the creation of artificial black-majority districts in order to increase black representation in local government. Guinier, on the other hand, proposes a system she calls "proportionate interest representation," which is similar to the electoral systems of continental Europe and which allows for a more effective representation of diverse political interests.

Following the controversy over her nomination, civil rights leaders argued that the president and the media had misinterpreted her ideas. Indeed, according to an article in the *New Yorker* (June 14, 1993), Guinier's writings "do not show her to be... a proponent of racial polarization, or an opponent of democratic norms. They do show her to be a provocative, interesting thinker, whose speculations could nourish what is a nascent debate [in the United States] about alternative electoral systems." Nonetheless, Guinier was not allowed to defend her writings before the Senate Judiciary Committee. She has since become one of the nation's leading spokepersons on racial and gender issues.

A graduate of Yale Law School, Guinier has had nearly two decades of experience in civil rights, including a key position in the U.S. Justice Department during the Carter administration. In 1996 she helped to found Commonplace, a nonprofit organization devoted to improving public discourse on racial issues. She has also published three books. She released *The Tyranny of the Majority* in 1994 – a discussion of the pros and cons of fixed majority rule. In *Becoming Gentlemen: Women, Law School, and Institutional Change* (1997), she and her coauthors examine the difficulties experienced by women, people of color, and many non-Europeans in American law and graduate schools, and they fault the aggressive Socratic method of teaching that is prevalent in these institutions. *Lift Every Voice: Turning a Civil Rights Setback into a New Vision of Social Justice* (1998) has been described by the *New York Times* as "a detailed if defensive memoir of her nomination fight and its implications."

Roanne Edwards

Africa

Guiziga (also known as the Gisiga and the Guizaga), ethnic group of West Africa.

The Guiziga primarily inhabit northern Cameroon, southwestern Chad, and northeastern Nigeria. They speak an Afro-Asiatic language in the Chadic group. Approximately 100,000 people consider themselves Guiziga.

See Also
Languages, African: An Overview.

North America

Gullah, an African American culture and language strongly influenced by West Africa.

The descendants of slaves (*see* SLAVERY IN THE UNITED STATES and TRANSATLANTIC SLAVE TRADE) who originated in West Africa, Gullah people have occupied the Sea Islands off the South Carolina and Georgia coasts since the late seventeenth century. After the Civil War they remained, the relative isolation provided by the islands preserving their cultural conditions. Although mainstream American culture has encroached on them during modern times, Gullah communities still existed during the late twentieth century (their numbers were estimated at 100,000 in 1979) in small farming and fishing villages, practicing many of the customs of their ancestors.

West African slaves were brought to the Sea Islands because of their knowledge of rice-growing, which greatly influenced rice-growing practices in South Carolina. The harsh conditions of the islands kept white settlement low and, by the late eighteenth century, more than 70 percent of the islands' inhabitants were black. In November 1861 plantation owners on the Sea Islands fled their plantations at the approach of United States Navy ships, effectively freeing the slaves who claimed the abandoned land as their own (*see* PORT ROYAL EXPERIMENT). Although the federal government did not allow them to obtain title for the lands, the period did provide the Gullah with experience in independent subsistence farming. In the years after the Civil War, because of falling cotton prices, more whites abandoned the Sea Islands, leaving the Gullah to inherit this land as well.

Like other African Americans in the South, the Gullah were often denied their civil rights, but their remote location allowed them to maintain their culture, which had its own civil practices. Gullah handcrafts have a distinctive African flavor. Gullah baskets, made from sweetgrass, favor a coiled design unlike European weaves, and experts believe them to be related to baskets made in SENEGAL and THE GAMBIA. The Gullah use palm-leaf brooms, fish with traditional cast nets of their own weaving, and retain a diet that is similar to the fare of their West African counterparts. Houses avoid the row-style layout typical of the United States, favoring instead the method of clustering homes around the main home, which belongs to a matriarch. The dead are buried near their mother, as in some West African societies. Although they are overwhelmingly Christian, the Gullah have incorporated many African cultural traits into their worship. For example, they are responsible for the 200-year preservation of an African funeral song. In 1996 Cynthia Schmidt, an ethnomusicologist, discovered a recording made in 1930 of a Gullah woman singing a folk song. Taking the recording to SIERRA LEONE, Schmidt traveled from village to village until a group of MENDE women recognized it and began to sing along with it. Researchers believe it is the oldest African song still sung by African Americans.

Gullah is the name not only of a people but also of their language (called Geechee in Georgia). A Creole form of English, it is a pidgin that has become the native language for its speakers. Gullah merges elements of several West African languages. Its vocabulary is predominantly English, but the syntax and grammar are more reflective of African languages. West African words that have been added to the English lexicon through Gullah include "goober" ("peanut"), "juke" ("disorderly"), and "hoodoo" ("bad luck" in Hausa). Linguists have linked Gullah most closely to KRIO, a Creole spoken in the African country of Sierra Leone.

The numbers of Gullah remaining on the Sea Islands began to dwindle during the twentieth century. In the 1920s mainland authorities constructed bridges to many of the islands. The economic opportunities associated with the war industries during World War II drew many Gullah away. In addition, in the 1950s and 1960s, developers began to purchase land on the island, developing the properties for tourism. Most vacationers know Hilton Head only as a resort, not as the home to a unique culture.

SEE ALSO
Food in Africa; Hausa Language; World War II and African Americans; Civil War, American; Creoles.

North America

Gumbel, Bryant Charles

(b. September 29, 1948, New Orleans, La.), African American journalist, sportswriter, and TV personality.

A member of the post-World War II baby boom, Bryant Gumbel was reared in Chicago, where his parents, Rhea LeCesne and Richard Dunbar Gumbel, were active in the Democratic Party. Graduating from Bates College in Maine in 1970, Gumbel began his career in 1971, writing freelance articles for *Black Sports* magazine, where he was quickly brought onto the staff. After working as a staff writer for eight months, his journalistic career accelerated and he became editor in chief.

Moving into television broadcasting in 1972, Gumbel appeared as a weekend sportscaster at KNBC-TV in Los Angeles. In 1976 he became the station's sports director, a position he held until 1980. During this time, NBC also utilized his talents as a pregame host for football, baseball, and other sports events. This work was awarded two Emmys, one in 1976, the other in 1978.

In 1981 the *Today* show promoted Gumbel from regular sports contributor to co-anchor with Jane Pauley. With this position, Gumbel achieved nationwide fame as a television personality. Among other projects, he created the teen-oriented magazine show *Mainstreet* in 1986. Gumbel's *Today* show broadcasts from the Soviet Union were honored in 1984 with the Edward R. Murrow Award for Outstanding Foreign Affairs Work. In 1993 he was recognized for his broadcasts from sub-Saharan Africa by TRANSAFRICA, UNICEF, and the NATIONAL ASSOCIATION OF BLACK JOURNALISTS.

Having achieved both fame and professional respect by his forties, Gumbel left NBC for CBS in 1997, where he signed a five-year contract that includes his own primetime news magazine show, several entertainment specials each year, and co-ownership in a production company.

SEE ALSO
World War II and African Americans; Baseball in the United States; Chicago, Illinois; Football, Professional; Television and African Americans.

Africa

Gurage (also known as Gerage and Gerawege), ethnic group of ETHIOPIA.

The Gurage primarily inhabit southwestern Shoa Province, Ethiopia. They speak a Semitic language in the Afro-Asiatic family. Approximately 2.5 million people consider themselves Gurage.

SEE ALSO
Languages, African: An Overview.

Africa

Gurma (also known as Gourmantché), ethnic group of West Africa.

The Gurma primarily inhabit northeastern GHANA, northern TOGO, and southern BURKINA FASO. They speak a Niger-Congo language. More than 1 million people consider themselves Gurma. The name Gurma also refers to a cultural and linguistic group comprising a number of related peoples, including the Basari, the BIMOBA, the KONKOMBA, the Gurma proper, and the Pilapila.

SEE ALSO
Languages, African: An Overview.

Africa

Gusii, an ethnic group of KENYA.

Also called the Kisii or Kosova, the Gusii are a Bantu-speaking people who inhabit the hills between LAKE VICTORIA and TANZANIA in western Kenya (*see* BANTU: DISPERSION AND SETTLEMENT). They are bordered on the west by the Nilotic-speaking LUO people;

on the east and southeast by the KIPSIGI and MAASAI; and on the south by the Tende people. They are closely related to the Bantu-speaking KIKUYU, the LUHYA, MERU, Embu, and KAMBA. The Gusii migrated to the Mount Elgon area from UGANDA and then, about 500 years ago, migrated south to the Kano plains, where they practiced a mix of PASTORALISM and agriculture. The expansion of the Luo peoples, beginning around 400 years ago, drove the Gusii to their present location, where they came to rely more heavily on agriculture. During the nineteenth century they fell victim to slave raids carried out by the neighboring Kipsigi (*see* SLAVERY IN AFRICA).

During their period on the Kano plains, the Gusii lived in individual family units. With their adoption of a settled agricultural lifestyle, however, they began to live in something akin to neighborhoods. Many believe that this clustering led to the establishment of clans. Family heads were still responsible for the day-to-day decisions within the individual family unit. Elders led the clans and resolved disputes, although they did not form a central government. The Gusii remained stateless, and family units enjoyed considerable autonomy.

The Gusii are one of Kenya's most economically diverse and largest ethnic groups, numbering approximately 1 million. Their fertile homeland is one of Kenya's most densely populated regions. Gusii farmers grow the subsistence crops of MILLET, maize, cassava, sorghum, YAMS, peanuts, and bananas. Pyrethrum and tea are grown as cash crops. In addition, many Gusii keep cattle, sheep, goats, chickens, and bees. Gusii crafts are popular, including baskets, pots, and "Kisii stools," whose seats are decorated with beads, designs, and soapstone carvings.

Robert Fay

Gustavus Vassa. Please see EQUIANO, OLAUDAH

Africa

Gutsa, Tapfuma (b. 1956, Salisbury, Rhodesia [now HARARE, ZIMBABWE]), Zimbabwean sculptor.

Tapfuma Gutsa is one of the best-known members of a "second generation" of Zimbabwean stone sculptors. Like members of the "first generation" – sculptors who got their start at the Rhodes National Gallery in the 1960s – Gutsa often draws on themes from SHONA culture. Formally, his pieces reflect more his Western art training and the influences of Picasso, Brancusi, and Matisse.

The son of a construction company owner, Gutsa grew up in the capital of colonial Rhodesia (present-day ZIMBABWE). He attended the Driefonten Mission School in order to study with a noted sculptor there, Cornelius Manguma. After completing school, Gutsa received the British Council's first grant to Zimbabwe. He used the funds to study at the London School of Art (1982-1985), where he received his diploma in sculpture. In Europe, his exposure to Western art traditions pushed him to search for his own style of abstract African art. He freely acknowledges, however, similarities between his works and Western abstract art. "The Western world has long borrowed from Africa," he writes; "I find no problem borrowing from them."

Gutsa's works range in theme from the political (*The Hidden Agenda*, 1991) to the intimate (*Listening to the Baby Kick*, 1989). Unlike the many Zimbabwean sculptors who carve primarily soapstone, he uses an array of materials, including wood, wire, porcupine quills, and egg shells. His sculptures have been shown in two New York exhibitions as well as in the prestigious Venice Biennale. He lives in Zimbabwe and has twice won the award for overall excellence from his country's National Gallery.

Christopher Tiné

SEE ALSO
Art and Architecture, African; Zimbabwe.

North America

Guy, Rosa Cuthbert

(b. September 1, 1925, Trinidad, West Indies), Caribbean American author and cofounder of the Harlem Writers Guild, known especially for her young adult fiction.

Over the last five decades, Rosa Guy has written books for children, teenagers, and adults, but she is best known for her novels for young adult readers. Guy places great importance on the power of communicating to teenagers through literature, and she has said of her books, "If I have proven to be popular with young people, it is because when they have finished one of my books, they not only have a satisfying experience – they have also had an education."

Guy was born in Trinidad but her parents emigrated to the United States when she was two, and she and her sister joined them five years later in Harlem. As a child, Guy found that her West Indian heritage made her an outsider in the African American community at the same time that her black skin made her an outsider in the larger society. After her parents' early deaths, Guy lived in an orphanage, and at age 14 she left school and took a job at a factory. Two years later, in 1941, she married Warner Guy, and the following year gave birth to a son, Warner Jr.

Although busy as a young working wife and mother, Guy began to study writing and drama in her free time. In the early 1940s she became part of the AMERICAN NEGRO THEATRE, a community theater group based in Harlem. A few years later she, John O. Killens, and two other black authors formed the writers' collaborative that became the HARLEM WRITERS GUILD. The guild provided an informal setting for aspiring Harlem writers to critique one another's work, and as its membership grew and its reputation spread, it became the most influential black literary organization of its time.

Guy's marriage ended in 1950, but throughout the next two decades, even as she took a variety of jobs to support herself and her son, she continued to write. Her one-act play *Venetian Blinds* was produced off-Broadway in 1954, and her first novel, *Bird at My Window*, was published in 1966. But Guy was inspired to write for teenagers after the assassinations of MALCOLM X and Martin Luther King Jr., which left her concerned about how the violence and racism in American society affected young people's lives. As a young adult writer, she is especially known for two award-winning trilogies. The first, which was published in the 1970s and begins with *The Friends* (1973), charts the friendship between a Caribbean American and an African American girl as they come of age. The Imamu Jones series, published in the 1980s, follows the title character, an African American teenage male detective.

Guy has also received acclaim for two adult novels, *A Measure of Time* (1983), set in Harlem during the HARLEM RENAISSANCE, and *My Love, My Love; or, the Peasant Girl* (1985), which was made into the 1990 Broadway musical *Once on This Island*. Her other books include several for younger children. Guy's books are popular not only in the United States but also with the large Caribbean population in Great Britain. Her work with the Harlem Writers Guild and her own fiction for adults and children have allowed her to influence several generations of black authors and readers.

Lisa Clayton Robinson

SEE ALSO
Literature, African American; Harlem, New York; Killens, John Oliver; King, Martin Luther, Jr.; Trinidad and Tobago.

Latin America and the Caribbean

Guyana (formerly British Guiana), an English-speaking nation on the northeastern coast of South America, bordered by the Atlantic Ocean, BRAZIL, SURINAME, and VENEZUELA; colonized by both the Dutch and the British.

INTRODUCTION

The Cooperative Republic of Guyana is one of the most diverse nations in South America. Ninety-four percent of Guyana's estimated 864,000 residents are East Indian (Indo-Guyanese), black (Afro-Guyanese), or mulatto (of African and European descent). Guyana is also one of the poorest nations in the Western Hemisphere, and many of its most impoverished citizens are Afro-Guyanese. Less than 40 percent of the country's population lives in urban areas, and those who do are concentrated on a coastal stretch of land that spans just 8 km (5 mi). Guyana has been plagued by political violence fueled by racial conflict. The country's largest racial group, the Indo-Guyanese, compose 51 percent of the national population and are disproportionately represented in the nation's oldest political party, the People's Progressive Party (PPP). Afro-Guyanese compose the second largest group and have traditionally supported the nation's second oldest political party, the People's National Congress (PNC). The PPP and PNC were the two most dominant political parties for the last half of the twentieth century.

Although the Indo-Guyanese represent the largest group in the country, African culture and African traditions predominate in Guyanese society. From the time the first African slaves were sold to Dutch SUGAR planters in 1657 to the period of authoritarian rule by Afro-Guyanese politicians after independence in 1966, blacks have played a major role in the development of modern Guyana. Forbes Burnham, a British-educated Afro-Guyanese, was head of state for 17 years (1968-1985). WALTER RODNEY, an Afro-Guyanese scholar and founder of the Working People's Alliance (WPA), was a popular intellectual before he was assassinated in 1980 as a result of his participation in the Guyanese democratic movement. Other prominent Guyanese include two internationally acclaimed artists, Edward K. Brathwaite, an Afro-Guyanese writer, and Philip Moore, an Afro-Guyanese wood sculptor.

Many of the most prominent Afro-Guyanese have been forced to live abroad because of the country's history of racial conflict and political violence. However, contemporary accounts of Guyanese society and politics often fail to give context to the historical background behind the racial conflict. Guyana's colonial economy – created first by the Dutch and later expanded by the British – was founded on a racially segregated labor force. African slaves worked primarily in bauxite mines, while East Indian indentured servants were employed on SUGAR and rice plantations. Although the colonial economy of the eighteenth and nineteenth centuries produced these racial cleavages, competition for political and economic dominance throughout the late twentieth century exacerbated them.

In spite of historical racial tensions in Guyana, the country has managed to create a rich and vibrant national culture. English is the official language and Christianity is the leading religion. But Guyana is a multicultural, multireligious country. Ninety-eight percent of the Guyanese population is literate. Cricket is the national pastime, but soccer and rugby are also popular activities. In addition to sports, theater is a leading cultural component of Guyanese society. For more than 20 years the Guyana Theater Guild has produced critically acclaimed plays. Obeah, a traditional African religion, is practiced widely in Guyana, and African music and dance are vibrant aspects of Guyanese culture. In contrast, Amerindian culture occupies a limited role in Guyana, maintained in small villages in the interior. Many Amerindians are poor and uneducated and have struggled to keep pace with the rapid changes in Guyanese society.

Amerindian Presence

In spite of their contemporary marginalization, the Amerindian population played an important role in Guyana's early history. Amerindians migrated from what is now Brazil and Venezuela into present-day Guyana around 900 B.C.E. They dispersed into coastal and interior communities, separated by language and geography. Those on the coast – the Arawak, Carib, and Warao – spoke three different languages and competed with one another for land and food. Those in the interior – the Akawaio, Arekuna, Macusi, Patamona, and Waiwai – spoke a Cariban dialect and had little contact with their coastal counterparts. Guiana, which means "land of waters," was initially ignored by European explorers because of the absence of silver and gold along its swampy coastline. On his third voyage to the Americas, in 1498, Christopher Columbus sighted Guiana but chose to sail past the region.

Dutch Colony and Conquest

Throughout the sixteenth century Dutch and Spanish explorers used Guyana as a temporary stopping ground for European vessels heading down the South American coast. In 1616 Holland built Essequibo, a permanent trading post 25 km (15 mi) upstream from the mouth of Guyana's Essequibo River. Subsequently several more Dutch settlements were constructed along the coast, including Berbice (created in 1627). Agricultural production soon became the leading industry in colonial Guyana. In 1623 alone, more than 15,000 kg (33,000 lb) of tobacco were exported from Guyana. Amerindian labor was an essential element in the colony's economic and demographic growth by the mid-seventeenth century. At this time, the Dutch assumed official control of Guyana (then called Guiana) with the Treaty of Munster. Although Amerindians worked on tobacco plantations, the Dutch were careful not to classify them as slaves. Colonial officials took precautions to treat the Amerindian community with considerable care, perhaps in an effort to prevent violent rebellion to colonial control. The relationship between the Dutch and the Amerindians was turbulent at times, but with the arrival of increasing numbers of European settlers, colonial officials were able to win the cooperation of Amerindian leaders. Agricultural production quickly outpaced the supply of labor as Amerindian workers proved unsuitable for the physically demanding work on colonial plantations. By 1657 colonial officials began replacing Amerindian workers with African slaves.

Slavery

Around 1658 Holland seized Portuguese slave ports along the West African coast and began transporting thousands of African slaves to Dutch colonies throughout the Caribbean and Latin America (*see* TRANSATLANTIC SLAVE TRADE). Under the leadership of the DUTCH WEST INDIA COMPANY, the slave population in Guyana grew from 2500 in 1663 to more than 14,000 in 1770. Through disease and violent skirmishes with European settlers, the Amerindian population, by contrast, steadily declined. Slaves became the primary source of labor on sugar and cotton plantations throughout the seventeenth century. Most came from ANGOLA and the REPUBLIC OF THE CONGO, and once in Guyana they worked long hours cutting, grinding, and processing sugar cane. Slave codes regulated all aspects of a slave's life, prohibiting freedom of movement and imposing severe punishments for acts of defiance. Slaves did manage to maintain some aspects of their traditional culture, including the Obeah religion.

As the plantation economy expanded, Dutch officials established a third settlement, Demerara, in 1746. British planters fleeing some of the less profitable islands in the Caribbean quickly outnumbered their Dutch counterparts in Demerara by 1760. Slave labor continued to dominate Guyana's labor force as sugar, rice, tobacco, and cotton exports surged. Although white planters in Guyana enjoyed steady profits from the colonial economy, life for slaves working on plantations rarely improved. Mortality rates were high, and discontent among slaves was a constant fear for Guyana's white minority. Several unsuccessful slave rebellions occurred throughout the eighteenth century, including the BERBICE SLAVE REVOLT in 1763, which involved more than 2500 slaves from two plantations on the Canje River. The insurrection, led by an African slave named Cuffy, who is now a national hero in Guyana, was an organized response to abuse by white plantation owners. The rebellion spread throughout Berbice, forcing nearly half of the settlement's white population to flee the country. Although British and Dutch troops were quickly able to restore order, the Berbice rebellion was a powerful reminder of the potential for mass slave resistance.

Control of Guyana changed hands four times between 1796 and 1814, before it was formally transferred to England at the London Convention of 1814. The three colonies of Essequibo, Berbice and Demerara were joined to create the colony of British Guiana

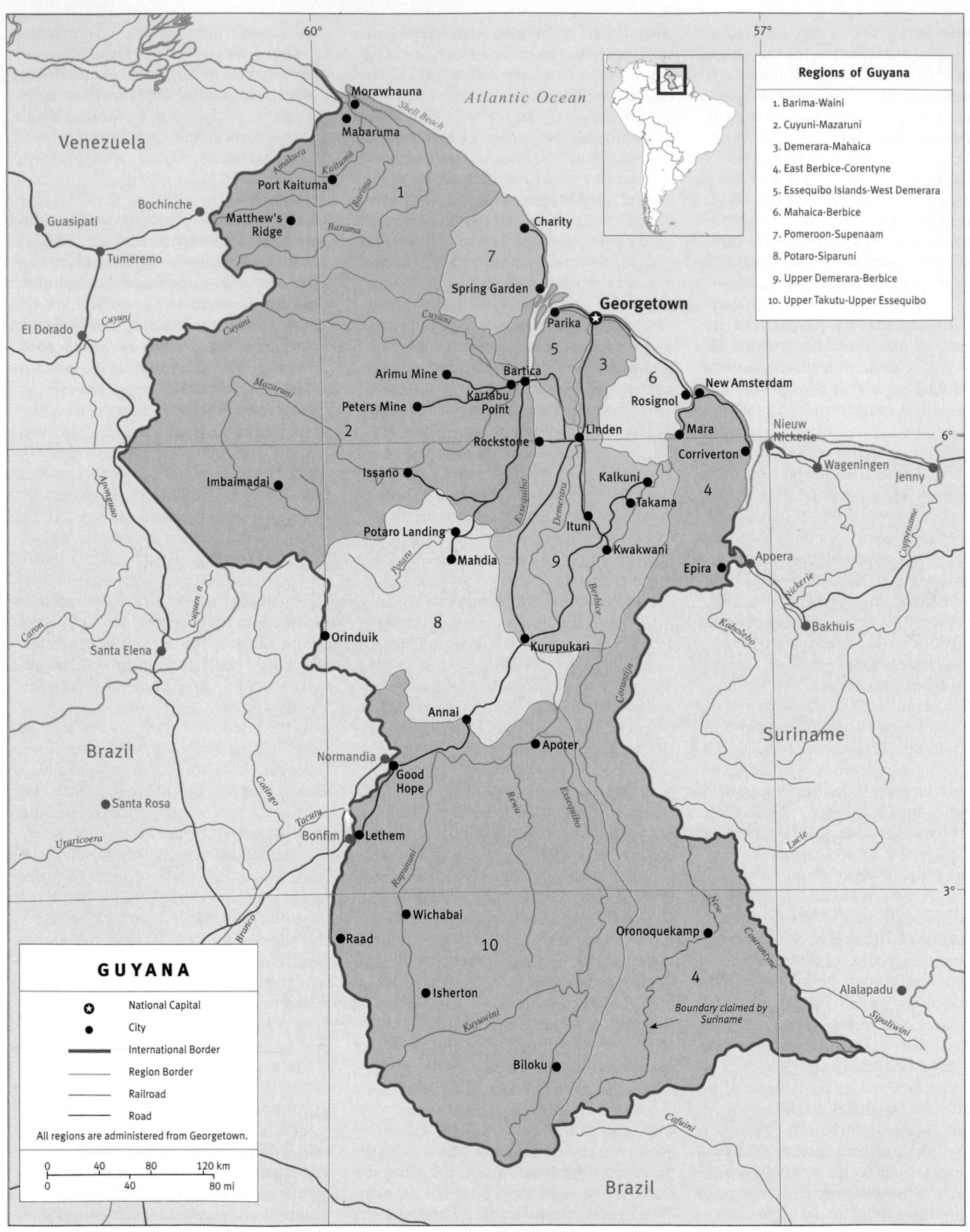

in 1831. By this time there were more than 380 sugar plantations and nearly 100,000 African slaves in the colony. A small mulatto and free black community existed during this period, but its members were treated little better than slaves. Nonwhites were legally excluded from many of the colony's political, economic, and social institutions. White planters dominated colonial society, and beneath them on the social hierarchy were European merchants, then free blacks and mulattos, and finally slaves.

However, white control experienced a series of blows in the 1820s and 1830s when slave rebellions in Demerara (1823) and JAMAICA (1832) revitalized the international antislavery movement. The demands for abolition by British abolitionists, a decline in international sugar prices, and a weakened planter influence in the British Parliament led to the abolition of slavery in 1834. After a four-year apprenticeship period, during which slaves were forced to remain on plantations under a form of indentured servitude, more than 100,000 slaves were freed in what was called British Guiana. As former slaves moved from plantations to free villages – economic cooperatives on abandoned estates – the colony experienced a labor shortage. Sugar and rice plantations were still the leading industries in post-emancipation British Guiana, and the migration of large numbers of Afro-Guyanese to urban areas threatened to destroy the colonial economy.

As white planters worked to replace Afro-Guyanese workers, they welcomed new immigrants from Europe and Asia. The Portuguese were the first to immigrate to British Guiana in the 1880s, but they quickly abandoned the plantations for commercial professions in urban areas. In addition, more than 240,000 East Indian indentured servants immigrated to British Guiana between 1840 and 1917, along with nearly 14,000 Chinese. The duration of most indentured contracts was five or seven years, and more than two-thirds of all East Indian workers chose to remain in British Guiana after their contracts expired. By the end of the nineteenth century, the economic system in British Guiana was segregated completely along racial lines. The Portuguese and Chinese were urban merchants, the Indo-Guyanese worked primarily on sugar and rice plantations, and the Afro-Guyanese working class were employed as bauxite miners.

The complexion of Guyanese society was permanently altered by the more than 300,000 immigrants who had arrived in the colony after 1840. As the immigrant population increased, so too did competition for access to the limited number of opportunities for upward social mobility. In the first decade of the twentieth century, that access was often determined by one's ability to assimilate into British culture. However, acceptance into the dominant culture did not come easily. White planters still controlled the political arena, and they used their monopoly in the legal and economic spheres to prevent nonwhites from gaining a foothold in colonial society. Nonwhites could not vote or hold political office. They were not represented on the colonial high court, and few earned enough money to join the upper strata of colonial society.

Organized Labor

At the beginning of the twentieth century most of the Afro-Guyanese population were working-class bauxite miners. Most were poor and uneducated, and their primary means of opposition was the labor strike. In 1905 stevedores in the capital city of Georgetown went on strike, demanding higher wages. On December 1 of that year (which became known as Black Friday), workers throughout the city joined together in a mass public protest that ended violently when police opened fire on the demonstrators. An ensuing riot engulfed the city and left 7 workers dead and more than 17 injured. The so-called Ruimveldt Riots marked the birth of the organized labor movement in British Guiana. World War I briefly interrupted the labor movement, as thousands of Afro-Guyanese soldiers joined the British in the "war to end all wars." But even though they returned home as heroes, little had changed in British Guiana. Many were forced back into treacherous conditions in the bauxite mines. In 1917 H. N. Critchlow, father of the country's labor movement, founded the British Guiana Labor Union (BGLU). The union, which represented Afro-Guyanese dockworkers, had 13,000 members by 1920.

Throughout the 1920s organized labor emerged as a powerful political force in colonial politics. Labor unrest was particularly pronounced in British Guiana, as Afro- and Indo-Guyanese workers protested the steadfast dominance of white planters with marches, boycotts, and strikes. Throughout the British Caribbean, trade unions became a driving force in the emergence of an anticolonial campaign waged by sugar, rice, and bauxite workers. British officials responded to the growth of organized labor by offering piecemeal changes. Colonial officials granted the BGLU legal standing in 1921, allowing the union to recruit members and collect dues. Seven years later British Guiana became a Crown colony, a designation that removed some power from the hands of local white planters and placed official control in the office of a governor appointed from London.

By the 1930s there was a small but vocal Afro-Guyanese middle class and an even smaller mulatto upper class. Most of them were employed as small-scale independent farmers or urban merchants. Gradual reforms were not enough to satisfy the demands of the new Afro- and Indo-Guyanese elite. They insisted on immediate reforms, and they relied on the strength of organized labor to convey their demands. In 1946 Cheddi Jagan, an Indo-Guyanese activist, and other labor organizers established the Political

Snack shop near the Timemri International Airport outside Georgetown, the capital of Guyana. *Henderson/Hutchison*

Affairs Committee (PAC), the first non-white political organization of its kind. Four years later Jagan and the PAC established the People's Progressive Party (PPP), a political party committed to socialism and independence from the British Crown. The Afro-Guyanese activist Forbes Burnham was the first chairman of the PPP.

Colonial officials responded to the founding of the PPP by granting universal adult suffrage and by establishing local representation at the municipal level. The PPP won 18 of the 24 seats available in the country's first general elections, held on April 27, 1953. In victory, Cheddi Jagan was named leader of the House and minister of agriculture. Five months later the British suspended the constitution, and British troops removed Jagan and the PPP from power on charges that they were planning on transforming Guyana into a communist state. Colonial officials appointed an interim government that governed the country between 1953 and 1957. During this period ideological and personal differences within the PPP led to Burnham's departure and his formation of a rival political party, the People's National Congress (PNC). When general elections were restored in 1957 and again in 1961, Jagan and the PPP emerged victorious in both campaigns.

Independence

In 1963 colonial officials introduced an electoral system based on proportional representation. The new system was intended to reduce the dominance of the PPP, but in another general election held in December 1964, the PPP won 45 percent of the popular vote. However, a coalition government engineered by Burnham and the United Force (TUF), a conservative political party, succeeded in capturing a majority in the electorate. The coalition removed Jagan and the PPP from power and Burnham became prime minister of Guyana. On May 26, 1966, Guyana achieved independence from Britain, and in 1970 Guyana became a Cooperative Republic. Under Burnham's leadership, sugar and bauxite corporations were nationalized and private enterprise was abandoned in favor of economic cooperatives. Burnham and the PNC recruited Afro-Guyanese for coveted civil service jobs. The civil service became an extension of the PNC and was expected to show loyalty to Burnham and the PNC. In this way, the PNC helped unite the Afro-Guyanese community.

During the 1970s and 1980s Burnham solidified his political power and that of the PNC, sometimes through acts of violence and intimidation. Burnham restructured Guyana's economy on principles of socialism and capitalism in an effort to increase the country's role in international commerce. It is widely believed that he was involved in the 1980 assassination of Walter Rodney, the Afro-Guyanese scholar and leader of the Working People's Alliance.

Burnham died in office on August 6, 1985. Vice President Desmond Hoyte succeeded him and gradually removed many of Burnham's more controversial programs. Hoyte pushed Guyana toward a market-oriented economy and encouraged foreign investment. On October 5, 1992, Guyana held its first free and fair elections since 1964. Jagan and the PPP regained control of the government, and Hoyte assumed leadership of the minority party in the newly created National Assembly. Cheddi Jagan died suddenly in March 1997, just months before scheduled elections. Janet Jagan, wife of Cheddi Jagan and one of the founders of the PPP, represented the party in the national elections. International election monitors performed an investigation and declared Janet Jagan winner of the December 1997 elections.

Present-Day Guyana

Jagan and the PPP have a difficult task ahead as they work to assuage racial conflict and ensure a peaceful political transition. Poverty remains a major concern as the country struggles to promote economic development. Guyana also faces long-standing border disputes with Venezuela and Suriname that will demand Jagan's attention. Despite the challenges, Guyanese from all racial backgrounds have begun a national dialogue designed to heal divisions and place the country firmly on a democratic path. The key to success will be the willingness of all parties to work together to secure peace and prosperity. A Guyanese proverb written in the Guyanese Creole language perhaps best illustrates the situation: "Contrary breeze ah mek crow and eagle light on one line." Translated in English, this reads: "When there is trouble, enemies are sometimes forced to get together to solve problems."

Alonford James Robinson, Jr.

See Also

Netherlands, The; Abolitionism in the United States; Brathwaite, Edward Kamau; Apprenticeship in the British Caribbean; Burnham, Linden Forbes Sampson; Free Village System; Religions, African, in Latin America and the Caribbean; Slave Rebellions in Latin America and the Caribbean; Slave Laws in Colonial Spanish America.

North America

Gwynn, Tony

Gwynn, Tony (b. May 6, 1960, Los Angeles, Calif.), African American professional baseball player, one of the best hitters in baseball history who batted better than .350 for three consecutive seasons (1993-1995) and became the first National League (NL) player in almost 60 years to accomplish the feat.

Anthony Keith Gwynn played baseball and BASKETBALL while a student at San Diego State University. He was selected by the San Diego Padres of the NL in the 1981 free-agent draft. After playing in the minor leagues he joined the Padres in 1982. In 1984 Gwynn, a left-handed hitter, led the NL in batting with a .351 average.

In 1987 Gwynn topped the league again with a .370 average, the highest NL mark since Stan Musial hit .376 in 1948. Gwynn then led the league in batting for the next two seasons, with averages of .313 and .336. He did not win the batting title from 1990 to 1993, but he maintained his excellent hitting, registering averages of .309, .317, .317, and .358. In 1994 the major league season ended in August because of a player strike, but Gwynn reclaimed the batting title by hitting .394 in the abbreviated campaign. This was the highest average in the major leagues since Ted Williams hit .406 in 1941. The following year Gwynn batted .368, making him the first NL player to top .350 in three consecutive seasons since Joe Medwick had achieved the feat from 1935 to 1937. Although best known for his hitting, Gwynn also became noted for his fine fielding, winning five Gold Glove Awards as one of the best defensive outfielders in the NL (1986, 1987, 1989-1991).

See Also

Baseball in the United States.

h

Africa

Ha, ethnic group of TANZANIA.

The Ha primarily inhabit northwestern Tanzania. They speak a Bantu language. Approximately 1.5 million people consider themselves Ha.

SEE ALSO
Bantu: Dispersion and Settlement.

Africa

Habyarimana, Juvénal

(b. March 8, 1937?, Gasizi, Gisenyi province, Ruanda-Urundi [present-day Rwanda]; d. April 6, 1994, near Kigali, Rwanda), president of RWANDA (1973-1994).

Juvénal Habyarimana was born in Gisenyi in northern Rwanda, into a prominent family of the Hutu ethnic group. He completed one year at Lovanium University (now the University of Kinshasa) Medical School in former Zaire (now the DEMOCRATIC REPUBLIC OF THE CONGO) before joining the army and enrolling in officers' training school in the Rwandan capital of Kigali. Rising quickly through the ranks, he served in a number of military roles between 1963 and 1973, including national guard chief of staff, commander of the national guard, and minister for the armed forces and police.

Backed by northern military officers, Habyarimana overthrew the civilian government of Grégoire Kayibanda in July 1973 and declared himself president. After creating the National Revolutionary Movement for Development (NRMD) as Rwanda's only legal party in July 1975, he shifted control of many sectors of the government to civilians, while retaining northern Hutu military men in key posts. In single-candidate presidential elections he was returned for five-year terms in 1983 and 1988.

For most of the 1980s Habyarimana's regime was criticized for its austerity measures, corruption, and the instigation of ethnic tensions. He was faced with pressure from international donors, opposition groups, and international human-rights agencies. Responding to the pressure, Habyarimana initiated a transition to multiparty democracy in July 1990. In October 1990 the Rwandan Patriotic Front (RPF), a rebel army consisting of some moderate Hutu and many rival Tutsi refugees living in Uganda, invaded northern Rwanda. The invasion sparked a civil war and resulted in thousands of civilian deaths, many at the hands of government security forces. Habyarimana and RPF leaders signed a peace accord in August 1993 but political and ethnic tension remained high. In April 1994, four months after he was installed for a 22-month term as transitional president, Habyarimana was killed when his plane was shot down over Kigali airport. It remains unknown who was responsible for his assassination, which sparked another, even deadlier, wave of ethnic violence.

SEE ALSO
Hutu and Tutsi; Kigali, Rwanda; Kinshasa, Democratic Republic of the Congo; Ethnicity in Rwanda: An Interpretation.

North America

Hackley, Emma Azalia Smith

(b. June 29, 1867, Murfreesboro, Tenn.; d. December 13, 1922, Detroit, Mich.), African American educator and singer who worked to promote African American musicians and performers.

Azalia Smith, the daughter of Corilla Beard and Henry Smith, was raised in DETROIT, MICHIGAN, after her mother's school was closed due to opposition from the white community and the family moved. She started taking piano lessons at age three, later studying violin and voice, and played professionally after school.

In 1883 Hackley became the first African American to attend Washington Normal School, taking education classes and supporting herself by teaching music lessons. After her graduation, she taught second grade until 1894, when she eloped with journalist Edwin Henry. They moved to Denver, where Hackley organized a branch of the Colored Women's League and earned a music degree from the University of Denver (1900). In 1901 she separated from her husband and left Denver.

Hackley settled in PHILADELPHIA, PENNSYLVANIA, working as a church musical director. She went on to form the all-black People's Chorus in 1904, which broke with convention and performed classical music instead of Negro spirituals. In 1905 Hackley sought additional voice training in Paris, an experience that inspired her to create the Hackley Foreign Scholarship Fund to raise money for black musicians to study abroad.

Hackley gave her farewell performance in 1911 and embarked on a lecture tour of universities. *The Colored Girl Beautiful* (1916), a book of her lectures, was published, complementing her self-published *A Guide in Voice Culture* (1909). In 1915 Hackley founded the Normal Voice Institute, designed to train music teachers. She left soon after to organize Folk Song Festivals across the country. The school failed, but she continued organizing choruses until her death.

Eric Brosch

SEE ALSO
Spirituals, African American.

Africa

Hadendowa (also known as the Hadendiwa and the Hendawa), ethnic group of SUDAN.

The Hadendowa primarily inhabit Sudan and ERITREA between the 'Atbarah River and the Red Sea. They speak an Afro-Asiatic language belonging to the Cushitic group and are one of the BEJA peoples. Approximately 600,000 people consider themselves Hadendowa.

SEE ALSO
Languages, African: An Overview.

Africa

Hadza (also known as the Hadzapi, the Kindiga, and the Tindiga), ethnic group of TANZANIA.

The Hadza primarily inhabit the region around Lake Eyasi. They speak a click language that linguists classify either as Afro-Asiatic or Khoisan. At the turn of the century, the Hadza were among the few groups in Africa to rely primarily on foraging for their food supply. The Hadza number at least 1000 people.

See Also
Languages, African: An Overview.

North America

Hagler, Marvelous Marvin

(b. May 24, 1954, Newark, N.J.), African American boxer, middleweight champion of the world in 1980.

Hagler, the eldest of seven children, was born on May 24, 1954, in Newark, New Jersey. His family moved to Brockton, Massachusetts, when he was 17. He won 57 amateur bouts, including the Amateur Athletic Union middleweight title in 1973. At five feet nine and a half inches tall, Hagler was a powerful 160-pound left-hander. He turned professional in 1973, winning his first 26 fights by knockout, and becoming middleweight champion of the world in 1980 by defeating Alan Minter. Hagler defended his title 12 times until his defeat by Sugar Ray Leonard in 1987. He retired in June 1988.

Alonford James Robinson, Jr.

Africa

Haile Selassie I

(b. July 23, 1892, Ejarsa Goro, Ethiopia; d. August 27, 1975, Addis Ababa, Ethiopia), last emperor of Ethiopia.

Haile Selassie I was born Lij Tafari Makonnen to Ras (Prince) Makonnen – the governor of Harer Province and a cousin, close friend, and advisor to Emperor Menilek II – and Yishimabet Ali. Young Tafari received a traditional religious education from Ethiopian Orthodox priests, who also taught him French.

Tafari proved his ability and responsibility in 1905 at age 13 when his father appointed him governor of one of the regions of Harer Province. Upon his father's death the following year, Tafari was summoned to the court of Emperor Menilek, who appointed him the governor of a small province. Tafari set out to modernize the government by instituting a paid civil service, lowering taxes, and creating a court system that recognized the rights of peasants. Menilek rewarded Tafari's success by giving him a larger province to govern in 1908.

Upon Menilek's death in 1913, his grandson Lij Yasu became emperor. Yasu, however, was considered too sympathetic toward Islam, which offended the dominant Amhara Christians. They began to see Tafari as their champion. In 1916 he and his supporters deposed Yasu and installed Menilek's daughter, Zawditu, reputedly Ethiopia's first empress. Tafari assumed the title of ras and served as her regent and heir apparent.

Tafari brought his modernization plan to the national level. In 1919 he created a centralized bureaucracy; two years later he installed the first courts of law. In 1923 he engineered a foreign affairs coup by securing Ethiopia's entry into the League of Nations. By 1928 his support was so strong that Tafari was able to pressure the empress to name him *negus* (king). Upon Zawditu's death in 1930, Tafari assumed the throne under his baptismal name, Haile Selassie I (Power of the Trinity). The coronation of Tafari, whose Dynasty claimed descent through Lebna Dengel from the biblical King Solomon, inspired Jamaican followers of Marcus Garvey to found a new religion, known as Rastafarianism, that idolized the emperor.

In 1931 Selassie introduced Ethiopia's first constitution, which proclaimed all Ethiopians equal under the law and the emperor, and established a parliament with a popularly elected lower house. The emperor still retained the power to overturn any decision that the parliament made. In 1935, however, Italian forces invaded Ethiopia. Although Selassie attempted to rally his forces, they proved no match for the better-equipped Italians. When defeat appeared certain, Selassie gave an impassioned speech before the League of Nations, pleading for help. None came, and in 1936 Selassie fled to exile in Great Britain.

During World War II Selassie helped the British liberate Ethiopia, and in 1941 a joint force of British soldiers and Ethiopian exiles restored Selassie to the throne. He spent much of the next decade rebuilding the country. He expanded Western education, in part by founding the country's first university, improved health care, and expanded the transportation network. However, Selassie left Ethiopian society – and most notably the feudal agricultural system – intact. This fact encouraged class distinctions and left many Ethiopians in poverty.

In the 1950s Selassie worked to consolidate his power in outlying areas, and the country's coffee exports created an economic boom that enhanced his popularity for a time. In 1952 Selassie's government annexed the province of Eritrea to provide Ethiopia with an outlet to the sea. In 1960 a group seeking democratic reforms led by students and Selassie's imperial guard staged a coup while the leader was in Brazil. Selassie quickly returned and the coup was put down by Loyalist troops.

After the coup attempt, Selassie, who had spent his life attempting to modernize Ethiopia, adopted a more conservative course. In addition he now focused on foreign policy, ignoring the increasing domestic problems that faced Ethiopia. Selassie commanded great respect throughout Africa as an elder statesman, embraced Pan-Africanism, and sought African unity. To that end, he was instrumental in establishing the Organization of African Unity (OAU), which was later headquartered in Addis Ababa.

Troubles at home demanded Selassie's attention, however. In 1962 the province of Eritrea sought independence from Ethiopia and Eritrean rebels took up armed struggle. The educated elite, seeking democratic reforms and jobs, began to demonstrate to demand change. A student protest in 1969 ended when soldiers opened fire, killing 23 and wounding 157. Continuing economic problems, high unemployment, and famine caused by prolonged drought led Ethiopians to demonstrate for higher wages and against the continuing economic woes. A military contingent led by junior officers deposed Selassie on September 12, 1974, after a gradual, bloodless coup. Selassie stepped down and was held under house arrest until his death on August 27, 1975.

Robert Fay

See Also
Addis Ababa, Ethiopia; Ethiopian Orthodox Church; Garvey, Marcus Mosiah; Jamaica; Rastafarians.

North America

Hair and Beauty Culture,

the traditions that have evolved around African American hair and skin care and style.

In his 1942 poem "Harlem Sweeties," Langston Hughes rhapsodizes about the rich variety of black beauty visible on a walk through Harlem's famed Sugar Hill, beauty that ranges from a "honey-gold baby / Sweet enough to eat" to a "cocoa brown, / Pomegranate-lipped / Pride of the town." His list captures the spectrum of colors in which African Americans come – and the diverse of ways in which black is beautiful.

The history of African American hair and beauty culture is rich and complicated, and reflects the complexities of African Americans' connections to both African and American cultures. At times, African American hair and beauty culture has been associated with the larger social trend toward assimilation into American culture, as blacks have adopted hairstyles and beauty techniques that reflect popular European standards of beauty. At many other stages, however, African Americans have used their West African roots and their own artistry to create styles and standards that reflect a uniquely black culture. Hairstyles have come to have cultural significance, and hairdressers serve a special function in the African American community.

The slogan "Black is beautiful" became a catch phrase during the 1960s, and is so common now that it has become almost cliché. But the argument that black is not beautiful – and in fact, that dark skin and stereotypically "black" features represent the exact opposite of beauty – was crucial to constructing the white American myth of racial difference. When African slaves were brought to the Americas, they encountered standards of beauty that privileged fair skin, straight hair, and thin features, in contrast to "African" dark skin, curly hair, and wider noses and mouths. Some slaves became proficient in European beauty care techniques by serving as barbers or beauticians for their owners, and some free blacks in both the North and the South made their living as hairdressers for white customers. For their own beauty and grooming rituals, however, most blacks chose to refer to African traditions, which included braiding hair in traditional African patterns and using berries and herbs for skin-care preparations.

After Emancipation, the demand for professional hair and beauty care within the black community began to grow. Some hairdressers worked out of their own homes, either full-time or in their spare time as a means of earning extra income; kitchen beauticians are one of the most established categories of African American entrepreneurs. But several black women owned their own beauty shops by the 1870s, and by 1885 there were 500 black barbers in Philadelphia alone. As the number of commercial establishments grew, barbershops and beauty parlors became increasingly important in the economic and social structure of black communities.

Not simply a place to get a haircut, barbershops and beauty parlors provided a place for people to gather and talk, sharing political insights, town gossip, and whatever else might be on their minds. Because these shops were often single-sex, they also provided their customers with a rare opportunity for gendered bonding. A first visit to the hairdresser's became a standard coming-of-age ritual, and as black men congregated in their barbershops and black women in their beauty parlors, the opposite sex became a celebrated topic of lively conversation. In these ways, beauty salons and barbershops came to provide a unique social function.

Because their workplaces were gathering points in many black communities, many salon owners and hairdressers became well-known community leaders. For example, RECONSTRUCTION congressmen Robert DeLarge and Joseph Rainey were both former barbers, and insurance company founders John Merrick and Alonzo Herndon had owned barbershops. Many hairdressers became known for the wisdom they dispensed with their services, assuming the role of town griot – knowing everything that was going on, and whose advice was best to follow.

The rise in professional shops coincided with a rise in commercial beauty products and treatments designed specifically for African American hair and skin. Some were welcome innovations, such as the development of chemical depilatories for men's shaving needs, because razor shaves often cause ingrown hairs in black men's curly beards. For much of the late nineteenth and early twentieth centuries, however, many of the new products seemed designed to make African Americans more European in appearance. Hairdresser and entrepreneur Madam C. J. Walker was the first self-made American woman millionaire; her empire included perfumes, toothpaste, soap, powders, and rouge in addition to shampoo, hair dressings, and hair pomades. Much of her fortune, however, was made from the Walker System, a hair-straightening technique that used hot combs to meet her customers' demand for straighter, smoother hair. The turn-of-the-century hair cream No-Kink advertised its purpose as clearly as contemporary products such as Bone Strait and Pretty-N-Silky, and the advent of chemical hair straighteners (or "relaxers") made it even easier for black women and men to approximate more closely European hairstyles.

At the same time that No-Kink conquered naturally curly black hair, Black-No-More, Dr. Fred Palmer's Skin Whitener, Shure White, and Black Skin Remover went after a larger target. The popularity of products claiming to make black hair straighter and black skin whiter – even when those claims proved patently false – pointed to troubling divisions within the black community. On the one hand, blacks were not the only consumers buying these products; many white Americans, both immigrant and native-born, used them to attain similar ideals. But for African Americans, anxieties over skin color were rooted in a national system that had first enslaved them based solely on color and then proved slightly less hostile to those whose appearance was closer to European standards.

Such discrimination began in slavery, when lighter-skinned blacks, often the owners' own children, were given favored jobs as house servants or plantation artisans while darker slaves served as field hands. Lighter-skinned African Americans were also disproportionately represented in the number of free blacks, and continued to be represented disproportionately among the educational, social, and economic elite of African Americans. Many blacks even argued that approximating European standards of beauty and grooming was necessary for African Americans to be accepted by white culture – and especially by potential white employers.

Some Black Nationalist leaders, such as the Universal Negro Improvement Association's Marcus Garvey, denounced this colorism within the black community; Garvey even refused to allow advertisements for hair straighteners and skin bleaches in the UNIA's newspaper, the *Negro World*. But the fact that many of the first black entertainers received "crossover" approval for their looks, such as Harry Belafonte, LENA HORNE, and DOROTHY DANDRIDGE, only reinforced the notion that lighter skin and straighter hair defined black beauty. The loudest protests against the use of European standards for black beauty ideals finally came during the 1960s as a direct result of the Civil Rights and BLACK POWER movements.

As black suddenly became beautiful, African Americans across the country began embracing hairstyles and beauty techniques that emphasized African American characteristics. Most memorable was the Afro, an extremely popular hairstyle for both men and women in the late 1960s and early 1970s that allowed natural, unrelaxed hair to grow in a crown above the head. For the first time, appearing as "black" as possible became a mark of status within the community, especially among younger African Americans. Hairstyles in particular were no longer regarded as personal aesthetic choices, but as political statements about how connected their wearer was to the black community and the black cause, and the size of an Afro became a source of pride.

Although the popularity of Afros eventually declined, the notion of hairstyle as a political litmus test introduced a new tension into African American hair and beauty culture that remains unresolved. Contemporary black women authors ALICE WALKER and BELL HOOKS eloquently discussed the continuing cultural significance of black hairstyles in their essays "Oppressed Hair Puts a Ceiling on the Brain" (Walker, 1988) and "Straightening Our Hair" (hooks, 1992); filmmaker Spike Lee's movie *School Daze* (1988) portrayed contemporary attitudes toward both hair and skin color. But the most important legacy of the "Black is beautiful" movement has been a new appreciation of the range of black beauty – all colors, shapes, textures, and styles.

The 1980s and 1990s saw a broad spectrum of African American hair and beauty styles. This included the resurgence of braids, often in designs that imitated traditional West African styles. Relaxed hair became popular again in a wide range of short and long styles, while the new jheri curl used a different chemical process to create loose, wet curls for both men and women. Women and men chose dreadlocks, twists, corkscrews, fades, and other styles that took advantage of black hair's natural texture. These decades also saw a growth in beauty care products designed for African Americans, especially in the number of mainstream cosmetic companies creating makeup that flattered black skin tone, and fashion magazines and runways finally showcased African American models with dark skin and natural hair.

Through all of the changes in African American hair and beauty culture, barbershops and beauty salons have retained their cultural status in the black community. Despite the economic depression in many black neighborhoods, hair salons remain among the most successful black businesses in most cities, and even African Americans who have moved to predominately white suburbs often return to black urban neighborhoods to get their hair done. Once they are there, the salon provides them with welcome reconnections to the black community.

In short, throughout centuries of changes in hair and skin care and beauty ideals, African American hair and beauty culture has been a vibrant, dynamic representation of the creativity and beauty inherent in African American culture.

Lisa Clayton Robinson

See Also

Slavery in the United States; Belafonte, Harold George (Harry); Women Writers, Black, in the United States; Civil Rights Movement; Free Blacks in the United States, 1619 to 1863; Garvey, Marcus Mosiah; Harlem, New York; Lee, Shelton Jackson ("Spike"); Universal Negro Improvement Association; Walker, Sarah ("Madam C.J."); Philadelphia, Pennsylvania; Film, Blacks in American.

Latin America and the Caribbean

Haiti, independent republic in the Caribbean, occupying the western third of the island of Hispaniola. Haiti is bounded on the north by the Atlantic Ocean, on the east by the Dominican Republic, on the south by the Caribbean Sea, and on the west by the Windward Passage, which separates it from Cuba.

Legend has it that Haitian *hougan* (or priest) Boukman spoke the following words at a Vodou ceremony in August 1791 as he prayed for Haiti's black slaves to rise against their French masters: "Hidden god in a cloud is there, watching us. He sees all the whites do... [and] our god that is so good orders vengeance; he will assist us. Throw away the thoughts of the white god who thirsts for our tears; listen to freedom that speaks from our hearts." One week later, the Haitian Revolution began. By the time it ended 13 years later, in 1804, Haiti had become the first black republic in the world, the second independent country in the Western Hemisphere, and the first country in the Western Hemisphere to abolish slavery and grant full citizenship to nonwhites. Haiti's former slaves became an inspiration for people of African descent across the world, particularly those who remained in slavery.

Early History

The Arawaks, the original inhabitants of the island Haiti shares with the Dominican Republic, called the island Ayti, meaning "land of mountains." When he arrived in 1492 Christopher Columbus named the island La Isla Española (the Spanish Island) in honor of his Spanish sponsors. The name later evolved into the present-day name Hispaniola. After an early settlement near Cap-Haïtien was destroyed by Native Americans, the Spanish settled the eastern half of the island and left the west unsettled.

French pirates operating from the island of Tortue hunted wild boar and other animals in Hispaniola to sell as food to passing ships. During their visits, the French recognized Hispaniola's potential as an agricultural center, and like the Spanish before them, they began importing African slaves to serve as forced labor. By 1697, when Spain formally ceded the western third of Hispaniola – the portion that later became Haiti – to France, the French had established a flourishing slave-plantation system throughout the colony. By the end of the next century Saint-Domingue (the French colonial term for Haiti) was the world's richest colony. By 1791 "the Pearl of the Antilles," as it was called, produced 60 percent of the world's coffee and 40 percent of its sugar.

Saint-Domingue's population at that time consisted of more than 450,000 black slaves, about 30,000 white French planters, and more than 25,000 free biracial people, who formed an important class in Saint-Domingue society. These *gens de couleur*, or mulattos – who were also called *sacatra, griffe, marabou, jaune, quateron*, and other terms, depending on their proportion of black or white ancestry – were descendants of French slaveholders and their black slaves. Many of them were wealthy landowners and slaveholders themselves, and shared more cultural connections with the French than they did with the slaves. But while they were initially accepted by French colonists, their affluence eventually threatened the whites.

By the 1780s new laws had been passed prohibiting free people of color from carrying firearms, excluding them from many political offices and occupations, and placing similar restrictions on their freedom. These laws were met with widespread resentment. Free people of color were caught between their distrust and dislike of whites and their desire to distance themselves from black slaves. As a result, tensions and suspicions among people of all three colors and classes ran very high.

News of the 1789 French Revolution affected all three segments of Saint-Domingue's society. While free people of color hoped France would force the white elite to reinstate their citizenship rights, whites hoped for the freedom to make Saint-Domingue an independent country, firmly under their rule. The first battle between these two groups came in early 1791, when freeman Vincent Ogé led a demonstration against the white government and was captured and executed. But neither the whites nor the freemen were fully aware of how the revolution's calls for freedom had affected the black slave majority. As the two segments of elites struggled for control, it was the slaves who took definitive action.

People shop in the markets of Port-au-Prince, Haiti's capital and chief commercial center. *Hatt/Hutchison*

Haitian Revolution

In late August a slave insurrection broke out in the north of the island. Within weeks, the slaves had destroyed most of the plantations, murdered many white citizens, and forced the surviving whites to flee the island. Several leaders quickly emerged from the rebellion: Jean-Jacques Dessalines, Henri Christophe, Alexandre Sabès Pétion, and above all, François Dominique Toussaint L'Ouverture. Toussaint was an ex-slave and the grandson of an African chief; he became the uprising's chief military strategist. Within the next several years, black, mulatto, French, Spanish, and English troops all found themselves fighting each other at various times for control of the island. The European troops were driven partly by greed over the island's former plantations, but also by their horror at the idea of a black state in the Americas – and their fear of the example it would set for their own slaves. But the black majority's drive for freedom was even

Seven years after helping to win Haiti's independence, in 1811 Henri Christophe (1767-1820) built an empire in the northern section of the country. Despite some progressive social and educational policies, Christophe's rule was brief, ending with his suicide in 1820. *CORBIS/Bettmann*

stronger, and by 1794 forces under Toussaint L'Ouverture (today known as "the Precursor") had freed the colony's slave population and rid it of its European presence.

By 1801 Toussaint ruled the entire island of Hispaniola, and that year a new constitution was created that declared him governor-general of the island for life. One year later, French forces under the leadership of Gen. Charles Leclerc again attacked the island; this time they captured Toussaint L'Ouverture, who was taken to France and died of pneumonia in prison. Leclerc's forces were initially successful, and most of Toussaint's generals were forced to surrender. But when the French forces, already weakened by disease, attempted to disarm the black population, rumors spread that this was a first step to the reimposition of slavery. This ignited the revolution yet again, and by September 1802 the war had again become widespread. A month later Dessalines and Christophe – Toussaint's two most important generals – turned against the French and were joined by the mulatto leader Alexandre Pétion. Leclerc died of malaria and was replaced by the notoriously brutal Gen. Donatien Rochambeau, who conducted large-scale massacres of the black population. Finally outside intervention proved to be crucial to the war, when England went to war against France in 1803. With France's attention thus divided, Dessalines's forces proved victorious: they pushed the French and many of the remaining white planters to Le Cap. After a massive evacuation in November 1803, France's rule over Saint-Domingue had ended. Dessalines, an African-born ex-slave, became the country's new leader, and in 1804 he renamed the island Haiti and declared it the world's first black republic.

After the Revolution

Haiti thus became a model for much of the black world, but the triumph of its fight for independence soon gave way to tremendous instability. As a free black nation that had revolted against its white colonizers, Haiti was regarded as an outcast – and indeed, as a threat – by most of the world, and so the new government received no assistance or support. In the struggle for freedom, most of the country's plantation infrastructure, the source of its former wealth, had been destroyed. In an attempt to bring order back to the country, Dessalines ordered all people who were not soldiers to become laborers on one of the former estates, and his decision to force the entire population to become farmers drastically affected Haiti's future.

His autocratic rule was widely resented, and divisions between the mulatto and black forces remained deep. On October 17, 1806, Dessalines was assassinated. Control was then split between the black general Henri Christophe and Alexandre Pétion, and their rule split the island by color and class, with Christophe ruling the north and Pétion declaring a mulatto-led republic in the south. Haitian blacks and mulattos already spoke different languages and practiced different religions – while most blacks spoke Creole (*see* Languages, Creole, in the Caribbean) and practiced Vodou, most mulattos spoke French and practiced Roman Catholicism (*see* Catholic Church in Latin America and the Caribbean). Now these cultural and racial differences translated to a temporary political split.

Christophe, a black ex-slave, ruled the northern part of Haiti, which was predominantly rural and black; and Pétion, a mulatto, controlled the southern half, which included many free people of color. Both Christophe and Pétion continued to encourage agriculture, giving out land grants from the former estates, and soon the island was dotted with small farms. In this manner, Haiti became one of the first Caribbean countries where most inhabitants owned and worked their own land. But because individual farmers generally practiced only subsistence agriculture, Haiti never again developed the large-scale plantation economy that could have brought much-needed capital to the island; instead, the majority of its population became peasant farmers.

After Christophe's death in 1820, Jean-Pierre Boyer, who had succeeded Pétion two years earlier, consolidated his power throughout the island. But as with Dessalines, his autocratic rule was widely resented, and in 1843 he was overthrown and exiled. In the chaos that followed, the eastern two-thirds of the island, which had been ruled by Spain but conquered by Haiti, declared its independence in 1844 as the Republic of Santo Domingo, now the Dominican Republic. The subsequent history of Haiti was characterized by a series of bitter struggles for political ascendancy between blacks and mulattos.

The palace of Roi Christophe at the Sans Souci Castle was constructed after the birth of the Haitian Republic in the beginning of the nineteenth century. This monument was one of the first edifices built by former slaves who won their freedom after the Haitian Revolution and for that reason has come to be seen as a symbol of liberty. *Hatt/Hutchison*

Beginning in 1844 the predominantly black army installed four black leaders in office, in an attempt to reduce the mulattos' influence in government. In 1849 the fourth of these leaders, Faustin Elie Soulouque, a black Haitian, proclaimed himself Emperor Faustin I. He ruled for ten years in a despotic manner until in early 1859 he was forced out of office by Nicolas Fabre Géffard, the son of a black father and mulatto mother. Géffard restored republican government, but he was in turn exiled in 1867, and so the struggle for control of the government continued. Between 1844 and 1915 Haiti was ruled by 22 dictators, each unable to address the extreme poverty and lack of education that characterized most Haitians' lives.

Early Twentieth Century

By the early twentieth century the political instability in the country began to worry the United States, which was concerned about French and German influences in Haiti and the security of the newly opened Panama Canal (*see* Panama). In 1915, during World War I, the United States invaded Haiti. Many Haitians resented the United States occupation and the insult to Haitian sovereignty, and rebels such as Charlemagne Péralte led armed resistance to U.S. rule. Black Haitians were also unhappy with the U.S. policy of favoring mulatto leaders, and 2000 Haitian citizens were said to have been killed in a 1920 protest.

The U.S. military occupation of Haiti ended on August 15, 1934. Although the country made many strides toward joining the larger international community in the years that followed, political instability continued to mark Haiti's internal affairs. The country's poverty was worsened by the Great Depression, and many Haitians sought work on the Dominican Republic's sugar estates. Haitians were not welcome in that country, however, and in 1937, 10,000 Haitian immigrants living in the Dominican Republic were rounded up and murdered (*see* Dominican-Haitian Relations).

In 1939 President Sténio J. Vincent, first elected in 1930, took steps to remain in office beyond the expiration of his second term and to augment his semidictatorial powers. However, when he was confronted with strong local opposition and U.S. disapproval, Vincent announced that he would not seek re-election. The Haitian legislature then elected Élie Lescot, another mulatto and a former minister to the United States, as president.

Following the Japanese attack on Pearl Harbor in December 1941, President Lescot, with unanimous approval of the legislature, joined the Allied forces in World War II by declaring war on Japan on December 8 and on Germany and Italy on December 12. Early in 1942 Haiti permitted U.S. antisubmarine aircraft to make use of the Port-au-Prince landing field. Haiti signed the charter of the United Nations on June 26, 1945, becoming one of the original members. But growing political disturbances in Haiti from the country's black majority led to the military overthrow of Lescot on January 11, 1946.

Lescot fled to Miami, Florida, and on August 16 the black leader Dumarsais Estimé was elected president. Estimé quickly replaced many mulatto government officials with black citizens. Under his leadership, Haiti signed the Inter-American Treaty of Reciprocal Assistance (also known as the Rio Treaty) in September 1947 and the charter of the Organization of American States (OAS) in April 1948. But in 1949 Haitian revolutionaries, with encouragement from the Dominican government, precipitated a domestic crisis and provoked Estimé to declare a state of siege on November 15. In May 1950, after he attempted to amend the constitution to allow him to succeed himself, Estimé was forced to resign, and a military junta ruled the country until elections were held on October 8. Paul E. Magloire, a soldier and member of the junta, won the presidency by a large majority.

The Magloire government encouraged foreign investment to strengthen the national economy and settled differences with the

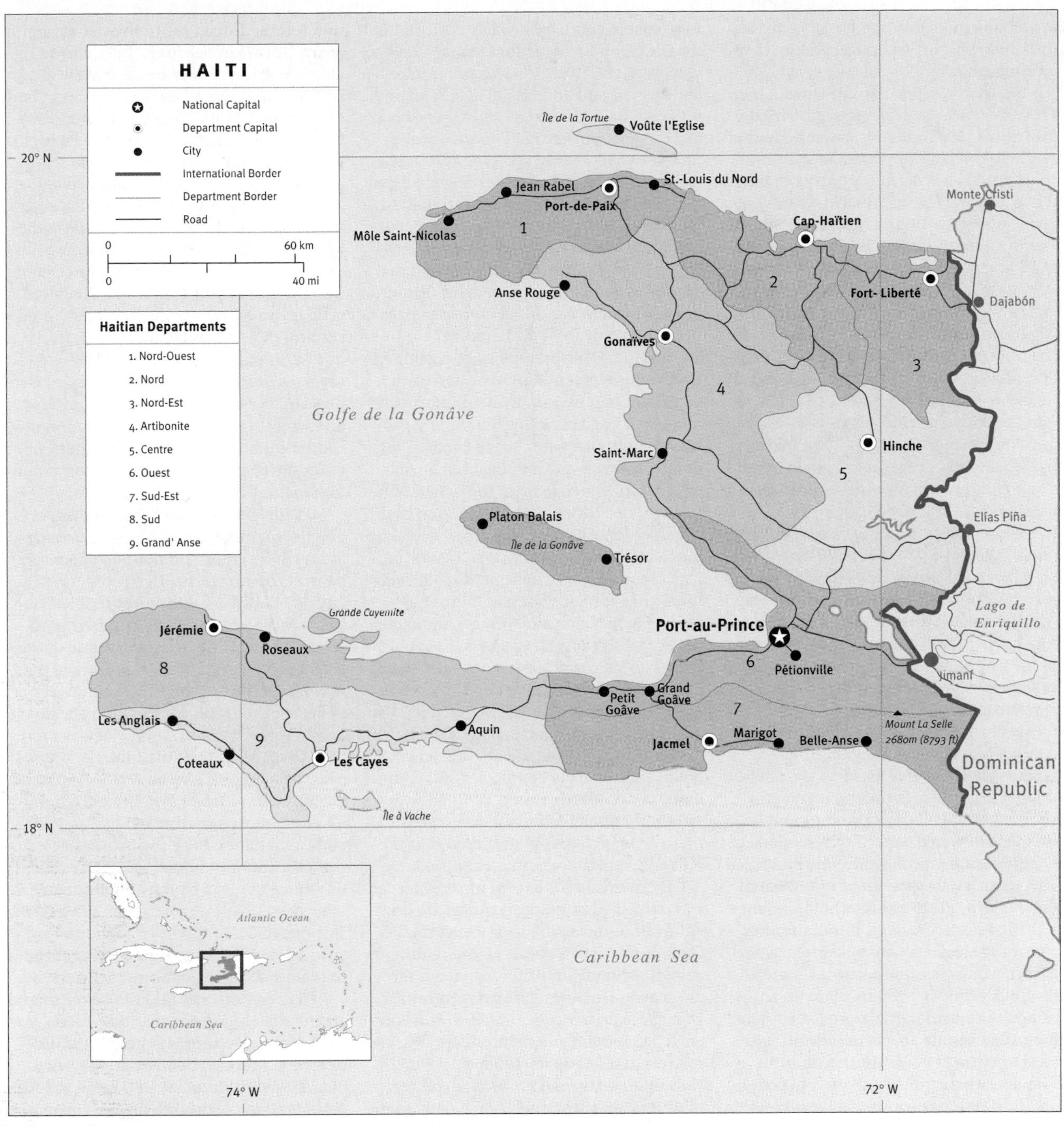

Dominican Republic. In 1956, however, controversy developed over the extent of Magloire's term of office, and in December of that year he relinquished all power. Political uncertainty followed until September 1957, when François Duvalier (known as "Papa Doc"), a former country physician who had been a member of the Estimé government, was elected president.

Second Half of the Twentieth Century Duvalier became the most powerful autocrat in Haitian history. Fear of political rivals led Duvalier to declare several of them outlaws. At his bidding, the legislature imposed a state of siege on May 2, 1958, and on July 31 authorized him to rule by decree. In this period Duvalier organized the Tonton Macoutes, an armed force under his personal control, which became responsible for the widespread harassment and killing of opponents to Duvalier's rule. Duvalier also astutely manipulated Haiti's historical and cultural legacy, declaring himself the protector of Haiti's "authentic" black culture and deliberately taking on the appearance of Baron Samedi, the Vodou master of the cemeteries, by wearing his iconic bowler hat and dark glasses. He dissolved the bicameral legislature on April 8, 1961, to form a new unicameral legislature. All the candidates for the new body elected on April 30 were Duvalier followers. On September 15 the legislature granted him extensive economic powers. U.S. aid was suspended in 1961 to demonstrate disapproval of Duvalier's policies.

On April 19, 1963, a military plot against Duvalier was uncovered and crushed. Haitian police invaded the Dominican embassy to seize government foes but withdrew when Dominican president Juan Bosch threatened to use armed force against them. The refusal of the Haitian government to permit the embassy refugees to leave the country safely led to a buildup of Dominican troops on the Haitian border. The troops withdrew on May 13, but Haitian exiles in the Dominican Republic made several unsuccessful invasions of Haiti in August in the hope of triggering a popular uprising. A severe hurricane on October 4, followed by a landslide on

November 10, caused about 5500 deaths and much property damage, adding to the country's misery.

A life term as president for Duvalier and a new red-and-black flag (to symbolize the link between Haiti and Africa) were authorized by a new constitution proclaimed in 1964. Rebel groups within the country remained active, despite the oppressive tyranny of Duvalier and the Tonton Macoutes. By 1967 the president had executed some 2000 political enemies and driven others into exile. In January 1971 the legislature amended the constitution to permit Duvalier to name his son, JEAN-CLAUDE DUVALIER, as his successor. The 19-year-old Duvalier (nicknamed "Baby Doc") became president after the death of his father on April 21, 1971.

In the early and mid-1970s Jean-Claude Duvalier consolidated his power. Advisors loyal to his father's regime still held important positions, and his mother exercised considerable influence. But an exodus of refugees to the Bahamas and to the United States during the late 1970s and early 1980s, a result of political oppression and deepening poverty, drew international attention to the Duvalier regime. In an attempt to hold on to power, Duvalier had his position reaffirmed for life by a constitutional revision in 1985. But as a result of rising opposition Duvalier fled Haiti in early 1986 and settled temporarily in France; a junta succeeded him.

Leslie Manigat was elected president in January 1988 but was ousted by the military in June. Lieut. Gen. Prosper Avril emerged from a subsequent power struggle as Haiti's president. Renewed political unrest, sparked by deteriorating economic conditions, led Avril to resign the presidency and flee in March 1990. During the interim presidency of Ertha Pascal-Trouillot, internationally supervised elections were held in December. Despite widespread predictions that the elections would be won by Marc Bazin, a former World Bank official close to the United States, they resulted in a landslide presidential victory for JEAN-BERTRAND ARISTIDE, a Roman Catholic priest and an outspoken advocate for the poor. After an unsuccessful coup attempt by Roger Lafontant, a former head of the Tonton Macoutes during the Duvalier regime, Aristide was inaugurated in February 1991. He was ousted by a military coup the following September and went into exile in the United States.

The OAS imposed sanctions on the new military regime, but negotiations for Aristide's return to office moved slowly. Of the thousands of Haitians who attempted to flee to the United States, more than half were sent back to Haiti by the U.S. Coast Guard. The United Nations (UN) imposed sanctions in June 1993, then suspended them in August after the Haitian military and Aristide agreed [illegible] a plan for his reinstatement as head of [illegible]cratic government by October 30. [illegible]tary government, led by Lieut. Gen. Raoul Cédras, refused to step down, and the UN reimposed sanctions in mid-October.

In December 1993 Aristide's prime minister and chief negotiator in Haiti, Robert Malval, resigned. Gasoline and oil shortages caused by UN sanctions left relief organizations unable to deliver food and medical supplies, although fuel was being successfully smuggled into Haiti from the Dominican Republic. In May 1994 the UN imposed broader sanctions, including a ban on international air travel, against Haiti's military rulers. The new sanctions, aimed at forcing them to step down and allow Aristide to return to power, permitted only food and medicine to be shipped into Haiti. In response to economic conditions worsened by sanctions and continued repression by the military, the number of Haitians fleeing the country and seeking political asylum in the United States greatly increased. An additional 20,000 refugees attempted to reach the United States in 1994. The UN passed a resolution that authorized member states to use all necessary means to facilitate the return of Aristide.

On September 16, 1994, the United States dispatched former president Jimmy Carter, Senator Sam Nunn, and former chairman of the Joint Chiefs of Staff Colin Powell to hold talks with Haiti's military leadership. Facing the threat of a U.S. invasion, the Cédras regime agreed to turn over power to President Aristide. Under the agreement General Cédras, Gen. Philippe Biamby, and chief of police Lt. Col. Michel François would retire and their positions would be filled with rightfully appointed individuals. In return the U.S. negotiators guaranteed that the embargo on Haiti would be lifted.

On September 19 a force of 20,000 U.S. troops arrived in Haiti to oversee the transition from dictatorship to democracy. Generals Cédras and Biamby were offered exile in Panama and they departed the country in October; François left for the Dominican Republic. The UN lifted its embargo in late September and President Aristide returned to Haiti on October 15, 1994. In November he named his former commerce minister, Smarck Michel, as the new prime minister. In keeping with Roman Catholic regulations that priests not hold public office, Aristide submitted his request to leave the priesthood that same month.

Aristide's return raised the hopes of many Haitians for peace, reconciliation, and economic revival. Haiti's economy, never very stable, was weakened to the point of collapse by the military takeover and subsequent international embargo. Much of Haiti's infrastructure – including port facilities, bridges, and roadways – had deteriorated. Millions of dollars in international aid were earmarked for the improvement and stabilization of Haiti, including the disbanding of the nation's police and military and the recruiting, training, and deployment of new members. As part of the effort, Aristide ordered the forced retirement of 43 senior army officers in February 1995, including all of the generals and lieutenants who had served under the military government that overthrew Aristide in 1991. In early 1995 U.S. forces left Haiti and a UN peacekeeping contingent took over.

Haiti staged general elections in June 1995, in which more than 10,000 candidates ran for 18 of 27 Senate seats, all 83 seats in the Chamber of Deputies, 134 mayoral posts, and positions in 565 local councils. The elections were an important test for the fledgling civilian government and about half of the country's 3.5 million registered voters cast ballots. International election observers and news outlets reported that the elections were peaceful but marked by chaos, confusion, and widespread violations of election procedures, including unopened ballots, poor ballot distribution, and lack of information for voters.

Makeup elections were held in August for people unable to vote in June, or for those areas where votes had not been counted because of administrative problems. The Lavalas Platform, a three-party coalition endorsed by Aristide, dominated both elections, winning over two-thirds of the legislative races and three-fourths of the mayoral elections. Most other parties refused to accept the results of the June elections and boycotted the makeup elections.

In October 1995 Prime Minister Michel resigned after clashes with Aristide and other government officials over Michel's support for economic reforms backed by the United States, including the privatization of state-owned companies such as electric and telephone utilities, banks, and the country's main port. The next month the United States suspended $4.5 million in economic aid, citing delays by Aristide's government in implementing the economic reforms.

In December 1995 Aristide's close friend and handpicked successor, René Preval, was elected president of Haiti in a landslide victory. Preval had been Aristide's prime minister at the time of the 1991 coup. Although Aristide was constitutionally forbidden to run for a second consecutive presidential term, many Haitians argued that he should have been able to make up for the three years he spent in exile by serving another three years in office.

After a wave of violence and political assassinations, President-elect Preval asked the UN in January 1996 to keep between 1000 and 1500 UN troops in Haiti for an additional six months. The 5800-member UN force had been scheduled to leave at the end of February. Preval was inaugurated as president of Haiti on February 7, 1996. In his last official act as president, Aristide restored Haiti's diplomatic relations with Cuba, which had been broken off in 1961 under diplomatic pressure from the United States. Rosny Smarth, an agronomist and member of the ruling Lavalas Platform, was selected as Haiti's new prime minister on March 6, 1996, becoming the country's third prime minister in less than a year.

The last U.S. combat units left Haiti at the end of April 1996, just as the United States froze about half of its economic aid to the country until the Haitian government was making progress in solving a series of murders of public figures. Haitian officials complained that the United States was asking too much of the country's recently assembled and inexperienced police force, and that U.S. intelligence agencies were not cooperating with the criminal investigations.

In one more blow, Smarth announced his resignation as prime minister in June 1997, after several months of strikes and protests against government austerity measures.

A former priest, Jean-Bertrand Aristide regained the presidency of Haiti in 1994 after having been overthrown three years earlier by a military coup. *Nicolas Jallot*

Smarth had been criticized by Aristide and others for following economic policies that aimed to reduce government spending and privatize state-owned industries. Austerity measures were required by international lending agencies as a condition for Haiti to continue receiving needed foreign aid. Smarth's critics contended that the poverty of Haiti requires government action to relieve the suffering of the poorest members of society, and determining how that segment can be helped remains Haiti's largest challenge for the next century.

Haiti's labor force currently consists of 2.3 million mostly unskilled workers. A few labor unions exist, and although they are legal, poverty and years of dictatorship have prevented labor groups from organizing. Industrial wages of $2 per day are the lowest in the Caribbean. The *petite industrie,* or handicraft industry, is an important source of income for many Haitians. Houses in the shantytowns of Port-au-Prince double as shops where artisans carve wood, weave cloth, or make a variety of other handicrafts to sell to tourists. Further industrialization in Haiti has been obstructed by an uncertain electrical supply, waste disposal problems, limited transportation, a lack of capital and skilled labor, and government policies. The country's poverty is reflected very seriously in its medical facilities, which have only one physician for every 6000 inhabitants; malaria, dengue, intestinal parasites, yaws, acquired immune deficiency syndrome (AIDS), and other infectious diseases are common.

Haiti's most serious social problems also stem from the disproportionate distribution of wealth, and some racial divisions continue between the small mulatto elite and the larger black population. Many mixed-raced Haitians still identify more strongly with the wealthy classes of other countries, especially France, than with poor Haitians. Underdeveloped social, economic, and political institutions – chiefly education – mean that there are still few mechanisms within the country to promote upward social mobility. Another problem preventing social cohesion is the physical isolation of rural communities; about 79 percent of Haitians have little contact with Port-au-Prince or other centers of cultural change.

But Haitians have also begun to find more common ground in celebration of their country's vibrant culture, which bridges races and fuses African, French, and West Indian elements. Haiti's prominent writers include historian Jean-Price Mars, novelists such as JACQUES ROUMAIN and JACQUES STÉPHEN ALEXIS, and poets such as RENÉ DEPESTRE, Ida Faubert, and MARIE CHAUVET. Most Haitian literature has traditionally been written in French, but Creole, which was once considered a social divider, was recognized as an official language in 1987. It is now being used in literature, drama, music, dance, and some schools and governmental functions. New writers in English are also emerging, such as Haitian-American novelist EDWIDGE DANTICAT, who has been called the next TONI MORRISON.

Prominent musicians and musical groups include BOUKMAN EKSPERYANS, Jean-Bapiste Nemours and Wéber Sicot, and MANNO CHARLEMAGNE. They have contributed to developing Haiti's own vital and dynamic culture, as have artists such as HECTOR HYPPOLITE, WILSON BIGAUD, and all those associated with the so-called Haitian primitivist movement (*see* HAITIAN ART). The country has several outstanding libraries and museums. The collection of the Brothers of Saint Louis de Gonzague (1912), the National Archives (1860), and the Bibliothèque Nationale (1940), all located in Port-au-Prince, contain rare works that date from the colonial period, and the National Museum (1983), located in Port-au-Prince, is devoted to Haitian history.

Haiti's rich cultural treasures are an appropriate extension of its history as one of the most influential nations in the world, particularly among people of African descent. Its legacy as the first country in which Africans were able to overthrow the system of race-based slavery remains a source of pride, and Haitians are optimistic about a more prosperous future that will fittingly reflect their remarkable past.

SEE ALSO

Transatlantic Slave Trade; Price-Mars, Jean; Nemours, Jean Baptiste and Sicot, Wéber; Slavery in Latin America and the Caribbean; Powell, Colin Luther; Cap-Haïtien, Haiti; Péralte, Charlemagne Masséna; Pétion, Alexandre; Port-au-Prince, Haiti; Literature, French Language, in Caribbean; Slave Rebellions in Latin America and the Caribbean.

Latin America and the Caribbean

Haitian Art

Many studies of Haitian art suggest that its central theme is national identity. Issues that are related to Haitian national identity – such as colonialism, national sovereignty, and nation building – are all seen as the underlying force behind the production of what has been called *l'Art Haïtien* (*see* HAITI). Thus, a number of artists from the early days of Haiti's independence in 1804 to the present have produced works that attempt to assert and reassess their country's sociocultural tradition.

The 1940s were a defining period in Haitian art history. At this time NÉGRITUDE – the ethnographical and literary movement that sought to affirm peasant culture, or Haiti's African cultural roots – began to spread beyond the limited world of intellectuals. The growing lower and middle classes, many of whom were the product of the long-suffering and oppressed peasant majority, became more aware of the importance of the Négritude writers. The famous Centre D'Art, for example, was founded in 1944 by Dewitt Peters with the support of Haitian artists and intellectuals. And the so-called popular artists, many of whom were affiliated with the center and who dominated Haitian visual culture from 1944 to 1950, were to a considerable degree the expressive voice of the hard-pressed, mostly urban lower classes. Many of these artists were themselves the children of peasants who had migrated to Haiti's cities. Such notable artists as Philomé Obin, WILSON BIGAUD, HECTOR HYPPOLITE, Rigaud Benoit, and Jasmin Joseph, among others, produced first-rate art, well known for its representation of VODOU, Haitian folklore, and history.

From 1804 to the United States Occupation

But the issue of national identity predates the Négritude Movement. Haitian rulers from HENRI CHRISTOPHE (who ruled from 1807 to 1820) to Florvil Hyppolite (from 1889 to 1896) have felt that the safeguarding of Haiti's historical memory (as well as that of their own rule) depended to some degree on the aesthetic contributions of artists. For instance, Christophe, who ruled the northern part of Haiti following independence and declared himself king, had himself heroically represented by the English painter Richard Evans. Subsequently, European-style portraiture, whether of national leaders and heroes or of elite families, became quite popular. And although much of their artistic legacy has either perished or remains undocumented, Haitian artists such as Colbert Lochard, Numa Desroches, Louis Rigaud, Thimoleon Déjoie, Normil Charles, and Edouard Goldman contributed to the development of a sense of national identity.

Some of the official art produced in the nineteenth century, aside from being derived from European neoclassical and romantic models, revealed some concern with blackness or at least, symbolically, with Vodou. Among the religious art created by Haitian artists, a portrait of Christ as a black man drew considerable attention. Moreover, in the Haitian cultural context the numerous ex-votos painted for the Catholic Church represented as much a devotion to Vodou as to Christianity. For instance, a government minister in the mid-1800s, after having recently recovered from a serious illness, had a "great mass" celebrated on the occasion of the "benediction and installation" of a painting of his "patron saint," Saint Jacques. In the Vodou cosmology, Saint Jacques represents Ogou Feray, the *lwa* (or spirit) of war. Interestingly, however, evidence suggests that there had been a long tradition of religious popular art in Haiti. The walls of *ounfo* (Vodou temples) were often covered with images or symbolic representations of various lwa.

If Haitian artists and their patrons officially tended to present an outwardly mainstream display of Catholicism to the public, their representation of national identity was at times more assertive. Leaving behind a promising artistic career in France, the sculptor Normil Charles returned to Haiti in 1912 in order to "contribute to the development of Haitian art." Inspired by a sense of patriotism, Charles created *Dans le rêve*, a sculpture of a "young négresse with a straight nose," symbolizing "Haiti asleep during the American occupation." Edouard Goldman, an actor as well as artist, would "reject all commissions coming from the Americans" in order to represent the "crucifixion" by the U.S. Marines of the resistance leader Charlemagne Péralte.

An Alternative Interpretation of Haitian Art

Thus far it would seem that the thematic content of the art produced by Haitian artists is overwhelmingly determined by cultural, sociopolitical, and historical issues. Yet to appreciate the full meaning of almost 200 years of art production, ranging from the classically oriented to the postmodern, it is necessary to venture beyond the preoccupation with Haiti's sociopolitical and cultural history. If the artists of the 1940s and 1950s in particular exhibit a distinct orientation in their art, other than the concern with national identity, it is the influence of modernism on their art. Even at its most "naive" and "primitive," Haiti's commodified, secular art necessarily reflects modern art's preoccupation with originality and individuality, separate from the influence of politics and society. Hence, sociohistorical issues might have ultimately preconditioned certain internal factors relating to, for instance, the

ABOVE LEFT: Depicting Haiti's ruler and his wife in a romantic, idealized style, *Le Roi Christophe et sa Femme Vont a l'Eglise de Milot* by Saint Louis Blaise reflects the optimism of that period in the country's history. *Christie's Images*

ABOVE: Haiti's folklore and festivals are often sources of artistic inspiration, as evidenced by this 1962 painting by Castera Bazile (1923-1966). *Christie's Images*

OPPOSITE: There has been a proliferation of Vodou-related art in Haiti since the late 1940s, when the religion was legalized. André Pierre, the artist of *Les Trois Esprits des Morts* (The Three Spirits of the Dead), was a Vodou priest before gaining recognition as a painter. *Christie's Images*

spiritual, the psychological, and even the sexual. But such internal factors, by themselves, also contributed to the shaping of Haitian art. It follows then that national identity or the focus on Négritude themes – that is, on Vodou, Haitian folklore and peasant customs, and so on – alone cannot account for the full range of meaning in Haitian art.

The tendency to tether particular Haitian artworks solely to the idea of national identity has often not only delimited arbitrarily their full meaning but also denied the artists their own agency and their art's individual expression. A case in point is Hector Hyppolite's *Maîtresse Erzulie*. The well-known painting depicts the profile of a full-length, voluptuous woman standing as if in the air among tree branches, colorful flowers, and staring birds. Those inclined to connect Haitian art to cultural or ethnographical issues would suggest that the birds are symbolic of protective spirits, and that the figure's pink headband is a definite clue that she represents Erzulie Fréda, the coquettish, luxury-loving lwa of love. Following this ethnographical tack, one might suggest that the flowers and the foliage, aside from being offerings to Erzulie, represent some imagined paradise that ironically offsets the artist's poverty on earth. But to limit one's interpretation solely to such a reading is to restrict the bounds of the painting's meaning and purpose.

Besides perhaps representing a spiritual incarnation, *Maîtresse Erzulie* is also the representation of an earthly icon. She is a marabout, a would-be delectable, swarthy woman popularized by the well-known sexist verses of the Négritude poet Emile Roumer. It is reported that Hyppolite had a certain fascination with the erotic. He enjoyed going to the movies to see what he euphemistically called "love pictures." Yet the figure in the painting seems unreachable. Her eye, shown in profile, does not make contact with the viewer. Her classically regal bearing and her aloofness suggest that she is perhaps upper class and thus symbolically unattainable to Hyppolite. Clearly issues of class, race, sexuality, and psychology – not just of national identity – filter into the meaning of the work.

Some of the so-called primitive artists of the 1940s were aware of the seductiveness of the idea of national identity and managed both to critique it and – for financial reasons – to package it into their art. Wilson Bigaud, an often witty painter who like Hyppolite was from the lower classes, conveys in his 1948 painting *Elite Dinner* that he was quite aware of the forces that contributed to the production of "primitive" art. The painting depicts a well-dressed couple and their daughter sitting at a sumptuously laid table. They seem to be engaged in a lively discussion about a typically "naive" picture, which is hung slightly above their heads next to a shuttered window. The wife, whose back is turned to her stolid, obliging servant, points directly to the picture's simplified depiction of a peasant. That the couple should be so solicitous vis-à-vis a fictitious peasant and, at the same time, oblivious to their servant points not only to Bigaud's biting irony but to his political consciousness. Is Bigaud suggesting that Négritude, as symbolized by the picture-within-his-picture, is merely the ideology of aesthetes who shut themselves in from the realities of the countryside? Whatever the case might be, the couple's impish little girl seems to be completely ignoring their pronouncements. She tosses a morsel of food to a lowly retinue of household animals.

A Critical Interpretation of National Identity

When in 1950 a group of artists broke away from the Centre D'Art to establish the Foyer des Arts Plastiques, they were not rejecting Négritude but simply affirming modernism. Their hope was that such affirmation would breathe new life into Négritude. The Realism of Cruelty style subsequently espoused by Dieudonné Cedor, René Exumé, and Denis Emil was essentially a kind of social realism that highlighted the plight of the downtrodden. It was, in short, Négritude with a political edge. Max Pinchinat, Lucner Lazare, Roland Dorcely, and Davertige all experimented with various styles of modernism, which they used as a kind of tinted lens through which to express Négritude themes. As conscious or unconscious practitioners of a decidedly modern art variant, the Foyer artists, as well as others of the same ilk from the Centre D'Art, faced a daunting obstacle: if modernism is ostensibly an autonomous, self-referential art, then the artists who so consciously aped it were at a disadvantage, as their faithfulness or moralistic duty to the idea of national identity undermined their modernism. Without an extensive supporting group of writers or critics to elaborate a discourse on their art, with the increasingly oppressive political conditions in Haiti, and without the material support of the elite, many of the artists who strove to bring the "light" of modernism to their work simply faded away or had to relinquish their homeland. Max Pinchinat, Lucner Lazare, and Roland Dorcely left Haiti in 1951 and spent most of their lives abroad. Lucien Price never fully recovered from a nervous breakdown in 1952 and died a year later.

Yet the artistic voices of Haiti were not silenced. In the 1970s a new group of popular artists – the Saint Soleil School – created a stir in Haitian art circles with their focus on personalized and Vodou-inspired themes. A number of artists, whether persevering in their own country or living abroad, have continued to express their sense of national identity, but often on very personal terms. Far from being the portraits of national leaders and heroes, Mario Benjamin's psychologically penetrating renditions of black faces, like Patrick Vilaire's oversized sculptural "thrones," are culturally ambiguous and, as such, disquieting. Ronald Bastien, in his mixed-media installation *Can Postmodern Art Breed Action?*, lays his body down on the gallery floor, in the shape of a cross, in a circle of white flour. His own body, thus, functions like a *vèvè* (a ritual diagram) across from a wall on which he has nailed 12 loaves of bread bearing the name of saints and postmodern artists. Hervé Télémaque, who has had perhaps the longest and most successful career among Haitian artists from the diaspora, rejects outright in his work any kind of facile rapprochement with Haitian visual culture. Yet when the sounds and sights of Haiti seem to dovetail with his pop imagery and colorfully illustrated contraptions, he readily filters them into his art.

If certain contemporary artists such as Télémaque, Bastien, and Benjamin gingerly venture into the rich field of Haiti's artistic legacy, others are more forthright in their appropriation. Both Paul Gardère and Edouard Duval-Carrié have critically appropriated some of the visual givens of popular Haitian art in order to recontextualize them, thereby producing often ironic representations of lwa, national heroes, or sentiments. Emmanuel Mérisier, who immigrated to the United States in the mid-1960s, has continued to pursue steadfastly some Négritude themes, but does so in a mastered, creolized expressionism that has eluded some of the Foyer artists' forays into various styles of modernism. Vladimir Cybil, unlike Mérisier, has pursued a different type of continuity. Cybil has created her *Haiti Meets Harlem* "series" as if to acknowledge the ideological support that African Americans have given to Haiti when it was occupied by the U.S. Marines. In this series Haitian historical anecdotes are correlated with, among other visual cues, loosely rendered fire escape motifs from Harlem tenements. Thus, the sense of historical and cultural continuity, which the Négritude writers strove for as they were privileging the African or black roots of Haiti, is also a part of Cybil's artistic agenda.

André Juste

See Also
Péralte, Charlemagne Masséna; Catholic Church in Latin America and the Caribbean.

François Dominique Toussaint L'Ouverture (1743?-1803), leader of the Haitian Revolution, is often depicted by Haitian artists, as in this imaginary portrait painted by Giradin in 1913. *Christie's Images*

Latin America and the Caribbean

Haitian Revolution, uprising in 1791 by black slaves on the Caribbean island of Hispaniola. It began as a rebellion against slavery and French plantation owners, but became a political revolution that lasted for 13 years and resulted in independence from France. By 1804 the revolution had destroyed the dominant white population, the plantation system, and the institution of slavery in the most prosperous colony of the Western Hemisphere. The colony then became the first independent black republic in the world, the Republic of Haiti.

The effects of the Haitian revolt spread far beyond the island. It contributed to the end of French colonial ambitions in the Western Hemisphere, which led France to sell its vast territory in North America to the United States in the Louisiana Purchase in 1803. Refugees from Haiti settled in Louisiana, helping to establish that area's distinct French Creole culture. The uprising also inspired fear of similar revolts in other slave-holding areas of the Caribbean and the United States. Slaveholders in these areas isolated Haiti to keep the idea of emancipation from spreading (*see* Abolition and Emancipation in Latin America and the Caribbean). Haiti's isolation continued for more than 200 years.

The island of Hispaniola in the West Indies was the first land settled by explorer Christopher Columbus, who landed on Hispaniola in 1492. This colony became the center of Spanish activity in the Americas until the Spanish explorer Hernán Cortés conquered Mexico in 1519. After that, Spanish attention turned to the highly developed civilizations of the American mainland, such as the Aztec and Inca empires, where gold and silver were available. Hispaniola was left behind, a sparsely settled Spanish colony where the native people, the Arawak, had died from warfare, forced labor, and the introduction of European diseases such as smallpox.

Within the next 150 years other European countries, notably England and France, settled the less populated Spanish colonies in the Caribbean. The western portion of Hispaniola was settled by French traders called buccaneers and in 1697 became the French colony of Saint-Domingue, which would later become Haiti. The eastern portion of the island remained Spanish and was called Santo Domingo (now the DOMINICAN REPUBLIC).

CAUSES OF THE REVOLT

By the late 1700s the French colony of Saint-Domingue had developed into the richest European colony in the Western Hemisphere. With an extensive system of SUGAR and coffee plantations based on African slave labor, Saint-Domingue exported more wealth than all of the British North American colonies combined. A lively trade developed between North America and Saint-Domingue: New England merchants supplied the island with equipment, food, and horses in exchange for molasses, a byproduct of sugar processing, that was made into highly profitable rum.

By 1789 Saint-Domingue's population consisted of about 450,000 black slaves, 40,000 whites, and 28,000 free blacks and mulattos (of African and European descent). The small white population was divided between an upper class of about 10,000 aristocrats and a middle class of about 30,000 shopkeepers, soldiers, artisans, and others. These two groups had little in common. Allied with the wealthy whites were the mulattos, many of whom were offspring of the white elite and wanted to share in their privileges. Yet the mulattos faced discrimination because of their racial background; in turn, they despised the black slaves, as did the whites.

While the upper-class whites enjoyed a life of indulgence and luxury in Saint-Domingue, the black slaves had a harsh existence. Laboring long hours in the fields of Saint-Domingue's sugar, coffee, and indigo plantations, many died of overwork and inadequate food. The death rate was high: more than 800,000 slaves were imported to the colony in the 1700s, yet in 1789 the population was about 450,000. Although officially protected by law from some abuse, in reality slaves could be tortured, mutilated, or killed by their owners (*see* CODE NOIR). Most of Saint-Domingue's slaves were recent arrivals from Africa, not born into slavery in the colony, so they retained both the memory of freedom and elements of their cultures. The African religion of Vodun or VODOU was widely practiced among the slave population, even though it was outlawed in the colony. Vodou gave the slaves a form of cultural expression and rallying point for protest against their oppressors.

THE REBELLION

The outbreak of the French Revolution in 1789 dramatically changed the wealthy French slave colony. The struggle that split France – between the old order, represented by the nobility and upper classes, and the revolutionary forces of the lower and middle classes – spilled over into the slave-holding colonies of the French West Indies. Saint-Domingue's white population was divided: the elites were loyal to the king, while the middle class supported the revolutionaries, or Jacobins. The mulattos, hoping to improve their lives, espoused the revolutionary ideals of liberty and equality for themselves, but not for the slaves. With the colony's rulers weakened by internal conflicts after a legendary Vodou ceremony in 1791 under the leadership of BOUKMAN, the black slaves rebelled against their owners, killing whites and destroying plantations and crops.

By 1793 the slave uprising had become a full-scale civil war. Seeking support to defeat the white elite, French revolutionary officials abolished slavery in the colony. Fierce fighting between the various groups continued, while Great Britain and Spain both sent invasion forces, hoping to take over the French colony.

In the midst of this confusion, a remarkable leader emerged in the colony. FRANÇOIS DOMINIQUE TOUSSAINT L'OUVERTURE, a former slave, took part in the slave revolt and, with other black rebel leaders, joined forces with the Spanish army against the French. Highly skilled in military tactics and politics, he rose to high rank within the Spanish army, but when France abolished slavery, he switched sides. Promoted to general in 1795 by French colonial officials, he helped drive out the Spanish.

By 1796 Toussaint ruled the colony as the French governor-general. Over the next four years, he forced the British troops to withdraw and defeated his internal rivals, especially a mulatto group in the south that was destroyed in a bloody race war. By 1801 he conquered Santo Domingo, the Spanish portion of the island, abolished slavery there, and proclaimed himself governor-general of the island for life. However, he did not declare independence but remained officially loyal to France. To rebuild the colony's economy, Toussaint demanded that both whites and blacks continue to produce their crops without slavery.

HAITIAN INDEPENDENCE

As Toussaint L'Ouverture took charge in Saint-Domingue, Napoleon Bonaparte became the leader of France. Napoleon sought to return Saint-Domingue to French control and reinstate slavery as a means of bringing the colony back to its former prosperity. Napoleon sent a large army to Saint-Domingue to replace Toussaint with a trusted white general. Toussaint was tricked onto a ship and taken to France, where he died in prison. However, the army that he had trained declared war on the French, led by two of Toussaint's subordinates, JEAN-JACQUES DESSALINES and HENRI CHRISTOPHE. After a bitter struggle, the former slaves defeated Napoleon's forces, massacred or drove all whites off the island, and changed the name of the colony to the aboriginal name "Haiti," which means "land of mountains." The Republic of Haiti, created by former slaves, declared its independence on January 1, 1804.

The new nation, however, faced continued division and economic hardship. Most of the plantation economy had been destroyed, and as much as half the population had fled or been killed. Dessalines declared himself leader for life, setting a precedent for many later Haitian rulers, but was assassinated in 1806. The following years in Haiti's history were marked by many years of violent struggles among different factions.

EXTERNAL EFFECTS

The Haitian revolt and independence had far-reaching effects on the United States, as well as other nearby countries and colonies. During the turmoil many refugees fled the island, pouring into seaports in the United States and the colony of Louisiana. These refugees from Saint-Domingue – white planters, mulatto artisans, and some African slaves – brought with them their language, religion, laws, newspapers, education, art, and their skills at growing sugar, all of which strongly influenced the culture of the Lower South.

The French failure to regain control over Saint-Domingue also influenced Napoleon to abandon efforts to build an empire in the Western Hemisphere. In 1803 France sold its North American province of Louisiana, a region of 2,100,000 sq km (more than 800,000 sq mi) west of the Mississippi River, to the United States.

The success of Toussaint L'Ouverture and the Haitians was a source of pride to many blacks in the United States and served as an example to some slaves who attempted unsuccessful uprisings in Virginia and South Carolina (*see* DENMARK VESEY CONSPIRACY). Southern slave owners, hearing of the massacres that preceded Haitian independence, were convinced that freeing slaves would result in a race war and became even less willing to end slavery peacefully. As the second independent nation in the Western Hemisphere (after the United States), Haiti gave support to Simón Bolívar, leader of the movement for South American independence from Spain in the early 1800s. In return, Bolívar made abolition of slavery one of the goals of his movement.

SEE ALSO

Slavery in Latin America and the Caribbean; Creoles; Religions, African, in Latin America and the Caribbean; Racial Question during Struggles of Independence in Latin America.

North America

Haley, Alexander Palmer (Alex)

(b. August 11, 1921, Ithaca, N.Y.; d. February 10, 1992, Seattle, Wash.), African American writer and journalist who authored two of the most influential books in the history of African American scholarship.

Alex Haley grew up in Henning, Tennessee, with maternal relatives who spent many hours telling family stories, some of which extended back to Africa. This exposure directed the course of much of Haley's work as an adult. Haley completed high school at age 15 and attended two years of college, but was uninspired by his studies and left school to join the United States Coast Guard, where he began writing to counteract the tedium of life at sea. When Haley retired from the service in 1959, he disembarked a mature, self-taught writer.

Haley settled in Greenwich Village, New York, determined to make his name as a journalist. After a period of hard work and obscurity, he broke into mainstream publications such as *Readers' Digest*, *Harper's*, and the *New York Times Magazine*. In 1962 he sold a Miles Davis interview to *Playboy* that began the magazine's famous interview series. Later that year *Playboy* commissioned Haley to interview MALCOLM X, an assignment that led to Haley's first book, his ghost-written *Autobiography of Malcolm X*.

The Autobiography of Malcolm X (1965) sold more than 5 million copies and changed the nation's opinion of the black nationalist leader. The book, which concludes with Malcolm X's reevaluation of the NATION OF ISLAM, highlights the complexity, compassion, and humanity of a figure whose public image might otherwise have remained monolithic and negative. The assassination of Malcolm X in 1965 increased public interest, and Haley's book became required reading in many college courses.

Soon after the publication of *The Autobiography of Malcolm X*, Haley began research for a second contribution to AFRICAN AMERICAN LITERATURE. The half-fictive, half-factual epic *Roots* (1977), which traces Haley's own maternal lineage back to an enslaved West African named Kunta Kinte, captured the attention of the nation. Haley took 12 years to write and research *Roots*, consulting relatives, archives, and libraries as well as a tribal historian from Kunta Kinte's village. At one point Haley even attempted to relive the Middle Passage experience of enslaved Africans by sleeping in the hold of a transatlantic ship.

Roots sold more than 8.5 million copies, was translated into 26 languages, and won 271 different awards. The Pulitzer Prize and National Book Award committees honored its contribution to American history, and ABC turned it into an eight-part television series, of which 130 million Americans watched at least one episode. *Roots* not only touched blacks whose histories resembled Haley's but also whites who were confronted by America's tragic past.

In the wake of the *Roots* phenomenon, two different plaintiffs accused Haley of plagiarism. Haley disproved one of the claims but settled the other out of court, conceding that, given his extensive and often unannotated notetaking, he had accidentally used material from Harold Courlander's book *The African* (1968). Critics also questioned Haley's method of presenting fiction as fact. Haley, however, repeatedly defended his methods as a necessary way of tapping the emotional poignancy of his subject.

Haley's career peaked with *Roots* – despite a television sequel *(Roots: The Next Generation*, 1979), a second, similar book-and-television project *(Queen: The Story of an American Family*, 1992), and a television drama about race and childhood in the American South (*Palmerstown U.S.A.*, 1980). These projects, along with a record called *Alex Haley Speaks*, which gave tips on constructing family genealogies, never achieved the success of Haley's second book. Haley worked on a long-delayed biography of Madam C. J. Walker that remained unfinished when he died from a heart attack in 1992.

Eric Bennett

SEE ALSO
Middle Passage, The; Davis, Miles Dewey, III; Television and African Americans; Walker, Sarah ("Madam C.J.").

North America

Hall, Arsenio (b. February 12, 1955, Cleveland, Ohio), African American comedian, producer, and star of the first successful African American late-night television talk show.

Arsenio Hall is a member of the influential Black Pack, a group of highly successful African Americans in the entertainment industry whose other members include EDDIE MURPHY, Robert Townsend, Damon and Keenan Ivory Wayans, and Paul Mooney. In the mid- to late 1980s, Hall and his syndicated television program revitalized late-night talk shows (*see* TELEVISION AND AFRICAN AMERICANS).

Arsenio Hall was born in the projects of Cleveland, Ohio, to Annie and Fred Hall. His father, a strict disciplinarian, was minister of Elizabeth Baptist Church. His parents divorced when Hall was five years old, and he cites their acrimonious relationship as the catalyst for his early attempts at entertainment. In the fall of 1973 he entered Ohio University in Athens, but soon transferred to Kent State University, where he subsequently received an undergraduate degree.

After garnering moderate success on the stand-up comedian circuit in Chicago, Hall moved to Los Angeles in early 1980. His break arrived in 1987 with his appearance on the *Tonight Show*, hosted by Joan Rivers. In late 1987 he was named host of the *Late Show*. After the cancellation of that show in 1989, Hall went on to star opposite EDDIE MURPHY in the film *Coming to America*. In January of that same year he began hosting the *Arsenio Hall Show*. The show popularized the barking chant ("woof, woof") in substitution for applause, and ushered in the casual, hip, urban talk show.

SEE ALSO
Chicago, Illinois; Los Angeles, California.

Europe

Hall, Stuart (b. February 3, 1932, Kingston, Jamaica), intellectual working in GREAT BRITAIN who helped found the New Left by prioritizing culture, race, and identity.

Stuart Hall, a founder of the New Left and the interdisciplinary field known as "cultural studies," has devoted his career to developing a framework for understanding issues of race, ethnicity, and cultural practice and their practical relationship to contemporary British politics.

Hall was born in 1932 to upwardly mobile, middle-class parents in JAMAICA. In 1951 he won a Rhodes scholarship to Merton College at Oxford University, which he has called "the hub, the motor, that creates Englishness." He earned a doctorate in American literature.

During the 1950s Hall became involved in West Indian and socialist politics. He was a founding member of the New Left Club and its publication *Universities and Left Review*. This journal merged with social historian E. P. Thompson's the *New Reasoner* in 1959 and became the *New Left Review;* Hall was its first editor. In this journal, Hall challenged the failure of the established Left to deal effectively with racism, imperialism, culture, and literature.

In 1964 Hall became assistant director of the Centre for Contemporary Cultural Studies at the University of Birmingham; in 1974, he became director. This position allowed him to help shape the new scholarly field of cultural studies, exploring connections among race, class, power, identity, and cultural practice in everyday life. He became a professor at the Open University in 1979.

In the 1980s Hall spoke out against "Thatcherism" – a term he coined to describe a New Right that, in his view, presented threats beyond those of traditional conservatism. He also was active in the Campaign for Nuclear Disarmament. In the 1990s he criticized Prime Minister Tony Blair's New Labour platform for its lack of principle and its deference to the New Right.

No mere critic, Hall is an active participant in contemporary British cultural politics. He insists that British identity is hybrid and can encompass the wide range of peoples who live in Great Britain. In a book dedicated to his work titled *Stuart Hall: Critical Dialogues*, the editors praised Hall for his ability to take on new issues.

Leyla Keough

North America

Hamer, Fannie Lou

(b. October 6, 1917, Montgomery County, Miss.; d. March 14, 1977, Ruleville, Miss.), African American civil rights activist who worked with the STUDENT NONVIOLENT COORDINATING COMMITTEE (SNCC) to secure voting rights for blacks and helped form the Mississippi Freedom Democratic Party.

The youngest of 20 children born to sharecroppers Ella and Jim Townsend, Fannie Lou Hamer began helping her family pick cotton at age six, and left school to work full-time in the fields only six years later. Despite her relative lack of education, Hamer spoke often of her love of reading. Her childhood was spent in poverty; her family lived without heat or plumbing and often lacked nutritious food. Hamer suffered a lifelong limp because one of her legs was broken in infancy and never treated. In 1944, after many of her siblings had moved North, she married local farmhand Percy Hamer. The two moved to a small house on a cotton plantation near Ruleville, Mississippi.

In the summer of 1962 Hamer went to a mass meeting organized by the Student Nonviolent Coordinating Committee, which had recently begun organizing in the Mississippi Delta, where poor blacks lived in some of the worst conditions anywhere in the United States. SNCC and other civil rights groups hoped to register and educate many of the more than 400,000 African Americans in Mississippi who were being denied their constitutional right to vote by a variety of means, including voter registration tests, poll taxes, and violent reprisals for political activity. Following the meeting, Hamer went along with 17 others to attempt to register to vote in Indianola, the county seat. Facing the registration test, which was administered in such a way as to ensure that black people never passed, Hamer and the others failed.

Returning home, Hamer refused to promise her white boss that she would stop trying to vote; he fired her and threw her off the plantation where she had lived and worked for 18 years. "They kicked me off the plantation," she later told friends, "they set me free. It's the best thing that could happen. Now I can work for my people." Hamer joined SNCC as a fieldworker, where she was soon seen by SNCC leader Robert Moses as a valuable asset because of her brilliant oratory and powerful singing. Hamer also became a living symbol of the dangers faced by civil rights workers after she was unfairly jailed and severely beaten in Winona, Mississippi (June 1963), while returning from citizenship classes. Eventually, due to the intervention of the FBI and the Justice Department, the jailers were tried for assaulting Hamer, but an all-white local jury later found the jailers not guilty.

In 1963 Hamer began working with the Council of Federated Organizations – a coalition of SNCC, the CONGRESS OF RACIAL EQUALITY (CORE), and the NATIONAL ASSOCIATION FOR THE ADVANCEMENT OF COLORED PEOPLE (NAACP) – on what was called the Freedom Vote. The first statewide voting rights effort, Freedom Vote provided Mississippi's unregistered black citizens with "freedom ballots," with which 80,000 of the citizens cast votes. During the next year, in addition to her SNCC work during FREEDOM SUMMER (when thousands of college students came South to assist in voter education and registration), Hamer and others founded the Mississippi Freedom Democratic Party (MFDP) in an attempt to force the state's traditionally all-white, racist Democratic party to integrate. At the same time, Hamer launched her own run for Congress as the MFDP candidate. Although she did not win the primary (and probably did not expect to), her candidacy and work with the MFDP brought her to national attention. When the MFDP was rebuffed in its attempt to seat delegates at the 1964 Democratic National Convention, Hamer appeared on television to "question America" about its failure to provide equal justice for all.

Over the next several years Hamer began to see results from her efforts. In 1965 Congress passed the Voting Rights Act, which theoretically ensured the rights of African Americans to register and vote. By 1968 Mississippi's convention delegation was no longer all-white. And in 1968 a black man, Robert Clark, was elected to the state legislature: the first black state congressman since RECONSTRUCTION. Hamer continued her involvement in civil rights work, branching out to issues of poverty and economic justice. From 1969 to 1974 she ran the Freedom Farm, a cooperatively owned and operated farm that provided poor blacks with both food and jobs.

Both HOWARD UNIVERSITY and MOREHOUSE COLLEGE awarded Hamer honorary degrees; her work was also recognized by the CONGRESSIONAL BLACK CAUCUS in 1976, and by her own hometown, Ruleville, shortly before her death. At Hamer's funeral, ANDREW YOUNG proclaimed that "[There is] no one in America [who] has not been influenced or inspired by Mrs. Hamer," and then he led the mourners in singing one of her trademark songs, "This little light of mine, / I'm gonna let it shine."

Kate Tuttle

SEE ALSO

Civil Rights Movement; Moses, Robert Parris; Voting Rights Act of 1965.

Hamid ibn Muhammad. Please see TIPPU TIP

Latin America and the Caribbean

Hamilton, Bermuda, a city in central BERMUDA, the capital of the British dependency, on Bermuda Island.

Hamilton is the chief port of Bermuda, on Hamilton Harbour at the eastern end of the Great Sound (an arm of the Atlantic Ocean). Tourism is the chief industry. Points of interest include the harbor, made a free port in 1956; Sessions House, containing government offices; and the fortification of old Fort Hamilton. The community was founded in 1790 and replaced Saint George as the colonial capital in 1815. Population (1990 estimate): 6000.

North America

Hammer, MC

(Stanley Kirk Burrell b. 1962, Oakland, Calif.), African American RAP artist whose flashy dance moves catapulted him to fame in the early 1990s.

MC Hammer debuted in 1988 with the self-produced *Let's Get It Started*. His style – frenetic beats and chanted lyrics – did not impress the hip hop cognoscenti, but the album sold more than a million copies and the stage was set for one of hip hop's biggest surprises. Buoyed by the genial dance floor anthem "U Can't Touch This" (based on Rick James's 1981 classic, "Superfreak"), *Please Hammer Don't Hurt 'Em* held the top spot on the charts for 21 weeks, becoming the biggest-selling rap album in history.

Hammer was a better entertainer than a rapper: his live shows were energetic spectacles, intricately choreographed events that highlighted the hugely popular dance routines of Hammer and his massive entourage. The artist's videos distilled the live experience into simple but effective blasts that found heavy rotation on MTV.

Hammer's good-natured dance music earned him continued – if diminished – success with *Too Legit to Quit* (1991). But *The Funky Headhunter* (1994) was an unexpected commercial failure: reacting to the current popularity of gangsta rap, Hammer abandoned his cheerful, energetic music and persona in a wholly unsuccessful effort to secure street credibility.

With his professional and financial life in disarray, the rapper filed for bankruptcy in 1996, claiming almost $14 million in debt. Although his career ended abruptly, Hammer's success paved the way for hip hop entertainment moguls like Bad Boy's Sean "Puffy" Combs.

Andrew Du Bois

SEE ALSO

Hip Hop in the United States; Combs, Sean ("Puffy").

North America

Hammon, Jupiter

(b. October 17, 1711, Oyster Bay, N.Y.; d. 1806?, Oyster Bay, N.Y.?), African American poet and the first published African American writer.

The following stanza is from Jupiter Hammon's poem "A Dialogue Entitled the Kind Master and the Dutiful Servant," published in 1786, when Hammon was in his seventies.

Dear Master, I will follow thee,
According to thy word,
And pray that God may be with me,
And save thee in the Lord.

Hammon had been a slave his entire life, and had served several generations of the Lloyd family on Long Island, New York. Many of his writings neither condemn nor even mention slavery; instead, they praise Christianity in the same manner as the evangelical hymns that were his models. But even when his words were not deliberately radical, they represented a radical act – Hammon became the first known African American to publish a piece of literature.

Hammon's owners were wealthy, and the few records of his life with them indicate that he was a favorite servant who worked as a clerk in their family business and was trained both as a farmhand and as an artisan. He was also allowed to attend school, and his formal education influenced his development as a poet. Like his masters, Hammon was a devout Christian, and was influenced by the religious revivals taking place in eighteenth-century New England. His extant writing reflects his deep spirituality, and his first published poem was written on Christmas Day, 1760.

"An Evening Thought. Salvation by Christ with Penitential Cries: Composed by Jupiter Hammon, a Negro belonging to Mr. Lloyd of Queen's Village, on Long Island, the 25th of December, 1760" was published as a broadside in early 1761, making it the first piece of literature published in the United States by a person of African descent. His second extant piece of poetry, published 17 years after the first, honors Phillis Wheatley, his contemporary and another African American slave poet. This poem, "An Address to Miss Phillis Wheatly [*sic*], Ethiopian Poetess, in Boston, who came from Africa at eight years of age, and soon became acquainted with the gospel of Jesus Christ" (1778), praises and encourages the younger poet. Hammon never mentions himself in the poem, but it appears that in choosing Wheatley as a subject, he was acknowledging their common and unlikely bond.

His other known writings include two more poems, three sermon essays, and a speech, *An Address to the Negroes of the State of New York,* which he gave before the African Society in New York on September 24, 1786. In this speech Hammon expressed his opinions on slavery most clearly. As an individual, he claimed he did "not wish to be free" – as one critic has observed, he felt "it was his personal duty to bear slavery with patience." But Hammon did add that he believed slavery was unjust, and would be "glad if others, especially the young negroes, were free." The speech was reprinted twice for a Pennsylvania Abolitionist society.

Hammon apparently remained a slave until his death. During the Revolutionary War he lived with his owners in Hartford, Connecticut; the family later returned to Oyster Bay, which is probably where Hammon died. His poetry is still often anthologized, in recognition of his role as a founder of the African American literary tradition.

Lisa Clayton Robinson

See Also
Slavery in the United States; Abolitionism in the United States; Literature, African American; American Revolution.

North America

Hammons, David

(b. 1943, Springfield, Ill.), African American artist known for towering basketball sculptures.

After growing up in the Midwest, David Hammons moved to Los Angeles in 1964 to study art. In the 1960s the progress of the Civil Rights Movement and the inception of the Black Power Movement encouraged artists of African descent both to produce a more racially conscious art and to challenge stereotypes of African Americans. After completing his studies in 1972, Hammons began to create prints of his body using margarine or grease. In 1975 he made Harlem his home and started forging sculptures from materials he collected on the street. He executed these assemblages in public spaces using such found objects as spades, chains, bottle caps, deflated inner tubes, barbecue bones, and African American hair in an effort to explore African American identity.

The spade is a recurring motif in Hammons's body prints and sculptures. He said, "I remember being called a spade once, and I didn't know what it meant; nigger I knew but spade I still don't. So I just took the shape, and started painting it." While Hammons tended to use the playing card symbol to represent a spade in his body prints, he used an upturned shovel as a spade in his sculptures. In these works Hammons transforms the spade into a black person's face. Another symbol frequently appearing in his work is an American flag in red, black, and green, Marcus Garvey's colors for the redemption of Africa.

Hammons installed his famous basketball series, *Higher Goals,* in vacant lots in New York City during the 1980s. The goals range from 9 to 17 m (30 to 55 ft) in height and are decorated with colorful bottle caps. Of *Higher Goals*, Hammons said, "It's an anti-basketball sculpture. Basketball has become a problem in the black community because kids aren't getting an education. They're pawns in someone else's game. That's why it's called *Higher Goals.* It means you should have higher goals in life than basketball." Hammons is also known for a controversial work called *How Ya Like Me Now?* (1988), which portrays African American politician Jesse Jackson as a white man with blond hair and blue eyes.

Aaron Myers

See Also
Garvey, Marcus Mosiah; Harlem, New York; Jackson, Jesse Louis; New York, New York; Racial Stereotypes; Los Angeles, California.

North America

Hampton, Lionel Leo

(b. April 12, 1908, Louisville, Ky.), African American multi-instrumentalist, the first jazz musician to play the vibraphone.

Lionel Hampton has been a tireless and swinging jazz soloist and bandleader since the 1930s. Although never changing his swing-derived style, he has remained open to new musical directions. During the 1940s his big band's shift from swing jazz helped create rhythm and blues (R&B). He later recorded a version of John Coltrane's "Giant Steps." In the 1990s a series of strokes hampered his playing, but Hampton has continued to tour and perform.

Hampton's family had moved to Birmingham, Alabama, while he was an infant, but in 1919 they joined the Great Migration and settled in Chicago. Hampton's mother secured his admission to Holy Rosary Academy, 150 km (90 mi) north of Chicago. There Hampton learned the rudiments of drumming. After transferring to another Catholic school in Chicago, he joined a youth band organized by Robert Abbott, owner of the *Chicago Defender* newspaper. Hampton's uncle, Richard Morgan – a Chicago bootlegger who became Bessie Smith's lover – bought Hampton a drum set and a xylophone.

During the 1920s Hampton played in several obscure bands. He made his recording debut in 1924 with Reb Spike's Legion Club Forty-fives. In 1930 Hampton traveled to California to join Les Hite's band, then the backup band for trumpeter Louis Armstrong. During a recording session, Armstrong noticed a vibraphone in the studio and asked Hampton to play it. The vibraphone – also called the vibes – is a xylophone with electrical fans mounted at the tops of the resonator tubes, allowing notes to be sustained longer than on a standard xylophone. That day, playing behind Armstrong on Eubie Blake's "Memories of You" and the popular "Shine," Hampton became the first jazz vibes player.

Hampton was also a capable drummer, though not a style setter on the order of Jo Jones or Chick Webb. In addition, he played piano with a unique "trigger-finger" style, playing rapid-fire, single-note melody lines. But his main instrument became the vibraphone. On up-tempo numbers Hampton relied on repeated short riffs – improvised melodic motifs – in hard-swinging and rhythmically driving solos. On ballads he revealed greater subtlety, demonstrating harmonic sophistication and a gift for melodic invention.

Hampton did not achieve fame until 1936, when clarinetist Benny Goodman added him to what became the Benny Goodman Quartet. During the late 1930s the group enjoyed phenomenal popularity. It included two black and two white musicians – Hampton and African American pianist Teddy Wilson, and Goodman and white drummer Gene Krupa – and played an important role in challenging racial segregation in the entertainment industry. At the same time, however, Goodman included neither Hampton nor Wilson in his all-white big band.

In 1940 Hampton left Goodman to organize his own big band. He soon had a major hit with "Flying Home" (1942), which featured a honking and growling Illinois Jacquet tenor saxophone solo that inspired countless R&B tenor sax players. But Hampton's primary musical contribution was the series of all-star sessions that he led for Victor Recording Company between 1937 and 1941. These small-group recordings feature a veritable who's who of swing-era jazz greats, including saxophonists Coleman Hawkins, Benny Carter, and Johnny Hodges, trumpeters Rex Stewart, Cootie Williams, and a young Dizzy Gillespie, guitarist Charlie Christian, pianist Nat King Cole, and drummer Jo Jones. Hampton's Victor recordings show the range and artistry of swing-era jazz.

James Clyde Sellman

See Also

Armstrong, Louis ("Satchmo"); Blake, James Hubert ("Eubie"); Carter, Bennett Lester (Benny); *Chicago Defender*; Chicago, Illinois; Cole, Nat ("King"); Coltrane, John William; Gillespie, John Birks ("Dizzy"); Great Migration, The; Hawkins, Coleman Randolph; Abbott, Robert Sengstacke.

North America

Hampton University, a private coeducational institution of higher learning established during Reconstruction to train African Americans teachers.

Between 1863, the year President Abraham Lincoln issued the Emancipation Proclamation, thus freeing slaves in the South, and 1868, the year Hampton Normal and Agricultural Institute opened its doors in Hampton, Virginia, thousands of African Americans had settled on the Virginia Peninsula. With the financial support of Northern philanthropists and religious groups, Samuel Chapman Armstrong, a white Brevet Brigadier General who commanded the United States Eighth and Ninth black troops during the Civil War, founded Hampton to help former slaves achieve self-sufficiency. Under Armstrong's guidance Hampton developed a system of industrial education that became the model for African American education in the post-Civil War era.

Armstrong's educational philosophy, known as the Hampton Idea, emphasized the cultivation of practical skills, a moral character, and a strong work ethic. Students were required to spend two full days of the week working on the school's farm and trade shops, where they applied their classroom knowledge of botany and arithmetic. Students also received social instruction in Christian morality, personal hygiene, and social etiquette. In the aftermath of slavery, these lessons were intended to help African American students become functioning members of society. From 1878 to 1923 Hampton also educated numerous Native Americans.

In the early twentieth century such African American leaders as W. E. B. Du Bois criticized Hampton because of its exclusively industrial curriculum. Du Bois claimed that black Americans needed higher education in order to progress beyond manual labor positions. An educational reform movement in the 1920s led to the elimination of elementary- and secondary-level courses and the implementation of college-level courses at Hampton. Between 1929 and 1930 Hampton raised its admission standards by requiring applicants to have a high school education, and changed its name to Hampton Institute. In 1932 Hampton became an accredited four-year institution, and in 1956 it organized a Division of Graduate Studies. In 1984 the school changed its name to Hampton University. Today Hampton has an enrollment of more than 5500 students pursuing degrees in some 50 areas of study.

Aaron Myers

See Also

Civil War, American; Du Bois, William Edward Burghardt (W. E. B.); Thirteenth Amendment of the United States Constitution and the Emancipation Proclamation.

North America

Hancock, Herbert Jeffrey (Herbie) (b. April 12, 1940, Chicago, Ill.), piano and keyboard player, composer, and group leader who has contributed to modal, free, and fusion jazz.

Since the 1960s Herbie Hancock has been, along with trumpet player Miles Davis, one of the most popular jazz musicians in the United States. As did Davis, he has played effectively in a wide range of styles, including modal, free jazz, and, most controversially, fusion or jazz-rock. Hancock first gained national acclaim in Davis's mid-1960s quintet along with Wayne Shorter (tenor saxophone), Tony Williams (drums), and Ron Carter (bass), but his talent was evident at an early age. He began studying piano at age 7 and performed with the Chicago Symphony Orchestra in a young people's concert when he was 11 years old.

After graduating from college in 1960, Hancock played piano professionally, including stints with tenor saxophonist Coleman Hawkins and trumpeter Donald Byrd. He moved to New York City in 1962 and later that year recorded his debut album, *Takin' Off*, which included the gospel-tinged soul jazz hit "Watermelon Man." Hancock recorded a series of classic Blue Note albums, including *Empyrean Isles* (1964), *Maiden Voyage* (1965), and *Speak Like a Child* (1968). His light touch and modal approach reflected the influence of white pianist Bill Evans. Several Hancock compositions, including "Maiden Voyage" and "Dolphin Dance," have become jazz standards.

Hancock joined the Miles Davis Quintet in 1963, and his distinctive piano stylings became an integral part of Davis's classic 1960s group. Although playing in a harmonically advanced modal style, Hancock and other members of the quintet moved steadily in the direction of greater harmonic freedom and rhythmic openness, reflected in classic recordings that include *E.S.P.* (1965), *Miles Smiles* (1966), and *Nefertiti* (1967). Hancock began playing electric keyboards with Davis in the late 1960s and, after leaving the Davis Quintet in 1971, continued to explore the possibilities of the electric piano and various synthesizers in his own band, Sextant.

In 1973 Hancock formed Headhunters, his most popular group, which merged the danceable rhythms of funk and rock with jazz. *Headhunters* (1973), the new group's first album, became a huge pop music success, especially the hit single "Chameleon." But many critics and fans of his earlier playing complained that Hancock had compromised his music to gain commercial success, views that the pianist dismissed as elitist.

In any case, Hancock never altogether left acoustic jazz. His later career has included the late 1970s V.S.O.P. (Very Special One-time Performance) tour – a reunion of the 1960s Davis Quintet with trumpeter Freddie Hubbard taking Davis's place – and piano duets with Chick Corea during the 1980s. His acoustic jazz score for the film *Round Midnight* won an Academy Award in 1986, and in the following year he toured as part of an all-star acoustic trio and quartet. In 1997 he released a well-received duet album with Wayne Shorter.

James Clyde Sellman

See Also

Soul Music; Davis, Miles Dewey, III; Gospel Music; Hawkins, Coleman Randolph; New York, New York.

North America

Handy, William Christopher (W.C.) (b. November 16, 1873, Florence, Ala.; d. March 28, 1958, New York, N.Y.), composer, cornet and trumpet player, bandleader, and self-described "father of the blues."

Although personally soft-spoken and unprepossessing, W. C. Handy titled his autobiography with a bold phrase that had long been associated with him, *Father of the Blues* (1941). But as Handy well knew, the blues, an African American musical genre of incalculable significance, was in no sense the creation of any one individual. More accurately, Handy's importance lay in his success as a promoter of African American music: popularizing the blues was his greatest accomplishment.

Handy took a loosely structured folk idiom performed by unschooled musicians and formalized it, in particular regularizing its most common 12-bar form. Handy explained that he took a music "already used by Negro roustabouts, honky-tonk piano players, wanderers, and others... from Missouri to the Gulf [of Mexico].... [and] introduce[d] this, the 'blues' form, to the general public."

His "Memphis Blues," published in 1912, is commonly regarded as the first blues to appear in sheet music. In fact, two other composers had published blues earlier that same year. Furthermore, musicologist Gunther Schuller argued that despite featuring two 12-bar blues-style strains, "Memphis Blues" was "not a blues at all" but rather "was closer to the cakewalk."

Handy was likewise not a JAZZ player. Record producer John Hammond observed that there "wasn't a note of improvisation" in Handy's recordings of "Memphis Blues" and "St. Louis Blues." Handy's early training was in European art music, and his formative professional experience came in brass bands and in African American MINSTRELSY. Handy first studied music with Y. A. Wallace, a FISK UNIVERSITY graduate who, despite the fame of the FISK JUBILEE SINGERS, "had no interest in the spirituals" and "made no attempt to instruct us in this remarkable folk music." Another influence was violinist Jim Turner, who came to Florence from Memphis, Tennessee, and organized a band. About this time Handy took up the cornet. He played with a number of brass bands, sang tenor in vocal quartets, and toured briefly with an amateur minstrel company.

But Handy's key professional experience was with Mahara's Minstrels. He was invited to join the troupe in 1896 as a cornet player earning $6 a week, which was good money during a severe national depression. After one season Handy was made leader of an orchestra of 42 musicians. However, his career choice brought criticism from friends and family. Minstrels, he explained, "were a disreputable lot in the eyes of a large section of upper-crust Negroes," although minstrel shows employed "the best talent of that generation."

Handy left minstrelsy in 1903 and spent five years leading a band in Clarksdale, Mississippi. It was then that Handy, now a trained professional musician, encountered the blues as if for the first time. He admitted that he took up such "low folk forms hesitantly. I approached them with a certain fear and trembling." But his interest deepened. Ultimately, he transformed American popular music by preparing the way for the blues craze of the 1920s and a more general dissemination of the blues that took place throughout the century, making it perhaps the world's most widely recognized music.

Handy then moved to Memphis and organized another band. Mayoral candidate Edward H. Crump hired the group in 1909, and Handy's campaign song, known as "Mr. Crump," later became "Memphis Blues." This song also led to Handy's involvement in the business side of music. After selling the rights to the song for $100, Handy realized that he had been cheated, and he resolved never to be cheated again. In partnership with lyricist and bank cashier Harry H. Pace, he formed Pace and Handy Music Company to publish sheet music. Pace and Handy had a lucrative hit with "St. Louis Blues" (1914), which became Handy's best-known composition and an American musical standard.

In 1918 Handy and Pace moved their company to New York City, and it became the leading publisher of music by black composers. The principals dissolved their partnership in 1920 but continued in the music business separately, Pace establishing BLACK SWAN RECORDS, the first black-owned record company, and Handy organizing Handy Brothers, Inc., a music publishing business, and the short-lived Handy Record Company. Although he continued to perform and compose, over the years Handy became increasingly active as a businessman and impresario.

Handy was forced to curtail his activities in the 1940s and 1950s as the result of blindness and a debilitating stroke, but throughout his long career he was a tireless ambassador for African American music. He organized concerts of black music for the Chicago World's Fair, the New York World's Fair, and the Golden Gate Exposition in San Francisco. He also published two musical collections, *Blues: An Anthology* (1926) and *Book of Negro Spirituals* (1938). Most of all, he understood music's healing power in a racially divided society. "Nothing," he wrote in his autobiography, "made me glow so much as seeing the softening effect of music on racial antagonisms."

James Clyde Sellman

SEE ALSO

Blues, The; Cakewalk, The; Memphis, Tennessee; New York, New York; Pace, Harry Hubert; Spirituals, African American.

Africa

Hani, Chris (b. June 28, 1942, Colimvaba, South Africa; d. April 10, 1993, Boksburg, South Africa), secretary-general of the SOUTH AFRICAN COMMUNIST PARTY; assassinated by right-wing whites.

At the time of his murder, Chris Hani (born Martin Thembisile Hani) was second only to Nelson Mandela among popular antiapartheid activists, and his militant rhetoric made him the favorite of SOUTH AFRICA's disaffected young blacks. His 1993 assassination occurred at the height of negotiations between the government and antiapartheid organizations and sparked days of rioting and violent government retaliation that threatened to disrupt the negotiating process – results that some felt reflected the assassins' goals. But the crisis instead proved the strength of Mandela's leadership, as the AFRICAN NATIONAL CONGRESS (ANC) appealed for calm and continued the talks.

Hani, who was born in the bantustan, or "black homeland," of Transkei and graduated from Fort Hare University in 1962, was a classics scholar turned freedom fighter. He joined the ANC Youth League in 1957 and in 1962 went into exile to join the ANC's newly formed paramilitary wing, Umkhonto we Sizwe (MK, the "spear of the nation"). Hani had his first contact with the SOUTH AFRICAN COMMUNIST PARTY (SACP) while working for the South African Congress of Trade Unions in Cape Town in the early 1960s. As a long-time ally of the ANC in the fight against APARTHEID, the SACP was one of Umkhonto's parent groups and helped secure much of its international support.

Known for his brilliance, energy, and charisma, Hani was drawn to his first military experience from exile as Umkhonto joined the battle against white rule in Southern Rhodesia (now ZIMBABWE). After serving two years in jail for weapons possession in BOTSWANA, Hani moved to LESOTHO, where he recruited and trained troops for sabotage missions into South Africa. He was named to the ANC's Executive Council in 1975 and selected as Umkhonto chief of staff in 1987. In 1990, after the government released Mandela from prison and reversed the bans on the ANC, SACP, and other groups, Hani returned to South Africa. He moved to Boksburg, a newly interracial suburb of Johannesburg, and called for an end to fighting. Hani's popularity was considered key to the recruitment of young blacks to the SACP, and in 1991 he was elected the party's secretary-general, replacing the ailing JOE SLOVO. He was a rising star in two major antiapartheid organizations, an important player in negotiations with the government, and commonly seen as a likely successor to Mandela. In April 1993, however, Hani was shot down outside his house by right-wing whites.

Hani's death brought days of mourning, protests, and strikes. At least seven people died in the resulting violence. But Mandela, Slovo, and President F. W. De Klerk called for the talks to continue, and unprecedented cooperation between the two sides served both to calm the turmoil and capture the killers. Two men, one a member of the AFRIKANER Resistance Movement and the other a former legislator allied with the pro-apartheid Conservative Party, were found guilty of Hani's murder in October 1993. In August 1997 the men applied for amnesty before South Africa's TRUTH AND RECONCILIATION COMMISSION.

Kate Tuttle

SEE ALSO
Antiapartheid Movement; Cape Town, South Africa; Johannesburg, South Africa; Mandela, Nelson Rolihlahla; De Klerk, Frederik Willem.

Europe

Hannibal, Abram (b. 1670, Eritrea; d. 1762?, St. Petersburg, Russia), African slave of Tsar Peter the Great, who became a major general and military engineer in Russia and was the great-grandfather of the poet ALEXANDER PUSHKIN.

Scholars agree that whether he was bought by Russians at the slave markets of Constantinople, or by the tsar himself in the Netherlands, Abram, who later asserted he was the son of an Ethiopian prince, entered Russia in 1700 and began his service with the royal court in 1705. Within two years Abram had won the favor of Tsar Peter I, known as Peter the Great, who became his godfather when he joined the Russian Orthodox Church. The newly baptized Abram Petrov served as the tsar's personal valet both in Russia and away from it during his military campaigns.

After nine years in the Court's service the tsar sent Abram to Paris for higher education. In 1718 he joined the French army to gain access to the best military engineering program, and during his service he was captured by the Spanish in FRANCE's war against SPAIN. Upon his release in 1722, he was promoted to lieutenant and continued to study mathematics and engineering in France for another year. The next year he returned to Russia and, with his advanced training, acquired a post first as an engineer and then as a mathematics tutor for one of the tsar's private guard units.

When Peter the Great died in 1725, Abram's fortunes began to decline. He became embroiled in the intrigues of Catherine the Great, and as a result of his role in the opposition to her succession, he was eventually exiled to Siberia for three years. In exile he began the work that distinguished him as an engineer. He built a fortress in Siberia and led several construction projects upon his transfer to the Baltic. After retiring from service in 1733, he returned to the Court in 1741, with the accession of Peter's daughter, Empress Elizabeth, who awarded him military promotions, engineering projects, and an estate near St. Petersburg to which he retired in 1762.

In the 1730s Abram took the surname Hannibal, possibly in preparation for his marriage to a Greek sea captain's daughter, which ended in divorce. In the course of the divorce proceedings, which took nearly two decades to finalize, he illegally married Christina Regina von Shoberg, the daughter of a German officer. The couple had 11 children and, in 1799, their granddaughter Nadezhda gave birth to Alexander Pushkin, the father of modern Russian literature. Though Pushkin never knew his great-grandfather, who died around 1762, he was enamored of his African heritage and wrote a fictionalized biography of Hannibal, *The Negro of Peter the Great* (incomplete version published in 1837).

Leyla Keough

SEE ALSO
Ethiopia; Russia and the Former Soviet Union; Netherlands, The.

North America

Hansberry, Lorraine

(b. May 19, 1930, Chicago, Ill.; d. January 12, 1965, New York, N.Y.), playwright whose award-winning play, *A Raisin in the Sun*, was the first by an African American woman to be produced on Broadway.

Lorraine Vivian Hansberry's parents were Carl Augustus Hansberry, a prominent real-estate broker in Chicago, and Nannie Perry, a schoolteacher who later devoted her life to activism. Hansberry was the youngest of four. Her father's victory in the Supreme Court case *Hansberry* v. *Lee* (1940) resulted in the repeal of restricted covenants (laws which prevented blacks from buying property in white areas), but enforcement did not follow the change in law, and her disappointed father left the United States and emigrated to MEXICO, where he later died.

Frustrated by her education at the University of Wisconsin, Hansberry only stayed for two years – long enough, however, to take courses in drama and stage design and to fall under the spell of Sean O'Casey's *Juno and the Paycock*: "The melody was one I had known for a very long while," she said. "I did not think then of writing the melody as I knew it – in a different key; but I believe it entered my consciousness and stayed there" (*To Be Young, Gifted and Black*, 1969). After briefly studying painting, she went to Harlem to work as a reporter and then as an associate editor at *Freedom*, a monthly headed by PAUL ROBESON. In 1953 she married Robert Nemiroff. He remained her active literary executor after she died of pancreatic cancer in 1965, despite their earlier, quiet divorce (1964).

Hansberry set *A Raisin in the Sun*, her most famous play, in familiar territory – the terrible living conditions produced for blacks by restricted covenants. It opened at the Ethel Barrymore Theatre on Broadway on March 11, 1959. Directed by Lloyd Richards and starring SIDNEY POITIER and RUBY DEE, it ran for 583 performances. *A Raisin in the Sun* was the first Broadway play directed by a black person in 50 years, and the first written by a black woman. Hansberry was the first black woman to receive the New York Drama Critics Circle Award (beating out Tennessee Williams, Eugene O'Neill, and Archibald MacLeish), and the youngest ever recipient. When it became a Columbia movie in 1961, the film received a nomination for Best Screenplay of the Year from the Screenwriters Guild and a special award at the Cannes Film Festival (1961); the musical, *Raisin* (1973), won a Tony Award. The play is widely anthologized and often revived. A second Broadway play, *The Sign in Sidney Brustein's Window* (1964), received mixed reviews, but private donations kept it running until the night Hansberry died. Posthumous productions orchestrated by Robert Nemiroff include *To Be Young, Gifted and Black* (1969) and *Les Blancs* (1970).

Sidney Poitier, *left*, starred in the 1961 film version of Lorraine Hansberry's play, *A Raisin in the Sun* (1959). *The Everett Collection*

Hansberry was prolific: *The Movement: Documentary of a Struggle for Equality; To Be Young, Gifted and Black: Lorraine Hansberry in Her Own Words*; and articles in the *Village Voice*, *Freedomways*, the *National Guardian*, and the *Black Scholar* are among her published work. In addition to the protests that her work embodied, she was a committed activist for black and gay rights, involved in the STUDENT NONVIOLENT COORDINATING COMMITTEE (SNCC), and a critic of the House Un-American Activities Committee.

SEE ALSO
Chicago, Illinois; Harlem, New York; Gay and Lesbian Movements in Latin America and the Caribbean.

Africa

Harare, Zimbabwe, capital of Zimbabwe.

Despite the absence of a port or river access, Harare has become one of Africa's most modern and prosperous cities. In 1890 Rhodesian settlers established what is today Harare at the base of a *kopje*, or small hill, that rose abruptly out of the rolling plain. Originally named Fort Salisbury, for a British member of Parliament, the settlement was proclaimed a municipality in 1897 and a city in 1935. The town slowly became the commercial and political hub of the settler colony, outpacing the southern town of Bulawayo as it drew on the agricultural productivity of the rich *highveld* land surrounding the city and the rail link to Beira in Mozambique. As part of the Rhodesian government's racial and land policies, inhabitants were increasingly segregated according to race and class, a division that persists unofficially today.

At independence Salisbury's name was changed to Harare to honor the Shona people the Harari, who inhabited the area before the settlers arrived. At the heart of the city are high-rise office blocks and government buildings. The city's industries and its more than 1 million residents are geographically divided. Light industries are located to the east of the city and heavy industries to the west, including the largest tobacco auction floor in the world. The middle- and lower-class residents live in the southern, high-density suburbs, while the upper class resides in the northern, low-density suburbs. The city grew substantially in the 1980s, and by the 1990s was recording a nearly 7 percent annual population growth, as droughts and poverty fed the rural exodus. Unemployment, at more than 30 percent, remains a problem in Harare, as does homelessness.

Eric Young

See Also
Beira, Mozambique.

Africa

Haratine, a social caste in Mauritania, Morocco, and the Western Sahara comprising black Moors, most of whom are former slaves.

The term *haratine* (Arabic for "plowmen") is commonly used throughout the northwestern Sahara to describe a low caste in Moorish society. In recent years the status of the haratine has become a controversial issue in Mauritania, at times affecting relations with neighboring countries. Officially, the haratine are black Moors who are either ancestors of slaves or former slaves themselves. Although slavery was formally abolished in Mauritania in 1960 and again in 1981, many haratine remain subservient to their former masters. Mauritanian officials have argued that these arrangements are completely consensual, but observers from the United Nations and international human rights groups, as well as Mauritanian groups such as El-Hor and Forces de Libération Africaine de Mauritanie (FLAM), claim that enslavement of some haratine persists in present-day Mauritania. In addition, they argue that the government, eager to "Arabize" its population, has systematically denied the haratine opportunities for economic and social advancement.

Most haratine are descendants of the Bambara, Fulani, Soninké, and Wolof peoples that once inhabited the western Sahara. Many of these groups fled south into the Senegal River valley when Berber migrants arrived in the third century. Those who remained were enslaved by the Berbers, and, centuries later, by the Moors. Under the Moors the haratine eventually adopted Islam, an Arab identity, and the Hassaniya Arabic language. Many slaves were freed prior to French colonization in the early twentieth century: some under Koranic law, which requires masters to free their slaves after five generations, others through marriage, and some by running away. Others – at least technically – were freed by the 1960 constitution. These former slaves and their descendants became known as haratine.

While some haratine have moved to cities and acquired education and employment, others continue to work for their former masters. Their status is ambiguous. Some, facing scant opportunities elsewhere, have remained where they can work for food. Other haratine have apparently benefited from staying with their former masters, inheriting land and livestock. But critics believe that many haratine have never been told that slavery was outlawed in Mauritania, and perhaps 100,000 are still effectively enslaved even though the edict abolishing slavery was reissued in 1981 by Col. Mohammed Khouna Ould Heydallah. During hearings before the United Nations and the United States Congress in 1994 and 1996, haratine representatives recounted tales of slave raids and produced receipts of slave purchases.

Racial tensions erupted into a cross-border crisis in 1989 when Moors, seeking grazing land for their herds, attacked blacks along the Senegal River, and Mauritania expelled large numbers of Senegalese nationals. Such tensions continued to spark sporadic violence throughout the 1990s, though some progress has been made; Col. Maouiya Ould Sid'Ahmed Taya, for instance, supported haratine candidates such as Fatma Zeina Mint Sbaghou in the 1996 parliamentary elections.

Elizabeth Heath

See Also
United Nations in Africa; Sahara Desert; Senegal; Taya, Maaouya Ould Sidi Ahmed; Senegal River; Human Rights in Africa; Islam and Tradition: An Interpretation; Slavery in Africa.

North America

Harlem Globetrotters, an all-black, Chicago-based touring basketball team whose virtuosity and comic antics on the court made them world famous.

Before the integration of professional basketball in the post-World War II era, the Harlem Globetrotters were considered one of the best basketball teams in the world. Founded as the Savoy Big Five, the team was rechristened by Abe Saperstein, who coined the name as a marketing gimmick and coached the Globetrotters from 1926 until his death in 1966. In 1927 the Harlem Globetrotters (they were neither from Harlem nor well-traveled) played their first game in Hinckley, Illinois, wearing red, white, and blue uniforms stitched in Saperstein's father's tailor shop. The team went on tour, playing local white and black teams, and later competed in tournaments; after finishing third in the *Chicago Herald American's* World Professional Tournament in 1939, the Globetrotters won the World Championship in 1940 and the International Cup Tournament in Mexico City in 1943.

In the mid-1940s, when the all-white National Basketball Association (NBA) began to integrate, the Globetrotters redefined their style of play to show off their mastery of trick shots, fancy behind-the-back passes, effortlessly evasive dribbling, and other basketball tricks. Soon this sort of skillful clowning dominated their performances; the Magic Circle – a pregame warm-up in which the Globetrotters passed the ball around a circle, displaying their impressive ball-handling skills to their theme song "Sweet Georgia Brown" – became their signature routine. By the 1950s demand for the Globetrotters was so great that Saperstein formed a second team to tour the western United States while the original squad remained in the East. By now the team had dispensed with tournaments and "genuine" competition in favor of barnstorming with college stars and, later, the all-white Washington Generals, chronic losers who were often dupes for the Globetrotters' pranks. As its popularity soared, the team finally began to live up to its name, touring Europe, North Africa, and South America in 1950 and 1951, and embarking on a goodwill tour of the Union of Soviet Socialist Republics (USSR) from 1958 to 1959.

Two legendary Globetrotters who played in the 1950s and 1960s, Meadowlark Lemon and Fred "Curly" Neal, were famous for hiding balls under their jerseys and dousing referees with water, then threatening to do the same to the spectators, only to shower them with buckets of confetti. Like the Globetrotters who preceded and followed them, they also occasionally kicked balls, spun them on fingers, and bounced them off other players' heads.

Reece "Goose" Tatum, another beloved Globetrotter, joined the team in 1942 as a center. From his position at the top of the key, he kept up a humorous monologue punctuated by silly facial expressions and noises, but he was also a proficient scorer known for an effective hook shot as well as his fake free throws.

Marques Haynes played with the Globetrotters from 1946 to 1953, and infuriated and baffled opponents with his dribbling skills. With one knee on the court or even lying down, he was able to maneuver the ball quickly between his legs and behind his back to evade defenders, moves that influenced later stars like Earvin "Magic" Johnson.

Another former Globetrotter went on to become one of the NBA's all-time greats. Wilt Chamberlain, then a young player who bypassed his senior year in college to play with the Globetrotters, played on the team as a seven-foot-one-inch guard from 1958 to 1959, a year he described as the "most fun" of his career. Other notable Globetrotters include Bob Karstens, who became the first nonblack Globetrotter in the mid-1940s (there have since been two others), and Lynette Woodward, who became the first female Globetrotter in 1985.

From the 1960s to the 1990s the Globetrotters rarely played any team other than the Washington Generals, and built steadily on a winning streak that lasted 24 years. The 8829-game streak was broken in 1995 when the KAREEM ABDUL-JABBAR's All-Stars beat the Globetrotters in an exhibition game in Vienna, Austria.

The Harlem Globetrotters have been the subject of three films, *Go Man Go* (1948); *The Harlem Globetrotters* (1951); and *The Harlem Globetrotters: Six Decades of Magic* (1988). In the 1970s they appeared in a television series and their own cartoon.

After 1966 the Globetrotters went through a series of owners before being purchased by former Globetrotter Mannie Jackson in 1993. Although the Globetrotters continue to amuse audiences in the United States and abroad, since the 1960s they have occasionally been criticized for their clownish antics, which some critics believe reinforce RACIAL STEREOTYPES.

Aaron Myers

SEE ALSO

World War II and African Americans; Chamberlain, Wilton Norman (Wilt); Johnson, Magic.

North America

Harlem, New York, political and cultural center of black America in the twentieth century, best known as the major site of the literary and artistic "renaissance" of the 1920s and 1930s.

Slaves to the Dutch West India Company, Africans built the first wagon road into Harlem in the seventeenth century, and in the next 200 years African slaves worked the Dutch and then English farms in Harlem. In 1790, 115 slaves were listed for the "Harlem Division," equal to one-third the population of the area.

But the evolution of Harlem into the political and cultural capital of black America is a twentieth-century phenomenon. Housing in Harlem, which was once a wealthy suburb of New York City, soared in value at the turn of the century, only to collapse beneath excessive real estate speculation in 1904 and 1905. Those years coincided with the completion of the Lenox Avenue subway line to lower Manhattan, facilitating the settlement of African Americans migrating from the South and the Caribbean in Harlem. Philip Payton's Afro-Am Realty Company leased large numbers of Harlem apartment houses from white owners and rented them to black tenants in neighborhoods that began at 135th Street east of Eighth Avenue and over the decades expanded east-west from Park to Amsterdam avenues and north-south from 155th Street to Central Park.

By 1930 the black population of New York had more than tripled, to 328,000 persons,

ABOVE RIGHT: Children from a Harlem dance school pose outside the studio of photographer Otis C. Butler, circa 1928. *Photographs and Prints Division, Schomburg Center for Research in Black Culture, The New York Public Library, Astor, Lenox and Tilden Foundation*

RIGHT: Not only the cultural and intellectual center of black life in the United States, Harlem has also served as a safe haven, a black community with strong connections among its inhabitants. *CORBIS/Bettmann*

THE HOUSE OF COMMON SENSE
HOME OF PROPER PROPAGANDA.
WORLD HISTORY
BOOK OUTLET ON
JOMO KENYATTA
HON MARCUS GARVEY
2,000,000,000
(TWO BILLION)
AFRICANS AND NON-WHITE PEOPLES
ETHIOPIA LIBERIA EGYPT SUDAN GHANA GUINEA CAMEROON TOGOLAND CONGO SOMALIA NIGERIA EAST NIGERIA
AFRICAN CHIEFS OF STATES
BLACK MAN'S GOD
REPATRIATION HEADQUARTERS
BACK TO AFRICA MOVEMENT
RECRUITING
REGISTER HERE!
HARLEM SQUARE
A HISTORY OF NEGRO PEOPLE IN AMERICA
LET GODS CHULLUN BY

OPPOSITE: From Marcus Garvey's Universal Negro Improvement Association to the National Memorial African Bookstore, pictured here in 1964, Harlem has long served as home to movements and ideas stressing African American self-reliance and self-esteem. *UPI/CORBIS-Bettmann*

TOP: Harlem marchers protest the East St. Louis race riots of 1917. In the World War I era African Americans faced mass violence in dozens of race riots across the country. *Photographs and Prints Division, Schomburg Center for Research in Black Culture, The New York Public Library, Astor, Lenox and Tilden Foundation*

ABOVE: "Take the A Train," written by Billy Strayhorn and made famous by Duke Ellington's orchestra, refers to the New York subway line that leads uptown to 125th Street, the gateway to Harlem. *Alex Pitt/Walkabout Pictures*

180,000 of whom lived in Harlem – two-thirds of all African Americans in New York City and 12 percent of the entire population. Between 1920 and 1930 the black population of Harlem increased by nearly 100,000 persons, developing middle- and upper-middle-class neighborhoods such as Striver's Row on West 139th Street.

The migration led to a political, cultural, and social community that was unprecedented in scope. The African Methodist Episcopal Zion Church, St. Philips' Protestant Episcopal Church, and Abyssinian Baptist Church moved north to Harlem. The *Amsterdam News* was founded in Harlem in 1919. The community also supported a vital literary and political life: by 1920 the trade union newspaper the *Messenger*, edited by A. Philip Randolph and Chandler Owen, was published in Harlem, as were the National Association for the Advancement of Colored People's (NAACP's) magazine the *Crisis*, edited by W. E. B. Du Bois and Jessie Fauset, and the National Urban League's magazine *Opportunity*, edited by Charles S. Johnson. Incipient political movements followed the establishment of a branch of the NAACP in 1910 and Marcus Garvey's Universal Negro Improvement Association in 1916. Flamboyant and charismatic, Garvey

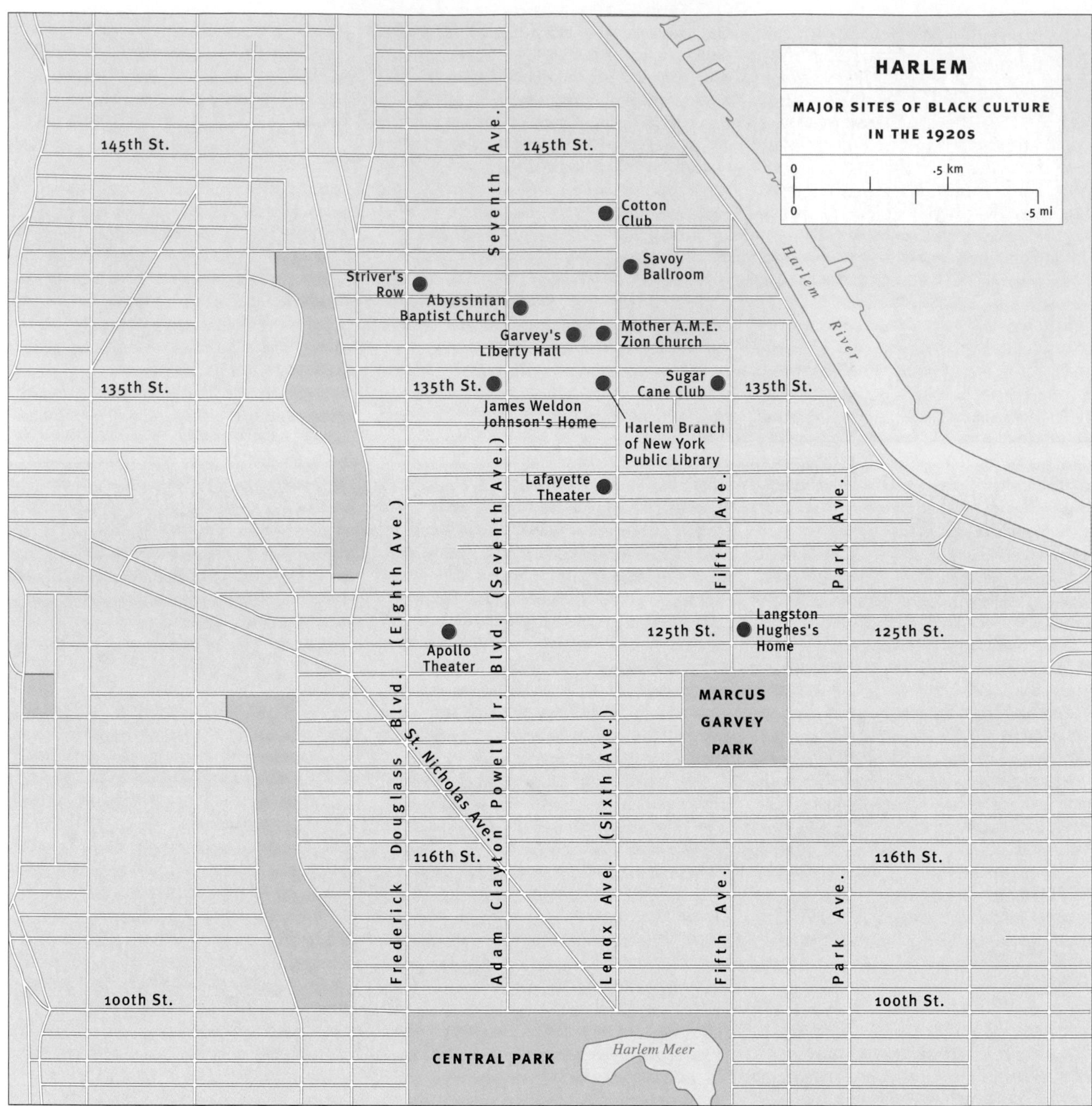

promoted both a back-to-Africa drive and the first popular Black Nationalist Movement. Harlem also nurtured a socialist movement led by H. H. Harrison, W. A. Domingo, and A. Philip Randolph.

Especially in the 1920s Harlem fostered pioneering black intellectual and popular movements as well as a dynamic nightlife centered on nightclubs, impromptu apartment "buffet parties," and speakeasies. Many of Harlem's cultural venues developed at this time, ranging from the Lincoln and Apollo theaters to the COTTON CLUB, Smalls Paradise, and SAVOY BALLROOM. In popular dance FLORENCE MILLS was one of the most celebrated entertainers of the 1920s, while in tap, Bill "Bojangles" Robinson was called "the Mayor of Harlem." In vaudeville BERT WILLIAMS broke the color line. In drama PAUL ROBESON was an honored figure for both his acting and singing.

In 1925 Alain Locke filled an issue of *Survey Graphic* magazine with black literature, folklore, and art, declaring a "New Negro" renaissance to be guided by "forces and motives of [cultural] self determination." The renaissance was led by writers such as JEAN TOOMER, LANGSTON HUGHES, COUNTEE CULLEN, CLAUDE MCKAY, NELLA LARSEN, and ZORA NEALE HURSTON, and Harlem became its symbol. In art AARON DOUGLAS, Richmond Barthé, and (later) Jacob Lawrence launched their careers.

In music Harlem pianists such as Fats Waller and Willie "the Lion" Smith began one of the most storied traditions of JAZZ in the world. In the 1920s it included big bands led by Fletcher Henderson, Duke Ellington, and Chick Webb and individual virtuosos such as Eubie Blake. Later, it included Charlie Parker, Bud Powell, ORNETTE COLEMAN, Thelonious Monk, and Miles Davis.

In the 1920s Harlem gained some political power and institutions. Arthur Schomburg's renowned collection of black literature and historical documents became a branch of the New York Public Library (*see* SCHOMBURG LIBRARY). Three years later Charles Fillmore was elected the first black district leader in New York City, and black physicians were admitted to the permanent staff of Harlem Hospital.

But such advances were modest. Harlem blacks owned less than 20 percent of Harlem's businesses in 1929, and the onset of the Depression quadrupled relief applications within two years. Blacks continued to be excluded from jobs, even in Harlem. The Communist Party and the Citizens' League for Fair Play organized a boycott of Harlem businesses that refused to hire blacks, but the boycott collapsed in 1934. A year later frustration erupted into a riot (*see* HARLEM RIOTS OF 1935) in which millions of dollars of property was damaged and 75 were arrested. By 1937 four African American district leaders were elected, and the Greater New York City Coordinating Committee for the Employment of Negroes was formed.

During World War II migration from the South and the Caribbean increased enormously, the direct result of the opening of defense industry jobs to blacks, for which the 1941 MARCH ON WASHINGTON – organized by A. Philip Randolph – was instrumental (*see* WORLD WAR II AND AFRICAN AMERICANS, and GREAT MIGRATION, THE). But racism persisted, and an incident of police brutality in 1943 precipitated a riot (*see* HARLEM RIOTS OF 1943) in which 6 African Americans were killed and 185 were injured. In 1944, on the heels of widespread efforts to improve race relations, Adam Clayton Powell Jr. was elected to the United States Congress and Benjamin Davis replaced him on the City Council.

The 1940s and 1950s brought further political cohesion and literary expression. Hulan Jack was elected the first black borough president in 1953. Through the 1970s Harlem was home to heralded writers such as novelist RALPH ELLISON, essayist JAMES BALDWIN, playwright LORRAINE HANSBERRY, and poets Audre Lorde and MAYA ANGELOU – many of them associated with the HARLEM WRITERS GUILD. Yet by 1960 middle class flight from Harlem produced a ghetto in large sections of the community. Half of all housing units were unsound, and the infant mortality rate was nearly double that in the rest of the city. Under the leadership of Harlem Youth Opportunities Unlimited (HARYOU), organized by Kenneth B. Clark, Harlem tried to draw federal funding into the area to rebuild the community and create jobs. The effort was largely unsuccessful, and in 1964, when an off-duty police officer shot a black youth, a riot ensued (*see* HARLEM RIOT OF 1964). One person was killed, and 144 were injured; stores were looted for several days.

In the 1950s MALCOLM X arrived to head the Harlem Mosque and soon created an independent religious and Black Nationalist Movement that declared itself ready to fight – "by any means necessary" – against white racism and violence toward African Americans. In 1965, however, Malcolm X was assassinated. His death made him a martyr for Black Nationalists even as his religious movement dissipated.

Percy Sutton was Manhattan borough president for 11 years beginning in 1966. In 1970 Charles Rangel was elected to the congressional seat vacated by Adam Clayton Powell Jr. By the late 1970s, however, deindustrialization and inflation led to widespread unemployment, while poverty, drugs, crime, and a deteriorating school system plagued the community for the next decade.

When, in 1989, Harlem's David Dinkins was elected mayor of New York, racial divisions briefly lessened and some parts of Harlem were revitalized. But Dinkins's defeat in the 1993 election cut short those efforts. In the more mercantilist environment of the late 1990s Harlem has turned to private development efforts by African Americans, such as the mall planned for 125th Street, as a means for rehabilitating an impoverished community.

Jim Mendelsohn

SEE ALSO

Slavery in the United States; Literature, African American; Apollo Theater; Barthé, Richmond; Blake, James Hubert ("Eubie"); Clark, Kenneth Bancroft; *Crisis, The*; Davis, Miles Dewey, III; Dinkins, David Norman; Du Bois, William Edward Burghardt (W. E. B.); Fauset, Jessie Redmon; Garvey, Marcus Mosiah; Great Depression; Harlem Renaissance; Henderson, Fletcher Hamilton, Jr.; Johnson, Charles Spurgeon; New York, New York; *Opportunity: Journal of Negro Life*; Socialism; Sutton, Percy Ellis; Lawrence, Jacob Armstead; Lincoln Theater; Locke, Alain Leroy; Lorde, Audre Geraldine; Monk, Thelonious Sphere; Parker, Charles Christopher ("Bird"); Powell, Adam Clayton, Jr.; Powell, Earl ("Bud"); Randolph, Asa Philip; Rangel, Charles Bernard; Robinson, Bill ("Bojangles"); Schomburg, Arthur Alfonso; Smith, Willie ("the Lion"); Waller, Thomas Wright ("Fats"); Ellington, Edward Kennedy ("Duke"); Art, African American; Communist Party USA, African Americans and the; Black Nationalism in the United States.

Harlem Renaissance

David Levering Lewis

The "Talented Tenth"

The Harlem Renaissance was a somewhat forced phenomenon, a cultural nationalism of the parlor, institutionally encouraged and directed by leaders of the national civil rights establishment for the paramount purpose of improving race relations in a time of extreme national backlash, caused in large part by economic gains won by African Americans during the Great War. W. E. B. Du Bois labeled this mobilizing elite the "Talented Tenth" in a seminal 1903 essay. He fleshed out the concept that same year in "The Advance Guard of the Race," a piece in *Booklover's Magazine* in which he identified the poet Paul Laurence Dunbar, the novelist Charles W. Chesnutt, and the painter Henry O. Tanner, among a small number of other well-educated professionals, as representatives of this class. The Talented Tenth formulated and propagated a new ideology of racial assertiveness that was to be embraced by the physicians, dentists, educators, preachers, businesspeople, lawyers, and morticians who comprised the bulk of the African American affluent and influential – some 10,000 men and women out of a total population in 1920 of more than 10 million. (In 1917, traditionally cited as the natal year of the Harlem Renaissance, there were 2132 African Americans in colleges and universities, probably no more than 50 of them attending "white" institutions. This minuscule vanguard of a minority – a fraction of 0.1 percent of the racial total – jump-started the New Negro Arts Movement, using as its vehicles the National Association for the Advancement of Colored People [NAACP] and the National Urban League [NUL], and their respective publications, the *Crisis* and *Opportunity* magazine.)

The Harlem Renaissance was not all-inclusive of the early twentieth-century African American urban experience. The potent mass movement founded and led by the charismatic Marcus Garvey was a parallel but socially different force related primarily through dialectical confrontation. Equally different from the institutional ethos and purpose of the Renaissance was the Black Church. An occasional minister (such as the father of poet Countee Cullen) or exceptional Garveyites (such as Yale-Harvard man William H. Ferris) might move in both worlds, but black evangelism and its cultist manifestations, such as Black Zionism, represented emotional and cultural retrogression in the eyes of the principal actors in the Renaissance.

When Du Bois wrote a few years after the beginning of the New Negro Movement in arts and letters that "until the art of the black folk compels recognition they will not be rated as human," he, like most of his Renaissance peers, fully intended to exclude the blues of Bessie Smith and the jazz of "King" Oliver. As board members of the Pace Phonograph Company, Du Bois, James Weldon Johnson, and others banned "funky" artists from the Black Swan list of recordings, thereby contributing to the demise of the African American-owned firm. But the wild Broadway success of Miller and Lyles's musical *Shuffle Along* (which helped to popularize the Charleston) and Florence Mill's *Blackbirds* revue flouted such artistic fastidiousness. The very centrality of music in black life, as well as of black musical stereotypes in white minds, caused popular musical forms to impinge inescapably on Renaissance high culture. Eventually, the Renaissance deans made a virtue out of necessity; they applauded the concert-hall ragtime of "Big Jim" Europe and the "educated" jazz of Atlanta University graduate and big-band leader Fletcher Henderson, and took to hiring Duke Ellington or Cab Calloway as drawing cards for fundraising socials. Still, their relationship to music remained beset by paradox. New York ragtime, with its "Jelly Roll" Morton strifes and Joplinesque elegance, had as much in common with Chicago jazz as Mozart did with "Fats" Waller.

Although the emergence of the Harlem Renaissance seems much more sudden and dramatic in retrospect than the historical reality, its institutional elaboration was, in fact, relatively quick. Because so little fiction or poetry had been produced by African Americans in the years immediately prior to the Harlem Renaissance, the appearance of a dozen or more poets and novelists and essayists seemed all the more striking and improbable (*see* Literature, African American). Death from tuberculosis had silenced poet-novelist Dunbar in 1906, and poor royalties had done the same for novelist Chesnutt after publication the previous year of *The Colonel's Dream*. Since then, no more than five African Americans had published significant works of fiction and verse. This relative silence was finally to be broken in 1922 by Claude McKay's *Harlem Shadows*, the first book of poetry since Dunbar.

Three Stages of Development, 1917 to 1935

Altogether, the Harlem Renaissance evolved through three stages. The first phase, ending in 1923 with the publication of Jean Toomer's unique prose poem, *Cane*, was deeply influenced by white artists and writers – bohemians and revolutionaries – fascinated for a variety of reasons with the life of black people. The second phase, from early 1924 to mid-1926, was presided over by the civil rights establishment of the NUL and the NAACP, a period of interracial collaboration between Zora Neale Hurston's "Negrotarian" whites and the African American Talented Tenth. The last phase, from mid-1926 to the Harlem Riot of March 1935, was increasingly dominated by the African American artists themselves – the "Niggerati," in Hurston's pungent phrase. The movement, then, was above all literary and self-consciously an enterprise of high culture well into its middle years. When Charles S. Johnson, new editor of *Opportunity*, sent invitations to some dozen young and mostly unknown African American poets and writers to attend a celebration at Manhattan's Civic Club of the sudden outpouring of "Negro" writing, on March 21, 1924, the Renaissance shifted into high gear. "A group of the younger writers, which includes Eric Walrond, Jessie Fauset, Gwendolyn Bennett, Countee Cullen, Langston Hughes, Alain Locke, and some others," would be present, Johnson promised each invitee. All told, in addition to the younger writers, some 50 persons were expected: "Eugene O'Neill, H. L. Mencken, Oswald Garrison Villard, Mary Johnston, Zona Gale, Robert Morss Lovett, Carl Van Doren, Ridgely Torrence, and about twenty more of this type. I think you might find this group interesting enough to draw you away for a few hours from your work on your next book," Johnson wrote almost coyly to the recently published Jean Toomer. Although both Toomer and Langston Hughes were absent in Europe, approximately 110 celebrants and honorees assembled that evening; included among them were Du Bois, James Weldon Johnson, and the young NAACP officer WALTER FRANCIS WHITE, the energetic literary entrepreneur. Locke, a professor of philosophy at HOWARD UNIVERSITY and the first African American Rhodes scholar, served as Civic Club master of ceremonies.

The nine defendants in the Scottsboro case arrive in New York in 1937, six years after their alleged crime and the same year the state of Alabama finally freed the youngest four defendants. *Photographs and Prints Division, Schomburg Center for Research in Black Culture, The New York Public Library, Astor, Lenox and Tilden Foundation/Morgan and Marvin P. Smith*

Two compelling messages emerged from the Civic Club gathering: Du Bois's, that the literature of apology and the denial to his generation of its authentic voice were now ending; and Van Doren's, that African American artists were developing at a uniquely propitious moment. They were "in a remarkable strategic position with reference to the new literary age which seems to be impending," Van Doren predicted. "What American literature decidedly needs at this moment," he continued, "is color, music, gusto, the free expression of gay or desperate moods. If the Negroes are not in a position to contribute these items," Van Doren could not imagine who else could.

White Artists and "the New Negro": World War I and its Aftermath

The African American had indisputably moved to the center of mainstream imagination with the end of the Great War, a development nurtured in the chrysalis of the Lost Generation – Greenwich Village Bohemia. Ready conversance with the essentials of Freud and Marx became the measure of serious conversation in MacDougal Street coffeehouses, Albert Boni's Washington Square Book Shop, or the Hotel Brevoort's restaurant, where Floyd Dell, Robert Minor, Matthew Josephson, Max Eastman, and other enragés denounced the social system, the Great War to which it had ineluctably led, and the soul-dead world created in its aftermath, with McKay and Toomer, two of the Renaissance's first stars, participating. Waldo Frank, Toomer's bosom friend and literary mentor, foresaw a revolutionary new America emerging "out of our terrifying welter of steel and scarlet."

Among the Lyrical Left writers gathered around *Broom*, *S4N*, and *Seven Arts*, and the political radicals

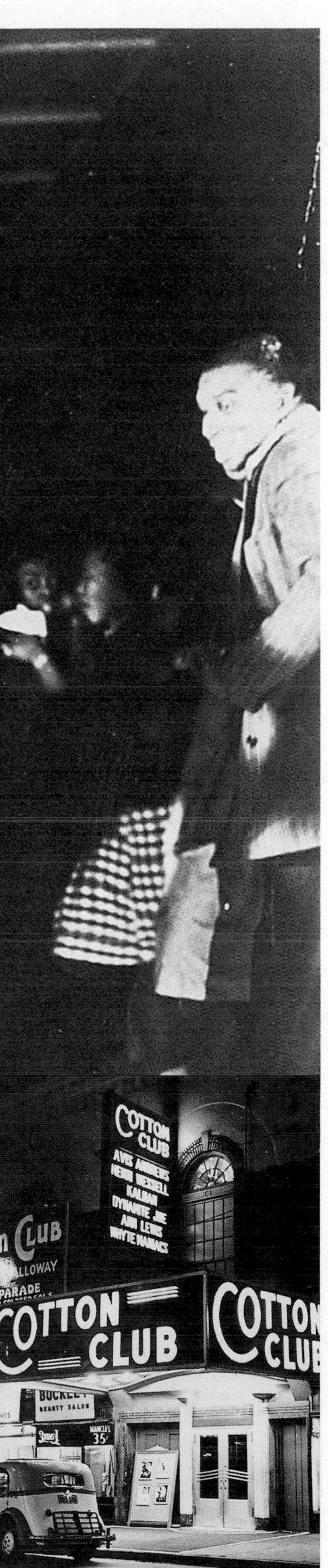

associated with *Liberator,* there was a shared reaction against the ruling Anglo-Saxon cultural paradigm. Bourne's concept of a "trans-national" America, democratically respectful of its ethnic, racial, and religious constituents, complemented Du Bois's earlier concept of divided racial identity in *The Souls of Black Folk.* From such conceptions, the Village's discovery of Harlem followed both logically and, more compellingly, psychologically. The African American, largely excluded because of race from all of the above, was a perfect symbol of cultural innocence and regeneration. He was perceived as an integral, indispensable part of the hoped-for design, somehow destined to aid in the reclamation of a diseased, desiccated civilization.

Theatrical Debut

Public annunciation of the rediscovered Negro came in the fall of 1917 with Emily Hapgood's production at the old Garden Street Theatre of three one-act plays by her husband, Ridgely Torrence. *The Rider of Dreams, Simon the Cyrenian,* and *Granny Maumee* were considered daring because the cast was black and the parts were dignified. From this watershed flowed a number of dramatic productions, musicals, and several successful novels by whites – yet also, with great significance, *Shuffle Along,* a cathartic musical by the African Americans Aubry Lyles and Flournoy Miller. Theodore Dreiser grappled with the explosive subject of LYNCHING in his 1918 short story "Nigger Jeff." Two years later the magnetic African American actor Charles Gilpin energized O'Neill's *Emperor Jones* in the 150-seat theater in a MacDougal Street brownstone taken over by the Provincetown Players.

In 1921 *Shuffle Along* came to the 63rd Street Theatre, with music, lyrics, choreography, cast, and production uniquely in African American hands; composer Eubie Blake's "I'm Just Wild About Harry" and "Love Will Find a Way" entered the list of all-time favorites. PAUL ROBESON made his theatrical debut in Mary Hoyt Wiborg's *Taboo.* In 1922 Clement Wood's sociological novel *Nigger* sympathetically tracked a beleaguered African American family from slavery through the Great War into urban adversity. T. S. Stribling's *Birthright* portrayed an African American male protagonist of superior education (a Harvard-educated physician) martyred for his ideals after returning to the South. In e. e. cummings's *The Enormous Room,* the black character "Jean Le Nègre" was another Noble Savage paradigm observed through a Freudian prism.

Striving toward a "black" aesthetic

But Village artists and intellectuals were aware and unhappy that they were theorizing about black American and spinning out African American fictional characters in a vacuum – that they knew almost nothing firsthand about these subjects. Sherwood Anderson's June 1922 letter to H. L. Mencken spoke for much of the Lost Generation: "Damn it, man, if I could really get inside the niggers and write about them with some intelligence, I'd be willing to be hanged later and perhaps would be." After he chanced to read a Jean Toomer short story in *Double-Dealer* magazine, Anderson helped Toomer's stories to appear in the magazines of the Lyrical Left and the Marxists, in *Dial, S4N, Broom,* and *Liberator.* His 1925 novel *Dark Laughter* bore unmistakable signs of indebtedness to Toomer, whose work, Anderson readily admitted, had given him a true insight into the cultural energies that could be harnessed to pull America back from the abyss of fatal materialism. Celebrity in the Village brought Toomer into Waldo Frank's circle.

Black Art and the American Mainstream

This was part of the background to the Talented Tenth's abrupt, enthusiastic, and programmatic embrace of arts and letters after the World War I. With white Broadway audiences flocking to O'Neill plays and shrieking with delight at *Liza, Runnin' Wild,* and other imitations of *Shuffle Along,* Charles Johnson and James Weldon Johnson, Du Bois, Fauset, White, Locke, and others saw a unique opportunity to tap into the American mainstream. Harlem, the Negro Capital of the World, filled up with successful bootleggers and racketeers, political and religious charlatans, cults of exotic character ("Black Jews"), street-corner pundits and health practitioners (Hubert Harrison, "Black Herman"), beauty culturists and distinguished professionals (Madam C. J. Walker, Louis T. Wright), religious and civil rights notables (the Reverends Cullen and Powell, Du Bois, Johnson, White), and hard-pressed, hardworking families determined to make decent lives for their children. Memories of the nightspots in "The Jungle" (133rd Street), of Bill "Bojangles" Robinson demonstrating his footwork on Lenox Avenue, of raucous shows at the Lafayette that gave Florenz Ziegfeld some of his ideas, of the Tree of Hope outside Connie's Inn, where musicians gathered as at a labor exchange, have been vividly set down by Arthur P. Davis, Regina Andrews, ARNA BONTEMPS, and Langston Hughes.

While Bohemia and the Lost Generation suggested to the Talented Tenth the new approach to the old problem of race relations, their shared premise about art and society obscured the diametrically opposite conclusions white and black intellectuals and artists drew from them. For the whites, art was the means to change society before they would accept it. For the blacks, art was the means to change society in order to be accepted into it. For this reason, many of the Harlem intellectuals found the white vogue in Afro-Americana troubling, although they usually feigned enthusiasm about the new dramatic and literary themes. The Talented Tenth convinced itself that the civil rights dividends were potentially greater than the liabilities. As Benjamin Brawley told James Weldon Johnson: "We have a tremendous opportunity to boost the NAACP, letters, and art; and anything else that calls attention to our development along the higher lines."

Johnson's preface to his best-selling anthology, *The Book of American Negro Poetry* (1922), proclaimed that nothing could "do more to change the mental attitude and raise his status than a demonstration of intellectual parity by the Negro through his production of literature and art." Jessie Fauset and her peers

OPPOSITE: A couple dances the jitterbug at Harlem's famed Savoy Ballroom, birthplace of the Lindy Hop. *Photographs and Prints Division, Schomburg Center for Research in Black Culture, The New York Public Library, Astor, Lenox and Tilden Foundation*
INSET: Bill "Bojangles" Robinson and Cab Calloway headline the white-owned Cotton Club, located at Lenox Avenue and 142nd Street in Harlem. *Culver Pictures*

reasoned, "Here is an audience waiting to hear the truth about us. Let us who are better qualified to present that truth than any white writer, try to do so." Fauset's *There Is Confusion* and Walter White's *The Fire in the Flint* (1924) were the first two novels of the Renaissance. Meanwhile, Langston Hughes published several poems in the *Crisis* that would later appear in the collection *The Weary Blues*. The euphonious "The Negro Speaks of Rivers" (dedicated to Du Bois) ran in the *Crisis* in 1921. With the appearance of McKay's *Harlem Shadows* and Toomer's *Cane* the next year, 1923, the African American officers of the NAACP and the NUL saw how a theory could be put into action. The young New York University prodigy Countee Cullen, already published in the *Crisis* and *Opportunity*, had his mainstream breakthrough in 1923 in *Harper's* and *Century* magazines. Two years later, with Carl Sandburg as one of the three judges, Cullen won the prestigious Witter Bynner poetry prize. Meanwhile, Paul Kellogg's *Survey Graphic* project moved apace under the editorship of Locke.

Wearing fur coats and standing by an elegant roadster, this couple was photographed by James VanDerZee, a noted chronicler of Harlem in the years between World War I and World War II. *"Couple in Raccoon Coats," 1932, James VanDerZee/© Donna VanDerZee*

World War I and the New Negro

Two preconditions made this unprecedented mobilization of talent and group support in the service of a racial arts-and-letters movement possible: demography and repression. The Great Black Migration from the rural South to the industrial North produced the metropolitan dynamism undergirding the Renaissance. The Red Summer of 1919, a period of socialist agitation and conservative backlash following the Russian Revolution, produced the trauma that led to the cultural sublimation of civil rights. In pressure-cooker fashion, the increase in its African American population caused Harlem to pulsate as it pushed its racial boundaries south below 135th Street to Central Park and north beyond 139th ("Striver's Row"). In the first flush of Harlem's realization and of general African American exuberance, the Red Summer of 1919 had a cruelly decompressing impact on Harlem and black America in general. Charleston, South Carolina, erupted in riot in May, followed by Longview, Texas, in July, and Washington, D.C., later in the month. Chicago exploded on July 27 (*see* Chicago Riots of 1919). Lynchings of returning African American soldiers and expulsion of African American workers from unions abounded. In the North, the white working classes struck out against perceived and manipulated threats to job security and unionism from blacks streaming north. In Helena, Arkansas, where a pogrom was unleashed against black farmers organizing a cotton cooperative, and outside Atlanta, where the Ku Klux Klan was reconstituted, the message of the white South to African Americans was that the racial status quo ante bellum was on again with a vengeance. Twenty-six race riots in towns, cities, and counties swept across the nation all the way to Nebraska. The "race problem" became definitively an American dilemma in the summer of 1919 and no longer a remote complexity in the exotic South.

Garveyism

The term *New Negro* entered the vocabulary in reaction to the Red Summer, along with McKay's poetic catechism – "Like men we'll face the murderous, cowardly pack / Pressed to the wall, dying, but fighting back!" There was a groundswell of support for Marcus Garvey's UNIA. Until his 1924 imprisonment for mail fraud, the Jamaican immigrant's message of African Zionism, anti-integrationism, working-class assertiveness, and Bookerite business enterprise increasingly threatened the hegemony of the Talented Tenth and its major organizations, the NAACP and NUL, among people of color in America (much of Garvey's support came from West Indians).

The Negro World, Garvey's multilingual newspaper, circulated throughout Latin America and the African empires of Britain and France. Locke spoke for the alarmed "respectable" civil rights leadership when he wrote, in his introductory remarks to the special issue of *Survey Graphic,* that, although "the thinking Negro has shifted a little to the left with the world trend," black separatism "cannot be – even if it were desirable." Although the movement was its own worst enemy, the Talented Tenth was pleased to help the Justice Department speed its demise.

Architects of the Harlem Renaissance

Du Bois, initially a Renaissance enthusiast, vividly expressed the farfetched nature of the arts-and-letters movement as early as 1926: "How is it that an organization of this kind [the NAACP] can turn aside to talk about art? After all, what have we who are slaves and black to do with art?" It was the brilliant insight of the men and women associated with the NAACP and NUL that, although the road to the ballot box, the union hall, the decent neighborhood, and the office was blocked, the small cracks in the wall of racism could be widened through the production of exemplary racial images in collaboration with liberal white philanthropy, the robust culture industry primarily located in New York, and artists from white Bohemia. If, in retrospect, then, the New Negro Arts Movement has been interpreted as a natural phase in the cultural evolution of another American group, such an interpretation sacrifices causation to appearance. The Renaissance was, in fact, a generation-skipping phenomenon in which a vanguard of the Talented Tenth elite recruited, organized, subventioned, and guided an unevenly endowed cohort of artists and writers to make statements that advanced a certain conception of the race, a cohort of men and women most of whom would never have imagined the possibility of artistic and literary careers.

Charles Johnson and his allies were able to make the critical Renaissance mass possible. Johnson assembled files on prospective recruits throughout the country, going so far as to cajole Aaron Douglas, the artist from Kansas, and others into coming to Harlem, where a network manned by his secretary, Ethel Ray Nance, and her friends Regina Anderson and Louella Tucker (assisted by gifted Trinidadian short-story writer Eric Walrond) looked after them until a salary or a fellowship was secured. White, the very self-important assistant secretary of the NAACP, urged Paul Robeson to abandon law for an acting career, encouraged Nella Larsen to follow his own example as a novelist, and passed the hat for artist Hale Woodruff. Fauset continued to discover and publish short stories and verse, such as those of Wallace Thurman and Arna Bontemps. Shortly after the Civic Club evening, both the NAACP and the NUL announced the creation of annual awards ceremonies bearing the titles of their respective publications, *Crisis* and *Opportunity.*

Opportunity Awards, 1925

The award of the first *Opportunity* prizes came in May 1925 in an elaborate ceremony at the Fifth Avenue Restaurant with some 300 participants. Twenty-four distinguished judges (among them Carl Van Doren, Zona Gale, Eugene O'Neill, James Weldon Johnson, and Van Wyck Brooks) had ruled on the worthiness of entries in five categories. The awards ceremony was interracial, but white capital and influence were crucial to success, and the white presence, in the beginning, was pervasive, setting the outer boundaries for what was creatively normative. Money to start the *Crisis* prizes had come from Amy Spingarn, an accomplished artist and poet, and wife of Joel Spingarn, chairman of the NAACP's board of directors. The wife of the influential attorney, Fisk University trustee, and Urban League board chairman, L. Hollingsworth Wood, had made a similar contribution to initiate the *Opportunity* prizes. These were the whites whom Zora Neal Hurston, one of the first *Opportunity* prizewinners, memorably dubbed "Negrotarians."

The May 1925 *Opportunity* gala showcased the steadily augmenting talent in the Renaissance – what Hurston characterized as the "Niggerati." Most of those whose talent had staying power were introduced that night: E. Franklin Frazier, who won the first prize for an essay on social equality; Sterling Brown, who took second prize for an essay on the singer Roland Hayes; Hurston, awarded second prize for a short story, "Spunk"; and Eric Walrond, third-prize winner for his short story "Voodoo's Revenge." James Weldon Johnson read the poem that took first prize, "The Weary Blues," Langston Hughes's turning-point poem, combining the gift of a superior artist and the enduring, music-encased spirit of the black migrant.

"Harlem: Mecca of the New Negro"

The measures of Charles S. Johnson's success were the announcement of a second *Opportunity* contest to be underwritten by Harlem "businessman" (and numbers king) Caspar Holstein, former *Times* music critic Carl Van Vechten's enthusiasm over Hughes and subsequent arranging of a contract with Knopf for Hughes's first volume of poetry, and, one week after the awards ceremony, a prediction by the *New York Herald Tribune* that the country was "on the edge, if not already in the midst of, what might not improperly be called a Negro renaissance" – thereby giving the movement its name. Priming the public for the Fifth Avenue Restaurant occasion, the special edition of *Survey Graphic*, "Harlem: Mecca of the New Negro," edited by Locke, had reached an unprecedented 42,000 readers in March 1925. The ideology of cultural nationalism at the heart of the Renaissance was crisply delineated in Locke's opening essay, "Harlem," stating that, "without pretense to their political significance, Harlem has the same role to play for the New Negro as Dublin has had for the New Ireland or Prague for the New Czechoslovakia." There was little amiss about America that interracial elitism could not set right, Locke and the others believed. Despite historic discrimination and the Red Summer, the Rhodes scholar assured readers that the increasing radicalism among African Americans was superficial. At year's end, Albert and Charles Boni published Locke's *The New Negro*, an expanded and polished edition of the poetry and prose from the *Opportunity* contest and the special *Survey Graphic*.

The New Negro (1926)

The New Negro carried several memorable works, such as the short story "The South Lingers On" by Brown University and Howard Medical School graduate Rudolph Fisher; the acid poem "White House(s)" and the euphonic "The Tropics in New York," by McKay, now in European self-exile; and several poetic vignettes from Toomer's *Cane*. Although the objective conditions confronting most African Americans in Harlem and elsewhere were deteriorating, optimism remained high. Harlem recoiled from Garveyism and socialism to applaud Phi Beta Kappa poets, university-trained painters, concretizing musicians, and novel-writing officers of civil rights organizations. "Everywhere we heard the sighs of wonder, amazement and sometimes admiration when it was whispered or announced that here was one of the 'New Negroes,'" Bontemps recalled.

The second *Opportunity* awards banquet, April 1926, was another artistic and interracial success. The William E. Harmon Foundation at the beginning of 1926 announced seven annual prizes for literature, music, fine arts, industry, science, education, and race relations, with George Edmund Haynes, African American official in the Federal Council of Churches, and Locke as chief advisers. That same year, the publishers Boni & Liveright offered a $1000 prize for the "best novel on Negro life" by an African American. Casper Holstein contributed $1000 that year to endow *Opportunity* prizes. Van Vechten made a smaller contribution to the same cause. Amy Spingarn provided $600 toward the *Crisis* awards. Otto Kanh underwrote two years in France for the young artist Hale Woodruff. There were Louis Rodman Wanamaker prizes in music composition.

The third *Opportunity* awards dinner was a vintage one for poetry, with entries by Bontemps, Sterling Brown, Hughes, Helene Johnson, and Jonathan H. Brooks. Eric Walrond's lush, impressionistic collection of short stories, *Tropic Death*, appeared from Boni & Liveright at the end of 1926, the most probing exploration of the psychology of cultural underdevelopment since Toomer's *Cane*. If *Cane* recaptured in a string of glowing vignettes (most of them about women) the sunset beauty and agony of a preindustrial culture, *Tropic Death* did much the same for the Antilles.

McKay, viewing the scene from abroad, spoke derisively of the artistic and literary autocracy of "that NAACP crowd." The Ministry mounted a movable feast to which the anointed were invited, sometimes to Walter and Gladys White's apartment at 409 Edgecombe Avenue, where they might share cocktails with Sinclair Lewis or Mencken; often (after 1928) to the famous 136th Street "Dark Tower" salon maintained by beauty culture heiress A'Lelia Walker, where guests might include Sir Osbert Sitwell, the Crown Prince of Sweden, or Lady Mountbatten; and very frequently to the home of Carl and Fania Van Vechten, to imbibe the host's sidecars and listen to Robeson sing or Jim Johnson recite from "God's Trombones" or George Gershwin play the piano. Meanwhile, Harlem's appeal to white revellers inspired the young physician Rudolph Fisher to write "The Caucasian Storms Harlem," a satiric piece in the August 1927 *American Mercury*.

The Ascendancy of Black Artists

The third phase of the Harlem Renaissance began even as the second had only just gotten under way. The second phase (1924 to mid-1926) was dominated by the officialdom of the two major civil rights organizations, with its ideology of civil rights advancement of African Americans through the creation and mobilization of an artistic-literary movement. The third phase, from mid-1926 to the end of 1934, was marked by rebellion against the civil rights establishment on the part of many of the artists and writers whom that establishment had assembled and promoted. Three publications during 1926 formed a watershed between the genteel and the demonic Renaissance. Hughes's "The Negro Artist and the Racial Mountain," which appeared in the June 1926 issue of the *Nation*, served as a manifesto of the breakaway from the arts-and-letters party line. Van Vechten's *Nigger Heaven*, released by Knopf that August, drove much of literate black America into a dichotomy of approval and apoplexy over "authentic" versus "proper" cultural expression. Wallace Thurman's *Fire!!*, which became available in November 1926, assembled the rebels for a major assault against the Civil Rights Ministry of Culture.

Hughes's turning-point essay had been provoked by Schuyler's essay in the *Nation*, "The Negro-Art Hokum," ridiculing "eager apostles from Greenwich Village, Harlem, and environs" who made claims for a special African American artistic vision distinct from that of white Americans. In a famous peroration, Hughes answered that he and his fellow artists intended to express their "individual dark-skinned selves without fear or shame. If white people are pleased we are glad... If colored people are pleased we are glad. If they are not, their displeasure doesn't matter either." There was considerable African American displeasure; and it was complex. Much of the condemnation of the license for expression that Hughes, Thurman, Hurston, and other artists arrogated to themselves was generational or puritanical, and usually both.

But much of the condemnation also stemmed from racial sensitivity, from sheer mortification at seeing uneducated, crude, and scrappy black men and women depicted without tinsel and soap. Thurman and associate editors John Davis, Aaron Douglas, Gwendolyn Bennett, Arthur Huff Fauset, Hughes, Hurston, and Richard Bruce Nugent took the Renaissance out of the parlor, the editorial office, and the banquet room. The focus shifted to Locke's

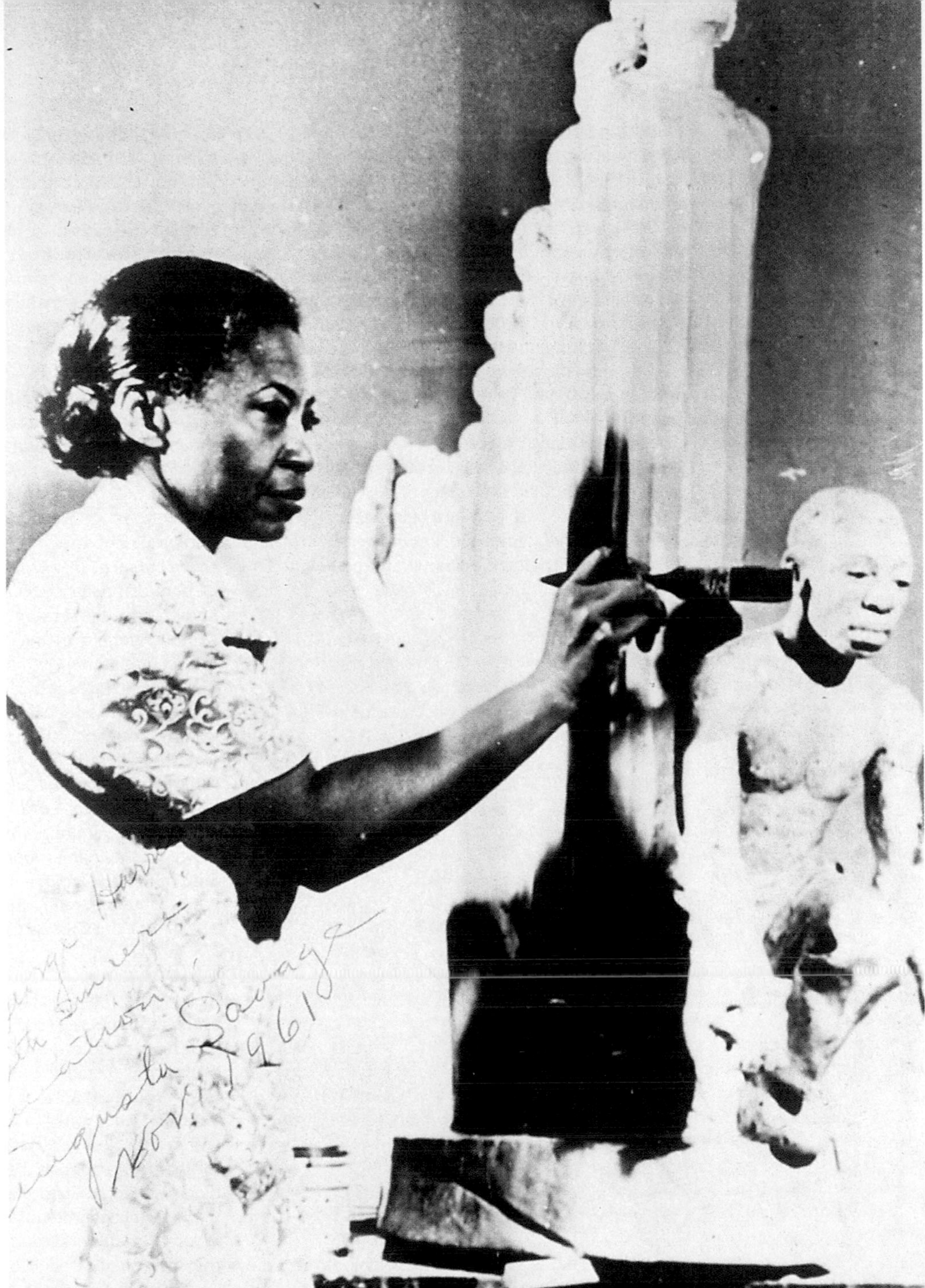

Sculptor Augusta Savage (1892-1962), who portrayed such African American leaders as W. E. B. Du Bois, Frederick Douglass, and Marcus Garvey, photographed by Morgan and Marvin P. Smith. She is working on a sculpture titled *Lift Every Voice and Sing* (1939).
Photographs and Prints Division, Schomburg Center for Research in Black Culture, The New York Public Library, Astor, Lenox and Tilden Foundation/Morgan and Marvin P. Smith

peasant matrix, "to the sorrows and joys of those outside the Talented Tenth. Let the blare of Negro jazz bands and the bellowing voice of Bessie Smith... penetrate the closed ears of the colored near-intellectuals," Hughes exhorted in "The Negro Artists and the Racial Mountain." Meanwhile, the deeper objections of the sophisticated to *Nigger Heaven* lay in its message that the Talented Tenth's preoccupation with cultural improvement was a misguided affectation that would cost the race its vitality. It was the "archaic Negroes" who were at ease in their skins and capable of action, Van Vechten's characters demonstrated.

The younger artists embraced Van Vechten's fiction as a worthy model because of its ribald iconoclasm and iteration that the future of African American arts and letters lay in the culture of the working poor and even of the underclass in bottom-up drama, fiction, music, poetry, and painting. Regularly convening at the notorious 267 House, the brownstone an indulgent landlady provided Thurman rent-free on 136th Street (alternately known as Niggerati Manor), the group that came to produce *Fire!!* saw art not as politics by other means – civil rights between covers or from a stage or an easel – but as an expression of the intrinsic conditions most men and women of African descent were experiencing. They spoke of the need "for a truly Negroid note," for empathy with "those elements within the race which are still too potent for easy assimilation," and they openly mocked the premise of the civil rights establishment that (as a Hughes character says in *The Ways of White Folks)* "art would break down color lines, art would save the race and prevent lynchings! Bunk!" Finally, like creative agents in society from time immemorial, they were impelled to insult their patrons and to defy conventions.

"The Criteria of Negro Art": A Symposium (1926)

To put the Renaissance back on track, Du Bois sponsored a symposium in late 1926, "The Criteria of Negro Art," inviting a spectrum of views about the appropriate course the arts should take. In a further effort to restore direction, his *Dark Princess* appeared in 1928 from Harcourt, Brace, a large, serious novel in which the "problem of the twentieth century" is taken in charge by a Talented Tenth International whose prime mover is a princess from India. But the momentum stayed firmly with the rebels.

Home to Harlem

Respectable black America was unable to ignore the novel that embodied the values of the Niggerati – the first Renaissance bestseller by a black author – McKay's *Home to Harlem,* released by Harper & Brothers in spring 1928. Its milieu is wholly plebeian. The protagonist, Jake, is a Lenox Avenue Noble Savage who demonstrates (in marked contrast to the book-reading Ray) the superiority of the Negro mind uncorrupted by European learning. *Home to Harlem* finally shattered the enforced literary code of the civil rights establishment. Du Bois confessed to feeling "distinctly like needing a bath" after reading McKay's novel about the "debauched tenth." Rudolph Fisher's *The Walls of Jericho,* appearing that year from Knopf, was a brilliant, deftly executed satire that upset Du Bois as much as it heartened Thurman. Fisher, a successful Harlem physician with solid Talented Tenth family credentials, satirized the NAACP, the Negrotarians, Harlem high society, and easily recognized Renaissance notables while entering convincingly into the world of the working classes, organized crime, and romance across classes.

Author of the line, "What happens to a dream deferred?," Langston Hughes was considered one of the defining authors of the Harlem Renaissance. Carl Van Vechten, a white photographer who chronicled many of the era's most notable African Americans, made this portrait in 1937. *Photographs and Prints Division, Schomburg Center for Research in Black Culture, The New York Public Library, Astor, Lenox and Tilden Foundation/Courtesty of the Van Vechten Trust*

Charles Johnson, preparing to leave the editorship of *Opportunity* for a professorship in sociology at Fisk University, observed that Renaissance artists were "now less self-conscious, less interested in proving that they are just like white people.... Relief from the stifling consciousness of being a problem has brought a certain superiority" to the Harlem Renaissance. McKay's and Fisher's fiction inspired the Niggerati to publish the magazine *Harlem* in November 1928. Editor Thurman announced portentously, "The time has now come when the Negro artist can be his true self and pander to the stupidities of no one, either white or black." *Harlem* won the collaboration of Locke and White, and lasted two issues. Roy de Coverly, George W. Little, and George S. Schuyler signed on, and Hughes contributed one of the finest short stories, based on his travels down the West Coast of Africa, "Luani of the Jungles," a polished genre piece on the seductions of the civilized and the primitives.

Quicksand

The other Renaissance novel that year from Knopf, Nella Larsen's *Quicksand,* achieved the distinction of being praised by Du Bois, Locke, and Hughes. Larsen would remain something of a mystery woman, helped in her career by Van Vechten and White but somehow always receding, and finally disappearing altogether from the Harlem scene, but *Quicksand* was a triumph of vivid yet economic writing and rich allegory. Its very modern heroine experiences misfortunes and ultimate destruction from causes that are both racial and individual. She is not a tragic mulatto but a mulatto who is tragic for reasons that are both sociological and existential. Helga Crane, Larsen's protagonist, was the Virginia Slim of Renaissance fiction. Angela Murray (Angela, in her white persona), the heroine of Fauset's second novel, was the Gibson Girl of Renaissance fiction.

The Blacker the Berry

Thurman's *The Blacker the Berry,* published by Macaulay in early 1929, was a breakthrough novel. For the first time in African American fiction, color prejudice within the race was the central theme of a novel. Emma Lou, its heroine (like the author very dark and conventionally unattractive), is obsessed with respectability as well as tortured by her pigment, for Thurman makes the point on every page that black America's aesthetic and spiritual center resides in the unaffected, unblended, noisome common folk and the liberated, unconventional artists. With the unprecedented Broadway success of *Harlem,* Thurman's sensationalized romp through the underside of Harlem, the triumph of Niggerati aesthetics over civil rights arts-and-letters was impressively confirmed. Another equally sharp smell of reality irritated establishment nostrils that same year when McKay's second novel, *Banjo,* was published, appearing only weeks after *The Blacker the Berry.* "The Negroes are writing against themselves," lamented the reviewer for the *Amsterdam News.* Set among the human flotsam and jetsam of Marseilles and West Africa, the message of McKay's novel was again that European civilization was inimical to Africans everywhere.

Twilight Years: The Great Depression

The stock market collapsed, but reverberations from the Harlem Renaissance seemed stronger than ever. Larsen's second novel, *Passing,* appeared. Its theme, like Fauset's, was the burden of mixed racial ancestry. Although *Passing* was less successful than *Quicksand,* Larsen's book again evaded the trap of writing another tragic-mulatto novel by opposing the richness of African American life to the material advantages afforded by the option of "passing." In February 1930 Marc Connelly's dramatization of Roark Bradford's book of short stories opened on Broadway as *The Green Pastures.* The Hall Johnson Choir sang in it, Richard Harrison played "De Lawd," and scores of Harlemites found parts during 557 performances at the Mansfield, and then on tour across the country. The demanding young critic and Howard University professor of English Sterling Brown pronounced the play a "miracle." After *The Green Pastures* came *Not Without Laughter,* Hughes's glowing novel from Knopf. Financed by Charlotte Osgood Mason (the often tyrannical bestower of artistic largesse nicknamed "Godmother") and Amy Spingarn, Hughes had resumed his college education at Lincoln University and completed *Not Without Laughter,* his senior year. The beleaguered family at the center of the novel represents black America in transition in white America. Hughes's young male protagonist learns that proving his equality means affirming his distinctive racial qualities. Not only Locke admired *Not Without Laughter,* the *New Masses* reviewer embraced it as "our novel." The Ministry of Culture decreed Hughes worthy of the Harmon Gold Medal for 1930. The year ended with Schuyler's ribald, sprawling satire *Black No More,* an unsparing demolition of every personality and institution in black America. Little wonder that Locke titled his retrospective piece in the February 1931 *Opportunity* "The Year of Grace."

Depression notwithstanding, the health of the Renaissance appeared to be more robust than ever. The first Rosenwald fellowships for African Americans had been secured largely due to James Weldon Johnson's influence the previous year. Since 1928, advised by Locke, the Harmon Foundation had mounted an annual traveling exhibition of drawings, paintings, and sculpture by African Americans (*see* ART, AFRICAN AMERICAN). The 1930 participants introduced the generally unsuspected talent and genius of Palmer Hayden, William H. Johnson, Archibald Motley Jr., James A. Porter, and Laura Wheeler Waring in painting. SARGENT JOHNSON, Elizabeth Prophet, and Augusta Savage were the outstanding sculptors of the show.

BLACK MANHATTAN (1930)

Superficially, Harlem itself appeared to be in fair health well into 1931. James Weldon Johnson's celebration of the community's strengths, *Black Manhattan,* was published near the end of 1930. "Harlem is still in the process of making," the book proclaimed, and the author's confidence in the power of the "recent literary and artistic emergence" to ameliorate race relations was unshaken. In Johnson's Harlem, redcaps and cooks cheered when Renaissance talents won Guggenheim and Rosenwald fellowships; they rushed to newsstands whenever the *American Mercury* or *New Republic* mentioned activities above Central Park. It was much too easy for Talented Tenth notables like Johnson, White, and Locke not to notice in the second year of the Great Depression that, for the great majority of the population, Harlem was in the process of unmaking.

The 1931 *Report on Negro Housing,* presented to President Hoover, was a document starkly in contrast to the optimism found in *Black Manhattan.* Nearly 50 percent of Harlem's families would be unemployed by the end of 1932. The syphilis rate was nine times higher than white Manhattan's; the tuberculosis rate was five times greater; pneumonia and typhoid were twice that of whites. Two African American mothers and two babies died for every white mother and child. Harlem General Hospital, the single public facility, served 200,000 African Americans with 273 beds. A Harlem family paid twice as much of its income for rent as a white family. Meanwhile, median family income in Harlem dropped 43.6 percent by 1932. The ending of Prohibition would devastate scores of marginal speakeasies and prove fatal to theaters like the Lafayette. In his letters to Charlotte Osgood, most of Locke's news was distinctly downbeat.

The writing partnership of two of his protégés, Hughes and Hurston, their material needs underwritten in a New Jersey township by "Godmother" Charlotte Mason, collapsed in acrimonious dispute. Marxism had a deep influence on Hughes in the aftermath of his painful breakup with Godmother, Locke, and Hurston. Beginning with "Advertisement for the Waldorf Astoria," published in the December 1931 *New Masses,* Hughes's poetry became markedly political. "Elderly Race Leaders" and "Goodbye Christ," as well as the play *Scottsboro, Limited,* were irreverent, staccato offerings to the coming triumph of the proletariat (*see* SCOTTSBORO CASE). The poet's departure in June 1932 for Moscow, along with 18 others, ostensibly to act in a Soviet film about American race relations, *Black and White,* symbolized the shift in patronage and accompanying politicization of Renaissance artists. An impatient Du Bois, already deeply alienated from the Renaissance, called for a second Amenia Conference to radicalize the movement's ideology and renew its personnel. James Weldon Johnson's autobiography, *Along This Way,* an elegantly written review of his sui generis public career as archetypal renaissance man in both meanings of the word, was the publishing event of the year. McKay's final novel also appeared that year. He worried familiar themes, but *Banana Bottom* represented a philosophical advance over *Home to Harlem* and *Banjo* in its reconciliation through the protagonist, Bita Plant, of the previously destructive tension in McKay between the natural and the artificial – soul and civilization.

The publication at the beginning of 1932 of Thurman's last novel, *Infants of the Spring,* had already announced the end of the Harlem Renaissance. The action of Thurman's novel is in the ideas of the characters, in their incessant talk about themselves, Booker T. Washington, Du Bois, racism, and the destiny of the race. Its ending is conceptually poignant. Paul Arbian (Richard Bruce Nugent) commits suicide in a full tub of water, which splashes over and obliterates the pages of Arbian's unfinished novel on the bathroom floor. A still legible page, however, contains this paragraph, which was, in effect, an epitaph: "He had drawn a distorted, inky black skyscraper, modeled after Niggerati Manor, and on which were focused on array of blindingly white beams of light. The foundation of this building was composed of crumbling stone. At first glance it could be ascertained that the skyscraper would soon crumple and fall, leaving the dominating white lights in full possession of the sky."

The literary energies of the Renaissance finally slumped. McKay returned to Harlem in February

1934 after a 12-year sojourn abroad, but his creative powers were spent. The last novel of the movement, Hurston's beautifully written *Jonah's Gourd Vine*, went on sale in May 1934. Charles Johnson, James Weldon Johnson, and Locke applauded Hurston's allegorical story of her immediate family (especially her father) and the mores of an African American town in Florida called Eatonville. Thurman died a few days before Christmas, 1934, soon after his return from an abortive Hollywood film project. Ignoring his physician's strictures, he hemorrhaged after drinking to excess while hosting a party in the infamous house at 267 West 136th Street. Four days later, Fisher expired from intestinal cancer by repeated exposure to his own x-ray equipment.

Locke's *New Negro* anthology had been crucial to the formation of the Renaissance. As the movement ran down, another anthology, English heiress Nancy Cunard's *Negro*, far more massive in scope, recharged the Renaissance for a brief period, enlisting the contributions of most of the principals (though McKay and Walrond refused, and Toomer no longer acknowledged his African American roots), and captured its essence in the manner of expert taxidermy. A grieving Locke wrote Charlotte Mason from Howard University, "It is hard to see the collapse of things you have labored to raise on a sound base."

Arthur Fauset, Jessie's perceptive brother, attempted to explain the collapse to Locke and the readers of *Opportunity* at the beginning of 1934. He foresaw "a socio-political-economic setback from which it may take decades to recover." The Renaissance had left the race unprepared, Fauset charged, because of its unrealistic belief "that social and economic recognition will be inevitable when once the race has produced a sufficiently large number of persons who have properly qualified themselves in the arts." Du Bois had not only turned his back on the movement, he had left the NAACP and Harlem for a university professorship in Atlanta after an enormous row over civil rights policy.

As the 1933 essay "Marxism and the Negro Problem" had made abundantly clear, Du Bois ruled out collaboration with American Marxists because they were much too racist. James Weldon Johnson's philosophical *tour d'horizon* appearing in 1934, *Negro Americans, What's Now?*, asked precisely the question of the decade. Most Harlemites were certain that the riot exploding on the evening of March 19, 1935, taking three lives and costing $2 million in property damage, was not an answer. By then, the Works Progress Administration (WPA) had become the major patron of African American artists and writers. Writers William Attaway, Ralph Ellison, Margaret Walker, Richard Wright, and Frank Yerby would emerge under its aegis, as would painters Romare Bearden, Jacob Lawrence, Charles Sebree, Lois Mailou Jones, and Charles White. The Communist Party was another patron, notably for Richard Wright, whose 1937 essay "Blueprint for Negro Writing" would materially contribute to the premise of Hughes's "The Negro Artist and the Racial Mountain." For thousands of ordinary Harlemites who had looked to Garvey's UNIA for inspiration, then to the Renaissance, there was now Father Divine and his "heavens."

In the ensuing years much was renounced, more was lost or forgotten, yet the Renaissance, however artificial and overreaching, left a positive mark. Locke's *New Negro* anthology featured 30 of the movement's 35 stars. They and a small number of less gifted collaborators generated 26 novels, 10 volumes of poetry, 5 Broadway plays, countless essays and short stories, 3 performed ballets and concerti, and a considerable output of canvas and sculpture. If the achievement was less than the titanic expectations of the Ministry of Culture, it was an arts-and-letters legacy, nevertheless, of which a beleaguered and belittled black America could be proud, and by which it could be sustained. If more by osmosis than conscious attention, mainstream America was also richer for the color, emotion, humanity, and cautionary vision produced by Harlem during its Golden Age.

"If I had supposed that all Negroes were illiterate brutes, I might be astonished to discover that they can write good third rate poetry, readable and unreadable magazine fiction," wrote one contemporary white Marxist. Nevertheless there were many white Americans – perhaps the majority – who found the African American artistic and literary ferment of the period wholly unexpected and little short of incredible. If the judgment of the Marxist observer soon became a commonplace, it was because the Harlem Renaissance demonstrated – finally, irrefutably, during slightly more than a decade – the considerable creative capacities of the best and brightest of a disadvantaged racial minority.

See Also

Slavery in the United States; World War I and African Americans; African Methodist Episcopal Zion Church; Amenia Conference of 1933; Atlanta, Georgia; Black Swan Records; Black Towns; Blake, James Hubert ("Eubie"); Blues, The; Brown, Sterling Allen; Calloway, Cabell (Cab); Chesnutt, Charles Waddell; Chicago, Illinois; *Crisis, The*; Du Bois, William Edward Burghardt (W. E. B.); Fauset, Jessie Redmon; Frazier, Edward Franklin; Garvey, Marcus Mosiah; Gilpin, Charles Sidney; Great Depression; Great Migration, The; Harlem Riots of 1935; Harlem, New York; Hayes, Roland Willsie; Henderson, Fletcher Hamilton, Jr.; Johnson, Charles Spurgeon; Johnson, William Henry; Joplin, Scott; Labor Unions in the United States; Lawrence, Jacob Armstead; Lincoln University (Pennsylvania); Locke, Alain Leroy; Mills, Florence; Morton, Ferdinand Joseph ("Jelly Roll"); Numbers Games; Oliver, Joseph ("King"); *Opportunity: Journal of Negro Life*; Porter, James Amos; Powell, Adam Clayton, Sr.; Prophet, Nancy Elizabeth; Robinson, Bill ("Bojangles"); Savage, Augusta Christine Fells; Socialism; Tanner, Henry Ossawa; Walker, Sarah ("Madam C.J."); Waller, Thomas Wright ("Fats"); Walrond, Eric Derwent; Washington, Booker Taliaferro; Woodruff, Hale Aspacio; Wright, Louis Tompkins; Ellington, Edward Kennedy ("Duke"); Jamaica; Trinidad and Tobago; Communist Party USA, African Americans and the; Film, Blacks in American; Black Church, The; West Indies; Passing in the United States.

North America

Harlem Renaissance Big Five,

one of the most successful all-black professional basketball teams in the 1920s and 1930s, the "Harlem Rens" added grace and style to the game of American basketball.

The Harlem Renaissance Big 5 was created in 1922 by Robert L. Douglass, a native of the Caribbean island of St. Kitts and a former professional BASKETBALL player with the New York Spartans. The team gained its name from its playing venue – the Renaissance Casino ballroom in Harlem, New York – where they dazzled fans with their innovative style of play. The Rens, as they were called, were one of the few all-black traveling professional basketball teams of that era. Formed five years before one of America's most famous all-black professional basketball teams, the HARLEM GLOBETROTTERS, the Rens provided African American men with the opportunity to compete against white athletes on an equal footing.

They toured the country competing against black and white teams, and in the process compiled one of the most impressive winning streaks in history. In 1934 the Rens won 88 consecutive games, and between 1932 and 1936 they won 473 games and lost only 49. Three years later they won the first World Basketball Tournament, held in Chicago, Illinois. In 1963 the entire team was inducted into the Professional Basketball Hall of Fame, including Charles T. "Tarzan" Cooper, John "Casey" Holt, Clarence "Fats" Jenkins, James "Pappy" Ricks, Eyre "Bruiser" Satch, William "Wee Willie" Smith, and William J. "Bill" Yancey.

SEE ALSO

Harlem, New York; St. Kitts and Nevis.

North America

Harlem Riots of 1935,

a New York City uprising caused by a combination of the disastrous economic effects of the GREAT DEPRESSION and job discrimination and police brutality.

On March 19, 1935, a white Harlem store owner accused a dark-skinned Latino boy, Lino Rivera, of shoplifting a knife. After a scuffle, in which ten-year-old Rivera struck a store clerk, the police arrested him. Rumors about the arrest and the police's treatment of the boy in custody spread throughout Harlem. Some people believed that the police had beaten or killed Rivera. Incited by streetcorner speakers, people began to riot, first attacking the store where Rivera had been arrested. They caused an estimated $2 million worth of damage, mostly to white-owned property. By the riot's end, 3 black people were dead and more than 200 wounded.

The riot may have been set off by Rivera's arrest, but Harlem's African American residents were already tense with frustration about their dire social and economic conditions and their treatment at the hands of whites. The GREAT DEPRESSION was unusually hard on Harlem, particularly because white store owners, most of whose businesses were frequented by African Americans, refused to hire African Americans as clerks. In 1933 African Americans had picketed and boycotted such stores, but in 1935 the store owners obtained an injunction against the picketing. Many Harlemites insisted that the police enforced the injunction with brutality.

After the riot, New York mayor Fiorello La Guardia established the Mayor's Commission on Conditions in Harlem, a biracial commission headed by the African American sociologist E. Franklin Frazier to investigate and propose solutions. The commission's report, "The Negro in Harlem: A Report on Social and Economic Conditions Responsible for the Outbreak of March 19, 1935," recommended antidiscrimination measures to be taken in city housing, relief agencies, the police department, and the hiring practices for municipal jobs. La Guardia appointed Alain Locke to implement the program and attempted to expand government services to Harlem, including public housing, facilities at Harlem Hospital, and special training for police. Conditions, however, remained tense throughout the decade and well into the 1940s.

Robert Fay

SEE ALSO

Frazier, Edward Franklin; Harlem, New York; Locke, Alain Leroy.

North America

Harlem Riots of 1943,

one of the first modern urban disturbances in which African Americans reacted violently to police brutality.

Marjorie Polite, an African American woman, was arrested on August 1, 1943, for causing a disturbance at the Braddock Hotel in Harlem, a predominantly black section of New York. Robert Bandy, a black soldier in uniform, demanded that the police release Polite. Reports about what happened next differ, but witnesses said that Bandy either grabbed the arresting officer's nightstick or struck the police officer and ran. In any event, police shot and wounded the fleeing Bandy. A rumor soon circulated that the police had killed an African American soldier trying to protect his mother.

A crowd of approximately 3000 African Americans, already frustrated by frequent police brutality, as well as housing and job discrimination, surrounded the Braddock, Sydenham Hospital, and the 28th police precinct, threatening the arresting officers.

Police lead away a bloodied African American man during the riots of 1943 in Harlem. At least 500 black people were arrested, 185 were injured, and 6 were killed. *CORBIS/Bettmann-UPI*

At approximately 10:30 PM, the crowd began breaking windows and setting fires. Despite efforts by Mayor Fiorello La Guardia and prominent African Americans to convince the rioters to stop, the violence continued until dawn. Six African Americans were killed, 185 injured, and 500 arrested.

City officials and African American leaders attempted to minimize the racial aspects of the riot, but La Guardia convened the Emergency Conference for Interracial Unity, which was charged with suggesting ways to reduce racial tensions in New York. He also ordered the establishment of the Office of Price Administration in Harlem to investigate alleged price gouging, and reopened the SAVOY BALLROOM, a popular nightclub that city officials had closed – many African Americans believed – unfairly. La Guardia's evenhanded response to the initial violence and his prompt institution of reforms garnered him further esteem from a Harlem population that already supported him.

Robert Fay

SEE ALSO

Harlem, New York; New York, New York.

North America

Harlem Riot of 1964,

an urban rebellion resulting from African American protest of police brutality.

At 10:30 pm on July 18, 1964, demonstrators rioted in Harlem to protest the fatal shooting of a 15-year-old African American, James Powell, by a white police officer. The protest, sponsored by the CONGRESS OF RACIAL EQUALITY (CORE), began peacefully, but later protesters began hurling missiles and Molotov cocktails at police and roaming the streets with bottles and bricks. The rioting in Harlem continued for four nights before spreading to Brooklyn's Bedford-Stuyvesant neighborhood. In all, one person was killed, more than 100 people were injured, and hundreds were arrested. Although smaller than the uprisings in urban African American communities later in the decade (Watts, Detroit), the Harlem Riot anticipated these uprisings.

Robert Fay

SEE ALSO
Harlem, New York.

North America

Harlem Writers Guild, influential African American writers' group based in Harlem, New York City.

Poet and essayist MAYA ANGELOU, mystery writer WALTER MOSLEY, and *Waiting to Exhale* author TERRY MCMILLAN are only three of the dozens of writers who have been part of the Harlem Writers Guild over the last five decades. Its first members, Rosa Guy, John O. Killens, Walter Christmas, and JOHN HENRIK CLARKE, began meeting in a Harlem storefront in the late 1940s to critique one another's stories. At that time, the mainstream American literary world had just started to take notice of black authors. Richard Wright's novel *Native Son* had been a bestseller a few years earlier, and many young African American writers who wanted to follow his lead created their own forums to discuss their work. The Harlem Writers Guild became one of these forums, and the membership soon outgrew the first storefront.

The Guild's members also shared a commitment to social change, and many of them were interested in incorporating political ideas into their art. The first novel published by a Guild member, Killens's *Youngblood* (1954), depicted four characters fighting for dignity in the segregated American South. Other novelists, like PAULE MARSHALL, wrote about the black experience in the West Indies and other parts of the African diaspora. Guild writers also identified with other political organizations and causes that were not focused only on race – for example, Christmas and Clarke both wrote for Communist periodicals, and other members were union organizers and Progressive Party supporters.

The Guild's focus on the connection between political action and art was an example of the philosophy that became the basis for the BLACK ARTS MOVEMENT. The Black Arts Movement, which is usually identified with the 1960s, emphasized the importance of social engagement for AFRICAN AMERICAN LITERATURE. These were the same kinds of ideas that the Harlem Writers Guild had already been exploring for over a decade, and the Guild soon became identified with the larger movement.

In 1965 the Guild and the New School for Social Research in New York City cosponsored a conference called "The Negro Writer's Vision of America," which more than a thousand people attended. The conference's widely publicized highlight was a debate between Guild founders Killens and Clarke and white scholar Herbert Aptheker and artist Walter Lowenfels on what role, if any, artists should play in the fight against racism. This was the exact question that Guild members and writers like them were trying to answer in their own careers, and they believed that artists did have a responsibility to include social issues in their work. Members during the 1960s included Maya Angelou, whose first published book, the autobiography *I Know Why the Caged Bird Sings,* became a bestseller in 1970; novelist CHESTER HIMES, known for his detective fiction set in Harlem; and Walter Dean Myers, an award-winning writer for children and young adults.

The Black Arts Movement declined in the 1970s, but the Guild continued as a forum for yet another generation of writers. Since 1988 Guild workshops have met at the Schomburg Center for Research in Black Culture of the New York Public Library. In 1991 Guild director William H. Banks Jr. began hosting "In Our Own Words," a weekly show featuring Guild members, for New York television station WNYE. The show was carried in six viewing areas in the United States and Canada, and this gave the Guild's latest writers a new forum. Former members Terry McMillan and Walter Mosley both became best-selling authors in the 1980s and 1990s, and in 1993 Maya Angelou was asked to compose and read a poem, *On the Pulse of Morning,* for the inauguration of United States President Bill Clinton.

Lisa Clayton Robinson

SEE ALSO
Guy, Rosa Cuthbert; Harlem, New York; Killens, John Oliver; Labor Unions in the United States; New York, New York; Wright, Richard; Schomburg Library; Communist Party USA, African Americans and the.

North America

Harper, Frances Ellen Watkins (b. September 24, 1825, Baltimore, Md.; d. February 20, 1911, Philadelphia, Pa.), African American writer and antislavery, women's rights, and temperance activist.

At her death in 1911, one memorial tribute said that Frances Ellen Watkins Harper "had acquired the title of 'Empress of Peace and Poet Laureate.'" As a lecturer, activist, poet, and novelist, Harper dedicated her life to promoting social uplift – of women, of African Americans, and of African American women in particular – in as many forums as she could find. In the process, she became one of the best-known and most respected black women of the nineteenth century.

Harper was born into a free black family in Baltimore. She was orphaned at the age of two and then raised by her uncle, Rev. William Watkins, director of Baltimore's prestigious Academy for Negro Youth. Harper herself attended the school, where she studied Greek, Latin, and the Bible. As a result, she was better educated than most other American women of her day, black or white. She began writing poetry as a teenager and started her career as a writer in 1845, when she reportedly published the poetry collection *Forest Leaves.* Her second career, as an activist, began almost a decade later.

This engraved portrait from *The Underground Railroad* (1872) by William Still shows poet and antislavery activist Frances Ellen Watkins Harper. *CORBIS*

Harper taught school for several years at Union Seminary in Ohio, and later in Pennsylvania. But in 1853, when her home state of Maryland passed a new law prohibiting free blacks from entering its borders, Harper was moved to action. In 1854 she moved to Philadelphia and became active in the antislavery movement. There Harper lived with WILLIAM STILL and his family, whose home was part of the UNDERGROUND RAILROAD. Within a few months, Harper became one of the few African American women to go on the antislavery lecture circuit. She proved to be such a popular speaker that over the next six years the Maine and Pennsylvania Anti-Slavery Societies sent her throughout New England, Ohio, and New York, and as far away as Detroit and Canada.

Audiences were often surprised by the petite black woman, nicknamed the "Bronze Muse," whom they encountered. Some complimented the fact that her speeches were "fiery" yet still "marked by dignity and composure" and "without the slightest violation of good taste." Others – unwilling to believe that a black woman could carry herself with intelligence and grace – accused her of being either a black man dressed as a woman or a white woman painted black. But her composure and bearing were precisely what made her a powerful symbol of black womanhood for much of the nineteenth century.

Harper often quoted original poetry in her lectures, and consequently her reputation as a poet spread as far as her speaking tours. Her second volume of poetry, *Poems on Miscellaneous Subjects* (1854), sold 10,000 copies between 1854 and 1857, and was then enlarged and reprinted. She published several more volumes of poetry and reprinted new editions of her poems many times. In the process, she became the most famous black poet of her time.

In 1860 she married Fenton Harper, a widower with three children. Their daughter, Mary, was born soon after, and Harper reduced her traveling for four years, during which she stayed at their Ohio farm. But her husband died in 1864, and she soon resumed her public schedule. The Emancipation Proclamation had ended slavery in 1863, but Harper still wanted to speak out on other social issues she found important. During the next few decades, she began to focus on racial uplift, moral reform, temperance, and women's rights.

Many of Harper's lectures were to women's clubs and associations, and some of her most popular speeches were on the rights and roles of women in general, and black women in particular. She worked in the American Equal Rights Association with white activists Elizabeth Cady Stanton and Susan B. Anthony. But when they began to criticize the Fifteenth Amendment, which gave black men the vote, because they felt that white women should have received it first, Harper's loyalty was to her race over her gender.

Harper continued speaking out in favor of women's rights, however, and was a member of the American Woman Suffrage Association and the National Council of Women. She also spoke at the International Council of Women in Washington, D.C., in 1888, and gave a lecture titled "Women's Political Future" at the Columbian Exposition in Chicago. But she remained committed to arguing for the particular needs of African American women. In 1893 Harper, Fannie Barrier Williams, Anna Julia Cooper, Fannie Jackson Coppin, Sarah J. Early, and Hallie Q. Brown together charged the World's Congress of Representative Women with overlooking black women. Harper belonged to the NATIONAL FEDERATION OF AFRO-AMERICAN WOMEN and helped found the NATIONAL ASSOCIATION OF COLORED WOMEN.

Harper was also active in the temperance movement. She lectured widely on the evils of alcohol, directed the Northern United States Temperance Union, and became the first black woman to be recognized on the Red Letter Calendar of the World Woman's Christian Temperance Union, which honored prominent temperance activists. Here again, Harper tailored her activism to reach the African American community. She directed the Colored Branches of the Philadelphia and Pennsylvania Woman's Christian Temperance Union, and in 1883 became national superintendent of temperance work among African Americans.

Throughout all of her political activism, Harper continued to write, and in the twentieth century she is best remembered as one of the earliest black women writers. Her story "The Two Offers" (1859) is considered the first published short story by an African American woman. In addition to short stories and poetry, Harper wrote three short novels that were serialized by church presses, and in all of these works, as one scholar points out, the major themes "are those that [Harper herself] expounded throughout her career: personal integrity, Christian service, and social equality."

These themes are all also present in Harper's best-known work, the 1892 novel *Iola Leroy,* which tells the story of a light-skinned African American woman who is raised believing she is white. She learns the truth under dramatically tragic circumstances but accepts and eventually welcomes the news, and devotes the rest of her life to racial uplift, working to improve the status of African Americans.

Iola Leroy has been criticized for its melodrama and its stereotypical portrayal of the Tragic Mulatto, but the novel can also be read as a blueprint for the intelligent, independent black woman activist that Harper encouraged others to become – and that she herself was. Contemporary reviewers called *Iola Leroy* the crowning effort of Harper's life. *Iola Leroy* was published when Harper was nearly 70, and she continued writing until a few years before her death in 1911.

Even during her lifetime, Harper was commemorated through F. E. W. Harper Leagues, Frances E. Harper Woman's Christian Temperance Unions, and chapters of other organizations that bore her name. Harper was also recognized by the Daughters of America and Patriots of the American Revolution. But her title as a Woman of Our Race Most Worthy of Imitation may have come closest to recognizing her signature achievement. Harper provided a model for the best of what any nineteenth-century woman could be – and as a black woman, who made a point of writing about and speaking to other black women, she set the standard for a generation of African American women's activism.

Lisa Clayton Robinson

SEE ALSO

Abolitionism in the United States; Literature, African American; American Anti-Slavery Society; Baltimore, Maryland; Brown, Hallie Quinn; Cooper, Anna Julia Hayward; Coppin, Frances (Fanny) Jackson; Fifteenth Amendment to the United States Constitution; Free Blacks in the United States, 1619 to 1863; Philadelphia, Pennsylvania; Thirteenth Amendment of the United States Constitution and the Emancipation Proclamation.

North America

Harper, Michael Steven

(b. March 18, 1938, Brooklyn, N.Y.), contemporary African American poet.

"Brother John," the first poem in Michael S. Harper's book *Dear John, Dear Coltrane* begins with the lines:

Black man:
I'm a black man;
I'm black; I am –
A black man; black –

Like much of Harper's poetry, "Brother John" takes its poetic form from African American music – especially JAZZ and the blues. "Brother John" also reflects Harper's trademark of writing about individuals who have influenced him, whether they be musicians, writers, or family. Finally, it reflects his interest in African American identity. Harper finds both sides of that identity equally important and has stated often that he is "both a black poet and an American poet."

Harper was born in Brooklyn and grew up in a predominantly white area of Los Angeles, where his teachers suggested that he was best suited for vocational education. Ignoring their recommendations, he went on to receive degrees from Los Angeles State College (now California State University at Los Angeles) and the University of Iowa, where he attended the prestigious Iowa Writers' Workshop. Harper published his poetry in several journals before *Dear John, Dear Coltrane,* his first book, was published in 1970. The book was nominated for the National Book Award and immediately established Harper as a nationally known writer.

Since then, Harper has published at least nine other volumes of poetry. Other volumes that received critical acclaim include *Song: I Want a Witness* (1972), *Nightmare Begins Responsibility* (1975), and *Images of Kin.* He has also received the National Institute of Arts and Letters Creative Writing Award, a Guggenheim Fellowship, and a National Endowment for the Arts grant. Since 1970 Harper has been a professor of literature and creative writing at Brown University.

Lisa Clayton Robinson

SEE ALSO

Blues, The; Los Angeles, California.

North America

Harrington, Oliver Wendell (Ollie) (b. February 14, 1912, Valhalla, N.Y.; d. November 7, 1995, Berlin, Germany), African American cartoonist and expatriate best known for creating the character Bootsie.

Known to friends as Ollie, Oliver Harrington was the eldest of five children born to Herbert Harrington and Eugenia Tarat. He graduated from high school in 1929 and moved to New York City during the HARLEM RENAISSANCE.

Harrington attended the National Academy of Design, where he studied painting and drawing. By 1932 his comic strips were being featured in black newspapers, including the *Pittsburgh Courier, New York Amsterdam News*, and *Baltimore Afro-American.* Bootsie, a cartoon character who mimicked the styles and trends in the urban black community, and who would become Harrington's most famous creation, first appeared in a comic strip called "Dark Laughter." In 1958 a collection of Bootsie comic strips was published as *Bootsie and Others.*

In 1940 Harrington received his bachelor's degree in fine arts from the Yale University School of Fine Arts. Two years later he became art director for the *People's Voice*, a weekly published by Adam Clayton Powell Jr. In 1943 he designed another comic strip, this one chronicling the adventurous life of a fictitious African American aviator named Jive Gray.

In 1944 Harrington traveled to ITALY and FRANCE as a war correspondent. After the war he took jobs as a journalist and book illustrator, and in 1946 created the public relations department for the NATIONAL ASSOCIATION FOR THE ADVANCEMENT OF COLORED PEOPLE (NAACP). In 1951 he moved to Paris, where he met RICHARD WRIGHT, another African American expatriate. After Wright's death in 1962, Harrington accepted a job illustrating classic novels and moved to East Berlin, where he met his wife, Helma Richter. He resided there for 13 years until his death.

Alonford James Robinson, Jr.

SEE ALSO
New York, New York; *Pittsburgh Courier*; Powell, Adam Clayton, Jr.

North America

Harris, Barbara Clementine (b. June 12, 1930, Philadelphia, Pa.), African American suffragan bishop of the Episcopal Diocese of Massachusetts, the first woman to be elected a bishop in the Episcopal Church and the worldwide Anglican communion or any church holding to apostolic succession.

On September 24, 1988, the Episcopal Diocese of Massachusetts elected Barbara Clementine Harris a suffragan (assistant) bishop to senior prelate David E. Johnson. Her election was a momentous and controversial event in the Episcopal Church. It departed from the traditional conception of apostolic succession – practiced by the Roman Catholic Church for nearly 2000 years as well as by the Anglican and Orthodox churches – in which bishops, because they are understood to be successors to Christ's original twelve disciples, must be male.

Yet Harris's groundbreaking role in the church went well beyond gender. An African American in a predominantly white church, she openly criticized church practices she believed to be contrary to social and economic justice. She was a bold advocate for the rights of women (including the right to choose abortion), gay men and lesbians, people of color, and other marginalized groups. She also had 15 years' experience ministering to prisoners, a nontraditional alternative to serving as a parish rector. As author Pamela Darling affirmed, "The idea of this diminutive, elegant, gravel-voiced, sharp-tongued, funny, iconoclastic, professional radical joining the Anglican gentleman's society that was the House of Bishops stretched everyone's imagination."

One of three children born to Beatrice (Price) Harris, a church organist, and Walter Harris, a steelworker, Harris grew up in PHILADELPHIA, PENNSYLVANIA, where her family attended St. Barnabas Church, an Episcopal parish. As a teenager she organized the church's Young Adults Group, the largest of its kind in the city. After high school she studied at Philadelphia's Charles Morris Price School of Advertising and Journalism, and in 1958 became president of Joseph V. Baker Associates, a black-owned public relations firm. She was also active in the CIVIL RIGHTS MOVEMENT, participating in voter rights campaigns and the historic Freedom March from Selma to Montgomery in 1965.

In 1968 Harris joined the Church of the Advocate, a mostly black Episcopal parish known for its civil rights activism. In 1974 she led the church's procession of the famed Philadelphia Eleven: the first American female deacons to be ordained Episcopal priests in defiance of church law. Although the Episcopal Church initially refused to recognize them, dissenting bishops ordained several other women and in 1976 the church officially permitted – but did not mandate – the ordination of women as priests and bishops.

Impelled by the new policy, Harris decided to follow her dream of becoming a priest. In lieu of a seminary degree, she devised her own program of theological studies, including coursework at Philadelphia's Metropolitan Collegiate Center (1976) and Villanova University (1977-1979). She read for holy orders under the supervision of her home diocese. She also gained pastoral experience by conducting religious services and counseling prisoners incarcerated in the Philadelphia County prison system. In 1980 she left her executive job at Philadelphia's Sun Oil Company (a position she had held since 1968) and was ordained a priest. In addition to her parish duties, in 1984 she became executive director of the Episcopal Church Publishing Company and began writing a politically charged column in the ecumenical journal *Witness.*

In September 1988 Harris was elected the first female Episcopal bishop, a move that incited fiery polemics among Episcopal Church traditionalists. In a bitter campaign to block her consecration, they faulted her educational and pastoral credentials as well as her political views, and tried to discredit her character and personal history. As a final countermeasure, a group of six bishops issued a signed statement declaring their refusal to acknowledge Harris as a bishop or "accept any episcopal actions performed by her."

But the Archbishop of Canterbury, Robert Runcie, soon issued a more positive statement. While he affirmed that the Anglican Church – and by association the Episcopal Church – "does not canonically accept the ministry of either women priests or bishops," he acknowledged that the barrier was a matter of ecclesiastical law and not doctrine. Runcie's statement paved the way for change, and in February 1989, to the jubilant acclaim of nearly 8000 onlookers in Boston's Hynes Auditorium, Harris was consecrated a bishop.

Many American women saw Harris's appointment as a major breakthrough. "Thanks in part to her ordination," said journalist Gustav Niebuhr, "laywomen and clergywomen started aiming higher." Since 1993 several women have joined Harris in the Episcopal House of Bishops, a leadership trend paralleled in other major Protestant denominations.

Roanne Edwards

North America

Harris, Patricia Roberts (b. May 31, 1924, Mattoon, Ill.; d. March 23, 1985, Washington, D.C.), first black American woman to serve as an ambassador, a cabinet secretary, and a law school dean.

Patricia Roberts Harris was born and raised in a working-class suburb of Chicago. She accepted a scholarship from HOWARD UNIVERSITY in Washington, D.C., where in 1943 she participated in one of the country's first student SIT-INS, at a whites-only cafeteria in a black neighborhood. She later attended law school at Washington's George Washington University, from which she graduated first in her class. In 1961 she joined the faculty of Howard Law School.

A lifelong Democrat, Harris served on several federal commissions concerned with minority rights. In 1965, largely on the strength of this work, President Johnson appointed her U.S. ambassador to Luxembourg. After a brief and noncontroversial posting, she returned to Howard in 1967 and in 1969 was named dean of the law school. Immediately after her appointment, students protested for greater power in university decisions. Harris took a strong stand against them and, when she felt she was not supported by the school's president, resigned. She had served as dean for one month. For the next eight years she practiced law in a Washington firm and continued her national party activities.

In 1977 President Jimmy Carter nominated Harris secretary of the Department of Housing and Urban Development (HUD). Her confirmation hearings were contentious, mostly because liberals feared her close connection to "the establishment" would make her unsympathetic to HUD's poor constituency. In a well-publicized reply to such fears, Harris told the Senate, "You do not seem to understand who I am. I'm a black woman, the daughter of a dining car waiter.... I am a black woman who could not buy a house eight years ago in parts of the District of Columbia." She was confirmed, the first black woman to direct a federal department. During her tenure, she secured greater funding for HUD, which she used to increase dramatically the number of new subsidized homes and to rehabilitate rather than destroy old homes. She also promoted grants to attract businesses to blighted areas and vouchers to give poor people greater choice in housing.

In 1979 Carter appointed Harris secretary of the Department of Health, Education, and Welfare (HEW), later the Department of Health and Human Services (HHS). At HEW her main task was protecting social programs from the budget cuts of the late 1970s. Her tenure was cut short by the election of Ronald Reagan in 1980.

In 1982 Harris ran for mayor of Washington against incumbent Marion Barry. In a bitter campaign, Barry depicted her as the elitist candidate of the middle and upper classes who had lost touch with Washington's large population of poor blacks. Harris was soundly defeated in the primary. For the next two years she taught law at George Washington University. She died of breast cancer a few months after the death of her husband.

See Also
Barry, Marion Shepilov, Jr.; Chicago, Illinois.

Latin America and the Caribbean

Harris, Theodore Wilson

(b. March 24, 1921, New Amsterdam, Guyana), one of the most recognized Afro-Caribbean novelists, poets, literary critics, and historians, of whom the Jamaican novelist John Hearne said, "No other British Caribbean novelist has made quite such an explicit and conscious effort... to reduce the material reckonings of everyday life to the significance of myth."

Wilson Harris is the author of more than 25 books of fiction, poetry, and literary criticism. His best-known works include the novels of *The Guyana Quartet* (1960-1963); *The Four Banks of the River of Space* (1990); the book of poems *Eternity to Season* (1954, 1978 second edition); and the collection of essays *The Radical Imagination* (1992). He published his first volume of poetry, *Fetish*, while serving as a government land surveyor in Guyana in 1951. *Palace of the Peacock*, the first novel of *The Guyana Quartet*, appeared in 1960 and makes use of the Guyanan landscape he came to know so well during his government appointment. During the 1970s and 1980s he visited various universities in the United States as guest lecturer or writer-in-residence.

In his fiction, poetry, and criticism, Wilson constantly evokes the landscape of his native country and its colonial past, with its multiple histories of exploration and exploitation, of discovery and extermination, and of a world traversed as much by the memory of the New World as by the trauma experienced by the colonized Amerindians, African slaves, and indentured laborers from Asia (*see* Colonial Latin America and the Caribbean, Slavery in Latin America and the Caribbean, and East Indian Communities in the Caribbean). As the literary critic Jean-Pierre Durix wrote, Wilson considers his mixed ancestry (Amerindian, African, and European) "as symbolic of a possible synthesis to overcome polarization."

Viewed in such a light, Wilson's notoriously difficult fiction stems from his determination to craft a new language and a narrative that attempts to retrieve Caribbean realities from the tyranny of the "status of victor and victim." He seeks to challenge the underlying linear and "straightforward" structure of all colonial narratives. Instead, using the stylistic devices of doubling and repetition, he transforms the static colonial hierarchies into more fluid structures and fragments that do not combine in any simple manner. He also appropriates the conventions of European modernism by imagining the fragments out of which the syncretic cultures of the Caribbean that have emerged since the arrival of the Europeans took their unique shape. By incorporating aspects of the African, Amerindian, and Asian historical experience, including that of the Middle Passage, Wilson reexcavates those subterranean forms of consciousness and artistic expression (such as the limbo) that had been occluded by the colonial experience but were nonetheless the source of unlimited vitality and regeneration. In *Quartets*, written on the eve of decolonization, Wilson uses Guyana's coastland and its hinterland to develop a new allegory that identifies and dramatizes the often violent effects of the nation's transition into modernity.

Aninydo Roy

See Also
Middle Passage, The; Literature, English Language, Caribbean; Jamaica.

Africa

Hartebeest, common name for a species of African antelope.

The hartebeest is characterized by a long, narrow head, shoulders higher than the hindquarters, and a cowlike tail. The curved, ringed horns, which are present in both sexes, do not grow directly out of the sides of the head but arise from a short central horn. Adults are 110 to 150 cm (3 ft 7 in to 4 ft 11 in) high at the shoulder and are brownish gray, with black markings on the face and a white or yellow patch on the rump. Hartebeests are keen-sighted, fleet-footed animals that can outdistance the fastest horses. They feed on grass and inhabit open plains or dry desert regions, being capable of going without water for several weeks at a time. **Scientific classification:** The hartebeest belongs to the family Bovidae. It is classified as *Alcelaphus buselaphus*.

North America

Hastie, William Henry

(b. November 17, 1904; d. April 14, 1976, Philadelphia, Pa.), African American lawyer and judge who was considered one of the best legal minds in twentieth century jurisprudence.

Both William Henry Hastie's father, a pension clerk, and mother, a teacher, taught him to oppose racial discrimination. The family moved to Washington, D.C., in 1916, where Hastie was valedictorian at Dunbar High School, one of the leading African American secondary schools in the country. He was senior class president at Amherst College in 1925, graduated as valedictorian again. After teaching for two years, he returned to school, earning a law degree from Harvard University in 1930.

Hastie practiced law in Washington with his father, fighting university segregation. At night he taught at Howard University Law School. Among his students, many of whom played important roles in the Civil Rights Movement, was Thurgood Marshall. From 1933 to 1937 Hastie was assistant solicitor at the United States Department of Interior, where he challenged racist policies and was instrumental in reorganizing the government of the Virgin Islands.

In 1937 Hastie moved to the Virgin Islands as the first African American to be appointed a federal district judge. He left the Virgin Islands in 1939 to become dean of Howard University, and in 1940 he advised the military on fighting discrimination in the U.S. armed forces. He returned to the Virgin Islands in 1946 as governor for three years.

Hastie was appointed by President Harry S. Truman to the Third District Court of Appeals in 1949, a position he held until his retirement in 1971, serving the last three years as chief justice.

SEE ALSO
Military, Blacks in the American; Virgin Islands (United States and British).

North America

Hastings, Alcee

(b. September 5, 1936, Altamonte Springs, Fla.), Democratic member of the United States House of Representatives from Florida (1993-).

Hastings was born in Altamonte Springs, Florida. He received a bachelor's degree from FISK UNIVERSITY in 1958, attended HOWARD UNIVERSITY from 1958 to 1960, and received a law degree in 1963 from Florida A&M University. He practiced law from 1964 to 1977. He was a circuit court judge for Broward County, Florida, from 1977 to 1979 and then was appointed to a federal judgeship by President Jimmy Carter. In 1988 Hastings was impeached on bribery charges by the U.S. House and removed from office by the U.S. Senate in 1989. He ran for secretary of state of Florida in 1990 and lost. When Florida's Twenty-third Congressional District was created in 1992, it included the agricultural area around Lake Okeechobee as well as a strip of land tying together black middle-class neighborhoods west of Palm Beach and Fort Lauderdale. Hastings ran to represent the district in the U.S. Congress. He won the general election with 59 percent of the vote and was returned to office in subsequent elections.

In the 105th Congress (1997-1999), Hastings served on the International Relations Committee and the Science Committee. He is also a member of the CONGRESSIONAL BLACK CAUCUS.

North America

Hatcher, Richard Gordon

(b. July 10, 1933, Michigan City, Ind.), African American public official.

Richard Gordon Hatcher was born into a large, low-income family, and his father, a factory worker, often struggled to support Richard and his 12 siblings. Despite a somewhat difficult childhood, Hatcher excelled in school and graduated from Indiana University with a bachelor's degree in economics and government in 1956. In 1959 he completed a law degree at Valparaiso University, and in 1961 was appointed deputy prosecuting attorney in Lake County, Indiana. He was active for many years in Gary, Indiana, politics. In 1963 he was elected to the City Council and four years later to the office of mayor. Hatcher was, with Carl Stokes of Cleveland, Ohio, one of the first two African Americans to be elected mayor of a major American city. Hatcher served five four-year terms as mayor until his defeat in 1987.

In 1972 Hatcher presided over the plenary session of the first National Black Political Convention held in Gary. He was chairman of the National Board of Directors for Jesse Jackson's Operation PUSH (People United to Save Humanity) from 1982 to 1984, national chairman of the Jackson for President Committee in 1984, and national vice-chair of the Jackson Presidential Campaign in 1988. In 1991 he formed the Hatcher and Associates law firm in Gary.

Hatcher received both the 1968 Gary Jaycees Award as Outstanding Man of the Year and the Loren Henry Award for civil rights in 1965. He holds honorary doctor of law degrees from Fisk, Duquesne, and Coppin State College. In 1991 he was honored in SOUTH AFRICA by Nelson Mandela for his antiapartheid activities. During the same year, Hatcher initiated work on the "black common market" program to assist black businesses throughout the United States.

Alonford James Robinson, Jr.

SEE ALSO
Antiapartheid Movement; Mandela, Nelson Rolihlahla; Fisk University; Jackson, Jesse Louis; Operation PUSH; Stokes, Carl Burton.

Africa

Hausa

an ethnic group comprising roughly 22 million native speakers of the HAUSA LANGUAGE, who live mainly in northern NIGERIA and southern NIGER.

In addition to those who speak Hausa as their mother tongue, many more use it as a lingua franca in Nigeria, Niger, and elsewhere. In total, there are about 50 million Hausa speakers (*see* LANGUAGES, AFRICAN: AN OVERVIEW). Hausa is therefore the most widely spoken language in Nigeria and the most widely spoken sub-Saharan African language. Hausa speakers include millions of ethnic FULANI.

The Hausa maintain a hierarchy distinguishing among chiefs, office holders, and commoners. Hereditary occupations also mark distinctions in rank. Hausa society is strongly patrilineal and patriarchal. Hausa men often marry non-Hausa women, and the Hausa thus tend to expand and assimilate outsiders.

The Hausa language belongs to the Chadic branch of the Afroasiatic language family. The first Chadic speakers are believed to have cultivated cereals such as MILLET and sorghum some 6000 years ago in the vicinity of LAKE CHAD. Chadic speakers subsequently brought their language and agricultural traditions to present-day Hausaland and merged with existing populations. Their descendants are the present-day Hausa.

The earliest Hausa states probably formed by 1200 C.E. The first towns apparently coalesced around traditional shrines, which attracted pilgrims and became centers for trade. An increase in traffic along the trans-Saharan trade routes to the Hausa towns expanded the commerce in slaves, gold, and cola nuts from the savanna and forest regions to the south. This thriving trade generated wealth that enabled the rulers of these towns to establish states. The seven "true" Hausa states – Biram, Kano, Rano, Katsina, Daura, Zazzau, and Gobir – which the Hausa consider the core of Hausaland – emerged during this period. Arabian horses obtained from trans-Saharan traders enabled the Hausa to raid southern groups for slaves, who provided a valuable source of labor. By the fifteenth century Kano was one of the most important trading centers in Africa, with a population perhaps approaching 50,000.

Contacts with the neighboring empires of Mali, Songhai, and Kanem-Bornu probably brought Islam to the Hausa towns as early as the end of the eleventh century. The migration of mostly Muslim Fulani pastoralists to Hausaland beginning in the fifteenth century brought an additional source of Muslim influence to the region. By the nineteenth century most rural Hausa had adopted Islam, but the Maguzawa, a rural Hausa subgroup, still maintain traditional African beliefs today.

At their peak, around 1650, the independent Hausa states stretched from the borders of Bornu in present-day northeastern Nigeria to the NIGER RIVER, and from the Jos Plateau north to the fringes of the Sahara. However, Hausa traders traveled to markets across West Africa, exchanging salt and leather goods from Hausaland for gold and other products of the forest zone. Hausa traders purchased slaves in regions such as ASANTE and Dahomey even after European powers banned the TRANSATLANTIC SLAVE TRADE in the early nineteenth century. Today a substantial Hausa diaspora persists in countries such as GHANA and Chad. Hausa communities in West African cities often live in separate districts known as *zongos*.

In the early nineteenth century Fulani warriors joined Hausa peasants and merchants under the leadership of USMAN DAN FODIO in a jihad, or holy war, to unite Hausaland under the SOKOTO CALIPHATE. The formerly independent Hausa states became emirates within the caliphate. Initially, Fulani rulers dominated the caliphate. Gradually, however, these Fulani adopted the Hausa language and customs and merged with Hausa elites to form a northern Nigerian ruling class best described as Fulani-Hausa. Under the stable rule of the caliphate, Hausaland prospered during the nineteenth century. Slaves owned by Fulani or Hausa nobles worked the fertile fields of Hausaland and produced a surplus that sustained a substantial number of artisan producers, including weavers, blacksmiths, and leather workers.

During the 1890s, as French troops in present-day Niger began to encroach on Hausaland, British troops conquered the bulk of the Sokoto Caliphate, partly under the premise of stopping the slave trade. Great Britain replaced the Islamic state as the supreme authority and implemented indirect rule over the region. The colonial administration permitted existing emirs to remain in office as long as they complied with British demands. The British slowly abolished agrarian slavery and encouraged the cultivation of cash crops such as cotton and peanuts.

The precolonial elites of Hausaland not only survived colonialism but have remained powerful since independence. Because they are Nigeria's largest ethnic group, the Hausa have played a dominant role in many of Nigeria's civilian and military governments. Today most Hausa speakers raise food and livestock or cash crops such as millet, sorghum, and peanuts. These farmers live mostly in villages and small towns. Fulani cattle manure provides a primary source of fertilizer. Many Hausa have also migrated to cities such as Kano and Lagos in search of more lucrative wage employment.

Ari Nave

See Also

Colonial Rule; Dahomey, Early Kingdom of; Ghana; Gold Trade; Kano, Nigeria; Lagos, Nigeria; Sahara Desert; Salt Trade; Songhai Empire; Cola; Trans-Saharan and Red Sea Slave Trade; Mali Empire.

Africa

Hausa Language, the main language of Niger and the northern parts of Nigeria, and commonly spoken in other parts of West Africa where groups of Hausa people have traveled for trade.

Hausa serves as a localized lingua franca, enabling peoples of different languages to communicate with one another. Like Swahili, Hausa features many words of foreign extraction: many Arabic loan-words appear, as the result of Islamic conquests, as well as many English words.

Hausa has a rich oral tradition, replete with animal stories, fables, proverbs, and mythic explanations. Hausa written literature began about 200 years ago, with the use of the Arabic script *(ajami),* especially for religious writing. There is much modern writing in Hausa, such as the well-known novels of Alhaji Abubakar Imam, as well as historical and political works. While many modern writings use the Roman alphabet, called *boko* in Hausa, most religious writing is still done in ajami. Although written poetry in Hausa has been strongly influenced by Arabic traditions, there is also much modern poetry, in the boko script, which is moving away from classical and religious styles.

Oral poetry, often called *waka,* is a very old tradition of the Hausa people. It is performed with music by professional singing poets, or *mawaka.* The subjects of poetry may be great men and rulers who pay the poets and performers, but poems may also be about farming, hunting, politics, and wrestling, and sometimes are specially made up for religious and ceremonial occasions. The most important musical instrument used with oral poetry is the talking drum, or *kalangu,* which can imitate the different tones of the human voice. Stringed instruments such as the *molo* and *garaya* also provide music with the poetry.

See Also

Swahili Language.

Latin America and the Caribbean

Havana, Cuba, capital city and chief seaport of Cuba, in the western part of the country.

The largest city in the West Indies, Havana is on the western side of the Bay of Havana, on the northern coast of the island of Cuba, about 145 km (about 90 mi) south of Key West, Florida. The Bay of Havana is one of the safest harbors in the world; a narrow strait affords entrance to the bay, which is navigable by oceangoing vessels. The eastern side of the outer entrance is dominated by Morro Castle, a sixteenth-century fortress. Castillo de la Punta, another old fortress, is on the western side of the strait. Numerous docks, warehouses, and related facilities occupy considerable frontage along the inner harbor, and a substantial part of the imports and exports of the island are handled through Havana. Sugar refining and tobacco processing are the principal industries. Other industries include distilling, food processing, and the manufacture of textiles. Havana is the most important rail, highway, and air terminus in Cuba, although international air service to Cuba is limited to connections with selected nations.

Founded in 1515 on the site of the modern town of Batabanó by the Spanish administrator Diego Velázquez, Havana was transferred to its present location in 1519. The excellent harbor and strategic location of the settlement made it the chief Spanish naval station in the Americas, the port at which Spanish treasure ships assembled before the voyage back to Spain. As a result, during the late sixteenth and early seventeenth centuries Havana was often under siege by English, Dutch, and French pirates. By the time of the French and Indian War (1754-1763) the city had been heavily fortified and enclosed within a wall, but in August 1762 Havana was captured by a British fleet. In the following year the city was restored to Spain in exchange for Spanish holdings in present-day Florida, and, under easier trade restrictions, Havana prospered as a commercial center.

There was a large influx of African slave labor to Cuba beginning in the late eighteenth century. The Spanish took advantage of the collapse of Haiti's plantation economy in the aftermath of the Haitian Revolution by expanding sugar production in Cuba. An unprecedented number of slaves from West Africa entered Cuba, primarily through the ports of Havana and Santiago de Cuba, from where they were dispersed to the rural sugar plantations. Although slaves had been imported to Cuba since the sixteenth century, they had only represented a small percentage of the population until the 1790s. By the 1840s people of Africa and their descendants comprised well over 50 percent of the island's population. Although the slave trade to Cuba was officially outlawed in 1853, an illicit trade continued up until the final abolition of slavery in 1886, reinforcing Cuba's strong African presence (*see* Transatlantic Slave Trade).

In February 1898 the second-class battleship USS *Maine,* at anchor in Havana Harbor, exploded and sank – probably after a spark ignited coal dust in an empty fuel bunker or detonated gunpowder stored on board – and during the ensuing Spanish-Cuban-American War, the port was blockaded by the United States fleet. Under the U.S. military administration, which assumed control of Havana after the defeat of Spain, Havana again flourished commercially. In addition, sanitary conditions were improved and many areas of the city were rebuilt and modernized.

Until the early twentieth century Havana's urban population consisted primarily of white Spanish and Creole elites. In the years following the Wars of Independence (1895-1898) and the Spanish-Cuban-American War, large numbers of blacks moved to Havana and other cities in search of opportunity, contributing to an increase in urbanization. Although Cubans of African descent played a central role in the Wars of Independence, representing more than half of the Liberation Army's soldiers, they found themselves squeezed out of jobs by increasing numbers of Spanish immigrants, whose arrival during the first decades of the twentieth century was subsidized by Cuban officials as a way to "whiten" Cuba's population (*see* Whitening). In Havana and other urban centers on the island, Afro-Cubans faced unemployment or working in the most menial, low-paying jobs, as bricklayers, dockworkers, shoemakers, and bakers. Such conditions fostered a rise in black protest and the creation in 1908 of the Partido Independiente de Color (PIC, Independent Party of Color) in Havana in order to defend the interests of the Afro-Cuban population. Two years later the PIC was declared illegal following the passage of a law prohibiting the formation of political parties along racial lines.

During the early twentieth century the Cuban government also sought to outlaw other African forms of cultural expression, including SANTERÍA, ABAKUÁS, and RUMBA. Although the literary-artistic movement AFROCUBANISMO led to increased interest in and respect for Afro-Cuban cultural traditions beginning in the 1920s, blacks continued to be denied entrance into white-collar jobs and public administration positions, with the exception of the police force or the army. Afro-Cubans were often refused service at hospitals and hotels. Although segregation was not legal, it was maintained in schools by high fees for private education, which forced children of African descent to attend poorly funded public schools. Some of these problems were resolved by the socialist revolution that in 1959 brought Fidel Castro to power and gave all Cubans equal access to education and medical care.

Havana is one of the oldest and most picturesque cities of the Western Hemisphere. Before the Cuban revolutionary leader Fidel Castro assumed power in 1959, it was a popular winter resort, particularly for tourists from the United States. The buildings of Havana are largely of white coral limestone. The original portion of the city, located near the inner entrance of the harbor, contains narrow, crooked streets, old houses with overhanging balconies, and various historic landmarks. Beyond the older section, Havana is essentially modern, with numerous magnificent residences, imposing public buildings and churches, beautiful parks and plazas, and broad, tree-lined boulevards. Many of the larger private homes have been turned into government offices, student residences, or other public facilities by the Castro government. Among the boulevards are the Paseo de Martí, better known as the Prado, the Avenida del Puerto, the Malecón, the Alameda de Paula, and the Avenida de las Misiones. Several of the drives, notably the Avenida del Puerto, extend along the edge of the bay.

Among Havana's notable buildings are the national capitol, a white limestone structure similar in design to the U.S. capitol; the Capitanía, administrative headquarters of the captain of the port; the presidential palace; and the University of Havana (1728). Besides Morro Castle, the outstanding historic landmarks are the former convent of Santa Clara, constructed in 1644; El Castillo de la Real Fuerza (called La Fuerza), a fortress built between 1565 and 1583 and once the headquarters of the Spanish colonial governors; the Cathedral of the Immaculate Conception, dating from 1656; the city post office, originally the Church of San Francisco, which dates from 1575; the Castillo del Príncipe, another old fortress, now used as the city jail; and the City Hall, a former palace of the colonial governors, completed in 1792 and generally regarded as the best example of Spanish colonial architecture in Cuba. Among the principal public parks of Havana are the Plaza de la Fraternidad, the Parque Central, and the Parque de Colón. The city has a number of notable educational and cultural institutions, including, besides the University of Havana, the former Catholic University of Saint Thomas of Villanova, now the Makerenko Institute for teachers, the Municipal Conservatory of Music, the National Museum, and the National Library.

Silhouetted against the Havana skyline, a young man dives into the harbor. *Jeanette Ortiz Osorio*

It is difficult to assess the number of blacks living in Cuba today, because censuses do not account for racial composition, reflecting the Cuban government's view that such divisions are not important. The last census taken before the Cuban Revolution indicated that 26 percent of Cuba's population was black or mulatto. Carlos Moore, an exiled Afro-Cuban scholar, contends that the true proportion of Cubans of African descent was closer to 35-45 percent. Observing that most of those who fled Cuba after the revolution were whites, Moore estimates that 60-70 percent of the island's current population is of African descent. Though the number of blacks living in Havana has not been estimated, the historic district known as Old Havana is predominantly black. According to a 1993 estimate, Havana's total population was 2,176,000.

Today Havana is a center of Afro-Cuban cultural activity. It is the home of the Afro-Cuban dance group Conjunto Folklórico Nacional, the Afro-Cuban jazz ensemble IRAKERE, and Cuba's most popular dance band, Los Van Van, all of whom have become international cultural ambassadors. Their repertoires reflect the influence of the Afro-Cuban community in Havana.

SEE ALSO

Slavery in Latin America and the Caribbean; Creole Affair.

North America

Hawkins, Coleman Randolph

(b. November 21, 1904?, St. Joseph, Mo.; d. May 19, 1969, New York, N.Y.), JAZZ musician, called the "father of the tenor saxophone," whose career spanned the years from early swing to post-bop jazz.

Famous for his landmark 1939 recording "Body and Soul" and as sideman in the big bands of MAMIE SMITH and Fletcher Henderson, Coleman Hawkins is credited with bringing the tenor saxophone into the jazz ensemble. When he began his long musical career in the early 1920s, the saxophone was, according to jazz historian Joachim Berendt, in "the category of strange noise makers." No previous player had explored the instrument's potential for carrying a song's melody, for mimicking the human voice, or for use in tonal experimentation.

Hawkins, known to his contemporaries as "Hawk" or "Bean," changed all that. Born in St. Joseph, Missouri, to a musically talented mother, Hawkins began piano lessons when he was five, studied cello at age seven, and started playing the saxophone by the time he was nine. His formal training also included classes at Washburn College in Topeka, Kansas. Hawkins played at weekend dances in KANSAS CITY, MISSOURI, as a young teenager, and at 17 joined the big band fronted by blues singer Mamie Smith. Two years later, in 1923, he followed her to New York City.

Hawkins left Smith to join the city's premier big band, led by Fletcher Henderson, the legendary bandleader considered by many to be the leading architect of the swing era in jazz. From 1923 to 1934 Hawkins played with Henderson's band, during which time he pioneered the saxophone as a solo instrument within the jazz ensemble. Especially on romantic ballads, his solos influenced scores of other musicians. "When I heard Hawk," the trumpeter Miles Davis once said, "I learned to play ballads." In addition to playing with Henderson, Hawkins recorded with fellow saxophonist Benny Webster in a smaller ensemble called the Chocolate Dandies.

In 1934 Hawkins left Henderson and New York for an extended European tour. He stayed for five years, playing throughout England, FRANCE, and the Netherlands. Only when World War II loomed in 1939 did he come back to the United States. Shortly after his return he recorded what would become his trademark song, "Body and Soul," a standard in which Hawkins's solo established him as the preeminent saxophonist of jazz. It was a best-selling record, his first in 20 years as a musician. From 1939 to 1940 Hawkins briefly fronted his own big band, but for the rest of his career he mostly worked solo, backed up by house musicians or playing in impromptu groups.

A lifelong innovator, Hawkins worked with musicians who were pioneering the new style known as bebop. He recorded "Woody 'n' You" in 1944 with Dizzy Gillespie and Max Roach, and later played with both Thelonious Monk and Miles Davis. In the last two decades of his life Hawkins recorded prolifically, toured Europe often, and continued to play in and around New York. He died in 1969 of liver disease. More than 500 people, including numerous jazz luminaries, attended his funeral.

Kate Tuttle

SEE ALSO

Netherlands, The; World War II and African Americans; Davis, Miles Dewey, III; Gillespie, John Birks ("Dizzy"); Henderson, Fletcher Hamilton, Jr.; Monk, Thelonious Sphere; New York, New York; Roach, Maxwell Lemuel (Max).

North America

Hawkins, Edler Garnett

(b. June 13, 1908, Bronx, N.Y.; d. December 18, 1977), minister and civil rights leader who led the Presbyterian Church's participation in the CIVIL RIGHTS MOVEMENT.

Born to Albert and Annie Lee Hawkins, Edler Garnett Hawkins received the bachelor of divinity degree from Union Theological Seminary in 1938. Upon graduation he entered the ministry and was the first pastor of Saint Augustine Presbyterian Church in the Bronx.

In 1964 Hawkins became the first African American moderator of the General Assembly of the United Presbyterian Church, the denomination's highest office. As a member of the Presbyterian Interracial Council, he promoted his church's involvement in the Civil Rights Movement. In 1970 he retired from the pastorate to join the faculty of Princeton Theological Seminary as professor of black studies.

Alonford James Robinson, Jr.

Africa

Haya, an ethnic group of northwestern TANZANIA.

The ancestors of the Haya first settled on the western shores of LAKE VICTORIA (in present-day Tanzania) during the period of Bantu Expansion. There they established numerous small, loosely affiliated communities, each of which had its own hierarchical political system based on a division between nobles and commoners. The Haya are believed to have been one of the first groups in the region to practice iron-working, a technology that made it possible for them to produce a sophisticated type of pottery called Urewe ware, around 500 B.C.E. The mainstay of their economy, however, was agriculture. Prior to the nineteenth century the Haya produced coffee and bananas for trade as well as for brewing banana beer.

During the nineteenth century many Haya communities formed alliances with the larger and more powerful Buganda Kingdom in the hope of securing protection from slave raids by Arab/Swahili traders from the East Coast. Instead of protecting the small Haya communities, however, the Baganda sought to accentuate internal divisions among the various Haya kingdoms as a means of securing new land for themselves. By 1891, when the Haya were brought under German COLONIAL RULE, their groups had been severely weakened and divided. Under German and British rule the Haya began growing tea and were encouraged to increase coffee production, both of which they processed at local plants. Through efforts to gain influence over coffee prices and agricultural policies in the 1930s, the Haya formed a powerful social and political group, the Buhaya Union. Today the Haya are the largest coffee producers in Tanzania and, along with the neighboring CHAGGA, some of the country's most prosperous farmers.

Elizabeth Heath

SEE ALSO

Bantu: Dispersion and Settlement; Buganda, Early Kingdom of; Iron in Africa; Swahili People; Indian Ocean Slave Trade.

North America

Hayden, Robert Earl

(b. August 4, 1913, Detroit, Mich.; d. February 25, 1980, Ann Arbor, Mich.), African American poet and educator.

Born Asa Bundy Sheffey, Robert Earl Hayden was adopted by William and Sue Ellen Hayden, who changed his name. Hayden spent a difficult childhood in the Paradise Valley ghetto of Detroit. He suffered from very poor eyesight and was in frequent conflict with his extremely strict and religious foster parents, who imbued in him the sense of sinfulness – particularly about his homosexual inclination, which would inform much of his poetry.

After graduating from Detroit City College (now Wayne State University) in 1936, Hayden worked on the FEDERAL WRITERS' PROJECT and as an editor and critic for the *Michigan Chronicle*, Detroit's leading African American newspaper. He became involved in Detroit's lively left-wing arts scene, reading his poetry at political demonstrations and union rallies. With help from Louis Martin, editor in chief of the *Michigan Chronicle*, in 1940 Hayden published a collection of his radical poetry, *Heart-Shape in the Dust*.

Hayden attended graduate school at the University of Michigan, where he studied poetry under W. H. Auden and wrote a number of historical poems about the slave era, including "Middle Passage" and "The Ballad of Nat Turner," for which he won the Hopwood Award in 1942. At this time, he converted to the Baha'i religion, which emphasizes the spiritual unity of humanity, and moved away from his earlier radical politics.

In 1946 Hayden joined the English Department at Fisk University. After teaching there for 23 years, he took a job at the University of Michigan, where he taught for the rest of his life. He published eight books of poetry, but it was not until the publication of his *Selected Poems* in 1966 that he received national recognition.

Although Hayden would, like many African American poets before him, sometimes use traditional forms such as the ballad and the sonnet, more often he wrote a sort of modernist collage, juxtaposing images, phrases, and rhythms. This ornate diction and combination of abstract but suggestive metaphors with homely local detail contributed to his reputation as a difficult and intellectual poet influenced by the modernism of T. S. Eliot and Auden.

The influence of Euro-American modernism on Hayden's poetry as well as Hayden's frequent declarations that he wanted to be considered an "American poet" rather than a "black poet" led to much criticism of him as a literary Uncle Tom by African American critics during the 1960s. Ironically, African American history, contemporary black figures such as Malcolm X, and African American communities, particularly Hayden's native Paradise Valley, were the subjects of many of his poems.

During the 1960s and 1970s Hayden adopted a simpler and more directly personal style, as in his "Elegies for Paradise Valley." In 1976 he became the first African American to be appointed Consultant in Poetry at the Library of Congress, an equivalent at the time to being named national poet laureate.

James Smethurst

See Also
Slavery in the United States; Detroit, Michigan; Labor Unions in the United States.

North America

Hayes, Roland Willsie

(b. June 3, 1887, Curryville, Ga.; d. December 31, 1976, Boston, Mass.), African American tenor whose pioneering recitals of German lieder and other classical music opened the concert stage for black singers (*see* Opera).

Born on the plantation where his mother had been enslaved, Roland Hayes grew up in extreme poverty, but sang in the local church choir and managed to complete the eighth grade. An Oberlin College student heard him sing, and urged him to pursue vocal training. Hayes was, he claimed, "born again" one evening when he heard recordings of opera singer Enrico Caruso and other classical artists.

Hayes attended Fisk University and was working as a waiter in Louisville, Kentucky, when the president of Fisk invited him to join the famous Fisk Jubilee Singers on a concert tour to Boston, Massachusetts. In Boston a benefactor arranged for voice lessons, and Hayes began studying with Arthur Hubbard in 1911. Hayes worked as a messenger for the John Hancock Insurance Company and sang in black churches. In 1920 he toured Europe, where he received positive reviews.

On December 2, 1923, Hayes presented a self-financed concert at Boston's Symphony Hall that won favorable attention and established him in a successful life-long career as an international recital artist. He sang French, Italian, and German songs around the world and was considered a master of German leider. Hayes had deep affection for African American folk music, and he introduced Negro spirituals to much of the world. He received many honors and awards, including the prestigious Spingarn Medal, the highest recognition of the National Association for the Advancement of Colored People (NAACP).

See Also
Spirituals, African American.

North America

Haynes, Elizabeth Ross

(b. July 30, 1883, Lowndes County, Ala.; d. October 26, 1953, New York, N.Y.), African American sociologist, social worker, and author concerned especially with black women workers.

The daughter of former slaves, Elizabeth Ross Haynes became a pioneering urban sociologist. She graduated valedictorian of the State Normal School (now Alabama State University) in 1900. She received an A.B. from Fisk University in 1903 and an M.A. in sociology from Columbia University in 1923.

After graduation from Fisk, Haynes taught school and worked for segregated branches of the Young Women's Christian Association (YMCA). In 1910 she married George Haynes, a sociologist and cofounder of the National Urban League; their son was born in 1912. After her marriage, Haynes continued to work in unsalaried positions.

From 1918 to 1922 Haynes worked for the United States Department of Labor, and from 1920 to 1922, she served as domestic service secretary for the U.S. Employment Service. Throughout her career, Haynes was especially concerned with black women workers. She published several important essays on this topic, including her 1923 master's thesis on black domestic workers.

In 1924 Haynes became the first African American woman elected to the national board of the YWCA. During this period she was also active in the black women's club movement, serving as chair of the Industry and Housing Department of the National Association of Colored Women (NACW). In 1935 she was elected coleader of the Twenty-first Assembly District in New York. In addition to her sociological writings, Haynes published *Unsung Heroes* (1921), containing biographies of several African Americans, and *The Black Boy of Atlanta* (1952), a biography of college president and banker Maj. Richard Robert Wright (1855-1947).

Lisa Clayton Robinson

North America

Haynes, Lemuel

(b. July 8, 1753, West Hartford, Conn.; d. September 28, 1833, Granville, Mass.), African American clergyman who ministered to white congregations.

Lemuel Haynes was born to a black father he never knew and a white mother who refused to acknowledge him. In his infancy he was made an indentured servant to a white family in Granville, Massachusetts, who treated him as one of their children. A serious and studious child, he received a common school education as well as a religious upbringing.

Haynes's indenture ended in 1774, whereupon he became a Minuteman in the Continental Army. During the Revolutionary War he fought at the siege of Boston and Fort Ticonderoga. After the war he studied Latin and Greek with local ministers and was ordained by the Congregationalists, apparently the first African American ordained by a mainstream white denomination. Throughout the next five decades he ministered to white congregations in New England and New York.

Haynes spoke little on race but did write a manuscript called "Liberty Further Extended," in which he claimed that the principles of the American Revolution should be "extended" to include the country's slave population. A Washingtonian Federalist, he opposed the War of 1812 and the presidencies of Thomas Jefferson and Andrew Jackson. He also intervened, in 1820, in the Boorne Case, a sensational trial of two brothers accused of killing their brother-in-law, who had been missing for seven years. Haynes's intervention on behalf of the brothers appeared to be for naught, and the brothers were sentenced to hang, until, five weeks before the hanging, the "murdered" brother-in-law appeared. The Boorne Case became famous as an example of the dangers of circumstantial evidence.

Haynes also received considerable attention for a sermon he preached rebutting Hosea Ballou's theory of universal salvation from a Calvinist perspective. Haynes's book *Universal Salvation, A Very Ancient Doctrine* ran some 70 editions. In 1804 Middlebury College awarded him an honorary master's degree; he was the first African American to receive that honor from any institution.

See Also
American Revolution.

North America

Haywood, Harry

(b. February 4, 1898, South Omaha, Nebr.; d. 1985, Chicago, Ill.), African American Black Nationalist and former Communist Party leader.

The son of former slaves, Harry Haywood moved with his family from Nebraska to Minneapolis, which he left to fight in the 370th Infantry in France during World War I. Settling in Chicago in the early 1920s, he supported himself as a bootblack, busboy, and bellboy. He was recruited into the African Blood Brotherhood, a secret Black Nationalist organization, and into the Young Workers League, both associated with the Communist Party of the USA (CPUSA).

Haywood was a leading proponent of Black Nationalism, self-determination, and the idea that American blacks are a colonized people who should organize themselves into a nation. From 1926 to 1930 he studied in the Soviet Union, where he met several anticolonial revolutionaries, including Vietnam's Ho Chi Minh. On his return to the United States in 1931, he was chosen to head the Communist Party's Negro Department and in 1934 was elected a member of its politburo. The Spanish Civil War took him to Spain in 1937, where he fought in a volunteer Communist brigade against Gen. Francisco Franco's fascist regime.

During World War II Haywood's belief in black self determination and territorial autonomy put him at odds with Communist Party policy, which, since the adoption of the Popular Front strategy in 1935, had gravitated away from support for a black nation in the American South. Haywood's agitation on "the Negro question" led to his expulsion from the Party in 1959.

Haywood lived in Mexico City from 1959 until 1963, when he returned permanently to Chicago. In his later years he supported several Black Nationalist movements, such as the Nation of Islam and the League of Revolutionary Black Workers, and he was highly critical of integrationists such as Martin Luther King Jr. and Jesse Jackson. His final years were spent in Chicago, out of the political limelight.

See Also

Chicago, Illinois; Jackson, Jesse Louis; King, Martin Luther, Jr.; Communist Party USA, African Americans and the.

Africa

Head, Bessie

(b. July 6, 1937, Pietermaritzburg, South Africa; d. April 17, 1986, Serowe, Botswana).

South African author and teacher Bessie Head was one of the great postwar African novelists. Her writings sound existential themes in unfamiliar terrain, treating such topics as personal and societal alienation, political exile, racial identity, and sexual oppression. She was particularly concerned with describing the institutionalization of evil.

Head was effectively an orphan. The child of a white woman and a black man, she was born in the mental institution in which her mother had been placed. Adopted by a white Afrikaner family when she was very young, she was later returned when her black features revealed themselves. She then lived with a black family, until she moved into an orphanage at age 13. In a few years she acquired a teaching degree, and taught school in Durban for two years, later leaving that position to work as a journalist for Drum Publications in Johannesburg.

Head became active in politics in the 1960s, eventually joining the Pan-Africanist Congress (PAC). She married Harold Head in 1961, and had a son. Following several arrests and continual harassment by Afrikaner authorities, Head moved with her son to Botswana, where she lived in the village of Serowe, working both as a schoolteacher and unpaid agricultural worker. Her experiences in political exile were extremely traumatic, provoking a nervous breakdown.

Head's first novel, *When Rain Clouds Gather* (1969), is the only work set in and developed from her experiences in South Africa. Her second novel, *Maru* (1971), addresses the issue of racism among blacks. Head focuses on the abuse of the Masarwa or Bushmen, considered slaves and outcasts within African society, by Serowe tribal people. As in Head's other novels, the antiracist sentiments expressed in *Maru* are not intended as a condemnation of the village of Serowe, but more as a broader reflection on the racial prejudices found throughout the world in many different societies. Head's third novel, the largely autobiographical *A Question of Power* (1973), is a portrait of her nervous breakdown, a condition she believes resulted from the ongoing psychological struggles she faced as both a woman and a political exile. This novel is often considered a milestone in the development and evolution of African literature, as it is one of the first African novels written from a largely personal and introspective point of view, focusing on the individual as opposed to broader societal issues. Furthermore, as a story written from a woman's perspective, *A Question of Power* gained the attention of feminists and established Head's reputation as a woman's author, although Head hesitated to embrace the feminist label for herself.

Head further established herself as a feminist with her short nonfiction piece, *The Collector of Treasures and Other Botswana Village Tales*, a collection of Botswana village stories told from a woman's perspective. These stories are decidedly optimistic and positive in tone, and serve to emphasize the inherent personal and communal strength of women in overcoming male oppressors. Head's major nonfiction work, *Serowe: Village of the Rainwind* (1981), is a history of Serowe, recorded as a series of interviews conducted by Head herself.

See Also

Women Writers in English-Speaking Africa; Durban, South Africa.

North America

Healy Family,

a highly accomplished American family of mixed race, many of whose members reached high-level positions in the Roman Catholic Church in the late nineteenth century.

Michael Morris Healy (1796-1850) was a white Irishman born in County Roscommon. During the War of 1812 he served the British Army in Canada, where he deserted. Within a few years he had resettled in rural Georgia, near Macon, and there acquired a plantation of more than 1000 acres. His many slaves worked the plantation, and in the late 1820s he became sexually involved with one of them, a teenage mulatto named Mary Eliza Smith. Together they had ten children, all of whom Healy publicly recognized. Under Georgia law, however, he was allowed neither to marry nor to free his common-law wife, nor could he free his children. Fearful that they would become slaves, he provided for his wife to be sent North should he die before her, and sent his children to the North for education and freedom.

James Augustine Healy (1830-1900), the eldest son, became the first black Roman Catholic priest and bishop in the United States. In 1837 Michael Healy had enrolled James in a Quaker school on Long Island, New York. Over the next few years, Michael Healy became acquainted with Roman Catholic bishop John Fitzpatrick of Boston. Fitzpatrick subsequently arranged for the Healy boys to enroll in the College of the Holy Cross, a new Jesuit school in Worcester, Massachusetts. James received his bachelor's degree from Holy Cross in 1849. At the time African Americans were not allowed to become priests in the United States, so James, declaring his intention to become a priest nonetheless, enrolled first in a Montreal, Canada, seminary and later in the Sulpician Seminary of Paris. In 1854 he was ordained a priest in Paris's Cathedral of Notre Dame.

When James Healy returned to the United States a short time later, Bishop Fitzpatrick made him his secretary as well as chancellor for the diocese of Boston. Although Fitzpatrick was aware of Healy's black heritage, neither he nor Healy, who was light-skinned enough to pass for white, made that heritage publicly known. By 1866 Healy became pastor of Saint James parish, home to Boston's largest Roman Catholic congregation. His white, Irish parishioners assumed he was white, and he became well known among them for his work on behalf of orphans, abandoned children, and unwed mothers. He was also instrumental in securing the right for Catholics to worship in orphanages, jails, and other institutions of Massachusetts. In 1875 Healy was made bishop of Portland, Maine, where he oversaw the construction of many churches and schools. During his tenure he did not attend or address the several national conferences held by African American Catholics.

Patrick Francis Healy (1834-1910) became the first black Jesuit, the first black president of a white college, and probably the first black American to earn a doctoral degree. Like his brother James, Patrick was light-skinned and entered Holy Cross, where he completed his studies in 1850. He was soon accepted into a Jesuit novitiate in Maryland and in 1852 took his vows. He taught briefly in Philadelphia, then returned to Holy Cross as a teacher for several years. In 1858 he continued his studies, first in Rome, then in Belgium, where in 1864 he was ordained a priest. The following year he earned a doctoral degree from the University of Louvain in Belgium.

In 1866 Patrick returned to the United States and became a professor of philosophy at Georgetown College, in Washington, D.C. By 1869 he was vice president, by 1873 vice rector, and on July 31, 1874, president – the first black president of a white college, although most people assumed he was white. During the next eight years, Patrick Healy transformed the school from a small college to a major university. Standards were raised, departments were added, and the curriculum was modernized. Healy authorized the construction of a massive building in the center of campus modeled after a building at the University of Louvain; after his death, the building was named Healy Hall. He did not, however, press for the admission of blacks to Georgetown – a right they would not gain until after World War II. Ill health forced him to retire in 1882.

Michael Augustine Healy (1839-1904) became a prominent officer of the United States Revenue Cutter Service, the precursor to the U.S. Coast Guard. Like his brothers, Healy attended Holy Cross, but as a teenager he ran away to work on a ship. His brothers brought him back and placed him in school in Montreal, but again he ran away. After being enrolled in school in Belgium and again running away, his brothers allowed him to pursue his naval career. By 1864 he had become an officer on a merchant ship. In 1865 he entered the U.S. Revenue Cutter Service and in 1883 received command of the cutter *Thomas Corwin*, which was charged with protecting American shippers and sailors near Alaska. He undertook several courageous rescue missions and explorations, received a citation from Congress for his bravery, and published *The Cruise of the Corwin*, a report of his Alaskan explorations.

In 1886 Michael Healy received command of the *Bear*, a ship made famous a few years earlier for a daring rescue mission at the North Pole. Healy took the *Bear* on several more bold missions. He also came to the aid of Alaska's native Inuits, whose hunting grounds had been encroached upon by whites and who were consequently under threat of starvation. Healy transported several herds of reindeer from Siberia to Alaska, providing a source of food and income for the Inuits. He also repeatedly intervened in disputes between whites and Inuits, once noting that in such matters, "the white men are always wrong."

Beginning in 1889 Michael Healy faced several widely publicized trials on charges of excessive cruelty in suppressing mutinies, treating sailors harshly on other occasions, and drunkenness while on duty. Originally exonerated, Healy was later convicted and court-martialed for his treatment of seamen, and was demoted. In the late 1890s, however, he was called back into service for several rescue missions. His bravery was widely celebrated and he was later given the command of several Revenue Cutter ships. He retired in 1903, a year before his death. Since that time, Healy has become known as one of the most colorful officers in Coast Guard history and is believed to have been the model for the protagonist in Jack London's *Sea Wolf* and a character in James Michener's *Alaska*.

Eliza Dunmore Healy (1846-1919) was a teacher and convent superior. She was born in Georgia and lived there until the death of her parents in 1850. After a brief stay with an older brother in New York, she was sent to St. Johns, Quebec, where, with her sister Amanda, she was cared for and educated at a boarding school and convent. After finishing her elementary education, Eliza Healy moved to Montreal, where she graduated from Villa Maria, another Catholic school. In Montreal she took her vows as a nun at the Congregation of Notre Dame and became known as Sister Mary Magdalene.

She taught at several Canadian schools before being appointed mother superior of a community of nuns in Huntington, Quebec, in 1895. The school run by the nuns had fallen deeply into debt, but in a few years Healy restored it to solvency. In 1903 she was made mother superior of a community of white nuns at Villa Barlow, a prestigious convent school in St. Albans, Vermont, attended by the daughters of elite New Englanders. She spent 15 years at Villa Barlow before her death from cancer.

The other surviving Healy children included Hugh Clark (1832-1900), who lived in New York; Alexander Sherwood (1836-1875), who received a doctoral degree in Europe and followed his brother James as chancellor of the diocese of Boston; Martha Ann (1838-1920), who like her sister Eliza became a nun but who later renounced her vows; Amanda Josephine (1845-1879), who also became a nun; and Eugene (1849-?), a professional gambler.

See Also

World War I and African Americans; Boston, Massachusetts; Philadelphia, Pennsylvania.

Latin America and the Caribbean

Hearne, John (b. February 4, 1926, Montreal, Quebec, Canada), Jamaican novelist and playwright.

Although writer John Hearne was born in Canada, his parents moved back to their native Jamaica when he was two. He attended Jamaica College, and after serving as a gunner in the Royal Air Force during World War II, a position he volunteered for "just to get out of the island," he went to Edinburgh University in Scotland, where he received an M.A. in history in 1950. For the next 12 years, Hearne moved back and forth between high school teaching jobs in London and Jamaica. The constant shift between the two cultures fueled his creativity, and he published five novels between 1955 and 1961.

Most of these novels were set on the fictional Caribbean island of Cayuna, which closely resembles Jamaica. While many other Caribbean writers portrayed working-class characters, Hearne's novels *Voices Under the Window* (1955), *Stranger at the Gate* (1956), and *Land of the Living* (1961) all featured middle-class characters, and so gave a different perspective on the class tensions in West Indian society. *The Faces of Love* (1957) and *The Autumn Equinox* (1959), on the other hand, focused on personal relationships set against the backdrop of Cayunan politics.

After this initial burst of activity, Hearne's novel-writing pace slowed when he became involved in other activities. He served briefly as an information officer in the Jamaican government, and then taught at the University of the West Indies in Kingston from 1962 to 1992, first in the department of Extra-Mural Studies, and then as chair of the Creative Arts Centre. Hearne published several plays in the mid-1960s, and in the early 1970s coauthored two novels with Morris Cargill under the joint pseudonym John Morris. His sixth novel, *The Sure Salvation*, was published in 1981.

Lisa Clayton Robinson

See Also

Literature, English Language, Caribbean; Kingston, Jamaica.

North America

Hedgeman, Anna Arnold

(b. July 5, 1899, Marshalltown, Iowa; d. January 17, 1990, New York, N.Y.), African American public servant and civil rights advocate.

Though born in Iowa, Anna Arnold Hedgeman grew up in Anoka, Minnesota, and later attended Hamline University in St. Paul, where she was the first black student in the school's history. She received her B.A. in 1922, but after finding teaching opportunities for blacks scarce in the North, she began teaching at a Southern black school, Rust College in Holly Springs, Mississippi. Though impressed with the resilience and determination of students who confronted terrible poverty and discrimination, Hedgeman was deeply discouraged by the South's rampant racism and deep-rooted segregation, and she left Rust to work in a series of positions with the Young Women's Christian Association (YWCA) in several cities.

Hedgeman's long career in public service included positions as executive director of the National Council for a Permanent Fair Employment Practices Committee, in the Federal Security Agency, and in the New York City mayor's cabinet. Hedgeman was the only woman on the organizing committee of the 1963 March on Washington.

Lisa Clayton Robinson

See Also
Fair Employment Practices Committee.

Africa

Hehe, ethnic group of Tanzania.

The Hehe primarily inhabit south central Tanzania. They speak a Bantu language. Approximately 700,000 people consider themselves Hehe.

See Also
Bantu: Dispersion and Settlement.

North America

Height, Dorothy

(b. March 24, 1912, Richmond, Va.), African American organizational leader, clubwoman, and activist; president of the National Council of Negro Women (NCNW).

For most of her life Dorothy Height has been a leader in influential African American women's organizations. Born in Richmond, Virginia, she grew up in Pennsylvania and graduated from New York University in 1933 with bachelor's and master's degrees in educational psychology. While employed as a social worker, she became a leader with the United Christian Youth Movement, which gave her the opportunity to travel widely and work alongside Eleanor Roosevelt.

In 1937 Height accepted a post with the Harlem Young Women's Christian Association (YWCA). She continued to hold leadership positions with the YWCA, first at the local and then at the national level, for the next 40 years. Among Height's accomplishments at the YWCA was her help in organizing the 1946 conference at which the association formally committed to integrating its programs.

Height continued to work with Roosevelt through the YWCA, and in November 1937, as she was escorting the First Lady to a function, she caught the attention of legendary black activist Mary McLeod Bethune. Bethune quickly became Height's mentor; through her, Height became involved with the National Council of Negro Women (NCNW), the coalition, founded by Bethune, of black women's organizations. As a clubwoman, Height was already active in a sorority and served as national president of Delta Sigma Theta Sorority from 1947 to 1956. A year after resigning that post, Height became the fourth president of the NCNW, a position she has now held for more than 40 years.

As leader of the NCNW, Height has traveled the world working to secure equal rights and justice for women and for people of color. Her special focus has been on elevating the status of African American women and strengthening the black family. Height has received more than 20 honorary degrees and more than 50 awards from local, state, and national organizations, including the Citizens Medal Award for distinguished service, presented to her by President Ronald Reagan in 1989.

Lisa Clayton Robinson

See Also
Black Women's Club Movement; Fraternities and Sororities, Black, in the United States.

North America

Hemings, Sally

(b. 1773, Bermuda Hundred, Va.; d. 1836), African American slave who may have been the mistress of Thomas Jefferson.

A woman at the center of controversy for the past two centuries, Sally Hemings was born the daughter of a mulatto slave woman, Elizabeth Hemings, and a free white man, John Wayles. Wayles was also the father of Martha Wayles, President Thomas Jefferson's wife, who died in 1782. Two years later Hemings, a slave in the Jefferson estate, accompanied the widowed Jefferson to France, where he served as ambassador and she tended his daughter, Martha. Although she could have claimed her freedom in Paris, Hemings returned with Jefferson to Virginia in 1789, remaining with him until his death in 1826. Jefferson's daughter, Martha, freed Hemings after her father's death, but she continued to work at Monicello until she died ten years later.

One of Jefferson's political enemies first aired public allegations that the two were sexually involved in 1802, starting what would become nearly 200 years of dispute over the relationship between Jefferson and Hemings. While Jefferson himself never denied the accusations during his lifetime, in the years since his death some of Jefferson's white descendants, and others to whom the idea of his relationship with Hemings is distasteful, have fought against the rumors. Lacking definitive scientific proof, the question of whether or not Hemings and Jefferson were lovers was for years open to interpretation and argument.

In 1998 speculation about the paternity of Heming's children, a subject of disagreement among scholars, prompted scientists to apply newly available DNA testing to the controversy. While it is impossible to claim with absolute certainty that Jefferson fathered Hemings's children, the results convinced scientists that it is extremely likely. The news confirmed both longstanding oral histories passed down by Hemings's descendants and the theories advanced by several prominent historians, such as Annette Gordon-Reed, whose book *Thomas Jefferson and Sally Hemings: An American Controversy* collected and presented the best available evidence on the subject. Others, both historians who had dismissed the Jefferson-Hemings relationship as rumor and white Jefferson descendants distressed at having new black relations (and new white ones, as some of those descended from Hemings's son Eston, who had passed as white), reacted with confusion and defensiveness.

In 1999 the Monticello Association, an organization of Jefferson's descendants, for the first time ever invited the Hemings descendants to their annual family gathering. Though it began in a spirit of warmth and reconciliation, the meeting soon degenerated into acrimony and anger, as the Monticello Association members refused to grant even honorary membership to the Hemings relatives. According to white novelist Lucian Truscott IV, a Jefferson descendant, the rejection of Hemings's descendants signals clearly that "in a really basic way, white people are scared to find out who their relatives are."

Kate Tuttle

North America

Henderson, Fletcher Hamilton, Jr.

[sometimes identified as James Fletcher Henderson] (b. December 18, 1897, Cuthbert, Ga.; d. December 28, 1952, New York, N.Y.), African American jazz pianist, composer, and arranger whose orchestra is considered the first true big band of the swing era.

Fletcher Henderson is regarded by most music historians as the architect of the big-band movement in jazz music. In his 30-year career he saw, and helped, jazz evolve from its RAGTIME and Dixieland roots to a polished, streamlined sound that hinted at the bebop and cool jazz styles that would follow. Though he began as a pianist, it was as a bandleader and arranger that Henderson's impact was most significant. His bands nurtured such influential talents as Coleman Hawkins, Louis Armstrong, Ben Webster, and Lester Young; his arrangements and compositions became the basis for hit records by Count Basie and the white bandleader Benny Goodman.

Born in Cuthbert, Georgia, Henderson's parents – his father was a school principal and his mother a pianist and music teacher – encouraged their son's talents, giving him piano lessons starting at the age of six. A good student, Henderson graduated from Atlanta University with a degree in chemistry in 1920, after which he traveled to New York City for graduate study. To support himself, he took a job with a music publishing and recording company run by African American musicians Harry Pace and W. C. Handy. Henderson led the house band, the Black Swan Troubadours, in accompanying the blues singer ETHEL WATERS. When Waters planned a tour in 1921, she took Henderson along as pianist, bandleader, and tour manager.

When Henderson returned to New York (having had his academic musical style loosened up by Waters, according to his biographers), he again worked as an accompanist for various artists, including the blues singer BESSIE SMITH. Henderson also began leading loose collaborations of musicians in nightly jam sessions. By 1923 a group of players had jelled into Henderson's first recognizable big band, which was based at the Club Alabam and later the Roseland Ballroom. Coleman Hawkins, the pioneering tenor saxophonist from Kansas City, joined Henderson when he moved to New York, and the coronetist and singer Louis Armstrong brought New Orleans style to the band.

In recordings such as "Sugar Foot Stomp," arranged by Don Redman and featuring Armstrong's searing solos, Henderson's band established the sound and feel that defined the era. Brass, wind (or reed), and rhythm instruments worked together in sections, often in a call-and-response pattern, and the syncopated, stomping beat made pop standards swing. As the big-band movement grew, however, Henderson's knack for attracting innovative talent began to break down. Known as a kind and friendly employer, he lacked the ambition and organizational drive of his burgeoning competition, which included Duke Ellington and Cab Calloway. By the mid-1930s Henderson's band began to dissolve.

Having fallen on hard times, Henderson sought a second career as an arranger. Always generous with other bandleaders – sharing, for instance, most of his musical library with the up-and-coming Count Basie – Henderson began selling compositions and arrangements to the white bandleader Benny Goodman. In 1939 and 1940, Henderson worked as Goodman's house arranger, and briefly as his pianist. Semiretired after 1940 due to declining health, Henderson scored a musical, "Jazz Train," and briefly led a sextet at a small bar in New York's Greenwich Village. He suffered a stroke in 1950, never fully recovered, and died in 1952.

Kate Tuttle

SEE ALSO

Armstrong, Louis ("Satchmo"); Basie, William James ("Count"); Blues, The; Calloway, Cabell (Cab); Young, Lester Willis ("Prez"); Handy, William Christopher (W.C.); Hawkins, Coleman Randolph; Kansas City, Missouri; New Orleans, Louisiana; New York, New York; Ellington, Edward Kennedy ("Duke").

North America

Hendrix, Jimi (b. November 27, 1942, Seattle, Wash.; d. September 18, 1970, London, England), African American musician, rock 'n' roll singer, and guitar virtuoso.

Jimi Hendrix taught himself guitar by listening to MUDDY WATERS, B. B. King, and Chuck Berry. After serving as a paratrooper in the army, he began his music career. Under the name Jimmy James, he played as a backup guitarist for many top rock 'n' roll and RHYTHM AND BLUES artists, including LITTLE RICHARD, Sam Cooke, B. B. King, WILSON PICKETT, Ike and TINA TURNER, and the ISLEY BROTHERS. Between 1962 and 1964 Hendrix began to captivate audiences with such guitar tricks as playing with his teeth, behind his back, and between his legs.

Aspiring to move out of the background, Hendrix formed a band called Jimmy James and the Blue Flames in 1965, and played coffeehouses in New York's Greenwich Village, where he was influenced by Bob Dylan. Chas Chandler, bassist for the popular group the Animals, discovered Hendrix in New York. In 1966, Chandler, who would later become Hendrix's manager, convinced him to accompany him to London by promising to introduce Hendrix to Eric Clapton. In London, Hendrix formed a band, a power trio called the Jimi Hendrix Experience, with drummer Mitch Mitchell and bassist Noel Redding.

The London rock world, hungry for a new trend, was consumed by Hendrix. His style of playing fascinated even such elite guitarists as Pete Townsend and Eric Clapton, who placed Hendrix's musicianship on a level above their own. Considered a true virtuoso, the left-handed Hendrix played a right-handed Fender Stratocaster strung upside down. He used new techniques, including distortion, "wah-wah," and feedback to add an electrifying sonic architecture to already accomplished songs. The Experience was one of the first integrated big-time rock bands that was led by an African American.

In 1967 the Experience released its first album, *Are You Experienced?*, which contained the hits "Hey Joe" and "Purple Haze," and featured Hendrix's famously expansive lyrics ("Scuze me while I kiss the sky"). In June 1967 the Experience made a dramatic debut in the American music scene at the Monterey Pop Festival. Because Hendrix and the Experience had not yet released *Are You Experienced?* in the United States, festival promoters were unwilling to book them until Paul McCartney of the Beatles persuaded them to do so. During their performance, Hendrix tore through a set of original compositions and eclectic covers, and closed the set by setting fire to his guitar.

On the strength of the Monterey performance Hendrix became a superstar. He began spending more and more time recording and founded his own studio, Electric Ladyland, in New York, where he associated with fellow musicians, including admirer Miles Davis. The Experience slowly unraveled as Hendrix pursued side projects. In 1969 he appeared at Woodstock, performing an unorthodox, distortion-filled guitar version of "The Star-Spangled Banner" that had fans raving and had "middle America," which saw his version as blasphemous, enraged. Following Woodstock, Hendrix formed the Band of Gypsies, an all-black band with Buddy Miles, a friend from the army, on drums and Billy Cox on bass. They released one album, a self-titled recording of a live performance. At age 27, Hendrix died in London of complications following barbiturate intoxication.

SEE ALSO

Berry, Charles Edward Anderson (Chuck); Cooke, Samuel (Sam); Davis, Miles Dewey, III; King, Riley B. ("B. B."); New York, New York.

North America

Henson, Josiah (b. June 15, 1789, Charles County, Md.; d. May 5, 1883, Dawn, Ont., Canada), preacher who founded a settlement for fugitive slaves in Canada.

Originally thought to be the model for Harriet Beecher Stowe's UNCLE TOM'S CABIN, Josiah Henson, born into slavery, demonstrated such loyalty and devotion that his owner, Isaac Riley, granted him exceptional privileges and responsibilities, allowing him to work as a Methodist Episcopal preacher. Through his meager salary as a preacher, Henson was able to save almost $300, which he hoped would buy his freedom. Riley agreed with Henson on a price of $450, but knowing that Henson was illiterate, Riley changed the contract to $1000 and then made plans to sell him. Henson learned of these betrayals and, fearing forced separation from his family, decided to escape to CANADA, settling in Dresden, Canada West (Ontario).

Henson became a British patriot while in Canada and led a volunteer brigade against William Lyon Mackenzie and the Americans in the 1837 Rebellion. In 1844 Henson was instrumental in planning a settlement for FUGITIVE SLAVES near Dawn, a township with a sizable black population. The Dawn Settlement was home to almost 500 blacks and included a vocational school called the British American Institute, as well as a commercial sawmill. Though it lasted for nearly 30 years, Henson's poor administrative skills left it continually in debt. Henson remained pastor of the British Methodist Episcopal Church at Dawn until his death.

Peter Hudson

SEE ALSO
Slavery in the United States.

North America

Henson, Matthew Alexander

(b. August 8, 1866, Charles County, Md.; d. March 9, 1955, New York, N.Y.), African American explorer, member of the 1909 expedition with American explorer Robert Peary that is generally credited with discovering the North Pole.

Matthew Henson's travels began when he was just a teen. He ran away from home after his parents' death and sailed around the world for six years as a hand aboard the merchant vessel *Katie Hines*.

Henson was working as a hat store clerk in WASHINGTON, D.C., in 1897 when Robert Peary hired him as a valet. He traveled with Peary on a survey expedition to Nicaragua in 1897 and accompanied him on seven polar expeditions. Henson quickly proved indispensable to Peary as a navigator in the Arctic and as a translator among the Inuit (also known as Eskimos).

On April 6, 1909, an expedition made up of Peary, Henson, and four Inuit claimed to be the first to reach the North Pole. Henson, who usually broke trail while pulling a sled, may have reached the Pole 45 minutes before Peary, although discovery of the North Pole is usually credited to Peary. In recent years, however, most scholars have concluded that the point the expedition reached was actually at least a few miles from the North Pole.

In 1912 Henson wrote *A Black Explorer at the North Pole*. In 1913 President Taft personally recommended Henson's appointment to the United States Customs House in New York City in recognition of his exploits in the Arctic. In 1944 Henson received a joint medal from the Congress of the United States, honoring the Peary expedition to the North Pole. He was also honored by President Truman in 1950 and admitted to the Explorer's Club, but he passed away in relative obscurity five years later. In 1986 Henson was commemorated on a postage stamp. Two years later he was reburied in Arlington National Cemetery in Virginia with full honors.

SEE ALSO
New York, New York.

Africa

Herero, ethnic group of NAMIBIA and BOTSWANA who suffered greatly from German colonialism.

The Herero, who now call themselves Ovaherero, are thought to have arrived on the central plateau of Namibia during the sixteenth century, migrating with other Bantu-speaking peoples from the area around LAKE VICTORIA. Some of these migrants settled in the northern Kaokoveld and became known as the Himba, while the rest continued south into east central Namibia. Politically decentralized, the seminomadic Herero recognized both matrilineal and patrilineal descent and inheritance systems. Like the SOTHO, to whom they are probably distantly related, the Herero placed great cultural and economic value on cattle, and still do today. Although women's agricultural produce provides much of their food supply, men's cattle herds are an important measure of wealth, especially in marriage and religious rituals (*see* PASTORALISM).

During the 1800s European missionaries began to live among the Herero, and many Herero women adopted long, European-style dresses and turban-like hats. Around the same time, competition for grazing land – especially after a drought in 1829-1830 – led to conflicts between the Herero and their neighbors to the south, the Oorlam. The Herero usually found themselves on the defensive until 1863, when the Herero, led by Maherero and armed with German-supplied weapons, launched a year-long "Freedom War."

The colonization of Namibia by GERMANY led to new clashes and, ultimately, the near destruction of the Herero. In early 1904 Samuel Maherero called upon Herero to attack German farms and outposts, on the grounds that German settlers had stolen these lands. Maherero specifically ordered that women, children, Englishmen, and Afrikaners be spared, a policy that the Herero followed. Although initially outnumbered, the Germans brought in reinforcements until their well-equipped army was double the size of the Herero's 10,000-troop force. After the Battle of Waterberg in August of 1904, the defeated Herero sought peace. But the peace accord meant little, as the Germans essentially sought to exterminate the Herero in what historians have called one of the bloodiest of all colonial wars. In three years the Herero population was reduced from 80,000 to 15,000. Their cattle herds decimated, many survivors fled to Bechuanaland, today known as Botswana.

The Herero who remained behind found themselves pushed onto a Herero "homeland" after SOUTH AFRICA occupied German South West Africa in 1915. Soon afterward the elder chiefs formed the Herero Council. The council would later play an important antigovernment role, repeatedly petitioning the United Nations for South African withdrawal. Although many Herero also joined the nationalist South West African National Union in the 1960s, the Herero Council itself was more conservative and ultimately endorsed the "internal settlement" arrangements proposed by South Africa, rather than the total independence demanded by the more radical nationalist group the South West African People's Organization, or SWAPO. In part this stance reflected the Herero leaders' fears of OVAMBO dominance in an independent Namibia. Today many Herero, especially the Himba, see themselves as discriminated against by the SWAPO- and Ovambo-dominated government, and in elections they have been more likely to support the opposition Democratic Turnhalle Alliance. The Herero now number around 100,000, or 7 percent of the Namibian population.

Eric Young

SEE ALSO
Afrikaner; Bantu: Dispersion and Settlement; Maherero, Samuel; South West Africa People's Organization; Christianity: Missionaries in Africa.

Latin America and the Caribbean

Hernández, Gaspar Octavio

(b. July 4, 1893, Panama City, Panama; d. November 13, 1918, Panama City, Panama), Afro-Panamanian modernist poet and journalist dubbed the "Black Swan."

Born in the Santa Ana district of Panama City, Gaspar Octavio Hernández would endure many hardships before vying with his contemporary Ricardo Miró (1883-1940) for the title of National Poet. Hernández's father left the family early on and never returned. By age eight Hernández was an orphan, working as a messenger boy first at a hotel and later at the Loan and Construction Company, where he would eventually rise to the positions of cashier and copier. Not long after, two of his brothers committed suicide within a three-month period, and Hernández assumed enormous responsibilities as principal provider for one of his siblings.

Hernández's affinity for literature was evident early in his childhood. By age 11, he had developed a voracious reading habit that gradually compensated for his leaving school after the third grade. He pored over newspapers he would find in the trash can at work and read the Spanish Romantic poets José de Espronceda and Gustavo Bécquer in books that had belonged to his mother. As his reading ability improved, his appetite for literature in general and poetry in particular steadily increased. From the classics and national poetry, he turned to modern languages, learning French from a Panama Canal worker who barely spoke Spanish so that he could read the French poet Charles Baudelaire in the original. By 1909 he began to study English, an interest sparked in part by United States involvement in the secession of Panama from COLOMBIA in 1903 and the building of the canal.

Remembered in Panama not just for his poetry but equally for his politics, Hernández composed a number of patriotic poems. The parades that ensued upon Panama's independence sparked his enduring pride in the new nation. He began to write for pro-independence newspapers that were now focusing their attention on an anti-imperialist campaign motivated by United States involvement in the country. He eventually directed several literary and political newspapers, including *La Estrella de Panama*. In addition, he held a civic office and became a founding member of the Intellectual Latin American Union of Panama.

Hernández was especially drawn to the Modernista movement in poetry (not to be confused with Modernism in English), which was popular in Latin America from the 1880s until the beginning of the Mexican Revolution in 1910. The genre was known for its precious language and its "art for art's sake" philosophy. Modernista poets like the Nicaraguan Ruben Darío were heavily influenced by the French Parnassian poets in Paris. Hernández himself adhered in his poetry to Modernismo's thematic tendencies and to its metric and strophic forms. A heavy drinker and self-proclaimed womanizer, he likewise embraced the bohemian lifestyle touted by Belle Epoque French poets and replicated by their Latin American counterparts.

In 1915 Hernández published his first volume of poetry, *Melodías del pasado* (Melodies of the Past), which exemplified his preoccupation with exotic themes, classical mythology, and white women. Indeed, in contrast to some of his Afro-Uruguayan (*see* LITERATURE, BLACK, IN SPANISH AMERICA) and Afro-Brazilian contemporaries (*see* LITERATURE, BLACK, IN BRAZIL), his poetry remained thematically obsessed with whiteness. "Ego Sum," which reflects his awareness of being black, is unique among his poems. A later prose collection, *Iconografía* (1916, Iconography), included chronicles, critical and doctrinal essays, biographies, and stories. In it, he relaxed the strident tone of precious odes to white women, classical gods (Aphrodite), and objects (swans, vases, etc.), and dedicated two poems to black Cuban violinist CLAUDIO BRINDIS DE SALAS. Hernández died at age 25 of tuberculosis. Today his bust appears in Santa Ana Square in Panama City. A Day of Journalism is named in his honor.

Joy Elizondo

North America

Herriman, George (b. August 22, 1880, New Orleans, La.; d. April 24, 1944, Los Angeles, Calif.), African American cartoonist whose strip *Krazy Kat* has been lauded by many as the greatest American cartoon.

George Herriman was born in New Orleans in 1880, but his family soon moved to California, perhaps because his light-skinned Creole parents hoped to pass as white and start life anew. Indeed, Herriman himself obscured his African descent all his life, earning the nickname "the Greek" from speculating coworkers. As a teenager Herriman contributed drawings to local newspapers. In his early twenties he moved to New York City and freelanced until white newspaper mogul William Randolph Hearst saw his cartoons and hired him for the *New York Evening Journal*.

During the first decade of the twentieth century, Herriman explored a number of characters and settings before developing *Krazy Kat*. The strip's main characters emerged from a cat and mouse he drew in the margins of his first success, *The Family Upstairs*. *Krazy Kat* gained independence on October 28, 1913, and ran until Herriman died in 1944.

Krazy Kat's title character, an androgynous cat, loves Ignatz, a married male mouse. Ignatz despises Krazy's affection and hurls bricks at him/her to make him/her go away. Krazy, however, has descended from Kleopatra Kat – an Egyptian for whom bricks were missives of love – and finds encouragement in the violence of Ignatz. Officer B. Pupp, a diligent and well-meaning dog who loves Krazy, attempts to curtail Ignatz's brick-throwing, but seldom succeeds.

The drama transpires in Coconino County, Arizona, a shifting, surreal desert landscape that was inspired by Herriman's own trip to Monument Valley. In addition to Krazy, Ignatz, and Pupp, Herriman introduced Mr. Wough Wuph Wuff, Don Kiyote, Osker Wildcat, Uncle Tomm Katt, and numerous other cleverly named characters.

Krazy Kat never achieved wide popularity among newspaper readers, though it attracted a highbrow following. Fans included Pablo Picasso, Charlie Chaplin, Walt Disney, F. Scott Fitzgerald, Frank Capra, H. L. Mencken, and Ernest Hemingway, and *Krazy Kat*'s lengthy tenure owed much to Hearst's personal love of the strip. Acceptance by the cultural mainstream grew after Herriman's death, as Krazy appeared in an animated series by Paramount Studios, in the tattoos and lyrics of rock 'n' roll stars, in a *Star Trek* episode, on T-shirts and postage stamps, in gallery shows and stage productions, and even in a novel. Throughout the twentieth century, cartoonists have considered *Krazy Kat* the founding father (or mother) of sophisticated comic strips.

Eric Bennett

SEE ALSO

Creoles; New Orleans, Louisiana; New York, New York.

Latin America and the Caribbean

Heureaux, Ulíses (b. October 21, 1845, Puerto Plata, Dominican Republic; d. July 26, 1899, Moca, Dominican Republic), among the most important figures of the Restoration War. Also known as Lilís, Heureaux dominated Dominican politics for more than 15 years – as elected president from 1882 to 1887 and by dictatorial imposition until 1899, when he was killed by his opponents.

Born in poverty to a Haitian father and a mother from the ANTILLES, Ulíses Heureaux was a principal political and military leader in the Restoration War (1863-1865) along with GREGORIO LUPERÓN. This conflict, which significantly involved Afro-Dominicans in a fight for their sovereignty and against the reinstitution of slavery for the first time, resulted in Spain's final withdrawal from the DOMINICAN REPUBLIC.

Heureaux became one of the most important political figures of the nineteenth-century Dominican Republic. He began his political career as the military leader of Gregorio Luperón's Partido Azul (Blue Party), opposing Buenaventura Baez's Partido Rojo (Red Party) during Baez's six-year regime from 1868 to 1874. Subsequently the presidency was limited to a two-year term; between 1876 and 1882 the Blue and Red Parties alternated control of the government. In 1876, following Luperón's orders, Heureaux defended the presidency of the Blue Party's Ulíses Espalliat. He later helped to bring an end to the term of the Red Party's Cesareo Guillermo with a coup d'état in 1879. In 1880 Heureaux became minister of the interior and police under Blue Party president Archbishop Fernando Arturo de Meriño. Heureaux served in that position until 1882, when he was elected president of the republic.

From 1883 to 1895 Heureaux consolidated and centralized his power, gaining more control and making decisions against the will and tradition of his party. He ended the previous practice of appointing only members of the party in power to the presidential cabinet, granting advisory positions to several members of the former Red Party. The president also attracted other nonaffiliated politicians to work for him and repressed the ones who did not accept his offers. He modified the constitution to extend the president's rule from two years to four, in opposition to Luperón's more democratic initiative of alternating power among different leaders. Heureaux's actions strengthened his power while damaging the solidarity of the Blue Party. The leader's autocratic decisions also deteriorated his relationship with Luperón, who later went into exile.

As president, Heureaux promoted the Dominican Republic as a politically stable country in order to attract foreign investment. This strategy proved effective as foreign capital fostered the development of the SUGAR cane industry and allowed telegraph lines, railways, and roads to be built. The economic improvement of the period was evident but was essentially based on international loans and dependence on United States capital. Moreover, Heureaux's supporters were the primary beneficiaries of his political, economic, and social decisions. He strongly repressed any kind of opposition to his government. Many of his political opponents were exiled, assassinated, imprisoned, bribed, or secretly surveyed by the police.

After 1895 the Dominican economy began to deteriorate due to accumulated debts and bad credit repayment. Heureaux's leadership and authority declined. The opposition grew and became stronger, and many of his allies abandoned him. When Heureaux was assassinated in 1899, the country was immersed in a deep economic and social crisis, which set the tone for the next century. His dictatorship served as a model for that of Rafael Leonidas Trujillo (1930-1961).

Mayda Grano de Oro

SEE ALSO
Trujillo, Rafael; Haiti.

North America

Highlander Folk School,

an interracial adult education center in Mounteagle, Tennessee, where some of the most important figures of the Civil Rights Movement studied.

In 1932 educator Myles Horton founded the Highlander Folk School. It was loosely modeled on Danish folk schools, which provided adult education, especially in history and government, to raise the consciousness of its students. Because of Horton's belief in education as an instrument for social change, Highlander offered leadership training courses to classes that were integrated in the segregated Tennessee of the 1930s, 1940s, and 1950s. Highlander focused on empowering ordinary citizens by teaching them the skills to organize and self-advocate. During the GREAT DEPRESSION, Highlander attempted to help the unemployed and impoverished in the nearby Cumberland Mountain communities. In the late 1930s and early 1940s Highlander worked with the southwide industrial union movement, and in the late 1940s it worked with the National Farmers Union. It is best known, however, for its association with the CIVIL RIGHTS MOVEMENT. Civil rights leaders Martin Luther King Jr., Rosa Parks, STOKELY CARMICHAEL, FANNIE LOU HAMER, ANDREW YOUNG, and Septima Clark all studied at Highlander.

Septima Clark became Highlander's director of education, and she developed the Highlander concept of CITIZENSHIP SCHOOLS, which proliferated in the South and provided instruction in everything from checkbook balancing to registering to vote to reading. But the main objective of the schools was to motivate its students to embrace political activism. As Horton said, students learned that they "couldn't read and write their way into freedom. They had to fight for that and they had to do it as part of a group, not as an individual."

Highlander's success in developing leaders within oppressed communities led to harassment, particularly from the Tennessee state government, which sought to close the school. In 1982 Highlander celebrated its 50th anniversary – confirming Horton's observation that "you can't padlock an idea."

Robert Fay

SEE ALSO
Clark, Septima Poinsette; King, Martin Luther, Jr.; Labor Unions in the United States; Parks, Rosa Louise McCauley.

North America

Hill, Anita Faye (b. July 30, 1956, Morris, Okla.),

African American lawyer and educator known for her controversial role in the Senate confirmation hearings of United States Supreme Court nominee CLARENCE THOMAS.

Born July 30, 1956, in Morris, Oklahoma, to Irma and Albert Hill, Anita Hill became valedictorian of her high school class. She completed a bachelor of science degree in psychology at Oklahoma State in 1977 and was one of 11 black students out of 160 graduates of Yale Law School in 1980. Her first position as a lawyer was at Ward, Harkrader and Ross, a WASHINGTON, D.C., firm in 1981. Later that year she became assistant to Clarence Thomas, who was head of the Office of Civil Rights at the U.S. Department of Education. In 1982 she joined him when he became chairman of the Equal Employment Opportunity Commission (EEOC).

In 1983 Hill left this job to join the faculty of Oral Roberts University as a law professor. In 1986 she accepted a position at the University of Oklahoma and received tenure in 1991. In October 1991 Hill testified in the nationally televised Senate confirmation hearings for Thomas's nomination to the U.S. Supreme Court (*see* HILL-THOMAS HEARINGS). Hill claimed Thomas had sexually harassed her while at the EEOC; Thomas denied the allegations. Despite Hill's assertions, Thomas was confirmed, but her testimony brought public awareness to the issue of sexual harassment and revitalized the feminist movement. Hill describes her professional relationship with Clarence Thomas and offers her account of the Thomas hearings in her book, *Speaking Truth to Power*, published in 1997.

In 1991 *Glamour* magazine honored Hill as Woman of the Year, and the National Coalition of 100 Black Women presented her with the Ida B. Wells Award.

Leyla Keough

SEE ALSO
Wells-Barnett, Ida Bell.

North America

Hill, Barney (b. July 20, 1922, Newport News, Va.; d. February 25, 1969, Portsmouth, N.H.),

African American who was reportedly the first person taken aboard a UFO.

Barney Hill, a United States postal employee from Portsmouth, N.H., and his European-American wife, Eunice ("Betty"), a state social worker, were participants in 1961 in the first and most famous case of reported abduction by aliens from outer space. Although there had been many alleged sightings of unidentified flying objects (UFOs) prior to this date, the few previous "contacts" were obviously hoaxes or delusions. The Hills, however, were sincere and credible witnesses whose experience established the pattern for future abduction narratives.

Barney Hill was born in Newport News, Virginia, the youngest of four children of Barney, a shipyard worker, and Grace Sills Hill. The Hills were descended from Peter J. Hill, a free black of Petersburg, Virginia. In 1923 the family moved to Philadelphia, where Hill graduated from South Philadelphia High School and attended Temple University before joining the U.S. Army. He married Ruby Horne of Philadelphia, and they became the parents of two sons, Barney III and Daryl. Following World War II, Hill began a lifetime career with the post office. At his re-marriage to Betty Hill he moved to her hometown of Portsmouth, New Hampshire.

On September 19, 1961, returning home from a Niagara Falls vacation, the Hills were driving south on U.S. Highway 3 near Concord, New Hampshire, when they were distracted by bright, moving lights from what they later described as a flying saucer. When they arrived home, they believed they had unaccountably lost two hours of time. Betty Hill dreamed of actually being taken aboard a landed spaceship. Barney suffered from ulcers and anxiety, particularly fear of rejection. They were referred in 1963 to Boston neurologist and psychiatrist Benjamin Simon, who hypnotized them both. The Hills reported supposedly repressed memories of physical examinations within the landed saucer. Short, gray-skinned, large almond-eyed humanoids in blue uniforms communicated by mental telepathy and took hair, nail, and skin samples. Too embarrassed to say so at the time, Barney Hill later admitted a sperm sample had also been taken.

Although they attempted to keep their alleged experience quiet, the Hills's sensational story was reported in *Look* magazine in October 1966, and JAMES EARL JONES portrayed Hill in a 1975 NBC television film, "The UFO Incident." Critics compared the case to occult initiation rites and centuries-old reports of abduction and ordeals with sexual implications. It was suggested that Barney's repressed memory was merely his hearing Betty's dream. Believers, however, emphasized the Hills's stability, even ordinariness; the fact that their stories came out only under hypnosis; and their reluctance to tell of their experience.

The Hills continued their community life in the Unitarian Church and the NATIONAL ASSOCIATION FOR THE ADVANCEMENT OF COLORED PEOPLE (NAACP) (of which both were life members). Barney served on the NAACP's New England Regional Board. He was also a member of the U.S. Civil Rights Commission, the Rockingham County Community Action Program, and the State Advisory Board of the Economic Opportunity Program. The Hills became the classic case of abduction, however, and most subsequent accounts are only variations of their report, particularly the physical descriptions of the so-called aliens. Barney Hill died in Portsmouth of a cerebral hemorrhage at age 46.

Richard Newman

North America

Hill, Henry Aaron (b. May 30, 1915, St. Joseph, N.C.; d. March 17, 1979, Haverhill, Mass.), African American scientist, first black president of the American Chemical Society.

Henry A. Hill was born in St. Joseph, Missouri. He completed a B.A. at Johnson C. Smith University in Charlotte, North Carolina, in 1936 and a Ph.D. in chemistry at the Massachusetts Institute of Technology (MIT) in 1942. In 1961 he became president and founder of the Riverside Research Laboratory. An authority in the fields of polymer chemistry and fabric flammability, he directed research on fluorocarbons.

In 1977 Hill became the first black president of the American Chemical Society and chaired the chemistry section of the American Association for the Advancement of Science. An advocate of chemical regulation and safety, Hill served on several government scientific groups.

North America

Hilliard, Earl (b. April 9, 1942, Birmingham, Ala.), Democratic member of the United States House of Representatives from Alabama (1993-).

Earl Hilliard was born in Birmingham, Alabama. He received a bachelor's degree from MOREHOUSE COLLEGE in 1964, a law degree from HOWARD UNIVERSITY in 1967, and a master's degree in business from Atlanta University in 1970. He was elected to the Alabama State House in 1974 and to the Alabama Senate in 1981. He served in the state Senate until being elected to represent Alabama's Seventh Congressional District in the U.S. Congress in 1992. He was reelected in 1994 and 1996. The Seventh District includes Selma, Montgomery, and parts of Birmingham. In the 105th Congress (1997-1999) Hilliard served on the Agriculture Committee and the International Relations Committee, and as vice chairman of the CONGRESSIONAL BLACK CAUCUS.

North America

Hill-Thomas Hearings (October 1991), a nationally televised event in which Anita Hill, an African American law professor, publicly brought charges of sexual harassment against African American judge and United States Supreme Court nominee CLARENCE THOMAS.

In recent U.S. history few events have elicited the publicity and public scrutiny of the Hill-Thomas hearings. Until the hearings, the issue of sexual harassment in the workplace had rarely received national attention.

In September 1991, upon the retirement of liberal African American justice THURGOOD MARSHALL, President George Bush nominated District Judge Clarence Thomas to the U.S. Supreme Court. Like all nominees, Thomas was required to defend his judicial and political record in confirmation hearings before the Senate Judicial Committee, and most observers believed the Senate would easily confirm him. Thomas offered a rare combination of qualities attractive to Bush: young, black, and staunchly conservative, Thomas consistently opposed governmental civil rights activity as well as AFFIRMATIVE ACTION. The fact that he had risen from rural poverty to power and prominence made him especially appealing to many African Americans. However, Thomas's quest to become the second African American Supreme Court judge soon erupted into a controversy that compelled – and divided – the country.

On September 23, 1991, University of Oklahoma law professor Anita Hill provided the Judicial Committee with a sworn statement that Clarence Thomas had sexually harassed her when she worked for him at the U.S. Department of Education and the Equal Employment Opportunity Commission (EEOC) during the early 1980s. Hill believed her statement, which she also gave to FBI investigators, to be confidential. Yet on October 6, 1991, her allegations against Thomas were broadcast on National Public Radio (NPR) and written up in *New York Newsday*. The following day Hill herself went public, voicing her allegations at a press conference broadcast live from the University of Oklahoma. Influenced by Hill's television appearance, on October 8 the Senate decided to postpone Thomas's confirmation until he and Hill had had the opportunity to present themselves before the Judiciary Committee.

The Hill-Thomas hearings, which took place from October 11 to 13, were broadcast nationwide on primetime television. Never before had the mainstream media so dramatically debated the issue of sexual harassment in the workplace. In the hearings Hill claimed that Thomas had repeatedly subjected her to explicit talk about his sexual and pornographic preferences. Like many victims of sexual harassment, Hill had kept her experience secret: she remained Thomas's employee, she argued, because she had feared reprisals and the prospect of finding herself jobless. Thomas denied the accusations. By the final day of the hearings a majority of the Senators, as well as the majority of Americans, believed Thomas, while Hill was perceived as untrustworthy and vindictive.

According to the authors of *The Lynching of Language* (1996), the verbal ploys of participants in the hearings powerfully shaped public opinion. Pivotal in this respect was Thomas's comparison of the hearings to a "high-tech LYNCHING" of himself by the white senators. Moreover, Judicial Committee members approached the hearings insensitive to the issue of sexual harassment and maintained their political loyalties to either Hill or Thomas. In the end, as *Lynching* authors attest, it was Hill who had to defend herself against a "deluge of... charges that impugned her professional competence, personal integrity, sanity, and sexual normalcy." The hearings over, the Senate confirmed Thomas in a 52-48 vote.

The Hill-Thomas hearings sparked heated discussion within the black community, some of which is reflected in two incisive anthologies: *Race-ing Justice, Engendering Power* (1992), and *Court of Appeal: The Black Community Speaks Out on the Racial and Sexual Politics of Thomas v. Hill* (1992). While many African Americans felt betrayed by Hill for accusing Thomas in public, others, such as Jesse Jackson, lauded her courage, calling her the Rosa Parks of sexual harassment. For most black commentators, the hearings ushered in a new era of public debate about the rights of blacks, especially those of black women in the workplace, and the dearth of African Americans in government institutions, especially the judicial bodies. Indeed, during the 12 years preceding the hearings only 2 out of 115 candidates appointed to the appellate courts were African American.

By late 1992 opinion polls indicated that most Americans believed Hill had told the truth. Throughout the United States women began to speak openly about their experiences of sexual harassment and to contest their underrepresentation in government institutions. According to California senator Dianne Feinstein, Hill's experience galvanized a record number of women (170) to run for Congress in the 1992 elections, resulting in four new women being elected to the U.S. Senate and a 68 percent increase – from 28 to 47 – in women in the House of Representatives. In addition, following the Hill-Thomas hearings the Senate finally enacted into law a previously vetoed civil rights bill that allows sexual harassment victims to "sue for damages in the amount of up to $300,000 per complainant." That more women than ever before are prevailing in such lawsuits signifies that the issue has finally gained a prominent place on the American political agenda.

Roanne Edwards

See Also

Hill, Anita Faye; Jackson, Jesse Louis; Parks, Rosa Louise McCauley.

North America

Himes, Chester **(b. July 29, 1909, Jefferson City, Mo.; d. November 12, 1984, Moraira, Spain), African American writer whose novels and autobiographies explore the absurdity of racism.**

An expatriate for the last 30 years of his life, Chester Himes never received the critical acclaim and popular following in the United States that he found in Europe. The indifference of his native land to his work probably would not have surprised him. In his 17 novels and two autobiographies, Himes never stopped exploring the violent, distorting effects – both personal and social – of racism in America. As his biographer Gilbert Muller writes, "Himes has one of the most radical, unforgiving, and coldly absurdist visions of the American experience in contemporary literature – a fact that contributes to his critical neglect." In the 1990s, however, with the appearance of several biographies and new editions of his work, Himes began to receive the recognition that eluded him in life.

Expatriate writer Chester Himes (1909-1984) is best known for his detective novels set in Harlem, New York. *CORBIS*

Himes was the last of three children born to educated, middle-class parents. His father, Joseph Himes, taught mechanical arts at several historically black institutions; his mother, Estelle Bomar Himes, was a music teacher. Himes was a good student, and after graduating from high school in Glenville, Ohio, in 1926, he enrolled in Ohio State University. Shortly before entering college, he fell down an open elevator shaft while working as a busboy, and suffered back injuries that would cause him pain for the rest of his life. Leaving school after one year due to "ill health and failing grades," Himes became involved in petty crime and drug use around Cleveland. In December of 1928, he was convicted of armed robbery and sentenced to 20 to 25 years in prison.

"I grew to manhood in Ohio State Penitentiary," Himes later wrote, and he also became a writer there. Before his release in 1936, he had several short stories published in magazines such as *Esquire*, one of which, "To What Red Hell," was based on a devastating fire in the penitentiary. Upon his parole, Himes quickly married his girlfriend, Jean Lucinda Johnson, and began seeking paid work as a writer. The Ohio Writers' Project, a New Deal agency, was one source of support, but Himes also had to work menial jobs. In 1940 he moved to Los Angeles, California, in the hope of writing for the movies – an unpublished novel about prison life (which would later be rewritten and published as *Cast the First Stone* [1952]) had been described as "cinematic" by a mentor.

But no studios would hire a black writer, and for the next four years Himes worked in California's burgeoning war manufacturing industries, where he found racist violence and discrimination. His California experiences inspired his first two published novels, *If He Hollers Let Him Go* (1946) and *Lonely Crusade* (1947). Critical and commercial neglect of the California novels, and of *Cast the First Stone*, contributed to his 1953 decision to leave the United States.

In Paris Himes found a dynamic community of African American expatriates that included fellow writers Richard Wright and James Baldwin. After producing two more semi-autobiographical novels, *The Third Generation* (1954) and *The Primitive* (1955), in 1956 Himes began writing detective novels for a French publisher. Originally taken on for money, these vivid, violence-laced dramas became the works for which Himes is most admired today.

Set in Harlem, *The Real Cool Killers* (1959), *Cotton Comes to Harlem* (1965), and *The Heat's On* (1966), among others, portray a black world full of contradictions – rich and poor, upstanding and corrupt, tragic and comic. Going beyond the limitations of the typical detective story, Himes wrote as much about the absurdity of racism and capitalist greed as he did about the crimes and double-crosses contrived for plot development. As critics noted and readers have always understood, Himes's Harlem, while nightmarishly violent and ugly, is also full of humor and life. As Himes wrote in his autobiography, "realism and absurdity are so similar in the lives of American blacks one cannot tell the difference."

In 1968, in ill health following a series of strokes, Himes moved to Spain with his second wife, the English writer Lesley Packard. There he wrote two autobiographies, *The Quality of Hurt* (1973) and *My Life of Absurdity* (1976). In the 1970s two of his detective novels were made into movies, and he received an award from the Carnegie Foundation. Himes died in Spain in 1984.

Kate Tuttle

See Also

Literature, African American; Harlem, New York.

North America

Hinderas, Natalie (b. June 15, 1927, Oberlin, Ohio; d. August ?, 1987, Philadelphia, Pa.), African American concert pianist and educator, one of the first African American classical instrumentalists to gain international prominence.

Following her recital debut at New York City's Town Hall in 1954, Natalie Hinderas established herself as a pianist of exceptional talent. Her playing has been described as both lyrical and technically brilliant and, on occasion, "super-bravura." She performed as a soloist with America's top orchestras and toured widely in Europe, Africa, Asia, and the West Indies. Known as a champion of piano music by black composers, she actively campaigned to expand opportunities for black artists at a time when most American conductors and music managers were reluctant to hire them.

Hinderas was reared and educated in Oberlin, Ohio. Her father was a professional JAZZ musician and her mother was a gifted pianist and conservatory music teacher. A child prodigy, Hinderas began playing piano at age three and later studied voice and violin. When she was eight years old, she was admitted to the Oberlin School of Music and performed publicly in a full-length piano recital. At age 12, she performed Grieg's Piano Concerto with the Cleveland Women's Symphony. After graduating with a bachelor's degree in music from Oberlin College in 1945, she studied with pianist Olga Samaroff at the Juilliard School of Music.

Following her successful debut recital in 1954, Hinderas continued to perform as a soloist while struggling for nearly two decades to break into the larger concert scene. In 1972 she debuted as a soloist with both the Philadelphia Orchestra and the New York Philharmonic, playing the Ginastera Piano Concerto. She toured widely throughout the United States and abroad and became known for her performances of such piano standards as Rachmaninoff's Second Concerto, the Schumann Concerto, and Gershwin's *Rhapsody in Blue*. She also taught piano at Temple University's College of Music, where her master classes were in great demand until her death in 1987.

Hinderas's performances and recordings of black piano music further guaranteed her importance in the classical music world. In 1971 she recorded *Natalie Hinderas Plays Music by Black Composers*, one of the first such anthologies, including works by R. Nathaniel Dett, WILLIAM GRANT STILL, Olly Wilson, and George Walker. Writing on Hinderas for the *American Record Guide* in 1993, Edward K. Hawkins said, "The untimely death of Natalie Hinderas in 1987 deprived us of an unrivaled exponent of piano music by black Americans.... She [displayed] a rare mastery of color and atmosphere." Among the many awards Hinderas received were the Levintritt Award and the Pennyslvania Governor's Award for the Arts.

Roanne Edwards

North America

Hines, Earl Kenneth ("Fatha") (b. December 28, 1903, Duquesne, Pa.; d. April 22, 1983, Oakland, Calif.), African American pianist and bandleader known as "the father of JAZZ piano."

Born to musical parents – his father played trumpet, his mother piano – Earl "Fatha" Hines has been largely credited with bringing piano from its solo RAGTIME roots into the jazz ensemble. He studied trumpet as a very young child and began piano lessons at the age of nine. After dropping out of high school, he played professionally around Pittsburgh, backing up singer Lois B. Deppe.

In 1923 Hines followed Deppe to CHICAGO, ILLINOIS, where a vibrant African American music scene was flourishing. Hines played with various big bands, including those led by Sammy Stewart, Jimmie Noone, and Carroll Dickerson. In 1927 Dickerson left his orchestra and was replaced by Louis Armstrong, who appointed Hines musical director. The ensemble, based at Chicago's Savoy Ballroom, became one of the city's most popular throughout the late 1920s. Hines also recorded with Armstrong's Hot Seven and other small groups; "Weather Bird" and "West End Blues" are his best-known numbers from this era.

In 1928 Hines founded his own orchestra, which played regularly at the Grand Terrace nightclub in Chicago. From there, his music was broadcast on radio nightly – whenever the band was not on tour – for more than ten years. While in residence, Hines fostered the careers of singers Billy Eckstine and SARAH VAUGHAN as well as bebop originators Dizzy Gillespie and Charlie Parker. In the 1930s he acquired the nickname "Fatha," according to most sources because he was the "father of jazz piano." (Hines told *Down Beat* magazine, however, that the nickname came from a drunken radio announcer in response to a lecture on sobriety from the pianist.) Hines continued to lead his own band well into the 1940s, producing such records as *Harlem Laments* and *Rosetta*.

Hines originated what was called a "trumpet style" on the piano. Influenced by the great New Orleans pianist Jelly Roll Morton, his work combined a strong rhythmic beat with active, idiosyncratic melodies. Hines was a continuous innovator, at one point hiring an all-female string section, and his band is consistently cited as an influence by his fellow musicians. Due to the wartime ban on pressing records during the years that his band included Gillespie and Parker, along with Freddie Webster and other key players, no recordings remain.

In 1948 Hines's orchestra disbanded and he joined Armstrong's All-Stars, which included trombonist Jack Teagarden. After touring worldwide with Armstrong for three years, Hines moved to the West Coast in 1951, where he played in small venues such as the Hangover Club in San Francisco, California. Although he never again led a large swing band, Hines continued to tour with small ensembles in Europe and played a series of solo concerts in New York City during the 1960s and 1970s. He never ceased performing, appearing in New York in 1982 and playing a gig in San Francisco the week before his death in 1983.

Kate Tuttle

See Also

Armstrong, Louis ("Satchmo"); Eckstine, William Clarence (Billy); Gillespie, John Birks ("Dizzy"); Morton, Ferdinand Joseph ("Jelly Roll"); New Orleans, Louisiana; New York, New York; Parker, Charles Christopher ("Bird"); San Francisco and Oakland, California.

North America

Hines, Gregory (b. February 14, 1946, New York, N.Y.), award-winning African American dancer and actor who reinvigorated tap dancing in the 1970s and 1980s.

Two years after beginning to dance at age three, Gregory Hines teamed with his brother Maurice to perform professionally. The brothers toured nightclubs and theaters nationwide as the Hines Kids. Hines studied tap dancing with Henry LeTang in New York City, and while touring he also learned from such dance legends as Honi Coles, Howard "Sandman" Sims, the NICHOLAS BROTHERS, and Teddy Hale.

In 1964 the brothers were joined onstage by their father, Gregory Hines Sr., who played drums. As Hines, Hines & Dad, they toured internationally and appeared on the *Tonight Show*. Tired from almost two decades of intermittent touring, however, Hines moved to California to pursue a career as a guitarist. In 1973 he formed Severance, a JAZZ-rock band, and released an album.

Returning to New York City, Hines debuted on Broadway in *Eubie* (1978), based on the life of pianist Eubie Blake. He was a major draw on Broadway and earned three Tony nominations for his lead role in *Sophisticated Ladies* (1980-1981). On television, he appeared on *Motown Returns to the Apollo* (for which he earned a Tony nomination) and hosted *Tap: Dance in America* (1989).

Hines combined his dramatic and dance experience in several movies, including *The Cotton Club* (1984), *White Knights* (with Mikhail Baryshnikov, 1985), *Running Scared* (1986), *Tap* (1989), and *A Rage in Harlem* (1991). In the late 1980s he also toured as a solo musical act and released his own album, *Gregory Hines*, produced by Luther Vandross. "There's Nothing Better than Love," Hines's duet with Vandross, reached the top of the RHYTHM AND BLUES (R&B) charts in 1987. In 1992 he won a Tony Award for his role as jazz pianist and arranger Jelly Roll Morton in *Jelly's Last Jam*.

SEE ALSO

Blake, James Hubert ("Eubie"); Morton, Ferdinand Joseph ("Jelly Roll"); Tap Dance; Television and African Americans; New York, New York.

North America

Hip Hop in the United States, an umbrella term for the youth culture that originated in the South Bronx, New York, in the 1970s.

Although hip hop includes GRAFFITI ART, BREAKDANCING, and RAP music, the name connotes more than the sum of these parts. Hip hop is a means of creative expression that gives voice to young, ethnic, urban populations. Says historian Tricia Rose, "Hip hop is a cultural form that attempts to negotiate the experiences of marginalization, brutally truncated opportunity, and oppression within the cultural imperatives of African American and Caribbean history, identity, and community."

In 1959 the city of New York began to construct the Cross Bronx Expressway. Designed to connect New Jersey and Long Island with Manhattan, the freeway project reflected the needs of white suburban commuters. By causing the destruction of numerous Bronx businesses and apartment complexes, the expressway project finished what the decline of federal assistance programs had begun, catapulting the Bronx into destitution. Longtime white residents fled to the suburbs, and slumlords bought up the devalued apartments that flanked the dusty and noisy construction sites.

A power outage in New York in 1977 and the looting and disorder that followed turned public attention toward the Bronx, and the borough became a national symbol of the inner city crisis. Bronx residents, primarily African and Caribbean Americans, received little external support as they attempted to live amid an economic wasteland. Hip hop culture emerged as a new, creative, and flexible value system in a landscape stripped of value. Although neighborhoods were ugly and neglected, fashion and art could embody pride, beauty, and self-respect.

Teenagers improvised. Black and Hispanic youths who had no dance halls and community spaces began dancing in the streets – first to disco, then to Jamaican-influenced DJ remixes, then to rap. DJs tapped into street lights to drive their booming sound systems. Young musicians, whose underfunded schools could provide no instruments, used stereo technology to make new sounds. Young artists painted on walls and subway cars instead of canvases. Breakdancing, rap, and graffiti art were all, in a sense, need-induced innovations, and each enriched the others. Graffiti artists designed posters, stage sets, and fashions for local DJs and rap musicians; breakdancers followed the rhythms of rap.

Many of hip hop's progenitors were trained in skills such as printing and radio repair, which quickly became obsolete in postindustrial New York. Unable to secure the kinds of jobs that had abounded ten years before, these craftspersons found artistic outlets for their workplace skills; graffiti replaced letterpress printing, rap replaced radio repair. Hip hop helped to ameliorate the archaic conditions of the inner city as the world approached the computer age.

Hip hop culture emphasized the new social allegiances of "crews" or "posses." Often interethnic, always panfamilial, crews and posses resembled gangs. Although a premium was placed on musical and artistic activities, gang-like rivalries characterized intergroup relations. Dancers and rappers held showdowns, competing against opponent performers, and graffiti artists sometimes defaced the murals of rivals. Hip hop culture included ongoing battles for local status, and creative conflicts often erupted into physical fights.

In the early 1980s hip hop culture exploded into the American mainstream. Breakdancing and rap gained nationwide popularity through movies, documentaries, music videos, and albums. The rampant merchandising that followed led some observers to suggest that the social and political power of hip hop died with commercialization.

From the beginning, however, hip hop artists maintained an often ambivalent relationship to consumer culture. Rap musicians both flouted and celebrated popular commodities. Although graffiti artists painted commercial icons such the Smurfs and Kodak film boxes, they often subordinated such images to their own massive, dynamic signatures. Breakdancers imitated Hollywood robots. Hip hop fashion mocked luxury companies such as Gucci yet sometimes celebrated conspicuous consumption. Members of hip hop culture neither panned nor unconditionally embraced white consumer society, though often they called attention to its artifice.

As rap artists accrued wealth and notoriety, the political impact of the hip hop ethos increased. Some rappers, such as PUBLIC ENEMY and NWA (Niggaz with Attitude), penetrated public consciousness with aggressive dissent that unnerved many members of the white establishment. Writer Kristal Brent Zook suggests that "there are persistent elements of Black Nationalist ideology which underlie and inform both rap music and a larger 'hip hop' culture. These elements include a desire for cultural pride, economic self-sufficiency, racial solidarity, and collective survival."

At the end of the twentieth century hip hop continues to represent the cultural movement that originally developed in the Bronx. Hip hop sensibilities, however, prevail across the nation and around the globe, comprising social conscience as well as artistic innovation.

Eric Bennett

SEE ALSO

Niggaz with Attitude; New York, New York.

Africa

Hippopotamus, African land mammal.

The third largest land animal in the world, common hippopotamuses (*Hippopotamus amphibius*) range from 2.9 to 5 m (about 9.5 to 16 ft) in length and weigh from 1000 to 4500 kg (about 2220 to 9000 lb). Pygmy hippopotamuses (*Choeropsis liberiensis*) range from 1.5 to 1.75 m (about 4.9 to 5.7 ft) in length and weigh from 160 to 270 kg (350 to 600 lb). Hippopotamuses are semiaquatic, spending their days in water. They feed on land vegetation at night, often taking corn and sugar cane from farms, where they may trample more crops than they eat.

Hippopotamuses traditionally have been hunted for their skin and for their canine teeth. Once populous throughout most of sub-Saharan Africa, they are now limited to areas near rivers and lakes. Highly territorial, hippopotamuses cause more human deaths than any other animal in Africa.

Robert Fay

Latin America and the Caribbean

Hispaniola, island located between Cuba and Puerto Rico.

With a total land area of 76,310 sq km (56 sq mi), it is the second largest island of the West Indies. Its territory is divided between Haiti, to the west, and the Dominican Republic, to the east. Christopher Columbus landed on the island in 1492 during his first voyage to the Americas (*see* Dominican-Haitian Relations).

Africa

Hlengwe (also known as Bahlengwe and Hlengue), ethnic group of southern Africa.

The Hlengwe primarily inhabit southwestern Mozambique, northeastern South Africa, and southeastern Zimbabwe. They speak a Bantu language and belong to the Tsonga cultural and linguistic group. Approximately 800,000 people consider themselves Hlengwe.

See Also

Bantu: Dispersion and Settlement.

Latin America and the Caribbean

Hodge, Merle (b. 1944, Curepe, Trinidad), Trinidadian novelist and critic.

Merle Hodge is one of the best-known Caribbean women writers. She was born and raised in Trinidad, and after graduating from high school in 1962 she received the Trinidad and Tobago Girls' Island Scholarship to study in England. There she received a B.A. in French from University College, London, in 1965, and a M.Phil in 1967. Her master's thesis was on the poetry of French Guianese Négritude writer Léon-Gontran Damas, and she later wrote several more scholarly studies of his work.

After graduation Hodge spent several years working as a baby sitter and a typist as she traveled across Europe, and during her travels she completed her first novel. *Crick Crack, Monkey* (1970) tells the story of Tee, a young girl who is forced to choose between her mother's family and her father's after her mother's death. The choice is complicated by color and class: one family is middle class and light-skinned, one darker-skinned and lower class. Hodge was not the first writer to portray the class and racial tensions in Caribbean society, but she was one of the first to use a female protagonist, and *Crick Crack, Monkey* won widespread praise.

Hodge returned to the Caribbean in the early 1970s and became a lecturer in French at the University of the West Indies campus in Mona, Jamaica. She also published many nonfiction essays, often about Caribbean women and Caribbean women writers. In 1979 she moved to Grenada after socialist leader Maurice Bishop's takeover of the government. Hodge was named director of the development of curriculum there and was responsible for creating socialist and adult education programs. After Bishop's assassination in 1983, she returned to Trinidad, where she continued her career as a lecturer and a literary critic. Hodge's second novel, *For the Life of Laetitia*, was published in 1993.

Lisa Clayton Robinson

See Also

Literature, English Language, Caribbean; Damas, Léon-Gontran; Bishop, Maurice; Trinidad and Tobago.

North America

Hodges, Johnny (b. July 25, 1906, Cambridge, Mass.; d. May 11, 1970, New York, N.Y.), African American jazz saxophonist who played for nearly 40 years with Duke Ellington's band.

A part of jazz's most celebrated band for nearly 40 years, Johnny Hodges became known as Duke Ellington's premiere soloist. Hodges's musical range included soaring, sensuous tones that one jazz critic described as being "draped over the notes like a lap rag" as well as snarling, blues-inflected tones inspired by his mentor, Sidney Bechet. Despite the variety of his creative expression, Hodges was also lauded for his consistent musical personality: he was considered the very model of a resourceful, self-assured, virtuosic jazz soloist.

As a child Hodges was given piano lessons, which he reputedly tried to avoid, turning instead to the drums. At age 13 or 14, he began teaching himself the soprano saxophone. When the great reed man Sidney Bechet played in Boston soon thereafter, Hodges's sister arranged for the two to meet. According to legend, Bechet promptly gave Hodges not only his first alto saxophone but also a series of lessons and a lifelong apprenticeship.

By his mid-teens Hodges was spending his weekends playing jazz in New York City. Through Bechet he had met Willie "the Lion" Smith, whose quartet he joined in 1924, and within four years Hodges had played in bands led by Smith, Bechet, and Chick Webb. In 1928 he left Webb to join Duke Ellington's band. For Ellington, Hodges played both alto and soprano saxophone as well as clarinet. He quickly became Ellington's most beloved soloist; his virtuosic range of expression inspired an English critic to say that "he seems to have an inexhaustible supply of ravishing melodic phrases in all moods and tempos."

Except for a four-year hiatus in the mid-1950s during which he led his own band, Hodges stayed with Ellington until his death. He also continued to record with smaller units, often with Ellington, as in the record "Hodge Podge." Hodges's work earned him recognition within the industry, and he was chosen best reed player ten times in a poll sponsored by *Down Beat* magazine. In addition to influencing the dozens of saxophonists who worked with him in Ellington's band, Hodges earned the admiration of bebop innovator Charlie Parker, who called him "the Poet." When Hodges died in 1970 Ellington, noting his "unique tonal personality," called the great saxophonist one of "the ever so few inimitables" of jazz.

Kate Tuttle

See Also

Bechet, Sidney Joseph; Boston, Massachusetts; Parker, Charles Christopher ("Bird"); Smith, Willie ("the Lion"); Ellington, Edward Kennedy ("Duke").

North America

Holdsclaw, Chamique (b. August 9, 1977, Flushing, N.Y.), University of Tennessee basketball player, poised to transform professional women's basketball, having completed a stellar collegiate career.

A native of Astoria, New York, Chamique Holdsclaw garnered state- and nationwide acclaim for her performance on the Christ the King High School team, a squad that won the Class-A state championship during all four years of her tenure. The team claimed a national championship and number-one ranking from *USA Today*, but sportswriters and coaches across the country focused on its precocious six-foot-two-inch forward, a complete player with offensive and defensive skills at both the guard and center spots. En route to 2223 high school career points, averaging 25 points and 15 rebounds per game, Holdsclaw faced a difficult decision: where to play college basketball.

Holdsclaw selected the University of Tennessee in Knoxville for its "great fan support, the tradition, and the togetherness of the team." The architect of that tradition, coach Pat Head Summitt, known for her ability to craft winning teams, offered a scholarship to Holdsclaw who became the Tennessee program's foundation. Between 1995 and 1998, over the course of Holdsclaw's freshman, sophomore, and junior years, the Lady Volunteers won three national championships, becoming the first women's team to win three consecutive National Collegiate Athletic Association (NCAA) titles.

In 1999 Tennessee lost to Duke University in the quarter-final round of the NCAA tournament. For Holdsclaw it was the first time her team had ended the season with a loss, but her senior year brought rewards as well. In December 1998 Holdsclaw became Tennessee's all-time scoring leader (she finished her collegiate career with 3025 points, more than any previous player for Tennessee's women's or men's teams). She also was selected as a first-team All American for the fourth straight year, a distinction she shares with just three other women.

Holdsclaw also won her second consecutive Naismith Award and was chosen to receive the 69th James E. Sullivan Award, presented annually to the nation's top amateur athlete. In addition, ESPN named Holdsclaw Female Athlete of the Year.

On May 12, 1999, the Washington Mystics chose Holdsclaw first in the Women's National Basketball Association (WNBA) draft. Few were surprised at her selection, although she was the only true rookie chosen in the top ten picks: the other nine were former professional players from the now-defunct American Basketball League. According to WNBA president Val Ackerman, Holdsclaw is "the player of the present… and the player of the future.

Some have compared Holdsclaw's future status to that of former Chicago Bulls star Michael Jordan. The comparison is not unfounded. They have brought grace, deft skill, and explosive athleticism to their respective leagues and, in the process, led a revolution in style and talent that will shape the next decades of basketball. Holdsclaw, who is able to create off the dribble, lead a fast break with the precision of a point guard, and soar above opponents to shoot a jump shot or grab a rebound, embodies a new force in women's basketball.

Sarah Russell

See Also
Jordan, Michael Jeffrey.

North America

Holiday, Billie (b. April 17, 1915, Baltimore, Md.; d. July 17, 1959, New York, N.Y.), African American JAZZ singer who influenced the course of American popular singing.

Billie Holiday lived two irreconcilably different lives: one as a consummate jazz artist, one as an emotionally traumatized victim of abuse. Her singing has inspired generations of musicians, and she is one of a few women – along with BESSIE SMITH, ELLA FITZGERALD, and SARAH VAUGHAN – to have attained the status of jazz legend. Jazz scholars treat her no less seriously than they do Louis Armstrong or Duke Ellington. Although Holiday had limited popular appeal during her lifetime, her impact on other singers was profound. In 1958 Frank Sinatra cited Holiday as "the greatest single musical influence on me" and "the most important influence on American popular singing in the last 20 years." On the other hand, Holiday's life story partakes of myth, for example, in the inaccuracies and exaggerations of her autobiography, *Lady Sings the Blues* (1959).

Holiday was also a profoundly tragic figure. Abandoned by her father, raised in poverty, and abused as a child, she claimed that she had become a prostitute by age 11. Throughout her life she remained barely literate, and she lacked self-esteem. Many of the men in her life victimized her and, when she was in her mid-twenties, one – trumpeter Joe Guy – introduced her to heroin. Holiday became addicted, and in 1947 she was imprisoned on narcotics charges.

In attempting to explain the power of Holiday's singing, musicologist Gunther Schuller bordered on the mystical. Her art, he wrote, "transcends the usual categorizations of style, content, and technique" and reaches "a realm that is not only beyond criticism but in the deepest sense inexplicable." Schuller underscored her "uncanny ability to go… beyond the song material [and to]… characterize it in whatever mood *she* happened to be in." Holiday linked her life and her singing. She said that it was easy to sing songs like "The Man I Love" or "Porgy" because, in her own words, "I've lived songs like that." Yet this sort of observation reinforces an unfortunate stereotype of jazz musicians as intuitive performers whose music simply mirrors their lives. Such an image – and the related theme of jazz artists as tortured and tragic figures – discounts the hard work and creative choices that go into jazz.

Although Holiday had no formal musical training, she pursued a far more demanding course of study in the late 1920s and early 1930s in such Harlem speakeasies as the Log Cabin, the Yeah Man, and the Hotcha.

African American singer Billie Holiday, nicknamed Lady Day by tenor saxophonist Lester Young, sang jazz with the weight of the blues. *Archive Photos*

She worked hard to perfect her singing. Her 1933 recording debut – a novelty number titled "Your Mother's Son-in-law" – reveals a vocalist still not in command of her art, but two years later she secured a long-term contract with Columbia Records.

Between 1935 and 1942 Holiday recorded her greatest work, including "I Must Have That Man," "I Cried for You," and "I'll Get By." She also recorded her best-known original, "God Bless the Child." Swing-era stars such as pianist Teddy Wilson and alto saxophonists Benny Carter and JOHNNY HODGES supported her performances, but her key collaborators were Teddy Wilson and tenor saxophonist Lester Young. Wilson's elegant style contributes to the classic quality of these recordings, and Young was Holiday's musical soul mate. He was renowned for his lyrical improvisations, and together the two achieved a rare musical intimacy. Young gave Billie Holiday her nickname, Lady Day, and she dubbed him Prez, the president of the tenor saxophone, a nickname that also stuck.

Holiday gained a reputation as a racial activist, although she never sought that role. In 1938 she joined clarinetist Artie Shaw's white big band for several months, which placed her in the forefront of those who were challenging racial segregation in popular music. Her most political act was singing the antilynching ballad "Strange Fruit" (1939), which became her signature piece. Columbia Records refused to record the song because the company feared alienating white record buyers, but at last permitted her to record it for tiny Commodore Records.

Holiday's style was simple and finely crafted. It was partly dictated by the nature of her voice. She had a limited range, and she compressed her singing into little more than an octave. Unlike Bessie Smith, she could not fill a hall with her voice, so she perfected the art of singing with a microphone. Her small voice conveyed an intimacy that more powerful singers could rarely approach. She was also highly improvisational. Even in stating a theme, Holiday reinvented and simplified the song's melody. Unlike most singers of the day, she used very little vibrato, but she employed other vocal embellishments – shifts in rhythm, especially singing behind the beat, and variations in pitch, including dips, scoops, and fall-offs.

During her lifetime these qualities worked against her. She rarely got to record the most popular songs of the day. She sang with a subtlety that did not win her great popularity, and record companies reserved the best material for their best-selling singers. In addition, music publishers and successful songwriters opposed having her record their best songs because she changed the written melodies.

Throughout her life Holiday resented the limitations of the "blues singer" label, and she was greatly disappointed when Doubleday published her autobiography under the title *Lady Sings the Blues*. She had wanted to name it *Bitter Crop*, from the final words of "Strange Fruit." Holiday – like her musical alter ego Lester Young – faced serious difficulties during the 1950s. Although she and Young did not collaborate regularly in these years, their lives remained linked. Personal problems hampered their performing abilities, and Holiday's voice, in particular, revealed the ravages of her personal life. In 1957 – on *The Sound of Jazz*, a television special – the two performed together in a moving rendition of "Fine and Mellow" that perfectly captured their vulnerability and their profound musical empathy. Holiday and Young died within four months of each other in 1959.

James Clyde Sellman

SEE ALSO

Antilynching Movement; Armstrong, Louis ("Satchmo"); Carter, Bennett Lester (Benny); Young, Lester Willis ("Prez"); Harlem, New York; Ellington, Edward Kennedy ("Duke").

Holidays. Please see FESTIVALS IN THE UNITED STATES

North America

Holmes, Larry (b. November 3, 1949, Cuthbert, Ga.), African American boxer, heavyweight champion from 1978 to 1985, whose comeback in the early 1990s led to an unsuccessful challenge against titleholder EVANDER HOLYFIELD in 1992.

Larry Holmes's long reign as champion was marred by conflicts among BOXING's governing bodies, which resulted in the recognition of as many as three different heavyweight champions at a time.

As a young boy Larry Holmes dropped out of school in Easton, Pennsylvania, and worked as a laborer while learning to box at a youth center. He turned professional in 1973, and after 26 straight victories defeated veteran Ken Norton for his first World Boxing Council (WBC) heavyweight crown in 1978. By mid-1979 he had made three successful title defenses. In October 1980 he defended his title against former boxing champion MUHAMMAD ALI.

Fighting frequently and successfully, Holmes built his record to 48 wins and no defeats by 1985, one victory short of the 49-0 record of heavyweight champion Rocky Marciano. Holmes then faced light-heavyweight champion Michael Spinks, who upset Holmes on points in 1985 and in 1986 beat him again in a split decision. Holmes returned to the ring to fight MIKE TYSON for the title in 1988 but was knocked out after four rounds. Supposedly retired, Holmes started boxing again in 1991 and defeated title contender Ray Mercer in early 1992. He was defeated later that year by defending champion Evander Holyfield.

Europe

Holt Decision, an English court decision made by Chief Justice John Holt in 1706 stating that Africans in Britain should be considered legally free.

In *Smith* v. *Gould* (1706), Lord Chief Justice John Holt freed a black slave from his West Indian owner, concluding that "common law takes no notice of Negroes being different from other men. By the common law no man can have property in another.... As soon as a Negro comes into England, he becomes free: one may be a villain [a serf] in England, but not a Slave." These comments became an important precedent in the eighteenth-century battle against slavery in England. This case, which became known as the Holt Decision, posited one solution to a legal predicament that had faced GREAT BRITAIN since its involvement in slavery: Did slaves who were brought to England by West Indian planters remain the property of those slaveholders? Or did these slaves become free upon entering England, which was generally upheld as a free land?

In the absence of parliamentary legislation, these questions had been answered in the English courts on a case-by-case basis; in most instances, courts decided in favor of West Indian slaveholders.

Holt's comments constituted one of the first legal views to refute slavery in Britain, and some judges did subsequently uphold the decision as a precedent. But others continued to rule that slavery could exist in England, and thus slaveholders were able to continue bringing their slaves to Britain. The Holt Decision became more influential later, when abolitionist GRANVILLE SHARP used it as a precedent for his arguments against slavery, which led to the landmark Mansfield Decision of 1772 that prohibited forcible repatriation of slaves from England to the West Indies.

Leyla Keough

North America

Holyfield, Evander (b. October 19, 1962, Atmore, Ala.), African American boxer, heavyweight champion of the world.

Evander Holyfield, the youngest of eight children, was raised by his mother, Annie Holyfield. When Evander was three, the family moved to Atlanta, Georgia. He began BOXING at the age of eight under the guidance of a local boys club, and although small for his age, he won several tournaments. He also played football but gave it up after he was relegated to the bench because of his small stature. On graduating from high school, he held a job fueling airplanes and during his off-hours pursued a disciplined training schedule.

In 1983 he won the light heavyweight championship at the National Sports Festival. The same year he won a silver medal at the Pan-American Games and the next year entered the Los Angeles Olympic Games as the favorite for the light heavyweight class. After crushing several opponents, he met New Zealand's Kevin Barry in the semifinals. Several times Barry fouled Holyfield, but when the referee called for a break to penalize the New Zealander, Holyfield, at almost the same moment, floored him with a left hook. In a controversial decision, Holyfield was disqualified. He eventually received the bronze medal.

After the Olympic Games, Holyfield fought as a professional. On July 12, 1986, he won an arduous 15-round victory over Dwight Muhammad Qawi that earned him the World Boxing Association (WBA) title. In 1987 he also won the world cruiser-weight title from the International Boxing Federation (IBF). Soon thereafter, Holyfield announced he would fight in the heavyweight class, where money and fame were more abundant, but where he, weighing about 210 lb, would have to fight opponents weighing more than 230 lb.

After a massive training program, Holyfield knocked out a series of larger heavyweights. Negotiations were soon under way for a much-anticipated fight with MIKE TYSON, the undisputed heavyweight champion. Tyson, however, suffered an embarrassing defeat at the hands of James "Buster" Douglas, and on October 25, 1990, Holyfield fought the out-of-shape Douglas for the crown. Holyfield won with a third-round knockout. With 25 professional victories and no losses, he was named the undisputed heavyweight champion of the world.

Holyfield's humility after his victory put him in sharp contrast with other boxers. Fans and journalists praised his proclamation of Christian principles, his respect for his mother, and his discipline. His reign as champion, however, was attended by controversy. While journalists called for a fight with Tyson, Holyfield instead fought an aging George Foreman. Holyfield won but not overwhelmingly. In the summer of 1991 Holyfield agreed to fight Tyson, but Tyson was accused (and later convicted) of rape and the fight was called off. Over the next year, Holyfield fought a lackluster Bert Cooper and another fighter past his prime, LARRY HOLMES. On November 13, 1992, Holyfield met Riddick Bowe. Large, young, and punishing, Bowe defeated Holyfield in a unanimous 12-round decision. Immediately after the fight, Holyfield announced his retirement.

In June 1993, however, Holyfield was back in the ring and earned the right to challenge Bowe for the title on November 6, 1993. The fight was again closely contested; it was also interrupted for 20 minutes when a skydiver sailed into the ring ropes. After 12 rounds, two judges sided with Holyfield, while the third judge declared the fight a draw – giving the fight and the IBF and WBA titles to Holyfield. The following April, in another 12-round decision, Holyfield lost, this time to undefeated Michael Moorer. Shortly after the fight, Holyfield was diagnosed with a life-threatening heart condition and announced his second retirement.

The heart condition, however, either cleared up or was a misdiagnosis, and Holyfield returned once more. Of three fights in 1995 and 1996, he won two and lost one before meeting Mike Tyson on November 9, 1996. With a convincing knockout of Tyson, Holyfield regained the heavyweight title a third time. In a highly publicized rematch on June 28, 1997, Tyson was disqualified for biting off a piece of Holyfield's ear.

SEE ALSO

Foreman, George Edward.

Africa

Homosexuality in Africa: An Interpretation, an overview of homosexuality in both traditional and modern African societies.

As more African nations turn to democracy, and as a human rights culture begins to take root across the continent, gay and lesbian Africans have recently become far more visible, often resulting in conflict within their conservative communities. Many African nationalist leaders believe, like President ROBERT MUGABE of ZIMBABWE, that homosexuality is "unnatural," "un-African," and a western colonial import. But there have always been forms of homosexuality and homophilic activity (affectionate relations – not necessarily erotic – between people of the same sex) in African cultures.

The ethnographer E. E. Evans-Pritchard found in his groundbreaking study of the AZANDE of southern SUDAN that both male and female homosexual relationships were common and sanctioned, particularly between men in military detachments. The same was true in ZULU king SHAKA's famous warrior *impis* (armies) of the mid-nineteenth century, in which young men were encouraged to engage in *hlobongo*, or thigh-sex, not only as a means of controlling their sexual urges in an environment devoid of women, but also to create intimacy and loyalty among the warriors. In the ancient kingdoms of RWANDA and UGANDA, homosexual activity was common as well, particularly in the royal courts; only with the advent of colonization and Christianity (*see* CHRISTIANITY: MISSIONARIES IN AFRICA) did it become stigmatized.

Anthropologists have also examined marriage between the NANDI women of KENYA, and of "Mummy-Baby" relationships in LESOTHO, where older women, whose husbands are migrant workers in the mines of SOUTH AFRICA, take younger women as their spouses. Modjadji, the "Rain Queen" of the LOVEDU in the Northern Province of South Africa, is a female hereditary leader who keeps as many as 40 wives. In southern Africa lesbian women are often considered traditional healers (*sangomas* or *inyangas*). Not only is their difference seen as something that gives them a special connection to the supernatural, their healer status also means they need not get married. This allows them to live independent lives as unattached women.

In parts of Muslim northern NIGERIA, there is a tradition of *yan dauda*, younger men who are available to older men as an option preferable to pre- or extramarital heterosexual sex. This tradition mirrors similar relationships that exist throughout the Islamic world. In many West African societies, notably the FANTE of GHANA and the WOLOF of SENEGAL, there are age-old traditions of cross-dressing, or transvestitism. In the city of Abidjan, in CÔTE D'IVOIRE, there has been a community of *woubis* (drag queens) for decades. In Central Africa, transvestites known as *kitesha*, like the North American berdaches or the Indian *hijras*, are believed to be of a third, hermaphroditic sex. In the Western Cape of South Africa there is a tradition of *moffies* (transvestites) in the Creole CAPE COLOURED community going back to the early nineteenth century; marriages between men have been common among migrant laborers in South African cities since the late nineteenth century.

It is important to note that, even though all of the above are examples of homosexual activity in Africa, it does not necessarily follow that their practitioners were or are "gay" or "lesbian" in the way this might be understood in the United States or Western Europe. "Gay" implies a particular form of self-identification that is specific to the twentieth century and to Western-style liberal capitalist society. Traditional African homosexual activity has its own specific features: perhaps most notably, it accommodates heterosexual gender roles in one way or another. Homosexuals are tolerated in many African cultures, but only so long as they play a specific gender role (by being, for example, a transvestite) or marry someone of the opposite sex and produce children – who are seen as a form of wealth – alongside their homosexual activity.

In homosexual "marriages" throughout Africa there is always a "man" and a "woman." In South African townships, homosexual men are either *injonga* (butch) or *skesana* (femme), and these roles are considered to be fixed and inviolable. Often, too, homosexuals are seen as freaks or supernatural beings with both male and female organs; in South Africa homosexuals are often known, pejoratively, as *stabane* (hermaphrodite).

Even though African communities often tacitly accommodate homosexuals, the law generally discriminates against them. According to the International Gay and Lesbian Human Rights Commission, most countries on the continent criminalize homosexual activity. For example, Article 214 of the Nigerian Penal Code imposes a maximum of 14 years' imprisonment on anyone who has "carnal knowledge of another person against the order of nature"; Kenya, Botswana, Zambia, and Uganda have similar prohibitions. What is significant about these prohibitions is that they are drawn from British colonial law – even though Great Britain itself decriminalized sodomy in 1967. While homosexuality in Africa predates the colonization of the continent, most of the formal prohibitions against homosexuality are in fact "colonial imports": the *sharia* laws that govern the Muslim states in the north, the penal codes that govern many of the former British colonies, and the powerful Christian doctrines against homosexuality that are often at the root of public anti-gay sentiment on the continent.

As in the West, though, younger homosexuals are beginning to assert their right to be "gay" or "lesbian," especially in urban settings. In cities such as Accra, Abidjan, Dakar, Lagos, Nairobi, Harare, Johannesburg, and Cape Town, there are burgeoning communities of gays and lesbians. In South Africa these communities grew more visible under the remarkably progressive African National Congress (ANC) government of President Nelson Mandela. South Africa has become the first country in the world to outlaw, explicitly, discrimination on the basis of sexual orientation. Section 8(3) of its May 1996 constitution states: "Neither the state nor any person may unfairly discriminate directly or indirectly against anyone on one or more grounds, including race, gender, sex, marital status, ethnic or social origin, color, sexual orientation, age, disability, religion, conscience, belief, culture, language and birth."

At his inaugural address in Cape Town in 1994 President Mandela himself stated that discrimination on the basis of sexual orientation would not be tolerated. The ANC has been persuaded – by some of its socially progressive leaders, including Mandela's successor Thabo Mbeki, and by gay activists within the liberation movement – that all human rights are equal and indivisible. The constitutional clause has already had much impact. A South African judge ruled in May 1998 that all laws making sodomy a crime or discriminating against homosexual practice were unconstitutional and had to be scrapped. "The expression of homosexuality," wrote Judge Jonathan Heher of the Johannesburg Supreme Court, "is as normal as that of its heterosexual equivalent, and is therefore entitled to equal tolerance and respect."

In landmark precedents, Supreme Court judges have also ruled that a lesbian mother could keep her baby (taken from her by a social welfare agency), and that the medical aid plan of the South Africa Police Services had to grant full benefits to the long-time companion of a lesbian police officer. In anticipation of constitutional challenges, institutions ranging from adoption agencies to life insurers have begun revising their policies to grant equality to gay people.

Not surprisingly, South Africa is gaining a reputation as a gay "mecca" in Africa. Given South Africa's history of apartheid, though, it is not surprising that black gay and white gay subcultures remain worlds apart. Because of its large white population, which has always had ties with the West, there has long been an active, mostly white gay subculture in places such as Johannesburg and Cape Town. Precisely because gay activism and gay subculture began during the apartheid years within the white community, gay equality still carries the stigma of being a "white" concern, and being "un-African." For this reason, even the progressive ANC has stopped short of advocating an acceptance of gay marriage in its policies, even though this is the logical consequence of the new constitution. Since the 1980s, though, significant black gay communities have developed in the townships and in the inner cities: Johannesburg, for example, boasts a vibrant black gay church, the Hope and Unity Metropolitan Community Church, with a congregation of more than 300. The founder of the South African black gay movement was Simon Nkoli, a political activist who was charged, along with several other leading South African revolutionaries, with high treason in 1986. His dual role as a gay activist and an antiapartheid activist was very important in securing equality for gay South Africans.

Spurred on by the South African experience, gay people in countries such as Namibia, Botswana, Zimbabwe, Swaziland, and even Kenya have begun lobbying for gay rights. But in stark contrast to the South African experience, these countries have responded with clampdowns and repression. In every instance the church has been a bulwark against gay activism. South Africa is unique in that many prominent church leaders have strongly supported gay equality – most notably Desmond Tutu, the Anglican archbishop and Nobel Peace Prize winner, who is now a world leader of the campaign to ordain gay priests into the church. In 1998 Tutu wrote that it is "the ultimate blasphemy" to make gays and lesbians "doubt that they were the children of God,"and that "if the Church, after the victory over apartheid, is looking for a worthy crusade, then this is it: the fight against homophobia and heterosexism."

This is a very different approach from, say, that of the president of the Swaziland League of Churches, Isaac Dhlamini, who declared that "[homosexuals] hate God. According to the Bible, these are the people who were thrown into the dustbin. The Bible says they should be killed." In Namibia, after the 1996 formation of a gay group, the Rainbow Coalition, the country's president, Sam Nujoma, told a women's conference that homosexuals had no place in the country. An official statement from the ruling South West Africa People's Organization (SWAPO) called on Namibians to "totally uproot homosexuality as a practise" and to "revitalize our inherent culture and its moral values which we have inherited for many centuries from our forefathers. We should not risk our people being identified with foreign immoral values."

This is a similar argument to the one used by Zimbabwean president Robert Mugabe, who declared in 1995 that "[homosexuality] degrades human dignity. It is unnatural and there is no question, ever, of allowing these people to behave worse than dogs and pigs. If dogs and pigs do not do it, why must human beings? We have our own culture, and we must rededicate ourselves to our traditional values that make us human beings." These comments were made after an international furor following the Zimbabwean government's refusal to allow a gay organization, Gays and Lesbians of Zimbabwe (GALZ), to exhibit at the high-profile Zimbabwe International Book Fair, even though the theme of the fair was "human rights." Following Mugabe's stand, the government has strategically deployed Zimbabwe's anti-gay laws (based, as noted above, on the colonial penal code) to drive black gay Zimbabweans back underground. Ironically, in 1997 the Zimbabwean state president, Rev. Canaan Banana, Mugabe's closest political colleague, was prosecuted on charges of sodomy and assault – for allegedly having forced himself repeatedly on one of his guards.

Mugabe is right about one thing: while homosexuality in Africa predates the colonization of the continent, the advent of a gay subculture – of people taking on identities as "gay" and "lesbian" and demanding their rights – is without doubt a new "Western" import. And this has caused a new form of tension in countries such as South Africa and Zimbabwe. Because of public discussion about homosexuality (as well as about acquired immune deficiency syndrome [AIDS]) in contemporary Africa, societies are being forced to talk about sex for the first time. This is a conversation that ends, logically, at a new analysis of gender and the roles that men and women play in both bedroom and society.

The tension is, ultimately, between two very different ways of dealing with homosexuality: the traditional approach, which finds ways of accommodating it and not talking about it, and the modern, "Western" way, which claims for homosexuals a public "gay" identity. The traditional approach is about finding a way to remain within one's family, while the modern approach – as seen in cities such as New York, San Francisco, and Amsterdam – is about leaving one's family and joining a new "family" of other gay people. Precisely because family is so important in African cultures, contemporary gay Africans usually try to find a middle way.

Mark Gevisser

See Also
Abidjan, Côte d'Ivoire; Accra, Ghana; Cape Town, South Africa; Colonial Rule; Dakar, Senegal; Harare, Zimbabwe; Johannesburg, South Africa; Lagos, Nigeria; Mandela, Nelson Rolihlahla; Nairobi, Kenya; Nujoma, Samuel; Swaziland; Tutu, Desmond Mpilo; AIDS in Africa: An Interpretation; Human Rights in Africa.

Africa

Hondo, Abid Mohamed Medoun (Med) **(b. May 4, 1936, Ain Ouled Beni Mathar, Mauritania), expatriate Mauritanian film director whose films focus on the experiences of Africans abroad.**

The son of farmers, Med Hondo was raised in the Atar region of Mauritania on the edge of the Sahara Desert. At age 18 he left home to attend cooking school in Morocco, after which he went to work as a chef in France. It was in France that he became interested in the performing arts.

Hondo began to work in the arts by acting for French theater companies. Frustrated by the roles they offered him, he soon formed a theater ensemble with the aim of producing plays that expressed feelings common among Africans in Europe, exile and estrangements. To earn extra income, however, he also took parts in movies and television. Through this work he became fascinated with film and taught himself how to use a movie camera. In early 1969 Hondo directed his first short film and by the end of the year completed his first full-length feature, *Soleil O*, which was well received on the international film festival circuit, including the Cannes Film Festival in France, the Locarno Film Festival in Switzerland, and the Festival Panafricain du Cinéma de Ouagadougou (FESPACO) in Burkina Faso.

Since 1969 Hondo has released five feature films, including *Les Bicots-nègres, vos voisins* (1973), the musical *West Indies* (1979), and *Sarraounia* (1986). Hondo's movies explore conditions of exile and alienation, often examining the case of African expatriates working in France, as in *Soleil O* and *Les Bicots-nègres, vos voisins,* or the problems of colonization, as in *West Indies* (1979). Through his films Hondo hopes to raise the consciousness of his audiences, particularly French audiences: "I decided to make films to bring some Black faces to the lily-white French screens.... For three centuries, a whole people has been led to believe that it was superior and such an ideology has not been eradicated in spite of the independence of African countries. People should be educated about the richness of the African heritage and the discrimination faced by immigrants in France. I hope my films explain Africa and the crucial and burning issues faced by Black people in Africa and abroad." Although Hondo's films have been critically acclaimed at film festivals, their general distribution has been severely limited by censorship in Africa and, in some cases, France.

Hondo is a prominent member of the Féderation Panafricain des Cinéastes (FESPACO), Comité Africain des Cinéastes (CAC), and the West African Film Corporation, in which he has done much to promote African cinema, particularly the production and international distribution of African films. Hondo brings a rare point of view to these organizations as one of the few African directors who works solely outside of Africa. In recent years Hondo has devoted much of his time to these organizations, as well as to continuing his own work on short films and documentaries.

Elizabeth Heath

See Also
Cinema, African.

Latin America and the Caribbean

Honduras, **republic in Central America, bounded on the north and east by the Caribbean Sea, on the south by Nicaragua, on the southwest by the Pacific Ocean and El Salvador, and on the west by Guatemala. Honduras is one of the largest Central American republics, with an area of 111,888 sq km (43,199 sq mi). The capital and largest city is Tegucigalpa (*see* Central America).**

Africa

Honeyguide, **common name for any of about 17 species of birds, mostly dull-colored, ranging from 9 to 20 cm (3.5 to 8 in) in length.**

All but two of the species are African. In all of the species whose breeding habits are known, the females lay their eggs in the nests of other birds, usually hole-nesting species such as woodpeckers and starlings. In some species, the chick kills the young of the host; in others the female punctures the host's eggs.

The name *honeyguide* is based on the habit of two species, the greater honeyguide and the scaly-throated honeyguide, of attracting the attention of humans or ratels (also known as honey badgers) and leading them to a bee's nest. After the human or ratel has torn open the nest, the bird feeds on scraps of beeswax and bee larvae.
Scientific classification: Honeyguides make up the family Indicatoridae of the order Piciformes. The Himalayan orange-rumped honeyguide is classified as *Indicator xanthonotus,* the greater honeyguide as *Indicator indicator,* and the scaly-throated honeyguide as *Indicator variegatus.*

North America

Hood, James Walker
(b. May 30, 1831, Kennett Township, Chester County, Pa.; d. October 30, 1918, ?), African American minister who published the first collection of sermons by an African American, *The Negro in the Christian Pulpit.*

A preacher's son, James Walker Hood was born May 30, in Kennett Township, Chester County, Pennsylvania. He was licensed to preach in New York in 1856 by the African Methodist Episcopal Zion Church (AMEZ) and, in 1860, was ordained deacon in New Haven, Connecticut. He did missionary work in Nova Scotia until his return to the United States in 1863.

In 1884 Hood published the first collection of sermons by an African American, *The Negro in the Christian Pulpit.* His other works include *One Hundred Years of the African Methodist Episcopal Zion Church* (1895) and *The Plan of the Apocalypse* (1900). Hood informally advised Theodore Roosevelt from 1901 to 1909. He died in 1918.

North America

Hooker, John Lee
(b. August 22, 1917, Clarksdale, Miss.), African American blues singer and guitarist.

John Lee Hooker's long blues career began at home, where he was influenced by his stepfather, a friend of such legendary

Blending both urban and country blues elements, John Lee Hooker became one of the style's most popular ambassadors by playing the blues on college campuses and in jazz and folk clubs.
A. Berliner/Gamma Liaison

bluesmen as Blind Lemon Jefferson and Charley Patton. Born in Mississippi, Hooker was playing and singing in Memphis nightclubs by the time he was a teenager.

In 1943 Hooker moved to Detroit, Michigan, where he worked in a factory and continued performing in clubs. Throughout the 1940s he made dozens of pseudonymous recordings for various small record labels. Influenced by the passionately expressive vocalists of the Mississippi Delta blues style, he integrated moans, groans, and howls into his more driving, electrified, urban blues sound.

Always a popular performer, Hooker sold a million records with "Boogie Chillun" (1948), and in the 1950s began working with a band, a departure from the traditional blues structure of one person with a guitar. In 1961 his song "Boom Boom" became a hit among teenagers – black and white – and helped bring a new audience to Hooker's urban blues. As the music historian Charles Kiel points out, Hooker helped popularize the blues by playing in settings – college campuses, jazz and folk festivals, and overseas venues – that were not usually frequented by bluesmen. As a result of his popularity and influence, Hooker was inducted into the Rock and Roll Hall of Fame in 1991.

Kate Tuttle

See Also

Blues, The; Jefferson, ("Blind") Lemon; Memphis, Tennessee.

North America

hooks, bell

(b. September 25, 1952, Hopkinsville, Ky.), African American feminist, critic, social activist, writer, and educator; one of the foremost African American public intellectuals.

Cited in *Booklist* as a "formidable feminist social and cultural critic," bell hooks is widely known for her pioneering and provocative scholarship on racism and sexism in the United States. A prolific essayist and the author of nearly 20 books, she has written on a range of issues, including feminist politics and the representation of race in film, television, and advertising.

In a 1995 interview with Carl Posey of *Essence* magazine, hooks affirmed that "fundamentally, my life is committed to revolutionary Black liberation struggle, and I don't ever see Black liberation and feminism as being separate." She has criticized both white, middle-class feminists and black liberation activists for neglecting women of color, and has encouraged African American women to "claim a critique of sexism" based on the black experience. Seeing class divisions among blacks as a principal obstacle to racial justice, in her 1996 book *Killing Rage: Ending Racism*, she wrote, "The ethic of liberal individualism has so deeply permeated the psyches of blacks... of all classes that we have little support for a political ethic of communalism that promotes the sharing of resources." She advocates coalitions between antiracist individuals, regardless of color and class, to counter what she has termed the "white supremacist capitalist patriarchy" of the United States.

Born Gloria Jean Watkins, bell hooks was one of seven children of Veodis Watkins, a janitor, and Rosa Bell Watkins, a domestic worker. hooks grew up in Hopkinsville, Kentucky, where her black schoolteachers approved of segregation and her family subscribed to rigid patriarchal values. Pivotal to her life was a violent quarrel she witnessed between her parents as a teenager, during which her father threatened her mother with a gun and temporarily forced her out of the family home. "When her heart broke, I felt mine breaking," wrote hooks of her mother in her memoir *Wounds of Passion* (1997). "Only unlike her I could not cry, I felt one of us had to be strong." An avid reader, hooks took refuge in poetry, learning to "enter these words as though they are flesh, a body of burning desire that can take me... through the pain and beyond." She also derived strength from the church women she knew, healers and preachers who, as she wrote in *Sisters of the Yam: Black Women and Self-Recovery* (1993), "worked with as much skill, power, and second sight as their black male comrades."

After high school, hooks left the South in search of a racially integrated environment where she could pursue her intellectual interests. In 1973 she graduated from Stanford University with a B.A. in English, and in 1983 she received her Ph.D., also in English, from the University of California at Santa Cruz. In 1981 she completed her first book – begun at age 19 – *Ain't I a Woman: Black Women and Feminism*, a groundbreaking polemic on the dual impact of racism and sexism on African American women. For her writing projects she adopted the pseudonym bell hooks – using the lowercase spelling in an effort to emphasize the substance of her books rather than their author – after her maternal great grandmother, a Native American named Bell Hooks.

Although hooks has been critical of the "conservatizing function" of academia, she has taught at Yale University, Oberlin College, and, since 1994, the City College of New York. In 1996 she published her first memoir, *Bone Black: Memories of Girlhood*, praised by Donna Seaman of *Booklist* as a "lyrical, deeply moving, and brilliantly structured autobiography of perceptions and ideas."

Roanne Edwards

See Also

American Indians; *Brown* v. *Board of Education*; Television and African Americans; Film, Blacks in American.

North America

Hooks, Benjamin Lawrence

(b. January 31, 1925, Memphis, Tenn.), lawyer, minister, civil rights activist, and executive director of the National Association for the Advancement of Colored People (NAACP).

After graduating from Howard University in 1944 and from DePaul University with a law degree in 1948, Benjamin Hooks worked as a public defender and a Baptist minister, serving from 1956 into the mid-1990s as a pastor of Memphis's Middle Baptist Church.

Through his legal and ministerial work Hooks became a prominent figure in the Civil Rights Movement and sat on the board of directors of the Southern Christian Leadership Conference from its founding in 1957 until 1977. In 1965 he became the first African American to become a criminal court judge in Tennessee. He was also the first black to sit on the Federal Communications Commission.

In 1977 he became executive director of the National Association for the Advancement of Colored People (NAACP) and became chairman of the Leadership Council on Civil Rights (LCCR) as well. A nationally recognized leader and the first African American to address both the Republican and Democratic national conventions, Hooks turned the attention of the NAACP to issues including national health insurance, welfare, urban problems, and the environment. He left the NAACP in 1992 and the LCCR in 1994 to return to Middle Street Church as a full-time pastor.

See Also

Leadership Conference on Civil Rights.

North America

Hope, John

(b. June 21, 1868, Augusta, Ga.; d. February 20, 1936, Atlanta, Ga.), African American university president and civil rights leader who founded the Atlanta University consortium and dedicated his life to achieving racial equality by improving black education.

John Hope's mother, Mary Frances, was a freed slave and his father, James Hope, a Scot. He graduated with honors from Worcester Academy in 1890, and received a scholarship to Brown University, where he graduated, also with honors, in 1894. He married Lugenia Burns, a social worker from Chicago; they became parents of two sons.

Hope was a teacher in Nashville at Roger Williams College, where he taught Greek, Latin, and the natural sciences from 1894 to 1898. His career reflected his belief that African Americans could achieve equality through higher learning. In 1898 he moved to Atlanta Baptist College, which in 1913 was renamed Morehouse College, where he was professor of classics.

In 1906 Hope became Morehouse's president. He was the only university president to join W. E. B. Du Bois's militant NIAGARA MOVEMENT in 1906. During his years in Atlanta he became well acquainted with Du Bois and the two became lifelong friends.

In 1929 Hope founded the Atlanta University consortium, which affiliated Atlanta University, Morehouse College, SPELMAN COLLEGE, and, later, Clark University and Morris Brown College. Hope was the group's first president. He also became president of the National Association of Teachers in Colored Schools and honorary president of the Association for the Study of Negro Life and History. He sat on the Advisory Board of the NATIONAL ASSOCIATION FOR THE ADVANCEMENT OF COLORED PEOPLE (NAACP) and on the Executive Committee of the Urban League of New York, and was a member of Atlanta's Commission on Interracial Cooperation.

SEE ALSO

Du Bois, William Edward Burghardt (W. E. B.).

North America

Hopkins, ("Lightnin' ") Sam

(b. March 15, 1912, Centerville, Texas; d. January 30, 1982), African American blues musician whose musical simplicity, lyrical originality, and colorful biography place him among the most respected and celebrated of his contemporaries.

As a child, Sam Hopkins met bluesman Blind Lemon Jefferson, whose talent as a performer inspired Hopkins to become a musician. During an adolescence that included cotton picking, gambling, and bootlegging, the young Hopkins developed his guitar playing by performing at parties, picnics, and saloons throughout Texas. Although he first collaborated with his cousin Alger "Texas" Alexander, he formed a duo with Wilson "Thunder" Smith in the mid-1940s after a talent scout directed Hopkins to Los Angeles. Hopkins became the "Lightnin'" to Smith's "Thunder" as the two recorded numerous sides on Aladdin Records.

Hopkins's lyrically improvisational music lent itself to solo performances, and he soon broke with Smith to develop further his freeform style. In the late 1940s and early 1950s he bounced from one label to the next, recording for whoever provided him money to support his wayward lifestyle. In the 1950s the ascendance of Chicago blues, which popularized electric ensembles, began to eclipse his career until white fans of folk discovered his apparently "authentic" sharecropper's sound. In 1959 he signed with Folkways Records and from then on held a position of high prestige with folk music audiences. He toured with white rock bands such as the Grateful Dead and appeared at Carnegie Hall in New York with folksingers Pete Seeger and Joan Baez.

In 1968 Hopkins became the subject of a documentary film, *The Blues According to Lightnin' Hopkins*, and in the next couple of years he recorded soundtrack music for the films *Blue Like Showers of Rain* and *Sounder*. Hopkins toured extensively throughout the 1970s and also recorded new albums. He again appeared at Carnegie Hall in 1979, was inducted into the Blues Foundation's Hall of Fame in 1980, and hardly slowed until his death from cancer in 1982.

Eric Bennett

SEE ALSO

Blues, The; Jefferson, ("Blind") Lemon; New York, New York.

North America

Hopkins, Pauline Elizabeth

(b. 1859, Portland, Me.; d. August 13, 1930, Cambridge, Mass.), pioneering African American novelist, essayist, short story writer, and editor.

Pauline E. Hopkins was the most prolific African American woman writer at the turn of the twentieth century. During her career as an editor and writer, she used essays, editorials, fiction, and biographies to promote her views on racial uplift and pride.

Hopkins was born in Maine and raised in BOSTON, MASSACHUSETTS. She won her first essay contest at age 15; the veteran abolitionist and writer WILLIAM WELLS BROWN presented her with the ten-dollar prize. As a young woman Hopkins became a playwright, actress, and singer with a family theatrical troupe, the Hopkins Colored Troubadors. But she eventually decided to take the government's civil service exam in order to have a steady income, and during the 1890s she worked as a stenographer. Her professional career as a writer and editor began in 1900 with the founding of *Colored American* magazine.

The journal was published by the Colored Cooperative Publishing Company in Boston, and Hopkins became a shareholder and member of the board of directors of this new company. She also published her first short story, "The Mystery Within Us," in its first issue, and in the same issue announced that she would edit the magazine's women's department. This was the beginning of an association with *Colored American* that lasted four years, during which Hopkins had an increasingly large influence on the journal's content.

In 1903 she became the magazine's literary editor. As an editor Hopkins was allied with other radical black journalists of her day, such as W. E. B. Du Bois and William Monroe Trotter, and she helped set the *Colored American*'s tradition of racial uplift and protest literature. She was one of the few women editors at the time, and her presence was both resented and downplayed by her male colleagues; as a result, some scholars believe that the extent of her influence is still underestimated.

Hopkins was also one of the magazine's major contributors. Her first novel, *Contending Forces: A Romance Illustrative of Negro Life, North and South*, was published by the Colored Cooperative Publishing Company in October 1900. Her next three novels were all serialized in *Colored American*. Over the next four years Hopkins contributed short stories, two series of biographical sketches on famous black men and women, and numerous editorials on social and political issues. She published so frequently that she used her mother's maiden name, Sarah A. Allen, as a pseudonym to prevent her own from appearing too often.

In her fiction Hopkins experimented with using elements of popular mainstream genres, such as the detective novel and the western, in narratives that emphasized black equality and the need for social justice. She was interested in the debates over intermarriage, MISCEGENATION, and contemporary scientific theories on inequalities among races, and she covered these in her fiction. She also used her novels and short stories as a vehicle for relating her own knowledge of great African civilizations. As a result, her fiction is characterized by complex plots that sometimes consider all of these issues within a single work.

It was the political beliefs in her editorials, however, that eventually led to her split from *Colored American*. Her antiaccommodationist views challenged one of the day's leading black intellectuals, Booker T. Washington. But in 1904, Washington supporters bought out the *Colored American*, and one month later the journal announced that Hopkins had regretfully resigned because of "ill health." This "ill health" did not keep her from immediately becoming affiliated with another journal, the *Voice of the Negro*, where she published articles on "The Dark Races of the Twentieth Century" and the "Negro Problem." But as a single woman trying to support herself and her aging mother through a career of speaking her mind, Hopkins found herself in an increasingly difficult position.

In 1905 Hopkins created her own publishing company – P. E. Hopkins and Co. – to publish *A Primer of Facts Pertaining to the Early Greatness of the African Race*. A decade later she attempted to begin another journal, *New Era*, that would replicate some of the successes and concerns of the original *Colored American*. But *New Era* failed after only two issues, and her last published work appeared in its final volume. After 1916 Hopkins resumed her stenography career in order to support herself. She was employed as a stenographer at the Massachusetts Institute of Technology (MIT) when she was killed by a fire in her Cambridge home on August 13, 1930.

During her lifetime Hopkins was never as well known as black male contemporaries such as Charles W. Chesnutt and Paul Laurence Dunbar. But as an editor and a writer, she used literature to spread her ideas as often and as far as she could. Her novels are available in new paperback editions, and with the resurgence of interest in early black women writers, Hopkins is receiving more of the recognition she deserves.

Lisa Clayton Robinson

See Also

Abolitionism in the United States; Literature, African American; Chesnutt, Charles Waddell; Du Bois, William Edward Burghardt (W. E. B.); Eugenics; Washington, Booker Taliaferro; Interracial Marriage in the United States; Accommodationism in the United States.

Africa

Hornbill, common name for any member of a family of birds found in Africa and Asia that have large but lightweight bills.

In certain small hornbills the bills may be brightly colored, reminiscent of those of the unrelated toucans of the tropical Americas. In some hornbills the bill is surmounted by a large projection called a *casque*.

Hornbills are relatively large birds, 61 to 152 cm (24 to 60 in) in length, and are black and white, gray, or dark brown in color. They are noted for their peculiar nesting habits. The female nests in a hollow tree, the opening of which she (helped by the male in some species) plasters over with clay mixed with salivary secretions, leaving only a small opening. While the eggs are being hatched, the male hornbill feeds the female through the opening in the tree.

Most hornbills live in trees and feed mainly on fruit, except for the ground hornbills of Africa. These large terrestrial birds feed on small animals of all kinds; the more northern species, the Abyssinian ground hornbill, also joins vultures in feeding on carrion. The ground hornbills are the only members of the family in which the females are not sealed into the nest hole.

The largest member of the family is the rhinoceros hornbill, so named because its large casque is upturned, hornlike, at the anterior end. It inhabits the Malay Peninsula and several islands of the East Indies.
Scientific classification: Hornbills make up the family Bucerotidae in the order Coraciiformes. The Abyssinian ground hornbill is classified as *Bucorvus abyssinicus* and the rhinoceros hornbill as *Buceros rhinoceros.*

North America

Horne, Lena (b. June 17, 1917, Brooklyn, N.Y.), African American singer and actress whose refusal to be cast in stereotypical roles helped transform the popular image of black women.

Lena Horne's father left home when she was only three, and her mother departed to pursue an acting career, leaving the child in the care of her paternal grandmother, a civil rights activist and suffragist in Brooklyn.

Horne's mother did return to take her daughter on tour with her. Eventually, her mother remarried and the family returned to New York, where Horne attended high school. But financial difficulties forced her to quit school and obtain a position as a chorus dancer at the Cotton Club in Harlem, New York. She was hired for her beauty, but she worked diligently to improve her singing by taking lessons, and she became known for her sultry voice. Horne then accepted a role on Broadway in *Dance with Your Gods* (1934) and afterward left the Cotton Club to sing with Noble Sissle's Society Orchestra in Philadelphia.

In Philadelphia she was reunited with her father, who subsequently played an important role in her life and career until his death in 1970. It was through her father that Horne met Louis Jones, whom she married in 1937. The couple had two children, Gail and Teddy, but divorced in 1941. Horne performed on Broadway in *Blackbirds of 1939* and became lead singer in Charlie Barnett's band in 1940. In 1941 she was a featured performer at the Café Society Downtown, where she became acquainted with both the singer and civil rights activist Paul Robeson and Walter White, an important figure in the National Association for the Advancement of Colored People (NAACP).

Horne left New York to perform at the Trocadero Club in California. Within a short time, she signed a Hollywood movie contract with Metro-Goldwyn-Mayer. She insisted her contract stipulate that she would not be cast in stereotypical black roles, and with her elegance and glamour, she became known for transforming the image of the black woman in film (*see* Film, Blacks in American). Her first role in 1942, like many that followed, was only a guest spot number in *Panama Hattie*, but the same year she played a leading part in *Cabin in the Sky*. In 1943 she was in three films: *I Dood It, Thousands Cheer*, and *Stormy Weather*, the title song of which became her trademark. It was on the set of *Stormy Weather* that Horne met Lennie Hayton. Though the couple married in 1947, the controversial interracial marriage was not publicly announced until 1950. She appeared in *Two Girls and a Sailor* (1944), *Broadway Rhythm* (1944), *Ziegfeld Follies* of 1945 and 1946, *The Duchess of Idaho* (1950) and *Meet Me in Las Vegas* (1956), her first speaking part. She also starred in the Broadway show *Jamaica* (1957) and appeared on several television shows in the 1950s (*see* Television and African Americans).

Horne has won many honors for her performances. She won a Grammy for the album based on her award-winning show *Lena Horne: The Lady and Her Music,* which began in 1981 and became the longest running one-woman show in Broadway history. In addition to the Kennedy Center Award for Lifetime Achievement in the Arts (1984), Horne received an honorary doctorate from Howard University as well as an Image Award and Spingarn Medal from the NAACP.

Leyla Keough

See Also

Civil Rights Movement; Philadelphia, Pennsylvania; White, Walter Francis.

North America

Horn, Rosa Artimus (b. 1880; d. 1976, Md.), preacher who led a popular Pentecostal church in Harlem and had a national radio broadcast.

Born to slave parents, Rosa Horn began preaching in Evanston, Illinois, and moved to New York City in 1926 in order to expand her ministry. In 1929 she founded the Pentecostal Faith Church for All Nations, which was also known as the Mount Calvary Pentecostal Faith Church.

Horn began radio broadcasting from her Harlem congregation in 1934, and her program, *You, Pray For Me Church of the Air,* attracted listeners from as far as the South and the Caribbean. As a child, James Baldwin attended her church, and she inspired him to become a preacher. During the Depression Horn opened the Gleaners' Aid Home, which provided food for the poor. From the 1940s through the 1970s Horn focused her charitable works primarily on providing vocational and religious training to poor youth.

See Also

Great Depression; Harlem, New York; New York, New York; Pentecostalism.

North America

Horse, John (also known as John Cavallo, Juan Cavallo, Cohia, Gopher John) (b. 1812, Florida; d. 1882, Mexico City, Mexico), nineteenth-century Afro-Native American leader.

John Horse was born in 1812 in Florida to Charles Cavallo, a Seminole tribesman, and a black woman living among the Seminole people of the then-Spanish territory. The Seminoles were an American Indian nation made up of Creek refugees and both free blacks (including numerous runaway slaves) and black slaves. While many Seminoles owned slaves – Charles Cavallo presumably owned Horse's mother – modern scholars describe the Seminole practice as more feudally based, with slaves enjoying relative liberty and self-determination (families, homes, and property) for giving a percentage of their harvest to their masters. Blacks even set up independent maroon communities, and Seminoles and blacks intermarried.

Little is known of Horse's early years. In 1818 he and his mother fled their home in the village of Sewanee to escape the advance of United States troops commanded by Gen. Andrew Jackson at the conclusion of the First Seminole War. Jackson's four-month-long march through central Florida was the culmination of almost seven years of hostilities between the Seminoles and U.S. forces – both military and armed settlers – precipitated by U.S. efforts to recapture escaped slaves and seize Florida from SPAIN. The invasion led Spain to cede the territory to the United States in 1819, and subsequently, the Seminoles were forcibly settled on reservations near newly erected military outposts.

By 1826 Horse himself was living in a village near Camp Brooke outside Tampa Bay. A trilingual speaker (Hitchiti, a Seminole language, Spanish, and English), he frequented the military camp throughout his teens and early twenties, selling the officers wild game, running errands for them, and serving as a guide on hunting trips. He married and began accumulating property and livestock.

Although life on the reservations was harsh – frequent kidnappings by slave hunters, drought, and low government rations – it was not until President Jackson signed the 1830 Indian Removal Act, calling for the removal of all Indian peoples to west of the Mississippi in Indian Territory (present-day Oklahoma), that the call for armed resistance arose again. A number of Seminoles, including a fiery and charismatic chief named Osceola, John Horse, King Philip, and Wild Cat, refused to leave their village, and the Second Seminole War exploded in 1835. During the war Horse served as a subchief, leading warriors and undertaking negotiations between the United States and the Seminole nation. Captured in 1838, he finally agreed to "emigrate," taking his family and more than 300 Indian and Black Seminoles. They arrived at Fort Gibson in Indian Territory in late June 1838.

Horse and the Seminole emigrants found their new "home" little better than the war-torn one they had left behind: land allotments for various relocated Indian groups were still in dispute; they were surrounded by proslavery whites and other hostile Indian nations; food was scarce; and the land was difficult to cultivate. However, in 1839, Horse traveled back to Florida to persuade the remaining Seminole resisters to relocate (perhaps seeing it as inevitable). Until 1842, when the war officially ended, he served the United States as a guide and negotiator.

When Horse returned to Indian Territory in 1843, he found his people still homeless and besieged by slave hunters, and the land gripped by drought. He made two separate trips to WASHINGTON, D.C., in 1843 and 1845 to petition for better land and recognition of Black Seminoles' freedom (one of the most contested issues in relocation negotiations), meeting with no success. In 1848 the U.S. attorney general declared the Black Seminoles not freedpeople, and therefore, Black Seminoles who had escaped from slavery were fair game for reenslavement. Although not personally threatened – his government service and father's will both rendered him free – Horse decided to defy orders to return many Black Seminoles to their former owners. In October 1849 he and his friend Wild Cat gathered up about 300 Indian and Black Seminoles and made a mass exodus to Mexico, finally crossing the Rio Grande near El Moral in Coahuila State in July 1850.

Upon arriving, Horse petitioned Mexican authorities for land, provisions, and tools. His request was granted, ironically, in exchange for assistance in Mexican efforts against Indian bands along the border. However, slave-hunting raids from Texas forced the Seminoles in Mexico farther and farther inland; they finally settled in Naciemento and Laguna das Parras. Horse himself was seized in 1852 in a Texas border town and released only after being ransomed by Wild Cat.

In the mid-1860s, when political unrest in Mexico and emancipation in the United States compelled some Mexican Seminoles to move back across the border to Indian Territory and Texas, Horse remained in Laguna. However, in 1873 he traveled to Washington again, lobbying both for land in either Indian Territory or Florida for the Seminoles in Mexico and on behalf of the Texas Seminoles, struggling because promised land and rations never materialized. He was visiting the Texas Seminoles living near Fort Clark in 1876 when he and another Black Seminole, Titus Payne, were attacked by unknown assailants. Payne died, but the elderly Horse recovered, traveling back to Naciemento the following year.

In the late 1870s ownership of the land containing the Seminoles' Naciemento settlement was disputed by an original owner's heir. At age 70 Horse rode to Mexico City to appeal to the Mexican government for formal recognition and protection of the Seminoles' land grant. His request was granted, and whenever the lands have been threatened, similar petitions have repeatedly been ratified by successive governments to the present. Soon after, Horse, the "father of his people," succumbed to pneumonia, dying in the capital on August 10, 1882. He was mourned from Indian Territory to Laguna.

Marc Mazique

SEE ALSO

Maroonage in the Americas; American Indians; Free Blacks in the United States, 1619 to 1863; Fugitive Slaves; Miscegenation; Seminole Wars.

North America

Horton, George Moses (b. 1797, Northampton County, N.C.; d. 1883?, Philadelphia, Pa.), African American poet.

George Moses Horton, who was enslaved for most of his life, has been called the first professional black poet in America. Even as a slave, Horton made money by composing poems for students at the University of North Carolina and became the first African American in the South to publish a book, receiving local fame as "the colored bard of North Carolina." But Horton's creative potential was continually frustrated by the limits on his freedom.

Horton was the property of three generations of the same North Carolina family before Emancipation in 1865. He had no formal education, but began creating poetry by composing verses in his head. His earliest patrons, university students, commissioned him to compose love poems for their sweethearts. Horton had not yet learned to write, but he dictated, the students transcribed, and he was paid in money and books.

Horton's talents were eventually noticed by white novelist Caroline Lee Hentz, who helped him learn to write, and by several professors at the university, who helped him publish his work. *Hope of Liberty* (1829) and *Poetical Works of George Moses Horton, the Colored Bard of North Carolina* (1845) were both issued in the hopes – never fulfilled – of raising enough money to purchase his freedom.

Horton's last collection, *Naked Genius* (1865), was published at the end of the Civil War, when he became legally free. Many of his poems dealt with traditional subjects such as love, religion, and death, but some, especially in later years, expressed antislavery themes. When Emancipation came, Horton was 70 years old and no longer able to pursue the career he might have had. He moved to Philadelphia and is thought to have died there in 1883.

Lisa Clayton Robinson

SEE ALSO

Slavery in the United States; Civil War, American; Philadelphia, Pennsylvania; Thirteenth Amendment of the United States Constitution and the Emancipation Proclamation.

North America

Hospitals, Black, hospitals established to serve African American patients who had previously been denied access to medical facilities.

Through the mid-1800s American hospitals routinely refused medical services to African Americans. During the antebellum period the only significant health care facilities for African Americans, "sick-houses" and "lying-in rooms," were set up on a few large Southern plantations by landed whites who had an economic stake in slave labor. The primary interest of the white population was in managing the health of the pregnant slaves, who reproduced the slave population, and of the slave children, who would provide the future work force for plantations.

The first hospital in America, a military facility built on Manhattan Island in 1658, provided services for West Indian Company blacks. But it was not until 1832 that a white-run civilian hospital, the Georgia Infirmary in Savannah, opened its doors to African Americans. It was the only such establishment in the United States. Demand was so great that 20 years later, whites in the same city opened another health care facility for blacks.

The major impetus for the establishment of hospital facilities for blacks in the mid- to late 1800s was the American government's desire to control diseases that were thought to be most prevalent among the African American population. Such illnesses included leprosy, syphilis (*see* Tuskegee Syphilis Experiment), and sickle cell anemia. The Freedmen's Hospital in Washington, D.C. (which later became Howard University Hospital), for example, was established in 1863 by the United States government to provide health care to former slaves, "freed men." A few other hospitals exclusively for blacks were established by whites in the late 1800s, including St. Agnes Hospital in Raleigh, North Carolina (1896), and MacVicar Infirmary in Atlanta (1900).

It was in the late 1800s that blacks themselves began setting up hospitals, many of them associated with black medical schools. Among these were the Tuskegee Institute's Nurse Training School in Alabama (1892), Provident Hospital in Baltimore (1894), and the Frederick Douglass Memorial Hospital in Philadelphia (1895).

The policy of white-run American hospitals to turn black patients away had egregious results, until the era of the Civil Rights Movement. In 1927, for example, a young man named George Moore was in an automobile accident in Alabama and sustained a critical fracture of his third cervical vertebra with a compressed spinal cord. His father, a black physician, observed that his son "was absolutely refused admittance to any hospital available in that territory on the ground that there were no hospital facilities for Colored patients, regardless of the severity of the disability." The boy died the following day from pneumonia, the result of rough handling while being moved from place to place in search of emergency medical care.

Similarly, in 1931, Juliette Derricotte, the dean of women at Fisk University in Nashville, Tennessee, died shortly after an automobile accident because she was unable to obtain medical care in a hospital. Instead she was given summary treatment at a white physician's office and then moved to the home of an untrained black woman, where black patients were sent because the local hospital would not admit them. Derricotte died several hours later after being rushed to a hospital that had a black ward 83 km (50 mi) away in Chattanooga.

Perhaps the most poignant measure of the difficulties posed by the lack of hospital care for black people was the 1931 fatal case of George White, whose son Walter was an administrator at the National Association for the Advancement of Colored People (NAACP). The fair-skinned black man was admitted as a patient in the white ward of an Atlanta hospital after being run over by a car. But he was quickly removed from the examination table and taken through a blinding rainstorm to the black ward across the street after the arrival of his daughter's dark-skinned husband alerted the staff to the fact that George White was not white.

The number of deaths among blacks in 1925 was one and a half times what it was for whites. Cases of needless suffering and wrongful death from lack of hospital care engendered the belief among black physicians, immediately upon their graduating from medical schools in the late 1800s, that hospitals were critically needed. Hospitals were crucial not only for the health of black Americans but also for the advancement of black physicians in the medical profession. Through the efforts of black physicians and civic-minded African Americans, some 40 black hospitals were established by 1900 in the United States, and by 1923 there were about 200, a number which only began to fill the need.

In the 1920s black physicians saw that it would be black medical associations like the National Medical Association (NMA) and the National Health Association (NHA) that would be critical in organizing support for adequate hospital facilities to serve the African American community. In 1927 the two organizations lobbied the white-dominated American Medical Association, the American Hospital Association, and the American College of Surgeons for financial assistance to implement a survey of black hospitals, which would, it was believed, illuminate the need for better facilities.

The survey results ran somewhat contrary to what had been intended, and although the black physician who completed the studies concluded that conditions were in many respects poor and hospitals in need of financial support, he also recommended that the many inferior hospitals be closed. Shortly afterward, the financial woes of the Depression slowed the efforts of the NMA and NHA. But through their continued work and with the financial help of white donors, the quality of health care in black hospitals improved by the 1940s, although the total number of black hospitals had been drastically reduced, from approximately 200 in 1923 to 124 in 1944.

The Civil Rights Movement, ironically, had the effect between 1945 and 1965 of further decreasing the number of black hospitals, which were seen as separating blacks from the rest of society. The opposition of the NMA and NAACP to segregated hospitals led to a legal battle in which the 1963 decision *Simkins* v. *Moses H. Cone Memorial Hospital* held that the Hill-Burton Act's separate-but-equal stance was not constitutional. In 1965 Congress passed Medicare and Medicaid legislation, in which hospitals were eligible for federal aid, but the 1964 Civil Rights Act had already made racial discrimination a factor in denying federal funding.

Since 1965 the need for black hospitals has decreased, because black patients and black physicians have gained access to white-run hospitals, and many black hospitals have closed. By 1990 the number of black hospitals in the United States had decreased to eight. Although it appears that their number will decrease further as the need for them disappears, the historically black hospitals were a great achievement of the black American medical profession, and a source of pride in the black community in an era when blacks were excluded from medical facilities.

Barbara Worley

See Also

Slavery in the United States; Great Depression.

Africa

Hottentot, a pejorative term used by Europeans in South Africa to describe pastoralists who speak Khoi, a clicking language; the ethnic group generally identified as the Hottentots is the Khoikhoi.

The first Europeans to encounter the cattle-herding people who later became known as Hottentots were the Portuguese explorers Bartolomeu Dias and Vasco da Gama, who stopped at the Cape of Good Hope in the fifteenth century. They and later European explorers and traders bartered tobacco and other goods for the pastoralists' livestock. It was at some point during these early stops that European travelers adopted the term *Hottentot* to describe the pastoralists, who referred to themselves as Khoikhoi or Kwena. Hottentot is derived from an old Dutch expression *hotteren-totteren*, which means to stammer or stutter; presumably the name was given in reference to the Khoikhoi's language, Khoi, which comprises implosive consonants frequently called clicks.

Europeans came to associate the term Hottentot with savagery and barbarism during the seventeenth and eighteenth centuries, when Dutch settlers on the Cape often clashed with the Khoikhoi over land and cattle. Frequently, the Dutch pressured the Khoikhoi to sell more cattle than they wanted to, and each side accused the other of stealing livestock. In 1659 and 1673 these conflicts erupted into wars that eventually forced the Khoikhoi to accept Dutch sovereignty.

The term Hottentot also came to be associated with particular physical types and cultural practices, which Europeans considered "exotic" and "uncivilized." In particular, Europeans were repulsed by the Khoikhoi custom of mixing red pigment with rendered seal fat and applying the mixture to their skin. Europeans were also shocked by what they viewed as the oversized buttocks and genitalia of Khoikhoi women. These characteristics supported Europeans' belief that the Hottentot were "oversexed" and degraded.

In the nineteenth century, European images of the Hottentot were further reinforced by traveling exhibitions. The most famous of these was an 1810 pay-per-view exhibit in London of Hottentot Venus – a caged South African SAN woman named Saartjie Baartman. After her death in 1815, Baartman's body was examined by Swiss anatomist Georges Cuvier, who later published a report of the autopsy. This report also became the basis for the Hottentot entry in his 1827 book, *The Animal Kingdom*, which claimed to give scientific evidence of the Hottentot's filthy and disgusting nature.

Today the term Hottentot is occasionally used by white South Africans to identify Africans who trace their ancestry to the original Khoikhoi inhabitants. In general, however, the term has fallen into disuse and the term Khoikhoi is more acceptable.

Elizabeth Heath

SEE ALSO

Explorers in Africa, 1500 to 1800; Pastoralism.

Africa

Houphouët-Boigny, Félix

(b. 1905 ?, Yamoussoukro, Côte d'Ivoire; d. December 7, 1993, Abidjan, Côte d'Ivoire), president of CÔTE D'IVOIRE (1960-1993).

Félix Houphouët-Boigny was the first president of the Côte d'Ivoire. Many people credit his political acumen and skillful leadership for the achievement of stability and economic prosperity in the country. The son of a BAULE chief, Houphouët-Boigny attended the prestigious École Normale William Ponty and the École de Médicine et de Pharmacie, both in Dakar, Senegal. After graduating in 1925, he practiced medicine and, at the same time, ran a coffee plantation. In 1940 he was appointed the canton chief of his family's home district; he subsequently turned his attention to politics, especially as they affected the Baule coffee farmers.

Confronted by the racist policies of the colonial government, Houphouët-Boigny organized fellow planters into the Syndicat Agricole Africain (SAA) to protest the colonial administration's race-based crop prices and use of forced labor, which only benefited European farmers. Although the SAA itself made little progress, it did provide Houphouët-Boigny with the backing necessary to take these concerns before the French Constituent Assembly, where he represented the newly formed Parti Démocratique de la Côte d'Ivoire (PDCI). In 1946, the assembly voted in favor of Houphouët-Boigny's bill to outlaw the forced labor system in all of France's colonies – a victory that guaranteed him popular support throughout French West Africa for years to come.

That same year Houphouët-Boigny joined with African assembly members from neighboring colonies to form the RASSEMBLEMENT DÉMOCRATIQUE AFRICAIN (RDA). Although the party had the initial backing of the French Communist Party, Houphouët-Boigny was afraid to alienate French President Charles de Gaulle and conservative planter interests at home, so he cut ties with the Communist Party in 1950. His support for de Gaulle's vision of a "federal community" in French West Africa won him a series of influential administrative posts, ranging from mayor of Abidjan to cabinet minister in France. But ever the shrewd politician, Houphouët-Boigny stopped advocating limited self-rule as soon as it became apparent that Ivoirians would accept nothing less than complete independence. When independence came in 1960, Houphouët-Boigny was easily elected president.

Over the next three decades Houphouët-Boigny ruled the Côte d'Ivoire as his personal kingdom. The country was technically a democracy; the one-party government held regular legislative and presidential elections. But Houphouët-Boigny used a combination of charisma, patronage, and low-key repression – primarily the jailing of dissident party members – to quell any serious opposition. At the same time, he maintained the appearance of accountability by holding public forums and allowing citizens to voice complaints. He would then choose a number of problems on which to lavish money, while blaming government officials for not having addressed the problems earlier.

A strong economy was central to Houphouët-Boigny's popularity. During the first two decades of independence, the "Ivoirian Miracle" owed much to the stable world markets for Côte d'Ivoire's two principal export crops, COCOA and coffee. Foreign investment, drawn by Houphouët-Boigny's free market policies, also contributed to economic growth, as did continued aid from the French government. A worldwide recession in the late 1970s and early 1980s, however, weakened both the economy and Houphouët-Boigny's popular support. Although the president was initially able to deflect criticism onto other officials, he was eventually pressured by opposition leaders and international donors to hold multiparty elections. The international donors, especially, were concerned about the health of the elderly president, and the possibility of the government's instability after his death. Houphouët-Boigny held multiparty elections in 1990 and won them, but even after being diagnosed with prostate cancer in June 1993 he refused to name his successor. He died on December 10, 1993 – the 33rd anniversary of the Côte d'Ivoire's independence – and was buried in his hometown of Yamoussoukro.

Elizabeth Heath

SEE ALSO

Colonial Rule; Dakar, Senegal; Yamoussoukro, Côte d'Ivoire.

North America

House, Son

(Eddie James House Jr.) (b. March 21, 1902, Riverton, Miss.; d. October 18, 1988, Detroit, Mich.), African American country blues singer and progenitor of the Delta blues tradition.

Eddie James House Jr. grew up primarily in New Orleans. After stints as a preacher, he became a Baptist pastor in Lyon, Mississippi, in the early 1920s, but his 1927 introduction to guitar acquainted him with a different lifestyle than that of a minister. He performed in various locales of the Mississippi Delta, playing at house parties and traveling medicine shows, and in 1929 served a brief sentence at the Parchman state prison. He then moved to Lula, Mississippi, where he studied further under the guitarist CHARLEY PATTON, who helped him record a few songs for the tiny Paramount label in Wisconsin in 1930.

House continued to play in the Delta in the 1930s and 1940s, often with his sidekick, Willie Brown. He was a strong influence on Robert Johnson, who sometimes joined him in playing. House later resented some of the attention paid to his talented disciple. Although he was recorded by Alan Lomax for the Library of Congress in 1942, House gave up the life of a Delta bluesman in 1943 and moved to Rochester, New York.

With the blues revival of the 1960s, many researchers grew interested in House, who had disappeared from the music scene. It was a major event, then for both House and the revival, when he was rediscovered. For the first time in his career, he played for white audiences, primarily at folk festivals and colleges. House also recorded again, and a 1965 session for Columbia documented an elderly bluesman still in full command of his powers.

SEE ALSO

Baptists; Blues, The; Johnson, Robert Leroy; New Orleans, Louisiana.

North America

Houston, Charles Hamilton

(b. September 3, 1895, Washington, D.C.; d. April 22, 1950, Bethesda, Md.), first chief counsel of the National Association for the Advancement of Colored People (NAACP) and vice dean of Howard University Law School; helped craft the legal groundwork and train lawyers for the Civil Rights Movement.

At Charles H. Houston's 1950 memorial service, his cousin, federal judge William H. Hastie, eulogized him as "the Moses of our journey." Referring to the hard-won victory against segregation, Houston's protégé and successor as NAACP chief counsel, Thurgood Marshall, described him as "the engineer of it all." In his work at both the NAACP and at Howard University Law School, which, according to historian Richard Kluger, Houston made into "a living laboratory where civil-rights law was invented," Houston was one of the most influential American lawyers of the twentieth century.

Born in Washington, D.C., in 1895, the only child of William and Mary Houston was raised in an atmosphere of racial and family pride. Houston graduated from the M Street School, the most academically rigorous black high school in the nation, and in 1911 entered Amherst College in Massachusetts. The only African American in the Amherst class of 1915, he studied diligently and was elected to Phi Beta Kappa.

After college Houston returned to Washington, where he taught part-time at Howard University until the United States entered World War I. Determined to avoid the menial service to which most black soldiers were subjected, Houston joined other black college men in pushing for a separate officers' training school for African Americans. The War Department complied by establishing a camp in Des Moines, Iowa, to which Houston reported in June 1917. He earned his commission as a second lieutenant and was sent to France in 1918, where he saw no action but did experience the racism that the segregated United States Army brought to Europe during the war.

Houston returned home during the Red Summer of 1919, named for its near-epidemic racial violence and lynchings. That fall he entered Harvard Law School, determined to "study law and use my time fighting for men who could not strike back." Houston excelled at Harvard. He was the first black student elected to the prestigious Law Review and after graduating was awarded a traveling scholarship for further study, which he spent in Madrid, Spain, completing his education in 1924.

Houston joined his father's law firm and began teaching evening classes at Howard University's law school. In 1929 Mordecai Johnson, Howard's first African American president, tapped Houston to revitalize the moribund institution, which had been denied accreditation by the American Bar Association. Houston closed Howard's legal night school, hired new faculty, coordinated guest lectures and workshops, and designed a curriculum aimed at his dream of "litigation against racism." He recruited bright young men throughout the South to attend the school, including future civil rights leaders Thurgood Marshall and Oliver W. Hill, telling them, "A lawyer's either a social engineer or he's a parasite." Due largely to Houston's boundless energy and exacting standards, the school was accredited in 1931.

Once he had established Howard as the nation's premier training ground for "capable and socially alert Negro lawyers," Houston was ready for a new challenge. He had served on the NAACP's Legal Committee and as informal adviser to NAACP secretary Walter White since the early 1930s. In 1934 he reluctantly agreed to assist in the defense of George Crawford, a black man accused of murder in Virginia, where African Americans were systematically excluded from jury duty. Houston lost the case (though the following year the Supreme Court of the United States ruled such jury discrimination unconstitutional) but saved Crawford from execution.

It was in the field of educational equality that Houston, who finally accepted White's invitation to become NAACP chief counsel in 1935, proved indispensable. With financial support from the Garland Fund (later called the American Fund for Public Service), the association commissioned the Margold Report, a rough blueprint for the fight. Houston agreed that education should be the primary battlefront, writing in a 1935 letter that "discrimination in education is symbolic of all the more drastic discriminations which Negroes suffer in American life." Reflecting Houston's understanding of political power and sensitivity to public opinion, his strategy differed from the Margold Report in its emphasis on gradual change and the building of legal precedent. He chose three primary targets: the different pay scales for black and white teachers; the disparity in transportation provided for black and white students; and the inequality in opportunity for graduate study at state-supported segregated institutions. It was the third approach that proved most successful, spawning the three Supreme Court cases that together provided the ammunition to topple *Plessy* v. *Ferguson*'s prescription for "separate but equal" accommodations.

The first, *Missouri* ex rel. *Gaines* v. *Canada*, involved Missouri's refusal to admit African American students to the state university's law school, offering applicants instead the choice of going out of state or attending a separate black law school yet to be established. The Court found in 1938 that such unequal provisions created an unfair "privilege… for white law students" that was denied African Americans. Though argued by Marshall, who had succeeded him as chief counsel, it was Houston's strategy and advice that helped win two cases in which inequality was less blatant. *McLaurin* v. *Oklahoma* concerned a lone black student who was segregated within the state's graduate school of education; and in Sweatt v. Painter, Texas provided a separate black law school that shared some facilities with the white institution. In both cases, eventually decided in 1950, the year of Houston's death, the court edged closer to overturning *Plessy*, ruling that intangible effects of inequality could violate a plaintiff's right to equal protection under the Fourteenth Amendment.

His health poor, in 1938 Houston stepped down as NAACP chief counsel. But he continued fighting for racial justice, as his biographer Genna R. McNeil says, "on diverse fronts." Returning to Washington, where he had served on the district's board of education from 1933 to 1935, Houston rejoined his father's law firm and began to focus on economic inequality. Representing two railroad unions, he challenged discriminatory actions by government negotiators and contractors. In 1944 he was appointed to the Fair Employment Practices Committee (FEPC), from which he resigned in 1945 in protest over its imminent disbanding. Already hospitalized for exhaustion once before, Houston suffered a serious heart attack in 1948. He died two years later, leaving behind his second wife, Henrietta, and their only child, Charles Hamilton Houston Jr.

Friends and associates remembered him as hard-driving and brilliant, a perfectionist whose passion was submerged beneath a dignified demeanor ("Lose your temper, lose your case" was one of many aphorisms his law students heard). For his work on behalf of school desegregation (which ultimately prevailed in 1954's *Brown* v. *Board of Education*), the NAACP posthumously awarded him its Spingarn Medal. In 1958 Howard University renamed its main law school building after the man who had written to one of his students, "The most important thing… is that no Negro tolerate any ceiling on his ambitions or imagination."

Kate Tuttle

See Also

Military, Blacks in the American; *Brown* v. *Board of Education*; Fourteenth Amendment to the United States Constitution; Hastie, William Henry; Johnson, Mordecai Wyatt; Labor Unions in the United States; Lynching; *Plessy* v. *Ferguson*; White, Walter Francis.

North America

Houston, Texas, **American city that is home to one of the largest African American populations in the South.**

Unlike many United States cities, whose black and white populations have followed markedly different patterns of demographic change, Houston has been home to a consistent proportion of African Americans since its founding in 1836. Because African American and white numbers grew roughly in sync – blacks never flooded the city in a mass migration – Houston blacks suffered less discrimination than blacks in many other Southern cities.

African Americans lived as slaves both in and around Houston until the end of the Civil War. Before the war many supported Houston's bustling commerce as dockworkers and road and railway builders, living under fewer restrictions than plantation slaves. After the war plantation slaves migrated to the city with hopes of better jobs but were often disappointed. Overt job discrimination persisted as late as the 1950s, and blacks who did obtain work earned less money than whites in comparable positions. Nevertheless, Houston's above-average economic prosperity touched its black population. The discovery of oil in 1901, the completion of a shipping channel in 1914 (which made Houston a deep-water port), and an economic boom in the 1970s all contributed to a higher standard of living for African Americans as well as whites.

Throughout the city's history, specific institutions and people reflected the ingenuity and strength of Houston's black community. Social societies and churches played a central role in surmounting the obstacles of RECONSTRUCTION, JIM CROW, and the CIVIL RIGHTS MOVEMENT. Antioch Baptist Church, founded in 1866, still operates today. In the 1920s and 1930s the weekly *Houston Informer* provided a rallying cry for black businessmen who competed with whites for black patrons. The founding of a college in 1927, which became Texas Southern University in 1947, also helped solidify community consciousness and pride.

From the Reconstruction successes of black businessman Richard Allen, who served in the state legislature, to the 1972 election of Barbara Jordan to the U.S. House of Representatives, numerous black Houstonians have overcome white oppression to gain elected offices. Meanwhile, black RHYTHM AND BLUES musicians – notably T-Bone Walker, Sam "Lightnin'" Hopkins, and Johnny Ace – embodied the cultural flavor of Houston's African American population.

Houston's economy bottomed out with the drop of oil prices in the 1980s, ending the relative prosperity of blacks during the 1970s. Studies show, however, that education is closing the gap between white and black economic opportunities. While African Americans continue to fill a disproportionate number of low-paying jobs, the number of black homeowners and professionals is on the rise.

Eric Bennett

SEE ALSO

Slavery in the United States; Civil War, American; Hopkins, ("Lightnin'") Sam; Jordan, Barbara Charline; Walker, Aaron ("T-Bone").

North America

Houston, Whitney (b. August 9, 1963, Newark, N.J.), African American singer, model, and film actress; one of the most successful musical performers in the United States.

Since the release of her debut album in 1985, Whitney Houston has enjoyed a meteoric musical career that has carried her into film stardom and made her an internationally recognized celebrity. With six albums, including three film soundtrack recordings, she continues to stun audiences with the power, range, and resilience of her voice. *New York Times* writer Stephen Holden has called her "the pop gospel equivalent of an Olympic athlete."

The youngest of three children, Houston grew up in East Orange, New Jersey, where her family settled after the Newark riots of 1967. Her mother, Emily "Cissy" Drinkard Houston, the lead singer of the soul group Sweet Inspirations, frequently brought young Whitney to the recording studios of some of the era's leading female gospel-turned-pop vocalists – Aretha Franklin and Whitney's cousins, Dee Dee and DIONNE WARWICK. Houston was particularly inspired by the emotional appeal of Franklin's voice and vowed early to do the same in her own singing. At age 12 Houston gave her first solo performance at Newark's New Hope Baptist Church. While in high school, she often performed with her mother in New York clubs and backed such singers as Lou Rawls and Chaka Khan. She also modeled for women's magazines such as *Vogue*, *Cosmopolitan*, and *Seventeen*.

In 1983 Houston met Arista Records founder Clive Davis, who signed her with Arista and proved instrumental in promoting her career. Houston's talent, coupled with a dynamic songwriting team that included Jermaine Jackson and composer Michael Masser, culminated in the record-setting 1985 album *Whitney Houston*, the sales of which topped all albums previously recorded by a black female vocalist. By 1995 Houston's first four albums had sold 66 million copies and won her myriad awards, including 12 American Music awards and five Grammy awards, three of which she received for the film soundtrack *The Bodyguard* in 1992.

In addition to singing, Houston has starred in several films, including *The Bodyguard* (1992), *Waiting to Exhale* (1995), and the *Preacher's Wife* (1996), in which she starred, opposite DENZEL WASHINGTON, as a church gospel choir director.

Roanne Edwards

SEE ALSO

Soul Music; Franklin, Aretha Louise; Jackson, Michael, and the Jackson Family; Newark, New Jersey; Rawls, Louis Allen (Lou).

North America

Howard University, predominantly black university located in Washington, D.C., that has the largest concentration of African American students and faculty of any university in the world.

Like many of the present 117 historically black colleges and universities (HBCUs), Howard was founded by whites. In 1866 ten members of the First Congregational Society of WASHINGTON, D.C., established the Howard Normal and Theological Institute for Education of Teachers and Preachers. The seminary, named in honor of the commissioner of the Freedmen's Bureau, Maj. Gen. Oliver Otis Howard, received its university charter from President Andrew Johnson in March 1867. Two months later the board of trustees shortened its name to Howard University and opened its doors to four young white girls – the daughters of some of the university's trustees and faculty.

Although FREDERICK DOUGLASS and Booker T. Washington were appointed to the university's private board of trustees in 1871 and 1907, respectively, very few African Americans were involved in either the administration or governance of the university during its early years. In addition, early financial support came from white sources: during the institution's first five years, it received most of its financial support from the Freedmen's Bureau. After the Bureau closed in 1872, the United States Congress agreed in 1879 to make an annual appropriation to the university.

Receiving money from Congress proved to be a mixed blessing. Congressional subsidies enabled the university to flourish, but often at the expense of freedom of thought and freedom of expression. Congress pressured university officials to monitor the activities and teachings of professors who were suspected of being communists or socialists. In the early 1940s several Howard faculty members, including English scholar Alphaeus Hunton, were investigated by the House Un-American Activities Committee. Although vindication eventually came for those faculty members who were investigated, serious questions were raised about the university's lack of autonomy.

Mordecai Johnson, appointed Howard's first black president in 1926, transformed the university into a major institution of higher learning. When Johnson first arrived at Howard, the university was composed of eight unaccredited schools and colleges, with a total enrollment of 1700 and a budget of $700,000. At his retirement 34 years later, Howard had ten nationally accredited schools and colleges, 6000 students, and an $8 million budget. The reputation of Howard's faculty grew during this time, when the university included scholars such as biologist Ernest E. Just, historian KELLY MILLER, writer Alain

Mordecai Wyatt Johnson became the first African American president of Howard University in 1926. *Photographs and Prints Division, Schomburg Center for Research in Black Culture, The New York Public Library, Astor, Lenox and Tilden Foundation*

Locke, sociologist E. Franklin Frazier, and economist Abram Harris Jr.

In 1960 Dr. James M. Nabrit, a leading constitutional lawyer and former dean of the Howard Law School, succeeded Johnson as president. Nabrit is credited with establishing the first systematic civil rights course at an American law school. Between 1969 and 1988 Howard continued to grow under the leadership of James E. Cheek and Carlton P. Alexis. In 1989 Franklyn G. Jenifer became the first Howard alumnus to serve as president.

Students at Howard also have been active participants in shaping both the university's curriculum and its direction. In the late 1960s student demonstrators demanded and won an African American Studies Department. In 1989 hundreds of student protesters forced Lee Atwater, chairman of the Republican Party, to resign from the university's board of trustees. Student activists were also successful in forcing the university's financial divestment from South Africa. In 1994 controversy erupted when a student group invited Khalid Abdul Muhammad, an outspoken official of the Nation of Islam, to speak on campus.

Since its beginnings Howard has educated more than 68,000 students, including diplomat Ralph Bunche, surgeon Charles Drew, author Zora Neale Hurston, U.S. Supreme Court Justice Thurgood Marshall, and Nobel laureate Toni Morrison. Today more than 12,000 Howard students, from all 50 states and more than 100 foreign countries, choose courses among 18 fully accredited schools and colleges. There are more than 70 major buildings located throughout the university's four campuses, including WHUR-FM and WHMM-TV, the first radio and television stations to be owned and operated by a black university in the United States. The university also features the Moorland-Spingarn Research Center, one of the largest and most comprehensive black research collections in the world.

Alonford James Robinson, Jr.

See Also
Bunche, Ralph Johnson; Bureau of Refugees, Freedmen and Abandoned Lands; Drew, Charles Richard; Frazier, Edward Franklin; Johnson, Mordecai Wyatt; Just, Ernest Everett; Locke, Alain Leroy; Moorland-Spingarn Research Collection; Nabrit, James Madison; Socialism; Washington, Booker Taliaferro; Communist Party USA, African Americans and the.

Latin America and the Caribbean

Howell, Leonard P., *see* Early Rastafarian Leaders.

North America

Howlin' Wolf (Chester Arthur Burnett)

(b. June 10, 1910, near West Point, Miss.; d. January 10, 1976, Hines, Ill.), blues musician who helped to import the rural music of the Mississippi River Delta to Chicago in the 1950s, thus making possible the creation of the new Chicago blues sound.

Howlin' Wolf was born Chester Arthur Burnett to plantation workers in Mississippi and as a youth worked in the fields himself. Throughout his childhood he was exposed to music from the Baptist church but did not take up the guitar until his teenage years. When Wolf was 18 he met bluesman Charley Patton, who instructed him in the rudiments of the genre. Another blues musician, Sonny Boy Williamson, whom Wolf knew as the husband of his half-sister, completed Wolf's education by teaching him to play the harmonica. During the 1920s and 1930s Wolf traveled the South, sometimes performing with blues veterans such as Robert Johnson, sometimes farming to support himself.

During World War II Wolf was drafted by the United States Army. When he returned from the service in 1945, he settled in West Memphis, Arkansas, where he started a band and secured work with local radio station KWEM. Wolf established himself as a charismatic disc jockey as well as a burgeoning blues star and caught the attention of promoter and musician Ike Turner, who encouraged producer Sam Phillips (later the owner of Sun Records) to record him. Phillips did, and sold the recordings to two different labels, Chicago-based Chess Records and the Bihari Brothers in California. The tremendous popularity of these recordings set the two companies at odds, and after legal negotiations, Wolf signed with Chess and moved to Chicago in 1953.

At Chess Records Wolf met bluesman and songwriter Willie Dixon, who composed many of Wolf's hits, including "Back Door Man," "Little Red Rooster," and "I Ain't Superstitious." Dixon meanwhile provided material for bluesman Muddy Waters, also of Chess Records, who became Wolf's local rival. Waters and Wolf – with the help of Dixon – at this time defined the Chicago Blues sound, each trying to outdo the other with rawness, intensity, and electric bravura. Wolf's performance style, which had always emulated Charley Patton's dramatic approach, became fully realized. He sang a harsh blend of gravelly bellows and falsetto howls, writhing on stage in the spirit of his music. In addition to Dixon's songs, Wolf popularized a number of his own compositions, including "Smokestack Lightning" and "Killing Floor."

Wolf's great popularity sustained him through the blues industry's lull during the late 1950s, and when British rock 'n' rollers such as the Rolling Stones and the Yardbirds began to popularize blues music among white listeners, Wolf experienced a resurgence of fame. He appeared with the Rolling Stones on the television show "Shindig," and toured Europe and America with the white groups who had appropriated his music. In the late 1960s he recorded *The London Howlin' Wolf Sessions*, joined by white guitarist Eric Clapton as well as members of the Rolling Stones and Ringo Starr of the Beatles.

In the 1970s Wolf scaled down his demanding tour schedule due to poor health. In the early 1970s he survived a heart attack and a car accident but kidney damage from the latter killed him in 1976. Wolf gave his last performance with bluesman B. B. King in November 1975. He was inducted into the Blues Foundation's Hall of Fame in 1980 and the Rock and Roll Hall of Fame in 1991.

Eric Bennett

See Also
World War II and African Americans; Baptists; Blues, The; Chicago, Illinois; Johnson, Robert Leroy; King, Riley B. ("B. B."); Television and African Americans; Williamson, Johnny Lee ("Sonny Boy").

Africa

Huddleston, Trevor (b. 1913, Bedford, England), British Anglican priest who became renowned for his opposition to apartheid, the South African government's rigid policy of racial separation.

Trevor Huddleston was ordained a priest in 1937 and entered the Community of the Resurrection Anglican order before being sent to South Africa in 1943 (*see* Christianity: Missionaries in Africa). As deacon of the Anglican Missions of Sophiatown and then Orlando (outside Johannesburg), he witnessed and protested against the injustices of apartheid. When the Native Resettlement Act of 1954 called for the destruction of Sophiatown to make way for a white suburb, he became chair of the Western Areas Protest Committee to support the blacks in defense of their homes. Despite his actions, Sophiatown was bulldozed in 1955 and the black residents were relocated to the black township of Soweto. Huddleston recorded the plight of Sophiatown in his 1956 book *Naught for Your Comfort*, a condemnation of South Africa's policy of persecution. He also worked with the African National Congress (ANC) to help bring about the Freedom Charter (the ANC's guiding statement of principles). He was later recalled to Great Britain, where he worked to focus international attention on the antiapartheid movement.

Huddleston served as bishop of Masasi in Tanzania from 1960 to 1968; bishop suffragan (bishop of a diocese within an archdiocese) of Stepney in London from 1968 to 1978; and both bishop of Mauritius and archbishop of the Indian Ocean from 1978 to 1983. He was vice president of the British Anti-Apartheid Movement from 1969 to 1981 and became chairman of the International Defense and Aid Fund for Southern Africa in 1983. He became founding patron of Action for Southern Africa in 1994.

See Also
Sophiatown, South Africa; Johannesburg, South Africa; Soweto, South Africa.

North America

Hudson, Hosea (b. 1898, Wilkes County, Ga.; d. 1988, Gainesville, Fla.), American union leader and communist activist who was a voice for African American workers during the Great Depression.

As a youth Hosea Hudson worked with his family on the sharecropping land where they lived and was, therefore, unable to attend school. In 1917 he married and began sharecropping land separately from his family. After boll weevils destroyed his crops, he moved with his new family to Atlanta in 1923. The next year he settled in Birmingham, Alabama, where he began his career in iron molding.

Hudson soon engaged in informal attempts to better the treatment of African American workers. But it was not until 1931, when he joined the Communist Party of the U.S.A. (CPUSA), that he became a public voice for worker's rights. Fired within a year from the Stockham Foundry and forced to find work under pseudonyms, he nonetheless continued to fight the Great Depression's devastating effects on African American workers. During the 1930s he strengthened his ties to the CPUSA while simultaneously working for the government on the Works Progress Administration (WPA). He also founded the Right to Vote Club in the struggle for African American enfranchisement. From 1940 to 1947 Hudson was an official in the United Steel Workers Local and the Birmingham Industrial Union Council, but eventually was expelled from any involvement in the organizations as a result of his CPUSA membership.

Forced to conceal his identity from this period until 1956 due to widespread anticommunist sentiment, Hudson lived in Atlanta and New York City. After moving to Atlantic City, he remained a CPUSA liaison while working as a janitor. Rediscovered by the American left in the early 1980s, Hudson was given the key to the city of Birmingham for his civil rights work. He remained politically active until his death in 1988.

See Also
Atlanta, Georgia; Great Depression; New York, New York; Labor Unions in the United States; Communist Party USA, African Americans and the.

North America

Hughes, Langston (b. February 1, 1902, Joplin, Mo.; d. May 22, 1967, New York, N.Y.), African American writer known especially for his poetry and for his use of Black Vernacular English, black cultural references, and black musical rhythms in his writing.

The following passage from "Harlem," a poem by Langston Hughes, has been described as a "virtual anthem of black America":

What happens to a dream deferred?
Does it dry up
like a raisin in the sun?
Or fester like a sore –
And then run?
... Maybe it just sags
like a heavy load.
Or does it explode?

As a poet, playwright, fiction writer, autobiographer, and anthologist, Hughes captured the moods and rhythms of the black communities he knew and loved – and translated those rhythms to the printed page. Hughes has been called "the literary explicator and interpreter of the social, cultural, spiritual, and emotional experiences of Black America," and this grand description is accurate for the role his writings have played in twentieth-century American literature.

Hughes was born in Joplin, Missouri, in 1902. His father, a lawyer frustrated by American racism, emigrated to Mexico when Hughes was a year old, and Hughes spent most of his childhood at his maternal grandmother's home in Lawrence, Kansas. His grandmother had been an activist for decades. Her first husband had been killed in the slave rebellion at Harpers Ferry (*see* John Brown); her second, Hughes's grandfather, was the brother of abolitionist John Mercer Langston and a participant in Kansas politics during Reconstruction. In his grandmother's home, Hughes was part of a close-knit black community, and he was always encouraged to read.

As a teenager Hughes lived with his mother in Lincoln, Illinois, and Cleveland, Ohio. In Cleveland he contributed to his high school literary magazine, was elected class poet his senior year, and graduated from high school in 1920. Hughes then spent a year in Mexico with his father. A poem he wrote on the train ride there, "The Negro Speaks of Rivers," was published in the June 1921 issue of *Crisis*, the official publication of the National Association for the Advancement of Colored People (NAACP). It is still perhaps his best-known poem, and it instantly confirmed his potential as a serious writer.

At his father's wish Hughes enrolled at Columbia University in New York in the fall of 1927, but he stayed only one year and spent most of his time in Harlem, in upper Manhattan. He took a series of jobs that included traveling down the west coast of Africa and then to Europe as a crew member on a merchant steamer. Hughes continued writing poetry during his travels, publishing much of it back home in black journals such as *Crisis* and the National Urban League's *Opportunity*. By the time he returned to the United States in 1924, his reputation was already established. He won first prize in *Opportunity*'s 1925 poetry contest for his poem "The Weary Blues," and the following year Alfred A. Knopf published *The Weary Blues,* Hughes's first volume of poetry.

By this time Hughes was recognized as one of the leading figures in the constellation of black writers, artists, and musicians in New York who created the Harlem Renaissance. Hughes's poetry was greatly influenced by the people and culture around him. He admired the narrative style of poets Carl Sandburg and Walt Whitman, but was also influenced by Paul Laurence Dunbar's poems written in black dialect, and he incorporated the rhythms of black speech into many of his poems. Above all, Hughes was influenced by black music, especially jazz and blues.

Hughes's poems are often "lyrical" in the musical sense of the word – many of them could easily be set to a rhythmic beat. They also incorporate some of the same subject matter found in many blues lyrics, and portray nuances of black life – including sexuality – missing in earlier black literature. In a 1926 essay titled "The Negro Artist and the Racial Mountain," Hughes eloquently defended the honest representations of black culture and the use of jazz, dialect, and other influences from the black vernacular that had become a trademark in the work of many Harlem Renaissance writers. As Hughes put it, "We younger Negro artists who create now intend to express our individual dark-skinned selves without fear or shame."

Hughes enrolled in Lincoln University in Lincoln, Pennsylvania, in 1927, and graduated in 1929. The next year he published his first novel, *Not Without Laughter.* After an argument with a white patron who had been supporting him financially, Hughes spent time traveling, making extended visits to Haiti, Russia, and Carmel, California. He had begun publishing in the Communist Party-sponsored journal *New Masses* even before he left the United States and wrote some of his most politically radical poetry while in Russia.

In Carmel Hughes wrote his first collection of short stories, *The Ways of White Folks* (1934). He finished the decade with several successful plays, including *Mulatto,* loosely based on his grandfather's family, which opened on Broadway in 1935 and became the longest running Broadway play by an African American until Lorraine Hansberry's *A Raisin in the Sun* 25 years later.

In 1940 Hughes published his first autobiography, *The Big Sea.* In it he discusses his childhood, his estrangement from his father, and other personal topics, but readers especially value its insider's portrayal of the Harlem Renaissance. Two years later he began writing a weekly column for the *Chicago Defender* that unexpectedly spawned his most popular literary character, Jesse B. Semple. "Simple," as he was called, was a fictional Harlem resident who had little education but many street-smart opinions on everything from World War II to American race relations. Simple became a representative for the black Everyman, and over the next 20 years, in addition to his column, Hughes published five books and an off-Broadway play that featured Simple, who has been called "one of the more original comic creations in American journalism."

Hughes also published more poetry and plays in the 1940s, and as lyricist for the 1947 Broadway musical *Street Scene* he earned enough money to buy the Harlem home where he lived for the rest of his life. In 1951 Hughes published one of his most important poetry collections, *Montage of a Dream Deferred,* which contained such well-known works as "Harlem" and "Dream Boogie."

Prolific and versatile, Langston Hughes (1902-1967) wrote plays, stories, novels, memoirs, and poetry that expressed the author's love and respect for his African American heritage. He is shown here in a 1936 photograph by Carl Van Vechten. *Library of Congress, Carl Van Vechten Collection*

During the 1950s Hughes published two more collections of short stories, another novel, several nonfiction works of children's literature, and his second autobiography, *I Wonder as I Wander* (1956).

In the 1960s Hughes wrote several successful Gospel plays, including *Black Nativity* (1961), which remains a holiday tradition in several cities, and *Jericho-Jim Crow* (1964), based on the CIVIL RIGHTS MOVEMENT. He also published anthologies of poetry, short stories, and humor, and the book-length poem *Ask Your Mama* (1962). When he died on May 22, 1967, he was at work on a new collection of poetry celebrating the Civil Rights and BLACK POWER movements, which was published later that year as *The Panther and the Lash.*

As a writer Hughes was prolific both in the genres he covered and the amount he produced, and he became the first African American author able to support himself completely by his writing. But his work was remarkable for much more than its quantity; Hughes's writing captured the essence of black America in a way black Americans felt it had not been captured before. As his biographer Arnold Rampersad said, "From the start, Hughes's art was responsive to the needs and emotions of the black world.... Arguably, Langston Hughes was black America's most original poet. Certainly he was black America's most representative writer and a significant figure in world literature in the twentieth century."

Lisa Clayton Robinson

SEE ALSO

Abolitionism in the United States; Blues, The; *Chicago Defender*; Children's Literature, African American; *Crisis, The*; Gospel Music; Harlem, New York; Lincoln University (Pennsylvania); New York, New York; *Opportunity: Journal of Negro Life*; Communist Party USA, African Americans and the.

Latin America and the Caribbean

Hugues, Victor (b. 1764, Marseilles, France; d. November 1826, Gironde, France, or Cayenne, French Guiana), the commissioner of the Revolutionary Convention in GUADELOUPE; Hugues rose to political prominence during the French Revolution.

Victor Hugues was the son of a baker from Marseilles, France. At age 12 he joined his uncle in Saint-Domingue (now HAITI) at the height of that island's colonial prosperity. After sailing the Caribbean as a corsair in search of English ships, in 1784 Hugues settled in Port-au-Prince, where he opened a bakery. In 1788, when the French king Louis XVI convened the Estates General in Versailles in an attempt to defuse rising anti-monarchical sentiment, Hugues was elected and returned to France to represent the *petits blancs,* or white shop owners and traders. He also became embroiled in the conflict between petits blancs and a mulatto class striving for legal recognition. In February 1791 Port-au-Prince was burned by armed members of the mulatto class, and Hugues, by his own estimation, lost seven-eighths of his worldly goods.

When the French monarchy was overthrown in August 1792, Hugues was still in France and used his position to defend vigorously his class interests against a Haitian mulatto-landowner alliance. He soon gained access to influential politicians completely unfamiliar with events in the colonies. In 1793 Robespierre took power. Hugues rose rapidly in Jacobin circles, coming to direct the Terror in the city of Rochefort.

Then, on February 4, 1794, the democratically elected National Convention abolished slavery in the French colonies. Although Marat, Robespierre, and the Société des Amis des Noirs had long argued for abolition, the decree was in many respects a purely tactical gesture of an embattled government. In 1793 a series of slave revolts in the towns of Baillif, Trois-Rivieres, and St. Anne had spread across Guadeloupe. In addition, news had reached France of an English invasion of the French-held Caribbean colonies. The Convention hoped that an emancipation declaration might encourage freed slaves to fight the English in gratitude.

Hugues was perfectly placed to take advantage of these events. Sensing the changing political winds, he made a bid for personal political power in support of the abolition decree. The Convention named him its emissary to reclaim the island of Guadeloupe from the British. On June 4, 1794, he arrived at Guadeloupe with 1150 men and quickly added freed slaves to his forces. After six months of assiduous fighting, amid rain and yellow fever, Hugues retook the island. In the process, more than 700 captured British sympathizers were guillotined or shot, including many *mûlatres* (or mulattos), of whom Hugues observed, "It pained us to see formerly free colored men [*hommes de couleur*] more enraged against the decree that abolished slavery than the colonizers themselves."

After expelling the English, Hugues was the master of the island in his capacity as commissioner for the Committee of Public Safety. He was quick to use the guillotine to put French revolutionary ideology into practice, executing or sending into exile those white landowners who had sided with the British. Hugues's Terror decisively weakened the hold of European landowning classes in Guadeloupe, in contrast to neighboring MARTINIQUE, where the white békés (or descendants of French colonists) dominate much of that island's economy to this day. Although Hugues for a time enforced juridical racial equality, he quickly instituted the quasi-slavery of enforced labor. He married a rich Creole Martinican woman and was soon accused of profiteering from the seized goods of both dead and exiled landowners and British ships. In 1798 the French government ended Hugues's now burdensome tenure as commissioner. In 1800 Hugues completed his transformation from liberator of the slaves to their nemesis. Arriving in FRENCH GUIANA as that colony's governor, he oversaw the implementation of Napoleon's decree of December 7, 1802, reestablishing slavery in the French colonies. Hugues went on to institute a virtual police state, ensuring that the black inhabitants of French Guiana would remain enslaved until abolition in 1848.

Nick Nesbitt

SEE ALSO

Port-au-Prince, Haiti; Slave Rebellions in Latin America and the Caribbean.

Africa

Human Rights in Africa

HUMAN RIGHTS IN AFRICA SINCE INDEPENDENCE

The term *human rights* has been problematic in Africa for the past 50 years, both conceptually and in its implementation. The term was born after World War II, in response to the atrocities committed in the Holocaust. However, at the time of the adoption of the Universal Declaration of Human Rights by the United Nations in 1948, nearly all of Africa was under COLONIAL RULE; thus, it was unable to participate in the drafting of the document that would define human rights globally for the next half-century. While colonialism in Africa entailed a comprehensive catalogue of human rights violations, Africa was excluded from the process of defining human rights as a part of international law.

HUMAN RIGHTS IN PAN-AFRICAN TREATY LAW

The human rights paradigm of the Universal Declaration is implicitly state-centered: the nation-state is recognized as both the greatest guarantor as well as the greatest threat to human rights. Before Africa could fit into this paradigm, modern African states had to be born. Most of them, under the banner of the right to self-determination, came into being in the 1960s. African leaders and scholars recognized early the potency and potential value of a Pan-African treaty incorporating international human rights law. But they also saw the differences between the communitarian and collectivist nature of African societies and the more individualistic societies of the West. An African human rights treaty would thus have to go beyond the Universal Declaration and reflect individuals as right-holders enmeshed in communities, with collective rights and specific duties to others. In 1961, a year when many African states gained independence, a conference on "rule of law" was organized in Lagos, NIGERIA. In the final document of this conference, known as the Law of Lagos, appears the first formal reference to a possible Africa convention on human rights. This convention would follow the model developed in Europe, the Americas, and the United Nations, and would include a tribunal to monitor and enforce its provisions.

As soon as it came into currency, however, the term "human rights" became a cold war battleground, and the debate over human rights within Africa took up the same themes. Many of the great leaders of African independence movements, such as SENEGAL's Léopold Senghor, TANZANIA's Julius Nyerere, and GHANA's KWAME NKRUMAH, were socialists. For them, the West's vision of "rights" (traced back to the American and French revolutions) was both suspect for its historical coexistence with colonialism and impoverished in its limitation to civil and political guarantees (even the most narrow of which were belied by United States treatment of blacks prior to the CIVIL RIGHTS MOVEMENT, a hypocrisy of which African leaders were acutely aware). "Rights" were an essential part of independence rhetoric, but African leaders in the decades after independence generally emphasized "economic and social" rights, that is, economic development and self-sufficiency, over "civil and political" rights, to which most of the Universal Declaration is devoted.

But the idea of an African human rights treaty persisted, and was given new life with a colloquium on human rights and development, held in 1978 in Dakar, SENEGAL. The first complete draft of the African Charter of Human and Peoples' Rights (African Charter) was finished by the end of 1979. In 1980-1981 the justice ministers of the ORGANIZATION OF AFRICAN UNITY (OAU) member states met in Banjul, THE GAMBIA, to approve the official version of what was also called the Banjul Charter. This draft was then adopted by the OAU Assembly of Heads of State in Government, in June 1981.

In a reflection of the political consciousness of African intellectuals, communitarianism, collective identities, individual duties, and economic development are all prominent in the African Charter. The charter contains substantial economic and social rights provisions, such as the right to education and health care. The rights of a people to self-determination and control over their natural resources and environment are also included. The individual duties mentioned in the African Charter include the duties to take care of one's parents, to avoid committing treasonous acts, and to promote the spirit of African unity.

Now ratified by 53 African countries, the African Charter went into force in 1986. It establishes the African Commission on Human and Peoples' Rights (African Commission) as a monitoring and enforcement body. The commission is composed of 11 independent African human rights experts who are elected by the OAU summit. It meets twice a year and is headquartered in Banjul. The commission's primary activities are, first, to promote the rights specified in the charter by examining reports submitted every two years by the states' parties, and second, to protect those rights by the hearing of cases brought by individuals and nongovernmental organizations (NGOs) against states' parties. While the commission got off to a slow start, it has become a major focus for human rights activities across the continent. Due in part to the active involvement of NGOs, the African Commission has been able to undertake a wide range of activities not specified in the charter. For example, it has held seminars and conferences and commissioned special reports on issues such as extrajudicial executions, prisons and detention conditions, and the status of African women.

The 1998 OAU summit meeting, held in OUAGADOUGOU, BURKINA FASO, approved an optional protocol to the African Charter that would establish an African Court of Human and Peoples' Rights. The court is intended to remedy some of the problems that the African Commission has had, such as lack of respect from states' parties. However, it is sure to face some of the same difficulties, such as insufficient material and financial resources.

HUMAN RIGHTS: EVENTS ON THE GROUND

Despite the progress made in creating a formal structure of African human rights law, the actual record of human rights in Africa has been grim. Violations fall into several general categories, touching nearly every aspect of Africans' daily lives. Tragically, those human rights violations associated with the most widespread and terrible suffering are those least responsive to international legal provisions and protections. Many of these violations are linked to colonialism's legacies: in other words, to the ethnic relations, political boundaries, and patterns of state power created under colonial rule.

One category of violations concerns civil and political rights. The African Charter, nodding to tradition, begins with these: rights to political participation, association, and freedom of speech, as well as freedom from arbitrary detention and right to a fair trial. SOUTH AFRICA under APARTHEID – a system that not only condoned but mandated racial discrimination – was the most outstanding example of comprehensive oppression and resulting social misery. In the rest of sub-Saharan Africa, most countries became one-party states upon independence, and those parties were headed by a single man. Many of these leaders, not without justification, argued that one-party rule was needed to build modern nation-states out of the ethnically diverse territories bequeathed by colonialism and to achieve rapid economic development on the "African socialist" model. They also argued that a one-party system embodied traditional, consensual African patterns of governance.

Whatever their philosophical justifications, most one-party states became highly repressive of civil and political rights. Opposition political parties and press freedom were unknown under even respected leaders such as JOMO KENYATTA of KENYA and Kwame Nkrumah of Ghana. In the most egregious cases, dictators such as IDI AMIN of UGANDA, JEAN-BÉDEL BOKASSA of the CENTRAL AFRICAN REPUBLIC, FRANCISCO MACÍAS NGUEMA of EQUATORIAL GUINEA, Kamuzu Banda of MALAWI, DANIEL ARAP MOI of Kenya, and MOBUTU SESE SEKO of the former Zaire (to name only a few) have brutally suppressed opposition, targeted specific ethnic groups for persecution, and ordered massacres. Among the countries that have not been ruled by a single, long-lived figure, many have suffered through a succession of coups d'état and military governments. NIGERIA, for example, has been governed by the military for almost all of its post-independence history.

While the need to build unity among diverse ethnic communities has served as a justification for political dictatorship, too often the lack of democratic process, combined with pervasive discrimination, only makes civil strife more likely, as one ethnic group monopolizes state power and systematically excludes others. In SUDAN, national unity seems a dim hope as the state, dominated by Muslim Arab northerners, wages a long-running war with southern black populations, who practice Christianity and traditional religions. The war has already cost hundreds of thousands of lives. An analogous conflict in MAURITANIA in the late 1980s drove tens of thousands of black Mauritanians over the southern border to Senegal. National unity is also a distant goal in RWANDA and BURUNDI, where tensions between the HUTU AND TUTSI deepened during the colonial era and resulted (after independence) in recurrent massacres in both countries, including the 1994 Rwandan genocide (*see* ETHNICITY IN RWANDA: AN INTERPRETATION and ETHNICITY IN BURUNDI: AN INTERPRETATION).

The OAU and the African Commission's effectiveness in combating civil and political violations has been limited by African states' reluctance to criticize one another. This contrasts with Europe, where the system of human rights law was shaped and given stature by a number of prominent state-against-state cases. Together, the many nondemocratic states in Africa have impeded the implementation of the African Charter. In addition, even now that the charter is in force and the commission has been established, Africa's human rights system suffers from the inadequate funding provided by the OAU. The commission's sessions, for example, originally lasted 14 days but have now been cut to 10 days by the OAU. The OAU also pays the salary of only one lawyer in the Secretariat.

Additionally, the human rights violations common in civil conflict are particularly difficult for international law to handle. A system of treaty law relies on state action to define punishable violations. Although widespread violations of the right to life are common in wars – as are incidents of torture, rape, mass displacement of populations, and destruction of property – assigning blame to either side may be nearly impossible. This task belongs in a "political" realm that international law must shun in order to preserve its legitimacy. International human rights law thus has not shown itself effective in situations of massive civil unrest. As remarkably few wars in Africa have been fought between recognized states, humanitarian law has overall offered relatively little protection.

Another category of human rights abuses are those that may be characterized as "customary" or "traditional" practices. The best-known example is female genital mutilation, also called female circumcision. Other traditional practices that are often considered to violate human rights include the levirate (the marrying of a widow to one of her brothers-in-law) and the giving or selling of young children to religious leaders (a practice known as *trikosi* in Ghana). Slavery also persists in some forms, particularly in Mauritania and Sudan. These practices, while not as devastating to the entire society as civic strife or systematic oppression, are resistant to abolition by law, since they concern no state action. Such traditions are typically long-standing and sometimes grounded in religious beliefs, and even where governments are willing to oppose them publicly, it is difficult to force an end to such practices by legal means.

The African Charter itself is deliberately ambiguous on customary practices, requiring only that African states "preserve positive African traditional values." The determination of which African values are positive and which are not is left for the African Commission to interpret. A great deal will depend on the cases brought before the commission and the arguments put forth by each side. It is unlikely that the commission would accept practices such as female circumcision or trikosi as "positive," but to declare them outright violations of the African Charter would be highly controversial, especially if these practices involve no direct state action. The African human rights system will probably not be the forum where these issues are addressed.

A last category of violations that must be mentioned concerns economic and social rights. The inclusion of these rights in the African Charter demonstrates their importance, in light of enduring poverty in Africa. But regional treaties have proven relatively ineffective remedies for economic ills. One difficulty is the lack of direct state action in such violations; the extent to which a government is responsible for its nation's poverty cannot be measured. Likewise, there are no objective standards for measuring the extent of economic and social rights violations. Lastly, African states often truly lack the financial resources needed to improve social services such as health care and education. As a result, the African Charter's articles on economic and social rights have meant little in practice. Only recently have they begun to form the basis of some litigation, which may result in concrete standards, at least for specific situations.

One development during the years since the drafting of the African Charter has been the general recognition of the *interdependence* of rights. In other words, the political oppression that has long plagued many African countries is now recognized as one of the factors contributing to the continent's failure to achieve greater economic success. Even financial institutions such as the World Bank and the International Monetary Fund, while they are loathe to speak of economic rights, can no longer overlook the clear relation between transparency and efficiency. They now speak of the need for "good governance," a euphemism for respect of civil and political rights.

The Future of Human Rights in Africa: Trends

The early 1990s saw a wave of democratization sweep Africa. The most dramatic example was South Africa, where the postapartheid government described its raison d'être as guaranteeing the human rights of the population. While democratic revolutions may have stalled in many other countries, a new momentum in African civil society promises to be the best guarantor of rights. NGOs have sprung up everywhere, dealing with the whole range of civil and political rights, combating traditional practices, and advocating for development. While not all of these organizations articulate their mission in terms of human rights, they have been vital to the development and support of the African regional system, and to human rights and development work at the national level. NGOs have provided staff for the commission's Secretariat and suggestions for its programs, and they constitute the overwhelming majority of complainants bringing cases. NGO representatives always make up the majority of the observers at the commission's sessions, and their participation has had a measurable impact on the human rights system's growth. Likewise, NGOs are intervening in nearly every issue at the national level, publicizing, litigating, and lobbying. If African states eventually fulfill the role of guarantor of human rights, it will be because of active prodding from NGOs.

Intergovernmental bodies themselves also offer reason for hope. The African Commission has grown more efficient in its administration and bolder in the implementation of its mission. It has handed down decisions against Nigeria, Malawi, Congo, Chad, and Cameroon, among others. It has taken missions to Mauritania, Senegal, Sudan, and Nigeria. Governments have recently shown a higher degree of interest in the commission's work, and become more cooperative. The OAU itself has begun to treat human rights as a priority, at least in rhetoric, and to incorporate them into peace accords.

Although the human rights situation in Africa remains grim, with especially widespread violations caused by civil wars, there are signs that the combined pressures from NGOs, from regional bodies such as the African Commission, and from forces outside the continent will together help bring about positive changes, both in the behavior of governments and in society itself. The definition of human rights will remain fluid and subject to debate, but Africa may yet use its innovative treaty provisions and distinctive philosophy of rights to make a global contribution.

Julia Harrington

See Also

African Socialism; Banda, Ngwazi Hastings Kamuzu; Christianity, African: An Overview; Congo, Democratic Republic of the; Dakar, Senegal; Education in Africa; Ethnicity and Identity in Africa: An Interpretation; Lagos, Nigeria; Law in Africa: Colonial and Contemporary; Nyerere, Julius Kambarage; United Nations in Africa; African Religions: An Interpretation; Female Circumcision in Africa; Slavery in Africa.

Latin America and the Caribbean

Human Rights in Latin America and the Caribbean

Latin Americans and Caribbeans of African descent number at least 150 million, yet few governments address their status with respect to internationally recognized civil, political, social, economic, and cultural rights. Moreover, the substantial violations and continuing inequality faced by blacks in the Americas are often concealed by the apparent intermixing and cohesion between groups and by the generalized denial that racism exists (*see* Race in Latin America and Myth of Racial Democracy in Latin America and the Caribbean: An Interpretation). (For more on human rights in the diaspora, *see* Human Rights in Africa.)

In 1948 the United Nations (UN) Universal Declaration on Human Rights and the Organization of American States (OAS) American Declaration of the Rights and Duties of Man established a framework of international principles that governments in the Americas agreed to guarantee as the minimum standards for ensuring dignity and well-being for citizens. In order to secure effective recognition and observance of human rights, governments in the Americas further developed these UN and OAS principles in international pacts, conventions, and treaties and in national constitutions and laws. The problems specifically affecting black communities in Latin America and the Caribbean today can be viewed from a human rights perspective in order to pressure governments to improve the living conditions in these communities or to make claims when the state is liable for human rights violations.

Historical Context

The European colonizers' preoccupation with the rights of black slaves was minimal. The few protections that existed were geared to prevent uprisings and slave escapes (*see* Slave Laws in Colonial Spanish America, Black Codes in Latin America, and Punishment of Slaves in Colonial Latin America and the Caribbean).

After the wars in the early nineteenth century that led to the independence of many states in Latin America and the Caribbean, slaves were offered freedom through the manumission and abolition laws that were issued throughout the continent (*see* Racial Question during Struggles of Independence). But the new nations did not honor the role that blacks had played in achieving independence and did not grant them special opportunities that might have helped counterbalance the toll of 300 years of slavery. Blacks found themselves as low-skilled, uneducated people of color in societies that had been structured bureaucratically, legally, and socially around castes and class divisions for more than three centuries (*see* Colonial Latin America and the Caribbean).

Today, 50 years after the signing of the Universal Declaration on Human Rights and the American Declaration of Rights and Duties of Man, in general, blacks in Latin America and the Caribbean continue to have lower living standards than nonblacks. In some cases they constitute a higher percentage of victims of civil and political rights violations than the rest of the population.

International Law

Besides the UN and OAS declarations, many countries in the region have signed other international instruments that are directly relevant to the situation of blacks in the Americas. These are the United Nations Declaration on the Rights of Persons Belonging to National or Ethnic, Religious and Linguistic Minorities (1992); the International Convention on the Elimination of All Forms of Racial Discrimination (1969); and the Convention against Discrimination in Education (1960). By signing these treaties states have committed to upholding certain minimum conditions of dignity and well-being for their populations. In addition these treaties are now so widely accepted that they have become standards to which human rights situations worldwide are compared. However, in most cases, a state that breaches its international obligations is met with consequences of a political and moral order rather than actual legal sanctions.

Article 1 of the International Convention on the Elimination of All Forms of Racial Discrimination carries a definition that is useful for understanding the concept of racial discrimination. It states that "the term 'racial discrimination' shall mean any distinction, exclusion, restriction or preference based on race, color, descent or national or ethnic origin which has the purpose or effect of nullifying or impairing the recognition, enjoyment or exercise, on an equal footing, of human rights and fundamental freedoms in the political, economic, social, cultural or any other field of public life."

Constitutional and Legal Provisions

Most recent constitutions in Latin America and the Caribbean recognize and incorporate international human rights standards into their provisions. Thus these standards have become assimilated as part of the principles used to govern the constitutionality of national laws. There are, however, differences among constitutional commitments to nondiscrimination and the recognition of blacks, depending on each country's particular history and its political and philosophical views. Cuba, for example, is the only country in the region whose constitution recognizes slaves and indigenous people as being among those who contributed to the making of the nation. The constitutions of most countries in the region claim to guarantee full equality for all citizens; some go further and expressly guarantee individual rights and freedoms regardless of race, place of origin, political opinion, creed, gender, language, disability, or economic or social condition.

A few countries have added a constitutional provision that recognizes their multiracial, multiethnic, or pluricultural identity as a nation and thus grants special recognition and rights to ethnic, racial, and/or cultural groups. Belize, Bolivia, Brazil, Colombia, Ecuador, Guatemala, and Paraguay all attest to official multiculturalism. Colombia is further distinguished by having recognized collective ownership and territorial rights for the black communities of the Pacific basin in its 1991 constitution. Brazil is the only country in the region that has a specific article in its constitution stating that racism is a crime punishable by law. Argentina issued an antidiscrimination law in 1988 and Brazil an antiracism law in 1997.

Despite the official claims to equality, nondiscrimination, and multiculturalism, particularly severe violations of these constitutional principles continue to occur. In all Latin American and Caribbean countries where people of African descent are not the majority, blacks fare much worse than the lighter-skinned population in terms of economic, social, and cultural rights such as access to education, health, employment, and land ownership. In Colombia and Brazil, especially, black communities have paid a high toll in terms of civil and political rights, with insidious violations to the right to life, physical integrity, and due process of law.

The Caribbean

In Trinidad and Tobago tensions with racial overtones have arisen because Indo-Trinidadians predominate in the private sector and in agriculture and Afro-Trinidadians are disproportionately represented in the civil service, police, and military. In Haiti two official languages are recognized: Creole, spoken by virtually all Haitians, and French, spoken by only 20 percent of the population. Yet those who speak, read, and write French have greater access to political and economic opportunities.

The Cuban Revolution especially benefited blacks by eliminating much previously existing structural racism through literacy programs, medical aid, and agrarian reforms. There was a perception that the political system would gradually erase any lingering manifestations of discrimination, yet whites and light-skinned mulattos continue to dominate the political leadership, diplomacy, tourism, and state bureaucracy sectors. Education continues to be Eurocentric, though the official persecution of Afro-Cuban cultural and religious manifestations has diminished with the influx of foreign tourists who come to see the "exotic" part of Cuba.

Central America

West Indian Afro-Creoles constitute a large minority in Costa Rica, Guatemala, Honduras, Nicaragua, and Panama (*see* Central America). Even though they are nationals of the countries in which they reside, they have faced tensions because of their skin color, origins, or native language. In some cases they still suffer from xenophobia, are resented for not being totally Hispanicized, and are restricted in their ability to obtain a bilingual education.

During the 1989 invasion of Panama by the United States (also known as Operation Just Cause), about 20,000 people of African descent lost their homes; 2000 or more died; and many disappeared. Today many are still homeless and unemployed or have not obtained any compensation for the loss of their property or family members. A positive outcome of the invasion is that it spurred unprecedented human rights activism and racial consciousness on behalf of Afro-Panamanians.

South America

Brazil: In South America's largest country, where people of African descent, according to official statistics, numerically represent close to half the population, racial discrimination has been illegal since 1951, but daily discrimination is still common. In 1995 the United Nations sent its Special Rapporteur on Contemporary Forms of Racism, Racial Discrimination, Xenophobia and Related Intolerance on an official mission to Brazil. When a human rights situation merits concern, it is the mandate of appointed experts (or Special Rapporteurs) from the United Nations Commission on Human

Rights (UNCHR) to examine, monitor, and report publicly on specific human rights themes or issues. Their international reports often prompt governments to adopt legislation and policies that comply with international standards. The Special Rapporteur sent to Brazil was to take firsthand cognizance of the related human rights situation and report it to the UNCHR in Geneva. In November 1995, after the rapporteur's visit, the president of Brazil publicly recognized that racism and discrimination existed, an official statement that was unprecedented (*see* Brazil, Blacks and Politics in: An Interpretation).

The UN official reported that blacks in Brazil are disproportionately absent from senior positions in government, the armed forces, and the private sector. Job access, according to the report, seems to depend on gradation of color: those with the darkest skin occupy the lowest-paid occupations, with black women at the bottom of the payroll scale. In terms of education, the report stated that 32 percent of blacks in Brazil are illiterate, compared with 14 percent of whites, with black women having the lowest level of education in the country. Additionally, educational materials generally portray people of African descent only as former slaves, servants, or manual workers, and Afro-Brazilian culture is officially presented as folklore.

Blacks are often the victims of violence at a level disproportionate to their percentage in the population. Blacks account for more than half, and in some regions up to 80 percent, of the murder victims, and street children, who are disproportionately Afro-Brazilian, are primary targets of death squads.

Afro-Brazilians are the main inhabitants of favelas (shantytowns) and constitute the majority of the homeless of large cities. The UN report also showed that many events in the daily lives of Brazilians tend to emphasize the notion that all blacks are servants, poor, or criminals. For example, blacks are requested to use service entrance elevators in apartment buildings where the wealthy reside and must show identity documents and justify their presence in residential areas. The media and advertising industries feature whites almost exclusively (*see also* Race and Class in Brazil: An Interpretation).

Colombia: The United Nations Special Rapporteur on Racism and Discrimination visited Colombia a year after his visit to Brazil and found that black communities were affected by persistent stereotyping, economic and social disparities, and grave human rights violations. The United Nations report (1997) points out that white supremacy is constantly reproduced through the many jokes and sayings in which Colombians identify blacks with ugliness, ignorance, evil, crime, and servility (*see* Complexities of Ethnic and Racial Terminology in Latin America and the Caribbean). In daily conversation, blacks are imagined as capable only of working in manual labor, sports, music, and domestic jobs. The rapporteur also commented that "the responses received were confused or an uncomfortable silence when one asked questions regarding the number or percentage of African-Colombians who serve in the army, the navy, the diplomatic corps, or in the Catholic Church hierarchy, as if these were unusual or inappropriate questions."

Moreover, black communities in the regions of Pacific Coast of Colombia have been caught between the crossfire of the armed forces, guerrilla groups, paramilitaries, and death squads active in Colombia. The report pointed out that in the cities of Buenaventura and Tumaco, death squads have been found to carry out "social cleansing" operations (*operaciones de limpieza social*) targeting young Afro-Colombians for murder on the assumption that they are all thieves. The rapporteur reported seeing street graffiti in Buenaventura that encouraged the killing of blacks, such as "Do your country a favor: kill a nigger and win a turkey." *("Hágale un favor a la pátria. Mate un negro y reclame un pavo.")*

In the rural areas of Chocó, mainly inhabited by Afro-Colombian descendants of emancipated and runaway slaves, forced displacement has become a major problem. Though it remains the region with the lowest per capita level of social investment and is last in terms of education, health, and infrastructure, its immense wealth in natural resources has recently attracted guerrilla forces and paramilitary groups. Since 1996 armed groups have violently displaced thousands of poor black Colombians from their homes and communities, causing a situation of extreme distress which, it seems, will not be resolved in the near future.

Ecuador: Most of the 1 million Afro-Ecuadorians, who constitute a minority in the country, live in the rural, northern coastal area and suffer widespread poverty. Discrimination is pervasive with respect to educational, professional, and economic opportunities. In 1997, following the example of the Afro-Colombians, black communities proposed legislation that would recognize territorial rights to their ancestral lands and provide equal opportunities in regard to education, employment, and political representation.

Peru: Blacks, who number between 6 and 10 percent of the total population of Peru, face particularly pervasive discrimination, racist attitudes, and social prejudice and are among the poorest groups in the country. The media portrays blacks as servants or individuals of questionable character. Blacks do not hold leadership positions in government, the diplomatic corps, business, the judiciary, clergy, army, navy, or air force. Employment advertisements in newspapers often request people of "good presence" (*buena presencia*) for managerial and professional positions as a way of excluding blacks and dark-skinned *mestizos* (of indigenous and European descent). Help-wanted advertisements seeking chauffeurs, cooks, doormen, butlers, maids, or pallbearers frequently state a preference for blacks (*"negros"* or *"morenos"*). Wealthy Peruvians consider it a status symbol to have black servants in their homes and black pallbearers at their funerals. Further, Afro-Peruvian human rights organizations report that the police routinely detain persons of African descent on unfounded suspicion of having committed crimes, and rarely act on complaints of crimes against blacks.

Suriname: Maroons (the descendants of former runaway slaves, also known as Bush Negroes) constitute a group in Suriname that has suffered grave human rights violations and has a limited ability to participate in decisions affecting their lands, cultures, traditions, and natural resources. In 1987 members of the Surinamese armed forces beat and tortured more than 20 unarmed Saramaka maroons in the presence of more than 50 maroon bystanders, including women and children. Seven males, including a 15-year-old boy, were then taken away in a military vehicle, blindfolded, and shot after they were first ordered to dig their own graves. The officials alleged, unfoundedly, that the maroons were members of the Jungle Commando, an armed rebel group persecuted by the government. In 1990 the Inter-American Commission on Human Rights issued a report finding the Suriname State responsible for the murders. The case was then sent to the Inter-American Court of Human Rights, where the government accepted responsibility in December 1991. The final 1994 judgment on reparations raised new questions of law that are unprecedented in the Inter-American human rights system.

This case is important because it is the first case of human rights violations affecting a surviving maroon community in the Americas to appear before an international court. Because the Surinamese government accepted state responsibility for the deaths of the Saramaka maroons, in the decision on reparations the position of the government and the court centered on the quantity, type, and form of the compensation owed by the state to the victims' families. First, the government of Suriname was not willing to recognize the distinct polygamous and matrilineal structure of the maroon society for the distribution of damages: it considered that polygamy was illegal; it said that damages should not be based on the tribe's customary norms but rather on principles of international law, however different; it argued that only individual damages and not community damages should be considered; and it did not recognize any distinct autonomy or territorial rights to the Saramakas.

Second, though the Inter-American Court accepted the polygamous structure as a basis for compensating family members, it did not accept the argument of the defense that stated that the Saramakas' identity and self-esteem as a people were degraded. The court therefore denied recognition of moral damages to the community. With respect to territorial rights, the court looked exclusively at the validity of a 1762 Dutch treaty, noting that "[n]o other provision of domestic law, either written or customary, has been relied upon to establish the autonomy of the Saramakas." Moreover, the court completely disregarded the principle established in Article 1 of the International Convention on the Elimination of All Forms of Racial Discrimination (stated above) by stating that "... the origin of the events... lies not in some racial issue but, rather, in a subversive situation that prevailed at the time... It is true that the victims of the killings all belonged to the Saramaka tribe, but this circumstance of itself does not lead to the conclusion that there was a racial element to the crime."

In the peace treaty of 1992, the Suriname government agreed to acknowledge the traditional land rights of the maroon communities, which had been recognized by the Dutch colonizers since 1762. Though the government created a council in 1995 that would oversee the peace treaty agreements, the government did not consult with the community's representatives when selling gold and timber concessions on traditional lands to multinational enterprises. However, by May 1995 at least 75 percent of the compensatory damages in the case (known as *Aloeboetoe et al.*), which were calculated at $453,102, had been made to nearly 50 members of the Saramaka community.

Liliana Obregón

See Also

Race and Class in Brazil: An Interpretation; Slavery in Latin America and the Caribbean; Pacific Coast of Colombia; Cuba; Catholic Church in Latin America and the Caribbean; Religions, African, in Latin America and the Caribbean; Education in Latin America and the Caribbean; Racial Question during Struggles of Independence in Latin America; Languages, Creole, in the Caribbean.

Africa

Hunde, ethnic group of the Democratic Republic of the Congo.

The Hunde primarily inhabit the Kivu Province of east-central Congo-Kinshasa. Other Hunde live in Rwanda and in southwestern Uganda. They speak a Bantu language and belong to the larger Kivu cultural and linguistic cluster. Approximately 200,000 people consider themselves Hunde.

See Also

Bantu: Dispersion and Settlement.

Africa

Hunkanrin, Louis

(b. November 25, 1886, Porto-Novo, Dahomey [present-day Benin]; d. May 28, 1964, Porto-Novo, Dahomey), journalist, educator, and early nationalist in French West Africa.

One of the earliest critics of French colonialism in Dahomey, Louis Hunkanrin spent most of his adult life imprisoned for challenging colonial policies and attempting to win new respect and rights for Africans in French West Africa. A descendant of the royal family of Porto-Novo, he received an exceptional early education and matriculated at the Ecole Normale in Senegal, where he graduated with a teaching degree in 1904. Immediately afterward he accepted a teaching position at a public school in Whydah and began vocalizing his criticism of France's arbitrary colonial policies.

Hunkanrin was dismissed from the school in 1909 after a series of disputes with the headmaster. He subsequently accepted a job at the Compagnie Française de l'Afrique Occidentale (C.F. A.O.), but in 1912 he was fired, tried, and convicted for insulting and threatening his superior. He was sent to prison in Dakar, where he became friends with Blaise Diagne and refined his critique of French colonial rule.

Hunkanrin returned to Dahomey in 1914. In articles written for local journals he railed against the racism and oppression of French colonialism. He also urged Africans to educate themselves; education, he claimed, was the only way for Africans to acquire equality with the French. Although he did not actually call for decolonization, the French colonial administration still considered him a threat. Hunkanrin consequently spent the next four years in hiding, traveling among Dahomey, Nigeria, and Senegal. He came out of hiding in 1918 after Diagne arranged for him to volunteer for military service in World War I, but his service was marred by a string of disputes that eventually resulted in a court-martial in 1921. Hunkanrin later severed ties with Diagne, who he claimed was taking monetary bribes to lure Africans into the military.

Hunkanrin returned to Dahomey in December 1921 and spent the next two years in prison for forgery. While in jail he helped organize the 1923 anticolonial demonstrations in Porto-Novo. The French administration then sent Hunkanrin into forced exile in Mauritania. Although he returned to Dahomey in 1933, he spent most of the next 23 years in jail, during which he was exiled to the French Sudan for challenging the Vichy government and supporting Charles de Gaulle's Free France campaign. He was finally released from jail after Dahomean independence in 1960. He died four years later, at which time the Dahomean government posthumously awarded him the title Grand Officier de l'Ordre National du Dahomey.

Elizabeth Heath

See Also

Colonial Rule; Dakar, Senegal; Nationalism in Africa; Porto-Novo, Benin.

North America

Hunter, Alberta (b. April 1, 1895, Memphis, Tenn.; d. October 17, 1984, New York, N.Y.), African American blues and cabaret singer, an early and enduring black recording star.

Alberta Hunter adapted her large and supple voice to a variety of musical styles and had one of the longest careers of any of the early female blues singers. She ran away from Memphis at age 11 to Chicago, hoping to work as a singer and send money to her mother. She became an immediate success, and as her reputation grew she appeared in nightclubs with such American jazz musicians as cornetist King Oliver and trumpet player Louis Armstrong. She also performed on Broadway, and in 1921 she made her first record. Hunter's best-known song was "Downhearted Blues" (1922), which she wrote. In 1923 African American blues singer Bessie Smith recorded the song, which then became widely known.

In 1927 Hunter traveled to London, where she sang opposite African American singer Paul Robeson in the British premiere of the musical *Showboat*, by American composer Jerome Kern. Hunter subsequently sang in Holland, Denmark, and France, becoming the first singer to perform American blues music in Europe. During World War II (1939-1945) and the Korean War (1950-1953), she toured the world in military entertainment shows. In 1955, when her mother died, she retired from singing. She studied to be a nurse and later worked in hospitals in New York City. In 1977 Hunter's singing talent was rediscovered, and at age 82 she renewed her singing career and became famous once again.

See Also

World War II and African Americans; Armstrong, Louis ("Satchmo"); Blues, The; Chicago, Illinois; Memphis, Tennessee; New York, New York; Oliver, Joseph ("King").

North America

Hunter, Clementine Clemence Rubin (b. December 1886, Clourtierville, La.; d. January 1, 1988, Melrose, La.), African American folk artist celebrated as the "Black Grandma Moses."

Clementine Hunter was born on a cotton plantation to Mary Antoinette Adams, a woman of Virginia slave ancestry, and

Janvier (John) Reuben, a man of Native American and Irish descent. She moved with her family from Hidden Hill to Melrose Plantation (formerly Yucca), near Natchitoches, Louisiana, while she was in her early teens. She remained at Melrose, first as a cotton picker, then as the plantation cook until 1970.

Hunter had two children, Joseph and Cora, with Charles Dupree. Dupree died in 1914, and Hunter married Emanuel Hunter in 1924. She bore five more children: Mary, Agnes, King, and two who died at birth. A widow by 1944, Hunter died at age 101 a few miles from Melrose, having outlived all of her children.

Hunter became a folk artist celebrated for her paintings of familiar scenes of Southern life when she was already well into her fifties. Although she received very little formal education and remained illiterate throughout her life, she became known as the "Black Grandma Moses" for her depiction of black rural Southern life, specifically that of Cane River Settlement on Isle Breville, Louisiana. Her art, quilts, and paintings depicted religious themes, scenes of plantation work and relaxation, wildlife, and abstracts. Hunter was prolific up until her death, having completed approximately 5000 paintings.

Hunter's first artistic medium was quilt-making. Her earliest piece is a quilt from 1938 depicting the rigors of plantation life. Her first painting dates from 1939. Her work began to draw positive attention in the late 1940s and greater admiration still in the 1950s. In 1955 she became the first African American artist to have a solo exhibition at the Delgado Museum (now the New Orleans Museum of Art). By 1973 her work was being shown at the Museum of American Folk Art in New York, and by the time of her death, she was considered one of the century's leading folk artists.

See Also
Art, African American.

North America

Hunter-Gault, Charlayne

(b. February 27, 1942, Due West, S.C.), African American journalist.

Charlayne Hunter-Gault first came to national attention in 1961, when she and Hamilton Holmes became the first black students to attend the University of Georgia, after a two-year-long court fight. Hunter-Gault received her B.A. in journalism in 1963.

After graduation, she took a job with the *New Yorker* magazine. In 1967 she received a Russell Sage Fellowship to study social science at Washington University, St. Louis, where she was an editor at *Trans-Action* magazine. She also became a reporter and anchorwoman for WRC-TV. In 1968 she joined the *New York Times*, where she created and managed a Harlem bureau. She spent several years as codirector of the Michele Clark Fellowship program for minority students in journalism at Columbia University. In 1971 she married Ronald Gault, with whom she has a son; she has a daughter from a previous marriage.

In 1978 Hunter-Gault began to work as a correspondent for *The MacNeil/Lehrer Report* on the Public Broadcasting Service (PBS); she became national correspondent for the show in 1983. Hunter-Gault's accomplishments have been widely recognized by her peers. In 1986 she received the George Foster Peabody Award for Excellence in Broadcast Journalism and the Journalist of the Year Award from the National Association of Black Journalists. She has also won the National Urban Coalition Award for Distinguished Urban Reporting and two national news and documentary Emmy Awards. Hunter-Gault published her autobiography in 1992, and in 1997 left PBS and moved to Johannesburg, South Africa. National Public Radio frequently broadcasts Hunter-Gault's reports on current events in various African countries.

Lisa Clayton Robinson

See Also
Johannesburg, South Africa; Harlem, New York.

North America

Hurley, Ruby

(b. November 7, 1909, Washington, D.C.; d. August 9, 1980, Atlanta, Ga.), civil rights leader who was the only full-time civil rights activist working in the Deep South in the 1950s.

Ruby Hurley began working in 1939 with the Washington chapter of the National Association for the Advancement of Colored People (NAACP). She became the National Youth Secretary of the NAACP in 1943, and during her tenure the number of youth councils and college chapters grew from 86 to more than 380.

Hurley transferred to Birmingham, Alabama, as regional secretary in 1951 in order to organize new NAACP branches throughout the South. One year later she became regional director. Hers was the NAACP's first full-time office in the Deep South. In 1955 she investigated the murders of Rev. George W. Lee and Lamar Smith, who were killed for participating in black voter registration drives in Mississippi. In the same year, with Medgar Evers, she investigated the murder of 14-year-old Emmett Till, traveling at personal risk, in disguise, to locate witnesses. She also helped register Autherine Lucy Foster, the first black student admitted at the University of Alabama.

When the NAACP was banned from operating in Alabama in 1956, Hurley relocated to Atlanta. There she became involved in disputes between the NAACP and the newer Student Nonviolent Coordinating Committee (SNCC) and the Southern Christian Leadership Conference (SCLC). She dedicated herself to defending the strategies of her generation of civil rights workers to the new generation of activists.

See Also
Atlanta, Georgia; Civil Rights Movement; Evers, Medgar Wylie; Lynching; Till, Emmett Louis.

North America

Hurston, Zora Neale

(b. January 7, 1891, Notasulga, Ala.; d. January 28, 1960, Fort Pierce, Fla.), African American writer and folklorist; author of *Their Eyes Were Watching God*, considered the first black feminist novel.

"I do not belong to the sobbing school of Negrohood who hold that nature somehow has given them a lowdown dirty deal and whose feelings are all hurt about it. Even in the helter-skelter skirmish that is my life, I have seen that the world is to the strong regardless of a little pigmentation more or less. No, I do not weep at the world – I am too busy sharpening my oyster knife."

This quotation from her essay "How It Feels to Be Colored Me" (1928) portrays Hurston's joyfully contrary view of herself in a world where being black was often perceived as a "problem" and portrayed that way even by black writers. Hurston considered her own blackness a gift and an opportunity. As an anthropologist and writer, she savored the richness of black culture and made a career out of writing about that culture in all its color and fullness. In the process she became a vibrant figure in the Harlem Renaissance and is now considered one of the defining authors of the African American literary tradition.

Hurston claimed to have been born in Eatonville, Florida, in either 1901 or 1910, but recent scholarship indicates that she was probably born in Alabama in 1891. She did, however, grow up in Eatonville, the first incorporated black town in the United States. Unlike many Southern towns, where African Americans lived under the constant specter of racial harassment or discrimination from their white neighbors, in Eatonville whites only passed through on the road to Orlando. Growing up in a town where she was surrounded by black culture and self-sufficient black people was fundamental to Hurston's work. It was to this organic African American community that she kept returning as an adult – literally, for her anthropological research on black folklore, and figuratively, in her novels and stories.

In her 1942 autobiography, *Dust Tracks on a Road,* Hurston recalled that in her family, her mother, who died when Hurston was 13, was the one who encouraged her to "jump at de sun." After her mother's death Hurston left home and school to work as a maid for a traveling theater company. Her further education came slowly and sporadically, and embarrassment over this probably led her to lie about her age. Hurston received a high school degree from Morgan Academy in Baltimore in 1918 and then took courses at Howard University intermittently until 1924. What was most likely her first published story, "John Redding Goes to Sea," appeared in *Stylus*, Howard's literary magazine, in 1921.

In 1925 Hurston moved to New York and soon became part of the convergence of African American writers, artists, and musicians in Harlem known as the Harlem Renaissance. She was an immediate success in Harlem literary circles: Alain Locke chose her short story "Spunk" for inclusion in his landmark 1925 anthology, *The New Negro*, and two of her pieces received awards from *Opportunity* magazine in May 1925.

Hurston received a scholarship to study anthropology at Barnard College, under then well-known Columbia University scholar Franz Boas. The only black student at Barnard, she received a B.A. in 1928 for research that focused on black folklore. She continued to write fiction, but in 1929 she also began a series of fieldwork trips to the American South, Haiti, and Jamaica to collect black folklore that formed the basis for much of her later writing. Hurston received Rosenwald and Guggenheim fellowships and private funding from a white patron to support her research. She wrote at least three books that focused exclusively on her findings: *Mules and Men* (1935), the first collection of black folklore by a black American; *Tell My Horse* (1938), materials on the religion Vodou gathered during travels to the Caribbean; and *The Florida Negro* (1938), which was funded by the Federal Writers' Project but never published.

Hurston's interest in black culture was also reflected in her fiction, which was often set in all-black communities and attempted to capture dialect and local life. She published four novels between 1934 and 1948, including what became her most famous work, *Their Eyes Were Watching God* (1938). But in the 1930s and 1940s Hurston's works were often considered anachronistic or offensive even by black audiences. Author Richard Wright accused her of portraying a "minstrel image" of African Americans – in contrast to more politically oriented books like his own *Native Son*.

Hurston also came under criticism from the African American community for some of her political beliefs. For example, her own positive experience within all-black communities made her an outspoken critic of integration. Many other African Americans have since come to agree with that view, but during Hurston's lifetime, black segregationists ran against the grain. And when she portrayed black characters not as victims of society, but as individuals who were as capable of succeeding and living and loving as anyone else, she was accused of being naïve and ignoring social realities.

By the 1940s Hurston's style was considered passé in the current literary scene, and she was no longer able to support herself as a writer. Largely forgotten, she returned to the South, and during the 1950s took a series of menial jobs while trying fruitlessly to find a publisher for several new works that she hoped to produce. On January 28, 1960, she died of a stroke in a Florida welfare home. She was buried in an unmarked grave.

In the 1970s Hurston's works underwent a dramatic literary renaissance, based largely on the power of *Their Eyes Were Watching God*. The story follows a black woman, Janie, through several black communities and several love relationships. Over the course of the novel, Janie comes to recognize and embrace her own identity. Long after *Their Eyes* had gone out of print, black women continued to circulate old paperback and xeroxed copies, and in the early 1970s Alice Walker published a widely read essay about Hurston and her work. *Their Eyes* was reprinted at the height of the women's movement, and black and white scholars alike embraced it as the first black feminist novel.

Since its rediscovery, *Their Eyes* has become one of the most frequently assigned novels on college campuses and one of the best-known works of African American literature. Moreover, Hurston's other books have been reprinted; scholar Robert Hemenway has written her biography; and Walker and other contemporary black women novelists freely acknowledge her influence on their work.

Folklorist, anthropologist, and writer Zora Neale Hurston (1891-1960) is perhaps best known for her book *Their Eyes Were Watching God* (1938), considered by many the first black feminist novel. *CORBIS*

A new generation of readers has been exposed to a writer who celebrated black culture and refused to portray blacks as victims; who saw the world as her oyster, and sharpened her knife.

Lisa Clayton Robinson

See Also
Literature, African American; Black Towns; Locke, Alain Leroy; Minstrelsy; New York, New York; *Opportunity: Journal of Negro Life.*

North America

Hutson, Jean Blackwell

(b. September 7, 1914, Summerfield, Fla.; d. February 3, 1998, New York, N.Y.), African American librarian who developed the Schomburg Center for Research in Black Culture into the world's largest collection of materials by and about people of African descent.

Born into a middle-class family, Jean Blackwell Hutson was the second African American (following Zora Neale Hurston) to graduate from Barnard College, and the first to receive a master's degree from Columbia University's School of Library Service. She was married to Andy Razaf, the song lyricist who collaborated with Thomas "Fats" Waller, and then to John Hutson, a library security guard. Their adopted daughter, Jean Jr., died in 1992.

Hutson joined the staff of the New York Public Library in 1936 and 12 years later was appointed head of its black collection, originally the private library of Afro-Puerto Rican bibliophile Arthur A. Schomburg, on 135th Street and Lenox Avenue in Harlem. Under her leadership, the library's holdings grew from 15,000 books to its present collection of more than 5 million separately catalogued items, including manuscripts, music, art, photographs, and clipping files. Hutson at first presided over a decaying Carnegie library building where the collection was housed, but through a personal campaign secured public money to construct a new facility after library officials had ignored her pleas for support.

Kwame Nkrumah invited Hutson to establish an Africana collection at the University of Ghana, which she did in 1964-1965. A friend of African American luminaries and a colleague of nearly everyone conducting research in black studies, Hutson not only transformed a small branch library into the research center of Harlem, but built an institution considered the world's finest in its field.

Richard Newman

See Also
Harlem, New York; Schomburg, Arthur Alfonso; Waller, Thomas Wright ("Fats"); Schomburg Library.

Africa

Hutu and Tutsi, groups living primarily in Rwanda and Burundi.

Most reference sources on Rwanda and Burundi estimate that both countries' national populations are approximately 85 percent Hutu, 14 percent Tutsi, and 1 percent Twa. Although these terms are commonly believed to refer to distinct ethnic groups, the people known as "Hutu" and "Tutsi" have lived in the same region and under the same political authorities for centuries. They have intermarried, speak the same language, and share many cultural practices. According to historical, linguistic, and cultural definitions of ethnicity, in other words, the Hutu and Tutsi are *not* distinct groups. Historically, the more important differences have been occupational and political: the agricultural people of this region have traditionally identified themselves as Hutu, while the Tutsi were traditionally the cattle-owning political elite. Even these categories were not immutable, however, at least not until European colonial rulers began using rigid "tribal" identities to define Africans' access to education, employment, and other resources. Since decolonization, violent civil conflicts in both Rwanda and Burundi have further polarized Hutu and Tutsi populations (*see* Ethnicity in Rwanda: An Interpretation and Ethnicity in Burundi: An Interpretation).

Susanne Freidberg

See Also
Colonial Rule; Decolonization in Africa: An Interpretation; Ethnicity and Identity in Africa: An Interpretation.

Africa

Hyena, African carnivore with a large head and neck; long, well-developed forelegs; and powerful jaws and premolars adapted for crushing bones. Each foot has four toes with nonretractible claws, well suited for running on the open plains, where hyenas feed on hoofed animals.

Of the three hyena species, the best known is the spotted, or laughing, hyena. Ranging south of the Sahara Desert, it is the largest and most robust of the hyenas, with a length of 1.8 m (5.9 ft) and a height of 90 cm (36 in) at the shoulder. Adults are brown-gray with dark brown or black spots. Named for their cry, which has been compared to hysterical human laughter, they also emit a striking howl that rises in pitch. Spotted hyenas were long thought to be only scavengers (warring African tribes abandoned their dead to the animals). Recently, hyenas have been found to be among the chief predators of herbivores, especially zebra and wildebeest. The hyenas attack in packs at night, ripping open the flanks of their prey and carrying off the carcasses.

Hyenas associate in clans centered around communal dens occupied by batches of young at varying stages of growth. Females conceive throughout the year, giving birth after 110 days to one or two cubs, which dig their own tunnels. Pair bonding is not evident; the female, larger than the male, selects her mating partners. The female sexual organs have an external resemblance to the male's, a phenomenon probably related to scent identification, which plays a large part when clan members encounter one another. A clan may consist of 10 or 12 females, 20 cubs, and a number of males on the fringe; it is strongly territorial.

The two other species – the striped hyena and the brown hyena – bear manes of coarse, erectile hair and are smaller and far less aggressive than the spotted hyena. The striped hyena, gray-tan with vertical stripes, ranges from East Africa north into Asia. It is largely a scavenger, often eating vulture-picked bones. The brown hyena, found in southern Africa, is dark brown with a gray head and striped legs. It feeds mainly on fish and crabs. **Scientific classification:** Hyenas belong to the family Hyaenidae. The spotted hyena is classified as *Crocuta crocuta,* the striped hyena as *Hyaena hyaena,* and the brown hyena as *Parahyaena brunnea.*

Latin America and the Caribbean

Hyppolite, Hector

(b. September 16, 1894, Saint-Marc, Haiti; d. June 9, 1948, Port-au-Prince, Haiti), one of Haiti's most famous artists, once called "the greatest of Haitian primitive painters," whose work contains deep religious, cultural, and political symbolism and drew an international audience to Haitian Art.

Hector Hyppolite's paintings drew international attention when art historian DeWitt Peters established the first art center in Haiti, which served as a catalyst for talented but unrecognized "naive" painters. Shortly after the center opened, Peters received a mysterious canvas from Philomé Obin depicting the arrival of United States president Franklin Roosevelt in Cap-Haïtien to lift the American occupation. This event led Peters to realize fully the museum's mission and the importance of Haitian painting as a vehicle for cultural and historical dissemination. Peters searched out Hyppolite and was startled by a sign he had painted on the door of a bar in Mont Rouis proclaiming "La Renaissance."

In his birthplace of Saint-Marc, Hyppolite practiced the profession of *houngan*, or priest (*see* Vodou) and lived on the meager sums he earned as a house painter. Upon moving to Port-au-Prince he set aside house painting and established a painting studio, which he advertised with the sign "Painting Depot Here." From 1945 to 1948 he produced some 70 important paintings a year. His success was due to the intriguing way in which he conveyed the subconscious through imagery. His brush strokes do not demonstrate the concern for aesthetic perfection shown by other Haitian artists such as his faithful companion, Rigaud Benoit, or Castera Bazile and Philome Obin. But the inventiveness of his work, its heterogeneity and its predominantly pink tinge, translate the Haitian spirit in a dreamy, poetic landscape that joins a subtle play of shades of light with a decided taste for the eclectic.

Much of Hyppolite's imagery came from his real and imagined travels: he claimed to have journeyed by foot from Dahomey in western Africa to ETHIOPIA, on the other end of the continent, and to the ancestral lands of SENEGAL and Abyssinia, earning his living by painting floral designs on chamber pots of local inns. From these travels and self-training emerged his imaginative artistic production.

Upon returning to FRANCE from Port-au-Prince with prized possessions purchased from the artist, André Breton exclaimed that Hyppolite's art would "revolutionize modern painting." Hyppolite's richness of design and boldness of expression fulfilled André Breton's prediction, as the surrealists found their utopian ideals embodied in Hyppolite's liberal display of his marvelous and heightened sense of the sublime.

Hyppolite drew inspiration from both the magical and spiritual realms, and his fascination with Vodou and the supernatural is unquestionably the source and sustenance of his aesthetic form. In *The Crucifixion,* for example, he blends the invisible realm of the spirits with a visible Christ who proclaims the redemption of the world. This painting, like his *Saint Francis and Christ Child* and *Jacob's Dream,* worked as much on subconscious as on conscious perception. His painting *Dream of an Angel* is a remarkable blend of Christian chromolithography and *vévés* (geometric designs evoking particular *loa,* or gods in Vodou).

In two of his paintings, Hyppolite's imagery embodies the sharp social distinctions of the Haitian caste system. *Portrait of a Habitant Woman* depicts a woman in stark peasant clothes; in the pensive *Seated Woman,* a figure is garbed in the sumptuous robe of an aristocrat, and the viewer's eye is drawn to her hand, which gestures toward her head.

In *Erzulie or Sirène,* Hyppolite takes the viewer back in Haitian history to the repressive plantation system, in which all representation of African deities was considered superstitious and potentially threatening and was strictly forbidden. The painting depicts Erzulie, a Vodou deity, in her aquatic aspect. Drawing upon a syncretistic logic, Hyppolite appropriated elements of Christian iconography – particularly symbols traditionally linked to the Virgin Mary – yet displaced this iconography by portraying a nude black deity. He thereby restored to Erzulie a dignity equal to that of her Roman Catholic counterpart.

Hyppolite's reputation eventually was on a par with that of the most renowned European artists. It is said that he acquired a remarkable celebrity in the great capitals of the occidental world and particularly with the subsequent special Expositions in Prague, New York, and Paris. Through his pioneering work, so-called naive art has been recognized as a serious genre, and one that conveys the culture and history of Haiti's people.

Paulette Smith

SEE ALSO

Dahomey, Early Kingdom of; Haiti; Port-au-Prince, Haiti.

i

Latin America and the Caribbean

Iansan (known as Iansan or Iansã in Brazil, and as Yansan or Oyá elsewhere), the orisha, or Yoruba deity, of the wind and the cemetery. She is one of the wives of Xangô. Her personality is forceful and tempestuous and her colors are russet and brown in both Cuba and Brazil. She does not get along with Oshún (*see* Orishas; Religions, African, in Latin America and the Caribbean; Santería; and Candomblé).

See Also
Oxum.

Africa

Ibadan, Nigeria, the capital of the Oyo state in southwestern Nigeria and the nation's second largest city.

Ibadan's development predates written history, though its modern composition traces back to wars between the Yoruba kingdoms during the 1820s, after which victorious armies of the Oyo, Ife, and Ijebu settled on the site. Scholars and traders brought Islam to the city in the mid-nineteenth century, and missionaries brought Christianity a few decades later. In 1893 Ibadan fell under British colonial rule, and by 1912 railroads linked the city both to Lagos in the south and Kano in the north.

Local industries include the manufacture of furniture and automobiles, brewing, canning, publishing, and tobacco processing. Yoruba handicrafts such as blacksmithing and ceramics, as well as weaving, spinning, and dyeing, retain important roles in the economy. These wares, along with locally produced food, are sold in Ibadan's numerous markets. As in many other Yoruba towns, most of the city's residents have traditionally made a living from farming. Today this is less common; farmers usually supplement their agricultural income with trade or artisanal work.

Ibadan University, founded in 1948, was Nigeria's first institution of higher learning. Although national economic troubles have undermined the university's world-class reputation, it continues to earn Ibadan the status of Nigeria's intellectual center. The Agodi Gardens, the Ibadan University Zoo, two stadiums, a technical institute, three institutes of agricultural research, and a branch of the National Archives all bolster Ibadan's reputation as cultural hub of the nation.

Today Ibadan is second in size only to Lagos, Nigeria's former capital. In 1995 the city's population had reached 1,295,000.

Eric Bennett

See Also
Kano, Nigeria; Lagos, Nigeria; Christianity: Missionaries in Africa.

Africa

Ibibio, ethnic group of Nigeria.

The Ibibio primarily live in the Cross River State of southeastern Nigeria. They speak a Niger-Congo language and number approximately 2 million.

See Also
Languages, African: An Overview.

Africa

Ibn Battutah (b. February 24, 1304, Tangiers, Morocco; d. 1368, Morocco), medieval North African jurist whose Saharan travels resulted in one of the most valuable early commentaries on African cultures.

Like most North Africans, Ibn Battutah (whose full name was Abu 'Abd Allah Muhammad ibn 'Abd Allah al-Lawati at-Tanji ibn Battutah) was ethnic Berber, and his family traced its ancestry to the nomadic Luwata tribe originating in Cyrenaica west of the Nile Delta. Born into the Muslim religious elite, he would have received a classical literary education in addition to rigorous studies in Islam.

Ibn Battutah wrote poetry in addition to traveling across Africa, Arabia, Asia Minor, India, and China. Most important of his works are his descriptions of the life and culture of peoples of the Niger Basin and Central Sahara, among the earliest and by far the most detailed. After Ibn Battutah returned from his voyages he recounted his observations to Ibn Juzayy, who recorded and edited them at Fès, in Morocco.

At age 21, Ibn Battutah set out on a pilgrimage across North Africa to Mecca, an obligation expected of all Muslims who can afford it. En route he visited Damascus and traveled throughout Syria to the borders of Asia Minor before joining the Muslim pilgrim caravan heading to Mecca, where he spent three years. He then made a visit to trading towns along the coast of East Africa, and returned to Mecca, after which he decided to go to India.

The Islamic brotherhood provided support for Ibn Battutah in his travels, supplying food and lodging as he moved from city to city throughout Asia Minor. He traveled across the Black Sea, visited Constantinople, and journeyed across the steppes of Central Asia. Wherever he traveled, rulers and wealthy people bestowed gifts on him, including many horses. He became quite rich and had many admirers. In India, the sultan was so fond of Ibn Battutah that he appointed him judge, a Malachite *qadi*, in Delhi, and later asked him to lead a royal envoy to the powerful Mongol emperor of China. A series of mishaps, however, left him separated from his ships and destitute for many months on the coast of Malabar. From there he sailed to the Maldive Islands, where he was again appointed judge. But after only a year there Ibn Battutah's curiosity took him in 1345 to see the "footprint of Adam" in Ceylon, where he climbed Adam's Peak.

After further journeys in Southeast Asia, Ibn Battutah finally visited China. He made the long journey home, after many years away from Morocco, returning through Sumatra, Malabar, Oman, Baghdad, Cairo, and Tunis, reaching Fès in 1349. He briefly contemplated taking part in the Crusades, and traveled to Grenada, Spain, in Andalusia.

It was toward the end of Ibn Battutah's travels that he undertook what was probably his most adventurous journey, across the Sahara to visit the peoples living along the bend of the Niger River. For three years, from 1352 to 1354, Ibn Battutah traveled by camel on ancient caravan routes from oasis to oasis, and through major market towns. He stayed for months at a time with rulers in the kingdoms of Mali and Songhai, as well as with TUAREG pastoralists living in the Niger River basin.

Ibn Battutah's description of the sultan of Mali at court is an excellent example of his keen eye for detail. "On certain days the sultan holds audiences in the palace yard, where there is a platform under a tree.... It is carpeted with silk and has cushions placed on it.... The sultan comes out of a door in a corner of the palace, carrying a bow in his hand and a quiver on his back. On his head he has a golden skullcap.... His usual dress is a velvety red tunic.... The sultan is preceded by his musicians, who carry gold and silver *guimbris* [two stringed guitars].... "

Ibn Battutah is the only traveler known to have visited all the Muslim-ruled lands of medieval times. He is estimated to have traveled up to 125,000 km (75,000 mi) in all, and his observations are renowned for their detail, credibility, and color.

Barbara Worley

SEE ALSO
Explorers in Africa Before 1500; Fès, Morocco; Nile River; Pastoralism; Sahara Desert; Songhai Empire; Tunis, Tunisia; Cairo, Egypt; Mali Empire.

Ibn Batuta. Please see IBN BATTUTAH

Ibo. Please see IGBO

Africa

Ibrahim, Abdullah (Dollar Brand or Adolphus Johannes Brand) (b. 1934, Cape Town, South Africa), prominent South African jazz pianist.

Adolphus Brand started studying piano as a young child. As a teenager in Cape Town he earned the nickname "Dollar" because he always carried United States currency to purchase the latest JAZZ albums from American sailors. His formidable musical talent landed him a spot in the Shantytown Sextet, a band strongly influenced by the American mainstream jazz trend toward leaner groups with the demise of the big-band sound. The Shantytown Sextet played in a style called *bebop mbaqanga*. In 1959 Brand, together with Hugh Masekela and Kippie Moeketsi, formed the Jazz Epistles, a group that won the jazz competition at the first Castle Lager Festival, held in Johannesburg in 1961.

In 1962, shortly after marrying the singer Sathima Bea Benjamin, Dollar Brand and the other members of the Jazz Epistles fled the oppressive APARTHEID policies of South Africa to settle in Zurich, Switzerland. There he caught the eye of Duke Ellington, who was on tour. Ellington introduced Brand to the American jazz scene, arranging for the South African musician to record an album and to play at the Newport Jazz Festival.

In 1968 Brand converted to Islam, changed his name to Abdullah Ibrahim, and returned to South Africa a world-famous musician. Of the more than 40 albums he recorded, his 1974 album *Mannenburg* is considered his best work, drawing on both the slow-tempo marabi South African style and American jazz elements. In 1976 Ibrahim fled apartheid oppression once again and settled in New York, where he formed the band Ekaya. With the erosion of apartheid in the early 1990s, Ibrahim returned to play music in South Africa. He remained one of the most respected jazz musicians during the 1990s, voted top jazz pianist by *Downbeat* magazine for three consecutive years.

Ari Nave

SEE ALSO
Cape Town, South Africa; Johannesburg, South Africa; Masekela, Hugh Ramopolo; South Africa; Ellington, Edward Kennedy ("Duke").

North America

Ice Cube (O'Shea Jackson) (b. June 1969, Los Angeles, Calif.), African American rap artist, actor, and music producer.

Musical artist Ice Cube was born and raised in South Central Los Angeles, one of the nation's toughest inner-city neighborhoods; both of his parents held jobs at the University of California at Los Angeles. Cube, as he is known, composed his first RAP, or metered, rhyming lyrics, in ninth-grade typing class, and found that his music, which combined violent fantasies and bawdy humor, was well received by peers. Within a few years he was rapping with a group, CIA, that performed at parties around South Central Los Angeles. In the mid-1980s, along with fellow rappers Eazy E., Dr. Dre, M.C. Ren, and DJ Yella, Cube formed the now-legendary group N.W.A. (usually spelled out as Niggaz with Attitude), whose gritty messages of anger and violence set them apart from the more politically minded East Coast hip hop artists.

Cube left N.W.A. in 1987 to pursue a degree in architectural drafting at the Phoenix Institute of Technology. After completing the one-year program, he returned to help with the production of N.W.A.'s seminal album, *Straight Outta Compton*, which marked the explosive emergence of "gangsta" rap, in which themes drew from life on the streets. After a bitter falling-out with band manager Jerry Heller, Cube left the group, this time heading to New York to collaborate with the Bomb Squad, producers for PUBLIC ENEMY.

The resulting album, *AmeriKKKa's Most Wanted* (1990), established Cube as a menacing solo force. His lyrics, although more articulate and intelligent than those of many rappers, were loaded with misogyny and nihilism, and the album was sharply criticized by the press. Despite limited radio and video play, the record went gold within its first two weeks of release. Cube defended his own words, and the genre, by saying, "Rap is the most positive thing for black kids because it gives information and talks about society, about black history." Cube used profits from his first album to form a multimedia corporation, through which he began producing records for other artists. In the same year, he received critical acclaim for his acting debut as a South Central gang leader in John Singleton's film *Boyz N the Hood*.

Cube's next album, *Death Certificate* (1991), expressed even more of his venomous rage, earning him the reputation of "America's angriest black man." His song "No Vaseline" lashed out against N.W.A.'s manager Heller as Cube defended himself against the group's accusations that he had betrayed them; the song was regarded as anti-Semitic. Another track, "Black Korea," was interpreted as a call to Los Angeles blacks to burn Korean-owned grocery stores. In an unprecedented

American rap artist Ice Cube starred as Doughboy in the John Singleton film *Boyz N the Hood* (1991). *The Everett Collection*

criticism, *Billboard Magazine* suggested that music stores "protest the sentiments" of the album. *Death Certificate* went platinum, and a year later, in the wake of the 1992 Los Angeles riots (in which many Korean-owned grocery stores were burned), Cube claimed to have delivered a prophetic message.

Following his conversion to the NATION OF ISLAM, Cube released his most popular album, *The Predator* (1992), in which he aimed his lilting, aggressive rhymes at crumbling school systems and corrupt police. His next album, *Lethal Injection* (1993), was less popular, and he took a break from rapping to produce debut recordings by Da Lench Mob and Kam. In 1995 he reemerged, forming the group the Westside Connection.

Cube continued his acting career, appearing in 1995 in Singleton's *Higher Learning*. He also starred in the 1997 blockbuster thriller *Anaconda*, and he wrote, produced, and starred in *Friday*, a lighthearted look at two men spending a day in South Central Los Angeles.

SEE ALSO

Hip Hop in the United States; Los Angeles Riot of 1992; Los Angeles, California; Niggaz with Attitude; Film, Blacks in American.

North America

Ice-T (Tracey Morrow)

(b. February 16, 1958, Newark, N.J.), African American rap singer, music producer, and actor.

One of the nation's most prolific and outspoken rap artists, Ice-T helped to pioneer the "gangsta" musical style, in which the turmoil of urban street life is exposed through blunt, explicit lyrics and a bass-heavy, fluid musical style.

Following the death of his parents in a car accident in 1968, Ice-T moved to South Central Los Angeles, where he attended high school. During this time he reportedly stole cars and wrote rhyming slogans for local street gangs. Ice-T took his name from Iceberg Slim, a local pimp who wrote novels and poetry and with whom Ice-T was personally acquainted. After high school Ice-T joined the army but returned to Los Angeles four years later, at which point he recorded "The Coldest Rap" on a local label to launch his musical career.

In 1984 Ice-T's first recording on a major label appeared, on the soundtracks for the low-budget hip hop films *Breakin'* and *Breakin' 2: Electric Boogaloo*, in which he also acted. A year later he formed his own record company, Rhyme Syndicate Productions, before signing with Warner Brothers in 1986. His first album, *Rhyme Pays* (1987), was the first ever to be voluntarily labeled with a warning about potentially offensive lyrics, but neither the warning nor mixed reviews hindered the success of the album, which sold more than 500,000 copies. Ice-T wrote and performed the title song for the film *Colors* (1987), which ensured his long-term popularity.

Ice-T's next album, *Power* (1988), included themes about death and street life, and thus anticipated the emergence of "gangsta" rap. The following year, he released the album *The Iceberg/Freedom of Speech... Just Watch What You Say* as a political commentary on hip hop censorship. In 1992 Ice-T released *Body Count*, recorded with his heavy-metal band of the same name. It featured the song "Cop Killer," which was cited by President George Bush and Vice President Dan Quayle as an incendiary threat to law-enforcement officials. While no police were harmed as a result of the song, Ice-T voluntarily pulled "Cop Killer" from the album.

Despite these sporadic "bad boy" episodes, Ice-T has become a major spokesperson for rap music. He has worked to change the problems he sings about: in 1988 he released an antigang video, and he later testified before a United States Congressional Committee about the gang problem in South Central Los Angeles. He has toured the nation's college campuses speaking about censorship and promoting antidrug and antiviolence campaigns.

Other highlights from Ice-T's musical career include his collaboration with Quincy Jones on the album *Back on the Block* (1990), which earned him a Grammy Award; and the release of *OG: Original Gangster* (1991), which is frequently hailed as his finest album. His later efforts, including *Return of the Real* (1996), have received mixed popular and critical acclaim.

In addition to his music career, Ice-T has appeared in several films, including *New Jack City* (1991), *Ricochet* (1991), *Trespass* (1993), and *Tank Girl* (1995). He has also written a book, *The Ice Opinion* (1994), in which he expresses his views on music, love, religion, and politics.

SEE ALSO

Hip Hop in the United States; Jones, Quincy Delight, Jr.; Los Angeles, California.

Africa

Idoma, ethnic group of NIGERIA.

The Idoma primarily inhabit Benue State of southeastern Nigeria and speak a Niger-Congo language. They are an ethnic group of roughly 800,000 people.

SEE ALSO

Languages, African: An Overview.

Africa

Idris I (Sidi Muhammad Idris as-Sanusi)

(b. 1890, al-Joghboub, Libya; d. May 25, 1983, Egypt), emir (king) of independent LIBYA and a leader in the struggle for decolonization from Italy.

Muhammad Idris was the son of Sayyid al-Mahdi, leader of the Sanusi, a powerful Islamic religious order. As heir to his father's position, Idris became the de facto ruler of the Libyan region of Cyrenaica, where the Sanusi order was based. Soon after he assumed leadership at age 22, Idris began negotiations with Italy for recognition of an emirate in Cyrenaica. In 1920, in return for a promise that Cyrenaicans would lay down their arms, Italy acknowledged Idris as the autonomous Sanusi emir of several oases. Many nationalists from both Tripolitania and Cyrenaica subsequently regarded Idris as the leader of the independence movement.

During World War II Idris risked reprisal from ITALY by allying with GREAT BRITAIN. Following the Allied victory he was installed as emir of Cyrenaica. Libyan support for the monarchy was in no way complete – some nationalists in Tripolitania sought a republic or simply opposed a Cyrenaican-dominated state, and some Cyrenaicans wanted autonomy. Nevertheless, under the constitution of October 1951, Idris was declared emir of Libya. Due to continuing disagreement over the choice of a capital city, Idris was forced to establish two royal cities in two regions.

After the discovery of oil in Libya, Idris continued to cultivate strong trade and military ties with the West, and authorized the construction of a giant oil pipeline. By the late 1960s Idris faced growing unrest over his alliances and priorities from a movement of young pan-Arab republicans, led by Muammar al-Qaddafi. Perhaps sensing the changing tide, Idris left the country in June 1969 for a long medical stay in Turkey. On September 1, 1969, a group of soldiers deposed the emir in his absence. Although Idris ultimately accepted the coup and handed over power peacefully, he was later tried in absentia and sentenced to death. Idris continued to live in exile in EGYPT until his death in 1983.

Marian Aguiar

SEE ALSO

Decolonization in Africa: An Interpretation; Qaddafi, Muammar al-.

Latin America and the Caribbean

Iemanjá (known as Iemajá in BRAZIL,

also called Yemayá or Yemoyá in CUBA and the United States), the mother of many of the ORISHAS, or YORUBA deities. Iemanjá is the orisha of the ocean. Her colors are blue and crystal, and she is propitiated with red roses. In Brazil she is honored on New Year's Eve in Rio de Janeiro, and on February 2 in BAHIA, when gifts of huge baskets full of flowers, perfume, and champagne are taken out to sea and put in the water for her (*see* RELIGIONS, AFRICAN, IN LATIN AMERICA AND THE CARIBBEAN; SANTERÍA; and CANDOMBLÉ).

SEE ALSO

Rio de Janeiro, Brazil.

Latin America and the Caribbean

Ifa, the divination system employed by *babalawos*, the priests or diviners of African-based religions in Cuba, Brazil, and elsewhere in Latin America and the United States. Ifa uses 16 palm nuts or a chain with eight curved disks, giving 256 possible signs, or *odu*, each with hundreds of verses with which to diagnose a client's situation or problem. The term *Ifa* is also used colloquially to identify the orisha, or Yoruba deity, Orúnmila, who speaks through the divination (*see* Orishas; Religions, African, in Latin America and the Caribbean; Santería; and Candomblé).

Africa

Ife, ethnic group of West Africa.

The Ife primarily inhabit southwestern Nigeria, although Ife populations can also be found in western Benin. They speak Yoruba, a Niger-Congo language, and are one of the Yoruba peoples. Approximately 1 million people consider themselves Ife.

See Also
Languages, African: An Overview.

Africa

Igala (also known as Igara), ethnic group of Nigeria.

The Igala primarily inhabit Benue and Kogi states in southeastern Nigeria. They speak a Niger-Congo language and are closely related to the Idoma people. Approximately 1 million people consider themselves Igala.

See Also
Languages, African: An Overview.

Africa

Igbo, one of the major ethnic groups in Nigeria, with roughly 17 to 20 million members concentrated in the southeastern part of the country.

Scholars believe that the Igbo language, which belongs to the Kwa subgroup of the Niger-Congo linguistic family, separated from related languages such as Yoruba, Igala, Idoma, and Edo several thousand years ago. There are some 30 Igbo dialects, which vary in their mutual intelligibility; Owerri Igbo and Onitsha Igbo are the most widely understood "standard" dialects. The traditional Igbo homeland lies on both sides of the lower Niger River, though most Igbo live to the east of the Niger between the Niger Delta and the Benue Valley. Igboland is one of Africa's most densely populated regions. Although Igbo speakers fall into more than a dozen subgroups, they share a common culture and have lived in the same area for thousands of years.

The Igbo have a long history of cultural achievement. Traditionally, they have excelled at metalwork, weaving, and woodcarving. Excavations at the village of Igbo-Ukwu have unearthed sophisticated cast bronze artifacts and textiles dating from the ninth century. Since ancient times, the Igbo have traded craft goods and agricultural products. Traditional Igbo religion varied regionally, but generally included a belief in an afterlife and reincarnation, sacrifice, and ancestor and spirit worship. The Igbo performed elaborate ceremonies marking funerals and other life passages.

Unlike some of their neighbors, the Igbo never developed a centralized monarchy. Chiefs or kings with limited powers ruled the villages of a few subgroups, such as the Nri, the Onitsha Igbo, and groups to the west of the Niger. Until the colonial era, however, most Igbo lived in autonomous, fairly democratic villages, where a complex structure of kinship ties, secret societies, professional organizations, oracles, and religious leaders regulated village society. This mix of overlapping institutions gave most Igbo some decision-making power and prevented any single person from gaining too much power.

Europeans arrived in the late fifteenth century, and by the late seventeenth century the area had become a major center for the slave trade. Many Igbo, especially those living along the Niger River, became traders who sold captives from the interior, including both interior Igbo and members of other ethnic groups. The British (and their North American colonists) played a key role in this trade during the 1700s. The British wanted to encourage "legitimate trade" in products such as palm oil, needed in British manufacturing. Igboland exported large quantities of palm oil after the British suppressed the slave trade in the early 1800s. Later in the century the British sought to establish effective control over Igboland, and the decentralized Igbo could not resist British advances. In 1885 the British established the Oil Rivers Protectorate, named for Igboland's abundant palm oil. By the 1890s the British had occupied the area. They imposed indirect rule (*see* Colonial Rule) in 1900 by appointing African warrant officers, who frequently lacked any standing in the Igbo communities they were supposed to oversee.

The decentralization and cultural openness of the Igbo made them prime targets for missionaries. Today most Igbo are Christian, and they have a high literacy rate. From the colonial period onward, the Igbo produced disproportionate numbers of civil servants and military officers. Educated Igbo played a central role in the struggle for Nigerian independence. Nigeria's first president, Benjamin Nnamdi Azikiwe, was an Igbo. When the country achieved independence in 1960, thousands of Igbo moved to cities all over Nigeria to work as civil servants and administrators. Members of other groups, especially in the north, came to resent the perceived Igbo dominance.

Rising ethnic tensions followed the discovery in the mid-1960s of large oil reserves mostly in or near Igboland. Many Igbo feared that plans to redraw the boundaries of Nigeria's internal administrative divisions would reduce their political clout and deprive them of revenue by placing the main oil-producing regions in divisions outside Igbo control. In 1966, following protests that the presidential election had been rigged, a group of Igbo military officers staged a coup. A countercoup by northern officers followed, along with a massacre of Igbo living in the north. In 1967 the military governor of the eastern region, Lt. Col. Odumegwu Ojukwu, declared the independent state of Biafra, dominated by the Igbo. Nigerian forces quickly forced the Biafran troops to withdraw to a small territory in Igboland, where hundreds of thousands of Igbo starved before Biafra surrendered to Nigerian troops in 1970.

The central government was largely magnanimous in victory. They failed to take reprisals against the Igbo and allowed Ojukwu to return from exile. While ethnic tensions remain, the Igbo are again integrated into Nigerian society. They play an important role in the oil-producing economy based in the cities of the southeast, though Igbo reside in cities throughout Nigeria. Some of Nigeria's leading writers are Igbo, including Nkem Nwankwo, Chinua Achebe, and Cyprian Ekwensi.

David P. Johnson, Jr.

See Also
Art and Architecture, African; Languages, African: An Overview; Transatlantic Slave Trade; Yoruba; Christianity: Missionaries in Africa.

Africa

Igede (also known as Egede and Igedde), ethnic group of Nigeria.

The Igede primarily inhabit Benue State in southeastern Nigeria. They speak a Niger-Congo language and are closely related to the Idoma people. Approximately 300,000 people consider themselves Igede.

See Also
Languages, African: An Overview.

Latin America and the Caribbean

Ignace, Jean (b. 1770, Guadeloupe; d. May 15, 1802, Baimbridge, Guadeloupe), co-commander, with the mixed-race Martinican colonel Louis Delgrès, of the 1802 revolt in Guadeloupe against the Napoleonic troops sent to reimpose slavery in the French Caribbean colony of Guadeloupe.

Few facts are known regarding Jean Ignace's life, and much speculation has surrounded this protean figure of Afro-Guadeloupean identity. Ignace has variously been perceived as a ferocious brute, a proto-independence fighter, a noble hero of the black race, a former maroon slave and Dessaline-like figure, and a brave though strategically naïve soldier. Born in Pointe-à-Pitre, most likely a free, mixed-race carpenter prior to the French abolition of slavery in 1794, he joined the colonial army sometime after the arrival of Victor Hugues in Guadeloupe in that same year.

The historical circumstances of Ignace and Delgrès's revolt itself are, however, fairly certain. On May 5, 1802, a fleet of ships under the command of the French general Richepance arrived in Guadeloupe. Like the troops of General Leclerc, who at the same moment were engaged in an unsuccessful struggle to retain the island of Saint-Domingue (present-day Haiti) for France, Napoleon wished through them to reactivate the economic productivity of slave labor. Following the 1794 abolition, a large number of black as well as *mulâtre* (mixed-race) troops had been incorporated into the French army in Guadeloupe, among them Ignace and Delgrès. Ignace himself rose from the rank of lieutenant in March 1795 to captain in November 1798. The revolt of May 1802 was precipitated when one of the highest ranking of Ignace's fellow mulâtre officers was denied promotion.

The revolt itself occurred only after it became clear to the black troops and their mixed-race leaders that Richepance intended to restore to power General Lacrosse. Ignace, then an officer with the rank of grenadier captain, had sent the once popular Lacrosse into exile the previous October when it appeared that Lacrosse was favorable to the reimposition of slavery. When Richepance failed to show the signs of respect demanded by protocol to the black troops who welcomed him, and when he then attempted to disarm them, Ignace and Delgrès fled with as many of their troops as they could gather. A series of battles ensued in which the badly outnumbered Guadeloupean soldiers attempted to stave off defeat and assert their refusal to reenter the bonds of slavery. A proclamation was issued by Delgrès (it was written by an aide) defending their cause, attacking Lacrosse, and stating their preference of death to the reimposition of servitude. Finally, Ignace and Delgrès split their troops. Delgrès remained on the western half of the island, escaping at night from Fort St. Charles (today Fort Delgrès) into the surrounding foothills of the volcano Soufrière and the plantation known as Habitation Danglemont. When on May 28, 1802, it became apparent that no further resistance was possible, Delgrès's troops mined the plantation with explosives, and upon the entry of the French, obliterated the entire plantation, along with women, children, and hundreds of soldiers from both sides.

Ignace, meanwhile, had returned to the area surrounding Pointe-à-Pitre in an attempt to create a diversion for Delgrès that would disperse Richepance's forces and draw them into fast-moving combat across unfamiliar terrain. Burning the towns of Trois-Rivières, Saint-Sauveur, and Capesterre as they went, they attempted to instigate the strategy that was to have such devastating effect in the concurrent battles in Haiti. Upon arriving in Pointe-à-Pitre, however, Ignace made the fatal decision on May 25, 1802, to withdraw with his troops into Fort Baimbridge just north of the city. The fort was nearly devoid of munitions and was soon surrounded by opposing forces. In the ensuing carnage, 675 soldiers died, including Ignace, who most likely committed suicide when faced with imminent capture. Ignace's head was subsequently exposed in Pointe-à-Pitre in the slave-owning tradition as an example to any who might consider similar resistance. Of the 250 surviving prisoners, all were executed and thrown into the ocean.

Their rebellion thus ended, all remaining participants were executed, exiled, or returned to slavery. A brutal repression and period of reaction followed in which it was made illegal even to discuss the events of May 1802. For the next 46 years the island of Guadeloupe returned to prerevolutionary social relations, including the immediate reimposition of the ownership of one human by another – although the word "slavery" remained taboo.

Nick Nesbitt

See Also

Maroonage in the Americas; Slavery in Latin America and the Caribbean; Dessalines, Jean-Jacques; Haiti; Abolition and Emancipation in Latin America and the Caribbean.

Africa

Ihetu, Dick ("Tiger")

(b. August 14, 1929, Nigeria; d. December 14, 1971?), Nigerian professional boxer.

Known as Dick Tiger, Ihetu won crowns as both a middleweight and a light heavyweight. Little is known of his childhood, but records show he began his professional career in 1952, compiling a record of 16 wins, 1 loss over the next four years. A strong counterpuncher, he was known for his left hook. In 1956 he moved to England, where his career at first faltered – he won five and lost four bouts in his first year there. But he soon regained his form, winning 13 out of 15 fights over the next two years and becoming the British Commonwealth middleweight titleholder along the way.

Ihetu first fought in the United States in 1959, and by 1962 had won the World Boxing Association (WBA) middleweight title by defeating the American Gene Fullmer in 15 rounds. He twice defended the title against Fullmer in 1963, fighting in Las Vegas and in Ibadan, Nigeria. In December 1963 he lost the title to Joey Giardello, an American boxer. Two years later Ihetu defeated Giardello to regain his title but lost it again in 1966. Now fighting as a light middleweight, Ihetu won the WBA title for that weight class (which comprises fighters from 73 to 80 kg [160 to 175 lb]) in December 1966, successfully defending it until May 1968, when Ihetu was knocked out for the first time in his career. He won his next three fights but retired in 1970 with a final record of 61 wins (26 by knockout), 17 losses, and three draws. He died the following year.

Kate Tuttle

See Also

Nigeria; Boxing.

Africa

Ijaw (also known as the Ijo), ethnic group of Nigeria.

The Ijaw primarily inhabit the Delta and Rivers states of southeastern Nigeria. They speak a Niger-Congo language possibly more ancient than others in the region and comprise several subgroups, including the Kalabari, the Nemba (Brass), and the Okrika. Approximately 400,000 people consider themselves Ijaw.

See Also

Languages, African: An Overview.

Africa

Ijebu, ethnic group of Nigeria.

The Ijebu primarily inhabit Ogun State, southwestern Nigeria. They speak Yoruba, a Niger-Congo language, and are one of the Yoruba peoples. Approximately 800,000 people consider themselves Ijebu.

See Also

Languages, African: An Overview.

Latin America and the Caribbean

Ilê Aiyê (founded 1974, Salvador, Bahia, Brazil), the original bloco Afro, a percussion-based music and dance troupe that initiated the "re-Africanization" of the Bahian Carnival.

Dissatisfied by the options available to Afro-Brazilians during Carnival, a group of young black petroleum workers from the working-class neighborhood of Curuzu-Liberdade organized Ilê Aiyê (Yoruba for House of Life) for the 1975 Carnival. The group's founder and president, Antônio Carlos dos Santos Vovô, cited three principal sources of inspiration: local Afro-Brazilian culture rooted in the Candomblé religion; the North American Black Power and soul movements and their Brazilian spinoffs; and the liberation of former Portuguese colonies in Africa such as Angola and Mozambique.

As a response to some elite Carnival groups who informally excluded people of color, Ilê Aiyê established a blacks-only membership policy, which it still maintains. Although Ilê Aiyê was criticized in the local press for "introducing racial politics" into the Bahian Carnival, it soon received moral support from established pop stars such as Gilberto Gil, who recorded a pop version of the group's first Carnival hit, "Que bloco é esse?" on his 1977 album *Refavela.* Caetano Veloso's praise song for the group, "Um canto de axé para o bloco do Ilê," was featured on his 1982 *Cores, nomes* album and was later included on David Byrne's popular compilation *Beleza Tropical.*

By the early 1980s Ilê Aiyê had emerged as a primary reference for Afro-Brazilians committed to political, social, and cultural affirmation while creating a viable model for subsequent *blocos Afros,* like Olodum, Malê Debalê, Araketu, and Muzenza. Its annual Carnival themes have paid homage to several African nations, including Senegal, Angola, Zimbabwe, Cameroon, and South Africa. In 1993 Ilê Aiyê's theme was Black America, which celebrated the legacy of key activists such as Marcus Garvey, Malcolm X, Fannie Lou Hamer, and Martin Luther King Jr. Each year in January the group sponsors a gala event called Noite da Beleza Negra (Night of Black Beauty), in which the band showcases new songs and the Carnival queen is chosen.

Ilê Aiyê has released three albums, all of them entitled *Canto Negro* (Black Song), featuring guest vocalists such as Gilberto Gil, Caetano Veloso, Martinho da Vila, and the Brazilian reggae singer Lazzo. In the 1990s, as Araketu and Olodum transformed into electric pop bands of international fame, Ilê Aiyê maintained a heavy, percussion-based sound as well as a resolutely Afrocentric ideological and aesthetic orientation.

Christopher Dunn

See Also

Soul Music; Garvey, Marcus Mosiah; King, Martin Luther, Jr.; Afoxés/Blocos Afros; Carnivals in Latin America and the Caribbean.

Africa

Ile de France. Former name of Mauritius.

Latin America and the Caribbean

Illescas, Sebastián Alonso de, former slave during the sixteenth century, leader of maroon community in Esmeraldas Province, Ecuador.

Sebastián Alonso de Illescas was a ladino slave (a slave who had lived for some time in Spain, who could speak Spanish, and who had been baptized). He had taken the name of his Spanish owner after his confirmation in Seville. In 1553 he and 22 other slaves were embarked with merchandise on a ship going to the Peruvian port of Callao, where colonization was burgeoning. During the trip between Panama and Callao, a strong thunderstorm wrecked the ship against the reefs off the coast of the Ecuadorian province of Esmeraldas. The slaves killed the Spanish crew, then escaped into the forest, where they developed what some historians have called the Republic of Zambos. (A *zamba[o]* is a mixed-race person from both African and Native American ancestry.)

Under the group's first leader, Anton, the maroons grew to dominate indigenous communities in the region. The maroons took indigenous wives and were already referred to by the Spaniards as mulattos by the end of the sixteenth century. In this context Sebastián Alonso de Illescas progressively affirmed himself as the new leader of the Esmeraldian zamba society. His rise was due to his ingenuity, his knowledge of the cultural habits of the Spaniards, and his skills as a political strategist. He knew how to use European firearms and learned at least one Native American language. Around 1600, after a series of confrontations between the community and soldiers of the colonial authority, the Spanish Crown designated Illescas's son as the first governor of the province of Esmeraldas. He was also named Sebastián de Illescas and had succeeded his father as leader.

"Official" Esmeraldian history is fashioned by Esmeraldian white and white-*mestizo* (of indigenous and European descent) elite. For this reason, Sebastián Alonso de Illescas and his companions are not celebrated in the province of Esmeraldas, as are white and white mestizo men, as heroes of the early history of the province (*see* Maroonage in the Americas and Ecuador).

Jean Muteba Rahier

Latin America and the Caribbean

Image of the Mulatta in Latin America and the Caribbean

The term *mulatta* is a social construction created by colonizers to signify the racial mixing of people of African and European ancestry with the intent of "whitening" African physical and cultural traits.

The image of the mulatta is inextricably tied to the violence of forced miscegenation of the female African slave by the European slaveholder beginning in the sixteenth century (*see* Slavery in Latin America and the Caribbean). In the European imagination the mulatta has come to signify the vulnerable yet highly sexualized woman whose sole ambition is to "better" herself by marrying a white European man and bearing children whose African ancestry is not physically apparent. By wishing to gain legal status for her mixed children in the colonies, the mulatta represents a threat to the racial purity of the European family. The image of the mulatta thus embodies a contradiction, fulfilling both the desire to whiten the Latin American and Caribbean population and the fear that non-Europeans will attain social and political privilege in the emerging nations (*see* Slave Laws in Colonial Spanish America and Colonial Latin America and the Caribbean).

Opposite: The appealing mulatta, often nude or partially clothed, is a frequent theme in the pictures of Brazilian artist Emiliano di Cavalcanti (1897-1976). His painting *Cinco moças de Guarantinguetá* (Five Girls from Guaratinguetá) is dated 1930. *Museu de Arte de São Paolo Assis Chateaubriand, Photo Luiz Hossaka*

This contradictory image of the mulatta was inscribed in the nineteenth-century literary imagination of Latin American readers by white abolitionist writers. For example, the Cuban antislavery novel *Cecilia Valdés* (1884), written by Cirilo Villaverde, centers on the image of an exceedingly attractive, lower-class mulatta who wishes to marry the son of a wealthy slave trader and landholder. The novel ties the antislavery theme to that of incest, since the protagonist is the illegitimate daughter of the landowner's son. The novel ends tragically with the death of the young man and the mulatta's insanity. His death signifies the end of colonial rule and her madness the marginalization of those of mixed race. Since abolitionism and independence often coincide in most Latin American and Caribbean nations, the contradictory image of the mulatta comes to represent the new republic, independent of the colonial power yet unable to accept and incorporate its African descendants into the social and political structures. The nation, moreover, is conceived through the secret, incestuous relationship between two people of differing social and racial origins. The dream of many Latin American and Caribbean liberators to create nations that contained a true mixture of races and cultures was tragically thwarted in the national literatures.

Because Latin American and Caribbean nations have traditionally associated social advancement with racial whitening, the image of the mulatta necessarily internalizes the racism practiced by those in power and forcefully denies what is African. The marginalization of blacks in the new nations created an underclass. The image of the mulatta in literature and the media in the twentieth century relegates the character to the roles of the domestic, the tropical nightclub dancer, and the prostitute. In all instances, the more contemporary image continues to uphold the characteristics of subservience and of a sexually provocative object. Visual images created by the mass media of the half-dressed tropical dancer are often used to attract foreigners, particularly to the Caribbean

nations, where the SUGAR and agricultural industries have been steadily replaced by the more profitable tourist industry.

To counteract this media-produced image of the mulatta, social and political movements throughout the Caribbean and Latin America have emphasized a sense of pride in the African heritage of their inhabitants. In Brazil, for example, the words "mulatto" and "mulatta" are highly offensive to black people because they have come to signify the crossing of a mule (the female slave) and a horse (the white Portuguese man). Black women in the arts portray themselves and their female ancestors as proud survivors of

ABOVE: In 1775 Le Masurier, an obscure French artist, painted three canvases depicting Creole and slave society on Martinique. In this scene a mulatta and her daughter take tea while dark-skinned slaves serve them. *Musée des Arts d'Afrique et d'Océanie, Paris. © Photo RMN*

LEFT ABOVE: Spanish artist Evaristo Valle's painting *Las morenas de azul* dates from 1929 and represents a pair of blue-clad mulattas in a West Indian sugar cane field. *Fundación Museo Evaristo Valle*

LEFT BELOW: For centuries the Caribbean woman of African descent has been objectified as a purely sexual being. *Jeanette Ortiz Osorio*

the violence inflicted upon them by slavery (*see* ART IN LATIN AMERICA AND THE CARIBBEAN). The image of the black grandmother and mother as the sustainer and promoter of nearly suppressed African traditions is beginning to supplant the racist image of the mulatta in literature, film, and the arts.

In her memoir-novel *When I Was Puerto Rican* (1993), an example of the revised image of the young black woman is portrayed by Esmeralda Santiago. In this autobiographical novel, Santiago lovingly reconstructs the Afro-Puerto Rican image as she traces the early life of a farm girl. The protagonist becomes highly educated and controls the definition of her destiny as an Afro-Caribbean woman. Along with a shift in the image of the mulatta in high culture, there is an equivalent change in social terms. An increasing number of black women have attained middle-class status through education. These women have organized themselves and met at international conferences, for example at the First Meeting of Black Women from Latin America and the Caribbean held in Santo Domingo in July 1992. Along with the continued revision of the image of the mulatta in cultural terms, it is hoped that there will be a parallel decrease of subservient and sexually derogatory roles assumed by the contemporary black woman both in the media and in actual life.

Flora González

SEE ALSO

Slavery in Latin America and the Caribbean; Abolition and Emancipation in Latin America and the Caribbean; Literature, Black, in Spanish America; Education in Latin America and the Caribbean.

Africa

Impala, slightly built African ANTELOPE that ranges from KENYA south to SOUTH AFRICA.

When frightened, impalas scatter, making leaps as long as 9 m (30 ft) and as high as

3 m (10 ft), which have the effect of startling and confusing LIONS and wild dogs, their main predators. Only male impala have horns, which are long, black, and of a graceful lyre shape. The impala stands 0.78 to 1 m (2.6 to 3.3 ft) high and is chestnut brown above and white below, with a distinctive black streak on each haunch.

Impalas inhabit the edges of forests within reach of water, grazing on plains grasses and browsing on shrubs in the forests, where they take refuge. During the dry season they form herds of sometimes hundreds of animals. After the dry season males compete for territory. During the mating seasons, which occur from March to June and from September to November, groups of females enter and remain in a male's territory. Males without territories stay together in a bachelor herd. **Scientific classification:** The impala belongs to the family Bovidae of the order Artiodactyla. It is classified as *Aepyceros melampus.*

Latin America and the Caribbean

Indentured Labor in the Caribbean, **the importation of South Asian labor into British colonies in the Caribbean shortly after the abolition of slavery in 1834. Most laborers came from India and worked on plantations for the duration of five-year contracts in exchange for wages and passage fare. Despite some laws designed to protect them, the laborers were greatly exploited. International humanitarian and labor groups pressured to end the system, and Indian laws in 1917 and 1922 effectively stemmed the flow of indentured labor from India (*see* EAST INDIAN COMMUNITIES IN THE CARIBBEAN).**

Africa

Indian Communities in Africa, **South Asian immigrants and their descendants in East Africa and SOUTH AFRICA.**

In 1972 Ugandan dictator IDI AMIN ordered the immediate expulsion of Asians (a term often used in East and South Africa to denote South Asians) from his country. Amin's policy on Asians was bolder than most in East Africa, but it played on existing tensions. It also raised questions about the future social, economic, and political roles of Asians in the African countries where they already had long histories. Besides UGANDA, these countries include MAURITIUS, KENYA, TANZANIA, MALAWI, and ZAMBIA.

EAST AFRICA

Although South Asians had been trading with people on the east coast of Africa since the first millennium B.C.E. (*see* SOUTH ASIA, AFRICANS IN), British colonialism transformed the relationship between these trading partners and their respective continents. The areas of India under control of the British East India Company during the nineteenth century provided support for the exploration and colonization of East Africa and Mauritius. In 1815 the British in Mauritius began importing Indian convict labor to rear silkworms. After 1834 they began importing indentured labor for road building and plantation work.

After the British Imperial East African Company was granted its royal charter in 1888, it encouraged Indian immigration to East Africa, primarily to provide indentured labor for railway construction. Most laborers were poor younger sons from middle castes or peasants released from land debts in their home villages. Many came from agricultural parts of the Indian regions of Uttar Pradesh, Bihar, and Madras. According to Indian colonial law, 40 women were recruited for every 100 men. For the most part, these Indians were not the ones who permanently settled in East Africa; only about one-fourth of them stayed beyond their term of service. The permanent South Asian community was made up of the traders, artisans, and professionals who arrived after the establishment of the indentured settlements, and particularly after World War I. They were Hindus, Muslims, Sikhs, and Christians, primarily from Gujarati- and Punjabi-speaking areas, as well as Konkani-speaking Goa.

Indians came to occupy the middle level of a three-tiered hierarchy in British colonial Africa – below white settlers and above Africans. In general, Indians enjoyed fewer restrictions on property ownership than Africans and better access to the resources needed for commercial enterprises, such as bank credit. Consequently, greater numbers of Indians were able to establish themselves as shop owners, hoteliers, commercial farmers, and export merchants. Although the economic mobility available to this group did not immediately foster anti-Indian sentiment among Africans, it did set the stage for later tensions.

By the early twentieth century white settlers and Africans alike were beginning to resent the Indian communities' control over important sectors of the economy. There were social tensions as well. Indians were accused of discriminating against non-Indians. In fact, the Indian community was itself not homogeneous, and caste, religious, and language identities regulated interpersonal relations within the community as race sometimes restricted relations outside of it.

Settlers successfully pressured for immigration regulations and the 1915 Crown Lands Ordinance, which restricted Indians from owning land in Kenya's fertile highland regions. Despite these measures, in the 1920s another wave of East African immigration began, this time bringing Indian accountants, teachers, technicians, and other professionals. The Asian population in East Africa swelled from approximately 34,000 in 1915 to 105,000 by 1939.

Indians were beginning to organize in East Africa, inspired in part by anticolonial resistance in India. The East African Indian National Congress, formed in 1914, demanded equal rights and, later, compensation for Indians' service in World War I. East African nationalist movements drew not only on the example of the successful anticolonial movement in India, which secured independence in 1947, but also on the active participation of some Indians in East Africa's nationalist organizations. Indians also defended African interests when, as members of colonial legislatures, they represented Africans in the years before that group won direct representation.

In 1959 Ugandan businessman Augustine Kamya led the first major anti-Asian boycott. In addition to the boycott, vandalism was directed at Asian traders, and Africans who defied the boycotts were also subject to violence. Asians faced a series of official and unofficial discriminatory policies throughout East Africa in the 1960s. Tanzania began nationalizing banking and trade firms in the 1960s and later effectively took over Asian businesses by seizing all rented buildings worth more than 5,833 British Pounds Sterling. As a result the Asian population dropped from 88,700 in 1961 to 52,000 in 1971. In Kenya, where in 1967 the government started restricting immigration as well as noncitizens' access to trade and work permits, the Asian population dropped from 176,613 in 1962 to approximately 105,000 in 1982. In Malawi, Asians' land was confiscated and noncitizens were deported; in 1968 Zambian president KENNETH KAUNDA banned noncitizens' businesses in both rural and urban areas. The most severe discrimination was evident in Uganda, where President MILTON OBOTE's nationalization scheme and restrictions on work permits drove down the Asian population by 35 percent between independence and his ouster in 1971 by General Amin. That same year Amin declared that all Asians had to leave the country within 90 days. Citizens and residents of Asian origin fled in terror from Uganda, forfeiting property and savings.

The Indians who left East Africa relocated in many places, but primarily Great Britain and India. In 1990 the Ugandan government under President YOWERI MUSEVENI offered repatriation and compensation for Asian exiles. Several hundred families have since returned to Uganda.

SOUTH AFRICA

The history of Indians in South Africa is distinct from that of Indians in East Africa, both because of the concentration of Indians in the Natal region and because of Indians' participation in the fight against APARTHEID.

The Dutch Cape Colony, founded in 1652 in the southern part of present-day South Africa, imported slaves from the Dutch East Indian Empire as well as from other parts

Indians in South Africa have faced a great deal of tension between themselves and both the black and white populations of this country.
CORBIS/Charles O'Rear

of Africa until the early nineteenth century. After Britain took over the colony in 1806 and outlawed slavery in 1834, indentured laborers were recruited from many parts of Asia, but especially India. Natal, and particularly the city of Durban, became a center for the Indian community in South Africa. Indians worked on sugar plantations and road and railway projects, in mines, and as domestics in British and AFRIKANER homes. As in East Africa, many of the immigrants were from rural regions of Uttar Pradesh and Bihar, but a good portion also came from Tamil and Telugu-speaking areas. More than 150,000 indentured workers arrived in Natal between 1860 and 1911.

Few laws protected indentured workers against exploitation by both recruiters and employers. Opposition to the recruiting of indentured labor in India led the British colonial administration there to ban recruitment to Natal for several years. After 1875 legal reforms in Natal improved the rights of these laborers who completed their five-year terms of service, encouraging more Indians to settle permanently. The colony's whites viewed the increasing Indian population with apprehension – in the words of a London journalist, they feared the colony "might soon be submerged in dusky waters." A Natal government commission recommended deportation and failing that, segregation.

The 1891 Immigration Act banned land grants to former indentured laborers, doing away with an incentive planters had used to maintain a stable work force. In 1895 the government imposed a tax on indentured and ex-indentured laborers and their families. Yet even as these measures encouraged indentured laborers to return to India, the population of "passenger Indians" – those who paid their own transport from India or Mauritius – increased. This group included large-scale merchants, many of them Gujarati Muslims, as well as petty traders, artisans, preachers, and teachers. By 1904 Indians outnumbered whites in Natal. Indentured labor was outlawed in 1911; this decision was influenced equally by pressure in British-held India over labor shortages and the exploitation of Indians and by South African settler resistance.

In the Afrikaner South Africa Republic, also known as the Transvaal, Indians were not allowed citizenship or property ownership. When the British took over the Afrikaner states at the end of the Boer War, they effectively maintained racial segregation in urban areas. Segregation, taxes, and the South African government's refusal to recognize anything but Christian marriages all galvanized the passive resistance campaign led by the Indian lawyer Mohandas Gandhi. Based in Durban, Gandhi had been teaching the *satyagraha*, a philosophy of nonviolent resistance, since 1894, when he became the first secretary of the Natal Indian Congress (NIC). The growing momentum of Gandhi's movement exploded in the 1913 strikes of Indian workers and defiance of discriminatory laws. The movement ultimately won the retraction of taxes and acknowledgment of Hindu and Muslim marriages.

The push for segregation and deportation (euphemistically termed repatriation, even though it would involve the forcible expulsion of people from their native land) continued, however. In 1914 the South African government began to offer free passage to Indians returning to India and, later, added payments as an extra incentive. The 1924 Class Areas Bill and 1925 Areas Reservation Bill, which were forerunners of later segregation laws, had the admitted aim of reducing the Indian population in Natal through the threat of segregation. Citing the stated goal of pushing Indians out of South Africa, politicians who sponsored such acts as the 1932 Transvaal Asiatic Land Tenure Act – which limited Indian trading by preventing Indians from acquiring property outside designated areas – introduced permanently the principle of statutory segregation. Despite this act, Natal's Indian community continued to grow.

The tensions between Indians and white traders, as well as poor Afrikaners, helped propel the NATIONAL PARTY to power in 1948. The National Party government's 1950 Group Areas Act was one of many laws that enforced racial segregation. In Durban alone the act forced 75,000 Indians to relocate and to relinquish valuable land outside the city. Some have argued that the National Party eased pressure for deportation in order to divert black opposition away from white domination; they point to the 1949 Indian-African race riots in Durban as evidence that this tactic worked.

Overall, however, political solidarity between Indians and Africans increased between the 1920s and the 1950s. Important Indian groups during this period included the NIC and the countrywide South African Indian Congress (1919). The NIC became a model for the AFRICAN NATIONAL CONGRESS (ANC). Both Indian organizations had links to high-profile "Coloured" and African activists such as Abdurrahman of the African Peoples' Organization, Bantu professor D. D. T. Jabavu, and ANC leader Rev. John L. Dube.

In addition, as the Indian community grew from its immigrant roots, it took on more of an urban character; contact between Indian and black workers, particularly in the labor movement, increased. Leaders such as Dr. Yusuf Dadoo and Nana Sita publicly supported the ANC, and activists such as Ahmed Kathrada received terms of life imprisonment for their activism to promote racial justice. In the 1970s the NIC, which had been defunct for several years, joined the ANC in mobilizing young Indians into political action against apartheid. Indian activists and lawyers filled gaps in the anti-apartheid struggle left by imprisoned or exiled ANC leaders, and later played a more direct role in the United Democratic Front, an antiapartheid alliance formed in 1983. In addition, India's newly independent government aided the ANC and appealed to the United Nations about Indians' mistreatment in South Africa. India was the first nation to cut ties with South Africa over the issue of apartheid.

Compared to the black population, however, South Africa's Indians enjoyed relative freedom, particularly after the National Party began easing restrictions in order to co-opt their support. During the late 1960s and 1970s Indians were given limited representation within the government and allowed to take middle-management, manufacturing, and service jobs that were prohibited to blacks.

In postapartheid South Africa, as in East Africa, the economic successes of Indians have caused tension. Polls in 1994 showed that the majority of Indian voters, a group that had previously supported the ANC, now leaned toward the National Party. This conservative shift has been attributed to an Indian fear of losing economic power to the growing black business class. Other analyses point out that it might take some time to overcome the legacy of apartheid – a system that not only distinguished groups by race but fostered conflict between them.

Marian Aguiar

SEE ALSO

Amin, Idi; Colonial Rule; Kérékou, Mathieu; Durban, South Africa.

Africa

Indian Ocean Slave Trade, the forced movement of people under bondage across the Indian Ocean.

The Indian Ocean slave trade is to a certain extent a misnomer, because it subsumes two historically and geographically distinct trades that happened to cross a single body of water. For over 1000 years, Arab traders transported African slaves across the Indian Ocean to the Arabian Peninsula, the Persian Gulf, and Asia. Centuries later they were joined by European slave traders who brought large numbers of Africans to the Mascarenes and other Indian Ocean islands, as well as to the Americas. Because the early Arab traders left few surviving records, it is difficult to estimate how many Africans they took across the Indian Ocean as slaves. It is likely, however, that about 7 to 10 million Africans traversed the Indian Ocean, compared to about 12 million Africans shipped across the Atlantic, though over a much longer period of time.

The Arab Indian Ocean Slave Trade

The earliest Arab traders probably voyaged to the east coast of Africa on *dhows,* small sailing ships developed during the first millennium B.C.E. Unlike the slave traders who crossed the Atlantic centuries later, Arab slave merchants were predominantly small dealers who transported fewer than 100 slaves at a time and usually also traded in other commodities, such as ivory, spices, and leather.

The first direct evidence of a sizable Indian Ocean slave trade dates to the seventh century C.E., when large numbers of East African male slaves labored on the plantations of the Abbasid Caliphate, in Mesopotamia. Slaves exported by Arab traders to southwest Asia, India, Indonesia, and China worked mainly as soldiers, concubines, and household servants. But African slaves were engaged in diverse occupations – in Bahrein and Lingeh, for example, they dove for pearls. Although legally they were assigned the status of chattel, Muslim law accorded slaves basic human rights. Thus, many slaves attained relatively high social status as concubines and bureaucrats, while others rebelled against the harsh conditions. In the late ninth century, for example, tens of thousands of African slaves in Abbasid revolted.

The Arab Indian Ocean slave trade went into decline for several centuries, as Arab and Asian demand for slaves was eclipsed by a demand for other African commodities, such as gold and ivory. It increased again in the late seventeenth century to meet a growing demand for labor on date plantations in Oman and, later, the sugar plantations on the Mascarene Island colonies. Large slave markets developed in ZANZIBAR and Pemba where, at the height of the trade, as many as 15,000 to 20,000 slaves passed through annually. The slave trade became so significant that in 1840, the sultan of Oman moved his seat of power to Zanzibar. In the East African interior, peoples such as the NYAMWEZI, YAO, NGONI, and Makua raided neighboring communities and sold their captives to Arab caravans, often in exchange for firearms. In addition to the many East African slaves sent to the distant shores of Arabia and the Persian Gulf, others remained as laborers on Arab plantations in East Africa, such as the Omani clove farms on Zanzibar.

Long after European countries outlawed the transatlantic slave trade in the early nineteenth century, Arab slave dhows continued to disembark from Zanzibar, Mombasa, and other depots, little hindered by the British fleet that patrolled the Indian Ocean seeking to enforce the prohibition on slaving.

The European Indian Ocean Slave Trade

European slave traders began operating in the Indian Ocean during the seventeenth century, when the settlement of the Mascarene Islands increased the demand for cheap labor. Some East African slaves during this period were shipped around the Cape of Good Hope and across the Atlantic to Caribbean colonies such as Saint-Domingue (present-day HAITI). During the eighteenth and nineteenth centuries, more and more East African slaves were sent to the Indian Ocean island colonies, such as Ile de France (in MAURITIUS), and Réunion. Although the vast majority of slaves ultimately would labor in the sugar cane fields, initially slaves built the islands' colonial infrastructures and cleared fields of rocks.

As the British attempted to impose controls on the West African slave trade at the beginning of the nineteenth century, European slavers grew to rely on East African markets to supply their ships. Mozambican slaves were primarily destined for BRAZIL and CUBA. At the height of the Indian Ocean slave trade to European colonies, as many as 15,000 slaves from Mozambique alone were exported annually. Similar numbers flowed through Zanzibar as well. The Indian Ocean slave trade did not, however, consist entirely of exports from the African mainland; in addition to slaves taken from MADAGASCAR, the Mascarene Islands also imported slaves from India and Malaysia.

Although the slave trade was formally abolished after Britain took possession of Mauritius in 1810, slavery remained an integral part of the economy until 1835. British agents signed a treaty with Radama, the Merina king of Madagascar, to eliminate Madagascar as a principal source of slaves in the Indian Ocean. But the Merina court did not have complete control over Madagascar, nor was it entirely invested in the abolition of slavery. The independent Sakalava kingdom of Madagascar continued to route East African and Comorian slaves through Madagascar before shipping them to Mauritius under a "free labour emigration scheme." Likewise, French traders shipped slaves from Mozambique to the many islands of the SEYCHELLES, and then introduced them "legally" to Mauritius as slaves that existed before the ban on the trade and property of French estate owners. Zanzibar and Kilwa also remained active export centers until the 1870s.

Impact of the Indian Ocean Slave Trade on East African Societies

The Indian Ocean slave trade provided one route for the introduction of Islam to East Africa, and it had many other lasting social consequences as well. Particularly as the slave trade escalated from the seventeenth through the nineteenth century, large regions of eastern, southern, and Central Africa suffered social disruption and depopulation. Although slavery had existed within Africa for centuries (*see* SLAVERY IN AFRICA), typically it was not a commercial enterprise but rather a means of extending kinship relations and increasing social status. External demand for slaves resulted in forced migrations; weaker groups fled from slave raiders pursuing the accumulation of wealth and power made possible by the new market-based trade. While raiders traded slaves for rifles and ammunition, violence spread across the East African interior, as missionary DAVID LIVINGSTONE observed when he visited the Lake Nyasa region in the mid-nineteenth century. Not long afterward, the need to abolish slavery and "pacify" the region became one of the primary justifications for the European colonization of East Africa.

Ari Nave

See Also

Comoros; Gold Trade; Ivory Trade; Malawi, Lake; Mombasa, Kenya; Mozambique; Transatlantic Slave Trade; Réunion.

Indomitable Lions. Please see CAMEROON LIONS

Africa

Infibulation, *see* Female Circumcision in Africa.

Latin America and the Caribbean

Influence of African Languages and Cultures on Colonial Languages in Latin America and the Caribbean

When enslaved black Africans were brought to the Americas and the Caribbean, their languages came into contact with European languages. At the same time, plantations brought together Africans from different ethnic and linguistic origins who did not share a common language. As a result, they became multilingual settings in which the slaves were led by circumstances to resort to using the rulers' languages as linguas francas and later as vernaculars, that is, languages used for day-to-day communication. Since the vast majority of African slaves who were brought to the New World were adults, and thus already fluent speakers of their local languages, this inevitably influenced the way that they spoke European colonial languages.

The European languages spoken in the colonies were already different from their metropolitan ancestors, as they were by-products of communication among European colonists who spoke diverse dialects and languages. They were further restructured when spoken by the Africans, especially during the peak of the plantation economy, as a result in part of two factors. First, racial segregation necessarily separated the languages spoken by African slaves from those spoken by European colonists. Second, high mortality rates, combined with the need for growing amounts of labor and the preference for African slaves, meant that overall the proportion of Creole slaves (those born in the colonies) kept decreasing while that of African-born increased. This growing disproportion of Creole and African-born slaves was inversely correlated with a decrease of fluent speakers of European languages. The result was the structural divergence of the varieties spoken by the Africans and their descendants.

A large proportion of the new vernaculars that developed and that are spoken today by the descendants of Africans are called Creoles (*see* LANGUAGES, CREOLE, IN THE CARIBBEAN). The term originated from the phrase "creoles' language," which referred literally to the ways that CREOLES (meaning here both Europeans and Africans born in the New World) spoke. Later, when the designation changed to "Creole language," it meant "the way of speaking that was typical of colonies," in the same way that the adjective "Creole" was used to describe vegetation and animals typical of the same places that were unknown in the Old World, for example, "Creole horse." Changing attitudes also led the term *Creole* to be used synonymously with the term *patois* in the Anglophone Caribbean, with patois retaining its original French meaning of "unintelligible language variety." Both Creole and patois became associated particularly with the descendants of Africans, whose restructured language varieties diverge the most from the European language varieties.

More recently, linguists have used the term *Creole,* without its negative connotations, to categorize several mixed vernaculars that are spoken primarily by descendants of Africans in the New World (and elsewhere) but are not identified by their speakers as separate languages. Examples are GULLAH, which is spoken in coastal South Carolina and Georgia, and Saramaccan, spoken in SURINAME. On the other hand, linguists have been reluctant to apply the term to vernaculars such as African American Vernacular English (or AAVE) in the United States and several varieties of Latin American Portuguese and Spanish spoken by African descendants, apparently because they are less restructured than the Creole varieties.

Several factors account for the less extensive divergence of these vernaculars. First, the linguistic restructuring of European languages is inversely related to the duration of the homestead phase of colonization. In areas with longer histories of colonization and slavery, Africans were more integrated into colonial society, and their vernaculars were more similar to those spoken by the whites they interacted with. Second, Creoles have typically developed where the Africans and their descendants were the majority during the colonial period. Third, rice fields and SUGAR cane plantations, which required more labor than tobacco and coffee plantations, seemed to have more segregated communities, which favored divergence of the vernaculars spoken by whites and blacks. Fourth, the most divergent Creoles also developed where the slaves communities were separated early from speakers of European languages. This occurred in the case of the Creoles spoken in Suriname, which the British traded to the Dutch 15 years after the colony's foundation. In this case, slaves originally brought to Suriname by the British, who had been acquiring English, found themselves with Dutch masters while retaining English as their lingua franca and later as a vernacular.

Thus, African American Vernacular English has remained close to white American Southern English because the speakers of both varieties interacted regularly with each other until the late nineteenth century, when the JIM CROW laws were passed, fostering a rigid separation of races. Elsewhere, although the Spaniards were among the first to have New World colonies, they launched into the sugar cane industry more than a century later than other European nations. They also taught Castilian Spanish while evangelizing their subjects. By the time the size of African labor increased significantly on the plantations, there was already a large black Creole population speaking the same kind of Spanish as the white Creoles. They served as models to the *bozal* slaves, the newcomers. All these factors made it difficult for Creoles to develop in the Spanish colonies, making Palenquero in COLOMBIA, for instance, rather special.

The linguistic situation of the Portuguese colonies is less clear. Portuguese Creoles developed in African countries such as CAPE VERDE, São Tomé, and GUINEA-BISSAU. But surprisingly, Papiamentu (which is overlain with Spanish influence) is the only Creole to have developed in the Portuguese colonies of the New World. Yet the Portuguese were among the earliest to cultivate sugar cane. A different kind of socioeconomic structure, which did not discourage the mixing of races, may account for this different development. To be sure, Creole-like varieties have been identified in BRAZIL, spoken by more segregated black communities, but these are small isolates.

It is safe to assume that the African linguistic influence on the structures of the vernaculars spoken by descendants of Africans is one of the factors that made them different from the vernaculars spoken by descendants of Europeans. However, what the influence consists of remains controversial. Positions vary depending both on how one defines *influence* and on what one compares these vernaculars with. These vernaculars have often been compared with educated varieties of the European languages, which ignores their histories. Before the Creole and seasoned slaves became the primary transmitters of the colonial languages, the model speakers were European farmers and indentured servants with whom the slaves worked side by side. Consequently, the European language varieties, some of which were nonnative, were nonstandard. Comparisons between the vernaculars spoken by the descendants of Europeans and those spoken by Africans' descendants reveal structural similarities, even though the patterns are not identical.

It is possible that the speech of Africans influenced that of their white counterparts. However, such structural similarities between European and African vernaculars are likely to have come from the colonial languages. They were modified and reshaped into the new vernaculars. For example, the linguistic structure known as serial verb construction, such as *Jaan swim kras di riba* – "John swam across the river" in Jamaican Creole (literally "John swam [and] crossed the river") – does not exist in European languages. However, there are constructions such as *go/come get your book* and *John swam and crossed the river* which are not too distant. Speakers of African languages in which serial verb constructions are common would have modified little to produce serial verb constructions in Creoles.

Such a conclusion may also be drawn from constructions such as *Mary think say Katie pretty* – "Mary thinks that Katie [is] pretty" – in which *say* has a function similar to *that* in English. However, the same African languages failed to produce such a construction in French Creoles. This raises the question of whether those who developed English Creoles would have restructured things as they did if colloquial English itself did not have a more conspicuous usage of *say* to report speech, as in *A man came to the door, says, "Hello, stranger."* AAVE also features constructions such as *He be mean every time I visit him,* which is a description of the state in which the subject is usually found but not necessarily of his personality. The fact that similar constructions are attested in Irish English suggests that African languages may often have been a decisive factor, favoring one particular alternative over others where there was variation, but they were not necessarily the sources of such peculiarities. They may have played this kind of role also in the selection of some sounds, for example, "t" for "th" in *throw*, which alternate in some other English dialects, so that the word can be pronounced either "trow" or "throw."

Some have argued convincingly that in domains that were controlled almost exclusively by the Africans themselves, such as cooking, folk medicine, and music, there is probably more African influence, in the sense of "apport from African languages," in the meanings of some words and in some social conventions regulating usage of language. The fact that nonlinguistic African influence has been identified in similar domains supports such a hypothesis, suggesting that African languages must have influenced the development of the vernaculars spoken by descendants of Africans in the New World differentially, depending on the contexts in which the vernaculars were used.

The adverb "differentially" opens up yet a new complex subject matter. First, African languages may have had more of an influence on narrative techniques, or the ways in which songs, stories, and other verbal performances are organized, than on the structural aspects of these vernaculars. Second, different sociohistorical ecologies, consisting of different ethnolinguistic mixes at different times, have favored different kinds of African influences. On the other hand, different African ethnolinguistic groups exerted different kinds and amounts of influence.

This last observation leads to the question of whether nonlinguistic and linguistic influences always go hand in hand. For example, reviews of Lorenzo Turner's work on Gullah nicknames (what are known as "basket names," or names that Gullah speakers often carry from childhood and are sometimes better known than their official names) reveal disparities between the identifiable sources of linguistic influence and the origins of the nicknames. In other words, the sources of structural influence on the languages do not often converge with those of the African basket names. This research also suggests that the names may have been retained from African languages after Gullah had already developed as a separate variety.

In conclusion, while there is no doubt that African languages and cultures influenced the languages spoken by descendants of Africans in the New World, the subject matter is a complex one, with more challenging questions than conclusive answers. This state of affairs may be the result of several factors in the legacy of slavery: Africans did not survive in complete isolation; nor did they develop by deliberate actions their new vernaculars and cultures, which were by-products of their responses to communicative and other social challenges in their daily lives. Therefore, they did not plan on retaining African substrate features. As carryovers, these found their ways naturally into the novel systems while the Africans were adapting to their new socioeconomic ecologies. Nevertheless, we still must understand the selection principles that led some linguistic features to influence the languages spoken in Latin America and the Caribbean but not others, regardless of whether they have African, European, or Native American origins.

Salikoko S. Mufwene

SEE ALSO

São Tomé and Príncipe; Black Vernacular English.

Europe

Initiative of Black Germans and Blacks in Germany (ISD, Initiative Schwarze Deutsche und Schwarze in Deutschland), a support organization for Afro-Germans and blacks in Germany, founded in 1986.

The Initiative of Black Germans and Blacks in Germany was formed in Berlin in 1986 as a support and advocacy organization for black Germans following publication of the book *Farbe Bekennen* (Showing Our Colors) on the Afro-German experience. ISD was the first attempt at self-organization by black Germans. The organization "affirms and encourages," as two of its founders have put it. Its aim is to break through the isolation experienced by Afro-Germans, increase the self-esteem of its members, and disseminate information on the situation of blacks in Germany. The group also maintains contacts with black communities elsewhere, including GREAT BRITAIN, FRANCE, the United States, and Africa, and publishes the magazine *Afro-Look*.

The group accepts men and women, in contrast to ADEFRA, a German organization for black women formed two years later. After the fall of the Berlin Wall in 1989, ISD established contacts with Afro-Germans in East Germany and supported efforts to set up similar groups there. Originally called simply the Black German Initiative, ISD changed its name around 1993 to emphasize its openness to all blacks in Germany, rather than merely those with German citizenship. Chapters of ISD now exist in most major German cities. Each year, ISD in Berlin sponsors a Black History Month, a program of lectures, events, and performances aimed at increasing awareness of African and black diaspora history and culture. Though it is impossible to give an exact membership figure for this loosely organized group, ISD events draw large audiences, and thousands participate in Black History Month.

Belinda Cooper

Africa

Inkatha Freedom Party, South African political party based in the KwaZulu-Natal Province.

Inkatha was originally formed as a ZULU cultural association, but for years it has been one of SOUTH AFRICA's most controversial political forces. Its leader, MANGOSUTHO GATSHA BUTHELEZI, was at one time a member of the AFRICAN NATIONAL CONGRESS (ANC), but has now become one of the ANC's most formidable rivals. Today, despite the widespread opinion that Buthelezi commands a corrupt and undemocratic – and strictly ethnocentric – organization, Inkatha remains the dominant party in KwaZulu-Natal Province.

Inkatha the political party has its roots in Inkatha Ya Ka Zulu (Zulu National Movement), a cultural organization founded in 1928. In 1974, some 20 years after the APARTHEID government designated Bantustans, or "Bantu homelands," for all the nation's major African ethnic groups, Buthelezi renewed Inkatha as Inkatha ye Nkululeko Ye Sizwe (National Cultural Liberation Movement). KwaZulu, like the other homelands, was partly self-governed, but Bantustan ministers were regarded as puppets of the national government. Most observers believe that Buthelezi revived Inkatha to undermine the Zulu king Goodwill Zwelithini, his only rival for power in KwaZulu.

Buthelezi, who had spoken out openly against apartheid, nonetheless supported the Bantustan system. He also emphasized that Inkatha, unlike many black South African political organizations, was pro-capitalist. During the 1970s Buthelezi often reminded audiences of his close ties with imprisoned ANC leader Nelson Mandela, but Inkatha criticized the ANC's support of student protests and presented itself as an alternative movement. Its less ideologically militant stance, stressing cooperation with the existing regime, made Inkatha palatable to South African whites as well as to Western governments. After the Soweto uprising of 1976, Buthelezi cooperated with the South African police to form antimilitant vigilante groups, thus confirming the suspicions of critics, especially within the Black Consciousness Movement, who had branded Buthelezi a government puppet.

The ANC officially broke with Inkatha in 1980, after Buthelezi leaked details of private meetings with exiled ANC leaders. The two organizations soon became bitter enemies. Never as large or as powerful as the ANC, Inkatha dropped its initially nonviolent stance, and armed Buthelezi supporters carried out strikes against ANC and United Democratic Front (UDF) supporters throughout the 1980s. Inkatha was reportedly responsible for dozens of assassinations at ANC funerals. In 1990 Inkatha became an official political party, the Inkatha Freedom Party; a year later reports emerged that it had received past support from the South African Security Police and Military Intelligence forces. Buthelezi, seeking a sovereign Zulu state, nearly forced a delay in the 1994 elections with Inkatha demonstrations and rioting. At the last minute he allowed his name to be placed on the ballot as a candidate for president in the national elections. Inkatha won 10.5 percent of the vote nationally and 43 legislative seats. Despite efforts by moderates within the party to oust Buthelezi, he remained Inkatha's leader.

Kate Tuttle

See Also

Mandela, Nelson Rolihlahla; Soweto, South Africa; Black Consciousness in Africa.

North America

Ink Spots, The, African American quartet famous for vocal harmonies that helped lay the foundations for doo-wop, rhythm and blues, and rock 'n' roll music.

Four porters at New York's Paramount Theater formed the Ink Spots in 1934. The group's career peaked in the 1940s but continued, with changes in membership, until the 1970s. The original lineup consisted of bass Orville "Hoppy" Jones, baritone Ivory "Deek" Watson, and tenors Slim Greene and Charlie Fuqua. Greene died shortly after the group's debut and tenor Jerry Daniels replaced him. The Ink Spots' first recording, "Swingin' on the Strings" (Victor Records, 1935), featured upbeat, walking-bass, scat-rich music reminiscent of the Mills Brothers. Bill Kenny succeeded Jerry Daniels in 1939 and it was then that the Ink Spots developed their groundbreaking sound. Kenny's sterling tenor lead vocal was backed by sparse and languid arrangements. Watson added lyricless lower-register harmonies and Jones provided spoken, bassy recapitulations of the lyrics of the song. A whole lineage of popular musicians, most notably Elvis Presley, imitated this effect. Many more imitated the Ink Spots' innovation of a guitar-riff introduction to a song.

Success for the group started in England, and transatlantic broadcasts of their concerts in Great Britain bolstered their following back home. The Ink Spots' first big hit in the United States was their recording "If I Didn't Care." Other songs that gained wide popularity included "We Three (My Echo, My Shadow, and Me)," "Maybe," "Java Jive," and "I Don't Want to Set the World on Fire." The group recorded with Ella Fitzgerald in the mid-1940s, appeared in the films *The Great American Radio Broadcast* (1941) and *Pardon My Sarong* (1942), and entertained American forces at home and in Europe during World War II. In 1952 Fuqua and Kenny split, each taking the Ink Spots name for his new ensemble. A third group, led by Stanley Morgan, also adopted the name, which led to a number of protracted lawsuits.

The Ink Spots remained active as a nostalgia act for more than two decades. Kenny, the last original member, died in 1978, and the charter group was inducted into the Rock and Roll Hall of Fame in 1989.

Eric Bennett

North America

Inner Cities in the United States commonly defined as urban ghettos or black ghettos; many white politicians and policy analysts portray the predominantly black inner city as the source of the nation's worst urban problems. To a great extent, however, the ills of the American city also reflect the consequences of suburbanization (*see* Los Angeles Watts Riot of 1965).

North America

Innis, Roy (b. June 6, 1934, St. Croix, United States Virgin Islands), civil rights activist and promoter of black nationalism and separatism.

Roy Innis moved from the U.S. Virgin Islands to New York City with his mother in 1946. He served in the army for two years during the Korean War, before returning to City College of New York as a chemistry major. In 1963 he began a 25-year involvement with the Harlem chapter of the Congress of Racial Equality (CORE), an interracial, nonviolent civil rights organization. He was first elected chairman and became the associate national director in 1968.

Innis was also the coeditor and founder of the *Manhattan Tribune*. He gained national publicity in 1973 when he participated in a televised debate with Nobel physicist William Shockley on the topic of black genetic inferiority. Through his work, Innis promoted Black Power as well as black nationalism and separatism, and encouraged self-defense over nonviolence.

See Also

Harlem, New York; New York, New York; Virgin Islands (United States and British); Black Nationalism in the United States.

North America

Institute of the Black World, research institute that focuses on education as an instrument of social change for African Americans.

The Institute of the Black World aims to foster racial equality, black self-understanding, and black self-determination. To achieve these goals, it organizes conferences, publishes articles, and distributes audiovisual resources, such as a taped lecture series. The institute trains scholars to conduct research and develop teaching materials for black children. In the 1990s, under the leadership of historian Vincent Harding, the institute created the Black Policy Studies Center to explore ways of improving African American education.

Located in Atlanta, Georgia, the Institute of the Black World was originally a part of the Martin Luther King Jr. Center for Nonviolent Social Change. In 1969 it became an independent organization and moved into a house where W. E. B. Du Bois once lived.

Aaron Myers

See Also

Du Bois, William Edward Burghardt (W. E. B.); King, Martin Luther, Jr.

North America

Interdenominational Theological Center, an ecumenical graduate school of theology in Atlanta, Georgia.

Six African American seminaries came together to form the Interdenominational Theological Center, whose mission is "to provide quality theological education for the predominantly black Christian churches." The center was chartered in 1958 through the cooperation of four Atlanta schools: the Morehouse School of Religion, founded at Morehouse College by the Baptist Church in 1867; the Gammon Theological Seminary, founded at Clark College by the United Methodist Church in 1869; the Turner Theological Seminary, founded at Morris Brown College by the African Methodist Episcopal Church in 1885; and the Phillips School of Theology, founded by the Christian Methodist Church in 1944. Twelve years later, the Johnson C. Smith Seminary of the Presbyterian Church and the Charles H. Mason Seminary of the Church of God in Christ joined the center.

Interdenominational Theological Center is one of the first institutions established through the cooperation of independent African American seminaries. The curriculum is geared toward students planning to serve in black churches. The school offers master's degrees in divinity, Christian education, and church music, and doctoral degrees in ministry and pastoral counseling. The center is also a part of the Atlanta University Center, which includes five other historically black colleges and universities in the city – Clark Atlanta University, Morris Brown College, Morehouse College, Morehouse School of Medicine, and Spelman College.

Lisa Clayton Robinson

See Also

Baptists; Mason, Charles Harrison; Black Church, The.

North America

Interracial Marriage in the United States, marriage between individuals of different races. Marriages of blacks and whites remain uncommon; during the nineteenth century such unions were classed with other forms of illicit interracial contact and labeled MISCEGENATION.

Latin America and the Caribbean

Irakere, a leading Cuban music ensemble, founded in the 1970s, that combines Afro-Cuban rhythms with elements of American JAZZ and rock music.

Since its founding in the early 1970s, Irakere has been Cuba's best-known and most popular jazz ensemble. Luis Tamargo writes that "Irakere's sound ranges seamlessly between acoustic and electronic music, combining incredible technique and wide conceptual enlightenment with ferocious groove." The group embodies the diverse styles of Cuban music, which is founded on the traditions of both Spanish and African peoples, who have inhabited the island since colonization. Cuban music has also absorbed influences from nearby countries such as MEXICO, HAITI, and the United States – perhaps most important, the influence of American jazz.

In the 1940s and 1950s celebrated American jazz trumpeter Dizzy Gillespie began to experiment with Afro-Cuban rhythms and to collaborate with numerous Cuban musicians, including trumpeter MARIO BAUZA, conga drummer Chano Pozo, and bandleader MACHITO (*see* AFRO-LATIN JAZZ). At the time of this cross-cultural musical fertilization, the future founder of Irakere, Jesus "Chucho" Valdés, was a boy beginning his studies in classical piano at the Havana Conservatory. Growing up, Valdés had a strong affinity for Gillespie's music, which he called "pure fire." During the 1960s he joined the government-sponsored Orquestra Cubana de Música Moderna (Cuban Modern Music Orchestra, OCMM), which was not a jazz ensemble. But around 1972 Valdés and a number of other musicians, including saxophonist PAQUITO D'RIVERA and trumpeter ARTURO SANDOVAL, left the OCMM to form Irakere. Together they sought a style that would be suited to the jazz sound they loved and to their aspiration to renovate Cuban popular music.

The band's name highlights the musicians' Afro-Cuban vision: Irakere is the YORUBA word for forest. As one critic explained, the Africans who brought a rich drumming tradition to Cuba were the descendants of great percussionists who lived in a forested region of Africa called Irakere. Percussion, in fact, has been central to the band's sound. Before Irakere, writes Luis Tamargo, popular Cuban music used only the country's basic percussion instruments, including the *tumbadora*, *bongó*, *pailas*, and *guiro*. Irakere also incorporated Afro-Cuban sacred instruments like the *batá* drums and the *chequeré*, as in its recording *African Mass* (1987), which powerfully mixes Yoruba and Carabalí polyrhythms.

Irakere's first hit came in 1974 with the song "Bacalao Con Pan." In 1977 Dizzy Gillespie, Stan Getz, and various other musicians, critics, and producers made their way to Havana and described Irakere's performance as "more musically exciting than any of the groups from which they have garnered their ideas." In 1978 a number of these Americans were instrumental in arranging for Irakere's appearance at the Newport Jazz Festival. The group won a Grammy Award for its self-titled debut on Columbia Records the following year. Although some members, including D'Rivera, Sandoval, and most recently Valdés, left the group to pursue solo careers, others continued to perform and record with Irakere, including bassist Carlos del Puerto and drummer Enrique Plá.

Over the course of its long career, Irakere has embraced a wide range of styles. In addition to exploring Cuba's rich and varied musical traditions, including SON, RUMBA, BOLERO, MAMBO, and Afro-Cuban religious music, the group has incorporated elements of FUNK, rock, and classical music. Although Irakere has undergone several personnel changes and experimented with many different musical styles, it continues to feature a jazz-oriented sound with polyrhythmic percussion.

Aaron Myers

SEE ALSO

Gillespie, John Birks ("Dizzy"); Cuba; Valdés, Jesús (Chucho); Pozo y González, Luciano (Chano); Music, Afro-Caribbean Secular; Music, Afro-Caribbean Religious; Music, Classical, in Latin America and the Caribbean; Havana, Cuba.

Africa

Iramba (also known as Anilamba), ethnic group of TANZANIA.

The Iramba primarily inhabit central Tanzania and speak a Bantu language. Approximately 500,000 people consider themselves Iramba.

SEE ALSO

Bantu: Dispersion and Settlement.

Africa

Iraqw, an ethnic group of central TANZANIA.

According to oral history, the ancestors of the Iraqw migrated to their present location from Mesopotamia (present-day Iraq). During this journey, the group developed a unique language that incorporated aspects of Nilotic, Cushitic, Khoisan, and Bantu languages (*see* LANGUAGES, AFRICAN: AN OVERVIEW). At least three different groups split from the main group; one of these, the present-day Iraqw, traveled down the Great Rift Valley and into the Mbulu and Hanang district of present-day Tanzania. There the Iraqw settled in scattered, locally governed villages, kept livestock, and cultivated subsistence crops.

During the nineteenth century the Iraqw avoided contact with merchants, missionaries, and other Europeans. Under German and British COLONIAL RULE, however, the Iraqw were forced to begin cultivating commercial crops, such as MILLET and maize. After independence the Iraqw attempted to reestablish their precolonial autonomy and resented intrusions by the Tanzanian government, especially attempts by President Julius K. Nyerere to relocate them into collectivized *ujamaa* villages. In recent years, however, the Iraqw have grown more receptive to government development projects as well as to commercial agriculture.

Elizabeth Heath

SEE ALSO

Nyerere, Julius Kambarage; Rift Valleys; Christianity: Missionaries in Africa.

Africa

Iron in Africa, the political, economic, and demographic history of the metal's influence on the continent.

Iron, a strong and malleable metal, can be shaped into the tools used in agriculture, hunting, forest clearing, conquest, and construction. Iron, in fact, facilitated the rise of Africa's early centralized states. Early in the twentieth century, scholars painted a succinct picture of the diffusion of iron working, from North Africa across the Sahara. The arrival of iron tools was thought to explain the rapid adoption of agriculture and the subsequent rapid Bantu dispersion across sub-Saharan Africa. Recent linguistic studies, combined with new archaeological discoveries, suggest a more complex history.

HISTORY OF METAL USE

Naturally occurring metals such as gold, silver, and bronze were probably used for ornamental purposes since about the eighth millennium B.C.E. Most metal is found in ores, however, and must be heated, or smelted, to remove the impurities. Iron smelting is a particularly complex process that is believed to have been discovered only a few times in the course of human history, or, perhaps, only once. Copper smelting first appeared in West Asia in the fourth millennium B.C.E. The earliest evidence of the more difficult process of iron smelting is found among the Hittites of West Asia and dates to the second millennium B.C.E.

It is generally believed that the use of metals diffused from West Asia to North Africa and that iron smelting was introduced during the seventh century B.C.E. to EGYPT by Greeks and Assyrians and to CARTHAGE by the Phoenicians. Egyptians were using naturally occurring copper by the fifth millennium B.C.E. and were smelting copper by the following millennium. Copper became an important trade item and the standard against which other objects were weighed. Bronze – copper mixed with tin – is found in Egypt as early as the third millennium B.C.E., and iron objects, probably imported, appear around 1400 B.C.E. Two avenues of diffusion have traditionally been suggested to explain the spread of iron smelting from North Africa to sub-Saharan Africa: along the Nile from Egypt, and across the trans-Saharan trade route from Carthage.

Diffusion from Egypt

When the iron-wielding Assyrians attacked Egypt in 670 B.C.E., Egypt's rulers fled south to NUBIA, establishing the city of Meroe (in present-day SUDAN) as their capital. Iron-working sites discovered at Meroe have yielded dates between the sixth and third century B.C.E. Contemporaneous iron slag has also been found at Aksum (in ETHIOPIA). However, there is insufficient data to prove that these sites represent a diffusion of smelting practices along the Nile. Archaeological excavations in the southern SUDAN have not produced evidence of iron smelting before 500 C.E.

A Trans-Saharan Diffusion

A second theory traces the diffusion of iron smelting across the Sahara Desert. Phoenicians brought iron-working technology to North Africa from the area of Lebanon when they established the city of Carthage (in present-day TUNISIA) during the ninth century B.C.E. Some scholars believe that Phoenician iron-working techniques diffused across the Sahara along established trade routes, and were adopted by Bantu-speaking populations in West Africa. Archaeologists supported the theory of iron diffusion across the Sahara by pointing out the lack of an indigenous copper industry in Africa prior to the appearance of iron, as it is widely believed that the production of copper and its related alloys is a prerequisite to the production of iron. Recent findings have established the presence of annealed copper at Sekkiret and Agades, NIGER, dating to the second millennium B.C.E. Equally ancient evidence of copper working has been found at Akjouj in MAURITANIA. This copper industry may have been a local invention or a product of cultural diffusion.

Several findings in West Africa support the claim of diffusion across the Sahara. Furnaces or other evidence of iron working that dates from the seventh to the fourth century B.C.E. have been found at sites in Niger, NIGERIA, CAMEROON, DEMOCRATIC REPUBLIC OF THE CONGO, and GABON. Thus iron smelting appears in West Africa at about the same time that it is believed to have reached North Africa. However, a furnace from the ninth century B.C.E. found at Do Dimmi, Niger, suggests that iron working in West Africa may have predated the arrival of the Phoenicians. But the evidence remains inconclusive, given that carbon dating, the method used to determine the age of the furnaces, provides only approximate information.

Independent Invention?

Evidence of early iron working has also been found in East Africa. For example, smelting furnaces in northwestern Tanzania and RWANDA have been dated to the ninth century B.C.E. Most sites, such as Urwew, near LAKE VICTORIA, date between 300 B.C.E. and 200 C.E. The scarcity of archaeological evidence, combined with the uncertainty of carbon dating during this era, makes it difficult to reconstruct with any certainty the exact origins of copper or iron smelting. The use of metals may have diffused from Egypt and North Africa or may have arisen independently, or both.

Scholars have noted that at least three distinct kinds of iron-smelting furnaces are found in Africa: bowl furnaces, low-shaft furnaces, and high-shaft furnaces. Early bowl furnaces are found throughout eastern and southern Africa. The more common low-shaft furnaces are present from West to southeastern Africa. A few later-dating high-shaft furnaces have also been found in West Africa, LAKE TANGANYIKA, LAKE MALAWI, and along the ZAMBEZI RIVER. This distribution gives few clues to the origin and development of iron-working technologies on the continent. Several furnaces do, however, show remarkable innovations in the shafts, bellows, and tuyeres (nozzles) to increase the temperature, allowing the iron bloom to reach higher carbon levels, thus effectively producing steel. Although the origins of iron working in sub-Saharan Africa remain unclear, it is known that iron smelting was firmly established among Bantu speakers in West Africa by the first half of the last millennium B.C.E.

Bantu Dispersion and Settlement

Iron working is associated with the spread of Bantu speakers eastward and southward beginning in the first millennium B.C.E. Numerous iron furnaces, dating between the sixth and the first century B.C.E, have been found along this route. Iron-smelting furnaces dating to the third or fourth century C.E. have also been found in KwaZulu-Natal and are viewed as markers of this migration. The importance of iron tools in fueling this rapid migration is still debated.

The Culture of Metallurgy in Africa

The importance of iron is depicted in many myths and folktales, such as YORUBA stories of Ogun, the god of iron, and the widespread depictions of African blacksmith-kings. The Italian explorer Cavazzi published a book in 1687 depicting the Ngongo king laboring at a furnace while musicians play. In many societies, such as that of the Montagnard of North CAMEROON, ironsmiths form distinct castes and pass on their specialized knowledge from generation to generation. Smiths are often identified with mystical powers, and the molding of the iron bloom is interpreted as a creative, transformative process, laden with symbolism and associated with rituals and taboos. Among the Barongo of TANZANIA, for example, the furnace is depicted as a womb, the iron as the offspring; the slag by-product is equated with a placenta. Modern smiths continue to produce iron products, particularly for ceremonial items such as axes. Indigenous smelting has become increasingly rare since the importation of large amounts of iron products during and since colonial times. Today a number of African countries have their own iron industries, and some, such as LIBERIA and Mauritania, are major iron exporters.

Ari Nave

See Also

Bantu: Dispersion and Settlement; Explorers in Africa, 1500 to 1800; Gold Trade; Nile River; Sahara Desert; Ancient African Civilizations; Ogum.

Africa

Isis, in Egyptian mythology, goddess of fertility and motherhood.

Isis was the daughter of the god Keb ("Earth") and the goddess Nut ("Sky"), the sister-wife of Osiris, judge of the dead, and mother of Horus, god of day. In the late fourth century B.C.E., the center of Isis worship, which was reaching its greatest peak, was on Philae, an island in the Nile, where a great temple was built to her during the Thirtieth Dynasty. Ancient stories described Isis as having great magical skill, and she was represented as human in form, frequently wearing the horns of a cow. Her personality was believed to resemble that of Hathor, the goddess of love and gaiety.

The cult of Isis spread from Alexandria throughout the Hellenistic world after the fourth century B.C.E. It appeared in Greece in combination with the cults of Horus and Serapis, the Greek name for Osiris. This tripartite cult was later introduced (86 B.C.E.) into Rome and became one of the most popular branches of Roman religion. It later received a bad reputation because of the licentiousness of some of its priestly rites, provoking efforts to suppress or limit Isis worship. The cult died out in Rome after the institution of Christianity; the last remaining Egyptian temples to Isis were closed in the middle of the sixth century C.E.

See Also

Nile River; Alexandria, Egypt.

Africa

Islam and Tradition: An Interpretation

Lamine Sanneh

The person who laid down the principle of tradition as an important part of the Muslim heritage was al-Shá'fí (d. 820), the great Muslim lawyer of Cairo. He believed that the community was central to maintaining tradition. Community for al-Shá'fí meant a group of recognized leaders and experts who use their knowledge to agree on something that affects public and personal life. Al-Shá'fí believed that such agreements carried the weight of truth, for in his view it was impossible for the community to agree in error. Error, he said, arose from separation, not from collective decision making. For al-Shá'fí, then, a living community was responsible for maintaining sound tradition.

However, al-Shá'fí was not just interested in tradition simply for the sake of protecting community interests. Rather, he defended the community because he saw it as necessary to preserving the tradition of the Prophet Muhammad. That tradition, called the *sunnah,* or custom of the Prophet, forms the superstructure of Muslim law, religion, ethics, education, worship, and devotion, and al-Shá'fí was largely responsible for making it the foundation of mainstream Islam. His book on the subject, called the *Risálah,* not only brought together the knowledge of a lawyer and a collector of tradition but it also brought about a major reform by streamlining local and regional deviations in the interpretation of Scripture and law. Al-Shá'fí simply soared in his steady drive to secure the authority of tradition for a Muslim community in serious danger of breaking up. He did this by setting up clear rules to uphold the authority of the sunnah. We may summarize these rules as follows: "1. The Prophet enjoys a special status (*wahy*) as God's approved messenger. 2. The Prophet's sunnah, therefore, has lying upon it the seal of divine approval. 3. The sunnah of the Prophet and the Koran, as the book of revelation, are always in agreement. 4. Therefore, conflict between the sunnah and the Koran cannot happen. 5. The sunnah can replace the Koran if the Koran has nothing to say on any subject. But even if the Koran has something to say, the sunnah can still provide complementary explanations."

Al-Shá'fí thus established the rule that no one was allowed to ignore tradition in Islam. He gave encouragement and a sense of unity to Muslims who were scattered in many different places and observing many different customs. Now everyone could agree on what Muslims should do and why.

Yet by making tradition so important, al-Shá'fí opened the door for people to fabricate stories about the Prophet, stories that even the most careful of scholars could not control entirely. For example, one story, or *hadíth,* claimed that the Prophet said, "Whatever is

A Bedouin man, facing Mecca, says his midday prayers along the Red Sea coast of the Sinai Peninsula, Egypt. *CORBIS/Jeffrey L. Rotman*

The mosque of al-Azhar in Cairo became a great center of Shiite Islamic learning. This excellent example of Fatimid architecture was built in the mid-tenth century during the reign of Gen. Jawhar al-Siqilli (the Sicilian). *Roger-Viollet*

said and found to be beautiful, it can be attributed to me," the sort of catch-all statement that is welcomed by the scrupulous and unscrupulous alike. In response, Muslim experts tried to organize the stories so that they could be included in official handbooks and collections. However, we must stress that such collections, called hadíth collections (*ahadíth*), were not simply ornamental; their words were borrowed by people to decorate an idea they liked. They were used to allow Muslims to overcome differences among themselves. It was for the sake of that sense of unity that many of the handbooks allowed sound or holy stories about the Prophet to exist alongside weak or even dubious ones. So these handbooks became an important resource for preserving Muslim unity across centuries and cultures.

Al-Shá'fí's success in establishing tradition enabled Muslims to make changes in their religious practices without losing touch with the past. In effect, al-Shá'fí created the idea of a living tradition, which allowed Islam to enter new cultures and societies outside the Arab heartland. That was how Islam came to Africa, where Muslims followed the advice of al-Shá'fí and another Muslim scholar, Imám Málik (d. 796) of Medina. Both scholars emphasized the importance of traditions about the Prophet. However, Imám Málik was more interested in what Muslims in Medina were actually practicing, while al-Shá'fí looked for rules that Muslims everywhere should follow. For example, Imám Málik would begin his account by saying something like, "This is the agreed on way of doing things among us," or "according to the way things are done among us," while al-Shá'fí surveyed the world of Muslims and pointed out contradictions in local practice and custom. Nevertheless, their approaches were complementary, and both stressed the central importance of the Prophet's sunnah.

Tradition: Its Supporters and Challengers

We must now consider the pressures and challenges that tradition faces in Muslim communities. It is natural that as Muslim traders and strangers entered African societies – first in North Africa, then in East and West – they would be wary of mixing freely with their non-Muslim hosts. As a result, these early Muslims lived in secluded quarters, making only occasional and necessary trading forays. The Muslim ritual code imposes restrictions of food, dress, and calendrical observance: it prohibits pork, strangled meat, and alcoholic beverages; forbids exposure of certain parts of the body at worship; and calls for observance of the Friday sabbath, the Prophet's birthday, and the two Islamic festivals of fasting and pilgrimage. In time, Muslims' observance of the ritual code left a marked impression on neighboring populations in Africa, and an attentive ruler would be quick to draw on that appeal to keep in step with his people. Some rulers converted at this stage, but only halfway – enough to explore the potential of the new religion while still enjoying the demonstrated advantages of the old. A shrewd ruler would take care not to step too far ahead of his people as a convert to an unknown or distrusted religion, nor lag behind as a resister of a growing faith. Some rulers, in order to hedge their bets, would thus pledge their children to the different religions in their realm.

Such calculations in the conversion process introduced novel ideas and practices into Islam, creating what the upholders of Muslim tradition call "a state between two states." They are referring to an indecisiveness they find objectionable, because it creates excuses for people who are ill informed or ill intentioned. But it was in this state that the once-secluded communities of traders and strangers broadened and took in the half-hearted and the compromising. Eventually scholars would object to compromises of Muslim tradition and call for reform. But by this time, enough teachers and lawyers would have been trained, and enough people would have converted to Islam, to make successful reform reasonably certain.

Those who want to uphold the Muslim tradition face the challenge of reconciling the rules of religion with the experiences of life. If they want to change and reform Muslim practice, they will have to determine if their own societies' Muslims agree with them. They just cannot take single-handed action simply because they think they know better than others what is right and wrong. So Muslim defenders of tradition have had to walk a narrow line between what the lawyers find in the rule books and what ordinary Muslims do in real life.

The African Dimension

Let us consider more concretely how Islam spread and became established in Africa, in light of the tension between the authority of tradition and the effects of practice.

When Islam first appeared in African societies, people were intrigued, curious, puzzled, perhaps even bewildered. But they were seldom hostile, in part because of the novelty, and in part because of the small numbers involved. The welcome Muslims thus received allowed them to flourish as minority communities. They usually established themselves along important trade routes, where their usefulness to their non-Muslim hosts was assured. In time these Muslim merchant communities grew in size and influence, attracting converts from the local population. Yet these converts continued to practice their old religions, because they saw no conflict with the new religion. It was only with time that Islam gently broke away from the old religions, but even then many converts continued to observe local customs (*see* African Religions: An Interpretation).

However, as knowledge of Muslim tradition increased and practice became less lax and better informed, some Muslims began to demand reform and a genuine break with the old customs. It typically took several generations for this reform phase to emerge, if it emerged at all. Reformers called attention to rules of faith and practice and called for sanctions against those guilty of mixing Islam and African customs. These sanctions were to be found in Muslim Scripture, law, and tradition. Only occasionally did reformist movements lead to *jihad*, or holy war. Reform was normally undertaken peacefully, such as when a charismatic Koranic schoolteacher or a holy person appeared in the land, and offered the community instruction for their uninitiated children. The children, once initiated into Islam, would be better informed than the older generation, and they would raise the standards of observance and conduct. By the time the next generation arrived, knowledge of religion and rules would have been generally improved. Some people would then decide to go to Mecca, the pilgrimage site in Saudi Arabia Muslims visit every year. While in Mecca pilgrims are introduced to other Muslims from all over the world, and that experience helps to strengthen the Muslim tradition back home.

Muslims approach the Great Mosque at Touba in Dakar, Senegal. *CORBIS/Nik Wheeler*

Eventually, important Muslim visitors would begin to visit the community. Their coming would demonstrate the worldwide nature of Islam, and upon their departure they would leave behind some religious objects, such as an illuminated manuscript of the Koran, a legal manual, handsomely bound volumes of the Prophet's sunnah, an embroidered turban or prayer rug, a picture of the Ka'ba (though never of the Prophet), some prayer beads, a silk gown, and so on. Eventually a ruler would emerge in the community who would undertake the pilgrimage, and return in triumph for having visited the holy city of Mecca. His personal example would inspire respect for Islam and give it a high political profile.

What is most interesting about the historical spread and consolidation of the Muslim tradition in Africa is not what happened when the rule books were first introduced nor what happened after reforms succeeded, but rather what happened in between, because it was then that African societies took Islam and adapted it to their own traditions. Islam emerged from that adaptation clearly marked by Africa, and also with clear proof that Africans had much to contribute to Islam. So Africa provided another element in the relationship between Islam and tradition.

Let us look at how this adaptation took place. Muslims, for example, are required to pray five times a day and to fast once a year during the month of Ramadan. The five daily prayers, including the congregation worship on the Friday sabbath, define the Islamic week. The fast of Ramadan is determined by the Islamic annual calendar, which is a lunar calendar, and thus approximately three weeks shorter than the solar calendar. So festivals of the Muslim calendar occur at a different time each year. The five daily prayers thus introduce a regular, daily habit in local Muslim observance, while the Ramadan fast breaks with the seasonal solar cycle and its agricultural customs and ceremonies. The members of peasant communities who converted to Islam would often find themselves absorbing Muslim feasts into a time period previously devoted to their agricultural solar festivals. They typically continued to observe these festivals but added Islamic content. For example, they would observe a new year's harvest thanksgiving at the customary time of the year but would make a tithe in compliance with the requirements of Islam.

Conversion to Islam was eased in other ways as well. For example, people would retain the local names of the old rituals marking the new year, rain, harvest, and so forth, but they would observe these occasions with prayers and rites based on the Koran and sunnah. If we take a long-range view, we may say that Islam undermines the old customs and will in time overthrow them. On the other hand, if we take a medium-term view, we may say that the old customs will co-opt Islam, as people adapt it in line with their own interests. Thus in Africa, dreams, dream interpretation, healing, and amulets belong as much to the Muslim religious tradition as they do to indigenous religious practice. We should not, therefore, draw too sharp a line between the two traditions.

Decorated with gold ink, this page from the Koran is written in Mabhribi, a North African language, and dates from around the beginning of the fourteenth century. *Courtesy of the Arthur M. Sackler Museum, Harvard University Art Museums, Gift of Paul S. Sachs, Esq. Photo by David Mathews.*

Asserting the Primacy of Tradition

The achievement of the Muslim "founding fathers," such as al-Shá'fí and Imám Málik, has given reform-minded Muslims the incentive to safeguard the Muslim tradition from harmful compromise. In Africa one such person was the Nigerian *shaykh* Usman dan Fodio (1754-1817), who reformed Muslim practice through the strict application of Muslim law and tradition. Yet he was not opposed to using African ways to achieve reform. Accordingly he used special dream techniques, called *salát al-istikhárah*, to authorize his followers to take action. In his own account, he speaks of how, in 1794, at the significant age of 40, the need for reform ripened into a command and an obligation, with dreams and visions steadying his resolve and clarifying his goals.

"When I reached forty years, five months and some days, God drew me to him, and I found the Lord of djinns and men, our Lord Muhammad.... With him were the Companions, and the prophets, and the saints. Then they welcomed me, and sat me down in their midst. Then the Saviour of djinns and men, our Lord Abd al-Qadir al-Jilani, brought a green robe embroidered

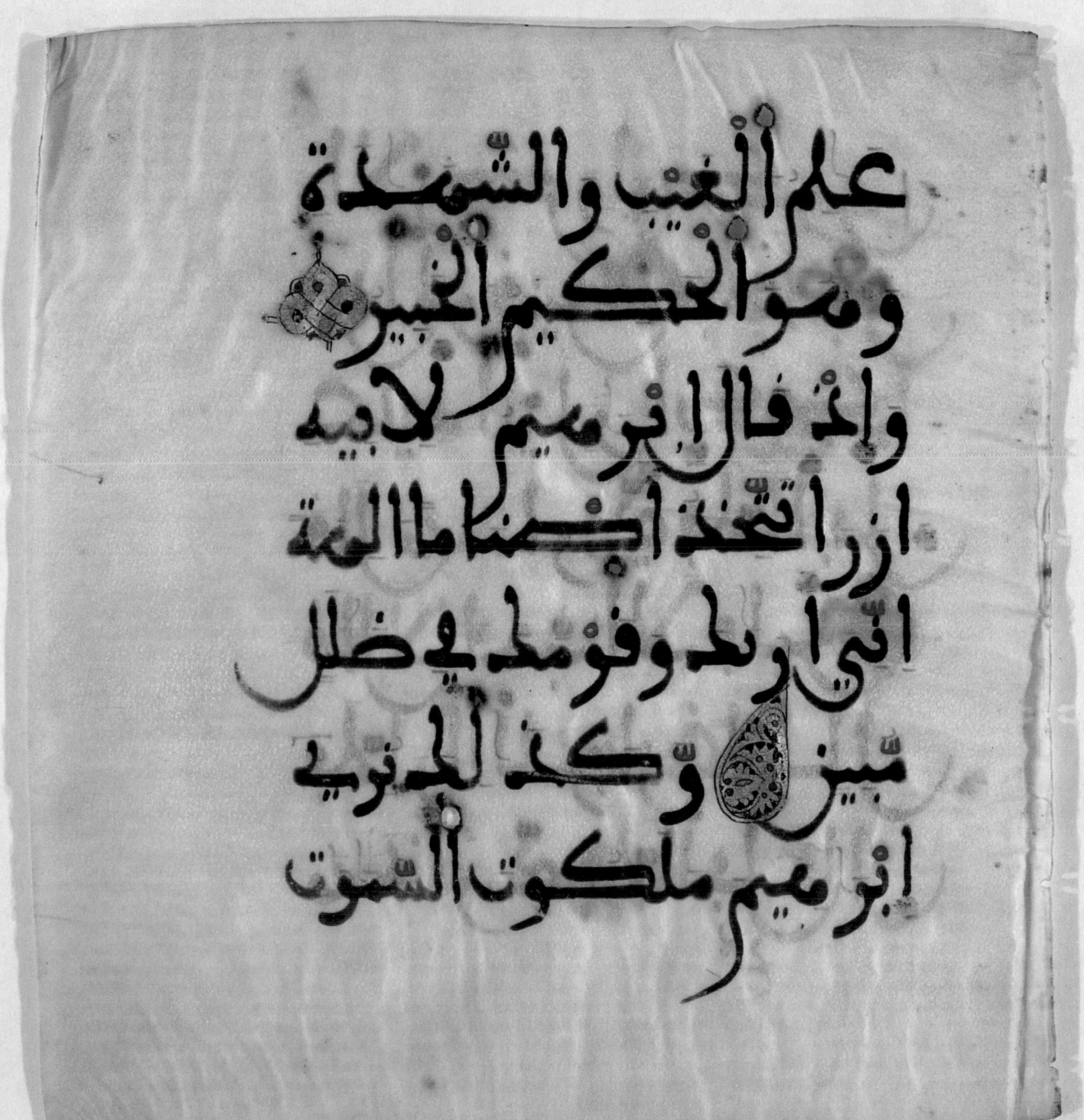

علم الغيب والشهدة
وهو الحكيم الخبير
واذ قال ابرهيم لابيه
ازر اتتخذ اصناما الهة
انى اريك وقومك في ضلل
مبين وكذلك نرى
ابرهيم ملكوت السموت

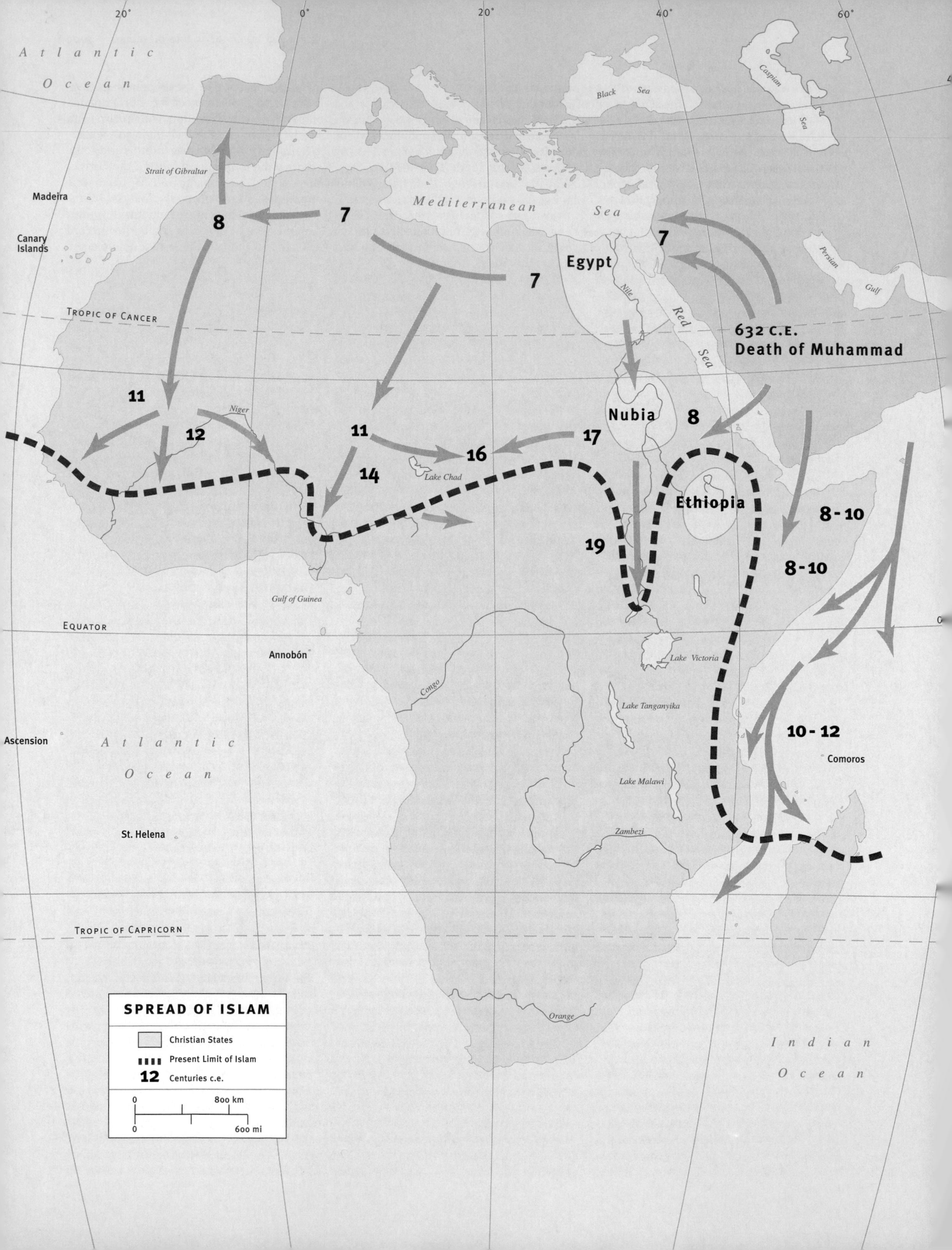

SPREAD OF ISLAM
Christian States
Present Limit of Islam
12 Centuries c.e.
0
800 km
0
600 mi
632 C.E.
Death of Muhammad
Atlantic Ocean
Mediterranean Sea
Black Sea
Caspian Sea
Persian Gulf
Red Sea
Indian Ocean
Strait of Gibraltar
Madeira
Canary Islands
Tropic of Cancer
Equator
Tropic of Capricorn
Egypt
Nile
Nubia
Ethiopia
Niger
Lake Chad
Gulf of Guinea
Annobón
Ascension
St. Helena
Congo
Lake Victoria
Lake Tanganyika
Lake Malawi
Zambezi
Orange
Comoros
7
7
7
8
8
11
11
12
14
16
17
19
8 - 10
8 - 10
10 - 12
20°
0°
20°
40°
60°

The veiling of women, one of the most recognizable of Islamic customs, probably originated as a secular practice in the Persian culture from which much of Islamic tradition springs.
Reuters/CORBIS

with the words 'There is no god but God; Muhammad is the Messenger of God'... and a turban embroidered with the words 'He is God, the One'... the Lord Abd al-Qadir al-Jilani... said, 'Dress him and enturban him, and name him with a name that shall be attributed exclusively to him.' He sat me down, and clothed me and enturbaned me. Then he addressed me as 'Imam of the saints' and commanded me to do what is approved of and forbade me to do what is disapproved of; and he girded me with the Sword of Truth, to unsheath it against the enemies of God. Then they commanded me... and at the same time gave me leave to make this litany that is written upon my ribs widely known, and promised me that whoever adhered to it, God would intercede for every one of his disciples."

The authority to reform the Muslim tradition was thus obtained. As a result, Usman dan Fodio decided to confront the compromising Muslims and their corrupt political leaders. Three years later, in 1797, we find the shaykh firmly set on the course of reform, and preparing to arm his followers for jihad. He commanded that this preparation for jihad was a sunnah, an order found in the tradition of the Prophet himself. During the months of preparation, the shaykh used prayer to inspire his disciples. His brother, Abdalláh dan Fodio, wrote that the shaykh "began to pray to God that He should show him the greatness of Islam in this country of the Sudan, and he set this to verse in his vernacular ode, *al-Qádiriyya* ['The Qadirite Ode'], and I put it into Arabic in verses." The shaykh coupled this experience with a decision to emigrate from his home in the HAUSA state of Gobir to Gudu. It was at that moment that he chose to launch his movement. He intended it to be an act of political defiance: the people of Gobir had been hostile to him and his disciples, and so he denounced them as infidels and enemies of God. Usman dan Fodio insisted on the territorial passage, the *hijrah*, as a condition of sound faith, and combined it with a call for personal sacrifice: "O brethren, it is incumbent upon you to emigrate from the lands of unbelief to the lands of Islam that you may attain Paradise and be companions of your ancestor Abraham, and your Prophet Muhammad, on account of the Prophet's saying, 'Whoever flees with his religion from one land to another, be it [merely the distance of] the span of a hand, will attain to Paradise and be the companion of Abraham and His Prophet Muhammad.'"

This denunciation of the political leaders in northern Nigeria was not a call for Muslims to retreat into prayer cells. The shaykh and his followers intended no flight from the world; they merely wanted to conquer it in order to change it. Religious discipline for them helped to safeguard sound tradition from compromise and error, and to warn the faithful that they should always be on guard against giving in to the world (*see* SOKOTO CALIPHATE).

But Muslim African leaders have also used less harsh methods to correct falling standards. In the FOUTA DJALLON region of GUINEA, for example, some local religious leaders in the late nineteenth century organized revival-type meetings that drew together numerous communities and taught them how to maintain proper standards. The centerpiece of these revival meetings was a form of devotion called "repeated prayer." The people repeated a litany about the tradition of the Prophet. The devotions were held in village congregations called *missidi*, and the discontented peasants, freed slaves, and poor people who attended were taught special prayers that were intended to inspire them. People came out of their prayers motivated to change the world by replacing those in power with people of their persuasion. They wanted change because they felt that the leaders of the day had abandoned the truth and followed their own ideas. However, the French colonial authorities feared these revivals might make the people revolt, and so sent troops to close down the main congregation at Diawia. That action frightened the other congregations, and people abandoned their farms and scattered. In this way the French proceeded to suppress Muslim religious activity in their colonies. They were determined that Muslims should become loyal subjects of the colonial empire, but Muslims instead became antagonized by COLONIAL RULE.

CONCLUSION

The leaders of the Muslim community have long recognized that the Muslim tradition will weaken unless they take steps to teach it to their children and support schools and teachers who can do that well. That is why many teachers and educators have taken responsibility for Islam, becoming active in Muslim communities as leaders of a unified, living tradition.

SEE ALSO

Cairo, Egypt.

The Jingere-Ber, or Great Mosque, at Tombouctou in Mali, was built around 1325. *Roger-Viollet*

Africa

Islamic Fundamentalism: An Interpretation

Although they have attracted much attention since the success of the Iranian Revolution of 1979, Islamic fundamentalist movements are not new, nor have they ever been prevalent among Islamic societies. When they do emerge, these movements are more symptomatic of profound societal crises than a direct outcome of Islamic political and legal thought as such, or a common feature of all Islamic societies. But fundamentalism is not the only possible response, because societies react differently to similar crises; a history of fundamentalist response does not necessarily lead to the recurrence of the phenomenon. For example, there are more Muslims in sub-Saharan Africa than in the Middle East – twice as many if one includes North Africa. Moreover, the Sudanic belt of sub-Saharan Africa experienced strong fundamentalist movements in the eighteenth and nineteenth centuries. Yet there is little indication of fundamentalism in this part of Africa at present, except in Sudan, though the region faces similar crises to those that have prompted fundamentalist responses in North Africa and elsewhere in the Muslim world.

Islamic fundamentalism can be seen as an expression of the right of Muslim peoples to political, religious, and/or cultural self-determination. Islamic fundamentalists claim to represent the free choice of their communities, whether in terms of demands for the strict application of *Shari'a* (Islamic law as a comprehensive way of life) by the state (when Muslims are the majority) or through voluntary compliance in social relations and personal lifestyle (when they are the minority). Much of the debate about Islamic fundamentalism tends to focus on the possibility or desirability of assertions of Islamic identity and self-determination in the abstract, with little attention to the underlying causes and dynamics of this phenomenon in the specific context of particular societies. For example, given the ideological orientation and political practice of fundamentalist groups in a variety of settings, it is pertinent to ask whether this approach is a legitimate means of realizing the right to self-determination in the modern context. A more basic question is whether fundamentalism is consistent with its own claims of exclusive representation of Islamic identity, political system, and legal order.

Defining or Identifying Islamic Fundamentalism

There is much debate about the appropriateness of using the term *fundamentalism*, as a product of Western Christian experience, to describe various religiopolitical movements in the presumably very different context of Islamic societies. This term was coined in the United States in the early decades of the twentieth century to refer to a Protestant group that published a series of 12 pamphlets between 1910 and 1912 under the title *The Fundamentals: A Testimony to the Truth*. But the origin of the term should not preclude its application to movements in the Islamic, Jewish, Hindu, or another religious tradition, if they share the same salient features and important traits.

The defining characteristic of the American Protestant fundamentalist movement was firm, principled, and militant opposition to the inroads that modernism, liberalism, and higher biblical criticism were making into the Protestant churches and the supposedly Bible-based culture of the United States at large. That movement called for the defense of a certain form of inherited religiosity that is based on the literal and categorical belief in, and understanding of, the fundamentals of the Protestant faith. Islamic fundamentalists hold sufficiently similar beliefs in relation to Islam and the Koran to justify using the term *fundamentalism* to identify these movements. Islamic movements in North Africa and the Middle East do use the corresponding Arabic terms (*Usuli/Usuliyya*) to describe themselves and their beliefs, and not simply as a matter of translation of the American term. The call to affirm and implement the "fundamentals" of the faith, as distinguished from its incidentals, is an established and recurrent theme in Islamic theological and political discourse, evidenced in the title of the book by al-Ashari (d. 935): *al-Ibanah 'an Usul al-Diyanah* (The Elucidation of the Fundamentals of the Religion). Other scholars who emphasized this theme in their work include al-Ghazzali (d. 1111), ibn Taymiya (d. 1328), and ibn Abdel Wahhab (d. 1787).

Like their Christian counterparts, Islamic fundamentalists see themselves as the moral guardians and saviors of their societies, which they condemn for their apostasy, godlessness, moral depravity, and social decadence. They see Islamic history as one of decline and fall, to be rectified at their hands to arrive at complete restoration and fulfillment of the divine design for all of humanity. Islamic fundamentalists share a profound mistrust of all notions of progress – gradual evolution or historical development – as antithetical to divine action and intervention in the world. As the select few, they see themselves as entrusted with discovering and implementing the will of God through the literal reading of the Koran, which they hold to be manifestly clear, unambiguous, and categorical, irrespective of the contingencies of time and place. Upholding the absolute sovereignty of God on earth, which they alone can discern and implement, Islamic fundamentalists reject the separation of Islam and state, and the sovereignty of the people. To them the state is simply an instrument for implementing the will of God, as expressed in the Koran; it does not exist for the people, as defined by secular constitutional instruments.

Fundamentalism in Islamic History

The Islamic legitimacy of the state has always been a cause of conflict and civil war since the death of the Prophet Muhammad in 632. For the majority of Muslims, the reign of the first four caliphs of Medina, western Arabia (namely, Abu Bakr, Umar, Uthman, and Ali), is generally accepted as an ideal Islamic state and community, but Shiite Muslims regard the first three of the caliphs as illegitimate usurpers of the position to which only Ali (the Prophet's cousin) and his descendants from Fatima (the Prophet's only surviving child) were entitled. Throughout his reign as the fourth caliph (656-661), Ali was locked in bitter civil war against the Umayyad clan and other factions, including some of his own supporters, known as al-Kawarij (secessionists), who condemned him for accepting mediation with the Umayyad. Upon Ali's assassination by one of the al-Khawarij in 661, the Umayyad clan founded a monarchy – contrary to Shari'a principles – that ruled the expanding Muslim empire from Damascus, Syria, until 750. The Abbasid (descendants of the Prophet's uncle) launched their successful challenge to the Umayyad Dynasty in the name of Islamic legitimacy, but the Abbasid state (750-1258) was also a monarchy ruling from Baghdad, Iraq, more in accordance with political expediency than Shari'a principles. The same was true of the other states of various sizes and duration that ruled Islamic societies since: from Spain, North and West Africa, and Central Asia to India, including the Ottoman Empire, which was abolished in 1923-1924.

The tension between Islamic legitimacy and political expediency was often mediated during different phases of history through mutual accommodation between *al-umara* (rulers) and *al-ulama* (scholars of Shari'a) whereby the former acknowledged the theoretical supremacy of Shari'a and the latter conceded the practical political authority of the rulers. Sometimes, rulers professed commitment to more rigorous implementation of Shari'a, as happened during the early Abbasid Dynasty, the Ibadi Khariji kingdom of Tlemsen, Morocco (761-909), Almoravid in Morocco and Spain (1056-1147), and the Ismaili Shia Fatimate Dynasty in parts of North Africa (969-1171). It is difficult to assess the scope and efficacy of those episodes of Shari'a application because of the lack of independent and sufficiently detailed historical sources. Nevertheless, it is reasonable to assume that the decentralized nature of the state and administration of justice in the past would not have permitted a systematic and comprehensive application of Shari'a that Islamic fundamentalists have demanded in the modern context.

The basic difficulty that has frustrated efforts to establish an Islamic state that would effectively implement Shari'a has been the lack of political and legal institutions to ensure state compliance. While the Ulama were supposed to be the guardians of Shari'a, they had no resort except appealing to the rulers' moral and religious sentiments. Another factor was that the Ulama were too concerned with safeguarding the unity of their Muslim communities, and the maintenance of peace and public order, to press their demands forcefully on rulers, especially in times of internal strife and external threat. The few scholars who expressly addressed legal and constitutional matters in their writings, such as those of al-Mawardi (d. 1058) in *al-Ahkam al-Sultaniya* (Principles of Government) and Ibn Taymiya in *al-Siyasa al-Shariiya* (Islamic Public Policy), confined themselves to elaborations of what ought to happen, in the form of advice to the ruler, rather than demands for application of Shari'a as an obligation of the state.

Most of Islamic history can therefore be seen as a record of aspirations to an ideal state that would faithfully and impartially implement Shari'a as a total way of life – aspirations frustrated by the realities of political expediency and security concerns. When the balance tilted too much in favor of the latter considerations, however, the intensity of demands for the application of Shari'a would rise, usually in the form of a local or regional fundamentalist movement.

The jihad movements of the Sudanic belt of sub-Saharan Africa represent a similar fundamentalist resurgence. These movements initially began in dispersed places, gradually influenced one another, and culminated in regional campaigns to found Islamic states. Examples of jihad movements in West Africa include those of Nasir al-Din in MAURITANIA (1673-1677), Malik Dauda Sy in Senegambia (1690s), and Ibrahim Musa, who was also known as Karamoko Alfa (d. 1751) in FOUTA DJALLON. This movement succeeded in setting up an Islamic state in 1776 under the leadership of Ibrahim Sori. Most successful and influential of the jihad movements in the central Sudanic belt is that initiated by USMAN DAN FODIO (d. 1817), who began his mission in 1774, achieved significant military success by 1808, and went on to control most of what is now northern NIGERIA and northern CAMEROON by 1830. This movement, known as the SOKOTO CALIPHATE, spread to parts of southern Nigeria and CHAD, as well as influencing other jihads in Senegambia to the west. Other jihad movements in the region include that of AL-HAJJ UMAR TAL (d. 1864) in the west, and Muhammad Ahmed "al-Mahdi" (d. 1885) along the Nile Valley in the east.

These and other jihad movements of the Sudanic belt of Africa varied greatly in their scope, intensity, and consequences. Some movements lasted for several decades and succeeded in establishing centralized and effective Islamic states in parts of present-day Nigeria, the Volta region, CÔTE D'IVOIRE, and GUINEA, while others were more in the nature of religious revivals, with little political or military success. Many jihad movements were uprisings of Muslim religious teachers and their followers against local military or landowning elites. The Islamic orientation of these movements also varied, as Islam was more of a mobilizing force than a religio-political program to some of them. Others, like that of al-Hajj Umar and SAMORY TOURÉ (d. 1900), forbade dancing and the use of tobacco, alcohol, and charms; prohibited pagan ceremonies and the worship of idols; and appointed Muslim scholars to enforce Shari'a even in non-Muslim areas under their control.

While usually driven by local political, economic, and security considerations, these jihad movements were also confronting the initial stages of European colonialism across the region. Like earlier cycles of Islamic fundamentalism, these African movements emerged in the context of societal crisis due to a combination of internal and external factors. Despite the recent history of jihad movements, there is little indication of fundamentalist resurgence in postcolonial sub-Saharan Africa except in Sudan, along the Nile Valley. Fundamentalist movements may yet emerge in response to the present crisis as an expression of their collective right to self-determination.

FUNDAMENTALISM AS SELF-DETERMINATION IN THE MODERN CONTEXT

Whatever may be the potential for resurgence of Islamic fundamentalism anywhere in the world today, it is clear that the internal and external contexts within which claims of Islamic identity and self-determination are made today are radically different from the way they used to be in the precolonial era. All Islamic societies are now constituted into nation-states that are part of a global political and economic system. They are members of the United Nations and subject to international law, including universal human rights standards, some of which are binding as customary international law even if the state is not party to relevant treaties. None of these nation-states is religiously homogeneous, politically insulated, or economically independent from the non-Muslim world. Even ostensibly purely Islamic and rich countries like Saudi Arabia are in fact vulnerable to economic, security, technological, or other forms of dependency on non-Muslim parts of the world.

Therefore, it is clear that the right to self-determination cannot mean that a people are free to do as they please in their own country. Whether legally as a matter of national constitutional law or international law in relation to other states, or because of pragmatic political and economic realities, the right of one people or group to self-determination is limited by the equal right of other peoples or groups to their own self-determination as well. It is neither legally permissible nor practically possible for a group of Muslims to force non-Muslims or fellow Muslims to accept and implement a specific view of Shari'a, whether as a matter of state policy or informal communal practice. Any attempt to force one's own views on others in the name of self-determination is itself a negation of that right as bases of the claim in the first place.

If and to the extent that Islamic fundamentalists usurp the right of other Muslims to express their views about the nature and implications of Islamic identity, or the desirability of enforcing traditional formulations of Shari'a, that cannot constitute legitimate exercise of the right to self-determination. Similarly, fundamentalist understandings of Islam and Shari'a that would violate the human rights of women, religious minorities, or any other individuals or groups cannot be allowed in the name of self-determination. But if fundamentalists are simply claiming the right to political participation and freedom of belief and expression and so forth, with due regard to the rights of others, then it is wrong to deny them that right simply because one strongly disagrees with their views (*see* FEMINISM IN ISLAMIC AFRICA and ISLAM AND TRADITION: AN INTERPRETATION).

Abdullahi Ahmed An-Na'im

SEE ALSO
Burkina Faso; Mahdist State; Nile River; United Nations in Africa; Almoravids; Alcohol in Africa.

Africa

Islamic Salvation Front (Front Islamique du Salut), an outlawed twentieth-century Algerian political party that advocates the establishment of an Islamic state.

Islam has been an important presence in ALGERIA since the seventh century, and during the twentieth century, Islamic groups played a critical role in the struggle against French colonial rule. The movement for an Islamic state in Algeria dates back to this struggle, but it gained momentum in the wake of the 1978 Iranian Revolution and the establishment of the Islamic Republic of Iran. In the 1980s the Islamic Salvation Front (Front Islamique du Salut, FIS) became the leading group in the call for an Islamic republic in Algeria.

University professor Abassi Madani and political leader Ali Benhadj founded the FIS at a time of widespread popular unrest, when food shortages and high unemployment accompanied growing anti-Western sentiment. In response to criticism of censorship, in 1989 the ruling party, the FRONT DE LIBÉRATION NATIONALE (FLN), legalized the FIS. Critical of the West and advocating a return to Islamic values, the FIS attracted many of those disaffected with the situation in Algeria, including numerous unemployed and alienated youth.

The FIS employed "Islamic police" to ensure observance of Islamic codes of behavior. Anti-Western sentiment extended to the international press, and the FIS was accused of sponsoring the murders of foreign journalists. Women activists and intellectuals who spoke out against the establishment of a conservative Islamic state also risked reprisal from the powerful group. Actions attributed to the organization have been difficult to verify. The group termed *Islamic Fundamentalism* by the West extends beyond official FIS actions. Some violent acts may have been committed by offshoot or rival groups, or members acting independently of the organization.

Dissent within the party emerged between the followers of Madani and the more militant followers of Benhadj, who called for a pan-Islamic republic. Nevertheless, the success of the FIS in the municipal elections of June 1990, where they won 850 of 1541 council seats, left no doubt about the popular appeal of the party. After the start of the next set of elections in December, the FIS accused the ruling party of fixing votes and demanded a presidential and parliamentary election. Violence erupted throughout the country, and Madani threatened a holy war against the state. In June 1991 Madani and Benhadj were arrested.

Even without its leaders, the party continued to gain power: in the first round of elections in 1992, the FIS won 188 of 232 seats. The military-led High Council of State stepped in to seize control from President CHADLI BENJEDID. The new government outlawed the FIS and then arrested its remaining leaders, interning some in a notorious desert concentration camp. In the period following, violent protests and acts of guerrilla warfare by FIS followers, including the 1992 bombing of the Algiers airport, were countered by equally extreme military crackdowns. Since 1992 other militant Islamic groups have moved into the void left by the FIS, now officially in exile. The FIS, meanwhile, has officially distanced itself from these groups, and in 1997, the leadership in exile called for all sides to lay down their arms and end the violence.

Marian Aguiar

SEE ALSO
Algiers, Algeria; Feminism in Islamic Africa; Islamic Fundamentalism: An Interpretation.

North America

Isley Brothers, an African American pop music group whose career has spanned five decades, evolving from 1960s soul to 1970s funk to 1980s pop.

As teenagers, O'Kelly, Ronald, and Rudolf Isley sang GOSPEL MUSIC with another brother, Vernon, until he died in a car accident in 1954. In 1956 the three remaining brothers moved from their home in CINCINNATI, OHIO, to New York City and struggled to establish themselves as an act. They released a series of unsuccessful singles on small New York labels before appearing at the APOLLO THEATER in Harlem and signing a contract with RCA Victor Records.

The Isley Brothers first reached a large audience in 1959 with "Shout," a soul music single that reflected the call-and-response style of gospel music as well as the Isleys' signature vocal style – O'Kelly and Rudolf backing Ronald's tenor lead. After an album with RCA the Isley Brothers switched to Atlantic and then Wand Records, a subsidiary of Scepter, with whom they released their second big hit, "Twist and Shout" (1962).

"Twist and Shout" was pure RHYTHM AND BLUES (R&B), and for the rest of the 1960s the Isleys recorded in this vein. Under pressure from Wand Records, they released insipid rewrites of "Twist and Shout" (such as "Surf and Shout") until they started their own label, T-Neck, in 1964. At that time few African American musicians controlled the production of their own music, and in the face of the high-budget competition of white companies, the venture floundered financially. T-Neck records was precocious in another way, capturing the early guitar innovations of JIMI HENDRIX, who backed the Isleys during the mid-1960s.

The Isley Brothers signed with Motown Records in 1965 and quickly sent "This Old Heart of Mine" up the R&B charts. By the end of the decade, however, they were prepared to change with the times. They replaced mohair suits with hipper fashions, and began writing songs that reflected the influence of JAMES BROWN and FUNK. The change in style was coupled with a change in roster when younger brothers Ernie and Marvin and cousin Chris Jasper joined the group. During the 1970s the Isley Brothers achieved the height of their success, combining dance rhythms with politically charged lyrics in songs such as "Fight the Power" (1975) and "Harvest for the World" (1976).

As the group's success waned in the early 1980s, the latecomers left to form their own group, Isley, Jasper, Isley. The charter members continued to record and perform until O'Kelly died of a heart attack in 1986. Thereafter Angela Wimbush, who later married Ronald, wrote and produced most of the duo's music. The Isley Brothers continued recording into the 1990s, having influenced popular music throughout the previous four decades. In 1992 they were inducted into the Rock and Roll Hall of Fame.

Eric Bennett

SEE ALSO
Soul Music; Harlem, New York; Motown; New York, New York.

Africa

Isoko (also known as Biotu, Igabo, and Urhobo), ethnic group of NIGERIA.

The Isoko primarily inhabit Delta state in southern Nigeria. They speak a Niger-Congo language and are closely related to the neighboring EDO people. Approximately 300,000 people consider themselves Isoko.

SEE ALSO
Languages, African: An Overview.

Africa

Issa (also known as Esa), ethnic group of the Horn of Africa.

The Issa primarily inhabit southern DJIBOUTI, northern SOMALIA, and Harer Province, ETHIOPIA. They speak SOMALI, an Afro-Asiatic language in the Cushitic group, and are considered part of the Dir clan of the Somali people. Approximately 400,000 people consider themselves Issa.

SEE ALSO
Languages, African: An Overview.

Europe

Italy, a country in southern Europe where people of African origin and descent have had a presence since ancient times.

The first recorded African migration to the Italian peninsula came in the aftermath of the conquest and destruction of CARTHAGE (146 B.C.E.). Among the 50,000 Africans that Scipio Africanus Minor brought to Rome as slaves was probably Terence (190-159 B.C.E.), the author of such theatrical comedies as *Andria* and *Hecyra*, whose talent led to his emancipation and to lasting fame in Latin literature. Roman culture's capacity to assimilate many foreign peoples and customs makes it difficult to detect the ethnic or racial origin of people mentioned in Roman texts; the region of birth or a person's name often provides the only clue. Still, there appears to have been a constant African presence in Rome, and in southern and central Italy.

In Latin the term *Africa* referred specifically to the region centered on Carthage in present-day TUNISIA and ALGERIA (*see* ROMAN AFRICA: AN INTERPRETATION). Both North Africans and sub-Saharan Africans (known in Latin as *Aethiopes*) went to Italy as enslaved prisoners of war and as free men and women, counting in their ranks two Roman emperors, Septimius Severus, a native of Leptis Magna in present-day LIBYA, and Marcus Opellius Macrinus. There were also countless craftsmen and traders from North Africa and sub-Saharan Africa. Ivory, wood, corn, fowls, wild animals, and spices were some of the African goods carried to Rome

Italian artist Titian painted this oil portrait of Laura di Dianti in about 1523. The work begins the convention of members of the nobility being depicted with young African servants. *Alinari/Art Resource, NY*

by sea in ships often manned by Egyptians. Animal trainers, boxers and wrestlers from ETHIOPIA were employed in Roman circuses, and black flutists were in great demand for private and public festivities.

By the fourth century so many African students appeared to be living in Rome that a special law was passed that made provisions for sending home those individuals who were too often seen at the theater. From the Berber town of Tagaste (present-day ALGERIA) in Africa where he was born, SAINT AUGUSTINE (354-430 C.E.) came to Rome to study and seek employment as a teacher. He later moved to Milan, where he set the foundations for his Christian philosophy. In addition to Saint Augustine, Saint Cyprian, Tertullian, and SAINT MAURICE are recorded among the early African Christians. Saint Maurice, whose cult is still alive in Northern Italy, Switzerland, and Germany, was an African general in the Roman legions who refused to kill fellow Christians – probably in 287 C.E. – and was executed with most of his soldiers by Emperor Maximian.

With the decline and fall of the Roman Empire, records of the African presence in Italy appear mainly in Muslim and Norman Sicily. Norman kings called themselves "kings of Africa," referring to the Roman province incorporating modern Tunisia and eastern Algeria. The Normans traded with the North African region, received tribute, and drafted soldiers. In 1154 the North African natural scientist, poet, and geographer al-Idrisi finished his monumental geography of the known world and submitted it, along with a world map engraved on a 300-pound silver plate, to Roger II, king of Sicily, who had commissioned it. At the invitatation of the Norman-Sicilian king, al-Idrisi compiled the most extensive and informative of medieval geographical treatises, including firsthand records of North and Central Africa. Johannes Morus was born in Sicily, probably a Muslim slave, and later became a member of the household of Frederick II and the vizier of Sicily under King Manfred. A member of the military class of the Saracens, Sicily's North African rulers, Johannes was very powerful and even challenged the authority of his king, an act that led to his assassination by fellow Saracens.

When the German emperor Frederick II conquered Sicily in 1222, his forces sent Saracens to a Muslim military colony at Lucera, in Apulia. Frederick selected his bodyguards from among them, and when he went back to Germany in 1231, "dark-skinned Aethiopes" are reported to have guarded his treasures. In his triumphal retinue marched many individuals of African descent, including his young black servants and Saracen women and girls. The idea of Africans parading after great men seems to have originated in the Orient, and Frederick revived a pattern of antiquity concerning blacks that was continued in Renaissance Italy. Often Muslim rulers donated African slaves to noblemen, and *mori neri* (black Moors) were found in courts and wealthy households in Venice, Florence, and Rome. The paintings of artists Paolo Veronese and Gian Battista Tiepolo portray Africans as house servants, or as a generic background for the nobility. In the Renaissance, Africans also appeared in Italian literature. Writer Masuccio Salernitano's *Novellino* (1475) included several erotic plots with African protagonists; Giraldi Cinthio's *Hecatommiti* (1566) first told the story of the Moor of Venice, and was Shakespeare's source for Othello; the Neapolitan poet Giambattista Marino wrote the sonnet "La bella schiava" (1614, The Beautiful Slave Woman).

At the same time, interest in Africa emerged in travel writing and geographic descriptions of the continent, such as Giovanni Cavazzi's account of his travels to the Kongo kingdom and ANGOLA. Most influential was the work of LEO AFRICANUS, published in 1550 in Venice – included were descriptions of Tombouctou (Timbuktu) and the sub-Saharan empires of Mali and Bornu. Born al-Hassan ibn Muhammad in Granada, SPAIN, he was given as a slave to Pope Leo X, who baptized him and set him up as an Arabic teacher and African historian.

In Renaissance Italy Africans came as slaves, to ports such as Genoa and Naples; as scholars; and as envoys, mainly to Rome and Venice. In both Venice and Naples, African communities developed in the sixteenth century. In Naples after 1578 the Congrega dei Catecumeni was instituted; its secular and religious members helped in arranging the baptism of slaves and protected them against ill treatment. From 1605 to the next century the Jesuits established a congregation that freed African slaves and exchanged them for Christian slaves held in North Africa. Some freed slaves worked as language teachers for Jesuit missionaries. In Sicily at San Fidelfo in 1526, Benedetto il Moro, the first black African canonized by the Catholic Church (1807), was born into a family of slaves. Benedetto was granted freedom at age 10 and at 21 joined a community of hermits, among whom he led an ascetic life. He became known as a miraculous healer and was renowned for his piety and religiosity.

Near the beginning of the Renaissance, contacts between Ethiopia and Italy intensified, and an Ethiopian messenger witnessed the 1395 coronation of Giovanni Galeazzo Visconti as duke of Milan. In 1402 Ethiopian ambassadors are recorded in Venice carrying "leopards and aromatic herbs." Ethiopians appear in many Vatican documents, especially after 1481, when Pope Sixtus IV turned the church of Santo Stefano Maggiore into an Ethiopian church, Santo Stefano degli Abissini, and its convent into an asylum for Ethiopian pilgrims. Santo Stefano became a cultural and religious center out of which came the first book printed in an Ethiopian language – *Psalterium Ethiopicum* (1513) – and, through the work of Abba Tesfa Sion, an Ethiopian New Testament and missal (1549). Santo Stefano helped in fostering the study of Ethiopian language and culture, especially through the scholarship of Abba Gregory, who resided there from 1649 to 1652.

In the wake of Portuguese exploration (*see* Explorers in Africa before 1500) of the African coastline, Rome and the Vatican played a crucial role in the relationship between Europe and Africa. The expansion of Christianity to Africa produced momentous developments in the history of Christianity (*see* Christianity, African: An Overview). Converted Christian rulers sought direct relationships with the pope. The Kongo Kingdom sent several ambassadors to Rome; in 1512 King Afonso sent his son Henry, who later became bishop of Utica and the Kongo; and in 1539 two more members of the Kongo royal family went to Rome to study church buildings and Renaissance culture. To commemorate another embassy from the Kongo, a sumptuous monument still stands in the Church of Santa Maria Maggiore in Rome, memorializing the death of Antonio Manuel de Vunda on the eve of Epiphany in 1608. In the Vatican Library a fresco represents Pope Paul V visiting him on his deathbed. In the wake of de Vunda's embassy, a new era in the relationship between the Catholic Church and Africa was inaugurated with the institution of the Congregatio de Propaganda Fidei, which fostered conversion to Christianity and directly coordinated missionary endeavors.

Italian Catholic institutions played their missionary role predominantly in such North African Muslim lands as Egypt, Ethiopia, and Sudan in the eighteenth and nineteenth centuries. Several Africans trained for the priesthood in Rome, notably the Ethiopian Tobia, who was consecrated bishop and translated a catechism into the Ethiopian scriptural language Geez. Within the larger movement for the emancipation from slavery, Catholic institutions such as the Collegio de Mori in Naples and the Istituto Mazza in Verona took an active role in the emanci-

TOP: An Italian official rides into Addis Ababa, Ethiopia, under a banner that asks, in Italian, "Whose is the power? Ours!" and hails Italian dictator Benito Mussolini (known as *Il Duce*). *CORBIS/Hulton-Deutsch Collection*

ABOVE: A New Orleans jazz band, Italian style, welcomes trumpeter Louis Armstrong to Rome in 1949. *CORBIS/Bettmann* pation and education of young Africans. Ransomed children would be brought by missionaries such as Nicola Mazza, the Genoese Nicola Olivieri, or the Neapolitan Ludovico da Casoria and sent to monasteries all over Italy. Monsignor Comboni brought the Sudanese antislavery figure Daniel Sorur Pharim Den to the Istituto Mazza in 1876. Daniel continued his studies in Rome and in Beirut, and was ordained as a priest in Cairo in 1887. He was a popular speaker and authored pamphlets in Italian, arguing for the need to fight the TRANS-SAHARAN AND RED SEA SLAVE TRADE, and was the only African active in the antislavery movement of the archbishop of Algiers, Cardinal Lavigerie.

After the 1884-1885 Berlin Conference, Italy embarked on a program of colonialism, which in the next four decades led to the establishment of protectorates and colonies in Ethiopia, ERITREA, SOMALIA, and Libya. At the outset of the Ethiopian expeditions, Italian propagandists for colonization exploited racist theories both of inferiority and exotic allure, finding their icon in Taitu, the Ethiopian queen after 1883. After Ethiopian king Menilek's victory over the Italians at Adwa in 1896, however, leftist anticolonialists alarmed the government by provoking disorders. At one meeting in Rome protesters cheered for Menilek; in Milan police and protesters clashed; and in Pavia protesters uprooted train tracks to prevent soldiers from joining their battalions.

With the rise of fascism, colonialism received a new impetus, and the rhetoric of patriotism often drew on racial stereotypes: "Faccetta nera" (Pretty Little Black Face) was the title song for Mussolini's 1935-1936 invasion of Ethiopia, in the last phase of the SCRAMBLE FOR AFRICA. Italian aggression in Ethiopia represented a violent denial of black independence, as well as of the long history of a Christian state, and provoked outrage among supporters of African anticolonial movements, bringing Africa to the center of world politics on the eve of World War II.

In the postwar era, Somalia maintained relations of cooperation with Italy, and numerous Ethiopians and Somali sought education in Italy up to the 1960s. Since the 1960s African immigrants, mainly from North Africa, have come to Italy, either to seek employment in Italy or to move on to FRANCE and GERMANY. An estimated 2 million immigrants have settled in Italy in the 1980s and 1990s, many of them illegally, and they face precarious economic and social conditions. In large cities such as Milan, Rome, and Turin, African communities have been growing, and Catholic and Muslim associations function as social and cultural centers for these immigrants. This new wave of immigration has changed Italian cities, and slowly the African community in Italy has acquired a voice through the institution of unions and the formulation of a political agenda focused on the recognition of legal immigrant status and the extension of civil rights to alien residents.

Alida Cagidemetrio

SEE ALSO

Algiers, Algeria; Explorers in Africa, 1500 to 1800; Ivory Trade; Kanuri; Kongo; Benedict of Palermo, Saint; Egypt, Ancient Kingdom of; Menilek II; Tombouctou, Mali; Christianity: Missionaries in Africa; Mali Empire; Ethiopic Script and Language; Berlin Conference of 1884-1885.

Africa

Iteso (also known as Elgumi, Teso, and Wamia), ethnic group of East Africa.

The Iteso primarily inhabit northeastern UGANDA and western KENYA. They speak a Nilo-Saharan language and are the second largest ethnic group in Uganda after the GANDA. Approximately 1.5 million people consider themselves Iteso.

SEE ALSO

Languages, African: An Overview.

Africa

Itsekiri (also known as Chekiri, Irhobo, Iwere, Shekiri, and Warri), ethnic group of NIGERIA.

The Itsekiri primarily inhabit Delta State in southern Nigeria. They speak a Niger-Congo language and are closely related to the EDO people, although today many speak YORUBA. Approximately 700,000 people consider themselves Itsekiri.

SEE ALSO

Languages, African: An Overview.

Africa

Ittu (also known as the Itu), ethnic group of ETHIOPIA.

The Ittu live mainly around Harer, Ethiopia. They speak OROMO, an Afro-Asiatic language, and are one of the Oromo peoples. There are approximately 1 million people who consider themselves Ittu.

SEE ALSO

Languages, African: An Overview.

Ivory Coast. Please see CÔTE D'IVOIRE

Africa

Ivory Trade, one of Africa's oldest, most lucrative, and now most controversial export trades.

Ivory is a form of dentin obtained mainly from ELEPHANT tusks. It is excellent for carving and is admired for its creamy color, smooth texture, and hardness. Long a symbol of luxury, it was used for furniture inlay, book covers, birdcages, brooches, scabbards, figurines, and boxes in ancient Egypt, Assyria (present-day ETHIOPIA), Crete, Greece, Italy, China, India, and Japan. Craftworkers in BENIN were well known for their skill at carving masks, statuettes, caskets, jewelry, bells, and rattles. Because ivory has been highly sought, the ivory trade has historically been lucrative. In the late twentieth century, however, declining African elephant populations, attributed to poachers, brought controversy to the trade.

Ancient Egyptians from the Sixth Dynasty (2420-2258 B.C.E.) onward used ivory extensively, obtaining most of their supply from the region of present-day SUDAN. The Romans in North Africa kept up a brisk trade in ivory following the demise of the Egyptian Empire. After Rome's decline, China and India became the largest importers of African ivory.

As Arab Islamic dynasties spread across North Africa in the seventh and eighth centuries, they established trade relations with peoples south of the SAHARA DESERT. Towns such as Koumbi Saleh, Gao, and Tombouctou (Timbuktu), became commercial centers where tusks were exchanged for salt, copper, gold, silk, and swords. European demand for ivory was sparked during the CRUSADES. Initially, ivory was exported to Europe primarily from North Africa, but in the late fifteenth century Portuguese merchant ships began trading European goods for ivory along the coasts of West and Central Africa.

Ivory also became an important trade commodity along East Africa's SWAHILI COAST, which stretches from SOMALIA to MOZAMBIQUE. From at least the fifteenth century, Swahili merchants exported ivory to India after obtaining it from inland peoples, such as the KAMBA of modern KENYA, the NYAMWEZI of TANZANIA, the YAO of MOZAMBIQUE, and the BISA of ZAMBIA. In the mid-nineteenth century the Omani rulers of ZANZIBAR sent trading caravans into the East African interior. These merchant caravans also traded in slaves, and in fact used slave labor to carry elephant tusks from the African interior to the coast.

One of the most famous Swahili traders was TIPPU TIP, a native of Zanzibar who established an inland trading empire that stretched from Zanzibar to the Lualaba River in the modern DEMOCRATIC REPUBLIC OF THE CONGO. In the nineteenth century the trade expanded further with the coming of European settlers and adventurers, many of whom subsidized their hunting expeditions by selling ivory and trophies in Europe.

At the same time industrial revolutions in Europe and the United States drove demand for ivory to unprecedented heights, supplementing the eastern demand. By the late 1800s Great Britain and the United States imported more than 1.5 million tons of ivory per year to be used for combs, piano

IVORY TRADE
Secondary city
Historical Centers of Ivory Trade
International border
The ivory trade ban Internationally Imposed by the Convention on International Trade in Endangered Species of Wild Fauna and Flora in 1989 was partially lifted for the indicated countries in 1997.
0
800 km
0
600 mi
Ancient Egypt imported ivory extensively from about 2400 B.C.E. onward.
Atlantic Ocean
Mediterranean Sea
Black Sea
Persian Gulf
Red Sea
Indian Ocean
Tropic of Cancer
Equator
Strait of Gibraltar
Gulf of Guinea
Ivory Coast
Swahili Coast
Mozambique Channel
Madeira
Casablanca
Oran
Tunisia
Morocco
Canary Islands
Tindouf
La'youn
Western Sahara (disputed)
Algeria
Libya
Benghazi
Alexandria
Egypt
Nile R.
Aswân
Al Jawf
Mauritania
Mali
Koumbi Saleh
Tombouctou
Gao
Niger
Faya-Largeau
Chad
Sudan
Port Sudan
Eritrea
Asmera
Djibouti
Senegal
Burkina Faso
Guinea
Sierra Leone
Liberia
Côte d'Ivoire
Ghana
Togo
Benin
Nigeria
Kano
Lagos
Niger R.
Lake Chad
El Fashir
Ethiopia
Somalia
Mogadishu
Cameroon
Central African Republic
Juba
Equatorial Guinea
Uganda
Kenya
São Tomé & Príncipe
Annobón
Gabon
Republic of the Congo
Democratic Republic of the Congo
Congo R.
Kisangani
Rwanda
Lake Victoria
Mombasa
Burundi
Cabinda (Angola)
Kalemie
Lake Tanganyika
Tanzania
Zanzibar
Kilwa Kisiwani
Comoros
Mtwara
Ascension
Lualaba R.
Lubumbashi
Angola
Lobito
Lake Malawi
Pemba
Antsiranana
Zambia
Malawi
Zambezi R.
St. Helena
Madagascar
Mozambique
Namibia
Zimbabwe
Beira
Botswana
Bulawayo
Toliara
Swaziland
Lüderitz
Johannesburg
Lesotho
Durban
South Africa
Cape Town
Port Elizabeth

keys, billiard balls, and fans. This frenzy for ivory in the late nineteenth century devastated Africa's elephant populations.

European colonial-era restrictions on Africans' indigenous hunting – intended to force Africans into wage labor and preserve elephant populations for European "safari" hunters – slowed the ivory trade. By the 1930s, however, ivory exports rose again. In the 1970s booming Asian economies fueled international demand, which, because of the advent of automatic weapons, was easily met.

The African elephant population declined from approximately 1.3 million to approximately 625,000 between 1979 and 1989, and ivory had doubled in price, from around U.S.$60 per kilogram (about U.S.$132 per pound) to between U.S.$120 and U.S.$300 per kilogram (about U.S.$264 to U.S.$660 per pound). In October 1989 the nations composing the Convention on International Trade in Endangered Species of Wild Fauna and Flora (CITES), responding to pressure from United States and European environmentalist and animal welfare lobbies, agreed to a complete ban on the ivory trade.

Many disagreed with the ban, however, citing the uneven distribution of elephants in Africa. For instance, in Kenya elephant populations were as low as 19,000, mostly because of poaching, but in SOUTH AFRICA, NAMIBIA, ZIMBABWE, and BOTSWANA, effective conservation programs resulted in elephant herds so large that they were damaging wild vegetation as well as farmers' fields (*see* WILDLIFE MANAGEMENT IN AFRICA). In these countries, elephant herds had to be culled regularly. The ivory from these culled animals represented an important potential source of income for these countries' governments. Not surprisingly, they protested the ban, arguing that they were being penalized for sound resource management.

In 1997 CITES partially lifted the ivory trade ban, allowing Botswana, Namibia, and Zimbabwe to sell their excess ivory stocks to Japan. By October 1997 critics of the lifting of the ban claimed that poaching had increased significantly throughout Africa.

Robert Fay

SEE ALSO

Roman Africa: An Interpretation; Gold Trade; Egypt, Ancient Kingdom of; Salt Trade; Swahili People; Tombouctou, Mali; Koumbi Saleh, Mauritania; Indian Ocean Slave Trade; Islam and Tradition: An Interpretation.

Africa

Iwa (also known as Awiwa and Mashukulumbwe), ethnic group of ZAMBIA.

The Iwa primarily inhabit northeastern Zambia. They speak MAMBWE, a Bantu language. Approximately 300,000 people consider themselves Iwa.

SEE ALSO

Bantu: Dispersion and Settlement.

Africa

Iyasu I, known as Iyasus the Great (1682-1706), one of the great warrior emperors of ETHIOPIA (1682-1706).

Iyasus I was the son of Emperor Johannes I and the grandson of Emperor Fasiladas. He came to the throne at a time of decline in imperial power that had begun during his grandfather's time. Through his brilliance as a military leader, Iyasus temporarily halted the trend of decline, reestablishing control over rebellious vassals and conquering areas to the south of his domain. In addition to his military and political exploits, Iyasus was a patron of arts and letters and sponsored buildings in the city of Gonder. He also attempted to settle doctrinal differences within Ethiopia's Coptic Church, but without long-lasting success. Iyasus was deposed by his son Takla Haymanot in 1706 and later assassinated. A series of ineffectual emperors followed until the middle of the nineteenth century, leading to a decline of imperial power and loss of territory for the empire.

SEE ALSO

Ethiopian Orthodox Church; Gonder, Ethiopia.

j

North America

Jack and Jill of America,

an American nonprofit philanthropic organization founded in 1938 as a play group for the children of Philadelphia's African American professional elite.

Jack and Jill was born during the GREAT DEPRESSION and grew out of the voluntary community work of upper-class African American women in PHILADELPHIA, PENNSYLVANIA, who wanted their children to have cultural opportunities, develop leadership skills, and form social networks in the midst of segregation.

By 1968 Jack and Jill had become a full-fledged national organization, and the first founded by African American women. It continues to sponsor educational, health, and cultural projects in inner-city neighborhoods. Jack and Jill publishes a national journal, *Up the Hill*, and has 187 local chapters in the United States.

Jalane Schmidt

North America

Jackson, George Lester

(b. September 23, 1941, Chicago, Ill.; d. August 21, 1971, San Quentin Prison, Calif.), African American anticapitalist revolutionary whose prison writings served as a manifesto for New Left activists in the 1970s.

George Jackson grew up on the West Side of Chicago, the son of Lester Jackson, a postal worker, and Georgia Jackson. He was the second oldest of five children. Street smart and rebellious, Jackson had several run-ins with the law for petty crimes by the time he was ten. In 1956 his family moved to Los Angeles, where Jackson's troubles with the law continued, including several arrests for robbery. Paroled in June 1960 after serving time for a gas station holdup, Jackson was arrested later that year for a gas station robbery that netted $71. Due to his previous convictions, he received an indeterminate sentence of one year to life. He was 19 and remained in prison for the rest of his life.

While in prison, Jackson studied the writings of Karl Marx, FRANTZ FANON, Mao Zedong, Fidel Castro, and others. He developed a critique of capitalism and racism that enabled him to see his criminal activity and his imprisonment within a political context. Jackson and several others organized study groups to help raise the political consciousness of African American prisoners. Jackson, who worked as a prison organizer for the BLACK PANTHER PARTY, aimed to channel the anger and rebellious spirit of African Americans toward political activism. His revolutionary philosophy cohered around a program of armed struggle directed at overthrowing the racist and imperialist establishment in the United States.

Over the years Jackson was repeatedly denied parole. Prison officials said that it was because of Jackson's disruptive behavior; Jackson and his supporters argued that it was due to his political activism.

On January 16, 1970, in response to the death of three black inmates, a white guard, John Mills, was killed in Soledad Prison. Jackson and two other black men, John Clutchette and Fleeta Drumgo, were accused of the murder. The facts of their alleged involvement have never been satisfactorily established. The three accused men became known as the Soledad Brothers and attracted international attention. *Soledad Brother: The Prison Letters of George Jackson* was published during this time and became a national bestseller. Many people protested that the Soledad Brothers were being framed due to their political activities. Angela Davis played a leading role in organizing support for their defense.

The trial dissolved into complete chaos on August 7, 1970, when Jonathon Jackson, younger brother of George, attempted to take over the courthouse and free the three accused. During the melee, Jonathon was shot to death, along with the judge and two of the inmates. A little more than a year later, on August 21, 1971, prison guards killed George Jackson. The official report said that Jackson was armed, that he had participated in a revolt, killing two white prisoners and three guards, and that he was attempting to escape. Supporters have noted several inconsistencies in the report and believe that prison authorities, fearful that Jackson had grown too powerful, set him up and murdered him.

SEE ALSO

Chicago, Illinois; Davis, Angela Yvonne; Los Angeles, California.

North America

Jackson, Jesse, Jr. **(b. 1965, Greenville, S.C.), Democratic member of the United States House of Representatives from Illinois (1995-).**

Jesse Louis Jackson Jr. was born in Greenville, South Carolina, to Jacqueline Brown and Jesse Jackson Sr., an African American minister and political activist. He graduated from North Carolina Agricultural and Technical State University with a bachelor's degree in 1987. He earned a graduate divinity degree from Chicago Theological Seminary in 1990 and a law degree from the University of Illinois in 1993. Jackson had been an activist and political organizer at the local and national levels since he was a teenager. Before his election to Congress, he was active in the National Rainbow Coalition. In that role he created programs to increase voter registration and to educate voters about the political process. Jackson was secretary of the Democratic National Committee's Black Caucus.

The Second Congressional District seat in Illinois was vacated when former Democratic representative Mel Reynolds resigned in October 1995. Jackson defeated three experienced politicians in the November Democratic primary and easily beat his Republican opponent in the general election to replace Reynolds. Jackson took office in December 1995 and was reelected in 1996.

The mostly black, heavily Democratic Second District covers the low-income and middle-class neighborhoods of Chicago's South Side and nearby suburbs. The South Side was once an important industrial center, but many factories have closed in recent years. Approximately half of the voters in the Second District are Chicago residents. In the 105th Congress (1997-1999), Jackson served on the Banking and Financial Services Committee and the Small Business Committee. He is a member of the Congressional Black Caucus.

See Also
Jackson, Jesse Louis.

North America

Jackson, Jesse Louis

(b. October 8, 1941, Greenville, S.C.), African American minister, founder of Operation PUSH and the National Rainbow Coalition, and twice candidate for president of the United States.

One of America's best-known and most respected black leaders, Jesse Jackson appeared on the national scene following the 1968 assassination of his mentor, Martin Luther King Jr. In the years since, Jackson has continued to work for racial and economic justice, international peace, and empowerment of society's outsiders. With projects like Operation Breadbasket, Operation PUSH, and the Rainbow Coalition, as well as political action – particularly his candidacy for the Democratic nomination for president in 1984 and 1988 – he has attracted fame, admiration, and criticism. For his work on behalf of racial and social justice, he has been awarded at least 40 honorary degrees, and for ten years he has been listed among the top ten men most admired by Americans. Despite all of Jackson's achievements, however, some commentators and biographers admit to a sense of disappointment because of what he has not accomplished.

Jackson was born to Helen Burns, an unwed teenaged mother, herself the child of an unwed teenaged mother. His childhood was marked by feelings of isolation and difference, according to his biographers. His biological father, Noah Robinson, was one of Greenville's most prosperous black citizens, while Jackson, along with his mother and grandmother, lived in relative poverty. Robinson's initial refusal to acknowledge Jackson (who took the name of his stepfather, Charles H. Jackson, upon being adopted by him in 1957) changed as Jesse grew into a promising athlete and scholar. Despite the material and emotional deprivations of Jackson's early life, one of his friends told biographer Marshall Frady, "Not only does Jesse believe in God, but Jesse believes God believes in him."

This self-assurance and sense of destiny was first tested at college. A football scholarship to the University of Illinois brought Jackson north in 1959, but after being denied the coveted quarterback position he returned south to the historically black North Carolina Agricultural and Technical State College. There he fulfilled his athletic and leadership potential, serving as the student body president as well as quarterback of the football team. It was also while he was at college that Jackson became involved in the Civil Rights Movement, first by protesting the whites-only local library system, then later by leading demonstrations against segregated restaurants, theaters, and hotels.

By the time Jackson graduated in 1964, he had decided to become a minister. Accepting a scholarship from the Chicago Theological Seminary, he returned to Illinois, this time with a family; he had married Jacqueline Brown the same year. In Chicago Jackson worked hard at his studies, and at first kept his distance from the local civil rights organizations, many of which were trying to recruit him as a potential leader. All that changed, according to Frady, when Jackson went to Selma, Alabama, in March 1965, to take part in a historic civil rights march led by Martin Luther King Jr., president of the Southern Christian Leadership Conference (SCLC). Leading a group of fellow divinity students, Jackson arrived in Selma, met King, and made himself noticed, as much for his obvious ambition as for his leadership skills.

Before long Jackson was working for SCLC. By 1966 he had left seminary to head the Chicago branch of Operation Breadbasket, an organization dedicated to improving the financial position of the black community; in 1967 he became its national chairman. Blessed with charm, energy, and a fiery oratorical style, Jackson soon found success and local fame as the man who pressured several large Chicago organizations into hiring more African Americans. Relations between Jackson and the SCLC leadership, which had been stormy at times due to competition among strong personalities, deteriorated further after King's assassination in April 1968. Accused by some of exaggerating his closeness to the slain civil rights hero, Jackson nevertheless quickly became a national figure, assumed by some to be King's natural heir. After the SCLC board selected Ralph David Abernathy as its next president, Jackson continued with the organization, even serving as mayor of the ill-fated antipoverty demonstration Resurrection City. In 1971 he left in order to begin a new project called Operation PUSH.

PUSH, which stands for People United to Serve Humanity, grew out of Operation Breadbasket and continued many of its themes, especially the theme of economic empowerment. Embellishing a line from one of King's speeches, Jackson provided PUSH with a catchy and compelling motto: "I Am Somebody." Jackson began attracting large and enthusiastic crowds to his weekly PUSH prayer meetings. As his influence and celebrity grew, so did his family, which soon included five children. With the addition of PUSH-Excel, a branch devoted to educational issues, and with a new emphasis on voter registration drives, Jackson became a powerful voice for minorities and the poor, appearing often in the national media and speaking on behalf of political candidates.

In 1983 Jackson declared himself a candidate for the presidential nomination of the Democratic Party. Emphasizing his compassion and fervor on behalf of the poor, the marginalized, and the downtrodden, he pledged to build a "rainbow coalition." Jackson had already been criticized for his support of the Palestinian Liberation Organization during a trip to North Africa and the Middle East in 1979. During the race for the 1984 election he faced renewed charges of anti-Semitism – for his association with the controversial Nation of Islam leader Louis Farrakhan and for his reference to New York City as Hymietown. Jackson apologized repeatedly for this remark and has since emphasized his distaste for all forms of bigotry, but the stigma remains.

Caught between the high expectations of the black community and the fear and indifference of the white mainstream, Jackson did not win the nomination in 1984. But he did amass far more delegates than anyone had predicted. In his speech before the Democratic Convention, his dramatic call to "Keep Hope Alive" electrified the crowd, and some commentators later called it the best political speech of the century. In 1986 Jackson founded the National Rainbow Coalition. Two years later he again sought the presidency and failed to be nominated, although this time he won several major primaries and, for a while, was the frontrunner. Although nominee Michael Dukakis did not ask him to be his running mate, despite that suggestion from several polls and advisors, Jackson worked hard to support the Democratic ticket, which eventually lost to George Bush and Dan Quayle. Beyond their simple success or failure, Jackson's presidential runs were significant: through them, he galvanized black voters, millions of whom he had helped to register prior to the election; he raised important social and racial issues on the national level; and, for the first time, he introduced the possibility that an African American could win the nation's highest office.

In the decade following the 1988 election, Jackson continued in leadership roles, although he has passed the political torch to his son, Jesse Jr., who is a congressman from Illinois. Despite the urging of supporters, Jackson chose not to run for mayor of Washington, D.C., where he and his family had moved in 1989. He left PUSH the same year. In 1990 he began serving as "statehood senator," a position created to lobby for statehood for the District of Columbia. Jackson also resumed the unaligned diplomacy he had begun in 1979 and that he had continued in 1983 when he had won the release of a black prisoner of war who was being detained in Syria. In 1991 Jackson's intervention was responsible for the release of hundreds of hostages being held by Iraqi president Saddam Hussein. In 1996 he returned to Chicago to resume leadership of PUSH. In 1999 Jackson once again assumed the role of roving ambassador and succeeded in securing from Slobadan Milosevic the release of three American soldiers taken prisoner on the border between Yugoslavia and Macedonia.

Kate Tuttle

See Also

Chicago, Illinois; Farrakhan, Louis Abdul; King, Martin Luther, Jr.; New York, New York; Poor People's Washington Campaign; Jackson, Jesse, Jr.

North America

Jackson, Jimmy Lee

(b. December 1938, Marion, Ala.; d. February 26, 1965, Selma, Ala.), African American civil rights activist whose death at the hands of Alabama state troopers inspired the march from Selma to Montgomery.

Jimmy Lee Jackson, a pulpwood cutter, had recently become the youngest deacon in the history of St. James Baptist Church in Marion, Alabama, before becoming a martyr in the struggle for civil rights. Born and raised in Marion, Jackson began to advocate for voting rights for African Americans as a participant in a local right-to-vote movement, led by Albert Turner. On February 18, 1965, Jackson and his family attended a nighttime rally at Zion's Chapel Methodist Church, held to protest the jailing of one of the Southern Christian Leadership Conference (SCLC) leaders, James Orange. Upon leaving the church, the congregation was attacked by state troopers and local police. Inside a nearby café Jackson was beaten and shot in the stomach while attempting to protect his mother and grandfather. Taken first to Perry County Hospital, Jackson was transferred to the Negro Good Samaritan Hospital in Selma, where he died eight days later due to the gunshot wound.

Martin Luther King Jr. preached at Jackson's funeral on March 3, criticizing the federal government for failing to protect its own citizens while spending millions of dollars to fight a war in Vietnam. Jackson's death caused activists to galvanize plans for a march from Selma to the state house in Montgomery. More than 500 African Americans began the march on March 7, 1965, and were savagely beaten back by police, some of them on horseback. The brutal encounter, which became known as Bloody Sunday, was televised across the nation and was critical to securing national support for voting rights legislation.

See Also

Civil Rights Movement; King, Martin Luther, Jr.

North America

Jackson, Joseph Harrison

(b. September 11, 1900, Rudyard, Miss.; d. August 18, 1990, Chicago, Ill.), African American Baptist leader who opposed Martin Luther King Jr. and the Civil Rights Movement.

As president of the 5-million-member National Baptist Convention U.S.A., Inc., from 1953 to 1982, Joseph H. Jackson was one of the most powerful black ministers of his day. Strongly opposed to the popular civil rights program and activity of Martin Luther King Jr., Jackson managed to continue his autocratic control of the denomination to which they both belonged. In 1960 Gardner C. Taylor, who was supportive of King, was elected to the presidency of the convention on a roll call vote, but Jackson refused to relinquish power. Consequently, King, Taylor, and other liberal activists withdrew to form the Progressive National Baptist Convention.

Born in Mississippi, Jackson attended Jackson College and Colgate-Rochester Divinity School. From 1922 to 1941 he served churches in Mississippi, Nebraska, and Pennsylvania. In 1941 he was called to Olivet Baptist Church in Chicago, Illinois, the largest black Baptist church in the country. In 1953 he was elected president of the convention, the governing body of thousands of autonomous congregations. He wrote several books, including a history of the convention.

Jackson eschewed political civil rights agitation in favor of black economic self-development, a position advocated by conservatives such as Booker T. Washington as well as radicals such as Marcus Garvey. In *Unholy Shadows and Freedom's Holy Light*, Jackson wrote, "Civil disobedience is a form of lawlessness and, is in reality, not far removed from open crime." Extending his idea of self-development, Jackson promoted African land development in Liberia. He died in 1990.

Richard Newman

See Also

Baptists; Garvey, Marcus Mosiah; King, Martin Luther, Jr.; Taylor, Gardner Calvin; Washington, Booker Taliaferro.

North America

Jackson-Lee, Sheila (b. 1950,

Jamaica, N.Y.), Democratic member of the United States House of Representatives from Texas (1995-).

Sheila Jackson-Lee was born in Jamaica, New York. She received a bachelor's degree in political science from Yale University in 1972 and a law degree from the University of Virginia in 1975. She was an attorney in Houston, Texas, from 1975 to 1987. She served as a Houston municipal court judge from 1987 to 1989 and sat on the Houston City Council from 1990 to 1995. In 1994 she ran for the U.S. Congress in the Eighteenth Congressional District of Texas and won with more than 70 percent of the vote. She was reelected in 1996 with nearly 80 percent of the vote.

The Eighteenth District includes many of the poorest parts of Houston. Federal judges ordered that the district be redrawn in 1995 because the 1990 redistricting had given the district too large a proportion of low-income minority voters. Office buildings and hotels in downtown Houston and the Texas Medical Center are major employers.

In the 105th Congress (1997-1999), Jackson-Lee sat on the Judiciary Committee and its Crime Subcommittee. She also sat on the Science Committee and its Basic Research and Space and Aeronautics Subcommittees. She is a member of the Congressional Black Caucus.

North America

Jackson, Lillie Mae Carroll

(b. May 25, 1889, Baltimore, Md.; d. July 5, 1975, Baltimore, Md.), long-time civil rights activist and Baltimore branch president of the National Association for the Advancement of Colored People (NAACP).

One of the women who helped revitalize a flagging NAACP in the 1930s was its Baltimore branch president, Lillie May Jackson. Known as "fearless Lil," she became involved in the association after her daughter, Juanita Jackson Mitchell, founded the Baltimore Young People's Forum in 1931. In her advisory role to her daughter's group, Jackson helped campaign for economic justice and voter education and against lynching. In 1935, around the same time that NAACP president Walter White recruited her daughter to serve as its first youth director, Jackson took over the association's Baltimore branch. With the help of her friend and fellow Baltimorean Thurgood Marshall, she soon transformed it into one of the nation's most active branches.

Membership in the Baltimore branch swelled to 20,000 during Jackon's tenure as president, and under her leadership voter registration among the area's African Americans nearly doubled by the late 1940s. The branch also played a national role, fighting segregation in a series of lawsuits that included *Murray* v. *Maryland* (1936), an important precursor to 1954's Brown v. Board of Education. After *Brown* outlawed school segregation, Jackson proved instrumental in seeing that the verdict was enforced in her home state. Jackson retired from the NAACP in 1970 but continued to work for human rights in Baltimore through her own organization, Freedom House, which served the city's poor. She died in 1975 at age 86, survived by four children, ten grandchildren, and nine great-grandchildren.

Kate Tuttle

See Also
Baltimore, Maryland; White, Walter Francis.

North America

Jackson, Luther Porter

(b. 1892, Louisville, Ky.; d. April 20, 1950, Petersburg, Va.), African American historian of the black American South and advocate of black voting rights.

Luther Porter Jackson was the ninth of 12 children born to Delilah and Edward Jackson, both former slaves. Inspired by his mother, who had become a schoolteacher after Emancipation, Jackson developed a keen interest in education. He earned bachelor's and master's degrees from Fisk University in Nashville, then taught at high schools and colleges in South Carolina and Kansas. By 1922 he was an instructor at the Virginia Normal and Industrial Institute (later Virginia State College) in Petersburg, where he spent the rest of his life.

Affected by the time he spent in South Carolina, Jackson published two studies about the education of Carolina blacks during the mid-1800s. He then focused almost exclusively on the history of black Virginians. Delving into courthouse records – wills, tax ledgers, marriage licenses, and property lists – he discovered previously unpublicized information about black life. The result was the pioneering *Free Negro Labor and Property Holding in Virginia, 1830-1860*, published in 1942.

Thereafter, Jackson published dozens of articles and books about the history of Virginia's blacks, prompting historian Carter G. Woodson to say of Jackson, "He knows more about Negro families in Virginia than any other man living." Along the way, Jackson received a full professorship from Virginia State and a doctoral degree from the University of Chicago.

Jackson was also a fervent supporter of black equality and an active fundraiser for the National Association for the Advancement of Colored People (NAACP). His Petersburg League of Negro Voters grew to become the Virginia Voters League, and his Petersburg Negro Business Association later became the Virginia Trade Association.

Not content with available data on black voters, he published yearly *The Voting Status of Negroes in Virginia*, and this effort, too, outgrew its beginnings: the Southern Regional Council commissioned him to conduct a larger study on voting rights, which was published in 1948 as the pamphlet *Race and Suffrage in the South since 1940*. Notorious for his long hours of work, Jackson died of a heart attack in 1950, his place secured as one of the most influential historians of Southern black life.

See Also
Woodson, Carter Godwin.

North America

Jackson, Mahalia

(b. October 26, 1911, New Orleans, La.; d. January 27, 1972, Chicago, Ill.), African American gospel singer who fused the varied musical traditions of New Orleans to become known as the "World's Greatest Gospel Singer."

Mahalia Jackson's father, John Jackson, worked on the New Orleans docks during the week and preached the gospel on Sundays. Her mother, Charity Clark, died at 25, four years after Jackson's birth. At her mother's death, Jackson moved in with her mother's sisters and began singing at Plymouth Rock Baptist Church. Later, she sang in Mount Moriah Baptist Church and in several other neighborhood churches.

In addition to singing traditional church hymns on Sundays, Jackson was exposed to the blues and jazz heard constantly in the streets of New Orleans. Musicians like Joseph "King" Oliver played on the bandwagons in her neighborhood and in the dance halls she frequented as a child. Although jazz bands were ever present, the two most profound influences on the young woman were blues singer Bessie Smith and the music of the sanctified church. She heard Smith's "Careless Love" and was instantly impressed by the down-home moans and shouts. Although Jackson refused to sing the blues because it was "the devil's music," Smith's contribution to Jackson's gospel style is unmistakable.

As a child Jackson lived next door to a sanctified church. She never converted to the Holiness Movement, but she was inspired by the joyous and spirited singing. The beat and bodily expression of the sanctified congregation stayed with Jackson throughout her career. She was frequently criticized for being crude and unsophisticated because of her handclapping and swaying, but she would always respond with Scripture. "As David said in the Bible, 'Make a joyful noise unto the Lord.'"

In 1927 Jackson moved to Chicago to live with her aunt, Hannah Robinson. She supported herself by working as a maid and laundress but continued singing in the choir at the Greater Salem Baptist Church. Jackson also studied beauty culture at C.J. Walker's and at the Scott Institute of Beauty Culture, eventually opening Mahalia's Beauty Salon. This was the first of several independent business ventures, which also included a florist shop and a chain of fried chicken restaurants. It did not take long for the choir director to recognize Jackson's talent, and she soon became the church's primary soloist. Together with the sons of the pastor of Greater Salem, Robert, Prince, and Wilbur Johnson, along with Louise Barry Lemon, Jackson formed the gospel quintet the Johnson Gospel Singers. At the time their style was very modern, with Prince Johnson playing a boogie-woogie piano patterned after Thomas A. Dorsey. The group supported itself by touring the local storefront churches and asking for donations at the end of its performances. By 1935 the group had broken up and its members were pursuing solo careers.

Jackson married Isaac Hackenhull in 1936. The marriage was strained from the beginning because Hackenhull, a graduate of Fisk and Tuskegee universities, wanted Jackson to take advantage of the financial opportunities available to jazz and blues singers. He convinced her to audition for *The Hot Mikado*, a jazz version of the Gilbert and Sullivan operetta. Although she got the lead by singing "Sometimes I Feel like a Motherless Child," she refused to participate in the show. Hackenhull did not understand Jackson's religious commitments, and Jackson did not approve of Hackenhull's gambling. These conflicts led to their divorce.

By the late 1930s Jackson had begun to garner some regional popularity. In 1937 she recorded her first 78 for Decca Records, which included "God's Gonna Separate the Wheat from the Tares," an adaptation of a New Orleans funeral song; the Baptist hymn "Keep Me Every Day"; and a modern gospel piece, "God Shall Wipe All the Tears Away." The record was a minor hit in the South and demonstrated Jackson's potential, but she did not record again until 1946. In the meantime she teamed up with Thomas A. Dorsey, the pianist, composer, and "father of Gospel Revival." Together they toured the country, Jackson's powerful contralto convincing congregations to purchase Dorsey's musical compositions. Jackson brought her enormous range of expression to Dorsey's gospel blues, providing the perfect medium for Dorsey's combination of Baptist hymns and gutbucket blues. As collaborators, they ushered in the era of modern African American gospel music.

A testament to the promotion of Jackson and Dorsey was her first recording for the Apollo label. The song, "Move On Up a Little Higher," sold more than 8 million copies. At once, Jackson's commercial viability and that of gospel music in general were established. From this point on she was the superstar of gospel music. Her talent and versatility were unequaled; her voice was comfortable and powerful whether singing a raucous blues growl or a sweet soulful ballad. Jackson recorded more than 30 albums in her career, including 12 million-selling singles.

By the early 1950s Jackson began to appeal to white fans with the help of Studs Terkel, who featured her music on his radio program. In 1951 she headlined a night of gospel stars that sold out New York's Carnegie Hall. She received the French Academy Award in 1953, prompting a European tour that established her as an international musical celebrity. She also appeared on the television shows of Dinah Shore and Ed Sullivan and hosted her own show on CBS from 1954 to 1955. At the 1958 Newport Jazz Festival, she received a standing ovation from the audience of jazz enthusiasts.

During the 1960s Jackson supported Martin Luther King Jr. and the CIVIL RIGHTS MOVEMENT by singing "We Shall Overcome" during her performances. She also preceded King at the March on Washington in 1963 with a rendition of "I've Been 'Buked and I've Been Scorned." At King's funeral in 1968 Mahalia sang his last request, the Dorsey standard "Precious Lord, Take My Hand." Politically, Jackson became close to Mayor Richard Daley of Chicago and the Kennedy family. She sang at John F. Kennedy's inauguration in 1961. After the assassinations of King and John and Robert Kennedy, Jackson no longer took part in politics. Her philanthropy continued and she established the Mahalia Jackson Scholarship Fund. She died of a heart attack in 1972.

SEE ALSO

Blues, The; Boogie Woogie; Chicago, Illinois; Dorsey, Thomas Andrew; Fisk University; Gospel Music; Hair and Beauty Culture; King, Martin Luther, Jr.; New Orleans, Louisiana; Oliver, Joseph ("King"); Tuskegee University; Walker, Sarah ("Madam C.J.").

North America

Jackson, Maynard Holbrook, Jr.

(b. March 23, 1938, Dallas, Tex.), three-time mayor of ATLANTA, GEORGIA, who helped bring the 1996 Olympic Games to the city.

By the time he was sworn in as Atlanta's mayor in 1974, Maynard H. Jackson Jr. had already captured the youthful energy of the capital of the New South, a city known for its relatively harmonious racial politics and pro-business attitude. At 34, Jackson, a Democrat, was not only Atlanta's first black mayor, he was also its youngest. But he was already a political veteran, having worked at Emory University's Community Legal Services Center on grassroots issues such as housing litigation and legal services for the poor, and he came from a family long prominent in Atlanta's history.

After serving the maximum of two consecutive terms allowed by Atlanta's city charter, Jackson stepped aside in 1982 for the new mayor, ANDREW YOUNG, the former ambassador to the United Nations, whom Jackson had recruited to succeed him. In 1990 Jackson was elected for a third term, during which he worked to bring the Olympic Games to Atlanta. Capitalizing on the city's upbeat image, strong corporate community, and international appeal – financial magazines consistently rate it among the best cities for business – Jackson won approval from the International Olympic Committee to host the Olympic Games in 1996. In addition, the city hosted the 1992 Democratic National Convention, attracting attention as a vibrant, successful, predominantly black city. In part because of health problems (he underwent cardiac bypass surgery in 1992), Jackson did not run for another term as mayor, stepping down in 1994.

Kate Tuttle

North America

Jackson, Michael, and the Jackson Family

superstar singer and his musical siblings, who together form the preeminent family of pop music in the 1970s, 1980s, and 1990s.

Joseph and Katherine Jackson, a working-class couple from Gary, Indiana, produced nine children, all of whom displayed considerable musical talent. Joseph encouraged his three eldest sons, Sigmund "Jackie" (b. May 4, 1951), Toriano "Tito" (b. October 15, 1953), and Jermaine (b. December 11, 1954) to practice the guitar and write songs. In the early 1960s the boys formed a trio that precocious youngsters Marlon (b. March 12, 1957) and Michael (b. August 29, 1958) joined, creating the Jackson Five. Although he was the youngest, Michael quickly became the focus of the act, deftly imitating the mannerisms of JAMES BROWN while singing with a sophistication and maturity that belied his young age.

The brothers won a talent contest in 1965 that led to a recording contract with the Indiana-based Steeltown Records. Then the Jackson Five toured regionally, opening for larger-name RHYTHM AND BLUES (R&B) groups. In 1967 the brothers took first place at an amateur night at Harlem's legendary APOLLO THEATER, and in 1969 they signed a recording contract with MOTOWN Records.

That year the Jackson family moved to Los Angeles, where Motown founder Berry Gordy carefully cultivated the image of the Jackson Five. Motown Records dressed the group in extravagant, hip outfits, choreographed their elaborate dance numbers, and provided them with musical material. The Jackson Five achieved success almost instantly, scoring number-one hit-singles with their first four releases: "I Want You Back" (1969), "ABC" (1970), "The Love You Save" (1970), and "I'll Be There" (1970).

In 1971, in response to MGM Records' solo recordings of 13-year-old Donny Osmond, Motown launched solo careers for Michael, Jermaine, and Jackie. Although Jermaine scored a Top Ten hit with "Daddy's Home" (1972), Michael was far and away the most successful of the three. His early solo hits include "Got to Be There" (1971) and "Rockin' Robin" (1972), as well as "Ben" (1972), an unlikely number-one soundtrack hit about a boy and his pet rat.

Meanwhile, the Jackson Five continued recording and performing as a group, and by the mid-1970s they had forsaken Motown's songwriters to produce and record hits of their own. They also covered classic pop and R&B songs from the 1950s and abandoned their earlier soul arrangements for the harder sounds of FUNK. In 1975, when their contract expired with Motown, four of the five brothers switched to Epic Records. Jermaine, who had married Berry Gordy's daughter, stayed with the old label to pursue a solo career. Steven "Randy" Jackson (b. October 29, 1962) replaced Jermaine, and the new group assumed a new name, the Jacksons. In 1976 and 1977 they starred in a self-titled CBS variety show, which introduced the Jackson girls Maureen "Rebbie" (b. May 29, 1950), LaToya (b. May 29, 1956), and Janet (b. May 16, 1966) to popular audiences. In 1978 the Jacksons released the album *Destiny*, which many fans and critics consider the best of the Jackson brothers' later work.

Michael's success as a solo performer continued with his appearance as the Scarecrow in *The Wiz* (1978), an African American remake of *The Wizard of Oz*. The movie led to his partnership with Quincy Jones, who composed the soundtrack, including Jackson's duet with DIANA ROSS, "Ease On Down the Road." Later that year Jones and Jackson collaborated on *Off the Wall* (1979), the solo album that established Michael as a sophisticated adult pop star. *Off the Wall* sold more than 7 million copies and included four Top Ten songs, including the number-one hits "Don't Stop 'til You Get Enough," and "Rock With You." Although Michael continued to perform with his brothers, this album signaled the beginning of a solo career that eclipsed the celebrity of the other Jackson children.

In 1982 Michael released another Jones-produced album, *Thriller*, which became the best-selling pop album of all time. *Thriller* incorporated the hoary oration of Vincent Price, the hard-rock licks of Eddie Van Halen, and the cooing of Paul McCartney, as well as the R&B, soul, and disco influences of Jackson himself. More than 40 million people bought the album, whose seven chart-topping singles included the number-one hits "The Girl Is Mine," "Billie Jean," and "Beat It." *Thriller* was a black landmark in the white-dominated market because Jackson's videos were the first by an African American to receive regularly scheduled rotation on MTV. The success of the album was bolstered by a well-planned marketing campaign that highlighted Jackson's dancing, fashion, musicianship, and commercial endorsement of Pepsi-Cola.

Although Jackson achieved this success as a solo performer, he continued to perform with his family throughout the 1980s. He also collaborated with Lionel Richie on the humanitarian hit "We Are the World" (1985), though he did not release a follow-up to *Thriller* until *Bad* (1987). Both *Bad* and Jackson's subsequent release, *Dangerous* (1991), sold well by standards of the industry, yet poorly in comparison to the global success of *Thriller*.

In the late 1980s and the 1990s Michael appeared to have increasing difficulty coping with celebrity, often withdrawing from the public eye. Numerous bouts of plastic surgery, allegations of pedophilia, and a secret marriage and publicized divorce with Lisa Marie Presley all exacerbated his public image as a troubled person. Despite high-visibility appearances on the *Oprah Winfrey Show* in 1993 (estimated 90 million viewers) and *Prime Time Live* in 1995 (estimated 60 million viewers), Jackson's career was considered in decline. His poorly selling 1995 album *HIStory–Past, Present and Future, Book I,* which anthologized old hits with new material, only seemed to underscore his waning popularity.

Michael's sister Janet achieved greater celebrity as Michael lost popularity. Although she had appeared in television programs in the 1970s and released her first solo album in 1982, Janet Jackson did not win considerable public attention until her quadruple-platinum album *Control* (1986). With *Janet Jackson's Rhythm Nation 1814* (1989), she topped the charts, won a Grammy, and sold more than 8 million records. She persevered as a major name in 1990s pop, scoring hit albums with *janet* (1993) and *The Velvet Rope* (1997).

None of the other Jacksons approached Michael's or Janet's level of success, although LaToya released solo albums in the early 1980s and appeared in *Playboy* magazine, and Jermaine recorded throughout the 1980s, working with Pia Zadora as well as with WHITNEY HOUSTON. Taken collectively, however, the Jackson family's career, spanning three decades, was the biggest pop-music phenomenon of the late twentieth century.

Eric Bennett

SEE ALSO

Soul Music; Jones, Quincy Delight, Jr.; Los Angeles, California.

North America

Jackson, Rebecca Cox

(b. February 15, 1795, Horntown, Pa.; d. May 24, 1871, Philadelphia, Pa.), African American preacher and spiritual visionary.

Rebecca Cox Jackson was born into a free family. Her mother, Jane Wisson (or Wilson), died in 1808. Nothing is known of her father. Later she began living with her elder brother, Joseph Cox, who was a tanner and preacher at Bethel African Methodist Episcopal (AME) Church in PHILADELPHIA, PENNSYLVANIA. She married a man named Samuel S. Jackson and cared for her brother's four children, remaining childless herself.

According to her spiritual autobiography, *Gifts of Power,* which was rediscovered and published in 1981, Jackson experienced in 1830 a religious awakening during a thunderstorm that changed her life. She soon became involved in the early Holiness Movement, an early form of PENTECOSTALISM that grew out of the Methodist Church. She began to hold prayer meetings with her friend Mary Peterson, attracting large crowds. This soon brought her into conflict with the AME Church, where some complained that she was a woman who was undermining the official authority of the church. Jackson was critical of the AME and denounced what she perceived to be its worldly "carnality." This judgment was based on a revelation that she claimed to have received that asserted that spiritual perfection demands celibacy.

Following her spiritual convictions, Jackson ultimately separated from her husband, her brother, and the AME Church. In *Gifts of Power* she details her prophetic visions, prayers, and spiritual healings. She describes, for example, receiving the gift of reading and writing instantaneously from God. In the late 1830s and early 1840s she began a career as an itinerant preacher, traveling throughout Pennsylvania, Delaware, New Jersey, New York, and southern New England. This travel led Jackson to the Shakers.

She first attended a prayer meeting with a Shaker community in Watervliet, New York. Shaker theology, which endorses celibacy, moral uprightness, and a dual-gender conception of deity, appealed to Jackson. After meeting with the Shakers, she recorded several visions in which the female face of God was revealed to her. She joined the Watervliet Society in June 1847 with her lifelong friend Rebecca Perot. She eventually became critical of the Shakers for being unwilling to spread their gospel to African Americans.

In 1851 Jackson and Perot left Watervliet to return to the black community of Philadelphia, where they practiced seance spiritualism. Never abandoning Shaker principles, they returned briefly in 1857 to the Watervliet community, where they soon acquired permission to found a primarily black, female Shaker "outfamily" in Philadelphia. Jackson spent the rest of her life with this community, which continued to prosper until it dissolved some 25 years after her death in 1871.

SEE ALSO

African Methodist Episcopal Church; Free Blacks in the United States, 1619 to 1863.

North America

Jackson, Reginald Martinez (Reggie)

(b. May 18, 1946, Wyncote, Pa.), African American baseball player, the sixth-leading home run hitter of all time (563) and the all-time career strikeout leader (2597).

Reggie Jackson (born Reginald Martinez Jackson) entered Arizona State University in 1964 and played football and baseball there before signing a baseball contract in 1966 with the Kansas City Athletics (known as the A's), who later moved to Oakland, California. Jackson joined the A's in 1967 after a brief period in the minor leagues. In 1969 he gained recognition as a power hitter when he had a career-high total of 47 home runs, with 118 runs batted in.

Jackson was traded to the Baltimore Orioles in 1976, then signed with the New York Yankees as a free agent the following season. He had his greatest success with the Yankees, leading the team to three East Division championships (1977, 1978, 1980), two American League pennants, and two World Series championships in 1977 and 1978. He hit four consecutive home runs in the fifth and sixth games of the 1977 World Series, each coming on a first pitch off four different Los Angeles Dodgers pitchers. That unprecedented performance under pressure earned Jackson the nickname "Mr. October." Jackson's brash public persona and dramatic performances on the field supported his claim that he was "the straw that stirs the drink." He retired after the 1987 season and was inducted into the Baseball Hall of Fame in 1993.

SEE ALSO

Baseball in the United States; Football, Collegiate; San Francisco and Oakland, California.

North America

Jackson, Shirley Ann

(b. August 6, 1946, Washington, D.C.), African American physicist; first African American chairperson of the United States Nuclear Regulatory Commission.

Shirley Jackson grew up in WASHINGTON, D.C., where her parents, Beatrice and George Jackson, encouraged her interest in science by helping her prepare science projects. After graduating first in her class at Roosevelt High School, Jackson was one of only 30 women to enter the Massachusetts Institute of Technology (M.I.T.) in 1964. She earned a B.S. degree in 1968 and a Ph.D. in 1973 from M.I.T., making her the first African American woman to earn a doctorate from that institution.

After graduating from M.I.T., Jackson joined the Fermi National Accelerator Laboratory in Batavia, Illinois, as a research associate (1973-1974, 1975-1976), and was a visiting scientist at the European Center for Nuclear Research in Geneva, Switzerland (1974-1975). From 1976 to 1991 she researched theoretical physics, solid state and quantum physics, and optical physics at AT&T Bell Laboratories. She became a professor in the Department of Physics at Rutgers University in 1991 while remaining a consultant in semiconductor theory at AT&T Bell Laboratories. She served as commissioner for the Nuclear Regulatory Commission before becoming its chair in 1995.

Jackson has received numerous awards and honors in both education and politics. She was elected a fellow of the American Physical Society, and she is a life member of the M.I.T. board of trustees. She advised the U.S. secretary of energy on the future of Department of Energy national laboratories, and she served on research councils for the

National Academy of Sciences and on the Advisory Council of the Institute of Nuclear Power Operations.

Robert Fay

North America

Jackson State Incident,

anti-Vietnam demonstration that turned into a race riot in which two black youths were killed.

On May 13, 1970, some 150 protesters gathered on the all-black campus of Jackson State College (now Jackson State University) in Mississippi to protest the VIETNAM WAR. The crowd was in an angry mood, their hostility fueled by the killing of four white students at Kent State University by National Guardsmen nine days earlier, and by the racially motivated murder, two days before, of six African Americans in Augusta, Georgia. While some of the young black demonstrators were content to chant slogans, others burned police barricades and threw rocks and bottles at passing white motorists. Local officials alerted the National Guard, which arrived in force on the campus when the demonstrations recurred the following day. Later that night, in the face of escalating violence, members of the Jackson police department and the Mississippi Highway Patrol fired into the crowd and killed 2 black students, wounding 12 others.

The Jackson State Incident took place at the height of the anti-Vietnam protest era, when violence and unrest gripped many American college campuses. The events at Jackson State reflected not only the national antiwar sentiment of college students but long-simmering racial conflicts. Jackson State students were protesting both President Nixon's plans to invade Cambodia and the racism of local police.

Throughout the 1960s the campus at Jackson State had seethed with tensions, not only between the students and the city's police, but also between the students and the school's own black administrators, who feared the possibility of losing state funding because of the campus turmoil. The problems were exacerbated by the frequent harassment of white motorists by neighborhood toughs, whom city police often mistook for Jackson State students.

After the shootings in 1970, local politicians and law enforcement agents tried to pass the blame off on the students, claiming that a sniper had caused the deaths. Survivors and family members of the victims took the issue to court, but no local police or National Guardsman was ever indicted.

Eric Bennett

North America

Jacobs, Harriet Ann

(b. 1813?, Edenton, N.C.; d. March 7, 1897, Washington, D.C.), African American writer known especially for her autobiography, which is the most significant African American slave narrative by a woman.

Harriet Jacobs states in the preface to her autobiography, *Incidents in the Life of a Slave Girl, Written by Herself,* published under the pseudonym Linda Brent in 1861, that she wanted her story to "arouse the women of the North to a realizing sense of the condition of millions of women at the South, still in bondage, suffering what I suffered." In this statement, which stresses her appeal to a female audience, Jacobs touches on one of her autobiography's most important features: Jacobs is the only African American woman slave to leave a long and detailed record of the particular ways in which slavery affected women, from sexual abuse to constraints on motherhood. For most of the twentieth century, however, scholars thought her narrative was a novel by a white author and ignored the book. It was not until the 1980s, when literary historian Jean Fagan Yellin used letters and manuscripts to prove that Jacobs had indeed written her autobiography "by herself," that readers rediscovered Jacobs as a key early African American writer.

Jacobs lived with her parents and younger brother until her mother's death, when Jacobs was six. She then was sent to live with her mother's owner, Margaret Horniblow, who treated her well and taught her to read and write. At her death, however, she willed Jacobs to her three-year-old niece, Mary Matilda Norcom, and at age 12 Jacobs was sent to live with the Norcom family. Her time with the Norcoms is a large part of her autobiography – especially the sexual harrassment she received from Dr. Norcom, the evil "Dr. Flint" in her narrative. Jacobs's narrative is very frank about Norcom's frequent sexual advances and threats, and makes explicit the particular hazards slave women faced, which are often only alluded to in men's slave narratives.

In 1829 and 1833 Jacobs gave birth to Joseph and Louisa Matilda, whose father was a white neighbor. This relationship only angered Norcom, and when he began to use her children, who were legally his property, as another means of controlling her, Jacobs decided to take a chance on running away. She hoped that if she was gone Norcom might sell her children to their father, and so in 1835 she ran away from the Norcom household.

Jacobs was first hidden in several Edenton homes by sympathetic black and white neighbors. But when it became apparent that it was going to be difficult for her to leave Edenton undetected, family members constructed a secret crawlspace in the house that belonged to her grandmother, who was free. The crawlspace was nine feet long, seven feet wide, and at its tallest, three feet high – but Jacobs hid in the tiny enclosure for the next seven years, a fact so harrowing that it may have been what led historians to suspect her autobiography was fictional.

In 1842 Jacobs was finally able to escape to New York. There she was reunited with her children, who had indeed been purchased by their father and sent to the North. In New York Jacobs worked as a nursemaid for a white family and became active in the antislavery movement. In 1850 her freedom was threatened when the Fugitive Slave Law stated that runaway slaves could and must be returned to their owners if apprehended in any part of the United States. The Norcom family sent agents to New York who attempted to kidnap her from her employers' home. Her employer finally secured her legal freedom by purchasing her from the Norcoms and emancipating her in 1853. That same year Jacobs began writing her autobiography, which she worked on at night after her child-care duties were done. The book was edited by white abolitionist Lydia Maria Child and received good reviews in the antislavery press when it was published in March 1861. But the outbreak of the Civil War one month later quickly stole readers' attention away.

During the war Jacobs and her daughter, Louisa, worked in the relief efforts for African American soldiers and newly freed slaves, first in Alexandria, Virginia, then in Savannah, Georgia. Increased violence and racial tension in the postwar South led them to Cambridge, Massachusetts, where Jacobs served as clerk of the New England Women's Club and ran a boarding house for Harvard University students and faculty. But by 1877, Jacobs and Louisa had returned to WASHINGTON, D.C., where Jacobs continued to work among the freed slaves while Louisa taught at several schools, including HOWARD UNIVERSITY. Jacobs lived with her daughter in Washington, D.C., until her death on March 7, 1897.

Since its rediscovery, Jacobs's autobiography has become required reading in English, history, African American studies, and women's studies courses around the country. In her narrative, Jacobs stated that she hoped to "add [her] testimony to that of abler pens to convince the people of the Free States what Slavery really is." The book she wrote is now recognized as one of the most valuable testimonies on what slavery really was, especially for the black women who endured it.

Lisa Clayton Robinson

SEE ALSO
Abolitionism in the United States; Boston, Massachusetts; Civil War, American; Fugitive Slave Laws; New York, New York; Slave Narratives.

Latin America and the Caribbean

Jagan, Cheddi (b. March 22, 1918, Port Mourant, British Guiana [present-day Guyana]; d. March 6, 1997, Washington, D.C.), author of five books and an advocate of socialism; a popular politician and a two-time prime minister (1961-1964 and 1992-1997) of the predominantly Indian country of Guyana.

Cheddi Jagan was born in 1918 on a sugar plantation in the English colony of British Guiana. The son of indentured servants from India, he became one of the most popular politicians in this predominantly working-class Indian nation. Although poor, Jagan's parents managed to send him to secondary school in the capital of Georgetown and from there to Howard University in Washington, D.C., where he enrolled as a premedical student. He supplemented his income by working part-time during the summers as an elevator operator and patent-medicine salesman in the Harlem area of New York City.

After graduating from Howard, Jagan attended the Northwestern University Dental School in Chicago, Illinois. While earning his degree Jagan met his wife, a white American nurse named Janet Rosenberg; they married in 1943. Together the couple began studying the principles of socialism, and when they returned to British Guiana a few years later, Jagan established a dental practice and organized labor groups in his spare time. His leadership potential surfaced almost immediately, and he was named head of the sugar, rice, and woodworkers' unions.

Jagan's career in politics began in 1947, when he was elected to the British Guiana Assembly. Three years later, disappointed with the colony's treatment of its predominantly Indian and black workers, Jagan and his wife formed the first modern political organization in the country, the People's Progressive Party (PPP). The PPP's support of socialist policies earned Jagan the label of "Communist threat" by the United States and Great Britain.

When a new constitution was passed in 1953, granting universal suffrage and increased home rule, Jagan became the minister of agriculture, lands, and mines, as well as leader of the House of Assembly. The socialist policies of the PPP captured the attention of outgoing British prime minister Winston Churchill, who believed that British Guiana was in the hands of Communist dictators. Churchill sent British warships and troops to depose Jagan and the PPP. Drawing inspiration from Mohandas Gandhi's defiance of British rule in India, Jagan and others responded by organizing similar civil disobedience campaigns. Jagan's activities led to his arrest and imprisonment for six months. Despite Churchill's attempts to weaken the PPP, it was victorious in the country's 1957 general elections, and Jagan and his wife were once again appointed to cabinet posts.

In 1961 the PPP captured a majority of the votes in the country's general elections, and as head of the PPP Jagan was named prime minister of British Guiana. Jagan's outspoken support of Cuba's communist leader, Fidel Castro, and his willingness to accept aid from the Soviet Union, threatened United States president John F. Kennedy. According to the *New York Times*, the Central Intelligence Agency (CIA) conducted a clandestine operation of wire taps, sabotage, and misinformation, all designed to bring down Jagan and his party. The efforts of the CIA are believed to have inspired the formation of two opposition parties, including one founded by black lawyer and former Jagan ally Forbes Burnham.

These subversive activities, combined with poor performance by Jagan and the PPP, led to their defeat in the general elections of 1964. Burnham replaced Jagan as prime minister and ushered in an era of authoritarianism and corruption. In the years immediately following Jagan's loss, the U.S. government encouraged Great Britain to delay granting the colony independence and urged it to alter the constitution to prevent Jagan from returning to power. But British Guiana achieved independence in 1966, becoming Guyana. Throughout Burnham's 21 years in office, Jagan spoke out against the government's corruption and called attention to the detrimental effect of its policies on the country's working-class Indian majority.

In 1985 Forbes Burnham died in office. In the general elections of 1992, Jagan defeated President Desmond Hoyte. Less ideologically driven, Jagan welcomed foreign investment and even began discussions with the United States to help mend the country's ailing economy. Jagan traveled the country and the world advocating economic reforms to benefit the poor and working class. He became an outspoken author, writing five books that are still popular today, including *The West on Trial: My Fight for Guyana's Freedom*. While in Washington, D.C., for heart surgery, Jagan died. He is survived by his wife, two children, and five grandchildren.

Alonford James Robinson, Jr.

See Also

Harlem, New York; New York, New York; Burnham, Linden Forbes Sampson.

Latin America and the Caribbean

Jamaica, the third largest island in the Caribbean, located in the Caribbean Sea between Cuba and the northern coast of South America; a predominantly black nation with cultural influences from Africa, Europe, Asia, and the Middle East.

Introduction

This Caribbean island of more than 2.5 million inhabitants is perhaps best known for its beautiful beaches and majestic views. Located a little more than 160 km (100 mi) from the United States, Jamaica is a popular tourist destination. It is known around the world for its music and culture, including reggae, dub poetry, and the Jamaican dialect of patois. Jamaica is a stable democratic nation with an emerging economy and a long history of social activism. Jamaicans are proud of their national heroes, men and women who have made significant contributions to freedom and democracy at home and abroad. They include social activists such as Marcus Garvey, Paul Bogle, George Gordon, and the slave leader Nanny; politicians such as Michael Manley and Alexander Bustamante; and artists such as reggae musician Bob Marley and authors Claude McKay and Una Marson.

The Standard History

Past accounts of Jamaica's history tend to emphasize the achievements of Europeans while minimizing, and even excluding, the accomplishments and influence of Jamaicans of African descent. There is ample evidence of the contributions to Jamaica's economic and political development by its indigenous or aboriginal population and, later, by its African slaves. But many history texts virtually ignore the early indigenous presence and begin recounting the island's history with the arrival of the European explorer Christopher Columbus in 1494. Yet Jamaica's indigenous inhabitants predated Columbus's arrival by at least 800 years. They lived in organized, hierarchically structured, polytheistic communities. Almost immediately the Spanish settlers set out to control the island through violence and eventually succeeded in eliminating the estimated 60,000 aboriginal inhabitants on the island.

By the early sixteenth century Jamaica became one of many islands in the Caribbean to be colonized by European nations. Spain, and later England, used its military might to dominate Jamaica's indigenous community as tobacco and sugar plantations spread across the island. When the pace of plantation production outstripped the supply of indigenous labor, Spanish settlers introduced African slaves into the colonial economy. By the mid-seventeenth century, slaves were the primary source of labor in colonial Jamaica.

Experts believe that over the course of the centuries-long transatlantic slave trade, more than 2 million African slaves passed through Jamaica on their way to destinations in North America, South America, and the rest of the Caribbean. Of the slaves who remained in Jamaica, most served as chattel labor on sugar plantations. Many risked their lives either to escape bondage or to organize others for rebellion. But past historical accounts often place a greater emphasis on the role of white abolitionists in the demise of slavery, neglecting the widespread and consistent slave insurrections on the island. By deemphasizing the prevalence of slave resistance, scholars risk devaluing the active role that Jamaicans of African ancestry played in the nation's political emergence. Scholars are beginning to acknowledge the accomplishments of Jamaicans of African descent, in addition to highlighting the African, as well as the indigenous, influence on the country's language, culture, and customs.

The Aboriginal Presence

The Taíno, often referred to as Arawak Indians, arrived in Jamaica from South America by canoe between 650 and 900 C.E. In journals, Christopher Columbus and his crew described the indigenous people in the Caribbean as uncivilized, primitive, and inept. Their society and leaders were portrayed as unsophisticated and disorganized, making colonization not only easy but necessary. However, contemporary scholars offer tangible evidence to refute these assertions. Recently discovered artifacts indicate that the Taíno in Jamaica lived in largely polytheistic communities. Experts also believe that their social structures left them vulnerable to more aggressive and more powerful groups, especially armed European explorers.

One of the most famous European explorers, Christopher Columbus, was informed in 1493 by the aborigines of Hispaniola (present-day Cuba) that the neighboring island of Yamaya (the Arawakan word for Jamaica) contained vast gold reserves. When Columbus landed at Saint Ann's Bay, Jamaica, on May 5, 1494 – his second voyage to the New World – his primary objective was acquiring gold. Although a small group of Taíno tried to defend their island, they were no match for Columbus and his military strength. After a brief offshore skirmish, most Taíno were forced to welcome the Europeans, providing them food, clothing, and shelter. Despite the language barrier, several Taíno even tried to help the Europeans find gold. But there was no gold in Jamaica, and Columbus left the island after about two months. Although he established a permanent settlement on the Caribbean island of Hispaniola, Columbus did not return to Jamaica for nine years.

On that occasion his storm-battered ships were unable to make it back to Spain from the American mainland, so they tried to sail to Hispaniola instead. But they began to take on water off the coast of Jamaica and found themselves stranded on the island in which they previously had little interest. Columbus turned to the Taíno for help. During their one-year stay the sailors bartered with the Taíno, exchanging European supplies for food, clothing, and canoes. Throughout that year Columbus and his crew endured starvation, illness, and mutiny. Despite these and other hardships the generosity of the Taíno kept most of the sailors alive, and on June 28, 1504, Columbus and more than 100 others were rescued by the Spanish. Two years later the Spanish would return to Jamaica to transform the island into a military and supply post for Spanish fleets in the Caribbean.

Spanish Conquest and Colonization

Spain's conquest and colonization of Jamaica began in 1506 when Juan de Esquivel was appointed governor of Jamaica. In *The Story of the Jamaican People*, authors Philip Sherlock and Hazel Bennett write that Esquivel's arrival "sounded the death knell for the Taínos." The Spanish settlers "hunted the native people mercilessly, enslaved those they caught and worked them to death on farms and in unproductive mines." In addition to indigenous slaves, many settlers brought their own African slaves with them, making slavery the island's leading source of labor by 1511.

Almost immediately the governor enacted policies designed to subjugate further Jamaica's indigenous population and its growing number of African slaves. For example, in 1511 the colonial policy known as *repartimiento* allowed all settlers to apply for the right to use any Taíno as a slave on their farms. Three years later another colonial policy, called *requerimiento*, instructed colonists to convert all aborigines to Christianity, a move that scholars today believe was designed to prevent resistance by teaching slaves obedience to the pope and to the Spanish Crown. They were thus unwavering in their attempts to dominate Jamaica's slaves. In a dramatic example, slave labor constructed the colony's first permanent settlement at New Seville, near present-day Saint Ann's Bay, including the governor's residence and more than 20 homes for settlers. Although slavery was not as extensively developed as it would be under the British, the Spanish settlers were deeply dependent on slave labor. By 1611, more than 100 years after the first Spanish settlement, colonial records indicate that there were 558 slaves in Jamaica, one for every colonist.

Although slavery emerged as an important institution in the growth of the colony, it was a relatively inefficient and small-scale enterprise under the Spanish. The number of slaves during nearly two centuries of Spanish occupation never exceeded 1000. Most slaves worked in groups of no more than five on small agricultural farms owned by settlers. These farms produced cassava, plantains, and cocoa, which were sold primarily to the crews of passing Spanish ships. But the arrival and departure of ships was so irregular that many of these items spoiled as they sat on Jamaican docks. Even though slaves were forced into the most physically demanding tasks, white settlers and white indentured servants often worked alongside their slaves, planting crops, tending to livestock, and tilling the soil. Nevertheless, slavery in Jamaica, as elsewhere, was characterized by harsh working conditions, high mortality rates, disruption of families, and severely oppressive living conditions.

The Earliest Free Blacks

The colonial records of 1611 show that there were 107 free blacks in the colony. It is not known for sure, but some of these free blacks may have arrived on passing European vessels. It is much more likely that most were runaway Taíno slaves who fled deep into the island's interior and formed independent communities that Spanish settlers called *palenques*. The palenques were the first in a long line of autonomous and self-governing communities comprised entirely of former slaves. Although details about these early free black communities are scarce, scholars believe that they existed in hard-to-reach areas in the Jamaican interior. Many of Jamaica's northern palenques were located near towns such as Nueva Sevilla (now New Seville) and Santa Gloria (Saint Ann's Bay). In the south they may have been scattered around towns such as Villa de la Vega (Spanish Town), Cayo de Carens (Port Royal), and Hato de Morante (Morant Bay). The presence of free blacks and their palenques was an early reminder to Spanish officials of the difficulty of recapturing runaways. Over the years colonial officials replaced runaways with European immigrants, most of whom were poor Jewish peasants willing to work the land.

Non-Europeans – both free and slave – comprised a large majority when the Spanish arrived in 1494, but by 1655 their numbers were reduced to less than 25 percent of the colony's total population of 6000. Many were killed during the initial Spanish invasion; others died from diseases introduced by European settlers; and some died from being overworked. Even the colony's white settlers faced tremendous challenges by 1655. Many were malnourished and unable to defend the island from frequent raids by pirates. There were less than 100 soldiers and only five cannons, not enough to sustain an armed defense.

British Conquest and Colonization

The year 1655 was pivotal in the colonial Caribbean. England, under the leadership of Gen. Oliver Cromwell, sought to extend its influence in the world by seizing the territorial possessions of its weaker European neighbors. Cromwell was aware of political and economic turmoil in Spain and chose to exploit Spain's weakness in April 1655 by attacking one of its most prized Caribbean possessions, the island of Hispaniola. However, the British were embarrassed when a small army of Spanish settlers on the island defeated the British Navy. Reeling from defeat, England turned its attention to the weaker and more vulnerable Spanish settlement on Jamaica. On May 10, 1655, an estimated 38 British warships arrived off the coast of Morant Bay. With the exception of a small army of a few hundred settlers led by the Spanish general Arnaldo Isasi, 8000 British soldiers encountered little resistance from the Spanish settlers as they seized the island.

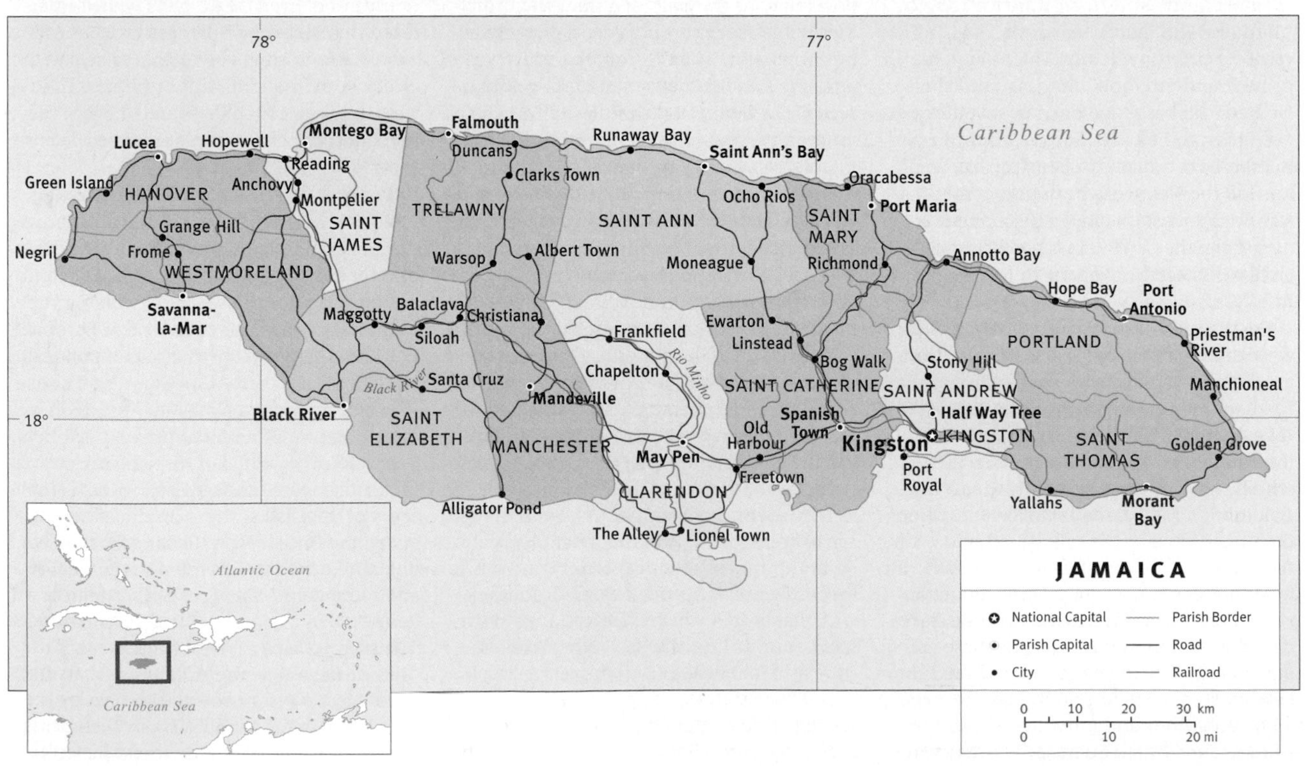
78°
77°
18°
Caribbean Sea
Lucea
Hopewell
Montego Bay
Falmouth
Duncans
Runaway Bay
Saint Ann's Bay
Oracabessa
Port Maria
Green Island
HANOVER
Reading
Anchovy
Montpelier
SAINT JAMES
Clarks Town
TRELAWNY
SAINT ANN
Ocho Rios
SAINT MARY
Grange Hill
Negril
Frome
WESTMORELAND
Warsop
Albert Town
Moneague
Richmond
Annotto Bay
Savanna-la-Mar
Maggotty
Balaclava
Christiana
Siloah
Frankfield
Ewarton
Linstead
Bog Walk
Hope Bay
Port Antonio
Priestman's River
PORTLAND
Black River
Santa Cruz
Chapelton
Rio Minho
Black River
Mandeville
SAINT CATHERINE
Stony Hill
SAINT ANDREW
Half Way Tree
Manchioneal
SAINT ELIZABETH
MANCHESTER
May Pen
Old Harbour
Spanish Town
Kingston
KINGSTON
SAINT THOMAS
Golden Grove
Port Royal
Freetown
CLARENDON
Alligator Pond
Yallahs
Morant Bay
The Alley
Lionel Town
Atlantic Ocean
Caribbean Sea
JAMAICA
National Capital
Parish Capital
City
Parish Border
Road
Railroad
0 10 20 30 km
0 10 20 mi

OPPOSITE: **The third-largest island in the Caribbean, Jamaica is a popular tourist destination, in part because of its natural beauty.** *CORBIS/Jan Butchofsky*

The Spanish tried to thwart the British victory by freeing all of the estimated 1500 slaves on the island. These *libertos,* as they are called in Spanish, fled into the mountains and joined the existing palenque communities. However, despite the Spanish actions, the former slaves' loyalties were divided. Only three major groups chose to form militias to support the Spaniards and Isasi. Located in the hills of Clarendon, Guanaboa Vale, and Rio Juana, these resistance fighters would later become the famous maroons of Jamaica. Among the libertos to emerge as leaders during this time were Juan de Bolas and Juan de Sierras. Juan de Bolas gained renown because he betrayed the Spanish by joining the British side. He was later murdered in revenge by libertos loyal to Isasi and the Spanish. But the British forces prevailed and Isasi and 68 others fled to Cuba in May 1660. Spain officially transferred Jamaica to Britain in 1670 under the Treaty of Madrid.

Britain moved quickly to transform Jamaica from a small-scale, cocoa producing economy dominated by small landholders to a sugar-producing plantation society fueled by large pools of slave labor. Gone were the days when whites worked next to black slaves on small farms. England sought to solidify white control further in 1662 by granting full British citizenship to Jamaica's white settlers. As citizens of the British Crown they were able to make their own laws and establish a political system that would exclude nonwhites for more than 200 years. Jamaica's new colonial government and officials back in London both benefited from the booming transatlantic slave trade. African slaves from the Gold Coast, the Bight of Benin, and the area that today is NIGERIA were sent to the Caribbean in exchange for sugar, rum, and molasses, which were in turn sent back to Europe for mass consumption. Experts believe that more than 10 million African slaves were bought and sold in the Americas. Jamaica became a major British port in the transatlantic slave trade, serving as a respite for vessels on their way to Barbados, South Carolina, Massachusetts, and New York. Nearly 2 million African slaves were transported through Jamaican ports alone.

In 1677 there were an estimated 9000 whites and 9000 black slaves in Jamaica. By 1739 there were 10,000 whites and nearly 100,000 black slaves. The slave trade changed Jamaican society, creating an identifiable social hierarchy complete with racial and occupational distinctions. A large proportion of European settlers in Jamaica during the mid-eighteenth century were common criminals and prisoners of war captured by Britain. Most were sent to Jamaica as indentured servants and relatively few were allowed to own land. In contrast, a small but powerful class of wealthy white landowners earned so much money from their Jamaican sugar plantations that they left the island to live lavishly at home in England. Slavery in Jamaica, therefore, was unique because of the high proportion of these so-called absentee owners. The plantation took center stage and wealthy white landowners relied on overseers, who were usually white lawyers or administrators, to run the estates.

Slavery and the Plantation Economy

Plantation life was extremely hard. Temperatures reached intolerably high levels, often leaving field hands dehydrated and emaciated. Heat stroke was a common cause of death. On most sugar plantations slaves were separated into three different work groups, or gangs. The "big gang" consisted of the strongest and healthiest adults. They cut, ground, and boiled the sugar cane, and once the harvest reached its end they were also forced to clear land and plant new cane. Young boys and girls were usually placed in the "second gang" alongside convalescents and pregnant women. They performed "lighter tasks" such as weeding cane. The third or "small gangs" were most often very young children who were supervised by an adult as they performed menial tasks, including gathering food for animals.

Although slaves shared a common physical experience, significant cultural and linguistic differences did exist among them. The largest proportion of slaves working on sugar plantations were Coromantees from the Gold Coast (Ghana) and Ibos from the Bight of Benin. In addition to the many languages and dialects spoken, slaves in Jamaica also worshiped different gods and practiced a wide array of social and religious customs. As time progressed, slave society was further complicated by a widening cultural and psychological gap between slaves who were born in Africa and then transported to Jamaica and slaves who were born on Jamaican soil (Creoles).

Gradually, those slaves who were born in Jamaica formed a Creole language that fused both African and English dialects. The contemporary Jamaican dialect of patois has linguistic roots in the Creole language of the slaves. In addition to language, slaves held on to a small set of religious beliefs and customs, including a form of worship known as Obeah. The practitioner of Obeah reportedly possessed magical powers and commanded enormous fear and respect on the plantation. Obeah was so entrenched in slave culture that British officials later outlawed it. But laws could not suppress Obeah worship, and it continued to be an influential part of the underground (secret) slave society.

Slave Resistance

Like religion, resistance to slavery played a central role in the underground slave society. Both public and hidden acts of resistance, such as foot dragging, arson, and running away, plagued the colony. Some scholars believe that organized resistance to slavery occurred more frequently and on a larger scale in Jamaica than anywhere else in the English-speaking Caribbean. What made slave resistance in Jamaica unique, they argue, is not simply the frequency of insurrection, but the sheer size of those insurrections. Slave rebellions in Jamaica involved not hundreds but thousands of slaves. A high slave-to-white ratio, a significant percentage of African-born slaves, absentee planters, and the work of black and white abolitionists all contributed to the frequency of resistance. In reaction, colonial officials imposed strict limitations on the activities and mobility of slaves. A series of laws called slave codes prescribed harsh punishments for disobedience. For example, runaways who were captured were publicly executed. Despite the best efforts of the colonists, thousands of slaves gained freedom by running away and hiding in the hills and mountains.

Maroons

The Spanish term for a runaway slave was *cimarrón,* and the term was reapplied to runaways during the period of British rule. The maroons, some of whom were the original *libertos* freed by the Spanish in 1655, caused substantial problems for colonial officials. Maroon militias, skilled in guerrilla warfare, proved to be a formidable military challenge for British soldiers. The maroons engaged the British in a protracted war that lasted nearly 50 years. During the war the maroon fighters were led by individuals such as CUDJOE, Accompong, Quao, and Nanny. The war ended in 1739 with a controversial treaty. In exchange for their freedom, the maroons promised to end all aggression against European settlers, harbor no more runaways, and help defeat future slave insurrections. The agreement led to the formation of several legendary maroon communities, including Trelawny Town, Nanny Town, and Clarendon. It also created divisions between maroons and slaves that widened whenever the maroons helped to put down a slave rebellion.

Free Blacks, Free Coloreds, and Religion

The maroons occupy a prominent place in Jamaica's history, but freedom was not limited to maroon communities. A small and politically powerless free black and free colored (a term used in Jamaica referring to people of partial African descent) community existed in the decades immediately preceding emancipation (1834). The secrecy of colonial society in the mid-nineteenth century makes it difficult to estimate the number of free blacks and coloreds in Jamaica. Colonial officials did not like to advertise to others the statistics on the number of free blacks and free coloreds in their society. Restricted to small towns at the edge of mainstream Jamaican society, free blacks and free coloreds united with white British abolitionists to teach slaves to read and write. They also converted thousands of slaves to Christianity. The Moravian, Baptist, and Methodist denominations were among the most popular with slaves. Moravian and Baptist missionaries established churches for slaves throughout Jamaica in the eighteenth and nineteenth centuries.

Religion became an ideological and a political threat to the institution of slavery. The teachings of white missionaries contradicted many of the tenets of slavery, including the notion that blacks were inferior to whites. As the presence of white missionaries grew – especially those who were also active abolitionists – they became a visible threat to Jamaica's slaveholding elite. Many were brutally attacked by white mobs, and others were forcibly expelled from the colony. The anti-abolitionist sentiment forced slaves to worship in secrecy. But despite the repressive tactics of white slaveholders, religion continued to serve as a catalyst for resistance.

The most visible manifestation of the influence of Christian missionization was the formation of independent black churches, especially the popular Native Baptist congregations. The ministers of these congregations were usually free blacks or coloreds. Many were trained by white Baptist missionaries and used the pulpit and their influence in the community to encourage dissent. Native Baptists became a central force in several organized resistance campaigns, including a number of slave rebellions.

The church was one of the few places where free blacks and coloreds could organize socially and politically. Black churches provided a "safe" space for both informal and formal discussions, including organized campaigns to enfranchise Jamaica's black majority. By 1830 a small free black and colored population occupied a middle level in Jamaican society. They served as a buffer between slaves and European settlers and were often subject to a unique set of constraints and challenges. Most free blacks and coloreds were barred from living on plantations, where they could encourage slaves to rebel. But they were not welcome in town. Most were forced to live on the outskirts of major towns such as Kingston and Montego Bay. Many of the most lucrative jobs in the city were reserved for whites, and free blacks and coloreds were relegated to positions as servants, porters, and shop hands. In many respects they were excluded from white society just like slaves. They were not allowed to serve in the all-white colonial legislature, were prohibited from testifying against whites, and were barred from sitting on juries. Free blacks and coloreds were even required to register themselves with local magistrates. In 1831 the Jamaican legislature allowed free blacks to vote, but they restricted the electoral franchise to those who owned property worth more than 100 British pounds. The restrictions, coupled with economic discrimination in major cities, eliminated most free blacks and coloreds from participating in the island's political affairs.

Emancipation and Apprenticeship

By 1831 Jamaica's white minority had dominated the colony's political, economic, and social affairs for more than 150 years. But the domestic crusade for freedom that had long existed in Jamaica began to find support from an international movement to abolish slavery. A drop in the world demand for sugar lowered prices and forced several sugar plantations into bankruptcy. British and American abolitionists continued to exert pressure on their governments, and religious leaders in England chastised the country for its participation in slavery. The biggest blow to slavery came one year later when more than 20,000 Jamaican slaves organized by Samuel Sharpe united to overthrow slavery. The insurrection, known as the Baptist War or Christmas Rebellion, was so large and violent that it sent shock waves throughout the world. The British government feared a massive revolution like the one in Haiti 30 years earlier. All of these pressures moved the British Parliament to abolish slavery on August 29, 1833. Up to 800,000 slaves were freed in British territories throughout the world – 311,000 in Jamaica alone (*see* Abolition and Emancipation in Latin America and the Caribbean).

Blacks and coloreds were no longer slaves, but neither were they full citizens. While white slave owners in Jamaica were compensated with more than 6 million pounds from the British government, blacks were forced to remain as "apprenticed laborers" on fledgling plantations. Apprenticeship was designed to soften the economic impact of emancipation on white planters throughout the British Caribbean. Fieldworkers were required to work for their former masters for six years, and those who did not work in the fields worked for four years. They were required to devote 40 hours per week of labor to white landowners in exchange for food, clothing, shelter, and a modest plot of land. But they were not compensated in cash. The remaining hours of the week were "free," and many blacks were allowed to cultivate their gardens and sell produce to other blacks in local markets.

In practice, the apprenticeship period was not remarkably different from slavery, and it evoked criticism from abolitionists in Britain. The policy proved to be inefficient and unprofitable and was ended in 1838. But after apprenticeship ended, blacks and coloreds faced new economic and political challenges. The average weekly working wage of a black plantation worker was a mere three shillings. In addition, blacks and coloreds were forced by white landowners to pay rent, sometimes up to one-third of their weekly pay. Those who could not afford the rents were evicted, and many of them were forced to settle in squatter camps outside urban centers such as Kingston. The predominantly white Jamaican legislature added to these difficulties by passing laws restricting the amount of land sold to blacks. Blacks were systematically excluded from purchasing land suitable for agricultural farming. The legislature also chose to restrict educational opportunities for blacks. Most blacks could not afford the tuition for Jamaica's primary and secondary schools and rarely advanced beyond the primary level. Money and other resources were routinely channeled to white schools and colleges, including the prestigious Jamaica College.

With the help of white missionaries, some blacks managed to purchase property at reasonable prices. Several large plots of lands were purchased by Moravian and Baptist missionaries and resold to local black congregations. The earliest and most famous of these so-called free villages was established in June 1838 in Sligoville, near Spanish Town. Some of the other leading free villages included Retreat Pen, and the Standfast, Birmingham, and Kettering estates. There were more than 2000 free villages by 1848, and by 1865 nearly 60,000 blacks owned more than 10 acres each. But property requirements still prevented most blacks from participating in the legislative affairs of the island. Fewer than 20,000 blacks met the requirements by 1865, and only 3000 of them were registered to vote.

European Immigration

Emancipation also set into motion demographic changes that altered Jamaica's social and political landscape. Although an estimated 90 percent of Jamaica's black workers were still working on plantations in the years immediately preceding emancipation, slavery no longer provided the steady stream of labor that the plantation economy demanded. Labor shortages in rural areas threatened the livelihood of white landowners. The influx of blacks to urban areas in search of employment also posed a threat to those wealthy whites who lived in town. The solution for the colony's white minority was to recruit nonblack workers from overseas.

Between 1834 and 1845 more than 4000 European indentured servants immigrated to Jamaica. Many of these new workers were from Germany, Scotland, Ireland, and England. They were employed as farmers and artisans on coffee and sugar plantations and in cattle pens. These new immigrants moved into cities occupied by a small but historic community of Jewish merchants. Jews immigrated to Jamaica as indentured servants in the sixteenth century and became leading traders in the colony. Up to 10,000 African indentured servants were also recruited between 1841 and 1867. But this was stopped after critics complained that it came too close to trafficking in slaves.

The largest group of indentured servants came from India. More than 20,000 Indians immigrated to Jamaica between 1845 and the end of World War I, when the program was terminated. Life for Indian indentured servants was quite different than it was for their European counterparts. They were housed in overcrowded, unsanitary conditions on plantations. Their length of servitude was expanded over time from one year to two years, and in some cases to as long as five years. Most came from northern India but others originated in Uttar Pradesh, the Central Provinces, Punjab, Bihar, and the North West Frontiers. They were concentrated on plantations in the parishes of Westmoreland, Saint Thomas, Saint Mary, Portland, and Clarendon and earned very low wages.

Racism made life difficult for most Indians. The Jamaican legislature passed laws prohibiting non-Christian marriages and outlawing non-Christian religions. Indians were not allowed to move into predominantly white areas, particularly in Kingston, where the white elite maintained close cultural distinctions between the city's various ethnic communities. Competition for unskilled jobs also caused increased tensions between blacks and Indians. Black workers often disparagingly called Indians "coolies," while Indians referred to blacks as "kafari," or infidels.

Chinese indentured servants faced similar challenges. Between 1854 and 1930, 6000 Chinese workers immigrated to Jamaica from China, Hong Kong, Panama, and the United States. Hundreds of Chinese workers died on Jamaican plantations from disease, malnutrition, and exhaustion. Like their black and Indian counterparts, Chinese indentured servants worked long hours in unsanitary conditions for meager wages. Although the number of Chinese immigrants remained relatively small throughout the nineteenth and twentieth centuries, the Jamaican legislature imposed quotas on Chinese workers. On January 7, 1931, colonial officials refused to accept Chinese immigrants who were above age 14. The growing wave of immigrants placed strains on the economy and increased competition for jobs. As blacks, coloreds, Indians, Chinese, and Arabs competed for limited opportunities, they developed their own prejudices. These prejudices increased as the plantation economy collapsed.

A Jamaican mother takes her family to church. *CORBIS/Daniel Lainé*

Economic Hardships

In 1846 the British Parliament equalized tariffs on sugar, thereby eliminating a lucrative source of income for colonial sugar producers. They eventually voted to eliminate all protective sugar duties, opening the sugar industry to competition. Sugar, rum, and coffee exports no longer enjoyed protection from the British government, and this had a devastating effect on the Jamaican economy. Many plantations were abandoned, leaving black and colored workers unemployed. Adding to the crisis was a series of droughts and earthquakes and a cholera epidemic that claimed 32,000 lives in 1850. Whites attempted to recoup their losses by squeezing black and colored workers. White landowners increased rents and imposed taxes on clothing, food, and basic necessities such as livestock and farming equipment. In addition, the 1840 Franchise Act was amended to include an inheritance tax that made it almost impossible for nonwhites to accumulate wealth. The Franchise Act excluded well-to-do blacks and coloreds from qualifying to vote because it raised the income requirement beyond their reach. Two years later the Master and Servants Act gave white employers the power to reduce wages and fire workers as they saw fit, without fear of punishment. In 1851 the legislature even tried unsuccessfully to pass a clause requiring literacy in order to vote.

Jamaica's black majority was strongly affected by these economic and political changes but had few institutional avenues for responding. There were few colored or black representatives in the legislature. There were even fewer registered black and colored voters. Among the exceptions was the colored politician George Gordon, an elected member of the legislature since 1840. He and black activist Paul Bogle stood at the forefront of the political consciousness that emerged in black communities throughout Jamaica during the last decades of the nineteenth century. Property restrictions on black voters, high property taxes, a virtually nonexistent educational system for nonwhites, and widespread racism all contributed to the Morant Bay Rebellion, a massive black protest orchestrated by Paul Bogle in 1865. The rebellion began as a protest by blacks in Morant Bay who were demanding economic and political reforms. A public demonstration on the city streets erupted into a violent confrontation with police. The fighting spanned one week and ended in a brutal military crackdown. Nearly 1000 black homes were burned to the ground and more than

600 protesters were flogged. Another 500 protesters were executed, including Bogle and Gordon, who are now national heroes in Jamaica.

The Morant Bay Rebellion marked a new chapter in the struggle for civil rights in Jamaica. The British Parliament sent a committee to Jamaica to investigate the actions of colonial officials. They found officials guilty of using excessive force and placed the administration of the island under the control of the British Crown. In response to the committee's report, Jamaica was designated a Crown colony in 1866 – a policy that stripped most of the formal political power from the hands of the colony's white elite. Subsequent reforms sought to incorporate nonwhites slowly into the political process. Jamaica's 22 parishes were reduced to 14, the judicial system was reformed, and the educational system was completely overhauled. Loans were provided to black and colored children to attend predominantly white grammar and secondary schools. (Free and compulsory primary education did not come until the 1970s.) Economic reforms also followed the Morant Bay Rebellion. By 1870 the Crown committed itself to rebuilding the colony's irrigation systems, leading to a reinvigoration of sugar production and the emergence of the banana industry, currently one of Jamaica's leading exports.

Economic and political reforms alleviated some of the pressures on blacks and coloreds but did not stop thousands from migrating to the United States, Panama, and other places in the Caribbean. Between 1888 and 1920 an estimated 146,000 Jamaicans left the country in search of better opportunities. The Great Depression, which began in 1929, contributed to the hardship, leading to the collapse of the Jamaican sugar and banana industries. Because of the resulting flow of migrants from Jamaica and other parts of the developing world, the advanced industrial nations placed strict quotas on immigration. This hampered the ability of Jamaicans to find employment overseas, forcing them to look at home.

Throughout the 1930s the country experienced a massive migration to urban areas such as Kingston and Saint Andrew. Many of these formerly rural agricultural workers settled in squatter camps and ghettos. Experts believe that nearly one-fifth of the entire rural population – 200,000 people – migrated to cities. Urbanization soon produced two Jamaican societies, divided by class, color, and culture. The tensions and prejudices within Jamaica's nonwhite majority increased as the country's white elite held on to power. It was during this period that several black activists emerged to lead another phase of the Jamaican civil rights movement.

Dr. Robert Love had been an early activist. Throughout the last decades of the nineteenth century Dr. Love, a long-time Jamaican resident who was born in the BAHAMAS, organized voter registration campaigns and encouraged blacks to become active in politics.

The civil rights movement progressed slowly until black activist Marcus Garvey returned to Jamaica in 1927 after being deported by the United States government for mail fraud. Garvey's UNIVERSAL NEGRO IMPROVEMENT ASSOCIATION (UNIA) and his Black Star shipping enterprise had made him one of the most influential blacks in the world, and his return to his native Jamaica was hailed as a triumph. While in Jamaica, Garvey encouraged the island's mostly poor and black working class to challenge the racist political and economic systems that had exploited them for so long. Garvey moved to England in 1935, but before he left Jamaica, he founded a workers' association and one of the country's first political parties. Garvey's race pride also inspired the formation of other black organizations devoted to racial consciousness, including the RASTAFARIANS, who in 1935 initiated a cultural and religious movement known as Rastafarianism.

In 1934 colored activist Alexander Bustamante joined the civil rights movement when he formed the Jamaican Workers' and Tradesmen's Union (JWTU). The union demanded higher wages and better working conditions by conducting marches and strikes. Laborers played an important part in the civil rights movement, broadening the coalition and giving the movement credibility among the country's mostly black working class. It also signaled the beginning of a trend toward associating workers' rights with Black Nationalism. It became increasingly difficult to separate demands for economic equality with those for racial equality.

The effort to secure better working conditions and higher wages made national headlines on May 1, 1938, when striking sugar workers at a factory in Frome (in Westmoreland parish) were attacked by the police. The ensuing riot engulfed Frome and spread to Kingston. Bustamante and another colored activist, Michael Manley, worked with colonial officials and rioters to restore calm. After weeks of violence the turmoil ended with 8 dead, 171 injured, and nearly 400 imprisoned for rioting. In the process, Bustamante and Manley emerged as the undisputed leaders of the Jamaican labor movement. But in the year following the riots they became bitter political rivals.

In 1938 Manley formed the People's National Party (PNP) and Bustamante established the Bustamante Industrial Trade Union (BITU). Bustamante was originally a member of the PNP but left in 1943 to form his own political party, the Jamaican Labor Party (JLP), which represented BITU members. The PNP initially emerged as a political party for the colored middle class but soon shed its aristocratic image and adopted socialist principles. In contrast, the JLP represented the interests of unskilled union members and was considered the voice of the working class. Although the ideological differences between the two political parties were limited, they soon became fierce competitors.

The size and political strength of organized labor grew so rapidly that Bustamante and Manley were considered two of the most powerful men in Jamaica in 1943. Their popularity with most of Jamaica's working class forced Britain to reconsider its historical presence in Jamaica and contributed to the British government's decision to construct a new constitution for Jamaica. The constitution, adopted on November 20, 1944, stripped Jamaica of its Crown colony status and implemented limited self-rule. Its political institutions were divided between two legislative chambers: a House of Representatives and a Legislative Council. The new constitution granted full suffrage to all adults and called for free and open elections. The country's first general elections took place on December 14, 1944. Bustamante and the JLP won most of the seats in the election, including 25 of the 32 in the House of Representatives. Manley transformed the PNP into a formidable opposition party.

ABOVE: Valentine "Willy" Best, a Jamaican Jonkonnu dancer, portrays the character known as Wild Indian. Wearing a feathered headdress, wire screen mask, and heart-shaped shield, he plays a rattling drum in performances of Jonkonnu, a traditional Jamaican festival art that combines music and dance as well as African and European influences. *J. Bettelheim*
OPPOSITE: Rastafarian bands like this one represent far more than the reggae music well known to many non-Jamaicans. Rastafarianism blends religious, political, and social philosophies to express opposition to the historic degradation of Africans in the Caribbean and worldwide. *CORBIS/Daniel Lainé*

INDEPENDENCE

The period between 1944 and independence in 1962 has been called the period of "constitutional decolonization." Partially in reaction to similar anticolonial sentiment in other Anglophone colonies, Britain gradually removed itself from the administration of Jamaica's internal affairs and passed several constitutional reforms that granted more local political control to native Jamaicans. In 1955 Manley and his PNP defeated Bustamante and his JLP in a general election. Three years later, on January 3, 1958, Jamaica joined the nine-member Federation of the West Indies. Britain had long insisted that it would only grant independence to a unified West Indies (or Caribbean) state and not to individual nations. But confusion and disputes over Jamaica's role in the federation led to its withdrawal from the group years later.

Jamaica moved quietly toward independence. The two-party system illustrated a democratic impulse that would carry the nation toward political freedom. On August 6, 1962, Jamaica became an independent nation but remained part of the Commonwealth of Nations. In the elections that year the JLP returned to power and Alexander Bustamante was elected the country's first prime minister. He retired five years later and passed power to Hugh Shearer. Over the next 13 years the JLP battled the PNP for political control. When Michael Manley was elected prime minister in 1972, he steered Jamaica down the path of socialism. Manley angered the United States government by embracing Fidel Castro, and he angered his political rivals by discouraging foreign investment. Although Manley's programs improved conditions for the poor and working class, his socialist policies also weakened the Jamaican economy and contributed to his defeat in the bitter elections of 1980. Manley was reelected prime minister in 1989 but retired because of poor health in 1992. Percival J. Patterson, former deputy prime minister and finance minister of the PNP, replaced Manley as head of the party. Patterson led the PNP to a landslide victory in the 1993 general elections.

THE PRESENT ERA

Even though many tourists know Jamaica only as a popular vacation spot, the island's history presents a compelling story of the triumph of freedom and independence. Jamaica's history, like most former European colonies, has progressed through various stages that include slavery, independence, and civil strife. However, what makes Jamaica's history so remarkable, especially in comparison to its colonial counterparts, is the consistent involvement of hundreds of thousands of slaves and former slaves – African and Creole – in the nation's relentless trajectory toward a democratic, black-ruled nation.

Only by providing a more balanced depiction of history can scholars present an accurate and fair commentary on some of the most pressing issues in the contemporary era. For example, the crime and street gangs that plague many of Jamaica's inner cities are often incorrectly attributed by some to the ignorance and apathy of its urban residents. However, a full understanding of the history of racial discrimination, persistent unemployment, and ethnic tension that have been present in Jamaica's largest cities, such as Kingston and Montego Bay, provides students of history with a wider view of the present landscape.

Poverty, homelessness, and crime are among the most immediate problems in need of attention. Jamaica's economy is still dependent on foreign consumers, and tourism is now one of its leading industries. In order to keep attracting foreign tourists, Jamaica has been forced to build lavish resorts suitable to American and European tastes. In the process, the concerns of many of the country's poorest residents have been ignored. It is a dilemma that many former Caribbean colonies now face, and it requires unique solutions. But as the past has shown, Jamaicans will continue to work together to solve many of the country's most demanding problems. As the country's national motto reminds us: "There is unity in diversity: out of many, one people."

Alonford James Robinson, Jr.

See Also

Ethnicity and Identity in Africa: An Interpretation; Maroonage in the Americas; Slavery in Latin America and the Caribbean; Garvey, Marcus Mosiah; Apprenticeship in the British Caribbean; Free Village System; Kingston, Jamaica; Marson, Una M.; Mooretown, Jamaica (Nanny Town); East Indian Communities in the Caribbean; Religions, African, in Latin America and the Caribbean; Languages, Creole, in the Caribbean; Protestant Church in Latin America and the Caribbean; Slave Rebellions in Latin America and the Caribbean; Slave Laws in Colonial Spanish America; Bustamante, Sir Alexander; Black Nationalism in the United States.

Latin America and the Caribbean

James, Cyril Lionel Richard

(b. January 4, 1901, Tunapuna, Trinidad; d. May 31, 1989, London, England), writer, historian, Marxist social critic, and activist who deeply influenced the intellectual underpinnings of West Indian and African movements for independence.

Cyril Lionel Richard James was born into an educated family in colonial Trinidad. At age nine he earned a scholarship to Queen's Royal College, in Port of Spain, Trinidad. He graduated in 1918 and taught English and history at the Queen's Royal College. Later he taught at the Government Training College for Teachers. During this time he met Alfred Mendes, who, with James, led an informal group of young intellectuals. James began writing and developing his political and literary ideas with this group, and in 1927 his short story "La Divina Pastora" was published by the British *Saturday Review of Literature*, a significant achievement for both James and Caribbean literature. "La Divina Pastora," in which a cocoa worker pleads with her patron saint for help with her romantic life, was notable for its clear portrayal of the rural poor.

James and Mendes founded and coedited a short-lived (1929-1930) literary magazine called *Trinidad*, which, with its successor magazine *Beacon*, became the foundation of Caribbean short fiction. "Triumph," James's next major story, appeared in *Trinidad* and was more controversial than "La Divina Pastora." In this story an exuberant, independent woman living in an urban slum, or barrack-yard, successfully plays her suitors off one another. Although James did not invent the barrack-yard stories, "Triumph" helped popularize them; today they are a fixture of Trinidadian literature and typically portray the violence and misery of barrack-yard life.

In 1932 James left Trinidad for England. A skilled cricket player, he became a writer about the sport for the *Manchester Guardian*, critiquing not just the sport but the social influences surrounding it. Much later he would publish *Beyond a Boundary* (1963), an autobiography, history of cricket, and dissection of the West Indies. During his stay in England, James became involved in socialist politics, gravitating toward a faction of anti-Stalinist Marxists. He applied Leon Trotsky's views about a worldwide workers' revolution to his colonial home. The result, in part, was *The Life of Captain Cipriani: An Account of British Government in the West Indies* (1932), in which he called for Caribbean independence.

Although hopeful about independence, James was troubled by and preoccupied with the rift between the comparative handful of educated blacks of the West Indies and the mass of ill-educated, lower-class citizens. In his first novel, *Minty Alley* (written 1927, published 1936), he developed these ideas by placing the middle-class narrator in dire financial straits. The narrator moves into a barrack-yard and gains a fuller understanding of lower-class life than he previously had. Critics praised James for giving less attention to the parts of lower-class life that strike middle-class readers as exotic or idiosyncratic, instead focusing on the aspects that express a commonality with middle- and upper-class life.

Following Italy's invasion of Ethiopia in the mid-1930s, James edited a journal of African opinion and headed an international group that advocated for Ethiopia. With political thinker George Padmore, he helped develop the theory of Pan-Africanism, his chief contributions being the play *Toussaint L'Ouverture* (1936), later called *The Black Jacobins*, and the history *The Black Jacobins: Toussaint L'Ouverture and the San Domingo Revolution* (1938). Both the play and the history deal harshly with the aftermath of the Haitian Revolution (1791-1804). White masters, James contends, have been replaced by black masters; freedom and equality are little regarded. As literature, the play has been criticized for using the leading historical figures as little more than megaphones for monologues rather than people with actions. African American actor Paul Robeson played Toussaint L'Ouverture in the 1936 production in London.

By 1938 James was well known, and he traveled to the United States on a speaking tour sponsored by a Trotskyist group. Although he later broke from the group, he stayed in America and in 1940 joined the newly created Worker's Party. James traveled among black sharecroppers and other black workers, lecturing and organizing throughout the 1940s. During this time he developed many of the views he would expand throughout his life, including the idea that because the world's nonwhite peoples vastly outnumbered the whites, they would eventually overcome their colonial subjugation. Furthermore, James believed that because many Africans and descendants of Africans were organized along communitarian lines, they would be ideally equipped for creating a new social order. James also hoped that blacks in the United States would help unite the Pan-African movement.

In 1952, with the anticommunist McCarthy era in full stride, the United States government placed James in detention at Ellis Island, New York. While the government mulled his radical views and decided his fate, he wrote *Mariners, Renegades, and Castaways: The Story of Herman Melville and the World We Live In* (1953). Although the main thrust of the work was a critique of Melville's *Moby Dick*, James used Melville's novel as a vehicle for sharp commentary on dictatorship and American democracy.

Expelled from the United States in 1953, James returned to Trinidad, where he joined the People's National Movement, a pro-independence group, and edited the *Nation*, the party's newspaper. This association did not last long. When in 1962 he fell into disfavor with the transitional West Indies Federation, he left Trinidad for England. He continued to write and lecture throughout Europe and, after he was allowed to return to the United States in 1968, in North America as well. For a time in the 1970s he taught at Federal City College in Washington, D.C. He lived the last years of his life in London. Three volumes of his collected works appeared as *The Future in the Present* (1977), *Spheres of Existence* (1980), and *At the Rendezvous of Victory* (1984).

See Also

Literature, English Language, Caribbean; Trinidad and Tobago.

North America

James, Daniel ("Chappie"), Jr.

(b. February 11, 1920, Pensacola, Fla.; d. February 25, 1978, Colorado Springs, Colo.), first African American four-star general.

Daniel James attended Tuskegee Institute, where he joined the segregated United States Army Air Corp. He served in World War II and in 1943 was commissioned a second lieutenant. He served again in Korea, leading a fighter plane squadron and devising tactics to support ground troops. During the Korean War he flew more than 100 combat missions and received the Distinguished Service Medal.

In 1957 James graduated from the Air Command and Staff College in Alabama. Nine years later, during the Vietnam War, he was promoted to deputy commander for operations of the Eighth Tactical Fighter Wing in Thailand. Speaking in favor of the war and encouraging blacks to serve made him a national figure. He was often criticized for not directly supporting the Civil Rights Movement, choosing instead to be an example of an individual overcoming barriers through persistence and service.

James became commander of the Wheelus Air Force Base in Libya in 1969. He achieved the rank of brigadier general in 1970, lieutenant general in 1973, and four-star general in 1975. In that capacity he commanded the North American Air Defense system during a critical time in the cold war. A heart condition forced his retirement in February 1978. He died later that month of a heart attack. During his military career, he was awarded the Legion of Merit, the Distinguished Flying Cross, and a Presidential Unit Citation.

See Also

World War II and African Americans; Military, Blacks in the American; Korean War; Tuskegee University.

North America

James, Etta (Jamesetta Hawkins)

(b. January 5, 1938, Los Angeles, Calif.), African American soul and rhythm and blues (R&B) singer.

Raised in California, Etta James – Jamesetta Hawkins at birth – began her singing career early. At age 5, she was the star of her church choir; by 14 she was singing professionally with a rhythm and blues band. In 1954 James recorded her first song, "Roll with Me Henry," a joking response to Hank Ballard and the Midnighters' ribald hit "Work with Me Annie." "Henry" was itself sexually suggestive enough to be banned by radio disc jockeys.

Throughout the late 1950s James recorded for Modern Records, producing the 1955 hit "Good Rockin' Daddy" and a series of less successful songs. In 1960 she signed with Chess Records, where she blossomed into a fully formed talent. Songs like "All I Could Do Was Cry" (1960) showed how her passionate, powerful voice could caress a ballad. Lighter, more pop-oriented numbers like "Pushover" (1963) also became hits.

James's drug addiction caused her to quit and resume recording periodically in the 1960s and 1970s, but she produced some of her best work during her healthy intervals in these decades. In 1967 she scored another series of hits, recorded at the legendary Muscle Shoals studio, which included "Tell Mama" and a remake of Otis Redding's "Security." After beating her heroin addiction in the mid-1970s, James returned to the music scene, recording and touring steadily. In 1993 she was elected to the Rock and Roll Hall of Fame.

Kate Tuttle

See Also

Soul Music; Los Angeles, California.

Latin America and the Caribbean

James, Norberto

(b. February 6, 1945, San Pedro de Macorís, Dominican Republic), Afro-Dominican writer; author of four collections of poetry, including *Sobre la marcha* (1969), *La provincia sublevada* (1972), *Vivir* (1982), and *Hago constar* (1983), none of which has been translated into English. He also wrote *Denuncia y complicidad* (1997), a book of literary criticism on two Dominican novels of the 1940s.

Norberto James was born on a sugar plantation into a community of English-speaking Afro-Caribbeans. As a youth his artistic talents led him to attend high school in the capital, Santo Domingo. There he studied music and painting, improved his Spanish, and met other artists. In 1963 a United States military intervention in the Dominican Republic overthrew then-president Juan Bosch, a novelist turned politician, in part because he attempted to renew diplomatic relations with Cuba. These circumstances both interrupted James's studies and prompted him to get involved in leftist politics. The event also convinced him to become a poet.

James cites Pablo Neruda and César Vallejo, two of the most important contemporary poets in all of Latin America, as major influences on his work. One of the principal themes of James's writing is a concern for political justice and collective well-being. Many of his poems reflect on personal experiences and on social conditions. Perhaps his best-known work is the 1969 poem "Los immigrantes," which invites the descendants of Anglophone West Indian immigrants to embrace a Dominican national identity.

James received a bachelor's degree from the University of Havana in 1978. He later enrolled in Boston University, where he earned a master's degree in 1985 and a doctorate in 1992, both in the field of Latin American literature. He is currently an educator and a writer residing in Wellesley, Massachusetts.

Marveta Ryan

See Also

Literature, Black, in Spanish America.

Africa

Jameson, Sir Leander Starr,

British administrator of the lands comprising present-day Zimbabwe in the late nineteenth century (*see* Rhodes, Cecil).

North America

Jamison, Judith

(b. May 10, 1944, Philadelphia, Pa.), African American dancer and choreographer; her work typically honors black women and African American cultural heritage.

Born on May 10, 1944, in Philadelphia, Pennsylvania, Judith Jamison started dancing at age 6 at the Judimar School of Dance. At 17, she left to study psychology at Fisk University in Nashville, Tennessee. After three semesters, she returned to Philadelphia to continue her dance training at the Philadelphia Dance Company (now the University of Arts).

After a 1964 appearance with Agnes de Mille's dance troupe in New York, Jamison joined the Alvin Ailey American Dance Theatre (AAADT) in 1965. Because of this company's financial difficulties, she danced in the Harkness Ballet's 1966 season. But in 1967 she returned to AAADT to become its premier dancer, and she toured the world dancing in roles such as *Cry* (1971), her signature dance, which Ailey choreographed to honor the strength and dignity of African American women. For her performances she won a *Dance Magazine* award in 1972.

Jamison left AAADT to perform with Gregory Hines in the 1980 Broadway musical *Sophisticated Ladies*. With encouragement from Ailey, she also began to choreograph her own pieces honoring her African heritage, such as *Divining* (1984) and *Ancestral Rites* (1989). These works, as well as others, including *Hymn* (1993), were performed by AAADT and the Jamison Project, the 12-member company she established in 1987.

Because of Ailey's failing health, Jamison returned to AAADT as artistic associate in 1988. When he died in 1989, she accepted the position of artistic director of his company. She has continued the company's performance of early works choreographed by African Americans.

Leyla Keough

See Also

New York, New York.

Africa

Jammeh, Yahya (b. 1965, Kanilai, the Gambia), president of the Gambia since 1994.

Yahya Jammeh was raised in a Jola Muslim community in the western Gambia. In 1984, a year after graduating from high school, he enlisted in the Gambian army, where he gradually rose through the ranks to become lieutenant. In 1994, after leading the coup that ousted President Sir Dawda Jawara, Jammeh promoted himself to captain and made himself head of state. He led a group of Gambian soldiers who had recently served in West African peacekeeping efforts in Liberia under the auspices of the Economic Community of West African States (ECOWAS) and who had not received their back pay. In July 1994, after installing a five-member Armed Forces Provisional Ruling Council, Jammeh declared himself chairman, suspended the constitution, and banned all political activity. He immediately announced his intention to return the Gambia to civilian rule "as soon as we have set things right." The young president created five civilian commissions of inquiry to investigate corruption charges and recover stolen government funds, detained and questioned many prominent businessmen and government officials (most of whom were later released), and installed a joint civilian-military government.

Despite its declarations supporting freedom of expression, the Jammeh regime has been criticized by international human rights groups for harassing and imprisoning journalists and for detaining dissidents for lengthy periods without trial (*see* Human Rights in Africa). On the other hand, Jammeh has support among some Gambians for his campaign to suppress a growing sex industry associated with European tourism and to restore a sense of pride and modesty among Gambian women. He has banned, for example, the importation of all skin lighteners and hair straighteners, products frequently used by Gambian prostitutes. Having survived two attempted coups, in November 1994 and again in January 1995, Jammeh gave in to pressure from Western donor nations and announced in early 1996 that the Gambia would hold open elections in October of that year. They were held on schedule, and Jammeh was elected president of the republic with more than 55 percent of the vote.

Robert Baum

See Also

Gambia, The; Jawara, Sir Dawda Kairaba; Tourism in Africa; Economic Community of West African States.

Latin America and the Caribbean

Janvier, Louis Joseph (b. May 7, 1855, Port-au-Prince, Haiti; d. 1919, Paris), Haitian politician and writer whose numerous political works defended the rights of blacks and the sovereignty of his homeland.

Highly educated, Louis Joseph Janvier obtained degrees in medicine and law and attended several prestigious academic institutions, including the Sorbonne, the Collège de France, and the Ecole des Sciences Politiques. While in Paris, he frequented the salon of the poet Leconte de Lisle, where he met famous French poets, including Coppée, Mallarmé, and Heredia.

During those years he wrote many articles that would eventually be published in several books. In *Les antinationaux* (1884, The Antinationalists), he vigorously defended the presidency of Lysius Félicité Salomon against the attacks of liberals. In *Haïti aux haïtiens* (1884, Haiti for Haitians), he lambasted Haiti's economic and political dependence on France and favored Protestantism as a means to achieve material progress. He defended mass public education and the protection of peasants in *Les affaires d'Haïti* and *Les constitutions d'Haïti* (1886, Haiti's Business, Haiti's Constitution).

Although he was a fierce patriot, Janvier lived outside Haiti for 28 years, from 1877 to 1905, after which he was appointed to diplomatic missions in Switzerland and England. In 1908 he made an unsuccessful bid for mayor of Port-au-Prince. After his defeat, he left again for London and Paris as an emissary of his country. He established his last residence in France, where he remained one of Haiti's most influential activist-writers until his death in 1919.

Martine Fernández

See Also

Salomon, Lysius Félicité; Literature, French Language, in Caribbean; Education in Latin America and the Caribbean.

Africa

Jarbah, Tunisia (also known as Djerba), an island off the southeast coast of Tunisia.

Legend has it that the island of Jarbah was the land of the lotus-eaters portrayed in Homer's *Odyssey* – a land where the sailors ate enchanted fruit and forgot everything but the beauty around them. Historians believe that the Jewish community on the island dates back to 500 B.C.E. Archaeological evidence shows that Carthaginians occupied this flat, fertile island in the Mediterranean Sea. Romans followed and named it Meninx. In 655 C.E. Arabs conquered the island, which they loosely ruled as part of the province of Ifriqiyya (present-day Tunisia and eastern Algeria).

The island became a center for the Kharijites, an Islamic sect popular among the many Berber inhabitants. By the eleventh century the Hafsid Dynasty ruled Jarbah from Tunis. The island's strategic location in the Mediterranean made it desirable to many different states. In 1284 the Spanish Aragones captured Jarbah; for the next four centuries control of Jarbah would pass between Hafsid, Spanish, and Sicilian-Norman rule. As the Hafsid Empire waned in the sixteenth century, the struggle for control of the island revived between the Islamic and Christian forces. First the Muslim corsair Darghut took the island, but then the Spanish staged a brutal conquest in 1560, seizing the Mediterranean prize.

Only a few years later the Ottoman Empire took possession of Jarbah, initiating a rule that would last more than 300 years. Some 300 mosques still remain on the island; the Ottomans constructed most of them during this time. Residents on the island cultivated the olive and date orchards for which the island became famous. By the nineteenth century these agricultural pursuits had replaced corsair activity as the focus of the island's economy, supplemented by a fishing and artisan industry. When the French claimed Tunisia as a protectorate in 1881, they also took Jarbah. Since Tunisian independence in 1960, Jarbah has been a major tourist attraction, and the government of Tunisia has built large hotels and an international airport to cater to the European visitors who flock to the beaches. The ancient Jewish community on the island has maintained a continuous presence through centuries of different rule, and Jarbah is home to a sizable Jewish population.

Marian Aguiar

See Also

Jewish Communities in North Africa; Tourism in Africa; Tunis, Tunisia; Carthage.

Africa

Jawara, Sir Dawda Kairaba (b. 1924, Barajally, the Gambia), first prime minister (1965-1970) and first president (1970-1994) of the Gambia.

Dawda Kairaba Jawara was born in Barajally, a small Mandinka community on the Upper Gambia River. The son of a Muslim merchant-farmer, he attended an elementary school in Bathurst that combined Islamic and Western education. After a brief stint working at the Royal Victoria Hospital in Bathurst, he attended Achimota College in the Gold Coast (present-day Ghana) and later studied veterinary surgery at the University of Glasgow. In 1954 he returned home and began work as a government veterinarian. The following year he became a Christian, took the name David, and married Augusta Mahoney, the daughter of a prominent Sierra Leonean in Bathurst. They had five children before divorcing in 1967.

Appointed the colony's principal veterinary officer in 1957, Jawara resigned two years later to enter politics. In 1959 he became one of the founders of the People's Progressive Party. The following year he was elected to the Gambian House of Representatives and in 1962 became minister of education and chief minister, succeeding his rival, Pierre S. N'Jie. His accession to the chief executive office marked the rise of the interior districts of the protectorate, dominated by Mandinka and Fula Muslims, and the decline of the urban, multiethnic groups of the coastal areas, which had dominated Gambian political life throughout the colonial period.

After Gambia's independence in 1965, Jawara was chosen prime minister; he also returned to his Islamic faith and to his Muslim name, Dawda. The following year he was knighted by Queen Elizabeth II. When the Gambia became a republic in 1970, Jawara was elected as president, and went on to be reelected in 1977 and 1982. In 1981, however, a coup attempt while he was out of the country – undertaken by members of the left-wing Movement for Justice in Africa – required the intervention of the Senegalese army. Shortly thereafter Jawara decided, despite little Gambian support, to join the Gambia with Senegal in 1982 in a loose confederation, of which he became vice president. ABDOU DIOUF, the president of Senegal, became president of the Senegambian confederation. Jawara retained political authority in the Gambia throughout the period of confederation and returned to the presidency after its dissolution, in 1989. In 1992 he won reelection to his fifth presidential term. Two years later, young officers of the Gambian military, led by YAHYA JAMMEH, overthrew Jawara's government and took control of the country. He lives in exile in the United Kingdom.

Robert Baum

SEE ALSO

Fulani; Senegal; Islam and Tradition: An Interpretation.

North America

Jazz, a twentieth-century African American music characterized by improvisation, a rhythmic conception termed *swing*, and the high value placed on each musician achieving a uniquely identifiable sound. Jazz musicians have consistently challenged musical boundaries and played leading roles in challenging racial discrimination.

Jazz is one of the crowning achievements of African American culture. It is a profoundly integrative genre, both musically and socially. Drawing on earlier traditions of New Orleans marching bands and RAGTIME-influenced society orchestras, jazz has continued to incorporate new musical influences, including the blues, GOSPEL MUSIC, Latin American music, European art music, and rock 'n' roll. African Americans have accounted for every significant musical advance in jazz, but the music has been open to all, regardless of race or nationality. During the first half of the twentieth century – a time of pervasive racial discrimination in the United States – jazz was strikingly democratic. Although far from perfect, the jazz world was remarkably successful in challenging racial segregation.

Jazz also reflects a continuing tension between individual freedom and group structure, as seen in the shifting emphasis between the spontaneously improvising soloist, on the one hand, and composed and arranged ensemble music, on the other. Successive jazz styles – including New Orleans, swing, bop, cool, hard bop, free jazz, jazz-rock, and neotraditionalism – have, to a considerable extent, reflected an increase in musical complexity, both in the playing of individual soloists and in the work of composers and arrangers. Jazz historians often liken the twentieth-century evolution of jazz to the changes that took place in European classical music – from eighteenth-century Bach inventions to Schönberg's 12-tone music of the twentieth century.

Although the historical development of jazz is often seen as a straightforward evolutionary process, it was complex and was powerfully influenced by the unique contributions of major innovators. A small number of creative and charismatic individuals were responsible for profound transformations in the music, most notably Louis Armstrong, Duke Ellington, Charlie Parker, Dizzy Gillespie, Miles Davis, John Coltrane, and WYNTON MARSALIS. The rapid dissemination of their new musical ideas suggests that, to a large extent, jazz musicians share a common artistic conception.

Over the course of the century jazz remained a dynamic tradition that profoundly influenced America and the world. Three characteristics have distinguished jazz throughout its history: (1) improvisation; (2) a distinctive rhythmic approach known as swing; and (3) an expectation that each jazz musician should attain a unique, individual sound through his or her distinctive improvisational approach to harmony, melody, and rhythm, and often through intentional variations or distortions of tone and timbre. The instrumental colorings and complex harmonies of jazz are evident in popular music and film scores heard by millions of people. Perhaps even more than AFRICAN AMERICAN LITERATURE or popular music – including the recent and pervasive genre of RAP – jazz has changed the cultural inflections of a great portion of the world.

NEW ORLEANS AND THE ORIGINS OF JAZZ

Jazz emerged in New Orleans around the turn of the twentieth century. New Orleans is distinctive among American cities for its French and Spanish colonial origins. As jazz historian James Lincoln Collier noted, it was "the most musical American city." Until the mid-1850s African-derived drum playing and dancing took place regularly in New Orleans's Congo Square. The city's population was diverse, combining French, Spanish, Caribbean, Anglo-American, Irish, German, and African elements.

Among African Americans the most significant division was between the poorer blacks and the more privileged, mixed-race CREOLES. Creoles lived downtown, in the French Quarter; blacks lived uptown, beyond Canal Street. Creole children generally received formal training in music. Creole musicians such as trumpeter Oscar "Papa" Celestin (1884-1954), clarinetist and soprano saxophonist Sidney Bechet, and saxophonist Barney Bigard (1906-1980) were able to read music and were expected to take part in well-established Creole musical traditions, including society dance bands for elegant Quadroon Balls. Black musicians – like cornetists Buddy Bolden, Joseph "King" Oliver, and Louis Armstrong – were less well schooled and emphasized playing by ear rather than reading music.

One primary catalyst for jazz was the growing contact among black and Creole musicians around the turn of the twentieth century, as JIM CROW segregation reduced the distinctions between blacks and Creoles. But jazz, which was commonly played in black honky-tonks and the bawdy houses, remained an outlaw music for relatively prosperous and upright Creoles. When Sidney Bechet cast his lot with jazz, he crossed a social as well as a musical divide.

THE MUSICAL ROOTS OF JAZZ

Jazz evolved from earlier forms of music, including minstrel show bands – such as the band led by African American cornetist and composer W.C. Handy – and ensembles on Mississippi River steamboats, like the one headed by African American pianist Fate Marable (1890-1947). Black and Creole marching bands – such as the Excelsior Brass Band, the Olympia Brass Band, and the Algiers Brass Band – were another source of jazz. In addition, many pianists played in the honky-tonks and brothels of Storyville, New Orleans's red-light district. Creole pianist Jelly Roll Morton recounted, "New Orleans was the stomping ground for all the greatest pianists in the country. We had Spanish, we had colored, we had white, we had Frenchmans, we had Americans, we had them from all parts of the world."

The blues, which has come to be closely connected with jazz, had little impact on jazz in its early years. At that time the blues was primarily a rural music. Jazz emerged in New Orleans and other urban areas. Blues musicians were mainly self-taught and self-accompanied performers. Some black jazz musicians, such as Buddy Bolden or King Oliver, were familiar with the idiom, but

ABOVE: Jazz is a recurrent theme in the work of artist Romare Bearden (1912-1988), as is evidenced in his 1987 collage *Opening at the Savoy*. *© Romare Bearden Foundation/Licensed by VAGA, New York, NY*
RIGHT: King Oliver's innovative Creole Jazz Band, *left to right*, Honore Dutrey, Baby Dodds, King Oliver, Louis Armstrong, Lil Hardin, Bill Johnson, and Johnny Dodds, plays in Chicago in 1923. *Archive Photos/Frank Driggs Collection*

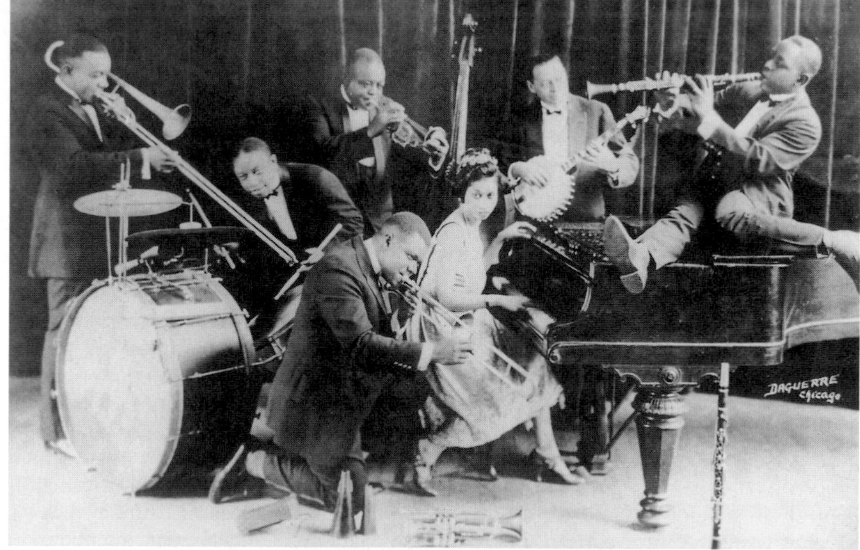

generally speaking the blues was seen as separate from jazz. "What's called jazz today," bassist Pops Foster (1892-1969) recounted, "was called ragtime back then.... From about 1900 on, there were three types of bands around New Orleans. You had bands that played ragtime, ones that played sweet music, and the ones that played nothin' but blues."

Ragtime, the main precursor to jazz, derived its name from its syncopated, or "ragged," time. Although now usually thought of as piano music, it was also performed by vocal ensembles and by instrumental groups. Until about 1920 the terms *ragtime* and *jazz* were used more or less interchangeably. Cornetist Buddy Bolden is said to have been the first musician to "rag the blues" for dancing around the turn of the century, thus creating jazz. Jelly Roll Morton, however, claimed to have invented both ragtime and, in 1902, jazz. In truth, no single musician created jazz; it was a collective effort of various black and Creole musicians.

The Role of Improvisation in Jazz

What separated jazz from ragtime was its emphasis on improvisation. Such ragtime composers as Scott Joplin saw ragtime as written music that should be played as it was written. Jazz was more freewheeling. Such jazz musicians as cornetist King Oliver made use of "freak" effects through the use of mutes, changes in embouchure, and unusual fingerings. As the influence of the blues gradually increased, New Orleans musicians adopted the blue notes and vocalized the instrumental sound of the blues. Almost from the start, however, jazz solos were more than just aural effects and ornamentation; they involved the creation of new melodic ideas.

Early jazz was characterized by collective, not individual, improvisation. Each instrument in the ensemble had a specific responsibility. The cornetist played mid-range variations on the melody. The clarinetist performed more intricate ornamentation in a higher register. The trombonist filled in punchy, rhythmic lines in a lower register, often punctuated by long descending slurs or smears created by rapidly extending the trombone's slide while playing, which gave rise to the term *tailgate trombone*. The drummer, pianist, and perhaps a banjo player or a tuba or bass player supplied the rhythmic underpinnings. New Orleans jazz maximized individual latitude, but, in the absence of extended individual solos, it also subsumed the individual within the group.

The two greatest exemplars of the New Orleans style were Oliver's Creole Jazz Band and Morton's Red Hot Peppers. The Creole Jazz Band made a series of classic recordings in 1923. The group included Oliver and his young protégé Louis Armstrong on cornets, clarinetist Johnny Dodds (1892-1940), trombonist Honore Dutrey (d. 1935), pianist Lil Hardin Armstrong, Warren "Baby" Dodds (1898-1959) on drums, and bassist Bill Johnson (1872-1972). The Red Hot Peppers recorded during the years 1926 to 1928 and featured Morton on piano and a shifting personnel that included such New Orleans musicians as trumpeter George Mitchell (d. 1942), clarinetist Omer Simeon (1902-1959), and trombonist Kid Ory. Morton's recordings reveal a deft balancing of textural variety and structural cohesiveness that earned him recognition as the first great composer in jazz.

The Transformation and Dissemination of Jazz

During the first quarter of the twentieth century, jazz moved out of New Orleans and reached much of the United States and Europe. Many prominent jazz musicians left New Orleans during the first two decades of the twentieth century and played a key role in disseminating jazz. In 1904 Jelly Roll Morton became an itinerant performer, playing with minstrel shows and vaudeville troupes in St. Louis and New York City as well as throughout the South. From 1911 to 1915 he lived in Chicago, where he performed with a small ensemble.

In 1918 King Oliver and clarinetist and soprano saxophonist Sidney Bechet left New Orleans for Chicago. Bechet traveled on to New York City, and in the following year he journeyed to Europe with an orchestra led by African American composer Will Marion Cook (1869-1944). In 1919 Kid Ory moved to California and in 1925 to Chicago. In 1922 Louis Armstrong left New Orleans for Chicago, where he joined Oliver's Creole Jazz Band. In 1924-1925 he moved to New York City, where he was featured in bandleader Fletcher Henderson's big band.

That New Orleans jazz musicians moved to Northern cities in these years is hardly surprising. In the 1890s and early 1900s Jim Crow segregation had tightened throughout the South. The first two decades of the twentieth century had witnessed the beginnings of the Great Migration, a vast movement of African Americans who left the South for greater opportunities in the urban North and West. Although jazz musicians were part of this larger movement, their wide-ranging travels reflect the popularity of jazz among blacks and whites in the United States and a growing audience abroad.

By the 1920s jazz bands and jazz-flavored dance bands were appearing in many cities. The 1912 recordings of New York City bandleader James Reese Europe (1881-1919) capture a bouncy, ragtime-influenced precursor to jazz. By 1919, several years before he moved to New York, Duke Ellington established a reputation in Washington, D.C., as a pianist and a leader of pickup bands that played at various dances and social functions. In 1922 he relocated to New York City and two years later took over a six-man band that became the nucleus of the Duke Ellington Orchestra. In 1923 Fletcher Henderson organized his first big band in New York City and a year later convinced Armstrong to join the group.

Two New Orleans musicians, Armstrong and Bechet, were central in transforming jazz from its focus on the collectively improvising ensemble to the individual soloist. Armstrong's and Bechet's lyrical extended solos established a new ideal for jazz and inspired countless musicians. Virtually every jazz trumpeter of the 1920s and 1930s was indebted to Armstrong. Bechet's influence, though less evident, was clear in the performances of clarinetist and tenor saxophonist Barney Bigard and alto saxophonist Johnny Hodges, who filled key roles in the 1930s Ellington Orchestra.

During the 1920s Armstrong and blues singer Bessie Smith established a tradition of jazz singing. During the 1930s Smith and Armstrong would be the two strongest influences on Billie Holiday, the greatest jazz singer of the swing era. In addition, Armstrong and bandleader Cab Calloway helped to popularize what came to be known as scat singing, in which the vocalist improvised by stringing together nonsense syllables.

Radio, Recordings, and the Spread of Jazz

In the early 1920s Chicago superseded New Orleans as a center of jazz. Many prominent jazz musicians found work in Chicago's speakeasies, where a thirsty public enjoyed alcoholic beverages, made illegal by Prohibition, courtesy of such gangsters as Dutch Schultz and Al Capone. Black jazz musicians – and the white New Orleans Rhythm Kings – inspired a number of young white Midwesterners, including cornet player Bix Beiderbecke, clarinetist Benny Goodman, and banjo player Eddie Condon, to try their hand at the music. Between 1925 and 1928 some of the decade's most important jazz ensembles recorded in Chicago, including Morton's Red Hot Peppers and Armstrong's brilliant Hot Fives and Hot Sevens.

By the late 1920s New York City had surpassed Chicago in its ability to attract America's best jazz musicians. While he was in New York City in 1924-1925, Armstrong had a major impact on Fletcher Henderson and his sidemen, including future tenor saxophone great Coleman Hawkins. Armstrong's virtuoso playing and his relaxed rhythmic feeling – the epitome of what came to be called swing – prepared the way for a new era in jazz. Fletcher Henderson applied Armstrong's innovations to the big band, which featured 12 to 15 members and helped lay the foundations for the swing era.

The center of jazz activity had shifted in part owing to New York City's emergence as the center of the nation's recording industry. The first true jazz recording was made in New York City on February 26, 1917, by a group of white New Orleans musicians who called themselves the Original Dixieland Jazz Band. Because of the discriminatory racial policies of recording studios, black jazz musicians did not record until several years later. Indeed, black musicians far from New Orleans often discovered jazz through the recordings of white jazz bands. In 1921 or 1922 Kid Ory's band became the first black jazz group to record. The first integrated recording session took place in 1923 in Richmond, Indiana, when Gennett Records brought the New Orleans Rhythm Kings together with pianist Jelly Roll Morton. In the late 1920s New York City emerged as the center of the American recording industry as well as the nation's jazz capital.

The dissemination of jazz also reflected the impact of radio broadcasting. By the mid-1920s radio broadcasts carried "live" jazz music hundreds of miles from the urban centers where it was played. Duke Ellington gained nationwide recognition after securing a long-term gig at New York City's prestigious Cotton Club in 1927, because the nightclub was wired to permit remote radio broadcasts.

The Emergence of Duke Ellington and the Ellington Orchestra

Duke Ellington's role in jazz history is, to use one of his favorite phrases, "beyond category." For almost half a century, from the 1920s to the 1970s, Ellington was the most significant composer and bandleader in jazz. At first his potential was less clear, but during a 1927-1931 stint at the Cotton Club, he evolved from a derivative pianist and pedestrian arranger into the preeminent composer in jazz. Ellington was initially inspired by Bubber Miley, a trumpet player who composed or co-composed some of the band's greatest early works, including "East St. Louis Toodle-oo" (1926) and "Black and Tan Fantasy" (1927).

At the Cotton Club, Ellington's creative abilities expanded steadily. He began to employ adventurous harmonies and voicings and experimented with radical changes in tempo and meter. He quickly recognized the importance of Hollywood in reaching a wider audience. The Ellington Orchestra appeared in such motion pictures as the Amos 'n' Andy film *Check and Double Check* (1930) and the all-black *Cabin in the Sky*

(1943). Ellington also challenged the creative limitations imposed by the three-minute 78 rpm recording and the notion that jazz was merely dance music. Ellington's most significant compositions were not his individual songs, but such ambitious suites as *Reminiscing in Tempo* (1935), the nine-minute film *Symphony in Black* (1935), and *Black, Brown, and Beige* (1943).

Swing

One Ellington song, "It Don't Mean a Thing If It Ain't Got That Swing" (1932), helped usher in the swing era, but Ellington's band was not a typical swing band. Swing is a difficult concept to define, in part because it has two distinct meanings. The more general meaning is a rhythmic feeling distinctive to jazz, a quality of rhythmic freedom found in most, if not all, jazz playing. Swing also refers to the popular jazz style of the 1930s that emphasized an even, four-beat rhythm and was often played by big bands of 12 or more members. The 1930s and early 1940s are often termed the *swing era.* Big-band swing arrangers commonly juxtaposed the various sections – trumpets, trombones, and saxophones – and employed riffs or short melodic phrases in call-and-response patterns to build climaxes and heighten rhythmic tension. Big-band music emphasized the ensemble over the individual soloist and was often reduced to cliché, which led a number of younger musicians to rebel against its stylistic limitations.

In a larger sense, swing is a subtle rhythmic feeling, the pulse that underlies almost all jazz playing. Swing involves a loosening of jazz rhythms from the constraints of the metronome. By means of accenting, attacking, and articulating notes, and through the use of silence, jazz musicians create the subtly displaced rhythms that characterize jazz. But swing varies by era and idiom. Early jazz musicians played rhythms that were looser or freer than those of ragtime but that retained a strong two-beat feel. The playing of an early jazz musician such as King Oliver would seem stiff and awkward to jazz musicians of the late twentieth century: younger musicians would not share Oliver's conception of swing.

Similarly, if Miles Davis or John Coltrane were transported back to play with the Creole Jazz Band, Oliver and his sidemen would regard their playing as distinctly unswinging. Many swing-era musicians complained that bop, the experimental jazz of the 1940s, did not swing. Most jazz musicians rate jazz that does not swing as poor jazz. Yet some very important jazz, including the experimental free jazz of pianist Cecil Taylor (b. 1929) and saxophonist Anthony Braxton (b. 1945), does not swing in any recognizable sense.

ABOVE: Willie "the Lion" Smith performs at a Friday Club jam session at the Park Lane Hotel in New York in 1939. *Charles Peterson/Archive Photos*
RIGHT: One of the greatest jazz vocalists of any era, Sarah Vaughn sings at a club in Los Angeles in 1950. *CORBIS/Joseph Schwartz Collection*

The Swing Era, 1930-1945

New York City became the principal center of swing music. Bandleader Fletcher Henderson pioneered the new swing sound, and by the early 1930s his big band was recording such hard-swinging compositions as "Hocus Pocus" (1934) and Coleman Hawkins's harmonically challenging "Queer Notions" (1933). The other notable center of swing was Kansas City, which featured such talented groups as Walter Page's Blue Devils, led by bassist Walter Page (1900-1957), the Bennie Moten (1894-1935) band, and later the great Count Basie Orchestra. In the early 1930s Moten's band was the most important in the Southwest. In 1932 the group traveled east and recorded such swing-era classics as "Moten Swing" and "Blue Room."

Black musicians were the principal innovators during the swing era, but, as was true of New Orleans jazz, white musicians often reaped the benefits. In 1935, when white clarinetist Benny Goodman made swing music a national fad, Moten was dead and Henderson had disbanded his orchestra. Although Henderson formed a new band between 1936 and 1939, his success was limited. The bands of Ellington, Basie, Calloway, Jimmie Lunceford, and drummer Chick Webb (1909-1939) had loyal black followings, but few white fans knew of them.

In the world of jazz, there was little question as to the superiority of black jazz musicians. Virtually all of the greatest talents in 1930s jazz were black, including alto saxophonists Benny Carter and Johnny Hodges; tenor saxophonists Coleman Hawkins and Lester Young; trumpeters Roy Eldridge (1911-1989) and Buck Clayton (1911-1991); trombonists Dicky Wells (1907-1985) and Trummy Young (1912-1984); pianists Fats Waller and Art Tatum; bassists Jimmy Blanton (1918-1942) and Walter Page; and drummers Jo Jones (1911-1985) and Webb.

Jazz Musicians and Racial Discrimination

The black musicians who found greatest favor with white audiences were those with a happy-go-lucky air and a ready grin, which often reinforced negative racial stereotypes. Waller, Calloway, and above all Armstrong epitomized the acceptable black entertainer. By the late 1930s, however, there were a number of successful challenges to racial

ABOVE: Widely credited as the architect of bop in the 1940s, trumpeter Dizzy Gillespie performs at the Monterery Jazz Festival in Monterey, California in the 1980s. *CORBIS/Craig Lovell*

LEFT: Jazz trumpeter Papa Celestin plays for his young grandson on the front porch of his house in New Orleans, Louisiana. *CORBIS/Bradley Smith*

segregation. Integrated recording sessions were common, and white jazz musicians regularly joined black players in jam sessions at Harlem's after-hours clubs. But until 1935, when Benny Goodman made Teddy Wilson (1912-1986) the pianist in his trio, white and black musicians did not perform together regularly in any working jazz band.

In 1936 Goodman added black vibraphonist Lionel Hampton to his small group, making it a quartet. During the late 1930s the Goodman quartet was the nation's most prominent interracial jazz group, but soon a number of other black musicians broke the color barrier by joining white swing bands. In 1938 singer Billie Holiday joined clarinetist Artie Shaw's band; in 1940-1941 singer LENA HORNE was part of saxophonist Charlie Barnet's band. Trumpeter Roy Eldridge was the featured trumpet soloist with drummer Gene Krupa's band in 1941-1942 and with Shaw's band in 1944-1945.

A number of liberal white journalists, concert promoters, and record producers aided black challenges to segregation. The 1938 and 1939 Spirituals to Swing Concerts organized by record and concert producer John Hammond brought an all-star cast of black musicians to New York City's prestigious Carnegie Hall. Hammond was an outspoken opponent of racial discrimination, as is evident in his late-1930s jazz criticism for the magazine *Downbeat*. Likewise, in the 1940s and 1950s jazz impresario Norman Granz forced many hotels and jazz venues to integrate.

Yet jazz performances were, in most cases, still segregated. For example, New York City's famed Cotton Club featured black entertainers but admitted only white patrons. Most of the dances at Boston's Roseland Ballroom were for whites only, although there were occasional blacks-only evenings. In general, white bands played for white audiences and black bands for black audiences, although white bandleaders – including Goodman, Barnet, Krupa, and Shaw – performed for blacks at such venues as Harlem's APOLLO THEATER. But some black jazz musicians actively resisted racial segregation. During the 1940s, for example, pianist Hazel Scott (1920-1981) included a clause in her contracts stipulating that promoters would forfeit their money if they separated the audience by race.

African American Women in Jazz

While the jazz community made significant challenges to racial discrimination, on gender issues its record was less impressive. Women have been involved in all aspects of jazz from its early stages, but their numbers have been few and their contributions largely unacknowledged. Males predominated in the music, and they did little to lessen the pervasive discrimination against women. African American women jazz performers thus found themselves outsiders even among their fellow black musicians.

The most important women in jazz have been vocalists, most notably Bessie Smith, Billie Holiday, Ella Fitzgerald, and Sarah Vaughan. But women have also served as jazz instrumentalists, bandleaders, composers, and arrangers. There have been numerous black female jazz pianists. Lil Hardin Armstrong enjoys the greatest historical prominence due to her recordings with King Oliver's Creole Jazz Band and Louis Armstrong's Hot Fives and Hot Sevens. In 1923 Cora "Lovie" Austin (1887-1972), the first female bandleader in jazz, became the first woman jazz instrumentalist to record.

Jazz pianist, composer, and arranger Mary Lou Williams saw Austin perform in Pittsburgh and recalled her excitement at "seeing this great woman sitting in the pit and conducting a group of five or six men, her legs crossed, a cigarette in her mouth, playing the show with her left hand and writing music for the next act with her right. WOW!"

Other important female jazz pianists include Hazel Scott, who combined jazz improvisation and classical music; Nellie Lutcher (b. 1912), who gained greatest recognition playing a jazz-inflected rhythm and blues (R&B); Beryl Booker (1922-1978), a talented bop-style improviser; Dorothy Donegan (1922-1998), an eclectic improviser who, like Scott, combined Art Tatum-like virtuosity, classical music, boogie woogie, and bop; Shirley Horn (b. 1934), a singer-pianist best known for her ballads; Marilyn Crispell (b. 1947), one of the most significant free-jazz pianists; and Geri Allen (b. 1957), one of the leading pianists in contemporary jazz.

African American women have less frequently filled other roles. In the 1930s the technically gifted trumpeter Valaida Snow (1903-1956) was dubbed the "Queen of the Trumpet." For several years following the 1939 death of Chick Webb, Ella Fitzgerald took over as the leader of Webb's big band. In the mid-1950s, trombonist Melba Liston (b. 1926) played in Dizzy Gillespie's big band and contributed several arrangements performed during the band's U.S. government-sponsored world tour. Alto saxophonist Elvira "Vi" Redd (b. 1928), arguably the finest female jazz saxophonist, plays in a bop-based style that reveals the influence of Charlie Parker. But Redd has made few recordings, preferring to devote herself to teaching music.

There were a number of all-female jazz bands, especially between the 1930s and the early 1950s. These groups suffered from being marketed as novelty acts. The best such group was the International Sweethearts of Rhythm, a racially integrated big band, which grew out of a student ensemble organized in 1939 at the Piney Woods Country Life School in Mississippi. Fronted by singer Anna Mae Winburn (b. 1913), the band featured such capable soloists as tenor saxophonist Viola Burnside (b. 1930?) and trumpeter Ernestine "Tiny" Davis (b. 1907). The group performed widely, including a 1945 tour of Europe and numerous radio broadcasts, but made few recordings before its 1949 breakup.

After the International Sweethearts of Rhythm disbanded, Winburn and Burnside each led all-female small groups. During the mid-1950s Beryl Booker headed an all-female trio. Since the 1950s all-female bands have been rare, although they have not disappeared altogether. In the late 1970s, for example, white jazz pianist Marian McPartland organized an all-female quintet, featuring alto player Vi Redd, which recorded the album *Now's the Time* (1977).

Big Bands and the End of the Swing Era

Jazz prospered during the Great Depression. The American public, white and black, wanted to escape the nation's depressed economy. Swing-era jazz, like 1930s Hollywood films, satisfied a national hunger for reassurance and uplift. During the Great Depression jazz enjoyed a truly national audience. No longer a music of brothels and speakeasies, it was almost respectable. Small-group jazz was still performed mainly in bars and nightclubs, but big bands appeared at such formal venues as theaters, ballrooms, and prestigious concert halls. Many big bands played for dancers at swank hotels, often making live broadcasts for one of the several radio networks.

Yet the lives of big-band musicians were far from glamorous. Many big bands did not secure long-term gigs at ballrooms or hotels; instead they toured, often to play a grueling series of one-night stands. Black musicians who challenged segregation by joining white bands faced particular hardships. In 1951 trumpeter Eldridge – after playing in several white big bands – insisted bitterly, "As long as I'm in America, I'll never in my life work with a white band again!... It's not worth the glory, not worth the money, not worth anything."

Life was nearly as taxing for all-black bands. When playing at white hotels, black musicians were required to use kitchen entrances and service elevators – and were not provided with accommodations – which forced them to confront the ugly realities of racial discrimination.

During the late 1940s a series of changes in the entertainment industry – including the emergence of television and the growing popularity of such solo vocalists as Frank Sinatra – led to the demise of most big bands and the end of the swing era. But the passing of the big-band era involved more than just a change in musical styles; it transformed the way in which jazz musicians learned their craft. The future of jazz lay not with big bands but with small ensembles that could provide more freedom for improvising soloists. The emphasis on tight ensemble playing and dance-music tempos left big band soloists few opportunities to challenge themselves. Nonetheless, big bands provided a musical apprenticeship for countless jazz musicians.

The Bop Era, 1945-1955

In the 1940s a number of younger musicians, especially in Harlem, began pressing at the boundaries of swing-era jazz. These musicians usually played in small combos at obscure nightclubs. They made no radio broadcasts and, due to a wartime shortage of the shellac used in pressing records, as well as a long strike by the American Federation of Musicians, they made almost no recordings before 1945. With the nation's attention fixed on World War II, few outside Harlem were aware of the new style known as bop.

Bop, as played by its greatest exemplars, alto saxophonist Charlie Parker and trumpeter Dizzy Gillespie, was a challenging music. Bop solos typically involved swirling cascades of notes, and bop tunes often used complex chord progressions – for instance, Parker's "Blues for Alice" (1951) – and tempos that were much faster than swing-era jazz – as in Gillespie's "Salt Peanuts" (1945) and "Shaw Nuff" (1945). Unlike big-band swing, bop was emphatically not for dancing. There were bop big bands, including those of singer Billy Eckstine, white clarinetist Woody Herman, and, above all, Gillespie, but only virtuoso dancers could negotiate their frantic tempos.

Gillespie's big band was also instrumental in introducing Afro-Latin jazz to an American audience. In 1948 Gillespie added Cuban conga drummer Chano Pozo to his orchestra and began playing such fiery pieces as "Manteca" (1947) and "Guarachi Guaro" (1948). Two other Cubans – Machito and his brother-in-law, arranger and trumpet player Mario Bauza – led the most important Afro-Latin jazz band of the 1940s, Machito and His Afro-Cubans. Machito's band made such influential recordings as "Tanga" (1949) and Chico O'Farrill's classic "Afro-Cuban Suite" (1950), which featured Charlie Parker as a guest soloist. So strong were the links between Cuban musicians and bop that many labeled Afro-Latin jazz Cu-bop.

Bop musicians idolized the improvising soloist, above all, the brilliant Parker and Gillespie. Other top soloists were pianists Thelonious Monk and Bud Powell, tenor saxophonist Dexter Gordon, drummers ART BLAKEY and Max Roach, and vocalists Ella Fitzgerald and Sarah Vaughan. The most important younger bop-style soloists to emerge in the 1950s were tenor saxophonist Sonny Rollins, pianist Hampton Hawes (1928-1977), and trumpeters Clifford Brown (1930-1956) and Lee Morgan (1938-1972). Bop musicians generally viewed themselves not as popular entertainers but as artists. They insisted that their music be taken seriously. But bop dismayed many listeners and older jazz musicians. In 1948, for instance, Louis Armstrong criticized the new style, referring to it as "that modern malice" of "young cats playing them weird chords" with "no melody to remember and no beat to dance to."

Some white record producers and fans sought refuge in the past, bringing several New Orleans jazz musicians out of retirement to perform in the old style. The movement, variously termed the *New Orleans revival* or the *traditionalist revival*, brought new attention to Kid Ory, clarinetist Omer Simeon, and trumpeters Bunk Johnson (1889-1949) and Papa Celestin. The most visible beneficiary of the New Orleans revival was Armstrong himself, who formed his traditionalist All Stars in 1947 and continued touring with the group into the 1960s. But as the original New Orleans jazz musicians died, the result was a slick commercial style, performed by and for whites, known as Dixieland.

Cool Jazz, Hard Bop, and Jazz in Hollywood

During the late 1940s the other main response to bop was cool jazz. Cool jazz slowed down bop's tempos and smoothed out its dissonances. Miles Davis's *Birth of the Cool* (1949-1950) and his late-1950s collaborations with arranger Gil Evans epitomized the cool style. Pianist John Lewis (b. 1920), a founding member of the MODERN JAZZ QUARTET (MJQ), was known for bringing elements of European classical music into such compositions as "The Queen's Fancy" (1953) and "Fontessa" (1956). The attempt to combine jazz and classical music came to be termed *third-stream music*, partly on the basis of the MJQ's album *Third Stream Music* (1960). Like Dixieland, however, cool was dominated by such white musicians as trumpeter Chet Baker, tenor saxophonist Stan Getz, and arranger Gil Evans.

Young black jazz musicians of the late 1950s preferred the raw-edged and dynamic style known as hard bop, the antithesis of cool. Hard bop embraced the harmonic innovations of bop but incorporated earthier harmonies inspired by the blues and gospel music. Cool jazz was an arranger's music, often played by large ensembles or orchestras. Hard bop was played in small groups, especially quintets. The key hard-bop groups were the Max Roach-Clifford Brown Quintet, the Horace Silver (b. 1928) Quintet, Art Blakey and the Jazz Messengers, and the Cannonball Adderly Quintet.

Beginning in the 1940s a number of jazz musicians sought to break through Hollywood's racial barriers. When composer WILLIAM GRANT STILL departed from the set of the all-black *Stormy Weather* (1943), Benny Carter stepped in. Carter served as an instrumentalist and arranger but received no screen credit. He worked on many films of the 1940s and 1950s and in 1958 began composing for television. He also aided other jazz musicians seeking careers in Hollywood, including trombonist J. J. Johnson (b. 1924) and tenor saxophonist Oliver Nelson (1932-1975). In the late 1950s Duke Ellington made his debut as a feature-film composer with *Anatomy of a Murder* (1959) and *Paris Blues* (1961). In the 1960s and 1970s Hollywood's most ubiquitous jazz musician was Quincy Jones, who composed music for such films as *In the Heat of the Night* (1967) and *The Wiz* (1978) as well as for television.

Jazz Experimentalists: Charles Mingus, Ornette Coleman, and John Coltrane

Jazz in the 1950s set the foundations for the free jazz – sometimes termed *avant-garde jazz* – of the 1960s. An important precursor of this atonal style, which dispensed with traditional chord progressions and melodies, can be found in the music of bassist and composer Charles Mingus. Mingus was iconoclastic, and his hard-to-label music attracted few disciples or imitators. Mingus avoided written scores; he sang the various parts to his musicians to achieve a looser, more spontaneous sound. In such compositions as "Wednesday Night Prayer Meeting" (1959), Mingus goaded his musicians into impassioned performances that joined basic gospel and blues harmonies with high-energy bop improvising. Although Mingus did not play free jazz, many of his sidemen did, most notably alto saxophonist Eric Dolphy (1928-1964).

Free jazz had its real beginnings in the work of alto saxophonist ORNETTE COLEMAN and pianist Cecil Taylor (b. 1929), and the experimental and often dissonant style takes its name from Coleman's *Free Jazz: A Collective Improvisation* (1960). Other significant free-jazz musicians were bandleader and arranger SUN RA; trumpeters Don Cherry (1936-1995) and Lester Bowie (b. 1941); pianist Marilyn Crispell; and tenor saxophonists Albert Ayler (1936-1970), Archie Shepp (b. 1937), and – after 1965 – John Coltrane. Of these, Coltrane had by far the greatest impact on jazz. Coltrane's sound on tenor was rather thin, and his improvisations were both meditative and impassioned. He became the greatest influence on tenor saxophonists since Coleman Hawkins and Lester Young.

Coltrane's music evolved out of hard bop. His hard-bop style, which jazz critic Ira Gitler characterized as "sheets of sound," can be heard on his albums *Blue Train* (1957) and *Giant Steps* (1959). During the late 1950s Coltrane and Miles Davis were instrumental in developing a new modal style of jazz playing. Modal jazz replaced the complex chord changes of bop with modes or tone rows, often played over extended two-chord vamps. Coltrane pioneered the style as a sideman on Miles Davis's *Kind of Blue* (1959) and on his own *My Favorite Things* (1960). In 1965 he embraced free jazz, adding two free-jazz musicians – drummer Rashied Ali (b. 1935) and tenor saxophonist Pharaoh Sanders (b. 1940) – to his group. Coltrane probed the outer reaches of tonality as part of a larger spiritual quest. In the notes for his album *A Love Supreme* (1964), he wrote that in 1957 he had experienced "a spiritual awakening, which was to lead me to a richer, fuller, more productive life.... I feel this has been granted through His grace. ALL PRAISE BE TO GOD.... This album is a humble offering to Him." Coltrane continued playing spiritually grounded free jazz until his death in 1967 of liver cancer.

Miles Davis: Modal Jazz and Jazz-Rock

Despite the importance of Coltrane's influence, the single most significant jazz musician from the late 1940s to the 1970s was trumpeter Miles Davis. Davis was a leader in cool jazz, and from 1952 to 1954 he led a number of seminal hard-bop sessions. In the late 1950s he pioneered modal jazz with *Kind of Blue* and a decade later ushered in the jazz-rock era with the album *Bitches Brew* (1969). Jazz-rock – sometimes termed *fusion* – combines jazz improvisation with the hard rhythms and electric instruments of rock music.

Bitches Brew exemplified the jazz-rock style, and it featured many musicians who would be significant in the 1970s, including saxophonist Wayne Shorter (b. 1933), guitarist John McLaughlin, keyboardists Chick Corea and Joe Zawinul, and drummer Jack DeJohnette (b. 1942). Former Davis sidemen went on to found several important jazz-rock units, including Shorter and Zawinul's Weather Report, Corea's Return to Forever, keyboardist Herbie Hancock's Headhunters, and Lifetime, led by drummer Tony Williams (1945-1997).

During his long career Davis led two bands, known as his classic quintets, which played particularly timeless music. In 1955-1956 Davis's first classic quintet featured Coltrane, pianist Red Garland (1923-1984), bassist Paul Chambers (1935-1969), and drummer Philly Joe Jones (1923-1985). From 1965 to 1968 his second classic quintet included Shorter, Hancock, Williams, and bassist Ron Carter (b. 1937). The latter group perfected an elliptical and rhythmically fluid style of modal jazz that inspired many jazz musicians in the 1980s and 1990s, most notably trumpeter Wynton Marsalis.

Wynton Marsalis and Neotraditionalism Since 1980

Since the early 1980s Marsalis has been the most prominent figure in jazz. A talented trumpeter and promising composer, Marsalis is also an outspoken defender of jazz. He has become the most articulate spokesperson for a younger generation of jazz musicians known as the Young Lions – so named because of their relative youth and vociferous pronouncements on jazz. Their music has been variously termed *modern mainstream, post bop,* and *classicism.* Perhaps a better label would be *neotraditionalism.* Just as the traditionalists of the 1940s harked back to the music of the first two decades of the twentieth century, so the neotraditionalists of the 1980s and 1990s embraced the hard bop and modal jazz of the late 1950s and early 1960s.

The Young Lions play acoustic jazz and condemn the electronic instruments and rock rhythms of jazz-rock. Where free jazz is abstract and often dissonant, the music of the neotraditionalists is tonal, often featuring familiar chord progressions and well-known jazz standards. Besides Marsalis, important neotraditionalists are trumpeters Terence Blanchard (b. 1962) and Roy Hargrove (b. 1969); pianists Mulgrew Miller (b. 1955) and Marcus Roberts (b. 1963); drummers Jeff "Tain" Watts (b. 1960) and Marvin "Smitty" Smith (b. 1961); and bass player Christian McBride (b. 1972). A second group of young jazz musicians has taken a strikingly different approach, open to a wider range of music, from free jazz to R&B. Such performers as pianist Geri Allen, alto saxophonist Donald Harrison (b. 1960), and tenor saxophonists David Murray (b. 1955) and Joshua Redman (b. 1969) combine a respect for past jazz styles with an active probing of musical boundaries.

In 1987 Marsalis was named the head of a new jazz program at New York City's Lincoln Center for the Performing Arts, giving him a visible pulpit from which to preach his version of the jazz gospel. Under his leadership Lincoln Center presented major retrospectives of such jazz masters as Armstrong, Bechet, and, above all, Ellington. Marsalis also composed a series of major works that call to mind Ellington's suites, including *In This House, On This Morning* (1993) and *Blood on the Fields* (1995), which in 1997 became the first nonclassical work to receive a Pulitzer Prize in music. The Lincoln Center jazz program and a comparable program instituted at Carnegie Hall in 1993 under trumpeter Jon Faddis (b. 1953) reveal the full acceptance of jazz as part of American high culture.

Jazz Today

Jazz musicians can be heard playing today in almost every style from the earliest beginnings of jazz. Because jazz has had such a short history, listeners can still hear, in person, many of the musicians who created the core traditions of jazz. During the 1970s several New Orleans musicians remained active who had recorded in the 1920s with King Oliver and Jelly Roll Morton. Pianist Eubie Blake – who composed "The Charleston Rag" (1899) – was a living link to the ragtime era who continued performing into the early 1980s, when he was 98 years old.

In the 1990s most of the older musicians of jazz derived from the swing or bop eras, although trumpeter Doc Cheatham (1905-1997), saxophonist Benny Waters (1902-1998), and Benny Carter all began recording in the 1920s. One could also hear leading cool, hard bop, modal, and free-jazz players. Because of its rapid evolution, jazz is not so much a linear sequence of styles as a crazy quilt. The creative improvisations and swinging music of several generations of jazz musicians, and their sharply contrasting juxtapositions, reveal both the continuity and the change that characterize jazz.

In defining their music, today's Young Lions invoke the conventions of hard bop and modal jazz. Their stylistic conservatism reflects, in part, a need for consolidation after the sweeping discontinuities of free jazz and jazz-rock. But neotraditionalism is by no means the final word in the evolution of jazz. Throughout its history, jazz has undergone profound and unexpected transformations in style, approach, and technique. As jazz critic Whitney Balliett has observed, jazz is the "sound of surprise," and, above all, that capacity to surprise underscores the continued vitality of the jazz tradition.

James Clyde Sellman

See Also

Adderley, Julian Edwin ("Cannonball"); Amos 'n' Andy; Armstrong, Lillian Hardin (Lil); Armstrong, Louis ("Satchmo"); Basie, William James ("Count"); Bechet, Sidney Joseph; Blake, James Hubert ("Eubie"); Blues, The; Bolden, Charles Joseph ("Buddy"); Boogie Woogie; Boston, Massachusetts; Calloway, Cabell (Cab); Carter, Bennett Lester (Benny); Chicago, Illinois; Coltrane, John William; Young, Lester Willis ("Prez"); Davis, Miles Dewey, III; Eckstine, William Clarence (Billy); Fitzgerald, Ella; Gillespie, John Birks ("Dizzy"); Gordon, Dexter Keith; Great Migration, The; Hampton, Lionel Leo; Hancock, Herbert Jeffrey (Herbie); Handy, William Christopher (W.C.); Harlem, New York; Hawkins, Coleman Randolph; Henderson, Fletcher Hamilton, Jr.; Jones, Quincy Delight, Jr.; Mingus, Charles, Jr.; Moten, Benjamin (Bennie); Kansas City, Missouri; Lunceford, James Melvin (Jimmie); Miley, James Wesley ("Bubber"); Minstrelsy; Monk, Thelonious Sphere; Morton, Ferdinand Joseph ("Jelly Roll"); New Orleans, Louisiana; New York, New York; Oliver, Joseph ("King"); Ory, Edward ("Kid"); Parker, Charles Christopher ("Bird"); Powell, Earl ("Bud"); Rhythm and Blues; Roach, Maxwell Lemuel (Max); Rollins, Theodore ("Sonny"); Waller, Thomas Wright ("Fats"); Ellington, Edward Kennedy ("Duke"); Pozo y González, Luciano (Chano).

Latin America and the Caribbean

Jazz, Afro-Latin, a musical fusion of Latin American music and African American jazz that emerged in the 1940s, combining Latin American rhythms with jazz improvisation.

Afro-Latin jazz, as popular music writer Scott Yanow observed, "has been the most consistently popular" jazz style since the swing era of the 1930s. The new style emerged in the 1940s, in particular through the experiments of Cuban musicians in New York City. "Cuban musicians," as *New York Times* music critic Ben Ratliff noted in 1998, "are known for complexity of rhythm more than harmony." The Cuban and Puerto Rican musicians who created Afro-Latin jazz made use of the rhythmic variety of Latin American music while drawing on the improvisational and harmonic complexity of African American jazz.

The creation of Afro-Latin jazz involved several prior historical and musical developments. Above all, it reflected the cultural maturity of Spanish Harlem, New York City's Latin American community. Musically, it grew out of new ensembles and rhythms, mainly derived from Cuba or the United States. Afro-Latin jazz grew out of various ensembles – swing-era big bands in jazz, the rumba bands that appeared in Latin American music during the 1930s, and the Cuban *conjunto,* a medium-sized group that featured two trumpets in the front line. Directly linked with the evolution of Afro-Latin jazz were such rhythms as the mambo and, above all, the clave beat (*see* Son).

Introduction

In the United States the English-speaking majority Americans perceived Latin music in somewhat condescending terms as lighthearted, good-time music. It had an image of being frivolous, fun, and slightly comic music – impressions that were encouraged by a variety of cultural stereotypes such as Brazilian singer Carmen Miranda's fruit-basket-on-the-head Hollywood persona. American pop music featured a series of "Latin" novelty songs that contained few authentic Latin American musical elements, including "When Yuba Plays the Rumba on His Tuba" (1931), "All Dressed Up Spic and Spanish" (1939), "I Came, I Saw, I Conga'd" (1941), and Cab Calloway's "Chili Con Conga" (1939).

Afro-Latin jazz changed that. The music of Machito (Frank Raoul Grillo) and Tito Puente was fiery, driving, and uncompromising. It was closely allied with experimental bebop or bop music; indeed, some jazz writers labeled it Cu-bop. Yet unlike American jazz, Afro-Latin music never disappeared into abstraction or intellectualized obscurity. Its stress on driving and danceable rhythms and on music grounded in recognizable harmonies ensured Afro-Cuban and later Afro-Brazilian jazz continued accessibility.

Although the Afro-Latin jazz audience has varied over the years, the music has never gone out of style.

Latin American Music and Immigrant Enclaves in the United States

Afro-Latin jazz first emerged in the 1940s in New York City, but the connections between the musical traditions of African Americans and Latin Americans date back much further, to the turn of the century or earlier. New Orleans, an active port that linked the Caribbean with the Mississippi River trade, and New York City, America's largest metropolis, were particularly important in the merging of African American and Latin American music. Jazz pianist Jelly Roll Morton noted the "Spanish tinge" that influenced early New Orleans jazz. Morton himself, in solo piano recordings such as "New Orleans Joys" (1923) and "Tia Juana" (1924), incorporated distinctly Latin rhythms in his playing. Similarly, the second strain of W. C. Handy's "St. Louis Blues" (1917) makes use of an Argentine TANGO rhythm.

The United States developed much closer ties with the Spanish-speaking Caribbean as a result of the Spanish-Cuban-American War (1898), which made PUERTO RICO an American colony and Cuba in essence an American protectorate. The early twentieth century brought increasing ties of trade and travel between the United States and various Caribbean nations. Immigrant communities – above all, the eastern portion of New York City's Harlem that was known as Spanish Harlem and later as El Barrio – also continued to grow. During the late nineteenth century Spanish Harlem was home to a variety of Spanish-speaking groups, with Cubans and Spanish Jews the most prevalent.

Set apart by language and culture, the inhabitants of Spanish Harlem and other Latin American neighborhoods retained close ties to their home countries. They also preferred familiar music and their own cultural celebrations. In the United States as a whole, Latin music became known through fads, novelty tunes, and dance crazes such as the RUMBA and the mambo. But in Caribbean immigrant communities, Latin music – undiluted by the larger commercial music industry – filled a well-established social function that had little to do with crossover success among the English-speaking majority. By the 1920s Latin Americans had emerged as a distinct sector of the American music market, one that supported numerous Latin music venues and specialty record stores as well as Latin bands and star performers.

Latin Music Puts Down American Roots

Between 1920 and 1930 a growing number of Cuban and Puerto Rican musicians arrived in the United States. In New York City, the band of Cuban Vicente Sigler played at such midtown hotels as the Astor and the Waldorf Astoria. Sigler's group was important in two regards. It brought together Cuban and Puerto Rican musicians for the first time, an important precondition for the development of a distinctly New York Latin music. And it provided invaluable experience for many Latin musicians, including such future bandleaders as Puerto Rican trumpeter Augusto Coen, Afro-Cuban flutist Alberto Socarrás, and Cuban violinist Alberto Iznaga.

During the 1920s and 1930s a growing number of Latin American musicians found work in African American jazz bands. In 1928, shortly after arriving in New York City, Socarrás recorded what appears to have been the first jazz flute solo, on a Clarence Williams recording of "Have You Ever Felt That Way?" During the late 1920s Socarrás and Coen were featured in *Blackbirds Revue* and *Rhapsody in Black*, which also brought them into closer contact with African American jazz musicians. During the 1930s Socarrás led a Latin big band at the Teatro Campoamor that drew upon African American jazz as well as Latin music. In 1920 trombonist Juan Tizol (1900-1984) came from Puerto Rico to Washington, D.C., as part of Marie Lucas's band.

Tizol played with Lucas's band at Washington's Howard Theater until he joined the Duke Ellington Orchestra in 1929. In so doing, Tizol – who was "white" by American racial categories – became one of the first Latin American musicians to begin the blurring of America's strict black-white dichotomy. When Ellington's band appeared in the Hollywood film *Check and Double Check* (1930), the studio insisted that Tizol and such light-skinned New Orleans Creole musicians as clarinetist Barney Bigard appear in blackface makeup.

Tizol wrote several pieces for the Ellington band, including "Perdido" (1942), which quickly became a jazz standard, and such Latin-tinged compositions as "Conga Brava" (1940) and "Bakiff" (1941). But Tizol's best-known piece was "Caravan" (1937). Like much of his writing, it conveys a Latin American feel, but its title is a reminder that American jazz musicians and the listening public viewed Latin influences primarily as exotica. In 1930 the young Afro-Cuban musician MARIO BAUZA arrived in New York City. During the 1930s Bauza worked in the bands of NOBLE SISSLE, Chick Webb (1909-1939), Don Redman (1900-1964), and Cab Calloway, and in the early 1940s, he played a seminal role in the creation of Afro-Cuban jazz.

Prior to the rise of Afro-Latin jazz, the most famous Latin musician in the United States was bandleader Xavier Cugat (1900-1990)(*see* MAMBO). Born in Gerona, Spain, Cugat moved at age five to Cuba, where he studied violin. By seven or eight, he was playing in various Havana cafés and accompanying silent films in a movie theater as part of a trio that included Cuban composer Moises Simóns on piano. In 1921 he emigrated to New York City and then moved to Los Angeles.

After working as a cartoonist for the *Los Angeles Times*, Cugat formed a tango orchestra that in 1927-1928, very early in the sound era, performed in two short films, playing such Latin American songs as "Estrellita" and "Cielito Lindo," as well as non-Latin music. During the 1930s and 1940s Cugat appeared in numerous Hollywood musical comedies. Until the mid-1940s he played a key role in defining Latin music for most Americans: he offered a sweet and inauthentic pastiche of American pop music flavored with Latin American elements, exemplified by such recordings as "The Rhumba-Cardi" (1940), featuring the singing of a young Dinah Shore. "To succeed in America," Cugat remarked, "I gave the Americans a Latin music that had nothing authentic about it."

Americans Encounter Authentic Cuban Music

All of that began to change, according to John Storm Roberts, on April 26, 1930, when Don Azpiazú's Havana Casino Orchestra played to a full house at New York's Palace Theater. For the first time, American audiences heard authentic Cuban dance music with a full Cuban rhythm section: maracas, congas, claves, timbales, bongos, and güiros. One of the songs Azpiazú (d. 1943) introduced that afternoon was Moises Simón's "El manicero" (The Peanut Vendor). By early 1931 that song, which Azpiazú recorded for RCA Victor, had become a national hit. Azpiazú and his band helped spur a nationwide rumba craze. Ironically, although Azpiazú introduced Americans to authentic Latin music, most of the songs that gained currency during the rumba fad were not rumbas at all: most were examples of the Cuban *son*.

Azpiazú set two other important precedents – one musical, one social. Prior to this time, Roberts explained, when Cuban dance orchestras recorded, they "repeated the sung melody in unison between verses." But when Azpiazú was in the studio to record "El manicero," one of his two trumpeters began playing variations on the theme, and Azpiazú encouraged him to continue doing so for the recording. "The resulting improvisations," Roberts noted, "were a major part of the record's success and perhaps the first Cuban *inspiraciones* to be recorded." Inspiraciones – vocal or instrumental improvisations – represented another step in the convergence of Latin music and jazz. Although he is little remembered today, Azpiazú also played an important role in challenging racial taboos. Roberts noted that he was "possibly the first Cuban bandleader to mix black and white musicians" and that he "broke the color bar in the U.S. in 1931" – four years before white clarinetist Benny Goodman added black pianist Teddy Wilson (1912-1986) to his trio.

Cubans, Puerto Ricans, and the Afro-Latin Jazz Fusion

Although the origins of Afro-Latin jazz were long and complex, the genre actually came into being quite suddenly during the early 1940s. The most important figures in creating the new music were brothers-in-law Machito and Mario Bauza. In 1940 Machito formed a Latin jazz big band, the Afro-Cubans. The following year Bauza joined the band as trumpeter and musical director. Machito and Bauza worked together for the next 35 years. In its early years the band featured three to four trumpeters and five saxophonists. It lacked the trombone section of a typical American big band, but what truly set Machito's band apart was its complete Afro-Cuban rhythm section, including bongos, congas, maracas, timbales, and a Latin American bass player. "Latin jazz," as Roberts observed in *The Latin Tinge*, "almost always involved a full Latin rhythm section: not merely a set of percussionists, but a bass player able to play the bass patterns called *tumbaos* that peg the percussionists."

The Afro-Cubans' first successful integration of Latin music and jazz was Bauza's composition "Tanga" the title of which derived from an African term for marijuana. Bauza and the band created the piece spontaneously during a 1943 rehearsal session, and it soon became the Afro-Cubans' theme song. In 1949 Machito and his Afro-Cubans recorded a version of "Tanga," featuring an impassioned solo by white tenor saxophonist Flip Phillips. That recording brought the band to the attention of a wider American audience. Also influential in this regard was the Afro-Cubans' recording of Arturo "Chico" O'Farrill's classic "Afro-Cuban Suite" (1950), which featured guest soloists Phillips, alto saxophonist Charlie Parker, and white jazz drummer Buddy Rich.

Machito and Bauza also brought the complex harmonies of bebop or bop into Afro-Cuban music. The Afro-Cubans – along with Dizzy Gillespie's big band – were instrumental in the emergence of Cu-bop. Machito's breakthrough performance took place on January 24, 1947, at New York's Town Hall in a concert that also featured Stan Kenton's popular white big band. Kenton was so impressed with the Afro-Cubans' sound that he borrowed Machito's rhythm section later that year when he recorded Simón's "El manicero."

Perhaps influenced by Machito's success, Gillespie decided to add a Cuban percussionist to his own big band. He turned to his old friend Bauza – his section mate in Calloway's band from 1931 to 1941 – for suggestions. Bauza recommended conga drummer Chano Pozo, and on September 29, 1947, when Gillespie's big band performed at Carnegie Hall, Pozo was featured on a new composition, "Cubano-Be, Cubano-Bop." In a lengthy middle section somewhat reminiscent of the *montuno*, the call-and-response passage of the Cuban *son*, Pozo and bongos player Lorenzo Salan set up a responsive rhythmic base for Gillespie's otherwise unaccompanied trumpet. Gillespie's solo demonstrated his unrivaled ability to bridge the realms of Afro-Cuban music and jazz.

Most American jazz musicians have found it difficult to negotiate Afro-Latin rhythms because of their inability to escape jazz's straight four-beat swing and to feel comfortable with the Cuban-derived three-two clave beat. The clave, the underlying ground beat in much of Afro-Latin jazz, is strongly syncopated rather than steady. The rhythmic patter is played across two four-beat measures, and it takes its name from the claves, the instrument on which it is most often played. In the first measure the musician strikes the claves on the first downbeat, on the second upbeat, and on the fourth downbeat. In the second measure, the rhythm is played on the second and third downbeats. The result is a loping, off-balance beat that defies American rhythmic conventions, especially in the three-against-four polyrhythmic feel of its first measure.

During the 1950s, in addition to Gillespie and Kenton, vibraphonist Cal Tjader emerged as the third important non-Latino in Afro-Latin jazz. Tjader, who was Swedish-American, first encountered Latin music when he joined pianist George Shearing's quintet in 1953. In that year the pianist decided to shift away from his bop-oriented style and to embrace Latin music; he hired American-born Willie Bobo on timbales and Cubans Mongo Santamaria on congas and Armando Peraza on bongos. In 1954 Tjader left Shearing and began his long career as a bandleader playing a cool version of Latin jazz.

Besides Cuban and American musicians, an increasing number of Puerto Ricans took part in the musical developments of these years. New York City's Puerto Rican community burgeoned in the post-World War II era, as the U.S.-sponsored industrialization scheme known as Operation Bootstrap promoted massive Puerto Rican migration to the city. Most Puerto Ricans settled in the area of Harlem that had long been called Spanish Harlem, but which among Puerto Ricans became known as El Barrio (*see* Afro-Latino Cultures in the United States). During the 1940s and 1950s the Puerto Rican influence could be seen in the emergence of two key bandleaders and musical innovators: Puerto Rican singer Tito Rodriguez and *timbalero* Tito Puente, who was born in New York City of Puerto Rican parents. Puente's band played an important role in popularizing the mambo, and during the 1950s introduced the chachachá. The most important Afro-Latin jazz venue of the post-World War II years was New York City's Palladium Ballroom, located on Fifty-second Street, then the hot spot of jazz in the city.

Latin American Developments: The Mambo and the Conjunto

Although the primary crucible of Afro-Latin jazz was New York City, Cuba contributed to the ongoing musical fusion. In Cuba the key setting for the creation of Afro-Latin jazz was Havana's active casino, dancehall, and nightclub scene. The famed Tropicana Nightclub was particularly important in the evolution of Cuban music. In the late 1940s pianist Bebo Valdés (b. 1918), the father of jazz pianist and bandleader Chucho Valdés, began a long tenure as the musical director and leader of the house band at the Tropicana. During the late 1930s and the 1940s Cuba contributed two important elements to the Latin-jazz fusion, the mambo and the conjunto.

The mambo was a new form of dance music that featured stronger syncopation and a considerably faster tempo than the traditional Cuban *danzón*. Music scholars are not certain who first created the mambo, but among those given the most credit are Afro-Cuban cellist Orestes López; his older brother, bassist Israel "Cachao" López; flutist Antonio Arcaño; Afro-Cuban *tres* player Arsenio Rodríguez; and bandleader Damaso Pérez Prado. The López brothers helped create the mambo rhythm while playing in various Havana nightclubs after joining Arcaño's band, Arcaño y sus Maravillas (the Marvels), in 1937. In short order, the two transformed the traditional danzón rhythm. By speeding the tempo and increasing the syncopation, they produced the mambo rhythm, which soon became popular both in Cuba and throughout the world.

During the 1940s the conjunto evolved out of the traditional Cuban *septeto*, which is made up of stringed instruments, percussion, and a single trumpet. The conjunto expanded the ensemble to include a second trumpeter, a pianist, a bassist, and a conga drummer. The key figure in the conjunto's popularity was Arsenio Rodríguez, the leader of Conjunto Casino. Some scholars also credit Rodríguez with a major role in popularizing the mambo rhythm. In Mexico, beginning in 1948, Cuban bandleader Pérez Prado began recording instrumental mambos with large ensembles inspired by American big bands, in which the trumpet, trombone, and saxophone sections replicated the musical interplay in the smaller conjuntos and septetos.

From the end of World War II to the Cuban Revolution, Havana had a vital jazz scene. Two of the key figures in Cuban jazz were bassist López and pianist Bebo Valdés. López popularized the *descarga* (meaning "discharge"), the Afro-Cuban jam session, generally involving medium-sized ensembles based on the conjunto. Valdés produced and played in countless descarga sessions throughout the 1950s. Another stalwart of Havana jazz was Afro-Cuban trumpeter Alfredo "Chocolate" Armenteros.

The Decline of Afro-Latin Jazz in the 1960s

In the 1960s Latin jazz drew on the music of a new culture – Brazil – and gained new popularity. The bossa nova (*see* Samba Schools) craze of the early 1960s reflected an Afro-Brazilian jazz, albeit one filtered through such white Brazilian and American musicians as composer Antonio Carlos Jobim, guitarist and singer João Gilberto, tenor saxophonist Stan Getz, and guitarist Charlie Byrd. Bossa nova is a cool and carefully modulated music, but its origins lie in the fiery Afro-Brazilian SAMBA. Although Brazilian musicians of African descent, such as bandleader GILBERTO GIL, did make notable contributions to the Latin-jazz fusion, bossa nova was largely performed by and for the white middle class.

Apart from the popularity of bossa nova, Afro-Latin jazz suffered a major eclipse in the 1960s. American jazz musicians largely lost interest in Latin American music. The jazz avant-garde, inspired by John Coltrane and ORNETTE COLEMAN, focused on expressing pure emotion and testing the absolute harmonic limits of their music. The jazz mainstream turned to the bluesy clichés of hard bop and soul jazz. For their part, many Latin American musicians retreated into traditional music and, above all, to the *típico* Cuban conjunto style. In 1974 arranger Louie Ramirez complained:

"Everybody who hires me wants two trumpets or two trumpets and one trombone. I say, why don't we use an oboe? But if it's not típico, it's no good.... [T]ípico music is two chords.... [M]usically, it's primitive! Aretha Franklin's drummer told me, 'You know, in the fifties,... you guys were doing some heavy things. Now you're kind of like CALYPSO bands.'"

Yet important developments in the 1960s prepared the way for a subsequent reawakening of interest in Latin jazz.

A number of Afro-Caribbean musicians – generally Cubans, Puerto Ricans, or their American-born children – continued to play Latin jazz through the 1960s. Besides such well-established figures as Machito, Tito Puente, and Tito Rodriguez, several key leaders emerged in the mid- to late 1950s and had a powerful impact on Afro-Latin jazz during the 1960s and beyond. The most important of these were Afro-Cuban conga player Mongo Santamaria and New York City-born pianist Charlie Palmieri (1927-1988). Santamaria played a fusion of Latin, jazz, and RHYTHM AND BLUES (R&B) that brought him mainstream popularity, including a Top Ten rendition of pianist Herbie Hancock's "Watermelon Man" (1963).

Palmieri never found such crossover success, but he had a powerful impact on Afro-Latin jazz. In 1958 he formed a highly influential flute-and-strings *charanga* band, Charanga Duboney, that featured four violins and Dominican JOHNNY PACHECO on flute. By 1960 Palmieri's band had inspired a charanga craze in New York City's Latin community. Later in the decade, Palmieri worked for Alegre Records as musical director on a series of descarga sessions by the Alegre All Stars, and in the mid-1960s he made several memorable albums in the then-popular "boogaloo" (or "bugalu") style that mixed Latin music with R&B. Beginning in the 1970s, Palmieri commenced a parallel career as a cultural historian and lecturer on the history of Latin American music. His younger brother, pianist Eddie Palmieri (b. 1936), is an important bandleader in his own right who, because of his angular playing and experimental compositions, is often regarded as the Thelonious Monk of Latin jazz.

In Cuba the 1960s were a time of social transformation in the aftermath of Fidel Castro's successful Cuban Revolution. But the creation of a socialist Cuba invoked the wrath of the staunchly anticommunist U.S. government. The United States imposed a trade embargo and cultural sanctions, and the Cuban government responded by marginalizing American culture, including contemporary jazz. For example, while serving in the Cuban military, trumpeter ARTURO SANDOVAL spent three and a half months in confinement because he had been caught listening to a Voice of America jazz broadcast.

This attitude would continue at least until the early 1970s, when Sandoval, pianist Chucho Valdés, saxophonist PAQUITO D'RIVERA, and several other musicians formed the jazz ensemble IRAKERE. Irakere revitalized Afro-Cuban jazz and soon became Cuba's most popular band. In 1977 Dizzy Gillespie and a number of other American jazz musicians visited Cuba, and Gillespie was able to perform with the band. But the U.S. government's intransigence has made it nearly impossible for these Cuban musicians to perform in the United States, unless – like D'Rivera and Sandoval – they defect and abandon their homeland.

SALSA AND AFTER: AFRO-LATIN JAZZ SINCE THE 1970S

During the 1960s Latin music turned inward and, in the traditionalism of the típico movement, sought out its roots. There was also a decreased interest in achieving crossover success. One by-product of the típico revival was a lessening of interest on the part of the non-Latino population. All that changed with the emergence of New York salsa music during the late 1960s and 1970s. Salsa soon became a blanket term for all Latin music – Machito and Tito Puente both returned to popularity during the salsa craze – but it began as a Cuban-based dance music aimed mainly at New York City's Puerto Rican population. The term *salsa* was popularized by a number of record companies that specialized in Latin music, above all FANIA RECORDS, founded in 1964 by Johnny Pacheco.

During the late 1970s trombonist WILLIE COLÓN led the Fania All Stars, which featured a two-trombone ensemble that was itself a variation on the two-trumpet Cuban conjunto. The Fania All Stars quickly came to epitomize the salsa sound. Although salsa was popular music rather than jazz, it made use of improvisation, and in the playing of instrumentalists such as Colón it retained a definite jazz tinge. Likewise as a leader on his own albums, Colón demonstrated his interest in breaking out of the restrictions of Cuban típico: his music ranged widely. He drew most heavily on the *jibaro* country music of Puerto Rico, but also incorporated Panamanian, Colombian, and Brazilian elements in his recordings.

For their part, non-Latino jazz musicians were by the 1970s better prepared to appreciate Latin music, the cumulative result of a musical dialogue that had extended over several decades. During the 1950s and 1960s jazz combo recordings often included a conga drummer, and *congeros* Candido Camero (b. 1921), Ray Barreto (b. 1929), Willie Bobo (1934-1983), and Ralph MacDonald (b. 1944) were in demand as session players. In the 1970s a number of American jazz artists went beyond Latin flavoring to record entire albums that featured Latin American music and rhythms. Thus Latin jazz trumpeter Luis Gasca joined tenor saxophonist Joe Henderson (b. 1937) on his Afro-Latin-flavored album *Canyon Lady* (1973). Singer Sarah Vaughan explored the music of Brazilians Milton Nascimento, Antonio Carlos Jobim, and Dorival Caynmi – with Caynmi providing the musical arrangements – on *I Love Brazil (Brazilian Romance)* (1977). Likewise tenor saxophonist Wayne Shorter (b. 1933) collaborated with Nascimento on the Brazilian-flavored *Native Dancer* (1974).

Individual Latin American musicians have also had a major impact on jazz since the 1970s. Brazilian percussionist Airto Moreira played in the jazz-rock or fusion band of trumpeter Miles Davis, on Weather Report's first album, and along with his wife, singer Flora Purim, in pianist Chick Corea's *Return to Forever*. Argentinian tenor saxophonist Leandro "Gato" Barbieri, whom musicologist Roberts described as "a kind of one-man Latin-jazz avant-garde," combined the polytonal experiments of free jazz with the rhythms, instruments, and musical forms of Argentina, Brazil, Cuba, and Peru. During the 1990s Cuban arranger Chico O'Farrill (b. 1921) led a well-received Latin-jazz big band, the Afro-Cuban Jazz Orchestra, which has appeared regularly at New York City's Birdland jazz club. Among the Latin American jazz musicians who have gained prominence in the 1980s and 1990s are Brazilian trumpeter Claudio Roditi, Cuban pianist Gonzalo Rubalcaba (b. 1963), Panamanian pianist Danilo Pérez, Peruvian drummer and percussionist Alex Acuña, and Puerto Rican saxophonist David Sanchez (b. 1968).

Although Cuban-American relations did not significantly improve in the 1990s, in musical terms the two countries drew closer than at any time since the revolution. Cuban musicians who have defected and settled in the United States in recent years, such as Arturo Sandoval and Paquito D'Rivera, have provided fresh infusions of Cuban musical culture. Moreover, the two nations have eased their hostility sufficiently to allow some cultural exchange to resume. After appearances at the Montreal and Montreux jazz festivals, pianist Rubalcaba was able to sign with Blue Note Records, giving his recordings American distribution, and he has had greater opportunities to tour in the United States. In 1996 the 79-year-old jazz pianist Ruben Gonzalez recorded his first album since the 1940s, *Introducing Ruben Gonzalez* (1996), which was released in the United States on World Circuit/Nonesuch Records. Two years later, Chucho Valdés, the jazz pianist and long-time leader of Irakere, received permission to perform two solo concerts at New York City's Lincoln Center.

Thus over the course of half a century, Afro-Latin jazz has evolved into a vital component of contemporary jazz. Afro-Latin jazz draws on the musical forms and rhythms of much of Latin America – including Argentine tangos, Brazilian sambas, Puerto Rican jibaros, and Trinidadian calypsos – but the most important contributions are Afro-Cuban. The three-two clave beat, the *son* song form, and the conjunto ensemble are all Afro-Cuban in origin. African American jazz has contributed larger ensembles, greater harmonic complexity, and, most important, a style of improvisation that complemented in the melodic realm the intricacy of Cuban percussion rhythms. The resulting fusion has proven its vitality for more than half a century, and its drive and passion continue to attract listeners and challenge musicians.

James Clyde Sellman

See Also

Nascimento, Milton; Calloway, Cabell (Cab); Coltrane, John William; Davis, Miles Dewey, III; Franklin, Aretha Louise; Gillespie, John Birks ("Dizzy"); Hancock, Herbert Jeffrey (Herbie); Handy, William Christopher (W.C.); Harlem, New York; Ellington, Edward Kennedy ("Duke"); Los Angeles, California; Monk, Thelonious Sphere; Morton, Ferdinand Joseph ("Jelly Roll"); New Orleans, Louisiana; New York, New York; Parker, Charles Christopher ("Bird"); Spanish-Cuban-American War, African Americans in the; Armenteros, Alfredo "Chocolate; Colombia; López, Israel ("Cachao"); Panama; Pérez Prado, Dámaso; Pozo y González, Luciano (Chano); Puente, Ernesto Antonio (Tito); Valdés, Jesús (Chucho); Brazil; Caymmi, Dorival; Santamaría, Ramón ("Mongo"); Trinidad and Tobago; Dance in Latin America and the Caribbean; Argentina; Havana, Cuba.

Blues singer "Blind" Lemon Jefferson holds his guitar. *Archive Photos*

North America

Jefferson, ("Blind") Lemon

(b. 1897, near Couchman, Tex.; d. 1930?, Chicago, Ill.), country bluesman who made some of the earliest blues recordings and profoundly influenced numerous subsequent blues musicians.

Blind Lemon Jefferson was born on a farm in Freestone County, Texas, where he spent his childhood. Although his mature songwriting suggests a familiarity with the visual world, Jefferson seems to have lost his sight at least by the time he was a teenager. Thereafter he devoted himself to music, a vocation that suffered little from his handicap. Jefferson began his career close to home, singing in the Shiloh Baptist Church in Kirvin, Texas, and playing his guitar in Wortham, Texas, at parties and on the street.

Sometime around 1915 Jefferson moved to Dallas and began performing full-time in the Deep Ellum neighborhood, mostly as a street musician. Some critics suggest that Jefferson's stentorian singing style arose to out-clamor the noise of the street. Jefferson did sing loudly, but he also sang with great mastery. He commanded a broad vocal range and sometimes performed gospel songs in addition to the blues. The intricacy and staggered rhythms of his guitar accompaniments also showed his superior musical skill. A body of lore grew about Jefferson's life as a blind performer, including the claim that he could recognize the clink of pennies in his tin cup and reject them as inadequate payment.

Jefferson earned enough money from his street performances to support a family; he reportedly married in the early 1920s and had a son. During these years he played throughout Mississippi and Alabama, as well as in Texas. Despite his blindness, he lived a rambler's life, likely carrying a gun and boot-legging liquor. He kept company with Leadbelly (William "Huddie" Ledbetter), who also lived the rough life of his songs.

In 1925 Jefferson caught the attention of Sammy Price, a music store owner who recorded a demo for him and sent it to Paramount Records. Paramount invited Jefferson to Chicago in 1925 or 1926 and began to record his extensive repertoire of original and folk material. His first Paramount recordings were gospel songs, released under the pseudonym Deacon L. J. Bates, but soon Jefferson was a premier name in secular race records.

Jefferson created a niche for male blues artists in an industry hitherto dominated by female performers such as Ma Rainey, Ida Cox, and Bessie Smith. Although he recorded only from 1926 to his death in 1929, he cut approximately a hundred sides and left a legacy of songs that later became standards of folk and blues, including "That Black

Snake Moan" (1926), "See That My Grave Is Kept Clean" (1928), "Corrina Blues" (1926), and "Match Box Blues" (1927).

During this phase of his life Jefferson became wealthy and well known. He could afford to own cars and hire chauffeurs, and at times employed young blues musicians, such as Leadbelly and T-Bone Walker. Within three or four years, however, near the end of his life, his celebrity had begun to wane.

Although uncertainty surrounds the date and details of Jefferson's death, the most common story is that he froze to death in March 1930 on the streets of Chicago. Allegedly, he got drunk and then lost, and his body was found in the snow the next morning. He was buried in Texas in a family plot next to his mother.

The Blues Foundation Hall of Fame inducted Jefferson in 1980. His music has influenced generations of performers, including Sonny Terry, Muddy Waters, Joe Turner, T-Bone Walker, and Josh White. Even the music of performers outside the blues genre, from Bob Dylan's to Louis Armstrong's, has reflected the influence of Jefferson's singing style and repertoire.

Eric Bennett

See Also

Armstrong, Louis ("Satchmo"); Blues, The; Ledbetter, Hudson William ("Leadbelly"); Rainey, Gertrude Pridgett ("Ma"); Walker, Aaron ("T-Bone").

North America

Jefferson, Mildred Fay (b. 1927, Pittsburgh, Tex.), African American physician and politician known for her opposition to abortion.

Mildred Jefferson received a bachelor's degree from Texas College in Tyler, Texas, then moved to Boston to continue her studies at Tufts University. She received a scholarship from a local synagogue to attend Harvard Medical School, which had just begun admitting women in 1945. In 1951 she became the first African American woman to graduate from Harvard Medical School.

Jefferson began her practice as a general surgeon, eventually becoming assistant clinical professor of surgery at Boston University Medical Center. In the early 1970s she became involved in politics because of her strong disagreement with the increasing liberalization of attitudes toward abortion. She became president of the antiabortion National Right to Life Committee (NRLC). She also served as a prosecution witness in the highly publicized trial of Boston doctor Kenneth Edelin, who was charged with manslaughter for performing an abortion.

Jefferson ran unsuccessfully as a candidate for the United States Senate from Massachusetts in 1982, 1984, 1988, and 1990.

Lisa Clayton Robinson

North America

Jefferson, William
(b. March 14, 1947, Lake Providence, La.), Democratic member of the United States House of Representatives from Louisiana (1991-). Jefferson was his state's first black congressman since the Reconstruction era of the 1870s.

Born in Lake Providence, Louisiana, William Jennings Jefferson was raised in poverty as one of ten children. He earned a bachelor's degree from Southern University and A&M College in 1969. He received a scholarship to Harvard Law School, where he earned his law degree in 1972. In 1996 he completed a master's degree in tax law at Georgetown University.

Jefferson served in the United States Army from 1969 until 1975. He worked as a clerk for a federal court judge (1972-1973) and as a legislative assistant to U.S. senator J. Bennett Johnston of Louisiana (1973-1975). Jefferson served in the Louisiana Senate from 1979 to 1991 and was an unsuccessful candidate for mayor of New Orleans in 1982 and 1986. In 1990 he was elected to the U.S. House to represent the Second District. He was returned to office in subsequent elections.

The heavily Democratic Second District covers most of the city of New Orleans. It is an ethnically diverse region rooted in the service industries, such as retail and hospitality services. The French Quarter is located in Jefferson's district. The Second District is home to Tulane University, the University of New Orleans, Loyola University, and Xavier University.

Before 1995 Jefferson sat on the Ways and Means Committee. When the Republicans took over the House in 1995, they cut the number of Democratic seats on the Ways and Means panel, causing Jefferson to lose his seat. However, he returned to the Ways and Means Committee in the 105th Congress (1997-1999). He is a member of the Congressional Black Caucus.

See Also

New Orleans, Louisiana.

North America

Jemison, Mae Carol
(b. October 17, 1956, Decatur, Ala.), African American astronaut, physician, and professor and the first African American woman to enter space.

Born to Charlie and Dorothy Jemison, a maintenance supervisor and a schoolteacher, Mae Carol Jemison was raised in Chicago, Illinois. Graduating from Morgan Park High School in 1973 at age 16, she entered Stanford University on a National Achievement Scholarship. She graduated in 1977 with two concurrent bachelor degrees, in chemical engineering and African/Afro-American Studies. She then entered Cornell Medical School, graduating in 1981, and interned briefly in Los Angeles, California.

Jemison joined the Peace Corps in January 1983 and worked as a medical officer in West Africa through July 1985. In 1987 she was accepted by NASA as an astronaut candidate, one of 15 who were accepted from among 2000 applicants. She completed a one-year training and evaluation program in August 1988 and became a science mission specialist, helping prepare the space shuttles for launch. She was the first black female astronaut to enter space, aboard the space shuttle *Endeavor* in September 1992. Retiring after six years with NASA, she started her own research, development, and constancy company, the Jemison Group, Inc., whose projects include ALAFIYA™, a satellite-based telecommunications system to improve health care delivery in West Africa, and The Earth We Share™, an international science camp for young teenagers.

The Mae C. Jemison Academy in Detroit, Michigan, teaches science and math to children in preschool through second grade. Jemison is also a professor in the Environmental Studies Program at Dartmouth College, where she heads the Jemison Institute for Advancing Technology in Developing Countries. She has received numerous awards and honors, such as the Essence Award in 1988 and the Gamma Sigma Gamma Woman of the Year Award in 1989; she lives in Houston, Texas.

See Also

Essence.

Jenné-Jeno, Mali. Please see Djenné-Djeno, Mali

Jenné, Mali. Please see Djenné, Mali

North America

Jessye, Eva (b. January 20, 1895, Coffeyville, Kans.; d. February 21, 1992, Ypsilanti, Mich.), African American choral director, composer, and educator, the first African American woman to gain international renown as a professional choral director.

A woman of many talents, Eva Jessye pursued a music career that spanned more than half a century and won her a reputation as "the dean of black female musicians." During the 1930s she gained international attention as director of the Eva Jessye Choir, which toured the United States and Europe and sang in the first production of George Gershwin's folk opera *Porgy and Bess* (1935). During the next three decades she led the choir in numerous revivals of the opera and in 1963 directed the choir for the historic March on Washington led by Martin Luther King Jr.

Jessye grew up in Coffeyville, Kansas, where, after the separation of her parents in 1898, she was reared by her grandmother and her mother's sisters. As a child she began singing, organized a girls' quartet, and, at age 12, helped composer Will Marion Cook copy music for his orchestra when he toured her hometown. At age 13 she began musical studies at Western University in Quindaro, Kansas. After earning a teaching certificate from Langston University in Oklahoma, she spent several years teaching music in Oklahoma schools, and in 1920 became the head of the music department at Morgan State College in Baltimore.

In 1922 Jessye moved to New York, where she studied privately with Will Marion Cook and the music theorist Percy Goetschius. Four years later she had established herself as director of the Original Dixie Jubilee Singers, later renamed the Eva Jessye Choir. In 1929 she went to Hollywood to train a choir to perform in the first black musical film, *Hallelujah* (1929, Metro-Goldwyn-Mayer), written and directed by King Vidor, and in 1934 she became choral director of Virgil Thompson's opera *Four Saints in Three Acts.* Achieving international fame as choral director of Gershwin's *Porgy and Bess,* she continued to tour with her choir for more than 40 years. A respected composer, she conducted her own music in both radio and stage performances and in 1972 directed her critically acclaimed folk oratorio *Paradise Lost and Regained* (composed in 1934) at the Washington Cathedral.

Jessye exerted considerable influence as a teacher. She held several teaching posts, lectured widely, and played an important role in the careers of such concert artists as Muriel Rahn, Andrew Frierson, and Lawrence Winters. In 1974 she established the Eva Jessye Collection of Afro-American Music at the University of Michigan in Ann Arbor, where she spent the last ten years of her life. She died of natural causes in Ypsilanti, Michigan, at age 97.

Roanne Edwards

See Also

King, Martin Luther, Jr.; New York, New York; March on Washington, 1963.

Latin America and the Caribbean

Jesus, Carolina Maria de

(b. 1914, Sacramento, Minas Gerais, Brazil; d. February 13, 1977, Parelheiros, São Paulo, Brazil), Afro-Brazilian writer, the first black woman from the FAVELAS, or squatter settlements, to write about the everyday struggles of the Brazilian poor.

In 1960 the diary of Carolina Maria de Jesus, an impoverished black woman, was published in BRAZIL, an event that brought her national and international celebrity. Titled *Quarto de Despejo* (Child of the Dark), the diary sold 90,000 copies within the first six months, making it the most successful book in the history of Brazilian publishing. It was translated into more than a dozen languages and attracted worldwide attention. The book also brought Jesus financial success, allowing her to move out of the favelas.

Her subsequent writings, including a second diary, *Casa de Alvenaria* (1961, I'm Going to Have a Little House), were not successful, and she soon drifted into obscurity. As scholar Robert M. Levine has said, "Ill-prepared for her meteoric rise to fame after her diary was published, Carolina Maria de Jesus went from being a woman reviled for her blackness, her illegitimacy, and her poverty to a woman mocked for her supposed ingratitude and lack of docility." Moreover, some have questioned the authenticity of *Quarto de Despejo*. In 1958 Jesus had shown her handwritten diary to the Brazilian journalist Audálio Dantes, who first published it in tightly edited form in the newspaper *Diário de São Paulo.* Then, after spending a year editing it again, Dantes succeeded in selling it to one of Brazil's most prestigious publishing houses.

Jesus grew up in Sacramento, in the backwoods of Minas Gerais, Brazil. Born out of wedlock, she was ostracized by her community, a stigma further compounded by her gender, color, and the fact that her mother worked cleaning house for prostitutes. From age 7 to 9 she attended primary school, where she learned to read and write. She spent the next four years on a *fazenda* (plantation), laboring without wages, while on her own improving her reading and writing skills. At age 16 she moved to Franca, near São Paulo, where she worked as a domestic servant. In 1947 she became pregnant, lost her job, and saw no option but to build a shack in São Paulo's Canindé favela. Although she lived in extreme poverty, she made time to write and in 1955 began her diary.

In *Quarto de Despejo*, Jesus describes the daily miseries of favela life and how she foraged in trashcans for food and clothing. She also affirms her independence as well as her pride in being black. Yet her diary contains profound contradictions. As Levine points out, "She hated her misery, she ached for a decent life for herself and her children, but at the same time she castigated her favela neighbors, harbored prejudices against northeasterners, and reviled fellow blacks." Jesus did not advocate resistance or revolution but seemed to accept the system that had left her impoverished. Indeed, it is the numbness of her existence that the diary most strongly conveys. It also reinforces many of the negative stereotypes held in the West about favela life. Numerous Western critics saw the diary as protest literature, revealing the corruption of the Brazilian political system.

The diary was published at a critical time in the history of Brazil. The early 1960s was a transitional period between the era of populist leader Getúlio Vargas (1930-1945) and the establishment in 1964 of a military dictatorship. As Brazilian scholar José Carlos Sebe Bom Meihy notes, "Carolina... in many ways was a model Vargas citizen. She was sober, she possessed an unbending work effort, and more than anything else she wanted to be a good mother for her children." Like many Brazilian critics, he does not see her diaries as protest literature. Jesus, who believed that the favelas should be eradicated, "never took part in community action within the favela; she wrote to escape," argues Meihy. "[Her diary] represents the traditional defensiveness of Brazilian black literature. She does not dwell on the question of racial identity. Rather, she sought to live in peace in a better world, the world of whites." But Meihy upholds the importance of Jesus's diary. "Her success cannot merely be explained as the work of journalists or editors," he says. "While Carolina rejected and fled favela life, she was also marked by it."

Roanne Edwards

See Also

Literature, Black, in Brazil; Women Writers, Black, in Brazil.

Latin America and the Caribbean

Jesus, Clementina de

(b. July 7, 1902, Valença, Rio de Janeiro, BRAZIL; d. 1987, Rio de Janeiro, Brazil), an Afro-Brazilian singer with a low-pitched, raspy voice and deep knowledge of obscure Afro-Brazilian genres such as *jongo, lundu,* and *samba partido alto.*

As an adolescent, Clementina de Jesus sang in the choir of the local church in the Oswaldo Cruz neighborhood and later participated in the Portela samba school. In 1940 she married and moved to Mangueira, home to a rival samba school. For the next 20 years she worked as a maid and sang only for family and friends. In 1964 the composer and impresario Hermínio Bello de Carvalho invited her to perform with the classical guitarist Turíbio Santos. Her professional debut coincided with an emerging interest in roots music among left-wing artists and intellectuals. In the following year she participated in the highly acclaimed musical showcase *Rosa de Ouro,* which was later released on two albums.

In 1966 she represented BRAZIL in the First Festival of Black Arts in Dakar, SENEGAL. In 1968 she recorded the album *Gente da Antiga* with two early innovators of SAMBA, PIXINGUINHA and João da Baiana. Two years later she finally recorded her first solo LP, *Clementina, cadê você?,* which was followed by *Clementina de Jesus-Marinheiro só.* In the Carnival of 1988, the Vila Isabel samba school commemorated the centennial year of abolition and paid homage to Clementina de Jesus in their winning theme song, "Kizomba, Festa da Raça."

Christopher Dunn

See Also
Samba Schools; Rio de Janeiro, Brazil; Carnivals in Latin America and the Caribbean.

North America

Jet, a popular African American weekly news magazine, sold in over 40 countries.

Jet's creator, John H. Johnson, founder of the Johnson Publishing Company, Inc., intended for the magazine to be a pocket-size (5 ¼ by 4 in) complement to *Ebony*, the leading black periodical of the day. Johnson modeled *Jet* on *Quick*, a complementary publication of the popular picture magazine *Life*. He envisioned a news digest for people who had neither the time nor inclination to read deeply on current issues, but who wished to remain well informed.

Jet won immediate popularity because of its concise coverage of important social, political, and sports events and of issues confronting the African American community. Within six issues of its founding, in November 1951, *Jet's* weekly circulation reached over 300,000. Its popularity grew steadily into the 1990s, by which time circulation had reached 900,000 per week. (It experienced literal growth as well, changing its format to 7 ½ by 5 ¼ in.) By 1997 *Jet* had over 1 million subscribers in over 40 countries, many of them in Africa.

Robert Fay

See Also
Ebony.

Africa

Jewish Communities in North Africa, communities of Jews who settled in North Africa in a number of migrations beginning before the Roman conquest.

Until the 1960s North Africa was home to one of the largest Jewish populations in the world. Egypt figures prominently in the Torah, which records a Jewish presence in Egypt as early as the second millennium B.C.E. In the sixth century B.C.E., the time of the first Jewish dispersion, Jews again sought refuge in Egypt, and it is believed that they accompanied Phoenician settlers to western coastal North Africa. Since then, Jewish communities have continuously inhabited the region now comprising Egypt, Libya, Tunisia, Algeria, and Morocco. The Muslims who conquered North Africa starting in the seventh century found Jewish, as well as Christian and animist, communities among the Berber- and Egyptian-speaking populations. Under early Muslim rule Jews were granted a special status as "people of the Scripture," and Islamic law allowed them to hold land, administer justice within their communities, and practice their religion. Under Muslim rule, Jews sometimes enjoyed tolerance, though at other times they faced anti-Semitic violence.

When the Almoravid and Almohad Islamic dynasties conquered the region of southern Spain known as Andalusia, North African Jewish communities established ties to their fellow Jews in Spain. From the fourteenth to the seventeenth century, these Spanish Jews, who spoke a Judeo-Spanish dialect called Ladino and were known as Sephardim, fled the terror of the Spanish Inquisition and the forced conversions of the Christian Reconquest. Many settled in North Africa.

Although these immigrants settled throughout the Maghreb and Egypt, particularly large Sephardic communities settled in Oran, Algeria, and in northern and coastal Morocco. They flocked to cities; in Morocco they lived in walled ghettos called *mellahs*. In some places, such as Tunisia, the first wave of Sephardic Jews integrated with existing Jewish communities. But many of the new immigrants were from a privileged background in Spain, and their cosmopolitan ways, their wealth, and their Judeo-Spanish language set them apart from existing Jewish communities. Wielding considerable influence in the trading centers of North Africa, they often occupied a higher class position than their counterparts who spoke Judeo-Arabic or Judeo-Berber languages. Throughout North Africa, Sephardic Jews developed the region as merchants, middlemen, and diplomats, and some even occupied prominent positions in Islamic dynasties. Arabic- and Berber-speaking Jews generally worked as artisans, tradesmen, jewelry makers, or small-scale farmers harvesting fruits and vegetables.

With the sixteenth-century conquest of much of North Africa by the Ottoman Empire, Jews in Algeria, Tunisia, Libya, and Egypt faced special taxes and discrimination. Once again, however, the relative privilege of different Jewish groups split their communities along lines of origin. For example, the Tunisian Grana, a cosmopolitan group of Jews who arrived from Livorno, Italy, in the late seventeenth century, often served as agents and middlemen for the Turkish corsairs. Jews from Eastern Europe, as well as some from other parts of the Ottoman Empire, settled in Egypt, where they established prosperous communities in Cairo and Tanta.

By the nineteenth century some Jewish communities were involved in the expanding trade with European powers. Their links with commercial interests might be one reason that colonized Jews at first enjoyed a relatively privileged position compared to their Islamic counterparts. In Algeria, where their population numbered 30,000 at the time of French colonization, Jews were even granted French citizenship in 1870, a move that generated anti-Semitic violence by French settlers and Muslims in cities around the country. During World War II, however, the rights Jews had gained disappeared when the Axis powers held forth in North Africa. Many Jews under the Vichy government were interned and forced into labor camps.

Jewish communities split over the issue of decolonization – in the words of Tunisian writer Albert Memmi, "The Jewish population identified as much with the colonizers as with the colonized." Despite this, many Jews took part in liberation struggles, and nationalist organizations such as the Algerian Front de Libération Nationale (FLN) promised tolerance under independent rule. Yet the tide turned against Jews as nationalist struggles took on an increasingly Muslim character, and many Jews either sided with the colonial governments or fled North Africa.

In Egypt, where a large Jewish community included those who had left Palestine during World War I, tensions increased with the rise of Zionism and Islamic nationalism. During the 1950s and 1960s in several North African states promoting an Islamic identity, Jews lost civil rights, and many of their places of worship were pillaged or seized. Numerous Jews left Egypt after the 1956 Suez War, and those who remained were imprisoned by the government in concentration camps during the 1967 Arab-Israeli war. Throughout North Africa, anti-Semitic violence increased after this war, and most Jews left for Europe, Israel, or the Americas. Today there are still Jews living in North Africa, but their communities are small and scattered.

Marian Aguiar

See Also
Roman Africa: An Interpretation; Decolonization in Africa: An Interpretation; Nationalism in Africa; Almohads; Almoravids; Cairo, Egypt.

North America

Jews, Black, groups that combine Black Nationalist and Pan-Africanist ideology with Jewish principles and symbols.

Black Jewish organizations are not affiliated with the African Americans who either converted to Judaism or were born Jewish, and although they often identify with Falasha, a group of Ethiopian Jews, they are a separate phenomenon. Also known as Black Hebrews, Black Jews refer to a range of often-militant religious groups who, through combining the philosophies of Black Nationalism and Pan-Africanism with idiosyncratic interpretations of Judaic history and teachings, identify themselves as God's chosen people.

Messianism figures prominently in their ideology; members often follow a charismatic leader who claims divine inspiration and promises an eventual redemption from the material and spiritual poverty of the United States. Motifs of freedom from bondage and slavery recur, and the plight of African Americans is paralleled with the biblical story of Exodus. They proclaim that African Americans were actually Hebrews before they were enslaved and robbed of their identities. Influenced by the calls for repatriation by Marcus Garvey and other black nationalists, many Black Jews proclaimed – and often attempted – a return to homelands in Israel, ETHIOPIA, or other parts of Africa.

As did Garvey's UNIVERSAL NEGRO IMPROVEMENT ASSOCIATION (UNIA), Black Jews have often adopted African-inspired symbols and rituals in an effort to mark their claims to an independent black nation. The Star Order of Ethiopians, Ethiopian Missionaries to Abyssinia – the force behind Chicago's Abyssinian Affair – is emblematic of this: members sold Abyssinian flags and bogus certificates of citizenship to finance their return to Ethiopia.

Perhaps the first Black Jewish group in the United States was the Church of the Living God, the Pillar Ground of Truth for All Nations, founded in the 1880s by the African American seaman and railway worker Prophet F. S. Cherry. It began in Chattanooga, Tennessee, before Cherry relocated it to Philadelphia. In addition to preaching black economic independence, Cherry taught that God and Jesus, as well as Adam and Eve, were black; that white Jews were false Jews; and that the white race was descended from Gehazi, a servant who was cursed with "skin as white as snow" by the prophet Elisha. Cherry's followers refused to acknowledge his death, believing instead that he had temporarily disappeared and would soon be back in spirit, leading the church through his son.

Another early black Hebrew organization was the Temple Beth-El congregation, better known as the Church of God and Saints of Christ, founded by William S. Crowdy in 1896. A former slave and cook on the Santa Fe Railroad, Crowdy was inspired by a vision he had in 1893 that, according to scholars Baer and Singer, told him he "was called by God to lead African American people back to their historic religion and identity." Based in Lawrence, Kansas, and Oneida, New York, until Crowdy moved it to Philadelphia, the Church's doctrines – the "Seven Keys" – were derived from his revelations. They suggested that black people were the lost tribes of Israel and, although the New Testament was also read and Jesus Christ recognized, promoted an adherence to the laws of the Hebrew Bible.

After Crowdy's death in 1908, the church continued to develop. Bishop H. Z. Plummer took it over, stressing collectivist principles and black economic self-sufficiency. He moved headquarters to Belleville, Virginia, where its members still live together on a 1000-acre plot of land, running a farm and school. In 1936 it had more than 200 tabernacles in the United States. The church currently lists 38,000 members, though the number of tabernacles had fallen to 53 in the United States and seven in SOUTH AFRICA.

In 1923 Arnold Josiah Ford, a Barbadian composer, musician, linguist, and theologian, founded Harlem's Beth B'nai Abraham congregation. After serving in the British Royal Navy's musical corps during World War I, he moved to Harlem and joined the Black Jewish Moorish Zionist Temple, founded by Leon Richelieu in 1899. Ford soon left Richelieu's congregation and founded the Beth B'nai Congregation. He also joined the UNIA and unsuccessfully attempted to persuade Garvey to institute Judaism as its official religion. With the decline of the UNIA, Ford devoted more time to his Beth B'nai Abraham congregation and to his efforts to repatriate blacks to Ethiopia. In 1930 Ethiopian ruler HAILE SELASSIE I granted Ford's congregation 800 acres of land for the establishment of a black colony. Ford soon left for Ethiopia, followed by 50 members of the temple. The colony survived only two years; internal squabbles, conflicts with the Ethiopian government, and hostility from Ethiopian whites destroyed it.

After Ford died in 1934, one of his students, Wentworth A. Matthew, founder of the Commandment Keepers, Holy Church of the Living God, Pillar and Ground of the Truth, became the most prominent Black Jewish figure in Harlem. His Royal Order of Ethiopian Hebrews, founded in 1936, had branches throughout the United States and the Caribbean. He also established the Ethiopian Hebrew Rabbinical College for training and ordaining the rabbis who continue his work today.

The most prominent Black Jewish organization today is probably Miami's Nation of Yahweh. Also known as the Temple of Love, it is only the most recent manifestation of its founder Yahweh Ben Yahweh's long spiritual career. Born Hulon Mitchell Jr. in Oklahoma, Ben Yahweh was a pampered child raised in the Pentecostal Church, and his holiness was proclaimed early by his mother. After incarnations as a civil rights activist, a Rosicrucian, a NATION OF ISLAM Minister, and a spiritual huckster in Atlanta, Mitchell settled in Miami, Florida, and founded the Temple of Love.

Its clean, white temples and its white-robed devotees stood out amongst the deterioration of the Miami ghetto of Liberty City, attracting both potential devotees and the local business community. Messages of black economic self-reliance, free from the "white devils" allegedly conspiring to commit genocide against African Americans, helped the rapid growth of the temple in Miami as well as in other United States cities. Through aggressive fundraising, the temple became not only an active force in Miami's civic culture, but a major real-estate holder, opening grocery stores, hotels, and schools.

In the late 1980s, however, the Nation of Yahweh was indicted on a series of charges developing from allegations of sexual and physical abuse, extortion, and murder. Former members claimed Ben Yahweh engaged in polygamy and pedophilia and incited members to go on killing sprees. In 1992 Yahweh Ben Yahweh was convicted for racketeering and murder charges. Although he remains in prison, his followers are still active. They maintain his innocence, claiming his incarceration was politically motivated.

At this time the exact number of Black Jewish organizations in the United States is unknown. It seems certain, however, that as long as social and economic conditions keep African Americans disfranchised, such groups will continue to thrive.

Peter Hudson

SEE ALSO

Pan-Africanism; World War I and African Americans; Garvey, Marcus Mosiah; Harlem, New York; Pentecostalism; Philadelphia, Pennsylvania; Black Nationalism in the United States.

North America

Jim Crow, the system of laws and customs that enforced racial segregation and discrimination throughout the United States, especially the South, from the late nineteenth century to the 1960s.

African Americans living in the South during the first half of the twentieth century saw graphic reminders of their second-class citizenship everywhere. Signs reading "Whites Only" or "Colored" hung over drinking fountains and the doors to restrooms, restaurants, movie theaters, and other public places. Along with segregation, blacks, particularly in the South, faced discrimination in jobs and housing and were often denied their constitutional right to vote. Whether by law or by custom, all these obstacles to equal status went by the name Jim Crow.

Jim Crow was the name of a character in MINSTRELSY (in which white performers in blackface used African American stereotypes in their songs and dances); it is not clear how the term came to describe American segregation and discrimination. Jim Crow has its origins in a variety of sources, including the Black Codes imposed upon African Americans immediately after the Civil War and prewar racial segregation of railroad cars in the North. But it was not until after Radical RECONSTRUCTION ended in 1877 that Jim Crow was born.

Jim Crow grew slowly. In the last two decades of the nineteenth century many African Americans still enjoyed the rights granted in the Thirteenth, Fourteenth, and Fifteenth amendments, along with the 1875 Civil Rights Act. But according to historian C. Vann Woodward, by the late 1890s various factors had combined to create an environment in which white supremacy prevailed. These included the reconciliation of warring political factions in the South, the acquiescence of Northern white liberals, and the United States' military conquest of nonwhite peoples in the Philippines, Hawaii, and Cuba.

Some of the earliest Jim Crow legislation came from the transportation industry. An 1890 law in New Orleans requiring separate railroad cars for black and white passengers was soon followed by regulations in other cities and states. Such laws, ostensibly written to "protect" both races, were given federal support when the United States Supreme Court ruled in PLESSY V. FERGUSON (1896) that "separate but equal" accommodations on Louisiana's railroads were constitutional. The ruling led to legalized segregation in education, public parks, and libraries.

Other Jim Crow laws did not specifically mention race but were written and applied in ways that discriminated against African Americans. Literacy tests and poll taxes, administered with informal loopholes and trick questions, barred nearly all African Americans from voting. For example, though more than 130,000 blacks were registered to vote in Louisiana in 1896, only 1342 were on the rolls in 1904.

Disfranchisement was often defended by invoking the mythology of Reconstruction, in which Southern whites claimed that unsophisticated black voters had been manipulated by Northern "carpetbaggers" who had moved south after the war. Jim Crow proponents also found ammunition in the incendiary propaganda of the Southern white press, which published sensational and exaggerated accounts of crimes committed by African Americans. As Woodward and other historians have pointed out, an atmosphere emerged of racist hysteria, which further fueled LYNCHING, antiblack rioting, and the rise of the Ku Klux Klan. In addition, early twentieth-century trends in scholarship, including the pseudoscience of EUGENICS, lent respectability to the view that blacks were inherently inferior to whites.

Jim Crow extended to deny private as well as public, or civil, rights to African Americans. Businesses routinely refused to serve blacks, and many white homeowners would not rent or sell property to African Americans. A strict, unwritten code of behavior governed interracial interaction. Under Jim Crow etiquette, African Americans were denied all social forms of respect. Whites addressed even adult black men as "boy," and all blacks were expected to show deference to all whites. The combination of constant personal humiliation, dismal economic opportunities (sharecropping consigned most rural, Southern blacks to perpetual poverty), and inferior segregated education for their children prompted thousands of African Americans to leave the South in the Jim Crow era. Waves of exodus culminated in the Great Migration north in the 1920s, 1930s, and 1940s, but many African Americans found conditions in the North little better.

A combination of factors led to the dismantling of Jim Crow starting in the late 1940s. Attention attracted by Gunnar Myrdal's 1944 book *An American Dilemma* made Jim Crow a national embarrassment. After more than a decade of litigation, the legal work of the NATIONAL ASSOCIATION FOR THE ADVANCEMENT OF COLORED PEOPLE (NACCP) began to bear fruit. Supreme Court decisions in SWEATT V. PAINTER (1949) and *McLaurin* v. *Oklahoma* (1950) started to break down the separate but equal standard set by *Plessy* and finally outlawed state-sponsored segregation in 1954's BROWN V. BOARD OF EDUCATION. Violent resistance by some white Southerners was met by a growing CIVIL RIGHTS MOVEMENT that used boycotts, SIT-INS, marches, and other forms of nonviolent protest to achieve goals such as passage of the 1964 Civil Rights Act and 1965 Voting Rights Act. But despite victories against segregation and discrimination, African Americans continued to face unequal opportunities, and new approaches, such as the BLACK POWER Movement, sought to repair the lasting damage of Jim Crow.

Kate Tuttle

SEE ALSO

An American Dilemma: The Negro Problem and Modern Democracy; Black Codes in the United States; Civil War, American; Fifteenth Amendment to the United States Constitution; Fourteenth Amendment to the United States Constitution; Great Migration, The; New Orleans, Louisiana; Racial Stereotypes; Thirteenth Amendment of the United States Constitution and the Emancipation Proclamation; Voting Rights Act of 1965; Spanish-Cuban-American War.

Latin America and the Caribbean

Jiménez, Blas (b. 1950, Santo Domingo, DOMINICAN REPUBLIC), Afro-Dominican writer whose published works include four collections of poetry: *Aquí... otro español* (1980), *Caribe africano en despertar* (1984), *Exigencias de un cimarrón (en sueños)* (1987), and *El nativo (versos en cuentos para espantar zombies)* (1996). None of these works has been translated into English.

Blas Jiménez grew up just outside the Dominican Republic's capital city, Santo Domingo. When he attended primary and secondary school, the educational system emphasized the Spanish legacy of Dominican culture. This Eurocentric image seemed foreign to Jiménez, who was a dark-skinned child of the lower classes. As a reaction against pervasive racism, he gradually came to identify with the extinct indigenous peoples of the island and with contemporary Haitians living in the Dominican Republic, since both were groups who had been oppressed because of their color and culture.

As a result of his academic achievement at a high school for agricultural studies, Jiménez received a student loan from the Agency for International Development to attend Texas A&M University. While studying for his bachelor's degree there, Jiménez read the literature of the HARLEM RENAISSANCE and of the AFROCUBANISMO and NÉGRITUDE movements. He was particularly inspired by the works of Haitian writer RENÉ DEPESTRE. All of these influences helped Jiménez to shape the Afro-Dominican identity expressed in his own writing. Many of his poems incorporate the rhythmic accents typical of Hispanic Caribbean negrista poetry of the 1930s. His poetry urges Dominicans and other Afro-Caribbean peoples to embrace African cultural values. It likewise condemns discrimination against people of African descent.

Jiménez currently lives in Santo Domingo. He maintains a weekly column in *Hoy*, one of the largest Dominican newspapers.

Marveta Ryan

SEE ALSO

Haiti; Literature, Black, in Spanish America; Education in Latin America and the Caribbean; Negrista Poets.

Africa

Johannesburg, South Africa, city in northeastern SOUTH AFRICA.

One of the largest cities in southern Africa, Johannesburg has a population estimated at more than 4.5 million. Its area, about 777 sq km (about 300 sq mi), comprises not only the city itself but more than 400 suburbs, as well as the townships where "non-whites" were forced to live under APARTHEID.

Situated on the Witwatersrand mountain range, the Johannesburg area was home only to scattered TSWANA settlements before 1886, when the discovery of gold deposits spurred the rapid immigration of speculators and diggers from other parts of southern Africa as well as from Europe. Within a decade Johannesburg had grown from a mining camp into an industrialized city of some 100,000 people, an estimated three-quarters of whom worked in the mines. For many years far more men than women migrated to Johannesburg, and many of them lived in workers' hostels. During and after World War II booming industrial growth spurred another wave of urban migration and the growth of Sophiatown and other shantytowns. By this time some of South Africa's largest labor unions were well established in Johannesburg.

After the NATIONAL PARTY began imposing apartheid policies in 1948, many of the Johannesburg shantytowns were destroyed, and blacks were relocated either to rural "bantustans" or to newly created townships outside the city. These areas were poorly serviced and soon became extremely crowded, often with as many as ten people sharing one room. The largest township, Soweto (with a current population estimated at between 2 and 4 million), was the site of a 1976 police massacre of peacefully protesting schoolchildren. Other townships housed the Asian and "Coloured" populations.

Since the dismantling of apartheid in the early 1990s, Johannesburg has become increasingly racially integrated. Great income inequality persists, and most of the city's black residents still live in Soweto, while the wealthy suburbs remain predominantly white. In addition, the freedom to move within the country has brought more job-seeking migrants to Johannesburg, straining already crowded conditions. Crime and pollution have become major problems in Soweto and other poor areas.

Johannesburg is now the capital of Gauteng, the richest of South Africa's nine provinces. The city is home not only to the mining industry but to the national stock exchange, a wide range of manufacturing industries, the international airport, and the University of Witwatersrand. Since 1994 the African National Congress has dominated Johannesburg's elected metropolitan council; some 32 percent of the council seats are held by women.

Kate Tuttle

See Also
Cape Coloured; Sophiatown, South Africa; Gold Trade; Soweto, South Africa.

North America

Johnson, "Blind" Willie (b. 1902, near Marlin, Tex.; d. 1947, Beaumont, Tex.), African American gospel bluesman who recorded best-selling religious race records in the late 1920s.

Willie Johnson's date of birth remains uncertain, as do the circumstances of the accident that took his sight at age seven. Allegedly, his stepmother threw lye water in his face during a domestic fracas. Johnson's blindness probably led him to cultivate his musical talent, as the handicap interfered less with this than with his interest in the ministry. By his teens Johnson was supporting himself as a musician, playing guitar, singing religious songs, and preaching on the streets of Waco and Dallas as well as in the Baptist churches of nearby towns.

Johnson married late in the 1920s, settled permanently in Dallas, and began to record with Columbia Records. All his best-known works have religious themes, and he is lauded as a major progenitor of gospel blues. It is believed that he also recorded at least two secular blues songs under the name of Blind Texas Marlin.

Most of Johnson's Columbia recordings are characterized by gravelly bass vocals – apparently affected – and artful slide-guitar, although some reveal his natural tenor voice and his aptitude as a fingerpicker. His basslike singing is often backed by a female vocalist, possibly his wife, Angeline. His most famous recordings include "Motherless Children Have a Hard Time," "Jesus Make Up My Dying Bed," and "Dark Was the Night and Cold Was the Ground," which was featured on the soundtrack of *The Gospel According to Saint Mark* and was interpreted by white guitarist and folk musician Ry Cooder for the film *Paris, Texas*. All of Johnson's records proved commercially successful.

Johnson ceased to record after the onset of the Great Depression in 1929. But he continued to perform until his death in 1947, the details of which are as obscure as those surrounding much of his life. According to his wife, Johnson died of pneumonia contracted by having slept in the wet ashes of his burnt-down house.

Eric Bennett

See Also
Baptists; Blues, The; Gospel Music.

North America

Johnson, Charles Richard (b. April 23, 1948, Evanston, Ill.), African American novelist, essayist, and screenwriter whose work challenges the concepts of time, history, language, and truth.

By the time Charles Richard Johnson finished his undergraduate degree at Southern Illinois University, he had already published two collections of drawings and had worked on an art program on the Public Broadcasting System (PBS) called *Charley's Pad*. Johnson stayed on to do graduate work at the university and received a Ph.D. in philosophy from SUNY-Stonybrook.

Johnson's influences are many and varied, ranging from Japanese Buddhism to Cervantes, and from Saint Augustine to Herman Hesse. But his primary mentors have been African American writers such as W. E. B. Du Bois, Jean Toomer, Richard Wright, and Ralph Ellison, as well as the novelist John Gardner, under whose supervision he worked for many years.

Among Johnson's many works are his novel *Oxherding Tale* (1982), which is an African American writer's slave narrative, and his sea story, *Middle Passage*, which received the 1990 National Book Award. He also published a collection of stories, *The Sorcerer's Apprentice* (1986), which explores and attempts to employ many of the philosophies he has studied, and a book of literary criticism titled *Being and Race: Black Writing Since 1970* (1988).

Johnson is considered an important contemporary American writer, constantly challenging his readers to question the constructs of time, history, language, and truth. His stylistic innovations offer a unique perspective on African American history, fiction, and philosophy. He teaches creative writing at the University of Washington in Seattle.

Rachel Antell

See Also
Literature, African American; Slave Narratives.

North America

Johnson, Charles Spurgeon (b. July 24, 1893, Bristol, Va.; d. October 27, 1956), African American sociologist, first African American president of Fisk University.

Charles Johnson's interest in sociology was sparked when his family sent him to Virginia Union University in Richmond, where he graduated with a B.A. in 1916. During his years at college Johnson came to suspect that racism is often closely intertwined with social and economic deprivation.

One year after completing college Johnson decided to enter graduate school at the University of Chicago to study sociology under the pioneering urban sociologist Robert Park. After attaining his Ph.D. in 1918, he published *The Negro in Chicago: A Study in Race Relations and a Race Riot* (1922). Johnson's report analyzed the causes of the 1919 Chicago race riot and warned of the possibility of further riots in Chicago because of continuing racial inequality. He became director of research for the National Urban League in New York City in 1921. He founded the league's magazine, *Opportunity: A Journal of Negro Life*, in 1923 and served as its editor until 1928.

From 1928 to 1947 Johnson served as chairman of the Department of Social Sciences at Fisk University in Nashville, Tennessee, where he continued to research how economic forces shape race relations. During this time he authored several books on black life and race relations, including *Shadow of the Plantation* (1934), *Growing Up in the Black Belt* (1941), and *Patterns of Negro Segregation* (1943).

Johnson was a consultant on race relations to three United States presidents: Franklin D. Roosevelt, Herbert Hoover, and Dwight D. Eisenhower. He served in the League of Nations in 1930 and worked with the U.S. Department of Agriculture from 1936 to 1937. In 1946 he became the first black president of Fisk. In this capacity Johnson continued to pursue his lifelong goal of "over-coming inequality in social and economic environments."

See Also
Chicago Riots of 1919; *Opportunity: Journal of Negro Life*; New York, New York; Richmond, Virginia.

Johnson, Earvin. Please see Johnson, Magic

North America

Johnson, Eddie Bernice (b. 1935, Waco, Tex.), Democratic member of the United States House of Representatives from Texas (1993-).

Eddie Bernice Johnson was born in Waco, Texas. She received a bachelor's degree in

1955 from St. Mary's at Notre Dame and a nursing degree in 1967 from Texas Christian University. She worked as a nurse until being elected to the Texas House of Representatives in 1972. She earned a master's degree in public administration in 1976 from Southern Methodist University. Johnson left the Texas House in 1977 when President Jimmy Carter appointed her regional director of the Department of Health, Education, and Welfare (HEW). She worked at HEW until 1981, then started her own business consulting firm in Dallas.

In 1986 Johnson was elected to the Texas Senate. As chair of the Texas Senate subcommittee responsible for drawing congressional districts for 1992, she created the new Thirtieth Congressional District, which subsequently elected her to Congress in 1992. In 1994 federal judges ruled the district unconstitutional because it was minority-based and ordered the Texas legislature to redraw it. The redistricting was completed in August 1996 and in November 1996 Johnson was easily reelected.

The Thirtieth District is now located entirely within Dallas County and includes portions of the cities of Dallas and Irving. The city of Dallas is a center of banking, insurance, and medical care in the Southwest. Electronic Data Systems, a manufacturer of computer semiconducters, is a major employer. Irving is home to the Dallas-Fort Worth Airport.

In the 105th Congress (1997-1999), Johnson sat on the Science Committee and the Committee on Transportation and Infrastructure. She also served as secretary of the CONGRESSIONAL BLACK CAUCUS.

North America

Johnson, Georgia Douglas

(b. September 10, 1877, Atlanta, Ga.; d. May 14, 1966, Washington, D.C.), African American poet and playwright; also known for the writers' workshops she hosted at her home during the HARLEM RENAISSANCE.

Although Georgia Douglas Johnson never lived in Harlem, she was the most famous woman poet of the fabled Harlem Renaissance. Her Washington, D.C., home became a salon for many of the Harlem writers associated with that literary movement, including LANGSTON HUGHES, ZORA NEALE HURSTON, JEAN TOOMER, and COUNTEE CULLEN, who often stayed with her while in the capital and held writers' workshops and discussions at her home. Johnson's own poetry and plays were popular among black audiences of the 1920s.

Johnson was born into a multiracial family (her mother was African American and Native American, her father was African American and English) in ATLANTA, GEORGIA. She graduated from Atlanta University's Normal School in 1896, studied music at the Oberlin Conservatory of Music and the Cleveland College of Music, and worked as a teacher and assistant principal in the Atlanta schools. In 1903 she married Henry Lincoln Johnson, a prominent Atlanta attorney, and it was her husband's affiliation with the Republican Party that led the family to WASHINGTON, D.C., in 1910, when he was offered a government post.

In Washington, D.C., Johnson had two sons and settled into the roles of wife and mother. But KELLY MILLER, a dean at HOWARD UNIVERSITY, read Johnson's writing and encouraged her to pursue her poetry. In 1916 Johnson's first published poems appeared in *Crisis*, the periodical of the NATIONAL ASSOCIATION FOR THE ADVANCEMENT OF COLORED PEOPLE (NAACP), and they were followed two years later by her first volume of poetry, *The Heart of a Woman.*

The poems in that book focused on romantic themes, Johnson's own favorite poetic subject. But when some black readers criticized the volume for ignoring racial issues, Johnson focused on race for the poems in her second book, *Bronze: A Book of Verse.* The new book fit thematically with the works of other Harlem Renaissance writers who were exploring race, and Johnson became identified with the larger movement. When her husband died in 1925, Johnson accepted an honorary government post in order to support herself and pay for her sons' higher education. But she continued to write, and it was after his death that she began hosting the writers' workshops in their 1461 South Street N.W. home that led to her reputation as a literary hostess.

Over the next three years several of Johnson's plays won prizes from the National Urban League's *Opportunity* magazine, and her second volume of poetry, *An Autumn Love Cycle,* was published in 1928. In 1926 Johnson began a weekly syndicated newspaper column, "Homely Philosophy," that ran in 20 papers across the country until 1932. Throughout the next three decades Johnson continued to write plays, short stories, and songs and to open her home to artists in need. She was turned down for several fellowships, however, and gradually lost the national influence she once had on the black literary scene.

When Johnson died of a stroke on May 14, 1966, cleaners discarded the unpublished manuscripts and papers she had been working on during the last 20 years of her life. But the poems and plays that she did leave behind have established her reputation as an important part of the African American literary tradition.

Lisa Clayton Robinson

SEE ALSO
American Indians; *Crisis, The*; Harlem, New York; National Urban League; *Opportunity: Journal of Negro Life.*

North America

Johnson, Helene

(b. July 7, 1906, Boston, Mass.; d. 1995), African American poet of the Harlem Renaissance; her work utilizes vernacular language and deals with issues of racial pride and female sensuality.

Helen Johnson, later nicknamed Helene by her aunt, was born July 7, 1906, in BOSTON, MASSACHUSETTS. As a child she spent time at her grandfather's house in Martha's Vineyard, but she grew up in Brookline, Massachusetts, where she did domestic work and attended high school. After graduating, she took classes at Boston University and wrote poetry as a member of Boston's Saturday Evening Quill Club.

By the time Johnson was in her early twenties, the periodical *Opportunity* had published several of her poems, for which she won three of the magazine's literary contests between 1925 and 1927. During this period her poems were also published in *Palms, Messenger, Fire!!,* and *Vanity Fair,* and in the anthology *Caroling Dusk* (1927).

Johnson and her cousin, the novelist DOROTHY WEST, moved to New York City in the late 1920s. Johnson attended the journalism program at Columbia University but never received a degree. Instead, she continued to write poetry and became associated with the writers and artists of the HARLEM RENAISSANCE. In her poems, she uses romantic and natural themes; she also utilizes vernacular language and deals with issues of racial pride and female sensuality. From 1927 to 1929 her poems were published in *Harlem* and the *Saturday Evening Quill*; and in 1931 her works were included in *The Book of American Negro Poetry.* Johnson's last published poems appeared in *Challenge: A Literary Quarterly* in 1934 and 1935.

Johnson married William Hubbel in 1935 and had one child, Abigail. After the couple's separation, Johnson lived in Massachusetts and New York City.

Leyla Keough

SEE ALSO
New York, New York; *Opportunity: Journal of Negro Life.*

North America

Johnson, James Weldon

(b. June 17, 1871, Jacksonville, Fla.; d. June 26, 1938, Wiscasset, Maine), diplomat, poet, novelist, critic, composer, and the first African American executive secretary of the NATIONAL ASSOCIATION FOR THE ADVANCEMENT OF COLORED PEOPLE (NAACP).

Few leaders have combined such keen intelligence with such varied talents as did James Weldon Johnson, whom his biographer Robert Fleming called "truly the 'Renaissance man' of the HARLEM RENAISSANCE." A leading literary and political figure, Johnson was instrumental not only in the growth of the NAACP but also in the formation and nurturing of a distinctly African American artistic community. Poetry, song lyrics, fiction, history, and editorials flowed from his pen and made him one of the great men of African American letters.

Born in Jacksonville, Florida, in 1871, Johnson grew up in a cultured household. His mother, a schoolteacher, had been born free in Nassau, Bahamas, and had spent much of her childhood in New York City. His father worked as headwaiter at a Jacksonville resort restaurant but still found time to read Plutarch; he was a self-educated man who spoke and read Spanish and enjoyed philosophical discussions. Both James and his younger brother, John Rosamond Johnson, were given music lessons at an early age, and their mother read to them at night from Charles Dickens and other Victorian novelists. Early trips to the Bahamas and New York supplemented Johnson's cosmopolitan upbringing.

After completing his education in Jacksonsville, where the black schools went only to the eighth grade, Johnson enrolled in Atlanta University both for preparatory and university classes. He spent seven years there, learning Latin and Greek, studying public speaking, singing with the Glee Club, and writing poetry. Upon his graduation in 1894, he took a job as principal of his old grammar school, a position he held for nearly eight years. As principal he added a ninth and tenth grade and visited white schools in search of ideas for improving his students' education. While working full-time as a principal, in 1895 Johnson launched a newspaper, the *Daily American*, which, though it was published for only eight months, gave him an opportunity to use his literary talents in the service of racial justice. At the same time he learned the law by apprenticeship with a local attorney and passed the bar exam in 1898.

Johnson's brother Rosamond, who had received formal musical training in Boston, convinced Johnson to collaborate with him in writing songs. In 1900 the two wrote "Lift Ev'ry Voice and Sing," the song that became known as the Negro national anthem. Two years later Johnson accompanied Rosamond to New York, where the brothers, along with Robert Cole, became a successful songwriting team. While there Johnson studied literature at Columbia University and met other African American artists such as Paul Laurence Dunbar and Will Marion Cook. In 1904 friends from Atlanta University invited Johnson to join the Colored Republican Club in New York, where his work for presidential candidate Theodore Roosevelt earned him a consulate post; he left for Puerto Cabello, Venezuela, in 1906.

Johnson's career as a diplomat lasted eight years, during which he served in both Venezuela and Nicaragua. With his excellent Spanish and elegant social manner, he became a popular figure in the racially diverse Latin American cities to which he was sent. Meanwhile, he continued to pursue literary work, beginning a novel that would eventually be titled *Autobiography of an Ex-Coloured Man* (published anonymously in 1912). In 1910 Johnson married the former Grace Nail, gaining companionship for the less enjoyable Nicaragua posting he began in 1909. When the Democrats regained the White House in 1914, Johnson resigned his consular duties, returned to New York, and turned his attention to literature.

He became a contributing editor at the *New York Age*, an African American weekly, writing sharp essays against racist violence, Jim Crow segregation, and the unequal treatment of blacks in the military. He also established a poetry section to showcase black literary talent. The political and the artistic realms were equally important and intertwined, Johnson argued, for "the world does not know that a race is great until that race produces great literature." To that end, Johnson not only continued to produce song lyrics and poetry (a collection, *Fifty Years and Other Poems*, came out in 1917) but also encouraged other African American writers to succeed.

Impressed with the multitalented young editor, the NAACP's Joel Spingarn and W. E. B. Du Bois asked Johnson to work with them. In 1916 he became the association's first field secretary, responsible for the formation of new branch offices throughout the country. While traveling in the South, Johnson recruited a young Atlantan, Walter White, who became one of the association's most important leaders. He also researched the lynchings and other racist violence that were beginning to increase in the years leading up to the Red Summer of 1919. Johnson himself had nearly suffered lynching when a group of white men saw him talking with a very fair-skinned black female journalist in 1901; only the woman's insistence that she herself was African American saved him. Upon visiting the site where a black man had been burned alive for a crime he believed the man could not have committed, Johnson realized, as he wrote in his autobiography, "that in large measure the race question involves the saving of black America's body and white America's soul."

Despite antilynching activities as varied as the Negro Silent Protest Parade in 1917 and the 1919 publication of *Thirty Years of Lynching* (the product of research by Johnson and White, among others), in 1922 the NAACP saw the defeat of the Dyer Bill, which would have made lynching a federal crime. Johnson had lobbied hard for its passage and was bitterly disappointed at its death by Southern Democratic filibuster and Northern Republican indifference. In his autobiography, though, he writes with characteristic optimism of the opportunity to make "the floors of Congress a forum in which [lynching was] discussed and brought home to the American people." While lynchings continued, their numbers did decrease dramatically following the public debate over the Dyer Bill.

In 1920 Johnson became NAACP secretary, the chief executive position within the association. His ten years in office were a decade of intense legal and organizational activity for the NAACP; for Johnson himself it also heralded a period of prodigious literary output. He edited three anthologies in the 1920s: *The Book of Negro American Poetry* (1922), *The Book of Negro American Spirituals* (1925), and *The Second Book of Negro American Spirituals* (1926). In addition, he published a second collection of poetry, *God's Trombones* (1927), and oversaw the republication, this time under his own name, of *Autobiography of an Ex-Coloured Man* (1927). After retiring from the NAACP in 1930, he published a work of social history, *Black Manhattan* (1930); a memoir, *Along This Way* (1933); and a collection of essays, *Black America, What Now?* (1934). A third poetry collection, *St. Peter Relates an Incident: Collected Poems* (1935), also appeared. In 1938, while vacationing in Maine, Johnson was killed in an automobile accident at age 67.

Kate Tuttle

See Also

Literature, African American; Antilynching Movement; Military, Blacks in the American; Boston, Massachusetts; Du Bois, William Edward Burghardt (W. E. B.); Lynching; National Association for the Advancement of Colored People; New York, New York; White, Walter Francis.

North America

Johnson, John Arthur (Jack)

(b. March 31, 1878, Galveston, Tex.; d. June 10, 1946, Raleigh, N.C.), first African American heavyweight boxing champion and controversial symbol of racial tensions in early twentieth-century America. Jack Johnson's athletic prowess and flamboyant lifestyle challenged codes of white supremacy and racial segregation in the boxing ring and in American society at large.

Born John Arthur Johnson, Jack Johnson was the son of Tina and Henry Johnson, a porter and school janitor. Johnson quit school after the fifth grade and went to work at a succession of menial jobs. He painted wagons, baked bread, trained horses, and loaded and unloaded ships on the docks of Galveston harbor. He became interested in boxing while working as a janitor at a local gymnasium.

Training and fighting locally, he quickly established a reputation as the best African American boxer in Galveston. He turned professional in 1897. In 113 fights over the next 35 years, he lost only 8. Though physically imposing and capable of unleashing a decisive knockout blow, Johnson was known for his defensive ingenuity and a compact, efficient style. He is still considered one of the great counterpunchers of all time.

A 1903 victory over "Denver Ed" Martin established Johnson as the unofficial black heavyweight champion. It was Johnson's desire, however, to prove himself against the very best competition, regardless of color. He was especially intent on undermining the reigning stereotype of African American fighters as being unable to take a punch. The leading white heavyweights, John L. Sullivan and Jim Jeffries, refused to fight Johnson, claiming that to do so would sully the sport's reputation.

Though Johnson was unable to gain a match against a white fighter in the United States, his reputation in international boxing circles mounted. On December 26, 1908, finally given the opportunity to compete for the heavyweight championship in a fight in Sydney, Australia, Johnson dethroned the reigning champion, Tommy Burns.

Johnson defended his championship against five white fighters over the next two years. Responding to the call of legions of fans anxious to restore boxing's traditional racial hierarchy, Jim Jeffries came out of retirement to challenge the African American champion.

Billed as "the Great White Hope," Jeffries fought Johnson in "the fight of the century" on July 4, 1910, in Reno, Nevada. Johnson soundly beat Jeffries. A series of race riots ensued around the country, sparked by angry whites fearful that millions of African Americans emboldened by Johnson's victory would strike out against their own subordinate status in American society.

Johnson was despised not simply for beating his white opponents, but for doing so in a manner that boldly defied white expectations of black docility and deference. He taunted, sneered, and even laughed at his opponents in the ring. In an era in which many prizefights took place in outdoor arenas, he took particular delight in having his gold front tooth gleam in the sun as he stood smiling triumphantly over a vanquished opponent. Writer Jack London spoke for many white fans when he urged Jim Jeffries to "wipe that smile off of Jack Johnson's face."

Johnson's personal life, in particular his penchant for highly publicized romantic attachments to white women, also was a flagrant violation of traditional racial norms. He married Etta Terry Duryea, a white woman, in 1911. After her suicide a year later, he married another white woman, Lucille Cameron.

In 1913 Johnson was convicted of violating the Mann Act, which forbade transporting women across state lines for immoral purposes. As a matter of course, Johnson had traveled with Duryea and Cameron across state lines; the mere fact that he had married these white women was deemed immoral. He fled the United States for FRANCE to avoid serving a prison term.

Johnson supported himself during his exile in France by conducting boxing and wrestling exhibitions. He returned to competitive boxing in HAVANA, CUBA, in April 1915, losing his heavyweight title to Jess Willard. After serving a year in prison on his return to the United States in 1920, Johnson spent the rest of his life writing, appearing in boxing exhibitions, and managing a series of business enterprises.

Johnson divorced Cameron in 1924 to marry another white woman, Irene Pineau. He died in an automobile accident in Raleigh, North Carolina, on June 10, 1946. He was inducted into the International Boxing Hall of Fame in 1990.

John Gennari

SEE ALSO
Miscegenation.

Europe

Johnson, Linton Kwesi

(b. August 24, 1952, Clarendon, Jamaica), black British poet who is one of the most prominent authors of dub poetry.

Drawing on his Jamaican roots, Linton Kwesi Johnson, also known as LKJ, pioneered DUB POETRY, using Jamaica's English-based Creole backed by REGGAE rhythms to voice the experience of racial injustice and resistance of blacks (*see* GREAT BRITAIN).

Linton Kwesi Johnson was born in rural Jamaica, where he lived with his grandmother. In 1963 he left Jamaica to join his mother in London's Brixton district. Johnson quit Tulse Hill School in Brixton at age 16 because he experienced racism. He continued to study independently and won admission to Goldsmith College at the University of London, where he earned a B.A. in 1973. Meanwhile, in 1970 he joined the Black Panther Youth League of Britain, which drew its inspiration from the Black Panthers in the United States.

In the early 1970s Johnson began to write poetry seriously. Attracted to the reggae music scene, he enlisted the band Rasta Love to accompany his poetry in 1972. At the same time, he began to publish in *Race Today*, a magazine dedicated to racial justice. The poems in Johnson's first publication, *Voices of the Living and the Dead* (1974), call on blacks to resist oppression in Great Britain. At a time when few were documenting the political struggles of blacks in Great Britain through art, Johnson published *Dread Beat and Blood* in 1975, which reflects his own experience growing up black and working-class in Brixton.

Johnson's work is radical and revolutionary, not only in the realities it depicts, but also in its use of Jamaican Creole and reggae rhythms. With his new style, Johnson was gaining a reputation as "one of Great Britain's most exciting and distinctive voices." He won the Cecil Day Lewis Fellowship in 1977 and was writer-in-residence at London Borough of Lambeth.

Wanting his poetry to be heard as well as read, Johnson released *Dread Beat and Blood* as an album called *Poet and the Roots* (1978). *Forces of Victory* followed in 1979. This album addresses racist politics and police oppression of black youth. It includes "Sonny's Lettah," a moving piece that depicts a young boy in prison who writes a letter to his mother apologizing for not taking care of his brother properly. In fact, the boy is in jail for killing the police officers who beat up his brother.

Inglan Is a Bitch, published in print in 1980, documents Johnson's impatience with the persistence of British racism. During the early 1980s Johnson spent a few years touring and working in journalism for *Race Today* and the British Broadcasting Corporation (BBC). He also launched his own record label called LKJ Records. In 1983 Johnson released the album *Making History*, a celebration of blacks in Great Britain that includes a poem about the BRIXTON RIOTS OF 1981 called "Di Great Insohreckshan."

For all his success in providing a view of black British life and his popularity among black Britons, Johnson is humble; in *Tings an Times* (1991) he writes:

me naw preach
mi naw teach
mi jus a show yu
ow me seit

Leyla Keough

SEE ALSO
Black Panther Party; Jamaica; Languages, Creole, in the Caribbean.

North America

Johnson, Magic

(b. August 14, 1959, Lansing, Mich.), African American professional BASKETBALL player who helped the Los Angeles Lakers become one of the dominant professional basketball teams of the 1980s and who is considered one of the greatest point guards and playmakers in the history of the National Basketball Association (NBA).

Earvin Johnson acquired the nickname Magic after a high school game in which he scored 36 points, grabbed 18 rebounds, and made 16 assists. At Michigan State University, the six-foot-nine-inch (2.06 m) Johnson helped the Spartans, the university team, win the National Collegiate Athletic Association (NCAA) championship in 1979.

Johnson left college after his second year (1979) to join the Los Angeles Lakers of the NBA. He helped lead the Lakers to five NBA championships (1980, 1982, 1985, 1987, 1988). Johnson was named the NBA's Most Valuable Player three times (1987, 1989, 1990). He played in many All-Star games and, at the time of his retirement, held the NBA record for assists (9921). Johnson helped the Lakers become one of the dominant teams in the NBA during the 1980s and is credited with helping revitalize fan interest in the NBA.

In the autumn of 1991 Johnson announced that he had tested positive for the virus that causes acquired immune deficiency syndrome (AIDS) and was retiring from the Lakers. He became a national spokesperson for AIDS awareness and prevention, and he established a foundation to promote AIDS research. His book *What You Can Do to Avoid AIDS* was published in 1992. After Johnson's poignant return to the 1992 NBA All-Star game, the Lakers retired his jersey number (32).

Johnson was a member of the United States basketball team that won the Gold Medal at the 1992 Summer Olympic Games in Barcelona, Spain, and served briefly on the President's Council on AIDS. He then announced his return to professional basketball, and in September 1992 he signed another contract with the Lakers. In November of that year, however, he once again announced that he would retire because of the controversy concerning his return to basketball. He subsequently became a television sports commentator and continued his efforts to become part of an NBA franchise ownership group.

Late in the 1993-1994 season, Johnson became head coach of the Lakers but resigned at the end of that season. He returned to the Lakers as a player in 1996, retiring again at the end of the season. In 1998 he hosted "The Magic Hour," a late night talk show on the Fox network. The show lasted only two months due to poor reviews and low ratings.

See Also

AIDS in the United States; Television and African Americans.

North America

Johnson, Mordecai Wyatt

(b. January 12, 1890, Paris, Tenn.; d. September 11, 1976, Washington, D.C.), the first African American president of Howard University.

Mordecai Wyatt Johnson received a bachelor of arts degree from Atlanta Baptist College (now Morehouse College) in 1911, after which he taught several courses there, including English, history, and economics. He then enrolled at the University of Chicago, where he took a second bachelor's degree, in social sciences, in 1913. A third bachelor's degree, in divinity, came from Rochester Theological Seminary three years later. For the next several years he served as pastor of a Baptist church in Charleston, West Virginia, and organized Charleston's first office of the National Association for the Advancement of Colored People (NAACP). In the early 1920s he returned to school, first at Harvard Divinity School, where he was awarded a master's degree in theology in 1922, then at Howard University, where he received a doctoral degree in theology in 1923. Supported by the Young Men's Christian Association (YMCA), he traveled throughout the Southwest studying black schools and became a noted orator.

At the time the trustees of Howard faced growing pressure from faculty, alumni, and students to appoint a black president. In 1926 Johnson received the trustees' unanimous nomination. As president, he advocated academic freedom inside the university and civil rights outside. He also proved adept in prying appropriations for Howard from the United States Congress, a task that required steady diplomacy with often hostile Southern Congressmen. In 1929 Johnson received the NAACP's Spingarn Medal. He retired in 1960.

North America

Johnson Products, **first black-owned firm to trade on the American Stock Exchange.**

In 1954 the 27-year-old George E. Johnson, then a laboratory worker in a cosmetics factory, perfected a mild lye and petroleum-based hair relaxer, or straightener, for African Americans. Until then relaxers were solely lye-based, which burned the scalp and actually damaged hair. Johnson borrowed $250 as a "vacation" loan, with which he and his wife, Joan, founded Johnson Products. They began by manufacturing and selling Ultra Wave Hair Culture for men. Johnson traveled throughout the United States to sell Ultra Wave to professional salons and hairdressers. Joan Johnson was responsible for finances and bookkeeping. Encouraged by Ultra Wave's success, Johnson Products introduced Ultra Sheen Hair products for women and sold them to haircare professionals.

By 1960 the Johnsons were confident enough to sell their products in the retail market, and within five years the company was grossing $2 million in sales annually, despite competition from less expensive brands. After the company introduced Ultra Sheen no-base cream relaxer in 1965, sales increased again, and in 1969 Johnson sold its first stock offering, of $10.2 million. In 1971 it became the first black-owned firm listed on the American Stock Exchange.

Johnson Products grossed $37.2 million in sales annually by 1975, and the company controlled 85 percent of the professional haircare market by 1975. It promoted black businesses by using black models and minority-owned advertising agencies, advertising in such publications as *Essence* and sponsoring the nationally syndicated television show Soul Train.

The success did not last, however, because Johnson's market share began to decline once a host of white-owned businesses entered the lucrative African American haircare market. By the mid-1980s Johnson Products was losing money. After Joan and George Johnson were divorced in 1988, their son, Eric, turned the company around financially. Joan Johnson, who controlled the company after the divorce, fired Eric and promoted two white men, Thomas P. Polke and Corey Meyer, to be president and director of operations. The move caused resentment among many family members and employees. In 1993 the white-owned Ivax Corporation, based in Miami, Florida, purchased Johnson Products for $67 million and promised to maintain Johnson's commitment to the African American community.

Robert Fay

See Also

Essence; Hair and Beauty Culture.

North America

Johnson Publishing Company, **the second largest black-owned company in the United States and the world's largest black-owned publisher.**

The Johnson Publishing Company of Chicago, a family-owned conglomerate of media outlets and beauty products, was founded in 1945 by John H. Johnson (b. January 19, 1918, Arkansas City, Mississippi). While working for Supreme Liberty Life Insurance Company in the early 1940s, Johnson collected and prepared a digest of news affecting the African American community for distribution among the company's upper managers. Realizing that this news digest could be marketed to African Americans, who were largely ignored by the mainstream press, he used his mother's furniture as collateral to borrow $500, with which he published the first issue of what would be called *Negro Digest*.

Similar in form to *Reader's Digest*, *Negro Digest* initially reprinted articles from other periodicals. Soon the magazine began publishing original articles and essays, notably in October 1943, with a piece written by First Lady Eleanor Roosevelt that was composed especially for *Negro Digest*. That issue doubled the magazine's usual circulation of 50,000. By the end of 1943 Johnson had an income that enabled him to pay for his mother's retirement.

The success of *Negro Digest* led Johnson to launch *Ebony* in 1945. It was modeled on the glossy picture magazine *Life* and sold well, growing steadily in circulation. Lack of advertising revenue and the production and distribution costs, however, nearly bankrupted the publishing company until Johnson obtained advertising from white-controlled businesses. *Ebony* went on to become the keystone of the Johnson Publishing Company and a familiar sight on coffee tables in African American homes nationwide; its circulation reached 2 million by 1996.

Negro Digest remained popular but its circulation stalled, hovering around 60,000. Its popularity lagged far behind that of *Ebony*. Johnson discontinued it in 1951 (although the company revived it in 1965, renamed it *Black World* in 1970, and discontinued it in 1976). In its place, Johnson launched *Jet*, a pocket-size (5½" x 4") weekly that offered society, entertainment, political, and sports reporting oriented to African American readers. Its editors aimed the magazine at readers who had neither the time nor the inclination to read deep analyses of current events but who wanted to remain well informed. *Jet* was an immediate success. After six issues, its circulation topped 300,000, and by 1997 *Jet*'s market covered more than 40 countries, and its weekly circulation surpassed a million.

Although some have criticized Johnson's omission of critical pieces about African Americans, none can deny the company's success. By the early 1990s it employed more than 2300 people. The total circulation of its publications was 3.25 million, and earnings were $325.7 million in 1996. Johnson's holdings include *Ebony, Jet, EM: Ebony Man,* and *Ebony South Africa,* Supreme Beauty Products, Ebony Fashion Fair, and Johnson Publishing Company Book Division. The company continues to be a family-run business, with John H. Johnson the publisher and chief executive officer; his wife, Eunice W. Johnson, the secretary-treasurer and producer-director of Ebony Fashion Fair; and his daughter, Linda Johnson Rice, the president and chief operating officer.

Robert Fay

See Also
Press, Black, in the United States; Chicago, Illinois; *Ebony*; *Jet*.

North America

Johnson, Robert Leroy

(b. May 8, 1911, Hazelhurst, Miss.; d. August 16, 1938, Greenwood, Miss.), African American country blues musician and Mississippi Delta legend.

The most influential bluesman in the music's history, Robert Johnson nonetheless remains an obscure figure, despite the efforts of numerous researchers to unearth more than a brief sketch of his life. Indeed, his photograph surfaced for the first time only in the late 1980s.

Johnson grew up in several different towns in the Delta and turned to music for self-expression. Charley Patton was an early influence on him, as was Son House, with whom he played as a supporting musician. Johnson became an itinerant musician after the manner of his heroes. He married at least twice and one of his wives later died in childbirth. It is presumed that like most Delta musicians, Johnson had a hard life; but his music was darker than most, with recurring references to the devil and double-dealing women.

The culmination of Johnson's career, and the basis for his posthumous reputation, were the recording sessions he did for Columbia in 1936 and 1937, considered to have produced one of the most important documents in American musical history. Alone with an acoustic guitar, Johnson set down a body of music characterized by richly textured lyrics and emotive guitar playing. One of his records, "Terraplane Blues," achieved modest local success, but most of the recordings were forgotten until the 1960s blues revival.

Part of the legend of Robert Johnson stems from his early death in 1938. Under mysterious circumstances, he died after playing a jook joint outside Greenwood, Mississippi. Some stories say that he was poisoned with bad whiskey, perhaps because of his penchant for married women, while others say that he was cursed by black magic and spent his final hours barking like a dog.

A lengthy catalogue of myths and rumors persists about Johnson, particularly regarding his dabblings in the supernatural. Perhaps the most famous story claims that he learned to play guitar in a deal with the devil, consummated in a late-night transaction at a crossroads outside Clarksdale, Mississippi. "Crossroads" is one of Johnson's most harrowing songs, and the events it recounts have permeated the folklore of rock and roll.

Johnson's songs have been covered by many of the biggest names in rock, including the Rolling Stones ("Love in Vain," "Stop Breaking Down"), Cream ("Crossroads"), and Captain Beefheart ("Terraplane Blues"). He also exerted a strong influence on the bluesmen who followed him, including Elmore James (whose signature song, "Dust My Broom," came from Johnson), Muddy Waters, and stepson Robert Jr. Lockwood.

Lending poignancy to Robert Johnson's legend is the fact that he was nearly discovered by the music industry while he was still alive. In 1938 the producer John Hammond wanted to invite Johnson to the historic concert he was promoting in Carnegie Hall, "From Spirituals to Swing," but was unable to find him. Still, Johnson's Columbia sessions remain a major influence on American music in the second half of the twentieth century.

See Also
Blues, The.

North America

Johnson, Sargent

(b. October 7, 1887, Boston, Mass.; d. October 10, 1967, San Francisco, Calif.), African American artist and sculptor whose work celebrated African American beauty and dignity.

Sargent Claude Johnson was the third of six children born to Anderson Johnson, a Swedish immigrant, and Lizzie Jackson, who was of Native American and African American descent. Both parents died before Johnson was grown, and he spent much of his childhood with relatives in and around Washington, D.C., then finally in an orphanage in Worcester, Massachusetts. As an adolescent he studied music. After graduating from high school, he continued his pursuit of music and other arts in Boston and Chicago.

In 1915 Johnson moved to San Francisco, where he enrolled at the A. W. Best School of Art and married Pearl Lawson, with whom he later had a daughter. From 1919 to 1923 he studied at the California School of Fine Arts, where his work received several prizes. Among his teachers were the sculptors Ralph Stackpole and Beniamino Bufano; the latter is often called Johnson's mentor. By this time Johnson was creating busts and portraits, mostly of people he knew, in several media, including ceramics, wood, and watercolor.

In the mid-1920s Johnson's work was exhibited throughout the San Francisco Bay Area. The praise he received led to support from New York's Harmon Foundation, which sponsored further exhibits. In these shows Johnson blended several materials into single sculptures of African Americans. Most of his works from this time are credited with demonstrating the beauty and grace of prominent black features such as full lips and kinky hair, as well as emphasizing African American complexions through the use of copper and redwood.

Buoyed by the Harmon-sponsored exhibits in New York, Johnson's sculpture soon became popular among African Americans, especially those who were active in the Harlem Renaissance of the 1920s and 1930s. Johnson also owed a measure of his popularity to his politics: light-skinned enough to pass for white, he refused to do so, instead embracing his African heritage. Recognition for his work soon spilled over the bounds of the black community, and he gained an international recognition for what he was calling "a strictly Negro art."

By the end of the 1930s Johnson was working for the Federal Arts Project, a Depression-era program for artists. He continued to live and work in San Francisco. Among his commissioned pieces were two eight-foot stone figures installed for the city's Golden Gate International Exposition, a large mosaic for a maritime museum, and a panel carved in relief for the California School for the Blind. During World War II (1939-1945) he created one of his best-known works, a large cast-stone frieze that adorns San Francisco's George Washington High School.

Beginning in 1945 Johnson made his first of several trips to Mexico, where he became influenced by Mayan and other native arts. In particular his study of Central American clay and ceramics led to similar uses in his work. By the 1950s he had largely abandoned his popular realistic sculptures for surreal and abstract art executed in vivid colors. His work continued, however, to explore racial themes. He increasingly incorporated wood and enamel, and by the 1960s he had added rock, bronze, and welded wire to his repertoire. During the last years of his career Johnson was plagued by ill health. He died of a heart attack in 1967. At the time of his death his work had been displayed in nearly 30 major exhibitions.

See Also

Great Depression; San Francisco and Oakland, California; Art, African American; Passing in the United States.

North America

Johnson, William Henry

(b. March 18, 1901, Florence, S.C.; d. April 13, 1970, Islip, N.Y.), African American painter who moved from expressionism to a "consciously naive" style to portray black life.

William H. Johnson began drawing when he was a child, encouraged by sympathetic art teachers. Determined to go to New York City to become an artist, he accompanied his uncle there in 1918 when they both took jobs as stevedores. He was able to send money home as well as save for his education. In 1921 he began five years of rigorous classical training at the National Academy of Design.

Winning numerous prizes at the academy, Johnson came to the attention of Charles W. Hawthorne, an influential instructor, who invited him to his Cape Cod School of Art on work-study programs during the summers of 1924, 1925, and 1926. Hawthorne also raised $1000 so that Johnson could spend a year studying in Paris. Hawthorne introduced his protégé to George Luks, a member of "The Eight," a group of realist painters who were later known as the Ashcan School. Luks contributed to Johnson's travel fund, but he also altered the young man's outlook. Luks's motto of "Guts! Life! Life! That's my technique!" fueled Johnson to explore modern expressionist methods of painting.

Reaching Paris in November 1926, Johnson visited Henry Ossawa Tanner, the successful black expatriate painter, who admired the younger man's talents. Johnson found the Paris art scene exciting. He was impressed by the dignity with which Paul Gauguin portrayed Tahitians, who were people of color. But the artist whose work most influenced him was Chaim Soutine, the expressionist painter whose first important exhibition was in Paris in 1927. Johnson now began to explore the portrayal of his own feelings expressionistically, using thick impasto for his simplified but churning forms and backgrounds. He even moved to Cagnes-sur-Mer in the south of France because Soutine had painted there.

Johnson's work during this important period includes *Young Pastry Cook* (1927-1928); two self-portraits (1929), one of which is now lost; *Landscape, Cagnes-sur-Mer* (1928-1929); and *Jacobia Hotel* (1930), painted in Florence, South Carolina, during a brief visit home. Exhibitions of his work in Paris (1927) and in Nice (1928-1929), however, did not garner much critical attention. Discouraged, Johnson returned to New York. He entered six paintings in the Harmon Foundation's 1930 competition and won the Gold Medal and $400 prize.

William Henry Johnson (1901-1970) painted this self-portrait in 1929, when he was working in southern France and absorbing the influence of French artist Chaim Soutine. *National Museum of American Art, Washington DC/Art Resource, NY*

After this success he returned to Europe in May and married Holcha Krake, the Danish potter and weaver he had met earlier in France. They moved to the fishing town of Kerteminde, Denmark, near the Krake family home. Later they traveled to the other Scandinavian countries and to North Africa. During this period Johnson painted Danish fishermen and Tunisian Arabs – people who worked close to nature. He described them as "primitive," and he believed that in painting them he could come closer to his own primitive essence.

Aware of the rising threats of fascism and war in Europe, the Johnsons sailed to New York in November 1938. They faced hostility in America as an interracial couple. Furthermore, the Great Depression had virtually destroyed the art market. Johnson fundamentally changed his style from expressionism to what he called "primitive," and what others termed "consciously naive." For subject matter, he turned to the black church and the African American rural scenes he had known as a young man. He painted flattened figures, using oil on burlap or board; he made greater use of primary colors; and he emphasized verticals such as trees, legs, fences, animals, and farm implements in his compositions.

Examples of Johnson's new naive style include *Going to Church* (1940-1941), *Climbing Jacob's Ladder* (1939), *Children at Ice Cream Stand* (1939), and *Jesus and the Three Marys* (1939). Johnson's work was not recognized, but he made a living on federal Works Progress Administration (WPA) art projects between 1939 and 1943. In the boom economy of World War II he worked at the Brooklyn Navy Yard. A fire in 1941 destroyed many of his paintings and personal possessions. His wife, Holcha Johnson, died in January 1943. Grief stricken, Johnson returned to his family in Florence, South Carolina, and after the war he traveled once again to Denmark.

By this time, however, Johnson's mind had been destroyed by syphilis, and he was sent to a New York State mental hospital at Islip on Long Island. More than 1000 of Johnson's paintings, drawings, and prints were threatened with destruction because he had left the warehouse rent unpaid for nine years. Mary Brady of the Harmon Foundation was able to rescue these works; when the foundation disbanded in 1967, she arranged for the transfer of Johnson's work to the National Museum of American Art in Washington, D.C.

Johnson lived until 1970. Unfortunately, he did not live long enough to see the eventual enormous popularity of both his expressionist and his "primitive" work. Johnson is now considered a major American artist and a preeminent portrayer of the African American experience.

Betty Gubert

See Also

World War II and African Americans; New York, New York; Art, African American.

North America

Johnson, William Julius ("Judy") **(b. October 26, 1899, Snow Hill, Mo.; d. June 15,1989, Wilmington, Del.), African American baseball player known for his intelligent, cool approach to the game as a third baseman in the Negro Leagues from 1918 to 1936.**

Judy Johnson was a gifted fielder and fine hitter who performed best in clutch situations. He also served as a manager for the Homestead Grays of Pittsburgh in 1930.

Johnson's father built a makeshift gym to train his son to become a prizefighter, but Johnson preferred baseball. He signed with the Philadelphia Hilldales in 1918 and spent winters playing in Cuba and Florida. In 1924 he batted .327 to lead the Hilldales to the first Negro World Series, where they faced the Kansas City Monarchs. He batted .364 in a losing cause in the series. In 1925 he upped his average to .392 in the regular season and helped the Hilldales overcome the Monarchs in the postseason with a key hit in game three. In 1929 he hit .416.

In 1930 the Great Depression forced the Hilldales out of business, and Johnson joined the Homestead Grays as third baseman and manager. One of Johnson's most famous moves as manager occurred that year during a game against the Kansas City Monarchs. After starting catcher Buck Leonard left the game with a cut hand, Johnson looked to the stands for a replacement and called on a boy he had seen playing on the local sandlot – future Hall of Fame catcher Josh Gibson. Johnson cultivated Gibson as a player along with two other future Hall of Fame members, Cool Papa Bell and Oscar Charleston. A year later Johnson left the Grays to manage the Darby (Pennsylvania) Daisies and in 1932 Johnson, as well as Bell, Charleston, and Gibson, joined Satchel Paige in the lineup of the Pittsburgh Crawfords. The Crawfords are considered by many to be the best of the Negro League teams and one of the greatest teams ever assembled.

Johnson retired after the 1936 season with an unofficial career batting average of .344. He later worked as a scout and coach for the Philadelphia Athletics, Philadelphia Phillies, and Brooklyn Dodgers. He was elected to the National Baseball Hall of Fame in 1975.

See Also

Baseball in the United States; Boxing; Gibson, Joshua; Paige, Leroy Robert ("Satchel").

North America

Joint Center for Political and Economic Studies, **a powerful and respected public policy institute, or think tank, in the United States specializing in political and economic issues affecting African Americans.**

Initially sponsored by Howard University and the Metropolitan Applied Research Center in 1969 and funded by a two-year $820,000 grant from the Ford Foundation, the Washington, D.C.-based Joint Center has developed into an independent nonprofit organization with an annual operating budget of more than $6.5 million. Its original mission was to provide policy consultants and political training to the new African American politicians who were elected after the Voting Rights Act of 1965. But the Joint Center soon began turning its attention to providing reliable reports and research about the African American community to politicians and public policy analysts.

The Joint Center's research is highly sought after. During the 1984 presidential campaign, Jesse Jackson's campaign office relied heavily on its data. Its research is also considered fair and accurate, as illustrated by a Mississippi voting rights lawsuit in which lawyers from both sides used the Joint Center's data to support their claims. In recent years the Joint Center has expanded its scope to provide economic analysis. President Eddie N. Williams, who took office in 1972, explains the shift this way: "Economic advancement must be the next big move in the life of African Americans. And the Joint Center must be as relevant to that movement as it has been to the black political movement in the community." In the late 1990s the Joint Center began planning a major conference for minority businesspeople to discuss United States economic policies, and publishing papers recommending African American job strategies for the twenty-first century.

Robert Fay

See Also

Jackson, Jesse Louis.

Africa

Jola, **an ethnic group of Senegal, the Gambia, and Guinea-Bissau.**

The Jola, numbering approximately 500,000 people, are the major ethnic group of the lower Casamance region of Senegal and are a significant minority group in the Gambia and Guinea-Bissau. Reflecting the irrationality of the partition of Africa, national boundaries often bisect Jola villages or separate the villages from their rice paddies. Described by agronomists as the best wet-rice farmers in West Africa, Jola farmers regularly produced substantial food surpluses until the frequent droughts of the last 30 years. Traditionally they have not formed states but have lived in communities governed by village councils and groups of elders, without formal political authorities. Since 1981 they have been one of the principal ethnic groups involved in the Casamance regional movement to secede from Senegal, a movement that has become particularly violent in recent years.

The name Jola is a relatively recent one, first applied to the people we know as Jola in the nineteenth century by Wolof sailors in response to French administrators' questions about the ethnicity of the people they encountered along the Casamance River. The Portuguese name for Jola, Floup, has been used to refer to the group since the beginning of the sixteenth century. Oral traditions suggest that the Jola or Floup originated in the coastal areas of central and northern Guinea-Bissau. They expanded to the north and west at the expense of the Bainounk, the earliest known inhabitants of the Casamance, many of whom were assimilated into various Jola communities. In the sixteenth century a substantial Jola kingdom, ruled by the Mansa Floup, dominated the southern Jola areas in Casamance and Guinea-Bissau. The growth in the slave trade destablilized this state, and the Jola assumed the stateless political organization that has characterized them ever since. Jola captives were sold into the transatlantic slave trade as early as 1500 and were taken initially to Spanish and Portuguese colonies off the coast of Africa, such as the Cape Verde Islands, and to Latin America. As the British became active in the slave trade in the seventeenth century, they took Jola captives to the Carolinas and Georgia, where they taught British settlers how to grow rice.

The French occupied most of the Jola lands in the nineteenth century, though the British occupied small areas in the northwest and the Portuguese occupied the southern Jola areas. Each colony practiced a different form of colonialism, and the Jola sought to minimize the disruption to their communities by migrating across colonial borders to avoid such burdens as military conscription, forced labor, and taxation. All three colonial powers found the Jola difficult to govern, reluctant to pay taxes, and often ready to resist. In 1942 a prophetic movement, led by a woman named Alinesitoué Diatta, contributed to open resistance to the pro-Nazi Vichy French government. She was arrested and charged with the crime of resisting colonial initiatives and causing embarrassment to the colonial administration. She died of starvation after a year of exile.

Since independence, many Jola have felt that the central government has neglected the Casamance region, separated from the rest of Senegal by the Gambia, and that the overwhelmingly Muslim peoples of northern Senegal have looked down on their adherence to traditional religion and Christianity (though some Jola profess Islam). This frustration finally led to open resistance beginning in 1981. Mass arrests by the Senegalese government and attacks by the guerrilla rebels on opponents of secession have both contributed to the escalating level of violence. The persistent drought that has affected Senegal since the 1960s, together with structural adjustment policies and consequent economic austerity since 1980, have also caused discontent among the Jola and generated support for rebel forces. In the neighboring Gambia, however, a Jola junior officer, Yahya Jammeh, became head of state after a military coup in 1995 and was recently elected president of the Gambia.

Robert Baum

See Also

Cape Verde; Colonial Rule; Gambia, The; Structural Adjustment in Africa.

North America

Jones, Absalom (b. 1746, Sussex County, Del.; d. February 13, 1818, Philadelphia, Pa.), African American minister and founder of one of the earliest black churches.

Absalom Jones was born a slave on the plantation of a Delaware businessman and farmer. From a young age Jones worked in his owner's house, where he received a basic education. During his teenage years he moved with his master to Philadelphia. By day he worked in his master's store, and at night he continued his education in a school for blacks. In 1770 he married another slave and in 1778, with the help of several Quakers and his father-in-law, bought his wife's freedom. Six years later he bought his own freedom.

Jones became active in Saint George's Methodist Episcopal Church, a Philadelphia congregation where whites and blacks worshiped together. He eventually became a lay preacher at Saint George's and met Richard Allen, also a lay preacher. The two men shared a lifetime of religious and community organizing in Philadelphia, which probably had the largest community of freed slaves in the country.

Due to Jones's and Allen's recruiting, large numbers of African Americans came to Saint George's between 1784 and 1786. The whites who controlled the church responded to the influx by declaring that blacks would no longer be allowed to worship on the main floor; instead, they would be relegated to the balcony. At one of the first services under the new seating arrangements, Jones sat in the front of the balcony but was told by ushers that blacks were required to sit in an even more remote location in the rear of the balcony. A scuffle ensued as ushers tried to force Jones to the back, at which point Jones, Allen, and the rest of the black congregation left the church. They never returned.

On April 12, 1787, Jones, Allen, and several other African Americans created the Free African Society of Philadelphia, which was probably the first independent black organization in the United States. The Free African Society helped the sick and gave support to widows and orphans. It also issued regular denunciations of slavery. With an emphasis on sobriety, marital fidelity, and opposition to gambling, it had a deeply religious flavor but was open to blacks of all denominations. In New York, Boston, Providence, and even Savannah similar mutual-aid societies for African Americans were inspired by and patterned after the Free African Society.

By 1791 Jones and Allen held regular Sunday services under what they called the African Church, one of the first black churches in North America free of white control. With help from Quakers, abolitionists, and Philadelphia's black community, the African Church began raising funds for a sanctuary in 1792. In 1793 a disastrous epidemic of yellow fever broke out, and the society suspended most of its operations while its members nursed the sick and dug graves for the dead.

After the epidemic the congregation faced a rift over whether to seek affiliation with white Methodism – most of the members of Saint George's had, after all, been Methodist –

Pictured here on a commemorative pitcher, Absalom Jones, lay preacher and cofounder of the Free African Society in 1787 in Philadelphia, became the first minister of St. Thomas's African Episcopal Church in 1794. *National Portrait Gallery, Smithsonian Institution/Art Resource, NY*

or reject Methodism altogether and affiliate with a church that treated blacks with greater equality. Most of the congregation decided to separate from the Methodists and eventually joined the predominantly white Episcopal Church of North America. When the sanctuary was finished in 1794 it was consecrated Saint Thomas's African Episcopal Church. Jones was its first minister. Allen, however, remained loyal to Methodism, left Jones and his parishioners, and later founded the African Methodist Episcopal Church (AME), the first denomination created specifically for African Americans.

Although leaders of the Episcopal Church waived requirements that Jones know Greek and Latin before ordaining him a deacon, they refused to let him or other blacks play a role in the government of the church. Unable to change the larger church, Jones instead focused his efforts on his congregation and other African Americans of Philadelphia. He soon became known for his oratory, his patient house-to-house ministration, and the school for blacks that he established at Saint Thomas's. (At the time, blacks were not entitled to public schooling in Pennsylvania.) The congregation grew and in 1804 Jones was ordained the first black priest in the United States.

Despite their differing ideology, Jones and Allen continued to work together. In 1798 they founded a black counterpart to the Masons. In the following years they submitted petitions to the Pennsylvania legislature and the United States Congress asking for an immediate end to slavery and abolition of the Fugitive Slave Law of 1793. During the War of 1812 Jones and Allen united with other black leaders to raise several thousand black troops, and in 1816 Jones helped consecrate Allen as the first bishop of the African Methodist Episcopal Church. In the last years of his life, Jones worked to condemn the American Colonization Society, which had recently been established to resettle blacks on the Liberian coast of Africa.

See Also

Liberia; Slavery in the United States; Abolitionism in the United States; Boston, Massachusetts; Free Blacks in the United States, 1619 to 1863; Fugitive Slave Laws; Philadelphia, Pennsylvania; New York, New York; Black Church, The.

North America

Jones, Bill T. **(b. February 15, 1952, Bunnell, Fla.), internationally acclaimed African American dancer, one of the foremost choreographers of contemporary dance theater.**

In the mid-1980s Bill T. Jones emerged as one of America's preeminent dancers and avant-garde choreographers. Rooted in the postmodern experimentation of the 1960s, his work often combines speech, song, dance, and mime as well as spontaneous movement. He infuses his art with candid autobiographical details in an effort to challenge audiences' ideas about tolerance, sexuality, death, and interracial romance, issues he has dealt with as a gay black man diagnosed in 1985 as HIV-positive. Jones "has a reputation for doing anything he wants, on and offstage," wrote dance critic Gus Solomons Jr. "Movement spills out of [his] powerful, instinctual body, driven by a fecund imagination."

The tenth of 12 children, Jones was reared and educated in Wayland, New York, a predominantly white agricultural community where his parents, then migrant farm workers, settled after moving from the Southeast. In 1970 he entered the State University of New York at Binghamton, where he excelled in track and theater and enrolled in movement classes with Trinidadian choreographer Percival Borde. Encouraged by his friend Arnie Zane, he began to study modern dance, particularly the pioneering techniques of choreographers Martha Graham, Merce Cunningham, and Alvin Ailey.

Jones and Zane, a white photographer and theater student, soon began a personal as well as professional partnership. In 1979, after successfully choreographing a variety of pieces for the American Dance Asylum, they settled in New York City. Influenced by postmodern choreographer and filmmaker Yvonne Rainer, Jones often incorporated spontaneous monologues into his solo pieces. When he and Zane performed in duets, they creatively emphasized their differences in race, size, and character and elaborated on each other's movements as a form of commentary, dialogue, or argument.

In 1982 Jones and Zane founded the Bill T. Jones/Arnie Zane Dance Company, a diverse troupe of dancers of all shapes, sizes, and ethnicities. Dance critic Tobi Tobias said, "Jones has always been addicted to unusual physical types; everyone in the company looks picked for body as well as for soul and technique." In 1983 the company debuted at the Brooklyn Academy of Music with the critically acclaimed *Intuitive Momentum*, a series of pieces set to the music of famed drummer Max Roach and pianist Connie Crothers. Attentive to stage design, Jones and Zane collaborated with such innovators as graffiti artist Keith Haring and fashion designer Willi Smith and soon gained recognition for work that was profoundly expressive and visually dazzling. In 1986 Jones and Zane received the coveted New York Dance and Performance (Bessie) Award.

With the death of Zane from AIDS in 1988, Jones focused his work on the themes of loss and mortality, producing and performing such celebrated solo pieces as *Absence* (1989) and the *Last Night on Earth* (1992). He also created pieces that affirm life and community, including *D-Man in the Waters* (1992), which earned him a second Bessie Award, and *Last Supper at Uncle Tom's Cabin/The Promised Land* (1990), a multimedia work that employs nudity as a metaphor for the common human condition and features, along with dance and music, the taped voice of Martin Luther King Jr.

African American dancer and choreographer Bill T. Jones received a prestigious MacArthur Fellowship in 1994. *Susan Kuklin*

In 1994 Jones and his dance company premiered *Still/Here*, a multimedia work about death and dying that ignited sharp controversy among journalists and cultural critics. Opening at the Brooklyn Academy of Music's Next Wave Festival, *Still/Here* incorporated videotaped testimonies of terminally ill people, including AIDS patients, whom Jones had been interviewing since 1992. Although the *New Yorker* dance critic Arlene Croce censured *Still/Here* as "victim art," *New York Times* columnist Frank Rich, who noted that AIDS is "part of art because it is part of life," wrote that Jones's *Still/Here* had captured "the story of our time." *Newsweek*'s Laura Shapiro considered the piece "so original and profound that its place among the landmarks of twentieth-century dance seems ensured."

No less complex than Jones's relationship to contemporary dance is his relationship to black culture. Since the early 1980s some black artists have openly questioned Jones's racial allegiances. Jones, who considers himself first and foremost an artist, has had to defend his 17-year partnership with Zane as well as his dance innovations, which have attracted mainly white avant garde audiences. Still, over the years Jones has won the respect of many black artists and intellectuals, including Maya Angelou, Dance Theater of Harlem founder Arthur Mitchell, and Jessye Norman, who considers him "the most soulful dancer I know."

In addition to creating works for his own company, Jones has choreographed for such companies as the Alvin Ailey American Dance Theater and the Boston Ballet and has applied his talents to opera and musical comedy. The recipient of a MacArthur Fellowship in 1994, Jones continues to perform throughout the United States and Europe, and in March 1997 premiered his *Ballets Mozart* with the Lyons Opera Ballet in France.

Roanne Edwards

See Also

AIDS in the United States; King, Martin Luther, Jr.; New York, New York; Roach, Maxwell Lemuel (Max).

North America

Jones, Gayl (b. November 23, 1949, Lexington, Ky.), African American novelist, poet, playwright, and literary critic.

When asked to describe her career, writer Gayl Jones calls herself a "storyteller," saying that for her, the term "always has its human connections." Jones's mother and grandmother were also storytellers, and she grew up captivated by the power of language; she wrote her first story in second grade. Throughout her career Jones's work has been known for its evocation of black vernacular speech and stories.

At Connecticut College, where Jones received a B.A. in English in 1971, she won awards for poetry and fiction. She went on to earn an M.A. in creative writing in 1973 and a doctorate in arts in 1975 from Brown University. Jones published her first play, *Chile Woman,* while in graduate school, and the year she received her doctorate she also published her first novel, *Corregidora. Corregidora* incorporated themes and motifs common to most of Jones's later work, such as the legacy of history for black families and the double specters of racism and sexism for black women. *Corregidora* also showed Jones's interest in incorporating black musical forms, such as JAZZ and the blues, into her narrative style, as well as her talent for capturing authentic black speech.

In 1976 Jones published her second novel, *Eva's Man.* The following year she published *White Rat,* a collection of short stories, several of which center on the tensions between heterosexuality and homosexuality. Her next three books were all narrative poems: *Song for Anniho* (1981), *The Hermit Woman* (1983), and *Xarque and Other Poems* (1985). In these poems Jones expands her discussion of racism to include other parts of the diaspora.

Jones was a professor of English at the University of Michigan, Ann Arbor, from 1975 to 1983. In 1983 she fled the United States after her husband, Bob Higgins (later Jones), was accused of firing on marchers at a gay rights event. For the next five years Jones and her husband lived in anonymity in Europe, and even after their return to the United States in 1988, Jones kept her whereabouts (her mother's home in Lexington, Kentucky) a closely guarded secret. In 1991 she published *Liberating Voices: Oral Tradition in African American Literature,* a book of literary criticism, and in 1998 she published the novel *The Healing,* which was released to widespread critical acclaim. However, media coverage of *The Healing*'s success led to personal tragedy.

Michigan authorities still had a warrant for Bob Jones's arrest, and after Gayl Jones granted a rare interview to *Newsweek,* the police were able to trace the couple to their hiding place in Kentucky. Both Joneses had reportedly spent the last several years in isolation, convinced that there was a racist conspiracy attempting to destroy them and their families. When authorities arrived at the home, the Joneses barricaded themselves inside, and when officers managed to enter, Bob Jones committed suicide by slashing his throat. Following a brief period of institutionalization, Jones once again adopted a quiet, private lifestyle. The 1999 publication of her novel *Mosquito* brought Jones a new wave of critical and popular admiration.

Lisa Clayton Robinson

See Also

Black Vernacular English; Women Writers, Black, in the United States; Blues, The.

North America

Jones, James Earl

(b. January 17, 1931, Arkabutla, Mississippi), African American stage, film, and television actor whose resonant bass voice is instantly recognizable.

In a long and successful career James Earl Jones has portrayed a wide range of characters in stage productions, motion pictures, and television. He transcended the limitations of his rural Mississippi childhood and became a much-loved actor with one of the most recognizable voices in the United States. His beginnings were far from auspicious. Not long after his birth, his actor father Robert Earl Jones abandoned the family. Young James was adopted and raised by his maternal grandparents. When he was five years old, his family moved to Michigan.

Jones's deep, resonant voice has reached countless millions of people, in particular as Darth Vader in the original *Star Wars* trilogy (1977, 1980, 1983), as father lion Mustafa in *The Lion King* (1994), and as the official voice of the telephone company Bell Atlantic. During his youth, however, Jones avoided speaking altogether for several years because of a pronounced stutter. "I was unable to talk from the age of eight to the age of 15," he recalled in a 1979 *Jet* magazine interview. "... I thought, if I can't say it, I just won't make an ass of myself... so I didn't talk." But while he was in high school, his English teacher discovered that Jones wrote poetry and took an interest in him, giving him the incentive to overcome his speech impediment.

In 1949 he entered the University of Michigan in Ann Arbor and majored in drama, although he had initially intended to study medicine. He graduated magna cum laude in 1953 and, after a stint in the military, moved to New York City. In 1957 he made his professional debut in New York City. During the 1960s he had a long association with Joseph Papp's New York Shakespeare Festival. Jones also gained prominence as part of an all-black production of Jean Genet's *The Blacks.* Over the years he tackled a wide range of Shakespearean roles, including Othello, King Lear, and Oberon in *A Midsummer Night's Dream.* In 1960 he won his first leading role, in Lionel Abel's *The Pretender.*

Jones found success in motion pictures as well as on stage (*see* FILMS, BLACKS IN AMERICAN). In 1966 he played the fictional boxer Jack Jefferson, who is closely modeled on Jack Johnson (1878-1946), in Howard Sackler's *The Great White Hope.* In 1968 the play moved to Broadway, and a year later Jones's portrayal earned him a Tony Award. Reprising the role in the 1970 movie version, Jones was nominated for an Academy Award as Best Actor and won a Golden Globe for best new male talent. In 1966 he made his television debut in the daytime drama *As the World Turns* (*see* TELEVISION AND AFRICAN AMERICANS). During the 1970s he pursued a busy schedule of film and stage acting with occasional television appearances.

In 1977 and 1978 Jones encountered controversy while playing the title role in *Paul Robeson,* a dramatic recounting of the singer-activist's life (*see* PAUL ROBESON). The play unintentionally sparked widespread opposition from the black intellectual community. Picketers appeared outside theaters during the production's tour, insisting that the play misrepresented Robeson's life, and prominent African Americans – including actor OSSIE DAVIS, civil rights activist CORETTA SCOTT KING, and writers JAMES BALDWIN and MAYA ANGELOU – publicly criticized the production. In retrospect, *Paul Robeson* has been credited with helping to reawaken interest in Robeson's life and accomplishments. In his 1993 autobiography, *James Earl Jones: Voices and Silences,* Jones noted that in recent years the play, under the sponsorship of MALCOLM X's daughter, Attilah Shabazz, has been "performed all over the country, without any form of protest."

Jones's long career has produced many finely honed performances. During 1985-1987 he won critical praise and a second Tony Award for his lead role in AUGUST WILSON's drama *Fences.* On television, he portrayed Alex Haley in *Roots: The Next Generations* (1979), the sequel to the 1977 miniseries *Roots.* Jones also appeared in such memorable films as John Sayles's *Matewan* (1987), Phil Alden Robinson's *Field of Dreams* (1989), and Darrel James Roodt's *Cry the Beloved Country* (1995).

Actor James Earl Jones, portraying singer and activist Paul Robeson in a one-man play, stands with a bust of Robeson. *CORBIS/Hulton-Deutsch Collection*

Since the late 1950s Jones has had a prolific and busy acting career. "I might cry for great dramas being written for me," he remarked in a 1980 interview, "but until one is, I'll take a crack at almost anything."

See Also

Haley, Alexander Palmer (Alex); *Jet*; Johnson, John Arthur (Jack); New York, New York; Film, Blacks in American.

North America

Jones, Lois Mailou

(b. November 3, 1905, Boston, Mass.; d. June 9, 1998, Washington, D.C.), African American painter known for her incorporation of French, Haitian, and African artistic influences.

At age four, Lois Mailou Jones began to copy paintings in the homes of wealthy white people for whom her mother, a beautician and hatmaker, worked. Her formal education began in her high school years, when she attended vocational drawing classes in the evenings and on weekends at the Museum of Fine Arts, Boston. She then studied textile design at the Boston Designers Art School before beginning a four-year program at the School of the Museum of Fine Arts, from which she was graduated in 1927 with honors in design.

Because she was black, Jones was denied a graduate assistantship and explored what appeared to be her only other option, teaching art at a black school. In 1928 she established an art department at Palmer Memorial Institute in Sedalia, North Carolina. At that time art departments at Southern black schools were virtually unknown. After seeing a student exhibition mounted by Jones in 1930, James Herring, who was attempting to establish an art department at Howard University, invited her to teach there. During her early years at Howard, Jones began to depict scenes of black life, especially ones that chronicled the injustices suffered by African Americans. She used her sabbatical leaves to travel to France, Haiti, and several countries in Africa. These trips would mark turning points in the subject matter and style of her artwork.

Realizing that to be considered an important artist one had to work in oils, Jones spent 1937 to 1938 at the Académie Julian in Paris, the alma mater of celebrated African American artist Henry Ossawa Tanner. She began to paint landscapes and street scenes, such as *Rue Norvins Montmarte* (1938), in an impressionistic manner inspired by French painter Paul Cézanne. Of her work at this time, one critic remarked, "Miss Jones wishes to confirm Cézanne but at the same time to add an original note of her own.... Sensuous color delicately adjusted to the mood indicates the artistic perceptiveness of this young woman."

In 1953 Jones married Vergniaud Pierre-Noël, a Haitian artist she first met in 1934 while a student in a summer design class at Columbia University. The following year, she went to Haiti and fell in love with the island and its dark people. She and her husband returned several times. Her best-known works from these sojourns depict Haiti's marketplaces and bazaars, as in *Les vendeuses de tissus* (1961). In contrast to the subdued color and diffused forms of her impressionistic French works, these paintings are characterized by vibrant colors and forms rendered in a flat, angular manner. In some of these works, the outlines of the figures' clothes and their belongings appear to be overlapping sticks. Jones also executed some works inspired by Vodou, a Haitian folk religion combining elements of Christianity and various African religions.

In 1971 Jones embarked on an extended journey through Africa. She visited more than a dozen countries and took more than 1000 photographs of contemporary and ancestral African art for Howard University's slide collection. This was not her first encounter with African art and artifacts; she had seen and painted African masks at Columbia University in 1934 and in Paris in 1938 (*Les fétiches*, for example). Her African-inspired

Les fétiches (1938) is an example of Lois Mailou Jones's incorporation of African themes. *National Museum of American Art, Washington DC/Art Resource, NY*

works have a colorful, hard-edged style reminiscent of some of her Haitian-inspired work, but they incorporate more abstract, geometric designs. One of these, *Moon Masque* (1971), is inspired by African mythology about the moon.

Between 1930 and 1977 Jones taught design, drawing, and watercolor to more than 2500 students, including such prominent African American artists as Elizabeth Catlett and David Driskell. Throughout her years as a teacher, Jones encouraged other African American artists to study and understand the context of African art. She once said, "Being basically a designer, I am always weaving together my research and my feelings – taking from textiles, carvings, and color – to press on canvas what I see and feel. As a painter, I am very dependent on design. With me design is basic." Because she had experienced repeated rejection and humiliation as a young black artist, Jones instilled in her students the hope that the "time will come when we will no longer need to attach the word 'black' to 'artist.' Let it be that black artists be referred to as 'artists' whose works are accepted universally on the strength of their merits." At the time of Jones's death in 1998, her work figured in many notable collections, including the Metropolitan Museum of Art, the Museum of Fine Arts in Boston, and the National Museum of American Art in Washington, D.C.

Aaron Myers

See Also

Art and Architecture, African; Boston, Massachusetts; Art, African American.

North America

Jones, M. Sissieretta ("Black Patti") (b. January 5, 1869, Portsmouth, Va.; d. June 24, 1933, Providence, R.I.), African American singer, a gifted soprano who rose to fame as a soloist and troupe leader during the last decades of the nineteenth century.

Sissieretta Jones came early to music. Her father was the pastor and choir director of their Portsmouth, Virginia, African Methodist Episcopal Church, and her mother was a soprano in the choir. She married at age 14 and began voice training the next year in Providence, Rhode Island. She continued her studies at the New England Conservatory in Boston, making her performance debut in that city in 1887. She acquired the nickname "Black Patti" from a newspaper review that praised her as an African American match for the renowned Italian soprano Adelina Patti.

National fame arrived with Jones's performance at the 1892 Grand Negro Jubilee at Madison Square Garden in New York City. Before an audience of 75,000, she sang selections from the opera *La Traviata* as well as the song "Swanee River." This combination of high opera and a popular repertoire continued throughout Jones's career. Racism kept Jones from ensemble roles in established white opera.

Jones toured the West Indies, South America, Europe, and North America as a soloist. She performed for the English royal family and four American presidents and appeared in New York with composer and conductor Antonin Dvořák in 1894.

In 1896 she formed her own troupe of African American entertainers, Black Patti's Troubadours. The group's performances drew on elements of vaudeville and minstrelsy, integrating opera selections into a musical comedy format. After 1916 she retired to Providence to care for her aging mother. She died there, penniless, in 1933.

See Also

Boston, Massachusetts; New York, New York.

North America

Jones, Quincy Delight, Jr. (b. March 14, 1933, Chicago, Ill.), African American arranger, composer, and entertainment industry executive who has worked in music, film, and television.

Quincy Jones has had several careers in popular entertainment, including roles as a big-band musician, composer-arranger, record company executive, producer of films and music videos, and partner in a television production company. He has emerged as one of the most influential figures in Hollywood. He commenced his music career in Seattle, Washington, where his family moved during the mid-1940s from Chicago, Illinois. He sang in a vocal harmony group directed by Joseph Powe, who had once been with Wings Over Jordan. After trying various instruments in his high school band, Jones settled on the trumpet.

As a teenager Jones played in local jazz and rhythm and blues (R&B) groups. He became acquainted with Ray Charles, an early musical influence, who moved to the Seattle area in 1950. Besides leading his own trio, Charles wrote and arranged for the five-member R&B vocal group in which Jones sang. Before he was 16, Jones had written his first suite, *From the Four Winds*, which later earned him a scholarship to Seattle University. Dissatisfied with the university's offerings, he moved to Boston, Massachusetts, and studied at Berklee School of Music.

Jones also found work in the big bands of Jay McShann (1949) and Lionel Hampton (1951-1953). While with Hampton, Jones played in a trumpet section that featured two superb jazz stylists, Clifford Brown and Art Farmer. Jones made his mark not by his playing but through his skilled arrangements. After leaving Hampton, he freelanced as an arranger and with his own big band led various recording dates, most memorably the sessions that produced *This Is How I Feel about Jazz* (1956). He provided arrangements for Count Basie, Billy Eckstine, Sarah Vaughan, Ella Fitzgerald, Dinah Washington, Tommy Dorsey, and others. In 1956 Jones helped organize and wrote many of the arrangements for a new big band for Dizzy Gillespie, touring Africa, Asia, and the Middle East under the auspices of the United States State Department – the first time a jazz group was chosen for such cultural diplomacy.

Jones settled in Paris for several years, where he studied arranging, organized a big band, and worked for Barclay Records as an arranger and producer. He also studied arranging with Nadia Boulanger. In 1961 he returned to the United States and became head of artists and repertoire (A&R) at Mercury Records. Three years later he became Mercury's first African American vice president. During this period Jones stopped playing the trumpet in order to devote his energies to composing and arranging. His music increasingly employed R&B and pop elements, including dance rhythms and electric instruments.

In the 1960s Jones moved to Los Angeles, California, and soon became one of the most successful composers and arrangers in the film industry. He followed in the footsteps of Benny Carter, the alto saxophonist, composer, and arranger who played a key role in challenging the color barrier in Hollywood during the 1940s and 1950s. According to Jones's biographer Raymond Horricks, white composer Henry Mancini aided Jones in his move into film music. Jones provided scores for many films, including *The Pawnbroker* (1965), *In the Heat of the Night* (1967), *The New Centurions* (1972), and *The Wiz* (1978). In 1974 he suffered a cerebral hemorrhage and underwent brain surgery. Upon recovering, he returned to work with undiminished vigor. He arranged and wrote music for numerous television programs of the 1970s, including *The Bill Cosby Show* (*see* Bill Cosby), *Ironside, Sanford and Son* (*see* Redd Foxx), and the miniseries *Roots*.

During these years, Jones further extended his role in the entertainment industry. In 1980 he established his own record label, Qwest. Later in the decade he expanded into movie producing. In addition to composing the film score, Jones served as one of the coproducers for the 1985 movie version of Alice Walker's novel *The Color Purple*. He also showed his ability to master popular musical styles and media, as in the hit albums and music videos that resulted from collaborations with Michael Jackson, including *Off the Wall* (1979), *Thriller* (1982), and *Bad* (1987).

Jones became a highly visible figure in American popular culture. In the mid-1980s he was one of the driving forces behind USA for Africa, producing the *We Are the World* (1985) album and video. In the 1990s his production company developed a number of television programs, including the hit series *Fresh Prince of Bel Air*, which debuted in 1990. Jones received his first Grammy Award from the National Academy of Recording Arts and Sciences (NARAS) in 1963, and by the mid-1990s he had received nearly two dozen Grammys, making him the most honored musician in the award's history. In 1997 he produced the televised Motion Picture Academy Awards ceremony.

Periodically, however, Jones has returned to his jazz roots. In 1964 he arranged and conducted *It Might As Well Be Swing*, an album that featured Frank Sinatra with the Count Basie Orchestra, and 20 years later he conducted and produced Sinatra's *L.A. Is My Lady*. In 1983 Jones conducted a big-band tribute to trumpeter Miles Davis, and in 1991 he appeared with Davis in one of the trumpeter's final public performances – a concert highlighting the collaborations between Davis and arranger Gil Evans – which was released on video and compact disc as *Miles and Quincy Live at Montreux* (1993).

More representative of Jones's musical vision, however, is the Grammy Award-winning *Q's Jook Joint* (1995), which pays tribute to the jook joint, a distinctly African American place for music, dancing, and socializing. Like Jones, this album – which features an eclectic mix of instrumental jazz riffs, R&B ballads, pop music and hip hop rhythms, and RAP vocals – is hard to categorize. "I'm all for de-categorizing the different musical pigeonholes," Jones has said. "Basically, they are all related anyway – blues, jazz, and gospel music, it's all the same thing."

James Clyde Sellman

SEE ALSO
Basie, William James ("Count"); Basie, William James ("Count"); Carter, Bennett Lester (Benny); Davis, Miles Dewey, III; Eckstine, William Clarence (Billy); Gillespie, John Birks ("Dizzy"); Haley, Alexander Palmer (Alex); Hampton, Lionel Leo; Hip Hop in the United States; Jackson, Michael, and the Jackson Family; Television and African Americans; Seattle, Washington; Film, Blacks in American.

North America

Joplin, Scott (b. November 24, 1868, rural eastern Texas; d. April 1, 1917, New York, N.Y.), African American composer and pianist properly known as the "King of Ragtime Writers."

Scott Joplin led the black musicians who, at the turn of the twentieth century, melded African American folk music with classical and Romantic European traditions to form RAGTIME, a march-based yet heavily syncopated style of popular music. His compositions fueled the ragtime craze that led thousands of middle-class whites to buy pianos, collect sheet music, and enjoy, for the first time, the pulse of black vernacular culture. While Joplin's energetic rags created a sensation in middle-class parlors, he also wrote more conventional classical music. He composed waltzes, tangos, operas, and ballet, yet, due to his tremendous success as a sheet-music scribe – and due to his race – he died with a reputation far smaller than the body of his work deserved.

Joplin spent his first years in the lawless RECONSTRUCTION countryside of East Texas's Red River Valley. His father was a laborer and former slave and his mother a free black from Kentucky. Both parents played musical instruments, and Joplin and his five siblings grew up amid fiddles, banjos, and song. When the family moved to Texarkana, Arkansas, in the mid-1870s, the city environment benefited Joplin's musical development. His mother worked as a domestic servant, and her white employers allowed her son to play their piano. Joplin's father, who had come to Texarkana for the good wage of railroad work, bought his son a used piano as soon as he could afford one.

Joplin earned a reputation throughout Texarkana's black community for his precocious musical skill. At age 11 he attracted the attention of a classically trained German musician who introduced him to the rudiments of music theory. As a teenager Joplin left home, probably to ride the new rail lines and play as an itinerant pianist in St. Louis, Memphis, and Dallas sporting houses and at the whistle-stop bars between.

In 1893 Joplin emerged as a well-practiced musician at the World's Columbian Exposition in Chicago, Illinois, where he probably played along the Midway Plaisance. Although white management excluded African Americans from the official program of concerts, black pianists entertained fairgoers along the exposition's bustling periphery. These Midway performances afforded a rare opportunity for middle-class whites to experience the lively music of African Americans. Although the ragtime craze was a few years away, the 1893 exposition – and fairs like it – sowed the seeds. While Joplin may have contributed some of the unofficial entertainment, he also listened to it, absorbing the influences of such great performers as "Plunk" Henry Johnson and Johnny Seymour.

At the same time Joplin met lifelong friend Otis Saunders, with whom he spent the next two years traveling the Midwest in a quartet that played many of Joplin's early compositions. By 1895 the two men were convinced that Joplin had composed songs that the public would buy. Joplin and Saunders settled in Sedalia, Missouri, and joined its local black music scene. In Sedalia, Joplin married Belle Jones, wrote pieces for the Queen City Band, took a course in composition at the George R. Smith College for Negroes, and, most important, began to peddle his compositions.

Joplin sold "Maple Leaf Rag" to white Sedalia businessman John Stark. Allegedly Stark doubted the salability of the tune but liked it so much that he took a chance and published it in 1899. "Maple Leaf Rag" was an instant hit, selling all of its 10,000-copy run and, by 1909, more than 500,000 copies. After the success of "Maple Leaf Rag," Stark moved his business to St. Louis, and Joplin, who had signed a contract with him, soon followed. Ironically the success of "Maple Leaf Rag" crippled the music scene from which it was born, as a number of influential Sedalia musicians followed Joplin to the city.

While Joplin's music deserved the enthusiasm it inspired, Stark's business savvy contributed significantly to the Joplin craze. Long before Joplin was well known, or even very prolific, Stark dubbed him the "King of Ragtime Writers." In addition to printing high-flown promotional rhetoric, Stark marketed Joplin's sheet music with covers that would appeal to the values of middle-class whites. While much contemporary music bore bawdy, racist caricatures, Stark opted for elegant line drawings. Nevertheless, racial ambivalence characterized even Stark's view of ragtime. The ragtime craze both

Scott Joplin (1868-1917) is considered the father of ragtime music, which blended African American and European styles into a wildly popular musical style that prefigured jazz. *Archive Photos/Frank Driggs Collection*

celebrated and questioned the "otherness" of African Americans; Stark himself proclaimed that Joplin combined "the skill of a Beethoven with the sentiment of a Black Mamma's croon."

In the first years of the new century Joplin published numerous rags with Stark, including "Peacherine Rag" (1901) and "The Entertainer" (1902). Joplin also embarked on more ambitious ventures, such as a folk ballet, *The Ragtime Dance* (1902), and his first OPERA, *A Guest of Honor* (1903), the text of which does not survive. Although these works demonstrated Joplin's growing maturity as a musician, they were rarely performed. Even Stark, whose money-making priorities often slackened for Joplin, dragged his heels when it came to publishing more complex music.

By 1906 both Stark and Joplin were facing new difficulties: Stark suffered economically as phonographs and player pianos usurped sheet music's appeal, while Joplin endured personal as well as financial loss. His first child died a few months after birth, and his marriage was in a state of deterioration. Belle died shortly thereafter, and Joplin decided to leave St. Louis.

After a period of meager productivity, during which he traveled to Chicago and Texarkana, Joplin relocated in New York, where the publishers of Tin Pan Alley provided a ready market for ragtime writers. While Joplin continued to write piano music, including the experimental "Wall Street Rag" and "Magnetic Rag," he devoted much of his time to larger projects. He wrote a study guide for up-and-coming ragtime pianists called *School of Ragtime* (1908), and in 1911 he began work on another opera, *Treemonisha*.

Joplin set *Treemonisha* in rural Arkansas during Reconstruction. Its moralistic plot contrasts the evil of ignorance with the hope of education, indicting the rural superstition that Joplin remembered from his childhood. *Treemonisha* contains some of Joplin's most beautiful music, but he never did see its full production. In 1913 a theater that had promised to stage *Treemonisha* backed out on him, and in 1915 he produced the show himself without costumes, sets, or even an orchestra in the LINCOLN THEATER in Harlem.

In 1916 Joplin began to exhibit advanced signs of syphilis, and in 1917 he died in a psychiatric ward, diagnosed with dementia. He worked through his final days and left behind several unfinished compositions. His last years in New York were marked by diminished popular recognition and the grand frustration of *Treemonisha.* His second wife, Lottie Stokes Joplin, organized a small funeral, and her deceased husband sank from popular consciousness over the following decades.

In 1950, however, scholars Rudi Blesh and Harriet Janis revived public interest in Joplin with their book *They All Played Ragtime: The True Story of an American Music.* In addition, pianist Joshua Rifkin made recordings of Joplin's rags that were released in 1970, introducing many people to the music. In 1973 the Hollywood blockbuster *The Sting* featured Joplin's music on its soundtrack, launching "The Entertainer" into frequent radio play. At the same time, interest in his later work grew, and in the 1970s three different productions of *Treemonisha* were staged. In 1976 Joplin was awarded a posthumous Pulitzer Prize.

Eric Bennett

SEE ALSO

Chicago, Illinois; Free Blacks in the United States, 1619 to 1863; Harlem, New York; Memphis, Tennessee; New York, New York; Racial Stereotypes.

North America

Jordan, Barbara Charline

(b. July 9, 1936, Houston, Tex.; d. January 17, 1996, Austin, Tex.), African American Texas state senator, United States congressperson, and educator, one of the foremost orators of the twentieth century.

Barbara Jordan was a political pioneer of her time, the first African American since 1883, and the first woman ever, to be elected to the Texas state Senate and the first Southern black woman to serve in the U.S. Congress. A spellbinding orator, she may be best remembered for the speech she gave as a member of the House Judiciary Committee that in 1974 determined the impeachment of President Richard Nixon. She stated that although the U.S. Constitution's clause "We the people" had not originally included her as an African American and as a woman, she had faith in the Constitution and refused to be "an idle spectator" to its "subversion" by the president.

Jordan was reared and educated in one of Houston's predominantly black districts, the Fifth Ward. She was the youngest of three daughters born to Benjamin Jordan, a warehouse laborer and part-time minister, and Arlyne (Patten) Jordan, a former church orator. The Jordans focused their lives on the local Good Hope Baptist Church. Yet Barbara felt constrained by the Jordan family's strict religious principles, and developed a close relationship with her maternal grandfather, John Ed Patten, a former minister who no longer attended church. In 1919 Patten had been imprisoned for shooting a white policeman in self-defense. After his release he set up a junk business, traveling around Houston on a mule-drawn wagon. Jordan was inspired by Patten's courage and independence and each Sunday helped him sort his rags and scrap iron, which the two of them sold to Houston merchants. Until his death in the early 1950s, Patten remained Jordan's key supporter, encouraging her always to follow her heart.

Jordan attended Phillis Wheatley High School, where she was an exemplary student. As a member of the debate team she won numerous awards, including the national Usher's Oratorical Prize. In 1953, determined to be a lawyer, she enrolled in the historically black Texas Southern University (TSU). She majored in government and, with the guidance of debating coach Tom Freeman, polished her oratorical skills. She also persuaded Freeman to include her in the all-male traveling debate team, despite his policy of never taking women on national tours.

College was a momentous time for Jordan. In BROWN V. BOARD OF EDUCATION (1954), the Supreme Court ended federal tolerance of segregation in U.S. educational institutions. Before *Brown* v. *Board of Education,* black debaters were customarily excluded from white debate contests; afterward, Jordan began traveling around the United States to debate white teams and became one of the first African Americans to tie white debaters from Harvard. Yet in Houston, most schools remained segregated. As Jordan said later: "I woke to the necessity that someone had to push integration along in a private way if it were ever going to happen." She wanted the best education possible in a nonsegregated setting, and on Freeman's advice decided to attend Boston University Law School.

In 1956 Jordan found herself one of two black women in a freshman law class of 600. She again realized the abysmal consequences of segregated education, and felt she was "doing sixteen years of remedial work in thinking." Within months of graduating from law school, she returned to Houston, this time with an eye to a political career. In 1960 she volunteered on the Kennedy-Johnson campaign. Campaign coworkers soon noticed her talent for public speaking, and she was put on the speech-making circuit for the Harris County Democrats.

Despite her widespread popularity among Houston's black and Chicano communities, Jordan lost her first two attempts to win a seat on the Texas state Senate in 1962 and 1964. However, following passage of the Civil Rights Act of 1964, the Supreme Court required Southern states to reapportion their electoral districts, and in 1966 Jordan, running against a popular white liberal, won a state Senate seat by a two-to-one margin. During Jordan's six years in the Texas Senate, she consistently advocated for the working-class constituencies that she represented. She was instrumental in setting up the Texas Fair Employment Practices Commission; she introduced the first Texas minimum wage bill; and she sponsored much of the state's environmental legislation.

In 1972 Jordan was elected to the U.S. House of Representatives, where she became a member of the Judiciary Committee and won national recognition for her moving indictment of Richard Nixon during the Watergate hearings. As a congressperson, she was neither confrontational nor radical in her politics, believing that she could best bring about change for her fellow African Americans by working within the system. As Jordan said of herself: "I am neither a black politician nor a female politician, just a politician."

In 1976 Jordan gave the keynote address at the Democratic National Convention. Many commentators believed that in 1978 she would run for governor or for the U.S. Senate; she was also mentioned as a possible candidate for the U.S. Supreme Court.

But in 1979 Jordan retired from Congress. Afflicted with multiple sclerosis, a neuromuscular disease, she returned to Texas and taught public policy at the University of Texas Lyndon B. Johnson School of Public Affairs. Between 1978 and 1996, the year of her death, she continued to devote herself to public service, acting as keynote speaker at the Democratic National Convention in 1992 and subsequently as chair of the U.S. Commission on Immigration Reform.

The numerous awards Jordan received include the Eleanor Roosevelt Humanities Award (1984) and more than 20 honorary doctorates from leading U.S. universities.

Roanne Edwards

SEE ALSO

Civil Rights Movement; Fair Employment Practices Committee; Houston, Texas; Congress, African Americans in.

North America

Jordan, June

(b. July 9, 1936, Harlem, N.Y.), African American poet, writer, and educator who intertwines personal and political issues in her creative work.

Since the publication in 1968 of her first poetry collection, *Who Look at Me,* June Jordan has pursued a successful career as poet, writer, educator, and activist. Along with eight volumes of poetry, she has published plays, political essays, and fiction for children and young adults. Her novel, *His Own Where,* was written entirely in Black English and was nominated for a National Book Award in 1972. Autobiographical elements figure prominently in her work, as do political and social issues. According to the *Norton Anthology of African American Literature* (1997), Jordan has sought throughout her career to redress the "long-neglected history of black women everywhere" and to critique "versions of feminism, both American and international, that do not adequately consider children, class, or race."

Jordan grew up in Brooklyn, New York, the only child of Mildred Jordan, a nurse, and Granville Jordan, a postal clerk. Jordan's parents, immigrants from JAMAICA, had high career aspirations for Jordan that placed her in a predominantly white world: she initially attended Midwood High School, where she was the only black among 3000 students, and she later enrolled in a New England preparatory school. As an undergraduate at Barnard College in 1955, she met and married Michael Meyer, a white anthropology student. These experiences made her acutely aware of her African American identity and the societal prejudices surrounding interracial marriage; they also inspired her to become an activist. During the 1960s she participated in the Freedom Rides and directed a Connecticut-based Search for Education, Elevation and Knowledge (SEEK) program. However, she soon found herself torn between family and political commitments, a development that, in part, led to her divorce from Meyer in 1965.

From 1966 onward Jordan raised her son single-handedly while writing and teaching English at several American universities. She has taught writing workshops for children and adults and is currently a professor of African American studies and women's studies at the University of California, Berkeley.

Roanne Edwards

SEE ALSO

Literature, African American; Black Vernacular English; Women Writers, Black, in the United States; Miscegenation; New York, New York; Feminism in the United States.

North America

Jordan, Michael Jeffrey

(b. February 17, 1963, Brooklyn, N.Y.), African American professional BASKETBALL player considered by many to be the best all-around player in the history of the sport.

Combining explosive athletic talent and a magnetic personality, Michael Jordan has achieved global popularity reminiscent of MUHAMMAD ALI. The fourth of five children, he was born to James and Deloris Jordan while his father was enlisted in an Air Force training program in Brooklyn. Returning to their home in Wallace, North Carolina, shortly after Michael's birth, the Jordans soon moved to nearby Wilmington. James worked as a mechanic and later an equipment supervisor at a General Electric plant, and Deloris was a customer service officer at the United Carolina Bank.

Jordan's father built a backyard basketball court when Michael was 13, but Michael did not excel in basketball until his junior year at Wilmington's Laney High School. As a sophomore he was cut from the varsity team because he was considered too small. By the fall of his junior year, though, Jordan had grown from five feet eleven inches (1.8 m) to six feet three inches (1.9 m) and was consistently beating his older brother Larry, who had dominated him since they were young boys.

After attending a summer all-star camp that showcased the nation's best high school players, Jordan was courted by numerous college coaches. He and his family chose the University of North Carolina (UNC) at Chapel Hill. Led by team stars James Worthy and Sam Perkins, the Tar Heels reached the finals of the 1982 National Collegiate Athletic Association (NCAA) championship. The freshman Jordan clinched the championship with the final shot that defeated Georgetown University, 63-62.

Jordan was voted the Atlantic Coast Conference Rookie of the Year for 1981-1982. The *Sporting News* named him College Player of the Year in both his sophomore and junior seasons. Combining the ability to score seemingly at will with a glove-like defensive presence learned from North Carolina coach Dean Smith, Jordan attracted the attention of the National Basketball Association (NBA).

In 1984 Jordan decided to forgo his senior season at UNC in order to enter the NBA draft, where he was selected as the third pick by the then-troubled Chicago Bulls. Before joining the Bulls, Jordan led the United States Olympic team to the Gold Medal in the 1984 Summer Games in Los Angeles. In his first professional season, the Bulls' record improved by 11 games and their attendance increased by 87 percent. Chosen as a starter in the midseason All-Star game, Jordan led the league in points scored with 2313 and was chosen as the NBA's Rookie of the Year.

Following his rookie season Jordan signed a contract with the Nike shoe company to create the *Air Jordan* sneaker. The Air Jordan sneaker became a huge popular success, fueled in part by an entertaining advertising campaign featuring Jordan and director Spike Lee. With his good looks and unassuming, natural charisma, Jordan became a highly marketable personality. He has since represented numerous companies and appeared in the feature film *Space Jam* (1996), achieving iconic status in international popular culture.

Jordan was forced to miss most of the 1985-1986 season due to a serious foot injury. He returned in time to play in a legendary playoff game against Larry Bird's Boston Celtics, scoring 63 points in a Bulls 135-131 loss. In the following season he led the league in scoring (an average of 37.1 points per game) and amassed a total of 3041 points, becoming only the second NBA player ever to score more than 3000 points in a single season. Jordan went on to win seven consecutive scoring titles, repeatedly capturing All-NBA and All-Defensive Team awards and winning the Most Valuable Player award in 1988, 1991, and 1992. He silenced critics who assailed his supposed "one-man show" style by leading the Bulls to three consecutive championships in 1991, 1992, and 1993. Jordan also played on the U.S. Olympic "Dream Team" that won the Gold Medal in Barcelona, Spain, in 1992.

Jordan's professional fortunes were eclipsed in 1993 by personal tragedy. In August, his father was slain in North Carolina by two teenage boys during a robbery. Jordan himself was reportedly linked to several underworld figures with whom he had accrued gambling debts. Despite almost single-handedly filling the NBA void left by the retirement of marquee players Larry Bird and Earvin "Magic" Johnson, Jordan announced his retirement from basketball, claiming he felt no connection to the game without his father, whom he called his best friend.

Embarking on a childhood dream, Jordan signed with the Chicago White Sox to play minor league baseball. After 127 games and a .202 batting average, he returned to the Bulls with 17 games remaining in the 1995 season. Jordan's basketball skills were rusty during the remaining games, but he returned the following season in prime form, wielding new offensive weapons. He led the Bulls to the best record in NBA history, 72-10, and to another championship. In 1996 he won MVP honors in the All-Star game, in the Finals, and for the regular season, becoming the first player to garner all three awards since Willis Reed in 1970. Led by Jordan and SCOTTIE PIPPEN, the Bulls won their fifth NBA championship in 1997 and their sixth in 1998. In 1998 Jordan's superb play won him his fifth regular season MVP award and his sixth Finals MVP award. At the peak of his career, following a labor dispute between NBA owners and players that resulted in a truncated 1998-1999 season, Michael Jordan retired from basketball and the Chicago Bulls in February 1999.

SEE ALSO

Baseball in the United States; Johnson, Magic; Lee, Shelton Jackson ("Spike"); Film, Blacks in American.

North America

Jordan, Vernon Eulion, Jr.

(b. August 15, 1935, Atlanta, Ga.), African American lawyer, business executive, former president of the NATIONAL URBAN LEAGUE and UNITED NEGRO COLLEGE FUND, and adviser to President Bill Clinton.

One of the most powerful, well-connected lawyers in the United States, Vernon Jordan has had a long, sometimes contradictory career. Few civil rights spokespeople of his generation have attained the kind of corporate and political influence Jordan has, an achievement enhanced by his position as a top adviser to and close friend of President Bill Clinton. Yet some critics have charged that the former NATIONAL ASSOCIATION FOR THE ADVANCEMENT OF COLORED PEOPLE (NAACP) field secretary and Urban League president has lost touch with his original goal, to improve the economic lives of African Americans.

The middle son of a postal clerk and his wife, a caterer, Jordan was deeply influenced by his mother's drive and business sense. As a child he sometimes accompanied her to catering jobs, where he observed Atlanta's white establishment, especially the Lawyer's Club. In an interview with the *New York Times*, Jordan talked about admiring the way the men dressed, spoke, and carried themselves. "I didn't necessarily like their views," he said, "but I think I learned from them."

After graduating with honors from David T. Howard High School in 1953, Jordan went to DePauw University in Indiana. Though the only black student in his class, Jordan excelled at DePauw, where he served in the student senate, won statewide honors in speaking contests, and played basketball. After college he went to law school at HOWARD UNIVERSITY; he graduated in 1960.

Jordan's early days as a lawyer in Atlanta were devoted to the cause of civil rights. While working as a law clerk for a local black attorney, Jordan helped organize the integration of the University of Georgia, personally escorting student Charlayne Hunter (now journalist CHARLAYNE HUNTER-GAULT) past a hostile white crowd. In the following decade Jordan served as Georgia field secretary for the NAACP, director of the Voter Education Project for the Southern Regional Council, head of the United Negro College Fund, and a delegate to President Lyndon B. Johnson's White House Conference on Civil Rights.

Always more identified with mainstream groups within the CIVIL RIGHTS MOVEMENT, in 1971 Jordan was named head of the National Urban League, one of the more conservative, established African American organizations. Under his leadership, the Urban League flourished. Jordan's experience in fundraising and with the business community helped him attract corporate sponsors, which allowed the organization to more than triple its budget and hire many more employees. At the same time Jordan joined the boards of many of the country's biggest corporations – including Xerox, American Express, and Dow Jones – where he was able to influence hiring policies and push for more jobs for blacks and women.

In 1981, following his recuperation from a May 29, 1980, shooting by a white supremacist, Jordan resigned from the Urban League to take a job with the Washington, D.C., office of Akin, Gump, Strauss, Hauer and Feld, an influential law and lobbying firm based in Dallas, Texas. This job, in addition to his membership in the corporate elite, and his long-standing friendship with President Bill Clinton, made Jordan one of Washington's most important power brokers. He has played a role in influencing the president's positions on foreign trade, budgetary issues, and AFFIRMATIVE ACTION, as well as key decisions on personnel. In 1998 Jordan's friendship with the president brought him once again into the news, this time in connection with allegations that Clinton, while carrying on a sexual relationship with a White House intern, Monica S. Lewinsky, had obstructed justice by asking Jordan to find Lewinsky a job in exchange for her silence about the affair. A corps of Republican congressmen used Jordan's taped deposition in their 1999 impeachment trial against the president, which ended in his acquittal. Known for his charm, elegant clothing, and impeccable manners, Jordan is described by many, including the president, as "larger than life."

Kate Tuttle

SEE ALSO
Atlanta, Georgia.

North America

Journal of Negro History, The,

a quarterly publication founded by Carter G. Woodson to correct through scholarship white racist views of African American history and culture.

Carter G. Woodson published the first issue of *Journal of Negro History* in January 1916. From its inception, the publication's scholarly articles discussed the full range of black experiences from the sixteenth through the twentieth centuries. Contributors highlighted the struggles and achievements of African Americans under slavery, for example, and discussed the abolitionist movement. They reviewed books and wrote biographies of African Americans from the past and present. One of the most important contributions of the *Journal of Negro History* to the body of scholarship on African Americans was its publication of primary source materials, which most white scholars believed did not exist. Revealing the existence of these sources thus facilitated African American primary research.

Woodson, who served as the editor of the journal until his death in 1950, encouraged writers of all types to explore African American history. While the majority of the contributors were African American men, Woodson included the work of white scholars whose interpretations of the African American past were historically accurate. He also published more articles by and about women than any other major contemporaneous historical journal. At the same time, Woodson strove to maintain a balance between amateur and professional writers.

Woodson and the authors he published changed the historiography of slavery by documenting facts, by, for example, interpreting slavery from the slaves' point of view, as opposed to the masters'. The journal's writers cited slave rebellions and slave flight as evidence that slavery was not a benevolent, civilizing system. Others documented the African cultural traditions preserved by enslaved blacks to refute the prevailing belief that African slaves had been cut off from their past. These interpretations began to be accepted more widely after 1950. Now, the *Journal of Negro History* continues to publish articles on African American history, although the more recent acceptance of black scholars and subjects in mainstream periodicals has lessened its influence.

Aaron Myers

SEE ALSO
Slavery in the United States; Maroonage in the Americas; Abolitionism in the United States; Fugitive Slaves; Woodson, Carter Godwin.

North America

Joyner-Kersee, Jacqueline

(b. March 3, 1962, East St. Louis, Ill.), African American heptathlete, one of the most successful track and field athletes of the twentieth century.

Jackie Joyner-Kersee was born to Mary Joyner, a nurse's assistant, and Al Joyner, a construction and railroad worker. The Joyners married in their early teens and raised their children in the impoverished Mississippi River city of East St. Louis. Joyner-Kersee studied modern dance before trying track and field. She and her older brother Al, who later won an Olympic Gold Medal in the triple jump, pushed each other to improve athletically. By the time she was 14, Joyner-Kersee had won the national junior championship in the pentathlon, a five-sport event combining running and jumping. In high school she won the junior pentathlon championship three more times and was an All-America selection for her state championship BASKETBALL team. Graduating in the top 10 percent of her class, she attended the University of California at Los Angeles (UCLA), which offered her a basketball scholarship.

Joyner-Kersee was soon a starting forward on the UCLA basketball team as well as a long jumper for the track team. She was spotted by Bob Kersee, an assistant track coach, who encouraged her to pursue track and field more fully. She qualified for the 1983 world track and field championships in the heptathlon, a two-day competition in which athletes compile points in the 100-meter hurdles, high jump, shot put, and 200-meter dash on the first day, and the long jump, javelin, and 800-meter run on the second day. A pulled hamstring kept Joyner-Kersee from finishing the 1983 championships. The following year she qualified for the United States Olympic team and at the Los Angeles Olympic Games won the Silver Medal in the heptathlon. She missed the Gold Medal by only hundredths of a second in the final event, the 800-meter run.

In 1985 she set a U.S. record in the long jump with a leap of 23 feet, 9 inches. The following year she married Bob Kersee, who continued to coach her after she graduated from UCLA. At the 1986 Goodwill Games in Moscow, Joyner-Kersee set a new world record in the heptathlon, scoring 7148 points – 200 more than the previous world record. She broke her own record less than a month later, in sweltering heat in Houston, with a score of 7161. At future meets often her only competition was her own record. In late 1986 she won the Sullivan Memorial Trophy, which is awarded to America's best amateur athlete. Her reputation for modesty and graciousness won her widespread popularity, and her popularity in turn made the heptathlon, previously little recognized in America, a widely watched track and field event.

At the 1988 Olympic Games in Seoul, Joyner-Kersee won the heptathlon Gold with another world record of 7291 points and took a Gold Medal in the long jump. She suffered several hamstring injuries over the next few years but recovered in time to win the Gold Medal in the heptathlon and the Bronze Medal in the long jump at the 1992 Olympic Games in Barcelona. In the 1996 Olympic Games in Atlanta, Joyner-Kersee was again the favorite to win the heptathlon, but after reinjuring her hamstring in the 100-meter hurdles, she was forced to withdraw. Off the track, she created a nonprofit association benefiting young people in East St. Louis and urban areas, and a sports marketing firm called JJK & Associates.

See Also
Track and Field in the United States.

Africa

Jugnauth, Anerood

(b. March 29, 1930, Palma, Mauritius), former prime minister of the Republic of Mauritius.

One of the most prominent Mauritian politicians, Anerood Jugnauth began his political career shortly after completing legal studies in Great Britain. Running as a candidate for the Independent Forward Bloc (IFB), he won a seat in the Legislative Assembly during the 1963 general elections. In 1966 he attended the Constitutional Conference in London, primarily to ensure adequate Hindu representation in the future government of independent Mauritius, and shortly thereafter was appointed minister of state for development. In 1967 newly elected prime minister Seewoosagur Ramgoolam appointed him minister of labour. But disagreements with the prime minister soon caused Jugnauth to resign, and he returned to law as a magistrate.

In 1971 Jugnauth reentered politics as a member of the newly formed Mouvement Militant Mauricien (MMM), a leftist socialist party founded by Franco-Mauritian Paul Bérenger. With many MMM leaders imprisoned during a government crackdown on the opposition, Jugnauth was able to quickly establish himself as an indispensable party asset, rising in the ranks to become party president in 1974. Winning a seat in Parliament in 1976, Jugnauth became leader of the opposition.

The MMM won a crushing victory during the 1982 general elections, its candidates winning all 60 elective seats. To ensure support from the Hindu community, Jugnauth, a Hindu, was appointed prime minister, while Bérenger became minister of finance. Conflicts between the two quickly arose over Bérenger's determination to maintain structural adjustment economic austerity measures and to make Kreol the official language. Jugnauth was forced to leave the MMM, and subsequently formed a new political party, the Mouvement Socialiste Militant (MSM).

In the 1983 elections Jugnauth's MSM party allied with two others to push the MMM from power. Jugnauth upheld the economic reforms he had previously opposed, and his administration presided over unprecedented economic growth and industrialization, making Mauritius one of the wealthiest countries in sub-Saharan Africa by the 1990s.

Jugnauth's regime was criticized, however, as both corrupt and undemocratic. In 1983 four members of the Mauritian Legislative Assembly, traveling under diplomatic passports, were arrested in Amsterdam airport for smuggling 20 kilos of heroin. A Mauritian commission of inquiry later implicated several other legislators in drug trafficking. The same legislation authorized press censorship with Jugnauth's support. Despite accusations of corruption, Jugnauth won the 1987 elections.

Over the next two years Jugnauth survived two assassination attempts. In 1995 an electorate tired of corruption allegations and hungry for new leadership voted overwhelmingly for Dr. Navin Ramgoolam, son of the late prime minister, ending Jugnauth's 13-year tenure.

Ari Nave

See Also
African Socialism; Structural Adjustment in Africa.

Africa

Juju

Juju, a musical genre originating among Nigerian pop musicians emphasizing speechlike layers of polyrhythmic drumming, a broad range of rhythmic and coloristic guitar patterns, and lyrics underscoring traditional Yoruba social values.

Juju music is an internationally popular musical expression growing out of a tradition of West African guitar-based popular music. The meaning of the term "juju" is unknown, though some historians have linked it to the sounds created by a tambourine. It emerged in the 1930s in southwestern Nigeria, where local Yoruba musicians began casually making music in bars (palm-wine shacks) with transient laborers and descendants of freed slaves from the Caribbean and South America. The musicians played guitars and banjos, sometimes supplemented by hand-held percussion instruments. Although early lyrics often drew on Yoruba folk sayings, juju songs later came to express thinly veiled anticolonial sentiments.

The first commercially available recordings appeared as 78s in the 1930s by musicians like Tunde King and J. O. Arabe. These recordings proved influential to Nigerian musicians after World War II (1939-1945). The compact disc compilation titled *Juju Roots: 1930s-1950s* clearly reveals the nature of the genre's evolution. Juju recordings from the 1940s and 1950s express a forcefully driving music with heavy emphasis on multiple, interlocking layers of polyrhythmic percussion intersected by electric guitar lines. In addition to a variety of hand-held percussion instruments (shakers, bells, rattles), the traditional Yoruba "pressure drum" (also called "talking drum," or *gangan* in Yoruba) was incorporated. The talking drum is a two-headed drum capable of producing a wide range of pitch variations imitating to some degree the tonal contours of spoken Yoruba. This instrument offered an ongoing parallel "commentary" to what a juju vocalist would sing, an ironic counterpoint or complementary expansion. The introduction of electrified guitars introduced a new spectrum of coloristic effects and rhythmic patterns, all at a volume capable of filling a large dance hall or concert arena.

The first major innovator in this heavily percussive and electrified style was I. K. Dairo. His bands, originally the Morning Star Orchestra and later, more famously, the Blue Spots, added accordion fills to complex guitar and drum-driven instrumental patterns. Song lyrics, tapping ancient Yoruba folkloric sources, began to comment sharply on social issues faced by increasingly cosmopolitan and Westernized urban audiences. By the 1970s Dairo became the first juju musician to attract international audiences. From the 1980s to the present Commander Ebenezer Obey and King Sunny Ade have developed individual styles building on the Dairo legacy. Obey's guitar playing has synthesized African American blues and rock styles with juju. Ade has introduced the pedal steel guitar, previously associated with American country music, to juju, along with songs extending to a half hour or longer. Both artists use sophisticated recording studio technology to create atmospheric electronic effects, furthering juju's evolution.

Norman Weinstein

See Also
Music, African; Nigeria; Blues, The.

North America

Julian, Hubert (b. September 20, 1897, Port of Spain, Trinidad; d. February 19, 1983, New York, N.Y.), West Indian-born aviator who was as famous for his daring publicity antics as for his flying expertise.

Hubert Julian, the son of Henry and Silvina (Lily) Hilaire Julian, owners of a cocoa plantation and a shoe factory, became one of the first African American pilots when he earned an aviation license at age 19. Instead of becoming a doctor, as his parents hoped, Julian lived a life of international intrigue as a pilot, arms dealer, and mercenary. Sent to school in England, he left Europe for Canada when World War I broke out. He earned a pilot's license in Canada and arrived in Harlem in the early 1920s with hopes of flying from North America to Africa.

Julian earned the name the "Black Eagle of Harlem" after a stunt in 1923 that typified his ability to parlay failures and defeats into publicity and monetary successes. Flamboyant and charming, he turned a failed parachute jump (he missed the mark, narrowly escaped electrocution, and was arrested for inciting a riot) into a media story. The newspaper coverage pleased his sponsors, as his stunts and schemes brought him national and international notoriety. In 1931, while training Ethiopian emperor Haile Selassie I's air force, Julian once again garnered notice when he crashed a plane bought especially for Emperor Selassie's coronation immediately before the scheduled event.

Julian kept himself in Rolls Royces and expensive clothes with the money he earned as a rum runner during Prohibition in the 1930s and later as an arms dealer. In the 1950s and 1960s he was continually arrested and denied a passport for supplying ammunition and weapons to groups that the United States government and the United Nations considered the "wrong" side of political conflicts in Central America (Guatemala), the Caribbean (Haiti, Cuba), and Africa (Congo, Nigeria). Once active with Marcus Garvey's Universal Negro Improvement Association (UNIA), Julian regularly expressed the sentiment that his deeds were "for the betterment of his race." He remained active in his business enterprises until the 1970s.

See Also

Congo, Democratic Republic of the; Garvey, Marcus Mosiah; Harlem, New York; Universal Negro Improvement Association.

North America

Julian, Percy Lavon (b. April 11, 1899, Montgomery, Ala.; d. April 19, 1975, Chicago, Ill.), chemist who pioneered the development of several synthetic drugs, including cortisone.

Percy Lavon Julian, the grandson of former slaves, was one of six children. His father, James Sumner Julian, a railway clerk, and his mother, Elizabeth Adams Julian, encouraged their children to pursue education, and each of the six achieved a master's, doctoral, or medical degree. In 1916 Percy Julian graduated at the top of his class from the private State Normal School for Negroes and entered Indiana's DePauw University. Because his prior schooling was inferior, DePauw required him to take high school courses alongside his full load of college credits. He also worked to support himself during this time. Nonetheless, he became a member of the Phi Beta Kappa honor society and graduated in 1920 as valedictorian.

Julian hoped to pursue a doctoral degree in chemistry, but while white members of his class with poorer academic records received graduate fellowships, he received no offers. Several universities told faculty members at DePauw that they rejected Julian because a black chemist with a doctoral degree would not be hirable in industry or academia. Reluctantly, Julian settled for a position teaching chemistry at Nashville's Fisk University. In 1922, however, he received an Austin Fellowship, which enabled him to attend Harvard University and study under the eminent chemist E. P. Kohler. Earning high marks, Julian graduated with a master's degree in organic chemistry in 1923. He then taught at West Virginia State College for Negroes and four years later was named professor and head of the chemistry department at Howard University.

In 1929 Julian received a fellowship from the Rockefeller Foundation and used it to study at the University of Vienna in Austria under Ernst Späth, an authority on natural substances who had won recognition for synthesizing nicotine and ephedrine. Julian helped Späth in his quest to synthesize hormones, vitamins, and other naturally occurring drugs – a quest that occupied Julian for the rest of his life. He left Vienna with a doctoral degree in 1931.

After Julian's brief return to Howard, his mentor at DePauw, William Blanchard, asked him to join the faculty there. Julian agreed and continued his studies into physostigmine, a drug used to prevent glaucoma-induced blindness. At the time chemists understood little about how physostigmine prevented blindness. They also were unable to find enough naturally occurring physostigmine to treat patients. Julian's research created a deeper understanding of how the drug worked, and, in a triumphant 1935 discovery, he found a method to replicate physostigmine synthetically. His work received praise from scholars worldwide.

Blanchard recommended that Julian be made head of DePauw's Department of Chemistry, but other professors demurred. Soon thereafter the Glidden Company, which manufactured paint, varnish, and chemicals, offered Julian a post as chief chemist, which he

Chemist Percy Lavon Julian works in his laboratory in the early 1940s. *Photographs and Prints Division, Schomburg Center for Research in Black Culture, The New York Public Library, Astor, Lenox and Tilden Foundation*

accepted in 1936. His appointment is considered a milestone for black industrial scientists. Working with soybeans (the substance he had used in synthesizing physostigmine), Julian pioneered the synthesis of Reichstein's Substance S, which enabled labs to mass-produce the drug cortisone at low cost. Cortisone is used to treat arthritis and other painful conditions.

Julian's team at Glidden also developed a new process for using soy protein in paints and papers that made large profits for the company. The protein had other uses: a fire-retarding foam derived from it was credited with saving many lives on ships and planes in World War II. Julian's team also performed groundbreaking syntheses of progesterone and testosterone, the female and male sex hormones.

In 1953 Julian left Glidden and founded Julian Laboratories, with offices in Chicago and Mexico City. The company specialized in the production of synthetic cortisone, first from soybeans, and then – after discovering that wild yams yielded even richer results – from yams. His labs were soon among the world's largest producers of drugs synthesized from yams. In 1964 he sold his company to the United States pharmaceutical company Smith, Kline, and French. He founded smaller companies in Chicago, continued his research, and became active in the Civil Rights Movement.

See Also

Chicago, Illinois.

Cross Cultural

Jungle (Drum and Bass), a frantic urban music form drawing on the slow dub bass lines of REGGAE, accelerated hip hop breakbeats, DANCEHALL toasting, and the delirious exuberance of "rave" techno dance music.

In 1991 black British producers began adding sped-up hip hop breakbeats (looped drum solos taken from FUNK songs) to the hyperactive genre of techno known as hardcore. Although the British rave dance scene was already on the wane, its doctrine of "Peace, Love, and Unity" still drew a multiracial crowd, and these hip hop mutations of hardcore brought more black youth to the events. Soon reggae influences such as dub echoes and sound effects, ragga bass lines, and dancehall toasting permeated the music, whose name quickly changed to "jungle." Many assert that the genre got its title because it was music designed for the urban jungle; others claim a Jamaican influence, as jungle refers to the Kingston ghetto where BOB MARLEY lived as a teenager.

A brief burst of popularity in 1992 saw proto-jungle songs hitting British Top Ten charts, and in backlash the scene quickly fled underground. Happy vocals and upbeat melodies were replaced with horror-movie sound bites, ultra-low dread bass, and the gangster swagger of dancehall, but the techno-futurism remained. The resulting mix was edgy and experimental, perfect for the tension and exhilaration of city living. Jungle's diverse roots and roughneck attitude yielded a broad crossover appeal, from white suburban ravers to Caribbean immigrants newly arrived in London. A strong Southeast Asian contingent joined the scene early on, as the jungle lived up to its namesake and accepted an abundance of youth cultures into its living mass. Black London deejay Moose notes, "It's not a black thing and it's not a white thing.... It's Jungle, a multicultural thing."

As the scene grew, it remained racially diverse, but, especially in the larger London venues, there was often a distinct black-white split on the dance floor. The reggae-techno hybrid meant that more blacks were attending raves, sparking a media panic in which jungle events were stigmatized by racist stereotypes of crack usage and violence. "Drum & bass" came to describe a cleaner strain catering to a white audience with music stripped of Caribbean influences. The term is now loosely synonymous with jungle, especially outside England. Jungle's popularity soon spread to other parts of Europe, and scenes emerged in Toronto, Montreal, New York, and Los Angeles by the mid-1990s. The racial reconciliation that jungle offered was espoused in the United States as well, although there the audience was primarily white.

The 1992 journey back to the underground was sparked again in 1994 when London "ragga" MC General Levy and M Beat's "Incredible" hit the Top 40 charts. This feat was repeated later in the year with Indian MC UK Apache and black British Shy FX's crossover hit "Original Nuttah." The sounds grew harder in response, and many junglist heavyweights continued to produce a bleak sound into the late 1990s.

Hybrid from its inception, jungle has splintered and become more complex. Intelligent jungle, ragga, darkside, hardstep, techstep, twostep, jazzy, and jump-up are just a few of the many subgenres the swiftly mutating form has created. Artists such as David Bowie and Björk have experimented with jungle-pop fusions, indicative of the genre's acceptance on a more mainstream level. While commercial jungle is readily available, the genre eschews stardom. Individual artists are less important than record labels or local deejays. Jungle remains primarily distributed on independent 12-inch singles for deejay usage and is most commonly heard at clubs or raves.

Jace Clayton

SEE ALSO

Hip Hop in the United States; Los Angeles, California; New York, New York; Jamaica; Kingston, Jamaica; London, Blacks in: An Interpretation.

North America

Just, Ernest Everett

(b. August 14, 1883, Charleston, S.C.; d. October 27, 1941, Washington, D.C.), African American biologist and educator who taught at HOWARD UNIVERSITY for more than 30 years.

Ernest Everett Just was one of the most respected scientists and teachers of his time. Only four years old when his father died, he and his siblings moved with their widowed mother, Mary, from Charleston to James Island, a nearby GULLAH community. There his mother worked in the phosphate fields – typically a man's job – and taught school.

Just grew up surrounded by mother's love of learning and by the natural beauty of James Island. Once he had exhausted the local educational opportunities, his mother helped send him to Kimball Union, a preparatory school in New Hampshire. Arriving in 1900, Just, the school's only black student, found a rich learning environment and a warm social one. He edited the school's yearbook, studied classics and oratory, and delivered the commencement address his senior year.

From Kimball Union, Just entered Dartmouth College in 1903, where he was again the only African American in his class. In contrast to his experience at Kimball, however, Just found himself socially isolated. Turning his attention to his studies, he switched his major from Greek to biology and graduated magna cum laude in 1907. He also minored in history and took several courses in sociology, then a new academic discipline.

Despite Just's having earned high honors at Dartmouth and being elected to Phi Beta Kappa, the pervasive racism in academia kept him from being offered any positions at predominantly white institutions. But MOREHOUSE COLLEGE and Howard University, historically black schools, both wanted him, and he accepted a job as instructor in English and rhetoric at Howard. In 1909 Howard's president, Wilbur Thirkield, persuaded Just to switch to teaching biology and zoology, as part of the liberal arts curriculum and as preparation for medical school. Three years later he was made a full professor. Just's popularity as a teacher was legendary, and his support of students extended beyond the classroom. In 1911 he helped Howard students form Omega Psi Phi, which became a national black fraternity.

Just began pursuing more advanced zoological research, spending summers at the Marine Biology Laboratory in Woods Hole, Massachusetts. He showed an affinity for the work, and focused on embryology and the fertilization of marine animal eggs. It was at Woods Hole that Just became the friend and colleague of Frank R. Lillie, a noted white scientist. In 1916, after four years of long-distance study and the publication of several papers, Just received a Ph.D. in zoology from the University of Chicago. He spent a total of 20 summers working at Woods Hole and published more than 50 scientific papers as well as an influential text, *Biology of the Cell Surface*.

Just's years at Howard were, according to his biographer Kenneth Manning, both a distraction from the research he loved and an expression of his deep commitment to the black community. As both Manning and Mary White Ovington, who profiled Just in her *Portraits in Color*, have pointed out, Just believed that African Americans should study science for the "objective" and "cold-blooded" rigor of the discipline. But Just also relished the opportunity to work in Europe, where racial prejudice was not nearly as prevalent. Beginning in 1929 he undertook a series of extended research tours to Italy, Germany, and France that lasted until 1940, when he and his German-born wife (he had divorced his first wife, a fellow Howard professor) were briefly held in Nazi-occupied France before returning to the United States.

It was his last trip. Already ill with pancreatic cancer, Just spent his final year mending rifts with the Howard administration, which resented his extensive travel, much of it funded by philanthropic foundations and his own family. As his health worsened, Just moved into his sister's Washington, D.C., home, where he died in 1941. In a tribute in the journal *Science*, Just's mentor Frank R. Lillie wrote that "an element of tragedy ran through all Just's scientific career due to the limitations imposed by being a Negro in America."

Kate Tuttle

k

Africa

Kaabu, Early Kingdom of, a historical kingdom centered in northeastern Guinea-Bissau.

Founded by Tiramakhan Traoré, a general of the Mali Empire, the Mandinka kingdom of Kaabu ruled the area that is presently known as northeastern Guinea-Bissau and southeastern Senegal from 1250 to 1867. For six centuries Kaabu dominated small chiefdoms throughout the region and enslaved their inhabitants. Initially the kingdom remained a dependency of Mali. Kaabu expanded slowly; many groups fled to the coastal lowlands, while others resisted Mandinka dominance. The kingdom was an important source of salt, gold, and slaves for Mali. It was socially stratified, with royal succession by matrilineal descent. In the late fifteenth and early sixteenth centuries Songhai assaults on Mali enabled Kaabu to assert its independence. At the same time Portuguese and other European slave traders demanded an increasing volume of slaves for the transatlantic trade. Kaabu expanded considerably through warfare that was intended to capture slaves for export. At its height the Kaabu Kingdom included 44 provinces that were providing troops and tribute.

When Portugal outlawed the slave trade in 1837, competition in the illicit slave trade increased. Kaabu provincial governors competed internally in intradynastic feuds that weakened the kingdom. The Islamic Fulani people, subject to heavy Kaabu taxation for generations, began to subvert the weakened kingdom through religious conversion and holy wars. Wars between Kaabu and the Fulani reached their apex in 1867 at the Kaabu capital, Kansala, when the Fulani Muslim religious leader Timbo Adbul Khudus and 12,000 soldiers forced Kaabu's final surrender.

Eric Young

See Also

Gold Trade; Transatlantic Slave Trade; Salt Trade; Songhai Empire; Slavery in Africa.

Africa

Kabila, Laurent-Désiré

(b. 1939, Jadotville [now Likasi], Belgian Congo [present-day Democratic Republic of the Congo]), African military leader and president of the Democratic Republic of the Congo.

In 1997 international attention focused on Laurent-Désiré Kabila when he led a seven-month rebellion in Zaire (now the Democratic Republic of the Congo) that toppled long-time dictator Mobutu Sese Seko.

Kabila's rapid rise to power followed nearly three decades of opposition to the regime of his predecessor, Mobutu. Kabila was born into the Luba ethnic group in the mineral-rich province of Katanga (present-day Shaba) in 1939. Little is known about his childhood. He attended university in France, where he studied political philosophy and became a Marxist, and in Dar es Salaam, Tanzania, where he befriended Yoweri Museveni, the future president of Uganda. He returned to the Belgian Congo shortly before it achieved independence (as the Congo) in 1960. Upon his return Kabila became a member of the North Katanga Assembly and a staunch supporter of Congo's first prime minister, Patrice Lumumba. After Lumumba's murder in 1961, Kabila and other Lumumba supporters fled to the Congolese borderlands, where they began organizing against the government.

In 1964 Kabila's rebel group received financial backing from Russia, China, and Cuba and staged an insurrection in the eastern provinces of the Congo. The rebellion briefly established a separatist state near Kisangani. In early 1965 Argentine revolutionary Che Guevara came to assist the rebellion but became frustrated with Kabila's leadership and left soon afterward. Later that year the Congolese army, led by Joseph Mobutu (later Mobutu Sese Seko), ended the rebellion. He seized control of the Congo in late 1965.

In 1967 Kabila cofounded the People's Revolutionary Party (PRP), a leftist rebel group that launched sporadic attacks against Mobutu and his regime. The group received funding from China and also supported itself by exporting gold and ivory. In the 1970s the PRP established a small socialist state in the South Kivu Province of Congo (by then renamed Zaire) near Lake Tanganyika. In 1975 Kabila and the PRP gained international notoriety when the group kidnapped three American students and a Dutch researcher from the nearby Gombe Stream Research Center founded by Jane Goodall. The PRP held the hostages for 67 days but released them unharmed after the PRP received an unspecified ransom. Two years later Mobutu's troops finally forced the PRP to abandon their mountain stronghold, and the rebel group fled into nearby Tanzania.

Kabila spent much of the 1980s in Tanzania, where he lived in relative obscurity. He sold gold mined in eastern Zaire in Dar es Salaam. At some point between 1980 and 1996 he developed ties with Museveni, president of Uganda, and Paul Kagame, Rwandan leader. Kabila disappeared in 1988, and many of his associates believed him dead.

Kabila returned to public view in 1996, after Mobutu's government attempted to expel hundreds of Banyamulenge rebels (closely related to the Tutsi of neighboring Burundi and Rwanda). The rebels resisted, and Kagame recruited Kabila to lead a rebellion against Mobutu's regime. Later that year, Kabila united Banyamulenge and other guerrilla groups into the Alliance of Democratic Forces for the Liberation of Congo-Zaire (AFDL) and vowed to overthrow Mobutu. The group enjoyed instant support among the disillusioned and impoverished Zairean population and, in town after town, Kabila's troops easily defeated Mobutu's army. In May 1997 Kabila and his army approached Kinshasa, the country's capital. The cancer-stricken Mobutu fled and Kabila's troops marched triumphantly into the city, where he renamed the country the Democratic Republic of the Congo and declared himself president on May 17.

Since taking power in the Congo, Kabila has had a mixed record. At first he was very popular among the Congolese, who applauded his promises to rebuild and revitalize the Congo and to end the rampant corruption that terrorized the citizenry and contributed to the country's decay. When Kabila imposed restrictions on civil liberties and political activity, however, he lost much of his initial popularity. Citizens complained that they had more freedom during the last years of Mobutu's regime and have accused Kabila of nepotism and promoting only his own ethnic group, the LUBA. Kabila has also faced international criticism for failing to hold democratic elections, limiting free speech, and arresting and threatening opposition groups. He has also been criticized for preventing a United Nations investigation into the disappearance of more than 100,000 Rwandan Hutu refugees, who may have been massacred by Kabila's largely Banyamulenge troops. Consequently, Kabila has lost millions of dollars of foreign aid that he had once hoped would help him rebuild the Congo. In response, Kabila has accused Western officials of hypocrisy for funding the brutal and autocratic Mobutu but refusing to support him, despite his promise to hold democratic elections by the year 2000.

Elizabeth Heath

SEE ALSO
Dar es Salaam, Tanzania; Gold Trade; Hutu and Tutsi; Ivory Trade; Kinshasa, Democratic Republic of the Congo; United Nations in Africa; Rwanda.

Africa

Kabré (also known as Kabyé), ethnic group of northern and central TOGO and adjacent parts of BENIN numbering around 450,000, or 1 million including closely related subgroups, such as the Logba and Losso, who speak mutually intelligible dialects.

Broadly defined, the Kabré are the second largest ethnic group in Togo, after the EWE. They dominate the country's military, and since Gen. GNASSINGBÉ EYADÉMA, an ethnic Kabré, seized power in 1967, they have dominated the government as well.

Researchers believe that the Kabré, who call themselves Lanmba, and related groups such as the Logba once occupied a broad band of territory across northern Togo and Benin. However, during the seventeenth and eighteenth centuries KONKOMBA, fleeing conquest by the DAGOMBA of modern northern GHANA, displaced the Kabré from their western territories. Meanwhile, Bariba fleeing the expanding kingdom of Dahomey drove them out of modern Benin. By the early eighteenth century the Kabré were concentrated in the densely populated La Kara region of Togo, where they live today. During the eighteenth and early nineteenth centuries the Kabré fell victim to slave raids carried out by the Bariba for their Dahomean overlords (*see* SLAVERY IN AFRICA).

Most Kabré raise MILLET, peanuts, YAMS, and other crops for subsistence. They build stone terraces to prevent erosion on their rocky hillside fields and have a reputation as hard workers. Traditionally, Kabré men also worked as blacksmiths, and Kabré women sold metal wares and agricultural produce to neighboring groups.

Until the late nineteenth century most Kabré lacked political structures beyond patrilineal descent groups and strong age-grade societies, though the Logba appointed officials to arbitrate disputes. A centralized chieftainship with limited powers emerged among the Kabré during the 1860s. The German colonial administration strengthened the powers of the Kabré chief.

The Kabré resisted German occupation but in 1897 were forced to surrender. The Germans relied heavily on Kabré forced labor to build railways and other infrastructure. They established valuable teak and mango plantations on the denuded slopes of La Kara. After World War I the French forcibly relocated many Kabré from this crowded region to relatively underpopulated regions of central Togo, and a voluntary southward migration of Kabré farmers continued into the 1990s. During the colonial period many Kabré men migrated seasonally to work in the cocoa plantations of southern Togo and the Gold Coast (present-day Ghana), and others, including Eyadéma, enlisted in the French military.

Under French and German COLONIAL RULE, the northern Kabré experienced little development. The region suffered persistent poverty, and many Kabré grew to resent the relative wealth of southerners such as the Ewe. Since 1967 many Ewe and other non-Kabré have come to resent Kabré domination of Togo's military and government.

Mark O'Malley

SEE ALSO
Dahomey, Early Kingdom of.

Africa

Kabwe, Zambia, a mining town in central ZAMBIA.

Known as Broken Hill before Zambian independence in 1964, the town of Kabwe grew around Broken Hill Mine, opened in 1902, an important source of zinc, vanadium, lead ores, and sulfuric acid. The mine prompted construction of the region's first railroad, which passed through Lusaka on its route to present-day ZIMBABWE. The railroad was extended north into the Copperbelt region soon thereafter. In 1924 a hydroelectric dam was built over the Mulungushi River to the southeast.

Following the construction of major trunk roads after the turn of the century, small numbers of European colonizers began to settle the region surrounding Broken Hill in order to grow maize and tobacco. The earlier inhabitants were displaced and forced to work as miners or tenant farmers. Migrants from a variety of ethnic groups arrived seeking employment; the town began to grow rapidly by 1927, when copper mining reached full production. Today approximately 170,000 people live in Kabwe.

Ari Nave

SEE ALSO
Lusaka, Zambia.

Kabye. Please see KABRÉ

Africa

Kabylia, a BERBER region in eastern ALGERIA whose inhabitants staged an important revolt against French colonialism.

At the time of the 1871 Great Revolt against the French, the Kabylia Berbers, who lived and farmed in the Tell mountain region in eastern Algeria, had enjoyed centuries of local governance. Even during the more than 250 years of Ottoman rule, Kabylia villages largely governed themselves, with decisions made by assemblies of adult men. Since the arrival of Islam in the seventh century, Islamic law had traditionally been integrated with customary law.

As the French moved into the region in 1850, leaders such as Bu Baghla and, later, Lalla Fatima led the Kabylia struggle to resist conquest. Although they were unable to stop French forces, the spirit of resistance endured, culminating in the revolt of 1871-1872, when leader Muhammad al-Hajj al-Muqrani proclaimed a jihad, or holy war, against the Christian invaders. About 150,000 Kabylias joined the rebellion, which spread toward Algiers. The French responded with military action, killing al-Muqrani and capturing his successor. Afterward, the French seized large amounts of fertile land, paving the way for colonial expansion.

The Kabylia is still known for its fierce independence. One of the most militant regions in the 1954-1962 anticolonial war, it is now home to many of Algeria's nationalist political and cultural leaders. After independence the Kabylias revolted against the efforts of the new president Ahmed Ben Bella to centralize power. Throughout the 1980s and 1990s they have been active in the national arena, opposing Arabization laws and policies and promoting Berber rights.

Marian Aguiar

SEE ALSO
Algiers, Algeria; Ben Bella, Ahmed; Colonial Rule.

Africa

Kadalie, Clements (b. 1896; d. 1951), South African trade union leader of the 1920s.

Born in Nyasaland (in what is now MALAWI), Clements Kadalie emigrated to Cape Town,

South Africa, where he became the most important black trade union leader of his day. In 1919 he assisted a strike of black dockers and later that year formed the Industrial and Commercial Union (ICU), originally consisting of 24 black and Coloured (mixed race) dockworkers. Kadalie became the national secretary of the ICU, which he reorganized in 1921 as he consolidated his influence in Cape Province. He tried to present the ICU as no more than a trade union and did not attempt to compete in political terms with the AFRICAN NATIONAL CONGRESS (ANC). He opposed the harsh handling by Prime Minister Jan Smuts of the 1922 miners' strike on the Witwatersrand, and he threw the support of the ICU behind the Nationalist-Labour Party of James Hertzog in the 1924 elections.

The Nationalist-Labour Party won, but Kadalie found that the new government was even more reactionary than that of Smuts. As a result, he became increasingly antiwhite and overtly political. By 1927 the ICU claimed more than 100,000 members and had become the largest South African trade union and black movement of the time. Kadalie moved the ICU headquarters to Johannesburg in 1927, but no white unions or organizations would enter into relations with the ICU except the Communist Party. Kadalie faced growing opposition from Communists and radicals within the ICU after the failure of several regional strikes and his reluctance to lead a nationwide strike. Although Kadalie expelled all Communists from the movement, his influence began to decline. He went to Geneva, Switzerland, in 1927 and then on to Great Britain in hopes of receiving international recognition of the ICU. When he returned to South Africa he found that his position in the ICU had been undermined. A split developed and in 1929 Kadalie resigned. The ICU became less effective and broke apart in 1933. Nevertheless, it provided a model for later mass movements. Kadalie remained active in small local unions until his death.

SEE ALSO
Cape Coloured; Cape Town, South Africa; South Africa; South African Communist Party.

Africa

Kagame, Paul (b. 1957, southern Rwanda), commander of the Rwandan Patriotic Front (RPF) and vice president and defense minister of RWANDA.

In July 1994 Paul Kagame led the guerrilla Rwandan Patriotic Front to power in Rwanda, overthrowing a government whose members had participated in a genocide that killed an estimated 1 million people. Kagame soon became the foremost figure in Rwandan politics.

In 1959 a Hutu revolution in the Belgian colony of Rwanda forced into exile thousands of Tutsi, including two-year-old Kagame and his family. Kagame grew up in a refugee camp in western UGANDA, where he attended school. As a young man he joined the rebel army of YOWERI MUSEVENI to fight against the dictatorship of MILTON OBOTE in Uganda. Museveni took power in 1986 and Kagame was awarded the post of chief of military intelligence. A year later Kagame and about 8000 other Uganda-based Tutsi founded the RPF guerrilla army with financial and military support from Museveni.

In 1990 Kagame was taking military courses in Fort Leavenworth, Kansas, when the RPF invaded Rwanda. When the RPF's leader was killed, Kagame flew back to take over. In 1993 the RPF and the government of Rwandan president Juvénal Habyarimana signed a peace accord calling for a transition to multiparty democracy and the repatriation of Rwandan Tutsi refugees. However, in April 1994, Habyarimana's plane was shot down over Kigali, Rwanda. His government immediately blamed the RPF (responsibility for the fatal crash was still undetermined years later), and Hutu militias began retaliating.

Over the next several weeks hundreds of thousands of Tutsi and Hutu moderates were killed by the militias, the Rwandan army, and civilians following orders. The RPF resumed its war against the government in mid-April. Due partly to the chaos caused by the genocide and partly to Kagame's skilled military leadership, the RPF advanced quickly on the capital. At the same time more than 1.5 million Hutu fled the country.

By the time the RPF took control of the government in early July, Kagame's leadership role was universally acknowledged. The RPF demonstrated Kagame's pledge to reunite Rwanda by appointing two Hutus as president and prime minister, Pasteur Bizimungu and Faustin Twagiramungu, respectively.

Kagame, as vice president and defense minister, was still regarded as Rwanda's de facto leader. His disciplined and pragmatic governance won praise in the West, but many Rwandan Hutu resented the predominance of Tutsi in the army and cabinet; numerous figures in these organizations were, like Kagame, from Uganda. Kagame's support of Laurent-Désiré Kabila's 1996-1997 rebellion against MOBUTU SESE SEKO in the former Zaire, now the DEMOCRATIC REPUBLIC OF THE CONGO (DRC), led to accusations of atrocities committed against Hutu refugees in the DRC by Rwandan forces.

Although postgenocide Rwanda depended heavily on foreign aid, Kagame did not hesitate to criticize or defy the West on issues concerning his own country's recovery. From the beginning he insisted that reconciliation between Hutu and Tutsi could only occur if those guilty of genocide were brought to justice. In 1998 he defended his government's executions of the first convicted criminals.

Leyla Keough

SEE ALSO
Habyarimana, Juvénal; Hutu and Tutsi; Kabila, Laurent-Désiré; Kigali, Rwanda.

Africa

Kaguru (also known as the Kagulu), ethnic group of TANZANIA.

The Kaguru inhabit the highlands of northeastern Tanzania. They speak a Bantu language. Approximately 250,000 people consider themselves Kaguru.

SEE ALSO
Bantu: Dispersion and Settlement.

Africa

Kagwa, Apolo (Kagwa) (b. 1869, Busoga; d. February 1927, Nairobi, Kenya), prime minister of Buganda (1889-1926).

Apolo Kagwa, originally a slave from Busoga, worked as a page for Kabaka Mutesa I, during a time when many Muslim and Christian missionaries were arriving in Buganda. Although Kagwa initially practiced Islam, he was later baptized in the Anglican Church.

After Mutesa I's death in 1884, religious civil war broke out in Buganda. Mutesa's successor, Mwanga II, purged many Christians from the Buganda court, but Kagwa survived. By 1887 he was commanding Buganda's royal guards. A year later Mwanga was overthrown; Kagwa fled to the neighboring Ankole Kingdom. In 1890 Kagwa returned to lead the Christian Party and help reinstate Mwanga, who in turn made Kagwa the *katikiro*, or prime minister. In this position Kagwa welcomed both the Church Missionary Society and the British East Africa Company, and signed the treaty making Buganda a British protectorate in 1894. When Mwanga rebelled against the British three years later, Kagwa helped to overthrow him. The king's infant son, Daudi Chwa, became the new *kabaka* (king), but Kagwa, as one of Chwa's three regents, effectively ruled Buganda for nearly two decades.

The British rewarded Kagwa's collaboration by promising to assure Protestant hegemony in Buganda and by granting Buganda considerable autonomy within the protectorate. Kagwa also received a vast tract of valuable land for his personal use. In 1905 the British knighted him.

After Chwa came of age in 1914, Kagwa came into increasing conflict with the new kabaka. His efforts to preserve Bugandan sovereignty also undermined his formerly friendly relations with the British. Ultimately Kagwa was forced to resign in 1926 after he challenged the British colonial administration's practice of dealing directly with GANDA chiefs rather than with him. He died a year later, reportedly after a fall.

Kagwa wrote extensively in Luganda.

His books on the history and culture of the Buganda kingdom are considered important early works of modern African historiography.

Ari Nave

See Also

Buganda, Early Kingdom of; Mutesa I; Christianity: Missionaries in Africa; Slavery in Africa.

Africa

Kahina (b. 575?; d. 702?), Berber priestess in the seventh century who led a campaign resisting Arab movement into North Africa.

In the seventh century the Arabs arrived in the land they called *Ifriqiya*, in present-day Tunisia, bringing Islam and seeking gold. The Jarawa Berbers in the Aurès mountains became the main force halting their progress through North Africa. The Jarawa were known for their military prowess, and although they offered nominal allegiance to the Byzantine Empire, they in fact ruled their own land. Their chief was the Kahina, a woman who, some said, was more than 100 years old and had two sons of two fathers, one Greek and one Berber. She might have been a Christian or a Jew, and some historians have attributed her resistance to religious fervor. Or she might simply have been a strong ruler who would rather burn down her own kingdom than let it fall into the hands of an outside force. There is little historical documentation of the Kahina's life, although she appears frequently in the legend and literature of the Berbers, the Arabs, and the Europeans, all groups that came to have a stake in the rich Mediterranean region.

In Arabic literature the Kahina appears as an Amazon, charging fiercely into battle with her long hair streaming behind. European writers depicted her as a romantic figure who fought heroically but in vain against marauding Islamic imperialists. All the stories tell how the Kahina, a traditional Berber prophetess, used divination to lead the Jarawa Berbers against the invaders. The Arab leader Hassan first reached the Aurès after defeating the Berber leader Kosaila in 686. The Kahina met the Arabs on the banks of the river Meskiana, after ordering the destruction of her own capital, Baghaya, so it could not be taken. She and the Jarawa were victorious and pursued the retreating Arabs to the town of Gabès, in present-day Tunisia. There the Arabs suffered such a defeat that they halted their advance for the next five years.

While the Arabs built the city of Tunis, the Kahina ruled the adjacent land in an uneasy stalemate. Stories tell of how she adopted an Arab captive during this time, a handsome man of remarkable nobility and bravery, and symbolically gave him her milk, making him her third son. She had a vision of the Arab future triumph and of her sons granted a place of honor among the enemy. Before the Kahina faced the Arabs a final time, she sent the three sons to swear allegiance to Hassan.

The Kahina then destroyed her kingdom rather than let the Arabs take it. But as she burned fields, cut down trees, and destroyed towns, she alienated her own people. When the Arabs attacked again, now bolstered by reinforcements from the East, they met a Berber force weakened by divisions. Hassan killed and took the head of the 127-year-old Kahina at the well that now bears her name, fulfilling her final prophecy of her defeat.

Marian Aguiar

See Also

Tunis, Tunisia.

Africa

Kakwa, an Eastern Sudanic-speaking ethnic group whose members inhabit a region that includes southern Sudan, northeastern Uganda, and northwestern parts of the Democratic Republic of the Congo.

According to oral tradition, the Kakwa migrated from East Africa into southern Sudan and then south into present-day Uganda and the Democratic Republic of the Congo, where they settled among and intermarried with the Madi, Bari, and Lotuke peoples. On the eve of European colonialism in the late nineteenth century, the Kakwa homeland was incorporated into Equitoria, a territory controlled by the Egyptian Khedive Isma'il until 1889. In 1890 much of the area became part of the Ugandan Protectorate.

Currently, approximately 86,000 Kakwa live in Uganda, while another 40,000 live in Sudan and 20,000 reside in the Democratic Republic of the Congo. Kakwa villages have traditionally been organized around a core of related men and their wives, and governed by councils of elders. Rural Kakwa depend primarily on agriculture for subsistence and income – corn, millet, and cassava are among their staple crops – but also raise cattle, which are valued as markers of prestige. Fishing is a significant economic activity among those Kakwa who live near the Nile. Many Kakwa observe the Muslim faith and follow the Malakite school of Islamic law.

Although the Kakwa are a relatively small minority in Uganda, comprising an estimated 1 percent of the total population, the ethnic group became well known when Idi Amin, a Kakwa by his father, became the Ugandan head of state after leading a coup to oust Milton Obote.

Kakwa in Sudan were among the members of Anya Nya, an insurgent group in Sudan's first civil war (1956-1972). As Obote's army chief and, later, as Uganda's president, Idi Amin supplied Israeli arms to Anya Nya. As president, Amin also recruited many Ugandan Kakwa into the armed forces and began to exterminate Acholi and Lango soldiers, who had previously dominated the military. When Amin was ousted in 1979, many Kakwa fled to Sudan to escape Acholi and Lango retribution; many also later allied themselves with Yoweri Museveni in opposing Obote's second regime.

Ari Nave

See Also

Egypt; Nile River.

Africa

Kalahari Desert, a semi-arid region in southern Africa inhabited by the Khoikhoi peoples.

Covering an area of approximately 712,250 sq km (about 275,000 sq mi), the Kalahari Desert spans southern Botswana, eastern Namibia, and northern South Africa. It stretches a maximum of 1300 km (800 mi) north to south and 1300 km (800 mi) east to west. Although it is not actually a desert (it is classified as a "thirstland"), the Kalahari is an arid region covered by grasses and brush, although tubers and bulbous plants grow there. Except for the Boteti River, the region is fed with no surface water (*see* Biogeography of Africa); thus Kalahari wildlife, which includes wildebeest, zebra, eland, giraffe, and elephant, must rely on waterholes.

The Kalahari, which is largely unsuitable for agriculture, was long inhabited only by the Khoikhoi peoples (often referred to as Bushmen), who lived by hunting, foraging, and raising livestock. Parts of the Kalahari have now been turned into national parks and game reserves. These have provided some employment for the desert's long-time residents but have also restricted access to their former hunting territory (*see* Tourism in Africa; Wildlife Management in Africa).

Robert Fay

See Also

Khoisan.

Africa

Kalanga (also known as Bakalanga and Kalaka), ethnic group of southern Africa.

The Kalanga primarily inhabit northeastern Botswana and western Zimbabwe. Others live in Mozambique. They speak a Bantu language and are closely related to the Shona people. Approximately 200,000 people consider themselves Kalanga.

See Also

Bantu: Dispersion and Settlement.

Africa

Kalenjin, a collection of ethnic groups in Kenya.

The term *Kalenjin* did not traditionally refer to a single ethnic group. Instead, it encompassed several Rift Valley peoples who spoke Southern Nilotic languages and were known to outsiders as "the Nandi-speaking peoples." These groups, who also share many cultural traits, forged a common identity in the years after World War II in anticipation of Kenyan independence. Today the Kalenjin comprise approximately 11 percent of Kenya's population. Groups that make up the Kalenjin include the Kipsigi, the Nandi, the Keyo, the Pokot, the Tugen, the Marakwet, the Sabaot, and the Terik.

The Kalenjin's origins remain uncertain. Some scholars believe that ancestors of the Kalenjin migrated from Ethiopia, arriving in the Mount Elgon area around the sixteenth century. The territorial expansion of the Maasai in the eighteenth century pushed the Kalenjin into the area where they now predominate, between the Rift Valley and Lake Victoria. Kalenjin myth names Misri, or Egypt, as their place of origin; their religious beliefs, based on sun worship, refer to the ancient Egyptian god Asiis.

Kalenjin peoples have traditionally practiced nomadic pastoralism, but many today, especially among the highland-dwelling Kipsigis and Nandi, are farmers. It is not uncommon for members of the same family to live in close proximity to one another yet practice different livelihoods. Staple food crops include millet, maize, beans, peas, and cassava; in the highlands, tea is an important cash crop. Nomadic pastoral Kalenjin peoples include the Tugen, Keyo, Marakwet, and Pokot, but even sedentary farming Kalenjin often keep cattle.

Kalenjin society is divided into patrilineal clans (*ortinuek*) as well as male and female age groups. Circumcision for both sexes has traditionally signified the passage to adulthood (*see* Female Circumcision in Africa). Politically decentralized, in precolonial times both nomadic and sedentary Kalenjin peoples vested decision-making responsibility in local councils of elders.

The Kalenjin unified in order to represent more effectively their interests to the British colonial government. Today they account for a smaller percentage of the Kenyan population than either the Kikuyu or the Luo. Nevertheless, they hold considerable political influence, largely because Kenya's president, Daniel arap Moi – himself a Kalenjin – has promoted their interests at the expense of larger groups, especially the Kikuyu.

Robert Fay

See Also
Great Britain; Rift Valleys.

Africa

Kamba, an ethnic group in Kenya.

The Kamba are a central Bantu-speaking people closely related to the neighboring Kikuyu. Before they migrated to their present location in the Ukamba Highlands, according to tradition, the Kamba resided around Mount Kilimanjaro in Tanzania. Although the majority of the Kamba practice Christianity, approximately 40 percent still practice the traditional Kamba religion, which is similar to that of the Kikuyu. Traditional Kamba believed in a supreme god, Ngai, and in *aimu,* or ancestral spirits.

The Kamba traditionally live in extended families on separate homesteads, each with its own agricultural plot. Several such homesteads make up a *utui* ("village"), which includes a common grazing area. The Kamba hold and inherit land patrilineally. The main political division in traditional Kamba society is the *mbai,* or "clan." The society historically has been organized by age grades, although this practice lost importance during the colonial period.

Although they mainly grow maize, millet, and sorghum today, many Kamba maintain a pastoral tradition and keep livestock. Trade has historically been an important element to the Kamba economy. Long-distance trade with Swahili traders along Kenya's coast was fruitful, especially because of Kamba access to ivory. Today Kamba craft products, such as woodcarvings, calabashes, and woven baskets, remain in demand both locally and internationally. In recent years, because of overpopulation and soil erosion, large numbers of Kamba have migrated to Nairobi and other urban areas to find work.

Robert Fay

See Also
Ivory Trade; Nairobi, Kenya; Pastoralism; Swahili Coast.

Africa

Kamberi (also known as the Kambari), ethnic group of Nigeria.

The Kamberi primarily inhabit western and northwestern Nigeria. They speak a Niger-Congo language. Approximately 100,000 people consider themselves Kamberi.

See Also
Languages, African: An Overview.

Africa

Kampala, Uganda, capital and largest city of Uganda.

Originally a settlement scattered across 7 hills on the northern shore of Lake Victoria, Kampala has grown into a city that spans nearly 50 hills and houses more than 800,000 people. The original settlement was known as Mengo, and during the nineteenth century it served as the royal seat for the Buganda *kabaka,* or king. English explorers such as Sir Richard Francis Burton came to the Buganda court at Mengo in 1862 and established diplomatic relations with Kabaka Mutesa I shortly thereafter. In 1890, seeking to establish British control over the source of the Nile, Capt. Frederick Lugard built a fort for the Imperial British East African Company on a hill near Mengo that was known as Kampala to the Bagandans and Fort Hill to the British. Four years later Great Britain formally claimed possession of the region. Eventually, the town around the fort grew to encompass Mengo.

From 1905 until 1962, the capital of the Ugandan Protectorate was relocated to nearby Nakesero Hill in Entebbe. Kampala, however, would remain Uganda's largest town, as well as its center for commerce and communication. Along with Jinja, Kampala grew to become a major industrial center with factories that process agricultural commodities, particularly sugar and cotton, and light manufacturing plants that produce consumer goods. By the 1930s a sewage and plumbing system had been constructed and several roads had been surfaced. When Uganda achieved independence in 1962, Kampala once again became the political capital.

Although Kampala's infrastructure deteriorated during the conflict-torn regimes of Milton Obote and Idi Amin, transportation and communication services have improved in recent years. Port Bell, a few miles to the south of the city, services the shipping industry along Lake Victoria. The city is also connected by major railroad lines to port facilities at Mombasa, Kenya.

Many of the hills of Kampala are crowned by cathedrals, churches, and mosques. Lugard's Fort, now a barrack, remains a hilltop landmark, as do Mulago Hospital and Makerere University. Elevation is also a marker of class; prosperous neighborhoods line the hilltops, while shantytowns dot the valleys. Extensive suburbs surround the city.

Ari Nave

See Also
Buganda, Early Kingdom of; Explorers in Africa Since 1800; Lugard, Frederick John Dealtry; Nile River; Burton, Sir Richard.

Africa

Kana (also known as Khana and Ogoni), ethnic group of Nigeria.

The Kana primarily inhabit River State in southeastern Nigeria. They speak a Niger-Congo language and are closely related to the Ibibio people. Approximately 300,000 people consider themselves Kana.

See Also
Languages, African: An Overview.

Africa

Kanembu, ethnic group of Chad.

The Kanembu primarily inhabit the northern shores of Lake Chad. They speak a Nilo-Saharan language and are closely related to the Kanuri people. Approximately 300,000 people consider themselves Kanembu.

See Also
Languages, African: An Overview.

Africa

Kano, Nigeria, or Kano City, a large city in northern Nigeria that serves as the capital of Kano State.

In the tenth century C.E., Bayajidda Abuyazid, said to be an exiled prince from Baghdad, is reputed to have founded seven Hausa city-states, of which Kano was one. Prehistoric stone tools discovered on the site, however, suggest that the city's actual history extends much further into the past. Scholars from the ancient Mali Empire brought Islam to Kano in the 1340s, and the city achieved great prosperity during the rule of Mohammad Rumfa (1463-1499). Walls built during that period still surround the old quarter of the city, and Rumfa's palace, located next to Nigeria's largest mosque, now serves as the emir's palace.

For centuries Kano was an important market town on trans-Saharan caravan routes. Cola and other products from the forested coastal areas of West Africa changed hands in Kano's market, as did Saharan salt, luxury goods from North Africa and Europe, and slaves. Kano's resident Hausa artisans also manufactured textiles as well as leather and metal goods for both long-distance and local commerce, while nearby villages produced most of the city's food supply. After the Fulani conquest of Hausaland in the early nineteenth century, Kano became the capital of an emirate within the Sokoto Caliphate. In the twentieth century Kano has retained a vital role in the regional economy but through different means. Today the primary crop is peanuts, or groundnuts, which are consumed locally and exported. The tanning and decoration of hides and skins, however, remains a major economic activity.

Most contemporary residents still claim to be Hausa, though sizable populations of Fulani and Abagagyawa also reside in Kano. The city has six major districts: Fagge; the Syrian Quarters and adjoining Commercial Township; Sabon Gari; the Nassarawa; Bompai; and the original walled area. These districts divide further into approximately 100 small neighborhoods (*unguwa*), each of which centers on a mosque and a market. Two hills, Dalla and Goron Dutse, dominate the oldest part of Kano. At their bases, water collects in pools that provide most of the clay used in constructing homes.

Kano is still a center of old-style textile making and leather- and metalworking. But it also hosts food industries, such as meat processing, canning, bottling, and the production of peanut and vegetable oils; light manufacturing, such as modern textiles, knit fabrics, plastics, pharmaceuticals, and furniture; and heavy industries, such as steel rolling and the production of chemicals, automobiles, and asbestos. In addition, Kano remains a hub of transport. Highways converge on the city; railroads run to Nguru, Lagos, and Port Harcourt; and the airport services major international flights.

Kano is also home to numerous schools and institutes, including Kano State Institute for Higher Education, an Arabic law school, Bayero University, a state polytechnic college, a commercial school, an agricultural research institute that focuses on peanuts, two libraries, and several teacher-training institutes.

Eric Bennett

See Also
Salt Trade; Islam and Tradition: An Interpretation; Trans-Saharan and Red Sea Slave Trade.

North America

Kansas City, Missouri, midwestern American city that was a major destination for black migrants from the South; distinguished as the birthplace of ragtime, and vibrant music scene for blues and jazz artists.

African Americans were slaves in area farm fields and on boats plying the Missouri River well before Kansas City was incorporated in 1853. While Kansas City grew around its stockyards and grain depot, a black community developed in the West Bottoms and North End. By 1880 African Americans numbered 8100 in Kansas City, or 14.5 percent of its population. By the turn of the century migration from the South and the Southwest had more than doubled that number. By then the growth of industry had forced most of the African American community to the north side of Kansas City. The black community would comprise 10 to 12 percent of the city's population for the next 70 years.

Segregation had been unofficially present since the 1870s, but in the twentieth century it became overt and still more devastating (*see* Jim Crow). African Americans were barred outright from many hotels and theaters. At the same time a vital music scene arose in the black community. At the turn of the century James Scott and others developed ragtime. In the 1920s a prolific jazz and blues scene began developing in dozens of bars, dance halls, nightclubs, and theaters. Big Joe Turner sang the blues in the 1920s. The Bennie Moten Orchestra became one of the important jazz bands in the country, and, by 1929, it featured pianist Will "Count" Basie, who would later take over the band and define the Kansas City sound: "four heavy beats to a bar." In the 1940s Lester Young, Chauncey Downs, and bebop founder Charlie "Yardbird" Parker pioneered variations in instrumental intonation, countermelody, and rhythmic displacement.

Most African Americans in Kansas City worked as laborers and domestics because of employment discrimination. Nonetheless, Dr. J. Edward Perry organized the Perry Sanitarium in 1910, and in 1919, the *Kansas City Call* newspaper was founded by Chester A. Franklin, a crusading black journalist. In 1920 the National Negro Baseball League was started, and the Kansas City Monarchs soon became one of its great teams, featuring Satchel Paige in the 1940s.

Discrimination, however, was entrenched and rampant. Even during the Depression, most federal work projects in the city excluded blacks from jobs. The black community developed a strong chapter of the National Association for the Advancement of Colored People (NAACP), led by journalist and civil rights leader Roy Wilkins, who later became its national director. Still, progress was modest at best until World War II. At a 1942 rally, 13,000 African Americans – nearly a third of Kansas City's black population – protested job discrimination; thereafter, black hiring increased.

Kansas City began to dismantle segregation in public parks and buildings in 1951 and in schools after the 1954 Brown v. Board of Education Supreme Court decision. But school efforts were largely unsuccessful when many whites fled to the suburbs. By 1964 sit-ins and other protests had integrated restaurants and other facilities. Earl D. Thomas and Bruce Watkins became the first black city councilors. Nonetheless, de facto segregation of schools and the neglect of the black community by city services led to increased activism in the late 1960s. The Black Panthers organized free breakfast programs and spoke out against continued racism. When Martin Luther King Jr. was assassinated in April 1968, the refusal of city authorities to close schools sparked a riot that left six people dead.

In the 1970s and 1980s the black community in Kansas City organized politically. Freedom, Inc., led efforts to elect African Americans, and in 1982 Alan Wheat became the first black United States congressman from Kansas City. A desegregation plan went into effect in 1984; this was followed by a court-ordered plan in 1990. In 1991 Emanuel Cleaver became the city's first black mayor. Despite these gains, loss of industry has produced widespread unemployment in the black community.

Jim Mendelsohn

See Also
World War II and African Americans; Basie, William

James ("Count"); Black Panther Party; Blues, The; Young, Lester Willis ("Prez"); Great Depression; King, Martin Luther, Jr.; Moten, Benjamin (Bennie); Negro Leagues; Paige, Leroy Robert ("Satchel"); Parker, Charles Christopher ("Bird"); Wilkins, Roy Ottoway.

Africa

Kanuri, an ethnic group of Nigeria, Niger, Chad, and Cameroon.

The Kanuri, today dispersed throughout four countries around Lake Chad, once ruled the powerful and centralized kingdom of Bornu. They speak a Nilo-Saharan language, which anthropologists believe originated in what is today the Sahara Desert, before climatic changes about 5000 years ago made the region dry and inhospitable. Kanuri oral histories, however, like those of many other Muslim groups in western Africa, claim that the group originated in Yemen. According to legend, their ancestor, Sayf, founded the Kanem Kingdom (in present-day Chad). His family, the Sefuwa Dynasty, would control Kanem and its successor, Bornu, for more than a thousand years.

By 1000 C.E., Kanem, dominated by the Kanembu people, was renowned throughout the Muslim world for its prosperity and trade connections. A regular stop for many trans-Saharan trade caravans, the capital city was also a popular resting point for Muslims who were traveling across the continent on the pilgrimage to Mecca. Beginning in the mid-thirteenth century, a series of disputes over succession ravaged the kingdom and made it susceptible to outside invaders. After several attacks, a rival group from the north called the Bulala invaded the kingdom in the fourteenth century and usurped power from the Sefuwa Dynasty.

Most Kanembu fled from the invaders and established a new kingdom southwest of Lake Chad in Bornu. Here they intermarried with indigenous Sao and Kotoko people to form the ethnic group known as the Kanuri. Bornu eventually recaptured Kanem and conquered surrounding regions. At its peak in the sixteenth century, the Bornu Empire stretched from Kano in present-day Nigeria around Lake Chad and north into the Fezzan of present-day Libya. Bornu's rulers traded salt from their lucrative mines at Bilma for gold and military equipment from the nearby Hausa. In addition, they imposed heavy taxes on their subjects. These revenues supported the jihads, or holy wars, that Bornu's kings, like many other West African rulers, launched during the sixteenth and seventeenth centuries to subdue the "heathen" groups living outside their territory and to acquire slaves. Bornu also conducted campaigns against neighboring kingdoms, imported firearms from North Africa, and one ruler, Idris Aloma, even hired Turkish mercenaries to train his army, a strategic move that enabled Bornu to defeat Songhai in the mid-1800s.

Bornu's military expansion sapped the kingdom's power. The constant military campaigns impoverished the Kanuri and caused popular discontent. In an effort to regain popular support, Bornu's rulers limited military action to slave raids and made the empire a center of Islamic learning. This decision, however, eventually contributed to Bornu's downfall. As rival armies continued to improve, Bornu became an easy target. During the nineteenth century Bornu lost its western Hausa territories to the Sokoto Caliphate; a Bornu tributary, the Damagaram Kingdom based in Zinder in present-day Niger, declared its independence from Bornu. In 1897 the kingdom finally fell to an invader from the east, Rabih. By 1900 the French had taken control of much of the area and killed Rabih.

Three different European powers – Great Britain, France, and Germany – divided the Bornu Empire between four different colonies – Nigeria, Niger, Cameroon, and Chad. (Great Britain and France divided the German territory after World War II.) The British and French disrupted the profitable trans-Saharan trade, subjecting the Kanuri to the colonial economy. Further, colonization divided the once-united Kanuri, although today most inhabit an area in northeastern Nigeria around the city of Maiduguri. The Kanuri now earn their income predominantly through commerce and agriculture. They produce guinea corn, millet, peanuts, and cotton, and they raise cattle.

Elizabeth Heath

See Also

Colonial Rule; Gold Trade; Kano, Nigeria; Zinder, Niger; Languages, African: An Overview; Salt Trade; Sokoto Caliphate; Songhai Empire; Djebar, Assia; Slavery in Africa; Trans-Saharan and Red Sea Slave Trade.

Africa

Kaonde (also known as Bakaonde, Kaundi, and Kunda), ethnic group of south Central Africa.

The Kaonde primarily inhabit the North West Province of Zambia and southeastern Congo-Kinshasa. They speak a Bantu language and are closely related to the neighboring Bemba and Luba peoples. Approximately 300,000 people consider themselves Kaonde.

See Also

Bantu: Dispersion and Settlement; Congo, Democratic Republic of the.

Africa

Karaboro (also known as Karakora), ethnic group of West Africa.

The Karaboro primarily inhabit northern Côte d'Ivoire and southwestern Burkina Faso. They speak a Niger-Congo language and are closely related to the Senufo people. Approximately 100,000 people consider themselves Karaboro.

See Also

Languages, African: An Overview.

North America

Karamu House, cultural center in Cleveland, Ohio, that provides support for interracial artistic endeavors.

In 1915 Russell and Rowena Jelliffe, two white graduates of Oberlin College, decided to open a center to provide recreational services for families moving to Cleveland from the rural South. Within a few years, their undertaking, known as the Playhouse Settlement, grew into a neighborhood center where people of all races were welcome. The center hosted various cultural events, with an emphasis on interracial theater productions. The first play, *Cinderella,* premiered in 1917.

By 1927 the name of the center had been changed to Karamu House, from the Swahili word meaning "festivity, banquet, and a place of joyful meeting." Karamu House became a model of the ways in which artistic endeavors can promote racial harmony. As the Jelliffes wrote, "The Karamu dream is fulfilled when every man has the full free right to live out his full potential, undeterred by any other man or group of men."

Karamu House became renowned for its theatrical productions and for the exposure it provided to African American performers and playwrights. A repertory company of actors, known first as the Dumas Dramatic Club, later as the Gilpin Players, and eventually as the Karamu Players, comprised the core cast for hundreds of productions over the years. Langston Hughes, a personal friend of the Jelliffes, premiered five of his works at Karamu House, including *Mulatto,* a play about miscegenation in the South that was later performed 373 times on Broadway. One of Karamu House's most successful productions, Kurt Weill's *Lost in the Stars,* ran for more than 100 performances. Some of the performers who got their start at Karamu House include Robert Guillaume, who later starred in *Benson,* his own television series, and Clayton Corbin, who went on to perform in *The King and I* on Broadway.

The Depression curtailed some of the activities at Karamu House, but funding from the Works Progress Administration kept the center alive. A fire destroyed the building in 1939, but ten years later contributions by donors helped the Jelliffes to rebuild. By the mid-1950s the theater had regained its popularity, and federal funding continued in recognition of the standard that Karamu House was setting. The rise of Black Nationalism in the 1970s led Karamu's leaders to shift to all-black productions, but by the 1980s interracial productions were reinstated.

Among the well-known figures to visit Karamu House over the years was Aleksei I. Adzhubei, the son-in-law of Soviet president Nikita Khrushchev. American officials had brought Adzhubei to Karamu House to prove to his delegation that "all is not Birmingham in the United States." The delegation of Russians who accompanied Adzhubei were at first convinced that the racial mixing at Karamu House had been staged specifically for their visit. After watching a play in the Karamu theater, however, they acknowledged the credibility of the organization and praised its success in integrating blacks and whites.

Currently, the Karamu Center encompasses two theaters, a studio for visual arts, a daytime nursery, rehearsal rooms, a dance studio, the Early Childhood Development Center, the Center for Cultural Arts and Education, the Drama Theatre for Youth, and the Langston Hughes Memorial Garden, with sculptures honoring 13 African American artists. Activities include drama, music, dance, and photography classes; courses for seniors, referred to as "most experienced adults," in quilting, crafts, sewing, and health screening; a community night theater; and continuous theatrical productions on the main stage. Local youth are also strongly encouraged to participate in order to fulfill the Jelliffes' intention to "extend and nourish the self-discovery that must initiate the learning process."

See Also

Swahili Language; Great Depression; Art, African American; Black Nationalism in the United States.

Africa

Karimojon (also known as the Karamojong), ethnic group of East Africa.

The Karimojon primarily inhabit northeastern Uganda and neighboring parts of Kenya and Sudan. They speak a Nilo-Saharan language. Approximately 500,000 people consider themselves Karimojon.

See Also

Languages, African: An Overview.

Africa

Kasavubu, Joseph (b. 1910?, near Tsehla, Belgian Congo; d. 1969?, Republic of the Congo), first president of the Republic of the Congo and former president of the Bakongo Alliance.

The first president of the independent Republic of the Congo, Joseph Kasavubu became involved in politics through his desire to empower the Kongo population. Originally trained as a Catholic priest, he dropped out of seminary in 1940 and soon entered the colonial civil service. While a civil servant, Kasavubu joined several Kongo cultural societies, many of which advocated the eventual reunification of the Kongo Kingdom. In 1955 he was elected president of the Bakongo Alliance (ABAKO), a cultural society with political leanings, and soon transformed the group into a serious political party advocating Kongo autonomy.

ABAKO's development coincided with the burgeoning independence movement and, as it was one of the few organized political parties and the dominant party in Léopoldville, Kasavubu soon became a key political leader. In the 1957 local elections he was elected mayor of a section of Léopoldville. Although he was arrested in 1959 after riots broke out in Léopoldville, he was soon reinstated.

In January 1960 Kasavubu participated in the Round Table Conference on Belgian Congo independence in Brussels. Soon after the Belgians nominated him to be president of the new Republic of the Congo and named Patrice Lumumba prime minister. This soon proved to be an uneasy alliance due to their vastly different political visions. Kasavubu hoped for a federal structure that might grant the Kongo population some autonomy, while Lumumba wanted a strong unitary state. The coalition was further strained by the chaos that erupted after independence. Although Kasavubu and Lumumba formally split in September 1960, both were unseated by a military coup led by Joseph Mobutu, later called Mobutu Sese Seko.

Kasavubu was reinstated in February 1961 and remained president until 1965. During this time he stabilized his position by deflecting difficult decisions to the prime minister. In 1965 Kasavubu was removed in a second coup d'état by Joseph Mobutu, and retired from politics.

Elizabeth Heath

See Also

Léopoldville.

Africa

Kasena (also known as Kassena), ethnic group of West Africa.

The Kasena primarily inhabit northern Ghana and southern Burkina Faso. They speak a Niger-Congo language and belong to the Grusi cultural and linguistic group. Approximately 200,000 people consider themselves Kasena.

See Also

Languages, African: An Overview.

Africa

Kaunda, Kenneth (b. April 28, 1924, Lubwe, Northern Rhodesia [present-day Zambia]), president of Zambia from independence in 1964 until 1991.

The eighth child of Malawian migrants, Kenneth Kaunda adopted the language of the Bemba people among whom he was raised. His parents were both teachers, and Kaunda followed in their footsteps as a teacher and headmaster from 1944 to 1947.

His political career began with involvement in the Northern Rhodesia African Congress. He was elected secretary in 1950 and rose quickly through the ranks. In 1953 he was elected secretary-general of the organization, which was renamed the African National Congress (ANC). Within a few months, his call for civil disobedience in opposition to the white-ruled Central African Federation led to his arrest. In 1955 he was again arrested and this time imprisoned. In 1957 Kaunda traveled to England under the auspices of the Labour Party to study the parliamentary system. He returned to Northern Rhodesia in 1958. Disillusioned with the moderate stance of the ANC leader Harry Nkumbula, Kaunda broke away and founded the Zambian African National Congress (ZANC). The colonial administration banned the ZANC in 1959 and imprisoned Kaunda.

Shortly after his release in 1960, Kaunda was elected president of the newly formed United National Independence Party (UNIP). He ran for a seat in the Legislative Assembly as a UNIP candidate during the 1962 elections. Kaunda took a ministerial post and established himself as the most powerful African in the government. In the face of civil disobedience organized by Kaunda and other nationalists, the British government finally acquiesced to demands for independence and abolished the Central African Federation in 1963. In the 1964 elections UNIP's victory won Kaunda the office of prime minister.

Zambia won independence on October 24, 1964, with Kaunda as president. He faced many obstacles, including ethnic partisanship that erupted in violence during the 1968 elections. Intolerant of opposition, Kaunda banned all political parties but UNIP in 1972 and made Zambia a one-party state. His policies, including nationalization of the copper industry and reliance on food subsidies for the poor, made Zambia increasingly dependent on revenues from copper exports. As president of a Front Line State (a country bordering the nations that were still under minority rule and subject to sanctions), Kaunda had to balance a commitment to majority rule against Zambia's vulnerability to economic sabotage and military attack. He served as chairman of the Organization of African Unity (OAU) from 1970 to 1971 and again from 1987 to 1988.

By the mid-1980s the Kaunda regime had

lost public support. With corrupt government officials and a failing economy, calls for a return to multiparty politics increased. Kaunda finally yielded and called for multiparty elections in 1991, in which Frederick Chiluba's Movement for Multiparty Democracy (MMD) defeated Kaunda's UNIP. In 1993 Kaunda announced plans for retirement from political life; however, during the following year he returned to challenge the MMD in the upcoming elections. As a response, Chiluba instituted constitutional amendments barring Kaunda from running by requiring that the candidates' parents be Zambian. The UNIP and other opposition parties boycotted the 1996 elections, and Chiluba consequently won reelection.

In August 1997 Kaunda suffered bullet wounds when police opened fire on his car. He charged the government with attempted assassination, and though evidence indicated that senior police officers had ordered his shooting, the government denied his charges. In October 1997 a group of drunken soldiers attempted a coup. Kaunda was accused of plotting the coup and was detained, despite a lack of evidence. He remains active as a leader of the opposition.

Ari Nave

See Also
Chiluba, Frederick; Nkumbula, Harry Mwaanga; Malawi; Nationalism in Africa.

Kavanga. Please see Kavango

Africa

Kavango, an ethnic group of northern Botswana, northeastern Namibia, and southern Angola.

The Kavango people are descendants of groups of ethnic Ovambo who split from that society during the seventeenth century and settled in the floodplain, in the northeast of what is today Namibia, and on the islands of the Okavango River. Known as Kavangoland, this area has a high seasonal rainfall, and the river's silt deposits make for rich and arable soil. The riverine environment also supports a variety of hardwood, nut, and fruit tree species. Papyrus growing in black-water pools produce leaves used for mats and thatch.

Organized into matrilineal, small-scale states, the Kavango complemented farming and cattle herding with iron smelting and trade. Slavery was common; the Kavango raided neighbors for slaves, used enslavement as a form of criminal punishment, and used slaves in trade. This trade was exacerbated by the expansion of the transatlantic slave trade into the area. Because the Kavango were geographically isolated and unfriendly toward visiting missionaries, they had limited contact with Europeans until Portuguese traders began arriving in the mid-1800s.

Eventually a few missions established themselves in the region and provided what little education was available during German colonialism and South African occupation. In addition to dividing Kavangoland, the colonial administrations of Bechuanaland, Angola, and South West Africa introduced taxation and European legal statutes, especially concerning the ownership of land that had previously been communal. In 1973 South Africa granted Kavangoland self-governing status with an administrative and commercial center at Rundu. In contemporary Namibia, the Kavango comprise just under 10 percent of the total population, and they are materially poor; hardwood timber and carvings are their most valuable exports.

Eric Young

See Also
Colonial Rule; South Africa; Slavery in Africa; Christianity: Missionaries in Africa.

North America

Keckley, Elizabeth (b. 1818, Dinwiddie Court House, Va.; d. May 26, 1907, Washington, D.C.), African American dressmaker, seamstress, and personal maid to President Abraham Lincoln's wife, Mary Todd.

Elizabeth Hobbs Keckley was born in Virginia, to Agnes, a slave of the Burgwell family, and George Pleasant, who was owned by a man named Hobbs. When she was in her teens, she was sold by the Burgwells to a slave owner in North Carolina by whom she was raped and had one child, George. Shortly thereafter, a Burgwell daughter, Anne Burgwell Garland, bought her and her son. They were taken to St. Louis, where she married James Keckley. She later found he had deceived her by claiming to be a free man, and the couple separated.

To support her owner's household, Keckley worked as a seamstress. She acquired many loyal customers, one of whom loaned her $1200 to buy her freedom in 1855. In 1860 she relocated to Baltimore and then moved to Washington D.C., where she opened a dressmaking business and set a goal to become a seamstress at the White House.

Keckley's dream was realized when Mary Todd Lincoln, President Abraham Lincoln's wife, recognized not only Keckley's talent for dressmaking, but also her quiet and good-natured personality and hired her as a personal maid and dressmaker. Keckley also became the first lady's close friend and traveling companion. The two shared a common sorrow in the loss of their sons; George died in August of 1861, fighting for the Union Army, and Willie Lincoln died a year later in 1862.

In 1862 Keckley established the Contraband Relief Organization, an organization of black women who assisted former slaves seeking refuge in Washington, D.C. In addition to moral support, Mary Todd Lincoln donated $200 to the organization; donations were also received from Frederick Douglass and Wendell Phillips.

When President Lincoln was assassinated on April 14, 1865, Keckley consoled Mary Todd Lincoln. In 1867, in order to raise money, Keckley helped her auction off her clothing in New York, which later led to scandal.

In another attempt to generate funds for Mary Todd Lincoln as well as herself, Keckley published her diaries in 1868, *Behind the Scenes; or, Thirty Years a Slave and Four Years in the White House*. Keckley recognized that the publication would invite criticism. However, she did not anticipate that the betrayal of her knowledge of the private lives of the Lincolns would elicit condemnation from Mary Todd Lincoln and disapproval from the African American community.

Because of this controversy, Keckley's business declined and she was ostracized from society. From 1892 to 1893 she left Washington to teach domestic science at Wilberforce University in Ohio. She returned soon after to spend the rest of her days at the Home for Destitute Women and Children in Washington, which she had helped to establish. She died there from a stroke May 26, 1907.

Because of Keckley's lack of formal schooling, the authorship of her memoirs is often questioned. Nevertheless, the information revealed in the book is upheld by scholars as an accurate source of information on her memories of the Lincoln White House.

Leyla Keough

See Also
Baltimore, Maryland; Civil War, American; New York, New York; Washington, D.C.

Africa

Keino, Kipchoge (b. January 17, 1940, Kipsamo, Kenya), Kenyan long-distance runner.

Kip Keino was the first of Kenya's world-class distance runners to make his mark on the world sports scene. He won Gold and Silver Medals at both the 1968 and 1972 Olympic Games, set long-standing world records in both the 5000- and 3000-meter races, and inspired a generation of Kenyan track and field athletes.

An ethnic Nandi, Keino was orphaned at age two and raised by his grandmother. His first racing success came in 1962, when he set a national record for the mile. In 1964, while working as a physical fitness instructor for a police academy, Keino participated in his first Olympic Games, where he finished fifth in the 5000-meter race. The following year he broke world records in both of his main events, the 3000- and 5000-meter races. Sports analysts see Keino's training on Kenya's mountainous terrain as one reason for his success in the next Olympic Games in 1968, which were held at Mexico City. There he won Gold in the 1500-meter race and Silver in the 5000-meter, and led a Kenyan team that garnered a total of eight Olympic medals.

In 1972 Keino repeated his two-medal performance, winning Gold in the 3000-meter steeplechase and Silver in the 1500. Soon runners worldwide were imitating his high-altitude training methods. Keino is renowned not only for his stellar track career – which he capped by serving as coach to the Kenyan national team starting in 1996 – but also for his personal beneficence. Since 1964 he and his wife, Phyllis, have taken into their home as many as 100 orphans and raised them as their own children. For this humanitarian work, *Sports Illustrated* named Keino one of its Sportsmen of the Year in 1987.

Kate Tuttle

See Also
Olympics, Africans and the; Track and Field in the United States.

Africa

Keita, Modibo (b. 1915, Bamako, Mali; d. May 16, 1977, Bamako, Mali), president of Mali (1960-1968).

The first president of Mali, Modibo Keita is often blamed for the economic problems that have afflicted the country since independence. A descendant of the Mandinka lineage that once ruled the ancient Mali Empire, Keita originally trained to be a schoolteacher. After his graduation from the William Ponty School in Dakar, he taught school, but he soon abandoned teaching for politics.

In 1945 Keita founded the Bloc Soudanais, a political party with socialist leanings. A year later the party joined the Rassemblement Démocratique Africain (RDA) – a multi-colony political party founded by Félix Houphouët-Boigny of Côte d'Ivoire – as the Union Soudanaise-RDA (US-RDA). As the US-RDA candidate, Keita won election to the territorial assembly of French Sudan (present-day Mali) in 1948, the French chamber of deputies in 1956, and the territorial assembly in 1957. Keita sought to build a state, the Mali Federation, incorporating several Francophone West African territories and linking French Sudan to the sea.In 1958 he was elected president of the federation (initially comprising French Sudan and Senegal). However, Houphouët-Boigny opposed the federation, and Léopold Sédar Senghor withdrew Senegal from the federation in 1960. Keita subsequently became president of an independent Mali Republic.

Mali inherited a weak, overwhelmingly agricultural economy from French colonial rule; Keita's strict anticolonialist and socialist policies only added to the country's economic difficulties. At first, Keita severed relations with France and pulled Mali out of the French-dominated Communauté Financière Africaine (CFA) franc zone. With the support of communist countries, Keita nationalized Mali's banks, transportation, and public services, and established village cooperatives. In addition, he imposed trade restrictions and tariffs that drove trade underground and depleted the national budget. Mali's economy rapidly deteriorated, and, against the wishes of his advisors, Keita negotiated Mali's readmission to the CFA in 1967.

Keita, however, placated his advisors with a series of political reforms styled after Mao Zedong's Cultural Revolution in China. He replaced the national legislature with a committee of radical supporters. He created a militant youth organization, the Popular Militia, to repress popular opposition. He also began purges of the government and military. In retaliation, army officers led by Lt. Moussa Traoré removed Keita in 1968 in a military coup d'état. Traoré imprisoned Keita, who died in custody on May 16, 1977.

Elizabeth Heath

See Also
African Socialism; Dakar, Senegal.

Africa

Kela (also known as the Bakela), ethnic group of the Democratic Republic of the Congo.

The Kela primarily inhabit the Kasai-Oriental region of central Congo-Kinshasa. They speak a Bantu language. Approximately 200,000 people consider themselves Kela.

See Also
Bantu: Dispersion and Settlement.

North America

Kennedy, Adrienne (b. September 13, 1931, Pittsburgh, Pa.), African American playwright.

Adrienne Kennedy was born Adrienne Lita Hawkins and grew up in Cleveland, Ohio. She received a B.A. in education from Ohio State University in 1953 and that same year married Joseph C. Kennedy and moved to New York.

Kennedy studied drama at several schools over the next decade, including Columbia University, the Theatre Wing of the New School for Social Research, and Circle in the Square Theatre School. Her first professionally produced play, *Funnyhouse of a Negro,* opened in 1964 and won both a Stanley Drama Award and a 1964 Obie Award. In 1967 she received a Guggenheim Memorial Fellowship and the first of several Rockefeller grants. Also in that year, her first full-length play, *The Lennon Play: In His Own Write,* was produced. In 1971 Kennedy became a founding member of the Women's Theater Council. She received a National Endowment for the Arts grant in 1973, and a Creative Artists public service grant and a Yale Fellowship in 1974.

Kennedy's best-known full-length play is *A Movie Star Has to Star in Black and White* (1976), and many of her one-act and full-length plays have been widely anthologized. Her other writings include several plays for children and her 1987 memoir, *People Who Led to My Plays.* In 1990 Kennedy received an American Book Award and the Lila Wallace-Reader's Digest Fund's Writers Award in 1994. She has taught at Yale, Princeton, Brown and Harvard universities and the University of California at Berkeley.

Lisa Clayton Robinson

See Also
New York, New York.

Africa

Kenya, East African country bordered by Ethiopia, Tanzania, Somalia, the Indian Ocean, and Uganda.

Fringed by coral beaches, crowned by Mount Kenya, and cut through by the majestic Rift Valley, Kenya's physical landscape is among the most beautiful and varied in Africa. It is a landscape made familiar to many in the West through novels, Hollywood films, and the country's well-developed tourist industry. But safari tours in Kenya's national parks provide little more than a glimpse of a country that has one of the world's longest histories of human habitation and an enormously diverse, and often divided, society.

British colonialism helped transform cultural differences into ethnic animosities, and it established enduring stratification between the land-rich and the land-poor. Rights to the fertile land in central Kenya, in fact, were at the heart of a bloody anticolonial uprising – the so-called Mau Mau Rebellion – and after independence, export crops produced on that land contributed to the young nation's economic prosperity. But years of economic mismanagement, corruption, and political repression, especially since the coming to power of President Daniel arap Moi in 1978, have dimmed Kenya's early promise. The country is now burdened with massive foreign debt, a failing infrastructure, accusations of widespread human rights abuses, and continuing ethnic tensions.

Early History

Millions of years ago the East African region now known as Kenya was the scene of early hominid evolution. Archaeological digs in the Rift Valley and around Lake Turkana, Kannapoi, and Allia Bay have uncovered remains of distant human ancestors, such as *Australopithecus boisei* and *Australopithecus anamensis*, and more recent and direct human ancestors, such as *Homo habilis* and *Homo erectus.* The latter are believed to be

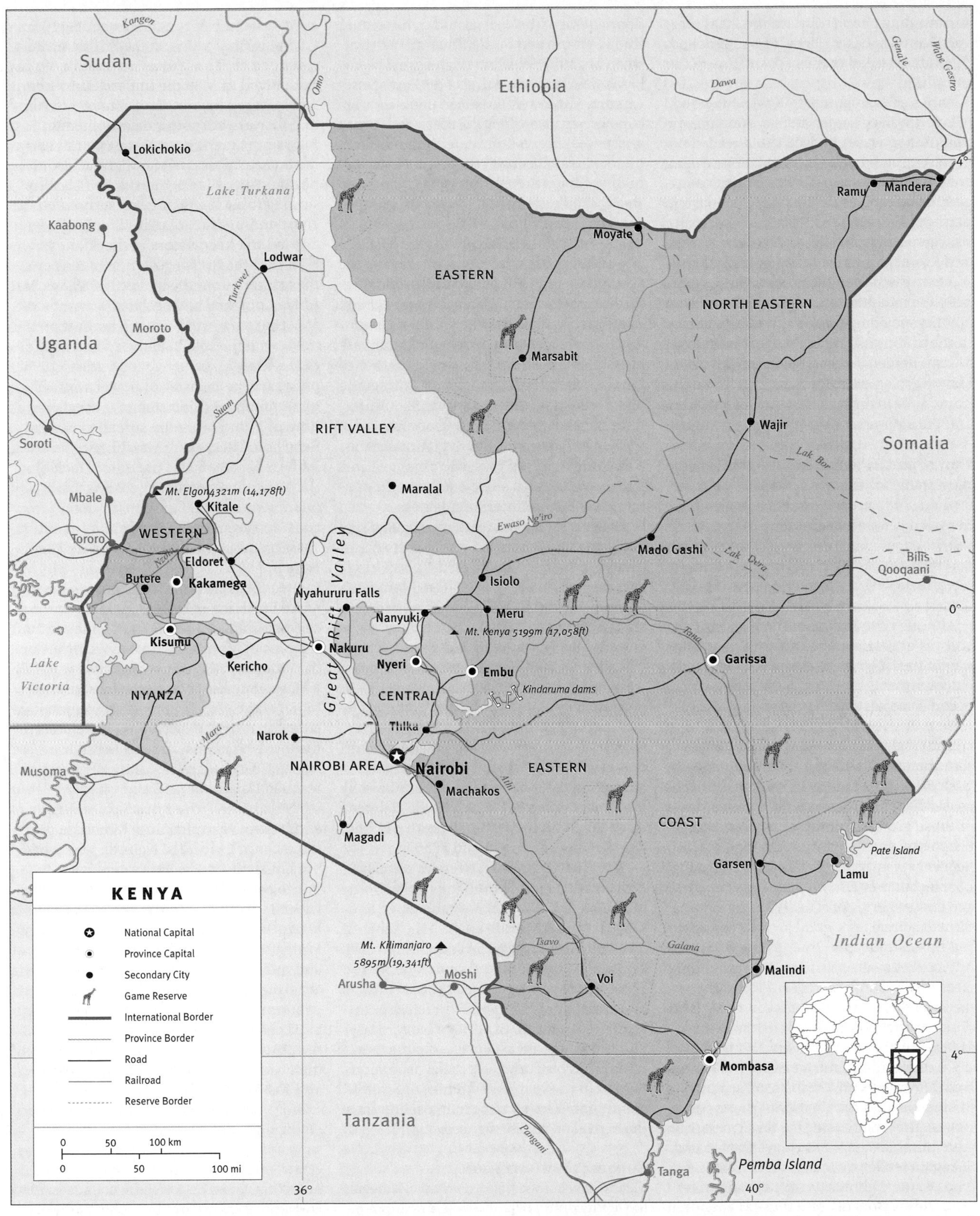

about 1.8 million years old. Archaeological research in Kenya's Malewa Gorge has also uncovered evidence of Stone Age tool making, dated at 238,000 B.C.E.

The earliest known human societies in the East African interior were KHOISAN speakers. Inhabiting the savanna, forests, and lakeshores, they used sophisticated stone tools to hunt, forage, and fish. Approximately 5000 years ago, speakers of Cushitic languages migrated south from Ethiopia and settled in the Rift Valley. These people cultivated dry land crops such as sorghum and MILLET and kept herds of sheep, goats, and cattle. About 3000 years ago, Bantu-speaking agriculturalists migrated east from the rain forests of Central Africa and settled in the vicinity of LAKE VICTORIA.

The constraints of a more arid climate and interaction with their Cushitic neighbors, led the Bantu speakers to take up grain farming and PASTORALISM. Bantu-speaking communities expanded and dispersed rapidly in East Africa, and they displaced or assimilated surrounding peoples. By around 2000 years ago, Bantu-speaking peoples had reached the Indian Ocean to the east and ZAMBIA to the south.

Other early migrants to Kenya included Nilotic-speaking herders from the SUDAN, who migrated in waves between 1000 and 2000 years ago, and the Eastern Cushitic-speaking ancestors of the pastoral OROMO and SOMALI peoples, who moved south from Ethiopia into northern Kenya around 1000 B.C.E. Eventually Bantu-speaking peoples, such as the KIKUYU and KAMBA, occupied much of central and southern Kenya, and Nilotic-speaking KALENJIN peoples predominated in western Kenya. The Nilotic-speaking TURKANA lived as nomads in the arid north, while the closely related MAASAI herded cattle in the fertile Rift Valley. Kenya's ecological diversity fostered the development of distinctive regional economies and cultural practices.

For centuries political organization in the Kenyan interior remained decentralized, and most trade occurred either locally, between farmers and herders, or between groups in Kenya's diverse ecological zones. Foodstuffs, salt, iron tools, and pottery were the primary goods traded among inland peoples, though ivory made its way through networks of traders to the coast, where it was exported.

Although the history of the East African coast is generally better documented than that of the interior (*see* SWAHILI COAST), the patterns of early settlement remain the subject of some speculation. Hunters and gatherers were probably the first inhabitants of the coastal regions; they were later joined at some point by Cushitic-speaking herders. The pastoral Oromo and Somali peoples in the coastal region are believed to be descendants of these groups. Finally, Bantu-speaking peoples migrated to the coast during the Iron Age. They were primarily farming and fishing people, but they also hunted, kept livestock, and engaged in regional trade. Their economy turned increasingly toward long-distance and sea-based trade, once merchants from the Arabian Peninsula began trading and settling along the East African coast. According to the second-century C.E. Greek source *Periplus of the Erythrean Sea*, this trade dates back at least 2000 years.

Generations of intermarriage between coastal Africans and Arabs produced the distinctive cultural identity of the SWAHILI PEOPLE. They were among the first East African adherents of Islam – a mosque excavated at Shanga, a settlement in the Lamu Archipelago, dates to the eighth century C.E. – and they were the creators of numerous independent coastal city-states. Ocean commerce in high-value goods such as RHINOCEROS horn, ivory, tortoise shell, gold, and slaves contributed to the prosperity of cities such as Mombasa, Malindi, Lamu, and Pate during what Swahili history refers to as the Golden Age, from the twelfth to the eighteenth century C.E.

The largest Swahili cities competed for domination of the coastal and transoceanic trades. At the end of the fifteenth century, when Malindi's power was waning and Mombasa's was rising, the arrival of the Portuguese explorer VASCO DA GAMA signaled a new era of power struggles along the coast. The Portuguese, seeking to dominate Indian Ocean trade routes, allied with the Swahili Dynasty in Malindi to take over Mombasa. The city was sacked once in 1505 but resisted Portuguese rule until 1529.

The Portuguese efforts to tax the Swahili city-states provoked revolts, prompting the Portuguese in 1593 to build the formidable Fort Jesus at the entrance of Mombasa Harbor, where its ruins still stand. The imam of Oman finally drove the Portuguese out of Mombasa in 1660, but the Portuguese held on to the fort itself until 1699. Although the Portuguese had few lasting effects on Swahili culture during their two-century-long occupation of the Kenyan coastline, they did introduce the New World crops of cassava, tomatoes, and maize, which have since become part of both coastal and interior cuisines.

The imam's victory over the Portuguese signaled growing Omani interest in East African trade but did not initially secure his control over the Kenya coastline. Instead, Mombasa's Mazrui clan, who themselves claimed descent from Omani settlers, took control of the city after the ouster of the Portuguese. They extended their influence through an alliance with the rulers of Pate, at that time the most powerful city-state in the Lamu Archipelago, but their allied forces were defeated by soldiers from Lamu in the early nineteenth century. The Mazrui were deposed and many were later driven out of Mombasa by the Omani sultan Sayyid Sa'id, who claimed all of the Swahili city-states north of Cape Delgado between 1820 and 1830.

After 1840 the sultan oversaw his East African trade empire from the capital he established in ZANZIBAR. A sizable navy and support from the British enabled the sultan to maintain his rule over the coast and to concentrate on developing inland trade routes. These caravan routes opened the East African interior not only to Swahili traders, but to Europeans as well. Exports of ivory, slaves, and hides, as well as cloves, sesame, and other crops produced on coastal plantations, helped to revive the economies of Swahili communities that had been in decline since the arrival of the Portuguese.

EUROPEAN COLONIZATION

Meanwhile, European powers had also begun to vie for control over the East African mainland. In the so-called SCRAMBLE FOR AFRICA, German claims to the mainland across from Zanzibar drove the British to claim the region directly to the north. The two countries agreed on the partition in Berlin in 1886, and the following year they met again to determine the sultan of Oman's holdings. They granted him all of the islands along the coast as well as a strip of coastline extending 16 km (10 mi) inland, which, in the British territory, extended as far north as the mouth of the Tana River. In 1888 the Imperial British East Africa Company obtained a royal charter to undertake economic development in East Africa north of Mount KILIMANJARO. This region itself possessed few natural resources besides fertile land, but the British were seeking to secure their interests both on the coast and in the Buganda Kingdom, and around the headwaters of the Nile.

In 1895 the British government took over the territory from the ineffectual British East Africa Company and declared it a protectorate. That same year Great Britain signed a treaty with the sultan, and assumed control of the coast in exchange for British £16,500 per year. The transfer of power sparked a nine-month rebellion along the coast, beginning in Mombasa – the so-called Mazrui Rebellion. The Swahili Mazrui clan took part in the rebellion, but so did others, including the Mijikenda people. The British subsequently transferred administration of the coast to the sultan of Omani. This administration continued until Kenyan independence in 1963.

Great Britain's initial objectives in the East Africa Protectorate were to make it economically self-sufficient and to build a railway from the port of Mombasa to Lake Victoria. For the latter task the British recruited not only Africans but also indentured laborers from India. Many of the Indian laborers remained after construction, becoming merchants in the towns that arose around the railway (*see* INDIAN COMMUNITIES IN AFRICA). The railway reached Nairobi in 1899 and was completed in 1901. In 1907 the British moved their administrative capital from Mombasa to the more centrally located Nairobi, which had previously been a railroad depot.

The completion of the railway, combined with the March 1902 transfer of Uganda's fertile eastern province to the East African Protectorate, spurred increased European and Indian settlement. The railway also enabled the British to bring in the troops needed to suppress resistance in several different parts of the interior. Between 1900 and 1908 the British troops put down uprisings among the NANDI, EMBU, GUSII, KIPSIGI, Bakusu, and Kabras peoples.

From the beginning, Kenya's white settlers enjoyed government representation and support far out of proportion to their numbers. The all-white Legislative Council, established in 1906, gave settlers a voice in colonial affairs. Even more important, the colonial government set aside Kenya's fertile highlands for settler farms. To create what became known as the White Highlands, the government declared pastures and fallow farmland to be unoccupied and thus available for white settlers. Only Africans working on settler farms were permitted to use land in the highlands, and they were subject to abrupt evictions. At the same time the government forced hundreds of thousands of Africans into crowded "native reserves," where farmland was often too poor and too scarce for households to support themselves.

Colonial rule in Kenya depended on defining and dividing "tribes." The government assigned Africans to reserve lands according to what "tribe" they claimed to belong to, and it appointed "chiefs" as tribal authorities. Since many of Kenya's ethnic groups had not historically recognized political powers higher than their village councils or clan elders, this attempt to rule "indirectly" through traditional authorities was, in many cases, not traditional at all. The British also drew on ethnic stereotypes to create a colonial division of labor: the Kikuyu, for example, were considered suitable for lower-level civil service, while the Maasai were preferred for police and military service.

One of the responsibilities of appointed chiefs was to recruit labor. The Native Authority Ordinance of 1912 authorized chiefs to recruit their subjects for up to two months of compulsory labor, either on public works projects or for a private employer, typically a white farmer. The Native Registration Act of 1915 helped prevent labor flight by requiring that all African adult males carry identification whenever they left the native reserves. During World War I about 195,000 were recruited to help as porters, of which an estimated 50,000 died from poor treatment. Another 10,000 served as soldiers.

The colonial government also used taxation to force Africans into wage labor. Men and women alike worked on the coffee and tea plantations of white settlers, while men predominated in the wage labor forces of Nairobi and Mombasa. Some women also migrated to the cities – beer-brewing and prostitution were among the few income-earning options open to them – but those who remained in rural areas often had to assume greater responsibility for farming.

The government of the protectorate based its plans for economic self-sufficiency on export crops such as coffee and tea that were produced by white settlers. By 1915 the settlers had still not proven to be productive farmers, but the Colonial Office still gave in to their requests for greater land tenure security, extending leases from 99 to 999 years. Kenya's new governor, Maj. Gen. Sir Edward Northey, encouraged British soldiers to settle and seized an additional 5186 hectares (12,810 acres) of land from native Kenyan peoples. In 1921 the protectorate became the Crown Colony officially named Kenya.

The World War I era saw the emergence of African political protest in Kenya. This protest was urban, led largely by the mission-educated elite, and moderate in tone. Its leaders, such as Harry Thuku of the Kikuyu Central Association, objected to colonial land and labor policies and called for intertribal unity. The colonial government arrested and detained Thuku in 1922 but not before his speeches had inspired a young mission-educated man named Jomo Kenyatta.

Kenya's Indians also began to pressure the colonial government for reforms. By the mid-colonial period many Indians had established shops and small businesses, but they objected to the urban segregation policies that barred Indians (and Africans) from living in certain neighborhoods, and to restrictions on Indian immigration. In 1923 the colonial government granted five seats on the Legislative Council to Indians and agreed to loosen segregation and immigrant restrictions. The highlands, however, remained reserved for whites. Meanwhile, European settlers pushed, with little success, for greater autonomy from the British Crown.

These men are members of the Maasai ethnic group, semi-nomadic pastoralists whose reputation as fierce warriors has sometimes led Europeans and other outsiders to romanticize them. *CORBIS/Patrick Bennett*

Excluded from the colony's political bodies as well as from most of the social services available to Europeans and Asians, many educated Africans put their energies into self-help associations, such as the Kavirondo Taxpayers' and Welfare Association and the Kikuyu Central Association (KCA). Although

LEFT: Nairobi women share information on family planning. *Betty Press*
BELOW LEFT: With its high rise buildings and modern amenities, Nairobi is a center of trade and tourism in East Africa. *CORBIS/The Purcell Team*

they were initially established to provide social services that Africans could not obtain from the government, the associations later became some of the driving forces of post-World War II nationalism.

During World War II Kenya was mobilized against the threat of an Italian invasion from Somaliland. Both Mombasa and Nairobi grew rapidly as laborers poured in, seeking work on the docks or in industry. Labor unions began to flex their muscles during this time: strikes rocked Mombasa in 1939 and again near the end of the war. In the countryside the compulsory labor policies used to secure workers for European farms also spurred protest. Although the administration had used the invasion threat as an excuse to ban African political activity, it attempted to appease unrest by agreeing to pay modest wage increases for urban workers. The administration also nominated Eliud Mathu, a politically prominent school principal, to an unofficial seat on the Legislative Council in October 1944. Africans gained an additional three seats (all unofficial) during the following year.

Mathu was supported by a group of Nairobi activists called the Kenya African Study Union (KASU). Their name was purposefully nonpolitical, but their goals – among them the return of settlers' land to Africans – were political. Still, KASU remained a small, elite organization until Jomo Kenyatta, by then a KCA leader, returned from university studies in Great Britain and assumed the presidency. Renamed the Kenya African Union (KAU), the group grew rapidly, attracting members from across the socioeconomic spectrum. Its leadership was divided between militant nationalists who wanted immediate independence and land handovers, and moderates like Kenyatta, who were willing to work for gradual Kenyan independence through constitutional reform.

By the early 1950s intermittent but escalating violence among Kenyans led the British to fear a general uprising and to suspect Kenyatta as the ringleader. Kenyatta denied any involvement, but in October 1952 he and approximately 100 other activists were arrested and jailed. The administration then declared a colony-wide state of emergency, in turn sparking the Kikuyu-dominated Mau Mau Rebellion. Support for the uprising in Nairobi was quickly crushed; afterward many of its organizers hid in the forests around the capital city. The Mau Mau Rebellion was aimed mainly at the British, but its forces also attacked African Loyalists. By the end of the fighting in 1956, the British had detained more than 80,000 Kenyans. Over 12,000 Africans and 100 Europeans had died. Great Britain won militarily but lost all faith in its future as a colonial power in East Africa.

Decolonization proceeded rapidly. The state of emergency ended in January 1960, and a delegation of Africans, including Tom Mboya and Jomo Kenyatta, traveled to London to negotiate a transitional constitution for Kenya, which was completed by February 1961. Also in 1960 the KAU was renamed the Kenya African National Union (KANU). The transitional constitution gave Africans the majority of seats in the Legislative Council and legalized political parties.

KANU candidates won a majority in the Legislative Council in 1961 but refused to form a government while Kenyatta remained in prison. Kenyatta was released in August of that year, whereupon he assumed the presidency of KANU. In general elections in May 1963, KANU was the overwhelming victor and Kenyatta became prime minister at Kenyan independence on December 12, 1963. Kenya officially became a republic one year later, with Kenyatta as its president.

Postcolonial Development and Nationhood

Kenya's first independent government proved moderate. Kenyatta favored free-market economic policies and close ties with the West. He instituted a plan for land distribution with the government purchasing European-owned farms and settling landless Africans on them. In the first ten years of independence approximately 150,000 formerly landless people were given 259,000 hectares (approximately 640,000 acres) of land. The extent and the nature of government reform rankled some of the more militant within KANU, however, which by 1965 was divided into two broad camps. Tom Mboya led the party's conservative wing, while fellow Luo, Oginga Odinga, Kenya's vice president since 1964, led the radical wing. In 1966 Odinga and many of his supporters left KANU and formed the Kenya People's Union (KPU). Kenyatta responded by expanding his government's detention and censorship powers, and merged the two legislative bodies into one. Minister of Home Affairs Daniel arap Moi became the new vice president.

In July 1969 Tom Mboya was assassinated in Nairobi by a Kikuyu man, aggravating tensions between the Luo and the numerically and politically dominant Kikuyu. Luo demonstrations in the western town of Kisumu gave Kenyatta an excuse to ban the KPU and place Odinga under house arrest, without charges, until 1971.

Throughout the 1970s the aged Kenyatta grew more reclusive and autocratic. But high world tea and coffee prices and a thriving tourist industry had brought Kenya relative prosperity, helping to assure the president's reelection to a third five-year term in 1974. He died in office in August 1978, and was succeeded by Vice President Moi despite opposition led by the nephew of Kenyatta, Njoroge Mungai.

Moi, an ethnic Kalenjin, made no immediate moves to end Kikuyu political dominance. For his administration he took the motto *Nyayo*, Swahili for "footsteps," indicating his wish to follow in Kenyatta's path. A year later, however, he banned ethnic associations and began doling out former Kikuyu properties to his Kalenjin supporters.

In 1982 discontented air force officials attempted a coup d'état. Moi subsequently reorganized the armed forces and outlawed all other political parties except KANU. Over the next several years, Moi further consolidated his hold on power. He replaced Kikuyu in his administration with fellow Kalenjin and eliminated press freedoms. Critics claim that Moi encouraged ethnic violence in order to divide his opposition.

Kenya in the 1990s

By the early 1990s Kenya had lost its reputation as one of Africa's most stable and prosperous countries. Pressure from foreign donors forced Moi to hold multiparty elections in 1992. But between the time of his victory that year and the 1997 elections (opponents claimed both elections were rigged) the president's regime did little to improve its record of corruption, ethnic favoritism, and human rights abuses. Before and after the 1997 elections, towns on the coast and in the Kikuyu regions – both opposition party strongholds – were violently attacked by what many believe were Moi's Kalenjin henchmen. Some of the 1997 candidates had campaigned for an end to "tribalism," but in April 1998 the human rights organization Amnesty International warned that ethnic tensions had made Kenya a "powder keg waiting to explode."

Kenya's liberal investment policies have created a relatively diversified agricultural export sector; Kenyan coffee, green beans, and fresh-cut flowers, for example, are known throughout Europe. But Kenya's economy overall has suffered not only from widely acknowledged government corruption but also from mounting debt and a crumbling infrastructure. Heavy rains associated with the 1997-1998 El Niño weather patterns inflicted especially severe damage on the road system. The trip from the capital, Nairobi, to the port city of Mombasa, once a five-hour drive, now takes two days to complete. Political instability has also hurt Kenya's tourist industry, one of the country's primary sources of foreign exchange. Future investment in and aid to Kenya remain in question, as the Moi government still has not undertaken substantive reforms.

Robert Fay

See Also

Bantu: Dispersion and Settlement; Buganda, Early Kingdom of; Decolonization in Africa: An Interpretation; Explorers in Africa, 1500 to 1800; Food in Africa; Gold Trade; Indian Communities in Africa; Ivory Trade; Languages, African: An Overview; Swahili Language; Mombasa, Kenya; Nairobi, Kenya; Nationalism in Africa; Nile River; Portugal; Rift Valleys; Sa'id Sayyid ibn Sultan; Salt Trade; Tourism in Africa; Lamu, Kenya; Christianity: Missionaries in Africa; Human Rights in Africa; Indian Ocean Slave Trade.

Africa

Kenya (Ready Reference)

Official Name: Republic of Kenya
Former Name: British East Africa
Area: 582,646 sq km (224,960 sq mi)
Location: Eastern Africa, bordering the Indian Ocean, between Somalia and Tanzania; bordered by Ethiopia, Somalia, Sudan, and Tanzania
Capital: Nairobi (population 1,504,900 [1990 estimate])
Other Major Cities: Mombasa (population 442,369 [1985 estimate]), Kisumu (population 167,100 [1984 estimate]), and Nakuru (population 150,000 [1991 estimate])
Population: 28,337,071 (1998 estimate)
Population Density: 48 persons per sq km (about 123 persons per sq mi [1995 estimate])
Population Below Age 15: 44 percent (male 6,248,260; female 6,109,443 [1998 estimate])
Population Growth Rate: 1.71 percent (1998 estimate)
Total Fertility Rate: 4.07 children born per woman (1998 estimate)
Life Expectancy at Birth: Total population: 47.5 years (male 47; female 48.1 [1998 estimate])
Infant Mortality Rate: 59.3 deaths per 1000 live births (1998 estimate)
Literacy (age 15 and over who can read and write): Total population: 78.1 percent (male 86.3 percent; female 70 percent [1995 estimate])
Education: Though not compulsory, the first eight years of primary school are free. In the early 1990s approximately 5.4 million pupils annually attended about 14,690 elementary schools, and about 614,000 students attended the more than 2750 secondary and teacher-training schools.
Languages: Swahili is the official language, although Kikuyu, Luo, and English are also widely spoken. Nearly all Kenyan ethnic groups have distinct languages.
Ethnic Groups: Of more than 30 ethnic groups in Kenya, the largest are the Bantu-speaking Kikuyu, Luhya, and Kamba; the Nilotic-speaking Luo; and the Paranilotic-speaking Kalenjin. Small numbers of Asians, Europeans, and Arabs reside in Kenya.
Religions: About 40 percent Protestant, 30 percent Catholic, and 6 percent Muslim. The remaining 24 percent follow traditional religions.
Climate: Kenya is divided into two almost equal parts by the equator. The region north of the equator is hot and receives comparatively little rain. The southern region falls into three meteorological zones. The coast is humid with an average annual temperature ranging from about 24° C (about 76° F) in

June and July to about 28° C (about 82° F) in February, March, and April; the highlands are relatively temperate; and the Lake Victoria region is tropical.

Land, Plants, and Animals: Kenya covers several well-defined topographical zones extending from the Indian Ocean coast upward to lofty mountain ranges that reach elevations of more than 3050 m (10,000 ft) above sea level. From a low coastal strip the terrain rises gradually to a broad, arid plateau that covers the largest portion of the country. The region west of the plateau contains great volcanic mountain chains, of which the principal peak is MOUNT KENYA (5199 m/17,058 ft). The southern and southeastern portions of the country are heavily forested, and in the west, the immense depression of the Great Rift Valley is demarcated by a succession of steep cliffs. The chief rivers of Kenya are the Tana and Galana (known as the Athi in its upper course). Besides a small portion of LAKE VICTORIA, Kenya contains almost all of Lake Turkana (formerly called Lake Rudolf).

Along the coast are forests containing palm, mangrove, teak, copal, and sandalwood trees. Forests of baobab, euphorbia, and acacia trees cover the lowlands to an elevation of approximately 915 m (approximately 3000 ft). Extensive tracts of savanna (grassland), interspersed with groves of acacia and papyrus, characterize the terrain from about 915 to 2745 m (about 3000 to 9000 ft). The principal species in the dense rain forest of the eastern and southeastern mountain slopes are camphor and bamboo. The alpine zone (above about 3350 m/11,000 ft) contains large senecios and lobelias.

The major animal species are the GIRAFFE, ELEPHANT, RHINOCEROS, ZEBRA, LION, other large cats, birds, and reptiles.

Currency: The Kenyan shilling

Gross Domestic Product (GDP): $45.3 billion (1997 estimate)

GDP per Capita: $1600 (1997 estimate)

GDP Real Growth Rate: 2.9 percent (1997 estimate)

Primary Economic Activities: Agriculture (26 percent of the GDP), small-scale mining and manufacturing, and tourism

Primary Crops: Sugar cane, corn, cassava, pineapples, sisal, cotton, cashew nuts on the coast and in the lowlands; potatoes, coffee, tea, cotton, cereal grains, beans, peanuts, tobacco in the highlands; also stockbreeding (cattle, goats, sheep, chickens) and dairy production

Industries: Small-scale mining (soda ash, salt, fluorspar, gold, garnets, limestone); large deposits of lead and silver have been discovered near Mombasa; small-scale food and raw material processing for local consumption; flour milling, cement manufacturing, oil refining, and small-scale consumer goods manufacturing

Primary Exports: Tea, coffee, petroleum products, canned pineapple, hides and skins, sisal, soda ash, and pyrethrum extract (used in insecticides)

Primary Imports: Crude petroleum, industrial machinery, motor vehicles, iron, steel, agricultural implements, pharmaceuticals, and fertilizer

Primary Trade Partners: Uganda, Great Britain, Rwanda, Pakistan, Japan, United States, United Arab Emirates, and Germany

Government: Kenya has a modified one-party parliamentary form of government. Executive authority is exercised by a president, elected for a five-year term by popular vote. President Daniel arap Moi has held office since 1978. A vice president and a cabinet are appointed by the president from members of the National Assembly, the legislative branch of government. The assembly consists of 188 directly elected members, the attorney general, the speaker, and ten members who are nominated by the president. The Kenya African National Union (KANU) was the nation's only legal political party from 1982 to 1991.

Robert Fay

SEE ALSO

Baobab Tree; Swahili Language; Moi, Daniel arap; Nairobi, Kenya; Mombasa, Kenya.

Africa

Kenyatta, Jomo

(b. 1894, Ichaweri, British East Africa [now Kenya]; d. August 22, 1978, Mombasa, Kenya), the first prime minister and first president of Kenya.

Jomo Kenyatta's life spanned almost the entire period of British COLONIAL RULE in the area that is now KENYA. Raised in the countryside near MOUNT KENYA and educated at a Church of Scotland mission school, Kenyatta became a leading member of the generation of African elites who rose in protest of oppressive colonial policies.

Kenyatta's political career began in 1922 when, while working as a civil servant in Nairobi, he joined the East African Association (EAA), a short-lived KIKUYU organization led by HARRY THUKU that was formed to regain stolen African lands from white settlers. Pressure from the colonial administration forced the EAA to disband in 1925 and reform as the Kikuyu Central Association (KCA). In 1928 Kenyatta became general secretary of KCA, and editor of its journal, *Muiguithania* (the Reconciler). *Muiguithania* publicized and gathered support for the KCA's demands, which included the return of confiscated land to Africans, improved social services, African representation on Kenya's Legislative Council (Legco), the repeal of hut taxes, and noninterference in Kikuyu customs, such as polygamy. The KCA also opposed a British proposal for "closer union" among Kenya, UGANDA, and Tanganyika (TANZANIA).

When Kenyatta traveled to England to protest the proposal (which the British government ultimately dismissed), his speeches and publications won increased support for Kenyan reform among members of Britain's Labour Party. Kenyatta spent 1931 to 1946 away from Kenya, a time of intellectual ferment for him. In addition to his activism, he attended classes at Moscow State University and received a degree in anthropology from the London School of Economics. His thesis, *Facing Mount Kenya*, a study of traditional Kikuyu customs and beliefs, became a bestseller in England after its publication and is still considered an anthropological classic. In addition, he helped organize the 1945 Pan-African Congress in Manchester.

Kenyatta found a radically different Kenya when he returned after World War II. The colonial government had banned the KCA, and in response, nationalist members of the KCA had formed the Kenya African Union (KAU), a multiethnic pro-independence organization, to which Kenyatta was elected president in 1947.

Growing anticolonial militancy in Kenya erupted in the 1952-1956 MAU MAU REBELLION. Mau Mau, a Kikuyu secret society that drew members from the KAU and other organizations, was committed to armed struggle to oust the British. Although excluded from Mau Mau, Kenyatta, under pressure from the colonial government, had denounced its activities, the government arrested him and some 150 other nationalists on October 21, 1952. In 1953 he was tried and convicted of "managing the Mau Mau terrorist organization" and sentenced to seven years in prison.

Although Mau Mau failed militarily, it brought international criticism to the colonial government's brutal crackdown – which cost more than 12,000 African lives – and pushed Britain to accelerate its plans for Kenyan independence. In 1960 the KAU was renamed the Kenya African National Union (KANU), and Kenyatta, still in prison, was elected its president.

After his release Kenyatta helped negotiate the terms of Kenya's independence at the London Conference in 1962. KANU won pre-independence elections in May 1963, and on independence day, December 12, 1963, Kenyatta became the country's first prime minister. The following year Kenya became a republic and Kenyatta its president, an office he held until his death in 1978.

Under his motto *Harambee* ("pulling together"), Kenyatta sought to unite Kenya and build a stable nation. He outlawed Kenya's opposition party in 1969 but also attempted to overcome ethnic divisions, appointing members of various ethnic groups to key government posts. He maintained friendly relations with Western nations, encouraged a free market economy, and promoted foreign investment and tourism, all of which helped the economy to grow five-fold between 1971 and 1981. Although most of the generated wealth was concentrated in the hands of a few – namely Kenyatta, his family, and their

Kenyan leader Jomo Kenyatta, who would become the first president of an independent Kenya in 1963, speaks at a 1961 news conference. *CORBIS/Bettmann*

close associates – the president faced little opposition during his time in office.

Robert Fay

See Also

Nationalism in Africa; Nairobi, Kenya; Tourism in Africa; Pan-Africanism.

Africa

Kérékou, Mathieu also known as Ahmed Kérékou (1933-), president of Benin (1972-1991, 1996-).

Born in Kouarfa in what was then Dahomey (part of French West Africa), Mathieu Kérékou attended schools in Mali and Senegal before enrolling in the French army and attending Fréjus Officers School in France. In 1961 he was commissioned second lieutenant in the Dahomean army, serving as aide-de-camp (military assistant) to President Hubert Maga (1961-1963) and close adviser to Kérékou's cousin Col. Iropa Maurice Kouandete, playing an important role in Kouandete's 1967 overthrow of Christophe Soglo's military regime.

After a series of attempted military coups and mounting chaos among civilian leaders in the early 1970s, Kérékou (then a major) seized power on October 26, 1972. He dismissed most senior army officers, imprisoned all three former presidents (who were eventually released in 1984), and established a government staffed entirely by army officers under the age of 40. Kérékou proclaimed Marxism-Leninism the official ideology of the state and changed the country's name from Dahomey to Benin in 1975. In 1979 he held elections, nominally converting Benin to civilian rule, while still ensuring his own power base.

Kérékou's policies of nationalization and government expansion remained in effect until the early 1980s, when economic woes and resulting internal strife forced him to agree to reforms, including privatization and reduction of government. He abandoned Marxism-Leninism in 1989, and in March 1991, faced with international and domestic pressure, allowed free elections. Defeated by Nicéphore Soglo, he publicly apologized for the abuses of his regime and received amnesty from the new government. He remained active in politics, and after Soglo failed to revitalize Benin's economy in his first five-year term, Kérékou was reelected president in March 1996.

See Also

Dahomey, Early Kingdom of.

Africa

Kerere (also known as Kerewe), ethnic group of Tanzania.

The Kerere primarily inhabit northern Tanzania, just south of Lake Victoria. Others live on Ukerewe Island in Lake Victoria itself. They speak a Bantu language. Approximately 100,000 people consider themselves Kerere.

See Also

Bantu: Dispersion and Settlement.

North America

Kerner Report, the 1968 report of a federal government commission that investigated urban riots in the United States.

The Kerner Report was released after seven months of investigation by the National Advisory Commission on Civil Disorders and took its name from the commission chairman, Illinois governor Otto Kerner. President Lyndon B. Johnson appointed the commission on July 28, 1967, while rioting was still underway in Detroit, Michigan. The long, hot summers since 1965 had brought riots in the black sections of many major cities, including Los Angeles (1965), Chicago (1966), and Newark (1967). Johnson charged the commission with analyzing the specific triggers for the riots, the deeper causes of the worsening racial climate of the time, and potential remedies.

The commission presented its findings in 1968, concluding that urban violence reflected the profound frustration of inner-city blacks and that racism was deeply embedded in American society. The report's most famous passage warned that the United States was "moving toward two societies, one black, one white – separate and unequal." The commission marshaled evidence on an array of problems that fell with particular severity on African Americans, including not only overt discrimination but also chronic poverty, high unemployment, poor schools, inadequate housing, lack of access to health care, and systematic police bias and brutality.

The report recommended sweeping federal initiatives directed at improving educational and employment opportunities, housing, and public services in black urban neighborhoods and called for a "national system of income supplementation." Reverend Martin Luther King Jr. pronounced the report a "physician's warning of approaching death, with a prescription for life." By 1968, however, Richard M. Nixon had gained the presidency through a conservative white backlash that ensured that the Kerner Report's recommendations would be largely ignored.

James Clyde Sellman

See Also

Chicago, Illinois; King, Martin Luther, Jr.; Los Angeles Watts Riot of 1965; Newark, New Jersey.

Africa

Keyo (also known as Elgeyo and Keiyu), ethnic group of Kenya.

The Keyo primarily inhabit the western shores of the Kerio River in northwestern Kenya. They speak a Nilo-Saharan language and are related to the Kalenjin people. Approximately 200,000 people consider themselves Keyo.

See Also

Languages, African: An Overview.

Africa

Khaldun, Ibn (b. May 27, 1332, Tunis, Tunisia; d. March 17, 1406, Cairo, Egypt), fourteenth-century North African scholar, considered to be one of the greatest Arab historians.

Ibn Khaldun wrote a monumental history of North Africa, the *Kitab al-Ibar*. But his most significant contribution, in the eyes of many contemporary scholars, is the *Muqaddimah*, perhaps the first systematic philosophical study of history and society.

Ibn Khaldun was born in Tunis to a family that for centuries had played a prominent political role in Andalusia, or southern Spain, before fleeing to North Africa to escape the Christian Reconquest. As a young man he received a formal education in the Koran, Arabic poetry, and Islamic law, preparing him for a life among the ruling class of North Africa. In 1349 both his mother and father died as the black plague ravaged Tunis.

As a young married man Ibn Khaldun joined the royal court in Tunis and later in Fès, Morocco. After a rebellion upset the court, he was accused of treason and imprisoned. This was the first of several times Ibn Khaldun would be ensnared in the intrigues of fourteenth-century court life, where dynasties rose and fell and intellectuals competed for royal favor. He was released after the sultan's death and went into exile in Muslim-held Granada, where he worked as a diplomat. He also developed a close but contentious relationship with Granada's prime minister and scholar, Ibn al-Khatib. The two men's eventual falling-out, followed by another accusation of treason, forced Ibn Khaldun to flee once again.

After years of negotiating the treacherous waters of dynastic service in the Maghreb, mostly as a diplomat and tax collector among the Berber confederacies, around 1375 Ibn Khaldun sought refuge at a Sufi shrine. He resigned from his royal duties and moved with his family into seclusion in a small town in Algeria. For the next four years he wrote *Muqaddimah*, which not only recounted the history of the region's Berbers and Arabs, but also outlined a method for the historical study of society. Many historians consider the work a masterpiece as well as the first study of its kind. It foreshadowed contemporary sociology by arguing that societies are held together by *asabiyah*, or "social cohesion," a characteristic that exists in everything from kinship relations to dynasties, and that may be amplified by the unifying force of religion.

While he was working on *Muqaddimah*, Ibn Khaldun began his history of North Africa, *Kitab al-Ibar* (Universal History). He continued writing after he returned to Tunis, but soon afterward he fell out of favor with the powerful imam, or religious leader, of the city's mosque. In 1382 he began a pilgrimage to Mecca. He stopped in the city of Cairo and remained there under the patronage of Egypt's Mamluk ruler. Tragically, his family died in a shipwreck en route to join him. While in Cairo Ibn Khaldun continued writing his massive history, taught at the famous Islamic university al-Azhar, became a grand Maliki judge, and once again became embroiled in dynastic politics.

In his remaining years Ibn Khaldun traveled farther through the Arab world, whose history he recorded for posterity. Finally he made his way to Mecca. In 1400 he traveled with Cairo's new sultan to the besieged city of Damascus, where the armies of the Tatar ruler Tamerlane had taken possession. Ibn Khaldun's reputation preceded him, and he enjoyed a hospitality not afforded to the conquered masses outside the camp's gates. After presenting the conqueror with a written history of North Africa, Ibn Khaldun returned to Cairo, where he lived until his death six years later.

Marian Aguiar

See Also

Fès, Morocco; Sufism; Mamluk State.

Africa

Khaled Hadj Brahim

(b. February 29, 1960, Oran, Algeria), Algerian singer considered to be the most prominent star of the contemporary North African music style Rai.

Khaled Hadj Brahim grew up in Oran, a cosmopolitan port city with a rich musical tradition. By age ten he was playing the harmonica, bass, guitar, and accordion, and with his first single, "La route du lycée" (1974, The Road to School), recorded at age 14, he emerged as an underground sensation on the Algerian pop scene. He took the name Cheb, or "young," Khaled, to mark himself as part of a youth culture ready to change Algeria.

During the late 1970s and the 1980s Khaled reworked Rai, an improvisational folk music that emerged from the bordellos and bars of Oran during the 1920s. Holding on to the sounds of the traditional instruments and the outspoken, often sexually provocative lyrics, Khaled added the Western sounds of drum machines, synthesizers, and electric guitars. The new Rai, which means "opinion" in Arabic, appealed to youths disenchanted with traditional romantic lyrics that had little to do with their lives. Rai spread throughout North Africa, where more than 60 percent of the war-ravaged population is under 25, and the fame of Khaled, "the King of Rai," spread with it.

Khaled's music was censored in Algeria until 1983, when the government relaxed controls on popular culture in an effort to undermine growing support for Islamic fundamentalism. Conservative Islamic leaders saw Khaled's music as corrupting and declared a *fatwa*, or death sentence, against him. In 1990 he bargained the profits for his record *Kutche* for a visa and fled to France.

Since his move, Khaled has again updated the sound of Rai, now incorporating African American jazz saxophone improvisations and hip hop "scratching," as well as other transcultural sounds, including Asian string arrangements, found in "world beat" music. His lyrics have also evolved and now include the experiences of the North African diaspora.

By the mid-1990s Khaled was a well-known pop figure in North Africa, the Middle East, South Asia, and Europe: his single "Aicha" sold more than 1.5 million copies and went gold in Europe. With his songs featured in the popular American films *Killing Zoe* and *The Fifth Element*, he began to win recognition in North America.

Marian Aguiar

See Also

Hip Hop in the United States; World Music, World Beat, and the Re-Africanization of Latin American Popular Music; Islamic Fundamentalism: An Interpretation.

Africa

Khama III (b. 1837?, Mushu, Bechuanaland [present-day Botswana]; d. February 21, 1923, Serowe, Bechuanaland), chief of the Bamangwato (Ngwato) tribe of the Tswana people (1875-1923) in Bechuanaland, who ensured that his people came under the protection of the British rather than the Boers (Afrikaners).

Known as Knainas "Khama the Good," Khama was baptized a Christian in 1860. In 1872 he attempted to seize the chieftainship from his father, Sekgoma I, because Sekgoma opposed Christianity, but he was forced into exile. Three years later he overthrew his father and became chief of the Bamangwato with his capital at Shoshong. He was a reformer who embraced the European values that were spreading through the region at this time. He abolished a number of old tribal customs, including circumcision, rainmaking, and bride-wealth (payment made by the groom to the bride's family), which he saw as anti-Christian, and allowed the London Missionary Society to establish a mission on his territory (*see* Christianity: Missionaries in Africa). He was opposed to Afrikaner attempts to expand into Bechuanaland from the independent Boer state of the Transvaal and in 1876 asked for British protection.

In 1885 Khama welcomed British general Charles Warren, who established the Bechuanaland Protectorate. In 1890 he assisted British colonialist Cecil Rhodes when Rhodes took a group of pioneer settlers north into what became Southern Rhodesia (present-day Zimbabwe). When the Ndebele under King Lobengula rose against the white settlers in 1893, Khama led his own troops against them in support of the settlers. However, he opposed Rhodes's plan to have Bechuanaland taken over by his own British South Africa Company. In 1895, accompanied by senior Tswana chiefs, Khama went to London and successfully petitioned for Bechuanaland to remain a British protectorate and not come under the control of the settlers. Although he retained substantial powers for himself, he was obliged to surrender a strip of his land for the construction of a railway.

See Also

Afrikaner; Christianity, African: An Overview.

Africa

Khama, Seretse (b. July 1, 1921, Serowe, Bechuanaland [now Botswana]; d. July 13, 1980, Gaborone, Botswana), first president of Botswana (1966-1980).

Born in Serowe of royal parents, Seretse Khama inherited the title of chief of the Ngwato (Bamangwato) people, who make up more than one-third of Botswana's population. When he violated the color bar by marrying a white woman in 1948, British authorities banished him from the country (1950) and deposed him as chief (1952). Allowed to return in 1956, he founded the Botswana Democratic party in 1962. Three years later, campaigning on a multiracial platform, the party was swept to power and Khama became prime minister. He was elected president in 1966 and was knighted the same year. Khama died in office.

Africa

Khartoum, Sudan, the capital city and commercial center of Sudan, located at the confluence of the White Nile and the Blue Nile rivers.

A city of close to half a million inhabitants in 1983, Khartoum is the center of Sudan's largest urban agglomeration, including the larger city and Islamic center of Omdurman and the slightly smaller industrial city of Khartoum North. Since the resumption of the Sudanese civil war in 1983 this urban region has absorbed approximately 1.8 million refugees; the urban region's population is now more than 3 million.

In the 1820s, when Uthman Bey led an Egyptian army to occupy the region on behalf of the Ottoman regime in Egypt (known in Sudan as the Turkiyya), Khartoum was a small farming village. Recognizing its strategic importance at the most important river junction in northeast Africa, Uthman built a fort there and made it his administrative center. In 1829 Muhammad Ali, viceroy of Egypt, designated it as the capital of the Egyptian Sudan. After the opening of the White Nile to riverine commerce, Khartoum became an important center for the slave and ivory trades. In 1885 the Mahdi's defeat of the Egyptian forces and the death of General Gordon at the Battle of Khartoum marked the end of the Turkiyya administration of the Sudan. The Mahdi destroyed the city and moved the capital across the river to Omdurman, which remained the capital until 1898.

When Horatio Kitchener led a British and Egyptian army to overthrow the Mahdist state in 1898, he rebuilt Khartoum and made it the capital of Anglo-Egyptian Sudan. Upon independence in 1956, Khartoum became capital of the Republic of the Sudan. Under colonial rule, Gordon College, the first institution of higher education in Sudan, was established at Khartoum. During the 1950s it became part of the University of Khartoum. Khartoum sits at the hub of Sudan's road and rail network and, together with Omdurman and Khartoum North, serves as the cultural, financial, and industrial center of the country.

In August 1998 the United States bombed a pharmaceutical plant in Khartoum. The United States government claimed that the plant manufactured chemical weapons, but neutral observers questioned these claims.

Robert Baum

See Also

Colonial Rule; Ivory Trade; Mahdist State; Nile River; Trans-Saharan and Red Sea Slave Trade.

Africa

Khoikhoi (also known as Khoekhoe, Namaqua, Khoi, and pejoratively as Hottentot), ethnic cluster of southern Africa.

The Khoikhoi comprise Khoisan-speaking pastoral groups, including the Nama. They live mainly in Namibia and South Africa. Traditionally they have based their livelihood on cattle herding and foraging.

Khoikhoi pastoralists were engaged in both foraging and cattle raising in northern Botswana more than 1000 years ago. Over the centuries they slowly migrated south to the Cape region in present-day western South Africa. When Europeans arrived in the mid-seventeenth century, they displaced the Khoikhoi population from their homeland in the Cape. Smallpox, introduced by the Europeans, decimated the Khoikhoi, who lacked natural resistance. Dutch settlers referred pejoratively to the Khoikhoi as Hottentots. The survivors either withdrew to marginal areas, mainly in present-day Namibia, or merged with other groups to form the Cape Coloured people. Some Afrikaner settlers intermarried with Khoikhoi, forming a population of Afrikaner-speaking Christians who today number around 30,000. Today the surviving Khoikhoi mostly live in arid districts of Namibia, where they continue to raise sheep and goats. Wage labor, however, earns the lion's share of income. Approximately 100,000 people consider themselves Khoikhoi.

Ari Nave

See Also

Hottentot; Pastoralism.

Africa

Khoisan, family of languages spoken primarily in southern Africa.

Khoisan languages, known for their click consonants, are spoken by both San foragers, pejoratively called Bushmen, and Khoikhoi pastoralists, often called Hottentots. The term refers collectively both to these groups and to the languages they speak. There are three distinct and mutually unintelligible Khoisan languages: Zhu, Khoi, and Qui. In ancient times Khoisan speakers are thought to have occupied most of southern and even East Africa, but the Bantu expansion either absorbed or displaced most of them (*see* Bantu: Dispersion and Settlement), particularly during the past 2000 years. Today the remaining Khoisan speakers, numbering approximately 200,000, live almost entirely in Namibia and Botswana.

Khoisan is not the only African language

family to contain click sounds. The NGUNI languages are Bantu languages in southern Africa that have absorbed click phonemes from Khoikhoi and San populations. In addition, the HADZA and Sandawe foragers of TANZANIA speak languages that use clicks. Many linguists classify these languages as Afro-Asiatic. However, other scholars believe these groups are linguistically and genetically related, though remotely, to the Khoisan, after thousands of years of separation.

While language is often used as a proxy for genetic relationships, there are clear cases where the two do not coincide. Khoisan and Bantu speakers have intermarried for centuries and often cannot be regarded as genetically distinct. Despite these ambiguities, Bantu and Khoisan continue to be used frequently as racial terms.

Ari Nave

SEE ALSO
Hottentot; Pastoralism; Languages, African: An Overview.

Africa

Kidjo, Angélique (b. July 14, 1960, Cotonou, Benin), Beninese singer and bandleader.

With music that blends African and Western influences, Angélique Kidjo has become a crossover star, winning worldwide popularity, as well as a role model for women and girls in her native BENIN. As one of nine children in a musical family, she remembers her older siblings singing folkloric Beninese songs as part of the Kidjo Brothers Band, in addition to songs by American rock 'n' roll stars. When Kidjo began making her own music, she was influenced both by the West African rhythms of her homeland and by the American soul and pop music she heard on the radio. As a solo singer she had developed a local following by the late 1970s.

But rather than stay in Benin, where she faced pressures to perform propaganda for the communist government, in 1983 Kidjo moved to Paris and studied JAZZ and OPERA. She quickly became involved in a Parisian musical scene bursting with expatriate Africans. The cross-cultural influences of jazz, gospel, FUNK, hip hop, and Western pop music are evident in *Logozo* (1991), Kidjo's first hit album. Two earlier albums, *Pretty* and *Parakou*, had limited success; *Logozo* was followed with *Ayé* (1994) and *Fifa* (1996). "Agolo," a song from *Ayé*, was nominated for a Grammy Award. With lyrics in FON, Mina, YORUBA, and Swahili as well as French and English, Kidjo sings about love, motherhood (she has a daughter, Naima), religion, and social issues.

Kidjo is a strong, charismatic performer, and she disputes the notion that, as an African woman, she should restrict herself to African material or project an "exotic" character. Yet her cultural roots run deep, from the influence of her childhood religion, VODOU, to her frequent trips home to Benin, which, as she says, she visits to "breathe the air of the country, to see my people, my mother, and pay respect to my ancestors."

Kate Tuttle

SEE ALSO
Swahili Language; Soul Music; Gospel Music; Hip Hop in the United States.

Africa

Kiga (also known as the Chiga and the Ciga), ethnic group of East Africa.

The Kiga primarily inhabit northern RWANDA and southern UGANDA. They speak a Bantu language, Kinyarwanda, and are sometimes considered a subgroup of the Hutu, to whom they are closely related (*see* ETHNICITY IN RWANDA: AN INTERPRETATION). Approximately 200,000 people consider themselves Kiga.

SEE ALSO
Bantu: Dispersion and Settlement; Hutu and Tutsi.

Africa

Kigali, Rwanda, capital city of RWANDA as well as its largest economic and urban center.

In the late fifteenth century the Tutsi kingdom of Rwanda occupied Kigali, which was a trade site for caravans traveling as far as the Indian Ocean. Under the German East Africa Company from 1899 to 1916 Kigali became an economic center. After Germany's defeat in World War I, the League of Nations granted Belgium a mandate to administer Rwanda as part of the territory of Ruanda-Urundi in 1923, and Kigali became an administrative center. The Belgians established mining operations near Kigali during the 1930s; revenue from the mines contributed to the city's growth. In 1962 Rwanda won independence and Kigali became the nation's capital.

The 1994 Rwandan civil war devastated Kigali. A series of massacres took place in the city, and one-third of the population was killed or fled. During the late 1990s displaced residents and other Rwandans uprooted by unrest congregated in Kigali. In 1997 Kigali had a population in excess of 300,000, most of them returned refugees. However, segregation has increasingly divided the Hutu and Tutsi residents of Kigali, and tensions between the two groups threaten to undermine the city's political and economic recovery (*see* ETHNICITY IN RWANDA: AN INTERPRETATION).

Kigali, spread over four hills in the central Rwandan highlands, is the only large city in this mostly rural nation. It boasts a modern business district, a technical college, and an international airport. Kigali is a center for tea and coffee exports, as well as a mining and manufacturing hub. Major roads radiate to most parts of Rwanda and to the railhead in UGANDA. In the late 1990s fighting and heavy rains blocked roads leading to DAR ES SALAAM, TANZANIA, and threatened the route to MOMBASA, KENYA, both important ports for Rwandan trade.

David P. Johnson, Jr.

SEE ALSO
Hutu and Tutsi.

Africa

Kikuyu, an ethnic group of KENYA.

The Kikuyu are the most populous – and most politically and economically powerful – ethnic group of present-day Kenya. An agricultural people who speak Gikuyu, a Bantu language, they have traditionally occupied the fertile highland areas between MOUNT KENYA and the Kenyan capital of Nairobi. Although they probably migrated to this area from the northeast around 1500 C.E., Kikuyu origin myths claim that their first ancestors, Gikuyu and his wife Mumbi, were given Kikuyuland by the god Ngai, who is believed to reside on Mount Kenya.

The Kikuyu are divided into nine clans, or *mihiriga*, which are in turn divided into subclans. The *mbari*, a residential group of families all descended from a common paternal ancestor, has historically been the most important landholding unit in Kikuyu society. The *muramati*, generally the first son of the first wife of his father, determines land distribution, though he has no greater rights to land than his brothers. Age and sex also have also figured importantly in Kikuyu social organization; groups of boys and girls are initiated into separate "generation sets" that in the past defined which generation of adults held political authority.

Land has long been vital to Kikuyu livelihoods. Precolonial Kikuyu societies practiced hoe cultivation, raising crops such as beans, sorghum, MILLET, peas, and yams. Land also holds important spiritual meaning. In his book *Facing Mount Kenya* (1978), JOMO KENYATTA, Kenya's first president and himself a Kikuyu, wrote of the land's spiritual impact on his people: "Communion with the spirits is perpetuated through contact with the soil in which the ancestors of the tribe lie buried."

Because the Kikuyu's land includes some of the best farmland in East Africa, they were not the only ones to appreciate its value, especially after British COLONIAL RULE was established in the late nineteenth century. Colonial land policies displaced many Kikuyu to make way for European settlers, creating a class of wage laborers who lived in overcrowded reserves and worked on European plantations or migrated to urban areas in the hope of finding other menial work.

In the 1920s this displacement inspired the first political protest against colonial rule. Such organizations as the Kikuyu Central Association were formed in an effort to regain confiscated Kikuyu lands. Later they came to protest other issues, including Christian missionaries' efforts to discourage traditional Kikuyu religious practices, such as polygamy and clitoridectomy (*see* FEMALE CIRCUMCISION IN AFRICA). Following World War II many dispossessed Kikuyu joined the MAU MAU REBELLION, a violent anticolonial revolt that cost more than 12,000 African lives but succeeded in hastening an end to British rule.

Although Kenyatta's official slogan was *Harambee*, meaning "all pull together," he favored his fellow Kikuyu, who developed into an economic elite during his presidency. Many of them became large landowners in the highlands. When Kenyatta died in 1978, his successor, DANIEL ARAP MOI, began to favor members of his own ethnic group, the KALENJIN. Gradually, this new favoritism eroded some of the privilege the Kikuyu had enjoyed. As Moi's regime became increasingly repressive in the 1980s and 1990s, the Kikuyu again formed one of the largest factions calling for an end to authoritarian rule. But the government-controlled media managed to keep the opposition divided, in part by appealing to other ethnic groups' fears of Kikuyu political domination. Mwai Kibaki, an ethnic Kikuyu, ran as the Democratic Party candidate in the December 1997 presidential election. He finished second to Moi but won few non-Kikuyu votes.

Robert Fay

SEE ALSO

Bantu: Dispersion and Settlement; Nairobi, Kenya; Christianity: Missionaries in Africa.

Africa

Kilimanjaro, the highest mountain in Africa.

Called Kilema Kyaro ("that which makes the journey impossible") by the local CHAGGA people, Mount Kilimanjaro is located in northeastern TANZANIA, near the border with KENYA. Kilimanjaro is a dormant volcano, its two peaks standing about 11 km (about 7 mi) apart, connected by a broad ridge. Kibo, the higher peak, rises to 5895 m (19,340 feet) above sea level, and the summit of Mawensi is 5149 m (16,892 feet) above sea level. Although Kilimanjaro lies 3° south of the equator, an ice cap covers the crater of Kibo year-round.

Kilimanjaro has a number of different vegetation zones on its steep slopes, ascending through tropical rain forests at its base and including moorlands, alpine meadows, and alpine desert. Chagga farmers grow coffee and plantains on the lower slopes of the mountain. In 1889 Kilimanjaro was scaled for the first time by German geographer Hans Meyer and Austrian mountain climber Ludwig Purtscheller. Kilimanjaro has become a highly popular destination for recreational hikers and mountain climbers and an important source of revenue for the Tanzanian government.

Robert Fay

North America

Killens, John Oliver

(b. January 14, 1916, Macon, Ga.; d. October 27, 1987, New York, N.Y.), African American writer and scholar whose politically engaged novels, essays, and screenplays exposed the racism of America in the decades after World War II and argued for new forms of African American independence and identity.

John Oliver Killens was born in Macon, Georgia, in 1916 to Charles Myles Sr. and Willie Lee Killens. He heard fanciful folktales as well as stories of the harsh realities of slavery from his great-grandmother. Between 1934 and 1936 he attended Edward Waters College in Jacksonville, Florida, and Morris Brown College in Atlanta. He moved to Washington, D.C., where he worked for the National Labor Relations Board and finished his B.A. at HOWARD UNIVERSITY. He studied to be a lawyer, then entered the army in 1942 and was stationed in the South Pacific.

After 1948, when Killens moved to New

Mount Kilimanjaro, Africa's highest mountain, rises to the clouds behind a small herd of zebras in Amboseli National Park in Kenya. © *David Keith Jones/ Images of Africa Photobank*

York City, his political work brought him into contact with a broader world of African American scholarship and art. He met Paul Robeson, and W. E. B. Du Bois and Langston Hughes, whose editorials he had admired as a boy. While studying at Columbia University and New York University, he wrote for the socialist newspaper *Freedom*. He founded the Harlem Writers Guild in the early 1950s and produced his first novel, *Youngblood*, in 1954.

Youngblood told the story of a contemporary African American family's hardships in segregated Georgia. Later novels *And Then We Heard the Thunder* (1963) and *'Sippi* (1967) dramatized racism in the armed forces and in the South. *The Cotillion; or, One Good Bull Is Half the Herd* (1971), a satire, addressed internal strife within the black community.

In 1964 Killens founded the Organization for Afro-American Unity with Malcolm X. Black Nationalism influenced much of his later work. Two of his novels received nominations for the Pulitzer Prize. Killens taught in universities and continued to write for national magazines until his death in 1987.

See Also
Slavery in the United States; World War II and African Americans; Literature, African American; Du Bois, William Edward Burghardt (W. E. B.); New York, New York; Socialism; Black Nationalism in the United States; Art, African American.

North America

Kilpatrick, Carolyn

(b. June 25, 1945, Detroit, Mich.), Democratic member of the United States House of Representatives from Michigan (1997-).

Carolyn Kilpatrick was born in Detroit, Michigan. She received an associate's degree in 1965 from Ferris State University in Big Rapids, Michigan, a bachelor's degree in 1968 from Western Michigan University in Kalamazoo, Michigan, and a master's degree in 1972 from the University of Michigan in Ann Arbor. After completing her master's degree she became a teacher in the Detroit public school system.

Kilpatrick's political career began in 1978 when she was elected to the first of nine terms in the Michigan state House of Representatives. During her tenure she served in the Democratic leadership and on the House Appropriations Committee. She was also a member of the Michigan Legislative Black Caucus. In 1994 she made an unsuccessful bid for the Michigan state Senate. Kilpatrick was elected in November 1996 to represent Michigan's Fifteenth Congressional District in the U. S. House.

The Fifteenth District includes parts of downtown Detroit and the suburbs of River Rouge, Hamtramck, and Grosse Pointe. The district includes both African American and white neighborhoods. Wide differences in housing conditions and income levels among the neighborhoods are importants issue in the district. Efforts to revitalize downtown Detroit are ongoing and have had some success in recent years.

Kilpatrick served on the Banking and Financial Services Committee in the 105th Congress (1997-1999), and was the interim vice chairperson of the Democratic Freshman Caucus. Kilpatrick is a member of the Congressional Black Caucus.

Africa

Kimbangu, Simon

(b. 1889, N'kamba, Belgian Congo [present-day Democratic Republic of the Congo]; d. 1951, Belgian Congo), founder and prophet of the Kimbanguist Church (now the Church of Jesus Christ on Earth), one of Africa's largest religious movements.

Born in the Belgian Congo, Simon Kimbangu attended a Baptist Missionary Society school. He later worked for the Society as a teacher and evangelist, but after healing an ailing woman in 1921, he heeded what he claimed were divine visions and initiated a ministry devoted to healing and preaching. He quickly developed a large following among his own ethnic group, the Kongo.

Preaching a message of forgiveness of enemies, obedience to authorities, and opposition to witchcraft and sorcery, Kimbangu's charismatic style filled churches throughout the region. Although supported by local Baptist missionaries, his popularity disturbed the Belgian authorities, who feared that the meetings were merely a pretext for a budding rebellion. In addition, some of his followers were said to support the ideas of Marcus Garvey and were urging audiences to overthrow the white colonial regime and create a Pan-African nation.

When questioned by the authorities Kimbangu did not reassure them, but rather reportedly spoke in tongues and told the story of David and Goliath. In September 1921 he was tried for sedition and sentenced to death. After Protestant missionaries protested, the sentence was commuted to life in prison, where Kimbangu spent the rest of his life. The Belgian authorities subsequently outlawed the Kimbanguist church and exiled many of its followers to distant provinces.

Nenetheless, many of Kimbangu's followers continued to spread the message of the church and, in their exile, created a multiethnic church. During the 1950s Kimbangu's son, Diangienda, reunited the various groups and established the Church of Jesus Christ on Earth (EJCSK). In 1960, after the independence of the Belgian Congo, the EJCSK became a national church and in 1969 became the first independent African church to become a full member of the World Council of Churches. Still active, the church claims a membership of four million people in the Democratic Republic of the Congo alone.

Elizabeth Heath

See Also
Colonial Rule; Garvey, Marcus Mosiah; Christianity: Missionaries in Africa.

Kimpa Vita. Please see Beatrice, Dona

Latin America and the Caribbean

Kincaid, Jamaica

(b. May 25, 1949, St. Johns, Antigua), contemporary Caribbean-American writer whose work has focused on the experience of colonization, immigration, as well as on mother-daughter relationships.

Jamaica Kincaid was born Elaine Potter Richardson, and as a child was greatly influenced by her mother, Annie Richards. At 16 years of age, after successfully completing a British education in Antigua, she moved to New York as an au pair.

After leaving her au pair job, working as a photographer's assistant, and briefly going to college, Richardson changed her name to Jamaica Kincaid and began establishing herself as a writer. After having pieces published in *Ingenue* magazine and the *Village Voice*, she caught the attention of William Shawn, the legendary editor of the *New Yorker*, who made her staff writer in 1976. In 1983 she published a collection of short fiction, *At the Bottom of the River*. These stories, which had previously appeared in the *New Yorker*, won the Morton Dauwen Zabel Award from the American Academy of Arts and Letters.

Kincaid's first novel, *Annie John* (1985), examines a childhood that begins as an idyllic relationship between mother and daughter, a connection that decays through mistrust and misunderstanding until the protagonist leaves her native Antigua. *Lucy* was published five years later and, in many ways, is thought to be a sequel to her first novel. The protagonist, Lucy, leaves Antigua, fleeing from her mother to become an au pair in New York. The plot of the novel centers on Lucy's relationship to Mariah, the white woman she works for, and their struggle to understand each other. In a key scene recalling the experience of colonial education, Kincaid presents a critical view of the history of colonization.

The Autobiography of My Mother (1996) was the third in Kincaid's series of mother-daughter narratives. It is the story of a young woman, Xuela Claudette Richardson, whose mother dies at birth. The experience of losing one's birth mother becomes a metaphor for the detachment from one's mother country. The novel is a chilling and tight monologue, a haunting expression of the protagonist's isolation, tracing the experiences of Xuela.

Kincaid's *My Brother* (1997) is a departure from her earlier books, in which she explored autobiographical themes in fiction. *My*

Brother is the story of Devon Drew, Kincaid's youngest brother, who died of acquired immune deficiency syndrome (AIDS) at age 33. Like her novels, Kincaid's memoir of her brother's death was praised for its stark honesty and lyrical language.

Kincaid also wrote *A Small Place* (1988), a book of essays about Antigua. Her short stories have appeared in the *New Yorker*, the *Paris Review, Harper's*, and *Rolling Stone*. She has taught creative writing at Bennington College and Harvard University. Married to the composer Allen Shawn, son of the *New Yorker* editor, Kincaid made news in 1995 when she resigned as staff writer of that magazine in protest of the editorial policies of Tina Brown.

Eva Stahl Brown

Writer Jamaica Kincaid in New York in 1985. *Neal Boenzi/New York Times Co./Archive Photos*

See Also
New York, New York; Antigua and Barbuda.

Africa

Kinga, ethnic group of Tanzania.

The Kinga primarily inhabit the northeastern shores of Lake Malawi in Tanzania. They speak a Bantu language. More than 100,000 people consider themselves Kinga.

See Also
Bantu: Dispersion and Settlement.

North America

King, Coretta Scott

(b. April 27, 1927, Marion, Ala.), widow of the slain civil rights leader Martin Luther King Jr. who is world renowned for her devotion to furthering his ideals.

Long active in the fight for civil and human rights, Coretta Scott King has become an international icon for her efforts to promote nonviolent social change.

The second of three children of Obadiah and Bernice (McMurry) Scott, King grew up in rural Alabama, where she helped her family harvest cotton and tend to their farm. Her father hauled lumber for a white sawmill owner, a job that enabled him to purchase and operate his own sawmill. The local white community resented her father's success: vandals allegedly burned his sawmill, and the Scotts's house, to the ground. King was deeply shaken by her family's trials. She dreamed of moving to the North and diligently focused on her education, enrolling in a local private high school, where she pursued her talent for music. In 1945 she won a scholarship to Antioch College in Yellow Springs, Ohio. She studied music and elementary education and in 1948 debuted as a vocalist at the Second Baptist Church. Also while at Antioch, she performed in a program with Paul Robeson, the renowned African American singer and civil rights activist, who encouraged her to pursue advanced musical training.

In 1951 King entered the New England Conservatory of Music in Boston on a scholarship. She struggled to support herself, living and working at a Beacon Hill boardinghouse. In 1953 she married Martin Luther King Jr., then a doctoral student in theology at Boston University. Her marriage to King was a pivotal point in her life: upon graduating from the conservatory, she returned with him to Montgomery, Alabama, where he worked as a pastor at Dexter Avenue Baptist Church. During the following years she reared their four children and stood by her husband at the forefront of the Civil Rights Movement. In 1962, following the King family's move to Atlanta, she taught voice lessons at Morris Brown College while continuing her civil rights work. Steadfastly loyal to her husband, she joined him in civil rights demonstrations throughout the South, led marches, spoke at rallies, and organized fundraising events at which she lectured and performed.

After the assassination of her husband in 1968, King continued to lead major demonstrations in support of striking workers and the poor, and organized marches to promote Dr. King's principles, such as the 20th anniversary March on Washington in 1983. In 1969, as a memorial to Dr. King, she founded the Atlanta-based Martin Luther King Jr. Center for Nonviolent Social Change, a center principally devoted to training people, especially students, in nonviolent social protest.

Serving as the center's president and chief executive officer, she has maintained a high public profile both in the United States and abroad, and traveled through southern Africa to protest APARTHEID. In 1986 she prevailed in her campaign to establish a national holiday honoring Dr. King.

Since then she has continued to campaign worldwide for human rights, social justice, and urban renewal programs for disadvantaged communities.

Roanne Edwards

SEE ALSO
Atlanta, Georgia; Boston, Massachusetts; King, Martin Luther, Jr.

North America

King, Don

(b. August 20, 1931, Cleveland, Ohio), controversial African American promoter of America's leading prizefighters.

Don King has emerged as the most powerful and controversial figure in American BOXING. By the late 1970s he had come to dominate the boxing industry, traditionally controlled by white brokers, and since then has raised millions of dollars for such prizefighters as MUHAMMAD ALI, LARRY HOLMES, Julio Cesar Chavez, and MIKE TYSON. He is a flamboyant public figure whose visibility has extended far beyond the field of boxing, and some commentators have likened him to the infamous gangster Al Capone. In 1997 *Sports Illustrated* noted, "King, who has beaten tax evasion charges and countless allegations of contract fraud over the years, is nothing if not resourceful."

The fifth of seven children born to Clarence and Hattie King, Don King was reared and educated in Cleveland, Ohio. After his father, a steelworker, died in a workplace explosion, King's mother moved the family to the predominantly black and poor Mount Pleasant, where the young King sold home-roasted peanuts and baked goods to help make ends meet at home. During high school and a year spent at Cleveland's Western Reserve University, he ran an illegal lottery, and by the late 1950s had amassed enough money to buy a nightclub.

Released from prison in 1971 after serving a four-year term for manslaughter, King began his career as a boxing promoter. His career took off in 1974 when he successfully arranged the famous "Rumble in the Jungle" match between star boxers Muhammad Ali and George Foreman in Kinshasa, Zaire (present-day DEMOCRATIC REPUBLIC OF THE CONGO). Since then he has negotiated contracts for some of the most celebrated boxing champions and title fights in the history of modern boxing.

In July 1997 the NATIONAL ASSOCIATION FOR THE ADVANCEMENT OF COLORED PEOPLE (NAACP) honored King with its President's Award for his role as a "philanthropist and sports pioneer who paved the way for minority athletes to make millions of dollars." In November 1997, Home Box Office (HBO) aired *Don King: Only in America*, a film based on Jack Newfield's unauthorized biography *Only in America: The Life and Crimes of Don King*, published in 1995.

Roanne Edwards

SEE ALSO
Kinshasa, Democratic Republic of the Congo; Foreman, George Edward.

North America

King, Martin Luther, Jr.

(b. January 15, 1929, Atlanta, Ga.; d. April 4, 1968, Memphis, Tenn.), African American clergyman and Nobel Prize winner, one of the principal leaders of the American Civil Rights Movement and a prominent advocate of nonviolent protest. King's challenges to segregation and racial discrimination in the 1950s and 1960s helped convince many white Americans to support the cause of civil rights in the United States. After his assassination in 1968, King became a symbol of protest in the struggle for racial justice.

EDUCATION AND EARLY LIFE

Martin Luther King Jr. was born in ATLANTA, GEORGIA, the eldest son of Martin Luther King Sr., a Baptist minister, and Alberta Williams King. His father served as pastor of a large Atlanta church, Ebenezer Baptist, which had been founded by Martin Luther King Jr.'s maternal grandfather. King Jr. was ordained as a Baptist minister at age 18.

King attended local segregated public schools, where he excelled. He entered nearby MOREHOUSE COLLEGE at age 15 and graduated with a bachelor's degree in sociology in 1948. After graduating with honors from Crozer Theological Seminary in Pennsylvania in 1951, he went to Boston University, where he earned a doctoral degree in systematic theology in 1955.

King's public-speaking abilities – which would become renowned as his stature grew in the CIVIL RIGHTS MOVEMENT – developed slowly during his collegiate years. He won a second-place prize in a speech contest while an undergraduate at Morehouse, but received Cs in two public-speaking courses in his first year at Crozer. By the end of his third year at Crozer, however, professors were praising King for the powerful impression he made in public speeches and discussions.

Throughout his education King was exposed to influences that related Christian theology to the struggles of oppressed people. At Morehouse, Crozer, and Boston University, he studied the teachings on nonviolent protest of Indian leader Mohandas Gandhi. King also read and heard the sermons of white Protestant ministers who preached against American racism. Benjamin E. Mays, president of Morehouse and a leader in the national community of racially liberal clergymen, was especially important in shaping King's theological development.

While in Boston, King met Coretta Scott, a music student and native of Alabama. They were married in 1953 and would have four children. In 1954 King accepted his first pastorate at the Dexter Avenue Baptist Church in Montgomery, Alabama, a church with a well-educated congregation that had recently been led by a minister, Vernon Johns, who had protested against segregation.

THE MONTGOMERY BUS BOYCOTT

Montgomery's black community had long-standing grievances about the mistreatment of blacks on city buses. Many white bus drivers treated blacks rudely, often cursing and humiliating them by enforcing the city's segregation laws, which forced black riders to sit in the back of buses and give up their seats to white passengers on crowded buses. By the early 1950s Montgomery's blacks had discussed boycotting the buses in an effort to gain better treatment, but not necessarily to end segregation.

On December 1, 1955, Rosa Parks, a leading member of the local branch of the NATIONAL ASSOCIATION FOR THE ADVANCEMENT OF COLORED PEOPLE (NAACP), was ordered by a bus driver to give up her seat to a white passenger. When she refused, she was arrested and taken to jail. Local leaders of the NAACP, especially Edgar D. Nixon, recognized that the arrest of the popular and highly respected Parks was the event that could rally local blacks to a bus protest.

Nixon also believed that a citywide protest should be led by someone who could unify the community. Unlike Nixon and other leaders in Montgomery's black community, the recently arrived King had no enemies. Furthermore, Nixon saw King's public-speaking gift as a great asset in the battle for black civil rights in Montgomery. King was soon chosen as president of the Montgomery Improvement Association (MIA), the organization that directed the bus boycott.

The MONTGOMERY BUS BOYCOTT lasted for more than a year, demonstrating a new spirit of protest among Southern blacks. King's serious demeanor and consistent appeal to Christian brotherhood and American idealism made a positive impression on whites outside the South. Incidents of violence against black protesters, including the bombing of King's home, focused media attention

OPPOSITE TOP: Photographed in 1963, King shakes hands with supporters from his car during a motorcade in Baltimore, Maryland.
Magnum Photos/Leonard Freed

OPPOSITE BELOW: Martin Luther King Jr. speaking from the Lincoln Memorial in Washington, D.C., at the 1957 Prayer Pilgrimage he helped orchestrate.
Archive Photos

on Montgomery. In February 1956 an attorney for the MIA filed a lawsuit in federal court seeking an injunction against Montgomery's segregated seating practices. The federal court ruled in favor of the MIA, ordering the city's buses to be desegregated, but the city government appealed the ruling to the United States Supreme Court. By November 1956, when the Supreme Court upheld the lower court decision, King was a national figure. His memoir of the bus boycott, *Stride Toward Freedom* (1958), gave a thoughtful account of that experience and further extended his national influence.

Civil Rights Leadership

In 1957 King helped found the Southern Christian Leadership Conference (SCLC), an organization of black ministers and churches that aimed to challenge racial segregation. As SCLC's president, King became the organization's dominant personality and its primary intellectual influence. He was responsible for much of the organization's fundraising, which he frequently conducted in conjunction with preaching engagements in Northern churches.

SCLC sought to complement the NAACP's legal efforts to dismantle segregation through the courts, with King and other SCLC leaders protested discrimination through the use of nonviolent action such as marches, boycotts, and demonstrations. The violent responses that direct action provoked from some whites eventually forced the federal government to confront the issues of injustice and racism in the South.

King made strategic alliances with Northern whites that would bolster his success in influencing public opinion in the United States. Through Bayard Rustin, a black civil rights and peace activist, King forged connections to older radical activists, many of them Jewish, who provided money and advice about strategy. King's closest advisor at times was Stanley Levison, a Jewish activist and former member of the American Communist Party. King also developed strong ties to white Protestant ministers in the North, with whom he shared theological and moral views.

In 1959 King visited India and worked out more clearly his understanding of Satyagraha, Gandhi's principle of nonviolent persuasion, which King had determined to use as his main instrument of social protest. The next year he gave up his pastorate in Montgomery to become co-pastor (with his father) of the Ebenezer Baptist Church in Atlanta.

SCLC Protest Campaigns

In the early 1960s King led SCLC in a series of protest campaigns that gained national attention. The first was in 1961 in Albany,

Written while he was imprisoned after the Birmingham civil rights march, King's eloquent "Letter from Birmingham City Jail" responded to white liberals who urged him to moderate his civil rights activities. *Ernst Haas/Hulton-Getty*

Georgia, where SCLC joined local demonstrations against segregated restaurants, hotels, transit, and housing. SCLC increased the size of the demonstrations in an effort to create so much dissent and disorder that local white officials would be forced to end segregation to restore normal business relations. The strategy did not work in Albany. During months of protests, Albany's police chief jailed hundreds of demonstrators without visible police violence. Eventually the protesters' energy, and the money to bail protesters out, ran out.

The strategy did work, however, in Birmingham, Alabama, when SCLC joined a local protest during the spring of 1963. The protest was led by SCLC member Fred Shuttlesworth, one of the ministers who had worked with King in 1957 in organizing SCLC. Shuttlesworth believed that the Birmingham police commissioner, Eugene "Bull" Connor, would meet protesters with violence. In May 1963 King and his SCLC staff escalated antisegregation marches in Birmingham by encouraging teenagers and schoolchildren to join. Hundreds of singing children filled the streets of downtown Birmingham, angering Connor, who sent police officers with attack dogs and firefighters with high-pressure water hoses against the marchers. Scenes of young protesters being attacked by dogs and pinned against buildings by torrents of water from fire hoses were shown in newspapers and on televisions around the world.

During the demonstrations King was arrested and sent to jail. He wrote a letter from his jail cell to local clergymen who had criticized him for creating disorder in the city. His "Letter from Birmingham City Jail," which argued that individuals had the moral right and responsibility to disobey unjust laws, was widely read at the time and added to King's standing as a moral leader.

National reaction to the Birmingham violence built support for the struggle for black civil rights. The demonstrations forced white leaders to negotiate an end to some forms of segregation in Birmingham. Even more important, the protests encouraged many Americans to support national legislation against segregation.

"I Have a Dream"

King and other black leaders organized the 1963 March on Washington, a massive protest in Washington, D.C., for jobs and civil rights. On August 28, 1963, King delivered the keynote address to an audience of more than 200,000 civil rights supporters. His "I Have a Dream" speech expressed the hopes of the Civil Rights Movement in oratory as moving as any in American history: "I have a dream that one day this nation will rise up and live out the true meaning of its creed: 'We hold these truths to be self-evident, that all men are created equal.'… I have a dream that my four little children will one day live in a nation where they will not be judged by the color of their skin but by the content of their character."

The speech and the march built on the Birmingham demonstrations to create the political momentum that resulted in the Civil Rights Act of 1964, which prohibited segregation in public accommodations as well as discrimination in education and employment. As a result of King's effectiveness as a leader of the American Civil Rights Movement and his highly visible moral stance, he was awarded the 1964 Nobel Prize for Peace.

Selma Marches

In 1965 SCLC joined a voting-rights protest march that was planned to go from Selma, Alabama, to the state capital of Montgomery, more than 80 km (50 mi) away. The goal of the march was to draw national attention to the struggle for black voting rights in the state. Police beat and tear-gassed the marchers just outside Selma, and televised scenes of the violence, on the day that came to be known as Bloody Sunday, resulted in an outpouring of support to continue the march. SCLC petitioned for and received a federal court order barring police from interfering with a renewed march to Montgomery. Two weeks after Bloody Sunday, more than 3000 people, including a core of 300 marchers who would make the entire trip, set out toward Montgomery. They arrived in Montgomery five days later, where King addressed a rally of more than 20,000 people in front of the capitol building.

The march created support for the Voting Rights Act of 1965, which President Lyndon Johnson signed into law in August. The act suspended (and amendments to the act later banned) the use of literacy tests and other voter qualification tests that had been used to prevent blacks from registering to vote.

After the Selma protests, King had fewer dramatic successes in his struggle for black civil rights. Many white Americans who had supported his work believed that the job was done. In many ways the nation's appetite for civil rights progress had been filled. King also lost support among white Americans when he joined the growing number of antiwar activists in 1965 and began to criticize publicly American foreign policy in Vietnam. King's outspoken opposition to the Vietnam War (1959-1975) also angered President Johnson. On the other hand, some of King's white supporters agreed with his criticisms of United States involvement in Vietnam so strongly that they shifted their activism from civil rights to the antiwar movement.

Black Power

By the mid-1960s King's role as the leader of the Civil Rights Movement was questioned by many younger blacks. Activists such as Stokely Carmichael of the Student Nonviolent Coordinating Committee (SNCC) argued that King's nonviolent protest strategies and appeals to moral idealism were useless in the face of sustained violence by whites. Some also rejected the leadership of ministers. In addition, many SNCC organizers resented King, feeling that often they had put in the hard work of planning and organizing protests only to have the charismatic King arrive later and receive much of the credit. In 1966 the Black Power Movement, advocated most forcefully by Carmichael, captured the nation's attention and suggested that King's influence among blacks was waning. Black Power advocates looked more to the beliefs of the recently assassinated black Muslim leader, Malcolm X, whose insistence on black self-reliance and the right of blacks to defend themselves against violent attacks had been embraced by many African Americans.

With internal divisions beginning to divide the Civil Rights Movement, King shifted his focus to racial injustice in the North. Realizing that the economic difficulties of blacks in Northern cities had largely been ignored, SCLC broadened its civil rights agenda by focusing on issues related to black poverty. King established a headquarters in a Chicago apartment in 1966, using that as a base to organize protests against housing and employment discrimination in the city. Black Baptist ministers who disagreed with many of SCLC's tactics, especially the confrontational act of sending black protesters into all-white neighborhoods, publicly opposed King's efforts. The protests did not lead to significant gains and were often met with violent counterdemonstrations by whites, including neo-Nazis and members of the Ku Klux Klan, a secret terrorist organization that was opposed to integration.

During 1966 and 1967 King increasingly turned the focus of his civil rights activism throughout the country to economic issues. He began to argue for redistribution of the nation's economic wealth to overcome entrenched black poverty. In 1967 he began planning a Poor People's Campaign to pressure national lawmakers to address the issue of economic justice.

Assassination

This emphasis on economic rights took King to Memphis, Tennessee, to support striking black garbage workers in the spring of 1968. He was assassinated in Memphis by a sniper on April 4. News of the assassination resulted in an outpouring of shock and anger throughout the nation and the world, prompting riots in more than 100 U.S. cities in the days following King's death. In 1969 James Earl Ray, an escaped white convict, pleaded guilty to the murder of King and was sentenced to 99 years in prison. Although over the years many investigators have suspected that Ray did not act alone, no accomplices have ever been identified.

After King's death, historians researching his life and career discovered that the Federal Bureau of Investigation (FBI) often tapped King's phone line and reported on his private

Photographed at a 1991 concert in the Netherlands, the blues guitarist B. B. King is pictured here with his guitar, nicknamed "Lucille." *CORBIS/Derick A. Thomas; Dat's Jazz*

life to the president and other government officials. The FBI's reason for invading his privacy was that King associated with Communists and other "radicals."

After his death, King came even more than during his lifetime to represent black courage and achievement, high moral leadership, and the ability of Americans to address and overcome racial divisions. Recollections of his criticisms of U.S. foreign policy and poverty faded, and his soaring rhetoric calling for racial justice and an integrated society became almost as familiar to subsequent generations of Americans as the Declaration of Independence.

King's historical importance was memorialized at the Martin Luther King Jr. Center for Social Justice, a research institute in Atlanta. Also in Atlanta is the Martin Luther King Jr. National Historic Site, which includes his birthplace, the Ebenezer Church, and the King Center, where his tomb is located. Perhaps the most important memorial is the national holiday in King's honor, designated by the Congress of the United States in 1983 and observed on the third Monday in January, a day that falls on or near King's birthday of January 15.

Anthony Badger

SEE ALSO

Baptists; Chicago, Illinois; Jim Crow; King, Coretta Scott; Mays, Benjamin Elijah; Nation of Islam; Nixon, Edgar Daniel; Parks, Rosa Louise McCauley; Poor People's Washington Campaign; Shuttlesworth, Fred L.; Communist Party USA, African Americans and the.

North America

King, Riley B. ("B. B.")

(b. September 16, 1925), one of the most successful bluesmen to emerge from the Memphis scene.

B. B. King has served as the prime ambassador of American blues. Although others may exceed his talent, King did more than anyone else to popularize the genre. After distinguishing himself on the RHYTHM AND BLUES (R&B) charts during the 1950s, he broke into the pop mainstream in the 1960s, touring with top-name rock bands. His success can be attributed to longevity as much as skill, something he himself admits: "I was 63 when my career hit its hottest stride." Having avoided the substance abuse and violence that took the lives of many of his peers, he continues to record and perform.

Born a sharecropper's son and raised on a plantation in Mississippi, King first found music through the church. After singing in a number of gospel groups, he left to play the blues in Memphis. He soon secured work at the famed WDIA radio station and began performing in bars and nightclubs. King the disc jockey was known as "the Blues Boy from Beale Street," then "Blues Boy," and then simply "B. B."

King's distinctive sound includes a robust vocal style and abbreviated, melodic guitar playing. In the tradition of call and response, King sings a line and follows it with a flourish of guitar. His riffs mimic patterns of speech, giving his performances an air of autonomous duet. Both his harmony, which uses abundant sixths, and his phrasing, which often subverts the beat, demonstrate the influence of jazz musicians such as Charlie Christian and Lester Young. King's lyrics depart from the popular blues themes of violence and sexual braggadocio. Instead, he emphasizes love, fidelity, security, reflecting his early days in gospel as well as his connection with soul.

After a series of hits on a Memphis record label in 1949, King attracted the attention of Ike Turner, who signed him to Los Angeles-based Modern Records. In 1952 King scored a number-one hit on the R&B charts with "Three O'Clock Blues." For the next ten years, he toured the circuit of small black clubs. In the mid-1960s, just as his career seemed to be winding down, the sounds of "British Invasion" bands, particularly Cream and the Rolling Stones, introduced blues to young white Americans and renewed King's popularity. He began recording and touring with these musicians, inspiring a comeback that culminated in his 1970 release "The Thrill Is Gone."

In the 1970s King toured the Las Vegas and dinner-club circuits, appeared in films, lectured at universities, received an honorary degree from Yale, and won awards for his prison-charity work. He also collaborated with musicians such as STEVIE WONDER, Steve Winwood, and Ringo Starr, though often with marginal results.

Although his recordings grew less reliably outstanding, his mainstream success persevered. Indeed, through both his television endorsements for companies such as Wendy's Hamburgers and Northwest Airlines as well as through his collaborative recordings, King gave the Memphis blues something hitherto unheard of – commercial importance. As an archetype, he paved the way for other blues musicians to become icons of mainstream culture. In 1987 he was inducted into the Rock and Roll Hall of Fame.

Eric Bennett

SEE ALSO

Soul Music; Blues, The; Young, Lester Willis ("Prez"); Gospel Music; Memphis, Tennessee.

Latin America and the Caribbean

Kingston, Jamaica, the capital city of Jamaica, home to more than 500,000 people of African, European, Asian, and Middle Eastern ancestry.

Kingston is situated on the southern side of the island of JAMAICA and is protected from the turbulent northeast trade winds by the vast Blue Mountain ranges. The city stretches for more than 80 km (50 mi). Modern Kingston includes a harbor that is 16 km (10 mi) long, the suburban community of Saint Andrew, and a common area in the middle of town called the Parade. Today Kingston is the largest and one of the most diverse cities in the English-speaking Caribbean. According to census figures, the Kingston metropolitan area was home in 1991 to 587,718 people of African, Asian, European, and Middle Eastern ancestry. The city's tremendous growth during the twentieth century produced severe overcrowding, persistent unemployment, and violent crime. Poverty has devastated Jamaica's black majority, and nowhere is this more evident than in the ghettos of Kingston. The city is also racially stratified, a byproduct of European colonialism, and it is struggling to deal with historical tensions between the city's black and brown residents.

Kingston has stood at the forefront of Jamaica's long march to democracy. The Kingston of today is a direct byproduct of the organized racial and cultural segregation that began more than 300 years ago. Many of the social and political changes that have swept Jamaica since 1692 occurred first in Kingston, often in reaction to organized political protests. The history of Kingston itself represents the legacy of chattel slavery and the efforts by black and brown Jamaicans to find freedom and equality in a nation haunted by the vestiges of colonialism.

Kingston was founded on July 22, 1692, after a large earthquake destroyed the coastal city of Port Royal. More than 2000 residents lost their lives in the quake and another 3000 died in its aftermath from hunger and disease. The survivors fled across the stretch of land known to locals as Hogs Crawle and founded what is now Kingston. From the beginning Kingston was firmly in the hands of the white elite, most of whom were SUGAR planters from England. The city was constructed to serve the social and economic interests of white planters. Residential segregation, beginning in 1692, served to reinforce (and in some cases reproduce) cultural separation.

During the first half of the 1700s Kingston saw an influx of Jewish merchants, white sugar planters, African slaves, and a small but significant free black and colored (of mixed African and European ancestry) community. One of Kingston's primary economic activities was as a trading post for the TRANSATLANTIC SLAVE TRADE. Sugar was produced in Jamaica by African slaves, then sent to New England, where it was made into rum and molasses. These goods were then exchanged for more African slaves. Although the growth of slavery changed the complexion of Kingston during the eighteenth century, white domination of the city's (and colony's) legal and political institutions confined the growing black majority to the periphery of town.

De facto segregation created social and cultural schisms that ensured the economic and social supremacy of white planters. Racial interaction was regulated by laws such as the Consolidated Slave Laws of 1792, which restricted the mobility and assembly of slaves, who were confined to rural sugar plantations. Coloreds were required to carry certificates of freedom, a practice repeated by British colonial officials in SOUTH AFRICA. But one of the most lasting policies enacted by whites in Jamaica involved legal distinctions between those free blacks and free coloreds who were *born* free and those who were *manumitted* (or formally emancipated).

These laws and institutions produced a rigid social hierarchy that privileged the city's white minority. Tensions developed between blacks and coloreds living in the lower strata of Kingston society. Initially, most coloreds tried to gain acceptance into white society by emulating white European culture. The coloreds favored those who were born with traditional European features, such as light skin, straight hair, and thin lips. But Kingston's social hierarchy never allowed them to gain full access. White indentured servants and Jews stood above them. By the end of the eighteenth century Kingston's policy of residential segregation had produced a cultural and social separation among the city's black, brown, and white residents.

During the nineteenth century Kingston underwent a series of dramatic changes. By 1820 it was the largest and richest city in the British West Indies. Whites continued to hold on to the legal and political institutions that guaranteed their privileged positions. But Kingston, like the rest of white Jamaica, had grown to fear the presence of runaway slaves – called maroons – who had established independent communities in the island's interior (*see* MAROONAGE IN THE AMERICAS). These fears were exacerbated in 1831, when a serious slave rebellion, led by a black slave named SAMUEL SHARPE along with more than 20,000 other slaves, occurred in the northwest parish of Saint James.

The end of slavery in 1834 marked a dramatic transformation in Kingston's society. Despite the fears of whites, emancipation did not bring an influx of former slaves into the city. Most blacks found few economic opportunities in Kingston and were forced to remain as workers on the sugar plantations. These blacks were precursors to today's peasant communities, and in the years immediately following emancipation they were confined to shantytowns in the outskirts of Kingston.

For the next 27 years most people in Jamaica experienced significant hardships as the island's economy collapsed. Wealthy whites returned to Europe and thousands of blacks and coloreds immigrated to places such as the United Kingdom, the United States, PANAMA, and CUBA. Those blacks and coloreds who remained in Kingston turned to selling homegrown produce in the small-scale markets that dotted the landscape. Although the economic crisis hit the wealthy as well as the poor, government policies in the 1860s targeting the poor aggravated an already difficult situation.

This led to discontent, which surfaced in 1865 when black activist PAUL BOGLE organized a massive demonstration in Morant Bay to protest the government's policies. Blacks in Kingston watched the events closely. After a violent police crackdown resulted in a riot, the British Parliament decided to make Jamaica a Crown Colony, placing the island under the direct rule of the British Crown. It also removed some of the power from the hands of the island's white minority, leading to transformations in Kingston's society.

Coloreds benefited most during the Crown colony period, and many now could afford to move into some of Kingston's most prestigious neighborhoods. But Kingston's black majority continued to find themselves locked out of the city's economy. Poor schools and rampant unemployment left many blacks disadvantaged. For example, in 1871, 60 percent of the city's population were illiterate, the majority of whom were black.

Kingston began to make an economic comeback in 1872, when it became the capital of Jamaica. Manufacturing provided jobs for some of the city's black residents, and the immigration of merchants from East India, China, and Syria boosted the city's recovery. Although a major earthquake in 1907 slowed development, Kingston continued to grow.

In the 1920s and 1930s Marcus Garvey led a black nationalist movement that brought conditions facing black workers to the forefront of national attention. During this period Kingston became the battleground for black nationalists, black religious organizations such as the RASTAFARIANS, trade unions, and political activists. Their activities eventually led to universal adult suffrage in 1944. This placed Jamaica on the path to independence and sparked the formation in Kingston of two major political parties: the Jamaican Labour Party (JLP) and the People's National Party (PNP).

Throughout the 1940s and 1950s both the JLP and the PNP competed for the support of Jamaica's black working-class majority. Alexander Bustamante and MICHAEL MANLEY and emerged as two colored politicians who spoke for the island's black and brown population. During this time Kingston symbolized the negative impact of white colonial rule, and it was the setting for continuous pressure on the British Crown for self-rule. Success came in 1962 when Jamaica was granted full independence.

After independence Kingston became the site of intense rivalry between supporters of the PNP and those of the JLP. Downtown Kingston was, and still is, divided by party Loyalists who lived in and controlled political enclaves or so-called garrisons. In the 1976 and 1980 national elections, hundreds of people died during violent confrontations in the garrisons of Kingston. Despite the violence, Jamaica has managed to champion the principles of democracy, and Kingston has come to symbolize a modern capital complete with administrative centers and a vibrant work force of civil servants.

Kingston remains racially segregated and many of its residents are still poor. But this capital city has survived two major earthquakes and has managed to transform its political institutions so that they welcome everyone in Jamaica. Kingston continues to deal with unemployment, crime, and overcrowding, as in many major cities throughout the world. But it does so today in the spirit of tolerance and inclusion, as reflected in the national motto: "There is unity in diversity. Out of many, one people."

Alonford James Robinson, Jr.

SEE ALSO

Slavery in Latin America and the Caribbean; Bustamante, Sir Alexander; Garvey, Marcus Mosiah; Abolition and Emancipation in Latin America and the Caribbean.

Africa

Kinigi, Sylvie (b. 1953?), prominent banker and first woman prime minister (1993-1994) of BURUNDI.

Sylvie Kinigi rose to prominence as a commercial banker and senior officer of Burundi's structural adjustment program. Kinigi, a Tutsi married to a Hutu, was appointed prime minister after Melchior Ndadaye, an ethnic Hutu, was elected president in June 1993. Kinigi and Agathe Uwilingiyimana, the premier of neighboring RWANDA, served at the same time as the first female prime ministers in Africa. Kinigi, a member of the former ruling Union for National Progress (UPRONA) party, was a political moderate, but her leadership was quickly eclipsed by events beyond her control.

In October 1993, after a military coup killed President Ndadaye and threw Burundi into violence, Kinigi sought asylum in the French embassy. Her appeals for international support convinced the military to return to its barracks, allowing Kinigi to recover her post. But when Ndadaye's successor was killed in a plane crash, conflict between the Tutsi-dominated military and Hutu militias flared again. Kinigi concluded that Burundi "entered into democracy without having the means of dealing with it. The process was too rapid. There was no time to form political leaders. So parties formed on the simple criterion of ethnicity." Amid growing ethnic conflict, in February 1994 Kinigi disbanded her cabinet, left Parliament, and returned to commercial banking.

Eric Young

SEE ALSO

Hutu and Tutsi; Structural Adjustment in Africa.

Africa

Kinshasa, Democratic Republic of the Congo, formerly Léopoldville, capital and largest city of the DEMOCRATIC REPUBLIC OF THE CONGO.

The administrative, cultural, and economic center of the Democratic Republic of the Congo, Kinshasa is located on the southern bank of the CONGO RIVER, opposite Brazzaville, in the Kinshasa region of the REPUBLIC OF THE CONGO. Although it is uncertain when people first settled in the area, Kinshasa was an important trading village and caravan stop, especially for the slave trade, during the height of the KONGO Kingdom in the fourteenth century. In 1881 explorer Henry Morton Stanley established a European trading center in the village and renamed it Léopoldville after LEOPOLD II of Belgium, who shortly thereafter claimed the area as part of his private colony, the Congo Free State. After the 1898 completion of a railroad between the city and the Atlantic Ocean port of Matadi, Kinshasa became the major shipping port from and to the railroad in the Belgian Congo. By 1920 Kinshasa's importance and size prompted Belgian authorities to make it capital of the Belgian Congo. After independence in 1966 the city was renamed Kinshasa, and it has since become the most populous city in the Congo. Although no reliable census data are available, it is estimated that Kinshasa has a population between 5 and 8 million and an annual growth rate of approximately 14 percent.

Since the colonial era, Kinshasa's economy has been supported by the shipping business between the Congo River and the railroad. It is also home to numerous factories that manufacture domestic and export goods such as textiles, beer, and cement. During MOBUTU SESE SEKO's reign, however, government corruption depleted most of the city's budget, and massive migration to the city overtaxed the few remaining resources. As a result there has been little effort to manage or maintain the city and almost no plan to deal with incoming populations. Unemployment is estimated at nearly 60 percent and most of the city's citizens live off commerce in the informal sector. Inadequate sanitation and housing in the city have contributed to public health problems, including major outbreaks of cholera and typhoid and widespread tuberculosis and malaria. In spite of these conditions, Kinshasa has developed a vibrant music scene and is known as the modern music capital of Central Africa.

In May 1997 LAURENT-DÉSIRÉ KABILA took control of the Democratic Republic of the Congo and promised, among other things, to eliminate corruption and revitalize the country. He ordered police officers and soldiers to stop robbing and harassing citizens, although it is uncertain that these orders were obeyed. Kinshasa's residents welcomed Kabila into the capital but later protested his restrictions on political demonstrations.

Elizabeth Heath

SEE ALSO

Brazzaville, Republic of the Congo; Transatlantic Slave Trade; Stanley, Sir Henry Morton.

Kioko. Please see CHOKWE

Africa

Kipsigi (also known as Kipsiki and sometimes erroneously labeled Lumbwa), ethnic group of KENYA.

The Kipsigi primarily inhabit the highlands of southwestern Kenya. They speak KALENJIN, a Nilo-Saharan language, and are considered a Kalenjin people. Approximately 1 million people consider themselves Kipsigi.

SEE ALSO

Languages, African: An Overview.

Africa

Kissi (also known as the Kisi), ethnic group of West Africa.

The Kissi primarily inhabit the borderlands of Liberia, Sierra Leone, and Guinea. They speak a Niger-Congo language. Some 400,000 people consider themselves Kissi.

See Also
Languages, African: An Overview.

North America

Kitt, Eartha Mae (b. January 26, 1928, North, S.C.), cabaret singer and stage and screen performer known for her seductive stage presence and her "sex kitten" style.

Born on a farm to poverty-stricken sharecroppers, William Kitt and Anna Mae Riley, Eartha Mae and her sister, Pearl, were abandoned by their mother at a young age. The two sisters were raised by a foster family until 1936, when they moved to New York City to live with their aunt. In New York Kitt attended Metropolitan High School (now the New York School of Performing Arts), and at age 16 was invited by Katherine Dunham to join her dance troupe. The group toured Europe and South America from 1946 to 1950, and while they were in Paris, Kitt was discovered by Orson Welles, who cast her in his 1951 production of Marlowe's *Dr. Faustus*. She returned to New York and performed at La Vie en Rose and the Village Vanguard, where she developed a sexy and sensual stage style. In 1952 she appeared in the Broadway show *New Faces of 1952* and in 1954 in the film version. She sang in nightclubs and cabarets from the mid-1950s through the 1960s.

During this period Kitt also worked in film, television, and the theater, as well as recording music. Her stage work included *Mrs. Patterson* (1954) and *Shinbone Alley* (1957). She appeared in the films *The Accused* (1957), *St. Louis Blues* (1958), and *Anna Lucasta* (1959). During this time she recorded two albums, *Bad But Beautiful* (1961) and *At the Plaza* (1965). In the 1960s she also had a stint as Catwoman in the TV series *Batman*. Some reviewers focused on her haughtiness and sophistication, while others gossiped about her alleged preference for white men and disdain for her rural past.

In 1968, while at a luncheon at the White House hosted by Lady Bird Johnson, Kitt publicly criticized American involvement in the Vietnam War by saying that juvenile delinquency and street crime were direct results of the war. She subsequently experienced a major loss of popularity and underwent personal investigations by the FBI and CIA. After that she performed mostly in Europe until the late 1970s. In 1978 she returned to Broadway to perform in *Timbuktu* and made an album, *I Love Men* (1984). She produced two autobiographies, *I'm Still Here* (1989) and *Confessions of a Sex Kitten* (1991). In 1993 a five-compact-disc retrospective of her work titled *Eartha Quake* was produced.

Kitt married William McDonald on June 6, 1960. They were divorced in 1965 and have a daughter, Kitt McDonald.

See Also
New York, New York; Film, Blacks in American; Television and African Americans.

Africa

Kiwanuka, Joseph (b. 1896?, Buganda; d. February 23, 1966, Rubaga, Uganda), the first African to serve as a Catholic bishop in the twentieth century and the first African doctor of canon law, who developed an African clergy and encouraged African leadership in religious and educational activities.

When Joseph Kiwanuka was a 12-year-old boy in the British colony of Uganda, a Catholic priest working as a missionary arranged for him to attend mission school, where he excelled. Kiwanuka went on to attend the seminary at Katigondo. After his ordination in 1929, he studied canon law in Rome and became the first African to earn the title doctor of canon law.

Missionaries in Africa, in effect, imposed a paternalistic and external Christianity on their African converts. During the colonial era Europeans largely considered Africans "inferior" and "backward," and they expected Africans simply to receive the Christianity that white Europeans conferred on them. However, Archbishop Streicher of the Catholic Church, perhaps sensing the changing nature of African society in the twentieth century, believed in the need to develop an indigenous and autonomous African clergy. Thus he trained Kiwanuka and others like him for leadership positions in the Catholic Church.

In 1939 Kiwanuka traveled to Rome for his consecration by Pope Pius XII. As a bishop, he was given charge of the Masaka district vicariate, a diocese staffed completely by African priests – an experiment of sorts – and he worked to help his diocese emerge from paternalistic, missionary Catholicism into an indigenous African expression of the faith. Bishop Kiwanuka encouraged lay participation in diocesan activities. He founded lay councils, to which local people were elected, as well as parents' associations for the church schools.

In 1961 Kiwanuka became Archbishop of Kampala in a ceremony that the king of Uganda attended. He participated in the Second Vatican Council from 1962 to 1965, which encouraged lay participation. He died in Rubaga in early 1966 after paving the way for the hundreds of African bishops who have followed in his footsteps.

Robert Fay

See Also
Christianity, African: An Overview; Kampala, Uganda; Great Britain; Christianity: Missionaries in Africa.

North America

Knight, Gladys (b. May 28, 1944, Atlanta, Ga.), African American soul and rhythm and blues (R&B) vocalist whose career spans more than 45 years.

Gladys Knight's parents sang in the famous Wings Over Jordan Choir and raised their daughter on the music of the black church. Knight joined the choir at the Mount Moriah Baptist Church in Atlanta at age four, toured with the Morris Brown Choir when she was five, and won the $2000 grand prize on the *Ted Mack Amateur Hour* at age eight. She also sang with family members, first informally but soon as an opening act for such big-name performers as Jackie Wilson and Sam Cooke. In addition to superlative singing, the Knight family displayed strong stage presence and savvy dance steps.

In 1961 Gladys Knight and "the Pips" (two cousins and a brother) released a version of Johnny Otis's ballad "Every Beat of My Heart" that attracted Atlanta-based Huntom records as well as Fury Records in New York. Following a legal fracas between the two labels, Knight and the Pips began to record singles with Fury, slowly establishing themselves on the R&B charts. They recorded and performed throughout the mid-1960s but did not meet with great success until they switched labels to a Motown subsidiary, Soul Records, in 1965. Their 1967 version of "I Heard It Through the Grapevine" reached number two on the pop charts and introduced them to mainstream audiences. Other hits included half a dozen albums and the hit single "Neither One of Us (Wants to Be the First to Say Goodbye)" (1972).

Despite their growing popularity, Gladys Knight and the Pips felt relegated by Soul Records to an undeserved second-tier status. When Motown moved from Detroit to Hollywood, the group opted to drop its affiliation, signing a contract with Buddah Records in 1973. After this change they hit their stride, releasing *Imagination*, a Grammy Award-winning album that included the smash single "Midnight Train to Georgia." By 1975 they had landed four more singles on the pop charts, and in 1976 Knight made her film debut in *Pipedream*.

Legal debacles with Motown in the late 1970s prevented Knight from recording with the Pips, and although she signed a solo contract with Columbia Records, her career seemed to be in decline. When the group reunited in 1980, however, they regained a name on the R&B charts with *About Love*. Likewise, Knight's 1985 collaboration with Stevie Wonder, Dionne Warwick, and Elton John on the number-one single "That's What

Friends Are For" evinced an enduring vitality. In 1985 she starred with Flip Wilson in the situation comedy *Charlie and Company;* in 1986 she appeared on an HBO special with Warwick and PATTI LABELLE; and in 1987 she and the Pips scored another major pop hit with "Love Overboard." Knight released a new album of solo material in 1995, called *Just for You,* and in 1996 was inducted into the Rock and Roll Hall of Fame.

Eric Bennett

SEE ALSO

Soul Music; Atlanta, Georgia; Cooke, Samuel (Sam); New York, New York; Black Church, The.

Africa

Kom (also known as Bikom and Nkom), ethnic group of CAMEROON.

The Kom primarily inhabit the highlands of North West Province, Cameroon. They speak a Niger-Congo language and are closely related to the TIKAR people. Approximately 150,000 people consider themselves Kom.

SEE ALSO

Languages, African: An Overview.

Komba. Please see KONKOMBA

Africa

Konaré, Alpha Oumar (b. 1946, Kayes, Mali), third president of MALI.

The winner of Mali's first multiparty elections, Alpha Oumar Konaré assumed the presidency in 1992. The son of a schoolteacher, he was born in the Kayes region of Mali. He received a doctorate in history from the University of Warsaw (Poland) in 1975. His dissertation explored the history of agriculture in the upper Niger basin under the MALI EMPIRE from the thirteenth through the seventeenth century. After graduation he returned to Mali to teach history, and soon took a position as head of the historic and ethnographic heritage division of the Ministry of Culture in the government of MOUSSA TRAORÉ. In 1979 he was appointed minister of youth, arts, and culture, but he resigned a year later after a dispute with the president. He returned to academia at that time.

Konaré became an advocate for democratization. In 1983 he founded a cultural cooperative called Jamana, which published an independent newspaper and political books such as his *Le concept du pouvoir en Afrique.* These publications, which Traoré's regime begrudgingly tolerated, reached a nationwide audience. In 1990, as popular unrest mounted, Konaré and his associates petitioned Traoré for democratic and multiparty elections and formed a pro-democracy party – the Alliance pour la Démocratie au Mali (ADEMA). ADEMA won instant support among student and labor groups; its actions were instrumental in the overthrow of Traoré. In the political reforms that followed, Konaré became the president of ADEMA, as well as its candidate in the 1992 national presidential elections. Konaré won the election by a landslide and assumed the presidency.

Despite his initial popularity, Konaré has faced numerous challenges. Most of these stem from the country's weak economy and the austerity measures demanded by international donors (*see* STRUCTURAL ADJUSTMENT IN AFRICA). These austerity measures have harmed large sectors of the Malian population, and like Traoré, Konaré has faced protests for imposing the measures. Spending cuts have also hit Mali's military, and disgruntled soldiers have launched several failed coup attempts against Konaré's government.

In addition to economic protests, Konaré has drawn criticism from opposition groups who have accused his government of thwarting the democratic process and have called for boycotts of recent elections. Despite these accusations, independent observers have attested to the fairness of the most recent elections. Konaré won reelection as president in 1997 and has stated that he will step down at the end of his second term in 2002.

Elizabeth Heath

SEE ALSO

Niger River.

Africa

Kong, precolonial DYULA kingdom spanning what are now northern CÔTE D'IVOIRE and southern BURKINA FASO.

The kingdom of Kong originated as a small trading settlement in the eleventh or twelfth century C.E. It eventually became the center of a kingdom whose influence reached as far as Djenné in present-day MALI. It reached its pinnacle in the eighteenth century. Warfare between the MALINKÉ Empire builder SAMORY TOURÉ and the French destroyed the city and its kingdom at the end of the nineteenth century.

Kong emerged as a trading center when MANDE merchants began trading in the territory of the surrounding SENUFO people. In the late fifteenth century a wave of Dyula traders moved to the area and brought with them their trading skills and connections. Kong became an increasingly important market for the exchange of northern desert goods such as salt and cloth and southern forest exports such as cola nuts, gold, and slaves. As Kong grew prosperous from trade, its early rulers – a group called the Tarawéré, apparently combining both Dyula and Senufo traditions – extended their authority over the surrounding region.

In 1710 Seku Wattara, a Dyula warrior, invaded the area and easily conquered the city of Kong with his cavalry. He established himself as ruler, and under his power Kong rose from a small city-state to an important regional power. During the 35 years of his reign Wattara unified the city-state with surrounding conquered regions, including the region centered on Bobo-Dioulasso. He imposed Dyula as the official language and Islam as the state religion. Wattara strove to increase his share of regional trade. Toward this end he put slaves to work in the manufacture of cloth. Wattara also used slave labor to cultivate rice, MILLET, sorghum, and cotton. Finally, he fostered trade by improving security along trading routes. By the end of his reign he had acquired a monopoly over a number of the southern trade routes.

Wattara died in 1745 and was succeeded by two able rulers – Koumbi Watara and Mori Maghari. Under their rule Kong continued to be a commercial center and also became a center of Islamic study. After the death of Maghari in 1800, his successors struggled with growing resistance from the kingdom's diverse ethnic and religious groups. Ultimately, however, Samory Touré destroyed the city of Kong when its rulers resisted his rule and refused to aid him in his campaign against French colonialists. Under COLONIAL RULE the Kong Kingdom was divided between two colonies – Côte d'Ivoire and Upper Volta (now Burkina Faso). The city of Kong, once the capital of the kingdom, became merely a small town after the French government routed the nearest rail line 70 km (45 mi) to the west.

Elizabeth Heath

SEE ALSO

Bobo-Dioulasso, Burkina Faso; Gold Trade; Salt Trade; Cola; Djenné, Mali; Islam and Tradition: An Interpretation; Trans-Saharan and Red Sea Slave Trade.

Africa

Kongo, the largest ethnic group in the DEMOCRATIC REPUBLIC OF THE CONGO and one of the largest in the southern REPUBLIC OF THE CONGO and northern ANGOLA.

Now dispersed throughout three countries in western Central Africa, the Kongo once comprised a highly centralized kingdom extending from the Congo to the Kwango and Kwanza rivers. The ancestors of the Kongo began settling small farming communities in the area sometime before the twelfth century. These communities became part of a semicohesive kingdom ruled during the fourteenth century from Mbanza Kongo, a prosperous farming village near the mouth of the Congo River. The Mbanza Kongo kings organized the surrounding communities into provinces, collected taxes and tributes, and instituted a monetary system based on shells, called *nzimbu,* which were farmed at the royal fisheries on the island of Luanda. In addition, the kings were responsible for protecting the kingdom and its people and performing religious rituals.

The first documented contact between the Kongo and Europeans occurred in 1483 when a Portuguese explorer, Diogo Cão, sailed into the mouth of the Congo River and encountered Kongo villages. He later took a group of Kongo emissaries back to PORTUGAL, who returned to Africa in 1491 with priests, soldiers, and European goods and had the Kongo king, Nzinga a Nkuwu, baptized. Although Nzinga a Nkuwu later abandoned Catholicism, his son, Nzinga Mbembe, later AFONSO I (or Alfonso), made Catholicism the state religion, invited missionaries to educate and Christianize his people, and renamed the capital São Salvador.

Afonso maintained strong trade relations with Portugal, exchanging slaves and ivory with the Portuguese for European luxury goods and guns. The slave trade, however, eventually took its toll on the Kongo Kingdom. Kongolese rulers met the Portuguese traders' huge demand for slaves by raiding neighboring peoples, such as the TÉKÉ and KUBA, who often retaliated. Embroiled in constant conflict, the Kongo became increasingly dependent on Portuguese assistance; by the time of the Jaga Wars (1568-1569), they managed to defeat the Jagas only with the help of the Portuguese mercenaries.

Weakened but intact, the Kongo Kingdom continued to do business with European slave traders, including the newly arrived Dutch. But Portuguese colonization of neighboring Angola led again to regional conflict, culminating in the 1665 attack at Ambuila. The Kongo Kingdom subsequently broke into factions, whose ongoing mutual raids generated a steady supply of slaves for Portuguese traders. In 1709, after considerable fighting, Pedro IV, a member of the Kimbangu clan who had won the support of Catholic missionaries by proclaiming DONA BEATRICE a false saint and sentencing her to death, assumed control of São Salvador. He reunited the scattered kingdom, which held together until the late nineteenth century. But it would never regain its former size or power.

Nevertheless, the Kongolese have remained fairly influential. During the colonial period the Kongo formed numerous churches – such as the Kimbanguist church founded by SIMON KIMBANGU – and social groups, many of which acted as early resistance organizations and later became political parties. Many Kongo attended either Catholic or Protestant mission schools and subsequently became one of the most highly educated ethnic groups in the Belgian Congo and Angola and generally one of the most active in the decolonization of both countries. JOSEPH KASAVUBU, head of the popular Association des Bakongo (ABAKO) in the Belgian Congo, became the first president after independence, and in Angola, the Kongo group Frente Nacional de Libertacão de Angola (FNLA) played an instrumental role in the liberation struggle between 1961 and 1974. Today the Kongo number over 5 million people and occupy significant administrative, political, and commercial positions in the lower Zaire region in the Democratic Republic of the Congo.

Elizabeth Heath

SEE ALSO
Congo River; Explorers in Africa Before 1500; Ivory Trade; Luanda, Angola; Transatlantic Slave Trade; Christianity: Missionaries in Africa; Slavery in Africa.

Africa

Konkomba, West African ethnic group numbering approximately 100,000 that occupies the upper basin of the Oti River in northern TOGO and adjacent GHANA.

The Konkomba, also called Kpokpokpam, have traditionally made their livelihood as fishers, subsistence farmers, and pastoralists. They are especially noted as cattle herders. Patrilineages and age-grade societies form the political units of the Konkomba clans.

Originally, the Konkomba are believed to have occupied much of northeastern Ghana. During the sixteenth century the DAGOMBA Kingdom, later subjugated by the ASANTE, established its capital on territory conquered from the Konkomba and drove them eastward into modern Togo. The Konkomba in turn displaced the ancestors of the KABRÉ, who withdrew to their present lands to the east. The Konkomba west of the Oti became vassals of the Dagomba, who sent Konkomba slaves as tribute to the Asante. Those to the east remained independent but still subject to slave raiding. During the 1900s the Konkomba were forced to abandon their northern territories by Chokossi invaders.

Historically, interclan conflict has divided the Konkomba and prevented political unity. However, many Konkomba clans united to resist German occupation in the insurrections of 1897 and 1898, which the Germans defeated with difficulty. Like other Togolese, the Germans conscripted them for forced labor. After World War I the Konkomba again faced political division. Those living west of the Oti came under the jurisdiction of the British, who backed the traditional power of Dagomba chiefs over their Konkomba vassals. Those to the east of the Oti fell within the borders of French Togo, and during the 1920s and 1930s, the Konkomba staged uprisings against French rule.

At the time of the pre-independence plebiscites in British and French Togoland, the Konkomba supported unification. Its defeat left them divided between Togo and Ghana, a division that has left lasting resentment. The vote deepened the enmity between the Konkomba and the Nanumba to the south, who opposed unification, and in 1981, the Togolese Konkomba joined their Ghanaian brethren in interethnic warfare against the Nanumba. In 1994 Konkomba demands for land rights and an end to their traditional subordination in Ghana provoked clashes with both the Nanumba and the Dagomba. The Konkomba have generally not shared in the patronage doled out by Gen. Etienne Eyadéma of Togo, and during the 1990s many joined the opposition to his regime.

Mark O'Malley

SEE ALSO
Eyadéma, Gnassingbé; Transatlantic Slave Trade; Pastoralism.

Africa

Kono, ethnic group of West Africa.

The Kono primarily inhabit SIERRA LEONE, LIBERIA, and GUINEA. They speak a MANDE language and are closely related to the VAI people. Approximately 300,000 people consider themselves Kono.

SEE ALSO
Languages, African: An Overview.

Africa

Konso, ethnic group of ETHIOPIA.

The Konso primarily inhabit the Gamo-Gofa Province of southwestern Ethiopia. They speak an Afro-Asiatic language and are closely related to the OROMO people. Approximately 100,000 people consider themselves Konso.

SEE ALSO
Languages, African: An Overview.

Africa

Konyaka, ethnic group of West Africa.

The Konyaka primarily inhabit northwestern CÔTE D'IVOIRE. Others live in southern MALI and eastern GUINEA. They speak a MANDE language. Approximately 2 million people consider themselves Konyaka.

SEE ALSO
Languages, African: An Overview.

Africa

Koranko (also known as Kouranko), ethnic group of West Africa.

The Koranko primarily inhabit SIERRA LEONE, GUINEA, and LIBERIA. They speak a MANDE language. Approximately 300,000 people consider themselves Koranko.

SEE ALSO
Languages, African: An Overview.

North America

Korean War (June 1951-July 1953), United States war with Korea that provided the impetus to carry through the planned integration of African American soldiers into all branches of the military.

Between 1948 and 1950 President Harry S. Truman and the U.S. War Department decided to eliminate segregation and racial discrimination from the military. Each branch of the armed forces was left to implement the policy on its own, however, and the pace of integration was sluggish. The air force began integrating the races in May 1949, but many old-line white officers predicted that blacks would embarrass themselves in integrated regiments.

The navy, while supposedly opening its jobs to all races, funneled 65 percent of its African American soldiers into the Steward's Branch, where they worked as waiters and cooks. The marine corps limited its integration mostly to athletic teams, and the army waited 21 months after Truman's order before eliminating racial quotas for recruiting. In the army African American men continued to be trained in segregated units.

The air of urgency surrounding the outbreak of the Korean War in June 1951 was instrumental in advancing the progress of integration within the military. At first the black soldiers who were sent to Korea fought in segregated units. The largest of these was the Twenty-fourth Infantry Regiment of the Twenty-fifth Infantry Division, which was ordered into a major battle within a week of arriving in Korea.

The Twenty-fourth Infantry helped push the North Koreans out of Yechon, an important transportation hub, in a victory that later served as a rallying cry for other regiments. A few of the Twenty-fourth Infantry's soldiers, including Pvt. William Thompson and Sgt. Cornelius Charlton, received the Congressional Medal of Honor for their efforts – but posthumously. Their performance raised questions among army leaders about the effectiveness of segregating battalions by race.

The United States' hasty entrance into the war provided a further push toward integration. Officers decided to fill some depleted white units, which had been weakened by heavy casualties suffered in the first months of the war, with black soldiers.

Yet many military leaders remained skeptical about integration. The leader of the United States/United Nations forces, Gen. Douglas MacArthur, was reluctant to accept integrated combat units. To allay these fears, a team of social scientists gathered in March 1951 to undertake Project Clear, a study of the effects of integration within the military. Project Clear found that integration raised morale among all troops, but particularly among black soldiers, and that it led to a better distribution of skills as well as improved performance by black soldiers. The report also noted fewer racial incidents within integrated troops than had occurred when units were separated by race.

Only after President Truman removed MacArthur from command in 1951, replacing him with Lt. Gen. Matthew B. Ridgeway, was permission secured to integrate all the forces. Meanwhile, the incorporation of blacks into white forces did not mark by any means an end to racial injustice. In 1951 THURGOOD MARSHALL of the NATIONAL ASSOCIATION FOR THE ADVANCEMENT OF COLORED PEOPLE found unusually frequent courts-martial for black soldiers.

Still, the overall effects of integration remained positive, and the consequences were soon felt back in the United States. Like their counterparts in Korea, military officials at domestic army bases found they could simplify their training procedures by eliminating racial separation. A few months after the outbreak of the war, the post commander at Fort Jackson, South Carolina, deemed it "totally impractical to sort [soldiers] out [by race]." Similarly, Gen. J. W. Cunningham desegregated his Alaskan forces.

The American public supported the integration of troops in Korea. African American newspapers were especially enthusiastic. Many Southern whites were critical of the trend, but the only political attempt to thwart integration came when Sen. Richard Russell of Georgia attached an amendment to a bill granting soldiers the choice to join an integrated unit. The bill was voted down.

By June 1952, just a year after the start of the war, the last all-black unit disbanded, and many units were fully integrated. The battlefield success of the racially mixed troops proved to military leaders that the needs of the service – not race – should determine soldiers' assignments, a message that carried over into the CIVIL RIGHTS MOVEMENT, which was to begin three years later.

SEE ALSO
Military, Blacks in the American.

Kota. Please see BAKOTA

Africa

Kotoko, ethnic group of West Africa.

The Kotoko primarily inhabit CAMEROON, CHAD, and NIGERIA. They speak an Afro-Asiatic language. Until its defeat in the 1400s, a Kotoko Kingdom ruled large areas of what are today northern Cameroon and northeastern Nigeria. From the fifteenth to the nineteenth century the Kotoko were vassals of the Bornu Kingdom, ruled by the KANURI people. Today about 150,000 people consider themselves Kotoko.

SEE ALSO
Languages, African: An Overview.

Africa

Kotokoli (also known as Cotocoli, Temba, and Tem), ethnic group of West Africa.

The Kotokoli primarily inhabit GHANA, TOGO, and BENIN. They speak a Niger-Congo language and belong to the GURMA cultural and linguistic group. Approximately 400,000 people consider themselves Kotokoli.

SEE ALSO
Languages, African: An Overview.

Kotonou, Benin. Please see COTONOU, BENIN

Africa

Koumbi Saleh, Mauritania (also Kumbi), twelfth-century capital of ancient Ghana.

Koumbi Saleh was the last capital of ancient Ghana (also known as Wagadu), a powerful and wealthy West Africa kingdom dominated by the Soninké people. The city's archaeological remains lie 320 km (200 mi) north of BAMAKO, MALI.

According to legend, Dyabe, son of the founder, Dinga, established the kingdom of Wagadu with Koumbi Saleh as its capital. Dyabe received permission to settle there from Bida, the black snake, on condition that each year Bida be given the most beautiful virgin in the city.

Eleventh-century scholar Abu Ubaydalla al-Bakri wrote that the city consisted of two distinct towns: a Muslim town and a royal compound. Archaeologists have confirmed the existence of the much larger and denser Muslim town, covering 2.5 sq km (an entire sq mi). Its wealthy Muslim traders prayed in the dozen mosques. A large main street 12 m (40 ft) wide ran the length of this settlement. A distinct, Soninké-dominated royal compound, less well built, probably existed 10 km (6 mi) from the main town. Approximately 15,000 to 20,000 people probably lived at Koumbi Saleh at its peak, when the town prospered from the sale of gold and slaves to trans-Saharan traders.

Sources state that the Almoravid Berbers destroyed the royal town in 1076. They may have brought Muslim rule to ancient Ghana. The larger town continued to prosper, even after Sumanguru, the Soso ruler of the Takrur Kingdom, conquered it in 1203. SUNDIATA KEITA, the ruler of ancient Mali, had his army destroy Koumbi Saleh in 1240.

According to the Wagadu legend, however, during the reign of Ghana's seventh king, the suitor of a sacrificial virgin killed Bida. Before dying the snake cursed Koumbi Saleh.

The curse ended the city's wealth in gold and extinguished its supply of water. The Soninké people dispersed as the desert consumed the city.

Ari Nave

See Also

Berber; Ghana, Early Kingdom of; Gold Trade; Soninké; Almoravids; Trans-Saharan and Red Sea Slave Trade; Mali Empire.

Africa

Kountché, Seyni (b. 1921, Fandou, Niger; d. November 10, 1987, Paris, France), military general and president of the Republic of Niger (1974-1987).

The son of wealthy Djerma, Seyni Kountché attended prestigious schools and joined the military after completing his studies in 1949. He quickly rose through the ranks. Under the presidency of Hamani Diori he won appointment to a series of powerful positions. Within months of his promotion to chief of staff, however, he led a military coup in 1974. He suspended the constitution and named himself president of the new regime.

Upon seizing control, Kountché enjoyed initial popularity. He moved to end the rampant corruption of the previous regime, whose officials had diverted food aid into private coffers during the severe famine and drought of the early 1970s. He chose to remain at the austere residence of the military chief of staff rather than occupy Diori's lavish presidential palace. Using military force to achieve humanitarian goals, Kountché immediately stopped the black market in food aid and distributed free seed to farmers. He increased revenues from Niger's uranium mines, the proceeds of which he initially allocated to the population of the drought-stricken countryside.

Kountché instituted Samariya, a new rural development project that attempted to teach villagers to increase food-crop production. The Société de Développement (Development Society), which followed this project in 1976, sought to increase communication between the national and local governments and to improve rural development projects. But the traditional elite soon co-opted the society, so that it offered little benefit for peasants, a failing that became increasingly common in the Kountché regime.

Kountché and his administration lost popularity within only a few years. An acerbic and authoritarian personality, Kountché lacked political charisma. His administration became increasingly enmeshed in internal military disputes, several of which culminated in coup attempts that were ruthlessly suppressed. Kountché subsequently gained a reputation as a bloodthirsty autocrat. He was accused of using spirit possession to undermine his rivals. After several attempted coups and other attacks, Kountché became increasingly suspicious; he frequently dismissed those he suspected of disloyalty. By 1980 he had a complete monopoly of political power in Niger, and his regime consisted almost entirely of his own civilian appointees, many of whom were his family members.

By the early 1980s Kountché had amassed a huge fortune from the state treasury, not unlike his predecessor Diori. The popularity of his regime dropped still further in the mid-1980s following a fall in the world price of uranium and continued drought. Niger experienced a severe economic crisis; the state froze spending and dismissed workers from many projects, including construction and mining. As the economy slowly improved after 1985, Kountché began to regain popularity. He adopted sweeping reforms such as a new, publicly ratified constitution in 1987. Stricken with illness, however, Kountché had to seek medical care in Paris, where he died of a brain tumor later that year.

Elizabeth Heath

See Also

Drought and Desertification.

Africa

Kpelle (also known as Guerzé, Nguerze, Ngere, and Pele), ethnic group of West Africa.

The Kpelle primarily inhabit northern and central Liberia. Representing about 20 percent of the population, they are the largest single ethnic group in Liberia. Kpelle also live in Sierra Leone and in Guinea, where they are sometimes called the Guerzé. Their total population is around 1 million. They speak a Mande language.

Most Kpelle cultivate rice as a staple. They also grow cassava, peanuts, and a variety of vegetables. Since the 1960s, however, large numbers of Kpelle have migrated to urban centers. Today around 15 percent of Kpelle live in cities such as Monrovia.

The patrilineal Kapelle have traditionally lived in several chiefdoms. While chiefs settle disputes and perform political functions, the Poro and Sande secret societies also enforce conformity to social conventions.

See Also

Languages, African: An Overview; Monrovia, Liberia.

Africa

Krio, an ethnic group of Sierra Leone.

Krio people (called Creoles in older sources) formed 10 percent of the Sierra Leone population in 1993. They are concentrated in the capital, Freetown, and its environs on the Sierra Leone Peninsula, on York Island, on the Banana Islands, and in Bonthe. There are small numbers of Krio in Senegal, Guinea, and Equatorial Guinea. The group's language, also called Krio, serves as a means of communication among the different peoples of Sierra Leone.

Krio society developed from the interaction between the various groups of early black settlers of Freetown and the Sierra Leone Peninsula. The first settlers arrived between 1787 and 1808. They were poor blacks from London (*see* London's Black Poor and the Sierra Leone Settlement Plan), ex-slaves who had either fought with the British in the American Revolution or had rebelled in Jamaica. These people were joined by "recaptives," people freed from slave-trading posts and vessels by the British anti-slave-trade campaign between 1808 and the 1860s. The Yoruba and Ibo and the Mende and Temne from the Sierra Leonean interior were among these recaptives, but others are said to have originated from as far away as Angola and Senegal.

At first the different groups retained quite separate identities. There were sharp divisions between the settlers from the West – who had adopted Christianity, Western habits, and the English language, – and the recaptives, who had never crossed the Atlantic.

The early Western settlers quickly established themselves as an elite class. They were successful traders, exporting palm oil and other agricultural goods produced in the interior and importing European goods. British administrators planned villages for the recaptives around Freetown, where they would farm as peasants, and this plan prevented the two groups from intermingling. Many recaptives resisted the peasant life, however; like Western settlers, some became wealthy from trade with the interior and in the capital. This common interest in commerce helped forge interaction between the settler elite and the recaptives, and by the 1840s recaptives were beginning to live beside and intermarry with the earlier settlers.

Most scholars agree that the Krio identity and language were well established in Sierra Leone by the 1870s. Their language includes elements of the older, Portuguese-based Creole used by coastal traders, in which the majority of words were derived from English and a large number of grammatical conventions and loan words were taken from African languages (especially Yoruba). Krio society adopted many elements of respectable Victorian British culture. British-style clothes were popular (although Edward Blynden led a movement for the adoption of African clothing styles toward the end of the last century), and most Krio embraced the values of Christianity and capitalism. There was, however, an important Muslim minority. Recent writers have stressed the African origins of Krio society. Important traditions such as the premarriage "asking ceremony" and the veneration of ancestors in the *awujoh* feast had origins in other African societies.

During the last third of the nineteenth century Krio businesses dominated Sierra

Leone; the Krio elite accrued wealth; and Sierra Leone served as an educational, religious, and commercial center on the West African coast. However, the colonization of the Guinean interior by the French after 1890 cut off Freetown from many of its former inland trading partners, and after the establishment of the British Protectorate over Freetown's more immediate hinterland in 1896, Krio power declined. Africans from the interior identified the Krio with European colonizers, and during the Mende uprising of 1898, for example, many Krio and Europeans were killed. The Krio also came into conflict with increasingly racist European administrators. In 1882 Krio held 18 of 40 senior government posts. By 1912 they held 15 of 92 such jobs. European and Syrian businessmen began to eclipse the Krio domination of trade.

Despite these setbacks, Krio politicians continued to exercise a powerful political influence through the first half of the twentieth century. Krio were important both inside the colonial government and in the growing nationalist movement. Krio leaders played an important role in the National Congress of British West Africa in the 1920s and the radical West African Youth League in the 1930s and 1940s. After World War II politicians from the interior assumed a dominant position in Sierra Leone, but Krio people have continued to exert an influence stronger than their number would suggest. This influence has at times been controversial.

See Also
Freetown, Sierra Leone; Blyden, Edward Wilmot; Nationalism in Africa; Igbo; Afro-Atlantic Culture: On the Live Dialogue Between Africa and the Americas.

Africa

Krobo (also known as Krobou), ethnic group of West Africa.

The Krobo primarily inhabit coastal Ghana and Côte d'Ivoire. They speak a Niger-Congo language and are closely related to the Adangbe people. Approximately 400,000 people consider themselves Krobo.

See Also
Languages, African: An Overview.

North America

KRS One (Laurence Kris Parker) (b. 1965, Brooklyn, New York), African American rap artist, self-styled "Teacher" of the hip hop nation.

KRS One was born Laurence Kris Parker and grew up in the South Bronx section of New York City. A graffiti artist turned rapper (*see* Rap), he founded the seminal rap group Boogie Down Productions (BDP) in 1986 with the disc jockey (DJ) Scott LaRock (Scott Sterling). Their first album, *Criminal Minded* (1987), combined LaRock's harsh, spare, reggae-influenced beats with KRS One's long-winded rhyme style on underground classics such as "9 MM Goes Bang" and "South Bronx." The album's gritty portrait of life on the streets (as well as the firearms that adorned its cover) influenced the gangsta rap movement that began in earnest two years later.

LaRock was fatally shot soon after *Criminal Minded* was released, but KRS One recruited a new production team for the second BDP album, *By All Means Necessary* (1988). The album retained some of the thuggish imagery of *Criminal Minded* but also explored the black radicalism suggested by its title, a riff on the words of Malcolm X: "by any means necessary." In tracks like "My Philosophy," "Stop the Violence," and "Illegal Business," KRS One affirmed his new persona – "The Teacher" – with scathing diatribes against institutionalized racism and black-on-black crime. Soon after, KRS One joined other rappers to form the Stop the Violence Movement, which addressed many of the same issues. *By All Means Necessary* stands as the most convincing political hip hop album to date.

In 1989 BDP's third album, *Ghetto Music: Blueprint of Hip Hop*, was released, and KRS One expressed his increasing Afrocentrism on a lecture tour of colleges and universities. BDP's fourth effort, *Edutainment* (1990), contained the hit "Love's Gonna Get 'Cha (Material Love)," but some critics complained that the group was running low on inspiration. After two more albums, KRS One dissolved BDP and embarked on a solo career, beginning with the highly acclaimed *Return of the Boom Bap* (1995). Since then, KRS One has maintained his status as hip hop's most committed voice. He has continued to release fairly successful solo albums, and in 1996 he founded the world's first school for hip hop culture, the Temple of Hip Hop.

Marc Mazique

See Also
Hip Hop in the United States; New York, New York.

Africa

Kru, a people of Côte d'Ivoire, Liberia, and Sierra Leone, and the broader linguistic group to which their language belongs.

The Kru people inhabit a homeland in coastal southeastern Liberia and neighboring Côte d'Ivoire. Some Kru have migrated to Sierra Leone to work as fishermen and dockworkers. Linguists use the group's name, Kru, to refer to a linguistic group within the larger Niger-Congo language family. Peoples speaking languages in this Kru group include the Bété, Dida, Grebo, Wobé, and the Kru people themselves. Speakers of Kru languages live in Ghana and Guinea in addition to the countries identified above.

The origins of the Kru people are unknown, although some historians believe that the group first migrated to the coastal areas in the early eighteenth century. There the Kru settled in loosely connected villages based on lineage and lived by hunting and subsistence farming. Although they lived along the coast, most Kru refused to take part in the Transatlantic slave trade, and they fought slave traders who attempted to capture Kru. During the late eighteenth and the nineteenth centuries Europeans frequently recruited the Liberian Kru, who were well known along the coast for their skillful seamanship, to work as sailors on European ships traveling between Europe and India. Other Kru worked as pilots and loaders along the coast.

During the late nineteenth and early twentieth centuries the Kru resisted domination by the Americo-Liberian elite in Liberia. In the early twentieth century a number of Kru became followers of William Harris, a Grebo missionary who had a religious vision while imprisoned by the Liberian government. Today many Kru continue to earn their living as sailors, longshoremen, fishermen, and dockworkers.

Elizabeth Heath

See Also
Americo-Liberians; Languages, African: An Overview.

Africa

Kuba, ethnic group of south central Democratic Republic of the Congo.

Although the origins of the Kuba are unknown, it is believed that they moved to the Kasai region in the Democratic Republic of the Congo after conflicts with the Portuguese and the Yaka, perhaps during the Jaga Wars, forced them away from their homeland near the mouth of the Congo River. During the sixteenth century they became skilled farmers and fisherpeople.

By the late sixteenth century the Kuba people had become a federation of 18 distinct groups. This federation became a cohesive kingdom during the reign of Shyaam, a chieftain from the dominant Bushong group, in the early seventeenth century. Shyaam established a capital, created an army, and appointed followers to state officers. He also encouraged the cultivation of valuable new crops such as maize, tobacco, cassava, and beans. The Kuba's very productive agriculture fostered population growth and commerce; by the eighteenth century they had established relations with people throughout the region between the Kwango and the Lualaba rivers. Despite the constant influx of new groups into the Kasai region, the Kuba were able to maintain this empire until the late nineteenth century. At this time invasions from neighboring groups significantly weakened the Kuba and probably would have destroyed the empire had King LEOPOLD II's Congo Free State not taken control of the area.

The Kuba remained fairly cohesive during the colonial period and were active in the independence movement in the 1950s. After independence they were eager to assert their own autonomy and, under the direction of Albert Kalonji, the Kuba led a short-lived South Kasai secession movement in 1960. Although South Kasai soon returned to the control of the central government, the Kuba have maintained their customary hierarchies while exercising considerable influence over provincial politics in South Kasai.

Elizabeth Heath

SEE ALSO
Colonial Rule; Portugal.

Africa

Kudu, common name for either of two antelopes that inhabit forested areas of Africa.

The greater kudu is one of the largest antelopes, measuring 1 to 1.5 m (3.3 to 5 ft) high at the shoulder. The animal is reddish brown to pale gray, with a longitudinal white stripe along the middle of its back and several transverse white stripes on each side. The male has long, spiraling horns, sometimes more than 1 m (4 ft) in length; the female is hornless. Greater kudus, found in the dry forests and dense brush from CHAD to SOMALIA and SOUTH AFRICA, are timid, gentle animals and feed on leaves, fruit, and grass. The lesser kudu is similar in color to the greater but measures only 90 to 105 cm (35 to 41 in) at the shoulder. This animal is found in dry, thick brushland in eastern Africa.
Scientific classification: Kudus belong to the family Bovidae. The greater kudu is classified as *Tragelaphus strepsiceros* and the lesser kudu as *Tragelaphus imberbis*.

SEE ALSO
Antelope.

Africa

Kukuruku (also known as northern Edo), ethnic group of NIGERIA.

The Kukuruku primarily inhabit northern Edo State in southern Nigeria. They speak a Niger-Congo language and are closely related to the neighboring EDO people. Some consider the name Kukuruku derogatory and prefer to be called northern Edo. The group numbers more than 200,000 people.

SEE ALSO
Languages, African: An Overview.

Africa

Kulango (also known as Babé, Kulamo, Koulango, Lorhon, and Nkoramfo), ethnic group of West Africa.

The Kulango primarily inhabit northeastern CÔTE D'IVOIRE and southwestern BURKINA FASO. Others live in GHANA. They speak a Niger-Congo language and are closely related to the LOBI people. Approximately 100,000 people consider themselves Kulango.

SEE ALSO
Languages, African: An Overview.

Africa

Kumasi, Ghana, the second largest city of GHANA and the former capital of the ASANTE Empire.

A major commercial and cultural hub, Kumasi is located in the rich tropical forests of south central Ghana. According to legend the first king of the Asante Empire, OSEI TUTU, established Kumasi as his capital around 1680. He is said to have negotiated for the land while sitting under a kum tree, hence the name Kumasi. As home to the Asante imperial palace and the Golden Stool, sacred symbol of the Asante nation, Kumasi was considered a princely city, *Osei-Krom*, and the center of Asante national culture. Tribute flowed to Kumasi from throughout the vast domains of Asante. The city also prospered because of its proximity to the gold fields and from its location at the hub of several north-south trade routes. HAUSA traders occupied the city's Muslim quarter, which served as a center for trade with interior regions.

When the British sacked Kumasi in 1874, it marked the first time an enemy army had entered the city in Asante history. But the city remained under Asante rule until 1896, when the British occupied the area and exiled the king. The Asante noblewoman YAA ASANTEWA led a national resistance struggle in 1900 that was centered in Kumasi. For three months the Asante besieged the British garrison at Kumasi but were eventually defeated. In 1902 the remaining Asante territory was declared a British protectorate, ruled from Accra by the governor of the British Gold Coast colony (present-day Ghana).

Under the British, Kumasi grew rapidly. A branch of the Bank of British West Africa opened there in 1908. Other firms followed suit. Ghana's two leading railways from Accra and from the port city of Sekondi-Takoradi intersected in Kumasi by the 1920s, as did the main east-west and north-south roads; the city thus served as a regional center for the Gold Coast's rich COCOA-growing and gold-mining regions. The British also turned Kumasi into a center for colonial administration and construction. Kumasi's population increased accordingly, rising from an estimated 3000 in 1900 to nearly 24,000 in 1924, and over 80,000 in 1948.

After Ghana achieved independence in 1957, Kumasi became capital of the Asante region. While Kumasi remains an important center for the trade of agricultural products, including cocoa, it is also a major manufacturing center. Half of Ghana's timber processing takes place in Kumasi. Manufacturing sectors include textiles and clothing, food processing, chemicals, and light consumer goods. Business, government, and finance are also important employers. The central market is the largest single market in Ghana. An important cultural center, the city is home to the Centre for National Culture, which holds crafts and many gold artifacts, as well as the University of Science and Technology at Kumasi, Wesley College, and the Komfo Anokye Teaching Hospital. The 1995 census listed the Kumasi population as 645,000. At its current growth rate of 2.5 percent, it is estimated that more than 730,000 people will live in Kumasi by the year 2000.

David P. Johnson, Jr.

SEE ALSO
Accra, Ghana; Gold Trade; Colonial Rule.

Africa

Kuria (also known as Kuriya and Tende), ethnic group of East Africa.

The Kuria primarily inhabit northwest TANZANIA and western KENYA, just to the east of LAKE VICTORIA. They speak a Bantu language. Approximately 400,000 people consider themselves Kuria.

SEE ALSO
Bantu: Dispersion and Settlement.

Africa

Kusasi (also known as Koussassi, Kusai, and Kusase), ethnic group of West Africa.

The Kusasi primarily inhabit northeastern GHANA and neighboring BURKINA FASO. They speak a Niger-Congo language and belong to the Molé-Dagbane cultural and linguistic group. Approximately 300,000 people consider themselves Kusasi.

SEE ALSO
Languages, African: An Overview.

Africa

Kush, Early Kingdom of, Egyptian name for ancient Nubia (*see* NUBIAN), site of highly advanced, ancient black African civilizations that rivaled ancient Egypt in wealth, power, and cultural development.

Although the world is familiar with the

material, architectural, and cultural achievements of ancient Egypt, few know of the neighboring kingdoms of Kush, civilizations centered to the south of Egypt in the area called Nubia (in present-day SUDAN). Over the course of ancient history, two great civilizations rose and fell in the region the Egyptians knew as Kush. Today the older of the two is better known by the name of a modern town in Sudan, Karmah (or Kerma), where the ruins of its capital stand. The more recent Nubian civilization is the kingdom usually known as Kush.

Before the late 1970s scholars saw Karmah and Kush as little more than Egyptian colonial outposts. Racist beliefs that black Africans were incapable of establishing advanced cultures and civilizations contributed to the misconception. Modern archaeologists have restored Karmah and Kush to their proper places among the great cultures in world history. Today scholars agree that Karmah and Kush were no mere copies of Egypt. Although at times during their history they borrowed, sometimes heavily, from Egyptian culture, they were indigenous, black African societies comparable to Egypt in importance, power, material wealth, and cultural development.

The civilizations of Karmah and Kush occupied the Nile Valley between present-day Khartoum (in Sudan) and Aswan (in Egypt). These areas were rich in natural resources such as gold, copper, diorite (a semiprecious stone), and the hard stone necessary for Egyptian building projects. They lay along trade routes connecting Egypt with West and Central Africa, and both civilizations grew wealthy from this trade.

Karmah

Even before the first pharaohs united Egypt around 3000 B.C.E., the black Africans of Nubia had developed one of the world's most advanced cultures. Recent archaeological finds have revealed that the region's people were producing sophisticated ceramics by 8000 B.C.E., even earlier than the people of Egypt. Indeed, it seems likely that Nubia contributed as much to ancient Egypt's development as Egypt did to Nubia's.

During Egypt's Old Kingdom (2575-2130 B.C.E.), Karmah Kingdom extended its rule over much of Nubia. Archaeologists divide Karmah's history into three periods: Early Karmah, 2400-2000 B.C.E.; Middle Karmah, 2000-1668 B.C.E.; Classic Karmah, 1668-1570 B.C.E. Each period can be distinguished by unique styles of pottery, tomb building, and burial practices. By 1700 B.C.E. the kingdom's capital had grown to a population of about 10,000. This complex society had several economic and social classes, with a king at the top, a priestly class, and an aristocracy. A firm agrarian base permitted the development of specialized occupations, including skilled artisans and an army. The town's eastern cemetery grew to about 30,000 graves.

Graves of the Early Karmah period were small and grew in size and complexity over time, suggesting that a distinct ruling class gradually accumulated wealth and power. An abundance of Egyptian articles in the graves indicates a greater contact between the two civilizations in the Middle Karmah period. The Classic Karmah period was the most prosperous for Karmah, which traded extensively with both the Egyptians at Thebes and the Hyksos people who dominated much of Egypt at the time.

Egypt had long viewed Karmah, which it called Kush, as a threat, particularly to its economic interests in Lower Nubia. Egypt controlled the area of Lower Nubia in times of political stability and withdrew from it during times of political or social upheaval. Egypt experienced such a period of upheaval beginning around 1700 B.C.E., when the Hyksos (most likely from present-day Syria) conquered lower, or northern, Egypt. The weakened armies of Upper, or southern, Egypt withdrew from Lower Nubia, which Karmah took over. Soldiers from Karmah fought on both sides in the warfare between the Hyksos and the Egyptians.

By 1570 B.C.E. the Egyptians began a national war of liberation, first against Karmah. During the war the pharaoh Kamose intercepted a message from the Hyksos ruler to the new king of Karmah inviting Karmah to join forces with Hyksos in a conquest of Egypt so that the two powers could share the spoils. To prevent such an alliance, Egypt reconquered Lower Nubia and then drove the Hyksos from Egypt. It then waged a series of attacks against Karmah until around 1450 B.C.E., when Egypt destroyed the kingdom and its capital. Egypt then occupied Nubia for approximately 500 years, and the Nubians (or Kushites) absorbed Egyptian culture.

Kush

Around 1075 B.C.E., when Egypt entered a period of instability, the governors of Kush attempted to assert their independence from Egypt. Egypt responded by invading and reoccupying Nubia in 1070 B.C.E. By the ninth century B.C.E., however, Egypt had disintegrated into several competing states, and Nubia regained its independence. Around 850 B.C.E. a kingdom arose to dominate Nubia from Napata, the former Egyptian colonial capital.

In about 750 B.C.E. King Piye of Kush invaded Egypt, then splintered into more than 11 independent principalities. Piye and his brother Shabaka conquered and united Egypt. Shabaka founded what is known as Egypt's Twenty-fifth Dynasty. For almost 100 years Egypt was ruled by a succession of Kushites, generally considered fair and benevolent rulers. This period represented the height of Kushite power, when Kush controlled an empire stretching from present-day Khartoum to the Mediterranean Sea.

Kush had absorbed much of Egypt's culture. Kushites worshiped many of the Egyptian gods, most importantly Amon. The Kushites believed that the *ka* (spirit or soul) of Amon resided at Jebel Barkal, just outside Napata. They constructed a temple to Amon there, around which developed a priestly class with great power. Kush's rulers considered themselves the true pharaohs of Egypt and maintained the ancient pharaonic traditions. Many Egyptians, however, considered the pharaohs of the Twenty-fifth Dynasty to be foreigners and rejected their legitimacy. In 674 B.C.E., during the rule of the Kushite pharaoh Taharqa, the Assyrians, whose empire was based in present-day Iraq, invaded Egypt and defeated Taharqa's army. Taharqa fled to Napata. Even though he attempted to retake Egypt, Taharqa and his successors failed. By about 663 B.C.E., Kush had permanently lost control of Egypt.

Subsequently, Egypt ousted the Assyrians and reestablished its forts in lower Nubia. Around 590 B.C.E. the Egyptian ruler Psamtik II invaded Upper Nubia, decisively defeating the Kushite army and possibly briefly taking Napata. The kings of Kush fled to the town of Meroë in about 590 B.C.E., although Napata remained an important religious center. Each king, until around 300 B.C.E., returned there to be crowned and to be buried.

The move to Meroë marked a cultural and political change in Kush. No longer preoccupied with the Egyptian borderlands, Kush began to face south and return to its Nubian roots. Meroitic replaced Egyptian as the official language, as did a unique form of writing, which scholars have yet to decipher. The god Apedemak, depicted as a man with a lion's head, supplanted Amon as the national deity. Meroë developed ironworking technology, which was new to Africa at that time. Today large and numerous slag heaps testify to the large-scale production of iron.

The first century B.C.E. was the high point of Meroitic culture and politics; after this Meroë began a slow decline. Several factors may have caused the decline: a rerouting of the trade between Egypt and West and Central Africa to bypass Meroë; soil erosion caused by cattle overgrazing; declining agricultural yields; and deforestation (probably due to the vast amounts of timber needed to fuel iron furnaces). The last known king of Kush, Yesbokheamani, ruled from approximately 283 to 300 C.E. After his death Kush's history remains unknown. The final reference to it comes from King Ezana of AKSUM (in present-day ETHIOPIA), who claimed to have sacked Meroë in 350 C.E.

Robert Fay

See Also

Khartoum, Sudan; Egypt, Ancient Kingdom of; Thebes, Egypt.

Africa

Kuti, Fela (b. October 15, 1938, Abeokuta, Nigeria; d. August 3, 1997, Lagos, Nigeria), Nigerian singer, saxophonist, bandleader, and composer.

One of Africa's best-known and most outspoken cultural figures for nearly 30 years was born Fela Ransome-Kuti, the son of a minister and his wife. After studying jazz and classical music in Great Britain, Fela – as he was popularly known – worked briefly for the Nigerian Broadcasting Corporation. In the late 1960s, while living in Ghana, Fela visited the United States, where he sampled various musical and political movements. He was particularly influenced by seeing James Brown in concert and meeting members of the Black Panther Party.

Returning to Nigeria in 1973, Fela – who had formed his band, Nigeria 70, three years earlier – began writing more overtly political songs. He attacked government corruption and took on wider social issues as well. One of his first hit songs, "Shakara/African Woman," criticized the use of white Western standards of feminine beauty in Africa. His signature sound – a blend of soul, jazz, highlife, and African percussion – was dubbed Afrobeat by Fela and spawned dozens of imitators. In the mid-1970s he opened a Lagos nightclub, the Shrine, where he presided over all-night dance parties for the next 25 years. Joined onstage by as many as 30 or 40 musicians and dancers at a time, Fela sang in a mostly English patois, his lyrics taking jabs at "all dem oppressors."

Long an irritant to authority figures, Fela's outspokenness brought him frequent harassment from the Nigerian government. In 1977 the army burned down his house, and his mother later died from beatings incurred during the same attack. After her death Fela announced the formation of his own party, the Movement of the People, and urged young Nigerians to get involved in public affairs. During an abandoned run for Nigeria's presidency, Fela announced that, if elected, he would make every Nigerian a police officer. That way, he said, "before a policeman could slap you he would have to think twice because you're a policeman too."

Fela's flamboyant ways also attracted attention. He often performed and conducted interviews wearing only his underwear. Although he avoided hard drugs, he was an enthusiastic user and proponent of marijuana, which led to several arrests during his lifetime. In 1978, already married though separated from his wife, he took 27 new brides, mostly singers and dancers with his band. In 1986, after serving 20 months in prison on drug charges, he divorced them all, saying he no longer believed in the institution of marriage.

By the 1990s, having achieved international fame and produced dozens of hit albums, Fela turned to religion. Probably already ill with acquired immune deficiency syndrome (AIDS), the disease that would kill him, he disappointed some fans and friends by not speaking out against the excesses of Nigeria's military government, which had recently imprisoned his brother, a pro-democracy activist. When he died in 1997, his family announced the cause of death, a rare admission in a country where AIDS is not often discussed publicly. In obituaries and editorials after his death, Fela was remembered as a giant, a genius, a hero, and an honest man.

Kate Tuttle

See Also

Soul Music; Afro-Beat; AIDS in Africa: An Interpretation.

North America

Kwanzaa, a holiday that African Americans celebrate during the final week of the year to reaffirm their African roots.

Kwanzaa, Swahili for "first fruits," is a secular holiday. Maulana Karenga, current chairman of the Black Studies Department at California State University at Long Beach, introduced this holiday in 1966 at the height of the Black Power Movement in the United States. At that time he was a graduate student and the head of US (United Slaves), a Los Angeles-based Black Nationalist group committed to learning about African history and teaching it to African Americans. After formulating the holiday, Karenga and members of US traveled around the country to promote it. Since then, the number of African Americans who observe the holiday has dramatically increased. In 1996, 13 million African Americans in the United States and 5 million people of African descent in other parts of the world were estimated to have celebrated Kwanzaa. Although Karenga designed the holiday to "give a Black alternative to the existing holiday," many African Americans who celebrate Kwanzaa also celebrate Christmas.

An elaborate and symbolic table setting is a central part of the Kwanzaa celebration. First, African Americans place on a table one of two items – a mat made of straw or a Kente-patterned textile – which represents the African American heritage in the materials of traditional African culture. Celebrants then put a seven-pronged candleholder in the center of the mat. The candleholder contains one central black candle that is flanked by three red and three green candles. Each candle stands for one of the seven principles Kwanzaa commemorates. Near the base of the candleholder, observers place a cup, which symbolizes the unity of all African peoples. Around these two centerpieces, vegetables, fruits, and nuts are arranged, which represent the yield of the first harvest.

The philosophical foundation of Kwanzaa is the seven principles collectively known as the *Nguzo Saba*. They include *umoja* (unity); *kujichagulia* (self-determination); *ujima* (collective work and responsibility); *ujamaa* (cooperative economics); *nia* (purpose); *kuumba* (creativity); and *imani* (faith). After researching cultures throughout the African continent, Karenga selected these Swahili-named principles because of their predominance in African history. The Nguzo Saba, according to Karenga, are the core principles "by which black people must live in order to begin to rescue and reconstruct [their] history and lives."

Each day before dinner celebrants light a candle and interpret its corresponding principle. In addition to explaining the principle and illustrating it through parables, African Americans discuss how to live according to the principle. After dinner, they blow out the candle. On the following day they light an additional candle along with the candle(s) from the preceding day(s), until the seventh day when all seven candles burn together.

While Kwanzaa's candle-lighting ritual tends to be solemn, the rest of the celebration is upbeat and festive. On each evening of the celebration, family and friends gather to eat and drink. A typical Kwanzaa feast may feature spicy oven-fried catfish or Creole chicken accompanied by a bean or rice dish, such as Hopping John or Jollof Rice, and completed by desserts such as fried candied sweet potatoes or sweet and tart lemon cake. All celebrants drink from the unity cup in reverence of their predecessors. They tell stories about their African ancestors, sing, and dance.

As part of the celebration family members exchange gifts of cultural significance, such as dashikis (African tunics). Another popular gift is a *Nia Umoja* figurine, also known as Kente Claus, which represents an ancient African storyteller. He wears a Kente cloth robe and has a neatly trimmed gray beard.

When he introduced Kwanzaa, Karenga urged that gifts as well as all decorations for the holiday be homemade, but in recent years there has been a proliferation of Kwanzaa merchandise. Since 1990 New York City has hosted an annual Kwanzaa Holiday Expo, which has attracted an increasing number of vendors. They sell publications such as cookbooks, how-to manuals, children's stories, and paraphernalia such as factory-made mats, mass-produced unity cups, and Taiwanese-made candleholders. Hallmark, which introduced a line of Kwanzaa greeting cards in 1992, is one of several major American corporations that market Kwanzaa-related merchandise.

Some African Americans have criticized the commercialization of Kwanzaa on the grounds that black-owned businesses are not the benefactors. Karenga argued that "We [African Americans] should be producing our own items for our own practice of the holiday." Other social critics have interpreted the commercialization of Kwanzaa as society's acknowledgment of the holiday's significance and the rising economic status of blacks. Even with this commercialization, Kwanzaa continues to be a cultural mainstay in the homes of many African Americans.

Aaron Myers

See Also

Swahili Language; Creoles; Black Nationalism in the United States.

Africa

Kweni (also known as Dipa, Guro, Gouro, Koueni, and Lo), ethnic group of Côte d'Ivoire.

The Kweni primarily inhabit west central Côte d'Ivoire. They speak a Mande language. Approximately 300,000 people consider themselves Kweni.

See Also

Languages, African: An Overview.

Africa

Kwere, ethnic group of Tanzania.

The Kwere primarily inhabit coastal Tanzania. They speak a Bantu language. Approximately 100,000 people consider themselves Kwere.

See Also

Bantu: Dispersion and Settlement.

l

Latin America and the Caribbean

Labat, Jean Baptiste (b. 1663; d. 1738), French priest who worked as a missionary in Guadeloupe between 1693 and 1705. His *Nouveau voyage aux îles d'Amerique* (1772, New Voyage to the Islands of the Americas) described the operation of plantations and the system of slavery in the French colony. While critical of some aspects of slavery, the work also recounts Labat's own participation in brutally punishing slaves who practiced African religions (*see* Colonial Critics of Slavery).

North America

LaBelle, Patti (b. October 4, 1944, Philadelphia, Pa.), African American singer whose career followed trends in popular music from soul music "girl-groups" in the 1960s through extravagant stage shows in the 1970s to synthesizer pop in the 1980s and 1990s.

Born Patricia Louise Holt, Patti LaBelle first performed for audiences as a teenager at Beulah Baptist Church in Philadelphia. In high school she formed a singing group, the Ordettes, with Cynthia "Cindy" Birdsong; later the two joined with Wynona Hendryx and Sarah Dash of the Del Capris to form the Bluebelles. The Bluebelles' music resembled that of many of their black female pop-singing contemporaries in terms of both repertoire and style. In fact the controversy over whether LaBelle actually recorded "I Sold My Heart to the Junkman" – attributed as her first hit – is unresolved. Some contend that the 1962 hit was cut by the Starlets.

Shortly after getting started, the Bluebelles changed their name to Patti LaBelle & the Bluebelles. In the mid-1960s they toured theaters throughout the East and Midwest, landing a number of songs on the R&B charts but failing to become superstars. In 1965 producer Jerry Wexler signed them with Atlantic Records, but even this breakthrough did not launch them onto pop charts. Soulful recordings of such standards as "Over the Rainbow" and "Danny Boy" earned LaBelle a steady following, yet the high quality of new compositions such as "Groovy Kind of Love" was often overlooked by mass audiences. In 1967 Cindy Birdsong left the Bluebelles and took Florence Ballard's place with the Supremes.

At the beginning of the 1970s LaBelle, persuaded by others, decided to change the group's look. She recruited Vicki Wickham, producer of Britain's hip television program "Ready, Steady, Go!," to oversee the rebirth of her career with the Bluebelles. Under Wickham's supervision, the group changed its name to the simpler, sleeker LaBelle and donned outrageous stage costumes with silver, feathers, leather, and much exposed flesh. The group's music followed their change in fashion, as they fused new hard rock sounds with old strains of R&B.

Despite its new look LaBelle remained on a low rung of stardom for the next two years. Although the flamboyant and defiant sexuality of its stage shows attracted a following among the gay male community, it remained a second-tier feature in the mainstream. Labelle nevertheless landed a gig at New York's Metropolitan Opera House in 1974, a first for a female African American group. And in 1975 the success of "Lady Marmalade" – which reached number one on the pop charts – caused sales of the album *Nightbirds* to break a million, propelling LaBelle to international fame. LaBelle flaunted its extravagant fashion and enjoyed its notoriety until 1977, when the group broke up over musical differences.

Patti LaBelle's career since the group's breakup has shown her ability to change with the times. In the 1980s and 1990s her solo albums sold as well as her group recordings ever had; meanwhile, she courted other media. She broke into television with appearances on *A Different World* and *Out All Night*, as well as on a special of her own. She appeared on Broadway with Al Green in *Your Arm's Too Short to Box with God*. She contributed hit songs to the soundtrack of the film *Beverly Hills Cop* and started her own line of perfume and cosmetics. In 1996 she released her autobiography, *Don't Block the Blessings: Revelations of a Lifetime*, and in 1997 won the Image Award of the National Association for the Advancement of Colored People (NAACP).

Patti LaBelle has employed her celebrity to social ends, sponsoring and speaking for the United Negro College Fund, civic programs in Philadelphia, and medical school scholarships for African Americans.

Eric Bennett

See Also

Philadelphia, Pennsylvania; Rhythm and Blues; Supremes, The; Television and African Americans.

North America

Labor Unions in the United States, the history of African Americans and organized labor, in which the attempt of black workers to unionize was met first with violent resistance and then began a slow process toward racial integration in the trade union movement.

The relationship between African Americans and organized labor in the United States has been both empowering and troubled. Unions have traditionally given vulnerable workers protection through the strength of collective bargaining. Yet African American unionizing efforts consistently met with resistance from both employers and the existing unions, which were white. Black workers who attempted to organize faced not only losing their own jobs and being blacklisted, but also violent actions by the police, militia, and vigilante groups. Although barred from white unions, black workers were still regarded as strikebreakers when they attempted to work during strikes, or as "union-busters" when they worked for lower pay than the union wage.

The eventual decision to integrate white unions was both moral and pragmatic. As the number of black workers swelled in the industrial sector during the two World Wars and some of the immense group of agricultural workers attempted to organize, national labor federations saw the benefit of shoring up union ranks with these workers. But membership did not necessarily mean that blacks held power within the union, or even that the entire union and its affiliates were racially integrated. African Americans carried on the fight for the desegregation of "Jim

Crow" unions through the Civil Rights Movement. The struggle continues for black representation in union leadership, union-secured grievance procedures to fight discrimination, and training for more highly skilled jobs.

The precursors of the labor unions that organized black workers existed as early as the antebellum period. These groups included benevolent societies, such as the New York African Society for Mutual Relief (1806); the Negro Convention Movement, which held annual meetings of black leaders during the 1840s and 1850s; and groups that promoted worker unity and industrial education, such as the American League of Colored Laborers (1850). Black workers also formed collectives, such as the Association of Black Caulkers, founded in 1858 in Baltimore, to protect themselves from the mob violence of immigrants who felt threatened by black employment. These groups sometimes engaged in unofficial bargaining for wage increases, as did the black waiters of the Waiter Protective Association of New York in 1853.

The formal unionization of black workers from the period following the Civil War to the present has followed two basic imperatives: integration of large white unions and separate organization of black-only unions. Most of the later unions sought the added strength of affiliation with a white-dominated federation, since, in the words of labor leader Isaac Myers in 1868, "Labor organizations are the safeguard of the colored man, but for real success, separate organization is not the real answer."

In 1869 a group of black leaders traveled to a convention of the National Labor Union to lobby for the organization of black affiliates. Although they were recognized as a delegation, they were unsuccessful at introducing integration into the white union. To fill the gap of black-worker representation in the labor movement, 214 African American delegates met the same year to create a confederation of autonomous black local and state unions, the Colored National Labor Union, with headquarters in Washington, D.C.

In 1869 the Philadelphia-based Noble Order of the Knights of Labor became the first white labor union to organize black members actively. By 1886 they had enrolled 60,000 African American workers, predominantly in the South. Yet it was clear that African Americans were second-class citizens in the union when in 1887 the Knights abandoned the 9000 black workers who had walked off the sugar plantations in Louisiana, thus leaving them open targets for militia and vigilante force.

Nevertheless, there were hopeful signs of a slow process of change as other unions integrated. Black workers still did not hold much power in integrated unions, but some African Americans made their way into the ranks of the leadership. In the 1890s African American miner Richard L. Davis became a member of the executive board of the United Mine Workers of American, a union in which more than half of the workers were black. He used the power of this position to fight against the segregation of the Southern affiliates and the exclusion of blacks from skilled jobs. Another African American labor leader, Benjamin H. Fletcher, organized the most powerful dockworkers' union in Philadelphia, the Marine Transport Workers Union, in 1913, as part of the socialist International Workers of the World's campaign to organize black workers.

As the Northern industrial centers bore the weight of a massive influx of black workers during the Great Migration north in the first half of the twentieth century, the distinction between unionized and nonunionized black workers became blurred in the growing climate of racial hatred. Many whites feared that blacks would take their jobs. With a few exceptions, racial differences overwhelmed worker solidarity, and the race riots of the Red Summer of 1919 made clear the demarcation lines between black and white.

In the South, despite the fatal risk of organizing farm labor, blacks forged labor unions to gain some measure of personal and financial protection. These efforts led to tragedy in Elaine, Arkansas, where sharecroppers, tenant farmers, and laborers had banded together to form the Progressive Farmers and Household Union of America. White planters responded to the unionizing efforts with official and vigilante violence that left 100 blacks dead and destroyed the union. Twenty years later, the Southern Tenant Farmers' Union would reclaim some measure of success by achieving national recognition for a massive protest in which 1700 evicted sharecroppers set up camp along Missouri's Highway 61.

The detrimental effects of the Great Depression were compounded for black workers, who were the first to be let go and the last to be hired. Desperate for work, many took nonunion jobs, undercutting the power of unions, while employed blacks faced animosity from unemployed white workers. Yet organizing efforts continued through the 1930s, gaining momentum in the latter part of the decade. After a long battle with the Pullman Company, A. Philip Randolph organized company porters into the Brotherhood of Sleeping Car Porters in 1928, and nine years later the Brotherhood became the first black affiliate of one of the most powerful unions of the era, the American Federation of Labor (AFL). Another prominent union, the Congress of Industrial Organizations (CIO), created in 1935, organized semiskilled and unskilled workers in mass-production industries with many black workers, such as steel, auto, rubber, and meat packing.

Despite the relatively progressive stance of these federations, blacks still found themselves barred from most of the skilled jobs, and many affiliates remained segregated. A plan to march on Washington, D.C., pressured President Franklin Roosevelt into signing an order banning racial discrimination in war employment and created the Fair Employment Practices Committee.

The progressive measures that these unions had achieved in the 1930s lost ground during the cold war. The expulsion of so-called communist organizations effectively meant the removal of affiliates that had been at the forefront of the fight for black workers. The short-lived National Labor Conference for Negro Rights attempted to fill this gap in 1951, until it too fell victim to the McCarthy Era purges.

The 1950s and 1960s saw an alliance forged between the Civil Rights Movement and the labor movement, and some have called organized labor the staunchest institutional supporter of civil rights legislation. After an indictment of racist practices led by A. Philip Randolph, the newly merged AFL-CIO announced its support for the struggle for civil rights and its promise to organize without regard to race. Despite this promise, the union refused to take measures against affiliates practicing segregation and was accused of perpetuating racist practices.

In response black labor activists organized the Negro American Labor Council in 1960 to promote civil rights in the American labor movement. Randolph and the council initiated the famous 1963 March on Washington for Jobs and Freedom, where Martin Luther King Jr. gave his famous "I Have a Dream" speech. In 1964 the last segregated affiliate of the AFL-CIO integrated.

Local 1199: Drug, Hospital and Health Care Employees Union brought the labor movement to a new sector of black workers: the predominantly poor, black, and female workers of the voluntary hospitals. The union attracted support from prominent civil rights leaders, including King, since Local 1199 was, in the words of Malcolm X, "not afraid of upsetting the applecart of those people who are running City Hall." In 1969 civil rights leaders rallied together for a massive protest in Charleston, South Carolina, for a labor dispute so contentious it ultimately led to federal mediation. The union's ultimate victory strengthened its ranks, and Local 1199 grew to a membership of more than 150,000 by the mid-1970s. More important, the shared struggle of the Charleston protest forged bonds between Southern civil rights leaders and those attempting to rework traditional unions to serve the needs of black workers.

Some African American workers, however, felt that their issues would forever be subsumed by white-dominated labor organizations. They sought a separate movement. With the rise of the Black Power Movement in the late 1960s, certain sectors of black labor became increasingly militant. In the automobile plants of the Northern industrial centers, a group of workers formed the League of Revolutionary Black Workers. Beginning with the idea that the issue of black labor was linked to a broader struggle for the decolonization of African Americans in a white supremacist society, this group connected organized labor to the ideologies of SOCIALISM and Black Power.

The leadership of large integrated unions such as the United Auto Workers responded to a perceived threat from radical elements by opening leadership positions to more moderate blacks and working with national black organizations. In the late 1960s national black organizations and labor unions worked together to develop several federally funded programs, including the Recruitment and Training Program (Workers Defense League), the Labor Education and Advancement Program (Urban League), and the Human Resources Development Institute (AFL-CIO). These programs brought blacks into apprenticeship programs in the 1970s, giving some workers a long-awaited upward mobility toward more highly skilled and better-paying jobs.

African American unemployment grew in the 1980s as a result of a national movement toward deindustrialization, an increased dependence on technology, and the shift of production out of the United States. Black workers were hit hard in the steel, auto, textile, and rubber industries as well as in the public sector, which had become the destination of more than half of the nation's black college graduates. In addition, unions had still not made inroads into the mostly nonunionized service sectors where many blacks were concentrated. Even so, by 1990, blacks were statistically more unionized than the rest of the work force.

Black participation in union leadership, affirmative action, protection from discrimination, and training for more highly skilled jobs (now high-tech jobs) have continued to be issues for the labor movement in the United States. Yet most proponents of organized labor still hold A. Philip Randolph's vision of worker solidarity across color lines: "The white and black workers... cannot be organized separately as the fingers on my hand. They must be organized altogether, as the fingers on my hand when they are doubled up in the form of a fist... If they are organized separately, they will not understand each other. They will fight each other, and if they fight each other, they will hate each other. And the employing class will profit from that condition."

Marian Aguiar

See Also
American Federation of Labor and Congress of Industrial Organizations; Civil War, American; Elaine, Arkansas, Race Riot of 1919; Jim Crow; King, Martin Luther, Jr.; National Urban League; Randolph, Asa Philip; Communist Party USA, African Americans and the; March on Washington, 1941.

Africa

Ladysmith Black Mambazo, a renowned South African musical group.

By improvising on traditional ZULU singing styles, the all-male a cappella choir Ladysmith Black Mambazo became an international sensation after a series of critically acclaimed albums in the 1980s and 1990s. Choral singer Joseph Shabalala formed the ten-member group with friends and relatives in 1962. With Shabalala as lead singer and composer, Mambazo includes seven bass singers, one alto, and one tenor. Since its formation, Mambazo has recorded some 40 albums, with songs in both Zulu and English.

The group's name reflects the Zulu roots of its members. "Ladysmith" is the Shabalala family's hometown in KwaZulu-Natal Province. "Black" refers to black oxen, the strongest animals on the farm, while "mambazo" is the Zulu word for ax, implying that the group could chop down rivals during singing competitions. Their artistic roots lie in a type of performance called *iscathamiya* – Zulu for "walking like a cat" – that combines dancing and call-and-response singing. Iscathamiya originated in the mines, where workers learned to "walk like a cat" and not bother the guards. At home on Saturdays, men would sing and dance late into the evening. Today teams of roughly ten men perform iscathamiya without instrumental accompaniment in competitions before judges.

After converting to Christianity in his youth, Shabalala blended church choral and Zulu singing, a style known as *mbube*. Mambazo generated a following through competitions and appearances on Radio Zulu. Their first release, *Amabutho* (1973), became the first African album to achieve Gold Medal status, with sales of over 25,000 copies.

Popular in South Africa, Mambazo remained largely unknown elsewhere until 1986, when American singer Paul Simon performed with them on his *Graceland* album, which fused African and Western pop music. With sales of more than 7 million, *Graceland* became one of the top-selling LPs of the decade and turned Mambazo into a musical phenomenon.

In 1988 Mambazo won the Grammy Award for Best World Music Recording with *Shaka Zulu*. Five other Mambazo albums have received Grammy nominations, including *How the Leopard Got His Spots* (1989), a collaboration with DANNY GLOVER; *Gift of the Tortoise* (1993); *Liph' Iqiniso* (1994); and *Thuthukani Ngoxolo* (1996).

Mambazo has appeared in several films, including two 1990 documentaries, *Spike Lee & Company – Do It A Cappella* and *Mandela in America*. They were also featured in *Waati*, a 1995 political drama. The group recorded soundtracks for various other movies, including *Moonwalker, A Dry White Season, Coming to America*, and *Cry the Beloved Country*.

In 1991 Mambazo began collaborating with Chicago's Steppenwolf Theatre Company in the production of two musicals, *Song of Jacob Zulu*, which opened on Broadway in 1993 and received six Tony Award nominations, and *Nomathemba*, based on Shabalala's first composition. Mambazo sang at the ceremony when Nelson Mandela and F. W. De Klerk, then president of South Africa, won the Nobel Peace Prize in 1993; at Mandela's inauguration as South African president in 1994; and before Queen Elizabeth during Mandela's 1996 state visit. Their 1997 album, *Heavenly*, broke new ground with gospel and RHYTHM AND BLUES numbers, as well as collaborations with Lou Rawls, Dolly Parton, and Bonnie Raitt.

David P. Johnson, Jr.

See Also
Christianity, African: An Overview; Mandela, Nelson Rolihlahla; South Africa; Gospel Music; Rawls, Louis Allen (Lou); De Klerk, Frederik Willem; World Music, World Beat, and the Re-Africanization of Latin American Popular Music; Nobel Prize.

North America

Lafayette Theatre, pioneering African American theater in Harlem that staged both serious drama and light entertainment.

Like many Harlem theaters, the Lafayette Theatre originally opened in 1912 for all-white audiences. A few years later black drama critic Lester Walton leased the theater and created a black stock company to bring meaningful dramatic theater to New York's black audiences. By 1916 the Lafayette Players, led by ANITA BUSH, had successfully produced plays by Shakespeare, Dumas, and Molière.

Eventually, the Lafayette adapted to its audience's taste for musical comedies and more lighthearted theater. The theater remained a center for black entertainment through the 1930s, when the Federal Theater Project brought more serious works back to the Lafayette stage. In 1967, at the height of the BLACK ARTS MOVEMENT, the New Lafayette Theatre opened in Harlem, honoring its namesake's commitment to producing theater with African American performers for African American audiences.

Lisa Clayton Robinson

See Also
Dumas, Alexandre, Père; Harlem, New York.

Africa

Lagos, Nigeria, the largest city in NIGERIA and its chief port.

Lagos, the most populous of Nigeria's cities and its former capital, forms the industrial, commercial, administrative, financial, and cultural heart of the country. Located on the Atlantic coast in southwestern Nigeria, the city occupies four islands – Lagos, Iddo, Ikoyi, and Victoria – and parts of the adjacent mainland, all connected by bridges. The main business district, the heart of the city, lies on southwestern Lagos Island.

The city was founded in the fifteenth century when the Awori, a subgroup of the YORUBA people, established a settlement on Lagos Island known as Oko. The kings of Benin, represented by local *obas*, or hereditary rulers, dominated Lagos from its founding until the mid-nineteenth century. Its first inhabitants engaged in fishing, hunting, and minor trading. Trade increased with the arrival of the Portuguese in 1472. Lagos did not, however, become a major trade center until the Lagos obas granted the Portuguese monopoly rights. As the slave trade flourished, the volume of trade at Lagos equaled and eventually surpassed that at the slave ports of Badagry and Porto-Novo.

Scholars disagree about whether the British ended the slave trade in Lagos primarily for moral reasons or mainly to reorient the economy to the British trade in palm oil, indigo, and cotton. The first decisive British move to end the trade occurred in an 1851 attack on the city that resulted in the ouster of the oba, Kosoko. Akitoye, a relative of Kosoko, succeeded him and signed an antislavery treaty with the British. Doubting the commitment of Akitoye's successor, Dosumu, to ending the slave trade, the British annexed the city in July 1861 and instituted COLONIAL RULE.

In 1864 Lagos became part of the British Gold Coast Colony (now GHANA). Its attachment to the Gold Coast lasted until 1886, when it became capital of a new protectorate that encompassed the surrounding region. Lagos became the capital of Southern Nigeria in 1906 and of the combined Protectorate of Nigeria (the colonial forerunner of the modern nation) in 1914.

During the period following Great Britain's annexation, Lagos became something of a melting pot. Europeans arrived in 1851, shortly after the defeat of Oba Kosoko. Missionaries from the Nigerian town of Badagry arrived next, followed by migrants from SIERRA LEONE, many of them former slaves taken from Yorubaland. After the declaration of Lagos as a free colony, escaped slaves from the interior began to settle there. The construction of a railway into the Yoruba interior in 1896 bolstered the city's commercial economy and attracted more migrants.

The city, as colonial capital, played an important role in the development of Nigerian politics. It was the home of such activists as Herbert Macaulay (called the father of Nigerian nationalism) and Nnamdi Azikiwe. At Nigerian independence in 1960, Lagos was named the national capital. In 1991 the capital was moved to Abuja, in central Nigeria.

Industries include automobile and radio assembly; textile, cosmetic, paint, and pharmaceutical production; food and beverage processing; and metalworking. In addition, the city features traditional markets for dyed cloth, herbs, and leather goods. The terminus of roads and rail lines leading to all parts of Nigeria, and the site of the country's main international airport, Lagos handles most of the country's trade.

As Nigeria's political stability and economy have deteriorated in recent years, an ever-growing stream of migrants has sought employment in metropolitan Lagos. Many have settled in overcrowded squatter camps on the edge of the city, where they are not included in Lagos's official population of nearly 1.5 million. The rapidly expanding population of greater Lagos, estimated at more than 10 million in 1997, has swamped the city's infrastructure and caused serious public health and pollution problems.

Andrew Burton

SEE ALSO

Abuja, Nigeria; Azikiwe, Benjamin Nnamdi; Benin, Early Kingdom of; Transatlantic Slave Trade; Porto-Novo, Benin.

Africa

La Guma, Alex **(b. February 20, 1925, Cape Town, South Africa; d. October 11, 1985, Havana, Cuba), South African writer who used his writing to give a voice to the black South Africans oppressed under APARTHEID, the official policy of racial segregation followed in South Africa from 1948 to the early 1990s. La Guma's work helped provide an artistic vision of cultural change that accompanied the efforts of the more celebrated antiapartheid political figures of South Africa, such as Nelson Mandela and STEPHEN BIKO.**

Born Justin Alexander La Guma in CAPE TOWN, SOUTH AFRICA, he was educated at the Cape Technical College and later, through correspondence courses, at the London School of Journalism. Influenced by the political principles and activities of his family, he participated in the union movement in South Africa, helping to organize a strike in the mid-1940s while employed as a factory worker. He also joined the Young Communist League, and in 1950 he was listed as a known Communist under the Suppression of Communism Act, a law used by the South African government to punish its critics. From 1955 to the early 1960s he worked as a staff journalist of the South African newspaper *New Age*. In 1960, during a state of emergency declared after the killing of 69 black South African protesters at a demonstration in Sharpeville, he was imprisoned for his political activities. In 1966 he emigrated to London, where he worked for the AFRICAN NATIONAL CONGRESS (ANC). He later served as an ANC representative in CUBA.

La Guma's short stories include "Nocturne," "Out of Darkness," and "Slipper Satin," published together in the edited collection *Quartet* (1963) by Richard Rive. They deal with the struggles of finding things of beauty and sensuality amid the trials of poverty, of prison life, of attempts to pass for white, and of participating in interracial relationships forbidden by law. La Guma is best known, however, for his novels, especially *A Walk in the Night* (1962), a short novel that traces the movement of the protagonist, Michael Adonis, toward criminality as he copes with poverty, police harassment, and racism in the workplace. The book is considered to follow in the tradition of American writer RICHARD WRIGHT, who portrayed social injustice against African Americans in vivid and brutal terms.

La Guma's novel *And a Threefold Cord* (1964), set in Cape Town during an unrelenting rainstorm, focuses on poor black families who live under bleak economic conditions. This culture of poverty encourages alcoholism, prostitution, illness, petty criminality, and violence, all of which lead to further destruction and harassment from police. The book thus emphasizes the ways in which the conditions of inequality and violence in South Africa were created by apartheid itself. The novel *The Stone Country* (1967) depicts life in a South African prison, the brutality of which serves as a metaphor for the experience of black South Africans living under apartheid. La Guma's other works include the edited volume *Apartheid: A Collection of Writings on South African Racism by South Africans* (1971), the autobiographical novel *In the Fog of the Seasons' End* (1972), the travel book *A Soviet Journey* (1978), and the novel *Time of the Butcherbird* (1979).

SEE ALSO

Antiapartheid Movement; Mandela, Nelson Rolihlahla; Sharpeville, South Africa; South Africa; South African Communist Party.

Africa

Lala, **ethnic group of ZAMBIA.**

The Lala primarily inhabit central Zambia. They speak a Bantu language and are related to the BEMBA people. Approximately 400,000 people consider themselves Lala.

SEE ALSO

Bantu: Dispersion and Settlement.

Africa

Lalibela, Ethiopia, **an Ethiopian town renowned for its ancient churches carved from solid rock.**

The first European visitor to describe the famous churches of Lalibela, cut from the living rock in the highlands of Lasta, was astonished. "It wearied me to write more of these works," he complained, "because it seemed to me that they will not believe me if I write more, and as to what I have already written, they will accuse me of untruth."

The 11 churches are regarded as one of the wonders of the world, excavated from solid rock with an immense underground maze of tunnels and passages. There are two main groups of churches, with another church dedicated to Saint George a short distance away. No one really knows when or why the houses of worship were constructed. Ethiopian tradition connects them with the most famous king of the Zagwe Dynasty, and the town, formerly known as Roha, has come to be known by that king's name. The *Life of Lalibela* describes how King Lalibela (who ruled from the late twelfth to the early thirteenth century) was carried away to the heavenly Jerusalem. There he was instructed to build the churches. Angels worked beside his men as they cut each one from the rock and then kept working through the night. However, the style in which the churches were made is remarkably similar to the surviving architecture of ancient AKSUM, and scholars have become intrigued by the possibility that some of the churches could be much older than the reign of Lalibela. Some of them may also have been constructed as palaces rather than as churches. They do not all follow the conventional alignment of churches to the east.

After the death of Lalibela his tomb and the city itself began to draw thousands of pilgrims. Although his dynasty was overthrown, Lalibela is still revered as a saint. The churches are seen as a New Jerusalem, with a river named Jordan and sites corresponding to the holy places of the great city. According to an Ethiopian saying, "If you do not wish to see Lalibela, you are like someone who has no desire to see the face of Christ."

SEE ALSO
Ethiopia.

Latin America and the Caribbean

Lamming, George (b. June 8, 1927, Carrington Village, Barbados), Barbadian novelist, critic, essayist, and educator.

George Lamming's first novel, *In the Castle of My Skin* (1953), is hailed as one of the masterpieces of Caribbean literature, and Lamming has followed that accomplishment with a long and varied career. Lamming grew up in BARBADOS, and was raised by a single mother; as one scholar has pointed out, it was Lamming who "gave to a Caribbean reality the important verbalization 'It was my mother who fathered me.'" After attending Roebuck Boys School, he won a scholarship to Combermere High School. There he met teacher Frank Collymore, who was also the editor of *Bim*, the influential new Caribbean literary journal, and who encouraged Lamming's writing ability. Collymore helped Lamming secure his first job in 1946 as a teacher at a Venezuelan boys' college in Trinidad.

Lamming remained there for four years before emigrating to Great Britain in 1950, on the same ship as the Trinidadian novelist SAMUEL SELVON (*see* LONDON, BLACKS IN: AN INTERPRETATION). During his first several years there Lamming wrote poetry and short fiction, which he published in *Bim* and broadcast in England through the British Broadcasting Company's radio program *Caribbean Voices.* But when *In the Castle of My Skin* was published, Lamming was immediately acclaimed as a brilliant novelist.

In the Castle of My Skin is a largely autobiographical account of a childhood in the Caribbean during the political protests and changes of the 1930s and 1940s. Lamming continued exploring themes of decolonization, Caribbean national reconstruction, and the Caribbean emigrant experience in four more books over the next seven years. In *The Emigrants* (1954), Lamming again followed a largely autobiographical theme by tracing the history of *In the Castle of My Skin*'s protagonist after he moves to England – in the process, portraying the common post-emigration struggles of many West Indians. *Of Age and Innocence* (1958) and *Season of Adventure* (1960) portray the fight for independence on a fictional Caribbean island, again emphasizing the common struggles among West Indian nations. Lamming's first nonfiction book, *The Pleasures of Exile* (1960), is a collection of essays on topics ranging from his travels to a discussion of Shakespeare's play *The Tempest,* and is considered an important early work of Caribbean literary and cultural theory.

In *The Pleasures of Exile,* Lamming's theme is "the migration of the writer from the Caribbean to the dubious refuge of a metropolitan culture." In the essay on Shakespeare, Lamming becomes one of the first contemporary authors to argue that the character Caliban represents the Caribbean perspective in the play, and that while canonical readings of *The Tempest* see Caliban as only an inarticulate savage, there is a need to reread the play from a Caribbean perspective – Caliban's perspective – to grasp new meanings in it. In the rest of his book, Lamming emphasizes literature's potential to define national culture, and the need for a separate Caribbean literature and Caribbean perspective on canonical literature that is different from that of the region's colonial powers. *The Pleasures of Exile* continues to be studied by scholars of Caribbean and postcolonial literature.

By this time Lamming had already won several major awards, including a 1955 Guggenheim Fellowship, which allowed him to travel to West Africa, and the 1957 Somerset Maugham Award for Literature for *In the Castle of My Skin.* After this first burst of activity, the pace of his literary output slowed considerably; Lamming's later books include two more novels, *Water With Berries* (1971) and *Natives of My Person* (1972), and the anthology *Cannon Shot and Glass Beads: Modern Black Writing* (1974). His poetry and essays continue to appear in journals and anthologies, however, and Lamming remains in demand as a lecturer and editor.

Lamming moved back to Barbados in 1974. During that same year the general secretary of the Barbados Workers' Union asked him to organize the opening of their first Labour College. Lamming spent the next year as a writer-in-residence at the University of Dar es Salaam and the University of Nairobi, and then the following year traveled to universities in India and Australia as the recipient of a British Commonwealth Foundation fellowship. He has also taught at the University of the West Indies at Mona (JAMAICA), the University of Texas at Austin, the University of Connecticut, the University of Pennsylvania, Cornell University, and the University of North Carolina, and he has directed the University of Miami's Summer Institute for Caribbean Creative Writing. A collection of some of his lectures, *Conversations. George Lamming: Essays, Addresses, and Interviews,* was published in 1990. Lamming's earliest novels still stand out as records of the Caribbean experience, and Lamming continues to be acknowledged as one of the most influential writers in the Caribbean literary tradition.

Lisa Clayton Robinson

SEE ALSO
Literature, English Language, Caribbean; Trinidad and Tobago.

North America

Lampkin, Daisy Elizabeth Adams (b. 1884?, Washington, D.C.?; d. March 10, 1965, Pittsburgh, Pa.), African American civil rights worker, newspaper executive, and national field secretary for the NATIONAL ASSOCIATION FOR THE ADVANCEMENT OF COLORED PEOPLE (NAACP).

Daisy Lampkin is best known for her work as national field secretary of the NAACP from 1935 to 1947. In addition to her NAACP service, she brought energy and passion to the *Pittsburgh Courier*, the nation's premier African American newspaper, as well as a host of clubs, organizations, and causes.

Historians are unsure of the date and place of Lampkin's birth, but it is known that she grew up in Reading, Pennsylvania, moved to Pittsburgh in 1909, and married William Lampkin in 1912. Around this time she became active in the Lucy Stone League, a women's suffrage organization, and in 1915 she became president of the Negro Women's Franchise League. By 1930, when she joined the NAACP as field secretary, she had been named vice president of the *Pittsburgh*

Courier and had served as a delegate to the 1926 Republican National Convention.

Lampkin's work for the NAACP was legendary. Named national field secretary in 1935, she is credited with bringing in new members – and new money – at unprecedented rates with her finely honed fundraising, recruiting, and speaking talents. Along with Walter White, then the NAACP's national secretary, Lampkin was influential in engineering the defeat of a racist Supreme Court nominee and in convincing THURGOOD MARSHALL, Roy Wilkins, and other future civil rights leaders to join the organization. Even after poor health forced her to step down from her post in 1947, Lampkin continued to work with the NAACP, serving on its board of directors. When she died in 1965, her obituary in the *Courier* dubbed her "Mrs. NAACP."

Lampkin was also active in the NATIONAL ASSOCIATION OF COLORED WOMEN, in which she served as vice president in the 1940s; the NATIONAL COUNCIL OF NEGRO WOMEN, on whose board of directors she sat; and Delta Sigma Theta, an African American sorority. After her death, the state of Pennsylvania honored Lampkin for her wide-ranging devotion to humanitarian and political efforts by proclaiming her house a historic landmark.

Kate Tuttle

SEE ALSO

Press, Black, in the United States; *Pittsburgh Courier*; Pittsburgh, Pennsylvania; White, Walter Francis; Wilkins, Roy Ottoway.

Africa

Lamu, Kenya, an Indian Ocean island with a Swahili port town of the same name.

Lamu was one of several coastal trading communities in Kenya where the blending of African and Arab cultures gave rise to SWAHILI LANGUAGE and culture. Although its origins are unclear, many believe that Lamu Town was founded in the fourteenth century C.E. as a trade post for Arab merchants, who later intermarried with Africans. The town saw its golden age between the seventeenth and nineteenth century, when it was an important depot for the export of gold, ivory, and, to a much lesser degree, slaves headed for Asia and the MIDDLE EAST. During this time Lamu Town produced many fine examples of Swahili art and literature, including famous wood carvings and poems, some of which remain in Lamu's museum.

Such abundance was not without cost, as rival leaders of neighboring Swahili communities, including Pate Island and Mombasa, sought to control Lamu. The *Pate Chronicle* tells of a long-running conflict between 1650 and 1812 that culminated in a joint attack waged by the Mazrui clan of Mombasa and a Pate force against Lamu. The Lamuites repelled the invasion.

Ironically, the victory marked the end of Lamu's independence; shortly afterward, Lamuites requested protection from the Omani Dynasty of ZANZIBAR, which subsequently controlled Lamu until the late nineteenth century, when the British imposed COLONIAL RULE. Lamuites continued to identify themselves as Arabs, and when Kenya achieved independence in 1963, many lobbied for autonomy from the *Mwafrika*, or up-country Africans, fearing that the ethnic KIKUYU in particular would dominate postcolonial business and government. Today, however, because Arabs are typically considered foreigners, Lamu's residents are more likely to call themselves Swahili.

Modern Lamu's economy runs on tourism. The island has become renowned for its slow pace, tranquil beaches, traditional Swahili architecture, and tolerance for bohemian lifestyles. Despite the constant influx of foreign visitors, donkeys and cows remain the primary modes of transportation on the island, as the streets are too narrow to accommodate automobile traffic.

Robert Fay

SEE ALSO

Gold Trade; Ivory Trade; Mombasa, Kenya; Great Britain; Swahili People; Tourism in Africa; Indian Ocean Slave Trade.

Latin America and the Caribbean

Lam, Wifredo (b. December 8, 1902, Sagua la Grande Provincia de Las Villas, Cuba; d. September 1, 1982, Paris, France), Cuban modern artist and the first internationally acclaimed Afro-Cuban painter and sculptor.

Throughout his career Wifredo Lam was active in major art movements, including surrealism and modernism, and was associated with many of the best-known figures in the art world of his day, including Pablo Picasso and André Breton. Lam's surrealist compositions make use of his Afro-Chinese and Cuban ancestry, and his most famous paintings, including *The Eternal Presence* (1945) and *The Jungle* (1943), present his mythic, erotic, and syncretic inheritances in a supernatural and symbolic way. He is arguably one of the most distinguished talents of the twentieth century.

Lam left CUBA in 1923 at age 21 to study at the Madrid School of Fine Arts. While he was in Europe, his painting was influenced by the experimental mode of the era, and his compositions became increasingly abstract. After visiting Picasso's studio in 1930, he established a relationship with the artist, apparently because Picasso himself was

Wifredo Lam (1902-1982), *The Jungle*. 1943. Gouache on paper mounted on canvas, 7'10 1/4" x 7'6 1/2" (239.4 x 229.9 cm). *The Museum of Modern Art, New York. Inter-America Fund. Photograph © 1999 The Museum of Modern Art, New York*

already involved in the so-called primitivist movement and had begun to incorporate African masks and design motifs into his own painting. This was a visual vernacular with which Lam was already familiar as a result of his Cuban roots. Picasso sponsored an exhibition of Lam's work in 1938 in Paris that began to establish Lam's reputation. By 1942 Lam had produced a series of paintings of women in tropical settings very much influenced by Picasso's style.

In 1941, during World War II, Lam was confined in an internment camp in MARTINIQUE along with prominent European intellectuals (including the surrealists André Breton and the anthropologist Claude Lévi-Strauss). Once he was able to procure his freedom after a month-long detainment, he returned to Cuba for the first time in nearly 20 years. There he rooted his work in the specificity of his own (and the island's) historical transculturation, or cultural mixing, drawing on Chinese, African, and indigenous influences to produce the most acclaimed work of his career. Lam was also closely associated with the artists of the NÉGRITUDE Movement in the French-speaking Caribbean, and with such literary figures as AIMÉ CÉSAIRE, all of whom wanted to plumb the depth of African heritage, spirituality, and liveliness in the Caribbean and oppose their findings to what they considered the moribund and stagnant intellectual life of Europe.

Although Cuba left its mark on his artistic work, Lam never remained in one place. He continued to live mostly in Cuba but also traveled frequently to other metropolitan centers of art in the West, including Paris and New York. He visited HAITI with Breton in 1945 to research VODOU in another effort to incorporate African spiritual traditions into his painting. It was in Haiti at the Centre d'Art that Lam became familiar with the work of another black painter, HECTOR HIPPOLYTE, who painted highly symbolic compositions of bright colors that incorporate motifs (flowers, animals, etc.) from Vodou. Lam eventually had an exhibit of his work in Port-au-Prince. In 1965 he moved to Albisola, Italy, where he remained for 17 years until his death.

Lam's style is easily recognizable for its mysterious, spiritual dimension, which proceeds from his debt to African religious traditions in the Caribbean, as exemplified by *Altar for Eleggua* (1944). His style is also known for the abstract, eroticized, and fetishistic representations of body parts and African masks that melt into and surge out of junglelike landscapes of camouflage in the tropics.

Bill Johnson-González

SEE ALSO

New York, New York; Port-au-Prince, Haiti; Haitian Art; Art in Latin America and the Caribbean; Religions, African, in Latin America and the Caribbean.

Africa

Lango (also called Langi), an ethnic group residing primarily in northern UGANDA. (Some scholars differentiate the Lango region from the Langi people, although Lango was divided into two districts, Lira and Apac, in 1974.)

The approximately 600,000 Lango speak an eastern Sudanic Chari-Nile language of the Nilo-Saharan family. The Lango are believed to have descended from a group of LUO speakers who fled from invaders of their Agore Mountains homeland around the mid-sixteenth century. Over the next two centuries this group moved south, en route adopting certain customs of neighboring peoples, including the BARI. By the time the migrants reached Mount Otuke in the mid-eighteenth century, they still spoke a Luo-based language but had developed distinctive social and political structures. Since this time they have adopted the ACHOLI language, although with dialectical distinctions. From here the group spread into present-day Lango district north of Lake Kwania.

The Lango are organized into exogamous patrilineages that comprise several clans. While Lango villages are inhabited by members of several lineages, a chief is typically chosen from the clan that dominates a particular village. Within each village, conflicts are mediated by a council of elders. Although the Lango have not historically recognized a centralized political authority, during the eighteenth and nineteenth centuries villages often formed military alliances, both to defend themselves against unfriendly neighbors and to wage raids for livestock and captives. By the mid-nineteenth century the Lango had grown accustomed to frequent warfare and had organized themselves into large fortified villages. Under British COLONIAL RULE, however, villages decreased in size in response to other pressures of economy and social life, including the need of pastoralists to live in dispersed groups and the pressures of living among large numbers of extended relatives.

The colonial administration encouraged cotton cultivation among the Lango, and it is still the primary source of livelihood for many rural Lango households, who typically also grow MILLET and sorghum for food. PASTORALISM remains important. Cattle, which are raised solely by men, are a mark of prestige as well as a form of brideprice.

The first prime minister of independent Uganda, MILTON OBOTE, was of Lango descent. He recruited many Lango into the military, hoping that ethnic allegiance would help minimize the chance of a military coup. When IDI AMIN took control of the government in 1971, he persecuted the Lango for their previous support of Obote. In the late 1970s Amin himself was ousted from power. Lango soldiers retaliated against Amin's KAKWA ethnic group, killing tens if not hundreds of thousands of individuals.

SEE ALSO

Languages, African: An Overview.

Africa

Languages, African: An Overview, languages indigenous to the African continent.

Estimates of the number of languages spoken in Africa range from 700 to 3000. Apart from Arabic, which is not confined to Africa, the most widely spoken African tongues are Swahili and Hausa, each with more than 20 million speakers. Several languages (often inaccurately termed dialects simply because they have few users) are spoken by only a few thousand people. On the average an African language has about 200,000 speakers; only a few dozen languages have more than a million speakers. Although very few African languages have written literatures, most have long-standing traditions of oral literature.

LANGUAGE GROUPINGS

According to the most recent and most widely accepted scholarly practice, the languages of Africa are grouped into four language families: Afro-Asiatic, Nilo-Saharan, KHOISAN, and Niger-Congo. Scholars have not firmly established that all of the languages classified in the Nilo-Saharan and Khoisan families are related to the other languages in their respective families. A language family is a group of related languages presumably derived from a common origin. A family is often subdivided into branches composed of more closely related languages. Some of the African linguistic families are believed to have a history of more than 5000 years.

THE AFRO-ASIATIC FAMILY

The Afro-Asiatic languages constitute the most important group of languages spoken in North Africa. The Semitic branch of the family includes languages spoken in Asia as well as in Africa. The Arabic language, the most widely spoken member of this branch, is the major language of North Africa (including MOROCCO, ALGERIA, TUNISIA, LIBYA, and EGYPT) and of SUDAN. Amharic (*see* AMHARA), which is spoken by more than 12 million people, is the official language of ETHIOPIA. The national epic of the Christian Ethiopian peoples, *Kebra nagast* (The Glory of the Kings), is written in ancient Ethiopic, or Ge'ez (*see* ETHIOPIC SCRIPT AND LANGUAGE), now no longer spoken. Ge'ez literature also includes several books of the Apocrypha not preserved in any other language. Other Semitic languages spoken in Africa include TIGRINYA in northern Ethiopia and ERITREA and Tigré in Eritrea.

Languages of the BERBER branch of the Afro-Asiatic family are spoken by a substantial portion of the population of Morocco, Algeria, and Tunisia; by scattered groups elsewhere in North Africa; and along the southern fringes of the SAHARA DESERT in West Africa. The Cushitic branch, confined to Ethiopia, SOMALIA, and parts of East Africa, includes such major languages as OROMO and SOMALI. The ancient Egyptian language (*see* EGYPT, ANCIENT KINGDOM OF) – which has no living descendant but which is still used in the rituals of the Coptic Christian Church of Egypt – was another branch of the Afro-Asiatic family.

A number of languages spoken largely in northern NIGERIA and CAMEROON form another Afro-Asiatic grouping known as the Chadic branch. By far the most important Chadic language is Hausa, one of the two most common indigenous languages of sub-Saharan Africa. Hausa is widely used in education and trade, even in regions far beyond its original borders. Several Hausa newspapers are published, and the body of Hausa literature is growing.

THE NILO-SAHARAN FAMILY

The Nilo-Saharan languages are found in a broken chain from the great bend of the NIGER RIVER in West Africa to Ethiopia, throughout most of the upper Nile valley, and in parts of UGANDA and KENYA. The westernmost member of this family is Songhai, spoken along much of the middle Niger River. The Saharan branch of this family includes languages spoken from northeastern Nigeria through CHAD to the east to the oasis settlements of Libya to the north. Although most of this area is sparsely populated, KANURI, the major language of the Saharan branch, is spoken by more than 4 million people.

Languages of the Chari-Nile branch are spoken in the southern part of Chad, in Sudan, in much of Uganda and Kenya, and in the northeastern corner of Congo-Kinshasa (formerly Zaire). Among the Chari-Nile languages are the NUBIAN languages, spoken along the Nile River near the southern border of Egypt and in scattered areas to the southwest. The Nubian alphabet was derived from that of the ancient Egyptian (Coptic) language. Nubian religious documents dating from the eighth century to the fourteenth century form the only literature of a living African language that was written before the modern period. In the southern Sudan and in northern Uganda and Kenya another important group of languages known as Nilotic belongs to the Chari-Nile branch. Prominent representatives are DINKA, NUER, SHILLUK, ACHOLI, LUO, and MAASAI.

The very small Maban and Komuz groups, and the single language FUR, also belong to the Nilo-Saharan family.

In many Nilo-Saharan languages, a system of noun suffixes indicates grammatical relationships. This system somewhat resembles the case system of Latin, but it is quite unlike that of any other family of languages in Africa. In the northern Nilotic languages, similar grammatical relationships are expressed by an extremely complex system of internal vowel changes; many of the vowel sounds themselves are unusually difficult for the learner. Various verbal constructions are indicated by series of suffixes in some Nilo-Saharan languages (for example, Kanuri) or by both prefixes and suffixes in others (for example, the southern Nilotic languages). Many of these languages have a characteristic passive construction that is used much more freely than its counterpart in English. For example, "He bought cloth" is usually expressed as "Cloth was bought by him." This sentence can be shortened to "Cloth was bought." The action (buying) and the object (cloth) form the basic part of the sentence; the person who performed the action is comparatively unimportant.

THE KHOISAN FAMILY

The Khoisan (or Click) languages constitute the smallest language family in Africa. Most of these languages are spoken by the KHOIKHOI and SAN peoples of southern Africa; the largest of them is Nama, with about 100,000 speakers. Far to the northeast in TANZANIA are two other possible representatives of this family: Sandawe, with about 70,000 speakers, and the much smaller HADZA. Some scholars, however, assign the Tanzanian languages to other families. The Khoisan languages are best known for the unusual click consonants characteristic of most of them. In some Khoisan languages nearly every word begins with a click. The production of these sounds involves a sucking action of the tongue. By the positioning of the tongue and the way air is released into the mouth, distinctive kinds of clicks are produced. When these languages are written, the clicks are represented either by otherwise unused letters such as C, Q, X, or by special symbols such as /, !, //. Some of the Khoisan languages have a system of grammatical gender, which is found elsewhere in Africa only in the Afro-Asiatic family.

THE NIGER-CONGO FAMILY

The Niger-Congo linguistic area comprises most of the African continent below the Sahara. About three out of four Africans speak languages that belong to the Niger-Congo family. Although migrations presumably separated certain branches of the Niger-Congo family more than 5000 years ago, languages in each of the branches have similar words for many common objects and actions. The Kordofanian branch is distantly related to the rest of the Niger-Congo languages and is considered one of the first branches to have separated. The Kordofanian languages number only about 30, all with relatively few speakers (*see* NUBA). They are found in a small area of the Nuba Mountains of Sudan, surrounded by languages of the Nilo-Saharan family and by Arabic. Languages in this branch share a few similar words with languages of other Niger-Congo branches and also show some striking resemblances in their grammatical structures.

Many linguists believe that the MANDE languages, spoken in many parts of West Africa, are the oldest offshoots of the parent Niger-Congo language spoken more than 5000 years ago. Three closely related major languages, MANDINKA, BAMBARA, and DYULA, are spoken from SENEGAL through much of MALI and northern GUINEA to northern CÔTE D'IVOIRE. Other important Mande languages are MENDE in SIERRA LEONE and KPELLE in LIBERIA. Small islands of Mande-language speakers are also scattered through areas farther east, as far as western Nigeria.

The largest branch of the Niger-Congo family is Benue-Congo, consisting of numerous language groups, most notably the Bantoid group, which contains the Bantu languages (*see* BANTU: DISPERSION AND SETTLEMENT). The Bantu languages have more speakers than all the rest of the Niger-Congo languages combined. Some of the more important Bantu languages are ZULU and XHOSA in SOUTH AFRICA; MAKUA in MOZAMBIQUE; NYANJA in MALAWI; SHONA in ZIMBABWE; BEMBA in ZAMBIA; MBUNDU in ANGOLA; Swahili and SUKUMA in TANZANIA; KIKUYU in KENYA; GANDA in UGANDA; Kinyarwanda in RWANDA (*see* ETHNICITY IN RWANDA: AN INTERPRETATION) and neighboring Congo-Kinshasa; Rundi in BURUNDI (*see* ETHNICITY IN BURUNDI: AN INTERPRETATION); KONGO in Congo-Brazzaville and Congo-Kinshasa; FANG and BULU in Cameroon; and TSWANA in southern Africa. Some Bantu-speaking authors are now beginning to produce literature in their languages. Languages from the other Benue-Congo language groups are spoken primarily in Nigeria. They include such major languages as YORUBA, IGBO, and EDO, which linguists previously classified in the Kwa branch of the Niger-Congo family.

The Kwa languages are found in a strip along the west coast of Africa from southeastern Nigeria to Liberia. This branch includes such important languages as EWE in TOGO and GHANA; the AKAN languages, including ASANTE and FANTE in Ghana; and ANYI and BAULE in Côte d'Ivoire. North of the Kwa language region, extending from western Nigeria into much of Côte d'Ivoire and BURKINA FASO, are the languages of the Gur branch, including MOSSI, BARIBA, and GURMA. The closely related Ubangi and Adamawa languages are spoken across north Central Africa. The Ubangi branch includes such important languages as AZANDE, BANDA, and NGBANDI. The Adamawa branch contains many subgroups, including MUMUYE.

Along the Atlantic coast of Africa, from Liberia to the desert north of DAKAR, SENEGAL, are several languages of the Atlantic branch. These include TEMNE in Sierra Leone, WOLOF in the vicinity of Dakar, and FULANI (also known as Ful or Fula), by far the most widely spoken. The two large concentrations of Fulani-speaking people are in Guinea and eastern Nigeria and Cameroon. Between these widely separated areas, Fulani-speaking people are scattered in numerous settlements. In southwestern Côte d'Ivoire and southern Liberia are the KRU languages. The Ijoid languages, including IBIBIO, spoken in the Niger delta, have proved difficult to classify, as have the DOGON languages, spoken in northeast Mali.

Tonality

With few exceptions, the languages of the Nilo-Saharan, Niger-Congo, and Khoisan families, as well as the Chadic languages and a few of the Cushitic languages in the Afro-Asiatic family, are tone languages – that is, distinctions in the pitch of a single syllable may differentiate completely different words or different grammatical functions of a word or of a prefix or suffix. For example, in a dialect of Jukun, a language of Nigeria, *kw??????* with a high pitch means "knife," *kw??????* with an intermediate pitch means "millstone," and *kw??????* with a low pitch means "chicken." In the same dialect, *ku bi* with both syllables on an intermediate pitch means "He came," but *ku bi* with the first syllable on a high pitch means "Have him come." In scores of Niger-Congo languages, different pronouns may differ only in pitch. Distinctions in pitch or tone have generally been ignored in writing, although they are often crucial to understanding what the writer intended to say. Tone is indicated by accent marks or other devices in only a relatively few modern grammars and dictionaries of African languages.

Other Language Families

Two other language families, Indo-European and Austronesian, are represented to some degree in Africa. The former group includes Afrikaans (*see* AFRIKANER) and English, both mother languages to many people in South Africa and Zimbabwe. English is also indigenous to Liberia, having been introduced there by liberated slaves who emigrated from the United States in the nineteenth century. MALAGASY, the language of the island of MADAGASCAR, is a member of the Austronesian group.

See Also

Congo, Republic of the; Congo, Democratic Republic of the; Hausa Language; Swahili Language; Nile River; Tigre; Songhai People.

Latin America and the Caribbean

Languages, Creole, in the Caribbean,

languages that usually develop within populations displaced by slavery and that are marked by the combination of African and European languages. Creoles are not corrupted or substandard versions of European languages but are full-fledged languages in their own right, and are regularly spoken in several countries, such as GUADELOUPE and HAITI.

This essay discusses the development and use of Creole languages in the Caribbean, along with the social and cultural factors that influence their evolution. In particular, it considers Guadeloupean and Martiniquais Creoles, Haitian Creole, and Papiamentu Creole.

The Development of Creole Languages in the Caribbean

Creole languages have usually evolved from two other, more simple linguistic forms: *jargons*, or languages with a small vocabulary and rather unstable grammatical forms; and *pidgins*, linguistic systems that are more stable than jargons but still rather simple in their grammar and vocabulary. Pidgin languages emerge from prolonged contacts between groups of people with no language in common (such as European slaveholders and their African slaves, or groups of slaves who spoke different languages and who were put together by slaveholders to work on sugar plantations). Unlike a jargon or a pidgin, however, a Creole is spoken natively by an entire speech community, often one whose ancestors were displaced geographically by slavery. In such circumstances the original linguistic and cultural heritage of these people was partially lost, and a new language, the Creole, emerged as a result.

If a Creole develops from a pidgin and particularly if this process is gradual, a phenomenon known as grammaticalization takes place. In grammaticalization a word becomes phonologically reduced and its use more generalized. Put differently, the original word's phonological structure is simplified, and its original, specific meaning becomes wider. This process often leads to an increased productivity of lexical items to fit the speaker's everyday needs. For example, in CAPE VERDEAN Creole the word for head is altered to carry a wider meaning:

Cape Verdean Creole: João mata kabesa
Literal transliteration: João killed head
Translation: João killed himself

Linguists have argued about the underlying influences that contributed to the development of Creole and pidgin languages. For the past 30 years there has been a debate between two schools of thought: monogenesis versus polygenesis. Proponents of monogenesis believed that Creole languages evolved from a single original language, thought to be an original Portuguese pidgin. Supporters of polygenesis, on the other hand, argued for multiple sources, claiming that different Creole language families have different origins.

Later, in the 1980s, two more opposing theories emerged. One group of scholars believed that the African languages were the substrata, or foundation, of current Creoles, and that they played the most important role in their development. A second group emphasized the primary role of European languages, seen as the superstrata of Creoles. (The distinction is clear: substratum refers to an African foundation, or underlying layer; superstratum carries with it the notion that European languages were the basis, and had African and indigenous elements added to them as conquest and slavery progressed.)

Finally, biogeneticists have stressed the role of the innate human language faculty. According to linguist Derek Bickerton, children born in the New World were usually exposed more to pidgin languages than to their parents' native language. Although the pidgin constituted an unstable and somewhat chaotic linguistic input, the children organized it into a Creole that became their native language. This new native language was thus a mix of the European and African languages. Sociogeneticists claim that social factors such as the political and economic contexts within which people communicate, not just biological ones, have influenced the emergence of Creoles.

Amid the gamut of linguistic theories, it is undisputed that the emergence of Creole languages is intertwined with the rise of the TRANSATLANTIC SLAVE TRADE, which gathered several European powers in the Caribbean area during the seventeenth century. Africans of diverse ethnic and linguistic groups were brought to the New World against their will and were forced to work on sugar plantations, often with slaves from other tribes to discourage communication and rebellion (*see* SLAVERY IN LATIN AMERICA AND THE CARIBBEAN and AFRICAN ETHNIC GROUPS IN LATIN AMERICA AND THE CARIBBEAN).

Various European nations dominated the Caribbean between the seventeenth and the nineteenth century, giving rise to a variety of Creoles in the Caribbean, including French-, Spanish-, or English-based Creoles. Among the English-based Creoles are Bahamian, Caymanian, Jamaican, Belizean, Virgin Islands Creole, and Barbadian. The Spanish-based Creoles include Papiamentu (spoken in ARUBA, Bonaire, and Curaçao). The French-based Creoles include Haitian, Lesser Antillean, Grenada Creole, and Trinidadian.

Given that both the so-called substrata (African) languages and the superstrata (European) ones played a role in the genesis of Creole languages, it is not surprising that similar linguistic features have been found among Caribbean Creoles. Linguists differ only as to whether the substrata or the superstrata played a greater role in Creole formation. The shared words found in various Creoles could also be explained by a common maritime vocabulary that settlers shared and that eventually permeated the various Creole languages.

Linguists have disagreed about which African languages have contributed to the Caribbean Creoles. Some have tried to separate Lesser Antillean Creoles (consisting primarily of languages spoken in Martinique and Guadeloupe) from Haitian Creoles on grounds both linguistic and sociohistoric. Indeed, scholars argue that Lesser Antillean

Creole originated in present-day St. Kitts (which was Saint-Christophe in the seventeenth century) from two substratal languages: the Kwa group of languages spoken on the Slave Coast, especially Gbe, spoken in present-day BENIN; and Western Bantu languages from the Congo and Angola area (*see* BANTU: DISPERSION AND SETTLEMENT). Other linguists have used demographic data to argue that the Bantu substratum was more important than the Kwa one in the Lesser Antilles, especially in Guadeloupe.

As linguist Karl Eland Gadelii has observed, when French colonists arrived in the Caribbean some kind of Spanish-Carib pidgin must have been spoken there, since Spain had previously invaded an area where the indigenous groups who are often classified as Carib lived. Caribs spoke several languages: Carib, Tupi, and Arawak. The Spanish-Carib pidgin was presumably later enriched with French words.

Since the French colonies were founded in the seventeenth and eighteenth centuries, we may expect that the French dialect spoken at that time differed from present-day French. It is also often observed that Creole languages contain a certain proportion of archaic words inherited from European languages, but these can be hard to distinguish from regional accents. It is usually claimed that French settlers in the New World came from the western parts of France, and more precisely from the regions west of an imaginary line running between Bordeaux, Paris, and Lille, and thus may have brought a distinctive form of French with them.

Other languages, such as Komanti, Luango, Papa, and Pzmbu, are used in the Caribbean by the descendants of maroons (or runaway slaves) during religious ceremonies (*see* MAROONAGE IN THE AMERICAS). Linguists claim that these languages have retained large portions of African elements, especially from Kikongo, Gbe, and Twi. In JAMAICA a group of maroons exists today who speak Jamaican Creole but are reported to make use of the African-based Maroon Spirit Language, as well as Kromanti, for ritual purposes.

The Use of Creoles

One of the primary characteristics of Creoles has to do with *diglossia*, particularly in the Caribbean. Diglossia means that the two languages in daily use, whether Creole and French, or Creole and Dutch, or Creole and English, are used alternately and in some contexts exclude each other. This is a consequence of the status conferred on the two types of languages. The European language is usually valued as the language of instruction, administration, literature, and social promotion, whereas the Creole is regarded as the language of the masses, intimacy, tales, and proverbs. The former is considered to be the language of abstraction and philosophy, whereas Creoles are considered languages of the concrete and of everyday life. The obvious inference is that European languages and Creoles would each have their specific spheres, and not be used simultaneously. But the reality is more complex; the coexistence of two languages can lead bilingual Creole speakers to practice *code switching* and *code mixing*. Code switching refers to the shift between the European language (French, Dutch, English, or Spanish) and the Creole language. Code mixing involves the transfer of linguistic elements, such as particular words, from one language to another.

Examples of Creoles in the Caribbean

Since Creole languages emerged in the context of the slave trade, they have always been accorded a lower status than their European counterparts, the languages of the conquerors. Creole languages were largely ignored until the nineteenth century, when linguists such as Hugo Schuchardt began to study them and speculate on their genesis and development. Recently some Creoles have become written languages, thereby attaining a higher status. Some have become the language of instruction in schools.

In the Caribbean, all Creoles are national languages but few are official languages: the Lesser Antillean French Creoles, discussed next, are all national languages, but only Haitian is an official language.

Guadeloupean and Martiniquais Creoles

Lesser Antillean French Creoles are spoken mainly on the Caribbean islands of Guadeloupe, Martinique, DOMINICA, and ST. LUCIA. Lesser Antillean Creole seems to have emerged in Guadeloupe and Martinique in the middle of the seventeenth century, with such contributing elements as French, various African languages, indigenously spoken Carib languages, and possibly other European languages. Currently in Guadeloupe 370,000 people speak Guadeloupean Creole, and in Martinique 390,000 people speak Martiniquais Creole. The different accents and vocabulary notwithstanding, linguists agree that Guadeloupean and Martiniquais are the same language.

Linguists who emphasize the superstratal elements of Creoles believe that Lesser Antillean originated when slaves attempted to speak the French spoken by whites. Between the 1680s and 1848 the settlements formed by early colonization gave way to a full-fledged plantation economy based on slave labor, and during this period African slaves largely came to outnumber Europeans. Scholars have debated whether Lesser Antillean Creole had already crystalized in more or less its current form by then, or whether the masses of African slaves who arrived later changed it. It is also assumed that by the time Lesser Antillean Creole developed, the subsequent groups of slaves tried to speak the Creole spoken by the earlier arrivals.

In 1848 slavery was officially abolished in the French Caribbean colonies, but former slaves continued to work in the SUGAR fields (*see* ABOLITION AND EMANCIPATION IN LATIN AMERICA AND THE CARIBBEAN). At the turn of the century workers from India and China joined their ranks, as did workers from Syria and Lebanon. In 1946 Guadeloupe and Martinique became French overseas departments (or Départements d'Outre-Mer), making them integral parts of France, a status they retain today despite separatist attempts during the 1960s and the 1970s (*see* MARTINIQUE and GUADELOUPE).

As Gadelii has noted, from a linguistic perspective the entire population of Guadeloupe and Martinique today has been "creolized," with the exception of the *métros* (people from France). Lesser Antillean Creole was taken to Dominica and St. Lucia later (as well as to other neighboring islands in the Caribbean "arch") by migrants from Guadeloupe or Martinique. Thus Dominica and St. Lucia have not experienced the emergence of local Creoles.

As far as the status of Lesser Antillean is concerned, the French government has declared Lesser Antillean a "regional language," which gives it the same status as languages such as Occitan, Alsacien, and Breton, the other surviving French regional languages.

Marie-Christine Hazaël-Massieux points out that while instruction in Lesser Antillean has been tried, the attempts have been too timid to initiate a widespread use of Creole in schools. Between 1970 and 1990, Lesser Antillean was "decreolized," that is, evolved in the direction of French and lost some of its distinctive Creole features. The explanation lies in its increasing visibility as a written language. Indeed, there are more and more writings in Guadeloupean Creole, including literary works, poetry, plays, short stories, and novels; reputable newspapers write entire sections in Guadeloupean. As people become accustomed to written Creole, their perceptions of the language change. But what emerges from these changes is a paradox. On the one hand, Lesser Antillean seems robust, with extensive oral and written use. On the other hand, it also seems threatened by French, which is influencing its linguistic features through French television and radio programs. The need to protect the Creole language is apparent, but the costs of this might be high.

Haitian Creole

Some linguists believe that Kwa languages form the main substratum in the genesis of Haitian Creole.

Bambi Schieffelin and Rachelle Doucet note that Haitian Creole is distinguishable from the other French-based Creoles by its high degree of instrumentalization and functionality, meaning that the language is not limited to particular spheres and has gained widespread usage in schools, the media, and public institutions. The government and the elites in Haiti have long claimed to promote Haitian. The 1918 constitution, for example, accorded it equal status with French. But many have complained that this legislation has not been adequately enforced and that Creole speakers are still discriminated against.

Nevertheless, public support has provided the conditions to turn Haitian into a written language. During the last four decades a large body of text was developed in this Creole, including textbooks on reading, mathematics, and elementary sciences, as well as plays, novels, and newsletters. Once it became a written medium, a relatively homogeneous form of Haitian Creole emerged naturally. Although the standardization of the language was based on a "neutral" variety (the dialect of Port-au-Prince), texts show that there are two variants. One variant – which linguists call a basilectal norm – is most commonly used by the rural masses who only speak Creole (or are "unilingual"), while the other – which has been called a mesolectal norm – is used by the media. The difference between the two varieties is most obvious at the level of written Creole. The users of the basilectal norm thus justify using this variety by invoking the communication needs of the rural unilingual masses. According to them, the use of their norm would facilitate access to written Creole by the rural masses and will open to them domains which have so far been reserved to the bilingual French and Creole speakers. With regard to the written form, "decreolization" has been noted to be pervasive throughout a number of texts. Decreolization, or the use of variants of Haitian Creole that are closer to French, manifests itself at many levels, including the syntactic level, and is most notable in administrative texts. In other words, in administrative texts written Haitian Creole is becoming more and more similar to French.

The educational reform launched in 1979 was a turning point in the development of written Haitian. After initiatives for adult literacy, it was the first time that the government produced a mass of texts in Haitian Creole (textbooks for reading, mathematics, and natural sciences). However, the state initiatives were not accompanied by the use of the commonly spoken variant of Creole in the administrative domain, where French is still often used. In addition, administrative texts written in Creole revealed the danger of decreolization when Haitian Creole is used in official settings. For instance, in pronouncing the word meaning "red," the sound /r/ is used instead of /w/ and results in "rouge" instead of the more distinctively Creole-sounding "wouj." The difference between /w/ and /r/ is highly symbolic in the Haitian orthography, as it marks Creole as different from French. When the difference is ignored and /r/ is used instead of /w/, Creole is effectively decreolized and becomes similar to French. This shows some of the conscious or subconscious pressures that are put on bilingual speakers of Creole and French.

Newspapers on the other hand (for instance *Bon Nouvel*) have a tendency to erase linguistic features from texts that are too rural or regional, hence provoking a relative homogeneity of the spelling.

In terms of speaker's attitude, there is a situation at work that linguists call "conflictual diglossia": the privileged master the two languages, Haitian Creole and French, but the unilingual only speak Creole and still value their African heritage as well as the French language inherited from the colonial past. The American occupation that took place between 1915 and 1934 reinforced the allegiance to French. Since the 1930s and the 1940s there have been actions valuing Creole, but these have not undermined the position of the French language.

Papiamentu Creole

Papiamentu is a Spanish-based Creole spoken by native inhabitants of the Leeward Islands of the Netherlands Antilles and of Aruba. A different English-based Creole is the vernacular of more than 80 percent of the population of Statia, Saba, and St. Martin. Papiamentu, however, is spoken by more than 80 percent of the population on the islands of Aruba, Bonaire, and Curaçao.

Hetty Kook and Goretti Narain provide an excellent description of the patterns of language use and the spheres in which Dutch and Papiamentu evolve: Dutch is still the official language on all six islands. However, it has retained the status of a foreign language. Television programs on the Leeward Islands and in Aruba are mostly broadcast in Papiamentu, English, or Spanish. The most popular papers are in Papiamentu, and of the eight newspapers in Curaçao, six are written in Papiamentu and two in Dutch. Most radio stations broadcast in Papiamentu.

Papiamentu is the only Spanish-based Creole in the Caribbean. In daily life the language is used by all social classes and is accorded a relatively high status. The differences in the Papiamentu spoken in the three islands are more striking at the written level: in 1982 Curaçao and Bonaire chose a more phonologically based spelling (built on the phonetic sounds of the words), whereas Aruba chose a more etymologically based spelling (grounded on the historical origins of the words).

At the beginning of the twentieth century Papiamentu was dropped from the school curriculum; in 1987 it was taught again as a subject in primary schools in Curaçao and Bonaire. Since 1979 primary schools in the Leeward Islands are entitled by law to use Papiamentu as the language of instruction in all grades. Most schools, however, still use Dutch as the language of instruction. The rationale is that the children should learn to read and write first in Dutch. Only after they master reading and writing in Dutch are they supposed to be prepared to read and write in Papiamentu. In most kindergartens in Curaçao, teachers speak only Papiamentu to the children and introduce Dutch only through songs and rhymes. But as soon as the children enter primary school, they are expected to speak and understand Dutch. However, Papiamentu is still respected by its speakers, and innovative projects in schools have attempted to give Papiamentu greater visibility and legitimacy.

The Future of Creole Languages

Creole languages in the Caribbean pose a paradox. As they gain status and power by becoming written languages and, in some cases, languages of instruction in schools, they undergo decreolization, meaning that their linguistic features come to approximate more closely those of the European language. Avoiding decreolization would mean adopting strict policies involving the precise description of the language, the production of textbooks, the organization of teacher training, and the publication of books in Creole to teach a variety of subject matters such as geography and history. Although some feel that the survival of Caribbean Creoles may be threatened by the coexisting European languages (French in particular), the history of languages provides reasons for optimism. Indeed, the French language itself was not a widespread or highly esteemed language before the eighteenth century; before the French Revolution, Latin was the language of prestige. It took very conscious and deliberate efforts on the part of the French government to give the French language the status it has gained today. The same could be done for the Caribbean Creoles with the support of the governments in the areas where they are spoken.

Marlyse Baptista

See Also

Netherlands Antilles; Slavery in Latin America and the Caribbean; St. Kitts and Nevis; Haiti; Port-au-Prince, Haiti.

North America

Larsen, Nella (b. April 13, 1891, Chicago, Ill.; d. March 30, 1964, New York, N.Y.), African American novelist of the Harlem Renaissance; landmark figure in the black women's literary tradition.

Nella Larsen's celebrity has followed an unusual trajectory. She was one of the most celebrated black novelists during the Harlem Renaissance and received several major awards for her writing, including the first Guggenheim Fellowship ever given to a black woman. She and her husband were also notable members of the Harlem social scene, and she was friends with most of the prominent Harlem writers of her time. After a public accusation of plagiarism and an equally public divorce, Larsen removed herself from the public eye and was effectively forgotten by acquaintances and audiences until after her death. But renewed interest in both the Harlem Renaissance and black women writers has brought her back to prominence, and Larsen is again celebrated as a key figure in the African American literary tradition.

Larsen was born Nellie Walker to a Danish mother and a West Indian father in Chicago. After her father's death when she was two, her mother married a Danish man and had a second daughter, making Larsen the only black member of her family. As a result, she always felt estranged from them, and in 1909 she left home to attend FISK UNIVERSITY. A year later she traveled to Denmark and spent the next two years living with relatives and studying at the University of Copenhagen. Larsen next studied nursing in New York, and in 1916 she returned south to Tuskegee Institute to become assistant superintendent of nurses there. But while she had come to feel most comfortable in all-black environments, she was still unhappy in the South, and in 1916 she returned to New York.

Larsen worked as a nurse and a children's librarian in New York over the next ten years. In 1919 she married Dr. Elmer Imes, a prominent physicist, and her marriage brought her into contact with the upper classes of New York's black society, including many of the writers who were already active in Harlem. She published her first two essays, both on Danish children's games, in 1920 in *The Brownies' Book,* a children's magazine that was an offshoot of the *Crisis,* the monthly magazine of the NATIONAL ASSOCIATION FOR THE ADVANCEMENT OF COLORED PEOPLE (NAACP). Encouraged by writers and artists around her, especially black writer Walter White and white patron Carl Van Vechten, in 1926 she began writing full-time.

Larsen's two novels, *Quicksand* and *Passing,* were published by the mainstream publisher Alfred A. Knopf in 1928 and 1929. Both novels deal with upper-class, mixed-race black women protagonists, reflecting the world Larsen found herself in, but they go beyond simply painting that world. Instead, they are complicated explorations of the ways in which race, gender, class, and sexuality all constrict the women's lives to varying degrees. In *Quicksand* the main character is a biracial Danish and black woman, like Larsen, who finds that she is not entirely at home in either Danish or African American society but who cannot find an alternative. And in *Passing,* the protagonists are two childhood friends who meet as adults and find that while one has settled into a safe life in the black bourgeoisie, the other has chosen to pass as white. That novel's tensions rise as the women find themselves drawn to one another yet jealous of one another's lives.

Quicksand and *Passing* were both well received. Larsen was awarded the Harmon Foundation's Bronze Medal for Literature in 1929 and the Guggenheim Fellowship in 1930, which she used to travel to SPAIN and FRANCE to research a third novel. But the charge of plagiarism came that same year, over the short story "Sanctuary" that Larsen had published in January 1930 in the prominent mainstream journal the *Forum.* Larsen's publisher supported her assertion that any resemblance between the plot of her story and one published in another magazine several years earlier was purely coincidental, as is probably true. But the damage still hurt Larsen's reputation and her confidence.

This was followed by the humiliation of her 1933 divorce, which stemmed from her husband's alleged affair with a white woman. Newspapers covering the story accused Larsen of being too preoccupied with her writing to be a good wife, and claimed that she had tried to commit suicide over the affair. While Larsen did not literally kill herself, she did close herself off from all contact with her former life. Spreading a rumor that she was moving to South America, she moved instead to New York's Lower East Side, where she lived alone and worked quietly as a nurse for the next 30 years. She was found dead in her apartment in 1964.

Despite the obscurity of the end of her life, Larsen's reputation and writings have been resurrected. Contemporary critics now regard her as one of the most sophisticated and modern novelists to emerge from the Harlem Renaissance, and her two books are regarded as landmark examples of black women's attempts to explain their complex identities – and the complicated forces circumscribing them – in fiction.

Lisa Clayton Robinson

SEE ALSO

Literature, African American; Women Writers, Black, in the United States; Chicago, Illinois; *Crisis, The*; Harlem, New York; New York, New York; Tuskegee University; White, Walter Francis.

Latin America and the Caribbean

Las Casas, Bartolomé de

(b. 1484, Seville, Spain; d. July 18, 1566, Madrid, Spain), Spanish bishop of the Dominican Order; recognized as one of the most significant chroniclers of the Spanish Conquest, he is famous for his defense of Amerindians and his initial promotion of African slavery. He is also read as a theologian, jurist, ethnographer, humanist, historian, politician, prophet, and biographer.

Bartolomé de Las Casas is a controversial figure whose prolific and complex writings continue to raise questions after five centuries of study and debate. Though known as the most unrelenting advocate of Amerindian interests before the Spanish Crown, he endorsed the colonial system and played a role in the slave trade. Throughout his life he denounced the violence and abuse that were inherent in Spanish policies toward Amerindians while he proposed more benevolent forms of colonization. As a strategic reformist, and in the hope of saving indigenous lives, he initially advocated that imported African slaves be used in place of Amerindian forced laborers. However, toward the end of his life Las Casas regretted his promotion of black slavery and was deeply troubled for having condoned *any* form of human bondage. Ironically, through his repentance, he became the first colonist of the sixteenth century to denounce the injustice of African slavery (*see* COLONIAL CRITICS OF SLAVERY).

Spanish chronicler and critic of the Spanish conquest, Bartolomé de Las Casas defended the exploited indigenous people from the Americas and endorsed the trade of African slaves. *Oronoz*

Bartolomé's father, Pedro Las Casas, was a colonist who traveled to the New World with Christopher Columbus and on one of his trips brought back an Indian slave as a gift for his son. In 1502 Las Casas sailed to Hispaniola to join his father and help him manage his land and business endeavors. In 1507 he returned to SPAIN, where he earned a law degree from the University of Salamanca and was ordained a priest in Rome. In 1510 he ventured back to CUBA, where the Spanish Crown rewarded him with an *encomienda,* a land grant that included the Indians who lived on the property. However, in 1514, after observing the suffering and deaths of thousands of Indians, he went through a profound spiritual transformation. Las Casas then gave up his encomienda and began to denounce the system of forced Indian labor.

In 1516, in a letter known as the *Memorial de Remedios,* Las Casas petitioned the Spanish king to send African slaves to the Americas to begin replacing the Indian laborers owned by the *encomenderos.* As a young man in Seville, Las Casas had known African people only under slavery and did not question the institution as understood in the political and economic context of the times. African slaves had been taken to the Spanish Antilles since the arrival of Christopher Columbus and were later requested by the Crown as a supposedly physically stronger and more trustworthy source of labor. For Las Casas, importing those who were already legitimate slaves in Spain meant the possibility of saving the lives and dignity of indigenous people in the Americas, who, he argued, were naturally free.

Las Casas's intended remedy backfired. As the prosperity of the islands grew and the need for labor increased, Indians were not freed from the encomienda system, and the importation of African slaves grew enormously through contraband and extended official licenses. Although Las Casas had acknowledged the failure of his proposal, in 1531 he was still requesting slaves to be imported for the benefit of the poor Spanish colonists. He managed to continue ignoring the moral question of black slavery until 1546, when he returned to Spain.

In his native Seville, during the process of rewriting his *Historia de las Indias,* Las Casas had access to previously uncirculated writings on the history of the Portuguese slave trade. He was shocked as he read and comprehended the parallels between Spanish Indian servitude and the commerce of African slaves. Before his death in 1566, Las Casas added several chapters to his work, declaring that although it was too late to rectify his own mistakes, he had awakened from his previous blindness. He hoped to alert others to an understanding of the injustice of slavery and urged a similar repentance.

Liliana Obregón

See Also

Transatlantic Slave Trade; Slavery in Latin America and the Caribbean; American Indians.

North America

Last Poets, The, American musical group whose style was a precursor to rap music.

Despite their name, many critics have argued that the Last Poets' innovative style made them the first RAP group. The Last Poets grew out of the BLACK ARTS MOVEMENT, a wave of socially and politically aware African American literature and art in the 1960s. Gylan Kain, Abiodun Oyewole, David Nelson, and conga player Nilija formed the Last Poets at a Harlem memorial gathering for MALCOLM X in May 1968. From the beginning their lyrics represented the type of radical poetry that flourished during the Black Arts Movement, and their music emphasized both the spoken word and African-inspired drumming. Author Darius James remembered the original Last Poets recordings this way: "The rhetoric made you mad. The drums made you pop your fingers. And the poetry made you sail.... Most importantly, they made you think and kept you 'correct' on a revolutionary level."

Disagreement in the early 1970s led to a split into two separate groups who both continued to use the Last Poets name, and confusion and disagreement over the two groups of Last Poets continued into the 1990s. But after adding new members, both groups continued to tour and record albums with the same musical structure and militant messages as the original Last Poets, arguing against racial oppression and in favor of BLACK POWER and social justice.

In the mid-1980s the Last Poets reached a new audience when younger rap musicians they had influenced began sampling, or quoting in their own music, pieces of the Last Poets' songs. The original Last Poets lineup reunited for a 1990 tour, and several new Last Poets albums were released in the 1990s.

Lisa Clayton Robinson

See Also

Harlem, New York.

North America

Latimer, Lewis Howard

(b. September 4, 1848, Chelsea, Mass.; d. December 11, 1928, Flushing, N.Y.), African American inventor and innovator in the electric lighting industry.

Lewis H. Latimer's father was an escaped slave from Virginia whom FREDERICK DOUGLASS and William Lloyd Garrison defended when his former owner tried to have him extradited. As a boy Latimer worked in his father's barbershop and peddled Garrison's newspaper, the *Liberator*.

Latimer joined the Union Navy during the Civil War, serving on the U.S.S. *Massasoit*

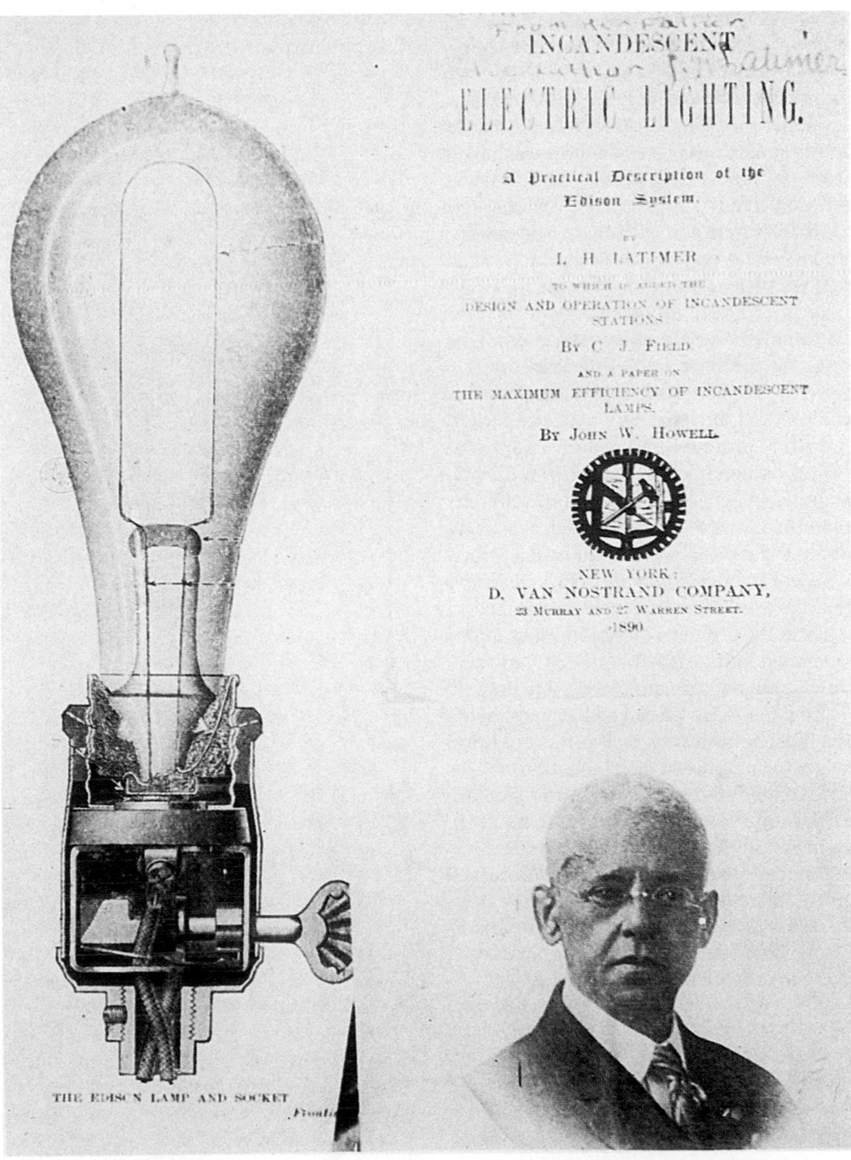

Inventor Lewis Howard Latimer's *Incandescent Electric Lighting* (1896) was one of the first textbooks published on electric lighting. *Photographs and Prints Division, Schomburg Center for Research in Black Culture, The New York Public Library, Astor, Lenox and Tilden Foundation*

on the James River in Virginia. After an honorable discharge in 1865, he found work with Crosby & Gould, a firm of patent lawyers. Although Latimer was hired as an office boy, he cultivated drafting skills in his spare time until he was qualified for blueprint work. In addition to drawing plans for other people's inventions, Latimer brainstormed his own, patenting in 1874 a "pivot bottom" for water closets on trains. His high-caliber draftsmanship impressed Alexander Graham Bell, whose 1876 telephone blueprints were drawn up by Latimer.

In 1880 Latimer left Crosby & Gould to work for the inventor Hiram Maxim, who ran the United States Electric Lighting Company in Bridgeport, Connecticut. The previous year Thomas A. Edison had invented the light bulb, and Maxim was one of Edison's prime competitors in the institutionalization of electric light. Under Maxim, Latimer supervised the installation of electric light in New York, Philadelphia, London, and Montreal. He also developed other inventions of his own, copatenting an electric lamp with Joseph V. Nichols in 1881, and, most important, refining light-bulb technology in 1882. Although Edison had invented electric light, Latimer made it more economically feasible by developing longer- and brighter-burning filaments, specifically ones derived from bamboo slivers and the cellulose of cotton thread.

In 1884 Latimer left Maxim, possibly due to racial discrimination, and worked for two other companies before joining Edison Electric Light (later General Electric). Latimer first served Edison as an engineer but eventually became Edison's expert witness in patent dispute lawsuits. His association with the legal side of the electricity industry continued in the early twentieth century, when he worked for the law firm of Hammer & Schwartz in New York. Latimer remained involved in the technical aspects of the industry, however, publishing *Incandescent Electric Lighting* in 1896, a definitive textbook on Edison's developments.

Latimer settled in Flushing, New York, a Queens neighborhood, at the end of the nineteenth century and lived there until his death in 1928. He was an active member of the local community, delivering a petition against school-board discrimination to New York mayor Seth Low in 1902 and teaching English and drafting to immigrants at the Henry Street Settlement in 1906. He also composed poetry and painted portraits. In 1918 Latimer helped form the Edison Pioneers, an honorary group of engineers who had worked for Edison, among whom Latimer was the only African American.

Eric Bennett

See Also

Civil War, American; *Liberator*, The; New York, New York; Philadelphia, Pennsylvania.

Latin America and the Caribbean

Latin America, Blacks and Indians in: An Interpretation

Peter Wade

The study of blacks and Indians in Latin America has, to a great extent, been divided into, on the one hand, studies of slavery, slavery-related issues, and "race relations" and, on the other, studies of Indians. Colonial historiography has brought the two together to some extent in synthetic overviews, but the divide is a deep-seated one. This essay explores why this divide exists. I argue that the roots of the split go back to the fifteenth century and have spread right through the colonial period, the republican period of nation building, and into the scholarship and politics of the twentieth century. I will also argue that such a division is not, ultimately, very helpful and only hides interesting contrasts and similarities between blacks and Indians in Latin America.

Africans and Indians in Colonial Latin America

When the Spanish and Portuguese arrived in the New World, Africans were a well-known category of person. Some of this derived from classical texts, religious sources, and travelers' tales; some of it derived from direct contact with Africa, by virtue of voyages of exploration down the West African coast from the 1430s, which had resulted in African slaves entering Lisbon from the 1440s. By 1552, 10 percent of the population of Lisbon was slave. In addition, the primary experience of the Iberian people (and other Europeans) with Africans was that of the Moors, both during the Crusades in the Holy Land and as a result of the Moorish occupation of the Iberian Peninsula, from which they were only finally expelled in 1492, after almost 800 years of continuous presence. Christianity had existed in Ethiopia since the second century, and African Christians had fought alongside Europeans in the Holy Wars: in medieval Europe cults formed around particular Ethiopian figures. Part of the motive for Portuguese explorations in Africa was the search for the legendary Christian kingdom of Prester John, and Bakongo kings in what is now Angola converted to Christianity as early as 1491. However, because of the long-standing Muslim presence in many areas of Africa – mainly those between the Saharan and sub-Saharan zones – the region as a whole tended to be seen as infidel territory and during the fifteenth century this status was reaffirmed in several papal bulls.

In contrast, the indigenous inhabitants of the Americas were a conundrum. There was a good deal of uncertainty about their status, whether they had the use of reason, whether they were real humans, whether they were brutal savages or, alternatively, represented some version of human existence before the biblical "Fall." Images in colonial discourse are rarely one-sided and with respect to Africans there was ambivalence – infidel or pagan versus Christian, slaves versus trading partners – but this was particularly evident with respect to native Americans. The dual image of the noble and the ignoble savage that was to flower in the eighteenth century was already captured in the constant representation of Indians as cannibals alongside the image of them as innocent beings.

Some of this ambivalence and the difference between Africans and native Americans is evident in the issue of slavery (*see* Slavery in Latin America and the Caribbean). At the time of European contact with Africans and Indians, slavery was considered a normal, if usually temporary, status. There was justification in the Bible and in Aristotelian philosophy for enslavement of the captives of a "just war" (such as one against infidels); Christians and Moors had enslaved each other, and slaves from the Balkans and the Black Sea area were being used in sugar plantations in Cyprus and Sicily. The conquistadors were keen on enslaving Indians in the New World, and they received some backing from the regal authorities. Indians could be legitimately enslaved if they were classed as cannibals or Caribs (from which the word "cannibal" derives) – which in the Caribbean context simply meant those who resisted Spanish rule. One reaction among Spanish thinkers and theologians was to label the Indians as "natural slaves," a category deriving from Aristotelian thought and designating a person incapable of autonomy. But there was little agreement on all this, and others in the clergy questioned whether a war could ever be "just" when waged against those who had never known Christianity and who had been defined as vassals of the Crown in Crown territory. The terrible brutality of the conquistadors and the manifest decline of the Indian population added strength to these arguments, as did contact with the Aztecs and the Incas, whose cities and rule of law were signs of "rationality." This was the substance of the famous 1550-1551 debates between Bartolomé de Las Casas and Juan Ginés de Sepúlveda; but already by 1542, slavery of Indians had been outlawed in Spanish colonies. Portugal followed suit in Brazil in 1570. Such legislation was often ineffective in rooting out slavery, which continued in many peripheral areas and especially in Brazil, where Indian slaves fed the northeastern sugar plantations (*see* Slave Laws in Colonial Spanish America).

For Africans and their descendants, in contrast, there was little questioning of the propriety of enslavement. There was legal provision for manumission (individual freedom), reflecting the concept of slavery as a temporary condition, and a good number of slaves became free through this means – mostly by self-purchase after years of saving. But it was not until slavery as an institution was challenged and dismantled during the early nineteenth century that black people as a category began to be freed in the Americas. During the early period of the slave trade Africa was infidel territory and the Portuguese had papal authority to wage a "just war" there; slavery was legitimated as a positive good for infidel Africans; and much of the enslaving was done by Africans themselves, thus masking the question of its legitimacy. Once the slave trade was well under way and the mines and plantations of the colonies so dependent on it, there was little incentive to question such a central institution.

Indians and Africans thus had different locations in the colonial order, both socially and conceptually. Indians were, officially, to be protected as well as exploited; Africans were slaves and, although they had rights enshrined in legislation, this was piecemeal and uneven – although the Spanish did produce a legal code in 1789 – and the main concern was with control rather than protection. This difference continued through the colonial period. Ideally, the Spanish would have liked to have maintained three separate categories: Spanish, Indians, and Africans; rulers, tributaries, and slaves. Indeed, the authorities talked of the *república de españoles* and the *república de indios*, the latter based on the Indian community, created and constrained by legislation. Such an ideal was undermined from the start by the possibility of slave manumission, which created the beginnings of a class of free blacks. It was also weakened by the fact that Spaniards' American-born offspring were no longer simply Spaniards, but *criollos* (Creoles). In addition, from early on, Indians moved into urban areas and Spaniards usurped Indian land, while some Indians became direct dependents of the developing rural *hacienda* (or plantation): both processes weakened the link of the Indians to the communities that, in great part, defined their identity as Indians.

Most of all, the ideal of separation was undermined by *mestizaje*, or mixture. The main meaning of this term is sexual mixture, but implied is the spatial mixture of peoples and the interchange of cultural elements, resulting in mixed and new cultural forms. Spaniards, Creoles, Indians, free blacks, and slaves interbred – destitute Spaniards with free black women, Indian princesses with aristocratic Spaniards, runaway slaves with Indian women, Spanish masters with slave women, free blacks with Indians and Creoles – and their offspring were recognized as mixed people of various kinds (*see* COMPLEXITIES OF ETHNIC AND RACIAL TERMINOLOGY IN LATIN AMERICA AND THE CARIBBEAN). Terminology was variable and dozens of labels existed, but *mulatto* was the term often used for someone of supposedly black-white mixture, *zambo* for black-Indian mixture, and *mestizo* for Indian-white mixture. Not all mestizos were "mixed," however, since an Indian who disavowed his or her origins could attempt to "pass" into this category. All these actually or nominally mixed people, in their turn, interbred with others. Some mulattos were slaves, but most mixed people were free and in many areas they soon outnumbered Spaniards, Creoles, Indians, and slaves.

Despite this proliferating mixture, the Spanish attempted to maintain categorical distinctions for whites and between Indians and the rest. *Indio* was a specific administrative category – in many ways a fiscal category, since the typical Indian was one who lived in an Indian community and paid tribute in labor or goods. It was also a census category, since it was important to enumerate Indians as a working and tributary population. In BRAZIL, where there was less in the way of a dense, sedentary Indian population that could be easily exploited through existing systems of political stratification, authorities were less concerned with maintaining strict barriers, but Indians still had a specific administrative status. In short, Indian was an institutionalized identity.

There was nothing comparable for blacks. The status of slave, of course, was very specifically defined and slave was a central census category. But many blacks were free and they fit into much vaguer categories that lumped together everyone who was not either white, Indian, or slave. Thus in New Granada (the basis of today's COLOMBIA), the residual census category was simply *libre* (free person), which included mestizos, zambos, freed blacks, and mulattos, and sometimes Indians who had evaded their formal Indian identity by leaving their communities. In Brazil, the middle category was free people, which, again, included a broad mixture of people. In CUBA, reference was usually made to *pardos* (literally, light browns), and sometimes also to *morenos* (dark browns). In MEXICO, while some local censuses used detailed categories such as mestizo, free mulatto, and free black, others simply classed all the racially mixed population as *casta*.

This system of socioracial stratification is often termed the *sociedad de castas*, after the term *castas* (breeds, castes), which was applied variously to the middle strata or everyone below the top strata. The term is not used for Brazil and there is evidence that the situation there was more fluid but basically similar. In this society, whites were at the top, Indians and blacks at the bottom, and positions in the middle were defined by various criteria of status, among which color and descent were important without being definitive. Thus occupation could influence one's "racial" classification in a census, as could the position of one's spouse – although the term *racial* might not be used, being signified, in Mexico for example, by the term *calidad*, or quality. People jockeyed for position, and transatlantic litigation might take place if someone who claimed to be white felt he had been insulted by being called a mestizo.

There has been debate about how open this system was in the Spanish colonies and, in particular, how important "race" was in defining position within it. John Chance and Magnus Mörner see a relatively open society in which race had a declining role to play as mestizaje made racial identifications more indeterminate. Jaime Jaramillo Uribe, Patrick Carroll, and Robert McCaa give a greater role to people's ideas about racial ancestry and identity. For Brazil, A.G.R. Russell-Wood talks of the emergence of a "meritocracy" during the eighteenth century, but admits that "the free colored had to fight to overcome… discrimination and prejudice," while James Lockhart and Stuart Schwartz say that in this period the merchant-planter elite saw the mixed middle strata as a threat in a social order in which "definitions of social conflict were often perceived in terms of color rather than economic class." It would appear that there is no single answer and that a lot depended on local factors, but it seems clear that ambiguity and room for maneuver were greatest in the middle ranges; for those at the bottom of the pile, labeled Indian and black (or worse, slave), there was less flexibility.

The point is that within this system, Indians had a relatively institutionalized position, whereas blacks did not: some were in the category of slave, others in that vague middle category of castes, pardos, or libres. It also seems that although both sets of people suffered great hardship in practical terms, Indians were seen in some sense as superior to blacks. This is evident from marriage regulations that allowed whites to marry Indians while restricting unions with blacks and mulattos. The authorities set out regulations in 1778 that forced whites under 25 years of age to seek parental approval of their marriage, thus impeding unions thought to be unsuitable. But intermarriage with Indians was not restricted, since "their origin is not vile like that of other castas." The Mexican Audiencia, or royal court, reviewing these regulations, commented on marriage between Indians and blacks or mulattos, recommending that parish priests be ordered to warn the Indian and his parents of the serious harm that "such unions will cause to themselves and their families and villages, besides making the descendants incapable of obtaining municipal positions of honor in which only pure Indians are allowed to serve."

In sum, then, Indians and blacks had different relationships to the official structures of bureaucracy. Since the relationship between law and social order is notoriously difficult to establish, it would be dangerous to argue that this difference translated directly into an identical difference in popular colonial perceptions of blacks and Indians, or in conditions of material welfare. Indeed, Indians were often treated extremely badly. But the laws themselves, especially those of the late colonial period, were in part a reflection of white elite concerns, and it is clear that the category Indian, for example, was not simply a legal fiction, but an everyday reality, reconstituted through daily practice.

Blacks and Indians in the New Republics

With independence the former Spanish colonies began to dismantle the administrative trappings of empire, although Brazil gained independence as an empire in its own right until it became a republic in 1891, while Puerto Rico and Cuba remained colonies of Spain until 1898. Under the pervasive influence of European liberalism, the status of Indian and, more particularly, Indian land came under attack. There were widespread moves to disestablish Indian communities and undermine the existence of a separate category of people who had a legal position distinct from that of simple citizens. These were frequently ineffective and in the Andes, as Olivia Harris argues, "there were strong local vested interests in maintaining a distinctive category of Indians." Legal discriminations against mixed bloods were gradually removed and by 1854 slavery was abolished in the new republics; it was retained in Brazil until 1888, in Puerto Rico until 1873, and in Cuba until 1886. However, ideas about race and about categories of people called Indians, blacks, or mestizos were by no means removed from the national panorama. Again, there was a distinct difference between the images of blacks and Indians in debates about the identity of the new nations – or empire in the case of Brazil.

Ideas about race (*see* Race in Latin America) were crucial elements in discussions about national identity in a world where European and North American nationalism already dominated the stage. Latin American elites wanted to emulate the modernity and progress of these nations and accepted in broad terms the tenets of liberalism, which saw in science, technology, reason, education, and freedom of the individual the underlying forces of progress. But these modern and progressive nations either had no significant black or Indian populations, or, in the case of the United States, kept them strictly segregated. In contrast, most Latin American countries had substantial numbers of mestizos, blacks, and Indians. Worse still, by the late nineteenth century the theories of human biology accepted in Western scientific racism relegated blacks and Indians to a permanently inferior status and condemned mixed-bloods as degenerate.

Latin American elites tried to deal with this contradiction by adapting Western theories of human difference and heredity (*see* Race: An Interpretation). The racial determinism of European theories was often avoided and emphasis placed instead on the possibility of improving the population through programs of "social hygiene," improving health and living conditions. Lamarckian theories about the hereditability of characteristics acquired during a single lifetime were popular, since these held out the hope of lasting improvement of "the race." The idea of the degeneracy of the mestizo was contested, and indeed in nations such as Colombia and Mexico, mixedness became a symbol of a distinctive Latin American identity, free from the slavish emulation of European or North American masters.

On the other hand, the type of mixedness invoked was often itself biased toward whiteness: European immigration was often encouraged or even sponsored by the state, and, more generally, the process of mixing could be seen as a progressive whitening of the population. Mixture would supposedly bring about the elimination of blacks and Indians and the creation of a mixed society that was at the distinctly whiter end of the spectrum. Such a vision was almost magical, since every instance of race mixture must logically be a darkening as well as a whitening. But the vision was sustained, on the one hand, by eugenic notions that white "blood" was stronger than other types and would naturally dominate in the mixture and, on the other, by immigration policies that tried to restrict the entry of blacks. These ideas and processes were common, in varying ways, to Brazil, Venezuela, Cuba, Argentina, and Colombia, among others.

In the attempt to delineate a distinctive national identity, reference could be made (or could not be avoided) to the historical roots of the nation. From the 1920s the Indian became a prime symbol of national identity in countries such as Mexico and Peru. Both countries created government departments for indigenous affairs; Peru recognized the "indigenous community" as a legal entity and Mexico created academic institutes dedicated to the study of indigenous peoples. In Brazil an agency was set up in 1910 for the "protection of the Indians." This, in broad terms, was the ideology of *indigenismo*. This term covers a variety of perspectives, but the central notion was that Indians needed special recognition and that special values attached to them. Very often it was a question of exotic and romantic symbolism, based more on the glorification of the pre-Columbian Indian ancestry of the nation than on respect for contemporary Indian populations. Thus the reality was often one of continued discrimination and exploitation. In addition, the future was generally seen as being integrated and mestizo in color.

Manuel Gamio, for example, who became director of the Instituto Indígena Interamericano in Mexico, undertook archaeological investigations of Teotihuacán and also began studies of contemporary Indian communities. At the same time his overall perspective was integrationist and conformed to the typical ideas of nation building based on education and incorporation. For Mexico, according to Alan Knight, "postrevolutionary indigenismo... represented yet another non-Indian formulation of the 'Indian problem'; it was another white/mestizo construct... part of a long tradition stretching back to the Conquest." In Brazil, as well, Antonio Carlos de Souza Lima states that "every indigenist project aimed to solve the problem of transforming the Indian from... 'savagery' to the superior stage of 'civilization.'" On the other hand, some *indigenistas* adopted much less integrationist positions. Peruvians José Carlos Mariátegui and Víctor Raúl Haya de la Torre, for example, took a more radical line, wedding socialism and indigenismo, and modeling the future nation on the supposedly socialist aspects of ancient Andean Indian culture. Such a view responded in part to the fact that a dense Indian population still lived in the Andes. Whatever the variety, however, the point remains that Indians were often seen as a special category, needing the specific attention of intellectuals, the state, and the church.

Blacks were much less likely to be symbolized in this way and were rarely held up as the symbols of a glorious heritage. Only in Cuba and Brazil, with their very large black populations, was there a positive revaluation of blackness in some quarters, although, again, this tended to be integrationist in tone, with the emphasis on the emergence of a mixed society in which a black input was valued as long as it was under control. Even then, the trend was mainly literary, with little discernible impact on government policy.

In Cuba during the 1920s and 1930s, there was a trend of Afrocubanismo in literary circles with authors such as Alejo Carpentier and Nicolás Guillén leading the way. Jean Franco argues that this was inspired by the European avant-garde view of primitivism as an alternative to scientific rationality. Afro-Cuban music was also making an impact within the country and internationally. Even though there were strong elements in these trends of the appropriation by whites of exotic aspects of black culture – blacks were an infrequent sight in the dance orchestras that played Afro-Cuban music – it was nevertheless a departure from the image of blacks as simply backward and inferior.

In Brazil, musicologist Mário de Andrade also accepted African musical elements as a valuable part of a mixed Brazilian national music, but it was Gilberto Freyre who really attempted to produce a vision of Brazil that went beyond the dilemmas created by scientific racism, which had branded the country as racially hybrid and therefore inferior. Policies of whitening through immigration still existed, but by Freyre's time, scientific racism was on the wane – in any case, some Brazilian thinkers had tried to avoid the most determinist versions of it. Freyre's aim was to redefine the Brazilian nation as mixed – and proud of it. Even so, his view was highly assimilationist. In his book *Brazil: An Interpretation,* for example, he stated: "Brazil stands today as a community from whose experiment in miscegenation other communities may profit. Probably in no other complex modern community are problems of race relations being solved in a more democratic or Christian way than in Portuguese America. And Brazil's experiment does not indicate that miscegenation leads to degeneration."

This declared Brazil actually to have benefited from race mixture, since this had solved problems of race relations. He also said that Brazilians generally feel that "nothing is sincerely or honestly Brazilian that denies or hides the influence of the Amerindian and the Negro": authentic Brazilian identity was therefore mixed. On the other hand, he declared, "Negroes are now rapidly disappearing in Brazil, merging into the white stock." And although "Brazil still has to face the problem of assimilating certain Amerindian tribes as well as those groups of Negroes whose culture remains largely African," this was not a major problem, since "the general tendency among broad-minded Brazilians [he admits that not all of them are] is to maintain, towards Africans as well as Indians, a policy of slow and intelligent assimilation, in which the assimilating group may incorporate into its culture certain values of general interest or artistic importance."

Some of this – not all – was very optimistic, indeed naive, when applied to the realities of Brazilian social structure and culture. But it was an attempt to redefine Brazilian identity as something other than a slavish copy of Euro-American nations and yet still "complex [and] modern"; it is, in effect, a redefinition of modernity away from whiteness toward hybridity – a move that prefigures more postmodern discussions and that also welcomes Latin America's hybrid nature.

The central point, however, is that the sort of redefinition of national identity attempted by some Cuban and Brazilian intellectuals and scholars was, in the Latin American context, limited in the way it dealt with blacks, as compared to Indians. Most important, perhaps, these attempts were at the level of image, representation, and literary and musical productions; they rarely involved state policy. Indigenista approaches generally did involve policy, thus continuing the tradition of reifying Indians as an object of official attention.

Blacks and Indians in Politics and Social Science

The different location of blacks and Indians in the political and imagined space of the nation has not received much attention from scholars, but it seems of great importance to discuss here. It has had significant political consequences and has also affected the way each category has become an object of study in academia. Colombia is a good example of this difference and its consequences. Indians in Colombia have suffered terrible discrimination and abuse and still suffer today. Yet legally and conceptually they have a special position. Legislation in 1890 reaffirmed the existence of Indian *resguardos* (reserves) and Indian councils to govern them. In 1941 the state created an institute of ethnology whose main purpose was to study Indian society and history. Since the beginnings of its academic institutionalization in the country in the 1940s, most anthropological work has focused on Indians. The premier Gold Museum in Bogotá focuses exclusively on pre-Columbian Indians, even though there were important gold-working traditions in the regions of Africa whence came a good part of the population of the country. Indian mobilization to fight for land and rights has been a significant force since the 1960s and important concessions – on paper at least – have been won. Legally, Indians, who form about 2 percent of the nation's population, now own about 22 percent of Colombia's territory in the form of reserves – although practical enforcement of that ownership is a different matter. In the 1991 constitutional reform, Indian groups won important rights, including the right to two seats in the Senate.

Blacks, in contrast, have, according to Nina de Friedemann, been made "invisible" in the nation – systematically ignored, marginalized, and belittled. I would argue that things are not quite so straightforward, in the sense that commentators on Colombian national identity have, for over a hundred years, always recognized the existence of blacks; but it is true that this has often only been to disparage them or caricature them in some way. It is certainly true that academically they have hardly been studied – not constituting the cultural "Otherness" that anthropology has sought among Indians – and that politically they have simply been seen as ordinary citizens, even while in practice they suffer racial discrimination. Black political mobilization has been much weaker than that of Indians, and in the 1991 constitutional reform, black groups fared much worse in terms of extracting concessions on land rights and cultural recognition – although in both respects they did make groundbreaking steps in the direction of being constituted as a specific cultural, political, and conceptual category within the nation.

This contrast, in my view, has its roots in the history I have outlined above and the result in academic terms has been the general separation of studies of blacks from those of Indians – with some notable exceptions such as Norman Whitten and Michael Taussig – and the relative neglect of blacks – with the main exception of Brazil where, even so, Indians have been the domain of anthropology, while blacks have generally been studied by sociologists. In the face of this, one tendency is to focus on blacks, bemoaning their neglect in academic circles compared to studies of Indians and seeking to redress it: this highlights the differences between "black" and "Indian" as categories. Another tendency is to see blacks and Indians as rather similar: both are seen as minorities in nation-states intent on a future of homogeneity; both are at the bottom of a ladder that represented parallel hierarchies of wealth, education, civilization, and race; both are inputs into the progressive, modernizing process of whitening the nation.

Neither perspective is wholly right or wrong. The point is to bring blacks and Indians into the same overall theoretical perspective, especially in the context of the Latin American nation, while also recognizing the historical, political, and conceptual differences that do exist between these categories. Blacks and Indians have both been characterized as Others, located in the spaces between, or liminal to, the nation, but they have fit in different ways into what I call the "structures of alterity" (or structures of difference). The apparent "invisibility" of black people in Colombia, for example, has not been due to a simple process of discrimination – Indians have, if anything, suffered even greater discrimination – but due to the precise mode of their insertion into the structures of alterity. They have not been institutionalized as Others in the same way that Indians have. Interestingly, however, there has been a relatively recent appearance of blacks on the public political stage in Colombia, Brazil, and Nicaragua, where constitutional measures recognize the special status of blacks in general or particular groups of blacks. In some sense, this corresponds to a relocation of "blackness" in structures of alterity in ways that make it look increasingly like "Indianness."

Blacks and Indians, Race and Ethnicity

Another way that the split between blacks and Indians has been introduced into social science is with the virtually unquestioned assumption that the study of blacks is one of racism and race relations, while the study of Indians is that of ethnicity and ethnic relations. The principal idea underlying this is that the category "Indian" does not depend on phenotypical signifiers, or observable physical characteristics. As mentioned above, during the colonial period, the identity "Indian" depended partly on being located in an Indian community; leaving that community, which might also involve leaving aside typically "Indian" clothing and language, was a step on the path to becoming a "mestizo." Studies in the twentieth century have reinforced this notion: "Indian" is a category defined by cultural signifiers (clothing, language, place of residence, etc.), and the boundary between Indian and mestizo is potentially crossable by manipulating those signifiers. In contrast, "black" is often seen as a category defined by more fixed phenotypical criteria that cannot be manipulated in the same way. In other words, one can presumably alter the language one speaks or where one lives, but not the color of one's skin.

There are two sets of problems here. The first is that it is wrong, in my view, to see Indians simply as an ethnic group or set of ethnic groups. The category "Indian" was an integral part of the colonial encounters within which the discourse of race emerged and, for example, the debates about the fate of the nation that took place in Colombia in the late nineteenth and early twentieth centuries talked in similar terms about the supposed failings of "Indian blood" and "black blood." From a macrohistorical perspective, then, "Indian" was a racial category and retains strong elements of this history.

The other set of problems relates to the microscale. There is no doubt that, on an individual level, "Indians" can become "mestizos"; it is also true, however, that "blacks" can become "mulattos." It is mistaken to assume that, just because racial signifiers are bodily, they are completely fixed. Part of this assumption comes from the classic United States case where racial identification has been very rigid and an attempt has been made to create very tightly bounded categories of black and white. Even there, "passing" occurs, so that an individual who is classed as black in some circumstances "passes" for white in others; and blacks may also lighten their skin and straighten their hair. Spike Lee, in his film *Jungle Fever,* cleverly plays with U.S. racial identifications by introducing a dark-skinned character who seems at first to be African American, but turns out, from his speech, to be Italian-American – and rabidly antiblack. The main point is that it is wrong to extrapolate from the U.S. case to racial identifications in general. The Latin American material shows that, for example, the same individual dressed shabbily or smartly will be identified with different color terms that locate the person on a scale between black and white. These terms are not dependent on phenotype alone, because the context of somatic features alters people's classification – and even perhaps perception – of these features. It is also widely reported that "the blacks" is often a term used more or less synonymously with "the poor," indicating again that economic status influences racial classifications. Thus identifications of "black" are malleable, as well as those of "Indian."

It is also worth bearing in mind, however, that such malleability is not complete. The Indian migrant from the highlands of Peru who becomes a domestic maid in Lima is on her way to becoming a mestizo woman, but her background is not forgotten; the term *cholo* is frequently used to identify people who are seen as "between" Indians and mestizos. Equally, people who, by local standards, have typically Indian or black somatic features have a hard job losing that identity, even if they are not publicly labeled as Indian or black. In Latin America, people are generally quite sensitive to the possibilities of ancestry that can be inferred from appearance, so such signifiers cannot be erased completely by changing other cues.

This is not to argue that the categories of black and Indian are therefore exactly the same in terms of the processes of identification they involve. Each category has a different history with different possibilities and modes of construction and transformation, modes that also depend on local contexts. The use of "race" to talk about black identity and "ethnicity" to talk about Indian identity is fair enough as long as it is recognized that the difference between them is not one of opposition between racial and ethnic classifications. Such an opposition separates phenotype from culture, as if the former were not itself culturally constructed. Both "Indian" and "black" are, in my view, categories that have aspects of racial and ethnic categorization.

In sum, then, I think it is necessary to bring blacks and Indians into the same theoretical frame of reference, while recognizing the historical differences between them and the consequences of these at a political level.

From *Race and Ethnicity in Latin America.* Pluto Press, 1997. Used with permission.

See Also

Christianity, African: An Overview; Explorers in Africa Before 1500; Transatlantic Slave Trade; Sahara Desert; Slavery in Latin America and the Caribbean; Eugenics; Lee, Shelton Jackson ("Spike"); Central America; Islam and Tradition: An Interpretation; Abolition and Emancipation in Latin America and the Caribbean; Colonial Latin America and the Caribbean; Black Codes in Latin America; Argentina.

Latin America and the Caribbean

Latin America, Blacks in, a history of people of African descent in the various countries of Latin America and the Caribbean.

The Latin American and Caribbean regions were the first areas of the Americas to be populated by African immigrants. African immigration to the Americas may have begun before European exploration of the region. Blacks sailed with Christopher Columbus even on his first voyage in 1492, and the earliest Spanish and Portuguese explorers were likewise accompanied by black Africans who had been born and reared in Iberia. In the following four centuries, millions of immigrants from Africa were brought to the New World as slaves. Today their descendants form significant ethnic minorities in several Latin American countries, and they are the dominant element in many of the Caribbean nations. Over the centuries black people have added their original contributions to the cultural mix of their respective societies and thus exerted a profound influence on all facets of life in Latin America.

Early Immigration and Slavery

Most of the earliest black immigrants to the Americas were natives of Spain and Portugal – men such as Pedro Alonso Niño, a navigator who accompanied Columbus on his first voyage, and the black colonists who helped Nicolás de Ovando form the first Spanish settlement on Hispaniola in 1502. The name of Nuflo de Olano appears in the records as that of a black slave present when Vasco Núñez de Balboa sighted the Pacific Ocean in 1513. Other blacks served with Hernán Cortés when he conquered Mexico and with Francisco Pizarro when he marched into Peru.

Iberian Blacks

Estebanico, one of the survivors of Pánfilo de Narváez's unfortunate expedition to Florida in 1527, was a black. With three companions, he spent eight years traveling overland to Mexico City, learning several Native American languages in the process. Later, while exploring what is now New Mexico, he lost his life in a dispute with the Zuñi. Juan Valiente, another black, led Spaniards in a series of battles against the Araucanian people of Chile between 1540 and 1546. Although Valiente was a slave, he was rewarded with an estate near Santiago and control of several Native American villages.

Between 1502 and 1518 Spain shipped out hundreds of Spanish-born Africans, called ladinos, to work as laborers, especially in the mines. Opponents of their enslavement cited their weak Christian faith and their penchant for escaping to the mountains or joining the Native Americans in revolt. Proponents declared that the rapid diminution of the Native American population required a consistent supply of reliable workhands. Free Spaniards were reluctant to do manual labor or to remain settled (especially after the discovery of gold on the mainland), and only slave labor could assure the economic viability of the colonies.

Beginning of the African Slave Trade

By 1518 the demand for slaves in the Spanish New World was so great that King Charles I of Spain sanctioned the direct transport of slaves from Africa to the American colonies. The slave trade was controlled by the Crown, which sold the right to import slaves (*asiento*) to entrepreneurs.

By the 1530s the Portuguese were also using African slaves in Brazil. From then until the abolition of the slave trade in 1870, at least 12 million Africans were forcibly brought to the Americas: about 47 percent of them to the Caribbean Islands and the Guianas; 38 percent to Brazil; and 6 percent to mainland Spanish America. About 4.5 percent went to North America, roughly the same proportion that went to Europe.

The greatest proportion of these slaves worked on plantations producing sugar, coffee, cotton, tobacco, and rice in the tropical lowlands of northeastern Brazil and in the Caribbean Islands. Most of them came from the sub-Saharan states of West and Central Africa, but by the late eighteenth century the supply zone extended to southern and East Africa as well.

Impact of Slavery

Slavery in the Americas was generally harsh, but it varied from time to time and place to place. The Caribbean and Brazilian sugar plantations required a consistently high supply of labor for centuries. In other areas – the frontiers of southern Brazil, Argentina, Venezuela, and Colombia – slavery was relatively unimportant to the economy.

To tame the wilderness, build cities, establish plantations, and exploit mineral wealth, the Europeans needed more laborers than they could recruit from among their own metropolitan masses. In the early sixteenth century the Spanish tried unsuccessfully to subjugate and enslave the native populations of the West Indies. Slavery was considered the most desirable system of labor organization because it allowed the master almost absolute control over the life and productivity of the laborer. The rapid disintegration of local indigenous societies and the subsequent decimation of the native peoples by warfare and European diseases severely exacerbated the labor situation, increasing the demand for imported workers.

African slaves constituted the highest proportion of laborers on the islands and around the Caribbean lowlands, where the native population had died. The same was true in the northeastern coastlands of Brazil – especially the rich agricultural area called the Reconcavo, where the seminomadic Tupinamba and Tupiniquim peoples resisted effective control by the Portuguese – and in some of the Leeward Islands, such as Guadeloupe and Dominica, where the Caribs waged a determined resistance to their expulsion and enslavement. In areas of previously dense populations, such as parts of central Mexico or the highlands of Peru, a sufficient number of the Native American inhabitants survived to satisfy a major part of the labor demands of the new colonists. In such cases African slaves supplemented coerced Native American labor.

Volume of Immigration

In Mexico (then called New Spain), the principal economic activity for the colonists in the early colonial period was mining. African slaves were imported to counteract the precipitate decline in the Native American populations. When the indigenous inhabitants recovered sufficiently to provide the required labor, the demand for expensive African slaves diminished. Between 1519 and 1650 Mexico imported about 120,000 African slaves, or slightly fewer than 1000 per year. From 1650 to 1810 Mexico received an additional 80,000 Africans, a rate of merely 500 slaves per year. Indeed, Mexican slave owners bought no more than 50,000 slaves during the entire eighteenth century, when the transatlantic slave trade was at its highest. Chile imported about 6000, about one-third of whom arrived before 1615; most were utilized in agriculture around Santiago. Argentina (mainly Buenos Aires) and Bolivia (mainly the mining areas around Charcas) brought in about 100,000 Africans. Import figures to all these areas were low compared with those for Brazil and the West Indies.

Throughout Latin America and the Caribbean the slave population declined at the astonishing rate of 2 to 4 percent a year; thus, by the time slavery was abolished, the overall slave population in many places was far less than the total number of slaves imported. The British colony of Jamaica, for example, imported more than 600,000 slaves during the eighteenth century; yet in 1838 the slave population numbered little more than 300,000. The French colony of Saint-Domingue (present-day Haiti) imported more than 800,000 Africans during the eighteenth century but had only 480,000 slaves in 1790, on the eve of the Haitian Revolution. Between 1810 and 1870 the Spanish colony of Cuba acquired about 600,000 slaves; in 1880, however, the Cubans had only 200,000 slaves and an entire Afro-Cuban population of 450,000. Altogether, the 4.7 million Africans imported to the Caribbean over the centuries had diminished to about 2 million in 1880.

Blacks in Colonial Society

In Latin America society was, in general, a three-tiered structure of castes, subdivided into classes. At the top were the Europeans;

in the middle were the free nonwhites; and at the bottom were slaves and Native Americans. Each caste had its own set of legal rights and social privileges, which varied from place to place. In the sugar-producing areas and other plantation-based economic units of Brazil, the Caribbean, and the lowlands of Mexico, Colombia, and Peru, the rights of slaves as well as free persons of color tended to be legally circumscribed. The greater the demand for labor, the more severe the coercion and discrimination exercised against the African sector of the population. In the coffee, cattle, and fishing areas of southern Brazil, PUERTO RICO, eastern Cuba, the interior of Argentina, and Venezuela, social mobility tended to be greater and internal class and caste distinctions more relaxed and less formal. In the towns and cities Africans filled occupational roles just as did other free members of society, although they tended to be concentrated in the more menial and unskilled tasks.

Most of the black population in Latin America and the Caribbean spent their lives in domestic service or as agricultural laborers. About 20 percent – both slave and free – were sailors, artisans, nursemaids, wet nurses, merchants, small shopkeepers, mining or sugar experts, or itinerant street vendors. Slavery was never only a form of labor organization or only an economic enterprise. It was a socioeconomic complex held together by law and custom. Regardless of their conditions, their hopes for freedom were strong, and slaves often revolted.

Emancipation

Throughout the history of slavery in the Americas, some masters voluntarily manumitted their slaves. In the Spanish colonies, slaves could purchase their freedom on a time-purchase plan called *coartación.* A similar scheme prevailed in Brazil and the sugar colonies of the Caribbean. Almost everywhere, female urban slaves constituted the majority of those who benefited from voluntary manumissions and self-purchase. The children of these women were also free. In addition, some free white fathers emancipated their children born of slave mothers; the state also emancipated slaves from time to time for a variety of reasons.

The Free Blacks

Because slavery played such an important role in the New World economy between 1600 and 1850, it overshadowed by far the number of Africans who came to the Americas as free persons. The first group of free, or semifree, Africans arrived in the early sixteenth century with the original European colonists. The second came during the nineteenth century, mainly as part of a British-sponsored attempt to provide an alternative source to African slave labor. Besides these free immigrants – of whom about 50,000 settled in the British and French West Indies – each slave society contained, almost from its beginning, an ever-expanding component of blacks who had been freed by manumission.

By the beginning of the nineteenth century this free population had become a fixture of every slave society in the Americas. In the New Granada provinces of what today are the independent states of PANAMA, Colombia, Venezuela, and ECUADOR, the free black population in 1789 was 420,000, whereas African slaves numbered only 20,000. Free blacks also outnumbered slaves in Peru, Argentina, and Brazil. In Puerto Rico they numbered nearly half the total population in 1812. In Cuba, by contrast, free blacks made up only 15 percent in 1827; in Saint-Domingue the ratio was even lower – 5 percent in 1789 – and in Jamaica it was a mere 3 percent in 1800. Thus, in plantation societies, opportunities for emancipation did not come easily, whereas in regions where the economy was more diversified, the free black and mulatto population expanded considerably.

The Campaign Against the Slave Trade

By the end of the eighteenth century the possibility of a general emancipation of all slaves began to emerge as a preoccupation of every slave society. By the sixteenth century Spanish missionaries such as Antonio Montesino and BARTOLOMÉ DE LAS CASAS had become critical of slavery, and in the seventeenth century English Quakers opposed both slavery and the slave trade. General disapproval developed only during the eighteenth century, however, when the rational attitudes of the Enlightenment combined with British Evangelical Protestantism to form the intellectual preconditions for the abolitionist movement.

The British abolitionists, aware that their compatriots transported the greatest number of African slaves to the New World, concentrated their efforts against the slave trade rather than slavery itself, feeling that the termination of the trade would eventually lead to the end of the institution. The abolitionist attack was spearheaded by Granville Sharp, a humanitarian who in 1772 persuaded the British courts to declare that slavery could not exist in England. The ruling immediately affected the more than 15,000 slaves brought into the country by their colonial masters, who valued them at approximately £700,000. In 1776 the British philosopher and economist Adam Smith declared in his classic economic study, *The Wealth of Nations,* that slavery was uneconomical because the plantation system was a wasteful use of land and because slaves cost more to maintain than free laborers.

By the 1780s slavery was being attacked, directly and indirectly, from several sources. Evangelicals condemned it on the grounds of Christian charity and the assumption of a natural law of common humanity. Economists opposed slavery because it wasted valuable resources. Political philosophers saw it as the basis of unjust privilege and unequal distribution of social and corporate responsibility. In 1787 Thomas Clarkson, an English cleric, joined Granville Sharp and Josiah Wedgwood, the famous English potter, to form a society for the abolition of the slave trade. The society recruited William Wilberforce as its parliamentary spokesman and in 1788 succeeded in getting Prime Minister William Pitt to set up a select committee of the Privy Council to investigate the slave trade. The year before, the society had established SIERRA LEONE in West Africa as a refuge for the "London black poor," and it achieved other successes.

Abolition of the Slave Traffic

A bill designed to restrict the number of slaves carried by each ship, based on the ship's tonnage, was enacted by Parliament on June 17, 1788; and that year the French abolitionists, inspired by their English counterparts, founded the Société des Amis des Noirs (Society of the Friends of Blacks). Finally in 1807, the British Parliament passed an act prohibiting British subjects from engaging in the slave trade after March 1, 1808 – 16 years after the Danes had abolished their trade. In 1811 slave trading was declared a felony punishable by transportation (exile to a penal colony) for all British subjects or foreigners caught trading in British possessions. Britain then assumed most of the responsibility for abolishing the transatlantic slave trade, partly to protect its sugar colonies. In 1815 Portugal accepted £750,000 to restrict the trade to Brazil; and in 1817 Spain accepted £400,000 to abandon the trade to Cuba, Puerto Rico, and Santo Domingo. In 1818 Holland and France abolished the trade. After 1824 slave trading was declared tantamount to piracy, and until 1837 participants faced the penalty of death.

Abolition of Slavery

The campaigns to abolish the trade exposed the abusive nature of slavery and led to the formation of the British Anti-Slavery Society in 1823. Long before that, the thrust for full emancipation of the enslaved Africans began with the successful revolt of the slaves in the French colony of Saint-Domingue in 1791 during the French Revolution. The radical French commissioner, Léger Félicité Sonthonax, emancipated all slaves and admitted them to full citizenship (1793), a move ratified the following year by the revolutionary government in Paris, which extended emancipation to all French colonies. This measure was revoked by Napoleon Bonaparte in 1802. Emancipation nevertheless remained permanent in Haiti, which won its independence under black leadership two years later. Elsewhere slaves worked for the disintegration of the system, but the official acts of emancipation lay outside their hands. Only in Haiti did they seize and hold political power.

During the struggle of Spain's American colonies for independence from 1810 to 1826, both the insurgents and the Loyalists promised to emancipate all slaves who took part in military campaigns. Mexico, the Central American states, and Chile abolished slavery once they were independent. In 1821 the Venezuelan Congress approved a law reaffirming the abolition of the slave trade, liberating all slaves who had fought with the victorious armies, and establishing a system that immediately manumitted all children of slaves while gradually freeing their parents. The last Venezuelan slaves were freed in 1854. In Argentina the process began in 1813 and ended with the ratification of the 1853 constitution by the city of Buenos Aires in 1861.

Brazil

Brazil suffered a long internal struggle over abolition and was the last Latin American country to adopt it. In 1864 the Brazilian emperor Pedro II emancipated the slaves that formed part of his daughter's dowry and acceded to the request of French abolitionists that the government commit itself to ending slavery. At the end of the disastrous Paraguayan War in 1870, more than 20,000 slaves were emancipated as a reward for their services. In 1871 the Brazilian Congress approved the Rio Branco Law of Free Birth, which conditionally freed the children of slaves. Until they were eight years old, such children remained in the custody of the mother's master. At that time the state could compensate the master for the emancipation of the child, or the master could elect to have the child work without wages for 13 years. This scheme failed to satisfy advocates of outright abolition, who won widespread support in the late 1870s. In 1884 dissatisfaction increased when it became known that in 12 years the Rio Branco Law had freed only about 20,000 slaves – less than 20 percent of those voluntarily manumitted. In 1887 army officers refused to order their troops to hunt runaway slaves, and in 1888 the Senate passed a law establishing immediate, unqualified emancipation.

The West Indies

Caribbean colonies required action by their European metropolises. In the British, French, Danish, and Dutch Antilles, economic problems in the early nineteenth century combined with the humanitarian and political pressures from Europe to weaken the planters' resistance to emancipation. West Indian SUGAR exports stabilized in volume and declined in price, driving production costs up. Meanwhile, the slaves became increasingly difficult to control. Emancipation became part of a general reform movement in Britain in the 1830s, and Parliament abolished slavery in 1834, instituting an apprenticeship program for ex-slaves, an arrangement that lasted until 1838. France and Denmark followed Britain's example in 1848, and the Netherlands did so in 1863. In every case emancipation resulted from the combined pressure of political reformers, humanitarian idealists, and believers in more efficient methods of production – a coalition that overwhelmed opposition from the colonial slave owners. Slaves also contributed to the disintegration of the system by actively revolting and by passively increasing production and administrative costs.

Largely under pressure from Cuban slave owners, Spain refused Puerto Rico's request that slavery be abolished on that island in 1812. In 1870 the Spanish Moret law freed the newborn offspring of slaves, all those more than 60 years old, and those who fought for Spain in the Ten Years' War in Cuba. Slavery in Puerto Rico was abolished in 1873, and in 1880 a system of gradual, indemnified emancipation was established in Cuba. The gradual system was abandoned in 1886, when the last 30,000 Cuban slaves were granted immediate emancipation.

Black Society after Emancipation

The black inhabitants of Latin America and the Caribbean were able to enjoy the rights of full freedom depending on their relative numbers, their economic or occupational roles, and the degree of their access to political power. In parts of Latin America where the black population was relatively small, cultural and genetic integration with the white or Native American majority over time blurred considerably the obvious ethnic distinctions.

In Mexico, Ecuador, Peru, Bolivia, Chile, Argentina, Paraguay, and Uruguay, the black sector constituted less than 1 percent of the population. In Central America, coastal Colombia, Venezuela, Brazil, and the Caribbean, the black concentration ranged from 2 percent (Honduras) to 99 percent (Haiti). People of mixed African, European, and Native American ancestry, however, had ceased to be counted as "black."

Prejudice Against Blacks

The rise of pseudoscientific racism and the popularity of social-engineering ideas among Latin American white elites militated against the social acceptance of the black population. The positivist followers of the French philosopher Auguste Comte thought Africans were far from ready for the stage of technical modernity and neglected them. Adherents of social Darwinism considered the African dimension of the pluralistic society a sign of fundamental weakness because they assumed the natural superiority of the white race. The preoccupation of Marxists with class conditions dulled their awareness of the problems of race and color. Thus, the Latin American elites of the nineteenth century refused to accept cultural pluralism because they feared sharing power with the domestic black populations. Several Latin American nations adopted laws prohibiting black immigration during the ninteenth century. In most areas the economic situation has not yet diversified or expanded sufficiently to allow blacks to move out of menial occupations. Most of them, therefore, remain in the lowest economic and social strata.

Assimilation of Latin Population

The prevalence of intermarriage precluded the historical development of a two-tiered society, and a racially mixed "colored" (as distinct from black) group frequently shared the legal and economic opportunities of the white elites. Race mixture in Latin America, however, is too complex for easy categorization. Centuries of contact among African, European, indigenous American, and Asian people have produced a socioethnic complexity in which status and racial designation depend on many factors.

When slavery collapsed, governments compensated not the ex-slaves, but the ex-slave owners. The black masses possessed neither the requisite economic base nor the skills to compete with the wave of new immigrants who poured into the southeastern part of South America. Between 1870 and 1963 the country of Brazil absorbed nearly 5 million European immigrants, a large number of whom had official or private sponsors who paid for their transportation and resettlement costs. Eighty percent of these immigrants settled in São Paulo and the southern states of the country, virtually inundating the resident black populations. Later economic expansion did not substantially improve the poor economic conditions of the blacks. Color and race contributed to the continued expulsion of Afro-Brazilians from occupations above the marginal and menial tasks assigned to servants, odd jobbers, porters, and other nonorganized groups.

In Argentina the impact of European immigration on the country's black people was even more dramatic. Between 1869 and 1914 the Argentine population increased from 1.8 to 7.9 million. During this period the total population in the city of Buenos Aires increased eight-fold, but its black population remained stable. In 1970 the Afro-Argentines numbered only about 4000 in a city population of 8 million. Most of the black men died in continuous wars, and a large number of Afro-Argentine women married European immigrants, thereby losing their ethnic identity.

Peasant and Maroon Communities

In the West Indies the situation was different. White immigrants to the islands were not numerous enough to swamp the Afro-Caribbean populations. In some countries, independent African American communities were established in remote areas by runaway slaves known as maroons. Maroon settlements were continually challenged by planters needing slaves. The maroons resisted in Palmares, Brazil (c. 1605-1695), and in ESMERALDAS, Ecuador (1570-1738). In Jamaica they signed (1796) a formal treaty with the British government after a series of conflicts and retained their independence until 1962. The maroons were the first black peasants in the West Indies.

The trend toward peasant production expanded greatly during the period after slavery. Ex-slaves bought up abandoned or bankrupt estates throughout the Caribbean. In BARBADOS and Antigua this was difficult, but in Cuba and Puerto Rico, land was available outside the sugar zones. Free peasant villages thus became a feature of Caribbean life. Blacks also entered commerce, the professions, and government. Throughout the nineteenth century and the first half of the twentieth century, Haiti remained the only independent black nation in the Americas. By 1962, when Jamaica, TRINIDAD AND TOBAGO, and other nations had become independent, there remained much to improve in the economic realm.

Culture

A strong African influence pervades music, dance, the arts, literature, speech forms, and religious practices in Latin America and the Caribbean. Africans, whether as slaves or free immigrants, brought a variety of African cultural influences to the New World. They came from too many places in Africa and were too scattered throughout the Americas to reestablish all the conditions of their homelands, but wherever possible, they did their best to reconcile reality with their beliefs. Like all other immigrant groups, they abandoned some aspects of their culture, modified others, and created new forms. This adaptation to local American conditions is called Creolization.

The number of Africans, their proportion in local society, and the length of time they spent in any one place were crucial in the development of an African American culture.

Regional Differences

In countries such as Argentina, Brazil, and Mexico, African immigrants were a minority having to deal with a vital and dynamic form of European society and culture. The African communities survived, and in some instances proliferated, but they did so against the stiff and relentless competition of the majority, or "high," culture. Aspects of the African ethnic subculture were eventually adopted by the mainstream. Nonetheless, in such societies, the African character of the African American culture is less pronounced than in societies where Africans formed the majority of the inhabitants.

In the essentially plantation societies of the Caribbean islands, people of African ancestry retained considerable control over their daily lives, despite the efforts of the politically dominant minority group to restrain and coerce them. The lack of cultural homogeneity as well as the paucity of the plantation elites provided an exceptional opportunity for the African masses to fashion their own society and influence the "high" culture.

Caribbean people speak variants of the standard European languages, which uniformly reflect West African speech patterns regardless of whether the spoken language is English, Spanish, French, or Dutch. The French spoken in Haiti constitutes a language of its own. In Curaçao, Aruba, and Bonaire, Papiamentu, a blend of Dutch, Spanish, and Portuguese, is one of the official languages. Nor are these Creole languages confined to the poorer, unschooled classes. Creole has now been accorded greater respect in the literature and political life of the islands.

Cultural Modifications

Official acceptance modifies some forms of culture. The Carnival is an example. Until the nineteenth century the annual celebration of Carnival was confined to the black population; the upper classes deplored Carnival and tried to destroy it as a public festival. By the early twentieth century it had attracted all classes and races, and currently it has official government support in the BAHAMAS, Cuba, Trinidad and Tobago, and Brazil. Although Carnival has become respectable, and its festivities are open to all races and classes, the chief participants of these Carnivals are still black. The same remains true for other folk festivals such as the Jonkonnu in Jamaica.

In some cases, however, the transition from low to high culture obscured the African origin, as in Argentina, where the TANGO was developed from dual African ancestry. One source is undoubtedly the Spanish fandango, but the fandango is really Moorish. The other source is a black dance called the *candombe*, the feature attraction of Afro-Argentine festivals during and after the period of slavery. Latin American music has always been deeply influenced by the vibrant rhythms and melodies that blacks brought with them from their African homeland. This is particularly true of Brazil; in fact, the first real music school in that country was founded by a black priest. Brazilian music is thoroughly imbued with African themes, and illustrious composers such as Heitor Villa-Lobos have long found inspiration in the black musical heritage. Many Caribbean musical styles have become widely known, including the MAMBO from Cuba, salsa from Puerto Rico, REGGAE from Jamaica, and CALYPSO from Trinidad.

Religious Practices

When it came to religion, African immigrants to Latin America and the Caribbean not only retained some of their original beliefs but also borrowed and modified religious rituals from the various European Christian churches they encountered there. Religious affiliation, however, is no longer restricted by race or color. A number of Christian groups such as the Seventh Day Adventists, Pentecostals, and Churches of God are predominantly black. On the other hand, religious sects of African origin – such as VODOU in Haiti; SHANGO in Trinidad and Tobago, Venezuela, and Brazil; SANTERÍA in Cuba and Puerto Rico; Kumina, Myal, Revivalist, and Rastafarianism in Jamaica; and UMBANDA, Macounda, and others in Brazil – are no longer only black.

Black Literature

African Americans have left a deep impression on the lore and literature of the New World. In some parts of Latin America, such as Brazil, popular tales and legends are to a great extent of African origin. Themes dealing with slavery have always been popular with black writers. Some, such as the Brazilian poet Luís Gama, were also active in the abolitionist movement. Antônio de Castro Alves was identified as the "poet of the slaves" for his treatment of slavery in his writings. JOÃO DA CRUZ E SOUSA, the son of emancipated slaves, is considered one of Brazil's greatest poets.

As nationalism intensified during the twentieth century, even more attention was paid to African origins. The Haitian poet JACQUES ROUMAIN stressed the value of his native (African) culture while expressing the pride and bitterness of his black ancestry. NICOLÁS GUILLÉN, one of Cuba's most eminent poets, wrote some of his best works as "black" poetry based on the rhythms of Afro-Cuban music. The novels, poetry, dance, and mime of Latin America and the Caribbean area have all incorporated African speech patterns, styles, or concepts and have tried to express the spirit of the black cultural heritage. In the Nobel Prize-winning poetry of Derek Walcott and the autobiographical short stories of JAMAICA KINCAID, an effort is made to reconcile the differences between the writers' native West Indian and adoptive white milieus.

Politics

The maroon settlements in the days of slavery were attempts to form black states; they were, in effect, states within states. Haiti, where slaves led by JEAN-JACQUES DESSALINES captured the governing apparatus in 1804, was only the second independent country in the Western Hemisphere (the first being the United States) and the first one ruled by blacks. As such, it became a symbol of black independence and a catalyst for Black Nationalism. Blacks in many other countries participated in politics within the prevailing political structures, but in some nations such activities were restricted. In Cuba, for example, a law forbade the organization of political parties based on race or color after 1911, and the military efforts of the Afro-Cuban leaders Pedro Ivonet and Evaristo Estenoz to reverse that decision ended in disaster in 1912. Government troops killed 3000 Afro-Cubans in Oriente Province, putting an end to black political resistance in Cuba. In Brazil, the Frente Negra Brasileira (Brazilian Black Front), founded in São Paulo in 1931, served as the national political voice of Afro-Brazilians but faded along with other political parties during the Vargas dictatorship of the 1930s and 1940s. In the British, French, and Dutch Caribbean, blacks have participated in politics for more than a century, and today hold local political power. Governments controlled by people of African ancestry have been in power in the Netherlands Antilles, Trinidad and Tobago, Barbados, St. Lucia, Grenada, St. Vincent and the Grenadines, Dominica, Antigua, St. Kitts and Nevis, and Jamaica. The Marxist government of Cuba has declared Cubans an Afro-Latin American people and has formed close ties with Angola, Ethiopia, and other African states.

Other Caribbean countries have also established contacts with the free nations of Africa, both directly and through United Nations agencies and other international organizations. Caribbean-African cooperation, however, has more frequently been based on shared ideology than it has on race or color.

Franklin W. Knight and Clayborne Carson

See Also

Transatlantic Slave Trade; Great Britain; Literature, English Language, Caribbean; Palmares: An African State in Brazil; Frente Negra Brasileira; Maroonage in the Americas; Portugal; Slavery in Latin America and the Caribbean; Abolitionism in the United States; American Indians; Eugenics; Miscegenation; Pentecostalism; Walcott, Derek Alton; Salsa Music; Gama, Luís Gonzaga Pinto da; Antigua and Barbuda; Rastafarians; Carnivals in Latin America and the Caribbean; Dance in Latin America and the Caribbean; Languages, Creole, in the Caribbean; Slave Laws in Colonial Spanish America.

Africa

Law in Africa: Colonial and Contemporary, the legal systems of the 48 countries of sub-Saharan Africa.

The most striking thing about the legal systems of the 48 countries of sub-Saharan Africa is that formally or informally, they are all based on two kinds of law. In addition to having overarching, substantial, and thoroughly modern legislative enactments on the books, virtually all of these countries also have some place for the recognition of what is called "customary law." Customary law is the law special to the many and various ethnic and religious groups that compose the population of African countries, "the ethnic mosaic." It is, in part, a remnant of precolonial legal ideas and practices but has been deeply changed. Today customary law exists in so greatly transformed a political, social, and economic milieu that its attribution to past "traditions" is more a claim to cultural-ethnic continuity, to legitimacy and political recognition, than it is a descriptor of historical fact.

In contrast, the modern legal sector is often a copy of (or an adapted version of) the statutes of the former colonial rulers. Thus in Francophone Africa one can expect to see various versions of French law; in Anglophone Africa, British law. In many countries there are also recent additions, statutory entries prepared by the local legal profession, some drafted as a matter of internal national policy, some required by the World Bank or the International Monetary Fund. Many of these transplants and insertions of law from elsewhere have elements that vary from the original models. The comparative study of African law, even in its modern sector, is a complex matter. The quantity of formal law material involved is enormous. But even more important are the questions of how the law is in fact implemented, who has access to legal institutions, and the like. As is true of legal institutions in general, none of this is self-evident from the law on the books.

Thus there is in every country a constitution, a shared national system of criminal law, and usually also considerable commonality in the law governing commercial transactions and institutions. But within this picture of apparent national homogeneity, there is considerable diversity. There are often major differences between urban and rural legal circumstances. In much of sub-Saharan Africa, most of the population lives in rural settings. There, in matters affecting marriage, inheritance, land law, family property, the rights of women and minors, as well as the rights of certain castes and occupational sectors, one is likely to find customary law governing local practices.

There are also great differences from one country to another, and within countries, in the nature of the available courts, the structure of the court system, and the effectiveness of the judiciary in processing cases and enforcing decisions, to say nothing of legislative and administrative bodies. Some countries have a highly developed bar, whose lawyers are in leadership positions and are very much in touch with their counterparts in other countries. In other African nations, the system of courts that exists on paper barely functions outside of urban settings. High court decisions may not be effectively communicated to lower, local courts, suggesting a pervasive lack of coherence in the institutional system. The judiciary may not be independent. In some countries there is more than inefficiency involved; courts may be used for the political ends of the government and its friends rather than as impartial implementers of the rule of law. There may be no effective system of public judicial accountability that might correct such abuses.

Colonial and Present-day Conceptions of Customary Law

European colonial governments recognized that there were organized communities in Africa before whites appeared on the scene. These communities had their own lawlike rules of family order, of property, of crime, of government, and so on, which, while not written down, were generally known and conformed to by the local groups to which they were pertinent. It would have been quite impossible to change all of these normative regimes immediately by decree when the colonial governments moved in. Moreover, there seemed no reason to make such changes as long as public order was maintained and other colonial objectives were served. What mattered most to the colonial rulers was that their own authority should be recognized as supreme, that African chiefs and princes should peacefully acknowledge their administrative subordination to the Europeans and realize that their own authority would be maintained only as long as they obeyed the colonial government. They were removed from office and replaced if they disobeyed.

Colonial governments wanted the taxes they imposed to be paid, the labor they recruited to be obedient, the roads kept in repair, and they wanted to suppress all collective violence. They often counted on "traditional authorities" in the countryside to maintain the requisite order. But those princes, chiefs, and clan leaders were not to exceed the authority delegated to them. The scope of that authority was greatly limited and altered by the colonial presence. The colonial authorities also appropriated land and other resources for governmental purposes, and they helped the settlers they invited into the colonies to acquire property as well. The laws that governed this kind of property were entirely different from the customary law that applied to the African population.

The position of chiefly subservience to the colonial government severely curtailed the authority of African leaders and removed a great many matters from their legal jurisdiction. Serious crimes were no longer within their authority, nor were certain appropriations of property. However, there remained a great deal in the existing, mundane normative regime of African peoples to which colonial governments, at least in the early decades of the century, were essentially indifferent and were willing to leave to the local authorities.

Those elements of local systems of normative order that were left to local communities to manage in their own "traditional" way, came to be known as customary law. The premise on which such a category rested was that there was another type of law in the land, namely the law of the central state and its officials. Only to the extent that the state was willing to recognize and enforce customary law did it have an official existence. Thus one can say that customary law in its modern form came into existence with colonial rule. To be sure, there were enforceable customs pertaining to kinship and property and the status of persons before colonial rule, and some of those customs persisted; but they were reclassified and rearranged in an important and radical way once they became part of a system of which customary law was only a subordinated segment.

Vast changes occurred among African societies from the beginning of colonial rule. Some of these alterations were the result of direct legislative or administrative intervention. For example, the practice of slavery was prohibited by colonial regimes (though it continued and continues in some places). Trials for witchcraft were forbidden and continued only unofficially. In many countries, only the currency issued and recognized by the state was legal tender.

Many shifts occurred without such dramatic legal interventions. For example, the introduction of Christianity altered many family relations, such as the legality of marriage, the legitimacy of polygamy, the legitimacy of children, and the like. A cash economy in European money made considerable inroads very rapidly. Cash cropping and paid labor became commonplace. The character of transactions changed. Eventually even land was bought and sold in areas where that had never been the case in precolonial times, or land was allocated by officials.

In many areas there came to be two kinds of land holding – land that was held under the "customary" rules of inheritance, and land that was self-acquired either through purchase or through official assignment. Inherited land was more or less entailed, self-acquired property that could generally be freely transferred. A precedent for these two parallel sets of rules had existed in many areas in precolonial times in that land pioneered (that is, first cultivated from bush) was treated as freely alienable by some ethnic groups even before the colonial period. But the addition of the possibility of purchase, and the change in the officials who might assign bush land, meant that the colonial version was considerably transformed from its predecessor. It is this kind of contextual change that very much alters what are currently identified as customary laws from what they were in a precolonial era. The legitimation of law by designating it as "traditional" and "customary" remained (and remains) attractive to local authorities, as it designated one domain that remained subject to their jurisdiction. The colonial authorities obviously found this delegation convenient. Today variants on this localism of political power and organization continue in many parts of Africa.

Three Periods of Constitutional Construction in Africa

The general legal picture since independence is further complicated by the fact that since the middle of the twentieth century, almost every country in Africa has experienced several radical changes of government with accompanying formal and constitutional legal transformation. Constitutions have often been replaced or revised. Some rough outlines of these shifts characterize many countries, though not all of them. South Africa, for example, does not fall within the general picture and has its own, no less complex, legal history.

As it is impossible to review the details of 48 different constitutional histories, African constitutional scholars have summarized matters in the following way: they recognize the importance of colonial-era law, but for them the true beginning of African constitutional law starts at independence – in the decades following the mid-century. At the moment of independence, "the first generation" of African constitutions begins. At that time most African countries adopted Euro-American constitutions, essentially carbon copied from the metropole and inspired by ideals of limited government power and representative democracy.

Subsequently, after a period of time, often following a coup, and there were many coups, everything changed. What came into being was a period of one-party systems and military dictatorships with accompanying constitutional alterations. The democratic designs of the independence movements were redesigned to accommodate the dictates of the centralized regimes that succeeded them. That was "the second generation" of constitutional development.

What has happened recently, certainly from the 1980s on, is that a new democratic wave has been under way. Many one-party regimes and military dictatorships have been overthrown or peacefully replaced. A new generation of constitutions has come into being in many countries, forming "the third generation" of constitutional design. Where they exist, these new constitutions embody principles of representative democracy and explicitly install political rights such as multiparty elections, freedom of speech and association, private property, limitations on the powers of government, and respect for human rights. The new constitutions are, once again, based on Francophone or Anglophone models.

The question has been asked why there has not been more innovative thinking among constitutional drafters, with attention to the special circumstances of Africa, its special history, and its characteristic institutions. The answer may be that these new constitutions are part of the political ambiance of post-cold war Africa. Influential international pressures have been exerted to encourage African countries to conform to democratic standards. It is difficult to tell how much the newest constitutions actually reflect the collective internal opinion of African nations themselves, and how much they are the result of external influences.

Democracy, Human Rights, and International Law in Africa

Anyone who knows something about the political history of the twentieth century will recognize that the sequence of constitutional regimes in Africa has been deeply influenced by international politics. During the cold war period foreign powers on both sides considered that they had policy reasons to support centralized regimes in Africa. More recently, with the breakup of the Soviet Union, the World Bank and the International Monetary Fund have made no bones about the conditions attached to their terms of credit and aid. "Structural adjustment" was an imposed condition that required a shrinking of government bureaucracies, the dismantling of government-owned enterprises, the installation of regimes of private property, and other market-oriented changes with their legal concomitants. There were political dictates as well. These spelled out the democratic principles enumerated above as necessary parts of the new constitutions, and also placed special emphasis on multiparty elections and individual human rights.

Multiparty elections have been staged in many countries, with international teams of inspectors trying to ascertain their openness. In the wake of one-party dictatorships or other forms of centralization, the elections have been welcomed by outsiders as visible indicators of progress toward democracy. In some countries elections may actually represent just such progress. But in other countries there is considerable question whether any such goal has been achieved. In some countries the new, multiple parties have been so numerous, and so often clientelist and ethnic in foundation, that up to this point there has been more fractioning of the electoral public than democracy manifest in these elections. But it may well be too early to judge. What the long-term result of the recent constitutional changes will be remains to be seen.

Some International Legal Commitments

Some African intellectuals feel strongly that the constitutional changes of the recent democratic wave, so focused on human rights pertaining to individual liberties, have not given enough attention to collective social and economic rights. They define help for excluded, impoverished, and/or unemployed categories of the population as a matter of "rights to development." They do not want to leave such matters to the chance playing out of market forces.

This attitude is in keeping with the international commitment of African states to what is known as the Banjul Charter. In June 1981 heads of state met under the auspices of the Organization of African Unity (OAU) in Nairobi and adopted the African Charter on Human and People's Rights. It came into force in 1986 when a majority of OAU member states had ratified it. Many of the same states had previously ratified the International Bill of Human Rights of the United Nations. Africans speaking of the Banjul Charter tend to emphasize the importance of social collectivities in African life and to distinguish African group emphases from what they see as Western individualistic conceptions of human rights.

Another international commitment of many African countries that may soon gain increased importance is environmental. For example, many African countries are signatories to the United Nations Convention to Combat Desertification. Its final draft text was presented to the international community in June 1994. This, like a number of other agreements, legally binds African countries to act through regional organizations of neighboring countries, such as the EAST AFRICAN COMMUNITY, the Economic Community for West African States (ECOWAS), and the Southern Africa Development Community (SADC). Such a regional emphasis recognizes that African nations have many supranational common interests. These will surely become more prominent in the future, whether they have to do with peacekeeping, the environment, population and public health, or migration and commercial matters. It is clear that the ongoing construction of African legal systems is anything but static at all of its multiple levels of institutional organization.

Sally Falk Moore

SEE ALSO

Christianity, African: An Overview; Colonial Rule; Environmental Movements in Africa; Ethnicity and Identity in Africa: An Interpretation; Nairobi, Kenya; United Nations in Africa; Structural Adjustment in Africa; Economic Community of West African States; Southern African Development Community; Human Rights in Africa; Slavery in Africa.

North America

Lawrence, Jacob Armstead

(b. September 7, 1917, Atlantic City, N.J.), the most acclaimed African American artist at the end of the twentieth century.

Jacob Lawrence has painted figurative and narrative pictures of the black community and black history for more than 60 years in a consistent modernist style, using expressive, strong design and flat areas of color. His parents, Jacob Armstead Lawrence of South Carolina and Rose Lee of Virginia, were part of the Great Migration, the movement of African Americans from the South to the promise of jobs in Northern industry during the two decades following the onset of World War I.

When Lawrence was two years old, his family moved to Easton, Pennsylvania. A few years later they moved to Philadelphia, where his father became a part-time dining-car cook on the railroads. After his parents separated in 1924, Lawrence, his mother, and his younger brother and sister moved to Harlem, where they joined relatives who had also relocated in the North.

During Lawrence's youth in Harlem his mother enrolled him in after-school arts and crafts classes held at the 135th Street Branch of the New York Public Library. Charles Alston, who taught art there, later moved to the Utopia Neighborhood Center, where Lawrence also enrolled. Using a variety of techniques, including collage and papier-mâché, the young Lawrence made colorful masks and cityscapes on the insides of cardboard shoeboxes. He was introduced to African American history in his classes, and he visited the exhibition of African sculpture held at the Museum of Modern Art in 1935.

Lawrence took classes at the Harlem Art Center and the American Artists School from 1936 through 1938, and in 1936 he also worked briefly for the Civilian Conservation Corps, one of the relief agencies set up by the Roosevelt administration to create employment for youth during the GREAT DEPRESSION. Among the older artists, Augusta Savage was probably the most influential on Lawrence's work. A dynamic sculptor, she believed her mission was to teach art to children and young people in Harlem, and she spearheaded the establishment of the Harlem Community Art Center in 1937, financed by the Federal Art Project (FAP) of the national WORKS PROGRESS ADMINISTRATION (WPA). She arranged to have Lawrence hired as a professional artist in 1938 in the easel section of the FAP.

Although he was still young as an artist, in his late teens and early twenties Lawrence participated fully in the activities at art centers and at Alston's studio at 306 West 141st Street. At this time Lawrence met his future wife, fellow artist Gwendolyn Knight. The intellectuals, writers, and artists who gave talks and readings at art centers were crucial to the development of Lawrence and other young Harlem artists such as Knight, ROMARE BEARDEN, and Bob Blackburn. Lawrence was particularly influenced by CLAUDE MCKAY and Alain Locke, but KATHERINE DUNHAM, COUNTEE CULLEN, and LANGSTON HUGHES also stand out in his memory.

In 1936 Lawrence was painting scenes of Harlem interiors and street life, using the flat style that was to become his lifelong trademark. During the next year he began his first narrative series with texts: 41 panels on the life of Toussaint L'Ouverture, the liberator of HAITI. Some of Lawrence's Harlem scenes were included in a 1937 group exhibition of the Harlem Artists Guild and then featured in his first solo exhibition, which was held in the next year at the Harlem YMCA. After a New York showing at the De Porres Interracial Center, his *Toussaint* series traveled to the Baltimore Museum of Art in 1939 for the exhibition *Contemporary Negro Art.*

During the late 1930s and the 1940s Lawrence worked on two other narrative series: FREDERICK DOUGLASS (1938-1939), comprising 32 paintings, and *Harriet Tubman* (1939-1949), comprising 31 paintings. For both he received support from the Harmon Foundation. There was support from the Julius Rosenwald Fund for *Migration* (1940-1941), a series of 60 paintings; and JOHN BROWN (1941-1942), a series of 22 paintings. Alain Locke, who had included Lawrence in his influential book *The Negro in Art* (1940), brought him to the attention of Edith Halpert, the prominent New York art dealer, who agreed to give Lawrence a show at her Downtown Gallery.

Halpert alerted publisher Henry Luce, who reproduced 26 pictures from the *Migration Series* in the November 1941 issue of *Fortune* magazine. The 60 panels were subsequently divided between the Phillips Collection in Washington, D.C., and the Museum of Modern Art in New York City. In 1942 Lawrence received another grant from the Rosenwald Fund to create a *Harlem* series of 30 genre paintings.

Lawrence and Gwendolyn Knight had married in 1941, but with the country at war, Lawrence was drafted into the United States Coast Guard in 1943, where he served until 1945. Even when he was in the service, he continued painting. After his discharge he used a Guggenheim Fellowship to paint a *War* series of 14 panels. In 1947 *Fortune* commissioned him to produce a series on rural life in the postwar South. In 1948 he illustrated *One Way Ticket* by Langston Hughes.

During the 1950s Lawrence continued to paint pictures in series. Even though he spent a year at Hillside Hospital in Queens for psychiatric treatment, he used the opportunity to paint a *Hospital* series of 11 panels, exhibited at the Downtown Gallery in 1950. In 1952 he painted his *Theater* series. During the CIVIL RIGHTS MOVEMENT of the mid-1950s, he turned again to black history and painted 30 panels of a projected 60-panel series entitled *Struggle: From the History of the American People,* which highlighted the contributions of African Americans.

Lawrence's first teaching job came in the summer of 1946 when Joseph Albers persuaded him to join the Summer Institute of his experimental arts school, Black Mountain College, in Asheville, North Carolina. In the summer of 1954 Lawrence taught at the Skowhegan School of Painting and Sculpture in Maine, and in the fall of 1955 he became an instructor at Pratt Institute in Brooklyn, where he stayed until 1970. In that year he was appointed visiting artist at the University of Washington in Seattle and in 1971 he became a full professor there, a position that he held until his retirement in 1986. He also held several visiting positions: Skowhegan in the summers, 1968-1972; Brandeis University as artist-in-residence in the spring of 1965; the New School for Social Research as part-time instructor, 1966-1969; the Art Students League, 1967-1969; and California State College at Hayward, 1969-1970.

In 1961 Lawrence began reworking earlier themes as prints. When he and Knight lived in NIGERIA in 1954, he painted scenes of the local market. He increasingly received commissions to design posters and prints. He designed two *Time* magazine covers, one of Jesse Jackson and one of Colonel Ojukwu, military governor of Biafra. He did a poster for the 1972 Olympic Games, and he completed the *George Washington Bush* series for the state of Washington in 1973. During the 1970s he began making paintings with the theme of building and carpenters, which to Lawrence symbolized the goal of constructing strong, integrated communities.

Major retrospective exhibitions of Lawrence's paintings have had national tours organized by the American Federation of Art in 1960, the Whitney Museum of American Art in 1974, and the Seattle Art Museum in 1986. The 60-panel *Migration Series*, organized by the Phillips Collection, circulated between 1993 and 1995. Murals on the themes of sports and work are on the walls of Kingdome Stadium in Seattle and the New York City subway system. Lawrence was honored by President Jimmy Carter in 1980, and he was inducted into the American Academy of Arts and Letters in 1994. In 1990 he received the National Medal of Arts from President George Bush.

Patricia Hills

SEE ALSO

World War I and African Americans; Alston, Charles Henry; Great Migration, The; Harlem, New York; Jackson, Jesse Louis; Locke, Alain Leroy; Philadelphia, Pennsylvania; Savage, Augusta Christine Fells; Tubman, Harriet Ross; Toussaint L'Ouverture, François Dominique; Art, African American.

North America

Lawson, James Morris

(b. September 22, 1928, Uniontown, Pa.), African American minister and civil rights leader who trained early civil rights activists in nonviolent resistance tactics.

Although he served as a low-profile leader of the CIVIL RIGHTS MOVEMENT, James Lawson's influence was profound and lasting. He first made his mark on the civil rights struggle by teaching Indian activist Mohandas Gandhi's nonviolent civil disobedience techniques during the Nashville, Tennessee, sit-in demonstrations of 1960. Lawson, an ordained minister and pacifist who in the early 1950s had gone to prison rather than fight in the KOREAN WAR, had traveled to India as a missionary after his release and studied Gandhi's tactics firsthand. A divinity student at Vanderbilt University when the sit-ins began, he was dismissed from the school when he refused to accede to the university's demand that he discontinue his organizing activities. Lawson's willingness to accept expulsion from the seminary rather than cease his civil rights work moved its sympathetic faculty members to pressure the university to provide him with an alternative educational institution to attend. The university eventually capitulated, but by that time Lawson had transferred to Boston University, earning a bachelor of sacred theology degree in 1960.

Though not as visible as other civil rights leaders, Lawson was involved with many of the well-known civil rights organizations and demonstrations of the Freedom Movement. He was an adviser to the STUDENT NONVIOLENT COORDINATING COMMITTEE (SNCC) and authored the organization's statement of purpose while attending its initial conference in April 1960. He led the direct action projects of the SOUTHERN CHRISTIAN LEADERSHIP CONFERENCE (SCLC), and he participated in the Freedom Rides, which were first sponsored by the CONGRESS OF RACIAL EQUALITY (CORE). In 1968, while serving as a pastor in MEMPHIS, TENNESSEE, he helped coordinate the garbage workers' strike, by which he hoped to highlight the lasting and adverse economic effects of segregation.

Robert Fay

SEE ALSO

Sit-Ins.

Africa

Laye, Camara

(b. January 1, 1928, Kouroussa, French Guinea [now Guinea]; d. February 4, 1980, Senegal), Guinean novelist considered a pioneer of modern West African literature.

With the 1953 publication of his autobiography *L'Enfant noir* (published in America as *The Dark Child* in 1954), Camara Laye was hailed as having "brought French African narrative prose finally into its own." Although he published only three more books, he is widely considered one of the most important African novelists to have written in French.

The son of a goldsmith, Laye was influenced in his childhood by both the local Koran and French schools he attended and by the traditional village life of Kouroussa, a town that still resonated with stories of the ancient MALI EMPIRE to which it once belonged. After attending secondary school in Conakry, the capital of GUINEA, he won a scholarship to study engineering in Argenteuil, France, outside Paris.

Away from his country for the first time and separated from his family and community, Laye began writing the memoir that became *L'Enfant noir*. The book recounts Laye's experiences in the village, at school, and in Conakry and ends as he boards the airplane that will take him to France. As critics have noted, some reviewers focused on issues outside the book itself: Americans and Europeans responded to its charming descriptions of traditional African life, and Africans condemned the absence of a critique of colonialism. But Laye's clear, elegant prose won over readers and such critics as Abiola Irele, who remarked that *The Dark Child*, in its portrayal of village life, presented "an image of coherence and dignity... in the self-contained African universe of [Laye's] childhood."

The success of his first book permitted Laye to quit his job as a mechanic and write full-time. His first novel, *Le regard du roi*, appeared in 1954 and was translated as *The Radiance of the King* in 1956. Telling the story of a white man's quest to find the African king he hopes will become his patron, it is a complex work interwoven with religious allegory, folkloric influences and, according to some critics, an echo of the European writer Franz Kafka's nightmarish world-view. Reviewers hailed it as "the great African novel."

After returning to Guinea in 1956 and marrying his high-school sweetheart, Marie, Laye worked as an engineer and later for the Ministry of Information. But Guinea's independence from France in 1958 and the subsequent rule of its first president, SÉKOU TOURÉ, brought disturbing changes to Laye's home country. His 1966 book, *A Dream of Africa* (*Dramouss* in French editions), openly attacked what its hero, Fatoman, called "a regime based on violence." Condemning both COLONIAL RULE and the regime that replaced it, Laye earned the hatred of Sékou Touré, and he and his family were forced into exile in neighboring SENEGAL soon after the book's publication.

Laye continued to write short stories, several of which were published in the literary magazines *Black Orpheus* and *Présence Africaine*. His last novel, *Le maître de la parole: Kuoma Lafolo Kuoma*, appeared in 1978 and was translated as *The Guardian of the Word* in 1980. It avoided contemporary politics, instead telling an epic tale set in the ancient Mali Empire. Drawing on the oral histories told by Guinean *griots* (storytellers), Laye used modern literary techniques to reassert what one reviewer called "the traditional African vision of the spiritual and the historic."

SEE ALSO

Conakry, Guinea; Literature, French Language, in Africa.

North America

Leadership Conference on Civil Rights,

an important American lobbying organization for civil rights legislation in the last half of the twentieth century.

The Leadership Conference on Civil Rights (LCCR) was formed in 1950 in response to the federal government's elimination of the Fair Employment Practices Committee (FEPC), an agency that had been created to end racially discriminatory hiring practices in the federal government. After failing to persuade the administration of President Harry S. Truman to revive the FEPC, Roy Wilkins and Arnold Aronson of the NATIONAL ASSOCIATION FOR THE ADVANCEMENT OF COLORED PEOPLE (NAACP) organized a conference in WASHINGTON, D.C., called the National Emergency Civil Rights Mobilization. Out of that conference, which was held on January 15, 1950, and was attended by 4000 African Americans representing more than 100 civil rights groups, came the LCCR, a broad coalition dedicated to lobbying Congress for the passage of civil rights laws and serving as an information clearinghouse for its member organizations.

The LCCR became a force in United States politics, mainly through the efforts of CLARENCE MITCHELL, its chief strategist, who was seen so often roaming the halls of Congress that he became known as "the 101st Senator." The LCCR played a pivotal role in the passage of the Civil Rights Acts of 1957, 1960, and 1964 and the VOTING RIGHTS ACT OF 1965 and its extension in 1976. The organization expanded its scope in the 1960s and 1970s, working with other minority groups such as women's, Asian American, and Latino organizations.

Robert Fay

SEE ALSO
Fair Employment Practices Committee; Wilkins, Roy Ottoway.

Africa

Leakey, Louis (b. August 7, 1903, Kabete, Kenya; d. October 1, 1972, London, England), British paleoanthropologist noted for his discoveries of fossil remains that greatly advanced the study of human evolution.

Even before he received his doctorate in anthropology from the University of Cambridge, Louis Leakey, the son of British missionaries to colonial KENYA, was convinced that human evolution began in Africa, not in Asia, as was commonly believed among his contemporaries. To prove his theory, Leakey focused his archaeological research on expeditions to Olduvai, a river gorge in Tanganyika (now TANZANIA). Though he found important fossils and Stone Age tools, Leakey had not found definitive evidence that Africa was the cradle of human evolution.

That changed on an expedition to Olduvai in 1959, when his wife, Mary Leakey, with whom he had worked since 1933, discovered the partial remains of a 1.75-million-year-old fossil hominid, which Louis Leakey classified as *Zinjanthropus* (later classified as *Australopithecus boisei*). From 1960 to 1963 the Leakeys unearthed other important discoveries, including the remains of another fossil hominid, which they classified as *Homo habilis* (Latin for "handy man"), claiming it was both the first member of the true human genus and the first true toolmaker. While the exact interpretation of the Leakeys' fossil finds is still debated, their significance to the field of physical anthropology is universally acknowledged and they are considered the best evidence yet that Africa was in fact the starting point for human evolution.

In his later years Leakey became increasingly interested in studying primate behavior as a way of understanding the behavior of human ancestors. He helped to engineer the funding and recruitment of groundbreaking researchers, including JANE GOODALL, who worked with chimpanzees in Gombe, Tanzania; Dian Fossey, who studied mountain gorillas in RWANDA; and Birute Galdikas Brindamour, who researched orangutans in the Sarawak region of Indonesia. His books include *Stone Age Africa* (1936) and *Olduvai Gorge, 1951-1961* (1965).

Robert Fay

SEE ALSO
Chimpanzee; Gorilla; Leakey, Mary Douglas Nicol.

Africa

Leakey, Mary Douglas Nicol (b. February 6, 1913, London, England; d. December 9, 1996, Nairobi, Kenya), British paleoanthropologist noted for her discoveries of fossil remains that greatly advanced the study of human evolution.

Mary Leakey's deep interest in the study of prehistory began at age 11, when she viewed cave paintings of the Dordogne in southern France. Although she later took courses in anthropology and geology at University College, London, and participated in excavations in England, she never earned a degree. In 1933 paleoanthropologist LOUIS LEAKEY asked her to illustrate a book he was writing. The two fell in love, married in 1936, and formed one of the most famous and most successful scientific collaborations of the twentieth century.

Although the Leakeys were partners, it was Louis Leakey's controversial theories that drove their research throughout much of their careers. During the 20 years that the Leakeys spent attempting to prove that human evolution occurred in Africa and not Asia, Mary Leakey developed rigorous excavation techniques that set the standard for paleoanthropological documentation and excavation. A tireless worker, after long days of carefully sifting the Olduvai earth for fossils she frequently spent the evenings sketching and cataloguing fossil fragments while enjoying Cuban cigars and single-malt whiskey.

Although Louis Leakey received most of the credit, Mary Leakey made their greatest discoveries. At Olduvai Gorge in 1959, she discovered the partial remains of a 1.75-million-year-old hominid. She later found the remains of another hominid, classified as *Homo habilis* (Latin for "handy man"), which many scientists believe was both the first member of the true human genus and the first true toolmaker. These finds demonstrated the antiquity of hominids in Africa, established the continent as the birthplace of the human species, and focused paleoanthropologic research in Africa. The fame that followed these finds led to frequent fundraising trips by Louis Leakey, which left Mary Leakey directing the research projects in Africa, a period in which she emerged from her husband's professional shadow.

In 1978 Mary Leakey made what she considered her greatest discovery: footprints of a human ancestor, dated to more than 3.6 million years earlier. The footprints indicated that bipedalism occurred well before the development of a large, complicated brain.

In 1983 Mary Leakey retired from fieldwork to her home in Nairobi, where she completed her analysis of the Olduvai fossil. Her autobiography, *Disclosing the Past*, was published in 1984.

Robert Fay

SEE ALSO
Nairobi, Kenya.

Africa

Leakey, Richard Erskine Frere (b. December 19, 1944, Nairobi, Kenya), Kenyan conservationist, fossil hunter, and political figure whose varied career has made him one of KENYA's most famous and controversial citizens.

Richard Leakey's parents, Louis and Mary Leakey, introduced him to paleoanthropology, the study of fossilized remains of extinct humanlike creatures called hominids. The elder Leakeys, whose discoveries at Olduvai Gorge in TANZANIA revolutionized theories of early human evolution, often took their son with them on their fossil-hunting expeditions. Richard Leakey left Nairobi's Duke of York School at age 17 to start a business leading wildlife photography safaris.

Although he had no formal training, Leakey began fossil hunting when he was only 19. His most famous discoveries were made in the area around Lake Turkana (formerly Lake Rudolf) in northern Kenya, where he uncovered more than 200 fossils of early hominids. These include an almost complete skeleton of an adolescent boy found at Nariokotome, on the western shore. The 1.6-million-year-old Turkana Boy is the most complete skeleton ever found from that period of human evolution. Leakey was also involved in the discovery of the 17-million-year-old jaw, teeth, and skull fragments of an apelike creature, *Sivapithecus*, a possible ancestor of both humans and apes. He has written about these and other findings in three books coauthored by Roger Lewin, *Origins* (1977), *People of the Lake* (1978), and *Origins Reconsidered* (1992).

Leakey's daughter Louise also participates in the "family business" of fossil-hunting expeditions, as has his wife, noted paleoanthropologist Maeve Leakey, who has made several important discoveries. In 1995 she discovered an approximately 4-million-year-old skeleton in the Lake Turkana region, the oldest known specimen of a hominid that walked upright.

Leakey served as the director of the National Museums of Kenya from 1968 to 1989, helping to establish it as one of the most prestigious in Africa. In 1989 Kenya's president, Daniel arap Moi, appointed Leakey director of the National Wildlife Services (NWS) of Kenya. One of Leakey's main duties as head of the NWS was to ensure the survival of Kenya's threatened and endangered wild animals, particularly the African elephant. Leakey took the controversial stance of supporting a total ban on the ivory trade, fearing that even restricted sale would invite poaching. Though he succeeded in reducing elephant poaching and the black-market sale of ivory, his views upset the many southern African nations that had thriving elephant populations as well as surplus stocks of ivory and needed the money that sale of those stocks would provide.

Leakey's conservation policies also caused tensions with Kenyan farmers and pastoralists. Only one-fourth of the wild animals in Kenya – elephants, zebras, and wildebeests among them – are confined to national parks, while the rest roam freely and thus may destroy crops, prey on vulnerable livestock, and injure and kill people. In addition, farmers and pastoralists living around the parks see little of the tourism revenue that the parks provide. Many believed that Leakey, who chose to reinvest the bulk of this tourism revenue into the national park system, was protecting animals to the detriment of Kenyan people.

These disagreements became bitter when officials in Moi's administration charged Leakey with racism, corruption, and mismanagement of the NWS. Leakey denied these claims, saying that his critics were upset at his refusal to allow mining and other commercial ventures in Kenya's National Parks. Leakey continued his efforts despite a 1993 plane crash that resulted in the loss of the lower half of both of his legs. In 1994, however, he resigned as director of the NWS, citing a "campaign of vilification" carried out by his opponents. After his resignation, Leakey grew increasingly disenchanted with Moi's government. In 1995 he helped found a new political party, Safina (Swahili for Noah's Ark), which has attacked corruption and political repression in Kenya.

Robert Fay

See Also

Elephant; Swahili Language; Leakey, Louis; Leakey, Mary Douglas Nicol; Pastoralism; Tourism in Africa; Wildebeest; Wildlife Management in Africa; Zebra.

Africa

Lebna Dengel (b. 1496, Ethiopia; d. September 2, 1540, Debra Damo, Ethiopia), ruler of the mainly Christian Ethiopian Empire at the time that Muslim invaders nearly conquered it.

Lebna Dengel assumed the throne at age 12, after the death of his father. During his early reign his mother, Helena, served as regent. In 1516 the Muslim sultanate of Adal rebelled against Ethiopian domination, but Lebna Dengel's forces defeated the rebellion. The queen regent, however, feared Muslim expansion and turned to Portugal for aid.

A Portuguese mission arrived in 1520. Some accounts suggest that the emperor sought a relationship with the Portuguese as a means of ending Ethiopia's isolation and acquiring European technology. Others sources imply that Lebna Dengel was unimpressed by the Portuguese visitors, whom he allegedly treated with cool disregard.

Sources also disagree about the nature of Lebna Dengel's reign. Some scholars emphasize his devotion to Christianity and claim that his rule was based on justice and mercy, while others assert that he was an arbitrary ruler who alienated the Ethiopian nobility. The latter may be more accurate, for the Adalites rebelled anew in 1527. Led by Ahmad Ibn Ibrahim, also called Grañ, Arabic for "left-handed," Adalite forces met little resistance. They swept through Ethiopia, destroyed monasteries, and forcibly converted much of the population to Islam. Lebna Dengel fled to a mountaintop monastery at Debra Damo, where he died in 1540. His son, Galawdéwos, defeated Grañ three years later with Portuguese assistance.

Robert Fay

Latin America and the Caribbean

Lecuona, Ernesto (b. August 7, 1896, Guanabacoa, Cuba; d. November 29, 1963, Santa Cruz de Tenerife, Spain), Cuban pianist and composer of classical and popular music who played an important role in bringing Afro-Cuban rhythms to an international audience.

Ernesto Lecuona, who gained international recognition in the 1920s, is widely considered to be one of Cuba's greatest composers. Famed for such classical masterpieces as *Malagueña* and *Andalucia Suite*, he produced more than 1000 works, including 176 pieces for solo piano and 37 orchestral scores. During the 1930s he founded the enormously popular rumba band Lecuona Cuban Boys, which helped to pave the way for Latin jazz and salsa. He also composed nearly a dozen Hollywood film scores, including the music for the 1947 film *Carnival in Costa Rica*.

Lecuona's compositions reflect three musical styles: pieces influenced by European classical styles, particularly the works of Spanish composers Isaac Albéniz and Enrique Granados; boleros and *criollas* inspired by Cuban folk sources; and works that delve into the rhythms and color of Afro-Cuban music. According to music critic Mark Holston, "Lecuona is known for the enduring melodic beauty of his most famous works and for his pioneering role in bringing West Africa-derived rhythms from the barrio to the concert hall." Lecuona was a gifted pianist with a technical and interpretative flair that recalled the great European pianists Chopin and Liszt. As a performer and composer, he knew well how to meld Afro-Cuban rhythms into both popular and classical idioms – a talent exemplified in the elegant *La camparsa* and *Danzas Afro-cubanas* for piano. He also composed numerous Afro-Cuban vocal works, popularized among the middle class by the Afro-Cuban pianist and singer Rita Montaner.

Educated in Cuba's National Conservatory, Lecuona debuted as a concert pianist at age 17 at New York City's Aeolian Hall. During the early 1920s he studied music in France with composer Maurice Ravel and toured widely as a pianist in Europe and the Americas. From the early 1930s on he spent a considerable part of his career performing with popular Latin bands, including his own group, Lecuona Cuban Boys, which recorded for Columbia and toured throughout Europe, the Americas, and the Middle East. He also performed with Machito, the famed Afro-Cuban musician and one of the founders of Afro-Cuban jazz. As Cuban musician Marco Rizo notes, "In the 1940s, [Lecuona] would be in concert at Carnegie Hall with a symphonic orchestra one night and be booked to perform at the La Conga cabaret with popular, jazz-leaning Latin bands… the very next evening." In 1943 Lecuona premiered his acclaimed *Rapsodia Negra* for piano and orchestra at New York's Carnegie Hall.

Lecuona was a musician of extraordinary versatility; he has often been compared to George Gershwin, a lifelong friend of the Cuban composer. Both wrote in classical, popular, and folk idioms – a talent which, according to Holston, "made their careers and contributions to global culture so profoundly influential and long lasting."

Roanne Edwards

See Also

Salsa Music; New York, New York; Jazz, Afro-Latin; Bolero; Music, Classical, in Latin America and the Caribbean.

North America

Ledbetter, Hudson William ("Leadbelly") (b. January 21, 1885, near Mooringsport, La.; d. December 6, 1949, New York, N.Y.), African American itinerant musician who played from a wide repertoire that centered on blues but included folk ballads, popular songs, and music from the American West.

As a child Leadbelly picked cotton with his parents, first as a sharecropper in Louisiana and then on land that his parents bought in Leigh, Texas. During his youth in Leigh, he demonstrated substantial musical talent. He played the accordion, mastered the 12-string guitar, and soon frequented the red-light district of neighboring Shreveport as a musician.

In his early twenties Leadbelly left home and was married, though not to the woman who mothered his two children. At this age he was already an inveterate rambling man, versed in violence, drink, and promiscuity. He settled in Harris County, Texas, and then moved to Dallas, where he met and formed a musical relationship with the great bluesman Blind Lemon Jefferson. When possible, Leadbelly supported himself with his music; otherwise he worked on farms and at other manual labor.

Throughout the next two decades Leadbelly had frequent skirmishes with the law. He was jailed in 1915 but escaped; he served a prison sentence from 1918 to 1925 for murder; and he returned to prison in 1930 until 1934 for attempted homicide. Both his stints in prison ended by means of his music. In 1925 he improvised a song that successfully begged the pardon of Gov. Pat Neff, who was visiting the penitentiary; and in 1934 Leadbelly shortened his sentence by impressing white folklorist John A. Lomax, who requested Leadbelly's release.

With the help of his son, Alan, John Lomax compiled folk recordings for the Library of Congress, traveling the south with new technology to capture America's oral traditions. In Leadbelly they found an immense repository of folk and original music, which they recorded and promoted in the East. John Lomax transformed Leadbelly's life, hiring him as a chauffeur and introducing him to white audiences.

Leadbelly cut commercial recordings and released "race records" but achieved his largest following on college campuses, at political rallies, and in the folk scene of Greenwich Village in the early 1940s. He collaborated with both white and black members of this crowd, including Woody Guthrie, Brownie McGhee, Sonny Terry, and Big Bill Broonzy. Like these musicians, Leadbelly became associated with left-wing politics and wrote such overtly political tunes as "Scottsboro Boys" (1938) and "Bourgeois Blues" (1938). In the 1940s he achieved greater celebrity by appearing on radio and in film. In 1949 he toured in Europe but returned to New York, where he died later that year.

Leadbelly had a rough and powerful voice, yet he could perform with subtle and surprising delicacy. He was a master of the 12-string guitar and accomplished on mandolin, accordion, piano, and harmonica. His work as a musician yielded approximately 70 original or highly reworked compositions in addition to scores of children's songs, Southern ballads, blues tunes, field hollers, and popular songs. In Europe Leadbelly influenced the skiffle bands that later culminated in the Beatles and the Rolling Stones. In the United States he inspired a generation of black bluesmen as well as white folk singers such as Joan Baez and Bob Dylan. In 1976 Gordon Parks Sr. made a biographical film about his life. In 1988 Leadbelly was inducted into the Rock and Roll Hall of Fame.

Eric Bennett

See Also
Blues, The; Jefferson, ("Blind") Lemon; Parks, Gordon, Sr.; New York, New York.

North America

Lee, Barbara (b. June 16, 1946, El Paso, Texas), Democratic member of the United States House of Representatives from California (1998-).

Barbara Lee was born in El Paso, Texas, and lived there until her family moved to San Fernando, California, in 1960. She earned a bachelor's degree from Mills College in 1973 and a master's degree in social welfare from the University of California at Berkeley in 1975. Shortly after earning her master's, Lee joined the staff of Congressman Ron V. Dellums, serving as his senior adviser and chief of staff before seeking election to the California legislature.

Prior to serving in the U.S. House of Representatives, Lee served in the California Assembly from 1990 to 1996, and the California Senate from 1996 to 1998. She was elected to Congress to fill the seat of Dellums, who retired during his 27th term. Lee vowed to "ensure that federal agencies have a good understanding of the needs of the district." One of her main concerns was to work closely with Pentagon officials to help convert the military bases in the San Francisco Bay Area to civilian uses. In the 105th Congress (1997-1999), Lee sat on the Committee on Banking and Financial Services and the House Science Committee.

Robert Fay

See Also
Dellums, Ronald V. (Ron).

North America

Lee, Canada (b. May 3, 1907, New York, N.Y.; d. May 10, 1952, England), African American prizefighter and actor noted for performing strong, nonstereotypical roles in the 1930s and 1940s.

As an African American actor, Canada Lee played nonstereotypical roles during the late 1930s and 1940s, when black actors and actresses were relegated to demeaning roles. Originally a boxer, he entered theater after being blinded in one eye in a fight in 1933. He began his acting career when he was cast in the role of Banquo in a black production of *Macbeth* funded by the Works Progress Administration (WPA) Negro Federal Theatre Project in 1936. The play was directed by Orson Welles and marked the beginning of Lee's casting in nontraditional roles.

Although *Macbeth* received some negative reviews (due more to the fact that a black cast was performing Shakespeare than to the acting), it gave Lee the needed exposure to continue in such roles. Through the WPA Negro Federal Theatre Project, he continued to experiment with the nontraditional, performing in Eugene O'Neill's *One Act Plays of the Sea* in 1937 and *Haiti*, by W. E. B. Du Bois, in 1938. Due to the "communist leanings" of the play *Haiti* and *Big White Fog* in 1940, the Negro Federal Theatre Project was halted by the House Committee on Un-American Activities (HUAC).

Nevertheless, Lee had gained enough exposure to be cast in the part of Drayton in *Mamba's Daughters* on Broadway in 1939. Further, the experience he gained with the Negro Federal Theatre Project led to his role as Bigger Thomas in *Native Son* in 1940 and 1941. Critics cite his portrayal of Bigger as the best role of his career. Because the play had an interracial cast, it became highly controversial.

Lee's visibility as a black actor doing unconventional roles inspired him to speak out against the limited casting of black actors and actresses in Hollywood and Broadway. Determined not to take stereotypical "handkerchief head roles," he decided to produce *On Whitman Avenue* to achieve that end. In 1947 the HUAC cited Lee's play as "left-wing."

Lee garnered even greater visibility when he portrayed Stephen Kumalo, a father whose son kills a white man, in the play *Cry, the Beloved Country*, produced by Zoltan Korda. Despite worldwide attention for his acting, Lee could not escape being black-listed and pursued by HUAC as well as by the Federal Bureau of Investigation for speaking out against stereotyping. He died in 1952, 45 years old and penniless.

See Also
Boxing; Du Bois, William Edward Burghardt (W. E. B.); Racial Stereotypes; Communist Party USA, African Americans and the; Film, Blacks in American.

North America

Lee, Jarena (b. February 11, 1783, Cape May, N.J.; d. ?), African American preacher; one of the most influential women in the early African Methodist Episcopal (AME) Church.

"And why should it be thought impossible, heterodox, or improper, for a woman to preach? seeing the Savior died for the woman as well as the man." In this quotation from her autobiography, Jarena Lee explains the belief that led her to become one of the first African American women preachers. Lee was born into a free black family and was hired out as an indentured servant at age 7. She converted to Christianity at age 21, and, after wrestling with spiritual doubts for several years, realized that she was serious about her faith and felt called by God to preach. But when Lee first asked to preach at Philadelphia's Bethel AME Church in 1809, Rev. Richard Allen dissuaded her because of her gender.

She became a minister's wife instead, marrying Rev. Joseph Lee in 1811 and giving birth to two children. But when her husband died in 1818, Lee returned to her original calling. This time Allen, impressed by Lee's oratorical abilities, supported her. As a woman she was still not allowed to become an official leader of a congregation, and so instead she became a traveling evangelist. As an itinerant preacher Lee traveled to churches, camp meetings, schoolhouses, and private homes across the Northeast, sharing her evangelical message with black and white audiences. Lee described her conversion, travels, and other experiences in her 1836 autobiography, which she revised and updated in 1849. She is still remembered as one of the first African American women preachers.

Lisa Clayton Robinson

See Also
African Methodist Episcopal Church; Free Blacks in the United States, 1619 to 1863.

North America

Lee, Shelton Jackson ("Spike") (b. March 20, 1957, Atlanta, Ga.), African American film director, writer, and actor.

Starting with the phenomenal popularity of *She's Gotta Have It*, Spike Lee has emerged as one of America's most successful filmmakers, garnering both good reviews and healthy box-office receipts for his movies. He has also attracted criticism; detractors have called him arrogant and paranoid and his movies incendiary, even racist. But controversy has not kept Lee from becoming a media icon, famous for his acting, fashion sense, and provocative public pronouncements on a variety of subjects.

Raised in the Fort Greene neighborhood of Brooklyn, New York, Lee is the eldest of five children born to Bill Lee, a jazz musician and composer, and Jacquelyn Lee, a schoolteacher. Both of his parents came from well-educated families, and Lee's childhood was rich in art, music, and literature. Like his father and grandfather before him, Lee attended Morehouse College in Atlanta, Georgia. It was at Morehouse that he first began to "dib and dab in super-8 filmmaking." These early experiments led to his enrollment at the Institute of Film and Television at New York University (NYU).

One of the few black students at NYU's film school, Lee attracted controversy with his short film *The Answer* (1980), a response to D. W. Griffith's classic silent film *Birth of a Nation*, which has become famous as much for its racist politics as for its cinematic excellence. Later student works included *Sarah* (1981), a loving depiction of Thanksgiving in Harlem, and Lee's last student film, *Joe's Bed-Stuy Barbershop: We Cut Heads* (1982), which garnered an award from the Academy of Motion Picture Arts and Sciences as well as screenings at prestigious film festivals.

Despite this early recognition, Lee received no offers from Hollywood after graduating from NYU, a situation he attributed to the systemic racism in the entertainment industry. While working at a film distribution company, he raised money to finance an independent film. In 1986, following the collapse of his plans for a movie about a bike messenger, Lee released his first feature film, *She's Gotta Have It*, a romantic comedy about a single black woman dating three men simultaneously. Critics praised the movie's style, intelligence, humor, and realistic portrayal of African Americans – something seldom seen in Hollywood productions – and it received the coveted New Film Award at the Cannes Film Festival.

For his next project Lee returned to a script he had written while at Morehouse. *School Daze* (1988) focused on conflicts between fair-skinned, upwardly mobile African American "wannabes" and darker, more Afrocentric "jigaboos" at a historically black university. Lee, who has appeared in nearly all of his films, costarred with Laurence Fishburne and Giancarlo Esposito in *School Daze*, which received mixed reviews but was financially successful.

It was Lee's third feature that received the most attention. *Do the Right Thing* (1989), set in the Bedford-Stuyvesant and Bensonhurst sections of Brooklyn, came in the wake of a series of racially motivated attacks against African Americans. Ending with a scene in which white police officers kill a black teenager, *Do the Right Thing* was met with alarm by many white critics and commentators who feared that it would incite rioting among African Americans. It did not. The movie, widely considered Lee's best film artistically, was a box-office success.

Attention from *Do the Right Thing*, combined with Lee's popular commercials for Nike and other products, made him a recognizable celebrity by 1990. With the increased exposure, Lee's comments on race relations, politics, other filmmakers, and even basketball sparked heated responses from many quarters. Despite the occasionally negative press, many credit Lee's visibility and the success of his first three films with inspiring a wave of African American filmmakers. Young directors such as John Singleton (*Boyz N the Hood*, 1991) and Matty Rich (*Straight out of Brooklyn*, 1991) began finding the financial and institutional support that had eluded Lee only a few years earlier.

Lee's next two films – *Mo' Better Blues* (1990) and *Jungle Fever* (1991) – were less well received critically, though each made money. In 1992 he released his most ambitious film, *Malcolm X*, a sweeping biography of the slain civil rights leader. *Malcolm X* attracted at least as much controversy as *Do the Right Thing*, particularly within the black community, some of which saw Lee as co-opting the Black Muslim hero's image. Lee, who had used security personnel from the Nation of Islam to guard the sets on previous films, responded with typical bravado. The film, starring Denzel Washington, received mostly favorable reviews but was criticized for its length and simplistic political message.

After *Malcolm X*, Lee made a number of movies – *Crooklyn* (1994), *Clockers* (1995), *Girl 6* (1996), *Get on the Bus* (1996), and *He Got Game* (1998) – that did not attract the critical or commercial attention that his earlier work did. Lee also continued to film commercials and music videos and command a film studio (40 Acres & A Mule, named for a broken promise the United States government made to former slaves after the Civil War [*see* Forty Acres and a Mule]) and a clothing store in his home neighborhood in Brooklyn. Lee's 1998 documentary *Four Little Girls*, about the victims of a 1963 church bombing in Birmingham, Alabama, was nominated for an Academy Award. In 1999 he released *Summer of Sam*, a drama set in the late 1970s.

Kate Tuttle

See Also
Slavery in the United States; *Birth of a Nation, The*; Civil War, American; Harlem, New York; Malcolm X; New York, New York; Film, Blacks in American; Afrocentrism.

Africa

Lega (also known as Rega), ethnic group of the Democratic Republic of the Congo.

The Lega primarily inhabit east central Congo-Kinshasa. They speak a Bantu language. Approximately 400,000 people consider themselves Lega.

See Also
Bantu: Dispersion and Settlement.

Latin America and the Caribbean

Légitimus, Hégésippe

(b. April 10, 1868, Pointe-à-Pitre, Guadeloupe; d. November 29, 1944, L'Angle-sur-Lánglin, France), founder and leader of the Guadeloupean Workers' Party (*Parti ouvrier de la Guadeloupe*); this socialist politician gave the black population of GUADELOUPE its first elected voice in that French colony's political process.

Hégésippe Légitimus was the son of a fisherman who lost his life at sea. He grew up in Pointe-à-Pitre and attended the *lycée* Carnot, where he came in contact with the ideas of the French socialist theoretician Jules Guesde. This political awakening led him to form a Committee for Republican Socialist Youth. After witnessing a mulatto overseer mistreat a black youth, he publicly took the defense of the latter in his first political gesture.

Légitimus entered public politics when Guadeloupe was in the throes of an extended economic crisis after the relative prosperity of the Second Empire (1852-1870). Following the abolition of slavery in 1848, this earlier period saw both the consolidation of SUGAR plantation capital in the hands of metropolitan owners and a rapid increase in economic activity following the lifting of foreign trade restrictions in 1861. The need for inexpensive labor, however, outlived slavery itself. When blacks refused the badly paid, quasi-obligatory work on the land where they had suffered, owners imported African, Chinese, and, in particular, East Indian workers rather than raise wages. In addition to this new labor competition, significant gains in local sugar production were undercut by worldwide overproduction of the commodity from 1885 onward.

FRANCE itself was producing more sugar beets than it could consume and was in no position to help a far-off colony. The combination of this extended crisis among the black working class and the gradual development of an embryonic black bourgeoisie supported the emergence of a black political movement in Guadeloupe.

In this context, Légitimus's political campaign, which began in 1891, marked the first appeal to black identity in Guadeloupean politics as grounds for electoral success. In that year he founded the socialist paper *Le peuple* with other students. This paper would later become, successively, *Le cri du peuple* and *La cravache*. Although he lost his first electoral battle in 1892, in 1894 he was elected to the regional council as *conseil général*, and his party won numerous local elections in 1896. His platform called for the organization of Guadeloupean workers into a distinct class that could then go on to dominate public office, "the possession of which can alone lead to the eviction of the capitalist bourgeoisie." In 1898 Légitimus defeated the mulatto politician Auguste Isaac in legislative elections to the departmental assembly that solidified the dominant role of the Workers' Party in the island's politics. This domination was to be short-lived. A split occurred in the Workers' Party that would terminally weaken it when Achille-René Boisneuf left to form the Liberal Party, accusing Légitimus of authoritarianism. Légitimus lost the electoral battle of 1902, regaining his seat from 1906 to 1914. The elections of 1910 were particularly acrimonious, marred by charges of absenteeism and fraud. This, along with Légitimus's continued support of the Guadeloupean working class and attacks on the colonial bourgeoisie, resulted in a two-year prison sentence and a five-year lifting of his *droits civiques* (civil rights) in February 1911, though this verdict was later commuted.

After his early successes, Légitimus had brought his once progressive party into contact with the property-owning classes so inimical to its original constituency. In an effort to overwhelm moderate mulatto political forces, this "worker-capital alliance" – which one commentator has termed a stratagem "against nature" – led Légitimus to support the French socialist Alfred-Léon Gérault-Richard, who eventually called in French troops against local protesters. By 1909, in fact, accusations of electoral fraud had so weakened him politically that Boisneuf was effectively able to replace him as the dominant force in the island's politics. From 1914 to 1936 Légitimus, though no longer an elected official, continued to defend Guadeloupe's black working class in both articles and speeches. In 1936 he moved to France, where he died in 1944.

Nick Nesbitt

SEE ALSO
East Indian Communities in the Caribbean; Abolition and Emancipation in Latin America and the Caribbean.

Africa

Lemurs, primates indigenous to MADAGASCAR.

Some time after a type of primate called "prosimians" first evolved in mainland Africa during the Eocene Epoch (about 58 million years ago), a group of them made the 400- to 550-km-wide (about 240-330 mi) crossing to Madagascar, possibly drifting atop vegetative rafts. Prosimians on the mainland became extinct approximately 30 million years ago, while those in Madagascar, an ecosystem devoid of large predators, evolved quite different adaptations from the mainland primates known as anthropoids, including monkeys, apes, and humans. Prosimians, including lemurs, are of particular interest to primatologists in part because they retain many characteristics once shared by early ancestors of the anthropoids and thus provide clues to both early primate behavior and the history of human evolution. These traits include fox-like features, smaller brains in relation to body size, hands less suited for grasping, an acute sense of smell, and nonstereoscopic vision.

Today the 32 surviving species of lemurs can only be found in Madagascar and the COMOROS, where they were probably imported by humans during the last millennium. At least 15 larger species of lemurs have become extinct since humans settled the island approximately 2000 years ago, due both to hunting and loss of habitation. The largest of these, archaeoindris, weighed between 160 and 200 kg (350 and 440 lb). The remaining species range considerably in size: an adult pygmy mouse lemur (*Microcebus myoxinus*) stands 4 cm (1.6 in) tall and weighs all of 30 gm (1.05 oz) while larger species such as the indri (*Indri indri*) can weigh as much as 7 kg (15.4 lb). Together these lemurs represent 13 percent of all primate species.

Lemurs are predominantly arboreal frugivores or herbivores, but smaller nocturnal species also eat insects. All but the indri have long, bushy, nonprehensile tails; the well-known ring-tailed lemur (*Lemur catta*) uses its tail for balance and to signal dominance. Lemurs' hind limbs are also quite long in relationship to body size and their second toes have an enlarged nail, particularly pronounced in the nocturnal aye-aye (*Daubentonia madagascariensis*).

With a body measuring 40 cm (15.6 in) long and a tail extending an additional 55 to 60 cm (21.4 to 25.7 in), the aye-aye was mistakenly classified as a rodent by a nineteenth-century French naturalist. It uses its long finger to tap on tree limbs and locate grubs by sound, and then, after chewing through the wood with ever-growing incisors, to hook and remove the larva. Because of its strange appearance, its taste for fruit crops, and the belief that it brings bad luck, the aye-aye is often killed when spotted. It is one of several severely endangered species of lemur in Madagascar.

Lemurs, along with other fauna such as chameleons, make Madagascar one of the seven most significant world centers of biodiversity. Recognizing the importance of lemurs in attracting tourism, the Madagascar government, in association with international agencies such as the World Wildlife Fund for Nature, has set up a number of protected reserves. Many of these reserves are ineffectual, however, due to a lack of infrastructure and resources. Lemurs are threatened primarily by a loss of habitat. With a high rate of population growth and a reliance on slash and burn agriculture, the human population of Madagascar continues to encroach on the forest upon which lemurs depend. Only a concerted and well-orchestrated conservation strategy will likely preserve the remaining species of lemurs.

Ari Nave

SEE ALSO
Tourism in Africa.

Africa

Lendu (also known as the Bale), ethnic group of eastern-Central Africa.

The Lendu inhabit the western shores of Lake Albert, mainly in the northeastern Democratic Republic of the Congo but also in northwestern Uganda. They speak a Nilo-Saharan language. More than 300,000 people consider themselves Lendu.

See Also
Languages, African: An Overview.

Africa

Lenje, ethnic group of Zambia.

The Lenje primarily inhabit south central Zambia. They speak a Bantu language and are closely related to the neighboring Tonga people. Approximately 200,000 people consider themselves Lenje.

See Also
Bantu: Dispersion and Settlement.

North America

LeNoire, Rosetta Olive Burton (b. August 8, 1911, New York, N.Y.), African American actress, theater executive, and social activist.

Encouraged by her godfather, the dancer Bill "Bojangles" Robinson, Rosetta LeNoire began to sing and dance at an early age. Robinson gave her the nickname "Bubbling Brown Sugar in a Crystal Ball," which she carried with her throughout her life. LeNoire began her career playing the First Witch in a Haitian *Macbeth*, a production directed by Orson Welles in 1936. Over much of her career, she played the roles of housemaids with a self-confident grace that inspired pride and respect. For over 50 years she performed on and off-Broadway. In her eighties, LeNoire appeared on television in such roles as Nell Carter's mother on *Gimme a Break* and the grandmother on *Family Matters*.

LeNoire was active in the creation of the Negro Actors Guild (NAG) and the Coordinating Council for Negro Performers (CCNP), both of which strove to aid black actors in financial need, create acting opportunities for blacks, and fight to eliminate demeaning portrayals of African Americans on television and on film. In 1968 LeNoire helped establish the Amas Repertory Theater in New York City. The purpose of Amas has been to encourage racial understanding through theatrical productions. Its most successful show, *Bubbling Brown Sugar*, an award-winning musical tribute to black music and culture, opened on Broadway in 1976.

See Also
Robinson, Bill ("Bojangles"); Television and African Americans; Film, Blacks in American.

Africa

Leo Africanus (al-Hassan ibn Muhammad al-Wizzaa al-Fasi, also known as Giovanni Leoni) (b. 1485?, Granada, present-day Spain; d. 1554?, Tunis, present-day Tunisia), a Moorish explorer who published an influential account of the western and central Sudan.

The son of a wealthy family, Leo Africanus was originally named al-Hassan ibn Muhammad al-Wizzaa al-Fasi. He was born in Spain but moved to Fès, Morocco, as a child. There he was educated and was later employed by

Published in 1584, this hand-colored map of Africa reflects information that travelers such as Leo Africanus brought to Europe. *CORBIS/Historical Picture Archive*

his uncle as a clerk. The first trip of Africanus to the western Sudan, around 1512, was part of a diplomatic and commercial mission to the SONGHAI EMPIRE led by his uncle on behalf of the rulers of Fès. During this trip Africanus traveled extensively throughout the region and visited its major trading cities, including Tombouctou (Timbuktu), Djenné, Gao, and Sijilmasa. He recorded his observations on all of the region's major states: the Songhai and Mali empires, the Hausa states and Bornu, as well as the Bulala state occupying the former Kanem Empire. This trip provided much of the research for his later publications.

Between 1516 and 1518 Africanus made several trips to EGYPT and possibly a trip to Constantinople. In 1518, during his return home from Egypt, Christian pirates captured the ship in which he was traveling near Tunis and took him as a hostage. The extent of his knowledge so impressed his captors that they presented him as a slave to Pope Leo X. The pope subsequently freed the Moor, who converted to Christianity and was baptized Leo Africanus. In addition, the pope encouraged Africanus to finish *The History and Description of Africa and the Notable Things Therein Contained*, a book the traveler had begun during his journeys in Africa. Africanus finished the book in 1526; it was eventually published in Italian in 1550. At the time this book was the most important account of West Africa published since IBN BATTUTAH'S book in 1350.

Africanus remained in ITALY for approximately 20 years. In that time he occasionally taught Arabic at Bologna University and also wrote on the lives of great Arab philosophers and physicians. Late in his life he returned to North Africa, where he may have reconverted to Islam. He died in Tunis between 1552 and 1560.

Elizabeth Heath

SEE ALSO

Kanuri; Tombouctou, Mali; Tunis, Tunisia; Djenné, Mali; Mali Empire.

Latin America and the Caribbean

León, Tania J. (b. May 14, 1943, Havana, CUBA), Afro-Cuban composer, conductor, and pianist, one of the first women to achieve international success as an orchestral conductor of classical music.

Tania León is an internationally acclaimed composer and conductor, and a leading exponent of contemporary classical music. Her musical style is versatile and innovative: she incorporates elements of jazz and gospel into her compositions as well as the rhythms and color of Afro-Cuban music. She debuted as a conductor at the Festival of Two Worlds in Spoleto, Italy, in 1971 – a time when there were few professional women conductors of classical music. Indeed, her unrelenting determination has been central to her career success. "It is not common for a woman of my skin color to conduct serious music, so I have to know the score inside out, or work twice as hard as male conductors," she told *Ebony* magazine in 1989. Since the 1980s she has served as a guest conductor-composer with orchestras in the United States and Europe. In 1993 she became an adviser to New York Philharmonic conductor Kurt Masur on contemporary music.

León grew up in HAVANA, CUBA, where she studied piano, violin, and composition at the Carlos Alfredo Peyrellado Conservatory. After graduation she spent several years performing as a pianist in Cuba and in 1967 emigrated to New York City. In 1969 Arthur Mitchell invited her to be the pianist for his dance troupe, DANCE THEATER OF HARLEM, an offer that led to her appointment as the troupe's music director. She wrote several ballet compositions for the troupe, including *Tones* (with Mitchell, 1970), *Beloved* (1972), and *Dougla* (with Geoffrey Holder, 1974) – all regularly performed by European dance companies. At the same time she earned a bachelor's degree in music (1971) and a master's degree in composition (1973) from New York University, and studied conducting with Leonard Bernstein and Seiji Ozawa at the Berkshire Music Center at Tanglewood.

In 1977 León founded the Brooklyn Philharmonic Community Concert Series, which she conducted for more than ten years. After leaving the Dance Theater of Harlem in 1980, she began touring the United States, PUERTO RICO, and Europe as a guest conductor. In 1985 she received the Dean Dixon Conducting Award. She also earned recognition as an innovative composer. From the mid-1980s onward she began to incorporate Latin American and African musical elements into her work; in 1991 she traveled throughout Central and South America to meet composers and research new sounds and styles. Discovering a wealth of material, she has since aspired to bring more Latin American music into Western concert halls. In 1994 she co-organized the American Composers Orchestra's Sonidos de las Americas (Sounds of the Americas) festival in New York City – a series of concerts, symposia, and master classes that featured the works of Mexican composers.

León has composed and recorded a wide variety of works for orchestra, chamber groups, and solo instruments. She has also written an award-winning opera, *Scourge of Hyacinths* (1994), based on a radio play by the Nigerian dramatist WOLE SOYINKA.

Roanne Edwards

SEE ALSO

Gospel Music; New York, New York; Jazz, Afro-Latin; Music, Classical, in Latin America and the Caribbean.

Africa

Leopold II (b. 1835, Brussels, Belgium; d. 1909, Brussels, Belgium), king of Belgium and infamous founder of the Congo Free State, later the Belgian Congo.

Son of Leopold I, the first king of independent Belgium, Leopold II ascended to the throne in 1865 intent on finding opportunities abroad to increase his power and personal wealth. Looking at first to the Far East, he was soon enticed by the stories of Henry Morton Stanley, an Anglo-American explorer, and the potential for wealth in the Congo basin of Central Africa. In 1876 Leopold organized an association to develop Central Africa and hired Stanley to lead an expedition to the CONGO RIVER and establish contacts with the peoples around the river. By 1884 Stanley had made 450 treaties with local chieftains on behalf of Leopold and had also constructed roads and railroads in the basin. As a result, Leopold was recognized as sovereign of the Congo Free State by the Berlin West Africa Conference (1884-1885). Leopold promised other European powers that his "exclusive mission... [was] to introduce civilization and trade into the Center of Africa."

Leopold claimed the Congo Free State as his personal empire, where he sold enormous concessions of land to companies for mining, rubber tapping, and speculation. During Leopold's reign the indigenous population of the Congo Free State was subject to land confiscation, forced labor, and the brutality of his military. Reports from Europeans, such as André Gide, who visited the Free States, eventually provoked international protest, and in 1906 Leopold was forced to institute modest reforms. Failing health and rising debts forced Leopold to turn the Congo Free State over to the Belgian government in 1908. He died in 1909.

Elizabeth Heath

SEE ALSO

Stanley, Sir Henry Morton; Berlin Conference of 1884-1885.

Africa

Léopoldville. Former name of KINSHASA, DEMOCRATIC REPUBLIC OF THE CONGO.

Latin America and the Caribbean

Léro, Etienne (b. August 3, 1910, Lamentin, MARTINIQUE; d. October 28, 1939, Paris, France), Martinican writer; coauthor of *Légitime défense*, an anticolonial journal.

In 1932 the Martinican student Etienne Léro published a single issue of the journal *Légitime défense* in Paris with a team of writers including René Ménil, Jules-Marcel

Monnerot, Maurice-Sabas Quitman, and Simone Yoyotte. The issue served as a cry to arms for the decolonization movement in the Francophone world. Condemning the "suffocation" of "this capitalist, Christian, bourgeois world," the writers of *Légitime défense* "call[ed] out to all those who are not yet killed, bought out, screwed, scholasticized, successful, decorated, rotten, provided for, decorative, prudish, marked opportunists; we call out to those who can still make a claim to life with some appearance of plausibility."

Légitime défense condemned the Antillean colored bourgeoisie for their desire to integrate within French society. The writers identified the consequent alienation of this group as unavoidable: "Progressively, the Antillean of color denies his race, his body, his fundamental and particular passions, his specific way of reacting to love and death, and comes to live in an unreal sphere determined by abstract ideas and the ideal of another people" (René Ménil). Léro's article "*Misère d'une poésie*" (The Misery of a Poem) condemns the literary corollary of this assimilationist Antillean ideology in the work of writers such as GILBERT GRATIANT and Daniel Thaly. The article instead invokes to its readers the work of the writers of the HARLEM RENAISSANCE, especially LANGSTON HUGHES and CLAUDE MCKAY.

In its 27 pages *Légitime défense* awkwardly mixed the discourses of surrealism, Hegelian Marxism, and Freudianism. In their opening manifesto the writers of *Légitime défense* freed themselves from submission to one ideology while submitting to a series of others: "We adhere to Marx's dialectical materialism, freed from any tendentious interpretations and victoriously exposed to the test of facts by Lenin. We are ready to conform in this domain to the discipline implied by such convictions. Regarding the concrete issue of the figured modes of human expression, we equally accept without reserve the surrealism to which – in 1932 – we unite our future.... As to Freud, we are ready to use the immense bourgeois-familial dissolving machine he set in motion." *Légitime défense* was quickly banned by the French government. Despite its shortcomings the manifesto marked a crucial step in the condemnation of colonialism and racism. It advanced the self-understanding of a Francophone African diaspora soon to be revolutionized by the journal's conceptual inheritor: NÉGRITUDE.

Nick Nesbitt

North America

Les Cenelles, a collection of romantic poems written by French Creole authors in New Orleans.

First published in 1845, *Les Cenelles* is a collection of 85 poems written by 17 New Orleans French Creole authors who were of mixed race and considered themselves a distinct class. The poems of *Les Cenelles* demonstrate the ways in which this hybrid group identified not with free or enslaved blacks or American whites but with France, and particularly the French romantic poets of the day. As Armand Lanusse, editor of *Les Cenelles*, wrote in the introduction, "We are publishing this collection to make known the works of several young lovers of poetry who... have had the good fortune to draw knowledge from the best sources of Europe."

The writers of *Les Cenelles* came from diverse backgrounds but found friendship through their common interest in literature. Armand Lanusse was the collection's most illustrious contributor as well as its editor. Born in 1812 in New Orleans, he was a teacher and civil rights pioneer known as an honest and caring man who helped found a school for orphans, and although his poems do not reflect it, he constantly lamented the plight of blacks. Lanusse published *L'Album littéraire*, a monthly anthology of the works of local poets, from which *Les Cenelles* emerged.

Other contributors to the collection included Valcour B., a French professor of classics known for his light, patriotic poems; Pierre Dalcour, a versatile contributor of 12 poems and friend of Victor Hugo; Nelson Desbrosses, who for a while lived in HAITI and studied VODOU; and Camille Thierry, who published several works of his own superb poetry and writing and who at one point left for Paris to escape the racial tension of Louisiana.

The themes of these poems are remarkably disconnected from the social conditions in New Orleans at the time. Slavery and the plight of blacks are barely mentioned, perhaps in part because of legislation prohibiting any written matter that might fuel discontent among people of color. Instead, *Les Cenelles* reflects themes popular in French romantic poetry of the time: suicide and death; love fulfilled, chaste, or unrequited; the glory of nature; and the wonder of faith. In his introduction, Lanusse evokes romanticism in noting that the poets "praised the charming ladies of Louisiana, whose beauty, grace, and loveliness will doubtless be preserved in all their marvelous purity by those who succeed them." Many of the poems are both philosophical and humorous; several include the word "Air" in the title, suggesting they were meant to be set to music.

Critics of *Les Cenelles* consider it remarkable that the poets so rarely drew from the social tension and racial turmoil then brewing in New Orleans, or from everyday life in the South. They note that in Haiti at the same time, another literary movement was taking place among blacks who wrote frequently about the alienation and patriotism around them. In *Les Cenelles*, as one critic asserts, "We read of nightingales, but not of mockingbirds. Live-oaks, cotton, and sugar cane are never mentioned. Slavery and racial relationships are passed over in silence."

"Cenelles" are holly or hawthorn berries, a name one scholar claims was chosen to describe the poems because holly is "indigenous and of modest growth," like the Creoles themselves. Another scholar and a descendant of one of the poets, R. L. Desdunes, attributes the title to how "a thorny shrub bearing white or colored flowers expresses... the difficulty of the undertaking for those who were forced to work in the midst of an environment so discouraging to their poetic inclinations."

Chuck Kapelke

SEE ALSO

Slavery in the United States; Creoles; Free Blacks in the United States, 1619 to 1863; New Orleans, Louisiana.

Africa

Lesotho, a small landlocked country in southern Africa, surrounded by the Republic of SOUTH AFRICA.

Lesotho is a mountainous, landlocked country with few natural resources apart from its water supply. It is extremely dependent on its only immediate neighbor, South Africa, for everything from food to energy to employment for hundreds of thousands of its citizens. It resisted incorporation into South Africa during its tenure as a British colony, thanks largely to a fierce nationalism that dates back to the formation of the Basutoland Kingdom in the early nineteenth century. Since achieving independence in 1966, Lesotho has suffered from political instability and oppression. Its relations with South Africa were strained during much of the late APARTHEID era, but the two countries' current governments are now on friendly terms. Their fates became even more closely linked in 1998 with the opening of Lesotho's Katse Dam, phase one of a massive hydroelectric project intended to bolster Lesotho's ailing economy both by making the country self-sufficient in electrical power and by generating revenue from water sales to South Africa.

PRECOLONIAL HISTORY

The earliest inhabitants of what is now Lesotho were the SAN, whose presence in southern Africa dates back at least 2000 years. These nomadic foraging societies were later joined by Bantu-speaking peoples, who emigrated into southern Africa as early as 300 C.E., bringing with them agriculture, animal husbandry, and ironworking techniques. By the sixteenth century both groups had a strong presence in the Caledon River valley, along present-day Lesotho's northern border. The San traded and even intermarried with the Bantu peoples, but by the nineteenth century, land-hungry Bantu speakers had driven the last of the foraging societies from the area. They had also developed a distinct language, SOTHO.

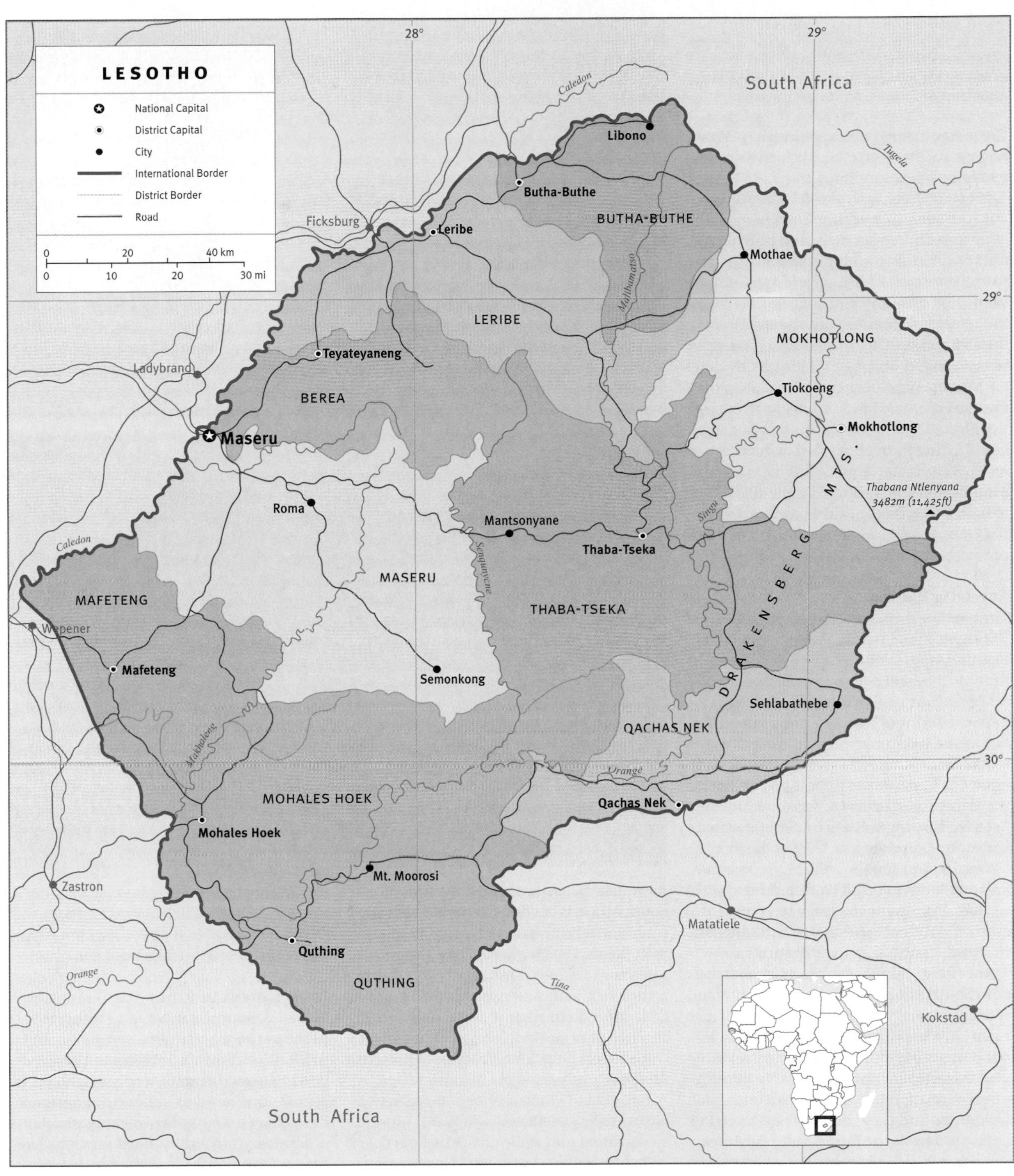

The Sotho speakers' collective identity and centralized political organization did not coalesce until the 1820s, when the ZULU's massive campaign of warfare and territorial expansion, known as the MFECANE, drove hundreds of Sotho clans north. The chief of the Sotho Kwena clan, MOSHOESHOE, relocated his people to the plateau of Thaba-Bosiu, in the foothills of the Drakensberg Mountains. From there they were able to fend off attacks from the many hostile groups migrating through the region between 1824 and 1831. Moshoeshoe granted peaceful refugees and even former enemies permission to settle in exchange for their allegiance. In this way the young Sotho leader expanded his small chiefdom of a few hundred souls into a substantial kingdom that, in the aftermath of the mfecane, covered all of present-day Lesotho and parts of what later became the AFRIKANER-controlled Orange Free State. The kingdom became known as Basutoland and its people were collectively referred to as the Basotho.

Moshoeshoe was a shrewd politician, and from his earliest contact with white settlers he understood that they could be pitted against rival clans and even against one another. He invited French missionaries into his kingdom in 1833 and enlisted their advice and diplomacy in dealing with aggression from the bands of mixed-race Kora people, who had acquired horses and guns from European settlers in the Cape Coast colony (now part of South Africa). Later, when the first Afrikaners began to cross into Basutoland during their

RIGHT: A Basotho man uses donkeys to carry food home to his family. *© Friedrich von Hörsten/Images of Africa Photobank*
BELOW RIGHT: A young man saddles a horse in the mountains of Lesotho. *CORBIS/Earl Kowall*

Great Trek inland to escape British rule, the presence of the missionaries helped to prevent a major armed conflict.

Moshoeshoe, fascinated by European culture, took to wearing European attire, attending church services, and practicing horseback riding and marksmanship. He won the respect of British administrators in the Cape Colony and successfully negotiated several treaties with the British in the 1840s and 1850s, intended to guarantee his sovereignty and prevent further Afrikaner encroachments. But after the creation of the Orange Free State in 1854, tensions between the Afrikaner and the Basotho escalated, culminating in open warfare, which began in 1865. The better-armed Afrikaners quickly assumed the upper hand. Moshoeshoe turned to his old friends, the British, for support. In response, they declared Basutoland a British protectorate in 1868.

Colonial Basutoland

Moshoeshoe died in 1870, and a year later the British unilaterally incorporated Basutoland into the Cape Colony. They expected, rightly, that Moshoeshoe's death would create a power vacuum in Basutoland. His successor, Letsie, commonly known not as the king but as the paramount chief, proved to be a weak ruler, and several lower-ranking Basotho chiefs mounted open rebellions against the Cape Colony government over the next decade. Basotho resistance culminated in a widespread uprising in 1880, following the colonial administration's efforts to confiscate firearms and auction off Basotho land to white settlers. Eventually the Cape government admitted defeat, and in 1884 the British reassumed authority over Basutoland.

The British, through their high commissioner in South Africa, administered Basutoland with an unusually free hand. Under what came to be known as the system of indirect rule, the Basotho's traditional political structures and laws remained largely intact. The British intervened on relatively few matters, aside from taxes and trade policy. They agreed to a Basotho proviso stating that no whites could acquire land in Basutoland and backed down from an effort to annex the kingdom into the newly formed Union of South Africa in 1910.

Under colonial rule, Basutoland was transformed from a relatively self-sufficient agrarian region – a net exporter of maize, wool, and sorghum – into a labor reserve for South Africa. By the 1930s more than half of adult male Sesothos worked on ranches and in mines in South Africa, where they earned only subsistence wages. The situation was no better at home, where the redrawing of colonial boundaries had made many of Basutoland's pastures and farmlands part of South Africa. What little arable land existed could scarcely meet the demands of a growing population. Most farmers in Basutoland were too poor to adopt more efficient farming techniques, and consequently could produce little more than what they needed for subsistence, at best. Many land-poor households came to rely on migrant laborers to purchase foodstuffs imported from South Africa.

Basutoland's long history of fierce nationalism coalesced after World War II around two leaders and their respective parties: Ntsu Mokhehle's Basutoland Congress Party (BCP) and the Basutoland National Party (BNP), led by Chief Leabua Jonathan. Both parties called for reforms to limit the powers of clan chiefs, and both drafted constitutions in anticipation of eventual independence. But while the BCP allied itself with nationalist groups like Nelson Mandela's African National Congress (ANC), the BNP carefully established relations with South Africa's white government. As a result, the BNP became the only party permitted to campaign among migrant Sotho workers in South Africa, which tipped the scales in its favor in the 1965 elections. The following year, on October 4, the British granted Basutoland full independence, making BNP leader Chief Jonathan the country's first prime minister.

Independent Lesotho

The new nation, renamed Lesotho, was perhaps the most underdeveloped country in all of southern Africa. Unemployment was high, and the impoverished agricultural sector continued to suffer from periodic droughts as well as the ongoing problems of land scarcity and soil exhaustion. The new government's clear inability to address the country's many pressing needs contributed to political strife, beginning almost immediately after British withdrawal. The primary tensions lay between members of the traditional hierarchy – the king, the royal family, and the chiefs – and representatives of the government bureaucracy. King Moshoeshoe II began campaigning for power beyond the primarily ceremonial responsibilities granted by the constitution. Chief Jonathan responded by placing the king under house arrest and restored his freedom and royal status in 1967 only after the king signed an agreement that he would abstain from further political activity. Other traditional leaders and BNP opponents suffered similar fates.

Lesotho citizens showed their dissatisfaction with the BNP-dominated government by voting for the BCP in 1970. Chief Jonathan immediately annulled the election results and declared a state of emergency. He also suspended the constitution and ordered the military to suppress all public demonstrations against the government. Many opposition politicians fled the country; others were arrested, and in some cases murdered. For the next 16 years Lesotho was essentially a police state.

Chief Jonathan's initially friendly relations with South Africa deteriorated in the 1970s. His main political rival, Ntsu Mokhehle, had received asylum in South Africa, where he and other opposition leaders organized the paramilitary Lesotho Liberation Army (LLA), a group that staged dozens of raids, assassinations, and other terrorist activities from 1979 to 1985. Meanwhile, Chief Jonathan had taken to harboring members of the banned African National Congress, a policy that led to several violent attacks on Lesotho by South African commandos.

In January 1986, South Africa imposed an economic blockade on Lesotho. Twelve days later, rebel Lesotho troops led by Maj. Gen. Justin Lekhanya overthrew Chief Jonathan's government and replaced it with a military council. The new regime repaired relations with South Africa by agreeing to stop sheltering ANC members; South Africa in turn pledged to end support for the LLA. But Lekhanya's domestic policies proved just as repressive as his predecessor's. In response to Moshoeshoe II's renewed campaign to expand his own political role, General Lekhanya initially granted the king greater legislative and executive powers, but then in 1990 had him dethroned and sent into exile. In 1991 Lekhanya was himself overthrown by military officers, who subsequently undertook political reforms. In 1993 the military government partially restored Lesotho's constitution and held the country's first general elections since 1970. Ntsu Mokhehle's Basotholand Congress Party won every seat in the General Assembly, and Mokhehle was named prime minister.

Mokhehle's government has since done little to reduce political violence. Despite the restoration of representational government, Lesotho's police and military units continue to act as rogue factions, making random arrests, violently suppressing strikes and protests, and allegedly assassinating dissident journalists and politicians. In 1992 Amnesty International cited the Lesotho police and military for human rights abuses, but those groups have not been held accountable for any crimes or violations.

In 1994 Moshoeshoe II's son and successor, King Letsie III, claimed to be responding to popular dissatisfaction with Mokhehle's leadership when he dissolved the National Assembly and attempted to seize control of the country. But both his own people and the international community condemned this action, and within a matter of weeks he restored power to Mokhehle's government.

Since independence, Lesotho has remained poor and highly dependent on foreign donors as well as on South Africa. Despite historically troubled relations between the two countries, Lesotho was a major labor source for South Africa's mining industry and agriculture well into the 1990s. In the mid-1980s it was estimated that more than 100,000 men – half of Lesotho's adult male labor force – worked as migrant laborers in South Africa; their remittances accounted for roughly 50 percent of Lesotho's gross national product. Cattle grazing and subsistence agriculture dominate Lesotho's domestic economy, but growth in these areas is limited by the fact that barely 10 percent of Lesotho's 30,350 sq km (12,140 sq mi) are suitable for farming.

Lesotho is now pinning its hopes for economic growth on the costly and controversial Highlands Water Project. Construction began in 1991; when completed, a network of dams and tunnels will link the Orange River in southern Lesotho to reservoirs 225 km (135 mi) north in South Africa, providing water for the city of Johannesburg and surrounding industrial areas. The World Bank and other international agencies have provided loans for the project, which is expected to cost over $3 billion and take until 2025 to be

Lesotho women carry bundles of wood on their heads. *CORBIS/Nazima Kowall*

A student points to the blackboard during an outdoor class in Lesotho, which has one of the highest literacy rates in Africa. *© G. Boutin/Explorer*

completed. Despite its apparent early benefits, the Highlands Water Project has many detractors in southern Africa and abroad. The project's massive dams will flood thousands of acres of the Orange River valley, submerging much of the region's limited supply of farmland and disrupting numerous ecosystems. As many as half of the several hundred poor farming families already displaced by the project have not been successfully relocated or compensated for their land.

In elections held in May 1998, the ruling Lesotho Congress for Democracy, the party of Prime Minister Pakalitha Mosisili, won 79 of the 80 parliamentary seats. Opposition groups, such as the Basutoland Congress Party, charged that the elections were rigged. An external audit in August produced evidence substantiating charges of electoral fraud. Widespread public unrest followed, including strikes and an army uprising. Fearing a coup, Mosisili invited the Southern African Development Community (SADC) to intervene militarily to restore order. In September 1998 some 800 South African and 200 Botswanan soldiers entered Maseru. Although SADC forces expected to encounter little opposition to their presence, Maseru residents treated the soldiers as invaders. Opponents of Mosisili's government, including members of Lesotho's army, called for a campaign of national resistance against the SADC "invaders." The dispute remained unresolved in October 1998, and there was a possibility that the SADC would be drawn into a protracted guerrilla war in Lesotho.

Andrew Hermann

See Also

Bantu: Dispersion and Settlement; Colonial Rule; Johannesburg, South Africa; Mandela, Nelson Rolihlahla; Nationalism in Africa; Christianity: Missionaries in Africa; Human Rights in Africa.

Africa

Lesotho (Ready Reference)

Official Name: Kingdom of Lesotho
Former Name: Basutoland
Area: 30,350 sq km (12,140 sq mi)
Location: Southern Africa; completely encircled by South Africa
Capital: Maseru (population 109,382 [1986 estimate])
Population: 1,970,781 (1996 estimate)
Population Density: 65 persons per sq km (about 169 persons per sq mi)
Population Below Age 15: 40 percent (male 420,526; female 419,059 [1998 estimate])
Population Growth Rate: 1.9 percent (1998 estimate)
Total Fertility Rate: 4.13 children born per woman (1998 estimate)
Life Expectancy at Birth: Total population: 53.97 years (male 52.18 years; female 55.81 years [1998 estimate])
Infant Mortality Rate: 78.3 deaths per 1000 live births (1998 estimate)
Literacy Rate (age 15 and over who can read and write): Total population: 71.3 percent (male 81.1 percent; female 62.3 percent [1995 estimate])
Education: Education is compulsory between ages 6 and 13. Nearly all of Lesotho's school-age children attend primary school. Christian missions under the direction of the Minister of Education operate most schools, which are free at the primary level. In the early 1990s nearly 362,700 pupils annually attended some 1200 primary schools, and about 53,500 pupils attended secondary and vocational schools. The National University of Lesotho (1966), in Roma, is attended yearly by about 1400 students and has a teaching staff of more than 200. The Lesotho Agricultural College (1955) is in Maseru. Lesotho has one of the highest literacy rates in Africa.
Languages: English is the official language, but Sesotho (southern Sotho), Zulu, and Xhosa are widely spoken.
Ethnic Groups: The vast majority of the population is ethnic Sotho; there is a tiny minority of approximately 1600 Europeans and 800 Asians.
Religions: Christian 80 percent; indigenous beliefs 20 percent
Climate: The climate is mild, with hot summer days in the lowlands relieved by cool nights. Winter can be cold, particularly in the mountains, and heavy snows occasionally occur. Precipitation falls mostly from October through April. In Maseru, located in the lowlands, average temperatures range from 14° to 28° C (57° to 82° F) in January and from -1° to 16° C (30° to 61° F) in July. The city averages 690 mm (27 in) of precipitation annually.
Lands, Plants, and Animals: Mostly highland with plateaus, hills, and mountains. Sixty-six percent of the land comprises meadows and pastures; less than 10 percent is arable.
Natural Resources: Water, agricultural and grazing land, some diamonds and other minerals
Currency: The loti
Gross Domestic Product (GDP): $5.1 billion (1997 estimate)
GDP per Capita: $2500 (1997 estimate)
GDP Real Growth Rate: 9 percent (1997 estimate)
Primary Economic Activities: Most of the labor force works in the service and industrial sectors; 86.2 percent of the resident population are engaged in subsistence agriculture, and roughly 60 percent of the active male wage earners work in South Africa. Manufacturing depends largely on farm products that support the milling, canning, leather, and jute industries.
Primary Crops: Corn, wheat, pulses, sorghum, barley; livestock
Industries: Food, beverages, textiles, handicrafts; construction, and tourism
Primary Exports: Clothing, furniture, footwear, and wool
Primary Imports: Corn, building materials, clothing, vehicles, machinery, medicines, and petroleum products
Primary Trade Partners: South Africa, Asia, the European Union, and South American countries
Government: Lesotho is a modified constitutional monarchy. Lesotho's king since 1996 (Letsie David Mohato, or Letsie III) is a hereditary monarch. But, under the terms of the constitution that came into effect after the March 1993 election, he has no executive or legislative powers. Under traditional law, the king can be elected or deposed by a majority vote of the College of Chiefs. Executive power is held by the prime minister. The legislative branch is a bicameral Parliament. The Senate consists of 33 members (the 22 principal chiefs and 11 other members

appointed by the ruling party), and the 65 members of the National Assembly are elected by popular vote. Lesotho has universal suffrage beginning at age 21.

Alonford James Robinson, Jr.

See Also
Maseru, Lesotho.

Africa

Lessing, Doris (b. October 22, 1919, Kermanshah, Persia [present-day Iran]), Anglo-African writer.

Raised in Southern Rhodesia (present-day Zimbabwe), Doris Lessing is one of the most prolific and celebrated authors writing in English today. Her work ranges from realistic early novels, many of which draw directly from her African childhood, to later books that experiment with literary genre (including science fiction) and form. In addition, Lessing has written poetry, drama, nonfiction, and a series of memoirs. Deeply influenced by her early exposure to racial, class, and sexual inequality, Lessing raises in her writing questions about politics, society, religion, work, and family – meditations at the heart of her most influential work, *The Golden Notebook* (1962).

Lessing, born Doris May Taylor, was the first child of her English expatriate parents. Her father, who had worked in a Persian bank after losing a leg in World War I, moved the family to a farm in colonial southern Rhodesia when Lessing was five. Lessing's father proved an unsuccessful farmer, and Lessing's childhood recollections describe both the anguish of feeling unloved by her homesick, disappointed mother and her growing awareness of social inequalities in colonial Africa. Lessing left high school at 14, later explaining that she "simply contracted out of the whole thing and educated [her]self."

After two marriages and two divorces, in 1949 Lessing moved from Salisbury (the Southern Rhodesian capital, now Harare, Zimbabwe) to London, England, taking with her only the youngest of her three children. She also brought the manuscript that would become her first novel, *The Grass Is Singing* (1950). Literary success came quickly; over the next ten years, Lessing published four more novels, in addition to stories, plays, reviews, and essays. She gained a reputation as a writer whose work probed both the personal and the political – particularly for women. The 1962 publication of *The Golden Notebook* made her a literary superstar and a feminist heroine, though Lessing herself, distrustful of movements since her split with the Communist Party in the early 1950s, refuses to align herself with feminism as an ideology. A structurally complex work, *The Golden Notebook* explores the interplay and disconnections among one woman's writing, relationships, politics, and childhood in Africa.

From 1952 to 1969, while continuing to produce other works, Lessing wrote a five-volume series of novels collectively titled *Children of Violence* in which she followed one woman's growth from domestic conformity in white-ruled Rhodesia through political and social awakening, disillusionment, and finally to self-sufficient individualism. Along with her interest in racial and gender politics and intergenerational relationships, Lessing began to draw from the teachings of Sufism, a mystical form of Islam. Hints of the supernatural in the series' last entry are expanded in the five-volume science-fiction series *Canopus in Argos: Archives* (1979-1983). Later novels include *The Good Terrorist* (1985), *The Fifth Child* (1988), and *Love, Again* (1996); works focused on Africa include *Collected African Stories* (1973), *Look Back in Laughter* (1992), and *Going Home* (1996). Lessing has published two volumes of her ongoing autobiography, *Under my Skin* (1994) and *Walking in the Shade* (1997). Critics praise Lessing's fierce, unsentimental honesty and her unique imagination, and many consider her one of the finest contemporary, Anglophone novelists.

Kate Tuttle

See Also
Colonial Rule; Women Writers in English-Speaking Africa; South African Communist Party.

Latin America and the Caribbean

Lewis, Arthur (b. January 23, 1915, Castries, St. Lucia, West Indies; d. June 15, 1991, Bridgeport, Barbados), West Indian economist, scholar, lecturer, writer, and government adviser who shared the 1979 Nobel Prize for Economics with the American Theodore Schultz for their pioneering research in economic development, with particular consideration of the problems of developing countries.

Arthur Lewis was the first black person to receive the Nobel Prize in a category other than peace. He once described his intellectual career as consisting of three phases: the history of world economics and development; industrial economics; and the economic problems of underdeveloped nations. In his Nobel lecture he suggested that the least developed countries should concentrate on increasing their regional trade rather than being heavily dependent on the continued growth of the most developed countries. He believed that in this way, underdeveloped nations could eventually accelerate their own economies even as growth in the more technologically advantaged nations slackened.

Lewis wanted to study engineering but decided it would be pointless since, at that time, neither the government nor white firms would hire a black engineer. A brilliant student, he received a bachelor of commerce degree with honors from Saint Mary's College in St. Lucia (1929) when he was 14 years old. He later received a scholarship for graduate study at the London School of Economics (Ph.D., 1937) and remained there as a professor from 1938 to 1947. In 1955, when he was a professor at the University of Manchester, Lewis published one of the first academic works in the area of applied developmental economics, *The Theory of Economic Growth*. During his life he was to write 11 books and more than 80 monographs and scholarly articles. His success as a scholar was recognized by the British government, who knighted him Sir Arthur William Lewis in 1963.

Lewis was a much sought after academic and economic advisor. He was professor emeritus at Princeton University in the United States from 1983 until his death, and held the following positions at Princeton as well: professor of public and international affairs, 1963-1968; James Madison Professor of Political Economy, 1968-1982; and Distinguished University Professor of Economics and International Affairs, 1982-1983. In addition, he was a professor of political economy at the University of Manchester from 1948 to 1958; vice-chancellor of the University of the West Indies from 1959 to 1963; president of the Caribbean Development Bank from 1970 to 1973; and president of the American Economic Association in 1983.

North America

Lewis, Carl (b. July 1, 1961, Birmingham, Ala.), African American track-and-field athlete who won a total of nine Gold Medals at the Olympic Games in 1984, 1988, 1992, and 1996, including four straight Gold Medal performances in the long jump.

Frederick Carlton Lewis came from a family of talented athletes and began to reveal his own gift in the 100-meter dash and the long jump while a student at the University of Houston. He qualified for the United States Olympic team for the 1980 Olympic Games in Moscow but was unable to compete because United States participation was canceled by President Jimmy Carter as a protest against the invasion of Afghanistan by the Union of Soviet Socialist Republics (USSR).

In 1981 Lewis won the James E. Sullivan Memorial Award, given annually by the Amateur Athletic Union of the United States (AAU) to the outstanding amateur athlete in the country. At the 1983 track-and-field world championships in Helsinki, Finland, he won the 100-meter dash and the long jump and was a member of the winning 4 x 100-meter relay team. The next year at the 1984 Olympic Games in Los Angeles, Lewis enjoyed his greatest performance. His feat of winning Gold Medals in the 100- and 200-meter dashes, the long jump, and the 4 x 100-meter relay had only been accomplished once before, by American athlete Jesse Owens at the 1936 Olympic Games in Berlin, Germany.

Lewis won the long jump and was a member of the winning 4 x 100-meter relay team at the 1987 world championships in Rome, Italy. Although he was beaten by Canadian athlete Ben Johnson in the 100-meter dash at the world championships, he was retroactively declared the winner when Johnson was disqualified the next year at the 1988 Olympic Games in Seoul, South Korea, for having used banned substances. Having placed second in the 100-meter dash at the 1988 Olympic Games, Lewis was declared the winner of this race upon Johnson's disqualification. Lewis also won the long jump and placed second in the 200-meter dash. At the 1991 world championships in Tokyo, Japan, he again won the 100-meter dash and was a member of the winning 4 x 100-meter relay team.

Lewis won two more Gold Medals at the 1992 Olympic Games in Barcelona, Spain, in the 4 x 100-meter relay and in the long jump. During the 1996 Olympic Games in Atlanta, Georgia, he won his fourth straight Gold Medal in the long jump. This victory made him only the fourth man to win nine Gold Medals at the Summer Games, after American swimmer Mark Spitz, Finnish runner Paavo Nurmi, and American athlete Ray Ewry. During his career Lewis also set numerous world records in his events. He was inducted into the U.S. Olympic Hall of Fame in 1985. He retired from competition in 1997.

See Also

Russia and the Former Soviet Union; Track and Field in the United States; Owens, James Cleveland ("Jesse"); Los Angeles, California.

North America

Lewis, Edmonia (b. 1845?; d. ?), believed to be the first woman sculptor of African American and Native American heritage.

Edmonia Lewis often drew upon her dual ancestry for inspiration. Her best-known work, *Forever Free* (1867, Howard University Gallery of Art, Washington, D.C.), was inspired by the Emancipation Proclamation. Created in marble, *Forever Free* depicts a man and a woman who have learned of their freedom. In an expression of gratitude, the woman kneels with her hands clasped; the man rests his foot on the ball that held them in bondage, raising his arm to display the broken shackle and chain on his wrist.

Little is known about Lewis's early life. Sources give differing birth dates – 1843 and 1845 – and birthplaces – Ohio, New York, and New Jersey. Her father was an African American, and her mother was a member of the Ojibwa community. In 1859 Lewis entered Oberlin College in Oberlin, Ohio, where she excelled at drawing. Known as Wildfire in the Ojibwa community, Lewis changed her name to Mary Edmonia during her time at Oberlin; she generally signed her sculptures and her correspondence with the name Edmonia. When a teacher at Oberlin missed some paintbrushes, Lewis was accused of the theft; she was also accused of attempted murder when two girls fell ill after drinking mulled wine, which Lewis allegedly served them. Although acquitted of both charges, she was not permitted to graduate.

In 1863 Lewis moved to Boston, where the abolitionist William Lloyd Garrison introduced her to sculptor Edward Brackett, who became her first mentor. Lewis's earliest sculptures were medallions with portraits of white antislavery leaders and Civil War heroes, which she modeled in clay and cast in plaster. Her *Bust of Colonel Robert Gould Shaw* (1865, Museum of Afro-American History, Boston, Massachusetts) depicted the young Bostonian who led an all-black battalion, the Fifty-fourth Massachusetts Volunteer Regiment, in battle against Confederate forces. Sales of replicas of the bust enabled Lewis to travel to Italy in 1865, where she established a studio in Rome.

The high point of Lewis's career was the completion of *The Death of Cleopatra* (1876, National Museum of American Art, Washington, D.C.), which created a sensation at the Philadelphia Centennial Exposition of 1876. Other sculptors generally depicted Cleopatra contemplating death; Lewis showed Cleopatra seated on her throne after death, her head thrown back. In her right hand Cleopatra holds the poisonous snake that has bitten her, while her left arm hangs lifelessly. This realistic portrayal ran contrary to the sentimentality about death that was prevalent at the time.

Lewis was reported as still living in Rome in 1911, but the date and location of her death are not known.

See Also

Abolitionism in the United States; American Indians; Boston, Massachusetts; Civil War, American; Fifty-fourth Regiment of Massachusetts Volunteer Infantry; Thirteenth Amendment of the United States Constitution and the Emancipation Proclamation; Art, African American.

North America

Lewis, Henry (b. October 16, 1932, Los Angeles, Calif.; d. January 26, 1996, New York, N.Y.), African American double-bass player and orchestra conductor; the first black to become a regular conductor of a major American symphony orchestra.

During a music career that spanned nearly five decades, Henry Lewis gained wide respect as a conductor, instrumentalist, and pioneer in the classical music world. At age 16 he joined the Los Angeles Philharmonic, becoming the first black instrumentalist in a major orchestra. In 1968 he became the first black to head a major American orchestra, the New Jersey Symphony, and in 1972 he debuted at the New York Metropolitan Opera, conducting Puccini's *La Bohème*.

Lewis began studying piano at age five and later learned to play the clarinet as well as several string instruments. After six years as a double-bassist with the Los Angeles Philharmonic Orchestra, he played with and conducted the Seventh Army Symphony while serving in the United States Armed Forces (1955-1956). He gained national recognition in 1961 when he was appointed assistant conductor of the Los Angeles Philharmonic under Zubin Mehta, a post he held until 1965.

After serving as a guest conductor of major symphony orchestras in the United States and abroad, Lewis moved to Newark, New Jersey, where in 1968 he became conductor and music director of the New Jersey Symphony – a small community ensemble. He transformed the ensemble into a nationally recognized orchestra that annually performed more than a hundred concerts, including outreach programs for local communities. From 1960 to 1979 he was married to famed opera singer Marilyn Horne, who considered him her "teacher and right hand." After retiring from the New Jersey Symphony in 1976, Lewis continued to tour as a guest conductor until his death from a heart attack at age 63.

Roanne Edwards

See Also

Los Angeles, California.

North America

Lewis, John (b. February 21, 1940, Troy, Ala.), African American civil rights leader and member of the United States House of Representatives.

John Lewis was one of ten children born to sharecroppers in Pike County, Alabama. He graduated from high school and entered the American Baptist Theological Seminary in Nashville in 1957. After graduating in 1961, he enrolled at Fisk University, where he earned a bachelor of arts degree in 1967.

While a seminary student, Lewis participated in nonviolence workshops taught by civil rights activist James Lawson. Lawson was a member of the Fellowship of Reconciliation (FOR), an organization committed to pacifism, and he made Lewis a field secretary. Working with Septima Clark, director of the interracial adult education center Highlander Folk School, Lewis became a leader in the Nashville Student Movement. He participated in sit-ins at segregated lunch counters, became a founding member of the Student Nonviolent Coordinating Committee (SNCC) in 1960, and helped organize the

John Lewis, chairman of the Student Nonviolent Coordinating Committee, and Hosea Williams of the Southern Christian Leadership Conference announce plans for demonstrations in Georgia in 1965.
CORBIS/Bettmann

Mississippi Freedom Summer in 1964 (*see* Civil Rights Movement).

During his tenure as national chairman of SNCC, Lewis delivered a powerful speech at the 1963 Civil Rights March on Washington, criticizing the federal government for its failure to protect the rights of African Americans. Two years later he marched with Dr. Martin Luther King Jr. from Selma to Montgomery, Alabama, in an effort to secure voting rights for African Americans. During the march a confrontation with police occurred, and Lewis was one of many beaten in what became known as Bloody Sunday.

Lewis's commitment to nonviolence strained his relationship with SNCC when the organization grew more militant under the leadership of Stokely Carmichael. Lewis resigned from SNCC in 1966 to become director of the Atlanta-based Voter Education Project (VEP). Under Lewis's leadership the organization led voter registration drives and helped elect black politicians throughout the South. In 1976 President Jimmy Carter appointed Lewis to the staff of ACTION, a government agency responsible for coordinating volunteer activities.

After Carter's defeat in 1980, Lewis returned to Atlanta and won a seat on the Atlanta City Council. He served in this capacity until 1986, when he defeated his friend and fellow civil rights activist Julian Bond in the Democratic primary for Georgia's Fifth Congressional District seat, a position Lewis assumed when he defeated his Republican opponent later that year. In Congress, Lewis has served on the Committee on Interior and Insular Affairs, the Committee on Public Works and Transportation, and the House Ways and Means Committee.

Alonford James Robinson, Jr.

See Also
Clark, Septima Poinsette; Freedom Summer; King, Martin Luther, Jr.; Lawson, James Morris; March on Washington, 1963.

North America

Lewis, Meade ("Lux")

(b. September 3, 1905, Chicago, Ill.; d. February 7, 1964, Minneapolis, Minn.), African American pianist who popularized boogie woogie.

In the 1930s and 1940s Lux Lewis worked alongside fellow boogie-woogie piano players Albert Ammons and Pete Johnson. Bringing this blues piano style to Carnegie Hall in New York City in 1938, Lewis raised the speedy rhythms and energetic solos of boogie woogie to new heights of popularity. His signature tune, "Honky Tonk Train Blues," was recorded in 1927 and was released by Paramount Records in 1929. Lewis's early musical mastery laid the foundation for New York City rhythm and blues and rock and roll. Lewis died in an automobile accident in 1964.

See Also
Blues, The; New York, New York.

North America

Lewis, Reginald F.

(b. December 7, 1942, Baltimore, Md.; d. January 19, 1993, New York, N.Y.), African American lawyer and businessman who managed the largest black-owned firm in the United States.

Although he disliked the sobriquet, Reginald Lewis was often called the "Jackie Robinson of Wall Street" and was considered "the man who broke the color barrier in large-scale mergers and acquisitions and leveraged buyouts." With his firm TLC, Lewis in 1987 orchestrated the largest offshore leveraged buyout in business history, paying $985 million for Beatrice International Foods. With subsidiaries in almost every continent, the renamed TLC-Beatrice International became the largest black-owned firm in the United States.

Lewis, whose parents separated when he was nine, grew up in a supportive, middle-class atmosphere in Baltimore, Maryland. By age ten, he had a job delivering the *Baltimore Afro-American* newspaper, and stored the money he earned in a tin can he labeled "Reggie's Treasures." Lewis excelled in football and hoped for a professional football career after earning a scholarship to attend Virginia State College (now Virginia State University). A shoulder injury ended his football career, and he began to concentrate on academics, graduating in 1965 with a degree in economics. He then entered Harvard Law School, graduating in 1968. After law school he worked with a number of New York law firms before opening the venture capital firm Lewis and Clarkson.

In 1983 Lewis started the TLC Group as a means to pursue greater business opportunities. In 1983 TLC acquired McCall Pattern Company for $22.5 million. McCall, an ailing business that had operated for more than a century, was at the time debt-ridden. Through cost-cutting measures, Lewis helped resuscitate McCall, and in 1987 he resold the company for $90 million. TLC's acquisition of Beatrice Foods (the parent company to Beatrice International) made him one of the most prominent African American businessmen.

Also a philanthropist, Lewis gave generously to many charities. His gift of $3 million to Harvard Law School in 1992 was the largest single gift the law school had received and was used to found the Reginald F. Lewis Fund for International Study and Research. The Reginald F. Lewis Center at Harvard was the first facility named for an African American. He also donated $1 million to Howard University in Washington, D.C., as well as significant amounts to his alma mater Virginia State University. Lewis was diagnosed with brain cancer in late 1992. Before his death of a cerebral hemorrhage in January 1993, he arranged for orderly transition at TLC Beatrice, naming his half-brother, former football star Jean S. Fugett, to succeed him.

See Also
New York, New York.

North America

Liberator, The,

publication of the American Anti-Slavery Society from 1831 to 1865; edited by William Lloyd Garrison, it was considered the most radical antislavery newspaper of the nineteenth century.

"I am in earnest – I will not equivocate – I will not excuse – I will not retreat a single inch – AND I WILL BE HEARD." These words, written on January 1, 1831, by famed white antislavery activist William Lloyd Garrison, launched the first issue of the *Liberator*, a radical antislavery weekly newspaper that stood at the pinnacle of American antislavery activism for 35 years. Widely considered the most militant and most passionate antislavery publication of the nineteenth century, it served more than 2000 subscribers, many of them African American, before it stopped printing in 1865.

Garrison and fellow activist Isaac Knapp created the *Liberator* in 1831 in an effort to expand their circle of influence in Boston, Massachusetts. Although a black antislavery organization had existed in Boston for several years, Garrison formed the New England Anti-Slavery Society in 1832, and then in 1834 established the American Anti-Slavery Society. His newspaper immediately gained respect and attention from the African American community. Approximately 400 of the newspaper's initial 450 subscribers were black, including James Forten, a prominent Philadelphian. After four years of publication, 75 percent of its subscribers were African

American, and Southern politicians, fearing the newspaper's impassioned demands for abolition, banned its circulation.

Officials in Columbia, South Carolina, offered a $5000 reward for the arrest and conviction of the paper's publishers. The Georgetown corporation of the District of Columbia prohibited blacks from removing the *Liberator* from the local post office. Those caught with the newspaper in their possession faced fines and imprisonment. Those who could not afford to pay the fines could be sold into slavery for four months. Despite these measures, the *Liberator* continued to command a small and loyal white following. Although most of its subscribers were literate free blacks, the newspaper was widely read and cited by white antislavery activists throughout the country.

Knapp left the paper in 1839 to pursue a career writing antislavery editorials. He published *Knapp's Liberator* in January 1842, but it quickly failed. By that time the *Liberator* had become the most prominent antislavery publication in America. It featured the writings of abolitionists such as Wendell Phillips, Oliver Johnson, and British activist George Thompson. During its tenure the newspaper called for the immediate and unconditional end to slavery, rejected the efforts of the American Colonization Society to resettle free blacks in Liberia, and urged Americans to boycott goods produced with slave labor.

In 1842 Garrison wrote that the United States Constitution was "a Covenant with Death and an Agreement with Hell." This served as the newspaper's motto until 1861, when he modified it to read, "Proclaim liberty throughout the land, to all the inhabitants thereof." The newspaper supported President Abraham Lincoln during the Civil War, urging him to free America's 4 million slaves.

The *Liberator* celebrated the end of slavery and the beginning of Reconstruction with its final issue on December 29, 1865. The Emancipation Proclamation and passage of the Thirteenth Amendment, which abolished slavery, persuaded Garrison to write in 1865, "Great and marvelous are thy works, Lord God Almighty!"

Alonford James Robinson, Jr.

See Also

Slavery in the United States; Abolitionism in the United States; Civil War, American; Free Blacks in the United States, 1619 to 1863; Thirteenth Amendment of the United States Constitution and the Emancipation Proclamation.

Africa

Liberia, a small West African country located on the Atlantic coast, bordered by Sierra Leone, the Republic of Guinea, and Côte d'Ivoire.

Liberia, the oldest republic in Africa, was once regarded by the West as the continent's most stable, prosperous, and peaceful country. One of only two African countries never colonized by a European power (Ethiopia is the other), Liberia's modern political foundation was built by free blacks who sailed there from the United States in the early nineteenth century. Since then, relations between Liberia's indigenous peoples and the African American settlers have rarely been easy. After more than 130 years of Americo-Liberian-dominated single-party rule, the First Republic was ended by a military coup in 1980, after which an unstable government faced a series of insurrections. Following a second revolt in 1989, throughout the early 1990s Liberia suffered from political chaos, civil unrest, famine, and violence. Some experts estimate that about 10 percent of Liberia's population died during that period while another 80 percent was dislocated.

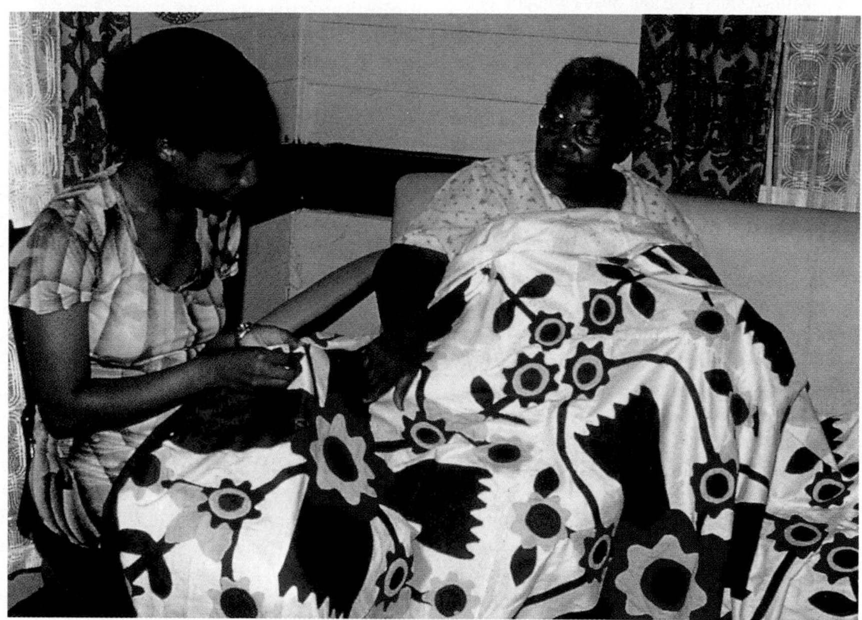

Liberian women stitch a colorful quilt. *Werner Gartung*

Early History

Anthropologists now believe that Liberia's first inhabitants were hunter-gatherers and ancestors of the Gola and Kissi peoples, both of whom are part of the Mel language group. They were joined by the Kruan people (the Kru, Kuwaa, Bassa, Kran, and Dei ethnic groups), who were migrating from the north and east, and later, around the fifteenth century, by people of the Mande language group, among them the Gio, Mano, Loma, Bandi, Mende, and Kpelle.

Traders from the savanna kingdoms of West Africa visited Liberia's early communities seeking spices, gold, and ivory. In the fifteenth century trade began to turn toward the coast, as European merchants came seeking Malaguetta peppers, gold, and, later, slaves. The chiefdoms of the Mande- and Mel-speaking groups in what is now northern Liberia met the demand for slaves by forging alliances and conducting raids on neighboring peoples. Other exports included rice, palm oil, and textiles. In return, the indigenous peoples received European firearms, knives, jewelry, and liquor.

American Settlement and the Commonwealth

The end of the transatlantic slave trade spawned the republic of Liberia. By the late eighteenth century the abolitionist movement in England had become a powerful force. Beyond their efforts to end the slave trade – a mission accomplished in Great Britain in 1807 – some abolitionists became interested in repatriation. In 1787, for instance, 1500 freed British slaves were settled in the English colony of Sierra Leone. Drawing partly on this example, a group of American abolitionists organized the American Colonization Society (ACS) in 1816. Although some other repatriation or colonization groups were run by people of African descent, the ACS administration was composed solely of wealthy white men, including such prominent members of society as former United States president James Madison and Kentucky congressman Henry Clay. As many historians have noted, the ACS's goal to relocate America's free black people united two disparate groups: those who saw the abolition of slavery and African resettlement as the best route to restoring African American dignity and freedom, and those who supported slavery as an institution and considered free blacks a threat to its existence.

In addition to soliciting funds from the U.S. government, the ACS began selling memberships to free American blacks, many of whom were farmers, professionals, or small businessmen. Memberships (which were lifelong and did not necessarily mean that the holder planned to go to Africa) cost $30; one ACS agent estimated that by 1825

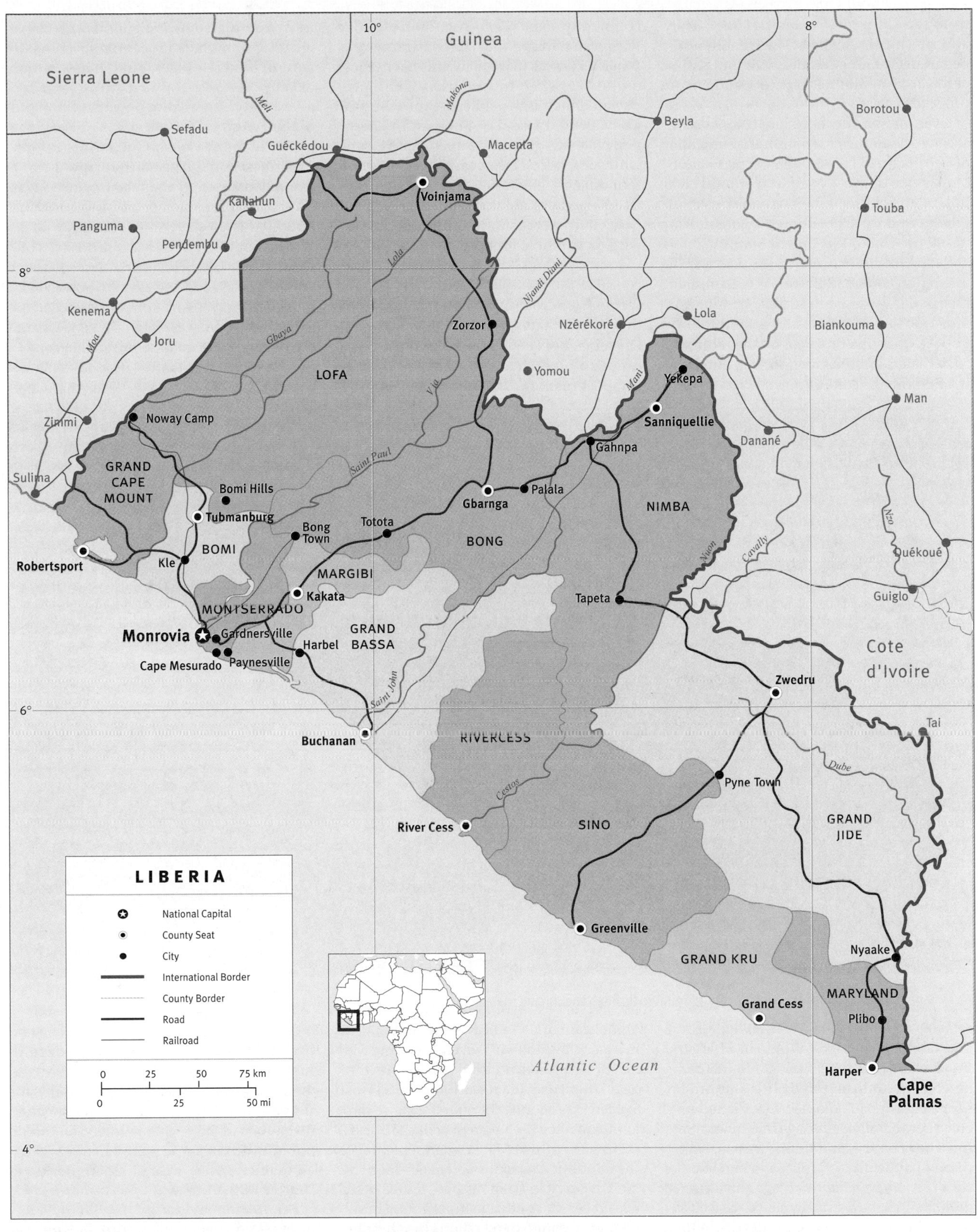

they had raised "not less than $50,000" through membership sales. In claiming that this money went into "the treasury of the Lord," the agent revealed the religious basis for much of the ACS's work; many colonizationists, black and white, were motivated at least in part by the desire to spread Christianity.

In 1820 the group launched its first ship, the *Elizabeth*, which sailed with more than 80 African American emigrants. After landing on the coast of what would become northwestern Liberia, many of the first arrivals died of tropical diseases to which they lacked immunity, and the group retreated to FREETOWN, SIERRA LEONE. In 1821 more settlers arrived and founded a town at Mesurado Bay. Controlled by ACS governors (all white until 1842) and supported by the U.S. military, in 1824 the Americans named their first settlement Monrovia, after U.S. president James Monroe, and the colony itself Liberia, from the Latin *liber*, meaning "free." They adopted a Plan of Civil Government and began negotiating treaties with indigenous chiefs to expand their territory and ensure the settlers' safety.

Over the next decade state colonization societies continued to sponsor the emigration of free blacks to Liberia, and the population of AMERICO-LIBERIANS grew to around 3000. In 1838 they formed the Commonwealth of Liberia and in 1839 adopted a constitution based on that of the United States.

Relationships between the settlers and the indigenous population were often strained. Liberian law excluded "tribal" people from most jobs and schools and attempted to impose Christian practices on them through such means as outlawing work on Sundays. In addition, the settlers (most of whom were artisans or semiskilled workers) had begun to establish a castelike system, in which the most wealthy and well educated formed an elegant and sheltered elite. But unlike Africa's European colonies, Liberia had no color bar that divided long-time inhabitants from newcomers, and thus it was possible (though difficult) for Africans to enter settler society. Moreover, intermarriage and informal multiple-marriage arrangements – as well as the children born to such unions – helped swell the Americo-Liberian population.

THE FIRST REPUBLIC

Compared to other African nations, independence came early for Liberia. Partly because of Americo-Liberian resistance to ACS authority, and partly because of the complexity of the colony's status in regard to European traders (who refused to recognize Liberia's power to regulate their activities), on July 26, 1847, the Americo-Liberians declared their independence from the ACS. They elected Joseph J. Roberts, the first nonwhite ACS governor, as president. Roberts, who served for eight years, oversaw the founding of Liberia University, in Monrovia, and helped expand the boundaries of the new country, most often through treaties with local ethnic groups.

In the second half of the nineteenth century Liberia began to receive diplomatic recognition from other nations, including the United States, HAITI, and GERMANY. Divisions between various factions of the Americo-Liberian community led to the establishment of two political parties, the Republicans and the True Whigs (both based on American parties of that era). Starting with the 1870 election of Edward James Roye, the True Whig Party (TWP), which was almost exclusively Americo-Liberian, became the dominant force it would remain for 110 years.

The early years of Liberian independence saw continued tensions between Americo-Liberians and indigenous peoples, who still held lower-class citizenship rights. These tensions resulted in rebellions by a number of groups, including the Kru Confederation in 1856 and the G'debo Kingdom in 1875. In 1873 the Liberian government extended some legislative representation to the indigenous peoples, thus somewhat calming the political waters. Historians estimate that the interior regions of Liberia, the areas most dominated by indigenous Liberians, were not truly under the central government's control until the 1920s. But the new nation also faced external threats from British and French colonizing powers at the end of the century.

Following the economic model of the American South, the settlers opted for plantation-style agriculture to produce sugar cane and coffee, often employing Africans liberated from slave ships. But they faced stiff competition from other producers of these commodities, and persistent economic shortfalls forced the new nation to seek foreign loans. Support from the United States and Great Britain was reciprocated by Liberia's acting as an African base for Allied armies during World War I, after Liberia declared war on Germany in 1917. After the war, foreign industries began arriving; the Firestone Tire and Rubber Company, which began operations in 1926, eventually became the country's largest private employer. In 1929 the American-led League of Nations investigated allegations of government-tolerated forced labor at the Firestone plant, a charge that led to the resignation of Liberian president Charles D. B. King.

The 1944 inauguration of William V. S. Tubman continued the unbroken chain of True Whig presidents. His 27-year-long tenure was characterized by openness to foreign investment, close ties with Western powers, and a gradual opening of political (though not economic) opportunities to previously disfranchised people. Under Tubman the administration of the interior regions was

A cross-bearer leads a procession of recent graduates through the streets of Monrovia, the capital of Liberia. *© G. Boutin/Explorer*

finally brought under the control of the central government. Tubman extended the vote to women in 1945 and to indigenous people in 1946, though Americo-Liberians continued to enjoy a representative advantage in the legislature.

Upon Tubman's death in 1971, his vice president of 19 years, William R. Tolbert Jr., assumed the presidency. In what some historians see as an effort to distinguish himself from Tubman, Tolbert attempted to reach out to the growing populist movement while maintaining support of the old-line establishment. Not surprisingly, both sides soon expressed distrust. Tolbert's foreign policy mixed the familiar dependence on the United States with new aims, such as establishing relations with the People's Republic of China and helping raise money for the ANTIAPARTHEID MOVEMENT in SOUTH AFRICA. For most Liberians, however, the more immediate concern was the domestic economy, which in the late 1970s was squeezed between declining world prices for Liberia's primary exports (rubber and iron ore) and rising import costs. Popular discontent over increasing food prices culminated in the 1979 Rice Riots, led by the Progressive Alliance of Liberians (PAL) and the Movement for Justice in Africa (MOJA).

Samuel K. Doe, Charles Taylor, and Civil War

On April 12, 1980, Samuel K. Doe, a master sergeant in the Liberian army, led 17 men to Tolbert's home and assassinated him. The men, former members of the People's Progressive Party, called themselves the People's Redemption Council (PRC) and declared themselves in charge of the government. Doe staffed his administration with fellow members of the Krahn ethnic group and pledged that his military rule would last only temporarily. A new constitution (written by Dr. Amos Sawyer, a University of Liberia professor who had been involved with MOJA) was approved by voters in 1984, and Doe promised that elections would be held the following year. But from the beginning Doe faced challenges from former PRC accomplices – who led at least two failed coup attempts – and when he and his newly formed National Democratic Party of Liberia (NDPL) won the 1985 elections, they were suspected of widespread vote fraud. Doe invited increasing charges of tribalism when he took revenge on the coup plotters by burning and sacking the towns of his rivals' ethnic groups.

A pattern of quick turnover and unexplained deaths in Doe's administration, coupled with heavy restrictions on press freedoms, prompted the United States to send in advisers in 1987 as a condition for continued foreign aid. Liberia's economic woes had heightened tensions throughout the country, and these had in turn strained relations with neighbors such as Sierra Leone and Guinea, which feared an influx of refugees. These fears, in fact, were justified. In late 1989 a group called the National Patriotic Front of Liberia (NPFL), led by Charles Taylor, a former government official facing arrest for corruption charges, launched an insurrection in Nimba County, on the border of CÔTE D'IVOIRE. Liberians fleeing the NPFL spilled into neighboring countries while shipments of smuggled arms crossed the borders in the opposite direction. Facing a threat to regional stability, the ECONOMIC COMMUNITY OF WEST AFRICAN STATES (ECOWAS) intervened in 1990, sending its multinational peacekeeping force (ECOMOG) to secure control of Monrovia. Much of the rest of the country was controlled by Taylor's NPFL.

Peace talks were held in THE GAMBIA in August 1990, but Taylor, who shortly thereafter declared himself the true president of Liberia, did not attend. Dr. Amos Sawyer was chosen as president of the so-called Interim Government of National Unity (IGNU). Meanwhile, a breakaway rebel group led by Prince Yormie Johnson had made surprising inroads into Monrovia and in September assassinated Doe. ECOMOG ultimately secured the capital again, but the hinterlands were still controlled by Taylor.

The next opposition force to enter the fray, the United Liberation Movement of Liberia for Democracy (ULIMO), led by Johnson, included some of Doe's former supporters. It crossed the border from Sierra Leone in 1991 and clashed repeatedly with Taylor's NPFL troops. Fighting continued and intensified as ECOMOG, attempting to subdue NPFL in the interior, retreated to Monrovia in 1992. Reports began appearing of NPFL's numerous human rights abuses, including the drafting of preteenaged boys as soldiers and the wholesale execution of civilians. The first half of 1993 was characterized by repeated skirmishes among ULIMO, the NPFL, and ECOMOG, which by then had abandoned its peacekeeping role and become an active combatant. After the breakdown of a July 1993 cease-fire, the United Nations established an observer mission in Liberia; at the same time, several new factions emerged, many of them based on ethnic affiliations and most of them armed.

The Council of State, 1997 Elections, and Beyond

Throughout the mid-1990s the major factions met in various configurations, their attempts at peacemaking prompted by the threatened removal of ECOMOG troops (which now included soldiers from NIGERIA, GHANA, Côte d'Ivoire, BURKINA FASO, and TOGO) and the implication that even more widespread war would result. As the United Nations (UN) Security Council increased its number of observers, each attempt to build coalitions failed. At an ECOWAS-sponsored meeting in Nigeria in August 1995, the combatants signed a peace accord, agreeing on plans for a council of state that would last until free elections could be held. Professor Wilton Sankawulo was pronounced chairman, with the main factional leaders, including Taylor, also serving.

Further hostilities plagued the council of state, including fighting between Taylor's forces and the predominantly Krahn defenders of the Doe regime, who had thrown their support behind Johnson's ULIMO. In August 1996, RUTH PERRY, a 57-year-old former senator, was chosen to replace Sankawulo as council chair, becoming the first African woman head of state in modern times. Following the reorganization of the council, elections were scheduled for July 1997. In a field of 13 political parties, Taylor's National Patriotic Party prevailed, awarding Taylor the presidency he had sought for nearly eight years. Within months of the election, several of Taylor's political rivals were found dead under suspicious circumstances.

Fifteen years of civil strife and warfare weakened Liberia's economy, which had been in decline even before Doe's 1980 coup. Before the war about half of Liberia's population lived in the countryside; subsistence farming and the export of iron ore, wood, and rubber were the dominant economic activities. Liberia had also long maintained a large shipping fleet due to its "open registry" policies for foreign ships. But the war, in addition to creating a huge refugee population and destroying the homes and businesses of hundreds of thousands of Liberians, disrupted rural food production. By 1997 the country was heavily dependent on food aid, and many regions faced a severe food shortage. The only people to benefit from the years of turmoil were the leaders of the armed factions who took advantage of the opportunity to make deals with foreign firms for diamond mining in the country's interior.

Kate Tuttle

See Also

Gold Trade; Ivory Trade; Doe, Samuel Kanyon; Taylor, Charles Ghankay; Tolbert, William Richard, Jr.; Monrovia, Liberia; Tubman, William Vacanarat Shadrach; World War I and African Americans; Abolitionism in the United States; Free Blacks in the United States, 1619 to 1863; Human Rights in Africa; Bassa of Liberia.

Africa

Liberia (Ready Reference)

Official Name: Republic of Liberia
Area: 99,067 sq km (38,250 sq mi)
Location: Western Africa, bordering the North Atlantic Ocean, CÔTE D'IVOIRE and SIERRA LEONE
Capital: Monrovia (population 421,058 [1984 estimate])
Other Major Cities: Buchanan (population 24,000 [1984 estimate])
Population: 2,771,901 (1998 estimate); due to civil war, hundreds of thousands of

Liberians are living as refugees outside the country.
Population Density: 31 persons per sq km (about 79 persons per sq mi)
Population Below Age 15: 45 percent (male 622,797; female 616,902 [1998 estimate])
Population Growth Rate: 5.76 percent (1998 estimate)
Total Fertility Rate: 6.09 children born per woman (1998 estimate)
Life Expectancy at Birth: Total population: 59.45 years (male 56.81 years; female 62.16 years [1998 estimate])
Infant Mortality Rate: 103.13 deaths per 1000 live births (1998 estimate)
Literacy Rate (age 15 and over who can read and write): Total population: 38.3 percent (male 53.9 percent; female 22.4 percent [1995 estimate])
Education: The Compulsory Education Act of 1912 provides for compulsory, free education for children between ages 6 and 16. However, government attempts to implement this law have been hindered by the scarcity of educational facilities and only a small minority of children receive education.
Languages: English is the official language but is spoken by barely one-fifth of the population. Most of the population speaks at least one language from the Niger-Congo language group of about 20 languages. Some of the more widely spoken languages are MANDE, West Atlantic, and Kwa.
Ethnic Groups: The majority of the population comes from one of 13 different ethnic groups. These groups include the Kpelle, Bassa, Gio, Kru, Grebo, Mano, Krahn, Gola, Gbandi, Loma, Kissi, Vai, and Bella. About 5 percent of the population are AMERICO-LIBERIANS who descended from former American slaves.
Religions: About 70 percent of the population adhere to indigenous beliefs. About 20 percent are Muslim and 10 percent are Christians.
Climate: The climate is tropical and humid, particularly during the rainy seasons of June to July and October to November. Annual rainfall varies from 2240 mm (88 in) in the interior to 5200 mm (205 in) along the coast. The average temperature in Monrovia is about 26° C (79° F) in January and 24° C (76° F) in July.
Land, Plants, and Animals: Liberia is mostly flat with some hills and low mountains in the northeast that reach elevations of about 900 to 1200 m (3000 to 4000 ft). The interior is heavily forested with cotton, fig, mahogany, ironwood, and various kinds of palms as well as rubber trees. Animals include pygmy HIPPOPOTAMUS, chimpanzees, elephants, buffalo, and monkeys.
Natural Resources: Minerals, such as iron ore, and forest products, such as wood and rubber. Liberia also has hydroelectric power plants on the Saint Paul River that provide a significant amount of hydroelectric power.
Currency: The Liberian dollar
Gross Domestic Product (GDP): $2.6 billion (1998 estimate)
GDP per Capita: $1000 (1997 estimate)
GDP Real Growth Rate: NA (1997 estimate)
Primary Economic Activities: Agriculture (70 percent of the population), services, industry, and commerce
Primary Crops: Rubber, coffee, cocoa, rice, cassava (tapioca), palm oil, sugar cane, bananas, and livestock
Industries: Rubber processing, food processing, construction materials, furniture, palm oil processing, iron ore, and diamonds
Primary Exports: Iron ore, rubber, timber, and coffee
Primary Imports: Mineral fuels, chemicals, machinery, transportation equipment, manufactured goods, rice, and other foodstuffs
Primary Trade Partners: United States, European Union, Japan, China, and South Korea
Government: Liberia is a constitutional republic in name; however, years of civil war have severely disrupted the government. In 1997 elections, CHARLES GHANKAY TAYLOR was elected president. Despite promises to establish a representative government, after taking office Taylor replaced much of the Liberian army and cabinet with loyalists. Fueled by conflict with opposition groups, Taylor's government remained unstable in 1999.

Elizabeth Heath

SEE ALSO
Chimpanzee; Elephant; Monrovia, Liberia.

Africa

Libreville, Gabon, capital of Gabon.

Since at least the seventeenth century, MPONGWE people have inhabited the northern bank of the Gabon Estuary. During the nineteenth century FANG people migrated into the area and became the predominant group numerically. In 1843 the French established a trading post and fort at the site of present-day Libreville. Six years later the French navy founded Libreville, meaning "free town," by granting plots of land to 52 freed slaves. In the subsequent years, during the SCRAMBLE FOR AFRICA, the French launched explorations and campaigns of conquest from Libreville into the interior. The town grew during the era of French colonialism (1887-1960) as the trading and administrative center of the Gabon colony.

In 1960 Libreville became the capital of independent Gabon. Four years later the city opened a deep-water port in the Owendo District. Today this port handles most of Gabon's imports and a large part of its exports. Libreville is the headquarters of the country's petroleum, uranium, and manganese companies. The city also has commercial fishing and lumber industries. Economically, Gabon's petroleum exporting center, Port-Gentil, overshadows Libreville. The 1970s oil boom, however, did finance the construction of several multistory buildings in Libreville's commercial district. These rise above the prevailing low-lying colonial-style architecture along the city's palm-lined boulevards. Since the mid-1990s the city's population has numbered approximately 350,000, including many non-Gabonese African migrant laborers and nearly 20,000 French expatriates.

Eric Young

SEE ALSO
Colonial Rule; Explorers in Africa Since 1800; Slavery in Africa.

Africa

Libya, a large North African country bordered by TUNISIA, ALGERIA, NIGER, CHAD, SUDAN, EGYPT, and the Mediterranean Sea.

In 1997 South African president Nelson Mandela visited the country of Libya and praised its leader, Col. Muammar al-Qaddafi, for his unceasing support during SOUTH AFRICA's struggle against APARTHEID. The international community was startled by this meeting of two of Africa's most prominent leaders, one a Nobel Peace Prize winner and the other, one of the West's most vilified enemies. But Mandela's visit only revealed to the West a picture of Libya already familiar elsewhere on the continent: that of a country as much African as Islamic. Often considered part of the Arab world, Libya is in fact one of Africa's largest and wealthiest nations, and for centuries its peoples have cultivated relations both across North Africa and south of the Sahara. Since coming to power in 1970, Qaddafi has provided both verbal and material support to a variety of African national movements as well as to governments ranging from IDI AMIN's dictatorship in UGANDA to THOMAS SANKARA's populist socialist state in BURKINA FASO. In 1997 Qaddafi initiated a plan for a Sahelian-Saharan economic treaty with at least nine African nations. Although many in the West view Libya's influence in Africa with concern, many poorer African nations have welcomed the oil-rich country's largesse.

The identity of Libya as an African nation was inscribed well before Qaddafi's tenure. Trade routes and political federations had long connected parts of Libya to EGYPT, to the western Islamic political entity of the Maghreb, and to sub-Saharan Africa. The concept of Libya as a distinct territory is fairly recent, arguably dating back only to the Italian colonial period. In fact, the contemporary nation comprises three historically distinct regions: Tripolitania, the cosmopolitan Mediterranean center of trade; Cyrenaica, historically linked to Egypt and the home of the powerful Islamic Sanusi sect; and Fezzan, the tribally ruled interior, linked by desert trade routes to sub-Saharan

Africa. The identities of these regions shaped their individual relationships to both of the powers that occupied their land during the last two centuries – the Ottoman Empire and Italy.

Tripolitania

Ancient Tripolitania existed under Punic and then Roman rule. While a Roman province, the fertile region exported olive oil and traded gold for slaves brought across the Sahara. As in much of North Africa, Roman presence was mainly limited to the coast, while the Berber inhabitants maintained autonomous rule inland. A stretch of desert passable only by camel divided Tripolitania from Cyrenaica to the east. By the second century coastal Tripolitania was linked by trade and Christian culture to western coastal Roman holdings such as Tunis; after the 395 C.E. split between the western and eastern Roman Empire divided Tripolitania from Cyrenaica, these links to the West grew stronger.

In the seventh century armies of Arabs moved through North Africa, bringing the new religion of Islam and dreams of conquest. Arab leaders took Tripolitania in 650 and from there expanded westward into the land they called Ifriqiya. Libya and Tunisia were ruled together, first by the Aghlabid emirs and then by the Fatimid Dynasty. Reviving ancient Roman irrigation systems, the Aghlabids developed the region's agriculture. Yet the main source of income continued to be the port of trade, where wool, leather, salt, and slaves passed through from the interior.

Despite the conversion of most Berbers to Islam, the Berber identity remained for the most part distinct from the urban Arab elite until the eleventh century, when the massive Hilalian migration began to sweep through the regions of Tripolitania and Cyrenaica. Driven by drought and famine, and motivated by the dynastic designs of the Fatimid rulers, the Hilalians moved westward from Egypt. The Banu Hilal continued westward to retake Tunis from the errant Fatimid proxy rulers, the Zirids, while

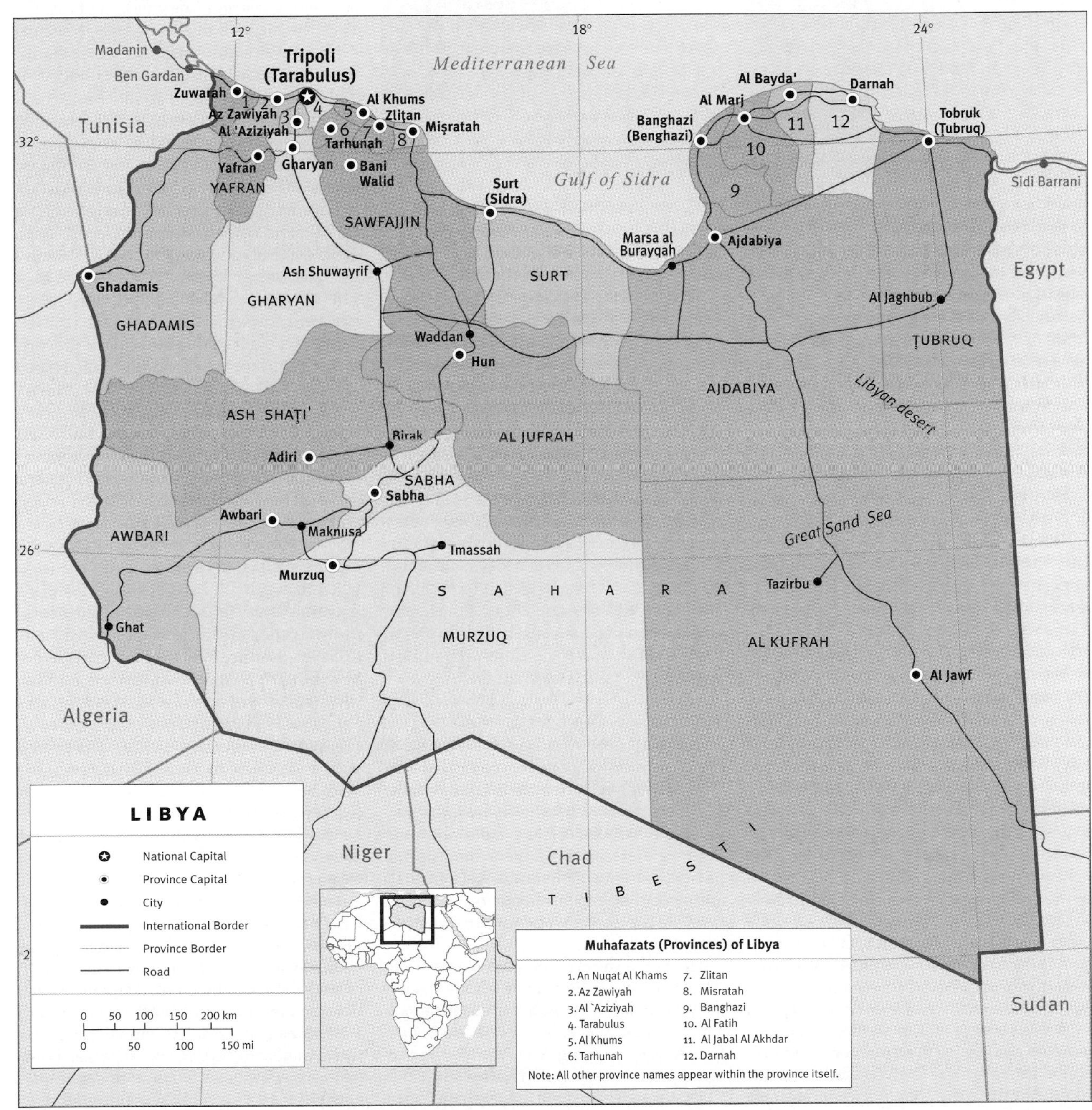

Muslim men offer Friday prayers at Badry mosque in Benghazi, Libya, where 97 percent of the population is Sunni Muslim. *Barry Iverson*

the Banu Salim remained in Tripolitania until the thirteenth century. Most historians trace the creation of an Arabic-speaking, Berber pastoral culture in the interior to this period of migration.

Along the coast, expanding Mediterranean trade in the eleventh century brought renewed struggles for control of strategic ports. In 1060 Normans from southern Italy took several ports near Tripoli. Under the 300-year reign of the Hafsids, Tripolitania developed thriving trades with both Christian Europe and the Moroccan-descended Andalusians of southern SPAIN.

CYRENAICA

Legend has it that Greeks from the island of Thera founded the city of Cyrene in 631 B.C.E. It became an intellectual and cultural center, home to schools of philosophy and medicine, and enriched by the fertile hinterlands' production of grain, wine, and the aphrodisiac silphium. Powerful African and Mediterranean rulers coveted the region known as Cyrenaica; it fell at different times under Egyptian, Persian, and finally, in 74 B.C.E., Roman rule. Cyrenaica also attracted immigrants and was home to a large population of Jews, many of whom had fled Palestine. In 115 C.E. a Jewish revolt leveled the city.

After the partition of the Roman Empire at the end of the fourth century, Christian Cyrenaica fell under the sphere of influence of the Egyptian Coptic Church, creating long-standing links between Cyrenaica and its eastern neighbor, Egypt. Three centuries later, Islam would create religious connections to the western Maghreb; in 642 Cyrenaica became the first of the three territories to come under Arab rule. Even while under rule from the west, Cyrenaica maintained political and economic ties to Egypt and later fell under the nominal control of a series of Egyptian Mamluk dynasties. BEDOUIN chieftains, however, maintained real political and economic control in Cyrenaica, taxing pilgrims and caravans en route to Egypt.

FEZZAN

In the arid interior region of Fezzan, oasis settlements grew up along the trade routes that linked the western Sudan to the Mediterranean. Some oasis communities irrigated farmland with stone-lined water channels; others profited from the trans-Saharan trade in gold, salt, ivory, and slaves. Unlike its neighbors, Fezzan did not fall under direct Roman rule, but chieftains did enter military and economic alliances with the Romans. In the seventh century Islam reached Fezzan almost 20 years after it had arrived at Cyrenaica. The Islamic Kharajite established a theocratic kingdom around the capital city of Zawilah. Later the Fezzan's trade routes fell under the control of the Bani Khattab.

THE OTTOMAN PERIOD

During the fifteenth and sixteenth centuries Christian and Muslim powers competed for control over Mediterranean maritime trade. North African ports became increasingly important as bases for corsairs, state-sponsored military ships that taxed and sometimes pillaged passing merchant vessels. In 1510 SPAIN captured Tripoli and put its naval base there under the protection of the Knights of St. John of Malta.

The same year that Spain took Tripoli, the Ottoman leader Khair al-Din seized the port of Algiers. The Barbarossa Brothers, as he and his successor were known, extended their holdings eastward along the coast until they captured Tripoli in 1551. The Ottomans sought to profit from the commerce through Fezzan, and sent armies to exact a yearly tribute. But Ottoman power remained concentrated mostly in coastal enclaves – particularly Tripoli – while the rest of the area that is now Libya was controlled by Islamic theocratic states and Berber confederacies.

Tripoli was home to a number of janissaries, special military troops who accompanied the Turkish conquerors and whose power rose as the region broke free of direct Ottoman rule. In 1611 the leader of a janissary corps, Dey Suleiman Safar, seized control of the government. By the end of the seventeenth century Tripoli had grown rich from corsair raids, and its population of 30,000 included janissaries, *cologhli* (the children of mixed Turkish and Arab descent), Jews, Muslims driven out of southern Spain, slaves from West Africa, and European Christians who had been captured by the corsairs.

During the next century Tripoli was ruled by a series of military leaders, some more independent than others from the Ottomans. One of the more autonomous rulers, Yusuf ibn Ali Karamanli, reasserted stronger control over Fezzan. Karamanli also alienated Great Britain, already antagonized by corsair activity, by assisting Napoleon Bonaparte in his 1799 Egyptian campaign. In the dawn of the new century Great Britain and the United States bombarded Tripoli to end the practice of forcing protection money from merchant and passenger ships. Deprived of a primary source of income, the Tripoli economy was thrown into crisis, and Karamanli borrowed heavily from French and British merchants. As people rebelled against stringent taxation, and the French and British blockaded Tripoli for lack of payment of debts, the region was thrown into civil war. In 1835 the Ottoman Empire stepped in to regain direct control.

Realizing the limited possibilities of maritime trade in the nineteenth century, the new Ottoman state turned south, looking to exploit the three long-standing trade routes between Tripoli and West Africa – one to what is now northern NIGERIA, one to Air and Kano in Hausaland, and one to Tombouctou (Timbuktu). On these routes, traders carried guns and European textiles to the interior in exchange for luxury goods such as ostrich feathers, gold, goatskins, and ivory. Until 1860, when slavery was effectively banned in the region, many slaves also traveled north along these routes.

The interior was far more difficult for the Ottoman Empire to control, particularly Fezzan, where the Awlad Slaiman fought to maintain autonomy. In 1842, with the death of leader Shaikh Abd al-Jalil, Fezzan also fell to Ottoman military control.

In nineteenth-century Cyrenaica, a land where wandering mystics known as marabouts possessed significant political and spiritual authority, a Sufi Islamic sect founded by Muhammad bin Ali al-Sanusi (1787-1859) transformed and unified the institutional

Men seated by a table of watermelons in Tripoli, the capital of Libya, a city whose history blends Mediterranean, Ottoman, and Egyptian influences.
CORBIS/Roger Wood

framework of long-distance commerce. Originally founded to promote a purified Islam, the Sanusi order built a series of lodges in Cyrenaica that operated as caravan watering holes in addition to serving as monasteries, schools, and social and commercial centers for the local populace. Under Sanusi's son Muhammad al-Mahdi, the order's influence spread southward. For trade caravans traveling between Benhazi and sub-Saharan market towns, the Sanusi lodges offered security and provisions along formerly impassible stretches. More important, they created a cohesive identity and social structure – what might be viewed as the prototype of the modern nation. Ultimately it was the Sanusi sect, not the Ottoman Empire, that forged a unified resistance to Italian colonization.

Italian Colonization

In the late nineteenth century European imperialism in North Africa gained momentum, shifting from economic domination to outright conquest. In part because ALGERIA, Morocco, and Tunisia had fallen under French control, Italy staked a claim to Tripolitania and its environs. As well as being a long-time trading partner with Tripoli merchants, Italy had been developing commercial interests in the city. Great Britain supported Italy in this endeavor, since an Italian Libya created a buffer state between French holdings and British-ruled Egypt. In 1911 Italy engineered a crisis in order to justify invasion – it accused the Ottomans of arming Libya's Arab Bedouins and then, asserting the need to protect Italian commercial interests, declared war.

The possession of Libya, however, was ultimately decided by conflicts in other parts of the world. In 1912 the Ottomans yielded Libya as part of a peace treaty concerning Balkan territories, but the Ottomans were allowed to keep official religious authority. This religious presence maintained Libya's strong ties with the Islamic world and was also a source of strength for the resistance. At first, fierce inland resistance meant that the Italian presence was confined mainly to the coast. In Fezzan the Bedouins, who had never fully accepted Ottoman control, were equally unreceptive to a foreign Christian presence.

In Cyrenaica, Sanusi followers formed a cohesive resistance, launching a military campaign in 1914 that continued after they officially allied themselves with Turkey and GERMANY during World War I. After the war the Sanusi strength ultimately forced Italy to grant some concessions in Cyrenaica, and IDRIS I retained a position as the Sanusis' political and religious leader.

In Tripolitania, Italian troops and colonists met with relatively little organized resistance, though some nationalists there did become involved in the Sanusis' resistance efforts. After considerable debate over a Sanusi-dominated anticolonial struggle, Idris accepted the emirate of Libya in 1922, thereby broadening his support among nationalists outside Cyrenaica. But threats of persecution forced him to flee to Egypt shortly afterward.

In 1923 Italy under Mussolini resumed war against the Sanusi, pacifying Tripolitania and Fezzan but again encountering strong resistance in Cyrenaica. Using Eritrean soldiers, the Italian army waged a brutal guerrilla war in the desert, cutting off supply lines, filling wells and killing livestock, confining Bedouins in concentration camps, and constructing a patrolled, barbed-wire barrier along 320 km (190 mi) of the Egyptian border. Italy finally established control over Cyrenaica in 1931, when Sanusi rebel leader Umar al-Mukhtar was captured and hanged. Cyrenaica and Tripolitania were then joined in a single colony called Libya, leaving Fezzan as a military territory.

With its colonial claims now established, Italy began investing in infrastructure, building roads, railways, and expanded ports. Promoting emigration to relieve unemployment and overcrowded cities at home, in 1938 Italy sent 20,000 settlers to Libya in a single convoy. These settlers, who within two years comprised 12 percent of the colony's population, benefited the most from the modernizing projects. Meanwhile, Libyans saw much of their best grazing and farming land confiscated and turned into settler-owned olive groves.

When World War II began, Libyan nationalists hoped that the defeat of Mussolini would bring the liberation of Libya. In Egypt, Idris committed troops – many of them veterans of the Italo-Sanusi war – to fight for the British. As the de facto leader of the Sanusi, Idris drew support for the Allies both from the traditionally rebellious Cyrenaica and, to a lesser extent, from the heavily occupied Tripolitania.

Several major World War II battles were fought in the Libyan Desert. In January 1943 the British took Tripoli; by the following month they had seized all of Libya. The British occupied Tripolitania and Cyrenaica, while the French held Fezzan. As the Allied powers debated the future of Italian colonial holdings, Idris returned to Cyrenaica and, with British support, established an independent emirate in Cyrenaica. An original plan for joint Italian, British, and French administration of Tripolitania, Cyrenaica, and Fezzan for ten years fell one vote short of adoption in the United Nations (UN). A UN resolution then called for the unification of the three provinces into an autonomous nation by January 1952 and created a National Constituent assembly to draft a constitution. Idris was declared king of the United Kingdom of Libya, a federal monarchy with a legislature made up of representatives of the three provinces, including elected senators and those nominated by the king. General elections were held on February 19, 1952. Libya became the first North African nation to achieve statehood.

A female art student paints a mural celebrating the twentieth anniversary of Libya's revolution. *CORBIS/Caroline Penn*

INDEPENDENCE

After independence, relations between the regions continued to be strained, as Idris had never truly centralized his authority. While Cyrenaica supported Idris and the Sanusi order, Fezzan looked to the tribal leadership of Sayf al-Nasr, and in Tripolitania the National Congress Party, led by Bashir al-Sadawi, attempted to establish a republican government. Not surprisingly, the monarchy viewed republicanism unfavorably and quickly outlawed the Congress Party as well as all other political parties. Republican sentiment was not, however, confined to Tripolitania. During the 1940s an organization of young nationalists in Cyrenaica called the Umar al-Mukhtar Club sought a republican government based on a pan-Arab vision of Libya. Ultimately, the threat to the monarchy would come not from the cosmopolitan nationalists of Tripoli, but from this pan-Arab identification.

The new nation was poverty-stricken and seemingly without major natural resources – a primary source of income came from the resale of scrap metal from World War II wrecks. Libya bartered military base rights in exchange for some economic aid, most significantly with the United States. The country's prospects changed dramatically, however, in June 1959, with the discovery of large amounts of high-quality petroleum in Cyrenaica.

As soon as a 167-km (100 mi) pipeline to the Mediterranean was completed, money

ABOVE: Libya's president Muammar al-Qaddafi, pictured here in 1986, the year the United States bombed his country in response to what the U.S. government saw as Libya's support of international terrorism. *CORBIS/Peter Turnley*

ABOVE RIGHT: Libyan soldiers display signs bearing the photograph of Muammar al-Qaddafi, the country's head of state since 1970. *CORBIS/Peter Turnley*

and oil began to flow. But most Libyans saw little of this new wealth, and within a few years popular resentment toward the national elites, combined with growing pro-Arab sentiment, exploded into widespread civil unrest. During the 1967 Arab-Israeli war, workers and students rioted in Tripoli and Benghazi. The violence spread to target Jews and the West, both seen as enemies of an Arab state. Finally, popular sentiment turned against the king.

Qaddafi and the "Popular Revolution"

On September 1, 1969, a group of young military officers, influenced by the political philosophy of Egypt's Gamal Abdel Nasser, seized power while the king was out of the country for medical treatment. Calling themselves the Revolutionary Command Council (RCC) of the Free Officers Movement, they declared the Libyan Arab Republic. Shortly after the bloodless coup, the RCC brought more than 200 top government officials, including the king, to trial for treason, some in absentia. By disbanding the Sanusi order and reorganizing administrative states to disrupt tribal affiliations, the RCC began to dismantle all remnants of the old Libya.

Within a year, a 27-year-old colonel named Muammar al-Qaddafi had risen to the top of the RCC. Ascetic yet charismatic, Qaddafi sought to unite Islamic principles with a reformist socialist economic and political policy. He cultivated relations with the Soviet Union, distanced himself from the West, and even forced the United States military to withdraw early from its Libyan base.

An enthusiastic proponent of Arab unity, Qaddafi proposed political unions with Egypt, Syria, Tunisia, Chad, Morocco, and Algeria. The most extensive discussions took place with Egypt and Syria. Hoping to combine Egypt's labor supply with Libya's potentially formidable oil industry, from 1972 to 1978 Qaddafi and Anwar al-Sadat discussed the merger of states. Ultimately, due to strong popular opposition and Qaddafi's anger over the 1978 Egypt-Israeli peace agreement, the proposal was jettisoned. In 1980 Libya embarked on a union with Syria under Hafiz al-Assad, agreeing to pay a billion-dollar debt to the Soviet Union for weapons. The deal fell through during diplomatic stasis over two hijackings. Libya was also one of the most militant founding members of the Organization of Petroleum Exporting Countries (OPEC).

During the same period Qaddafi launched the "popular revolution," a massive internal restructuring of national and local government that was intended to fight bureaucratic inefficiency and the lack of public interest and participation in government. Qaddafi created "people's committees" that in principle would take over and run the government. By 1973 there were more than 2000 such committees, filled by popular election in selected geographical areas as well as in universities, businesses, government administrations, and the broadcast media. "Revolutionary committees" were instituted to oversee the perpetuation and evolution of revolutionary ideals, as described in Qaddafi's *The Green Book*, published in 1976.

In volume two of *The Green Book*, published in 1978, Qaddafi, by then the "Leader of the Revolution" and the controller of the military, attacked democracy, private trade, and property. A second phase of restructuring brought worker management of state enterprises, including retail trading, and a limit on one private dwelling. Securing economic control of Libya's resources, Qaddafi nationalized the oil industry, ultimately gaining control of about 70 percent of the industry. Banks were also nationalized.

These reforms met with considerable resistance. The middle class opposed his economic reforms, and many professionals and technocrats left the country. A number of Islamic leaders opposed what they perceived to be an appropriation of Islam for Qaddafi's own purposes and resented the nationalization of endowed Islamic properties. Qaddafi's international reputation, already lacking, further declined after a number of prominent exiles were assassinated and several men accused of international terrorism were given shelter in Libya. Finally the army, from which Qaddafi had originally emerged as a leader, unsuccessfully attempted a coup in August

1980, hoping to regain some of the power he had amalgamated.

Qaddafi also made many enemies through his foreign policy. Relations between Libya and Chad were strained. Claiming rights from before the colonial period, Libya occupied the mineral-rich Aouzou Strip and used it as a base to aid rebels in the Chadian civil war. Qaddafi at first supported Sudanese president Jaafar al-Numayri, who was later accused of coup attempts. He also backed Idi Amin to the bitter end, supplying Amin with weapons and troops and granting him asylum when he fled Uganda in 1979. In 1981 two Libyan aircraft were shot down by the United States. Five years later, as tensions grew between the two countries over trade restrictions and alleged Libyan support for terrorism, the United States attacked Libya and subsequently instituted a trade embargo. The UN ordered a ban on arms sales and flights to Libya in April 1992, after Qaddafi refused to extradite suspected terrorists in the bombing of a U.S. airliner over Scotland.

Despite sanctions, European companies have taken up much of the slack left by American companies. Libyan standards of living, including housing, education, social services, and health care, were among the highest in Africa during the 1980s and 1990s. Qaddafi sponsored large infrastructure projects such as railways and the Great Man-Made River project, a $30-billion effort to transport subterranean water in the southern desert to the heavily populated Mediterranean coast. In the late 1990s Qaddafi experimented with liberalization but also arrested 1500 businessmen on charges of corruption. Despite five unsuccessful coup attempts and considerable international animosity, he remains firmly in place as leader of Libya.

Marian Aguiar

See Also

African Socialism; Roman Africa: An Interpretation; Algiers, Algeria; Eritrea; Gold Trade; Ivory Trade; Jewish Communities in North Africa; Kano, Nigeria; Mandela, Nelson Rolihlahla; Nationalism in Africa; Morocco; United Nations in Africa; Russia and the Former Soviet Union; Italy; Qaddafi, Muammar al-; Sahara Desert; Sahel; Salt Trade; Sufism; Tombouctou, Mali; Tunis, Tunisia; World War II and African Americans; Mamluk State; Marabout; Tripoli, Libya; Banu Hilal and Banu Sulaim; Sadat, Anwar al-; Trans-Saharan and Red Sea Slave Trade; Nobel Prize.

Africa

Libya (Ready Reference)

Official Name: Socialist People's Libyan Arab Jamahiriya
Area: 1,759,540 sq km (679,358 sq mi)
Location: Northern Africa; borders Mediterranean Sea, Egypt, Tunisia, Republic of Sudan, Chad, Niger, and Algeria
Capital: Tripoli (population 1,500,000 [1994 estimate])
Other Major Cities: Banghazi (population 800,000 [1994 estimate])
Population: 5,690,727 (1998 estimate)
Population Density: 3 persons per sq km (about 8 persons per sq mi); more than 85 percent of the people live in urban areas.
Population Below Age 15: Total population: 48 percent (male 1,399,354; female 1,351,442 [1998 estimate])
Population Growth Rate: 3.68 percent (1998 estimate)
Total Fertility Rate: 6.18 children born per woman (1998 estimate)
Life Expectancy at Birth: Total population: 65.44 years (male 63.21 years; female 67.78 years [1998 estimate])
Infant Mortality Rate: 59.5 deaths per 1000 live births (1996 estimate)
Literacy Rate (age 15 and over who can read and write): Total population: 76.2 percent (male 87.9 percent; female 63 percent [1997 estimate])
Education: Primary education in Libya is free and compulsory. In the early 1990s some 1,239,000 pupils were enrolled annually in primary schools, and about 215,500 students attended secondary, vocational, and teacher-training schools. Libya has five universities.
Languages: Arabic is the official language, although Berber is sometimes spoken and English and Italian are used in trade.
Ethnic Groups: The indigenous population of Libya is mostly Berber and Arab in origin; about 17 percent of the population consists of foreign workers and their families from the Mediterranean region and South Asia.
Religions: Islam is the state religion, and about 97 percent of all Libyans are Sunni Muslim. A small number are Roman Catholic.
Climate: Climatic conditions in Libya are characterized by extreme heat and aridity. Desert and subdesert regions have little precipitation. On the coast the annual rainfall rarely exceeds 400 mm (16 in).
Land, Plants, and Animals: About 90 percent of Libya is made up of barren, rock-strewn plains and sand sea, with two small areas of hills rising to about 900 m (about 3000 ft) in the northwest and northeast. In the south the land rises to the Tibesti massif along the Chad border.

Most of Libya is either devoid of vegetation or supports only sparse growth. Date palms and olive and orange trees grow in the scattered oases, and junipers and mastic trees are found in the higher elevations. Wildlife includes desert rodents, hyena, gazelle, and wildcat. Eagles, hawks, and vultures are common.
Natural Resources: The principal resource of Libya is petroleum. Others include natural gas, gypsum, limestone, marine salt, potash, and natron.
Currency: The Libyan dinar
Gross Domestic Product (GDP): $38 billion (1997 estimate)
GDP per Capita: $6700 (1997 estimate)
GDP Real Growth Rate: 0.5 percent (1997 estimate)
Primary Economic Activities: The economy depends on revenues from the oil sector, which makes up about one-third of GDP. Libya was traditionally an agricultural country, although farming was restricted primarily to the coastal regions; livestock raising has also been important.
Primary Crops: Tomatoes, wheat, potatoes, barley, citrus fruits, dates, and olives; livestock includes sheep, goats, cattle, camels, and poultry.
Industries: Petroleum, food processing, textiles, handicrafts, and cement
Primary Exports: Crude oil, refined petroleum products, and natural gas
Primary Imports: Machinery, transport equipment, food, and manufactured goods
Primary Trade Partners: Italy, Germany, Spain, France, United Kingdom, Greece, Egypt, Turkey, Tunisia, and Eastern European countries
Government: Libya is governed under a constitution adopted in 1977 by the General People's Congress (GPC). Power is delegated to the head of state, or Revolutionary Leader, currently Col. Muammar Abu Minyar al-Qaddafi; five members of the General Secretariat of the GPC; and 16 members of the General People's Committee, led by a secretary (premier), currently Abd al Majid al-Qa'ud. Libya is organized into 46 municipal and 186 Basic People's Congress administrative units.

Marian Aguiar

See Also

Qaddafi, Muammar al-; Sudan; Tripoli, Libya.

Africa

Lilongwe, Malawi, capital of Malawi.

In 1904 the colonial administration of Nyasaland built an administrative office and police post in the Bwalia region. Originally referred to as both Bwalia and Lilongwe, the post was strategically located at the crossroads of two of the colony's most important roadways. In 1921 it became the capital of the larger Central Province. The following year a hospital was built, just before an influenza epidemic that resulted in thousands of deaths.

Early on an Indian community developed, mostly traders whose families had come to southern Africa as indentured laborers. The east bank of the Lilongwe River became known as the city's Indian Quarter, and by 1932 Lilongwe was home to more than 20 Indian-owned stores and a mosque.

With the opening of the Imperial Tobacco Company plant in 1930, Lilongwe became a major tobacco-growing region, producing dark-fired tobacco, an American variety. By 1931 the commercial activity warranted the opening of a Standard Bank branch.

Although Lilongwe was located at the center of a major tobacco-producing region, most of the colony's economic activity was centered in the city of Blantyre, and Zomba was the administrative capital. In 1964 the prime minister of newly independent Malawi, Kamuzu Banda, decided to make Lilongwe the nation's official capital, partially in an effort to stimulate the regional economy. Pursuing plans he developed while in prison for his anticolonial protests years earlier, he sought funds to construct the University of Malawi in Lilongwe and eventually obtained them from the South African government.

Lilongwe became the official capital in 1975. The new and modern Capital Hill district, home to the Parliament, Supreme Court, and other government buildings, contrasted sharply with Old Lilongwe. Although Banda also constructed an enormous state house in Lilongwe, he continued to reside in the presidential palace in Blantyre. With a population of 234,000 (1991 estimate), Lilongwe is the second largest city in Malawi after Blantyre.

Ari Nave

See Also

Banda, Ngwazi Hastings Kamuzu; Indian Communities in Africa.

Africa

Lilse (also known as the Lyela), ethnic group of Burkina Faso.

The Lilse primarily inhabit west central Burkina Faso. They speak a Niger-Congo language and belong to the Grusi cultural and linguistic group. Approximately 200,000 people consider themselves Lilse.

See Also

Languages, African: An Overview.

Latin America and the Caribbean

Lima Barreto, Afonso Henriques de (b. May 13, 1881, Rio de Janeiro, Brazil; d. November 1, 1922, Rio de Janeiro, Brazil), Afro-Brazilian writer and novelist and a pioneering critic of Brazilian racism in the early twentieth century.

Lima Barreto was born in Rio de Janeiro exactly seven years before the abolition of slavery in Brazil. Both his parents were mulattos. His father worked as a typographer; his mother was a schoolteacher. In 1888 his mother died of tuberculosis; a year later his father was dismissed from his job. Thanks to the protection of his godfather, a viscount, Barreto was able to complete his studies. He enrolled in the college Escola Politécnica but never received a degree, a fact that some would attribute to a direct order from a racist professor. For the remainder of his life, Barreto worked for various newspapers and magazines. He resigned in protest from one of them, the political weekly *A.B.C.*, when it published an article against blacks.

His first novel, *Recordações do escrivão Isaías Caminha*, was published in 1909, and his best-known work, *Triste fim de Policarpo Quaresma* (translated as *The Patriot*, 1978) first appeared in 1916. Both were written during the time when he studied European realist and social fiction. Like the author himself, the characters in Barreto's novels often lived in the suburbs of Rio de Janeiro and were lower or lower-middle class. Mulatto characters were often protagonists in his novels, such as the title characters in *Clara dos Anjos* (written in 1904; published posthumously) and *Recordações do escrivão Isaías Caminha*.

Occasional bouts of depression and struggles with alcoholism caused Barreto on two occasions to be interned in an asylum for the mentally ill, an experience that inspired the novel *Cemitério dos vivos* (1922, Cemetery of the Living). Barreto died of a heart attack at age 41. His novels were influential in the development of Brazilian Modernism in the 1920s and the social novel of the 1930s. Yet he had to publish many of his books himself; his work was recognized only posthumously. At three different times in his life he applied for membership to the prestigious Brazilian Academy of Letters and each time was rejected.

The Brazilian novelist Machado de Assis, also a mulatto, was the founder of the academy and the writer with whom Barreto was fated to be contrasted. Their writing, and their politics, were indeed quite different. Barreto rejected grammaticism and formalism, choosing a colloquial style of writing. At a time when the style of Brazilian writing was judged by its proximity to European Portuguese, he shocked literary circles by writing "as people spoke" and incorporating Brazilianisms into his writing, as in the very title of the novel *Bruzundangas* (1922). His writing was criticized for its "carelessness" and "ugliness," yet he anticipated the Modernist debate over whether an independent Brazilian Portuguese actually existed.

Seventy years before the black movement tried to demystify the notion of Brazilian identity, Barreto had attempted precisely that. The novel *Triste fim de Policarpo Quaresma* is largely a parody of Brazilian nationalism, illustrated through the life of Quaresma, the title character. Quaresma undertakes a systematic study of "authentic" Brazilian folklore only to discover, to his dismay, that the songs and dances he exalted were all of foreign origin. His search for Brazilian cultural roots then leads him to the glorification of indigenous Tupinambá customs. Meanwhile, Quaresma is oblivious to the plight of Anastácio, a black man who had worked for him for 30 years.

Barreto's criticism of *indigenism*, in *Triste fim de Policarpo Quaresma* and elsewhere, was based on the awareness of a contradiction: the movements that surfaced at the turn of the century claimed a distant, archaic "Indianness" as the basis of Brazilian national identity, ultimately excluding the African component of the Brazilian population.

Barreto also wrote fervently against certain forms of modernization, such as skyscrapers, the cinema, and the republican regime. His attack on soccer in a series of newspaper articles between 1919 and 1921 is sufficient to illustrate his thinking. Barreto condemned the imitation of a foreign sport and founded a League Against Soccer. Barreto's wrath was directed at more than merely copying the foreign; he was also angry about the racism of early Brazilian soccer, which, as an elite practice, prohibited the participation of blacks and mulattos. His writing was especially heated when a national debate considered whether blacks should be allowed to represent Brazil in an upcoming game in Argentina. The Brazilian president in effect intervened and declared that it would not be in the best interest of Brazil's image if people of color represented the country in international competitions. Barreto responded bitterly: "Our only revenge is that the Argentineans don't distinguish us based on color; to them, we are all monkeys."

Marcos Natalí

See Also

Machado de Assis, Joaquim Maria; Rio de Janeiro, Brazil; Abolition and Emancipation in Latin America and the Caribbean; Literature, Black, in Brazil.

Latin America and the Caribbean

Lima, Jorge Mateus Vicente (b. April 23, 1895, União dos Palmares, Alagoas, Brazil; d. November 16, 1953, Rio de Janeiro), Brazilian poet, novelist, essayist, painter, critic, professor, doctor, and politician; as a writer he is best known for manipulating inherently Brazilian themes while exploring Afro-Brazilian culture, folklore, and regionalism and for his place in the vanguard of 1920s Brazilian culture.

Jorge de Lima was the son of José Mateus de Lima, a wealthy businessman, and Delmira Simões Lima. He studied humanities at Maceió, the seaport capital city of Alagoas State, and earned a degree in medicine, which he practiced in Maceió and Rio de Janeiro. He went on to become a university professor and local politician in Rio de Janeiro.

Lima's talent for writing emerged at an early age. He published his first poems, including "O Acendedor dos Lampiões" (1907, The Street Lamp Lighters), in a small literary paper he produced while still in secondary school. He spent his childhood living either at the stately house of a sugar plantation or the family's second home in the city. These experiences inspired much of his literary work. Both his father and his maternal grandfather were white abolitionists who refused to accept slave labor on their plantations. In this environment Lima developed a keen interest in the figure of the black slave.

Although he started writing poetry as a Parnassian (a late-nineteenth-century literary movement to practice art for art's sake), in 1925 Lima took an active role in the Modernist (or avant-garde) movement that emerged in the northeast part of the country. His most celebrated poem, "Essa nega fulô" (1928, That Black Girl Fulô), was his first major manifestation of formal experimentation, marking his rupture from the formalism of the romantics. The poem boldly explores dynamics of power and sexuality in the relationship between a slave, her mistress, and her master. Here, as in other works, the poet re-creates colloquial and regional speech patterns with strongly rhythmic musicality (*see* LITERATURE, BLACK, IN BRAZIL).

Nicola Cooney

SEE ALSO
Slavery in Latin America and the Caribbean; Rio de Janeiro, Brazil; White Abolitionists in Brazil.

Africa

Limba, ethnic group of SIERRA LEONE.

The Limba primarily inhabit northwestern Sierra Leone. Others live in GUINEA. They speak a Niger-Congo language and are related to the neighboring TEMNE people. Approximately 400,000 people consider themselves Limba.

SEE ALSO
Languages, African: An Overview.

North America

Lincoln, Abbey (b. August 6, 1930, Chicago, Ill.), African American actress and JAZZ vocalist, arranger, and composer.

Although she calls herself a "late bloomer," Abbey Lincoln has excelled both musically and dramatically for more than 40 years. Born Anna Marie Wooldridge and raised in a family of 12 children in a small Michigan town, Lincoln began her show business career as a singer. Under the stage name Gaby Lee, she sang in nightclubs in California and Hawaii throughout the early 1950s. Her carefully crafted image as a seductress helped earn her a small role in the 1956 film *The Girl Can't Help It*.

In the late 1950s Lincoln (rechristened Abbey Lincoln by her manager) met the jazz drummer Max Roach, with whom she moved to New York City. There she met Thelonious Monk, John Coltrane, and other avant-garde members of the black musical world. Lincoln married Roach in 1960, the same year she sang in his *Freedom Now Suite*, a musical celebration of the CIVIL RIGHTS MOVEMENT. The 1960s saw Lincoln's return to the screen in groundbreaking roles in such movies as *Nothing But a Man* (1964), with Ivan Dixon, and *For Love of Ivy* (1968), with SIDNEY POITIER. Critics praised both performances for their stereotype-shattering realism.

In the 1970s, facing the shortage of movie roles available to African American women as well as the end of her marriage to Roach, Lincoln left the United States and toured Asia and Europe as a solo singer. She also visited Africa, where she took the African name Aminata Moseka. Returning to New York in 1981, she joined M-Base, a group of young jazz musicians, and began recording again. Lincoln's 1991 album *You Gotta Pay the Band* won acclaim for both her voice and her songwriting talent.

Kate Tuttle

SEE ALSO
Coltrane, John William; Monk, Thelonious Sphere; New York, New York; Racial Stereotypes; Roach, Maxwell Lemuel (Max); Film, Blacks in American.

North America

Lincoln Theatre, popular African American theater in Harlem from approximately 1910 to 1930 that catered to New York's Southern immigrants.

In the decades before the Harlem Renaissance, when many Harlem theaters admitted only whites, the Lincoln Theatre's open-admissions policy made it the hot spot for Harlem's African American audiences. On 135th Street at Lenox Avenue, the Lincoln catered to the community's working-class Southern immigrants. It was known for its live entertainment and lively audiences, who often participated in the onstage action with loud and witty running commentary. Pianist Thomas "Fats" Waller got his start at the Lincoln, and "Mother of the Blues" Ma Rainey, "Empress of the Blues" BESSIE SMITH, JAZZ musician Duke Ellington, and vaudeville entertainer BERT WILLIAMS all performed there before it became a movie theater and later a church.

Lisa Clayton Robinson

SEE ALSO
Harlem, New York; Rainey, Gertrude Pridgett ("Ma"); Waller, Thomas Wright ("Fats"); Ellington, Edward Kennedy ("Duke").

North America

Lincoln University (Missouri), a public, coeducational, predominantly black university in Jefferson City.

Like many of the United States' oldest black colleges and universities, Lincoln University was founded at the end of the Civil War. While many of these schools were established by white benefactors, Lincoln was founded by black Civil War veterans. Soldiers and officers of the 62nd and 65th United States Colored Infantries together gave $6400 to endow the school, which was intended "for the special benefit of the freed African-Americans."

Classes met for the first time on September 17, 1866, in an old frame building in Jefferson City, Missouri. Three years later the school moved several miles to its present campus. For the first few decades elementary and high school classes were offered in addition to teacher-training and general college courses. Lincoln added an industrial and agricultural program in 1891 and its first graduate programs in 1940.

Lincoln has been a part of Missouri's state educational system since 1879. The United States Supreme Court's 1954 BROWN V. BOARD OF EDUCATION of Topeka, Kansas ruling, which prohibited segregated public educational institutions, led Lincoln to affirm that it welcomes qualified students of all backgrounds, not simply African Americans. But Lincoln adds that "as a historically black university, particular attention continues to be given to African-American students from both within and outside Missouri." The university also actively recruits minority faculty and staff.

Currently, Lincoln offers a range of liberal arts and sciences degree programs. Its most popular majors are business, computer science, engineering technology, nursing science, and teacher education. The school is also committed to developing distance-learning and continuing education programs, and admits without any academic preconditions students who have completed a minimum high school core curriculum.

Lisa Clayton Robinson

SEE ALSO
Civil War, American.

North America

Lincoln University (Pennsylvania), the oldest black institution of higher learning in the United States, located in Oxford, Pennsylvania.

Even though slavery was still legal when Lincoln University was founded, its motto has always been "If the Son shall make you free, ye shall be free indeed." Lincoln was founded in 1854 by John Miller Dickey, the white pastor of the Oxford Presbyterian Church in Oxford, Pennsylvania. Two years earlier Dickey had tried to help a black student, James Amos, gain admission to Princeton Theological Seminary and a Philadelphia Presbyterian seminary. When Amos was rejected from both schools because of race, Dickey decided that the solution was to create an institution for black men.

His school became the first in the United States dedicated to providing post-secondary instruction for African American students. It was originally named Ashmun Institute,

Mary McLeod Bethune and W. E. B. Du Bois speak with Lincoln University president Horace Mann Bond after receiving the university's Alpha Medallion in 1950. *CORBIS/Bettmann*

in honor of the first governor of LIBERIA, but after the AMERICAN CIVIL WAR it was renamed in honor of President Abraham Lincoln. Lincoln's first classes were in liberal arts, law, medicine, and theology, and the school awarded its first baccalaureate degree in 1868.

During the first 100 years of the university's existence, Lincoln alumni comprised 20 percent of the black physicians and more than 10 percent of the black lawyers in the United States. Poet LANGSTON HUGHES and Supreme Court Justice THURGOOD MARSHALL were both Lincoln graduates. Lincoln alumni have become United States ambassadors, mayors, federal judges, college and university presidents, and pastors of prominent churches.

In the twentieth century Lincoln has also gained a strong reputation for training African leaders. Nnamdi Azikiwe, Nigeria's first president, graduated in 1930, and KWAME NKRUMAH, Ghana's first prime minister, graduated in 1939. NAMIBIA's first independence government cabinet had six Lincoln University graduates. Many African students continue to come to the United States to study at Lincoln.

Lincoln's international reputation has been supplemented by its own commitment to international studies. In 1961 the U.S. State Department sponsored Lincoln's African Languages and Area Studies program, and from 1963 to 1971, Peace Corps volunteers to Africa and the Caribbean were trained on Lincoln's campus. In recent years Lincoln established the Center for Public Policy and Diplomacy, the Center for the Study of Critical Languages, and the Center for the Comparative Study of the Humanities, all of which are part of the university's international studies curriculum.

HORACE MANN BOND, a Lincoln alumnus, became the university's first black president in 1945. In 1953 Lincoln became coeducational, and its current president, Niara Sudarkasa, is the first African American woman to lead the university. Today approximately 1400 students from a variety of national, social, and economic backgrounds are enrolled.

Lisa Clayton Robinson

SEE ALSO

Azikiwe, Benjamin Nnamdi; Slavery in the United States.

Africa

Lion, a carnivorous cat found primarily in East and southern Africa whose regal appearance has earned it the nickname "king of the beasts."

Lions belong to the family Felidae and are classified as *Panthera leo*. Muscular, with short legs and long bodies, males grow from 1.7 to 2.5 m long (about 5.6 to 8.2 ft), stand approximately 1.23 m high (about 4 ft), and weigh between 150 to 250 kg (about 330 to 550 lbs). Females grow to approximately 1.5 m long (about 5 ft), 0.9 to 1.0 m high (about 3 to 3.5 ft), and weigh between 120 to 180 kg (about 265 to 390 lbs). Lions have short coats that range in color from buff yellow to brown, and males possess the species' most distinguishing physical feature, the mane. The average life span is 12 years for males in the wild, 16 for females in the wild, and as long as 30 years in captivity.

Lions differ from other cats in that they live in social groups, known as prides, that can contain anywhere from four to forty members. Prides are usually made up of several generations of females and their cubs, and one to six outside males who lead the pride for as long as they can repel the challenges of other males. Lions are polygamous and can breed throughout the year, although females only have cubs in the wild every two or three years. Gestation averages 108 days and produces a litter of between one and six cubs, although two to four is the average. Lionesses bond closely and often suckle their young communally. At about three years of age males are expelled from the pride, as are some females at that age. Adolescent males roam in bachelor groups until they are about five years old, when they challenge males for leadership of a pride. Often, after ousting a rival, the new pride leader will kill his rival's cubs to eliminate competition for any offspring he may sire.

Prides are territorial and males mark their territory by urinating on trees, bushes, or the ground. They also roar to announce their territory. Lions' roars can reach as loud as 114 decibels and can be heard for a distance of up to 9 km (about 5.6 mi). A pride's territory can range from 20 to 400 sq km (about 8 to 150 sq m), depending on the availability of game. Pride members spend the day in small groups, rejoining for the hunt, usually in the evening and early morning.

When game is plentiful, lions hunt for only two to three hours each day and rest for as much as 20 hours. Lionesses do much of the hunting and prefer hoofed herd animals such as WILDEBEEST, ZEBRA, gazelle, and ANTELOPE. When game is scarce, lions have been known to hunt BABOON, buffalo, and HIPPOPOTAMUS and to scavenge. Lions hunt by ambush, stalking their prey, flushing it, and chasing it a short distance before bringing it down with their weight and strangling it by biting and clamping its throat. Males eat first, then lionesses, and finally cubs, who often starve in times of scarcity. After a successful hunt, lions gorge, eating as much as 40 kg (about 88 lbs) of meat. They can then go for up to a week without hunting again.

Although lions used to roam throughout Africa, they are now largely restricted to national parks, such as Maasai Mara in KENYA, SERENGETI NATIONAL PARK in TANZANIA, and Kruger National Park in SOUTH AFRICA, largely because of human encroachment on their habitat. Although they are relatively secure in the parks and are considered valuable because of the tourist revenue they generate, scientists believe they could become threatened in the near future.

Robert Fay

Latin America and the Caribbean

Lisboa, Antônio Francisco ("Aleijadinho") **(b. August 29, 1730, Villa Rica do Ouro Preto, Minas Gerais, Brazil; d. November 18, 1814, Villa Rica do Ouro Preto, Minas Gerais, Brazil), the most famous sculptor and architect of colonial Brazil.**

Antônio Francisco Lisboa, better known by his nickname "Aleijadinho" (the Little Cripple), distinguished himself as an artist in Minas Gerais, Brazil, during the baroque and rococo artistic periods. The Minas Gerais variant of the baroque and rococo styles is distinct because, unlike the coastal states of Rio de Janeiro and Bahia, whose frequent contact with Portugal kept the art and architecture of those provinces in tune with European artistic developments, the location of Minas Gerias in the interior largely insulated it from European influences. Minas Gerais was also a more recently settled province, and it had few convents or monasteries of the regular orders, which would have otherwise encouraged the duplication of European architectural designs.

During the colonial era in Latin America, the church was the center of social life and the principal patron of the arts. Virtually all of Aleijadinho's works have religious themes, because they were commissioned by churches in Minas Gerais, whose construction was made possible by the province's lucrative mining industry.

Aleijadinho was the son of a Portuguese architect named Manuel Francisco Lisboa and a slave named Isabel. As a mulatto growing up in colonial Brazil, he faced some restrictions, but otherwise his youth was relatively unburdened. His father recognized Antônio Francisco as his son and instructed him in the fundamentals of architecture. Aleijadinho also learned architecture and design from other artists in Villa Rica, including the painter João Gomes Baptista. He began to carve wood, sculpt in stone, and draft building plans at age 14. Beyond what Aleijadinho was taught by his mentors in Minas Gerais, he was also exposed to European art through book illustrations and engravings of buildings and paintings by European artists. He reinterpreted some of these forms in his own work, giving birth to a uniquely Brazilian version of the rococo style. Some of the distinguishing elements of Aleijadinho's work include the use of soapstone, which until then had rarely been employed; a church plan synthesizing the rectangular, linear forms of the traditional Portuguese designs with a more curvilinear Italian-influenced design; the execution of an ornate, circular relief sculpture on the façade of the church above the central door, a type of ornamentation previously reserved only for the interior; and the unprecedented use of cylindrical towers topped with elegant bulb-shaped forms.

In addition to sculpting statues, pulpits, and altars, Aleijadinho designed churches and decorated their interiors, usually by means of ornamental reliefs. He often worked in collaboration with the painters Francisco Xavier Carneiro and Manoel da Costa Ataíde, also of African descent. In part or whole, Aleijadinho's most famous works are the churches of São Francisco de Assis in Ouro Preto and São João de Rei; Nossa Senhora do Carmo in Sabará; and Bom Jesus de Matosinhos in Congonhas dos Campo, Aleijadinho's masterpiece. Bom Jesus de Matosinhos is a pilgrimage church and houses a set of 66 life-size wooden figures carved by Aleijadinho that represent the scenes from the Last Supper and the Stations of the Cross. The stairway leading to the church features 12 massive yet dynamic statues of the Old Testament prophets executed by Aleijadinho.

Many of Aleijadinho's best-known works, including his Prophets, were done after he contracted a debilitating and painful disease in his forties. The disease, which has frequently been labeled as leprosy, caused severe scarring, atrophy, and disfigurement. His appendages shriveled, he lost fingers and toes, and eventually he had to have his three assistants strap the chisel and mallet to the stumps of his gnarled hands. His appearance became so deformed that he

Known as "Aleijadinho" (little cripple), Lisboa created some of his most famous sculptures after losing the use of his hands to a crippling disease. In the later part of his life his assistants strapped tools to his wrists so that he could continue to work. *CORBIS/Genevieve Naylor*

hid himself from public view, traveling and working behind curtains. Although in a state of physical deterioration, he worked with increasing intensity during the last three decades of his life. He died in 1814 at age 84, never having traveled or worked beyond the state of Minas Gerais.

In an artistic career lasting more than half a century, Aleijadinho produced a vast oeuvre that includes some 80 sculptures as well as the design and decoration of numerous churches. In addition, a number of works are believed to have been executed by Aleijadinho, most notably the church of Santa Ifigênia for Chico Rei, but there is no documentation or signature to verify these attributions. Most of Aleijadinho's work is concentrated in the city of Ouro Preto (formerly Villa Rica), which is today a Brazilian national monument. In the words of art historian Pál Kelemen, "Aleijadinho carried Brazilian rococo to its fullest flowering.... A rare human story lives in his masterpieces; his gift was genius."

Aaron Myers

See Also
Rio de Janeiro, Brazil; Art in Latin America and the Caribbean.

Africa

Lissouba, Pascal (b. 1931, Tsingidi, Belgian Congo [present-day Republic of the Congo]), president of the Republic of the Congo (1992-).

Pascal Lissouba was born in Tsingidi, in the southern part of the country, a member of the Nibolek ethnic group. Trained in Tunisia and France as an agronomist, he received a doctoral degree in biology from the University of Paris. After the Republic of the Congo became independent in 1960, he served simultaneously as prime minister and minister of trade, industry, and agriculture (1963-1966). Between 1966 and 1977 Lissouba held various professional and ministerial positions in Brazzaville, the capital of the Republic of the Congo. He was arrested and sentenced to life in prison for complicity in the 1977 assassination of President Marien Ngouabi, a sentence that was later reduced to exile. Returning to the Republic of the Congo, Lissouba became the leader of the Pan-African Union for Social Democracy (French acronym, UPADS) political party, and took 61 percent of the vote in a runoff contest to win Congo's presidential election in August 1992.

Strikes, violent civil unrest, and a changing coalition of opposition parties threatened Lissouba's regime from the start. In 1993 hotly contested legislative elections caused several months of armed conflict. After civil war was averted through international intervention, Lissouba's UPADS and allied parties retained a shaky legislative majority, but his short-term success collapsed as fighting broke out in Brazzaville again in November 1993. Fighting continued into 1994 as armed forces loyal to Lissouba battled independent partisan militias. Although a mediation force was set up after a 1994 cease-fire, it has been difficult to disarm the ethnic-based factions.

See Also
Brazzaville, Republic of the Congo.

North America

Liston, Charles ("Sonny")

(b. May 8, 1932, St. Francis County, Ark.; d. December 30, 1970, New York, N.Y.), African American heavyweight boxer known for his strength and stamina.

Sonny Liston was born to a poor Arkansas cotton farmer who had 25 children from two marriages. In 1945 Liston moved with his mother to St. Louis, where his juvenile delinquency graduated into adult crime. In 1950 he was sentenced to 19 months in prison for armed robbery. A chaplain at the prison guided Liston into boxing and, after his release, Liston won the Golden Gloves championship in 1953.

Liston went 14 and 1 as a professional before returning to prison for assaulting a policeman in 1956. Upon his release, he amassed a 33 and 1 record with 23 knockouts and was named the number-one heavyweight contender in 1960. In a 1962 fight he knocked out the heavyweight champion Floyd Patterson in the first round. In a 1963 rematch he again knocked Patterson out in the first round.

Liston was known for his physical presence, his left hook, and an impressive capacity to take punches. In 1964, though, he fought Cassius Clay and was knocked out in the seventh round. In a 1965 rematch, the newly renamed Muhammad Ali knocked Liston out in the first round. Liston continued to box until six months before his death. He had a career record of 50 and 4, with 39 knockouts.

North America

Literature, African American

Although black Americans responded to their enslavement and the denial of their humanity in a number of ways, the emergence of African American literature reflects the centrality of writing to the project of seeking freedom and equality in the United States. At first, because of the European Enlightenment's stress on writing as the most visible sign of the ability to reason, literature presented a way for Africans in America to prove their humanity and demonstrate a capacity for artistic creation and imaginative thought. Later literature developed into a vehicle through which African Americans could voice not only their rejection of slavery and institutionalized racism but their desire for freedom and recognition as full citizens of the United States. In the twentieth century African American literature has continued to be a means through which to right the historical record and counter the absence or distortion of black people in historical representation.

Reading, Writing, and Black Humanity: The Story of Phillis Wheatley

Phillis Wheatley was the first African American to publish a book and the first to achieve international recognition as a writer. Her significance to the history of African American literature, however, extends beyond these milestones. Wheatley was born in Africa and transported to the United States as a young child in 1761. With the instruction and encouragement of her master and his family, Phillis learned English quickly and began to study the Bible as well as scholarly works in Latin and Greek; within four years of her arrival in Boston, Massachusetts, she was writing verse. Her first published poem, which appeared in 1767, was quickly followed by others, and her notoriety – not simply as a poet but as an African poet – rose.

In the eyes of colonial Boston society the very idea of an African poet was something of a contradiction in terms. Poetry was considered the highest form of human expression, and black Africans were not considered capable of the depth of feeling necessary for such artistic achievement. Before Wheatley's work was accepted by a publisher, both she and her manuscript were subjected to examination by 18 of Boston's most prominent gentlemen. The men's attestation that "the POEMS specified in the following Page were... written by PHILLIS, a young Negro Girl, who was but a few years since, brought an uncultivated Barbarian from *Africa*, and has ever since been, and now is, under the Disadvantage of serving as a Slave in a Family in this Town" was reprinted as part of the prefatory material to Wheatley's collection. When *Poems on Various Subjects, Religious and Moral, by Phillis Wheatley, Negro Servant to Mr. John Wheatley, of Boston, in New England* was published in the fall of 1773, the letters that preceded Wheatley's poetry were meant to assure readers of the authenticity of her work. These documents speak to the tremendous impact Wheatley's supporters knew her poetry would have on its white audience, most of which would not be prepared to believe a black person capable of producing such verse.

Indeed, the impact of the collection was tremendous, not only for Phillis Wheatley herself but for the history of African American letters. Reviewers argued that the publication of her poems illustrated the humanity of the young poet and insisted that if she was, as her poetry demonstrated, capable of improvement and artistic expression, she should not be enslaved. The fact that Wheatley was given her freedom soon after the publication of *Poems on Various Subjects* suggests the extent to which her writing was not simply an intellectual pursuit: the author used writing to gain access to her humanity and to free herself from the dehumanizing institution of slavery. Although Wheatley's poems have been criticized because their subject matter is not explicitly political, the very fact that Wheatley was writing made a political statement: the poetry provided her gateway to recognition as a human being. Along with other early African writers like Olaudah Equiano, whose autobiography *The Interesting Life of Olaudah Equiano, or Gustavus Vassa, the African, Written by Himself* was published in 1789, Wheatley proved that blacks could command written language and represent themselves effectively through writing.

Antebellum Writers in the Urban North and the Tradition of Protest

As the American Revolution reinforced Enlightenment ideas about the importance of written communication, reading, writing, and print were increasingly seen as technologies of power. Colonists turned to written texts in the form of pamphlets and broadsides as a medium of public expression. The fact that the country had formed itself through one written document, the Declaration of Independence, and negotiated the terms of its existence through another, the Constitution, caused writing and publication to become associated with legitimacy in the new nation. In this environment the ability to read and write took on special significance: it became a marker for citizenship.

At the beginning of the nineteenth century free blacks living in urban areas of the North used writing to highlight the disparity between the condition of people of African descent in the United States and the republican principles laid out in the Declaration of Independence. The writers used literature not only to call for the abolition of slavery in the United States but also to point to the particular needs of the free black population and to voice their demands for full citizenship and equal participation in the life of the republic. The most outspoken and militant of these voices belonged to David Walker. Published privately in Boston by its author, Walker's *Appeal, in Four Articles; Together with a Preamble to the Colored Citizens of the World, but in Particular, and Very Expressly to Those of the United States of America* delivered a furious indictment of American slavery and racism. The content of Walker's *Appeal*, which called for a series of violent black uprisings, shocked white readers. Equally disturbing was Walker's ability to get his pamphlet into the hands of its intended audience, the "colored citizens" of the South.

The *Appeal* is representative of an important moment in the history of African American letters. In the late 1820s and throughout the 1830s free blacks crafted and distributed literature that was intended to combat charges of racial inferiority, validate their calls for social justice, and alert their audience to the disparity between American ideals and racial inequality. Much of this writing emerged from literary societies formed by free blacks to support reading, writing, and literary discussion in their communities. This surge in literary activity coincided with the publication of the first African American newspaper, *Freedom's Journal*. The paper quickly became a primary publishing venue for "Original Communications," including poetry and occasional pieces, editorials and letters to the editors, testimonials, and appeals and addresses, all of which were considered "literature" in the early nineteenth century.

In part because late twentieth-century definitions of "literature" differ so radically from those of the early nineteenth century, the rich store of writings that free blacks contributed to newspapers has seldom found its way into anthologies of antebellum African American literary work. Yet newspapers provide a remarkable record of the early literary efforts of African Americans and the beginnings of a tradition. One impediment to studying the poetry and prose that appears in the earliest black newspapers and the abolitionist press is that much of it was published anonymously. As the unsigned broadsides and pamphlets of the Revolutionary era illustrate, recognition of individual authorship was not a priority in the early United States. Furthermore, anonymity and the use of pen names often provided a degree of protection that allowed black writers to speak their minds more freely. This was especially true for black women. Socially imposed constraints of both race and gender would have prohibited black women from engaging in public and political discussion. But the abundance of publications by "A Young Lady of Color" or "A Colored Lady" attest not only to the wide variety of writing submitted by African Americans but also to the ability of black women to circumvent socially imposed norms through publication.

The Slave's Story

In the 1830s growing unrest among the slave population of the South combined with the proliferation of abolitionist forces in the North to produce a new direction in African American literature: the fugitive slave narrative. Written by former slaves who recorded the transition from the slave South to the free North, slave narratives documented the physical and spiritual horrors of their authors' lives in slavery. The narratives were often the result of collaborative work between the former slave and a white abolitionist, whose job it was to shape the story into a narrative that would promote the abolitionist mission. Narratives were advertised in the abolitionist press and sold at antislavery meetings; their popularity was not limited to the United States but extended throughout the English-speaking world.

Of the numerous accounts of slavery written by former slaves, the best known was written by Frederick Douglass. By the time the *Narrative of the Life of Frederick Douglass, An American Slave, Written by Himself* was published in 1845 Douglass was an abolitionist speaker well known for his rhetorical skill. As evidenced by the narrative's subtitle, Douglass broke with the tradition of having a white abolitionist coauthor or transcribe his narrative: the book was indeed "Written by Himself." This announcement of intellectual independence and literary authority became increasingly common as black authors such as William Wells Brown, Henry Bibb, and James W. C. Pennington self-consciously chose to take control of their own stories.

Douglass's *Narrative* is best known for the association it makes between literacy and freedom. Selected as a boy to go to Baltimore, Maryland, as a servant, Douglass was taught the rudiments of literacy by his mistress. For Douglass, learning to read was a decisively political act; literacy was, in his words, "the pathway from slavery to freedom." Although the slave narratives have been mined for their adherence to this "literacy equals freedom" paradigm, black feminist scholars have recently questioned its failure to distinguish between the conditions and results of literacy for men and women. *Incidents in the Life of a Slave Girl*, written by Harriet Jacobs and published in 1861, underscores different uses of literacy by male and female slaves. Through the pseudonym and character of Linda Brent, Jacobs's narrative outlines the particular injustices faced by enslaved black women as well as their strategies of resistance. Jacobs's account of the sexual violation of black women by white men was a daring literary effort. By speaking out about her sexual exploitation in slavery and revealing her use of her own sexuality as a weapon against such exploitation, Jacobs risked offending her white audience and reinforcing stereotypes that associated black women with unbridled sexuality.

The First African American Literary Renaissance

The strategies Jacobs develops to facilitate the telling of her story – such as her use of the name "Linda Brent" and her masking of important persons and places – illustrate the complexity of her position as an author and the techniques African American writers were incorporating into their work in the 1850s and 1860s. In 1853 Frederick Douglass published his historical novel *The Heroic Slave* in his newspaper, *Frederick Douglass' Paper*. The same year saw the publication of William Wells Brown's *Clotel; or The President's Daughter*, a story of the light-skinned woman reputed to be Thomas Jefferson's daughter by his slave mistress. Five years later Brown published *The Escape; or, A Leap for Freedom* (1858), the first drama written by an African American. In 1859 Martin R. Delany, a black journalist whose Pittsburgh newspaper the *Mystery* was rich in literary content, wrote *Blake; or the Huts of America*. The novel's hero, who leads a slave revolt in the South, is the first black nationalist hero in African American literature. To this literary outpouring Harriet E. Wilson contributed the autobiographical *Our Nig; or Sketches from the Life of a Free Black* (1859), the first novel published in the United States by a black woman.

On the eve of the Civil War the first African American literary magazines were published. The *Anglo-African Magazine* included literature by some of the most prominent black intellectuals of the time. To this magazine FRANCES ELLEN WATKINS HARPER contributed two important pieces in 1859: "Our Greatest Want" and the short story "Two Offers." Another important literary magazine of the time, the *Repository of Religion and Literature and of Science and Art* (1858), appeared under the auspices of the AFRICAN METHODIST EPISCOPAL CHURCH. That magazine's rich literary content serves as a reminder that the distinction between secular and religious interests was not so clearly drawn in the mid-nineteenth century as it is today.

LITERATURE OF THE "NEW NEGRO"

Although African Americans were officially free in the period just after the Civil War known as RECONSTRUCTION, the times were not conducive to their literary efforts. Slavery had been abolished, but the place and position of the newly freed slaves and those African Americans who had been free before the Civil War had not been determined. Paradoxically, the dissolution of the promises of Reconstruction marked a significant revival in the production of black literature and literary activity in the black community. At the end of the nineteenth century personal testimonies continued to be powerful tools through which to share the trials and triumphs of black life. Especially popular were the autobiographies of former slaves, whose determination to succeed in the face of obstacles facilitated their rise from the material poverty of their youth. *Up From Slavery* (1901) by Booker T. Washington is the classic example of this type of narrative. Although Washington's belief in industrial education and his acceptance of the political status quo in the South are troublesome from the vantage point of the late twentieth century, his text must be seen in its historical context. At the turn of the century black authors sought to revise the stereotypes that filled the white imagination and dominated plantation fiction, blackface, MINSTRELSY, and vaudeville acts. Advances in educational opportunities for black children brought the need for literature that accurately portrayed the history and aspirations of African Americans. Biographies of nineteenth-century black leaders such as Frederick Douglass and Martin Delany and histories such as *The History of the African American Episcopal Church* (1891) by Daniel Payne and *History of the Negro Race in America from 1619-1880* (1893) by GEORGE WASHINGTON WILLIAMS, as well as the collection *A New Negro For A New Century* (1900), to which Booker T. Washington and Fannie Barrier Williams contributed essays, sought to present a "New Negro" to the world. These texts inspired pride in African American communities while communicating to white readers the contributions black Americans had made to the nation.

Although black historian RAYFORD LOGAN identified the two decades between 1890 and 1910 as "The Nadir of Black Experience," a characterization justified by a historical record of widespread lynching and segregation, the literary outpouring by black women writers at the turn of the century underscores the reasons why the same period was labeled the "Woman's Era." Motivated by the desire to alter their public image and bolstered by the sense of community and achievement that membership in women's clubs offered, black women's literary contributions during this time ranged from fiction and poetry to autobiography and investigative reporting. A sampling of titles published in 1892 alone gives some sense of the variety of literature black women were writing at the end of the nineteenth century: *Iola Leroy; or, Shadows Uplifted* by Frances E.W. Harper, *A Voice from the South by a Black Woman of the South* by Anna Julia Cooper, *From Darkness Cometh the Light; or, Struggles for Freedom* by Lucy Delaney, and *Southern Horrors: Lynch Law in All Its Phases* by Ida B. Wells. Other important contributions include the essay "The Importance of Race Literature" (1895) by VICTORIA EARLE MATTHEWS, *The Work of Afro-American Women* (1894) by Gertrude Mossell, and *Contending Forces* (1900) by Pauline Hopkins.

The most influential voice of the early twentieth century belonged to W. E. B. Du Bois, whose *The Souls of Black Folk* (1903) stands as the preeminent text of modern African American cultural consciousness. In *Souls* Du Bois employed various modes of writing and challenged the formal boundaries of several disciplines to define black experience and the place of black culture in America. Calling Negro spirituals the only "true American music" and locating the creation of African American art as central to the future status of black people in the United States, Du Bois issued a challenge to black writers to create literature that would celebrate the vital and significant world in which they lived. In addition to advancing education and suffrage causes, Du Bois argued, African Americans needed to make artistic contributions to American culture. The problematic exploration of racial identity and the conflicted relationship of "the Negro" to "the American" are identified by Du Bois with the term *double consciousness*, and this term has remained a significant subject of African American literature throughout the twentieth century. Two important texts that highlight the influence of Du Bois's formulations are *The Autobiography of an Ex-Colored Man* (1912) by JAMES WELDON JOHNSON and *Invisible Man* (1952) by RALPH ELLISON.

THE HARLEM RENAISSANCE

Recent critical work by literary historians has revealed the extent to which the term "HARLEM RENAISSANCE" inaccurately describes the literary and cultural phenomenon that took place not only in the area of New York City called Harlem but nationwide and, to some extent, worldwide in the decade between 1919 and 1929. But New York and particularly Harlem were central to the movement. In part on the strength of newcomers who took part in the Great Migration of black people from the rural South to the urban North, Harlem in the 1920s fostered a sense of racial unity and pride. This environment inspired a new sense of confidence among African American artists and gave rise to a boldly creative period in the history of African American letters.

The parameters of the movement were put forth in two pivotal anthologies. In 1922 JAMES WELDON JOHNSON edited *The Book of Negro Verse*, a collection that highlighted the poetry of younger poets. In his preface to the volume Johnson urged new black artists to reject dialect verse in favor of "a form expressing the imagery, the idioms, the peculiar turns of thought, and the distinctive humor and pathos" of black Americans. He pushed the artists to create literature that explored "the widest range of subjects and the widest scope of treatment" so as to give voice to "the deepest emotions and aspirations" of African Americans. In 1925 Howard University professor Alain Locke combined the essays, stories, and artwork of older and younger artists, both black and white, to create *The New Negro*, a volume that announced a fresh vision and new sense of independence in African American art. Most influential was Locke's own essay entitled "The New Negro," which proclaimed the "new self-respect and self-dependence" of the black community. Arguing that the "Old Negro had long become more of a myth than a man," Locke challenged young artists to create new and diverse portraits of black life.

The New Negro marked the height rather than the beginning of the Harlem Renaissance. In 1923 *Cane* by JEAN TOOMER captured through innovative poetry and prose the many and varied attributes of black life in the United States Toomer's work depicted the lyrical language and mystical setting of rural Georgia along with the beauty and ugliness of black folk life there. The book also identified the isolation and dislocation of urban blacks in WASHINGTON, D.C., and

Chicago. Filled with racial self-awareness but also racial self-consciousness, *Cane* illustrated the literary excellence and experimentation that would distinguish the Harlem Renaissance. Other important writers of the period included LANGSTON HUGHES, whose poetry drew heavily from jazz and the blues, musical forms that he considered the most authentic and insistent expressions of art to come from the black community; COUNTEE CULLEN, for whom the Harlem Renaissance meant the freedom to experiment with forms of poetry that merged racial awareness with the traditional poetic formats of English Romantic authors Keats and Shelley; GEORGIA DOUGLAS JOHNSON, who published two volumes of poetry during the 1920s; and CLAUDE MCKAY, whose collection of poetry, *Harlem Shadows* (1922), contained the militant sonnet "If We Must Die." Written in 1919 in response to the racial violence and urban unrest of that year, this poem sounded a note of defiance against racism that was repeated throughout the Renaissance.

While the focus of many black writers at the beginning of the Harlem Renaissance was on poetry, authors increasingly turned their attention to fiction in the second half of the decade. In 1928 and 1929 respectively, *Quicksand* and *Passing* by NELLA LARSEN were published; both novels address the limitations imposed by sexuality and class as well as race on their female protagonists. Other well-received novels of the Harlem Renaissance include *Home to Harlem* (1928) by Claude McKay, *There is Confusion* (1924) by Jessie Fauset, *The Blacker the Berry* (1929) and *Infants of the Spring* (1932) by WALLACE THURMAN, *Not Without Laughter* (1930) by Langston Hughes, and *Black No More* (1931) by George Schuyler. Although her most widely acclaimed novel, *Their Eyes Were Watching God*, was not published until 1937, ZORA NEALE HURSTON was an important part of the Harlem Renaissance: she published several short stories in the 1920s and collaborated with other Harlem Renaissance figures to launch the literary magazine *Fire!!*. Like that of other female novelists of the time, Hurston's daring exploration of black female selfhood opened the way for black female writers of the 1970s and 1980s to explore the tangled web of race, sex, and class in which black women struggled to know themselves.

MODERNISM, NATURALISM, AND URBAN REALISM: 1940-1960

The stock market crash of 1929 brought an abrupt end to the reckless fun associated with the Jazz Age, drying up the financial resources of white patrons and the prosperity of the publishing industry that had been so crucial to buttressing black authors. In the wake of the crash came the GREAT DEPRESSION of the early 1930s, which fueled the less celebrated aspects of urban living that were captured in African American literature of the 1940s and 1950s. In 1940 *Native Son* by RICHARD WRIGHT burst onto the scene to wide critical acclaim. As a Book-of-the-Month-Club selection, Wright's story of Bigger Thomas and the alienating, environmental forces that shaped him and determined the course of his life was a commercial success. Drawing from Marxism and social protest theories as well as traditions of naturalism and realism, this direct, powerful novel had a deep impact on the course of African American literature. Wright's gritty portrayal of urban living and victimization by negative social forces asserted his conviction that black art and so-called social protest were synonymous. *Native Son* issued a new challenge to black writers to document the living conditions of urban blacks and make protest the narrative mode of their writing.

RALPH ELLISON's *Invisible Man* (1952) made a radical departure from the tradition of social protest embodied by Richard Wright's fictional work, signifying Ellison's fundamental disagreement with Wright's portrayal of Bigger Thomas as a powerless victim of his bleak surroundings. Ellison found the inspiration for his story in African American musical forms like JAZZ and the blues as well as black folklore; bringing these together with African American cultural values and his knowledge of the Western literary tradition, Ellison created a portrait of the paradoxical status of African Americans in the United States. The unnamed narrator of *Invisible Man* moves from the South to the North through a series of episodes that illustrate his naivete when faced with racial issues as well as the alienation that results from that naivete. Another prolific writer from this period, JAMES BALDWIN, shared Ellison's conviction about the limitations of ideological fiction and his interest in the paradox between the failed promises of American democracy and those aspects of the African American psyche that position black Americans as an integral part of American life. An essayist as well as a novelist, Baldwin wrote the semiautobiographical *Go Tell It on the Mountain* (1953), a novel that tells the story of a young black man's coming of age and explores the effects of fear, hatred, love, and sexuality on the psyches of African Americans.

Although critical perspectives of the period have tended to focus on the work of Wright, Ellison, and Baldwin, other significant black authors emerged in the 1940s and 1950s. Many rejected the militant edge associated with social protest writing or the bleakness of naturalism and realism while striving to create powerful portraits of black urban life in poetry, prose, and drama. The 1946 novel *The Street* by Ann Petry is often compared to Wright's *Native Son*, but Petry's presentation of a female protagonist and her interest in the ways that gender marks the black experience make *The Street* a very different work. The first collection of poetry published by Gwendolyn Brooks, *A Street in Bronzeville*, as well as the author's later novella *Maud Martha* (1953) captured the sounds and rhythms that defined the lives of poor blacks in the ghettos of Chicago. According to Brooks material for poetry was everywhere in the urban landscape: "If you wanted a poem," she once said, "you had only to look out a window." Inspired by African American experience but influenced by white modernist poets like Carl Sandburg, Hart Crane, and W. H. Auden, poet Robert Hayden used black history to create his poem "Middle Passage" (1945), which imaginatively recreates the rebellion aboard the slave ship *Amistad*. In 1959 *A Raisin in the Sun* by LORRAINE HANSBERRY opened on Broadway to critical acclaim and won the New York Drama Critics Award. Anticipating the concerns and interests of writers of the BLACK ARTS MOVEMENT, the play explores the African roots of African American identity and culture.

THE BLACK ARTS MOVEMENT

The social and political upheaval of the 1960s was accompanied by a change in the black literary and cultural movement. Seeking equal treatment in the United States, the black freedom movement of the 1960s looked to redefine how black people were seen and how they saw themselves. The writers of the Black Arts Movement wished to create politically engaging expression that would match the charged atmosphere of the period. They turned to the black community for inspiration and defined their goals in broadly collective political and social terms: rather than a movement focused on intellectual exchange between the black elite, the writers of the Black Arts Movement sought to communicate with the masses. According to Addison Gayle Jr., whose introduction to *The Black Aesthetic* (1971) serves as a critical and theoretical guide to the Black Arts Movement, the role of the black artist was to "provide us with images based on our own lives."

This new generation, represented by writers such as AMIRI BARAKA (LeRoi Jones), SONIA SANCHEZ, and LARRY NEAL, welcomed the fact that their work was not accepted by the mainstream. Larry Neal's "The Black Arts Movement," published in 1968, the year of the assassination of Martin Luther King Jr., served as a manifesto for these young writers. They were to look to their African ancestors as a source of inspiration, eschew white, middle-class values, create new themes, and shape new forms. Through their writing they were to distance themselves from what Neal and others referred to as the white aesthetic, the "Euro-American cultural sensibility" that the movement's leaders felt had too heavily influenced black writers who came before them. The members of this new generation aesthetically aligned themselves in opposition to those European-American concepts of art that influenced the work of Ernest Gaines, James Baldwin, Ralph Ellison, Gwendolyn Brooks, and JOHN OLIVER KILLENS and, in their opinion, had strangled black cultural and literary creativity.

African American Literature after the 1970s

Criticism of the Black Arts Movement of the 1960s has centered on its tendency to ascribe to all blacks the same backgrounds, desires, and goals; feminist scholars also challenged the movement's articulation of blackness almost purely in male terms. The questions that arose in response to these challenges have been addressed through the writing of African Americans since the 1970s. The authors of this period have celebrated the multiplicity and complexity of African American identities. Crucial to this effort has been the recovery work being done by historians and social scientists as well as creative and critical writers. Of particular interest to today's black writers has been the experience of slavery, which has been used as a means of better understanding the present. Notable examples of literature that draw on the slave's experience include the *Autobiography of Miss Jane Pittman* (1971) by Ernest Gaines, *Corregidora* (1975) by Gayl Jones, *Oxherding Tale* and *Middle Passage* by Charles Johnson, *Song of Solomon* (1977) and *Beloved* (1987) by Toni Morrison, *Dessa Rose* (1986) by Sherley Anne Williams, and *Mama Day* (1988) by Gloria Naylor. Other authors have traveled even further into the past to forge connections between African Americans and the continent of Africa. While Alice Walker chose Africa as the setting for parts of her three most recent novels, other writers such as Ntozake Shange and Ishmael Reed have used fiction to illustrate the ways that African rituals and myths remain central to African American life.

The veritable explosion of writing by African American women is the most significant development in African American literature since the 1970s (*see* Women Writers, Black, in the United States). The relative success of three novels published in 1970 – *I Know Why the Caged Bird Sings* by Maya Angelou, *The Third Life of Grange Copeland* by Alice Walker, and *The Bluest Eye* by Toni Morrison – identified the existence of a market for black women writers. Mining their own experience and the experiences of their ancestors, these and other black women writers changed the direction of African American literature by introducing new themes. The authors' primary focus on the black community rather than on the relationship between blacks and whites allows them to make inquiries into the parameters of motherhood, the dynamics of class difference among blacks, and the ambiguous expectations of sexuality and love.

Critical acclaim for the literature of both male and female black writers has been second only to the authors' appeal to a diverse reading public. Recent Pulitzer Prize winners include Alice Walker (1983), August Wilson (1986, 1990), Rita Dove (1987), and Toni Morrison (1988); Morrison was also the first African American to be honored with the Nobel Prize for Literature (1993), and in 1994 Poet Rita Dove was named the United States Poet Laureate. In 1992 books by Terry McMillan, Toni Morrison, and Alice Walker appeared on the *New York Times* bestseller list at the same time, signaling the centrality of black writers to mainstream American culture.

Elizabeth McHenry

See Also

Slavery in the United States; Abolitionism in the United States; Amistad Mutiny; Bibb, Henry Walton; Press, Black, in the United States; Blues, The; Brooks, Gwendolyn Elizabeth; Chicago, Illinois; Civil War, American; Cooper, Anna Julia Hayward; Delany, Martin Robison; Du Bois, William Edward Burghardt (W. E. B.); Fauset, Jessie Redmon; Free Blacks in the United States, 1619 to 1863; *Freedom's Journal*; Gaines, Ernest J.; Great Migration, The; Harlem, New York; Hayden, Robert Earl; Hopkins, Pauline Elizabeth; Jacobs, Harriet Ann; Johnson, Charles Richard; New York, New York; King, Martin Luther, Jr.; Locke, Alain Leroy; Payne, Daniel Alexander; Petry, Ann Lane; Pittsburgh, Pennsylvania; Schuyler, George S.; Slave Narratives; Washington, Booker Taliaferro; Wells-Barnett, Ida Bell; Williams, Sherley; Wilson, Harriet E. Adams; Spirituals, African American.

Latin America and the Caribbean

Literature, Black, in Brazil,

literature written in Portuguese by authors of African descent.

Black literature in Brazil has passed through roughly three stages of development: in the 1700s black authors adopted European literary forms; at the time of abolition, literature was used as a tool for raising political consciousness; and, more recently, we have observed the period of Brazilian Négritude. Contemporary writers blend demands for social justice with African aesthetic principles.

Black and mulatto Brazilian authors of the eighteenth and nineteenth centuries followed the dictates of Eurocentric literary models. Domingos Caldas Barbosa (1738-1800), a member of the literary school of Arcadismo, the neoclassical aesthetic dominant in Portugal and its colonies, was the first to incorporate black themes into classical models. He integrated words from the African and *mestiço* colonial vocabularies in his work and created poetry that could be set to music canticles. José da Natividade Saldanha (1795-1830), another important Afro-Brazilian poet influenced by Arcadismo, published his *Poemas dedicados aos amigos e amantes do Brasil* in 1822. Luís Gonzaga Pinto da Gama (1830-1882), abolitionist and son of Luiza Mahin (c. 1835), the leader of the last great slave revolt in Salvador da Bahia, composed satirical poetry attacking the pretentiousness of a Brazilian society that idolized European values. He provoked his readers by suggesting that the traditional standard of beauty should be modeled on the black, not the white, woman (*see* Image of the Mulatta in Latin America and the Caribbean). The playwright, poet, and fiction writer Antonio Gonçalves Texeira e Souza (1812-1861) wrote about slavery in his novel *O filho do pescador*. Joaquim Maria Machado de Assis (1839-1908), regarded as one of the greatest Brazilian novelists, was the author of *Dom Casmurro* (1900) and *Memorias postumas de Bras Cubas* (1881) and one of the founders of the Brazilian Academy of Letters. Machado de Assis was a gifted mulatto writer who remained silent about slavery during the height of abolitionist debate. His poetry contains only marginal references to blacks, and he has been criticized for the absence of black themes in his work. At the end of the century João da Cruz e Sousa (1861-1898), the son of slaves, achieved recognition as Brazil's most important Symbolist poet. He was the author of *Broqueis* (1893), *Missal* (1893), *Evocações* (1898), and *Ultimos sonetos* (1905). In the latter work Cruz e Sousa ambiguously addressed blackness, but his writing was not directed primarily at a black audience.

Afonso Henriques de Lima Barreto (1881-1922), a social novelist often compared to the French writer Honoré de Balzac (1799-1850), was the "great voice of the black in Brazil," "a kind of 'ethnic conscience,'" according to Clovis Moura. He was critical of the racist, paternalistic, and corrupt white elite of Rio de Janeiro and sought to portray black characters as social activists. His works include *Recordações do escrivão Isaías Caminha* (1909), *Triste fim de Policarpo Quaresma* (1916), and *Numa e a ninfa* (1915).

Lino Guedes (1897-1951), poet and the son of ex-slaves, is considered the precursor of Négritude in Brazil. Stigmatized by slavery, he believed that blacks could improve their status in Brazilian society by assimilating the education and values of the white elite (*see* Whitening). A journalist who worked at São Paulo's largest newspaper, Guedes also was active in the black press. He published *O Canto do cisne preto* (1927), *Resurreição negra*, *Negro preto*, and *Cor da noite* (all published in 1932), among other works.

Solano Trindade (1908-1974) was a black poet who used language accessible to the common person. He criticized black marginalization and wrote political poems such as "Canção aos Palmares," which recalls the resistance of runaway slaves in the *quilombos* (maroon settlements) (*see* Palmares: An African State in Brazil). He was one of the founders of the Centro de Cultura Afro-Brasileira, a cultural institution created in Recife, Brazil, in 1937 with the goal of promoting educational awareness about the social and political conditions of Afro-Brazilians. His best-known books are *Poemas d'uma vida simple* (1944) and *Cantares ao meu povo* (1961).

Carlos de Assumpção's (b. 1927) popular work *Protesto*, with its signature poem of the same name, recalls the contributions of black men to the building of Brazil and laments their exclusion from Brazilian society. It is regularly quoted, even today, in civic programs and gatherings.

Some critics described Eduardo de Oliveira (b. 1926) as the most gifted poet since Cruz e Sousa. A member of the Brazilian Négritude Movement, Oliveira declared, "I am a piece of Africa tossed out on the road of the world."

The writer, playwright, and activist Abdias do Nascimento (b. 1914) founded the Black Experimental Theatre. He also wrote the drama *Sortilegio*, which blends aspects of classical Greek drama with performance elements of the Afro-Brazilian religion Candomblé. In *Sortilegio,* Nascimento examines the protagonist's struggle with the conflict between his African heritage and the forces urging assimilation. Nascimento's theatrical work is sometimes compared to the Black Arts Movement in the United States. He is also a prolific writer – the author of more than 20 books – and the editor of a magazine on diasporic culture titled *Thoth: Pensamento dos povos afros e afrodescendentes* (1997-) (*See* Brazil, Blacks and Politics in: An Interpretation).

Deoscoredes Maximiliano dos Santos (b. 1918), known as Mestre Didi, was the first to write the traditional tales of the Yoruba people as told in Brazil. His ability to write these tales stems from his knowledge as a descendant of African royal lineage, his special position as a religious leader entrusted with the oral traditions of the Ketu people, and his position as the high priest of the Cult of Egungun (Cult of the Ancestors). His books include *Contos negros da Bahía* (1961, Black Stories from Bahia), *Contos de Nagô* (1963, Nagô Stories), and *Contos de Mestre Didi* (1981, Master Didi's Stories).

Oliviera Silivera (b. 1941) is of the "new poets" school and his work is reminiscent of that of Solano Trindade. He is the author of several volumes of poetry, including *Banzo* and *Pelo Escuro*.

The decline of the military dictatorship in 1978 marked the beginning of a new period of free expression following an era of obligatory "racial democracy." Although contemporary Afro-Brazilian literature deals with universal themes, its distinctiveness resides in its recognition that racial identity is related to the quality of life in Brazil. Afro-Brazilian literature examines a number of themes of social importance, such as hunger, illiteracy, abandoned street children, poverty, health, unemployment, institutionalized violence, color politics, miscegenation, and forgotten black historical figures. The decision to treat social concerns in a literary context emerges from the African aesthetic tradition that views art and life as inseparable. Afro-Brazilian literature also follows African tradition in the presentation of certain fundamental beliefs about the nature of the universe and the forces within it that influence the destiny of humanity. Consequently, Afro-Brazilian religious tradition is a frequent source of metaphorical allusions, imagery, themes, characterizations, and rhetorical devices. Literature by black women has been increasing during the last two decades, and works treating both race and gender are an emerging side of Brazilian literature.

Oswaldo de Camargo (b. 1936), a journalist for São Paulo's newspaper *O Jornal da Tarde*, is the author of *Um homem temta ser anjo* (1958), *15 Poemas negros* (1961), and *O carro do exito*. He anthologized black Brazilian poetry in his groundbreaking work *A razãao da chama* and wrote a history of black literature in Brazil titled *O negro escrito*.

Cuti (Luiz Silva, b. 1952) is a prolific, accomplished writer of poetry, theater, and short stories. He advocates that Afro-Brazilian literature adhere to an African aesthetic system. His short stories make ample use of irony, paradox, ambiguity, and the twists of fate commonly associated with literature of the African diaspora. Cuti's poetry incorporates such devices as call and response, repetition, and contrasting metrical lines similar to those heard at Afro-Brazilian religious observances. An activist within the Movimento Negro Unificado (Black Unified Movement), he is also the founder of the important literary organization Quilombhoje (1980) and of the annual anthology of black literature *Cadernos Negros*.

Márcio Barbosa (b. 1959), author of the novel *Paixões crioulas* (Creole Passions), writes about people living at the margins of society and how they cope with the conflicts between intersecting worlds: the worlds of dream and reality, visible and invisible, and Afrocentric and Eurocentric.

Edimilison de Perreira Almeida (b. 1962) captures the history and African traditions of Minas Gerais, a state in eastern Brazil with a rich colonial history, in compressed, elegant verses. His works include *O livro de falas ou Kalunbungu* and *O lapassi e outros ritmos de ouvido*.

The above-mentioned authors indicate the immense wealth of themes, styles, and personalities within Afro-Brazilian literature. However, in addition to these writers, many others struggle to find their audience. Although Afro-Brazilians have expressed their activism and creativity since colonial times through literary writing, it is only now that these authors are gaining prestige and renown in Brazil and abroad. Black literature in Brazil, now in the process of gaining the recognition it deserves, promises to be a vigorous, vital force of expression in the future.

Carolyn Richardson Durham

See Also

Maroonage in the Americas; Slavery in Latin America and the Caribbean; Yoruba; Rio de Janeiro, Brazil; Saldanha, José da Natividades; Teatro Experimental do Negro; Teixeira e Souza, Antonio Gonçalves; Abolition and Emancipation in Latin America and the Caribbean; Transculturation, Mestizaje, and the Cosmic Race: An Interpretation; Myth of Racial Democracy in Latin America and the Caribbean: An Interpretation; Women Writers, Black, in Brazil; Salvador, Brazil.

Latin America and the Caribbean

Literature, Black, in Spanish America, literature written by authors of African descent in Spanish America, often about the black experience.

Afro-Hispanic literature is a growth area in African diasporic and Latin American studies (*see* Research on Afro-Latin America). Among knowledgeable people, it is no longer assumed that blacks in Latin America have no uniqueness of expression peculiar to their circumstances (*see* Literature, English Language, Caribbean; Literature, French Language, in Caribbean; and Literature, Black, in Brazil). While Afro-Hispanic literature, like black literature of the United States (*see* Literature, African American), is primarily culture-specific, the idea of being black transcends national boundaries. The commonality of the black experience in the Americas was discussed elegantly by Martha Cobb in her pioneering work, *Harlem, Haiti, and Havana: A Comparative Study of Langston Hughes, Jacques Roumain, and Nicolás Guilllén* (1979). In her analysis Cobb delineated four thematic links – confrontation, dualism, identity, and liberation – that unify the black experience and are manifested in experiential images of linkage throughout the diaspora. For Cobb, confrontation occurs in an alien and hostile society; dualism conveys the sense of one's own concept of self as it enters into conflict with societal impositions; identity addresses the question of "Who am I?"; and, finally, liberation is the political and psychical act by which the self overcomes the previous constraints. These thematic concerns are essential to interpretations of Afro-Hispanic literature from the critical postures of Négritude, that is to say, from a point of view that affirms and celebrates African culture and values.

This brief discussion begins with Uruguay, whose black literary trajectory is representative of other traditions in the Americas, and ends with Cuba, at the other geographical pole. Afro-Uruguayan literature was born on a note of social protest as blacks in that country recognized early on that they were not equal to their white counterparts despite what the laws of Uruguay professed. In the black journal *La conservación* in 1872, Tomás Oliviera questioned the national commitment to liberty and justice in a poem titled "A los hombres de color."

Periodicals were the key to black literary development in Uruguay, as they were in neighboring ARGENTINA. Black-sponsored outlets published the first poems, plays, and essays of writers who were not able until later to have individual collections edited. The literary and political magazine *Nuestra Raza*, which began publishing in San Carlos in 1917 and continued in Montevideo from 1933 to 1948, is exemplary of this trend. Two of Uruguay's most prominent black writers, VIRGINIA BRINDIS DE SALAS (1908-1958) and PILAR BARRIOS (1899-1974), penned their first works in *Nuestra Raza* and other journals, such as *Revista Uruguay* and *Rumbos*. Brindis de Salas, the first major contemporary black woman writer in Spanish America, subsequently published *Pregón de Marimorena* (1946) and *Cien cárceles de amor* (1949). (Although Brindis de Salas claimed the Cuban violinist Claudio José Domingo Brindis de Salas [1852-1911] as a distant relative, they were not related.) Barrios authored *Piel negra* (1947), *Mis cantos* (1949), and several other volumes of poetry. The works of Brindis de Salas and Barrios incorporate Cobb's four thematic concepts of confrontation, dualism, identity, and liberation while bringing to the foreground other issues such as gender and the exploitation of blacks throughout the diaspora. In *Pregón de Marimorena*, for example, Brindis de Salas establishes a dialectical relationship between victimization and resistance in her interpretation of the experiences of a female street vendor. Though poor and black, Marimorena maintains her dignity and sense of personhood.

Officially, black existence is purported to have been less problematic in Uruguay and Spanish America than in the United States, for example because of the supposedly "benign" nature of slavery and the absence of racism. It has also been said that these countries are racial democracies in which social conflicts arise out of class conflict rather than racial oppression. From the perspective of committed Afro-Hispanic writers, however, a different picture emerges. In both creative writing and the genre of the essay, they have constantly questioned the notion that class is more important as a determinant of social status than race. Much of this self-analysis is contained in relatively unknown newspapers and periodicals.

Afro-Argentine periodicals helped to foster and sustain the literary tradition of that country. It is in the pages of journals like *El Unionisita* (1877) and *La Broma* (1879) that GABINO EZEIZA (1858-1916), Argentina's most important black poet, began to publish poems written in the popular *payador* fashion, an oral poetic form traditional among gauchos that employed the DÉCIMA structure. Ezeiza subsequently published more than a dozen collections of poetry. Several other Afro-Argentine writers, who were unable to transcend the pages of periodicals, remain obscure or anonymous.

With the exceptions of CHILE, PARAGUAY, and BOLIVIA perhaps, where most traces of blacks have disappeared, the national literary trajectories of this ethnic group in South America have been documented, or are in the process of being documented. In PERU the black literary tradition has been enhanced by the late NICOMEDES SANTA CRUZ (1925-1992), the leading black popular poet in South America. Nicomedes, a decimista in the tradition of Ezeiza, published short stories and poetry. He is best known for *Ritmos negros del Perú* (Black Peruvian Rhythms), a culturalist interpretation of Peruvian society. Santa Cruz voluntarily exiled himself to Spain for economic and political reasons, but his international renown has continued to grow since his death in 1992.

COLOMBIA, of course, has a long black literary tradition that includes such distinguished writers as CANDELARIO OBESO (1849-1884), JORGE ARTEL (1909-1994), Carlos Arturo Truque (1924-1970), ARNOLDO PALACIOS (1924-), and MANUEL ZAPATA OLIVELLA (1920-), the dean of Afro-Colombian letters. Colombian writers form a part of the same thematic matrix as their counterparts from the Southern Cone (Argentina and Uruguay) and writers throughout the Afro-Hispanic diaspora, while emphasizing postcolonial concerns such as place and displacement. In addition to the themes outlined by Martha Cobb, black writers in Colombia and Spanish America foreground issues dealing with language and environment as they attempt to situate themselves in the Americas. While poetry is a popular genre of black Colombian writers, their novels have enjoyed greater success. Their concerns are both rural and urban, popular and official. The first novels of Zapata Olivella (*Tierra Mojada* [1947, The Drenched Earth]), and Palacios (*Las estrellas son negras* [1949, The Stars Are Black]), interpret the plight of dispossessed rural populations. These early works set the tone for later ones whose objective was giving voice to the marginalized. Olivella's most outstanding works include *Changó, el gran putas* (1983, Chango, The Baddest SOB), the best literary interpretation of the African diaspora in the Americas. Among other prose works by Palacios is his autobiographical account of growing up in the Choco, *Buscando mi madre de Dios*. As the leading Afro-Hispanic literary figure, Olivella has also written plays, short stories, autobiographies, and the most profound interpretations of *mestizaje* (miscegenation), ethnicity, and cultural hybridity in Latin America, *Las claves mágicas de América* (1989) and *La rebelión de los genes* (1998).

The best-known black text in ECUADOR, and one of the first major Afro-Hispanic novels, is *Juyungo* (1943), by ADALBERTO ORTIZ (1914-). This groundbreaking work interprets issues of race, class, and caste in that country and is representative of Afro-Hispanic novels of similar concerns throughout the diaspora. Ortiz wrote an experimental novel, *La envoltura del sueño*, in 1972.

NELSON ESTUPIÑÁN BASS (1915-) has dominated the Afro-Ecuadorian literary scene in recent decades. A prolific writer, Bass has produced poetry, drama, and novels, his strongest suit. His best-known work, *Cuando los guayacanes florecían* (1954), treats the Carlos Concha rebellion phenomenon, an uprising of poor and disfranchised workers (1913-1916) in ESMERALDAS, a traditional black area located in the western part of the country. His other novels include *El ultimo río* (1967, The Last River). His entire literary production examines critically the assumption that class, rather than race, governs social relationships in Ecuador. Antonio Peciado Bedoya (1941-) showed a great deal of promise with *Jolgorio* (1961) and *Tal como somos* (1969) but has published little in recent years.

The African diaspora in VENEZUELA has produced several writers of international stature, including JUAN PABLO SOJO (1908-1948) and Antonio Acosta Marquez (1952-). Sojo shares with Adalberto Ortiz the distinction of being the first to publish black novels in Spanish America. His novel *Nochebuena negra* (1943, Black Christmas) interprets the experiences of indentured workers in the Barlovento region and their quest for "place." Acosta Marquez is a declamatory poet of *décimas* in the oral traditions of Gabino Ezeiza and Nicomedes Santa Cruz. *Yo pienso aquí, donde estoy* (1977), his poetic masterpiece, places the historical black experience at the center of Venezuelan national discourse, imposing a layer of blackness upon the "*café con leche*" (coffee with milk, an allusion to racial democracy) surface of that country.

Much Afro-Hispanic literature is culture-specific, but not all. Costa Rica's QUINCE DUNCAN (1940-) is a case in point. Of the Afro-Hispanic writers residing in CENTRAL AMERICA, Duncan is the most impressive. He has consistently interpreted the experiences of immigrants from the WEST INDIES and indigenous black Costa Ricans in their confrontations with white society. Duncan won the prestigious Editorial Costa Rica Prize in 1978 for *Final de calle*, an anonymously submitted work not dealing with the black experience. Although *Final de calle* has been widely praised, Duncan's most acclaimed novel, *Los cuatro espejos* (1973, The Four Mirrors), an examination of the Afro-Costa Rican psyche, is his best work.

BLAS JIMÉNEZ (1950-) has emerged as the leading Afro-Hispanic literary figure in the DOMINICAN REPUBLIC. While a number of writers in that country maintained the "vacillating mulatto" image and never acknowledged the African dimension of their heritage, Jiménez articulated early on his identity as a black writer. He is the author of several volumes of poetry, including *Aquí, otro español* (1980), *Caribe africano en despertar* (1984), *Exigencias de un cimarrón (en sueños)* (1987), and *El nativo* (1996). Not since the late Juan Sanchez Lamouth (1929-1968) has such a strong Afro-Dominican poetic voice been heard. Norberto James Rawlings (1945-) is also a black Dominican poet of international renown, but he has been reluctant to embrace black themes as forcefully as Jiménez.

While many Dominican writers worked under the widely held assumption that only Haitians are black, Jiménez proclaimed his African identity in a variety of popular and learned verse forms. Letting it be known that Haitians are not the only blacks in the Dominican Republic, he made the negative portrayal of the Haitian by mainstream writers one of his primary concerns (*see* DOMINICAN-HAITIAN RELATIONS). Many works by Jiménez question the predominance of the Spanish over the African heritage in Dominican culture as well. By posing this question, Jiménez has opened the door to a closer examination of self-identity in that country.

The Afro-Panamanian CARLOS GUILLERMO WILSON (also known as Cubena) (1941-), who resides in the United States and enjoys an international reputation, has published short stories, poetry, and two acclaimed novels, *Chombo* (1981) and *Los nietos de Felicidad Dolores* (1991, Felicidad Dolores's Grandchildren). All of his works interpret the African diasporic experience. On a more specific level, Cubena criticizes the treatment of Afro-Panamanians by the dominant, *mestizo*-based (of European and indigenous descent) culture.

Gerardo Maloney (1945-) is the most outstanding Afro-Panamanian writer living in Panama. A strong advocate of Afro-Panamanian culture, he is primarily a poet. In poems such as "Amo a mi raza," "Cambios," "Cogiéndolo suave," "Igualdad," and "El conductor," which have been translated and published in the *Afro-Hispanic Review*, Maloney presents an entire ethnic group in contention with a society of which it forms a part; ultimately, it triumphs owing to will and the human spirit. Maloney's works have appeared in the *Revista Nacional de Cultura* in Panama City; in *Afro-Hispanic Review*, a literary journal based in the United States; and in two anthologies, *Juega vivo* (1984) and *Obra selecta* (1994).

NICOLÁS GUILLÉN (1902-1989) is recognized as CUBA's leading poet of the twentieth century. His writings span several decades and include highly acclaimed early contributions such as *Motivos del son* (1930), his first major collection; *Songoro cosongo* (1931), which interprets the question of ethnicity in Cuban poetry; and *West Indies, LTD.* (1934), an exercise in protest and Afro-Cuban subject creation. Subsequent volumes, which include *La rueda dentada* and *El diario que a diario* (1972), treat a variety of poetic themes.

Guillén has overshadowed MARCELINO AROZARENA (1912-1996), another outstanding exponent of NÉGRITUDE. Perhaps Guillén's greatest achievement is adapting social themes to popular poetic forms, such as the Cuban SON. He has become the best known of a group of stellar Afro-Antillean poets (*see* AFROCUBANISMO).

NANCY MOREJÓN (1944-), a disciple of Guillén and a poet of international stature, is successful due to her ability to combine questions of black identity, feminism, and revolutionary ideology in an outstanding manner. A great deal of Morejón's recent fame can be attributed to the 1985 bilingual anthology *Where the Island Sleeps Like a Wing* (reissued 1997), translated by Kathleen Weaver. This text is a compilation of the best selections from earlier volumes such as *Mutismos* (1962), *Amor, ciudad atribuida* (1964), *Parajes de una época* (1979), and *Octubre imprescindible* (1982). Morejón has to her credit, as well, a number of critical studies devoted to poetry and to Nicolás Guillén.

Morejón's recent poetry continues to maintain a balance between the aesthetic and the social, as evinced in *Paisaje celebre* (1993), a volume whose provocative imagery implicitly seeks distance from aspects of daily reality. This text, according to William Luis, "also underscores a coming to terms with a struggle within, regarding her poetry and position in the revolution."

In the final analysis Afro-Hispanic writers can be as specific or as encompassing as necessary. As creative artists, though, they bear the heavier burden of knowing themselves as well as the dominant others. Afro-Hispanic writers have not traditionally been given the same consideration in publications, such as histories, anthologies, and critical studies, as their counterparts in Spanish America. This is due, in many cases, to concerns other than those associated with the quality of any given text. The diversity and caliber of authors and texts contained in this brief summary are written testimony to the fact that the Afro-Hispanic voice remains an integral component of the literary fabric of the Americas.

Marvín Lewis

SEE ALSO

Slavery in Latin America and the Caribbean; Pacific Coast of Colombia; James, Norberto; Panama; Preciado Bedoya, Antonio; Haiti; Transculturation, Mestizaje, and the Cosmic Race: An Interpretation; Myth of Racial Democracy in Latin America and the Caribbean: An Interpretation; Brindis de Salas, Claudio.

Latin America and the Caribbean

Literature, English Language, Caribbean, written works of the English-speaking islands of the WEST INDIES, GUYANA, and BELIZE.

Although the literature of the Anglophone Caribbean has much in common with the literatures of Latin America and African America in the United States, over the course of time it has developed a identity of its own (*see* LITERATURE, AFRICAN AMERICAN; LITERATURE, BLACK, IN SPANISH AMERICA; and LITERATURE, BLACK, IN BRAZIL). An offshoot of the African oral literary tradition (most island inhabitants came from West Africa) and shaped by its Asian and European roots, the earliest Anglophone Caribbean literature can be traced to the proverbs, riddles, and *kheesas* (tales) of African and Indian literature respectively (*see* EAST INDIAN COMMUNITIES IN THE CARIBBEAN).

Jean Baptiste Philippe's *Free Mulatto* (1824) was one of the first works of Caribbean Anglophone literature. It was followed by several SLAVE NARRATIVES that were published before or after the emancipation of the slaves in 1834. These narratives – *The History of Mary Prince* (1831), *The Narrative of Ashton Warner* (1831), *The History of Abu Bekr* (1834), *The Narrative of James Williams* (1838), and *The Narrative of John Monteith* (1853) – describe the inhuman conditions of slavery and dramatize the lives of Africans in the Caribbean (*see* TRANSATLANTIC SLAVE TRADE).

The Barbadian poet and critic EDWARD KAMAU BRATHWAITE suggests that the anonymous narrative *Hamel the Obeah Man* (1827) may offer the first complex portrayal of the African in the Anglophone Caribbean. However, Maxwell Philip's novel *Emmanuel Appadocca: A Tale of the Boucaneers* (1854) may very well be the first fictional narrative published by a person from the Anglophone Caribbean. Through language that reveals his rich understanding of European and classical literatures, Philip stakes a moral claim against a person (his father) and two systems (slavery and colonialism) that made him an orphan. The novel began a tradition in fiction of creative resistance and defiance of the combined forces of slavery, colonialism, and dispossession; this tradition is very much alive today. In an illuminating introduction to the new edition of the novel, the critic William Cain argues that *Emmanuel Appadocca* should be seen as a "companion piece to such manifestly antislavery texts as UNCLE TOM'S CABIN and FREDERICK DOUGLASS's *The Heroic Slave*."

The next major work published by an Anglophone Caribbean author was MARY SEACOLE's *Wonderful Adventures of Mrs. Seacole in Many Lands* (1857). In the book Seacole recounts her extensive travels, during which she practiced medicine and set up her own business. Secure enough in her womanhood to strike out independently in the colonial world, Seacole expressed her conviction that women could navigate life on their own. The author recalls, "It was from a confidence in my own powers, and not at all from necessity, that I remained an unprotected female."

Following Seacole's *Wonderful Adventures*, several works were published between 1857 and 1900. One of the most important of these was Horatio Nelson Huggins's *Hiroona*, a collection of Carib children's stories (*see* DOMINICA) from the island of St. Vincent that was published eventually by Huggins's family in Trinidad. Although the book was only published in 1937, evidence suggests that it was composed around 1885. Literary critic Paula Burnett calls *Hiroona* "the Caribbean's first epic poem." Of equal interest was Jean-Ch de Saint Avir's *The First Two Martyrs of Trinidad* (1885), which was serialized in a Trinidadian newspaper and eventually published as a book. Like *Hiroona*, this tragedy in four acts drew on the activities of the Amerindians who went to Santo Domingo in 1513 to flee the tyranny of the Spanish conquerors (*see* COLONIAL LATIN AMERICA AND THE CARIBBEAN).

The twentieth century saw the rise of a more sustained tradition in Anglophone Caribbean literature. In the first 30 years of the century several prominent novels were published. The Jamaican poet and novelist Thomas MacDermot (1870-1933, better known as Tom Redcan) published *Beeka's Buckra Baby* (1903) and *One Brown Girl And 1/4* (1909). Three other significant novels of this period were *Rupert Gray: A Tale of Black and White* (1907) by Stephen Nathaniel Cobham; *Jane's Career* (1913) by Herbert de Lisser (1878-1944); and *Those That Be in Bondage* (1917) by A. R. F. Webber (1880-1932). These novels spoke to what GEORGE LAMMING (1927) in another context called "the peasant" aspects of Caribbean life. Together with other works, these novels paved the way for a Caribbean renaissance of the 1930s. This flowering of the islands' arts and culture was intimately tied to the rise of Caribbean nationalist parties, decolonization, and labor movements.

Coming on the heels of the GREAT DEPRESSION of 1929 and a rise in the social and political consciousness of Caribbean people, the works of the Caribbean renaissance offered a deeper and more penetrating exploration of the society. Relying on a mixture of naturalist and realist literary techniques – often depicting social conditions instead of psychological issues – these novels had an important impact on society. Beginning with *Black Fauns* (1935) by Alfred Mendes, and *Minty Alley* (1936) by C. L. R. James, this period culminated in the achievement of political independence that brought colonialism to its formal conclusion. Necessarily, political independence ushered in a new phase of writing that was much more political.

The 1940s through the 1960s saw the publication of works such as *Corentyne Thunder* (1941) and *Children of Kaywana* (1952) by Edgar Mittleholzer; *Gurudeva and Other Tales* (1943) by Seepersad Naipaul; *New Day* (1949) by Vic Reid; *Crown Jewel* (1952), which was set in the 1930s, by Ralph de Boissiere; *The Hills Were Joyful Together* (1953) and *Brother Man* (1954), one of the first books to depict the RASTAFARIANS in JAMAICA, by ROGER MAIS; *Orchid House* (1953) by Phyllis Allfrey; *The Brighter Sun* (1952) by Sam Selvon; *Poems of Resistance* (1952) by MARTIN CARTER; *In the Castle of My Skin* (1953) and *Of Age and Innocence* (1958) by Lamming; and the early Trinidadian novels *The Mystic Masseur* (1957) and *The Suffrage of Elvira* (1958) by V. S. Naipaul.

Five important magazines that provided publication opportunities for Caribbean writers were also created in the early period: *Trinidad* (1929), published in Trinidad and edited by Mendes and James; *The Beacon* (1931), published in Trinidad and edited by Albert Gomes; *Bim* (1942), published in BARBADOS and edited by Therold Barnes and Frank Collymore; *Focus* (1943), published in Jamaica and edited by Edna Manley; and *Kyk over Al* (1945), published in British Guiana (now Guyana) and edited by A. J. Seymour. Many of the writers who achieved major recognition in the post-1960 era (Lamming, Derek Walcott, and Wilson Harris, to name a few) got their starts in these magazines.

Anglophone Caribbean literature blossomed in the 1960s, and many new and exciting talents were discovered. New writers included the Guyanese Wilson Harris (*Palace of the Peacock*, 1960) and Ismith Khan (b. 1925) (*The Jumbie Bird*, 1961) and the London-based Naipaul (*A House for Mr. Biswas*, 1961), both from Trinidad and Tobago. Other outstanding contributors to the emerging Caribbean literature were Michael Anthony (b. 1932) (*Year in San Fernando*, 1965); Lamming (*A Season of Adventure*, 1974); the Jamaican poet and novelist Sylvia Wynter (b. 1928) (*The Hills of Hebron*, 1966); DOMINICA-born JEAN RHYS (*Wide Sargasso Sea*, 1966); and MERLE HODGE (*Crick, Crack Monkey*, 1970). Finally, this period also saw the publication of classics such as *Rights of Passage* (1967) by Brathwaite – the first part of a poetic trilogy that subsequently appeared as *The Arrivants* (1973) – and *In a Green Night* (1962), *The Castaways and Other Poems* (1965), *Another Life* (1973), and *The Fortunate Traveler* (1981), by Walcott.

Interestingly enough, most Caribbean Anglophone writers had to go abroad (primarily to England) to achieve literary recognition and to gain a sympathetic audience. Many found the British Broadcasting Corporation radio program Caribbean Voices – hosted by Una Marson and Henry Swanzy – an important forum in which to read their works and reach a wider audience. Naipaul, Lamming, the Panamanian-born Jamaican Andrew Salkey (b. 1928), and myriad other Caribbean writers had their works read over this program and were able to reap some monetary reward for their work. EARL LOVELACE, ERNA BRODBER, and Walcott, who had remained in the islands to pursue their craft, gradually began to gain fame and acceptance in the metropolis as fellow Caribbean writers abroad piqued international interest in Caribbean literature and art.

Although the literary historian Lloyd Brown placed the birth of modern Anglophone Caribbean poetry in the 1940-1960 period, poets such as Brathwaite and Walcott began to enjoy international prestige in the years 1960 to 1990. Brathwaite won the prestigious Commonwealth Prize for Poetry in 1987 and the Neustadt International Prize for Literature in 1994. One critic notes that Brathwaite's "poetry, prose fiction, historiographical essays, and literary criticism, all reflect a scheme of thought wherein language is seen as a means of communication, a vehicle of cultural identity [and] a principal instrument for liberation from the vestiges of colonial education." On the other hand, the more personalized poetry of Walcott revealed an intensely private response to the Anglophone experience and culminated in the publication of *Omeros* (1992), an epic poem that drew its inspiration from Homer. This work brought Walcott's genius to the attention of the world and led to his winning the 1993 NOBEL PRIZE for Literature. Walcott, a prolific playwright, also published plays such as *Ti-Jean and His Brothers* (1958) and *Dream on Monkey Mountain* (1967) (*see* THEATER IN THE CARIBBEAN).

In the 1980s women writers from the Caribbean began to receive as much attention as their male counterparts. At the First International Congress of Caribbean Women Writers, which took place at Wellesley College in 1988, many well-known Anglophone Caribbean writers found a platform to display their talents to the world. This conference brought to the fore remarkable writers such as Brodber (*Myal*, 1988); Hodge (*For the Life of Laetitia*, 1993); Glaseda Honeyghan (*Father Sleeps with the Mudpies*, 1988); JAMAICA KINCAID (*Annie John*, 1983); MICHELLE CLIFF (*Abeng*, 1984, and *No Telephone to Heaven*, 1987); Rosa Guy (*Bird at My Window*, 1966); Lorna Goodison (*I'm Becoming My Mother*, 1986); MARLENE NOURBESE PHILIP (*She Tries Her Tongue*, 1989, and *Harriet's Daughter*, 1988); Olive Senior (*Summer Lightning and Other Stories*, 1986); Beryl Gilroy (*Frangipani House*, 1986); Opal Adissa Palmer (*Bake Face and Other Guava Stories*, 1986); Valerie Belgrave (*Ti Marie*, 1988); Dionne Brand (*Sans Souci and Other Stories*, 1988); Joan Riley (*The Waiting Room*, 1989); and ZEE EDGELL (*Beeka Lamb*, 1982).

In the 1990s the acceptance and achievements of Caribbean writers continued to rise. Kincaid's success persisted (*The Autobiography of My Mother*, 1996); Lawrence Scott's *Witchbroom* (1992) was shortlisted for the Commonwealth Writers Prize for 1993; and Lovelace won the Commonwealth Prize for Literature with *Salt* (1997). Important literary journals began to pay more attention to the region's literary production. The influential journal *World Literature Today*, for instance, devoted its autumn 1994 issue to the life and work of Brathwaite, while *Callaloo* devoted its winter 1995 volume to the work of Harris. Meanwhile, younger talents such as Patricia Powell, Willi Chen, Mikeda Silvera, Neil Bissondath, Brodber, and others have begun to invigorate the tradition with new approaches to the literature.

In such hands the literature will certainly continue to flourish.

Selwyn Cudjoe

See Also

Great Britain; Naipaul, V. S.; Slavery in Latin America and the Caribbean; Douglass, Frederick; James, Cyril Lionel Richard; Walcott, Derek Alton; Harris,Theodore Wilson; Marson, Una M.; Reid, V.S.; St. Vincent and the Grenadines; Trinidad and Tobago; Mittelhölzer, Edgar Austin; Selvon, Samuel.

Africa

Literature, French Language, in Africa

The Colonial Legacy

French is the official language of 19 states in Africa, from Senegal in the extreme west through the republics that border the Congo River in the heart of the continent to the island of Madagascar in the Indian Ocean. The privileged position of French in this area is a direct consequence of European colonialism, which often brought together within the same administrative boundaries and under one colonial power different ethnic groups, each with its own language and forms of sociopolitical organization and cultural expression. As a result, the language of the European colonizer assumed in each territory a commanding position due as much to its promotion by official policy as to the advantage it enjoyed as the only common language among the colonized African population.

The French controlled most of the Sahel region in West Africa as well as much of the West African coast and the Congo basin in Central Africa. The territories comprised within this area were grouped for administrative convenience into two federations, Afrique Occidentale Française (French West Africa) and Afrique Equatoriale Française (French Equatorial Africa). Within this vast expanse, covering an area several times the size of metropolitan France, French was imposed as the dominant language. The Belgians also ensured the further spread of the language in Africa south of the Sahara by using French rather than Flemish to administer their colonies in the Congo (today the Democratic Republic of the Congo) and present-day Rwanda and Burundi. The ethnic diversity of the various independent states that have emerged from the French and Belgian colonial empires has obliged most of them, even after independence, to retain French as the language of administration. In nearly every former French African colony the French language remains dominant in education and the formal areas of economic activity.

It is this consequence of the colonial experience that gives meaning to the terms "Francophone" or "French-speaking" Africa. These terms, by convention, now refer to these countries, even though the regular use of standard French is limited in reality to the few Africans who have received a Western education and who constitute, at most, 10 percent of the entire population. The use of French as the language of a restricted elite raises some serious social and cultural problems; these disadvantages are, however, offset to some extent by the advantages of French as an international language widely understood in the advanced industrial world, with a rich literary tradition. Moreover, the literary and cultural legacy of French has favored its development in Africa not only as a medium of practical communication but also as a means of self-expression, especially in the symbolic mode represented by literature. It was indeed inevitable that, having acquired the language of the colonizer, Africans would use that language to explore the very conditions that enabled them to claim its literary heritage.

In order to grasp the themes and formal strategies of Francophone African literature, it is important to note that, historically, this literature has been closely tied to metropolitan French literature, which has served as a national resource for France and an instrument of cultural domination in the colonies. The educational policy pursued under French (and, to some extent, under Belgian) colonial rule ensured that Africans who received an education in these colonies had sustained contact with the French literary tradition. The works of the great authors of the classical and romantic periods, which form the accepted canon, occupied a central place in the education of generations of Francophone Africans, and have provided them with early models for literary uses of the French language. Moreover, modern French literature, spanning the period from the late nineteenth century to the present day, provides a contemporary idiom to which the aspiring writer is obliged to relate. The total body of French literature has thus effectively functioned as a comprehensive reference for Francophone African literature.

Within this general framework, the "colonial" or "exotic" literature produced by native French writers whose themes and settings concerned other peoples and cultures assumed a special relevance for the Western-educated Africans. The consistently negative image of Africa and of African life that this literature presents served to confirm the principles of colonial ideology, with its wholehearted devaluation of Africa. Thus, the representation of Africa as an inhospitable landscape in Pierre Loti's *Le roman d'un Spahi* (1882, The Romance of a Spahi) is given a moral implication for its indigenous populations. Beyond this thematic focus, the exotic and colonial literature pointed to the formal problems of representing in French the manners, values, and thought processes of non-Western peoples, in particular Africans.

The African Response: Négritude

Given this background, Francophone African literature emerged both as a derivation from the broad stream of the French literary tradition and, more specifically, as a response to the ideological implications and formal challenge of its exotic and colonial manifestations. Ironically, it was a black West Indian, René Maran, whose novel *Batouala* (1921) marked the genesis of a new African literature in French. Maran labeled it an authentic novel of black African life ("un véritable roman nègre"). Maran won the Prix Goncourt, France's highest literary prize, in 1921, thus bringing the novel's account of French colonial methods in Africa to a wide audience. What gives distinction to Maran's work, however, is the effort to present an inside view of African life and customs in language appropriate to the setting. Maran pursued this direction in his subsequent work, drawing on and extending the African folktale tradition in a series of animal stories, culminating in the highly symbolic novel *Le Livre de la brousse* (1934, The Book of the Bush). Léopold Sédar Senghor has called Maran the "precursor of Négritude," in recognition of the exemplary value of his work for a whole generation of Francophone African writers and intellectuals and the impetus it lent to the emergence of the literary and cultural movement of Négritude, of which Senghor himself has been the most prominent advocate.

Poetry

The concept of Négritude provides the fundamental thematic ground of Francophone African literature, which has served as the most vital channel of the black cultural renaissance known under this name. The origins of Négritude as a movement lie in the experience, common to black people, of slavery, colonialism, and racism and in the lived predicament arising out of black people's historic confrontation with the Western world and the white race. The term itself was coined by the West Indian poet Aimé Césaire. He first used it in his long poem *Cahier d'un retour au pays natal* (1939, Notebook of a Return to My Native Land) to designate a collective consciousness of black people of their membership in a racial and historical community with a grounded connection to Africa and to its cultural values and spiritual inheritance. These ideas provided a unifying theme for the black poets, predominantly Caribbean, represented in Senghor's *Anthologie de la nouvelle poésie nègre et malgache de langue française* (1948, Anthology of New Black and Malagasy Poetry in the French Language). In this publication's preface, titled "Orphée noir" (Black Orpheus), the French philosopher Jean-Paul Sartre elucidated the term and its ramifications and launched Négritude as a distinctive literary movement.

Senghor subsequently devoted his career to the elaboration in theoretical terms of

Négritude as a concept implying a fundamental racial endowment of black people, but it is primarily in his own poetry that we gain a full sense of its relation to experience. The feeling of cultural discomfort of the individual between two worlds – stemming from a pained response to the pressures and contradictions of French colonialism – unfolds in many of the poems in his early volumes *Chants d'ombres* (1948, Shadow Songs) and *Hosties noires* (1948, Black Offerings) into a sentiment of exile in the world, while other poems enact the self-recovery implied by a recall and revaluation of the poet's African forbears. In *Ethiopiques* (1960) Senghor gives resonance to this second theme in a celebration of Africa, restored to consideration as a distinctive human environment, sustained by original social manners and cultural values, and as a spiritual universe. This last aspect of his poetry finds elaboration in his later work, notably the *Elégies majeures* (1978, Major Elegies), in which a profoundly meditative note predominates.

Senghor's poetry seeks to establish Africa as a poetic landscape, one with an immediate relevance for himself and the black race, but also with a universal significance.

I know that the arrogance of these hills
calls to my pride.
Standing on the jagged summits crowned
with fragrant gum trees,
I seize the navel's echo beating the
rhythm of their song
A lake of deep water sleeps in its watchful
crater.
I know that only this rich black-skinned
plain
Is worthy of the plowshare and the deep
flow of my virility.

The combative tone that dominates David Diop's single volume *Coups de pilon* (1956, Hammer Blows) registers the African poet's disaffection with the Western world, dictating a militancy that progresses toward a vision of restoration through revolt. A similar commitment animates the poetry of Bernard Dadié in *Afrique debout* (1950, Africa Rise Up), accompanied by a romantic evocation of Africa, a theme reproduced in more serene accents in Birago Diop's *Leurres et lueurs* (1960, Lures and Glimmers) and Lamine Diakhaté's *Primordiale du sixième jour* (1963, Primordial of the Sixth Day). A more personal note, in an entirely different tonality, runs through the almost tortured explorations of the inner self, against the background of a violent history and a traumatic present, in Tchicaya u Tam'si's *Le mauvais sang* (1955, The Bad Blood). Tchicaya u Tam'si's broadens and intensifies this exploration in the collections that have followed, such as *Feu de brousse* (1957, Brush Fire), *A triche-coeur* (1958, To Cheating Heart), and *Epitomé* (1962, Epitome). Tchicaya u Tam'si's poetic work lies in the outer reaches, as it were, of Négritude and serves as a bridge between the poets involved in that movement and the generation of younger poets that has emerged since the 1960s, whose preoccupations are related more directly to the social and moral dilemmas of post-independence Africa.

This generation includes such accomplished poets as Malick Fall, Ibrahima Tall, Francis Bebey, and Veronique Tadjo. The outstanding voice is without question that of Jean-Baptiste Tati-Loutard, whose work has taken Francophone African poetry to perhaps its highest point of accomplishment. His first volume, *Poèmes de la mer* (1968, Poems of the Sea), introduced his grave tone and the broad scale of his imagery. Subsequent volumes have amply confirmed this richness, notably *La tradition du songe* (1985, The Tradition of the Dream), a collection informed by a powerful sense of the cosmic dimension of individual life and human history.

Drama

The poetry of Francophone Africa has maintained a firm engagement with history, a feature of the literature that is even more evident in the dramatic works. The influence of Aimé Césaire's plays has often been suggested as the decisive factor in the orientation of Francophone African drama toward heroic subjects. However, Senghor's evocation in his dramatic poem *Chaka* (Shaka) of the Zulu emperor's passion (*see* Shaka) provides an important precedent for the dramatization of Shaka's heroic career and tragic destiny by Francophone African writers as diverse as Abdou Anta Kâ, Seydou Badian, and, in overtly expressionist terms, Tchicaya u Tam'si Senouvo Zinsou effects a critical inversion of the Shaka theme in his play *On joue la comédie* (1984, Performing Comedy) in order to challenge its contemporary significance in African politics. Beyond these works, Cheik Ndao fully exemplifies the conventions of historical drama in *L'Exil d'Alboury* (1969, The Exile of Alboury), which marries the rhetorical structure of French classical drama with the spectacular appeal of traditional African festivals.

Bernard Dadié's plays occupy a prominent place in the dramatic repertory of Francophone Africa. His *Béatrice au Congo* (1970, Beatrice in the Congo), which celebrates a female historical figure in the early phase of the African encounter with Europe (*see* Dona Beatrice), has assumed the status of a classic. A contrasting vein to these historical plays and their heroic action is offered by the comedies of Guillaume Oyono-Mbia, beginning with *Trois prétendants...un mari* (1964, Three Suitors...One Husband), plays that center on the often incongruous responses of characters to the culture conflict generated by colonial status.

More recently, Werewere Liking has introduced a new form of theater that seeks to deploy the ritual potential of theater as a means of social therapy and moral reform in a secular context. From this point of view her first play, *La Puissance d'Um* (1979, The Power of Um), inaugurated a new reconnection to the traditional legacy of aesthetic form and creation of meaning. Although the dramatic literature is still limited, innovations such as that of Werewere Liking appear to be on the horizon in Francophone Africa, for they are inherent in the vitality of theater movements in places such as Côte d'Ivoire and Congo-Brazzaville.

Prose

In contrast to drama, Francophone Africa has generated an abundance and variety of prose works with a remarkable energy of production. Despite its indifferent beginning in such works as Bakary Diallo's *Force bonté* (1926, A Great Deal of Good), Félix Couchoro's *L'Esclave* (1929, The Slave), and Ousmane Socé's *Karim* (1935) – works regularly cited as the earliest embodiments of the prose narrative form in Francophone Africa – the novel as a genre has developed an extremely strong profile in the region. Birago Diop's transpositions of the traditional tales in the three collections he published represent an effort not only to put a personal stamp on a communal resource but also to establish a new convention of narrative in full communication with the oral tradition. The Western novel has, however, presented a readily available model that African writers have conveniently adopted. Paul Hazoumé's imaginative reconstitution of the court atmosphere in ancient Dahomey in *Doguicimi* (1938, Doguicimi: The First Dahomean Novel) represents the first serious effort by an indigenous African to adapt the French language to the African experience in an extended narrative form.

It was Camara Laye's lyrical recall of his childhood in his autobiography *L'Enfant noir* (1953, The African Child), however, that signaled the advent of narrative as a mature form in Francophone Africa. Laye's work is the first and most accomplished in a category that includes Bernard Dadié's *Climbié* (1956) and Aké Loba's *Kocoumbo, L'Etudiant noir* (1960, Kocoumbo, the Black Student), works that explore the developing consciousness of young Africans severed from their African backgrounds and made aware of their diminished condition as colonial subjects. The subjective focus of these works assumes an intensity of statement in Cheik Hamidou Kane's *L'Aventure ambigüe* (1960, Ambiguous Adventure), an introspective novel that endows the drama of colonial alienation with a metaphysical dimension. Amadou Hampaté Bâ's *L'Etrange destin de Wangrin* (1973, The Fortunes of Wangrin) strikes a similar note in a far more varied and extended register than Kane's novel. Along with its dramatic organization and its thematic foundation in myth, the special vigor of expression Hampaté Bâ employs in his depiction of the ambiguous condition of his subject makes this work one of the most original in the literature.

However, the exceptional impact of these two works may obscure the tendency of Francophone African writers toward a more documentary and critical approach in their fictional representation of the African world both during the colonial period and after. The novels of Mongo Beti and Ferdinand Oyono exemplify this approach. Their fierce satires are intended to demonstrate the violent logic of the colonial encounter; in Oyono's *Une vie de Boy* (1956, Houseboy) the plot moves inexorably toward a tragic outcome.

Ousmane Sembène aligns the protest theme in his novels closely with the ideological tenets and literary tradition of socialist realism, as demonstrated by his most acclaimed work, *Les Bouts de bois de Dieu* (1960, God's Bits of Wood), which builds its epic narrative upon a real historical event developed in the novel as a signal moment of collective heroism. Ousmane Sembène has extended the social criticism of his early work to the post-independence period in *Le Mandat* (1965, The Money Order) and *Xala* (1973). These works connect with the theme first introduced in Malick Fall's *La Plaie* (1967, The Wound), a novel about a social outcast in the new political order.

This orientation toward what one might call a new realism, focused on the peculiar failure of will and purpose in post-independence Africa, has predominated in recent Francophone African fiction. The searing imagination that Yambo Ouologuem displays in presenting his disenchanted vision of African destiny in *Le Devoir de violence* (1968, Bound to Violence) provides the most extreme instance of the preoccupation with the African condition in its new post-independence configuration. While a sober appraisal of contemporary tensions in Africa also motivates Amadou Kourouma's *Les soleils des indépendances* (1968, The Suns of Independence), its primary claim to attention resides in its creative recasting of the French language to reflect the subjectivity of the Africans whose dilemmas the novel explores. The uncompromising light that these works project on the new African reality is broadly evident in such novels as Henri Lopes's *Le Pleurer-rire* (1982, The Laughing Cry), Alioum Fantouré's *Le cercle des tropiques* (1972, Tropical Circle), Williams Sassine's *Le jeune homme de sable* (1979, The Young Man of Sand), and Tierno Monénembo's *Les crapauds-brousse* (1979, The Bush Toads). The dystopian element that unites these works finds its culmination in the nightmarish world the late Sony Labou Tansi created in the five novels he published between 1979 and 1988. The close correlation between the formal complexities of these novels and their deep probing of the present African reality suggests that the novel represents today the strongest area of achievement in Francophone letters.

Literature by Women

The remarkable entry of women writers into the field since the late 1970s has also altered the landscape of Francophone African literature. While the social novels of Aminata Sow continue mainly to reflect the influence of Ousmane Sembène, as in *La grève des battus* (1979, The Beggars' Strike), others writers have introduced a somewhat different emphasis related to the specific concerns of women. The outstanding work here is Mariama Bâ's *Une si longue lettre* (1979, So Long a Letter), in which the narrative of the novel extends its focus beyond the problem of polygamy to encompass a whole range of issues related to the process of modernization in Africa. The novel is also distinguished by the fact that the writer lends her heroine a discretion that convention associates with a female sensibility. The tone of Mariama Bâ's novel does not, however, represent the only female voice in Francophone Africa. Women's writing exhibits a variety that ranges from Nafissatou Diallo's anxious interrogation in her autobiography, *De Tilène au Plateau* (1975, A Dakar Childhood), to the combative feminism of Calixthe Beyala's two works, *C'est le soleil qui m'a brûlée* (1987, The Sun Hath Looked Upon Me) and *Tu t'appelleras Tanga* (1988, Your Name Shall Be Tanga).

Conclusion

Given the nature of modern African experience, it was inevitable that the literature of the continent should be focused on the encounter with Europe and its far-reaching consequences even in the post-independence period. As with parts of Africa dominated by other European powers, the literature that has emerged from the former French colonies has served primarily as a comprehensive testimony to the colonial experience – to the objective facts that constitute this historical experience as well as the inward effects that give it human significance. This historical consciousness provides the broad perspective within which Yambo Ouologuem situates his work, mentioned above. The same historical perspective unfolds in *Cette Afrique-là* (1963, That Africa), by Jean Ikellé-Matiba; in *Monné, outrages et défis* (1990, Monnew: A Novel), by Amadou Kourouma; and in *Entre le lys et le flamboyant* (1997, Between the Lily and the Flame Tree), by Henri Lopes. In these works, the Francophone African experience appears in its full historical span, and in relation to the French, who are represented not merely as conquerors and colonizers, but as a national community defined by a language and culture with which a significant segment of the African population has been profoundly involved.

Abiola Irele

See Also

Congo, Republic of the; Dahomey, Early Kingdom of; Senghor, Léopold Sédar; Ousmane Sembène.

Latin America and the Caribbean

Literature, French Language, in Caribbean,

poetry, prose fiction, and essays in French by writers hailing principally from Haiti, Martinique, and Guadeloupe; a few of the authors whose work fits in this category also come from French Guiana and Dominica.

The term "Francophone Caribbean literature" can in theory refer to any work in French from the Caribbean area, including the works of white French writers born or living in the region. The most prominent example of such a writer is Saint-John Perse (1887-1975), born in Guadeloupe to a family that had been living in the Caribbean since the seventeenth century. Perse's poetic works evoked images of his island birthplace. However, Francophone Caribbean literature has come to represent mainly the works of writers living in the Caribbean whose ethnic origins are other than French, for it this group that presently dominates the cultural scene in the Francophone Caribbean.

Although there exist cultural similarities between Haiti and the rest of the French-speaking Caribbean, Haitian Francophone literature is often considered to constitute a separate category in this genre. This is largely the result of two factors: Haiti's nearly mono-ethnic population (95 percent of Haitians are of African descent, whereas the rest of the Francophone Caribbean is considerably more diverse) and the diverging path Haiti took from the rest of the Caribbean following the Haitian Revolution (1791-1804), led by Toussaint L'Ouverture. If Haitian literature in the nineteenth century mimicked works of French Romanticism, it is clear that Haitian writers assumed their own voice in the twentieth century. Exposure to white racism during the United States occupation (1915-1934) shook some of Haiti's intellectuals out of their complacent Francophilia. Led by Jean Price-Mars (1876-1969) and his pioneering essay "Ainsi parla l'oncle" (1928), they began to seek their identity in Haiti's African roots. Peasant life, Creole expressions, and Vodou started to appear together with a Marxist perspective in novels such as *Gouverneurs de la rosée* (1944; translated as *Masters of the Dew*, 1947) by Jacques Roumain (1907-1944). René Depestre (b. 1926), considered Haiti's greatest living novelist despite the fact that he has been exiled from the country since age 20, continues to evoke the myths and ways of Haiti even in his recent works written in France; these works include *Alléluia pour une femme-jardin* (1981) and *Eros dans un train chinois* (1990). Women's voices, Marie Chauvet's in particular (in *Fille d'Haïti* [1954], for example), have also been resonating on the Haitian literary scene since the 1950s. Of the most recent generation of writers, Gary Victor (b. 1958), a deputy minister in the government of Jean-Bertrand

ARISTIDE before the coup, has been most successful. Like those of many of his predecessors, Victor's works (such as *Sonson Pipirit: profil d'un homme du peuple* [1988]) constitute an artful blend of Vodou, politics, and acerbic social commentary.

Works in French from Martinique, Guadeloupe, and French Guiana constitute a second category of Francophone Caribbean literature because of the parallel political and, to a lesser extent, cultural development of these overseas departments of France. In the nineteenth century and early years of the twentieth, the Francophone literature of the French overseas departments was dominated by the so-called doodooist works of the mulatto bourgeoisie. Doodooist writers tended to exoticize their islands in the same way that European travel writers did. They painted idyllic pictures of life in Martinique and Guadeloupe without evoking the scars left on the islands and their people by slavery. Since World War II, the literature of Martinique and Guadeloupe has been informed by two dominant literary movements: NÉGRITUDE and CRÉOLITÉ. It was – somewhat paradoxically – in Paris, France, that the Martinican AIMÉ CÉSAIRE (b. 1913), the French Guianese LÉON-GONTRAN DAMAS (b. 1912), and the Senegalese Léopold Sédar Senghor (b. 1906) developed the notion of Négritude. It was Césaire's landmark poem "Cahier d'un retour au pays natal" (1947; translated as *Notebook of a Return to my Native Land*, 1947) that brought Négritude to the Caribbean. Négritude writers of the Caribbean explicitly rejected the doodooists' slavish attachment to French customs as well as their disdain for the darker-skinned Africans, whom they considered to be inferior. Césaire, Damas, René Ménil, and others attempted in their works to reconcile their African past with their Caribbean present. This attachment to African values would be rejected by a subsequent generation of Francophone Caribbean writers, and the first to do so was EDOUARD GLISSANT (b. 1928), author of *Le discours antillais* (1981) and *Caribbean Discourse* (1989). The quest for an African identity was also abandoned by a group of writers who form the Créolité movement (for example, Jean Bernabé et al., *Eloge de la créolité* [1989; issued in a bilingual edition in 1993]). In both the theoretical works and fictional works (such as PATRICK CHAMOISEAU's 1992 Prix Goncourt-winning *Texaco*) of this younger generation, identity is sought and found in the Caribbean itself.

There are writers of note from throughout the twentieth century whose works do not fall into either the Négritude or the Créolité category. The realist works of the Martinican writer JOSEPH ZOBEL (b. 1915) focus on the brutality of plantation existence in Martinique in the early twentieth century (in *La Rue cases-nègres* [1950]). The Guadeloupean MARYSE CONDÉ (b. 1937) has written novels set in Africa, the Caribbean, and the United States but is less concerned with the search for identity in these places than with broader questions of human justice.

Today there is an offshoot of Francophone Caribbean literature that could be called Caribbean exile literature. Many writers with strong connections to the Francophone Caribbean are living and writing elsewhere. Haitian writers who fit this description are Dany Laferrière, who lives in Quebec (*Comment faire l'amour à un nègre sans se fatiguer* [1983; translated as *How to Make Love to a Negro*, 1987]), and EDWIDGE DANTICAT (b. 1969), who lives in Brooklyn, New York, and writes in Creole-inflected English (in *Krik? Krak!* [1996]). The Guadeloupean writer Gisèle Pineau (b. 1956) describes the alienating experience of being brought up in Paris by her Creole-speaking grandmother in *L'Exil selon Julia* (1996), while DANIEL MAXIMIN (b. 1947) attempts to reconcile existence in France with his Guadeloupean heritage in *L'Isolé soleil* (1981; translated as *Lone Sun*, 1989). These expatriate writers both expand and challenge the definition of Francophone Caribbean literature, and in so doing breathe new life into the literary production of the region.

Richard Watts

SEE ALSO

Senghor, Léopold Sédar; Slavery in Latin America and the Caribbean; Toussaint L'Ouverture, François Dominique; Languages, Creole, in the Caribbean.

Cross Cultural

Literature in Eighteenth-Century Britain and the United States

Although literacy was denied to the vast majority of English-speaking people of African descent during the age of slavery, a fortunate and determined few wrote or dictated their stories in the eighteenth century. Almost all such Anglophone blacks were subjects of the British monarch before the AMERICAN REVOLUTION, and many remained so during and after that event, though others became subjects of the new government of the United States.

The first two known English-language publications by blacks appeared in North America in 1760. The prose *Narrative of the Uncommon Sufferings, and Surprizing Deliverance of Briton Hammon, a Negro Man*, published in Boston in 1760 by Briton Hammon, perhaps a free man, recounts his providential reunion with his owner or employer after many years of captivity and adventure. That same year, in New York, JUPITER HAMMON (1711-1800?) (no relation to Briton), who was a slave his whole life, published the poem "An Evening Thought. Salvation by Christ, with Penitential Cries: Composed by Jupiter Hammon, a Negro Belonging to Mr. Lloyd." However, neither work seems to have influenced the early tradition of black literature written either by black authors or by whites who recorded their words. Although the two Hammons anticipated the use of the Bible and the Christian theme of liberation from spiritual or physical captivity (and often from both) treated by most subsequent black authors, later writers did not seem to know the work of either Hammon.

Other examples of eighteenth-century, English-language black works that apparently remained unknown to contemporary black writers include *The Life and Confession* (Worcester, Massachusetts, 1786) by Johnson Green and *Sketches of the Life of Joseph Mountain, a Negro* (New Haven, Connecticut, 1790) by Joseph Mountain. Commonly called "as-told-to" tales, these confessional narratives might be called "as-told-for" tales because whites taking down the story may have changed the facts. The earliest known poem by a black writing in English, "Bars Fight," by LUCY TERRY PRINCE (1730?-1821), was not published until 1855, though it was originally created around 1745.

English-language black literature developed into a tradition after blacks began to win freedom from slavery. This began in GREAT BRITAIN with the 1772 decision in London by Lord Mansfield, Lord Chief Justice of the King's Bench, in the case of James Somerset, in light of which blacks in England became arguably the freest people of their color in the world. Mansfield ruled that slaves like Somerset who had been brought to England by their owners could not be legally forced to return to the colonies. Mansfield's judgment was received as an emancipation proclamation, widely accepted to mean that a slave was free as soon as he or she set foot on English soil.

At the end of 1772, perhaps capitalizing on the attention that blacks gained with the Mansfield decision, JAMES ALBERT UKAWSAW GRONNIOSAW (1710?-1775?) published in Bath *A Narrative of the Most Remarkable Particulars of the Life of... an African Prince, Written by Himself*, an "as-told-to" tale. Gronniosaw's work, which recounts his kidnapping in Africa, slavery in New Jersey, and poverty as a free man in England, went through many transatlantic editions before the end of the century. The attention Mansfield brought to the subject of British slavery may also at least partly explain the publication of the poem "Ode," by Francis Williams, a black man, in Edward Long's *History of Jamaica* (London, 1774). A defender of slavery, particularly in the West Indies, Long reproduced Williams's poem in hopes of disproving arguments that Africans were capable of creating literature when given the benefit of education. But Long's attempt to discredit Williams, and by extension all black writers, backfired almost completely. Without Long's attack, we would know virtually nothing of Williams and have no certain example of his work.

Slave traders brought PHILLIS WHEATLEY (1753?-1784) from Africa to North America when she was around eight years old (*see*

TRANSATLANTIC SLAVE TRADE). The year after the Mansfield decision, Wheatley came from Massachusetts with her master to London to try to recover her health and to find a publisher for her *Poems on Various Subjects, Religious and Moral* (London, England, 1773). Boston publishers – who would not believe that she could write poetry – had rejected the work. One of her poems, "A Farewell to America," locates the figure of Temptation in England – probably a reference to the Mansfield case and the opportunity for self-emancipation it would give her when she reached London. She was freed, "at the desire of my friends in England," shortly after her return to Boston. The first English-speaking black author of a book, Wheatley saw her poems reprinted on both sides of the Atlantic, but she was unable to find an American publisher for a proposed second volume of writings.

Other black writers quickly acknowledged Wheatley's contribution to the English-language black tradition. In 1778 IGNATIUS SANCHO (1729?-1780) wrote privately to the Philadelphia Quaker Jabez Fisher that Wheatley was a "Genius in bondage" and said of her work, "Phillis's poems do credit to nature – and put art – merely as art – to the blush." Sancho's letter was first published posthumously in *Letters of the Late Ignatius Sancho, an African* (1782). Also in 1778 Jupiter Hammon published *An Address to Miss Phillis Wheatly, Ethiopian Poetess, in Boston* (Hartford, Connecticut, 1778), a work that apparently remained unknown to Wheatley or any other black writer.

Sancho's *Letters*, however, became widely known on both sides of the Atlantic. Born during the Middle Passage, Sancho eventually became the valet of the duke of Montagu, who established Sancho as a Westminster grocer when he retired from his service. During his life Sancho gained international celebrity as the friend and correspondent of Laurence Sterne, author of the comic novel *Tristram Shandy*. He is the first known black British patron of white artists and writers, whose work he helped publish and distribute. He also published letters on current events in the newspapers under both his own name and the name "Africanus," in support of the king and the British side in the American Revolution. His posthumously published letters increased Sancho's fame as a letter writer, a devoted husband and father, a wit, a man of feeling, an abolitionist, and a critic of art, literature, and politics. In addition, Sancho composed music. He also wrote plays, now lost, and a theory of music, also lost.

The Mansfield judgment focused public attention on the legal status of people of African descent in Great Britain and its North American colonies, like Gronniosaw, Wheatley, and Sancho, who were British subjects yet not ethnically English, Scottish, or Welsh. The ideological conflict during the American Revolution added to the controversy surrounding their status, and during the crusade in the 1780s and 1790s to end British involvement in the slave trade with Africa, their status as writers and thus human beings became an issue. The number and overtly political nature of black English-language publications greatly increased in response to these historical developments.

In 1776 the DECLARATION OF INDEPENDENCE signed in Philadelphia offered nothing to the nearly 500,000 blacks in North America, or 20 percent of the total population. (The 500,000 blacks in the British West Indies, more than 90 percent of the population, were unaffected by either the Mansfield ruling or the Declaration of Independence.) The contrast between the legal status of blacks in the Mother Country and in the colonies underscored the hypocrisy of the white North American colonists demanding liberty for themselves while enslaving others.

Given English-speaking blacks' association of England with potential liberation, many of the eighteenth-century blacks whose voices we can recover, either directly or through intermediaries, sided with the British rather than the Americans. Many took advantage of British promises of emancipation for the refugee slaves of colonial rebels (but not for refugees from Loyalist masters). For every Johnson Green or the more famous CRISPUS ATTUCKS (1723?-1770) who joined the American rebel cause, many more blacks chose the British side. One example is John Marrant (1755-1791), a slave-owning free black whose *A Narrative of the Lord's Wonderful Dealings with John Marrant, a Black* (London, 1785) and *A Journal* (London, 1790) recount his postrevolutionary missionary work in Canada, America, and England.

In the period known as the "first emancipation" – during and after the American Revolution, when an antislavery movement in the Northern American states developed – blacks, including Prince Hall (1735?-1807), LEMUEL HAYNES (1753-1833), and BENJAMIN BANNEKER (1731-1806), wrote and published poems, sermons, petitions, tracts, and letters expressing their faith and hope that the promise of the Revolution would be extended to their people. Notable among these writings are Haynes's (perhaps significantly) unpublished and incomplete "Liberty Further Extended: Or Free Thoughts on the Illegality of Slave-Keeping" (1776?) and Banneker's published letter to Thomas Jefferson (Philadelphia, 1792), both of which challenge white Americans to apply to blacks Jefferson's words in the Declaration.

The failure of black Americans' hopes is implicit in *A Narrative of the Life and Adventures of Venture, A Native of Africa: But Resident above Sixty Years in the United States of America. Related by Himself* (New London, 1798) by Venture Smith (1729?-1805). The *Narrative* seems to reflect Smith's disillusion at the end of the century with the failed promises of the "first emancipation." Smith identifies himself as only a "resident" of the country, which, the anonymous voice in the preface to his story reminds us, has denied him the citizenship and thus the opportunities that might have allowed him to rival the achievements of Benjamin Franklin or George Washington. Smith's text is the only example of a work written or dictated by a black during the period that is entitled a "narrative" but is not a story of conversion, and his reference to the "Christian land" in which he lives is clearly ironic.

The Americans' victory against the British in 1783 led to a great and very visible increase in the numbers of free blacks accompanying their Loyalist former masters as they left the former 13 colonies for Canada and London. Joining them were many former slaves who had emancipated themselves by enlisting in the British forces in the war. The sight of unemployed and impoverished blacks in London prompted the project for resettlement in SIERRA LEONE, West Africa, beginning in 1787 (*see* LONDON'S BLACK POOR AND THE SIERRA LEONE SETTLEMENT PLAN), and contributed to the growing demand for the abolition of the transatlantic slave trade. Among the former slaves emancipated and evacuated from the American South by the withdrawing British troops who then resettled in Sierra Leone or elsewhere in the British Empire, David George (1743?-1810?) and Boston King (1760?-1802) published slave narratives while they lived in Africa, and George Liele (1751?-1825) published his after he went to JAMAICA.

In 1787 OTTOBAH CUGOANO (who also went by the name John Stewart or Stuart) made the most overt challenge to slavery by an English-speaking black in *Thoughts and Sentiments on the Evil and Wicked Traffic of the Slavery and Commerce of the Human Species, Humbly Submitted to the Inhabitants of Great-Britain, by Ottobah Cugoano, a Native of Africa* (London). In 1770 fellow Africans kidnapped Cugoano, who was about age 13, from his home on the coast of present-day GHANA and sold him into slavery to Europeans, who transported him to GRENADA. At the end of 1772 he was brought to England, where he gained his freedom. In his jeremiad Cugoano raised the most overt and extended challenge to slavery ever made by a person of African descent. He is also the first English-speaking African historian of slavery and the slave trade and the first English-speaking black in Great Britain or North America to criticize European imperialism in the Americas.

His works, full of acknowledged and unacknowledged debts to the writings of others, demonstrate that he saw the struggle against the slave trade as a kind of group project. His recognition of Marrant and Gronniosaw as his predecessors also helped establish a tradition of black English-language writing by converts to Christianity. In *Thoughts and Sentiments* Cugoano refutes the proslavery arguments that slavery was divinely sanctioned; that Africans gladly sold their own families into slavery (though he acknowledges African complicity in the slave trade); that Africans were especially well suited for slavery; and that West Indian slaves lived better lives than the European poor. Cugoano believed that slaves had not only the right but also the obligation to rebel: "It is the duty of every man to deliver himself from rogues and villains if he can." The "enslavers of men are the servants of the devil" and the breakers of God's law and thus "the only men that others have any right to enslave." According to him, every Briton shared the blame for the evil of slavery, and if it continued, Great Britain faced divine retribution. He also condemned European imperialism throughout the world and especially in the Americas.

Cugoano's friend and occasional collaborator, OLAUDAH EQUIANO, also known as Gustavus Vassa (1745?-1797), published *The Interesting Narrative of the Life of Olaudah Equiano, or Gustavus Vassa, the African, Written by Himself* (London, 1789), the first full account of the slave trade and slavery published by a former slave. Equiano's work, with nine British editions between 1789 and 1794, is the longest and most significant publication by an African in Great Britain in the century. It is a spiritual autobiography, captivity narrative, travel book, adventure tale, narrative of slavery, economic treatise, and apologia (justification and vindication of one's life), among other things. Appearing amid the mass national petitioning movement that began in 1788 against the slave trade, the *Interesting Narrative* amounts to a petition against the trade, beginning with an address to the members of both houses of Parliament and virtually ending with a petition to the queen. Equiano sold his *Interesting Narrative* by subscription, that is, by convincing buyers to commit themselves to purchasing copies of his book prior to its publication, usually requiring at least partial payment in advance to cover living and production costs. The list of subscribers published at the front of his book served to link Equiano with the larger movement against the slave trade by including names of others who had already attacked in print or from the pulpit the invidious practice.

By 1789 a recognized tradition of black English-language authors had been established, with new writers aware of and acknowledging the works of their predecessors. Jupiter Hammon and Sancho acknowledged and praised the poetry of Wheatley, and Cugoano referred explicitly to the works of Gronniosaw and Marrant. The subscription lists for Equiano's *Interesting Narrative* connect the author and his work explicitly and implicitly with the black writers in English of the preceding 15 years. Subscribers included Cugoano; Sancho's son William; the Countess of Huntingdon, associated with Gronniosaw and Wheatley; and the Reverend William Aldridge, Marrant's editor.

Alongside the tradition of black English-language literature created by black authors by the end of the eighteenth century, proponents and opponents of the slave trade and slavery were also creating a canon of black English-language writers. Although Wheatley, Williams, and Sancho rarely openly addressed the abolition of the slave trade or of slavery itself, the arguments of the 1780s and later by abolitionists and their opponents about the literary and intellectual capacities of Africans often referred to these three writers. Already dead by the 1780s, and thus not able, as were Cugoano and Equiano, to engage in the controversy themselves, Wheatley, Williams, and Sancho, with their obvious literary ambitions, provided a focus for the late eighteenth-century debate over the innate intelligence and even humanity of blacks. Thomas Jefferson's comments in *Notes on the State of Virginia* (1787) exemplify the kind of attacks defenders of the slave trade, ignoring critical acclaim, made on the achievements of black English-language writers: "Religion indeed has produced a Phillis Wheately [*sic*]; but it could not produce a poet.... [Ignatius Sancho] has approached nearer to merit in composition.... [T]hough we admit him to the first place among those of his own colour who have presented themselves to the public judgment, yet when we compare him with the writers of the race among whom he lived, and particularly with the epistolary class, in which he has taken his own stand, we are compelled to enroll him at the bottom of the column."

The outbreak of the French Revolution and the subsequent Terror (1789-1794) made the British reluctant to pursue major social reforms lest they lead to revolutionary results, and the slave revolts in the West Indies, especially HAITI, during the 1790s seemed to justify conservative fears. Later in the decade, the threat posed by Napoleonic France to national survival eclipsed all other issues. However, agitation for abolition revived in 1804 when the war resumed against Napoleon, who had reintroduced slavery in the French Caribbean colonies. The British legally abolished the slave trade in 1808, and in 1838 nonindigenous slavery ended in the British Empire. By the end of the eighteenth century the increasing economic value of cotton in the American South halted the spread of emancipation in the United States, delayed for three generations until the end of the inevitable American Civil War. However, black writers of the eighteenth century contributed significantly to the abolition of slavery in the British Empire and established a tradition on which black Americans drew in their own struggle for freedom.

Vincent Carretta

SEE ALSO

Middle Passage, The; Slavery in the United States; Abolitionism in the United States; Boston, Massachusetts; Civil War, American; Philadelphia, Pennsylvania; Slave Narratives.

North America

Little Richard (Richard Wayne Penniman) (b. December 25, 1932 or 1935, Macon, Ga.), African American musician; rock and roll pioneer.

Born Richard Penniman, Little Richard was one of 12 children in a family divided by the religious concerns of some – many were Seventh Day Adventist preachers – and the more secular interests of others – his father was a bootlegger. Richard was kicked out of the house at age 13 for reasons that remain unclear but that probably relate to his precocious and adventurous sexuality. He was taken in by a white family who owned the Tick Tock Club in Macon, where he began his musical career.

American musician Little Richard performs during a Rock and Roll Hall of Fame show in 1995. *CORBIS/Neal Preston*

After several years of playing around the South and recording in Atlanta and Houston, Little Richard sent a demonstration tape in 1955 to Specialty Records, a RHYTHM AND BLUES label based in Los Angeles. Specialty found the tapes promising and arranged a recording session in New Orleans. This turned out to be one of the germinal sessions of rock and roll. Little Richard's explosive vocal energy heralded a new style, far removed from the conventional jump blues he had been playing.

Most of these songs were filled with barely concealed sexual imagery (even after cleaning up the lyrics), made more outrageous by Little Richard's falsetto squeals. One of them was "Tutti Frutti," featuring the immortal introduction: "A-wop-bop-a-lu-bop, a-wop-bam-boom." Other hits quickly followed, including "Long Tall Sally," "Rip It Up," "Lucille," and "Good Golly Miss Molly." Little Richard became a sensation, touring nationally and appearing in Hollywood movies about rock and roll, of which the most popular was *The Girl Can't Help It* (1956), named after one of his compositions.

In retrospect, Little Richard's popularity is startling. He may have modeled his outrageous stage persona in the tradition of effeminate black male entertainers wearing makeup, such as Billy Wright. While the sight of an African American man wearing makeup and singing about barnyard sex unnerved some, both black and white teenagers loved it. Almost as soon as Little Richard created a new hit, Pat Boone would produce a less soulful cover rendition of it. But American youth preferred and respected the Originator, as Little Richard sometimes calls himself.

In 1957, while performing successfully at the top of the American music industry, Little Richard quit rock and roll after a trip to Australia, following a religious conversion that he believed alerted him to the immorality of rock 'n' roll. After becoming an ordained Seventh Day Adventist minister, he toiled away in obscurity for several years. Little Richard returned to rock 'n' roll in the mid-sixties and toured in Europe with the Beatles and the Rolling Stones, who were among the artists directly influenced by his work. Since that time, he has moved back and forth between his church life and preaching and the world of rock 'n' roll.

In 1986, Little Richard was inducted into the Rock and Roll Hall of Fame; that same year he appeared in the film *Down and Out in Beverly Hills.* He was honored with a Grammy Award for Lifetime Achievement in 1993, and in 1994 he was among the recipients of the Rhythm and Blues Foundation's Pioneer Award.

See Also

Atlanta, Georgia; Blues, The; Houston, Texas; New Orleans, Louisiana; Los Angeles, California.

North America

Little Rock Crisis, 1957, an early crisis in the Civil Rights Movement that began in 1957 when whites in Little Rock, Arkansas, rioted in protest against the integration of Central High School; in so doing they – and Arkansas governor Orval Faubus – challenged the supremacy of the federal courts, and President Dwight D. Eisenhower reluctantly sent in United States troops to maintain order (*see* Daisy Lee Gatson Bates).

Africa

Livingstone, David

(b. March 19, 1813, Blantyre, Lanarkshire, Scotland; d. May 1, 1873, Chitambo, Barotseland [in present-day Zambia]), Scottish missionary and physician who explored much of southern Africa.

Born to a poor Scottish family, the devout young David Livingstone entered the London Missionary Society (LMS) in 1838 with the intent of studying medicine and then traveling to China, a dream cut short by the 1839-1842 Opium War. But when his services were solicited by missionaries working in southern Africa, he turned his sights to that region, and four months after his ordination in November 1840 he set sail for Cape Town.

From 1841 until 1857 Livingstone journeyed throughout southern Africa as a member of the LMS, traveling through the Kalahari and working among the Tswana. In 1844, while on his way to Mabotsa, he was attacked by a lion; one of his arms would remain permanently impaired.

In 1845 Livingstone married Marry Moffet, the daughter of one of his mentors, Robert Moffet. Marry initially accompanied him on his journeys but, in poor health and concerned for their child's schooling, she returned to England in 1852. Livingstone continued his travels north and west, reaching the Atlantic coastal town of Luanda (in present-day Angola) in 1854. Next he traveled east to the Zambezi River, where he named Victoria Falls. In addition to spreading Christianity, he encouraged forms of commerce that could replace slave trading, which was still widely practiced in many of the areas he visited. He declared it was "extremely desirous to promote the preparation of raw materials of European manufacture in Africa, for by that means we may not only put a stop to the slave trade but introduce the Negro family into the body of corporate of nations, no member of which can suffer without others suffering with it."

In 1856 Livingstone returned to England. His book *Missionary Travels and Researchers in South Africa*, published in 1857, brought the issue of slavery to the forefront of public consciousness. Two years later he returned to Africa to head a British government-sponsored expedition that led to the European discovery of a number of southern African sites, including Lake Nyasa (now Lake Malawi). Although this expedition resulted in major cartographic revisions in Europe, the British authorities considered it a failure and ended it in 1863.

After crossing the Indian Ocean to Bombay, Livingstone returned to Britain and, with his brother Charles, wrote *Narrative of an Expedition to the Zambezi and Its Tributaries* (1865). This account of the slave trade around Lake Nyasa is credited with helping to convince many missionaries in the following decades to dedicate themselves to the elimination of the slave trade and the spread of Christianity.

In 1866 Livingstone set out to find the source of the Nile, traveling the Rovuma River to the north of Lake Nyasa and reaching Lake Tanganyika in 1869. When expedition deserters claimed that Livingstone had been killed by Africans en route, the American journalist Henry Morton Stanley embarked on a widely publicized eight-month "rescue mission," which ended when he found Livingstone in Ujuji, in present-day Democratic Republic of the Congo.

Livingstone and Stanley explored the area north of Lake Tanganyika until parting company in 1872. For two more years Livingstone unsuccessfully searched for the source of the Nile before dying in Chitambo, Zambia. His heart was buried beneath the tree where he died, and the rest of his remains lie in Westminster Abbey.

See Also

Cape Town, South Africa; Christianity, African: An Overview; Kalahari Desert; Malawi, Lake; Luanda, Angola; Nile River; Stanley, Sir Henry Morton; Christianity: Missionaries in Africa; Indian Ocean Slave Trade; Slavery in Africa.

North America

LL Cool J (also known as James Todd Smith) (b. January 14, 1968, Queens, New York), African American hip hop pioneer, actor, and sex symbol whose 15 years of success make him rap's longest-running superstar.

LL Cool J – short for Ladies Love Cool James – was raised in Hollis, Queens, a neighborhood that also produced the early rap masters who formed Run-DMC. *Radio*, his 1985 debut album, sported such signature songs as "Rock the Bells" and "I Can't Live Without My Radio." It sold more than 1 million copies. The kid in the sneakers, gold chains, and Kangol hat rapped over spare, programmed beats that were sometimes splashed with rock guitar. In an art form founded on cocky sparring, LL Cool J was the king of the boast. Fans admired him for his cherubic looks and smooth style as well as his lyrical skills.

While *Bigger and Deffer* (1987), LL's second release, contained one of the all-time great battle raps, "I'm Bad," it also revealed the MC's softer side in "I Need Love," the first rap love ballad. His next album, *Walking with a Panther* (1989), succeeded commercially but not critically; Public Enemy's black nationalist politics were then in vogue, and critics protested LL's conspicuous materialism. The next year, in a furious rebuke to naysayers, he released *Mama Said Knock You Out.* "Don't call it a comeback," he warned on the title track and added: "I've been here for years/ I'm rockin' my peers/ Puttin' suckers in fear." The album, produced by Marley Marl, continued LL's history of hits: chart successes, such as "Around the Way Girl," "Jingling Baby," the bass-heavy "Boomin' System," and the title track, pushed album sales past the 2 million mark.

LL suffered a rare commercial failure with *14 Shots to the Dome* (1993), but as his hip hop credibility started to drop, he branched out. LL Cool J performed at Bill Clinton's 1993 presidential inauguration; starred in the popular television sitcom, *In the House*; and acted in a string of feature films. In 1995 he returned to rap music with *Mr. Smith*, a multi-platinum success that garnered little critical acclaim but earned him two Grammy Awards. With *I Make My Own Rules* (1997), a best-selling autobiography, LL confirmed his status as hip hop's preeminent superstar.

Andrew Du Bois

See Also
Hip Hop in the United States.

North America

Llewellyn, James Bruce

(b. July 16, 1927, New York, N.Y.), African American entrepreneur who managed some of the most successful black businesses in the United States.

J. Bruce Llewellyn was born in Harlem to Jamaican immigrant parents who instilled a strong sense of ambition, work ethic, and motivation in their son. While he was young, his family moved to the predominantly white middle-class suburb of White Plains, New York. Here, Llewellyn worked at his father's restaurant and bar while also selling magazines and Fuller brush products on his own.

When he was 16, Llewellyn enlisted in the United States Army. Since he was too young for combat, he was sent to Rutgers University to study engineering for training as an aviation cadet. He completed Engineer's Officer Candidate school with the rank of second lieutenant. By 1948 he had left the military, and with his earnings from the army, he opened a liquor store in Harlem. He used the proceeds from the store to finance his education at City College of New York in the mid-1950s. After receiving his undergraduate degree, Llewellyn entered the School of Business at Columbia University and then New York Law School, where he received a law degree in 1960.

Throughout the 1970s and 1980s, Llewellyn achieved impressive results in business by combining service to the black community with service to the larger public. "My father always told me that brains and education can defeat prejudice in society," was Llewellyn's understated analysis of his own success as a businessman. Among his accomplishments are the transformation of Fedco, a small chain of fledgling supermarkets, to a chain of 27 stores and sales of $85 million by 1983; the control of 36 percent of the Coca-Cola Bottling Company of New York; the management of the Overseas Private Investment Corporation (OPIC) under President Jimmy Carter; and ownership of a televison station. Llewellyn is the only person to have four companies placed on the Black Enterprise list of the 100 largest black businesses in its 20-year history. In addition to his various business concerns, he is active in several service organizations.

See Also
Harlem, New York.

Africa

Loango, Early Kingdom of,

kingdom of the Vili people during the eighteenth century in the area of the present-day Republic of the Congo and Gabon.

From the fourteenth to the nineteenth century the Vili people, an ethnic subgroup of the Bantu-speaking Bakongo, ruled the kingdom of Loango that was also known as Brama. Its center was on the coast of the present-day Republic of the Congo. However, it controlled a vast coastline stretching from Angola's Cabinda enclave to an area that was approximately 200 km (120 mi) north, into the area known today as Gabon. Loango's territory also extended roughly 200 km inland, with the kingdom's influence through trade stretching even farther into the interior.

The exact origins of the Loango Kingdom are unclear. Linguistic evidence and oral histories suggest that the Bakongo, Vili, Téké, and Woyo all had a common origin. According to this view, the Vili migrated from the Nguunu Kingdom in the interior to the coastal plains in the late fourteenth century. Archaeological evidence suggests that the area was previously inhabited, perhaps by the Bongo "Pygmies," who held a respected position in the Loango court.

During its early history Loango remained subordinate to the Kongo Kingdom, to which Loango paid tribute through much of the fifteenth century. With the decline of the Kongo Kingdom, the independence of the Maloangos, the semi-divine kings of the Loango, increased. The Loango traded ivory, copper, and slaves with Dutch and Portuguese merchants for salt and European manufactured goods. They also traded copper, dyewood, and ivory along the coast with the Mpongwe in the north and the Bakongo in the south. After 1630 the Dutch assumed a dominant position in the transatlantic slave trade with Brazil and parts of the Caribbean, and began purchasing slaves from Loango. Loango's power reached its peak in the 1700s. The kingdom's extensive trade routes converged on Loango Bay. The town of Buali, with a population of approximately 15,000 in the late 1700s, served as the capital.

The kingdom had a decentralized but strictly hierarchical structure. Those in line for succession to the crown first served as governor of each of the kingdom's four provinces. Potential heirs changed provinces each time a king, or Maloango, died. The king appointed local officials, most of whom were members of the royal family, for life terms of office. These local chiefs collected taxes, mobilized armies in time of war, and oversaw the systems of justice. Most Vili lived in towns of about 100 people. They grew a variety of crops on the fertile land, including maize, sorghum, and cassava. They also hunted in the forest, fished the rivers and coastal areas, produced salt, and wove reeds.

By the late eighteenth century the Loango Kingdom had begun to fragment and the king's authority waned. The abolition of the slave trade and the opening up of the interior by European merchants broke the Loango trade monopoly by the late 1800s. In 1883 Pierre Savorgnan de Brazza secured a treaty from the Loango ceding their sovereignty to the French. Under French colonial rule, the region's center of trade shifted to Pointe-Noire, with its modern harbor at the terminus of the Congo-Ocean railway. While the formal authority of the descendants of the Loango royalty disappeared, many held positions in the colonial administration. Many have maintained influential political positions in the Congo since independence in 1960.

Eric Young

See Also
Ivory Trade; Kongo; Pygmy.

Africa

Lobi, an ethnic group living in Burkina Faso, Côte d'Ivoire, and Ghana.

The Lobi speak a Voltaic language and live between the Black Volta (Mouhoun) and White Volta rivers. Ethnographic accounts trace the Lobi's original homeland to Ghana, where pressure from the neighboring Mamprusi, Dogamba, and Gonjas peoples forced them to migrate in the late eighteenth century. Over the next 200 years the Lobi moved slowly north, periodically settling among and assimilating with groups such as the Lorhon, Téuessué, and Touna. En route they avoided the conquests of both the Mandinka ruler Samory Touré and the Kong Kingdom. In the late nineteenth century the Lobi temporarily settled in northern Côte d'Ivoire. Residing in self-governing matrilineal villages, they lived from hunting and periodic raids on neighboring groups. Although the region was home to Islamic Mande communities, the Lobi largely retained their animist practices.

The Lobi were relatively unaffected by European colonization until a 1901 French "pacification" campaign brought colonial rule to northern Côte d'Ivoire. Some Lobi groups continued to migrate during the colonial era. According to some reports, the Lobi evaded French administrators by migrating extremely slowly, approximately 1 km (0.62 mi) a year, until they finally settled in the Kulanog region of Upper Volta (present-day Burkina Faso), one of the country's more fertile areas. Today most Lobi live in Burkina Faso. Rural Lobi support themselves from cash crops such as cotton and peanuts as well as from raising livestock (*see* pastoralism). Smaller subgroups of the Lobi still live in Côte d'Ivoire and Ghana.

Elizabeth Heath

See Also
Languages, African: An Overview.

WINOLD
REISS

North America

Locke, Alain Leroy

(b. September 13, 1885, Philadelphia, Pa.; d. June 9, 1954, Washington, D.C.), African American philosopher, intellectual, and educator; editor of *The New Negro*, the anthology credited with defining the Harlem Renaissance.

In his introduction to *Alain Locke: Reflections on a Modern Renaissance Man*, Russell J. Linnemann points out that though Locke was trained as a philosopher at Harvard, Oxford, and Berlin Universities, "anthropology, art, music, literature, education, political theory, sociology, and African studies represent only a few of his wide range of intellectual pursuits." Linnemann goes on to hypothesize that this extraordinary breadth of intellectual activity is "the primary reason why a biography of him has not yet been written.... Few if any potential biographers who might wish to examine the scope of his thought, assess his often provocative contributions, and place them within the context of the appropriate disciplines, would have the intellectual breadth or depth to fulfill the task properly." The title of Linnemann's edited volume gets to the heart of Alain Locke's legacy: while he is often best remembered for his role in the Harlem Renaissance, the scope of his work makes him a Renaissance man in all senses of the term.

Born into Philadelphia's black elite, Locke was the only child of schoolteacher parents who were both descended from established free black families. By high school he was an accomplished pianist and violinist in addition to being an excellent student. In 1904 Locke became one of the few African American undergraduates at Harvard University, where he was elected to Phi Beta Kappa and received a B.A. in philosophy magna cum laude in 1907. That same year he became the first African American to be awarded a Rhodes Scholarship, which he used to continue studying philosophy at Oxford University and the University of Berlin.

He remained the only African American Rhodes scholar until the 1960s, and the achievement brought him national publicity in both the black and white presses. Locke returned to the United States in 1911, and in 1912 joined the faculty of Howard University as a professor of philosophy and English, a position he held for the rest of his life. He took a sabbatical in 1916-1917 to complete his Ph.D. in philosophy at Harvard, and became the chair of Howard's philosophy department upon his return. As a philosopher Locke was highly respected, and he has been called one of the most important philosophical thinkers of his day. But his best-remembered accomplishments come from his scholarship on literature and art.

1925 pastel portrait by Winold Reiss of Alain Locke, scholar and author active during the Harlem Renaissance. *National Portrait Gallery, Smithsonian Institution/Art Resource, NY*

In 1923 Locke began contributing essays on a range of subjects to *Opportunity*, the journal of the National Urban League. These essays gained him even wider prominence as a rising black intellectual, and in 1925 he was asked to edit the March issue of the *Survey Graphic*, a national sociology magazine, which was planned as a special issue devoted entirely to race. Locke decided to turn the issue into a showpiece for the gifted young African American writers then gathering in Harlem. The resulting journal, subtitled *Harlem: Mecca of the New Negro*, included poetry, fiction, and essays by W. E. B. Du Bois, James Weldon Johnson, Langston Hughes, Countee Cullen, Jean Toomer, and Anne Spencer – many of them writers who were touted as the new generation in African American art, the best and the brightest black America had yet produced.

The issue was an outstanding success. Locke expanded it into a book, and *The New Negro*, published eight months later, immediately became the definitive anthology of the Harlem Renaissance. In addition to writers featured in the magazine special, *The New Negro* included poetry and fiction by Claude McKay, Zora Neale Hurston, Angelina Grimké, and Jessie Fauset; essays by scholars William Stanley Braithwaite, Kelly Miller, J. A. Rogers, and E. Franklin Frazier; and striking artwork by Aaron Douglas. The book was widely interpreted as a resounding rebuttal to the argument that African Americans were not capable of great literature and art. As Braithwaite later said, *The New Negro* was "a protest against the imposed limitations of the spirit of the Negro artist... and [marked] the assumption of his membership in the wide realm of human vision and imagination."

Locke's intellectual interest in African American art and its relationship to black culture remained clear long after *The New Negro*'s publication. Like many black intellectuals of his day, Locke was intrigued by the question of just how much influence Africa had on African America. He believed that one of Africa's clearest legacies came through the visual arts, and argued that even though it was impossible to trace many direct lines of cultural descent to Africa, there were still undeniable artistic connections that should keep the African American from considering himself "a cultural foundling without his own inheritance." In fact, Locke saw defining this artistic connection as an important step in defining African American culture.

As a result, Locke became a leading critic and collector of both African and African American art. In an era when African art was being hailed by whites for being "primitive" and "pure," Locke insisted on documenting its technical artistry. As one of the earliest critics of black art, he was especially vocal in encouraging black colleges to train more scholars in the field, and as a collector he was responsible for greatly enlarging Howard University's art collection. He also became a scholar on black folk music, and even as he pointed out African influences on African American music, he was among the earliest critics to argue for African American music's importance to American music as a whole. Locke called black music "the closest America has to a folk music," and noted that it had become "one of the main sources of America's serious or classical music" and "almost as important for the musical culture of America as it is for the Negro."

Locke documented these interests in several books. In the 1930s he established the Associates in Negro Folk Education, dedicated to publishing scholarly books on African American subjects geared toward interested adult learners. Through it he published *Negro Art: Past and Present* and *The Negro and His Music*, both in 1936, and the comprehensive, illustrated volume *The Negro in Art: A Pictorial Record of the Negro Artists and the Negro Theme in Art* in 1940, which remains his most celebrated work after *The New Negro*.

In 1935, at age 50, Locke published his first article on philosophy. By then, most observers agreed that the Harlem Renaissance was over, and Locke appeared to make a seamless transition from his focus on literary and art criticism to new work that used philosophy to explore larger questions about race and culture. He was especially interested in the concepts of cultural relativism and cultural pluralism, which emphasize both the fundamental equality among different cultures and the usefulness of identifying commonalties among cultures. His philosophy has been described as an effort to "direct the collective energies of all peoples towards a transcendental approach to interactions in which differences of race, culture, values and ideas are respected and appreciated."

In 1942 Locke coedited an anthology on global race relations, *When Peoples Meet: A Study in Race and Culture Contacts*, which is considered the best legacy of his later intellectual work. He planned an even larger volume entirely on African American cultural identity. Called *The Negro in American Culture*, Locke envisioned the work as his magnum opus and worked on it for years between lectures, teaching, and other publications. But when he died from complications from heart disease in June 1954, it was left unfinished. Margaret Just Butcher, a Howard University colleague's daughter, did complete and publish a version of it, but most scholars agree that it cannot be considered Locke's work.

Even without that final volume, the sum of Locke's books, essays, articles, and lectures has been more than enough to establish his place in the history of American and African American arts and letters. Locke made a career of thinking about black culture in innovative ways, and in the process he became one of the most important black intellectual leaders of the twentieth century.

Lisa Clayton Robinson

See Also

Art and Architecture, African; Braithwaite, William Stanley Beaumont; Du Bois, William Edward Burghardt (W. E. B.); Fauset, Jessie Redmon; Frazier, Edward Franklin; Free Blacks in the United States, 1619 to 1863; Grimké, Angelina Weld; Harlem, New York; *Opportunity: Journal of Negro Life*; Philadelphia, Pennsylvania; Rogers, Joel Augustus.

North America

Logan, Rayford (b. January 7, 1897, Washington, D.C.; d. November 4, 1982, Washington, D.C.), African American historian who worked for the equality of black people throughout the world.

After graduating Phi Beta Kappa from Williams College in 1917, Rayford Logan enlisted in the United States Army. He was demobilized from the all-African American 93rd Division as a lieutenant, and remained in France for five years as an expatriate and an activist for Pan-Africanism. He returned to America in 1924 to agitate for civil rights and to pursue an academic career. His scholarship was dedicated to promoting the equality of black people around the world, and as a civil rights activist, he helped coordinate the 1963 March on Washington.

Logan received a master's degree in 1932 and a Ph.D. from Harvard in 1936 while teaching at both Virginia Union University (1925-1930) and Atlanta University (1933-1938). He assisted in Carter G. Woodson's Association for the Study of Negro Life and History and W. E. B. Du Bois's *Encyclopedia of the Negro*. Logan was a professor of history at Howard University from 1938 and chair of the History Department until his retirement in 1965.

Logan was honored extensively for his work on freedom and equality. He received honorary doctorates from Williams College (1965) and Howard University (1972), was appointed commander of the National Order of Honor and Merit by Haiti in 1941, and was awarded the Spingarn Medal from the National Association for the Advancement of Colored People (NAACP) in 1980. In addition, he served as coeditor of the *Dictionary of American Negro Biography*.

Alonford James Robinson, Jr.

See Also

Association for the Study of Afro-American Life and History; Du Bois, William Edward Burghardt (W. E. B.); Woodson, Carter Godwin.

Africa

Logo, ethnic group of the Democratic Republic of the Congo.

The Logo primarily inhabit northeastern Congo-Kinshasa; some also live in western Uganda. They speak a Nilo-Saharan language. More than 200,000 people consider themselves Logo.

See Also

Languages, African: An Overview.

Africa

Loke (also known as Loko, Ugep, and Yakö), ethnic group of Nigeria.

The Loke primarily inhabit Cross River State in southeastern Nigeria. They speak a Niger-Congo language and are closely related to the Ibibio people. Approximately 200,000 people consider themselves Loke.

See Also

Languages, African: An Overview.

Africa

Lokele, ethnic group of the Democratic Republic of the Congo.

The Lokele primarily inhabit the west bank of the Lualaba River in east central Congo-Kinshasa. They speak a Bantu language. Approximately 200,000 people consider themselves Lokele.

See Also

Bantu: Dispersion and Settlement.

Africa

Loko (also known as the Lokko), ethnic group of Sierra Leone.

The Loko primarily inhabit northwestern Sierra Leone. They speak a Mande language and are closely related to the Mende people. Approximately 200,000 people consider themselves Loko.

See Also

Languages, African: An Overview.

Africa

Loma (also known as Toma), ethnic group of West Africa.

The Loma primarily inhabit Liberia. Others live in Sierra Leone and Guinea. They speak a Mande language and are closely related to the Mende people. Approximately 200,000 people consider themselves Loma.

See Also

Languages, African: An Overview.

Africa

Lomé, Togo, capital and by far the largest city of Togo.

Lomé lies on the Atlantic coast in the southwestern corner of Togo. The metropolitan population was estimated at 750,000 in 1992, with an annual growth rate of roughly 6.5 percent since 1981, though population estimates vary widely.

Indigenous merchants founded Lomé in 1880. The town's founding families belong to Anlo, Mina, or "Brazilian" Ewe subgroups that historically traded with Europeans along the coast to the east or west, unlike the farmers and fishers of the region surrounding Lomé. The merchants chose the site, just outside the newly drawn border of the British Gold Coast (today Ghana), primarily to skirt British duties on goods imported for sale in the interior. The founding families have dominated Lomé down to the present day, and the city remains a commercial center and a transshipment point for the interior.

In 1882 German merchants began operations in Lomé, and Germany claimed Togo in 1884. The Germans chose Lomé as the colonial capital in 1897. With the completion of the colony's only dock for seagoing ships in 1904 and a railway network radiating from Lomé to the interior of Togo in the following years, Lomé drew business and Mina merchants away from the older port of Anécho. Many of these merchants were female, and Lomé's wealthy market women remain among the most powerful members of the city's economic elite.

After World War I (1914-1918), Lomé became the capital of French Togo. The city grew steadily and acquired an electrical grid and water supply. The characteristic pastel-colored architecture of central Lomé dates from this period. In 1933 French troops brutally repressed demonstrations against attempts to tax the city's market women. After World War II (1939-1945), an export boom drew migrants from throughout southern Togo and fueled rapid urban expansion that continued through the first two decades of independence.

During the sudden expansion of the phosphate trade in the late 1960s and 1970s, Lomé's population tripled, and export revenues funded the construction of a new central market hall (1967), the city's first modern port (1968, since repeatedly expanded), a university (1970), and a 3000-seat conference hall (1972), along with high-rise hotels, office buildings, and industrial facilities. Extremely low land prices have encouraged sprawl, but as a consequence, unlike most African cities, Lomé largely lacks segregated luxury quarters or slums. A lack of modern sanitation or effective building codes, however, has led to severe erosion and the pollution of the city's lagoon and water supply.

Gen. Gnassingbé Eyadéma gained power in 1963 by assassinating Sylvanus Olympio, a member of Lomé's commercial elite, and the city has been a center of opposition to his military rule. During the late 1960s and 1970s, prosperity and favorable policies won Eyadéma support among the powerful market women, but during the 1980s and early 1990s, government austerity sparked unrest on the streets of the city. More recently, booming transshipment trade with BURKINA FASO, NIGER, and MALI through the expanded port has contributed to an economic upturn. It remains to be seen whether prosperity will win Eyadéma renewed support among Lomé's merchants.

Mark O'Malley

SEE ALSO
Eyadéma, Gnassingbé.

Europe

London, Blacks in: An Interpretation

After three generations, being black has finally become a way of being British.

In the early 1970s I took a job at the London bureau of *Time*. Freshly arrived in town, I had set out on foot from Bayswater Road to the Time Life Building, on New Bond Street. Soon I was desperately lost and desperately trying not to show my desperation. It was that time of the morning when the only people who were on the street were people who worked on the street, and they all seemed to speak that alien tongue known as cockney. This was my first time in England, where I was to live for the next few years, but I might as well have been in Vladivostok: I couldn't understand a word they were saying. Finally, I saw a black face, and, out of habit, eagerly approached: at last, in this strange land, a *brother*. The man was cleaning the sidewalk outside of a men's clothier's, dousing the pavement with soapy water and sweeping it over the curb. Could he possibly tell me how to find New Bond Street, I asked him. The man stared at me quizzically – and when he opened his mouth, he sounded exactly like every other workman I'd encountered.

I was dumbstruck – it was as if the voice was the work of an unseen ventriloquist. Though I must have known better, I had, on some unreflective level, always assumed that my black compatriots *sounded* black because they *were* black: I'd assumed (I cringe to relate now) that the shape of our African lips had something to do with our characteristic consonants and vowels. Black comedians like Godfrey Cambridge could "do" a white voice – they delighted in it – but you didn't think they could really keep it up for very long. I spent the next weeks studying English blacks as they spoke, mesmerized by the sight of protuberant lips forming sounds – whether plummily R.P., or blurry and filled with glottal-stops – that were indistinguishable from those of their white counterparts. It took a while for the novelty to wear off. My initial travels through black London, then, were for me a succession of spit-takes: black people who sounded English without even trying.

What bliss it was to be black and living in London! How free you felt, even walking down the street, from the mundane prejudices of race-obsessed America: the reflexive, purse-clutching wariness you routinely encountered. Here was a country where the boundaries between the races were down. Or so, for a time, I could imagine. I eagerly sought out London's island immigrants: the Trinidadians in Ladbroke Grove; the Barbadians in Finsbury Park, Nottinghill Gate, and Shepherd's Bush; the Jamaicans (who then made up – as they continue to do – more than two-thirds of the West Indian population) concentrated in Brixton. As I soon learned, the history of Britain's West Indians – as a substantial presence, rather than the occasional anomaly – went back only to 1948, when a boatload of nearly 500 Jamaicans docked at Liverpool. Postwar England had a pressing need for manual labor, and the West Indians provided a convenient source. There had, of course, been people of African descent in England for centuries; the National Portrait Gallery currently has an exhibition devoted to IGNATIUS SANCHO, who corresponded with Sterne and was painted by Gainsborough; and long before Enoch Powell, Queen Elizabeth I demanded that all the blacks in England pick up and leave. But this was the first time they had established themselves as a genuine collective presence, in numbers that grew to 200,000 within a decade and a half. Black London – and it was in London that the great majority of them pooled – was born. The Jamaican poet LOUISE BENNETT called the process "colonization in reverse."

The presence of the black *gastarbeiter* inevitably caused a certain unease among the natives. You wanted to be good hosts, of course, but you were hard-pressed to know what to do when the guests forgot that they *were* guests. And that was the trouble with those postwar West Indians. You'd welcomed them into your home (*so* nice they could stop by), but now the hour was getting late. And though you'd turned up the lights, noisily switched on the Hoover, even asked if you could call them a cab – done everything you politely could – they still didn't get the message: *you can all go home now*. That's when the sense of panic began to rise.

The blacks arrived in a time of "overemployment," but as the 1960s wore on, so-called overemployment turned to underemployment, and a new and newly disaffected generation found itself out of luck and out of place. If many of them had no jobs, though, they had their folkways; and in the contest of cultures, bangers-and-mash finally wasn't any match for curry goat. That sense of cultural difference was itself the cause of further unease. Britain had always had its own internal ethnic clashes, but they were familiar and, for the most part unthreatening, the stuff of music-hall caricatures – "When Ah take a couple o' drinks on a Sa'day night, Glasgow belongs tae me!"

Gradually, my enthusiasm for the Afro-Saxon diaspora soured into frustration at its marginality and powerlessness. I'd arrived from a land where JAMES BROWN and JIMI HENDRIX – and Miles Davis and John Coltrane – ruled; where an entire generation, so it seemed, had with pen and brush taken up the task of self-representation. In London, the only cultural vitality seemed to come from forms that were borrowed, essentially unmodified, from the Caribbean. I would visit London's leading black bookstore, the New Beacon, and find that nearly everything on the shelves was from the West Indies or America. "How can they be English?" John La Rose, the poet and publisher who ran the store, used to say to me about his fellow expatriates. "Their entire culture is West Indian."

On Saturdays, the younger generation of Britain's recent immigrants would gather at some vacant house that had recently been "liberated" for the occasion, the electricity and gas reconnected for an evening's bacchanalia. It was called "goin' blues," and although the venue changed from week to week, you rarely had to ask where it was held: you could hear it half a block away, as the reggae thudded through the adjoining council housing. You paid your 20 pence at the door and entered into the sweltering, Caribbean heat. The floors trembled from the enormous bass loud-speakers. Upstairs, people queued for hot food and for Johnny Walker served in Coke cans. Everybody was smoking ganja; you could get high just from breathing. But what always struck me was how joyless it all seemed: nobody spoke or even laughed. Expressions were hard, affectless. The only white man I ever saw was the one distributing cocaine and ganja. "Him not white," an acquaintance told me, "him da *pusher* mon, dat all." Otherwise, the only words you'd hear spoken all night were in the injunctive mood: "Pass da ganja," and (if you accidentally brushed by someone in the crowded room) "Don't touch me, mon." Not jubilation but escape was the order of the night. And their language itself was another means of escape. *"Da rotted kayan"* were the police; *"da monkeys"* or *"da natives"* were the English; *"Babylon,"* with a pleasing semantic symmetry, could refer either to England or to JAMAICA. There was even a peculiar nomenclature for cognition: a Jamaican friend used to tell me, "Da monkey understands. But da black mon *over-stands.*" The one thing they all could overstand was that, no matter how many drinks on a Saturday night, London did not belong to them.

The Emergence of a Black British Culture

Twenty-five years later, a culture that is distinctively black and British can be said to be in full flower, both on the streets and in the galleries. "What we had before was the Afro-Caribbean presence in Britain," says Stuart Hall, a professor of sociology at the Open University, who is, among other things, black Britain's leading theorist of black Britain. "But the emergence of a black British culture can now be seen. For the first time, being black is a way of being British."

This development is partly a reflection of social engineering: in the aftermath of the riots that swept Brixton and other black neighborhoods in 1981, employment measures like Section 11 were adopted, accelerating the placement of blacks in public-sector jobs and helping to create something of a black middle class, however tiny. It's partly a reflection of the entrepreneurial ethos of Thatcherism itself. And it's partly a reflection of the liminal status of a new generation that was always looking both ahead and behind. "You know that if you go into a smart boutique on Oxford Street," Hall says, "one of the things you will find is a very smart, good-looking black woman. Blacks become objects of desire in curious ways, with some secret umbilical connection to what's cool or exotic or sexy, or to the body or to music – all the things that Puritan English culture both reviled and desired. They've turned marginality into a very creative art form – life form, really – and they've done so at the level of youth culture, of music, of dress. They've *styled* their way into British culture. Which isn't hard, of course – it's one of the most unstylish places in the world."

Among those who have styled their way into British culture is Ozwald Boateng, the first black tailor, he says, to hang out his own shingle on Savile Row, and, at 30, the youngest. His parents came from the Asante region in Ghana, and he has a West African's dark-chocolate skin, though at six feet three inches he's tall for a Ghanaian. More than Boateng's blackness, his brashness makes him an anomaly on the street: Slick Rick meets Paul Stuart. Even the shop's décor – the mustard-yellow walls, the purple carpet, the cerise velvet that drapes the freestanding dressing room – seems a deliberate affront to the staid establishments that surround it. But what makes him so subversive, sartorially speaking, is his conservatism. "Balance" is Boateng's rallying cry as a maker of men's suits, and I'm impressed, too, by his ability to strike a balance between bland assimilation and strident racial self-assertion. He tells me that he's "a big believer in being Asante," but he also declares, "I love the whole pompous cast of English tradition." He recounts an annual occasion when the tailors from Savile Row have a formal, sit-down dinner. "And all the Lords, and everyone – it's a men's club. Really a staunch British organization. And every so often there would be a toast to the Queen, so you'd stand up: 'The Queen, the Queen!' It's like totally fantastic." You sense in Boateng a deliciously camp devotion to the ways of little England: he finds them – well, fetching. And how, I inquire, did he dress at this congregation of the sartorial centurions, the last guardians of tradition? Did he wear gray flannel? Boateng appears to be aghast at the possibility. "Actually," he says, squaring his shoulders, "I wore a black velvet suit with a slight glitter in it."

To see what's new here, it helps to talk to someone who has succeeded under the terms of the older covenant, and can remind you that in the more rarefied circles of London society you're still unlikely to encounter a black face. The dress designer Bruce Oldfield, whose clients included the Princess of Wales, was adopted as a child by a white woman who lived in rural England. "I don't think I really saw black people en masse until I was about 21, when I came to London and lived in Brixton," he says. At any rate, the visible signs of Oldfield's Jamaican heritage are pretty discreet. "I have a great rapport with Arabs, because they think I'm an Arab," he tells me, with a low, mischievous chuckle. "Which is handy, because they've got a lot of money, and they like buying flashy frocks." These days, Oldfield has left Brixton far behind, and the London he inhabits is essentially color-free. "I mean, if I go into a trendy restaurant, like the Caprice or the Ivy, I don't see many black people," he says. "I just don't see black people where I go. I'm rarely in a house where there's another black person, socially." He speaks of all this matter-of-factly, and yet it's clear that he sees himself, finally, as an interloper in the circles he moves through. "English society is very compartmentalized," he says. "There are black people who cross over, obviously – there'll be an interior decorator, a designer, people like me." Yet there's all the difference in the world between thinking that you belong and thinking that you've crossed over. Oldfield doesn't quite manage a smile when he tells me, "I cross over because I'm amusing and witty and charming."

As you'd expect, a lot of the recent cultural ferment associated with black London happens much closer to street level. You feel that energy when you page through some of the black newspapers, like the weekly *Voice* (which claims to have 200,000 readers) and the more bourgeoisie *New Nation*. And you feel it even in the crudely satiric *Skank*, which is produced by and addressed to younger blacks. *Skank* has a less than reverential attitude toward black celebrities (devoting an entire page to the splayed nostrils of the Birmingham-based black boxer Chris Eubank, which it likens to King Kong's); and it spoofs such historic episodes of black resistance as the 1981 Brixton riots, by offering "the Brixton Riots '95 role playing game." ("Feel the tension as you try to light that petrol bomb! Feel your pulse race as you try to find a hiding place for that brand new 48 inch Dolby stereo, laser colour TV and video you happily found lying in Dixons!") Then, there was a scabrous cartoon sequence entitled "Lunch Box Christie," which focused on the runner Linford Christie's supposedly outsized endowment. (Christie sued the magazine, but only because the cartoon also implied that he took drugs to increase his athletic performance.)

Skank is published by the X Press, which is otherwise exclusively a book-publishing house. The press's founder, Dotun Adebayo, was born in Nigeria and came to Britain when he was six; his father taught physics at the University of London, though he has since retired and returned to Nigeria. The Adebayos are a textbook story of upward mobility: during one period, Dr. Adebayo had five children at university in England at the same time. Dotun Adebayo himself studied philosophy at the University of Essex; his brother Diran, a successful novelist, attended Oxford. Dotun Adebayo, like others of his generation, has a strong sense of mission – the familiar first-generation drive to fulfill the longings of the immigrant parents. "I drive a very old car, but it happens to be a Jaguar," he told me. "The reason I have it is my father, and his dream. He always wanted a Jaguar XJ-6. My father came back over to this country recently, and I didn't even tell him I had this car. I just told him I'd pick him up. He was so proud. He said, 'Ah, Dotun. When I lived in England, I always wanted this car.' It didn't matter that he'd spent thirty years here without achieving what he wanted to achieve – he had actually achieved it for the next generation. So that the onus is now on us to do something."

Adebayo's first big score as a book publisher was Victor Headley's *Yardie* – pulp fiction about Jamaican gangster life. "Basically, we postered the whole of Brixton," he recalls. "You woke up one morning and everywhere you looked in Brixton it said '*Yardie.*' Within a few weeks, we'd sold thousands and thousands of copies." The X Press has now published 51 titles, most by black British authors, and most delightfully lurid and action-packed. (The titles include *Rude Gal*, *Curvy Lovebox*, and *The Ragga and the Royal.*) The success of these books shows that there is a black reading public – though Adebayo would argue that black London is something that is in the process of being created. "You need to go outside London and see the other inner cities, and then you will realize there is a black London," he told me. "The black people in Manchester are Mancunians first, black people second. There's no link point over there. In the circles I move in – and I move in circles from ragamuffin kids to intellectuals, or what have you – there is definitely an urge to create a black London."

In the main, the black London that existed in the 1960s and 1970s was bound by what

Stuart Hall calls a "transistor culture" – by certain kinds of music and the radio stations that played them. Though blacks in Britain have always been known for the music they brought with them from the islands (like SKA and REGGAE and its rougher offspring, ragga), it is only relatively recently that these musical styles have evolved beyond their precursors. Today, the mores of the black British club scene have drifted far from those island moorings.

You can get a sense of just how far at Rampage, a movable feast held one recent Friday at the S.W.1. Club, near Victoria Station. By quarter past ten, there's already a line of young working-class blacks all the way down the block and around the corner. They queue relatively quietly, chatting in small groups. Inside the small foyer, everyone is halted for a serious security check, scanned by metal detectors and thoroughly patted down by bouncers with headsets. Then they pay their eight pounds cover charge and proceed up a flight of steps and into a large rectangular room. It is furnished sparely, with just a few tables and chairs – nowhere near enough to accommodate a crowd that will grow to a thousand or more by midnight, but by then everybody will be bumping and grinding to garage and house, hip hop, jungle, and even some rhythm and blues (R&B). At first, men face each other, dancing, but in postures that are menacing rather than erotic. It's as if they were shadowboxing to the heavy bass beat. Few couples dance together; instead the genders divide and watch each other, with the men engaged in active display. A man moves in and out of another man's space, mimicking and exaggerating the other's moves. Again, it's pretend sparring; occasionally a shoulder knocks a shoulder.

The hair stylist Daniel ("Er, I still use 'Daniel X,'" he says sheepishly, "but my friends tell me it's *such* a cliché") fluently explains the vitality of the popular-music scene to me. "I was really disturbed when I first heard Jungle, because they took some of my favorite reggae tunes and just speeded them up," he says. "The vocals sounded like Mickey Mouse. I was like 'That tune's sacred! How dare you play it at that speed?' They'd double the speed, sample stuff, then put a chant over it, like 'I'll kill your mother.' It took me a little while to come around." Now Daniel speaks of jungle music with the zeal of a convert. He distinguishes with scholastic precision between Jungle (the drum-and-bass kind of thing that has crossed over, to the point where musician David Bowie, in his fifties, has a couple of Jungle tracks on his new album) and *Jungle* Jungle, which remains hard-core and all black. But that's not the point. The point is that Daniel himself is about to put out a Jungle track in a couple of months, on his label, Ticking Time Records. Daniel sees a musical world rife with possibility; and should he fail there are multitudes behind him.

In no small measure, black culture simply is youth culture in London today. Bizarre as it first seems, speaking with a Jamaican inflection has become hip among working-class white kids. If blacks are only 1.6 percent of the population, the percentage of wiggers – white wannabes – seems considerably higher. It would be a mistake, though, to come to any hasty conclusions. Imitation and enmity have an uncanny ability to coexist. Paul Gilroy, a leading theorist of black British culture and a professor at Goldsmiths' College, at the University of London, tells me about white skinheads who beat up blacks and then go home and listen to the RAP group PUBLIC ENEMY. It's as if they can't decide whether they want to bash blacks or be blacks.

British Identity: The Contest Between Race and Class

And there you have the central contradictions of post-Thatcherite England: the growing cultural prominence of black culture there doesn't mean that racism itself has much abated. The police recently bugged the apartment of the young white thugs suspected of killing a 17-year-old black student, Stephen Lawrence, and found them hashing over various ways of killing blacks – even demonstrating the right moves with their kitchen knives. Just last week, a report by the Office for Public Management finds that the Royal Navy has "a level of awareness of cultural diversity which is 10 or 20 years behind that of society at large and which can reasonably be said to constitute institutional racism." The same investigation concluded that in the RAF, blacks were routinely excluded from honor guard or VIP details: "An unwritten rule summarised as 'no blacks, Pakis, spots or specs' governed basic assumptions about how things should 'really' or 'normally' be."

Nor are the better off necessarily better disposed. At a dinner party at a Suffolk manor house, a group of fairly well-to-do Englishmen discuss their hopes and fears for postelection Britain, while a fly-on-the-wall documentary-maker Paul Watson films the group he has convened. The guests – a sales director at a real estate company, a Lloyds insurance broker, a restaurant owner, and so forth – talk spiritedly about, inter alia, the disagreeableness of blacks. ("I would encourage the black minorities to move back to their country of origin," one says.) Controversy ensued when the documentary was shown on Channel 4, but the participants have few regrets: one of them, a baronet's son named Henry Erskine-Hill, says, "I would think our opinions are representative of the views of a great many people." Erskine-Hill was asked by a newspaper if he was a racist. "It depends what you mean by racism," he sagely replied.

What's clear is that British identity itself remains, as Stuart Hall would say, a contested space. A few years ago, Norman Beresford Tebbit, who was one of Margaret Thatcher's ministers and a onetime chairman of the Tory Party, complained that when Britain's cricket team played one of the West Indian teams, "our blacks" tended to root for the wrong side. How could they be truly British if they weren't rooting for the British team? And it's perfectly true that most black Brits fail the so-called Tebbit test; collective allegiances don't always align themselves altogether neatly. In Britain the challenge is to figure out a vocabulary for addressing the intersections of racial and national identities.

"The trouble is, all of our language on race and race relations has always been borrowed from the United States, and there are reasons why that's wrong," Trevor Phillips complains to me, in a crisp Oxford English with just the faintest lilt to it; he spent his childhood between Guyana and North London. "Effectively, Caribbean Americans behave in the United States as classical immigrants do and succeed as classical immigrants do – Koreans, say. Here, we behave like black Americans in Northern cities. Our experience is just the same as that of the blacks who migrated from the South to Chicago – all the way down to welfare dependency and so forth."

The statistics *are* pretty dire. The unemployment rate among Afro-Caribbeans is around 25 percent – and, in some parts of London, closer to 50 percent. The fraction that belongs to the professional class is only 2 percent. Despite the fact that Afro-Caribbeans make up only 1.2 percent of the population, moreover, a recent survey indicated that there may be as many as 61,000 racially motivated assaults against Afro-Caribbeans over the course of a year.

Phillips, a man whose velvety burnt-sienna skin is accented by copper-framed glasses, is the chairman of the Runnymede Trust, and is regarded by many black Brits as a leading cultural broker. As influential as he is at present, he is likely to become more so in the near future. For one thing, he's a friend of Tony Blair's and is said to be in line for a position of some importance. Rumor has him as the chairman of the London Arts Board – or even, once the city's council system of governance is overhauled, as mayor. The possibility of his being raised to a peerage has also been mentioned. Perhaps not surprisingly for such an insider, he doesn't see how separatist ideologies will ever prosper among English blacks.

"I think most black people in this country are embarrassed by the idea of being separate," he says. "Our neighbors don't come to lynch us, by and large. And, you know, we go out with their daughters, for Christ's sake." The saving grace of a class-bound society, after all, is that the right class credentials can often override other obstacles.

"The one thing that saves me on the street with the police," Dotun Adebayo tells me, "is they hear my accent and then they think, 'Hang on, this isn't your typical black bus driver or minicab driver,' and take you a bit more seriously." And class is distinguished more by the way you speak than by anything else. In fact, the most tangible racism you'll find here is from the working classes. They're the ones who are going to fight you on the street. Whereas with the middle classes it can be, 'Oh, gosh, you went to Oxford as well? Oh, jolly good.'" The novelist Caryl Phillips, who grew up between St. Kitts and England, where he studied at Cambridge, tidily describes the relationship between sociolelect and skin color: "In the States, until I open my mouth I look as if I fit in. In Britain, it's only when I open my mouth that I fit in."

That situation can lead to some cultural contortions. Yvonne Brewster, artistic director of the black theatre company Talawa and a recent O.B.E. ("for services in the arts"), tells me about what she dubs the "raffia ceiling." She says, "Lynford Christie will say to you, 'I cannot drive my Porsche.' The man is a millionaire, but he could get arrested for stealing the car. That's why someone like the boxer Chris Eubank dresses up like a kind of antediluvian English toff, with plus-fours and a monocle, so he is easily identifiable. You know, there's method to his madness. Even if they stop him with his Mercedes-Benz, they say, 'Ah, it's Chris Eubank, drive on.' In this country there's absolutely no chance of burning that raffia ceiling. If you put your head above the parapet you're likely to get it cut off."

For Yvonne Brewster, a member of Jamaica's "mulatto elite," there was never anything abstract about the vagaries of race and class in her new country. "My father had two farms, one in Portland and one in St. Thomas, and there was a man who used to do the horses in St. Thomas," she recalls. "He used to call me Miss Yvonne. Anyway, he came over here as a migrant, because there was no future for him in Jamaica and he didn't have any education. I was over here studying, and I was at Tottenham Court Road underground station and he saw me and came up and hugged and kissed me." That the laborer should have presumed on the solidarity of color and acquaintance horrified her, and, in her vulnerable state, she recoiled. "I suppose what flashed through my mind was that in Jamaica this man wouldn't even come within six feet of me," she says. "Anyway, I never saw the man again." She breaks off, and I notice that there are tears in her eyes.

Yet if the boundaries of class seem higher in England, those of race seem far more permeable. I'm always struck at the social ease between most blacks and whites in London streets. I was recently near the Brixton market, across the street from the entrance to its open-air section, and two men – tall, coal black, muscle-bound – came loping toward a small young white woman who was walking by herself in the opposite direction. What happened then was, well, nothing. The needle on the anxiety meter didn't so much as quiver. Throughout the area, blacks and whites seemed comfortable with one another in a way that most American urbanites simply aren't and never have been. "The advantage we have here in England is that you are more likely to be accepted for who you are," one black Londoner tells me. "People don't judge you as to who your partner is or who your friends are. I have this white girlfriend who lives in Brixton. We were going shopping in a market and I met some Lisson Grovers. They had never ever met me with a white woman. They took it really well. They were like, 'Yeah, O.K.'" Annie Stewart, the editor of the *Voice*, says, "I think something like 40 percent of our men have a relationship with a white woman. You find a second generation of blacks here who are more integrated than the first generation."

Some of this sense of belonging is simply a matter of racial dispersion. The labour minister of parliament (MP) Bernie Grant points out, "Even in my area, Tottenham, housing is dispersed among the various races – blacks are mixed with whites and Asians and Cypriots, and it's all one big cosmopolitan bundle." Americans who imagine Brixton to be analogous to Harlem are always surprised to see how large its white population is. London is where 70 percent of Britain's blacks reside, but its blackest neighborhoods are almost never more than two-thirds black, and usually they're substantially less.

All this sounds like a good thing, and yet blacks in London often speak enviously of the salience of race in America. "I love going to New York because I can walk down the street and the place is full of black people," says Ekow Eshun, who is the 28-year-old editor of *Arena* magazine – a sort of English *Details*. "A lot of the identity of the city is forged on the basis of that. The whole young black generation – the whole hip hop thing – is very, very alive in New York, and it has a marked effect on the character of the city." So part of the romance with America that you find in black Britain has to do with a sense that America has, racially speaking, a critical mass.

The allure of America isn't just that of indelible blackness. It's also the allure of class mobility. Of all the black Londoners I've spoken to, Trevor Phillips delivers the most impassioned homage to America, and it's in precisely these terms: "I think the thing about the West Indians in the United States is – and I know it's probably not fashionable to say this – but it's the openness of American society. There is, I think, genuine social mobility if you're ready for it." He's convinced of this because of his father's fortunes. His father left school at 13 and had never learned to write other than in block capitals; in England, he worked in the post office. Trevor remembers visiting his father at work one day, in a large sorting office largely manned by blacks. "They were all wearing Post Office uniforms, blue jackets with red piping, and then across the floor comes a white man wearing a suit, a gray suit, and my father simply said to me, 'That's one of the guv'nors,' meaning that it's one of the bosses. The way he said it signified two things: that no matter what I, George Phillips, do – no matter how much people respect me, no matter how well I know my job – I will never be one of them." Then his father came to New York, got a job as a security guard at Columbia University, and decided, for some reason, to go to night school and learn bookkeeping. "In a year, I think, he had become the treasurer of a little think tank in Columbia called the American Assembly. This guy goes to the United States, he gets some education at the age of 57, gets his qualification, and he ends his life signing Henry Kissinger's expenses for one of those think tanks." And Phillips is practically swelling in the recitation – there's a nearly evangelical fervor to his voice now – and he looks at me as if to say: How can you not love a country like that?

Like many other British blacks, it must be said, he has a slightly romantic view of black America. "The idea that my children could grow up in a place where all the kinds of rich people, the people who call the shots, who feel comfortable in their skins, are black. That's the greatest advantage I could give them." It's a seductive image, this land where blacks call the shots, and one I often hear yearningly invoked by black Brits. They'd disavow it, but I gradually begin to detect an implicit fantasy of black America as a Cotswald village populated by Oprah Winfrey, Bill Cosby, Michael Jordan, Terry McMillan, Spike Lee, Michael Jackson, Quincy Jones, Vernon Jordan, and dozens more of their ilk. ("Yo, Trev – I know this is kind of last minute, but Oprah, Quincy, Bill, and I were thinking about snagging a bite at Sylvia's and then maybe popping over to the Senate to try and talk some sense into them about the new education bill. Care to join us?") *That's* their American fantasy, and it seems unsporting to demur.

Black British Art

What's curious is that, while black Londoners look yearningly across the Atlantic, their American counterparts in the arts increasingly turn to them for inspiration. Thelma Golden, a curator of contemporary art at the Whitney Museum, is voluble on the subject of how much more vibrant – how much more advanced – the arts scene in London is compared to its New York counterpart. "In a way, I'd much rather be a black curator in London than in New York, because the excitement and sophistication there is extraordinary, way ahead of what's happening here in New York," she told me.

"Most thinking people don't know that there is a huge creative upsurge going on in the young black generation," Stuart Hall says. Hall was born and educated in Jamaica, came to England in 1951, as a Rhodes Scholar, and has watched three successive generations learn what it means to be black and British. But clearly the word is getting out, in part because of people like Hall himself. A soft-spoken man in his early sixties, with warm light-brown skin, a close-cropped gray beard, and a gentle manner, he is a tutelary figure for dozens of artists who constitute, in a free-form way, a postmodern black arts scene. He himself has played a central role in this development; indeed, for some he has nearly a guru-like status. "People are like, 'Tell us your stories, Obi Wan Kenobi,'" the black photographer David A. Bailey says. But Hall's characteristic tone is far from oracular. What he brings to London's postmodern black arts scene is really a set of emphases; for him, identities are things we make up, but not just out of any old thing. As he puts it, "Identities are the names we give to the different ways we are positioned by, and position ourselves in, the narratives of the past."

Today, Hall and his wife live in Mowbray House, a three-story yellow-brick Victorian situated in Kilburn. Hall's high-ceiling, book-lined study is on the second floor; on the way you pass by a patrician-looking portrait of his nearly white grandfather. Amid volumes by Jane Austen and Henry James are books with titles like *The Photographs of Rotimi Fani-Kayode* and *Race and the Education of Desire*. There's a poster for Isaac Julien's 1986 film *Looking for Langston* and another for the 50th anniversary staging of a C. L. R. James play, produced by Yvonne Brewster. Hall's movements are cautious, and he uses a cane to get around – he's in chronic pain – and yet he grows animated when he talks about the coalescence of a new artistic vanguard in black London, one that's devoted to reinventing the very idea of British identity.

He shows me some photographs of the late Rotimi Fani-Kayode, who settled in London from a prominent Yoruba family in Nigeria, and, Hall says, managed to use all the elements of his cultural heritage with "a kind of equal weight and yet at the same time to transform each by the presence of the other." Still, it isn't insignificant that Fani-Kayode's principal subject was the black body. "What's happened with the new generation is that they begin to acknowledge their own blackness," Hall argues. "They've begun to paint and photograph their own bodies. They can live with their own bodies – this is a very important turning point." This inward turn has meant leaving behind a "progressive" convention of the 1980s: using "black" to refer indifferently to all nonwhites, including South Asians. "People don't use 'black' in quite that way any longer, because they want to identify more precisely where they come from, culturally," Hall says. That moment of self-reflexivity plays out in all sorts of ways: Sonia Boyce's four-panel drawing "Lay Back, Keep Quiet, and Think of What Made Britain So Great" (1986) positions her own brown visage in a wallpaper pattern that was designed to mark the 50th year of Victoria's reign; filmmakers like Isaac Julien and John Akomfra produce visual meditations on memory and migration; multimedia artists like Keith Piper use computer-abetted installations to reflect on the politics of image. All these artists acknowledge their indebtedness to Hall, and yet for him the real significance of the new black arts scene is that it isn't, any longer, a black arts scene. "It's reached the point where a lot of artists who began by identifying themselves with ethnic minority groups have fought off the 'burden of representation' – the idea that they have to speak on behalf of their entire race. They're moving outward into engaging in a more culturally diverse mainstream. They're questioning and diversifying that mainstream."

Black British in Power

The challenge of questioning and diversifying the mainstream is something that Lord Taylor of Warwick knows intimately, and, as we sat in the Peer's Guest Room of the House of Lords, he told me about the contrasts between his own career and that of his father, Derief Taylor. His father was a champion cricket player from Jamaica who went on to play for Warwick; he was also a qualified accountant. When he retired from the playing field, however, he could only find work doing menial labor. "He was always striving to improve himself," Lord Taylor says, "and then he reached a kind of ceiling and began to sort of see his ambitions through me." Taylor, for his part, went on to become the first black to be head pupil at Mosely Grammar School, in Birmingham, and the first black to win the Gray's Inn Advocacy Prize, and – when the criminal evidence (amendment) bill is enacted – he will be the first black to create British law.

"Some tea, milord?" a florid-faced servant murmurs. Lord Taylor – England's only, though not its first, black Lord – graciously murmurs assent.

And yet the story of his ennoblement – he has enjoyed this salutation for less than six months – isn't an altogether edifying one. It seems that when the Tory Party put him up for a vacant seat in Cheltenham, vociferous protesters came from the party locals – retired colonels and other stalwarts, who had a hard time seeing themselves represented by the son of a Jamaican cricketeer and laborer. He was forced to stand aside. That episode embarrassed the National Party, and Prime Minister John Major sought to make the best of things by arranging for him to receive a peerage. "None of the parties have a good record on race, one has to be honest about that," Lord Taylor admits.

Ultimately, though, he believes that black Britain's destiny belongs to black Britain – something that does give him pause. "Trevor's right – I think the aspiration thing is part of Asian culture, but certainly is not part of the Afro-Caribbean culture here," he says. "If you read the Afro-Caribbean newspapers, week by week it tends to be gloom and doom – deaths in police custody, unemployment, some black person taking her company to the industrial tribunal because of being sacked or not getting the right job. And all that sort of thing. And we all identify with it. Just because we're professionals, we all identify with it."

As is true of so many of black London's illuminati, Lord Taylor has a corresponding fascination with the global preeminence of America's black superstars. "We have media and showbiz people who have made it, but they're few in number – no more than ten or eleven – and they don't have the global standing of their American counterparts," Lord Taylor says. He goes on to tell me that as a child in England he took inspiration from a magazine for American blacks. "Many of my positive black role models came from *Ebony* – people like Muhammad Ali, Martin Luther King, Jesse Jackson, Quincy Jones. You know, it was always the elitism, but that encouraged me, because I could see that there were and are successful black people. That was the sweet part of it. The sad part of it was they were all American. They were untouchable in that sense." Having long cherished a fantasy of appearing in *Ebony* himself, Lord Taylor says he was jubilant to learn recently that *Ebony* would be featuring him and his family in its May edition.

There are moments – for me, this was one – when an American visitor to black London feels caught in a time warp. Their numbers are small, their achievements still, somehow, measurable. "Just a few weeks ago," Lord Taylor recalls, "an editor at *Ebony* calls me and says, 'Lord Taylor, could you fax me a list of the 50 top black chairmen of companies in England?' I just fell about laughing, and he couldn't understand what the joke was, and I said, 'I can try to get you five,' because they just don't exist. The big companies do not have black directors. That's the whole point." Ekow Eshun says, "The frustrating thing about Britain is that the black presence in this country is decades behind America, especially in terms of high culture." I see what he means, and yet that isn't my reaction. So I'm left struggling to understand why black Britain seems to me at once 20 years behind the times and 20 years ahead, somehow both pre-and post-nationalist. No doubt both temporal impressions are illusory. Yet perhaps what is most heartening about black London is the hope it offers of a consciousness that is cultural rather than racial – that has the capacity to acknowledge difference without fetishizing it, the freedom to represent without having to be representative. In the unending Kulturkampf between irony and solidarity, irony seems to be ahead in black London, at least on points.

As Lord Taylor of Warwick could attest, many things have changed since the 1960s, when a Tory parliamentary candidate could triumph with the slogan "If you want a nigger neighbor, vote Labour." And many things haven't. "I'm also going into business," Lord Taylor had told me when we spoke. "I'm going to be a sort of corporate headhunter, joining one of the top firms in the world." He was girding himself for the challenge, which he discussed with Dale Carnegie gumption: "A lot of it will be networking – meeting the right people." Even after being raised to the peerage, he'd had more than his share of meeting the wrong people. He recalled an encounter with a woman at a formal cocktail party a few months ago. "So you're Lord Taylor," she said, studying him coolly. "I'll bet you do a good limbo." Today Taylor's entry in the latest edition of *Dod's Parliamentary Companion* appears directly above that of another life baron, one Norman Beresford Tebbit. Make of that what you will.

Henry Louis Gates, Jr.

See Also

Jungle (Drum and Bass); Brixton Riots of 1981; Coltrane, John William; Davis, Miles Dewey, III; *Ebony*; Jackson, Michael, and the Jackson Family; James, Cyril Lionel Richard; Jones, Quincy Delight, Jr.; Jordan, Michael Jeffrey; Jordan, Vernon Eulion, Jr.; King, Martin Luther, Jr.; Lee, Shelton Jackson ("Spike"); Rhythm and Blues; Winfrey, Oprah Gail; St. Kitts and Nevis; Jackson, Jesse, Jr.

Europe

London's Black Poor and the Sierra Leone Settlement Plan,

a disastrous British attempt in 1786 to settle some of London's poor blacks in Sierra Leone.

In 1786 white abolitionists, the British government, and blacks themselves designed a plan to settle a large number of London's poor blacks in Sierra Leone in Africa. Scholar Folarin Shyllon claims that both the plan and its collapse were demonstrations of English racism and oppression. Other experts argue that many motives – primarily humanitarian but also monetary – led the parties involved to join the scheme, and that they all contributed to its breakdown.

After the American Revolution, hundreds of black Loyalists flooded to the streets of London in hopes of gaining the freedom and the financial compensation they had been promised. The black Loyalists were American blacks who had served in the British military forces against the revolution or who, following the war, had responded to the British promise of manumission. They acquired their freedom, joining the approximately 10,000 free blacks already present in England, but compensation was harder to collect. Since blacks were banned from the learning of trades by a 1731 law, which prevented them from gainful employment, many turned to begging. Exacerbating the situation were the rapidly growing population and the industrial revolution, which forced many working-class people – both black and white – out of their jobs. This prompted whites to resent the presence of the black poor because of the economic competition they posed.

In this context Granville Sharp and other white abolitionists joined in an effort to help the blacks by creating in 1786 the Committee for the Relief of the Black Poor. The organization raised money for needy blacks, opened a hospital for the sick, and offered financial assistance for sending blacks home to the West Indies or Africa. However, the committee soon became monetarily overextended.

In May 1786 the committee and the English government, hard-pressed to cope with the situation, welcomed the recommendation of Henry Smeathman, an eccentric and ambitious businessman and botanist, to settle the black poor in Sierra Leone, an area previously explored by the British. Three years earlier Granville Sharp himself had written a memorandum outlining a plan to relocate the poor blacks to Africa. Sharp's intent was humanitarian; he imagined an ideal religious and political community of free blacks, which would attest to the "civilization" of Africa and blacks. Though just six months earlier Smeathman had rejected a proposal for a penal colony in Sierra Leone by claiming that the land and climate were not viable, he now wrote to the committee extolling the virtues of the area. He claimed that, for just £14 per person, the blacks could be carried to Sierra Leone and provisioned for three months. His plan outlined how, after establishing a community, these blacks could provide a base for trade in raw materials to Great Britain and thereby provide the British government with a profit. The government, abolitionists, and the blacks themselves were eager to make this proposal a reality.

Smeathman did not live to see his plan carried out; he died in July 1786. By this time the committee had come to realize that he had deceived them. They learned that the land in Sierra Leone was not suitable and blacks there would be in danger of falling prey to slavers. The committee suggested alternative projects, but the blacks who had already signed up for Sierra Leone did not want to change the planned destination and insisted on the original plan.

The scheme seemed doomed from the beginning. The departure date was set for October 1786, but because of administrative difficulties, many delays occurred. The blacks boarded a month late, in November, and only one-third of the expected 750 showed up. In order to get more blacks involved, the government decreed a Vagrancy Act, which made black beggars choose between Sierra Leone or jail. Some scholars claim that the government used the scheme to get rid of numerous undesirables. For example, the British put white prostitutes on board who were ostensibly the wives of the blacks.

The blacks who went on board were forced to remain there until the ships departed in February 1787. In the meantime, 50 people died from disease that had spread easily on the ships; those on board had not been provided with promised new, clean clothing because the money for it had been pocketed by corrupt officials. Olaudah Equiano, an educated African in London who was hired in November 1786 to be the commissary for supplies, reported this corruption; he was dismissed from his duties.

The convoy finally set sail in February, but one ship was damaged in a storm before even leaving the English Channel. While that ship was being repaired, the other two ships could do nothing but wait in Plymouth Bay, England, where at least 20 blacks decided against the venture and disembarked. Numerous blacks had backed out of the project even earlier, having taken their £14 and gone into hiding. When all the ships were finally able to depart in April, fewer than 500 people were on board, only about 350 of whom were black.

As a result of the delay in England, the ships landed in Sierra Leone on the eve of the rainy season. Agreements to buy and occupy the land were made with local chieftans. However, the settlers found the land unarable. They were also unable to put up proper housing. Within three months one-third had died from dysentery and fever; others had been captured by either local or European slave traders and sold into slavery, and still more had run away. By September only 130 were left. In March 1788 Granville Sharp sent another group of blacks to replenish the settlement, called Granville Town; 30 of the 60 new settlers made it to Sierra Leone and the community was revived for a time. But when the agreements made with local chiefs proved precarious, local Africans burned down Granville Town in December 1788, and the town's inhabitants scattered.

Sharp did not want to give up on the settlement; he wanted to prove that trade with Africa in goods and not in slaves could be profitable to Europeans, and he sought government funds to begin again. In 1790 he supported the creation of the Sierra Leone Company, which was incorporated by an Act of Parliament in 1791. Thomas Peters, a black Canadian, led the effort to resettle 1000 blacks from Nova Scotia to Sierra Leone in 1792. Sierra Leone became a British Crown Colony in 1808 and by 1811 the population of the settlement reached a respectable 2000 because of the emigration to Sierra Leone by freed slaves, maroon communities (escaped slaves from the Americas), and other Africans.

Leyla Keough

See Also

Transatlantic Slave Trade; Great Britain; Maroonage in the Americas.

Latin America and the Caribbean

López, Israel ("Cachao")

(b. September 14, 1918, Havana, Cuba), Afro-Latin jazz bassist renowned for his role in creating two popular musical styles, the mambo and the *descarga.*

Between the 1920s and the 1950s the Afro-Cuban bassist Israel López – who takes his nickname, "Cachao," from his grandfather's surname – was a key figure in Cuban jazz, most significant for his role in transforming the staid ballroom music known as *danzón* into the upbeat, wildly syncopated mambo. Of course, few stylistic developments in music can be attributed to a single individual or innovation. Afro-Cuban *tres* player Arsenio Rodríguez and Afro-Cuban bandleader Damaso Pérez Prado were also important in shaping the mambo, and during the 1950s Puerto Rican *timbalero* Tito Puente popularized the style among non-Latinos. But the musical innovations of Israel López were of central importance in the evolution of the mambo. After the Cuban Revolution, however, when López defected to the United States with his family, he discovered that there was no American audience for his music. After years of journeyman gigs, first at birthday parties and weddings and eventually at hotels and nightclubs, López regained widespread popularity in the 1990s.

López's Spanish forebears, all reportedly professional musicians, settled in Havana around the turn of the century. López revealed his own talents at an early age and secured his first paying gig when he was only eight years old, playing contrabass in a pit band that accompanied silent movies at a theater. He told *Washington Post* correspondent Gigi Anders that he had to take a wooden soapbox to the orchestra pit in order to reach the strings on his instrument. When Anders asked why he had chosen the bass, López replied, "Because it's the most important instrument... [t]he foundation.... An orchestra without a bass cannot speak.... "

By age 12 López was a bassist with the Havana Philharmonic, although he still required a soapbox to reach his instrument. At about the same time he and his younger brother, the cellist Orestes López, began playing in Havana nightclubs and dance halls. In 1937 the two joined flutist Antonio Arcano's las Maravillas (the Marvels). In short order, the two transformed the traditional danzón rhythm. By upping the tempo and making much greater use of syncopation, they played a key role in the creation of the mambo rhythm, which became popular not only in Cuba but worldwide.

In the late 1950s López helped achieve a second musical breakthrough when he combined Cuban music with the improvisational spontaneity of the American jam session. To his surprise, the new music, which became known as descarga (Spanish for discharge), won a large popular following. As he explained, "I thought, 'Nobody will like this.' It was a very explosive, spontaneous treatment. We were trying to advance our music... [but we were certain that] people would think we were loco."

Yet López has also been a significant conservator of Cuban musical traditions. "For me," he noted, "what counts most is the preservation of our roots, to have something... to pass on to the next generation." In 1990, two decades after his most recent recording session, he recorded an album that traced the history of Afro-Cuban music, from its origins in the danzón to the driving rhythms of modern Afro-Cuban jazz. The album, *Cachao: Master Sessions, Volume I* (1994), quickly ascended *Billboard*'s Latin and tropical jazz album charts.

In 1994 López was invited to open National Hispanic Heritage Month by performing on the steps of the Library of Congress. That year he was inducted into *Billboard* magazine's Latin Music Hall of Fame, and in 1995 he won a Grammy Award from the National Academy of Recording Arts and Sciences (NARAS) for *Cachao: Master Sessions, Volume I.* He was also the subject of the 1994 film documentary *Cachao: Como su ritmo no hay dos* (Cachao: Like His Rhythm There Is No Other), produced and directed by actor Andy Garcia. López continues to make his home in Miami, but his active musical career takes him to New York City and throughout much of the Caribbean – with the exception of his homeland, due to the continued political animosities between Cuba and the United States.

James Clyde Sellman

See Also

New York, New York; Pérez Prado, Dámaso; Puente, Ernesto Antonio (Tito); Puerto Rico; Dance in Latin America and the Caribbean.

North America

Lorde, Audre Geraldine,

(b. February 18, 1934, New York, N.Y.; d. November 17, 1992, St. Croix, Virgin Islands), African American poet, essayist, and feminist who is known for works that intertwine the personal and the political.

Audre Geraldine Lorde, the youngest daughter of Frederic Byron and Linda Bellmar Lorde, was born in Harlem and grew up in Brooklyn. Her understanding of herself as an outsider developed early, as her parents, who had immigrated from Grenada and planned to return until the Depression destroyed that hope, never accepted New York as home. Lorde herself always felt displaced both in her parents' strict household and at school. After high school, she attended Hunter College from 1954 to 1959. Lorde's self-identification as a poet and a lesbian was affirmed during this time, when she spent a year as a student at the National University in Mexico. Upon her return to New York, she became involved with the Harlem Writer's Guild and, more actively, with "gay-girl" culture in Greenwich Village.

Lorde received a B.A. from Hunter College in 1959 and a master of library science from Columbia University a year later. During the 1960s she worked as a librarian, becoming the head librarian at the Town School Library from 1966 to 1968. Lorde married Edward Ashley Rollins and had two children, Elizabeth and Jonathan. Although she revealed little about her marriage, which ended in divorce in 1970, she made motherhood one of the great themes of her writing.

In 1968 Lorde was awarded a grant from the National Endowment for the Arts and published her first book of poetry, *The First Cities.* For six weeks that spring, she served as poet-in-residence at Tougaloo College in Mississippi. Despite the brevity of her stay at the historically black college, Lorde credited this period with defining the rest of her career. She wrote most of the poems for *Cables to Rage* (1970) at Tougaloo, discovered her love of teaching, found a black community that accepted her, and met the woman who would become her long-term partner.

Lorde again returned to New York to write and teach. She offered courses on poetry at City College and on racism at Lehman College and John Jay College. In 1973 *From a Land Where Other People Live* was nominated for a National Book Award for poetry. Next came the more expressly political *New York Head Shop and Museum* (1974). *Coal* (1976), which was published by W. W. Norton, brought Lorde a broader readership and also marked the beginning of a long association with white poet Adrienne Rich. Lorde explored the relationship between African mythology and the experiences of the black diaspora in *The Black Unicorn* (1978), widely held to be the masterpiece of her career. Two more books of poetry, *Chosen Poems, Old and New* (1982) and *Our Dead Behind Us* (1986), followed.

Like her poetry, Lorde's prose intertwined social criticism with personal revelation. *The Cancer Journals* (1980) detailed her terrors during treatment for breast cancer. Her childhood and early adulthood were the subject of a "biomythography" titled *Zami: A New Spelling of My Name* (1982). *Sister Outsider: Essays and Speeches* (1984) established Lorde as an important feminist theorist. Her continuing struggle with cancer and decision to forgo invasive treatments were chronicled in her last book, *A Burst of Light* (1988). After Lorde died of cancer in 1992, her life and work were celebrated at the Cathedral of St. John the Divine in New York City.

"As a forty-nine-year-old black lesbian feminist socialist mother of two, including one boy, and a member of an interracial couple," Audre Lorde said, "I usually find myself a part of some group defined as other, deviant, inferior, or just plain wrong." Through poetry, prose, and speeches, Lorde devoted her career to celebrating all of the elements of her identity and to offering very personal protests against racial and sexual oppression.

Lawrie Balfour

See Also

Literature, African American; Great Depression; Harlem Writers Guild; Harlem, New York; New York, New York.

Africa

Loroupe, Tegla (b. 1973, near Kapenguria, Kenya), Kenyan long-distance runner.

When Tegla Loroupe emerged from the pack to finish first in the New York City Marathon in 1994, she was the first black African woman to have won a major marathon anywhere in the world. Because she came from Kenya, a country that was renowned for its male marathoners – and, according to Loroupe and others, a country renowned for its patronizing view of women as athletes or professionals – her victory was all the sweeter.

Now a hero to many Kenyan women and girls, Loroupe grew up with six brothers and sisters on her parents' farm near the Uganda border. She learned to run in the ways that many Kenyan children do – by having to travel six miles each way to school daily and by helping herd her family's cattle. A member of the Potok ethnic group, Loroupe has been described by the American press as feeling somewhat discriminated against by Kenya's running establishment, which is dominated by ethnic Nandis.

In 1992 Loroupe began spending part of the year training in Germany with her new coach. In 1993 she entered and won the Advil Mini-Marathon in New York City, a 10-km race. The next year she ran in the New York Marathon, her first attempt at a complete marathon. Surprising nearly everyone, Loroupe burst from her position well behind the leaders to run a fast second half, finishing with a winning time of 2 hours, 27 minutes, and 37 seconds. Her second win in New York, in 1995, came just two weeks after the death of her older sister, who had helped raise her. This was a poignant victory that endeared Loroupe to the city, which she now calls "my second home." Back home in Kapenguria, she received a hero's welcome, including a parade, with gifts of land, cattle, and sheep. She has won the praise of Kenya's women, one of whom told Loroupe that she has "made women in Kenya proud."

Kate Tuttle

See Also

Kenya; New York, New York.

North America

Los Angeles, California, an American city of both promise and frustration for the waves of black immigrants who came looking for work.

People of African descent formed a majority among those who founded the riverside outpost El Pueblo de Nuestra Señora La Reina de Los Angeles in 1781. Twenty-six "negroes and mulattos [of African and European descent]," sixteen Native Americans, and two Spaniards settled an area that held, 200 years later, the fastest growing urban population in the United States. The history of Los Angeles entails themes of rapid change as well as racial diversity, and the interweaving of these themes has made the city a fickle haven for blacks. The City of Angels continues to be a bittersweet refuge, a place where the prevalence of disillusionment matches the persistence of hope.

The Spanish founded Los Angeles as an outpost, and for 80 years it remained a predominantly Mexican town. Neither Mexico's break from Spain nor the United States' conquest of California much disturbed life in a place as far afield as El Pueblo. Throughout the eras of Spanish (1781-1821) and Mexican (1821-1848) rule, men of African descent participated in the governing of the town and were treated as social equals by Mexicans and whites.

Once under United States jurisdiction, Los Angeles attracted increasing numbers of fugitive slaves. With a population of only 1250 in 1840, the town promised isolation and obscurity. The California Gold Rush of 1848-1849 (centered on San Francisco and Oakland, California) left Los Angeles untouched, so during the 1850s and 1860s its seclusion continued to attract runaway slaves. The financial success of fugitive Biddy Mason contributed to the town's good reputation among blacks. Mason, who accumulated wealth from real estate ventures, invested her fortune in community organizations for African Americans.

Aboard America's new railroads, black porters spread news of the merits of Los Angeles to other parts of the country. By the time of the Los Angeles housing boom, in the late 1880s, African Americans were arriving in Los Angeles at a steady rate. In 1887 the black publisher of the *California Eagle*, John J. Niemore, bolstered immigration by imploring Southern sharecroppers to come to the flourishing town. Between 1870 and 1910 the number of blacks grew from 100 to 7500, but the white population grew even faster, so the overall percentage of blacks became lower. Nevertheless, the black community comprised enough people to disturb local whites. As the African American population grew, so did the discrimination against them.

The ethnic makeup of Los Angeles, however, comprised more than black and white. With its Mexican origins and relative proximity to Asia, Los Angeles hosted large Hispanic, Japanese, and Chinese American populations – groups that often bore the brunt of a hatred felt solely by blacks in other cities. Sometimes nonwhites united against oppression, but often prejudice and competition left the groups at odds with one another. The complicated racial calculus that developed at the turn of the twentieth century still characterizes Los Angeles today.

In spite of mounting racial tensions, the years between 1900 and 1920 represented a golden age for blacks in Los Angeles. Thirty-six percent of the African American population owned private homes, compared with only 11 percent in New Orleans and less than 3 percent in New York City. After 1900 small black-owned businesses appeared along Central Avenue in downtown Los Angeles, and the population exploded from 936,000 in 1920 to 2,208,000 in 1930.

In 1903 a group of blacks, led by the investor, promoter, and businessman Theodore Troy, established the Los Angeles Forum, an organization intended to direct community growth and help black immigrants adjust. Many of the forum's members had arrived as immigrants themselves, late in the 1880s. The older generation feared that the newcomers might tarnish the image of an already marginal black community and made efforts to curb uncouth behavior. The forum preached a doctrine of respectability and assimilation, emulating the philosophical stance of Booker T. Washington. Members oversaw police raids on "dens of vice," trained newcomers in the conduct that maximized white tolerance, and tried to forestall the growth of the ghetto that had formed around the Central Avenue Hotel.

Despite the efforts of the forum, white discrimination abounded by the end of the World War I. After 1917 housing "covenants" – ordinances that mandated segregation – squeezed most African Americans out of white neighborhoods, while the Ku Klux Klan harassed any who remained.

Although blacks inhabited a number of Los Angeles neighborhoods at the turn of the century, whites soon pressed them into the Central Avenue ghetto. By 1930 approximately 70 percent of black residents inhabited the overcrowded neighborhood of South Central Los Angeles. Exclusion from swimming pools, parks, restaurants, and theaters compounded the discomfort of the ghetto. Furthermore, whites denied black people clerical, white-collar, and industrial jobs, leaving domestic and personal service as the main employment opportunities.

The Central Avenue strip, however, embraced culture alongside scarcity. During the 1930s and 1940s nightlife so flourished that some looked to the neighborhood as a second Harlem. The tenor saxophonist Dexter Gordon began his career in the Central Avenue nightclubs; Nat "King" Cole and

Duke Ellington often played in them. Church congregations swelled, restaurants opened, businesses proliferated. Even in the sphere of politics, some African Americans benefited from the consolidation of the black population, obtaining strong support from the sheer number of black voters in the district. The Republican Frederick Roberts served in the state assembly from 1919 to 1933; the Democrat Augustus Hawkins, whose tenure lasted until 1962, replaced him.

World War II opened numerous industrial jobs to African Americans. The black community fared better than the Chinese and Japanese Americans, who suffered wartime prejudice because of Japan's Axis affiliations. Franklin Delano Roosevelt's liberal legislation also helped blacks. The president established the Fair Employment Practices Committee to root out the discriminatory hiring policies of military contractors, and although the commission was titular and weak, its federal endorsement encouraged many African Americans. Taking the president's lead, groups organized and fought for themselves.

The self-ordered attack on discrimination fostered cooperation between blacks and Mexican Americans, and the Zoot Suit Riots of 1943 strengthened the alliance. When white American soldiers and sailors attacked African and Mexican American youth who wore the loose-fitting and colorful fashion of the time, the ethnic communities united in self-defense. Black and Mexican leaders founded a multiracial coalition that included newly formed special-interest groups as well as the National Association for the Advancement of Colored People (NAACP) and the National Urban League. The coalition remained strong for a number of years, curbing zoot-suit violence, protesting job discrimination, and, after the war, aiding Japanese Americans as they relocated from concentration camps. Like many other socially progressive organizations, however, the coalition faltered during the Red Scare of the late 1940s and early 1950s.

Despite the relative abundance of industrial jobs during the war, most blacks were still working as domestic and personal servants in 1950. After the war whites reclaimed the dwindling opportunities in industry. Nevertheless, African Americans continued to emigrate from other regions of the United States, increasing the black population by 450,000 between 1950 and 1960. Widespread unemployment, overcrowded ghettoes, and worsening police brutality accompanied this growth in population. In 1965 the Los Angeles Watts Riot erupted from the combination of these factors, demonstrating just how volatile South Central Los Angeles had become. While the larger, denser ghetto was conducive to violence, however, it simultaneously enabled black politicians to climb further up the local political ladder. In 1963 a retired police officer, Thomas Bradley, won a seat on the City Council.

During the Civil Rights Movement the black community fought for equal opportunity housing with some success. In 1968 the Open Housing Act obviated the exclusive housing "covenants" that had hitherto enforced residential segregation. But as the Open Housing Act enabled middle-class blacks to escape from the ghetto, it deprived the ghetto of many exemplary citizens. Community leaders – who in an earlier day would have led antidiscrimination groups – now moved to the suburbs. The class rift became even more apparent as black performers like Eddie Murphy, Bill Cosby, and Michael Jackson gained national and international fame in the 1980s.

Although such entertainers failed to facilitate the amelioration of ghetto conditions, black politicians abounded. Thomas Bradley continued to navigate the channels of power in Los Angeles, becoming mayor in 1973. He fought to improve conditions along Central Avenue and to eliminate racial discrimination in municipal jobs. He also campaigned against police brutality but met with less luck, and the worsening conditions of the 1970s seemed beyond his control. Unemployment for African Americans rose to 40 percent by 1980; acquired immune deficiency syndrome (AIDS) took hold; and drug abuse skyrocketed.

Grim and violent conditions in Los Angeles became the subject of new forms of film and music in the mid- and late 1980s. A film by director John Singleton, *Boyz N the Hood,* portrayed the brutality of life in South Central Los Angeles and was nominated for an Oscar. The music of rappers like NWA and Ice Cube offered similar glimpses and received comparable praise. Though written about the ghetto and for the ghetto, the music and films attracted national interest.

LEFT: A family relaxes in Los Angeles, home to more than one million African Americans. *Alex Pitt/Walkabout Pictures*

ABOVE: Immigrant builder Simon Rodia began the four Watts Towers in 1921. The towers are decorated with 70,000 mussel shells, as well as fragments of glass, mirror, and tile. *CORBIS/Robert Holmes*

The Los Angeles Riot of 1992 showed that conditions in South Central had continued to decay. An instance of unpunished police brutality – similar to that which had sparked the Watts Riot – reflected the unhealthy stasis of the past 30 years. Following the acquittal of four officers accused of extreme violence against an African American citizen, Rodney King, rioters destroyed lives, jobs, and blocks and blocks of South Central businesses. Unlike the rioters of the 1960s, whose violent acts were tempered with political savvy, the 1992 participants looted indiscriminately and laid waste their own neighborhood.

Black rioters targeted innocent Korean store owners, looting their stores and startling the nation into an awareness of Los Angeles' pathological condition.

In 1913, before a large crowd in Los Angeles' Temple Auditorium, W. E. B. Du Bois had proclaimed that "[o]ut here in this matchless Southern California there would seem to be no limit to your opportunities, your possibilities." In 1965 a participant in the Watts riot replied, "Everywhere they say 'go to California! California's the great pot o' gold at the end of the rainbow.' Well, now we're here in California, and there ain't no place else to go, and the only pot I seen's the kind they peddle at Sixtieth and Avalon." African Americans in Los Angeles have witnessed the validity of both these observations at every stage of the city's growth. The city's history comprises dreams, and dreams deferred.

Eric Bennett

See Also

AIDS in the United States; World War I and African Americans; World War II and African Americans; American Indians; Bradley, Thomas (Tom); Cole, Nat ("King"); Du Bois, William Edward Burghardt (W. E. B.); Gordon, Dexter Keith; Harlem, New York; Jackson, Michael, and the Jackson Family; Los Angeles Watts Riot of 1965; Mason, Biddy Bridget; Niggaz with Attitude; New Orleans, Louisiana; New York, New York; Washington, Booker Taliaferro; Ellington, Edward Kennedy ("Duke").

Men try to salvage what they can from a South Central Los Angeles building burned during the 1992 riots. *CORBIS/Joseph Sohm; ChromoSohm Inc.*

North America

Los Angeles Riot of 1992, one of the first major urban insurrections since the 1960s. This riot shocked many suburban Americans who had come to believe that the days of explosive racial tensions were behind them.

Like the Los Angeles Watts Riot of 1965, the 1992 rioting was sparked by an act of antiblack police brutality. On March 3, 1991, Los Angeles police officers stopped a car driven by a 34-year-old African American named Rodney King, who, they said, was speeding. According to the officers, King emerged from his automobile in an aggressive manner that suggested he might have been high on drugs. Before handcuffing King, the police delivered some 56 blows and kicks and a number of shocks from a stun-gun to the fallen body of the suspect. A bystander captured the beating on videotape, and within two days the footage was being broadcast all over national television.

King brought charges of brutality against four of the policemen, and the officers, who claimed they had acted in self-defense, were tried before a predominantly white jury in a white middle-class suburb of Los Angeles. On April 29, 1992, all four men were acquitted. Within two and a half hours of the verdict, a crowd of furious protesters had gathered at the corner of Florence and Normandie streets in South Central Los Angeles, and through the next day and night the rioting exploded across 130 sq km (50 sq mi) of South Central. At the same time, smaller disturbances were erupting in San Francisco, Seattle, Atlanta, Pittsburgh, and other cities.

President George Bush called in 4500 United States Army troops to quell the rioting, which ended on Friday, May 1. In three days of turbulence more than 50 people were killed, almost 400 injured, and about 17,000 arrested. The city incurred an estimated $1 billion worth of damage.

Unlike the race riots of the 1960s, the 1992 uprising resulted in considerable black-on-black violence as well as the looting of many black-owned shops. Korean shopkeepers were also prime targets of the rioters' rage, as one minority community attacked another. Writing about the riot in a 1992 essay, "Learning to Talk of Race," the philosopher Cornel West suggested that "what we witnessed in Los Angeles was the consequence of a lethal linkage of economic decline, cultural decay, and political lethargy in American life. Race was the visible catalyst, not the underlying cause." In a 1992 interview with the *CovertAction* Information Bulletin, labor historian Mike Davis offered a similar opinion, calling the riot "a hybrid social revolt with three major dimensions. It was a revolutionary democratic protest characteristic of African-American history when demands for equal rights have been thwarted by the major institutions. It was also a major postmodern bread riot – an uprising of not just poor people but particularly of those strata of poor in southern California who've been most savagely affected by the recession [of the early 1990s]. Thirdly it was an interethnic conflict – particularly the systematic destroying and uprooting of Korean stores in the Black community." The 1992 riot represented a rude awakening for many Americans who had assumed that after two relatively quiet decades, the days of large-scale urban race riots had been put behind them.

Eric Bennett

See Also

Atlanta, Georgia; Pittsburgh, Pennsylvania; San Francisco and Oakland, California; Seattle, Washington.

North America

Los Angeles Watts Riot of 1965, the first major racially fueled rebellion of the 1960s, an event that foreshadowed the widespread urban violence of the latter half of the decade.

With the arrest of a 21-year-old African American, Los Angeles' South Central neighborhood of Watts erupted into violence. On August 11, 1965, a Los Angeles police officer flagged down motorist Marquette Frye, whom he suspected of being intoxicated. When a crowd of onlookers began to taunt the policeman, a second officer was called in. According to eyewitness accounts, the second officer struck crowd members with his baton, and news of the act of police brutality soon spread throughout the neighborhood. The incident, combined with escalating racial tensions, overcrowding in the neighborhood, and a summer heat wave, sparked violence on a massive scale. Despite attempts the following day aimed at quelling anti-police sentiment, residents began looting and burning local stores. In the rioting, which lasted five days, more than 34 people died, at least 1000 were wounded, and an estimated $200 million in property was destroyed. An estimated 35,000 African Americans took part in the riot, which required 16,000 National Guardsmen, county deputies, and city police to put down.

Although city officials initially blamed outside agitators for the insurrection, sub-

There were "civil disturbances" in more than 40 cities in each of the summers of 1966 and 1977 and in 125 cities after the assassination of Rev. Martin Luther King Jr., on April 4, 1968.

sequent studies showed that most of the participants had lived in Watts all their lives. These studies also found that the protesters' anger was directed primarily at white shopkeepers in the neighborhood and at members of the all-white Los Angeles police force. The rioters left black churches, libraries, businesses, and private homes virtually untouched.

The Watts Riot was the first major lesson for the American public on the tinderbox volatility of segregated inner-city neighborhoods. The riot provided a sobering preview of the violent urban uprisings of the late 1960s and helped define several hard-core political camps: militant blacks applauded the spectacle of rage; moderates lamented the riot's senselessness and self-destructiveness; and conservative whites viewed the uprising as a symptom of the aggressive pace of civil rights legislation.

The Watts Riot changed California's political landscape and damaged a number of political careers, including that of Governer Edmund G. "Pat" Brown. The liberal Brown lost his office to challenger Ronald Reagan, in part because Reagan was able to pin the blame on the incumbent for the riot.

Eric Bennett

See Also

Los Angeles, California.

Watts residents make their way through rubble in the aftermath of the 1965 riots. *Archive Photos*

North America

Louis, Joe (b. May 13, 1914, Chambers County, Ala.; d. April 12, 1981, Las Vegas, Nev.), one of the greatest boxers in modern history, widely viewed by white Americans as a symbol of racial harmony and by black Americans as a symbol of black triumph in a racist society.

Joseph Louis Barrow was born on a sharecropper's farm near Lafayette, Alabama, the seventh of eight children. His father, Munroe Barrow, was committed to a psychiatric hospital soon after Louis's birth. The family was told a short while later that Munroe had died, but in fact he lived for two more decades. Lillie Barrow remarried another farmer, and when Louis was ten the family followed the Great Migration north to Detroit, where his stepfather found work. Because of Louis's poor schooling in the South, he attended school in Detroit with students much younger than himself. He was reportedly humiliated by the experience and developed a stammer. Later he attended a trade school to study carpentry, but his real interest lay in BOXING. He spent hours watching boxers spar at a local gym, and after leaving school at age 17, he began training on his own.

Louis lost his first amateur bout but racked up an impressive string of victories over the next three years. They included more than 40 knockouts and only a handful of losses. In 1934 he won a national amateur title in the light heavyweight division, then opted for professional boxing. John Roxborough and Julian Black, two African American businessmen who were also involved in illegal gambling and running numbers, agreed to manage Louis. They encouraged him to drop Barrow from his name, thereby making it easier to remember. They also hired Jack Blackburn, a former lightweight fighter and well-regarded trainer. Discovering that Louis had little foot speed, Blackburn encouraged him to use a flat-footed shuffle. The shuffle and Louis's compact punches, became his signature traits.

Roxborough and Black were also keenly aware of how much the white public hated the first African American heavyweight champion, Jack Johnson. Johnson, who reigned from 1908 to 1915, offended whites by gloating over his defeated (often white) opponents and by having relationships with white women. Louis's managers counseled him to be a gentleman in the ring and shy with the press; he was also to avoid drinking, smoking, and being seen alone with white women in public. Publicly, Louis followed this advice, and whites, who nicknamed him the Brown Bomber, widely championed his modesty and dignity. Even white Southerners hailed him as a nonthreatening black man. Privately, although Louis neither drank nor smoked, he enjoyed an active nightlife as well as discreet romances with both black and white women.

Louis's professional career was nothing short of brilliant. In his first year he won more than 20 fights without a loss, typically with white opponents. His many knockout victims included former heavyweight champions Primo Carnera and Max Baer in 1935. Boxing was the only major sport that then allowed blacks to compete against whites, and many African Americans lived vicariously through Louis's punishing blows to whites. After a victory by Louis, entire black neighborhoods were known to burst into spontaneous celebration.

On June 19, 1936, Louis met the German fighter Max Schmeling, a former world champion, in New York's Yankee Stadium. At the time Adolf Hitler's fascism was encroaching on Europe, and the press seized on the fight to portray Schmeling as a representative of authoritarianism and Louis as a symbol of democracy. To a lesser degree, Louis was also touted as a symbol of racial harmony and of the possibilities of upward mobility in America. In the 12th round, Schmeling knocked out the heavily favored Louis, dealing him his first professional defeat. Hitler cited Schmeling's victory as proof of the superiority of the Aryan race.

His popularity reduced, Louis rebounded to seven straight victories and the right to fight heavyweight champion James Braddock on June 22, 1937, in Chicago's Comiskey Park. Braddock knocked Louis to the ground early in the fight, but Louis recovered and in the eighth round sent Braddock to the canvas with a sharp punch. Louis, only 23 years old, became heavyweight champion of the world. The fight was followed, one year to the day later, with a rematch against Schmeling. With the possibility of a European war looming, the second Louis-Schmeling fight took on even more significance than the first. In the first round Louis scored a stunning knockout, making him one of the most popular athletes in America and, indeed, much of the world.

By the early 1940s, however, Louis was deeply in debt as a result of poor investments, gross financial mismanagement by his handlers, a habit of giving money away freely, and high living. To pay his creditors, he accepted a challenge to his title every month for most of 1940 and 1941, a number of contests unheard of among boxing champions. Many of the contenders posed Louis little challenge, prompting reporters to call the fights the Bum of the Month Club. The matches, however, were not all easy; Billy Conn, for one, all but destroyed the champ before Louis mustered an incredible last-round knockout.

In 1942, with World War II under way, Louis entered the United States Army and boxed in nearly 100 exhibition matches for troops. Although to that point he had rarely taken political positions, he now protested racial segregation in the armed services and refused to sit on segregated military buses. After the war he resumed his professional career. In a 1947 fight Jersey Joe Walcott knocked him down twice, but Louis won a victory in a controversial split decision. Louis settled the controversy in a rematch by knocking out Walcott.

In 1949, a few months before turning 35, Louis retired with only the loss to Schmeling on his record. His finances, however, were in even worse shape than before, and in 1950 he returned to the ring. He compiled several victories but lost twice, once to heavyweight champion Ezzard Charles and, in a knockout on October 26, 1951, to Rocky Marciano. After the Marciano fight, Louis retired for good. His final record was 68 wins, 54 by knockout, and 3 losses.

Louis's personal life was in shambles. He was divorced three times before marrying Martha Jefferson in 1959. Overwhelmed by his debts, he tried professional wrestling, then established an unsuccessful chain of fast-food restaurants before entering a deal with alleged Mafiosi to promote boxing. He would later admit that he used cocaine in the late 1960s, and in 1970 he was committed to a psychiatric hospital after suffering paranoid delusions. In his final years he worked in Las Vegas as a greeter and companion to wealthy guests. Despite his failings, Joe Louis remained one of America's most loved sports heroes.

See Also

World War II and African Americans; Military, Blacks in the American; Detroit, Michigan; Great Migration, The; Johnson, John Arthur (Jack).

North America

Louisville, Kentucky,

an American city to which black Kentuckians gravitated after the Civil War, hoping to escape lynch mobs and white vigilante violence. Louisville blacks overcame many of the resulting urban problems – overcrowding and economic discrimination – by starting strong private schools.

From its founding in 1778 until the civil rights advances of the late twentieth century, Louisville provided safety and security for African Americans, but only in comparison to the rest of Kentucky. In the antebellum period the slaves of Louisville, who worked as stevedores, draymen, factory workers, and domestics, suffered relatively less than their counterparts on plantations. After the Civil War many rural blacks opted to weather Reconstruction under the protection of a larger population. During the late nineteenth century vigilante whites rampaged through the Kentucky countryside, burning black homes, hanging freed blacks, and driving the fearful to the city.

The merits of Louisville were limited for African Americans. While town whites murdered blacks less often, they discriminated on all fronts – education, employment, housing, and civil rights. The only mitigating factor was the strength of the black community. A tenacious lineage of African American leaders arose to protest inequalities, starting with Henry Fitzbutler, who fought Jim Crow laws in the 1870s and 1880s, and including journalist Frank Stanley Sr. and politician Charles W. Anderson, both of whom protested segregation in the 1920s. A deep rift within the black community, however, between accommodationists and black nationalists, recurred in successive generations of black leaders, reflecting the extraordinary passion of – and the extraordinary challenges before – activists in Kentucky.

Despite extreme and often violent white opposition, Louisville blacks made large strides toward equality through education. Enduring segregation, lack of resources, and even the torches and clubs of whites, Louisville's blacks made school a priority. During Reconstruction the Freedmen's Bureau founded numerous private schools for blacks, since white leaders skimped on black education. Through these efforts African Americans often matched the public programs of whites; in 1869, and then again in 1907, a greater proportion of blacks than whites attended classes.

While white people in the 1950s and 1960s staunchly resisted school desegregation, a busing mandate in 1975 heralded full integration for Louisville schools. After a long history of white dissent and trouble making, the outcome of the mandate was surprisingly mild. As historians Lowell H. Harrison and James C. Klotter write: "Increasingly, whites who had decried integration would find themselves cheering the sporting accomplishments of a black high school or college player on their favorite team." In the 1980s and 1990s traces of discrimination remained in Louisville, but athletic stereotyping had superseded lynching and overt racism had changed from a rule to an exception.

Eric Bennett

See Also

Bureau of Refugees, Freedmen and Abandoned Lands; Civil War, American; Lynching; Black Nationalism in the United States; Accommodationism in the United States.

Africa

Lourenço Marques. Former name of Maputo, Mozambique.

Africa

Lovedu (also known as the Lobedu), ethnic group of South Africa.

The Lovedu primarily inhabit northernmost South Africa. They speak a Bantu language closely related to Sotho and they share many cultural traits with the Venda. Approximately 200,000 people consider themselves Lovedu.

See Also
Bantu: Dispersion and Settlement.

Latin America and the Caribbean

Lovelace, Earl (b. July 13, 1935, Toco, Trinidad), Trinidadian playwright, novelist, journalist, and poet.

Earl Lovelace has been described as an author whose writing and work display an uncommon love for himself as a black man, for his language, for his people, and for their potential greatness. Lovelace is one of the few prominent Caribbean writers who has chosen to remain based in the islands, and his work draws heavily on Trinidadian dialect, traditions, and culture.

Lovelace was born in Trinidad in 1935 but spent much of his childhood in Tobago with his maternal grandparents. He returned to Trinidad as a teenager, where he graduated from Ideal High School in Port of Spain in 1953. After graduation he took a job as a proofreader for the *Trinidad Guardian.* Within a few years, he began a career in the civil service, working for the Departments of Forestry and Agriculture and studying at the Eastern Caribbean Institute of Agriculture and Forestry from 1961 to 1962. But even as he held these positions, he began a second career as a writer.

In 1962 Lovelace's first play, *The New Boss,* premiered in Matura, Trinidad. While still working full-time as an agricultural assistant, Lovelace next went on to write a novel. *While Gods Are Falling* won the 1964 British Petroleum Independence Literary Award, an annual award that honored an unpublished novel by a Trinidadian or Tobagian which was either set in the West Indies or about West Indians; the novel was published one year later to critical acclaim. As his first book, *While Gods Are Falling* established a theme that runs throughout Lovelace's work: the search for heroes and heroic figures in West Indian culture.

In 1966 Lovelace was awarded the Pegasus Literary Award for outstanding contributions to the arts in Trinidad and Tobago. Over the next several years, Lovelace and his family moved back and forth between the United States and Trinidad as he continued his education and his career. He spent the 1966-1967 academic year at Howard University, and after returning to Port of Spain to write for the *Trinidad and Tobago Express* he published his second novel, *The Schoolmaster,* in 1968. Lovelace returned to Washington, D.C., between 1971 and 1973, this time to teach at the University of the District of Columbia and to earn a master's degree in English at Johns Hopkins University. At the end of that stay he settled in Trinidad.

Lovelace had four more plays produced in rapid succession in Port of Spain and Saint Augustine: *My Name Is Village* (1976), *Pierrot Ginnard* (1977), *Jestina's Calypso* (1978), and *The New Hardware Store* (1980). His next two novels, *The Dragon Can't Dance* (1979) and *Wine of Astonishment* (1982), were also made into stage versions. By this time Lovelace had become professor of literature and creative writing at the University of the West Indies in Saint Augustine. His plays were often performed by local townspeople rather than professional actors, and were celebrated as folk dramas that both represented and engaged the community.

In 1980 Lovelace won a Guggenheim Fellowship and participated in the International Writing Program at the University of Iowa. In 1986 he received a grant from the National Endowment of the Humanities during a semester at Hartwick College in New York. His collection of short stories, *A Brief Conversion and Other Stories,* was published in 1988. Lovelace's plays have been produced in the United States and England in addition to Trinidad and Tobago, and his work continues to attract an international audience.

Lisa Clayton Robinson

See Also
Literature, English Language, Caribbean; Trinidad and Tobago.

Europe

Lovers' Rock, the first distinctively British variant of reggae, a fusion of soul elements and female vocalists into lush, romantic ballads.

Lovers' rock emerged in the mid-1970s as an alternative to heavy roots reggae being played in London clubs. Soundman Lloyd Coxsone anticipated lovers' rock by playing an occasional soul record in his reggae sets. The crowds enjoyed the opportunity for a close, slow dance. Coxsone teamed up with musician Dennis Bovell of the reggae band Matumbi to produce a reggae version of one of Coxsone's crowd-pleasing soul tunes. Featuring 13-year-old singer Louisa Mark, the resulting hit, "Caught in a Lie," broke new ground for British reggae. Its enormous success led Bovell to create a record label called Lovers' Rock, which would come to define the emergent sound. From the late 1970s through the early 1980s black women's lovers' rock topped British reggae charts and exerted a strong influence on reggae production in England and Jamaica.

With its easy melodies, soft soul string arrangements, and sensual reggae bass lines, lovers' rock began to outsell much of the heavier roots reggae in British markets. Female audiences were quick to embrace the form because it offered themes of love and marriage largely neglected by the male-dominated Rastafarian roots reggae lyrics. Lovers' rock allowed women to fashion a sophisticated self-image through music that was fully independent from Rastafarian preoccupations with Africa, Babylon, and mystic dread. For the first time in reggae history, female voices were given precedence over males, and this led to a sharp increase in the number of black female musicians, producers, and record-label owners.

After her 1980 hit record *Hopelessly in Love,* Carroll Thompson was able to open a production company. Brown Sugar, a popular all-female group, mixed the usual romantic lyrics with "conscious" songs that dealt with black pride and cultural awareness. Singer-actress Janet Kay ushered British reggae into mainstream acceptance with a hit single that reached the number-two slot in British pop charts. Just as lovers' rock enjoyed success outside of reggae markets, several of its top performers crossed over into jazz, funk, and soul projects throughout the 1980s. Brown Sugar's Caron Wheeler went on to join the black British group Soul II Soul; Carroll Thompson moved into funk-soul while still recording lovers' rock; and many others have followed the path toward black American popular music. In Jamaica, lovers' rock was applied to any melodic, romantic reggae, such as the tales of lonely love sung by Gregory Isaacs.

Many music critics have neglected lovers' rock because of its tendency toward sentimental themes. Regardless of critical attention, significant record sales prove the genre's importance. Lovers' rock opened the doors for women in reggae further than they had been opened before. In contrast to the male-oriented lyrics or outright macho boasting of much reggae, lovers' rock explored black sexuality from the female's viewpoint. Lovers' rock made reggae relevant to the experience of black British women through a shift in themes and the addition of American soul.

Jace Clayton

See Also
Soul Music; Rastafarians.

North America

Lowery, Joseph Echols (b. October 6, 1924, Huntsville, Ala.), leader of the Southern Christian Leadership Conference (SCLC) from 1977 to 1997.

One of the founding members of the Southern Christian Leadership Conference in 1957, Joseph Lowery was part of a core group of ministers, including Martin Luther King Jr., Fred Shuttlesworth, and Ralph Abernathy, who were integral to the Civil Rights Movement of the 1960s. Yet it was not until 20 years later, when he became president of the SCLC, that Lowery gained celebrity as an outspoken leader who moved the desegregation organization fully into the international political arena.

Lowery brought a wealth of activist experience to his position as the president of the SCLC. Ordained by the United Methodist Church, he had used his ministry in Mobile, Alabama, from 1952 to 1961 to sponsor lower- and middle-class housing developments. He then became one of the central organizers for the SCLC in the Montgomery, Birmingham, and Selma, Alabama, desegregation campaigns. In 1962 he received national recognition as one of four ministers sued for libel over a *New York Times* advertisement exposing racism in the Montgomery city government. Lowery and the others were ultimately acquitted in a landmark Supreme Court ruling on libel that reversed an earlier Alabama court decision.

In 1977 Lowery, then a pastor of Central United Methodist Church in Atlanta, was elected president of the SCLC. The election was contentious, and supporters of incumbent Hosea Williams accused Lowery of wanting to create a "middle-class clique of blacks." Despite the original view of Lowery as part of the more moderate faction of the SCLC, he led the organization beyond traditional civil rights issues with an unflinching outspokenness.

Throughout the 1970s and 1980s Lowery was an active leader in both the national and international arenas. He vocally opposed APARTHEID in SOUTH AFRICA and in 1978 launched a protest against a Mississippi energy company buying coal from that country. He moved into the national spotlight in 1979, when he led a group of African American clergy to Lebanon to meet with Yasir Arafat, leader of the Palestinian Liberation Organization. Lowery called for the establishment of a Palestinian homeland recognized as a nation by Israel, and a reduction in United States aid to Israel. In the 1980s Lowery criticized U.S. policy in Central America and used the SCLC to assist Haitian refugees in seeking political asylum.

Lowery also maintained the traditional concerns of the SCLC. During the 1970s he directed marches to free the "Wilmington Ten," a group accused of conspiring to murder segregationists, and to free Tommie Lee Hines, a mentally retarded young black man accused of raping a white woman. Lowery revived the SCLC economic empowerment program OPERATION BREADBASKET, which promoted support for black-owned businesses. During this time he also established Crusade for the Ballot, a campaign that carried on the drive for Southern black voter registration begun by the organization during the 1960s (*see* VOTING RIGHTS ACT OF 1965).

Marian Aguiar

SEE ALSO

Abernathy, Ralph David; King, Martin Luther, Jr.; Shuttlesworth, Fred L.; Haiti.

Africa

Lozi (also referred to as the Silozi, Rozi, Tozvi, Malozi, Barotose, Rotse, Rutse, or Kololo), an ethnic group living primarily in ZAMBIA.

The Lozi are a politically prominent ethnic group of Zambia, though they number only about 380,000 people in a country of some 10 million. They inhabit Barotseland, in the Zambezi River basin of the Western and Southern Provinces.

The Lozi speak Silozi, a central Bantu language. They probably migrated from the Congo Basin, as their culture and language are similar to those of the LUNDA, who originated there. Other scholars have argued for LUBA origins, but this is a fine point, since the Lunda themselves maintain a tradition of Luba origin. It is believed that the Lozi, originally calling themselves the Luyi or Luyana, migrated sometime during the seventeenth century to the floodplains of the ZAMBEZI RIVER (in present-day Zambia), where they may have displaced Khoisan speakers.

There the Luyi, as they were then known, established a powerful expansionist kingdom that extended its control over neighboring groups, partly to satisfy the constant need for additional agricultural labor in the fertile floodplains of the Zambezi. At the height of its power the kingdom encompassed more than two dozen neighboring ethnic groups. An elaborate social hierarchy developed, including serfs, commoners, and a ruling class. However, the kingdom lacked clear lines of succession and suffered from frequent dynastic disputes. One such dispute around 1830 so weakened the kingdom that invading Kololo from the south (also known as the Makololo) were able to conquer the Luyi. The Kololo were a Sotho-speaking group who were fleeing ZULU expansion. The Kololo called the subjugated Luyi the Barotse. When the Barotse regained control in 1864, they assimilated their previous conquerors and became known as the Lozi.

From an early date the Lozi cultivated relations with Europeans. DAVID LIVINGSTONE visited the kingdom on his explorations during the mid-nineteenth century, and other missionaries followed. Later, agents of CECIL RHODES's British South Africa Company (BSAC) signed a treaty with Lewanika, the Lozi ruler at the time. Lewanika, concerned with internal political struggles as well as possible Portuguese encroachment, entered into the agreement in order to consolidate his power. The treaty granted the BSAC full mineral rights in return for military protection. Ultimately the British Foreign Office forced the BSAC to renegotiate the treaty and relinquish its monopoly rights. The Lozi king was recognized as the legitimate ruler over the Barotseland Reserve, the center of Lozi power.

The Lozi today continue to cultivate the fertile floodplains of the Zambezi. They alternate their location between two permanent villages as the waters of the Zambezi rise and recede with the seasons. Consequently, they have an elaborate and precise system of land tenure. Fishing and cattle husbandry are also important economic activities. Unlike most African peoples, the Lozi lack clans and a formal system of lineage. For most purposes descent is traced bilaterally, that is, through both parents. The Lozi remain politically prominent partly due to their early cooperation with European colonial powers and their subsequent privileged access to education. Consequently, they retain a disproportionately high representation in the civil service and government. Many Lozi also have sought to establish a separate Lozi nation. While Lozi separatists failed to win British support for independence and secession from Zambia, in 1964 KENNETH KAUNDA, president of the newly independent Zambia, signed a treaty recognizing the Lozi king's partial sovereignty within the borders of Barotseland. In 1969 Kaunda rescinded the treaty, but Lozi demands for autonomy persist.

Ari Nave

SEE ALSO

Christianity: Missionaries in Africa.

Africa

Luanda, Angola, the capital of ANGOLA and a major port city.

Luanda has long been the commercial, political, and cultural hub of Angola. During the sixteenth century royal shell fisheries of the KONGO operated on an island off the coast of what is today the city of Luanda, until Paulo Dias de Novães claimed it as a Portuguese dependency in 1576.

From 1589 until Angolan independence Luanda was the seat of Portuguese colonial administration, except for a brief period of Dutch occupation between 1641 and 1648. The town also served as the center of the Portuguese slave trade, giving it a Creole culture, in which Europeans, *mestiço* (those of both African and Portuguese parentage), and Africans mixed. Brazilian independence and the end of the slave trade in the nineteenth century sent Luanda into a period of stagnation; not until the 1940s did the city begin to regain its former dynamism. The colonial administration had built a modern business district in the city's lowlands to accommodate Portuguese immigrants, pushing resident Africans into *musseques*, or shantytowns, in the surrounding hills. New economic prosperity drew Africans from the countryside, increasing the city's population to 500,000. Like many other African capitals, Luanda became the center of African nationalism, especially among the mestiços and educated elite.

Angolan independence reinvigorated cultural life in Luanda, including the annual

Carnival festival held along the city's wide, palm-lined boulevards. But war in the countryside between government and NATIONAL UNION FOR THE TOTAL INDEPENDENCE OF ANGOLA (UNITA) forces also brought an influx of thousands of refugees, severely taxing the city's social services and infrastructure. Today, although the war appears to be over, conditions for many of Luanda's approximately 3 million residents remain difficult. Unemployment is high, and even wage workers must often seek secondary sources of income in petty trade. In recent years crime has increased and the central market, Roque Santeira, teems with illegal goods from South Africa. Luanda is among the 30 busiest ports in the world, exporting coffee, cotton, and diamonds.

Eric Young

SEE ALSO

Nationalism in Africa; Transatlantic Slave Trade; Portugal; Afro-Atlantic Culture: On the Live Dialogue Between Africa and the Americas.

Africa

Luapala, ethnic group of south Central Africa.

The Luapula primarily inhabit northwestern ZAMBIA and neighboring parts of the DEMOCRATIC REPUBLIC OF THE CONGO. They speak a Bantu language and are closely related to the BEMBA people. Approximately 100,000 people consider themselves Luapula.

SEE ALSO

Bantu: Dispersion and Settlement.

Africa

Luba, one of the largest ethnic groups of the DEMOCRATIC REPUBLIC OF THE CONGO and ZAMBIA.

One of the earliest ironworking groups in Central Africa, the ancestors of the Luba were farmers who occupied the Lake Kisale region around the fourth century. These communities slowly grew into small farming and trading chiefdoms. Between 1300 and 1400 these chiefdoms came under the control of the Nkongolo Dynasty, which was then conquered in the early 1400s, according to oral history, by a fierce huntsman named Ilunga Kalala. He expanded the kingdom westward, taking control of the vital trade routes between East and Central Africa in addition to copper mines, lakeside fishing, and palm oil industries in the region. The Luba also began participating in the slave trade, which added to their prosperity and dominance in the region.

By the 1700s the Luba Empire spanned the northern end of the Upemba depression, across the CONGO RIVER, along the Invua River, and the shores of LAKE TANGANYIKA. Its preeminence, however, was to be short-lived. In the 1850s Arab-Swahili and ivory traders from the west and east coasts began encroaching on Luba territory. The Luba briefly established relations with two of the most powerful traders – MSIRI and TIPPU TIP – by trading the kingdom's ivory reserves, but relations soon fell apart. Frustrated with the Luba's elaborate tribute system, which allowed a percentage of all ivory to go to village chiefs, Tippu Tip began raiding the villages for prisoners, which he used to extort ivory.

Unlike the Luba, Tippu Tip's and Msiri's armies possessed guns. In order to acquire guns themselves, the Luba traded slaves, at times selling their own people because they lacked the military power to conduct raids on others. Coupled with an outbreak of smallpox, apparently introduced to the region by Tippu Tip's men, the slave trade soon took a visible toll on the Luba population. It also fostered animosity and discontent, leading to the eventual breakup of the Luba kingdom into factions. By the time Belgian king LEOPOLD II took control of the area in 1885, the Luba kingdom had been reduced to two small factions.

The Luba faced harsh treatment under Belgian COLONIAL RULE. After an ill-fated rebellion against Belgian officers in 1895, large numbers of Luba men were forced to work in the Katanga mines, where many perished. Nevertheless, Luba factions waged numerous rebellions throughout the colonial period. The most famous of these was the drawn-out insurrection led by Kasongo Nyembo that lasted from 1905 to 1917, after which Nyembo was arrested and exiled.

During the independence movement the Luba factions again split, this time on the issue of the Katanga secession. One faction, led by Ndaye Emanuel, supported the secession led by Moise Tshombe, while another, led by Kisula Ngoye, resisted the secession. After the end of the secession and the 1965 military takeover of Mobutu Sese Sekou, Ngoye's faction became the official liaison between the Luba and the central government in Zaire (now the Democratic Republic of the Congo). Today the Luba number more than 4 million and are one of the largest groups in the mineral-rich Katanga Province.

Elizabeth Heath

SEE ALSO

Ivory Trade; Iron in Africa; Mobutu Sese Seko; Transatlantic Slave Trade; Tshombe, Moise-Kapenda.

North America

Luca Family Singers, a troupe of African American musicians who traveled the midwestern and eastern United States in the mid-nineteenth century performing secular as well as religious music.

John W. Luca was born in 1805 in Milford, Connecticut. Although his formal training was in shoemaking, he also acquired a musical education that, combined with his substantial natural aptitude, won him a job as a chorister at a Congregational church in New Haven. There he met and married the equally talented Lisette Lewis, with whom he had four sons. In the 1840s the Luca parents began performing alongside their children and Mrs. Luca's sister. Their son Cleveland evinced the most talent; he later achieved renown as a master pianist. He also sang, as did Alexander, a violinist; Simeon, a violinist; and John Jr., a cellist and bassist. John Sr. eventually gave up performing in order to manage the engagements of his talented family.

The Luca Family Singers won regional success and then achieved national attention in May 1853 at an Antislavery Society concert in New York. Thereafter they toured Pennsylvania, Ohio, and New York, generating considerable acclaim. In 1854 Simeon died and Jennie Allen, a contralto from New York, joined the group. In 1859 the Lucas teamed with a white family troupe, the Hutchinsons, who performed a similar act. Both groups drew from an eclectic repertoire, combining comic and temperance songs with classical European arias.

Upon the invitation of the president of LIBERIA in 1860, Cleveland left the group and went to Africa, where he composed Liberia's national anthem. The troupe disbanded, but its members continued to pursue music individually.

Eric Bennett

North America

Lucy Foster, Autherine (b. October 5, 1929, Shiloh, Ala.), African American civil rights activist who sued to integrate the University of Alabama.

Autherine Lucy Foster attended public schools in Alabama and did her undergraduate work at Selma University and Miles College in Birmingham. After her graduation in 1952, she and Pollie Myers, an activist for the NATIONAL ASSOCIATION FOR THE ADVANCEMENT OF COLORED PEOPLE (NAACP), applied to the University of Alabama. The two women were accepted but then rejected when the university learned that they were not white. With the backing of the NAACP, they went to court and successfully charged the university with racial discrimination. While Foster was reaccepted, the university rejected Myers again, claiming that a child she had had out of wedlock rendered her an unfit student.

Foster's enrollment at the University of Alabama was met with violent anti-integration demonstrations, burning crosses, and a rioting mob that pelted Lucy with rotting food and death threats. For this, Foster was suspended "for her own safety." Again Foster sued and won, but the decision was preempted by her expulsion on the grounds that she had maligned school officials by taking them to court. Lucy and the NAACP decided to drop the case.

For many years Foster had trouble finding work as a teacher because of the controversy. She and her husband, Hugh Foster, and their five children moved throughout the South, with Foster speaking on civil rights issues. She finally was hired for a teaching position in Birmingham in 1974. In 1988 Foster's expulsion was overturned by the University of Alabama and she enrolled there, receiving an M.A. in elementary education in 1992.

Rachel Antell

See Also
Civil Rights Movement.

Africa

Lugard, Frederick John Dealtry (b. January 22, 1858, Fort St. George, Madras, India; d. April 11, 1945, Abinger, Surrey, England), British administrator and soldier who pioneered the system of "indirect rule" in colonial Africa.

A son of missionary parents, Frederick Lugard was born in India in 1858. He was educated in England and trained briefly at the Royal Military College, which he left at age 21 to join the British army. While in the army he was posted to India and also served in Afghanistan, Sudan, and Burma (present-day Myanmar). In the late 1880s he left the army to fight slavery in East and Central Africa. In 1888 Lugard led his first expedition in Nyasaland (present-day Malawi) and was seriously injured in an attack on Arab slave traders. A year after he established the territorial claims of British settlers, in the hire of the British East African Company, Lugard explored the Kenyan interior. In 1890 he led an expedition to the Buganda Kingdom in present-day Uganda. Lugard negotiated an end to the civil war in the kingdom and established a British protectorate. He returned to England in 1892, where he denied accusations that his mission had used excessive force to subdue the Buganda rulers.

Lugard returned to Africa two years later. In 1894 the Royal Niger Company hired him to secure treaties from groups like the Borgu, who lived along the Niger River in Nigeria, in order to block a French colonial advance from the west. Lugard next worked briefly for the British West Charterland Company in the Bechuanaland protectorate (present-day Botswana). His work attracted the notice of the British government, which appointed him leader of the West African Frontier Force; their mission was, again, to block French expansion.

In 1900 Lugard was appointed high commissioner of Northern Nigeria. His experiences in Northern Nigeria influenced his later theories of colonial rule in Africa. By 1904 Lugard had conquered the Sokoto Caliphate – until then the largest African state south of the Sahara – and much of the surrounding territory. Lacking resources, however, he had to devise a practical and inexpensive method of ruling this vast region. Consequently, Lugard took advantage of the elaborate administrative structure of the Sokoto Caliphate and hired the precolonial rulers to serve as local administrators. Under this system, which came to be known as indirect rule, African rulers were expected to lead the African populations, collect taxes, and enforce "traditional" laws. Because Lugard's system was successful in Northern Nigeria, British administrators used indirect rule throughout their African possessions. Lugard achieved a reputation as a leading authority on colonial administration.

In 1907 Lugard accepted the post of governor of Hong Kong, but he returned to Africa in 1912 to oversee the unification of Southern and Northern Nigeria. Indirect rule faced its greatest challenge and perhaps revealed its major weakness when societies lacking hierarchical, centralized rulers, such as the Igbo of southeastern Nigeria, resisted Lugard's system. Nevertheless, Lugard persevered and declared Nigerian unification complete in 1914.

Lugard retired from the colonial service in 1919 but remained active in colonial policymaking. In 1922 he published *The Dual Mandate in British Tropical Africa*, which outlined his theories of colonial rule in Africa. From 1923 to 1939 he served as the British representative on the League of Nations Permanent Mandates Commission. He also served as chairman of the International Institute of African Languages and Cultures. Lugard received the title of baron in 1928 and thenceforth was known as Baron Lugard of Abinger. He died in 1945.

Elizabeth Heath

See Also
Buganda, Early Kingdom of; Kenya; Scramble for Africa.

Africa

Lugbara (also known as Logbara and Lugbwari), ethnic group of east Central Africa.

The Lugbara primarily inhabit southern Sudan, northwestern Uganda, and the northeastern Democratic Republic of the Congo. They speak a Nilo-Saharan language. The term *Lugbara* refers to both the Lugbara people, numbering around 300,000 people, and to a larger cultural and linguistic group that includes the Lendu, the Madi, and the Lugbara proper.

See Also
Languages, African: An Overview.

Africa

Luhya, ethnic group of Kenya and Uganda.

Unlike other ethnic groups in Kenya, such as the Kikuyu and the Maasai, the Luhya is not homogeneous. Its subgroups, however, speak a common Bantu language and share cultural and ethnic traits that distinguish them from such neighboring ethnic groups as the Nilotic-speaking Kalenjin to the north and east, the Luo speakers to the south, and the Teso to the west. The Luhya comprise about 18 subgroups, some of which straddle the Kenya-Uganda border, though the majority live in Kenya.

The Luhya traditionally have occupied the area between the southern side of Mount Elgon and the easternmost shore of Lake Victoria. Although scholars are uncertain about Luhya origins, they believe that Bantu speakers migrated into the region by the end of the first millennium c.e. Between the sixteenth and eighteenth century this population absorbed a series of newcomers, including other Bantus and peoples related to the present-day Kalenjin and Maasai, who gradually became Bantuized. Luhya tradition holds that they are descended from Mugoma and Malaba, who were created by Wele, the supreme being.

Although 94 percent of the Luhya profess Christianity, they have blended Christian and indigenous beliefs. Ancestor worship is common among the Luhya, and families offer sacrifices to dead ancestors and call on them for assistance in times of distress. The Luhya also believe in and practice magic and witchcraft. Historically, the Luhya shared a tract of land with their extended families in scattered homesteads and cultivated individual plots. The next most important social unit in Luhya society is the *oluhia* (clan), a territorial group tracing its descent patrilineally from a single famous ancestor, from whom the clan takes its name.

Traditionally, the Luhya are primarily agriculturists, but they also keep cattle, sheep, and goats. Farmers customarily practice hoe cultivation, though ox-drawn plows have become more common. Staple crops include corn, sorghum, finger millet, beans, peas, sweet potatoes, and bananas. In addition, many Luhya grow cash crops, such as sugar cane, cotton, and coffee. Population density is one of the highest in Kenya, and the division of land among heirs has fragmented most farms into small plots that make commercial farming difficult. In addition, communal grazing lands in many areas have been put into cultivation, which has reduced the number of cattle owned. This combination of factors has made the Luhya one of Kenya's poorest ethnic groups, causing a significant percentage of Luhya to migrate to urban areas in search of employment.

The only centralized government in Luhya history occurred in the kingdom of Wanga, named after the leader of the Tiriki clan who founded the kingdom in the seventeenth century. Over the next two centuries the kingdom ruled two dozen clans, but most Luhya remained outside of it. British colonialists, who preferred indirect governance through indigenous rulers, declared the king's residence its first provincial headquarters and named King Mumia the "paramount chief" over all the subgroups of the Luhya. This arrangement did not last, as most of the subgroups declined to recognize Mumia's authority, and the British abolished the office of paramount chief on Mumia's death in 1926. The only other attempt at Luhya unity occurred in 1940 with the founding of the Abaluyia Association, a tribal welfare organization set up on the lines of the Luo Union and others.

Shortly before and after Kenya achieved independence in 1963, the Luhya strongly supported the Kenya African Democratic Union (KADU), which at the time opposed the ruling Kenya African National Union (KANU). KADU disbanded in 1964, however, and merged with KANU. Kenyans had no viable political alternative until the revival of multiparty elections in the 1990s. Many believe that the Luhya will now support the Forum for the Restoration of Democracy (FORD-Kenya), because that party's presidential candidate, Michael Kijana Wamalwa, is a Luhya.

Robert Fay

See Also

Bantu: Dispersion and Settlement; Christianity, African: An Overview.

Africa

Lumumba, Patrice (b. 1925, Onalua, Belgian Congo; d. January 17, 1961, Katanga Province, Republic of the Congo), Congolese independence leader and first prime minister of the Democratic Republic of the Congo.

A charismatic and energetic statesman, Patrice Lumumba became politically active as a young postal worker when he organized the Stanleyville (now Kisangani) postal worker's union. In October 1958 he became involved with national politics, founding the Mouvement National Congolais (MNC), Congo's first national political party. In December Lumumba took an MNC delegation to the All-African People's Conference in Ghana, where he met with Pan-Africanists and African nationalists and became friends with Kwame Nkrumah, Ghana's first African prime minister. Influenced by the spirit of nationalism and anticolonialism that pervaded the conference, Lumumba returned to the Republic of the Congo a militant, ready to demand independence.

Lumumba made the first public appeal for independence in January 1959. On October 31 he was arrested and held responsible for riots that broke out after a meeting of the MNC. From jail he and his nationalist supporters organized a boycott of the December local elections. Although the Belgian government had proposed a five-year decolonization plan, Lumumba and the MNC wanted immediate independence and believed a five-year plan would give Belgium the opportunity to install a puppet regime. In fact, Lumumba was released from jail in time to participate in the Round Table Conference in Brussels, where the Belgians ultimately agreed to grant independence within six months.

In May 1960 the Belgians selected Lumumba to be prime minister under Joseph Kasavubu, who was to be president. From the beginning relations were strained. Lumumba wanted a strong centralized state free of outside interference and hoped to make the Republic of the Congo the leader of a Pan-African Union of African States. Kasavubu, a federalist, took a more moderate stance and wanted to maintain close connections with Belgium and the West. This tension was evident from the nature of their June 30 independence ceremony speeches; Kasavubu thanked King Boudouin I for independence, and Lumumba reminded the king of the atrocities of Belgian colonialism.

Shortly after independence, the government faced widespread military revolt, and the Katanga province, supported by Belgian troops and Western businesses, seceded. Belgium immediately sent in military troops to restore order; Lumumba, fearing a reinstatement of colonial rule, quickly broke diplomatic relations with Belgium. He appealed to the United Nations (UN) for military intervention, which arrived on July 14, 1960. Lumumba, however, soon lost faith in the UN mission, which he suspected was interested in protecting Belgian and other Western business interests, and turned to the Soviet Union for assistance. This action caused a complete split with Kasavubu, who dismissed Lumumba in September 1960.

Lumumba contested his removal until Kasavubu was also pushed out of office, in a military coup led by Col. Joseph Mobutu (later Mobutu Sese Sekou), who, ironically, Lumumba himself had named army chief of staff. Mobutu ordered the arrest of Lumumba. Although Lumumba, using UN protection, avoided arrest for several months, he was finally caught in January 1961 and was murdered in Katanga. It is uncertain who killed Lumumba, but there is evidence that Mobutu, working in affiliation with the United States Central Intelligence Agency (CIA) and Moise Tshombe, the leader of the Katanga secession, may have been responsible. To this day Lumumba remains one of the country's national heroes.

Elizabeth Heath

See Also

Mobutu Sese Seko; Nationalism in Africa; Pan-Africanism; Tshombe, Moise-Kapenda.

North America

Lunceford, James Melvin (Jimmie) (b. June 6, 1902, Fulton, Mo.; d. July 12?, 1947, Seaside, Oreg.), jazz bandleader and arranger whose big band helped define the swing era of the 1930s.

Regarded as the most exciting band of its time, Jimmie Lunceford's big band was known for its precise arrangements and smoothly polished choreography. Light, swinging hits such as "My Blue Heaven" reflected the perfectionism and charm of the band and its leader. Raised in Denver, Colorado, Jimmie Lunceford graduated from Fisk University in Nashville, Tennessee, in 1926. After doing graduate work in New York City, he taught high school music and physical education in Memphis. It was there that he put together his first band, originally called the Chickasaw Syncopators.

Soon renamed the Jimmie Lunceford Orchestra, the band toured the Upper Midwest and Great Lakes region for several years before making its first New York appearance at Harlem's fabled Cotton Club. For the next decade the orchestra dominated the city's lively big-band scene. Although Lunceford's group featured talented and dynamic musicians, it became famous more for its playful sound and vibrant stage presence than for its musical virtuosity. Instead of playing any of the several instruments he had studied, Lunceford acted as the band's conductor, head arranger, and business leader, keeping the group together during more than ten years of frequent national and international touring and dozens of recordings for the Decca and Columbia labels.

Despite Lunceford's discipline and leadership, the band lost key members in the early 1940s, including arrangers Sy Oliver and Willie "the Lion" Smith, and began a decline from which it never recovered. Nevertheless, it continued working until 1947, when Lunceford died following a publicity appearance in Oregon. The band soon folded for good, but Lunceford's work has gone on to influence countless jazz ensembles.

Kate Tuttle

See Also

Harlem, New York; New York, New York; Smith, Willie ("the Lion").

Africa

Lunda, an ethnic group that formed one of the most powerful states in Central Africa during the seventeenth and eighteenth centuries, and which continues to exert considerable influence in the Shaba Province of the Democratic Republic of the Congo, northern Zambia, and eastern Angola.

According to some oral histories, the Lunda were founded around 1450, when a group from the LUBA royal family broke off to found their own kingdom to the west of the Lake Kisale region. In other histories the Lunda existed prior to 1450, but did not develop into a highly centralized state until the marriage between Chibunda Ilunga, the chief of the loose confederation, and Rweej, a Luba queen. Chibunda Ilunga then began a process of centralization that eventually united the fragmented villages under the leadership of one chief, the *mwata yamvo*, who assumed control of political and religious life. By the seventeenth century the Lunda had developed a cohesive kingdom and a complex administration, enabling them to assume economic control over the region.

Originally agriculturalists, the Lunda became more involved in trading during the seventeenth century, when a route developed between middle Kwango and upper Kasai. Keen to extend his empire and increase his prestige, the king moved the Lunda capital to northern Kasai and assumed control of one end of the trade route. The Lunda increased their agricultural production to trade foodstuffs such as maize, cassava, millet, and bananas for valuable goods such as salt, copper, cloth, and tobacco. At first lacking a sufficient population to cultivate the available farming land, the Lunda began raiding from neighboring villages and put the captives to work on plantations. In addition, they colonized remote villages and forced them to pay crop tributes to the Lunda king. These practices were soon used to supply slaves for the even more profitable Atlantic trade.

During the eighteenth century the Lunda began selling slaves to the Portuguese for European goods and became one of the largest suppliers of slaves in Central Africa. In 1850 a slave trader estimated that one-third of all slaves traded in the previous century had been sold by the Lunda kingdom. Most of the slaves were Kete or Luba captives from border fights or slave raids. But the Lunda also sold Lunda criminals into slavery and, in fact, protested the end of the Portuguese slave trade on the basis that they would have to resort to killing the criminals if they could no longer sell them.

As the Lunda profited from the slave trade, they expanded throughout the Luapula valley and in the late eighteenth century became involved with the IVORY TRADE. This venture was short-lived, because the intensive ivory trade quickly devastated the regional ELEPHANT population. Soon afterward, Belgium's king LEOPOLD II assumed control of the area, and many of the Lunda living in the newly contrived Congo Free State were forced to work in the nearby copper mines.

Nevertheless, the Lunda remained fairly cohesive throughout the colonial period, due in part to Belgian policies that used the preexisting state structures to facilitate COLONIAL RULE. In the 1950s Lundas in the Belgian Congo, led by Moise Tshombe, formed CONAKAT, a political group opposed both to Belgian colonialism and to what they perceived as the growing political dominance of the Luba and the CHOKWE peoples. After independence, CONAKAT also opposed the Democratic Republic of the Congo government headed by President JOSEPH KASAVUBU and Prime Minister PATRICE LUMUMBA, and led the Katanga secessionist movement in 1960, which took the central government two years to crush. After 1965 Mobutu Sese Sekou, ruler of Zaire, quickly crushed subsequent secession attempts but appointed many Lunda to privileged positions in his own government. Nevertheless, Lunda diamond traders living in Zaire (now the Democratic Republic of the Congo) and Angola have long evaded the efforts of both states to appropriate control over their informal but highly lucrative cross-border commerce.

Elizabeth Heath

SEE ALSO
Mobutu Sese Seko; Transatlantic Slave Trade; Portugal; Tshombe, Moise-Kapenda.

Africa

Luo, ethnic group of KENYA and TANZANIA.

Around the sixteenth century the ancestors of the Luo people began migrating from the Bahr al-Ghazal region, south of the Nile, and settling on the eastern side of the LAKE VICTORIA basin. They continued arriving in a steady stream until the nineteenth century. Practitioners of PASTORALISM, they spoke a western Nilotic language now known as DhoLuo, which is distinct from the languages spoken by most of their neighbors. By the late 1990s the Luo had become Kenya's second largest ethnic group, numbering approximately 2.7 million. Much smaller numbers of Luo live in Tanzania.

Although most rural Luo now depend primarily on farming and fishing for subsistence, livestock are still highly valued in Luo culture. Cattle are their most important animals, used in bride wealth transactions and religious ceremonies as well as for food and skins.

Luo farm households typically grow staple food crops such as maize, millet or finger millet, sorghum, beans, peas, and cassava as well as cash crops such as cotton, coffee, tobacco, and sugar cane. Women do most of the farming, especially in the many households whose male members migrate to seek paid employment.

Historically, Luo society has been politically decentralized, governed by clan leaders and knit together by ties of patrilineal kinship and marriage. Rural Luo live in scattered homesteads (*dala*) and cultivate land inherited from a patrilineal ancestor. Unlike many ethnic groups in Kenya, the Luo do not form strict groupings based on age or sex and do not typically practice circumcision. Most rites of passage are considered private.

Customary Luo religion featured a central deity, Nyasae or Nyasi, the creator of humanity and the universe. It also emphasized ancestor worship and "free Jok," spirits associated with specific diseases or natural disasters that had to be exorcised by prophets known as *jabilo*. Today approximately 90 percent of Luo are Christians, but many still engage in customary rituals. Luo funerals are still extravagant affairs, reflecting the time-honored role of ancestor worship in unifying lineages. In addition, Luo have founded a number of independent Christian churches.

During the colonial period Luo nationalists allied with the Kikuyu to form the Kenya African National Union Party. Since independence, however, the Luo's numerical strength has not translated into significant political power. Although some Luo have served in high-level posts, particularly former vice president OGINGA ODINGA and cabinet minister TOM MBOYA, they have been the exception.

Robert Fay

SEE ALSO
Nationalism in Africa; Nile River; Sugar; Millet; Christianity: Independent and Charismatic Churches in Africa; Female Circumcision in Africa.

Latin America and the Caribbean

Luperón, Gregorio

(b. September 8, 1839, Puerto Plata, Dominican Republic; d. May 21, 1897, Puerto Plata, Dominican Republic), Afro-Dominican political and military leader who helped restore the sovereignty of the Dominican Republic from Spain during the War of Restoration (1863-1865).

Gregorio Luperón grew up in the rural area of Jamao, DOMINICAN REPUBLIC, where as an adolescent he worked as a wood cutter. His early intellectual development was fostered by a man named Don Pedro Eduardo Dubocq, who tutored him and gave him access to his small library. At age 18, he began working as an auxiliary commander at the military base Puesto Cantonal de Rincón. In 1861 Spain annexed the Dominican Republic (*see* COLONIAL LATIN AMERICA AND THE CARIBBEAN) and in protest Luperón moved to the United States. He soon returned to the Dominican Republic and enlisted in the War of Restoration. After serving as a general of one of the provincial regiments, he accepted a position as vice president of the Central Government (1864-1865).

Following the restoration of the republic in 1865, Luperón continued to serve as both soldier and statesman. In 1876 he accepted a post as a minister of war and navy, and in 1879 he agreed to serve as the country's provisional president. While in office (October 6, 1879-September 1, 1880), he restructured the local administration and the military, and resolved many of the country's foreign and domestic debts. Through these and other reforms, Luperón stabilized the government and helped bring about economic prosperity. He also helped ratify a new constitution in 1880, which mandated elections every two years. Suceeded by Fernando Arturo de Meriño as president, Luperón subsequently served as a diplomat in Paris.

Luperón remained active in the political affairs of the country, running in 1893 as a Liberal Party candidate against Ulíses Heureaux, another black hero of the War of Restoration. Luperón withdrew his candidacy and later attempted to incite a revolutionary movement to overthrow Heureaux, who had declared himself dictator. Luperón then went into exile in St. Thomas. In 1896 Heureaux pardoned Luperón in recognition of his ailing health and allowed him to return to the Dominican Republic. Luperón died the following year of throat cancer. Today he is one of the Dominican Republic's most celebrated heroes of independence.

Aaron Myers

Africa

Lusaka, Zambia, capital city of Zambia; also name of the district in the Central Province surrounding the capital city.

Lusaka was named for a Lenje headman, Lusaakas, who settled the area in the late nineteenth century. In the 1890s the region fell under the control of Cecil Rhodes's British South Africa Company. Originally called Lusakas Village, the name was later shortened to Lusaka. The village developed around 1905, located on the rail line that connected the mines of Broken Hill (now Kabwe) with Southern Rhodesia (present-day Zimbabwe) and South Africa. In the following year the European-owned Northern Copper Company sold land, which it had confiscated from Africans, to European immigrants, who used the land to establish maize farms around Lusaka.

Because of Lusaka's central location within the colony, the capital of Northern Rhodesia was moved from Livingstone to Lusaka in 1935. The city began to expand rapidly. Despite the efforts of urban planners, it developed idiosyncratically, as housing and businesses were quickly constructed independently of planning codes. After Northern Rhodesia gained independence in 1964, Lusaka became the capital of independent Zambia. With travel restrictions on Africans lifted, large numbers of migrants began to arrive from the country-side, including many Nyanja speakers from the east. High copper prices supported an economic boom, and as both government and private-sector employment grew, Lusaka's population doubled in the years from 1963 to 1969.

Today approximately a million people live in Lusaka, which has expanded to incorporate several once-rural townships. The city is Zambia's major transportation hub: it is the site of the main international airport, and it lies at the intersection of the north-south railway (connecting to TanZam railway) and the major east-west and north-south highways of the country. In addition to being the seat of government, Lusaka is the center of Zambia's commerce and finance and the site of the country's leading university. Thirty miles to the south, the suburb of Kafue is a leading industrial center.

Ari Nave

See Also
Rhodes, Cecil.

North America

Lutheranism, a Protestant denomination with a long but little known presence in African American life.

A Protestant sect founded by German theologian Martin Luther during the Reformation, Lutheranism soon spread to the United States, where it has had a long but negligible relationship to black life. In 1699 a black man now known only as Emmanuel was the first person to be baptized in the Lutheran Church in New York City. Limited numbers of African American slaves in the pre-Emancipation South encountered the religion through the small Lutheran planter community. Black preachers such as Daniel A. Payne, the African Methodist Episcopal bishop, were occasionally trained by Lutherans, but because of the racism pervasive in the Lutheran Church (as well as in other largely white denominations), they usually joined independent black Baptist or Methodist congregations. This remained true throughout the nineteenth century despite short-lived efforts to create autonomous black Lutheran churches.

In the twentieth century there was something of a Lutheran religious revival among African Americans in Northern cities. The emigration of black Lutherans since the 1920s from the Danish West Indies where Lutheranism has been the state religion spurred the development of a number of African American congregations. In addition, the Civil Rights and Black Power Movements inspired the formation of the Association of Black Lutheran Clergyman in 1968, as well as "A Harare Message by Black Lutherans," in 1986, a document applying the questions of black identity and autonomy to the Afro-Lutheran experience.

Peter Hudson

See Also
Methodist Episcopal Church; African Methodist Episcopal Church; Baptists; Civil Rights Movement; Payne, Daniel Alexander.

Africa

Luthuli, Albert John (b. 1899; d. July 21, 1967), South African leader and Nobel laureate.

Born in Southern Rhodesia (now Zimbabwe), the son of well-respected members of the Zulu ethnic group, Albert John Luthuli was educated at the mission school in which he later taught (1921-1936). In 1936 he was elected chief of the Zulu Abasemakholweni tribe in Groutville. Luthuli joined the African National Congress (ANC), a black political group, in 1946 and took an increasingly active role in campaigns to abolish apartheid, the system of racial segregation in South Africa.

In 1952 he was removed as chief by the South African government, which opposed his activities, and was forbidden to enter major South African cities and towns for one year. That same year he was elected president-general of the ANC. Because of his continued political activities, he was restricted to his farm in Groutville for two years in 1953 and again in 1959 for five years. For his nonviolent resistance to South African apartheid policies, Luthuli was awarded the 1960 Nobel Peace Prize. In 1964 the government extended its restrictions against him for another five years. His autobiography, *Let My People Go,* was published in 1962.

North America

Lynching, mob execution, usually by hanging and often accompanied by torture, of alleged criminals, particularly African Americans.

Apart from slavery, lynching is perhaps the most horrific chapter in the history of African Americans. Although lynching, defined as execution without the due process of law, has been used against members of many different ethnicities, the vast majority of victims have been African American men, mostly in the Southern states, during a 50-year period following Reconstruction. Despite its stated justification – that lynching is merely a response to crime – in most cases victims had not been convicted, or even charged with, a specific crime. As historian W. Fitzhugh Brundage has noted, lynching was not only "a tragic symbol of race relations in the American South" but also "a powerful tool of intimidation." A constant and unpredictable threat, lynching was used to maintain the status quo of white superiority long after any legal distinction between the races remained.

Because of its unpredictability and extra-legal nature – black men knew that they could become victims at any time, for any reason – lynching cast a shadow greater than its 3386 known black (mostly male) victims between 1882 and 1930. It is almost certain that these numbers are understated.

Despite groundbreaking research into lynching by historians and sociologists, many cases were never recorded. Even those that were well documented rarely reveal the names of the perpetrators; as scholar Robert Zangrando points out, coroners' reports typically attributed the murder to "parties unknown," even though "lynchers' identities were seldom a secret."

More than an epidemic of racially targeted violence, lynching has become a symbol of the most disheartening aspects of American race relations. For many African Americans, there is no more potent reminder of their history of slavery, subjugation, and pain at the hands of white society. In music – most notably JAZZ singer Billie Holiday's "Strange Fruit" – literature, and painting, black artists have explored this brutal and complex crime. As many scholars have pointed out, lynching was directed not only at a particular victim, but at all black people.

The History of Lynching

Lynching has its roots in the lawless early days of prerevolutionary America. Lacking an established system of courts, jails, and legal rights, mobs often attempted to maintain social order by executing alleged criminals. From its beginning, though, lynching was also a means of controlling people deemed marginal by society's mainstream. Although slaves were often beaten, whipped, and sometimes killed by white slaveholders, systematic violence against African Americans in the form of lynching was not prevalent before the Civil War and Emancipation.

In the five years that followed the Civil War (1861-1865), a series of constitutional amendments conferred several rights upon African Americans: freedom from slavery, legal recognition as United States citizens, and, for men, the right to vote. At this time Reconstruction – primarily an effort to reunite the country – began, and the federal government, dominated by Northern Republicans, maintained a presence in the South and established agencies to oversee the transition from slavery to freedom. But after their emancipation, blacks faced a threat of social violence. With white supremacy challenged throughout the South, many whites sought to protect their former status by threatening African Americans who exercised their new rights. Southern blacks, particularly political and religious leaders, became the targets of white violence. But as Republican resolve weakened, Reconstruction waned, and white Southern Democrats were able to engineer limits on state and federal rights for African Americans.

Incidents of lynching increased even as Reconstruction faltered. Although good statistics on lynching were not kept before 1882, historians believe that the numbers grew throughout the 1870s and 1880s, peaking around 1892, which saw 230 victims, 161 of them African American. From that year on, white victims of mob execution sharply and steadily decreased, while blacks in the South continued to be lynched in large numbers (for instance, in 1900, 106 African Americans were lynched, compared to 9 whites). From its frontier roots, when it took the place of legal law enforcement, lynching became almost entirely a Southern, racial phenomenon – in which, as historians have pointed out, mob execution was really about social control, not crime control.

With the rise in racially motivated mob execution, an ANTILYNCHING MOVEMENT was born. Its foremost voice was Ida B. Wells-Barnett, an African American who in the early 1890s published several influential pamphlets detailing the horrors of lynching. Her statement that many of the alleged rapes that led to lynchings were actually consensual interracial encounters caused Wells-Barnett to be vilified by Southern whites, and she was forced to flee her home city of Memphis on threat of lynching. Many of her potential supporters, middle-class black clubwomen, saw Wells-Barnett's bold and passionate rhetoric as unfeminine and supported her cautiously.

In 1909, when the NATIONAL ASSOCIATION FOR THE ADVANCEMENT OF COLORED PEOPLE (NAACP) was founded, an end to lynching was named as one of the organization's top priorities from the start. In 1917 the NAACP staged the Negro Silent Protest Parade in New York City to criticize the federal government's lack of commitment to ending lynching. The Dyer Bill, which would have made participating in a lynch mob a federal crime, was first introduced in 1918 by Leonidas Dyer, a white Republican congressman from Missouri. Over the next ten years, the NAACP, led by JAMES WELDON JOHNSON and Walter White, lobbied heavily for its passage, which was repeatedly blocked by Southern Democrats in the Senate. Despite its legislative failure, the Dyer Bill debate allowed the NAACP to educate the white American public about the amount and severity of racial violence that was going unpunished.

ABOVE LEFT: **A crowd of white people gathers around a tree from which two black men are hanging, lynched by vigilantes in Marion, Indiana, in 1930.** *CORBIS/Bettmann*

ABOVE: **George Bellows's 1923 lithograph *The Law Is Too Slow* expresses the drama and pain of a lynching scene.** *Art Resource, NY*

The number of lynchings began to decrease in the twentieth century, especially during the 1920s; by the late 1930s the annual victim count was in the single digits. Although some African Americans were still lynched in the following decades, lynching was more or less ended by 1965. Historians have different explanations for the decline in lynching, among them increased public awareness, national pressure on the South, and the growing exodus of African Americans from the region in THE GREAT MIGRATION of the 1930s and 1940s.

The Significance of Lynching

Starting in 1882, scholars at the Tuskegee Institute began collecting data on lynching, including documenting every known case of mob execution. Because of the availability of this detailed information, sociologists and historians have been able to study the phenomenon of lynching and to try to

LYNCHING VICTIMS 1868-1935

Year	Blacks	Year	Blacks
1868	291	1907	58
1869	31	1908	89
1870	34	1909	69
1871	53	1910	67
1882	49	1911	60
1883	53	1912	61
1884	51	1913	51
1885	74	1914	51
1886	74	1915	56
1887	70	1916	50
1888	69	1917	36
1889	94	1918	60
1890	85	1919	76
1891	113	1920	53
1892	161	1921	59
1893	118	1922	51
1894	134	1923	29
1895	113	1924	16
1896	78	1925	17
1897	123	1926	23
1898	101	1927	16
1899	85	1928	10
1900	106	1929	7
1901	105	1930	20
1902	85	1931	12
1903	84	1932	6
1904	76	1933	24
1905	57	1934	15
1906	62	1935	18

understand this most extreme form of racial violence.

Early theories about lynching emphasized the economic and political threats that African Americans posed to the superior status of poor whites in the period following the Civil War. Historians such as Arthur Raper suggested that lynch mobs were made up of marginalized white men who murdered black men out of fear and frustration. Most historians today recognize that lynchers were, in fact, as W. Fitzhugh Brundage says, not "isolated deviants" but instead "representative... members of society." In the collected testimony of some Southern sheriffs, jailers, and lawyers – typically the people most likely to be in a position to prevent lynching – several mention that they would release the prisoner to the mob after noticing several of the town's leading citizens among it.

Some historians have proposed a new interpretation of lynching, seeing it as a political and economic tool. Marxist historians have suggested, for instance, that rich white businessmen supported lynching, as it helped cement the racial hatred that could work to their advantage. Such scholars reasoned that without racism to divide poor blacks and whites from each other, workers on both sides of the color line could unite against their capitalist oppressors.

Although some scholarship, especially in the late nineteenth and early twentieth centuries, focused exclusively on lynching as an economic and political event, many historians now also consider social and psychological factors in mob executions. Historian Jacquelyn Dowd Hall, who has written about the antilynching movement, argues that lynching was intimately linked to white men's fears about black men's sexuality. While interracial sex was a staple of the prewar South (slaveholders regularly raped their female slaves), it was part of the white South's code of honor that white women must be protected from the supposed threat of black men. So, while less than 30 percent of the black lynching victims had even been accused of sexually assaulting white women, defenders of lynching continued to claim that the practice was necessary to prevent rape.

Lynching's basis in the sexual fears of white society would account, more than cotton prices or other economic reasons, for the extreme brutality with which many lynchings were carried out. It was not uncommon for lynching victims to be castrated. Many were burned alive. Other common tortures were to have their eyes gouged out, their fingers severed, or their teeth pulled out – with the white lynch mob taking home various body parts as souvenirs.

As antilynching activist Ida B. Wells-Barnett pointed out, the emphasis on rape as a justification for lynching only served to reinforce racist stereotypes of black men as sexual predators and to put them "beyond the pale of human sympathy." The sexual excuse for lynching helped perpetuate both the racial and gender inequalities in American society. Lynching reflected a value system that put white men at the top of a hierarchy, above both the white women lynching was said to protect and the black men it was meant to intimidate. In this system, black women's humanity was ignored – although their vulnerability to sexual assault by white men continued to remind black men that they could not protect their wives, mothers, sisters, and daughters. Historian Patricia Schechter says of Wells-Barnett's work that it proves that lynching was "both about sex and not about sex." That is, most lynchings were not directly the result of rape accusations, but all of them served to remind both whites and blacks, men and women, where they stood in Southern society.

The Legacy of Lynching

Despite the end of lynching, African Americans continued to suffer from inferior legal status. Subject to discriminatory segregation under the South's Jim Crow laws, blacks were unable to choose freely where to work, live, eat, or go to school. Until the Civil Rights Movement of the 1960s, most Southern African Americans could not exercise their constitutional right to vote. If they no longer faced the threat of death at a hangman's noose, they were still vulnerable to being beaten, fired from their jobs, or arrested for whatever infractions a white person might accuse them.

Increasingly, the criminal justice system – which had been, in lynching days, an accused man's one hope for safety – began to seem another arena of unfairness. Still treated as second-class citizens, black men were often tried, convicted, and executed on shaky charges. Only a strong defense and nationwide publicity saved the defendants in the Scottsboro affair – young black men who had been accused of having sex with white women – from such a lynching-like fate. Many scholars have called this sort of unequal application of the death penalty "legal lynching."

Kate Tuttle

See Also

Slavery in the United States; Literature, African American; Black Women's Club Movement; Civil War, American; Fifteenth Amendment to the United States Constitution; Holiday, Billie; Memphis, Tennessee; Miscegenation; New York, New York; Racial Stereotypes; Scottsboro Case; Tuskegee University; Wells-Barnett, Ida Bell; White, Walter Francis; Thirteenth Amendment of the United States Constitution and the Emancipation Proclamation; Art, African American.

North America

Lynch, John Roy (b. 1847?, Louisiana; d. November 2, 1939, Chicago, Ill.), politician and lawyer, first African American to deliver the keynote address at the Republican National Convention.

Born a slave and freed at the end of the Civil War, John Lynch became active in Republican party politics in 1867. His prominent career began with his election to the Mississippi legislature in 1869. Lynch became its Speaker in 1872.

As a United States congressman in 1873, Lynch supported the Civil Rights Bill of 1875. He lost his seat in 1876 but regained it after contesting the election; he was defeated in 1882, but two years later he gave the keynote address at the Republican National Convention. He went on to practice law and write *The Facts of Reconstruction* (1913).

See Also

Civil War, American.

m

Africa

Maasai, an ethnic group of Kenya and Tanzania.

The Maasai have a long tradition of PASTORALISM, though today some are adopting settled life. They speak a language of the Eastern Nilotic Maa grouping, which also includes the languages of the Arusha and Baraguyu (or Kwafi) peoples of Tanzania. Maasai origins are uncertain; however, some scholars believe that their ancestors migrated to the Rift Valley from what is now southern SUDAN sometime before 1000 C.E. These migrants practiced an agro-pastoral economy, growing sorghum and MILLET in addition to keeping cattle and other livestock. Most of them gradually adopted a strictly pastoral economy as they became dependent on neighboring farming communities in the Rift Valley highlands.

At its height, Maasailand ranged from Lake Turkana in the north to central Tanzania in the south (roughly to the latitude of Dar es Salaam). The Maasai were reputed to be fierce and disciplined warriors who could effectively defend their territory and stock or raid the stock of other groups. Trading caravans from coastal areas were wary enough of the Maasai reputation to avoid Maasailand entirely.

In the nineteenth century Maasai subgroups – most notably the pastoral IlMaasai and the agricultural Iloikop – participated in a series of wars over contested grazing rights. In addition, in the late nineteenth century the IlMaasai fought the War of Morijo, a struggle between Lenana and Sendeyo, sons of a famous *oloiboni* (ritual leader), Mbatian. Lenana ultimately defeated Sendeyo, but by the time the conflict was resolved the Maasai had been militarily debilitated. A series of droughts and associated diseases in the 1880s and 1890s further weakened the group. Both the Maasai and their herds suffered – the former from smallpox, the latter from bovine pleuro-pneumonia and rinderpest. These misfortunes left them vulnerable to the British and Germans, who imposed colonial rule at the end of the nineteenth century.

The British held a mixed view of the Maasai lifestyle. Although they disapproved of the unproductive way the Maasai treated the land, they also romanticized the Maasai lifestyle and warrior tradition. The Maasai adhered to their traditional way of life even after the British limited the Maasai range through the Treaties of 1904 and 1912. These treaties reserved the best-watered and most fertile of Maasailand for European settlers, and relocated the Maasai to reserves in what are today the Kajiado and Narok Districts in Kenya.

Young Maasai males traditionally subsist entirely on milk, meat, and blood from their herds. Blood is obtained by making a vertical slit with an arrow in the animal's jugular vein in such a way that the wound can be closed again. Women, children, and older men customarily supplement their diets with agricultural products such as corn and beans. Maasailand sees two rainy seasons – a long rainy season from March to May and a short rainy season from November to December.

Traditional Maasai society is governed by a series of age-based groupings, especially among males. Males between the approximate ages of 15 and 30 are junior *murran*, or warriors, whose responsibility it is to protect the herds. During this period, the murran live in a separate area called *manyata* and are prohibited from marrying. After age 30 they become senior warriors for approximately 15 years. During this time they live among the rest of the Maasai and serve as a sort of home guard, and have the option of marrying. Following this stage, men become junior elders. After another interval of approximately 15 years, they become senior elders, who make decisions for the group.

Historically, the Maasai are pastoral, and the two distinct rainy seasons in the Rift Valley keep them moving with their herds in search of water and pasture. Land is traditionally considered communal; wealth is determined by the number of cattle owned, and families brand their cattle to differentiate them. Traditional Maasai live in temporary camps called *inkangitie* (*enkang* in the singular), composed of huts, called *kraals* or *bomas*, made of wooden poles plastered with dung. Kraals include a corral for the cattle.

After Kenyan independence in 1964, significant portions of the most fertile and well-watered areas of Maasailand were taken by the government and distributed to other ethnic groups. The Maasai today face problems of overgrazing and soil erosion as they find themselves more and more constrained. The governments of both Kenya and Tanzania have encouraged them to abandon their communal land ownership practices and nomadic existence in favor of private property, either for ranching or for farming.

Robert Fay

SEE ALSO

Colonial Rule; Dar es Salaam, Tanzania; Languages, African: An Overview; Great Britain; Germany; Rift Valleys.

Africa

Maathai, Wangari (b. April 1, 1940, Nyeri, Kenya), renowned Kenyan environmental activist, scholar, and one-time presidential candidate.

Wangari Maathai grew up in a farming family in Nyeri in what was then colonial KENYA's "white highlands." Her parents sent her to Loreto Limuru Girls School, and her teachers there helped her get a scholarship to Mount Scholastica College in Kansas. After graduating with a B.S. in biology in 1964, Maathai attended the University of Pittsburgh. She returned to Kenya in 1966 for graduate study at the University of Nairobi, and in 1971 became one of the first women in sub-Saharan Africa to earn a doctorate (in veterinary medicine). After receiving her Ph.D., Maathai went to work as a professor at the University of Nairobi, eventually becoming the head of the faculty of veterinary medicine there.

Dr. Maathai is most famous for her environmental activism (*see* ENVIRONMENTAL MOVEMENTS IN AFRICA). She founded the Green Belt Movement in 1977, which aimed to prevent or reverse deforestation and also to improve women's economic status by hiring women to plant trees. The women earned 50 Kenyan cents (about U.S.$.04) for every tree that lived longer than three months and at the same time helped replenish local firewood supplies and preserve soil fertility. Since its founding, the Green Belt Movement has been responsible for the planting of approximately 15 million trees and now oversees more than 1500 tree nurseries and offices in 30 African countries. Although it originally received funding from the Mobil Oil Corporation, it later won support from the United Nations and a number of international donor agencies.

Maathai's environmental activities have led to conflicts with the Kenyan government. In 1989, for example, she objected to the proposed construction of a 62-story building (which would have been the tallest building in Africa) in Nairobi's Uhuru Park. She took her protest abroad, lobbying organizations that provided financial assistance to Kenya. Kenyan president DANIEL ARAP MOI ultimately canceled the project, but he also labeled Maathai a subversive and expelled the Green Belt Movement from its Nairobi office.

Maathai's outspokenness brought an end to her marriage – her businessman husband, like many of his peers, objected to her high profile – and frequent government harassment, including beatings and jailings. Still, her political activism broadened in the 1990s. She ran as the Liberal Party's presidential candidate in 1997, but because of her low-key campaign, as well as incorrect news stories near election day reporting that she had pulled out of the race, she did not garner much support.

Maathai has won several international awards, including the Goldman Prize (for environmental activists), the Africa Prize for Leadership, and the Better World Award. She runs the Green Belt Movement from her home in Nairobi.

Eric Bennett

SEE ALSO

Nairobi, Kenya; United Nations in Africa.

Africa

Maba (also known as Fertit, Mandala, and Wadain), ethnic group of north Central Africa.

The Maba primarily inhabit Ouaddai Province in eastern CHAD. Others live in SUDAN. They speak a Nilo-Saharan language. More than 200,000 people consider themselves Maba.

SEE ALSO

Languages, African: An Overview.

North America

Mabley, Jackie ("Moms")

(b. March 19, 1897, Brevard, N.C.; d. May 23, 1975, White Plains, N.Y.), African American vaudeville performer and comedian, the first African American woman to establish herself as a single act in standup comedy.

Jackie "Moms" Mabley rose to national recognition as a standup comedian in the early 1960s. A pioneer of social satire, she strongly influenced such contemporary black comedians as Richard Pryor and WHOOPI GOLDBERG. Author Elsie A. Williams said that Mabley "found a unique way to connect herself to her audience... often breaking propriety and breaching established lines of decorum, across gender, race, and class." Mabley was also known for her compassion and kindness to others – qualities that earned her the endearing sobriquet "Moms" – and focused her humor on the pain and dissonance of black life.

Born Loretta Mary Aiken, Mabley grew up in a large family in Brevard, North Carolina. Her father ran several businesses while her mother presided over a large household that included boarders. When Loretta was 11 her father, a volunteer firefighter, died when his fire truck overturned and exploded.

Loretta underwent additional trauma when, as an adolescent, she was raped twice: first by an older black man and later by the town's white sheriff. Both rapes resulted in pregnancies. Encouraged by her grandmother to make a life for herself, she left her babies in the care of two women and departed for Cleveland, Ohio, where she lived with a minister's family.

In Cleveland, Mabley befriended a number of local entertainers, including the Canadian Jack Mabley, who became her boyfriend. "He took a lot off me," she would later say, "the least I could do was take his name." After singing and dancing in local shows, she began performing throughout the country on the Theater Owners Booking Association (TOBA), a circuit of white- and black-owned theaters catering to African American audiences. Traveling the vaudeville circuit she experienced overt racism and demeaning working conditions and deflected her pain through satirical wit that drew heavily from black folk traditions. As black comedian Godfrey Cambridge observed, "The line that leads to Moms Mabley, NIPSEY RUSSELL, BILL COSBY, and myself can be traced to the social satire of slave humor, back even through minstrels, through countless attempts to cast off that fantasy."

Mabley's career took off when in 1921 the husband-wife vaudeville team Butterbeans and Susie invited her to perform with them in PITTSBURGH, PENNSYLVANIA. She accompanied them to New York and soon began entertaining at nightclubs, including Harlem's COTTON CLUB, where she appeared on bills with Duke Ellington, Count Basie, Louis Armstrong, and Cab Calloway. Mabley also performed in early black theater, and collaborated with HARLEM RENAISSANCE writer ZORA NEALE HURSTON in the Broadway play *Fast and Furious: A Colored Revue in 37 Scenes* (1931).

In her comedy routines Mabley adopted a stage persona based loosely on her own grandmother but with a distinctly cantankerous and sassy edge. She was known for her folksy humor and ribald jokes and affectionately referred to her audience as her "children." Mel Watkins, author of a recent study on African American humor, noted, "The guise [of a granny] provided the buffer or intermediary necessary to quell resistance to a woman doing a single comic routine." It also endeared her to both black and white audiences.

Onstage Mabley became famous for her gaudy housedresses, floppy hats, and oversized clodhoppers. Audiences especially appreciated her spicy, innuendo-laden quips such as "A woman is a woman until the day she dies, but a man's a man only as long as he can"; and "The only thing an old man can do for me is bring a message from a young one."

From 1939 until the 1960s Mabley regularly performed at Harlem's APOLLO THEATER. She also won roles in the films *Killer Diller* (1947) and *Boarding House Blues* (1948), a social commentary on struggling black entertainers in which she starred as a boardinghouse matron. During the 1960s she recorded more than 20 albums of her comedy routines and appeared on television shows hosted by Harry Belafonte, Mike Douglas, Merv Griffin, and Bill Cosby. A year after starring in the feature film *Amazing Grace* (1974), Mabley died of natural causes at age 78.

Roanne Edwards

SEE ALSO

Armstrong, Louis ("Satchmo"); Basie, William James ("Count"); Belafonte, Harold George (Harry); Calloway, Cabell (Cab); Cambridge, Godfrey MacArthur; Pryor, Richard Franklin Lenox Thomas; Minstrelsy; New York, New York; Ellington, Edward Kennedy ("Duke").

Latin America and the Caribbean

Maceo y Grajales, Antonio

(b. June 14, 1845, Majaguabo, San Luis, Oriente province, Cuba; d. December 1896), Cuban black war hero who fought in the Ten Years' War and the Spanish-Cuban-American War.

Antonio Maceo's father was Venezuelan but had lived many years in CUBA. His mother, Mariana Grajales, a Cuban, has become a legend, since eight of her sons and her husband died in the struggle for Cuban independence. At an early age,

Maceo took an interest in the political affairs of the country; he became a mason at age 19.

When landowner Carlos Manuel de Céspedes's call to overthrow the Spaniards, the Grito de Yara of 1868, sparked the beginning of the TEN YEARS' WAR, Maceo was among the insurrectionists. By mid-January 1869, three months later, his military exploits had earned him the rank of commander; soon after he became a lieutenant colonel. Careful, thoughtful, and quick thinking, Maceo became a true genius of guerrilla warfare, which he learned from Máximo Gómez. He mastered the art of the false defeat: pretending his troops had been routed, he would lead them to retreat in such a way as to ambush the pursuing troops. The insurrectionary forces were divided on the issue of abolition (*see* ABOLITION AND EMANCIPATION IN LATIN AMERICA AND THE CARIBBEAN). Maceo, an Afro-Cuban proud of his racial heritage, favored abolition and freed the slaves on territory liberated by his army. His courage and inspirational leadership made him a revered military figure, even respected by the Spanish. One of his famous mottoes was "Liberty is not begged for, it is conquered."

The divisions on the issue of abolition haunted Maceo. The more conservative of the rebel factions often accused him of favoring black officers and of hiding his true aim, the establishment of a separate black republic, like HAITI. Whites in conservative opposition factions, especially landowners who had slaves, often raised the possibility of Cuba's becoming another Haiti in order to undermine the more radical factions of the separatist movement; the Spanish raised the issue to discredit the movement altogether. Maceo either ignored these blatant comments or responded with dignified and eloquent statements that reiterated his basic position: Cuba's independence required the sacrifice and commitment of all Cubans and would benefit all Cubans – black, white, and mulatto.

Maceo was eventually put in charge of all forces in Oriente province. However, like Gómez, he felt the insurrection should go westward, to all of Cuba, thus crippling the economic viability of the Spanish war effort. Maceo actually tried to pursue this course, but when his success in going westward resulted in high casualties, he stopped. The rest of the war left those areas intact. Despite internal differences, bickering, and racism among rebel factions, Maceo's brilliance during the war was consistent. His stature further increased when the war was over. The Zanjón Peace Treaty in February 1878 inspired Maceo's Protest of Baraguá the following month. Maceo claimed that the treaty sold the Cubans short; that because neither abolition nor independence had been achieved, it was not a peace treaty but a truce. Although most Cubans had grown weary of the war, they admired Maceo's principled stance. Along with Calixto García and others, Maceo launched La Guerra Chiquita (The Little War) in August 1879, which lasted less than a year.

A hero in the war for Cuba's independence, Antonio Maceo y Grajales honored his African heritage in his unwavering commitment to the abolition of slavery and equal rights for all Cubans. *Photographs and Prints Division, Schomburg Center for Research in Black Culture, The New York Public Library, Astor, Lenox and Tilden Foundation*

Shortly after this unsuccessful effort, Maceo left Cuba. In exile in the 1880s he continued to conspire to renew the Cuban independence struggle, but every attempt ended in failure. For some years he farmed and pursued business ventures in Costa Rica. During this period he returned once to Cuba in 1890, where he was greeted like a hero by Cubans from all walks of life. By 1892 JOSÉ MARTÍ had formed the Cuban Revolutionary Party and actively sought out Maceo, along with Máximo Gómez, to be his top military commanders. Maceo again fully dedicated himself to the cause, raising funds over the next few years in several countries. In April 1895, after an abortive attempt months earlier, he landed in Oriente province to initiate Cuba's second major war for independence, under the political leadership of Martí (*see* SPANISH-CUBAN-AMERICAN WAR).

The rebels quickly achieved military success under Gómez and Maceo. This time the war succeeded in moving westward. In a period of 90 days Maceo's troops covered about 1667 km (1000 mi, from one end of the island to the other), fought 27 battles, burned and destroyed 59 towns, and captured more than 2000 rifles, 80,000 rounds of ammunition, 3000 horses, and even two cannons. One United States military historian called it "the most audacious military feat of the century." Maceo's achievement brought him international renown.

Gómez, however, needed Maceo back in Oriente province, and while attempting to return, Maceo and his troops were ambushed. Maceo was shot and killed. It was December 1896, and despite Spanish predictions to the contrary, Cuba's insurrection, even without Maceo, continued to flourish. The Bronze Titan, as he was known, had received more than 25 bullet wounds during his military career.

Maceo was one of the great figures of the Latin American independence movement, like Simón Bolívar, San Martín, and others. His commitment to Cuba's independence was total, as was his vision of racial equality. Cuba had finally abolished slavery in 1886, but discrimination remained widespread. Estimates suggest that between 60 and 80 percent of blacks and mulattos were among the ranks of the Cuban insurrectionary forces. Maceo was not the only black officer: Flor Crombet, Guillermo Moncada, Quintín Banderas, Cecilio González, Pedro Díaz, and José Maceo (Antonio's brother) also distinguished themselves, but none achieved his fame. In particular, Maceo became both symbol and inspiration for Afro-Cubans. At the turn of the century and later, many African Americans who had come to know Maceo's exploits gave their sons Maceo as a first name.

Alan West

Latin America and the Caribbean

Machado de Assis, Joaquim Maria **(b. June 21, 1839, Rio de Janeiro, Brazil; d. September 29, 1908, Rio de Janeiro, Brazil), Afro-Brazilian playwright, poet, and one of the most famous Latin American novelists; his biting works studied the contradictions of late nineteenth-century Brazilian society.**

Machado de Assis was the son of a mulatto house painter and a Portuguese Azorian woman. His parents were free employees attached to a wealthy white family in Rio de Janeiro, with whom they also lived as retainers. When Machado's mother died of tuberculosis in 1849, the family remained connected to the estate, maintaining a complex relationship in which dependence was the price for access to certain benefits and opportunities. (This early, ambiguous social position would later be seized by critics, who saw it as a distinguishing trait both of Machado's life and of his writings.) Machado's youth was marked by early signs of his frail health – stuttering, nearsightedness, severe nervousness, and epilepsy would accompany him throughout his life – and by access to education afforded by the protection of the owner of the estate. His vast literary knowledge, however, was largely self-taught.

Machado's education permitted him to perform various jobs related to publishing. At 20 he was already writing for newspapers, such as *Correio Mercantil* in Rio de Janeiro. There he distinguished himself as a chronicler,

Brazilian writer Machado de Assis was known for his sense of humor and cynical views of late nineteenth-century society in Rio de Janeiro. He authored five major novels. *Oronoz*

literary critic, poet, and journalist and soon became acquainted with the most important intellectuals of his time. In 1869 he married a well-to-do white Portuguese woman who would later inspire several of his characters, most notably Carmo in *Memorial de Aires* (1908).

With various forms of bureaucratic employment securing his well-being, Machado de Assis published six books during what is called his Romantic period, among them *Helena* (1876) and *Iaiá Garcia* (1878). Between 1878 and 1880 he turned his attention to poetry and wrote some of the most anthologized poems in the Portuguese language. He is best remembered for the novelistic production that followed this period, when the ambiguous realism for which he is known would flourish. Novels such as *Memórias Póstumas de Brás Cubas* (1881, Posthumous Memoirs of Brás Cubas); *Quincas Borba* (1892), *Dom Casmurro* (1900), and *Esaú e Jacó* (1904) continue to be read as the most acute dissections of the late nineteenth-century upper classes. He was, according to Brazilian literary critic Roberto Schwartz, a master of exposing, with profound irony, the relationships among classes in the Brazilian Empire and the early First Republic (*see* BRAZIL). However, in none of Machado's novels are blacks or mulattos the protagonists. Even in works that refer to slavery, whites are the focus.

For this and other reasons, the critic David Haberly suggests that Machado's work was a "highly evasive and ambiguous journal of his passage from nonwhiteness to whiteness." A common criticism of Machado has been that the passage from poor mulatto child to respectable intellectual figure required masking his past, distancing himself from any form of black culture, and avoiding social causes related to blacks, most importantly abolitionism. His fiction is said to be dominated by a profound skepticism concerning the possibility of transformative action and an overwhelming pessimism regarding the human condition. For other readers his skepticism, pessimism, and irony are themselves forms of criticism related to Machado's tenuous status as a nonwhite man in a racist, elitist society.

In 1896 Machado de Assis founded the prestigious Brazilian Academy of Letters, of which he was also the first president. During his lifetime he was already considered the greatest Brazilian novelist, a reputation that would survive him. He died at age 69 of a cancerous ulcer.

Machado's death provoked an outburst of praise exceeding the approbation accorded any other Brazilian writer, but the heated debates that surfaced at the time anticipated the polemic nature of his legacy. Not surprisingly, though the quality of his writing is rarely questioned, some of the most enduring disputes concern racial issues.

In a newspaper article published only 20 days after Machado's death, Hemétrio José dos Santos, while recognizing the brilliance of the deceased writer, claimed that his silence on the most important issue of his day, slavery, could not be ignored. Beginning at his death and continuing into the present, Machado has been fiercely attacked for this alleged silence.

As much as his writings' approach to race, Machado's own racial politics have been the subject of discussion. White abolitionist JOAQUIM NABUCO strongly criticized a reference to Machado as a mulatto, published shortly after his death (*see* WHITE ABOLITIONISTS IN BRAZIL). Nabuco insisted that Machado would have forfeited his fame rather than reveal a racial background he sought so vigorously to conceal. "I would not have called him a mulatto," wrote Nabuco. "And I believe that nothing would hurt him more than this classification.... Machado was white to me and I believe he thought of himself in the same way. Whatever alien blood there might have been, it in no way affected his purely Caucasian character. I, at least, saw in him only the Greek." David Haberly, for one, claims it was precisely this that should be seen as Machado's "most astonishing fictive achievement."

Marcos Natalí

SEE ALSO

Slavery in Latin America and the Caribbean; Rio de Janeiro, Brazil.

Africa

Machel, Graça (b. 1945, Portuguese East Africa [Mozambique]), Mozambican minister of education and international human rights advocate.

The youngest of six children, Graça Machel, née Simbine, was a leading figure in MOZAMBIQUE's war for independence. She became a prominent national and international figure not only as an education and human rights advocate but also as the wife of the late Mozambican president Samora Machel (d. 1986).

In the early 1970s Graça Machel received a scholarship to study romance languages at the University of Lisbon, Portugal. She soon became involved in clandestine work for the Mozambican opposition group FRONT FOR THE LIBERATION OF MOZAMBIQUE (FRELIMO) and in 1973 went to TANZANIA to join the war for independence. After some time in the "liberated zones" of Mozambique, she returned to Tanzania, where Samora Machel was also working with FRELIMO, to run FRELIMO's school. In 1974 she was a member of the team that negotiated Mozambique's independence. The following year she became minister of education and the only female cabinet member in independent Mozambique, while Samora Machel, now her husband, became president.

As minister of education, Machel promoted universal elementary education, a goal that was severely undermined by the war with MOZAMBICAN NATIONAL RESISTANCE (RENAMO) as well as by the country's persistent poverty. After holding her cabinet position for 14 years, Machel left the government and later chaired the United Nations Study on the Plight of Children in Situations of Armed Conflict in 1990. She also established the Foundation for Community Development, a nonprofit organization in Mozambique working to eliminate poverty and protect women and children. In September 1996 it was disclosed that Graça Machel had become romantically involved with long-time friend Nelson Mandela, then president of South Africa; the two were married on Mandela's 80th birthday in July 1998.

Eric Young

SEE ALSO

Machel, Samora Moises; Mandela, Nelson Rolihlahla; Human Rights in Africa.

Africa

Machel, Samora Moises (b. January 29, 1933, Chilembene, Portuguese East Africa [present-day Mozambique]; d. October 19, 1986, Mbuzini, South Africa), revolutionary leader and former president of Mozambique.

Samora Machel was one of Africa's most famous revolutionary figures, known for his charisma and disciplined character. As a revolutionary leader and as president of MOZAMBIQUE, Machel created a cult of personality wrapped in Marxist ideology and populism.

Like many of the Mozambican nationalist leaders, Machel was a southerner who attended Catholic schools in his youth. He trained as a nurse and worked in Maputo's central hospital before joining the nationalist group FRONT FOR THE LIBERATION OF MOZAMBIQUE (FRELIMO), led by Eduardo Mondlane, in 1962. After receiving military training in ALGERIA the following year, Machel returned to lead many military operations during the war for independence. As the war progressed, Machel became commander of Nachingwea, FRELIMO's military training camp in TANZANIA; in 1966 he became FRELIMO's secretary of defense and, in 1968, commander in chief. Shortly after the assassination of Eduardo Mondlane in 1969, Machel assumed the presidency of FRELIMO.

In 1975 Machel became president of independent Mozambique. Throughout his presidency Machel remained a Marxist, though most observers agree that his politics drew little on academic theories. Instead, he relied heavily on his oratorical skills at mass rallies, where his speeches attacking capitalism and imperialism had great popular appeal. Routinely he presented "enemies of the people" to be judged by the masses and used medical analogies to illustrate his arguments. He considered scientific socialism a universal theory that could be applied to Mozambique, with the help of a strong centralized state and *poder popular*, or popular power, despite the unique nature of the Mozambican revolution. But Machel's plan to create a laboratory of scientific socialism was confounded by the war against the insurgent group MOZAMBICAN NATIONAL RESISTANCE (RENAMO), which consumed more and more of the president's time.

As the war against RENAMO escalated, Machel sought to open up Mozambique while still maintaining control over society. He turned to the West for military assistance and tried to make peace with SOUTH AFRICA. He loosened state control of the economy and eased restrictions on religious groups, especially the Catholic Church. At the same time Machel waged several political "*ofensivas*" (offensives), imposing severe penalties for corruption, stealing, and collaborating with the enemy. He increasingly appealed to patriotism rather than class identity and brought many veterans of the liberation struggle back into the government and military. Although Machel rarely left the capital and fell increasingly out of touch with local realities, he continued to hold mass rallies and media events to build on his *poder popular*.

Machel died in October 1986 when his plane crashed in South Africa. The circumstances of the crash remain suspicious: many contend that the South African government was involved, while others blame the negligence of the Soviet pilots. Machel continues to be revered and honored throughout Mozambique. He was succeeded by his foreign minister, JOAQUIM CHISSANO, and survived by his second wife, GRAÇA MACHEL, a prominent international human rights and child welfare activist.

Eric Young

SEE ALSO

African Socialism; Maputo, Mozambique; Nationalism in Africa.

Latin America and the Caribbean

Machito (Frank Raoul Grillo)

(b. 1909?, HAVANA, CUBA; d. April 15, 1984, London, England), Afro-Cuban bandleader and vocalist, one of the founders of Afro-Cuban JAZZ.

The son of a cigar manufacturer, Frank Raoul Grillo was the first son born to a family that had three daughters, hence his lifelong nickname, Machito, or "little man." He had his first musical experiences as a child, dancing and singing with workers at his father's company. After he grew up, he played bongos and tumbadora in various Cuban bands, including the Sexteto Nacional. In the autumn of 1937 he left CUBA for New York City, where he sang and played maracas with a number of Latin bands, including a stint as the lead singer in Xavier Cugat's orchestra. In 1940 Machito organized his big band, the Afro-Cubans, and the following year his brother-in-law MARIO BAUZA joined the band as music director, a position he held for 35 years.

Machito credited Duke Ellington as his principal inspiration and recounted that in the beginning his band sounded like "a combination of the Duke and Glenn Miller, but we quickly went into our own style." The Afro-Cubans' first successful integration of Latin music and jazz was Bauza's composition "Tanga," the title of which derived from an African term for marijuana. "Tanga" soon became the band's theme song. During the late 1940s and early 1950s Machito's performances and recordings increased the American audience for Afro-Cuban jazz. The band also brought the unfamiliar new harmonies of bebop or bop into Afro-Cuban music. Machito's Afro-Cubans – along with Dizzy Gillespie's big band – were instrumental in the emergence of what some dubbed Cubop. Machito's breakthrough performance occurred on January 24, 1947, at New York's Town Hall in a concert that also featured Stan Kenton's popular white big band. Kenton was so impressed with the Afro-Cubans' sound that he borrowed Machito's rhythm section later that year when he recorded Moises Simón's "El manisero" ("The Peanut Vendor").

Among Machito's significant early recordings was a 1949 version of "Tanga" featuring an impassioned solo by white tenor saxophonist Flip Phillips that brought the band considerable attention beyond New York City. Also influential was Machito's recording of Arturo "Chico" O'Farrill's classic "Afro-Cuban Suite" (1950), in which the Afro-Cubans performed with soloists Phillips, Charlie Parker, trumpeter Harry "Sweets" Edison, and white jazz drummer Buddy Rich. Machito's orchestra maintained its popularity through the 1950s and into the early 1960s. After several lean years the band regained its popular following during the salsa craze of the 1970s and 1980s.

One of Machito's finest later albums was *Afro-Cuban Jazz Moods* (1975), a suite composed and arranged by Chico O'Farrill that featured Dizzy Gillespie as guest soloist. The Afro-Cubans maintained a busy touring schedule into the 1980s, appearing in jazz festivals and clubs as well as on the salsa circuit. In 1984 Machito suffered a fatal stroke during a gig at Ronnie Scott's, London's premier jazz club. He was the subject of Carlos Ortiz's documentary *Machito: A Jazz Legacy* (1987).

James Clyde Sellman

SEE ALSO

Gillespie, John Birks ("Dizzy"); New York, New York; Parker, Charles Christopher ("Bird"); Ellington, Edward Kennedy ("Duke"); Mambo; Salsa Music.

Africa

Macías Nguema, Francisco

(b. January 1, 1924, Mongomo region, Spanish Guinea [present-day Equatorial Guinea]; d. September 1979, Malabo, Equatorial Guinea), president and self-proclaimed Unique Miracle of EQUATORIAL GUINEA.

Born, raised, and educated in the Mongomo region of Equatorial Guinea, Francisco Macías Nguema as president relied on family connections and repression to maintain his dictatorship. As a youth, his Catholic teachers noted his paranoia, megalomania, and feelings of inferiority. In 1944 he began working for the Spanish colonial administration, which in 1960 appointed him mayor of Mongomo. In the 1960s he joined a series of nationalist parties, although he never directly opposed Spain, and was elected to Parliament and appointed minister of public works. With support from conservative Spanish interests, he won the presidency shortly before Equatorial Guinea became independent in October 1968.

Soon afterward Macías Nguema used an allegedly faked coup d'état attempt as a pretext for executing his opponents. His paranoia and cruelty defined his rule for the next 11 years. Arbitrary arrests, executions, tortures, and atrocities were conducted by his presidential militia, the national guard, and the militant youth movement – all controlled by his family members from Mongomo. An estimated one-third of the country's population fled to GABON, CAMEROON, and SPAIN from Macías Nguema's regime in Equatorial Guinea, which the human rights group Amnesty International called "among the most brutal and unpredictable in the world." Macías Nguema outlawed the word "intellectual," destroyed fishing boats to prevent smuggling and escape from Bioko Island, and decreed that all citizens replace their Christian names with African ones. He proclaimed himself the Unique Miracle and president-for-life of Equatorial Guinea. In 1979, after directly threatening the integrity of the National Guard, his nephew, TEODORO OBIANG NGUEMA MBASOGO, who was head of the guard, succeeded in overthrowing, trying, and executing Macías Nguema, describing him as "an envoy of the Devil and president of sorcerers." Stories remain that Macías Nguema is still alive.

Eric Young

SEE ALSO
Nationalism in Africa.

Latin America and the Caribbean

Mackandal (b. 1715?, Guinea Coast, Africa; d. 1758, Haiti), a semimythical priest, prophet, and revolutionary maroon (runaway slave) leader in Saint-Domingue (now HAITI).

Though little is known about Mackandal's early life, and much of the information about him is shrouded in myth, this famous maroon has become a legendary figure. Most prominent historians do not mention him, but he has become a symbol of Haitian national identity, and all schoolchildren in Haiti learn about his life.

Mackandal is said to have come to the French-ruled colony of Saint-Domingue (now Haiti) around 1750. Slave traders had bought him on the coast of GUINEA, in Africa, and he was taken to the colony, where he worked as a field hand (*see* SLAVERY IN LATIN AMERICA AND THE CARIBBEAN).

According to accounts of his life, Mackandal did not submit to slavery for very long. He soon escaped to the woods, becoming a *marron* (a fugitive slave) (*see* MAROONAGE IN THE AMERICAS). Prizes were offered for his capture but he escaped all ambushes. It is also said that Mackandal was a learned man, that he could read and write in Arabic, and that, as a Muslim, he carried a Koran.

Unlike some other rebel slaves, Mackandal is said not to have used outright violence against slave owners. Instead, it is held that he favored poisoning, and his knowledge of books made him aware of poisonous fruits, foods, herbs, and plants. He attacked white slave owners and disobedient blacks by poisoning their drinking water, while supplying antidotes to the slaves. It is also said that he could give a special poison to nursing black nannies; the poison purportedly would not harm the nannies but would kill the white babies. According to documents uncovered by scholar Joan Dayan, more than 6000 people may have been poisoned in what was called the "great fear of 1755."

Because Mackandal escaped capture despite a high bounty on his head, the legend of his invulnerability spread. It is said that no bullet could kill him, that the French soldiers could not catch him because he could transform into a bird and fly away, and that he could appear and suddenly disappear, as if swallowed by a cloud.

After living in freedom for a few years, protected by the silence and assistance of slaves who helped hide him and supplied him with food, Mackandal was finally captured by the French in an ambush. He was convicted of the creation and distribution of poison. In order to destroy the myths surrounding him, and thus decrease his influence on the slave population, the French executed Mackandal in public so that everyone could witness his death. He was burned alive and his ashes were dispersed to the winds so that no one could take his cadaver and say that he had been resurrected. But onlookers claimed that as he was being burned alive, Mackandal shouted out some fierce words in an African language and a firebird flew out of his mouth.

Mackandal's spirit has indeed survived, both as a national symbol and as a spirit believed to communicate with the living: in the most famous example, it is said that Mackandal's spirit warned JEAN-JACQUES DESSALINES, Haiti's revolutionary leader, about his impending betrayal and death in October 1806. The figure of Mackandal has remained part of Haitian history and literature. Partly mythical, partly historic, Mackandal is seen as one of the great combatants for Haiti's independence.

Paulette Poujol-Orion

Maconde. Please see MAKONDE

Africa

Madagascar, republic in the Indian Ocean, located 390 km (242.3 mi) off the coast of MOZAMBIQUE. Madagascar is made up of Madagascar Island, Africa's largest island and the fourth largest island in the world, and several small islands.

More than 1600 km (994.2 mi) long and 570 km (354.2 mi) wide, Madagascar has a total area of 587,040 sq km (226,658 sq mi). The island is both geographically and demographically complex. Some 14.8 million people of Southeast Asian, African, and Arabic descent, along with more recent Indian and Chinese immigrants, are distributed throughout the island's six microclimates. Eighteen ethnic groups are traditionally identified, each associated with a geographical area. Farmers cultivate predominately patty rice for subsistence. Coffee, cloves, and vanilla are the main cash crops.

A mountain plateau runs along the length of Madagascar, rising steeply from the Indian Ocean on the east and sloping more gently to the western shores. The ridge causes a rain shadow, capturing the moisture of the tradewinds. Consequently, the east coast receives the largest share of the island's rainfall and is home to tropical rain forests, such as Masoala Peninsula, rich in endangered fauna and flora. Many cash crops, including vanilla, cloves, and coffee, are grown here. Antsirnana province to the north has fertile volcanic soils, allowing a number of important crops to be grown. Only 29,000 sq km (11,000 sq mi) of the island's soils are arable. The northwest region is another important agricultural district. Despite the excellent soils, the southwest lacks precipitation and is used primarily to graze cattle. The area is also rich in minerals and semiprecious stones. Antananarivo, the densely populated capital, is located in the central highlands. Extensive *swidden* agriculture, a farming method that involves cutting and burning a forested area to clear fields for crops, and the resulting erosion have deteriorated the land where cattle are now grazed. The southern plateau contains the oldest rock formations on the surface of the earth, dating from 1500 million years ago.

The island of Madagascar separated from the African mainland during the Late Jurassic or Upper Cretaceous period, about 130 million years ago. The resulting isolation led to the evolution of remarkable endemic species. Most famous, perhaps, are the island's population of tarsiers, LEMURS, and lorises. These primates retain many primitive features of early hominoids. Tenrecs, civets, mongooses, and bats add to the unique wildlife of the island. Five percent of the entire world's species can be found in Madagascar, 90 percent of which are endemic to the island. To combat the loss of biodiversity, the World Wildlife Fund (WWF) began a debt-for-nature exchange program, setting up conservation projects. The island's unique biogeography is matched only by its colorful history, including the synthesis of a singular blend of African and Asian cultures.

PRECOLONIAL HISTORY

Due to sparse physical evidence, scholars debate the details of the island's human history. Linguistic and cultural evidence suggests that the earliest migrants came to the island from Indonesia around the second or third century C.E. in outrigger canoes. The exact route taken by these pioneers is unclear. The consensus among scholars is

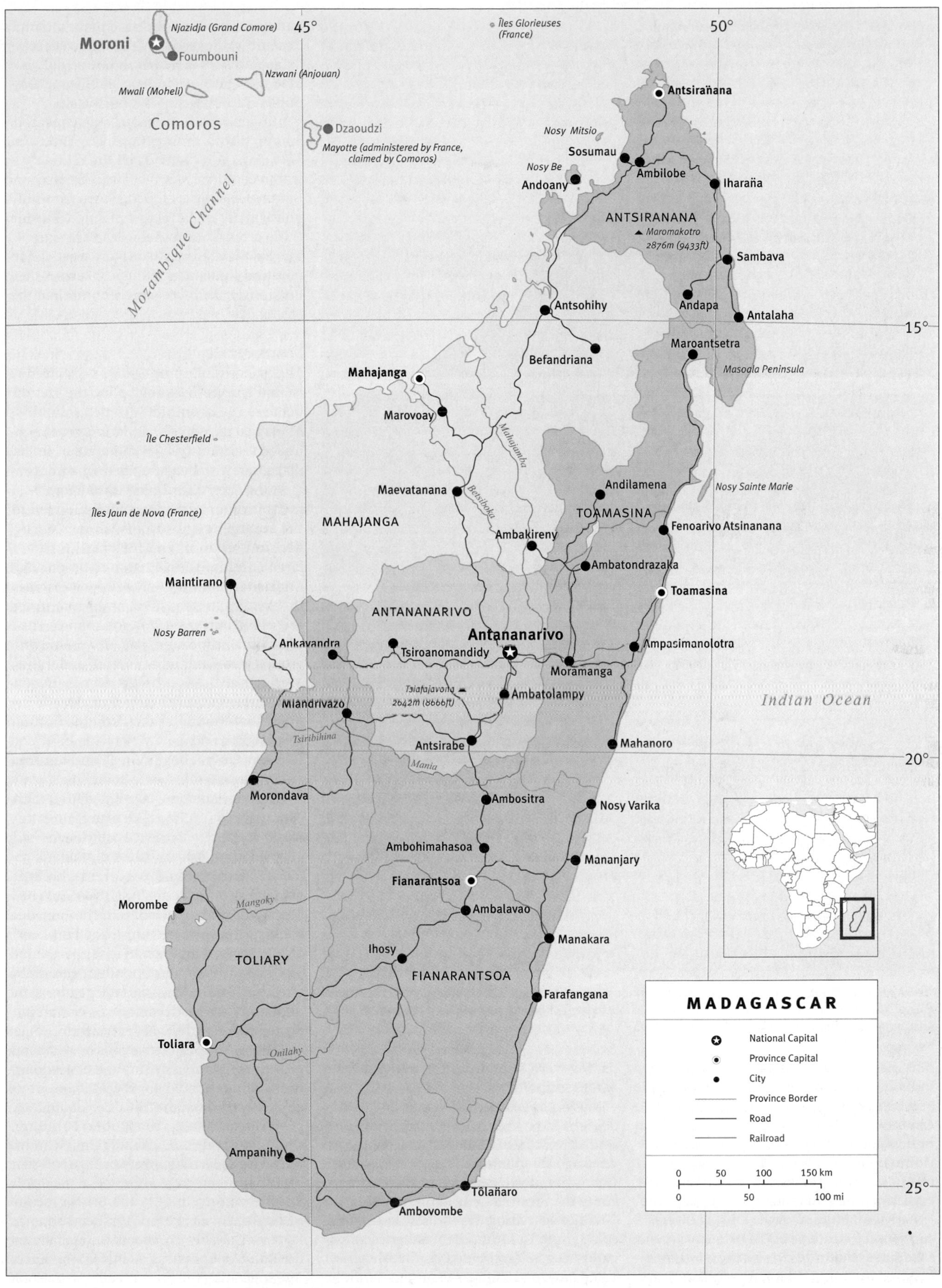
MADAGASCAR
National Capital
Province Capital
City
Province Border
Road
Railroad
0 50 100 150 km
0 50 100 mi
Moroni
Foumbouni
Njazidja (Grand Comore)
Nzwani (Anjouan)
Mwali (Moheli)
Comoros
Dzaoudzi
Mayotte (administered by France, claimed by Comoros)
Îles Glorieuses (France)
Mozambique Channel
Indian Ocean
Antsirañana
Nosy Mitsio
Sosumau
Ambilobe
Nosy Be
Andoany
Iharaña
ANTSIRANANA
Maromakotro 2876m (9433ft)
Sambava
Andapa
Antalaha
Antsohihy
Befandriana
Maroantsetra
Masoala Peninsula
Mahajanga
Marovoay
Mahajamba
Île Chesterfield
Maevatanana
Betsiboka
Andilamena
Nosy Sainte Marie
TOAMASINA
Fenoarivo Atsinanana
Îles Jaun de Nova (France)
MAHAJANGA
Ambakireny
Ambatondrazaka
Toamasina
Maintirano
ANTANANARIVO
Antananarivo
Nosy Barren
Ankavandra
Tsiroanomandidy
Ampasimanolotra
Moramanga
Tsiafajavona 2642m (8666ft)
Ambatolampy
Miandrivazo
Tsiribihina
Antsirabe
Mahanoro
Mania
Morondava
Ambositra
Nosy Varika
Ambohimahasoa
Mananjary
Fianarantsoa
Morombe
Mangoky
Ambalavao
Manakara
Ihosy
TOLIARY
FIANARANTSOA
Farafangana
Toliara
Onilahy
Ampanihy
Tôlañaro
Ambovombe
45°
50°
15°
20°
25°

TOP: **A group of buildings in Madagascar's mountainous central plateau.** *CORBIS/John Corbett; Ecoscene*
ABOVE: **The inhabitants of Madagascar, the world's fourth largest island, share a heritage that blends African, Arabic, and Indonesian influences.** *CORBIS/Chris Rainier*

that they traveled along the coast of the Indian Ocean Rim, as Indonesian linguistic and cultural traits can be found in southern India, Arabia, and eastern Africa. More radical routes have been suggested; Tom Hobman of New Zealand sailed from Indonesia directly to Madagascar in a traditional craft to support his thesis of a direct route.

Early inhabitants survived using diverse subsistence strategies. The extensive use of swidden agriculture over long periods has resulted in large-scale deforestation. Early inhabitants grew rice, YAMS, toro, and arrowroot. PASTORALISM, foraging, and particularly fishing were also important activities of earlier inhabitants.

Muslim traders of Arab, Bantu, and Persian descent, known as Antolalotra, began to settle in northern Madagascar around 1000 years ago, adopting the MALAGASY language. Goods produced in Madagascar were traded along the SWAHILI COAST and in Arabia.

While searching the Indian Ocean for a spice route to India, the Portuguese navigator Diego-Diaz landed on the island in 1500, naming it Ile Saint Laurent. With the coming of Europeans, Islamic dominance over trade declined. The Portuguese, French, and English all made subsequent attempts to settle Madagascar, with limited success. Large numbers of pirates, however, did make Madagascar their home, establishing a republic, Libertalia, in the northeast.

Indigenous monarchical rule appeared among three ethnic groups, the Antimoro, SAKALAVA, and MERINA, by the mid-sixteenth century. Later the BARA, BETSILEO, and BETSIMISARAKA developed similar forms of political organization. As in feudal Europe, these groups competed with each other. The Sakalava expanded to the west, incorporating smaller chiefdoms. Likewise, the Betsimisaraka increasingly controlled the east coast.

MERINA RULE

After successfully employing an expansionist and empire-building policy, the Merina became the dominant ethnic group in Madagascar. While the Merina never controlled the country in its entirety, the Merina dialect grew to become the lingua franca.

Along the central plateau the implementation of patty rice cultivation led to the emergence of surplus, an increased division of labor, and the creation of large chiefdoms. In 1780 the Merina ruler Andrianampoinimerina began coalescing these chiefdoms into an empire centered around his throne at Ambohimanga. The Betsileo, Bezanozano, and Sihanaka ethnic groups were later incorporated under the Merina political umbrella. A brilliant general and accomplished political leader, Andrianampoinimerina instituted taxation laws, courts, and a network of administrators to maintain his hegemony. Land tenure and marriage rules were codified into law.

His son, Radama I, continued his father's expansionist policies, incorporating the Sakalava Empire to the west during the early 1820s. Ramada established diplomatic relations with the colonial forces who were vying for power in the Indian Ocean. The Merina court benefited from the continual conflicts between the British and French as Madagascar remained an essential source of vital supplies for dependent colonial outposts like Bourbon and the nearby island of MAURITIUS. Madagascar was also an important source of slaves for nearby colonies.

The British courted relations with Radama, providing military advisors and educational training in exchange for access to resources and a promise to abolish slave trading. The governor of MAURITIUS, Robert Farquher, sent a general to advise Radama, who in return signed a trade treaty in 1816 and sent his two brothers to be educated in the nearby English colony. In 1817 the British recognized Radama as king. With their support Radama was able to conquer the Manabe and the Boina, eliminating all major resistance. After defeating the French in the Napoleonic Wars, the British controlled the Indian Ocean; however, the French continued to solicit

A man from the Mahafaly ethnic group visits the tomb of his father. Although Madagascar is home to at least 18 major ethnic groups, nearly all share common Malagasy characteristics, including ancestor worship and the erection of stone monuments to the dead. *CORBIS/Chris Hellier*

relations with both Radama and his Sakalava and Betsimisaraka rivals.

Radama was succeeded by his wife, Ranavalona. The queen killed any potential rival to the throne and took an anti-Christian, anticolonial stance. Christians were persecuted and previous treaties with European powers were declared null and void. In 1857 she exiled all Europeans. Ranavalona was a skilled politician who attempted to assert Malagasy independence from colonial powers. Ultimately, however, she was not successful.

With the death of Ranavalona in 1861, her son, Prince Rakoto, ascended to the throne as Radama II, reinstating the foreign policies of his namesake. Ramada II signed treaties with both the British and French, ensuring Europeans the right to purchase property and guaranteeing them the right to religious freedom. His strong pro-European stance met with popular resistance and led to his assassination in 1863. Radama's widow, Rasoherina, became queen. She abolished the absolute monarchy and appointed a prime minister, Rainilaiarivony, whom she married. Rainilaiarivony had a long political career, notably marrying Rasoherina's two successors.

Colonial History

With the opening of the Suez Canal in 1869, British strategic interest in Madagascar waned. The island continued to interest the French as a potential colony. They used an unremarkable property dispute as an excuse to take control of the island, instigating armed conflict and placing a naval blockade around the island. A settlement was reached in 1885, granting greater authority to the French. Neither side was satisfied with the outcome and tensions continued to rise. Within a few years France demanded that the Merina court cease any foreign relations and allow the French navy to establish a permanent presence. The prolonged conflict came to a head in 1895 when French and Malagasy troops entered into combat. Meeting minimal resistance, France secured a surrender in September of that year.

In 1896 Madagascar was formally declared a French colony, a status the island would retain for 64 years. Slavery was abolished and more than a million people were emancipated. From 1896 to 1905 Gen. Joseph Simon Galliéni governed Madagascar, stamping out anti-European sentiment through force. He exiled Ranavalona to Algeria and brought 7000 troops to quell any resistance. Under Galliéni's tenure a number of educational, social, and health programs were instituted. He also demanded a head tax from all Malagasy, payable in currency or labor. Despite his having made some improvements in infrastructure, resistance to French rule grew, culminating in the formation of a nationalist political party, the Vy Vato Sakeliak (VVS). In 1915 VVS leaders and hundreds of members were imprisoned.

In 1942, two years after the fall of France during World War II, the British government, fearful that the Japanese would seize Madagascar, dispatched an expeditionary force to the island. In 1943 the British surrendered control to the Free French government. Political reforms were instituted and in 1946 Madagascar had representation in the French Parliament. Merina members of the Mouvement démocratique pour la rénovation malgache (MDRM) won all three seats. Minority fears of Merina domination led to the formation of the Parti des déshérités de Madagascar (PADESM). Conflicts between MDRM and PADESM members led to riots in 1947. According to the PADESM, two MDRM secret societies – the Parti Nationaliste Malgache (PANAMA) and the Jeunesse Nationale (JINA), founded by Manja Jaona – instigated the conflict. The riots developed into a low-level guerrilla conflict lasting one year, during which between 80,000 and 100,000 people were killed by a fierce French suppression. MDRM leaders were either killed or imprisoned.

Despite tax and labor incentives, French attempts to develop a plantation economy in Madagascar largely failed. Nor did any

Farmers in Madagascar construct terraces for the rice they farm as their primary subsistence crop. Other crops include coffee, cloves, and vanilla, which are mostly raised for export. *CORBIS/Chris Hellier*

significant industries develop. The Malagasy population resented and resisted French rule and administrative practices, which they felt lacked legitimacy. Although many French companies mined Madagascar's natural resources, such recalcitrance undermined the ability of the French to alter the traditional Malagasy economy and create a fiscally successful colony.

Independence

By the end of World War II Malagasy political leaders were demanding greater autonomy, with an eye cast toward independence. In 1958 Madagascar was granted status as an autonomous state of the French Community. Independence came in 1960.

Philibert Tsiranana became the first president in 1959, leading the Parti social démocrate (PSD) on a pro-Western, anticommunist platform. Ethnic antagonisms shaped the political domain in post-independent Madagascar, with the PSD representing broad-based côtier (non-Merina) interests and the Parti du congrès de l'indépendance de Madagascar (AKFM) lobbying for Merina demands, led by Richard Andimanjato.

Tsiranana remained in office until 1972, when discontent turned into riots. Thirty-four people were killed, leading Tsiranana to relinquish power to Gen. Gabriel Ramanantsoa, who established a five-year transitional government to write a new constitution. However, continued ethnic conflict between the Merina and côtiers, a poor economy, and internal fractures led to a coup in 1975. Ramanantsoa was forced to hand over the reins of power to Col. Richard Ratsimandrava, who was assassinated only six days later. Gen. Gilles Andriamahazo stepped in, establishing martial law and banning political parties. Four months later, on June 15, 1975, Andriamahazo stepped down and a "supreme revolutionary council" (CSR) was established by Lt.-Cmdr. Didier Ratsiraka, a PADESM founder.

Ratsiraka formed the socialist Democratic Republic of Madagascar, serving as its only president until he was ousted in 1992. Martial law was lifted but the press continued to be censored. Essential industries, such as banks, were nationalized. Whereas independent Madagascar had previously taken a strong anticommunist stance, Ratsiraka's government pursued a policy of nonalignment, courting relations with the Union of Soviet Socialist Republics (USSR) and the Democratic People's Republic of Korea, and publishing his own "little red book." To demarcate a change in political policy, a Second Republic was declared.

Elections were held in 1977 in which Ratsiraka's Avant-garde de la révolution malgache (AREMA), the only party legal under the constitution, won the majority of seats in the National Popular Assembly. His party won the vast majority of seats again in 1983.

During the 1970s and 1980s bands of unemployed youths, the Tanora Tonga Saina (TTS, Revolutionary Youths) and the Zatovo Western Andevo Malgasy (ZOAM, Young Slave Cowboys of Madagascar), formed to commit petty crime and extortion. A reactionary group of kung fu devotees formed vigilante bands, attacking and killing 100 to 250 TTS members before the government intervened. Ratsiraka banned kung fu, and government forces attacked the martial arts centers, killing the leader, Pierre Mizael Rakotoarijaona, and hundreds of devotees.

Social unrest continued in 1986 and 1987. Students protested proposed educational reforms. Famine in the south instigated violent riots. Ethnic tensions mounted and several Indians were killed. Despite these turbulent years, Ratsiraka was elected once again in 1989, although with less support. In 1990 multiparty elections became legal once again.

Contemporary Madagascar

With the collapse of the Soviet Union, Ratsiraka looked increasingly to the West. France agreed to cancel $750 million of dept in return for naval access. In exchange for loans, the International Monetary Fund (IMF) demanded economic liberalization.

However, popular resistance to these austerity measures, such as the elimination of rice subsidies, prevented their immediate implementation.

A free press was also reinstated. The ability to express political dissent led to a general strike and a series of large demonstrations in 1991, organized by the Forces vives (FV), a coalition of opposition parties and labor unions. When Ratsiraka refused to meet the coalition's demands for his resignation, it created a provisional government, assigning ministers who began to take their post in various government buildings. Ratsiraka's army and civil servants refused to intervene, but several provisional ministers were arrested and other coalition leaders were murdered.

A number of large and violent demonstrations ensued. Finally, on October 31, 1991, an agreement was reached. Ratsiraka retained a ceremonial title as president but relinquished all power. A provisional government developed a new constitution and held elections on November 25, 1992. Albert Zafy became the first president of the Third Republic.

In July 1996 Zafy was impeached for violating the constitution, although he immediately ran for president in the next election only a few months later. Capturing 50.71 percent of the votes, Ratsiraka beat out Zafy's bid for the presidency in the December elections, taking office February 9, 1997. Pascal Rakotomavo was appointed prime minister on February 21.

The economy of Madagascar has suffered both from environmental degradation and fractured, unstable government. The World Bank in 1994 estimated the per capita gross national product (GNP) to be $200, making Madagascar one of the poorest countries in the world. The current government is working to strengthen the economy, liberalizing the market and instituting programs to increase agricultural output and make the country self-sufficient. Seventy percent of public-sector industries are to be privatized. Tourism is also being increasingly developed.

Ari Nave

See Also
Antananarivo, Madagascar; Russia and the Former Soviet Union; Ranavalona I, Queen; Tourism in Africa; Indian Ocean Slave Trade.

Africa

Madagascar (Ready Reference)

Official Name: Republic of Madagascar
Former Name: Malagasy Republic
Area: 587,040 sq km (226,658 sq mi)
Location: Southern Africa; island in the Indian Ocean, east of Mozambique
Capital: Antananarivo (population 1,052,835 [1993 estimate])
Other Major Cities: Toamasina (population 127,441), Mahajanga (100,807), and Fianarantsoa (99,005) (1993 estimate)
Population: 14,462,509 (1998 estimate)
Population Density: 24 persons per sq km (about 62 persons per sq mi)
Population Below Age 15: 45 percent (male 3,272,236; female 3,196,565 [1998 estimate])
Population Growth Rate: 2.8 percent (1998 estimate)
Total Fertility Rate: 5.76 children per woman (1998 estimate)
Life Expectancy at Birth: Total population: 52.8 years (male 51.7; female 54.1 [1998 estimate])
Infant Mortality Rate: 90.5 deaths per 1000 live births (1998 estimate)
Literacy Rate (age 15 and over who can read and write): Total population: 80 percent (male 88 percent; female 73 percent [1990 estimate])
Education: Six years of primary school are compulsory. Nearly all children from 6 to 11 attend school, and 18 percent from 12 to 17 are enrolled in secondary school.
Languages: There are two official languages, Malagasy – a language of Malayo-Indonesian origin – and French.
Ethnic Groups: In the interior, around 27 percent of people belong to the Merina (Hova) group and another 12 percent belong to the related Betsileo; both groups are descendants of emigrants from Malaysia and Indonesia around 2000 years ago. The coastal areas are more diverse, with many people of mixed descent; distinct ethnic groups there include the Betsimisaraka, Tsimihety, Sakalave, and Antaisaka.
Religions: About 52 percent of the population adhere to indigenous beliefs. About 41 percent is Christian and 7 percent Muslim.
Climate: The eastern region receives abundant rainfall, in some places more than 3050 mm (120 in) annually. The interior's central plateau is drier, with the arid south and southwest receiving less than 380 mm (15 in) of annual precipitation. The coasts are tropical, with high heat year round. A temperate climate, with warm summers and cool winters, prevails inland. Average temperatures in Antananarivo, the inland capital, range from 16° to 26° C (61° to 79° F) in January to 9° to 20° C (48° to 68° F) in July.
Land, Plants, and Animals: Madagascar, the world's fourth largest island, rises from sea level at its coastline to altitudes of more than 2800 m (around 9400 ft) on its mountainous plateau. It is bordered by the Indian Ocean to the east and the Mozambique Channel to the west. Many rivers cross the island's interior, including the Betsiboka, Tsirivihina, Mangoky, and Onilahy. Tropical rain forests dominate eastern Madagascar, while the drier west consists of savanna woodlands and grasslands and the extreme southwest is desert. Known for its unusual and varied animal life, the island is home to lemurs, a primate family.
Natural Resources: Rich in minerals, Madagascar produces chromite, graphite, mica, bauxite, quartz, salt, coal, and semiprecious stones. The island's best soil is found along the coast and its major rivers. It also has abundant fish.
Currency: The Malagasy franc
Gross Domestic Product (GDP): $10.3 billion (1997 estimate)
GDP per Capita: $730 (1997 estimate)
GDP Real Growth Rate: 3 percent (1997 estimate)
Primary Economic Activities: Agriculture, including fishing and forestry (33 percent of GDP); industry, particularly processing of agricultural products and textile manufacturing (15 percent of GDP); some 96 percent of total labor force does not receive money wages, working mostly in subsistence agriculture.
Primary Crops: Coffee, vanilla, sugar cane, cloves, cocoa, rice, cassava, beans, bananas, and peanuts
Industries: Meat processing, soap, breweries, tanneries, sugar, textiles, glassware, automobile assembly, and petroleum refining
Primary Exports: Coffee, vanilla, cloves, shellfish, sugar, and petroleum products
Primary Imports: Petroleum, consumer goods, and food
Primary Trade Partners: France, Germany, Japan, United Kingdom, Italy, and the Netherlands
Government: Since 1993 Madagascar has been a multiparty democracy with a president, prime minister, and bicameral Parliament. President Didier Ratsiraka, elected in 1996 and in office since 1997, is the current president. The Parliament consists of a Senate and a National Assembly.

Kate Tuttle

See Also
Antananarivo, Madagascar.

Africa

Madagascar, Ethnicity in

Africans are often categorized as members of a specific tribe associated with fixed cultural traits. The people and culture of Madagascar stand in stark contrast to such oversimplified portrayals. Although scholars frequently identify between 18 and 21 distinct ethnic groups in that country – each associated with a distinct territory and dialect – a common Malagasy culture overshadows these distinctions. This Malagasy culture is a product of interaction among the people and ideas of Indonesia, Africa, Arabia, and elsewhere.

Cultural, linguistic, and genetic evidence testifies to a migration from Indonesia early in the first millennium B.C.E. For example, Malagasy, the language spoken by virtually all the island's inhabitants, is a Malayo-Polynesian language related to the Ma'anyan spoken in Borneo. Linguists estimate that it took approximately 1500 to 2000 years for Malagasy to diverge from the ancestral Ma'anyan language to its present state. But how and when such Indonesians arrived in Madagascar is a topic of much scholarly debate. Given the difficulty of a direct transoceanic voyage, many historians have argued that the immigrants must have traveled around the coasts of India, Arabia, and East Africa, which would explain the Bantu, Arabic, and Sanskrit cognates found in Malagasy. Others have argued that several distinct migrations took place, including a coastal route and a direct route, which would explain why the highland people of Madagascar appear to retain more Indonesian traits while people on the coast show evidence of having had greater contact with African and Arabic populations. A group known as the Vazimba are believed to have inhabited Madagascar prior to the arrival of the neo-Malagasy, who are thought by some researchers to have been people of African and/or paleo-Indonesian descent who were absorbed by newer arrivals from Indonesia. Others suggest the Vazimba were Malagasy who lived in stateless societies that were enveloped by more complex social systems.

While it is unclear exactly when the Malagasy population absorbed different cultural traits, Indonesian and African influences such as the practice of terraced rice cultivation and the social importance of cattle are evident in contemporary Malagasy culture. The numerous distinct ethnic groups share this culture. These groups include the MERINA, BETSIMISARAKA, BETSILEO, Amtambahoaka, Antaimoro, Bezanozano, Sihanaka, SAKALAVA, Makoa, Antakarana, BARA, Tsimihety, Mahafaly, Antandroy, Antaifasy, Antaisaka, Tanala, and Antanosy. Ancestral worship prevails among all ethnic groups, and historians have noted the similarity between Malagasy stone monuments and those used in Indonesian ancestral worship. Some variation in religious rituals exists, however, among the different ethnic groups. The Merina, for example, are known for their practice of *famadihana*, or "turning of the dead," where ancestral bones are removed from their tombs and reshrouded after a celebration. Tomb carvings vary from group to group and African influences can be found within the religious practices of the Sakalava, such as spirit possession.

The ethnic distinctions that do exist are partly a product of ecology. Permanent terraced rice cultivation prevails where ecologically possible, particularly among the Merina and Betsileo. In some cases the permanent plots are rain-fed; in others irrigation channels have been built. Cattle are raised throughout the island. In addition to providing meat, particularly for funeral celebrations, they are used to fertilize and trample fields. Cattle also play an important role as bride price, a payment a groom makes to his bride's family. Cattle raising is particularly important among the Bara and Antakarana, who live in drier and rockier areas. In addition to labor-intensive rice cultivation, Malagasy grow manioc, sweet potatoes, taro, beans, Irish potatoes, maize, and other produce. Along the coast, fishing contributes significantly to the economy, particularly among the Vezo Sakalava. Arab and Swahili traders have had a particularly important impact along the southeastern coast, home of the Antambahoaka and Antaimoro, where Malagasy was first transcribed into the Arabic script.

Ethnicity is not the only or even the most important variable defining social relations or events. Many cultural distinctions occur at the regional or family level, such as familial ritual taboos (*fady*). Ethnic divisions are also cross-cut by class and underlaid by caste. For example, the Merina distinguish between commoners (*Hova*), aristocrats (*andrianal*), and slaves (*andevo*). About half of the Malagasy population, particularly the Merina, practice Christianity (25 percent being Catholic and 21 percent Protestant) in some form, often combining Christian and traditional beliefs. The majority of people, however, continue to follow traditional practices of ancestral worship, which vary slightly between ethnic groups. The funerary poles of the Bara, for example, differ in appearance from those built by the Vezo, a group of Sakalava fishermen.

Many ethnic groups, including the Sakalava and Betsileo, have a history of centralized kingship. During the nineteenth century the monarchs of the largest ethnic group, the Merina, employed a powerful army to bring two-thirds of the island under their control by the time of French colonial occupation. One legacy of this empire is the persistent distinction between the Merina and all other peoples, who are collectively referred to as *côtier*. The Merina-côtier distinction has historically been correlated with geography, the Merina living in the central highlands and the côtier, meaning coastal, living along the island's littoral regions. But it is also imbued with racist and ethnocentric overtones, the latent claim being that the Merina are more closely related to Indonesians and superior, and the côtier are more African and less sophisticated. As with all ethnic and racial categories, some individuals and groups hold ambiguous positions. The Betsileo, for example, are distinctly non-Merina, yet their highland culture distinguishes them from the côtier population.

Despite the salience of a pan-Malagasy culture, ethnic and racial cleavages, particularly the Merina-côtier distinction, play an important role in framing contemporary political affiliation. For example, the Parti des Déshérités de Madagascar was formed by côtiers to fight against Merina political domination and establish a federalist government. Côtiers are also known as *déshérités*, alluding to their sense of disinheritance from land and culture long ruled by the Merina.

Ethnicity in contemporary Madagascar is further complicated by the arrival of more recent immigrants from the COMOROS Islands. More than 70,000 Comorians lived in Madagascar until 1973, when many began to return to their country of origin, no longer enjoying the privileged status that had been previously accorded French citizens. Race riots in Mahajanga left more than 1000 Comorians dead in 1976, after which all but some 20,000 people left Madagascar. The remaining Comorian population live predominantly in the capital city, Antananarivo. Approximately 10,000 people of Chinese descent, mostly from the Canton Delta, also live in Madagascar. The Chinese community is heavily involved in the retail trade. Muslim immigrants from India and Pakistan also comprise a population of approximately 15,000, locally referred to as Karana. Like the Chinese, they are associated with wholesale and retail commerce. The Chinese were also subject to racial violence in 1986 and 1987. When Gen. Gabriel Ramanantsoa took control of Madagascar, Chinese and Indo-Pakistanian enterprises were nationalized.

Ari Nave

SEE ALSO

Antananarivo, Madagascar; Bantu: Dispersion and Settlement; Indian Communities in Africa; Swahili People.

Africa

Madi, ethnic group of east Central Africa.

The Madi primarily inhabit northwestern UGANDA. Others live in southern SUDAN. They speak a Nilo-Saharan language and are related to the LUGBARA and BONGO peoples. Approximately 200,000 people consider themselves Madi.

SEE ALSO

Languages, African: An Overview.

Africa

Madikizela-Mandela, Winnie (b. September 26, 1936, Bizana, Pondoland, South Africa), South African antiapartheid activist and advocate for women's rights worldwide.

Winnie Madikizela-Mandela is perhaps the most famous and controversial woman in SOUTH AFRICA. Known for years as one of the most outspoken members of the ANTI-APARTHEID MOVEMENT and the wife of the imprisoned AFRICAN NATIONAL CONGRESS (ANC) leader Nelson Mandela, she later made international headlines when she defended herself at the TRUTH AND RECONCILIATION COMMISSION against charges of murder and torture. Despite lingering questions about her role in late apartheid-era crimes, Madikizela-Mandela remains an influential figure in South African politics and commands a strong following among the nation's poor.

Nomzamo Winifred Zanyiwe Madikizela was the daughter of Colombus Madikizela, a headmaster and cabinet minister in the Transkei homeland government, and Gertrude Madikizela, a teacher. Winnie Madikizela lost her mother at age 9, and afterward she and her seven sisters and their brother were raised by aunts. At age 16 she left home to attend the Jan Hofmeyer School of Social Work in Johannesburg, and after graduation in 1956 she became Baragwanath Hospital's first African medical social worker.

As a student Winnie Madikizela became acquainted with young ANC members. Although initially she was not politically active, during her early career as a social worker she became increasingly interested in both antiapartheid and women's liberation causes. In 1957 she met Nelson Mandela, then the ANC's secretary-general; soon she joined the ANC Women's League and the Federation of South African Women. Mandela was on trial for treason at the time, but after a brief courtship he and Madikizela married in June 1958.

That same year, while pregnant with her first child, Madikizela-Mandela was arrested while participating in a women's anti-pass law demonstration (*see* PASS LAWS). The arrest cost her her job. Madikizela-Mandela's first daughter, Zenani, was born in 1959 and her second, Zindziswa, in 1960. The following year the ANC was outlawed and the Mandela family was forced underground, seeking refuge on a farm in Rivonia. In 1962 they were found: Nelson Mandela, who had been organizing Umkhonto we Sizwe (Spear of the Nation), the ANC's armed wing, was arrested, tried, and sentenced to life imprisonment.

Nelson Mandela was sent to ROBBEN ISLAND, and Winnie Mandela was officially confined to the Orlando district of Soweto. She was able to visit her husband but only with the government's permission. Winnie Mandela was arrested in 1967 for ignoring her confinement orders and resisting arrest. Later charged under the Suppression of Communism Act, she spent 17 months in solitary confinement and was then placed under house arrest.

Despite the restrictions on her movements, Mandela continued her work for the banned ANC. She was particularly active in parents' groups, especially after hundreds of schoolchildren were killed by security forces during the 1976 Soweto uprising. She arranged funerals and support groups to help the aggrieved parents and helped found the nationwide Black Parents' Association. But within months of the uprising she was again jailed under the Internal Security Act and subsequently banished to Brandfort, in the Orange Free State.

Over the next several years Mandela was repeatedly arrested – sometimes twice a day – for defying orders. On Christmas Day, 1985, after visiting her husband, she was pursued by police in a car chase, which was captured on camera by the international press. Broadcast worldwide, Winnie Mandela's persecution became emblematic of the harassment endured by black South Africans under apartheid.

In February 1990 Nelson Mandela was released from prison, and Winnie Mandela accompanied him as he walked out the door. Several months later, however, she was charged with involvement in the 1988 kidnapping of four youth activists and the murder of a fifth, the 14-year-old James (Stompie) Moeketsi Seipei. Her bodyguards at the time, a group of young men known as the Mandela Football Club, were charged with the murder. In 1991 Winnie Mandela was found guilty of kidnapping and an accessory to assault, but after appeal her six-year sentence was reduced to two and suspended. That year she was also elected to the ANC's National Executive. In April 1992 she and her husband separated; they divorced in 1996.

In South Africa's first democratic election in 1994, Nelson Mandela was elected president, and Winnie – now going by the name Madikizela-Mandela – was elected to Parliament. Highly critical of the government, she was unseated a year later but remained popular, especially among South Africa's poor, whom she claimed to champion. She was considered a strong candidate for the country's deputy presidency in 1997, but her testimony before the Truth and Reconciliation Committee that year failed to clear her name. Lacking support within her own party, she pulled out of the race but continued to speak out against racism and economic injustice. In October 1997 she was a keynote speaker at the MILLION WOMAN MARCH in Philadelphia, Pennsylvania.

Jessica Hochman

SEE ALSO

Johannesburg, South Africa; Mandela, Nelson Rolihlahla; Soweto, South Africa.

Magwe. Please see BÉTÉ

Africa

Mahdist State, an Islamic state that dominated present-day SUDAN from 1885 to 1898.

Muhammad Ahmad ibn Abd Allah, a NUBIAN born near Dongola, organized an Islamic popular movement that culminated in the founding of the Mahdist state. Muhammad Ahmad was born in 1844 and received a classical Islamic education before leaving home to study with a leading Sufi teacher of the Sammaniyah order. In 1870 he began to teach on his own, gathering students at Aba Island on the White Nile.

In 1878 Abd Allah ibn Muhammad Adam, a BAGGARA Arab, visited Muhammad Ahmad. Abd Allah accepted his acquaintance as more than a teacher of Islamic mysticism; he thought that this religious leader was the Mahdi (guided one), a messianic figure who would cleanse the world of corruption, unite the world in an egalitarian and just Islamic state, and prepare the world for the end of time. Throughout the Sudanic region of Africa there had been widespread expectation that the Mahdi, awaited since the first appearance of conflict among Muslims in Medina in the mid-seventh century, would return during the thirteenth Islamic century (1785-1882 C.E.). In 1881 Muhammad Ahmad had a series of visions that convinced him that he was indeed the Mahdi. Initially he revealed this only to a limited number of followers, but within a few months he was confident enough to teach publicly.

At the time that Muhammad Ahmad began to teach, the government of the Turkiyya, the Egyptian state affiliated with the Ottoman Empire, had lost its credibility with many Muslims. Deeply in debt to European creditors and under the control of the British, the Turkiyya seemed dangerously dependent on non-Islamic and secular powers. Many Muslims saw the lavish lifestyle of the Turkiyya court, its imposition of a host of taxes not sanctioned by Islamic laws, its acceptance of usury in direct contradiction of Koranic prohibitions, and its British-prompted interference with the slave trade in southern Sudan (*see* SLAVERY IN AFRICA) as signs of the Egyptian administration's corruption and abandonment of Islamic principles.

Modeling himself after the prophet Muhammad, the Mahdi performed the *hijra* (emigration) in 1881 from Aba Island to the Nuba Mountains. He called on the faithful to support him in a military struggle against the Turkiyya. In a little more than a year he won control of the province of Kordofan. In January 1885, after a long siege, the Mahdist forces captured and razed Khartoum. It was during the siege of Khartoum that General Gordon, a British officer and former governor-general of the Sudan, was killed. The Mahdi moved the Sudanese capital from Khartoum to the Islamic center of Omdurman on the west bank of the Nile, where he proclaimed the Mahdist state.

The Mahdi died later that year without leaving a solid political structure in place to guide his successors. Perhaps his emphasis on the imminence of the "end of days" led him and his advisors to avoid making decisions about the future. During his short period of governance the Mahdi used the Koran and the traditions (*sunnah*) concerning the prophet Muhammad as his primary legal guide. He saw his own interpretations of tradition as superior to those of the established Islamic legal schools and issued a series of written and oral decrees concerning many aspects of religious, social, and economic life.

After the death of the Mahdi, Abd Allah became Khalifat al-Mahdi (the successor to the Mahdi) and the head of the Mahdist state. He proclaimed his intention to follow the teachings of the Mahdi in governing Sudan. However, he faced armed threats to his regime, both from followers of the Mahdi who refused to follow Abd Allah and the various European powers interested in controlling the Nile valley. He left in place many of the burdensome forms of taxation that had provoked the Mahdist uprising. He failed to carry out land reform; corruption remained widespread. Gradually, support for the Mahdist state diminished. In 1898 Lord Kitchener led a combined British and Egyptian force that reconquered the Sudan and eliminated the Mahdist state.

Robert Baum

See Also
Egypt; Khartoum, Sudan; Nile River.

Africa

Maherero, Samuel (b. 1856?; d. March 14, 1923, Serowe, Bechuanaland Protectorate [Botswana]), son of a prominent Herero chief and an early nationalist leader of Namibia.

Samuel Maherero, born Uereani Maherero, was the first son of Chief Maherero, who between 1860 and 1889 led the Herero in a series of wars with the Nama. Vehemently opposed to settlement by Europeans, particularly Afrikaners and Germans, in what is today Namibia, the elder Maherero repeatedly and unsuccessfully requested British "protection" during his reign. He finally gave in to German occupation in 1885.

Samuel and his brothers were educated at the Rhenish mission school in Otjimbingwe in the early 1860s. Samuel's brother, Wilhelm, the chief's second son and intended heir, was killed in battle with the Nama. Thus when his father died in 1890, Samuel Maherero assumed the chieftainship – a succession that divided the Herero, as some believed that one of his cousins should have become chief.

For the next two years Maherero continued in his father's footsteps, leading his people in wars against the Nama. To gain support among the Germans, Maherero ceded large tracts of land held by Eastern Herero to the Germans, and allowed them to station troops at Okanhandja, the Herero capital. However, German settlers continued to take land from the Herero and in 1904 Maherero, supported by his people and many younger chiefs, reversed his allegiances. In January, Maherero ordered his warriors to attack German soldiers and male settlers. He exhorted the Herero and other African groups to "rise up and let the whole of Africa fight against the Germans... let us die fighting rather than die as a result of maltreatment, imprisonment, or some other calamity." The Herero nearly defeated the Germans in two major battles, but at the Battle of Waterburg in August overwhelming German forces crushed the Herero revolt. Maherero fled with 1500 soldiers to Bechuanaland, now Botswana, where he died in exile in 1923.

Eric Young

See Also
Afrikaner.

Mahfouz, Naguib. Please see Mahfuz, Najib

Africa

Mahfuz, Najib
(b. December 11, 1911, Cairo, Egypt), Egyptian novelist; the first Arab to win the Nobel Prize for Literature.

Upon presenting the Nobel Prize for Literature to Najib Mahfuz in 1988, the Swedish Academy of Letters announced, "Through works rich in nuance – now clear-sightedly realistic, now evocatively ambiguous – [Mahfuz] has formed an Arabian narrative art that applies to all mankind." The academy stated that Mahfuz's body of writing "speaks to us all" by addressing universal themes such as injustice, the desire for freedom, and the place of the individual in society.

Critics have described Mahfuz's literary career as a journey through the history of the European novel. Over four decades he has written approximately one book a year. Scholars claim that his early works resemble the romanticism of Victor Hugo. Mahfuz fully admits the influence of Sir Walter Scott in *Radubi* (1943), in which he uses the history of ancient Pharaonic Egypt as an allegory for the later British occupation. His best-known work, the three-volume *Cairo Trilogy* (1956-1957) – a depiction of the changes in urban society through three generations of various Cairene families from 1917 to 1944 – is often compared to the social realism of Charles Dickens.

The 1981 English-language release of *Midaq Alley* (1947) brought Mahfuz's work to an American audience. The characters in this novel include a man who maims beggars so that they can make more money; a young beauty who chases a life of wealth only to find that she must prostitute herself to obtain it; a dentist who digs up graves to obtain teeth for his practice; and a youthful idealist who bets all on love and loses. These characters and his descriptions of their lives expand the Western view of Egypt as an exotic land, as depicted by authors such as T. E. Lawrence, Gustave Flaubert, and E. M. Forster. Mahfuz's later works are said to have been influenced by modern novelists such as James Joyce and Virginia Woolf.

Through the realistic description of the everyday trials and tribulations of lower- and middle-class Egyptians in Cairo, Mahfuz's works offer insight into Arab society and help to bridge the cultural divide between the Western and Arab worlds. Though some see Mahfuz as a writer who upholds – and even defends – the status quo, novels such as *The Thief and the Dogs* (1961) and *Miramar* (1967) express critical views of the Egyptian leader Gamal Abdel Nasser's dictatorship. Other writings attack the former Egyptian monarchy and the era of British colonialism. As a result of his support of Anwar al-Sadat's peace treaty with Israel in 1979, Mahfuz's books were banned in several Arab countries. He came into conflict with some Muslims after the publication of *Children of Gebelawi* (1959), a book about the human quest for religion, in which the main characters were based on canonical figures such as Adam, Eve, Moses, and the prophet Muhammad. The book was banned in Egypt for its unorthodox use of religious figures, and Islamic fundamentalists are said to have threatened Mahfuz's life. An Islamic militant probably acted on this threat when he stabbed Mahfuz in the neck in an assassination attempt on October 14, 1994, the anniversary of his receipt of the Nobel Prize.

Mahfuz survived and continued his quiet and methodical life in Cairo. He had grown up in one of that city's oldest quarters, Gamaliyya, a place, like those he often portrays in his writing, full of small alleyways, monumental mosques, and tall minarets. After finishing his philosophy degree at the University of Cairo, he followed in his father's footsteps and became a civil servant. He worked in the ministry of Islamic affairs, as director of censorship in the Department of Art, and for the State Cinema organization. When Mahfuz retired in 1971, he continued to write novels, screenplays, and short stories and supplemented his income by writing for the newspaper *Al Ahram*. Writing remains a necessity in Mahfuz's life. As he once said, "If the urge to write were ever to leave me, I would want that day to be my last." The large body of work he has already produced has made him an icon of modern Arabic literature – a tradition that he helped create. The Egyptian writer Sonallah Ibrahim said, "You cannot picture Egypt without the Pyramids and neither can you conceive of Arabic literature without Najib Mahfuz."

Leyla Keough

See Also
Sadat, Anwar al-.

Mailman, The. Please see Malone, Karl

Latin America and the Caribbean

Mais, Roger (b. August 11, 1905, Kingston, Jamaica; d. June 21, 1955, Kingston, Jamaica), Jamaican novelist, playwright, and activist.

Roger Mais is one of the pioneers of the contemporary West Indian literary tradition. He was born into a middle-class, mixed-race Kingston family but spent most of his childhood in Jamaica's Blue Mountains before returning to Kingston, where he graduated from Calabar High School in 1922. For the next 15 years he worked intermittently as a civil servant, an insurance salesman, and even an overseer on a banana plantation. He kept returning to jobs in journalism, however, and through his writing became involved in the Jamaican nationalist movement.

Mais was an early supporter of the People's National Party (PNP) and its leader, Norman Manley. By the early 1940s he was publishing short stories, poetry, plays, and essays in the PNP's journal, and in 1944 he was jailed for four months after writing the essay "Now We Know," which criticized British colonialism. While in prison, Mais began work on what would become his first novel. In 1951 he emigrated to Paris, where his circle of friends included RICHARD WRIGHT, JOHN HEARNE, and other black expatriate writers. There he finished the novel he had begun in the Kingston jail.

The Hills Were Joyful Together (1953), which portrayed life in a Kingston tenement yard, was the first realistic fictional depiction of Jamaica's black working-class majority. Mais's second novel, *Brother Man* (1954), is a parable about a Rastafarian leader who becomes a Christ-figure, and his third, *Black Lightning* (1955), also draws on biblical imagery in its portrayal of a modern-day Samson. Just as his career as a novelist began to develop, however, ill health forced Mais to return to Kingston, and in June 1955 he died of cancer, his "fascist disease."

Lisa Clayton Robinson

SEE ALSO

Literature, English Language, Caribbean; Manley, Norman Washington; Rastafarians.

Africa

Maka, ethnic group of West Africa.

The Maka primarily inhabit southern CAMEROON, northern EQUATORIAL GUINEA, and northern GABON. They speak a Bantu language and are closely related to the BETI people. Approximately 100,000 people consider themselves Maka.

SEE ALSO

Bantu: Dispersion and Settlement.

Africa

Makeba, Miriam Zenzi

(b. March 4, 1932, Prospect, SOUTH AFRICA), South African singer and political activist who helped introduce South African music to the world.

Throughout her life and singing career, Miriam Makeba has used her voice, which journalist Michael A. Hiltzik described as having "the clarity of a Joan Baez with the timing and throaty authority of a SARAH VAUGHAN," to draw the attention of the world to the music of South Africa and to its oppressive system of racial separation, APARTHEID. Makeba became an indirect victim of South African policies at the age of 18 days when she began serving a six-month prison term with her mother for illegally selling traditional Swazi homemade beer as a result of economic necessity. For eight years Makeba attended the Kilmerton Training School in Pretoria, where she sang in the school choir. During her teenage years Makeba assisted her mother with the domestic work she did for white families.

She also pursued singing, and in 1950 joined an amateur Johannesburg group called the Cuban Brothers. In 1954 Makeba caught the notice of a successful professional South African group, the Black Manhattan Brothers, an 11-piece band that toured South Africa, Rhodesia (now ZIMBABWE), and the Belgian Congo (now the DEMOCRATIC REPUBLIC OF THE CONGO). Makeba left the Manhattan Brothers in 1957 to become a member of a touring revue show, African Jazz and Variety; this stint led to a successful recording career in South Africa.

With her appearance in the semidocumentary, antiapartheid film *Come Back, Africa* (1959), Makeba, already a major star in southern Africa, drew the attention of international audiences. As a result she attended the premiere of *Come Back, Africa* at the 1959 Venice Film Festival in Italy.

After the festival Makeba traveled to London, where she met African American performer and civil rights activist Harry Belafonte, who had requested a private screening of the film. Struck by Makeba's mixture of traditional African rhythms and popular musical forms, Belafonte called the artist "the most revolutionary new talent to appear in any medium in the last decade" and became her sponsor and promoter in the United States. Through Belafonte, Makeba appeared on the *Steve Allen Show*, which led to performances in nightclubs around New York City and recordings of the music of South Africa. Some songs became hits in the United States, including "Patha Patha," "Malaika," and "The Click Song," which earned Makeba the nickname of "the click-click girl."

Makeba's music also contained a political component – the denunciation of apartheid. Her criticism of the system earned Makeba the enmity of the South African government, which revoked her passport when she attempted to return for her mother's funeral in 1960. Makeba pressed the issue of apartheid, nevertheless. In 1963 she addressed a United Nations special committee on apartheid, characterizing South Africa as "a nightmare of police brutality and government terrorism" and demanding an international boycott of her homeland. In response, the South African government banned Makeba's music from South Africa.

Marriage to African American civil rights activist STOKELY CARMICHAEL (later Kwame Turé) derailed her career in the United States. Carmichael, who at the time was involved with the BLACK PANTHER PARTY and who had popularized the phrase "BLACK POWER," was considered by many in mainstream society to be a revolutionary. The entertainment industry virtually blacklisted Makeba. According to one account, her record company never called her in to record again after the marriage. As Makeba said in her 1987 autobiography *Makeba: My Story*, "My concerts were being canceled left and right.... What does Stokely have to do with my singing?" She and Carmichael eventually moved to GUINEA in West Africa.

Makeba's career continued outside the United States, however, and during the 1970s and 1980s she toured Europe, South America, and Africa and was a fixture on the jazz festival circuit, appearing regularly at the Montreux Jazz Festival, the Berlin Jazz Festival, and the Northsea Jazz Festival. In 1977 she traveled to LAGOS, NIGERIA, to serve as the unofficial South African representative at Festac, a Pan-African festival of arts and culture. In 1982 "Mother Africa," as she was known, reunited with South African trumpeter Hugh Masekela, to whom Makeba was married from 1964 to 1966.

Continuing her activism, in 1975 Makeba served a term as a United Nations delegate from Guinea. In addition, she was awarded the Dag Hammerskjöld Peace Prize in 1986. In 1987 American musician Paul Simon invited Makeba to perform on his *Graceland* tour, which reintroduced her to a United States audience, reigniting her career there.

In 1990 Makeba finally returned to South Africa. In 1991 she released *Eyes on Tomorrow*, which was recorded in a Johannesburg studio and featured such musical lights as Dizzy Gillespie, singer NINA SIMONE, and Masekela. That same year Makeba gave her first live performance in South Africa since her departure more than 30 years earlier. She has continued to record and tour.

SEE ALSO

Antiapartheid Movement; Johannesburg, South Africa; Masekela, Hugh Ramopolo; Belafonte, Harold George (Harry); Gillespie, John Birks ("Dizzy").

Africa

Makonde, ethno-linguistic group of southeastern Africa.

The Makonde of TANZANIA and Maconde of MOZAMBIQUE live in the coastal regions to the north and south of the Ruvuma River, respectively, also known as the Umakonde.

Although distinct peoples, the two groups share a history shaped in part by their harsh, remote environment.

It is believed that the Makonde and Maconde, traveling in *litawa*, or small kin groups, migrated to the region in the late eighteenth or nineteenth century from the undulating grassy plain, or *ndonde*, to the west of the present-day Maconde of Mozambique. Driven primarily by pressures for more land, these migrants also had to contend with NGUNI slave raiders from the interior. For protective purposes they settled on the plateaus rather than in the river valleys, and lived in scattered homesteads rather than villages. On the dry land they cleared, they practiced stump cultivation, in which tree stumps were left in place to promote the fast regeneration of the land for maize, millet, and sorghum, still their primary crops.

In addition to their common history of migration, the Makonde and Maconde share certain forms of social and political organizations. Both have matrilineal systems of inheritance and succession, and both still live in small, loosely associated litawa communities where authority lies with lineage elders. They also share many religious beliefs and initiation rites. On the other hand, the Maconde and Makonde languages are markedly different, in part due to the geographical separation created by the Ruvuma River, as are their perceptions of each other. The Makonde tend to see the Maconde as unclean and warlike, often referring to them as *Mawia*, a pejorative term that connotes a subordinate relationship. The Maconde, for their part, generally accepted this characterization, building a warrior myth into their culture.

The Umakonde was greatly affected by the Arab and European slave trades, because it was both a source of slaves itself and a route between the populous LAKE MALAWI region and the coast, where many people were sent to French plantations in MAURITIUS and RÉUNION. With the arrival of European missionaries and colonialists in southeast Africa, the Umakonde region became marginalized. The people, many already Muslim, rejected missionary proselytization, and the region offered little to attract settlers. Although communities in the Umakonde were required to provide laborers and taxes to the colonial administrations of Tanganyika and Portuguese East Africa (Mozambique), they otherwise remained isolated from foreign influence.

Makonde marginalization led many to join and become senior members of the TANU nationalist movement in Tanzania. Maconde formed the backbone of the FRONT FOR THE LIBERATION OF MOZAMBIQUE (FRELIMO) forces fighting Portuguese colonial rule in Mozambique and are still an influential interest group in independent Mozambique. In addition to a growing political role, the Makonde and Maconde have become famous for their woodcarving. Usually made of blackwood (*mpingo*), Makonde sculptures are often haunting, mysterious portrayals of humans and their spiritual ancestors.

Eric Young

SEE ALSO
Transatlantic Slave Trade; Indian Ocean Slave Trade.

Africa

Makua, ethnic group of southeastern Africa.

The Makua primarily inhabit southwestern TANZANIA and also live in neighboring parts of MALAWI and northern MOZAMBIQUE. They speak a Bantu language and are closely related to the neighboring MAKONDE people. Approximately 6 million people consider themselves Makua.

SEE ALSO
Bantu: Dispersion and Settlement.

Africa

Malabo, Equatorial Guinea, capital of EQUATORIAL GUINEA.

Much more a town than a city, this small, somewhat run-down capital, after years of dereliction, has recently enjoyed some prosperity from Equatorial Guinea's newfound oil revenues. In 1827 British traders founded the town and named it Clarence City. It was located on the northern beaches of Bioko Island, known then as Fernando Pó, at the base of a volcanic cone (present-day Mount Malabo). Renamed Santa Isabel in 1843, the town served as the administrative and commercial center of Spain's only colony in sub-Saharan Africa; it became best known as "death's waiting room," because of the oppressive tropical climate and disease.

By 1960 the town's population had reached nearly 20,000. But after Equatorial Guinea's independence in 1968, there was a rapid departure of 7000 Spanish residents. Following years of dictatorial rule, this exodus nearly destroyed the town's economy, which had been sustained primarily by a small fishing industry, a distillery, and other small businesses. Port capacity, around 300,000 tons per year, has been grossly under-utilized, especially since the 1976 departure of 25,000 Nigerian cacao plantation workers.

In 1973 the town was renamed Malabo, after a BUBI paramount chief. Its population has grown to approximately 50,000, many of them ethnic FANG, who dominate employment in the national government. With little economic growth, new construction has been limited to a luxury hotel, a central bank, and a high school. Functioning public utilities are few, electrical outages are common, daily newspapers do not exist, most restaurants and hotels are closed, and prices are high. But Malabo is home to a lively marketplace as well as the presidential palace and a Roman Catholic gothic-style cathedral that was begun in 1916. A recent oil boom has created new wealth for the city's small ruling elite and has helped to revitalize the town; cars are again common on Malabo's few paved roads.

Eric Young

SEE ALSO
Nigeria.

Africa

Malagasy, the most widely spoken language of MADAGASCAR and, along with French, one of two official languages.

Although Madagascar lies off the coast of East Africa, its inhabitants speak Malagasy, a non-tonal Malayo-Polynesian language of the Austronesian family of languages. All the inhabitants of Madagascar, except for a small number of very recent immigrants, speak one of 18 closely related and mutually intelligible dialects. These dialects are sometimes grouped into three larger families defined by geography: the Merina-Betsileo dialect spoken on the plateau, the east and north coast variant, and the west and southern vernacular. Malagasy dialects are distinguished primarily by lexical, rather than syntactical, differences.

The lack of linguistic divergence over a vast area and the similarity of Malagasy to Indonesian languages provide important clues to the history of the peopling of Madagascar. Malagasy is most closely related to Ma'anyan, a language spoken in southeast Borneo, and is also related to Malay, Javanese, Balinese, and Minangkabau. This and other evidence has led scholars to conclude that Madagascar was settled by Indonesians approximately 2000 years ago. Researchers arrived at this date in part by estimating the time it would take for the two languages to diverge from a common ancestor.

Interestingly, while Malagasy borrowed heavily from neighboring cultures, adopting words from Arabic, Swahili, and Bantu, the reverse is not true. For example "Alarobia," meaning Wednesday, is clearly of Arabic origin. Less pronounced but equally important are grammatical borrowings, such as the employment of "ho"/"h-" to mark the future tense, a Bantu trait. This suggests that proto-Indonesians came into extensive contact with African and Arab populations in Madagascar, but not en route.

About 500 years ago Malagasy was first transcribed into the Arabic script that is still used among the Antaimoro. Most people, however, write Malagasy in the Roman script, originally adopted by monks under Radama I in the 1820s. Some English and French words have also been adapted by

Malagasy speakers since the Merina Empire. For instance, *boky* refers to a book and *savony* derives from the French word for soap, *savon*. Due to French COLONIAL RULE from 1895 until 1960, French is also an official language of Madagascar.

Ari Nave

SEE ALSO

Swahili Language.

Africa

Malagasy Republic. Former name of MADAGASCAR.

Africa

Malawi, landlocked country in east southern Africa bordering TANZANIA, MOZAMBIQUE, and ZAMBIA, with the third highest population density (95 people per sq km) of any African country.

Surrounded by countries rich in diamonds and gold, Malawi is known for humbler resources: fertile albeit densely populated land, a vast lake, and an abundant labor supply. Historically, the fortunes of Malawi's primarily agrarian societies have been shaped by regional patterns of trade, warfare, and conquest but also marked by the careers of ambitious if paternalistic "saviors." In precolonial times years of violent slave raids were followed by the arrival of the Scottish missionary DAVID LIVINGSTONE, determined to rescue the region's peasants from enslavement and paganism. British colonialists followed, taking away farmland and imposing high taxes, but they were eventually pushed out by Malawian nationalists, led by the Western-educated physician Hastings Kamuzu Banda. During the three decades' rule of this self-proclaimed "paternal despot," the chasms between rich and poor, ruler and ruled, grew wider than anywhere else on the continent. Multiparty elections in 1994 finally replaced the ailing Banda; today's Malawians wait to see whether democracy and regional stability will help the country climb out of continuing poverty.

EARLY HISTORY

Archaeological evidence suggests that Malawi has been inhabited for more than 50,000 years. The earliest human remains – dated to between 4000 and 10,000 years ago – together with linguistic evidence, suggest that these early residents were foragers and the ancestors of TWA, Fula, and perhaps contemporary KHOISAN speakers, such as the SAN of southern Africa. Bantu-speaking immigrants settled in the area of present-day Malawi approximately between the first and fourth centuries C.E., probably displacing the existing populations. The Bantu migrants relied primarily on shifting (or "swidden") agriculture, and are thought to have introduced ironworking as they spread throughout the region during the following centuries. Sometime between the thirteenth and fifteenth centuries C.E., a second wave of Bantu migrants, possibly of Shaba and LUBA origin, reached Malawi from areas to the north.

Shifting cultivation, while still practiced in some areas, gave way to more sedentary, intensive forms of agricultural production. This shift, combined with the resulting increase in population density, fostered the development of allied kingdoms, beginning with the fifteenth-century Maravi (or Malawi, in Portuguese) Confederacy. The Maravi kings formed a federation of several distinct kingdoms, including the Lundu, located in the present-day Shire Valley and the Undi, who lived west of Lake Nyasa (now Lake Malawi). They came to rule over most of the territory that is now known as central and southern Malawi as well as parts of Mozambique and Zambia. These hereditary kings came from the Phiri clan, and their principal charge was to collect and store grain as tribute and to redistribute it during times of famine. The kings also controlled the trade in ivory and iron, materials that were in particular demand among Swahili traders.

Portuguese merchants arrived at the lower reaches of the ZAMBEZI RIVER in the sixteenth century. Along with arms, ammunition, textiles, and glass beads, the Portuguese introduced manioc (also called cassava), a carbohydrate-rich tuber that, unlike MILLET and bananas, could be stored for significant periods of time. Manioc quickly spread throughout Africa and became one of the dominant subsistence crops.

More immediately, however, Africans in the Zambezi River region were faced with Portuguese efforts to gain control over the river's lucrative gold and ivory trades. In response, Maravi kings sent troops north to establish alternative routes to the Indian Ocean, conquering a large section of MAKUA territory in Mozambique. The cannibalism of the Lundi soldiers, in particular, terrorized their neighbors into subjugation. Portuguese troops sent to quell the Lundi in 1592 met with defeat. Ultimately one king, Kalanga, collaborated with the Portuguese to help defeat the Lundu in 1622, in return for unhindered access to Indian Ocean markets.

Toward the close of the seventeenth century YAO and Ngoni moved into the region from the south, acting as brokers of slaves, firearms, and other commodities between European, Swahili, and Arab merchants and various African suppliers. With its trade monopoly undermined, the Maravi Confederacy disintegrated into numerous independent chiefdoms. Its people also fell prey to slave raiding by the well-armed Yao. In the eighteenth century a group of Mavari known as the Chewa split off and migrated to the west. The Chewa would eventually become the largest ethnic group in present-day Malawi.

The slave trade between the Lake Nyasa region and Indian Ocean ports such as Mombasa expanded rapidly during the late eighteenth and early nineteenth centuries. Maravi communities continued to suffer from slave raids by neighboring groups, particularly the Ngoni. By the mid-nineteenth century Swahili, Ngoni, and Yao traders had introduced Islam to the region, and 10,000 slaves were passing annually through the slave depot at Nkhota Kota, ruled by an Arab sultan. The merchants had also introduced vast quantities of firearms, making struggles for control over diminishing supplies of ivory and slave labor increasingly violent.

The Scottish explorer and missionary David Livingstone remarked on this violence when he first arrived in the region in the 1850s. He and other members of the London Missionary Society established the Livingstonia Mission in the northern highlands as well as several mission schools. The missionaries won many converts among the groups subjected to slave raids and conquest, and they encouraged them to take up "legitimate" forms of entrepreneurial activity, such as cultivating cotton and other cash crops. They also lobbied European government officials to intervene in order to abolish slavery. In the late nineteenth century other missionary groups became active in the region, including the Free Church of Scotland, the Dutch Reformed Church of South Africa, and the Roman Catholic Church. Today approximately 35 percent of the population practices Christianity.

COLONIALISM

In 1889 the British South Africa Company (BSAC), headed by CECIL RHODES, received a royal charter to find and exploit Malawi's mineral resources in return for a commitment to hedge Portuguese influence in the region. The Crown took control when it created the Nyasaland Districts Protectorate in 1891. Many groups preyed upon by Yao slave raiders welcomed British intervention, but the Yao, Chewa, and others resisted colonization. Capt. FREDERICK JOHN DEALTRY LUGARD, a notorious colonialist, was called on to establish control over the sultan of Karonga, who fought to maintain his valuable trade in slaves. In 1893 the region was renamed the British Central African Protectorate and finally Nyasaland in 1907.

Nyasaland's mineral resources proved disappointingly scarce, leading the British colonial administration to focus instead on agricultural commodities, especially tea. White settlers were given large tracts of land in the fertile highlands to establish tea, coffee, and tobacco plantations. During the early colonial period large numbers of Lomwe refugees, fleeing Portuguese rule in Mozambique, arrived in the British colony, where they remained to become the second largest ethnic group of contemporary Malawi. The landless Lomwe immigrants had no choice but to work as laborers in return for minimal tenancy rights on European plantations, a system referred to as *thangata.* People from the less productive lands of the north also migrated to work on European estates, driven by the need to pay colonial taxes.

In addition, many men (and a few women) from Nyasaland migrated to Rhodesia (*see* Zimbabwe) and South Africa, where they worked in and around the gold, diamond, and copper mines. These populations were actively recruited by both the Rhodesian and the South African Native Labour Bureaus, even after the governor of Nayasaland enacted legislation in 1911 to curtail the colony's labor outflow.

Massive land appropriation by white settlers, labor outmigration, and high taxes combined to create conditions of hardship and discontent in much of Nyasaland. These conditions, as well as more immediate outrage at World War I conscription, led the African clergyman John Chilembwe to mobilize followers in an armed rebellion. It was quickly put down and Chilembwe was killed, but he was remembered as a hero by later anticolonial activists.

In 1944 a multiethnic coalition of independent African churches and associations formed the Nyasaland African Congress (NAC). The NAC demanded rights to organize labor and to have direct representation in the Nyasaland legislature. The NAC also adamantly opposed Britain's proposed creation of a Central African Federation, a political entity encompassing Nyasaland and southern Rhodesia, where some 100,000 Nyasa workers had migrated to work in the mines. While colonial authorities argued that the federation would facilitate regional economic development and allow Africans greater political representation, NAC believed it would simply strengthen the foothold of southern Africa's white settlers and recreate colonial rule in a more permanent guise.

Despite protests in both Nyasaland and Rhodesia, the Central African Federation was established in 1953, with several seats in the Legislative Council allocated to Nyasas. The NAC, having so far failed to achieve many of its demands for reform, became increasingly militant during the 1950s and ultimately committed to independence. In 1957 the organization's youthful but disorganized leadership invited the respected Nyasa-born physician Kamuzu Banda, who was in Ghana at the time, to become NAC's president. Within two years the charismatic Banda had transformed NAC into a mass movement. In 1959 work stoppages and other forms of civil disobedience led the colonial administration to imprison Banda and other NAC leaders, ban the NAC itself, and declare a state of emergency.

Published by the antislavery missionary, explorer, and physician David Livingstone in *The Life and Explorations of Dr. Livingstone* (1871), this etching of slaves being led to market was intended to stir British sentiment against the slave trade in East Africa. *Hulton Getty/Liaison Agency*

Independence, Nationhood, and the Banda Regime

Upon their release several months later, the NAC leadership quickly created the Malawi Congress Party (MCP), with Banda as its chief, and resumed its campaign of civil disobedience. By this time Great Britain had accepted decolonization as inevitable and agreed to universal adult voting rights. In the first assembly elections held in April 1961, the MCP won a majority of seats.

Nyasaland won internal self-governance in January 1963 and became the independent nation of Malawi in July 1964. Banda became the prime minister and quickly established a highly autocratic government, staffed by a large number of European expatriate bureaucrats and advisors. Within months of coming into office, Banda's cabinet members were accusing him of being too slow to "Africanize" the government. In response, Banda fired three ministers, and three others resigned. Of these six, five ultimately fled the country and the other one remained under house arrest. Disenchanted citizens led a small revolt in 1965 and again in 1967, only to be quickly suppressed by security forces.

Banda instituted constitutional amendments in 1966, establishing Malawi as a one-party republic; he named himself president and head of the military. With the ability to dissolve the Legislative Assembly at will, Banda had consolidated power to the point where he was, in effect, the state. In 1971 he became "life-president." Political opposition was ruthlessly stamped out, the press was heavily censored, and Banda continually reshuffled his government to prevent any minister from cultivating a power base. As head of the MCP, he also dictated who ran in the single-party elections.

Until 1994 Banda reigned over Malawi; he was often portrayed in the Malawian press as a benevolent monarch or even as a savior. He pursued a pro-Western, anticommunist foreign policy and attempted to nurture a market-based economy. During the 1970s there was an influx of foreign capital, much of it from South Africa and white-ruled Rhodesia, in the plantation and manufacturing sectors, and the construction of the modern new capital in Lilongwe.

Yet despite substantial financial assistance from abroad and a relatively stable political climate, Malawi remained one of the world's poorest countries. While a small elite prospered under Banda's rule, most of the population worked in agriculture and suffered from droughts in the late 1970s and early 1990s. The country's economic decline was exacerbated when Mozambique, itself suffering from civil war, dramatically increased the export taxes it charged on freight transported through the country. This effectively eliminated Malawi's primary access to world trade, the Indian Ocean port of Nacala.

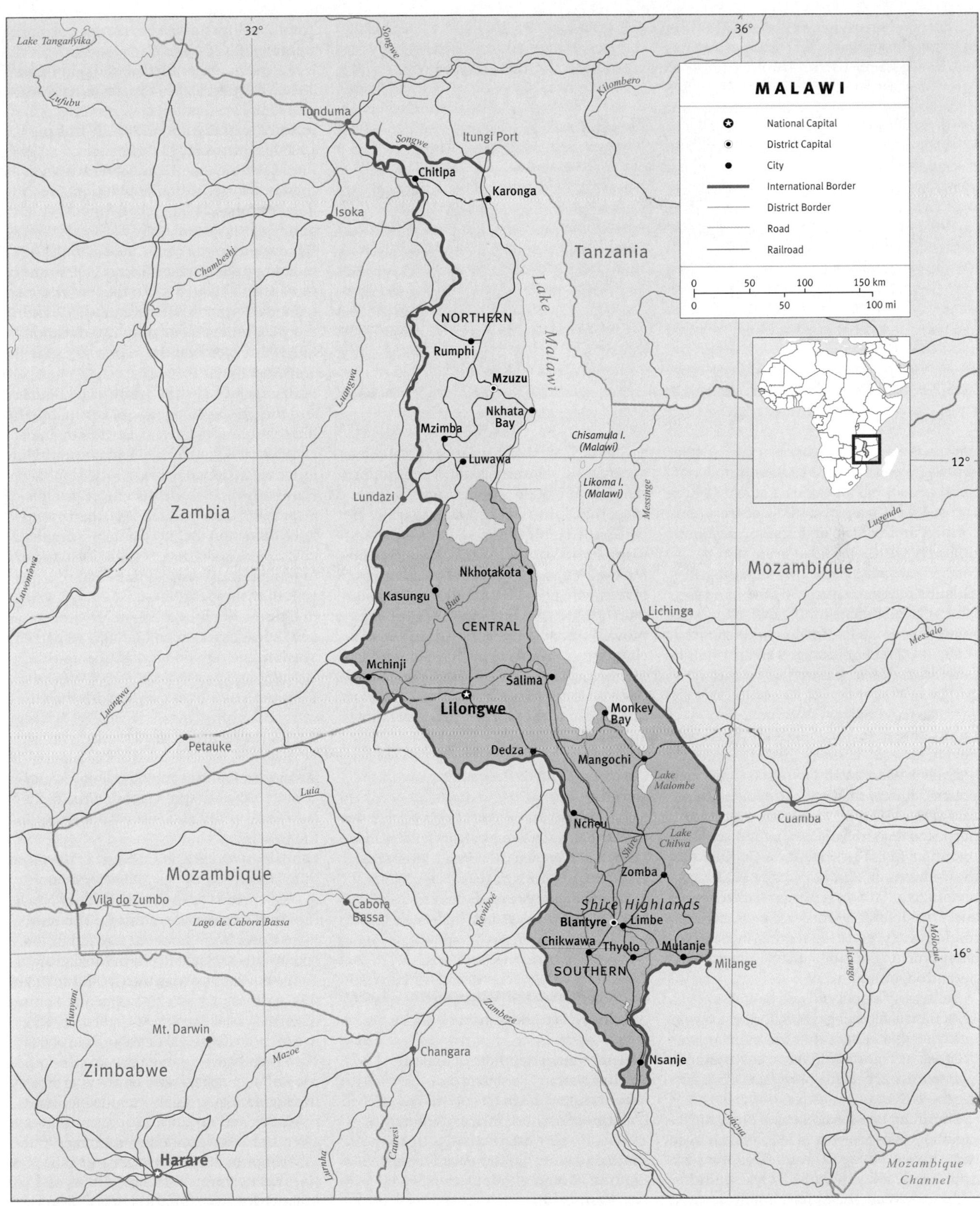

Banda's relations with South Africa isolated Malawi politically from the rest of Africa. Arguing that APARTHEID could only be overcome through dialogue, Banda ignored international sanctions in allowing thousands of Malawian workers to migrate annually to the South African mines. He also allowed South African tourists (who were barred from traveling almost everywhere else in Africa) to enter Malawi. Banda initially established relations with the Portuguese colonial government of Mozambique, in return for the construction of the Nacula railway and other investments, yet he later welcomed a representative of the anti-colonial movement FRELIMO to Malawi. During Mozambique's drawn-out civil war Malawi also hosted thousands of refugees.

For years Banda's ability to maintain power and sustain the economy depended on his pragmatic regional diplomacy, as well as on the international community's willingness to overlook his record of corruption and brutality. But this era ended abruptly when donor agencies declared in 1992 that nonhumanitarian aid would be conditional upon Malawi's compliance with

A Malawi woman rinses clothes before hanging them out to dry. *CORBIS/Gina Glover*

international human rights standards. Earlier that year organizations such as Amnesty International and the Roman Catholic Church accused the Banda government of executions, torture, and the use of detention without due process. Civil unrest grew, and newly formed opposition groups, including the Alliance for Democracy (AFORD) and the United Democratic Front (UDF), demanded multiparty elections. In January 1993 more than 100,000 people staged an anti-Banda demonstration in Blantyre.

The Period Following Banda

Banda agreed to a referendum, which was held in June 1993; the results left no doubt that the public wanted a return to multi-party politics. Shortly thereafter, the constitution was amended, first permitting opposition parties to register and then later rescinding the office of life-president. In October of that same year, Banda became ill and was hospitalized in South Africa. A three-person presidential council took control and made several additional constitutional amendments, including the elimination of detention without trial.

Multiparty elections were held in May 1994. Banda, receiving only a third of the vote, finally stepped down after more than three decades as leader of Malawi. In his place Bakili Muluzi became president, representing the UDF.

The ailing Banda, along with other MCP members, was arrested in 1995 and charged with the 1983 alleged murders of political opponents; all were ultimately acquitted within the year. The Muluzi administration has been slow to institute real policy changes; the 1996 announcement of an independent anticorruption agency has yet to be realized; the press remains largely influenced by government interests; and the police are still charged with detaining and torturing dissidents without trial. The government also continues to control the Malawi Broadcasting Corporation (MBC), the sole radio station.

Although the Banda era is over, Malawians' struggle with poverty is not. The economy remains one of the poorest in the world, exacerbated by the extreme disparities between the country's rich and its poor – a disparity second only to Brazil's. Despite Malawi's ongoing effort to attract foreign investment, agriculture still employs about four-fifths of the working population and provides most of the country's foreign exchange earnings. As in the past, the fortunes of this small land-locked nation are tied to those of its neighbors, and especially to South Africa's capacity to generate regional trade and industrialization.

Ari Nave

See Also

Banda, Ngwazi Hastings Kamuzu; Decolonization in Africa: An Interpretation; Front for the Liberation of Mozambique; Gold Trade; Ivory Trade; Malawi, Lake; Lilongwe, Malawi; Iron in Africa; Mombasa, Kenya; Swahili People; Zambia; Christianity: Missionaries in Africa; Human Rights in Africa; Indian Ocean Slave Trade.

Africa

Malawi (Ready Reference)

Official Name: Republic of Malawi
Former Name: Nyasaland
Area: 118,484 sq km (45,747 sq mi)
Location: Southern Africa; borders Zambia to the west, Mozambique to the south and west, Tanzania to the northeast
Capital: Lilongwe (population 395,500 [1994 estimate])
Other Major Cities: Blantyre (population 446,800 [1994 estimate])
Population: 9,840,474 (1998 estimate)
Population Density: 95 persons per sq km (about 247 per sq mi [1995 estimate])
Population Below Age 15: 46 percent (male 2,249,108; female 2,228,934 [1998 estimate])
Population Growth Rate: 1.66 percent (1998 estimate)
Total Fertility Rate: 5.6 children born per woman (1998 estimate)
Life Expectancy at Birth: Total population: 36.59 years (male 36.64 years; female 36.54 years [1998 estimate])
Infant Mortality Rate: 133.7 deaths per 1000 live births (1998 estimate)
Literacy Rate (age 15 and over who can read and write): Total population: 56.4 percent (male 71.9 percent; female 41.8 percent [1995 estimate])
Education: In the early 1990s about 1.4 million pupils attended some 2900 primary schools and about 31,500 students attended secondary schools. However, in 1995, after the government made primary education in Malawi free, enrollment in primary schools grew to 3 million.
Languages: English is the official language and the primary language of instruction in the schools. Chichewa, a Bantu language, is the national language, and a number of other Bantu languages are widely spoken.
Ethnic Groups: Principal ethnic groups include the Chewa, the Nyanja, the Tumbuka, the Ngoni, and the Yao. Remaining inhabitants, principally settlers of British and Indian origin, form less than half of 1 percent of the population.
Religions: About 55 percent are Protestant, 20 percent Roman Catholic, 15 percent Muslim; the remainder practice traditional religions.
Climate: The climate varies with the elevation. The low-lying Shire Valley is hot and humid with temperatures averaging from 21° C (69° F) to 29° C (84° F). The highlands are more temperate. Annual rainfall averages about 2300 mm (about 90 in) in the highlands and about 800 mm (about 30 in) in the lowlands.
Land, Plants, and Animals: Part of the Great Rift Valley runs through Malawi from north to south. In this deep trough lies Lake Nyasa, the third largest lake in Africa. The Shire River flows from the southern end of the lake to the Zambezi River in Mozambique. To the east and west of the Great Rift Valley the land rises to form high plateaus. South of Lake Nyasa lie the Shire Highlands, which rise to more than 2700 m (more than 9000 ft). Thin forest covers large parts of the country. Baobab, acacia, and conifers grow in the highlands. Animals include elephants, rhinoceroses, giraffes, zebras, monkeys, antelope, hippopotamuses, snakes and other reptiles, birds, insects, and fish.
Natural Resources: The resources of Malawi are almost entirely agricultural and timber-based. Mineral wealth is slight, although some marble and limestone are produced.
Currency: The Malawian kwacha
Gross Domestic Product (GDP): $8.6 billion (1997 estimate)
GDP per Capita: $900 (1997 estimate)
GDP Real Growth Rate: 6 percent (1997 estimate)

Primary Economic Activities: Agriculture (45 percent of GDP; 43 percent of employment), industry (30 percent of GDP; 16 percent of employment in manufacturing, 7 percent of employment in construction), services (25 percent of GDP) (1995 estimate)
Primary Crops: Tobacco, sugar cane, cotton, tea, corn, potatoes, cassava (tapioca), sorghum, pulses; cattle and goats
Industries: Tea, tobacco, sugar, sawmill products, cement, and consumer goods
Primary Exports: Tobacco, tea, sugar, coffee, peanuts, and wood products
Primary Imports: Food, petroleum products, semimanufactures, consumer goods, and transportation equipment
Primary Trade Partners: United States, South Africa, Germany, Japan, United Kingdom, and Zimbabwe
Government: Malawi is a multiparty parliamentary republic, with an elected president (Bakili Muluzi since May 21, 1994), who is both the head of government and the head of state. Cabinet ministers are responsible to the president, who is elected to a five-year term by universal adult suffrage. The 177-member unicameral parliament, the National Assembly, is popularly elected to five-year terms. Political parties include the ruling party: United Democratic Front as well as Alliance for Democracy, Congress for the Second Republic, Malawi Congress Party, Malawi Democratic Party, People Democratic Party, and the Social Democratic Party.

Robert Fay

See Also
Baobab Tree; Elephant; Giraffe; Hippopotamus; Malawi, Lake; Rhinoceros; Rift Valleys; Zebra.

Africa

Malawi, Lake, or Lake Nyasa, the third largest and southernmost of the African Rift Valley lakes, and home to hundreds of species of fish.

The ninth largest lake in the world, Lake Malawi is 584 km (about 365 mi) long and 16 to 80 km (about 10 to 50 mi) wide, with a total area of 30,800 sq km (about 11,430 sq mi) or about 8 percent of the total area of Malawi. It is about 706 km deep (about 2310 ft). Most of Lake Malawi is located in Malawi, although some extends into Tanzania. It forms most of Malawi's northern border with Tanzania and its eastern border with Mozambique.

Lake Malawi is integral to the Malawian economy. Malawi, a landlocked state, depends on the lake for water, transportation, electricity, irrigation, tourism, and fish. Lake Malawi is home to more than 200 species of fish, most from the Cichlid family, and many of them are found nowhere else. Hippopotamuses also inhabit the lake. Fish provides approximately 70 percent of the animal protein consumed by Malawians, most of whom live in rural areas. In addition, fishing is an important industry in Malawi. An estimated 230,000 Malawians are employed by fishing or fishing-related industries, which are threatened by decreasing fish populations. In 1987 the commercial fish catch was 88,586 tons, of which 101 tons were exported. By 1991 the commercial fish catch was 63,000 tons, of which only 3 tons were exported. In 1992, although the catch was 69,500 tons, Malawi exported no fish.

Robert Fay

See Also
Hippopotamus; Rift Valleys.

North America

Malcolm X (Malcolm Little; later El-Hajj Malik El-Shabazz) (b. May 19, 1925, Omaha, Nebr.; d. February 21, 1965, New York, N.Y.); a leading figure in the twentieth-century movement for black liberation in the United States, and arguably its most enduring symbol.

Malcolm X has been called many things: Pan-Africanist (*see* Pan-Africanism), father of Black Power, religious fanatic, closet conservative, incipient socialist (*see* Socialism), and a menace to society. The meaning of his public life – his politics and ideology – is contested in part because his entire body of work consists of a few dozen speeches and a collaborative autobiography whose veracity is often challenged. Gunned down three months before his fortieth birthday, Malcolm X's life was cut short just when his thinking had reached a critical juncture.

Malcolm's life is a Horatio Alger story with a twist. His is not a "rags to riches" tale, but a powerful narrative of self-transformation from petty hustler to internationally known political leader. The son of Louisa and Earl Little, who was a Baptist preacher active in Marcus Garvey's Universal Negro Improvement Association, Malcolm and his siblings experienced dramatic confrontations with racism from childhood. Hooded Klansmen burned their home in Lansing, Michigan; Earl Little was killed under mysterious circumstances; welfare agencies split up the children and eventually committed Louisa Little to a state mental institution; and Malcolm was forced to live in a detention home run by a racist white couple. By the eighth grade he left school, moved to Boston, Massachusetts, to live with his half-sister Ella, and discovered the underground world of African American hipsters.

Malcolm's entry into the masculine culture of the zoot suit, the "conked" (straightened) hair, and the lindy hop coincided with the outbreak of World War II, rising black militancy (symbolized in part by A. Philip Randolph's threatened March on Washington for racial and economic justice), and outbreaks of race riots in Detroit, Michigan, and other cities (*see* Detroit Riot of 1943). Malcolm and his partners did not seem very "political" at the time, but they dodged the draft so as not to lose their lives over a "white man's war," and they avoided wage work whenever possible. His search for leisure and pleasure took him to Harlem, New York, where his primary sources of income derived from petty hustling, drug dealing, pimping, gambling, and viciously exploiting women. In 1946 his luck ran out; he was arrested for burglary and sentenced to ten years in prison.

Malcolm's downward descent took a U-turn in prison when he began studying the teachings of the Lost-Found Nation of Islam (NOI), the black Muslim group founded by Wallace D. Fard and led by Elijah Muhammad (Elijah Poole). Submitting to the discipline and guidance of the NOI, he became a voracious reader of the Koran and the Bible. He also immersed himself in works of literature and history at the prison library. Behind prison walls he quickly emerged as a powerful orator and brilliant rhetorician. He led the famous prison debating team that beat the Massachusetts Institute of Technology (M.I.T.), arguing against capital punishment by pointing out that English pickpockets often did their best work at public hangings! Upon his release in 1952 he renamed himself Malcolm X, symbolically repudiating the "white man's name."

As a devoted follower of Elijah Muhammad, Malcolm X rose quickly within the NOI ranks, serving as minister of Harlem's Temple No. 7 in 1954, and later ministering to temples in Detroit and Philadelphia, Pennsylvania. Through national speaking engagements and television appearances, and by establishing *Muhammad Speaks* – the NOI's first nationally distributed newspaper – Malcolm X put the Nation of Islam on the map. His sharp criticisms of civil rights leaders for advocating integration into white society instead of building black institutions and defending themselves from racist violence generated opposition from both conservatives and liberals. His opponents called him "violent," "fascist," and "racist." To those who claimed that the NOI undermined their efforts toward integration by preaching racial separatism, Malcolm responded, "It is not integration that Negroes in America want, it is human dignity."

Distinguishing Malcolm's early political and intellectual views from the teachings of Elijah Muhammad is not a simple matter. His role as minister was to preach the gospel of Islam according to Muhammad. He remained a staunch devotee of the Nation's strict moral codes and gender conventions. Although his own narrative suggests that he never entirely discarded his hustler's distrust of women, he married Betty Sanders (later Betty Shabazz) in 1958 and lived by NOI rules: men must lead, women must follow; the man's domain is the world, the woman's is the home.

On other issues, however, Malcolm showed signs of independence from the NOI line. During the mid-1950s, for example, he privately scoffed at Muhammad's interpretation of the genesis of the "white race" and seemed uncomfortable with the idea that all white people were literally devils. He was always careful to preface his remarks with "The honorable Elijah Muhammad teaches.... " More significant, Malcolm clearly disagreed with the NOI's policy of not participating in politics. He not only believed that political mobilization was indispensable but occasionally defied the rule by supporting boycotts and other forms of protest. In 1962, before he split with the NOI, Malcolm shared the podium with black, white, and Puerto Rican labor organizers in the left-wing, multiracial hospital workers' union in New York. He also began developing an independent Pan-Africanist and, in some respects, "Third World" political perspective during the 1950s, when anticolonial wars and decolonization (*see* DECOLONIZATION IN AFRICA: AN INTERPRETATION) were pressing public issues. As early as 1954 Malcolm gave a speech comparing the situation in Vietnam (*see* VIETNAM WAR) with that of the MAU MAU REBELLION in colonial KENYA, framing both of these movements as uprisings of the "darker races" creating a "tidal wave" against United States and European imperialism. Indeed, Africa remained his primary political interest outside of black America. He toured EGYPT, SUDAN, NIGERIA, and GHANA in 1959, well before his famous trip to Africa and the Middle East in 1964.

Although Malcolm tried to conceal his differences with Elijah Muhammad, tensions between them erupted. The tensions were exacerbated by the threat that Malcolm's popularity posed to Muhammad's leadership and by Malcolm's disillusionment with Elijah upon learning that the NOI's moral and spiritual leader had fathered children by former secretaries. The tensions became publicly visible when Muhammad silenced Malcolm for remarking after the assassination of President John F. Kennedy that it was a case of the "chickens coming home to roost." (Malcolm's point was that the federal government's inaction toward racist violence in the South had come back to strike the president.) When Malcolm learned that Muhammad had planned to have him assassinated, he decided to leave the NOI.

On March 8, 1964, he announced his resignation and formed the Muslim Mosque, Inc., an Islamic movement devoted to working in the political sphere and cooperating with civil rights leaders. That same year he made his first pilgrimage to Mecca and took a second tour of several African and Arab nations. The trip was apparently transformative. Upon his return he renamed himself El-Hajj Malik El-Shabazz, adopted from Sunni Islam, and announced that he had found the "true brotherhood" of man. He publicly acknowledged that whites were no longer devils, though he still remained a Black Nationalist (*see* BLACK NATIONALISM IN THE UNITED STATES) and staunch believer in black self-determination and self-organization.

During the summer of 1964 he formed the Organization of Afro-American Unity (OAAU). Inspired by the ORGANIZATION OF AFRICAN UNITY (OAU), made up of independent African states, the OAAU's program combined advocacy for independent black institutions (e.g., schools and cultural centers) with support for black participation in mainstream politics, including electoral campaigns. Following the example of PAUL ROBESON and W. E. B. Du Bois, Malcolm planned in 1965 to submit to the United Nations a petition that documented human rights violations and acts of genocide against African Americans. His assassination at the Audubon Ballroom in New York – carried out by gunmen affiliated with the NOI – intervened, and the OAAU died soon after Malcolm was laid to rest.

Although Malcolm left no real institutional legacy, he did exert a notable impact on the CIVIL RIGHTS MOVEMENT in the last year of his life. Black activists in the CONGRESS OF RACIAL EQUALITY (CORE) and the STUDENT NONVIOLENT COORDINATING COMMITTEE (SNCC) who had heard him speak to organizers in Selma, Alabama, in February 1965 began to support some of his ideas, especially on armed self-defense, racial pride, and the creation of black-run institutions. He also gained a small following of radical Marxists, mostly Trotskyists in the Socialist Workers Party (SWP). Malcolm convinced some SWP members of the revolutionary potential of ordinary black ghetto dwellers, and he began to speak more critically of capitalism. Was Malcolm about to become a civil rights leader? Could he have launched a successful Pan-Africanist movement? Was he turning toward Marxism? Scholars and activists have debated these issues, but no firm answers are possible.

Ironically, Malcolm X made a bigger impact on black politics and culture dead than alive. The Watts Rebellion occurred and the BLACK POWER Movement emerged just months after his death, and his ideas about community control, African liberation, and self-pride became widespread and influential. His autobiography, written with Alex Haley, became a movement standard. Malcolm's life story proved to the BLACK PANTHER PARTY, founded in 1966, that ex-criminals and hustlers could be turned into revolutionaries. And arguments in favor of armed self-defense – certainly not a new idea in African American communities – were renewed by Malcolm's narrative and the publication of his speeches. Even after the death of Martin Luther King Jr., when the civil rights leader was celebrated as an American hero by many blacks and whites, Malcolm's image loomed much larger in inner-city communities, especially among young males.

Despite the collapse or destruction of Black Nationalist organizations during the mid-1970s, Malcolm X continued to live through the folklore of submerged black urban youth cultures, making a huge comeback thanks to RAP music, black-oriented bookstores, and Afrocentric street vendors. The 1980s were a ripe time for a hero like Malcolm X, as racism on college campuses increased, inner cities deteriorated, police brutality cases seemed to rise again, and young black men came to be seen as an "endangered species." Malcolm's uncompromising statements about racism, self-hatred, community empowerment, and his background as a "ghetto youth" made him the undisputed icon of the young.

The recirculation of Malcolm as icon during the late 1980s and the 1990s got its biggest boost from the commercial marketplace, as retailers, publishers, and Hollywood cashed in on the popularity of hip hop music and culture. As Afrocentrism achieved respectability among black urban (and suburban) professionals, Malcolm's face and name became a central staple among the "Afro-Chic" products that made up their casual attire. The rush to purchase "X" paraphernalia affected not only African Americans but also suburban whites, Latinos, and Asian Americans, who were dubbed the X Generation and were fascinated with black youth cultures. Ad agencies boldly marketed "X" products without even mentioning Malcolm. "Malcolmania" reached its high point with the release of Spike Lee's cinematic rendering of Malcolm's autobiography in 1992. Following Lee's lead, retailers sold millions of dollars worth of "X" caps, T-shirts, medallions, and posters emblazoned with Malcolm's name, body, or words.

Not surprisingly, the selling of Malcolm X in the 1990s generated pointed debate among African Americans. Some argued that marketing Malcolm undermined his message, while others insisted that the circulation of his image has prompted young people to search out his ideas. Some utilized his emphasis on black community development to support a new African American entrepreneurialism, while others insisted on seeing him as a radical democrat devoted to social justice. His anti-imperialism has dropped out of public memory, whereas his misogyny has been ignored by his supporters and spotlighted by his detractors. However these disputes evolve, it appears that Malcolm X's place in U.S. history, and in the collective memory of African Americans, is secure. Ironically, some of his centrality can be attributed to the mutability of his own viewpoint. Because his ideas were constantly being renewed and rethought during his short career, Malcolm has become a sort of tabula rasa, or blank slate, on which people of different positions can write their own

Malcolm X speaks to a crowd at a prointegration rally in Harlem, New York, in May 1963. *CORBIS/Bettmann*

interpretation of his politics and legacy. Chuck D of the rap group Public Enemy and Supreme Court Justice Clarence Thomas can both declare Malcolm X their hero.

Robin Kelley

See Also

World War II and African Americans; Du Bois, William Edward Burghardt (W. E. B.); Garvey, Marcus Mosiah; Haley, Alexander Palmer (Alex); Hip Hop in the United States; King, Martin Luther, Jr.; Lee, Shelton Jackson ("Spike"); Los Angeles Watts Riot of 1965; Randolph, Asa Philip; Afrocentrism; March on Washington, 1941; Dance in the United States; Shabazz, Hajj Bahiyah Betty.

Europe

Maldoror, Sarah (Sarah Ducados) (b. 1939, Candou, France), French film director of Guadeloupean descent, considered one of the most important women directors in African and Caribbean cinema.

Born in France as Sarah Ducados, Sarah Maldoror has primarily made films about Africa and the Caribbean. She has won praise for her positive portrayals of African women and their role in liberation movements.

Raised in southern France, Maldoror attended the Centre d'Art Dramatique de la Rue Blanche in Paris. Frustrated by the lack of acting roles for black women, she and her colleagues Toto Bissinthe, Timité Bassori, and Ababacar Samb formed an independent theater company, the Compagnie d'Art Dramatique des Griots. During the mid-1950s Maldoror directed several plays for the company, including Aimé Césaire's *La Tragédie du roi Christophe*. She became friends with several exiled African militants, including Mario de Andrarde, a leader of the Angolan Popular Movement for the Liberation of Angola (MPLA). Andrarde convinced Maldoror to use her production talents to promote African liberation movements.

In 1961 Maldoror won a scholarship to study film at the Gorki Studio in Moscow. After graduation two years later she went to Africa to assist with the production of the movies *The Battle of Algiers* and *Elles*. During this time she began writing the script that became her 1971 debut film, *Monangambee*, about the life of Angolan writer and activist Jose Luandino Vieira. Highly acclaimed, this short film enabled Maldoror to raise funding for her second and more ambitious work, *Des fusils pour Banta*, a documentary about women in Amílcar Cabral's liberation troops in Guinea-Bissau. Although completed, the film was never released, which Maldoror attributes to a disagreement with her financial backer, the Algerian government.

In 1972 she released her best-known film, *Sambizanga*. Adapted from Vieira's *The Real Life of Domingos Xavier*, the film explores men's and women's roles in the Angolan independence struggle through the story of one married couple. *Sambizanga* received awards at the 1972 Carthage Film Festival and the 1973 Festival Panafricain du Cinéma de Ouagadougou.

Since *Sambizanga*, Maldoror has produced several feature films, including *Un Dessert pour Constance* (1981). But short films and documentaries have comprised the majority of her subsequent work. Her documentaries on Aimé Césaire (*Un Homme, Une Terre*, 1977) and Christiane Diop (*Portrait de Madame Diop*, 1986), the editor of *Présence Africaine*, have been especially well received. Maldoror finished her latest documentary, *Léon G. Demas*, in 1994, and has since been lecturing on film at universities in the United States and France.

Elizabeth Heath

See Also

Cinema, African; *Présence Africaine*; Algeria; Angola; Guadeloupe.

Latin America and the Caribbean

Malê, a term used to describe Muslim slaves and freed blacks in colonial Brazil (*see* African Ethnic Groups in Latin America and the Caribbean).

Africa

Mali, a landlocked country in West Africa bordered by Senegal, Mauritania, Algeria, Niger, Burkina Faso, Côte d'Ivoire, and Guinea.

Mali, formerly the French Sudan, is a country best known for its ancient kingdoms and empires. Controlling the rich trans-Saharan trade in gold and slaves, kingdoms such as Ghana, Mali, and Songhai achieved prosperity and cultural advancement. During the period of colonialism, however, the French imposed an economic dependence on cash crops that left the country vulnerable to drought and the vagaries of the world market. Since independence, successive governments have attempted development strategies ranging from Marxist state-led development to market-oriented liberalism. However, the structural weakness of the country's overwhelmingly agricultural economy has left Mali one of the poorest countries in the world. In recent years economic liberalization has attracted new foreign investment to Mali. It remains to be seen whether this investment will bring renewed prosperity to modern Mali, whose history is surely one of the richest in Africa.

Early History

Evidence of the human presence in Mali dates back to the neolithic period, when lush savanna and grasslands covered the area. Detailed rock paintings portray the life of the early hunters and pastoralists, and their adaptations to the climatic changes that began around 6000 B.C.E. Over subsequent centuries the whole region became more arid, while the north became a desert. Much of the population shifted south and gradually began cultivating crops. By 500 B.C.E. the agriculturalists of the Niger and Senegal river valleys had developed the ability to work metal, including copper, iron, and gold. The production and exchange of these metals was the basis of prosperity in ancient trading centers such as Djenné-Jeno and the kingdom of Ghana (not to be confused with the modern nation of Ghana).

Around 400 C.E. the Soninké, a Mande people of the upper Senegal Valley, established trade contracts with the northern nomads. During the following centuries their kingdom, Ghana, extended from present-day southeastern Mauritania into western Mali and northern Guinea. It controlled the exchange of southern gold for northern salt and copper as well as luxury goods from North Africa. The empire, with a capital at Koumbi Saleh, reached its peak in the eleventh century but declined after 1076 as a result of attacks by the Almoravids. These Muslim invaders converted the Soninké to Islam and seized control of their trade centers. Though Almoravid control lasted less than 20 years, it wrecked the economy of the kingdom, which gradually disintegrated over the next century. An offshoot of Ghana, known as Soso, dominated the remnants of the kingdom in the early thirteenth century.

The kingdom of Mali soon conquered the remainder of Ghana and surrounding regions. According to Mandinka oral traditions, Sundiata Keita, a Mandinka chief who controlled the Bouré gold mines, overthrew Soso's harsh ruler in 1230 and gained control of the lucrative trans-Saharan trade. At its peak in the early fourteenth century under Mansa Musa I, Mali extended from the Atlantic Ocean to Gao on the middle Niger. Like Ghana, Mali grew rich and powerful from its central location and its trading centers – Gao, Tombouctou (Timbuktu), Djenné, and Audaghost – as well as its control of the valuable southern gold mines. Politically, the empire was a federation of conquered kingdoms united under the rule of one king, the *mansa*. After the mid-fourteenth century succession disputes and struggles among the empire's vassals weakened the empire. As the power of the mansa eroded, Mali lost the ability to collect revenue from the rich trade caravans crossing its territory. During the fifteenth century Mali's peripheral territories began to secede. The empire had all but disintegrated by the mid-sixteenth century.

The rulers of Songhai, a former tributary to Mali centered at Gao, took advantage of the empire's dissolution. In 1465 Songhai ruler Sonni Ali Ber conquered much of former Mali. His successors, including Muhammad Askia and Askia Dawud, gained control of the region's gold and salt mines and the trade routes passing through Tombouctou and

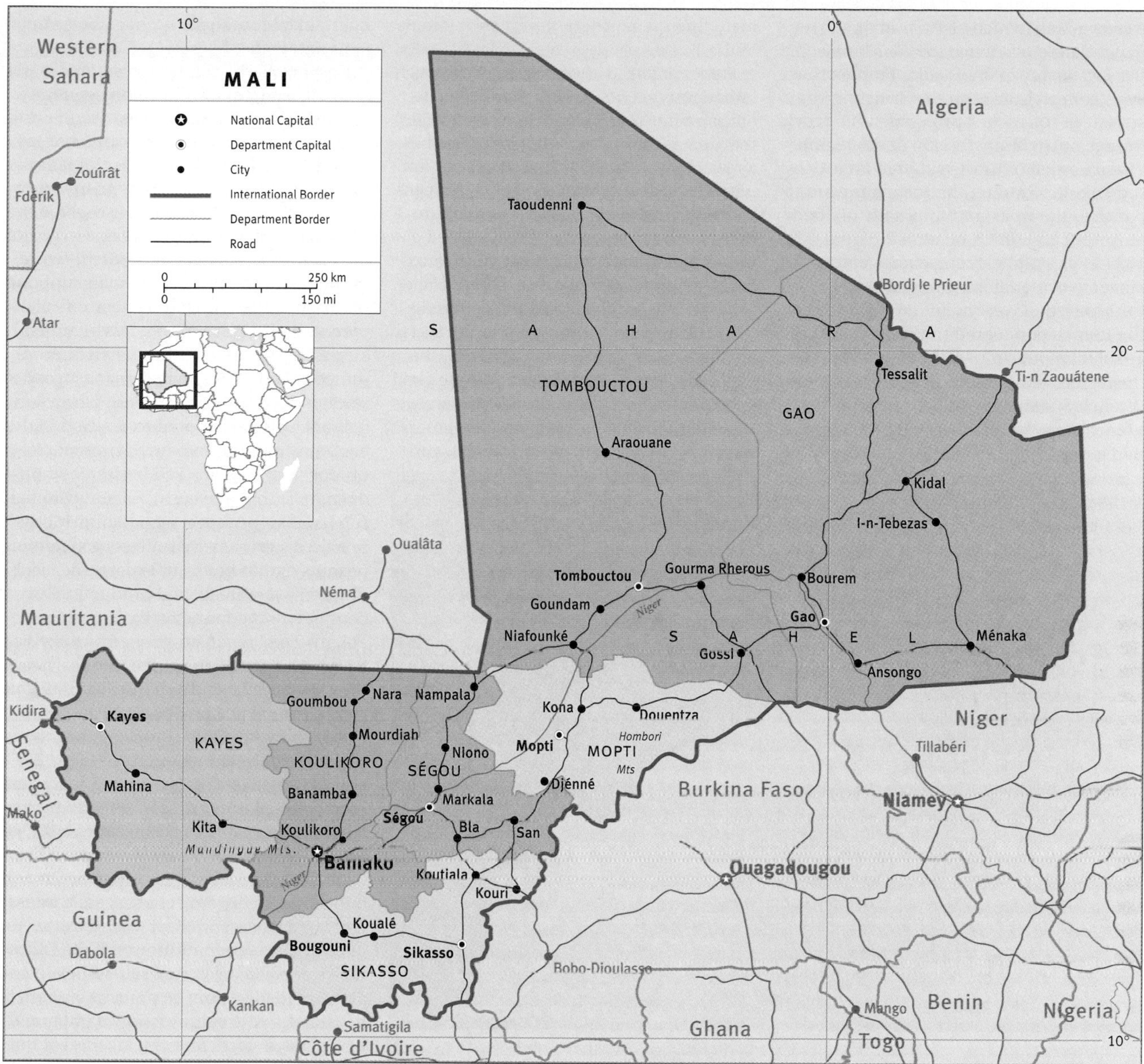

Djenné. Songhai became a major center of Islamic scholarship. Frequent succession disputes, however, shook Songhai. This instability, as well as its control over Saharan gold and salt mines, made it an attractive target for the Moroccan ruler Mansur. In 1589 Mansur hired 4000 soldiers to cross the Sahara and conquer Songhai. Equipped with firearms, the Moroccan army easily defeated the Songhai forces, who were armed only with hand weapons, near Gao. The Songhai ruler, Askia Ishaq, surrendered and offered to pay Morocco an annual tribute. Mansur, enraged by Ishaq's meager tribute, sent another commander to the region with the order to demolish the Songhai ruler and army. The Moroccans crushed the Songhai Empire, which fragmented into several smaller units. Morocco retained control of the Niger bend around Tombouctou until 1737. In that year, Tuareg tribes defeated Morocco; they seized control of the Niger bend region and its rich trans-Saharan trade.

Meanwhile, after the collapse of Songhai, a series of states emerged to the west along the upper Niger and upper Senegal rivers. Around 1650 the Bambara kingdom of Ségu arose along the upper Niger near the site of the modern town of Ségou. Its territory included much of the western part of present-day Mali, and it periodically expanded as far east as Tombouctou. Slaves were taken from western Ségu to Atlantic coastal ports in exchange for firearms and other European goods. Another Bambara state, Kaarta, controlled the Niger Valley between Ségou and Tombouctou after about 1750. During the early nineteenth century the expansionist Fulani Muslim theocracy of Macina defeated both Bambara states. Macina exported slaves taken from the region both across the Sahara and down the Niger to the Sokoto Caliphate.

Between 1850 and 1864 the Tukulor Sufi scholar al-Hajj Umar Tal, armed with European weaponry, conquered most of the territory (present-day Mali), including the remnants of the Bambara states, Macina, and the Tuareg stronghold of Tombouctou. However, Umar's Tukulor followers were motivated more by greed than by religious fervor or a desire for political stability. After his death in 1864 his followers fought for control of the vast realm. His son, Ahmadu Seku, struggled to retain control of the Tukulor Empire, based at Ségou, but his Bambara and Fulani subjects staged repeated rebellions, and the Tukulor rivals continually challenged his authority.

French Conquest and Colonial Rule

The French explorer René Caillié visited Tombouctou in 1828. His published account generated increased European interest in the region.

During the mid-nineteenth century the French expanded into the region to control trade routes leading to their coastal base in Senegal. In 1855 the French constructed a fort on the Senegal River in present-day western Mali, which al-Hajj Umar subsequently attacked. At first the French accepted the sovereignty of the Tukulor Empire. However, competition with the British in the SCRAMBLE FOR AFRICA prompted the French to seek outright possession of the region. When French outposts suffered attacks by the Tukulor Empire, the French moved to conquer the weak and internally divided empire. The French occupied Bamako in 1883 as part of their campaign against the kingdom of Mandinka warrior SAMORY TOURÉ to the south. Over the following decade the French conquered the remnants of the Tukulor Empire. In 1892 the French claimed the region as the colony of Soudan Français (French Sudan), which became a part of French West Africa in 1895. By 1898 France had conquered the whole of modern Mali, including the northern desert strongholds of the Tuareg.

France enforced its COLONIAL RULE through indigenous agents. Although most local officials came from traditional ruling families, the French chose many of these officials as a reward for their loyalty to colonial authorities. Throughout the colonial era, Africans viewed many "native" agents with apprehension and mistrust, since they carried out unpopular French policies, including tax collection and the recruitment of forced labor. Nevertheless, colonial positions offered a few Africans limited opportunities for social advancement. Unlike other Africans, the children of colonial administrators often had access to Western education. Ultimately this group formed a small but elite group of *assimilés* ("assimilated" Africans), and many, like MODIBO KEITA, became prominent nationalist figures.

Despite Mali's scant resources, France was determined to make the colony generate income. As in other colonies, French officials conscripted forced African labor for various state projects, such as the railroad to Dakar, completed in 1924. As in Upper Volta (present-day Burkina Faso), French Sudan also exported wage laborers to French plantations in Senegal and Côte d'Ivoire. In the world wars, French Sudan supplied troops for France, including nearly 49,500 men in World War I alone. Having fought alongside the French, these men later returned to French Sudan to demand an end to second-class status for Africans in the colony.

France also attempted to develop Mali's economy and implemented projects to produce export crops and bolster food production. During the early years of colonial rule, Malian peasants who had formerly practiced subsistence farming began farming peanuts (groundnuts) for export. The yields, however, were small, and production was confined to the more fertile regions of the colony. The French government conceived a vast scheme to irrigate the middle Niger River delta region and make the land suitable for cotton and rice production. The project, overseen by the Office du Niger, began on a small scale near Baguineda in the 1920s and expanded during the 1940s. The scheme requisitioned thousands of forced African laborers; it irrigated 44,500 hectares (109,960 acres) of formerly arid land that was farmed by forcibly relocated peasants. The French initially called the project a success because it created a peasant-based cash-crop sector of the Malian economy. However, the Office du Niger failed to become self-sufficient and accounted for nearly 30 percent of French subsidies to the colony prior to independence. The project's forced relocation of the peasantry increased African resentment of French colonial rule.

French rule faced resistance throughout the colonial period. Tuareg nomads in the north fought French policies that would have forced them into a sedentary lifestyle. Meanwhile, Muslim religious leaders protested the domination of the non-Muslim French "infidels." The most famous of the Muslim leaders was Shaykh Mohammed al-Tishiti Hamalla, who founded the Hamallist religious movement and led a series of violent revolts between 1922 and 1946. Urban trade unions and other voluntary associations organized secular opposition

TOP: Malian farmers lead their reluctant animals onto a ferry on their way to the market at Djenné. *CORBIS/Nik Wheeler*

FAR LEFT: A street vendor peddles a variety of household goods in Bamako, capital and largest city of Mali. *CORBIS/Nik Wheeler*

LEFT: Women gather for the weekly street market in Djenné, Mali, which has been a trading town since the Middle Ages. *Wolfgang Kaehler, 1999*

to French colonial rule. Civil servants generally formed the earliest associations, such the teachers union of Mamadou Konaté in Bamako, which sought to influence French policy in the colony. Later, labor leaders rallied African workers against the *indigénat,* the colonial legal system that limited the rights of Africans and imposed the forced labor obligations. These associations were the forerunners of postwar political parties.

After World War II France allowed each of its colonies to form political parties and elect two delegates to the French National Assembly. In Mali, Modibo Keita and Mamadou Konaté founded the Bloc Soudanais in 1946. The party, which eventually joined the multicolony RASSEMBLEMENT DÉMOCRATIQUE AFRICAIN (RDA) as the Union Soudanaise-RDA (US-RDA), professed Marxism and anticolonialism. Although the US-RDA enjoyed popular support, the French government preferred the moderate Parti Progressiste Soudanais (PPS).

The establishment of universal suffrage enabled the US-RDA to defeat the PPS easily in the 1956 elections. Keita, the party's leader, won election to the territorial assembly and to the French National Assembly. As independence approached, Keita attempted to organize a Mali Federation against the wishes of the French government. The federation would have united Senegal, Mali, Upper Volta, Dahomey (present-day BENIN), and Côte d'Ivoire. This attempt to provide duty-free access to the sea for Mali failed; on September 22, 1960, Keita became president of an independent Republic of Mali.

A Tuareg family camped outside Tombouctou, Mali, makes dinner. *CORBIS/Wolfgang Kaehler*

INDEPENDENT MALI

Although many of Mali's neighbors at first relied heavily on French advisers, Keita pursued a different path. In 1960 he declared Marxism to be the official ideology of the country's only legitimate party, the US-RDA. Keita aimed to end Mali's economic dependence on France and achieve industrialization through state ownership of the economy. He withdrew Mali from the Communauté Financière Africaine (CFA, the Franco-African monetary union); established a nonconvertible currency for Mali; and severed diplomatic relations with France. These actions effectively cut Mali off from significant import and export markets. Over the next few years Keita's government brutally repressed opposition. Although Keita cultivated ties with the Soviet bloc, communist aid failed to prevent the economy's collapse by the mid-1960s.

Threatened with financial disaster, Keita negotiated readmission to the CFA in 1967. The agreement required a devaluation of the Malian franc and subjected the Malian economy to French influence. The resulting price increases aggravated the hardships of ordinary Malians. Keita responded to protests by creating the People's Militia, a radical youth organization based on Mao's Red Guard, which combed the streets, harassing critics. Keita also replaced the National Assembly with a committee of supporters.

These actions antagonized Mali's powerful army. In 1968 a group of Malian junior officers petitioned Keita to dissolve the People's Militia. When Keita refused to take immediate action, the group overthrew him. These soldiers, led by Lt. Moussa Traoré, disbanded Keita's government and replaced it with the Comité militaire pour la libération nationale (CMLN). Traoré promised to revert to civilian rule after stabilizing the economy.

Traoré, however, focused primarily on maintaining political stability. Confronted by internal factions, public unrest, and repeated coup attempts, Traoré decided to continue Keita's state-led economic policies rather than further antagonize Keita's former supporters. His economic strategy went little beyond an effort to improve relations with France and other Western donors. Between 1968 and 1974 a series of droughts ravaged the country, especially the northern Tuareg region. Mali received considerable aid from Western donors. Meanwhile, Traoré replaced the CMLN with a civilian government. He introduced a new constitution and in 1976 declared a one-party state. As the candidate of the only legal political party, he won election as president in 1979.

In 1980 Western donors, including the World Bank and the International Monetary Fund (IMF), aiming to reduce Mali's reliance

The great mosque at Djenné is the third to stand on the present site. The first was erected around 1300. The current adobe structure was completed in 1907. *Wolfgang Kaehler, 1999*

on foreign aid, compelled Traoré to enact economic liberalization, such as privatizing nationalized businesses, and to impose strict austerity measures. Accordingly, Traoré's government started to privatize businesses, trim the civil service, reduce government salaries, and deny students both financial aid and jobs. Students, teachers, and laid-off workers protested the reforms; the government repressed numerous riots and arrested dozens of protesters. Meanwhile, during the mid-1980s another drought devastated the overwhelmingly agricultural economy. Again the Tuareg north was hardest hit. In 1987 Traoré bowed to public demands and suspended the austerity program.

The IMF immediately suspended financial aid to Mali. For a year Traoré attempted to get by without the much-needed aid. In the months that followed, Mali was unable to pay government workers and students, and again protests rocked Bamako. Although Traoré's promise to return to IMF strictures in 1988 brought renewed financial aid, the government still failed to meet monthly payrolls.

Both state-led development in the 1960s and 1970s and IMF-mandated austerity during the 1980s failed to ease Mali's economic woes. As a result of French colonial policy, Mali depended on cash crops, primarily cotton and peanuts, for export income. Mali was not the only producer of these crops, and supplies tended to glut the world market while export earnings fell. Economic disaster ensued when imports became more expensive, as petroleum did during the 1970s and early 1980s, or when drought disrupted Mali's harvest, as it did repeatedly in the 1970s and 1980s. Mali thus faced a chronic inability to pay for needed imports, including the manufactured goods necessary for its economic development.

Political challenges, in the meantime, distracted Traoré from the country's desperate economic situation. Beginning in the late 1980s Traoré faced a rebellion by northern Tuareg, who blamed the government for indifference to their plight during the drought. Dissatisfied with the government's failure to reduce economic hardship, protesters began demanding multiparty democracy and free elections. Traoré's ambivalent response spurred the formation of pro-democracy movements, including Alpha Oumar Konaré's Alliance pour la démocratie au Mali (ADEMA). Protesters organized massive prodemocracy rallies despite government bans, and in 1991 Traoré's government retaliated with a violent crackdown that killed 106 people and injured more than 700.

In response to public demands, military leader Lt. Col. Amadou Toumani Touré overthrew and arrested Traoré and members of the president's regime. Touré installed a temporary government and guided the nation toward elections. An assembly drafted a new constitution and electoral code, approved in a 1992 referendum. In the presidential elections that followed, ADEMA won by a landslide. Konaré became president of the third republic of Mali.

As president, Konaré has faced ongoing economic and political challenges. Mali's poor economy and the austerity measures imposed by the IMF and World Bank continue to generate unrest. Despite the unpopularity of the economic austerity, Konaré has continued the measures and weathered the unpopular 50 percent devaluation of the CFA franc in 1994. Mali has finally earned the approval of the international financial community: in 1997 the IMF praised Mali as a successful example of structural adjustment. The country's adherence to IMF policy has attracted new foreign investment that has helped Mali become Africa's second largest cotton producer and the continent's third largest exporter of gold. However, IMF policies have ensured that foreign investors will reap most of the benefit from this economic upswing, and it is uncertain whether the living standards of Malians will improve.

The political situation in Mali remains troubled. Rival parties continually accuse Konaré's ruling party, ADEMA, of electoral fraud. Opposition parties have protested national election codes and have boycotted almost every election since 1992. Nevertheless, opposition boycotts have lacked credibility, and independent observers have generally validated the country's electoral process.

Elizabeth Heath

See Also

Bamako, Mali; Colonial Rule; Dakar, Senegal; Drought and Desertification; Explorers in Africa Since 1800; Ghana, Early Kingdom of; Gold Trade; Djenné-Djeno, Mali; Iron in Africa; Morocco; Askia Muhammad; Nationalism in Africa; Niger River; Transatlantic Slave Trade; Pastoralism; Salt Trade; Songhai Empire; Soninké; Structural Adjustment in Africa; Sunni Ali; Tombouctou, Mali; Caillié, René-Auguste; Djenné, Mali; Traoré, Moussa; Koumbi Saleh, Mauritania; Senegal River; Islam and Tradition: An Interpretation; Trans-Saharan and Red Sea Slave Trade; Mali Empire.

Africa

Mali (Ready Reference)

Official Name: Republic of Mali
Former Name: French Sudan
Area: 1,240,192 sq km (478,841 sq mi)
Location: West Africa; borders Algeria, Niger, Burkina Faso, Côte d'Ivoire, Guinea, Senegal, and Mauritania
Capital: Bamako (population 880,000 [1993 estimate])
Other Major Cities: Ségou (population 85,000), Mopti (75,000), Sikasso (73,050), Kayes (50,000), and Gao (40,000) (1993 estimate)
Population: 10,108,569 (1998 estimate)
Population Density: 9 persons per sq km (about 23 persons per sq mi)
Population Below Age 15: 47 percent (male 2,405,624; female 2,383,728 [1998 estimate])
Population Growth Rate: 3 percent (1998 estimate)
Total Fertility Rate: 7.02 children born per woman (1998 estimate)
Life Expectancy at Birth: Total population: 47.03 years (male 45.67 years; female 48.43 years [1998 estimate])
Infant Mortality Rate: 121.72 deaths per 1000 live births (1998 estimate)
Literacy Rate (age 15 and over who can read and write): Total population: 31 percent (male 39.4 percent; female 23.1 percent [1995 estimate])
Education: Annual primary school enrollment in the early 1990s was about 375,000, only about 15 percent of the eligible population. Approximately 88,600 were enrolled in secondary schools and 6700 in institutions of higher education in Bamako, including a teacher's college, an agricultural institute, and schools of administration, medicine, and engineering.
Languages: French is the official language; most of the population speaks Bambara; numerous other African languages are spoken, including Peul, Songhai, and Tamasheq (Tuareg Berber).
Ethnic Groups: Mali's ethnic majority is Mande. Other groups include Bambara, Boboi, Bozo, Diawara, Dioula, Dogon, Fulani, Khassonke, Malinké, Marka, Maure, Minianka, Sarakole, Senufo, Somono, Songhai, Tuareg, Tukulor, and Wassalunke.
Religions: Ninety percent of the population is Muslim, 9 percent adhere to indigenous beliefs, and 1 percent is Christian.
Climate: More than half of the country (in the Saharan north) is hot, dry, and dusty. Average temperatures range from about 24° to 32° C (about 75° to 90° F) in the south and higher in the north. Annual rainfall from June to October decreases from about 1400 mm (about 55 in) in the south to some 1120 mm (44 in) at Bamako and less than 127 mm (less than 5 in) in the north.
Land, Plants, and Animals: Most of Mali consists of low plains broken occasionally by rocky hills. In the southeast the Hombori Mountains rise to 1155 m (3789 ft), and in the southwest the Bambouk and Mandingue mountains are separated by an area of sandy lowlands north and northwest of the Niger River, which cuts an arc across Mali. The northern third of the country lies within the Sahara, while the west is a part of the Sahel, a semi-arid transitional zone. In the southern Saharan zone of Mali are found mimosa and gum trees; in the central region, thorny plants; and in the south, kapok, baobab, and shea trees. Animals include cheetah, oryx, gazelle, giraffe, warthog, lion, leopard, antelope, and jackal.
Natural Resources: Fish, gold, phosphate rock, kaolin, salt, limestone, uranium, bauxite, iron ore, manganese, tin, and copper deposits
Currency: The Communauté Financière Africaine franc
Gross Domestic Product (GDP): $6 billion (1997 estimate)
GDP per Capita: $600 (1997 estimate)
GDP Real Growth Rate: 6 percent (1997 estimate)
Primary Economic Activities: Agriculture (49 percent of GDP, 80 percent of employment); services (34 percent of GDP, 19 percent of employment); industry: 17 percent of GDP, 1 percent of employment) (1995 estimates)
Primary Crops: Cotton, millet, rice, corn, vegetables, peanuts, cattle, sheep, and goats
Industries: Light consumer goods, food processing, construction, phosphate, and gold mining
Primary Exports: Cotton, livestock, and gold
Primary Imports: Machinery and equipment, foodstuffs, construction materials, petroleum, and textiles
Primary Trade Partners: Francophone West Africa and European Union (France especially)
Government: A constitution, approved by popular referendum in January 1992, established Mali as a multiparty republic with a president directly elected to a five-year term. The president, currently Alpha Oumar Konaré, appoints the prime minister, currently Ibrahim Boubacar Keita, who selects the other members of the Council of Ministers. The unicameral National Assembly consists of 129 deputies elected to five-year terms. Since the legislative elections in mid-1997 – which opposition parties boycotted – the Assembly has been dominated by Konaré's party, the Alliance for Democracy in Mali.

Barbara Worley

See Also

Bamako, Mali; Baobab Tree; Sahara Desert; Konaré, Alpha Oumar; Songhai People; Malinké.

Africa

Mali Empire, a West African empire that flourished between the thirteenth and the early sixteenth century, incorporating most of present-day Mali, Senegal, and the Gambia as well as southern Mauritania, eastern Guinea-Bissau, and eastern Guinea.

Mali arose as a small kingdom along the upper Niger River. Oral accounts state that the kingdom came into existence before the year 1000 C.E.; however, if this is true, it must have been a vassal of the empire of Ghana. Mali probably gained independence with the breakup of Ghana in the early twelfth century. During the thirteenth century Mali conquered several of its neighbors. The empire reached its zenith during the fourteenth century, when it ruled over a vast West African domain stretching from the Atlantic coast to the middle Niger below Gao. During the fifteenth century Mali began a slow decline. It ceased to exist by the early eighteenth century.

After the collapse of ancient Ghana, the kingdom of Mali, ruled by the Keita Dynasty, arose among the Mandinka (Malinké) people in the region of Kangaba, spanning the borders of present-day Mali and Guinea. During the twelfth century Mali fell under the dominance of the kingdom of Soso (also known as Susu or Sosso, names carried today by a Guinean people). In 1230 a king named Mari Diata came to the throne and threw off the oppressive Soso yoke. According to the Arab geographer Ibn Khaldun, Mari Diata waged a war of expansion between 1230 and 1234. He conquered Soso and its dependent states with the aid of an alliance of Mandinka chiefs. Celebrating his success and bravery, people began to call him Sundiata, or "lion prince." Mali's power increased after Sundiata gained control of vital trans-Saharan trade routes and the gold mines of Bouré on the banks of the Tinkisso River (in present-day Guinea). Revenues from the gold trade supported the growth of Mali.

The Mandinka alliance coalesced into a federation. The early Mali Empire may have had a number of capitals. Ibn Khaldun stated during the fourteenth century that the empire's capital was a city named Mali, while the sixteenth-century Arab geographer LEO AFRICANUS named Niani (in present-day Guinea) as the capital. Some historians claim that Kangaba was the original capital of Mali, prior to Niani. Others maintain that the original capital of Mali was Djariba (or Dioliba), also in present-day Guinea. Scholars remain uncertain about whether the empire maintained several capitals simultaneously for defensive reasons or occupied a succession of capital cities.

A complex system of lineages and other kin groups, organized geographically, formed the basis of the empire's social and political organization. Slave labor produced the food surpluses that underlay the power of Mali's rulers and lineage chiefs. Slaves lacked kinship ties, and Mali's ruling elite prized slaves for their loyalty. Slaves played an important role in Mali as royal administrators and soldiers. Indeed, a court slave, Sakura, ruled the empire for a decade, from 1298 to 1308.

Apart from Sakura, a series of unspectacular monarchs carried the title *mansa*, or king, after Sundiata died in 1260. Mali's most famous and powerful king, known as MANSA MUSA I, ruled from 1307 to 1337. During his reign Mali reached its height of power and its greatest geographical extent. Mansa Musa's spectacular *hajj*, or pilgrimage to Mecca, spread the fame of Mali throughout the Islamic world and even in Europe, where Mali appeared on contemporary maps for the first time. On his way to Mecca in 1324, he spent so much gold in Cairo that the precious metal suffered a serious loss in value.

Following the death of Mansa Musa in 1337, Mali began to decline in power. The Arab geographer and historian IBN BATTUTAH recorded divisive succession struggles during his visit to Mali in the mid-fourteenth century. A series of ineffective and autocratic rulers depleted the state's treasury and weakened its military prowess. The empire's internal weakness inspired outlying provinces and neighboring peoples to challenge its power. At about the time of Mansa Musa's death, the empire's easternmost province, Songhai, broke away, and over the following two centuries conquered much of Mali's former territory. Meanwhile, the MOSSI attacked Tombouctou (Timbuktu). Despite this, Mali persisted into the sixteenth century as a powerful kingdom within its original Mandinka homeland in the upper Niger basin. Portuguese explorers of the fifteenth century continued to record the existence of a Mali whose power continued to extend to the Atlantic coast. Likewise, Leo Africanus visited the region in the early sixteenth century, depicting a Mali of reduced but still substantial size.

In 1542 the Songhai invaded the city of Mali, forcing its rulers to flee temporarily. While Mali kings returned to power, the BAMBARA kingdoms of Ségu and Kaarta gradually absorbed much of Mali's remaining territory during the seventeenth century. By the eighteenth century Mali had ceased to exist, but the Keita Dynasty continued to rule as provincial chiefs in their ancestral home, Kangaba.

Ari Nave

SEE ALSO

Ghana, Early Kingdom of; Gold Trade; Songhai Empire; Sundiata Keita; Tombouctou, Mali; Cairo, Egypt; Slavery in Africa; Malinké.

Africa

Malinké (also known as Mandinka), ethnic group of West Africa.

The Malinké are the second largest ethnic group in GUINEA, where they primarily inhabit upper Guinea in the east central part of the country. Some Malinké also reside in neighboring regions of MALI and CÔTE D'IVOIRE. They speak a MANDE language. The Malinké are closely related to the MANDINKA of THE GAMBIA and SENEGAL. Some scholars believe that they are both subgroups of a single Mandinka people, while others maintain that the Malinké constitute a separate ethnic group. Approximately 2.5 million people identify themselves as Malinké.

SEE ALSO

Languages, African: An Overview.

Malinké. Please see MANDINKA

North America

Malone, Karl (b. July 24, 1963, Summerfield, La.), African American professional BASKETBALL player, one of the sport's best players in the power-forward position.

With his combination of strength, speed, and effective shooting, Karl Malone ranked consistently among National Basketball Association (NBA) leaders in scoring and rebounding during the 1980s and 1990s.

Malone was educated at Louisiana Tech University, where he led the basketball team in scoring and rebounding in each of the three seasons he played there. At Louisiana Tech he was nicknamed the "Mailman" for his ability to deliver great performances under pressure. Malone was selected by the Utah Jazz in the first round of the 1985 NBA draft and quickly established himself as one of the league's best players. For six consecutive seasons, beginning in 1987-1988, he averaged at least 27 points and 10 rebounds per game.

Malone's baskets often resulted from passes from his teammate John Stockton, a guard who became the NBA career leader in assists in 1995. The two athletes, who began playing together in the 1985-1986 season, formed one of the most consistently productive guard-forward combinations in basketball history. Malone played in numerous NBA All-Star games and was a member of the United States national basketball teams, known as Dream Teams, that won Gold Medals at the 1992 Olympic Games in Barcelona, Spain, and the 1996 Olympic Games in Atlanta, Georgia. Malone was named the NBA's Most Valuable Player (MVP) for the 1996-1997 season after averaging 27.4 points and 9.9 rebounds per game. He and Stockton led the Jazz to the NBA Finals at the end of both the 1996-1997 and 1997-1998 seasons; both times, the Jazz lost to the Chicago Bulls.

Africa

Mambila (also known as Bang, Mambere, and Tongbo), ethnic group of West Africa.

The Mambila primarily inhabit Gongola State in NIGERIA and neighboring northwestern CAMEROON. They speak a Niger-Congo language. Approximately 200,000 people consider themselves Mambila.

SEE ALSO

Languages, African: An Overview.

Latin America and the Caribbean

Mambo, an Afro-Cuban dance music that emerged in the 1940s, prompting a major dance fad (*see* DANCE IN LATIN AMERICA AND THE CARIBBEAN) and providing one of the principal foundations for AFRO-LATIN JAZZ.

According to musicologist John Storm Roberts, mambo was "a truly American-Latin hybrid." While reflecting Cuban rhythmic innovations and a performance style shaped by the nightclubs of New York City's vibrant Latino community, it incorporated the ensemble format of swing-era JAZZ bands. Mambo's origins lie in Cuba's African-derived religious traditions, and the term itself most likely derives from the peoples of the present-day REPUBLIC OF THE CONGO or ANGOLA. It is not known who first adapted this Afro-Cuban religious music as vernacular dance music, although scholars credit four Cuban musicians with particularly important roles in developing and popularizing mambo: *tres* player and bandleader ARSENIO RODRÍGUEZ, bandleader DÁMASO PÉREZ PRADO, bassist Israel "Cachao" López, and his brother, the cellist Orestes López.

In Cuba mambo was played by such small ensembles as flutist Antonio Arcaño's band, Arcaño y sus Maravillas (Arcaño and the Marvels), which in the late 1930s and early 1940s featured the López brothers. But in 1948 Pérez Prado, an expatriate living in Mexico City, began recording instrumental mambos with an American-style big band. However, it was in New York City that the big band mambo sound truly crystalized. The bands of MACHITO, Marcelino Guerra, and José Curbelo performed infectious and driving mambo rhythms that quickly gained favor with dancers at the Palladium Dance Hall and other Latin music venues. Typically, the style juxtaposed the band's various sections – trumpets, trombones, and saxophones – and made use of extensive call-and-response passages that built to a climax of intensity.

During the 1950s Puerto Rican *timbales* player and bandleader Tito Puente, who became known as the "King of the Mambo," brought the driving big-band mambo style to its musical peak, in particular in his album *Dance Mania* (1958). Machito, Puente, and Tito Rodriguez (1923-1973) also incorporated jazz-style instrumental solos into their arrangements, creating a fusion known as Afro-Latin jazz. But the closing of the Palladium in 1966 marked the end of the mambo era and of the dominance of the American-style big band in Latin music.

During the 1960s Latin musicians emphasized more traditional sounds, which became known as *típico*, played by smaller ensembles such as the flute-and-strings *charanga* or the two-trumpet *conjunto*. But during the late 1960s and 1970s, with the rise of SALSA MUSIC, the term *mambo* (or mambo section) began to be used in reference to an instrumental interlude played over a repetitive one- or two-chord vamp in a salsa performance (*see* SON). But mambo is more than a historical footnote; it remains important in Latin American music. Above all, in helping to catalyze Afro-Latin jazz and salsa music, mambo played a vital role in popularizing Latin American music throughout the world.

James Clyde Sellman

SEE ALSO
Cuba; New York, New York; Afro-Latino Cultures in the United States; López, Israel ("Cachao"); Puente, Ernesto Antonio (Tito); Music, Afro-Caribbean Religious.

Africa

Mambwe, ethnic group of East Africa.

The Mambwe primarily inhabit ZAMBIA and TANZANIA. They speak a Bantu language and are related to the BEMBA people. Approximately 300,000 people consider themselves Mambwe.

SEE ALSO
Bantu: Dispersion and Settlement.

Africa

Mamluk State, a state founded by Turkish and Circassian slaves that ruled present-day Egypt, Palestine, and Syria from 1250 to 1517.

As early as the eighth century Turks from central Asia were recruited to serve in armies of the MIDDLE EAST and North Africa. The Islamic rulers of these lands took recruits from afar so that local ties would not compromise their loyalty. These soldiers, who underwent rigorous training, came to be called *Mamluks,* meaning "one who is owned" in Arabic. The Mamluks had great influence in the empires they served and often rose to the highest ranks, numbering among the closest advisers of the sultans. But strict rules prevented them from passing their position or their property to heirs, another attempt to assure undivided loyalty to their empires.

Nevertheless, these rules failed to produce the intended subservience among Mamluks serving as emirs, or commanders, for the Ayyubid sultan al-Malik al-Salih Ayyub. Ayyub ruled EGYPT and Syria from 1240 to 1249. When he died in 1249, the Mamluks of his regime seized power, murdered his heir, and created a vast state that eventually stretched from Arabia, Syria, and Egypt to parts of LIBYA and NUBIA.

Historians divide Mamluk history into two periods, each named for the ruling Mamluk regiment. During the first period, that of the Bahri Mamluks (1250-1382), Turkish sultans created a state far more centralized than its Ayyubid predecessor. The first and perhaps most renowned sultan, Baybars (r. 1260-1277), had previously led forces in two wars to defend the Holy Lands – he defeated the Europeans at the Crusade of Saint Louis (1249-1250) and drove the Mongols from Palestine (1259-1260). The Mamluks brought stability to the region and revived the caliphate (under their own control) in Cairo by offering refuge to the uncle of the Baghdad caliph, who had been ousted by the Mongols in 1258. The Bahri sultans made Cairo a center for trade between South Asia and the Mediterranean, and the thriving economy supported artistic and literary expression. Because the Mamluk state encompassed the holy cities of Mecca, Medina, and Jerusalem, the Mamluk capital, Cairo, became the intellectual, religious, and economic center of the Islamic world.

According to historians, the Mamluk state gradually declined during the second period, that of the Burji sultans (1382-1517). Its population decimated by the plague, the state faced economic decline and maintained its power only by imposing heavy taxes that further undermined the economy. Some scholars argue that ethnic favoritism toward Mamluk soldiers of Circassian descent also diminished the state's power. The Mamluks could not prevent Portugal from seizing control of the lucrative Red Sea trade around 1500, and their weakened army suffered defeat by the Ottoman sultan Selim I at the Battle of Marj Dabiq in Syria in 1517.

Under Ottoman rule the Mamluks continued to hold a powerful position in Egyptian society. With Ottoman decline in the late seventeenth century the Mamluks returned to power and ruled over Egypt as an autonomous region under Ottoman suzerainty; when Napoleon invaded in 1798, he faced Mamluk armies. The Mamluks finally lost power in 1811, as Muhammad Ali gained control of Egypt. A record of their former glory remains in the beautiful Mamluk architecture that still lines the streets of Cairo.

Leyla Keough

SEE ALSO
South Asia, Africans in; Crusades; Cairo, Egypt.

Africa

Mamprusi (also known as Mampruli and Mamprussi), ethnic group of West Africa.

The Mamprusi primarily inhabit northeastern GHANA and neighboring southern BURKINA FASO. They speak a Niger-Congo language. They are closely related to the Dagomba people. They ruled over a powerful kingdom roughly from the fourteenth to the eighteenth century. More than 200,000 people consider themselves Mamprusi.

SEE ALSO
Languages, African: An Overview.

Africa

Mande (also called Manding and Mandingue), a linguistic group of West Africa.

The Mande group is a subset of the larger Niger-Congo language family. Nearly 20 million people in West Africa speak Mande languages, and the linguistic group incorporates dozens of ethnic groups sharing traditions and common cultural features. Mande groups include the Soninké, BAMBARA, DYULA, MENDE, and Malinké. Mande speakers are found in all of the following countries: MALI, MAURITANIA, SENEGAL, THE GAMBIA, GUINEA-BISSAU, GUINEA, SIERRA LEONE, LIBERIA, CÔTE D'IVOIRE, and BURKINA FASO.

Mande speakers have inhabited the western SUDAN, at the headwaters of the Niger and Senegal rivers, since at least 5000 B.C.E. In this region they first domesticated many of the most important crops of sub-Saharan Africa, including MILLET, sorghum, African rice, peanuts, okra, COLA, and perhaps cotton. Many Mande groups remain skilled agriculturists. Later, Mande speakers developed gold mines, including those in the Bambouk region of the upper Senegal. These mines provided a source of wealth for empires founded by Mande speakers, including ancient Ghana, or Wagadu (fifth through eleventh century C.E.), and ancient Mali (thirteenth through sixteenth century C.E.). Both ancient Ghana and ancient Mali prospered from trade with the Tuaregs and Moors, whose trans-Saharan trade caravans brought salt, textiles, and cloth in exchange for gold and slaves exported by the Mande empires.

These trade connections also exposed Mande speakers to Islam. Most of the larger Mande groups in the Niger and Senegal basins converted to Islam between the twelfth and nineteenth century. The rise of hierarchical and Islamized states in the Niger and Senegal basin may have encouraged the emigration of less centralized Mande-speaking groups who practiced traditional religions. By the seventeenth century Mande groups such as the Mende and the DAN had spread toward the Guinea Coast between present-day Senegal and Côte d'Ivoire.

Mande speakers fall into two broad cultural and linguistic groupings: the Mande-tan and the Mande-fu. Most Mande-tan groups, known as the "nuclear Mande," still live in the original Mande territory near the upper Niger River in present-day Mali. These groups, such as the Bambara, Soninké, and Malinké share a hierarchical social structure, including nobility, various castes, and ranks. In these predominantly Muslim societies, farmers usually occupy elevated positions, while *nyamakalya* – specialists such as blacksmiths, potters, leatherworkers, and bards – occupy lower social strata.

Many of the Mande-fu groups, such as the Mende and Dan, have decentralized and relatively egalitarian societies, and most are not Muslim. Some scholars think that these people spread the practice of agriculture to the forest regions of West Africa. The Mande-fu are also known as "peripheral Mande," that is, Mande speakers who live outside the original Mande territory. Although the peripheral Mande groups exerted tremendous influence on the regions to which they moved, they generally did not form major empires; one of the few exceptions was the short-lived MANDINKA Empire of SAMORY TOURÉ in the late nineteenth century.

The DYULA are also considered peripheral Mande, though they are more recent migrants from the Mande homeland, and their language and culture belong to the Mande-tan group. Beginning under the kingdoms of Ghana and Mali, Mande-tan speakers established new and lucrative long-distance trade routes to the forest regions of the south. These Dyula, whose name means "trader" in their Mande language, introduced Islam to the forest region. Their trade is believed to have fostered the development of centralized kingdoms, such as Bono, among the AKAN. The Dyula are unique among the Mande because of their primary economic focus on trade.

Elizabeth Heath

SEE ALSO

Ghana, Early Kingdom of; Gold Trade; Gold Trade; Languages, African: An Overview; Niger River; Salt Trade; Soninké; Tuareg; Senegal River; Islam and Tradition: An Interpretation; Trans-Saharan and Red Sea Slave Trade; Mali Empire; Malinké.

Africa

Mandela, Nelson Rolihlahla

(b. July 18, 1918, Mvezo, South Africa), former president of South Africa, winner of the Nobel Peace Prize, and former head of the African National Congress.

The first black president of SOUTH AFRICA, Nelson Mandela became a worldwide symbol of resistance to the injustice of his country's APARTHEID system. Imprisoned for more than 27 years, and before that banned from all public activity and hounded by police for nearly a decade, Mandela led a struggle for freedom that mirrored that of his black countrymen. After his 1990 release from the Robben Island prison, his work to end apartheid won him the 1993 Nobel Peace Prize (which he shared with South African president F. W. De Klerk) and then the presidency itself a year later.

Mandela's father, Chief Henry Mandela, was a member of the Thembu people's royal lineage; his mother was one of the chief's four wives. Mandela grew up in Qunu, a small village in the Eastern Cape. At age seven he became the first member of his family to attend school. When his father died two years later, Nelson – the Christian name he had acquired at school – was sent to live with Chief Jongintaba Dalindyebo, the regent, or supreme leader, of the Thembu people. From the regent, Mandela said, he learned that "a leader... is like a shepherd. He stays behind the flock, letting the most nimble go on ahead, whereupon the others follow, not realizing that all along they are being directed from behind."

Mandela finished his secondary education at Healdtown, a missionary school where an emphasis on English traditions molded students into "Black Englishmen." Only as a student at Fort Hare University did Mandela begin to question the injustices he and all black South Africans faced. Fort Hare was considered an oasis of black scholarship; it was also a training ground for future leaders (lawyer and antiapartheid activist OLIVER TAMBO was Mandela's classmate, and FREEDOM CHARTER originator Z. K. Matthews taught there). But a dispute with the adminstration over students' rights caused Mandela to leave Fort Hare in his second year; at the same time he broke with the regent rather than accept an arranged marriage.

Jobless when he arrived in Johannesburg in 1941, Mandela found work assisting a lawyer – a job arranged by activist WALTER SISULU – while finishing his bachelor's degree by correspondence from the University of South Africa. His political education continued as well, as he met members of the Communist Party of South Africa and, more important, the AFRICAN NATIONAL CONGRESS (ANC). Of his decision to join the ANC in 1943, Mandela later wrote that he was motivated by "no epiphany, no singular revelation, no moment of truth, but a steady accumulation of a thousand slights." Soon afterward

A South African justice swears in Nelson Mandela as president of South Africa in 1994. *CORBIS/Paul Velasco; ABPL*

Former South African president Nelson Mandela greets supporters of the African National Congress after a meeting with local political leaders outside Durban in May 1995. *CORBIS/AFP*

Mandela and a group of fellow ANC members, including Walter Sisulu and Oliver Tambo (with whom Mandela formed South Africa's first black-run law firm), founded the ANC Youth League.

Mandela also worked as the volunteer-in-chief of ANC's Campaign for the Defiance of Unjust Laws, in which about 9000 volunteers defied selected laws and consequently were imprisoned. As a result, the NATIONAL PARTY government banned him from all public gatherings in 1952 and again from 1953 to 1955. When, in 1960, the government banned the ANC outright in the wake of the police massacre of demonstrators in Sharpeville township, Mandela and several thousand apartheid opponents were detained. A consistent voice for nonviolence, Mandela at this point decided that "it was wrong and immoral to subject [his] people to armed attacks by the state without offering them some kind of alternative." Consequently, in 1961 he went underground and he helped create the ANC's paramilitary wing Umkhonto we Sizwe (Spear of the Nation), which carried out acts of sabotage against the government. Captured in August 1962, Mandela was charged with traveling outside the country without a passport and inciting workers to strike. At his trial he acted as his own lawyer, arguing not that he was innocent but rather that the South African government had used the law "to impose a state of outlawry" upon him. Several months into his five-year sentence, Mandela was charged with treason and in 1964 was sentenced to life in prison without the possibility of parole.

Until 1982 Mandela was imprisoned on ROBBEN ISLAND, South Africa's most notorious prison, located just offshore from Cape Town. Initially he lived in a cell measuring seven by seven feet, could write and receive only one letter every six months, and was forced to break rocks in the prison yard for hours daily. By the early 1980s South Africa's apartheid government, faced with international sanctions, began to make gestures toward Mandela, its most famous political prisoner, including moving him to Pollsmoor Prison – a much less brutal environment than Robben Island – in 1982. The negotiations unfolded gradually over the next decade. In 1985 President P. W. Botha publicly stated that he would release Mandela provided he "rejected violence as a political instrument," a deal designed to alienate Mandela from other ANC leaders. Mandela rejected the offer. In 1988 he was transferred to a private facility at Victor Verster Prison, where talks continued in secret. F. W. De Klerk succeeded P. W. Botha as president in 1989, and within a few months he lifted the 30-year-long ban on the ANC. On February 2, 1990, he announced Mandela's release from prison.

Freedom brought new challenges. During his imprisonment Mandela's wife, WINNIE MADIKIZELA-MANDELA (whom he had married in 1958 following the end of his first marriage), had been accused of crimes that included ordering the torture and murder of her enemies. In 1991 Mrs. Mandela was convicted of kidnapping and accessory to assault in the death of a Soweto teenager. The couple, who have two daughters (Mandela has three older children from his first marriage), separated in 1992.

Mandela succeeded Oliver Tambo as president of the ANC in 1992. In September 1992 he and De Klerk agreed on a framework within which to negotiate a transition to multiracial democratic rule. The Record of Understanding they signed in December 1993 provided for a new constitution and free elections to be held April 27, 1994. With black South Africans voting for the first time in their lives, the ANC won handily, and Mandela was inaugurated as president on May 10, 1994. Since assuming office he has earned a reputation as an international peacemaker, helping to mediate conflicts both in Africa and abroad. In addition, Mandela has worked to strengthen South Africa's economy by pursuing international trade agreements and foreign investment. In 1997 Mandela, who has always indicated that he would not run for reelection in 1999, stepped down as ANC leader and was succeeded by THABO MBEKI. On his 80th birthday on July 18, 1998, Mandela married GRAÇA MACHEL, the widow of Mozambican president Samora Machel. In September 1998 Mandela received the Congressional Gold Medal in a ceremony at the United States capitol. He was the first African to receive this award.

Kate Tuttle

SEE ALSO

Cape Town, South Africa; Johannesburg, South Africa; Machel, Samora Moises; Mozambique; Sharpeville, South Africa; Botha, Pieter Willem; De Klerk, Frederik Willem.

Africa

Mandija (also known as the Mandja and the Mandjia), ethnic group of the Central African Republic.

The Mandija primarily inhabit the central part of the CENTRAL AFRICAN REPUBLIC. They speak a Niger-Congo language and are closely related to the GBAYA people. Approximately 200,000 people consider themselves Mandija.

SEE ALSO

Languages, African: An Overview.

Africa

Mandinka (also known as Mandingo), ethnic group with substantial populations in SENEGAL, THE GAMBIA, GUINEA-BISSAU, and GUINEA and smaller clusters in MALI, SIERRA LEONE, LIBERIA, and CÔTE D'IVOIRE.

The Mandinka are the largest ethnic group in the Gambia; the dominant ethnic group in the Casamance region of southern Senegal; a major ethnic group in eastern Guinea-Bissau; and the dominant group in Guinea, where they are the largest group in the north-eastern part of that country. They are closely related to other MANDE-speaking peoples who trace their ancestry to the MALI EMPIRE, which first emerged under the leadership of SUNDIATA KEITA in the thirteenth century. According to oral traditions, Sundiata sent one of his primary generals, Tiramakhan Traoré, to expand Mali's domains to the west. As connections with Mali became more tenuous, distinctive Mandinka cultures developed in the Senegambia area (including Senegal, the Gambia, and Guinea-Bissau) and in the region of upper Guinea (the northeastern third of Guinea).

Some scholars regard the populations in Senegal, the Gambia, and Guinea-Bissau as an ethnic group distinct from the populations in eastern Guinea and northwestern Côte d'Ivoire. Nevertheless, the term "Mandinka" is widely used to refer to both these groups of people, and there is little doubt that they speak closely related languages and have similar customs and a shared ancestry in the Mali Empire.

Like other Mande groups, the Mandinka emphasize patrilineal descent and live in extended family compounds within larger villages. As with most of the peoples of the western SUDAN (a region extending from CHAD to Senegal between the northern desert and the southern forests), their traditional social organization included a system of hereditary castes. This included the freeborn, who were primarily farmers; slaves, who worked in a variety of capacities; and a cluster of special occupational groups, including metalworkers, griots (praise singers), potters, and leather workers, among others. Traditionally, marriage outside one's caste was forbidden. Each village quarter was dominated by a single patrilineage (an extended-family group recognizing descent along the father's line) and occupational group, which governed its own affairs and, until the massive conversion of the Mandinka to Islam in the late nineteenth century, its own set of spirit shrines. The senior man from the most senior lineage was the chief of a particular village and served as an intermediary with the regional Mandinka officials. Age grades of men who were circumcised and initiated together provided an important source of village unity. Both men and women are circumcised (*see* FEMALE CIRCUMCISION IN AFRICA) in Mandinka society, and the Mandinka have introduced these practices to a number of neighboring peoples. Traditionally, gender roles were quite distinct. Women performed the bulk of the agricultural labor, while men dominated long-distance trade, hunting, and warfare.

When Tiramakhan Traoré led the ancestors of the Mandinka westward, they conquered a large area along both shores of the Gambia River and southeastward toward the highlands of the FOUTA DJALLON. As the kingdom of Mali weakened in the fifteenth century, the western Mandinka states became more autonomous, initially as part of the kingdom of Kaabu. Small groups of Mandinka, known as Guellwar, married into some of the leading Wolof and Serer ruling families and became an important influence in the political development of WOLOF and SERER coastal states. With the expansion of the Atlantic trading system from the sixteenth century, Mandinka kingdoms along the Gambia River, including Niumi, Barra, and Kombo, became increasingly powerful. With easy access to European musketry, gunpowder and iron in exchange for slaves, gold, and ivory, these riverine Mandinka states became independent and highly militarized. The Mandinka became the primary slave raiders in the region.

With the suppression of the slave trade in the early nineteenth century, the Mandinka states of Senegambia shifted their primary economic activity to peanut production. Still, they had large military and important martial traditions. Competition over land and over the procurement of domestic slaves for peanut production led to frequent warfare. Eventually, by mid-century two factions emerged in the Mandinka states, separated into a reformist Muslim faction and a faction of adherents of Mandinka religious traditions, known as the SONINKÉ. In the 1860s Ma Ba Diakhou led the first of several jihads, or holy wars, aimed at converting the remaining Mandinka and their neighbors to Islam. Later jihads were directed by Mandinka clerics against the non-Muslim JOLA. From the 1870s through the 1890s the Mandinka leader SAMORY TOURÉ built an empire based in northern Côte d'Ivoire and extending from present-day eastern Guinea to western GHANA. The French did not finally conquer Touré's Mandinka state until 1898.

The British, given their strong commercial interests along the Gambia River, became increasingly involved in the maintenance of the peace in that region. Armed interventions followed and a protectorate was established over the Mandinka areas, which the British governed through appointed "customary" chiefs. The French and Portuguese occupied Mandinka territories to the south of the Gambia and encouraged peanut cultivation. In all three areas Islam became an increasingly important part of a new form of Mandinka cultural identity. Indeed, the neighboring Jola, who were taught about Islam mostly by Mandinka teachers, refer to Islam as "the path of the Mandinka." In southern Senegal Mandinka traders became important to local commerce; they were often appointed as local administrators, given continued resistance by other southern Senegalese peoples to the establishment of French authority. In Senegal and the Gambia, however, the Mandinka were slow to avail themselves of a Western education, given its association with Christianity.

Since independence the Mandinka have played a dominant role in the political life of Guinea and the Gambia. The nationalist leader SÉKOU TOURÉ, a Mandinka, ruled Guinea from its independence in 1958 to 1984. A Mandinka, Sir Dawda Jawara, served as the Gambia's head of state from shortly before independence until 1995, when a Jola officer, YAHYA JAMMEH, seized control of the government. In neighboring Senegal, Mandinka political influence was more muted, though several Mandinka have risen to prominence in the Senegalese military. In Guinea-Bissau the Mandinka were the last major ethnic group to abandon the Portuguese and align themselves with the national liberation movement. Today the Mandinka number more than 4 million.

SEE ALSO
Gold Trade; Ivory Trade; Jawara, Sir Dawda Kairaba; Nationalism in Africa; Transatlantic Slave Trade; Kaabu, Early Kingdom of.

Africa

Manga, ethnic group of West Africa.

The Manga primarily inhabit southeastern NIGER and neighboring sections of NIGERIA and CHAD. They speak KANURI, a Nilo-Saharan language, and are sometimes considered a subgroup of the Kanuri. The Manga number approximately 600,000 people.

SEE ALSO
Languages, African: An Overview.

Africa

Mangbetu (also known as Manbetu), ethnic group of Central Africa.

The Mangbetu primarily inhabit the northwestern DEMOCRATIC REPUBLIC OF THE CONGO. They speak a Nilo-Saharan language. The Mangbetu consist of several subgroups, whose cultural and linguistic diversity reflects the Mangbetu history of absorbing neighboring peoples. Approximately 500,000 people consider themselves Mangbetu.

SEE ALSO
Languages, African: An Overview.

Latin America and the Caribbean

Mangueira, Estação Primeira da, one of the oldest and most traditional SAMBA SCHOOLS in Rio de Janeiro, BRAZIL.

The first samba school to be created was Deixa Falar, which was established in Rio de Janeiro's Estácio de Sá neighborhood in 1926. But Mangueira is one of the oldest samba schools that still remains active. Samba composer CARTOLA and several friends established Mangueira on April 28, 1928, bringing together several earlier and less formal groups known as *blocos*. Today the Mangueira samba school remains the pride of the Rio de Janeiro FAVELAS (or shantytown) where it is headquartered. Mangueira has won several of the highly coveted annual Carnival competitions, most recently in 1997 when it shared first prize with the Beija-Flor school.

Ben Penglase

SEE ALSO
Afoxés/Blocos Afros; Rio de Janeiro, Brazil; Carnivals in Latin America and the Caribbean.

Africa

Manjaco (also known as Mandyako and Manjago), ethnic group of West Africa.

The Manjaco primarily inhabit GUINEA-BISSAU, THE GAMBIA, and southern SENEGAL. They speak a Niger-Congo language and are related to the neighboring JOLA people. Approximately 200,000 people consider themselves Manjaco.

SEE ALSO
Languages, African: An Overview.

Latin America and the Caribbean

Manley, Edna (b. 1900?; d. 1987), Jamaican sculptor, publisher, editor, and writer of British descent and the mother of Jamaica's former prime minister Michael Manley. Her artwork fuses Afro-Caribbean and European elements (*see* Art in Latin America and the Caribbean).

Latin America and the Caribbean

Manley, Michael

(b. December 10, 1924, St. Andrew, Jamaica; d. March 6, 1997, Kingston, Jamaica), prime minister of Jamaica (1972-1980, 1989-1992).

The son of a prominent Jamaican politician and an English sculptor, Michael Manley was born into a family of privilege. His father, Norman Washington Manley, was founder of the democratic People's National Party (PNP), prime minister of Jamaica from 1959 to 1962, and a leader in the Jamaican independence movement. The fair-skinned Michael Manley was a member of Jamaica's colored, or mixed-race, community, and he grew up around many of the most influential elites in Jamaica. He was educated at the London School of Economics and served as a freelance journalist for the British Broadcasting Corporation (BBC) upon graduation in 1949.

His privileged background notwithstanding, Manley dedicated his career to improving life for all Jamaicans. Returning from London in 1952, he accepted a position as organizer of Jamaica's National Workers Union. In 1962 he was appointed to a senator's seat and five years later was elected to Parliament. Manley's political career was influenced by his father's commitment to the PNP and its progressive political policies. In 1969 Manley succeeded his father as president of the PNP and three years later was elected prime minister of Jamaica.

During the 1972 election for prime minister, Manley captured the hearts of many voters when he publicly acknowledged Jamaica's African roots. He often wore traditional African clothing and carried a staff reportedly given to him by Haile Selassie I, then emperor of Ethiopia. Called the Rod of Joshua, the staff symbolized African pride and moral authority.

As prime minister, Manley steered Jamaica toward socialism. He nationalized the bauxite industry, spoke out against economic dependency on foreign investment, and angered the United States government by embracing Cuba's communist president Fidel Castro. Though Manley's socialist policies improved life for many poor Jamaicans, they also weakened Jamaica's economy. By 1980 the nation stood near bankruptcy. The United States government, angered by his ties to Castro, reportedly worked secretly to remove Manley from power. He was defeated by conservative politician Edward Seaga in the violence-stricken elections of 1980.

After a nine-year hiatus, Manley was reelected prime minister in 1989. His socialist leanings tempered, Manley embraced the principles of free-market capitalism, liberalized the economy, and welcomed foreign investment. His term was cut short in 1992 when he was diagnosed with prostate cancer. He died in 1997 at his home in Kingston, leaving a wife and five children.

Alonford James Robinson, Jr.

See Also

Cuba; Kingston, Jamaica.

Latin America and the Caribbean

Manley, Norman Washington

(b. July 4, 1893, Kingston, Jamaica; d. September 2, 1969, Kingston, Jamaica), prime minister of Jamaica (1959-1962), one of the founders of the People's National Party and an early champion of independence for Jamaica.

Norman Manley was born to colored parents – a term used to describe persons of mixed racial heritage – during the time of British colonialism in Jamaica. His father, Thomas Albert Samuel Manley, was a leading produce trader who did business with companies in the United States. His mother, Margaret Shearer, was the fair-skinned daughter of Irish and colored parents. Margaret and Thomas had four children, including Norman, and they settled in an upper-middle class, predominantly white Jamaican community known for its conservatism.

Manley was just seven years old when his father died, in 1900. His mother worked hard to maintain the family's middle-class status, sending him to elementary school and then on to Jamaica's most prestigious secondary school, Jamaica College. Manley excelled at Jamaica College both as an athlete and a debater. In 1914 he was awarded a Rhodes Scholarship, which allowed him to study at Oxford University in England. The scholarship also provided him with the opportunity to join his siblings, who were already living in London. While in London he met his aunt, Ellie Shearer Swithenbank, and her daughter and his future wife, Edna Swithenbank.

With World War I raging, Manley and his brother Roy enlisted in the British army. The brothers fought in the war and in 1916 Roy was killed in battle. That same year Manley returned to England physically and emotionally scarred. He suffered another setback three years later with a nervous breakdown. But he was able to recover and reenroll at Oxford, this time studying to be a lawyer.

In 1921, just months after he received his law degree, Manley married Edna Swithenbank. The couple moved to Jamaica in 1922. Although Edna's unhappiness with the rural island inspired her to return to England in 1923, she and Manley were reunited a year later when she agreed to give the struggling colony a second chance. In Jamaica Manley became an influential lawyer. He represented some of the most powerful Jamaican businesses and in 1932 earned the highly distinguished title of King's Counsel.

The 1930s were marked by a growing labor movement in Jamaica. Confrontations between colonial officials and mostly black Jamaican laborers engulfed the nation in 1938. Manley and others responded to the labor movement by forming the socialist People's National Party (PNP). Under Manley's leadership the PNP stood at the forefront of labor politics. The PNP pushed for universal adult suffrage and was among the first groups to demand independence from the British Crown.

For years Manley's PNP battled the Jamaican Labour Party, which was under the leadership of William Alexander Bustamante, Manley's cousin. Throughout the 1940s and 1950s Manley remained an influential politician and leader of the PNP. He was elected prime minister in 1959 and served until 1962. He remained a public figure until February 1969, when he resigned as president of the PNP and passed the reins to his son, Michael Manley. Seven months later, at age 76, he died of natural causes. He was named a National Hero in Jamaica.

Alonford James Robinson, Jr.

See Also

Bustamante, Sir Alexander.

North America

Manumission Societies, eighteenth-century antislavery organizations that advocated the gradual emancipation of slaves through legislation.

Manumission societies emerged after the American Revolution as advocates for an end to the slave trade and the gradual abolition of slavery. Manumission, which entailed the formal release of a slave, was the most common path to freedom, and it could occur either privately, by an individual slave owner, or officially, by state law.

The Pennsylvania Abolition Society, formed in 1775 by the Quakers, is considered the first manumission society. On the eve of the Civil War, there were an estimated 154 manumission societies throughout the United States; 130 of those were located in the South. The membership and policies of these societies varied dramatically. Slave owners who expressed a desire to improve conditions for slaves were given membership in New York and Virginia but were excluded in Pennsylvania and Rhode Island. The New York and Pennsylvania Manumission Societies sponsored schools for free blacks, including the African Free School in New York City.

Nine manumission societies gathered in 1791 to submit a petition to the United States Congress urging it to limit the slave trade. Three years later the American Convention for Promoting the Abolition of Slavery and Improving the Condition of the African Race met in Philadelphia to report on local efforts to end slavery. The convention met annually until 1806 and sporadically until 1832. It was formally dissolved in 1838.

Manumission societies were an important part of the antislavery movement in both America and Great Britain. Although they pressed for gradual emancipation, they were instrumental in achieving manumission legislation in several states immediately following the American Revolution. Several Northern states, like New York, New Jersey, and Pennsylvania, adopted policies that freed the children of current slaves once they reached a particular age (generally 21 or 25). In the South no states changed their laws to require mandatory manumission, but several states changed their laws to make manumission easier, including Delaware, Maryland, and Virginia.

Alonford James Robinson, Jr.

See Also

Slavery in the United States; Transatlantic Slave Trade; Abolitionism in the United States; American Anti-Slavery Society; Civil War, American; Free Blacks in the United States, 1619 to 1863; New York, New York; Philadelphia, Pennsylvania.

Africa

Manyika, ethnic group of southern Africa.

The Manyika primarily inhabit Mozambique and Zimbabwe. They speak a Bantu language and are closely related to the Shona people. Approximately 200,000 people consider themselves Manyika.

See Also

Bantu: Dispersion and Settlement.

Latin America and the Caribbean

Manzano, Juan Francisco

(b. 1797?, Cuba; d. July 19, 1853, Havana, Cuba), Cuban poet, autobiographer, playwright, and novelist who wrote the first and only known autobiographical account of black slavery in Latin America, *Autobiografía de un esclavo* (English, 1840; Spanish, 1937).

Juan Francisco Manzano did not give his date of birth in his autobiography, but sources indicate that he was born a slave in a country province in Cuba around 1797. He was initially recognized for his poetry, and his collection of poems, *Poesías líricas (Cantos a Lesbia)* (1821), was the first book by a black poet to be published in Cuba. Manzano wrote this book only three years after he learned to read and write. He continued to write poetry after its publication, but copies of some of his works are no longer extant, including his second collection, *Flores pasajeras* (1830). However, the poems published in contemporary literary journals and newspapers of his day have been collected and republished.

Prior to the abolition of slavery in Cuba in 1886, Manzano's autobiography was the only published account written by a slave. Manzano wrote the autobiography at the suggestion of Domingo Del Monte (1804-1853), a wealthy patron of Cuban letters and an activist in the reformist movement for better treatment of slaves. Although Del Monte's privileged political and class position kept him from being an abolitionist, he agitated for more humane treatment of the slaves because he felt that the condition of slavery had base and immoral effects on slave and master alike. Del Monte also aided in the publication of the most important antislavery novel of Latin America, Anselmo Suárez y Romero's *Francisco* (1880). (Suárez y Romero was the editor of the manuscript of Manzano's autobiography taken to London for publication.) In 1830 Del Monte became a protector of Manzano and invited him to literary gatherings where Manzano was able to recite his poems, such as his famous 1836 sonnet "Mis treinta años," a reflection on the suffering he had endured in the first 30 years of his life under slavery. Del Monte was also instrumental in publishing Manzano's work in his literary magazines, such as *La Moda* and *El Pasatiempo*, and in helping Manzano purchase his freedom. Del Monte took up a collection among wealthy Creoles on the island, raising enough money for Manzano to be granted his freedom in 1836.

Del Monte then convinced Manzano to take the risk of publishing an autobiography. Many critics feel that Manzano followed Del Monte's suggestions as to the content of the autobiography, leaving out direct indictments of the institution of slavery and focusing instead on the inhumane mistreatment he suffered under the masters he served, indicting in particular his second mistress.

As a free black, Manzano incurred some risk of censorship and punishment in writing about prominent citizens, but he completed the autobiography in 1839. Although the book was not published in Spanish until 1937, a translation of it was published in England in 1840 by Richard Madden, an English writer and friend of Del Monte. The autobiography was originally conceived as a two-part work, only the first part of which survives. Manzano's letters to Del Monte reveal that he had intended to save descriptions of some of the more interesting events of his life for the second part, or for a novel about Cuban society. The second volume of the autobiography disappeared while in the hands of Ramón de Palma, a person with perhaps some connection to Manzano's former masters.

Manzano took his name from the husband (Don Juan Manzano) of his first mistress, Doña Beatriz de Justiz, the marchioness of Santa Ana, who apparently treated him very well. His second mistress, the marchioness of Prado Ameno, inflicted cruel punishments on him with little pity.

After being widowed by his first wife, Marcelina Campos, in 1835 Manzano married María del Rosario Díaz, whom he called Delia, a light-skinned young mulatto whose father had been white. Once he was freed in 1836, Manzano worked in Havana at various small trades, as a cook, tailor, and confectioner. His literary production declined in this period, and after the 1840 publication of the autobiography, he wrote one play, *Zafira*, in 1842. In 1844 he and Del Monte were both falsely accused by Plácido (the pseudonym of Gabriel de la Concepción Valdés, another free black Cuban writer) of being involved in La Escalera, a movement among free blacks and mulattos to overthrow the Spanish colonial government. Manzano was jailed and released in 1845; he died in Havana eight years later. In 1937 a Spanish edition of the autobiography was published, based on a manuscript found in the National Archives in Havana.

Bill Johnson-González

See Also

Slavery in Latin America and the Caribbean; Conspiración de la Escalera; Abolition and Emancipation in Latin America and the Caribbean; Literature, Black, in Spanish America.

Africa

Mapanje, Jack (b. 1944, Kadango, Malawi), Malawian poet and linguist imprisoned nearly four years for his politically charged poetry.

Jack Mapanje, one of Africa's most respected poets and a scholar of linguistics, became an internationally recognized victim of censorship when the regime of Malawi's president, Dr. Hastings Banda, imprisoned him without charges or trial in 1987. The human rights monitoring group Amnesty International declared him a political prisoner, and other groups, including those devoted to human rights and artistic freedom, launched a letter-writing campaign that resulted in his 1991 release.

Mapanje attended local Catholic schools as a child, then received a bachelor's degree from the University of Malawi and a Ph.D. in linguistics from University College, London. While in London he wrote his first collection of poetry, *Of Chameleons and Gods* (1981), which contained much veiled criticism of the repressive Banda government but was not one of the many books that the government banned.

At about the time *Of Chameleons and Gods* was being published, Mapanje returned to Malawi and became chair of the Department of Languages and Literature at Chancellor College, Malawi's national university. Soon after, he formed the Linguistic Association of the SOUTHERN AFRICAN DEVELOPMENT COMMUNITY (which at the time included ANGOLA, BOTSWANA, LESOTHO, Malawi, MOZAMBIQUE, SWAZILAND, TANZANIA, ZAMBIA, and ZIMBABWE). Mapanje also edited *Oral Poetry from Africa: An Anthology* and *Summer Fires: An Anthology of Modern African Poetry*, both published in 1983.

Of Chameleons and Gods was reprinted in 1987. Although there is disagreement as to whether the book was officially banned, it was removed from circulation in Malawi, and the Banda administration had Mapanje arrested and sentenced him to prison.

Mapanje was held incommunicado in Malawi's Mikuyu prison. Almost immediately, organizations such as Africa Rights Monitor, Amnesty International, PEN International (a writers' group), and the Linguistics Association of Great Britain (several of whose members had known Mapanje as a graduate student) protested his imprisonment. A petition and thousands of letters were sent to President Banda, whose government had already been implicated in the deaths of political prisoners. While it was never acknowledged that Mapanje's 1991 release was influenced by the campaign on his behalf, many believe that the publicity saved the poet's life.

The Chattering Wagtails of Mikuyu Prison, published in 1993 after Mapanje moved to England with his family, contains several poems describing his detention. In "Scrubbing the Furious Walls of Mikuyu," Mapanje confronts the ghosts of past political prisoners. Among the blood and dead insects he washes from the cell's walls, Mapanje encounters scrawled messages, the "barbarous squiggles" that led him to ask, "How long did this anger languish without / charge without trial without visit here and / what justice committed?" Another poem, "To the Unknown Dutch Post-card Sender," was written in prison; in it Mapanje thanks the stranger whose card slipped past the prison censors to send "waves of hope and reason / To hang on to the fetid walls of these / Cold cells.... "

After Mapanje moved to England, the British government sponsored him as a writer-in-residence, and he lectured widely on linguistics and Malawi's political situation. Visiting Malawi after the downfall of the Banda regime in 1995, Mapanje wrote that only legal, financial, and spiritual atonement would begin to repair a country wounded by 33 years of "fear, lies and suspicion."

Kate Tuttle

SEE ALSO
Banda, Ngwazi Hastings Kamuzu; Malawi; Human Rights in Africa.

Africa

Mapfumo, Thomas (b. July 2, 1945, Marondera, Zimbabwe), prominent chimurenga musician from ZIMBABWE.

Thomas Mapfumo created *chimurenga* music, a new style that drew on SHONA traditions of music as a form of resistance to confront colonial oppression in Rhodesia (present-day Zimbabwe), then under white-minority rule. Raised in the rural household of his grandparents, themselves traditional musicians, Mapfumo learned traditional Shona music at an early age. The young Mapfumo played the mbira (thumb piano) and drums during his grandmother's performances at beer parties.

To obtain a better education, Mapfumo moved to Salisbury (present-day Harare). His musical repertoire expanded as he discovered other African, European, and American musical styles, including the music of Nat "King" Cole, OTIS REDDING, and Elvis Presley. In Salisbury he sang in a number of local bands, covering popular tunes by Sam Cooke and the Beatles, whose lyrics he sang in Shona. In 1973 Mapfumo formed the Hallelujah Chicken Run Band (most of the band members worked in a chicken run) and began to record African rock singles. The band released a Shona chimurenga, or war, song in 1974, and it was an immediate hit.

Returning to Salisbury in 1976, Mapfumo formed the Black Spirits and recorded chimurenga music that supported the Zimbabwean liberation struggle. His lyrics criticized the colonial regime and encouraged people to rebel. When the Black Spirits disbanded, Mapfumo joined the Acid Band. When the colonial administration realized in 1977 that Mapfumo's chimurenga music was a call for rebellion, they detained him and banned the Acid Band. Despite their efforts, Mapfumo formed the band Blacks Unlimited in 1978 and continued to perform and record. Since Zimbabwean independence in 1980, Mapfumo has continued to play traditional Shona music, using his music to lobby for political reform. He has also helped set up cooperative music labels to support local musicians.

Ari Nave

SEE ALSO
Harare, Zimbabwe; Cole, Nat ("King"); Cooke, Samuel (Sam); Chimurenga Music.

Africa

Maputo, Mozambique, capital of MOZAMBIQUE and major port.

Maputo, formerly Lourenço Marques, is Mozambique's political and economic center. In 1544 Portuguese sailors landed in the far south of what would become Mozambique. The settlement served as little more than a trading post until the Portuguese erected a fort in 1787. Slowly it grew into a town and in 1907 became the official capital of the colony of Portuguese East Africa. With its deep harbor and access to northern SOUTH AFRICA, Lourenço Marques prospered as a hub of commercial and administrative activity. Furniture, processed food, and textile and cement factories were built, often with forced labor. In the early 1900s up to one-third of the local Africans were employed as domestic workers, while thousands more were put to work filling in the coastal marshes to create more land for industry and what would become the business and government district. White-washed Portuguese colonial buildings, concrete high-rises, and a Catholic cathedral reputedly built by former prostitutes stood astride wide boulevards.

During the nationalist era Lourenço Marques was a center of clandestine political work and intellectual protest, but there were few urban demonstrations or terrorist attacks. In 1975 the victorious FRONT FOR THE LIBERATION OF MOZAMBIQUE (FRELIMO) changed the name Lourenço Marques to Maputo, and the city became the capital of independent Mozambique. In the 1980s war with the MOZAMBICAN NATIONAL RESISTANCE (RENAMO), although it never reached Maputo, wreaked havoc on the city's economy and population. Immigrants from the war-ravaged countryside poured into the capital, quickly overtaxing its limited resources. The streets, buildings, sewers, and power systems of the "cement city," as Maputo's city center became known, deteriorated with the rapidly growing population, which now numbers between 1 and 1.2 million. Maputo's harbor, once Africa's second busiest port, is today clogged with silt and wrecked ships. As in the colonial era, Maputo's inhabitants have resorted to a variety of strategies, both legal and increasingly criminal, to survive in the cement city.

Eric Young

Africa

Marabout, populist Islamic spiritual and political teachers in North and West Africa.

The term *marabout* has had a number of different meanings. Originally, the Arabic *murabit* denoted a resident of the *ribat*, the twelfth-century fortified monasteries of North Africa. As Islam spread throughout the region now comprising LIBYA, TUNISIA, ALGERIA, MOROCCO, and the Sahara, the meaning of *marabout* evolved to include first the disciples of any Islamic teachers, then those who belonged to Sufi fraternities, and finally, the mystical spiritual teachers of the Maghreb.

The history of the marabout leaders and their followers reveals one way in which Islam became integrated with traditional North and West African beliefs and modes of political power from the seventh century through the twentieth century.

Historians have characterized the teachings of the marabout as "populist" mysticism. In North Africa it has been seen as a BERBER counterpart to the elite intellectual Islam of urban Arab migrants. Many marabout were renowned for their miracles and magic and had such popular currency that colonial historians later designated them "local saints." Yet the marabout were also priests and scholars of the Koran, focusing with varying degrees of asceticism on the spiritual beliefs of Islam.

Throughout the Maghreb the marabout grew in influence until they and the sects that grew around them were an integral part of regional social and political structures. Some marabout remained wandering mystics, bringing the teachings of Islam to rural communities. Others were at the center of religious orders that vied for power against the Islamic dynasties controlling portions of North Africa.

The marabout had a particularly strong impact on the region that is now Morocco. In the twelfth century they were persecuted as heretics by the Almoravid Dynasty. The subsequent Almohad Dynasty tolerated the marabout, allowing the tradition to flourish in northwest Africa. The marabout gained political as well as spiritual power during the period of Marinid decline in the fifteenth and sixteenth centuries, but with the subsequent rise of Mawlay Ismâ'il and his dynasty, they again faced persecution.

The beliefs and practices of the marabout throughout the Maghreb differed as widely as the Berber-speaking communities where they lived. Contemporary historians often describe marabout teachings as incorporating pre-Islamic Berber spiritual beliefs. Some marabout followers, such as the Darqâwa of Morocco, used traditional music and dance as well as ascetic practices such as solitude, fasting, and prayer. The Hamâdsha, a marabout tradition by the end of the seventeenth century, incorporated such practices as ecstatic trances and self-mutilation. New teachings were mixed with traditional beliefs; West African musical and dance influences, for example, could be found in the celebrations of the Gnawa marabout following.

Whatever the individual variants, the marabout had a profound political and social impact on North Africa into the twentieth century. They created a populist political and social structure from which anticolonial movements in the nineteenth and twentieth centuries could garner power. In mid-nineteenth century Morocco the Kattaniyin marabout actively opposed close relations with the French. In Libya historians cite the marabout influence as a foundation for the Sanusi order, an Islamic sect that was a prominent force in the anticolonial struggle. Today in North Africa the domed white tombs of these mystics are the sites of pilgrimage, and small buildings of a similar architecture are sometimes called marabout.

In West Africa the marabout were seen alternately as allies and as threats to organized Islam. Their version of Islam had the potential to coexist, if not combine, with non-Islamic beliefs, and they were accused of undermining a more "pure" form of Islam. As such, there were movements against maraboutism, for example, the twentieth-century Wahhabiyya revivalist movement in CÔTE D'IVOIRE. Yet the marabouts, along with Muslim traders, played one of the most significant roles in the spread of Islam in West Africa. Their role in the Islamicization of Africa is now beginning to receive recognition by historians.

Marian Aguiar

SEE ALSO

Sahara Desert; Sufism; Almohads; Almoravids; Islam and Tradition: An Interpretation.

Europe

Maran, René

(b. November 5, 1887, Fort-de-France, Martinique; d. May 9, 1960, Paris, France), French writer and poet who wrote the first "véritable roman nègre" (real Negro novel) and was a leading figure in the development of French black literature.

In 1890 René Maran's parents took him to GABON, in Africa, where his father was offered a colonial post. In 1894 he was sent to France to study, and there he contributed to several journals and published his first collection of poems, *La maison du bonheur* (1909, The House of Happiness). After graduating from high school, he returned to Africa to work in the Bangui colonial office and to continue his literary pursuits. During this time he published the poetry collections *La vie intérieure* (1912, Interior Life) and *Le visage calme* (1922, Serene Expression). The crowning of his career came with the publication of his novel *Batouala* (1921), for which he was awarded the prestigious Goncourt Prize. *Batouala* not only brought him well-deserved fame but also earned him many political enemies, since in the book he denounced social injustices taking place in equatorial Africa due to colonial domination.

Forced to resign from colonial service in 1923, he settled in Paris, where he met with African American authors LANGSTON HUGHES, Gwendolyn Bennett, and others (*see* LITERATURE, AFRICAN AMERICAN); joined the Ligue universelle pour la défense de la race nègre (Universal League for the Defense of the Black Race); and collaborated with newspapers and reviews such as *Présence Africaine* and *Jeune Afrique*. Until his death in 1960 he continued to publish many literary works in which he developed the ideals of brotherhood, equality, and justice for blacks, making him, as Léopold Sédar Senghor said, "the true precursor of NÉGRITUDE," a Caribbean literary movement rooted in black consciousness.

Martine Fernández

SEE ALSO

Bangui, Central African Republic; Colonial Rule; Senghor, Léopold Sédar; Martinique.

Latin America and the Caribbean

Marcelin, Frédéric

(b. January 11, 1848, Port-au Prince, Haiti; d. 1917, Paris, France), Haitian politician and writer who helped to forge a national literature through his novels, which depicted a native's perspective on Haitian society.

Coming from a rich family of merchants, Frédéric Marcelin was educated in Paris and in his mid-twenties was elected as a member of Parliament in HAITI. Reelected in 1882, he became closely aligned with the government's National Party, a link that would eventually secure him the directorship of the Haitian Treasury Department from 1892 to 1894. Using his extensive knowledge and experience in political affairs, he wrote several books, including the autobiographical pieces *Au gré du souvenir* (1913, Along Memory) and *Bric à Brac* (1913, Junk), and the technical works *La Politique* (1887, Politics) and *Finances d'Haïti* (1911, Haiti's Finances).

Marcelin, however, was better known for his literary work. He was the first to write "real" Haitian novels that focused on Haitian society and politics, marking the end of the literary period of Romanticism, highly influenced by French realities. In *Autour de deux romans* (1903, Around Two Novels), he elaborated on his theory that defended the development of a national literature. Unlike the previous Romantic period, this theory placed traditional Haitian customs at the forefront and provided a more realistic depiction of the society's mentality and socioeconomic situation at the turn of the nineteenth century. His nationalistic commitment would eventually lead him to found the review *Haïti littéraire et sociale* (Literary and Social Haiti), in 1905, which he would direct for most of his life.

A political moderate, he discouraged any revolution or opposition to the government, a view espoused in his novel *Thémistocle Epaminondas Labasterre* (1901). However, in a subsequent novel, *La vengeance de Mama* (1902, Mama's Revenge), he shifted his opinions and started advocating a possible transformation of society through education. Through his political views, literary talent, and poignant style, Marcelin is undoubtedly a central figure in Haiti's literary world, and in his search for a national identity he foreshadowed many themes that are being explored by contemporary Haitian authors.

Martine Fernández

See Also

France; Literature, French Language, in Caribbean; Education in Latin America and the Caribbean.

North America

March on Washington, 1941,

a protest planned by A. Philip Randolph, who canceled the march after President Franklin D. Roosevelt established the Fair Employment Practices Committee to eliminate discrimination in World War II defense-industry hiring.

See Also

Randolph, Asa Philip.

North America

March on Washington, 1963,

a massive public demonstration that articulated the goals of the Civil Rights Movement.

The 1963 March on Washington attracted an estimated 250,000 people for a peaceful demonstration to promote civil rights and economic equality for African Americans. Participants walked down Constitution and Independence avenues, then – 100 years after the Emancipation Proclamation was signed – gathered before the Lincoln Monument for speeches, songs, and prayer. Televised live to an audience of millions, the march provided dramatic moments, most memorably the Reverend Martin Luther King Jr.'s "I Have a Dream" speech.

Far larger than previous demonstrations for any cause, the march had an obvious impact, both on the passage of civil rights legislation and on nationwide public opinion. It proved the power of mass appeal and inspired imitators in the antiwar, feminist, and environmental movements. But the March on Washington in 1963 was more complex than the iconic images for which most Americans remember it. As the high point of the Civil Rights Movement, the march – and the integrationist, nonviolent, liberal form of protest it represented – was followed by more radical, militant, and race-conscious approaches.

The march was initiated by A. Philip Randolph, international president of the Brotherhood of Sleeping Car Porters, president of the Negro American Labor Council, and vice president of the AFL-CIO, and was sponsored by five of the largest civil rights organizations in the United States. Planning for the event was complicated by differences among members. Known in the press as "the big six," the major players were Randolph; Whitney Young, president of the National Urban League (NUL); Roy Wilkins, president of the National Association for the Advancement of Colored People (NAACP); James Farmer, founder and president of the Congress of Racial Equality (CORE); John Lewis, president of the Student Nonviolent Coordinating Committee (SNCC); and Martin Luther King Jr., founder and president of the Southern Christian Leadership Conference (SCLC). Bayard Rustin, a close associate of Randolph's and organizer of the first Freedom Ride in 1947, orchestrated and administered the details of the march.

It was Randolph who first conceived of a march on Washington. In 1941 his threat to assemble 100,000 African Americans in the capital helped convince President Franklin D. Roosevelt to sign an executive order banning discrimination in the defense industries and creating the Fair Employment Practices Committee. More than 20 years later, Randolph revived his idea. His primary interest, as always, was jobs – African Americans were disproportionately unemployed and underpaid. In a December 1962 meeting, Randolph and Rustin began planning the March on Washington for Jobs and Freedom.

While Randolph (and the NUL's Young) focused on jobs, the other groups centered on freedom. Both SNCC and CORE were organizing nonviolent protests against Jim Crow segregation and discrimination. In 1963 King's SCLC was waging a long campaign to desegregate Birmingham, Alabama. The violence Sheriff "Bull" Connor and his men visited upon peaceful demonstrators in Birmingham brought national attention to the issue of civil rights. As Rustin later said, credit for mobilizing the March on Washington could go to "Bull Connor, his police dogs, and his fire hoses."

By June, King had agreed to cooperate with Randolph on the march. The older, more conservative NAACP and NUL were still ambivalent. After winning Randolph's promise that the march would be a nonviolent, nonconfrontational event – a promise that dismayed the more militant CORE and SNCC leaders, who had also joined with Randolph – the NAACP's Wilkins pledged his support. In addition, white supporters such as labor leader Walter Reuther and Jewish, Catholic, and Presbyterian officials offered their help. The date was set for August 28, 1963.

Operating out of a tiny office in Harlem, Rustin and his staff had only two months to plan a massive mobilization. Money was raised by the sale of buttons for the march at 25 cents apiece, and thousands of people sent in small cash contributions. The staff tackled the difficult logistics of transportation, publicity, and the marchers' health and safety. Attention to detail was crucial, for the planners believed that anything other than a peaceful, well-organized demonstration would damage the cause for which they would march.

On August 28 the marchers arrived. They came in chartered buses and private cars, on trains and planes – one man even roller-skated to Washington from Chicago. By 11 o'clock in the morning, more than 200,000 had gathered by the Washington Monument, where the march was to begin. It was a diverse crowd: black and white, rich and poor, young and old, Hollywood stars and everyday people. Despite the fears that had prompted extraordinary precautions (including presigned executive orders authorizing military intervention in the case of rioting), those assembled marched peacefully to the Lincoln Monument.

After the national anthem and an invocation by Archbishop Patrick O'Boyle came the speeches. Although the official march goals included an endorsement of Kennedy's civil rights bill – in part because the administration had officially cooperated with the march – some of the most passionate speeches criticized the bill as incomplete. John Lewis, the 23-year-old president of SNCC, promised that without "meaningful legislation" blacks would "march through the South." (His original text, edited to avoid controversy, had continued, "through the heart of Dixie, the way Sherman did. We shall pursue our own scorched earth policy and burn Jim Crow to the ground nonviolently.") The speech written by CORE's James Farmer, imprisoned in Louisiana, was read by Floyd McKissick. Farmer said the fight for legal and economic equality would not stop "until the dogs stop biting us in the South and the rats stop biting us in the North." By the time Young and Wilkins spoke, the crowd was quieted by the heat. When Mahalia Jackson took the stage to sing "I've Been 'Buked and I've Been Scorned," the crowd revived.

King, the last speaker of the day, was introduced by Randolph as "the moral leader of our nation." King's speech, eloquent on the page, was electrifying when delivered. With the passionate, poetic style he had honed at the altar, King stirred the audience and built to his reportedly extemporaneous "I have a dream" finale.

The rally concluded with Rustin's reading of the march's ten demands – which included not only passage of the civil rights bill but also school and housing desegregation, job training, and an increase in the minimum wage – and the marchers' pledge, followed by a benediction from Dr. Benjamin E. Mays, president of Morehouse College. The march ended at 4:20 in the afternoon, ten minutes ahead of schedule. As marchers returned to the buses that would take them home, the organizers met with President Kennedy, who encouraged them to continue with their work.

Although white racists decried it as a sentimental appeal to mainstream white America, the March on Washington was a success. It had been powerful yet peaceful and orderly beyond anyone's expectations, including those of the organizers themselves. Yet it was, according to most historians, the high tide of that phase of the Civil Rights Movement that looked to white support and government solutions. The bombing, just three weeks later, of the Sixteenth Street Baptist Church in Birmingham, Alabama, which resulted in the deaths of four young black girls, reminded African Americans of the depth and violence of segregationist America. Increasingly, young African Americans turned to the Black Power Movement or to the Nation of Islam (whose leader, Malcolm X, had criticized the march) in their search for freedom and strength.

Kate Tuttle

See Also

American Federation of Labor and Congress of Industrial Organizations; Harlem, New York; Randolph, Asa Philip; King, Martin Luther, Jr.; Mays, Benjamin Elijah; Sixteenth Street Baptist Church (Birmingham, Ala.); Thirteenth Amendment of the United States Constitution and the Emancipation Proclamation; Wilkins, Roy Ottoway; Young, Whitney Moore, Jr.

Africa

Margi (also known as Marghi), ethnic group of Nigeria.

The Margi primarily inhabit the Adamawa and Borno states of northeastern Nigeria. They speak an Afro-Asiatic language in the Chadic group. Approximately 200,000 people consider themselves Margi.

See Also

Languages, African: An Overview.

North America

Markham, Dewey ("Pigmeat") (b. April 18, 1906, Durham, N.C.; d. December 13, 1981, New York, N.Y.), African American comedian best known for his famous line "Here Come de Judge."

Dewey Markham ran away from home at age 13 to join the circus, the beginning of a six-decade-long career as a stage performer. After six years with the circus, he became a regular with minstrel shows, singing, dancing, and honing his comedy skills. He gained his nickname "Pigmeat" from a song he performed called "Sweet Papa Pigmeat."

In the 1930s Markham branched out to Broadway and eventually to Hollywood, where he starred in all-black films. During his long career, he also recorded 16 albums, which combined his talents for comedy and singing the blues. In the 1950s and 1960s Markham appeared frequently on television talk and variety shows. It was during an appearance on the hit comedy *Laugh-In* that he unveiled his legendary skit, "Here Come de Judge." The punchline became an overnight sensation.

See Also

Blues, The; Minstrelsy; Television and African Americans; Film, Blacks in American.

Latin America and the Caribbean

Marley, Bob (b. February 6, 1945, Rhoden Hall, Jamaica; d. May 11, 1981, Miami, Fla.), Jamaican singer and songwriter whose name invokes reggae music, the tenets of Rastafarianism, and, more broadly, the struggle of the economically and politically oppressed.

The first global pop star to emerge from a developing nation, Bob Marley has won fans from nations around the globe who share his vision of redemption and freedom and love his innovative blend of American and Caribbean music.

Bob Marley was born Robert Nesta Marley in rural Rhoden Hall in the parish of St. Ann, Jamaica. His mother was a Jamaican teenager and his father a middle-aged captain in the West Indian regiment of the British Army. Marley's parents separated when he was six and soon thereafter he moved with his mother to Kingston, joining the wave of rural immigrants that flooded the capital during the 1950s and 1960s. Marley and his mother settled in Trench Town, a west Kingston slum named for the sewer that ran through it.

There Marley shared quarters with a boy his age named "Bunny" Neville O'Riley Livingston. The two made music together, fashioning a guitar from bamboo, sardine cans, and electrical wire and learning harmonies from local singer Joe Higgs. Like a number of their contemporaries, Marley and Bunny listened to radio from New Orleans; and like their peers they adopted the sounds of rhythm and blues, combined them with strains of a local musical style, *mento,* and produced a new music called ska. Although encouraged by his mother to learn a craft, Marley soon abandoned an apprenticeship as a welder to devote himself to music.

Peter McIntosh (later Peter Tosh) joined Bunny and Marley's musical sessions, bringing with him a real guitar. In the early 1960s the three formed a harmony group, the Wailing Wailers; meanwhile, Marley recorded a few songs with producer Leslie Kong, to whom local ska celebrity Jimmy Cliff had introduced him. Marley's earliest recordings received little radio play but strengthened his desire to sing.

Joined by Junior Braithwaite and two backup singers, the Wailing Wailers recorded on the Coxsone label, supervised by local sound-system superstar Clement Dodd. The group became Kingston celebrities in the summer of 1963 with "Simmer Down," a song that both indicted and romanticized the lives of Trench Town toughs, known as "rude boys." The Wailing Wailers recorded more than 30 singles in the mid-1960s, reflecting – and sometimes leading – the evolution of reggae, from mento to ska to rocksteady.

In 1963 Marley's mother moved to Delaware, expecting that her son would follow her and begin life anew. Marley did make a prolonged visit in 1966, working jobs for Chrysler and DuPont; yet his heart lay back home, where his new wife, the Jamaican Rita Anderson, and his old passion – the music of the island – both remained. When he returned to Jamaica in 1967, he converted from Christianity to Rastafarianism and began the mature stage of his musical career. Marley reunited with Bunny and Peter Tosh, and together they called themselves the Wailers and began their own record label, Wail 'N' Soul. They abandoned the rude-boy ethos for the spirituality of Rastafarian beliefs and slowed their music under the new rocksteady influence.

Although the Wailers soon cohered as a group, they did not find success beyond Jamaica for a few years. In 1970 bassist Aston "Family Man" Barnett and his drummer – together considered the best rhythm section on Jamaica – joined the Wailers. With this addition the group attracted the attention of Island Records, a company that had started in Jamaica but moved to London. In 1971 they recorded *Catch a Fire,* the first Jamaican reggae album to enjoy the benefits of a large budget and widespread commercial promotion. *Catch a Fire* sold modestly, better in Europe than America, but well enough to sustain Island's interest in the Wailers.

During the early 1970s the band recorded an album each year and toured extensively, slowly breaking into the European and American mainstream. They played shows with American superstars Bruce Springsteen and Sly and the Family Stone, and in 1974 British rocker Eric Clapton scored a hit with "I Shot the Sheriff," a Marley composition. In 1975 the Wailers made their first major splash in the United States with "No Woman No Cry" as well as an album of live material. At this point, Peter Tosh and Bunny left the band, which took the name Bob Marley & the Wailers.

Although Marley had melded politics and music since the early days of "Simmer Down," as his success grew he became increasingly political. His 1976 song "War" transcribed a speech of Haile Selassie I, the Ethiopian king upon whom the Rastafarian sect was based. In addition to Rastafarian spirituality and mysticism, his lyrics probed the turmoil in Jamaica. Prior to the 1976 elections, partisanship inspired gang war in Trench Town and divided the people against themselves. By siding with Prime Minister Michael Manley – and by singing songs of a political bent – Marley angered some Jamaicans. After surviving an assassination attempt in December, he fled to London until the following year.

When Marley returned to Jamaica in 1978, he performed in the One Love Peace

Concert, which sought to ameliorate existing political conflicts. During his set Marley orchestrated a handshake between political opponents Manley and Edward Seaga, a highly symbolic moment.

Marley's activism extended beyond Jamaica, and people from developing nations around the world found hope in his music. In 1980 Bob Marley & the Wailers had the honor of performing at the independence ceremony when Rhodesia became ZIMBABWE. The group's concerts in the late 1970s attracted enormous crowds in West Africa and Latin America as well as in Europe and the United States.

Bob Marley died at age 36 from a cancer that began in his toe and spread throughout his body. His memory was honored by the Jamaican government and he was given a national funeral. During Marley's lifetime his music became closely associated with the movement toward black political independence that was then prominent in several African and South American countries. His songs have remained popular, and for many they symbolize the hopes of the downtrodden for worldly redemption and spiritual transcendence. The conviction and sincerity of Marley's performances, and his unique, melodic songwriting have influenced many pop artists, including STEVIE WONDER and Eric Clapton. He was inducted into the Rock and Roll Hall of Fame in 1994.

Eric Bennett

SEE ALSO

New Orleans, Louisiana; Kingston, Jamaica; Rastafarians.

Cross Cultural

Maroonage in the Americas,

the forming of communities by escaped slaves in North America, Latin America, and the Caribbean.

From the beginning of New World slavery in the sixteenth century through abolition in the nineteenth century, male and female slaves escaped from plantations and established semi-independent, self-governing communities. These communities were often located in inaccessible areas such as forests, swamps, and mountains. They were known variously as *palenques, quilombos, mocambos, cumbes, mambises, ladeiras,* and *maroons*. Over time the term *maroon* – derived from the Spanish *cimarrón*, which, in turn, is based on a Taíno Indian word meaning "fugitive" – became the standard word for an individual escaped slave or a community of escaped slaves. The phenomenon of escaped slaves forming communities, known as *maroonage*, represented a common response to slavery throughout the New World. Maroon communities ranged in size from small bands that came together for less than a year to powerful groups of thousands that survived for generations or even centuries.

Current scholarship on maroonage in the Americas recognizes two categories of rebellion: *petit maroonage* and *grand maroonage*. Petit maroonage refers to the short-term absenteeism of an individual slave or a small group of slaves, while grand maroonage refers to the formation of more stable, longer-lasting communities by large groups of escaped slaves. In both cases, escaped slaves remained relatively close to plantation society, conducting occasional raids to obtain food and arms, among other supplies. The maroon groups at times traded with local communities. In contrast to petit maroon groups, grand maroon societies tended to remain in one well-defended location, where they cultivated various crops for their own sustenance and for clandestine trading purposes.

Generally, the longer a slave eluded slavery, the harsher the punishment upon his or her recapture. Recaptured maroons faced whipping and reenslavement at best, and at worst they feared the amputation of a leg, castration, suspension from a meat hook through the ribs, or death. These forms of punishment, however, did not deter slaves from seeking freedom from the abusive treatment, overwork, and malnutrition experienced on plantations.

Most escaped-slave communities in the United States represented only petit maroonage. As documented by Herbert Aptheker in his 1939 publication, *Maroons Within the Present Limits of the United States*, more than 50 maroon communities existed in South Carolina, North Carolina, Virginia, Louisiana, Florida, Georgia, Mississippi, and Alabama between 1672 and 1864. One of the most noted maroon communities in the United States was located in the Dismal Swamp between Virginia and North Carolina; some 2000 fugitive slaves and their descendants lived there. Yet even this community was small compared to many of the maroon communities of Latin America and the Caribbean. For example, the quilombo of Palmares, BRAZIL, was composed of a group of several small villages. In the mid-seventeenth century Palmares is thought to have had a population of at least 11,000 and perhaps as high as 20,000.

Slave communities in North America lacked several of the demographic factors and environmental conditions that facilitated grand maroonage. Maroon communities tended to be more numerous and longer-lived where the slave population was predominantly African and where it outnumbered the white population. The United States imported a much smaller number of African slaves relative to its overall population than did countries in Latin America or the Caribbean, where African slaves were usually worked to death and then replaced by new, African-born slaves. The United States also favored slave reproduction over slave importation, producing a more assimilated and acculturated slave population. Blacks born into slavery were less likely to rebel and escape than their African-born counterparts. In addition, although the country had an extensive wilderness conducive to maroonage, few parts of the United States had the tropical climate that allowed fugitive slaves in Latin America and the Caribbean to survive with little clothing and shelter year round. The limited opportunities for maroonage in the United States further diminished in the nineteenth century as the white population increased and spread out to settle and develop the land.

Grand maroon communities in Latin America and the Caribbean struck directly at the foundations of plantation society. Slave owners and state officials feared maroon raids and their repercussions: loss of livestock and property, desertion of slave laborers, undermining of slave discipline, and inciting of slave rebellions. European powers organized armed forces known as *rancheadores* in Spanish colonies and *capitões-do-mato* in Brazil for the explicit purpose of capturing runaway slaves and vanquishing their communities. However, the ubiquity and strength of maroon communities forced colonial officials in Brazil, COLOMBIA, CUBA, ECUADOR, JAMAICA, MEXICO, and SURINAME to forge treaties with them. These arrangements recognized the autonomy and territorial claims of the maroons in exchange for an end to maroon hostilities toward the plantations and maroon assistance in returning runaways. The extent of maroon cooperation with European authorities varied, ranging from close collaboration to collapsed alliance ending in war, and peace treaties were broken repeatedly by both sides.

Like the relations between maroons and colonial officials, those between the maroons and Amerindians also varied from one country and historical period to another. From the time of their arrival in the New World, European settlers attempted with varying degrees of success to pit Indians and blacks against one another. Initially, colonial authorities employed slaves as soldiers to drive Indians out of certain territories. Later they often paid Indians to track down FUGITIVE SLAVES or to assist them in antimaroon expeditions. Lured by monetary rewards and the granting of freedom, free and enslaved blacks also participated in the colonial effort to crack down on maroons.

Colonial governments in Latin America and the Caribbean called on Indians to seize maroons more often than they called on maroons to help them control indigenous populations. Some governments in these countries even brought in Indians from other provinces for the explicit purpose of handling maroon insurgency; the Miskito Indians of NICARAGUA and HONDURAS were recruited by the Jamaican government to capture maroons and destroy their communities on that island. The Miskito Indians ultimately enslaved many of the maroons that they captured.

Despite the opposition created between the two groups, there was some association and cooperation between maroon settlements and Native American communities, which after being driven inland during the early stages of colonization sought protection from European violence and diseases in inaccessible areas. In the sixteenth century slaves from a shipwreck joined and intermarried with Amerindians in Ecuador and formed the settlement known as ESMERALDAS. In less tightly knit alliances, Amerindians provided maroons with information about impending colonial attacks on their communities and traded colonial goods for foods cultivated by maroons. Though there were occasions when Indians and blacks united against colonial forces, in general fugitive slaves in the Americas could not trust Native Americans.

Recognizing their precarious state of existence, maroon communities took extreme measures to ensure their safety. Escaped slaves strategically established their communities in remote, inhospitable areas. They carefully hid the paths leading to their settlements and set dangerous booby traps. In Suriname maroons were reported to have dug a single sunken path down which they rolled logs and boulders to crush approaching soldiers. The quilombo of Palmares in northeastern Brazil, the most populated maroon colony, successfully defended itself from colonial attacks for almost a century

ABOVE RIGHT: A colored aquatint after a painting by French artist François-Jules Bourgoin, dating from about 1795, depicts maroons waiting to ambush French soldiers on the Dromilly estate, Trelawny. *Courtesy of the National Library of Jamaica*
RIGHT: In his account of the war in Suriname between maroon slaves and the Dutch from 1772 to 1777, Captain John Gabriel Stedman included this engraving of a maroon family stolen from the Loango area of West Central Africa. *Image of the Black Project, Harvard University*
BELOW: A late nineteenth-century illustration from Wilhelm Joest's "Ethnographisches und Verwandtes aus Guyana" shows two women paddling a canoe on the Marowyne River. Maroon women still sit in this posture, legs outstretched, while working at tasks ranging from sewing to preparing food. *From Joest 1893, plate 4/Courtesy Richard and Sally Price*

TOP: Saramaka children, descendants of an eighteenth-century maroon (fugitive slave) community in Suriname, dance to the accompaniment of a kinsman, who sings and slaps his thighs. *Richard Price*
ABOVE RIGHT: Maroon women of the Saramaka people hoe the ground as they prepare to plant rice in Upper Pikilio, Suriname. *Richard Price*
ABOVE: Two men carry an oracle past a Saramaka mother and her newborn child; the oracle had been consulted frequently during the woman's pregnancy. *Sally Price*

with its sophisticated fortifications. Beyond constructing a barrier of earthen walls around the quilombo, the inhabitants covered the surrounding terrain with pointed stakes and pitfalls lined with wooden spikes that made approaching the quilombo from any angle nearly impossible. Palmares repelled Portuguese attacks until its final destruction in 1694. Almost always outnumbered and outarmed, maroons made extensive use of guerrilla tactics, ambushing and withdrawing with agility and speed.

Maroon communities also had to be on guard against internal dissension. Since the security of the entire community would be jeopardized by the desertion of one member, traitors were commonly punished with death. As a safety measure, new members were often required to serve and stay within the boundaries of the maroon settlement for an extended period of time – as long as two years, for example, in Cuba.

Personal disputes involving relationships between men and women also posed a serious threat to maroon communities. Although some female slaves escaped from slavery on their own, male maroons often abducted female slaves from the plantations. All maroon communities had many more men than women, since more male than female slaves were imported to the New World. In addition, the physical toll of warfare with colonial forces and maroon life resulted in a low fertility rate. To keep maroon communities from being exposed or torn apart as a result of conflicts between men over women, severe consequences were prescribed for adulterers. In Palmares, for example, the penalty for adultery was death.

Many maroon settlements prescribed a similar division of labor between the sexes. Women farmed and processed food and cared for children and the elderly. They were often spiritual leaders among maroons, harnessing supernatural powers to protect community

members and bring good fortune. Men, on the other hand, were largely responsible for hunting, surveillance, and defense of the settlement.

While historians have debated the extent to which maroon communities replicated African patterns of culture, kinship, and political organization, a strong maroon heritage nevertheless endures today in some parts of Latin America and the Caribbean. Although economic and industrial development during the nineteenth and twentieth centuries absorbed or displaced many maroon communities, some have survived until the present time. These include ethnic groups such as the Garífuna of Honduras, the Djuka and Saramaka of Suriname, and various communities throughout Brazil, such as Oriximiná and Rio das Rãs. The city of San Basílio in Colombia and the region known as Cockpit Country in Jamaica also host major maroon-descended populations. These communities reflect the syncretic character of the various cultures and traditions of the different African peoples that founded and defended them. Past maroonage leaders – such as Zumbi of Palmares in Brazil and Nanny of Mooretown in Jamaica – have become sources of inspiration for many contemporary Afro-Latin American and Afro-Caribbean movements.

Aaron Myers

See Also

Palmares: An African State in Brazil; Mooretown, Jamaica (Nanny Town).

Africa

Marrakech, Morocco, a city in western Morocco.

The city of Marrakech, called the Red City for the color of its clay walls, was founded in the eleventh century as a base camp for the armies of the Islamic Dynasty of the Almoravids. The Almoravids fortified the settlement at the foot of the Atlas Mountains and made Marrakech the capital of an empire that stretched east to Algiers, south to the Senegal River, and north to the Ebro River in Spain. In 1146, when the Almohads seized power, they massacred the inhabitants of Marrakech. Under the Almohads, Marrakech flourished as an Islamic cultural center, attracting scholars from throughout North Africa and Moorish Spain. It is said that during this time, the entrance to the famed Koutoubia mosque was surrounded by a hundred booksellers.

During the subsequent Berber Dynasty of the Marinids, the political capital shifted to the city of Fès. Marrakech was left under semiautonomous rule, and the vestiges of the Almohads' glorious past fell to ruin; it is said that the Almohad palace became a poultry house. By the early sixteenth century a Berber confederation called the Hintata ruled in Marrakech and faced regular incursions by the Portuguese. They were later conquered by the Sa'dians, who used Marrakech as a center for their Saharan trade and revived the Islamic scholarship that had marked the city's past. They built the famed El-Badii palace, which is considered one of the wonders of the Islamic world.

Beginning in 1664, under the reign of the Alwites, Marrakech entered a period of civil unrest as it was plundered by armies and became a hotbed of rebellious sentiment. Although conflict tapered off after the mid-eighteenth century, Marrakech never regained its status as an imperial city.

In 1912, as the French moved to secure political control over Morocco, a resistance leader named al-Hiba led a revolt from the Sahara and briefly captured the city. He was forced out by the French, who established their protectorate over Morocco in the same year. The French used the city of Casablanca as their main commercial base but also built a modern quarter, called Gueliz, in Marrakech.

Since independence in 1956, the city has continued to serve as a marketplace for trade from the Sahara and the Atlas Mountains. Mining outside the limits of the city has become an important industry, yielding lead, zinc, copper, molybdenum, and graphite. Marrakech has continued to produce the traditional handicrafts of Morocco, including leather goods and carpets, in addition to fruit, vegetables, and date palms from the thousand-year-old groves surrounding the city. Marrakech also attracts a significant number of tourists. Many of the tourists are drawn by Morocco's famous palaces and mosques, as well as by tales of its legendary past. To cater to these visitors, the Club Med hotel downtown has set up large Berber tents on its terrace. For both tourists and locals, all roads lead to Place Jâmi' al-hanâ, a vast bazaar at the heart of Marrakech.

Marian Aguiar

See Also

Algiers, Algeria; Casablanca, Morocco; Fès, Morocco; Sahara Desert.

Marrakesh, Morocco. Please see Marrakech, Morocco

Latin America and the Caribbean

Marrero Aristy, Ramón

(b. June 14, 1913, San Rafael del Yuma, Dominican Republic; d. July 17, 1959), Dominican fiction writer, journalist, historian, and diplomat.

Although poverty prevented Ramón Marrero Aristy from attending school regularly, he studied on his own. As a young man, he wrote stories while he worked as the storeroom clerk of a sugar plantation. Some of his early stories were published in a newspaper in the capital city of Santo Domingo, and the newspaper soon hired him as a writer. During his career he worked as an editor of three newspapers, *La Opinión*, *Listín Diario*, and *La Nación*. He also directed the illustrated review *Babeque*.

Marrero worked for the government of Rafael Trujillo, who dominated the Dominican Republic from 1930 to 1961. Despite his lack of support for the Trujillo dictatorship, Marrero served twice as the state secretary of labor. He also held diplomatic posts in France and the United States.

Marrero wrote two collections of short stories, *Perfiles agrestes* (1933) and *Balsié* (1938), and three volumes of history, titled *La República Dominicana* (1957). He is best known for his 1939 novel *Over* (not available in English). It describes the exploitation of Afro-Caribbean peoples by Americans and Europeans in the Dominican sugar industry, a discussion that indirectly criticized Trujillo's economic policies. Surprisingly, the novel was published in the Dominican Republic, but the government banned it days after its release.

It is widely believed that Marrero was assassinated because of suspected involvement in anti-Trujillo plots, but the details of his death remain unconfirmed.

Marveta Ryan

North America

Marsalis, Wynton

(b. October 18, 1961, New Orleans, La.), African American trumpeter who excels in both jazz and classical music; a leading advocate of the acoustic, bop-based jazz mainstream and the most prominent figure in contemporary jazz.

Trumpeter Wynton Marsalis is the leading figure in contemporary jazz. He burst onto the jazz scene as part of Art Blakey's 1980 edition of the Jazz Messengers. More than an inventive and talented musician, Marsalis has become the de facto spokesman for the neoclassical movement in jazz that emerged in the early 1980s, drawing inspiration from acoustic jazz styles that antedate the free jazz and jazz-rock of the late 1960s and 1970s. He has also worked effectively as a jazz educator, particularly for his four-part Public Broadcasting System (PBS) series *Marsalis on Music*, which won a Peabody Award in 1996.

Besides achieving acclaim as a musician, Marsalis emerged in the 1980s as an outspoken and controversial figure in America's ongoing dialogue on race and culture. His ideas on jazz and African American culture are indebted to the thinking of Albert Murray and Murray's intellectual disciple, Stanley Crouch. Murray and Crouch share a black-centered social vision, but they reject nationalism and repudiate the separatist legacy of Malcolm X and the radicalism of Amiri Baraka. Crouch, in particular, has become Marsalis's mentor and has contributed liner essays for several of his recordings.

Marsalis is part of a family of active jazz musicians, including his father, pianist Ellis Marsalis (b. 1934); his older brother, saxophonist Branford (b. 1960); and his younger brothers, trombonist Delfeayo (b. 1965) and drummer Jason (b. 1976). He was named for jazz pianist Wynton Kelly (1931-1971). Moreover, he was born in New Orleans, the historic birthplace of jazz. He received his first trumpet when he was 6 years old from white New Orleans trumpeter Al Hirt. At age 12, after hearing a record by legendary jazz trumpeter Clifford Brown (1930-1956), Marsalis began to take his own trumpet playing seriously.

During his high school years Marsalis played in a wide range of ensembles. He joined New Orleans marching bands and, together with his brother Branford, took part in a local funk unit called the Creators. His formal training involved both jazz and classical music. While in high school, he played first trumpet with the New Orleans Civic Orchestra. At age 14 he performed as featured soloist with the New Orleans Philharmonic Orchestra. After high school he attended the Juilliard School of Music in New York.

In 1980 Art Blakey asked Marsalis to join the Jazz Messengers for a summer tour. Soon the young trumpeter became the group's musical director. One year later Marsalis decided to leave Juilliard in order to tour again with Blakey. During 1981 he left Blakey temporarily to join V.S.O.P., pianist Herbie Hancock's acoustic group, featuring bassist Ron Carter (b. 1937) and drummer Tony Williams (1945-1997), all of whom were part of the classic 1960s combo of trumpeter Miles Davis.

Marsalis quickly established a considerable reputation in jazz circles. During his stint with Blakey he emulated past Jazz Messengers' trumpeter Freddie Hubbard (b. 1938), but by 1981 his playing recalled the mid-1960s Miles Davis, albeit with much greater technical virtuosity. By the late 1980s Marsalis had established his own identity by revisiting jazz history, going all the way back to the 1920s. His mature style combines post-bop harmonies with the melodic sensitivity of trumpeter Louis Armstrong and the penchant for mutes and "freak" effects of cornet players Joe Oliver and Bubber Miley.

In 1981 Columbia Records signed Marsalis to an unprecedented contract for both jazz and classical music recordings. Later that year he formed his own band, the Wynton Marsalis Quintet, which included his brother Branford. The group recorded several albums, including the widely praised *Black Codes (from the Underground)* (1985). In 1985 Branford Marsalis and other members of the band quit to tour with the rock singer Sting. But by early 1986 Wynton had organized a new and equally talented group, the Wynton Marsalis Quartet, featuring pianist Marcus Roberts (b. 1963). Over the years it grew into a septet that provided a perfect vehicle for Marsalis's talents as a composer and arranger.

In 1987 Marsalis became cofounder and artistic director of Jazz at Lincoln Center, a program of New York City's prestigious Lincoln Center for the Performing Arts. The new position gave him an unrivaled ability to shape the critical understanding of jazz. He has presented major retrospectives of the music of past jazz masters, including Louis Armstrong and Sidney Bechet, but above all he has emphasized the towering role of Duke Ellington. Marsalis's position at Lincoln Center also broadened his own writing talents.

Marsalis, as director of the Jazz at Lincoln Center program, agreed not only to direct the Lincoln Center jazz band, but also to compose and present one significant new work per year. These commissioned works suggest that his study of Ellington's music has shaped his own composing and arranging. In 1993 Marsalis introduced the first of these new works, *In This House, On This Morning,* a musical evocation of Sunday services at an African American church. In the following year he debuted *Blood on the Fields,* an oratorio for three singers and a 14-piece orchestra, his most ambitious piece thus far. *Blood on the Fields* recounts the story of two Africans, Leona and Jesse, who are captured and sold into slavery in the American South but who ultimately find love and escape to freedom together. In 1997 *Blood on the Fields* became the first nonclassical work to receive a Pulitzer Prize for music.

Marsalis is one of the few jazz musicians whose classical and jazz performances are equally acclaimed. In 1984 he won a Grammy Award from the National Academy of Recording Arts and Sciences (NARAS) for his classical debut album, *Trumpet Concertos* (1983). His widely praised second jazz album, *Think of One* (1983), also received a Grammy Award in 1984 for best jazz recording, making Marsalis the first artist to win Grammy Awards in two different musical categories in a single year. In 1995 he debuted his first string quartet, *(At the) Octoroon Balls,* at the Lincoln Center, and the following year he released *In Gabriel's Garden,* which he recorded with Anthony Newman on harpsichord and organ and the English Chamber Orchestra.

James Clyde Sellman

See Also

Slavery in the United States; Armstrong, Louis ("Satchmo"); Bechet, Sidney Joseph; Davis, Miles Dewey, III; Hancock, Herbert Jeffrey (Herbie); Ellington, Edward Kennedy ("Duke"); Miley, James Wesley ("Bubber"); Murray, Albert L.; New Orleans, Louisiana; Oliver, Joseph ("King").

North America

Marshall, Paule (b. April 9, 1929, Brooklyn, N.Y.), African American writer known for novels that incorporate Caribbean-American heritage and feature black women protagonists.

The Norton Anthology of African American Literature calls Paule Marshall's *Brown Girl, Brownstones* "the novel that most black feminist critics consider to be the beginning of contemporary African American women's writings." Marshall grew up a voracious reader but was primarily exposed to white male authors. When she finally read African American authors Paul Laurence Dunbar and Richard Wright, she felt that black women's voices were missing. In her own novels and short stories, she incorporated the language and lessons she had learned from the women around her, and she in turn inspired younger black women writers such as Alice Walker and Ntozake Shange.

Marshall was born Valenza Pauline Burke to parents who had recently immigrated to New York from Barbados and was raised in a close-knit West Indian community. In a 1983 essay titled "The Making of a Writer: From the Poets in the Kitchen," she credited her mother and her mother's neighborhood friends with being her most important teachers. As a child, she listened as these women, the "poets in the kitchen," gathered around their kitchen tables at the end of each work day to talk; "there she learned," as one critic has written, "the basic skills that characterize her writing – trenchant imagery and idiom, relentless character analysis, and a strong sense of ritual." West Indian dialect and culture are prominent in Marshall's writing, as are the conflicts that face Caribbean-American immigrant families like her own.

In 1953 Marshall graduated cum laude from Brooklyn College and was inducted into Phi Beta Kappa. Illness had forced her to take a two-year break in the middle of college; during that period she began writing fiction to relieve her boredom. Soon after her graduation, she was hired as a writer for *Our World,* a popular 1950s African American magazine. Despite the sexism she encountered as the only woman on the staff, she was able to travel to the Caribbean and South America on assignments. The experience piqued her interest in a writing career, and she began writing *Brown Girl, Brownstones.* In 1957 she married her first husband, Kenneth Marshall, and a year later gave birth to her son, Evan-Keith. Over her husband's strong protests, she hired a babysitter for her son so that she could finish her novel. *Brown Girl, Brownstones* was published in 1959.

The novel tells the story of Selina Boyce, an adolescent girl growing up in a New York West Indian community much like Marshall's own. The novel broke new ground in its portrayal of a Caribbean immigrant family, its use of a black girl as its protagonist, and its exploration of gender dynamics within the black community. Selina comes of age as she observes the roles her parents play and decides what kind of woman she will be. Marshall said later that as she wrote the novel, she thought of it not as something she would publish, but as an attempt to "untie [her] own knots." *Brown Girl, Brownstones* was well reviewed when it appeared, but it did not become a commercial success until the surge of interest in black women writers in the early 1970s. By then Marshall had been writing for over a decade.

In 1960 she received a Guggenheim Fellowship, which supported her while she wrote *Soul Clap Hands and Sing* (1961), a collection of four novellas, each of which portrays an elderly black man in a different part of the diaspora. Set on a fictional island, Marshall's next novel, *The Chosen Place, The Timeless People* (1969), was called "the best novel to be written by an American black woman, one of the two important black novels of the 1960s, and one of the four or five most impressive novels ever written by a black American." Marshall had divorced her husband in 1963 and had begun teaching part-time at several universities. In 1970 she married a Haitian businessman and began to divide her time between New York and Haiti.

Both Caribbean and American settings are featured in Marshall's third novel, *Praisesong for the Widow* (1983), which portrays an

African American woman who is profoundly changed by her stay in the islands during a cruise. Also in 1983, Marshall published a short-story collection, *Reena and Other Stories*. Her fourth novel, *Daughters* (1991), features a young professional Caribbean-American woman learning to understand her father and her heritage.

Marshall has taught at Yale, Columbia, Cornell, and Oxford universities and has won numerous prizes and awards, including in 1992 the prestigious MacArthur Prize Fellowship. Her work celebrates black immigrant communities, Afro-diasporic culture, and black women in ways that broke new ground in African American literature.

Lisa Clayton Robinson

See Also

Women Writers, Black, in the United States; New York, New York.

North America

Marshall, Thurgood

(b. July 2, 1908, Baltimore, Md.; d. January 24, 1993, Bethesda, Md.), first black United States Supreme Court justice, founder of the NAACP Legal Defense and Educational Fund; lawyer whose victory in *Brown* v. *Board of Education* (1954) outlawed segregation in American public life.

When Thurgood Marshall died in 1993, he was only the second justice to lie in state in the Supreme Court's chambers. Chief Justice Earl Warren, who had written the opinion in Marshall's most celebrated case, Brown v. Board of Education, was the other. This honor capped the outpouring of praise for the Court's first black justice, a man who, said one of his former law clerks, "would have had a place in American history before his appointment" to the Supreme Court.

Indeed, Marshall's tenure as chief counsel for the National Association for the Advancement of Colored People (NAACP) and founder of its Legal Defense and Educational Fund made him one of America's most influential and best-known lawyers. His 30 years of public service – first as a federal appeals court judge, then as America's first black solicitor general, and finally as the first black U.S. Supreme Court justice – came after he had already helped millions of African Americans exercise long-denied constitutional rights.

Marshall once said that his father told him, "If anyone calls you nigger, you not only have my permission to fight him, you got my orders." Both of Marshall's parents – William, who worked as a dining steward at an all-white private club, and Norma, a grade school teacher – instilled in their son racial pride and self-confidence. As a child, Marshall later recalled, he was a "hell-raiser," whose high school teacher punished him by sending him to the school's basement to read and copy passages from the United States Constitution. It was valuable training for the future lawyer, who claimed that by the time he graduated he could recite nearly the entire document by heart. From Baltimore's Douglass High School, Marshall entered Lincoln University in Oxford, Pennsylvania, where he won respect as a debater and graduated with honors in 1930.

Denied admission to the University of Maryland's all-white law school – an institution whose segregation he later challenged and defeated in *Murray* v. *Maryland* (1936) – Marshall entered the law school at Howard University. There he met Charles H. Houston, the school's vice dean, who became the NAACP's first chief counsel and the first black man to win a case before the U.S. Supreme Court. Shortly after graduating magna cum laude in 1933, Marshall went to work for Houston at the NAACP, replacing him as chief counsel in 1938.

From Houston, Marshall absorbed the lesson that lawyers could be "social engineers." Since its inception in 1909 the NAACP had challenged racial inequality, winning many local cases involving inadequate segregated schools. But Marshall was the architect of a new strategy that increasingly attacked segregation itself. Plessy v. Ferguson (1896), a case involving segregated public railroads in Louisiana, had decreed segregation to be constitutional as long as facilities for both races were equal. In a series of cases concerning graduate education, Marshall and the NAACP began asking whether separate could ever be equal. Each victory – in *Murray* and other law school cases such as *Gaines* v. *Missouri* and Sweatt v. Painter – brought the Supreme Court closer to toppling *Plessy*'s "separate but equal" formula.

The case that finally ended legal segregation in America was *Brown* v. *Board of Education*. Drawing on psychological and sociological evidence, Marshall argued that the mere fact of racial separation, even without gross inequality, irrevocably harmed African American children. The Court unanimously agreed. In *Brown* (1954) and its companion decision, *Brown II* (1955), the Supreme Court outlawed state-imposed segregation and set guidelines for eradicating it, a process that was neither quick nor easy nor complete. But despite often violent resistance to desegregation, the constitutional impact of Marshall's victory in *Brown* was enormous and lasting.

Thurgood Marshall brought 32 cases before the Supreme Court; he won 29 of them. He had an even more impressive record as a judge for the U.S. Court of Appeals, a position to which President John F. Kennedy appointed him in 1961. Of the 112 opinions he wrote for that court, not one was overturned on appeal. In 1965 President Lyndon B. Johnson appointed Marshall solicitor general of the United States – in essence, the nation's chief counsel. Two years later Johnson nominated Marshall to fill the Supreme Court vacancy left by Justice Thomas C. Clark. The first African American to serve as solicitor general or a Supreme Court justice, Marshall said he hesitated to take on the roles, not wanting to abandon his friends in the Civil Rights Movement. But, he said, "when one has the opportunity to serve the Government, he should think twice before passing it up."

On the Court, Marshall wrote important majority opinions in *Bounds* v. *Smith* (1977), which defended prisoners' rights to legal assistance and libraries, and *Stanley* v. *Georgia* (1969), which protected the rights of individuals to possess pornography. His opinion in *Stanley* illustrates the common sense and clarity for which Marshall was famous: "If the First Amendment means anything, it means that the state has no business telling a man, sitting alone in his own house, what books he may read or what films he may watch." Known as the

Representing defendant Walter Lee Irvin, *third from left*, at his second trial for rape are, *left to right*, Paul C. Perkins, Jack Greenberg, New York attorney for the National Association for the Advancement of Colored People (NAACP), and Thurgood Marshall, chief counsel for the NAACP. *CORBIS/Bettmann*

"great dissenter," he stood firmly for the rights of poor people and minorities and against the death penalty even as the Court grew more conservative in the 1980s. Marshall continued to fight for educational equality, writing a 63-page dissent in *San Antonio School District* v. *Rodriguez*, a 1973 case in which the majority decided that unequal funding of urban and suburban school districts, based on their disparate tax bases, was constitutional. Marshall disagreed, asserting "the right of every American to an equal start in life."

Gruff and sometimes intimidating from the bench, Marshall was known in private life as a warm man and a brilliant storyteller. When he announced his retirement in 1991, even his most conservative colleagues expressed their respect and affection for the 83-year-old justice. After Marshall's death in 1993, Paul Gewirtz, his former law clerk and a professor at Yale Law School, wrote in remembrance that Marshall, growing up among discrimination, segregation, and racist violence, "had the capacity to imagine a radically different world... the strength to sustain that image in the mind's eye and the heart's longing, and the courage and ability to make that imagined world real." Marshall himself, when asked by a reporter how he wished to be remembered, was characteristically plainspoken, saying, "He did the best he could with what he had."

Kate Tuttle

See Also
Baltimore, Maryland; Houston, Charles Hamilton; Lincoln University (Pennsylvania); NAACP Legal Defense and Educational Fund.

Latin America and the Caribbean

Marson, Una M.

(b. February 6, 1905, Sharon Village, Jamaica; d. May 6, 1965, Kingston, Jamaica), Jamaican writer and activist.

In England, her adopted home for almost 20 years, Una Marson is remembered as "Britain's first black feminist." She was born in a rural village in Jamaica in 1905, the daughter of a pastor. She received a scholarship to the prestigious Hampton School, a girls' boarding school, and after graduation moved to Kingston, where she supported herself as a social worker and began publishing poetry and plays.

In 1928 Marson founded and edited the magazine the *Cosmopolitan,* an early feminist publication that championed Jamaican women. It soon folded but her writings continued to receive notice; in 1930 she received the Institute of Jamaica's Musgrave Medal for *Tropic Reveries,* her first collection of poetry. In 1932 she became one of the first of many twentieth-century Caribbean writers who emigrated to London, seeking wider horizons.

Marson continued publishing her plays and poetry in England. She also worked as secretary to the League of Coloured Peoples and as private secretary to exiled Ethiopian emperor Haile Selassie I, and founded the influential radio show *Caribbean Voices* of the British Broadcasting Corporation (BBC). At the same time she became involved with many British women's organizations, including the Women's Freedom League, the Women's Peace Crusade, and the Women's International Alliance. Marson was one of the first people in Britain's women's movement to address the particular concerns of women of African descent.

In 1936 Marson returned to Jamaica for two years and while there helped found *Public Opinion,* an influential newspaper that was associated with the Jamaican nationalist movement. After returning to England in 1938 for another nine years, she finally went back to Kingston in 1947, where she continued to work as a publisher, journalist, and social activist until her death in 1965.

Lisa Clayton Robinson

North America

Martha and the Vandellas,

rhythm and blues group of female vocalists who recorded hits for Motown Records throughout the 1960s.

Martha Reeves (b. July 18, 1941, Alabama) was working as a secretary for the Hitsville Studio of Motown Records in Detroit, Michigan when singer Mary Wells failed to show for a recording session. Reeves, who had sung in area talent shows with a group of friends, the Del-Phis, summoned the other members of the group; they filled in at the scheduled recording of "There He Is (At My Door)." In addition to Reeves, Roselind Ashford, Annette Sterling, and Gloria Williams sang at this formative session, although Williams left the group after the single flopped. The three remaining women formed the group called Martha and the Vandellas. They backed other Motown acts (most notably Marvin Gaye) and began recording their own material.

Martha and the Vandellas first achieved pop-chart success in 1963 with the release of "Come and Get These Memories." Thereafter Reeves and Ashford, along with Betty Kelly, who had replaced Annette Sterling, inched their way up the charts with each successive hit, a climb that culminated in 1964 with "Dancing in the Street." This upbeat song reached number two of the Top 40, and it took on political significance as an anthem for the decade's urban race riots. Earlier minor hits included "Heat Wave" and "Quick Sand" (both 1963).

In the late 1960s the group underwent further changes in its roster, but when Reeves became ill, the Vandellas disbanded in 1968. They reunited in 1970 and worked together until Reeves launched a solo career around 1972. Motown had moved to Los Angeles, California, and Reeves, who had stayed behind in Detroit, had little luck on her own. She recorded and performed throughout the 1980s, but the peak of her career seemed to be over.

The Vandellas reunited in 1989 and performed and recorded in the 1990s. Reeves published an autobiography, *Dancing in the Streets* (1994), which describes the Motown milieu in which she began her career.

Eric Bennett

See Also
Los Angeles, California; Motown.

Latin America and the Caribbean

Martí, José

(b. January 28, 1853, Havana, Cuba; d. May 19, 1895, Cuba), poet, journalist, political activist, diplomat, writer of fiction, essayist, art and literary critic, and playwright.

José Martí is one of the major figures of nineteenth-century Latin America. He is regarded by Cubans across the political spectrum as the father of Cuba's independence. His collected works span some 28 volumes and include exquisite poetry, insightful essays on Walt Whitman and Ralph Waldo Emerson, impassioned political analysis, and a remarkable book of children's literature, *La Edad de Oro* (1889).

While still an adolescent, Martí embraced the cause of Cuban independence, founding the newspaper *La Patria Libre* in 1869. He was imprisoned and then banished for writing a letter denouncing a Spanish fellow student. After 1871 Martí spent a great deal of his life outside Cuba (Mexico, Guatemala, Spain) and most of the years between 1881 and 1895 in New York, where he dedicated himself to the Cuban independence movement as a brilliant orator, journalist, fundraiser, and political leader. He often wrote for the *New York Herald,* and his essays and articles on the United States dealt with issues of racism, social inequality, United States imperial aims in Latin America, American culture, and even Chinese funerals.

In 1892, while still in New York, Martí founded the Cuban Revolutionary Party (PRC) to lead the struggle for Cuban independence. In creating the PRC, he envisioned a vehicle for establishing a civilian republican regime on the island. In 1895 he returned to Cuba to fight in the war against Spain and died in a minor skirmish that year (*see* Spanish-Cuban-American War).

Martí was one of the central figures of the modernist movement in poetry. His *Ismaelillo* (1882) is considered the first modernist book of poems and was followed by the *Versos sencillos* (1891), a seminal work. His other poetry, known as *Versos libres, Flores del*

Poet, essayist, and political activist José Martí (1853-1895) is often referred to as the father of Cuban independence. *Oronoz*

destierro, and *Versos varios*, was published posthumously. As a journalist, Martí's work is unparalleled, reflecting a heartfelt mix of poetic imagery, insightful analysis, dense allusions, and exquisite description.

Martí's writings on race are numerous and varied. He wrote about racism against indigenous peoples, blacks, Chinese, and Italians. In general, these works deal with racism in Latin America or Cuba and in the United States. In the latter essays, particularly "Los indios en los EEUU" and "El problema negro," Martí wrote convincingly about the pervasive racism in the United States after the abolition of slavery.

Few denunciations of racism have been written with the passion, intelligence, poetry, and eloquence shown by Martí. He not only saw racism as destructive and degrading but also as a divisive element in society. Having lived through the Ten Years' War (1868-1878), a failed attempt to win independence from Spain, he was aware of how the lack of unity had damaged the Cuban independence cause. This concern stayed with him as he organized, fought, and died in the second war for independence, the Spanish-Cuban-American War (1895-1898). In essays such as "Nuestra América," and even more so in "Mi raza," Martí energetically addressed racial tensions and divisions. In the latter essay he wrote: "A man is more than being white, more than a mulatto, more than black. A Cuban is more than being white or mulatto or black. On the battlefields, dying for Cuba, both black and white souls have ascended to the heavens." The essay ends as follows: "In Cuba there is great nobility of character, in blacks and whites."

Three criticisms can be made of Martí's views on race: first, that they were too abstract. Martí's views still owe a huge debt to the Enlightenment, and his view of race was expressed from the standpoint of humanity, an abstract universal concept. Second, this abstract universalism carried over into his nationalism. His appeals to Cuban national unity made him see racial perspectives as divisive and distracting from the great common goal of achieving Cuban independence. This is understandable, given the historical circumstances within which he operated. Third, as a result of these two appeals, to humanity and nationhood, the historical specificity of blacks in Cuba is not addressed, which some critics have called a discourse of negation or denial. As Enrique Patterson has pointed out, in 1895 Afro-Cubans fought as humans and as Cubans, but as soon as the war was over they were treated again as blacks.

Still, Martí's thoughts on blacks and racism in general formed an essential part of Cuban discourse on race. His appeal to humanity and nationhood, despite his attempt to transcend difference and the lack of specificity in his critiques, is nonetheless a key component in understanding the history of civil and human rights of the Afro-Cuban population of the island.

Alan West

See Also
New York, New York.

Latin America and the Caribbean

Martínez, Gregorio

(b. March 12, 1942, Nazca, Peru), important Peruvian writer, university professor, and journalist of African and indigenous descent (*see* Literature, Black, in Spanish America).

Gregorio Martínez grew up in Nazca, a coastal region of Peru that has profound African roots. His intellectual development was enriched by his African and indigenous heritage, his education at the Universidad de San Marcos in Lima, Peru, and his experience as a journalist. His culture and personal experiences constitute the main source of his fiction and literary language and have forcefully shaped his idea about the role of writing in developing societies. He was once quoted as saying, "I see literature as a mirror"; for Martínez writing is a means to reveal the economic and political conditions of Afro-Peruvians and other oppressed social groups in Peru.

Martínez's first novel and his most important work to date, *Canto de sirena* (1977, Mermaid's Song), is based on the personal testimony of Candelario Navarro, an elderly Afro-Peruvian man. The work, more than a biography of Navarro, manages to capture the cultural and historical trajectory of Afro-Peruvians. The narrative quickly became an important literary piece in South American literature, was translated into French and Italian, and was adapted to film.

Martínez also published a collection of short stories titled *Tierra de caléndula* (1975, Land of Calendula); an anthology of stories and reflections based on Afro-Peruvian and indigenous mythology called *La gloria del Piturrín y otros embrujos de amor* (1986, Piturrin's Glory and Other Bewitchments of Love); and *Crónica de músicos y diablos* (1991, Chronicle of Musicians and Devils), a novel that continues the development of Négritude in his fiction. He also wrote scripts for short films, including *Dale golpe a ese cajón* (1979, Play That Rhythmical Box), about the Afro-Peruvian percussion instrument; *Cómo matar al lobo* (1983, How to Kill the Wolf); and *Candico* (1985).

Carlos L. Orihuela

Latin America and the Caribbean

Martinique,

former French colony and present-day overseas department of France in the Caribbean, situated among the Lesser Antilles halfway between Puerto Rico and Trinidad, with St. Lucia directly to the south and Dominica directly to the north.

At the time of French colonization in the mid-1600s, Martinique's inhabitants were Indians who are known as the Carib, who had migrated into the Caribbean from South America and had displaced the Arawak, probably the earliest inhabitants of Martinique. The Carib first came into contact with Europeans when Christopher Columbus landed on Martinique on June 15, 1502, during his fourth voyage to the Americas. Unclaimed by Spain, Martinique and the surrounding islands attracted the attention of the French in the seventeenth century. In 1635 an expedition led by Pierre d'Esnambuc overcame Carib resistance and established a French foothold at Saint-Pierre. (This city became and was to remain the capital of Martinique until the volcanic eruption of Mount Pelée in 1902 destroyed the city, killing 30,000 of its inhabitants.) Following the success of d'Esnambuc's mission, France claimed Martinique as a colonial possession. Except for the periods 1762-1763, 1793-1802, and 1809-1815, when the British disputed and temporarily wrested ownership of the island from the French, the island has remained under French control.

Unlike other French colonies in Africa and Southeast Asia, which had sizable indigenous populations, Martinique's Caribs were largely decimated by disease following Columbus's arrival. Thus the island's sparse inhabitation necessitated an imported population. Initially, the French tried to populate the island with settlers from France. But the French who went to Martinique rarely found the opportunity for economic wealth that was promised them, and left within a few years of arriving. Those who stayed were the plantation owners who had managed to claim the best lands. These colonizers soon found themselves in a bind, since they could not attract field workers from overseas. The importation of slaves would serve as the solution to the colonizers' problems, at least initially. In 1640, during the reign of Louis XIII and Cardinal Richelieu in France, slaves were brought to Martinique for the first time (principally from SENEGAL) to work in the SUGAR cane fields. Very quickly the numbers of slaves brought from Africa to the Caribbean soared. It is estimated that from 1722 to 1788, the years during which the TRANSATLANTIC SLAVE TRADE was most active, some 600,000 slaves were forcibly displaced to the Caribbean on French ships. However, in spite of the large numbers of slaves arriving in Martinique from Africa, their numbers on the island increased slowly. This was the result of an astonishingly high mortality rate. Because of the hazardous working conditions on the plantations and regular outbreaks of yellow fever and smallpox, many slaves died before reaching age 40.

Still, the slave population did grow, especially in relation to the number of colonizers. Whereas in 1789 there were 12,000 whites, 65,000 slaves, and 5000 free men of color in Martinique, in 1848 there were only 9000 whites to 73,000 slaves and 39,000 free men of color. In May of that year, slaves revolted in Martinique. The revolt was spurred not only by the population imbalance but by certain external factors: (1) the impoverishment of sugar plantation owners (known as *békés*), due to the increased production of sugar beets in Europe; (2) the abolition of slavery in the neighboring English colonies in August 1834; and (3) the antislavery activism of VICTOR SCHOELCHER in Martinique. Slavery was officially abolished in the French colonies one month later (*see* ABOLITION AND EMANCIPATION IN LATIN AMERICA AND THE CARIBBEAN). This is considered a critical moment in the history of the island. The historian Armand Nicolas has referred to the events of May 1848 as the "birth of the Martinican people," since those who constituted the overwhelming majority of the island's population assumed, for the first time, an active role in Martinique's political destiny.

In the years following the abolition of slavery, the békés were forced to make the transition from a slave economy to a capitalist one. Still eager to use inexpensive labor, they kept many of their former slaves on the plantation by offering them a modest wage and even more modest housing. They also imported indentured labor from abroad: from 1852 to 1884, 9080 Africans (principally from the Congo), 25,509 East Indians, and approximately 1000 Chinese workers were brought to Martinique. This last wave of laborers, along with the more recent arrival of immigrants from Syria and Lebanon, brought to Martinique the ethnic and cultural diversity that the CRÉOLITÉ movement celebrates today. As a result of the new arrivals, the plantation system remained in existence into the twentieth century and can be seen in the film version of Joseph Zobel's novel *La Rue cases-nègres* (1983, Sugar Cane Alley), which depicts working conditions not that different from those in the days of slavery. But even the importation of indentured laborers could not keep the plantation system intact indefinitely. Because of competition from the sugar beet industry in Europe and exports of rum and bananas, supplemental income declined and some békés were forced to give up their plantations. Moreover, increasing numbers of former slaves and their descendants abandoned the harsh life of the plantations for the cities and mostly for the new capital, Fort-de-France. It is here, in the late nineteenth century, that a mulatto bourgeoisie (the children of the mixed-race unions that had taken place on the plantation since the seventeenth century) and a black underclass began to coalesce.

The twentieth century has witnessed dramatic changes in Martinique. Politics, once the exclusive domain of békés, opened up to the descendants of slaves. In 1945 AIMÉ CÉSAIRE, the black poet, politician, and intellectual, ran for the position of Martinican deputy to France's parliament. In a surprising upset he won, and Césaire has been a force in Martinican politics ever since, both as deputy and as mayor of Fort-de-France. He helped stimulate Martinique's cultural renewal with the publication of *Cahier d'un retour au pays natal* in 1939. Although

TOP: The market bustles in Fort-de-France, the capital of Martinique. *Robert Fried/D. Donne Bryant Stock Photo*

ABOVE: In the fishing village of Marin, Martinique, citizens pull a boat ashore. *Robert Fried/D. Donne Bryant Stock Photo*

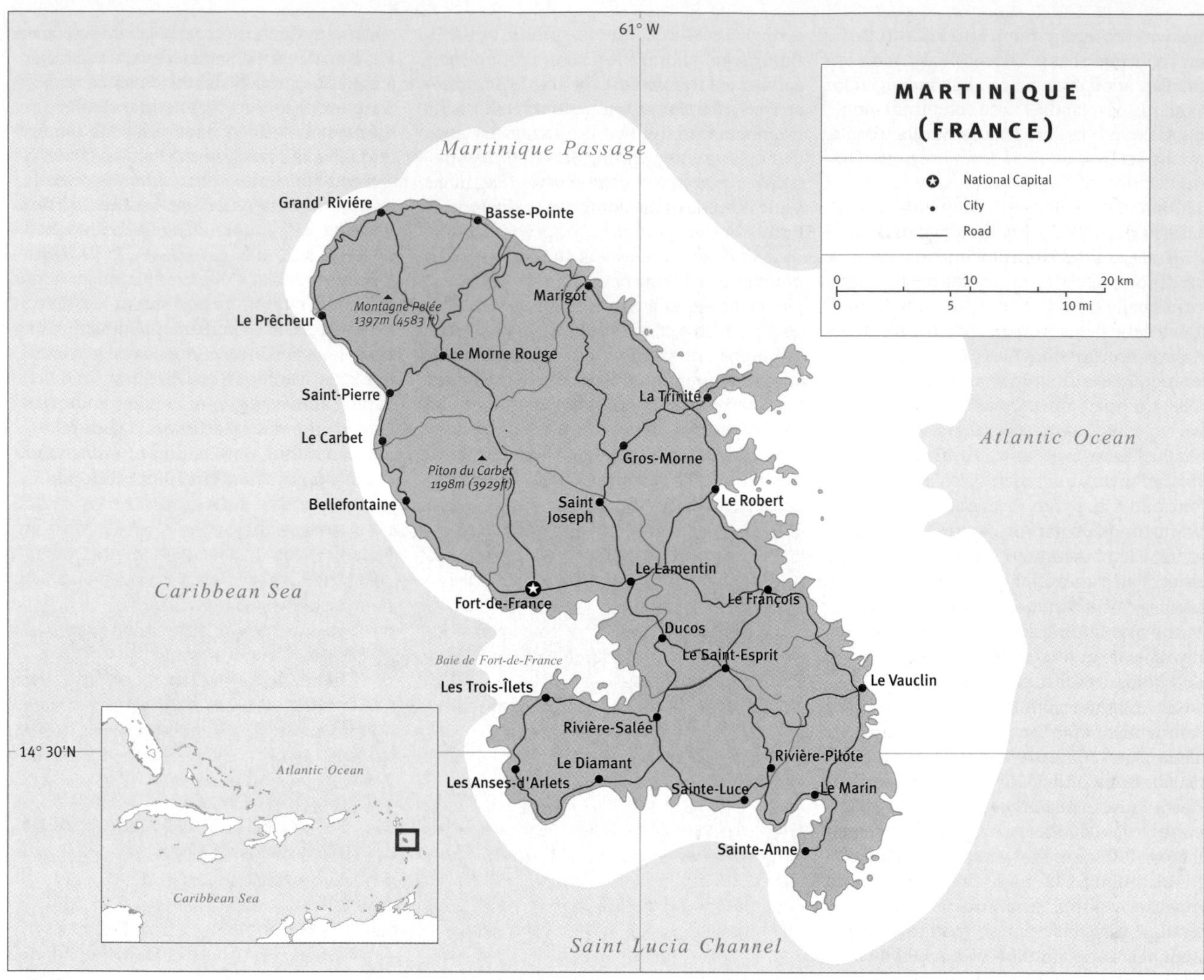

Césaire sought to promote the cultural singularity of the Caribbean and its inhabitants in his poetry and in the Négritude ideology he helped create and disseminate, his politics have always been assimilationist. Césaire supported Martinque's change in status on March 19, 1946, to French overseas department, effectively making the island an integral part of France.

Since that time, Césaire has never called for Martinique's independence from France. For this reason, he has come under fire from a younger generation of intellectuals – most notably Edouard Glissant and Raphaël Confiant – who argue that the descendants of slaves and indentured laborers in Martinique will never have a culture of their own until all official ties with France are severed. But the independence forces have had trouble convincing a populace that recognizes the extent to which it is dependent on France. Today most of Martinique's trade is with the French mainland, and Martinique receives massive subsidies from France. But as with all French departments, whether in the Caribbean or on the mainland, Martinique has gained a degree of autonomy through the decentralization of the French political system that took place in the 1980s. It remains to be seen, though, if these changes will suffice to keep the forces of independence at bay on an island whose inhabitants generally consider themselves to be more Caribbean than French.

Richard Watts

See Also

France; Zobel, Joseph; Garifuna; Trinidad and Tobago.

North America

Martin, Sallie

(b. November 20, 1886; d. June 8, 1988, Pittsfield, Ga.), gospel singer who was an influential proponent of gospel music throughout the twentieth century.

After leaving the eighth grade, Sallie Martin moved to Atlanta, Georgia, and joined the Fire Baptized Holiness Church in 1916, where she learned to sing in the spontaneous and spirited manner of the church's sanctified folk. In 1932 she met Thomas A. Dorsey, the "Father of Gospel Music," at Ebenezer Baptist Church. This meeting spawned an eight-year business relationship, during which Martin traveled the country singing and promoting Dorsey's songs as well as organizing gospel choruses. Together they founded the Gospel Singers Convention, later known as the National Convention of Gospel Choirs and Choruses. Martin and Dorsey severed their relationship in 1940, after which Martin went on to form her own singing groups and publishing company.

For a brief period she teamed with Roberta Martin to form the Martin and Martin Gospel Singers. After that she created the Sallie Martin Singers, one of the first all-female gospel groups. Ruth Jones, later known as Dinah Washington, sang and played piano for the group. Martin toured with the group throughout the 1940s until the mid-1950s to promote the songs of the Martin and Morris Publishing Company, which she co-owned with songwriter Kenneth Morris.

"Just a Closer Walk with Thee" was their most successful song, helping Martin and Morris to become the largest African American-owned gospel publishing company. Martin remained a pillar in the gospel community for over 60 years, always stubbornly representing the old-time gospel music in the face of many new trends. Her raw and rough style of singing influenced performers such as Willie Mae Ford

Smith, Alex Bradford, J. Earl Hines, and Clara Ward.

See Also

Dorsey, Thomas Andrew; Gospel Music.

Africa

Masekela, Hugh Ramopolo

(b. April 4, 1931, Witbank, South Africa), noted South African trumpeter.

Born in a coal-mining town near Johannesburg, trumpet player Hugh Ramopolo Masekela is one of Africa's most influential contemporary jazz musicians. His father was a health inspector and sculptor. Masekela attended mission schools. Introduced to the trumpet by antiapartheid activist Father Trevor Huddleston, a British Anglican priest, Masekela was soon caught up by the musical innovation sweeping South Africa in the 1950s. By mixing American jazz with traditional African rhythms and melodies, he became one of the leaders in creating a new cosmopolitan style. He played with the Father Huddleston Band, the Jazz Dazzlers, and a number of prominent musicians, including pianist Dollar Brand, now known as Abdullah Ibrahim.

By the 1960s South African jazz had become intertwined with the struggle against apartheid. Masekela went to London, where he attended the Guildhall School of Music, and then traveled to New York City, where he attended the Manhattan School of Music from 1960 to 1964. From 1964 to 1966 he was married to another South African musical exile, the legendary singer Miriam Makeba. In 1968 Masekela, then living in New York City, recorded his first commercial hit, "Grazing in the Grass." In 1987, along with the band Ladysmith Black Mambazo, he joined Paul Simon's Graceland tour, which highlighted South African music.

In the early 1990s Masekela returned to a postapartheid South Africa and began urging young South Africans to rediscover their musical roots. He was appointed codirector of the State Theatre in Pretoria in 1995. A year later he joined a gala performance in London before Queen Elizabeth II. He also bought a jazz nightclub, J & B Junction, in the trendy Johannesburg suburb of Yeoville.

David P. Johnson, Jr.

See Also

Johannesburg, South Africa; Makeba, Miriam Zenzi; Pretoria, South Africa; South Africa; New York, New York.

Africa

Maseru, Lesotho, capital of Lesotho.

Maseru grew from settlements established by the Basuto during the nineteenth century under the reign of Moshoeshoe. The city was officially founded in 1869, after the British declared Basutoland a protectorate (*see* Colonial Rule) and established their administrative capital on the top of Griffith Hill, in the center of present-day Maseru. Initially the capital consisted of nothing more than the house of the governor's agent, James Henry Bowker.

Maseru remained the administrative capital after Basutoland became a British colony in 1884. In 1905 the Bloemfontein-Natal railway reached the town, stimulating the export of agricultural produce and the recruitment of labor to work in the gold and diamond mines of Transvaal and Witwatersrand. At the time 960 people lived in Maseru. During this period Anglican and French Protestant missionaries built a number of churches and schools, such as Saint James's Church and Saint Catherine's, a teacher training school. In 1913 legislation prohibiting tenant farming in South Africa sparked a wave of migration of rural Basotho to the capital in search of work. By the 1920s the population had grown enough to warrant the publication of two weeklies.

Like many other colonial cities in southern Africa, Maseru maintained segregation through a variety of laws. By the 1950s a shantytown known as the "Dark City," because of its lack of street lights, had developed on the outskirts of Maseru. Residents referred to the southwest portion of town, where the houses were whitewashed, as the "White City." But both of these nicknames reflected the racial segregation of residential areas.

Maseru became the capital and the only major urban center of independent Lesotho in 1966, with a population of approximately 15,000. Following independence, there was a rapid influx of people to Lesotho who were looking for wage labor. By 1993 the city's population had grown to 180,000. The economy continues to center on the processing and export of livestock and agricultural products, and many of the city's residents depend on the remittances of migrant laborers who are working in South Africa.

See Also

Gold Trade; Christianity: Missionaries in Africa.

Africa

Masire, Quett Ketumile Joni

(b. July 23, 1925, Kanye, Botswana), president of Botswana (1980-).

Quett Ketumile Joni Masire was born in Kanye in southeastern Botswana, the eldest son of a minor headman of the Bangwaketse ethnic group. He spent his youth as a herdsboy, attending local schools until completing a teaching certificate in South Africa in 1949. He worked as a teacher, administrator, and newspaper correspondent. At that time Botswana was a British protectorate known as Bechuanaland. In 1958 Masire was elected to the Bangwaketse Tribal Council. In 1961 he won the Kanye South seat on Bechuanaland's newly formed Legislative Council.

In January 1962, with Seretse Khama, he cofounded the Botswana Democratic Party (BDP), a moderate party supported by many whites, chiefs, and rural people, and served as the party's secretary-general and publications editor. He was appointed deputy prime minister in March 1965 and, after taking an active part in Botswanan independence negotiations, became vice president and minister of finance under President Khama after independence in 1966.

Much of Botswana's economic stability has been attributed to Masire's role as minister of development planning from 1967 to 1980, when he oversaw government investment in mining, with distribution of profits into other sectors of the economy. Following the death of Khama in July 1980, the National Assembly appointed Masire president. Known primarily for his astute economic practices, Masire has also demonstrated sound foreign policy with neighboring powers, especially South Africa. Masire was reelected in 1984, 1989, and 1994. Recent challenges to his government have included a recession, growing unemployment, and student unrest.

North America

Mason, Biddy Bridget

(b. August 15, 1818, Hancock, Miss.; d. January 15, 1891, Los Angeles, Calif.), African American philanthropist, entrepreneur, and founder of the oldest church in Los Angeles.

Born into slavery to unknown parents and raised on John Smithson's plantation in Hancock, Mississippi, Biddy Mason was given by her owners as a wedding gift in 1836 to Robert Marion Smith and Rebecca Crosby Smith. After converting to Mormonism in 1847, Smith's family and their slaves made the 2000-mile trek to Utah. Traveling with her three daughters, Ella, Ann, and Harriet, who were probably fathered by her owner, Mason acted as midwife, nurse, and caretaker for the caravan. After four years in Salt Lake City, Smith took the group to a new Mormon settlement in San Bernardino, California. Smith had apparently forgotten that California was declared a free state in 1850, and under this law Mason and her family were manumitted on January 1, 1856.

Now free, Mason moved to Los Angeles, where she worked as a nurse. By 1866 she had saved enough money to purchase property in downtown Los Angeles at 331 Spring Street. This became a base for her philanthropic work and a haven where the poor and homeless could find safety and food. Mason soon purchased a commercial building, which she leased to tenants from whom she earned a substantial income.

With this money she helped found the First African Methodist Episcopal Church, now the oldest church in Los Angeles. There Mason operated a nursery and food pantry. She was the first black female property owner and philanthropist in Los Angeles.

At the time of her death in 1891 Mason was buried in an unmarked grave. In 1988 a tombstone was erected by Mayor Tom Bradley of Los Angeles. In 1989, November 16 was declared Biddy Mason Day, and a large timeline depicting the highlights of Biddy Mason's life was dedicated on the wall of the Spring Center in Los Angeles.

See Also

Bradley, Thomas (Tom); Los Angeles, California; Mormons.

North America

Mason, Charles Harrison

(b. September 9, 1866, near Bartlett, Tennessee; d. November 28, 1961, Detroit, Michigan), African American religious leader and founder of the Church of God in Christ, the largest black Pentecostal denomination.

Charles Mason was born to Jerry and Eliza Mason, former slaves who were poor tenant farmers in Shelby County, Tennessee. In 1879 the family moved to a plantation in Plummersville, Arkansas. Mason was converted to evangelical Christianity as a child, after a seemingly miraculous recovery from yellow fever, which killed his father. He was baptized by his brother, a Baptist preacher. After reading Amanda Smith, a black evangelist, Mason believed himself sanctified, or free from sin, which he saw as a necessary act of divine grace following conversion.

Along with Charles P. Jones, Mason began to preach the doctrines associated with the controversial Holiness Movement. Both were expelled from the Baptist Church for heresy. Mason attended Arkansas Bible College for three months in 1882 but was educated more by the spirituality of former slaves. In 1895 Mason and Jones founded the Church of Christ in an abandoned cotton gin building in Mississippi. They were attacked by racist whites, but publicity surrounding the attack brought new members to the fledgling church. In 1897 Mason and Jones changed the name to the Church of God in Christ (COGIC), a title Mason claimed was revealed to him by God on the street in Little Rock, Arkansas.

In 1907 Mason traveled from Memphis to Los Angeles to investigate the Azusa Street Revival, a religious phenomenon in which participants experienced glossolalia, or speaking in tongues, and which marked the beginning of the worldwide Pentecostal movement. The revival was presided over by William J. Seymour, an African American, but the ecstatic outpouring described as "Spirit baptism" fell upon whites as well as blacks. Mason returned home a believing Pentecostal but failed to convince Jones, who left to found the Church of Christ (Holiness) U.S.A.

Pentecostalism spread rapidly around the world, appealing especially to the poor and oppressed and gaining countless members internationally. The early movement in the United States continued the interracialism of Azusa Street. Many white Pentecostal ministers came to Mason for ordination, because COGIC was already legally incorporated. By 1914 segregation had been reestablished through white initiative, and white Pentecostals went their separate way. COGIC flourished under Mason's charismatic leadership. Today it has nearly 5 million adherents, and among African American churches is second in size only to the Baptists.

Richard Newman

See Also

Baptists; Los Angeles, California; Pentecostalism; Seymour, William Joseph.

Africa

Massa (also known as Banana and Masa), ethnic group of West Africa.

The Massa primarily inhabit southern Chad and northern Cameroon. They speak a Niger-Congo language but some ethnologists believe that they are Nilotic in origin. Approximately 200,000 people consider themselves Massa.

See Also

Languages, African: An Overview.

Massachusetts Fifty-fourth Colored Infantry. Please see Fifty-fourth Regiment of Massachusetts Volunteer Infantry

Africa

Massawa, Eritrea, major Red Sea port and the second largest city of Eritrea.

Massawa's varied Arab, Turkish, and Italian architecture reflects the Horn of Africa's long history of trade and foreign occupation. Heavily damaged during Eritrea's roughly 30-year war for independence, which ended in 1993, the city soon began rebuilding its port and industries.

Earliest references to the fishing village of Massawa date to the ninth century C.E. By the eleventh century Massawa was a major port, linked to interior kingdoms by caravan routes. It was also a center of Islamic scholarship and law. The sultan of the nearby Dahlak Islands governed Massawa through the fourteenth century. By the sixteenth century both the Portuguese and the Ottoman Turks were seeking control of the strategically located port; the Turks won, occupying Massawa in 1557 and exercising at least nominal control until the early nineteenth century. The Egyptians occupied Massawa from 1813 to 1823, while Britain and France vied for influence as well.

In 1885 Italian troops occupied the city. The colonial capital of Eritrea was located in Massawa until 1900, when it was changed to Asmara. Most of Massawa was destroyed by an earthquake in 1921, but the Italians rebuilt it into one of the biggest naval facilities on Africa's eastern shoreline by World War II. After the British took over Massawa late in the war, much of the port's infrastructure was dismantled and sold.

During the Eritrean war for independence from Ethiopia during the 1980s and early 1990s, Massawa was the site of major battles. It was heavily bombed in 1990. Both during and after the war, food arrived in Massawa to provide famine relief. Since independence in 1993, Massawa's economy has rebounded, and the Eritrean government is hoping that the city's historic architecture and Red Sea location will draw tourists. By the late 1990s Massawa had a population of roughly 25,000.

David P. Johnson, Jr.

See Also

Asmara, Eritrea; Egypt.

Africa

Matakam, ethnic group of West Africa.

The Matakam primarily inhabit northern Cameroon and northeastern Nigeria. They speak an Afro-Asiatic language in the Chadic group. Approximately 200,000 people consider themselves Matakam.

See Also

Languages, African: An Overview.

Latin America and the Caribbean

Matanzas, Cuba, capital of Matanzas province on Matanzas Bay, near Havana.

Matanzas province was the center of the Cuban sugar industry during the nineteenth century. By the 1820s slaves imported from West Africa to work on rural sugar plantations constituted a majority of the province's population. By growing their own crops or hiring out their services, some slaves saved enough money to purchase their own freedom. Others abandoned plantations and formed escaped slave communities called *palenques* (*see* Maroonage in the Americas), such as those reported during the first half of the nineteenth century along the northern coast, interior mountains, and southern swamplands of the province. Slaves in Matanzas also expressed their desire for freedom by revolting in 1825, 1835, and 1843 (*see*

Slave Rebellions in Latin America and the Caribbean).

While much of the enslaved population lived in a rural setting, most of the free black and mulatto population lived in the city of Matanzas during the nineteenth century. At this time most free black females worked as laundresses and seamstresses and most free black males worked as masons, tailors, and day laborers, among other vocations. Many of them were members of *cabildos de nación*, all-black mutual aid societies organized according to African ethnic origins. Some free Cubans of color, such as the mulatto poet Gabriel de la Concepción Valdés, distinguished themselves on the thriving artistic scene in Matanzas.

The city's Afro-Cuban population gradually increased after passage of the Moret Law in 1870, which freed the offspring of slave women born after 1868 as well as slaves reaching age 60, and the abolition of slavery in 1886, when many ex-slaves moved to urban centers in search of jobs and housing. Matanzas has a population of 123,843 (1993 estimate), most of which is of African descent. The city is home to the rumba dance ensembles Los Muñequitos de Matanzas and AfroCuba de Matanzas and continues to be, as it was in the nineteenth century, a major center of Afro-Cuban cultural activity.

Aaron Myers

See Also

Slavery in Latin America and the Caribbean; Cuba; Valdés, Gabriel de la Concepción ("Plácido"); Havana, Cuba.

Africa

Matengo, ethnic group of southeastern Africa.

The Matengo primarily inhabit Tanzania and Mozambique. They speak a Bantu language and are closely related to the Nyasa people. More than 200,000 people consider themselves Matengo.

See Also

Bantu: Dispersion and Settlement.

Latin America and the Caribbean

Mateo, Liborio (b. San Juan de la Maguana, Dominican Republic; d. June 27, 1922, Bánica, Dominican Republic), Afro-Dominican founder of a dissident religious movement known as *liborismo.*

Liborio Mateo established a religious community in San Juan de la Maguana, in the southern Dominican Republic, shortly after a storm devastated the area in 1908. He and many of his followers were Afro-Dominicans. While not directly confronting authorities with protest or destruction of property, they established a community that functioned autonomously, both politically and economically. Beginning in 1910, when Mateo was ordered arrested (but managed to escape), authorities, urged by the Roman Catholic Church, stepped up efforts to crack down on the liborismo movement. Official hostility was motivated in large part by distrust of the group's political and cultural separateness and rumors of alleged immoral activities connected to its religious practices. It was only when confronted with this government repression that the group became armed in self-defense. With the fall of President Ramón Cáceres (1906-1911), the community's relations with the government improved. In fact, the government of President Eladio Victoria solicited Mateo's support in containing a rebellion in the southern part of the country. Following the United States occupation of the island (1916-1924), authorities again sought to crush the movement, which retreated into hiding in a mountain range. In 1922 the National Police defeated the movement in a bloody confrontation that left many dead, including Mateo.

Liborismo reflected one response by poor Afro-Dominicans to their economic and political marginalization. Half a century later, a movement emerged in Palma Sola, inspired by liborismo, which again met with harsh government repression.

Mayda Grano de Oro

Africa

Matsoua, André

(b. January 17, 1899, Mandzala-Kinkala, Moyen-Congo; d. January 13, 1942, Brazzaville, Moyen-Congo), founder of a self-help organization that developed into a messianic cult opposing French colonialism.

André Matsoua was a renowned civil servant, soldier, and labor organizer whose work continued even after his death. As a youth he studied to become a priest but in 1919 decided to join the colonial customs service. He later traveled to France and joined the army, serving in North Africa during World War I. In 1926 he settled in Paris, where he became involved in labor-union organizing and founded Amicale, a self-help organization. Seeking recruits and financial contributions, the movement spread to the French Moyen-Congo, where the colonial administration, upset by Matsoua's outspoken opposition to the discriminatory *indigénant*, or indigenous, classification of many Congolese, arrested him in 1929.

Although Matsoua was by then a legal French citizen, an African "traditional" court in Brazzaville sentenced him to three years in prison and a decade in exile in Chad. Six years later he escaped, was soon caught, escaped again, and found his way to Paris. When World War II began, he entered the military and served until he was wounded. French officials arrested him in the hospital and repatriated him to Moyen-Congo. Convicted again, he was imprisoned for life but soon died. Many allege that he was murdered and was secretly buried by prison officials.

The followers of Amicale, many of them ethnic Lari, like Matsoua, refused to accept his death. He became a potent anti-French symbol and the posthumous leader of a messianic cult, nationalist in character and organization, not unlike Kimbangouism or Lassy Zepherin's N'Zambie-Bougie movement. Many Lari refused to pay taxes, participated in civil disobedience, and twice "elected" the dead Matsoua to the colonial legislative assembly. In the late 1950s Fulbert Youlou convinced many that he was Matsoua's rightful heir and was elected prime minister. Matsoua's legacy again played a role in the 1992 elections, when Bernard Kolelas appealed to Matsoua's followers.

Eric Young

See Also

Brazzaville, Republic of the Congo.

North America

Matthews, Victoria Earle

(b. May 27, 1861, Fort Valley, Ga.; d. March 10, 1907, Brooklyn, N.Y.), African American author, journalist, and social reformer.

Although she lived only to age 45, Victoria Earle Matthews left an important legacy to black women. Born a slave on a plantation in Georgia in 1861, she moved to New York City with her mother, Caroline Smith, an escaped slave who returned from the North to retrieve her family after the Civil War.

Matthews attended Grammar School 48 in New York but had to leave school and do domestic work to help support her family. She continued to educate herself, reading in the library of the family for whom she worked and attending lectures. Shortly after her marriage in 1879, she began writing essays and short stories for periodicals like *Waverly* and *New York Weekly*. Under the pen name Victoria Earle she wrote *Aunt Lindy*, a novel about a Georgia slave who kills her former master after the Civil War (1893). She also was a freelance writer for the *New York Times* and several black newspapers. While on the staff of *New York Age*, she compiled and edited a collection of Booker T. Washington's speeches, *Black Belt Diamonds: Gems from the Speeches, Addresses, and Talks of Booker T. Washington* (1898).

In 1892 Matthews helped antilynching crusader Ida Wells-Barnett organize women from large cities into women's clubs. Matthews founded her own organization, the Woman's Loyal Union of New York City and Brooklyn, bringing together teachers, journalists, businesswomen, and homemakers to work toward social and political goals.

At the first national conference of black women in 1895, Matthews gave an address titled "The Value of Race Literature" about preserving the contribution of blacks to culture. Conference members created the National Federation of Afro-American Women, and Matthews joined the board and wrote for its newspaper, *Woman's Era*. The federation grew quickly and merged with the National Colored Women's League to become the National Association of Colored Women in 1896. Matthews served as its national organizer from 1897 to 1899.

Matthews also served as the New York State organizer for the Northern Federation of Women's Clubs. Later that year she toured the South, investigating the condition of black women in the cities. After the death of her 16-year-old son, she further devoted her time to the welfare of women and children. In 1897 she created the White Rose Mission, a community center and shelter for young, inexperienced women from the South.

Matthews was an exceptional speaker. Inspired by the teachings of the Episcopal Church, she lectured on social responsibility, charity, and self-improvement. She was recognized for her speeches by the Society of Christian Endeavor in San Francisco, where she gave an address, "The Awakening of the Afro-American Woman," in 1897.

She expanded the White Rose Mission in 1905, creating the White Rose Travelers' Aid Society. Members watched the docks and rescued Southern women and children from Northerners who exploited them. Matthews helped organize similar societies along the coast from New York to Virginia. At the White Rose Home for Working Girls, she amassed a library of black literature and history that she used in her lectures and teachings. She died in March 1907 of tuberculosis.

See Also

Antilynching Movement; Press, Black, in the United States; Civil War, American; New York, New York; Washington, Booker Taliaferro; Wells-Barnett, Ida Bell.

Africa

Matumbi, ethnic group of Tanzania.

The Matumbi primarily inhabit east central Tanzania. They speak a Bantu language. Approximately 100,000 people consider themselves Matumbi.

See Also

Bantu: Dispersion and Settlement.

Africa

Mau Mau Rebellion, an anticolonial rebellion that took place predominantly among the Kikuyu ethnic group in British-ruled Kenya, ultimately accelerating the process of Kenyan independence.

Defendants hold identification numbers in a 1953 trial of those suspected of fighting in the anticolonial Mau Mau rebellion. At its height between 1952 and 1956, the rebellion claimed the lives of more than 12,000 Africans and 100 Europeans. The British colonial government hanged an estimated 1000 Africans convicted of participation. *CORBIS/Hulton-Deutsch Collection*

The British had used the term *Mau Mau* as early as 1947 to refer to the intermittent but escalating Kikuyu violence that was taking place in both rural and urban areas of colonial Kenya. Later it came to describe the anticolonial guerrilla movement that launched a four-year revolt beginning in 1952. The movement's grievances centered on colonial land policies, which confiscated prime farmland for white settlers while relegating Africans to overcrowded "tribal reserves." Although the origins of the term *Mau Mau* are still debated, in the Gikuyu language it means "greedy eating." Many participants in the rebellion rejected the label, instead favoring such names as Kiama Kia Muingi (the Community's Party), Muhimu (Swahili for "important"), the African Government, and the Kenya Land Freedom Army.

Although Mau Mau's leaders and most of its members were ethnic Kikuyu, the movement also attracted small numbers of supporters from other ethnic groups. Few disagree with the basic facts surrounding the rebellion, but interpretation remains contentious, suggesting that Mau Mau was a diffuse movement with objectives that varied among members. What is certain is that the British reaction to Mau Mau was severe and bloody but largely futile, because afterward Great Britain only hastened its plans for decolonization.

Despite the fact that the movement sought to end British rule in Kenya, most of the violence occurred between Mau Mau members and Africans who they believed had cooperated treasonously with the British. In 1950 the British banned Mau Mau activities, particularly the secret oath-taking that committed members to oppose the colonial government. In October 1952, however, the pro-British senior chief Waruhiu was assassinated, an act the colonial government viewed as an escalation of Mau Mau violence, and officials responded with a counterinsurgency program to restore "law and order." British authorities immediately arrested some 150 nationalist political and labor leaders, including Jomo Kenyatta, who they believed was the movement's supreme leader and strategist, and declared a state of emergency. By mid-November more than 8000 Africans had been arrested and sent to detention camps, a number that climbed to more than 80,000 before the rebellion's end.

The announcement of the state of emergency mobilized Mau Mau forces, which left the Kikuyu reserves en masse for the dense forests of the Aberdares Mountain range and Mount Kenya. The forests provided excellent cover, from which Mau Mau insurgents conducted nighttime hit-and-run raids on settlements of whites or Loyalist Kikuyus. Although Mau Mau forces totaled as many as 30,000, they were ill-equipped. Their arsenals consisted of small arms (pistols, shotguns, rifles, and machine guns stolen from the British or purchased illegally), *pangas* (African machetes), spears, and bows and arrows. With no outside support, they depended on noncombatant (mostly women) Kikuyus for supplies, arms, and ammunition. The British responded with regular army troops, engineers, artillery, naval forces, bombers, and jet fighters.

Great Britain began to turn the military tide of the rebellion with Operation Anvil in April 1954. Approximately 25,000 troops occupied Nairobi and screened the city's entire African population, detaining more than 15,000 Africans without charges or trial. After effectively eliminating organized resistance in the city, British troops drove 100,000 Kikuyus from the white highlands onto already overcrowded reserves, while at the same time driving Land Freedom Party members out of the reserves and into the forests. Many suspected Mau Mau members were beaten or killed outright.

By the end of the military phase of the rebellion in 1956 (the state of emergency was not lifted until 1960), Mau Mau and related events had claimed the lives of more than 12,000 Africans (approximately 1000 of whom the British hanged) and 100 Europeans. Though militarily defeated, Mau Mau had broken British resolve in Kenya and cost the government approximately £60 million. Furthermore, international criticism of its repressive tactics convinced Great Britain to accelerate its departure from Kenya rather than risk another conflict.

Debate continues over the significance of Mau Mau. Initially the British government described it as a movement by Africans who, unable to adapt to the social changes associated with modernization, reverted to their barbaric roots. This view held until the mid-1960s, when scholars declared Mau Mau a peasant liberation movement. Others cast it as a Kikuyu religious movement because of the secret membership oaths, while still others maintain that it was both a political and religious organization. Most agree that the rebellion was never as unified as the British believed, and that it was a "movement" only in the sense that the inequities of the colonial system inspired widespread resistance.

Robert Fay

SEE ALSO
Decolonization in Africa: An Interpretation; Swahili Language; Nairobi, Kenya.

Europe

Maurice, Saint (Saint Maurice d'Agaune) (d. 287 C.E.?), Christian martyr and saint.

According to Christian legend, Maurice, the first Christian saint to be explicitly represented as an African, was a *primicerius* (a high-ranking officer) in the Roman army whose legion was massacred by the Romans in the late third century for refusing to participate in a pagan ritual.

Maurice and his legion, all baptized Christians, were recruited for military service in Thebaid, an Egyptian province on the Upper Nile (near the present-day border between EGYPT and SUDAN). Thebaid, with its capital at Thebes, was the southernmost region of the Roman Empire, then ruled by co-emperors Diocletian (284-305) and Maximian (240-310).

In 287 Maximian, commander of the Roman army in Gaul, led his troops, which included Maurice's legion, in a military campaign against insurgents in Gaul. On the eve of battle, the army camped at Octodurum (in what is now Martigny, Switzerland), and Maximian ordered his soldiers to participate in a sacrifice to the Roman gods to ensure their success in battle. Maurice, refusing to betray his Christian convictions, moved his legion to a camp at Agaunum (now Saint-Maurice-en-Valais) to avoid participating in the ritual. Maurice and three other Theban officers – Exuperius, Innocent, and Candidus – refused Maximian's orders to return to Octodurum, and, in retaliation, the Roman emperor decimated the Theban legion, ordering every tenth soldier killed in an attempt to force the remaining legionnaires to take part in the sacrifice. When these soldiers continued to disobey, the legion was decimated a second time.

Sculptor Michael Helwig depicted Saint Maurice, patron saint of the Holy Roman Empire, in knight's armor with lance and shield, on an early eighteenth-century altarpiece in Germany. *Image of the Black Project*

In the first written account of the legend, recorded by Bishop Eucherius of Lyons between 443 and 450, Maurice, spokesman and leader of the Theban legion, is said to have offered Maximian this remonstrance: "We are your soldiers, but are also servants of the true God. We owe you military service and obedience; but we cannot renounce Him who is our Creator and Master, and also yours even though you reject him. In all things which are not against His law we most willingly obey you, as we have done hitherto.... We have taken an oath to God before we took one to you: you can place no confidence in our second oath if we violate the first.... We have arms in our hands, but we do not resist because we would rather die innocent than live by any sin."

At this Maximian ordered the entire legion – said to have numbered between 3000 and 6000 – put to death.

While Maurice's dignified words are widely thought to be the invention of Bishop Eucherius, and while the legend's death toll is thought to be exaggerated, the celebration of this version of the story helps to explain the popularity and importance of this much-revered saint in the European Christian tradition. From around 380 onward, Saint Maurice has been honored in religious societies with cultic zeal. As the patron saint of Savoy, Sardinia, and several towns, and as the protector of infantry soldiers, sword smiths, weavers, and dyers, he has inspired cathedrals, monuments, and religious art. In 962 Emperor Otto the Great, who was anointed in a cathedral devoted to Saint Maurice, nominated him patron saint of the Holy Roman Empire. His saint's day is September 22.

Though often described as "the first black saint," Saint Maurice was not represented as a black man until 1240, when construction (begun in 1211) was completed on the Cathedral of Magdeburg, which houses his relics and contains a life-size stone statue of him clad in chain mail and with dark skin and unambiguously African features. Before the sculpting of this figure, and for a long time afterward, there were no other comparably explicit representations of black saints.

Europeans had been in direct contact with sub-Saharan Africans since at least the twelfth century; contemporary religious literature describes Christians of African origin as "blacks," "aethiops," or "Moors." However, the stigma associated with Africans at that time led artists who rendered black biblical figures – such as the QUEEN OF SHEBA and the black king who followed the Star of Bethlehem to the birth site of Jesus – to shy away from representing them as Africans, instead depicting them either as white or as having swarthy complexions and white features.

Similarly, before 1240 Saint Maurice was depicted as a white man. Most medieval accounts of him did not confront the issue of his race, even though his land of origin was well known. It was not until 1160 that an account by a German cleric in Regensburg explicitly described Saint Maurice as "the leader of the Moors," perhaps indicating a shift in the way in which Saint Maurice was being conceptualized among European Christians.

It may have been Archbishop Albert II of Magdeburg or his stepbrother, Wilbrand, who prompted the first representation of Maurice as an African. Albert II was a strong supporter of the Saint Maurice cult and a highly educated patron of art. For the work on the statue at Magdeburg, he chose stonemasons from a school of artists greatly influenced by French forms of naturalistic delineation. Albert was interested in more than representational accuracy. He saw conversion of the heathens to the east as his religious and political duty, and seized on the Saint Maurice legend as a banner under which to expand the Christianizing influence of the German Empire. With Albert's help, Maurice's militaristic image, coupled with the idea that he had overcome the stigma of his non-European origins through his martyrdom, developed into a convincing symbol of the Church's conversion mission. In this way Saint Maurice became a political symbol of imperial power, serving a primarily political, rather than religious, function as the embodiment of the power and values of the empire.

The shift toward representations of Saint Maurice as a black man was also doubtlessly encouraged by the growing public prevalence of Moors in the entourage of the German emperor Frederick II, a leader with a special affinity for and fascination with Africa. Frederick employed African political advisers and soldiers and thus helped to expose and accustom Europeans to the physical appearance of Africans. His interest in and employment of Africans, and Maurice's role as an effective political symbol, led to more depictions of the saint as black. As the influence of the Holy Roman Empire grew, representations of Maurice as an African spread beyond Magdeburg and across the empire on into the sixteenth century.

Phillipe Wamba

See Also

Roman Africa: An Interpretation; Thebes, Egypt; Nile River; Germany; Europe.

Africa

Mauritania, a country of northwest Africa bordered by Senegal, the Western Sahara, Mali, Algeria, and the Atlantic Ocean.

Situated between North and sub-Saharan Africa, precolonial Mauritania was a land of salt mines and caravan routes, and a meeting ground between the powerful empires of the western Sudan and the Arab and Berber dynasties of the north. During the colonial era French rule effectively divided northern and southern Mauritania. Independence reunited the country geographically, but internal racial tensions and several cross-border conflicts have contributed to political instability and drained the country's limited resources.

Early History

Archaeologists date the earliest human presence in Mauritania to 5000 B.C.E., when the region's grasslands were home to nomadic hunter-gatherer communities. By the time the Saharan climate began turning increasingly arid around 2500 B.C.E., sedentary agricultural peoples had established themselves in Mauritania, but many, including the ancestors of the Wolof and Tukulor, would eventually migrate south to the relatively lush Senegal River valley. The peoples who remained in the desert practiced either nomadic pastoralism or, where possible, agriculture. Archaeological records indicate that some of Mauritania's earliest farmers cultivated millet, a drought-resistant crop; later agricultural societies relied on irrigation or lived near oases, where they cultivated dates and palms.

The Berbers began migrating to the area from North Africa in the third century C.E. The region's inhabitants were subsequently integrated into Berber society, often as slaves (*see* Trans-Saharan and Red Sea Slave Trade) or vassals, though most were not converted to Islam. Over the next several centuries three Berber clans – the Lemtuna, Messufa, and Djodala – came to dominate trade in the western Sahara in slaves, gold, ivory, and copper. By the ninth century these three clans, together known as the Sanhadja Confederation, controlled the trade routes between Koumbi Saleh (the capital of ancient Ghana), Aoudaghost, and Tombouctou as well as the northwestern Sahara salt mines. But the Sanhadja's decentralized authority structure, combined with internal conflicts between the unconverted nomadic pastoralists and the Muslim merchants, made them vulnerable to attacks.

In 990 armies from the Ghana Empire attacked and seized control of Aoudaghost, one of the Berbers' primary trading centers. In 1039 the religious scholar 'Abd Allah ibn Yasin, founder of the Almoravid movement, declared a jihad (holy war) against the "heathen" Sanhadja Berbers. By 1054 'Abd Allah ibn Yasin and his followers had converted the Berbers to a stricter form of Islam – Malekite Sunni – and replaced the crumbling Sanhadja Confederation with a theocratic empire. The Almoravids also took control of Aoudaghost and other market towns, as well as major trade routes across the western Sahara. The Almoravids' conquests eventually extended their influence to Morocco, southern Spain, and parts of the Ghana Empire and present-day Senegal. Even after they were pushed out of Europe, the Almoravids ruled Mauritania until the mid-thirteenth century.

Arab groups moved southward from North Africa in the eleventh century, and the Beni Hassan group reached the western parts of the Sahara Desert in the mid-thirteenth century. Although they shared the Berbers' Islamic faith and nomadic way of life, their traditions of caravan raiding, warfare, and tribute collection brought them into conflict with the western Sahara's long-time inhabitants. Tensions between Berbers and Arabs increased in the mid-seventeenth century, during a three-decade period known as the Char Bobha. Oral traditions offer varying accounts of the nature and extent of the Char Bobha conflict, but it culminated in a jihad launched in 1673 by Nasir al-Din, a Berber cleric. After four years of fighting, the Islamic reformers – most of them Berbers – were defeated by the *hassan* warriors. These years of conflict established the social hierarchy that would come to define Moorish society: hassan Arabs, who controlled trade and political power, occupied the top tier, above the *zawiya*, or Berber religious scholars. Below them were the *znaga*, or tribute-paying Berber herders and oasis farmers. Lower still were the haratine (former slaves) and *abid* (slaves), most of whom were black.

The seventeenth century also saw the arrival of more European merchants. The Portuguese had been trading guns for slaves with the hassan since the mid-fifteenth century (many of these slaves were bound for sugar plantations on the Portuguese-held islands of São Tomé and Príncipe) and had built a fort at Arguin (north of present-day Nouadhibou). But now Dutch, French, and Spanish merchants came looking for Mauritanian gum arabic, which was used in textile manufacturing. The hassan elite took advantage of rivalries among the Europeans to secure gifts and annual payments, as well as lucrative trade deals. Due to the region's treacherous coastline and desert climate, most European merchants conducted business with the hassan in the port town of Saint-Louis in northern Senegal, and most European missionaries avoided Mauritania altogether. The French referred to the entire region as a "vacuum."

Although France acquired territorial rights to Mauritania in the 1814 Treaty of Paris, the colonial administration in Dakar posed little challenge to Moorish hegemony until the twentieth century. For the most part, the French limited their concerns to the fertile Senegal River valley region, which they administered from Saint-Louis, and rarely ventured into the northern interior except when Arab rulers threatened to disrupt the gum arabic trade. One of the few to take an interest in the northern region was French governor Louis Faidherbe (1854-1861 and 1863-1865), whose expeditions produced the

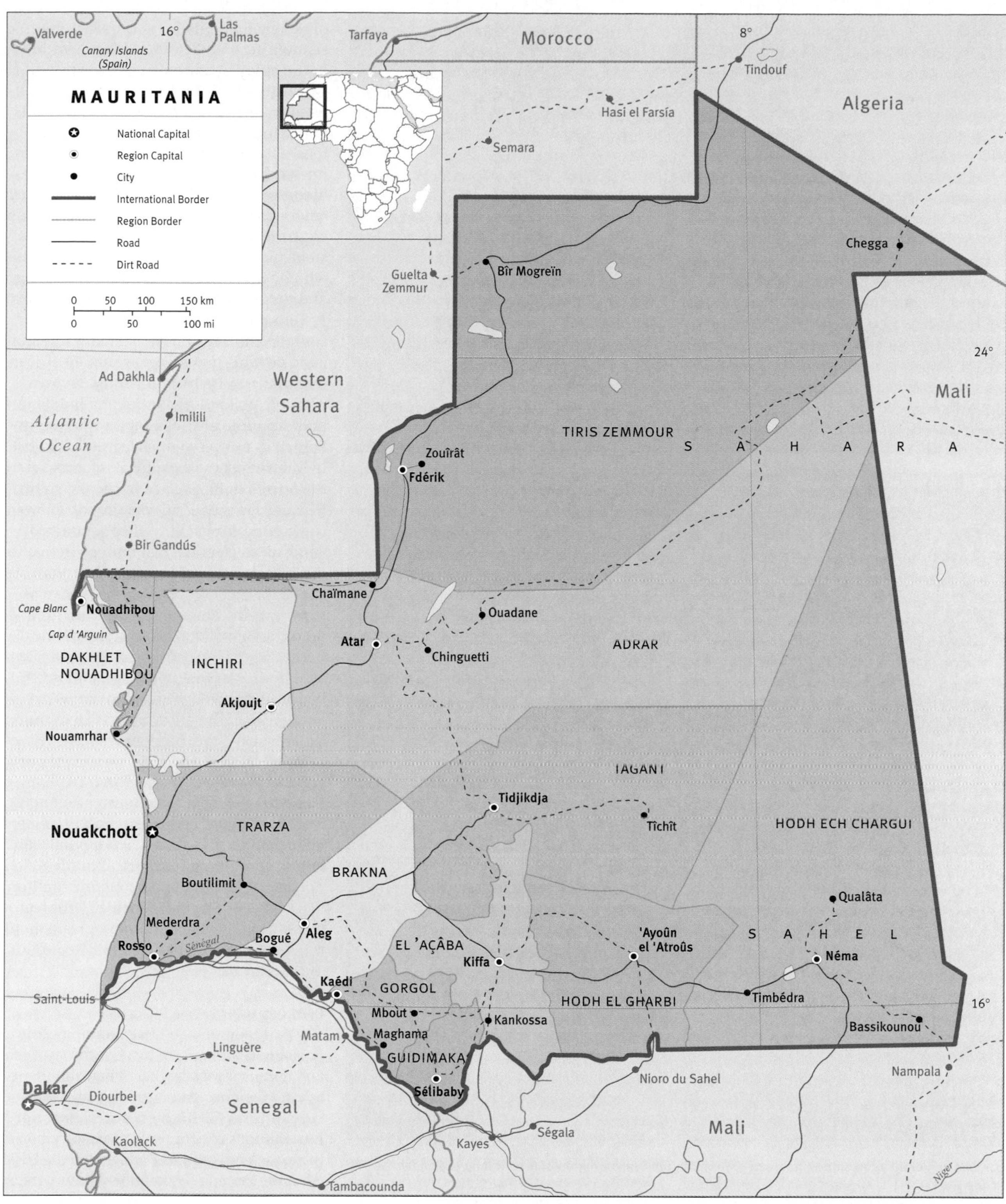

first comprehensive map of northern Mauritania. During Faidherbe's governorship the French also conquered a number of kingdoms in the north, but subsequent administrations did little to secure these claims.

Colonial Rule

In 1899 France reassessed its growing West African empire and decided that further efforts needed to be taken to secure Mauritania, which, though mostly desert, served as an important link between Senegal and Morocco. The task of "pacification" fell to Xavier Coppolani, a colonial administrator with extensive knowledge of northwest Africa. Coppolani sought to weaken potential Moorish resistance by pitting rival hassan groups against each other while simultaneously securing alliances with the zawiya. Coppolani foresaw employing the zawiya as colonial agents, allowing France to administer the colony cheaply, with a minimum of French personnel.

By 1902 Coppolani had secured French control over much of southern Mauritania through a combination of negotiation and military threat. Coppolani then convinced the French government that complete pacification required a campaign in the more northerly Adrar region, a stronghold of Moorish rebellion. But before his army could set out, Coppolani was killed by followers of the Sahrawi religious leader Cheikh Ma el-Ainin. The French campaign into

TOP: Women of all ages enjoy a game of *golorgal* in the Brakna region of Mauritania. *L. Goodsmith/The Image Works*
ABOVE: A boy prepares tea in Rosso, Mauritania. *CORBIS/Bernard and Catherine Desjeux*

Mauritania floundered after Coppolani's death and little progress was made until 1909, when a new military leader, Henri Gouraud, launched an aggressive military campaign against Ma el-Ainin's army. Gouraud's army defeated Ma el-Ainin in July 1909 and successfully secured the entire region by the end of 1912.

Northern and southern Mauritania experienced COLONIAL RULE very differently. In the sparsely populated north the French hired zawiya chiefs to collect taxes and stationed a few troops there to ward off hostile nomads, but otherwise did little to develop the territory. In contrast, they devoted considerable resources to the southern region, where a larger sedentary peasant population and better soil could support the production of export crops, such as peanuts, indigo, and tobacco. The south was governed as part of Senegal, and its French-built public schools groomed young Africans for jobs in the colonial administration.

During World War II all of Mauritania suffered from a series of debilitating droughts, depleting the colony's already tenuous food supply. The war made grain imports impossible, at least until near-famine conditions convinced France to send the colony emergency supplies. The wartime hardship contributed to the discontent among the small but vocal Mauritanian educated elite, who began protesting both conscription and the harsh and arbitrary colonial penal system known as the *indigénat.*

At the end of World War II France responded to growing unrest throughout its African colonial empire by abolishing its most punitive policies (including the indigénat) and expanding African representation in French as well as colonial legislative bodies. In Mauritania these political reforms led to the formal unification of north and south, because France's 1946 constitution allowed the colony, long a virtual appendage of Senegal, to elect its own representative to the French National Assembly. Mauritanians chose Horma Ould Babana, a zawiya of the Idaw Ali clan and founder of Entente Mauritanienne, the colony's first political party. Babana's socialist leanings soon alienated both zawiya and hassan, and in 1951 he was defeated by Sidi el Moktar n'Diaye, a member of the more conservative Union Progressiste Mauritanienne (UPM). The UPM became the colony's dominant party and its president, MOKTAR OULD DADDAH, a French-educated lawyer from a prominent marabout family, became its most prominent politician. Ould Daddah's background won him supporters among both Arab-identified northern Moors and Francophone southern blacks. Backed by the French government, in 1961 Ould Daddah became president of the newly independent Islamic Republic of Mauritania.

INDEPENDENCE

Since independence Mauritanian politics have been dominated by regional conflicts and domestic racial strife. At first abundant coastal fisheries and untapped iron ore and copper reserves in the northern interior raised hopes of economic prosperity, and the leadership of Ould Daddah and the UPM (later the Parti du Regroupment Mauritanien, or PRM) kept internal divisions to a minimum. France initially provided considerable economic and military aid, both valued during the years when Mauritania was not even recognized by its powerful northern neighbor, Morocco, and was not on friendly terms with most members of the Arab League.

Ould Daddah won diplomatic recognition from Morocco in 1969, in part through a campaign to Arabize Mauritanian institutions. He made Hassaniya Arabic the official language of schooling and government in

1966 – a move that brought protests of Arab domination from the southern black minority. In the early 1970s Ould Daddah made appeals to national unity and pride by "Mauritanizing" the economy: he nationalized the iron mines and other industries, and introduced a new currency, the ouguiya, in place of the West African franc.

In 1975 Mauritania was swept up in the long-running dispute over the neighboring Spanish colony of Western Sahara. In November of that year Ould Daddah and King Hassan II met in Madrid and agreed to divide the territory between them as soon as Spanish forces withdrew. The resultant Madrid Agreement, however, ignored the demands of the Algerian-backed Sahrawi liberation organization, POLISARIO, as well as an earlier 1975 verdict by the International Court of Justice that called for an independent Western Sahara. When Ould Daddah sent the Mauritanian army to occupy the Tiris al-Gharbia territory in 1976, Polisario retaliated.

Over the next two years Polisario guerrillas attacked Mauritania's railroads, cities, and iron ore industry. The economy was further debilitated by heavy military spending and declining world prices for iron ore, Mauritania's primary export. As military support from Morocco and France failed to stop the attacks, Mauritanians themselves, many of whom had Sahrawi relatives, grew increasingly impatient with the war and with their president. In July 1978 a group of army officers overthrew Ould Daddah. The leader of the new military government, Col. Mustapha Ould Mohammed Salek, pledged to bring peace.

Morocco's determination to take over the Western Sahara, however, prevented a quick end to the conflict. Although Polisario and Mauritania signed a cease-fire soon after Salek's takeover, Moroccan troops based in Mauritania refused to abide by it. As the situation continued to deteriorate, France threatened to pull its military aid, and Polisario warned that it would end the cease-fire. Mauritanian military officers, concerned with the threat of renewed warfare, stepped in, and on April 6, 1979, Col. Mohamed Khouna Ould Haidalla and Ahmed Ould Boucek overthrew Salek.

Haidalla led the new government, with Boucek as prime minister and Salek retained as a figurehead president. After the death of Boucek in May, Haidalla assumed his position and replaced Salek with a fellow officer, Lt. Col. Mohamed Mahoud Ould Ahmed Louly. In July of that year Polisario ended its cease-fire. Confronted by a costly and unwinnable war, Haidalla accepted the counsel of fellow military officers as well as the ORGANIZATION OF AFRICAN UNITY (OAU) and renounced Mauritanian claims to Western Saharan territory. On August 5, 1979, Mauritania negotiated a peace settlement with Polisario.

The end of the Western Saharan conflict, however, did not bring tranquility to Mauritania. In 1980 Haidalla exiled several military officers, installed a civilian government, drafted a new constitution, and promised multiparty elections in the near future. Haidalla also announced a new ban against slavery, which, although it had been banned since the colonial era, remained a persistent problem in the northern interior. But he retreated from political liberalization after a coup attempt in mid-1981. He ordered military troops to arrest political opponents and drew on the Islamic legal code, the *Shari'a*, to justify restrictions on civic freedoms. Meanwhile, Morocco's leaders accused Haidalla, a native of Western Sahara, of aiding Polisario's ongoing fight against Moroccan occupation. Amid allegations of government mismanagement and corruption, in December 1984 Haidalla was ousted in a military coup led by Col. Maaouya Ould Sidi Ahmed Taya.

Taya immediately cracked down on government corruption and profiteering, and undertook a series of economic reforms agreed to in an International Monetary Fund/World Bank structural adjustment program. Taya also released many political prisoners, relaxed the imposition of the Shari'a, and scheduled Mauritania's first multiparty municipal elections for December 1986.

Taya's actions won favor with France as well as with some Mauritanians, but they failed to appease growing discontent among Mauritania's blacks. In April 1986 the Forces de Libération Africaine de Mauritanie (FLAM) published *The Manifesto of the Oppressed Black Mauritanian*. This pamphlet accused both the government and Mauritanian Moors of "systematic discrimination and hostile acts" toward blacks, and demanded an end to racial discrimination in public schools and government jobs. Taya responded by arresting 30 prominent black citizens and dismissing all government and military employees suspected of FLAM sympathies. Racial tensions heightened after October 1987 when Taya, claiming to have discovered a coup plot, arrested 51 Tukulors and dismissed more than 500 Tukulor officers from the Mauritanian army. Three officers received death sentences.

Mauritania's racial tensions sparked an international crisis in April 1989, when two Senegalese farmers were allegedly killed in a grazing-rights dispute with Mauritanian herders in the Senegal River valley border region. Riots broke out in Dakar, and in both countries Senegalese and Mauritanian expatriates were attacked. Dozens died in Senegal, more than 200 died in Mauritania, and tens of thousands fled. As the countries airlifted each other's citizens home, black Mauritanians accused their government of using the crisis to expel blacks, and to justify the torture and murder of opposition leaders. Despite foreign mediators' efforts to resolve the crisis, Senegal and Mauritania broke diplomatic relations in August 1989.

In early 1991 Taya responded to pressures both at home and abroad for political reform. He resumed diplomatic relations with Senegal and granted amnesty to political prisoners, most of whom were black. He also eased restrictions on political associations and parties, and held a national referendum on a new constitution. Although the constitution still concentrated enormous power in the presidency, it was approved, and in January 1992, Taya defeated Ahmed Ould Daddah (brother of Moktar Ould Daddah) in the country's first multiparty presidential election. Opposition parties accused Taya of fraud, and a month later several of them boycotted national assembly elections, allowing Taya's Democratic and Social Republic Party (DSRP) to win a majority.

After the 1992 elections Taya attempted to placate the opposition by appointing several blacks to his cabinet. But his regime is still criticized for discriminating against blacks, as well suppressing national census results that many believe would increase parliamentary representation of the black-dominated southern regions. Human rights groups have also accused the Mauritanian government of tolerating slavery, especially in the northern interior, and of persecuting Mauritanians who speak out against the practice (*see* HUMAN RIGHTS IN AFRICA). Press censorship persists, and fundamentalist Islamic groups have been systematically denied the right to free speech. Although the discovery of new iron ore deposits in the mid-1990s has bolstered Mauritania's economy, hardships resulting from structural adjustment austerity measures have prompted periodic protests, including bread riots in Nouakchott in January 1995. Nevertheless, Taya kept his promise to hold parliamentary elections in 1996 and 1997; despite boycotts by the large opposition groups, a small number of opposition politicians have won seats and growing influence in the national government.

Elizabeth Heath

SEE ALSO

Sahrawi; Colonial Rule; Dakar, Senegal; Explorers in Africa Since 1800; Ghana, Early Kingdom of; Gold Trade; Ivory Trade; Transatlantic Slave Trade; Salt Trade; São Tomé and Príncipe; Structural Adjustment in Africa; Taya, Maaouya Ould Sidi Ahmed; Tombouctou, Mali; Nouakchott, Mauritania; Koumbi Saleh, Mauritania; Christianity: Missionaries in Africa.

Africa

Mauritania (Ready Reference)

Official Name: Islamic Republic of Mauritania
Area: 1,030,700 sq km (397,955 sq mi)
Location: Northern Africa; borders the North Atlantic Ocean, SENEGAL, MALI, ALGERIA, and the WESTERN SAHARA

Capital: Nouakchott (population 550,000 [1992 estimate])
Other Major Cities: Kaédi (population 74,000), Nouadhibou (70,000) (1992 estimate)
Population: 2,511,473 (1998 estimate)
Population Density: 3 persons per sq km (about 5 persons per sq mi)
Population Below Age 15: 46 percent (male 584,303; female 583,526 [1998 estimate])
Population Growth Rate: 2.52 percent (1998 estimate)
Total Fertility Rate: 6.41 children born per woman (1998 estimate)
Life Expectancy at Birth: Total population: 49.9 years (male 46.95 years; female 53.11 years [1998 estimate])
Infant Mortality: 78.22 deaths per 1000 live births (1998 estimate)
Literacy Rate (age 15 and over who can read and write): Total population: 37.7 percent (male 49.6 percent; female 26.3 percent [1995 estimate])
Education: The government of Mauritania attempts to provide free primary education. These efforts, however, have been hindered by the nomadic practices of the people. In the early 1990s only 55 percent of all eligible children were attending primary school.
Languages: Hasaniya Arabic is the official language. Poular, Wolof, and Soninké are also recognized as national languages.
Ethnic Groups: The majority of the population is Moors (of mixed Arab and Berber ancestry), many of whom lead nomadic lives.
Religions: Islam, which is the state religion, is practiced by more than 99 percent of the population.
Climate: Except for a narrow strip in the south along the Senegal River, the country lies entirely within the Sahara Desert. Daytime temperatures in most of the country average near 37.8° C (100° F) during the day for more than six months of the year, but the nights are cool. Annual rainfall varies from less than 130 mm (less than 5 in) in the north to about 660 mm (26 in) in the Senegal Valley.
Land, Plants, and Animals: In Mauritania there are mostly flat Sahara plains with some hills. The elevation varies from about 150m (500 ft) in the southwest to about 460 m (about 1500 ft) in the northeast. Few animals and little plant life thrive in the northern region. Lions and monkeys inhabit the region near the Senegal River.
Natural Resources: Mauritania's natural resources include iron ore, gypsum, fish, copper, and phosphate.
Currency: The ouguiya
Gross Domestic Product (GDP): $4.1 billion (1996 estimate)
GDP per Capita: $750 (1996 estimate)
GDP Real Growth Rate: 6 percent (1996 estimate)
Primary Economic Activities: Agriculture (47 percent of population), industry, and commerce
Primary Crops: Millet, sorghum, root crops, dates, and livestock
Industries: Fish processing and mining of iron ore and gypsum
Primary Exports: Iron ore, fish, and fish products
Primary Imports: Foodstuffs, consumer goods, petroleum products, and capital goods
Primary Trade Partners: Algeria, China, United States, France, Germany, Spain, and Italy
Government: Mauritania is a constitutional republic that obtained its independence from France on November 28, 1960. The executive branch is led by President Col. Maaouya Ould Sidi Ahmed Taya and the Council of Ministers. The president is elected by popular vote for a six-year term. The legislative branch is bicameral, consisting of the 56-seat Senate, or Majlis al-Shuyukh, whose members serve six-year terms, and the 79-member National Assembly, or Majlis al-Wajani, whose members serve for five years. The judicial system is based on Islamic (Shari'a) courts, special courts, and state security courts; the state security courts are being phased out. Though politics often falls along tribal lines, some fledgling political parties include the Democratic and Social Republican Party, the Union of Democratic Forces-New Era, and the Assembly for Democracy and Unity.

Elizabeth Heath

See Also

Soninké; Taya, Maaouya Ould Sidi Ahmed.

Africa

Mauritius, African island republic in the western Indian Ocean, located 800 km (497 mi) east of Madagascar and 200 km (124.3 mi) northeast of Réunion. The country includes the island of Mauritius; the island of Rodrigues to the east; the Agalega Islands to the north; and the Cargados Carajos Shoals to the northeast.

The small, volcanic island of Mauritius remained unsettled until the seventeenth century. More than 1.1 million people, descendants from India, Africa, Europe, and China, now claim the island as their home. Although Mauritius was initially discovered by Arab seafarers, European colonialism and mercantile economic forces later brought colonists, soldiers, slaves, indentured laborers, and traders to the island, resulting in a remarkably diverse mixture of people and cultures. In recent years Mauritius has transformed itself from an obscure sugar plantation colony into a major European tourist destination boasting a strong, rapidly expanding and diversifying economy overseen by a stable, democratic political regime.

Precolonial History

Given its proximity to Madagascar, it has been suggested that proto-Malagasy (early Indonesian settlers) reached Mauritius en route to the larger island. However, there is no direct evidence to support such claims. Arab traders were clearly among the first to reach Mauritius. The renowned geographer Al Sharif El-Edrissi drew a map in 1153 that clearly demarcated the island of Mauritius with the name Dina Mozare. According to some sources, he named the island Domingo Fernandez after himself but later changed the name to Ilha do Cirne (Island of the Swan). Mauritius, Réunion, and Rodrigues were named the Mascarene Islands after the Portuguese captain Pero Mascarenes.

Dutch Rule

Admiral Van Warwijk took possession of the island for the Dutch Crown in 1598, renaming it Mauritius after the *stadhouder* (governor) of the Netherlands, Maurice of Nassau. Not until 1638 did the Dutch attempt to settle Mauritius. Twenty years later the colonists abandoned their fledgling settlement, after hunting the famous dodo bird to extinction. In 1664 the Dutch returned to Mauritius in a second attempt to establish a permanent colony but failed to make the settlement a profitable venture and left the island once again in 1710. When the Dutch departed, they left behind slaves, sugar cane, deer, rats, and monkeys, all of which they had introduced.

French Rule

In 1715 Dufresne d'Arsel laid claim to Mauritius for Louis XV, renaming the land Ile de France. However, settlement efforts would wait until 1722, when the French East India Company assumed administrative control of the island. For the next 13 years the colony made little progress toward establishing a productive, viable community. With the arrival of Mahé de Labourdonnais in 1735, Ile de France began to flourish. Labourdonnais oversaw the construction of the harbor during the 11 years of his administration, setting the stage for Port Louis to become the bustling urban center of the Mascarene Islands. He introduced manioc (cassava) from Brazil to ensure a reliable food source. Labourdonnais also advocated the establishment of sugar as the island's main cash crop, entrusting the construction of the first local sugar cane factory to his brother. By 1786 the island boasted ten sugar factories, but it was not until the next century that sugar would dominate the economy.

The population of the island grew exceptionally diverse. To build the port and shipping yard, Labourdonnais brought architects and skilled workmen from Madras, India, while dockworkers and sailors came from Pondicherry, India. Large numbers of slaves were brought from Mozambique, Madagascar, and Kilwa, and a smaller number from India and Malaya. Used in every aspect of the economy, from agriculture to the shipping industry, slaves greatly outnumbered the rest of the population from the colony's inception.

Women wash and rinse clothes in a narrow canal on Mauritius. *CORBIS/Wolfgang Kaehler*

Several governors succeeded Labourdonnais and the colony's population continued to grow. After the Seven Years' War (1756-1763), the French East India Company sold Ile de France back to the French Crown and it remained a Crown Colony until the French Revolution. In 1790 news of the revolution reached Ile de France, along with a call to form a legislative assembly. Colonists were unprepared to accept the 1794 decree that outlawed slavery. When members of the revolutionary government arrived in Ile de France to enforce compliance, they were expelled under threat of violence. Ile de France remained semi-autonomous until the arrival of Charles Mathieu Isidore Decaen in 1803, appointed governor by Napoleon. Although Decaen began enforcing Napoleonic law, slavery remained in full force until 1810, when the British invaded and took control. The island was then again called Mauritius.

British Rule

The British captured Mauritius to assure access to vital sea-lanes and protect their growing interests in India. They had little concern for the internal workings of Mauritian society, leaving the daily affairs of the colony to the Franco-Mauritian aristocracy. The abolition of the slave trade throughout the British Empire in 1808 did, however, have a dramatic effect on Mauritian society, where slavery was abolished in 1835. French slaveholders argued that the government had to compensate them for their loss of valuable property, and they eventually received some £2 million. Slaves were required to work for their former owners as paid laborers for a four-year period, providing the plantation owners time to locate other sources of cheap labor. Not surprisingly, once freed of their obligation to work the plantations, the former slaves fled the fields en masse, establishing themselves in towns, in coastal fishing villages, and on marginal, unclaimed farmlands.

Even before slavery was abolished, the Franco-Mauritian plantation owners had made contingency plans to locate cheap labor. From 1834 until 1909 hundreds of thousands of Indians – primarily from Calcutta, Madras, and Bombay – migrated to Mauritius as indentured laborers.

Although slavery had been abolished, policies such as the "double cut" and vagrancy laws subjugated indentured laborers. Under the double cut, for example, laborers lost two days' wages for every day absent from work. Despite extremely low pay, many Indian immigrants chose to remain after their five-year indenture in the sugar fields. Colonial authorities promoted permanent settlement by encouraging the immigration of women and by eliminating free return passages to India.

The large-scale Indian immigration sparked demand for local trade, a niche partially filled by Gujarati Muslims. A significant number of Chinese traders also immigrated to Mauritius during the nineteenth and twentieth centuries, primarily from the Canton region. By 1861 more than 2000 Chinese were reported to live throughout the island, dominating the retail trade sector.

Thus, by the beginning of the twentieth century the main constituencies of the contemporary Mauritian population had established themselves. Immigration and emigration slowed and the population stabilized. Indians, an extremely heterogeneous group, came to comprise two-thirds of the population.

Mauritian Nation Building

The twentieth century brought a series of political and social reforms as Mauritians looked to improve their conditions. Trade unions gained power and several political parties were formed, including the Labour Party. Between 1937 and 1943 there were labor disturbances on plantations and the docks – in some instances leading to violence – indicating a population weary of subjugation and anxious for political representation.

In 1947 a new constitution granted suffrage to all literate adults, followed by universal adult suffrage in 1958. As a result of these changes, Indo-Mauritians for the first time were granted greater influence through representation on the Legislative Council. Political parties quickly formed along ethnic lines with the Labour Party, led by Seewoosagur Ramgoolam, representing the Hindu majority, the Parti Mauricien Sociale Démocrate (PMSD) speaking for the interests of whites and Creoles, and the Muslim Action Committee articulating the demands of the Muslim community.

A series of constitutional conferences took place in London during the 1960s amid rumblings for independence. Afraid of a Hindu-dominated government, the PMSD hoped to block independence in favor of an "association" with Britain. To their disappointment, the British guaranteed the Labour Party support for independence in exchange for the Chagos Archipelago (islands located 1930 km [1199 mi] northeast of Mauritius), which includes the Diego Garcia atoll. Disputes over the sovereignty of Diego Garcia, where the United States maintains a military base, are still unresolved.

To alleviate fears by minority groups of Hindu dominance, an electoral system was designed to ensure minority representation. Nevertheless, many Franco-Mauritians and middle-class Creoles emigrated to South Africa, Australia, and England prior to independence, fearing that their positions of privilege would be undermined. Ethnic tensions mounted in the weeks prior to independence, leading to a violent clash between Hindus and Creoles.

Under the leadership of Ramgoolam and the Independence Party, Mauritius obtained sovereignty on March 12, 1968. The formation of the Mouvement Militant Mauricien (MMM), a socialist opposition party, combined with the threat of labor strikes, led to the passing of the Public Order Act in 1971 and later to a state of emergency. Leaders of the MMM were held by the police without trial, and the 1972 election was postponed. The press was censored and public assembly was banned. But by 1976 the MMM had

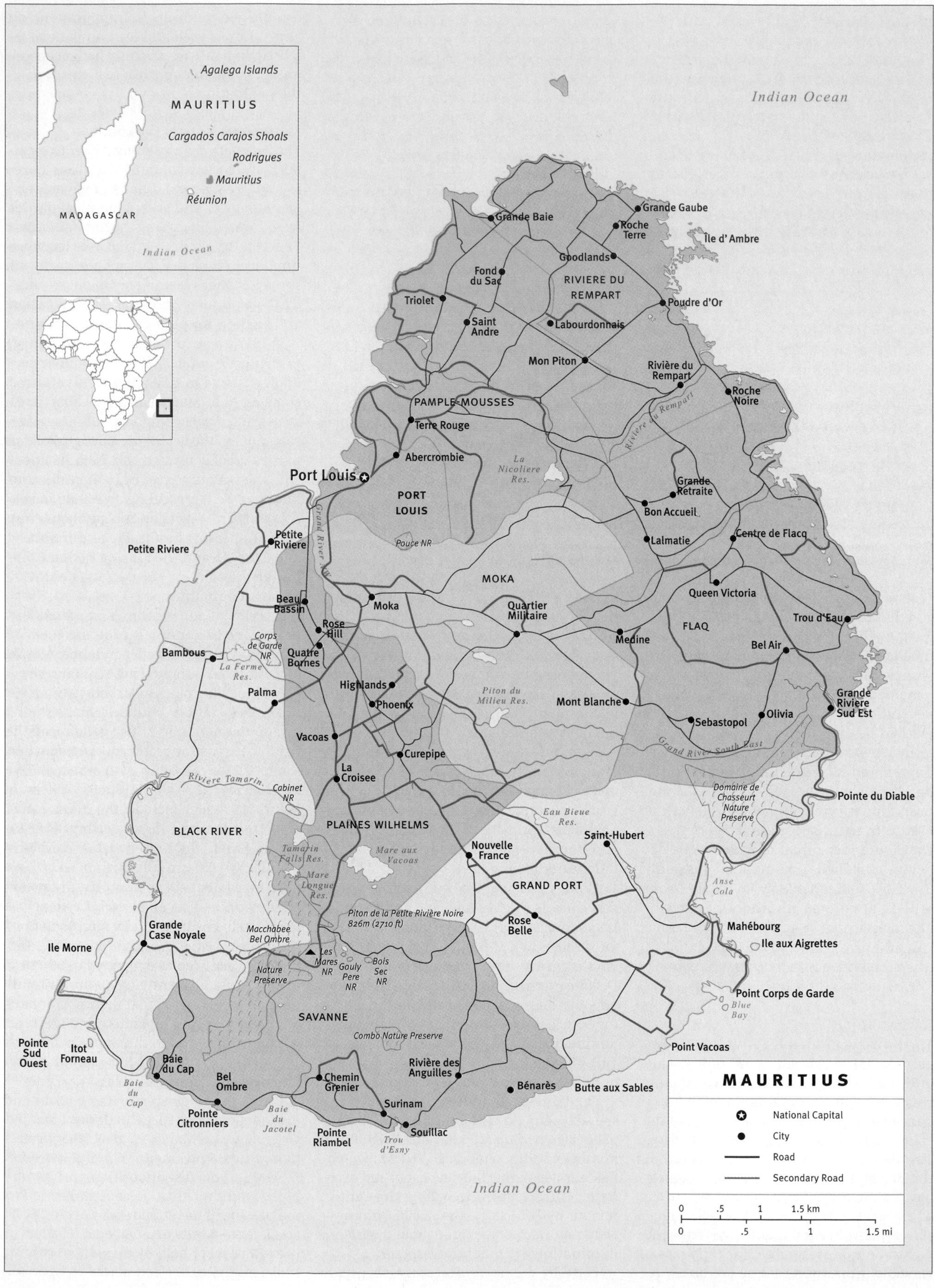
Agalega Islands
MAURITIUS
Cargados Carajos Shoals
Rodrigues
Mauritius
Réunion
MADAGASCAR
Indian Ocean
Indian Ocean
Grande Gaube
Grande Baie
Roche Terre
Île d'Ambre
Goodlands
Fond du Sac
RIVIERE DU REMPART
Triolet
Poudre d'Or
Saint Andre
Labourdonnais
Mon Piton
Rivière du Rempart
Roche Noire
PAMPLEMOUSSES
Terre Rouge
Rivière du Rempart
Abercrombie
La Nicoliere Res.
Port Louis
PORT LOUIS
Grande Retraite
Bon Accueil
Petite Riviere
Petite Riviere
Grand River
Pouce NR
Lalmatie
Centre de Flacq
MOKA
Queen Victoria
Beau Bassin
Moka
Quartier Militaire
Trou d'Eau
Rose Hill
FLAQ
Corps de Garde NR
Medine
Bambous
Quatre Bornes
Bel Air
La Ferme Res.
Highlands
Palma
Piton du Milieu Res.
Phoenix
Mont Blanche
Grande Riviere Sud Est
Olivia
Sebastopol
Vacoas
Grand River South East
Curepipe
La Croisee
Riviere Tamarin
Cabinet NR
Domaine de Chasseurt Nature Preserve
Pointe du Diable
Eau Bieue Res.
PLAINES WILHELMS
BLACK RIVER
Saint-Hubert
Tamarin Falls Res.
Nouvelle France
Mare aux Vacoas
Mare Longue Res.
GRAND PORT
Anse Cola
Piton de la Petite Rivière Noire 826m (2710 ft)
Rose Belle
Grande Case Noyale
Macchabee Bel Ombre
Mahébourg
Ile Morne
Ile aux Aigrettes
Les Mares NR
Gouly Pere NR
Bois Sec NR
Nature Preserve
Point Corps de Garde
Blue Bay
SAVANNE
Combo Nature Preserve
Point Vacoas
Pointe Sud Ouest
Itot Forneau
Baie du Cap
Rivière des Anguilles
Bel Ombre
Chemin Grenier
Bénarès
Butte aux Sables
Baie du Cap
Surinam
Pointe Citronniers
Baie du Jacotel
Souillac
Pointe Riambel
Trou d'Esny
Indian Ocean
MAURITIUS
National Capital
City
Road
Secondary Road
0 .5 1 1.5 km
0 .5 1 1.5 mi

obtained significant support, winning 34 of 70 seats in the Legislative Assembly.

In June 1982 the MMM, in coalition with the Parti Socialiste Mauricien (PSM), swept the election, winning all 60 Mauritian seats in the assembly. ANEROOD JUGNAUTH became prime minister, but within a few months internal quarreling split his coalition – the first of many Mauritian political alliances to collapse as quickly as it formed. Nevertheless Jugnauth served as prime minister until 1995. Despite a rapidly changing political landscape, Mauritius's democratically elected prime ministers have served long and relatively stable tenures.

CONTEMPORARY EVENTS

The initial socialist leanings of the MMM and other parties have never significantly tempered the country's devotion to free-market economics. After the initial economic difficulties of the 1970s, the International Monetary Fund (IMF) and the World Bank introduced a structural adjustment program providing loans in exchange for compliance with a number of economic-stabilization policies, including currency devaluation. These measures proved largely successful, leading to significant economic growth and prosperity in the 1980s and 1990s. Exports increased; deficit spending was radically reduced; inflation was brought under control; and the gross domestic product (GDP) dramatically rose. Formed in 1972, the Export Processing Zone (EPZ) has been quite successful in attracting foreign investment through a number of tax and fiscal incentives, particularly in the production of knitwear. In 1988 the EPZ accounted for 58.8 percent of the nation's export earnings. The country also opened a stock exchange in 1989 and off-shore banking facilities in 1990.

While underemployment is pervasive, unemployment is minimal. Indeed, labor shortages have led many Mauritian textile firms to recruit laborers from East Asia. Despite these successes, the economy remains dependent on sugar prices (sugar accounts for 32 percent of export earnings) and the importation of foreign goods, particularly fuel and food. Tourism is another leading industry, ranking third after sugar production and textile manufacturing. Some 400,000 tourists visit Mauritius annually. However, much of the foreign exchange earned through tourism is spent on the importation of products to build and maintain the industry itself.

Primary education is free, compulsory, and relatively enforced in Mauritius. Ninety-four percent of children attend primary school, leading to one of the lowest rates of illiteracy in sub-Saharan Africa (estimated to be 17.1 percent). Economic reforms have had significant social impact. The creation of the EPZ has drawn many more women into the work force, forcing a reevaluation of gender roles and family structure. Traditional values are also changing as children become more economically independent and freed from family pressures.

In December 1995 Dr. Navin Ramgoolam, son of Sir Seewoosagur Ramgoolam, became prime minister in a coalition formed with Paul Berenger's MMM party. By July 1996 the coalition broke down and Berenger left the government, reconfirming an established Mauritian political tradition of unstable coalitions. Despite the political turbulence, the government shows no sign of shifting away from its commitment to free-market economics.

Ari Nave

SEE ALSO

Indian Communities in Africa; Transatlantic Slave Trade; Great Britain; Structural Adjustment in Africa; Tourism in Africa; Réunion; Indian Ocean Slave Trade.

Grass sun umbrellas line the beach at St. Geran, Mauritius. *CORBIS*

Africa

Mauritius (Ready Reference)

Official Name: Republic of Mauritius
Area: Mauritius Island, 1865 sq km (720 sq mi); includes Rodrigues and the Agalega Islands, and the Cargados Carajos Shoals, 2040 sq km (787 sq mi)
Location: Islands in the western Indian Ocean, west of MADAGASCAR
Capital: Port Louis (population 142,850 [1992 estimate])
Population: 1,168,256 (1998 estimate)
Population Density: 554 persons per sq km

(1436 persons per sq mi)
Population Below Age 15: 26 percent (male 155,917; female 152,563 [1998 estimate])
Population Growth Rate: 1.2 percent (1998 estimate)
Total Fertility Rate: 2.2 children born per woman (1998 estimate)
Life Expectancy at Birth: Total population: 70.9 years (male 67.0 years; female: 74.7 years [1997 estimate])
Infant Mortality Rate: 16.5 deaths per 1000 live births (1998 estimate)
Literacy Rate (age 15 and over who can read and write): Total population: 82.9 percent (male 87.1 percent; female 78.8 percent [1995 estimate])
Education: Education has been a high priority of the Mauritius government since the early 1980s; the country has one of the highest literacy rates in Africa.
Languages: English is the official language, but French, Hindi, and Creole – a French patois – are more commonly spoken. There are also speakers of Urdu, Hakka, and Bojpoori.
Ethnic Groups: More than 60 percent of Mauritians are Indian immigrants and their descendants. Another 25 percent are Creole (of mixed African and European heritage). There is a small ethnically Chinese population.
Religions: About 52 percent of the population is Hindu, and around 28 percent is Christian (mostly Roman Catholic). Another 16 percent is Muslim.
Climate: The climate is tropical; the weather is warm and dry during the winter months (May through October) and hot, wet, and humid in the summer (November through April). Average annual rainfall ranges from about 1000 mm (40 in) on the coast to about 5000 mm (200 in) in the central plateau. Strong cyclones occur often during the summer. The average annual temperature on the coast is 23° C (73° F).
Land, Plants, and Animals: The main island of Mauritius is volcanic in origin and rises from a narrow coastline to jagged mountains ringing the central plateau. Its highest elevation, Piton de la Petite Rivière Noire, is 826 m (2710 ft). Coral reefs circle the coastline, except at Port Louis, the capital, which has a deep-water harbor. The lushly forested interior has many lakes and small streams.
Natural Resources: Fertile, arable soil and fish
Currency: The Mauritian rupee
Gross Domestic Product (GDP): $11.7 billion (1996 estimate)
GDP per Capita: $10,300 (1996 estimate)
GDP Real Growth Rate: 5.4 percent (1996 estimate)
Primary Economic Activities: Agriculture, food processing, manufacturing, and tourism
Primary Crops: Sugar cane (grown on 90 percent of cultivated land), tea, peanuts, tobacco, and vegetables
Industries: Food processing, textiles, leather goods, chemicals, metal products, and electronic components
Primary Exports: Textiles and SUGAR
Primary Imports: Food, petroleum products, and chemicals
Primary Trade Partners: European Union, United States, South Africa, and Japan
Government: Though formerly a constitutional monarchy, since 1992 Mauritius has been a constitutional republic. It is headed by a president elected by a legislative body, the National Assembly, and a prime minister appointed by the president. Cassam Uteem has been president since 1992; in 1995 Navin Ramgoolam became prime minister. Major parties include the coalition of the Mauritius Labor Party (MLP) and the Mauritian Militant Movement (MMM), which currently dominates the National Assembly and executive branch. An opposition party, the Mauritian Socialist Movement (MSM), controls about 20 percent of the votes in the assembly.

Kate Tuttle

SEE ALSO
Indian Communities in Africa.

Latin America and the Caribbean

Maximin, Daniel (b. April 9, 1947, Saint-Claude, Guadeloupe), Guadeloupean novelist whose lyrical, allusive works express Caribbean life in a literary invocation of poetry and prose, Creole and French, and past and present.

Although he has lived in FRANCE for most of his adult life, Daniel Maximin's novels constitute a return to the cultural origins of Guadeloupe and, more generally, of the Caribbean. His first novel, *L'Isolé soleil* (1981; Lone Sun, 1989), a work that contains "the totality of Antillean history," according to AIMÉ CÉSAIRE, covers, in compelling, dreamlike narratives, the signal events in the history of GUADELOUPE – from LOUIS DELGRÈS's slave rebellion of 1802 to African American activist Angela Davis's stay in Guadeloupe in 1969.

Maximin employs a number of different genres (poetry, epistolary writing, and narration) in a multitude of voices to recount two centuries of the history of Guadeloupe and MARTINIQUE in relation not only to France and Africa but to the rest of the Americas. The follow-up to this novel, *Soufrières* (1987), confines itself to five days in the life of the island, but uses the geological history of Guadeloupe as a starting point for a contemplation of personal histories. Maximin's most recent novel, *L'Ile et une nuit* (1995, The Island and One Night), further telescopes time, taking place over the seven hours of a hurricane's assault on the island of Guadeloupe. Maximin continues nonetheless to explore the histories and inner lives of the same characters from the previous two novels as they endure the hurricane.

Maximin's novels do more than recount personal, political, or geological histories in fictional form. In a style full of word-play that can be likened to improvisational JAZZ, Maximin endows each character with a singular writing voice that is reflected most strikingly in the graceful and strong voices of the women of his novels. It is this ease with multiple voices and styles that most clearly distinguishes his work from that of his eminent contemporary, EDOUARD GLISSANT, and confirms his importance in the realm of the Caribbean novel. Since completing his studies in comparative literature at the Sorbonne in 1969, Maximin has taught literature and ethnography at the university and secondary levels. He has been affiliated with the journal *Présence Africaine* over the past 30 years and continues to produce programs for Radio-France that are transmitted throughout the Francophone world.

Richard Watts

SEE ALSO
Présence Africaine; Davis, Angela Yvonne; Literature, French Language, in Caribbean; Slave Rebellions in Latin America and the Caribbean.

North America

Mayfield, Curtis (b. June 3, 1942, Chicago, Ill.), African American singer and composer whose work as a solo artist and with the group the Impressions combined music with political messages.

A self-taught guitarist, Curtis Mayfield led his first group, the Alphatones, at age 14. One year later, his childhood friend Jerry Butler invited him to write music and lyrics for the Roosters, a quintet that later changed its name to the Impressions. In 1958 they recorded their first RHYTHM AND BLUES hit, "For Your Precious Love," on Vee Jay Records. Their music was influenced by the CIVIL RIGHTS MOVEMENT, as evidenced by some of their most popular songs, including "People Get Ready" (1965) and "We're a Winner" (1968).

In 1970 Mayfield left the group to become a full-time songwriter and producer. His record *Curtis* was one of the most successful African American music albums of the year, and his compositions for Hollywood's *Superfly* (1972) brought him superstardom. Mayfield then wrote and produced for television and such films as *Claudine* (1974) and *Let's Do It Again* (1975). In 1977 he composed the soundtrack for a film in which he also appeared, titled *Short Eyes*.

Mayfield took part in an Impressions reunion tour in the late 1980s and composed songs for *The Return of Superfly* and *I'm Gonna Get You Sucka* (1989). Popular since his early days with the Impressions in Japan, Mayfield has toured there and in Europe extensively. In August 1990, before opening an outdoor performance in Brooklyn, New York, he was paralyzed from the neck down by a falling lighting rig. He was honored in 1994 at the Grammy Awards show with a Grammy Legend Award.

See Also
Television and African Americans.

North America

Maynor, Dorothy Leigh

(b. September 3, 1910, Norfolk, Va.), African American opera singer, choral director, and founder of the Harlem School for the Arts.

Dorothy Leigh Maynor (originally Mainor) was born to John J. Mainor, a pastor, and Alice (Jeffries) Mainor. At age 14 she enrolled at Hampton Institute, where she studied with the goal of becoming a public school teacher. During her college years Maynor's focus increasingly shifted toward vocal training and the study of piano and orchestral instruments. After graduating, she decided to pursue a second degree in music from Westminster Choir College in New Jersey, and then spent four years in New York continuing her musical studies privately under Wilfried Klamroth and John Alan Houghton.

In 1939 Maynor made her solo singing debut at the Berkshire Musical Festival in Tanglewood, Massachusetts, for which she received widespread acclaim. The performance was soon followed by a New York debut at Town Hall, where reviewers called her "one of the most remarkable soprano voices of [her] generation." She went on to perform in concert halls across the United States, Europe, and Australia, with a repertoire that included lieder, Bach, Handel, spirituals, and opera arias.

In 1964 Maynor retired as a concert artist to fulfill her dream of establishing a school to create opportunities for African American youth. She founded the Harlem School for the Arts, which offered a comprehensive cultural education, and provided instruction in the visual and performing arts of piano, painting, string orchestra, classical and modern dance, and voice.

Rachel Antell

See Also
Hampton University; New York, New York; Spirituals, African American.

North America

Mays, Benjamin Elijah

(b. August 1, 1894, Ninety-Six, S.C.; d. March 28, 1984, Atlanta, Ga.), African American educator and Baptist minister.

Benjamin Mays was the son of Hezekiah and Louvenia Carter Mays, both former slaves. After attending Virginia Union University in Richmond, Virginia, he transferred to Bates College in Maine, where he earned a bachelor's degree in 1920. The following year he was ordained as a Baptist minister. He then attended the University of Chicago's Divinity School, earning a master's degree in 1925 and a Ph.D. ten years later. In 1934 Mays assumed the deanship of Howard University's school of religion, where he revitalized a moribund program. In six years under his administration, enrollment increased, the quality of the faculty improved, and the library grew. In addition, the school achieved the American Association of Theological Schools' highest rating.

In 1950 Mays became president of Morehouse College in Atlanta, Georgia; he served in that position until 1967. Although he enhanced the quality of the faculty and the campus at Morehouse, Mays valued even more his relationship with students, particularly with Martin Luther King Jr., who attended Morehouse from 1944 to 1948. Mays and King developed an almost father and son relationship. King later said that Mays was his "spiritual mentor and my intellectual father." Mays had encouraged King's civil rights activities, although critics attacked Mays's moderate views and his denunciation of such organizations as the Black Panther Party for Self-Defense.

In addition to his work in black higher education, Mays was a scholar of the Black Church, and together with Joseph W. Nicholson authored a survey of the Black Church in 12 cities, *The Negro's Church* (1933). In 1938 he published a study of how God figured in the lives of blacks, *The Negro's God as Reflected in His Literature.* Mays was also active in the National Baptist Convention and participated in a number of ecumenical groups, including the National Council of Churches and the World Council of Churches. Mays worked with these groups to facilitate interracial understanding and to promote a more active commitment to racial justice on the part of Christian churches.

After retiring from Morehouse in 1967, Mays was elected to the Atlanta Board of Education, becoming its president in 1970. In 1982, in recognition of his life of service to the African American community, the National Association for the Advancement of Colored People awarded Mays its highest honor, the Spingarn Medal. He died in Atlanta in 1984.

Robert Fay

See Also
Black Panther Party; King, Martin Luther, Jr.; Black Church, The.

North America

Mays, Willie Howard

(b. May 6, 1931, Westfield, Ala.), African American baseball player who is a member of the Baseball Hall of Fame and who ranks third in total career home runs.

Known as the "Say Hey Kid," Willie Mays played in the major leagues for more than 20 years, amassing a record of achievements that rank him among the best ever to have played the game. His 660 home runs give him the third highest all-time record, behind only Henry "Hank" Aaron (755) and Babe Ruth (714). Mays was not only a great hitter and base runner; his work in center field was also superb, earning him 12 Gold Glove awards. Considered by many to be the best all-around baseball player in the history of the game, as well as one of its most popular players, Mays was inducted into the Baseball Hall of Fame in 1979, the first year in which he was eligible.

Born into an athletic family – his father and grandfather had both been baseball players, and his mother had been a track star in high school – Mays took to sports early, excelling in both football and basketball in high school. His school had no baseball team, however, and this prompted him to seek a place on the Black Barons, the Negro League team of Birmingham, Alabama, when he was just 17. The Negro League was baseball's all-black alternative to the all-white American and National leagues. Quickly becoming a star, Mays was signed by the New York Giants, a National League team, in 1950; he joined their minor league affiliate just after graduating from high school.

After short stints with the Giants' farm clubs in New Jersey and Minneapolis, Mays joined the major league team near the beginning of the 1951 season. Despite his early difficulty in facing big-league pitching, Mays ended the year with 20 home runs and 68 runs batted in, and sportswriters regarded his fielding as "phenomenal." Not only was Mays named Rookie of the Year in 1951, but his team also won the pennant (though they lost the World Series to the New York Yankees). Missing most of the next two seasons due to army service, Mays returned to the Giants in 1954. Led by his 41 home runs and .345 batting average, the Giants won the World Series that year, and Mays was named Most Valuable Player. (He was MVP again in 1965.) In Game One of the 1954 World Series with the Cleveland Indians, Mays made a particularly brilliant and game-saving bare-handed catch that has become one of the sport's legendary moments.

By the late 1950s Mays had led his league in base stealing and had won the first of 12 fielding awards for his work in center field. He was becoming a public star, immensely popular with fans and teammates not only for his obvious talent but also for his personal charm. He played, according to an article in *Time* magazine, "with a boy's glee, a pro's sureness, and a champion's flair."

Willie Mays played for the Giants – who moved from New York to San Francisco, California, in 1958 – until 1972. At that time he was traded to the New York Mets. When he retired from baseball at the end of the

1973 season, he had amassed not only 660 home runs but also 3283 total hits and a lifetime batting average of .302. After his election to the Hall of Fame in 1979, he was banned from professional baseball-related work in a controversial move by then commissioner Bowie Kuhn because he had been employed as a spokesperson for a gambling casino, but this ban was later lifted by commissioner Peter Ueberroth. Since 1986 Mays has served as special assistant to the president of the Giants organization.

Mays, who grew up in the segregated American South, seemed to have little interest in serving as a spokesperson for racial justice. At times he faced criticism within the African American community for his silence on issues like civil rights. Had Mays been born 20 years earlier, he might have spent his entire career playing in the Negro League, where team members traveled on broken-down buses, endured racist harassment, and often had to work second jobs to support themselves. But Mays, who entered major-league baseball just four years after Jackie Robinson broke the color line, was able to exercise his talents in front of a nationwide, integrated audience, and he became one of the sport's most celebrated stars.

Kate Tuttle

See Also

Track and Field in the United States; Aaron, Henry Louis (Hank); Baseball in the United States; Civil Rights Movement; Football, Professional; Jim Crow; Negro Leagues; San Francisco and Oakland, California.

Africa

Mazrui, Ali A. (b. February 24, 1933, Mombasa, Kenya), a prominent African scholar whose indictment of Western colonialism has sparked controversy.

Ali Mazrui was born into the prominent Mazrui clan of Mombasa, which ruled the city during the eighteenth century. His father, Al'Amin Ali Mazrui, was chief Kadhi, Kenya's highest-ranking Islamic judge. After attending primary and secondary schools in Mombasa, Mazrui earned a B.A. from the University of Manchester in 1960. He earned an M.A. from Columbia University in New York City in 1961 and a doctorate from Oxford University in 1966.

While working on his dissertation, Mazrui began teaching political science in 1963 at Makerere University in Kampala, Uganda. He was named dean of the Faculty of Social Sciences in 1967, a position he held until 1973. A favorite of Idi Amin in 1971, Amin's first year in power, Mazrui soon lost favor because of his outspokenness, and was told to "shut up" or move out of Uganda. In 1973 Mazrui moved to the United States, where he has taught at several universities, including the University of Michigan and Cornell University in New York. He has also held an at-large professorship at the University of Jos in Nigeria.

Mazrui established his scholarly reputation by publishing his first three books in 1967: *Toward a Pax Africana,* which he based on his dissertation; *The Anglo-African Commonwealth;* and *On Heroes and Uhuru-Worship;* each received favorable reviews. He has continued to publish extensively, authoring more than 20 books and more than 100 journal articles and editing several scholarly and reference works. His most popular and controversial work was a nine-part television series produced in 1986 for the British Broadcasting Company (BBC) and the United States' Public Broadcasting System (PBS), *The Africans: A Triple Heritage.* Mazrui, who both wrote and hosted the show, sought to balance what he considered prevailing pro-Western views of Africa with a purely African perspective on the continent's history and contemporary trends. Conservatives criticized him for anti-Western bias, a charge Mazrui denied.

Kate Tuttle

Africa

Mbaka (also known as the Bwaka, the Ngbaka, and the Gbwaka), ethnic group of Central Africa.

The Mbaka primarily inhabit the Lobaye prefecture of northwestern Congo-Kinshasa and neighboring parts of the Central African Republic (CAR). Historically, many of leaders of the CAR have been Mbaka, including Barthélemy Boganda, David Dacko, and Jean-Bédel Bokassa. The Mbaka speak a Niger-Congo language and number around 300,000 people.

See Also

Congo, Democratic Republic of the; Languages, African: An Overview.

Africa

Mbala, ethnic group of the Democratic Republic of the Congo.

The Mbala primarily inhabit southwestern Congo-Kinshasa. They speak a Bantu language and are related to the Kongo people. Approximately 200,000 people consider themselves Mbala.

See Also

Bantu: Dispersion and Settlement.

Africa

Mba, Léon (b. February 9, 1902, Libreville, Gabon; d. November, 27, 1967, Paris, France), leading nationalist and first prime minister and president of Gabon.

Léon Mba, a Fang from the estuary region of western Gabon, was the son of a village chief and the brother of Gabon's first Roman Catholic priest. He ultimately eclipsed the power and fame of both his father and brother as one of Gabon's most prominent nationalist figures and the country's first prime minister.

After completing a Catholic primary education, Mba served in the colonial administration as an interpreter. During the 1920s he was active in nascent nationalist groups advocating for African rights, and became known as an expert in Fang customary law. In 1924 the French colonial administration appointed him canton chief of Libreville's Fang quarter. Mba's advocacy of the Bwiti religion, however, earned him the enmity of French missionaries and officials. In 1933, after being convicted of participating in banned Bwiti practices, he was exiled to prison in Oubangui-Chari (the present-day Central African Republic), where he worked as a prison financial agent and wrote on Fang culture.

On his return to Gabon in 1946, Mba became involved in nationalist politics. He was among the founders of the Comité Mixte Gabonaise, a left-wing nationalist party. During the early 1950s, together with representatives of the Mpongwe and southern groups, Mba founded a new party opposing the leading nationalist, Jean-Hilaire Aubame, a Conservative supported by traditional northern Fang. In 1956 Mba won election as mayor of Libreville. Ultimately, Mba's alliance prevailed in national elections, and in 1959 he became prime minister, a post he retained when Gabon became independent the following year. In 1961, under a new constitution, he assumed office as president.

In the early years of his rule Mba worked to increase the power of the presidency relative to the legislature. His growing authoritarianism disenchanted many and spurred a coup d'état in 1964. France intervened to restore Mba to the presidency. Upon his reinstatement Mba moved to monopolize power, repress opposition, and create a de facto one-party state. Mba's handpicked successor, Albert-Bernard Bongo, assumed power when Mba died in November 1967.

Eric Young

See Also

Bongo, Omar; Colonial Rule; Nationalism in Africa; Libreville, Gabon; Christianity: Missionaries in Africa.

Africa

Mbeki, Thabo (b. June 18, 1942, Idutywa, Transkei, South Africa), South African activist who became president of South Africa in 1999.

The son of Govan Mbeki, a prominent African National Congress (ANC) leader,

Thabo Mbeki was born in Idutywa, in a region of southeastern South Africa then known as the Transkei. He joined the ANC Youth League as a young teenager in 1956. He attended Lovedale secondary school near Alice until a strike closed the school, then returned to the Transkei region and graduated from Saint John's High School in Umtata in 1959. He moved to Johannesburg and enrolled as a correspondence student in economics with the University of London.

While in Johannesburg, Mbeki was elected national secretary of the African Students' Association. The organization eventually collapsed following the arrest of many of its members by the South African government. In 1960 the South African government banned the ANC and other organizations that were active in opposition to apartheid, the government's system of forced segregation of the races. Mbeki then worked underground as an opposition organizer. He left South Africa illegally in 1962, on instructions from the ANC. He went first to Southern Rhodesia (now Zimbabwe), then to Tanzania, and finally to Great Britain. There he studied at the University of Sussex, where he received a master's degree in economics in 1966. He worked for the ANC out of London from 1966 until 1970, when he went to the Union of Soviet Socialist Republics (USSR) for military training.

In 1971 Mbeki served as assistant secretary of the ANC's Revolutionary Council in Lusaka, Zambia. He undertook missions for the ANC to Botswana, Swaziland, and Nigeria during the 1970s. In 1975, at age 33, he became the youngest member of the ANC's National Executive Committee. Three years later he became political secretary to ANC president Oliver Tambo. In the early 1980s Mbeki assumed the position of director of the ANC's information office, where he played a significant role in focusing the international media's attention on apartheid. In 1989 he was named head of the ANC's department of international affairs.

After the ban on the ANC was lifted in 1990, Mbeki returned to South Africa to participate in negotiations with the government over the future of the country. He succeeded Oliver Tambo as national chair of the ANC in 1993. Free multiracial elections were held for the first time in South Africa in 1994, with the ANC gaining the support of the majority of voters. On May 10, 1994, Mbeki was sworn in as first deputy president in the new government headed by Nelson Mandela. Five years later, Mandela having retired, Mbeki ran for president. He and the ANC won a landslide victory in South Africa's second all-race elections.

See Also

Johannesburg, South Africa; Lusaka, Zambia; Mandela, Nelson Rolihlahla; South Africa.

Africa

Mbembe (also known as the Tigong), ethnic group of West Africa.

The Mbembe primarily inhabit Taraba State in eastern Nigeria and western Cameroon. They speak a Niger-Congo language and are closely related to the Ibibio people. More than 100,000 people consider themselves Mbembe.

See Also

Languages, African: An Overview.

Africa

Mbochi, a major ethnic group of northern Republic of the Congo.

Since Congolese independence the Mbochi people of northern Congo have emerged as a powerful political force, even though they make up only around 12 percent of the national population. Little is known about their early history, but it is believed that the Mbochi are descendants of Bantu speaking groups who migrated to the fluvial basins of the Mossaka, Likouala, and Sangha rivers from the western bank of the Congo River during the middle of the eighteenth century. They established hereditary fishing rights, controlled riverine trade, and engaged in fishing, hunting, and boat building. Oral history suggests that the Mbochi came from a common ancestor named Ndinga, though today the Mbochi divide themselves into several subgroups, including the Kouyou, Makoua, Likouala, Bangala, and Bonga.

During the transatlantic slave trade as well as the colonial era, the Mbochi re-mained relatively isolated in the dense forest of northern Congo, though the French recruited many Mbochi men into the colonial army. In postcolonial Congo, the Mbochi rose to prominence when Marien Ngouabi became president in 1969. Although Ngouabi was a northerner, he was of the Mbochi subgroup Kouyou, and intranorthern disputes broke out and continued until Denis Sassou-Nguesso, a Mbochi, took over in 1979. Since then Sassou-Nguesso, surrounded by Mbochi military men, has ruled the Republic of the Congo, except for an interlude of elected government between 1992 and 1997. Because the north remains relatively poor and underdeveloped, many Mbochi have migrated to Brazzaville, the capital, seeking employment.

Eric Young

See Also

Bantu: Dispersion and Settlement; Brazzaville, Republic of the Congo.

Africa

Mbole, ethnic group of the Democratic Republic of the Congo.

The Mbole primarily inhabit north central Congo-Kinshasa. They speak a Bantu language. Approximately 200,000 people consider themselves Mbole.

See Also

Bantu: Dispersion and Settlement.

Africa

Mboya, Tom (b. August 15, 1930, Kilima, Mbogo Kenya [near Nairobi]; d. July 5, 1969, Nairobi, Kenya), Kenyan labor activist and nationalist leader.

Tom Mboya, the son of a poor Luo sisal cutter, realized that he had a "keen sense of the political" while attending mission schools near Nairobi. He became politically active through the labor movement – the only legal avenue for social protest in colonial Kenya – while working as a sanitary inspector.

Elected secretary of the African Staff Association in 1951 and founder of the Kenya Local Government Workers Union in 1952, Mboya had an initial goal of better working conditions for Africans. Soon, however, the British colonial government's repressive response to the Mau Mau uprising convinced him that economic improvements were not enough. At a time when many nationalist leaders were detained in concentration camps, Mboya became a leader in the independence struggle, with strong support from Kenyan workers. After spending two years at Oxford University studying industrial relations, Mboya was elected to Kenya's Legislative Council in 1957.

Mboya and Oginga Odinga founded the Kenya African National Union (KANU) in 1960. Its president, nationalist hero Jomo Kenyatta, became president of Kenya at the time of the country's independence in December 1963, and he appointed Mboya minister for economic planning and development. As minister Mboye sought to rally international support for a Marshall Plan for Africa.

Compared with many Kenyan political figures, Mboya was a politically inclusive Pan-Africanist. He encouraged what he termed "positive tribalism" – that is, seeking in one's ethnic identity a sense of community, security, and history – but he opposed "negative tribalism," especially when it fostered ethnically based political divisions. Unfortunately, he was assassinated in Nairobi in 1969 by a Kikuyu man. This did, in fact, aggravate existing Kikuyu-Luo tensions.

Robert Fay

See Also

Mau Mau Rebellion; Nairobi, Kenya; Pan-Africanism.

Africa

Mbundu, major ethnic group in ANGOLA.

According to oral histories, the people who now call themselves the Mbundu came from three different Bantu-speaking groups who, in the fifteenth century C.E., migrated to the northern coast of what is today Angola. They came from central and east Central Africa, bringing with them iron-making, agricultural, and new hunting skills as well as a unifying belief in divine kingship. Their diverse and decentralized political systems gradually coalesced into centralized kingdoms organized around *ngola*, or lineage emblems, which were inherited through matrilineal succession, though historians continue to debate the reasons for this transformation. By 1500 the Ndongo monarchy, with its capital at Kabasa, was the largest and most prosperous of the kingdoms, built on a mixed economy of agriculture, artisanry, and trade.

The Mbundu's proximity to the coast and their control over trade routes brought them into early and extensive contact with the Portuguese. The Mbundu initially called the Portuguese *Ndele*, or "masters of the white birds," for the white sails that powered their ships. In 1520 a royal Portuguese decree called for the conversion of the Mbundu to Christianity, and Catholic missionaries established a mission near present-day Luanda. Unlike rulers of the KONGO kingdom to the north, however, the Ndongo king was indifferent to Christianity, preferring only to trade with the Portuguese. He treated the mission with disdain and outlawed the preaching of the gospel. In the late sixteenth century Portugal appointed Paulo Dias de Novias (grandson of navigator Bartholemu Dias) proprietor of the coastal Mbundu territory, thus inaugurating a military conquest of the region. The Mbundu resisted Portuguese invasions until 1669, when, after a three-month siege, Portuguese troops overthrew the Ndongo capital.

The primary objective behind the conquest of Mbundu territory was to acquire slaves for the TRANSATLANTIC SLAVE TRADE, conducted at the time by Portuguese traders and their African middlemen, primarily the Imbangala people of Kasanje. Although Mbundu rulers such as Queen NZINGA resisted, the slave trade destroyed most existing Mbundu kingdoms. It also created other kingdoms, such as the Matamba and Kasanje, that centered on the slave trade. With the abolition of the slave trade and the new demand for coffee and SUGAR in the nineteenth century, Mbundu men and women became increasingly alienated from their land and were forced to work on agricultural estates. Meanwhile, centuries of interaction with the Portuguese had created a distinct Afro-Portuguese group of Mbundu, many of whom were *assimilados*, those who had "assimilated" Portuguese culture. Assimilados held an elite social status, creating a divide within the Mbundu between the primarily urban, educated assimilados and the rural Ambakista speakers.

The Mbundu were among the front-runners of early supporters of African nationalism in the 1950s and 1960s. With Portuguese Marxists and Afro-Portuguese intellectuals, educated Mbundu provided the core membership for the nationalist POPULAR MOVEMENT FOR THE LIBERATION OF ANGOLA (MPLA). When Angola won independence in 1975, the Mbundu-dominated MPLA gained control of the government and military. Since then, most senior political, military, and business positions have been held by Mbundu, including Angola's past and current presidents AGOSTINHO NETO and JOSÉ EDUARDO DOS SANTOS. Today the Mbundu are the second largest ethnic group in Angola, comprising approximately 25 percent of the total population. Many of them earn their livelihood in Luanda or in commercial farming.

Eric Young

SEE ALSO

Bantu: Dispersion and Settlement; Luanda, Angola; Iron in Africa; Nationalism in Africa; Portugal; Christianity: Missionaries in Africa; Afro-Atlantic Culture: On the Live Dialogue Between Africa and the Americas.

North America

McClendon, Rose

(b. August 27, 1884, Greenville, S.C.; d. July 12, 1936, New York, N.Y.), African American actor who promoted African American theater, playwrights, and actors.

Rose McClendon, born Rosalie Virginia Scott, moved to New York City with her family around 1890 where, in 1904, she married Henry Pruden McClendon, a chiropractor who also worked as a porter.

McClendon directed and acted in dramatic performances at Saint Mark's African Methodist Episcopal Church, but her professional acting career began with a scholarship to the American Academy of Dramatic Arts in 1916. Her first role was in *Justice* (1919) and she appeared in *Roseanne* (1924) with Charles Gilpin and, later, PAUL ROBESON. She achieved critical acclaim for her performance in *Deep River* (1926) with Jules Bledsoe. In Paul Green's Pulitzer Prize-winning *In Abraham's Bosom* (1926) she won a *Morning Telegraph* acting award. She also acted in *Porgy* (1927), *House of Connelly* (1931), *Never No More* (1932), *Black Souls* (1932), *Roll Sweet Chariot* (1934), *Brainsweat* (1934), *Panic* (1935), and LANGSTON HUGHES's *Mulatto* (1935), the first dramatic play by an African American to appear on Broadway.

McClendon promoted African American theater as a board member of the Theatre Union and as director of the Harlem Experimental Theatre. With Dick Campbell, she organized the Negro People's Theatre and co-headed this project when it was incorporated into the federal relief agency, the WORKS PROGRESS ADMINISTRATION, in 1935.

McClendon contracted pneumonia and died on July 12, 1936. After her death, Campbell established the Rose McClendon Players community theater group in her honor. In 1946 Carl Van Vechten instituted the Rose McClendon Collection of Photographs of Distinguished Negroes at Yale University.

Leyla Keough

SEE ALSO

African Methodist Episcopal Church; Gilpin, Charles Sidney; New York, New York.

North America

McCoy, Elijah J. (b. May 2, 1843, Colchester, Canada; d. October 10, 1929, Eloise, Mich.), African American inventor with whom the saying "the real McCoy" gained popularity.

Elijah McCoy was one of 12 children born to runaway slaves who had used the UNDERGROUND RAILROAD to escape slavery in Kentucky. Living in extreme poverty, McCoy's parents emphasized education to their children as the surest means of betterment. When he was 15, McCoy's parents sent him to study mechanical engineering in Edinburgh, Scotland, training that was impossible for blacks to get in the United States. After finishing his schooling in Scotland, McCoy returned to the United States with the hope of obtaining an engineering job.

Although a trained engineer with impressive credentials, McCoy was unable to find work in his field because of his race. He was forced to accept a job as a locomotive fireman with the Michigan Central Railroad, a position that required no engineering knowledge, only that he shovel coal into the engine and apply oil in the moving parts of the machine. McCoy found the work unchallenging and sought other more productive forms of occupation.

It had long been considered a problem that railroad engines were unable to lubricate themselves. When in need of lubrication, the machines had to be shut off entirely, causing a loss in time and money. As this was a regular necessity, the industry found profit nearly impossible to realize. In his free time McCoy began to consider solutions to this problem, and after two years he developed the "lubricating cup" for steam engines. According to McCoy, the cup allowed for the "continuous flow of oil on the gears... thereby do[ing] away with the necessity of shutting down the machine."

McCoy received a patent for his lubricating device in 1872. The lubricating cup was essential to industries throughout the world, and those in possession of the valuable cup were said to have "the real McCoy." The lubricating cup was his most successful and best-known invention, although McCoy also obtained patents for an automatic sprinkler and an ironing table, eventually acquiring 58 patents in his lifetime.

See Also
Fugitive Slaves.

North America

McDaniel, Hattie **(b. June 10, 1895, Wichita, Kans.; d. October 26, 1952, Woodland Hills, Calif.), African American singer, actress, and radio performer, the first black ever to win an Oscar for her role as Mammy in *Gone With the Wind.***

Hattie McDaniel appeared in more than 300 films and, despite her considerable talent, was limited to mainly housemaid roles, as were most black actresses of the 1930s and 1940s, including Louise Beavers, Ethel Waters, and Lillian Randolph. Although McDaniel's housemaid roles often exemplified the stereotypes blacks abhorred, she transformed many of these roles into sassy, independent-minded characters. In a Hollywood that enshrined white stars at the expense of black performers, she became the first black ever to win an Academy Award – as Best Supporting Actress for her "Mammy" role in the 1939 film *Gone With the Wind.*

Hattie McDaniel grew up in Denver, Colorado, the 13th child of Henry McDaniel, a Baptist preacher, and Susan (Holbert) McDaniel, a church singer. Her talents for singing and drama were apparent from an early age. Encouraged by a teacher, she often sang and recited poetry at her predominantly white elementary school. At age 13 she began performing in black minstrel shows – billed as "Denver's favorite soubrette" – and took the lead in high school plays and musical performances. In a contest sponsored by the Woman's Christian Temperance Union, she won a gold medal for her moving rendition of "Convict Joe," an Alexander Murdoch poem about a man ruined by drink. Based on this success, she quit high school to tour full-time with minstrel groups along the West Coast, mainly with her father's Henry McDaniel Minstrel Show. When her father retired from performing in 1916, McDaniel supported herself clerking in a Denver bakery.

In 1920 McDaniel began touring with the Melody Hounds, a musical ensemble led by one of Denver's top black musicians, George Morrison. Traveling from Portland to El Paso, she received popular recognition as a singer and vaudeville performer, and in 1924 made her radio debut with Morrison in Denver. She was also a talented songwriter and recorded many of her own songs on the Okeh and Paramount labels in Chicago.

By the late 1920s McDaniel's theater bookings were dependent on the Theater Owners Booking Association (TOBA), and in 1929, when TOBA went bankrupt, she was left stranded and broke. Seeking work as a performer at the Club Madrid in Milwaukee, she was hired as a ladies' washroom attendant. When finally the club invited her to sing, she won immediate success and soon after set her sights on Hollywood.

Arriving in Los Angeles in 1931, McDaniel visited film studios looking for work while washing "three million dishes on her way to stardom." She also performed weekly on Los Angeles radio, where she became popularly known as Hi-Hat Hattie, a bossy, effervescent maid "who continually forgets her place." In 1932 she won her first, uncredited film role as a Southern house servant in Fox's *The Golden West.* Numerous offers followed and in 1934 she was chosen to play the washerwoman Aunt Dilsey, a lead part in Will Rogers's film *Judge Priest.*

By the late 1930s she had become a widely recognized Hollywood "Mammy" with two distinct film personae. As her biographer Carlton Jackson points out, while "she was much too servile in *The Little Colonel* for the liking of many blacks, she was much too independent in *Alice Adams* for numerous whites." Indeed, with the exception of the 1941 film *In This Our Life,* in which McDaniel's character, Minerva Clay, openly confronts racial issues, her film roles alternated between subservient and cantankerous maids. Although McDaniel relished her success, her film personae weighed heavily on her. During the 1940s she spent much time defending herself before the National Association for the Advancement of Colored People (NAACP), which claimed that she was perpetuating a stereotype. The NAACP particularly criticized her role in *Gone With the Wind,* in which Mammy spoke nostalgically about the Old South.

From 1947 to 1952 McDaniel was the host of *The Beulah Show,* a nationally broadcast radio program later transferred to television. She portrayed Beulah, an ebullient Southern maid, yet this time without using dialect and entirely on her own terms. Beulah was also the first radio program in which a black played the starring role. Praised by the NAACP and the National Urban League, *The Beulah Show* attracted nearly 20,000 listeners weekly and finally provided McDaniel with a role in which she could truly be herself. Suffering from breast cancer, she died in 1952 at age 57.

Roanne Edwards

See Also
Baptists; Chicago, Illinois; Minstrelsy; Racial Stereotypes; Los Angeles, California; Film, Blacks in American.

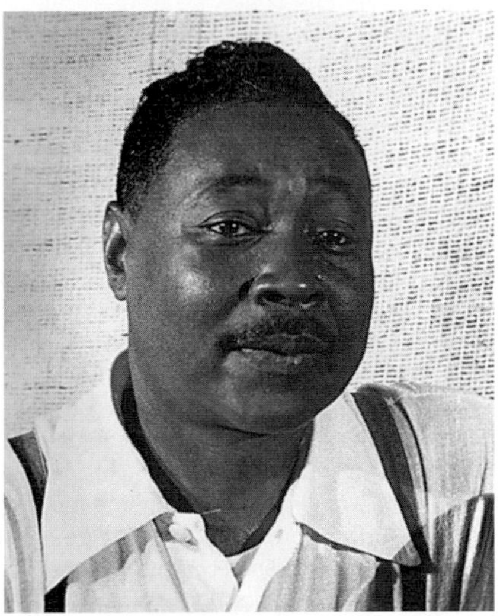

Jamaica-born poet and novelist Claude McKay became a pivotal figure in the Harlem Renaissance. *CORBIS*

Latin America and the Caribbean

McKay, Claude

(b. September 15, 1889, Sunny Ville, Jamaica; d. May 22, 1948, Chicago, Ill.), Jamaican poet, essayist, and novelist who was one of the founders of both modern African American literature and modern Jamaican literature.

Claude McKay's work as a poet, novelist, and essayist heralded several of the most significant moments in African American culture. His protest poetry of the second and third decades of the twentieth century was seen by may of his contemporaries as the premier example of the "New Negro" spirit. His novels were sophisticated considerations of the problems and possibilities of Pan-Africanism at the end of the colonial era, influencing writers of African descent throughout the world. His early poetry in Jamaican patois, and his fiction set in Jamaica, are now seen as crucial to the development of a national Jamaican literature.

McKay's Early Life

McKay's parents, Thomas Francis McKay and Hannah Ann McKay, were prosperous farmers by the standards of the town. Through the efforts of his brother Uriah Theodore, a schoolteacher, and Walter Jekyll, an expatriate Englishman who became McKay's patron and who was particularly important in encouraging McKay's literary ambitions, McKay received more formal education than was typical for a child of a farming family. He became a police constable (or "constab") in Kingston in 1911.

McKay's Early Writing

McKay published two collections of poetry, *Songs of Jamaica* and *Constab Ballad,* in 1912. These poems emerged largely out of McKay's experience as a constab, which

McKay found, along with urban life in general, to be alienating. He felt uncomfortably located between the Jamaican elite and the great mass of the urban poor. Many of the concerns of McKay's later work, such as the opposition of the city and the country, the problems of exile, and the relation of the black intellectual to the common folk, appear first in these poems.

McKay moved to the United States in 1912 to attend Tuskegee Institute. After brief stints at Tuskegee and Kansas State University, he left for Harlem. There he wrote poetry while holding several menial jobs, including working on a railroad dining car. This period of McKay's work is best remembered for his militant protest sonnets, notably "If We Must Die," considered by such contemporaries of McKay as James Weldon Johnson and Walter White to be the beginning of the Harlem Renaissance. McKay also wrote many poems of exile, such as "Flame-Heart" and "The Tropics in New York," in which he nostalgically invokes a tropical landscape and the desire to return to a remembered community. Even many of the protest sonnets can be considered exile poems, since a break between the poem's speaker and his original community is often at the root of the speaker's anger. Much of McKay's early poetry was collected in the book *Harlem Shadows* (1922).

McKay and Communism

In 1919 McKay moved to Europe, where he became increasingly involved in the new communist movement. McKay saw in communism an alternative to racism, poverty, and colonialism. He worked on Sylvia Pankhurst's pro-communist newspaper *Worker's Dreadnought* in London. On his return to New York in 1921, he became coeditor (with Mike Gold) of the radical journal the *Liberator*. After personal and aesthetic disagreements with Gold and the other members of the *Liberator* editorial board, McKay left the journal in 1922. As a delegate to the Fourth Congress of the Communist International (Comintern) in 1922, McKay declared that the "Negro Question" was central to the world revolutionary movement. He moved again to Europe in 1923 and remained in Europe and North Africa until 1934.

In his two novels of the 1920s, *Home to Harlem* (1928) and *Banjo* (1929), McKay investigated how the concepts of race and class worked in a world dominated by capitalism and colonialism, and how cosmopolitan and rural black communities can be reconciled to each other. *Home to Harlem* was more commercially successful than any novel by an African American author to that point. Its plot revolves around an intellectual Haitian expatriate, Ray, and an African American longshoreman and World War I veteran, Jake. Ray worries constantly and feels isolated from the African American community as a result of his European education. Jake is spontaneous and direct. Ray and Jake work for a time as dining car workers, becoming close friends. Ray appears again in *Banjo* with another "natural" black character, the African American musician Lincoln Agrippa Daily (or "Banjo"). *Banjo* is set in the old port of Marseilles and features a shifting group of black longshoremen, sailors, and drifters from Africa. In both novels McKay articulates the need for the exiled black intellectual to return to the common black folk. This theme is taken even further in McKay's final novel, *Banana Bottom* (1933). The protagonist of *Banana Bottom* is Bita Plant, a European-educated Jamaican woman who returns to her native village in Jamaica. In the course of the novel, Plant rejects European culture and the Jamaican elite, choosing instead to rejoin the farming folk.

McKay's Later Career

McKay returned to the United States in 1934. During the 1920s and early 1930s he moved further away from the communist movement, becoming at last an active anticommunist. His final books, the autobiographical *A Long Way from Home* (1937) and the sociological *Harlem: Negro Metropolis* (1940), were in large part attacks on the Communist Party of the United States of America (CPUSA). McKay also sharply criticized black intellectuals for either being intimidated or deceived by the CPUSA in the late 1930s and early 1940s. While working as a member of the Works Progress Administration's Federal Writers' Project in New York during the late 1930s, McKay attempted without success to organize an anticommunist writer's group in Harlem. Throughout this work, McKay became increasingly isolated from the mainstream of black artists and intellectuals.

McKay's interest in Roman Catholicism grew significantly during the 1940s, and he officially joined the Catholic Church in 1944. At this time he wrote much new poetry which he failed to get published, a failure he blamed on the influence of the CPUSA.

James Smethurst

See Also

World War I and African Americans; Harlem, New York; Tuskegee University; White, Walter Francis; Kingston, Jamaica; Communist Party USA, African Americans and the.

North America

McKinney, Cynthia

(b. March 17, 1955, Atlanta, Ga.), Democratic member of the United States House of Representatives from Georgia (1993-).

The first black woman elected to the House of Representatives from the state of Georgia, Cynthia McKinney was born in Atlanta, Georgia. She was the daughter of J. E. "Billy" McKinney, a civil rights activist and a member of the Georgia state legislature for more than 20 years. McKinney earned a bachelor's degree in international relations from the University of Southern California in 1978. She taught political science at various Georgia colleges and universities and then received a master's degree in 1994 from Tufts University.

McKinney was elected to the Georgia House in 1989, where she served alongside her father. She was part of the state legislative committee that reorganized the state's voting districts in 1992 to create two new black-majority districts. In 1992 she was elected to represent one of these new districts – the primarily urban and Democratic 11th Congressional District of Georgia. In September 1994 a federal appeals court ruled that McKinney's district was unconstitutional. While the appeal was pending in the U.S. Supreme Court, the 1994 election continued with the existing boundaries and McKinney was reelected. In July 1995 the Supreme Court ruled that the 11th District must be redrawn. Resultant changes in district boundaries in 1995 placed her in the newly drawn Fourth District, from which she was reelected in 1996. In the 105th Congress (1997-1999), McKinney served on the International Relations Committee and the Banking and Financial Services Committee. She is a member of the Congressional Black Caucus.

North America

McKinney-Steward, Susan Maria Smith

(b. 1847?, Brooklyn, N.Y.; d. March 7, 1918, Wilberforce, Ohio), physician; the third African American woman to earn a medical degree and the first in New York State.

As a child, Susan Maria Smith McKinney-Steward trained and performed as an organist. Her early training qualified her for teaching positions, and she taught school in Washington, D.C., and New York City, using the proceeds of her New York teaching to pay tuition for medical school.

McKinney-Steward began medical study at the New York Medical College for Women in 1867. She specialized in homeopathic medicine and graduated as class valedictorian after three years. After receiving her degree, she achieved wealth and a local reputation as a successful Brooklyn physician with an interracial clientele. McKinney-Steward excelled especially in pediatric care and the treatment of childhood diseases. Outside her medical practice, she agitated for social reform, advocating female suffrage and temperance. Until the early 1890s she remained the organist for the African Methodist Episcopal (AME) church where she regularly worshiped.

Both of McKinney-Steward's husbands were ministers. She was married to South Carolina minister William G. McKinney in 1871 until his death in 1894. In 1896 McKinney-Steward married United States Army chaplain

Theophilus Gould Steward. She moved with him to army bases in Montana, Nebraska, and Texas. By 1906 husband and wife had both found positions at the AME's Wilberforce University in Ohio, McKinney-Steward as college physician.

In 1911 McKinney-Steward joined luminaries including W. E. B. Du Bois at a Universal Race Congress in London, where she delivered a paper on "Colored American Women." She died in 1918, at WILBERFORCE UNIVERSITY.

SEE ALSO
African Methodist Episcopal Church; Du Bois, William Edward Burghardt (W. E. B.); New York, New York.

North America

McMillan, Terry

(b. October 18, 1951, Port Huron, Mich.), African American novelist and short story writer known for realistic portrayals of contemporary black life.

The success of the 1995 film version of her 1992 novel *Waiting to Exhale* established Terry McMillan as one of the most popular contemporary black authors. The story, which portrays four successful black women struggling with their romantic relationships, careers, and families, touches on all of the themes for which McMillan's work is known – and with which her readers readily identify. She is especially liked as an author for her down-to-earth, conversational writing style, which has been described as "tough and sexy."

McMillan grew up in a factory town 100 km (60 mi) northeast of DETROIT, MICHIGAN, the oldest of five children. Her mother divorced her alcoholic, abusive husband when McMillan was 13 and supported her family as a factory and domestic worker. The only book in their home was the Bible, and at school McMillan was exposed only to white authors. Then when she was 16, she discovered JAMES BALDWIN during a part-time job at a library and realized that "if we [African Americans] did have anything important to say... someone would actually publish it."

McMillan graduated with a degree in journalism from the University of California at Berkeley in 1979, then studied screenwriting at Columbia University in New York. She published her first short story in a campus literary magazine as an undergraduate, and in New York joined the HARLEM WRITERS GUILD. While working by day as a typist, she wrote the short story that became the first chapter of her first novel, *Mama* (1987). *Mama* was published by the mainstream firm Houghton Mifflin, but McMillan chose to arrange a publicity tour herself, contacting colleges and bookstores and scheduling appearances in areas that would attract black readers. Even Houghton Mifflin agreed that her grassroots approach had a strong impact on sales, and *Mama* was reprinted three times in its first two months of publication. As has been noted in *Black Women in America: An Historical Encyclopedia*, the "conventional wisdom among [commercial publishing houses] had been that black people do not buy books. McMillan proved that when someone reaches out to them, black readers are indeed there." McMillan has become one of the first black authors to achieve large-scale success with a predominantly black audience.

Her subsequent novels – *Disappearing Acts* (1989), *Waiting to Exhale*, and *How Stella Got Her Groove Back* (1996) – each added to her reputation and success. *Waiting to Exhale* became a bestseller in its first week of publication and remained on the *New York Times* Bestseller List for months. McMillan's work has been celebrated and criticized for the same strong feature – its honesty in portraying black people and black relationships, especially between men and women. A frequent complaint when the film *Waiting to Exhale* was released was that it portrayed black men too negatively. Some readers have also objected to her use of profanity. But most of her readers find her semiautobiographical novels relevant because they identify with the characters. McMillan has avoided stereotypical "problem" novels about African Americans and instead presents middle-class, educated black characters working through common challenges, speaking in familiar language. In the process she has become one of the most successful contemporary black authors, and one the *Norton Anthology of African American Literature* calls "in many ways the apotheosis of the renaissance in writing by African American women." In 1998 *How Stella Got Her Groove Back* was made into another successful film.

Lisa Clayton Robinson

SEE ALSO
Literature, African American; Women Writers, Black, in the United States.

North America

McNair, Ronald

(b. October 12, 1950, Lake City, S.C.; d. January 28, 1986, Cape Canaveral, Fla.), the second of six African American astronauts.

Despite a background of poverty and segregation, Ronald McNair earned a Ph.D. in physics from the Massachusetts Institute of Technology (M.I.T.) in 1976. After working as a physicist at Hughes Research Laboratories, he became a mission specialist astronaut with the National Aeronautics and Space Administration (NASA) in 1978. His second flight into space ended in tragedy when the space shuttle *Challenger* exploded 73 seconds after takeoff on January 28, 1986; McNair and the six other astronauts on board died in the explosion. His father, Carl McNair, has created a fund for the Ron McNair Science Playground in New York City.

Alonford James Robinson, Jr.

North America

McQueen, Thelma ("Butterfly")

(b. January 8, 1911, Tampa, Fla.), African American actor and dancer known for her exaggerated roles as a domestic worker.

Thelma McQueen was born in Tampa, the child of a maid and a stevedore. In New York City she developed her interests in ballet and modern dance. Through the "Butterfly Ballet" in *A Midsummer Night's Dream*, McQueen earned her nickname "Butterfly" and her major break as an actress. After this part came others, all with McQueen earning the praise of critics. It was in a Benny Goodman-Louis Armstrong musical, "Swingin' the Dream," that she was spotted by David O. Selznick, who cast her as Prissy the maid in *Gone With The Wind* (1939). The role of Prissy immortalized McQueen with her line, "Lawdy, Miz Scarlett... I don't know nuthin' 'bout birthin' babies!"

It was her comic role as the flustered maid, or some variation of it, that McQueen would continue to play for most of her career, to uniformly fine reviews. Yet, while her great talent was widely acknowledged, she could not find roles that were not demeaning stereotypes. As one film critic observed, McQueen was fated "to act stereotypes or starve." She soon tired of playing roles that she called "dumb colored maid parts" and, in frustration, walked out of Jack Benny's radio show. For this she was boycotted for more than a year by casting agents. Refusing to play stereotypes, McQueen left acting altogether by the early 1950s.

After leaving acting, she occasionally took small roles in projects but mainly held jobs as a waitress and a factory worker, and finally opened her own restaurant in Augusta, Georgia. In the early 1970s she returned to college to receive a bachelor of arts degree in Spanish at age 64. McQueen then dedicated herself to community-based projects in New York City that aid black and Hispanic children in Harlem. Although McQueen appeared occasionally in films in the 1970s and 1980s, such as *The Mosquito Coast* (1986) with Harrison Ford, she preferred to serve in roles that aided her community.

SEE ALSO
Armstrong, Louis ("Satchmo"); Harlem, New York; New York, New York; Racial Stereotypes.

North America

McRae, Carmen (b. April 8, 1922, New York, N.Y.; d. November 10, 1994, Beverly Hills, Calif.), African American singer internationally known for her JAZZ and pop repertoire and unique lyrical projection.

Born in Harlem in 1922, Carmen McRae studied classical piano as a youth, although singing was her first passion. When she won an amateur contest at the APOLLO THEATER, her singing career was launched. McRae was greatly influenced by BILLIE HOLIDAY, a lifelong friend and mentor. She dedicated her albums and most of her nightclub performances to Lady Day's memory. In her later years McRae's original style similarly influenced singers BETTY CARTER and Carol Sloane.

In the early 1940s McRae performed with bandleaders Benny Carter, Earl Hines, and Count Basie. While she was married to Kenny Clarke, she made her recording debut as Carmen Clarke with Mercer Ellington's orchestra in 1946-1947. When Ellington's group disbanded in 1948, McRae spent several years in nonmusical jobs. She also performed solo, accompanying herself as an intermission pianist, and met jazz accordionist Matt Mathews. Their association led to McRae's first solo recordings in 1953-1954. In 1955 McRae signed with Decca Records, having achieved popularity at Minton's Playhouse in Harlem.

From the 1950s onward, McRae toured internationally, developing significant popularity in Japan. Her best-known recordings were *Skyliner* (1956) and *Take Five* with Dave Brubeck (1961). McRae also acted in the films *Hotel* (1967) and *Jo Jo Dancer Your Life Is Calling* (1986). Her wide-reaching talents won six Grammy Award nominations and the National Endowment for the Arts' National Jazz Masters Fellowship Award in 1994. She died in 1994.

SEE ALSO

Basie, William James ("Count"); Carter, Bennett Lester (Benny); Harlem, New York; Hines, Earl Kenneth ("Fatha").

North America

Medical Associations, professional organizations that unite physicians for the purpose of promoting the interests, standards, and goals of medical research and practice.

The advancement of black physicians and nurses in the United States, as well as the gradual improvement of health care for the African American community, has been largely a result of the persistent vigilance, lobbying, fundraising, and political influence of medical associations established by blacks in the field of medicine. Racial segregation, announced as the official policy of the American Medical Association (AMA) in 1872, was for many years in the United States the major obstacle for graduating black medical students looking for clinical experience and appointments on the staffs of quality hospitals.

In 1870, for example, three black physicians were refused membership in the Medical Society of the District of Columbia, an all-white organization. The biracial National Medical Society (NMS), was organized as a result. Because of a technicality, however, members of the NMS were not permitted to attend conventions of the AMA even as late as the 1950s. This was due to AMA rules that permitted only one majority association to attend from each locale.

As a result of rigorous medical standardization programs initiated in the early twentieth century by the AMA and the American College of Surgeons, organizations dominated by white physicians, the total number of black medical schools was reduced from ten in 1900 to two in 1923 – Meharry Medical College and HOWARD UNIVERSITY School of Medicine. The demise of black medical schools was accompanied by the closing of the university-affiliated hospitals attached to them, which served large populations of African Americans in their local communities. In the 1920s the number of independent black-run hospitals was also in danger of being reduced as a result of the same standardization programs.

After nearly 25 years of struggling to integrate the AMA, black physicians began organizing their own medical associations, starting with the Atlanta-based National Medical Association (NMA, founded in 1895). By the 1920s there were more than 50 black or mostly black medical associations in the United States. Among the earliest black medical associations were the Medico-Chirurgical Society of the District of Columbia (1884); the Lone Star State Medical Association in Galveston, Texas (1886); the Palmetto State Medical Association in South Carolina (1896); the Old North State Medical, Dental and Pharmaceutical Society in North Carolina (1897); and the Philadelphia Academy of Medicine and Allied Sciences in Philadelphia (1900).

In 1910 the NMA helped promote awareness of the importance of quality hospitals for the advancement of black physicians by conducting a survey of eight black hospitals. In 1923 the National Hospital Association (NHA) was formed to regulate and improve education and care in BLACK HOSPITALS, which began an era of black hospital reform.

The goals outlined in the NMA's original charter were to unite African American physicians toward building their collective political and legislative influence; to help them network and share the results of their research; to build a library of medical publications; and finally, to help the black community itself, by educating African Americans about health care for their families. At Harlem Hospital in New York, for example, there were landmark successes in incorporating black medical professionals as a result of vigorous efforts by the NMA and especially the NHA in the 1920s and 1930s.

In 1920, when 75 percent of Harlem Hospital's patients were black, there were no black doctors or nurses. In 1923 Harlem Hospital hired three black nurses; in 1925 it hired five temporary black physicians, and by 1932 it had 55 full-time black physicians and 14 black interns. The NMA has worked hand in hand with the NATIONAL ASSOCIATION FOR THE ADVANCEMENT OF COLORED PEOPLE (NAACP) to lobby for funding and legislation to end discrimination against African Americans, and has remained active in the 1990s health care debate to ensure that African Americans receive quality health care.

Barbara Worley

Latin America and the Caribbean

Medina y Céspedes, Antonio (b. June 13, 1824, Havana, CUBA; d. 1885, Havana, Cuba), Afro-Cuban poet and playwright.

Born to free parents, Antonio Medina y Céspedes received a modest but formal elementary school education. At age 12 he became an apprentice tailor in order to help his family after the death of his father. After completing his occupational training he secured a position as a tailor at the Tacón Theater, the most prestigious theater in Havana at the time. This job had a great impact on him, not only because it gave him the occasion to meet important members of the Cuban intelligentsia but because it likely influenced his future work as a playwright.

According to Francisco Calcagno, the Cuban educator and author of *Diccionario biográfico cubano* (1886, Cuban Biographical Dictionary) and *Poetas de color* (1886, Black Poets), Medina formed friendships with Afro-Cuban poets GABRIEL DE LA CONCEPCIÓN ("PLÁCIDO") VALDÉS and JUAN FRANCISCO MANZANO, both of whom were directly or indirectly implicated in the La Escalera Conspiracy, the 1844 island-wide slave uprising. It may be inferred that Plácido's life and work had an impact on Medina's *Poesías* (1851), since, like Plácido, Medina frequently utilized sarcastic fables and poems to criticize society's double standard with regard to race.

While working at the Tacón Theater and providing for his 13 children, Medina pursued an education and in 1850 became a certified elementary schoolteacher. Immediately thereafter he founded a school for people of color, Nuestra Señora de los Desamparados. The school rapidly gained recognition and became a cultural center for people of color. Medina directed his school until 1878, educating important figures such as the future senator Juan Gualberto

Gómez (*see* Education in Latin America and the Caribbean).

Together with the Afro-Cuban poet Anselmo Font, in 1856 Medina founded the first Cuban literary journal by people of color, *El Rocío*. This journal, of which only one issue was published, aimed to improve the education of women and to entertain. In addition to *El Rocío*, Medina also founded *El faro* (1842), the first newspaper for people of color, and made literary contributions to other important newspapers and journals.

Medina's plays, published in Havana and staged by local theatrical companies, included two dramas: *Jacobo Girondi* (1880) and *Lodoiska o La Maldicion* (1882). He also wrote a *zarzuela* (comic Spanish operetta), *Don Canuto de Ceibamocha o El Guajiro Generoso* (1858). Through his promotion of education as a tool to fight racial inequality in colonial Cuba, Medina served as literary mentor and cultural pioneer for other Afro-Cuban intellectuals. Although his contributions are still in need of rigorous study and recognition, he was, together with the poets Plácido and Manzano, the politicians Isidro Acea and Gómez, and the scientist Manuel del Socorro Rodríguez, among the most outstanding black intellectual figures of his time (*see* Literature, Black, in Spanish America).

Sonia Labrador Rodrigués

See Also

Conspiración de la Escalera; Havana, Cuba.

North America

Meek, Carrie (b. 1926), Democratic member of the United States House of Representatives from Florida (1993-).

In 1992, at age 66, Carrie Meek became the oldest woman elected to Congress. Meek was born in Tallahassee, Florida, the daughter of sharecroppers and the granddaughter of slaves (*see* Slavery in the United States). After receiving a bachelor's degree in 1946 from Florida A&M University and a master's degree in 1948 from the University of Michigan, Meek worked as an administrator for Miami-Dade Community College from 1949 to 1992. Her political career began in the Florida State House, where she served from 1979 to 1982; she also served in the Florida State Senate from 1982 to 1992. Meek was elected to represent Florida's 17th Congressional District in 1992 after winning the Democratic primary election with 83 percent of the vote. She was returned to office in subsequent elections.

Florida's 17th District, created to be a black-majority district, takes in the northern part of Miami as well as a corridor of black neighborhoods south of Miami. The heavily Democratic district also includes sizable white and Hispanic populations.

In the 105th Congress (1997-1999), Meek served on the Appropriations Committee. She is a member of the Congressional Black Caucus.

North America

Meeks, Gregory (b. September 25, 1953, Far Rockaway, N.Y.), Democratic member of the United States House of Representatives from New York (1998-).

Drawing support from across the political spectrum, former New York State assemblyman Gregory Weldon Meeks won election to the U.S. House of Representatives, replacing the retiring Rev. Floyd Flake. Meeks, a lifetime resident of New York City, was born in Harlem and grew up in public housing projects in East Harlem. The son of a cab driver and a homemaker, he developed an interest in politics in his youth and participated in student government groups at Julia Richman High School. After graduating from Richman High School in 1971, he attended Adelphi University, graduating in 1975. He then earned a law degree from Washington, D.C.'s Howard University Law School.

Meeks began his public service in 1978 as an assistant district attorney in the Borough of Queens. In 1980 he became a special assistant narcotics prosecutor for the City of New York. In addition, he served as assistant counsel of the State Investigation Commission from 1982 to 1984 and judge of the State Workers Compensation Board from 1985 to 1987, becoming the board's supervising judge in 1987. In 1992 he left the State Workers Compensation Board to run for the New York Assembly. In 1997 he successfully ran for Congress. In the 105th Congress, Meeks sat on the House Banking and Financial Services Committee, the Subcommittee on Financial Institutions and Consumer Credit, and the Subcommittee on Domestic and International Monetary Policy.

See Also

Harlem, New York; New York, New York.

Africa

Mehafaly (also known as Mahafali), ethnic group of Madagascar.

The Mehafaly primarily inhabit southwestern Madagascar. They speak Malagasy, a Malayo-Polynesian language, and are closely related to the Sakalava people. Approximately 200,000 people consider themselves Mehafaly.

See Also

Languages, African: An Overview.

Africa

Memmi, Albert (b. 1920, Tunis, Tunisia), a Tunisian writer whose work developed a social theory of colonization.

Albert Memmi was born to a poor Jewish family in Tunis, the capital city of Tunisia. His position as a non-Muslim gave him some privilege in what was then a French protectorate, and as a young man he was educated at an exclusive French secondary school. Yet as a Jew from the ghetto and as a Tunisian, he suffered his own indignities. After Germany occupied Tunisia in 1942, Memmi was interned in a forced-labor camp. He used his intermediate position between the dominated majority and the dominating minority to gain insight into the social structure of colonization. "I know the colonizer from the inside almost as well as I know the colonized," he would later write, reflecting on his background as a North African Jew.

In his autobiographical first novel, *La Statue de sel* (1953, The Pillar of Salt), Memmi embarked on a discussion of colonial identity that would thread throughout all his fiction and political essays. The novel told the story of an alienated young man growing up in Tunisia and deciding ultimately to leave. Its fluid prose won Memmi public recognition, and he received the Prix de Carthage and the Prix Fénéon. His next novel, *Agar* (1955), explored the metaphor of the "mixed" marriage, describing a couple's relationship that encapsulated the historical relations between the West and non-West.

The issues of identity explored in this second novel continued to fascinate Memmi, who experienced an unsuccessful mixed marriage in his own life. His third and most famous work, *Portrait du colonisé* (1957, Portrait of the Colonized, or The Colonizer and the Colonized), published six years before Frantz Fanon's *Wretched of the Earth*, was a landmark in the study of the psychology of colonization. The book provided insight into the complexities of the colonial relationship, in which the positions of colonizer and colonized begin to define each other. "The colonial system manufactures colonialists, just as it manufactures the colonized," Memmi wrote. A source of inspiration across Africa, *Portrait du colonisé* was found throughout the continent in the prison cells of interned anticolonialists.

In his next two works, the two-part *Portrait d'un Juif* (1962 and 1966, *Portrait of a Jew*) and *L'Homme dominé* (1968, *Dominated Man*), Memmi broadened the range of his analysis to include European Jews, the "black man," the proletariat, and women. He sought to create a philosophy of domination, revealing the structural causes of problems such as racism. In *Jews and Arabs* (1974), he explored Zionism and the foundation of a Jewish state as a liberating response to Jewish marginalization.

During the 1980s and 1990s Memmi published a number of books that further explore the nature of oppression. In the words of critic Gary Wilder, "His readers confront autobiography driven by philosophy which unfolds as sociology – sometimes represented in fiction as a form of history." Memmi has taught sociology at the University of Paris, and he founded a research group on North African literature at the Ecole Pratique des Hautes Etudes in Paris.

Marian Aguiar

SEE ALSO
Jewish Communities in North Africa; Tunis, Tunisia; Tunisia.

North America

Memphis, Tennessee, Southern American city just north of the Mississippi Delta that developed as a result of the cotton trade, hosted the first urban blues scene, and is home to one of the largest and poorest black populations in the South.

A visitor to Memphis today can still discern the mark of cotton brokerage on the fronts of abandoned offices and warehouses; she can visit the National Civil Rights Museum at the Lorraine Motel, where Martin Luther King Jr. was assassinated; she can hear old and new blues on Beale Street, and eat barbecued pork ribs in the restaurant owned by blues singer B. B. King.

Memphis sits on a bluff overlooking the Mississippi River and was probably named for its geographical similarity to Memphis, Egypt, which flanks the Nile. Its proximity to the Mississippi River has played a key role in the city's 200-year history. In the antebellum period regional slave trading and cotton commerce centered on the riverside town. Even after the Civil War, the economy of Memphis depended on the transport and sale of cotton as well as other goods.

The geography of Memphis often caused serious problems for poor African Americans, whom whites pushed onto the least valuable land – swampy bayou that drains poorly and breeds tropical disease. The status of Memphis as a port town, however, has contributed to its bustling cultural milieu and its historic centrality to black music in the American South.

White people founded Memphis in 1819. Early black residents worked as domestic servants, artisans, or laborers in river commerce; most voted freely and lived as citizens. In 1834, however, the local government stripped blacks of their rights and in 1840 repealed a ban on the slave trade. Memphis became a center of slave trading and remained so until the Civil War, when the Union Army took the city in 1862.

During and after the war many African Americans gravitated to Memphis, filling the freedpeople's camps of the Union Army. Blacks often roused the hatred of white immigrants – Germans, Irish, and Italians – who competed for the same jobs and living quarters. The changing racial climate of RECONSTRUCTION encouraged some cooperation along class lines, and in the 1860s and 1870s blacks formed political coalitions with foreign-born whites. Yet the alliance was short-lived. JIM CROW laws and the PLESSY V. FERGUSON decision of the United States Supreme Court encouraged racism among lower-class whites.

Yellow fever epidemics in 1877 and 1878, caused by mosquito-infested Memphis swampland, hastened the deterioration of good relations between blacks and their white neighbors. Well-off whites, whose residency began in days of greater racial tolerance, fled the mosquito-infested neighborhoods; white immigrants from poor regions of Arkansas, Mississippi, and Tennessee replaced them, introducing a new, provincial racism. For African Americans, civil rights diminished and segregation proliferated as the century reached its end.

While the yellow fever epidemics hurt Memphis in many ways, they did spell some prosperity for entrepreneurial blacks. Robert Reed Church Sr., a local businessman, bought many properties that had been vacated during the late 1870s. Church accrued exceptional wealth from his saloons and real estate holdings, becoming one of the first African American millionaires. He returned much of his wealth to the black community, founding an auditorium and a park to facilitate social events and recreation.

Through the efforts of black clergy and other African American businessmen, Memphis blacks developed an economic community of their own. Beale Street, which stretched along the Memphis waterfront, soon came to symbolize African American independence in the Jim Crow era of racial violence and discrimination. Both honest businesses and seedy clubs lined the concourse, attracting black doctors, lawyers, gamblers, and blues musicians.

In fact, Beale Street became known as the home of the blues, when musician W. C. Handy arrived in 1908, introducing music of the Southern countryside, popularizing this new sound, and founding a company that published the first blues sheet music. Beale Street became a black haven in a racist city and state, attracting itinerant blues musicians such as Memphis Minnie and Robert Johnson. Historians Margaret McKee and Fred Chisenhall write, "On Beale you could find surcease from sorrow; on Beale you could forget for a shining moment the burden of being black and celebrate being black; on Beale you could be a man, your own man; on Beale you could be free." Although Beale Street suffered immensely during the GREAT DEPRESSION, it survived to produce master bluesmen after World War II. Performers such as B.B. King and Memphis Slim emerged from Beale Street clubs in the 1950s.

Memphis in the early twentieth century showcased black cultural prosperity, yet it also reflected the poor state of African American political life. Irish-American Edward H. "Boss" Crump dominated Memphis politics from the late 1920s until 1954. Although he never became mayor himself, Crump consolidated power and assembled a formidable political machine. All the while he maintained an ambivalent and paternalistic relationship with the black community of Memphis. He oversaw massive voter registration campaigns,

Rhythm and blues singer Rufus Thomas works as a deejay at a Memphis, Tennessee, radio station. *CORBIS/David Reed*

enfranchising a large segment of the African American population. Yet in the single-party politics of Crump's Memphis, the power he bestowed on blacks served only his ends; and as a staunch segregationist, his generosity was predicated on the submissiveness of his black constituents.

Under the Crump administration few African Americans gained any political power. When Crump died in 1954, however, his self-serving registration drives ultimately set Memphis blacks ahead of blacks in other cities. In 1963 as many African Americans as whites were registered to vote, and throughout the 1950s and 1960s black candidates began to run for office. African American political victories came slowly. Blacks voters comprised a minority, and within that minority there was much competition. Furthermore, white candidates often ran for office using racist rhetoric. The most successful black politician of the era, Harold Ford, did not win his congressional seat until 1974. W. W. Herenton, the first black mayor of Memphis, won office only in 1987.

Despite the languor of conventional political channels in Memphis, the city played an active role in the CIVIL RIGHTS MOVEMENT. Through the power of the church and the success of voter registration drives, blacks secured the vote. Through SIT-INS and demonstrations, they gained access to segregated business and schools. One of the most tragic events of the Civil Rights Movement, the assassination of Martin Luther King Jr., occurred amid the strike of Memphis's predominantly black sanitation workers in 1968. After addressing a rally at Mason Temple, the city's largest black church, King was shot dead at the Lorraine Motel.

Census data in the 1990s showed that blacks in Memphis were among the poorest in the nation. Despite the success of black politicians, Memphis suffered from a limited economy. The city's dependence on service industries and commerce – instead of industry or new technology – left it with few well-paying jobs for blue-collar blacks.

Eric Bennett

SEE ALSO

Nile River; Slavery in the United States; World War II and African Americans; Blues, The; Church, Robert Reed, Sr.; Civil War, American; Ford, Harold Eugene; Handy, William Christopher (W.C.); Johnson, Robert Leroy; King, Martin Luther, Jr.; King, Riley B. ("B. B."); Black Church, The.

Africa

Mende, ethnic group of SIERRA LEONE and LIBERIA.

There are roughly 1.5 million Mende in Sierra Leone (mainly in the southeast), comprising some 30 percent of the population, and approximately 30,000 in neighboring Liberia.

The Mende probably originated among the Mani peoples, who moved from the West African savanna into coastal and forest regions between the thirteenth and sixteenth century. Mende tradition holds that they entered their present homeland from the south. The genealogies of most Mende ruling families extend back only to the late eighteenth century; before this, the Mende probably had little political structure beyond local lineages.

The arrival of MANDE-speaking invaders from the north, together with an increase in population and the advantages of political and military alliances at the time of the slave trade, shaped the emerging Mende state system during the eighteenth century. By the late nineteenth century there were approximately 70 Mende chieftaincies. Observers identified two types of Mende states: those defined territorially and those defined by loyalty to a particular chief. In both cases, chiefly authority depended primarily on military prowess and the support of subordinate chiefs. Secret societies, called *Poro* or *Wonde* for men and *Sande* or *Bundo* for women, supported chiefly authority and government. These societies combined training in civic and military matters with religious and initiation rites.

Until the British abolished the slave trade in 1807, the Mende engaged in predatory warfare to capture slaves, and the slave trade was an important source of wealth and power for Mende chiefs. Agriculture, especially rice and oil palm cultivation, provided the basis for the people's livelihood. Nineteenth-century Mende settlements were either undefended, food-producing communities inhabited largely by slaves, or fortified towns inhabited by warriors and their families. Throughout the nineteenth century the Mende were involved in a complex system of war and trade among themselves and with their African and European neighbors.

After the British declared the Protectorate of Sierra Leone in 1896 – thus assuming partial control over much Mende territory – the Mende and the British came into conflict. Disputes over British authority and hut-tax collection began in various parts of the protectorate. The Mende particularly resented British attempts to restrict Mende control over the harvesting of palm oil. In April 1898 the Mende, organized by their Poro societies, rose and killed Europeans and Africans in European dress throughout their territory.

In the first decades of the twentieth century a rail line connected Mendeland to the coast and facilitated palm oil exports, which dominated the Mende economy. As road and rail connections improved, larger towns developed in the palm-oil-producing regions. Agricultural production continued to be based on slavery until the 1920s. In the 1930s maize, COCOA, and coffee emerged as important export crops, and diamond mining began in the area around the city of Bo, in Sierra Leone. Since the 1980s there has been some small-scale gold mining in the region.

The Mende are one of the two largest groups in Sierra Leone. (The TEMNE are roughly equivalent in number.) Occupying the most developed region of the country outside the capital, Freetown, and producing the bulk of the country's cash crops, the Mende acquired increasing wealth and influence in pre-independence Sierra Leone. The Mende people were a powerful component in the Sierra Leone People's Party, which led that country to independence in 1961. After independence the dominance of Mende politicians contributed to ethnic and political tensions in Sierra Leone.

Alistair Chisholm

SEE ALSO

Freetown, Sierra Leone; Gold Trade; Transatlantic Slave Trade.

Latin America and the Caribbean

Mendieta, Ana (b. 1948, Havana, Cuba; d. September 8, 1985, New York, N.Y.), Afro-Cuban American artist who explored themes of identity and exile in her work.

Ana Mendieta was born in CUBA and emigrated to the United States with her family in 1961. She received an M.A. in painting (1972) and an M.F.A. in multimedia and video (1977), both from the University of Iowa. Though she sought to achieve the approval of the mainstream art world, her work as a Cuban and a feminist (she belonged to AIR, a feminist art cooperative) was created on the margins of conventional and avant-garde art (*see* ART IN LATIN AMERICA AND THE CARIBBEAN).

The uprootedness of exile made Mendieta seek out the earth, literally. She crafted her work outdoors, often using her body as the medium or its gunpowder outline imprinted on the earth, evoking the gestures of Palo Mayombe rites. Critic Luis Camnitzer characterized Mendieta's conception of her relationship to the earth and to the physical world: "... she would talk about her attraction to earth as the outgrowth of the fact that she lacked a homeland, that she had been 'taken from the womb.' She would also express a mystical belief in an energy that flows through everything and in the healing power of spiritually charged objects." These beliefs and Mendieta's work with tree roots also reflected her interest in SANTERÍA and other Afro-Cuban religious practices (*see* RELIGIONS, AFRICAN, IN LATIN AMERICA AND THE CARIBBEAN).

In 1980 Mendieta returned to Cuba for the first time and visited Jaruco, a forest not far from Havana. In Jaruco there are caves where the indigenous population of Cuba once lived. Mendieta used the rocks of the caves to carve her "earth works," which she would then photograph. In some cases she would use the photographs to create etchings. The forms and figures are reminiscent of Taíno petroglyphs, ancient stone sculptures, and cave drawings. By molding the earth, Mendieta was not only fashioning or recreating her own roots but creating her own mythology and cosmos as an artist. By photographing this work, she endowed it with a permanence that such art would not ordinarily have (erosion and time would either change or deface the creations) and gave it a distance that revealed the impossibility of ever returning to authentic origins. Through her cave sculptures, Mendieta made her own origins.

Mendieta died after falling from her apartment on the 34th story. Whether her fatal fall was an accident, murder, or suicide has never been fully determined. Her husband, artist Carl André, was acquitted in 1988 on charges that he played a role in her death.

Alan West

See Also
Havana, Cuba.

Latin America and the Caribbean

Mendive, Manuel (b. 1944), Cuban artist whose paintings and multimedia performances are inspired by Afro-Cuban religion and mythology (*see* Art in Latin America and the Caribbean).

Latin America and the Caribbean

Mendizábal, Horacio (b. 1847, Buenos Aires, Argentina; d. 1871, Buenos Aires, Argentina), Afro-Argentine Romantic poet whose work addressed the black presence in Argentina and struggles for racial equality.

Relatively little is known about the life of Horacio Mendizábal. He was born to an upper-class family and received a better education than most of his contemporaries. His father, Rosendo Mendizábal, served as a representative in Argentina's provincial legislative body. Mendizábal managed to publish his first book of poetry, *First Verses,* in 1865, while he was still a teenager. Like many Afro-Argentine artists, he embraced national themes with a penchant for Romantic overtones in poems like "Alerta" (Alert) and "Arjentina [*sic*]." *First Verses* was even dedicated to then president Domingo F. Sarmiento. In the same vein, Mendizábal composed two poems in honor of black Argentine military heroes Col. Domingo Sosa and José María Morales, who were still relatively unknown to white Argentines.

With the publication in 1869 of his second book, *Hours of Meditation,* Mendizábal began to write less about love and nature and more about equality and justice, expanding somewhat his treatment of Afro-Argentine concerns. Like many Argentines of his time, he gravitated toward all things European, as evidenced in *Hours of Meditation*'s bilingual text in Italian and French, with Mendizábal's Spanish translations. However, his awareness of wider struggles for racial equality and national independence is evident in sonnets he dedicated to United States president Abraham Lincoln, Afro-Cuban poet "Plácido," and Mexican president Benito Juárez, of indigenous heritage.

Although he was left out of literary histories of Argentina, George Reid Andrews calls Mendizábal "the only black [Argentine] author of any note" in his study of Afro-Argentine history. Marvín Lewis emphasizes Mendizábal's varied lyric forms, including the madrigal, ode, silva, sonnet, acrostic and dolora. In poems like "My Song," Mendizábal embodied both the late Romantic aesthetic of Latin American poetry and a willingness to confront nineteenth-century liberalist rhetoric with its racist contradictions. The sense of social responsibility reflected in his verse stems from convictions that ironically led to his death. While tending to the sick in the yellow fever epidemic, he succumbed to the illness and died at age 24.

Joy Elizondo

See Also
Valdés, Gabriel de la Concepción ("Plácido").

Africa

Mengistu, Haile Mariam (b. 1937, Kefa Province, Ethiopia), former president of Ethiopia.

Haile Mengistu was born into Ethiopia's ruling class. He attended the Holeta Military Academy and graduated as a second lieutenant in 1966. He participated in the military coup that ousted Ethiopian emperor Haile Selassie I in 1974, and was elected vice chairman of Ethiopia's new ruling body, the Provisional Armed Forces Coordinating Committee (commonly called the Derg), which proclaimed Ethiopia a socialist state (*see* African Socialism). Mengistu eliminated all of his rivals – according to some sources he personally executed some of them – and assumed chairmanship of the Derg in 1977. After the adoption of a new constitution in 1987 Mengistu became president, a post he held until 1991.

To solidify his hold on power, Mengistu eliminated political opposition among civilians in a murderous campaign known as the Red Terror. By this time, however, the government faced rebellions in the breakaway regions of Eritrea and Tigray, as well as a Somalian incursion into the disputed region of Ogaden. The disastrous and failed collectivization of Ethiopia's farms coincided with one of the worst droughts in Ethiopian history. The ensuing famine took the lives of more than a million people and inspired widespread if muted opposition. The collapse of the Soviet Union, Mengistu's main source of military and financial support, further weakened the Mengistu regime.

In May 1991, with rebel forces advancing rapidly on Addis Ababa, Mengistu resigned and fled to Zimbabwe, where he had been given asylum. He survived an assassination attempt as well as Ethiopian calls for his extradition. Political instability in Zimbabwe forced Mengistu to seek asylum in North Korea in 1998.

Robert Fay

See Also
Drought and Desertification; Addis Ababa, Ethiopia; Somalia.

Africa

Menilek II (b. August 17, 1844, Ankober, Shewa, Ethiopia; d. December 12, 1913, Addis Ababa, Ethiopia), one of Ethiopia's greatest emperors, who defended Ethiopia's independence and transformed the country into a modern nation-state.

Menilek II's birth name was Sahle Mariam. His father, Haile Malakot, was king of Shewa, the heartland of the Amhara people in present-day central Ethiopia, and his mother was Wayzaro Ejegayahu, a court servant who later married Haile Malakot. His father's death in 1855 during a military campaign by Ethiopian emperor Tewodros II – whose victory ended Shewa's autonomy – brought Sahle Mariam to Tewodros's court, where the emperor held all of his potential rivals. There he received a traditional church education (*see* Ethiopian Orthodox Church). Sahle Mariam escaped in 1865, returned to Shewa, deposed Shewa's governor, Bezzabbeh, and at 21 years of age, declared himself *negus* (king) of Shewa, though he recognized the Emperor Tewodros II as his overlord.

Sahle Mariam expanded Shewa's borders south and east into Oromo and Somali territory through warfare and diplomacy, and under his rule Shewa became the largest and most powerful kingdom of Ethiopia. At Tewodros's death in 1868, first Teke Giogis (1868-1872) and then Yohannes IV (1872-1889) ruled as emperor. Although he was forced to recognize Yohannes as emperor, Sahle Mariam retained Shewa's autonomy by compromising with Yohannes and maintaining good relations with the more powerful of Ethiopia's nobility. He cultivated relations with European powers and secured their help in importing firearms, developing the best-equipped army in northeast Africa.

After Yohannes's death in 1889, Sahle Mariam was the most powerful leader in Ethiopia, and he moved quickly to seize the throne, assuming the title Negus-Negast ("king of kings," or emperor) of Ethiopia and the imperial name Menilek II. This name emphasized his claim to descent from the

Israelite king Solomon and the QUEEN OF SHEBA, whose son, Menilek, according to legend, was the first emperor of Ethiopia.

In 1889 Menilek II signed the Treaty of Wichale, granting Italy control of the coastal region that became ERITREA and establishing ties between Italy and Ethiopia. However, the version of the treaty in Amharic (the Ethiopian imperial language) differed from the Italian version on one important point. According to the Amharic version, Italy had offered to act as Ethiopia's intermediary with foreign powers, while according to the Italian version, Ethiopia agreed to become a protectorate of Italy. After learning of the differences in wordings, Menilek declared the treaty void, and Italy invaded in 1895.

Ethiopia united behind Menilek in the face of the Italian invasion. After some setbacks, Menilek's forces won an overwhelming victory at the Battle of Adwa in 1896, and the Italians were forced to recognize Ethiopian independence. Other European powers followed suit. Menilek's Ethiopia was the only traditional African state to repel successfully conquest by European colonial powers. By 1899 Menilek had extended Ethiopia's borders to roughly their present position.

Menilek spent his final years of rule promoting modernization in Ethiopia. His wife, Empress Taitu, founded a new capital city, Addis Ababa, which featured paved streets, hospitals, and secular schools. Menilek drove the first automobile in Ethiopia. He founded government ministries like those of European nations and replaced hereditary territorial rulers with trained civil servants. He created an Ethiopian standing army, streamlined the tax system, created a national currency, imported the nation's first printing press, and promoted the use of telephones. In addition, Menilek commissioned a rail line from Addis Ababa to the seaport at Djibouti City, which a French firm completed in 1917, four years after his death.

Robert Fay

SEE ALSO
Djibouti, Djibouti.

North America

Mennonite Church, a Protestant denomination known for its pacifism and religious tolerance that has attracted few people of African descent.

Facing religious persecution in Europe, Menno Simons, a pacifist associated with the Reformation in Switzerland and Germany, fled to North America in the late seventeenth century. Menno and his followers, who became known as the Mennonites, settled in parts of Pennsylvania and Canada's Northwest Territories, and after the Civil War, in the Great Plains – areas in which they had little contact with the black populations of North America.

By 1886, Mennonite missionary Heinrich V. Wiebe had established schools in North Carolina for black children. The first African Americans to join the church, Robert and Mary Elizabeth Carter and their son, Cloyd, did so in the same year. Despite efforts directed by African American Mennonite James Henry Lark during the Civil Rights era to increase the church's black membership, today there are only an estimated 3500 black Mennonites in a total Mennonite population of 350,000.

Peter Hudson

SEE ALSO
Civil War, American.

Latin America and the Caribbean

Mento, Jamaica's first indigenous popular musical form, a synthesis of various folk traditions commonly referred to as Jamaican calypso in its heyday during the 1940s and 1950s.

Mento derived from Afro-European folk forms and emerged in the 1930s with its own distinct sound. Reminiscent of Trinidadian CALYPSO but drawing on different roots, mento was JAMAICA's first music to achieve national recognition. Its strongest origins lie in the music of Afro-Protestant Revival or Pocomania churches. During the mid-nineteenth century the hybridization between Christian and African forms of worship launched the "Great Revival." Revivalist/Pocomania hymns layered complex African rhythms with European melodic structures but remained primarily percussive.

Exerting near-equal influence on mento were Jamaica's secular quadrille bands. Quadrille began as a European ballroom dance played by Jamaican slaves, who slowly added African elements and appropriated the European social music for their own enjoyment. Martial fife-and-drum music, another Afro-European form, lent elements to mento, as did African drumming styles, such as Burru, which survived untouched by European influence in rural JAMAICA.

Mento successfully blended these disparate traditions into a kind of "generic folk music" that was easily accessible to Jamaicans from different musical settings. Unassociated with a church, ethnicity, or region, mento provided a common musical ground and quickly became Jamaica's national music. Mento bands sported a flexible lineup, ranging from small-sized orchestras to trios comprising harmonica, a singer, and drums. The most common format was a multiperson ensemble with several percussionists and banjo and guitar players, accompanied by a few musicians playing thumb-pianos, fifes, or brass instruments. Mento sounds similar to up-tempo calypso, although its heritage is far too complex to be considered derivative. The popularity of Trinidadian calypso led mento singers to associate themselves with calypso, and misleading band names such as Reynolds Calypso Clippers, the Calypsonians, and Bedasse Calypso Quintet were common. Mento lyrics were lighthearted, often with bawdy undertones or explicit sexual themes.

Jamaican music was first recorded on ten-inch mento 78 rpm records, which then received radio play alongside American RHYTHM AND BLUES. These initial mento records were recorded in Jamaica but manufactured entirely in London. Mento's grassroots popularity led Jamaicans to establish their own record labels and production facilities by the 1960s, in perfect time for Jamaica's independence in 1962 and the emergence of SKA music. By this time interest in mento was on the wane and the genre was disparagingly associated with its deep rural roots. The Jamaican innovations on American rhythm and blues would lead to ska, which soon overshadowed mento.

Jace Clayton

SEE ALSO
Slavery in Latin America and the Caribbean; Trinidad and Tobago; Protestant Church in Latin America and the Caribbean.

Latin America and the Caribbean

Mercado, Tomás de. *See* COLONIAL CRITICS OF SLAVERY.

Europe

Mercer, Mabel Alice Wadham (b. February 3, 1900, Burton-on-Trent, England; d. April 20, 1984, Pittsfield, Mass.), influential British-American cabaret singer.

Mabel Mercer was born and spent her early years in Britain with her mother, an English variety actress. Her father, who died before Mercer was born, was an American JAZZ musician.

Mercer acquired entertainment experience in her family's vaudeville troupe. Later, she performed at Bricktop's, the legendary Paris cabaret, from 1931 to 1938. Upon her arrival in the United States in 1938, Mercer immediately made a favorable impression in New York City, where she first performed at the club Ruban Bleu. She held extended engagements in New York at Tony's and the Byline Room, as well as the St. Regis Room and the Cafe Carlyle.

Mercer's voice was less noteworthy than her delivery and presentation. She articulated each song's nuances through her precise diction and her ability to convey the emotional tone of the lyrics. She is also known for the regal poise she assumed by singing while seated on stage.

Mercer influenced many singers, including Frank Sinatra, BOBBY SHORT, Nat "King"

Cole, and Billie Holiday. In 1974 *Stereo Review* presented her with its first Award of Merit, subsequently renaming it the Mabel Mercer Award. In 1981 Mercer received an award from the American Society of Composers, Authors and Publishers at a Whitney Museum tribute concert. In addition, she was honored with the Presidential Medal of Freedom in 1983. After her death from respiratory arrest in 1984, the Mabel Mercer Foundation was founded to promote cabaret singing as an art form.

See Also

Great Britain; Cole, Nat ("King"); New York, New York.

North America

Meredith, James H.

(b. June 25, 1933, Kosciusko, Miss.), African American who in 1962 became the first black student to enroll at the University of Mississippi; this landmark event and the attention surrounding his 1966 "walk against fear" were central events of the Civil Rights Movement.

While attending the all-black Jackson State University in Jackson, Mississippi, James Meredith applied to the all-white University of Mississippi. Rejected because he was black, he sued for admission, and after a series of appeals the university was ordered to admit him. Gov. Ross Barnett, with support of the state legislature, vowed to block Meredith. On September 30, 1962, federal marshals escorted Meredith to the Ole Miss campus in Oxford, Mississippi. Approximately 3000 whites rioted in protest. More than 23,000 United States troops restored order by the next morning. But two people had been killed and 160 injured. Meredith attended classes and graduated the following year.

After studying at Ibadan University in Nigeria and at the Columbia University School of Law, in 1966 Meredith returned to Mississippi to stage a 225-mile march from Memphis, Tennessee, to Jackson, Mississippi. By completing this "walk against fear," Meredith hoped to inspire blacks to vote in the upcoming primary elections. He was shot on the second day of his march and, although he was not seriously injured, was hospitalized and unable to complete the march. Major civil rights organizations, most notably the Southern Christian Leadership Conference (SCLC) and the Student Nonviolent Coordinating Committee (SNCC), started from the spot of the shooting and finished Meredith's march to Jackson. Significant was SNCC member Stokely Carmichael's use of the phrase "Black Power" during the march, which signaled a schism between moderate and militant civil rights groups.

In 1968 Meredith unsuccessfully tried to unseat Congressman Adam Clayton Powell Jr. He lectured about racial justice and published a memoir, *Three Years in Mississippi*, as well as numerous pamphlets and other publications. He also became active in several business ventures. In the late 1980s he allied himself with the Republican Party, serving in 1989 as a domestic policy adviser to conservative Southern senator Jesse Helms. In 1991 he endorsed former neo-Nazi and Ku Klux Klan Imperial Wizard David Duke in Duke's unsuccessful bid to become governor of Louisiana.

In 1995, once again living in Mississippi, Meredith began teaching literacy and standard English to African American boys and men, whose material and social progress, Meredith believed, had been stunted by their use of Black Vernacular English. Critics charged that Meredith's plan would do little more than undermine African American culture.

Robert Fay

See Also

Black Vernacular English; Carmichael, Stokely; Memphis, Tennessee; Powell, Adam Clayton, Jr.; Black Power.

Latin America and the Caribbean

Merengue: Music, Race and Nation in the Dominican Republic

Considered a national symbol since mid-century, *merengue* has played a significant role in the negotiation of racial and national identity in the Dominican Republic. Since the independence of the Dominican Republic in 1844, ruling classes have propagated a Eurocentric notion of national identity despite a largely African-derived ethnic population, estimated at 80 percent mixed African and European, 15 percent black, and 5 percent white. The music of the Dominican Republic reflects its Afro-Hispanic ethnicity. A plethora of neo-African forms, indispensable to rural religious ceremonies, predominate. These include *palos, congos,* and *sarandunga* drumming of the Afro-Dominican religious fraternal organizations and a celebratory processional form called *gagá* performed on one-note trumpets and percussion during Holy Week.

Less prevalent than the neo-African forms, highly European-influenced music such as the improvised sung poems called *chuines* and *tonadas* are also significant in the soundscape. Lying between the extremes of African and European influence is a large repertory of syncretic music such as merengue. The cleavage between the Dominican Republic's dominant Hispano-centric ideology and its African-derived reality has caused mixed feelings similar to the "socialized ambivalence" that anthropologist Melville Herskovits noted in Haiti. Herskovits wrote that this predicament is caused by a Haitian's "possession by the gods of his [African] ancestors... despite his strict Catholic upbringing," and that his "desire to understand and worship the gods of his ancestors" is followed by "utter remorse after having done this." While North American ethnographer Erika Bourguignon wrote that "ambivalence is essentially disruptive... to successful self-identification," W. E. B. Du Bois argued that "double-consciousness" cut both ways, sometimes widening, rather than limiting, people's horizons: the African American "ever feels... two warring ideals in one dark body," but while this may "seem like the absence of power,... it is not weakness, – it is the contradiction of double aims." Complex feelings engender multifaceted creativity, and merengue's multiple meanings have given it special aesthetic and political relevance.

Dating to the mid-nineteenth century, the earliest references to merengue describe it as ballroom dance music related to the pan-Caribbean *danza,* which had developed from the stately European contredanse. Merengue was distinguished by the fact that it was danced by independent couples (instead of in groups) and by Afro-Caribbean rhythmic tinges. After a short heyday in Dominican ballrooms, merengue was rejected by the elites both because of its dance style, considered lewd, and because of its African elements. The rural Dominican majority, however, adopted merengue and infused it with even more African influences. Merengue variants with differing instrumentations developed in several areas of the Dominican Republic, but only the Cibao region's version gained prominence. By the early twentieth century *merengue típico cibaeño* (Cibao-style folk merengue), performed on the *tambora* (a double-headed drum), the *güira* (a metal scraper), the button accordion, and the alto saxophone, was the top social dance in Cibao's countryside and barrios (working-class urban neighborhoods).

The Dominican Republic experienced severe economic difficulties in the early twentieth century; as a result, its European creditors threatened to send battleships to collect unpaid debts. United States president Woodrow Wilson found the possibility of a European military presence in the Caribbean unacceptable, and, evoking Theodore Roosevelt's Corollary to the Monroe Doctrine (which called for the United States to thwart European military presence in Latin America), he ordered a U.S. invasion of the Dominican Republic on May 5, 1916. In the following year the Marines established a military government that ruled the country until 1924. Dominicans did not take the U.S. occupation sitting down: rural populations waged guerrilla warfare, while the urban upper-classes mounted an international program of protest on the diplomatic front. Associated with the diplomatic campaign, virulent cultural nationalism fomented the embrace of all things Dominican. At the same time, however, Dominicans were attracted to North American popular culture that the Marines brought. These competing tendencies were at the crux of the occupation's musical repercussions.

At the outset of U.S. occupation, upper-class Dominicans rejected both local Afro-Caribbean genres and modernistic North American imports in favor of European-influenced forms such as the waltz, polka, and danza. But the mood of resistance created a mood consonant with musical nationalism, and composers in the Cibao city of Santiago began to write art music based on merengue and other local forms. Influenced by this trend, the leader of Cibao's top dance band, Juan Espínola, gained fame by performing refined arrangements of merengue for ballroom dancing. By the 1920s and 1930s salon dance bands became influenced by JAZZ-tinged popular music that the Marines had introduced. The jazz vogue, however, did not meet a wholly favorable reaction in the face of anti-Yankee sentiment that reigned after the occupation. In 1933 the Santiago bandleader Luis Alberti had the original idea of taking the bite out of jazz's popularity by fusing merengue with big-band jazz. This new merengue style soon found a permanent though small place in the Cibao dance band repertoires. It was precisely the neocolonial experience that piqued the Cibao elites' interest in merengue; prior to the occupation, they had rejected local forms.

Meanwhile, rural and urban barrio dwellers in the Cibao region continued to dance to accordion-based merengue. Two types of merengue típico cibaeño were current (and both are still played today): a three-part sectional form and a one-part form called the *pambiche*. While it is probable that both existed already before the U.S. occupation, the pambiche is often said to have originated during this period. As the story goes, U.S. Marines sometimes went to local fiestas but were unable to dance merengue correctly, combining fox trot with merengue steps. Imitating the North Americans, Dominicans in the town of Puerto Plata created a dance called "Yankee-style merengue" (*merengue estilo yanqui*), which was accompanied by a syncopated tambora rhythm. The new dance became associated with a song about a fabric called Palm Beach (as in the Florida city), and the new style, called pambiche. Just as its name Dominicanizes "Palm Beach," the anecdote about its origin demonstrates an ironic commentary that turns occupation-era power relations on their head: Dominicans could not contend with U.S. military might, but their superiority on the dance floor was unquestioned. They even created a new genre out of the Marines' choreographic ineptness!

The Dominican dictator RAFAEL TRUJILLO rose to power in 1930. Even though he had African blood and his grandmother was of Haitian descent, Trujillo espoused a racist idea of Dominicanness that excluded explicit links to Africa and Haiti from officially sanctioned national culture. The extremity of Trujillo's anti-Haitianism was epitomized in his 1937 massacre, evocative of the Nazi Holocaust. From 12,000 to 40,000 Haitians residing in the Dominican Republic were killed. Also like the European fascists, Trujillo believed that folklore can be a potent symbol of the nation, and in 1936 he brought Luis Alberti's band, renamed Orquesta Presidente Trujillo, from Santiago to the capital city of Santo Domingo to play big-band arrangements of merengue at high-society balls. All of the country's dance bands were required to perform newly composed merengues praising the dictator, and this national music became a staple of radio broadcasts. In keeping with the party line, scholars argued that merengue is of Spanish origin. This view was of course influenced by Trujillo's racist ideology, but it also issued from the fact that merengue's European melodies, harmonies, and instrumentation set it apart from Afro-Dominican ritual drumming, whose links to African culture are more explicit.

After Trujillo was assassinated in 1961, the Dominican Republic opened to outside influences as never before. Bandleader JOHNNY VENTURA and arranger Luis Pérez incorporated salsa elements and rock 'n' roll performance style into an exuberant, faster merengue that abandoned jazz-band instrumentation in favor of a smaller *conjunto* (combo) format consisting of tambora, güira, piano, electric bass, singers, and two to six wind instruments. Massive emigration ensued in the decades that followed, and by 1990 an estimated 900,000 Dominicans (12 percent of the country's population) were estimated to be living in New York City alone. Escalating transnational intercourse was reflected in merengue's continued assimilation of outside influences ranging from disco and RAP to Haitian and South American sources. Access to the transnational Latin music markets gained new audiences for merengue among non-Dominicans; it even usurped salsa's position as the most requested Latin Caribbean dance by the late 1970s. Bandleaders Wilfrido Vargas and Juan Luis Guerra led the way in the internationalization of merengue. Merengue became an important marker of identity for Dominicans in the diaspora, serving as a form of resistance to Anglo hegemony.

In spite of growing urbanization and modernization, accordion-based merengue remained vital in the late twentieth century. While rural groups and those playing for tourists stuck to the traditional style, groups in the Cibao city of Santiago developed a new form of típico merengue that added conga drums and electric bass to the traditional lineup of accordion, saxophone, tambora, and güira. These groups became more and more popular during the merengue boom, and in the late 1990s they performed alongside top merengue bands in luxurious nightclubs throughout the Dominican Republic and in the diaspora. Because it is allied with both tradition and modernity, Dominicans sometimes call this music merengue típico moderno (modern folk merengue). In a parallel trend, urban musicians adopted aspects of rural merengue. In the late 1990s, for example, the New York City-based Dominican bandleader Fulanito gained fame with his dramatic juxtaposition of merengue accordion riffs, allied with rural authenticity, with quintessentially urban hip hop and house music.

Young Dominicans began to challenge Dominican Eurocentrism in the post-Trujillo era. While some city dwellers still associated Afro-Dominican culture with drumming and spirit possession with backward lifestyles that are best left behind, others, especially artists and intellectuals, embraced the philosophy that "black is beautiful." The question of origin became central to a debate that developed between conservative Dominicans, insisting on the republic's Hispanic identity, and those who celebrated the country's African heritage. The traditional faction claimed that merengue had little or no African influence, while progressive thinkers celebrated its African-derived aesthetic. Bandleader Juan Luis Guerra spoke eloquently about merengue's African elements without negating its syncretic nature (*see* TRANSCULTURATION, MESTIZAJE, AND THE COSMIC RACE: AN INTERPRETATION): "Unequivocally, you can't take merengue out of Africa. No matter how much you may want to, you can't take it out of Africa. Forget it: the rhythms are African, period. Of course there are these influences, which are melodic: the melodies are European, the harmony, just like in jazz."

Large numbers of Dominicans continue to live in the countryside; the 1991 population was estimated at 45 percent rural. While commodified genres such as merengue predominate in rural as well as urban recreational contexts, the rich repertory of uncommodified drumming styles associated with African-influenced religious rituals flourishes in rural areas. Perhaps the most striking aspect of Dominican music culture as a whole is the degree to which urban, mass-mediated, transnational music coexists with local, rural, orally transmitted music. In spite of Eurocentric values, which had long relegated this repertory to a marginal status, rural sacred music had influenced commodified music already in the 1950s, when rural prayers called *salves* were incorporated into urban popular songs.

In the 1970s urban musicians forged new musical ground by blending Afro-Caribbean ritual drumming with rock and jazz. Spearheading this movement was the group Convite. Like the Dominican-Haitian communal work teams after which it is named, Convite was a collaborative effort dedicated to serving the community. In addition to being a musical ensemble, Convite investigated, educated, and politicized: group members conducted ethno-musicological fieldwork and held workshops to promote their musicopolitical agenda. In the 1980s and 1990s bandleaders such as Tony Vicioso, José Duluc, David Almengod, and Edis Sánchez continued the movement that Convite had navigated, traversing the rural-urban divide as well as boundaries of social class by undertaking collaborative musical and cultural ventures with rural musicians and religious leaders in several regions of the country. This musical movement sorely lacked recording opportunities due to conspicuous disinterest on the part of the music industry. Top merengue musicians such as Juan Luis Guerra, Sergio Vargas, and Kinito Méndez, however, began to show limited though high-profile interest in Afro-Dominican drumming in the 1990s; Méndez, for example, included palos music on one of his hit CDs.

Merengue's history includes periods resembling Adornoesque fantasies of mass culture in the service of the state as well as periods in which the music was clearly oppositional; repeatedly enlisted in opposition to neocolonial hegemony in the transnational arena, the music has generally been allied with the status quo within the Dominican Republic. As the recent incorporation of Afro-Dominican ritual drumming into merengue illustrates, however, merengue's multivalent quality renders it serviceable to variegated musicopolitical agendas, assuring it a continued role in the ongoing negotiation of race and nation in the Dominican Republic.

Paul Austerlitz

See Also

Salsa Music; New York, New York; Music, Afro-Caribbean Secular; Haiti; Religions, African, in Latin America and the Caribbean.

Africa

Merina (also known as Antimerina, Hova, and Ovah), largest ethnic group of Madagascar.

The Merina primarily inhabit the north central highlands of Madagascar. They speak Malagasy, a Malayo-Polynesian language. They tend to dominate Madagascar politically and economically (*see* Madagascar, Ethnicity in). Approximately 3 million people consider themselves Merina.

Africa

Meru, an ethnic group in Kenya.

The Meru are a Bantu-speaking ethnic group that numbers approximately 1 million and occupies the fertile eastern slope of Mount Kenya. The Meru are a loose grouping of peoples, rather than one unified people. They include a number of distinct subgroups. Culturally, they are closely related to the nearby Kikuyu people, although Meru traditions claim that they migrated to their present location from Kenya's coast.

Clans organized traditional Meru society and landholding patterns, and families lived in scattered homesteads. An age-set system bound members closely together, as did the *Njuri Ncheke*, or local council of elders. Comprising a group's leading elders, the Njuri Ncheke enforced cultural norms and punished those who strayed. Although economic and political modernization have eroded the authority of this council, the Meru and local police have recently sought to reinstate the Njuri Ncheke to discipline their youth.

Because they inhabit a mountainous region, the Meru have historically practiced terrace agriculture as a method of soil conservation. They raise millet, beans, sorghum, maize, and potatoes for subsistence, as well as coffee, tea, and cotton as cash crops. In addition, the Meru grow the controversial cash crop miraa. A stimulant derived from the bark and leaves of an evergreen tree, it is quickly replacing other cash crops as its market expands from northeastern Africa and the Middle East to Europe, the United States, and Canada. Critics condemn its addictive qualities, its bad health consequences, and its unwholesome appeal to Meru boys, many of whom quit school to enter the lucrative miraa trade.

Robert Fay

North America

Messenger, The (1917-1928), Harlem-based monthly magazine of radical black opinion.

In 1917 A. Philip Randolph and Chandler Owen, Southerners who had migrated to New York City, were hired to edit the *Hotel Messenger*, then a newsletter for a labor union of hotel and restaurant employees. A few months into their tenure they accused the union, in print, of overcharging its members for uniforms. The union boss was duly enraged and fired Randolph and Owen, whereupon they moved down the street and in November 1917 began publishing *The Messenger*. It was the self-proclaimed "Only Radical Negro Magazine in America."

The *Messenger* attacked everybody. It proclaimed that the teachings of Booker T. Washington were accommodationist, that the writings of his rival W. E. B. Du Bois ignored class struggle, and that the messages of Marcus Garvey were unrealistic in their exclusion of whites. More generically, conservative black ministers were condemned for promising that the meek would inherit the earth, as were black Republican politicians who had done nothing to end underpayment of black workers, disfranchisement of black voters, or lynching of black people.

In the place of these leaders of the "Old Crowd," the *Messenger* advocated the rise of a Negro of the "New Crowd": uncompromising, socialist, at one with workingmen of all colors, and armed and ready to defend himself when assaulted. His totems were the Russian Revolution and the Industrial Workers of the World (IWW).

Published sporadically at first, the *Messenger* became a monthly in 1919. In its first two years the United States Postal Service revoked its second-class mailing permit and the U.S. Justice Department investigated it for sedition. Still, the *Messenger* managed a peak circulation at the turn of the decade of about 20,000. In 1923 a disillusioned Owen left the magazine, while Randolph maintained it in title; in deed, he focused much of his attention on his Brotherhood of Sleeping Car Porters (BSCP).

Concurrent with the weakening of both the American socialist movement and the IWW, the *Messenger*'s radicalism mellowed. Its editorials celebrated black business and reached out to a wider audience. In 1925 the financially struggling *Messenger* became the official organ of the BSCP, which discontinued it in 1928.

See Also

Du Bois, William Edward Burghardt (W. E. B.); Garvey, Marcus Mosiah; Labor Unions in the United States; New York, New York; Randolph, Asa Philip; Socialism; Washington, Booker Taliaferro; Accommodationism in the United States.

Latin America and the Caribbean

Mestre Bimba (b. Manuel dos Reis Machado, 1900, Bahia, Brazil; d. 1974, Bahia, Brazil), opened the first academy that formally taught capoeira, an Afro-Brazilian martial art, in Salvador, Bahia, in 1932.

Mestre Bimba initially called the martial art that he taught *luta regional* (or regional fighting), and this style has since come to be known as *Capoeira Regional*. Mestre Bimba was one of the capoeira *mestres* (or masters) who was influential in the legalization of capoeira. After his group performed for President Getúlio Vargas, the Brazilian leader declared that capoeira was Brazil's national sport.

Ben Penglase

See Also

Salvador, Brazil.

Latin America and the Caribbean

Mestre Pastinha (b. Vicente Ferreira Pastinha, 1889, Brazil; d. 1982, Bahia, Brazil), highly influential and respected master of capoeira, an Afro-Brazilian art form that combines dance and martial arts.

Mestre Pastinha is said to have learned capoeira as a young boy from an African-born Brazilian named Benedito. He opened his capoeira academy in 1941 in Salvador, BAHIA, and worked to preserve the traditional form of capoeira, which he termed *Capoeira Angola*.

SEE ALSO
Salvador, Brazil.

North America

Methodist Episcopal Church,

American Protestant denomination whose initial progress in ministering to African Americans was thwarted by segregationist policies.

When the Methodist Episcopal Church formally separated from the Anglican Church on Christmas Eve, 1784, it was declared that within a year, all slaves owned by Methodists would be set free. The church soon drifted from this position, however. "On the local level it was not expedient to free slaves," writes religious scholar Richard E. Wentz. "Preachers began to develop a theological position that concerned itself only with the saving of souls and left social ethics to the government." Individual parishes were allowed to develop their own positions regarding slavery, but the questions it provoked haunted the church well into the next century.

By the 1830s a number of Northern congregations had left the church because this ambivalent posture conflicted with their own abolitionist stance. In the South, Methodist planters vehemently fought for the institution that was the foundation of their economy. To further protect themselves from attacks by abolitionist Methodists, in 1844 they convened the Methodist Episcopal Church, South.

The church's wavering position on slavery did not halt its growth among African Americans. The Methodist itinerant clergy, following the teachings of founder John Wesley ("All God's children had a soul," he once wrote, "and the only problem was to find it and save it"), took it upon themselves to seek black audiences. By the time of the convening conference of 1784, of the 51 societies that met, 36 included black members. Francis Asbury (1745-1816), the first elected Methodist bishop, helped to recruit black members out of his desire for a racially inclusive church and a belief in indigenous evangelism. Asbury ordained Harry Hosier, the first African American Methodist preacher, and dedicated Philadelphia's African Methodist Episcopal (AME) Church and New York's African Methodist Episcopal Zion (AMEZ) Church. Even so, the institutional segregation of the church and its general reluctance to ordain black clergy stymied its growth among African Americans until the Civil War, and prompted the rise of independent churches such as the AME and AMEZ.

After the war African American membership in the Southern church plummeted, and those who remained formed the Colored Methodist Episcopal Church. This new church, alongside both the independent congregations and the main body of the church, grew rapidly in the postbellum era. The social programs for recently emancipated blacks, established by the Northern missionaries flocking to the South, helped to swell African American membership.

This growth was not sustained. When the fractured church decided to regroup in the early twentieth century, the position of African Americans within it was hotly debated. Amid protest from black and white Methodists, at the 1939 Uniting General Conference segregation was written into the Methodist constitution, and all African American members were regulated to a central jurisdiction that existed until the late 1960s. After 1939 the black Methodist population did not increase – despite a rise in the national African American pop-ulation – and the number of black churches declined. In 1968 the United Methodist Church was formed from a merger of the Methodists and the Evangelical United Brethren Church. During the Uniting Conference that established the new church, the question of race – this time framed in discussions about approaches to inclusivity – was again an issue.

Since then the representation of African Americans in the Methodist hierarchy has increased, including the election in 1984 of the first black woman bishop, Rev. Leontine Kelly. The most radical efforts to eliminate racism within the church and return it to its original commitment to social justice have come from the Black Methodists for Church Renewal, founded in 1968. Their work has led to antidiscriminatory legislation and various development projects within African American communities.

Peter Hudson

SEE ALSO
Race: An Interpretation; Slavery in the United States; Abolitionism in the United States; African Methodist Episcopal Church; African Methodist Episcopal Zion Church; Civil War, American.

Latin America and the Caribbean

Mexico, **republic of North America sharing a border with the United States and GUATEMALA and home to a significant African population since colonial times.**

Mexico prides itself on being a nation of *mestizos*, people of indigenous and European descent. This intermixing is said to reflect Mexico's ethnic harmony and its so-called cosmic race (*see* TRANSCULTURATION, MESTIZAJE, AND THE COSMIC RACE: AN INTERPRETATION). Too often, however, these homogenizing beliefs call on the nation's ethnic minorities to assimilate into a dominant culture and obscure the social and political marginalization that they continue to face. Furthermore, the existence of Afro-Mexicans is often denied by an image of the nation as principally a mixture of European and Indian. In fact, Afro-Mexicans have played an important role in Mexican history and remain a significant though often overlooked minority.

ORIGINS AND EARLY SLAVERY

The African presence in what is today known as Mexico dates to the first of the Spanish incursions in the New World. When the conquistador Hernán Cortés came ashore in the area of Veracruz in 1519, a free black man named Juan Garrido was with him. Garrido may have participated in the conquest of the Aztec capital Tenochtitlán and was a known participant in several expeditions in other parts of New Spain after Cortés toppled Tenochtitlán. He is also said to have been the first person to farm wheat in Mexico. Free blacks, however, were uncommon in early Mexico; more common were the several African slaves who also accompanied Cortés and his invading army. Little is known about what role these slaves played in the conquest and immediate postconquest periods.

As Spanish settlers arrived in Mexico in the mid-1500s, they relied heavily on Amerindians for labor in mines and on plantations; but even then settlers supplemented the labor base with a small but steady stream of African slaves. In the first 60 years after the fall of Tenochtitlán, between 30,000 and 40,000 slaves arrived in Mexico. Some of these were Hispanicized slaves, Africans who had been enslaved in Spain for some time before arriving in the New World. Most were imported directly from Africa. Regardless of origin, the slaves were mostly male: typically three men were imported for every woman because they were seen as better suited for work in the mines. This ratio forced many enslaved African men to seek Amerindian mates, beginning a process of MISCEGENATION that would continue throughout Afro-Mexican history. Such intermixing had further implications. Since under Spanish law freedom followed the mother's line, the children of an enslaved man and a free woman would be freeborn. Thus if the slave population was to grow, the Spaniards would fuel it with infusions of slaves from Africa instead of with reproduction in Mexico.

By the late 1500s European settlement in Mexico had grown rapidly, and with it, commerce and the demand for slave labor (*see* COLONIAL LATIN AMERICA AND THE CARIBBEAN). Vast stores of copper and silver had been discovered; large ranches had been carved from the land; a nascent SUGAR industry was flowering; textile works were established; and fisheries were being exploited. Inexpensive labor was essential to maintaining the incredible profitability of these ventures. Although Mexico's Amerindians were the original draftees for this labor, abysmal conditions, more general mistreatment at the hands of their Spanish overlords, and sweeping European diseases had decimated their ranks by the late 1500s. Many Spanish reformers, such as Bartolomé de Las Casas, argued against the harsh treatment of the Indians and suggested that Africans be imported. The reformers' logic seemed to be that Africans had already proven themselves in Spain and elsewhere to be better adapted to European disease and labor. Businessmen in New Spain heartily agreed, throwing in their (dubious) opinion that a single African laborer could do the work of three or four Indians. Before the end of the sixteenth century the Spanish Crown made the enslavement of Amerindians illegal but allowed African enslavement and importation to continue. Africans thus became all the more important to business in New Spain.

The Peak and Decline of Slavery

The Mexican slave trade, both the domestic trade and the importation of new slaves, reached its peak between 1580 and 1640, when imports from Africa averaged better than 1000 slaves a year and two out of every three slaves bound for Spanish America were destined for Mexico. Most of the slaves arrived at the port of Veracruz, on Mexico's Caribbean coast. From there they were sent to Mexico City and points beyond, although many were kept in the vicinity of Veracruz to work the fisheries and ports. It is estimated that by the mid-1600s Afro-Mexicans, enslaved and free, totaled slightly fewer than 150,000. Historian Gonzalo Aguirre Beltrán has estimated that in the 1500s and 1600s Afro-Mexicans outnumbered whites two to one, but natives outnumbered blacks and whites combined thirty to one.

By the early 1700s the Afro-Mexican population began to decline, partly because of Spanish reforms that limited (but certainly did not halt) the slave trade. A large number of Afro-Mexicans also succumbed to foreign diseases; although more resistant to most illnesses than Amerindians, Africans were nonetheless vulnerable to yellow fever, syphilis, and tuberculosis. It was also not uncommon for slaves to be worked to death, as their native predecessors had been.

A more subtle but perhaps more pervasive cause of decline was the Spanish preference for light skin. In Mexico, as elsewhere in the Spanish Empire, social status was tightly linked with skin color: the lighter the better. Thus an Afro-Mexican improved his or her social status by taking a lighter-skinned partner, preferably a white, but lacking that, a mestizo or Indian. The children of such a union, typically lighter-skinned than their Afro-Mexican parent, were thus assured of a marginally better social caste than the darker-skinned parent. The Spanish custom of importing few African women only accelerated the process by which Africans mixed with Amerindians. Moreover, because the few women slaves who were imported typically worked as domestic servants in Spanish households, they often were taken as concubines by their masters – leading to a further "lightening" of the race and diminishing the number of potential Afro-Mexican couples.

Black Life, Black Resistance

Afro-Mexicans, whether slave or free, were subject to the harsh rigidity of the Mexican caste system, in which they were the lowest rung. Blacks had no right to attend school; were barred from some orders of the Roman Catholic Church; could not travel on their own at certain times of day; could not carry weapons; and in some cases were forbidden to marry and raise a family. Punishment for violating these and similar laws often took a dreadful corporal form: the severing of a hand, foot, or ear; having hot wax or fat

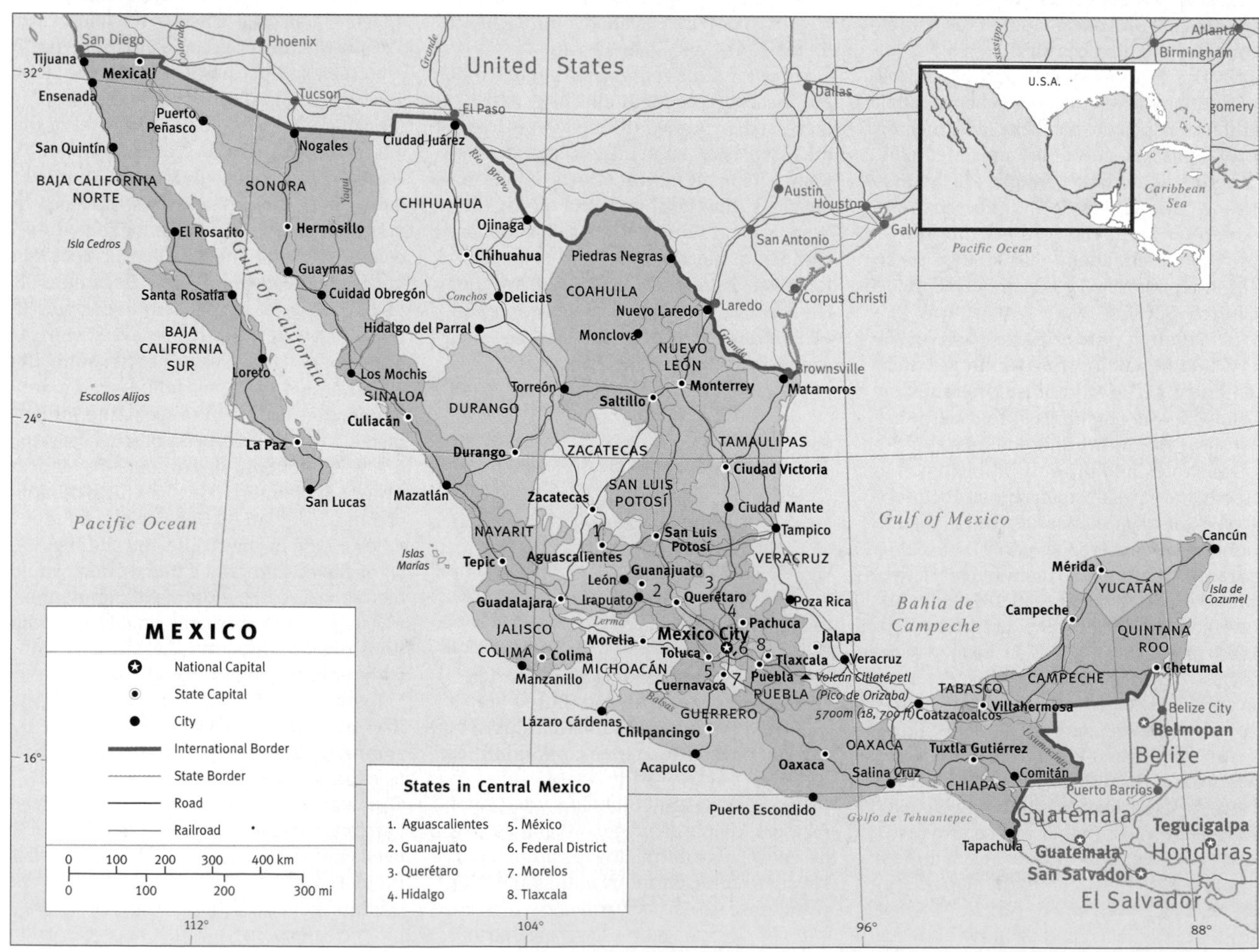

In 1763 Mexican artist Miguel Cabrera (1695-1768) painted a series of 16 canvases illustrating the results of intermarriage between different ethnic groups. In this picture the offspring of a "Negro" and an "Indian" is a "China cambuja." *Oronoz*

dripped onto the skin; or, for men, castration (*see* Punishment of Slaves in Colonial Latin America and the Caribbean).

Life in bondage, of course, had additional cruelties. Slaves could be bought and sold at will. On arrival in Mexico or on being sold to a new owner, slaves were stripped of their names and given names identifying them as belonging to their masters. Slaves were typically branded for identification, and sometimes as punishment. They were denied their religion and baptized as Christians.

From the earliest parts of the colonial era, Afro-Mexicans rebelled against these and other indignities. In the mid-1530s a group of slaves in the area of Mexico City revolted. After a brief period of fighting, they were caught and beheaded, and their heads were displayed in a public plaza as a warning to others. Escape was a more common form of resistance. Aided by the rugged and often little-explored geography of Mexico, escaped slaves often banded together and formed communities called *palenques*. Most of the palenques quickly succumbed to colonial attacks but some survived, and a few plagued Spaniards by periodically raiding colonial settlements. One of the most successful palenques was established in the late 1500s near present-day Orizaba, inland from Veracruz. Under the leadership of an Afro-Mexican runaway named Nyanga Yanga, the *palenqueros* rebuffed all Spanish attacks and were so persistent in their counterattacks that Spanish officials signed a truce with them in 1612. The palenque was thereafter a free settlement (*see* Maroonage in the Americas).

In the early and mid-1700s, also in the region inland of Veracruz, slaves working the profitable Atlantic sugar mills revolted, prompting further rebel activity. When colonial officials could not contain the outbreaks, negotiations followed; in return for helping Spain in its battles against Great Britain, the Afro-Mexicans were given their freedom. Similar uprisings, and with them the creation of palenques, occurred around the Pacific ports of Acapulco and Huatulco. Because Spanish settlement was lighter on the Pacific coast, many of these African communities lasted longer than their Atlantic counterparts. With time the mostly male palenqueros intermingled with nearby Amerindian women, and the communities began to grow with a mixed-race population.

OPPOSITE: ***Abrazo de la memoria*** **(Embrace of Memory), 1990, Cualjincuilapa, Guerrero, Mexico.** *Tony Gleaton*
ABOVE LEFT: ***La Boda de Maurillio y Teresa*** **(The Marriage of Maurillio and Teresa), 1989, Corrallero, Oaxaca, Mexico.** *Tony Gleaton*
ABOVE RIGHT: ***Mi Hija no vivó mas que un tiempo corto, veinte años atras*** **(My Daughter Lived Only a Short Time, Twenty Years Ago), 1991, Corallero, Oaxaca, Mexico.** *Tony Gleaton*

Slaves also found a small measure of protection in Spanish laws requiring the humane treatment of slaves. For example, although harsh punishments could be meted out for crimes – even trivial crimes – the law required that punishment be linked to a particular crime; cruelty for cruelty's sake was forbidden. Spanish law also preserved the right to marriage in most instances. Perhaps more important, slaves were given several routes to freedom through the Siete Partidas, the Spanish legal code dating from medieval times that governed not only enslaved blacks but also enslaved Jews, Arabs, and others in the Iberian Peninsula. Slaves could buy their own freedom, usually through installments at an agreed-upon price. If the slaveholder later tried to change the price or disputed that payments were made, there was at least the possibility for the slave to take legal recourse against his or her owner. Freedom could also be bought for a slave by another party. And slaveholders were allowed to free their slaves more or less at will. Still, just because a good offer was made for a slave's freedom, the slaveholder was not obliged to sell. As long as a slaveholder wanted to keep a slave, he could do so. Moreover, many progressive elements of the Siete Partidas were simply ignored or amended in New Spain. For example, in the Old World slaves who married freedpeople were given their freedom; however, because in the New World so many African slaves married (free) Amerindians, as early as the 1520s local officials got rid of this route to freedom (*see* SLAVE LAWS IN COLONIAL SPANISH AMERICA).

INDEPENDENCE AND EMANCIPATION

By the end of the 1700s, much to the despair of the Spanish state, the races of New Spain had become intermixed. A complex system of caste distinctions based on skin color had evolved alongside this intermixing, and much of it was codified in law, such as prohibitions against marriage between castes. As with most caste systems, far more people occupied the lower rungs of the Mexican system than the upper, and by the late 1700s and early 1800s several elites began to give voice to the discrimination inflicted on the mass of people. Two of the most prominent such spokesmen were JOSÉ MARÍA MORELOS and Miguel Hidalgo, a pair of vocal priests who called on colonial leaders in the early 1800s to end the caste system and, along with it, slavery. Their cries went unheeded, but anger over the caste system and, more generally, colonialism had reached such a point that revolution was now almost inevitable.

In 1810 Hidalgo led the rebellion that prompted Spain to accede to Mexican demands for independence in 1821. Many historians believe that a troop of Afro-Mexicans under Hidalgo, the Batallón de los Morenos, began the revolution. Among the revolution's other early leaders was VICENTE GUERRERO, a Mexican of partial African descent who was known as El Negro Guerrero and, for his calls to end caste and slavery, "the people's champion." Guerrero played a key role in rallying nonwhites to revolt and would later become Mexico's second president. It was also Guerrero who, in 1829, officially abolished slavery.

Mexico's new leaders hoped that the country's citizens would think of themselves not as blacks or Indians or mestizos but rather as Mexicans. To this end, they banned racial discrimination and forbade the Church to classify parishioners on the basis of race. They also eliminated questions about race from the national census. This development had some unfortunate consequences. For example, the mere presence of blacks in Mexico has often been denied in the last century and a half, and studies of Afro-Mexican life languished until the mid-1900s. Because of the ban on racial determination in the census, even the number of Afro-Mexicans is unknown. (The last official count was in 1810, when Afro-Mexicans made up slightly more than 10 percent of the population.)

CONTEMPORARY AFRO-MEXICANS

In the nineteenth and twentieth centuries the process of miscegenation continued steadily. Officials and intellectuals even used the phrase *mejorar la raza* ("to improve the race"), which in practice meant diluting the Afro-Mexican gene pool with the lighter-skinned Amerindian gene pool in order to create a lighter race. Almost never did mejorar la raza mean "tainting" the white race with African blood. The ideology of WHITENING also penetrated what used to be the lower castes – that is, among the darker-skinned Amerindians and mestizos – who were often prejudiced against marrying someone of even darker skin (*see* COMPLEXITIES OF ETHNIC AND RACIAL TERMINOLOGY IN LATIN AMERICA AND THE CARIBBEAN).

Still, gradual miscegenation had caused Afro-Mexicans to dwindle to slightly more than 5 percent of the population in 1950, by one estimate. By 1995 another estimate judged

Afro-Mexicans at .5 percent, or just under 500,000, of Mexico's almost 100 million people. Other estimates place the figure in 1995 as high as 4 or 5 percent, or up to 5 million Afro-Mexicans. The number of Mexicans with at least some degree of African ancestry is almost certainly much higher.

Beginning in the 1940s and 1950s interest in Afro-Mexicans slowly revived, urged largely by the pioneering studies of Gonzalo Aguirre Beltrán. Beltrán's work in turn gave impetus to recognition of Afro-Mexicans by the government, which in 1991 gave its support to a project called Nuestra Tercera Raíz (Our Third Root), intended to further the study of Afro-Mexicans. Today the largest Afro-Mexican settlements are in the Pacific region known as Costa Chica, where escaped slaves from Acapulco and Huatulco established palenques. Other black settlements are near Veracruz and, to a lesser degree, in the northern desert states of Coahuila, Zacatecas, and Sinaola and in the southern Yucatán and Quintana Roo. The Afro-Mexican population in Coahuila is supplemented by the descendants of escaped North American slaves who intermarried with Seminole Indians (*see* SEMINOLE WARS, JOHN HORSE).

SEE ALSO

Transatlantic Slave Trade; Slavery in Latin America and the Caribbean; Yanga; Slave Rebellions in Latin America and the Caribbean; Garrido, Juan: A Black Conquistador in Mexico.

Africa

Mfecane (Zulu, "crushing"), period of warfare and forced migrations among the peoples of southern Africa; in SOTHO it is known as the *difaqane.*

The mfecane was initiated by the ZULU under their aggressive military leader, SHAKA. In 1818 he embarked on a great expansion of his realm in what is now the South African province of KwaZulu-Natal, and during the next ten years his depredations evicted several other peoples from their lands, setting off large-scale migrations and ultimately resulting in the formation of several new kingdoms. The Basotho nation was thus created by King MOSHOESHOE, who gathered his refugee followers in a defensible area of present-day LESOTHO.

The NDEBELE marched north under Mzilikazi to carve out a kingdom on land previously occupied by the SHONA in modern ZIMBABWE. The NGONI, led by Zwangendaba, also marched through the Shona country, where they destroyed Changamire in 1834 before they resumed their 20-year, 1600-km (1000-mi) trek into present-day TANZANIA. Soshangane took his Ndwandwe followers into present-day MOZAMBIQUE, where he founded the powerful Gaza Empire. The Kololo, a Sotho group, were led by Sebetwane into modern ZAMBIA, where they settled after defeating the Lozi. In addition to these major groups, which clashed with one another at various times on their wanderings, setting off ripple effects in all directions, the Afrikaners, or Boers, were on their Great Trek during the same period. By 1840 the mfecane was for the most part over.

SEE ALSO

Afrikaner; South Africa.

Africa

Mfengu (also known as Fingo and Mfingo), ethnic group of SOUTH AFRICA.

The Mfengu primarily inhabit Eastern Cape Province, South Africa. Others live in ZIMBABWE. They speak XHOSA, a Bantu language. More than 1 million people consider themselves Mfengu.

SEE ALSO

Bantu: Dispersion and Settlement.

North America

Mfume, Kweisi (b. October 24, 1948, Turners Station, Maryland), congressman, civil rights leader, and president of the National Association for the Advancement of Colored People (NAACP).

The eldest of four children, Kweisi Mfume (born Frizzell Gray) was raised in a poor community just outside BALTIMORE, MARYLAND, by his mother and stepfather, Mary and Clifton Gray. After years of physical abuse, Mary Gray left her huband in 1960 and moved the family to a neighborhood closer to the city. Four years later she was diagnosed with cancer and within a short time learned that the disease was terminal. Mfume and his sisters were devastated by the news and suffered another traumatic blow when she died, literally, in the arms of her only son. In his autobiography, *No Free Ride*, Mfume recalls just how difficult it was losing his mother. After his mother's death, Mfume quit high school and began working to support his three sisters. Disillusioned, he also began hanging out on the streets, becoming a gang leader and fathering several illegitimate children.

Disappointed with his reckless lifestyle, Mfume made a decision to change his life when he was 22 years old. He earned a high school equivalency diploma and graduated magna cum laude from Morgan State University in 1976. In the early 1970s he began working as a disc jockey on local radio stations, where he developed an interest in politics. He changed his name from Frizzell Gray to Kweisi Mfume (which means "conquering son of kings" in the African language spoken by the IGBO) and in 1978 won a seat on the Baltimore City Council.

Mfume honed his political skills and in 1986 won the seat in the Seventh Congressional District vacated by the legendary black politician Parren J. Mitchell. Mfume served five terms in Congress, eventually becoming leader of the CONGRESSIONAL BLACK CAUCUS (CBC). On February 20, 1996, he left Congress to become president and chief executive officer of the NATIONAL ASSOCIATION FOR THE ADVANCEMENT OF COLORED PEOPLE (NAACP), the nation's oldest and largest civil rights organization. As president of the NAACP, Mfume has eliminated the organization's six-figure debt and has worked to revitalize its image among young African Americans.

Alonford James Robinson, Jr.

North America

Miami Riot of 1980, the first major American race riot since the CIVIL RIGHTS MOVEMENT, an event that heightened American awareness of the volatility of neglected urban enclaves.

Violence erupted in Dade County, Florida, on the night of May 17, 1980, when residents of Liberty City, a predominantly African American neighborhood, learned of the verdict in a case of white-on-black police brutality. Furious blacks threw bricks, rocks, and bottles at white suburban motorists who had to drive through Liberty City to reach a main Miami highway. Rumors of whites shooting children in retaliation fueled the violence. Black mobs attacked white derelicts and white motorists who tried to flee their damaged cars on foot.

Meanwhile, a nominally peaceful protest, sponsored by the NATIONAL ASSOCIATION FOR THE ADVANCEMENT OF COLORED PEOPLE (NAACP), failed to produce a speaker. Soon, the frustrated crowd joined in the violence, attacking the Dade County Department of Public Safety headquarters as well as local white-owned businesses.

Joining forces with Miami police, the National Guard restored order with roadblocks and guns. By the time the rioting ceased the following morning, 855 people had been arrested and $80 million of property damage had been incurred. In the skirmishes between blacks and white motorists, eight white people and ten African Americans had died.

The acquittal of five white policemen who had been accused of beating a black motorist to death sparked the violence. In December 1979, police officers had pursued an African American motorcyclist, Arthur McDuffie, in a high-speed chase. Although the officers claimed that the chase ended when McDuffie crashed his motorcycle and died, the coroner's report concluded otherwise. One of the pursuing officers cleared up the story, testifying that five of his fellow policemen had beaten McDuffie with their flashlights. According to his testimony, the officers murdered McDuffie after McDuffie forcefully resisted arrest. An all-white jury acquitted the officers after brief deliberation.

For the Miami police the McDuffie case was one incident in a history of unpunished malfeasance and neglected allegations. Stories – some verified, some not – of roadside sexual harassment, physical assault, and even murder tarnished the department's reputation. Because African Americans in Liberty City faced tough competition for jobs (due to a growing Cuban population) and a dwindling tax base (attributable to white flight to the suburbs), the community readily burst into violence on the conclusion of the McDuffie case.

The 1980 riot shattered the illusion that the racially motivated uprisings of the 1960s were a thing of the past. Like the LOS ANGELES RIOT OF 1992, the Miami conflagration awakened many suburban and middle-class Americans to the explosive potential of impoverished inner-city neighborhoods.

Eric Bennett

North America

Micheaux, Oscar

(b. January 2, 1884, near Murphysboro, Ill.; d. March, 25, 1951, Charlotte, N.C.), African American filmmaker, novelist, businessman, and pioneer best known for his dramatic films about African American life.

Oscar Micheaux was born in 1884, the fifth of 13 children. At age 17 he went to Chicago, where he worked as a shoeshine boy and Pullman porter. In 1904 he used his savings to buy a homestead in South Dakota on land newly opened to settlement. Micheaux's experiences as an African American settler in the rough-and-tumble environment of the South Dakota frontier provided him with material for several of his most important books and movies.

Micheaux's first creative work was the 1913 novel *The Conquest: The Story of a Negro Pioneer*. This novel followed the adventures of a self-made black settler caught between his love for a white woman and the perceived demands of his racial identity. A similar plot defined Micheaux's longer novel *The Homesteader* (1917). Micheaux used the proceeds from *The Conquest* to start a Sioux City business, the Western Book and Supply Company, which published several of his novels.

When black filmmakers George and Noble Johnson negotiated unsuccessfully with Micheaux to film *The Homesteader* in 1919, the writer's interest turned to making movies (*see* FILM, BLACKS IN AMERICAN). He filmed *The Homesteader* himself, and subsequently renamed his business the Micheaux Book and Film Company. He went on to produce, write, and direct more than 30 films – the exact number remains unclear – over the next three decades. The first African American feature-length sound movie, *The Exile* (1931), was a Micheaux creation. Another Micheaux film, *Body and Soul* (1924), featured singer and actor PAUL ROBESON in his first American appearance on screen.

The budgets for Micheaux's many films came from the director's own entrepreneurial efforts. He personally transported prints from town to town, sometimes for a single showing, and edited his movies on the road. To raise money from theater owners, Micheaux asked his actors to give private performances of scenes from upcoming productions. At the height of his success, branch offices of Micheaux's film company opened in New York and Chicago.

Many of Micheaux's films have been lost. Those that survive today include *Within Our Gates* (1919), *Body and Soul*, and *God's Stepchildren* (1937). Micheaux's works dramatized individual characters' struggles against prejudice within the black community as well as in opposition to outer racism. Booker T. Washington's doctrines of industry, self-sufficiency, and accommodation to whites profoundly influenced Micheaux's world-view and art.

African American reviewers in Micheaux's own time sometimes criticized his films for their perpetuation of negative stereotypes, idealization of interracial relationships, and blindness to the problems of a black lower class. Recent scholars such as BELL HOOKS and Joseph Young have defended Micheaux's portrayals of black women and a black middle class as subversive antidotes to the racial myths of Micheaux's era.

Micheaux returned to writing novels in the last decade of his life. Another retelling of his pioneer memories appeared in 1944 as *The Wind from Nowhere*. Three more books followed. Micheaux continued to address African American concerns while framing them within the familiar narratives of white mainstream writing. The three-hour epic *The Betrayal*, his final film, failed commercially at its release in 1948. Micheaux died in 1951.

SEE ALSO

American West, Blacks in the; Chicago, Illinois; New York, New York; Racial Stereotypes; Washington, Booker Taliaferro; Accommodationism in the United States.

Africa

Micombero, Michel (b. 1940,

Buriri province, Ruanda-Urundi [BURUNDI]; d. July 17, 1983, MOGADISHU, SOMALIA), army captain and former president of Burundi who threw the country into genocide.

Born in the southern Burundian province of Buriri, Michel Micombero attended a local Catholic school before entering the military in 1960. In 1962 the newly independent government of Burundi recalled him from the Ecole Royale military academy in Brussels to head the gendarmerie. In 1965 the constitutional monarch King Mwambutsa put Micombero in control after a coup attempt left the serving prime minister hospitalized. A year later the king was ousted by his teenage son, Prince Ndizeye, who asked Micombero to form a new cabinet. After appointing a cabinet that included five army officers, in November 1966 Micombero, age 27, effectively carried out a bloodless coup d'état. He deposed both the young king and the official prime minister and proclaimed a republic with himself as president.

Micombero changed the political dynamics of ethnic identity in Burundi. A socially low-standing Tutsi-Hima of mixed Tutsi-Hutu parentage from the south, he did not participate in the clan conflicts between the northern Bezi and Batare that had long dominated Burundian politics. Once in office, Micombero surrounded himself with family members and others from Buriri, appointing them to top positions in the government, the judicial system, the army, and state-run businesses. He used the sole legal party, the Union for National Progress (UPRONA), as a base of support for the military as well as a tool for promoting "Micombérisme," a vague ideology advocating revolutionary socialism, democratic centralism, and hard work. By supporting fellow Tutsi southerners who lambasted northern "moderate" Tutsi and warned of a Hutu peril, Micombero heightened tensions between the Hutu and the Tutsi.

In 1972 Micombero sent troops to quell an attempted Hutu uprising, resulting from what the Hutu considered to be ongoing discrimination and repression. But the Tutsi-dominated army, influenced by extremist politicians and fearing a replay of the Rwandan revolution in which the Hutu overthrew the Tutsi, became an errant force, and between April and September between 100,000 and 200,000 Barundi died, most of whom were Hutu. Although the extent of Micombero's personal involvement in the killing is debated, he did nothing to stop it. In 1976 a member of his "family corporation," Col. JEAN-BAPTISTE BAGAZA, overthrew Micombero in another bloodless coup. Micombero sought asylum in Somalia, where he later graduated from the university with a degree in economics. He died of a heart attack in 1983.

Eric Young

SEE ALSO

Hutu and Tutsi; Rwanda; Ethnicity in Burundi: An Interpretation.

Africa

Middle Congo. Former name of the REPUBLIC OF THE CONGO.

Cross Cultural

Middle East, a region comprising the present-day countries of Israel, Jordan, Lebanon, Syria, Iraq, Iran, and the Arabian Peninsula that has imported slaves and drawn migrants from Africa since ancient times.

Because the Mediterranean Sea, the Red Sea, and the Indian Ocean have always been active trading zones between Africa and the Middle East, an African presence has existed in the Arabian Peninsula, the Persian Gulf, and other parts of the Middle East since ancient times. Even before the emergence of Islam in the seventh century C.E., Arabs had contact with the Africans of "Habash," a term used to refer to ETHIOPIA and the Horn of Africa. After the early Islamic jihads, or holy wars, brought them into contact with larger areas of Africa, Arabs referred to the entire region west of Ethiopia and south of the Sahara as "al-Sudan," meaning the land of the blacks. They referred to the East African coast and its people as Zanj. Poets and leaders of African descent were famous in the Middle East from pre-Islamic times, and Africans numbered among the prophet Muhammad's companions. Many Africans ended up in the Middle East as a result of the slave trade across the Red Sea and the Indian Ocean. Most of these slaves were concubines, domestics, or eunuchs, although some labored as agricultural workers. In contrast to the Americas, these slaves did not leave distinct communities of descendants. Most scholars believe that the peoples of the Middle East gradually accepted the slaves' descendants into their communities through intermarriage. The expansion of Islam continues to bring many Muslims from Africa and the African diaspora to the Middle East in the twentieth century.

AFRICANS IN THE MIDDLE EAST FROM ANTIQUITY TO THE EARLY ISLAMIC PERIOD

Even in pre-Roman times, Ethiopians journeyed to the Arabian Peninsula and the Persian Gulf for trade. According to the anonymous writer of *Periplus of the Erythraean Sea*, which dates from the first century C.E., African merchants, sailors, and adventurers had already established these routes to trade ivory, rhinoceros horn, tortoise shell, and slaves for lances, hatchets, swords, and many kinds of small glass objects. Some scholars suggest that in pre-Islamic times there was a large African population in the Hijaz (the area of Mecca and Medina). They claim that this accounts for the "green" Hijazis – recognized as darker than most Arabs – many of whom gained fame as tribal leaders, entertainers, and poets.

Warfare also brought many Africans to the Arabian Peninsula in ancient times. The Byzantines enlisted Ethiopian Christians to defend Yemen from Persian invaders during the sixth century C.E. Ethiopian deserters from these wars anointed their own king, Abraha, who may have led a failed attempt to capture the trading post of Mecca. In 570 Persians conquered this region, but many Ethiopians remained.

Arab men held Ethiopian women as concubines in the Middle East. In pre-Islamic times, children born of a slave mother and an Arab father generally remained slaves, though the father could manumit and recognize the child as part of his family. During pre-Islamic and early Islamic times, several well-known poets of African slave origin came to be known collectively as *Aghribat al-Arab*, meaning Crows of the Arabs. The famous pre-Islamic poet and warrior Antara was born of an Ethiopian slave mother named Zabiba and an Arab father from the Abs tribe. After valiantly defending his father's tribe in battle, Antara was recognized by his father as a legitimate son. Other recognized sons of slaves also became leaders. A contemporary of the prophet Muhammad, Khufaf ibn Nadba, was born to a black slave mother, yet he became the chief of his Arab father's tribe.

Since many Arabs identified blackness with slave status, Africans faced widespread prejudice, which they often internalized. Troubled by his color, Antara wrote, "Enemies revile me for the blackness of my skin, but the whiteness of my character effaces the blackness." Like Antara, many of the poets wrote of blackness as an affliction. A black slave named Suhaym (d. 660), meaning little black man, wrote,"the lord has marred me with blackness." The slaves were equally disturbed by their lack of Arab lineage. Abu Dulama (d. 776?), a black jester for the early Abassid caliphs whose name means father of blackness, claimed of the Crows: "we are alike in color; our faces are black and ugly, our names shameful." However, the black poet Nusayb ibn Raba (d. 726), recognized as one of the most gifted of this group, celebrated his own victory over racist limitations: "Blackness does not diminish me, as long as I have this tongue and this stout heart. / Some are raised up by means of their lineage; the verses of my poems are my lineage! / How much better a keen-minded, clear-spoken black than a mute white!"

Other African poets of the era included a slave, al-Hayqutan, who lived during the Umayyid Caliphs' reign (661-750); Nusayb al-Ashgar the Younger (d. 791), who was a poet of the Caliph Harun al-Rashid's court; and Daud ibn Salm (d. 750?). A black singer, Said ibn Misja (d. 705?), was considered the greatest musician of his time. For unknown reasons, historians record few black poets and entertainers in the Middle East after the tenth century.

Africans were known to be among the prophet Muhammad's companions; thus, they hold an honorable status in Islamic history. The Ethiopian Bilal ibn Raba was a freed slave who fought on behalf of Muhammad in Arabia, Pakistan, and India; he was the first *muezzin*, the chanter of the Islamic call to prayer. Another companion of the Prophet was Abu Bakra, an Ethiopian slave who joined the Muslims when they came to the oasis town of Taif. He converted to Islam and was manumitted by the Prophet himself; later, he settled in Basra, where he died in 672. The Prophet is known to have had close relations with Africans in Ethiopia as well; when early Muslims were persecuted in Mecca, he sent them to find refuge in that country. Many of the early leaders of Islam had African heritage. For instance, an Ethiopian concubine was the paternal grandmother of Umar, the second Caliph of the Islamic commmunity, who reigned from 634 to 644.

AFRICAN SLAVES AND FREED AFRICANS IN THE MUSLIM MIDDLE EAST FROM THE EIGHTH TO NINETEENTH CENTURY

For centuries in the Middle East and North Africa, peoples defeated in battle had to send slaves as a tribute or payment to the victors. In 652 C.E. a pact between Muslims and Nubians required an annual levy of 360 black slaves in exchange for peace. The Arab Islamic conquest of much of northern Africa beginning in the late seventh century seems to have expanded the slave trade and brought more African slaves to the Middle East. According to Islamic jurists, however, slaves could not be taken from Dar al-Islam, or, the Land of Islam, but only from Dar al-Harb, the Land of War. It became commonly accepted that this land of war was all non-Islamic lands, where indiscriminate raiding could occur, under the assumption that these were jihads, or holy wars. The purchasing of slaves from non-Muslim lands, where no official agreement existed, could occur legally. In practice, raids often occurred in lands where an agreement did exist and sometimes on Muslim peoples. However, as Africans converted to Islam in the tenth century, the supply of slaves decreased, because Islam prohibits the enslaving of fellow Muslims (although if a slave converts to Islam, a master is under no obligation to free him or her). Despite this, the slave trade continued well into the nineteenth century.

Slaves were brought to the Middle East mostly from East Africa. Traders transported them down the Nile to EGYPT, where they crossed the Red Sea, or the traders led them to ports on the Indian Ocean, from which ships carried them to the Arabian Peninsula, Iraq, or Persia. Slave traders also led some slaves across the Sahara to North African ports, then shipped them across the Mediterranean Sea. It is said that certain African Muslims would purchase slaves to sell on their way to Mecca, to pay for their pilgrimage to the Holy Land.

These slaves were often sold to work in Arabia, the lands of the Persian Gulf, or later, Turkey and other parts of the Middle East.

Some slaves were taken through the Middle East en route to other parts of Asia, such as India or even China. Both Jews and Christians in the Middle East could hold slaves according to Islamic law, as long as the slaves were not Muslim.

Most African slaves brought to the Middle East were females sold for domestic use or concubinage. According to Islamic law, when a concubine had a child by her master, the child was a free person who took on his father's name and status; the mother could not be sold by her master and would be manumitted upon his death. No doubt, many African women and their children in the Middle East became free in this manner. Most African female slaves were taken as concubines, but if taken as a legal wife (as was the case with many Ethiopians), they and their descendants were free.

African male slaves were purchased by the upper and sometimes middle classes to serve in the household. African men also served rulers as bodyguards or palace staff and, less often, as soldiers. Slaves taken from Central Asia and the Caucasus generally served as slave-soldiers, or *mamluks*, while African, Armenian, Greek, and other Christian slaves, called *abd*, mostly fulfilled domestic or commercial purposes. African slaves sometimes labored as construction workers in cities or as agricultural workers, miners, and pearl fishers. In the ninth century a large number of black slaves were put to work in southern Iraq to collect salt from coastal flats. At the same time East African slaves worked in western Persia producing sugar. These Africans united in a force of 15,000 men led by a slave, Rihan ibn Salih, and revolted against the ruling Abassids in 868. The Zanj Revolt, as it is called, briefly established an independent African-ruled state called Dawlat al-Zanj. Arabs dissolved this threat to their dominance within a year.

Many male African slaves suffered castration so that they could be sold in the Middle East as eunuchs. Eunuchs were needed as custodians at holy sites, such as the Kaaba in Mecca, or to guard tombs; they were also used as confidential servants and palace staff. Most of the time they were bought to guard the harems of the sultan and of the elite. The black eunuchs of the Ottoman palace in Istanbul were powerful and wealthy. The chief black eunuch, or *kizlar agasi*, meaning chief of the girls, was entitled to own slaves himself (including concubines) and was entrusted with financial tasks. He alone had unencumbered access to the sultan at all times, and served as the confidential messenger between the sultan and the vizier. Eunuchs who were dismissed or retired became free members of society. One eunuch became a tax collector for the port of Jiddah, another became the governor of Aden. Still others were able to purchase their freedom and go on to study, travel, donate to public works, and even marry.

Muslim law did not make racial distinctions among slaves. However, as the white slave supply dwindled beginning in the sixteenth century and became practically nonexistent in the nineteenth century, Middle Easterners became so dependent on Africa for slaves that *abd* came to mean black man in many Arabic dialects. Slavery persisted in the Middle East through the nineteenth century; it was increasingly a racial institution, imposed exclusively on people of African origin. Africans continued to serve as slaves in parts of the Middle East into the twentieth century, when slavery was banned.

Generally, manumitted slaves became "clients" of their former masters; often, even if not related, they would take the names of their masters and acquire the status of their lineages. There is some evidence that communities of African people emerged in Arabian and Persian cities such as Jiddah, Mecca, and Aden in the Red Sea area; Muscat, Basra, Bushire, and Bandar Abbas in the Persian Gulf; and inland at Shiraz. People of African origin worked as merchants, dockworkers, clerks, agricultural laborers, shopkeepers, and civil servants. In the 1860s and 1870s European travelers to Arabia remarked on the communities of Arabized Africans. English traveler William Palgrave noted that the Wahabi ruler, Faisal, employed an African freedman as his treasurer. Palgrave also wrote of a community of mixed African and Middle Eastern background, called *khudayriyya*, meaning little green ones, who worked in and around Riyadh. He claimed that these communities held equal rights with the Arab populations.

But generally most scholars note the lack of a visible African community in the Middle East. They speculate that many slaves died as a result of disease and, in Iran, as a result of the high altitudes. Some scholars note that the lack of a black community may be the result of the Africans' dispersal and confinement to remote places and their marginalized status as former slaves or descendants of slaves. The most compelling thesis seems to be that no large community exists because most slaves were concubines or eunuchs, and as a result the black population could not replenish itself. With high rates of manumission and subsequent intermarriage with Arab populations, children of freed slaves often became indistinguishable members of society.

In the late nineteenth century European colonial powers occupied Africa and forced the Ottoman Empire to suppress the slave trade to the Middle East. Subsequently, the Ottomans attempted to ban slavery within the empire. The Hijaz rebelled against the Ottoman attempts at abolition. Citing the fact that the Koran recognized slavery, they declared a holy war against their Ottoman rulers in 1855. This rebellion was defeated in 1856, but the Hijaz population was exempted from the Ottoman abolition decree in 1857. Abolition was completed in the Middle East in the 1920s under League of Nations mandates, though it was only when nations emerged in the region, mostly after World War II, that they enacted individual decrees outlawing slavery.

Africans and African Americans in the Middle East in the Postcolonial Era

In the twentieth century Africans have continued to come to the Middle East, most visibly as pilgrims making the hajj to Mecca. Many Africans have also sought refuge in the Middle East. Idi Amin has lived in Saudi Arabia since he fled Uganda in 1979. Writers have also traveled there; James Baldwin, for example, spent many years in Istanbul, Turkey, in the 1960s. While an Ethiopian Orthodox Christian presence has existed in Jerusalem for centuries, a large-scale migration of Ethiopian Jews to Israel fleeing discrimination in Ethiopia began in 1984 and continued in the early 1990s. A problem of discrimination against this Jewish population developed in the 1990s.

In recent decades Africans from Sudan, Ethiopia, Eritrea, Nigeria, and other countries have remained in Saudi Arabia after completing their pilgrimage. Many have traveled from there to other parts of the Arab Middle East to search for work in the oil fields, in the region's wealthy cities, or as domestic servants for the elite. Even though most of these Africans are Muslim, government authorities generally have not welcomed these "overstayers," as they are called. In 1998 the Saudi government forced the return of all illegal foreign workers to their countries of origin. It is unlikely that the Saudi government can entirely stop the movement of African workers to the Arabian Peninsula until the demand for cheap labor subsides.

High-profile visits by African Americans to the Middle East have impacted United States politics, particularly since the 1960s. The emergence and popularity of the Nation of Islam created a community of Black Muslims in the United States and stimulated an interest in Islam among African Americans. After Malcolm X went on a pilgrimage to Mecca in 1964, he disassociated himself from the Nation's brand of Islam and converted to orthodox Islam, changing his name to an Islamic one: Malik El Hajj Shabazz. In 1979 the U.S. ambassador to the United Nations, Andrew Young, was forced to resign after it became known that he had held secret meetings with the Palestine Liberation Organization (PLO). When other black leaders, including the Reverend Jesse Jackson, showed their support for Young in the Middle East that same year and met with Yasser Arafat, the leader of the PLO, they faced the criticism that these meetings demonstrated anti-Semitism.

Perhaps because of their shared history as victims of slavery and colonialism, Africans and African Americans have been able to bridge the gulf between Western powers and the Arab world and to act as mediators in regional crises. In 1983 Jesse Jackson negotiated the release of an African American hostage in Syria. In 1998 United Nations secretary general KOFI ANNAN negotiated an agreement with Iraq's Saddam Hussein that averted the threat of war between Iraq and the United States. Blacks from Africa, the Americas, and other parts of the world continue to travel to the Middle East, as Muslims for the pilgrimage or as tourists and visitors. Thus the ancient connection between people of African origin and the peoples of the Middle East continues today.

Leyla Keough

SEE ALSO

Colonial Rule; Ivory Trade; Nile River; Nubian; South Asia, Africans in; Sahara Desert; Jackson, Jesse Louis; Indian Ocean Slave Trade; Indian Ocean Slave Trade; Islam and Tradition: An Interpretation; Trans-Saharan and Red Sea Slave Trade; Slaves, African, in Iraq.

Cross Cultural

Middle Passage, The, term used to describe the transatlantic slave voyages between Africa and the Americas that claimed the lives of approximately 1.8 million slaves over a period of about 350 years.

The Middle Passage was a physical and psychological nightmare for an estimated 12 million slaves who were packed like animals aboard slave vessels. This middle or second leg of the TRANSATLANTIC SLAVE TRADE marked the beginning of a terrifying experience. OLAUDAH EQUIANO, a former slave turned antislavery activist, captured his experience aboard a slave vessel in his autobiography: "When I looked round the ship... and saw... a multitude of black people of every description chained together, every one of their countenances expressing dejection and sorrow, I no longer doubted my fate; and, quite overpowered with horror and anguish, I fell motionless on the deck and fainted."

Typically, Equiano and others were shackled in pairs, the right arm and leg of one chained to the left leg and arm of the other. Men were separated from women, but all were confined below deck and packed into "slave quarters" throughout the ship's belly. These quarters were no more than six feet long and not high enough to allow an individual to sit upright. Conditions were miserable. Slaves were forced to lie naked on wooden planks, and many developed bruises and open sores. The unbearable heat below deck, mixed with the human waste and vomit, produced an overpowering stench. The unsanitary conditions were breeding grounds for diseases like dysentery, smallpox, and measles. Close to 5 percent of the slaves aboard these vessels died from disease, and many more died from malnutrition. Slaves were fed twice a day rations of fish, beans, or yams that were prepared in large copper vats below deck. Those who refused to eat, hoping to starve themselves to death, were force-fed.

Slaves were sometimes allowed, in small groups, to come on deck for exercise. Women and children were often permitted to roam freely, a practice that opened opportunities to the ship's crew for abuse and rape. Occasionally some slaves managed to break free from their shackles and organize mutinies. There are more than 250 documented cases of rebellion at sea, including the AMISTAD MUTINY, an unsuccessful revolt that was the subject of a film by director Steven Spielberg in the fall of 1997.

Resistance was not limited to mutiny. Instances of Africans in war canoes attacking slave vessels near the African coast are known. Eyewitness reports tell of slaves hanging or starving themselves to death during the Middle Passage. Some captives jumped overboard to escape slavery.

Millions of Africans were forced to endure the dehumanizing Middle Passage as they were transported into slavery in the New World. Of these millions, Toni Morrison wrote: "Nobody knows their names, and nobody thinks about them. In addition to that, they never survived in the lore; there are no songs or dances or tales of these people. The people who arrived – there is lore about them. But nothing survives about – *that*."

Alonford James Robinson, Jr.

Latin America and the Caribbean

Mighty Sparrow (Francisco Slinger) (b. July 9, 1935, Grandroy Bay, GRENADA), one of Trinidad's most popular CALYPSO singers.

According to Caribbean scholar Peter Manuel, Mighty Sparrow is "[one of the] two most important figures in modern Trinidadian culture," rivaled only by the late ERIC WILLIAMS, the long-time head of the People's National Movement and a popular prime minister. Born in Grenada as Francisco Slinger, the singer made his name in Trinidad's Carnival, the long celebration ending with Lent for which most calypso music is produced.

Mighty Sparrow has a strong voice and is an effective performer. He is also a capable songwriter. He has won more of the island's prestigious calypso competitions – the National Calypso Monarchy (for the best performer of the year) and Road March (for the most popular party song) – than any other performer. His first popular success was "Jean and Dinah" (1956). In 1957 he paid tribute to the wild Carnival spirit:

The biggest bacchanal is in Trinidad
Carnival,
Regardless of color, creed, or race,
Jump up and shake your waist.
So jump as you mad, this is Trinidad;
We don't care who say we bad.

The lyrics are vintage Mighty Sparrow, verbally playful and incorporating less social commentary than ribald humor.

Manuel noted that Mighty Sparrow's lyrics are "consistently clever, pithy, and catchy." For example, his song warning of the dangers of cocaine abuse is titled "Coke Is Not It." Although not a profound social critic, Mighty Sparrow has repeatedly distilled the mood of the nation in his topical songs. One of the most highly regarded of his many albums is *King of the World* (1984).

James Clyde Sellman

SEE ALSO

Trinidad and Tobago; Carnivals in Latin America and the Caribbean.

Africa

Mijikenda, ethnic group of KENYA.

The Mijikenda primarily inhabit coastal southeastern Kenya. Others live in TANZANIA. They speak a Bantu language and comprise several subgroups, including the GIRIYAMA, the DURUMA, and the DIGO of Tanzania. Approximately 1 million people consider themselves Mijikenda.

SEE ALSO

Bantu: Dispersion and Settlement.

Latin America and the Caribbean

Milanés, Pablo (b. February 24, 1943, Bayamo, Cuba), Afro-Cuban protest singer, representative of the Nueva Trova (New Song) movement of the 1960s and 1970s.

Pablo Milanés was born on February 24, 1943, in Bayamo, a historically important town in the eastern part of CUBA, to a poor mulatto family. When he was only five years old his mother took him to amateur contests on radio programs, where he sang *boleros* (a Cuban genre of romantic ballads) and *rancheras* (a style of Mexican song). In 1949 his family moved to Havana, where he began to play the guitar, taking lessons sporadically at the Havana Municipal Conservatory. Working in menial jobs and studying at night, he began playing in 1959 in the Del Rey Quartet, which specialized in American hymns of African American influence. He wrote his first songs in 1963. In 1964 he switched to Los Bucaneros Quartet, which had a broader repertoire. He also sang as a soloist, collaborating with composers of the "feeling" movement (romantic ballads of the 1950s and 1960s) or sometimes joining singers such as Omara Portuondo. His first hit song, written in 1965, was "Mis 22 años" (My 22 Years).

In 1966 he was obligated to serve in the UMAP centers (Unidad Militar de Ayuda a la Producción, or Military Unit of Production Assistance), a forced labor system created by the Cuban government to rehabilitate and reeducate those alienated from the revolution, such as homosexuals, hippies, and so on. In 1967 he was transferred to perform his required military service. That same year he wrote his first politically motivated song, "Yo vi la sangre de un niño brotar" (I saw a child's blood running). Through Omara Portuondo he met Silvio Rodríguez, another luminary of the Nueva Trova movement (New Song, a genre of Cuban protest music), with whom he established a solid friendship that continues to the present. They realized that they had many similar ideas about the future of the new Cuban song. In February 1968 they appeared together, along with Noel Nicola, in the first concert of the Protest Song Center.

His compositions continued to reflect everyday life as well as political concerns. "Yo no te pido" (I Don't Ask You) and "Para vivir" (To Live) are examples of the former; songs reflecting a political content include "Si el poeta eres tu" (If You Are the Poet), composed after Cuban revolutionary hero Ernesto "Che" Guevara's death, with lyrics by author Miguel Barnet, and "Su nombre puede ponerse en verso" (His Name Can Be Written in Verse), dedicated to Ho Chi Minh.

Unlike most singers in the Nueva Trova, Milanés has frequently ventured into other musical styles, both in concerts and recordings. His talents extend to singing the Cuban Son, old trova songs, and "feeling," a Cuban musical style influenced by Jazz.

Milanés draws more on Cuba's traditional musical styles, such as *son*, *guaguancó* (see Rumba), *guajira*, and bolero than does Silvio Rodríguez or other representatives of the genre. Of the leading figures of the Nueva Trova, he is the only nonwhite. In some of his songs he has specifically addressed issues of race: among them, "Nelson Mandela: sus dos amores" (Nelson Mandela: His Two Loves) and "Háblame de colores" (Speak to Me of Colors). He has recorded more than 30 LPs and CDs, and his songs have been interpreted and recorded by more leading figures of other countries than those of any other Nueva Trova singer.

Cristobal Diaz-Ayala

See Also

Havana, Cuba.

North America

Miley, James Wesley ("Bubber")

(b. April 3, 1903, Aiken, S.C.; d. May 20, 1932, New York, N.Y.), African American trumpeter who was one of the first great soloists in Jazz and who, as a member of the Duke Ellington band, was largely responsible for its early "jungle" sound.

Bubber Miley – along with Louis Armstrong, Sidney Bechet, and Bix Beiderbecke – was one of the great jazz soloists of the 1920s. Miley's career, like that of Bechet, illustrates the importance of professionalism in securing long-term success in jazz, something that Armstrong and Duke Ellington, each in his own way, clearly understood. Ironically, however, much of Ellington's early renown as a composer and bandleader was a direct product of Miley's contributions to the Ellington orchestra.

Born in Aiken, South Carolina, Miley moved with his family to New York City in 1909. He began playing music in public school, initially trombone, then cornet. During 1918 he joined the United States Navy and served for 18 months, including the final months of World War I. In 1920, after his discharge from the navy, he began playing professionally. The following year he joined the Jazz Hounds, the group that had accompanied blues singer Mamie Smith on many of her recordings, including "Crazy Blues" (1920), the song that initiated the blues craze of the 1920s. In the fall of 1923 Miley joined banjo player Elmer Snowden's Washingtonians, which soon came under the leadership of its pianist, Duke Ellington.

The addition of Miley transformed the Washingtonians, giving them an instantly recognizable sound. Prior to Miley's arrival, the group had often played "sweet" dance music. Ellington recalled, "Our band changed character when Bubber came in. He used to growl all night long, playing gutbucket on his horn. That was when we decided to forget all about the sweet music." In particular, Miley's playing reflected the influence of the great New Orleans cornet player Joe "King" Oliver. Oliver's playing was suffused with a deep blues feeling. He combined his gift for melody with the use of a plunger mute; by variously positioning the rubber cup of a toilet plunger over the bell of his instrument, he could alter the sounds and produce vocal-like growling effects.

Miley adopted this technique – combining the plunger mute with a straight mute inserted directly into the cornet's bell – and raised it to an expressive art. Most important, he did not use the plunger mute strictly for novelty effects; he made it an expressive element of the music, intrinsic to the emotional content of the melody. Miley became the most prominently featured soloist in the early Ellington band. He also taught trombone player Joe "Tricky Sam" Nanton everything that he knew about mutes. During the mid- to late 1920s the two provided a distinctive tonal quality, commonly referred to as the "jungle-music sound," for which the early Ellington band became well known.

Miley and Nanton's musical influence is particularly evident in many of Ellington's recordings between 1926 and 1928 – for example, the various renditions of the slow-tempo "Black and Tan Fantasy" (1927), particularly the Victor Records version, on which Miley played what may be his greatest recorded solo. He opened on a keening high b-flat, which he held for four long measures before tumbling downward in a brilliant, bluesy cascade of plunger-muted notes. "It is also a highly dramatic solo," musicologist Gunther Schuller concluded, "equal to anything achieved up to that time by the New Orleans trumpet men. And perhaps none of them ever achieved the extraordinary contrast produced by the intense stillness of the four-bar-long high b-flat, suddenly erupting, as if unable to contain itself any longer, into a magnificently structured melodic creation."

Miley's superb improvisation may even have influenced the great Louis Armstrong. Eight months after Miley recorded this solo on "Black and Tan Fantasy," Armstrong took a strikingly similar approach in his classic improvisation on "West End Blues" (1928), entering on a high b-flat that he held for four tension-building measures before falling away in a cascade of notes. Armstrong did not directly copy Miley's solo: after the first four measures, their note choices, phrasing, and rhythms were quite different, and Armstrong's bravura open horn sounded completely different from Miley's plunger-muted growl. Yet the two solos share a remarkable similarity in their ways of building and releasing dramatic tension.

Miley also created some of the Ellington band's most memorable melodies. It is difficult to determine who was responsible for many pieces in the band's early repertoire. However, Gunther Schuller and Ellington biographer John Edward Hasse agree in assigning Miley a key role in creating some of the group's signature pieces, including "Black and Tan Fantasy," "East St. Louis Toodle-Oo" (1926), "Creole Love Call" (1927), and "The Mooche" (1928). Late in 1927 the Ellington band secured a long-term gig at the Cotton Club, New York City's most prestigious nightclub, and by the following year it emerged as the nation's foremost jazz ensemble.

But early in 1929 Ellington forced Miley, his most celebrated soloist, out of the band. Miley's heavy drinking and increasing unpredictability had at last exhausted Ellington's patience. Ellington scholar John Edward Hasse wrote that on occasion Miley did "not show up for several days," missing performances and recording sessions. As his replacement, trumpeter Charles "Cootie" Williams, explained, "[E]very time some big shot come up [to the Cotton Club] to listen to the band, there wasn't no Bubber Miley, and [Ellington] had the whole band built around Bubber Miley."

After leaving Ellington, Miley joined the Noble Sissle band on a 1929 trip to Paris. During the early 1930s he played with several other ensembles and briefly led his own group before succumbing to tuberculosis, aggravated by alcoholism, in the spring of 1932. He was 29 years old.

Miley left an enduring legacy within the Ellington band. Many of his compositions remained an active part of the band's repertoire, and Tricky Sam Nanton showed Cootie Williams the secrets of Miley's plunger mute technique. Through the years Ellington brass players passed on this knowledge to succeeding generations of musicians, maintaining a living link to the band's first famous soloist.

James Clyde Sellman

See Also

World War I and African Americans; Armstrong, Louis ("Satchmo"); Bechet, Sidney Joseph; Blues, The; New Orleans, Louisiana; New York, New York; Oliver, Joseph ("King"); Ellington, Edward Kennedy ("Duke").

North America

Military, Blacks in the American,

African Americans serving in various branches of the United States armed services and in every military conflict, often in the face of white resistance.

In 1948, as a result of President Harry S. Truman's Executive Order 9981, the U.S. military became the first major American institution to undertake racial integration. Although the military did not welcome the change, over the years it made great strides toward eliminating racial segregation and discrimination. Today large numbers of African Americans serve in the armed forces because – to a much greater extent than the larger society – the various branches of service reward ability regardless of race or class. For much of American history, however, white Americans resisted the admission of blacks to the military. Like other parts of the African American past, the story of blacks in the American military is closely entwined with the historical American realities of slavery and racism.

African Americans in the armed forces have faced conditions that varied widely over the years and from branch to branch within the services. Their story encompasses three major themes: first, black efforts to gain the right to serve and their changing reception within the various services; second, the service records and combat experiences of African American soldiers; and third, the complex impact of black military service on other aspects of American society and African American life. For African Americans, the most significant American military conflicts were the American Revolution (1775-1783), the Civil War (1861-1865), World War I (1917-1918), and World War II (1941-1945). Each of these wars had a profound impact on African American life as well as on the nation as a whole, and each involved significant numbers of black soldiers. African Americans, largely unsung, have played a part in every military conflict in American history.

The Role of African Americans in Colonial Militias

In the early seventeenth century British colonists, conscious of their vulnerability, welcomed slaves and free blacks into the provincial militias that defended their settlements from Native American, French, or Spanish attack. But as white colonists came to fear slave rebellions more than foreign aggression, they began to exclude African Americans from military service. Virginia passed such a law in 1639; Massachusetts, in 1656; and Connecticut followed five years later, after a joint rebellion of Native Americans and slaves near Hartford. In wartime, however, whites were receptive to black volunteers. Black militiamen fought and died in King William's War (1689-1697), Queen Anne's War (1702-1713), and the French and Indian War (1754-1763), as well as in countless skirmishes with Native Americans.

Slaves who distinguished themselves in battle were often granted their freedom, but most did not escape bondage in this manner because they had few opportunities to demonstrate their heroism. In what would be an enduring pattern, white commanders relegated black soldiers to support positions such as laborers and teamsters. As Lt. Col. (Ret.) Michael Lee Lanning observed in *The African-American Soldier* (1997), it was only when whites felt immediately "threatened by outside enemies" that they welcomed blacks in "armed positions," and black soldiers consistently found themselves "fighting and dying for a culture which did not recognize them as equals."

At sea, on the other hand, African Americans experienced much greater acceptance. Because of intolerable living conditions aboard ship, many white seamen deserted. Free blacks and runaway slaves, however, welcomed the comparative freedom and relative equality of pay, and they were therefore willing to endure the hardships faced by American merchantmen, whalers, and privateers. Although few blacks served as officers or ship captains – the most notable exception being black Massachusetts captain and ship owner Paul Cuffe – black seamen served in racially integrated crews. A similar tradition of racial openness would continue in the U.S. Navy until the late nineteenth century.

African Americans in the American Revolution

Black soldiers also played their part in the American Revolution, although the role of Crispus Attucks, the most celebrated black Revolutionary hero, has been misunderstood. In 1770, when Attucks and four whites were killed in the Boston Massacre, they did not die in the cause of American independence, a political goal that would not emerge until several years later. Rather, they were involved in a labor struggle. Attucks's role in leading a mob against British soldiers reflected rising anger at soldiers who were taking jobs in their off-duty hours and augmenting their pay at the expense of Boston workingmen. It would thus be more accurate to view Attucks as an early martyr in the American labor movement.

African Americans, especially those who were slaves, faced a difficult choice between siding with the patriots, whose leaders included prominent slaveholders such as George Washington and Thomas Jefferson, or with the British Loyalists. Late in 1775 Virginia's royal governor John Murray, the earl of Dunmore, tried to take advantage of implicit racial divisions by offering freedom to any slave who joined the Loyalist forces. Although Lord Dunmore organized one black regiment, a surprisingly small number of slaves answered his call – probably 2000, although higher figures have been reported.

But the threat of a wholesale slave exodus to the British led patriot leaders to reconsider their original policy of excluding black soldiers. Ultimately, some 5000 African Americans, both free blacks and slaves, joined the Continental Army, and many others served in local militias. Most of those who were slaves won their freedom in the process. These black soldiers proved their courage under fire, and many died in the struggle for American independence, beginning with Prince Estabrook, a black militiaman killed at Lexington Green on April 19, 1775.

In 1775, after the Battle of Bunker Hill, the Massachusetts legislature particularly commended African American militiaman Salem Poor, declaring that "in the person of this said Negro centers a brave and gallant soldier." Black sailors in the fledgling American navy also saw extensive action, including service aboard John Paul Jones's *Bonhomme Richard* in its 1778 victory over the British *Serapis*. Lemuel Haynes, a black soldier from Connecticut and later a Congregational minister, dramatically broadened the patriots' own logic of liberty and inalienable rights in "Liberty Further Extended." This essay, written around 1776 though long unpublished, offers an early natural-rights argument against slavery.

Black Gains and Losses from the Revolution to the Civil War

Revolutionary ideals gave impetus to the abolition of slavery in the North – beginning

A hand-colored lithograph from about 1865 is titled *Major Martin R. Delany USA. Promoted on the Battle Field for Bravery.* With that promotion, Delany became the highest-ranking African American in the American military. *National Portrait Gallery, Smithsonian Institution/Art Resource, NY*

with Vermont in 1777 and concluding with a plan for gradual emancipation that New Jersey ratified in 1804 – certainly the most significant consequence of the Revolutionary War for African Americans. At the same time, however, Southern slavery became more entrenched and the military more firmly whites-only. The Militia Act, passed by Congress in 1792, was restrictively understood to limit militia service to "able-bodied white male citizen[s] between the ages of 18 and 45." In 1798, in the act that formally organized the U.S. Marine Corps, Congress expressly excluded "Negroes, mulattos [of African and European descent], and Indians" from serving. The Marines remained lily-white until the manpower crisis of World War II.

African Americans encountered a very different reception in the army and the navy, the nation's principal military branches. The navy remained a bastion of opportunity for African Americans, in large part because it had to compete with the expanding fleet of American merchant vessels and fishing and whaling ships. Thus many blacks fought as sailors against the Barbary States (1801-1805) and in the War of 1812 (1812-1815); at the end of the latter, fully 10 percent of the U.S. Navy was black. On land, however, blacks had a far less prominent role, although black explorers did play an important part in westward expansion. The Lewis and Clark Expedition (1804-1805) included one African American, Capt. William Clark's slave, York. Black MOUNTAIN MEN and fur trappers – such as Jim Beckwourth and Pierre Bonga – gained extensive knowledge of the mountainous West and later served as scouts and guides for the military.

In peacetime the services once again sought to exclude African Americans. In 1820 the U.S. Army ordered that no blacks be accepted as recruits, and in 1839 the navy ordered that African Americans not exceed a maximum of 5 percent of total naval manpower, a policy that was often ignored yet unambiguously revealed the beginning of racial discrimination at sea. During these years at least some blacks thought it better to oppose the United States and its military. In the First Seminole War (1816-1818) and Second Seminole War (1835-1842), the Native American forces included many escaped slaves, maroons who had taken refuge with Florida Seminoles and who fought courageously against a numerically superior U.S. Army (*see* SEMINOLE WARS). During the Mexican War (1846-1848), however, just a handful of African Americans served in the U.S. Army, principally as servants to white officers or in support roles.

THE MILITARY ROLE OF AFRICAN AMERICANS IN THE CIVIL WAR

The Civil War offered significant numbers of African Americans the chance to prove themselves in combat. At the outset the war gave every appearance of being strictly a white man's fight. President Abraham Lincoln specifically refused to accept black recruits for the Union Army. "Colored men were good enough to fight under Washington," remarked a frustrated FREDERICK DOUGLASS, "but they are not good enough to fight under McClellan." However, Union forces advancing through the slave states attracted large numbers of blacks who sought freedom and refuge and who confronted Union commanders with a significant tactical, legal, and moral problem. Southern slaveholders who were noncombatants regularly appealed to Union commanders demanding the return of their slave property. Army commanders faced with such pleas discovered that no set policy or precedent existed to guide them.

Gen. Benjamin Butler, a Massachusetts abolitionist and political appointee, argued that if Southerners chose to regard runaway slaves as property, those slaves should be considered "contrabands of war" and, in light of their obvious strategic value, should not be returned. Soon these contrabands were put to work in support roles, and eventually some were outfitted with discarded Union equipment to serve as sentries to protect other African Americans. On the Sea Islands off the coast of Georgia, Gen. David C. Hunter began organizing contrabands into military units as early as May 1862. That August, Hunter's successor, Gen. Rufus Saxton, received authorization from the War Department to recruit, arm, and train 5000 African American volunteers under the leadership of white officers. That unit, named the First South Carolina Colored Volunteers, was the first African American regiment organized in the war, although it was not called into active duty until January 31, 1863.

In 1863 – through the diligent efforts of Northern black leaders, most notably Frederick Douglass, and because of a growing manpower shortage in the North – President Abraham Lincoln issued the

Emancipation Proclamation, which set the Union on the path to dismantling slavery and authorized African American military recruitment. This change in policy did not alter the profound racial hostility of many Northern whites, evidenced in the Draft Riots of 1863 that erupted in various Northern cities, most seriously in New York City, where a massive race riot by whites against blacks resulted in as many as 1200 fatalities.

Nonetheless, Douglass, Martin R. Delany, Rev. Henry Highland Garnet, and other African American leaders enthusiastically engaged in recruiting black volunteers. Black leaders even accepted that the new black regiments were to be commanded by white officers, although eventually Delany – commissioned a major in 1865 – became the nation's first African American field officer. The most celebrated black regiment was the Fifty-fourth Massachusetts Volunteers, subject of the 1989 film *Glory*. Like their white counterparts, African American women also took part in the Civil War, although mostly in support roles. The nation's two most prominent black women were actively involved in the struggle: Sojourner Truth worked as a nurse in a field hospital, and Harriet Tubman performed valuable service as a scout and Union spy.

As historian Eric Foner pointed out, African American soldiers "played a crucial role not only in winning the Civil War, but also in defining the war's consequences." Even more important, they helped to transform the black community. In the course of military service, many former slaves learned to read and write, and a considerable number of black soldiers acquired the fundamentals of leadership, including, during Reconstruction, 60 state legislators, 41 delegates to state constitutional conventions, 3 lieutenant governors, and 4 congressmen. For African Americans as a group, the war instilled a new confidence. Thus in 1865 black troops of the Fifty-fourth Massachusetts marched into Charleston, South Carolina – that city of planter-aristocrats and secessionist "fire-eaters" that had started the war – singing "John Brown's Body."

Reconstruction and the Late Nineteenth Century

Black soldiers were prominent in the U.S. military forces that occupied the defeated South during the early years of Reconstruction, at least until 1867, when Southern complaints led President Andrew Johnson to phase most of them out. Moreover, the contributions of the 180,000 black Union Army volunteers – accounting for 9 to 10 percent of the total Union Army enrollment – provided a compelling case not only for Emancipation, accomplished by the Thirteenth Amendment (1865), but for granting African Americans citizenship through the Fourteenth Amendment (1868) and for extending the suffrage to black males through the Fifteenth Amendment (1870). Indeed, when President Abraham Lincoln cautiously endorsed the idea of black suffrage, he proposed a limited extension to "the very intelligent" and to "those who serve our cause as soldiers."

The late nineteenth century was a time of heightened racial animus on the part of white America, marked by a sharp increase in the lynching of African Americans and the development of Jim Crow social segregation and black disfranchisement throughout the South. Black wartime contributions faded quickly from white memories. White harassment cut short the military careers of James Webster Smith and Henry O. Flipper, the first two African American cadets at the U.S. Military Academy at West Point. Smith was dismissed before graduating; Flipper graduated in 1877, earning a commission as a lieutenant, but four years later was court-martialed and dishonorably discharged. Nearly a century passed before the army exonerated him and made his discharge honorable.

Peacetime reductions in defense spending after the Civil War resulted in the disbandment of almost all of the army's black regiments. But unlike peacetime reductions in years past, the U.S. Army did not wholly abandon African American soldiers. Until World War I it maintained four black units, the 24th and 25th Infantry and the Ninth and Tenth Cavalry Regiments. These regiments served mainly in the Far West and became known by Native Americans as buffalo soldiers.

The Spanish-Cuban-American War and the "Philippines Insurrection"

All four African American units played a prom-

Henry O. Flipper was the first African American to graduate from the U.S. Military Academy at West Point. *CORBIS/Bettmann*

inent role in the Spanish-Cuban-American War (1898-1899). The regimental quartermaster for the Tenth Cavalry was the young captain John J. Pershing, whose nickname, "Black Jack," derived from his service with African American troops. The Tenth fought gallantly at the Battle of San Juan Hill, and in a speech several months later Pershing declared, "We officers of the Tenth Cavalry could have taken our black heroes into our arms. They had fought their way into our affections as they have fought their way into the hearts of the American people."

After the war the army's four permanent black regiments – later augmented by two regiments of black volunteers – were ordered to the Philippines (1899-1902) to join in the jungle fighting between U.S. troops and Filipino freedom fighters that had erupted shortly after the Spanish capitulation. The so-called Philippines Insurrection, an undeclared and unpopular jungle war fought against an elusive enemy, had much in common with the later conflict in Vietnam. It was also potentially divisive for African Americans, since the Filipino freedom fighters were dark-skinned people seeking freedom from oppression. Moreover, white American troops in the Philippines consistently referred to the Filipino nationalists as "niggers."

In the United States some black newspapers emphasized the similarities between the Filipinos and African Americans. The *Colored American* of Washington, D.C., observed that both groups were "struggling for the right of liberty and the pursuit of happiness." However, most African Americans stood by their country. When white newspapers questioned the ability of blacks to fight their racial "brothers," African American soldiers were adamant in their patriotism. "We are American citizens," one man in the Twenty-fourth Infantry declared, "and we have at heart the interests of our native land in the same manner as do all Americans."

In late November and December 1899 on the island of Luzon, some 350 men of the Twenty-fourth participated in one of the most successful operations of the war. After marching more than 500 km (300 mi) through uncharted jungle, they captured rebel commander Daniel Tirona and his thousand-man force. Gen. Elwell S. Otis commended the Twenty-fourth for its accomplishments despite "the difficulties encountered and the discomfort suffered by the troops."

In the U.S. Navy, however, conditions for African Americans deteriorated significantly by the turn of the twentieth century. The navy, once the most receptive branch of the military, deliberately acted to reduce the number of black sailors. Service heads and ship captains justified the new policies as inevitable, given the navy's shift from sailing vessels that required a large and relatively unspecialized crew of common seamen to steamships that relied on more highly trained engineers, gunners, and other specialists. Naval officers argued that blacks lacked the intellectual or technical capabilities to master the high technology of steam engines, and black sailors found themselves increasingly confined to work as stewards or messmen in ships' galleys. With the "pacification" of the Philippines, even those positions became fewer. Around the time of World War I the navy began recruiting allegedly more tractable Filipino messmen.

The Early Twentieth Century and World War I

Thus the United States entered the twentieth century with a whites-only Marine Corps, a largely white navy, and a segregated army. After returning from duty in the Philippines, the nation's four black army regiments resumed their isolated postings in the Far West. The Tenth Cavalry served with distinction in Gen. "Black Jack" Pershing's Punitive Expedition (1916-1917) against Mexican revolutionary leader Pancho Villa, riding 1210 km (750 mi) in the first four weeks of the ten-month operation. On January 9, 1918, members of the Tenth made the last cavalry charge against Native Americans in the history of the American West.

In general, however, African Americans learned to expect little in the way of recognition or justice from any branch of the armed forces. In the Southwest the buffalo soldiers encountered steady racial harassment and intimidation, including LYNCHING, yet no white citizen was ever punished for engaging in such assaults. In the 1906 Brownsville Affair, President Theodore Roosevelt ordered the discharge without honor of 167 black enlisted men after a Texas shooting incident in which the men quite likely had no part. The men – of Companies B, C, and D of the Twenty-fifth Infantry – had served with distinction in CUBA and the Philippines, yet their exemplary record counted for little.

African Americans found greater opportunities as the nation mobilized for its 1917 entry into World War I, an ongoing conflict in Europe since August 1914. Ultimately, 200,000 black soldiers would be deployed to Europe, some serving with the American Expeditionary Force and others detailed to the French Army. But almost 90 percent of those troops were relegated to service and labor battalions far behind the lines. Curiously, the War Department did not order its four black regiments – the U.S. Army's most experienced soldiers – to Europe; they remained at their posts along the Mexican border. The army did organize two black combat divisions, the Ninety-second and Ninety-third Divisions, but when the Ninety-third arrived in France, General Pershing, the supreme American commander, turned it over to the French army. As Col. William Hayward, commander of the 369th Infantry Regiment and part of the Ninety-third Division, wrote, "Our great American general simply put the black orphan in a basket, set it on the doorstep of the French, pulled the bell, and went away."

Both the Ninety-third Division and the French inadvertently benefited from white Americans' unwillingness to serve with blacks. With the French, the Ninety-third experienced far greater acceptance and more equal treatment than the U.S. Army then provided. The unit served heroically throughout the remainder of the war, suffering a casualty rate of 35 percent. The 369th Infantry Regiment spent 191 days on the front lines – longer than any other American unit – during which time it neither gave up an inch of Allied territory nor lost a single soldier through capture. Although no black soldiers were awarded the Congressional Medal of Honor during the war, in the 369th alone 171 officers and men received either the Croix de Guerre or the Legion of Merit from the French government. The 369th included Lt. James Reese Europe, the black society musician from New York City who organized the regimental band. Lieutenant Europe was the first black officer to lead troops into combat in World War I, and he and his band also introduced the French to African American music, catalyzing a lasting French fascination with JAZZ.

The Colored Officers Training Camp and the 1917 Houston Mutiny

African American leaders faced great difficulties in gaining recognition for black soldiers. In light of the service academies' hostility to black cadets, the NATIONAL ASSOCIATION FOR THE ADVANCEMENT OF COLORED PEOPLE (NAACP) pressed for the establishment of a training school for black officers. Joel E. Spingarn, a white member of the NAACP board of directors, coordinated the effort that established the Colored Officers' Training Camp at Fort Dodge in Des Moines, Iowa. Over the course of the war, Fort Dodge trained and commissioned 639 African American officers. However important the achievement of these officers was in symbolic terms, it did little to alter the reality of racial imbalance. During the war African Americans comprised 13 percent of active-duty military manpower, but a mere seven-tenths of 1 percent of the officer corps.

Black aspirations were dealt a further setback when members of the Third Battalion of the Twenty-fourth Infantry took part in the Houston Mutiny of August 23, 1917, the first race riot in American history in which more whites than blacks died. The violence left 16 whites and 4 black soldiers dead. After hasty courts-martial, 19 more African American soldiers were executed for their part in the mutiny, and numerous others received lengthy jail sentences. Ironically, military historian Lt. Col. (Ret.) Michael Lee Lanning, author of *The African-American Soldier*, concluded that a key factor in the riot was the previous transfer of 25 of the battalion's most senior sergeants to Des Moines to attend the Colored Officers Training Camp, leaving only one experienced company first sergeant and seriously undermining battalion discipline. In the years to come, this incident effectively undermined any proposal to increase the role of black troops.

World War II

During World War I challenges to racial injustice were fitful and fruitless, but in World War II the nation faced a crisis of such magnitude that it swept away much of the rationale for exclusion and segregation. At the outset, however, African Americans encountered an all-too-familiar resistance from the white majority. In 1941, as the United States began to mobilize for war, there were few opportunities for African Americans in the booming defense industry. In response, black labor leader and civil rights activist A. Philip Randolph organized a massive March on Washington Movement, and President Franklin D. Roosevelt, who was eager to head off the protest, signed Executive Order 8802, banning racial discrimination in defense industry and federal government hiring. Executive Order 8802 also established the Fair Employment Practices Committee to implement and oversee the new policy. Randolph's victory would be the first of many during the war years.

Throughout the war the NAACP stressed the need for a "Double-V campaign," meaning victory over fascism overseas and over racism at home. In fact, World War II set in motion a process of change that would not only integrate the armed services, but would transform the whole of African American life and indeed remake the nation. Above all, World War II greatly accelerated the Great Migration that first began in the early decades of the twentieth century. Between the 1940s and the 1960s millions upon millions of African Americans would leave the South for newly opened, high-paying factory jobs in urban areas in the North and West.

Within the armed services World War II offers a long list of firsts, advancements, and breakthroughs. Initially, the opportunities for blacks remained few. The army's mobilization plan on the eve of World War II would have allowed African Americans to contribute only 6 percent of total army manpower, and few African American soldiers were given combat assignments. For example, Dorie Miller, who shot down two enemy aircraft, and possibly downed two more, during the Japanese attack on Pearl Harbor, was a messman ineligible for military training. Moreover, he was ignored for months after the battle; only after concerted protests in the African American press did Miller receive a Navy Cross and an invitation to speak to the 1942 graduating class at the Great Lakes Naval Training Center. Miller was then assigned to the aircraft carrier USS *Liscome Bay,* but a year later, when a Japanese submarine sank the ship, the black hero of Pearl Harbor died as a messman.

Throughout the war the official American policy was "not to intermingle colored and white enlisted personnel in the same regimental organizations." On the other hand, in 1940 President Franklin D. Roosevelt did commit the nation to establishing combatant and noncombatant black units in each branch of the armed forces. A year later the army activated the first black tank battalion, the 758th Tank Battalion. On March 7, 1942, the U.S. Army Air Corps commissioned its first black pilots, part of the all-black Ninety-ninth Pursuit Squadron – the famed Tuskegee Airmen – that Col. Benjamin O. Davis Jr. would command. On June 1 the U.S. Marine Corps admitted African Americans for the first time in its 144-year history, taking as its first recruit a former Nashville, Tennessee, dogcatcher named George Thompson. A month later the army accepted the first black women for the Women Auxiliary Army Corps (WAAC), later simplified to the Women's Army Corps (WAC). Nonetheless, African American soldiers never accounted for more than 8.7 percent of army manpower, and only 15 percent of that number received combat assignments.

The U.S. Navy, in contrast to its record in the late eighteenth and early nineteenth centuries, remained the service most obdurate on racial issues. Secretary of the Navy Frank Knox and senior naval officers resisted assigning African American sailors to any but the most menial shipboard duties, as servants to officers, in construction battalions, or as messmen or stewards in ships' galleys. The navy did not commission its first group of black officers, known as the Golden Thirteen, until March 17, 1944. Three days later it finally commissioned the USS *Mason*, an antisubmarine ship and the first navy vessel manned by black sailors under the command of white officers, at last providing African Americans with an official opportunity for naval combat. The navy would not order the desegregation of its shore facilities until after the end of the Korean War (1950-1953). Understandably, therefore, during World War II African Americans represented only 5 percent of the navy's total manpower.

Integrating the Military from World War II to the Korean War

In contrast, the U.S. Army began to take steps to challenge the assumptions of Jim Crow segregation. In 1941 it began integrating its officers' candidate schools. In July 1944 the War Department prohibited discrimination in transportation and recreational facilities on all army bases. On a Texas military base not long after this directive was issued, Lt. Jackie Robinson – who would soon become the first African American to break the long-standing color bar in major-league baseball – refused to go to the back of a bus, resulting in his court-martial and complete vindication. Lieutenant Robinson's refusal to abide southern Jim Crow practices was by no means an isolated example. Indeed, the pride and confidence of African American military veterans and their unwillingness to endure further discrimination would help provide the impetus for the Civil Rights Movement of the 1950s and 1960s.

On December 26, 1944, during the worst days of the Battle of the Bulge, the army issued a directive requesting African American volunteers to be integrated into white combat units, a request that clearly marked the beginning of the end for the Jim Crow army. But no service branch welcomed the prospect of integration. The persistent delaying tactics of the various service heads outraged African Americans, whose pressure in 1948 moved President Harry S. Truman to order the integration of America's armed forces and to establish the President's Committee on Equality of Treatment and Opportunity in the Armed Services.

During the Korean War the first integrated American combat units saw action, and they proved that racial prejudices and enmities fall away quickly under the pressure of battle. By the war's end more than 90 percent of black troops were serving in integrated units. The only regrets that African Americans expressed about this process concerned the disbandment of the four historic black regiments, which thus closed a part of black history reaching back to the end of the Civil War. Above all, the Korean War transformed the U.S. Marine Corps. At the start of that conflict, only 1075 of the nation's 74,279 marines were Africans Americans, and of that 1075, nearly half (427) were stewards. In the space of two years the Corps changed from the most segregated branch of the armed forces to one approaching complete integration. The United States disbanded its last segregated unit in 1954, the year in which the Supreme Court issued its pivotal decision in Brown v. Board of Education. Thus when the nation had scarcely begun its effort to end segregation in public schools, racial integration was nearly an accomplished fact in the armed forces.

Integrating the Military from the Korean War to Vietnam

Integration proceeded, not always smoothly, through the 1950s and 1960s. The military made great strides toward integrating its rank and file, but progress was much slower with respect to the officer corps, although undeniable gains were made there as well. Moreover, during the Vietnam War (1960-1973), African American soldiers faced a new problem; rather than being excluded from combat, they now found themselves almost inevitably condemned to it. African Americans, as Lt. Col. (Ret.) Michael Lee Lanning observed, were "13.5 percent of

the military-age population [and] 10.6 percent of the total force in the war zone," but accounted for "20 percent of U.S. battlefield casualties." It was, as one black soldier remarked, "the kind of integration that could kill you."

The Vietnam War was the first war in which African American leaders gradually turned against the federal government, which they had long regarded as African Americans' best ally. Paradoxically, as Lieutenant Colonel Lanning noted, the first black leaders to come out against the war were not, generally speaking, those who advocated nonviolence. Thus the militant and often bellicose MALCOLM X spoke out against the war as early as 1964; the Reverend Martin Luther King Jr., on the other hand, did not voice his opposition until 1967.

Far more quickly than most civil rights activists, African American soldiers in Vietnam came to doubt the wisdom of their political and military leaders. Black soldiers, along with Mexican-Americans and working-class whites, faced the most dangerous and thankless combat assignments. Regardless of race, these combat troops came in many ways to share a common outlook. They questioned military discipline, sometimes challenged orders, and generally developed a cynical attitude toward military authority and political leaders. On the other hand, soldiers "in country" learned that they needed to count on one another regardless of race. Indeed, in a war where the difficulty in knowing the enemy and the obduracy of the high command were equally legendary, combat troops discovered that they could not really count on anyone else.

AFRICAN AMERICAN SOLDIERS IN THE ALL-VOLUNTEER ARMY

During the war Americans black and white came to mistrust the draft, which had been established by the Selective Service Act of 1948. In response, President Richard M. Nixon approved a proposal for an all-volunteer military, and the army inducted its last draftees in mid-1973. The new policy resulted in a sharp increase in the proportion of African Americans in military service. Many blacks joined the military because it offered jobs, training, and educational and other benefits, while in the larger society African Americans faced an unemployment

TOP: Wounded members of the 369th Infantry, also known as the Harlem Hellfighters, ride up Fifth Avenue in New York City in 1919 after their return from fighting in France. The parade was led by James Reese Europe's Harlem Hellfighters band. *CORBIS/Bettmann*
MIDDLE: The United States Marine Corps admitted its first black recruit on June 1, 1942. These marines pause for a moment on the treacherous beach of Iwo Jima in the South Pacific, March 1942. *Archive Photos*
LEFT: Issued in 1948, President Harry S. Truman's executive order integrated the United States armed forces. The first combat units, such as this one on the Chongchon River in 1950, saw action in the Korean War. *CORBIS*

rate significantly higher than that of the white majority. But critics argued that the phrase "all-volunteer" misrepresented what was in fact an economic draft, in which the lack of alternatives forced a disproportionate number of blacks into military service. Thus in 1972 about 17 percent of the army was African American, but by 1981 that figure had nearly doubled to one-third. The navy continued to be the least congenial service for blacks; nonetheless, the proportion of black sailors also essentially doubled, from 6.4 to 12.0 percent. Only the U.S. Air Force lagged in its ability to attract African Americans, posting a much smaller increase, from 12.6 to 16.5 percent.

At the same time the military did not measure its success in achieving racial integration in merely quantitative terms. It also confronted much thornier problems of prejudice and discriminatory attitudes, and it made an unprecedented effort to redress past injustices. Since the 1970s military historical commissions have reexamined the records of various courts-martial, disciplinary hearings, and recommendations for service awards in which the original decisions may have been tainted by racial prejudice and discrimination.

Thus in 1972 the army exonerated the 167 black soldiers punished in the 1906 Brownsville Affair. Four years later it provided an honorable discharge for Lt. Henry O. Flipper, and in 1977, the 100th anniversary of Lieutenant Flipper's graduation from West Point, the military academy unveiled a bust in his honor. In 1991 President George Bush presented family members of Cpl. Freddie Stowers with a "long overdue" Medal of Honor for his heroism on September 28, 1918, while serving in the Ninety-third Infantry Division in France, making Corporal Stowers the first black soldier granted a Medal of Honor for service in World War I.

In 1996 the Department of Defense decided to honor seven African Americans with Medals of Honor for their heroism during World War II. During the war itself not one African American soldier was judged worthy of the nation's highest military honor. In a White House ceremony on January 13, 1997, President Bill Clinton presented the Medal of Honor to the only survivor among the seven recipients, Lt. Vernon J. Baker. On April 5, 1945, Lieutenant Baker had led his 25-man platoon against heavily fortified German positions. He killed two Germans in an observation post and led his men on to destroy six German machine gun nests and kill 26 German soldiers. Only Lieutenant Baker and six of his men survived the assault. In presenting the medal, President Clinton declared: "History has been made whole again, and our nation is bestowing honor on those who have long deserved it. They were denied their nation's highest honor, but their deeds could not be denied, and they cleared the way to a better world."

When journalists asked Lieutenant Baker how he had felt about defending his country in a Jim Crow army, he replied, "I was an angry young man. We were all angry. But we had a job to do, and we did it."

The Persian Gulf War and After

The Persian Gulf War (1991) was the first war in the nation's history in which the top military commander, Gen. Colin L. Powell, chairman of the Joint Chiefs of Staff, was black. Moreover, Gen. Cal Waller, an African American, was second in command to Gen. Norman Schwarzkopf in Operation Desert Storm, as the Pentagon designated the allied war effort. African Americans were also heavily overrepresented in U.S. forces in the war zone. Although only 12 percent of the military-age population, African Americans accounted for 26 percent of the troops in the Gulf.

Between the early 1980s and the late 1990s the proportion of African Americans in the military remained relatively constant. In 1996 African Americans comprised about 21.9 percent of the total enlisted forces – 30.2 of the army, 18.5 percent of the navy, 17.1 percent of the marines, and 16.8 percent of the air force – all well above the proportion of African Americans in the total population. There is an obvious reason for the prevalence of blacks in the military. As General Powell observed: "The Army was living the democratic idea ahead of the rest of America. Beginning in the fifties, less discrimination, a truer merit system, and leveler playing fields existed inside the gates of our military posts than in any Southern city hall or Northern corporation."

Although some problems remain, particularly the relative shortage of blacks within the officer corps, at the start of the twenty-first century African Americans have achieved a level of equality in the armed forces that the larger society cannot yet approach.

James Clyde Sellman

See Also

Slavery in the United States; Maroonage in the Americas; World War I and African Americans; World War II and African Americans; Abolitionism in the United States; American Indians; Baseball in the United States; Beckwourth, James Pierson; Civil War, American; Davis, Benjamin O., Jr.; Delany, Martin Robison; Fifteenth Amendment to the United States Constitution; Fifty-fourth Regiment of Massachusetts Volunteer Infantry; Fourteenth Amendment to the United States Constitution; Free Blacks in the United States, 1619 to 1863; Fugitive Slaves; King, Martin Luther, Jr.; New York City Draft Riot of 1863; Powell, Colin Luther; Randolph, Asa Philip; Spanish-Cuban-American War, African Americans in the; Thirteenth Amendment of the United States Constitution and the Emancipation Proclamation; Tubman, Harriet Ross; Vietnam War; March on Washington, 1941.

North America

Millender-McDonald, Juanita

(b. September 7, 1938, Birmingham, Ala.), Democratic member of the United States House of Representatives from California (1996-).

Juanita Millender-McDonald earned a bachelor's degree from the University of Redlands and a master's degree from California State University, Los Angeles. She taught in the Los Angeles School District and received national recognition when she served on the National Commission on Teaching and America's Future. In 1990 she became the first black elected to the Carson City Council. During her second year on the council, she was elected mayor pro tem for Carson. In 1992 she won a seat in the California State Assembly.

After Representative Walter R. Tucker III resigned as U.S. Representative for California's 37th Congressional District, Millender-McDonald announced her candidacy for the vacant seat. She defeated eight other candidates in the March 1996 Democratic primary. In the general election, she ran unopposed. She was sworn into office on April 16, 1996, and was immediately assigned to the Transportation and Infrastructure Committee and the Small Business Committee. She retained these posts in the 105th Congress (1997-1999) and is a member of the Congressional Black Caucus.

See Also

Los Angeles, California.

North America

Miller, Cheryl

(b. January 3, 1964, Riverside, Calif.), African American basketball player, one of the greatest female basketball players.

Cheryl Miller was a four-time All-American in high school and scored 105 points in a single high school game in 1982. Her high school team had a win-loss record of 132-4 during her four years there. In 1982 Miller enrolled at the University of Southern California (USC), where she became a four-time collegiate All-American. For three consecutive years she won a Naismith Award as the nation's outstanding female basketball player (1984-1986). In 1983 and 1984 Miller led USC to the National Collegiate Athletic Association (NCAA) women's basketball championship and was named Most Valuable Player (MVP) of the tournament both years. She finished her collegiate career with averages of 23.6 points per game and 12 rebounds per game, and in her four years of play there, USC's win-loss record was 112-20. She was the first basketball player at USC – male or female – to have a jersey number retired (an honor whereby future players do not wear the number).

Miller also starred on the United States national basketball teams that won Gold Medals at the 1983 Pan American Games in Caracas, Venezuela; the 1984 Olympic Games in Los Angeles; and the 1986 Goodwill Games in Moscow. After graduating from USC in 1986, Miller was drafted by several professional basketball leagues, including the United States Basketball League, a men's league. In the late 1980s Miller suffered knee injuries that prevented her from continuing her playing career. From 1986 to 1991 she worked as an assistant coach at USC and as a television sports commentator. She became the head coach of the USC women's basketball team in 1993 but after two seasons she left to resume her broadcasting career. In 1995 Miller was inducted into the Basketball Hall of Fame.

See Also
Basketball; Television and African Americans.

North America

Miller, Kelly (b. July 18, 1863, Winnsboro, S.C.; d. December 29, 1939, Washington, D.C.), African American educator and scholar who sought to achieve a middle ground between the conservatism of Booker T. Washington and the radicalism of W. E. B. Du Bois.

Kelly Miller was the sixth of ten children born to a slavewoman and a freedman who served in the Confederate Army during the American Civil War. He was educated at missionary schools and in his mid-teens was admitted to the Fairfield Institute, a preparatory school in Winnsboro, South Carolina. Earning a scholarship to Howard University in Washington D.C., Miller finished his preparatory education there and entered Howard's bachelor's program while working as a clerk for the federal government. He graduated in 1886 and continued to work as a clerk. In addition, he studied math and physics privately with a mathematician at the United States Naval Observatory.

On the strength of this relationship, in 1887 Miller became the first African American admitted to Johns Hopkins University in Baltimore, Maryland. A tuition increase in 1889 prevented him from completing his graduate studies but after a short stint as a high school teacher in Washington, D.C., he was appointed professor of mathematics at Howard. In 1894 he married Annie May Butler, a Baltimore teacher, with whom he had five children.

Miller soon became interested in the emerging field of sociology and its application to the study of race relations. By the mid-1890s he had relegated his mathematical pursuits to a secondary status and published extensively on the current and future state of African Americans. His writings earned him a joint appointment as professor of mathematics and sociology. At the time, Booker T. Washington's philosophy – that blacks should receive an industrial rather than a liberal education and seek accommodation rather than confrontation with whites – had achieved widespread acceptance among whites and many blacks.

Although Miller praised Washington for encouraging blacks to apply themselves where and when they could, he criticized him for denigrating higher education. When W. E. B. Du Bois and other black scholars founded the Niagara Movement in opposition to Washington, Miller appraised the movement equally sharply, saying that the radicals were right for trying to return higher education to greater esteem, but that they went too far in their condemnations of industrial schooling. In one of his many articles, Miller wrote that "the subject of industrial and higher education is merely one of ratio and proportion, and not one of fundamental controversy." Because of his importance as a centrist, Miller was courted by both camps; neither, however, completely trusted him.

In 1907 Miller became dean of Howard University's College of Arts and Sciences. In the hope of enrolling more students, he oversaw a controversial addition of sciences – including applied (industrial) sciences – to the mostly classical curriculum. He traveled widely and recruited students throughout the country; as a result Howard's enrollment increased dramatically. In addition, he oversaw the donation of Howard alumnus Jesse E. Moorland's private library to the school, forming the core of what would become the Moorland-Spingarn Research Collection. Miller was prominent in prodding Howard's board of directors to allow blacks to govern the school. Since its founding, Howard had always had a white president. On many occasions Miller himself was mentioned as a potential candidate for the post, and so influential was he at Howard that the school was sometimes called Kelly Miller's University. When an African American (Mordecai W. Johnson) was finally appointed to the presidency in 1926, Miller was overlooked, perhaps because of his stinging criticism of incompetent and racist white university presidents. J. Stanley Durkee, the last of these presidents, demoted Miller, who never completely recovered his lost power.

Miller wrote and published his opinions on a variety of issues. He refuted the argument that blacks' problems were due to genetic inferiority; he critiqued and then opposed the migration of blacks from rural areas to highly competitive cities; and he condemned the racial discrimination of white labor unions (his anti-union stance grew to include opposition to black unions as well). He also published a weekly column in the 1920s and 1930s in more than 100 newspapers. At its peak the column reached as many as half a million readers. In his later years he was disturbed by the large number of radicals appointed at Howard and urged a government investigation on the teaching of communism there. He was rebuked by Mordecai W. Johnson, Howard's first black president, for attempting to restrict freedom of speech. Miller retired from Howard in 1934 and died of a heart attack in 1939.

See Also
Civil War, American; Du Bois, William Edward Burghardt (W. E. B.); Eugenics; Johnson, Mordecai Wyatt; Labor Unions in the United States; Moorland, Jesse Edward; Washington, Booker Taliaferro; Communist Party USA, African Americans and the.

Africa

Millet, a variety of grass that is a staple crop throughout much of Africa.

The term *millet* is used to describe several species of the *Poaceae* (grass) family, which people first began cultivating in Africa approximately 4000 years ago. Millet plants produce flowers called racemes, which yield small edible seeds. Generally, the seeds are hulled, and cereals are then made from them. Millet plants range in height from 0.3 to 1.3 m (about 1 to 4 ft), except for pearl millet (*Pennisetum americanum*), the tallest of all the millet species, which can produce stalks ranging from 1.5 to 3 m (about 5 to 10 ft) and yields the largest seeds.

Several kinds of millet are cultivated in Africa, among them pearl and finger millet (*Eleusine coracana*). It is a particularly valued grain crop in arid regions, because it grows relatively quickly (in approximately 60 to 80 days) and can tolerate both drought and poor soil. It is also higher in protein than most of Africa's other staple starch crops, such as rice, maize, and cassava, and its bland taste combines well with other foods and spices. Porridge made from boiled millet flour (once ground primarily by women by hand, though now increasingly machine-milled) is the core of many traditional African dishes, typically accompanied by spicy sauces made from a combination of vegetables and fish, meat, or peanuts. Millet can also be used to brew beer.

Robert Fay

North America

Million Man March, a 1995 Washington, D.C., rally organized by Nation of Islam minister Louis Farrakhan and Benjamin Chavis to draw attention to the social conditions of African Americans and to urge black men to assume control over their lives.

The Million Man March emerged from Nation of Islam minister Louis Farrakhan's call for a Day of Atonement that would draw attention to the social and economic problems plaguing African American males. On October 16, 1995, approximately 900,000 black men congregated in WASHINGTON, D.C., to hear speeches from black luminaries such as Rosa Parks, Jesse Jackson, and MAYA ANGELOU. Farrakhan provided the keynote address. He asked black men to assume responsibility for themselves, their families, their communities, and America as a whole instead of placing the blame for their conditions on outside forces. Primarily organized by Benjamin Chavis, former executive director of the NATIONAL ASSOCIATION FOR THE ADVANCEMENT OF COLORED PEOPLE (NAACP), it was the single largest gathering of African Americans in history – surpassing in size the 1963 MARCH ON WASHINGTON.

Despite the numbers, from its inception the march drew severe criticism. It was denounced on the basis of Farrakhan's reputation as an anti-Semitic firebrand. Both men and women within the black community criticized the males-only policy and the undue emphasis placed on males as leaders within the African American community. (This eventually led to the organizing of a MILLION WOMAN MARCH in Philadelphia on October 25, 1997.) Others scorned the Nation of Islam's brand of black capitalism. And with its emphasis on individual responsibility as the means of racial uplift, it was charged with overlooking the systemic problem of racism within American social, economic, and political institutions.

While the long-term effects of the march have yet to be determined, immediately afterward it reinvigorated African American grassroots activism. It was also seen as an attempt by Farrakhan to move the Nation of Islam into the mainstream of American politics through development of a secular, coalition-based movement inclusive of the broad spectrum of African American political thought.

Peter Hudson

SEE ALSO

Chavis, Benjamin Franklin, Jr.; Farrakhan, Louis Abdul; Jackson, Jesse Louis; Parks, Rosa Louise McCauley.

North America

Million Woman March, a 1997 grassroots-organized PHILADELPHIA, PENNSYLVANIA, march of more than a million African American women seeking to build coalitions within the black community.

Asia Coney and Phile Chionesu do not command the same attention on the American political scene as NATION OF ISLAM minister Louis Farrakhan or former NATIONAL ASSOCIATION FOR THE ADVANCEMENT OF COLORED PEOPLE (NAACP) chairman Benjamin Chavis. Yet the two female, Philadelphia-based African American community activists organized a march whose size eclipsed that of Farrakhan and Chavis's much-publicized MILLION MAN MARCH (1995). On October 25, 1997, an estimated 1.5 million women congregated on Philadelphia's Benjamin Franklin Parkway for the Million Woman March. Under the slogan "Repentance, Resurrection and Restoration," the march aimed to forge black economic, social, and political coalitions that could rebuild an African American community quickly losing gains made during the CIVIL RIGHTS MOVEMENT.

Although the march was endorsed by the Nation of Islam, traditional African American political institutions such as the NAACP were not involved in its organization. It relied instead on grassroots activist networks, independent black media, and the Internet. Keynote speeches were delivered by United States Representative Maxine Waters, South African activist WINNIE MADIKIZELA-MANDELA, and Tynnetta Muhammad, the widow of Nation of Islam founder ELIJAH MUHAMMAD. Waters drew the loudest cheers for a statement that summed up the significance of the event. "America, be placed on notice," she proclaimed. "We know who we are. We understand our collective power. Following today, we will act on that power."

Despite such bold proclamations, the immediate impact of the march was unclear. Its major accomplishments may have been to draw attention to the declining social conditions of African Americans in the post-Civil Rights Movement era and to demonstrate solidarity among black women. Organizers hoped to repeat the event in the year 2000, and Farrakhan asked for a massive rally uniting the Million Man March and the Million Woman March on October 16, 2000, the fifth anniversary of the Million Man March.

Peter Hudson

SEE ALSO

Chavis, Benjamin Franklin, Jr.; Farrakhan, Louis Abdul; Waters, Maxine Moore.

North America

Mills Brothers, an African American pop vocal quartet that became famous in the 1930s for its ability to imitate JAZZ instruments.

The four Mills brothers were born to a musical family in Piqua, Ohio. Their paternal grandfather had sung with the Sourbeck Jubilee Singers. As children, John Jr., Herbert, Harry, and Donald performed professionally at local social events. In 1925 the boys – then between ages 10 and 15 – auditioned to appear on Cincinnati radio station WLW and won a prolonged broadcasting contract.

During the next few years they became station regulars and adopted stage names in accord with station sponsors – the Tasty Yeast Jesters (Tasty Yeast) and the Steamboat Four (Sohio Motor Oil) – but also achieved renown as Four Boys and a Guitar. Their success caught the attention of talent scouts from New York City, and in 1930 they signed a three-year contract with CBS Records, at the time an unusually long contract for African American musicians. The Mills Brothers' debut album in 1931 won them instant acclaim. Their single "Tiger Rag" sold a million copies and in 1932 they performed with Bing Crosby in *The Big Broadcast*, the first of the numerous films in which the quartet appeared.

Much of the Mills Brothers' popularity originated from arrangements in which they simulated a full instrumental ensemble by singing as horns. The only accompaniment came from John Jr.'s guitar playing; the rest of their rich sound comprised saxophone, trumpet, and tuba imitations, as well as tight, sweet, four-part harmonies. Throughout the 1930s they scored hit after hit with this formula, including "You Rascal You," "Good-Bye Blues," and "Swing It Sister." In the 1940s the quartet adopted conventional pop arrangements yet maintained their popularity – their 1942 hit, "Paper Doll," sold 6 million copies. Meanwhile, they undertook collaborations with some of the era's top African American musicians, such as Duke Ellington, Cab Calloway, and ELLA FITZGERALD.

The Mills Brothers remained together until 1982 but not without changes in their roster. The oldest brother, John Jr., died in 1935; his father then filled his role as bass vocalist, and exbandleader Bernard Addison played guitar. At times the three remaining brothers performed as a trio. By the end, the group had recorded almost 2500 songs.

The Mills Brothers' legacy involved social as well as musical accomplishments. Their vocal styles were a historic first, as were the terms under which they recorded them for white record companies. And their popularity among audiences of different races was unprecedented and influenced the formation, and mainstream acceptance, of doo-wop and RHYTHM AND BLUES (R&B) groups in the 1950s.

Eric Bennett

SEE ALSO

Calloway, Cabell (Cab); New York, New York; Ellington, Edward Kennedy ("Duke"); Film, Blacks in American.

North America

Mills, Florence (b. January 25, 1896, Washington, D.C.; d. November 1, 1927, New York, N.Y.), African American musical comedy singer and dancer; one of the most celebrated black entertainers of the Jazz Age and the HARLEM RENAISSANCE.

Florence Mills, who rose to stardom in the early 1920s, joined performing to a crusade for racial justice. She expressed a profound race consciousness and a conviction that her career could advance the status of

African Americans. "The stage is the quickest way to get to the people," she said in an interview with London's *Daily Express* in 1927. "My own success makes people think better of other colored folk."

Rejecting an offer to join the *Ziegfeld Follies,* America's leading white musical revue, she helped create a rival all-black musical revue in the heart of Broadway. She also broke through Broadway's racial barriers, performing in some of New York City's leading white vaudeville theaters, including the Palace Theater, where she was the first black ever to headline. Yet her principal goal was to foster opportunities for black entertainers and to remain true in her art to her black roots. "Harlem loves Florence Mills," wrote journalist Dudley Nichols in 1926. "She is the melodious, impish spirit of the Afro-American embodied piquantly."

The youngest of three daughters of John and Nellie (Simon) Winfrey, Mills grew up in Washington, D.C.'s poverty-stricken Goat Alley. Her mother and father, former slaves and tobacco workers from Virginia, worked as a laundress and a day laborer to make ends meet. It was the golden age of vaudeville, and Mills, a child prodigy, began singing and dancing at local black theaters at age three.

In 1903, under the guidance of RAGTIME singer AIDA OVERTON WALKER, Mills sang "Miss Hannah from Savannah" in a touring production of BERT WILLIAMS's and George Walker's musical *Sons of Ham.* Although her talent won her recognition and much-needed family income, she suffered racial exploitation performing as a "pickaninny" with a white vaudeville team. In 1910 she began touring the East Coast with her two sisters and faced the difficult travel conditions imposed on blacks by segregation. Eventually she found herself in Chicago, where gangster-controlled cabarets welcomed black clientele and the new jazz music. She sang with Cora Green and Ada "Bricktop" Smith at the Panama Cafe, a notorious cabaret in the city's red-light district. She also met and married the dancer "Slow Kid" Thompson; they would have a devoted and lifelong relationship.

Mills's career took off in 1921 when she replaced Gertrude Sanders in the black musical comedy *Shuffle Along,* by NOBLE SISSLE and Eubie Blake. Performed off-Broadway in New York, the musical introduced white audiences to the ebullient, fast-paced rhythms of authentic black song and dance and heralded the beginning of the HARLEM RENAISSANCE.

Dainty and elfin, Mills dazzled listeners and critics with her "flute-like" voice and quick, frolicking dance steps. Impressed by her talent, the white promoter Lew Leslie hired her as a nightly performer at the Plantation Club (so named to inform would-be patrons that its entertainers were black). The club drew a variety of famed black performers, including Will Vodery and his orchestra, and in 1922 Leslie turned his nightclub show into a Broadway musical group called the Plantation Review. Mills starred in the show and received effusive praise from New York critics.

In 1923 the Plantation Review cast performed in the musical *Dover Street to Dixie* at the Pavilion in London. Hostile to the visiting black Americans, British entertainers threatened to demonstrate in the theater on opening night. However, Mills's poignant rendition of "The Sleeping Hills of Tennessee" left the British audience enchanted; their opposition to the Review immediately subsided. For many British critics the Review's performance was nothing short of high art. American Alexander Wollcott described Mills as "a slender streak of genius five feet tall." Another reviewer wrote that she was "by far the most artistic person London had ever had the good fortune to see."

When Mills returned to London in 1926, this time in the widely acclaimed musical *Blackbirds of 1926,* she became the toast of British society. The Prince of Wales saw the revue more than a dozen times, and many artists and intellectuals of the period mentioned Mills in their writings and personal diaries. "Anything she did was super," wrote one critic, "whether spotlighted solo singing... or high-stepping in a smashing full-dress suit, her top hat at a rakish angle, jauntily swinging a malacca cane."

For Mills the London visit proved an auspicious time to voice openly her feelings about racial prejudice. British journalist Hannen Swaffer, who heard a speech Mills gave in the Picadilly Cabaret, wrote that "her eloquent plea for tolerance made an impression on many minds." Her title song, "I'm a little Blackbird, Looking for a Bluebird" – which for Mills contained a message about the quest for racial equality – became a hit with British and American audiences alike. "Few realized it, but the number was a protest song," noted black American journalist Alvin White. "There were no hidden meanings, no dramatic phrases, just simple words that told of the poignant yearnings of black women everywhere."

Throughout her short life Mills worked relentlessly; eventually she became seriously ill. Unable to continue her British tour, she sailed back to New York, where on November 1, 1927, she died following an operation for appendicitis. Her funeral on November 6 was an elaborately planned public event. More than 5000 people filled the Mother AFRICAN METHODIST EPISCOPAL ZION CHURCH in Harlem, while 150,000 more lined the streets to witness the funeral cortege and pay homage to the beloved "blackbird," who had never forgotten her heritage.

Roanne Edwards

SEE ALSO

Great Britain; Blake, James Hubert ("Eubie"); Chicago, Illinois; Harlem, New York; Smith, Ada "Bricktop.

North America

Milner, Ronald (b. May 29, 1938, Detroit, Mich.), African American playwright and producer prominent in the Black Theater movement of the 1970s.

With training from Harvey Swando's writing workshop at Columbia University, plus a wealth of creative material from his childhood in inner-city DETROIT, MICHIGAN, Ronald Milner produced his first play, *Who's Got His Own,* off-Broadway in 1966. Three years later, as one of four African American playwrights in the production *A Black Quartet,* he helped inaugurate the Black Theater Movement. With connections to the BLACK POWER Movement, the Black Theater Movement promoted plays allowing African Americans to represent their lives on stage.

With *What the Wine-Sellers Buy* (1973) Milner achieved national recognition, and followed with *Jazz Set* (1980), *Checkmates* (1987), and *Don't Get God Started* (1987). He worked closely with fellow playwright Woodie King Jr., cofounding the theater company Concept-East in 1962 and coediting the *Black Drama Anthology* in 1971.

Marian Aguiar

Africa

Mina (also known as the Popo), ethnic group of West Africa.

The Mina primarily inhabit southern TOGO and southern BENIN. They speak a dialect of EWE, a Niger-Congo language, and are sometimes considered an Ewe subgroup. The Mina are the descendants of GA and FANTE migrants. Approximately 400,000 people consider themselves Mina.

SEE ALSO

Languages, African: An Overview.

Latin America and the Caribbean

Minas Gerais, state in southeastern BRAZIL whose extensive gold and diamond deposits resulted in an influx of slave labor during the eighteenth century.

MINAS GERAIS: AN OVERVIEW

Minas Gerais was a densely forested region sparsely inhabited by Tupi and Guarani Indians before the arrival of Europeans in the seventeenth century. At that time explorers and *bandeirantes* (slave raiders) moved inland from São Paulo in search of Indian slaves as well as precious stones and metals. In the early 1690s they discovered large deposits of gold in the mountainous region in the central western part of the state, near the present-day city of Belo Horizonte. During the gold rush that ensued, the population boomed, from only a few inhabitants in the 1690s to 30,000 by 1709 and to 500,000 by the end of the century.

Competition over mining sites became fierce, sometimes resulting in violent conflicts. This led the Portuguese Crown to establish the *capitania* of Minas Gerais (Portuguese for "general mines") in 1720, and to create an administrative headquarters in Vila Rica (est. 1711), now known as Ouro Preto. At about this time two civilian rebellions occurred in protest of having to pay *quintos*, a royal tax of 20 percent: the Revolta de Pitangui (1719) and the Revolta de Felipe dos Santos (1720). In 1729 diamonds were discovered in the region surrounding the city of Tejuco (present-day Diamantina), to the north of the gold-mining region. The wealth generated by gold and diamonds during the eighteenth century (more than 2 million pounds of gold and 3 million carats of diamonds) enabled miners in Minas Gerais to finance the construction of churches, homes, and public buildings in the rococo and baroque styles popular at the time.

By the 1770s the production of gold began to decrease, and numerous mining ventures fell into debt. Many smuggled their finds to avoid having to pay taxes to the Crown, and faced harassment and tightening restrictions from government officials. The colonizers' frustration culminated in the Inconfidência Mineira in 1788-1789. This was an independence movement launched by members of the elite class in Ouro Preto who, influenced by the ideas of the European Enlightenment, were discontent with the colonial status of Minas Gerais. Provincial authorities exposed the conspiracy against the Portuguese Crown and executed its leader, Joaquim José "Tiradentes" (tooth-puller) da Silva Xavier, who became a symbol of the nationalist spirit.

After a period of stagnation the economy of Minas Gerais recovered in the mid-nineteenth century with the cultivation of coffee in the southern part of the state and the growth of cattle ranching and dairy farming in its central, southern, and western areas. Since then Minas Gerais, along with Rio de Janeiro and São Paulo, has been one of the nation's three most economically and politically powerful states. Today Minas Gerais accounts for nearly half of Brazil's coffee production and, with the country's largest cattle population, almost one-third of the nation's milk production. Faithful to its name, mining and the processing of metals such as iron ore and steel continue to be a major part of the economy of Minas Gerais.

The Arrival of the Slaves and the Growth of the Black Population

The state of Minas Gerais is the one exception to the generalization that Africans were concentrated and exerted an influence only in the coastal regions of Brazil. Gold and diamond prospectors brought large numbers of African slaves to Minas Gerais during the eighteenth century to work in the mines. While prospectors arriving from Portugal brought slaves from Africa with them for this purpose, those already living in Brazil tended to rely more heavily on Indian slaves. In 1708 these two groups clashed in the interior of Minas Gerais in the Guerra dos Emboabas, *Emboabas* being the term used by Brazilian-born prospectors to refer to the Portuguese. With the help of free and enslaved black soldiers, the Portuguese prospectors defeated the Brazilians the following year, thus also largely ending the use of Indian slaves.

While some slaves came with prospectors from other parts of the colony, especially Bahia and Pernambuco via the San Francisco River, many were imported directly from Africa for the explicit purpose of mining. Between one-fourth and one-third of all the slaves entering Brazil in the eighteenth century were destined for Minas Gerais. Slave traders categorized slaves according to their *nações* (nations), which referred to the part of Africa from which they embarked (and not necessarily the diverse regions from which different slaves came). The Minas, slaves that embarked from the Gold Coast (including Ghana, Benin, and Dahomey), tended to be experienced in and knowledgeable about mining (unlike the prospectors) and made up the bulk of the slave population in Minas Gerais. After the Minas slaves, the predominant "nations" included Congos, Cabindas/Benguelas, and Angolas, among others. The prevalent ethnic groups in this diverse body of slaves were Sudanese (*see* Sudan) during the first part of the eighteenth century and Bantu during the second part of the eighteenth century. At the end of the eighteenth century the number of Bantu imports was more than double the number of Sudanese imports.

By the second decade of the eighteenth century African slaves constituted the majority of the population of Minas Gerais. This population increased quickly, and by the last quarter of the eighteenth century the population of African descent in Minas Gerais, including free and enslaved blacks, was more than three times the size of the white population. Although the free black population increased steadily over time, slaves continued to constitute the majority of the black population through the end of the eighteenth century. Miscegenation had occurred since the beginning of slavery in Minas Gerais and resulted in a mulatto (of African and European descent) population that, by the early nineteenth century, was more numerous than the African-born population.

The growth of the mining industry in Minas Gerais during the eighteenth century resulted in a high influx of African slaves and funded the construction of numerous churches. The religious procession taking place in front of this colonial church in Mariana, Minas Gerais, is known as Virgen das Rosas. *Sue Cunningham/SCP*

During the later colonial period and the early years of the empire, which was created in 1822, some free members of the growing mulatto population in Minas Gerais gained social prominence. This small group of mulattos owned slaves, helped fund the construction and decoration of churches, and participated in the artistic life of their towns, distinguishing themselves as musicians, composers, and artists. For example, Ouro Preto was home to the famous mulatto sculptor Antonio Francisco Lisboa (1730-1814), known as Aleijadinho (Portuguese for "the little cripple"), whose religious sculptures adorn the city's historic churches. Despite their successes, the mulatto population was often accused of engaging in contraband commerce, harboring runaways, and providing escaped slave communities with supplies and information. Notwithstanding the inaccuracy of many of these claims in relation to mulattos, black brotherhoods such as those of Nossa Senhora do Rosário had a close relationship with escaped slaves, to whom they offered help and protection.

Working Toward Freedom

Although slaves were concentrated in the mining regions for much of the eighteenth century, over the course of the century they became increasingly involved in other economic activities in order to acquire their freedom. The calendar year included a month's worth of holidays, most of them Catholic holidays, on which slaves could work to earn money to purchase their *cartas de alforria* (manumission documents). To this end, some slaves grew their own crops or raised livestock. Many male slaves intermittently worked as carpenters, blacksmiths, barbers, cooks, and tailors. Records from this era in Minas Gerais also mention the prevalence of *negras de tabuleiro*, black female street vendors who moved between a village and its surrounding plantations or mines, or both, selling food products.

There were also opportunities to win free time and even freedom while working in the mines. Some prospectors allowed their slaves to take the remainder of the day off after finding a certain amount of gold. In the diamond fields some prospectors gave freedom to those slaves who found diamonds of a certain size (20 carats according to a 1734 law). In evasion of end-of-the-day inspections, some slaves smuggled small quantities of gold or diamonds away from mining sites by concealing these goods between their toes, in their ears, or in their mouths. Others hid gold or diamonds while on the job and later returned to collect them. The slaves then sold the gold and diamonds to contraband dealers in the hope of eventually accumulating enough money to purchase their freedom. Their success at achieving manumission is reflected in the fact that the provincial government attempted to restrict the granting of cartas de alforria out of the fear that the growing number of free blacks and mulattos would take over the province.

Although slavery in Minas Gerais was no more benign than in any other part of the colony, it was easier to achieve manumission in that province than, for example, on the sugar plantations in the northeast. Manumission was, however, still a long and arduous process that lasted an average of four to six years. Nor was it equally available to all who sought it: both in Minas Gerais and in Brazil as a whole, Brazilian-born slaves were favored over African-born slaves for manumission, and female slaves tended to win or be granted their freedom more easily than male slaves. In the city of Diamantina, the famous slave woman Xica da Silva not only won her freedom, but through her personal charm attained, however briefly, a position of social prestige.

Asserting Freedom: Quilombos and Slave Revolts

Although manumission had become commonplace by the end of the 1720s, many slaves simply escaped. The diamond-mining region and the region surrounding the cities of Vila Rica and Araxá were both major refuges for escaped slaves, who as early as 1711 organized themselves into communities known as *quilombos* (*see* Maroonage in the Americas). In the eighteenth century alone there were more than 125 documented quilombos in Minas Gerais. The most famous one was Quilombo do Ambrósio (named after its leader), also known as Quilombo do Campo Grande, which emerged sometime in the mid-1720s. It was located near the present-day city of Cristais and was unsuccessfully attacked twice (in 1741 and in 1743) before being overthrown in 1746. It then relocated to the region surrounding the present-day city of Ibiá, where it was finally destroyed in 1759. This quilombo contained some 10,000 members and lasted for nearly 35 years.

Quilombos comprised a diverse group of slaves of various origins: some mulatto slaves, some free blacks, and in a few cases, Indians and poor whites. They usually acquired what they needed by raiding nearby towns or plantations. These raids inspired great and widespread fear in the colonizing population. In Minas Gerais, some escaped slaves subsisted by collecting gold in hidden streams or abandoned mining sites and using it to purchase food, arms, and other goods. Some slaves, such as the legendary Chico Rei, mined gold on their own in order to purchase the freedom of enslaved family members and friends.

Escaped slave communities posed the greatest threat to the colonial social order in Minas Gerais, not only because of their raids and attacks on colonial society, but because they provided a compelling impetus for the enslaved to escape. These communities were repeatedly attacked by *capitães do mato* (bush captains), government-sponsored slave-catching regiments that were first formed in Minas Gerais in 1715. While the prospectors in Minas Gerais viewed the Indians as an obstacle to their lucrative plans, capitães do mato often employed Indians to help them track down escaped slaves and attack quilombos because of their familiarity with the land. Blacks and mulattos also worked as capitães do mato.

Though escaping and forming quilombos was the most common form of slave resistance in Minas Gerais, the state did experience a few slave revolts during and after the gold rush. One of the earliest slave risings in Minas Gerais occurred 1719 and was known as the Inconfidência Quilombola (*see* Slave Rebellions in Latin America and the Caribbean). On the night of March 30, taking advantage of the fact that most of their owners and their owners' families were at church, the rebelling slaves looted houses for firearms. Colonial officials discovered the plot and prepared defenses around the churches. When the revolting blacks arrived at the churches, the colonial regiments were able to defeat them. Two other significant rebellions occurred in Catas Altas, in 1735, and in Ouro Preto, in 1821. Both of these resulted in several deaths and the executions of their black leaders.

Abolition and the Transition to Freedom

Although the neighboring states of São Paulo and Rio de Janeiro were leading abolitionist centers, Minas Gerais did not become extensively involved in the abolition movement during the 1870s and 1880s (*see* Abolition and Emancipation in Latin America and the Caribbean). In Ouro Preto, then the capital, students from the Escola de Minas and the Escola de Farmácia founded an emancipation society in 1882, which was called the Sociedade Abolicionista Ouropretana. Their primary activity was the production of antislavery propaganda. In provincial assembly meetings, politicians Theodomiro Alves Pereira and Ignacio Antonio de Assis Martins advocated the emancipation of the slaves in Minas Gerais. Prominent religious figures, such as Bishop Antonio Maria Corrêa de Sá e Benevides and his successor, Dom Silverio Gomes Pimenta, both from the city of Mariana, frequently condemned slavery. Small-scale abolitionist activism occurred in several cities in Minas Gerais, including Barbacena, Cataguases, and Guanhães.

Following abolition in 1888, the freedpeople demanded food and clothing from their former owners, who refused their requests. Anticipating a violent outburst from the slaves, the colonial government quickly organized the recently freed blacks into military defense units known as the *guarda-negras* (black guards). Later that year, in order to diminish the number of unemployed blacks in the cities, the colonial government made military service an obligation for all able-bodied former slaves. However, these were preventive measures against Afro-Brazilian rioting, rather than preparatory measures for Afro-Brazilian integration.

The Brazilian government did little to facilitate former slaves' transition to freedom. Lacking the means to compete effectively with whites, Afro-Brazilians were forced into menial and often dangerous jobs. Because of their debased socioeconomic status, they were denied access to medical care, education, and decent housing. In the 1930s and 1940s, during the Getúlio Vargas era, low-income housing became available and allowed a number of black families residing in shacks on the outskirts of urban centers in Minas Gerais to live in healthier and more centrally located homes. Toward the middle of the twentieth century, however, inflation kept many black families from being able to continue living in these homes. Black communities in Minas Gerais still contend with illiteracy as well as poor health, which is reflected in high infant mortality rates and a shorter life expectancy than for Brazilians of European descent.

Despite these problems, blacks in Minas Gerais have found an inspirational figure in MILTON NASCIMENTO. Hailing from Minas Gerais, Nascimento has become one of the most famous musician-singers in contemporary MPB (Música Popular Brasileira). Black heritage, unity, and liberation are reccurring themes in his songs. Nascimento's most complete expression of these themes was his *Missa dos Quilombos* (1982, Mass of the Quilombos), written with Dom Pedro Casadáliga and Pedro Tierra, prominent figures in the Brazilian church's liberation theology movement. The album synthesizes Afro-Brazilian rhythms with Catholic hymns in commemoration of the suffering and resistance of African slaves in Brazil. In the song "Em Nome de Deus" (In the Name of God), Nascimento invokes the power of the African deity XANGÔ:

To liberate Quilombos Palmares.
In the name of a people continually
dragged into
Suppressive exile over the ocean.
Who established its own palm groves
Its free republic
Of runaway slaves.

By celebrating Afro-Brazilian history and calling for political change, Milton Nascimento's music has become a source of pride and hope for blacks in Minas Gerais and throughout Brazil.

Aaron Myers

SEE ALSO

Bantu: Dispersion and Settlement; Dahomey, Early Kingdom of; Lisboa, Antônio Francisco ("Aleijadinho"); Rio de Janeiro, Brazil; Religious Brotherhoods in Latin America.

North America

Mingus, Charles, Jr.

(b. April 22, 1922, Nogales, Ariz.; d. January 5, 1979, Cuernavaca, Mexico), African American bassist, bandleader, and composer who foreshadowed free JAZZ but grounded his music in the black gospel and blues traditions.

Charles Mingus was a temperamental iconoclast, a virtuoso bassist, and a man who protested racial injustice through his music. His compositions reveal his deep involvement in the musical experimentation of the 1940s known as bop, in which young black musicians significantly expanded the harmonic boundaries of jazz. He drew upon the legacy of older jazz styles and the rich African American traditions of blues and gospel music, but he created a jazz world uniquely his own. Few jazz musicians gain renown for their compositions. Apart from Mingus, critics identify only three great jazz composers: Jelly Roll Morton, Duke Ellington, and Thelonious Monk. Of these, Mingus is the most contemporary and the least appreciated. His intensely personal music seemed to look both backward and forward. He invoked the origins of jazz by grounding his compositions in the blues, the music from which jazz emerged. He also made extensive use of collective improvisation, a playing style that was characteristic of New Orleans jazz of the early 1900s but that had virtually disappeared from mid-twentieth century jazz. On the other hand, his work anticipated the dissonance and openness of the free jazz that appeared in the 1960s.

The titles of Mingus's compositions are some of the most striking in jazz. He repeatedly addressed issues of racial injustice, as in "Haitian Fight Song" (1955), "Prayer for Passive Resistance" (1960), and "Remember Rockefeller at Attica" (1974) (*see* ATTICA UPRISING). He also revealed a lively humor – as in his take on Oscar Hammerstein II and Jerome Kern's "All the Things You Are," which he titled "All the Things You Could Be By Now If Sigmund Freud's Wife Were Your Mother" (1960).

Mingus's family moved shortly after his birth to Watts, the principal black neighborhood of Los Angeles. His mother died when he was six months old, and his father remarried. His stepmother introduced him to the fervent gospel music of the Holiness Church. Such Mingus compositions as "Wednesday Night Prayer Meeting" (1959) and "Better Git It in Your Soul"(1959) reveal the continuing influence of the religious music that he had heard as a child, not only in the titles, but also in their ecstatic, bluesy quality.

In grade school Mingus began playing the trombone, then the cello, and finally the bass. Hearing Duke Ellington in a late-night radio broadcast was what inspired his interest in jazz. In 1939 he began taking lessons from jazz bassist Red Callender (1916-1992), and later he studied with ex-New York Philharmonic bassist Herman Rheinshagen. As a teenager, Mingus was part of the jazz scene that flourished along Los Angeles' Central Avenue, along with such aspiring musicians as tenor saxophonist Dexter Gordon (b. 1923) and drummer Chico Hamilton (b. 1921). But like other young musicians of the 1940s, Mingus found it difficult to gain a foothold in jazz.

In 1942 Mingus played with clarinetist Barney Bigard (1906-1980), and in 1943 he toured with trumpeter Louis Armstrong's big band. But the changing musical tastes of the latter half of the 1940s put an end to the big bands that had provided work for many young musicians. In 1946 Mingus made his recording debut with an octet playing several of his early, Ellington-influenced compositions. That year he took a more secure job with the United States Post Office. In 1947 he toured with Lionel Hampton's big band, but during 1948-1950 he returned to post office work, playing jazz and rhythm and blues (R&B) gigs freelance.

Mingus's breakthrough came with a 1950-1951 stint with the Red Norvo Trio, composed of white vibraphonist Norvo, white guitarist Tal Farlow, and Mingus. The small group offered a showcase for his early playing style, which combined the virtuosity of style-setting jazz bassist Jimmy Blanton (1918-1942) and the harmonic sophistication of bop. As he recounted in his searing autobiographical novel, *Beneath the Underdog* (1971), the months of touring with the interracial trio brought Mingus face to face with the harsh realities of racial discrimination. He left the group after an incident in which a white bass player temporarily took his place for a television broadcast in New York City.

Despite that unpleasant racial incident, Mingus decided to relocate to New York City in 1951. There he played with such jazz musicians as alto saxophonist and bop innovator Charlie Parker, swing piano master ART TATUM, and white pianist Lennie Tristano, a cool jazz pioneer. But in 1952 Mingus returned to working at the post office. In that year, with drummer Max Roach, he founded Debut Records (1952-1957), his first of many attempts to exert greater control over the business side of music. The label's crowning achievement lay in recording a 1953 concert at Toronto's Massey Hall that featured the finest bop group ever assembled: Parker, trumpeter Dizzy Gillespie, pianist Bud Powell, Roach, and Mingus.

Mingus contributed numerous compositions to the Jazz Composers Workshop during 1953-1955, and in 1955 founded his own repertory group, the Jazz Workshop. During this period he moved beyond his bop-based approach and reached his mature playing style. Earlier he had played steady, harmonically complex single-note lines and had soloed with hornlike virtuosity; now he simplified his approach. He played more slowly, using varied rhythms that were less metronomic. He emphasized simpler, more basic harmonies and made effective use of pedal points, in which the bass plays a single note for an extended period. His compositional style simplified as well, moving away from the rapid chord changes of bebop and harking back to the basic essence of the blues – as can be heard on such albums as *Blues and Roots* (1959).

During 1955-1960 Mingus perfected a unique approach to composition. In the interest of spontaneity, he largely abandoned standard musical notation. He introduced new compositions by playing them at the piano and then singing the various parts to his sidemen. He preferred emotional immediacy to precision ensemble playing, and he introduced a degree of dissonance that foreshadowed the free jazz of alto saxophonist ORNETTE COLEMAN, pianist Cecil Taylor (b. 1929), and, after 1965, tenor saxophonist John Coltrane. An important early example of his new style is found in *Weary Blues* (1957), a collaboration with poet LANGSTON HUGHES.

Mingus, like Ellington, composed works with specific musicians in mind, and he encouraged his sidemen to find their own styles rather than copy someone else's. From the 1950s to the 1970s his ensembles provided a training ground for such key musicians as multi-instrumentalists Eric Dolphy (1928-1964) and Rahsaan Roland Kirk (1936-1977), alto saxophonist Jackie McLean (b. 1932), tenor saxophonist Booker Ervin (1930-1970), pianist Roland Hanna (b. 1932), and drummer Dannie Richmond (1935-1988).

Mingus's most productive period was in 1959-1960, when he recorded such important albums as *Blues and Roots*, *Mingus Ah Um* (1959), *Mingus Dynasty* (1959), and *Mingus Presents Mingus* (1960). During the 1960s he continued trying to wrest control of jazz from record companies and concert producers. He protested the conservative booking policies of the Newport Jazz Festival by organizing a counter-festival that featured swing trumpeter Roy Eldridge (1911-1989), free jazz saxophonist Ornette Coleman, and Max Roach. This effort led to the formation of the Jazz Artists Guild, which sought to give musicians greater artistic control, but the organization disbanded in rancor after a 1962 concert in New York City's Town Hall turned into a costly failure. Mingus then formed Charles Mingus Records (1964-1965), but when it failed, he left jazz for three years.

Mingus resumed his musical career in 1969 and in the mid-1970s recorded two notable albums, *Changes One* (1974) and *Changes Two* (1975). In 1977 he was diagnosed with amyotrophic lateral sclerosis (Lou Gehrig's disease) and within a year was confined to a wheelchair. Although he could no longer play the bass, he continued to compose music. In the last year of his life Mingus collaborated with white pop singer Joni Mitchell on the album *Mingus* (1979). President Jimmy Carter honored him along with other leading jazz musicians at a 1978 White House reception.

Since his death, Mingus's legacy has endured through the efforts of his former sidemen, jazz scholars such as Gunther Schuller, and above all his widow Sue Mingus. His large-scale composition *Epitaph*, which was never performed during his lifetime, had its premiere in 1989 and appeared on compact disc the following year. Former Mingus sidemen in the George Adams-Don Pullen Quartet, the Mingus Dynasty Band, and the Mingus Big Band have kept alive Mingus's musical spirit and repertory. In 1993 Mingus became the first African American composer to have his papers preserved by the Library of Congress, which acquired an extensive collection of his musical and literary writings, including the 1000-page manuscript for *Beneath the Underdog*.

James Clyde Sellman

SEE ALSO

Armstrong, Louis ("Satchmo"); Blues, The; Coltrane, John William; Gillespie, John Birks ("Dizzy"); Gordon, Dexter Keith; Gospel Music; Hampton, Lionel Leo; New York, New York; Rhythm and Blues; Ellington, Edward Kennedy ("Duke"); Los Angeles, California; Monk, Thelonious Sphere; Morton, Ferdinand Joseph ("Jelly Roll"); New Orleans, Louisiana; Parker, Charles Christopher ("Bird"); Powell, Earl ("Bud"); Roach, Maxwell Lemuel (Max).

Africa

Minianka, ethnic group of West Africa.

The Minianka primarily inhabit northeastern CÔTE D'IVOIRE and southern MALI. They speak SENUFO, a Niger-Congo language, and are generally considered a Senufo subgroup. Approximately 400,000 people consider themselves Minianka.

SEE ALSO

Languages, African: An Overview.

Latin America and the Caribbean

Mini-Jazz, a form of popular music in HAITI that was based on *compas* music and was heavily influenced by American rock and JAZZ.

In the 1960s middle-class Haitian youth began listening to rock 'n' roll music broadcast on American radio stations. FRANCE, seeking to open up the Haitian buying market, inundated the island with records and subsequently a rock craze was born among the well-off youth. The term *yeye* came to describe the young rock bands formed at that time. Taken from the Beatles' lyric "she loves you, yeah, yeah, yeah," yeye embraced an unexpected middle-class optimism in the early years of dictator FRANÇOIS DUVALIER's reign.

In 1963 United States president John F. Kennedy decreased American government aid to Haiti, seeking to persuade Duvalier to leave office. As a result, tourism slowed to a trickle and the emergent Haitian nationalism rejected foreign cultural influences. Yeye responded to the aggressive cultural climate by incorporating native *compas* music. The setup of yeye bands included electric guitars and bass, drums, and a horn section. American pop songs were played alongside Haitian classics, but the main emphasis was on teenage themes of sports, dancing, and lighthearted romance. The small size of yeye bands drastically altered the compas sound, as compas was traditionally played in orchestras or large ensembles. The fusion led to a distinct new sound that was called mini-jazz. The versatility of mini-jazz's small bands brought live compas to school events, house parties, and other small social events. "Mini" referred to the miniskirt fad and associated the sound with stylistic newness, rather than diminutive size.

When Duvalier declared himself president-for-life in 1964, the unprecedented optimism of yeye deepened with mini-jazz. Political terror escalated while the bands continued producing what was essentially teenage dance music. Avoiding political suspicion was crucial to survival during the height of François Duvalier's reign. This could be seen directly in Haitian popular music, as many bands sought to avoid any form of confrontation. The mini-jazz ensemble Shleu-Shleu, for example, popularized the use of nonsense names, and within months numerous bands had sprung up bearing nonsense syllables in lieu of an actual title.

JEAN-CLAUDE DUVALIER, François Duvalier's son and 1971 successor, heavily patronized the mini-jazz ensemble Bossa Combo. During the mid-1970s the band used its favor with the dictator to develop mini-jazz into a critical form: they incorporated lyrics with mild, often allusive elements of social critique and precipitated an interest in Haitian musical history. A period of stylistic experimentation followed. Tabou Combo, the most famous mini-jazz band, now performs an international mix, with heavy influences from ZOUK, American RAP, and FUNK, and a lead vocalist who sings in French, Spanish, English, and Haitian Creole. Founded in 1968 as Los Incognitos, the band soon opted for a more Haitian-sounding name. The success of its 1974 hit single "Haiti" brought compas mini-jazz into the international spotlight. With a drummer incorporating rock and Brazilian SAMBA beats and an all-American horn section, Tabou Combo crossed over into a number of markets, as did many of the mini-jazz bands of the 1980s. Like many other Haitian artists, activists, intellectuals, and musicians, Tabou Combo emigrated to New York to escape Duvalier's repressive regime.

Today Coupé Coupé is one of the few bands continuing to produce traditional compas mini-jazz – a move facilitated by the band members' residence in Haiti. Haitians living outside the country have incorporated more non-Haitian influences, partly because they have had easy access to synthesizers and other electronic instruments. The New York All-Stars is a Tabou Combo side project that combines rap with Haitian ra-ra, or Carnival music; the Brooklyn-based Ra-Ra Machine employs a similar fusion.

Jace Clayton

SEE ALSO

New York, New York.

North America

Minstrelsy, the most popular nineteenth-century American vernacular entertainment, featuring white performers mimicking blacks; it reinforced negative stereotypes of African Americans yet preserved aspects of black humor and performance style.

During the Middle Ages minstrels were servant-performers who entertained their patrons by playing music, singing, telling stories, juggling, or performing comic antics and buffoonery. In the antebellum United States, the term referred to comic performers, almost always white, who wore blackface makeup – generally burnt cork – and mimicked African Americans. The most popular entertainment of that century, minstrel shows had a powerful impact on American culture; in particular, they served to "codify the public image of blacks as the prototypical Fool or Sambo," as Mel Watkins observed in his *On the Real Side: Laughing, Lying, and Signifying: The Underground Tradition of African-American Humor.*

During the decades before the Civil War minstrel companies found great success in GREAT BRITAIN, Australia, and elsewhere in the English-speaking world. Minstrelsy helped to create misleading and highly demeaning stereotypes of African Americans. Yet it also captured something of the distinctive qualities of African American humor and song, especially during the late nineteenth century, when a number of African American minstrel troupes appeared. Although black minstrel companies were largely trapped by the stereotypes of white minstrelsy, they nonetheless provided an important showcase for black performing talent and served as a springboard for black participation in the twentieth-century entertainment industry.

In the 1820s a number of white actors began to include brief sketches of Southern blacks as part of their acts. In Cincinnati, Edwin Forrest, who became one of America's most prominent actors, made himself up as a black man and portrayed a plantation slave on stage. During two tours of the United States, the well-known British actor and comedian Charles James Mathews collected characteristic American types that he later presented in *A Trip to America*, a one-man show that included a blackface rendition of what became a popular minstrel song, "Possum Up a Gum Tree."

The career of Thomas D. "Daddy" Rice marked the true beginnings of American minstrelsy. In about 1828 Rice began impersonating a black man during the intermissions in a minor drama of the period. His act featured a song and dance that became known as "Jim Crow." Rice claimed that he based his sketch on a song and dance he had seen performed, in the words of Mel Watkins, by a "crippled and deformed black hostler or stable groom." The chorus of the song was simple:

Wheel about an' turn about an' do jes so,
An' eb'ry time I wheel about, I jump Jim Crow.

Rice dressed his Jim Crow character in the long blue coat and striped pants associated with another popular stereotype, the stage Yankee. Rice's sketch won him such acclaim that he quickly added additional blackface characters and music to his performances. Another African American source for Rice's minstrel act was the black street vendor and singer known as Signor Cornmeali, or "Old Corn Meal." Signor Cornmeali traveled about New Orleans with horse and cart, selling cornmeal and singing such songs as "Rosin Up the Bow" and his own "Fresh Corn Meal" in a rich baritone alternating with a resonant falsetto. Thomas "Daddy" Rice heard Cornmeali in 1837 and soon added a sketch titled "Corn Meal" to his minstrel act.

The notion of a minstrel troupe emerged as a response to a severe depression that began in 1837, an economic downturn that continued into the early 1840s and hit theatrical performers particularly hard. In 1842 four out-of-work white minstrels – Frank Brower, Dan Emmett, Frank Pelham, and Billy Whitlock – met in a New York City hotel and decided to work together as the Virginia Minstrels, the nation's first true minstrel troupe. The company concentrated exclusively on blackface comedy. The Virginia Minstrels, from their first performance in 1843, were a sensation and within a year had begun a well-received tour of England. Despite its great success, however, the troupe broke up while still touring abroad as a result of personal disagreements.

With the demise of the Virginia Minstrels, the Ethiopian Serenaders emerged as the nation's foremost minstrel company. In 1848 the Ethiopian Serenaders hired an African American dancer, William Henry Lane, known as Master Juba. Apart from Lane, Thomas Dilward was the only other African American known to have worked as a minstrel before the Civil War. Dilward was a singer and dancer, but his chief attraction lay in his diminutive height; he was reportedly about 91 cm (3 ft) tall. Lane, on the other hand, was widely recognized as a gifted dancer. English author Charles Dickens declared unequivocally that Lane was the "greatest dancer known," and in his *American Notes* described the black dancer in action: "Single shuffle, double shuffle, cut and cross-out: snapping his fingers, rolling his eyes, turning in his knees, presenting the backs of his legs in front, spinning about on his toes and heels... all sorts of legs and no legs – what is this to him?" Lane's performances, by all accounts, represented the first time many whites had seen authentic African American dance.

Besides being a master of the Irish jig, Lane incorporated distinctly African American elements in his performances, including what would later be known as tap dancing and the hand jive. Indeed, Lane is commonly regarded as the father of tap dancing. He also utilized the dance style known as "patting juba," in which a dancer sets complex rhythms through hand clapping, foot stomping, and striking his hands against different portions of his body. (Juba was a title or nickname commonly conferred on slaves who showed talent in music or dancing; it derived from the African Gioube, an intricate step dance with many variations.) Lane first began performing professionally with white minstrels in 1845 and appeared with several companies before joining the Ethiopian Serenaders for their 1848 tour of England. At the end of this tour Lane elected to remain in England, where he died in 1852 at age 27.

The troupe that had the most enduring legacy and the greatest impact on the conventions of minstrel performance was Christy's Original Band of Virginia Minstrels, founded in 1843 by Edwin P. Christy. In 1847 this company began a ten-year run in New York City and soon became as popular in the city as P. T. Barnum's Museum. Christy's Minstrels introduced many "Ethiopian songs" that mimicked or evoked an African American style, especially the compositions of Stephen C. Foster, including "Old Folks at Home," "Massa's in de Cold, Cold Ground," and "My Old Kentucky Home" – the types of songs for which Foster is best remembered. Ironically, in 1851 Foster asked that his name be removed as the composer of "Old Folks at Home" because he feared that being associated with such a song might injure his reputation as a serious songwriter. But a year later he had a change of heart. Insisting on his responsibility for popularizing such music, Foster announced that he would "establish [his] name as the best Ethiopian songwriter" in the country.

In addition to popularizing many of Stephen Foster's most memorable songs, Christy's Minstrels also established minstrelsy's standard three-act format. The first act opened with a general walkabout of the costumed minstrels or with a cakewalk – a traditional African American dance that stressed flamboyant improvisation. Then came a long routine in which the minstrels sat in a semicircle and engaged in a rapid-fire comic exchange interspersed with popular dances and love songs. The key figures in this part of the show were the interlocutor, the most proper and sophisticated character, who acted as the master of ceremonies and straight man, and two outrageously costumed endmen, who served as the focal points of mischief and mayhem. The second set, known as the olio, employed a variety show format, presenting a mix of music, dance, and novelty numbers highlighted by a farcical "stump speech." The final act was a theatrical – originally a freewheeling plantation skit, but after the mid-1850s typically a send-up of some serious drama – marked by broad slapstick and innumerable pratfalls. During the 1850s most other minstrel companies adopted the Christy Minstrels' program.

In performance, minstrels exuded an energy bordering on the manic, as Robert C. Toll vividly recounted in *Blacking Up: The Minstrel Show in Nineteenth Century America*: "They burst on stage in makeup [that] gave the impression of huge eyes and gaping mouths. They dressed in ill-fitting, patchwork clothes, and spoke in heavy 'nigger' dialects. Once on stage, they could not stay still for an instant. Even while sitting, they contorted their bodies, cocked their heads... and twisted their outstretched legs.... [T]heir... seemingly compulsive movements charged the entire performance with excitement."

In *Black Literature in White America*, Berndt Ostendorf argued that despite its reliance on demeaning caricature, minstrelsy introduced white Americans – if only indirectly – to the "influence and influx of black American culture." Perhaps more immediately important, minstrelsy was a response to profound strains within white society.

During the 1840s and 1850s the United States received its first massive influx of European immigrants. To many native-born Anglo-Americans these newcomers seemed frighteningly alien. At the same time American society had clearly acquired the beginnings of a working class: although the permanence of its membership was a matter of debate, it was without question growing. Profound economic dislocations accompanied America's Industrial Revolution, as seen in national depressions during the late 1830s and early 1840s and the mid- to late 1850s and in the strikes and conflicts of the early labor movement. And the ever-present and highly divisive political issue of slavery threatened to set white Americans against one another.

In an atmosphere marked by political acrimony and social tension, minstrelsy had a vital unifying function for white Americans. By constructing an image of happy-go-lucky plantation slaves and irresponsible free black dandies, minstrel shows made light of slavery and emancipation as political issues and denied the human suffering that the institution exacted daily. In addition – much like their medieval counterparts – antebellum minstrels and their absurd antics served not only to entertain, but also to reassure their patrons of their own superiority. By defining blackness so ludicrously, antebellum minstrels constructed a cultural "other" over whom all whites – whether immigrant or native-born, urban or rural, working class or well-to-do – could feel superior. Thus minstrelsy provided indirect but not inconsequential grounds for white social and political unity – at the expense of African Americans.

Although a greater number of African Americans took part in minstrelsy during the Civil War, the first influential black minstrel troupes appeared during the RECONSTRUCTION era. In 1865-1866 an African American company known as Brooker and Clayton's Georgia Minstrels toured in the Northeast, billing itself as "the Only Simon Pure Negro Troupe in the World." From 1866 to 1872 British minstrel dancer Sam Hague toured England with a troupe of black minstrels billed as Sam Hague's Slave Troupe of Georgia Minstrels. A short time later African American minstrel performer Charles Hicks organized yet another company of "Georgia Minstrels." As black minstrel troupes proved their popularity and profitability, their ownership and management generally fell into the hands of whites. By the mid-1870s the most successful black minstrel troupes were all white-owned.

These prestigious companies toured throughout the United States and in Canada, the British Isles, Germany, Australia, New Zealand, and Java. They typically featured large casts and played in prominent venues and major cities, often traveling in their own railroad cars. Although there were a number of less prestigious, black-owned minstrel troupes, these were generally smaller and less likely to travel in such comfort. Black-owned companies tended to appear in less desirable venues and in the smaller towns and cities of America's hinterland. Notable black-owned troupes included Johnson's Plantation Minstrels, which also appeared as the Black Baby Boy Minstrels or as Lew Johnson's Original Tennessee Jubilee Singers, and companies organized by prominent black minstrels such as Billy Kersands, Bob Height, and James Bland. Below these professional troupes were many amateur minstrels.

Minstrelsy provided invaluable experience for countless African American composers, comedians, and musicians. W. C. Handy, who later gained fame as the composer of "St. Louis Blues," worked for many years as a cornet player and bandleader with Mahara's Minstrels. James Bland – best remembered for composing "Carry Me Back to Old Virginny" and "Dem Golden Slippers" – was a particularly prolific minstrel composer. The talented African American minstrel and dramatic actor Sam Lucas also composed numerous minstrel songs, of which "Grandfather's Clock" remains the best known.

Numerous twentieth-century black performers also had experience with minstrelsy. Vaudeville comedians BERT WILLIAMS and Ernest Hogan got their start by serving as endmen in minstrel troupes. Blues singer Gertrude "Ma" Rainey was a featured performer with the Rabbit's Foot Minstrels, a company that also included a young dancer who would one day be recognized as the greatest of all female blues singers, BESSIE SMITH. New Orleans jazz musicians such as pianist Ferdinand "Jelly Roll" Morton and trumpeter Bunk Johnson did stints playing in minstrel companies. And modern jazz trumpeter John Birks "Dizzy" Gillespie made his first public performance in 1929 playing in the pit band for a minstrel show put on by his elementary school.

Although black performers found opportunities in minstrelsy, they also found themselves trapped by its restrictive racial conventions. However, as author Mel Watkins cautioned, if African Americans adopted "many of the epithets and referents of minstrel humor, they did not necessarily accept [its] general racist connotations." In *On with the Show: The First Century of Show Business in America,* Robert C. Toll noted that "most early black minstrels did not wear burnt cork, although the endmen used blackface as a comic mask." In a sense, blackface was like the exaggerated facial makeup of the circus clown – with the obvious difference that minstrelsy created a comic mask that ridiculed an entire race.

During the late nineteenth century, as racial hostilities sharpened throughout the United States, white audiences came to expect that all minstrels, black as well as white, should appear in blackface, and the practice became general among black troupes. Although some black performers may have resisted using blackface, the great African American dancer and comedian Bert Williams found it liberated him as a comedian. Recalling his first experience in blackface, Williams said, "Then I began to find myself. It was not until I was able to see myself as another person that my sense of humor developed."

By the turn of the century professional minstrelsy was in decline. Vaudeville – its generally accepted advent being B. F. Keith's opening of the nation's first vaudeville theater in Boston in 1882 – gradually supplanted minstrel shows as America's foremost entertainment. George M. Cohan and Sam Harris's Minstrels, the last full-fledged minstrel company to appear on Broadway, had brief runs in 1908 and 1909. Yet minstrelsy did not simply disappear. Even today its legacy remains extensive and complex. Long after vaudeville became the principal popular entertainment in major cities of the Northeast, minstrel companies continued to tour the small towns of that region and widely through the South and Midwest. Amateur minstrel performances, black as well as white, continued well into the twentieth century.

Many have criticized minstrelsy for its demeaning stereotypes and its nostalgia for plantation slavery. But the minstrel legacy was not wholly negative. Minstrelsy had a powerful impact on vaudeville. Many early vaudeville performers had their first professional experience in minstrel companies. The routines of many black vaudeville comedians – including STEPIN FETCHIT, Jackie "Moms" Mabley, Dewey "Pigmeat" Markham, Mantan Moreland, and Bert Williams – clearly reflected the influence of minstrelsy.

Minstrelsy helped transform American humor and, to a lesser extent, African

American popular music. Minstrels' energy and verbal inventiveness – including fast-paced repartee, puns, double entendres, and assorted malapropisms – had a major impact on an emerging American comic tradition, as can be seen not only in such vaudeville comedians as Williams and Mabley but also in literature, above all in the humor of Mark Twain. Evan Esar's *The Comic Encyclopedia* observed that minstrelsy's endmen, the most popular minstrel characters, were "chiefly responsible for turning riddle wit in America into gags." During the twentieth century their comic legacy would help shape not just vaudeville but also American musical theater, motion pictures, radio, and television.

The musical legacy of minstrelsy is less obvious, but also important. Admittedly, the songs of black minstrels – no less than those of their white counterparts – perpetuated extreme stereotypes of African Americans. Minstrel song lyrics featured degrading heavy dialects, and they tended to invoke a warm nostalgia for the bygone days of plantation slavery. But the key musical contribution of black minstrels lay not as much in their compositions as in their overall performance style. Like the dancing of William Henry Lane, the musical performances of black minstrels introduced a measure of authentic African American culture to a wider audience.

Black minstrel companies often featured renditions, in harmony, of spirituals, jubilee songs, and sentimental ballads. The singing of such professional entertainers – along with performances by college-trained choirs, such as the Fisk Jubilee Singers – had a profound influence on subsequent vocal harmony groups, evident in secular singing no less than in gospel quartets. Professional minstrels and college choral groups offered slick versions of African American music, but they nonetheless provided an eye-opening experience for white audiences, and they inspired countless young African American singers and performers. At age 15, W. C. Handy played his first amateur minstrel show in Florence, Alabama – his hometown – as first tenor in a vocal quartet. In his autobiography, *Father of the Blues,* Handy recalled how professional minstrels served as models for his own group of amateurs: "We had seen the famous Georgia Minstrels in Florence.... We were all acquainted with Billy Kersands, the man who could 'make a mule laugh'.... We had seen Sam Lucas and Tom McIntosh walking at the head of the parade in high silk hats and long-tailed coats. We had an idea of how the thing should be done, but I suppose our trouble was lack of experience."

The passage of more than 50 years had not dimmed Handy's awareness of the importance of black minstrelsy. "All the best black talent," he recalled, "the composers, the singers, the musicians, the speakers, the stage performers – the Minstrel Show got them all."

James Clyde Sellman

See Also

Slavery in the United States; Blues, The; Cakewalk, The; Civil War, American; Gillespie, John Birks ("Dizzy"); Handy, William Christopher (W.C.); Labor Unions in the United States; Mabley, Jackie ("Moms"); Markham, Dewey ("Pigmeat"); Morton, Ferdinand Joseph ("Jelly Roll"); New Orleans, Louisiana; Racial Stereotypes; Rainey, Gertrude Pridgett ("Ma"); Tap Dance; Television and African Americans; New Orleans, Louisiana; New York, New York; Film, Blacks in American; Spirituals, African American.

North America

Miscegenation, a term for sexual relations across racial lines; no longer in use because of its racist implications, the word was invented in 1863 for political purposes and was created from two Latin words: *miscere* (to mix) and *genus* (race).

The word "miscegenation" was coined by two Democrats in the presidential election campaign of 1864 in an attempt to embarrass and discredit the Republican incumbent running for reelection, Abraham Lincoln. In an anonymous pamphlet that appeared in December 1863 entitled *Miscegenation: The Theory of the Blending of the Races Applied to the American White Man and Negro*, the authors played on white fears of interracial sex by pretending to issue a Republican-sponsored booklet advocating racial mixing and amalgamation. The real authors were David Goodman Croly, managing editor of the *New York World*, a staunchly Democratic paper, and George Wakeman, a *World* reporter.

Sex across the color line was an obsession of white America, particularly the stereotype of black men's alleged craving for white women, and of believers in Anglo-Saxon "racial" superiority, who feared that "mongrelization" was degenerative. In fact, black-white sex existed from the beginning of the slave trade in the sixteenth century, virtually always on the initiative of Europeans, who held Africans in their total power. During the notorious Middle Passage between Africa and the New World, for example, black women and children were allowed mobility on board ship so that white sailors could have unlimited sexual access to them.

Sex played a role in the gradual differentiation of Africans from other indentured servants in Virginia, a process that culminated around 1700 in the unique North American phenomenon of chattel slavery, by which people were legally defined as property. The very first case in this sequence of events was a sexual one: in 1630 Hugh Davis was sentenced by the Virginia court to a whipping "for defiling his body in lying with a Negro." Even though it was a white man who was convicted and punished for the act, the case shows the early eroticization of racial differences.

The interracial sexual pattern in the antebellum South is clear: because slaves were property, like animals or objects, they had no rights, and all black women were sexually available to all white men. In addition, African American marriage and parenthood were not recognized in law, and there was no recourse for sexual abuse in the courts, government, church, or press. Virtually every plantation produced children of mixed race: the 1860 federal census classified 588,532 persons as mulattos. A minuscule number of white fathers recognized their children and provided for them; some parents encouraged the fairest skinned to run away and hide their racial identity by passing for white. Most mixed-blood slave children were simply worked and sold like all other slaves.

The white South combined the permissive sexual exploitation of black women by white men with a fanatic "protection" of white women from black men. In both cases, the ideology was that people of African descent were closer to nature and savagery, but the real reason was probably economic: legally, a child was slave or free depending on the status of the mother. All white women were free and nearly all black women were slaves.

The uniqueness of chattel slavery prohibited in North America (except for New Orleans) the emergence of mulattos as a distinct third group between black and white, as existed in the West Indies, Latin America, and South Africa. American slavery was race and color based, but it would have become weakened ideologically and economically if it had allowed any deviation from the one-drop rule, that is, the belief that any black ancestry made a person black.

Miscegenation was about marriage as well as sex, since sexual relationships were legitimized by marriage. Therefore, interracial marriage was prohibited, a law upheld by the United States Supreme Court in *Pace* v. *Alabama* (1883). That decision was not overturned until well after the modern Civil Rights Movement had begun, in *Loving* v. *Virginia* (1967), when 16 states still had laws prohibiting interracial marriage. Civil rights and voting rights were extended to African Americans before the right was granted both to whites and blacks to marry (and have legitimate sexual relationships) across the color line.

Richard Newman

See Also

Middle Passage, The; Slavery in the United States; Transatlantic Slave Trade.

Latin America and the Caribbean

Misik Raisin, the highly political Haitian "roots music" revival spearheaded by Boukman Eksperyans and its fusion of Vodou and *ra-ra* music.

Misik raisin (or "roots music") appeared on Haiti's music scene in the late 1970s. The

Jamaican-based philosophy of Rastafarianism and roots REGGAE had a profound impact on a new generation of middle-class Haitian musicians. Reggae musician BOB MARLEY's stirring message of Afrocentrism, black cultural autonomy, and strong political commitment inspired Haitians to seek out their own version of roots music. The roots musicians used traditional Haitian Vodou as a common national heritage to engender community against dictatorship and imperial control. The up-tempo dance music of the ra-ra festival (second in size only to Haiti's Carnival) also became part of misik raisin's repertoire.

The band Boukman Eksperyans is the best known of the Haitian roots reinterpreters. BOUKMAN was a slave leader and Vodou priest active in Haiti during the late eighteenth century. He led a successful slave insurrection that relied on Vodou's power to unify slaves of various African ethnicities (*see* HAITIAN REVOLUTION). Boukman Eksperyans titled its 1991 album *Vodou Adjae* (meaning "concerned Vodou"). It abandoned the all-popular *compas* sound in favor of Vodou drumming and the rhythms of ra-ra music. The title track, "Se Kreyo'l Nou Ye" ("We Speak Creole"), came into usage as an anthem of Creole Haitian pride. The government harassed performers of misik raisin for their aggressively political lyrics accompanied by Vodou rhythms.

The music of Boukman Eksperyans played a role in the ousting of President General Prospère Avril in 1990. Its song for Carnival that year, "Kè m pa sote" ("My heart doesn't leap / I'm not afraid"), caused great commotion whenever it was played. The group's popularity prevented the government from forbidding them access to Carnival performances; their oblique lyrics promoted fearlessness against an unnamed enemy and the military government was thus unsure how to respond. The song won Carnival awards, and countless other misik raisin and ra-ra bands incorporated it as a kind of populist national anthem. A week after Carnival, "Kè m pa sote" was sung in support of a strike protesting the unprovoked murder of a young girl by Avril's military. The government publicly labeled Boukman Eksperyans "a band of paranoid frauds and idiots," which only gave the strikers added determination. The grassroots strike swelled into a large-scale uprising that ended with Avril's ousting.

Thus, out of the political noninvolvement of compas came misik raisin, a powerful new movement inextricably tied to political developments in Haiti. Boukman Eksperyans sang songs in support of democratically elected president JEAN-BERTRAND ARISTIDE, as did many fellow musicians. Aristide's overthrow by military coup led to renewed efforts to quell misik raisin. Because of the international fame it gained after the release of its 1991 album *Vodou Adjae*, Boukman Eksperyans was essentially safe from physical harm, although the government tormented members with surveillance, harassment, and edicts of silence. The military threw tear gas at a 1993 Boukman Eksperyans concert. Audiences worldwide loved the African-influenced drumming of misik raisin, and bands such as Boukman Eksperyans received greater recognition than their less "ethnic"-sounding compas predecessors. The group's 1992 album *Kalfou Danjere* ("Dangerous Crossroads") topped world music sales charts.

Jace Clayton

SEE ALSO

Jamaica; Rastafarians; Carnivals in Latin America and the Caribbean; Afrocentrism.

North America

Mitchell, Clarence Maurice, Jr.

(b. March 8, 1911, Baltimore, Md.; d. March 18, 1984, WASHINGTON, D.C.), lobbyist to the United States Congress for the NATIONAL ASSOCIATION FOR THE ADVANCEMENT OF COLORED PEOPLE (NAACP).

Less visible than many of his NAACP colleagues, Clarence Mitchell nonetheless had a major impact on the lives of African Americans. Known as "the 101st Senator," the long-time NAACP lobbyist was instrumental in the passage of both the Civil Rights Act of 1964 and the VOTING RIGHTS ACT OF 1965, the two most significant successes of the CIVIL RIGHTS MOVEMENT. Mitchell, a 1932 graduate of Lincoln University in Pennsylvania and the husband of JUANITA JACKSON MITCHELL, an NAACP official, joined the NAACP staff following his work with the NATIONAL URBAN LEAGUE and the FAIR EMPLOYMENT PRACTICES COMMITTEE (FEPC).

Formed in 1941 to eliminate employment discrimination, the FEPC was dissolved in 1946. While acting as the NAACP's labor secretary, Mitchell continued to fight for economic fair play, founding the National Council for a Permanent FEPC in 1949, and participating the following year in the Leadership Conference on Civil Rights, a group with representatives from more than 50 civil rights organizations. Mitchell began his legislative work as part of this struggle, quickly becoming the association's chief lobbyist, a position he held until his retirement in 1978. The veteran lobbyist became a lawyer himself in 1962, when he completed four years of night school at the University of Maryland Law School. In 1968 the NAACP awarded Mitchell the Spingarn Medal and in 1980 he was honored with the Presidential Medal of Freedom, the nation's highest nonmilitary decoration. After his death in 1984, the city of Baltimore, Maryland, renamed its courthouse after him.

Kate Tuttle

SEE ALSO

Baltimore, Maryland; Lincoln University (Pennsylvania).

North America

Mitchell, Juanita Jackson

(b. January 2, 1913, Hot Springs, Ark.; d. July 7, 1992, Baltimore, Md.), civil rights lawyer; first African American woman admitted to the Maryland bar; and first national youth director of the NATIONAL ASSOCIATION FOR THE ADVANCEMENT OF COLORED PEOPLE (NAACP).

By the time Juanita J. Mitchell received her law degree in 1950, she had already spent nearly 20 years working for civil rights on the local and national levels. Born to racially conscious parents – her mother, LILLIE MAE CARROLL JACKSON, was president of the state conference of NAACP branches – Mitchell earned a degree in education from the University of Pennsylvania in 1931. Upon graduation she returned to her native Baltimore to help African Americans struggling with both the economic devastation of the GREAT DEPRESSION and the persistence of LYNCHING and other racist violence. Hoping to alleviate some of their suffering, Mitchell founded the City-Wide Young People's Forum of Baltimore in 1931 and served as its president until 1934. In 1935 Walter White, then executive secretary of the NAACP, recruited Jackson to head that organization's newly created youth program, a position she held until her 1938 marriage to Clarence M. Mitchell Jr.

After the birth of four sons, Mitchell entered law school at the University of Maryland, from which she graduated in 1950. That same year she became the first African American woman to be admitted to the bar in her state. As a lawyer, she continued the work she had begun as an organizer: improving the lives of African Americans. She filed lawsuits that helped integrate public beaches and schools, represented students arrested during SIT-INS in the 1960s, and continued to direct voter registration drives. By the time she died in 1992 at age 79, Mitchell had been recognized by the NATIONAL COUNCIL OF NEGRO WOMEN – which she had helped found with MARY MCLEOD BETHUNE – the NAACP's Youth/College Division, and the Maryland Women's Hall of Fame.

Kate Tuttle

SEE ALSO

Baltimore, Maryland; Mitchell, Clarence Maurice, Jr.; White, Walter Francis.

North America

Mitchell, Loften (b. April 15, 1919, Columbia, N.C.), African American playwright and novelist who portrayed the court case that ended school segregation in his play *A Land Beyond the River.*

Loften Mitchell grew up in Harlem, where as a young man he began working in theater with the Rose McClendon Players. In 1943 he completed an A.B. at Talladega College in Alabama and studied playwriting with John Glassner at Columbia University.

Mitchell's play *A Land Beyond the River*, which depicted a court case ending school segregation, was met with critical acclaim in 1957. His prolific literary output includes *The Photographer* (1962), *Ballad of Bimshire* (1963), *Ballad for the Winter Soldiers* (1964), *Tell Pharaoh* (1967), and the successful musical co-written with Rosetta LeNoire, *Bubbling Brown Sugar* (1976).

Mitchell also taught at the State University of New York at Binghamton, published the novel *The Stubborn Old Lady Who Resisted Change* (1973), and wrote two histories of drama, *Black Drama: The Story of the American Negro in the Theatre* (1967) and *Voices of the Black Theatre* (1975).

Marian Aguiar

See Also
Harlem, New York; LeNoire, Rosetta Olive Burton.

Latin America and the Caribbean

Mittelhölzer, Edgar Austin (b. December 16, 1909, New Amsterdam, British Guiana [now Guyana]; d. May 5, 1965, Farnham, Surrey, England), well-known and controversial Afro-Guyanese novelist who lived and died in exile but used Caribbean and Creole history and themes in his work.

Edgar Mittelhölzer has been called the father of the novel in the English-speaking Caribbean (*see* Literature, English Language, Caribbean). He was the first Caribbean author to make a living entirely by his writing, and he remains the most prolific Caribbean novelist to date, even though his career was cut short by his suicide at age 55.

Mittelhölzer was born into a mixed-race, middle-class family in Guyana and had Swiss, German, French, English, and African heritage – although his father's resentment of their black blood shaped his childhood. He attended the well-known Barbice High School, and by the time he was 19 his love for movies, detective fiction, and the Buffalo Bill stories had convinced him that he "had to be a writer."

For his first decade as a writer he received mainly rejection slips, but he supported himself with menial jobs and continued writing until his first novel, *Corentyne Thunder*, was published in 1941. Shortly after that he moved to Trinidad, where he lived for several years before deciding that he needed to leave the Caribbean to achieve true success as a writer. In 1947 he emigrated to London, and so became one of the first of many Caribbean writers who have gone to London to find success "in exile" (*see* Great Britain).

Mittelhölzer's success was represented by his brisk publishing pace. *A Morning at the Office*, his second novel, was published in 1950, and he went on to publish at least one novel each year until his death. In 1952 he began writing full-time; that same year he moved to Canada on a Guggenheim Fellowship. He spent the next three years in Barbados before returning to England in May 1956. By that time his books included the first two volumes of his Kaywana trilogy, which is often considered his most celebrated work.

The Kaywana books trace the saga of one Guyanese family from the colonial period to the mid-twentieth century, and they have been praised for their elegant interweaving of Guyana's history into the family's story. While several of his books are set abroad, many others also treat Caribbean themes, particularly the tangled connections between races and classes in West Indian society.

Mittelhölzer himself, however, said that his two main themes were "sex and religion," and the adultery, rape, incest, and other recurring sexual themes in his work led one book (*The Piling Clouds*) to be initially classified as pornography, and consequently rejected. But his works also included many characters who were in psychological torment or who were suicidal, a tragic reflection of his own life. He attempted suicide twice before setting himself on fire in his Surrey home in May 1965.

Lisa Clayton Robinson

See Also
Creoles; Trinidad and Tobago.

Africa

Mkapa, Benjamin (b. 1938, Ndanda, Tanzania), president of Tanzania (1995-).

Born in Ndanda in the Masasi District of southeastern Tanzania, the last of four children, Benjamin Mkapa attended local schools before completing a bachelor's degree at Makerere University in Uganda in 1962. He worked as a district administrative officer in Dodoma and Dar es Salaam for one year before joining the foreign service in 1963. Having joined the ruling party, the Tanganyika African National Union (TANU), Mkapa was appointed managing editor of the party's newspaper in May 1966. In July 1974 he was promoted to press secretary for President Julius Nyerere. Mkapa served briefly as the first director of Shihata, the Tanzanian news agency, in 1974 before becoming high commissioner to Nigeria (1976-1977).

In a series of rapid promotions and reassignments resulting from cabinet reshuffles, Mkapa held a succession of important government posts in the late 1970s and the 1980s. Initially appointed to Parliament in 1977, he was elected to represent the Masasi District in 1985. He was elected to the central committee of TANU's successor, the Revolutionary Party of Tanzania (Chama Cha Mapinduzi, or CCM), in 1987 and received the party's nomination for president in July 1995. In October 1995 he took 62 percent of the vote in Tanzania's first multiparty elections and began his five-year term as president in November 1995.

See Also
Dar es Salaam, Tanzania; Nyerere, Julius Kambarage.

Africa

Mobeur (also known as Mavar and Mober), ethnic group of West Africa.

The Mobeur primarily inhabit southeastern Niger and northeastern Nigeria. They speak an Afro-Asiatic language in the Chadic group and are closely related to the Kanuri people. Approximately 400,000 people consider themselves Mobeur.

See Also
Languages, African: An Overview.

Mobutu, Joseph-Désiré. Please see Mobutu Sese Seko

Africa

Mobutu Sese Seko (b. October 14, 1930, Lisala, Belgian Congo; d. September 7, 1997, Rabat, Morocco), former president and long-term dictator of Zaire (now the Democratic Republic of the Congo).

Once the personification of the African autocrat and shrewd cold-war politician, Mobutu Sese Seko fled Zaire on May 17, 1997, after three decades in power. Known as a corrupt and brutal dictator for most of his reign, he abdicated power after rebels conquered Zaire within a span of six months. Dying of cancer and politically unpopular, Mobutu lacked the support necessary to maintain control.

The son a Ngbaka chief, Mobutu was educated by Belgian missionaries. In 1950 he joined the colonial army, the Force Publique, and within six years rose to the rank of sergeant. He left the army in 1956 and became a columnist for the Léopoldville (now Kinshasa) newspaper, *L'Avenir*. Three years later he received a fellowship from the colonial administration to study at the Institute of Journalism and Social Sciences in Brussels, Belgium. Because of his studies Mobutu missed most of the independence movement in the Belgian Congo, but he did attend the Round Table Conference in Brussels, where, it is widely believed, he spied on fellow Congolese for the Belgian government. He returned to the Belgian Congo before independence and was appointed army chief of staff by the new prime minister, PATRICE LUMUMBA.

Shortly afterward, Mobutu took advantage of a rift between President JOSEPH KASAVUBU and Lumumba to make his own bid for power. With support from the United States Central Intelligence Agency (CIA), he helped overthrow and track down Lumumba. It is believed that Mobutu ordered Lumumba's murder in January 1961.

Mobutu returned Kasavubu to power in February 1961 and for the next four years led military operations against regional rebellions. Not content to stay behind the scenes, he staged another coup d'état and on November 25, 1965, seized permanent control of the government.

For the next 32 years Mobutu ruled over the Congo. Spending the first five years centralizing authority, Mobutu held and easily won presidential elections in 1970. After these elections, however, he created an autocratic state maintained by an elaborate system of terror and corruption coupled with unpredictable generosity. At times Mobutu would force political opponents into exile, only to invite them back later to be pardoned. In some instances his opponents would be publicly executed; in others they would be co-opted and brought into the president's inner circle of well-paid advisers.

Mobutu justified his dictatorial power, as well as all his economic and social policies, by referring to an ideology that he called *authenticité* and that others called Mobutuism. Exalting the superiority of African "authentic" traditions, he portrayed himself as a traditional chief and changed his name to Mobutu Sese Seko Kuku Ngbendu waza Banga, which meant "the all-powerful warrior who, because of his endurance and inflexible will to win, will go from conquest to conquest leaving fire in his wake." He adopted his trademark leopard-skin cap and wooden walking stick topped with an eagle, a symbol of power that allegedly took the strength of eight normal men to carry. He ordered all citizens to adopt African names and dress and renamed the Republic of Congo, Zaire. In 1973 he undertook the "Zaireanization" of the economy, in which he nationalized foreign businesses, including the valuable copper and diamond mines. Much of the revenue from these enterprises financed Mobutu's luxurious lifestyle (including villas on the French Riviera, yachts, and limousines) and accumulated in his private bank account (once estimated at $5 billion).

Despite his infamous corruption and brutality, Mobutu received generous financial and military support from Western powers, especially FRANCE and the United States, who were eager to maintain a barrier to the "communist threat" in Central Africa. Western banks and construction companies were equally eager to help Mobutu realize his elaborate development plans, such as the Inga dam, which was projected to generate one-third of the world's hydroelectricity. The dam and many other projects failed, as Mobutu and his friends pocketed the funds.

During the 1980s mounting debts and the fall in world copper prices plunged Zaire into economic crisis. Food shortages, unpaid government salaries, and a decaying infrastructure all contributed to popular discontent. After a 1990 massacre of students at a pro-democracy rally at the University of Lubumbashi, France and the United States – no longer so inclined to support Mobutu once the cold war was over – demanded political reforms. Mobutu agreed to create a multiparty state and national assembly but repeatedly undermined efforts to carry out these reforms. In 1991 Etienne Tshisekedi was named prime minister, and though dismissed shortly afterward, was reinstated in 1992. For the next two years Mobutu, angered by Tshisekedi's popularity, avoided the capital and spent his time in his various homes in Africa and Europe. Mobutu did resume a more active role in 1994 when Kengo wa Dondo, a close associate of the president, was appointed prime minister. In addition, civil conflict in neighboring RWANDA returned international attention to Mobutu. This renewed authority, however, was to be short-lived.

In October 1996 the Alliance of Democratic Forces for the Liberation of Congo-Zaire, led by LAURENT-DÉSIRÉ KABILA, began an offensive that conquered virtually the entire country within six months. Already sick with prostate cancer, Mobutu was also politically weak and thus unable to rally support at home from distant treatment centers in Europe. Despite some external aid, Mobutu's demoralized forces melted away and he returned to Zaire too late to reverse the situation. Nevertheless, he refused to accept defeat until Kabila's army threatened to take over Kinshasa in May, when he fled the capital with his family. Refused entrance in France and TOGO, Mobutu finally found refuge in MOROCCO, where he died less than four months later on September 7, 1997.

Elizabeth Heath

SEE ALSO

Kinshasa, Democratic Republic of the Congo.

Latin America and the Caribbean

Modernism from Afro-America: An Interpretation of Wifredo Lam's Paintings

The history of art has, to a large extent, been a Eurocentric story, a Western construction that has excluded, diminished, and decontextualized a good part of the aesthetic production of the world. It is becoming increasingly urgent – especially for Latin Americans – to deconstruct this version of art history in search of more decentralized, integrative, contextualized, and multidisciplinary discourses (*see* ART IN LATIN AMERICA AND THE CARIBBEAN). Some time ago the literary critic Etiemble invalidated "any theory which is based exclusively on European phenomena," and his remark has a tinge of urgency in our field.

This article analyzes the work of the Afro-Cuban painter and sculptor WIFREDO LAM (1902-1982), a paradigmatic figure in Latin American modernism and the first artist for whom African culture appears in its own right as a decisive factor of expression. Lam's work will be discussed not, as many critics have done, as a product of surrealism, primitivism, or cubism, but rather as a pioneering expression of Afro-Cuban and Afro-Caribbean culture and a means by which this culture came to influence and infiltrate European avant-garde art. This is what Lam must have meant when he said that he was a "Trojan horse." This new approach to Lam does not imply nonrecognition of his academic training, the influence of Picasso and surrealism, or his status as a participant in the European avant-garde movement. He himself once surprised me during an interview when he showed me a picture of a work, which was African in appearance, and commented: "You need to have seen a lot of Poussin to do this."

The perspective in this article also implies a recognition of Western culture as characteristic of the world today, as a result of the global expansion of industrial capitalism, which for the first time integrated the world into a global system centered in Europe. Many elements of Western culture have ceased to be "ethnic" and have become internationalized as intrinsic elements of a world shaped by the development of the West. The very idea of "art" as a self-sufficient activity based on aesthetics, a definition dating from no earlier than the end of the eighteenth century, is also a product of Western culture. The traditional art of other cultures, as well as that of the West from earlier epochs, was a different type of creation, determined by functions of a religious, representational, or commemorative nature.

The difficulties of deconstructing Eurocentrism are many. Even though much of postmodernism introduces a diversification in the center-periphery and hegemony-subordination oppositions, it is itself a Western mode of thought imposed by the "center" and thereby reproduces Western domination. The center, disguised as relativism, "threatens to supplant the periphery in its alternative role," as scholar Nelly Richard has pointed out, and to deprive it of oppositional force by integration. Much of contemporary interest in difference is itself Eurocentric, a move from the dominator toward the dominated: in this equation the "other" is always us. In all events, subordinate cultures must exploit for themselves the opportunities offered by this new situation and by the rhetoric of decentralization. One of the unavoidable challenges is to transform the dominant culture to their advantage, de-Eurocentralizing it without depriving it of its contemporary relevance, introducing into it new discourses based on hybridization and transformation.

The intercultural dialogue implicit in Lam's work is an example of the cultural diversity inherent in the Caribbean nationalities. These nationalities are part of the Western trunk, and European culture lies at their origins, although they are modulated from within by very active non-Western ingredients. Western culture is not foreign to the Caribbean, unlike African or Asian countries, which to a certain extent are divided between their traditional cultures and Western culture imposed by colonialism. Thus, for Lam, the academic, cubist, or surrealist poetics were part of a familiar tradition. His contribution was to make a qualitative turn and base his art on those elements of African heritage that are alive in Cuban culture. In this sense his work reproduces the plurality characteristic of the Caribbean, centering it on the African component, which indeed determines the profile of the region.

The son of a Cantonese immigrant and a mulatta, Lam was raised in Sagua la Grande, CUBA. His godmother was a priestess in the chapter of Santa Barbara (Changó), and he grew up in a region strongly marked by Afro-Cuban traditions such as SANTERÍA and *palo monte*, although he was never formally initiated into any such traditions. He left Cuba in 1923, heading first to SPAIN, where he acquired a classical artistic training and earned a living by painting portraits. Toward the end of the 1920s Lam produced some works in the style of Spanish surrealism tinged with academicism. However, in Paris, where he settled in 1938, he consolidated himself as a late modernist, with the support of Picasso. His painting from 1938 to 1940, although based to a large extent on African masks and geometry, was reminiscent of Picasso and in general of the School of Paris. At that time Lam also began to develop a passion for the traditional art of Africa and became a permanent collector of such pieces.

The features that most attracted Lam to Picasso – the African element and certain surrealist-like expressive deformation – would subsequently become decisive in his own painting. Picasso was interested in African art in terms of geometry, as a constructive synthesis of the human image. The Spanish painter's most expressive paintings or surrealist works were based less directly on African geometry, which inspired colder and more abstract pieces. Lam managed to link both sides, a process that would engender the personal style that was to characterize his subsequent work. He developed this process in France in works dating from 1940, such as *Portrait, Homme-Femme,* and *Symbiosis;* and from 1941, for example, in his illustrations for André Breton's *Fata Morgana.* At the same time Lam was becoming powerfully influenced by surrealism. Although he never actually joined the surrealist movement, he used surrealistic features, such as double eyes, in his paintings and began to depict mythological, fantastic, and more carnal figures than his earlier schematized characters from African geometry.

Lam returned to Cuba in 1942. The cultural mood introduced by surrealism had encouraged him to express his own world, the world of his culture, in an exercise of modernity. His arrival in Cuba marked his encounter with that world in reality. This arrival did not produce any sense of astonishment, but a feeling of belonging. It was the confirmation of, and final encounter with, his own space. It was a "*retour au pays natal,*" in the sense of the moving poem by Martinican poet and intellectual AIMÉ CÉSAIRE. Indeed, back in Cuba Lam found his cultural universe as a personal artistic universe. The return occurred at the right moment: fascinated by African and what was then called "primitive" elements thanks to modern art, he had begun to give outward expression to those aspects of himself. This came about through his direct contact with Afro-Cuban traditions, greatly facilitated by the Cuban folklore specialist LYDIA CABRERA, who helped familiarize Lam with the myths, liturgies, and representations of that world. As FERNANDO ORTIZ writes, "the Afroid world is in Lam and in all his environment"; it is not some diffuse feeling, a dream, a sense of longing, or something in a museum. While "ethnographic" artists such as Joseph Beuys looked to Africa to obtain a distance from their own cultures in order to transform them, Lam's approach aimed at moving more deeply into Cuban culture, thus reaffirming it. Unlike many ethnologists who engage in "participant observation," Lam emerged from his immersion in Afro-Cuban folklore as an "observant participant" whose ethnographic material became a subject with which he established a relationship from within the very culture itself.

From 1942 Lam's works became the vehicle for his own, definitive kind of expression, the first vision ever of modern art from the standpoint of Africa. His art became dominated by a figuration that, although indebted to cubism, distanced itself from the analytical breaking down of forms, and moved toward invention, with the object of communicating, rather than strictly representing, a mythology of the Caribbean. There is a baroque gathering of natural and fantastic elements in these works whose message is – as Desiderio Navarro writes – the unity of life, a vision characteristic of Afro-Cuban traditions, where everything is interconnected because everything – gods, energies, human beings, animals, plants, minerals – is full of mystical force and depends and acts on everything else. This message questions and ultimately deconstructs standard Western oppositions between beauty and ugliness, good and bad, life and death, creation and destruction. As Cuban writer ALEJO CARPENTIER wrote, Lam had come from the "fixed" world of the West to another kind of world, "one of symbiosis, metamorphosis, confusion, vegetable and telluric transformations."

A major element in Lam's works is the god Eleguá, the only god whose basic image was used by Lam in nearly all his pictures (*see* ORISHAS). Eleguá is the trickster, the principle of uncertainty, who stands in opposition to Orula-Ifa, the principle of structure and accumulated wisdom. He is the master of doors and crossroads, he opens and closes everything but is unpredictable and mischievous. Similarly, in Lam's works everything seems to change into something unexpected; his art is a metamorphosis, "a praise of osmosis," as he entitled one of his paintings. Eleguá's influence is also apparent in the displacement of vision in Lam's art and in its representation and embodiment of a cultural crossroads.

Thus Lam had come a long way from pure cubism. Picasso and other modern artists had sought inspiration in African masks and statues essentially to achieve a formal renovation of Western art. They remained unaware of the context of these objects and their religious meanings and functions. In his "Picasso period" of 1938-1940, Lam emulated this geometric interpretation of African art. However, under the influence of surrealism, his own personal world became activated in a way that was to foster a more internal manipulation of those forms. As a modern artist, Lam displaced the focus from forms to meanings, in a coherent, natural, and spontaneous manner. He was attempting to create for himself, and within the context of a more personal imagery, that which the creators of the masks themselves had sought: the construction of something both fantastic and natural. Lam's art was an abstract approximation, through the necessarily different resources and functions of easel painting and modern Western art, to the mystical sense expressed in the masks.

Despite the fact that Lam's painting is often described as a set of symbols, there is no precise or direct encoding of Afro-

Cuban religious elements, which are always referred to indirectly. As Lam himself said, "I do not tend to use an exact symbology." Given the degree of decomposition, mixing, and processing of the sources, there is no strict quotation of specific kinds of masks (although some, such as the *gbon*, can still be recognized). A stricter symbolic codification appears only in a few large oil works from the second half of the 1940s, such as *Eternal Presence, The Wedding, Belial,* and *Annunciation,* which are also characterized by a greater figurative naturalism and by their expressionist aggression.

The displacements that occur in Lam's work were often proclaimed in a polemical manner. His art, like that of many surrealist painters, is often very challenging to bourgeois good taste, as he himself admitted when he said he wanted to create "hallucinating figures that can cause surprise and trouble the minds of the exploiters." Such an ingenuous program can only be understood in a figurative sense, as poetics. Lam had a preference for certain aggressive forms such as thorns, horns, and teeth (which sometimes filled an entire picture, as in *Escolopendras),* grotesque shapes alluding to repulsive animals, snakelike forms, and deformities. He viewed this attempt to shock as a Third World offensive against established taste and, in the final analysis, against what he called the "aristocratic" Western aesthetic. But Lam acted from within the context of modernity and even classicism, which he never abandoned, but rather reoriented. Lam created a non-Western space within the Western tradition, decentralizing, transforming, and de-Europeanizing it. The irony of the fact that the cultured "exploiters" now hang Lam's pictures in their drawing rooms is rather like the problem posed by the glass that is "half full" or "half empty." Such ambivalence and contradictions are part of the postcolonial culture games, particularly those of the immigrant in the power centers, who is absorbed by the center and at the same time infiltrates and transforms from within.

The polemical synthesis characteristic of Lam's art is evident in the very concept of certain of his works; for example, in those dated between 1949 and 1961 that show women sitting in poses reminiscent of academic paintings, with their hands arranged in a conventional expression of "good manners." But these elegant ladies are endowed with a most "savage" mixture of masks, tails, horns, manes, and thorns, with all those kinds of animal and plant references that enabled Lam to create his mythological figures. These pieces can be seen almost as an allegory of Lam's work and of his aesthetic stand.

Just like Eleguá, Lam's work is at the crossroads. His work not only infiltrates modernism, it participates in it. More accurate than Lam's view of himself as a Trojan horse is the metaphor of the horse of Santería, Candomblé, Vodou, and other Afro-American religions. The horse is the name given to the initiated, "ridden" by a deity, who appropriates the body, voice, and whole being of the initiated in order to manifest himself or herself in a possession trance that is the major liturgical event in these religions. Lam became an orisha riding the horse of modernism and making it utter new words. By using the artistic language of modernism, Lam's voice became legitimized by the centers of power, and it communicated from them.

Syncretism, to a greater or lesser extent, has always been a path to resistance and affirmation on the part of subordinates. A historical example of syncretism, comparable to Lam's achievement, was the identification of African gods with Catholic saints by slaves in Latin America who were forced to become Christians, a strategy that combined resistance and appropriation. In this way, the adoption of Christianity was like pushing a door that was already open, and that led to Africa. Similar to Lam, although the slaves worshiped their own deities in the shape of Catholic figures, they also incorporated the Catholic religion into an inclusive system in which Santería and Candomblé practitioners worship all gods and saints simultaneously. Syncretism, in both examples, is a strategy of participation, a resignification and pluralization against hegemony, although the fact that Lam used the language of modernism limits his audience to those familiar with elite Western art. Lam's modernism even inclined him toward a view of himself and Afro-Cuban culture as primitive and exotic. However, this in no way diminishes his achievement.

Gerardo Mosquera

See Also

Art and Architecture, African; Afrocubanismo; Candomblé; France; Santería; Transculturation, Mestizaje, and the Cosmic Race: An Interpretation; Catholic Church in Latin America and the Caribbean; Religions, African, in Latin America and the Caribbean; Orishas.

North America

Modern Jazz Quartet (MJQ),

American jazz quartet that was one of the first and most important ensembles to combine group jazz improvisation with elements of classical music.

The Modern Jazz Quartet, also known as the MJQ, was formed in 1952 by John Lewis on piano and director of the ensemble; Milt Jackson on vibraphone; Percy Heath on double bass; and Kenny Clarke on drums. The quartet evolved from the Milt Jackson Quartet (1951), which included Lewis, Clarke, and bassist Ray Brown, veterans of the 1946 big band of trumpeter Dizzy Gillespie. Drummer Connie Kay replaced Clarke in 1955. The quartet's refined ensemble sound, closely aligned with the style known as cool jazz, eventually came to be known as third-stream music.

Lewis's compositions featured his own understated, melodic playing layered against Jackson's freer, more rhythmically complex solos. The group recorded many of Lewis's compositions, including "Versailles" (1956), "Three Windows" (1957), and "England's Carol" (1960), as well as pieces by American composer Gunther Schuller and French composer André Hodeir. The quartet favored dressing in tuxedos and performing in concert halls over the usual nightclub venues.

During its more than 20 years the group annually disbanded during the summer, allowing members to play in other ensembles. Formally dissolved in July 1974, the MJQ reunited for a concert in November of that year and in later years for occasional tours. In the early 1980s the MJQ resumed playing together for several months a year. The group's albums include *Fontessa* (1956), *The Modern Jazz Quartet* (1957), *The Modern Jazz Quartet and Orchestra* (1960), *The Last Concert* (1974), and *Together Again!* (1982). Kay passed away in 1994 and was succeeded by drummer Albert "Tootie" Heath, brother of Percy Heath, in 1995.

See Also

Gillespie, John Birks ("Dizzy").

Africa

Mogadishu, Somalia, capital city of Somalia.

To most outside Somalia, Mogadishu is known as a city wracked by civil war. For centuries, however, it was a prosperous port and market town. Mogadishu was founded on the Benadir coast of modern-day Somalia by Arab and Persian settlers in the tenth century. It was one of many port towns in that region that participated in the trade between East Africa, Arabia, the Indian subcontinent, China, and Southeast Asia. Like Lamu, Mombasa, Zanzibar, and other East African coastal cities, Mogadishu became influenced by Swahili culture, traces of which are still apparent in the city's language.

Mogadishu, also called Hammawein or Xamar Weyne, was at first governed by a loose federation of families, mostly of Arab and Persian origin but later including Arab-influenced Somali clans such as the Hawiye. Although Islam arrived in Somalia around the seventh century, the ruling families of the tenth century were responsible for widespread conversion.

By the thirteenth century trade in gold from southern Africa had made Mogadishu a prosperous city, and political power had been consolidated under the rule of the Fakhr al-Din Sultanate. Once primarily an entrepôt for coastal commerce, Mogadishu now also traded in goods from the hinterlands, such as livestock, leather, ivory, and slaves. The famed traveler IBN BATTUTAH visited the city in the fourteenth century.

The Muzaffar Dynasty ruled Mogadishu in the late fifteenth and early sixteenth centuries. The city fought off the Portuguese, who were expanding their sphere of influence all along the SWAHILI COAST, but by the end of the seventeenth century it had been taken over by another foreign power, the sultan of Oman. Mogadishu, following the lead of Mombasa to the south, attempted to throw off the yoke of Omani rule in 1825. But unlike Mombasa, Mogadishu refused offers of British protection, and in 1828 faced Omani reprisals alone. Sa'id Sayyid ibn Sultan of ZANZIBAR then had jurisdiction over the city.

In 1892 Sa'id Sayyid ibn Sultan agreed to lease the port of Mogadishu to Italy for 25 years in return for an annual rent of 160,000 rupees. In a later treaty, the Italians bought the city outright, and Mogadishu became the administrative capital for their colony in southern Somalia. They built the city's cathedral, as well as a government school.

Mogadishu became a center of the nationalist activities of the Somali Youth League (SYL), founded in 1943. During a 1947 SYL demonstration, Italian police opened fire and launched grenades into the crowd, provoking a riot and killing several demonstrators. In the violence that ensued, 51 Italians were killed.

Mogadishu became the capital of independent Somalia, despite efforts by groups from northern Somalia to have the capital located in a northern political center such as Hargeysa. Already a major port and Somalia's largest city, Mogadishu grew rapidly through the 1960s and 1970s. Although much of the urban economy centered on the export of primary commodities such as fruit, meat, and animal hides, the city developed a number of light industries, including milk processing, soft-drink bottling, and textile production.

By the 1980s political instability under the military dictatorship of Maj. Gen. Mohammad Siad Barre was beginning to consume Mogadishu. In 1989 his troops bombarded Mogadishu for four weeks, leaving more than 50,000 dead and three-quarters of the city in ruins, and massacring 50 youths of the Issaq clan.

Siad Barre fled Mogadishu in early 1991, but he left a violent legacy. Soon after his overthrow, a schism in the opposition group known as the United Somali Congress (USC) led to a three-month battle between faction leaders Gen. Mohammad Farah Aidid and Ali Mahdi Mohamed. Following a devastating famine in 1992, United Nations (UN) troops (*see* UNITED NATIONS IN AFRICA) occupied the city in order to prevent armed factions from interfering with the distribution of relief aid. After what many considered an unsuccessful mission, the UN pulled out in 1994.

Since the early 1990s more than 12,000 have been killed and 40,000 injured from the violence in Mogadishu, and 400,000 have fled the city. Although Mogadishu's markets are once again busy, much of the city's infrastructure is still in ruins. The conflicts during the early 1980s left a generation of orphans, many of whom have joined violent gangs. Even in the midst of this violence, many in Mogadishu continue to struggle to maintain a peaceful existence. One such person, the charismatic Elman Ali Ahmed, ran the Mogadishu-based Gunman Project from the early stages of the conflict until his death in 1996, giving hundreds of the city's youths choices outside of war by teaching them the technical skills necessary to build the city's future.

Marian Aguiar

SEE ALSO

Gold Trade; Ivory Trade; Mombasa, Kenya; Nationalism in Africa; Sa'id Sayyid ibn Sultan; Somalia; Swahili People; Lamu, Kenya; Aidid, Mohammad Farrah; Siad Barre, Muhammad; Indian Ocean Slave Trade; Islam and Tradition: An Interpretation.

Africa

Moi, Daniel arap (b. 1924, Karing'wo Village, Baringo Rift Valley District, Kenya), second president of KENYA and one of the last of a generation of postcolonial African "big men," authoritarian rulers known for their human rights abuses.

Daniel arap Moi is a member of the Tugen, a subgroup of the KALENJIN, a relatively small ethnic group famous for producing many of Kenya's champion long-distance runners. Moi has displayed a different kind of stamina. President since 1978, he is also Kenya's longest-serving legislator, having joined the Legislative Council (now the National Assembly) in 1955 and retained his seat two years later in Kenya's first elections. Previously, Moi worked as a schoolteacher, rising to become headmaster of the Kabarnet Intermediate School in 1948, where he taught many current members of the National Assembly.

In 1960 Moi was one of the Kenyan representatives to the Lancaster House Conference in London, which negotiated the terms of Kenyan independence. Shortly afterward he became the national chairman for the Kenya African Democratic Union (KADU), a rival political party to then-president JOMO KENYATTA's party, the Kenya African National Union (KANU). KADU dissolved in 1964, and Kenyatta recruited Moi into his cabinet of ministers.

Moi began as Kenyatta's minister of education but quickly widened his influence. He became minister of local government, then minister for home affairs, which gave him responsibility for internal security, police, and immigration. In 1967 he became Kenya's vice president following the ouster of OGINGA ODINGA.

As Kenyatta's health declined during the 1970s, Moi began overseeing day-to-day government operations. When Kenyatta died on August 22, 1978, Moi succeeded him, despite opposition from many KIKUYU in the Kenyatta administration. On assuming the presidency, Moi, who lacked Kenyatta's charisma and broad-based support, outlined a policy for his government. He called it *Nyayo*, or "footsteps," implying his intention to continue Kenyatta's policies. These included an emphasis on national unity as opposed to tribalism; the gradual "Kenyanization" of the economy, which consisted of replacing noncitizens with Kenyans; a market economy; close economic ties with the West, especially with GREAT BRITAIN; and political nonalignment. But after this program failed to address high unemployment, inflation, and constant political infighting, members of the Kenyan air force attempted a coup in 1982. Loyal soldiers defeated the rebels but only after a bloody battle and extensive property damage. Moi immediately sought to tighten control over the government and to eliminate opposition, real or imagined.

Moi replaced high-ranking Kikuyus in government and parastatal industries. Claiming that ethnic conflicts caused much of the political instability in Kenya, he outlawed ethnically based political organizations. A series of parliamentary measures in the mid-1980s further consolidated his power over the civil service and the judiciary. Taking advantage of colonial-era laws that limited press, speech, and political freedoms, he censored the press and jailed editors and activists who criticized him or his policies. Allegations of torture and illegal imprisonment, combined with a recession in the late 1980s, contributed to Moi's declining popularity.

By the early 1990s student groups and churches were holding demonstrations calling for increased freedom of speech and a multiparty political system. Security forces often met such protests with violence. In response, many Western aid donors, who had overlooked Moi's repressive tactics during the cold war, began to demand political reforms and respect for human rights as a condition of continued aid. Although Moi habitually criticized the foreign media and organizations for "meddling" in Kenya's internal affairs, he succumbed to international pressure and in 1992 authorized multiparty elections and restored partial judicial independence.

Thanks in part to a highly fragmented political opposition, Moi managed to win the 1993 presidential election with a mere 36 percent of the popular vote. Since then his political legitimacy has, if anything, further deteriorated, especially after a series of mass killings in areas of concentrated political opposition raised suspicions of government-sponsored terrorism.

Moi held presidential elections in late December 1997. While Kenyans of every political stripe had become fed up with his regime, his tactics of divide and rule among ethnic groups helped him win a fifth term as president.

Robert Fay

See Also
Human Rights in Africa.

Africa

Mombasa, Kenya, second largest city of Kenya and the main port of East Africa.

Mombasa, with a 1994 population of more than 640,000, is the largest port city in East Africa and the second largest city in Kenya. It is located on a bay in the Indian Ocean and serves Kenya, northeastern Tanzania, Uganda, Rwanda, and Burundi. Originally founded on the island of Mombasa, the city now sprawls over the adjacent mainland, which is connected to the island by a causeway, a bridge, and ferries. Mombasa's modern deep-water port, Kilindini, handles transoceanic shipping, while smaller vessels, including wooden dhows engaged in coastal trade and fishing, frequent the Old Mombasa Harbor. Mombasa also has a sizable industrial zone, with sugar and oil refineries and other factories.

Mombasa was founded in the eleventh century by Arabs who exchanged cloth, beads, metal goods, silks, and porcelain for gold, ivory, and slaves brought from the African interior. By the fifteenth century Mombasa had surpassed Kilwa as the primary trading center in East Africa. Transplanted Arabs mixed with the Bantu-speaking African inhabitants, eventually creating the Swahili culture and language. Architecture in Mombasa still shows distinct Arab influences, featuring narrow streets, tall houses, and several mosques.

In 1498 the Portuguese explorer Vasco da Gama was the first European to visit Mombasa; six years later the Portuguese, seeking greater control over lucrative Indian Ocean trades, captured the city. But Portuguese rule was tenuous at best. Constant challenges from the Omani Dynasty prompted the construction of Fort Jesus in 1593, which today is a historic landmark and tourist stop.

In 1740 a local Swahili clan, the Mazrui, captured Mombasa, then lost it to the Omani sultan of Zanzibar in 1832. Even after the British established colonial rule over Kenya in 1887, the sultan maintained nominal control of the city. The completion of the Uganda Railway in 1902 linked Mombasa to Lake Victoria.

During the 1950s Mombasa became a favorite tourist destination for European settlers from Zimbabwe (then Rhodesia) and South Africa. Tourism grew into a vital part of the Mombasa economy in the 1970s and 1980s, and the city attracted more than 250,000 visitors annually. But ethnic violence in Mombasa beginning in August 1997 quickly diminished the number of tourists. This followed a general decline of tourism nationwide, which many experts blamed on disintegrating infrastructure, increased ethnic violence, and the declining quality of services. By March 1998 hundreds of workers in the tourist industry were being laid off each week. Industry watchers anticipated that the downturn would continue until at least the year 2000. Nevertheless, Mombasa will likely hold onto its position as East Africa's most important port well into the twenty-first century.

Robert Fay

See Also
Gold Trade; Ivory Trade; Great Britain; Portugal; Swahili People; Tourism in Africa; Indian Ocean Slave Trade.

North America

Monk, Thelonious Sphere

(b. October 10, 1917, Rocky Mount, N.C.; d. February 17, 1982, Weehawken, N.J.), African American jazz pianist and composer noted for his highly individual compositions and angular and rhythmic style of playing.

Thelonious Monk was one of the great iconoclasts of jazz. He has long been classed among the main creators of bebop or modern jazz in the 1940s, along with alto sax player Charlie Parker, trumpeter Dizzy Gillespie, drummer Kenny Clarke, and guitarist Charlie Christian. Many also emphasize Monk's importance as a precursor of free jazz; jazz scholar Joachim Berendt notes that "what leads to Ornette Coleman, John Coltrane, Eric Dolphy, and all the other avant-gardists of jazz was heard for the first time in his music." Although Monk had some formal instruction, he was essentially self-taught and never really fit within any larger movement or style. Still, in going his own way, he ultimately took much of the jazz world with him.

Monk was born in North Carolina but moved with his family to New York City when he was an infant. He first became interested in playing piano when he was five or six years old. Growing up, he lived near the great Harlem stride pianist James P. Johnson, and Monk himself initially played in the stride style. In effect, the stride piano style divides the piano keyboard into three ranges. The pianist's left hand covers the two lower ranges, alternating single bass notes at the bottom with chord clusters struck higher up. The term "stride" comes from the characteristic bouncing "oom-pah, oom-pah" of the pianist's "striding" left hand. While the left hand sets up a propulsive beat and outlines the tune's harmonic structure, the pianist's right hand plays the melody, adds ornamentation, and improvises solo lines.

Throughout his performing career, Monk continued to display hints of the stride piano style of his youth. But he soon began moving further, not just away from the stride style, but beyond the conventions of swing jazz in general. His explorations coincided with the experiments of a generation of young jazz players who were in the process of creating bebop or modern jazz. Monk himself became a part of these efforts during

Known for his irregular rhythms and jarring harmonies, American jazz pianist and composer Thelonious Monk was one of the creators of bebop, or modern, jazz during the 1940s. *The Everett Collection*

his 1940-1943 stint in the house band of Minton's, a New York City jazz club and bop incubator. There he played with Charlie Christian, Dizzy Gillespie, and Don Byas, among others. Impromptu recordings made at Minton's reveal a pianist strongly influenced by the stripped-down melodic swing of Teddy Wilson. These early recordings also capture some of the irregular rhythms and jarring harmonies that would characterize Monk's mature playing.

Monk played briefly with Lucky Millinder in 1942 and two years later joined Cootie Williams's short-lived big band, which had recorded two Monk compositions, "Epistrophy" and his most famous piece, "'Round Midnight." Monk enjoyed much wider recognition, and had his recording debut, after joining tenor saxophonist Coleman Hawkins, who consistently supported creative younger players. Nonetheless, during a period when other bop musicians found growing acceptance – in fact, near pop-culture celebrity during the short-lived bebop craze of the late 1940s – Monk continued to play in obscurity.

In certain respects, his compositions and solos are forbidding. The chord progressions are unexpected and sometimes jarring, the melodies often agitated and edgy. In an era in which jazz soloists strove to play more and more notes at ever faster tempos, Monk's lines were spare, with open space between the notes and phrases. And the tempos he played in were often remarkably slow. Between 1947 and 1952 he recorded several sessions for Blue Note that were later acclaimed by jazz musicians and listeners alike – featuring such classic Monk compositions as "Ruby My Dear," "Well You Needn't," "'Round Midnight," and "Straight No Chaser" – but he remained too "far out" for widespread acceptance until the latter half of the 1950s.

Monk did not alter his style between 1947 and the end of his life. But after 1955, when he began recording for Riverside Records with jazz producer Orrin Keepnews, jazz at last caught up with him. In 1956 Monk recorded his outstanding *Brilliant Corners* album, praised in *Downbeat* magazine by jazz critic Nat Henthoff. Monk's talent was finally recognized in 1957, when he played an extended gig at the Five Spot, then one of New York City's premier jazz clubs. At the Five Spot, Monk performed with a quartet that featured tenor saxophonist John Coltrane. Under the pianist's tutelage, Coltrane began his own rapid growth toward musical greatness.

During the 1960s Monk established a long-standing quartet featuring Charlie Rouse on tenor saxophone, which recorded regularly for Columbia Records. In his later years Monk suffered psychiatric problems that led to his effective retirement in 1973, though he made occasional appearances to the end of the decade. Since his death, jazz musicians have continued to embrace his music. It has become almost de rigueur for jazz players to include at least one Monk tune in their recording sessions and nightclub sets.

James Clyde Sellman

See Also

Coltrane, John William; Gillespie, John Birks ("Dizzy"); Harlem, New York; Hawkins, Coleman Randolph; New York, New York; Parker, Charles Christopher ("Bird").

Africa

Monrovia, Liberia, the capital of Liberia.

In 1821 the first African American settlers in the area that would become the Republic of Liberia purchased land from King Peter, an indigenous leader, to establish a settlement at Mesurado Bay. They called the small town, set on a rocky hilltop on the banks of the Mesurado River, Christopolis, "city of Christ." Three years later they renamed it Monrovia, after then United States president James Monroe. Monrovia grew quickly. Settlers with adequate means built houses with columns and verandas that reflected the architectural traditions of the American South, from which many of them had come.

Traditionally the home of Americo-Liberians, through the years Monrovia became an important center of both commerce and government, as well as the home of the University of Liberia and the presidential palace. In contrast to the Liberian countryside, where indigenous languages and religious beliefs prevail, by the late 1980s Monrovia boasted a population of more than 3 million people, about 80 percent of whom were Christian.

Following the outbreak of civil war in December 1989, Monrovia became a magnet for refugees fleeing violence in the hinterlands. Analysts estimate that about 100,000 rural Liberians sought refuge in the capital during the early 1990s. Fighting between rival rebel groups (including Charles Taylor's NPFL and Prince Johnson's ULIMO Parties) finally spilled into Monrovia in 1997, causing severe damage as well as many civilian casualties. In 1997 the transitional government headed by Ruth Perry made plans to help Monrovia's internal refugees return to their home counties.

Kate Tuttle

See Also

Christianity, African: An Overview; Taylor, Charles Ghankay.

Latin America and the Caribbean

Montejo, Esteban (b. 1860; d. 1973), Cuban runaway slave whose life story was recorded by author Miguel Barnet.

As a child, Esteban Montejo escaped the sugar plantation to live as a maroon until the abolition of slavery in 1885. His memories were published by the Cuban writer Miguel Barnet in *A Maroon's Biography* (1966), considered a pioneering work of the Latin American testimonial genre (*see* Abolition and Emancipation in Latin America and the Caribbean). The first part of the book gives one of the most detailed descriptions of the harsh working and living conditions of slaves on the sugar plantations. Montejo's account of his survival as a solitary runaway affirms that hunger and lack of shelter were preferable to the life of a slave.

In the last part of the book Montejo narrates his experience in the Cuban Liberation Army during the War of Independence (1895-1898) (*see* Spanish-Cuban-American War). His account underscores the important role played by the Afro-Cuban officials and soldiers, particularly Antonio Maceo. This section of the book also describes the racial discrimination within the Cuban army, which anticipated the racial disputes among Cuban political parties in the early twentieth century (*see* Partido Independiente de Color). Montejo's life in the nineteenth century is presented as an allegory of Cuban liberation from Spain and the socialist revolution, though this is attributed to Barnet's mediation in compiling the narrative.

Juan Otero-Garabis

See Also

Maroonage in the Americas; Slavery in Latin America and the Caribbean; Maceo y Grajales, Antonio.

Latin America and the Caribbean

Monte y Aponte, Domingo del (b. 1804; d. 1853), white Cuban intellectual and patron to the principal antislavery writers of the period such as Anselmo Suárez y Romero, Cirilo Villaverde, and the black poet Juan Francisco Manzano.

North America

Montgomery Bus Boycott, the year-long protest in Montgomery, Alabama, that galvanized the American Civil Rights Movement and led to a 1956 United States Supreme Court decision declaring segregated seating on buses unconstitutional.

In December 1955, 42,000 black residents of Montgomery began a year-long boycott of city buses to protest racially segregated seating. After 381 days of taking taxis, carpooling, and walking the hostile streets of Montgomery, African Americans eventually won their fight to desegregate seating on public buses, not only in Montgomery, but throughout the United States.

An empty bus makes its rounds of the city during the Montgomery, Alabama, bus boycott in 1956.
CORBIS/Bettmann-UPI

The protest was first organized by the Women's Political Council as a one-day boycott to coincide with the trial of Rosa Parks, who had been arrested on December 2, 1955, for refusing to give up her seat to a white man on a segregated Montgomery bus. By the next morning, the council, led by JoAnn Robinson, had printed 52,000 fliers asking Montgomery blacks to stay off public buses on December 5, the day of the trial. Meanwhile, labor activist E. D. Nixon, who had bailed Parks out of jail, notified Ralph Abernathy, minister of the First Baptist Church, and Martin Luther King Jr., the new minister at Dexter Avenue Baptist Church, of her arrest. A group of about 50 black leaders and one white minister, Robert Graetz, gathered in the basement of King's church to endorse the boycott and begin planning a massive rally for the evening of the trial. Graetz offered his support from the pulpit of his predominantly white Lutheran church. The Montgomery Chapter of the National Association for the Advancement of Colored People (NAACP), which had been looking for a test case for segregation, began preparing for the legal challenge.

The issue of segregated seating had long been a source of resentment in Montgomery's black community. African Americans were forced to pay their fares at the front, and then reboard the bus at the back. They faced systematic harassment from white drivers, who sometimes pulled away before black passengers could reboard. On the bus blacks sat behind a mobile barrier dividing the races, and as the bus filled, the barrier was pushed backward to make room for white passengers. No black person could sit in the same row as a white, and whites had priority in this middle "no-man's land."

On the morning of Parks's trial, buses rumbled nearly empty through the streets of Montgomery. Police officers with shotguns roamed in search of imaginary "Negro goon squads" who they believed were forcing blacks to stay off the buses. After Parks lost her case and was convicted of violating the segregated seating laws, black leaders met again to organize an extension of the bus boycott. To this end they formed the Montgomery Improvement Association (MIA) and elected King as its president. That evening, 7000 blacks crowded into Holt Street Baptist Church, where King inspired the audience with his words: "There comes a time when people get tired of being trampled over by the iron feet of oppression."

With this speech, King was able to spark the black residents' collective outrage into a grassroots movement that would sustain the boycott. The Montgomery Bus Boycott followed King's credo of nonviolent resistance, even in the face of a police crackdown and attempts by white supremacists to undermine the protest. Montgomery police threatened to arrest taxi drivers giving discount rates to the black riders, and when the MIA arranged carpools, the police systematically harassed drivers, arresting them for allegedly going too fast or too slow. Meanwhile, the boycott leaders squared off at the bargaining table with the local officials. The MIA presented its modest demands for bus seating by race, with no mobile area, and "Negro routes" with black drivers. They were met with unconditional refusal.

Many white supremacists joined the White Citizen's Council, one of many racist citizens' organizations that would gain power throughout the South in the 1960s. Convinced that there was an outside mastermind of the movement, they focused their attention on terrorizing boycott leaders. Vigilante groups set off bombs at black homes and churches. In addition, there were several police sweeps, and twice King joined the other black protesters in Montgomery's crowded jails. In one attempt to sabotage the boycott, the Montgomery *Advertiser*, a white newspaper, planned to put out a false story that the boycott had ended. King and other leaders, warned in advance of the story, traveled late that night to the rural jook joints where black workers went to dance and drink. Thus forewarned, African Americans continued to stay off the local buses. Shortly after, the *Advertiser* announced that Montgomery was on the verge of a "full scale racial war."

Even as the protesters and black leaders were confronted with escalating violence, they maintained both nonviolent resistance and their exhausting day-to-day schedule without public transportation. At the same time the MIA moved ahead on the legal front. On February 1, 1956, shortly after a bomb went off in King's home, the MIA filed a federal suit against bus segregation in the names of four black women.

In the spring protesters led by E. D. Nixon turned the tables on the local government and caught the attention of the national press. Indicted under a statute that prohibited boycotts "without just cause or legal excuse," leaders presented themselves at the courthouse rather than waiting to be arrested. The national press came down to cover the scene of black leaders marching into the courthouse while hundreds cheered them on. As protesters walked to work through the summer of 1956, the issue of civil rights took center stage in the national consciousness. After the March trial of the MIA, King appeared on the cover of *Time* magazine and the *New York Times Magazine*.

In June a federal court ruled segregated seating unconstitutional, and the case went on appeal to the U.S. Supreme Court. Meanwhile, King and the MIA leadership went to the Montgomery court to try to stave off an injunction against the carpools. They were in court when they were handed a notice from the Associated Press wire announcing the Supreme Court decision that ruled segregated seating on public buses unconstitutional. King addressed a euphoric crowd that night, and over the next week, celebrities such as singer Mahalia Jackson and New York minister Gardner C. Taylor came to Montgomery to celebrate. On December 20, 1956, when the federal ruling took effect, an integrated group of boycott supporters, including King, Abernathy, Fred Gray, and Glenn Smiley, rode the city buses.

The Montgomery Bus Boycott had implications that reached far beyond the desegregation of public buses. The protest propelled the Civil Rights Movement into national consciousness and Martin Luther King Jr. into the public eye. In the words of King: "We have gained a new sense of dignity and destiny. We have discovered a new and powerful weapon – nonviolent resistance."

Marian Aguiar

See Also

Abernathy, Ralph David; King, Martin Luther, Jr.; Nixon, Edgar Daniel; Parks, Rosa Louise McCauley; Robinson, JoAnn Gibson; Taylor, Gardner Calvin.

Latin America and the Caribbean

Montserrat, country in the Caribbean Sea, southeast of Puerto Rico and about halfway between Guadeloupe and St. Kitts and Nevis.

A nineteenth-century visitor to Montserrat wrote in a letter home that "no island in these seas is bolder in its general aspect, more picturesque, more beautiful in the details of its scenery... it has the fatal gifts of beauty." The island's beauty earned it its reputation as the Emerald Isle of the Caribbean.

Montserrat's earliest residents were most likely Ciboney Amerindians who arrived on the island between 500 B.C.E. and 500 C.E. after migrating north from Venezuela. They were later succeeded by Taíno Arawak Amerindians, and the Taíno were followed by the Carib, who named the island Alliouagana, or "land of the prickly bush." On November 11, 1493, Christopher Columbus and his crew were the first Europeans to see the island during their second voyage to the Caribbean. Columbus immediately renamed the mountainous island Santa Maria de Monserrate, after a Spanish abbey set in the mountains outside Barcelona.

The first permanent European settlers on Montserrat were English settlers who migrated from nearby St. Kitts and Nevis in 1632. Within months they were followed by a group of Irish Catholic colonists who had recently fled the British settlement in Virginia because of religious persecution. Montserrat soon became known as a safe haven for those seeking religious freedom; Irish Catholic settlers from other British colonies began to settle there. At the same time it became a common destination for many Irish Catholics who did not come voluntarily but were forced into indentured servitude and exile by British rulers at home.

The Irish laborers were forced to work on the island's small farms and plantations, growing tobacco, cotton, and indigo. But when sugar cane was found to be a profitable crop in the 1650s, there were not enough Irish workers to fill the demand for sugar plantations. British Montserratians turned to the same labor force that was being exploited by colonists across the Americas: African slaves. The first black slaves probably arrived in Montserrat in 1651. Within 20 years there were about 1000 black slaves on the island, and by 1729 that number had grown to 5858, with blacks outnumbering whites five to one.

Rumors of planned slave uprisings roused fear among Montserratian whites in 1768 and 1770 – each supposedly intended to coincide with Saint Patrick's Day, a holiday when many whites would have been caught off guard. Neither uprising took place, but it was not surprising that Montserrat slaves wanted their freedom. Montserrat laws forbade slaves to become coopers, smiths, tailors, sawyers, masons, or shinglers, and while they were allowed to keep small gardens for their own use, they were forbidden to plant indigo, ginger, coffee, cotton, and cocoa. Their exclusion from the most profitable trades and crops ensured that few slaves were able to make extra money that might have allowed them to purchase their freedom. It also meant that most Montserratian blacks were relegated to laboring in the sugar fields, a condition that remained constant even after slavery was finally abolished in 1834 (*see* Abolition and Emancipation in Latin America and the Caribbean).

As the nineteenth century proceeded, it became clear that Montserrat's economy could not depend on sugar alone. In 1897 three-fifths of the island's cultivated land was still planted in sugar cane, but because the industry was no longer profitable, planters began experimenting with such crops as limes, coffee, tomatoes, silkworms, and cotton. Limes and cotton were the most successful, and for the first few decades of the twentieth century, they formed the backbone of Montserrat's economy. But the change in crops did not change the fact that most Montserratians worked as poorly paid field laborers on white-owned estates. Black workers were understandably frustrated by this status quo, and in the 1930s laborers in Montserrat, like laborers throughout the Caribbean, began unionizing.

As the unions became more powerful, union members were able to fight for political changes. For most of the nineteenth century and the beginning of the twentieth century, Montserrat's governing council was entirely appointed. This factor had allowed the white minority to retain political power, but by the 1940s Montserrat's black majority began insisting on change. In 1951 elections were held under universal adult suffrage for the first time. Union leader W. H. Bramble was elected to the council and became Montserrat's first chief minister.

Montserrat is one of several British colonies that have not pushed for increased independence. Montserrat's culture, while not necessarily British, is an unusual mix of African and Irish elements. Citizens celebrate Carnival and Saint Patrick's Day, and while calypso and other Afro-Caribbean musical forms are extremely popular, Montserratian folk music and dance also have roots in Irish step dances and *bodhrans*. For a time Montserratians enjoyed the increased financial stability associated with being a British dependency. The island was a popular vacation destination for both British and American tourists, and British stars such as Elton John, the Rolling Stones, and Sting recorded at a famous studio on the island. Tourism was the island's most important economic sector.

The late twentieth century, however, brought disaster to the island. Montserratians rebuilt their island after Hurricane Hugo struck in 1989, only to be faced with an even more devastating disaster in the 1990s: the eruption of the Soufrière Hills volcano. The Soufrière Hills eruptions began in 1995 and reached their worst level in the summer of 1997. Between June and August of that year 20 people were killed, thousands more evacuated, and much of the southern two-thirds of the island was destroyed, including the capital, Plymouth. In mid-1998 it remained unclear when volcanic activity would cease and when Montserratians might be able to begin the difficult process of rebuilding their homes.

The volcanic eruptions cast uncertainty on all aspects of Montserratian life, including the country's relationship with Great Britain. Many critics claimed that the British government should have done more to relocate residents before the eruptions and to help victims after the disaster. It remains to be seen how Montserrat will be able to recover from this difficult chapter in its national history.

Lisa Clayton Robinson

See Also

Slavery in Latin America and the Caribbean; Carnivals in Latin America and the Caribbean; Slave Rebellions in Latin America and the Caribbean.

North America

Moody, Anne (b. September 15, 1940, Centerville, Miss.), African American civil rights activist and writer.

The daughter of sharecroppers, Anne Moody was educated in the segregated schools of rural Mississippi and began her college career at Natchez Junior College on a basketball scholarship. She later transferred to Tougaloo College in Jackson, Mississippi, where she became active in the Civil Rights Movement.

From 1961 to 1963 Moody served as an organizer for the Congress of Racial Equality (CORE) in Mississippi, then considered to be the state with the most violent and most dangerous white resistance to civil rights activities in the South. She participated in direct action protests, including the first sit-in demonstration at a Woolworth's lunch counter in Jackson, Mississippi. In 1964, the same year she graduated from Tougaloo, she began fundraising for CORE. From 1964 to 1965 she also worked for Cornell University as its civil rights project coordinator. Her civil rights activities soon cooled, however, because of her frustration with the changing nature of the movement, in particular its shift toward Black Nationalism.

But Moody is best known for her autobiography, *Coming of Age in Mississippi* (1968), which received the Best Book of the Year Award from the National Library Association in 1969. One of the most widely read works to come out of the Civil Rights Movement, this moving book traces her life from the poverty and racism of the rural Mississippi Delta through her educational struggles and civil rights activities up to the 1963 March on Washington. In 1975 Moody published *Mr. Death*, a book of short stories.

Robert Fay

See Also
Sit-Ins; March on Washington, 1963; Black Nationalism in the United States.

North America

Moore, Audley ("Queen Mother")

(b. July 27, 1898, New Iberia, La.; d. May 2, 1997, New York, N.Y.), American black nationalist and Harlem civil rights leader.

Born in rural Louisiana, Audley Moore and her family experienced the terror of racism in its most brutal form with the LYNCHING of her paternal grandfather. Her parents died when Moore was in the fourth grade, and by the time she was 15 she had to raise and support herself and her two sisters as a hairdresser.

Her family's suffering and the racism she faced pushed Moore to political activism. In New Orleans she joined Marcus Garvey's militant UNIVERSAL NEGRO IMPROVEMENT ASSOCIATION, inspired by Garvey's Black Nationalism and pride in blacks' African heritage. Part of THE GREAT MIGRATION from the rural South to the urban North, Moore and her sisters moved to Harlem in the 1920s. Moore became a prominent organizer for the Communist Party, particularly in defense of the Scottsboro Boys, eight young men in Alabama who were wrongly convicted of rape and sentenced to death. Through the party, she fought on behalf of black tenants and for black political representation, but because of the racism she encountered within the party she eventually resigned.

Moore continued her political activity by fighting for education for the poor and becoming a leader in the movement demanding REPARATIONS from the federal government for the labor of blacks under slavery. She stated: "Ever since 1950, I've been on the trail fighting for reparations. They owe us more than they could ever pay. They stole our language, they stole our culture. They stole us from our mothers and fathers and took away our names from us. They worked us free of charge 18 hours a day, 7 days a week, under the lash, for centuries."

Moore promoted PAN-AFRICANISM and was one of the founders of the Universal Association of Ethiopian Women. In 1972, on one of her many visits to Africa, she was honored by the the ASANTE people of GHANA as "Queen Mother." In 1989 Moore was among the black women honored at the Corcoran Gallery of Art, where "I Have A Dream," an exhibition of one of these prominent women, was on display. Moore participated in the MILLION MAN MARCH in 1995.

In a life that spanned some six decades of activism, Moore exemplified Nelson Mandela's dictum, which she often referred to: "The struggle is my life."

Leyla Keough

See Also
Mandela, Nelson Rolihlahla; Slavery in the United States; Garvey, Marcus Mosiah; Harlem, New York; New Orleans, Louisiana; Scottsboro Case; Communist Party USA, African Americans and the; Black Nationalism in the United States.

North America

Moore, Harry Tyson

(b. November 17, 1905, Houston, Fla.; d. December 25, 1951, Mims, Fla.), teacher, political activist, and Florida state coordinator of the NATIONAL ASSOCIATION FOR THE ADVANCEMENT OF COLORED PEOPLE (NAACP), whose murder was never solved.

The victim of a bombing on Christmas night, Henry Tyson Moore was only 46 when he died, but in his short life he accomplished much. Trained as a schoolteacher, he worked for the Brevard County, Florida, school system from 1925 until 1946, when his NAACP-supported campaign to secure equal pay for African American teachers cost him his position as superintendent of the area's Negro High School. Following the loss of his job, Moore continued to work for the state branch of the NAACP, focusing not only on economic and educational equality but also on voter registration and the fair enforcement of laws. When in November 1951 a white sheriff shot two black handcuffed defendants, killing one, Moore demanded that the sheriff be indicted for murder.

On December 25 of that year, a bomb exploded under the bedroom of Moore's house, killing him instantly (his wife, Harriet, died a few days later). Neither local law enforcement nor the Federal Bureau of Investigation (FBI) was able to solve Moore's murder. Documents unveiled when Florida's governor reopened the case in 1991 reveal that the FBI's initial investigation focused solely on African American suspects, including all 600 people who attended Moore's funeral. To date, no one has been charged with the crime, which a 1952 editorial in the *Nation* described as "part of a clear pattern of open force directed against the struggle of racial minorities to win full rights as citizens."

Kate Tuttle

North America

Moore, Richard Benjamin

(b. August 9, 1893, Hastings, Christ Church, Barbados; d. August 18, 1978, Barbados), activist and intellectual who was a leading figure in black socialism and labor politics in the United States.

Richard Moore became a political activist when he immigrated to New York in 1901. He joined the Socialist Party in 1918 and became a member of the AFRICAN BLOOD BROTHERHOOD (ABB), a secret organization with ties both to Black Nationalism and the Communist Party USA.

In 1921 Moore left the Socialist Party because of its indifference to African American concerns. Soon after he joined the Workers Party, the Harlem branch of the Communist Party. In 1925 he was elected to the executive board and council of directors of the American Negro Labor Congress (ANLC), a national organization of black radicals, and became a contributing editor to the ANLC's the *Negro Champion*. In 1931 Moore became vice president of the International Labor Defense (ILD), which was formed to resolve legal problems caused by labor disputes and racism. Moore and the ILD became well known for defending the SCOTTSBORO CASE, in which nine black boys were sent to prison for raping two white girls, although doctors determined that no rape had taken place.

Moore founded the Pathway Press and the Frederick Douglass Historical and Cultural League in 1940. In 1942 he established the Frederick Douglass Book Center, an Afro-American and Caribbean bookstore, which was a well-known intellectual center in Harlem until it was burned in 1968. The Communist Party expelled him in 1942 for his "Negro Nationalist way of thinking."

Throughout his life Moore was dedicated to the independence of Caribbean nations. He was invited by BARBADOS to participate in its independence celebration in 1966.

Moore fought ceaselessly to end racism. In 1960 he published *The Name "Negro" – Its Origin and Evil Use*. He strongly promoted the term "Afro-American," which, he felt, "proclaims at once our past continental heritage and our present national status."

See Also
Harlem, New York; Socialism; Communist Party USA, African Americans and the; Black Nationalism in the United States.

Latin America and the Caribbean

Mooretown, Jamaica (Nanny Town), former maroon community in the Blue Mountains of Jamaica. Now known as Mooretown, Nanny Town was destroyed by colonial officials in 1734 and is now a symbol of slave resistance.

Nanny Town was one of five major eighteenth-century maroon communities in Jamaica. Located in the inaccessible Blue Mountain range of Portland parish, Nanny Town was home to the Windward or Eastern maroons. The town and its destruction by the British in 1734 have become a powerful symbol of slave resistance. The town's legendary leader was an African chief named Nanny: her mysterious life and death have become an integral part of Jamaican history.

According to legend Nanny was the wife or sister of the legendary maroon Cudjoe. She is described in myths as possessing impressive magical powers. Local oral tradition recalls how she was able to repel bullets fired from European guns, and how she could capture colonial soldiers in her boiling cauldron.

Although historians are not sure if Nanny actually existed, most agree that the town named in her honor was a reality. It had been attacked by colonial militias several times, but it fell victim to a massive European offensive in 1734. That year, according to colonial history, Captain Stoddart led a small army by night into the maroon community and set up portable swivel guns high above the town's sleeping residents. Firing down on the unsuspecting maroons, Stoddart killed most of them before they could mount an organized resistance. According to colonial history Nanny Town was sacked and many of its survivors chose to commit suicide rather than suffer the humiliation of defeat.

The maroons have their own version of the events at Nanny Town. According to maroon legend lookouts spotted Stoddart and his army as they approached. The town was evacuated and maroon fighters hid themselves along the path to the town, lying in wait as the white soldiers passed. When they reached Nanny Town they found an empty village. Disappointed and tired, they chose to set up camp and sleep throughout the night. Once the soldiers were asleep the maroons set upon the town, throwing burning candles onto the tents and setting the town afire. The terrified soldiers chose not to fight and instead leapt over the surrounding cliffs to their death. Historians currently believe that the truth lies somewhere in between these two accounts.

Nanny Town was never resettled after the confrontation in 1734. The maroons who survived the attack fled into the mountains, and many joined forces with Cudjoe and his army. Some believe that Nanny Town is haunted by ghosts. The legend of Nanny Town, and the controversy surrounding its demise, continue to add fuel to the powerful tales of slave resistance in Jamaica.

Alonford James Robinson, Jr.

See Also

Maroonage in the Americas.

North America

Moorhead, Scipio (fl. 1773, Boston, Mass.), African American slave and artist known primarily for his painting of Phillis Wheatley.

Despite Scipio Moorhead's position as a slave in the home of Rev. John Moorhead, a Presbyterian minister in Boston, he managed to develop his artistic talent. Sarah Moorhead, a painter who was the wife of the minister, probably provided some instruction.

Attributed to Moorhead is the painting of African American poet Phillis Wheatley that inspired the engraved frontispiece of her book of poetry. The volume, *Poems on Various Subjects, Religious and Moral,* was published in London in 1773 and provoked public debate concerning the intellectual abilities of those of African descent.

Unfortunately, no signed works by Moorhead are known to exist. It is believed to be Moorhead whom Wheatley immortalized with her 1773 poem "To S.M., A Young African Painter, on Seeing His Work." The poem describes two paintings presumably by Moorhead, *Aurora* and *Damon and Pythia.*

Matthew Goff

North America

Moorland, Jesse Edward (b. September 10, 1863, Coldwater, Ohio; d. March 20, 1939, New York, N.Y.), African American minister; Young Men's Christian Association (YMCA) leader devoted to achieving social progress in leadership positions through the Congregational Church and the YMCA.

After attending Northwestern Normal University in Ada, Ohio, Jesse Edward Moorland enrolled in Howard University's Department of Theology. He graduated from Howard with a master's degree in 1891 and was ordained a minister in the Congregational Church. In that year he also became secretary of the Colored Branch of the YMCA in Washington, D.C. He moved to Nashville, Tennessee, in 1893 to become pastor of Howard Church. In 1896 he became pastor of Cleveland's Mount Zion Congregational Church. He struggled to make Congregationalism a "practical, muscular Christianity" that directly addressed social needs.

Returning to the YMCA in 1898, Moorland served as administrator and fundraiser for its Colored Men's Department in Washington, D.C. He raised more than $2 million for 29 new YMCA buildings for black communities throughout America. In 1914 he became senior secretary of the YMCA's Colored Men's Department. Under his leadership, the department expanded significantly its number of college student chapters and city associations. He retired in 1923.

Moorland collected a substantial library of books by and about people of African descent. His collection, the largest of its time, went to Howard University and formed the basis of the Moorland-Spingarn Research Center.

Moorland continued his efforts with black social organizations such as the National Health Circle for Colored People. In 1907 he joined the Executive Committee of Howard University's Board of Trustees, which he chaired in the 1930s.

See Also

Moorland-Spingarn Research Collection.

North America

Moorland-Spingarn Research Collection, comprehensive collection of scholarly materials by and about people of African descent, housed at Howard University.

The Moorland-Spingarn Research Center (MSRC) is a research facility located in Founder Library at Howard University in Washington, D.C. It aims to collect, organize, preserve, and make available valuable resources on the history and culture of Africans and people of African descent. The MSRC's holdings chronicle the experiences of people of African descent in Africa, the Americas, and other parts of the world from the sixteenth century through the present.

The MSRC is composed of two divisions: Library and Manuscript. The Library Division houses more than 175,000 books, periodicals, and microforms in numerous languages. This body of literature includes rare works by early black writers such as David Walker, Phillis Wheatley, and Frederick Douglass and first-edition works by twentieth-century black authors, including W. E. B. Du Bois, Richard Wright, and Alice Walker. The Library Division also features special resources such as theses on black subjects by students from other colleges and a vertical file collection covering an array of people and events.

The Manuscript Division is a collection of primary source materials divided into four departments: manuscripts, music, oral history, and prints and photographs. The manuscript department contains the correspondences, writings, and memorabilia of more than 160 African American people and organizations. The music department's collection covers more than 400 black composers, starting in the eighteenth century. Its sheet music, songbooks, and recordings span all musical genres, including classical, spiritual, and jazz. The oral history department brings together over 700 transcripts of the speeches made by participants in the Civil Rights Movement. The prints and photographs department houses over 50,000 images dating from the 1800s to the present.

The MSRC is named for its two benefactors, Jesse E. Moorland (1863-1939) and Arthur B. Spingarn (1878-1971). Moorland was a minister, YMCA executive, and collector of materials about African American culture and history, with an emphasis on the history of slavery. After inheriting a book collection from an uncle, he began collecting books, pamphlets, and manuscripts about black men and women as well as portraits and engravings. As a member of the Board of Trustees at Howard University, he advocated the establishment of an African American research library at the university and in 1914 decided to donate his private library of more than 3000 items to Howard. At that time it was regarded as the most extensive collection of materials in the world by and about people of African descent. The collection became known as the Moorland Foundation, a Library of Negro Life, and established Howard University as the center of black scholarship.

Arthur B. Spingarn was a lawyer, NAACP officer, and collector of books by black authors. A European American, he began collecting books by black authors in response to white scholars' claim that people of African descent would continue to be viewed as inferior until the day a black man could read a book by a black author. The books he accumulated explored topics in every academic field of study and were written in all major African and European languages. In 1946 Spingarn donated his eclectic collection to Howard University. From then until his death, Spingarn sent Howard a copy of every book by a black author he could find.

While Moorland and Spingarn laid the foundation for the research library, scholar-librarian Dorothy Porter Wesley (1905-1995) reorganized and expanded its holdings through her own collecting efforts. For patrons of the library, she was an invaluable resource with a profound knowledge of black history and culture. In 1973 associate Letitia Woods Brown said that Porter Wesley "has the broadest understanding of Black bibliography of anyone living. If it has been written or even spoken about, Dorothy Porter knows." The same year another associate, Benjamin Quarles, stated that "without exaggeration, there hasn't been a major history book in the last 30 years in which the author hasn't acknowledged Mrs. Porter's help."

After serving as the director of the Moorland Foundation for 43 years, Porter Wesley retired in 1973 and the library's name was changed to the Moorland-Spingarn Research Center. Largely through the efforts of Porter Wesley, the MSRC has become one of the most valuable resources for the study of the black experience.

Aaron Myers

See Also
Du Bois, William Edward Burghardt (W. E. B.); Moorland, Jesse Edward; Wesley, Dorothy Burnett Porter.

Latin America and the Caribbean

Morales, José María

(b. August 14, 1818, Buenos Aires, Argentina; d. October 23, 1894, Buenos Aires, Argentina), one of the highest-ranking Afro-Argentine military leaders and a musician, poet, and politician.

José María Morales was the son of a military man who fought in the Battle of the Patricios in 1807 against the British forces. His father's continued participation in Argentina's independence and civil wars forced Morales to leave school early and work as a tinsmith. In 1838 Morales followed his father's example, setting out for Montevideo to fight with the Unitarians (who envisioned a centralized political system based in Buenos Aires) in exile against the Argentine leader Juan Manuel Rosas. Rosas enjoyed widespread support in the black community – including the support of Domingo Sosa, another rising Afro-Argentine military figure and a contemporary of Morales – in part because his opposition to Buenos Aires's white Creole elite allowed for a more socially diverse society. Yet Rosas's highly authoritarian government sparked opposition, especially among some middle-class blacks, including Morales. Argentina's civil war lasted until 1852, when the Unitarians finally marched triumphantly into Buenos Aires and Rosas went into exile in England. The Unitarians assumed control of the city and province of Buenos Aires, establishing it as the seat of a highly centralized national government at the expense of the political power of the other provinces.

The future colonel Morales continued to serve in many battles, including the war against Paraguay (1865-1870) and the so-called Conquest of the Desert, the war against the Indians who lived in the southern plains of the country (1879-1880). Having held a variety of military posts, as a gunrunner, battlefield soldier, commander, and military strategist, he went on to become chief of conscription. In 1874 Morales became a regional representative in the Buenos Aires legislature during the presidency of Nicolás Avellaneda (1874-1880), serving for three terms. He took part in the convention to reform the constitution of Buenos Aires in the late 1870s and later participated in yet another revolution, this time against President Miguel Juárez Celman in 1890. Shortly before his death he was named head of the National Penitentiary by President Carlos Pellegrini (1890-1892).

Despite his many accomplishments and the fact that he became a hero within Afro-Argentine communities, literary critic Marvín Lewis points out that today Morales appears more frequently in the often ignored Afro-Argentine sources than in military history books. Historian George Reid Andrews explains that mythologizing black patriot martyrs was a convenient way of writing them out of the history that followed the wars: "By claiming an almost complete destruction of the black male population through military service, the nation's historians were able to ignore the fact that many of those soldiers returned alive from the wars to contribute to Buenos Aires's cultural, social, and demographic development." Horacio Mendizábal, perhaps the most famous Afro-Argentine poet, dedicated two poems to Morales in *First Verses*, "¡Alerta!" and "Conmemoración de la Batalla de Cepeda." Another compatriot, Jorge Miguel Ford, in his biographical volume, *Beneméritos de mi estirpe* (Outstanding Members of My Race), included Morales as one of a number of prominent Afro-Argentine military figures, writers, composers, and intellectuals.

Joy Elizondo

Latin America and the Caribbean

Moré, Beny

(Bartolome Maximilliano Moré) (b. August 24, 1919, Santa Isabel de las Lajas, Cuba; d. February 19, 1963, Havana, Cuba), Afro-Cuban singer and bandleader regarded by many critics as the greatest popular singer Cuba has ever produced.

Beny Moré was one of Cuba's greatest singers and entertainers. Cuba's musical culture draws upon the dual legacy of Africa and Europe. Moré was not only a talented vocalist, he was a master of both the Afro-Cuban and the more European-derived musical traditions. He was a superb interpreter of a wide range of musical styles, including the son, the mambo, the rumba, the bolero, and the Spanish-derived rural music known as *guajiro*. Early in his career he sang both up-tempo songs and ballads, but by the 1950s he was concentrating primarily on ballads, especially boleros and slow-tempo *son*. In *Salsa!*, Hernando Calvo Ospina writes that Moré was "the greatest *son* musician of all time." Music writer Spencer Harrington has observed that in the three decades since his death, no Cuban singer has been able to replace him.

As a teenager Bartolome Maximiliano Moré moved to Havana, where he performed as a street singer, making ends meet by taking various odd jobs. In 1945 he toured Mexico with the band of Miguel Matamoro and remained behind when the band returned to Cuba. Before departing Mexico, Matamoro advised Moré to change his name: *bartolo* meant donkey in Mexican slang. Moré took the name Beny. Two years later he was given a contract by RCA-Victor Mexico. RCA paired Moré with a number of large orchestras, notably that of fellow Cuban expatriate Dámaso Pérez Prado. In these early recordings Moré showed himself to be a mature vocalist. Harrington notes that Moré's "signature vocal technique" was an impressive upward glissando in which he "would hold a note, then slide up the scale to a higher note and hold it" in turn.

After a series of influential and popular recordings in Mexico, Moré returned to Cuba in 1953, where he assembled his own big band, featuring musicians like trumpeter Alfredo "Chocolate" Armenteros and trombonist and arranger Generoso "El Tojo" Jimenez. Although Moré could not read music, he composed two of his most popular songs, which others then transcribed into musical notation: "*Bonito y sabroso*" and "*Que bueno baila usted*." His orchestra established itself as Cuba's quintessential big band, and for the rest of his life he toured the country with it. Moré remained in Cuba after the Cuban Revolution and died of cirrhosis of the liver six months short of his 44th birthday.

James Clyde Sellman

See Also
Armenteros, Alfredo "Chocolate."

North America

Morehouse College, America's only historically black, all male liberal arts college; Martin Luther King Jr.'s alma mater.

Morehouse College, located in Atlanta, Georgia, has conferred bachelor's degrees on more African American men than any other private college in the nation. Each year it educates nearly 3000 students from more than 40 states and 18 foreign countries. It provides a balanced liberal arts education in the social sciences, mathematics, natural sciences, arts, humanities, and business. But Morehouse is perhaps best known for the achievements of its distinguished alumni, who include Martin Luther King Jr., Olympian Edwin Moses, filmmaker Spike Lee, former Atlanta mayor Maynard Jackson, activist Julian Bond, and several United States congressmen.

The college was founded in 1867 as the Augusta Institute to train blacks for professions in teaching and ministry. Three ministers, William Jefferson White, Richard C. Coulter, and Edmund Turney, organized the institute and conducted its first classes in the basement of Springfield Baptist Church, which today ranks as the oldest independent African American church in the country. Twelve years later the institute moved to the basement of Friendship Baptist Church in Atlanta and changed its name to the Atlanta Baptist Seminary.

In 1906 John Hope became the first African American president of the college. Hope, a Phi Beta Kappa graduate of Brown University, led the college during an era of unprecedented growth. Under his leadership the college was renamed Morehouse in 1913, in honor of Henry L. Morehouse, the white secretary of the Northern Baptist Home Mission Society.

Morehouse College gained an international reputation for excellence in 1940 when another African American, Benjamin Mays, assumed the presidency. Mays, considered by many to be the father of the Civil Rights Movement, was a mentor and friend to Martin Luther King Jr. While Mays was president, from 1940 until 1967, the number of faculty members grew and the percentage with doctoral degrees tripled.

During Mays's tenure the term "Morehouse Man" came to symbolize an elite group of young men – confident, intelligent, and honest leaders. Morehouse men were the best educated and, often, the most prominent African American men in the country. It is what many refer to as the "Morehouse Mystique," an image that has brought criticism that the college is an elitist institution catering exclusively to the black middle class. Despite this criticism, Morehouse has managed consistently to provide a high-quality education for students from all backgrounds.

As one of 109 historically black colleges and universities (HBCUs) in the United States, Morehouse continues to contribute to the education and empowerment of the entire African American community. Morehouse is a member of the Atlanta University Center (AUC), the oldest and largest consortium of historically black, private institutions of higher education in the world. It is located in downtown Atlanta and comprises six

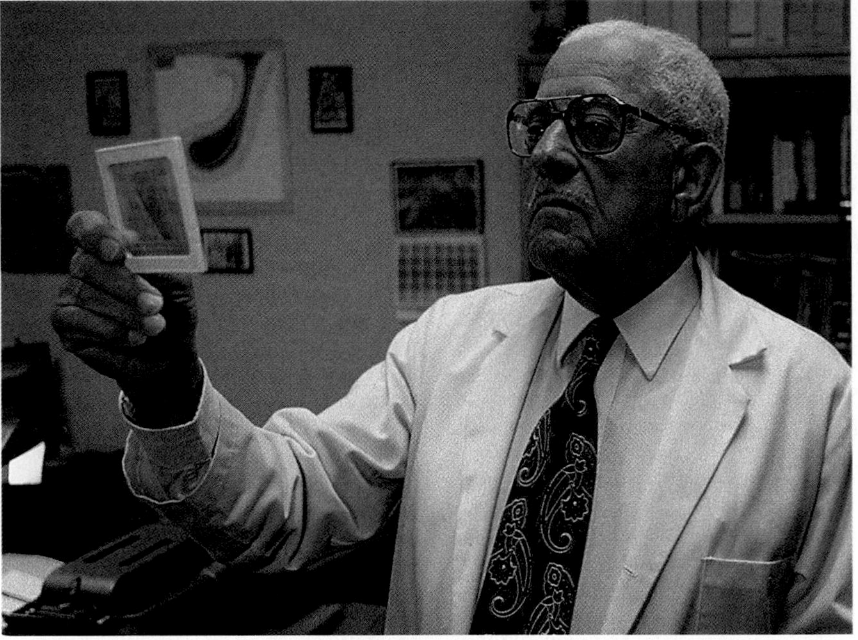

TOP: Graduates of Morehouse College, Spelman College, and Atlanta University at the schools' combined commencement in 1968. *CORBIS/James L. Amos*
ABOVE: Morehouse Professor Frederick Mapp, a specialist in freshwater biology, studies a transparency in his laboratory. *CORBIS/Bob Krist*

interlinked campuses represented by six independent black institutions: Clark Atlanta University; the Interdenominational Theological Center; the Morehouse School of Medicine; Morehouse College; Morris Brown College; and Spelman College.

Alonford James Robinson, Jr.

See Also

Jackson, Maynard Holbrook, Jr.; King, Martin Luther, Jr.; Lee, Shelton Jackson ("Spike"); Mays, Benjamin Elijah.

Latin America and the Caribbean

Morejón, Nancy

(b. 1944, Havana, Cuba), Afro-Cuban poet, historian, translator, and literary critic; the best-known black woman poet in Spanish America.

Nancy Morejón grew up in a working-class district of Havana known as Los Sitios. As a young child she was discouraged by her parents from observing the Santería religion (a traditional Yoruban-based Cuban faith). Nevertheless she absorbed Santería's musical rites, like performances of neighborhood rumba bands through members of her extended family. (Rumba is an Afro-Cuban song and dance form that synthesizes Bantu-derived rituals and rhythms. It was later modified into a ballroom dance.) She is particularly interested in Afro-Cuban religious forms as modes of cultural expression. In her article "Las poéticas de Nancy Morejón," she explains that she incorporates Santería themes and motifs in her literary work. References to Yoruba deities such as Eleggua and Oshun are abundant in her poetry (*see* Orishas).

Morejón's parents, though not formally educated, emphasized her education from an early age and instilled in her a love for reading. She first read poetry in her father's collection of books by Cuba's national poet, Nicolás Guillén. As a consequence she developed an early appreciation for poetry and languages. By age 13 she had mastered English, translating for her family during her cousin's wedding to a Protestant North American minister. Taking advantage of the free education available as a result of the Cuban Revolution (*see* Cuba), she went on to study French language and literature at the University of Havana. In an interview with Lucía Suárez, Morejón highlighted the importance of knowing several languages, saying, "[It] gives you the opportunity to see other literary worlds and compare different methods of doing literature."

In 1962 Morejón published her first collection of poems, titled *Mutismos* (Silences). These poems illustrated her fundamental poetic concerns and provided her with a foundation and aesthetic framework for decades to come: a kind of self-examination of her role as a black woman and as a young writer against the backdrop of the climactic changes of the Cuban Revolution. Literary critic William Luis notes that these early poems are marked by intimate self-examination as well as Morejón's proud assertion of her Afro-Cuban roots (*see* Afrocubanismo). In 1964 she published *Amor, ciudad atribuida* (Love, Attributed City) and in 1967 another poetry collection titled *Richard trajo su flauta* (Richard Brought His Flute). During the late 1960s Morejón began to experiment with the more conversational and less abstract style that characterizes many of the works of other revolutionary poets. In addition, she focused on collective political and historical themes as manifested through race, gender, and Afro-Cuban religions in her personal experience, as literary critic Miriam DeCosta Willis points out.

In 1979 Morejón published *Parajes de una época* (Places of an Era), which renews her commitment to the revolution while placing less emphasis on racial pride and Afro-Cuban themes. Luis attributes this shift in the author's writing to growing nationalist tendencies in Cuba at that time, in part exacerbated by the intensification of the conflict with the United States. In 1982 Morejón published *Cuadernos de Granada* (Grenada Notebook) and in 1984 *Piedra pulida* (On Polished Stone).

From a critical standpoint Morejón's 1993 collection, *Paisaje célebre* (Famous Landscape), a finalist in the international poetry competition of Pérez Bonalde, represents the most recent stage of the author's poetry and a relative break with her previous work. As Luis writes, *Paisaje célebre* "underscores a coming to terms with a struggle within, regarding her poetry and position in the revolution." With this book Morejón emerges as an independent Cuban writer whose poetry is informed but not dominated by race and revolutionary politics.

In addition to poetry Morejón has written important works of literary criticism, including a crucial study on the poetry of Guillén titled *Nación y mestizaje en Nicolás Guillén* (Nation and Racial Mixture in Nicolás Guillén). Until 1995 she directed the editorial house Ediciones PM, of the Pablo Milanés Foundation, a multimedia nonprofit center for the promotion and support of all artistic expression that "contributes to the preservation of the cultural identity of the Cuban nation." Morejón continues to write poetry and literary criticism while residing in Havana. She often travels to Europe, Latin America, Africa, the Caribbean, and the United States. Her poetry has been translated into many languages.

Joy Elizondo

See Also

Literature, Black, in Spanish America; Religions, African, in Latin America and the Caribbean; Exú; Oxum.

Latin America and the Caribbean

Morel Campos, Juan

(b. May 16, 1857, Ponce, Puerto Rico; d. May 12, 1896, Ponce, Puerto Rico), Afro-Puerto Rican composer and musician; critical figure in the development of the *danza*, a musical style that incorporates Afro-Caribbean and European elements.

Juan Morel Campos was born in the city of Ponce, the main cultural center of Puerto Rico during the nineteenth century. He studied music and composition with Manuel G. Tavárez, the most acclaimed Puerto Rican composer of his time. His musical production was varied and rich, and included *zarzuelas* (Spanish light opera), masses, symphonies, waltzes, marches, and danzas. It was through his danzas that Morel Campos made his most important and lasting contribution to classical music in Latin America (*see* Music, Classical, in Latin America and the Caribbean). Of the 550 works attributed to him, approximately half of them are danzas for piano, including *No me toques, El torbellino, Felices días,* and *Vano empeño.*

Morel Campos created a distinct national style by modifying the classic European molds. For his creative compositions he is considered the father of the *danza puertorriqueña.* Like other composers in Cuba, Mexico, and Brazil, he transformed classical styles by incorporating Afro-Caribbean styles and folk-rhythmic formulas in his compositions.

In 1882 Morel Campos founded the Firemen's Band of Ponce, one of the first bands in Puerto Rico. He conducted many concerts in Ponce and in various towns around the island at a time of national awakening and cultural enthusiasm. He also toured South America with a company of zarzuelas.

Unfortunately, Morel Campos's production ended prematurely when he suffered a stroke while conducting the overture of an opera in Ponce. He died a few days later before reaching age 40.

Carlos Dalmau

Latin America and the Caribbean

Morelos, José María

(b. September 30, 1765, Valladolid, New Spain [present-day Mexico]; d. December 22, 1815, San Cristóbal Ecatepec, New Spain), mulatto leader of the Mexican wars of independence (1810-1821).

José María Morelos y Pavón was born in Valladolid, New Spain – what is now the city of Morelia in the Mexican state of Michoacán (the city was named in his honor). Educated there, he worked as a scribe and accountant from 1779 to 1799, when he began studies for the priesthood. The Catholic Church had long forbidden blacks, mulattos, and *zambos* (Afro-Indians) to become priests.

A former priest who played an important role in winning Mexican independence, José María Morelos practiced progressive racial policies in his military command. *Oronoz*

However, Morelos's baptismal record had been tampered with – he was originally designated a mulatto, but the record later indicated that he was white – and throughout his life the leader maintained that he was of Spanish (white) descent. In all likelihood his parents paid the local priest to make the change in his baptismal record so he would receive more favorable treatment in New Spain's rigid caste system (*see* COLONIAL LATIN AMERICA AND THE CARIBBEAN).

Morelos's studies took him to the College of San Nicolás, where he met Miguel Hidalgo y Costilla (1753-1811), future leader of the Mexican independence movement. On completing his religious education in 1796, Morelos became an auxiliary priest; in 1799 he was ordained as a full priest. For the next decade he was parish priest in a string of towns in present-day Michoacán: Churumuco, La Huacana, Carácuaro, and Nocupétaro.

In September 1810 Hidalgo initiated the Mexican struggle for independence with a call to Indians, *mestizos* (persons of indigenous and European descent), and Afro-Mexicans to overthrow Spanish rule and the white-dominated caste system. Morelos soon joined Hidalgo, who charged the former with raising troops in southern Mexico. Morelos spent the latter part of 1810 mustering men and weapons. While in this position of authority he encouraged social change within the movement. He abolished slavery and the caste system in his ranks and prohibited his followers from describing themselves with racial terms like "mulatto" or "Indian." Racial conflict nonetheless stirred among his men. When two officers tried to incite blacks to slaughter whites in the army, Morelos had the instigators shot (*see* RACIAL QUESTION DURING STRUGGLES OF INDEPENDENCE IN LATIN AMERICA).

In 1810 and 1811 Morelos entered the first of his conflicts against the Spanish royalist army, which included a long-running siege of the port town Acapulco. Although Acapulco would not succumb to his troops for two more years, Morelos achieved far-reaching victories throughout the rest of south central Mexico. By the time Hidalgo was executed by a Spanish firing squad in midsummer of 1811, Morelos was the clear heir apparent of the revolt.

Morelos's successes in south central Mexico continued through 1813. At the end of the year he convened a Supreme Congress that vested him with executive power for the insurgent provinces. In short order, however, he suffered a series of battlefield defeats, including significant setbacks in his hometown of Valladolid in December 1813, in Puruarán in January 1814, and in Tlacotepec in February 1814. Morelos spent much of the last two years of his life protecting the rebel congress as it fled from one town to the next in the face of royalist advances.

On November 5, 1815, at Temalaca in what is now the state of Guerrero, Morelos was captured during one such protective run. He was immediately taken to Mexico City, tried, found guilty, and condemned to death. His execution on December 22 marked the end, for several years, of the organized rebellion. His legacy to Afro-Latin Americans remains complex. Morelos is largely heralded for his progressive social policies, for his martyrdom, and for taking difficult positions (such as denying his black heritage) in order to advance worthy anticaste positions. However, some latter-day critics have argued that his attempts to abolish slavery and the caste system were little more than gambits to win support for his anti-Spanish army; they also question whether Morelos would have made such bold moves if he had won control of all of Mexico.

SEE ALSO

Complexities of Ethnic and Racial Terminology in Latin America and the Caribbean; Catholic Church in Latin America and the Caribbean.

North America

Morgan, Garrett Augustus

(b. March 4, 1875, Paris, Ky.; d. July 27, 1963, Cleveland, Ohio), African American inventor and community leader who invented the gas mask and the automatic traffic signal.

At age 14 Garrett Augustus Morgan moved to CINCINNATI, OHIO, and became a handyman. In 1895 he moved to Cleveland, where he worked as a sewing machine repairman. There he developed several successful enterprises: a sewing machine repair service in 1907, a tailor shop in 1909, and a hair-straightening company in 1913. The most important of his various inventions was a "breathing device" that served as the prototype for the modern gas mask. In 1914 the National Safety Device company awarded the Morgan Safety Hood First Grand Prize.

On July 25, 1916, Morgan demonstrated the use of his invention by wearing it as he, along with others, rescued 24 trapped workers from a smoke-filled tunnel beneath Lake Erie. The city of Cleveland awarded Morgan a gold medal for his heroism, which led to a contract from the United States Navy to develop his hood for combat use. It was used in World War I and by fire departments throughout the country, although some canceled their orders when they discovered that the inventor was black.

In 1922 Morgan patented the three-way automatic traffic signal. Before this time, traffic signals had no yellow caution light. Morgan's signal gave drivers warning to slow down before a red stop light. Noting the marked improvement in traffic safety, the General Electric Company bought the rights to his invention in 1923 for $40,000 and developed today's standard three-way traffic light.

In addition to his work on safety devices, Morgan was involved in civil rights work. From 1920 to 1923 he published the African American newspaper *Cleveland Call,* and he was a long-standing member of the Cleveland branch of the National Association for the Advancement of Colored People (NAACP).

See Also
World War I and African Americans.

North America

Morgan, Sister Gertrude

(b. April 7, 1900, Lafayette, Ala.; d. 1980), African American artist and preacher whose religious folk art and colorful personality made an invaluable contribution to the street culture of New Orleans.

Sister Gertrude Morgan became an evangelist and moved to New Orleans in 1939 at age 39. She took the title Sister in the 1950s when, with two other street missionaries, she founded a church and an orphanage.

Morgan began painting in 1956, concentrating primarily on religious visions and biblical scenes. She believed that she was mystically married to Jesus Christ, which she symbolized by dressing entirely in white. Her paintings frequently depicted her with Jesus as bride and groom, often with herself in black before and in white after the marriage. As a street preacher she eschewed the formal art world, preferring to make folk art with any material at hand, including styrofoam, cardboard, lampshades, and jelly jars. Her work frequently includes calligraphy that communicates a spiritual message or a biblical verse. All her inspiration, she felt, came from God. "He moves my hand," she said. "Do you think I would ever know how to do a picture like this by myself?"

Among her most famous works is a series of illustrated scenes from the Book of Revelations, which she called "charters." She also made fans, which she distributed during her prayer meetings. In 1971 her original prayer compositions were set to music and were released as an album, *Let's Make a Record.*

See Also
New Orleans, Louisiana.

North America

Mormons, indigenous American religious group with an ambivalent history regarding people of African descent.

The recent rapid growth of the Church of Jesus Christ of Latter-Day Saints (commonly known as the Mormons) among the black populations of Africa, the Caribbean, and Brazil has reversed a long-standing trend within the church. Mormons traditionally have refused to ordain people of African descent to the priesthood, a status conferred on all adult males. Indeed, when Mormon missionaries tried to settle in Nigeria in the 1960s – in itself a radical departure from the usual practice of avoiding missionary work in predominantly black communities – they were denied residency visas by the Nigerian government because of their discriminatory policies.

Founded in 1830, the Mormon Church adopted an explicitly racist doctrine that claimed that the skin tones of black people were the sign of a curse that God placed on the descendants of Cain and Ham for refusing to follow his will. The Mormons believed that as punishment for this wickedness, people of African descent were condemned to perpetual servitude. In the first decade after the church was organized, only about half a dozen African Americans joined – and those who did are remembered more for being expelled from the church than for their work within it. While Elijah Abel became a respected elder, others, such as Black Peter and William McLary, were expelled for having revelations that competed with those of the church leaders.

After the Mormons established themselves in Utah in 1844, church leader Brigham Young further affirmed a ban on black ordination and approved An Act in Relation to Service. The act reversed the church's surprising abolitionist stance and legalized black slavery, making Utah the only slave state in the American West. After Emancipation following the Civil War, the subordinate status of people of African descent within the church remained unchanged, but the Mormon position on race was confused as missionaries ventured into the wide world. A black man thought to be Native Hawaiian was ordained by mistake, as were two elders later revealed to have African ancestry.

Only during the Civil Rights Movement did the church become more flexible, primarily through the work of outsiders. Although Mormon elders were resistant, in 1963 the small but active Utah chapter of the National Association for the Advancement of Colored People pressured the church into issuing a proclamation in support of civil rights. Two years later the Mormon-dominated Utah legislature enacted legislation favoring nondiscriminatory treatment in housing and employment. In 1971 three black people were allowed positions within the famous Mormon Tabernacle Choir, and the Mormons' Brigham Young University began recruiting black students, although largely for its athletic teams. In 1978 the Mormons finally lifted their ban on ordaining black males, but the church remains mostly white.

Peter Hudson

See Also
Civil War, American; Thirteenth Amendment of the United States Constitution and the Emancipation Proclamation.

Africa

Morocco, hereditary monarchy in the northwest of Africa, bounded on the north by the Mediterranean Sea, on the east and southeast by Algeria, on the south by Western Sahara, and on the west by the Atlantic Ocean. The southeastern boundary, in the Sahara, is not precisely defined.

Morocco is a nation known by its cities. Marrakech, Rabat, Fès, Casablanca, and Tangier all played crucial roles in the nation's dynastic history, serving as political, economic, and cultural capitals of the kingdoms that mapped what is now Moroccan territory. For centuries these cities also provided vital centers for the commerce in goods and ideas that came from the Islamic world and Christian Europe as well as sub-Saharan Africa. In the nineteenth century, as European investment poured in, Morocco's cities held perhaps too much appeal: the gravitation of people and resources toward urban areas, especially on the coast, sapped the vitality of the rural agricultural economy on which urban prosperity had always depended. After becoming perilously indebted to Europe, Morocco fell under French control in the early twentieth century. Even as French colonial planners (*see* Urbanism and Urbanization in Africa) attempted to impose functionality and racial segregation on Morocco's cities, European and American artists, writers, and wanderers were drawn by a vision of the "exotic" beauty of Morocco. Today Morocco's economy still depends largely on agriculture, but its cities remain dynamic commercial centers as well as destinations for migrants seeking a better life and travelers in search of legends.

History

The Berber people have lived in the region of present-day Morocco since about the second millennium B.C.E. Although a

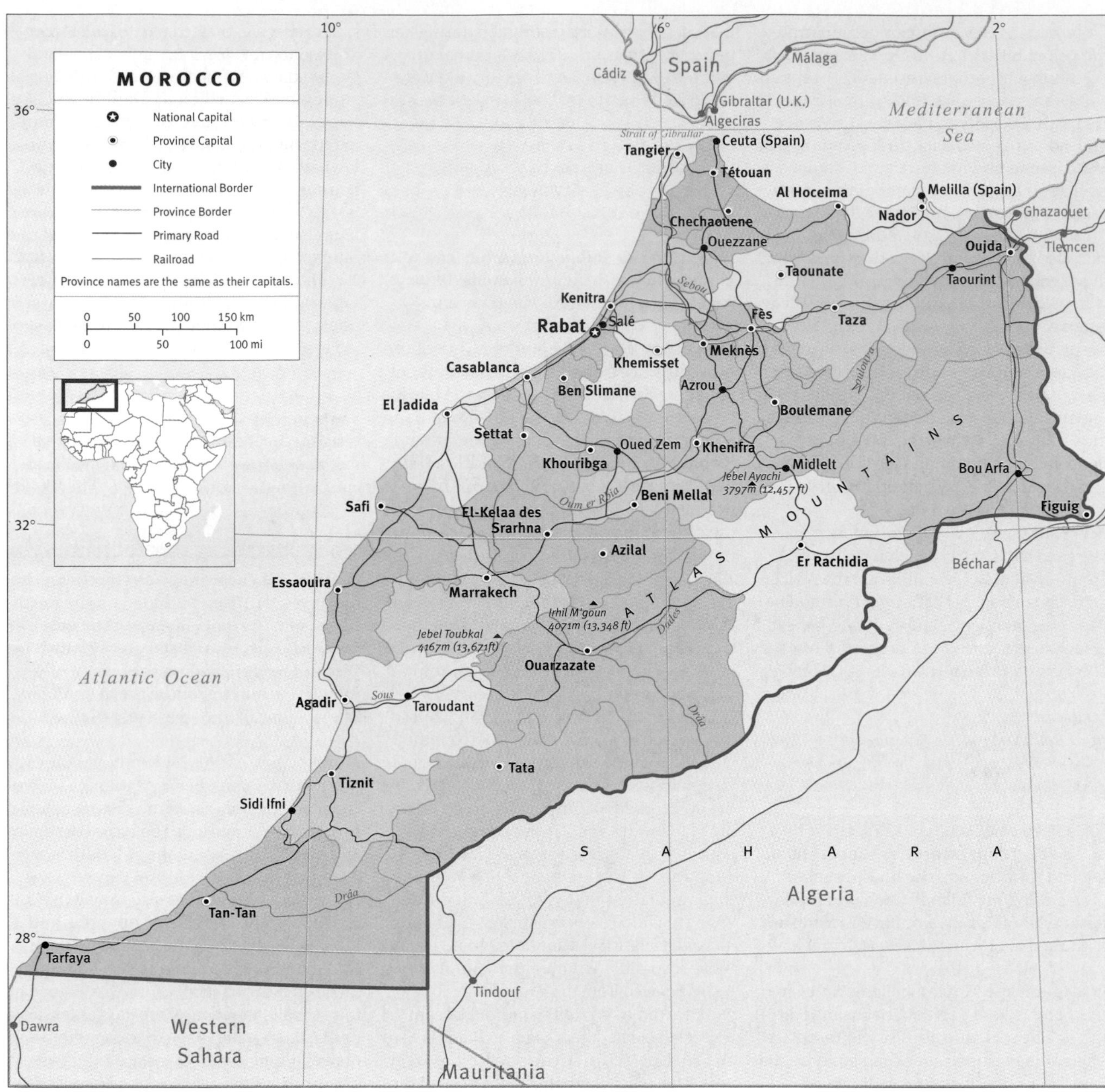

number of dynasties flourished on Moroccan soil, they were all influenced by Berber political traditions, such as decentralized rule by confederacies. Berber confederacies sometimes helped to direct the course of Moroccan history, as strong Berber rulers mounted religious or political reform movements. At the same time the Berber identity itself was shaped by migrations and invasions from Romans, Arabs, Europeans, and Africans of the Sahara.

When the Romans came to northern Africa in the second century B.C.E., they sought control of the region they called Mauretania Tingitana through alliances with Berber confederacies. By the first century B.C.E. Roman cultural influences were felt mostly in the cities, where immigrants from the larger Roman world brought to North Africa the religions of Christianity and Judaism. After the Vandals, a Germanic tribe, conquered Roman holdings to the east (in what is now ALGERIA and TUNISIA), the Berbers resumed control of the Moroccan region.

Although Arab raiders had first passed into the coastal plains beyond the Taza Gap of the Atlas Mountains in 683 C.E., most Berbers did not convert to Islam until Musa ibn Nusayr pushed west the border of the region the Arabs called Ifriqiya. Morocco then fell under the political and religious leadership of the Umayyad Dynasty, which was based in Damascus. As the Berbers converted to Islam and intermarried with Arabs, they became an important military force for Islamic incursions into southern SPAIN.

IDRIS I was one of the strongest Berber rulers, bringing the region under definitive Islamic rule. According to one legend, he founded twin Arab and Berber cities at Fès; another legend credits Idris with founding one city and his son, Idris II, with founding its twin. With the opening of al Qarawîyîn University in 859, the city of Fès flourished as a center for learning, attracting Muslims from southern Spain and Ifriquiya. Some historians credit the Idris Dynasty with creating around Fès the first Moroccan state, but it did not control the entire area comprising present-day Morocco: some territory remained under the control of Umayyad emirs in southern Spain or the Fatimid Empire in eastern Ifriquiya, and several Berber confederacies maintained autonomous rule in neighboring territories. During the ninth century Idris's kingdom fragmented as Idris II followed the Berber tradition of succession, dividing the kingdom among seven sons rather than passing it on whole.

Two hundred years later a religious reformation generated another empire and metropolis. The Almoravids began as a confederacy of religious warriors, Berbers who founded a brotherhood in secluded fortified retreats. They secured their economic prosperity by exerting control over portions of the trans-Saharan trade routes. In 1062 the Almoravids founded the city of Marrakech as their capital, and by the end of the century they had pushed the borders of their empire east to Algiers, south to the Senegal River, and north to the Ebro River in Spain.

During the next century the Almoravids' political power waned. In 1146 the Almohads massacred the inhabitants of Marrakech and seized control of the region. Although the Almohads ruled through a centralized Islamic theocracy, they incorporated Berber traditions of rule, such as representative government and tribal councils. They also sponsored an intellectual renaissance, and even after the Almohads moved their throne to Andalusian Spain, philosophers and scientists such as Ibn Bajja (Avempace), Ibn Tufayl, Ibn Rushd (Averroës), and the great explorer Ibn Battutah came to live in Morocco. At the same time that Morocco's cities became centers of Islamic scholarship, the face of the countryside was also changing as the Hilalian, originally Bedouin Arabs, settled the Maghreb, bringing with them Arabic culture and language.

In 1212 the Almohads were defeated on European soil by the Spanish, who were engaged in a Christian reconquest of Spain, and by the Marinids, a dynasty rising from the Zenata Berber confederacy in northwestern Africa. For 50 years the region was engaged in war, in part over the trans-Saharan gold and salt trades with the western Sudan. The Spanish and Portuguese took advantage of the instability to capture coastal enclaves such as Tétouan and Ceuta, which were seen as key locations to the reconquest of Granada. A branch of the Marinids, the Wattasids, held onto Tangier, and when Granada fell in 1492, they received thousands of fleeing Spanish Muslims and Jews.

This period marked the rise of the mystical Marabout tradition. Begun as a philosophic tradition perpetuated by wandering Sufi mystics, the marabouts gained a populist foothold in Morocco during the period of Marinid decline. During the fifteenth and sixteenth centuries these "men of the soil" became the political leaders of small republics in Morocco.

In the late sixteenth century another power rose in the south and became a major trade empire along the trans-Saharan trade route. The Sa'dians, originally Arab nomads, took Marrakech and Fès, defeating the Wattasids as they waged a holy war against Christians. Once established, the Sa'dians resisted the incursions of both the Ottomans, who held North Africa to the east, and the Portuguese. In 1591 one of the strongest Sa'dian rulers, Ahmed al-Mansur (1578-1603) conquered a portion of the gold-rich Songhai Empire, including Gao and Tombouctou (Timbuktu). Although after the initial looting Ahmed al-Mansur did not find as much gold as he had anticipated, he nevertheless took Songhai captives for his army. Moroccan rule in the Sahara never went uncontested, but Ahmed al-Mansur's leadership unified Morocco as a political entity. With the wealth acquired in military campaigns, Ahmed al-Mansur sponsored a golden age of cultural revival.

For a short period after the death of Ahmed al-Mansur, the state was divided under the rule of rival sultanates, until Mawlay al-Rashid and his successor, Mawlay Isma'il, founded the Alawid Dynasty. They raised their grand palace in Meknès and filled the ranks of the 150,000-strong professional army with slaves captured in the western Sudan as well as Berber, European, and Turkish mercenaries. Although confederacies beyond the Atlas Mountains paid tribute, the Alawids directly controlled and taxed only the coastal areas near Fès and Marrakesh.

After the death of Mawlay Isma'il in 1727, political control was wielded by the elite personal guard of his former army through a series of puppet sultans. Beginning in the early nineteenth century a new European influence spread in Morocco: speculation and investment. France, Great Britain, Germany, and Spain – nations whose influences were previously contained – benefited from a series of trade agreements with Morocco. France became Morocco's major creditor; Great Britain built railroads; and Germany acquired the largest amount of foreign-held property. Spain, meanwhile, held several coastal regions, including Ceuta, which it had acquired from the Portuguese in 1580, and a portion of western Sahara that had

Moroccan horsemen brandish elaborately ornamented guns as they gallop in a Fantasia, a traditional Arabic equestrian event. *CORBIS/Robert van der Hilst*

been placed under a Spanish protectorate in 1884. Relations with Europe were often tense. After France invaded neighboring Algeria in 1830, resistance leader ABD AL-QADIR used Morocco as a base for anticolonial activities, prompting skirmishes on the border and, finally, French bombardment of Tangier and Essaouira. The sultan clashed with Spain over the borders of Ceuta, and, following a threat of war, Morocco was forced to cede the enclave of Ifni.

Morocco's internal economy was transformed at this time. As agricultural exports to Europe boomed during the AMERICAN CIVIL WAR, Morocco increased European imports such as textiles and leather, displacing the traditional markets for goods produced locally. When European demand for grain declined, a trade imbalance developed and Morocco's rural economy stagnated. Migrants flocked to the port cities looking for work, further undermining the once dynamic relationship between the cities, with their craft industries, and the rural areas, which had provided raw materials as well as markets for urban goods. Meanwhile, a small, elite Moroccan population benefited from trade with the Europeans and emerged as a powerful bourgeois class.

ABOVE: Dressed in traditional finery, a Berber man awaits his wedding. *CORBIS/Robert van der Hilst*
LEFT: A Berber bride wears her robe and jewelry at an engagement festival in Imilchil, Morocco. *CORBIS/Nik Wheeler*

As Morocco's economy increasingly fell under foreign control, Sultan Mawlay Hassan I took steps to maintain sovereignty. He reorganized the Moroccan army, enacted a series of modernizing reforms, and even secured European guarantees for Morocco's independence at the Madrid Conference of 1880. His son and successor, Abd al-Aziz, attempted to Europeanize the court and introduced an unpopular land taxation. But the monarchy fragmented in the face of regional rebellions, rival court systems, and popular discontent. European creditors stepped in to enact a series of trade agreements that, among other stipulations, allowed foreigners to hold property and exempted them from local taxes.

France moved to occupy Morocco in 1904, after ceding its claims on EGYPT to Britain, its claims on LIBYA to Italy, and granting some Moroccan territory to Spain. The Germans, ignored in this divvying-up of North Africa, sought to undermine French authority by encouraging nationalist resistance, which nearly led to war in 1904 and again in 1911. After negotiations, the Germans agreed to a French protectorate in Morocco. With little alternative, the sultan of Morocco acquiesced, signing the Treaty of Fès in 1912.

FRENCH RULE AND MOROCCAN RESISTANCE

The treaty gave France control of Morocco's foreign relations, police powers, and finances. Although it stripped the sultan of most of his powers, it did grant him the right to veto protectorate legislation, a right that would become critical during the nationalist struggle. The treaty left about a tenth of the country under Spanish control, including parts of present-day WESTERN SAHARA, and granted Tangier special status as an international zone. Some parts of the south were also left under semi-independent Berber control, but France moved quickly to suppress dissident groups, particularly Marabout rulers in the Atlas Mountains.

Industrialization and modernization in early twentieth-century Morocco brought more railroads, electricity, and irrigation. Most of these benefits were enjoyed primarily by the protectorate's European population, who appropriated the richest agricultural land and established elite, European-only neighborhoods in the cities and towns, including the commercial port of Casablanca. Protectorate administration was based in Rabat.

Abd al-Krim led the first major anticolonial revolt in the Spanish-held northern coastal area, where he founded the Rif Republic. In the French territory two separate movements merged by 1930: the Salafiya religious reform movement and the secret reformist organizations led by French-educated students in Rabat and Fès. Protonationalists harnessed the popular resentment provoked by French attempts to divide Berbers and Arabs and in 1934 founded the reformist Comité d'Action Marocaine (CAM; Moroccan Action Committee). Three years later Moroccans in Meknès rioted when town water was diverted to irrigate settler land. The French responded swiftly, exiling nationalist leader Muhammad 'Allal al-Fasi.

Internal tension was diverted during World War II (1939-1945), when more than 40,000 Moroccans served in the French army. The sultan, who called for full support for the French at the start of the war, refused to approve the subsequent French Vichy government's anti-Jewish measures. In 1942 American troops occupied the country, using it as a supply base for the Allied forces.

In 1944 the Hizb al-Istiqlal (Independence Party), known as Istiqlal, drafted a manifesto of independence. The French responded by arresting the leaders on accusations of Nazi collaboration. After French troops fired on crowds demonstrating in Fès, the French government, hoping to appease the outraged Moroccan populace, gave Sultan Sidi Muhammad permission to make his first visit to the Spanish Zone and Tangier. The sultan took the opportunity of a public appearance in Tangier to emphasize Morocco's ties to the rest of the Arab world rather than to France. Later the sultan used his veto power to halt the resident general's decrees that granted France more power. French troops, with the help of some Berber opposition factions, surrounded Fès and Rabat in 1951, forcing the sultan into temporary submission. Two years later they again surrounded Rabat, this time forcing the sultan out of office.

Opposition to French rule increased rapidly during the early 1950s, especially after a trade-union protest in Casablanca over the allegedly French-planned assassination of a union leader led to hundreds of arrests in 1952. By this time Istiqlal had more than 80,000 members and several hundred thousand sympathizers, including many from Berber communities. The French government, meanwhile, was increasingly preoccupied with civil unrest in colonial Algeria.

The 1955 French-Moroccan Agreement gave Morocco independence from the French, although the Spanish areas were ceded later – Tarfaya in 1958 and Ifni in 1969. In March 1956 the sultan became the king of independent Morocco, presiding over an appointed legislature, the Consultative Assembly.

TOP: A worker bags salt at the saltworks at Souk El Arsa Du Rhaul, Morocco. *© J. Joffre/Explorer*
ABOVE: Lengths of dyed cloth billow over the Street of Dyers in the famous bazaar of Marrakech, Morocco. *CORBIS/Robert Holmes*

Independent Morocco

Four years later the political alliance that won independence fragmented, as Istiqlal broke into conservative and socialist factions. Hassan II ascended to the throne amid growing antimonarchist sentiment and dissolved Parliament. After two unsuccessful military coups against him, Hassan II revived popular support through his aggressive tactics to claim contested territories.

The territories at stake included coastal enclaves and the Spanish Sahara. Although it had ceded the enclaves of Tarfaya and Ifni following Morocco's independence, Spain had held onto Ceuta and Melilla as well as phosphate-rich territory in the Sahara. Until 1970 Hassan II refused to recognize Mauritania, claiming the iron-ore rich region as a sphere of influence. He waged a war against Spain for the Western Sahara, and in 1975, after the United Nations (UN) declared that the territory should be self-determined, he organized the Green March that sent 350,000 unarmed people across the border to occupy the land and effectively claim it for Morocco. But even after Spain ceded Spanish Sahara to a joint Moroccan-Mauritanian administration the next year, King Hassan was still faced with the liberation group Polisario, who waged a guerrilla campaign for an independent state, the Saharan Arab Democratic Republic. The leaders of the independence movement won the support of Algeria, Libya, and, later, a number of foreign governments.

In the early 1980s the kingdom of Morocco undertook a program of structural adjustment in response to the demands of the International Monetary Fund (IMF) to improve the balance of foreign debt. As a result, basic food prices skyrocketed, workers declared a general strike, and a series of riots swept through the cities of Morocco, killing an estimated 200 people and injuring 5000 others. Human rights observers both inside and outside Morocco accused King Hassan at this time and later of using brutal methods, such as torture and detention without trial, to quash antimonarchist sentiment from socialist and Islamist groups as well as dissent from separatist Shrawi, or Western Sahara, groups. The UN scheduled a 1998 referendum for self-determination for Western Sahara, which is currently occupied by UN peacekeeping forces. Due to disagreements over eligibility, the referendum was postponed repeatedly.

Morocco approved a new constitution in 1992 and held a parliamentary election the following year. Despite the initial victory of the left-wing Socialist Union of Populist Forces, accusations of election fraud arose, and Loyalist parties ultimately carried the day. Although Morocco is once again attracting foreign investment in areas such as phosphate mining, export agriculture, and tourism, the nation currently faces rising unemployment and a decline in agricultural growth following a 1995 drought as well as civil unrest over the issue of the Western Sahara. King Hassan's death in July 1999 inspired days of mourning in Rabat, as some 20 heads of state gathered to pay their respects. Soon thereafter Hassan's son and heir, Mohammed VI, assumed the throne of one of the world's oldest monarchies.

Marian Aguiar

See Also

Casablanca, Morocco; Roman Africa: An Interpretation; Explorers in Africa Before 1500; Fès, Morocco; Gold Trade; Marrakech, Morocco; Nationalism in Africa; United Nations in Africa; Portugal; Rabat, Morocco; Sahara Desert; Salt Trade; Structural Adjustment in Africa; Tombouctou, Mali; World War II and African Americans.

Africa

Morocco (Ready Reference)

Official Name: Kingdom of Morocco
Area: 446,550 sq km (about 172,413 sq mi); the southeastern boundary, in the Sahara, is contested; within Morocco are the Spanish exclaves of Ceuta and Melilla.
Location: Northern Africa; borders the Mediterranean Sea, Algeria, Western Sahara, and the Atlantic Ocean
Capital: Rabat (population 1,472,000 [1990 estimate])
Other Major Cities: Casablanca (3,210,000), the country's largest city and main seaport; Marrakech (1,517,000) and Fès (1,012,000), both important trade centers; and Tangier (554,000), a seaport on a bay of the Strait of Gibraltar (1990 estimates)
Population: 29,114,497 (1998 estimate)
Population Density: 67 persons per sq km (about 172 persons per sq mi); the population has almost an equal number of urban and rural dwellers. Most Moroccans inhabit the Atlantic coastal plain.
Population Below Age 15: 36 percent (male 5,398,592; female 5,200,660 [1998 estimate])
Population Growth Rate: 1.89 percent (1998 estimate)
Total Fertility Rate: 3.5 children born per woman (1997 estimate)
Life Expectancy at Birth: Total population: 68.51 years (male 66.49 years; female 70.64 years [1996 estimate])
Infant Mortality Rate: 52.99 deaths per 1000 live births (1998 estimate)
Literacy Rate (age 15 and over who can read and write): Total population: 43.7 percent (male 56.6 percent; female 31 percent [1995 estimate])
Education: Schooling is compulsory in Morocco for children between ages 7 and 13, but significantly fewer girls than boys attend classes, and less than 40 percent of secondary-school-age Moroccans actually attend secondary school. Arabic is the main language of instruction, and French is also used in secondary schools. Traditional higher education is centered in Fès at al Qarawîyîn University, and modern higher education is offered at Mohammed V University, Mohammed Ben Abdellah University, Cadi Ayyad University, Hassan II University, and Mohammed I University.
Languages: Arabic is the official language. Berber languages, French, and Spanish are also spoken.
Ethnic Groups: Arab-Berber, 99.1 percent; European (mostly French), 0.7 percent; Jewish, 0.2 percent
Religions: Islam is the established state religion of Morocco. Almost the entire population is Sunni Muslim. The monarch is the supreme Muslim authority in the country. About 1 percent of the population is Christian, and less than 0.2 percent is Jewish.
Climate: Along the Mediterranean, Morocco has a subtropical climate, tempered by oceanic influences that give the coastal cities moderate temperatures averaging about 16.4° C (61.5° F) in January and 22.5° C (72.5° F) in August. Toward the interior, the mean temperature is 10° C (50° F) in January and 26.9° C (80.5° F) in August. At high altitudes temperatures of less than -17.8° C (0° F) are not uncommon. Rain falls mainly during the winter months, with precipitation heaviest in the northwest: about 955 mm (about 37.5 in) in Tangier and less than 102 mm (4 in) in the Sahara.
Land, Plants, and Animals: Morocco has an area of highlands, called Er Rif, that parallels the Mediterranean coast. The Atlas Mountains extend across the country in a southwestern to northeastern direction, while a region of broad coastal plains stretches along the Atlantic Ocean. South of the Atlas Mountains, plains and valleys merge with the Sahara along the southeastern borders of the country. Morocco has many rivers, including the Moulouya and the Sebou.

The mountainous regions of Morocco contain extensive forests, including large stands of cork oak, evergreen oak, juniper, cedar, fir, and pine. Moroccan wildlife includes the gazelle, wild boar, panther, baboon, wild goat, fox, rabbit, otter, squirrel, and horned viper.
Natural Resources: Morocco's resources are primarily agricultural, but mineral resources are also significant. Among the latter the most important is phosphate rock; other minerals include coal, iron, lead, manganese, petroleum, silver, tin, and zinc. Cork is a major forest product of Morocco.
Currency: The Moroccan dirham
Gross Domestic Product (GDP): $107 billion (1997 estimate)
GDP per Capita: $3500 (1997 estimate)
GDP Real Growth Rate: -2.2 percent (1997 estimate)
Primary Economic Activities: Morocco is primarily an agricultural country but is also a leading producer of phosphate rock.
Primary Crops: The principal crops of Morocco are cereals, particularly wheat and barley, plus potatoes, tomatoes, melons, olives, grapes, pulses, dates, sugar cane, and sugar beets. Livestock includes sheep, goats, and cattle; fishing yields pilchard, tuna, mackerel, anchovies, and shellfish.
Industries: Phosphate rock mining and processing, food processing, leather goods, textiles, construction, and tourism
Primary Exports: Food and beverages, semiprocessed goods, consumer goods, and phosphates
Primary Imports: Capital goods, semiprocessed goods, raw materials, fuel and lubricants, food and beverages, and consumer goods
Primary Trade Partners: European Union, Japan, United States, Libya, India, Saudi Arabia, United Arab Emirates, and Russia
Government: Morocco is a hereditary monarchy governed by a king, currently Mohammed VI, who appoints the prime minister, currently Abderrahmane Youssoufi, and cabinet. Under the constitution of 1972 Morocco has a unicameral legislature called the Chamber of Representatives. Deputies for 206 seats are chosen by direct universal suffrage; deputies for the remaining 100 seats are named by local political and economic groups. The major political parties are the Istiqlal (Independence Party), the Popular Movement, the National Rally of Independents, and the Constitutional Union. The king has the power to call for a reconsideration of legislative measures and to dissolve the legislature. Morocco's provinces are administered by governors who are appointed by the king. Each province is divided into *cercles,* which are subdivided into *circonscriptions* (constituencies).

Marian Aguiar

See Also

Casablanca, Morocco; Fès, Morocco; Marrakech, Morocco; Rabat, Morocco; Sahara Desert.

North America

Morrison, Toni

(b. February 18, 1931, Lorain, Ohio), African American writer; one of the most celebrated twentieth-century American writers and the first black woman and first African American to receive the NOBEL PRIZE for Literature.

"I'm interested in how men are educated, how women relate to each other, how we are able to love, how we balance political and personal forces, who survives in certain situations and who doesn't and, specifically, how these and other universal issues relate to African Americans. The search for love and identity runs through most everything I write." In this excerpt from a 1992 interview, Toni Morrison gives one description of the complex range of issues she explores in her work. Morrison is widely recognized as one of the most influential American writers, and her novels are taught in literature and history courses and in women's and African American studies programs across the country and around the world. She has received numerous honorary degrees, prizes, and awards, including the Nobel Prize for Literature. Above all, Morrison is known for her rich, lyrical prose, which fuses the rhythms and imagery of African American speech and music with other literary influences to create a discourse of its own. In a 1977 interview, she said that it "seemed to [her] Black people's grace has been what they do with language." Morrison is unparalleled in her ability to capture that grace on the page.

Toni Morrison was born Chloe Anthony Wofford in Lorain, Ohio, a small, racially mixed steel town. Her grandparents were all originally from the South, and Morrison credits her family with giving her a rich foundation in the language and rhythms of African American culture. She has said she was born into a family of storytellers, and considers her father's folktales, her mother's singing, and her grandmother's NUMBERS GAMES all examples of the uniquely black language she absorbed as a child. After graduating with honors from Lorain public schools, she received a bachelor's degree from HOWARD UNIVERSITY in 1953. In 1955 she earned a master's degree in English Literature from Cornell University, where she wrote her thesis on alienation in the works of William Faulkner and Virginia Woolf. She taught at Texas Southern University for two years before accepting a teaching position at Howard.

While teaching at Howard, Morrison married Jamaican architect Harold Morrison and gave birth to two sons. She later said it was the "powerlessness" she felt during her years as a wife and mother of small children that led her to begin writing. In 1964 Morrison and her husband divorced, and she took a job in Syracuse, New York, as a textbook editor for Random House. In 1968 she moved to Random House's trade division in Manhattan, becoming its first black woman senior editor. There she focused on black authors and edited books by Angela Davis, TONI CADE BAMBARA, GAYL JONES, and MUHAMMAD ALI. Morrison continued writing her own fiction at night, after her sons were asleep, and in 1970 published her first novel, *The Bluest Eye.*

The Bluest Eye tells the story of a nine-year-old black girl in a 1940s Ohio town who prays for blue eyes, thinking they will stop the emotional, physical, and sexual abuse she receives from her peers and the adults around her. Morrison became part of a new generation of black women writers, including Jones, Bambara, and ALICE WALKER, who were interested in telling black women's stories and stories set wholly within the black community. *The Bluest Eye* received critical praise, and Morrison became sought-after for book reviews and articles on black literature and culture. Her next novel, *Sula* (1973), was nominated for the 1975 National Book Award in fiction. Set in another Ohio town between World War II and the Korean War, *Sula* is about the classic forces of good and evil, set within the context of a friendship between two black women and the community that surrounds them. Morrison truly rose to prominence as a novelist, however, with her third book, *Song of Solomon* (1977).

Like both of her earlier novels, *Song of Solomon* is set mainly in a Midwestern town – one of Morrison's innovations in African American fiction, which is traditionally set in either the urban North or the rural South. But in contrast to the earlier works, *Song of Solomon*'s main character is male, and the book has been described as incorporating more traditionally Western and male themes of flight, journey, and violence into its narrative of a particular black community and a particular black family. *Song of Solomon* became a Book-of-the-Month Club selection, the first novel by a black author to be so chosen since *Native Son* (1940), by RICHARD WRIGHT. It also won the National Book Critics Circle Award and secured Morrison appointments to the American Academy of Arts and Letters and the National Council of the Arts. Twenty years after its publication, the book was again featured as a national book club selection – this time, for the popular television feature Oprah Winfrey's Book Club.

Morrison's next novel, *Tar Baby* (1981), received similar acclaim. It is the first of her novels to be set primarily outside the United States (on a Caribbean island) and in the present, and to feature several white main characters. *Tar Baby* was also a bestseller. But Morrison's fifth novel, *Beloved* (1987), is her most celebrated work to date. *Beloved* is loosely based on a news clipping that Morrison had read years earlier while editing a book on black history: the true story of Margaret Garner, a slave who ran away with her four children. When she was captured, she tried to slit her children's throats, and succeeded with one of them, rather than see them returned to slavery. In its fullness, *Beloved* becomes a novel about slavery, history, community, possession – and ultimately love. *Beloved* was another national bestseller, was internationally reviewed, and won the Pulitzer Prize for Literature in 1988.

Morrison has said that *Beloved* is the first novel in a trilogy about love. The second novel in that trilogy, *Jazz,* was published in 1992. Set in New York during the HARLEM RENAISSANCE, the novel pieces together the story of a love triangle in a narrative form that imitates the rhythms of JAZZ music. The third novel, *Paradise,* was published in 1998. It portrays the lives of the townspeople of Ruby, Oklahoma, who believe their community is "the one all-black town worth the pain," and the women who inhabit the abandoned convent just outside town, whom the townspeople wish to exclude from their Eden. In 1993 Morrison received the Nobel Prize for Literature for her six novels. She was the first African American and the first black woman of any nationality ever to receive the prize.

Morrison has taught at several universities and in 1989 was named the Robert F. Goheen Professor in the Council of the Humanities at Princeton University. Her reputation as one of the most influential American writers rests not only on her fiction, but also on her work as a literary and cultural critic. Her essays and speeches have been included in numerous journals and books, and in 1992 she published her first volume of literary criticism, *Playing in the Dark: Whiteness and the Literary Imagination.* That same year she edited *Race-ing Justice, En-Gendering Power,* a collection of essays on the HILL-THOMAS HEARINGS. In 1996 she coedited a second essay collection, *Birth of a Nation'hood: Gaze, Script and Spectacle in the O. J. Simpson Case* (*see* SIMPSON, O.J.). Morrison has also written a play, *Dreaming Emmett,* first produced in New York in 1986.

Through all of these works Morrison has had a tremendous impact on both the American and the African American literary landscapes. Her novels are widely accessible to readers and internationally praised for the quality of their prose; yet they remain dedicated to exploring nuances of African American culture and language. In Mari Evans's 1984 book *Black Women Writers,* Morrison states that for her, the best art "is unquestionably political and irrevocably beautiful at the same time," a standard that many readers believe she has met in all of her work.

Lisa Clayton Robinson

SEE ALSO

Slavery in the United States; Literature, African American; Women Writers, Black, in the United States; Davis, Angela Yvonne; Winfrey, Oprah Gail.

North America

Morrow, Everett Frederick

(b. April 20, 1909, Hackensack, N.J.), business leader and Republican who was the first African American appointed to a White House staff position.

Everett Frederick Morrow graduated from Bowdoin College in 1930, and then worked as a field secretary for the NATIONAL ASSOCIATION FOR THE ADVANCEMENT OF COLORED PEOPLE (NAACP).

In 1952 Morrow became a consultant to Dwight D. Eisenhower's Republican presidential campaign. In 1955 he became the first African American White House staff member, when Eisenhower appointed him administrative officer for the Special Projects group, a position with little real responsibility. Morrow tried to use his position to turn Eisenhower's attention to civil rights matters, but he was largely frustrated in these efforts. He also campaigned for Richard Nixon's unsuccessful 1960 election bid. In 1964 Morrow became the first African American to work as a corporate executive for Bank of America.

North America

Morton, Ferdinand Joseph ("Jelly Roll")

(Ferdinand Joseph La Menthe) (b. October 20, 1890, New Orleans, La.; d. July 10, 1941, Los Angeles, Calif.), early JAZZ pianist and composer who since his death has risen to the highest tier of critical acclaim for his mastery of the piano.

Composer and pianist Ferdinand "Jelly Roll" Morton shown in 1938 when he traveled to Washington, D.C., to record for Library of Congress archivist and music historian Alan Lomax. *AP/Wide World Photos*

Jelly Roll Morton was born to fair-skinned Creole parents in New Orleans, and all his life he considered himself more white than black. His father, who left the family when Morton was young, played trombone, as did Morton's stepfather, Ed Morton. Morton received guitar lessons by age 6 but soon abandoned guitar for piano. At age 12 he began playing piano in the bordellos of New Orleans's Storyville district, and as a teenager he traveled the gulf coast, mingling with famous regional musicians, including RAGTIME pianist Tony Jackson. Morton also received some formal musical training at St. Joseph's Seminary College in St. Benedict, Louisiana.

Beginning with his trip to the St. Louis World's Fair in 1904, Morton embarked on a decade of itinerant music making that carried him throughout the South and to New York and Chicago. He played with vaudeville troupes and minstrel shows, supplementing his income with profits from pool hustling, card playing, and pimping. Indeed, his notoriety as a swindler, braggart, and womanizer often preceded his reputation as a musician.

Morton settled in Chicago from around 1911 until 1915, playing music with a small ensemble. He published "Jelly Roll Blues" in 1915, an accomplishment that set him apart from other JAZZ pianists of the time. While his performances evinced high passion and spontaneity, Morton made music with a composer's fastidious mind. Even when fast and improvised, his playing reflected rational, intentional calculations. In 1915 he uprooted once more, traveling up and down the West Coast until he resettled in Chicago in 1923.

In Chicago Morton observed the new and thriving recording industry and decided to cut his own takes. In 1923 and 1924 he recorded as a solo pianist, and from 1926 to 1930 he led the ensemble Red Hot Peppers, featuring such legendary players as clarinetist Johnny Dodds and trombonist Kid Ory. Morton recorded some of his most famous compositions with this group, including "Kansas City Stomps" and "Smokehouse Blues." Critics often describe Morton's style in these recordings as orchestral; instead of backing the melody with chords and steady rhythm in the bass, he created one or two lines of counterpoint in which his left hand emulated a trombone for the cornet of his right.

Morton moved to New York in 1928 and began running an all-girl revue that doubled as a prostitution racket. He continued to record, but both the advent of big-band music and the onset of the GREAT DEPRESSION diminished his popularity. He moved to WASHINGTON, D.C., in 1935, managed a nightclub, and eventually worked with folklorist Alan Lomax on a set of recordings for the Library of Congress. In the hours of collected footage, Morton expounds on his playing style and reconstructs a history of jazz. Although many of his observations have historical and musicological value, his arrogance and hyperbole limit the recording's veracity, as in his claim that he "invented jazz in 1902," the year he turned 12.

Morton moved to LOS ANGELES, CALIFORNIA, toward the end of his life and died in 1941, with the bulk of his popularity seeming to have passed. Throughout his life he had managed his career poorly, often spoiling business relationships with displays of arrogance and pomp. He is now recognized as a musical genius, however, and jazz pianists today cite his direct influence on their style, approach, and repertoire.

Eric Bennett

See Also

Chicago, Illinois; Minstrelsy; New Orleans, Louisiana; New York, New York; Ory, Edward ("Kid").

Latin America and the Caribbean

Morúa Delgado, Martín

(b. November 11, 1856, Matanzas, Cuba; d. April 28, 1910, Havana, Cuba), Afro-Cuban author, journalist, activist, and statesman.

Poverty and racism forced Martín Morúa, the son of a Spanish immigrant father and an ex-slave mother, to leave school and find work. He managed to educate himself, often by purchasing books with part of his salary. His experiences working in a barrel factory led him to become a labor activist. Besides organizing workers in several Cuban cities, Morúa made speeches and wrote newspaper and magazine articles on workers' rights, thus launching his career as a political leader and a journalist.

In the nineteenth century paid readers read books aloud to factory workers while they engaged in nonmechanical tasks like rolling cigars. Even before slavery had been abolished, Morúa was the first man of African descent to become a professional reader in Cuba. He also became the first reader of color in New York, when he worked in a tobacco factory there years later.

Along with his work in defending workers' rights, Morúa dedicated himself to the struggle for Cuban independence and the abolition of slavery. His labor and political activities displeased the Spanish colonial government that ruled Cuba at the time (*see* Colonial Latin America and the Caribbean). He was arrested and held briefly as a political prisoner in 1881. Soon afterward, he left the country.

Morúa continued his political activism as he traveled through Panama, Mexico, Jamaica, and the United States. He worked as a journalist and learned French, English, and other languages. Part of his exile was spent in New York, where he developed the skill of translating into English.

Upon returning to Cuba in 1890, he deepened his commitment to political struggle through the written word. He soon founded the newspaper *El Tribuno.* (He had already started a journal in Matanzas in 1879 and a magazine in Key West, Florida, during the 1880s.) He also established the magazine *La Nueva Era* to deal with the new social situation created by the 1886 abolition of slavery. He expressed dissatisfaction with Cuban antislavery novels, especially the most famous one, *Cecilia Valdés* (1882), by Cirilo Villaverde. To stress the need for racial equality, Morúa wrote two novels about slavery and racism: *Sofía* (1891) and *La familia Unzúazu* (1901). He also translated a biography of Toussaint L'Ouverture, hero of the Haitian Revolution.

In 1898 Morúa joined the Cuban revolutionaries in their war against Spain. Two years later he helped to set up the Cuban Republican Party and was elected to serve as a delegate to the Constitutional Convention. Morúa was later appointed the founding secretary of the municipality of Palmira. Eventually he became a senator and advanced to the post of president of the Senate. In 1909 the president of Cuba appointed him minister of agriculture, commerce, and labor. As architect and advocate of the Ley Morúa – a law that discouraged the organization of political parties along racial lines – he argued staunchly for integrationism, which caused considerable controversy. Still, Morúa was such a respected citizen and important historical figure that in 1956, Cuba celebrated the centennial of his birth.

Marveta Ryan

See Also

Slavery in Latin America and the Caribbean; New York, New York; Toussaint L'Ouverture, François Dominique; Abolition and Emancipation in Latin America and the Caribbean.

North America

Moseley-Braun, Carol

(b. August 16, 1947, Chicago, Ill.), lawyer and public official; first African American woman to serve as a United States senator.

Carol Moseley-Braun, the oldest of four daughters, was born to Edna Moseley, a medical technician, and Joseph Moseley, a Chicago police officer who dreamed of being a successful jazz musician. Reared a Roman Catholic on Chicago's South Side, Moseley-Braun graduated in 1969 from the University of Illinois at Chicago with a B.A. in political science. Three years later she finished a J.D. at the University of Chicago Law School. While in law school, she met and eventually married Michael Braun, also a lawyer. Moseley-Braun gave birth to Matthew, her only child, in 1977, and in 1986 she and her husband divorced.

Moseley-Braun served in the Illinois State Legislature from 1978 to 1987, and she was the first African American to serve as that body's assistant majority leader. In 1992 she ran for the U.S. Senate against two-term incumbent Alan Dixon, who had voted to confirm Clarence Thomas's nomination to the Supreme Court. She won the Democratic primary in March 1992 and went on to win the election in November over Republican candidate Richard S. Williamson. Moseley-Braun's victory made her the fourth African American and the first African American woman to serve in the U.S. Senate. Sworn in to the 103rd Congress on January 3, 1993, she was one of six women who served in the U.S. Senate during that session.

Throughout her career Moseley-Braun has commanded attention for her legislative leadership in sponsoring progressive bills on education and for her ability to build successful coalitions. However, due to allegations of personal and financial misconduct, in November 1998 she lost her Senate seat to conservative Republican Peter Fitzgerald.

See Also

Chicago, Illinois; Thomas, Clarence.

North America

Moses, Robert Parris

(b. January 23, 1935, New York, N.Y.), African American civil rights activist; first Student Nonviolent Coordinating Committee (SNCC) worker in Mississippi.

Inspired by student sit-ins in 1960, 25-year-old Harvard Ph.D. candidate and middle-school teacher Bob Moses left his New York teaching job to join the Civil Rights Movement, where he led the effort of the Student Nonviolent Coordinating Committee (SNCC) to register black voters in Mississippi. Many civil rights workers had believed that Mississippi was too dangerous a place to attempt to organize. His courage and stoicism made Moses an almost mythical figure to other civil rights workers, who stood amazed by stories such as the one in which a bloodied Moses accompanied prospective black registrants to the county courthouse just minutes after being beaten by whites.

Disturbed by competition between SNCC and other civil rights organizations in Mississippi, Moses helped found the Council of Federated Organizations (COFO), an umbrella organization that coordinated all of Mississippi's civil rights organizations. As COFO's project director in September 1963, he developed the Freedom Vote, a mock gubernatorial election in which 80,000 blacks voted to protest their disfranchisement. Encouraged by the turnout, COFO launched Freedom Summer the following year, a massive voter registration and education project. Later in 1964 Moses helped establish the Mississippi Freedom Democratic Party, which challenged the all-white Mississippi Democratic delegation to the Democratic National Convention.

In 1982, believing that math literacy was the key to modern citizenship, just as literacy and voter registration had been the keys to citizenship in the 1960s, Moses founded the Algebra Project, a program in which students use concrete examples from their lives to master abstract algebraic concepts. He brought the Algebra Project to the Mississippi Delta in 1992, thereby helping to empower a new generation of Mississippi blacks.

Robert Fay

Africa

Moshoeshoe (b. 1786?; d. 1870), founder and first king of the Basotho nation.

Born in Menkwaneng, the son of a Sotho leader, Moshoeshoe began to gather together refugees from the upheaval in southeastern Africa known as the MFECANE in the early 1820s. Retiring to an impregnable mountaintop known as Thaba Bosiu (Sotho for "mountain of the night"), he fought off marauding tribes, but more often used his formidable diplomatic skills to defend his growing number of Basotho people.

In the early 1830s French missionaries arrived in the region. While continuing to support the traditional customs and religion of the Sotho, Moshoeshoe welcomed the missionaries and sought their advice in dealing with the British and the Afrikaners, or Boers, who were seeking to colonize southern Africa. Fearing Afrikaner settlement on his lands, he asked for British protection, but an alliance with the government of the Cape Colony was not enough to prevent armed incursions by settlers into Basotho territory.

Fighting between the Basotho and the Afrikaners continued until the 1860s, resulting in the loss of some Basotho land. In 1868 Moshoeshoe arranged for Basutoland to become a British protectorate, thereby saving it from the Afrikaners and other European settlers. When Moshoeshoe died in 1870, he ruled roughly 150,000 people in what was essentially a federal state. Basutoland eventually became the independent nation of LESOTHO.

SEE ALSO

Afrikaner; Christianity: Missionaries in Africa.

North America

Mosley, Walter (b. January 12, 1952, Los Angeles, Calif.), African American novelist known for his detective fiction.

Walter Mosley was born to an African American father and a Jewish mother in South Central Los Angeles, where he lived until he left for college in Vermont. After college he worked a series of jobs, including caterer, potter, and computer programmer. In 1981 he moved to New York and began taking graduate writing courses at the City College of New York. There he completed *Gone Fishin'* and *Devil in a Blue Dress*, two novels that centered on the same Los Angeles protagonist, a working-class African American named Easy Rawlins.

Although *Gone Fishin'* did not sell, the rights to *Devil in a Blue Dress* were soon purchased by Norton, which published the book in 1990. *Devil* portrayed the Easy Rawlins character as a private investigator, and Mosley seemed to have found a strong voice as an author of detective fiction. After *Devil* he published four more Easy Rawlins books: *A Red Death* (1991), *White Butterfly* (1992), *Black Betty* (1994), and *A Little Yellow Dog* (1996).

Although Mosley's fiction falls into a category that many consider subliterary – detective fiction – his depth of character, researched historical details, and realistic dialogue transcend the cliches of the genre. He portrays the complexity of the Los Angeles African American community between the late 1940s and mid-1960s, and does so with nuance and at times painful realism. Mosley's novel outside the series, *R. L.'s Dream*, evinces a similar level of sophistication in its speculative portrayal of bluesman Robert Johnson.

Mosley's books experienced a boom in sales during the 1992 presidential campaign, when Bill Clinton cited them as among his favorites. Mosley has been included in the *Norton Anthology of African American Literature*, compared to renowned detective novelist Raymond Chandler, and praised as a superior writer of his generation. A film version of *Devil in a Blue Dress*, directed by Jonathan Demme and starring DENZEL WASHINGTON, was released in 1998.

Eric Bennett

SEE ALSO

Literature, African American; Johnson, Robert Leroy; Los Angeles, California.

Africa

Mossi, a kingdom and the largest ethnic group in BURKINA FASO, whose members also live in CÔTE D'IVOIRE, GHANA, TOGO, and BENIN.

Although the origin of Mossi society is debated, oral tradition claims that the kingdom was founded by Ouédraogo, the son of a Mamprusi princess from Gambaga (in present-day Ghana), and a MANDE hunter. Ouédraogo (meaning "stallion," after the horse that his mother rode to find her husband) migrated north as a young man with a group of DAGOMBA followers and founded the village of Tenkodogo, site of the first Mossi kingdom. Ouédraogo later sent three of his sons and a cavalry to acquire new territory in the Volta River basin region; by the fifteenth century his descendants had established more than 20 kingdoms and had assimilated numerous peoples, including the Nioniosse, Ninsi, Gurunis, DOGON, and Bisa. The most important dynasty was founded in Ouagadougou in 1495 by Ouédraogo's grandson, Oubry, who called himself the *mogho naaba*, "king of the world," a title that was adopted by subsequent Ouagadougou kings.

Mossi expansion into the SAHEL met with challenges from the empire of Songhai, led first by SUNNI ALI and then his successor, ASKIA MUHAMMAD. Askia's jihad against the Mossi, who observed a form of ancestor worship, failed to win Mossi conversion to Islam. Although many Mossi traders did convert later, even today Burkina Faso remains less Islamized than its Sahelian neighbors.

By the eighteenth century the Mossi had developed a complex hierarchy, ruled by the nobles, or *nakombse*, who claimed direct patrilineal descent from Ouédraogo. The ruler of Ouagadougou exercised loose authority over the kings (*naaba*) of the four other largest kingdoms – Tenkodogo, Yatenga, Boussouma, and Gurma – who in turn collected tribute from smaller kingdoms. Mossi society also distinguished between the *talse* (commoners) and *yemse* (slaves). Among the *talse*, those lineages who claimed descent from the original settlers were known as the *tengabiise* (children of the earth); this indigenous status gave them privileged claims to land as well as responsibility for harvest rites.

Most Mossi kingdoms supplemented agricultural production with trade. Caravans brought gold and COLA from the south and salt and livestock from the north. The region's predominant traders were the *yarse*, assimilated Mande Muslims who paid the naaba annual tributes in return for market space in Mossi towns and safe passage through the region. In the late eighteenth century some Mossi kingdoms also participated in the TRANSATLANTIC SLAVE TRADE, but many slaves were diverted to the royal court in Ouagadougou after the European abolition of the trade.

In the late nineteenth century the mogho naaba repeatedly rebuffed French efforts to establish a protectorate over the Mossi region, but these kings finally fled the French conquest of Ouagadougou in 1896. Within the colony of Upper Volta (present-day Burkina Faso), the Mossi royal hierarchy was used by the French to administer COLONIAL RULE. Where necessary, the French replaced recalcitrant naaba with more willing collaborators, thus undermining, though never destroying, the basis of nakombse authority.

In 1932 the French dismantled the bankrupt Upper Volta and annexed much of the Mossi region to Côte d'Ivoire, thereby facilitating the flow of labor to the southern colony's plantations. After thousands of Mossi volunteered to fight in World War II, Mossi chiefs convinced France to reunite Upper Volta, a move that increased their own political clout as independence approached. After independence in 1960 the Mossi were crucial in the election of Burkina Faso's first president, Maurice Yaméogo. The current mogho naaba remains a respected figure in Ouagadougou society. Today the Mossi constitute more than half the population of Burkina Faso. Known for their traditions of migration, hundreds of thousands of the approximately 5.5 million Mossi move seasonally for farming work in neighboring countries, especially Côte d'Ivoire.

Elizabeth Heath

See Also

Colonial Rule; Gold Trade; France; Ouagadougou, Burkina Faso; Salt Trade; Songhai Empire; Slavery in Africa.

North America

Moten, Benjamin (Bennie)

(b. November 13, 1894, Kansas City, Mo.; d. April 2, 1935, Kansas City, Mo.), African American jazz bandleader who popularized the "Kansas City" sound in big-band jazz.

In his youth Moten played baritone saxophone in Kansas City brass bands. Switching to the piano, he studied ragtime with two of Scott Joplin's students. In 1918 he formed the ragtime trio B.B.&D. Moten's band toured the Midwest through the 1920s, settling in New York near the end of the decade. By the beginning of the 1930s Moten's group included a roster of intensely talented musicians and arrangers. Those who later acquired fame as independent artists included singer Jimmy Rushing, tenor saxophonist Ben Webster, trumpeter Oran "Hot Lips" Page, and pianist and bandleader Count Basie.

Key early Moten recordings, such as "Elephant's Wobble" and "Crawdad Blues" (1923), showcased his band's tight ensemble playing and heavy, percussive beat. The band's characteristic sound wed stellar solo passages and instrumental riffs to a distinctive underlying flow. Important later recordings included "Moten Stomp" (1927), "Kansas City Breakdown" (1928), "Lafayette" (1932), and "Prince of Wails" (1932).

Moten died in 1935 during an operation to remove his tonsils. Members of his band regrouped as the Count Basie Orchestra in 1936.

See Also

Basie, William James ("Count"); New York, New York.

North America

Moton, Robert Russa

(b. August 26, 1867, Amelia County, Va.; d. May 31, 1940, Holly Knoll Capahosic, Va.), African American educator and lawyer, and the successor to Booker T. Washington as president of Tuskegee Institute.

The son of Book and Emily (Brown) Moton, Robert Moton enrolled in the Hampton Institute in 1885. After his junior year he taught in Cottontown, Cumberland County, and subsequently obtained a license to practice law. He returned to Hampton in 1889 and finished his senior year to become assistant commandant in charge of the male student cadet corps. He was appointed "major" commandant, a position he retained for 25 years. In 1900 he was elected president of the National Negro Business League and was reelected for the next 20 years.

Moton's first wife, Elizabeth Hunt Harris, died in 1906, only one year after their marriage. He had four children with his second wife, Jennie Dee Booth.

Moton's working relationship with Booker T. Washington began in 1908, the year of his second marriage, when he accompanied Washington on several tours through the Southern states to promote the Hampton-Tuskegee model of racial advancement through vocational education and interracial cooperation. Their routine consisted of singing "Negro melodies" led by Moton, followed by a speech from Washington.

When Washington died in 1915, Moton assumed many of Washington's roles as race leader, advising the federal government on racial policies and Negro appointments, consulting philanthropists in the distribution of educational funds, and steering organizations serving the cause of racial advancement.

As president of Tuskegee from 1915 until 1930, Moton increased its endowment from $2.3 million to $7.77 million, introduced college-level coursework, and improved the administrative structure. Moreover, he ensured that Tuskegee's vocational curriculum kept up with the changing employment world.

Moton received honorary degrees from several colleges and universities, including Oberlin, Williams, Harvard, Virginia Union, Wilberforce, and Howard. In 1930 he won the Harmon Award for contributions to better race relations, and in 1932 the National Association for the Advancement of Colored People honored him with the Spingarn Medal for distinguished service.

See Also

Hampton University; Howard University; Tuskegee University; Washington, Booker Taliaferro; Wilberforce University.

North America

Motown

black-owned record company that became the most commercially successful and culturally influential record company of the 1960s, producing a distinct musical style that appealed to audiences across racial boundaries.

The Supremes, the Temptations, the Four Tops, Smokey Robinson and the Miracles, Martha and the Vandellas, the Contours, and the Jackson 5, as well as solo artists Mary Wells, Marvin Gaye, and Stevie Wonder were some of Motown's leading popular acts. This collection of musical talent produced scores of hits, including "My Girl," "Stop! In the Name of Love," "Shop Around," "I Heard It Through the Grapevine," "Baby, I Need Your Loving," and "Dancing in the Street." These songs captured the spirit of an era and became – as the company motto promised – the "Sound of Young America."

Berry Gordy Jr. founded the company in Detroit, Michigan, in 1959 with the support of a family loan of $800. Gordy, who worked briefly at the Ford Motor Company, named the company Motown after Detroit's "Motor Town" nickname. He believed that the efficiency of the automobile assembly line could be applied to the music industry.

Gordy designed his "hit factory" in a modest two-story home on West Grand Boulevard in Detroit. His concept involved finding young talent from local neighborhoods and transforming these amateur musicians and singers into professional artists. Gordy set up a separate Artist Development Department, which was often referred to as the company "charm school," to teach performers how to sing, dance, and comport themselves in the public spotlight. Legendary bandleader Maurice King led the musical instruction. Cholly Atkins, a veteran choreographer, taught the synchronized black dance steps that became an integral part of Motown's signature style. Maxine Powell instructed performers on the etiquette of celebrity life – including how to dress, greet dignitaries, and behave on stage. With this schooling, Gordy's young artists, many of whom were just out of high school, exuded the confidence of seasoned entertainers.

The "Motown Sound" has always been difficult to define yet easy to recognize. Motown songs often combine strong bass lines and a gritty back beat with call-and-response vocals and clever lyrics about the trials and joys of teenage romance. The music's magic resulted from the combined efforts of skilled songwriters, producers, and musicians. Gordy, a talented songwriter, gained early fame writing songs for Jackie Wilson, including "Reet Petite" (1957) and "Lonely Teardrops" (1958). He mentored other Motown writers and producers in the art of romantic storytelling through popular song.

In 1959 Gordy signed a new group, the Miracles, to the label. In February 1961 their song "Shop Around" became the company's first million seller. Smokey Robinson, the lead singer, quickly became one of Motown's most prolific songwriters. He composed top hits, including "My Girl," "The Way You Do the Things You Do," and "You've Really Got a Hold on Me." Motown's innovative studio musicians, also known as the Funk Brothers, created the company's unique "sound." The original members included James Jamerson on bass, Earl Van Dyke on keyboards, Benny "Papa Zita" Benjamin on drums, Robert White on guitar, and Thomas "Beans" Bowles on saxophone.

With such a powerful array of creative talent, the Motown recording studio soon lived up to its ambitious nickname: "Hitsville, U.S.A." Early hits included Barrett Strong's "Money (That's What I Want)" (1959) and the Marvelettes' "Please Mr. Postman" (1961). In 1962 Motown developed enough new acts to send its own road show, the Motortown Revue, on a national tour. The tour, the first sponsored solely by a black-owned record company, was a music industry first. The Revue's roster, which included Mary Wells, the Contours, Martha and the Vandellas, the Supremes, the Miracles, "Little" Stevie Wonder, Marvin Gaye, and the Marvelettes, testified to the company's rich potential. From 1961 to 1972 Motown performers sent over 100 songs to the Top Ten of the popular music charts, including 31 number-one hits.

The key to Motown's success was the company's ability to produce music that appealed to audiences across racial boundaries. No Motown group exemplified this skill more than the Supremes, the company's most commercially successful group. The Supremes first reached number one on the pop charts with their song "Where Did Our Love Go?" in the summer of 1964. A string of hits followed, including "Baby Love," "Come See About Me," "Stop! In the Name of Love," and "I Hear a Symphony." The songwriting team of Eddie Holland, Lamont Dozier, and Brian Holland – known as Holland-Dozier-Holland – masterminded the Supremes' unique sound. Diana Ross, Florence Ballard, and Mary Wilson became international celebrities through national television appearances and world tours. Ross left the group in 1970 to pursue a solo singing career and film acting.

By the late 1960s and early 1970s Motown music had moved beyond carefree teenage themes to address the political and social struggles of the Civil Rights Movement and the Vietnam War. Stevie Wonder was the first Motown artist to address social issues through song in 1966, when he recorded a cover version of Bob Dylan's song "Blowin' in the Wind." Wonder's moving interpretation spoke to the challenges of the Civil Rights campaign. The Supremes recorded "Love Child" (1968) and "I'm Livin' in Shame" (1969), both of which depicted the problems of urban ghetto life. The Temptations also recorded a series of "message" songs, including "Ball of Confusion (That's What the World Is Today)" (1970) and "Papa was a Rollin' Stone" (1972). Edwin Starr's song "War!" (1970) became one of the strongest anti-Vietnam War anthems on the airwaves.

In 1971 Marvin Gaye produced his groundbreaking album *What's Going On*, which commented not only on the Vietnam War but also on ecology, racism, and urban violence. Motown Records also founded the Black Forum label, which produced spoken-word recordings on political and literary subjects. Black Forum releases included *Free Huey!* (1970), *Writers of the Revolution* (1970), *The Congressional Black Caucus* (1972), and Martin Luther King Jr.'s speech *Why I Oppose the War in Vietnam*, which won a Grammy Award in 1970 for Best Spoken-Word Recording.

In 1972 the Motown Record Company announced its plans to relocate its headquarters from Detroit to Los Angeles, California. Gordy wanted to expand into filmmaking as well as record producing. Motown's first feature film was *Lady Sings the Blues* (1973), starring Diana Ross. Ross's moving portrayal of Billie Holiday won her an Academy Award Best Actress nomination. Other Motown feature films include *Mahogany* (1975) and *The Bingo Long and the Travelling All-Star and Motor Kings* (1976). In the early 1980s Motown produced television specials, including "Motown 25: Yesterday, Today, Forever" (1983), which first featured Michael Jackson's famous "moonwalk" dance. In 1988 Gordy sold Motown to MCA, Inc., for $61.9 million. The Motown label is currently owned by Polygram Records and features groups such as Boyz II Men.

Suzanne Smith

See Also

Jackson, Michael, and the Jackson Family; Robinson, William ("Smokey"); Film, Blacks in American.

North America

Mound Bayou, Mississippi, an intentional community in the Mississippi wetlands that illustrated, at the height of its prosperity, the possibilities of black self-help. By applying the philosophy of Booker T. Washington, cofounder Isaiah Montgomery gained national attention for the success of his experiment there.

Freedmen Ben Green and Isaiah Montgomery founded Mound Bayou in 1888 on the rich alluvial land halfway between Memphis, Tennessee, and Vicksburg, Mississippi. The site flanked a new railroad line and cost little because of its swampy ground and thick underbrush. Green and Montgomery intended the settlement to be a refuge from discrimination and a place where freedpeople could live independent and self-sustaining lives.

Mound Bayou grew quickly; by 1907, 400 families, totaling about 8000 residents, populated the town. Mound Bayou townsfolk earned money by clearing and selling swampland hardwood and by cultivating cotton on the fertile soil. The capital accrued from this work underwrote a dozen businesses, a newspaper, two private schools, ten churches, a bank, and a cottonseed oil mill. The Mound Bayou community governed itself through town-hall meetings, and, by means of effective local democracy, enforced prohibition, outlawed premarital cohabitation, banned prostitution, and dealt with a negligible crime rate.

Although Isaiah Montgomery played an instrumental role in these successes, his interests extended beyond the settlement. He won an office in the state government by adopting a position of accommodation from which he advocated the temporary disfranchisement of African Americans for the sake of later gains. Sympathetic with Montgomery's rhetoric, Booker T. Washington became his friend and President Theodore Roosevelt appointed him to a position collecting monies in Mississippi for the federal government.

Montgomery, however, continued to devote most of his attention to Mound Bayou. When hard times hit after 1910, Montgomery's connections with the white establishment proved a mixed blessing. White philanthropists, including Andrew Carnegie and Julius Rosenwald, subsidized the town's bank and cottonseed oil mill, which had faltered from the economic shifts induced by World War I. Since the citizens of Mound Bayou prided themselves on their success in maintaining self-help and economic independence, the subsidies undermined the town's founding philosophy.

Despite perennial attempts to reinvigorate the economy, Mound Bayou struggled through the rest of the twentieth century and failed to regain the prosperity of its first 25 years. The Mound Bayou experiment exemplified both the possibilities and limits of self-help, both the pride of black independence and the inescapable burden of economic dependency.

Eric Bennett

See Also

World War I and African Americans; Washington, Booker Taliaferro.

Africa

Mount Cameroon, the highest mountain in West Africa.

At 4095 m (13,435 ft), Mount Cameroon is the highest peak in West and Central Africa. It is part of a volcanic chain that runs southwest to northeast, including both the Equatorial Guinean islands of Annobón (or Pagalu) and Bioko, and the mountain range that extends northeast of Mount Cameroon, creating a natural frontier between Cameroon and Nigeria. The volcanoes formed in two stages: first around 110 million years ago, when the continents of Africa and South America divided, and second, 80 million years ago, when the continental plate of Africa rotated to its present position. Mount Cameroon last erupted explosively in 1959, though a fissure eruption occurred in 1982. In 1986 the volcano emitted carbon dioxide at Lake Nyos, killing 1700 people in the surrounding valleys.

In the rich soils of the mountain, people grow bananas, cacao, coffee, oil palms, rubber trees, and tea. The southern slope of the mountain, facing the sea, records a mean annual rainfall of more than 400 in (1000 cm), making it one of the wettest places in the world. The cities of Buea and Limbe both lie on the mountain's south side. The Carthaginian explorer Hanno is believed to have sighted Mount Cameroon, which he called the Chariot of the Gods, around 500 B.C.E.; he wrote of "a land full of fire [and] in the middle was a lofty fire larger than all the rest touching seemingly the stars."

Eric Young

See Also

Equatorial Guinea; Carthage.

Africa

Mount Kenya, or *Kirinyaga* in Swahili ("mountain of whiteness"), the second highest mountain in Africa.

An extinct volcano located in central KENYA, Mount Kenya reaches 5199 m (17,058 ft) at its summit. The mountain features several vegetative zones and is surrounded by forest up to about 3200 m (10,500 ft). The KIKUYU and the Embu and Meru peoples have traditionally inhabited the area, farming the fertile lower slopes. Now part of Mount Kenya National Park, the mountain has become a popular destination for both recreational climbing and wildlife viewing and is a valuable source of revenue for the Kenyan government.

Robert Fay

North America

Mountain Men, fur trappers, Indian interpreters, and trailblazers who became mythical emblems of the American Western frontier.

According to historian Kenneth W. Porter, any account of the early nineteenth-century fur trade that left out African Americans would be "so incomplete as to give a false impression." Sadly, such false impressions run rampant. When Hollywood filmed the life of the famous black trapper James P. Beckwourth (1798-1866), a white man played the lead.

Mountain men, who trapped animals for their valuable fur, roamed the mythic American West, stock characters representing independence, courage, and self-reliance. They were, in many cases, the first non-Native Americans to explore the vast territory unsettled by Europeans. Starting in the early 1800s, several fur companies sought men to travel into the upper Midwest and the Rocky Mountains. Beckwourth and Edward Rose were among the black men who went. Although most of these adventurers were porters and trappers, George Bonga, descended from African slaves and Chippewa Indians, became an important fur trader in his own right during the 1830s.

Bears, wolves, and snakes made the work treacherous, and many mountain men died of exposure to the harsh western winters. Many Native Americans fought to defend their land against the interlopers who sought to profit from it. But the fur trade offered some black men more freedom and independence than they found in more settled parts of the country, and their experience with Indian cultures was not always antagonistic. Some black mountain men, like Beckwourth and Bonga, married Native American women.

Even after the fur trade declined, the mountain men remained, putting their skills to use as interpreters, Indian agents, guides, army scouts, and soldiers. The African Americans among them became some of the first blacks in the American frontier West.

Kate Tuttle

SEE ALSO

Beckwourth, James Pierson.

North America

MOVE, a countercultural organization founded in PHILADELPHIA, PENNSYLVANIA; its activities led to two controversial clashes with police in 1978 and 1985, resulting in the imprisonment or death of more than two dozen members.

MOVE was founded in 1972 by Vincent Leaphart, an African American handyman. Leaphart believed that various problems plaguing American society, such as crime, substance abuse, and violence, grow out of humanity's growing alienation from the natural world through technology and various social institutions. He advocated a lifestyle based on the "principle of natural law," which involved observances such as eating only uncooked, unprocessed foods, living without electric heat, letting one's hair grow naturally, and rejecting "man's [corrupt] laws." Donald Glassey, a white leftist graduate student at the University of Pennsylvania, befriended Leaphart – who began calling himself John Africa – and collected his ideas into a manuscript called *The Guidelines*.

The Guidelines circulated throughout the Powelton Village section of Philadelphia, attracting a small number of disciples, mostly students from surrounding universities, relatives of John Africa, working-class folk from the community, and veterans of various radical groups, including the Black Panthers. Although the group's membership was predominantly African American and its activities often focused on racially charged issues such as police brutality against blacks, a few sympathizers and members like Glassey were white. All followers, emulating their leader, took "Africa" as their surname. The group was first named the Christian Movement for Life; John Africa eventually shortened the name of his new "family" to MOVE. Glassey purchased a house on North 33rd Street, and, although not all members lived there, the house became MOVE's communal residence.

MOVE's early activities included protests against city and school board policies, police brutality (rampant under law-and-order Mayor Frank Rizzo, 1971-1979), and pollution and other environmental abuses. They picketed the Philadelphia Zoo, comparing the caging of animals to the Jewish Holocaust and the treatment of blacks during times of slavery. Meanwhile, MOVE's neighbors on North 33rd Street had their own complaints: rats, rotting garbage, fecal odor, unclothed children, the 50 to 60 stray animals adopted by the "family," and increasingly violent arguments with group members (with MOVE usually gaining the upper hand). The complaints finally led to a court-ordered inspection that Rizzo hesitated to enforce, especially after he received reports that the organization was stockpiling food and weapons at the house in anticipation of an invasion.

After a politically embarrassing ten-month delay, Rizzo had a four-block area surrounding the MOVE house blockaded by police, cutting off all food, water, and supplies to the house. Supporters somehow smuggled provisions to the group. Three months later, on August 8, 1978, Rizzo sanctioned a police raid, during which five police officers and firefighters were wounded and one police officer was killed. One MOVE member, Delbert Africa, was beaten by police while he was trying to escape (local television news crews captured this beating on videotape). After the house was evacuated, it was immediately seized, condemned, and razed by the city. Rizzo blamed the group and a hostile media presence for the violence. The group briefly dispersed, with some members going underground to avoid various weapons and conspiracy charges, while others remained to work toward the release of members who had been detained after the 1978 showdown.

In 1980, after a controversial trial in which compelling evidence suggested that "friendly fire" may have been the cause of the officer's death, nine MOVE members (including Delbert Africa) were convicted of manslaughter charges stemming from the confrontation and were sentenced to terms of 30 to 100 years. The three police officers charged with beating Delbert Africa were acquitted in 1981 by a judge, before the case could go to a jury trial.

That same year John Africa returned to Philadelphia to face weapons and conspiracy charges and was acquitted. Soon after, the family regrouped and moved into a house at 6221 Osage Avenue. Nearly two years passed before problems with neighbors arose again. A community delegation appealed to the new city administration, now led by Philadelphia's first black mayor, Wilson Goode, who had been elected in November 1983. Goode, fearful of another deadly showdown, avoided any direct action against the group, and even delayed the arrests of several MOVE members for outstanding warrants. But he was eventually forced into action because of political pressure from the community and the media, and because of reports that bunker-like additions were being built around the house. He authorized a hastily planned raid on the MOVE house on May 13, 1985.

The police attempted to break into 6221 Osage Avenue from neighboring houses but failed. Then they dropped a bomb on the house from a helicopter, presumably in an effort to make an opening in the roof for tear gas. A fire started, but police intentionally allowed it to burn, hoping to disable the rooftop bunkers. The blaze soon grew wildly out of control, spreading to neighboring houses and adjoining city blocks. In the end, the fire had consumed 61 homes and killed 11 MOVE members, including John Africa and five children. Only two of the members in the house escaped the blaze: Ramona Africa, who was eventually imprisoned for seven years on conspiracy and riot charges, and Birdie Africa, a 13-year-old boy.

Two grand jury investigations – city-commissioned and independent – found that the decision to drop the bomb had been "unconscionable," and they exposed a police cover-up concerning the use of C-4, a military-grade explosive, in the bomb. But no criminal charges were ever filed against Goode, other city officials, or any of the police officers involved.

Wrongful death lawsuits by relatives of the deceased and by surviving MOVE members (including Ramona Africa, released in 1992) against the city have already led to nearly $5 million in damages, with more suits pending. There are at least three dozen active MOVE members either still in prison or living in the Philadelphia area.

Marc Mazique

See Also
Slavery in the United States; Black Panther Party.

Latin America and the Caribbean

Movimento Negro Unificado,

an organization created in the 1970s to fight racial discrimination against blacks in Brazil.

The Movimento Negro Unificado (Unified Black Movement, or MNU) was created on June 18, 1978, in São Paulo, Brazil, by a group of Afro-Brazilians, among whom were political activists, journalists, artists, and athletes. The MNU was conceived during a phase when Brazil's military regime, which took power in a 1964 coup, was conducting a transition to democracy. The military government was therefore allowing political organizations and social movements to organize freely. It is likely that international decolonization and independence movements, especially in Africa, and the Civil Rights Movement in the United States influenced the upsurge of a black movement in Brazil (*see* Black Consciousness in Brazil).

In a context where routine police violence against blacks was one of the public faces of racial discrimination, the torture and assassination of a black taxi driver, Robson Luz, is considered to have been the decisive impulse for the creation of the MNU. Flavio Carranca, Hamilton Cardoso, Vanderlei José Maria, and Abdias do Nascimento were some of the leaders of the MNU at the time of its creation. On July 7, 1978, the MNU organized its first public act, gathering some 2000 participants in downtown São Paulo.

The MNU is a national organization, bringing together associates from all over Brazil. Around 300 people participated in the MNU's first national assembly, which took place in Rio de Janeiro on September 10, 1978. The MNU is made up of several independent bodies, including action groups, municipal coordinating committees, state coordinating committees, the National Executive Commission, and a National Congress. Each body has a certain amount of autonomous power, and decisions are taken only with the agreement of all the members of the groups, instead of just the national coordinating committee. It is a decentralized structure that reserves to the activists the power to decide which programs will be developed by the MNU. The National Congress has limited power to interfere with the other bodies; it is responsible only for defining the MNU's general policy.

The MNU was preceded by a number of Afro-Brazilian groups, newspapers, and events during the 1970s. These included groups such as Grupo Evolução, the Center for Black Culture and Art, and Quilombhoje; events like the First Meeting of Black Entities of São Paulo and the First Week of Black Art and Culture; and publications such as *Jornegro* and *Cadernos Negros*. In *Orpheus and Power* (1994), scholar Michael Hanchard comments on the significance of the MNU: "For the first time in Brazil, the advocacy of a race-class position was not marginalized by the Afro-Brazilian intelligentsia, and in fact had come to supplant accommodationist, assimilationist paradigms as the dominant position of the black movement. What was missing, by the later part of the 1970s, were events to propel these intellectual and political positions into forms of praxis."

The organization holds a comprehensive view of the problem of racial discrimination in Brazil. Unlike the Frente Negra Brasileira (the Brazilian Black Front) of the 1930s, Teatro Experimental do Negro (Black Experimental Theater), which was active from 1944-1968, and other precursors, the MNU deals with the racial question in all its aspects: political, social, cultural, and economic. Therefore, the MNU combines a broad range of activities in order to carry on its political project, ranging from grassroots rights education to public campaigns. For instance, the movement participated in the 1979 campaign for amnesty of political prisoners in Brazil. In this case the MNU made a statement protesting the exclusionary social-economic process that particularly victimizes the black population and in part explains the disproportionate number of Afro-Brazilians in the country's penal system. The MNU's concerns embraced topics as diverse as police violence, job opportunities for blacks, agrarian reform, education, health, and housing.

MNU women carried out educational programs in Bahia, for instance. Furthermore, the MNU supported individual candidates in electoral campaigns, such as Benedita da Silva, who in 1982 was elected as a city councilor in Rio de Janeiro and then in 1986 became the first black woman elected to the National Congress. The MNU also embraced questions related to black women and homosexuals and gay and lesbian movements in Latin America.

After its birth and ascendance during the late 1970s and early 1980s, the MNU began to decline. Its reduced impact on the national political arena is in part attributed to poor material resources and to the proliferation of competing groups. The MNU was never financially self-sufficient and relied on donations in order to carry out its activities. Its organizational diversity, which made unity difficult to achieve, was another factor relevant to the progressive decrease in the MNU's action: the independence of the MNU's action groups often generated internal conflict.

Nevertheless, among the groups that have been responsible for building the black movement in Brazil, the MNU is the organization that came closest to the mass-based claims and aspirations of its proponents, and represents a rupture in the history of Brazil's black movements. It moved away from an elitist and academic approach to the racial question, and instead took a more pragmatic and cross-class approach. The coalitions that the MNU made with political parties produced progress in terms of the acceptance of the racial question by career politicians. From the end of the 1970s onward, all the leftist political parties included special policies directed to the black population in their platforms, and many of these policies were in fact implemented. When Leonel Brizola was elected governor of the state of Rio de Janeiro in 1982, he nominated quite a few activists of the black movement as heads of governmental secretariats during his mandate. For instance, Carlos Alberto Cão was appointed secretary of labor; Edialeda Salgado Nascimento was the minister of social promotion; and Carlos Magno Nazareth headed the military police. The MNU was fundamental in introducing new challenges to racial discrimination and inequality in Brazil.

Michelle Gueraldi

See Also
Gay and Lesbian Movements in Latin America and the Caribbean; Rio de Janeiro, Brazil.

Africa

Mozambican National Resistance

(Mozambique National Resistance), Mozambican opposition movement and later political party.

The Resistência Nacional Moçambicana, or Mozambique National Resistance (RENAMO), emerged in the late 1970s as the Mozambican National Resistance (MNR) and in 1980 became a South African instrument to destabilize MOZAMBIQUE. The movement was organized by Rhodesian Security Forces and Portuguese Mozambicans who recruited disaffected Mozambicans, many of them former African members of the Portuguese colonial armed forces. Its initial objective was to undermine the Mozambican-based Zimbabwean freedom fighters, but when ZIMBABWE became independent in 1980, the South African government transferred the MNR to SOUTH AFRICA. The South African government viewed the fall of white-ruled colonial regimes in ANGOLA, Mozambique, and Zimbabwe, combined with rising internal unrest, as the beginning of a "total onslaught" on the APARTHEID regime and saw the MNR as an instrument to keep the Mozambican government weak and dependent.

Under South African instruction RENAMO set out to destroy the Mozambican economy, targeting railways, health centers, schools, bridges, administrative posts, roads, and other elements of the infrastructure. RENAMO initially relied on violent coercion to recruit new members, but over time many rural people voluntarily joined or provided other forms of support, due to their disaffection with the socialist policies of the ruling party, the FRONT FOR THE LIBERATION OF MOZAMBIQUE (FRELIMO).

Despite waning South African support (due to international pressure and domestic reform), by the late 1980s RENAMO numbered between 15,000 and 20,000 troops and had brought the Mozambican government to its knees. Negotiations concluded with a 1992 cease-fire and demobilization. By the national elections in 1994, RENAMO had transformed itself into a political party and the primary opposition in Mozambique's new multiparty political system. As a political party, RENAMO continued to lack a coherent ideology other than superficial calls for democracy, a free market economy, individual freedoms, and the reinstatement of traditional authorities.

Eric Young

Africa

Mozambique, republic on the eastern coast of southern Africa, bounded on the north by TANZANIA; on the east by the Mozambique Channel of the Indian Ocean; on the south and southwest by SOUTH AFRICA and SWAZILAND; and on the west by ZIMBABWE, ZAMBIA, and MALAWI.

Mozambique's history has been marked by strife. Conflicts that existed between the numerous indigenous societies were exacerbated by the initial expansion of regional kingdoms in the eighth century as well as by Portuguese imperialism beginning in the sixteenth century. Eventually, Mozambicans turned against the Portuguese in a long and bloody war for independence. However, Mozambique had to defend its hard-won independence from Rhodesia (now Zimbabwe), South Africa, and an indigenous insurgency movement. The government's survival came at the cost of abandoning its socialist development policies and of turning to the West for assistance. Although a fragile peace has recently come to Mozambique, external involvement continues to be central to the country's political and economic life.

EARLY HISTORY

In the third century C.E., as Bantu-speaking people migrated to the area now known as Mozambique, they replaced descendants of the KHOIKHOI of southwestern Africa. The character of the societies that emerged was defined largely by geography. In the south, the Chopi, Tonga, and Tsonga ethnic groups, all descendants of larger groups in eastern SOUTH AFRICA, were typically organized into village-sized chiefdoms. In the central regions, around the ZAMBEZI RIVER, lived the Barue, Maravi, Makua-Lomwe, SHONA, and TONGA (to be distinguished from the southern group of the same name). These groups, however, were not internally homogeneous, and they included a variety of forms of organization. The Maravi, for example, were composed of a series of decentralized kingdoms (the CHEWA, Nyanja, Chipeta, Zimba, Nsenga, and Nyassa), while the Makua-Lomwe were organized around clans, which often made alliances against the invading Maravi. Further north were the Makonde and Yao, living in isolation among the hills of the Mueda Plateau.

As early as the eighth century, Arab traders entered the region, particularly in the north and along the Zambezi River. They brought ceramics, cloth, beads, glass, salt, and metal goods to be traded for gold, palm oil, rhinoceros horn, and ivory. With the cooperation of African chiefs, this trade expanded, and in the fifteenth century trading stations were founded along the Zambezi. Not long after the Arab traders established themselves, the Shona of Zimbabwe became a major influence in central Mozambique. Prior to the eleventh century, Shona influence was negligible, but the predominance of the Karanga subgroup of the Shona changed this. Steeped in the royal cult powers of the Mwari spirit, the creator and sustainer of life, Nyatsimba Mutota, who became known as the Munhumutapa (the Pillager), tried to conquer the Zambezi valley. Although the Munhumutapa was unsuccessful, his son carried on the war that ultimately destroyed small kingdoms and chieftainships and dislocated populations throughout Mozambique, south of the Zambezi River and north of the Save River.

EARLY ARAB AND PORTUGUESE INFLUENCE IN MOZAMBIQUE

After Portuguese explorer VASCO DA GAMA arrived in 1497, increasing Arab economic preeminence and Shona military dominance in Mozambique were met by Portuguese expansion. The Portuguese initially confined their activities to trade along the coast for supplies while en route to the Far East. Soon, however, they ventured inland in search of gold and ivory. Jesuit priests brought Christianity, and African chiefs proved amenable to the demands of the Portuguese, who had taken over domestic and international trade. The Portuguese gradually fragmented and dismantled the Munhumutapa Kingdom through material enticement and force. More important, using land ceded to them by the Munhumutapa in 1629, the Portuguese introduced settlers to Mozambique and the system of *prazos*, or leaseholds. The prazos were a semifeudal system of land tenure in which the land remained the property of the Crown but could be leased for a fixed time, usually three lifetimes. The leaseholders were expected to provide for their own defense with the proceeds from the land, which included the right to use the inhabitants of the land for labor.

The prazos system was an affordable way for Portugal, the poorest European imperial power, to expand its influence, but the system also gave wide-ranging independence to the leaseholders, the *prazeros*. The prazos developed into Africanized autonomous kingdoms, ruled by families of Afro-Goan-Portuguese descent and sustained by slave armies. The prazeros and their African collaborators also played a prominent role in sustaining the slave trade, which reached its height in the 1820s and 1830s after GREAT BRITAIN banned slave trading, providing approximately 15,000 slaves annually to BRAZIL (around 10 percent of the annual Atlantic trade at the time). During the middle of the nineteenth century Mozambique south of the Zambezi effectively came under the control of the NGUNI warlord Soshangane and his Gaza Empire. With the independence of the prazeros in the Zambezi valley, and the de facto control of southern Mozambique by Soshangane, the Portuguese changed tactics to save their "overseas province" when the SCRAMBLE FOR AFRICA began in earnest in the late 1800s. Fearing British or German encroachment, the Portuguese government conquered the land, then gave large concessions to charter companies to occupy it. By the BERLIN CONFERENCE OF 1884-1885, Portuguese colonial forces maintained at least a minimal presence in most of what is today Mozambique. While some groups surrendered to Portuguese colonial rule, many others, particularly in the Zambezi valley and on the Mueda Plateau, fought extended wars of resistance.

PORTUGUESE COLONIALISM

Violence and neglect characterized Portuguese

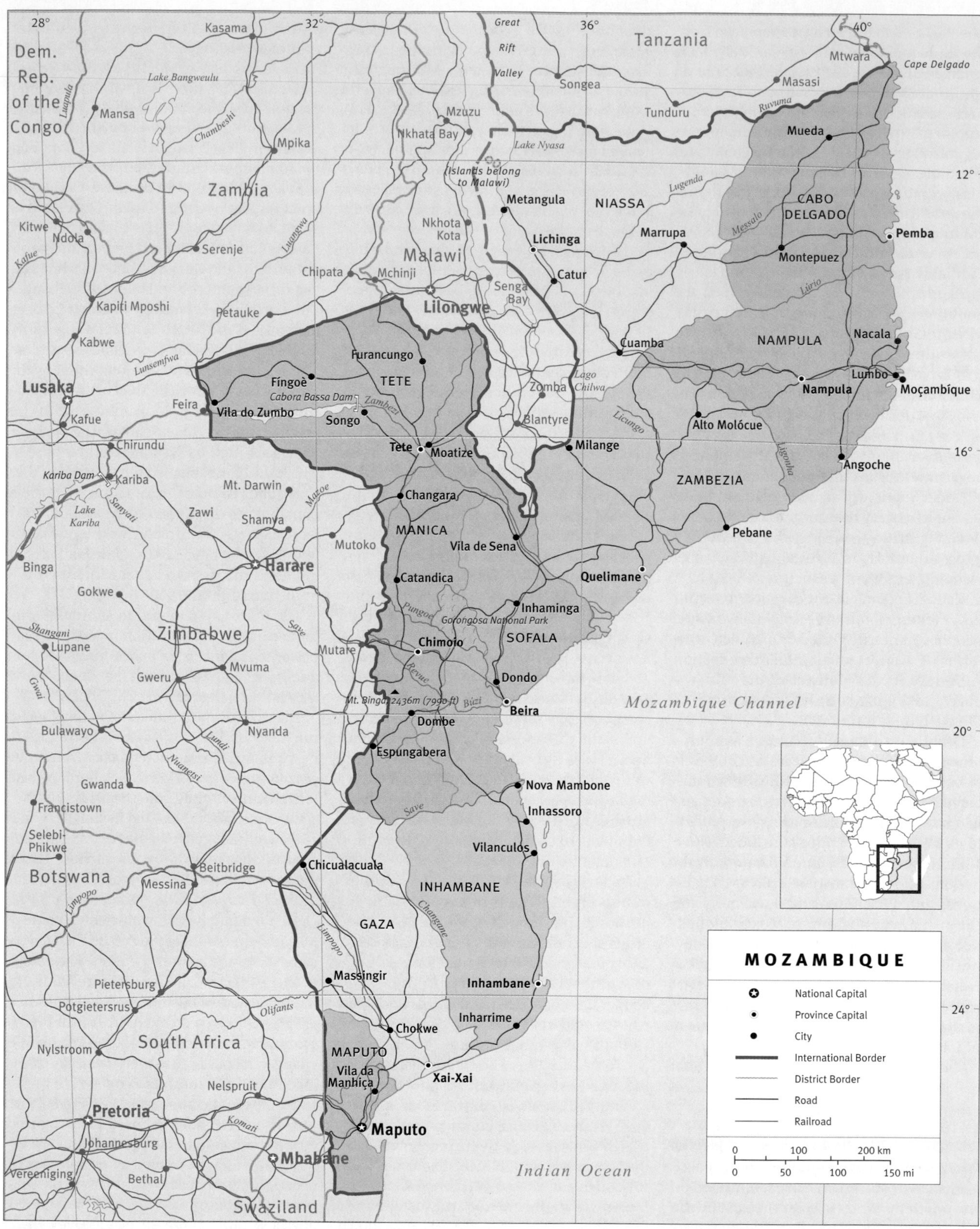

colonialism in Mozambique. In addition to centralizing administrative control over the territory for the first time, the Portuguese dictator Antonio Salazar (1932-1968) instituted a system of forced labor, avoidable only through attaining an *assimilado* (assimilated) status through education and land ownership or employment outside the colony. (Migration to South African mines became a prominent feature in Mozambique's economy at this time.) Africans were forced to work on large plantations harvesting SUGAR, tea, and other agricultural products. Few Africans in Mozambique gained the status of assimilado, and Salazar's ideology of "Lusotropicalism," which advanced the notion that Portugal was uniquely capable of creating a nonracial society, was a myth created to sustain domestic Portuguese support for its overseas possessions (though the ideology did curtail more blatant race-based policies). Thus, when Marcello Caetano replaced Salazar, educational, health, and skilled employment opportunities for Africans were almost nonexistent and repression was commonplace.

The Struggle for Independence
Organized opposition to Portuguese colonialism was initially fragmented. Rural discontent was allowed no legal form of expression. Instead, opposition groups formed among students in Lisbon, Portugal, and Paris, France, and among exiles in Southern Rhodesia, Malawi, and Tanzania. In 1962 the fragmented opposition united to form the Frente de Libertação de Moçambique (Front for the Liberation of Mozambique, or FRELIMO) under the leadership of Eduardo Mondlane. Mondlane and FRELIMO used nationalist appeals that highlighted the evils of Portuguese colonialism to bring the disparate groups together. Its leaders also concluded that independence would be won only through armed struggle, given Portuguese intransigence in granting greater equality, rights, and freedoms to Africans. In 1964 the war for independence began in northern Mozambique.

The war spread quickly in the north, facilitated by sanctuaries of the insurgents in Tanzania, minimal Portuguese presence, and FRELIMO's Chinese military training. Stiffening Portuguese resistance and a resettlement program that denied FRELIMO vital local support soon slowed FRELIMO's progress. To maintain its momentum, FRELIMO opened a second front, in the northwestern Tete Province, catching the Portuguese off guard. Initial FRELIMO gains, however, were again frustrated for a number of reasons: in 1969 FRELIMO president Mondlane was assassinated by the colonial secret police; many FRELIMO bases were destroyed in a major Portuguese counterinsurgency offensive; resettlement programs were intensified; the Cabora Bassa dam project flooded much of the upper Zambezi River, making it difficult for FRELIMO to move south; and African recruitment into the colonial armed forces was accelerated.

Under the leadership of Samora Machel, FRELIMO survived the Portuguese counteroffensive and by the early 1970s had moved into the Zambezi valley, ultimately claiming "liberated zones" in approximately one-fourth of the country. Before FRELIMO had a chance to win the war, the Portuguese military, increasingly frustrated because it was simultaneously fighting counterinsurgency wars in Angola and Guinea-Bissau, overthrew the Caetano government in April

ABOVE RIGHT: The bridge over the Zambezi River, Mozambique, indicates efforts to modernize the transportation system. *CORBIS/Jon Spaull*
RIGHT: A child drinks from a water spout in Mozambique. Years of civil turmoil have severely damaged the country's education system. *CORBIS/Liba Taylor*

1974. The new military government in Lisbon brought the war in Mozambique to an end and agreed to a transition to independence.

A Luta Continua (The Struggle Continues)

The coup d'état in Lisbon did not bring peace to Mozambique. Soon after independence in June 1975, Mozambique closed its border with Rhodesia and began supporting Zimbabwe African National Union (ZANU) insurgents by providing sanctuary from which to launch their war for independence against Rhodesia. In response, the Rhodesian regime attacked refugee camps and military training bases inside Mozambique and created the Mozambican National Resistance (MNR), later known as the Resistência Nacional Moçambicana or Mozambique

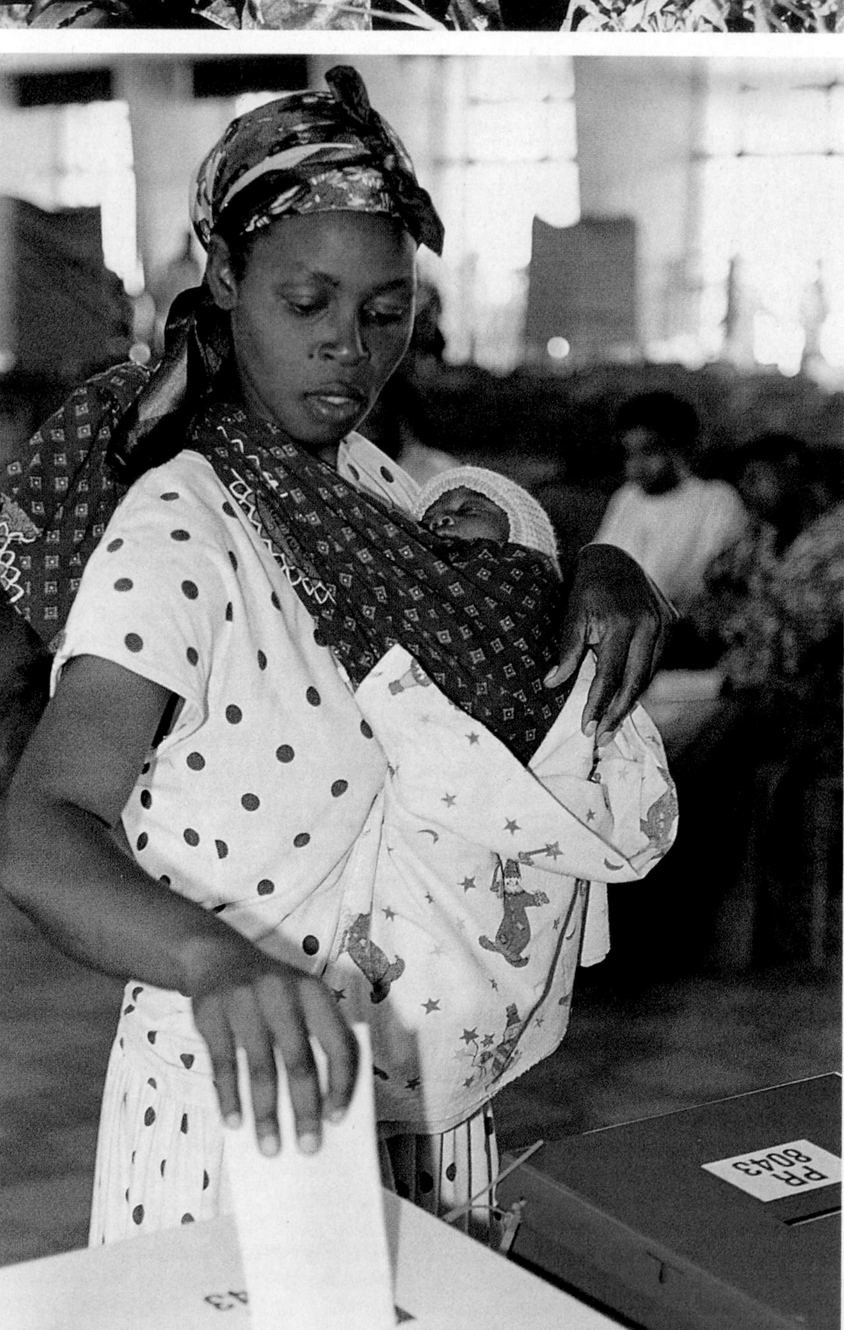

ABOVE LEFT: Two Mozambican soldiers guard a civilian convoy from attack by Mozambican National Resistance guerillas in 1985. *Reuters/CORBIS*
LEFT: A young Mozambican mother casts her ballot during the country's first multiparty elections in October 1994. *Reuters/Juda Ngwenya/Archive Photos*
ABOVE: A land mine found outside Dombe in Mozambique during the war for independence from Portugal, which lasted from 1964 to 1975. *CORBIS/Gary Trotter; Eye Ubiquitous*

National Resistance (RENAMO), to destabilize Mozambique. At the same time, in the late 1970s, FRELIMO sought to implement wide-ranging socialist policies as well as to consolidate its power throughout the country. FRELIMO thus conceived of the battle as one with two fronts: one was a defensive strategy to protect itself from Rhodesian, South African, and international imperialism; the second was an offensive for the creation of a new society. *A Luta Continua* (The Struggle Continues) became a popular slogan with dual connotations.

When Zimbabwe won its independence, RENAMO was transferred to South Africa, where it was employed by the apartheid government to further destabilize Mozambique and pressure the FRELIMO government to cease its support for the antiapartheid African National Congress (ANC). In the early 1980s, with vital South African support, RENAMO carried out attacks on administrative posts, health centers, schools, and infrastructure projects throughout central Mozambique. RENAMO boosted its numbers through forced recruitment, but it also attracted support from rural populations increasingly alienated by FRELIMO's policies of scientific socialism. The government's efforts to mechanize agricultural production on collectivized state-run farms increased rural hardship, especially after a cycle of severe floods and droughts in the late 1970s and early 1980s. FRELIMO's opposition to traditional chiefs and nonscientific beliefs, such as beliefs in witchcraft, spirit mediums, and superstition, also antagonized large parts of society.

Neither the Soviet-backed Mozambican military, with assistance from Zimbabwe, Tanzania, and Malawi, nor a 1984 nonaggression pact with South Africa stemmed the RENAMO onslaught. When President Machel was killed in a mysterious plane crash in South Africa in 1986 (Machel was survived by his wife, GRAÇA MACHEL, a prominent human rights advocate), Mozambique was on the brink of disintegration. FRELIMO was unable to defend Mozambique and largely failed in its attempt to build a new economic and social order.

STRUCTURAL ADJUSTMENT AND PEACE

Growing domestic pragmatism and changes in the international environment ultimately brought the war in Mozambique to an end. The more pragmatic and less ideological president JOAQUIM CHISSANO slowly turned the country toward the West for economic and military assistance. After the Soviet Union collapsed, Britain, Portugal, and the United States became the primary supporters of the beleaguered FRELIMO government. Support did not come without conditions, particularly from the International Monetary Fund (IMF) and World Bank, which tied the financing of Mozambique's economic structural adjustment program to political liberalization. At FRELIMO's Fifth Congress, in July 1989, the party dropped its Marxist-Leninist ideology and opened party membership to business and religious leaders. Later that year the president submitted to the Popular Assembly a new constitution permitting multiparty elections.

The government also entered into negotiations with RENAMO. In 1992, after protracted negotiations, the parties signed the General Peace Agreement, which called for an immediate cease-fire; the demobilization of the militaries; the creation of a new, national military; and elections in 1994. The entire process was closely monitored by the United Nations, which also observed the reelection of Chissano as president. FRELIMO came to dominate the new Assembly of the Republic, while RENAMO became the official opposition.

The cost of peace in Mozambique has been rising crime and corruption. Mozambique is a major shipment point for drugs to South Africa, and a profusion of weapons has facilitated the rise of armed banditry throughout the country. Unemployment and the rising costs accompanying economic liberalization have led to corruption. Both crime and corruption have hurt an already weak economy that is only slowly recovering from the war. Prawns and shrimp remain the largest export; the tourism industry, which seeks to attract visitors to its beaches and to Gorongosa National Park, is growing slowly; and the country remains massively in debt and dependent on international donor assistance.

Eric Young

SEE ALSO

African Socialism; Bantu: Dispersion and Settlement; Christianity, African: An Overview; Explorers in Africa Before 1500; Gold Trade; Ivory Trade; Machel, Samora Moises; Nationalism in Africa; Transatlantic Slave Trade; United Nations in Africa; Portugal; Mozambican National Resistance; Salt Trade; Structural Adjustment in Africa; Tourism in Africa.

Africa

Mozambique (Ready Reference)

Official Name: Republic of Mozambique
Area: 799,380 sq km (308,641 sq mi)
Location: Southern Africa, bounded on the north by TANZANIA; on the east by the Mozambique Channel of the Indian Ocean; on the south and southwest by SOUTH AFRICA and SWAZILAND; and on the west by ZIMBABWE, ZAMBIA, and MALAWI
Capital: Maputo (population 1,098,000 [1991 estimate])
Other Major Cities: Beira (population 299,300 [1990 estimate]) and Nampula (202,600)
Population: 18,641,469 (1998 estimate)
Population Density: 20 persons per sq km (53 persons per sq mi)
Population Below Age 15: 45 percent (male 4,129,779; female 4,232,091 [1998 estimate])
Population Growth Rate: 2.57 percent (1998 estimate)
Life Expectancy at Birth: Total population: 45.37 years (male 44.22 years; female 46.55 years [1998 estimate])
Infant Mortality Rate: 120.26 deaths per 1000 live births (1998 estimate)
Literacy Rate (age 15 and over who can read and write): Total population: 40.1 percent (male 57.7 percent; female 23.3 percent [1995 estimate])
Education: Due to civil instability and the limited number of trained teachers, in the early 1990s only about 1.2 million pupils attended primary schools and just over 150,000 students went to secondary schools.
Languages: Portuguese is the official language, though Swahili and various Bantu languages are spoken commonly.
Ethnic Groups: Mozambique has ten major ethnic groups, including the Makua-Lomwe (which accounts for nearly 50 percent of the northern population), Tsonga, Malawi, SHONA, and YAO.
Religions: Indigenous beliefs, 50 percent; Christian, 30 percent; Muslim, 20 percent
Climate: Mozambique has tropical savanna with a dry season lasting from April to October. July (winter) temperatures range from an average of 21° C (70° F) in the north to 18° C (65° F) in the south. January (summer) temperatures average about 27° C (80° F). Although rainfall can be irregular, the northern regions receive around 1500 mm (about 60 in) annually, as opposed to 750 mm (about 30 in) in the south.
Land, Plants, and Animals: Two-fifths of Mozambique is coastal lowland. Inland the land rises to the western low hills and plateaus to the far western mountains, including Mount Binga's 2436 m (7992 ft) peak. Northwest Mozambique's Angonia Plateau lies in the Great Rift Valley. Flowing from the western highlands to the Mozambique Channel are several rivers, including the Zambezi; other major rivers include the Ruvuma, Save, and Limpopo. With landscapes ranging from grassland to tropical rain forest, Mozambique is home to many species, including ZEBRA, buffalo, RHINOCEROS, GIRAFFE, LION, and ELEPHANT.
Natural Resources: Mineral resources include coal, iron, salt, tantalite, diamonds, asbestos, bauxite, copper, manganese, titanium, natural gas, and soil.
Currency: The metical (Mt)
Gross Domestic Product (GDP): $14.6 billion (1997 estimate)
GDP per Capita: $800 (1997 estimate)
GDP Real Growth Rate: 8 percent (1997 estimate)
Primary Economic Activities: Agriculture, industry, and services
Primary Crops: Cotton, cashew nuts, sugar cane, tea, cassava, corn, rice, and tropical fruits
Industries: Food, beverages, chemicals (fertilizer, soap, paints), petroleum products, textiles, cement, glass, asbestos, and tobacco
Primary Exports: Shrimp, cashews, cotton, and sugar
Primary Imports: Food, clothing, farm equipment, and petroleum
Primary Trade Partners: South Africa, United Kingdom, France, Japan, and Portugal
Government: Following a new constitution in 1990, a multiparty republic was instituted. In the executive branch, the prime minister, currently Pascal Mocumbi, is head of government, while the president, currently JOAQUIM CHISSANO, is chief of state. The People's Assembly, a unicameral national legislature, is directly elected. In the 1994 elections, the FRONT FOR THE LIBERATION OF MOZAMBIQUE (FRELIMO) won a slight majority; the main opposition party, the

Mozambique National Resistance (RENAMO), won full legal recognition only in 1992.

Kate Tuttle

See Also

Bantu: Dispersion and Settlement; Swahili Language; Maputo, Mozambique; Mozambican National Resistance; Rift Valleys; Zambezi River.

Latin America and the Caribbean

Mozambique, Luis de,

Panamanian slave who in the mid-sixteenth century led a maroon settlement located in the San Blas Mountains (*see* Panama).

Africa

Mphahlele, Es'kia (b. 1919,

Marabastad Township, Pretoria, South Africa), South African writer best known for his autobiography *Down Second Avenue* (1959), which portrays his early life as a black South African. The characters in his fictional works are drawn with vivid realism and are portrayed not as victims but as survivors who overcome the harshness of their lives.

Born Ezekiel Mphahlele (in 1977 he changed his first name to Es'kia) in Marabastad Township, Pretoria, Mphahlele was educated at Adams Teaching Training College. He became a teacher, but in the early 1950s he was banned from teaching because of his opposition to the Bantu Education Act of 1953, which segregated classrooms by race. In the mid-1950s he worked as an editor for the literary journal *Drum,* and in 1956 he obtained a master's degree from the University of South Africa. Mphahlele went into exile from South Africa in 1957. He subsequently lived in Nigeria, where he was an editor for the periodical *Black Orpheus;* in Kenya; in Zambia; and in the United States, where he attended the University of Denver and taught at the University of Pennsylvania. He returned to South Africa in 1977 and later became a professor at the University of Witwatersrand.

Mphahlele's first book, *Man Must Live* (1947), is a collection of short stories about black life in South Africa. *Down Second Avenue,* his second and most famous work, achieved great critical and popular success and is considered a classic of South African literature. *The Wanderers* (1971) is an autobiographical novel dealing with themes of exile. His novel *Chirundu* (1979) focuses on the conflicts felt by a fictional African politician. *Afrika My Music* (1984) is another autobiographical work, describing Mphahlele's exile and return to South Africa. His novel *Father Come Home* (1984) is concerned with the suffering caused by the Natives Land Act of 1913, which restricted blacks from residing in certain areas in South Africa. Mphahlele's other books include the critical works *The African Image* (1962) and *Voices in the Whirlwind and Other Essays* (1972). A collection of his letters, *Bury Me at the Marketplace,* was published in 1984.

MPLA. Please see Popular Movement for the Liberation of Angola

Africa

Mpondo (also known as the Amapondo and the Pondo), ethnic group of South Africa.

The Mpondo primarily inhabit Eastern Cape Province, South Africa. They speak Xhosa, a Bantu language in the Nguni group. Approximately 2 million people consider themselves Mpondo.

See Also

Bantu: Dispersion and Settlement.

Africa

Mpongwe, ethnic group of northwestern Gabon.

Some historians believe that the Mpongwe migrated to the northwest coast of present-day Gabon from the interior around 2000 years ago, while others contend that they migrated during the tenth century C.E. The Mpongwe's own legends hold that their ancestors emerged spontaneously from the ground.

The Mpongwe and the neighboring Orungu share many ethnolinguistic similarities. Their languages both belong to the Myènè group, whose speakers say *myènè,* "I say that," to initiate conversation. As a result of migrations throughout the centuries, the Mpongwe formed numerous clans, each headed by an *oga,* or chief. According to tradition, the Ndiwa were the first of the clans to reach the coast. The clans of the Mpongwe traded extensively among themselves and probably with the Loango Kingdom to the south. The Mpongwe fished, hunted, and grew yams and other crops. Each settlement included a few artisans who made utensils and religious paraphernalia. The Mpongwe were also accomplished sailors who traveled in dugout canoes along the coast as far north as the Cameroon River.

In the sixteenth century, as competition for trade with European ships increased, the interior Orungu forced many of the Mpongwe clans toward the Estuary of Gabon. Slaveholders themselves, the Mpongwe became extensively involved as middlemen in the transatlantic trade in slaves and other commodities. The incursions of the Orungu and a Dutch massacre of the Ndiwa clan in 1698 began to undermine Mpongwe hegemony in the estuary region. Mpongwe dominance was further eroded in the early nineteenth century when the Fang migrated to the region and a subsequent low birthrate and smallpox epidemic cut the Mpongwe population by between one-third and one-half. But as traders and entrepreneurs, the Mpongwe prospered. Their access to mission schools earned them an elite status within the French colonial bureaucracy; this, in turn, permitted them to become an instrumental part of the Gabonese nationalist movement. Since independence the Mpongwe have continued to play a preeminent role in the country's political and economic life. Today the Mpongwe number around 60,000.

Eric Young

See Also

Colonial Rule; Transatlantic Slave Trade; Loango, Early Kingdom of; Slavery in Africa.

Africa

Msiri (also known as Mwanda, Msidi, and Moshidi, born as Ngelengwa) (b. 1820s,

Tanzania; d. 1891, Katanga region, Democratic Republic of the Congo), trader, founder, and ruler of the Yeke (Garenganze) Kingdom in southern Central Africa.

The son of a Sumbwa chief and trader, Msiri started his career on the trade routes forged by his father between East and Central Africa. In 1856 he negotiated with Mwata Kazembe, chief of the Lunda Empire, for the right to settle and trade in south Katanga.

There Msiri used alliances with local ruling families and firearms acquired from traders to build his own empire, the Yeke, or Garenganze. By 1870 Msiri's empire extended throughout Katanga. He also built his trade networks by forging ties with Tippu Tip, a Swahili trader, as well as many other East African merchants, to whom he exported slaves, ivory, and copper in return for cloth and firearms.

In 1880, after the death of his father, Msiri proclaimed himself *mwami,* or king, of the region. For the next six years he was the most powerful ruler in what is now the southern Democratic Republic of the Congo. His empire extended over former Luba and Lunda states, including areas formerly controlled by Mwata Kazembe, the salt springs of Mwashya and the Lualaba River. The stability of this empire, however, was short-lived. Revolts in newly acquired territories, coupled with colonial advances, weakened Msiri's control. He tried to deter the Europeans, but they were intent on acquiring the mineral-rich land. In 1891 he was shot by a Belgian soldier after he refused to negotiate with representatives of the Congo Free State, to whom he declared, "I am the master here, and so long as I live, the Kingdom of Garenganze shall have no other."

Elizabeth Heath

See Also

Ivory Trade; Swahili People; Slavery in Africa.

Africa

Mswati III (b. 1968), formerly Makhosetive, *ngwenyama* (paramount chief or king) of Swaziland (1986-).

The second youngest of at least 67 sons of King Sobhuza II, Makhosetive was only 15 years old when chosen by his ailing father to succeed him to the throne. According to tradition, he was not to be crowned king until he turned 21; in the meantime, royal duties were to be attended to by a regent, one of Sobhuza's wives. In 1983 Makhosetive was called away from his studies at Sherborne, England, to quell unrest generated by the removal of Queen Mother Dzeliwe as regent and the installation of Queen Ntombi. Further disputes between royal factions led to his coronation as King Mswati III in April 1986, three years earlier than expected. In May 1986 Mswati dismissed the Liqoqo, the traditional advisory council to regents, which had assumed greater powers than was customary. In July 1986 he dismissed and charged with treason Prime Minister Prince Bhekimpi and several government officials for their role in the ejection of Queen Regent Dzeliwe, though he eventually pardoned those who were convicted.

Following the confirmation of his kingship when he turned 21, Mswati faced increasing demands by opposition leaders for transition to a multiparty democratic state in which the monarchy would only serve a ceremonial function. Mswati refused these demands and again dismissed his prime minister. Today Swaziland's economy suffers from the withdrawal of large multinational corporations that looked on the small nation as a safe investment in the midst of the political volatility in neighboring South Africa and Mozambique during the 1980s. Criticism of the royal family, with its monopoly on agricultural lands and its lavish spending on luxuries, has intensified. A January 1996 eight-day pro-democracy strike by timber and sugar workers prompted Mswati to agree to hold forums on the future of the monarchy, but he insisted that he would not be forced to cede power.

Africa

Mubarak, Hosni (b. May 4, 1928, al-Minufiyah governate, Egypt), president of Egypt.

Hosni Mubarak's life largely parallels that of his predecessor and mentor, Anwar al-Sadat. Both were sons of minor government officials, and both were born in the Nile Delta region of Egypt. Both pursued careers in the military, which seized political control of Egypt from the royal family in a 1952 coup. Each was considered weak and politically vulnerable when he assumed the presidency, and each emerged as a strong leader who solidified his hold on power. Yet Mubarak's career differed from Sadat's in several important ways.

Mubarak graduated from the Cairo Military Academy in 1949. He then attended Egypt's Air Force Academy and received advanced flight and bomber training at the Frunze General Staff Academy in the Soviet Union. He rose to prominence after the purge of air force leadership that followed its ignominious defeat in the 1967 Six-Day War with Israel. During this period he served as director of the Egyptian Air Force Academy. In 1971 Sadat named Mubarak air force commander. Many credit Mubarak with rebuilding the air force in the wake of the Six-Day War. He also received much of the credit for the air force's strong performance in the Yom Kippur War of 1973, when combined Egyptian and Syrian forces launched a surprise attack against Israel. Sadat promoted Mubarak to the rank of air marshal in 1974 and to vice president in 1975, a position he held until Sadat's assassination on October 6, 1981.

After assuming office Mubarak pursued a course of moderation. He upheld the Camp David Accords, the 1979 peace treaty between Egypt and Israel that stated that Israel would return portions of the Sinai Peninsula to Egypt in April 1982. Israel's invasion of Lebanon later that year, however, strained relations with Egypt. Meanwhile, Mubarak worked to improve Egypt's relationship with other Arab states since conditions had deteriorated in the wake of the accords. He also sought to reclaim Egypt's prominence among Arab nations by mediating between Arab states and Israel and by brokering Arab League support for military action against Iraq after its 1990 invasion of Kuwait. Mubarak sent approximately 40,000 Egyptian troops to support the anti-Iraq coalition during the 1991 Persian Gulf War. He also figured prominently in the 1993 deal between Israel and the Palestinian Liberation Organization.

Though Mubarak won reelection in 1987 and 1993, he also faced a series of crises, including an assassination attempt in 1995 from which he emerged unharmed. In addition, Mubarak faces threats from Islamic fundamentalist opposition groups, most notably the Muslim Brotherhood and the Islamic Group. Just before parliamentary elections in 1995, Mubarak arrested several leaders of the Muslim Brotherhood, including some who were candidates in the election. He has imposed martial law in Egypt and resorted to repression to quell violence by Islamic fundamentalists, though with little lasting effect. In late 1997 in the Valley of the Kings in Luxor, members of the Islamic Group attacked and killed dozens of foreign tourists. The attack crippled Egypt's tourism industry, which attracted more than $3 billion per year in foreign currency.

Robert Fay

See Also

Nile River; Tourism in Africa; Sadat, Anwar al-; Islamic Fundamentalism: An Interpretation.

Africa

Mugabe, Robert (b. February 21, 1924, Zvimba, Rhodesia [now Zimbabwe]), revolutionary leader and president of Zimbabwe.

A teacher by training and politician by practice, Robert Mugabe has been Zimbabwe's preeminent political leader for nearly two decades. Born, raised, and trained as a teacher at Kutama Mission in northwestern Zimbabwe, he taught at the mission school between 1941 and 1943. After holding several other brief teaching jobs around Zimbabwe (then Southern Rhodesia), he won a scholarship to Fort Hare University College in South Africa, where he was introduced to literature on communism, Marxism, and Gandhian passive resistance. He completed his bachelor's degree, returned to and taught in Zimbabwe, then taught in Northern Rhodesia (Zambia) and later in Ghana.

In 1960 Mugabe returned home to enter politics. He first joined the nationalist group the Zimbabwe African People's Union (ZAPU), but in 1964, after several arrests and a falling-out with its leadership, Mugabe went to Tanzania and joined the newly formed Zimbabwe African National Union, or ZANU, which inaugurated the war for independence that same year.

On returning to Southern Rhodesia, Mugabe was again arrested. He spent most of the next decade in prison, earning bachelor's degrees in law and administration while there. While Mugabe was in prison, ZANU members elected him to replace Ndabaningi Sithole as party head; his position as such was contested until 1976, when the military wing of ZANU recognized him as leader. After four more years of war, Mugabe and ZAPU leader Joshua Nkomo entered into negotiations with the Rhodesians, concluding with Zimbabwe's independence in April 1980. In elections just prior to independence, Mugabe and ZANU won by a landslide and Mugabe became prime minister.

Since independence Mugabe has proven to be a highly pragmatic leader. After the war he called for reconciliation and has taken care not to offend Western governments or the white community of Zimbabwe, whose skills and wealth the country needed. Although he has often espoused socialism, he has maintained an essentially free-market economy. At the same time Mugabe has consolidated his power. He put considerable pressure on Nkomo and the ZAPU party until 1987, when they agreed to join ZANU, creating the ZANU-Patriotic Front (ZANU-PF). With the creation of an executive presidency the same year, opposition, official or otherwise, effectively came to an end. In elections in 1990 Mugabe won 78 percent of the popular vote; ZANU-PF has remained the de facto ruling party, typically winning all but a handful of parliamentary seats.

Elitism and cronyism have become the norm in Mugabe's government. The Zimbabwean parliament has served as little more than a rubber stamp, and the president and his few advisers retain a tight grip on the most powerful ministries, such as defense, home affairs, and justice. In several corruption scandals Mugabe has intervened to halt the prosecution of close associates and family members. Few within or outside government dare oppose him in the face of broad though increasingly apathetic popular support and the bureaucracy's powerful patronage system. The lack of an obvious successor has caused considerable speculation in political circles and the press, as Mugabe, the dominant political force in Zimbabwe, begins to show his age.

Eric Young

See Also

African Socialism.

North America

Muhammad, Elijah (Elijah Poole) (b. October 1897, Sandersville, Ga.; d. February 25, 1975, Chicago, Ill.), leader of the Nation of Islam; black separatist.

The sixth of seven children of William and Mariah Poole, Elijah was the favorite of his siblings, parents, and grandfather, and was perceived by them as being destined for greatness. It was his grandfather who named him after the biblical Elijah, and throughout his childhood he was teasingly referred to as "the Prophet."

Aside from sharecropping and working at a sawmill, William Poole pastored at two Baptist churches. Young Elijah was exposed to the ministry from a tender age. He took an avid interest in Christian theology, but his father's fire and brimstone sermons caused him to question what seemed like a dour intrepretation of spirituality. It was many years before he would break away from Christianity completely, and ironically it was his father who first introduced him to the Nation of Islam.

When he was around ten years old, he left school out of economic necessity and began chopping firewood with his sister. Until this point he had lived in relative shelter from the brutal racist practices of the region. This ended when he witnessed, as an adolescent, the lynching of an 18-year-old acquaintance. On another occasion, as he was walking home from work, a white man taunted him with the severed ears of a black person. The horror of these two incidents, he later recounted, made him ripe for black separatist ideology. "I had seen enough of the white man's brutality in Georgia to last me 26,000 years."

Elijah's youth and early adulthood were marked by a pattern of floating jobs and long periods of unemployment. In 1923, married with two children, he migrated to industrial Detroit. But even in the years before the Depression there was an economic downturn in many large cities. With the pressure of three more children to support and little prospect of work, he went through a period of listlessness and heavy drinking.

It was at this time that his father, on a spiritual quest of his own, started speaking to Elijah and his brothers about the Islamic movement. In 1931 Elijah attended his first Islamic meeting and met its leader, Wallace D. Fard. He became fully immersed in the movement, abandoning his "slave owner" surname. He was initially called Karriem, and later Muhammad. Within the year he became Fard's top assistant. As the Muslim movement grew more prominent in the black community, it became a target for government investigation, and Fard's leadership began to suffer. In 1933, in an attempt to remove himself from the negative spotlight, Fard named Muhammad Supreme Minister and gave him full administrative power.

Despite continual police hostility and subsequent relocation to Chicago, the Nation of Islam under Muhammad prospered and evolved. Rather than shunning the technology of Western culture, as Fard had encouraged, Muhammad invested in radios and modern farm equipment. In order for black separatism to succeed, he believed, total economic independence was crucial. In 1945 the Nation purchased 140 acres of farmland in Michigan. Two years later a Nation-owned grocery store, restaurant, and bakery opened in Chicago.

As the Nation's influence spread throughout various black communities around the United States, Muhammad began to live a more luxurious lifestyle that seemingly contradicted the Muslim creed of stringency and humility. He purchased cars and real estate and apparently had sexual liaisons with a number of young women in the movement. When Malcolm X was murdered after leaving the movement, there were many who believed that Muhammad's violent denunciation of his one-time protégé had instigated the assassination.

As a leader in the quest for black nationalism, Muhammad was, for a long time, considered a hostile force by the United States government. He served a jail sentence for draft evasion during World War II and was wired by the FBI for more than two decades. Nevertheless, by the time of his death in 1975, his conservative approach made him seem moderate compared to other radical groups of the Civil Rights era. His emphasis on black self-suffiency rather than overthrow of the government made him an appealing ally to such local officials as Mayor Richard Daley, who in 1974 declared March 29 "Honorable Elijah Muhammad Day in Chicago."

Suzanne Albulak

See Also

World War II and African Americans; Baptists; Chicago, Illinois; Civil Rights Movement; Detroit, Michigan; Fard, Wallace D.; Black Nationalism in the United States.

Africa

Muluzi, Bakili (1943-), president of Malawi (1994-).

Bakili Muluzi was born in Machinga in southern Malawi (at the time called Nyasaland) and was educated in Great Britain and Denmark. He entered Parliament in 1975 after rising through the ranks of the ruling Malawi Congress Party (MCP), and held posts as the minister of education and party secretary-general during the next several years.

In 1982, having recently been demoted to a less prestigious post at the ministry of transport and communications, and fearing that President Hastings Kamuzu Banda might have him killed because he was gaining power in the party, Mulazi left the MCP for private business. He served for several years as deputy head of the national Chamber of Commerce, slowly gathering his forces until 1992, when he founded the United Democratic Front, the first political alternative under Banda's dictatorship.

Banda was forced to hold a referendum on one-party rule in June 1993 following widespread protests and a 1992 decision by Western donors to suspend their support of Malawi's repressive regime and its poor human rights record. A majority of the voters approved of reform, and a new constitution providing for a multiparty system was adopted in May 1994. Muluzi defeated Banda in the country's first multiparty elections held that month. Muluzi's stated aims for his administration were to combat poverty and corruption, liberalize the economy, and improve Malawi's human rights situation. He immediately freed political prisoners and shut down three prisons that were reportedly the sites of many tortures.

See Also

Banda, Ngwazi Hastings Kamuzu.

Africa

Mumuye, ethnic group of Nigeria.

The Mumuye primarily inhabit Taraba State in eastern Nigeria. They speak a Niger-Congo language. Approximately 400,000 people consider themselves Mumuye.

See Also

Languages, African: An Overview.

Africa

Mundang (also known as the Moundang), ethnic group of West Africa.

The Mundang primarily inhabit northern CAMEROON, southwestern CHAD, and northeastern NIGERIA. They speak a Niger-Congo language and are closely related to the SARA people. More than 100,000 people consider themselves Mundang.

SEE ALSO
Languages, African: An Overview.

Latin America and the Caribbean

Muñequitos de Matanzas, Los, a family-based Cuban musical group founded in Matanzas in 1952 and renowned for its folkloric presentations of Afro-Cuban music and dance, especially the RUMBA.

For more than four decades Los Muñequitos de Matanzas have sought to preserve and strengthen traditional Afro-Cuban song and dance (*see* DANCE IN LATIN AMERICA AND THE CARIBBEAN). Founded in 1952 as Guanguanco Matancero, the group adopted its current name – which in English means the little dolls of Matanzas – a year later, after recording a hit song by that name. The group's music is highly percussive, with layers of complex rhythms played on congas, maracas, wooden box drums, and cylindrical wooden *claves.* Over the percussion, vocalists perform call and-response choruses that alternate with the lead singer's improvisations. Beyond drawing attention to Cuba's rich legacy of folk music and dance, the troupe was also an important influence on the rise of SALSA MUSIC in the 1960s. With the growing popularity of world music during the 1980s and 1990s, the troupe has gained a much larger, international following.

Los Muñequitos de Matanzas is a family-based musical troupe, and many of its members have remained together for decades. The group is currently in its third generation. Its original dancer, Diosdado Ramos, is its current director. His son also danced with the group, and his grandson, Luis Deyvis Ramos (b. 1988), has recently emerged as a crowd-pleasing dancer in his own right. Musical director Jesus Alfonso Miro and his son Ivan Miro are both drummers in the group. Los Muñequitos also features the father-and-son vocalists Israel Berriel Gonzalez and Israel Berriel Jimenez.

As its name implies, Los Muñequitos de Matanzas has its roots in Matanzas, a musically influential city located in western Cuba, which has an extensive African legacy. In its role as cultural conservator, the group performs music and dances that reflect various African religious traditions and rituals. But the rumba and its variants continue to be the group's trademark.

James Clyde Sellman

SEE ALSO
Cuba; Matanzas, Cuba; World Music, World Beat, and the Re-Africanization of Latin American Popular Music.

North America

Murphy, Carl (b. January 17, 1889, Baltimore, Md.; d. February 26, 1967, Baltimore, Md.), publisher of the influential *Baltimore Afro-American.*

Carl Murphy's father, John Henry, began publishing the *Baltimore Afro-American* in 1892. Murphy graduated from HOWARD UNIVERSITY in 1911, and then attended Harvard, where he received an M.A. in German in 1913.

After teaching German at Howard, Murphy resigned in 1918 to work for the *Baltimore Afro-American.* He assumed leadership of the newspaper when his father died in 1922, and retained that position until 1961. When he retired, the paper's circulation had risen to 200,000, and his company owned newspapers in several other cities.

Murphy served on the board of directors of the NATIONAL ASSOCIATION FOR THE ADVANCEMENT OF COLORED PEOPLE (NAACP) in 1931. In 1955 he received the NAACP's Spingarn Medal for his dedication to civil rights and education.

North America

Murphy, Eddie (b. April 3, 1961, Brooklyn, N.Y.), African American comedian and actor.

Eddie Murphy first achieved fame in the United States in 1980 as a featured performer on the popular television show *Saturday Night Live (SNL)* at age 20. He was already a veteran of comedy clubs, where he had been performing since age 15. *SNL*'s sketch comedy format proved the perfect vehicle for Murphy's hard-edged comedic characterizations and at times unflattering celebrity impersonations. Murphy became *SNL*'s biggest star.

In 1982 Murphy released *Eddie Murphy*, an album of his standup material, which earned a Grammy nomination. Murphy capitalized on his popularity, taking his first film role later that year in *48 Hours*, which was well received critically and commercially. The success of *48 Hours* led to a costarring role with former *SNL* cast member Dan Ackroyd in *Trading Places*, which was among the top ten earning films of 1983. *Eddie Murphy: Comedian*, another comedy album, won a Grammy. By 1984, when he left *SNL* to pursue a film career full-time, Murphy was considered one of Hollywood's leading box office attractions.

Murphy has often achieved box-office success at the expense of critical acclaim. *Beverly Hills Cop* (1987) broke box-office records, which prompted Paramount Pictures to sign him to a $25 million six-film contract. Sequels to *48 Hours* and *Beverly Hills Cop*, on the other hand, were poorly received critically and enjoyed only modest commercial success. Critics panned Murphy's first attempt at writing and directing, *Harlem Nights* (1989). In addition, the success of *Coming to America* (1988) was diminished when in 1990 writer Art Buchwald successfully sued Murphy and Paramount Pictures for stealing his idea for the screenplay. Murphy's career rebounded in the 1990s with such films as *Boomerang* (1992) and a remake of *The Nutty Professor* (1996), which earned Murphy critical and popular acclaim.

SEE ALSO
Film, Blacks in American.

North America

Murray, Albert L. (b. May 12, 1916, Nokomis, Ala.), African American writer whose work depicts the history of the blues in language that intertwines rhythm and the vernacular.

Adopted by Albert Lee Murray and his wife, Mattie James Murray, Albert Murray grew up in Magazine Point outside Mobile, Alabama. Often characterized as a member of the "Talented Tenth," Murray excelled academically and won a scholarship to Tuskegee Institute in 1935. Following his graduate study at the University of Michigan, he returned to Tuskegee to teach English and theater. In 1943 he enlisted in the United States Air Force and was in the service until 1962, when he retired as a major. During the years of his retirement Murray has lived mostly in New York City but has been a visiting professor in various universities, including Colgate, Barnard, Columbia, Emory, the University of Massachusetts at Boston, and Washington and Lee.

Like his late friend and Tuskegee classmate RALPH ELLISON, Murray is interested in the cutural complexity of America, especially in regard to African Americans. He strongly contends that African culture permeates American life. His first published work, *The Omni-Americans* (1970), is a compilation of essays in which he criticizes theories contending that African Americans are subservient to white social infrastructures. He views African American culture as an advantageous extension of the American self. In his second work, *South to a Very Old Place* (1971), Murray adds autobiographical appeal to his social theory. The book guides the reader through the South from New York to Mobile with Murray as mediator. *South to a Very Old Place* centers on balancing and understanding the relationship between black and white, oral tradition and journalism, and past and present.

Other works include a collection of public lectures given at the University of Missouri, titled *The Hero and the Blues* (1973), which emphasizes the natural synthesis of blues ballads and prose. *Train Whistle Guitar* (1974) was the first of a fiction trilogy, followed by *The Spyglass Tree* (1991) and *Seven League Boots*. These novels trace the life of a bright young man named Scooter, Murray's fictional alter ego. *Train Whistle Guitar* won the Lillian Smith Award for Southern Fiction; its intertwining of rhythm and use of vernacular is attributed to the author's passion for the blues and his efforts to place them on the page. *Stomping the Blues* (1976) pays homage to Murray's tenet of the "vernacular imperative," transcending everyday life into aesthetic. Within this framework, Murray transforms the rhythmic, improvisational, style of JAZZ and the blues into prose.

Good Morning Blues (1985), the autobiography of Count Basie as narrated by Murray, is his ultimate tribute to the aesthetic, as he steps into the shoes of a black jazz artist. In *The Blue Devils of Nada* (1996), a collection of essays, Murray analyzes some of his favorite artists (Duke Ellington, Ernest Hemingway, ROMARE BEARDEN), using tenets of both blues and prose in American culture.

Eva Stahl Brown

SEE ALSO

Literature, African American; Basie, William James ("Count"); Blues, The; New York, New York; Tuskegee University; Ellington, Edward Kennedy ("Duke").

North America

Murray, Pauli (b. November 20, 1910, Baltimore, Md.; d. July 1, 1985, Pittsburgh, Pa.), African American lawyer, teacher, poet, women's rights advocate; first African American woman Episcopal priest.

A pioneer in fields previously inaccessible to women and African Americans, Pauli Murray was the first African American to be awarded a doctorate in juridical science from Yale University. A freedom rider in the 1940s who later led student SIT-INS in WASHINGTON, D.C. restaurants, Murray graduated at the top of her class at HOWARD UNIVERSITY. Nominated by the NATIONAL COUNCIL OF NEGRO WOMEN as one of the 12 outstanding women in Negro life in 1945, she was the recipient of many honorary degrees and was a founding member of the National Organization for Women. In 1977 she was the first African American woman to be ordained as a priest of the EPISCOPAL CHURCH.

The daughter of a racially mixed, middle-class family, Murray was the fourth of six children born to Agnes Georgianna Fitzgerald Murray and William Henry Murray. When Murray was 3 years old, her mother died as a result of a cerebral hemorrhage. Three years later, while Murray and her siblings were in the care of their aunt, their father was committed to a mental institution, where he died in 1923.

Murray received an A.B. at Hunter College in 1933 as one of four black students in a class of 247 women. Unsuccessful in breaking the color line at the University of North Carolina at Chapel Hill (where she was later awarded an honorary degree and honored with a scholarship in her name), she was accepted at the Howard University Law School, where she was the only female in the class of 1944. Murray completed an LL.M. at the University of California at Berkeley in 1945, after she was denied entrance to the all-male Harvard Law School. In 1976 she graduated from the General Theological Seminary with an M.Div. degree.

A writer since her early adolescence, Murray was a resident of the MacDowell Colony at the same time as JAMES BALDWIN in the early 1950s. In 1956 she documented her interracial family history in *Proud Shoes: The Story of an American Family*. Her collection of poetry, *Dark Testament and Other Poems*, appeared in 1970.

While teaching in Accra, GHANA, Murray coauthored the first textbook on law in Africa, titled *The Constitution and Government in Africa*. THURGOOD MARSHALL lauded her book *States' Law on Race and Color* (1951) as a bible for lawyers battling segregation.

Murray died of cancer in 1985. Her autobiography, *Song in a Weary Throat: An American Pilgrimage*, appeared posthumously in 1987 and received the Robert F. Kennedy Book Award and the Christopher Award.

Africa

Musa (called Mansa ["king"] Musa) (d. 1337), ruler of MALI (1312-1337) whose wealth was legendary throughout the Middle East and Europe.

A grandson or grandnephew of the warrior king Sundiata, who first established Mali as a major empire in the thirteenth century, Musa extended it still further and ruled it at the height of its extent and power. The pivotal event in Musa's reign was his famous pilgrimage to Mecca (1324-1325). It involved a retinue of thousands, including 500 slaves bearing golden staffs; 100 camels, each loaded with 135 kg (300 lb) of gold; and such lavish spending in Cairo that the price of gold plummeted and took a dozen years to recover.

On his return Musa brought with him numerous Muslim scholars and artisans. With their help he attempted a systematic conversion to Islam of the sub-Saharan population; built splendid mosques, introducing Asian architecture; and spread Islamic law and civilization. Tombouctou (Timbuktu), during his reign, became the unquestioned cultural center and commercial metropolis of western Africa.

SEE ALSO

Sundiata Keita; Tombouctou, Mali; Cairo, Egypt; Islam and Tradition: An Interpretation; Islamic Fundamentalism: An Interpretation.

Africa

Museveni, Yoweri (b. 1944), revolutionary military leader and president of UGANDA (1986-).

While many contemporary African leaders have come to power through force of arms, few have since won as much international acclaim for their diplomacy and effective governance as Uganda's president Yoweri Museveni. His political career began when he was a secondary school student, helping Rwandan pastoralists who were living in Uganda to organize against forced relocation. In 1967 Museveni entered Dar es Salaam University in Tanzania, where he became president of the University Students' African Revolutionary Front (USARF) and became friends with many future African leaders. Later he traveled to recently liberated areas in northern MOZAMBIQUE, gaining firsthand experience in guerrilla warfare with the FRONT FOR THE LIBERATION OF MOZAMBIQUE (FRELIMO).

Returning to Uganda, Museveni began working in MILTON OBOTE's administration as a research assistant. When IDI AMIN ousted the Obote government, Museveni fled to TANZANIA, where he formed a guerrilla group, the Front for National Salvation (FRONASA). Museveni joined the Tanzanian forces when they invaded Uganda and expelled Amin in 1979. After serving in the short-lived governments of Yusufu Lule and Godfrey Binaisa, he ran for president in 1980 but lost by a wide margin to Obote.

Claiming that the elections were fraudulent, Museveni, together with former president Yusuf Lule, created the National Resistance Movement/Army (NRM/A). Disillusioned by Obote's thirst for power above all else, Museveni's NRM/A launched a campaign to undermine the Obote regime, particularly through the sabotage of transportation and communication channels in the Luwero triangle. Museveni made a concerted effort to avoid direct confrontations with Obote's soldiers in an effort to conserve his limited troops. By the beginning of 1983 the NRM/A controlled about 10,360 sq km (some 4000 sq mi) outside Kampala, and their ranks had swelled to several thousand volunteers.

In 1985 Obote fled when one of his generals, Tito Lutwa Okello, marched on Kampala. Okello remained in power only a short while, however, as NRM/A troops began an offensive against Okello's supporters. Despite a cease-fire brokered by Kenya's president, DANIEL ARAP MOI, the fighting continued until NRM/A troops finally invaded Kampala in January 1986.

Museveni became president in 1986 and immediately outlawed opposition parties. He has denied accusations that Uganda has become a one-party state, declaring, rather, that he has created a "no-party" state, in which candidates may run for office as individuals. Museveni's distinctive approach to leadership, outlined in his Ten Point Program, stresses democratic processes and respect for human rights but permits no multiparty politics. Arguing that Western-style political parties in Africa only foster ethnic and religious conflict, he has instead focused on decentralizing and democratizing the structure of Uganda's government, instituting village-level councils to allow for a degree of grassroots participation. In order to foster national unity, Museveni has also reinstituted Uganda's traditional monarchies, although each monarchy is vested with ceremonial powers only.

Museveni came to power as a professed socialist, but he has since adhered closely to the market reforms mandated under Uganda's structural adjustment program. Although many Ugandans remain extremely poor, the country's rapid economic growth in the 1990s earned Museveni's economic pragmatism high praise from the World Bank and other international donors. In addition, many Asians expelled by Idi Amin have accepted Museveni's invitation to return to Uganda and reclaim their properties, and this has helped to reinvigorate the country's manufacturing, trade, and commercial farming sectors.

In 1996 Museveni received a large majority of votes in what were considered free and fair elections, despite the continuing ban on political parties. The relative peace that has prevailed during his leadership has won him broad support from Ugandans, even if his human rights record is still criticized by international organizations such as Amnesty International. He also faces ongoing challenges from rebel groups, particularly in the poorer northern and eastern regions of Uganda. So, like his predecessors, Museveni has relied on his military force to remain in power. Moreover, while he has reduced the size of the armed forces, he has provided support to his regional allies, such as RWANDA's defense chief, PAUL KAGAME, and LAURENT-DÉSIRÉ KABILA, the president of the DEMOCRATIC REPUBLIC OF THE CONGO.

While Museveni's willingness to intervene militarily has raised concern in some circles of the international community, it has also earned him considerable respect within Africa, where he has already chaired the ORGANIZATION OF AFRICAN UNITY. He has written several books, including an autobiography, compilations of his presidential speeches, and essays on obstacles to African development.

Ari Nave

SEE ALSO

Kampala, Uganda; Kenya; Pastoralism; Rwanda; Structural Adjustment in Africa; Socialism; Human Rights in Africa.

Africa

Musgu (also known as Mousgoum and Musgum), ethnic group of West Africa.

The Musgu primarily inhabit northern CAMEROON, southwestern CHAD, and northeastern NIGERIA. They speak an Afro-Asiatic language in the Chadic group. More than 100,000 people consider themselves Musgu.

SEE ALSO

Languages, African: An Overview.

Africa

Music, African, the rich musical traditions of African peoples south of the Sahara.

MUSICAL STYLE

Although diverse, African music has certain distinctive traits. One is the use of repetition as an organizing principle. For example, in the mbira music of the SHONA people of ZIMBABWE, a repeated pattern is established by the interaction of various parts, and the musician develops an improvisation out of this core pattern. Another common characteristic is polyphony (the simultaneous combination of several distinct musical parts). African music also has a conversational quality, in which different voices, instrumental parts, or even the parts of a single player are brought into lively exchange. One of the most common types of music making is call-and-response singing, in which a chorus repeats a fixed refrain in alternation with a lead singer, who has more freedom to improvise.

There are many different modes of expression in African music. In West Africa drum ensembles consisting of three to five musicians who play interlocking patterns are common. In the ensemble each drummer uses a special method of striking the drum head to produce varying pitches and timbres – distinctive sounds also known as tone colors – to distinguish the drum from all the others. Such ensembles often include rattles and an iron bell, which is struck with a stick to produce a repeated pattern called a timeline. This pattern penetrates the dense texture of the ensemble and helps the drummers to play their patterns at the correct time. In the *akadinda* xylophone music of the Baganda, two groups of three players each face one another across one xylophone. The first group plays a repeated pattern in octaves, and the second group fills in the missing beats with an interlocking pattern. The resulting tempo may approach 600 beats per minute. In eastern, central, and southern Africa groups of musicians play sets of stopped flutes or trumpets, each person contributing a single note in strict rotations with the others. The alternation of the parts creates a rich polyphonic texture. This kind of ensemble technique, sometimes called hocketing, was described by European observers as early as the fifteenth century. Hocketing also plays an important role in the music of both the SAN people of the KALAHARI DESERT and the forest-dwelling peoples of Central Africa.

Among the southern African peoples, polyphony is most highly developed in vocal music. In traditional ZULU choral music, individual voices enter at different points in a continuous cycle, overlapping in a complex and constantly shifting texture. The same technique may be used in solo vocal performances, during which a singer will jump from one entrance point to another to create a polyphonic texture. A wide variety of vocal qualities is used in African music, and it is common for sound-producing objects, such as jingles, rattles, and membranes made of spider web, to be attached to instruments to produce a "sizzling" effect.

INSTRUMENTS

A wide variety of instruments is used in African music. Drums are among the more popular instruments and are made in a variety of shapes and sizes. Materials such as wood, gourds, and clay are used to construct drum bodies. Drum membranes are made from the skins of reptiles, cows, goats, and other animals. Important types of drums include drum chimes, in which a set of drums tuned to a scale is mounted in a frame and played by a team of drummers; friction drums, in which sound is produced by rubbing the membrane; and the West African hourglass-shaped tension drum, which is sometimes called a talking drum because it can be used to imitate the tonal contours of spoken language.

Other important percussion instruments in African music include clap-sticks, bells, rattles, slit gongs, struck gourds and clay pots, stamping tubes, and xylophones. The lamellaphone, an instrument unique to Africa, consists of a series of metal or bamboo strips mounted on a board or box. The instrument is held in the hands or on the player's lap, and the free ends of the strips are plucked with thumbs or forefingers. Lamellaphones are used throughout Africa and are also referred to as *mbira, kalimba*, or *likembe*.

African stringed instruments include the musical bow, lute, lyre, harp, and zither. Professional musicians among the MANDINKA people of THE GAMBIA play the *kora*, a 21-string harp-lute. The *xalam*, a plucked lute, is a close relative of the African American banjo. It is used in SENEGAL by WOLOF praise singers, whose songs revere important people. The musical bow, which consists of a string stretched between two ends of a flexible stave, plays a particularly important role in the traditional music of southern African peoples, such as the San, XHOSA, and Zulu.

TOP LEFT: A trio of drummers in Sakété, Benin, accompany ritual dancing in honor of the Yoruba god of thunder, Xangô. *Fundação Pierre Verger*
TOP RIGHT: People dancing at a Kinshasa nightclub in 1957. *CORBIS/Studio Patellani*
ABOVE: The balo, a xylophone-like instrument made from gourds and wooden keys, is played here by a Bobo man in Burkina Faso. *CORBIS/Charles & Josette Lenar*

The flute, whistle, oboe, and trumpet are among the African wind instruments. Transverse and end-blown flutes made from bamboo, reeds, wood, clay, bones, and other materials are used throughout the sub-Saharan region. Trumpets, often associated with royalty, are made from animal horns or wood and are also widely used. Clarinets from the savanna region of West Africa are made from guinea-corn or sorghum stems, with a reed cut from the surface of the stem at one end. Double-reed instruments, such as the HAUSA *algaita,* originated from the shawms of North Africa.

AFRICAN MUSIC IN SOCIETY

Professional musicians played a crucial role as historians in the kingdoms that developed from the tenth to the twentieth century in various parts of Africa. Among the MANDE people of western Africa, professional bards, or griots, still recount the histories of powerful lineages and offer counsel to contemporary rulers. Among the YORUBA of NIGERIA, an incompetent or evil king often first heard the public's command to abdicate from his "talking drummers." When Ugandan government troops invaded the palace of the *kabaka* (king) of Buganda in the 1970s, they made sure that the royal musical instruments were destroyed first. In his memoirs, the kabaka described the royal drums as the "heart" of his kingdom.

Music continues to play an important role in African societies. It is a medium for the transmission of knowledge and values and for celebrating important communal and personal events. Music is often combined with speech, dance, and the visual arts to create multimedia performances. Even in societies with well-developed traditions of professional musicianship, the ability of all individuals to participate in a musical event by adding a voice to the chorus or by adding an appropriate clap pattern is assumed to be part of normal cultural competence.

Important stages of an African person's life are often marked with music. There are lullabies, children's game songs, and music for adolescent initiation rites, weddings, title-taking ceremonies, funerals, and ceremonies for the ancestors. Among the Yoruba of Nigeria, the mother of twins must perform a special repertoire of songs, and in GHANA there are songs for teasing bedwetters and for celebrating the loss of a child's first tooth.

In many African religions sound is thought to be one of the primary means by which deities and humans impose order on the universe. In West Africa drummers play a crucial role in possession-trance ceremonies, in which the gods enter or "ride" the bodies of devotees. A competent drummer must know scores of specific rhythms for particular gods and be responsible throughout the performance for regulating the flow of supernatural power in ritual contexts. In Zimbabwe, Shona mbira musicians create an environment that encourages the ancestral-spirit possession that is considered a necessary part of healing.

Music is also used to organize work activities. KPELLE men in LIBERIA use a form of vocal hocketing to coordinate their machete blows while clearing dense brush for rice fields. The forest-dwelling peoples of Central Africa use singing and vocal cries to coordinate the movements of hunters through the brush. In southern Africa herders use flutes and other instruments to help control the movement of cattle.

POPULAR MUSIC

African popular music is a blend of African, European, African American, and Middle Eastern musical traditions. In most parts of Africa popular music was pioneered by workers drawn into expanding colonial economies during the early twentieth century. The subsequent development of popular-music styles has been strongly influenced by the electronic mass media. The international popularity of African music increased in the 1980s, in part because of the participation of African musicians on albums by popular music stars such as Paul Simon, Peter Gabriel, and David Byrne.

The most influential style of popular music within Africa is Congolese guitar band music, also known as *soukous.* Influenced by Afro-Cuban music, this style developed in the towns of Central Africa and is now played by groups in such cities as KINSHASA, DEMOCRATIC REPUBLIC OF THE CONGO; Brazzaville, REPUBLIC OF THE CONGO; and Paris, France. Proponents of soukous include Franco and L'Orchestre OK Jazz, Rochereau, Mbilia Bel, Papa Wemba, and Loketo.

In the late nineteenth century a style called highlife began to develop in Ghana. There are two types of highlife groups: dance bands, in which musicians play an Africanized version of Western ballroom-dance music, complete with trumpets and saxophones; and guitar bands, which usually include several electric guitars and a set of percussion instruments. In Nigeria, the Afro-beat style of Fela Anikulapo-Kuti, formerly a highlife

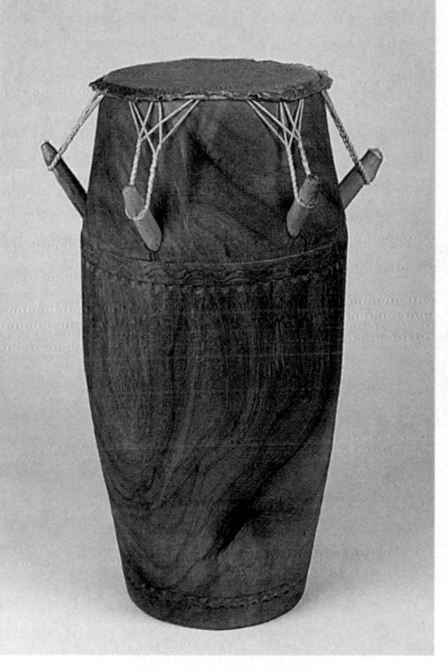

LEFT: A young member of the Gwi ethnic group in Botswana plays the mbira, sometimes called a thumb piano. *CORBIS/Peter Johnson*
CENTER: Drums are the most common type of musical instrument found throughout Africa. *CORBIS/James Marshall*
RIGHT: Wind instruments, such as the one played by this man in Tangier, Morocco, are common in many varieties of African music. *CORBIS/Patrick Ward*

Wearing robes and headwraps designed to echo the South African flag, this choir sings at Nelson R. Mandela's 1994 inauguration. *CORBIS/Peter Turnley*

musician, is strongly influenced by the African American music of JAZZ. Yoruba musicians developed a variant of guitar-band highlife called JUJU, which uses traditional proverbs and praise poetry and features the talking drum. Popular stars of juju music include KING SUNNY ADE and Chief Commander Ebenezer Obey. In Zimbabwe, THOMAS MAPFUMO and guitarist Joshua Sithole helped to develop a style called *jiti*, transferring Shona mbira patterns to the electric guitar. This style played an important role in the songs of resistance disseminated during the struggle for independence (1957-1980) against the white-controlled Rhodesian government.

The tradition of professional griots in the savanna region of West Africa is carried on by musicians such as YOUSSOU N'DOUR of Senegal and Salif Keita of MALI. These musicians make use of traditional instruments such as the xylophone and the kora (a harp-lute) in addition to using electric guitars. Their vocal styles often reflect the influence of Islam on the music of the savanna region.

SOUTH AFRICA is home to some of the best-known styles of African popular music. *Mbaqanga,* which was developed in the segregated black townships created under apartheid, is the most popular form of dance music. Contemporary mbaqanga groups, such as the Soul Brothers and Mahlathini and the Mahotella Queens, employ a lead singer and chorus, electric guitar and bass, drum set, and some combination of saxophone, accordion, and organ. The Zulu male choral style *isicathamiya* ("a stalking approach"), performed by LADYSMITH BLACK MAMBAZO, draws upon traditional wedding songs, African American choral styles, and Wesleyan church hymns.

Chris Waterman

SEE ALSO
Brazzaville, Republic of the Congo; Buganda, Early Kingdom of; Sahara Desert; Uganda; Kuti, Fela; African Religions: An Interpretation.

Latin America and the Caribbean

Music, Afro-Caribbean Religious, music performed within a religious context.

Afro-Caribbean religious music exhibits extraordinary diversity and richness, which are made all the more conspicuous by the adverse conditions under which they were created. As in traditional music cultures in Africa, distinctions between sacred and secular genres are often ambiguous, and performance of explicitly devotional music may serve an important role as social recreation. In many respects, however, Afro-Caribbean religious music genres constitute a relatively discrete category, spanning a continuum from Creole styles, which include overtly Westernized genres, to those that bear no evident Euro-American influence.

Many of the most significant and distinctive types of Afro-Caribbean sacred music are associated with syncretic religions such as SANTERÍA and VODOU, which clearly reflect their African roots. Typically, such religions

TOP: A man dressed in a cowboy hat and red tail coat directs a Rara band in the town of Dessalines, Haiti. *Dolores Yonker, Ph.D.*
ABOVE: Drums "sleep" propped against a wall in Archaie, Haiti, gathering strength to lead a Rara procession the next day. *Dolores Yonker, Ph.D.*

combine European and African elements, identifying African deities with Christian saints, and reflecting other, superficial aspects of Christian worship. However, music genres associated with these religions often exhibit no Western influence either in style or content; indeed, it is in such music that the greatest influence of African music is to be found. This influence is reflected in the use of call-and-response vocal style; the emphasis on rhythm; the use of percussion-based ensembles (typically featuring two or three drums); the fondness for syncopation and polyrhythm; and the tendency for pieces to be structured on repetition of short, rhythmically complex ostinatos. At the same time such music genres seldom correspond directly to modern counterparts in Africa, because they are products of transculturation processes involving slaves and free Afro-Caribbeans of different African ethnic backgrounds, and because they have been creatively rearticulated and modified by generations of performers, although on primarily African-derived aesthetic lines. While such neo-African music styles have been of particular interest to scholars, much research relating them to their African sources remains to be done.

Neo-African religious music genres are particularly prominent and diverse in CUBA, where their survival was facilitated by various factors, including the late importation of slaves (continuing until the 1860s) and relatively lenient Spanish manumission laws. From early in the colonial period such policies led to the presence of a substantial free black population, many of whose members formed ethnically based societies called *cabildos,* in which they were able, despite intermittent repression, to practice their traditional religions, together with their associated music and dance. The most widespread of these religions is Santería (also called *Lucumí*), which can be seen as a particularly dynamic efflorescence of the international phenomenon of Yoruba-derived religion. Santería worship centers on ceremonies in which songs and dances are used to honor the deities and, ideally, induce spirit possession. Typically, three instrumentalists play relatively standardized rhythms on hourglass-shaped *batá* drums while a vocalist leads devotees in responsorial singing. The rhythms, dances, and lyrics (sung in a somewhat garbled, archaic YORUBA dialect) are all associated with particular spirits (ORISHAS) in the Yoruba pantheon. A more festive kind of Santería event is the *bembé,* whose distinctive music features improvised solos played on the single-headed drum of the same name. Yoruba-derived religious music also includes that of the *iyesá cabildos,* deriving from a related West African regional tradition.

Congolese-derived religious practices have also flourished in Cuba, where they are sometimes grouped under the name Palo. Although Palo is in many respects less formalized as a religion than Santería, its repertoire of songs and dances is prodigious, and may have been influential in the evolution of the secular Afro-Cuban music and dance form RUMBA. Another Afro-Cuban religious sect with a distinctive music tradition is *arará,* which, like the Rada traditions of Haiti and Trinidad, evidently derives from the old Dahomean port town of Alada. Also still vital is the music tradition of the *abakuá* secret societies, whose songs and dances reenact Carabali-derived mythology (of the Ibo ethnic group). Starting with the monumental works of Cuban anthropologist Fernando Ortiz (1881-1969), such Afro-Cuban religious music genres have received a fair amount of scholarly attention and continue to be actively performed by devotees and folkloric groups, both in Cuba and in places like New York City. In Cuba today, Santería flourishes with great vigor and has been essentially tolerated by the Communist government.

Haiti is another stronghold of neo-African religious music, especially that associated with the complex religion known to outsiders as Vodou, which syncretizes Congolese and Yoruba traditions with those of Benin/Dahomey. Since the Haitian Revolution (ending around 1804), such religions and associated music styles have resiliently withstood repression by the Catholic Church and the mulatto elite, although their practice in many communities has been curtailed in recent decades by American-based Protestant evangelism. Despite the negative publicity associated with Vodou, its associated music, dance, and mythology traditions are comparable in richness to those of Santería, with which it shares many features. Vodou music thrives in a variety of regional forms, many of which have yet to be documented. The religion and its music are also perpetuated by ethnic Haitians in the neighboring Dominican Republic, alongside a less standardized set of neo-African religious music that reflects Congolese influence. These Dominican traditions, however, are considerably weaker than in Haiti and Cuba and occupy little legitimacy in the more Afro-phobic national ideology.

Neo-African religions and their music are somewhat less prominent in the English-speaking Caribbean, due to such factors as the earlier cessation of slave imports (in 1807); the limited numbers of free blacks during the slave period (ending in 1838); the more intensive presence of Protestant churches in sociocultural life; and, perhaps, the greater intolerance of pagan and syncretic practices on the part of missionaries and colonial authorities. Nevertheless, several neo-African religious traditions did survive and were reinforced in the mid-nineteenth century by the immigration of African indentured workers, particularly Yorubans. Such workers were the evident source for the Afro-Trinidadian sect known as Shango, or orisha worship, whose songs, dances, instruments, and practices, although of evident Yoruba derivation, differ substantially from those of Santería. Similarly, Congolese indentured immigrants appear to have contributed to the Jamaican *kumina* sect, which survives in eastern parts of that island. By contrast, the Jamaican religious tradition of *kromanti* appears to derive from the older practices established by maroons (escaped slaves). The most extensive and culturally autonomous maroon societies of the Caribbean Basin are those of the former Dutch colony of Suriname, where neo-African music styles of the Kwinti, Njuka, Saramaka, and other groups have flourished unimpeded by legal or Christian repression. However diverse, all these traditions, like Santería and Vodou, center on performance of songs and dances in neo-African style, with texts abundant with African words used to invoke spirit possession. Other neo-African, West Indian music genres, such as Guyanese *cumfa* and *kwe-kwe* (queh-queh) and the "big drum dance" from Carriocou (an island of Grenada), do not involve possession trance but honor spirits of departed ancestors. Aside from Surinamese maroon religions, most of these West Indian neo-African sects were repressed, with varying degrees of vigor, until around the 1960s; British authorities also attempted to ban all drumming in most of their West Indian colonies. While such persecution no longer occurs, neo-African religions and music genres in independent West Indian countries have, on the whole, found relatively little public recognition, whether among state culture ministries or popular opinion, where more "Creole" notions of cultural identity tend to dominate.

In the English-speaking Caribbean, more widespread than neo-African religions are acculturated, Creole Protestant sects whose theologies and devotional practices reflect a more Western orientation. Accordingly, their associated music styles lie somewhere closer to the middle of the African-versus-European spectrum. In this category would fall the Jamaican *pocomania* (pukimina) and Revival Zion sects and the Trinidadian Spiritual Baptists (Shouters). The music styles of these sects, which bear certain affinities to American gospel music, typically consist of English-language Protestant hymns rendered in a vigorously rhythmic style, often accompanied by animated clapping and drumming. Spirit possession may occur, although the trance is less likely to be associated with African deities. With colonial repression over, the neo-African features of such sects, along with the popularity of faiths like Santería, appear in many respects to be increasing rather than declining.

Peter Manuel

See Also

Music, African; Dahomey, Early Kingdom of; Maroonage in the Americas; Merengue: Music, Race and Nation in the Dominican Republic; Rumba; New York, New York; Abakuás; Regla de Palo; Jamaica; Music, Afro-Caribbean Secular; Trinidad and Tobago; Transculturation, Mestizaje, and the Cosmic Race: An Interpretation; African Ethnic Groups in Latin America and the Caribbean; Catholic Church in Latin America and the Caribbean; Orishas; Protestant Church in Latin America and the Caribbean; Slave Laws in Colonial Spanish America.

Latin America and the Caribbean

Music, Afro-Caribbean Secular

The Caribbean Basin has proved to be an extraordinarily fertile site for musical creation, with several forms of modern Caribbean popular music coming to enjoy global renown and appeal. These musics can be regarded as "Creole" products in the sense that they are uniquely Caribbean idioms distinct from Old World predecessors. Most can be characterized as Afro-Caribbean in the sense that their most distinctive features derive from African influences. More specifically, they are products of syncretic transculturation involving African- and European-derived features, and can be seen as occupying various points on a stylistic continuum ranging from neo-African genres on one end to more purely European-derived idioms on the other.

Although the Caribbean is perhaps best known for its commercial popular musics, the field of Afro-Caribbean secular music has comprised a considerably broader range of expressive idioms. Various forms of work songs, although less often heard today, flourished throughout the region and constituted one of the most common forms of Creolized musical expression. Some of these, such as Haitian *combite* (konbit) songs chanted responsorially by communal work teams, retain a strong neo-African flavor and are still performed today. Another traditional category of Afro-Caribbean secular music comprises the diverse processional music associated with Carnival festivities, most of which commenced as European pre-Lenten occasions but came to be dominated by Afro-Caribbean celebrants. While some of these musics, such as Trinidadian camboulay, have died out, others, such as the Cuban conga, still survive. The conga (as distinct from the drum of the same name) consists of a processional dance, accompanied by animated Afro-Cuban drumming and singing, performed by costumed participants in *comparsa* processions during that island's Carnival (now held in July). Another vibrant Carnival music is Haitian *rara* (and the derivative Dominican *gaga*), comprising processional groups based around players of bamboo tubes called *vaksin*, which are blown in hocket technique to produce complex interlocking melodies, in a manner closely related to similar contemporary practices in West Africa. English-speaking West Indian islands have their own Carnival tradition musics, some of which, like the "mummies" of St. Kitts and Nevis, include fife-and-drum music that appears to blend European military drumming and African flute-and-drum traditions.

While such occasion-specific musics are of considerable interest and originality, it is in the realm of recreational social dance music that the greatest richness and diversity of Caribbean music are to be found. As with Afro-Caribbean religious musics, many of these genres, such as Cuban RUMBA and Puerto Rican bomba, are free from any particular European stylistic influence, deriving overwhelmingly from African sources (although their lyrics tend to be in European or local Creole languages rather than the African languages encountered in SANTERÍA or VODOU musics, for example). At the same time they differ from their African counterparts in having evolved through centuries of interethnic syncretism among Africans of different regions, and through being creatively transformed by generations of Afro-Caribbean musicians. In that sense such musics are best regarded as "neo-African." They tend to reflect with particular clarity the quintessential features of African music, including call-and-response singing, reliance on repetition and ostinato, and an emphasis on rhythm, including off-beat phrasing and, often, polyrhythm. Aside from still-vital genres like Cuban rumba, colonial accounts attest to a wide variety of such musics flourishing in the past throughout the Caribbean, including now-obscure forms like bamboula and calinda.

Most traditional Afro-Caribbean dance musics, however, reflect some degree of stylistic syncretism with European influences. In many cases these have involved rendering European-style melodies, whether vocally or on instruments like violin or guitar, with a more syncopated and animated rhythmic accompaniment provided on percussion instruments. When black musicians were hired to play European quadroons, waltzes, jigs, and other genres, the resultant music often acquired a distinctive Afro-Caribbean flavor, still manifest in genres like Trinidadian "heel-and-toe."

One prominent set of Creole social dance musics emerging from the early nineteenth century was that comprising the local varieties of contredanse, contradanza, danza, and related idioms. The nucleus of this cluster appears to have been the Franco-Haitian *contredanse*, which formed the basis for the subsequent Haitian *méringue*, the early Dominican *merengue*, the Cuban *contradanza* (known elsewhere as the *habanera*) and the subsequent *danzón*, and the derivative but distinctive Puerto Rican *danza*. Most of these idioms could be rendered either in refined parlor styles for white elites or in more vigorous and rhythmic styles by dance bands, typically consisting of black or mixed-race musicians. These genres were significant both for their subdued but insistent Afro-Caribbean lilt and their gradual transition from line dances to ballroom-style couple dances. As such, they were vehicles both for the Afro-Caribbeanization and the choreographic liberalization of Creole music culture, features that made genres like the habanera popular in nineteenth-century Europe as well.

With the spread of recording technology around 1900, Afro-Caribbean popular musics rapidly evolved into a set of unique and dynamic genres. Most of these styles were products of creative cross-fertilization, at once borrowing features from one another and from European and especially American popular music while influencing these latter musics in their turn. Almost all of these music genres have derived their most distinctive features from Afro-Caribbean sources, and have been created and performed largely by black or mixed-race artists. Most, from RUMBA to REGGAE, encountered vigorous opposition from negrophobic, Eurocentric elites. Several, however, eventually came to be accepted as national musics, thus playing crucial roles in the emergence of Creole national and cultural identities and legitimizing the Afro-Caribbean presence therein.

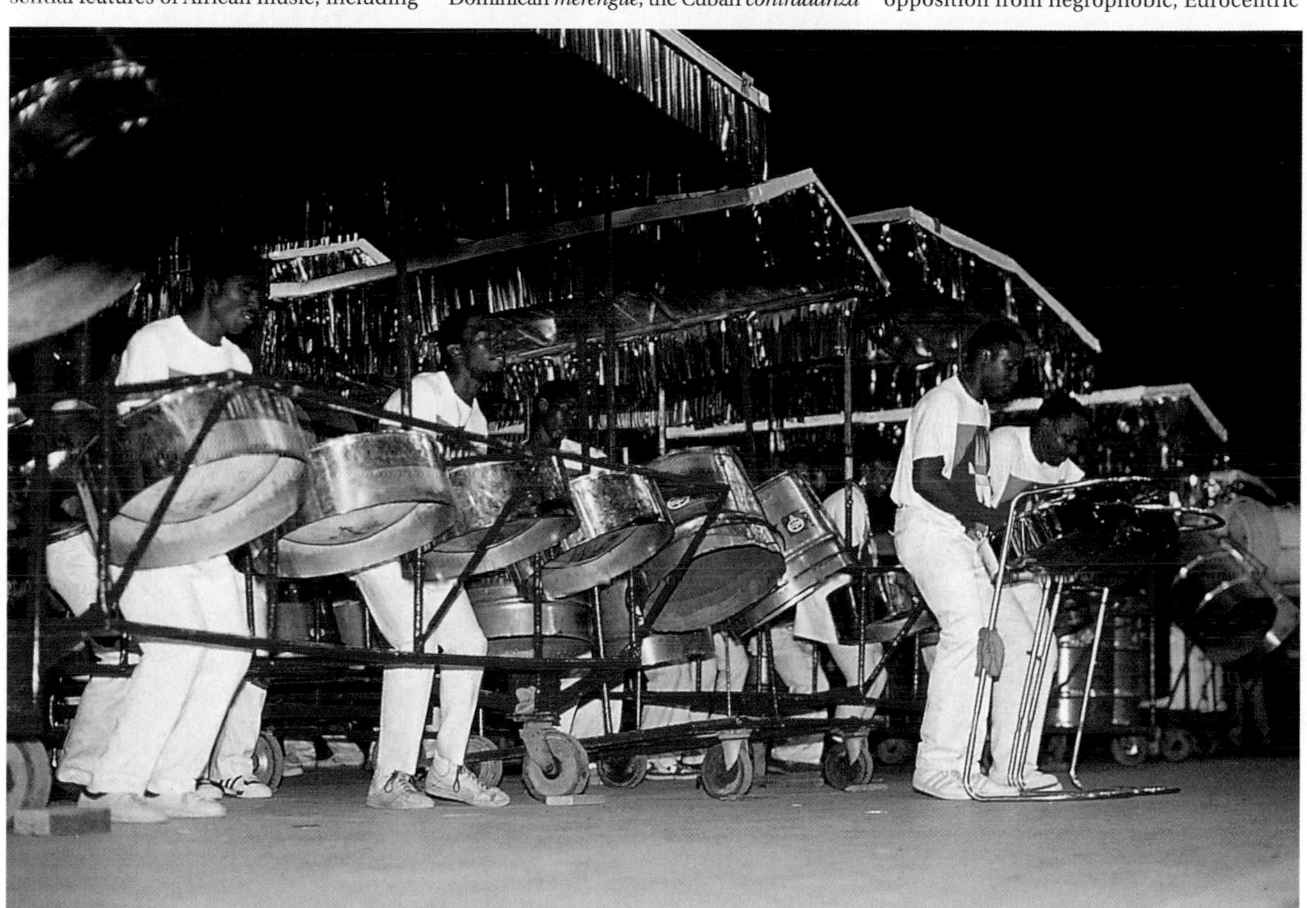

The Amoco Renegades compete in a steel drum band contest as part of Carnival in Port of Spain, Trinidad and Tobago. *Photo © 1988 Alex Castro*

CUBA has been the most musically influential island in the region, both by virtue of its relative size and, perhaps, the particularly balanced and felicitous nature of its syntheses of Afro-Caribbean and European-derived elements. By the nineteenth century Cuba hosted a thriving Creole music culture comprising neo-African genres

ABOVE: A Jamaican man plays banjo at a backyard party. *CORBIS/Bradley Smith*
RIGHT: Walfrido Ballerino, the leader of the Conga San Pedrito, plays the *corneta china* during Carnival in Santiago de Cuba in 1987. *J. Bettelheim*

like rumba as well as more Europeanized styles like the contradanza (habanera). The development of the more syncopated and rhythmic danzón out of the contradanza typified the gradual, if then controversial, Afro-Cubanization of the island's popular musics. Such tendencies became more pronounced in the early twentieth century with the emergence of the SON, which synthesized Spanish-derived chordal harmonies and instruments (especially the guitar and guitar-like *tres*) with Afro-Cuban features, including the use of the clave rhythmic cell, the progression to an extended call-and-response section (the *montuno*), and the use of the bongo and the marimbula, an enlarged bass version of African lamellophones like the mbira. By the 1920s the *son*, although played primarily by black musicians, was increasingly accepted as the nation's most popular dance music. In subsequent decades the *son* became in some respects more Westernized, adopting jazz harmonies and larger ensembles, including piano and additional brass instruments; at the same time it acquired a more Afro-Cuban flavor through the use of faster tempi and a generally more percussive flavor reminiscent of the rumba. Such tendencies were epitomized in the MAMBO, which emerged in the 1950s as a largely instrumental adaptation of up-tempo Cuban rhythms to jazz big-band format. In the 1940s and 1950s the innovations of ARSENIO RODRÍGUEZ, the Conjunto Casino, Félix Chapotin, and others established the essential form of the modern *son*, which remains the stylistic basis for what is now called "salsa." By this time Cuban genres like the *son*, the mambo, and the chachachá had become thoroughly international, flourishing among Latino communities in New York and elsewhere, and throughout much of urban Africa. Dance music based on the modern *son* has continued to flourish in Cuba since the 1950s, and it took on a new life in New York and elsewhere from the 1960s under the new label "salsa," especially as linked to the sharpened socio-political consciousness of Caribbean Basin Latinos during the 1960s and 1970s.

By the late nineteenth century Cuba's sister Spanish colony of PUERTO RICO had developed its own thriving Creole music culture, encompassing both neo-African forms like bomba and the more Europeanized danza, which, however, retained a subtle Afro-Caribbean syncopation. In the early twentieth century Cuban popular musics, especially the *son* and bolero, took root in Puerto Rico, especially as performed and composed by black and mulatto artists. Meanwhile, the *plena* had emerged as a lively, syncopated, informal topical song genre, rooted in lower-class social life. The 1940s saw the adaptation of big-band format to somewhat diluted versions of the plena, but the genre regained its proletarian, Afro-Caribbean flavor in the 1950s in the music of bandleaders RAFAEL CORTIJO and Mon Rivera. Since then, however, salsa and merengue have dominated the Puerto Rican popular music scene. For its part, the Dominican merengue has become similarly international while retaining some Afro-Caribbean flavor in its animated rhythms and its frequent use of a call-and-response second section. As merengue and salsa become increasingly popular among all social classes and are increasingly performed by white and mixed-race musicians, salsa, *son,* and merengue have come to be less exclusively regarded as Afro-Latin, although their Afro-Caribbean characteristics and origins remain clear.

By the 1950s distinctive forms of Afro-Caribbean popular music had also emerged in the French Caribbean. The Creolized biguine of MARTINIQUE enjoyed some international popularity, although the Haitian compas bands of Nemours Jean-Baptiste and Weber Sicot had larger local constituencies. These bands laid the foundation for the emergence of modern Haitian compas, as well as the electric guitar- and brass-dominated "MINI-JAZZ" groups that emerged in the 1960s and 1970s. Haitian popular musics, as well as the ZOUK emerging in the 1980s from Martinique and GUADELOUPE, retain a strong Afro-Caribbean flavor in their rhythms, their use of Creole patois and local proverbs and expressions, and, in some cases, specific melodies, rhythms, and other features derived from local neo-African musics such as Guadeloupian *gwo-ka* drumming.

Neo-African musics in the English-speaking West Indies have been somewhat less resilient than those in the French and Spanish Caribbean, such that the urban popular musics emerging in these areas have reflected somewhat less overt Afro-Caribbean character. Trinidadian CALYPSO evolved from around 1900 as a Creole urban folk idiom whose style reflected only a subtle Afro-Caribbean rhythmic flavor. Nevertheless, it has been performed largely by black musicians and is regarded by some as a perpetuation of African-derived satirical or topical song traditions; further, SOCA, which emerged in the latter 1970s as a dance-oriented variant of calypso, has a more animated rhythmic character, reflecting both Afro-Caribbean as well as East Indian inspiration. For its part, the Jamaican popular music that evolved in the 1950s and 1960s as SKA was informed less by local Creole or neo-African musics than by American RHYTHM AND BLUES. However, with the evolution of reggae around 1970, Jamaican popular music became at once more indigenous and more distinctively Afro-Caribbean both in style and in lyric content. DUB and DANCEHALL, which largely replaced "classic" reggae by the mid-1980s, illustrate even more clearly how a regional popular music can become more distinctively Afro-Caribbean by evolving in a new direction rather than by returning to local neo-African roots. In this sense, as well as in stylistic parameters, dancehall's development has paralleled that of Afro-American hip hop music. As the Caribbean region and its emigrant communities increasingly become involved in the globalization of world culture, many Afro-Caribbean musics at once cross-fertilize and modernize while continuing to regenerate themselves through inspirations from traditional neo-African musics.

Peter Manuel

SEE ALSO

Merengue: Music, Race and Nation in the Dominican Republic; Nemours, Jean Baptiste and Sicot, Wéber; Hip Hop in the United States; New York, New York; Afro-Latino Cultures in the United States; Bolero; Dominican Republic; Salsa Music; Jamaica; Music, Afro-Caribbean Religious; Trinidad and Tobago; East Indian Communities in the Caribbean; Haiti; Plena and Bomba; Transculturation, Mestizaje, and the Cosmic Race: An Interpretation; Carnivals in Latin America and the Caribbean; Dance in Latin America and the Caribbean; Languages, Creole, in the Caribbean.

Latin America and the Caribbean

Music, Classical, in Latin America and the Caribbean,

the influence of African musical traditions and artists of African descent on Latin American classical music.

INTRODUCTION

The African presence in Latin America has had a significant effect on the development of its classical or art music. During the colonial period (early 1500s to 1820s), as SPAIN and PORTUGAL imported African slaves into the region, African idioms, folk traditions, and musical instruments came to form an integral part of Latin American popular music. In addition, as historian Darién J. Davis has noted, "Contact among Europeans, aborigines, and Africans created a mixed people – Afro-Creoles – and facilitated a distinct New World culture through mestizaje, or the combining of elements of distinct cultures." In some countries of the New World, composers and musicians of African descent were at times able to pursue musical careers within the military or the church – institutions that provided a means of social mobility to nonwhites. Nowhere is this more evident than in BRAZIL, where composers of African descent dominated the country's musical life during the eighteenth century and part of the nineteenth century.

Between 1810 and 1830 Latin America was beginning to free itself from the political dominance of Spain and Portugal. This development considerably influenced musical composition and performance in the emerging nations and culminated, during the late nineteenth century, in musical nationalism: Latin American composers consciously sought to differentiate their music from classical European styles by incorporating local folk idioms into their works. By the 1860s Latin America had all but abolished the institution of slavery. Only Brazil, PUERTO RICO, and CUBA continued to receive African slaves until the late 1880s, thus reinforcing the African influences in their music. By the turn of the century many blacks were able to participate more fully in the musical life of Latin American societies.

In countries with a substantial African presence, such as Brazil, Cuba, and other Caribbean countries, composers, black and white, liberally incorporated the rhythms, folklore, and popular music of their countries' Afro-Creole heritage. For some prominent composers, such as AMADEO ROLDÁN (Cuba) and Heitor Villa-Lobos (Brazil), Afro-Creole traditions were the principal source of inspiration and thus a significant component in the expression and affirmation of their countries' national identities. As musicologist Nicolas Slonimsky notes, "The creative musician occupies an exalted place in the social fabric of the Latin-American countries. He is the pride of the nation... [and] serves his country by enhancing its cultural prestige."

AFRO-CREOLE MUSICIANS AND MUSICAL TRADITIONS IN THE COLONIAL ERA

In colonial Latin America and the Caribbean, the African presence in classical music dates from the sixteenth century, when Spanish and Portuguese colonists introduced African slaves into the region. Although Latin American slavery was no less brutal than its counterpart in the United States, Spanish and Portuguese rulers did institute laws of manumission that eventually enabled a sizable number of black slaves to buy their freedom. In colonial Brazil and VENEZUELA, composers of African descent had a highly influential role in their country's musical life. In other countries, such as Mexico, the African presence made itself felt mainly through the works of important artists of Spanish descent. For example, composers Gaspar Fernandes (c. 1566-1629), Gutiérrez de Padilla (c. 1590-1664), and the poet Sor Juana Inés de la Cruz (1651?-1695) all drew from Afro-Hispanic musical traditions for their religious *villancicos* (settings for voice and instrumental accompaniment, written for church festivals).

In Brazil, as early as 1610, Portuguese noblemen and church conductors began to organize both black slaves and freedpeople into choral and instrumental groups. According to music scholar Claver Filho, such "musical groups from the townships and sugar estates were numerous... not only in the first two centuries of the Colony but later also." The Portuguese colonizers provided musical instruction in the form of such Jesuit-run schools as the Conservatorio dos Negros. These schools greatly benefited composers of African descent, a significant number of whom flourished as professional musicians in Pernambuco, MINAS GERAIS, and Rio de Janeiro. Although these composers did contend with racial discrimination, their profession gave them a measure of status in Brazilian colonial society. As Filho said, "It was above all the mulattos (of African and European descent) who best produced theatrical matter, composed military music and especially religious music, in a display of serious-minded professionalism."

Luiz Álvares Pinto (1719-1789), José Joaquim Emerico Lobo de Mesquita (1740-1805), and José Mauricio Nunes Garcia (1767-1830) had outstanding careers as composers of church music, the predominant musical genre of the colonial era. Garcia, the most distinguished eighteenth-century Brazilian composer, is considered the "father of Brazilian music." As chapelmaster of Rio de Janeiro Cathedral from 1798 to 1808, he produced a wealth of liturgical music, influenced by the late baroque and classical Viennese styles. During the early nineteenth century he was appointed chapelmaster of the royal chapel of Dom João VI and became famous for his improvisational skills at the keyboard. He also taught some of Brazil's leading young musicians, including Francisco Manuel da Silva, composer of the Brazilian national anthem, a work later orchestrated by the noted Afro-Brazilian composer Antonio de Assis Republicano (1897-1960).

Musicians of African descent also pursued successful careers in Venezuela. Like Brazil, colonial society in Venezuela was divided into whites (in this case of Spanish descent), people of mixed Afro-European descent, slaves, and Indians. During the latter half of the eighteenth century a group of Venezuela's most significant church-music composers formed around the composer Juan Manuel Olivares at the Academia de Música. According to musicologist Gerard Béhague, most of the younger composers of the [group] Escuela de Chacao were "free mulattos, since the circumstance of exercising the music profession put them in a privileged social position." Prominent Escuela members of African descent included José Francisco Velásquez (c. 1755-1805), José Antonio Caro de Boesi (c. 1760-1814), Juan José Landaeta (c. 1780-1812), and Lino Gallardo (c. 1775-1837).

Postcolonial Latin America and the Roots of Musical Nationalism

Toward the end of the colonial period, as Latin America's classical music left the confines of the church, professional composers began to focus on secular forms of music. Some colonial-era composers had already written secular villancicos and operas, the first of which was produced in 1701 in Lima, Peru. With Latin America on its way to political independence, new foreign influences entered the region, particularly that of the European Romantic tradition. While composers of instrumental music looked to Liszt, Chopin, and other European virtuosos, opera composers sought inspiration in such Italian masters as Rossini, Bellini, and Verdi.

For much of the nineteenth century Latin American art music was judged according to the stylistic conventions of European music. National conservatories and theaters for opera performance were established, but they were mostly dominated by foreign music professionals and visiting celebrities. By the 1860s, however, Latin American composers began to reveal elements of a national musical style. Like their European counterparts, they sought inspiration in folk and popular music, some of which was derived from African traditions.

Ignacio Cervantes (1847-1905) was Cuba's most important nineteenth-century composer. He transcended the regnant conventions of European classical music that had inspired a plethora of superficial salon pieces throughout Latin America. He wrote works centered on the rhythmic patterns of the *contradanza*, a popular Cuban dance based on African-derived syncopations. Similar innovations were employed by Ernesto Elorduy (1853-1912, Mexico), Juan Morel Campos (1857-1896, Puerto Rico), Felipe Villanueva (1862-1893, Mexico), and Alberto Nepomuceno (1864-1920, Brazil).

The reigning master of Brazilian opera, Antônio Carlos Gomes (1836-1896), who was of African descent, also found inspiration in indigenous material. He achieved world renown in 1870 when his opera *Il guarany* premiered at La Scala in Milan, Italy. Gomes gave *Il guarany* a Brazilian subject and setting, and a later opera, *Lo schiavo* (1888), was inspired by the liberation struggle of black slaves in Brazil. Although Gomes's works reflect a European style, Claver Filho considers his piano piece *A caiumba* (1857), a dance based on the African *congada*, "the first composition that ushered in Brazilian pre-nationalism."

Musicians of African descent were among the region's leading instrumentalists, including the violinists José Pedro de Santana Gomes (1834-1908, Brazil), Claudio J. D. Brindis de Salas (1852-1917, Cuba), and José Silvestre White (1836-1918, Cuba). White gained world fame as a violinist and composer after the American pianist Louis Moreau Gottschalk, impressed with White's talent, persuaded his family to send him to Paris for musical studies. In 1856 White won the Prix de Rome and began touring widely in Europe, South America, and the Caribbean. In 1875 he debuted with the New York Philharmonic, reputedly the first black to perform with an American orchestra. He had not come to the United States intending to perform: he had been expelled from Cuba by the government after his performance of "La bella cubana" – his own composition, written in support of the Cuban insurgents during the Ten Years' War (1868-1878) against Spain – incited the Havana audience to protest Spanish domination.

African Traditions in Latin American Musical Nationalism

During the late nineteenth and early twentieth centuries Latin American musical nationalism developed in full force, a movement that emerged contemporaneously with similar trends in Russia and various central European countries. Nationalist composers, like many writers and thinkers of the time, looked to their countries' historical roots in order to create a distinctly national form of expression in art music. In many Latin American countries musical nationalism was also a reaction to centuries of colonial domination in the arts.

Peter Wade, author of *Race and Ethnicity in Latin America*, notes that Brazil and Cuba, with their large black populations, were the Latin American countries most inclined to see blacks "as symbols of a glorious heritage." Indeed, many composers of nationalist art music in Brazil and Cuba were inspired first and foremost by their countries' African heritage. In countries where *mestizo* (of indigenous and European descent) or Indian folk traditions were most prevalent – Ecuador, Peru, Bolivia, Chile, and Uruguay – these traditions became the principal basis for art music. Yet even countries with relatively small black communities have evinced an African influence in some of their classical music. In Argentina, for example, the tango inspired the classical works of the composer Astor Piazzolla (1921-1992).

Mestizo musical traditions strongly influenced the nationalist composers of Mexico, Colombia, Venezuela, and Panama, but several of these composers also deliberately sought material from African sources. Roque Cordero (b. 1917, Panama), who is of African descent, based some of his early works on Afro-Panamanian folklore; José Rozo Contreras (b. 1894, Colombia) found inspiration in the Afro-Colombian folk music of the Pacific and Atlantic coastal areas, enclaves of black and Caribbean cultures. In Venezuela, the Afro-Caribbean musical tradition served as source material for the nationalist composer Juan Bautista Plaza (1898-1965), while in Mexico, Silvestre Revueltas (1899-1940) based songs and an orchestral piece, *Sensemayá* (1938), on the rhythms of verse by the renowned Afro-Cuban poet Nicolás Guillén.

Among countries of the Caribbean basin, Cuba was at the forefront of musical nationalism with the founders of its modern school of composition, Amadeo Roldán (1900-1939) and Alejandro Garcia Caturla (1906-1940). In the 1920s Roldán and Caturla became the principal musical exponents of Afrocubanismo, an artistic and literary movement that looked to Cuba's urban black culture as a basis for new musical and literary forms. Roldán and Caturla also played a central role in the expression of Cuban nationalism in the arts – a response, according to music scholar Peter Manuel, to "the late persistence of Spanish rule, its replacement in 1902 by a thinly disguised North American domination, and above all, the ambivalence toward nationalistic struggles on the part of the Cuban bourgeoisie."

Both Roldán and Caturla used Afro-Cuban folk rhythms and dance music, such as the RUMBA, conga, danzon, and SON, as their principal source materials. They endeavored to give stature to the popular urban music often denigrated by Cuban elites and distorted in American commercial music. Roldán, who was of African descent, was particularly inspired by Afro-Cuban ritual music, as reflected in his string quartet *Poema negro* (1930) and ballet *La rebambaramba*, a work in which he collaborated with the eminent Cuban ethnomusicologist ALEJO CARPENTIER. Roldán's orchestral piece *Rítmica V* is quintessential African-derived art music. Describing the work, music critic Octavio Roca wrote, "Never before or since Roldán's day have Afro-Cuban rhythms been so exuberantly integrated into the fabric of a symphony orchestra."

Though Caturla was of Spanish descent, he devoted himself to researching and incorporating Cuba's black cultural traditions into his works. As well as using Afro-Cuban rhythms, he attempted to synthesize white and black elements of Cuban folk music. In his *Berceuse campesina* for piano, for example, he employed African-based rhythms in the left hand with *guajiro* (Hispanic peasant) melodies in the right. His most important work, *Yamba-O*, is a symphonic poem based on African-derived ritual music.

Composers in other Caribbean countries also produced works inspired by African musical traditions. Haitian composer Justin Elie (1883-1931) wrote several pieces that reflect the ceremonial music of the VODOU ritual, while Ludovic Lamothe (1882-?), called "the black Chopin," delved into Haitian folklore for some of his piano compositions.

It was in Brazil that African-derived musical traditions were most widely explored in the creation of art music. Among Brazil's many composers who saw Afro-Brazilian folk traditions as essential to their musical roots were Heitor Villa-Lobos (1887-1959), Oscar Lorenzo Fernândez (1897-1948), Francisco Mignone (b. 1897), Camargo Guarnieri (1907-1993), and José Siqueira (b. 1907). In their compositions, all five employed the varied and complex rhythms of Afro-Brazilian dances, such as the *batuque*, congada, *jongo*, and SAMBA and, in this respect, they contributed to preserving these rhythms in musical literature. According to musicologist Nicolas Slonimsky, "[Guarnieri] and other Brazilian composers have elevated the *samba* to an art form, as distinctive as any of the European dance forms used in classical music."

Villa-Lobos, Brazil's most celebrated composer, traveled throughout Brazil researching and collecting Afro-Brazilian folk songs. Later trained in the European classical tradition, he made it his foremost goal to shape Afro-Brazilian folklore into a classical art form. In his works he used elements of popular song as well as complex rhythmic patterns and a variety of percussion instruments traditional in Afro-Brazilian ritual music. His experimental piece *Bachianas brasileiras*, in which he applied Bach's contrapuntal technique to Afro-Brazilian folk melodies, was cited by music critic Mark Holston as "one of the most successful marriages of indigenous idioms and the European classical tradition ever accomplished."

African Influences in Contemporary Latin American Art Music

Latin American musical nationalism continued until the 1950s, outlasting its European counterpart by more than 20 years. It compelled the region's composers to reflect deeply on what distinguished their nations' musical idioms from the European idiom and to adapt Western musical forms to their own cultural setting, language, and temperament. At the same time some composers, taking the lead from such European neoclassicist composers as Stravinsky and Schönberg, returned to the classical ideal in music, which strictly separated classical music from popular and folk genres. Thus, by the mid-twentieth century a strong countercurrent to musical nationalism had developed in Latin America and the Caribbean, where many composers once again cultivated a predominantly European musical language.

Yet the late twentieth century witnessed the revival of a more eclectic approach to classical music among some Latin American composers. For example, the Afro-Cuban composer Tania León and the Cuban jazz trumpeter ARTURO SANDOVAL created classical compositions that fuse elements of several musical genres, including AFRO-LATIN JAZZ and folk music. "Nothing is as special as the immense task of creating," noted the contemporary Afro-Peruvian composer and vocalist SUSANA BACA. "In other words, to take, transforming with illusion, the old toward the new, the forgotten toward the dreamed."

Roanne Edwards

SEE ALSO

Slavery in Latin America and the Caribbean; Blackness in Latin America and the Caribbean: an Interpretation; Rio de Janeiro, Brazil; León, Tania J.; Brindis de Salas, Claudio.

Latin America and the Caribbean

Muslim Uprisings in Bahia, Brazil, a series of rebellions against slavery that took place during the early nineteenth century.

Most African Muslims who arrived in BRAZIL did so during the first half of the nineteenth century. Primarily HAUSA and YORUBA, and less frequently Bornu, NUPE, and FULANI, they were brought to work on the sugar plantations of the northeastern state of BAHIA and its capital, Salvador (*see* AFRICAN ETHNIC GROUPS IN LATIN AMERICA AND THE CARIBBEAN). Bahia practically monopolized the Brazilian slave trade from the BIGHT OF BENIN ports, where most Muslims embarked (*see* TRANSATLANTIC SLAVE TRADE). At least 354,100 slaves, including a significant number of Muslims, were imported from that area between 1791 and 1850. Most had been made prisoners during political and religious conflicts within present-day NIGERIA, mainly successive revolts leading to the demise of the Yoruba Empire of Oyo and the jihad (Muslim holy war) begun by USMAN DAN FODIO in Hausaland in 1804.

In Brazil Muslim slaves were known as *malê*, from the Yoruba *imale*, because Yorubas predominated in the Muslim community in the 1820s and 1830s. There is evidence that Muslims in Bahia may have forged at least two rebellions and two important conspiracies, and that they may have been involved in other revolts and conspiracies, more than 20 of which happened during the first half of the nineteenth century in the region.

In May 1807 an extensive Hausa conspiracy was uncovered before the planned rebellion could occur. Organized under a complex hierarchy of leaders, the rebels planned to surround the city of Salvador and seal out food provisions; conquer the hungry city; make contact with Muslim slaves in the northern province of Pernambuco; and establish a kingdom in the country's backlands. In the city itself, Roman Catholic churches would be stormed and the images of saints gathered in a public square and burned. Whites would be massacred and black Creoles and mulattos enslaved.

In 1814 slave fishermen revolted with the help of runaway urban slaves and freedpeople. More than 200 men put fire to fishing nets and warehouses, attacked a village near the capital, and tried to reach the plantation area, killing more than 50 people before being overpowered by troops. Rebel ranks were again overwhelmingly Hausa but included a few Nupe, Bornu, and Yoruba. Their principal leader was described as a *malomi*, or priest, the term *malomi* certainly being a variation of *malam*, a Hausa word for Muslim preacher. That Muslims contributed to the episode is confirmed by confiscated papers written in Arabic. Three months later the Hausa were again conspiring in Salvador and surrounding runaway communities. Their leader was the same malomi who had led the previous rebellion. Besides the Hausa, other African "nations" and even Indians were said to have been involved, but the scheme was discovered and dismantled by the government.

A more serious movement, which came to be known as the Malê Rebellion, took place ten years later. On January 25, 1835, some 600 rebels fought for nearly four hours in the streets of Salvador, and at least 70 died – against 9 killed in the opposing camp.

Some have suggested that this movement, which was led by Muslim preachers, was a continuation in Bahia of the Fulani jihads. This interpretation overemphasizes the continuity of African traditions to the exclusion of the Bahian context. Jihadic ideology may have inspired some of its leaders, but this does not make the movement itself a jihad, much less a continuation of the Fulani jihad. Of the very few Fulani among the Bahian slaves, none was involved in this movement. Most Muslims in Bahia in 1835, including their leaders, were Yoruba and secondarily Hausa. In contrast to the conspiracy uncovered in 1807, nothing in the records of the trials of the leaders indicates a particularly violent opposition to Roman Catholicism and its symbols. During the uprising the Africans, among whom there were non-Muslims, did not attack any of the large number of churches of Salvador. There is no reason to believe that the rebels sought to establish an Islamic state or saw the movement as a jihad of the sword; at the same time the uprising did not lack a religious, even ritualistic, dimension. A strong process of conversion to Islam was under way at the time of the rebellion, particularly among the more numerous Yoruba slaves and freedpeople. And the rebellion was planned to begin at the end of the Islamic festival of Ramadan, probably after the Lailat al-Qadr festival of 1250 A.H. (January 25, 1835).

The repression that followed disrupted and dispersed the Muslim community. Four rebels were executed, hundreds whipped and imprisoned, the freedpeople deported back to Africa, and numerous slaves sold outside Bahia. Anywhere in Brazil, and particularly in Bahia, blacks found with Muslim writings were immediately viewed as suspect. The Malê Rebellion had a tremendous repercussion throughout Brazil: local and federal laws were passed to improve slave control, including the death penalty for slaves accused of killing masters, overseers, or members of their families. The repression against Muslims and the hardening of slave laws were mild compared to conditions in other countries and colonies in the Americas, and these events occurred at a time when a liberal discourse, including some steps toward abolitionism, were prevailing in Brazilian society and government.

João José Reis

See Also

Oyo, Early Kingdom of; Abolition and Emancipation in Latin America and the Caribbean; Catholic Church in Latin America and the Caribbean; Salvador, Brazil.

Latin America and the Caribbean

Mutabaruka

(Allan Hope) (b. 1952, Kingston, Jamaica), poet and producer best known for recording his poetry, influenced by Rastafarian and Black Power ideologies, to reggae rhythm tracks.

Mutabaruka's literary and musical career began when he became affiliated with Rastafarianism in the 1970s. He published three poetry collections during that decade, all marked by his imaginative handling of Jamaican colloquial speech patterns, his praise of Africanisms in Jamaican culture, and his fiery condemnations of Western politics and materialism. The release of his first recordings in 1982 signaled the start of a new career as a "dub poet" (a poet writing and performing poetry within the context of reggae instrumental music). Inspired by the example of poet Linton Kwesi Johnson, Mutabaruka sought to arouse his audiences to take political action to counter what he perceived as the destructive actions of hypocritical authorities. But his recording of "Revolutionary Poets" revealed a self-critical examination of that stance ("revolutionary poets/have all gone to the/creative art centre/ to watch/the sufferin/of the people"), and, although sympathetic to Rastafarianism, he has emphasized feminist themes and produced recordings of feminist dub poets antagonistic to Rastafarianism's traditional patriarchalism.

His albums blend a "Back to Africa" vision with a pantheistic "Back to Nature" sensibility; his reggae-anchored poems attack aspects of Western civilization, such as processed foods and other things that are antithetical to what in his perception belong to ancient and indigenous African civilization. A comprehensive overview of his recording career is offered on a compact disk, *Mutabaruka: The Ultimate Collection* (Shanachie Records).

Norman Weinstein

See Also

Literature, English Language, Caribbean; Dub Poetry; Feminism in Africa: An Interpretation; Rastafarians.

Africa

Mutesa I

(Mutesa Walugembe Mukaabya) (b. 1838?; d. October 1884, Nabulagala, Buganda, in present-day Uganda), kabaka (king) of the Buganda kingdom from 1856 until his death.

When the Bugandan king Suna II died in 1856, his son Mutesa I ascended to the throne – over more senior and apparently competent brothers – with the help of prominent Bugandan chiefs who hoped to become more powerful under a weak monarchy. Initially unpopular, Mutesa quickly consolidated his authority, partly through a brutal campaign of executions that continued throughout his reign. Many of his political rivals were burned alive.

Mutesa presided over Buganda during a period of increasing contact with Arab-Swahili merchants from Zanzibar and European explorers in search of the Nile River. Threatened by an expansionist Egypt to the north, he actively sought diplomatic relations with potential allies. He sent an envoy to meet the sultan of Zanzibar and invited English missionaries to his court; he also adopted the Muslim faith and learned to speak Arabic. He declined circumcision, however, as Bugandan culture opposed body modification. Furthermore, when some 200 men refused to eat meat killed by Mutesa's butcher on the grounds that it had not been ritually cleansed according to Muslim law, he had them executed.

Depicted as an aggressive and witty strategist, Mutesa used cunning political maneuvers to avoid annexation by Egypt. In 1873 the Egyptian khedive, Isma'il Paha, hired the British general Charles George Gordon to take control of the regions to the south of Egypt. When Gordon made plans to establish a fort in Mutesa's territory, Mutesa invited the troops to visit his capital. An army of some 150 soldiers was greeted by an enormous gathering of Bagandans, recruited and armed by Mutesa. Once the army was settled in the capital, Mutesa arranged for their porters to leave. Immobilized, the troops found themselves essentially captured by Mutesa. Ultimately, Gordon abandoned plans to conquer Buganda and instead recognized the kabaka's sovereignty.

Toward the end of his reign, Mutesa became very ill. Because his own sons had died of disease and his brother had been killed, he began maneuvers to ensure that his prime minister, Prince Mwanga, would succeed him. Despite the administration of an unknown pharmaceutical by Arabs at the court, Mutesa died. He was buried in a makeshift lead coffin at Muzibuazaalapanga Palace in Buganda.

Ari Nave

See Also

Buganda, Early Kingdom of; Explorers in Africa Since 1800; Swahili People; Christianity: Missionaries in Africa.

North America

Mutual Benefit Societies,

black American organizations that provide financial and social support otherwise denied to African Americans; these societies were especially active during the nineteenth century.

First formed near the end of the eighteenth century, mutual benefit societies represent one of the oldest and most durable kinds of African American self-help organizations.

The earliest known mutual benefit society, the Union Society of Newport, Rhode Island, was founded in 1780. Blacks soon founded similar societies in Boston and Philadelphia.

Most mutual benefit societies formed to provide financial assistance: benefits for members who were unable to work because of illness; funeral and burial expenses; pensions for widows and orphans; and low-interest loans. In addition to financial aid many societies attempted to provide social uplift, encouraging temperance, discouraging fighting and profanity, and expelling members convicted of a crime. One organization in Charleston, South Carolina, realizing that blacks were often jailed unfairly, established extended benefits for those members. By the 1820s most organizations had similar membership requirements.

Blacks originally formed their own societies because organizations founded by whites excluded them, although some black societies also restricted membership based on color and gender. The Brown Fellowship Society of Charleston admitted only light-skinned members, forcing the excluded members to form the Free Dark Men of Color. Similarly, women frequently founded their own societies when men excluded them from their societies or when mixed societies denied women equal rights.

Mutual benefit societies became one of the most popular forms of organization for free blacks during the nineteenth century. By 1840 Philadelphia had 106 mutual aid societies with nearly 8000 members – half of Philadelphia's black population. Societies also organized in several Southern cities, including Baltimore, Washington, D.C., Richmond, Charleston, and New Orleans, although Southern societies were less common than their Northern counterparts because of restrictions that local Southern governments imposed on free blacks. Slaves were categorically forbidden by whites to join, although some joined despite the laws, notably the slave Frederick Douglass. Evidence also suggests that slaves themselves formed such societies for mutual benefit and burial.

Mutual benefit societies flourished after the Civil War, especially in the South, to provide social welfare services for black Americans. Newly freed blacks were particularly vulnerable to economic hardship, because the federal government offered few social welfare programs and excluded African Americans from programs that were available. In 1910 mutual benefit societies in Mississippi had a combined membership of 80,000, almost equaling the number of black church members in the state.

Southern whites criticized mutual benefit societies, believing that such organizations – especially those that met secretly – were plotting the overthrow of the Jim Crow South. Many black ministers also objected to the growing influence exercised by mutual benefit societies, though many societies were affiliated with churches, because they believed that the societies were drawing members away from the churches. Black leaders such as W. E. B. Du Bois and Booker T. Washington, however, praised these organizations, citing the value of the services they provided.

Mutual benefit societies, especially small ones, declined in importance after the Great Depression; with largely aged memberships, societies began losing money by paying an increasing amount of benefits with no corresponding rise in income, as younger members could no longer afford the dues. In addition, the social welfare programs developed during the New Deal eliminated much of the need for mutual benefit societies. Even as they declined, many mutual benefit societies remained active in the late twentieth century and provided support for blacks living in the rural South and within immigrant groups.

Robert Fay

See Also

Baltimore, Maryland; Boston, Massachusetts; Civil War, American; Du Bois, William Edward Burghardt (W. E. B.); Free Blacks in the United States, 1619 to 1863; New Orleans, Louisiana; Richmond, Virginia; Washington, Booker Taliaferro; Philadelphia, Pennsylvania.

Mwanda. Please see Msiri

Africa

Mwere (also known as the Mwera), ethnic group of southeastern Africa.

The Mwere primarily inhabit Tanzania. Others live in Malawi and Mozambique. They speak a Bantu language and are closely related to the Yao people. Approximately 400,000 people consider themselves Mwere.

See Also

Bantu: Dispersion and Settlement.

Africa

Mwezi II (also Gisabo, Kisabo, or Kissabo) (b. 1845; d. 1908), king of Burundi who used collaboration with the Germans to solidify his rule.

Born Gisabo, Mwezi II Gisabo became the king, or *mwami*, of Burundi in 1860 upon the death of his father, Ntare II. Although tradition dictated that the king had near absolute power, several of Ntare II's sons had actively rebelled, sparking dynastic feuds over succession and territory that continued throughout Mwezi II's reign. The explorer Sir Richard Francis Burton observed that Mwezi II could "gather in a short time a large host of warriors who are the terror of the neighboring tribes"; but still the king was constantly frustrated in his attempts to consolidate authority.

Mwezi II welcomed the arrival of German troops in Burundi in the late 1890s, hoping that the Germans would help him vanquish his opponents and control his unruly chiefs. This strategy proved only partially successful. Convinced that the king was a threat to German interests, Captain von Beringe led a military campaign against him, which the governor of German East Africa opposed. The governor ordered that all chiefs in Burundi be treated as subordinate to Mwezi II as long as he recognized German authority, thus fulfilling Mwezi II's original aspirations. In response, the chiefs revolted against both the Germans and Mwezi II, who with considerable German assistance, brought them under control, satisfying German hopes of establishing "indirect rule" in the colony. But Mwezi II died in 1908, and his son Mutanga II proved much less useful to the Germans, as he was unable to prevent rebellion among his subordinates.

Eric Young

See Also

Burton, Sir Richard.

Africa

Mwinyi, Ali Hassan (b. 1925, Dar es Salaam, Tanganyika), president of Tanzania (1985-1995) who initiated the country's transition to a multi-party system.

Born in Dar es Salaam (in what was then Tanganyika), Ali Hassan Mwinyi spent his youth on the island of Zanzibar, his parents' birthplace, attending local schools before earning a degree from the University of Durham in England in 1956. He was an early member of the Afro-Shirazi Party (ASP), the nationalist party that led Zanzibar to independence in 1963 and cooperated with the Tanganyika African National Union (TANU) after the 1964 federation of Zanzibar and Tanganyika into Tanzania.

Mwinyi left his job as a schoolteacher and administrator in 1964 and served in a number of Zanzibari and Tanzanian ministerial positions until 1977, when he resigned from his post as Tanzanian minister of home affairs as a matter of principle after several deaths resulted from the unauthorized conduct of junior security officers under his charge. After serving as ambassador to Egypt from 1977 to 1982, he returned to the Tanzanian cabinet, first as minister of natural resources and tourism (1982-1983), then as minister of state in the administration of Aboud Jumbe. Mwinyi succeeded Jumbe as both vice president of Tanzania and president of Zanzibar in 1984.

Mwinyi was elected president of Tanzania in November 1985 and reelected to another five-year term in 1990. He succeeded Julius

K. Nyerere, who had been president of Tanzania since 1963. Nyerere had implemented a form of collectivized self-help SOCIALISM, *Ujamaa*, in the hopes that Tanzania could build a productive economy through the energies and skills of its people rather than through foreign aid. Nyerere's experiments largely failed and, as a result, Mwinyi inherited a huge national debt and an economy in shambles. During his first term Mwinyi focused on converting Tanzania to a free market economy and privatizing state companies. In addition, he adopted International Monetary Fund (IMF) reforms in exchange for new grants, despite resistance within the Socialist Revolutionary Party of Tanzania (Chama Cha Mapinduzi, or CCM). Although Mwinyi's austerity measures were successful in his first term, he lost control of government spending in his second term and broke with the IMF in 1994.

During his second term Mwinyi targeted corruption and inefficiency. He dismissed many government officials, but in 1994 a tax-evasion scandal involving many government officials demonstrated that his anticorruption efforts had not succeeded. He also initiated the transition to a multiparty state. Under the terms of Tanzania's constitution, Mwinyi was barred from seeking a third term. He completed his term in 1995 after the election of Augustine Mvema, leader of the National Convention for Construction and Reform (NCCR).

Elizabeth Heath

See Also

Dar es Salaam, Tanzania; Nyerere, Julius Kambarage.

Latin America and the Caribbean

Myth of Racial Democracy in Latin America and the Caribbean: An Interpretation

"There's no racism in Brazil!" Manuel declared with a dismissive wave of his glass. "Here we're all equal! How could there be racism when people of all colors intermarry and have children?" We were leaning against the counter in a small bar in a working-class town on the outskirts of Rio de Janeiro. Pointing to his brown skin and short frizzy hair, he said, "I have the blood of all races in me – white, black, Indian. How could we be racists?"

Litanies about "racial democracy" can be heard throughout Latin America. The key, racial democrats argue, is that in contrast to North America's pattern of categorizing people as either black or white, in much of Latin America people fall somewhere in between these extremes, along a broad color spectrum. Venezuelans, for example, often say theirs is a *café con leche* country: 70 percent of all Venezuelans are *pardos*, of mixed African and non-African origin, descended from the 100,000 slaves forced to work on coastal cacao plantations before the nineteenth century (*see* VENEZUELA). About 40 percent of all Brazilians are mulattos, that is, people with some degree of descent from the more than 3.5 million slaves who once sweated in that country's SUGAR and coffee plantations; and at least a quarter of all Colombians are partially descended from the 200,000 slaves brought to toil in the cane fields and pan for gold in New Granada, the former Spanish colony composed of present-day COLOMBIA, Venezuela, and ECUADOR (*see* SLAVERY IN LATIN AMERICA AND THE CARIBBEAN). Even in the Andean country of Ecuador, up to a tenth of the population is descended from the 100,000 slaves sent there centuries ago. According to racial democrats, the presence of so many mixed-bloods promotes fraternal race relations.

The reality is less sanguine. People on the lighter end of the color-race continuum hold strong prejudices against those toward the darker end. Mulattos, anxious to maximize their distance from people darker than themselves, can be as racist as whites. One Brazilian mulatta recalls her childhood in this way: "I didn't know my place, but I knew I wasn't black. Blacks were dirty, and I was clean; blacks were stupid, and I was intelligent; blacks lived in the slum and I did not; and above all, blacks had thick noses and lips, and I didn't. I was a mulatta; I still had hopes of being saved."

Such attitudes have direct consequences for blacks' life chances. In Colombia virtually no graduate from middle-class secondary or law schools is black, while two-thirds of the slum dwellers near Cartagena are. In Venezuela most dark-skinned people work in the lowest-paying jobs, such as domestic service, informal labor, stevedoring, and sharecropping. In BRAZIL blacks are concentrated in the low-paying service sector, working as janitors, porters, laundresses, day laborers, domestic servants, and in other, similar positions. Jobs asking for applicants of a "good appearance" (read, "of light complexion"), such as receptionist, secretary, bank teller, or low-level federal employee, are effectively closed to blacks.

So strong is antiblack sentiment in Latin America that for much of the region's history, those toward the lighter end of the color spectrum have sought to "bleach" blacks right out of existence. If, as Richard Jackson has put it, whites in the United States tried to get rid of blacks "through extermination," in Latin America they attempted to do so "through amalgamation." As early as 1835 Cuban historian José Antonio Saco was already proclaiming that "the only remedy for making us respectable is whitening." "WHITENING" meant eliminating Africa's racial heritage by means of miscegenation. In practical terms, this required the importation of Europeans and restrictions on the immigration of blacks. Throughout the twentieth century the governments of Colombia, Venezuela, ARGENTINA, Ecuador, and Guatemala (*see* CENTRAL AMERICA), among others, passed such racist, antiblack immigration legislation.

Costa Rica, for example, refused citizenship in the 1930s to the West Indians who came to work on its railroads and banana plantations, and denied them the right to live outside certain provinces. In PANAMA racism was intensified during the construction of the Panama Canal, because United States supervisors treated West Indian workers the same as lighter-skinned Panamanians. This enraged the latter, who proceeded between 1920 and 1940 to ban any further black immigration, refuse blacks citizenship, and threaten to expel them. In the early twentieth century Brazilian newspapers were up in arms at the suggestion that North American blacks be encouraged to migrate to their country. Such immigration, the editor of the *Getulino* wrote, would "be the death blow to the mathematical process of the disappearance of the black race of Brazil."

If racial democracy has any meaning at all, it refers to the fact that Latin American societies make some provision for better treatment of people of visibly mixed ancestry. Mulattos usually enjoy at least some advantages over blacks, but their status varies greatly throughout the hemisphere. Shunted aside from the most respectable professions, such as medicine, law, academia, upper-level government, and the officer and diplomatic corps, Brazilian mulattos are still able to enter a secondary occupational tier as schoolteachers, journalists, artists, clerks, and low-level officials in municipal government and tax offices. Mulattos get promoted more easily and earn more than their black counterparts. Marriages between whites and mulattos are less stigmatized than those between whites and blacks.

In contrast, for much of the last 200 years in CUBA – at least until the Cuban Revolution in 1959 and, some say, even afterward – only the smallest minority of the lightest-skinned mulattos have been able to attain positions of prestige; most have faced the same sort of discrimination as darker-skinned Cubans. In the nineteenth century rural mulattos and blacks were mainly agricultural laborers, while their urban counterparts were prevented from entering the navy, air force, and various food-handling occupations. The segregation introduced by U.S. occupation early in this century, affecting mulattos and blacks equally, dovetailed neatly with white attitudes so that even after the United States no longer directly implemented segregationist rules, whites continued to keep many of them in force. Ten years before the 1959 revolution, mulatto workers were still primarily "hewers of wood and drawers of water." Whether such patterns have survived in revolutionary Cuba is open to furious debate. Official sources and some observers claim that racism has been eradicated, but contrary claims made by black nationalists Eldridge Cleaver, Robert Williams, and Carlos Moore have become virtually legendary. Most observers of revolutionary Cuba concur that there is essentially no difference in status between blacks and mulattos.

Two societies, two patterns of mixed-blood status. Any explanation of the difference should take into account the experiences of free mulattos in Brazil and Cuba during the long night of slavery. In Brazil free mulattos remained so economically vital throughout the slave era that the white ruling class had little choice but to concede some social mobility to them. This concession nurtured among Brazilian mulattos a willingness after the abolition of slavery to play the role of buffer between whites and blacks.

In Cuba, by contrast, a small, economically marginal, politically vulnerable free mulatto population found itself the victim, in the nineteenth century, of harsh repression at the hands of a jittery slaveholding elite. This experience forged among many Cuban mulattos a deep-seated resentment against whites and a willingness to fight on the side of the slaves for abolition. This, in turn, reinforced whites' hostility toward the mulattos, and rendered unworkable a Brazilian-style white-mulatto alliance after slavery was ended.

Marvín Harris has argued that at the very inception of the Brazilian colony, planters needed free mulattos as overseers, slave catchers, foot soldiers and gunmen, cattle hands and subsistence farmers. Slaves could not be used for these functions, and a labor shortage in Portugal meant that not enough whites were available either. (The rate of white immigration remained static throughout the entire colonial period.) Slaveholders manumitted mulattos in such numbers that by the late eighteenth and early nineteenth centuries, free people of color represented, in virtually every province of the country, between half and two times the size of the white population.

Many of these mulattos were employed in militias to protect the property of white slaveholders. By distinguishing themselves in this service, mulattos found ample opportunity for promotion through the ranks. Mulatto farmers also had a stake in slave society. Many of them worked small parcels of land to supply nearby sugar plantations with food. A surprisingly large number of these poor farmers, up to 77 percent of them in one locality, owned one or two slaves. Add to this that most of them depended on large slaveholders for land rights, credit, and protection, and it is not hard to see why rural mulattos identified with the slave system and were unwilling to fight against it.

By the eighteenth century many mulattos had migrated to the burgeoning cities of Salvador (*see* BAHIA), São Luis, and Rio de Janeiro, where they found opportunities as self-employed artisans and petty merchants. On the eve of abolition, mulattos outnumbered free blacks in urban artisanal occupations by more than 4 to 1, and, not surprisingly, feared that the end of slavery would threaten their position in the labor market.

From such favored positions in urban areas, Brazilian mulattos readily advanced into the arts, letters, and liberal professions, including medicine. While slavery was still in force, free mulattos could become engineers, civil servants, and lawyers. And at the culmination of their careers, they could buy a certificate of whiteness.

A historical bargain had been struck: in exchange for at least some social recognition and advancement, mulattos threw in their lot with the white elite against the blackest members of society. As early as the seventeenth century mulattos helped Portuguese slaveholders expel Dutch invaders. During the Pernambucan independence rebellion of 1817-1823, mulatto leaders proclaimed support for slavery. And during every major slave revolt of the nineteenth century mulattos sided with the whites. So reliable were mulattos, in fact, that at the height of the sugar boom, the rate of manumission increased steadily and free mulattos played an important role in local militias.

Support for slavery was most striking in the period leading up to abolition in 1888. Though a few prominent mulattos, like ANDRÉ REBOUÇAS and Luis Gama, were abolitionists, most of the mulatto political elite studiously refrained from taking a stand, while others, such as the baron of Cotegipe, were strongly anti-abolitionist. Only the combination of international pressure, the growing expense of slaveholding in many regions of the country, and massive slave rebellion finally broke the back of Brazilian slavery.

That mulattos "sat out" the abolition of slavery entered, it seems, into the popular consciousness of many working-class blacks. The elderly black men and women I spoke with in 1988 found no place for mulattos in their recounting of the story of abolition, even those who believed that abolition was a gift from the white masters. As one told me, "The mulattos were sitting pretty up on high. They never cared for the slave, even if they shared his blood. They wanted only to forget him."

The process of abolition thus strengthened ties between whites and mulattos, and allowed whites to continue counting on mulatto support in efforts to exclude blacks from social power. As long as dark-skinned blacks were forced to remain in the lowest-paying jobs, mulattos would gladly take up the slack in the skilled trades, petty commerce, and the professions. In exchange, mulattos pledged allegiance to white values, modes of behavior, and physical aesthetics. "Let us not seek to perpetuate our race," wrote a Brazilian mulatto leader in the 1920s, "but, yes, to infiltrate ourselves into the bosom of the privileged race, the white race."

Cuba's was a different story. An economic backwater of the Spanish Empire until the late eighteenth century, its inhabitants occupied themselves primarily with cattle raising and producing food to provision the Spanish ships and troops passing through the port of Havana. Until the sugar boom of the eighteenth and nineteenth centuries, slavery was a fairly minor institution on the island.

Mulattos never established themselves as key actors in the Cuban economy. The Cuban mulatto population grew not from the slaveholders' economic needs, but from the desire of the Spanish Crown to people the colony as thickly as possible in order to ward off the territorial pretensions of the French and British. Only a small though visible percentage of mulattos migrated to Havana, where limited opportunities as artisans and small merchants awaited them.

The absolute number of Cuban mulattos always remained relatively small. Unlike Portugal, which was hard-pressed to send migrants to Brazil, Spain provided a small but steady flow of settlers to Cuba before 1800. By the end of the eighteenth century free nonwhites accounted for only about 20 percent of Cuba's population. Numbering far fewer than whites and lacking a sizable, skilled, literate urban contingent, Cuban mulattos remained vulnerable both socially and politically.

Immediately after the HAITIAN REVOLUTION of 1791-1804, Cuba's sugar industry began to prosper, requiring hundreds of thousands of slaves. By mid-century free nonwhites, mainly mulattos, numbered just over 200,000, only half the number of slaves on the island and a quarter of the whites. These ratios spelled political trouble for the mulattos. The sudden influx of slaves at the very moment that slavery was being abolished in much of the hemisphere – as well as Cuba's geographic proximity to HAITI – made Cuban slaveholders more than a little nervous.

The planters were haunted by the specter not just of a slave revolution, but of a mulatto-led slave revolution. As far as the Cuban elite was concerned, the events in Haiti were the handiwork of mixed-bloods who had been coddled by the decadent French. In 1845 Vicente Queipo, attorney general of Cuba, declared in no uncertain terms that Cuba's leaders had learned "the severe lesson of the neighboring island of Santo Domingo, whose loss depended a great deal on the close intimacy in which the white inhabitants of the French part lived with their slaves, and the numerous colored population resulting from this foreboding association."

Regardless of the accuracy of this perception of Haitian history, it led to a full-scale attack on the rights of mulattos. An 1809 decree banned freedpeople and mulattos from teaching at or attending Cuban schools, followed soon after by laws prohibiting them from owning land, serving in the militia, and traveling without special passes. The most dramatic change, and undoubtedly the cruelest blow, was the government's reclassification of mulattos after 1841 as belonging to the same category as blacks: *gente de color.* This act accelerated other laws restricting interracial marriage, so that by the 1860s all interracial marriages were prohibited.

Such antimulatto legislation and color classifications left an indelible mark on the consciousness of the mixed-blood population. In the Cespedes Rebellion of 1868, which called for the end of Spanish rule and freedom for the slaves, one observer estimated that two-thirds of the fighting men were "of color other than black, all shades of brown predominating" (*see* TEN YEARS' WAR). These were men of little means, who, in contrast to the mulattos of Brazil, owned no slaves. Ten years later, in yet another revolt that included the call for abolition, the so-called Guerra Chiquita (Little War), mulattos again figured prominently.

The end of slavery in 1886, however, did not bring about an improvement in the condition of mulattos. Throughout the 1890s, in Havana and the sugar-producing areas, mulattos continued to be victims of the same racism as blacks.

In Brazil throughout much of the twentieth century, mulattos identified their ultimate interest as incorporation into, rather than rejection of, the established system of race relations. This identification did not prevent many of them from keenly resenting their exclusion from the highest echelons of power, a resentment periodically translated into mulatto-based social and political organizations. Such groups, however, have characteristically avoided calling for a distinct black identity, aiming instead to improve chances for assimilation. The Brazilian Negro Front of the 1930s insisted in one of its publications that "the problem of the Brazilian Negro is that of definitive, total integration of the Negro in all aspects of Brazilian life."

Brazilian mulattos often redirected their resentment away from dominant whites and toward other vulnerable groups, a tendency reinforced by job competition with foreign immigrants. In the 1930s mulatto newspapers adopted a virulently antiforeign, anti-immigrant stance, as when *O Clarim da Alvorada* denounced "the colonies of foreigners, who organize themselves and discriminate." Nearly all of the limited number of mulatto politicians active in the last generation adopted similar postures, doing their best to blend into mainstream party politics and avoid being pulled into the political orbit of the small but growing black consciousness movement (*see* BRAZIL, BLACKS AND POLITICS IN: AN INTERPRETATION).

By contrast, a strong mulatto and black political movement emerged in Cuba at the beginning of the twentieth century. The PARTIDO INDEPENDIENTE DE COLOR (Independent Party of Color; PIC) was founded in 1908. Unlike the Black Brazilian Front, the PIC demonstrated sensitivity to the concerns of rural dark-skinned blacks by calling for land distribution to poor tenants in the densely black province of Oriente. In 1912 PIC leaders led rural blacks in a revolt against the white oligarchy. In the hysterical repression that followed, more than 3000 blacks and mulattos lost their lives. The slaughter seared the consciousness of Cuban mulattos in ways entirely unknown to people of color in Brazil. The memory of the massacre was still alive in small villages in Oriente Province as recently as 1968.

In the aftermath of the bloodshed urban blacks and mulattos limited their demands to the urban area, yet they continued to work together toward achieving common objectives. The Organización Celular Asteria, formed in the 1930s, argued that "since half of all Cubans were Negroid, the same percentage of government jobs must be held by Afro-Cubans." Also in the 1930s the Committee for the Rights of the Negro brought blacks and mulattos together to fight racist employment policies and to demonstrate against segregation at public beaches and parks. Given such a strong nonassimilationist political tradition, it is not surprising that in the 1950s blacks and mulattos joined the Communist Party in droves.

The jury is still out on the impact of the Cuban Revolution on race relations in that country. The revolution did eliminate the visible, legal pillars of racism, and it seems to have enjoyed the support of poor blacks and mulattos. Declaring its own version of racial democracy, the government has made race and racism taboo subjects, and no race-based political movements (or any other for that matter) have been allowed to emerge.

Brazil, on the other hand, has witnessed the emergence of an entirely new kind of black movement over the past two decades. Though still largely middle-class, intellectual, and mulatto-based, the black consciousness movement no longer calls for assimilation, but rather black pride and power (*see* BLACK CONSCIOUSNESS IN BRAZIL). Buried in Brazilian whites' strategy of selective privilege – generally successful in dividing mulattos from blacks, thereby conquering them both – lies the seed of its own destruction. Put simply, while white society holds out the promise of acceptance to mulattos, it fails to fulfill it.

My barroom companion Manuel once told me, "There is a saying in Brazil: If you're not white, you're black. That's not really true, you know. Here you can be other things. Like me. I'm a *moreno* [brown]. But to a white man, I'm a moreno only if he likes me. If he doesn't like me, I'm a mulatto, or I'm even a *preto* [black]. They play a game, you know? I guess the real saying should be, If you're not white, you lose." Herein lies a glimmer of the consciousness that has led an entire generation of mulattos to become activists in black consciousness movements, a process that has begun to undermine the hold of the myth of racial democracy.

John Burdick

From *NACLA Report on the Americas* 25, no. 4 (February 1992): 40-45.

SEE ALSO

Frente Negra Brasileira; Cleaver, Eldridge Leroy; Williams, Robert Franklin; Cartagena de Indias, Colombia; Gama, Luís Gonzaga Pinto da; Rio de Janeiro, Brazil; Abolition and Emancipation in Latin America and the Caribbean.

n

NAACP. Please see NATIONAL ASSOCIATION FOR THE ADVANCEMENT OF COLORED PEOPLE

North America

NAACP Legal Defense and Educational Fund, the major organization by which African Americans have, through law, achieved advances in civil rights in the twentieth century.

Created in 1940 by the NATIONAL ASSOCIATION FOR THE ADVANCEMENT OF COLORED PEOPLE (NAACP), the NAACP Legal Defense and Educational Fund (LDF) pioneered the field of public interest law, using the courts to gain and expand civil rights for African Americans when other avenues were blocked. The LDF was most visible during the 1940s, when its first director, future Supreme Court justice THURGOOD MARSHALL, led it in the fight against legal segregation in the South. Its victories laid the groundwork for, and inspired the participants in, the CIVIL RIGHTS MOVEMENT. After overcoming legalized segregation in the courts, the LDF fought against the backlash of angry Southern state governments, several of which attempted to challenge the LDF's right to practice in their states. It worked to strengthen and protect those rights through the courts, by lobbying and providing scholarships to help African Americans attend law schools.

The LDF is most famous for arguing before the Supreme Court in 1954's landmark *Brown* v. *Board of Education of Topeka, Kansas,* which ended legal segregation in United States public education. *Brown,* however, marked the culmination of the strategy to desegregate public education. Since shortly after the end of RECONSTRUCTION (about 1877), the South had been a one-party region, dominated by the Democratic party and its white supremacist policies. Southern states were able to retain their segregationist policies because voters returned the same representatives, who gained seniority and influence in both houses of Congress and blocked any federal civil rights legislation proposed. In response, CHARLES HAMILTON HOUSTON – called the Moses of the Civil Rights Movement – developed in the mid-1930s, as head of the NAACP's legal department, the strategy that gained civil rights for blacks through the courts by indirectly attacking segregated public education. Houston believed that suing for greater African American participation in graduate schools would be less incendiary to segregationist whites than directly attacking public schools, because the number of people attending graduate programs at that time was low.

Houston aimed to force Southern states to strengthen black public schools or eliminate them by underscoring the high cost of maintaining two "separate but equal" school systems. The strategy proved effective by as early as 1938, when the NAACP's legal department successfully argued *Missouri* ex rel. *Gaines* v. *Canada.* The Court determined in *Gaines* that Missouri's proposal to provide financial aid so that Lloyd Gaines could attend an out-of-state law school while denying him admission to an in-state, whites-only law school was not equal treatment under the Constitution, and violated the Fourteenth Amendment.

The NAACP, because it lobbied and issued propaganda, was ineligible for non-profit status. Thus, its contributors could not deduct donations to the NAACP from their tax returns. In 1939 NAACP secretary (its highest position) Walter White attempted to attract contributors by creating a separate organization to administer the NAACP's charitable activities. On March 20, 1940, the NAACP created the LDF. Although created to be independent of the NAACP, the boards of directors for each organization were interlocked, and the LDF was largely guided by the same principles as the NAACP. Director-counsel Marshall, a former student of Houston's and an NAACP lawyer, continued the NAACP legal department's strategy at the LDF. With Marshall executing Houston's strategy, the LDF won a number of graduate school desegregation cases, including *Sipuel* v. *Board of Regents of the University of Oklahoma* (1948), *McLaurin* v. *Oklahoma State Regents* (1950), and SWEATT V. PAINTER (1950), all of which contributed to *Brown,* the final assault on segregated education.

Earl Warren, writing for the Court in *Brown,* worded the decision ambiguously, directing schools to desegregate "with all deliberate speed." Many Southern states emphasized the "deliberate" rather than the "speed," maneuvering to slow integration. The LDF, therefore, began concentrating on ensuring that states complied with *Brown,* as in *Cooper* v. *Aaron* (1958), in which the Court ordered the desegregation of the Little Rock, Arkansas, Central High School. The Supreme Court did not order complete school desegregation, however, until 1968, with *Green* v. *County School Board of New Kent County.*

Brown ended one era for the LDF and it began another era, as African Americans began to demand equal access to all public facilities and equal treatment before the law, and the protest moved from the courthouses to the streets. The LDF, which had set the agenda in the fight against legal segregation, now yielded to civil rights activists and organizations, representing their members when they were arrested for participating in SIT-INS, protest marches, and rallies.

In addition to attempting to block integration, Southern governments reacted to *Brown* by attacking the NAACP and the LDF, which it saw as the catalysts of all the activism and protest. According to Jack Greenberg, an LDF lawyer who became its director after Thurgood Marshall left in 1961, almost every Southern state "passed laws and started legislative investigations... to put the NAACP and the LDF out of business." South Carolina's legislature prohibited schools from hiring NAACP members. Arkansas, Florida, Georgia, Louisiana, North Carolina, Tennessee, Texas, and Virginia all followed suit. Virginia's attempt to outlaw the NAACP ended in *NAACP* v. *Button,* in which the Supreme Court ruled that the NAACP had a first amendment right to pursue public interest law.

Although the LDF, which fully separated from the NAACP because of threats to its tax-exempt status, is best known for its fight against school segregation, it also sought changes in other areas. In its earliest days, despite a small budget and the threat of violence posed by angry whites, LDF lawyers often traveled to small Southern towns to represent accused African Americans and make certain they received fair trials. Many of those local cases became Supreme Court cases, such as *Shepherd and Irvin* v. *Florida* (1950), in which the LDF successfully argued that a defendant must be tried in a bias-free venue. In *Smith* v. *Allwright* (1944), the Supreme Court ruled that primary elections excluding blacks were unconstitutional. *Morgan* v. *the Commonwealth of Virginia* outlawed segregated accommodations on interstate buses. In *Shelley* v. *Kraemer* (1948), the Court ruled that covenants prohibiting blacks from purchasing homes were unconstitutional.

In the late twentieth century the LDF's efforts continued in the courtroom and beyond. In court, it worked to end discrimination in employment, education, and in the criminal justice system. Among the issues it championed were fair employment practices, AFFIRMATIVE ACTION in employment and education, and ending the death penalty, which its studies indicated was applied disproportionately to black defendants. It has also formed and strengthened coalitions of civil rights groups to monitor the enforcement of civil rights laws, report civil rights abuses, and inform the American public about areas of need. The LDF, with its lasting and profound influence, has successfully pioneered a style of civil rights law that numerous agencies have emulated, as seen in those agencies with the phrase "legal defense fund" in their titles.

Robert Fay

See Also
Brown v. *Board of Education*; Fourteenth Amendment to the United States Constitution; White, Walter Francis; Little Rock Crisis, 1957.

North America

Nabrit, James Madison, Jr.

(b. September 4, 1900, Atlanta, Ga.; d. December 27, 1997, WASHINGTON, D.C.), civil rights attorney and university president who became the first African American United States Delegate to the United Nations.

James Madison Nabrit Jr. was born to the Reverend James Madison Nabrit and his wife, Gertrude. He graduated from MOREHOUSE COLLEGE in 1923 and from Northwestern University Law School in 1927. In 1930 he moved to Houston, where he worked as a civil rights lawyer. Nabrit joined the faculty of HOWARD UNIVERSITY Law School in 1936, where, in 1938 he taught the first formal civil rights course in any law school in the United States. While a teacher and administrator at Howard from 1936 to 1960, Nabrit was involved in numerous civil rights cases, including *Bolling* v. *Sharpe*, in which he and attorney George E. C. Hayes challenged segregation in the public schools of the District of Columbia. *Bolling* was ruled on by the Supreme Court in conjunction with *Brown* v. *Board of Education*, wherein the Court found segregation to be unconstitutional. In 1960 Nabrit became the president of Howard University, a post he retired from in 1969. He took a leave of absence from 1965 to 1967 to serve on the United States delegation to the United Nations. In 1966 President Lyndon Johnson appointed Nabrit to the second highest post in the U.S. mission, deputy to the chief delegate.

See Also
Atlanta, Georgia.

Latin America and the Caribbean

Nabuco, Joaquim

(b. August 19, 1849, Recife, Pernambuco, BRAZIL; d. January 17, 1910, Washington, D.C.), Brazilian politician, author, and abolitionist whose 1883 book, *O abolicionismo*, one of the most influential abolitionist works of its time, catalyzed Brazil's abolition movement.

Born into an aristocratic and politically active family, Joaquim Nabuco spent the first eight years of his life on his family's large sugar plantation in the northeastern province of Pernambuco. He later moved with his parents to Rio de Janeiro, then attended the prestigious law academies of São Paulo and Recife. At the former, he met Antônio de Castro Alves, the "Poet of the Slaves," and abolitionist RUI BARBOSA. Between 1873 and 1876 he made several trips to Europe and the United States, where he learned about abolitionists such as William Lloyd Garrison, in the process strengthening his belief in abolition.

Nabuco opposed slavery for moral reasons. At age 8 he became aware of the cruelties of slavery when a slave from a nearby plantation approached him and begged to be purchased by Nabuco's family, explaining that his master often punished him. When Nabuco was 20, he returned to the plantation where he had grown up, and reflected: "The sacrifice of the poor blacks who had incorporated their lives into the future of that property no longer existed except perhaps in my own memory." Nabuco recalled that it was then that he "resolved to devote my life, if it was given to do so, to [this] generous race."

Nabuco had become familiar with abolitionist activities at a young age. His father, José Tomás Nabuco de Araújo, a prominent politician and advocate of gradual emancipation, was instrumental in passing the so-called Free Womb Law, which freed all children born to slave women. While in law school, Nabuco composed his own abolition treatise and, in a case in which he eloquently critiqued slavery and capital punishment, saved from the death penalty a young black man accused of murdering several people.

Following the death of his father in 1878, Nabuco was elected to the Brazilian Parliament and initiated his abolitionist campaign by introducing bills providing for a gradual end to slavery. After their rejection, in 1880 Nabuco founded the Sociedade Brasileira contra a escravidão (Brazilian Antislavery Society) and the monthly bulletin *O abolicionista* (The Abolitionist). The organization's manifesto declared: "Slavery has been for [Brazil] only an impediment to progress; it is a tree whose roots sterilize the physical and moral soil wherever they extend." The Sociedade Brasileira contra a escravidão used propaganda to fight slavery, attacking the government and appealing to the patriotic sentiments of the people.

Nabuco was defeated in the 1881 parliamentary elections and spent the next three years in London writing his book *O abolicionismo* (1883), a comprehensive analysis of the slave trade, slavery, and the abolition movement in Brazil. The publication of this book renewed the antislavery movement in Brazil, sparking emancipation movements in the provinces of Amazonas and Rio Grande do Sul.

Nabuco returned to Brazil in 1884 and resumed his abolition campaign. He was elected to the Brazilian Parliament in 1885. That year he became an outspoken critic of the Saraiva-Cotegipe, or Sexagenarian, Law, which freed slaves aged 65 and older. Although this law liberated the oldest slaves – and, not coincidentally, the least economically valuable – Nabuco feared that plantation owners would use it to abandon the old and infirm, and argued that the nation was in need of more radical reforms.

Nabuco lost the 1886 elections, but an article he had written, about the death of two slaves who had been sentenced to 300 lashes, inspired a bill to outlaw corporal punishment of slaves. The bill became a law later that year and, with the threat of whipping removed, slaves abandoned plantations in large numbers. The military soon complained about having to pursue runaway slaves, and was absolved of this responsibility. Responding to these and other pressures, Princess Isabela freed Brazil's slaves on May 13, 1888, by signing the Lei Aurea (Golden Law). Nabuco remained active in politics and died in 1910, after five years of service as an ambassador in the United States.

Aaron Myers

See Also
Transatlantic Slave Trade; Slavery in Latin America and the Caribbean; Rio de Janeiro, Brazil; Abolition and Emancipation in Latin America and the Caribbean; Free Womb Laws.

Africa

Nago

(also known as the Nagot), ethnic group of BENIN.

The Nago primarily inhabit southern Benin. They speak YORUBA, a Niger-Congo language, and are one of the Yoruba peoples, although they have increasingly assimilated with the surrounding GOUN people. Approximately 200,000 people consider themselves Nago.

SEE ALSO
Languages, African: An Overview.

Latin America and the Caribbean

Nagô, a term often applied to slaves and freed blacks in Brazil who originally came from the Yoruba-controlled parts of present-day Nigeria (*see* AFRICAN ETHNIC GROUPS IN LATIN AMERICA AND THE CARIBBEAN).

Latin America and the Caribbean

Naipaul, V. S. (b. August 17, 1932, Chaguanas, Trinidad), Trinidadian expatriate novelist and essayist, known especially for works that explore the experience of South Asians in the Caribbean (*see* EAST INDIAN COMMUNITIES IN THE CARIBBEAN).

When writer V. S. Naipaul was asked by a Jamaican newspaper interviewer whether he considered himself British or Trinidadian, his answer was "[n]ot Trinidadian.... One was born there, but there's no importance in that. They don't understand literature there." Because of statements like this one, and because he has spent his entire adult life living in England, some have criticized Naipaul for being alienated from his West Indian roots. He has also been accused of similar insensitivity in his essays on India, his parents' homeland, and on other Asian and African countries. But despite these ideological criticisms of his work, Naipaul is acknowledged as one of the best writers of his generation, and a good part of this reputation is based on his books about the Caribbean.

Naipaul is unusual among contemporary Caribbean writers, however, in that his work is not centered on the black Caribbean experience. Instead, it focuses on the South Asian and Caribbean culture that he himself came from, but he is quick to point out the common effects of colonization on both communities. Naipaul was born in Chaguanas, a small sugar cane-growing village, and moved to Port of Spain at age six. After graduating from Queens Royal College in 1949, he won a scholarship to attend University College, Oxford. The opportunity to go to England was "a dream come true" for him, and he never returned home to stay.

One of his first jobs after leaving Oxford was writing and editing for the British Broadcasting Corporation's *Caribbean Voices,* which was already an outlet for such emerging Caribbean writers as EDWARD KAMAU BRATHWAITE and GEORGE LAMMING. Naipaul published his first novel in 1957, and within five years he had completed five books, including the novels *Miguel Street* (1959) and *A House for Mr. Biswas* (1961) and the essay collection *The Middle Passage* (1962). These three books established his position as a chronicler of the West Indian experience.

In *A House for Mr. Biswas,* widely considered his masterpiece, Naipaul chronicles a South Asian Trinidadian man's struggle to own a home. In the process, Naipaul also outlines the existing social and economic conditions on the island that made that struggle so difficult. A year after the book's publication, the government of Trinidad and Tobago awarded Naipaul a scholarship to spend seven months studying Caribbean culture and history. The result was *The Middle Passage,* a combination of historical narrative and travel narrative covering five Caribbean countries. Naipaul's criticisms of Trinidad as "unimportant, uncreative, cynical" and the entire Caribbean as "the Third World's third world" are often repeated as proof of his unwillingness to understand the Caribbean. However, he has also been praised for creating a valuable collection of insights into the West Indies from an insider's perspective.

The Mimic Men (1967) and *Guerrillas* (1975) present similarly cynical fictional accounts of the Caribbean independence and Black Power struggles of the 1960s. As his career progressed, Naipaul traveled farther abroad for his novels and travel books, setting them in England, India, Africa, and even the United States. Books such as *India: A Wounded Civilization* (1977) and *A Bend in the River* (1979) solidified his reputation, and Naipaul has won numerous honors and awards for his work. For all Naipaul's pessimism it is undeniable that he writes about the Caribbean with an honesty and a wealth of observed detail and insight that many consider unparalleled. Anthologies and critical studies of West Indian literature acknowledge Naipaul as one of the region's most important writers.

Lisa Clayton Robinson

SEE ALSO
Great Britain; Literature, English Language, Caribbean; Jamaica; Trinidad and Tobago.

Africa

Nairobi, Kenya, capital and largest city of KENYA.

The largest city between Cairo and Johannesburg, with an estimated 1990 population of 1.5 million, Nairobi sits at an elevation of approximately 1,660 m (about 5,450 ft) in the highlands of southern Kenya. It was founded in 1899 by the British, at the 317th-mile peg of the railroad they were constructing between the Indian Ocean port city of Mombasa and Lake Victoria. Named for a nearby MAASAI watering hole, Enkare Nairobi ("cold water"), it became a stopping point for the railway project's 32,000 workers (many of them from India) and eventually grew into a small town. In 1905 the British declared Nairobi the capital of the British East African Protectorate, which they moved from Mombasa.

Around 1900 Indian merchants in the town established a small bazaar, which soon became the main marketplace for nearby KIKUYU farmers to sell their produce. European settlers, drawn by the fertile hinterlands and temperate climate, also came, as did big game hunters. In 1919 Nairobi was declared a municipality; it earned city status in 1954. By that time Nairobi had become the center of Kenya's growing agro-processing industries, and had developed large working-class neighborhoods. Kikuyu migrants, many of whom had been educated at mission schools and held municipal jobs, began to organize politically in the city in the 1920s.

During the 1950s Kikuyu protest solidified into a nationalist movement across all ethnic groups and was centered in Nairobi. When the government declared a state of emergency during the MAU MAU REBELLION, approximately 15,000 Africans were arrested in Nairobi and sent to detention camps. With Kenyan independence in December 1963, Nairobi became the national capital.

Under President JOMO KENYATTA, the city's economy flourished. But the urban population grew by only 4 percent each year during the 1970s, creating a severe labor shortage. Shantytowns proliferated and were subject to periodic bulldozing. The capital city is now home to many secondary schools as well as the University of Nairobi, but employment has grown increasingly scarce for Kenya's educated youth. In the mid-1990s Nairobi was shaken repeatedly by protests against President DANIEL ARAP MOI's authoritarian regime.

Although Kenya's tourist industry has suffered from the country's recent political unrest, Nairobi is still a prime destination for tourists to East Africa, who are attracted by the abundance of modern conveniences, including cafés, bars, bookstores, and museums, as well as the proximity of game parks such as Amboseli, Tsavo, and Maasai Mara. Nairobi is also Kenya's most industrialized city, and its skyscrapers house the headquarters of many foreign corporations.

In August 1998 a bomb rocked the United States Embassy in Nairobi. The blast destroyed much of the embassy building and caused an adjacent office building, the Ufundi Cooperative House, to collapse, killing 247 Kenyans and 10 Americans. Some 5000 people were injured. The bombing further threatened Kenya's tourist industry, a major source of foreign exchange.

Robert Fay

SEE ALSO
Johannesburg, South Africa; Victoria, Lake; Mombasa, Kenya; Tourism in Africa; Cairo, Egypt.

NALC. Please see NEGRO AMERICAN LABOR COUNCIL

Africa

Nalu (also known as the Nalou), ethnic group of West Africa.

The Nalu primarily inhabit GUINEA, GUINEA-BISSAU, SENEGAL, and THE GAMBIA. They speak a Niger-Congo language and are closely related to the neighboring JOLA people. Approximately 200,000 people consider themselves Nalu.

SEE ALSO
Languages, African: An Overview.

Africa

Nama (also known as the Namakwa), ethnic group of southern Africa.

The Nama primarily inhabit western BOTSWANA and southern NAMIBIA. They speak a KHOISAN language and are considered part of the KHOIKHOI group of peoples, pejoratively known as the Hottentots. Approximately 100,000 people consider themselves Nama.

SEE ALSO
Hottentot.

Africa

Namib Desert, the world's oldest desert and the only true African desert south of the equator.

Lying along Africa's west coast, the Namib Desert stretches from Namibe in ANGOLA south through NAMIBIA to the Olifants River in Cape Province, SOUTH AFRICA, extending some 1900 km (about 1200 mi) from north to south. The Namib reaches eastward about 130 to 160 km (about 80 to 100 mi) from the Atlantic Ocean to the foot of the GREAT ESCARPMENT of southern Africa. The Benguela Current, which carries icy Atlantic water from Antarctica to the African coast, helps to cool the desert. The collision of cold water with warm air creates a dense fog that causes a hazard to ships in the area, now known as the Skeleton Coast. The current also provides moisture for the coastal region of the desert, supplementing the scant 10 mm (0.4 in) of rain it averages yearly.

Though many describe the landscape as barren, the Namib in fact supports a variety of vegetation, including Tumboa (*Welwitschia mirablisis*). Numerous forms of wildlife also inhabit the desert, including antelopes, ostriches, zebras, jackals, and large flocks of birds along the coast. Several indigenous groups practice PASTORALISM, including the Ovahimba and Obatjimba Herero, who herd goats between waterholes in the north, and Topnaar Nama (Khoikhoi), who graze sheep and cattle along the Kuiseb River in the central Namib region. In addition, the desert is the largest source of diamonds in the world.

Some parts of the Namib Desert are spectacularly scenic. The Sossusvlei region, located in the Namib-Naukluft National Park, is known for its huge sand dunes, some of which rise as high as 60 to 240 m (about 200 to 800 ft) and span 16 to 32 km (about 10 to 20 mi) in length. The Namib-Naukluft National Park is also home to the Naukluft Mountains and Sesriem Canyon.

Robert Fay

SEE ALSO
Antelope; Herero; Ostrich; Zebra.

Africa

Namibia, country on the southwest coast of Africa.

The history of Namibia, one of Africa's newest independent countries, has long been shaped by its geography. For centuries few African populations inhabited its two vast deserts, the Namib and the Kalahari, while European vessels avoided its rough coastline. The region was still sparsely populated when missionaries and, later, traders finally arrived in the eighteenth century, but its inhabitants fiercely resisted German settlement and colonization, resulting in one of Africa's bloodiest colonial wars of suppression.

SOUTH AFRICA wrested control of the mineral-rich South-West Africa from Germany in 1915, but its occupation proved no less repressive and discriminatory than European colonialism had been. Land and labor policies that were aimed at creating a cheap migrant labor supply for the region's diamond and gold mines fostered nationalist sentiment and, ultimately, armed struggle. The war between South Africa and nationalist forces, fueled by international cold war rivalries, finally ended with Namibian independence in 1990. Today land distribution in Namibia is still highly stratified, and labor unions remain a powerful political force. In addition, the government's efforts to harness the natural resources needed to support Namibia's growing population and economy have met with protests from its neighbors and international groups.

PRECOLONIAL HISTORY

Despite the challenges of the harsh climate, the SAN people were living in the arid region of present-day Namibia as early as 8000 B.C.E. Often referred to as BUSHMEN, they were a nomadic, foraging people living in small communities on the central plateau. They gradually assimilated with their southern neighbors, the Khoi, to become the KHOIKHOI people. Between the ninth and fourteenth centuries C.E., Bantu speakers migrated to the region (*see* BANTU: DISPERSION AND SETTLEMENT). Armed with iron tools and weapons, they began pushing the Khoikhoi into the Kalahari and established sedentary societies based on a combination of agriculture, PASTORALISM, and mining. Some were small and decentralized chieftainships, such as the Masubia and Mafue of the Caprivi.

In the north of the country, however, the OVAMBO and the KAVANGO built small, loosely federated kingdoms, in which each clan had a centralized authority and hereditary system of succession. They traded copper, iron ore, salt, and agricultural products, and controlled trade routes throughout southwest Africa. Reaching the height of their power during the seventeenth and eighteenth centuries, the eight Ovambo clans engaged in mutual cattle raids as well as periodic skirmishes over land and water sources. Meanwhile, the cattle-raising HERERO migrated farther south on the central plateau, where they established a centralized state. Typically residing in self-sufficient homesteads, the Herero needed great tracts of land to graze their large herds, occasionally bringing them into conflict with neighboring groups, including the Ovambo and Khoikhoi.

Although Portuguese sailors erected a stone cross on the coast of Namibia in 1484, few Europeans ventured much farther inland until the Dutch East Indies Company conducted a brief exploration of the region in the 1650s. The greatest natural barrier to European intrusion was the rough, inaccessible coastline, much of which became known as the Skeleton Coast because of the number of vessels that shipwrecked on its rocks. Although American, British, Dutch, and French sealing and whaling ships frequented the Namibian coast in the 1700s, only a few Europeans actually settled there, most of them traders who took up residence among the Khoi people in present-day southern Namibia. Seeking ivory, the merchants brought firearms, which the Ovambo and Herero clans used in their struggles for regional domination and to defend their herds. Over time, communities of mixed Khoi and European descent, particularly the Oorlams and Rehoboth, also established a prominent presence. They traded firearms for cattle with the Nama, whom they soon came to dominate.

In the early 1800s British, American, Finnish, and German missionaries stepped up their activities in Namibia. With their own rifle factory at the Otijibingue mission trading post, the missionaries quickly came to dominate regional commerce, trading firearms and luxury items for cattle and ivory. As roads were constructed farther inland, missionaries also settled in Windhoek, at that time a kingdom composed of Afrikaners, Nama, and Herero. By the 1850s the discovery of diamonds in the southern Namib Desert was luring increasing numbers of European miners and traders, including Portuguese from nearby ANGOLA.

To meet the booming demand for slaves, ivory, and cattle, the Ovambo raided their

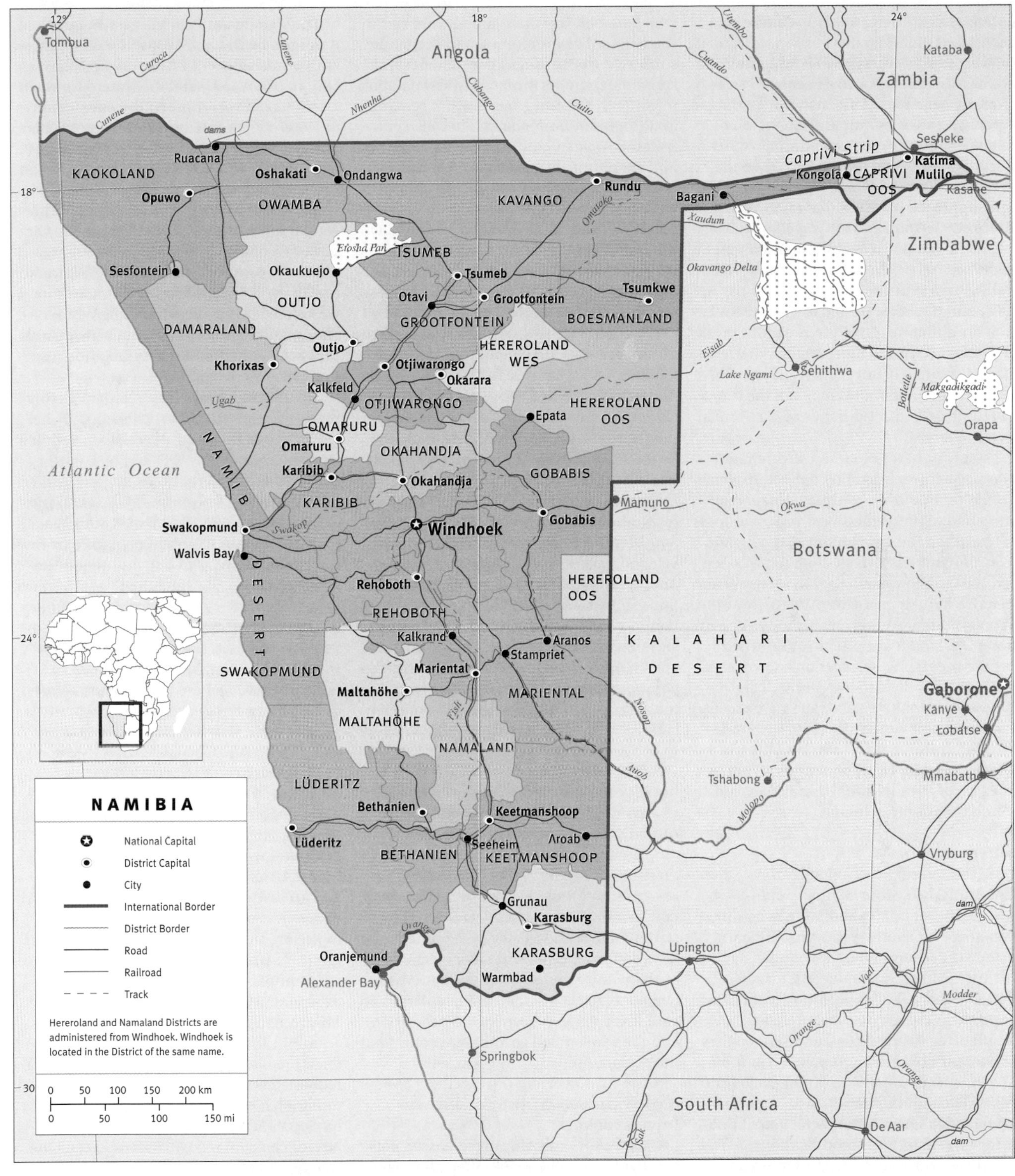

neighbors and nearly wiped out the region's ELEPHANT populations. At the same time, however, these lucrative trading activities were undermining the Ovambo's economic independence. To satisfy their desires for European goods, Ovambo leaders raised taxes among their people, forcing thousands of young men to migrate to diamond-mine operations in the south. Ovambo leaders were often able to exploit the tensions among Portuguese, German, and British South African commercial interests in Namibia, until European powers came together at the BERLIN CONFERENCE OF 1884-1885. There they drew the borders of present-day Namibia and declared it a German colony.

German Colonization and Genocide

Due to their isolation and diplomatic skills, the Ovambo avoided falling under direct European rule until after World War I. But floods, drought, locusts, and a rinderpest epidemic in the 1890s did create severe hardship, and pushed even more Ovambo away from their homeland in search of paid employment. By the second decade of the twentieth century, as many as 10,000 Ovambo and Kavango migrated south annually, and another 2000 went north each year to work on plantations in Angola.

Meanwhile, expanding European settlement in the southern part of the colony began pushing the Nama into Herero territory, leading to wars between the two groups. The German colonial administration introduced a system of private land ownership, initially setting aside 25 percent of the colony's land for Africans. But even this portion was gradually eroded as concession companies, the German Crown, and settlers acquired more property from local Africans through direct purchases, treaties, and the extension of credit. Sporadic resistance to German COLONIAL RULE mounted until 1904, when the Herero, led by Chief SAMUEL MAHERERO and supported by the Nama and Damara, attacked German towns as well as the colonial headquarters at Okahandja. After negotiations the Germans initially appeared willing to accept the Herero's surrender in 1904, but they soon turned to a strategy of tacit annihilation. Over the next four years they engaged in the most genocidal war in Africa's colonial history: nearly 80 percent of the Herero and more than half the Nama and Damara died at the hands of the German colonial forces.

The annihilation led to a severe labor shortage in the mines and on ranches, which turned to recruiting contract workers, or those tied to their employer through a strict contract that the state enforced, among the Ovambo and Kavango, who had not been involved in the war, as the Germans were selective in their genocide. After the war the colonial administration created more African "reserves" and instituted a South African form of geographic segregation known as the Red Line. This divided the country between the south, a "white area" where rights to live and work were determined by the administration through pass laws, and the north, where local African leaders were permitted a degree of autonomy as long as they completed the required labor.

South African Occupation

In 1915, after war broke out in Europe, South Africa quickly overran German South-West Africa. Five years later South Africa assumed a mandate for South-West Africa under the League of Nations, effectively annexing the territory. Afrikaners replaced German settlers, and the new administration maintained its predecessor's repressive policies. The Ovambo, the Bondelswaart, and Rehobothers all encountered violent police retribution after unsuccessful revolts in the 1920s and 1930s. The administration also imported South Africa's policies of racial discrimination, with slight local modifications.

After World War II the United Nations changed the status of the colony from a mandate to a trust territory, thereby making South Africa responsible for preparing for its independence. But South Africa had other plans. The colonial administration established a democratic system for the territory's white community but remained in control of defense, foreign affairs, "native policy," and the infrastructure, including the mining industry, harbors, and railways.

South Africa also called on the German, Finnish, British, and South African missions – which had always maintained close ties to the colonial government – to help instill subservience. Through their schools and sermons, churches promoted the separation of white from black, master from servant, and Christian from pagan. They also confiscated African land for private farming and ranching, and used African contract laborers on church estates.

The colonial economy rested on commercial farming, fisheries, and mining. On the central plateau large white-owned farms depended on African labor to raise cattle, grains, and horticultural products. In Walvis Bay, the fishing industry's catches (primarily pilchard and mackerel) accounted for approximately one-quarter of South-West Africa's income. South African and Western multinationals controlled the mining industry, extracting large quantities of diamonds from the restricted-access Diamond Area in the southwest as well as uranium, copper, lead, and zinc from other parts of the territory. Despite its mineral wealth and nearly total integration into the South African economy, South-West Africa itself remained underdeveloped, and most of its African population poor. Productivity in the countryside was limited by the contract labor system, which bound a large proportion of the working-age Ovambo male population to jobs in the mines and on the plantations. Living in overcrowded compounds and earning only 5 percent of the average white worker's wages, contract laborers were typically granted only two weeks of home leave annually.

South African rule increasingly divided the African population. Employing the 1923 Group Areas Act, the government pushed Africans onto reserves, ultimately creating ten "homelands" for the "indigenous peoples" based on the blueprint provided by APARTHEID. Although South African capital flowed into the colony, Africans' economic status deteriorated as they were pushed onto less productive land. Ultimately, 93 percent of the colony's population inhabited 40 percent of the land, while white settlers (who comprised only 7 percent of the population) and the white-ruled government controlled the remainder.

Nationalism and the Struggle for Independence

Resistance to South African race-based policies emerged in the 1950s. After 1948, when the first blacks graduated from secondary school, youths began protesting the government's discriminatory educational policies. Churches such as the African Methodist Episcopal (AME) Church, no longer as willing to help the government carry out these policies, backed the students as well as workers' growing demands for labor policy reforms. In the early 1950s newly formed mineworkers' unions staged strikes in Luderitz, led by the Ovamboland People's Organization (OPO) and its founder, ANDIMBA TOIVO JA TOIVO.

Three main anticolonial movements had emerged by the late 1950s: the OPO; the student-based South-West African National Union, or SWANU; and the Herero Council, an elite, relatively conservative association of Herero leaders. These and many smaller groups staged numerous protests against South Africa rule, often employing Gandhian methods of passive resistance. The largest demonstration occurred when the authorities sought to relocate Africans living in the Old Location quarter of Windhoek to an area known as Katutura, or "the place where no one lives." Eleven African demonstrators were killed by the police, and the Windhoek Shooting, as the event became known, both radicalized the Namibian population and provoked international outcry.

In 1959, in an attempt to create a truly nationalist political party, leaders of the OPO created the South-West Africa People's Organzation, or SWAPO, led by SAMUEL NUJOMA. In the early 1960s SWAPO and SWANU joined forces, but SWANU continued to identify SWAPO with the Ovambo and, fearing Ovambo dominance, broke from the coalition. SWAPO also petitioned the United Nations (UN) and the ORGANIZATION OF AFRICAN UNITY (OAU) for recognition as the sole representative of the people of South-West Africa, recognition it won in 1962. In 1966, however, the International Court of Justice reversed the decision and refused to denounce South African occupation.

That same year SWAPO's small military wing, the People's Liberation Army of Namibia, or PLAN, started the war for independence. Although PLAN enjoyed great popular support, the insurgents were at a disadvantage fighting on flat, open ground against the large and well-armed South African army. South Africa also used laws such as the Terrorism Act of 1967 to suppress African resistance and put many SWAPO leaders in prison. In 1969 the UN declared that the territory would henceforth be referred to as Namibia, from the Nama word *namib*, or shield, coined by the nationalist leader Mburumba Kerina some years before.

In 1971 the International Court of Justice declared South African occupation illegal, requested withdrawal, and called on the international community to impose sanctions on South Africa for its conduct. The UN also once again recognized SWAPO as the sole representative of the Namibian people. While South Africa began a dialogue with the UN, it also began to seek an "internal settlement." In 1975 and 1976 the South African government brought 11 leaders of the African homelands, though not SWAPO or other nationalist groups, to the Turnhalle Conference. There it proposed a political system for an independent Namibia that would provide the white community, considered an ethnic group, with veto power over national decisions as well as continued control over most of the economy.

South Africa's proposals satisfied neither the international community nor most Namibians. The late 1970s saw increasing confrontation between South Africa and PLAN, which had received arms and training from the Eastern bloc, China, and North Korea. During this time South Africa established military checkpoints and a restrictive curfew in the northern "war zone" of Ovamboland, Caprivi, and Okavango; increased African conscription into the army; attempted to co-opt many traditional chiefs by expanding their authority; and undertook development projects aimed at winning popular support.

Meanwhile, SWAPO pushed the international community, in particular the so-called Contact Group – GREAT BRITAIN, CANADA, FRANCE, the United States, and West Germany – to pressure South Africa to abide by UN resolutions 385 (of 1976), which called for a cease-fire and withdrawal, and 435 (of 1978), which called for elections and independence. But recently elected conservative governments in the United States and Great Britain showed little interest. Instead, South Africa held internal elections that ensured the victory of the Democratic Turnhalle Alliance, or DTA, an alliance of minor ethnic-based parties led by the white community.

Fighting continued between South Africa and PLAN and its supporters during the mid-1980s. Not until 1987, when Angolan and Cuban forces defeated South Africa at the Battle of Cuito Cuanavale, was South Africa finally forced back to the negotiating table. SWAPO meanwhile toned down its rhetoric advocating "scientific socialism," aiming to calm international and especially South African fears that independence would bring a Marxist takeover and economic nationalization. Indeed, during much of the struggle the exiled SWAPO leadership had increasingly advocated development policies and political solutions acceptable to the international community, forcing these ideas upon the more radical PLAN leadership and the labor unions that remained inside Namibia.

In 1988 the Contact Group successfully linked the withdrawal of Cuban military forces from Angola with the South African withdrawal from Namibia. In 1989 South Africa agreed to implement UN resolutions 385 and 435, and set elections for the following year. In November 1989 SWAPO won a majority of the seats to the assembly charged with writing a constitution for an independent Namibia.

A San man, with his bow and arrows over his shoulder and a cargo of gourds, rides his bicycle through the Namibian bush. *CORBIS/Anthony Bannister; ABPL*

POLITICS AND THE ECONOMY IN INDEPENDENT NAMIBIA

Namibia became independent on March 21, 1990. Sam Nujoma became president and immediately began promoting private-sector growth and foreign investment. The International Monetary Fund (IMF) and World Bank have since provided substantial loans for a wide range of development projects, while foreign firms have stepped up investment in diamond and uranium mining in the southern Namib Desert. In other ways, however, Namibia's economy has changed little. It continues to export much of its beef, fish, and agricultural produce to South Africa, and the Namibian dollar is tied to the South African rand. Although some assembly ministers are pushing the government to follow up on SWAPO's wartime promises of land reform, most large cattle ranches remain in the hands of a small minority of whites, and 5 percent of the population still controls more than 70 percent of the GDP. The average white earns 14 times more than the average black.

In 1994 elections SWAPO increased its representation in the assembly, at the expense of the opposition party DTA, from 57 percent to 72 percent of the seats. But dissatisfaction with SWAPO and Nujoma has mounted. International donors have criticized Nujoma's plans to run for a third term as president (which the constitution does not permit) as well as his government's

LEFT: A camel thorn tree stands surrounded by water in the Namib Desert after the heaviest rain in 30 years. *© Friedrich von Hörsten/Images of Africa Photobank*

BELOW: Diamonds have long been one of Namibia's most valuable natural resources and remain an important source of export revenue. *Jason Lauré*

lavish spending on limousines, helicopters, and presidential jets. While the public has criticized the elite privileges extended to members of Parliament, strong labor unions have prevented significant cuts in the large state bureaucracy.

Some of Namibia's greatest economic and political challenges lie in the realm of natural resource management. In an effort to compensate for perennially uneven rainfall patterns, the government has begun steps to siphon river water from the Okavango, and expects to provide residents of Walvis Bay with desalinated seawater by 1999. It has even discussed a pipeline from the CONGO RIVER. Meanwhile, however, a government plan to build the highest hydroelectric dam in Africa on the Kunene River threatens to displace the Himba people, who have voiced strong opposition to the project.

Livestock and wildlife issues have also generated domestic and international controversy. Neighboring Botswana's 140-km-long (about 85 mi) Northern Buffalo Fence, which runs partially along the Namibian border, was built to prevent the cross-border transmission of cattle-lung disease. But this fence – like many private fences built by ranchers – has created a barrier to wildlife in search of water, and large numbers of animal deaths have provoked outcry from wildlife conservationists. International animal-rights groups have also pushed the Namibian government to stop RHINOCEROS-culling as well as the annual killing of thousands of seals, practices that produce significant revenue for the government.

Eric Young

SEE ALSO

Afrikaner; Gold Trade; Kalahari Desert; Ivory Trade; Iron in Africa; Namib Desert; Nationalism in Africa; Windhoek, Namibia; Transatlantic Slave Trade; United Nations in Africa; Germany; Portugal; Salt Trade; Wildlife Management in Africa; African Methodist Episcopal Church; South West Africa People's Organization; Christianity: Missionaries in Africa.

Africa

Namibia (Ready Reference)

Official Name: Republic of Namibia
Former Name: South-West Africa
Area: 824,268 sq km (about 318,252 sq mi)
Location: Southwestern Africa; borders ANGOLA, ZAMBIA, BOTSWANA, SOUTH AFRICA, and the Atlantic Ocean
Capital: Windhoek (population 125,000 [1990 estimate])

Population: 1,622,328 (1998 estimate)
Population Density: 2 persons per sq km (about 5 persons per sq mi)
Population Below Age 15: 44 percent (male 362,310; female 354,386 [1998 estimate])
Population Growth Rate: 1.6 percent (1998 estimate)
Total Fertility Rate: 4.9 children born per woman (1998 estimate)
Life Expectancy at Birth: Total population: 41.48 years (male 41.73 years; female 41.24 years [1998 estimate])
Infant Mortality Rate: 66.7 deaths per 1000 live births (1998 estimate)
Literacy Rate (age 15 and over who can read and write): Total population: 38 percent (male 45 percent; female 31 percent [1960 estimate])
Education: Officially compulsory for nine years; in the early 1990s about 349,200 students attended primary schools and 84,600 attended secondary schools.
Languages: English, Afrikaans, and German are the official languages; Afrikaans is the most widely spoken. Indigenous languages include Oshivambo, Herero, and Nama.
Ethnic Groups: About 50 percent of the population belong to the Ovambo cultural group. Other principal ethnic groups include the Kavango, the Herero, the Damara, the Khoikhoi, and the San.
Religions: About 80 to 90 percent of the population are Christian (mainly Lutheran), and about 10 to 20 percent adhere to indigenous beliefs.
Climate: Namibia has a hot, dry, desert climate. Average rainfall ranges from 50 mm (about 2 in) in the Namib Desert along the coast to about 560 mm (about 22 in) in the north. Average temperatures in Windhoek vary from 17° C (63° F) in January to 6° C (43° F) in July.
Land, Plants, and Animals: Namibia is located mostly on a high plateau, with the Namib Desert along the coast and the Kalahari Desert in the east; its highest point is about 2606 m (8550 ft) in elevation. Vegetation is sparse in both deserts. A woodland savanna is found in the central plateau, and forests in the northeast. Animals include elephants, rhinoceroses, lions, giraffes, zebras, and hartebeests.
Natural Resources: Diamonds, copper, uranium, zinc, lead, gold, tin, lithium, cadmium, salt, vanadium, suspected deposits of natural gas, oil, coal, and iron ore; Namibia's waters also have over a million metric tons of fish.
Currency: The Namibian dollar
Gross Domestic Product (GDP): $6.2 billion (1996 estimate)
GDP per Capita: $3700 (1996 estimate)
GDP Real Growth Rate: 3 percent (1996 estimate)
Primary Economic Activities: Livestock raising and subsistence agriculture (60 percent of employment), mining (32 percent of GDP), industry and commerce (20 percent of employment)
Primary Crops: Millet, sorghum, peanuts, and livestock
Industries: Meat packing, fish processing, dairy products, and mining
Primary Exports: Diamonds, copper, gold, zinc, lead, uranium, cattle, processed fish, and karakul skins
Primary Imports: Food, petroleum, machinery, and equipment
Primary Trade Partners: South Africa, Germany, Switzerland, United Kingdom, and United States
Government: Namibia is a constitutional republic. The executive branch is led by President Sam Nujoma. The bicameral legislative branch consists of the 26-member National Council and the 72-member National Assembly, both currently dominated by President Nujoma's party, the South West Africa People's Organization (SWAPO).

Lisa Clayton Robinson

See Also

Elephant; Giraffe; Hartebeest; Lion; Nujoma, Samuel; Windhoek, Namibia; Rhinoceros; Zebra.

Africa

Nandi, ethnic group of Kenya.

The Nandi primarily inhabit the highlands of western Kenya. They speak a Nilo-Saharan language and are one of the Kalenjin peoples. More than 400,000 people consider themselves Nandi.

See Also

Languages, African: An Overview.

Latin America and the Caribbean

Nascimento, Abdias do

(b. March 14, 1914, Franca, São Paulo, Brazil), Afro-Brazilian playwright, poet, educator, artist, and political activist; one of the leading figures of Brazil's black movement.

Abdias do Nascimento grew up in Franca, São Paulo, where his father was a shoemaker and his mother worked as a sweetmaker, cook, and seamstress. Very early, he distinguished himself as an excellent student, and by age 13, he was teaching primary school and working as an accountant for local farmers. Nascimento served in the army from 1930 to 1936, during the early years of the Getúlio Vargas administration. At this time he began his career as a black activist by joining the Frente Negra Brasileira (United Black Front). In 1937, when Vargas established the Estado Novo dictatorship, the Frente Negra was shut down, along with all other political organizations.

Nascimento's first major Afro-Brazilian project was the Teatro Experimental do Negro (TEN) (Black Experimental Theater), which he founded in 1944. For the next 24 years he worked as its director and as a playwright. He created TEN in order to redefine the role of blacks in Brazilian theater. TEN trained the first generation of Afro-Brazilian actors and actresses and won critical acclaim for its productions of Eugene O'Neill's *Emperor Jones* and Nascimento's *Sortilégio* (Black Mystery).

TEN also served as a vehicle for Nascimento's political activism. From 1949 to 1951, TEN published *Quilombo: Black Life, Problems, and Aspirations*, a journal promoting the Afro-Brazilian freedom struggle through various Afro-Brazilian-centered articles, biographies, and illustrations. As an extension of TEN, Nascimento convened the Comité Democrático Afro-Brasileiro (Afro-Brazilian Democratic Committee) in 1945 in order to lobby the Brazilian Congress to enact antidiscrimination legislation. He was president of the 1945 and 1946 National Convention of Blacks, held in São Paulo and Rio de Janeiro, respectively, which drafted a bill defining and urging the banning of racial discrimination. With the help of TEN, Nascimento also organized the Primeiro Congresso do Negro Brasileiro (First National Congress of Brazilian Blacks, 1950). These conferences paved the way for the passing of the Afonso Arinos Law of 1951, which made racial discrimination illegal yet classified it as a misdemeanor rather than a crime.

In 1968, four years after a military dictatorship suspended many individual and collective rights, Nascimento sought exile in the United States. There he traveled and lectured extensively, gaining recognition for his role in the black movement in Brazil. He was a lecturer at the Yale School of Dramatic Arts in 1969 and was a visiting scholar at Wesleyan University from 1969 to 1970. From 1971 to 1981 he was a member of the faculty of the State University of New York, Buffalo, where he created the chair of African Culture in the New World and taught at the Puerto Rican Studies and Research Center. In 1976-1977 he taught at the University of Ife's Department of African Languages and Literatures in Ile-Ife, Nigeria. He returned to Brazil in 1981 and was named professor of black studies at the Pontifical Catholic University in São Paulo, where he founded the Afro-Brazilian Studies and Research Institute (IPEAFRO).

In addition to his work as a scholar, Nascimento devoted himself to painting while in exile. Just before his departure from Brazil, he founded the Blacks Arts Museum in Rio de Janeiro in 1968 and began to create his own artwork. He uses bold, unmodulated colors and geometric forms in his paintings to depict scenes from African and Afro-Brazilian mythology. The inspiration for many of his works is the Afro-Brazilian religion of Candomblé. Nascimento's wife, Elisa Larkin Nascimento, who has collaborated with him on many publications, said that her husband's painting "expresses, in artistic terms, his role of adding to Afro-Brazilian human rights demands, and develops... the dimension of African cultural heritage vital to rescuing and recovering Afro-Brazilian identity and human dignity" (*see* ART IN LATIN AMERICA AND THE CARIBBEAN).

While in exile Nascimento also participated in and helped organize many Pan-African conferences. These included the Sixth Pan-African Congress (Dar es Salaam, TANZANIA; 1974), the Encounter for African World Alternatives (Dakar, SENEGAL; 1976), and the Second World Festival of Black and African Arts and Culture (Lagos, Nigeria; 1977). He also played a major role in all three of the Congresses of Black Culture in the Americas (held in Cali, COLOMBIA, in 1977; PANAMA in 1980; and São Paulo, Brazil, in 1982).

An artist, educator, and politican, Abdias do Nascimento has worked on diverse fronts to increase awareness of and respect for Afro-Brazilian culture. *Photo by Américo Vermelho*

Nascimento has also been deeply involved in electoral politics, mainly through the Partido Democrático Trabalhista (PDT), led by Leonel Brizola. In the 1940s Nascimento, along with Brizola, cofounded the Rio de Janeiro branch of the Brazilian Labor Party (PTB), and helped create a black caucus within the party to work for Afro-Brazilian interests. During Nascimento's exile, the PTB was reorganized and renamed the Partido Democrático Trabalhista. At this point, at his urging, the party identified the issue of racial discrimination as one of its major priorities. In 1981 the PDT founded the National Black Movement Secretariat, making it the first political party in the country with a committee dedicated to fighting racism and addressing the needs of the Afro-Brazilian community.

Nascimento's academic, artistic, and political experiences while in exile prepared him for increased political activism upon his return to Brazil in 1981. The centrality of Afro-Brazilian concerns in his political agenda was evident during his campaign for office in 1962, when he unsuccessfully ran for Rio de Janeiro's City Council, using the slogan "Don't vote white [a phrase in Portuguese that also means 'don't cast a blank ballot'], vote black – Abdias." In 1982 Nascimento was elected to the House of Deputies and became the first federal congressman to defend systematically the civil rights of Afro-Brazilians. In a 1983 bill he encouraged the House of Deputies to create a Committee on African Brazilians. He advocated that November 20, the anniversary of the death of ZUMBI – the leader of the famous *quilombo* Palmares (*see* MAROONAGE IN THE AMERICAS) – be declared National Black Consciousness Day, and proposed that racial discrimination be declared a crime against humanity. He also pressed the issue of affirmative action as compensation for centuries of persecution and discrimination. In terms of employment, Nascimento's bill proposed setting 20 percent hiring quotas for Afro-Brazilian men and women and offering incentives to private businesses to eliminate racial discrimination. The bill also called for the creation of scholarships for Afro-Brazilian students and the inclusion of African and Afro-Brazilian histories in school textbooks.

In the years leading up to the 1988 constitutional assembly, Nascimento stressed that racism and racial discrimination were not merely black communal concerns, but issues of national significance. Partly as a result of his efforts, the 1988 constitution included provisions that recognized the multiethnic character of Brazilian society, defined racism as an "imprescriptable and non-bondable crime," and determined the boundaries of lands that were formerly quilombos.

In 1990 Nascimento was elected to the Senate as a delegate from Rio de Janeiro State. Soon thereafter he became a member of the Rio de Janeiro State Council of Culture. The following year the governor of Rio de Janeiro created the Secretariat for the Defense and Promotion of Afro-Brazilian Peoples (SEAFRO), the first state agency of its sort, and appointed Nascimento as its state secretary.

In February 1997 Nascimento was reelected to represent Rio de Janeiro State in the Senate. As a congressman and senator, he has addressed not only Afro-Brazilian issues, but also international issues concerning Africans. He has addressed relations between SOUTH AFRICA and Brazil and defended efforts of Portuguese-speaking countries in Africa to achieve national liberation. In addition to his political accomplishments, he has written or edited more than 20 books, plays, and collections of essays on Afro-Brazilian culture and politics. Nascimento's achievements in such diverse fields have led some scholars to call him the twentieth century's most complete African intellectual.

Aaron Myers

SEE ALSO

Dakar, Senegal; Dar es Salaam, Tanzania; Lagos, Nigeria; Palmares: An African State in Brazil; Pan-Africanism; Rio de Janeiro, Brazil.

Latin America and the Caribbean

Nascimento, Milton

(b. October 26, 1942, Rio de Janeiro, Brazil), a gifted Afro-Brazilian vocalist and composer who achieved international success and critical acclaim for his otherworldly fusions of jazz, rock, and classical music with the popular traditions of MINAS GERAIS, his home state in the interior of BRAZIL.

Milton Nascimento is noted for his extraordinary vocal range and rich timbre. Caetano Veloso has written that "Milton Nascimento's falsetto is one of the most beautiful sounds produced today by the human species." Elis Regina, the legendary vocalist who recorded several of his songs, simply remarked: "If God sang, it would be with the voice of Milton."

Nascimento was adopted as an infant by a family in Rio de Janeiro that had employed his deceased mother. The family later moved to Três Pontas, a small town in the mountainous interior of Minas Gerais. Like most musicians of his generation, Nascimento was deeply inspired by the emergence of bossa nova (*see* AFRO-LATIN JAZZ) in the late 1950s. In 1963 he moved to the state capital, Belo Horizonte, where he met future collaborators Márcio and Lô Borges, who turned him on to the Beatles.

In 1967 Nascimento gained national attention at the Second International Song Festival in Rio de Janeiro. He was selected best performer of the festival, and his song "Travessia" received second prize. Nascimento was subsequently invited to tour the United States, where he released an album, *Courage*, featuring Herbie Hancock (keyboards) and Airto Moreira (percussion). In 1975 he returned to the United States to record a landmark fusion album, *Native Dancer*, with saxophonist Wayne Shorter. In the meantime a cohort of musicians known as the *clube da esquina* (corner club) had coalesced around him. This group, which included Wagner Tiso, Toninho Horta, Fernando Brant, and the Borges brothers, produced two beautiful and eclectic double albums in the 1970s.

Throughout this period Nascimento recorded Spanish-American songs of the Nueva Canción movement and explored Afro-Catholic traditions of Minas Gerais, such as the *reisada do congo*. In 1982 he composed and produced the *Missa dos Quilombos*, a choral work celebrating the legacy of black resistance to slavery (*see* SLAVE REBELLIONS IN LATIN AMERICA AND THE CARIBBEAN) and racial oppression, which combines Afro-Brazilian rhythms and Roman Catholic hymns. Remarking on the melancholic and introspective nature of his region's musical traditions compared to upbeat Afro-Bahian music of the coast, Nascimento cites the history of gold and diamond mining dating to the eighteenth century: "The blacks who came from Africa to BAHIA worked on the land, while those who went to Minas Gerais worked *inside* the land."

Following a long journey up the Juruá River, Nascimento became sensitized to the plight of indigenous peoples of the Amazonian rain forest whose lives are disrupted and threatened by deforestation. His 1990 recording, *Txai*, features clips of indigenous music with poignant songs about the destruction of the rain forest and the cultural identities it sustains. Nascimento has continued to record with international musical luminaries such as Pat Metheny, Paul Simon, Quincy Jones, Peter Gabriel, and James Taylor. In 1997, after a life-threatening bout with diabetes, he released a triumphant comeback recording, *Nascimento*, which received a Grammy Award for the Best World Music album.

Christopher Dunn

SEE ALSO

Hancock, Herbert Jeffrey (Herbie); Jones, Quincy Delight, Jr.; Rio de Janeiro, Brazil; Catholic Church in Latin America and the Caribbean; World Music, World Beat, and the Re-Africanization of Latin American Popular Music.

North America

Nash, Diane Bevel

(b. May 15, 1938, Chicago, Ill.), African American civil rights activist, a founder of the Student Nonviolent Coordinating Committee (SNCC), and one of the few female leaders of the CIVIL RIGHTS MOVEMENT.

Diane Nash attended HOWARD UNIVERSITY and then transferred to FISK UNIVERSITY in Nashville, where she confronted Southern racial segregation and became active in the young Civil Rights Movement. She cofounded the STUDENT NONVIOLENT COORDINATING COMMITTEE (SNCC) in Raleigh, North Carolina, in April 1960. In February 1961 in Rock Hill, South Carolina, she was a member of the first group arrested for civil rights protest who refused to pay bail and remained in prison as a symbol of the plight of blacks in America.

Nash soon became SNCC's head of direct action. After marrying fellow civil rights activist James Bevel, taking his last name as her middle name, Nash moved to Georgia in 1962. There she worked with the SOUTHERN CHRISTIAN LEADERSHIP CONFERENCE (SCLC), a civil rights organization led by Martin Luther King Jr., which coordinated civil rights activities. SCLC awarded Bevel and Nash the Rosa Parks Award in 1965.

SEE ALSO

King, Martin Luther, Jr.; Parks, Rosa Louise McCauley.

Africa

Nasser, Gamal Abdel

(b. January 15, 1918, Alexandria, Egypt; d. September 28, 1970, Cairo, Egypt), former prime minister and president of EGYPT, and a leading proponent of Third World and pan-Arab unity.

Gamal Abdel Nasser is widely considered one of Africa's greatest modern leaders. Although his leadership style was highly authoritarian and some of his foreign policy decisions had disastrous consequences, he was lauded not only for ending British colonial rule and implementing ambitious social reforms in Egypt, but also for his support for Third World independence movements worldwide.

Nasser was born in Alexandria. He went to primary school in the village where his father, a postman, worked, then attended secondary school in Cairo, where he participated in street protests against the British. He briefly attended law school before entering the Royal Military Academy. Graduating in 1938, he received a commission as a second lieutenant.

While serving in the SUDAN, Nasser and three other officers formed the Free Officers, a secret organization that aimed to overthrow the British as well as the Egyptian monarch, Farouk I. In July 1952 the Free Officers deposed King Farouk and installed the Revolutionary Command Council, led by Nasser. He initially kept a low profile, naming the older and more experienced Maj. Gen. Muhammad Naguib head of state. In the spring of 1954, however, Nasser deposed Naguib and declared himself prime minister.

Nasser's first major accomplishment was the 1954 Anglo-Egyptian treaty, which provided for the gradual British pullout of troops from the SUEZ CANAL Zone. Later that year he survived an assassination attempt by a member of the Muslim Brotherhood who disapproved of the treaty's terms; Nasser responded with a harsh crackdown on the group. Throughout his career he would repeatedly use this tactic to block opposition.

Nasser won international renown at the 1955 Bandung Conference in Indonesia, where, along with other African and Asian leaders, he called for Third World decolonization and solidarity within the Non-Aligned Movement. Nasser first demonstrated his nonalignment to the West in September 1955, when he announced an arms purchase agreement with Czechoslovakia. The following year, a month after Nasser was elected president, the United States withdrew its offer of $270 million to subsidize construction of the ASWAN HIGH DAM; Nasser responded by nationalizing the Suez Canal. When Israel attacked Egypt in October 1956, British and French forces joined in, and ultimately crippled the Egyptian air force. Nasser ordered the sinking of 40 vessels, rendering the canal impassable. The United Nations (UN), with the support of both the United States and the Soviet Union, subsequently arranged for the withdrawal of the British, French, and Israeli forces and undertook repairs to the canal, now an acknowledged Egyptian possession.

The Suez Crisis, as it came to be called, enormously increased Nasser's popularity among Arab countries. Although in his *Philosophy of the Revolution* (1954) he wrote of wishing to lead all the world's Arabs, Africans, and followers of Islam, he was best known for his efforts to achieve Arab unity, creating the United Arab Republic, a union of Syria and Egypt, in 1958. Syria, however, split from the union in 1961.

Within Egypt, Nasser's regime brought a true revolution. The Free Officers ousted the landholding elites who, along with Europeans, had traditionally dominated the government, and nationalized their land. Nasser's land policies prohibited any individual from owning more than 100 *feddans* (104 acres). Crucial to his vision for improving the lives of Egyptians was the Aswan High Dam, completed in 1968, which provided for irrigation of the fertile Nile Delta as well as inexpensive hydroelectric power. Egypt's industries, educational programs, and medical services all expanded during the Nasser era, and women gained more civil rights.

Yet Nasser increasingly depended on repressive tactics, such as censorship, the prohibition of political parties, and detention of political enemies. Furthermore, the birth rate in Egypt remained high, thwarting the efforts to create a higher standard of living.

Throughout the first half of the 1960s Egypt disguised its moderate stance toward Israel with belligerent public rhetoric, though among Arab leaders Nasser urged restraint. By 1966, however, Palestinian raiders were launching attacks in Israel from bases in Jordan, Syria, and Lebanon. On November 13, 1966, Israel struck a Palestinian base in Jordan, killing 18 and wounding 54. Nasser, under pressure from his fellow Arabs, requested the removal of UN troops, which had been stationed in the Sinai Peninsula since the Suez Crisis, and Egypt closed the Gulf of Aqaba to Israeli shipping. On June 6, 1967, Israel launched a simultaneous strike at Jordan and Egypt in what would be called the Six-Day War, crippling Egypt's air forces on the ground and routing its army. Nasser resigned, only to return at the urging of the Egyptian people, who took to the streets in a show of support. He never reclaimed the luster of his early years, however, and he began a conservative shift that his successor, Anwar al-Sadat, continued prior to his historic visit to Jerusalem in 1977 to discuss solutions to Arab-Israeli conflict.

Robert Fay

SEE ALSO

Nile River; United Nations in Africa; Great Britain; Cairo, Egypt; Sadat, Anwar al-; Alexandria, Egypt.

Latin America and the Caribbean

Natera, Ramón

(d. November 1923, San Pedro de Macorís, Dominican Republic), the leading guerrilla war general during the Dominican Republic's war with United States occupation forces (1917-1922).

Motivated by both economic and strategic military interests, the United States initiated in 1916 an eight-year occupation of the Dominican Republic. From 1916 to 1920 the United States introduced a number of reforms and programs meant to change the Dominican political, economic, and social structure. While some members of Dominican society cooperated with the United States, others resisted. In the eastern part of the country, opposition to the U.S. presence led to a five-year war between hundreds of guerrilla soldiers and U.S. Marines. Gen. Ramón Natera emerged as the most important leader of the guerrilla troops, which consisted primarily of peasants and sugar workers who had been displaced from their homes or jobs as a result of the U.S. occupation.

Little is known about Natera's life before the U.S occupation. He was briefly captured by U.S. Marine forces in 1918 while attempting to seize the town of Hato Mayor, but escaped the following day when a band of guerrilla soldiers attacked the marines guarding him. Other American attempts to capture or kill Natera failed. He eluded the larger and better equipped U.S. forces by staying in an undisclosed location apart from his soldiers and because civilians kept him informed of American plans and troop movements.

One of Natera's boldest actions came in September 1921, when he and his soldiers abducted the British manager of La Angelina sugar estate, Thomas J. Steele. They released Steele two days later after he agreed to their demand to make clear to U.S. officials in Washington the political goals of the guerrillas – that the United States end its occupation of the country. The United States responded by increasing troops in the region.

Despite increased military activity by the U.S. Marines, Natera's revolutionary campaign continued. He gained support from the elite Congreso Nacionalista del Seibo (National Congress of Seibo), which issued a public statement in November 1921 arguing that the insurgents in the east were merely acting in response to the harsh treatment they received from the U.S. Marines. As a result, the United States reversed its policy and began to arrange for amnesty for those revolutionary insurgents who surrendered, and many did. In the beginning of May 1922, U.S. District Commander Lyman and Natera met and arranged a cease-fire. On May 5, 1922, Natera surrendered; he brought his troops in three days later. In November 1923 he was shot to death during a dispute with a *guarda campestre* (rural guard), ending a life dedicated to restoring the Dominican Republic's independence.

Aaron Myers

North America

National Association for the Advancement of Colored People,

an interracial membership organization, founded in 1909, that is devoted to civil rights and racial justice.

Founded February 12, 1909, the National Association for the Advancement of Colored People (NAACP) has been instrumental in improving the legal, educational, and economic lives of African Americans. Combining the white philanthropic support

that characterized Booker T. Washington's accommodationist organizations with the call for racial justice delivered by W. E. B. Du Bois's militant Niagara Movement, the NAACP forged a middle road of interracial cooperation. Throughout its existence it has worked primarily through the American legal system to fulfill its goals of full suffrage and other civil rights and an end to segregation and racial violence. Since the end of the Civil Rights Movement of the 1960s, however, the influence of the NAACP has waned, and it has suffered declining membership and a series of internal scandals.

The NAACP was formed in response to the 1908 race riot in Springfield, the capital of Illinois and the birthplace of President Abraham Lincoln. Appalled at the violence that was committed against blacks, a group of white liberals that included Mary Ovington White and Oswald Garrison Villard, both the descendants of abolitionists, issued a call for a meeting to discuss racial justice. Some 60 people, only 7 of whom were African American (including W. E. B. Du Bois, Ida B. Wells-Barnett, and Mary Church Terrell), signed the call, which was released on the centennial of Lincoln's birth. Echoing the focus of Du Bois's militant all-black Niagara Movement, the NAACP's stated goal was to secure for all people the rights guaranteed in the Thirteenth, Fourteenth, and Fifteenth Amendments to the United States Constitution, which promised an end to slavery, the equal protection of the law, and universal adult male suffrage.

The NAACP established its national office in New York City and named a board of directors as well as a president, Moorfield Storey, a white constitutional lawyer and former president of the American Bar Association (ABA). The only African American among the organization's executives, Du Bois was made director of publications and research, and in 1910 he established the official journal of the NAACP, the *Crisis*. With a strong emphasis on local organizing, by 1913 the NAACP had established branch offices in such cities as Boston, Kansas City, Washington, D.C., Detroit, and St. Louis.

A series of early court battles – including a victory against a discriminatory Oklahoma law that regulated voting by means of a grandfather clause (*Guinn* v. *United States*, 1910) – helped establish the NAACP's importance as a legal advocate, a role it would play with overwhelming success. The fledgling organization also learned to harness the power of publicity in its 1915 battle against D. W. Griffith's inflammatory *Birth of a Nation*, a movie that perpetuated demeaning stereotypes of African Americans and glorified the Ku Klux Klan.

With its membership growing rapidly –

from around 9000 in 1917 to around 90,000 in 1919 – and with more than 300 local branches, the NAACP leadership soon included more African Americans. The writer and diplomat James Weldon Johnson became the association's first black secretary in 1920, and Louis T. Wright, a surgeon, was named the first black chairman of its board of directors in 1934; neither position was ever again held by a white person. Meanwhile, the *Crisis* became a voice of the Harlem Renaissance, as Du Bois published works by Langston Hughes, Countee Cullen, and other African American literary figures.

Throughout the 1920s the fight against lynching was among the association's top priorities. After early worries about its constitutionality, the NAACP strongly supported before the U.S. Congress the Dyer Bill, which would have punished those who participated in or failed to prosecute lynch mobs. Though Congress never passed the bill, or any other antilynching legislation, many credit the resulting public debate – fueled by the NAACP's report *Thirty Years of Lynching in the United States, 1889-1919* – with drastically decreasing the incidence of lynching.

When Johnson stepped down as secretary in 1930, he was succeeded by Walter F. White, who had been instrumental not only in his research on lynching (in part because, as a very fair-skinned African American, he had been able to infiltrate white groups) but also in his successful block of segregationist judge John J. Parker's nomination by President Herbert Hoover to the U.S. Supreme Court. Though some historians blame Du Bois's 1934 resignation on White, the new secretary presided over the NAACP's most productive period of legal advocacy. In 1930 the association commissioned the Margold Report, which became the basis for its successful drive to reverse the "separate but equal" doctrine that had governed public facilities since the Plessy v. Ferguson decision in 1896. In 1935 White recruited as NAACP chief counsel Charles H. Houston, the Howard University law school dean whose strategy on school-segregation cases paved the way for his protégé Thurgood Marshall to prevail in 1954's Brown v. Board of Education, the decision that overturned *Plessy.*

During the Great Depression of the 1930s, which was disproportionately disastrous for African Americans, the NAACP began to focus on economic justice. After years of tension with white labor unions, the association cooperated with the newly formed Congress of Industrial Organizations (CIO) in an effort to win jobs for black Americans. Walter White, a friend and adviser to First Lady Eleanor Roosevelt – who was sympathetic to civil rights – met with her often in attempts to convince President Franklin D. Roosevelt to outlaw job discrimination in the armed forces, defense industries (which were booming in anticipation of U.S. entry into World War II), and the agencies spawned by Roosevelt's New Deal legislation. Though this effort was not initially successful, when the NAACP backed labor leader A. Philip Randolph's March on Washington movement in 1941, Roosevelt agreed to open thousands of jobs to black workers and to set up a Fair Employment Practices Committee (FEPC) to ensure compliance.

OPPOSITE: First Lady Eleanor Roosevelt charts a program in 1947 with NAACP executive officers *clockwise from top left* Walter White, Roy Wilkins, Thurgood Marshall, and James McClendon. *Library of Congress*

LEFT: By the late 1940s, when this poster urged blacks to join the NAACP, the organization could boast half a million members. *Library of Congress*

ABOVE: This flag flew from NAACP headquarters on Fifth Avenue in New York City whenever a lynching took place. *Library of Congress*

The NAACP joined with civic and religious groups to organize the 1917 silent protest parade in Harlem. About 8000 African American men, women, and children marched down Fifth Avenue, silently bearing signs protesting the racist violence of the recent East St. Louis riot and the continuing scourge of lynching. Marchers questioned as well the bitter irony of the United States's entrance into World War I – a war meant to "make the world safe for democracy" – while the government continued to tolerate racial injustice at home. *CORBIS/Bettmann*

Throughout the 1940s the NAACP saw enormous growth in its membership, claiming nearly half a million members by 1946. It continued to act as a legislative and legal advocate, pushing (albeit unsuccessfully) for a federal antilynching law and for an end to state-mandated segregation. By the 1950s the NAACP Legal Defense and Educational Fund, headed by Marshall, secured the second of these goals through *Brown* v. *Board of Education,* which outlawed segregation in public schools. The NAACP's WASHINGTON, D.C., bureau, led by lobbyist Clarence M. Mitchell Jr., helped advance not only integration of the armed forces in 1948 but also passage of the Civil Rights Acts of 1957, 1964, and 1968 as well as the VOTING RIGHTS ACT OF 1965.

Despite such dramatic courtroom and congressional victories, the implementation of civil rights was a slow, painful, and sometimes violent process. The unsolved 1951 murder of Harry T. Moore, an NAACP field secretary in Florida whose home was bombed on Christmas night, was just one of many crimes of retribution against the NAACP and its staff and members during the 1950s. Violence also met black children attempting to enter previously segregated schools in Little Rock, Arkansas, and other Southern cities, and throughout the South many African Americans were still denied the right to register and vote.

Arising out of frustration at the continuing lack of equality and justice, the CIVIL RIGHTS MOVEMENT of the 1960s echoed the NAACP's moderate, integrationist goals, but leaders such as the Reverend Martin Luther King Jr. of the SOUTHERN CHRISTIAN LEADERSHIP CONFERENCE (SCLC) felt that direct action was needed to obtain them. Though the NAACP was opposed to extralegal popular actions, many of its members, such as Mississippi field secretary Medgar Evers, participated in nonviolent demonstrations such as SIT-INS to protest the persistence of JIM CROW segregation throughout the South. Although it was criticized for working exclusively within the system by pursuing legislative and judicial solutions, the NAACP did provide legal representation and aid to members of more militant protest groups.

Led by Roy Wilkins, who had succeeded Walter White as secretary in 1955 the NAACP cooperated with organizers A. Philip Randolph and BAYARD RUSTIN in planning the 1963 MARCH ON WASHINGTON. With the passage of civil rights legislation the following year, the association had finally accomplished much of its historic legislative agenda. In the following years the NAACP began to diversify its goals and, in the eyes of many, to lose its focus. Rising urban poverty and crime, de facto racial segregation, and lingering job discrimination continued to afflict millions of African Americans. With its traditional interracial, integrationist approach, the NAACP found itself attracting fewer members, as many African Americans became sympathetic to more militant, even separatist, philosophies, such as the beliefs espoused by the BLACK POWER Movement.

Wilkins retired as executive director in 1977 and was replaced by Benjamin L. Hooks, whose tenure witnessed the Bakke case (1978), in which a California court outlawed several aspects of AFFIRMATIVE ACTION. At around the same time tensions between the executive director and the board of directors – tensions that had existed since the association's founding – escalated into open hostility that threatened to weaken the organization. With the 1993 selection of the Reverend Benjamin F. Chavis (now Chavis Muhammad) as director, new controversies arose. In an attempt to take the NAACP in new directions, Chavis offended many liberals by reaching out to NATION OF ISLAM leader Louis Farrakhan. After using NAACP funds to settle a sexual harassment lawsuit, Chavis was forced to resign in 1995 and subsequently joined the Nation of Islam.

Now headed by KWEISI MFUME, former congressman and head of the CONGRESSIONAL BLACK CAUCUS, with JULIAN BOND acting as chairperson of the board, the NAACP has focused in recent years on economic development and educational programs for youth, while also continuing its role as legal advocate for civil rights issues. The organization currently has more than half a million members.

Kate Tuttle

SEE ALSO
Slavery in the United States; World War II and African Americans; Abolitionism in the United States; American Federation of Labor and Congress of Industrial Organizations; *Birth of a Nation, The*; Boston, Massachusetts; Chavis, Benjamin Franklin, Jr.; *Crisis, The*; Detroit, Michigan; Du Bois, William Edward Burghardt (W. E. B.); Evers, Medgar Wylie; Farrakhan, Louis Abdul; Fifteenth Amendment to the United States Constitution; Fourteenth Amendment to the United States Constitution; Hooks, Benjamin Lawrence; Houston, Charles Hamilton; Kansas City, Missouri; King, Martin Luther, Jr.; Labor Unions in the United States; Mitchell, Clarence Maurice, Jr.; Moore, Harry Tyson; NAACP Legal Defense and Educational Fund; New York, New York; Racial Stereotypes; Randolph, Asa Philip; Terrell, Mary Eliza Church; Thirteenth Amendment of the United States Constitution and the Emancipation Proclamation; Washington, Booker Taliaferro; Wells-Barnett, Ida Bell; White, Walter Francis; Wilkins, Roy Ottoway; Wright, Louis Tompkins; Little Rock Crisis, 1957; March on Washington, 1941; Accommodationism in the United States.

North America

National Association of Black Journalists (NABJ), American organization, founded in 1975, of black reporters, editors, and managers of media outlets.

Based in WASHINGTON, D.C., the NABJ encourages black employment in journalism and fair reporting about blacks. The group has used its monthly *NABJ Journal* and its regular conferences to increase communication among black journalists; to monitor and publicize institutionalized racism; and to advocate an increase in the number of blacks who manage newspapers, magazines, and television and radio networks and stations. The NABJ offers scholarships to young blacks interested in journalism, and it finances exchanges between African and African American journalists. In the mid-1990s the NABJ had nearly 3000 members.

SEE ALSO
Television and African Americans.

North America

National Association of Colored Women, African American women's organization, the first national black organization in the United States.

The familiar slogan of the National Association of Colored Women (NACW), "Lifting As We Climb," sums up its century-long commitment to service, uplift, and advancement in the African American community. The NACW grew out of the network of local black women's clubs and organizations that began to develop in the United States in the late nineteenth century to promote racial progress by providing necessary social services in black communities. These clubs were formed by women who firmly believed that improving conditions in individual black homes would have positive effects on the social, educational, and economic advancement of the entire African American community (*see* BLACK WOMEN'S CLUB MOVEMENT).

In 1895 a widely reprinted editorial by a white Southerner, which accused black women of being dishonest and immoral, led club leaders across the country to realize that they needed to work together in their efforts to protect and advance the race and the cause of black womanhood. In July of that year 100 women from organizations in ten states met in Boston to begin planning a national coalition of black women. One year later the NACW was officially formed, making it the first national African American organization. Within a few years the NACW had 5000 members; by 1916 it had grown to 50,000 members and more than 1000 local clubs.

The slogan "Lifting As We Climb" was coined by the NACW's first president, Mary Church Terrell, who explained that "self-preservation demands that [black women] go among the lowly, to whom they are bound by ties of race and sex," and that NACW members had "determined to come into the closest possible touch with the masses of our women, through whom the womanhood of our people is always judged." This statement points out a key feature of the original black women's club movement: the NACW's members were overwhelmingly middle-class, educated women, and thus in a class and social situation different from many of the women and families whom their programs were designed to help.

NACW members planned to solve this division by raising as many women as they could to their own level of relative material comfort. Teaching middle-class values became one of their early priorities, and the NACW's first programs included temperance societies and classes on housekeeping and child-rearing. Club members were also dedicated to protecting the most vulnerable members of their communities, the very young and the very old. By the turn of the century clubs all over the country had begun establishing kindergartens and homes for the aged. These facilities were generally staffed by NACW volunteers, and members held fundraisers to gain additional money for their projects.

While NACW members believed that the progress of the race could and should begin in the home, they were also fully aware of the constant outside injustices faced daily by black women and men. Club members supported the passage of the Nineteenth Amendment, which gave women the right to vote, and they played a key role in the antilynching campaign of the 1920s. Individual branches also led boycotts of segregated facilities and expressed other protests against racial injustices. By the time prominent activist MARY MCLEOD BETHUNE became president of the NACW in 1924, the organization had grown to 100,000 members, who were involved in social reform programs across the country.

In the next few decades, however, the NACW began to decline in influence. During the GREAT DEPRESSION, the government finally began providing many of the services the black community had received from the NACW. And after Bethune founded the NATIONAL COUNCIL OF NEGRO WOMEN in 1935, the NACW was no longer the only national black women's association. In 1957 the NACW changed its name to the National Association of Colored Women's Clubs (NACWC), and narrowed its focus to educational and social services, such as providing college scholarships for young black women. The NACWC celebrated its centennial in 1996, with approximately 40,000 members in 1500 clubs, retaining its original commitment to uplifting the black community.

Lisa Clayton Robinson

SEE ALSO
Antilynching Movement; Boston, Massachusetts; Terrell, Mary Eliza Church.

North America

National Council of Negro Women, influential African American women's organization founded by Mary McLeod Bethune.

The National Council of Negro Women (NCNW), one of the largest and most prominent black women's groups of the twentieth century, was the inspiration of civil rights and women's rights leader Mary McLeod Bethune. In 1924, after almost two decades of activism in clubs and organizations dedicated to black women's issues, Bethune became president of the NATIONAL ASSOCIATION OF COLORED WOMEN (NACW), then the country's leading association of African American women. But five years later, she was announcing her dream of creating a larger coalition of black women's groups, modeled after the mainstream National Council of Women. As Bethune wrote in a letter to her friend Mary Church Terrell, "Such an organization will, I believe, make for unity of opinion among Negro women who must do some thinking on public questions; it will ensure greater cooperation among women in varied lines of endeavor; and it will lift the ideals not only of the individual organizations, but of the organizations as a group."

After almost six years of planning, Bethune's vision was realized when the National Council of Negro Women held its founding meeting in Harlem on December 5, 1935. Several groups were initially hesitant about joining the NCNW – including Bethune's former organization, the NACW – because of fears that it might detract from the prestige or power of individual groups. But representatives from 29 groups, including religious, political, and professional organizations, sororities, and even the NACW, ultimately attended the founding meeting.

Members of the NCNW quickly began to speak out on issues they felt were important to African Americans in general and black women in particular. Their public insistence on opening more federal jobs to African Americans and their documentation of discriminatory hiring practices in government factories during World War II helped lead to the establishment of the national FAIR EMPLOYMENT PRACTICES COMMITTEE (FEPC). They also fought for integration of the military and desegregation of schools and other public facilities. In addition to their work for racial and social equality at home, the NCNW spoke out on international affairs. NCNW delegates were present at the founding of the United Nations (UN), and have since attended all UN proceedings as official observers. By the mid-1950s the council's 11 national departments included Archives and Museum, Citizenship Education, Education, Fine Arts, Human Relations, International Relations, Labor and Industry, Public Relations, Religious Education, Social Welfare, and Youth Conservation.

In 1957 DOROTHY HEIGHT became the fourth president of the NCNW. Height has continued to hold that post for more than four decades, and under her administration the NCNW became a nonprofit organization, allowing it to receive grants from such sources as the Ford Foundation and the United States Department of Health, Education and Welfare. During the last 30 years the NCNW has sponsored such programs as Operation Sisters United, Youth Career Development, the FANNIE LOU HAMER Day Care Centers, Project Woman Power, the NCNW Leadership Development Project, and the national Black Family Reunion celebrations. In 1975 a grant from the Agency for International Development enabled the NCNW to establish an international department, making it possible for African American women to coordinate their efforts with those of black women across the diaspora. The NCNW was instrumental in the founding of the National Archives for Black Women's History, and in 1974 Height and the NCNW were able to oversee the unveiling of the Bethune Memorial Statue in Washington, D.C., a long-overdue tribute to the organization's extraordinary founder.

Lisa Clayton Robinson

SEE ALSO
World War II and African Americans; Bethune, Mary McLeod; Harlem, New York; Terrell, Mary Eliza Church.

North America

National Federation of Afro-American Women, early African American women's organization that became part of the National Association of Colored Women.

The National Federation of Afro-American Women was an early attempt to unite some of the many black women's organizations that had formed throughout the United States during the nineteenth century (*see* BLACK WOMEN'S CLUB MOVEMENT). In many cities, black women had formed clubs and associations to provide social services for the elderly, young, and poor in their communities. At the same time black women's clubs worked to uplift the public image of African American womanhood, since black women had long been portrayed as oversexed, unintelligent creatures. In July 1895, after a white editor published a letter in a Missouri newspaper that he then forwarded to papers in the United States and England, accusing "all Afro-American women of having no sense of virtue and of being altogether without character," 100 black women activists from across the country came together for a conference in BOSTON, MASSACHUSETTS, to strategize about coordinating their efforts.

The National Federation of Afro-American Women was formed at that meeting. MARGARET MURRAY WASHINGTON, the "lady principal" of Tuskegee Institute and wife of educator Booker T. Washington, became its first president, and 36 clubs from 12 states joined the federation. But even as the federation was beginning its work, the National League of Colored Women, a similar organization, was founded in Washington, D.C. In an effort to return to the goal of national cooperation, in 1896 the National Federation of Afro-American Women and the National League of Colored Women merged to form the NATIONAL ASSOCIATION OF COLORED WOMEN, which remains active today.

Lisa Clayton Robinson

SEE ALSO
Tuskegee University; Washington, Booker Taliaferro.

National Football League (NFL). Please see FOOTBALL, PROFESSIONAL

Africa

Nationalism in Africa

Between 1951 and 1980 nationalist movements – efforts toward establishing national sovereignties unfettered by colonial rule – toppled European colonial governments throughout Africa. The names of these movements' leaders are legendary: KWAME NKRUMAH in GHANA; GAMAL ABDEL NASSER in EGYPT; JOMO KENYATTA in KENYA; Léopold Sédar Senghor in SENEGAL; Julius Nyerere in TANZANIA; AMÍLCAR CABRAL in GUINEA-BISSAU; and Nelson Mandela in SOUTH AFRICA. More recently, in 1993, ERITREA won a decades-long struggle for independence from ETHIOPIA, arguably showing that nationhood is still a viable goal for African regions seeking political autonomy.

African nationalism was born out of opposition to the injustices of COLONIAL RULE and thus was inseparable from the struggle for decolonization. Since race had provided European powers with a rationale for colonial domination, racial identification was one important source of anticolonial solidarity and nation building, but it was certainly not the only source. Participants in independence struggles sought to reclaim appropriated lands, rid themselves of poverty and burdensome taxation, and gain the civil liberties enjoyed by citizens of the colonizing countries themselves – England, France, Portugal, Belgium, Italy, and (on much smaller scales) Germany and Spain.

The advantages of national sovereignty were debated among African leaders, particularly in France's colonies in West and Central Africa. There, leaders such as Senghor of Senegal and Félix Houphouët-Boigny of Côte d'Ivoire advocated not complete independence but rather "association" with France (a comparable option was not given to the English colonies). These leaders had enjoyed the privileges accorded to *assimilés* (French-speaking Africans whose education qualified them for French citizenship) and believed their countries would benefit both economically and strategically from continued close ties with France and neighboring Francophone territories. In 1958 French president Charles de Gaulle allowed France's African colonies to vote on their proposed membership in an international French community of semiautonomous countries;

all but Guinea voted in favor of the revised political alliance.

Although Guinea's 1958 vote was anomalous – and owed much to the charisma and organizing talents of labor activist and political leader Sékou Touré – the aspirations of the colony's people to achieve independence were not unique. The motivation for decolonization was in part economic: Touré's movement depended on convincing Guinea's peasants, market women, wageworkers, and youth – all citizens who had never enjoyed opulence under colonial rule anyway – that they could only ultimately escape poverty if their colony achieved independence. But when Touré proclaimed, "We prefer poverty in freedom to opulence in slavery," he underscored the fact that it was the desire for autonomy that ultimately propelled nationalist movements throughout Africa.

Nationalism in Africa

Scholars have long debated the meaning of African nationalism. For many years the dominant view was that nationalism was a European political ideal promoted by Africa's Westernized, educated elite. According to the dominant view, this elite used the European concept of the nation to forge unity among disparate African groups and thereby build a cohesive resistance to colonialism. This analysis is certainly well founded. Nineteenth-century African social reformers such as James Africanus Horton in Sierra Leone and Edward Wilmot Blyden in Liberia as well as twentieth-century political theorists like Albert Memmi, Frantz Fanon, and Amílcar Cabral were educated in Europe or at least studied European texts. Colonialism introduced to Africa European versions of Christianity, modernity, socialism, democracy, and citizenship. It also brought irreversible changes: borders partitioned the continent into distinct colonial states; mining, plantation agriculture, and urbanization transformed the landscape; and new communication and transportation systems brought together once distant communities. Unable to reverse the changes brought by colonial rule, Africans sought a new model for the organization of their society, one that would be recognized in the international arena that colonization had introduced. The nation provided that.

But clearly, Western-educated elites were not the only participants in nationalist movements. To understand nationalism in Africa, we must examine the forms of mass mobilization behind the political motivations and parties – the movements that stood behind the famous names. Two strains of grassroots resistance stand out in Africa's history of nationalist struggle. The first type of resistance drew its inspiration from identities forged before and during the colonial period – identities based on ethnicity, religion, and language in particular. This resistance mobilized to reclaim or reinstate places or institutions considered crucial to those identities, such as sacred homelands or preexisting forms of political and spiritual authority. The second type of resistance came out of the labor movements, whose members included railroad workers, miners, civil servants, and dockworkers as well as agricultural workers. These movements mobilized to claim the rights demanded by workers worldwide, such as fair wages, pensions, and equal employment opportunities. The different kinds of resistance movements sometimes clashed over methods and goals, but moments of unity, or at least collaboration, between them convinced the European powers that decolonization was inevitable.

Identity and Nationalism in Libya and Kenya

The history of Libya provides a clear example of a struggle for independent statehood that drew its power from traditional identity, in this case the religious identity of Islam. Libyan nationalism was expressed in three arenas. There was an urban-based movement in the city of Tripoli and an Egyptian-based pan-Arab movement, which by 1950 was attracting support in several parts of North Africa. But the Islamic brotherhood of the Sanusi order arguably provided the most important foundation for anticolonial resistance. Founded in the nineteenth century, prior to colonization, the brotherhood constructed lodges and schools throughout the Cyrenaica region that became gathering places for residents and long-distance caravan traders alike. The gathering places were much more than simply meeting points, and the social and political structure they provided helped create a cohesive regional identity that would later prove a persistent source of resistance to Italian colonial control.

Nationalists in the city of Tripoli had lived under a European-controlled economy and held a more secular, republican ideal of the nation than did the leaders of the Sanusi order. Nevertheless, the Tripolitanians saw the advantage of cooperation with the powerful Sanusi, and so in 1922 they appointed the head of the order, Idris I, as the leader of their collective nationalist movement.

After independence in 1951 Idris assumed the throne of the United Kingdom of Libya, but the idea of a republic was not forgotten. The successful challenge to the monarchy came from a coup led by Muammar al-Qaddafi that drew upon pan-Arab sentiments generated by Gamal Abdel Nasser's revolution in neighboring Egypt. Thus in Libya two traditional political and cultural movements identified with Islam played dominant roles in both the anticolonial struggle and the establishment of a republic.

In Kenya, as in Libya, the nationalist movement was not homogeneous. But cultural identity played a crucial role in the Kikuyu people's anticolonial struggle, which culminated in an event the British referred to as the Mau Mau Rebellion. In the late 1940s the Kikuyu guerrilla movement began with uprisings on Kikuyu reservations around the country and sporadic violence against white settlers' plantations that had appropriated prime Kikuyu farmland. The group expanded its goals, however, and began to fight for an end to British colonial rule. The colonial government responded with a declaration of emergency, mass arrests, and military force. More than 80,000 people were detained and 12,000 killed in the conflict, among them only about 100 Europeans.

The Kikuyu movement used oaths, songs, and prayers to unite and mobilize its members in a culturally meaningful way. To the British colonial government, however, the oath taking simply proved that Mau Mau adherents were barbaric and that their violence represented an atavistic protest against progress. Not all Kikuyu supported Mau Mau; indeed, those Kikuyu who had benefited themselves by taking on colonial administration duties under British rule (known as Loyalists) were among the guerrillas' main victims.

It is important to realize that the Kikuyu-dominated Mau Mau uprising was not the only expression of anticolonialism in Kenya. Other regional rural rebellions, moderate urban-based political associations, and labor unions contributed to the anticolonial cause. Yet as historian Frederick Cooper has observed, even the groups that sought a constitution based on a Western model invoked the "discipline and patience of the Kikuyu elder" as model qualities for political activism. Thus the parallel movements retained, or at least acknowledged, the traditional Kikuyu principles – in this case following the wisdom of respected elders. The man who finally took up the nationalist banner, Jomo Kenyatta, was himself a Kikuyu but headed a multiethnic political party, the Kenya Africa Union, and considered himself a Pan-Africanist. Yet Kenyatta's own scholarly work on the history and culture of the Kikuyu, published in his 1938 monograph, *Facing Mount Kenya*, provided early evidence of how important ethnic identity was to Kenyans' perspectives on their new nation-state.

Labor and Nationalist Movements

The rise of labor movements as vehicles of nationalist mobilization corresponded with the rapid expansion of colonial bureaucracies and import-export infrastructures during and after World War II. Workers protested both colonial labor policies and broader economic conditions. During the war, workers found themselves caught between shortages of imported goods and high inflation on the one hand and an acceleration of export production on the other; profits derived from the increased production benefited only the colonizers and a small group of indigenous elite. As a result, a wave of strikes swept through many colonies. Wartime labor

Kenya's prime minister Jomo Kenyatta pictured on the eve of independence in 1963 with former Mau Mau field marshall Mwariama. *CORBIS/Bettmann*

protests included major strikes by miners and industrial workers in the British Copperbelt colonies. For example, in 1935 a wave of strikes spread through the mines in northern Rhodesia.

Soon after World War II the labor movements gained momentum, fueled both by the rising expectations of mission-educated, urban-based civil servants and the challenging idealism of veterans returned from service abroad. The year 1945 saw a large-scale strike in Dakar, SENEGAL, and a colony-wide strike of government and railway workers that paralyzed NIGERIA for a month. Two years later railway workers organized a massive transnational strike in French West Africa, a protest immortalized by Ousmane Sembène's novel *God's Bits of Wood*. In the same period a wave of strikes swept through East Africa's port cities, including MOMBASA, KENYA (1947); DAR ES SALAAM, TANZANIA (1947); and ZANZIBAR (1948).

Although these strikes were prompted by immediate economic concerns, they also challenged the fundamental terms of colonial labor policies and, by extension, colonial rule itself. For example, as Cooper points out, negotiations regarding a minimum wage in Dakar brought into question the different standards of living available to Africans and Europeans. This forced the French to face the inherent contradiction between their racially stratified colonial labor policies and their rhetoric of assimilation. As one African labor negotiator in Saint-Louis put it, "Your goal is to elevate us to your level; without the means, we will never succeed."

Although most union leaders were educated, male, and often from relatively elite backgrounds, their movements needed, and found, community support. According to Cooper, "Each of these strike movements took place in a particular milieu, and it was the ability of workers to draw on the resources and solidarity of communities that made them so effective." Social connections provided an important basis for the organization of these strikes; the early protests, such as the one in Rhodesia in 1935, were organized through social connections and religious organizations rather than trade unions. In the 1947 Mombasa strike, for example, word of protests spread through the Swahili-speaking area where most of the workers lived. Tapping into local channels of communication, such as meetings in homes and dance societies, the labor struggle spread as a truly grassroots movement. Later, these channels were formalized, with mass assemblies called to organize the protests.

The history of nationalism in Ghana provides one of the best examples of the nexus between the labor movement and the nationalist movement. Between 1937 and 1947, Ghana, then called the Gold Coast, witnessed a series of small strikes, most of which were led by former servicemen returned from service in World War II. The unrest culminated in 1947 with a wave of strikes involving more than 46,000 workers from the railway, gold mines, and other industrial sectors. During the same period farmers protested government intervention in cocoa production. To protest goods shortages and high prices, Nii Kwabena Bonne II, a local chief turned businessman, organized a wide-scale urban boycott of European- and Syrian-owned businesses in Accra, Kumasi, and other cities. At the same time leaders such as Kwame Nkrumah were going further and articulating nationalist agendas.

The British colonial governments, which had originally viewed African trade unions with suspicion, soon realized that organized unions with which they could negotiate presented a far less threatening possibility than mass mobilization for independence. As a result, by 1948 the British sought to invest official bargaining power in trade unions that did not espouse overtly political agendas. In some cases the British revised their opinions about unions previously considered hostile. The United Gold Coast Convention (UGCC), which distanced itself from more militant urban workers, was one such union to come into British favor.

As the labor movement split in the late 1940s between those in favor of labor reform and those who sought full decolonization, many of these militant urban workers ultimately threw their lot in with Nkrumah and the Convention People's Party (CPP). Railway union leaders Anthony Woode and Pobee Biney allied themselves with this group, helping to build massive popular support for the nationalist cause. Over the next ten years Nkrumah led the nationalist demonstrations and elections that dismantled the British colonial state in 1957.

In the Portuguese colonies large-scale labor movements developed in the 1950s. Responding to the fascist Portuguese ruler António Salazar's harsh colonial labor practices, including forced labor, labor organizers in Guinea-Bissau allied with the growing antifascist movement in Portugal itself, which included communist groups. Nationalists organized around labor struggles led by Amílcar Cabral's Partido Africano da Independencia da Guine e Cabo Verde (PAIGC, 1956), staging a series of general strikes. The PAIGC's size and militancy grew in 1959, after Portuguese troops massacred striking dockworkers in Bissau. Four years later the PAIGC's guerrilla actions exploded into full-scale anticolonial war in Guinea-Bissau, with clandestine operations based on the islands. The PIAGC ultimately won independence in Guinea-Bissau in 1974 and in Cape Verde a year later.

Contemporary Nationalism

Once independence had been achieved, many of Africa's postcolonial governments invoked their national identities to justify their administration's agendas. Many of the changes were made in the name of economic development, with approaches varying from the socialism of Guinea and Tanzania to the free-market path of Côte d'Ivoire (*see* individual country entries for more information). All too often, African bureaucratic or military elite leaders proved as despotic and unaccountable as the colonial administrations they replaced. Some postcolonial regimes outlawed the organizations that had helped win the nationalist struggles. In Libya, for example, the Sanusi order was outlawed under Qaddafi and its role suppressed in official history books. In Guinea, Touré had enormous popular support when he became the country's first president in 1958, but during the 1970s thousands fled the country in response to the police and army brutality of his paranoid, one-party regime. Although labor unions continued to exercise a degree of political clout in a number of countries – such as Ghana and its northern neighbor Upper Volta (now Burkina Faso) – economic stagnation in the years after independence highlighted the fact that the unions of urban wage and salary workers represented only a fraction of the population in these countries. Many people lived in rural areas and did not benefit at all from policies aimed at pacifying the "labor elite." In Kenya, as in several other countries where ethnic identity had informed nationalist movements, postcolonial political groups were quickly divided along tribal lines. In short, many of the ideals of the nationalist struggles proved more difficult to achieve than independence itself.

Since the end of the cold war and the speedup of economic globalization, political turmoil both in Africa and elsewhere has led many to question the meaning of nationalism and the future of the nation-state. But these concepts have not lost relevance in Africa. In South Africa the African National Congress (ANC) finally achieved its long-standing goal: the transformation of the nation to one in which all races are afforded equal rights. In Central Africa, Laurent-Désiré Kabila's 1997 overthrow of Zairean dictator Mobutu Sese Seko proved that an era of cold war-enforced balances of power in the region had definitely ended. One of Kabila's first actions as self-proclaimed president was to change the country's name from Zaire – a name associated with Mobutu, since he chose it for the former Belgian colony in 1965 – to the Democratic Republic of the Congo. Whether or not Kabila had any intention of establishing a democracy soon became questionable, but by changing the name of the entire country he demonstrated that the image of national liberator was still significant in contemporary Africa. Finally, when tensions over trade and a disputed border between Eritrea and Ethiopia erupted into armed conflict in mid-1998, the two countries – whose citizenries are linked by language, religion, and even family ties – justified their actions as the defense of national sovereignty. All these events demonstrate that national movements and national identity remain dynamic concepts in contemporary Africa.

Marian Aguiar

See Also

Accra, Ghana; African Socialism; Bissau, Guinea-Bissau; Cabral, Amílcar; Christianity, African: An Overview; Côte d'Ivoire; Dakar, Senegal; Ethnicity and Identity in Africa: An Interpretation; Houphouët-Boigny, Félix; Kumasi, Ghana; Mandela, Nelson Rolihlahla; Nyerere, Julius Kambarage; Race: An Interpretation; Senghor, Léopold Sédar; Pan-Africanism; Qaddafi, Muammar al-; Ousmane Sembène; Urbanism and Urbanization in Africa; Tripoli, Libya; Islam and Tradition: An Interpretation.

North America

National League for the Protection of Colored Women,

an early twentieth-century organization, designed to aid African American women, that eventually became part of the National Urban League.

The National League for the Protection of Colored Women grew out of the Associations for the Protection of Negro Women, an organization founded by white social worker Frances Kellor in 1902 to help black women workers in New York. By the turn of the century many African Americans had started migrating to Northern cities from the South in search of economic opportunity, but 90 percent of urban black women found work only in low-paying domestic service jobs. Some agents had begun meeting black women travelers at train stations and docks and taking advantage of their precarious economic situation by coercing them into signing unfair contracts or encouraging them to engage in prostitution. The Associations for the Protection of Negro Women established travelers' aid networks in Baltimore, Washington, Richmond, and Savannah to prepare women passing through those cities for what they might find in the North. The organization also set up employment agencies in black neighborhoods and worked with the White Rose Mission, the Young Women's Christian Association, and other agencies to provide safe lodging houses for African American women.

The first affiliated branch of the Associations for the Protection of Negro Women was located in Philadelphia and was run by Mrs. S. W. Layten, a black activist. In 1906 the organization became the National League for the Protection of Colored Women, opening up additional branches in Baltimore, Washington, D.C., and Chicago, and extending its travelers' aid service to Memphis and Norfolk. In October 1911 the National League for the Protection of Colored Women merged with several other African American social welfare organizations to form the National League on Urban Conditions Among Negroes, which in turn became the National Urban League.

Lisa Clayton Robinson

See Also

Baltimore, Maryland; Chicago, Illinois; Great Migration, The; Memphis, Tennessee; New York, New York; Philadelphia, Pennsylvania; Richmond, Virginia; Washington, D.C.

Latin America and the Caribbean

National Movement of Street Children

(Movimento Nacional de Meninos e Meninas de Rua, or MNMMR), an organization established in Brazil in 1985 that represents the interests of street children, many of whom are of African descent.

North America

National Negro Labor Council,

American organization that was formed in 1951 to promote the cause of black workers and was labeled a "Communist-front organization" by the House Committee on Un-American Activities.

In 1951 the National Negro Labor Council (NNLC) was established to end discrimination against blacks in hiring, in promotions, and within labor unions themselves. Within five years, however, the organization had succumbed to attacks by the United States House Committee on Un-American Activities (HUAC). The collapse of the NNLC indicates the extent to which cold-war, anticommunist hysteria in the United States pervaded the ranks of organized labor and undercut the fledgling movement to advance the cause of the black worker.

In the late 1940s one of the most powerful American unions, the Congress of Industrial Organizations (CIO), had purged from its ranks a number of affiliate unions because of alleged Communist leanings. Several of these affiliates had been the leading advocates within the CIO for racial equality, and had histories of promoting job opportunities and increased union representation for black workers. The expulsion of these affiliates left a dearth of black proponents in the labor movement.

In 1950, 900 predominantly black labor delegates from various unions met in Chicago to air the problems of African American workers, who faced discrimination not only on the job but also in their own unions as well. The next year 23 newly formed Negro Labor Councils, representing industrial centers around the country, forged a permanent vehicle of advocacy, the National Negro Labor Council.

Working under the guiding principle that "blacks would attain first-class citizenship only if black workers organized to fight for full economic opportunity," the NNLC also promised to fight police brutality and segregation of housing and public facilities. Local NLCs targeted large corporations such as the Ford Motor Company, Sears-Roebuck, and the Detroit Tigers to force fair hiring and promotion practices, while the national council pushed for fair employment practices clauses in union contracts. Throughout the 1950s the NNLC supported black workers in a number of important strikes, including those against International Harvester in Chicago (1952) and Louisiana sugar cane plantations (1953). In the well orchestrated "Let Freedom Crash the Gateway to the South" campaign of 1954, the NNLC anticipated hiring discrimination at a new General Electric plant in Louisville, Kentucky, and organized an extensive workers' training program. When the plant opened, it attempted to exclude blacks workers for lack of training, a common tactic of employment discrimination. The workers, with certificates from night classes to prove their qualifications, forced General Electric to reconsider. Despite the relatively successful outcome of these efforts, there was still firm resistance to reform in many industries. American Airlines, for example, refused to hire black pilots and stewardesses in spite of the national attention that the NNLC drew to the airline's discriminatory practices.

The NNLC became a highly visible force in the labor movement and attracted support from the likes of PAUL ROBESON. One of the key features of the NNLC was its links to progressive unions, to black-worker bastions of mainstream unions, such as Detroit's UAW Local 600, and to the unions that had been expelled from the CIO. These associations led to charges that the NNLC was controlled by the Communist Party – accusations that came from not only organized labor, but from African-American organizations themselves, including the NATIONAL ASSOCIATION FOR THE ADVANCEMENT OF COLORED PEOPLE (NAACP) and the NATIONAL URBAN LEAGUE. In 1952 and again in 1956, the HUAC and the Subversive Activities Control Board charged the NNLC with being "a Communist-front organization." Although the Communist Party may well have had some adherents within the ranks of the NNLC, the degree to which the party controlled the organization is open to debate. Unable to meet the legal costs of defending itself before HUAC, the organization voted to disband in 1956.

Marian Aguiar

SEE ALSO

American Federation of Labor and Congress of Industrial Organizations; Chicago, Illinois; Labor Unions in the United States; Communist Party USA, African Americans and the.

Africa

National Party,

South African political party known for its harsh apartheid policies.

Conservative Afrikaners, the descendants of Dutch colonial settlers in SOUTH AFRICA, founded the National Party (NP) in 1914, just four years after the birth of the Union of South Africa. The party, first led by General J. B. M. Hertzog, primarily sought to defend Afrikaner interests against British domination. In addition, the NP's founders were in favor of maintaining racial segregation laws that had prevailed in the Afrikaner republics, as opposed to the more liberal policies of the British.

In the beginning the NP was not overtly racist. Indeed, the antisegregationist AFRICAN NATIONAL CONGRESS (ANC) favored the NP over the more conservative South African Party in 1924 elections. But in 1934 a new leader, Dr. D. F. Malan, launched what he called the Purified National Party, from which the modern NP grew. The new NP came to power in 1948, and immediately instituted laws that formalized and extended the racial inequality that was traditional throughout most of the country. These included acts that restricted where black South Africans could live, denied their children an equal education, and prohibited interracial marriages. In addition, the NP rescinded voting rights for Coloured (mixed race) citizens.

Although black South Africans had faced injustice for years, the new laws – commonly referred to by the Dutch word APARTHEID ("apartness") – represented a harsher, more systematic oppression. During the more than 40 years during which the National Party held power, it continued to defend apartheid, at times violently, until growing internal dissent and international economic pressure forced President P. W. Botha to initiate minor reforms, beginning in the late 1970s. His legalization of trade unions and mixed marriages outraged the party's right wing, which defected and formed the Conservative Party. Objections also came from South Africa's ANTIAPARTHEID MOVEMENT, which sought the complete dismantling of the system, not merely reforms.

F. W. De Klerk, the NP member who had succeeded Botha as president in 1989, surprised many by freeing Nelson Mandela, the ANC leader imprisoned for treason in 1962. In addition, De Klerk, who promised a "new South Africa," lifted the long-standing ban on opposition parties, including the ANC, the PAN-AFRICANIST CONGRESS, and the South African Communist Party, and began negotiating with these and other groups. The talks led to a new constitution and, in 1994, South Africa's first multiracial, democratic elections. With the white electorate now reduced a mere 15 percent of the vote, the NP lost its long hold on the presidency and the legislature. Under De Klerk, who has tried to shed the taint of apartheid, the NP reached out to Indian and mixed-race South Africans, winning more than 60 percent of their votes in 1994. By the late 1990s, however, its support had dwindled drastically.

Kate Tuttle

SEE ALSO

Afrikaner; Mandela, Nelson Rolihlahla; Botha, Pieter Willem; De Klerk, Frederik Willem.

Europe

National Socialist Sterilization Policies in Germany,

policies of "racial hygiene" implemented by the National Socialist (Nazi) government of Germany (1933-1945) involving the sterilization of black Germans.

The precise number of blacks in Germany when the Nazi government took power is unknown. Probably a few hundred black citizens of former German colonies and black foreign nationals were present in the country. More significantly, however, the post-World War I occupation of the German Rhineland by French troops, including black soldiers from the French colonies, had resulted in the birth of an estimated 500 to 800 children of mixed race (popularly referred to as "Rhineland bastards") to German women. In contrast to their policy toward Jews, the Nazis did not attempt to exterminate this small minority, though mixed-race Germans did suffer harassment and persecution in the Third Reich. The Nazis' main concern with regard to blacks, however, was racial mixing. They aimed to prevent this through a policy of sterilizing the Rhineland children.

The Nazis' eugenic theories (like similar theories popular throughout Europe and the United States in the early twentieth century) included ideas of racial purity and genetic "health," promoted through the sterilization of the supposedly unfit. Proponents of what the Nazis termed "racial hygiene" believed that mixing races created weak, genetically inferior offspring. German doctors "proved" the inferiority of biracial children in pseudo-scientific experiments. The Nazis' 1933 Law for the Prevention of Offspring with Hereditary Defects authorized forcible sterilization in certain cases. The sterilization of black Germans took place separately, however, under the aegis of "Special Commission 3," established in 1937. Though the policy supposedly required parental permission for the operations, the Nazis seem to have coerced most parents to comply. They carried out the entire program in secrecy, sterilizing some 385 of the Rhineland children. The 1986 book *Farbe Bekennen* (*Showing our Colors*, 1992) includes interviews with two survivors of the period.

Belinda Cooper

See Also
France; Eugenics.

Africa

National Union for the Total Independence of Angola

(União Nacional para a Independência Total de Angola), a leading nationalist group, insurgency movement, and opposition party in Angola.

After splitting with other nationalist parties over ideology and strategy, Jonas Savimbi created the National Union for the Total Independence of Angola, or UNITA, in March 1966. With its base in the southern town of Jamba, and in the south and east of Portuguese-ruled Angola, UNITA gained most of its domestic support from the Ovimbundu ethnic group.

Although its ideology was often unclear, in general UNITA promoted democracy, capitalist development, and the recognition of African ethnic identities and customs. With military aid from South Africa, the United States, and several Western European countries, the movement built one of the largest armies in Africa. In areas under its control, UNITA reinvigorated chieftainships, established a barter economy, mined diamonds for international export, and maintained strict army discipline.

During the war to overthrow Portuguese colonialism, UNITA often fought the other two major nationalist parties, the Popular Movement for the Liberation of Angola, or MPLA, and the National Front for the Liberation of Angola. In 1974, when Angolan independence seemed inevitable, UNITA allied briefly with these groups. But the alliance soon fell apart, and in 1975 South Africa supported UNITA in its drive to take the capital, Luanda. The following year UNITA abandoned the cities and launched an insurgency war against the Marxist-Leninist MPLA government that lasted until 1992.

In the late 1980s UNITA entered into negotiations to end the war. The negotiations resulted in elections in 1992, but when it became obvious that Savimbi would lose, UNITA accused the government of electoral irregularities and attacks on demobilized UNITA soldiers, and again took up arms. In 1994 UNITA was forced by international pressure to negotiate, and it has since been slowly integrated into the government and military. In early 1997, 70 elected UNITA deputies and several ministers began serving in a government of national reconciliation, although sanctions remained on UNITA's activities.

Eric Young

See Also
Luanda, Angola; Nationalism in Africa; Savimbi, Jonas Malheiro.

North America

National Urban League,

an interracial social service organization that attempts to obtain full participation in American society for African Americans through lobbying, research, and direct social services.

Unlike organizations such as the National Association for the Advancement of Colored People (NAACP), which has been judged by how successfully it has fought for blacks' civil and political rights, the National Urban League (NUL) has pursued less measurable goals. Since its founding in 1911, the organization has used the tools of scientific social work to offer programs to help African Americans. The NUL originally provided direct services to African Americans who had migrated from the rural South to Northern cities. Later in the century, as social conditions changed, the organization increased its scope. It undertook sociological research that disputed commonly held misconceptions about African American inferiority; began to lobby businesses, labor unions, and the government; and embraced direct protest during the Civil Rights Movement as a means of gaining greater social and economic participation for African Americans.

At its inception the NUL modeled its social services on white charitable organizations of the day, such as settlement houses, charitable agencies, and immigrant aid societies, and adapted them to blacks' needs. As many African Americans moved north during the Great Migration, the NUL worked through local affiliates to help them adjust to urban life. The affiliates taught basic skills such as behavior, dress, sanitation, health, and homemaking. The NUL also sponsored community centers, clinics, kindergartens, day care, and summer camps. League workers provided individual care to African Americans in a range of areas, including juvenile delinquency, truancy, and marital adjustment.

The Great Migration increased demands on the NUL, and the organization soon had affiliates in nearly every industrial city in the United States. The NUL began offering vocational training to immigrants, urging businesses to hire blacks and attempting to persuade unions such as the American Federation of Labor (AFL) to accept black members. The NUL achieved its primary aim of improving employment opportunities for blacks, but such gains were temporary: at the end of World War I returning soldiers put many blacks out of work again.

During the Great Depression the NUL broadened its scope still more under the leadership of Lester B. Granger. While continuing to offer vocational training and social services to urban blacks, the NUL sought to persuade the federal government to include blacks in President Franklin Roosevelt's New Deal programs. The organization lobbied the federal government to end discrimination in allocating government benefits. During World War II the NUL fought to desegregate wartime employment and the armed forces, supporting A. Philip Randolph's plan for a March on Washington. In exchange for Randolph's calling off the march, Roosevelt issued Executive Order (E.O.) 8802, which barred discrimination in defense industries and in federal agencies, and established the Fair Employment Practices Committee

PERSONS LIVING BELOW THE POVERTY LEVEL 1959-1990

Year	Total (In Millions)	Percent	Blacks (In Millions)	Percent
1959	39.5	22.4	9.9	55.1
1970	25.4	12.6	7.5	33.5
1980	29.3	13.0	8.6	32.5
1990	33.6	13.5	9.8	31.9

* Persons are classified as being above or below the poverty level using the poverty index, based on the Department of Agriculture's 1961 Economy Food Plan. Poverty thresholds are updated every year. In 1990 the weighted average poverty threshold for a family of four was $13,359.

Sources: *Encyclopedia of African-American Culture and History* (1996): "Persons Living Below the Poverty Level, 1959-1990" (Table 5.1); *Statistical Abstract*, 1992.

Vernon Jordan announces his resignation as president of the National Urban League in 1981, a year after he was wounded in an assassination attempt. *CORBIS/Bettmann*

(FEPC), which was responsible for implementing E.O. 8802.

The NUL also sought to shape public and private opinion through its research. Its sociological studies – published independently and, from 1923 to 1949, in its journal, *Opportunity* – took an explicitly scientific approach to social problems. NUL leaders criticized the NAACP's journal, the *Crisis*, believing it to be too "subjective." *Opportunity* also published black writers and artists such as Gwendolyn Bennett, Langston Hughes, James Weldon Johnson, and Countee Cullen.

In the 1960s, under Whitney M. Young Jr., the NUL expanded its traditional social service approach by strengthening its commitment to civil rights. It embraced direct action, promoted community organization, and sponsored leadership development and voter education and registration projects. It helped organize two important events of the Civil Rights Movement: the March on Washington in 1963 and the Poor People's Campaign in 1968. Toward the end of the 1960s the NUL attempted to revitalize ghettos by calling for a domestic Marshall Plan.

Following Whitney Young's death in 1971, Vernon Jordan became president of the NUL. Jordan helped to begin programs in health, housing, education, and job training. In 1975 the NUL began to publish a journal, the *Urban League Review*, and began issuing an annual report, *The State of Black America*. In 1982 Jordan was succeeded by John Jacobs.

When the federal government cut social programs in the 1980s, the NUL responded by emphasizing self-help and seeking solutions to new and continuing problems facing African Americans, including high rates of teen pregnancy, families headed by single women, declining quality of public schools, and crime. Under Hugh Price, who became NUL president in 1994, the Urban League tackled the consequences of welfare "reform," the rollback of affirmative action programs, and the persistence of racial discrimination and exclusion in the workplace. A communications veteran, Price has been a strong national voice on behalf of economic opportunity and equality.

Robert Fay

See Also

World War II and African Americans; American Federation of Labor and Congress of Industrial Organizations; *Crisis, The*; Granger, Lester Blackwell; Jordan, Vernon Eulion, Jr.; Labor Unions in the United States; *Opportunity: Journal of Negro Life*; Poor People's Washington Campaign; Randolph, Asa Philip; Young, Whitney Moore, Jr.; March on Washington, 1963; March on Washington, 1941.

North America

National Welfare Rights Organization, coalition of poor Americans, mostly black and mostly women, who demanded better welfare assistance from state governments and the federal government in the late 1960s and early 1970s.

By the mid-1960s the Civil Rights Movement in the United States had achieved several of its basic political goals: blacks could vote, eat at integrated lunch counters, and send their children to integrated schools. Many activists, however, believed such gains were of little value as long as most blacks lived in poverty. Among these activists were several black women in Los Angeles, New York, and other cities who received Aid to Families with Dependent Children (AFDC, or welfare). Separately and somewhat spontaneously, they organized fellow welfare recipients to demand better benefits and treatment from welfare agencies.

To coordinate and spread their protests, George Wiley, a black chemistry professor and former worker for the Congress of Racial Equality (CORE), created the Poverty Rights Action Center in 1966. The following year the office evolved into the National Welfare Rights Organization (NWRO), with headquarters in Washington, D.C. With help from the NWRO, women receiving welfare gathered by the dozens or hundreds, went to the local welfare office, and demanded money for basic needs – such as clothes for school – that were not being met by their welfare benefits. If refused, they held a sit-in. The strategy won better benefits for large numbers of women. The NWRO, in turn, received valuable publicity and thousands of dollars from the antipoverty agencies of Lyndon Johnson's Great Society as well as from private donors.

In the late 1960s the NWRO held mass marches and rallies to publicize its demands, which now included livable grants for all welfare recipients, access to daycare, and programs for job training. Although these goals went mostly unmet, the NWRO did succeed in ending the intrusive investigations that were often a prerequisite for receiving benefits. Partly due to the NWRO and partly to the programs of the Great Society, many women previously reluctant to apply for welfare now did so, and were accepted. Others who had been denied relief earlier were finally accepted. Welfare rolls, with about 750,000 participants in 1960, were at 3 million by 1972.

The NWRO had a peak membership of about 100,000. As such, it was one of the first large-scale attempts by poor black women to take control of their political and economic future. However, while the women on welfare exercised great power locally, the NWRO's national staff, who were primarily white, male, and middle class, dominated many of the NWRO's important decisions. By the early 1970s relations between national and local offices had grown increasingly strained over the question of how much autonomy to give locals. That question, though, was eclipsed by a broad public backlash against welfare programs that emerged at the end of the 1960s. After 1970 the NWRO had few important successes; by 1972 it was badly in debt; and by the mid-1970s it was defunct.

See Also

Brown v. Board of Education; Sit-Ins; Voting Rights Act of 1965; Los Angeles, California; New York, New York.

North America

Nation of Islam, religious movement based on black separatism; founded around 1930 in Detroit, Michigan.

The Nation of Islam (NOI) was established in Detroit at the beginning of the Great Depression, by Wallace D. Fard, a door-to-door silk salesman. In addition to selling his wares, he spread his message of salvation and self-determination throughout Detroit's black neighborhoods. He held the first meetings in people's homes, but the movement soon grew big and Fard rented halls for his gatherings. Far from adhering to strict Islamic law, NOI under Fard was an eclectic mix of philosophy that borrowed from earlier black Muslim movements, Christian Scripture (largely to debunk Christianity), and Fard's Afrocentric interpretation of the story of Origin. The organization attracted many followers because of its angry rejection of white society.

Fard wrote two manuals, *The Secret Ritual of the Nation of Islam*, which is still used as a blueprint for oral instruction, and *Teaching for a Lost-Found Nation of Islam in a Mathematical Way*, written in a coded language that a select few are able to decipher. He also established the University of Islam, the Muslim Girls Training Corps – an instruction center that trained females to follow the tenets of proper Muslim womanhood – and the Fruit of Islam, a militaristic unit that served as Fard's bodyguard faction and enforced the Nation's laws.

When word reached white authorities that Fard was preaching about the Western "blue-eyed devil" whose civilization would soon perish, the Nation was deemed subversive. The hostile relationship between the movement and law enforcement (including ultimately the FBI) would continue for the next several decades. In 1931 Fard was investigated and detained by the Detroit police department for endorsing a sacrificial killing performed by a fringe member of the movement. There is no evidence to indicate that Fard was involved in the murder. Despite the fact that the victim was black, the charge against Fard was exacerbated when authorities found a pamphlet in his possession calling for the annihilation of "white devils."

Fard apparently had the foresight to know that his presence in the Nation would potentially lead to its demise. In 1933, months before he was told to leave Detroit or face incarceration, Fard began preparing his young right-hand man, Elijah Muhammad, for leadership. Fard's departure and his replacement by Muhammad led to internal strife within the movement. The Nation of Islam splintered, and within a couple of years Muhammad's trusted circle, including his family, moved to Chicago. The Temple of Islam No. 2 was built and later became the national headquarters of the Nation.

Under Muhammad the Nation was able to put into practice the concept of black economic self-sufficiency, a premise that Fard had envisioned but never fully realized. Because of their highly disciplined lifestyle, Muslims were hired more readily than other blacks. A good portion of their salary went into the Nation's coffers. One decade later, in 1945, members had pooled enough earnings to invest in 57 hectares (140 acres) of farmland in rural Michigan. In subsequent years more than 100 temples flourished nationwide, and Muslim-owned bakeries, grocery stores, and other small businesses were opened in African American communities.

During its early days the NOI tended to attract Southerners who had migrated north and had little formal education. The appeal of the movement was not just self-sufficiency but the structured lifestyle, with its emphasis on marriage, family, strict diet, and hygiene. In particular, the image of womanhood in the Nation of Islam was acclaimed for "purity, domesticity, and piety." Muhammad carried on Fard's program of providing female members with an education that included classes in nursing, gymnastics, cooking, sewing, child rearing, and the proper approach to gender relations. While its women seemed to be put on a pedestal, NOI has nevertheless been criticized over the years for being ambiguously caught between glorification and objectification of females.

By the 1950s NOI did begin to resemble a nation. Complete with its own national flag and anthem, militaristic marches and salutes, the movement was, in essence, a military theocracy. The structure and ritual, and the promise of salvation from the "grave" – the soulless, dog-eat-dog world outside the Nation – appealed to many poor blacks, particularly convicts in jail. One of those recruited from prison was a young man named Malcolm Little. Like all inductees into the movement, Little discarded his "slave" surname; he became known as Malcolm X. Recognized as a brilliant orator, Malcolm X quickly rose through the ranks of the Nation. He had arrived at an opportune time. The early rumblings of the CIVIL RIGHTS MOVEMENT were beginning as a result of the government's failure to satisfy African American demands for equality. The Nation would soon be competing with other black movements for members. Malcolm's charisma and the advent of television brought the movement greater visibility than ever before. NOI actively began to recruit black, middle-class professionals. Not only was Muhammad interested in incorporating their skills for the betterment of the Nation, but he was also adamant that their expertise not be wasted in "the white man's world."

By the late 1950s NOI's separatist beliefs stood in contrast to the growing Civil Rights Movement, which sought integration. The primary focus of NOI was economic self-sufficiency, and by the early 1960s some,

ABOVE: Elijah Muhammad, *right,* talks with Malcolm X, *center,* during a Nation of Islam convention in Chicago. *AP/Wide World Photos*
ABOVE RIGHT: Benjamin Chavis, *right,* chats with Louis Farrakhan at the African American Leadership summit in Washington, D.C., in November 1995. *CORBIS/Jacques M. Chenet*
RIGHT: Elijah Muhammad speaks at a black Muslim convention in Chicago in 1966. *CORBIS/Bettmann*

including Malcolm X, criticized the interest in financial gain and the money-and-wealth fixation among the upper ranks of the movement. In 1964, discontented with Muhammad's political philosophy and allegations that the leader had fathered several illegitimate children, Malcolm broke away from the Nation to form his own religious organization. One year later he was assassinated.

Critics of Muhammad claimed that his violent denunciation of Malcolm X in speeches and in the Nation's newspaper, *Muhammad Speaks*, incited the murder. The Nation has continued to prosper economically, but there has not been another surge in membership since the 1960s. In 1975, after Elijah Muhammad's death, his son Wallace Deen Muhammad was named supreme minister. However, two months into his leadership he declared that whites were no longer viewed as evil and would be allowed into the movement. This shift, as well as a move toward the more orthodox Sunni Islam, shocked and alienated a large group of followers. The Nation splintered into several alliances, and by 1978 national spokesman Louis Farrakhan led a group that resurrected the original Nation of Islam teachings of Black Nationalism and separatism.

Despite his controversial persona, Farrakhan in the 1990s has been credited with reaching out to non-Muslim black religious leaders and activists in order to effect positive change in inner cities. In 1995 he successfully orchestrated the MILLION MAN MARCH, an event that brought together many people and organizations of opposing political viewpoints.

There is no official information on the size of NOI membership as of 1998. Various sources estimate that it numbers between 10,000 and 100,000.

Suzanne Albulak

SEE ALSO
Chicago, Illinois; Detroit, Michigan; Farrakhan, Louis Abdul.

Nat Turner's Rebellion. Please see TURNER, NAT

Africa

Naudeba, ethnic group of West Africa.

The Naudeba primarily inhabit Burkina Faso. They speak a Niger-Congo language and are related to the Mossi people. Approximately 100,000 people consider themselves Naudeba.

See Also

Languages, African: An Overview.

Africa

Naude, Beyers (b. 1915, Roodepoort-Maraisburg, South Africa), South African Afrikaner minister in the Dutch Reformed Church (DRC) and opponent of apartheid, South Africa's rigid policy of racial segregation.

Born near Johannesburg, Beyers Naude was the son of a DRC minister whose family moved to Graaff-Reinet in southwestern South Africa in 1921. Naude obtained a master's degree in languages and a degree in theology from the University of Stellenbosch School of Theology in 1939. That same year he became an assistant minister at a DRC chapter in Wellington, Western Cape province. He married at this time and joined the Afrikaner Broederbond, a secret organization dedicated to the promotion of Afrikaner nationalism and white rule in South Africa.

Naude remained an orthodox DRC minister and supporter of the National Party, which promoted apartheid, until 1960. He was horrified by the Sharpeville Massacre of March 21, 1960, when 69 blacks were killed by police during a demonstration against apartheid's pass laws, which forced nonwhites to carry identity papers and restricted their movement. After much reflection and Bible study Naude decided that apartheid was unjust and immoral, and he began to preach accordingly. As a result, he was strongly criticized by the DRC, and he resigned as moderator of his congregation (the highest local position) in 1963. Naude also left the Broederbond and founded the Christian Institute, which sought to unite all churches and languages in an effort to reconcile blacks and whites in South Africa. He edited the Institute's controversial publication *Pro Veritate*. In addition to opposing apartheid, Naude denounced the use of violence. For the rest of the 1960s he was bitterly attacked by right-wing members of the DRC, and both his home and the Christian Institute were searched by the security police.

In 1972 Naude traveled to Germany and Great Britain, where he was asked to preach at Westminster Abbey; the following year his passport was withdrawn. In 1974 he was awarded an honorary doctorate of law by the University of the Witwatersrand in Johannesburg and received the Reinhold Niebuhr Award for "steadfast and self-sacrificing services in South Africa for justice and peace" (shared with Soviet dissident Andrei Sakharov). In 1975, after a three-year government investigation, the Christian Institute was deprived of its income from abroad and its activities were greatly restricted. In 1977 Naude was banned for five years by the government, which meant he was confined to his home area, not allowed to attend meetings, and could not be quoted anywhere in South Africa. He was awarded the Swedish Free Church prize for reconciliation and development and another award by the Bruno Kreisky Foundation for "untiring work in race relations." In 1980 he broke away from the DRC to be admitted to the African Reformed Church, its separate black equivalent. In 1982 his banning order was renewed for a further three years, but it was lifted in 1984. In November of that year he became secretary general of the South African Council of Churches and in that capacity traveled to Europe, the United States, and Zimbabwe.

See Also

Johannesburg, South Africa; Sharpeville, South Africa.

North America

Navarro, Theodore "Fats" (b. September 24, 1923, Key West, Fla.; d. July 7, 1950), African American jazz trumpeter who helped pioneer the genre of jazz known as bebop during the 1940s.

Theodore "Fats" Navarro was considered one of the foremost jazz trumpeters of the 1940s, helping to pioneer the new style of jazz known as bebop, which featured quick tempos and highly complex musical phrasing. Navarro, with the help of Dizzy Gillespie, toured with several famous musicians in his career, including Billy Eckstine, Lionel Hampton, and Coleman Hawkins. Navarro was a big man who at one point weighed more than 136 kg (300 lb), earning him the nickname "Fat Girl." Despite an addiction to heroin and a severe case of tuberculosis, Navarro continued to record until his 1950 death.

Zebulon Miletsky

See Also

Eckstine, William Clarence (Billy); Gillespie, John Birks ("Dizzy"); Hampton, Lionel Leo; Hawkins, Coleman Randolph.

Navy. Please see Military, Blacks in the American

North America

Naylor, Gloria (b. January 25, 1950, New York, N.Y.), African American writer whose novels depict different African American communities and often incorporate elements of magical realism.

Gloria Naylor, recalling the influence that Toni Morrison's work has had on her own life, remembers discovering that for "a young black woman, struggling to find a mirror to her worth in this society, not only is your story worth telling but it can be told in words so painstakingly eloquent that it becomes a song." The realization was a turning point for Naylor, who, at age 27, began "gathering the authority within" to write her own stories.

Naylor's stories draw upon the legacy of her parents, former cotton sharecroppers in Mississippi who had migrated north; her father found a job as a transit worker and her mother as a telephone operator. After graduating from high school in 1968, Naylor traveled as a missionary for the Jehovah's Witnesses in New York City, North Carolina, and Florida. She returned to New York after seven years, completing a bachelor's degree in English at Brooklyn College in 1981 and a master's degree at Yale University in Afro-American Studies in 1983.

While she was still an undergraduate, Naylor began to write about the many different black communities to which her parents' stories and her own travels had brought her. Her first short story, "A Life on Beekman Place," was published in *Essence* magazine in 1980 and became a cornerstone for the novel she developed as her master's thesis, *The Women of Brewster Place* (1982). The novel portrays a disparate group of African American women who, having found themselves on a dead-end street in the inner city, explore their differences and draw upon their shared strength to survive. "All the good men are either dead or waiting to be born," one character comments, and with an unswerving gaze, Naylor looks at the brutality of relationships forged in the wake of oppression. *The Women of Brewster Place* received the American Book Award for best first novel of 1983.

Naylor's next novel, *Linden Hills* (1985), also derives narrative from place, this time an affluent community set on a hillside. As two young men, Willie and Lester, explore the sloping spiral of streets descending from Linden Hills, Naylor uses the structure of Dante's *Inferno* to portray a middle-class community obsessed with material gain. Wealth flows toward the bottom of the hill, and the successive line of identical sons, undertakers named Luther and Nedeed, rules from the house at the base. Naylor's novel is not only a critique of materialism, but also a feminist story of women's unwritten history, as Nedeed's wife, Willa, banished to the basement for producing an unidentical son, garners strength from the dusty testimonies of her predecessors.

Naylor develops the theme of spirituality in her third novel, *Mama Day* (1988), which explores the composition of individual belief. Again, Naylor juxtaposes disparate African American experiences, as George travels with his wife, Cocoa, from New York to the island of Willow Springs, the home of healer

Mama Day. Naylor relies on the legacy of African American healers and conjurers to create an ambiguous narrative in which both the characters and the readers are left to grapple with the notions of the real, the magical, and the process of fiction itself.

Naylor's fourth novel, *Bailey's Café* (1992), brings magic to New York City, where it enters the lives of a group of people who gather in a café. With a narrative that resonates with the blues, Naylor depicts the hard lives of the café patrons. As in *Mama Day*, Naylor blurs the line between the real and the magical, placing a magical dock behind the real café.

Naylor has taught at numerous colleges, including George Washington, New York, Princeton, Cornell, and Boston Universities. She won a Guggenheim Fellowship in 1988.

Marian Aguiar

See Also

Blues, The; *Essence*; New York, New York.

Africa

Ndau (also known as Buzi and Vandau), ethnic group of southern Africa.

The Ndau primarily inhabit southeastern Zimbabwe and south central Mozambique. They speak a Bantu language and are closely related to the Shona people. More than 100,000 people consider themselves Ndau.

See Also

Bantu: Dispersion and Settlement.

Africa

Ndebele, ethnic group of Botswana, South Africa, and Zimbabwe.

The founder of the Ndebele was Mzilikazi, head of the Khumalo Dynasty. His people spoke a Nguni language like that of the Zulu. In 1838, under constant Zulu attack and after a falling-out with the Zulu leader Shaka, Mzilikazi led his kinsmen to the area around present-day Bulawayo, Zimbabwe, in Shona territory. The region became known as Matabeleland and ultimately comprised a kingdom of around 10,000 sq km (3900 sq mi) as the Ndebele raided the Shona for cattle. The kingdom included both hereditary chieftainships, which were linked to the king through kin ties, and independent chieftainships, or *izinduna*, which maintained militias and paid allegiance to the king, first Mzilikazi and later his son Lobengula. Through intermarriage and the incorporation of Shona villages, the Ndebele adopted the Shona *Mwari* cult, in which the High God, or Mwari, speaks through oracles. Although the Ndebele built their capital at Bulawayo, most lived in villages, growing maize and other subsistence crops and herding cattle.

The Ndebele Kingdom began to disintegrate in 1893 when a war broke out between King Lobengula and the British South African Company over Ndebele cattle raiding. In 1896 the two sides reached an uneasy peace after Lobengula burned down Bulawayo and died without leaving a successor, but subsequent Ndebele leadership was divided and relatively weak. Under Rhodesian colonial rule the Ndebele were forced onto reserves, though the colonial administration considered the Ndebele able warriors and recruited many of them into the colonial army, the Rhodesian African Rifles. Although many of the early nationalist leaders were Ndebele, the war for independence was fought primarily by Shona-dominated opposition groups.

Today the Ndebele people number approximately 2 million and live in northern South Africa, eastern Botswana, and Zimbabwe. Although they are the second largest ethnic group in Zimbabwe, they account for only around 15 percent of the total population and hold few senior political, military, or corporate posts. Many Zimbabwean Ndebele believe that the Shona have tried to keep them poor and weak, despite evidence that development projects and assistance are equitably distributed to the Matabeleland provinces. Ndebele promote their interests through regional associations, although the Mwari cult is also an important part of Ndebele identity. The Ndebele have recently become renowned for their artwork, typically brightly colored geometric patterns that women paint on the exterior walls of their houses.

Eric Young

Africa

N'Djamena, Chad, the capital of Chad, its largest city, and its economic center.

N'Djamena lies at the confluence of the Logone and Chari rivers close to the border with Cameroon and 80 km (50 mi) southeast of Lake Chad. Known as Fort Lamy from its establishment up to September 1973, when President François Tombalbaye Africanized all French place names, N'Djamena acquired its present name from a small Kotoko fishing village called Am-Djamena that was founded on the site by the nineteenth century. In 1900 the French defeated and killed the Sudanese slaver Rabih al-Zubayr at the Battle of Kousseri, across the Chari River from Am-Djamena. That same year, for strategic reasons, the French built fortifications on both sides of the river: Fort Kousseri at the battle site and Fort Lamy on the site of Am-Djamena. The latter was named after the French soldier Major Lamy, who had also died in the battle.

Fort Lamy became the colonial capital under French rule. However, it remained a small town throughout the colonial period. Located at the center of cotton-growing, livestock-keeping, and fishing areas, it witnessed rapid growth after independence in 1960 as the national capital and an important market center. In 1958 Fort Lamy had a population of just 53,000, but by 1972 it had grown to 130,000. Chad's intermittent warfare during the 1970s and 1980s drove many refugees to seek security and economic opportunity in the capital. In 1990 the official population estimate was 728,000; the population is 95 percent Muslim.

N'Djamena is Chad's main financial and industrial center. Meat processing is the most important single industry in the city. N'Djamena sits at the hub of Chad's road network. Roads extend east into Sudan and southwest into Cameroon and Nigeria, whose ports handle Chad's seaborne trade. The city remains a major transit center on the east-west pilgrimage route to Mecca. The town is divided into two sections: a modern commercial center and a bustling African township. Much of N'Djamena's infrastructure was damaged as a result of faction fighting during Chad's long-running civil war. Although most of this damage had been repaired, some was still in evidence in the mid-1990s.

Andrew Burton

See Also

Tombalbaye, François; Rabih.

Africa

Ndowe, a coastal people of Equatorial Guinea, Cameroon, and Gabon.

Ndowe is a name broadly given to the Bantu-speaking coastal people of Equatorial Guinea. The two primary Ndowe ethnic groups, who speak the Kombe language, are the Boumba, including the Banga and Bapuku people, and the Bongue, including the Kombe, Bomoudi, Asangon, Muiko, and others. The Spanish referred to all of them as *playeros*, or "beach dwellers."

Historians believe that these groups began arriving on the coast from the upper Ubangui River between the twelfth and fourteenth century. Settling along the Mbini, or Muni, River and its affluents and the beaches, they fished, hunted, and grew cassava, malanga, and plantains. Living in scattered village communities linked by lineage and clans, they were increasingly dominated by the more politically centralized Fang, and were prevented from settling inland. Despite frequent conflicts, intermarriage between the Ndowe and the Fang was common, as it was between the Ndowe and the Bayele "Pygmies." The most unifying force among Ndowe communities was the transethnic Bwiti religion, adopted at the end of the 1800s, which promotes "one-heartness" among its followers.

When European slave traders became increasingly active in the region during the late fifteenth century, the Ndowe first fled inland but later returned to act as middlemen between the Fang and Europeans. Foreign diseases and the return of the Fang following the end of the slave trade decimated the Ndowe. Under Spanish COLONIAL RULE in Equatorial Guinea, the Ndowe's subordinate position vis-à-vis the Fang was sustained, though they were also protected from Fang dominance. At the 1967 Constitutional Conference the ethno-nationalist Ndowe Union advocated for Ndowe representation. But soon after independence the following year, the Ndowe became a subject of the Fang-dominated government's repression.

Eric Young

SEE ALSO

Bantu: Dispersion and Settlement; Transatlantic Slave Trade; Pygmy.

North America

Neal, Larry (b. September 5, 1937, Atlanta, Ga.; d. January 6, 1981, Hamilton, N.Y.), African American poet, essayist, and editor who helped develop the aesthetic theory of the Black Arts Movement.

An important contributor to the development of the BLACK ARTS MOVEMENT, Larry Neal received his B.A. from Lincoln University (1961) and his M.A. from the University of Pennsylvania (1963). Using bebop and the blues as aesthetic references, he published the books *Black Boogaloo: Notes on Black Liberation* (1969) and *Hoodoo Hollerin' Bebop Ghosts* (1971). In addition to founding several journals, Neal, with AMIRI BARAKA, founded Harlem's Black Arts Repertory Theater and edited the seminal nationalist anthology *Black Fire* (1968).

Peter Hudson

SEE ALSO

Blues, The; Harlem, New York; Lincoln University (Pennsylvania).

Africa

Nefertiti, a queen of ancient EGYPT.

Nefertiti was one of the most powerful women in the history of Egypt. Scholars generally believe that she exercised priestly powers previously reserved for the pharaoh alone. However, our knowledge of Nefertiti comes almost exclusively from the archaeological record, which allows few firm conclusions and leaves much room for speculation.

Nefertiti's origins are uncertain, although many believe she was a princess from the MIDDLE EAST. She was the chief wife of the pharaoh Akhenaten, who reigned from 1353 to 1336 B.C.E. Akhenaten's rule is famous because of the religious reforms that he and Nefertiti instituted. Some scholars believe that Nefertiti was primarily responsible for these reforms. The royal couple established monotheism in Egypt by abandoning the Egyptian pantheon and instituting the worship of the sun god Aton and requiring all Egyptian people to do the same.

By all accounts Nefertiti believed devoutly in Aton, and some scholars believe that her devotion may have contributed to her loss of power. Such religious innovation was controversial in Egypt, which had a powerful priestly caste that pressured Akhenaten to revert to traditional religious beliefs. The woman with whom Akhenaten had six daughters and who, in Akhenaten's words, was "the Hereditary Princess, Great of Favor, Mistress of Happiness... Great and Beloved Wife of the King... Nefertiti" largely disappears from the historical record in the twelfth year of his reign. Many scholars believe she retired to the northern palace at Amarna after a confrontation with Akhenaten in which she proved unwilling to abandon exclusive worship of Aton. Nefertiti is perhaps best known from the painted limestone bust that was discovered at Tell el-Amarna, the ruins of the ancient capital, Akhetaton, from which she reigned until her fall from grace.

Robert Fay

Latin America and the Caribbean

Negrista Poets, a group of Latin American and Caribbean poets, mostly white and middle class, who incorporated black themes of folklore, religious practices, music, and dance in their work. Writing principally from the 1930s through the 1950s, the group included such writers as LUIS PALÉS MATOS and Emilio Ballagas of PUERTO RICO and Ramón Güirao and José Zacarías Tallet of CUBA.

First and foremost, *negrista*, or "blackish" poetry, also known as *poesía negroide* (negroid poetry) or *afroantillano* (afro-antillean, the term preferred by Luis Palés Matos), should not be confused with *poesía negra*, or black poetry. Though some studies group authors of so-called blackish and black poetry, poesía negra – also identified as *poesía mulata* (mulatto poetry, the term preferred by Afro-Cuban poet NICOLÁS GUILLÉN), *afrocubanista* (*see* AFROCUBANISMO), or Afro-Hispanic – generally refers to poetry written mostly by black and mulatto authors that reflects a social and cultural investment in black communities. In contrast, negrista poetry, or the *negrismo* movement more generally, refers to works by mostly white, middle-class writers who exoticized blacks and mulattos in their poems. Both definitions represent an extreme; many poets fell somewhere in between on the spectrum.

In 1925 the Puerto Rican poet Palés Matos published "Black Town," which in the view of some scholars initiated the negrista poetry movement. Others cite earlier poems published in the 1920s, such as "The African Dancer," by Emilio Ballagas, or "Black Man and Black Woman," by Llorens Torres. In any case, as literary critic Leslie Wilson notes, negrista poetry conjures racist stereotypes of "pseudo-African rhythms and expressions... grotesque gestures and simian capers for provoking white laughter... jiving, high-stepping Black carousers... and sinewy, vivacious, voluptuous, and carefree Black and mulatto women who light the lamps of love."

Caricaturesque portrayals of blacks emerged in negrista poetry that were fashioned largely to satisfy a growing penchant for African themes in art and literature, sparked by nineteenth-century scholars who had written of their travels to Africa. Wilson explains that scholars like the German Leo Frobenius "thronged to Dark Africa to drink from its bountiful fountain of human knowledge and artistic inspiration." Ethnographic narratives about sub-Saharan Africa and anthologies of oral literature of African kingdoms like Benin, Mali, and Songhai, compiled by European travelers, captured the attention of artists and intellectuals both in Europe and in Latin America, resulting in a burgeoning audience for all things African. Negrista poetry exoticized black themes, incorporating them as curiosities for a largely white, elite audience. The thematic and formal characteristics of much of this poetry included the use of "black" musical forms as a basis for linguistic and literary experiments; onomatopoeic words; African words, allusions to a mythical Africa; oral histories; and religious practices, dances, and beliefs.

In contrast, black poetry generally resisted the folkloric in favor of a poetics that denoted a social and linguistic collective history. Thus it was not a poetry that imitated or recreated superficial cultural expressions or racist stereotypes, but one that tried to invoke a social and cultural authenticity in relating everyday black and mulatto experiences. Still, such divisions between blackish and black poetry were not always well defined in the 1940s and 1950s. As Wilson observes, Guillén himself wrote folkloric poems at one point in his career, and one of the negrista poets, Emilio Ballagas, published a poem that advocated racial harmony and solidarity with his Afro-Cuban compatriots.

In the 1930s Cuban scholar Fernando Ortiz's anthropological studies in Latin America as well as the dominance of Afro-Cuban music throughout the world contributed to the popularity of negrismo as an intellectual and artistic movement. Unlike NÉGRITUDE in the Francophone Caribbean, negrista poetry tended to essentialize black and mulatto stereotypes. While Négritude represented a key movement for black pride and political independence for MARTINIQUE and GUADELOUPE, negrismo's political implications are more ambiguous. Early on, in the 1920s, many negrista poets remained essentially aloof to everyday black and mulatto experiences, preferring to portray blacks with mythical or comical connotations. However, in Cuba, for example, when middle-class artists began to feel the pressure of the Gerardo Machado dictatorship in the 1930s, they ironically turned to Afro-Cubans, targets of much discrimination at the time, as models for forging a national identity. Influenced by Afrocubanismo and by the HARLEM RENAISSANCE, some negrista poets, like Emilio Ballagas, would invoke mulatto nationalism. Still others, Palés Matos in particular, argued for a Pan-Caribbean or Antillean identity but remained focused on technical poetic innovation rather than the social status of Afro-Cubans. Thus some links between early blackish poets and black poets were established, though the two were distinct movements that implied very different sociocultural viewpoints. Negrista poets, by most scholars' accounts, stereotyped blacks in their writings. Such portrayals mostly affirmed elite ideas about blacks and the "popular classes," yet they were influential in ushering Afro-Caribbean themes to the forefront of emerging national identities.

Joy Elizondo

SEE ALSO
Benin, Early Kingdom of; Ortiz, Fernando; Songhai Empire; Image of the Mulatta in Latin America and the Caribbean; Mali Empire.

Cross Cultural

Négritude, neologism coined by Martinican poet and statesman AIMÉ CÉSAIRE in Paris in the 1930s in discussions with fellow students LÉOPOLD SÉDAR SENGHOR and LÉON-GONTRAN DAMAS.

The concept of Négritude represents a historic development in the formulation of African diasporic identity and culture in this century. The term marks a revalorization of Africa on the part of New World blacks, affirming an overwhelming pride in black heritage and culture, and asserting, in Marcus Garvey's words, that blacks are "descendants of the greatest and proudest race who ever peopled the earth." The concept finds its roots in the thought of Martin Delany, EDWARD WILMOT BLYDEN, and W. E. B. Du Bois, each of whom sought to erase the stigma attached to the black world through their intellectual and political efforts on behalf of the African diaspora. Early in this century French Caribbean politicians such as HÉGÉSIPPE LÉGITIMUS, René Boisneuf, and Gratien Candace affirmed the right and necessity of blacks to enter into the global community as equals, while historians such as Oruno Lara strove to "edify a more beautiful past, drawing upon our heritage of sacrifice and probity." The inspiration for Césaire's term comes most directly, however, from the example of the HARLEM RENAISSANCE, in which writers such as LANGSTON HUGHES and CLAUDE MCKAY explored and revindicated the richness of black culture. Léopold Senghor himself referred to McKay as "the true inventor of [the values of] Négritude.... Far from seeing in one's blackness an inferiority, one accepts it, one lays claim to it with pride, one cultivates it lovingly." Like the evolution of the term "black" in the United States, Négritude took a stigmatized term and turned it into a point of pride.

As a historical movement, Négritude received two competing interpretations. Césaire's original conception sees the specificity and unity of black existence as a historically developing phenomenon that arose through the highly contingent events of the African slave trade and New World plantation system (*see* TRANSATLANTIC SLAVE TRADE). This formulation was gradually displaced in intellectual debate by Senghor's essentialist interpretation of Négritude, which argues for an unchanging core or essence to black existence. As this later formulation gained currency, it was widely attacked, all the more so as Senghor, then president of an independent SENEGAL, came to use the term ideologically to justify his own political platform. Senghor's Négritude nonetheless served to reverse the system of values that had informed Western perception of blacks since the earliest voyages of discovery to Africa. Césaire's developmental model of Négritude, on the other hand, continues to offer a model for the ongoing project of black liberation in all its fullness, at once spiritual and political.

First used by Césaire in his 1939 poem "Cahier d'un retour au pays natal" (Notebook of a Return to My Native Land), Négritude refers to a collective identity of the African diaspora born of a common historico-cultural experience of subjugation. Césaire writes, "Négritude, not a cephalic index, or a plasma, or a soma, but measured by the compass of suffering." Both the term and the subsequent literary and cultural movement that developed equally emphasized the possible negation of that subjugation via concerted actions of racial affirmation, of which the HAITIAN REVOLUTION (1791-1804) is the prototype. In succeeding decades the term became a focus for ideological disputes among the black intelligentsia of a Francophone world in the process of decolonization, and writers such as Senghor, FRANTZ FANON, (*see* LITERATURE, FRENCH LANGUAGE, IN CARIBBEAN), and the Anglophone WOLE SOYINKA each weighed in with his own reformulations and critiques of Césaire's concept. Négritude as a concept encompassed and distilled a wide range of previous historical moments, in turn generating a diverse field of debate that has, in its use of the term, extended, and at times even contradicted, Césaire's original intervention.

ORIGINS OF NÉGRITUDE
The historical origins of Négritude can be traced to the various forms of cultural expression in the French Caribbean that find their roots in the African continent, practices that were transmogrified by the experience of THE MIDDLE PASSAGE and slavery. Like the North American spirituals first championed in *The Souls of Black Folk*, by W. E. B. Du Bois, a variety of arts and practices served as refuges for Afro-Caribbean pride and African culture: the dances called *calenda, bamboula,* and *laghia* (*see* DANCE IN LATIN AMERICA AND THE CARIBBEAN); the drumming and songs of the *bel-air, Gwoka,* and *léwoz* (*see* MUSIC, AFRO-CARIBBEAN SECULAR); Creole culinary arts; the *Kric-Krac* folktales; and the multitude of practices arising from Haitian VODOU.

Forced underground by the violence and racism of slavery, this proto-Négritude manifested itself less as overt, self-proclaimed affirmation than through the concrete, positive production of cultural, religious, and aesthetic practices. In addition, black slaves at times responded to the threat of annihilation with self-affirmation in the form of overt resistance: feigned laziness, ignorance, or incompetence; theft; poisoning of animals and burning of buildings; escape into maroon communities (*see* MAROONAGE IN THE AMERICAS), and organized revolts (*see* SLAVE REBELLIONS IN LATIN AMERICA AND THE CARIBBEAN).

The social dynamics of a Caribbean society created through the institution of slavery and its vehicle, the plantation (in its French variant, *l'habitation*), resulted in a powerful ideological valorization of and identification with a highly centralized metropolitan French culture. For commentators such as EDOUARD GLISSANT, this identification explains the success and longevity of a French colonial project that, in his estimation, continues to this day in the very Martinique that Aimé Césaire helped to integrate juridically in 1945. This overwhelming cultural identification points to the radicality of Césaire's revalorization of African, rather than French, culture. The Franco-centric cultural reference also explains why literary models for Négritude must be sought elsewhere in the African diaspora. No equivalent of OLAUDAH EQUIANO's 1789 slave narrative, *Interesting Narrative of the Life of Olaudah Equiano...* , or the various autobiographical narratives of Anglophone authors such as PHILLIS WHEATLEY, OTTOBAH CUGOANO, and Frederick Douglass, appears to have survived in French Antillean letters. The French Code Noir of 1685 (*see* BLACK CODES IN LATIN AMERICA) had forbidden blacks to read or write, and remained in effect through 1848. The authors PATRICK CHAMOISEAU and RAPHAËL CONFIANT have described how, in a century and a half of literary production preceding Césaire, Martinican writing was characterized by a triple rupture. "From oral to written [production], a rupture of enunciation; from the Creole language to French, a rupture of language; from the storyteller to the writer, a temporal-spatial rupture." The result was a literature entirely subordinated to a "French cultural superego," mimetically echoing succeeding French literary fashions (Romantic, Parnassian, then Symbolist poetry), mired in the tradition of literary exoticism (*doudouisme*).

Despite the fundamental importance of the German philosopher Hegel for both Césaire and subsequent participants in the Négritude debate such as Fanon, Richard Wright, and Jean-Paul Sartre, an insidious aspect of Hegel's philosophy decisively marked the development of proto-Négritude thought in the nineteenth century. Hegel notoriously exempted blacks from the processes of historical development in his *Philosophy of History*, stating that their "condition is capable of no development of Culture, and as we see them at this day, such they have always been." Hegel's thesis participated in the development of a biological racism, whose main proponents in the French tradition were the doctor J. J. Virey, the biologist Georges Cuvier, and the writer Joseph-Arthur de Gobineau. This field of thought articulated a belief in the inferiority of blacks based on supposed physical and intellectual traits, furthermore presupposing the existence of discrete "races" that modern genetics has repeatedly disproved. In response, writers such as Alexander Crummell, Martin Robison Delany, and Edward Wilmot Blyden sought to rescue the image of Africa for New World blacks. Delany organized the first scientific expedition to Africa from the Western Hemisphere and is acknowledged as the founder of Black Nationalism in America, while Blyden undertook the revalorization of African history after Hegel's blanket condemnation, developing as well an early form of Pan-Africanist thought that prefigures the championing of African culture enacted in Césaire's Négritude. Du Bois continued this turn to Africa and initiated reflection upon the formal continuities of African diasporic culture. The fruits of that more general reflection informed Du Bois's critique of North American racism in works such as *The Souls of Black Folk* in ways strikingly similar to Césaire's later critique of the specific forms of French racism as found in Martinique and Paris. Though not well known to Césaire in 1939, intellectual forerunners like Du Bois, Delany, and Blyden thus anticipated that aspect of Négritude that strives for the revalorization of Africa in French Caribbean culture.

Certain lone figures in the French Caribbean also participated in the affirmation of black culture. The early years of the French Third Republic (1871-1940) witnessed profound changes in Martinican and Guadeloupean culture. Economies previously based on the production of sugar cane were thrown into a long decline that would continue into this century, after the introduction of cheaply produced sugar beets undercut global sugar prices, making competition impossible. This recession, combined with the presence of a black proletariat and nascent middle class following the abolition of slavery in the French colonies in 1848, paved the way for the novel success of black socialist politicians such as Légitimus of Guadeloupe. Martinican politics remained dominated through this period by members of the white land-owning *béké* class, such as Ernest Deproge and Osman Duquesnay. In contrast, a relatively small béké population in Guadeloupe led that island's elected positions to be filled by representatives of the mulatto bourgeoisie, such as Gerville-Réache, Sarlat, Auguste Isaac, and Emile Réaux. The electoral defeat of the mulatto Isaac by Légitimus in 1898 signals the triumph of black electoral politics in the region, foreshadowing Césaire's 50-year dominance of Martinican politics as both mayor of Fort-de-France and Martinican representative in the French General Assembly. If Légitimus's early affirmation of racial pride and solidarity predated the Négritude movement by three decades, his recourse to race baiting in electoral politics soon reduced him to inflammatory diatribes against mulatto politicians, whom he referred to as "parasites" and "yellow politicians." Other black Guadeloupean politicians, such as René Boisneuf and Gratien Candace, continued the processes initiated by Légitimus in the years before the emergence of Négritude. Candace, along with Césaire one of the leading black political figures in French politics of the twentieth century, was one of the first black colonial leaders to begin questioning French racial and colonial hegemony.

World War I had brought blacks from the French Caribbean colonies of Martinique, Guadeloupe, and French Guiana to Europe. Already benefiting from full French citizenship since 1848, they, along with Senegalese blacks, fought beside metropolitan and black American soldiers (*see* World War I and African Americans) and sent representatives to the French parliament following the war. Blaise Diagne of Senegal and Candace organized the first Pan-African Congress with Du Bois in 1919, immediately following the armistice. Though only tentative steps were taken in condemning colonialism at the congress, it nonetheless marked the beginnings of a truly international solidarity among members of the African diaspora.

In addition, a series of journals, publications, and organizations appeared that prefigure the Négritude of Aimé Césaire. In 1924 Kojo Tovalou Houénou of Benin founded the Ligue universelle de défense de la race noire, which two years later would change its name to the Comité de défense de la race nègre. The league's journal, *La Voix des Nègres*, quotes Légitimus's revindication of black pride: "We honor and glorify ourselves in using the word 'Black' [Nègre] with a capital B." In 1927 Lenis Blanche founded an Association des étudiants guadeloupéens, while the Comité de défense confusingly changed its name again to become the Ligue de défense de la race nègre, arguing in its journal, *La Race Nègre*, for collaboration between (Francophone) black intellectuals and workers and calling for a student-led Pan-Africanism. In 1928 the Internationale Syndicale Rouge published in Moscow *L'Ouvrier Nègre*, in defense of "the disinherited son of the proletarian family." In 1931 the Ligue split, and Tiémoko Garan Kouyaté founded, with the Martinican communist Trissot, the journal *Le Cri des Nègres*. This black communist journal vigorously defended Antillean workers, and its circulation was severely limited by the French authorities.

In the realm of black cultural production, *La Dépêche africaine*, published from 1928 to 1930 with the participation of René Maran and the Nardal sisters, saw its mission as forming a "juncture between Negroes of the entire world" via the valorization of black aesthetic and intellectual production. In 1928 the publication of Jean Price-Mars's *Ainsi parla l'oncle* (So Spoke the Uncle) was the first overt condemnation of the colonial identification with French culture, which had led, in Price-Mars's famous formulation, to a "collective boveryism," or romanticized yearning for French cultural products and the denigration of African-derived culture such as Haitian Vodou. In 1931 the *Revue du monde noir* valorized black cultural production, positioning itself as a moderate, pro-assimilationist voice. Far more radical, the revue *Légitime Défense*, founded in 1932 by the Martinican Etienne Léro, combined in its single published issue discourses of Surrealism, Hegelian Marxism, and Freudianism in its vehement condemnation of French colonialism, racism, and capitalist exploitation. Despite a certain lack of depth in its analysis and the immaturity of its poetic texts, it marked a fundamental step in the assertion of black identity in the Francophone world. In 1934 the 21-year-old student Césaire, along with Gilbert Gratiant, Léonard Sainville, Paulette Nardal, and Césaire's fellow student Senghor, founded the review *L'Etudiant Noir*. More moderate in tone than *Légitime Défense*, it nonetheless contains Césaire's first published text, the poem "Nègreries," in which he clearly prefigures Négritude in his forceful, affirmative use of the stigmatized term "nègre," refusing the assimilation of blacks into French society in favor of "emancipation."

Throughout the 1920s the triumph of Russian Bolshevism was followed closely throughout the African diaspora. Though the French Communist Party long regarded colonialism as strictly subsidiary to the triumph of European proletarian revolution, journals such as *Les Continents* (founded in 1924 by René Maran and Kodjo Touvalou) and, in particular, *L'Action coloniale* (founded in 1918 by Maurice Boursaud) were fundamental in articulating a preliminary Marxist condemnation of colonialism. An increasing social and juridical permeability between colonized and colonizer helped make possible the rapid changes in black consciousness that occurred through the 1920s and 1930s.

The HARLEM RENAISSANCE was also central to Césaire's concept of Négritude. Césaire wrote a dissertation on the movement in the 1930s, and LANGSTON HUGHES, CLAUDE MCKAY, JAMES WELDON JOHNSON, JEAN TOOMER, and COUNTEE CULLEN were already well known among the Paris-based Antillean intelligentsia when Césaire arrived there in 1931. The Jamaican McKay in particular, in works such as *Banjo*, expressed a keen perception of the fractures dividing black cultures along lines of pigmentation and class. Indeed, Senghor has gone so far as to cite McKay as the spiritual founder of Négritude: "Claude McKay can rightfully be considered the true inventor of Négritude. I speak not of the word, but of the values of Négritude.... Far from seeing in one's blackness an inferiority, one accepts it, one lays claim to it with pride, one cultivates it lovingly." Léon-Gontran Damas's 1930 collection of poems, *Pigments*, powerfully appropriated many of McKay's insights, its violent condemnation of racial division and colonialist assimilation serving as the most immediate spur to Césaire's invention of Négritude. In Haiti a similar renaissance occurred during the 1920s and 1930s, as journals like the *Revue indigène* and writers such as JACQUES ROUMAIN, Emile Roumer, and Jacques Stéphen Aléxis developed the racial revindication articulated in Price-Mars's *Ainsi parla l'oncle*.

The work of another Caribbean, Marcus Garvey, though unknown to Césaire in 1939, prefigures the concept of Négritude in more than one respect. Garvey's critique of an assimilationist black middle class announces that of French Antilleans such as Léro and Césaire, while his revalorization of African culture is similar to both Césaire's and Senghor's subsequent development of Négritude. "Negroes," Garvey implored, "teach your children that they are direct descendants of the greatest and proudest race who ever peopled the earth." In 1933 the Jamaican Leonard Percival Howell founded the Rastafarian movement, striving to "construct the black race economically, the better to serve God." Elsewhere in the Caribbean, Cuban poets allied with the *Revista de Estudios Afrocubanos*, while Nicolas Guillén in particular, and the Cuban painter WIFREDO LAM, sought to explore and valorize their African heritage (*see* AFROCUBANISMO).

Certain European intellectuals were central to the elaboration of Négritude. The fashionable interest in African art and culture that arose in 1920s Paris in the work of Pablo Picasso, the writers Jean Cocteau, Blaise Cendrars, and André Gide, and the composer Darius Milhaud made reference to an often vague amalgam known as "l'art nègre." Too often, little effort was made to differentiate between the cultural traditions of regions as diverse as Dakar, Senegal, BAHIA, BRAZIL, and HARLEM, NEW YORK, in deference to a putative "black soul." Nonetheless, this movement created a climate of receptivity in which intellectuals such as André Breton and Sartre would quickly recognize the importance of Négritude in the 1940s. Anthropologists also turned to Africa and its diaspora in these years. Maurice Delafosse, in his 1927 work *Les Nègres*, applied to African culture the methods of ethnographic analysis. The German Leo Frobenius's *History of African Civilization* was translated into French in 1936 and avidly read by both Césaire and Senghor. "We knew by heart chapter II of the first book of the History," Senghor has written, "entitled 'What does Africa mean to us?' a chapter adorned with lapidary phrases such as this: 'The idea of the "barbarous Negro" is a European invention, which in turn dominated Europe until the beginning of this century.'" Frobenius's work, along with Oswald Spengler's *The Decline of the West* (1918), provided Césaire and Senghor with a conception of history in which a tired, defeated West might be superseded by more vital African diasporic cultures.

Césaire's revindication of the term "nègre," though mirroring parallel processes occurring in the North American adoption first of "black," then "African American" as self-designations, occurred in a specific historical and linguistic environment. In 1939, when Césaire's poem appeared, the term "noir" ("black") roughly corresponded to the socially valorized North American "negro." The traditional French Caribbean identification with metropolitan French culture also meant, in the view of commentators like Frantz Fanon, that black Antilleans were largely alienated from their African roots. In Fanon's words, the Antillean black until 1939 conceived of Africa as "a country of savages, of barbarians, of natives, of 'boys'.... The African was a nigger [nègre] and the Antillean a European." In France during the 1920s and 1930s, "nègre," particularly in its adjectival form, was used more or less interchangeably with "noir" ("l'art nègre," "la musique nègre"). In Martinique, however, the term "nègre" shared a functional similarity with the racist North American epithet "nigger." A. James Arnold credits Césaire with being the first black intellectual outside Africa to have taken the humiliating term "nigger" and boldly transformed it into the proud term "black." The specificity of Césaire's intervention and affirmation arises from this highly specific historical conjuncture of self-alienation, in which, Fanon states, "haunted by impurity, overwhelmed by sin, ridden by guilt, [the Antillean] lives the drama of being neither white nor black [nègre]."

In addition to its historical importance, Césaire's coining of the term "Négritude" possesses a philosophical dimension later developed in the work of Fanon (1952) and Sartre. Theoretically, and in contradistinction to the uses and abuses that the term would undergo in succeeding decades, Négritude in Césaire's poem possesses a decidedly objective status, as the poet refuses to affirm the unity of black identity. Previous articulations of black identity in the Francophone world opted uniformly for the latter. Earlier in the century – to cite two relevant examples – Hégésippe Légitimus had affirmed with pride his status as "nègre," while Oruno Lara in his 1921 *History of Guadeloupe* proclaimed his pride to be a "writer of the black race." Lara states that his book – a little-known precursor to Négritude – is "the image of the painful and formidable creation of an American continent wrought with African tears and blood," written to serve "our advancement." The first black historian of the region and author of the 1923 novel *Questions de couleur: Blanches et noires* went on to affirm that "If, born yesterday, we seem to have neither a past, nor civil status, it was up to one of us to edify a more beautiful past, drawing upon our heritage of sacrifice and probity."

Césaire's concept of Négritude, in contrast to these and many other postulations of black identity that came before it, objectifies the self-alienation of colonized black subjects through an act of creation: the neologism. In Césaire's usage, an alienated black identity is forced to confront itself as a reified object:

ma négritude n'est pas une pierre,
sa surdité ruée contre la clameur du jour
ma négritude n'est pas une taie d'eau morte sur l'œil
mort de la terre
ma négritude n'est ni une tour ni une cathédrale
elle plonge dans la chair rouge du sol
elle plonge dans la chair ardente du ciel
elle troue l'accablement opaque de sa droite patience.

(my Négritude is not a stone, its deafness dashed against / the clamor of the day / my Négritude is not an opaque spot of dead water / on the dead eye of the earth / my Négritude is neither a tower nor a cathedral / it plunges into the red flesh of the soil / it plunges into the ardent flesh of the sky / it pierces opaque prostration with its upright patience.)

This conception postulates Négritude as self-estrangement, a fact or quality that confronts the black subject as an object. Such a gesture initiates a movement in Césaire's poem toward a self-consciousness that breaks the bonds of subjugation through a grappling with negativity in the form of self-alienation. Négritude "is not" the lifeless object society has reduced it to (stone, spot, or even tower). Instead, it is active, creative, and liberatory ("plunging," "piercing" through the world that had enchained it in subjection). Césaire applies to the realm of black subjectivity Hegel's insight that "alienation" is in fact a transformational process in which the individual's so-called "natural" existence – in this case the ideological subjugation of blacks – is concretely negated for an artificial, self-created one: "[The self's] actuality consists solely in the setting-aside of its natural self.... The self knows itself as actual only as a transcended self." Césaire's neologism is at once the naming and active instantiation of the very process it describes, tracing the liberation of black subjectivity through a confrontation with racism and colonialism. Négritude is thus for Césaire the self-created object that negates the very objectivity of black existence itself – where humans are reduced to pure animal-objects (slaves) – in a becoming-human. Humans, following Marx's articulation of Hegel, "distinguish themselves from animals as soon as they begin to produce.... " In the concept of Négritude, Aimé Césaire produced the material, textual objectification of black self-consciousness, a program for self-understanding and liberation.

The Growth of Négritude as a Movement

When Aimé Césaire returned to Martinique in 1939, the term "Négritude" was known and used only by the small circle of black intellectuals who had surrounded Césaire in Paris, in particular Senghor and Damas. Césaire's "Cahier" was itself virtually unknown, having appeared only in an obscure Parisian review, *Volontés*. During the occupation of Martinique by the Nazi-controlled Vichy government, Césaire, along with his wife, Suzanne, René Menil, and Aristide Maugée, edited from 1941 to 1945 the journal *Tropiques*. The journal enacted a profound refusal of white European cultural values and references in favor of those of the African diaspora. Unlike Césaire's earlier historicizing use of the term "Négritude," articles such as "What Does Africa Mean to Us?" argued for a biologically based notion of black identity inherited from Frobenius, in which a black "biological reality" is invoked to account for black identity. During this period, as A. James Arnold has argued, both Césaire's and Senghor's uncritical reliance upon a sanguinary ideology of African "blood" resonates disturbingly with fascist doctrine of the era (*see* Eugenics). At the same time *Tropiques* appealed nondogmatically to a heterogeneous field of influences, invoking those elements of a European aesthetic heritage (surrealism, the French poets Rimbaud and Lautréamont) whose iconoclastic work could be appropriated as a tool in refashioning black Caribbean culture.

In 1947 Damas published an anthology of poetry from the French colonies, and in the following year Senghor published a similar collection, *Anthologie de la nouvelle poésie nègre et malgache*. In addition to Césaire, Damas, and Senghor, a number of black Francophone poets and writers produced works that participated indirectly in the project of Négritude, reflecting upon the vicissitudes of black existence. Paul Niger, David Diop, and Guy Tirollien all explored diasporic psyches damaged by colonialism and the contradictions of a dual African and European heritage. The novels of Cheikh Hamadou Kane (*L'Aventure ambiguë*), Mongo Béti (*Pauvre Christ de Bomba*), and Ousmane Sembène (*La Femme noire*) articulated the various forms of alienation encountered by colonized African subjects.

Senghor's 1948 anthology featured a preface by Jean-Paul Sartre, "Black Orpheus," that is largely responsible for establishing the concept of Négritude at the center of postwar Francophone debate regarding black identity. Sartre's position as the dominant postwar Francophone intellectual caused the Négritude debate to focus on his articulation of the concept, with subsequent participants often defining their use of the term in relation to his analysis. Sartre's text develops the Hegelian category of negativity in relation to black consciousness, building on the Russian philosopher Alexandre Kojève's influential lectures on Hegel's master/slave dialectic. Sartre endorses the notion of a racial essence ("The black soul is an Africa from which the black [nègre] is exiled amidst the cold buildings of white culture and technology"), grounding this conception within the undeniable visibility of skin color: "A Jew, a white among whites, can deny that he is a Jew, declaring himself a man among men. The black cannot deny that he is black nor claim for himself an abstract, colorless humanity: he is black. Thus he is driven to authenticity: insulted, enslaved, he raises himself up. He picks up the word 'black' [nègre] that they had thrown at him like a stone, he asserts his blackness, facing the white man, with pride."

Fanon critiques Senghor's famous statement "Emotion is black as Reason is Hellenic," indicting Césaire and Senghor's glorification of the irrational as a "regressive process" in his 1952 study *Black Skin, White Masks*. He then proceeds to attack Sartre's interpretation of Négritude as what the latter termed an "antiracist racism." Fanon critiques Sartre's reduction of Négritude to "the weak pole (or antithesis) of a dialectical progression" from within the very Hegelian perspective Sartre invokes: "For once, this born Hegelian [Sartre] had forgotten that consciousness needs to lose itself in absolute night, this being the only requirement for the attainment of self-consciousness." Fanon violently refuses Sartre's vision of an instrumentalized black identity dissolved in the Hegelian *aufhebung* (sublation) of a "raceless society," asserting: "I am not a potentiality for something. I am fully that which I am."

In 1947 Alioune Diop of Senegal began in Paris the journal *Présence Africaine* with the backing of the Parisian and colonial intelligentsia, including Gide, Sartre, Albert Camus, Césaire, and many others. The journal was fundamental in articulating the parameters of African diasporic culture, addressing a global audience of English and French speakers in more than a half century of publication. In addition, *Présence Africaine* sponsored a series of celebrated conferences uniting black scholars of the world, at the Sorbonne in 1956 and in Rome in 1959. In 1966 *Présence Africaine* also sponsored the First World Festival of Negro Arts in Dakar, Senegal. By the time Senghor organized the Colloquium on Négritude in 1971, Négritude had itself become a highly contested term, whose interpretation had rigidified into a largely ideological concept.

During the postwar period the concept of Négritude developed along two opposing lines of interpretation. The first sustains the notion as a cultural, historically developing process. This, we have seen, was implicit in Césaire's original conception of the term, and he increasingly abandoned any notion of Négritude as based on a genetic or "blood" inheritance: "My Négritude has a ground. It is a fact that there is a black culture: it is historical, there is nothing biological about it." Similarly, recent interpretations of Fanon's work have underlined its historical dimensions; in this view, the author of *The Wretched of the Earth*, following Hegel's 1804 *Phenomenology of Spirit*, undertakes a veritable phenomenology of black consciousness as it moves from immersion in the immediacy of experience to self-consciousness and fully historical, human existence. In contrast, Senghor's notion of Négritude, and the general reception and critique of the concept in West Africa following Senghor, focused on the putatively "African" characteristics of emotion, intuition, and artistic creativity as opposed to a Western, or "Hellenic," rationality.

Senghor elaborates his conception of Négritude in various texts collected in the five-volume work *Liberté*. Dismissing without engaging the scientific invalidation of races, Senghor constructs a typology of an "eternal... black soul" based on the categories of "emotion," "rhythmic attitude," "humor," and "anthropopsychism." This last trait refers to the unmediated relation of the "black soul" to the phenomenological world, the "eternal... essential" trait, Senghor affirms, of the black soul. Though this early formulation dates from 1939, Senghor continued to defend and develop this conception of an "african personality" in the 1966 text "Négritude is a Humanism of the Twentieth Century," arguing tautologically for the objective existence of such a category [the "african personality"], since it had been accepted as a given over "60 years" of ethnological and sociological investigation. In this text Senghor further elaborates his articulation of an immediate black apprehension of phenomena, invoking the philosophers Henri Bergson and Pierre Teilhard de Chardin. Senghor's Négritude is, to use his own term, an ontology, or study of the being of blacks in the world, a fundamentally ahistorical, transcultural determination of the constituents and commonalities of "blackness" in African diasporic societies. In 1969 he refers to it as a modification of the Hedeggerian Dasein, a "Neger-sein" or "black being." As Senghor himself pointed out in 1993, this ontological definition of Négritude has become the accepted one: in the standard French *Robert* dictionary, we find the definition "The ensemble of characteristics, of manners of thinking, of feeling, proper to the black race; belonging to the black race." There follows a quotation of Senghor. No mention is made of Césaire's act of neologism. Senghor's Négritude reverses the stigmatization of blacks derived from the nineteenth-century racialism of Gobineau, Lucien Lévy-Bruhl's concept of a prelogical "primitive mentality," and fictional works such as Paul Morand's stereotype-laden novel, *Magie noire* (1928). Senghor's postulation of an African ontology is echoed in works such as Placied Tempel's *La Philosophie bantoue* (1949). In turn, philosophers such as Marcien Towa (*Essai sur la problématique philosophique dans l'Afrique actuelle,* 1971) and Paulin Hountondji (*Sur la "Philosophie africaine,"* 1977) have questioned whether traditional African philosophies can truly sustain such ontological interpretations.

Due to Senghor's overwhelming cultural and political influence in West Africa (he was president of Senegal from its independence in 1960 till 1979), it is precisely this ontological conception of Négritude that fueled attacks by writers such as Stanislas Adotevi. Adotevi's 1972 study *Négritude et négrologues* argues against a Senghorian racial explanation for African suffering in deference to a Marxist model of global capitalist exploitation. The Anglophone African nations received Négritude primarily as a politicized, ideological movement. Writers such as Es'kia Mphahlele, in *The African Image* (1962), and Wole Soyinka, in *Myth, Literature, and the African World* (1976), attacked a perceived cultural imperialism on the part of Francophone African intellectuals, the latter stating that "the tiger does not stalk about crying his tigritude." Senghor, responding to these attacks in 1969, points to the Anglophone historical derivation of Négritude from the African American writers of the Harlem Renaissance.

In the French Caribbean, Césaire's notion of Négritude has been developed and extended by another of his students, the writer Edouard Glissant. Glissant's notion of "antillanité," developed in works such as the 1981 *Caribbean Discourse*, envisages an opening of black experience to the entirety of global culture. Like Césaire's earlier critique of cultural assimilation, Glissant argues against subsuming or dissolving an African and Creole Martinican identity in the economic and cultural imperialism of a North American-led "New World Order," without, on the other hand, limiting that region to a stifling provincialism. Other Antilleans have been more critical of aspects of Césaire's concept. The Guadeloupean author Maryse Condé critiques the notion of a return to Africa by black Antilleans in novels such as *Heremakonon* (1976). Her 1974 article "Négritude césairienne, Négritude senghorienne," while drawing attention to Césaire's neologism, offers a trenchant warning against the fetishization of blackness: "The Black (Nègre) does not exist.... [Négritude] is a sentimental and empty trap. Starting from an illusory 'racial' community founded upon a heritage of suffering, it obliterates the true problems that have always been of a political, social, and economic nature.... Our liberation will come through the knowledge that there will never be any Blacks (Nègres). There has only ever been human exploitation." Condé's critique implies that Césaire's Négritude cannot remain a mere invocation to black identity politics; instead, the shock of its alienating gesture must serve to illuminate the very constructedness of "blackness" itself.

More recently, Jean Bernabé, Patrick Chamoiseau, and Raphaël Confiant attacked what they see as the mythologization of Africa in Césaire's Négritude, affirming instead the heterogeneous status of Antillean culture, with its French, Hindu, Chinese, Amerindian, and African elements. This attack reaches its apex in Confiant's 1993 polemic against Césaire, *Une traversée paradoxale du siècle.*

The concept of Négritude represents a fundamental development in notions of African diasporic identity and culture in this century. The African and Antillean controversies around the term's reception and its rigidification into a politicized, ideological category initiated one of the fundamental debates in postwar global black thought, while Senghor's elaboration of the term itself constituted a radical reversal of dominant racialist discourse in the West. Finally, Césaire's historicizing phenomenological use of the term remains largely unexplored, implying for the black subject a developmental model of enlightenment that sustains and advances the transformational project of black liberation, pointing beyond the circularity of identity politics toward the elusive instantiation of a fully realized utopian freedom.

Nick Nesbitt

See Also

Béti, Mongo; Dakar, Senegal; Alexis, Jacques Stéphen; Fanon, Frantz; France; Pan-Africanism; Price-Mars, Jean; Ousmane Sembène; Senegal; Pan-African Congress of 1919; Delany, Martin Robison; Douglass, Frederick; Du Bois, William Edward Burghardt (W. E. B.); Garvey, Marcus Mosiah; Slave Narratives; Cuba; Guillén, Nicolás; Rastafarians; Guadeloupe; Haiti; Martinique; Spirituals, African American; Languages, Creole, in the Caribbean; Black Nationalism in the United States; Howell, Leonard P.

North America

Negro American Labor Council,

AFL-CIO splinter group of black workers who organized in 1960 to pressure the federation to end discrimination in its affiliate unions, and who became a driving force behind the 1963 March on Washington.

In May 1960, after the AFL-CIO refused to impose sanctions against affiliate unions practicing discrimination, 75 African American trade unionists formed the Negro American Labor Council (NALC). Under the leadership of A. Philip Randolph, president of the Brotherhood of Sleeping Car Porters, the new organization set out to accelerate the unionization of black workers and to put blacks into positions of union leadership. The broader aim of the group was to end discrimination against blacks in hiring and promotion.

By 1961 membership in the NALC had swelled to 10,000 across the nation. That year Randolph presented a series of demands to the AFL-CIO Executive Council. Asserting that the status of black workers in the labor movement was that of "second class citizenship," he called on the federation to end discrimination within its ranks. This would require, he said, not only ending the color bar in affiliate unions and desegregating unions, but also placing African Americans on the AFL-CIO Executive Council and fighting to abolish barriers to employment training programs. The AFL-CIO's immediate response was to censure Randolph, and its officers charged that he himself had created the breach between blacks and labor with his accusations. At its fall convention, the federation passed a series of civil rights resolutions that vowed an end to discrimination in the union. The AFL-CIO refused to meet the NALC demands fully, however, and left the decision to desegregate a voluntary one for the affiliates.

In one of the group's most important achievements, Randolph and the NALC first envisioned a massive march on Washington to demand jobs. The movement led to the 1963 March on Washington for Jobs and Freedom, where Martin Luther King Jr. gave his famous "I Have a Dream" speech. The AFL-CIO refused to support the march publicly, but other powerful unions, such as the United Auto Workers, did put their force behind it. The 1963 March on Washington solidified alliances between the leaders of the NALC and those of the CIVIL RIGHTS MOVEMENT, which was expanding rapidly in the South.

Marian Aguiar

SEE ALSO

American Federation of Labor and Congress of Industrial Organizations; King, Martin Luther, Jr.; Labor Unions in the United States; Randolph, Asa Philip; March on Washington, 1963.

North America

Negro Ensemble Company,

longest-running black theater company in the United States.

The Negro Ensemble Company was founded in New York City in 1967 by actor-director-playwright Douglas Turner Ward, actor Robert Hooks, and white manager Gerald Krone. Their intent was to provide a space where black playwrights "could communicate with an audience of other Negroes, better informed through commonly shared experience to readily understand, confirm, or reject the truth or paucity of [their] creative explorations." This was during the height of the BLACK ARTS MOVEMENT, and many other companies shared the vision of creating theater by black people for black people. But while others were committed to theater with strong nationalistic and political messages, the Negro Ensemble Company produced a much wider spectrum of plays, including family dramas, folk musicals, and plays from African and Caribbean perspectives.

The company was criticized by more militant artists for its less political messages and for its early support from mainstream white sources such as the Ford Foundation. Its broader appeal, however, gave it staying power. In addition to producing plays, the company also offered actor training programs and playwrights' workshops. The Negro Ensemble Company's most successful productions included Joseph Walker's *The River Niger* (1972), which went to Broadway and won a Tony Award for Best Play of the Year; Charles Fuller's Pulitzer-Prize winning *A Soldier's Play* (1982); and Samm-Art Williams's *Home* (1979), which also became a Broadway success.

Lisa Clayton Robinson

North America

Negro Leagues

Baseball is said to be America's national pastime, but only since the spring of 1947 can it be said to have become truly national. That year Jack Roosevelt Robinson entered the Brooklyn Dodgers lineup, becoming the first African American to play major league baseball since Moses Fleetwood "Fleet" Walker and his brother Weldy played for Toledo in 1884. The exclusion of African Americans from major league baseball paralleled their treatment in other areas of American society. And, like other segregated African American institutions, Negro baseball leagues recognized and developed the talent of black people in their full humanity.

EARLY PROFESSIONAL TEAMS

During the JIM CROW period baseball became one of the most thriving institutions of African American life. Professional teams began forming in the 1880s, including the Philadelphia Orions (1882), the St. Louis Black Stockings (1882), and the Cuban Giants (1885). Under the management of S. K. Govern, the Cuban Giants were immensely successful, spawning numerous African American teams named the Giants, including the Columbia Page Fence Giants, the Chicago Leland Giants, the Brooklyn Royal Giants, and even the Cuban X Giants. The "genuine" Cuban Giants competed in the predominantly white Middle States (minor) League from 1889 to 1891, along with another African American team, the New York Gorhams (or Gothams). In 1886 and 1887 African American baseball leagues were formed but soon folded.

BARNSTORMING

During the height of Jim Crowism, from 1890 to 1920, successful African American baseball teams played outside formal leagues, "barnstorming" the nation. Teams such as the Indianapolis ABCs and the Lincoln Giants went to any town or city that could field an opposing team and promise financial return. The major problem for barnstormers was dependence on white booking agents who controlled the sporting activities in major cities. Games between barnstorming teams were quite lucrative, because they allowed fans to watch black teams face anyone who would play, including teams comprising white major and minor leaguers.

THE NEGRO LEAGUES

At the turn of the century Andrew "Rube" Foster, a star pitcher for several African American teams, envisioned a baseball league for blacks that would rival the white Major League, eventually forcing full recognition and inclusion of African American ballplayers. With partner John Schorling, in 1911, Foster formed the Chicago American Giants and set the foundation for the creation of a "Negro baseball league." In February 1920 Foster founded the Negro National League (NNL) with the owners/representatives of the Indianapolis ABCs, the Chicago Giants, the Kansas City Monarchs (owned by white promoter J. L. Wilkinson), the St. Louis Giants, the Detroit Stars, and the Cuban Stars. As the first enduring professional sports league managed by African Americans, the NNL was widely successful. With players such as sluggers Oscar Charleston, John Henry Lloyd, and the great "Smokey Joe" Williams, the new, mostly Midwestern league garnered much fanfare and popular support in African American communities. In 1923 the Eastern Colored League (ECL) was formed by white booking agent Nat Strong, leading to a feud with the NNL. Tensions were alleviated in 1924 when owners in each league agreed to a system based on the Major League, with split schedules and the two best teams meeting for a "black World Series." During the mid-1920s league teams such as the Birmingham Black Barons and the Cuban Stars enjoyed success in both league play and the ever-fruitful barnstorming circuit.

Both leagues failed, however, soon after Foster's leadership was cut short by mental illness in 1926 and his death in 1930. The ECL folded in 1928 and the NNL in 1931. In 1932 black baseball thrived mainly in the Southern Negro League (which had been a lesser league prior to that year) and in Latin America, where great ball players were welcome regardless of race.

THE REVIVAL OF THE NEGRO LEAGUES

In 1933 the Negro National League was revived by Pittsburgh "numbers" banker Gus Greenlee and several other African American owners. Even though the Great Depression was a catastrophe for black communities, the wealth of Greenlee and other "gangsters" allowed the league to flourish. Beginning with six teams and later expanding to eight, the NNL boasted some of the best baseball talent ever to play the game. Greenlee's Pittsburgh Crawfords competed with the great Homestead Grays for the best local players. Often winning the battle, the Crawfords possessed five future Hall of Fame players at one time: James "Cool" Papa Bell, Oscar Charleston, Josh Gibson, Judy Johnson, and Leroy "Satchel" Paige.

When Greenlee instituted an East-West All Star game to be played each year in Chicago, the amassed talent drew crowds of 30,000 to 40,000, becoming a major social event of the Jim Crow era. The enormous popularity of black baseball led white businessmen to form the Negro American League in 1937, which brought the ever-popular Kansas City Monarchs back into league play. That same year Dominican Republic president RAFAEL TRUJILLO brought future Hall of Famers Satchel Paige, Josh Gibson, and Cool Papa Bell to play on his own team, but they returned to the Negro Leagues the following year.

During this period Latin America was an important arena for baseball because in the winter the best Negro Leaguers played in such nations as CUBA, the DOMINICAN REPUBLIC, and MEXICO with stars of the Major League. Excelling alongside and against white players exposed the lie that African Americans were inferior baseball players. From Latin America, Negro Leaguers moved on to spring training, which was based in the American South. Steadily traveling northward, teams would barnstorm until they reached their home cities. On the way, they would often compete against barnstorming major leaguers.

NEGRO BASEBALL LEAGUES

Negro National League I

Birmingham Black Barons	1925, 1927-1930	Cleveland Elites	1926	Louisville White Sox	1931
Chicago American Giants	1920-1931	Cleveland Hornets	1927	Memphis Red Sox	1924-1925, 1927-1930
Chicago Giants	1920-1921	Cleveland Tate Stars	1922	Milwaukee Bears	1923
Columbus Buckeyes	1921	Dayton Marcos	1920, 1926	Nashville Elite Giants	1930
Cuban Stars	1920, 1922	Detroit Stars	1920-1931	Pittsburgh Keystone	1922
Cleveland Browns	1924	Indianapolis ABC's	1920-1926, 1931	St. Louis Giants	1920-1921
Cleveland Cubs	1931	Kansas City Monarchs	1920-1931	Toledo Tigers	1923

Negro National League II

Bacharach Giants (Atlantic City)	1934	Columbus Blue Birds	1933	New York Black Yankees	1936-1948
Baltimore Black Sox	1933-1934	Columbus Elite Giants	1935	New York Cubans	1935-1936, 1939-1948
Baltimore Elite Giants	1938-1948	Detroit Stars	1933	Philadelphia Stars	1934-1948
Brooklyn Eagles	1935	Harrisburg-St. Louis Stars	1943	Pittsburgh Crawford	1933-1938
Cleveland Giants	1933	Homestead (Pa.) Grays	1935-1948	Washington Black Senators	1938
Cleveland Red Sox	1934	Nashville Elite Giants	1933-1934	Washington Elite Giants	1936-1937
Cole's American Giants (Chicago)	1933-1935	Newark Dodgers	1934-1935		
		Newark Eagles	1936-1948		

Eastern Colored League (American Negro League, 1929)

Bacharach Giants (Atlantic City)	1923-1929	Harrisburg (Pa.) Giants	1924-1927	Newark Stars	1926
Baltimore Black Sox	1923-1929	Hilldale (Philadelphia)	1923-1927, 1929	Philadelphia Tigers	1928
Brooklyn Royal Giants	1923-1927	Homestead (Pa.) Grays	1929	Washington Potomacs	1924
Cuban Stars East	1923-1929	Lincoln Giants (New York)	1923-1926, 1928-1929		

Negro Southern League

Cole's American Giants (Chicago)	1932	Indianapolis ABC's	1932	Monroe Monarchs	1932
		Louisville Black Caps	1932	Montgomery Grey Sox	1932
Columbus Turfs (Ohio)	1932	Memphis Red Sox	1932	Nashville Elite Giants	1932

East-West League

Baltimore Black Sox	Spring 1932	Cuban Stars	Spring 1932	Homestead (Pa.) Grays	Spring 1932
Cleveland Stars	Spring 1932	Hilldale (Philadelphia)	Spring 1932	Newark Browns	Spring 1932

Negro-American League

Atlantic Black Crackers	1938	Cleveland Bears	1939-1940	Kansas City Monarchs	1937-1950
Baltimore Elite Giants	1949-1950	Detroit Stars	1937	Louisville Buckeyes	1949
Birmingham Black Barons	1937-1938, 1940-1950	Houston Eagles	1949-1950	Memphis Red Sox	1937-1941, 1943-1950
		Indianapolis ABC's	1938-1939		
Chicago American Giants	1937-1950	Indianapolis Athletics	1937	New York Cubans	1949-1950
Cleveland Buckeyes	1943-1948, 1950	Indianapolis Clowns	1943-1950	Philadelphia Stars	1949-1950
Cincinnati Buckeyes	1942	Indianapolis Crawfords	1940	St. Louis Stars	1937, 1939, 1941
Cincinnati Tigers	1937	Jacksonville Red Caps	1938, 1941-1942	Toledo Crawfords	1939

Researchers estimate that African American teams won 60 percent of these games.

Demise of the Negro Leagues

The Negro National League folded in 1948, due in great part to Jackie Robinson's integration of the major leagues. Although the Negro American League lasted until 1960, in its later years it failed to capture the imagination of black ticket buyers, who were now watching former Negro Leaguers in the Major Leagues including Monte Irvin (NL: Newark Eagles, ML: New York Giants); Roy Campanella (NL: Baltimore Elite Giants, ML: Brooklyn Dodgers); "Satchel" Paige (NL: Philadelphia Stars, ML: Cleveland Indians); Henry "Hank" Aaron (NL: Indianapolis Clowns, ML: Milwaukee Braves); and Willie Mays (NL: Birmingham Black Barons, ML: New York Giants).

African American baseball players have had a profound impact on major league baseball by bringing to center stage the showmanship and skill that characterized the Negro Leagues. The legacy of vision and excellence proffered by the Negro Leagues has been recognized recently by many Americans and has emerged as a source of great pride, as well as an unavoidable embarrassment to those who permitted the system of exclusion.

See Also
Aaron, Henry Louis (Hank); Baseball in the United States; Gibson, Joshua; Mays, Willie Howard; Numbers Games; Paige, Leroy Robert ("Satchel"); Robinson, Jackie; Baseball in Latin America and the Caribbean.

North America

Negro National Anthem,

the African American national hymn.

"Lift Ev'ry Voice and Sing," popularly considered the Negro national anthem, was composed in 1900 at the Colored

High School in Jacksonville, Florida, by JAMES WELDON JOHNSON and his brother, J. Rosamond Johnson. It is a 34-line poem that expresses the difficulty African Americans have experienced in reaching the present, exemplified in such lines as "Stony the road we trod." Despite acknowledging the pain and disappointment faced by black Americans, the song is essentially a hymn of faith in God, to whom it says, "Thou has brought us thus far on the way," and the Johnsons' lyrics express both hope for the future and American patriotism.

Richard Newman

Latin America and the Caribbean

Nemours, Jean Baptiste and Sicot, Wéber, **musicians who contributed to the development of Haiti's first national pop music. Nemours was a Haitian bandleader during the 1950s and 1960s, a saxophonist, composer, and inventor of the Haitian musical form *compas-direct.* Sicot, initially in Nemours's band, went on to have a career of his own as one of Haiti's most influential musicians.**

During the summer of 1955 Haitian bandleader Jean Baptiste Nemours initiated a transformation of Haitian popular music by creating a new dance rhythm that he called the *compas-direct* (direct beat). At first compas sounded quite similar to the Dominican merengue, which was enormously popular in HAITI at that time (*see* COMPAS). Nevertheless, ethnomusicologist Gage Averill notes an important distinction between the repeated rhythmic pattern of the *tambora* (conga-like drum) in merengue and that of its cousin, the *tanbou*, in compas music. He explains that the pattern on the tanbou is shifted forward one eighth note in compas, spilling over into each following measure. This shift creates an even stronger forward propulsion in compas than is found in the Dominican merengue.

Nemours's composition "Tioule 3" (c. 1955) is generally accepted as the first fully developed example of compas music. The song's orchestration (tanbou, saxophone, accordion, and bass), its rhythms and harmonies, and its use of ostinati and dialogue between instruments all combine to create a form of Haitian popular music that was to endure for decades to come. One Haitian journalist describes Nemours's pioneer status in these terms: "Jean Bapiste Nemours was the first Haitian maestro to grasp the significance of show business. Producing an extremely commercial music, he succeeded in imposing his rhythm at the very outset."

Nemours was not alone in his attempt to corner the market on Haitian music. He had many imitators and rivals, including former bandmate Wéber Sicot. Nemours and Sicot played together briefly in a band called Conjunto International, eventually splitting up in order to form their own groups. In 1958 relations between the two musicians became irreparably strained when Sicot coined a new dance rhythm that was almost indistinguishable from Nemours's compas-direct. He called his rhythm *kadans ranpa* (from *rempart*, meaning "defense" or "fortification"). From that point on, their relationship was strictly competitive, the two composers constantly striving to imitate and outdo the other. Occasionally their rivalry resulted in the outright piracy of material. Wagmer Lalanne, Nemours's former keyboardist, explains: "If we heard Sicot make a good song, we picked it up. So when we hear on the radio the Sicot song 'Cadence rampas numero un,' Nemours said, 'By God, that's a very good song. We'll pick up the same song and ours will beat it.'" Nemours's promise held true when his band scored the biggest hit in the country by stealing "Cadence rampas," changing only the lyrics and renaming it "Compas cabane choucune."

The *epòk polemik Nemou ak Siko* (period of controversy between Nemours and Sicot), as it is referred to in Haiti, was marked by a continuous argument between the two artists over whose band was superior. Sicot was widely considered the better musician, and often corroborated this opinion, lashing out at Nemours in his songs:

You have to stop trying to fool serious people
Because every Haitian knows good music.
From when you start until you finish, it's a single saxophone honk!...
You have no shame! You can't play a solo!
("Deux guidons")

Nemours, on the other hand, was considered to be the originator of compas and used this prestige to his advantage in his song "Rhythme commercial," which portrays Nemours as a productive, fruit-bearing mango tree at which others, namely Sicot, throw rocks out of jealousy. Nemours borrowed this image from the Haitian proverb, "One only throws rocks at mango trees that are full":

The tree that's bearing fruit
It's at him they're throwing rocks
But let's halt all this jealousy, truly!
Nemours is a mango tree
Defying time, always yielding fruit
They're throwing rocks all the time, at him!

In 1964 the rivalry between Sicot and Nemours culminated when the two bands resolved to play a soccer game in order to decide once and for all which group was better. The resulting match took place in March of that year and drew a crowd of more than 35,000 people. It is perhaps fitting that the game ended in a draw (1-1). Today Nemours and Sicot are both considered important figures in the development of compas, Haiti's first national pop music.

Gordon Root

SEE ALSO
Merengue: Music, Race and Nation in the Dominican Republic.

Latin America and the Caribbean

Netherlands Antilles, **a part of the kingdom of the Netherlands consisting of five islands in the Caribbean Sea. Curaçao and Bonaire, located north of VENEZUELA, constitute one island group, and St. Maarten, St. Eustatius, and Saba, located east of the Virgin Islands, constitute a second.**

The present-day kingdom of the Netherlands consists of three separate states: the Netherlands, the Caribbean island of ARUBA, and the five Caribbean islands that together compose the Netherlands Antilles. Many European nations competed to be part of the fifteenth- and sixteenth-century European invasion of the Caribbean, and most of them were hoping to establish control of islands that contained either gold or fertile soils that would facilitate plantation farming. But the Dutch had a simple, unique need that led them to establish Caribbean colonies: salt. The herring industry was an important part of the Dutch economy, and salt was required to cure the fish. This salt had traditionally come from the Spanish Iberian Peninsula, but conflicts between the Netherlands and Spain in the 1500s led Spain to outlaw that trade. The Dutch needed to find a new region of the world that could furnish a suitable salt supply. The result of their quest changed the kingdom and the six Caribbean islands that were destined to become part of it.

The six islands are geographically divided into two distinct groups. The first of these contains Aruba, Bonaire, and Curaçao, all located 66 km (40 mi) off the coast of Venezuela. Although Aruba has been a separate state since 1986, it was a part of the Netherlands Antilles for 250 years before that. As a result Aruba shares many linguistic and cultural traditions with Bonaire and Curaçao, and the three islands are still often referred to collectively as the ABC islands. St. Maarten, St. Eustatius, and Saba, all about 830 km (500 mi) northeast of the first group and east of the Virgin Islands and PUERTO RICO, are often called the three Ss. The five islands that today comprise the Netherlands Antilles do have significant differences as a result of their geographical separation. Many of the differences and similarities between them can be traced to the islands' precolonial and colonial histories.

Like most Caribbean islands, all five of the islands in the Netherlands Antilles had significant indigenous Amerindian populations for centuries before Christopher Columbus and other European explorers reached the region. At the time of Columbus's arrival in the Caribbean at the end of the fifteenth century, Aruba, Curaçao, and Bonaire

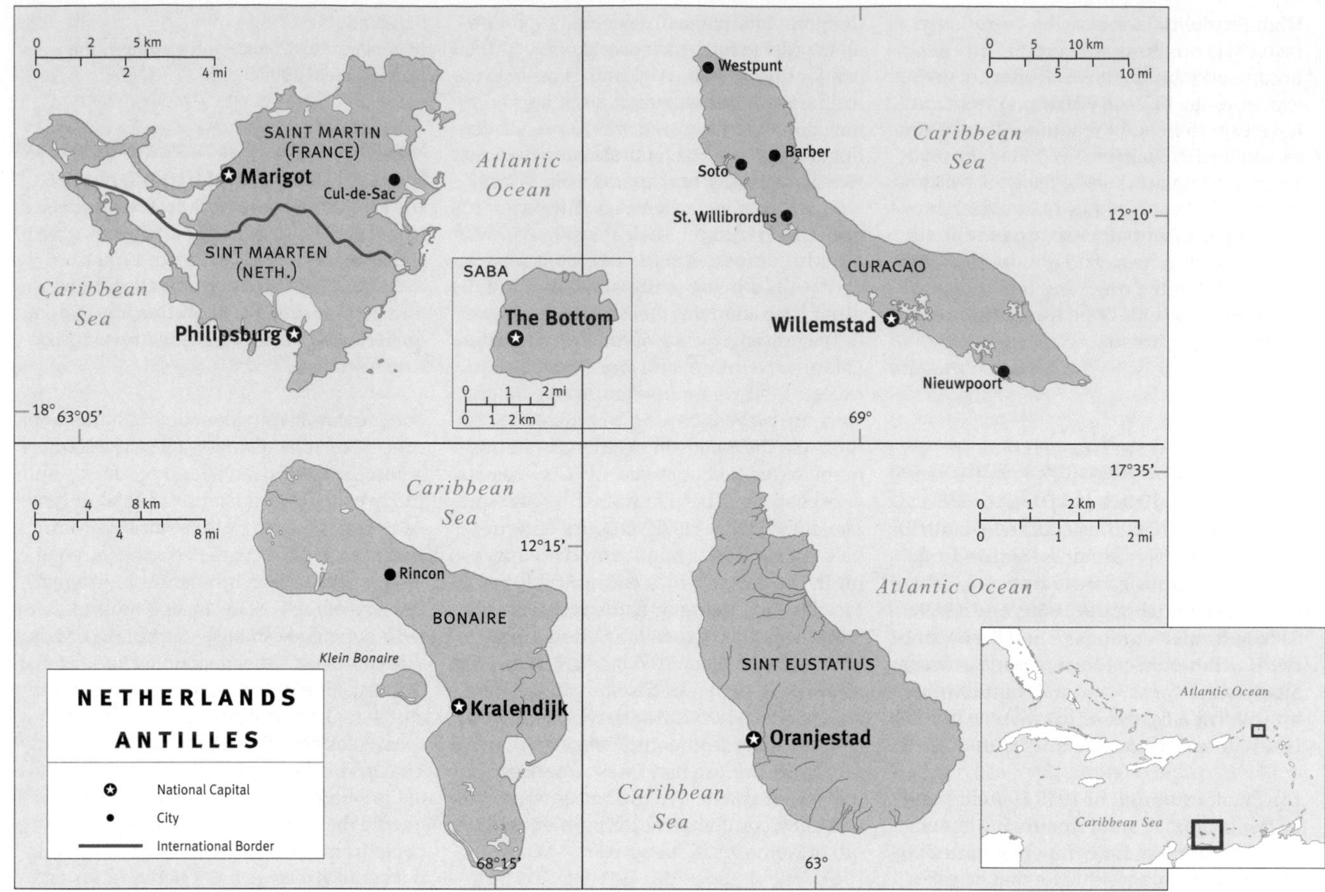

were inhabited by Caiquetíos Arawak Indians, who were primarily peaceful farmers and fishermen. St. Maarten, St. Eustatius, and Saba were uninhabited when they were first discovered by Europeans, but there was evidence that they too had once been inhabited by the Arawaks. Most likely those Arawaks had been taken into slavery by the Caribs, a second Amerindian tribe, and the Arawaks who lived in the ABC islands would soon meet the same fate at the hands of the Spanish.

The soils in all of these islands were generally poor, and so the Spanish declared them *islas inutiles* ("useless islands"). The Spanish captured many of the Arawaks on Bonaire and Curaçao in order to bring them to work on Spanish plantations on more profitable islands; they chose to let St. Maarten, St. Eustatius, and Saba remain uninhabited. The abundant salt deposits off the coasts of Bonaire, Curaçao, and St. Maarten made these islands quite appealing to the Dutch, who began eyeing them in the early seventeenth century.

The Dutch made their first move in 1631, sending a group of colonists to settle on St. Maarten. In 1634 Dutch colonists occupied Curaçao, and after a brief battle with the small group of Spanish settlers already on the island they were granted control of Curaçao and Bonaire. Meanwhile, the Dutch settlers on St. Maarten spread to St. Eustatius in 1636 and from there to Saba in 1640. Although a conflict arose with France over the island of St. Maarten in 1638, it was resolved amicably with each power agreeing to keep control of one side (and with the French side changing its spelling to Saint Martin). With their foothold in the Caribbean established, the Dutch immediately focused on the commodity that had attracted them – salt.

Salt mining, which involved long hours of standing in the ocean and manually sifting salt from the water, was extremely difficult work. There were not nearly enough Dutch colonists willing to do it, and so the Dutch turned to African slaves as a captive labor force. Slaves from ANGOLA and Congo composed the first group of Africans in the Netherlands Antilles, arriving in Curaçao as early as 1639. The Dutch West India Company, the Netherlands' slave-trading enterprise, grew so rapidly during that period that the Dutch became the second largest slave-trading power in the Atlantic by the 1640s (*see* TRANSATLANTIC SLAVE TRADE).

Curaçao quickly became one of the Dutch West India Company's main bases of operation because of the valuable convenience of the island's natural deep-water harbor. Slaves arriving in Curaçao were taken to Venezuela and other parts of the South American mainland. St. Eustatius provided a second port for shipments to that region of the Dutch Caribbean. The slave trade was ultimately more important to the economy of the Netherlands Antilles than slavery itself. In 1700 there were approximately 4000 slaves on Curaçao and Bonaire, with another 250 on St. Maarten and 750 on St. Eustatius. One hundred years later there were 4000 slaves on St. Maarten, 5000 on St. Eustatius, and 750 on Saba, with similar gains on Curaçao and Bonaire. While these figures represent a dramatic increase, the numbers of slaves were still much smaller here than they were on many Caribbean islands.

The numbers stayed relatively low because none of the islands in the Netherlands Antilles had soil fertile enough for large-scale plantation farming. The Dutch added Aruba to their holdings in 1686 but chose to send very few settlers and almost no slaves to that island. As a consequence Aruba had virtually no slave or African presence at all. Slaves in the rest of the Netherlands Antilles worked primarily in the salt mines, as domestic servants, or as laborers on the small tobacco plantations that Dutch planters had been able to establish on St. Maarten, St. Eustatius, and Saba.

Some historians have claimed that slavery was milder in Dutch colonies than in some others, but it is clear that Dutch slaves also resisted their captivity. In 1750 a group of slaves on a Curaçao plantation led an armed revolt; the rebels burned several buildings and were about to march on the main settlement at Willemstad when the colony's Dutch governor sent a military detachment of white soldiers and free blacks to recapture them. Several of the rebels drowned themselves to avoid being returned to slavery. A second revolt happened on Curaçao in 1795, when 50 slaves on one plantation decided to go on strike. Within days the rebellion, whose leaders were named Tula and Carpata, had grown to include more than 1000 slaves. This time it took several days before the militia was able to end the uprising. When the struggle was finally over, 29 slaves were executed. While there were no more open slave rebellions after that one, slaves continued to use the limited legal opportunities they had to protest mistreatment by cruel masters and to express their unhappiness with their treatment.

The slaves' voices were often ignored by the Dutch, but outside influences gradually intervened. When the French freed their slaves on Saint Martin in 1848, the remaining slaves on the Dutch half of the island simply declared that they were free too; Dutch slaves on St. Eustatius and Saba soon followed their lead. It was nearly impossible for the Dutch to do anything about the declarations, since slaves from those islands could so easily escape to nearby free territories. The Dutch agreed to let these former slaves remain free and concentrated instead on maintaining slavery in the ABC islands. But abolitionist sentiment at home and from Roman Catholic missionaries who had come to the islands to work with the slaves made the Dutch goal difficult. In 1863 slavery was finally abolished in all of the Netherlands Antilles (*see* Abolition and Emancipation in Latin America and the Caribbean).

By the time of emancipation the salt industry on the islands was in decline, and so the newly free black majority in the Netherlands Antilles needed other methods of making a living. There were a few jobs on aloe and sisal plantations and at plants that produced sand for construction or fresh water for the island's dry interior areas. But the economic situation in the islands had grown so bleak by the turn of the century that many Antilleans began migrating to Cuba in search of jobs in the booming sugar cane fields. Just then, however, new developments completely changed the economic structure of the Netherlands Antilles.

In 1907 oil was discovered in nearby Venezuela. Shell, a Dutch-British petroleum company, immediately began looking for suitable sites from which to refine and export the oil, and the Netherlands suggested Curaçao because of its excellent harbor. The first refinery on Curaçao was built in 1917. Within a few years refineries were sprinkled across Curaçao and Aruba; special tankers had been designed to carry thousands of tons of oil to the islands every day; and, above all, new workers were being recruited to fill the plentiful jobs. Oil jobs paid better than those in farming or fishing, and so Antilleans from all six islands arrived to work in the refineries. Even after this migration there were still more jobs to be filled, and so immigrants from other countries, especially Grenada and other neighboring islands in the Anglophone Caribbean, began arriving to work in the Dutch refineries.

Oil brought increased prosperity to most Antilleans, and with prosperity came increased demand for autonomy and political power. Throughout colonial history the Netherlands had been governed exclusively by appointed representatives of the Dutch Crown, giving blacks no political voice at all. But in 1941 the Dutch queen Wilhelmina finally promised that the Dutch East and West Indies – an empire that at the time included the Netherlands Antilles, Indonesia, and Suriname – would be granted self-government at the end of World War II. In 1948 the first important step toward political autonomy came when the appointed government of the Netherlands Antilles was replaced by a new government, called the Staten, elected through universal adult suffrage. In 1950 a new statute was introduced that granted the Netherlands, Suriname, and the Netherlands Antilles each equal status as separate partners in the kingdom of the Antilles. All three countries signed the statute in 1954.

Suriname declared full independence from the kingdom of the Netherlands in 1975, but most of the population of the Netherlands Antilles was content to stay under the Dutch Crown. More pressing problems arose in governing and unifying the home state. In May 1969 labor tensions stemming from the oil refineries led to several days of rioting, burning, and looting in downtown Willemstad that eventually had to be subdued by Dutch marines. Unemployment figures for that year ran as high as 20 to 25 percent, a sign that the oil-industry miracle was no longer working for all Antilleans.

Tourism had played a minor role in the country's economy since the 1920s, but from the 1960s on there was a serious attempt to expand that industry. This proved an excellent move when the worldwide collapse of oil prices in the 1980s put the refineries into jeopardy. By then several of the Netherlands Antilles – most notably Aruba and St. Maarten – already had well-established tourist industries that gave the country's economy a small buffer. But during the 1980s Arubans became convinced that their island would be more successful without official ties to the other Netherlands Antilles. Aruba was granted its status as a separate state within the kingdom in 1986.

In the early 1990s there was discussion of dividing the remaining Netherlands Antilles into two more separate states – one composed of Bonaire and Curaçao and the other of St. Maarten, St. Eustatius, and Saba – a measure that made sense to many politicians and voters. The islands had developed very different cultures as a result of the hundreds of miles that separated them; they did not even share a common language. While Dutch is the official language across the Netherlands Antilles, people on Bonaire and Curaçao speak Papiamento and Spanish, and residents of the other island group speak English. The distribution of the country's population was also significant: in 1992, 155,000 of the Netherlands Antilles' 190,000 residents lived on Curaçao and Bonaire, and those islands' large, urban populations had some very specific needs. But a 1993 referendum on the question of political division was resoundingly defeated. This led to the resignation of the country's first female prime minister, Maria Liberia-Peters, who had supported the measure.

As the Netherlands Antilles enter the twenty-first century, the islands' residents are determined to maintain the unification of their country. Daily life is still very different for a refinery worker in Curaçao and a fisherman on tiny Saba, but the five islands share a common history under the Dutch flag and some aspects of a common culture that blends Dutch and African elements. Many Caribbean traditions, such as the Carnival celebration (*see* Carnivals in Latin America and the Caribbean), are also a part of the Netherlands Antilles culture. The warm Papiamento phrase *bon bini* ("welcome") has been adopted as a general introduction to all of the Netherlands Antilles.

Lisa Clayton Robinson

See Also

Congo, Democratic Republic of the; Slavery in Latin America and the Caribbean; Virgin Islands (United States and British); Languages, Creole, in the Caribbean.

Europe

Netherlands, The, a Western European country in which blacks have had a presence for centuries.

As early as the sixteenth century a small population of Africans and people of African descent resided in the Netherlands as servants and laborers, military servicemen, and intellectuals. Black military recruits served in the Dutch army in Suriname and Indonesia and fought for the Dutch in World War II. Black Surinamese intellectuals, who have studied in the Netherlands, have challenged racism in Dutch society, the Dutch view of its colonies, and the self-image of tolerance and pluralism that is prevalent among the Dutch.

However, a significant black presence in the Netherlands did not exist until the 1950s. With the arrival of blacks from former Dutch colonies, the Netherlands has faced the consequences of its past involvement in the slave trade and colonialism. In the 1960s Moroccans and other North Africans entered the Netherlands to work in Dutch industry. When Suriname attained independence in 1975, many Surinamers migrated to the

Netherlands to retain their Dutch citizenship. While the Netherlands is known as a country of refuge and home to one of the most comprehensive social benefits systems in EUROPE, the continued presence of these ethnic minorities has revealed the limits of Dutch tolerance. However, the Dutch government has attempted to accommodate these migrants by promoting multiculturalism and addressing issues of economic disparity and racial discrimination.

SLAVES AND FREEDMEN

The Dutch had little direct contact with Africans until they began trading slaves in the late sixteenth century. Before this, their ideas about blacks derived largely from SPAIN, which ruled the Netherlands until the Dutch revolted in the sixteenth century. Images of blacks appeared in Dutch heraldry as early as the thirteenth century. In the Saint Nicholas tradition of the Dutch, a black boy called Zwarte Piet, meaning Black Pete, accompanies Santa Claus on his nocturnal rounds. As the tale goes, it is Black Pete who slides down the chimney to give children candy if they are good or to steal the children away if they are bad. This image of blacks was not controversial until large numbers of blacks emigrated to the Netherlands in the 1970s.

During the seventeenth century the Dutch became the leading slave traders on the west coast of Africa. Over the course of their involvement in the slave trade, which peaked in the late seventeenth century and ended in the early nineteenth century, the Dutch transported several hundred thousand slaves to the Americas. Founded in 1602, the Dutch East India Company brought slaves from the Dutch holding in Elmina, in present-day GHANA, and several other Dutch posts on the west coast of Africa, to the Dutch holdings in the Cape Colony (today part of SOUTH AFRICA) and Indonesia. The Dutch West India Company, founded in 1621, brought slaves from West Africa, mostly from Elmina, to Dutch colonies in BRAZIL (collectively called Dutch Brazil), Suriname, ARUBA, and the NETHERLANDS ANTILLES – a group of islands including St. Maarten, St. Eustatius, Saba, Bonaire, and Curaçao.

The Dutch brought hundreds of blacks from Africa or the Caribbean to the Netherlands as slaves, servants, and students. A privateer carried the first known group of Africans to the Zeeland region of the Netherlands in the late sixteenth century. Local authorities ruled that these Africans, seized from a Portuguese slave ship, could not be kept as slaves in the Netherlands and must be freed. Though slavery was legal in the Dutch colonies, the Dutch did not condone it in the Netherlands proper. While some Dutch brought slaves to the Netherlands, courts often ruled in favor of those slaves who petitioned for freedom.

Church and city documents record manumissions, baptisms, and marriages of blacks as early as the sixteenth century. For instance, Jan Kompanie was the slave of Admiral de Ruiter in Zeeland for a few years during the early seventeenth century. The admiral then freed Kompanie and the former slave returned to Africa. In many cases, freed blacks married white Dutch spouses. Tabo, a freed slave, opened a tobacco store and changed his name to Adriaan de Bruijn ("the Brown"). He later married a Dutch woman, Wolmetje Bakkers. Louis Alons, described as "a Negro from Curaçao" in the Sappemeer town marriage register, wedded a Dutch woman in 1779. Interestingly, documents do not mention his children's ethnicity.

Africans also worked in the Netherlands as servants. These blacks, in costumes with feathered turbans, appear in seventeenth- and eighteenth-century portraits of the royalty and upper classes. In the late eighteenth century blacks served the bourgeoisie of Groningen. The Dutch in this region had connections with trading companies in the colonies.

During this period children of white Dutch men and black Caribbean and Surinamese women often traveled to the Netherlands for schooling, as did other Surinamese blacks. For instance, in 1767 the Dutch Reformed Church in Paramaribo, the capital of Suriname, sent Jeboa, the son of a chief of the Aucaner people, for schooling in Amsterdam. The Aucaner were one of the communities of maroons, or independent descendants of escaped slaves (*see* MAROONAGE IN THE AMERICAS), in the Dutch colonies.

By the eighteenth century the Dutch seafaring empire was in decline, and the British had come to dominate the transatlantic slave trade. Both the West India Company and the East India Company lost profits when the French and English gained hold of Dutch trade routes and colonies. The British abolished the slave trade in 1808, and the Netherlands followed suit in 1814. In reality the Dutch slave trade had become unprofitable and was all but finished by the 1780s. In 1863 the Dutch outlawed slavery in their colonies.

SOLDIERS AND SAILORS

As early as the seventeenth century the Dutch employed blacks in military roles, mainly in the colonies. The first blacks to be employed in the military were musicians – mainly drummers and buglers – as a sort of curiosity. The Dutch West Indian Army organized a contingent called the Black Rangers of Suriname in 1772 to fight maroon revolts. After the abolition of the slave trade many former slaves from Suriname traveled to the Netherlands for training as members of colonial armies. Blacks served in the East Indian Army in Indonesia from the early nineteenth to the twentieth century. Noting that these West Africans and West Indian blacks were Europeanized and Christianized, local Indonesians called them Blanda Itam, meaning Black Hollanders. In Dutch colonial societies these black servicemen formed a community separate from both the white Dutch, who gave them lower pay and fewer benefits than white soldiers, and from the peoples whom they policed. Still, in Suriname and Indonesia, these soldiers often took local wives and settled after their retirement from service. Some Black Hollanders, and even some Black Rangers, fought for the Netherlands against Indonesian independence in 1949. In modern Indonesia 75 families who are descended from the Black Hollanders hold annual reunions.

Jan Kooi, a West African, joined the Dutch East Indian Army in 1882 and became a corporal. Kooi suffered wounds while saving the lives of a commander and a lieutenant. At age 33 he became the first Black Hollander to be decorated by the Dutch authorities. Kooi returned to Holland after his service in Indonesia was over. Blacks from Indonesia and Suriname also fought with the Dutch army against the Germans in World War II.

INTELLECTUALS

Blacks from throughout the Dutch Empire traveled to the Netherlands to acquire an education. Some became well-known intellectuals. For example, JACOBUS ELISA CAPITEIN studied at the University of Leiden. Although he believed in equality for blacks, he was acclaimed by Dutch colonists and slave traders because his dissertation condoned slavery as a means for Africans' conversion to Christianity. In 1742 Capitien became the first known black Protestant minister. He served as a missionary in the West Indies.

Another black man who impressed Europe with his intellectual abilities was ANTON WILHELM AMO. The West Indian Company brought Amo as a boy from the Gold Coast (present-day Ghana) to the Netherlands during the early eighteenth century and presented him to the duke of Wolfenbüttel in Germany. The duke named him Anton Wilhelm and educated him. Amo knew at least six languages, earned a doctorate, and lectured in Europe on philosophy for a time, but he eventually returned to Africa. The sons of African kings also came to the Netherlands for education or other purposes. Aquasie Boachi, the son of King Kwaku Dua of ASANTE, entered the Dutch military during the early nineteenth century at the expense of the Dutch colonial ministry. He attended boarding school in the Netherlands, frequented the highest social circles, and befriended the crown prince Willem III of the Netherlands.

In the twentieth century, with the development of independence movements in the colonies, black intellectuals from Suriname came to the Netherlands to attend university and often used their learning to challenge Dutch conceptions of Suriname. Anton de Kom, a Surinamer known as a radical socialist and anticolonial agitator, studied in Amsterdam and wrote *We, Slaves of Suriname*

(1934), the first history of Suriname. De Kom married a Dutch woman and was forbidden to return to Suriname to settle because the Dutch feared he would start a revolt. More recently, Rudolf Asveer Jacob van Lier, a Surinamer of African and Jewish descent, attended the University of Leiden and the Sorbonne in Paris. After his studies he became chair of the department of sociology at Leiden and wrote *Frontier Society* (1971), a classic sociological study of Suriname.

From 1900 to 1950 Surinamers and Antilleans who entered the Netherlands were mostly from the elite class. They came for an education and planned to return to Africa. Many of these people of African descent, however, remained and settled in the Netherlands.

Postwar Immigrants

It was not until after World War II and decolonization that substantial numbers of Africans and peoples of African descent migrated to the Netherlands. Two of the largest migrant groups were Moroccans and Surinamers. Each group arrived under different circumstances.

The Dutch recruited Moroccans, along with other peoples of the Mediterranean region, as "guest workers" to fill the postwar labor shortage in the 1960s. The government treated them as temporary inhabitants of the Netherlands and they acted as such; they did not invest in housing and worked only to save money to take back to Morocco. As the labor shortage in the Netherlands disappeared, however, unemployment began to rise. In 1968 the government restricted labor migration and decided that migrants who returned home would lose their residence permits. Thus, in the 1970s, instead of returning to their native lands, many laborers remained in the Netherlands and, in the 1980s, brought their families to join them. In the 1990s Moroccans constituted one of the largest immigrant groups in the Netherlands, with nearly 200,000 people.

Surinamers began coming to the Netherlands in significant numbers beginning in 1954, when they gained Dutch citizenship with the incorporation of Suriname into the kingdom of the Netherlands. The 1954 charter incorporated Aruba and the Dutch Antilles into the kingdom as well. All three colonies had internal self-rule. Many of the first Surinamers who arrived were elite, but as transportation costs dropped, laborers and others began to migrate. By 1973 the Surinamese and Antillean immigrant population in the Netherlands was approximately 40,000 to 45,000.

In 1973 Surinamers voted for independence from the Netherlands, to take effect in 1975. However, about 40 percent of Surinamers opposed independence, partly due to the advantages of Dutch citizenship. Beginning in 1974 many migrated to the Netherlands to retain Dutch citizenship. In order to discourage last-minute mass migration, the Dutch decided to allow a five-year transition period during which borders were open to Surinamers. But political instability in Suriname in the 1980s impelled more Surinamers to migrate to the Netherlands as political refugees. Within a few years more than 200,000 Surinamers, almost one-third of the entire population of Suriname, resided in the Netherlands. In the 1990s Surinamese migration steadied at about 6000 immigrants yearly. In 1995 the Surinamese population of the Netherlands was 296,000; almost 40 percent of these people had been born in the Netherlands.

Emigration of people of African descent from the Dutch Antilles and Aruba largely depends on the economic situation on the islands, but it tends to be at a lesser rate than from Morocco or Suriname. Aruba gained its independence in 1986, but, in contrast to the trend in Suriname, migration to the Netherlands increased little. The oil industry in Curaçao kept many Curaçaoans employed on the island. Still, in 1994 there were 82,000 people of Antillean origin in the Netherlands.

Other Africans have migrated to the Netherlands since 1960. Tunisians and other North Africans migrated with Moroccans as laborers in the 1960s. In the early 1970s about 300 Ugandans of Asian origin sought refuge in the Netherlands when dictator Idi Amin exiled them. About 20,000 refugees from Ghana and Cape Verde migrated in the 1980s. Ethiopians have also sought refuge in the Netherlands.

The Surinamers and Moroccans were not the first postcolonial migrants to the Netherlands. After Indonesian independence in 1949, approximately 300,000 people migrated to the Netherlands from Indonesia; 180,000 were of mixed Dutch and Asian background. The Dutch government dealt with that population with a policy of assimilation.

This was not the case with the newcomers in the 1960s and 1970s. Because migrant workers and even Surinamese or Antillean migrants were originally considered temporary – they were there for an education, or to make money, and would then return to their homelands – the Dutch made little effort to assimilate them. Most immigrant children were educated in their own language, under the assumption that they would return to their country of origin. It was not until the late 1970s that the Dutch government started to acknowledge that many of these newer immigrants were permanent residents.

The Dutch government has responded to the newcomers in a number of ways. The Netherlands is one of the world's most densely populated nations. It also has one of the world's most comprehensive social security systems. The government has tried to restrict immigration rather than extend all benefits to those who enter. Since the 1980s it has been increasingly difficult for Surinamers and North Africans to get entry visas. In addition, the Dutch have restricted economic and labor migration and tightened the criteria for asylum seekers in order to make emigration unattractive.

Since the nineteenth century the Dutch government has divided its population into "pillars" (*zuilen*), according to religious orientation. Traditionally, all Dutch have belonged to one of three pillars – Roman Catholic, Protestant (mostly Dutch Reformed Church), or nonreligious (humanist). Children attend schools according to their religious orientation. Though the pillar system has been in decline since the 1960s, the principle that each religious or cultural group should retain a distinct existence has remained the basic assumption of Dutch pluralism. However, the immigrant population of the Netherlands is so diverse that organization into one pillar or even separate pillars according to national origin has largely failed. For instance, the Surinamese population consists of peoples of African, South Asian, and Indonesian descent; long-standing conflicts exist among these peoples in Suriname. The biggest criticism of pillarization (*verzuiling*) is that it ignores racial discrimination and economic or educational disadvantage and that it promotes segregation in instances such as school choice.

Government policy in the 1980s and 1990s attempted to address immigrants' economic disadvantages and generally acknowledged immigrants as a permanent population – as "minority groups." Since the 1980s the government has developed a two-tiered strategy of socioeconomic integration and cultural pluralism. The state has extended social security benefits to legal foreign residents. Affirmative action policies have aimed to decrease socioeconomic disadvantages and institutional discrimination in housing, education, and employment. The government has begun to promote education in both the migrants' own language and Dutch. At the same time an integration course has encouraged assimilation. Heavily subsidized by the government, the 500-hour, 18-month course aims to teach Dutch ways to immigrants – from acceptable business attire to behavior on public transportation – in order to increase their chances of getting jobs and "fitting in." Some immigrants feel that the course has benefited them, but few believe it should be made mandatory for all immigrants, as some government officials proposed in 1997.

The Netherlands has led the European Union (EU) in extending citizenship to immigrants. Many have gained Dutch citizenship without abandoning citizenship in their country of origin and are thus dual citizens. This law also allows foreigners who are residents in the Netherlands for three years to vote and run for office in municipal elections. In the 1986 elections, 330,000 new voters made a significant difference in election results and gave a boost to the socialist Labour Party.

Despite these government efforts, many immigrants face unemployment and poor living conditions. About 80 percent of the residents of the Amsterdam district of Bijlmermeer – known as "the biggest ghetto in Europe" – are minorities; most are Surinamers, Moroccans, or Turks. It is estimated that 10,000 illegal immigrants from Ghana also reside in the neighborhood. In the 1970s the government put up public housing in the area for incoming Surinamers, but now this housing development is dilapidated. Drugs, crime, and racial violence abound. Even so, some people insist that certain parts of the neighborhood are safe. They point out that the various cultural communities in Bijlmermeer coexist harmoniously.

Problems such as those in Bijlmermeer have led some people to oppose the government's liberal social benefits policies. As Dutch unemployment has increased since the 1970s, many Dutch have voiced resentment at the immigrants' demands for space and resources and have viewed the immigrants as a burden. As a result, discrimination in employment, housing, education, and political life has become commonplace. In addition, some have blamed immigrants for the rise in crime and drug trafficking. Although fascist and racist groups have not taken hold in the Netherlands as they have in other European countries, far-right parties gained ground with promises to restrict immigration in 1994. Tolerance of immigrants seemed to be waning. That year the government gave police the right to stop and search people suspected of being illegal immigrants and implemented a stricter screening process for those seeking political asylum. Immigrants and liberals feared that these policies would lead to a police state in the Netherlands.

Historically, the Dutch have taken pride in their tolerance of religious and cultural differences. But some Dutch have reacted to immigrants with racism and discrimination, forcing others to doubt the Dutch reputation as an unprejudiced society. Racist imagery, such as Santa Claus's helper, Black Pete, still lingers just barely out of sight, and racist ideas, though discouraged, are present. To be sure, the Dutch, more than most Europeans, have attempted to engender peaceful coexistence between peoples, and many immigrants have become Dutch citizens. The Dutch face a choice between clinging to the attitudes that supported the slave trade and colonialism and embracing people of African or Caribbean descent as fellow Dutch citizens in a peaceful, multicultural society.

Leyla Keough

SEE ALSO

Colonial Rule; Ethiopia; Morocco; Transatlantic Slave Trade; Tunisia; Uganda.

Africa

Neto, Agostinho

(b. September 17, 1922, near Catete, Angola; d. September 10, 1979, Moscow, Soviet Union), physician, poet, nationalist leader, and president of ANGOLA.

The son of a Methodist minister, António Agostinho Neto received his high school education in Luanda. In 1947, after spending three years in the government health service, he traveled to PORTUGAL to attend medical school on a Methodist Church scholarship. While there he met his Portuguese wife, Maria Eugénia da Silva, and other students from Portuguese Africa, including future nationalist leaders AMÍLCAR CABRAL of GUINEA-BISSAU and Eduardo Mondlane of MOZAMBIQUE. He also became involved in the youth organization of the Portuguese opposition movement. Between 1952 and 1962, during various stays in prison for his political activity, Neto began writing poetry. The publication of his nationalist poetry and his subsequent detention delayed his graduation from medical school until 1958.

By mid-1957 Neto had joined the recently formed opposition group the POPULAR MOVEMENT FOR THE LIBERATION OF ANGOLA (or MPLA). He fit in well with the MPLA's educated, middle-class leadership, which was dominated by Africans of the Kimbundu ethnic group, whites, and mestiços (those of mixed race). Despite his religious upbringing, Neto soon adopted the movement's Marxist-Leninist and Stalinist rhetoric. After escaping from detention in PORTUGAL, in 1962 he was elected MPLA president while in exile in the DEMOCRATIC REPUBLIC OF THE CONGO. Thereafter, Neto was consumed with trying to gain international support for the movement and its struggle, writing little poetry after the 1963 publication of the collection *Sacred Hope.*

In 1975, after Portugal withdrew from Angola, the MPLA succeeded in gaining control of the capital. Neto, after 20 years in exile, became president of independent Angola. But ongoing conflict between the former nationalist movement NATIONAL UNION FOR THE TOTAL INDEPENDENCE OF ANGOLA (UNITA) and the MPLA quickly overshadowed Neto's political, organizational, and intellectual skills. A civil war soon consumed the country and an unsuccessful coup d'état in 1977 threatened Neto's leadership. Although Neto remained beholden to the Soviet Union and CUBA for both their military assistance and their aid for his socialist development policies, he also encouraged business ties with the West.

Neto's poetry, always more about nationalism and exile than about politics, often spoke of hope, and as such became part of modern Angola's political lexicon and literary canon. In 1979 Neto died of cancer in a Moscow hospital. He was succeeded as president by JOSÉ EDUARDO DOS SANTOS.

Eric Young

SEE ALSO

African Socialism; Luanda, Angola; Nationalism in Africa.

North America

Newark, New Jersey, city in which slavery was gradually abolished beginning in 1804, so that by the time Newark incorporated in 1836, a small, free black community had already formed. African Americans established the Clinton Memorial AFRICAN METHODIST EPISCOPAL CHURCH in 1822 and founded an auxiliary of the AMERICAN ANTI-SLAVERY SOCIETY in 1834. Four years later the Colored School – later the Baxter School – was founded.

Newark, New Jersey, remained ambivalent about its black community and its commitment to the Union cause in the Civil War. In 1863 the New York City Draft Riot spread to Newark, where whites blamed and then attacked blacks as the cause of their conscription in the Union Army.

After 1870 African Americans migrated to the city from the South and worked as unskilled laborers. Black leaders such as James Baxter fought to integrate schools well into the twentieth century, even though segregation had been outlawed after an 1884 New Jersey Supreme Court decision.

As Newark evolved into an industrial city with substantial immigrant populations, the African American community grew. By 1910 it had reached 10,000 people – five times the 1870 total. African Americans could rarely get industrial jobs, except as occasional strikebreakers. Because unions excluded them, they organized their own labor actions, as Prosper Brewer did in a 1917 black dockworkers' strike of Port Newark.

The black community developed its own institutions. Newark's first black paper (*see* PRESS, BLACK, IN THE UNITED STATES), the *Appeal*, began in 1902, and the Newark branch of the NATIONAL ASSOCIATION FOR THE ADVANCEMENT OF COLORED PEOPLE (NAACP) was established in 1914. In 1919 an Urban League chapter formed out of the Negro Welfare League of Newark. The Community Hospital of Newark was founded in 1927.

During World War I the industrial job market opened to African Americans. Black migration to Newark increased significantly; nearly 22,000 blacks arrived between 1920 and 1930. Housing segregation, which had begun in 1870, increased dramatically in this decade, leading to de facto segregation of schools and concentrating many African Americans in the Hill District, one of the poorest ghettos in the United States. A JAZZ scene developed around the Orpheum and Paramount theaters and the Kinney

Poet, playwright, and novelist Amiri Baraka, a Newark native, organized the Committee for a United Newark to aid the city's black community.
The Everett Collection

and Skateland nightclubs, where Jimmy Lunceford and Ella Fitzgerald performed.

During the Great Depression of the 1930s, the unemployment level among African Americans quickly reached twice that among whites. New Deal programs fundamentally shifted black political allegiance to the Democratic Party, resulting in Guy Moorehead's election as the first black Democrat to the state assembly in 1938.

With the outbreak of World War II, jobs in war-related industries further opened to blacks, and the African American community began its most profound expansion. Between 1940 and 1960 the community more than tripled in size, to 34 percent of the total Newark population. White flight then created a population decline. By 1970 African Americans were 54.2 percent of the Newark population.

With the exception of city councilor and political boss Irvine Turner, Newark had little black political representation before the mid-1960s, and conditions in the city were extreme. Corrupt government, high unemployment, crime, and especially police brutality against African Americans were rampant problems. The predominantly white school board resisted integration and failed to rescue an increasingly desperate school system. In the early 1960s the black community became more politically organized, more insistent on the need for change, and more frustrated with each successive failure to improve conditions. The Newark chapter of the Congress of Racial Equality (CORE) fought housing discrimination and police brutality. The Newark Coordination Council attacked discrimination in city jobs and contracts. The more radical Newark Community Union Project used rent strikes and sit-ins to push for enforcement of building codes. In 1966 playwright and black nationalist Amiri Baraka, a Newark native, organized the Committee for a United Newark, which focused on education and other issues vital to the survival of the black community. A year later the first National Conference on Black Power convened in Newark.

Nonetheless, by 1967 Newark had the highest percentage of substandard housing and the second highest crime and infant mortality rates in the country. In July continual frustration with poverty and racism erupted into one of the bloodiest and most devastating racial insurrections in recent U.S. history. Sparked by an incident of police brutality, the four-day riot left 23 people dead and more than $10 million in property damage. A second riot followed the assassination of Martin Luther King Jr. one year later.

Although reform-minded Kenneth Gibson was elected the first black mayor of Newark in 1970, the history of Newark from 1960 to 1980 is the history of one of the poorest urban black communities in the nation. Gibson further integrated the school board and secured some federal funding for building projects and jobs. Yet in 1983 nearly one-quarter of all black families in Newark still lived in poverty. This number was reduced only slightly in the ensuing 15 years. Sharpe James defeated Gibson as mayor in 1986, and Donald Payne became the first black representative from New Jersey in 1988; but Newark remains a city with difficult and challenging problems in the areas of housing, crime, education, and unemployment.

Jim Mendelsohn

See Also

World War I and African Americans; World War II and African Americans; Civil War, American; Great Migration, The; King, Martin Luther, Jr.; Lunceford, James Melvin (Jimmie); National Urban League; New York City Draft Riot of 1863.

North America

New Deal, President Franklin Delano Roosevelt's domestic reform program of 1933-1941, which, though inconsistent in its treatment of African Americans, greatly strengthened black hopes for racial justice.

The New Deal, a reform effort unparalleled in American history, took shape during the troubled times of the Great Depression. It gave substance to President Franklin Delano Roosevelt's vague campaign promises to restore hope and revive the United States economy. When he took office in March 1933, Americans had already endured more than three years of the worst economic depression in the nation's history. African Americans, in particular, had suffered the brunt of the hardship. In the early 1930s nearly one in three African American families was receiving some form of public assistance, and roughly half the black workers in New York City, Chicago, Philadelphia, and Detroit were unemployed.

During his first hundred days in office, Roosevelt secured passage of a record number of programs, and he continued implementing domestic reforms until the onset of World War II. Temporary initiatives included the Works Progress Administration (WPA) and Public Works Administration (PWA), which created work projects for the unemployed, and the Federal Emergency Relief Administration (FERA), which offered federal assistance to individuals in need.

The New Deal also sought more far-reaching reforms. A wave of Great Depression-era bank failures led to the Federal Deposit Insurance Corporation (FDIC), which guaranteed bank deposits. The Securities Exchange Commission (SEC) was established to regulate the stock market, whose 1929 collapse had triggered the Great Depression. The Tennessee Valley Authority (TVA) and the Rural Electrification Authority (REA) were development projects aimed primarily at the South and the West. Roosevelt flirted briefly with national economic planning in the National Recovery Administration (NRA), but with the Social Security Administration (SSA) he left a lasting mark.

Although their need was particularly great, African Americans found themselves shortchanged by Roosevelt's New Deal. The social security system, which excluded agricultural workers, had nothing to offer the South's black sharecroppers. Many Southern landowners, rather than share Agricultural Adjustment Administration (AAA) subsidies with their sharecroppers as the enabling legislation intended, evicted their tenants and kept the entire payment for themselves. Overt racial discrimination was evident in the segregated camps of the Civilian Conservation Corps (CCC) and in the hiring and housing policies of the TVA. NRA guidelines permitted lower wages for blacks than for whites doing the same work. Although a 1935 executive order banned discrimination in WPA projects, a cut in the WPA budget in 1937 helped bring on the sharp downturn of 1937-1939, known as the Roosevelt Recession, which jeopardized many black families.

In general, the Roosevelt administration recognized blacks in ways that were more symbolic than substantive. Yet Roosevelt appointed an unprecedented number of African American advisers. His Federal Council on Negro Affairs, known informally as the Black Cabinet, included William H. Hastie, Robert C. Weaver, and Mary McLeod Bethune. In 1939 First Lady Eleanor Roosevelt played a prominent role in arranging an Easter Sunday recital by famed black contralto Marian Anderson at Washington's Lincoln Memorial after the Daughters of the American Revolution had refused to let Anderson perform at a concert hall owned by the organization.

Politically, the New Deal solidified Roosevelt's Democratic coalition into a force that dominated American politics for more than a generation, but for African Americans the political results were less clear. In Northern cities blacks achieved greater political influence. In the 1936 presidential election, they rallied around Roosevelt and the New Deal. Their support represented a political shift of historic proportions; Northern black voters became a cornerstone of the liberal-labor coalition that challenged the dominance of Southern conservatives in national politics. During the 1930s, however, most African Americans still lived in the South, where disfranchisement effectively deprived them of any political voice. Yet the New Deal had particularly important political consequences for Southern blacks (*see* VOTING RIGHTS ACT OF 1965).

The New Deal encouraged political activism among African Americans in the South. In 1934 groups of black citizens organized in South Carolina and Georgia to try to vote in whites-only Democratic primaries. In Arkansas a number of black and white sharecroppers formed the Southern Tenant Farmers Union to press the federal government to enforce protections written into the Agricultural Adjustment Act of 1933. Student activism in the 1930s and the growth of the industrial labor movement frequently facilitated interracial alliances in support of economic reform. During the New Deal era, the NATIONAL ASSOCIATION FOR THE ADVANCEMENT OF COLORED PEOPLE (NAACP) undertook major organizing drives among Southern blacks, building black membership, supporting voter registration efforts, and initiating the legal campaign against unequal education that laid the groundwork for the 1954 BROWN V. BOARD OF EDUCATION decision.

New Deal programs and policies often accommodated the racial status quo. But African Americans responded to the democratic rhetoric of the New Deal – and the unprecedented expansion of federal power it envisioned – in ways that created an atmosphere conducive to organizing and mobilizing for full citizenship rights. Indeed, the roots of the modern CIVIL RIGHTS MOVEMENT can be traced to the black political activism of the New Deal era.

James Clyde Sellman

SEE ALSO

World War II and African Americans; Chicago, Illinois; Detroit, Michigan; Hastie, William Henry; New York, New York; Philadelphia, Pennsylvania; Weaver, Robert Clifton.

North America

New Negro, The, **a term indelibly associated with the African American artistic and political activity of the 1920s, above all the HARLEM RENAISSANCE; the term was substantially defined by *The New Negro*, an anthology edited by Alain Locke.**

SEE ALSO

Locke, Alain Leroy.

North America

New Orleans, Louisiana,

the most European and African of North American cities, in which French, Spanish, Creole, African, and English cultures have blended to produce distinctive music, cuisine, and festivals. This cultural synthesis distinguishes the history of the city from other, more common patterns of urban growth in the United States.

New Orleans spent a century under European rule before it was purchased by the United States. Jean Baptiste, Sieur de Bienville, the governor of the French colony of Louisiana, founded the city in 1718. In 1767 it was ceded to SPAIN. In 1800 FRANCE reclaimed sovereignty, and in 1803 Napoleon sold all of the Louisiana Territory, including New Orleans, to the United States.

Slaves labored in New Orleans and its surrounding plantations from the first years of French rule. In 1721 more black male slaves than free white men lived in the city, and until the massive European immigration of the 1830s and 1840s, nonwhite residents formed the majority. A large number of slaves arrived in New Orleans between 1719 and 1731, most of them abducted directly from SENEGAL. The influence of African culture, therefore, was stronger in Louisiana than in the British colonies, whose slave populations often stopped over in the British West Indies for a generation or two.

Slavery in New Orleans also differed from the English practice in other ways. Owners admitted to sexual liaisons with slaves, often taking financial responsibility for their mistresses and offspring. Unlike Yankee slavery, in which whites drew a firm line between the two races, the New Orleans system produced a third caste, that of mixed-blood CREOLES. French and Spanish fathers treated their Creole children equitably, often sending them to Europe for their education and making them legal heirs. Although the French and Spanish governments attempted to limit this propagation of a privileged Creole class with a series of *code noir* laws, citizens frequently ignored the legislation. By the time of the Civil War, New Orleans hosted a considerable Creole population, some of whose members owned slaves themselves.

When the United States purchased New Orleans in 1803, it obtained a thriving and culturally distinct crossroads. Spanish and French sensibilities intermingled with African and Caribbean ones, producing syncretic religions and innovative cuisine. Black Creoles and slaves combined African beliefs, Haitian rituals, and Catholic pageantry into the baleful religion of VODOU. New Orleans Catholics celebrated Mardi Gras with an African air of Carnival delight, donning lavish costumes and feasting on Creole food. Throughout the year slaves congregated in the city's Congo Square, the only place in America where masters permitted the performance of Afrodiasporic music and dance. At Congo Square, African rhythms mingled with European melodies in the foreshadowings of blues and JAZZ.

The upper-class black Creoles also forged new paths: NORBERT RILLIEUX invented a vacuum pump for refining sugar; Victor Séjour wrote plays; Alexandre Chaumette, James Derham, and Charles Roundanez practiced medicine; Edmond Dédé composed and directed music; Eugene Warbourg sculpted. In 1850 nearly 85 percent of black CREOLES in New Orleans possessed the skills to be classified as doctors, clerks, teachers, and skilled workers. Educated Creoles proliferated as merchants and dominated the trades of cabinet making, carpentry, cigar manufacturing, masonry, and plastering. These middle-class blacks distanced themselves from the black African slave culture and founded Roman Catholic churches based on European models.

Despite the assimilation of the Creole community, discrimination intensified toward the middle of the nineteenth century. The Dred Scott decision of the United States Supreme Court in 1857 impinged on black freedom everywhere. By the start of the Civil War, new laws restricted the mobility of free blacks and limited the manumission of slaves. Hundreds of free people of color served in the Confederate Army, reflecting this growing white domination. (After the Union takeover of the city in 1862, however, the majority of black soldiers fought on the side of the North.)

Although Republican law makers enfranchised African Americans in New Orleans during RECONSTRUCTION, conservative whites soon voted these politicians out of office. Democrats won power in 1867, intent on "redeeming" the state. New white leaders segregated accommodations and schools, and, after the U.S. Supreme Court decision of PLESSY V. FERGUSON in 1896, they pushed for the segregation of public transit. The historian Caryn Cossé Bell writes, "Radical Reconstruction's promise of freedom, opportunity, and equal citizenship had ended in a nightmare of semiservitude, Jim Crow laws, and disfranchisement." The growing tension led to the New Orleans Riot of 1900, which was sparked by an instance of police harassment and marked by rampant violence of whites against blacks.

While Reconstruction-era politics strained relations between blacks and whites, it also upset relationships within the African American community. The educated Creoles, whose racism often rivaled that of whites, suddenly found themselves grouped with black freedpeople. African American leaders had to contend with internal prejudice and resentment to direct this larger community.

Amid the growing discrimination, however, African American culture flourished. In the last quarter of the century blacks created secret societies and social lodges, opened theaters, played baseball, and founded three colleges. SPASM BANDS roamed the streets, and music developed in the form of blues and RAGTIME. By the end of the century presentiments of jazz filled the air of Storyville, the red-light district of New Orleans. Musicians improvised and embellished musical styles until those styles emerged, by World War I, as jazz. Jazz fused complex melodies – played by Creoles who could read music – with the rhythms that pulsed from Congo Square. Performers like King Oliver, Sidney Bechet, and Louis Armstrong helped to make the new sounds nationally popular, and by 1925 the form was evolving in the cities of the North.

Later in the century other music developed in New Orleans. The rock 'n' roll singer and pianist Antoine "Fats" Domino was a native, as were the gospel singer MAHALIA JACKSON and the jazz musicians Branford and WYNTON MARSALIS.

After the Riot of 1900, which marked the height of the city's racial discord, blacks fought a slow battle for civil rights. A branch of the NAACP formed in the 1920s, under the leadership of A. P. Tureaud, a Creole activist. Over the following three decades, the chapter won gains in housing desegregation and salary equalization for teachers, and expanded voting rights and access to Louisiana State University.

The kind of police harassment that had precipitated the Riot of 1900 persisted through the 1950s, and city landlords continued to discriminate by color. Although a moderate mayor, Chep Morrison, helped to curtail police racism, he opposed the desegregation of schools, transportation, and lunch counters. The NAACP, however, won these gains in the late 1950s and early 1960s. After the passage of the U.S. Voting Rights Act of 1965, political victories for African Americans became far more common, and New Orleans elected its first black mayor, Dutch Morial, in 1978.

These changes in the political sphere reflected the major demographic shift that came with the advent of the suburbs. New Orleans's location on the Mississippi Delta had restricted the city's growth for 200 years, because most of the surrounding land was useless swamp. Using modern technology, developers drained marshlands and built new neighborhoods, and white residents moved in as soon as they could. Between 1950 and 1975 the greater metropolitan area doubled in geographic sprawl, and the white population of the city itself declined drastically.

New Orleans lost a good deal of its tax base as whites fled to the suburbs, yet the city did not die the death of many Northern industrial towns. Through the end of the twentieth century the distinctive food, music, and annual Mardi Gras celebration attracted droves of tourists. The historians Arnold R. Hirsh and Joseph Logsdon contend that "the delicate cultural amalgam that gave us jazz, a unique cuisine, and a love for public festivals is beleaguered but not yet obliterated."

Eric Bennett

SEE ALSO

World War I and African Americans; Armstrong, Louis ("Satchmo"); Baseball in the United States; Bechet, Sidney Joseph; Black Codes in the United States; Blues, The; Civil War, American; Domino, Antoine ("Fats"), Jr.; *Dred Scott* v. *Sanford*; Free Blacks in the United States, 1619 to 1863; National Association for the Advancement of Colored People; Oliver, Joseph ("King"); Voting Rights Act of 1965.

North America

Newton, Huey P.

(b. February 17, 1942, New Orleans, La.; d. August 22, 1989, Oakland, Calif.), cofounder of the American black nationalist organization the Black Panther Party.

Huey Newton grew up in Oakland, California, a place that would become the West Coast center of the American black nationalist movement. While attending Merritt College in Oakland, he met BOBBY SEALE, and the two began to work together on a project to diversify the school's curriculum. Inspired by nationalist struggles in the Third World and revolutionaries such as Fidel Castro and Mao Zedong, Newton became critical of the racist oppression of blacks in the United States and the capitalist system he saw as underpinning that exploitation (*see* SOCIALISM).

As a response to the condition of black America, Newton and Seale founded the BLACK PANTHER PARTY for Self-Defense, later simply called the Black Panther Party. "We want land, bread, housing, education, clothing, justice and peace," concluded the organization's ten-point program, which Newton coauthored. Patrolling black neighborhoods with shotguns, which were deemed legal as long as they were visible, the Panthers set themselves up as monitors of the police. These "justice patrols" sought to inform African Americans of their rights and to counteract a history of police brutality against blacks. Not surprisingly, the Panthers developed a hostile relationship with the police, with Newton becoming a magnet for police antagonism.

On October 28, 1967, Newton was charged with the murder of a police officer and the wounding of another. He pleaded innocent, and the trial provoked an intensive "Free Huey" campaign, drawing thousands to Black Panther rallies and rapidly boosting Panther membership and visibility. Viewed by many as a political prisoner, Newton continued to address political issues from prison.

In 1970, after his 1968 conviction was overturned because of procedural errors, Newton left prison to return to the Black Panther Party. He found the party weakened by regional conflict, in part because of disputes about the militant programs of Eldridge Cleaver, who influenced an East Coast-based movement. Leading a West Coast faction, Newton advocated political education and programs that he believed would link the Panthers to the broader African American community.

As his prominence in the Panthers declined, conflict with the law continued to trouble Newton. In 1974 he was accused of killing a woman and fled to CUBA. Three years later he returned to face the murder charge, which after two hung juries the state eventually dropped. He was retried and convicted for the 1967 murder of the policeman, but the conviction was later overturned.

In 1980 Newton received a Ph.D. in social philosophy from the University of California at Santa Cruz; he wrote a thesis titled the "War Against the Panthers – A Study of Repression in America." Newton's life began a downward spiral after the Panthers finally disbanded in 1982. Rumors about drug abuse surrounded him, and he was arrested in 1989 for embezzling funds from an Oakland children's nutritional program founded by the Panthers. He served six months of jail time. Later that year he was killed in what was believed to be a drug-trade related incident.

Marian Aguiar

SEE ALSO

Nationalism in Africa; Cleaver, Eldridge Leroy; San Francisco and Oakland, California; Black Nationalism in the United States.

North America

New York African Society for Mutual Relief, **New York City's first African American mutual benefit society.**

While some scholars believe that the New York African Society for Mutual Relief began meeting secretly in 1784, it was officially founded by Peter Williams Jr., a carpenter and talented public speaker, in 1808, the year of the society's first public meeting and the printing of its constitution. Its mission, like that of other MUTUAL BENEFIT SOCIETIES, was to provide a pool of resources from which members and their families could draw benefits otherwise denied to African Americans, such as burial insurance and financial aid in times of sickness. The society also provided financial assistance to widows, orphans, and the disabled. Its membership constituted a diverse segment of New York's African American community, but its leaders were mainly merchants and ministers. The society was formally incorporated on March 23, 1810, an event that was commemorated in an annual parade until around 1830.

An important safety net for many struggling African American families and small businessmen, the society quickly became a valuable source of financial aid for the needy, despite its own troubles. In 1812, for example, the society became financially strapped when one of its officers went bankrupt, but it was able to raise the funds needed to save itself from ruin. By 1820 the society was financially stable enough to invest in real estate and to build a regular meetinghouse on Orange (now Baxter) Street, which also served as a school and a stop on the UNDERGROUND RAILROAD. The society also bought properties at 27 Greenwich Avenue and 41 West 66th Street, which it rented to raise money for its relief activities.

By the 1850s the society's importance had waned with the sudden proliferation of African American organizations and the lessening need for assistance among its 65 increasingly secure members. The society continued to raise money through its properties, however, and after the NEW YORK CITY DRAFT RIOT OF 1863, in which many African Americans were hard hit, the society's leader at the time, abolitionist Charles B. Ray, provided much-needed financial assistance to many of the victims.

One of the first African American organizations of its kind, the New York African Society for Mutual Relief provided a blueprint for later African American civic organizations, including the Clarkson Society, the Dorcas Association, the Wilberforce Benevolent Society, and the Phoenix Society. It attracted many prominent black community leaders of the nineteenth century, including William Hamilton, believed to be a black descendant of Alexander Hamilton; Philip Bell, editor and publisher of the *Colored American*; Abraham Lawrence, president of the Harlem Railroad; and Samuel E. Cornish, who with John Russwurm founded *Freedom's Journal*, the first African American newspaper in the United States.

In the 1920s much of the society's work began to be shouldered by two related organizations, the William Hamilton Society and the Eato Aid Society, each named after past New York African Society presidents. Despite a diminishing role, the New York African Society for Mutual Relief remained active until the 1950s.

Robert Fay

SEE ALSO
Freedom's Journal; Russwurm, John Brown; Williams, Peter, Jr.

North America

New York City Draft Riot of 1863, the Civil War's most violent urban insurrection, largely directed at black Americans.

In Northern American cities like Toledo, Cincinnati, Harrisburg, and Detroit, the economic and social disruption caused by the Civil War led to violence directed at free Northern blacks, but the New York City Draft Riot of 1863 was by far the most violent. Factors contributing to the riot were labor unrest, unfair draft laws in an unpopular war, ethnic tensions, and disruptive street gangs. Before the 1840s New York City's blacks held most of the city's jobs as longshoremen, hod carriers, brick makers, barbers, waiters, and domestic servants. Irish immigrants, particularly those arriving after 1846, competed with blacks for these unskilled jobs and eventually gained control of the occupations, leaving many blacks to work only as strike breakers.

The animosity between New York's whites and blacks was further intensified by the Emancipation Proclamation. Democratic politicians used it to their advantage by claiming, paradoxically, that Republicans would transport freedpeople to New York to replace white workers while lazy blacks lived on relief services provided by industrious whites. Shortly after President Abraham Lincoln issued the Emancipation Proclamation, Congress passed the Conscription Act, which had a provision allowing a draftee to decline service for a $300 fee. This financial arrangement widened class divisions.

The three-day riot began on July 13 as a protest against the Conscription Act. After the protesters, many of them Irish laborers, destroyed draft headquarters, they roamed the streets, at times razing entire city blocks, cutting telegraph lines, tearing up railroad tracks, and causing factories and shops to close. They assaulted the offices of the *New York Tribune*, trying to find the pro-Union editor Horace Greeley, and they attacked the home of the city's provost marshal.

The mob then split into groups. Some destroyed mansions; others attacked the mayor's house in a failed attempt to level it. Still others targeted New York's black residents with intense violence. They terrorized blacks, burned the Colored Orphan Asylum, and looted the Colored Seamen's Home. They raided and destroyed homes; they shot, stomped, clubbed, burned, and hanged black victims. Eleven blacks were killed by rioters. Most blacks fled the city, but a few desperately sought the sanctuary of police-station jail cells. Union army regiments – including some men returning from the Battle of Gettysburg – finally restored order.

Though New York City merchants raised $50,000 to pay black victims and rebuild the Colored Orphan Asylum, the psychic scars remained. By 1865 New York's black population had decreased by 20 percent, from 12,472 to 9,945, because of the fear arising from the three nights of rioting in July 1863.

Robert Fay

SEE ALSO
Civil War, American; Thirteenth Amendment of the United States Constitution and the Emancipation Proclamation.

North America

New York Manumission Society, antislavery organization of white males who supported the gradual abolition of slavery and the betterment of African Americans.

MANUMISSION SOCIETIES emerged after the AMERICAN REVOLUTION to advocate for the end of the slave trade and the gradual abolition of slavery. Manumission, which entailed the formal and legal release of a slave, was the most common path to freedom. It could occur either privately, by an individual slaveowner, or officially, by state law. One of the most active and best organized proponents was the New York Manumission Society, founded by Quakers on January 25, 1785, in Lower Manhattan. Although many of its members were slaveholders, the New York Manumission Society actively pushed for better treatment of slaves and pursued legal action on behalf of slaves who had been mistreated or enslaved illegally.

Under the guidance of John Jay and Alexander Hamilton, the New York Manumission Society was a leader in the education of blacks in New York City for 64 years. In 1787 the society established the AFRICAN FREE SCHOOL in New York City to provide primary education for free blacks. The school emphasized reading, writing, and arithmetic and provided specialized training in navigation to encourage seafaring as a career for blacks. In addition to teaching basic skills, the black faculty of the school provided moral and religious instruction to its students, some of whom became prominent in the black community. Among this influential group of teachers were James McCune Smith, IRA ALDRIDGE, Peter Williams Jr., and ALEXANDER CRUMMELL.

By 1809 the African Free School was the largest in the city, and by 1814 it had educated more than 2300 black students. The society closed its doors in 1849 and donated its financial resources to organizations in New York that were committed to the antislavery movement.

Alonford James Robinson, Jr.

SEE ALSO
Slavery in the United States; Transatlantic Slave Trade; Abolitionism in the United States; New York, New York; Williams, Peter, Jr.

North America

New York, New York

The first Africans arrived in New Amsterdam in 1626 as slaves to the Dutch West India Company. As early as 1630 the community had free blacks, and in 1644 a group of slaves was given conditional freedom. They settled in what is now Greenwich Village, which remained a black neighborhood for nearly 200 years.

Nightclubs line 52nd Street in New York City in 1941. In the mid-1940s 52nd Street was a hotbed of bop, beginning with the 1944 appearance of a quintet co-led by trumpeter Dizzy Gillespie and bassist Oscar Pettiford. *CORBIS/Bettmann*

In 1664 the English took over New Netherland and renamed it New York, instituting a still more severe form of slavery. Africans began to organize and to battle slavery in the early eighteenth century. In 1704 Elias Neau established the first school for blacks in British North America, and in 1712 slaves rebelled but were brutally suppressed, as was a suspected slave rebellion in 1741, when 29 blacks were executed.

Abolitionist sentiment grew. A 1787 law began eliminating slavery, and in that same year free blacks founded the African Free School, which future black leaders Henry Highland Garnet and Alexander Crummell attended. In 1800 the African Methodist Episcopal Zion Church (AMEZ) was founded, and in 1809 the Abyssinian Baptist Church started. After 1820 many African Americans lived in the infamous Five Points slum and areas north and west of the Hudson River. In 1827 slavery was finally abolished, and the first black newspaper in the United States began – *Freedom's Journal,* edited by John Russwurm and Samuel Cornish. The abolitionist movement gained momentum in 1835, when David Ruggles organized the New York Committee of Vigilance.

At the same time immigrants from Europe pushed African Americans out of the skilled labor force and rioted against blacks in 1834 and 1835. The 1840s and 1850s were characterized by widespread discrimination against African Americans, and during the Civil War poor whites rebelled against conscription, venting their anger during the 1863 draft riot: 11 African Americans, including children, were murdered by marauding white mobs, who also burned down the Colored Orphan Asylum. Many African Americans fled to Brooklyn.

The African American community continued to develop its institutions, notably T. Thomas Fortune's newspaper the *New York Age* in 1870. But African Americans were excluded from most unions and hence from much of the growing industrial labor market. By 1890 the 33,000-person community lived in the old and new Tenderloin districts between 20th and 53rd Streets and eventually the San Juan Hill district (so named for its racial fights) between West 61st and West 63rd Streets.

In 1898 New York consolidated five boroughs into itself, including Brooklyn, the third largest city in the United States. Brooklyn's black population was 10,287 by 1890.

The 1904 collapse of the housing market in Harlem led the black community of Manhattan to resettle there. Philip Payton's Afro-Am Realty Company was instrumental in that move, as was a new migration of African Americans from the South and the Caribbean. From 1900 to 1920 the black population of New York nearly tripled, making New York the largest black community in the United States. Harlem quickly became the cultural and political epicenter of black America. The AME Zion, St. Philip's Protestant Episcopal, and Abyssinian Baptist Church relocated to Harlem. In 1919 the influential *Amsterdam News* was founded there. From Harlem, the National Association for the Advancement of Colored People's *Crisis* and the National Urban League's *Opportunity* magazines published pioneering black literature and editorials. In the 1920s Harlem nurtured a socialist movement, led by H. H. Harrison, W. A. Domingo, and (later) A. Philip Randolph, while Marcus Garvey's enormously popular Universal Negro Improvement Association promoted not simply a back-to-Africa drive but the first black nationalist movement.

In 1925 Alain Locke edited an issue of *Survey Graphic* magazine, filling it with poetry, art, essays, fiction, and folklore and declaring a "New Negro" renaissance: through cultural expression, African Americans would be "a new figure on the national canvas and a new force in the foreground of affairs." The issue signaled a brief but intense interest in Harlem and African America, from nightclubs such as the Cotton Club to the literature of Jessie Fauset, James Weldon Johnson, Jean Toomer, Langston Hughes, Countee Cullen, Claude McKay, Wallace Thurman, Nella Larsen, Zora Neale Hurston, and Arna Bontemps. Eubie Blake, Fats Waller, and Duke Ellington developed a jazz tradition that over the decades brought Charlie Parker, Bud Powell, Ornette Coleman, and Miles Davis to New York. In politics, Charles Fillmore became the first black district leader in 1929.

The Depression brought much of this momentum to a halt. African Americans were thrown out of work in disproportionately larger numbers than white New Yorkers. Discrimination and segregation became more pronounced, leading to the 1935 Harlem riot, when thousands of frustrated Harlemites destroyed more than $2 million of property. The disturbance led to greater black political organization. Four black district leaders were elected. In 1937 black leaders formed the Greater New York City Coordinating Committee for the Employment of Negroes, an activist organization that used boycotts to force the hiring of African Americans.

Beginning with World War II, African Americans from the South and the Caribbean poured into Harlem and Brooklyn – especially after A. Philip Randolph organized the 1941 March on Washington, which opened defense industry jobs to blacks. In 1943, however, frustration with racism led to another Harlem riot, in which 6 African Americans were killed and more than 180 injured. This event galvanized citywide efforts to improve race relations. One year later Adam Clayton Powell Jr. was elected to the United States Congress and Benjamin Davis to the city council.

The 1940s saw the consolidation and growth of Brooklyn's Bedford-Stuyvesant neighborhood into the most populous black community in New York – but also an impoverished ghetto that reached into Crown Heights and Brownsville by 1960. Caribbean immigration shifted to Brooklyn until, by 1970, 40 percent of all African Americans in the city lived in Brooklyn. The population shift led to increased black political strength, and in 1968 state assemblywoman Shirley Chisholm was elected to the U.S. Congress.

Harlem developed as a political, religious, and literary mecca in the 1940s and 1950s.

Hulan Jack became the first black Manhattan borough president in 1953. In the 1950s Malcolm X built the Harlem Mosque into one of the most dynamic centers of the Nation of Islam and spearheaded a black nationalist movement to defend black Americans with force against white racism and violence. In 1965 Malcolm X was assassinated; his death led to a call for still greater black power as well as the decline of his movement. From the 1940s through the 1970s Harlem nurtured some of the most powerful and original literary voices in the United States, including Ralph Ellison, James Baldwin, Lorraine Hansberry, Amiri Baraka, and Audre Lorde. In the late 1970s black New York also developed a vital new musical tradition – rap – notably through

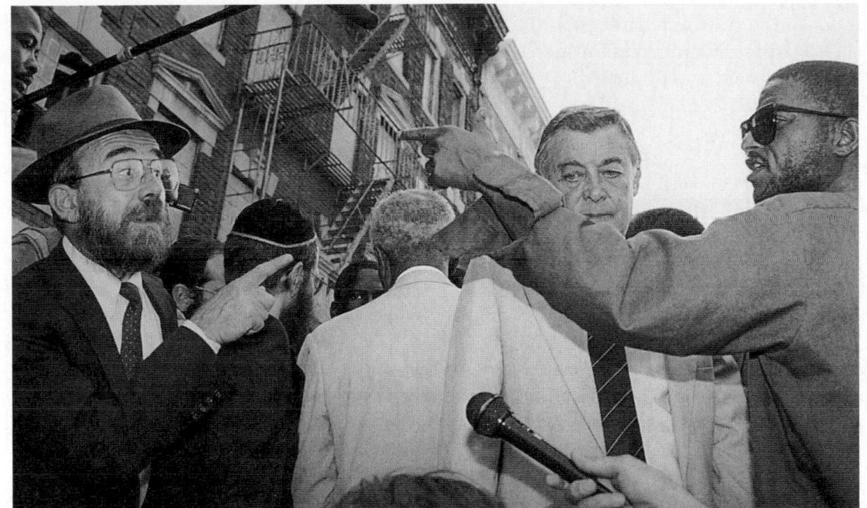

such pioneers as RUN-DMC, Grandmaster Flash, and PUBLIC ENEMY.

In 1970 Charles Rangel was elected to the congressional seat vacated by Adam Clayton Powell Jr. Percy Sutton was Manhattan borough president for 11 years, beginning in 1966. But the African American community had not advanced into other citywide offices, and widespread unemployment and poverty once again increased frustrations. A 1977 power brownout led to looting in Brooklyn that was reminiscent of the 1935 Harlem riot.

OPPOSITE: Two black workers tighten a rivet during construction of the Holland Tunnel into New York City in 1924. *CORBIS/Bettmann*
LEFT: Relations between African Americans and Hasidic Jews became strained after the Crown Heights incident in 1991. *AP/Wide World Photos*
BELOW LEFT: This engraving shows a mob setting fire to a house on Lexington Avenue during the 1863 New York City draft riots. *CORBIS/Bettmann*

In 1989 David Dinkins was the first African American to be elected mayor of New York. But Dinkins inherited severe problems, notably crime and a deteriorated school system. In 1993 Dinkins was defeated for reelection in a city that was newly polarized along racial lines after the 1991 Crown Heights incident – in which the accidental death of a black boy, killed by a Hasidic driver in a motorcade, led to the murder of a rabbinical student by a black mob.

Jim Mendelsohn

SEE ALSO

Blake, James Hubert ("Eubie"); Civil War, American; Coleman, Ornette; *Crisis, The*; Davis, Miles Dewey, III; Dinkins, David Norman; Fauset, Jessie Redmon; *Freedom's Journal*; Garvey, Marcus Mosiah; Grandmaster Flash, Melle Mel, and the Furious Five; Great Depression; Harlem Renaissance; Harlem Riots of 1935; Harlem Riots of 1943; Harlem, New York; Locke, Alain Leroy; Lorde, Audre Geraldine; National Association for the Advancement of Colored People; New York City Draft Riot of 1863; Opportunity: Journal of Negro Life; Parker, Charles Christopher ("Bird"); Powell, Adam Clayton, Jr.; Powell, Earl ("Bud"); Randolph, Asa Philip; Rangel, Charles Bernard; Sutton, Percy Ellis; Waller, Thomas Wright ("Fats"); Ellington, Edward Kennedy ("Duke"); Black Nationalism in the United States.

North America

New York Slave Conspiracy of 1741, **an alleged insurrection planned by New York City's black slaves and white poor, which highlighted the fear whites had of violent slave rebellions and the punitive measures they enlisted to prevent them.**

Between May 11 and August 29, 1741, following years of increasing paranoia among white New Yorkers, 30 blacks and 4 whites were executed for allegedly planning an insurrection against slaveholders. Scholars disagree about whether a conspiracy existed. The trial's record contains evidence of widespread dissatisfaction, unrest, and sporadic violence among blacks, but it provides no conclusive evidence of an actual insurrectionary plot. What seems clear is that the charges, and the executions that followed, grew out of New York whites' mounting fear of the city's blacks.

White New Yorkers' fear was fueled by a series of events. Two dozen slaves participated in the NEW YORK SLAVE REBELLION OF 1712, killing 9 and wounding 7. Many whites believed rumors that slaves had poisoned the city's water supply in 1740. In response, they drank only bottled water for months. White New Yorkers also felt threatened by the relatively high concentration of slaves in the city. Blacks represented about 20 percent of the city's 11,000 residents. In the colonies, only Charleston, South Carolina, had a higher proportion of blacks. In 1739 slaves in Charleston rebelled, and white New Yorkers associated that incident with Charleston's similarly high concentration of slaves. Further, many white men had left New York to fight in the "King's War" against Spain. Those who remained felt more vulnerable.

The widespread discontent that had existed among the black and white poor, who were adversely affected by an economic depression throughout the colony, increased during the winter of 1740-1741. More than 3 m (10 ft) of snow had fallen on the city, and over 100 km (60 mi) of the Hudson River had frozen. Commerce in the city virtually stopped. Supplies dwindled, and merchants raised food and heating fuel prices beyond the reach of the poor. The wealthy, who were able to afford the price increases, passed the winter comfortably (as did their slaves). Many of the poor long remembered the merchants who profited by the scarcity, as well as the uncharitable among the wealthy.

Finally, a series of fires from mid-March into April 1741 persuaded many whites that blacks were plotting an insurrection. First, Fort George, a government complex, burned to the ground. A week later a resident's house caught fire. Eight more fires occurred by April 5, some of suspicious origin. No conclusive evidence tied blacks to the fires, but one resident claimed to have heard a slave repeating, "Fire, Fire, Scorch, Scorch, A LITTLE, damn it, BY-AND-BY," which she believed indicated that blacks were responsible for the fires.

One hundred and fifty slaves were charged with the capital crime of conspiracy. The subsequent trial was marred by coercion and bribes. When investigators could find no conclusive evidence that a conspiracy existed, they began seeking witnesses who could link the fires to a planned uprising. Many slaves confessed after being tortured or promised rewards. The most damaging testimony came from Mary Burton, a servant indentured to an innkeeper named Hughson who had been granted immunity by prosecutor Daniel Horsmanden. Burton stated that several slaves had met frequently at her employer's house, and that she heard them "talk frequently of burning the fort and that they'd go down to the Fly and burn the whole town. My master and mistress [the innkeeper and his wife] said they'd aid and assist them as much as they could."

The Hughsons, two other whites, and 104 blacks were convicted. Of the 30 slaves executed, 13 were burned to death and 16 hanged. All four whites were hanged. Authorities pardoned 33 of the slaves, returning them to their owners. The remaining 72 slaves confessed, pleaded for mercy, and were pardoned and deported.

Robert Fay

North America

New York Slave Rebellion of 1712, a rebellion against inhumane treatment that resulted in harsher slave codes in New York.

On April 6, 1712, about 25 American Indian and black slaves in colonial New York City retaliated against harsh treatment by their masters. They set fire to an outhouse, then lay in ambush, killing nine men and wounding seven others as they came to extinguish the fire. The slaves then fled to the woods. Within two days more than 40 had been arrested and 6 had committed suicide before arrest.

Twenty-seven slaves were convicted of murder and sentenced to death, although much of the evidence used to convict them was suspect; 18 were acquitted. Six, including a pregnant woman, were reprieved. Historians disagree on the exact number of people executed, but it is likely that approximately 20 people were hanged, including a pregnant woman. Three more were burned to death, one was hung in chains until he died, and one was broken on the wheel.

Shortly after the rebellion, New York's legislature toughened its slave codes. Slaves gathering in groups of three or more were subject to 40 lashes, and such crimes as burning barns, outhouses, stables, and stacks of corn or hay were all made punishable by death. Wanting to avoid similar uprisings, the Massachusetts legislature passed a law forbidding slave importation, and the Pennsylvania legislature placed an import duty on blacks that effectively ended their importation.

Robert Fay

See Also
American Indians; New York, New York.

Africa

Ngala (also known as Bangala and Mangala), ethnic group of Democratic Republic of the Congo.

The Ngala primarily inhabit northwestern Congo-Kinshasa and neighboring Congo-Brazzaville. Other Ngala live in Angola. They speak a Bantu language, Lingala, which serves as a means of communication among different peoples in western Congo-Kinshasa. Approximately 400,000 people consider themselves Ngala.

See Also
Bantu: Dispersion and Settlement; Congo, Republic of the.

Africa

Ngandu, ethnic group of the Democratic Republic of the Congo.

The Ngandu primarily inhabit central Congo-Kinshasa. They speak a Bantu language. Approximately 200,000 people consider themselves Ngandu.

See Also
Bantu: Dispersion and Settlement.

Africa

Ngbandi, ethnic group of Central Africa.

The Ngbandi primarily inhabit the northwestern Democratic Republic of the Congo and the southern Central African Republic. They speak a Niger-Congo language. Approximately 200,000 people consider themselves Ngbandi.

See Also
Languages, African: An Overview.

Africa

Ngindu (also known as Ngindo), ethnic group of Tanzania.

The Ngindu primarily inhabit Tanzania. They speak a Bantu language. More than 200,000 people consider themselves Ngindu.

See Also
Bantu: Dispersion and Settlement.

Africa

Ngombe, ethnic group of the Democratic Republic of the Congo.

The Ngombe primarily inhabit northwestern Congo-Kinshasa along the Congo River. They speak a Bantu language. Approximately 200,000 people consider themselves Ngombe.

See Also
Bantu: Dispersion and Settlement.

Africa

Ngonde, ethnic group of southeastern Africa.

The Ngonde primarily inhabit the Northern Province of Malawi. Others live in eastern Zambia and southwestern Tanzania. They speak a Bantu language and are closely related to the Nyasa people. Approximately 200,000 people consider themselves Ngonde.

See Also
Bantu: Dispersion and Settlement.

Africa

Ngoni (also known as Angoni, Abangoni, Mangoni, and Wangoni), ethnic group comprising approximately a dozen distinct peoples.

The Ngoni are a Bantu-speaking NGUNI group who, before the nineteenth century, inhabited the area of present-day Natal in SOUTH AFRICA. Starting in 1818 the Ngoni began to flee north as Shaka Zulu's army undertook its campaign of expansion. Led by their chief, Zwangendaba, they traveled through present-day MOZAMBIQUE and crossed the ZAMBEZI RIVER in 1835. Traversing ZAMBIA, they settled on the southeastern shores of LAKE TANGANYIKA.

Adopting the military strategies of the ZULU, the Ngoni dominated most of the groups they encountered while spreading northward in the wake of the Zulu expansion. Their large, compact villages – which, for defensive purposes, were inhabited by 2000 to 3000 adults – were strategically clustered and were surrounded by a buffer zone. A centralized political hierarchy, led by a hereditary chief, also contributed to their military success. But the Ngoni could not conquer the BEMBA or Bisa, despite frequent raids. These groups, having acquired guns through the sale of ivory and slaves to Swahili and Arab merchants, were able to stand their ground.

When Zwangendaba fled in 1845, the Ngoni splintered and dispersed. Under the leadership of Zwangendaba's son, Mpezeni I, a large group migrated south and in 1880 subdued the CHEWA and Nsenga of southeastern Zambia and the adjacent areas of Malawi and Mozambique. Although these and other groups came under the political umbrella of the Ngoni, they retained their ethnic identity and much of their culture. The Ngoni themselves soon faced an overpowering military force of British colonial troops, who conquered the area in 1897 and banned slave trading. The colonial administration appointed the grandson of Mpezeni I to administer local government as the Ngoni Native Authority.

Today three-quarters of the more than 1 million Ngoni live in Malawi. About 350,000 live in Zambia, another 170,000 inhabit Tanzania, and a small number live in northwestern Mozambique. Having been pacified by the British colonial authorities, the Ngoni gradually assimilated into the local culture. As a result, the Ngoni have almost lost their original language, and today speak primarily Nyanja except during religious ceremonies and royal praises. They have become matrilineal cultivators of maize and herders of cattle.

Ari Nave

SEE ALSO

Ivory Trade; Shaka; Swahili People; Indian Ocean Slave Trade.

Africa

Ngouabi, Marien (b. December 31, 1938, Ombélé, Moyen-Congo [Republic of the Congo]; d. March 18, 1977, Brazzaville, Republic of the Congo), army officer and president of the Congo (1968-1977) who was assassinated by rivals.

Born into a chiefly lineage, Marien Ngouabi proved to be a popular political moderate during his term as president of the REPUBLIC OF THE CONGO. He attended the Général Leclerc school for veterans' children in Brazzaville, hundreds of miles from his hometown in northeastern Congo (then the French colony of Moyen-Congo). Later he joined the French colonial military in OUBANGUI-CHARI (present-day CENTRAL AFRICAN REPUBLIC); became a sergeant; served in suppressing the BAMILÉKÉ rebellion in CAMEROON; and received military training in FRANCE. He was arrested twice during his early years as an officer, first for criticizing French policies in Cameroon and later for joining riots in Brazzaville. Acceptance into the French officers' academy, St. Cyr, however, redeemed his military career.

In 1963 Ngouabi became commander of the parachute corps in the newly independent Republic of the Congo. As he became more active in the ruling party, then-president Alphonse Massemba-Debat began to fear the charismatic captain's popularity and influence, and so he demoted and later arrested Ngouabi. This arrest led to a mutiny, Massemba-Debat's resignation, and Ngouabi's release and takeover in 1968. To assuage the radical left and gain support among his MBOCHI ethnic kinsmen, Ngouabi established a "vanguard" party (the Congolese Workers Party, or PCT), proclaimed a "people's republic," and adopted scientific socialism. In theory, socialism would be rationally planned and implemented thoroughly throughout the country.

Ngouabi increasingly employed the security apparatus to crush opposition while also attempting to broaden the government's popular appeal by reestablishing the national assembly. An ideological moderate in Congolese terms, he tried to please all sides through a belated incorporation of southerners into his government. But this move alienated many radical northern military officers. A number of these officers – including current president DENIS SASSOU-NGUESSO – are alleged to have plotted the still unsolved assassination of Ngouabi in March 1977. Brig. Gen. J. Yhombi-Opango succeeded Ngouabi.

Eric Young

SEE ALSO

African Socialism; Brazzaville, Republic of the Congo.

Ngugi, James. Please see NGUGI WA THIONG'O

Africa

Ngugi wa Thiong'o (Ngugi, James) (b. January 5, 1938, Kamiriithu, Kenya), Kenyan writer whose fictional work depicts events in colonial and postcolonial KENYA and whose essays emphasize the role of language and culture in the process of decolonization in Africa.

During a critical time in Kenyan history Ngugi wa Thiong'o's fiction brought to life the struggle for independence and the task of nation building (*see* NATIONALISM IN AFRICA). He integrated Marxist-Leninist beliefs into his writing, depicting the lives of Kenyan peasants and workers with an aesthetic finesse that for the most part avoided the doctrinaire yet at times landed him in trouble with Kenyan authorities. His vivid characterizations of women illustrate the range of women's roles in national struggles. Yet, for many, what has set Ngugi apart has been his decision to radicalize his contribution to Kenyan culture by writing in his native language of Gikuyu rather than English, the colonial tongue.

Ngugi was born into a polygamous family in a village near Limuru Town in Central Province, Kenya. While attending a prestigious British-sponsored high school, he witnessed the intensifying independence struggle of the Kenyan people against the British colonial government in a guerrilla war that came to be called the MAU MAU REBELLION. The war came very close to home for Ngugi. His mother was arrested and tortured for his brother's involvement with the guerrillas, and his stepbrother, a deaf mute, was shot by soldiers simply because he did not hear their order to stop. Ngugi later incorporated many of these experiences into his fictional work.

After completing an undergraduate degree at Makerere University, Ngugi traveled to England to enroll at the University of Leeds. His first two novels were written there. *Weep Not Child* (1964) portrays a young Kenyan man who pursues a Western education while his village suffers the ravages of the war of independence. In this novel Ngugi revealed how personal tragedy is interconnected with the larger tragedy of the ancestral lands lost and resources plundered under COLONIAL RULE. Like many of Ngugi's later works, the novel draws on KIKUYU myth, most significantly the story of creation, and emphasizes the connection between the people and the land of Kenya.

The River Between (1965), written first but published second, portrays the conflicted relationship between two villages representing traditional African beliefs on the one hand and Christianity on the other. In this novel a mission-educated character tries unsuccessfully to synthesize the Christian world-view with the Gikuyu, even as he comes to understand the ultimately destructive force Christianity will have on his own culture (*see* CHRISTIANITY: MISSIONARIES IN AFRICA).

Ngugi did not complete his master's thesis, which focused on Caribbean literature, because he refused to make the designated revisions. Instead, he spent his time studying Marxism and reading the works of national liberation writers such as FRANTZ FANON. When he returned to Kenya in 1967, he became the first black African member of the University of Nairobi English Department. A year later, citing the need for the newly independent nation to develop a national culture, he coauthored a successful proposal to abolish the English Department and replace it with a Department of Literature focusing primarily on national literature and indigenous oral tradition, with reference to other writings of Africa, the African diaspora, and the Third World.

With his third and best-known novel, *A Grain of Wheat* (1967), Ngugi revealed his sophistication as an artist. The novel portrays several characters in a village whose intertwined lives are transformed by the 1952-1960 state of emergency in Kenya. As events unfold, compromises are forced, friendships are betrayed, and romantic loves are tested. The narrative of *A Grain of Wheat* is interwoven with myth as well as allusions to real-life leaders of the nationalist struggle, such as JOMO KENYATTA. Ngugi explores the psychology of his characters yet employs a shifting narrative voice to evoke a strong sense of community. He did not hesitate to portray harshly those Kenyans, specifically the Home Guard, who made compromises with the colonial government for their own personal gain.

In 1969 Ngugi resigned from his post in Nairobi to protest the lack of academic freedom. After two years of teaching in the United States at Northwestern University, he returned to the department in Nairobi and published a collection of essays, *Homecoming: Essays on African and Caribbean Literature, Culture, and Politics* (1972). In one essay he implicated the missionary church in bolstering colonial authority in Kenya, and shortly after, he dropped the Christian name James in favor of the name Ngugi wa Thiong'o.

His next novel, *Petals of Blood* (1977), criticized the elite post-independence leaders and the role that capitalism had played in creating a Kenyan society increasingly polarized between rich and poor. Although *Petals of Blood* painted a harsh picture of the Kenyan government, it was not the work that raised the ire of the Kenyan authorities. Rather it was Ngugi's work in popular theater that landed him in prison. During the 1960s and 1970s he had written several plays, including *The Black Hermit* (1968; produced 1962), and cowritten others, including the critically acclaimed *The Trial of Dedan Kimathi* (1976; produced 1974) and the Gikuyu play *Ngaahika ndeenda* (1980, I Will Marry When I Want). When *Ngaahika ndeenda* was used as a political organizing tool, a call to arms for exploited Kenyan peasants, the government imprisoned Ngugi for a year in 1977-1978.

While in prison, Ngugi made the decision to write in Gikuyu. He explained his reasons in a later collection of essays, *Decolonising the Mind* (1983), in which he discussed how language carries ideology, and how national culture is endangered when the colonial language supplants the indigenous: "Language carries culture, and culture carries, particularly through orature and literature, the entire body of values by which we perceive ourselves and our place in the world.... Language is thus inseparable from ourselves as a community of human beings with a specific form and character, a specific history, a specific relationship to the world."

Caitaani Mutharaba-ini (1980, Devil on the Cross), begun on a roll of toilet paper hidden from the guards in prison, portrays a gruesome contest between participants at the Devil's Feast, who compete for the title of greatest criminal. The party symbolically represents a nation cannibalized by greedy individuals, both Kenyan and foreign. The heroes are the Kenyan peasants and workers, some of whom later heard the work read out loud in villages. Ngugi followed this with another play, *Maitu njugira* (1981, Mother, Sing for Me), never officially performed but seen by many in public rehearsals, and the essay collection *Writers in Politics* (1981).

During a book tour in 1982, Ngugi was forced to remain in England after he learned that he would be arrested if he returned to Kenya. That year he wrote his next novel, *Matigari ma Mjiruumgi* (1986, Matigari), which quickly became an underground success in Kenya. By this time his work commanded such a presence that the Kenyan government waged a campaign to route out the rebel leader Matigari, a man said to be inciting revolutions throughout the Kenyan countryside, only to discover that he was merely a fictional character.

From his home in New York, where he teaches at New York University, Ngugi has continued to write on cultural imperialism and the necessity for social and economic justice. He has designated the role of literature as a life force in this struggle: "The very act of writing is a social act: writing about somebody for somebody. Writing reflects a community wrestling with its environment to make it yield the means of life."

Marian Aguiar

SEE ALSO

Christianity, African: An Overview; Decolonization in Africa: An Interpretation; Theater, African; African Religions: An Interpretation.

Africa

Nguni, southern African ethnic groups that speak related Bantu languages and inhabit southeast Africa from Cape Province to southern MOZAMBIQUE.

Historians believe that the ancestors of contemporary Nguni were the first Bantu speakers to arrive in southeastern Africa, some time after the second century C.E. Linguists point to the use of "clicks" in Nguni languages as evidence not only of the antiquity of the migration but also of the early migrants' likely assimilation of KHOISAN speakers, whose language uses similar phonemes. No other Bantu languages use "clicks." The large number of cognates between Nguni languages and Swahili also suggests that the Bantu migrants traveled south via Africa's east coast. Today most Nguni languages are not mutually intelligible. Some of the more prominent Nguni ethnic groups include the XHOSA and the ZULU of SOUTH AFRICA, the SWAZI of SWAZILAND, the NDEBELE of ZIMBABWE, and the NGONI of MALAWI.

The Nguni peoples are thought to have lived for centuries in scattered patrilineal chiefdoms, cultivating cereal crops such as millet and raising cattle. The current geographic distribution of Nguni peoples largely reflects the turbulent political developments and population movements of the nineteenth century. In the 1820s the cattle-herding Zulu, led by their king SHAKA, embarked on an aggressive campaign of conquest and expansion known as the MFECANE. Shaka's large and well-armed armies conquered a number of neighboring peoples and sent others fleeing. Some Nguni groups adopted the Zulu's methods of warfare and used them to subjugate the peoples in whose territory they ultimately settled. The Ndebele of Zimbabwe are one such group; the Soshangane of MOZAMBIQUE are another. The Swazi Kingdom was also established during this period.

Even before the *mfecane*, trade and colonialism made their mark on the regions inhabited by Nguni peoples. From the sixteenth century onward European merchant vessels frequented trading posts on the coast of present-day southern Mozambique, seeking goods such as gold, ivory, and slaves. The Portuguese, in particular, brought maize from the New World, which soon became a staple crop in much of southeastern Africa, and which some historians argue contributed to both population growth and the eventual rise of complex states in the region. Nguni cattle-herding groups such as the Xhosa traded their livestock for the guns and tobacco of European settlers from the Cape Colony (in present-day South Africa).

During the nineteenth century European expansionism brought the Xhosa and other Nguni groups into conflicts with both migrating Afrikaners and British troops. Many communities lost land and cattle. The discovery of diamonds in the 1860s and gold in the 1880s provided an even greater motive for European conquest of Nguni-occupied lands. By the turn of the century many men from Nguni communities were migrating to work in the gold mines near Witwatersrand.

In rural areas many Nguni peoples still herd cattle and cultivate cereal crops, as well as a variety of cash crops. But a significant proportion of many Nguni groups' populations now either live in cities or depend on earnings from seasonal migrant labor in the mines.

Ari Nave

See Also

Afrikaner; Gold Trade; Ivory Trade; Languages, African: An Overview; Swahili Language; Trans-atlantic Slave Trade.

Africa

Nguru (also known as Ngulu and Wanguru), ethnic group of Tanzania.

The Nguru primarily inhabit the coastal highlands of northeastern Tanzania. They speak a Bantu language. Approximately 200,000 people consider themselves Nguru.

See Also

Bantu: Dispersion and Settlement.

North America

Niagara Movement (1905-1910), African American political action organization founded by W. E. B. Du Bois and William Monroe Trotter.

At the start of the twentieth century no African American voice carried such authority with both black and white audiences as that of Booker T. Washington. The founder of Tuskegee Institute, he presided over a network of membership organizations, including the Afro-American Council and the National Negro Business League, that worked to promote racial uplift among black Americans. Some African Americans, however, were dissatisfied with Washington's message of accommodationism, which counseled economic self-help and patience. Washington's critics demanded that black American citizens be granted the same civil rights enjoyed by whites. The militant Niagara Movement was a direct response to Washington's cautious approach to racial justice; though short-lived, it was an important step in the formation of modern African American protest movements.

Both W. E. B. Du Bois and William Monroe Trotter, the movement's organizers, had long opposed Washington's philosophy. Trotter, the editor of the *Boston Guardian*, an African American daily newspaper known for its militant editorials, had publicly rebuked Washington at a meeting in Boston in 1903; after the meeting, Trotter was jailed for nearly causing a riot. That same year Du Bois had published in his classic book *The Souls of Black Folk* an essay condemning Washington for his acceptance of lowered expectations for African Americans. In 1904 Du Bois had joined Washington on the Committee of Twelve, a coalition that met to discuss solutions to the problems facing black Americans. But the preponderance of Washington's allies on the committee and its general air of conservatism caused Du Bois to resign the following year.

Trotter and Du Bois first met in the spring of 1905, while the latter was investigating charges that Washington had been using financial pressure to control the mainstream black press. Trotter proposed that he and Du Bois collaborate further, this time in creating, as he said, a "national 'strategy board' for defensive and offensive and constructive action." Together with C. E. Bentley and F. L. McGhee, two midwestern activists, Du Bois and Trotter planned a conference to be held in upstate New York later that year. Du Bois sent invitations to nearly 60 men whose anti-Washington feelings were known, asking them to join in "organized, determined and aggressive action on the part of men who believe in Negro freedom and growth."

Because they had difficulty finding hotel accommodations on the United States side of Niagara Falls, Du Bois, Trotter, and the 27 other men who came met across the river in Canada. Du Bois was chosen as secretary and Trotter as chairman of the committee on press and public opinion. The group also issued a Declaration of Principles, which stated that the movement sought economic justice, educational equality, fully protected suffrage, and an end to racial segregation. They argued that "persistent manly agitation is the way to liberty." In advocating direct action for African American civil rights, the Niagara Movement placed itself in direct opposition to Booker T. Washington's cautious stance. Though never naming Washington, the declaration further said, "We refuse to allow the impression to remain that the Negro-American assents to inferiority, is submissive under oppression and apologetic before insults."

Even before the Niagara members met, spies from the Washington camp had tried to infiltrate the movement, though they were stymied by the change in location. After the first meeting the black press, which typically championed Washington, kept mention of the Niagara Movement from its pages. Though the movement grew to include 170 members in 34 states, by 1906 it was already in trouble. Trotter and Du Bois clashed on the inclusion of women, which Trotter opposed, and feuds within Boston's black community further unbalanced the *Guardian*'s editor. In 1907 Trotter resigned his chairmanship of the press committee. The following year neither Du Bois nor Trotter attended the annual conference. In 1908 Trotter started his own group, the Negro-American Political League, and by 1909 Du Bois was asking remaining Niagara contacts to consider joining the newly formed National Association for the Advancement of Colored People (NAACP).

Historian Stephen R. Fox cites three reasons, in addition to the tensions between Du Bois and Trotter, for the collapse of the Niagara Movement: Washington's opposition; a persistent lack of money, stemming in part from the white philanthropic world's loyalty to Washington; and a racial message too militant for its own time. At its 1906 meeting in Harpers Ferry, Du Bois had written that the Niagara Movement claimed for black Americans "every single right that belongs to a freeborn American, political, civil, and social; and until we get these rights we will never cease to protest and assail the ears of America." This plea for racial justice was later voiced by the NAACP and other groups, and resonated during the Civil Rights Movement of the 1960s; but in 1905 few Americans were ready to hear it.

Kate Tuttle

See Also

Press, Black, in the United States; Du Bois, William Edward Burghardt (W. E. B.); *Guardian, The*; Tuskegee University; Washington, Booker Taliaferro; Accommodationism in the United States.

Africa

Niamey, Niger, capital and largest city of Niger.

The administrative, economic, and cultural capital of Niger, Niamey is located on the left bank of the Niger River in the south-western part of the country. The city's early history is subject to dispute. Some claim that it was originally a Songhai fishing village named after the local Niami tree, while others believe it was founded by a Djerma chief named Kouri Mali. Nevertheless, most historians agree that small groups of Djerma, Hausa, and Wazi peoples coexisted in the Niamey area prior to European colonialism. In 1926 the French moved the capital of Niger from Zinder to Niamey in order to facilitate trade with other French colonies along the Niger River.

Since the colonial era Niamey has served as a crossroads, linking Niger's regional towns and farming areas, such as Agadez and Zinder, to West African cities such as Abidjan and Lagos. Trade between the city and neighboring countries suffers, however, from the poor state of the region's roadways, which are often impassable during the rainy seasons. Although it is expected that Niamey will greatly profit from the trans-Saharan highway now under construction, many critics believe that the government should instead spend the money to construct a railway linking Niamey to the BURKINA FASO capital of Ouagadougou, which is already connected to Abidjan by rail. Although the French had planned to construct such a railway during the colonial era, it was never completed.

Niamey is also home to several minor factories that produce bricks and textiles and process grains, much of which is exported. The city has an estimated population of 700,000 people and an annual growth rate of approximately 10 percent.

Elizabeth Heath

SEE ALSO

Abidjan, Côte d'Ivoire; Colonial Rule; Lagos, Nigeria; Ouagadougou, Burkina Faso; Songhai Empire; Zinder, Niger.

Latin America and the Caribbean

Nicaragua, republic and largest nation in Central America. Called "the land of lakes and volcanoes," it contains regions of thick rain forests, rugged highlands, and fertile farming areas. The largest lakes in Central America and a chain of volcanic peaks dominate its western heartland, the center of its population and economy. Severe earthquakes have destroyed Managua, its capital and largest city, twice in the twentieth century (*see* CENTRAL AMERICA).

Most of Nicaragua's black population was historically concentrated in the country's southeastern corner, known as the Mosquito Coast. These children attend school in that area. *Julio Etchart/Still Pictures*

North America

Nicholas Brothers (Fayard, b. 1918, and Harold, b. 1924, Philadelphia, Pa.), African American tap dancers who performed in Hollywood musicals in the 1930s and 1940s.

Fayard and Harold Nicholas began dancing in Philadelphia in the 1930s. Rising to stardom as a tap-dancing duo, they appeared in the musicals *Tin Pan Alley, Stormy Weather, Down Argentine Way,* and *The Big Broadcast of 1936.* The pair performed with such contemporary stars as JOSEPHINE BAKER, LENA HORNE, Gene Kelly, BILL ("BOJANGLES") ROBINSON, and Cab Calloway. In the late 1940s, with tap dance's popularity waning in the United States, the Nicholas Brothers moved to Europe. They gave a royal command performance for the king of England in 1948 and performed at the inauguration of United States president Dwight D. Eisenhower in 1955.

Marian Aguiar

SEE ALSO

Calloway, Cabell (Cab); Tap Dance.

Nicholas, Fayard. Please see NICHOLAS BROTHERS

Africa

Niger, a West African country bordered by BURKINA FASO, BENIN, NIGERIA, CHAD, LIBYA, ALGERIA, and MALI.

Straddling the SAHARA DESERT and the SAHEL, the fragile environment of Niger has shaped the lives of its peoples from the earliest days to the present. Niger's early societies enabled their people to sustain themselves even in times of drought through such means as shifting cultivation and participation in trans-Saharan trade networks that supplemented local production. These practices preserved the fragile Sahel and buffered against famine. During the twentieth century, however, French colonialism forced Nigeriens to abandon such centuries-old techniques in order to produce cash crops. This left Nigeriens more vulnerable to drought and dependent on unreliable global commodity markets. French colonial neglect and the demands of the global market economy have perpetuated Nigerien poverty, ecological vulnerability, and political instability since independence. As a result, Nigeriens, like other peoples of the Sahel, struggle to meet their social and ecological needs amid the pressures of the global economy.

EARLY HISTORY

Thinly populated and peripheral to the major kingdoms of West Africa, Niger, along with its early history, has frequently been ignored in comparison to the nearby great empires – Mali, Ghana, and Songhai. Niger has a rich history of its own, however. The human presence in the region dates back at least 60,000 years. Archaeological evidence suggests that pastoralists settled in the north central regions of the country during a time of frequent rainfall more than 7000 years ago. These groups migrated southward and adopted settled agriculture, based on the cultivation of MILLET and sorghum, around 2500 B.C.E., when the Sahara region became more arid. By 1000 C.E. two empires had started to develop along the borders of present-day Niger – Songhai to the west and Kanem-Bornu to the east. Both empires periodically extended their rule over parts of present-day Niger. Nomadic TUAREG people controlled the northern two-thirds of Niger for much of this period.

The strength and prosperity of these empires were based on their ability to control the lucrative trans-Saharan and trans-Sudanic trade in slaves, valuable metals, and salt. Their security depended on maintaining a successful symbiosis with the nomadic groups – Tuareg, TOUBOU, and FULANI – who led the caravans. Attacked by Moroccan invaders in 1591, the Songhai Empire gradually disintegrated into separate city-states, many of them subject to Mali. Refugees from this invasion settled in present-day Niger. Kanem-Bornu, although weakened by a series of succession disputes, recovered sufficiently to remain an important player in the region for the next three centuries. Meanwhile, in Hausaland to the south, the expansion of trade had led to the rise of the HAUSA states as independent centers of power by the fifteenth century.

During the nineteenth century external aggressors reconfigured the region's geopolitics. Fulani warriors launched jihads ("holy wars") and began attacking the Hausa states in the early nineteenth century; they eventually conquered most of the northern states. This drove many Hausa to flee northward into present-day Niger. The jihads produced a new state – the SOKOTO CALIPHATE – and attracted various adventurers who wanted to build their own empires from the remnants of disintegrating states or to conquer existing ones. Sokoto's attacks on Kanem-Bornu allowed Damagaram, initially a tributary to Kanem-Bornu, to establish autonomous power over much of central Niger. Allied with Tuareg traders, Damagaram took control of much of the trans-Saharan trade from its base at Zinder, and by the late nineteenth century had declared its independence from Kanem-Bornu. During the 1890s RABIH, a slave trader, conquered Kanem-Bornu and Bagirmi and merged the two to create his own empire, including parts of southeastern Niger. These new powers, however, proved short-lived. Both Damagaram and Rabih's empire soon succumbed to a new invader – the French.

FRENCH COLONIALISM

In the late nineteenth century the French began a frantic scuffle (see SCRAMBLE FOR AFRICA) to claim the West African interior before Great Britain could. Having already established colonies on the coast, both European powers wished to extend their possessions inland. In particular, the French sought this region to establish an empire extending from the Mediterranean to the REPUBLIC OF THE CONGO and from the Red Sea to the Atlantic. In addition, both powers sought control of the valuable resources – gold, valuable minerals, and salt – carried by the lucrative trans-Saharan trade caravans that traversed the region. France dispatched several missions to the area to determine the extent of British influence and to seize control of any and all available land.

After securing treaties with several smaller groups, France launched the Mission Afrique Centrale in order to conquer most of southern Niger. As part of this operation, a military party led by Voulet and Chanoine seized food and supplies from drought-stricken local populations, and responded to local resistance with a brutal scorched-earth policy that killed thousands. The French conquered Damagaram, seized Zinder, defeated Rabih in 1900, and concluded by claiming possession of the region.

Although France controlled most of the sedentary groups by 1900, northern nomadic groups such as the Tuareg and Toubou successfully resisted France until 1922. French COLONIAL RULE, which attempted to control and regulate subject populations, threatened the lifestyle of the nomads, whose unrestricted movement was a clear threat to French hegemony. Eventually France launched a military mission into the Sahara expressly to control and tax the trade caravans. Predictably, the Tuareg resisted for years. The two groups seized animals and supplies from one another, filled in wells, and destroyed crops. The French, however, had a larger army, aided by sedentary Tuareg, many of whom were servants of the Tuareg nomads. Eventually the French defeated the Tuareg, many of whom fled their devastated homeland for temporary exile in Nigeria. Having subdued the Nigerien populations, France declared Niger a colony in 1922.

By this time, however, France's attempts to exploit the Nigerien colony had already destroyed much of the local economy. When the French first seized Niger, most of its "sedentary" farmers and herders actually engaged in seminomadic behavior; small family groups migrated every year (within a small area) in order to allow the fragile Sahel land to regain fertility for future use. The French considered these farming techniques disorderly, wasteful, and ill-suited to the export crops they hoped to cultivate in Niger.

As a result, the French blocked access to the land in order to prevent nomadic movement, forcing people to move to larger sedentary villages that were responsible for export crop production on nearby state-owned plantations. The French imposed taxes to force farmers to work on the plantations and instructed them to cultivate as much as possible and to leave no land fallow. In addition, the French, having already experienced drought in the Sahel, attempted to impose a strict storage program among the farmers. The program required farmers to allocate a percentage of their personal crops to regional storage bins; this created resentments and broke down the centuries-old technique for dealing with drought. Within 20 years these colonial policies had devastating effects: land had become sterile and arid, and thereafter farmers could grow little more than peanuts.

When the French finally imposed taxes and tariffs (payable in French currency) on the trans-Saharan trade caravans that passed through Niger, they undermined this ancient economic institution as well. Because there was a severe shortage of French currency in the colony, traders often could not pay the exact amount in the requisite currency. Consequently, the French forced the traders to overpay. To add insult to economic injury, the French army also seized goods and camels, which were not only symbolic of traders' nomadic lifestyles, but integral to their economic prosperity. Furious with the policy, many traders abandoned the trans-Saharan routes and moved their business across the border to British-controlled Nigeria, whose ports offered easy access to world markets. Again, in an attempt to exploit the local economy, France had destroyed the prospect of future revenues.

Consequently, in 1922, when France formally declared Niger a colony, the colonial administration no longer saw much value in the economically ruined country. They invested very little in its social or infrastructural development. Underdeveloped and supported by a meager one-crop economy, Niger became an undesirable posting among the West African colonies. As a result, the colonial administration relied more heavily on indigenous rulers in Niger than they did in more profitable colonies. Because the French built only a few schools and provided little opportunity for Nigeriens to obtain a modern education, Niger lacked the sizable elite of indigenous but Westernized *assimilés* that developed in many coastal colonies. Instead, in Niger the colonial government essentially left local administration to indigenous rulers, who received little French scrutiny so long as they produced the required taxes and crops. This system encouraged authoritarian rulers who exploited their subjects. The French government did little to intervene, despite recurrent criticism.

At the Brazzaville Conference of 1944, France moved to give colonies more autonomy. The immediate beneficiaries of this new policy in Niger were its tiny percentage of educated elite. This clique, led by individuals like HAMANI DIORI, organized to promote its own political and economic interests and to protest French colonial neglect. In 1946 members of this circle founded the Parti Progressiste Nigérien (PPN), an affiliate of the RASSEMBLEMENT DÉMOCRATIQUE AFRICAIN (RDA). They were joined by small numbers of workers in the urban centers of Niamey and Zinder. By 1949, however, PPN's core elite had essentially marginalized the workers' concerns.

By 1956 two other political parties had formed in Niger: the Bloc Nigérien d'Action (BNA) and the Union Démocratique Nigérienne (UDN), later renamed Sawaba ("Freedom"). Hamani Diori emerged victorious in the 1958 elections for president, and he retained this post when Niger gained independence in August 1960. Diori outlawed Sawaba, which drew its support largely from the Hausa, Niger's largest ethnic group. Diori and the mostly Djerma PPN elite would continue to dominate Nigerien politics until 1974.

INDEPENDENCE

During the first five years of independence, Diori concentrated on consolidating his own power. Faced with an attempted military coup in 1963 and attacks by members of Sawaba, he used French advisers and troops to repress opposition, despite student and union protests against French neocolonialism. Diori limited cabinet appointments to fellow Djerma, family members, and close friends. In addition, he acquired new powers by declaring himself the minister of foreign and defense affairs.

As internal affairs settled and Niger experienced a slight economic boom, Diori dismissed many of the government's French advisers – a move that both satisfied popular demands and further centralized government power in the presidency. He attempted to bypass the traditional elite with a rural development program aimed at collectivizing farms and introducing modern agricultural techniques, but the traditional elite undermined this effort. In 1971 a French firm began mining Niger's uranium deposits in the northern desert region. The exploitation of this valuable resource raised hopes for economic improvement.

But Diori faced a number of new problems that ultimately led to his downfall. His relationship with France suffered for the first time when his government voiced dissatisfaction with the level of investment in uranium production. Meanwhile, the price of peanuts, Niger's main export crop, plummeted. Economic deterioration coincided with an increasingly severe drought during the early 1970s. These economic difficulties forced the government to reduce funding to schools, universities, and civil servants – moves that met with violent student and union protests.

Diori managed to maintain order until the devastating drought reached its peak in 1973. Popular unrest escalated into riots when evidence emerged that Diori and members of his administration were enriching themselves with diverted foreign food aid. The situation continued to worsen until April 1974, when a group of military leaders led by SEYNI KOUNTCHÉ toppled the government and imprisoned Diori, a move that won overwhelming popular support.

Kountché declared himself president of a transitional government and immediately provided relief to the drought-stricken areas. He distributed free seed and stopped black-market sales of food aid. In addition, he devised a new program – called Samariya – through which he attempted to revitalize the

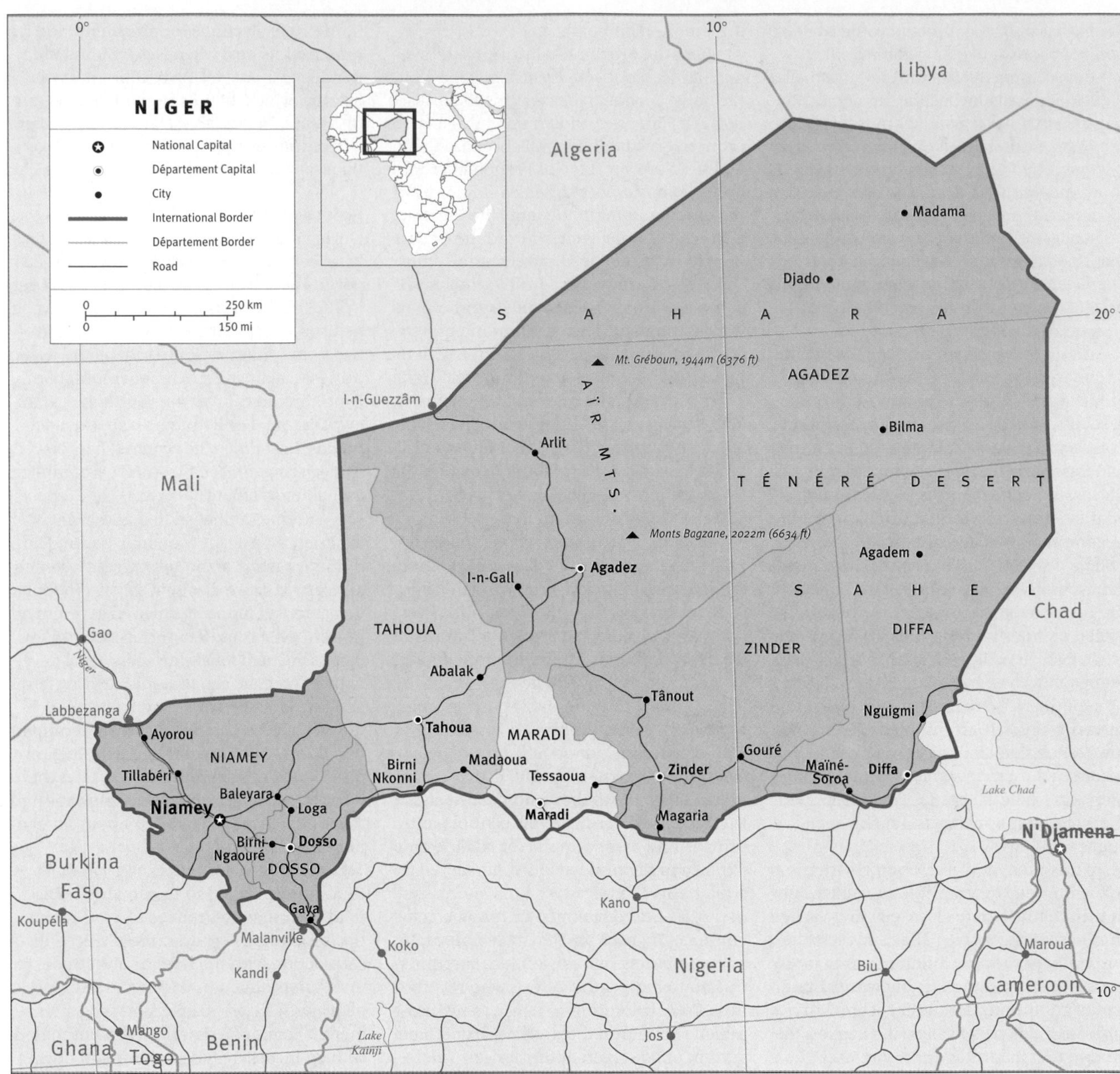

rural economy. Modeled on "traditional" Hausa youth groups, the program initiated new public works projects in the villages and attempted to increase food production through collectivized farms. Like Diori, Kountché bypassed the traditional elite and targeted rural development aid directly to the peasantry. But his programs had little success. Samariya failed to increase crop production, and the traditional elite again blocked attempts to undermine their power in rural areas. The program also ignored the nomadic Tuareg, whose pastoral economy had not recovered from the years of drought. Nonetheless, a rise in uranium prices in the wake of the 1973-1974 Arab oil embargo brought an economic recovery that bolstered Kountché's regime.

Over the course of his rule Kountché confronted growing popular opposition and attempted coups with an increasingly authoritarian style. In an effort to maintain control, he dismissed most military advisors and replaced them with family members and friends, who in turn faced dismissal whenever Kountché suspected them of threatening his power. After 1979 uranium prices plummeted and Niger faced a fiscal crisis.

To conserve state resources Kountché halted state development projects, including construction and mining projects that employed a large sector of the Nigerien population. Popular opposition increased as the economy declined, but Kountché put down expressions of dissent, such as a 1983 student strike. A new drought in 1984 intensified Niger's economic woes as uranium prices continued to decline. The return of normal rains in 1985 and an infusion of international assistance brought a slow economic recovery during the late 1980s.

The Transition Toward Democracy

In 1986 Kountché was diagnosed with a brain tumor; he spent the last year of his life in a Paris hospital. During this period Niger was governed by the chief of staff of the armed forces, Ali Saibou, who assumed the presidency upon Kountché's death in November 1987. Though he continued many of Kountché's policies, the more liberal Saibou took steps to introduce consitutional rule; a referendum approved his proposed constitution in 1989. That year Saibou founded a ruling party, the Mouvement National de la Société de Développement, and, in the wake of single-party elections, he declared himself the legitimate leader of Niger.

Like his predecessor, however, Saibou resorted to repression. Although he permitted greater personal freedom and public protest, he had inherited a national government that was teetering on bankruptcy. Beginning in 1990 foreign lenders forced Saibou to accept austerity measures and structural adjustment plans, including

ABOVE LEFT: The lifestyle of nomads in Niger, such as the Tuareg and the Toubou, has been threatened by both colonial and postcolonial regimes, which have attempted to suppress the nomads' movements in the Sahel. *CORBIS/Tiziana and Gianni B*
ABOVE RIGHT: A barber stands in front of a sign advertising the kinds of haircuts he offers. *CORBIS/The Purcell Team*

privatization of state enterprises and cuts in student scholarships and civil servant salaries. The cuts prompted student and union demonstrations; the military dispersed them by shooting into the crowds. Meanwhile, the army suppressed a Tuareg rebellion in the northern countryside. A brutal military raid at Agadez in 1990 left hundreds of Tuaregs dead, including many innocent civilians.

In response to domestic and international pressures, Saibou declared a new multiparty system and invited both progovernment and opposition delegates to convene at a national conference in Niamey in 1991. Led by André Salifou, a prominent Nigerien scholar, the conference declared itself sovereign and implemented massive reforms. Saibou subsequently renounced most of his political power, and the conference named Amadou Cheiffou prime minister of the new transitional government. Cheiffou assumed presidential duties. He helped orchestrate a new emergency grant from France that saved the government from bankruptcy and made possible the first multiparty presidential election in Nigerien history in 1993.

Mahamane Ousmane won the presidency in this election, and Mahamadou Issoufou was elected prime minister. Within a year of his election, however, Issoufou resigned because differences with the president made it impossible for him to implement desired economic and social reforms. Ousmane held new parliamentary elections in December 1994, and opposition leader Hama Amadou was elected. For the next year, personal attacks between Ousmane and Amadou paralyzed government while bankruptcy loomed and internal unrest mounted, particularly among students and northern Tuareg rebels. Consequently, in January 1996 Ousmane disbanded the general assembly and unconstitutionally designated a new prime minister.

In the midst of this crisis, Col. Ibrahim Barré Mainassara staged a military coup. International donors responded by suspending foreign aid. Unable to pay civil servants, military troops, and government administrators, Mainassara appeased the international donors by promising elections. He introduced a new constitution and held presidential and parliamentary elections in 1996. Mainassara easily won the contested November presidential election and declared himself president of the Fourth Republic of Niger. Although the larger opposition parties had boycotted the parliamentary elections, a coalition of smaller opposition parties, the Comité du Soutien d'Ibrahim Barré (later renamed the Rassemblement pour la Démocratie et le Progrès), won the majority in the general assembly.

After the elections Mainassara promoted interregional cooperation and trade. He strongly supported the Economic Community of West African States (ECOWAS). In 1997 he cofounded a new organization to promote economic cooperation among states of the Sahara and Sahel. On April 9, 1999, Mainassara was assassinated at the airport of the capital city Niamey. Two days later the army announced the formation of a National Reconciliation Council, which would rule for nine months; the dissolution of all national institutions, including the National Assembly and the Supreme Court; and the appointment of Maj. Daouda Malam Wanke as president.

Elizabeth Heath

See Also

Camel; Ghana, Early Kingdom of; Morocco; Niamey, Niger; Salt Trade; Songhai Empire; Structural Adjustment in Africa; Djebar, Assia; Zinder, Niger; Trans-Saharan and Red Sea Slave Trade; Mali Empire.

Africa

Niger (Ready Reference)

Official Name: Republic of Niger
Area: 1,267,000 sq km (489,189 sq mi)
Location: Inland West Africa; borders Algeria, Libya, Chad, Nigeria, Benin, Burkina Faso, and Mali
Capital: Niamey (population 398,265 [1988 estimate])
Other Major Cities: Zinder (population 120,900), Maradi (113,000), Tahoua (51,600), and Agadez (50,200) (1988 estimate)
Population: 9,671,848 (1998 estimate)
Population Density: 7 persons per sq km (about 19 persons per sq mi); 90 percent of the population lives near the southern border.
Population Below Age 15: 48 percent (male 2,374,482; female 2,277,176 [1998 estimate])
Population Growth Rate: 2.96 percent (1998 estimate)
Total Fertility Rate: 7.3 children born per woman (1998 estimate)
Life Expectancy at Birth: Total population:

41.52 years (male 41.83 years; female 41.21 years [1998 estimate])
Infant Mortality Rate: 114.39 deaths per 1000 live births (1998 estimate)
Literacy Rate (age 15 and over who can read and write): Total population: 13.6 percent (male 20.9 percent; female 6.6 percent [1998 estimate])
Education: In the early 1990s Niger had some 368,700 pupils in primary schools, 74,300 in secondary schools, and 2400 in vocational and teacher-training schools. Only about 25 percent of primary-school-aged children receive an education. Advanced training is given at the University of Niamey.
Languages: French is the official language. Hausa, the first language of over half the population, is also used as a trade language by a large number of Nigeriens (*see* HAUSA LANGUAGE). Other spoken languages include Temasheq (Tuareg Berber), Djerma (Songhai), Fulani, and Arabic.
Ethnic Groups: More than half the population is HAUSA. Other ethnic groups include the Songhai, FULANI, TUAREG, Beriberi (KANURI), Arab, Tubu, and Gourmantche. There are about 4000 French expatriates.
Religions: 85 percent are Sunni Muslims; fewer than 1 percent are Christian; and the remainder practice traditional religions.
Climate: Rainfall (June through October) is minimal over most of Niger; the southern farming zone receives an average of 820 mm (32 in) per year. Average annual temperature at Niamey is 29.4° C (85° F).
Land, Plants, and Animals: The northern half of the country is in the Sahara Desert and has little or no vegetation; the SAHEL region south of the Sahara is semi-arid brush country; the extreme south is partially forested. The Air Mountain range is located in the center of Niger, in the southern Sahara. The NIGER RIVER flows through the western part of the country, and LAKE CHAD lies on the southeastern border. Wildlife on protected reserves include elephants, hippopotamuses, giraffes, and lions; gazelles, hyenas, and vipers are widespread, and monkeys are found in the Air Mountains.
Natural Resources: Gold, uranium, coal, iron ore, tin, and phosphates
Currency: The Communauté Financière Africaine franc
Gross Domestic Product (GDP): $6.3 billion (1997 estimate)
GDP per Capita: $670 (1997 estimate)
GDP Real Growth Rate: 4.5 percent (1997 estimate)
Primary Economic Activities: Agriculture (farming and animal husbandry, 38.5 percent of GDP, 90 percent of employment), industry, and other services
Primary Crops: Cowpeas, cotton, peanuts, millet, sorghum, cassava (tapioca), rice; cattle, sheep, and goats
Industries: Cement, brick, textiles, food processing, chemicals, slaughterhouses, and other small, light industries; uranium mining
Primary Exports: Uranium ore, livestock products, cowpeas, and onions
Primary Imports: Consumer goods, primary materials, machinery, vehicles and parts, petroleum, and cereals
Primary Trade Partners: France, Nigeria, Côte d'Ivoire, Italy, Germany, and Japan
Government: Niger is nominally a constitutional multiparty republic, but events in 1999 threatened that form of government. Under normal circumstances the president appoints the prime minister and his cabinet, the National Salvation Council. The unicameral 83-seat National Assembly is elected by proportional representation for five-year terms. However, in April 1999 President Ibrahim Bare Mainassara, who took power in a 1996 military coup and who was elected president later that same year, was assassinated. The army vested power in a National Reconciliation Council – slated to rule for nine months – and appointed Maj. Daouda Malam Wanke as president.

Barbara Worley

SEE ALSO
Elephant; Giraffe; Gold Trade; Hippopotamus; Hyena; Lion; Iron in Africa; Niamey, Niger; Sahara Desert; Songhai Empire; Zinder, Niger.

Africa

Nigeria, country with the world's largest black population, located on the Atlantic coast of West Africa, sharing borders with BENIN, NIGER, CHAD, and CAMEROON.

The NIGER RIVER is Nigeria's most remarkable physical feature, as well as the source of its name. But Africa's most populous nation did not even have a name before the late nineteenth century, nor for that matter a national identity. Rather, British colonization brought together three vast and culturally distinctive regions – north, southeast, and southwest – and at least 250 different language groups, more than any other African country (*see* LANGUAGES, AFRICAN: AN OVERVIEW). Generously endowed as well with natural resources such as crude oil, gas, coal, iron, limestone, columbite, and tin, Nigeria in its early postcolonial years was viewed as a potential middle-level economic power. Since independence in 1960, however, corrupt military rule has conspired with religious as well as ethnic fractiousness to all but dissipate the nation's early promise.

Following independence Nigeria was rocked by political crises: disputed elections led to widespread violence, then to a coup and countercoup, then to ethnic tensions that exploded into the 30-month Biafran War (1967-1970). In the nearly three decades since the Biafran War, promised returns to democratic civilian rule have been repeatedly thwarted by military-sponsored coups, crackdowns on opposition groups, and electoral maneuverings. Many of Nigeria's most esteemed intellectuals have left the country, while others have faced severe state persecution. By the late 1990s many Nigerians viewed head of state Gen. SANI ABACHA's ostensible democratic transition with great skepticism. In mid-1998 Abacha's sudden death, followed a month later by the equally unexpected death of one of his greatest rivals, the imprisoned businessman Moshood Abiola, left the country's political future even more uncertain.

EARLY SOCIETIES IN NORTHERN NIGERIA

The best evidence of early civilizations in northern Nigeria is provided by the NOK terracotta heads, named after a village of the Jaba people in northern Nigeria. The highly stylized figurines, at least 2500 years old, point to a thriving Iron Age culture in a wide swath of northern Nigeria.

Also important among the groups that established some of the northern region's largest and most enduring states were the HAUSA. During the first millennium C.E. they were village-dwelling cultivators and artisans, living on the belt of open woodland and grass savanna known as the SAHEL, on the southern edge of the Sahara. After about 1000 C.E. the rise of Hausa statehood coincided with the building of walled cities known as *birane*. The kings who resided within the birane were charged with warding off external aggression, in return for which they collected taxes from commoners.

Economic and cultural life in the early Hausa states was deeply shaped by trade. Hausa farmers and artisans – weavers and dyers, smiths and leatherworkers – produced goods for local markets as well as long-distance caravans. From southern forested regions these caravans brought ivory, gold, and slaves. From the north they brought desert salt, goods from the Mediterranean and, beginning around the ninth century, Islam.

Only after the thirteenth century did Hausa rulers begin to convert to Islam. In the centuries following, cities such as Kano and Katsina became centers for Islamic scholarship as well as commerce, but many Hausa commoners were little affected by Islamic culture until the early nineteenth century, when a jihad, or crusade, led by the FULANI cleric USMAN DAN FODIO, created a vast Islamic empire, with its headquarters in Sokoto. Triggered in 1804 by the attempts of King Yunfa of Gobir to stem the cleric's growing popularity, the jihad defeated most of the Hausa kings by 1810, putting Usman dan Fodio and later his son MUHAMMAD BELLO in control of the largest state in nineteenth-century West Africa, spanning some 400,000 sq km (154,440 sq mi). This period also marked the ascendancy of the Fulani, a numerical minority in the north.

Another important precolonial state in northern Nigeria was Kanem Borno (*see*

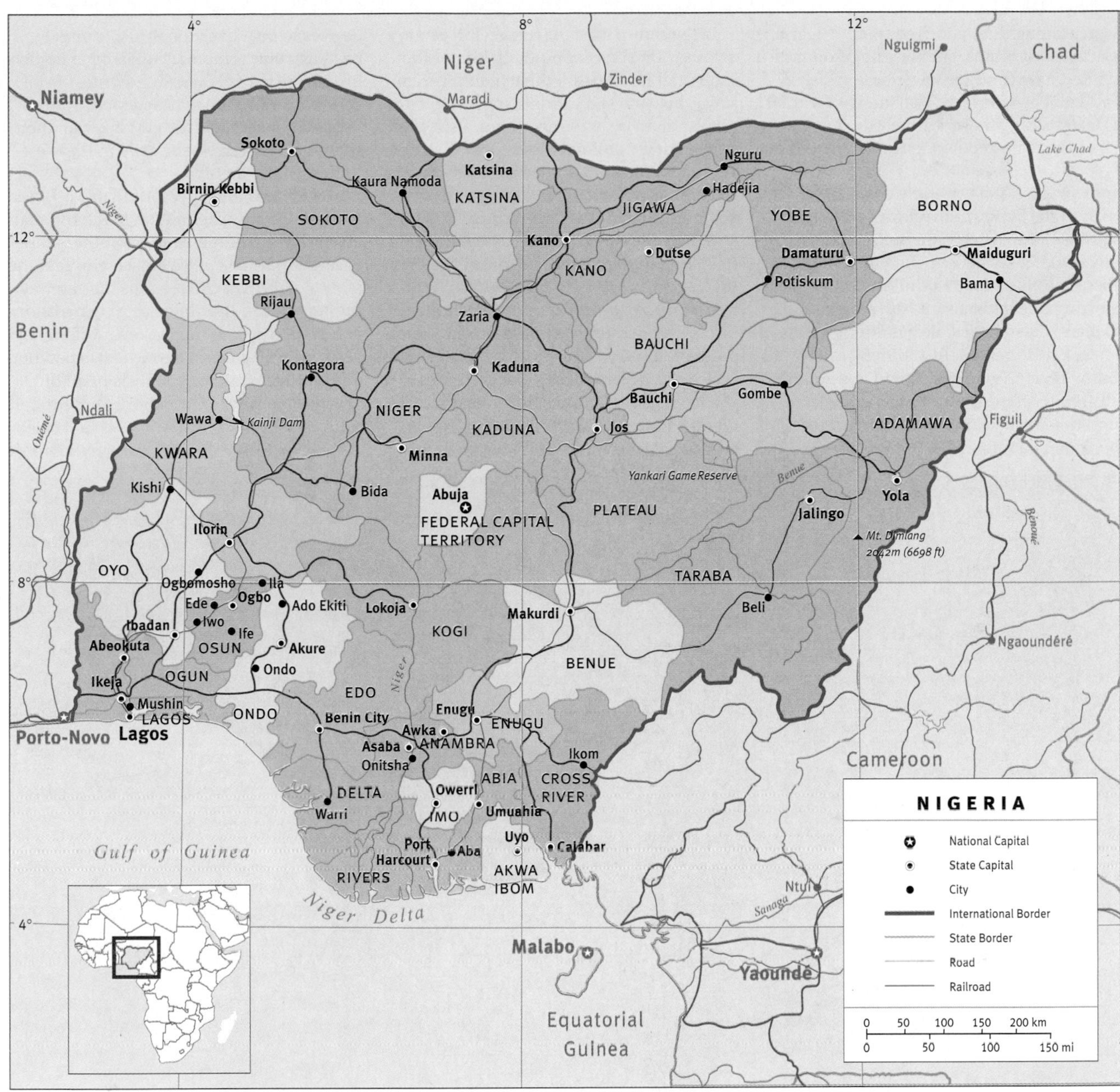

Kanuri). Founded between 700 and 800 C.E., it went through periods of growth and contraction, but at its peak, under the leadership of Idris Alooma (1571-1603), the ruling Sefawa Dynasty of Kanem Borno extended its control as far as the region of Fezzan, in modern Libya.

Northern Nigeria was also home to a multitude of other ethnic groups and cultures, including the Tiv, Jukun, the Idoma, the Igala, the Igbira, and the Nupe. Some, such as the Jukun, developed centralized forms of government, while others – notably the Idoma – remained politically decentralized.

Early Societies in Southern Nigeria

The Yoruba peoples of southwestern Nigeria claim a common ancestry in Ile-Ife. The spiritual epicenter of the Yoruba is the home of one of the most magnificent traditions of bronze casting, dating back to the eleventh century. Among the several highly urbanized Yoruba kingdoms that arose beginning in the fourteenth century, Oyo, on the northern fringe of the forest, was best located for commerce both with Hausaland and with coastal traders, including, eventually, European slave ships. By the early eighteenth century the Oyo cavalry had conquered many neighboring kingdoms, including Dahomey (in present-day Benin).

The ancient Benin Empire of the Edo people, with its capital in a city of the same name, was already an extensive political and military force when Portuguese traders came ashore in the fifteenth century. Highly influenced by the artistic traditions of Ile-Ife, Benin architecture and court life deeply impressed fifteenth-century Dutch traders as well. The long tradition of internal slavery that evolved from the kingdom's formidable martial history enabled Benin to play an important role in the transatlantic slave trade.

In southeastern Nigeria the Igbo maintained a largely decentralized and republican mode of political organization based on clan units. Apart from the Igbo's philosophical disposition against absolutist powers, the dense tropical swamp covering much of Igboland acted as a natural obstacle to expansionist schemes and the formation of centralized states. Instead, Igbo communities handled decision making and judicial matters at open village congresses attended by all eligible citizens. However politically decentralized, the Igbo were united in their reverence for the powerful oracle at Arochukwu, named the Long Juju by Europeans. This oracle once represented the final adjudicator of cases in Igboland.

The Igbo practiced both farming and trade, and by the fifteenth century Igbo merchants were trading throughout southern Nigeria. Certain Igbo clans, such as the Aro, made a reputation for themselves as fierce slave raiders. The Igbo were also known for their artisanry; bronze works unearthed at Igbo-Ukwu have been dated to the ninth century.

European Contact and Conquest

Although the Portuguese were the first Europeans to arrive in the region that is now Nigeria, it was the British – entering the picture only in 1553 – who were to play the starring role in the drama of colonization as well as Nigeria's birth as a modern nation-state. British merchants, initially interested in the region's gold, ivory, and pepper, soon shifted their attention to the slave trade and quickly became the dominant foreign commercial interest in Nigeria.

In the early part of the nineteenth century, as Great Britain reaped the fruits of the Industrial Revolution, the need for African slaves became subordinate to the need for African markets and raw materials. After Great Britain outlawed the transatlantic slave trade in 1808 – a decision driven less by humanitarian considerations than by economic logic – that need translated into a vague policy of territorial acquisition. For British merchants based around the Oil Rivers on the coast, the top priority was to penetrate the hinterlands and establish direct links with the primary producers of palm oil, thereby dispensing with coastal African middlemen. But they faced stiff challenges from both the threatened middlemen and from nature. King Ja Ja of Opobo, for example, deployed a number of strategic devices to beat back the British campaign, including direct shipment of his oil to Europe. In 1887, when Ja Ja was lured onto a British vessel "to talk," he was arrested, sent to the Gold Coast (now Ghana) for trial, then sentenced to a five-year exile in the West Indies, where he died.

Malaria was the other formidable obstacle to Great Britain's exploration of the Nigerian interior. In 1830 the Lander brothers discovered that the Oil Rivers were in fact the mouth of the Niger River, thus the gateway to the interior. But the several expeditions that tried to ply this highway met with many fatalities. Macgregor Laird's 1832 expedition up the Niger claimed the lives of all but 9 of the 48 Europeans. A major breakthrough came, however, in 1854, when W. B. Baikie's expedition into Fulani country in the north

demonstrated the prophylactic effects of quinine; not a single person died. British trading companies began moving operations inland soon afterward.

In 1861 Lagos became the first territory of present-day Nigeria to be annexed by the British. Thenceforth, British colonial acquisitions followed two patterns – so-called treaties of protection signed between British officials (or merchants acting in that de facto capacity) and local rulers, or conquest. Violence and trickery were essential to both approaches, since many customary rulers were assured of tragic consequences if they refused to sign. Evidence abounds, too, that the British officials often misrepresented the letter and import of the treaties, while exaggerating reports about impending threats from neighboring communities.

Trading concerns played an extensive role in the formal colonial subjugation of Nigeria. Faced with strong French competition in the north in the 1870s, a number of British trading firms, under the leadership of George Taubman Goldie, merged in 1879 to form the United African Company. By 1882 the company had secured enough treaties of protection to reestablish British supremacy. Goldie subsequently attended the BERLIN CONFERENCE OF 1884-1885, where he argued for British control in northern Nigeria. In 1886 the English Crown, reluctant to commit the resources needed to administer the vast region, gave a royal charter to Goldie's company. In return for shouldering the cost of running the territory, the company, now renamed the Royal Niger Company, was granted a trade monopoly. But as the cost of administration escalated – and in the face of renewed French designs on the territory – the company's charter was revoked in 1900. The company's Frederick Lugard was then appointed high commissioner of the protectorate of Northern Nigeria.

That same year Great Britain formalized its control over most of what is modern Nigeria. But it continued to administer the area as two separate units, the colony and protectorate of Southern Nigeria (so named in 1906 after a merger of Lagos and southern Nigeria) and the protectorate of Northern Nigeria, until 1914, when they were joined. Lugard, who became the first governor-general of an amalgamated Nigeria, was the architect of indirect rule – the policy of ruling colonies through the structures of customary authority. Given Nigeria's vast size and malarial climate, indirect rule offered an innovative solution to a real problem, namely the dearth of colonial officers willing to serve there.

Lugard had applied indirect rule quite successfully in the north, where the Sokoto Caliphate, the century-old Fulani empire, had established a highly centralized, hierarchical administrative order. Indirect rule elsewhere in Nigeria, however, ran into formidable problems. Although the Yoruba recognized long-standing monarchies, they resisted turning their traditional administrative structures over to the goals of British colonialism. In Igboland, the absence of even rudimentary states led the British to the misadventure of appointing warrant chiefs. These "invented" chiefs, usually little respected within their communities, became power-drunk and corrupt, in turn provoking their subjects' revolt. One of the fiercest revolts was the Aba Women's Tax Riots of 1929. Responding to rumors that their commerce would be taxed, Igbo market women organized themselves and attacked both British officials and their appointed minions. The colonial police escalated the violence, killing 50 women and wounding many more.

The colonial government made an early decision to seclude the largely Islamic northern region from the influences of Western education and Christianity. The logic was that Islam had established a stable system that was at once universal and – if provoked by proselytizers – capable of great violence. And while Islam had penetrated the southwestern region, it had not won over many converts among the Yoruba, who, like the Igbo, adhered to a variety of traditional religions (*see* AFRICAN RELIGIONS: AN INTERPRETATION).

OPPOSITE: Oba (or King) Akenzua II of Benin, in full regalia including coral garment and headpiece, plays only an advisory role in government. *Werner Forman/Art Resource, NY*

ABOVE LEFT: Kano horsemen, famous for their riding skills and their horses' elaborate, padded armor, attend the Durbar festival in Nigeria. *Jason Lauré*

LEFT: Pedestrians and vans crowd a street market in Lagos, the capital of Nigeria. *CORBIS/Daniel Lainé*

The preservation of the north's "cultural purity," however, deprived northerners of access to Western education – the key to employment in the colony's growing civil service. In addition, the north's isolation fostered a cultural and political divide that later shaped Nigerian nationalism. Some northern leaders, hardly enamored of the prospect of southern domination, found themselves in the odd position of advocating continued colonial rule.

Colonialism dramatically altered economic and social relations in Nigeria. The installation of an internal communication system and transportation grid facilitated trade and travel, and the expansion of the cash economy aided the emergence of a wider system of division of labor. As coal and tin mines, ports, and railways drew laborers from the countryside (sometimes through conscription), they fostered the development of urban working classes, whose mass strikes in the 1940s and 1950s would force the colonial government to grant wage increases. As the cities grew, they also became increasingly multiethnic.

In rural areas the colonial administration promoted the production of crops needed by British industries. The decades of colonial rule saw a steady growth in the volume of export crops – palm oil and other palm produce from the southeast, COCOA from the southwest, and peanuts from the north. But customary land ownership patterns and farming methods did not change dramatically. This was in part because the British had no desire to alienate those who traditionally exercised control over land distribution – elders, lineage heads, chiefs – and partly because of the reluctance of banks and other financial institutions to invest in commercial farms or other indigenously run enterprises.

This reluctance to encourage Nigerian entrepreneurship was also apparent in commerce. Initially, British trade firms made use of Nigerian middlemen in the export trade, feeding the growth of an already vibrant class of indigenous businesspeople. But as these firms progressively marginalized Nigerian traders, they bred resentment and contributed to the deepening of nationalist sentiments in many parts of the colony.

The early stages of nationalist revolt against entrenched British rule took the form of localized skirmishes like the Aba Women's Riots, provoked by specific grievances. But an embryonic nationalist movement began to emerge around World War I, bolstered by the first Pan-African Congress, convened by W. E. B. Du Bois in Paris in 1918-1919 (*see* PAN-AFRICAN CONGRESS OF 1919). In response to early nationalism, British officials either denied that the agitators for independence represented popular sentiments or, paradoxically, insisted – as did Sir Hugh Clifford, then governor of Nigeria – that the very idea of "nation" in the colonies was absurd.

The emergence in the 1930s of BENJAMIN NNAMDI AZIKIWE, a charismatic American-educated newspaper editor, broadened and transformed the nationalist struggle. Azikiwe's publications made him a prominent advocate for independence, and the political party he founded in 1944, the National Council of Nigeria and the Cameroons (NCNC), became one of the largest nationalist organizations, albeit one supported primarily by fellow Ibo from the southeast. In the southwest nationalist support rallied around Obafemi Awolowo and his party, the Action Group.

The British, meanwhile, oscillated between a policy of divide and rule – encouraging the divisions already apparent in the regionalist nature of early political parties, and playing especially on the north's fear of domination by southern civil servants and intellectuals – and a recognition of the need to prepare for inevitable decolonization. Reforms in the late 1940s through the 1950s allowed Nigerians limited political representation, but southerners pushed for full autonomy. Yet northern political leaders, under the auspices of the Northern People's Congress (NPC), opposed a motion calling for independence by 1956, and agreed to support self-rule only after constitutional concessions were made to the north. On October 1, 1960, after years of constitutional conferences, Great Britain lowered the Union Jack, ushering in Nigerian independence.

EARLY INDEPENDENCE AND CIVIL WAR

Nigeria inherited the British-style parliamentary system, with Azikiwe as the first governor-general (and, from 1963, president); ABUBAKAR TAFAWA BALEWA of the NPC as the prime minister, exercising executive power; and Obafemi Awolowo as the opposition leader. The Northern, Western, and Eastern Regions constituted the country's tripartite structure, until the Mid-Western Region was created in 1963. Owing partly to the conservative nature of the coalition that formed the first national government, independent Nigeria proceeded cautiously. Professing nonalignment, it stayed close to Great Britain on a number of foreign policy issues, with the understandable exception of white rule in southern Africa. For a nation expected to assume the leadership of the black world, the rhetoric of its leaders was remarkably tame. In economic policy as well, the country continued to ply the route of a primary commodity export economy, ensuring that Great Britain remained an important trade partner as well as an aid donor.

Soon after independence, however, efforts by the government at modest industrial development were, like much else in the country, drowned in the din of raucous politics. The coalition government seemed racked by mutual incomprehension, and many politicians began using their offices to enrich themselves and their supporters. Massive electoral rigging, especially in the 1965 Western Region parliamentary elections, unleashed widespread violence and paved the way for a military coup d'état on January 15, 1966. Prime Minister Balewa and several other politicians were killed, and army commander Johnson Aguiyi-Ironsi, from the Eastern Region, became head of state.

Six months later northern army officers launched a countercoup, and installed YAKUBU GOWON as the country's new ruler. During Gowon's nine-year term Nigeria was rocked by a series of tumultuous events, beginning with the massacre of Ibo people throughout the Northern Region. When the Ibo then began pushing for a separate state, Gowon announced instead the creation of a 12-state structure, calculated to weaken the petroleum-rich Eastern Region. The governor of the Eastern Region declared its secession and created a new name, the Republic of Biafra; within weeks a civil war had begun.

The 30-month-long Biafran War cost an estimated 1 million lives – the majority of them civilians who died of famine in the blockaded east – and ended with Biafra's surrender in January 1970. Gowon then announced a policy of "reconciliation, reconstruction, and recovery" and plans for a gradual transition to civilian rule. He also opened the government's coffers – flush with money since crude oil exploitation began shortly before the war – to fund the reconstruction of the country's war-damaged infrastructure, as well as a number of new "white elephant" projects. The government almost entirely neglected the agricultural sector, however; so even as the economy enjoyed unprecedented growth, it grew increasingly dependent on imported food and capital goods, and foreign loans. Moreover, much of the new wealth was concentrated in relatively few hands, and much of the state funding for development projects was funneled toward the north. In years to come, this inequitable distribution of wealth would become a major grievance of Nigeria's smaller and less politically influential ethnic groups.

Shortly after Gowon declared that the 1976 date he set for elections was "unrealistic," he was removed in a coup on July 29, 1975, and replaced by Murtala Muhammad, another northern officer. Muhammad set out to stem corruption by dismissing several public servants and adopted a bold new foreign policy, mustering other African nations to back AGOSTINHO NETO'S POPULAR MOVEMENT FOR THE LIBERATION OF ANGOLA (MPLA). After only months in office, the popular Muhammad was assassinated on February 13, 1976. Muhammad's chief of staff, Yoruba officer OLUSEGUN OBASANJO, kept his predecessor's promise and handed over power to a democratically elected government on October 1, 1979.

DEMOCRACY DELAYED

The new government, modeled after the United States presidential system, was headed by Shehu Shagari, another northerner.

In December 1983, following national elections that the opposition charged were extensively rigged, he was overthrown and replaced by military officer Muhammadu Buhari, who was himself deposed two years later in a palace coup led by Ibrahim Babangida. By this time a worldwide recession had brought Nigeria's oil boom to a definitive end, and the country was deeply indebted. Babangida's adoption of World Bank-prescribed austerity measures forced communities and individuals to rely less on government handouts but also caused great hardship. During the 1980s urban streets and marketplaces grew increasingly crowded with hawkers and petty traders, many of them women, struggling to earn an income.

After several years of promising a transition to democratic rule, Babangida agreed to presidential elections in 1993, then promptly annulled the victory of the opposition candidate, wealthy businessman Moshood Abiola. Babangida's hand-picked transition government was soon ousted by Sani Abacha, his own defense minister. Even in the face of mounting international criticism, Abacha proved as repressive as any of his predecessors. He jailed the popular Abiola in 1994, and in 1995 his regime hanged the environmental and human rights activist Ken Saro-Wiwa, along with eight Ogoni colleagues. They had been jailed on trumped-up murder charges, but it was widely recognized that the group's demands for Ogoni statehood and protests against Shell Oil's environmentally destructive practices in Ogoniland were the real reasons they were silenced (*see* ENVIRONMENTAL MOVEMENTS IN AFRICA).

Abacha announced an elaborate democratic transition program when he first took office but repeatedly delayed elections. Many critics doubted his pledge to hand over power to an elected government by October 1998, especially after all five registered political parties invited Abacha to continue in office as their "consensus candidate." On June 7, 1998, death vetoed Abacha's self-succession bid. To the relief of many observers, Abacha's successor, Gen. Abdulsalam Abubakar, appeared determined to retrieve Nigeria from its status as an international pariah. Abubakar met with several opposition and foreign diplomats, promised to respect the election timetable, and released many political prisoners. The anticipated release of Moshood Abiola raised hopes across the country and prompted a meeting on July 7 among Abiola, Nigerian government officials, and U.S. State Department representatives. Abiola, who was known to be in poor health, fell gravely ill during the meeting. He died within hours – like Abacha, of apparent cardiac arrest. At least 50 people died in riots that occurred after his death. Although an autopsy conducted by an international team of pathologists confirmed that Abiola died of natural causes, many of his followers remained suspicious and bitter. In the tense climate following Abiola's funeral, opposition leaders urged Abubakar to transfer power to a transitional "national unity" government, led by eminent citizens from all regions. Instead, the military leader announced a new transition program calling for the military's withdrawal on May 29, 1999. Abubakar held true to his word and handed over the reins of government, on schedule, to the newly elected president, Gen. Olusegun Obasanjo.

Whatever happens on the political front, two sad results of long-time military rule are already apparent. The first is the flight of Nigerian brain power. The country's universities are today a shadow of their former selves, and many of the country's most famous intellectuals, such as Nobel Prize-winning author WOLE SOYINKA, are in exile. The second consequence of ongoing military rule is the sharp rise in violence within Nigerian society. Lingering ethnic tensions, far from abating, have been exacerbated by religious fanaticism and by the widening material gap in a country that many still see as the great hope of Africa – if it puts its house in order.

Okey Ndibe

SEE ALSO

Colonial Rule; Babangida, Ibrahim Gbadamosi; Dahomey, Early Kingdom of; Decolonization in Africa: An Interpretation; Ethnicity and Identity in Africa: An Interpretation; Gold Trade; Ivory Trade; Kano, Nigeria; Lagos, Nigeria; Law in Africa: Colonial and Contemporary; Lugard, Frederick John Dealtry; Nationalism in Africa; Oyo, Early Kingdom of; Pan-Africanism; Sahara Desert; Salt Trade; Saro-Wiwa, Kenule Beeson; Sokoto Caliphate; Yoruba; Du Bois, William Edward Burghardt (W. E. B.); Christianity: Missionaries in Africa; Islam and Tradition: An Interpretation; Slavery in Africa; Trans-Saharan and Red Sea Slave Trade; Abiola, Moshood Kashimawo Olawale.

Africa

Nigeria (Ready Reference)

Official Name: Federal Republic of Nigeria
Area: 923,768 sq km (356,669 sq mi)
Location: West Africa, on the Gulf of Guinea, bordered by BENIN, NIGER, CHAD, and CAMEROON
Capital: Abuja (population 107,129,469 [1997 estimate])
Other Major Cities: Lagos (official population 1,347,000 [1992 estimate], the metropolitan area has an estimated 10 million residents), Ibadan (1,295,000), Niger (2,482,000 [1991 estimate]), Bauchi (4,294,000), Sokoto (4,392,000), Kano (5,632,000), and Ondo (3,884,000)
Population: 110,532,242 (1998 estimate)
Population Density: 137 persons per sq km (356 per sq mi)
Population Below Age 15: 45 percent (male 24,871,855; female 24,661,134 [1998 estimate])
Population Growth Rate: 2.96 percent (1998 estimate)
Total Fertility Rate: 6.09 children born per woman (1998 estimate)
Life Expectancy at Birth: Total population: 53.55 years (male 52.68 years; female 54.45 years [1998 estimate])
Infant Mortality: 70.2 deaths per 1000 live births (1997 estimate)
Literacy Rate (age 15 and over who can read and write): Total population: 57.1 percent (male 67.3 percent; female 47.3 percent [1995 estimate])
Education: In the early 1990s Nigeria had 14.8 million pupils enrolled in primary schools and more than 3.6 million in secondary schools. Institutions of higher education include the University of Ibadan, Ahmadu Bello University, the Obafemi Awolowo University, the University of Lagos, and the University of Nigeria.
Languages: English is the official language. Hausa, YORUBA, Ibo, and FULANI are also spoken.
Ethnic Groups: Hausa and Fulani in the north, along with Yoruba in the southwest and Ibos in the southeast, together make up 65 percent of population. Other ethnic groups include the EDO, IJAW, and IBIBIO in the south, the NUPE and TIV in the central part of the country, and the KANURI in the northeast.
Religions: Muslim 50 percent; Christian 40 percent; indigenous beliefs 10 percent.
Climate: Nigeria has two distinct climatic zones: high humidity and heavy rainfall along the coast, and dry and dusty conditions in the north. The temperature varies considerably with the season, as does rainfall, of which there is far less in the north than in the south.
Land, Plants, and Animals: Along the coast the Niger delta region, mangrove forests and swamps extend inland some 100 km (some 60 mi). North of the coast is a forested belt, rising to the Jos Plateau. Farther north is a savanna region and a semidesert zone in the extreme north. Vegetation zones in Nigeria parallel the climatic zones. In the south the well-watered zone is partly covered by dense tropical forests containing hardwoods such as mahogany and obeche and abundant oil palms. In the plateau and savanna regions forests give way to grasslands and such hardy trees as the baobab and the tamarind. In the extreme northeast semidesert vegetation prevails. CROCODILES and snakes are found in the swamps and rain forest zones. Most large animals have disappeared from heavily populated areas. Some ANTELOPE, camels, and hyenas live in the north.
Natural Resources: Petroleum, tin, columbite, iron ore, coal, limestone, lead, zinc, and natural gas
Currency: The naira (N)
Gross Domestic Product (GDP): $132.7 billion (1996 estimate)
GDP per Capita: $1,300 (1996 estimate)

GDP Real Growth Rate: 3.3 percent (1996 estimate)
Primary Economic Activities: Agriculture, mining, manufacturing, and services
Primary Crops: Yams, cassava, sorghum, rice, millet, maize, sugar cane, taro, plantains, peanuts, palm oil, chiles and green peppers, tomatoes, palm kernels, cotton lint, cacao beans, livestock, and poultry
Industries: Crude oil, coal, tin, columbite, palm oil, peanuts, cotton, rubber, wood, hides and skins, textiles, cement and other construction materials, food products, footwear, chemicals, fertilizer, printing, ceramics, and steel
Primary Exports: Oil, cocoa, and rubber
Primary Imports: Machinery, transportation equipment, manufactured goods, chemicals, and food
Primary Trade Partners: United States, Europe, and Japan
Government: Nigeria has been a military government since 1983, and its 1979 constitution remained in force until May 1999. In June 1998 the country's repressive president, Gen. SANI ABACHA, died suddenly. His replacement, Gen. Abdulsalam Abubakar, pledged to hold elections and transfer power to a civilian government on May 29, 1999. A former military leader, Gen. Olusegun Obasanjo, won the nationwide elections in February 1999 with 62 percent of the vote; he assumed the office of president in May 1999. The National Assembly, consisting of a 593-member House of Representatives and a 91-seat Senate, was dissolved following the military coup in 1993.

Barbara Worley

SEE ALSO
Abuja, Nigeria; Camel; Baobab Tree; Hausa Language; Hyena; Lagos, Nigeria; Niger River.

Latin America and the Caribbean

Niger, Paul (Albert Beville)

(b. December 21, 1915, Basse-Terre, Guadeloupe; d. June 22, 1962, Sainte-Rose, Guadeloupe), one of the most powerful writers of the NÉGRITUDE movement and an outspoken critic of French colonialism.

Paul Niger completed his primary schooling at the Lycée Carnot in the French Caribbean island of GUADELOUPE. He then traveled to Paris, France, where he studied at the Lycée Louis-le-Grand and the Ecole Nationale de la France d'outre-mer. While in Paris, he became part of a circle of black intellectuals such as AIMÉ CÉSAIRE and LÉOPOLD SÉDAR SENGHOR before the war. He also fought for the French resistance following the installation of the Nazi-supported Vichy regime.

Niger subsequently began a career as a colonial administrator in Dahomey (now BENIN), MALI, and NIGER in 1944. This experience led him to an increasingly violent condemnation of French colonialism (*see* COLONIAL RULE). In turn, he celebrated a somewhat mythical, essentialized Africa in poems such as "Or j'avais renoncé à prononcer ton nom" (1959). Niger was a frequent contributor to the journal *Présence Africaine* in the postwar years. In 1954 he published a collection of poems entitled *Initiation*, in which his violent condemnation of colonialism announces the coming explosion of African independence of the late 1950s:

L'Afrique va parler,
J'entends chanter la sève au coeur
du flamboyant

(Africa is going to speak, / I hear the sap sing from the heart of the flame tree)

Niger fought for the decolonization and independence of the French Overseas Departments (FRENCH GUIANA, MARTINIQUE, and GUADELOUPE) during the late 1950s as part of the Front des Antilles-Guyane organization. France's De Gaulle government banned him from Guadeloupe in the early 1960s. Niger was one of the authors of the pro-independence text produced by the Congress for the Independence of the Antilles, held April 22 and 23, 1961. In 1962, while attempting to return to Guadeloupe clandestinely, Niger died in a plane crash in Sainte-Rose, Guadeloupe.

Niger's last writings (*Les puissants* [1956] and *Les grenouilles du Mont Kimbo* [1964]) describe both his experience of colonialism and his vision of a future liberation from the domination of colonialist exploitation.

Nick Nesbitt

SEE ALSO
France.

Africa

Niger River, the third largest river in Africa.

The Niger River is located in western Africa, originating in GUINEA and running generally east through MALI, NIGER, and NIGERIA, where it discharges into the Gulf of Guinea in the Atlantic Ocean. The third largest river in Africa, it flows for approximately 4180 km (about 2600 mi). Its chief tributary is the Lokoja River in Nigeria.

The Niger is an important travel artery in Mali, Niger, and Nigeria and is a source of fish, including carp, Nile perch, and catfish. In Mali the river's inland delta is the country's richest agricultural region. In Nigeria the Niger River delta constitutes one of the world's largest wetlands and contains one of Africa's largest mangrove forests. It is also the location of some of Africa's largest petroleum and natural gas deposits, which are critical to the Nigerian economy. Pollution caused by the oil and natural gas industries has damaged farms, fisheries, and mangrove stands and provoked protests from local peoples such as the Ogoni. The Movement for the Survival of the Ogoni People, led by the late Ken Saro-Wiwa until his execution in 1995, has become one of the biggest environmental movements in Africa.

Robert Fay

SEE ALSO
Environmental Movements in Africa; Saro-Wiwa, Kenule Beeson.

North America

Niggaz with Attitude, Los Angeles rap group that brought "gangsta rap" to a mass audience.

Niggaz with Attitude (N.W.A.) was formed in Compton, California, in 1987 and included Eazy-E (Eric Wright), MC Ren (Lorenzo Patterson), ICE CUBE (O'Shea Jackson), Dr. Dre (Andre Young), and Yella (Antoine Carraby). Recording for Eazy-E's own Ruthless Records, N.W.A. made its debut with one of the most important albums in RAP history. *Straight Outta Compton* (1988) was powered by the innovative production of Dr. Dre (whose career in rap had started with the World Class Wreckin' Cru, a synthesizer-oriented dance group), which emphasized the heavy, loping beats of 1970s soul and FUNK.

Members of the "gangsta rap" group Niggaz with Attitude included, *left to right*, Eazy-E, Dr. Dre, MC Ren, and Yella. Ice Cube, not pictured, was an early member of the group before launching a solo career. *CORBIS*

The group's rhymes – especially those of Ice Cube – helped reinvent rap lyrics through the unflinching portraits of gang life that they created. While rap lyrics had traditionally been built around ebullient (if violent) boasts, songs like "Dopeman" told graphic stories of drugs and gangs and "bitches and ho's" without apology. "F – tha Police" – a block party anthem during the summer of 1989 – was condemned by law enforcement officials nationwide, including the Federal Bureau of Investigation (FBI). Despite receiving scant radio play, *Straight Outta Compton* sold more than 2 million copies, and N.W.A.'s gangsta rap style made Los Angeles the capital of the hip hop world for years to come.

Soon after the release of the band's debut album, Ice Cube quit the group, and N.W.A. became even more reliant on Dr. Dre's production skills. But despite being ignored by commercial radio and many critics, the band's next album, *Efil4zaggin* (1991) – the title was written backward – went immediately to the top of the album charts.

After N.W.A. disbanded in 1992, each of its members pursued solo careers. Despite several attempts, MC Ren and Yella never achieved much success on their own. But Eazy-E, embroiled in an explosive public feud with Dr. Dre, found success with an anti-Dre album titled *It's On (Dr. Dre) 187um Killa* (1993). Eazy-E continued to release albums and run Ruthless Records (which found huge success with Cleveland's Bone Thugs-N-Harmony); he died of acquired immune deficiency syndrome (AIDS) in 1995. Dr. Dre went on to cofound Death Row Records, where he released his wildly successful solo debut, *The Chronic* (1992); Dre's menacing yet accessible beats also powered the meteoric rise of Death Row's young stars TUPAC SHAKUR and SNOOP DOGGY DOGG.

Ice Cube established himself as one of hip hop's most important voices with *Amerikkka's Most Wanted* (1990); his success continued with solo and collaborative albums throughout the 1990s. He has acted as well, starring in John Singleton's *Boyz N the Hood* (1991) and F. Gary Gray's *Friday* (1995), for which he was also the screenwriter. *The Player's Club* (1998) was Cube's directorial debut (*see* FILM, BLACKS IN AMERICAN).

Andrew Du Bois

SEE ALSO

AIDS in the United States; Soul Music; Hip Hop in the United States; Los Angeles, California.

Africa

Nile River, the longest river in the world and the principal source for Egyptian agriculture.

From its major source, LAKE VICTORIA in east Central Africa, the Nile flows generally north through UGANDA, SUDAN, and EGYPT to the Mediterranean Sea for 5584 km (3470 mi). From its remotest headstream, the Ruvyironza River in BURUNDI, the river is 6671 km (4145 mi) long. The river basin has an area of more than 3,349,000 sq km (1,293,049 sq mi).

The Ruvyironza, regarded as the ultimate source of the Nile, is one of the upper branches of the Kagera River in TANZANIA. The Kagera follows the boundary of RWANDA northward, turns along the boundary of Uganda, and drains into Lake Victoria. On leaving Lake Victoria at the site of the now-submerged Ripon Falls, the Nile rushes for 483 km (300 mi) between high rocky walls and over rapids and cataracts, at first northwest and then west, until it enters Lake Albert. The section between the two lakes is called the Victoria Nile.

The river leaves the northern end of Lake Albert as the Albert Nile, flows through northern Uganda, and at the Sudan border becomes the Bahr al Jabal. At its junction with the Bahr al Ghazal, the river becomes the Bahr al Abyad, or the White Nile. At Khartoum the White Nile is joined by the Blue Nile, or Bahr al Azraq, so named because of the color of the water. The Blue Nile, 1529 km (950 mi) long, gathers its volume mainly from Lake T'ana, in the Ethiopian Highlands; it is known here as the Abbai. From Khartoum the Nile flows northeast; 322 km (200 mi) below that city, it is joined by the 'Atbarah River. During its course from the confluence of the 'Atbarah through the Nubian Desert, the Nile makes two deep bends. It enters the Mediterranean Sea by a delta that separates into the Rosetta and Damietta distributaries. The Nile River valley is home to a host of wildlife, including the Nile CROCODILE, hippopotamuses, more than 300 species of birds, and numerous fish species.

Europeans considered the source of the Nile one of the last great mysteries on earth until the mid-nineteenth century, when a series of expeditions brought British and German explorers into the Lake Victoria region for the first time. These explorers included the Englishmen John Hanning Speke, who reached Lake Victoria in 1858 and Ripon Falls in 1862, and Sir Samuel White, who sighted Lake Albert in 1864; a German, Georg August Schweinfurth, who explored (1868-1871) the western feeders of the White Nile; and a British American, SIR HENRY MORTON STANLEY. In 1875 Stanley sailed around Lake Victoria; in 1889 he traced the Semliki River and reached LAKE EDWARD and the Ruwenzori Range.

For thousands of years the Nile's yearly flood, the result of August rains in the Ethiopian highlands and the runoff from snowmelt in the Mountains of the Moon, flooded the Nile delta in Egypt. As the floodwaters receded, a heavy layer of silt remained. The intensive irrigated agriculture in the fertile Nile River valley supported one of the world's earliest civilizations and in more recent times earned Egypt the title "Breadbasket of the Middle East."

The first dam on the Nile, the High Dam, was built in 1902 and heightened in 1936. The Makwar Dam, now called the Sennar Dam, was built across the Blue Nile south of Khartoum following World War I (1914-1918) to provide storage water for cotton plantations in the Sudan. A dam at Jabal Awliya was constructed on the White Nile south of Khartoum in 1937. But the Aswan High Dam, which opened in the early 1970s, has most dramatically transformed the ecology and economic role of the Nile. It created one of the world's largest reservoirs, Lake Nasser, and allowed the Egyptian government to produce hydroelectric power, control flooding, and minimize droughts. But it has severely reduced sedimentation deposits that the floodwaters once brought to the delta and has increased the river's salinity. Consequently, the Nile delta has become less fertile, forcing Egyptian farmers to increase the use of chemical fertilizers.

The lack of sedimentation has had other harmful effects, such as erosion of the river's banks. The silt in the floodwaters also fed into the coastal waters of the Mediterranean Sea, nourishing the algae blooms and sea-bottom detritus that in turn fed sardines, shrimp, and other sea creatures. Since the Aswan High Dam's opening, fish and shrimp catches have declined significantly.

Robert Fay

SEE ALSO

Hippopotamus; Khartoum, Sudan; Nubia; Aswan High Dam.

Africa

Nimeiri, Gaafar Muhammad al- (b. January 1, 1930, Wad Nubawi, Omdurman, Sudan), president of SUDAN (1971-1985).

Gaafar Muhammad al-Nimeiri came to power after a military coup in 1969. Born in 1930 in the Omdurman area of central Sudan, he attended the Sudan Military College and graduated in 1952, four years before Sudanese independence. After 1960 he belonged to a small group of politically active military officers who were strongly influenced by pan-Arabist and socialist thought. In 1966 he graduated from the United States Army Command College at Fort Leavenworth, Kansas. Upon his return to Sudan, Nimeiri became director of the Gebeit training school, where he had ready access to the newest members of the Sudanese officer corps.

In 1969 Nimeiri and five other officers overthrew the civilian government of Ismail al-Azhari. Nimeiri was promoted to major general and was chosen as prime minister and chairman of the Revolutionary Command Council. This group included military officers and a number of civilians seeking socialist, communist, and/or pan-Arabist political programs. Nimeiri's government nationalized banks and some industries, carried out limited land reform, and expanded the rights of organized labor. In 1970 Sadiq al-Mahdi, a conservative Muslim leader, substantial landholder, and direct descendant of the Mahdi (*see* MAHDIST STATE) led an unsuccessful attempt to overthrow Nimeiri. In 1971 Communists briefly succeeded in removing him from office, but Nimeiri returned to power. Later that year he was elected president with more than 98 percent of the vote.

Once securely in power, Nimeiri established a political party, the Sudanese Socialist

Union, and began negotiations to end the Sudanese civil war with the Anya-Nya guerrilla organization, which had been fighting for southern regional autonomy. In 1972 Nimeiri concluded a peace settlement, the Addis Ababa Agreement. This granted regional autonomy to southern Sudan, which was predominantly non-Muslim. The agreement brought peace to southern Sudan for 11 years. Embittered by the role of Sudanese Communists in the 1971 coup, Nimeiri began to shift to a more market-oriented economic program and sought cordial relations with the United States and other Western powers. He denationalized the banks and developed economic policies that encouraged Western and Arab investment in Sudan, and he purged his government of leftists suspected of supporting the 1971 coup.

In 1976 another unsuccessful coup associated with Sadiq al-Mahdi impressed Nimeiri with the power of Islamic opposition. In 1981 he formed an alliance with the Muslim Brotherhood and, in 1983, imposed Islamic law throughout the country. In direct violation of the Addis Ababa Agreement, he dissolved the southern Sudanese government and divided the region into three provinces. This provoked a mutiny of southern Sudanese troops and led directly to the revival of the southern Sudanese secessionist movement. In 1985, while undergoing a medical examination in the United States, Nimeiri was overthrown in a bloodless military coup. Since his ouster he has lived in exile in Egypt.

Robert Baum

Latin America and the Caribbean

Nina Rodrigues, Raimundo

(b. December 4, 1862, Vargem Grande, Maranhão, Brazil; d. July 17, 1906, Paris, France), one of the first social scientists to study Afro-Brazilian culture, particularly Brazilian religious syncretism.

Raimundo Nina Rodrigues was trained as a medical doctor and graduated from the medical school of Bahia. He was also interested in the study of anthropology, sociology, and criminology. He became a professor of general pathology and forensic medicine at the medical school in the early 1890s and was a pioneer in Afro-Brazilian ethnology and forensic medicine. He founded *Forensic Medicine* magazine and was a member of the Forensic Medicine Society of New York and of the Société de Medico-Psychologique de Paris.

Rodrigues identified two distinct African "cults," which he termed the Iorubanos and the Malês. He devoted most of his attention to the Iorubano cults, which he felt were more strongly influenced by Catholicism. These originated from the Candomblé Gêgê-Nagô, whereas the Malês were thought to be associated more with Islam.

Among his most important works are *O animismo fetichista dos negros da Bahianos* (1935, The Fetishist Animism of Bahian Blacks), *Os Africanos no Brasil* (1932, Africans in Brazil, a posthumous collection of his papers); and *As raças humanas e a responsabilidade penal no Brasil* (1958, The Human Races and Penal Responsibility in Brazil).

Rodrigues's works embrace theories of scientific racism and social Darwinism broadly held by the Brazilian intellectual elite of his time. He viewed racial mixing and the black presence in Brazil more generally as hindering the nation's progress. His views greatly influenced a national immigration policy that discriminated against Africans and Asians while encouraging European immigrants (*see* whitening). Rodrigues also applied his theory of racial inferiority in the field of forensic medicine. In 1894 he published a book stating that the "degenerates," that is, the Negroes and Indians, should have only attenuated criminal responsibility, given the allegedly different capacities of what he believed to be inferior races. Rodrigues also influenced generations of students of Afro-Brazilian culture. He died in 1906 while in Paris.

Michelle Gueraldi

North America

Nixon, Edgar Daniel

(b. July 12, 1899, Robinson Springs, Ala.; d. February 25, 1987, Montgomery, Ala.), African American civil rights leader and organizer of the Montgomery Bus Boycott.

E. D. Nixon's struggle to organize African Americans in Montgomery, Alabama, illustrated several sources of tension within the United States Civil Rights Movement: social class, the roles of the labor movement and the church, and older versus newer leadership. Nixon was the son of Wesley Nixon, a tenant farmer turned Primitive Baptist preacher, and Susan Chappell Nixon. Having little formal education, Nixon began to work full-time at age 13, and worked for 41 years as a Pullman car porter.

A supporter of African American labor union leader A. Philip Randolph, Nixon became president of the Brotherhood of Sleeping Car Porters Montgomery chapter in 1938. Despite white hostility, he also organized a registration drive for black voters in Montgomery.

When the middle-class Montgomery branch of the National Association for the Advancement of Colored People (NAACP) failed to support the 1943 voter registration drive actively, Nixon organized poorer African Americans to gain control of the local chapter, and he was elected its president in 1945 and 1946. After he became president of the state NAACP in 1947, the national NAACP leadership, embarrassed by Nixon's homespun demeanor and sixth-grade education, orchestrated his 1949 reelection defeat. The following year Nixon was also ousted from the presidency of the NAACP Montgomery chapter.

Nixon spearheaded a plan to challenge Montgomery's segregated public transportation system, and when Montgomery NAACP secretary Rosa L. Parks was arrested for refusing to relinquish her bus seat to a white patron, it was Nixon who posted her bail and called for a bus boycott. As treasurer of the Montgomery Improvement Association, organized to end discrimination on the buses, Nixon resented the association's president, the Reverend Dr. Martin Luther King Jr., who was associated with Montgomery's African American middle class, and who, Nixon believed, did not properly credit him and the masses of poor African Americans for the boycott's ultimate success.

Following a number of unsuccessful attempts to regain leadership roles, an embittered Nixon withdrew from public life.

Jalane Schmidt

See Also

King, Martin Luther, Jr.; Parks, Rosa Louise McCauley; Randolph, Asa Philip.

Africa

Nkomo, Joshua

(b. June 19, 1917, Semokwe Reserve, Southern Rhodesia, now Zimbabwe; d. July 1, 1999, Harare, Zimbabwe), nationalist leader and politician in Zimbabwe.

From humble beginnings, Joshua Nkomo rose to become a leading nationalist figure and prominent politician in independent Zimbabwe. After attending elementary school in Southern Rhodesia, Nkomo traveled to South Africa for high school in Durban and college in Johannesburg. He returned to Rhodesia in 1947, becoming a social worker for the railways and then secretary of the Railway Worker's Association. An effective organizer, in 1952 Nkomo was elected president of the Southern Rhodesia African National Congress, or ANC, and represented African opinion in the Central African Federation.

After the ANC was banned, Nkomo, in London, was elected president of the new Rhodesian National Democratic Party, or NDP, in absentia in 1960. The NDP was also banned, re-forming as the increasingly militant Zimbabwe African People's Union, or ZAPU, with Nkomo as president. Soon afterward many of his cohorts left ZAPU to form the Zimbabwe African National Union, or ZANU. From 1964 to 1974 Nkomo remained either in confinement or restricted to certain areas, rarely appearing in public. Nevertheless, his stature grew as ZAPU built a conventional army and carried out attacks on the Rhodesian establishment. After his release Nkomo worked hard to negotiate a peaceful transition to independence; fought to retain his position in ZAPU in the face of opposition from younger, more militant members; and, later, led ZAPU from ZAMBIA in its fight against the Rhodesian regime.

In the transition to independence, ROBERT MUGABE and ZANU disavowed Nkomo, leading to ZAPU's electoral defeat. Nkomo became the minister of home affairs but was soon forced from office when Mugabe cracked down on opposition parties, particularly ZAPU. Outside of government he retained a huge popular following among the NDEBELE people in southern and western Zimbabwe. In 1988, with the creation of the united ZANU-PF, Nkomo reentered the government as a senior minister and as one of two vice presidents. He transferred his allegiance to ZANU-PF and, although promoting development in Matabeleland, remained strongly aligned with the policies of Mugabe and ZANU. When Nkomo stepped down from his government positions in late 1997 in ill health, the question of who would succeed him as the de facto leader of the Ndebele remained unclear. Nkomo died at age 82 in July 1999.

Eric Young

SEE ALSO

Johannesburg, South Africa; Nationalism in Africa; Durban, South Africa.

Africa

Nkrumah, Kwame

(Francis Nwia Kofi Nkrumah) (b. September 21, 1909, Nkroful, Gold Coast [present-day Ghana]; d. April 27, 1972, Bucharest, Romania), leading nationalist and prime minister of the Gold Coast from 1952 until its independence in 1957; later prime minister (1957-1960) and president (1960-1966) of independent GHANA.

Leader of the first sub-Saharan African colony to gain independence, Kwame Nkrumah was a towering figure in the Pan-African movement and a tireless advocate of an independent AFRICAN SOCIALISM. Nkrumah was born into a NZIMA family in the southwestern Gold Coast. His father was a goldsmith and his mother a retail market trader. A baptized Roman Catholic, Nkrumah attended the Roman Catholic mission school in the nearby town of Half Assini and graduated from another Roman Catholic school in Sekondi. He studied teaching at Achimota College. After teaching in the early 1930s Nkrumah considered becoming a Jesuit priest, but decided to study in the United States instead. He earned degrees from Lincoln University and the University of Pennsylvania. Nkrumah's political philosophy began to develop as he studied the international socialism of Marx and Lenin, the African nationalist writings of American leader Marcus Garvey, and the nonviolence of Mohandas Gandhi. He also met W. E. B. Du Bois and GEORGE PADMORE, leading advocates of Pan-Africanism.

When he moved to England in 1945 to earn a doctorate degree from the London School of Economics, Nkrumah became secretary of the West African Students Union and helped organize the fifth Pan-African Congress in Manchester. He also wrote three pamphlets on fighting colonialism and met other future leaders, including JOMO KENYATTA of KENYA and Kamuzu Banda of MALAWI. In 1947 Nkrumah returned to Africa to become secretary general of United Gold Coast Convention (UGCC), a party calling for self-government in the Gold Coast, at the invitation of its leaders, including Joseph B. Danquah. Membership in the party increased as Nkrumah toured the region, urging Africans to unite. In 1948 the British colonial governor, Gerald Creasy, blamed rioting and looting on the party's activities and ordered the arrests of Danquah and Nkrumah. Police found a Communist Party membership card in Nkrumah's possession, but it was not signed and Nkrumah denied ever having joined the party, calling himself a Marxist-socialist and nondenominational Christian. Later that year he established the *Accra Evening News*. In 1949 Nkrumah broke with the UGCC because its middle-class leaders distrusted his more radical populism; he formed the Convention People's Party (CPP), which advocated mass action in the form of boycotts, strikes, and civil disobedience to gain independence.

This strategy led to Nkrumah's arrest and imprisonment on charges of "subversion" and "sedition," which won him widespread public sympathy. In February 1951 the CPP won 34 of the 38 popularly contested seats in the Legislative Assembly. Consequently, the British administration released Nkrumah from jail. On the next day, Governor Charles Arden-Clarke summoned him to Christiansborg Castle in Accra and asked him to lead the new government in cooperation with the colonial administration. He took office as prime minister in 1952 and guided the country to independence on March 6, 1957, with the name Ghana. In 1960 a new constitution made Ghana a republic, with Nkrumah as president.

At first the Nkrumah administration was widely popular. Nkrumah brought Africans into the government, offered free education, provided scholarships for study abroad, built hospitals, and paved roads. But the borrowing necessary to pay for domestic spending pushed Ghana into debt. His government abandoned its 1959 Development Plan two years later in the face of mounting financial problems. Meanwhile, Nkrumah became increasingly autocratic. He introduced laws enabling the government to jail without trial people who were labeled security risks. In 1961 Nkrumah strengthened his grip on the CPP. Later that year he introduced a law under which anyone found guilty of insulting Nkrumah faced a three-year prison term. Economic troubles, worsened by falling COCOA prices, generated labor unrest and a general strike in 1961. Following the strike Nkrumah assumed command of the armed forces and dismissed all foreign officers. In 1964 Nkrumah declared Ghana a one-party state, and his government tightened censorship. Several assassination attempts prompted Nkrumah's increasing isolation, a substantial increase in the internal security apparatus, and the number of political prisoners.

While the situation within Ghana deteriorated, Nkrumah continued to advocate Pan-Africanism internationally. From 1960 to 1963 Ghanaian troops served with United Nations forces in Congo-Kinshasa. Ghana became a charter member of the ORGANIZATION OF AFRICAN UNITY in 1963. Also that year Nkrumah published his book, *Why Africa Must Unite*. On February 24, 1966, while Nkrumah was visiting Beijing and Hanoi in an effort to end the Vietnam War, a military coup ousted him from office. He went into exile in GUINEA. He wrote *Handbook for Revolutionary Warfare* (1968) and *Class Struggle in Africa* (1970). Nkrumah died in 1972 while seeking cancer treatment in Romania.

David P. Johnson, Jr.

SEE ALSO

Accra, Ghana; Banda, Ngwazi Hastings Kamuzu; Congo, Democratic Republic of the; Danquah, Joseph Kwame Kyeretwi Boakye; Nationalism in Africa; Pan-Africanism; Du Bois, William Edward Burghardt (W. E. B.); Garvey, Marcus Mosiah; Lincoln University (Pennsylvania).

Africa

Nkumbula, Harry Mwaanga

(b. January 1916, Maala, Northern Rhodesia [present-day ZAMBIA]; d. October 10, 1983, Lusaka, Zambia), prominent Zambian nationalist and leader of the African National Congress (ANC).

Harry Mwaanga Nkumbula is considered a father of Zambian nationalism. After working as a schoolteacher and being influenced by GEORGE PADMORE's *How Britain Rules Africa*, Nkumbula became the secretary of the Mufulira Welfare Association and later the cofounder of the Kitwe African Society. Welfare associations were precursors to formal political parties; they provided black Zambians with an opportunity to mobilize against colonial authorities. After studying in UGANDA, Nkumbala moved to England and earned a degree from the London School of Economics. While he was in London, he associated with such African nationalist figures as KWAME NKRUMAH, JOMO KENYATTA, and Hastings Banda, who were all to achieve political prominence in later years.

In 1951 Nkumbula returned to Northern Rhodesia and became president of the African National Congress (a separate entity from the South African organization of the same name). He led the moderate ANC campaign against the formation of the Central African Federation, the consolidation of Northern and Southern Rhodesia. When his ANC campaign failed and the Central African Federation was established in 1953, Nkumbula's prestige began to fade. In 1955 he and future Zambian president KENNETH KAUNDA were jailed for distributing ANC literature. Following his release, Nkumbula campaigned for the adoption of a new constitution and universal adult suffrage.

In 1958 Nkumbula lost the support of his colleague Kaunda, who broke with the more moderate ANC to form the United National Independence Party (UNIP). In 1959 Nkumbula was elected to the legislative council. However, he was clearly eclipsed by Kaunda by the time the two nationalists attended the 1961 London constitutional conference on the future of the Central African Federation.

The ANC lost much of its support to Kaunda's UNIP. But following the 1962 election, the ANC joined the ruling coalition with the UNIP, and Nkumbula received a ministerial appointment. He remained active in politics and joined the UNIP in 1973. He died on October 8, 1983, at age 67.

Ari Nave

SEE ALSO
Banda, Ngwazi Hastings Kamuzu; Nationalism in Africa.

NNLC. Please see NATIONAL NEGRO LABOR COUNCIL

Cross Cultural

Nobel Prize, awards granted annually to persons or institutions for outstanding contributions made during the previous year in the fields of physics, chemistry, physiology or medicine, literature, international peace, and economic sciences.

Generally considered the world's most prestigious awards, Nobel Prizes come from a trust fund established by the Swedish chemist, inventor, and philanthropist Alfred Bernhard Nobel. As designated in Nobel's will, the Royal Swedish Academy of Sciences awards prizes for physics and chemistry; the Nobel Assembly at the Karolinksa Institute awards prizes for physiological or medical works; the Swedish Academy awards prizes for literature; and the Norwegian Nobel Committee selects the winner of the peace prize. In 1968 a new prize for economics was established and endowed by the National Bank of Sweden.

The first Nobel Prizes were awarded on December 10, 1901, but it was not until 1950 that a black person was a recipient. An American from Detroit, Dr. Ralph J. Bunche, was the first black man to receive the distinguished prize for his work as a United Nations mediator; his efforts led to the 1949 Arab-Israeli armistice agreement. Since then eight other remarkable blacks have received a Nobel: ALBERT JOHN LUTHULI, 1960 Peace Prize; Martin Luther King Jr., 1964 Peace Prize; Sir William Arthur Lewis, 1979 Economics Prize; Bishop Desmond Tutu, 1984 Peace Prize; WOLE SOYINKA, 1986 Literature Prize; Derek Walcott, 1992 Literature Prize; TONI MORRISON, 1993 Literature Prize; Nelson Mandela, 1993 Peace Prize. Nobel Prize winners receive a cash award, a gold medal, and a diploma.

Liliana Obregón

SEE ALSO
Mandela, Nelson Rolihlahla; Tutu, Desmond Mpilo; Bunche, Ralph Johnson; King, Martin Luther, Jr.; Walcott, Derek Alton; Lewis, Arthur.

Africa

Nok, ancient African culture.

The name Nok was given to the culture of a group of people who lived in what are now the northern and central parts of NIGERIA, in the area north of the confluence of the Niger and Benue rivers, from the fourth century B.C.E. to the second century C.E. Remains of this culture were first discovered in the area of the Jos Plateau, and similar artifacts have been found in the middle valley of the Benue River.

The Nok were also the earliest people yet known in this part of Africa who made iron tools and weapons. They also produced very fine sculpture, usually of human forms, in terra cotta (baked clay). These magnificent pottery heads and figures are the earliest known sub-Saharan African sculptures. It is believed that the Nok had a well-organized economy and administrative system, and that their culture influenced later peoples of the region.

SEE ALSO
Iron in Africa; Niger River.

North America

Noone, Jimmie (b. April 23, 1894, New Orleans, La; d. April 19, 1944, Los Angeles, Calif.), African American musician who was considered one of the great first-generation JAZZ clarinetists and who was influential in the development of swing music.

Jimmie Noone began playing clarinet around 1910 in New Orleans, taking lessons from Lorenzo Tio Jr. and Sidney Bechet (who was himself only 13 years old at the time). In 1915 Noone got his first professional job playing in Buddy Petit's Young Olympia Band. During his stint with Petit's band, Noone befriended Freddie Keppard, whose band, the Original Creole Orchestra in Chicago, he joined in 1917. From 1920 to 1926 he played with Doc Cooke's Dreamland Orchestra, at the same time studying classical clarinet. Noone led his own bands in Chicago between 1927 and 1931, the most famous of which was Jimmie Noone's Apex Club Orchestra, which performed at the Apex Club on Chicago's South Side.

Noone's style differed from that of Johnny Dodds and Bechet, two other great New Orleans clarinetists, in that it was smoother and more romantic. His style had a major influence on the swing music that was popular in the 1930s, in particular the music of fellow clarinetists Bennie Goodman and Jimmy Dorsey.

Between 1927 and 1931 Noone and his bands recorded many songs that are considered classic examples of Noone's clarinet virtuosity. Noone led several bands in Chicago throughout the 1930s. In the early 1940s he moved to southern California, where he played on several famous radio programs, recordings of which are available. He was playing in a band led by "Kid" Ory when he died of a heart attack.

Robert Fay

SEE ALSO
Bechet, Sidney Joseph; Chicago, Illinois; New Orleans, Louisiana; Ory, Edward ("Kid").

North America

Norman, Jessye (b. September 15, 1945, Augusta, Ga.), African American OPERA singer.

Jessye Norman is a dramatic soprano whose rich voice is recognized for its strength, warmth and intensity, dynamic coloration, affective depth, and impressive range – from the E above high C to the E below middle C. She is one of five children from an educated and musical family. Her mother, Janie (King), is an amateur pianist. Her father, Silas, an insurance broker, often sang in Augusta's Mount Calvary Baptist Church, the site of Norman's earliest singing performances.

Norman entered HOWARD UNIVERSITY in 1963 on a full-tuition scholarship to train under voice instructor Carolyn Grant, and received her B.Mus. degree cum laude in 1967. The following year she won the International Music Competition in Munich. This showing won her a 1969 operatic debut with the Deutsche Oper and many subsequent performances before German and Italian audiences. The glowing reviews from these European recitals, her 1972 United States appearances, and her recordings for Philips Records attracted a sellout crowd to her January 21, 1973, New York debut in the Great Performers series at Lincoln Center.

Norman is an internationally recognized performer and is considered to have excellent stylistic and linguistic command of the French, German, and Italian compositions of the operatic canon. She has broadened her performance repertoire by reintroducing lesser-known works, including significant interpretations of theater songs and AFRICAN AMERICAN SPIRITUALS, to the appreciation of audiences and critics alike. In addition to performing as a recording artist, guest orchestral soloist, and recitalist, Norman directs master classes.

Jalane Schmidt

North America

North Carolina Mutual Life Insurance Company, the first black-controlled American company to gross more than $1 billion.

Seven men founded the North Carolina Mutual Provident Association by investing $50 each, on April 1, 1899. The founders intended for the Durham-based company to provide insurance for black people. The company initially offered mostly inexpensive industrial insurance. Workers could insure themselves against sickness and death for as little as three cents per week, a sum that yielded correspondingly small benefits.

By the summer of 1900 Mutual nearly faced bankruptcy, leading five of the original seven investors to withdraw. The two remaining investors lent the company personal funds: they were John Merrick, a businessman and the company's president, and Aaron Moore, a physician, its secretary. They promoted Charles C. Spaulding to general manager, and by the end of 1902 the company showed a profit. By 1906 the company had quadrupled its customer base and expanded within North Carolina and later into South Carolina. By 1913 it raised $100,000 to meet the requirement of a higher state deposit.

Mutual's success drew national attention to the Durham area because the company's growing economic base enabled it to invest in numerous business ventures, like Merrick-Moore-Spaulding Land Company, dealing in real estate (1907); Mechanics and Farmers Bank (1908) with a branch in Raleigh, which opened in 1922; Banker's Fire, a fire insurance company (1920); Mutual Building & Loan Association (1921); the National Negro Finance Corporation (1924); and the Mortgage Company of Durham (1929). All of these firms delivered economic services to blacks and furthered economic development of Durham's black community.

In part because rising cotton prices led to black prosperity during World War I, Mutual's life insurance in force grew from $5 million to $26 million under Spaulding, who became president in 1918 and renamed it North Carolina Mutual Life Insurance Company in 1919. By 1926, however, after expanding north to follow the migration of African Americans, Spaulding realized that new costs exceeded new revenue. He decided against further expansion until the company was once again secure. Mutual did not grow again until 1938.

Spaulding's retrenchment plan and Mutual's conservative investments in real estate, government bonds, and mortgage loans protected the company. For example, in 1929 Mutual's life insurance in force reached $39 million and remained above $33 million during the Depression. The company was ready to take advantage of the wartime recovery during World War II, during which time its life insurance in force jumped from $51 million to $100 million. This growth yielded dividends to its investors for the first time. It also allowed Mutual to compete with mainstream insurance companies, which were beginning to sell to blacks at standard rates, luring black customers from black-controlled companies. The movement toward racial solidarity in the 1960s brought many blacks back to Mutual from the white companies, strengthening its position in the overall insurance market. When urban riots put pressure on white-controlled companies to invest in black businesses and communities, between 1969 and 1971 companies like General Motors, IBM, Procter and Gamble, Atlantic Richfield Company, Sun Oil, and Chrysler bought more than $400 million in insurance contracts from Mutual, helping to make it the first black-controlled company to gross $1 billion. It continued its rise, growing tenfold between 1970 and 1990.

Robert Fay

SEE ALSO

World War I and African Americans; World War II and African Americans; Great Depression; Great Migration, The; Spaulding, Charles Clinton.

Northern Migration. Please see GREAT MIGRATION

Africa

Northern Rhodesia. Former name of ZAMBIA.

North America

Northrup, Solomon (b. 1808?, Minerva, N.Y.; d. 1863?, Glens Falls, N.Y.), author of a best-selling story of his kidnapping and years of slavery.

In 1841 Solomon Northrup, a free black, was kidnapped in New York and sold to slave traders. He spent the next 12 years as a slave in Louisiana. In 1852 he met Samuel Bass, a Canadian carpenter. Bass contacted the former owner of Northrup's father, who traveled to Louisiana to free him. Inspired by UNCLE TOM'S CABIN, Northrup wrote the story of his enslavement, with the help of David Wilson. *Twelve Years a Slave: Narrative of Solomon Northrup*, published in 1853, was an immediate success. His book described the daily acts of resistance that most slaves directed against their owners.

SEE ALSO

Free Blacks in the United States, 1619 to 1863; New York, New York; Slave Narratives.

North America

Norton, Eleanor Holmes (b. June 13, 1937, Washington, D.C.), District of Columbia delegate to the United States House of Representatives, first woman chair of the Equal Employment Opportunity Commission (EEOC).

Eleanor Holmes Norton has devoted much of her professional life to defending human rights and combating racial and gender discrimination. A graduate of Yale University law school, in the 1960s Norton became active in the CIVIL RIGHTS MOVEMENT, joining the STUDENT NONVIOLENT COORDINATING COMMITTEE (SNCC) and the Mississippi Freedom Democratic Party. From 1965 to 1970 she was a highly visible lawyer for the American Civil Liberties Union in New York City, where she specialized in controversial free speech cases. She represented VIETNAM WAR protesters, Ku Klux Klan members, and politicians, most notably Alabama's segregationist Governor George Wallace, then a presidential candidate who had been denied a permit to hold a rally.

Norton's activist credentials led to her appointment as chair of the New York City's Human Rights Commission (HRC) in 1970, an agency charged with ending discriminatory practices in the workplace and schools. Her seven-year HRC record, which ranged from reforming workmen's compensation laws to helping women sportswriters gain access to the press box at hockey games, prompted then-President Jimmy Carter to appoint her chair of the EEOC in 1977, a post she held until 1981. Norton emphasized bureaucratic reform during her tenure at EEOC, cutting a 130,000-case backlog in half.

Despite the negative publicity surrounding her failure to file tax returns from 1982 to 1988, Norton was elected District of Columbia Delegate to the U.S. House of Representatives in 1990, where she waged an uphill battle to maintain the autonomy of the D.C. government.

Robert Fay

SEE ALSO

New York, New York.

Latin America and the Caribbean

Nossa Senhora Aparecida, the patron saint of Brazil, an invocation of the Virgin Mary who is represented as black.

The devotion to the Virgin Mary, the mother of Jesus Christ, has for centuries been common in Catholicism and arrived in Latin America with the first Portuguese and Spanish conquerors in the sixteenth century. An image of the Virgin Mary, Nossa Senhora da Esperança, was present in the ship that took Pedro Álvares Cabral and the first Europeans to Brazil in 1500. Another image popular in Portugal, that of Nossa Senhora da Glória, is believed to have been taken to Brazil in 1503.

In the colonial period that followed, variations of the devotion to the Virgin Mary spread throughout Brazil. Slaves of African descent were particularly devoted to Our Lady of the Rosary and Our Lady of Lampadosa, while those of mixed blood preferred Our Lady of Mercy. In the state of Bahia, where most of the population is of African descent and religious practices of African origin have historically been strongest, the preference is for Our Lady of the Conception and Our Lady of Candeias. Both of these invocations of the Virgin Mary have been associated with certain *orixás* of the Afro-Brazilian religion of Candomblé.

Although at first part of European colonialism, Catholicism was appropriated in different ways by the less powerful, and in the process was often transformed into a new practice that can only be called partially European. In sixteenth-century Mexico, for instance, the devotion to Our Lady of Guadalupe combined Spanish Catholic practices with indigenous religious traditions. The Virgin of Guadalupe, who is believed to have appeared to the Indian Juan Diego in 1531, has since been represented with dark skin and indigenous features.

In Brazil the lesser-known image of Our Lady of Brazil also has indigenous features. Yet in a country with such a significant population of African descent, it should not come as a surprise that the patron saint would be represented with black skin. The invocation of Nossa Senhora Aparecida (Our Lady of Aparecida) dates from the eighteenth century. In 1717 three fishermen, Domingos Garcia, João Alves, and Filipe Pedroso, were fishing in the Paraíba River near the town of Itaguaçu in the state of São Paulo. After little success, they threw their net into the river and upon withdrawing it found a sculpture of the Virgin Mary with its head missing. After a second attempt they found the image's head, and for the remainder of the day the fishermen caught an extraordinary number of fish.

The sculpture they found was a black image of the Virgin. It had most likely originally been painted in colors, but the time under water had caused its color to darken, an effect that would be enhanced by the smoke from candles in the first oratories where the image was housed.

More than ten years after its discovery, a small chapel was built for the image. Stories about extraordinary events involving the image circulated and drew increasingly larger crowds to pray at the site. A larger chapel was built in 1743, and in 1930, Pope Pio XI declared Our Lady of Aparecida the patron saint of Brazil. The image, and the church that houses it, are currently the objects of great devotion, and some 7 million pilgrims visit the icon every year. The climax of these pilgrimages occurs on October 12, when more than 200,000 pilgrims descend on the city of Aparecida.

However, Our Lady of Aparecida is not the preferred object of devotion of black Brazilians. Historically, saints such as Benedict, Efigênia, Onofre, Gonçalo, and Anthony of Catagerona, all of whom have been represented in traditional hagiography as black or of mixed race, have been more popular among Brazilians of African descent. Among the invocations of the Virgin, the white Our Lady of the Rosary has been preferred.

Marcos Natalí

See Also

Nossa Senhora do Rosário; Religions, African, in Brazil; Catholic Church in Latin America and the Caribbean; Orishas.

Latin America and the Caribbean

Nossa Senhora do Rosário,

a Catholic invocation of the Virgin Mary and the patron saint of Brazilian blacks.

The devotion to Nossa Senhora do Rosário (Our Lady of the Rosary) began in France in the thirteenth century, when Saint Dominick claimed that the Virgin Mary had appeared to him and demonstrated a new form of prayer: the rosary. In the following centuries, the devotion gained popularity, especially in the Iberian Peninsula. A large number of *irmandades* (brotherhoods), Catholic associations providing various forms of support for their members and performing charitable deeds, were formed in connection with this invocation of the Virgin Mary.

African slaves taken to the Portuguese colony of Brazil worshiped a number of Catholic saints, with particular preference for saints of African origin such as Saint Benedict. There is disagreement, however, over the reasons for the special devotion of Africans in Brazil to Our Lady of the Rosary. The fact that many Africans from Angola and the Congo might have already been familiar with Our Lady of the Rosary from interactions with Portuguese missionaries in their homelands could have affected the rapid spread of the invocation among slaves in Brazil.

Since colonial times, people of African descent, whether slave or free, have used the brotherhoods devoted to Our Lady of the Rosary to form their own independent associations. These were some of the first collective black organizations in Brazil, some founded as early as 1522. The irmandades of Our Lady of the Rosary were usually comprised entirely of blacks, and most declared explicitly that the leader should be black as well. During slavery they were the only legal black organizations.

The irmandades represented, in effect, a relatively autonomous religious sphere that unavoidably acquired political significance. In 1683 a group of these organizations asked the Portuguese king to grant the freedom of all slaves in Brazil. When the king did not meet the demand, many irmandades gathered funds to purchase the freedom of slaves and guaranteed a network of support for blacks. Although the adoption of Catholicism did imply a distancing, to different degrees, from African religions – which had by this time been prohibited – the irmandades also played a fundamental role in maintaining African traditions of music and dance. The yearly festivals held by the irmandades in honor of their patron saints have for centuries involved the staging of elaborate traditional black dances and processions known as *reisados* and *congadas*.

In the twentieth century Our Lady of the Rosary has become the patron saint of Afro-Brazilians. In 1980 more than 115 parishes were dedicated to her in Brazil, more than to the country's official patron saint. Among the most beautiful are those in the former mining town of Ouro Preto; in the state of Minas Gerais; and the church of Nossa Senhora do Rosário dos Homens Pretos do Alto da Cruz, an important center for Brazil's black irmandades.

Marcos Natalí

See Also

Congo, Democratic Republic of the; Benedict of Palermo, Saint; Religions, African, in Brazil; Catholic Church in Latin America and the Caribbean; Religious Brotherhoods in Latin America.

North America

Notorious B.I.G. ("Biggie Smalls") (Christopher Wallace)

(b. 1972, New York, N.Y.; d. March 9, 1997, Los Angeles, Calif.), African American rap artist murdered in 1997.

Notorious B.I.G.'s debut album, *Ready to Die*, appeared on Sean "Puffy" Combs's Bad Boy Entertainment music label in 1995. The record was a critical and commercial success, exhibiting the rapper's lyrical talents through a series of taut, first-person narratives chronicling life as a hustler on the streets of New York's Bedford-Stuyvesant neighborhood. The grim humor of B.I.G.'s lyrics emphasized the claustrophobia of his ghetto universe; on "Warning," he raps, "There's gonna be a lot of slow singing / and flower bringing / If my burglar alarm starts ringing." Songs like "Suicidal Thoughts" and "Things Done Changed" helped create one of "gangsta rap's" most sophisticated personas, a strange brew of subdued self-loathing and energetic violence. In B.I.G.'s world, the sexual boasting typical of hip hop became an occasion for self-parody, as on "#!*@ Me (Interlude)," a skit describing a sexual encounter complicated by the rapper's prodigious girth.

Soon after the success of his debut album, B.I.G. found himself immersed in a simmering feud with Los Angeles gangsta rap label Death Row Records, in a manifestation of hip hop's growing coastal animosity. Death Row star TUPAC SHAKUR claimed that B.I.G. and Combs were behind a 1994 robbery in which Shakur was shot five times in the chest. The violent climate turned fatal in September 1996, when Shakur was murdered in a mysterious Las Vegas drive-by shooting; some suggested that the Bad Boy Entertainment crew was involved. Soon after, in March 1997, Notorious B.I.G. was gunned down while making an appearance in Los Angeles.

B.I.G.'s posthumously released double album, *Life After Death* (1997), topped the *Billboard* album charts and sold more than 7 million copies, thanks to radio-friendly songs like "Mo Money Mo Problems" and "Hypnotize." Death has only enhanced B.I.G.'s legend: Sean "Puffy" Combs's "I'll Be Missing You," a tribute to his fallen friend, was one of the best-selling singles of 1997.

Andrew Du Bois

SEE ALSO

Hip Hop in the United States; Los Angeles, California; New York, New York; Combs, Sean ("Puffy").

Europe

Nottingham and Notting Hill Riots, 1958, the first riots involving white-on-black violence in Great Britain after large-scale immigration of West Indians to that nation began in 1948.

Between August 23 and September 2, 1958, after a summer of isolated, racially charged incidents between whites and blacks in Great Britain's cities, whites attacked West Indians and their properties in the city of Nottingham in the English Midlands and in London's Notting Hill neighborhood. White working-class teenagers committed most of the violence in both riots. But a wider population was also involved – specifically, adult whites who lived at the edge of poverty and felt that West Indian immigrants threatened their jobs.

Beginning in 1948, the British government and various employers had welcomed West Indians to Great Britain as workers. As the number of immigrants grew, however, many white British, fearing for their own jobs, came to resent this new population. Some whites joined fascist and racist groups such as Oswald Moseley's Union Movement, which called for the deportation of West Indians. In this hostile environment, West Indians faced discrimination that left them unemployed, with inadequate or overcrowded housing, and without places to socialize.

Blacks complained of harassment in the St. Ann's district of Nottingham, especially during the summer of 1958. Late on August 23, a Saturday, these tensions exploded. That night, a black man allegedly hassled a white woman in a pub. A fight broke out between whites and blacks and spilled into the street. After this altercation, more than 1000 whites attacked blacks with sticks, bricks, and stones. Some blacks retaliated, but most, shocked and frightened, hid in their homes. Several people suffered serious injuries. Sporadic events occurred the next day; by Monday the riot had subsided.

The following weekend whites gathered again to attack West Indians, but most blacks stayed indoors. The crowd turned on itself and on the police, whom many of these whites blamed for protecting the West Indians rather than "their own." The next weekend, on September 6, a crowd of 200 whites attacked the houses of blacks.

A parallel series of violent incidents occurred in London. On August 23, the same day that violence broke out in Nottingham, police apprehended nine white youths cruising the streets of London's Notting Hill neighborhood "nigger hunting" – a practice in which whites, usually teenagers, would search for and attack individual blacks. In Notting Hill a week later, on August 30, an argument between a West Indian man and his white wife drew the attention of a group of white men, who proceeded to attack some of the man's friends. The next day these same white men assaulted the woman with milk bottles and other objects and called her a "nigger lover"; police intervened to protect her. But by this time a white crowd was already rioting. The police responded by escorting most of the black residents out of the area. The next day a group of about 100 white teenagers – who were soon joined by some 300 others – gathered and attacked police officers and the few black individuals they could find.

The worst rioting in Notting Hill occurred on the following day, September 1. Although the previous conflict had remained local, news had since spread, and whites across London went to Notting Hill to "nigger hunt." Blacks also gathered to support their friends and relatives. Whites chased and attacked blacks, set their houses ablaze, and smashed store windows. Most blacks stayed indoors, but some organized to defend themselves. Collecting an arsenal of knives, bottles, glass, and other makeshift weapons, they retaliated against the whites. Police arrested three white men and eight black, including Baron Baker and Michael de Freitas, who went on to become activists for racial equality.

Police regained control the following day, and within a couple of weeks a tense calm had returned. Officers arrested more than 100 people during the riots, over two-thirds of whom were white. Judges reprimanded them with fines or prison sentences. Despite the threat of punishment, isolated racial incidents continued to occur in London and other cities.

After the riots, conservative parliamentarian Cyril Osborne led a legal battle for restricted immigration. He and other lawmakers suggested the deportation of West Indians as the solution to racial violence. In 1962 the government passed the Immigration Act, which restricted West Indian immigration. Others called for campaigns to alleviate racism in British society, and in 1965 the government instituted a Race Relations Act to fight discrimination, though many liberals and blacks claim that the act was largely ineffective.

Sadly, the events of 1958 were part of a long history of racial violence in Britain. In recent years race riots continued to erupt in British cities (*see* BRIXTON RIOTS OF 1981 and RIOTS IN GREAT BRITAIN, 1985).

Leyla Keough

SEE ALSO

Great Britain.

Europe

Notting Hill Carnival, an annual outdoor celebration in London of British black culture that has grown to be one of the largest street festivals in all of Europe.

The Notting Hill Carnival is the largest and most prominent public event in Great Britain organized by and primarily for the black community. The Carnival has grown from a small West Indian community event to a celebration of multicultural London.

The Notting Hill Carnival takes its inspiration from Carnival of Trinidad. Trinidadian immigrants began celebrating Carnival in London during the 1950s. In Notting Hill the Carnival first took place as a summer street parade in 1965. In the following years other West Indians joined Trinidadians in Notting Hill for one collective event. This neighborhood, home to many black Britons, was the site of the first widely publicized white-on-black violence in Great Britain (*see* NOTTINGHAM AND NOTTING HILL RIOTS, 1958), so the Carnival carried special significance as an effort to reclaim the streets of the neighborhood for a peaceful black celebration.

At the first official Carnival in 1965, one steel drum band played and 500 people attended. The festival grew in the late 1960s. With some government funding, participants were able to better organize the Carnival and offer prizes in band contests and costume competitions. The five official "disciplines" of Carnival are the steel drum bands (*see* AFRO-CARIBBEAN SECULAR MUSIC), CALYPSO performers, "mas" (masquerade) bands, mobile sound systems, and static sound systems. Each mas band focuses on a specific theme, and preparations for costumes often begin months in advance. Sometimes the themes are political; at other times they reflect the West Indians' African heritage. Mas bands are usually led by mobile sound systems on trucks called "Soca [a fusion of Soul and Calypso] on the move." The static sound systems stay on the perimeter of the parade route and usually play REGGAE, techno, and JUNGLE (DRUM AND BASS) music. Each discipline has a seat on the official Carnival board. The disciplines represent the basic elements of the Carnival, but the festival is far from formal.

In fact, the spontaneity that reigns during the festival has sometimes resulted in clashes when the police have attempted to restrain revelers and establish order, often with severe methods. In the 1970s, as tension between blacks and whites in Great Britain was on the rise, the Carnival became a site of confrontation. Riots occurred at the Carnivals of 1976, 1979, and 1989. Over-policing was a problem: in 1979, 10,000 police (half of the entire London police force) were present at the Carnival. Since one of the Carnival's purposes was to reclaim the streets for blacks, many participants resented heavy-handed and sometimes brutal efforts by police to assert control. After each Carnival during this era, delicate negotiations took place when police and some conservative white residents of Notting Hill asked that the Carnival be moved to another outdoor area, to an indoor arena, or canceled altogether.

Despite these troubles, the Carnival has survived, and as it has won greater acceptance among British whites, the event has become less violent. What began as a West Indian event is now embraced by all of London. In 1997 close to 2 million people, including visitors from all over the world, crowded the streets for the celebration.

Leyla Keough

See Also

Trinidad and Tobago; Carnivals in Latin America and the Caribbean.

Africa

Nouakchott, Mauritania, the largest city and the capital of Mauritania.

Nouakchott is one of Africa's younger capital cities. Positioned halfway between St. Louis, in SENEGAL, and Nouadhibou, in northern Mauritania, it sits slightly inland from the Atlantic coast. It was originally a small fishing village frequented by desert traders traveling northward from Dakar, and became the capital of Mauritania in 1959. Colonial Mauritania had previously been governed from St. Louis and did not have a separate capital. As independence approached in the 1950s, however, French and Mauritanian officials debated which of the colony's few towns – most of which were located in the remote interior or along the Moor-dominated northern coast – would be a suitable national capital. After much deliberation, Mauritania's most prominent politician, MOKTAR OULD DADDAH, and his advisers chose the centrally positioned Nouakchott, aiming to bridge the divide between the country's southern and northern regions. The city's construction, carefully planned to accommodate the national government and a population of 15,000, began in early 1958 and was completed by the time of Mauritanian independence in November 1960.

During the first years of independence, Nouakchott remained a fairly small town, inhabited primarily by civil servants. But employment-seeking migrants soon flooded in, and by 1969 the city's population exceeded its expected size. High rates of urban migration continued throughout the 1970s, especially after a series of droughts forced thousands of farmers and nomads from the interior into Nouakchott, where they took up residence in makeshift shanties on the edge of town. Today Nouakchott has an estimated 600,000 residents – nearly 25 percent of the country's population. Although the 1986 completion of the Friendship Port brought an influx of business, Nouakchott's infrastructure is sorely inadequate relative to the population's demand for water, housing, and other services. The city also faces the unusual problem of encroaching sand dunes.

Elizabeth Heath

See Also

Dakar, Senegal; Drought and Desertification.

Africa

Ntare II (d. 1852), considered the first monarch of present-day Burundi.

Although fifth in a line of Burundian kings, Ntare II is widely regarded as the first monarch of the nation, because it was during his reign that the kingdom expanded to the borders of present-day Burundi. Born Rugaamba, he ascended the throne upon the death of his father, Mwambutswa I, and took the name Ntare, meaning "skin of the lion."

Ntare II conquered outlying chieftainships until his own kingdom included parts of present-day RWANDA and TANZANIA, establishing himself in history as one of Burundi's most powerful kings. Although the spoils of his victories went to his sons, several of them ultimately rebelled. The families of these rebellious sons became known as the Batare clan, and the family of Ntare II's successor son, Gisabo Mwezi IV, became known as the Bezi. Conflicts between the two clans influenced Burundian politics long before the conflicts between the HUTU AND TUTSI. Ntare II died in 1852.

Eric Young

Africa

Nuba, an ethnic group of south central Sudan.

The Nuba, numbering somewhat over a million people, inhabit a mountainous area in the southern part of Kordofan Province in Sudan. They are distantly related to the peoples of southern Sudan, and they represent a minority in the predominantly Arab province of Kordofan. The languages of the Nuba belong to the Kordofanian group, a distant branch of the Niger-Congo family, though most Nuba also speak Arabic.

It appears that the Nuba retreated into the mountains to flee persistent slave raiding by BAGGARA and Kababish Arabs beginning in the sixteenth century. In their mountainous environment the Nuba practiced intensive agriculture, employing terraced fields, manure-based fertilizers, and irrigation systems in order to maximize their production of MILLET, sorghum, cotton, onions, sesame, and a variety of vegetables. During the period of the Anglo-Egyptian Condominium, they began growing peanuts, peppers, and corn.

Interesting conclusions may be drawn from an overview of gender and age distinctions in Nuba society. Both men and women do farm work, though men are responsible for clearing the land and herding livestock. Southern Nuba trace descent matrilineally, while central and northern Nuba families are patrilineal, perhaps as a result of their greater interaction with patrilineal Arab communities. Unlike neighboring groups, the Nuba have never practiced either male or female circumcision. Traditionally, headmen and rain priests exercised relatively weak authority within Nuba communities. Age sets – cohorts of similar age who undergo initiation together and share an age-based status – were an important source of social authority.

Until the intensification of the Sudanese Civil War in the 1980s, most Nuba lived in small, kin-related villages. During the war their minority status has made them especially vulnerable to attacks by the Sudanese military, and many Nuba have sought refuge in the Khartoum metropolitan area.

Robert Baum

See Also

Khartoum, Sudan; Languages, African: An Overview; Indian Ocean Slave Trade.

Africa

Nubia, a historical region encompassing present-day southern Egypt and northern Sudan.

What was Nubia? This has always been a controversial question. The controversy stems from difficulties in determining the origin of the name Nubia, the time when Nubia first appeared in history, and its geographical limits. There is general agreement among most scholars that the name derives from *nob*, the Nubian word for gold, and is linked to the importance of gold to the Nubians.

However, recent research is looking into other possibilities. The modern Nubian word *kiji* means "fertile land, dark gray mud, silt, or black land"; the sound of this word is near to the Egyptian name Kish or Kush, referring to the land south of Egypt. It is believed that the name Kush also meant "the land of dark silt" or "the black land." This was the Egyptian (*see* EGYPT, ANCIENT KINGDOM OF) name for Nubia.

We know from ancient and recent analogies that peoples do not always adopt the name attributed to them by others. Therefore it is likely that the Egyptian's Kushites had their own name for their home, which must have had the same meaning as Kush: the black land. It was Nubia, the black land, the Sudan of today, which is a straightforward Arabic translation: *sud* is the plural form of *aswad*, meaning "black"; *an* means "of the"; thus, Sudan means "of the blacks." In modern Nubian, *nugud* means "black." So do *nuger*, *nugur*, and *nub*. This suggests that Kush, Nubia, and Sudan all mean the same thing – the "black land" and/or the "land of the blacks."

It is evident both historically and archaeologically that Nubia's boundaries have fluctuated through time. In other words, there were times when Nubian rule and cultural influence were limited to lower and middle Nubia, in the Sudanese-Egyptian borderlands; at other times Nubia covered all of present-day northern Sudan, while its cultural influence extended to an even vaster territory.

However, in modern times, Nubia typically refers to the region along the NILE RIVER between the first cataract (just south of Aswan in Egypt) and present-day Ed Debba in Sudan, where Nubian speakers live today. The region borders the Nubian Desert to the east and the Libyan Desert to the west. Land suitable for farming is confined to scattered plots along the riverbanks. Modern Nubians live in the region's many *irki* (villages or communities), which are distributed unevenly on both sides of the Nile and on islands within the course of the river, wherever there is land suitable for cultivation.

From this description it is obvious that Nubia is not rich in resources. Why then was Nubia subject to repeated raids and domination by its neighbors, especially Egypt to the north? First, Egypt tried to expand its authority over Nubia to secure its southern frontier. Second, Egyptians greatly desired Nubian natural resources, in the form of gold, copper, diorite stones used to build royal monuments, and African animal products. Third, the Egyptians sought African slaves for many purposes.

The trade in natural resources and slaves between Egypt and the African interior, together with the fertile riverine ecology of the Nile and its banks, encouraged settlement in Nubia from early times. And despite the scarcity of land for cultivation, agricultural activities were and still are the basis of the subsistence economy of most Nubians. To compensate for the limited quantity of land, the Nubians adopted intensive rather than extensive cultivation. Moreover, in recent years the Nubian economy has increasingly relied on income from Nubians working outside their country, particularly in the MIDDLE EAST.

Nubia has never been the exclusive domain of any one group of people. Foreign conquerors, alien merchants and adventurers, and both friendly and hostile nomads have always interacted with and settled among the indigenous peasant population of Nubia and have contributed significantly to its cultural development. Hence the present population is the product of a long and fairly continuous mingling of the ancient inhabitants with newcomers from a variety of places.

In the seventh century Arab tribesmen settled in Nubia and intermarried with the indigenous population. During the sixteenth century the Ottoman sultan Salim sent garrisons into Nubia, composed largely of soldiers from Bosnia, Circassia, Hungary, and Kurdistan. They were stationed at Aswan, Gasr Ibrim, and Sai to protect Egypt's southern borders. Their descendants (known as *al-Kushaf*), born of Nubian women and speaking only the Nubian language, regarded themselves as Bosnians or Turks rather than Nubians and claimed special privileges on this basis as late as the nineteenth century. Consequently, one can say that Nubian society now consists of a mixture of indigenous as well as Arab and Turkish elements.

Other groups of non-Nubians inhabit the area. They are small in number and made up of descendants of slaves and nomadic and seminomadic groups. Descendants of slaves who have been living with Nubians for generations and are accustomed to their ways of life can be regarded culturally as Nubians. They work mainly in domestic service and farming. Other non-Nubians in the region include Arab tribes, mainly Bisharia and Gararish, who raise camels. They play an important role in the Nubian economy and society. During the nineteenth and early twentieth centuries, Arab camel drivers provided the only means of transporting heavy loads, but during the late twentieth century the Arabs have been obliged to adopt a settled life beside the Nile and have begun to cultivate small plots leased from the Nubians. They have no land rights, and although they use the Nubian language to communicate with Nubians, they are linguistically and culturally distinct from them. This ethnic diversity reflects Nubia's ancient history as a cultural crossroads.

Ali Osman Mohammad Salih

SEE ALSO

Kush, Early Kingdom of; Nubian.

Africa

Nubian, the primary ethnic group of the middle Nile Valley from Aswan in EGYPT to the region of Dongola in northern SUDAN.

Archaeological evidence suggests that hunters and gatherers occupied the middle Nile region by the Mesolithic period, more than 10,000 years ago. Farming, both of Egyptian and Sudanic crops, became important in the region by 3000 B.C.E. When pharaonic Egypt occupied Nubia between 1970 and 1520 B.C.E., Egyptian culture increasingly influenced Nubia. Nubia regained its independence in the eleventh century B.C.E. A new Nubian kingdom, centered at Napata, adopted an Egyptian model of the monarchy, including royal brother-sister marriages. In 742 B.C.E. Pianchi, king of Napata, conquered Egypt and founded the Twenty-fifth Dynasty, which ruled Egypt for nearly a century. Soon after the conquest the Nubian capital shifted to Meroe. The Meroe kingdom developed its own form of writing as well as a technologically sophisticated iron industry. Around 300 C.E. the Ethiopian kingdom of AKSUM invaded Meroe and defeated its forces.

During a long period of political instability in Nubia, Coptic Christianity, similar to the Christianity practiced in Egypt (*see* ALEXANDRIA, EGYPT) and Ethiopia (*see* ETHIOPIAN ORTHODOX CHURCH), became an important influence in the region. By the sixth century two small states, Makuria and Alwa, dominated the region. The Muslim conquest of Egypt in 639 isolated Christian Nubia from most of the Christian world, but the Nubian states were able to resist the Arab armies. Gradually, Islam became important and intermarriage between Nubians and Arabs became common. By the end of the fifteenth century an Arab confederacy had conquered the Nubian states, which thereafter remained overwhelmingly Muslim. However, unlike their neighbors in the Nile Valley to the south, the Nubians resisted complete Arabization and maintained their Nilo-Saharan languages and elements of their own culture. In the nineteenth century Ottoman-ruled Egypt conquered Nubia until the MAHDIST STATE assumed control during the 1880s. In 1898 southern Nubia became a part of the Anglo-Egyptian Sudan, while the north was incorporated into Egypt.

Beginning in 1897 successive dams built at Aswan by the British displaced Nubians from their homeland. Many relocated to Egyptian cities. During the 1960s the construction of the new ASWAN HIGH DAM flooded a large part of the Nubian homeland and forced 100,000 Nubians to seek refuge around Aswan in Egypt and in the cities of Sudan, including Khartoum. The forced relocation of the Nubians to Arabic-speaking regions created a shared Nubian ethnic identity, whereas previously linguistic and regional distinctions had divided Nubians. On the other hand, relocation led to the gradual disappearance of the ancient Nubian languages; today more and more Nubians communicate in Arabic. The Nubians number around 1 million people, with about half of them located in Egypt and the other half in Sudan.

Robert Baum

See Also

Ethiopia; Khartoum, Sudan; Egypt, Ancient Kingdom of; Iron in Africa; Nile River.

Africa

Nuer, a major ethnic group of southern Sudan.

Until the Sudanese civil war intensified in the 1980s, most Nuer occupied an area of swamps and low-lying plains from the White Nile (*see* Nile River) eastward to the Ethiopian escarpment, and relied on cattle keeping as their primary economic activity.

Before the colonial conquest the Nuer did not form states or have recognized paramount chiefs. Instead, councils of village elders and religious specialists called leopard-skin priests exercised primary authority. Leopard-skin priests served as arbiters of feuds between Nuer clans and villages. Their homes served as a sanctuary for those fleeing possible retribution from rival clans. They had the power to curse those who refused to attempt to resolve a dispute in good faith. For ordinary decision making, the Nuer convened community assemblies in order to reach a consensus. Under Anglo-Egyptian colonial rule (1898-1956), government officials appointed a series of local "chiefs," but the Nuer did not recognize their legitimacy.

Since they inhabited the Sudd – the largest swamp in the world – and the surrounding plains, the Nuer had to develop a complex mode of adaptation to a difficult environment. Before warfare and government population control interfered, Nuer inhabited small, kin-related villages along narrow ridges of high ground during the rainy season. After the rains ended, the Nuer left these settlements and moved with their herds across the rich pasturage land that emerged alongside the receding floodwaters. By the peak of the dry season, they arrived with their cattle to graze in the permanent river valleys of Nuerland. During the rainy season women planted a crop of millet. Men hunted and fished and controlled cattle keeping, the dominant economic activity. Cattle provided most necessities of Nuer material culture. Not only did the Nuer rely on cattle as a source of meat and milk, but they used the skin, bones, and internal organs of cattle for beds, tools, musical instruments, and weapons. They used cow dung for cooking fuel and for plastering their homes. The sacrifice of cattle played an important role in most Nuer rites of passage, birth, initiation, marriage, and death. During male initiation young men received an "ox-name" to mark their entrance into the ranks of cattle owners.

Nuer religion centered on a supreme being, known as Kwoth Nhial. The Nuer associated lesser spirits, also known as kwoth, with the celestial realm (spirits of the above) or with the earthly realm (spirits of the below). All the powers of lesser spirits originated with Kwoth Nhial. This religious category of lesser spirits became a major source of innovation in Nuer religion in the nineteenth and twentieth centuries. The Nuer assimilated lesser deities of the Dinka and other neighboring peoples, even the authority of the Mahdi (an Islamic reformer) and Jesus, into their religion as spirits of the above.

At the time that the Ottoman government of Egypt (the Turkiyya) established its first contacts with the Nuer, in 1841, Dinka and Azande expansion was driving the Nuer eastward. The slave raiding and warfare of the mid- to late nineteenth century accelerated that process. It also produced a new type of Nuer leader, the prophet, who claimed direct revelation from spirits of the above. Prophets became important military and spiritual leaders at a time of endemic warfare. The most famous of these was Ngundeng. His son Gwek led Nuer opposition to the British in the early twentieth century. The Nuer resisted British occupation until the 1930s, when the British had to use airplanes and machine guns to subdue them. By 1956 the Nuer had joined the armed struggle for southern Sudanese autonomy, within a Sudanese federal state, or independence. They continue to participate in the Sudanese civil war, both as a source of soldiers for the secessionist movement and as victims of raids by government forces. Large numbers of Nuer have been forced from their homelands to seek refuge near Khartoum. Estimates place the present population of the Nuer at around 1 million.

Robert Baum

See Also

Ethiopia; Mahdist State; Trans-Saharan and Red Sea Slave Trade.

North America

Nugent, Richard Bruce (also known as Richard Bruce and Bruce Nugent) (b. July 2, 1906, Washington, D.C.; d. May 27, 1987, Hoboken, N.J.), African American writer and artist of the Harlem Renaissance.

The son of Richard Henry and Pauline Minerva Nugent, Richard Bruce Nugent left Washington, D.C., with his recently widowed mother at age 13 and moved to New York City, where he attended Dunbar High School. To support himself, Nugent worked as an errand boy, bellhop, designer, and elevator operator, as well as a "secretary and a confidance man for a modiste."

Openly gay at age 19, Nugent went by the name Richard Bruce to protect his mother from public embarrassment about his homosexuality. Though his gay identity cost him friendships, Nugent associated with gay and bisexual contemporaries Langston Hughes, Carl Van Vechten, E. M. Forster, and Alain Locke. His dramatic "ultimate bohemian" style was the basis for Wallace Thurman's character Paul Arbian in *Infants of the Spring* (1932), the roman à clef that satirized figures of the Harlem Renaissance. Jessie Fauset chaffed at Nugent's "rather too deliberate eccentricities."

Nugent's first published poem, "Shadows," appeared in *Opportunity* magazine before Countee Cullen reprinted it in *Caroling Dusk: An Anthology of Verse by Negro Poets*, in 1927. Locke published Nugent's short story "Sahdji" in *The New Negro* in 1925. Nugent later developed "Sahdji" into a play, published as *Sahdji – An African Ballet* in Locke's anthology *Plays of Negro Life* (1927); the play was produced in 1932.

Nugent published the first explicitly gay short story written by an African American, titled "Smoke, Lilies and Jade," in the sole issue of *Fire!!*, a controversial journal he founded with Zora Neale Hurston, Hughes, Thurman, and Aaron Douglas. Two years later Nugent and Thurman coedited another journal, *Harlem*. Nugent's bold, often erotic illustrations were showcased in *Harlem* as they were in *Fire!!*, *Opportunity*, and *Crisis*, well-known publications of the period. His series *Drawing for Mulattoes* appeared in 1927. A talented illustrator and painter, he had shows at the Harmon Foundation in 1931 and 1936. While Nugent's work was well received, Thurman characterized his drawings as "nothing but highly colored phalli."

In his later years Nugent amassed a substantial collection of Afro-Americana. In the 1960s he cofounded the Harlem Cultural Council with Romare Bearden. He appeared on stage in *Porgy*, and in 1984 (three years before his death) in the documentary film *Before Stonewall*. Director Isaac Julien celebrated the artistic contributions of Bruce Nugent and other African American gay men of the Harlem Renaissance in his 1992 film *Looking for Langston*.

See Also

Fauset, Jessie Redmon; Locke, Alain Leroy; New York, New York; *Opportunity: Journal of Negro Life*.

Africa

Nujoma, Samuel (b. May 12, 1929, Etunda, South West Africa [Namibia]), nationalist politician and first president of Namibia.

By the time Namibia achieved independence in 1990, the nationalist leader Samuel "Sam" Nujoma, known for his fiery rhetoric, had matured into a seasoned and charismatic but not unanimously popular politician. As a young boy Nujoma attended the Finnish Mission Primary School while helping his father tend cattle around his home in southern Namibia. As a teenager he traveled to Walvis Bay and, later, to Windhoek, where he lived with relatives and attended secondary school. In 1955 he began working for the South African Railways. Although he was later fired for participating in labor union activities, his job at the railway company enabled him to meet leading Namibian nationalists and to travel throughout southwestern Africa, where he witnessed the injustices of South African control over the territory.

In 1959 Nujoma joined the Ovamboland People's Organization (OPO) and the South West African National Union, both of which were active in the nationalist movement. His prominent role in boycotts against the forced removal of blacks and Coloureds from Windhoek suburbs quickly brought him to the forefront of the movement and made him vulnerable to government retribution. Also in 1959, Nujoma fled South West Africa, remaining in exile for 30 years as president of the successor to the OPO, the South West African People's Organization, or SWAPO.

In his first decade as SWAPO president, Nujoma gained support for the movement and organized the nationalist leaders. When the armed struggle for independence began in 1966, he turned his attention to managing the guerrilla war, though he continued to travel extensively to African, Scandinavian, and Eastern bloc countries and to the United Nations (UN). During the 1970s Nujoma, an increasingly shrewd politician, reorganized SWAPO and its military to ensure his leadership. In the 1980s he intensified his international efforts to win independence for Namibia. To further the cause, he toned down his socialist rhetoric and relaxed ties to the Eastern bloc.

In 1989 Nujoma returned to Namibia a hero. Shortly thereafter Namibians elected him to the National Assembly, a seat he relinquished in 1990 when the assembly unanimously elected him president. Since independence Nujoma and his SWAPO-dominated National Assembly have upheld a policy of reconciliation, permitting white Namibians to control much of the economy. But a strong labor movement and high unemployment are persistent threats to Nujoma's leadership, and his lavish spending on presidential limousines, helicopters, and jets has sparked criticism. The United States and other Western donors have condemned extravagant government spending in Namibia and have urged Nujoma to limit his time in office to two five-year terms, but Nujoma had not yet groomed a successor as of 1999.

Eric Young

See Also
Windhoek, Namibia; South Africa; South West Africa People's Organization.

North America

Numbers Games, **a form of gambling that was widespread among inner-city African Americans from the end of the nineteenth century until the 1970s, when state-run lotteries were established.**

Also known as the "policy racket" or just "numbers," numbers games have influenced the lives of many African Americans as both an economic activity and a source of hope. Until the birth of state lotteries in the 1970s, "policy stations" – where bets were made and winners awarded – usually appeared on every block of black neighborhoods in Northern cities. Poet Claude McKay called the numbers "the greatest industrial phenomenon in Harlem." Indeed, by the 1960s numbers games comprised an estimated 60 percent of the neighborhood's financial transactions.

In numbers games a player tries to guess the numbers of the day; historically, the source of winning numbers has taken various forms. At the end of the nineteenth century, when numbers games first achieved widespread popularity, racketeers provided such numbers themselves, often drawing numbered balls from a drum-shaped container. As the policy racket became more established, managers began taking numbers from outside sources that could not be manipulated. Until the 1960s Harlem bettors would wager on the last three numbers of the total volume of New York Stock Exchange trade. From the 1960s through the 1990s, bets were placed on harness-racing numbers.

In some places city governments attempted to curtail gambling by ordering that newspapers round off such numbers. In others, however, local officials accepted the existence of the games. In Kingston, New York, where bettors wagered on the United States Treasury balance, the local newspaper printed the daily balance in their sports section.

The policy racket involved a constant exchange of money between bettors and a managerial hierarchy: runners, who took the bets; collectors, who oversaw the rackets' daily management; and bankers, who backed the operations. The policy rackets were profitable endeavors – lower managers generally took 10 percent on winnings and bankers took 25 percent. Some policy bankers won esteem in the communities that supplied their wealth by investing in philanthropic programs.

In the 1920s banker Casper Holstein was a sponsor of the Harlem Renaissance, supporting an Elks Lodge and contributing money to *Opportunity* magazine. Numbers games also supported the community simply by providing extra income to the businesses that fronted them. To avoid police crackdowns, many centers of operation were fronted by newsstands, barber shops, liquor stores, and other small businesses.

Bettors' techniques for choosing lucky numbers engendered much lore. The popular "dream books" assigned specific numbers to words and images, allowing gamblers to translate their thoughts and experiences into bets. Players also took numbers from the hymn boards in churches, the license plates of crashed cars, and the suggestions of children; they bet on the dates of births, deaths, and other significant events. Some male gamblers favored numbers that dream books assigned to sexual acts and parts, especially when attractive women took the bets.

What began in the early 1900s as locally run operations had by mid-century been widely co-opted by white organized crime. Although the numbers continued to thrive, profits increasingly left the communities that generated them. In the 1970s and 1980s most policy racket activity was replaced by state-run lotteries. Through the end of the century, however, numbers games remained popular in urban centers as an unofficial form of betting.

Eric Bennett

See Also
Harlem, New York; *Opportunity: Journal of Negro Life.*

Africa

Nunuma **(also known as Nanoumba, Nibulu, Nouna, and Nounouma), ethnic group of West Africa.**

The Nunuma primarily inhabit the Northern Province of Ghana. Some also live in southern and west central Burkina Faso. They speak a Niger-Congo language and belong to the Grusi cultural and linguistic group. More than 500,000 people consider themselves Nunuma.

See Also
Languages, African: An Overview.

Africa

Nupe, **ethnic group of Nigeria.**

The Nupe primarily inhabit west central Nigeria, along the Niger and Kaduna rivers. They speak a Niger-Congo language related to Yoruba and Igbo. Approximately 1 million people consider themselves Nupe.

See Also
Languages, African: An Overview; Niger River.

Africa

Nwapa, Flora **(full name Florence Nwanzuruahu Nkiru Nwapa) (b. January 18, 1931, Oguta, Nigeria; d. October 16, 1993, Enugu, Nigeria), Nigerian author of children's books and novels dealing with the transformation of women's roles.**

Nigeria's best-known woman writer, Flora Nwapa was also a teacher, businesswoman, and government official. Her multiple careers echo the complicated lives of her fictional female characters: women who grow beyond the traditional ambitions of wife and motherhood to seek economic and personal independence. Nwapa changed her society through business as well as art, founding Tana Press Limited and Flora Nwapa Books. She was, in fact, the first African woman to own and operate a publishing house.

Nwapa was the eldest daughter in a large and relatively wealthy IGBO family; her mother was a teacher and her father an agent with the British-owned United Africa Company in Nigeria. She attended Christian schools in Oguta and Lagos, including Queen's College, from which she graduated in 1951. After teaching for a year, she studied briefly in London before entering University College in Idaban, Nigeria. She graduated in 1957 with a bachelor's degree in English, history, and geography. The following year she earned a diploma in education from the University of Edinburgh, Scotland. Back in Nigeria, then on the brink of independence, Nwapa worked for the next seven years as an education officer, college teacher, and university administrator.

After traveling to the United States for further study in 1965, Nwapa returned to Lagos, where, with the help of novelist CHINUA ACHEBE, she found a publisher for her first novel, *Efuru* (1966). Nwapa, who later said that she never planned to become a writer, had begun the book while working as a teacher and quickly realized that she had "a good story to tell." Like many of her subsequent novels, *Efuru* was about a woman struggling with the traditional roles of wife and mother. Between the publication of *Efuru* and *Idu* (1970), Nwapa served as minister of Nigeria's East Central State during the turmoil of the Nigerian Civil War (also called the Biafran War). Her 1980 short story collection, *Wives at War*, describes the importance of women to the Biafran cause, both as family wage earners and as expert bargainers who negotiated with the enemy for needed supplies. She married and had her second child (the first was born while Nwapa was single). A third child was born in 1971, and shortly thereafter Nwapa, at the suggestion of writer CHRISTOPHER OKIGBO, began writing children's books.

Nwapa's government career continued after the war; she was appointed commissioner for health and social welfare in 1971 and later headed the Commission for Lands, Survey, and Urban Development. Her belief that Nigerian women deserved a greater role in politics was inspired by both modern feminism and Igbo political traditions, in which priestesses held great power. Establishing her own publishing house in 1977, Nwapa took control of her literary career, which many critics believe reached its peak in the 1980s.

One Is Enough (1981) attacks multiple marriage – a widespread custom in Nigeria – and features a heroine who chooses single motherhood over subservience. *Women Are Different* (1986) reasserts women's need for economic independence, as does *Wives at War* (1980), a collection of short stories that deals with the disintegration of traditional society following civil strife. Since her death in 1993, Nwapa has been hailed as a literary pioneer who gave eloquent voice to the lives of African women.

Kate Tuttle

SEE ALSO
Education in Africa; Lagos, Nigeria; Feminism in Africa: An Interpretation.

Latin America and the Caribbean

Nyabinghi, ceremonial music of the Rastafarian faith played at ritual meetings called groundings or grounations; often refers to ceremonies held to mark special occasions.

The birth of Rastafarianism in JAMAICA in the late 1930s brought with it the need for a liturgical music based on African sources, rather than the European-influenced Jamaican folk music. Dissatisfied with the Revivalist Afro-European hymns rewritten with Rastafarian lyrics, Rastas turned to the drumming of the rural Burru men for inspiration. The Burrus originally worked on plantations but relocated to urban centers as agricultural work declined. Considered disreputable by mainstream Jamaicans, the Burrus found fraternity among the equally downtrodden Rastafarians. The two groups shared close proximity while living in West Kingston ghettos. Burru music was performed at Christmas time and to welcome released prisoners back into the community. Burru featured a West African rhythmic base with sung and chanted accompaniment. Rastas swiftly embraced Burru drumming as their own liturgical music. The Burrus in turn adopted Rastafarianism, and with this exchange the two groups combined into one.

Music of the neo-African Kumina cult also influenced the evolution of Rastafarian nyabinghi. Kumina drumming styles were closely related to Burru, although esoteric religious beliefs and ceremonies involving animal sacrifice greatly hindered Kumina's accessibility. Kumina differed enough from Burru so that when Burru evolved into nyabinghi, significant aspects of both forms had been altered in nyabinghi's distinct sound.

Nyabinghi uses three drums: the bass (used for timekeeping), the *funde* (used for syncopation), and the repeater (featured in improvisational solos). Religious nyabinghi is called "churchical" and employs slow, ponderous drumming. The secular version, known as "heartical," relies on a lighter, faster sound. The term *nyabinghi* originally meant "death to the white oppressors and their black allies." Passage of time softened the definition into "death to evil forces." The music is played continually throughout Rastafarian grounation ceremonies, often called "reasonings," where believers discuss biblical Scripture and philosophy, often sharing a "chalice" filled with *ganja*, or marijuana (considered a holy sacrament by many Rastafarians).

Nyabinghi has exerted a profound influence on REGGAE music. Renowned Rasta drummer COUNT OSSIE held lengthy open jams in Kingston during the late 1940s. The prolonged nature of nyabinghi gave musicians space and opportunity to explore the synthesis of American RHYTHM AND BLUES within nyabinghi's loping percussive framework. The founding members of the Skatalites, the seminal band of SKA, all developed their skills at Ossie's legendary sessions. In 1960 Ossie's nyabinghi drumming and melodic arrangements were used on the Folks Brothers' hit ska single "Oh Carolina."

Ossie was happiest recording traditional nyabinghi and went on to produce several albums with his band, the Mystic Revelation of Rastafari. His prolific career ended with his 1976 death. By this time roots reggae's emphasis on Rastafarian beliefs fostered the development of nyabinghi groups Ras Michael and the Sons of Negus and Light of Saba. Roots reggae songs featuring nyabinghi influences surfaced regularly. BOB MARLEY's "Rastaman Chant" is an excellent example of the churchical style fused with reggae.

Jace Clayton

SEE ALSO
Kingston, Jamaica; Rastafarians.

Africa

Nyakyusa (also known as Niabiussa, Sochile, and Sokile), ethnic group of TANZANIA.

The Nyakyusa primarily inhabit southwestern Tanzania. They speak the same Bantu language as the NGONDE people of MALAWI and are closely related to the NYASA people. Approximately 600,000 people consider themselves Nyakyusa.

SEE ALSO
Bantu: Dispersion and Settlement.

Africa

Nyamwezi, one of the largest ethnic groups in TANZANIA.

The ancestors of the Nyamwezi are believed to have first inhabited their current homeland in the Tabora region of western Tanzania around the first millennium C.E., during the period of Bantu expansion. There, they established more than 30 small, loosely linked chiefdoms but never unified into a centralized kingdom. Over several centuries the Nyamwezi established farming villages throughout the region and gradually assimilated neighboring peoples, such as the SUKUMA, into their chiefdoms. These people were apparently given land and political security by local chiefs in exchange for tribute and allegiance, but were not required to adopt Nyamwezi religious customs, which were centered on ancestor worship and divination.

By the eighteenth century the Nyamwezi began taking part in trade between the African interior and the East African coast. They carved out a trade route from the Great Lakes region of East Africa to Bagamoyo, a port on the mainland opposite the island of ZANZIBAR, and soon became one of the biggest suppliers of ivory, copper, and wax to coastal Arab/Swahili traders. When ivory became scarce during the late nineteenth century, the Nyamwezi used guns they had acquired through trade to conduct slave raids in the eastern CONGO RIVER basin and then sold their hostages into the INDIAN OCEAN SLAVE TRADE in Zanzibar. Some powerful Nyamwezi slave traders, such as MSIRI and Mirambo, even established their own trading empires deep within the Central African interior. For ordinary Nyamwezi slave raiding raised the possibility of retaliation, and many moved from their scattered farms into walled villages. Nevertheless, the Nyamwezi remained active traders, and it is estimated that by the late nineteenth century more than 15,000 Nyamwezi traveled to the coast each year. The journey had become a rite of passage among young men, especially chiefs, who were expected to lead a caravan at least once before they could be considered adults in the chiefdoms.

In 1891 the German East Africa Company colonized the area now called Tanzania. The Germans restricted trade and forced Nyamwezi and other peoples to cultivate export crops such as tea, coffee, and cotton. Nyamwezi chiefs were made into local agents of the colonial administration, responsible for carrying out the COLONIAL RULE and colonial labor policies of the Germans and later the British, who renamed the colony Tanganyika. This role often cost them the respect of their followers. Many chiefs also became unpopular when they denounced the pro-independence Tanganyikan African National Unity party led by Julius K. Nyerere because they believed it threatened their power. After independence the 1962 constitution abolished chiefdoms as a political office, and few Nyamwezi disputed the edict.

Today most of Nyamwezi in the Tabora region live in farming villages and raise cattle. Under Nyerere, many were forced into *ujamaa* villages, but most maintained subsistence crops on their family farms and returned to them in the early 1980s.

Elizabeth Heath

SEE ALSO
Bantu: Dispersion and Settlement; Ivory Trade; Nyerere, Julius Kambarage; Swahili People.

Africa

Nyanja (also known as Nianja, Niassa, and Wanyanja), ethnic group of southern Africa.

The Nyanja primarily inhabit southern MALAWI, eastern ZAMBIA, central MOZAMBIQUE, and eastern ZIMBABWE. They speak a dialect of CHEWA, a Bantu language, and are closely related to the Chewa people. More than 2.5 million people consider themselves Nyanja.

SEE ALSO
Bantu: Dispersion and Settlement.

Africa

Nyankore (also known as Ankole, Banyankole, Nkole, and Nyankole), ethnic group of UGANDA.

The Nyankore primarily inhabit southwestern Uganda. They speak a Bantu language. They had formed a centralized kingdom, known as Ankole, before the British imposed COLONIAL RULE in 1901. The Nyankore comprise two main subgroups: the majority are Iru, traditionally peasant farmers, while a minority are Hima, traditionally the pastoralist ruling elite. Approximately 1 million people consider themselves Nyankore.

SEE ALSO
Bantu: Dispersion and Settlement; Pastoralism.

Africa

Nyasa, ethnic group of TANZANIA.

The Nyasa primarily inhabit southwestern Tanzania. Some also live in northwestern MOZAMBIQUE. They speak a Bantu language. The term *Nyasa* is also sometimes used to refer to the inhabitants of MALAWI, particularly the NYANJA. Approximately 500,000 people consider themselves Nyasa.

SEE ALSO
Bantu: Dispersion and Settlement.

Africa

Nyasaland. Former name of MALAWI.

Africa

Nyerere, Julius Kambarage (b. March 1922, Butiama, Tanganyika [present-day Tanzania]), independence leader and first president of TANZANIA.

Called both "Father of the Nation" and "Mwalimu" (which means teacher), Julius K. Nyerere is to many the founder of present-day Tanzania. Lauded for his role in building a nation free of ethnic and civil conflict, he also bears much responsibility for the dire state of Tanzania's economy. The leader of one of the most unified nationalist movements in all of Africa, Nyerere guided Tanzania through a peaceful transition to independence, and then pursued an ambitious plan to build a self-reliant socialist economy. He stepped down from the presidency when it became obvious that this plan had failed, but since then has continued to be one of the most influential people in Tanzania and East Africa.

The son of a minor chief of the Zanaki, one of the smallest ethnic groups in Tanzania, Nyerere excelled in primary school and was thus permitted to study at colonial Tanganyika's only secondary school, which was in Tabora. He later received a scholarship and attended Makerere University in UGANDA. He graduated with a teaching degree in 1945 and taught for several years in the city of Makerere, where he helped organize a branch of the Tanganyikan African Association, a civic organization. In 1949 he left Africa to attend the University of Edinburgh. After three years he returned to Tanganyika with a degree in economics and history, ready to take a leading role in the emerging anticolonial movement.

In 1953 Nyerere became president of the Tanganyikan African Association and a year later transformed it into the more overtly political Tanganyika African National Union (TANU). TANU's goal, Nyerere announced, was to win full self-governance for Tanganyika and to build a nation free of ethnic and racial divisions. He began traveling throughout the colony to encourage grassroots support for the nascent movement. By 1957 TANU was the single largest organization in the country, and Nyerere had become the voice of Tanganyika's independence movement.

When in 1958 the British colonial government announced open elections for the Tanganyika Legislative Council, Nyerere protested electoral rules that reserved two-thirds of the seats for Europeans and Asians, restricted African voter registration, and effectively excluded TANU candidates from being elected to the council. Britain responded by replacing the colonial governor, who held new and reformed elections in 1960. This time TANU candidates won a majority and Nyerere was named chief minister in 1960. For the next year Nyerere helped outline and implement the transition to independence and on December 9, 1961, was named prime minister of independent Tanganyika. Surprisingly, Nyerere stepped down after only a month to restructure TANU. But ten months later he was elected again, this time as president of Tanganyika.

During his first term as president, Nyerere sought to do away with the divisive structures of COLONIAL RULE and to build a sense of national identity. He immediately declared Swahili the national language, making

Tanganyika the only African nation with an indigenous African official language. He even translated Shakespeare's *Julius Caesar* and *The Merchant of Venice* into Swahili. Shortly afterward, he persuaded the neighboring and politically fragile island of ZANZIBAR to unify with Tanganyika; the agreement created the United Republic of Tanzania in 1964.

After the government reaffirmed confidence in Nyerere in 1965 and declared him head of a one-party state, he began developing his vision of a uniquely AFRICAN SOCIALISM, combining Maoist principles with "traditional" African values of hard work, egalitarianism, and above all, *ujamaa*, or "familyhood." In his famous February 7, 1967, Arusha Declaration, Nyerere explained how socialism would create a self-reliant nation of peasants. He outlined a plan to resettle Tanzania's primarily rural population to large, collectivized ujamaa villages where, Nyerere believed, their combined efforts would improve productivity and resource distribution. After few people moved voluntarily, the government became more forceful, and by 1977 more than 80 percent of the population had been resettled.

Although the program did improve rural access to clean water, health care, and schools, it failed to produce sufficient food to feed the country's population, and the low state-mandated crop prices deepened rural poverty. By 1985 Nyerere had realized the necessity for reform. He took public responsibility for the economic failure, announcing, "I failed. Let's admit it." He stepped down to allow his successor, ALI HASSAN MWINYI, to implement the reforms required by the International Monetary Fund and other international donors. Nevertheless, Nyerere remained the head of Chama Cha Mapinduzi (CCM, formerly TANU) until 1990, when he retired to his modest house in Butiama, where he now lives with his wife and seven children.

Although Nyerere has slipped into the background of Tanzanian politics, he has continued to play an active role in the country's diplomatic affairs. While president, he often called for a new "moral" order in international politics. He supported nationalist movements in MOZAMBIQUE and ANGOLA and was one of the first to lead an anti-APARTHEID boycott of SOUTH AFRICA. In addition, he initiated the military overthrow of Uganda's IDI AMIN in 1979, which returned to power the democratically elected MILTON OBOTE.

Since stepping down, Nyerere has also spoken out against structural adjustment, which he believes forces developing nations to deprive children of food and education in order to pay off debts. He has criticized the "new world order," which he has said concentrates the world's wealth in the hands of a few. In 1995 he acted as mediator of failed peace talks between Burundi's former democratic leader Sylvestre Ntibantunganya and rebel leader PIERRE BUYOYA. He also organized an East African trade embargo of Buyoya's military government. He remains a strong advocate of greater regional cooperation and has at times spoken of the need for Tanzania and neighboring nations to unite and form an East African Federation.

Elizabeth Heath

SEE ALSO

Burundi; Swahili Language; Nationalism in Africa; Structural Adjustment in Africa; Uganda.

Africa

Nyoro (also known as Banyoro and Runyoro), ethnic group of UGANDA.

The Nyoro primarily inhabit western Uganda. They speak a Bantu language and historically constituted the centralized kingdom of Bunyoro. More than 1.5 million people consider themselves Nyoro.

SEE ALSO

Bantu: Dispersion and Settlement.

Africa

Nzima (also known as Amanya, Appolonian, Assoko, Nzema, N'zima, and Zéma), ethnic group of West Africa.

The Nzima primarily inhabit southwestern GHANA and southeastern Côte d'Ivoire. They speak a Niger-Congo language and belong to the AKAN cultural and linguistic group. Approximately 400,000 people consider themselves Nzima.

SEE ALSO

Côte d'Ivoire; Languages, African: An Overview.

Africa

Nzinga (Dona Anna de Sousa) (b. 1581?, Portuguese Angola [present-day ANGOLA]; d. December 17, 1663, Angola), a queen of the MBUNDU in Angola and a leading opponent of Portuguese colonialism.

Nzinga, daughter of King Kiluanji of the Ndongo, was born during a time of war between the Portuguese and the Mbundu of the Ndongo Kingdom, in what is today Angola. When the people deposed Nzinga's father for his autocratic rule, his eldest son Mbandi, though illegitimate, succeeded him. Mbandi killed Nzinga's son to quell any chance of opposition and drove Nzinga out of the kingdom, but when the Portuguese soon thereafter invaded, he turned to her for support. In Luanda in 1622, Nzinga negotiated in the interest of her half-brother, and the Portuguese agreed to recognize the Ndongo Kingdom and withdraw their forces in exchange for the kingdom's release of Portuguese prisoners and assistance in the slave trade. At the same time Nzinga received a Jesuit baptism (becoming Dona Anna de Sousa), hoping that this would solidify her contacts with Portuguese traders.

After the Portuguese reneged on their agreements, Mbandi sought to establish an independent treaty for his protection. In response Nzinga rallied her many supporters, forged an alliance with the warlike and reputedly cannibalistic Jaga people to the south, and killed Mbandi, the traitor and executioner of her son. It is for this alliance that she is often known as the Cannibal Queen, though the extent of her cannibalism remains in question. When forced from her land in 1629 by a Portuguese military expedition, Nzinga built a sizable army of her own, employing Jaga slaves, whom she promised would be freed after their service. As the transatlantic slave trade gained momentum, Nzinga sought out politically and economically advantageous alliances while preventing the expansion of European control. Maintaining uneasy relations with the Jaga and accepting escaped slaves, she established her kingdom at Matamba, and from there she launched attacks on the Ndongo king Ari, whom she considered a puppet of the Portuguese.

From 1639 to 1648, in alliance with the Dutch and the KONGO, Nzinga increased her attacks on the Portuguese, forcing them back to their forts along the coast. According to a Dutch military attaché, Queen Nzinga wore men's clothes and kept a harem of men, dressed as women, whom she called her "wives." She was also the primary military strategist for the coalition of troops and led her own warriors into battle. But her alliances ultimately disintegrated under severe Portuguese military pressure, and Nzinga retreated to Matamba in 1656, where she eventually agreed to peace terms. She died in 1663 and was succeeded by her sister, Dona Barbara.

Eric Young

SEE ALSO

Luanda, Angola; Transatlantic Slave Trade.

O

OAU. Please see ORGANIZATION OF AFRICAN UNITY

Latin America and the Caribbean

Obá,

a YORUBA deity, or orisha, who is the senior wife of Changó. On the advice of Oshún, Changó's favorite wife, Obá cut off her ear to make Changó a soup that Oshún told her would tie her husband to her forever. Changó was so disgusted with the ear soup that he repudiated Obá. Obá dances with her hand cupped over her missing ear (*see* ORISHAS; RELIGIONS, AFRICAN, IN LATIN AMERICA AND THE CARIBBEAN; SANTERÍA; and CANDOMBLÉ).

Latin America and the Caribbean

Obaluaiyé

(known as Omolú in Brazil and as Obaluaiyé or Babaluaiyé in Cuba and the United States), the orisha, or Yoruba deity, of smallpox and infectious diseases. In BRAZIL he is covered from head to toe with raffia so as not to be seen, and his initiates are said to be people with unfortunate, difficult lives. He is thought to be very ugly and disfigured by disease. He is a feared orisha. In CUBA he is represented by San Lázaro, and his initiates wear burlap or purple (*see* ORISHAS; RELIGIONS, AFRICAN, IN LATIN AMERICA AND THE CARIBBEAN; SANTERÍA; and CANDOMBLÉ).

Africa

Obasanjo, Olusegun

(b. March 5, 1937, Abeokuta, in Ogun State, NIGERIA), former military officer and head of state; writer, agricultural reformer, and international activist; president of Nigeria (1999-).

Olusegun Obasanjo was born to a Christian YORUBA family that lacked the means to send him to college. He excelled at the provincial Abeokuta Baptist High School, however, and when he enlisted in the army in 1958 it was partly with an eye toward further schooling. During his tenure as a soldier he studied in both India and England.

Obasanjo specialized in engineering and rose through the ranks of Nigeria's Engineering Corps. Later, while serving as head of state, he credited this military training for the systematic clarity of his thought. Between 1959 and 1976 Obasanjo advanced from second lieutenant to chief of staff, supreme headquarters. During this time he led Nigerian forces in the country's civil war (1969-1970), and he accepted the surrender of the Biafran troops in 1970.

Obasanjo was devoted to military service but appeared to have a limited appetite for power. He claimed that his ascendance to head of state after Murtala Muhammad's assassination in 1976 was "not my will." This reticence distinguished Obasanjo as the only Nigerian leader ever to relinquish power peacefully, which he did three years later.

Obasanjo's regime faced the task of preparing Nigeria for civilian rule. He oversaw the Constituent Assembly that drafted the constitution and ensured that the transition occurred according to the initial timetable. He also worked to integrate Nigeria's profusion of trade unions into the National Labor Congress. After the 1979 election Obasanjo duly handed over power to the elected government.

Obasanjo retired from the government and military service and took up farming in his home region. He made this move partly out of concern for the country's agricultural development, which suffered, in his view, from a lack of esteem for farming and farmers in Nigeria. He also continued his studies, at the University of Ibadan.

Although Obasanjo refrained from involvement in domestic politics, he wrote critical essays about subsequent Nigerian regimes and began involving himself with international affairs. In 1989 he published *Constitution for National Integration and Development*, a book advocating a one-party government rather than the multiparty system he himself had helped to install a decade before. That same year Obasanjo began publishing *Africa Forum*, a self-promotional magazine that was part of his failed campaign to become secretary general of the United Nations. In the late 1980s and early 1990s he served on the Commonwealth Eminent Person's Group, which pressed for justice in SOUTH AFRICA. In 1990 he won the Africa Prize for Leadership for leading the search for a sustainable end to hunger.

Obasanjo, though not directly active in politics, remained a steady critic of Nigerian political life. As a consequence, the repressive Nigerian military government imprisoned him in 1995 under charges of "concealing treason." He was sentenced to death, but after international protest the sentence was commuted to 15 years in prison. He was released in June 1998 after the death of Gen. SANI ABACHA. Gen. Abdusalam Abubakar assumed the role of president and, following the death of a popular opposition figure, Moshood K. O. Abiola, announced a timetable for elections and a return to civilian rule. In the February 1999 elections General Obasanjo ran for the presidency against Olu Falae and won. Obasanjo's inauguration took place as scheduled on May 29, 1999.

Eric Bennett

SEE ALSO

Abeokuta, Nigeria; Abiola, Moshood Kashimawo Olawale.

Latin America and the Caribbean

Obeso, Candelario

(b. 1849, Mompox, COLOMBIA; d. 1884, Santa Fé de Bogotá, Colombia), Afro-Colombian poet and writer; a precursor of black poetry in Colombia and one of the first in Latin America to use nonstandard Spanish in his literary work.

Candelario Obeso was born three years before the Colombian government abolished slavery. The illegitimate son of a white lawyer and a mulatto (of African and European descent) laundry woman, Obeso was raised by his mother in the small town of Mompox along the banks of the Magdalena River. At age 17 he moved to Bogotá to study at a military academy. Just one year after his arrival a military coup closed down the academy, and Obeso then entered the recently inaugurated National University. Even though he never graduated, Obeso received a teaching certificate and started writing his first poems.

In 1871 Obeso released his first novel, *La familia Pygmalión* (The Pygmalion Family), in which he ridiculed a family that got him imprisoned for a love affair. Obeso then published articles and poems in Bogotá's most important newspapers and magazines; he gradually gained notoriety. The 1876 civil war interrupted his literary career. He enlisted as a government soldier and fought in the Battle of Garrapata, in which his brave efforts led to his appointment as lieutenant colonel.

The crowning event of his literary career came in 1877 with the publication of *Cantos populares de mi tierra* (Popular Songs of My Land), a collection of 16 poems that employed the linguistic particularities of blacks from the Caribbean coast to depict the daily activities of the Caribbean poor. Obeso initiated a literary tradition in which blacks spoke in their own voices about their ambiguities, struggles, and contradictions. He was one of the first poets to present blacks as fully human and in a positive light, challenging the racial, social, and cultural inequalities of his time.

Despite his artistic and military accomplishments – which landed him a diplomatic post in FRANCE and a high military position in PANAMA, both of which lasted just a few months – he faced many tribulations in his life in Bogotá. Being black, poor, and from the coastal lands, Obeso was often discriminated against in a city that prided itself on its white and European heritage. He aspired to join society's privileged ranks but met stark opposition that prevented him from improving socioeconomically. To make a living for his companion Zenaida and himself, he continued publishing his works, including the play *Secundino el zapatero* (1880, Secundino, the Cobbler), and he used his remarkable polyglot ability to teach languages and to translate texts into Spanish.

Obeso died tragically at age 35 as a result of a self-inflicted gunshot wound. It is uncertain if the wound was accidental. Some claim that a life mired by financial burdens and a feeling of despondency over his unrequited love for an upper-class woman led him to commit suicide. In any case, with Obeso's untimely death Colombia lost one of its most original poets and its first major writer of African descent.

Alberto Arenas

SEE ALSO

Abolition and Emancipation in Latin America and the Caribbean; Literature, Black, in Spanish America.

Africa

Obiang Nguema Mbasogo, Teodoro (b. 1942, Acoacan, Equatorial Guinea), president of EQUATORIAL GUINEA (1979-).

Born to the Esangui (FANG) ethnic group at Acoacan in mainland Equatorial Guinea, Obiang Nguema went to secondary school in Bata and underwent military training at Saragossa Military Academy in SPAIN from 1963 to 1965. His uncle Francisco Macías Macías Nguema was elected Equatorial Guinea's first president in 1968, and Obiang Nguema was appointed military governor of the island of Fernando Po. In 1975 he became the tyrannical President Macías Macías Nguema's personal aide-de-camp (military assistant). Early in 1979 one of Obiang Nguema's brothers, who complained about not receiving the wages he was due, was executed on Macías Macías Nguema's orders, and Obiang Nguema began plotting the overthrow of his uncle. In August 1979 Obiang Nguema, then a lieutenant-colonel, seized power with the support of the Supreme Military Council. Obiang Nguema proclaimed an amnesty for refugees overseas and released an estimated 5000 political prisoners, but his close identification with the Macías Macías Nguema regime (even after Macías Macías Nguema's trial and execution) meant that most were still afraid to return home.

After being sworn in as president in October 1979, Obiang Nguema continued his uncle's policies of absolute personal control and extensive corruption. He took over companies he coveted, executed opponents, and ruled through a single-party state. A series of coup attempts was harshly subdued. A new constitution approved by 95 percent of the voters in 1982 provided for a return to civilian government after a seven-year transitional period, but it also gave Obiang Nguema nearly total powers as president. In 1985 and 1986 the United Nations Human Rights Commission complained of repeated flagrant violations of human rights in the country.

In 1987 Obiang Nguema ended his ban on formal political activity and announced the establishment of the official single legal party, the Democratic Party of Equatorial Guinea (PDGE). In 1988 he began taking steps to consolidate his power by arresting opposition leadership. As the sole candidate in 1989, he was reconfirmed for another term. A new constitution legalized opposition political parties in 1991 and 1992, but Obiang Nguema, at the time living in exile outside the country, placed restrictions that eliminated most of the opposition. By mid-1993, 13 small opposition parties had been recognized, and a number of opposition leaders had received amnesty. Soon thereafter, however, Obiang Nguema again arrested many of the important leaders, postponed the elections, and enabled his party (the PDGE) to easily win 68 out of the 80 seats in the unicameral House of People's Representatives, as the opposition boycotted the elections.

SEE ALSO

Macías Nguema, Francisco; Human Rights in Africa.

Africa

Obote, Milton (b. December 28, 1924, Akoroko Village, Lango District, Uganda), prime minister of Uganda from 1962 to 1970 and two-time president of Uganda, from 1966 to 1971 and 1980 to 1985.

Born in the LANGO district of UGANDA to a family of nine children, Milton Apollo Obote established a pattern of scholastic achievement at an early age. After attending Busoga College, Obote enrolled at Makerere University College. Although he was an excellent student, he was expelled in 1949 on the grounds that he had engaged in subversive political activities on campus. The British colonial administration subsequently prevented Obote from accepting scholarships offered to him by universities in the United States and Germany. Frustrated, he traveled to KENYA, where he worked odd jobs and became active in the Kenya African Union, a banned nationalist group. While Obote was suspected of having helped organize the Mau Mau resistance movement, IDI AMIN, who succeeded Obote as leader of Uganda, was suppressing the Mau Mau movement as an officer in the British colonial force known as the King's African Rifles.

Shortly after returning to Uganda in 1957 Obote was elected to the Central Legislative Council for Lango District, where he gained a reputation for outspoken opposition to colonial dictates. As president of the Uganda National Congress Party (UNCP) he called for decolonization, despite fellow Langos' fears that an independent Uganda would be dominated by the more numerous Baganda ethnic group. After internal divisions led to the collapse of the UNCP, Obote founded the Uganda People's Congress (UPC), a party composed primarily of ethnic Lango and ACHOLI.

After Obote was elected as prime minister in 1962, Uganda gained independence. The federal constitution recognized the a priori territories associated with Uganda's major ethnic groups, including the ancient kingdom of Buganda. As the Baganda constitute the single largest ethnic group and consequently held significant political sway, Obote formed a coalition with Mutesa II, the king of Buganda. Mutesa II was elected president while Obote retained the more powerful post of prime minister.

Obote's career as head of government was beset with difficulties from an early date. The Uganda Army mutinied in 1964, as did the armies of Kenya and TANZANIA. While the leadership in these other countries dealt harshly with the insubordination, Obote gave in to the demands of the military leadership, establishing a precedent for the armed forces to dictate political policy and ultimately leading to instability for years to come. In 1966 he was implicated in a gold and ivory smuggling scheme with Gen. Idi Amin. It was discovered that Obote had ordered Amin to provide secret support to Simba rebels in the Congo. Several ministers moved against Obote, ordering an investigation of Amin's activities. Obote preemptively eliminated the political challenge by ordering the arrest of the cabinet ministers who had initiated the investigation. He then implemented a new constitution to secure himself greater powers and promoted Amin to the position of army chief of state. He then declared himself executive president at the expense of Mutesa II. When Mutesa II ordered national government officials to leave Buganda, Obote instructed Amin to attack the Bugandan palace, forcing the king to flee to London. In 1967 Obote introduced yet another constitution that eliminated the sovereign status of Ugandan kingdoms, including Buganda.

With his political legitimacy weakened, in 1969 Obote finally began to outline a political platform, described as the "Move to the Left," in which he proposed socialist reforms in the hopes of cultivating a Ugandan nationalist identity and improving the economy. In 1969 Obote narrowly survived an assassination attempt made while he was attending a UPC conference in Kampala. Several Baganda were arrested and convicted, although Obote declined to sign the execution orders. Meanwhile, relations were deteriorating between the president and Amin. Despite the fact that Obote placed the general under house arrest (for misappropriating military funds), Obote returned from a summit in Singapore in 1971 to find that Amin had staged a coup d'état. Exiled to Tanzania, Obote attempted an unsuccessful counter coup in September 1972.

Amin was eventually forced out of office when Tanzania invaded Uganda in 1979. The following year Obote regained the presidency in allegedly rigged elections. Although he was able to make some initial repairs to the gutted Ugandan economy with the support of foreign aid, the festering ethnic conflicts of Amin's rule continued, especially in the army. Nor did Obote's own government abstain from the violence. Faced with numerous insurgency groups, particularly Yoweri Museveni's National Resistance Army/Movement, Obote responded with a harsh military campaign to suppress the rebellions, particularly in the Luwero Triangle. The human rights group Amnesty International reported widespread use of torture on civilians, and the United States Congress received reports in 1984 that as many as 100,000 people had died after Obote took power for a second time.

In 1985 Obote was again ousted by his own army chief of staff, this time Tito Okello. He fled to Zambia, where he remains exiled today.

See Also

Congo, Republic of the; Buganda, Early Kingdom of; Decolonization in Africa: An Interpretation; Gold Trade; Ivory Trade; Kampala, Uganda; Mau Mau Rebellion; Nationalism in Africa; Human Rights in Africa.

Africa

Odinga, Oginga

(b. October 1911?, Sakwa, Central Nyanza, East African Protectorate [present-day Kenya]; d. January 20, 1994, Kisumu, Kenya), Kenyan nationalist and first vice president of Kenya.

After his death in 1994 Oginga Odinga was described by Kenyan president Daniel arap Moi as a "patriotic citizen," ironic praise for a man who spent most of his career in opposition to the government. As Moi also noted, Odinga was a nationalist as well, a teacher who became a leading member of the independence struggle while president of the Luo Union from 1952 to 1957. In addition, he was one of the first Africans to be elected directly to the colonial government's legislative council.

In 1960 Odinga, with fellow Luo Tom Mboya, founded the Kenya African National Union (KANU). After Kenya achieved independence in December 1963, Odinga served briefly in Jomo Kenyatta's administration, first as minister for home affairs and then as vice president. But Odinga's political beliefs lay considerably to the left of Kenyatta's, and in 1966 he resigned to form the Kenya People's Union (KPU). In 1969 Kenyatta banned the KPU and placed Odinga in detention for two years. After his release Odinga was blocked from political office until Moi "rehabilitated" him in the early 1980s.

Odinga then became an outspoken critic of Moi and a leading agitator for multiparty elections, earning an expulsion from KANU in 1982. In 1988 he organized the Forum for Restoration of Democracy and in 1992 was that party's candidate in Kenya's first multiparty presidential election, in which he finished third. He was the official leader of the opposition in parliament until his death in 1994.

Robert Fay

Africa

Ogot, Grace

(b. 1930-), Kenyan author of short stories and novels; the first female writer from Kenya to win international attention. She is one of the most widely read short-story writers from that country.

Born Grace Emily Akinyi in the village of Butere in western Kenya, Grace Ogot received her early education in local schools before training as a nurse in Uganda and England. After working as a nurse in the 1950s in Kenya and Uganda, Ogot's career followed several different routes, although her writing continued to draw on her nursing experience.

Ogot worked as a broadcaster and scriptwriter for the British Broadcasting Corporation in London in 1959 and 1960 and later as an announcer on a weekly radio magazine program in the Luo and Kiswahili languages for the Voice of Kenya broadcasting company. Her career moved in a literary direction in the early 1960s, and she wrote most of her works in English. Her first novel, *The Promised Land* (1966), explores the issue of marriage in modern Kenya, especially a woman's relationship to her husband. It also considers the relation of past and present in traditional and modern medicine. In her work Ogot focuses on the preservation of family and on the sacrifices made to achieve that goal. She is also committed to showing the truths embodied in traditional law and folk wisdom. Both of these issues appear as themes in her short-story collections *Land Without Thunder* (1968) and *The Other Woman* (1976).

In 1975 and 1976 Ogot lived in New York City, first as a delegate to the General Assembly of the United Nations (UN) and then as a member of the Kenya delegation to the United Nations Educational, Scientific and Cultural Organization (UNESCO). The short-story collection *The Island of Tears* (1980) reflects her UN experiences as well as her interest in the common ancestry of African Americans and Africans. Ogot later became involved in politics and served in the National Assembly, the legislative branch of Kenya's government, from 1983 to 1992. Her other works include the novella *The Graduate* (1980) and the Luo-language novel *Miaha* (1983; translated as *The Strange Bride*, 1989).

See Also

Women Writers in English-Speaking Africa; New York, New York.

Latin America and the Caribbean

Ogum

(known as Ogum in Brazil and as Ogun in Cuba and the United States), the orisha, or Yoruba deity, of iron, knives, the forge, and war. Ogum is the former lover of Oshún, has a terrible temper, and inhabits the forest, where he can be alone. In Brazil his color is blue; in Cuba and the United States he wears green and black. Dogs and the truth are sacred to Ogum, and because he owns the knife, he eats first in the sacrifice (*see* Orishas; Religions, African, in Latin America and the Caribbean; Santería; and Candomblé).

Africa

Okebu

(also known as Ndu), ethnic group of east Central Africa.

The Okebu primarily inhabit northwestern Uganda, northeastern Congo-Kinshasa, and southern Sudan. They speak a Nilo-Saharan language. Approximately 300,000 people consider themselves Okebu.

See Also

Congo, Democratic Republic of the; Languages, African: An Overview.

Africa

Okigbo, Christopher

(b. August 16, 1932, Ojoto, Nigeria; d. August 1967, Nsukka, Nigeria), Nigerian poet.

Born in Ojoto, a small village in eastern Nigeria, Christopher Okigbo was the fourth of five children of a Catholic school teacher of Igbo heritage. He attended Catholic schools, the Umuahia Government College (secondary school), and the University of Ibadan, receiving a degree in classics in 1956. He worked as a teacher, an editor, a librarian at the University of Nsukka, and as secretary to the Nigerian minister of research and information; he was also the West African editor of the journal *Transition*. He published two volumes of poetry – *Heavensgate* (1962) and *Limits* (1964) – as well as poems in the journals *Horn*, *Black Orpheus*, and *Transition*. His work shows the influence of Igbo mythology and the American modernists as well as his training in Greek and Latin.

Offered the poetry prize at the 1966 Dakar Festival of Negro Arts, Okigbo declined it because he thought it racially exclusive to black writers. "There is no such thing as Negro art," he said. Deeply committed to political change, he resisted the 1930s neologism Négritude, a concept introduced by Aimé Césaire and Léopold Sédar Senghor that describes a particular mode of black experience and artistic expression. He also showed little interest in the opinions of critics and literary theorists. He was planning to establish a publishing house along with Nigerian writer Chinua Achebe when he was killed while fighting on the Biafran side during the Biafran war of independence from Nigeria. His collected poems were published as *Labyrinths with Path of Thunder* (1971).

See Also

Senghor, Léopold Sédar.

Africa

Okri, Ben

(b. March 15, 1959, Minna, Nigeria), prize-winning Nigerian-British author whose work incorporates elements of magical realism and social commentary.

Ben Okri, the son of a British-educated tenants' lawyer, was born in Nigeria to parents of the Urhobo ethnic group. Through his father's work, Okri was exposed to the world of the dispossessed; through myths and folktales as well as Western classics, he discovered the landscape of the imagination. He finished school at age 14 and went on to spend the next five years writing. His first publication was an article on a rent edict, but he soon turned to writing short stories for Nigerian women's journals and evening papers.

In 1978 Okri went to England to study philosophy and English at the University of Essex. Two years later he published his first novel, *Flowers and Shadows*. In chronicling a son's discovery of his businessman father's legacy of corruption, the story depicts the moral disintegration of contemporary Nigeria. His next work, *The Landscapes Within* (1981), was a novel Okri described as a "double mirror" of two realities: the psychic world of the artist and the chaos of daily life. Although *The Landscapes Within* gives an account of what Okri has called "the violent relations" of Nigeria, it marked a shift toward his growing preoccupation with the spiritual world.

During the next six years Okri worked as a journalist for BBC Television's African department and as a poetry editor for *West Africa* magazine. His short stories and poetry received growing recognition and were published in prominent journals such as *Paris Review*, *New Statesman*, *Firebird*, and *PEN New Fiction*. In 1986 he published *Incidents at the Shrine*, a collection of short stories that won the *Paris Review* Aga Khan Prize for Fiction, and, the following year, the Commonwealth Writers Prize for Africa. Set in the seamy urban underworld of Nigeria and England, *Shrine* blurs the boundaries between the "real world" and the world of the dream. In Okri's next collection, *Stars of the New Curfew* (1988), Okri moved further into the literary realm known as magical realism.

Okri's Booker Prize-winning novel *The Famished Road* (1991) is told from the viewpoint of Azaro, who is an *abiku*, a child believed to be caught in a cycle of death and rebirth. Set in the squalor of the ghetto, the novel's experimental storyline, which Okri characterizes as "open toward infinity," mirrors the cyclical and eternal nature of the abiku cycle. Okri continued the story of Azaro in *Songs of Enchantment* (1993), setting even more of the narrative in the spiritual world.

The novel *Astonishing the Gods* (1995) recounts a man's transformative explorations of an enchanted island. Okri's most recent works are *Birds of Heaven* (1996), *Dangerous Love* (1996), and *A Way of Being Free* (1997).

Marian Aguiar

Africa

Olajuwon, Hakeem

(b. January 21, 1963, Lagos, Nigeria), Nigerian-born basketball player.

One of the first African professional basketball players in the United States, Hakeem Olajuwon did not take up the game until he was 15. The third of six children, Olajuwon had been a standout high-school soccer player. The 2.06 m (6 ft, 9 in) teenager was discovered by the coach of the Nigerian national basketball team, and by age 17 he was receiving recruitment offers from several United States colleges. Olajuwon chose the University of Houston, which he entered in 1981. Sitting out one year to gain weight and focus on the sport's fundamentals, Olajuwon, soon nicknamed "the Dream," was starting at center by his sophomore year. Twice he took his team to the final four of the National Collegiate Athletic Association (NCAA) basketball tournament. At the end of his junior year Olajuwon entered the draft of the National Basketball Association (NBA).

Now 2.13 m (7 ft) tall and weighing 107 kg (235 lb), Olajuwon was the first player chosen in the 1984 NBA draft. As a rookie for the Houston Rockets he soon established himself as one of the league's best players, averaging 20.6 points and 11.9 rebounds per game. Over the next decade Olajuwon played in 12 All-Star games and won Most Valuable Player for the league (1993-94 season) as well as for the playoff finals (1993-94, 1994-95). In 1996 he was named one of the NBA's 50 greatest players of all time. Despite his intelligent play and brilliant athleticism, Olajuwon's criticism of management has earned him a mixed reputation, and his Nigerian accent has denied him the lucrative endorsement contracts lesser NBA stars enjoy.

Kate Tuttle

See Also

Nigeria; Basketball.

North America

O'Leary, Hazel Rollins

(b. May 17, 1937, Newport News, Va.), African American public official, first female secretary of energy.

Hazel O'Leary was raised by her father, Russell E. Reid, a physician, and by her stepmother. She earned a B.A. from Fisk University in Nashville, Tennessee, in 1959, and a J.D. from Rutgers University Law School in 1966.

From 1974 to 1980 O'Leary worked in the Federal Energy Administration (later part of the Department of Energy), reaching the position of chief of the Economic Regulatory Administration. She worked at her own energy consulting firm from 1980 to 1989. She was president of Northern States Power Company in 1993, when President Bill Clinton appointed her secretary of energy.

Robert Fay

North America

Oliver, Joseph ("King")

(b. May 11, 1885, Donaldsville, La.; d. April 8, 1938, Savannah, Ga.), African American cornetist and bandleader; pioneering figure in New Orleans- and Chicago-style jazz.

Joseph Oliver was born in Donaldsville, Louisiana. After his family moved to New Orleans he learned to play the trombone from local street musicians. He soon switched to the cornet and trumpet, and by 1907 Oliver had begun to play professionally with various local brass bands.

From 1916 to 1919 Oliver played in Edward "Kid" Ory's band. Ory gave him the moniker "King" because he was the best cornetist in the most popular jazz band in New Orleans. In 1918 Oliver was courted by bassist/banjoist Bill Johnson to join his band in CHICAGO, ILLINOIS. A year later Oliver moved to Chicago, where he became first cornetist in Johnson's Creole Jazz Band. Oliver soon assumed the leadership of the band, taking the group to California from 1920 to 1921.

Returning to Chicago, Oliver solidified the Creole Jazz Band with powerful new members, creating one of the most important ensembles in the history of jazz. From 1922 to 1924 the band included Louis Armstrong on cornet, Honore Dutrey on trombone, Johnny Dodds on clarinet, his brother Baby Dodds on drums, Lil Hardin (Armstrong) on piano, and Bill Johnson on bass and banjo. Featuring a "wa-wa" cornet sound and polyphonic four-to-the-beat rhythmic attack, such performances as "Dipper Mouth Blues," "Riverside Blues," and "Snake Rag" influenced a new generation of jazz musicians that included many aspiring white performers.

The Creole Jazz Band disbanded after Armstrong left. Oliver then recorded several duos with the great Jelly Roll Morton during 1924. From 1924 through 1927 Oliver led the Dixie Syncopators, made up of former Creole Jazz Band members along with trombonist "Kid" Ory and clarinetist and saxophonist Barney Bigard. From 1930 until 1937 he led several bands on tours of the Midwest and the South, but did not play after 1931 due to painful gum disease. Oliver retired from music in 1937.

SEE ALSO

Armstrong, Lillian Hardin (Lil); Armstrong, Louis ("Satchmo"); Morton, Ferdinand Joseph ("Jelly Roll"); Ory, Edward ("Kid").

Latin America and the Caribbean

Oller, Francisco (b. 1833, Bayamón, Puerto Rico; d. 1917), Afro-Puerto Rican painter who traveled to Spain and France in the 1850s, where he was influenced by impressionist painting. Among his most noted paintings is *El Velorio* (*see* ART IN LATIN AMERICA AND THE CARIBBEAN).

Latin America and the Caribbean

Olodum, an internationally acclaimed Afro-Brazilian Carnival association whose music celebrates black history and protests racial discrimination (*see* CARNIVALS IN LATIN AMERICA AND THE CARIBBEAN).

Olodum was founded in Salvador, BAHIA, BRAZIL, on April 25, 1979. That year marked the beginning of the *abertura* (opening), the gradual return to democracy after 15 years of military rule in Brazil. Many rights were curtailed during this period and, as a result, Carnival became an increasingly important occasion for voicing political concerns and asserting cultural pride. The 1970s in Salvador, Bahia, witnessed the emergence of *blocos Indios* (Indian Carnival associations) and *blocos Afros* (African Carnival associations), whose presentations at the annual pre-Lent Carnival celebration revolved around indigenous and African themes. Olodum emerged out of this bloco Afro movement just as abertura was paving the way for increased social, political, and cultural activism. Olodum's name comes from Olodumaré, the name of the supreme YORUBA deity.

Drum, voice, and liberation ideology are the foundations of Olodum's music. Every February Olodum brings together some 200 large *surdo* bass drums and smaller, high-pitched *repique* drums in a thunderous and irresistibly kinetic presentation. The group is at the center of a sea of some 4000 elaborately costumed performers who accompany the booming percussion with short call-and-response phrases. The occasion is Carnival, and for Olodum, the most famous of Salvador's blocos Afros, the theme is black history.

Olodum's yearly Carnival themes focus on black history and contemporary black political movements in Africa and in the

Members of Ilê Aiyê, the original *bloco Afro* or percussion-based music and dance troupe that began emphasizing African themes in Bahian Carnival, created a model for organizations like Olodum.
Vantoen Pereira, Jr./Contexto

African diaspora. In 1981, for example, Olodum developed its music, lyrics, and costumes around the history of Guinea-Bissau and its revolutionary black leader during the 1970s and 1980s, Amílcar Cabral. Then, in 1986, Olodum's parade celebrated the black culture and history of Cuba. Olodum has also frequently explored Afro-Brazilian heritage. In 1998 Olodum's Carnival theme was *A Revolta dos Búzios – A Rota da Liberdade*, in commemoration of the 200th anniversary of this slave revolt, the first in a string of slave rebellions in Bahia that lasted through the first part of the nineteenth century (*see* Slave Rebellions in Latin America and the Caribbean).

One of the masterminds behind Olodum is João Jorge Santos Rodrigues. He was a member of Ilê Aiyê, the first bloco Afro (established in 1974), before joining Olodum in 1983. He helped rescue Olodum from disorganization and debt and, as a scholar of African history, has provided much of the black historical information that has inspired Olodum's songs and Carnival presentations. In addition to serving as Olodum's president, Rodrigues has distinguished himself as one of the leading defenders of Afro-Brazilian interests. In the early 1990s he established contacts with human rights organizations and universities in the United States to gain support for and to promote a broader understanding of the Afro-Brazilian struggle against racial discrimination.

Another creative force in Olodum was musical director Neguinho do Samba (Antonio Luis Alves de Souza). In the mid-1980s he mixed Afro-Caribbean rhythms, including Jamaican reggae, with Brazilian samba to create a new genre of music known as samba-reggae, which quickly became the dominant musical form at Bahian Carnival. In 1995, after 12 years with Olodum, Neguinho do Samba left the group.

Olodum's success in Brazil caught the attention of American songwriter Paul Simon, who invited Olodum to collaborate on his 1991 album, *The Rhythm of the Saints*. This union brought Olodum international recognition, which led to tours outside of Brazil and collaboration with other famous musicians, including Jimmy Cliff and Michael Jackson. Some critics have lamented the elaboration of Olodum's percussion-and-voice formula to include horns, synthesizers, and longer singing arrangements. The group's message, however, remains centered on the black communities in Brazil and abroad.

Olodum's activities go well beyond Carnival and music. When not performing, Olodum has been the spearhead of black protests and demonstrations in the city of Salvador. The group has engaged in protests against police brutality targeting Salvador's black population. Internationally, Olodum spent more than ten years calling for the release of Nelson Mandela and an end to apartheid in South Africa. With the end of apartheid, Olodum raised concern over the internal conflict in Angola.

Over the years Olodum has evolved into a community organization that serves the people in its immediate vicinity as well as the general black community in Salvador. It has launched several community uplift programs, including a health campaign to prevent the spread of diseases such as acquired immune deficiency syndrome (AIDS) and cholera as well as an effective clean-up program in the neighborhoods of Maciel and Pelourinho. Olodum was instrumental in lobbying for a $12 million bill, which was passed in 1993, to restore some 450 historic buildings in Pelourinho. Olodum has also attempted to address the high level of unemployment in the Maciel-Pelourinho neighborhood, in part by building a factory in 1993 where instruments, clothing, and Olodum paraphernalia are manufactured. Olodum also manages a reggae bar and the Africa Bar, where the group performs regularly.

Profits from Olodum's factory and bars help to fund the Olodum Creative School, established to provide an education to people of all ages who otherwise might not be able to afford one. The school's courses are designed to give students of African descent a greater sense of Afro-Brazilian history, which is largely omitted in the traditional Brazilian curriculum, and to equip them with the social and technical skills that will make them better job candidates. The school also develops the artistic talents of its students through courses in dance, music, and theater and an extracurricular youth samba group called Banda Mirim (established in 1983). Olodum has taken hundreds of homeless children off Salvador's streets, enrolled them in its school, and launched efforts to improve their self-esteem and prepare them for fuller participation in Brazilian society.

As an extension of these educational activities, Olodum organizes and participates in seminars, speeches, and conferences on various issues affecting the black community in Brazil and in other parts of the world. It has its own publishing house (established in 1994) that prints books and a monthly journal called *Bantu Nagô*. Olodum is an outstanding example of how Carnival organizations, in particular blocos Afros, have become building blocks for black economic and political power.

Aaron Myers

See Also

Mandela, Nelson Rolihlahla; Jackson, Michael, and the Jackson Family; Afoxés/Blocos Afros; Jamaica; Salvador, Brazil.

Latin America and the Caribbean

Olorun, the supreme god of the Yoruba pantheon. Olodumaré, also known as Olorun, is the sky god to whom all of the orishas answer, and he is mentioned first in all prayers. He is somewhat remote because he is busy, which is why the orishas do most of the work dealing with human beings (*see* Orishas; Religions, African, in Latin America and the Caribbean; Santería; and Candomblé).

Africa

Olympics, Africans and the

At the 1996 Summer Olympic Games, held in Atlanta, Georgia, African athletes brought home 34 medals, 11 of them gold. The African continent, however, which sent teams from 52 nations to the Atlanta games, has had a shorter history of Olympic participation than Europe or the Americas, and one marked by exclusion alternating with triumph.

The first African country to claim a gold medal in the modern Olympic Games was South Africa, which won gold in 1908 for the 100-meter race. South African athletes – until 1992, only whites were permitted to participate – also won gold in cycling in 1912, tennis in 1912 and 1920, wrestling in 1928, and swimming in 1952. Gold medals for weightlifting went to the Egyptians in 1928, 1936, and 1948. In 1960 the barefoot Ethiopian marathoner Abebe Bikila became the first black sub-Saharan athlete to win a gold medal, and his victory began an era in which Africans dominated international long-distance running. A Moroccan, Abdesiam Rhadi, finished second that year. Also in 1960 Egyptians won medals in wrestling and boxing, a Senegalese athlete running for France won the bronze in the 200-meter race, and Ghanaian welterweight Clement Quartey won a silver medal in boxing.

African nations, many of them recently freed from colonial rule, participated in great numbers in the 1964 and 1968 Summer Olympic Games, held in Tokyo and Mexico City, respectively. In Tokyo not only did Bikila repeat his gold-medal performance, but Kenyan Wilson Kiprugut won a bronze in the 800-meter race, the first medal for his country, which has since become known for its middle- and long-distance runners. Boxers from Nigeria and Ghana also collected bronze medals. In 1968, 25 newly independent African nations sent athletes to Mexico City, where high altitude proved treacherous for many world-class runners – but not those who had trained in the highlands of Ethiopia and Kenya. Kenyan Naftali Temu won gold in the 10,000-meter race and bronze in the 5000-meter race. His countrymen Kip Keino and Benjamin Jipcho finished first and second in the 1500-meter event, and Africans

AFRICAN OLYMPIC GOLD MEDALISTS

Year	Name	Country	Event
Track and Field (Men)			
1908	Reginald Walker	South Africa	100m
1920	Bevil Rudd	South Africa	400m
1988	Paul Ereng	Kenya	800m
1992	William Tanui	Kenya	800m
1968	Kipchoge Keino	Kenya	1500m
1988	Peter Rono	Kenya	1500m
1968	Mohamed Gammoudi	Tunisia	5000m
1980	Miruts Yifter	Ethiopia	5000m
1984	Said Aouita	Morocco	5000m
1988	John Ngugi	Kenya	5000m
1996	Venuste Niyongabo	Burundi	5000m
1968	Naftali Temu	Kenya	10,000m
1980	Miruts Yifter	Ethiopia	10,000m
1988	Brahim Boutaib	Morocco	10,000m
1992	Khalid Skah	Morocco	10,000m
1996	Haile Gebrselassie	Ethiopia	10,000m
1928	Sydney Atkinson	South Africa	110m Hurdles
1972	John Akii-Bua	Uganda	400m Hurdles
1968	Amos Biwott	Kenya	3000m Steeple Chase
1972	Kipchoge Keino	Kenya	3000m Steeple Chase
1984	Julius Korir	Kenya	3000m Steeple Chase
1988	Julius Karviki	Kenya	3000m Steeple Chase
1992	Matthew Birer	Kenya	3000m Steeple Chase
1996	Joseph Keter	Kenya	3000m Steeple Chase
1912	Kenneth McArthur	South Africa	Marathon
1960	Abebe Bikila	Ethiopia	Marathon
1964	Abebe Bikila	Ethiopia	Marathon
1968	Mamo Wolde	Ethiopia	Marathon
1996	Josia Thugwane	South Africa	Marathon
Track and Field (Women)			
1992	Hassiba Boulmerka	Algeria	1500m
1992	Derartu Tulu	Ethiopia	10,000m
1984	Nawal el Moutawakel	Morocco	400m Hurdles
1996	Fatuma Roba	Ethiopia	Marathon
1952	Esther Brand	South Africa	High Jump
1996	Chioma Ajunwa	Nigeria	Long Jump
Swimming and Diving (Women)			
1996	Penny Heyns	South Africa	100m Breast Stroke
1996	Penny Heyns	South Africa	200m Breast Stroke
Boxing			**Weight Class**
1920	Clarence Walker	South Africa	Bantam Weight
1924	William Smith	South Africa	Bantam Weight
1932	Lawrence Stevens	South Africa	Lightweight
1948	Gerald Dreyer	South Africa	Lightweight
1996	Hocine Soltani	Algeria	Lightweight
1932	David Carstens	South Africa	Light Heavyweight
1948	George Hunter	South Africa	Light Heavyweight

also won the 3000-meter steeplechase and finished second in the 800-meter and 4 x 400-meter relays. In addition, Africans won 4 medals in boxing.

It was also in the 1960s that African politics – and the worldwide Black Power Movement – first influenced the Olympic Games. After the International Olympic Committee (IOC) decided in 1968 to readmit South Africa, which had been excluded in 1964 for its APARTHEID policies, a group of 32 African nations planned a boycott of the Mexico City games. Several non-African nations, such as ITALY, Sweden, Denmark, and Norway, joined their protest. Kenya's Kip Keino, who won 2 medals in Mexico City, said before the games, "I'd prefer to give up all hope of a medal than have to run with South Africans, who regard my black brothers and colored brothers as second-class citizens." Finally the IOC decided to retain the ban against South Africa.

Again in 1972 it took the threat of boycott by not only African but African American athletes to force the IOC to keep similarly racist Rhodesia (now ZIMBABWE) from participating in the Olympic Games. The 1972 Munich games yielded medals for Kip Keino, fellow Kenyan Mike Boit (who won bronze in the 800-meter race), Ugandan John Akii-Bua (who won gold in the 400-meter hurdles), and the Kenyan 4 x 400-meter relay team, which won gold. As they did in Mexico City, Africa's boxers did almost as well as its runners, winning 7 medals. Africa has continued to produce world-class track-and-field athletes, including women runners who won gold in 1984 and 1992. In 1988 Africans won 5 gold medals – with 4 going to Kenyan athletes and 1 to a Moroccan. The 1992 games, held in Barcelona, yielded 5 gold medals out of a total of 25 for African athletes, including Namibian sprinter Frank Fredericks, who won 2 silver medals.

The 1996 Summer Olympic Games saw Africa's best showing ever, with African nations taking home 10 gold medals. Perhaps most inspiring was the victory of Nigeria's soccer team in a sport long dominated by South America and Europe. Fredericks again won 2 silver medals, while Ethiopian HAILE GEBRSELASSIE won gold in the 10,000-meter race. Nigerian Chioma Ajunwa, gold medalist in the long jump, and Fatuma Roba, Ethiopian marathon winner, were two of the African women to shine in Atlanta. As one African sports fan told the *New York Times*, after decades of exclusion and controversy, 1996 was "the year of the black athlete."

Kate Tuttle

SEE ALSO

Egypt; Ethiopia; Kenya; Morocco; Namibia; Senegal; Track and Field in the United States; Uganda; Keino, Kipchoge; Black Power.

Africa

Ometo, ethnic group of ETHIOPIA.

The Ometo primarily inhabit southwestern Ethiopia. They speak an Afro-Asiatic language in the Cushitic group and are considered one of the SIDAMO peoples. Approximately 1 million people consider themselves Ometo.

SEE ALSO

Languages, African: An Overview.

Africa

Omotoso, Kole (b. April 21, 1943, Akure, Western State, Nigeria), Nigerian novelist, poet, and critic who has maintained a commitment to address the common people of Africa.

Kole Omotoso was born into a YORUBA family in the Western State of NIGERIA. Inspired by his uncle, the author Olaiya Fagbamigbe, and evenings spent listening to Yoruba folktales, after an education in local schools Omotoso published stories while at King's College in Lagos. He earned a bachelor of arts degree in French and Arabic from the University of Ibadan in 1968 and a docorate in modern Arabic literature from the University of Edinburgh in Scotland in 1972. He returned to Nigeria to write and teach and took a post as professor at the University of Ibadan in 1976.

Influenced by the Nigerian writer WOLE SOYINKA, Omotoso's increasingly political writings have dealt with issues affecting Africa's future from the perspective of ordinary people. Omotoso believes in the power of the arts to bring social change. He contributes frequently to magazines and newspapers and has written novels, plays, short stories, essays, and literary criticism. Focusing on Nigeria and Africa, Omoto's works address interracial marriage, the effects of poverty on children, communism, SOCIALISM, the Nigerian civil war, and criticisms of materialism and neocolonialism – especially the relationship of Africa's colonial past to its postcolonial economic problems and ethnic discord.

The tireless Omotoso was a founder of the Association of Nigerian Authors and served as its national secretary and its national president. He also helped found the Union of Writers of the African Peoples in Accra, GHANA, and worked as an editor of *Afriscope* and *Ch'Indaba Magazine*.

In 1991 he made a controversial decision to leave Nigeria for SOUTH AFRICA, which was then still a white-ruled APARTHEID state. He took a position as professor at the University of the Western Cape, and his writings after 1991 addressed the transition to majority rule in South Africa and the implications of the South African experience for the rest of the continent of Africa.

Robert Fay

SEE ALSO

Accra, Ghana; Ibadan, Nigeria; Lagos, Nigeria.

Latin America and the Caribbean

O'Neale, Charles Duncan (b. 1879: d. 1936), a black activist in Barbados during the 1920s and 1930s. O'Neale was the first leader of the Democratic League, the country's first political party, founded in 1924 (*see* BARBADOS).

North America

O'Neal, Shaquille (b. March 6, 1972, Newark, N.J.), African American basketball player, one of the greatest players of the 1990s.

Shaquille O'Neal attended high school in San Antonio, Texas, where he led the school BASKETBALL team to the state championship. O'Neal then entered Louisiana State University (LSU) in 1989. He quickly became a dominating player in college basketball, and he averaged 21.6 points and 13.5 rebounds per game over three seasons. In his last year at LSU he led the nation in blocked shots and was second in rebounding.

In 1992 he entered the National Basketball Association (NBA) draft and was the first player chosen by the Orlando Magic, then a recent expansion team. Although his inexperience was evident in his first professional year, O'Neal's high level of play made him a nearly unanimous choice as rookie of the year for the 1992-1993 season. That year he led the season's rookies in points (23.4), rebounds (13.9), and blocked shots (3.53) per game, and he was second overall in the league in rebounds and eighth overall in scoring. During the 1993-1994 season O'Neal's play continued to improve. He led the NBA in field-goal percentage (.599) and finished second in points (29.3) and rebounds per game (13.2). In 1994 he was also a member of the United States national basketball team known as Dream Team II, which won the gold medal at the world basketball championships in Toronto, Ontario, in Canada.

In the 1994-1995 season O'Neal led the NBA in points per game (29.3) and finished second in field-goal percentage (.583) and third in rebounds per game (11.4). He also led the Magic to the NBA Finals, where the team lost to the Houston Rockets. O'Neal's success continued in the 1995-1996 season, when he was selected as an All-Star for the fourth consecutive year. After the season he played for the U.S. national basketball team at the 1996 Olympic Games in Atlanta, Georgia. In July 1996 O'Neal signed as a free agent with the Los Angeles Lakers; he powered the team to playoff appearances in the 1996-1997 and 1997-1998 seasons. O'Neal appeared in his fifth All-Star game in 1998.

O'Neal also became popular as an entertainer. In 1993 *Shaq Diesel,* a best-selling RAP music album, was released. The following year he acted in the motion picture *Blue Chips.* In 1994 he issued a second rap album, *Shaq Fu – Da Return,* and an action-oriented home video game, *Shaq-Fu,* which stars O'Neal as a kung fu warrior. Further entertainment projects included the albums *You Can't Stop the Reign* (1996) and *The Best of Shaquille O'Neal* (1997) as well as a role in the 1997 movie *Steel.*

Cross Cultural

Opera, musical theater that originated in seventeenth-century Florence, Italy; numerous African Americans have risen to prominence within the genre.

Early ninteenth-century African American opera singers and performers were crossover artists. Barred from all major American stages, they transgressed the boundaries between high and low culture by playing the marginal American concert stages and opera houses that permitted them, as well as minstrel and vaudeville shows. Careers were short lived, usually lasting only two or three years – the length of time it typically took for the novelty of seeing a black singer to wear off on white audiences. Europe often proved a more hospitable climate for African American artists.

Nonetheless, a number of black performers rose to prominence in the American opera scene. Elizabeth Taylor Greenfield – "The Black Swan" – toured North America and England with an African American troupe in the 1850s and 1860s. During the same period the multitalented Luca family included opera in their performances, as did the Hyers Sisters – renowned for their renditions of the works of Verdi and Donizetti. Sissieretta Joyner Jones was the most celebrated opera performer of the time. Known as "the Black Patti" after white soprano Adelina Patti, she gave a recital at the White House for President Benjamin Harrison. Jones outlasted her contemporaries – extending her career to 15 years – by forming, in 1896, the Black Patti Troubadours, which mixed opera with musical theater and offered a vehicle to showcase her talents. Similarly, soprano Nellie Brown Mitchell's career lasted almost ten years, thanks to her creation of the Nellie Brown Mitchell Concert Company.

Until the color bar that prevented African Americans from performing on America's greatest stages was lifted, recitals were the quickest way to success for black performers. In 1955 contralto MARIAN ANDERSON, thanks to her unmatched talent and the breadth of her repertoire, became the first African American to perform at New York City's Metropolitan Opera, after years of dazzling audiences on recital stages. Anderson's performances, like those of her predecessor, the tenor recitalist Roland Hayes, opened the stages to other opera singers. Both Anderson and Hayes incorporated the concert spiritual – an indigenous African American contribution that fused European art music with black spirituals – into their recitals.

Throughout the mid-twentieth century blacks were usually cast in secondary roles, confined to playing marginal dark-skinned characters. This began to change in 1966. The era of the African American diva began when Mississippi-born soprano Leontyne Price performed at the opening of the new Metropolitan Opera House at New York City's Lincoln Center. By the 1980s the concept of

William Franklin and Lillian Evanti sing here in the second act of *La Traviata*, produced by the National Negro Opera Company in 1944. *Library of Congress*

the African American diva had been well established by the glamorous sopranos JESSYE NORMAN and KATHLEEN BATTLE.

African American opera companies have developed alongside individual artists. Organizations such as the Colored American Opera Company and the Theodore Drury Opera Company staged productions in the early twentieth century. This work was followed by productions by the Imperial Company, the National Negro Opera Company, the Dra-Mu Opera Company, and the Harlem Opera Company. With the establishment of Opera/South and the National Ebony Opera in the 1970s, black productions flourished. Their mandate was to create opportunities for professionals working in the field.

By the early 1990s mainstream American stages began to reconsider early compositions written by African Americans and to stage productions that conveyed the tragedy and triumph of the black experience. Duke Ellington's *Queenie Pie* and Leroy Jenkins's *The Mother of Three Sons* were among the first to take part in this mainstream revival. These compositions are part of a body of African American work that includes long-neglected pieces by composers like Harry Laurence Freeman, writer of 14 grand-style operas including the *Octoroon* and the early JAZZ opera, *The Flapper*, and RAGTIME innovator SCOTT JOPLIN, who attempted to create an indigenous African American opera in *Treemonisha*. Anthony Davis, founder of the instrumental group Episteme, is the dominant figure in late twentieth-century African American opera composition. His *X: The Life and Times of Malcolm X*, *Under the Double Moon*, and *Amistad* have all reached well-known United States halls, bringing a contemporary flavor to traditional opera.

Peter Hudson

SEE ALSO

Hayes, Roland Willsie; Minstrelsy; New York, New York; Jones, M. Sissieretta ("Black Patti"); Ellington, Edward Kennedy ("Duke"); Spirituals, African American.

North America

Operation Breadbasket, organization formed by the SOUTHERN CHRISTIAN LEADERSHIP CONFERENCE (SCLC) and later led by Jesse Jackson that put pressure on corporations to hire blacks and support black businesses.

In 1962 Operation Breadbasket was established by the SCLC to put "bread, money, and income into the baskets of black and poor people." With the mandate of improving the economic conditions of African Americans, Operation Breadbasket organized black consumers to press for jobs and to encourage and expand black-owned businesses. In its first campaign in ATLANTA, GEORGIA, the organization won a commitment from local companies to create 5000 jobs over the next five years.

After establishing affiliates in several Southern states, the organization expanded north. In 1966 Jesse Jackson, then a student at Chicago Theological Seminary, helped found the Chicago chapter, which directed protests at several dairy companies and supermarket chains to demand that they hire black workers and support black-owned businesses. Although the protesters were able to secure promises of employment for black workers from several major corporations, they had trouble ensuring compliance. The A&P supermarket, for example, promised 770 permanent jobs and 1200 summer jobs in May 1967, but did not deliver until another protest was launched in 1970.

As Operation Breadbasket expanded across the country in 1967, Martin Luther King Jr. appointed Jackson to be its national director. From then on the group became increasingly identified with Jackson's high-profile leadership. Under Jackson, Operation Breadbasket took on a number of projects, among them a free breakfast program and the 1968 Poor People's Campaign in WASHINGTON, D.C. The organization also became a voice in local and national politics, opposing welfare cuts and supporting electoral candidates.

By 1971 the group had started to collapse under the weight of too many projects, too few resources, and charges of financial corruption. Some criticized Jackson for using Operation Breadbasket as his own personal power base in CHICAGO, ILLINOIS, and faulted him for the failure of the group to act like a true national organization. That year Jackson left the SCLC, dissolving the Chicago chapter and forming OPERATION PUSH (People United to Save Humanity). Since then Operation Breadbasket has continued as a subsidiary operation of the SCLC but has never regained the momentum it had during the 1960s.

Marian Aguiar

See Also
Jackson, Jesse Louis; King, Martin Luther, Jr.; Poor People's Washington Campaign.

Operation People United to Save Humanity.
Please see Operation PUSH

North America

Operation PUSH, organization founded by Jesse Jackson in 1971 to promote economic security for black workers and businesses and to provide assistance to African American urban youth.

Jesse Jackson left Operation Breadbasket, the economic arm of the Southern Christian Leadership Conference, in 1971 to found Operation People United to Save Humanity (PUSH). Like Operation Breadbasket, the new organization set its sights on strengthening the economic security of African Americans. Under Jackson's charismatic leadership, Operation PUSH organized boycotts for black consumers to press for minority employment and support for black-owned businesses.

Over the years Operation PUSH expanded its mission and focused on national issues like education and national politics. In the late 1970s Jackson brought national attention to the subject of minority education and raised money for an elementary school education program called PUSH for Excellence, or PUSH/EXCEL. Despite substantial federal and private support, the education program foundered because of poor administration. Following accusations of shady business alliances and embezzlement, the organization scaled down and, by the early 1980s, had reduced its agenda to consciousness-raising.

Operation PUSH, which was largely dependent on Jackson's powerful personality for its success, lost momentum when he left to run in the 1984 presidential election primaries. Jackson remained a spokesperson for the organization through the 1980s, however, keeping Operation PUSH afloat through his fundraising efforts. Returning to a more active role in 1991, Jackson turned the group toward the issues that had been a part of his election campaign, including the crises of acquired immune deficiency syndrome (AIDS) and urban violence. In 1993 Operation PUSH began a program in Chicago to promote education and employment opportunities for minority youth.

Marian Aguiar

See Also
AIDS in the United States; Jackson, Jesse Louis.

North America

Opportunity: Journal of Negro Life, the National Urban League's early publication, which documented the social and economic conditions of African Americans and provided a forum for young writers and artists, many of whom became famous during the Harlem Renaissance.

Founding editor Charles Spurgeon Johnson intended that *Opportunity* not only publicize the projects and staff of the National Urban League (NUL), but also provide information about and analysis of the social and economic conditions that faced blacks. The journal's scientific approach was meant in part to serve as a counterweight to the National Association for the Advancement of Colored People (NAACP) publication *Crisis*, which NUL leaders considered too "subjective." Through articles addressing northern migration, Negro intelligence, and the influence of Marcus Garvey, the magazine became one of the most respected black publications in the United States. During World War II Johnson's successor, Elmer A. Carter, devoted significant space to discussions of the contradiction between blacks fighting overseas in a "war for democracy," and their exclusion from democracy at home.

Opportunity also published black authors who had difficulty selling their work to white publications, including such stars of the Harlem Renaissance as Langston Hughes, Countee Cullen, James Weldon Johnson, Claude McKay, Angelina Weld Grimké, and Sterling Brown. *Opportunity* also sponsored literary contests and social events that introduced writers to editors and publishers.

Opportunity never earned enough to cover production costs. In 1923, the journal's first year of operation, circulation was only 4000. By 1927 it had peaked at 11,000. Although in 1949 circulation stood around 10,000, *Opportunity*'s publishers ended the journal's production, citing persistent deficits and the availability of other journals to continue its work.

Robert Fay

See Also
World War II and African Americans; Brown, Sterling Allen; *Crisis, The*; Garvey, Marcus Mosiah; Great Migration, The.

Africa

Organization of African Unity, organization of African nations created to promote continental peace, unity, and cooperation.

The Organization of African Unity (OAU) works to resolve conflicts between nations and to coordinate political, economic, cultural, scientific, medical, and defense policies. The OAU has 53 member nations. Its headquarters is in Addis Ababa, Ethiopia, where it was founded on May 25, 1963.

At the time of the organization's founding, African leaders disagreed about what kind of organization the OAU should be. Some leaders pushed for the creation of a central government that would unite all of Africa under one authority. However, many of the nations had just recently gained independence from colonial rule and their leaders opposed the idea (*see* Decolonization in Africa: An Interpretation; Nationalism in Africa). The leaders eventually reached a compromise but in so doing created an organization that is controlled by its member nations, leaving it with little power to act on its own.

Since its founding, the OAU helped strengthen ties between African nations and settle disputes. But it also faced many problems that undermined its ability to achieve its goals. In the 1990s new leadership helped the OAU gain increased influence.

Structure

The OAU has three major governing bodies – the Assembly of the Heads of States and Governments, the Council of Ministers, and the General Secretariat. The assembly consists of a representative from each member nation. It meets once a year to discuss policy and consider recommendations from the Council of Ministers. Each year a different African leader becomes chair of the OAU and handles disputes among member nations. The Council of Ministers is headed by the foreign ministers of each member nation. It meets at least twice during the year to recommend policies and actions to the assembly. The General Secretariat runs the day-to-day operations of the organization. It is headed by a secretary general, who helps build consensus among member nations.

Problems in the OAU

Throughout its history the OAU has been troubled by disputes among its member nations. In 1975 the organization's members became divided over which side to support in the Angolan civil war. In this conflict rival factions fought for control of Angola, which had won independence from Portugal in 1974. One faction, the Popular Movement for the Liberation of Angola (officially known as Movemento Popular de Libertação de Angola-Partido de Trabalho, or MPLA), was backed by Cuba and the Soviet Union. The other two, the National Front for the Liberation of Angola (Frente Nacional de Libertação de Angola, or FNLA) and the National Union for the Total Independence of Angola (União Nacional para a Independência Total de Angola, or UNITA), were supported by the United States, its Western allies, and South Africa. In a December 1975 vote to decide which side to support, half of the nations chose one side, half the other.

The split in the OAU continued during a series of wars, including the 1977 and 1978 invasions of the Katanga Province in Zaire (now the Democratic Republic of the Congo) by Angolan-backed forces, Somalia's war with Ethiopia in 1978, and the conflicts between Uganda and Tanzania in 1978 and 1979. In

1981 the same nations that had supported the MPLA government in Angola also recognized the Western Sahara as an independent state and admitted it into the OAU. Morocco and other states that had supported the UNITA/FNLA side of the Angolan conflict did not approve of this move, and Morocco temporarily withdrew from the OAU. The OAU's strength was sapped further by an accelerating economic decline in Africa during the 1970s and 1980s.

Successes of the OAU

Despite its problems the OAU has scored a number of successes over the years. It mediated a border dispute between Algeria and Morocco in 1964 and 1965. It also mediated the border conflicts of Somalia with Ethiopia and Kenya from 1968 to 1970.

In 1963 the OAU formed the African Liberation Committee to channel financial support to movements trying to defeat Portuguese colonial rule in Guinea-Bissau, Angola, and Mozambique. Those movements were victorious in 1974. It also supported movements against white minority rule in South Africa, Zimbabwe, and Namibia. South Africa was excluded from OAU membership until 1994, when white minority rule and apartheid (the policy of racial segregation) ended.

The organization sent an observer mission to the United Nations (UN) in 1963. (An observer mission allows representatives of a nation or organization that is not a member of the UN to participate in UN discussions. Members of observer missions cannot vote on UN actions.) The OAU also coordinated collective action among African nations at the UN. It promoted decisions that led to South Africa being barred from participating in the UN's General Assembly in 1974, and to the admission of the People's Republic of China to the UN in 1971. In 1986 the OAU established the African Commission on Human and People's Rights to monitor human rights practices in member nations.

Recent Developments

In the 1990s the OAU experienced a revival, partly due to the election of Salim Ahmed Salim of Tanzania as its secretary general in 1989 for a four-year term. Salim was one of Africa's most respected statesmen and brought increased authority and prestige to the post. He was reelected in 1993 and 1997.

Under Salim's leadership the OAU established a new mechanism for conflict resolution and a peace fund in 1992 to deal with a growing number of conflicts. In 1993 the OAU sent peacekeepers to Liberia to support other peacekeeping missions trying to end a civil war. In 1994 African nations ratified an OAU initiative to establish an African Economic Community that would promote trade between African nations and remove tariffs and other restrictions that hamper commercial exchange. The African Economic Community would also work to establish a common currency in Africa. But these goals are not likely to be achieved until well into the twenty-first century.

The OAU received another boost when South Africa became a member in 1994. South Africa has been a major force for peace, democracy, and economic development in Africa since 1994, when apartheid ended in that country. With Salim's leadership and South Africa's influence, the OAU has the chance to become a stronger and more effective organization in the future.

See Also

Addis Ababa, Ethiopia; Angola; Mozambique; Somalia; Human Rights in Africa.

Latin America and the Caribbean

Orishas

Orishas, a pantheon of deities in the traditional Yoruba religion of Nigeria and in Yoruba-derived religious traditions in the African diaspora. The name for these deities is spelled differently in different languages and cultural areas – orisa in Yoruba, orixá in Portuguese, and orisha in Spanish – and orishas are also often known colloquially as *santos*, or saints.

The orishas are not equal to the sky god (Olodumaré), nor do they supplant him. Rather they are semi-independent divinities capable of working their own will with or without propitiation (often in the form of offerings) or supplication by human beings. They are believed to act in accordance with the wishes of Olodumaré, but they often appear autonomous in their behavior and in how they are worshiped and propitiated. Although their names are the same in all areas, they are spelled differently. For reasons of consistency this essay uses the most common Cuban spelling, unless otherwise indicated.

The religion based on the worship of the orishas is known by several names. In urban Brazil, especially Bahia, Rio de Janeiro, and São Paulo, one form is called Candomblé and another Umbanda. There is a significant difference between these two in that Umbanda incorporates a great deal of the spiritism, or European philosophy developed by the French writer known as Alan Kardec, with a complicated pantheon of spirits that are not orishas. Spiritism is a type of spiritual practice that originated in France in the mid-nineteenth century and combines healing, the summoning of disincarnated spirits, and the practice of charitable activities. Further, in Umbanda humans negotiate neither with God nor with the orishas, who are considered too remote, but rather with lesser spirits.

Farther north in Brazil, in Recife, the religion is known as Xangó; in Trinidad the same term is spelled Shango. Both Xangó and Shango refer to a specific orisha, Changó (see below). In the United States and Cuba the orisha religion is called Santería, a colonial term imposed by the Spanish and maintained in academia and journalism. Terms more frequently used by practitioners in the United States and Cuba are *Regla de Ocha* or *Ocha* or simply, "the religion."

Divination constitutes one of two primary activities in the orisha religion. The divination system most frequently used is the 16-cowrie shell system (*dilogun*). It is through this system that the orishas speak and their will can be determined. Typically the diviner throws the cowrie shells onto a special tray. Each orisha corresponds to a specific number and sign, which is indicated by the way the cowrie shells fall. In this manner the diviner ascertains the problem or situation facing the practitioner, what is causing the problem, and which orisha will help.

Another more complicated system of divination is Ifa, the tool of the high priests, the *babalawos*. Ifa divination contains 256 signs, or *odu*, and each sign contains hundreds of verses, each potentially pertaining to the individual's destiny. Here the position of the cowrie shells, or often the position of several necklaces tossed onto a sacred tray, determines which odu is to be interpreted and applied to the particular question or problem put to the babalawo. Ifa divination is consulted in all major life changes, such as birth, marriage, and death. Ifa divination can be used for everyday consultations, but also for determining the destiny of the person in a ritual called *Mano de Orúnmila* (Hand of Orúnmila) for men and *Kofa* for women. Ifa divination relays the words and advice of the orisha Orúnmila, who also is in charge of the 16 cowries. Orúnmila never comes to earth, however, and speaks only through ifa divination. Apparently Orúnmila was insulted by the youngest of his 16 sons, who refused to bow to his father (denying him the appropriate greeting to a senior family member in Yoruba culture) and who believed himself as wise and talented as his elder. Orúnmila removed himself to heaven and refused to come back. After being entreated by his children to return to earth, Orúnmila sent instead 16 palm nuts, which would speak in his absence. The palm nuts became the basis of the system of divination known as Ifa.

Through further divination the diviner determines what type of offering should be given to the orisha to ensure his or her help. An offering is called an *ebo*. This cycle of divination and ebo represents the fundamental daily custom of worship in the orisha religion. Since the orishas are embodiment of the forces of nature and manifestations of energy, it is this energy that is harnessed through ebo to work on behalf of the practitioner.

The other major activity in the orisha religion is possession. The orishas visit the earth and, to do so, they must borrow the body of a devotee who has been ritually prepared and trained to receive them. Mediums can enter a trance state and begin channeling the orisha at any time, whenever the orisha wants to come, but this activity mostly occurs within

LEFT: Macumba worshipers prepare food for the orishas before a ceremony inducting a novice into their temple in Rio de Janeiro.
CORBIS/Stephanie Maze
BELOW LEFT: A woman in an elaborate ceremonial costume participates in a Camdomblé religious ritual in Belém, Pará, Brazil.
CORBIS/Barnabas Bosshart

the context of a party for the orisha. At these parties, called *festas* in Brazil and *tambors* in the United States and Cuba, people gather to hear drumming and singing, and specific members of the group, or "house," dance.

In Brazil festas are highly choreographed performances. The members of the house dance in a circle (*roda* or *roça)*; the women wear fine traditional dress consisting of several heavily starched petticoats under a brightly colored full skirt and a lace blouse. They are then wrapped with a large cloth (*pano da costa*), which extends from chest to knees, and finally the costume is tied just under the armpits and tightly across the breasts with a long strip of cloth. The head is always covered with a scarf, often made of lace.

The dancers dance in order of length of time initiated. Songs and dances specific to the orishas are performed in a predetermined order. Interestingly, the order corresponds to that of the Cuban tradition. After the songs have been performed to each orisha, and generally not before, the dancers begin falling into trance and become possessed by their orishas. In Brazil most mediums present become possessed with their orishas.

At this point the mediums are cared for by special priestesses called *ekedes,* whose role is to take care of the belongings of the persons in trance, to bring them out of trance when necessary or at the orders of the house leader, to wipe the sweat off their faces as they dance, and to adjust their clothing. Ekedes go through an initiation process similar to that of a medium, but unlike the medium their head is not shaved, as it was determined through divination that they were not destined to become possessed. In the Cuban tradition there is no official role analogous to the ekede, but frequently a medium brings trusted assistants who essentially perform the same function with him or her.

After the orishas appear and possess their mediums, they dance a little bit and then are taken away from the scene of the dancing and are dressed in ritual clothing specific to their attributes and colors. They are subsequently brought back out to dance and to dispense advice to those present. In the United States and Cuba the orishas are allowed to remain as long as they want at a tambor, and individual supplicants seek their advice. In Brazil, however, the orishas speak much less to individual guests, and they are not free to come and go but are handled skillfully by the ekedes. Each orisha dances for a few songs only, and then leaves. In the Cuban tradition generally only one or two orishas come and take possession of a medium at a tambor, and they stay much longer, being the center of attention while they are at the tambor.

Each orisha has certain attributes corresponding to a natural phenomenon. Changó is represented by lightning and thunder; Oyá or Yansa by the wind; Oko by the farm or agriculture in Cuba and the United States and by the home in Brazil; Agayú by the volcano; Ochún by the river and sweet water; and Yemayá by the sea (in Trinidad these aspects of Yemayá and Ochún are reversed). Many orishas live in the forest and can be worshiped in wooded areas or urban parks. These include Osain, the herbalist and doctor, and Ochosi, the hunter. Ogun, the solitary warrior, divinity of iron and the forge, can be found wherever transportation facilities, especially train tracks and stations, are located, and in contemporary times is thought to inhabit airports. Elegguá, the trickster, is the lord of the crossroads. His offerings are frequently taken to a crossroads.

The warrior orishas include Elegguá, Ogun, and Ochosi. Members of the religion in the Cuban tradition who have not yet been initiated into the priesthood can be dedicated to, or "given to," these orishas, along with Osun, the guardian of one's destiny, in a ritual known as "giving the warriors." There does not appear to be an analogous initiation in Brazil. In fact, Elegguá in Brazil, where he is known as Exú, is treated completely differently than he is in Caribbean culture. This is one of the most interesting discrepancies in a comparative study. In the Cuban tradition Elegguá is a trickster and causes many problems, such as car trouble or other problems in travel, or inexplicable confusions. He is the orisha of choices, and he must be propitiated first, before all other orishas, so that he is kept content and so that he does not play disruptive jokes. Although considered dangerous, he is something of a childlike orisha in that he likes toys and candy. He manifests in his devotees at tambors, is taken along on vacations, and is kept close to his keepers – inside the house behind the door to guard the home, where practitioners can ask him for protection before exiting.

In Brazil, however, Exú is thought of as quite maleficent. There he also lives behind the door or preferably outside at the front gate. He is also propitiated first, but this is done in order to send him away so that he will not disrupt rituals and festas. He is sent away at least three hours before a festa begins: for example, the ceremony to propitiate Exú usually takes place at approximately five o'clock in the afternoon for a nine o'clock festa. In Brazil Exú is regarded with absolute respect mixed with a little terror. The idea of giving him candy and toys and keeping him nearby is met with horrified looks. Speaking to him or propitiating him by spraying rum on him prior to leaving the home is thought to cause problems by "calling" him.

The African deities known as orishas have their own particular colors, symbols, and ritual garments. These two members of a Candomblé in Belém are dressed as Omolú, *left*, and Xangó. *CORBIS/Barnabas Bosshart*

The orishas all have their favorite foods, colors, and numbers. Offerings as well as material culture adhere to these specific preferences. A typical food offering for Changó might be okra cooked with cornmeal; for Oxun of Brazil one might cook a dish of black-eyed beans or for Ochun of Cuba, a pastry soaked in honey. The food and colors of Obatalá (Oxalá in Brazil) are all of the strictest purity and white, such as the whites of eggs and cocoa butter. Oyá or Yansa uses brown, and Babaluaiyé, the orisha of smallpox, uses purple and burlap in Cuba and the United States, and raffia in Brazil.

Material culture in the orisha religion is quite rich. Practitioners of Ocha, from the very earliest initiations, all wear strings of beads in the specific colors of the orishas. Generally a newcomer starts with five necklaces, called *elekes,* which correspond to Obatalá (white), Changó (red and white), Ochún (yellows, gold, and coral with possibly a few single green and blue beads), Elegguá (black and red), and Yemayá (blue, crystal, and silver). Bead wearing in Brazil is at once more casual and more formal: casual wearing of the beads can be observed among nonmembers who simply are fond of the religion from the outside, and initiates wear long, heavy strings, often of 21 strands held together at points by larger beads. The colors in the two areas are very similar; the notable exceptions are the beads for Ogun (green and black in the Cuban tradition and dark blue in Brazil). In Brazil, further, one does not wear beads for Exú.

Costumes for the orishas are very elaborate in both the Brazilian and the Cuban tradition. In the Cuban initiation the novice must have seven new white outfits consisting of a full petticoat, an overskirt, and a lace blouse. During the party for the new initiate on the third day, he or she wears a very elaborate costume in the colors of the orisha to whom the initiate is dedicated. These clothes are usually in nineteenth-century colonial style, with long full skirts, puffed sleeves, and tight waists for the women; the men wear tunics with loose pants. The preferred fabric is heavy satin; the costumes are decorated with sequins, lace, and appliqués and are often heavily and beautifully beaded. In Brazil the preferred decoration is lace, as lace making is a skill that remains fairly common, although the process is increasingly expensive, as are the fabrics. Clothing design in Brazil, as described above, is an intriguing combination of the colonial with the African: colonial skirts and blouses are worn below an African pano da costa, which is tied on top. In both traditions the legs are covered for modesty.

The orishas have Catholic saints to which they correspond as well. Changó, for example, corresponds to Saint Barbara in most areas. Other correspondences are not uniform and vary regionally, even within the same country. The linking of orishas to saints occurred from the entry of the orisha religion into the diaspora. Most slave-receiving areas were Catholic, and slaves were required to embrace the faith of their masters. Since Catholicism already had an established group of saints, it was easy for slaves to view the saints as manifestations of their orishas and worship them in this guise. The orishas, therefore, are also known from colonial times as the saints *(los santos* or *os santos).* This subterfuge has caused the religion in all areas, particularly Trinidad, often to be described in academic discourse as "syncretic," that is, a melding of two traditions (*see* Colonial Latin America and the Caribbean).

The more research scholars do, however, the clearer it becomes that the two traditions are not melded at all but are kept very strictly apart. For example, in Ocha homes there may be an altar to the Catholic saints and family ancestors on which are placed glasses of water, crucifixes, images of saints and pictures of deceased relatives, candles, and flowers. In another space, on the floor, there may be a shrine to the *egun,* the ancestral African dead. For the egun there may be candles, servings of food, coffee, rum, and cigars. But the two shrines are never under any circumstances combined. Also, at *missas,* or seances in which non-orisha spirits are contacted, all manifestations of the orisha religion, such as the elekes, are removed.

In Brazil Candomblé ceremonies have no Catholic saints represented whatsoever, although one might see an image or a lithograph of a saint corresponding to the orisha who rules the house. Special Catholic masses figure in Candomblé and Ocha ritual festivity, but these are always held in separate spaces. Masses on the first Friday of every month are held at the Church of Nosso Senhor do Bomfim in Bahia in honor of Oxalá, who corresponds loosely to Jesus Christ. However, it is unclear that the mass is being said for Christ, since it is Oxalá who is mentioned in the homily, and fireworks are set off (a common means in Brazil to attract the attention of the orishas). In the ritual context, however, no Catholic processes or imagery appear.

Kathleen O'Connor

See Also

Rio de Janeiro, Brazil; Trinidad and Tobago; Exú; Ogum; Catholic Church in Latin America and the Caribbean; Oxalá; Oxum; Xangô.

Orixás/Orishas. Please see Orishas

Africa

Oromo, an ethnic group of Ethiopia and Kenya.

The Oromo, sometimes known as the Galla (a term they find insulting), speak a language that belongs to the Eastern Cushitic family of Afro-Asiatic languages, similar to Somali. They occupy an area that extends from the southern highlands of Ethiopia in the north, to the Ogaden and Somalia in the east, to the Sudan border in the west, and across the Kenyan border to the Tana River in the south. Although they are the largest single ethnic group in Ethiopia, their division along regional and religious lines has historically prevented them from uniting to block Amhara domination in Ethiopia.

The Oromo originated in present-day southern Ethiopia. During the sixteenth century c.e. the then almost exclusively pastoralist Oromo began to expand northward into the Ethiopian highlands. After their migration to the relatively lush highlands, home to the agricultural Amhara and Tigre people, many of the northern Oromo adopted agriculture. The main crops grown by the Oromo are teff, wheat, and barley.

The Oromo migration fostered regional differences that contributed to the development of 16 subgroups. While the northern Oromo practice agriculture, the southern Oromo groups, including those in Kenya, generally practice pastoralism.

More than half of the Oromo are Sunni Muslims, while some practice Christianity. Other Oromo still practice the traditional Oromo religion. Members of the Boran subgroup follow the prototypical traditional Cushitic religion. The Boran worship and offer sacrifices to Waqa, who created and sustains life. Priests called *qaallu* belong to a sacred lineage among the Boran and represent Waqa on earth.

During the twentieth century the Oromo subgroups began to unite behind a nationalist movement to resist Amhara dominance in Ethiopia, and many Oromo define themselves not as Ethiopians but as Oromo. After the overthrow of the regime of Emperor Haile Selassie I in 1974, the new Marxist government, led by Haile Mariam Mengistu, gave the Oromo more political prominence.

In 1991 a coalition led by the mostly Tigrean Ethiopian People's Revolutionary Democratic Front, which included organizations representing other ethnic groups, including the Oromo People's Democratic Organization, overthrew the Mengistu regime. However, the Oromo comprise a number of factions. Groups such as the United Oromo People's Liberation Front and the Oromo Liberation Front have sought either independence from Ethiopia or the imposition of Islamic law in Ethiopia.

Robert Fay

See Also

Languages, African: An Overview.

Africa

Oron (also known as Oro), ethnic group of Nigeria.

The Oron primarily inhabit Cross River State in southeastern Nigeria. They speak a Niger-Congo language and are closely related to the Ibibio people. More than 100,000 people consider themselves Oron.

See Also

Languages, African: An Overview.

Latin America and the Caribbean

Ortiz, Adalberto (b. 1914, Ecuador), light-skinned Afro-Ecuadorian writer, painter, poet, teacher, and diplomat. Along with Manuel Zapata Olivella and Quince Duncan, he is one of the most recognized Afro-Spanish American writers.

When Adalberto Ortiz was three months old, his mother and grandmother abruptly left Esmeraldas with him for Guayaquil to escape from the civil war, *La Guerra de Concha,* or the "revolt of the Esmeraldian colonel Carlos Concha" against the national government in Quito. His father stayed in Esmeraldas. After the escape his mother joined a convent, and Ortiz grew up with his maternal grandmother. He discovered his father in Esmeraldas when he was 11 years old. Due to family financial constraints he had to work at a young age. An assiduous reader, he soon developed a taste for literature. In 1928 he obtained a scholarship to study in the Colegio Normal Juan Montalvo in Quito, which was one of the most exclusive schools in the country. He spent most of his academic holidays in Esmeraldas. He obtained his diploma as a schoolteacher in 1937.

During a boat trip from Guayaquil to Esmeraldas in 1937, Ortiz had the opportunity to read Emilio Ballagas's *Antología de poesía Negra* (Anthology of Black Poetry). The reading of that text marked, in his own words, the awakening of his interest in writing negrista poetry – a genre that tries to "convey the rhythm and musicality" of black speech – which he did while teaching in various schools in Esmeraldas. Ortiz was greatly influenced by and participated actively in the Grupo de Guayaquil or Generación del 30 (Group of Guayaquil or Generation of the 1930s), which was a group of innovative writers residing in Guayaquil who had a great impact on modern Ecuadorian literature.

In 1939 Ortiz moved back to Guayaquil, taught in a correctional school, and wrote his first novel, which is also his most famous: *Juyungo: Historia de un negro, una isla y otros negros* (translated as *Juyungo: A Classic Afro-Hispanic Novel* by Jonathan Tittler and Susan Hill, Washington D.C.: Three Continents Press, 1982). After many difficulties with Ecuadorian publishing companies, the first edition came out in Mexico in 1943.

From 1944 on, with the inauguration of the first government of José María Velasco Ibarra, Ortiz pursued a diplomatic career. He was first sent to Mexico for more than three years as the secretary of the Ecuadorian embassy there. While in Mexico he published *Tierra, son y tambor* (1944) and *Camino y puerto de la angustia* (1945), two collections of poems. His diplomatic career also took him to Panama, Paraguay, and Argentina.

Ortiz has published to date nine tales or novels and eight collections of poems. *Juyungo* has been reedited numerous times in Spanish since 1943, and it has been translated into French, German, Russian, Croat, and English. The central themes Ortiz addresses in his work are those of black, Indian, and white interracial relations and processes of identity formation. While *Juyungo* expresses some Marxist views, over time Ortiz became less and less preoccupied with political engagement. In *El espejo y la ventana* (1967), he portrays the decadence of an Ecuadorian mulatto (of African and European descent) family that immigrated to the coastal city of Guayaquil. In this work he explores the psychological dimensions of racial identity in an Ecuadorian social context. More recent publications include *La envoltura del sueño* (1982), *Niebla encendida* (1984), and *Poemas de Adalberto Ortiz* (1985). In 1995 he received a literary prize, Premio Eugenio Espejo.

For more than 30 years Ortiz has also been a renowned painter, exhibiting his work numerous times in Guayaquil and Quito.

Jean Muteba Rahier

See Also

Literature, Black, in Spanish America; Negrista Poets.

Latin America and the Caribbean

Ortiz, Fernando (b. July 16, 1881, Havana, Cuba; d. April 10, 1969, Havana, Cuba), Cuban scholar, scientist, sociologist, musicologist, writer, linguist, ethnologist, social psychologist, journalist, anthropologist, legal expert, and criminologist.

Fernando Ortiz's intellectual legacy is one of astonishing breadth and erudition. Cuban scholar Juan Marinello has likened him to a third discoverer of Cuba, after Columbus and Humboldt. A Cuban-American critic has called him "Mr. Cuba." The claim is no exaggeration: he is one of a great line of Caribbean intellectual figures such as Eugenio María de Hostos, José Martí, Pedro Henríquez Ureña, Frantz Fanon, and C. L. R. James.

Along with the work of Lydia Cabrera, Ortiz's seminal works deal with the African traditions that have uniquely shaped the identity of Cuban music, religion, society, and culture. His major theoretical contribution is the concept of *transculturation,* a term used to describe the rich, textured, and sometimes bloody encounter between two or more cultures that mutually transforms them. It provides a refined framework for understanding the complexity and diversity of Caribbean culture, history, and identity.

While a meticulous social scientist, Ortiz created work that was unique in its creativity, expressiveness, and freedom of form. He wrote ingeniously about different themes, using a *contrapunteo,* or contrapuntal method, that allowed for solid research with immense literary flair. Ortiz created a discourse that blurred the boundaries among essay, history, and narrative.

Born of a Spanish father and Cuban mother, Ortiz spent most of his youth in Menorca (1882-1895), then returned to the island to study law at the University of Havana. He eventually obtained a degree in law from the University of Barcelona (1900) and a doctorate in law one year later from the University of Madrid.

In Madrid he began his first criminological investigations, observing prisoners in jail using the positivist scientific theories of Cesare Lombroso and Enrico Ferri. This marked the beginning of Ortiz's interest in the social behavior of both individuals and groups, a lifelong pursuit that over time shifted from a more narrow scientific to a historical-humanistic methodology.

Ortiz held a wide variety of professional positions over the years. In 1902 he worked in the Cuban consulate in Italy, where he met Lombroso and Ferri as well as Marxist sociologist Alfonso Asturaro. From 1906 to 1908 Ortiz was a lawyer for the district court of Havana, and from 1908 to 1917 he was a professor in the School of Public Law at the University of Havana.

During this period he wrote and edited a prolific body of work, often engaged with his political life. Beginning in 1910, along with Ramiro Guerra, Ortiz codirected (and later directed) the magazine *Revista Bimestre Cubana,* until it ceased publication in 1959. By 1915 he had joined the Liberal Party, and in 1917 he became the party's representative in the Chamber of Deputies. Five years later, disgusted with the corruption and political chaos of the country, he retired from the chamber but kept active politically. In 1924 he founded the Sociedad de Folklore Cubano, as well as the magazine *Archivos de Folklore Cubano* (1924-1929). By this time the Machado dictatorship (1925-1933) was in power. Ortiz, who fervently opposed the regime, spent from 1931 to 1933 in Washington, D.C., involved in the anti-Machado struggle, returning to the island after the dictator fled. In 1936 Ortiz founded the Institución Hispanoamericana de Cultura and edited its magazine, *Ultra* (1936-1947). A year later he founded the Sociedad de Estudios Afrocubanos, which also published a journal, *Estudios Afrocubanos* (1937-1940 and 1945-1946). Ortiz was also active during the 1940s in organizing intellectuals against fascism.

In 1942 he inaugurated an ethnographic seminar at the University of Havana and continued publishing as well as lecturing widely, penning four books in that period. In the 1950s Ortiz published eight books totaling more than 3500 pages, almost all related to the themes of Afro-Cuban music and culture; he continued to lecture internationally and was awarded honorary doctorates from many prestigious universities.

In 1961 he was designated a member of the National Commission of the Cuban Academy of Sciences and during the 1960s continued working on the third volume (*Los negros curros*) of his trilogy *Hampa afrocubana*, which remained unfinished at the time of his death.

Ortiz was influenced by positivism in the beginning of his career; he was concerned with the terrible problems that beset Cuba: poverty, unemployment, racism, crime, political corruption, and fragmentation. His intellectual formation was within a largely white and Hispanophile cultural elite, which had little interest in or appreciation of the black population of the island and was deeply influenced by the legal and criminological studies of the time.

Ortiz's first book, *Los negros brujos* (1906), revealed a certain Eurocentric and white bias as he saw blacks as "outside" of societal norms. And yet Ortiz admitted that without blacks there would be no Cuba, in the truest sense of the word. Speaking of the book some 40 years after its publication, Ortiz said it was motivated by the absolute lack of sociological research on blacks in Cuba. It was also the first major book published on the island to use the term *Afro-Cuban*. Ortiz's discourse on identity began a major shift in white Cuban discourse on identity and race. Furthermore, the book, as well as his subsequent research, dispelled the notion of a monolithic black culture in Cuba. While the YORUBA influence is perhaps the strongest, there are Abakuá, Arará, Carabalí, Congo, WOLOF, and Bantu influences that are by no means insignificant.

Aside from some legal writings, research on the indigenous roots of Cuban culture, and a long historical tome on the seventeenth century, the bulk of Ortiz's writing focused on Cuba's African traditions. His research delved into linguistics (*Glosario de afronegrismos*), economics (*Contrapunteo cubano del tabaco y el azúcar*), racism (*El engaño de las razas*), history (*Los negros esclavos*), music (*Africanía de la música folklórica de Cuba*), and dance and theater (*Los bailes y el teatro de los negros en el folklore de Cuba*), as well as other fields of study. His best-known work is *Contrapunteo cubano del tabaco y azúcar* (1940; Cuban Counterpoint: Tobacco and Sugar, 1947, 1995), in which he elaborates the concept of transculturation, his most influential contribution (*see* TRANSCULTURATION, MESTIZAJE, AND THE COSMIC RACE: AN INTERPRETATION). Ortiz's work was a constant reminder to whites in Cuba that the contribution of Afro-Cubans was not merely limited to the provision of cheap labor in a plantation economy but was essential to Cuba's identity in its patterns of socialization, cuisine, language, productivity, worship, and play.

But Ortiz's legacy is more than one of the devoted scholar doing meticulous research. He lectured widely, wrote about current affairs, and was very active in the fight to combat racism in Cuba. He belonged to a generation of reformist intellectuals that could be highly critical of Cuban society, including Carlos Loveira, Miguel de Carrión, Ramiro Guerra, and Medardo Vitier. The next generation would include such revolutionaries as Ruben Martínez Villena, Julio Antonio Mella, Juan Marinello, and Nicolás Guillén, all of whom had close relations with Ortiz.

Ortiz's work has also illuminated complex issues of contemporary Caribbean culture in the work of scholars such as STUART HALL, EDOUARD GLISSANT, and Antonio Benítez-Rojo. In addition, his influence has reached beyond a geographical sphere to inflect the work of Latino writers in the United States such as Guillermo Gómez-Peña, Juan Flores, and Gloria Anzaldúa, who struggle with the issues of borders, cultures, and migration.

Alan West

SEE ALSO
Congo, Republic of the; Afrocubanismo; James, Cyril Lionel Richard; Washington, D.C.; Abakuás; Music, Afro-Caribbean Secular; Race in Latin America; Religions, African, in Latin America and the Caribbean; Afro-Latin America, Research on.

Africa

Orungu, ethnic group and historical kingdom of GABON.

The Orungu developed a prosperous kingdom in the eighteenth century during the height of the TRANSATLANTIC SLAVE TRADE in the region. Scholars debate the exact origin of the Orungu, though most agree that they came from the south, probably as an offshoot of the Eshira, and migrated into the Ogooué River delta in the early seventeenth century.

Like the MPONGWE, the Orungu speak a Myènè language: both groups say *"myènè,"* or "I say that," to initiate conversation. The Orungu also share a number of cultural practices with the Mpongwe, including iron working and boatbuilding. In the seventeenth century, in an attempt to dominate trade with Europeans, the Orungu drove many of the Mpongwe clans toward the Gabon Estuary. By 1700 they succeeded in gaining direct access to European traders. The Orungu clans at Cape Lopez organized a kingdom sustained by its control of trade through the mouth of the Ogooué River. There were approximately 20 Orungu clans; one of them held the line of succession to the kingship, and another exercised control over maritime commerce in such goods as ivory, beeswax, dyewood, copal, and ebony.

By the 1760s the Orungu were trading slaves. The Orungu monarchs grew rich and increasingly powerful through their taxation of the slave trade on the Nazareth and San Mexias rivers. In 1853 the Orungu monarchy under King Ombango-Rogombe agreed to abandon the slave trade, but in fact the Orungu moved their operations to more protected points upriver in an attempt to continue the trade clandestinely. This attempt failed, but most Orungu proved unwilling to return to the farming and fishing ways of their ancestors. The king had become dependent on the slave trade and was unable to maintain the tradition of royal patronage as the trade declined, and the kingdom disintegrated. In 1873 King Ntchengué signed a treaty granting the French a post on Orungu territory. Due to their hostility toward European missionaries in the 1800s, few Orungu obtained a western education. This limited their influence in the colonial administration or postcolonial politics. Today the Orungu are one of Gabon's smaller ethnic groups, numbering around 10,000 people.

Eric Young

SEE ALSO
Ivory Trade; Languages, African: An Overview; Iron in Africa; Christianity: Missionaries in Africa.

North America

Ory, Edward ("Kid") (b. 1889, St. John Baptist Parish, La.; d. January 23, 1973, Hawaii), African American musician, jazz trombonist, and band leader; pioneer of New Orleans-style jazz.

Born on a farm near New Orleans, Edward "Kid" Ory arrived on the music scene of New Orleans in 1917. Joining up with cornetist Joe "King" Oliver and clarinetist Johnny Dodds, he led several prominent bands in New Orleans. He carried the tradition of New Orleans-style JAZZ to California in 1919, leading Kid Ory's Brownskinned Babies and Kid Ory's Original Creole Jazz Band in the Los Angeles and San Francisco Bay Area.

Ory's Sunshine Orchestra recorded such hits as "Ory's Creole Trombone" and "Society Blues" in June 1922. With these recordings, Ory's band became the first African American group to make all-instrumental jazz records. Ory moved to Chicago in 1925, where he participated in some of the most significant sound recordings of the period, alongside Louis Armstrong in "Muskrat Ramble" (1926), with "Jelly Roll" Morton in "Doctor Jazz" (1926), and with King Oliver in "Every Tub" (1927).

Ory's style was distinctive: expressive and highly rhythmic, incorporating glissando runs of the early tailgate trombone style. With his recorded compositions, including "Muskrat Ramble," he left the sounds of New Orleans-style jazz as his legacy to music history. In 1930 Ory left the music scene for ten years, returning to California to work on a poultry farm and in a railroad office. He regained some prominence when he performed on an Orson Welles radio broadcast in 1944. He toured until 1966, when he retired to Hawaii.

Marian Aguiar

SEE ALSO
Armstrong, Louis ("Satchmo"); Chicago, Illinois; Los Angeles, California; Morton, Ferdinand Joseph ("Jelly Roll"); New Orleans, Louisiana; Oliver, Joseph ("King"); San Francisco and Oakland, California.

Africa

Osei Tutu (b. 1650?, present-day Ghana; d. 1717, Pra River, present-day Ghana), founder and first king of the ASANTE nation.

Following a model established by the earlier AKAN military states, Denkyira and Akwamu, Osei Tutu forged Asante into a powerful state that dominated most of present-day GHANA, except the coast, for 200 years. Tripling the area under Asante control, Osei Tutu gained the Asante access to (but not control of) the ocean, where they could trade directly with the Europeans to exchange slaves and gold for guns.

According to legend Osei Tutu was named after the shrine of Otutu, where his mother had prayed for a child. Obiri Yeboa, ruler of Kwaman (an Asante chiefdom) and Osei Tutu's uncle, sent the young man as his heir for training at the court of Denkyira, the state that then ruled over the Asante. A love affair with the Denkyira king's sister forced Osei Tutu to flee to Akwamu, a neighboring state to the east. There he met Okomfo Anokye, an Akwamu priest who became his lifelong friend and adviser. After observing the political institutions of the powerful kingdoms of Denkyira and Akwamu, Osei Tutu determined to unite the Asante into a single state. Succeeding his uncle, he ascended to the stool of Kwaman around 1670 and combined the various Asante chiefdoms into a military alliance under his leadership, though the other chiefs retained rights and privileges. From 1698 to 1701 Asante crushed Denkyira. In 1701 Asante won sovereignty over Elmina Castle, a Dutch trading post, which paid tribute to Asante and offered the nation access to the lucrative slave trade.

To unify the new nation, Osei Tutu and Anokye created a state structure that endured for 200 years. They made Kwaman, renamed Kumasi, the kingdom's capital. They borrowed the Denkyira concept of a sacred stool for the monarch: according to legend the Asante Golden Stool descended from heaven onto Osei Tutu's knees. The stool became a revered symbol of Asante nationhood. In addition, Osei Tutu established the Odwira (yam) Festival, in which the bones of enemies were displayed and Asante solidarity celebrated. He also created a bureaucracy to administer the newly conquered vassal states. Osei Tutu died in 1717 during a battle on the Pra River in which Akyem Kotoku defeated Asante.

David P. Johnson, Jr.

SEE ALSO

Gold Trade; Kumasi, Ghana; Transatlantic Slave Trade; Yams.

Latin America and the Caribbean

Ossie, Count (Oswald Williams) (b. 1928, St. Thomas Parish, Jamaica; d. October 18, 1976, Kingston, Jamaica), Jamaican drummer and composer; leader of the Mystic Revelation of Rastafari band, best known for recordings combining Afro-Jamaican musical ritual rhythms.

Count Ossie, whose given name was Oswald Williams, was drawn to hand drumming accompanied by chanting as a young child. Since his impoverished family could not afford to buy him a drum, Ossie did his first drumming on discarded tin cans. Through informal contacts with Rastafarian drummers, Count Ossie began to gain enough proficiency on his instrument to start his own drumming band, the Count Ossie Group, in the 1950s. He would have been one of many obscure drummers using a "Back to Africa" concept if not for a historic collaboration with singer/producer Prince Buster (Cecil Bustamante). The result was "Oh Carolina," the first Jamaican recording to combine Rastafarian ritual music SKA, and REGGAE. Count Ossie's drum rhythms undergirding this pop music hit on several continents greatly influenced the evolution of ska and reggae, inspiring scores of musicians to incorporate these African-tinged sounds. Jam sessions organized by Count Ossie attracted major Jamaican pop and jazz musicians. Two recordings by Count Ossie and his Mystic Revelation of Rastafari band in the 1970s, *Grounation* and *Tales of Mozambique*, combine chanting, storytelling, spoken poetry, jazz sax improvisations, and ritual drumming, telling tales to catalyze Afrocentric consciousness. After successfully touring the United States, Count Ossie died in a tragic accident at the National Arena, Kingston, at age 48.

Norman Weinstein

SEE ALSO

Jamaica; Kingston, Jamaica; Rastafarians.

Africa

Ostrich, common name for a large, flightless bird formerly found in the MIDDLE EAST but now found in fragmented populations in east, west, and south Africa.

The ostrich makes up the family Struthionidae and the order Struthioniformes, classified as *Struthio camelus.* Ostriches are the largest and strongest of living birds, attaining a height from crown to foot of about 2.4 m (about 8 ft) and a weight of up to 136 kg (300 lb). Male ostriches are black, with white wings and tail. The white feathers of the male, which are large and soft, are the ostrich plumes of commercial value. The female is a dull grayish brown.

Ostriches can run up to 65 km/h (about 40 mph). The males are polygamous and travel about in hot, sandy areas with three or four females, or in groups of four or five males accompanied by mates and young. The females lay their yellowish white eggs together in a single large depression in the sand. The eggs weigh about 1.4 kg (about 3 lb) each and have a volume of about 1.4 liters (about 3 pints). The male sits on them at night, and the female incubates them by day.

Ostrich feathers have been exported from Africa for many centuries. Medieval caravan traders carried them across the SAHARA DESERT to sell in Europe, where knights wore the plumes in their helmets. In the nineteenth century ostrich feathers adorned women's hats and dresses. Ostriches were bred and raised for their plumes in SOUTH AFRICA, ALGERIA, Australia, FRANCE, and the United States, but as styles changed after World War I and demand dropped, ostrich farms almost disappeared. In recent years, however, there has been renewed interest in ostrich farming.

Robert Fay

Africa

Ouagadougou, Burkina Faso, the capital and largest city of BURKINA FASO, with a population of approximately 750,000.

The MOSSI people founded Ouagadougou in the early fourteenth century, at a time when Mossi warriors were expanding their control over the savanna region south of the NIGER RIVER. Located on a plateau irrigated by tributaries of the White Volta River, the site was suitable for agriculture. It would become an important market for caravans moving between the forests and the Sahara. According to Mossi oral history, the settlement was originally called Woge Zabra Soba Koumbemb' tenga, or "Honored Chief Zabra Soba's Village," but MANDE traders altered the name, using *Ouaga* for Woge, and *dougou*, their word for village.

By the sixteenth century Ouagadougou had become the capital of the most powerful of the Mossi states and home of the Mossi king whose title, the Mogho Naaba, meant "king of the world." Nineteenth-century European explorers were unimpressed by Ouagadougou's mud-brick, thatched-roof architecture. In 1888 Captain Louis Binger wrote, "I did not have to wait long to find out the true state of affairs.... What was acknowledged as a palace and seraglio was nothing but a group of miserable huts surrounded by heaps of filth.... "

As European powers raced to colonize Africa in the late nineteenth century, France made claims on the Mossi region. The Mogho Naaba Wobogo, however, refused French offers to make his kingdom a protectorate, so French troops took the city by force on September 5, 1896. When Ouagadougou's residents resisted, the French set the town afire. Wobogo fled, and the French later appointed his brother, Sighiri, as the new Mogho Naaba.

The French built a garrison for African soldiers at Ouagadougou, which was originally part of the larger French colony of Haut-Sénégal-Niger. Roman Catholic missionaries arrived soon afterward. By 1904 the town's population had swelled to 8000, only 12 of whom were European. Unlike coastal cities such as Dakar or Abidjan, the arid and remote town of Ouagadougou attracted few European settlers. But during World War I the population skyrocketed to nearly 20,000. In 1919 the French declared Upper Volta a separate colony and made Ouagadougou its capital. Using some 2000 Mossi laborers recruited by the Mogho Naaba, the French built a capital with wide, tree-lined streets, and they drained swamps to create a fresh water supply.

Upper Volta was dissolved and administered from the Côte d'Ivoire in 1932. No longer a colonial capital, Ouagadougou's economy languished, and its population declined. At the end of World War II, however, Mossi chiefs successfully lobbied to have France reconstitute Upper Volta as a separate colony, and Ouagadougou once again became its capital. In 1955 the rail line from the port city of Abidjan, Côte d'Ivoire, reached Ouagadougou, further reducing the city's isolation.

Ouagadougou remained the capital when Upper Volta (present-day Burkina Faso) won independence in 1960. Over the next three decades the city was the site of frequent labor unrest and several coups d'état. Despite the instability Ouagadougou grew rapidly, attracting migrants from the countryside as well as from the neighboring countries. The city now has an international airport, a university, and a two-story central market; major industries include textiles, a brewery, and several agricultural product processing plants. Every other year the city hosts the famous African film festival, FESPACO. The Mogho Naaba, now only a ceremonial king, still lives in Ouagadougou. The weekly reenactment of the Mossi empire's founding, staged outside the Mogho Naaba's palace, is a popular tourist attraction.

David P. Johnson, Jr.

See Also

Cinema, African; Dakar, Senegal; Explorers in Africa Since 1800; Scramble for Africa; Sahara Desert; Tourism in Africa; Christianity: Missionaries in Africa.

Africa

Oubangui-Chari. Former name of Central African Republic.

Africa

Ouédraogo, Idrissa (b. 1954, Banfora, Upper Volta [present-day Burkina Faso]), Burkinabé film director.

Idrissa Ouédraogo is widely considered one of the leading members of a new generation of African filmmakers. The son of a civil servant, Ouédraogo studied English at the University of Ouagadougou in the capital city of Burkina Faso. But forays into playwriting soon piqued his interest in film, and he enrolled in the Institut Africain d'Éducation Cinématographique de Ouagadougou, Burkina Faso's film institute. He later studied film at the Gorki Institute in Russia and at the Institut des Hautes Études Cinématographiques (IDHEC) in Paris. He graduated from the IDHEC in 1985 but remained in France to pursue a Ph.D. under the direction of anthropologist Jean Rouche.

As a film director Ouédraogo has produced a number of widely acclaimed films. He is one of the most technically accomplished film directors in Africa. His first film to receive international attention was *Yam Daabo*, which opened at the 1986 Cannes Film Festival in France. Other internationally recognized films by Ouédraogo include *Zan Boko* (1988), *Yaaba* (1989), *Tilai* (1990), *Samba Traoré* (1992), *Afrique mon Afrique* (1994), and *Kini and Adams* (1997). The latter film – his first in English – was the opening feature at the 1997 Festival Panafricain du Cinéma (FESPACO) in Ougadougou.

Ouédraogo's fluid style and skillful film technique have prompted critics to compare him to the French film director Jean Renoir. Ouédraogo's films have also won praise for their sensitive portrayals and astute criticisms of Burkinabé society. Although many of his films take place in rural Mossi villages, *Zan Boko* examines life in Ouagadougou, and *Kini and Adams* is shot in an industrializing region of southern Africa.

Elizabeth Heath

See Also

Cinema, African; Ouagadougou, Burkina Faso.

Africa

Ousmane, Mahamane (b. 1950), president of the Republic of Niger from 1993 to 1996.

A statistician and economist by training, Mahamane Ousmane was not involved in politics until he founded the Convention Démocratique et Sociale-Rhama (CDS) in Zinder, Niger. With the support of the town's wealthy Hausa merchants he was able to organize a coalition of opposition parties, the Alliance des Forces du Changement (AFC), and defeat the ruling Mouvement National de la Société de Développement (MNSD) in 1993 presidential elections.

As president, Ousmane's lack of political finesse and charisma eventually alienated many of his allies. He also faced a number of problems familiar to his predecessors – state bankruptcy, unrest among the Tuareg, labor protests, and severe droughts. In order to obtain vital funding from international donors, Ousmane was forced to enact structural adjustment austerity measures, which only increased popular discontent. Although his government both helped stabilize the economy and signed a peace treaty with Tuareg rebels, opposition to Ousmane's leadership mounted. In the 1995 parliamentary elections opposition candidates won a majority in the General Assembly and political rival Hama Amadou was elected prime minister. Fighting between the two leaders grew so fierce that government activities came to a virtual standstill and Ousmane contemplated dissolving the assembly and unconstitutionally nominating a new prime minister. The threat of this action, coupled with the decline in world prices for uranium, Niger's major export, prompted Lt. Col. Ibrahim Bare Mainassara to overthrow the government in a military coup on January 27, 1996.

Elizabeth Heath

See Also

Drought and Desertification; Zinder, Niger; Structural Adjustment in Africa.

Africa

Ousmane Sembène (b. 1923, Cassamance region, Senegal), Senegalese novelist and film director; considered one of Africa's leading film directors.

Ousmane Sembène is a pioneer and foundational figure in the history of cinema in Africa. During a career that has spanned 30 years, Ousmane Sembène has revolutionized African film through changes in film subject and cinematic language. His film style has influenced numerous film directors and has set standards for the premier organization of African film directors – La Fédération Panafricaine des Cinéastes (FEPACI).

Born in 1923 in the Cassamance region of Senegal, Ousmane Sembène received only three years of formal education. He was dismissed from primary school after he struck the headmaster. In 1942 he enlisted in the army and was sent to fight with French troops in World War II. Ousmane Sembène's experiences in Europe made him keenly aware of the inequalities of the colonial system, and he began to participate in anticolonial movements, such as the 1947 Dakar-Niger railroad strike, after returning to Senegal. In 1948 he moved to France, where he worked as a docker. While in France, Ousmane Sembène began to experiment with writing.

Ousmane Sembène's interest in writing first began when he realized that there was a lack of literature by African writers available in Europe. Through literature he hoped to correct some of the misperceptions that Europeans held about Africans. He published his first book, *Le Docker noir*, in 1956, and his second book, *O pays mon beau peuple*, a year later. After an injury Ousmane Sembène dedicated all of his attention to writing and returned to Africa to travel and write. During his travels Ousmane Sembène confronted the limited accessibility of literature caused by illiteracy and became interested in film. Believing that film had the potential to reach a wider audience, he enrolled in the Gorki Studio in Moscow in 1961. After he completed his training, he returned to Senegal and began work as a film director.

His first movies, *Barom Sarret* (1963) and *Niaye* (1964), were highly acclaimed by critics and received prizes at film festivals. In 1966 Ousmane Sembène finished the first feature-length film to be produced in sub-Saharan Africa – *La Noire de....* He soon established his own studio and devised a balance between writing and directing his own films, and producing documentaries to provide funding for his films. While working on his early films, Ousmane Sembène also created a way to overcome distributional problems and a lack of theaters by initiating film tours that allowed him to travel to the villages in Senegal and show his movies. These techniques were lauded by FEPACI and were soon adopted by other African film directors.

The tours also helped him in his efforts to create an African cinematic language. He aspired to develop a filmic vocabulary that addressed the problems posed by multiple African languages and dialects. His developments toward an African cinematic language can be clearly seen in *Le Mandat* (1968) and *Xala* (1974). In *Le Mandat*, Ousmane Sembène attempts to integrate pictures, images, and gestures as a vital part of the story text. By supplementing the text in this way, Ousmane Sembène was able to communicate the overall plot of the movie even though he chose to have actors speak in Wolof, one of four major languages in Senegal. In *Xala*, Ousmane Sembène continued to supplement the narrative, this time with a series of symbols used in conjunction with each character to explicate the finer points of the narrative that might be lost between different languages. The filmic language developed in these films became the model for FEPACI film directors.

Since completing his landmark film, *Xala*, Ousmane Sembène has worked on larger films about historical events in Senegal. *Ceddo* (1977) examines the religious wars in Africa during the seventeenth and eighteenth centuries. His next film, *Camp de Thiaroye* (1987), explores the conditions that preceded the massacre of Senegalese infantrymen, veterans who had served in the French army in World War II, by the French army in Thiaroye. *Camp de Thiaroye* won the Jury Special Award at the Venice Film Festival in 1989.

In recent years Ousmane Sembène has concentrated on his newest, and to many film critics, his most ambitious film – *Guelwaar*. In *Guelwaar* Ousmane Sembène addresses the problem of food aid diversion by the government in postcolonial Africa, specifically in Senegal. He finished the film in 1994, but the Senegalese government has prevented Ousmane Sembène from releasing and showing *Guelwaar* in Senegal. The film has had only minor distribution and screening in other areas of the world.

Elizabeth Heath

See Also

Cinema, African.

Africa

Ovambo, the largest ethnic group of Namibia and southern Angola.

The Bantu-speaking Ovambo (or Owambo) migrated from Central Africa in the seventeenth century, settling in an area that today spans northern Namibia and southern Angola. Organized into eight matrilineal clans, the Ovambo lived in small villages where extended families raised cattle and cultivated millet, sorghum, and beans. The Ovambo are closely related to the Kavango and possibly to the Herero, as most share a belief in a supreme being, the Kalunga, and the tradition of a holy fire of ritual significance.

Highly productive farmland, the development of a flourishing metal-working industry, and participation in the long-distance caravan trade in salt, copper, and iron ore brought prosperity to the Ovambo. Over time the eight clans formed a loose federation of kingdoms, each with its own hereditary system of succession. Although European influence in Namibia grew during the 1800s, Ovamboland saw relatively few Europeans apart from the establishment of a Finnish mission. The region remained isolated during the brief era of German colonial rule, and in 1915, when South Africa occupied Namibia, Ovamboland became a self-governing "homeland."

During the 1930s Ovambo men began to migrate to work as contract laborers in the mines of southern Namibia and South Africa. Their experiences of unjust labor policies and racial discrimination helped build support for groups in the Namibian nationalist movement, particularly the Ovambo People's Organization, led by Andimba Toivo ja Toivo, which later became the South West Africa People's Organization, or SWAPO. At independence, Sam Nujoma, leader of SWAPO, became the president of Namibia, and the Ovambo have since come to dominate the national government. The Ovambo are the largest ethnic group in Namibia, numbering around 650,000, or approximately half the population. Many Ovambo men still earn their livelihoods as migrant mine laborers, and women continue to farm the land.

Eric Young

See Also

Bantu: Dispersion and Settlement; Iron in Africa; Nujoma, Samuel; Christianity: Missionaries in Africa; Salt Trade.

Africa

Ovimbundu, the largest ethnic group of Angola.

The Ovimbundu, "people of the mist," are the largest ethnolinguistic group in Angola, comprising approximately 40 percent of the national population. Although most of the 2 million Ovimbundu today speak umBundu, historically they separated themselves into regional-political subgroups, including the Bailundu, Bié, Dombe, Ganda, Huambo, Hanha, Caconda, Ciyaka, Sambu, and Sele. This was a result of migration patterns and the emergence of numerous kingdoms.

In the sixteenth and seventeenth centuries peoples migrating to the Benguela Plateau from the north and east settled in the fertile central highlands of Angola and forged a common Ovimbundu identity. After the introduction of maize as the staple crop in the seventeenth century, Ovimbundu women became the farmers while men engaged in hunting, trading, and raiding neighboring groups for cattle and women as slaves. By the late eighteenth century 22 centralized kingdoms had emerged among the Ovimbundu, dominated by the Bié, Bailundu, and Ciyaka. Many built forts in large granite and sandstone outcroppings scattered around the highlands. Although there was often a degree of popular democracy within the kingdoms, an Ovimbundu king played the role of lead hunter, senior diplomat, judge, diviner, and high priest of the warrior cult.

These kingdoms owed their wealth to commerce as well as to agriculture. They actively participated in the transatlantic slave trade and took advantage of Portuguese and Afro-Portuguese military expeditions between 1773 and 1775 to consolidate their power vis-à-vis their rivals. After slave trading was abolished, they became involved in the caravan trade in ivory and wild rubber between the interior African kingdoms – such as the Chokwe, Lozi, and Lunda – and the Portuguese settlements.

Although politically not united, many Ovimbundu resisted the Portuguese colonial policies of taxation, forced labor, and land acquisition. In 1902 the Bailundu fought the Portuguese in the so-called Bailundu War, but the Portuguese successfully suppressed the revolt and other forms of resistance. Meanwhile, new rail and road systems marginalized the Ovimbundu. As their role as caravan traders waned, their dependency on the colonial administration and the cash economy grew, and many Ovimbundu men migrated to jobs on northern coffee plantations. Ovimbundu kings, deprived of their primary sources of wealth and authority, became little more than symbolic leaders.

When nationalism swept Angola in the 1960s the Ovimbundu found a voice in the National Union for the Total Independence of Angola (UNITA) movement, which they have dominated ever since under the leadership of Jonas Savimbi. The movement operated from Huambo, the historical capital of the Bailundu. After Angolan independence in 1975, UNITA fought the government over its socialist policies and perceived ethnic discrimination within the Mbundu-dominated Angolan government. As part of the peace effort in the early 1990s, Ovimbundu politician Marcelino Moco was appointed prime minister, though he was sacked four years later after UNITA had renewed the war. After nearly two decades of war the highlands of the Ovimbundu remain a site of poverty and massive popular dislocation.

Eric Young

See Also

Ivory Trade; Nationalism in Africa; Savimbi, Jonas Malheiro; Slavery in Africa.

North America

Owen, Chandler (b. April 5, 1889, Warrenton, N.C.; d. 1967?, Chicago, Ill.), coeditor of the socialist magazine the *Messenger* and, later, Republican Party activist.

Graduating from Richmond's Virginia Union University in 1913, Chandler Owen left the South for New York City to become a fellow of the National Urban League (NUL). He studied at the New York School of Philanthropy and then at Columbia University. During this time he met another young migrant from the South, A. Philip Randolph. Randolph exerted a great influence over Owen, convincing him to sever ties with the NUL and, in 1916, join the Socialist Party.

The following year Owen and Randolph coedited the *Hotel Messenger*, a newsletter of a local hotel and restaurant employees' union. A few months into their tenure they criticized the union for overcharging its members for uniforms. Their reward was a swift dismissal, to which they responded by founding the *Messenger* in late 1917.

In the *Messenger*, Owen and Randolph praised the Russian Revolution, opposed World War I, advocated the more radical elements of unionization (as exemplified by the Industrial Workers of the World), and promoted the Socialist Party. Owen also played a large role in the magazine's effort to have Marcus Garvey, whose back-to-Africa views he opposed, deported to his native Jamaica.

By 1923, however, Owen had grown disenchanted with radical socialism. He left the *Messenger*, settled in Chicago, and became managing editor of the *Chicago Bee*, a black newspaper. Though he continued to advocate unionism – through the *Bee* he supported Randolph's efforts to organize the railroad porters – he became increasingly involved in Republican politics. He ran unsuccessfully as a Republican for a seat in the United States House of Representatives in 1928.

Owen then became involved in public relations. Before and during World War II he wrote about black anti-Semitism for the Anti-Defamation League of B'nai B'rith. Although he had reservations about the civil rights record of President Franklin D. Roosevelt, he set them aside and wrote on race relations for the U.S. War Department. The department distributed millions of copies of his pamphlet *Negroes and the War* (1942), in which he reminded blacks of the liberties they would lose if Hitler won. Owen also stressed the gains blacks had made under Roosevelt's New Deal programs.

During and after the war Owen continued to rise in the Republican Party. In his later years he was an important speechwriter and campaigner for several Republican politicians, including presidential candidates Wendell Wilkie, Robert Taft, and Dwight Eisenhower, as well as Illinois governor William Stratton and U.S. Senator Everett Dirksen.

See Also

World War I and African Americans; World War II and African Americans; Brotherhood of Sleeping Car Porters; Garvey, Marcus Mosiah; Labor Unions in the United States; *Messenger, The*; Randolph, Asa Philip; Socialism; New York, New York.

North America

Owens, James Cleveland ("Jesse") (b. September 12, 1913, Oakville, Ala.; d. March 31, 1980, Tucson, Ariz.), African American sprinter, winner of four gold medals in the 1936 Olympic Games, and in his time heralded as "the world's fastest human."

James Cleveland Owens was the tenth of 11 children of Henry and Emma Fitzgerald Owens, who worked as sharecroppers. As a child Jesse Owens was chronically ill, probably because of poor diet, substandard housing, and inadequate clothing. During several winters he contracted pneumonia, which he was forced to endure since his family lacked money for a doctor or medicine. In the early 1920s the Owens family left the South as part of the Great Migration and settled in Cleveland, Ohio, where Owens's father and three brothers found work in the steel mills. For the first time in his life Owens was able to attend school regularly.

In a racially integrated junior high school a white physical education teacher named Charles Riley noticed Owens's athletic ability and began coaching him in track and field. After Owens entered a vocational high school Riley continued to coach him. Owens's success was immediate: school records in the 220-yard and 100-yard sprints and the long jump fell to his smooth stride.

In 1932 he made an unsuccessful attempt to join the United States Olympic Team, but by 1933 his dominance of the sport was undeniable. At a high school meet in May 1933 he set a world record in the long jump with a leap of 7.41 m (24 ft 3¾in) – an improvement of more than 76.2 mm (3 in) on the old mark. A month later he helped his high school to a national track title with another world record in the long jump and a 9.4-second 100-yard dash, which tied the world record. Cleveland welcomed him home with a celebratory parade.

Owens was the first member of his family to graduate from high school. Although by most accounts his educational preparation was minimal, he was recruited aggressively by colleges around the country because of his athletic prowess. Despite the fact that he was urged by the black press to choose a less discriminatory school, Owens chose to stay near home. He entered Ohio State University in Columbus, where he was barred from living on the whites-only campus, and where he and other black athletes were forced to ride to meets in cars separate from their white teammates.

By the spring of 1934 Owens was on academic probation, which prompted his coach to set up public speaking engagements for him – perhaps to bolster his confidence, or perhaps in the belief that an African American could not be helped academically. Whatever the motivation, the chance to develop and display his charisma and charm was fortuitous; it was a strength he would rely on the rest of his professional life. In May 1935 Owens broke five world records at a single meet, earning him the title among sportswriters of "the world's fastest human."

The 1936 Olympic Games in Berlin were embroiled in controversy long before the athletes arrived. The Amateur Athletic Union (AAU) threatened a United States boycott to protest the treatment of German Jews under Adolf Hitler, and black journalists were inflamed by Nazi claims of Aryan racial superiority. The American Olympic Committee, however, overruled the AAU and sent athletes to the games. To many American blacks Owens symbolized a rebuttal to Nazi racism, and he became a symbol that gained all the more importance after German boxer Max Schmeling delivered a surprising defeat to black American Joe Louis in early 1936.

Owens delivered an outstanding Olympic performance. He won gold medals for the 100-meter and 200-meter sprints, the 400-meter relay, and the long jump, in which he set a record that lasted 25 years. When Hitler refused to invite Owens and other black victors to shake his hand (an invitation that had been extended to several German athletes), the press seized on the snub and the International Olympic Committee rebuked the German leader.

Owens was welcomed home to a series of triumphal parades, but before long he was again confronted with American racism – forced to enter through back doors and ride at the back of buses – and he found that no jobs were open to him. As he later told an interviewer, "I wasn't invited up to shake

TOP: Shown here at a 1937 track meet, Jesse Owens was one of the greatest athletes of all time, whose four gold medals at the 1936 Olympic Games stood as an unparalled accomplishment for nearly 50 years. *CORBIS/Bettmann*

ABOVE: ***Left to right***, Owens with Ralph Metcalfe, Foy Draper, and Frank Wykoff, his teammates on the gold-medal winning 400-meter relay team. German dictator Adolph Hitler left the stadium early to avoid having to congratulate the team. *CORBIS/Bettmann*

LEFT: Owens set a new world record with his 8m 6cm (26ft 5in) longjump at the 1936 Olympic Games. *CORBIS/Bettmann*

hands with Hitler, but I wasn't invited to the White House to shake hands with the president, either." He was initially given several offers for public appearances, but most opportunities dissolved or were bogus. Failing to graduate from Ohio State, Owens relied on low-income jobs and the few personal appearances he could muster for money – including carnival races against horses.

He started a laundry business that failed, then returned to Ohio State. After four semesters, however, his grades were no better than they had been in his first effort. He withdrew. By the 1940s Owens was able to rely on public speaking for his income; he eventually opened his own public relations firm. In his later years Owens abstained from the CIVIL RIGHTS MOVEMENT. His conservative response to the BLACK POWER salute of Tommie Smith and John Carlos at the 1968 Olympic Games in Mexico City won him derision as an "Uncle Tom" by young black activists, but others continued to admire him for his entrepreneurial achievements.

North America

Owens, Major (b. June 28, 1936, Collierville, Tenn.), Democratic member of the United States House of Representatives from New York (1983-).

Owens received a bachelor's degree from MOREHOUSE COLLEGE in 1956 and a master's degree in library science from Atlanta University in 1957. Before entering politics he worked in New York at the Brooklyn Public Library and as director of the Community Media Library Program at Columbia University. From the mid-1960s through the early 1970s Owens served in a number of community service posts, eventually leading up to a five-year stint as New York City community development commissioner. In 1974 Owens won a seat in the New York Senate. In 1982 he was elected to succeed SHIRLEY CHISHOLM as the U.S. representative from New York's Eleventh Congressional District.

The Eleventh District encompasses the central Brooklyn neighborhoods of Flatbush, Crown Heights, and Brownsville. The local population is mainly black, and voters are overwhelmingly Democratic. Owens won his reelection campaigns with ease every two years beginning in 1984. He received 92 percent of the vote in 1996.

In Congress Owens chaired the Education and Labor Committee's Subcommittee on Select Education and Civil Rights. His other committee assignments placed him on the Education and the Workforce Committee and the Government Reform and Oversight Committee. In the 105th Congress (1997-1999) he was the ranking member of the Workforce Protections Subcommittee of the Education and the Workforce Committee. He is also a member of the CONGRESSIONAL BLACK CAUCUS.

SEE ALSO
New York, New York.

Latin America and the Caribbean

Oxalá (known as Obatalá in CUBA and the United States; and in BRAZIL as Oxalá or by other avatars, such as the youthful Oxaguian and the elderly Oxalufon), is the white orisha, or YORUBA deity, meaning that everything around him must be pure white. He had a role in creating the world, but drank too much palm wine, became drunk, and began making deformed people. All those with deformities are sacred to Oxalá, and his initiates do not drink alcohol or wear dark-colored clothing (*see* ORISHAS; RELIGIONS, AFRICAN, IN LATIN AMERICA AND THE CARIBBEAN; SANTERÍA; and CANDOMBLÉ).

Latin America and the Caribbean

Oxóssi (known as Oxóssi in BRAZIL and as Ochosi in CUBA and United States), the hunter orisha, or YORUBA deity. His assistance is sought in connection with any trouble with the law or the police (*see* ORISHAS; RELIGIONS, AFRICAN, IN LATIN AMERICA AND THE CARIBBEAN; SANTERÍA; and CANDOMBLÉ).

Latin America and the Caribbean

Oxum (known as Oxum in BRAZIL and as Ochún or Oshún in CUBA and the United States), the riverine orisha, or YORUBA deity, of beauty, feminine ways, and reproduction. Women pray to Oxum when they want to bear children. She is vain and represents the spirit of happiness; she is fond of mirrors and perfume. The queen of sorceresses wears yellow and gold and is the favorite woman of XANGÔ as well as the youngest orisha (*see* ORISHAS; RELIGIONS, AFRICAN, IN LATIN AMERICA AND THE CARIBBEAN; SANTERÍA; and CANDOMBLÉ).

Latin America and the Caribbean

Oxumaré (also known as Oxunmaré; seen mostly in Brazil, rarely in CUBA and the United States), the orisha, or YORUBA deity of the rainbow, Oxumaré is represented with serpents. Oxumaré is a hardworking and patient orisha who assists those who want to be rich (*see* ORISHAS; RELIGIONS, AFRICAN, IN LATIN AMERICA AND THE CARIBBEAN; SANTERÍA; and CANDOMBLÉ).

Africa

Oyo, Early Kingdom of, precolonial West African state.

Oyo was the most powerful of the YORUBA states during the peak of its power between roughly 1650 and 1750 C.E. Its capital, the town of Oyo, was situated slightly to the north of present-day Oyo in NIGERIA. Legend has it that Oyo's first *alafin*, or ruler, was a son of Oduduwa, the mythical ancestor of the Yoruba people. In the sixteenth century Oyo began its ascent to power under the alafin Orompoto, who established a cavalry and maintained a trained army. During the first half of the eighteenth century Oyo subjugated the neighboring kingdom of Dahomey, but in 1818 Dahomey regained its independence from Oyo. Numerous internal disputes, war with Dahomey, and an invasion by the FULANI from the north contributed to the collapse of the empire soon afterward. In the mid-1830s the old town of Oyo was destroyed by a Fulani invasion, and the capital was subsequently relocated to its present site. In the treaty of 1888 after the Yoruba civil wars of the middle part of the century, Oyo, along with much of Yorubaland, was placed under British rule.

SEE ALSO
Dahomey, Early Kingdom of.

P

North America

Pace, Harry Hubert

(b. January 6, 1884, Covington, Ga.; d. July 26, 1943, Chicago, Ill.), music publisher and founder of the first African American recording company.

Harry Pace began his printing and business career in 1903, opening a company in Memphis with former teacher W. E. B. Du Bois. Together they produced *Moon Illustrated Weekly* (1905), the first illustrated African American journal. Pace met composer W. C. Handy in 1908, and they formed one of the most enduring African American music companies, Pace and Handy Music Co. (1909). Pace went on to establish Pace Phonograph Company, issuing records by such artists as Alberta Hunter and Ethel Waters under the label of Black Swan. With the bankruptcy of the company in 1923, Pace returned to insurance work, expanding Chicago's Supreme Liberty Life Insurance Co. into the largest black-owned business in the North.

Marian Aguiar

See Also

Black Swan Records; Du Bois, William Edward Burghardt (W. E. B.); Handy, William Christopher (W.C.).

Latin America and the Caribbean

Pacheco, Johnny

(b. March 25, 1935, Santiago de los Caballeros, Dominican Republic), Afro-Dominican bandleader, composer, singer, flutist, and percussionist who played an important role in creating New York salsa music during the 1960s and 1970s; an important Latin music record producer and cofounder of Fania Records.

Johnny Pacheco made his mark during the 1960s and 1970s as part of New York City's Latin music scene. Pacheco's father, Rafael Azarías Pacheco, was a prominent clarinetist and conductor of the Orquesta Santa Cecilia, a leading Dominican orchestra. In the late 1940s the family moved to New York City. Johnny Pacheco learned to play saxophone, flute, and percussion in high school. In 1959 Pacheco joined the pianist Charlie Palmieri (1927-1988) as the flutist in the newly formed group Charanga Duboney.

Charanga Duboney, featuring a Cuban-style charanga flute-and-violins front line, inspired an early 1960s charanga craze among Latino New Yorkers (*see* Afro-Latino Cultures in the United States). In September 1959 Pacheco left Palmieri to organize his own charanga. With the album *Pacheco y su Charanga* (1961) he introduced the *pachanga*, an energetic dance style that combined elements of the charanga and the chachachá.

During the mid-1960s when the pachanga fell out of favor with the Latin music audience, Pacheco turned to the Cuban *conjunto*, a traditional ensemble that featured a two-trumpet front line, as a new formula for success (*see* Son). His group, Pacheco y su Nuevo Tumbao, was a Cuban-style conjunto that featured pianist Eddie Palmieri (b. 1936), the younger brother of Charlie Palmieri. The band renewed interest in traditional Cuban music among New York City's Latino population, spearheading what became known as the *típico* movement. More than a musical style, típico reflected, as John Storm Roberts wrote, a "prevailing rhetoric of roots, purity, and a concept (related to the growth of Latino political awareness) of 'community music.'"

Over the years Pacheco continued to play traditional, Cuban-influenced music. At the same time he was instrumental in broadening the Cuban musical legacy. In part his success was a matter of historical timing. As a result of the successful revolution led by Fidel Castro and a United States embargo on trade with Cuba, there were few new musical influences coming from the island, allowing Pacheco and other Latino musicians in New York City to develop their own sound.

In 1964 Pacheco turned his attention from musical performance to the recording business. He established his own record company, Fania Records. In partnership with Gerald "Jerry" Masucci, he helped shape a Latin music style that Fania Records marketed as salsa music. At the outset the company's prospects were hardly promising. The only group signed to the label was Pacheco's own, and the two partners delivered their records to music stores out of their car trunks. Although the company started with little money and few resources, it quickly built a reputation for excellence among Latino listeners.

As Fania's musical director, Pacheco recorded many of the major talents in Latin music, including trombonist Willie Colón, percussionist Ray Barreto, singer/songwriter Rubén Blades, and vocalists Celia Cruz, Hector Lavoe, and Pete "El Conde" Rodriguez. For several years Pacheco led the Fania All Stars, before Willie Colón assumed the leadership. The Fania All Stars, with its irresistibly danceable, percussion-driven sound, epitomized salsa music. Blades, who sang with the Fania All Stars for six years before launching a solo career, brought an innovative social consciousness to his lyrics. Through the influence of Blades and other songwriters, salsa music came to reflect closely the realities of life in El Barrio, New York City's poor Latino community. During the 1970s the salsa sound gained a following throughout Latin America and with a broad range of non-Latino listeners as well.

New York Times music critic Peter Watrous noted that for more than a decade Fania Records was "extraordinarily consistent, comparable to Motown at its peak in popular music or the Blue Note label for jazz." Changing musical tastes brought hard times for the independent label, and Fania ceased operations in the 1980s. For some time Pacheco seemed to fall from sight as well. In 1992, however, the label was resurrected and reissued several albums under his leadership. Pacheco's legacy extends well beyond both his musical career and his entrepreneurial achievements. During the 1960s and 1970s his music and the albums that he produced for Fania Records expressed a growing pride in Latino identity and were an important counterpart of other contemporaneous forms of Latino empowerment.

James Clyde Sellman

See Also

New York, New York; Dance in Latin America and the Caribbean.

Latin America and the Caribbean

Pacific Coast of Colombia,

very humid forested lowland in the western portion of Colombia between the Andes and the Pacific Ocean where black culture is predominant. This region, which covers approximately 46,619,784 sq km (18,000 sq mi), is also one of the most biodiverse areas in the world. It is one of the rainiest places on earth, with a mean annual precipitation ranging from 2000 mm (79.4 in) to almost 13,000 mm (516 in). It is also one of the most isolated and poorest areas of Colombia.

The Pacific coast of Colombia has a relatively low population density and few major urban centers. According to the 1993 national census the region had fewer than 1 million inhabitants – about 3 percent of Colombia's population. Although there is no official estimate of its ethnic composition, more than 90 percent of the area's inhabitants are black and mulatto. Indians comprise about 5 percent and *mestizos* (people of Indian and European descent) a smaller percentage of the region's population. Approximately half the population lives in small towns and villages, and to a lesser extent in scattered dwellings along the rivers, the coast, and the four roads that connect the lowlands with the Andes. The other half inhabits the coast's three cities: Buenaventura, Quibdó, and Tumaco. Buenaventura is the largest of them, with about 200,000 inhabitants. Trade from the Panama Canal and coffee production hastened the growth of this port, through which most of Colombia's imports and exports pass. Quibdó is an inland city, located on the Atrato River. It is the capital of the department of Chocó, the only independent political entity that lies entirely in the lowlands. In the South three departments – Valle, Cauca, and Nariño – extend into the lowlands, but all have their capital cities (Cali, Popayán, and Pasto) in the Andes.

Prior to the arrival of the Spanish conquerors the area was inhabited by the Kuna and Embera peoples, among other indigenous groups. The conquest of this region was launched from the western Andean cities enclaves, among which Popayán was the most important, in an effort to seize the area's gold riches. Although military expeditions into the lowlands began in the sixteenth century, they took a long time to be successful. The mines in the area of the Telembí River, where the town of Barbacoas was the nucleus, first yielded a steady supply of gold shortly after the mid-seventeenth century. Only at the very end of that century was gold production consolidated in the upper Atrato and San Juan river drainages, the present Chocó, with Novitá and Citará (now Quibdó) as its major centers. The mining frontier expanded throughout the eighteenth century, forming small and provisional settlements. In this way small, valuable areas were brought under Spanish dominion while large territorial extensions were still uncontrolled by the Spanish Empire.

From the outset mining was carried out by slave labor. The fact that the Andean cities had developed a mining economy that had already begun to use African slaves favored the rapid spread of this form of labor. This subsequently fueled the slave trade, especially in the early eighteenth century, when this commerce reached its height in the viceroyalty of New Granada, now Colombia (*see* Colonial Latin America and the Caribbean). The example of the region that is now constituted by the department of Chocó illustrates this point: the number of slaves increased from 821 in 1717 to 4000 by 1738. Until 1770 the increase in the lowland black population was due primarily to purchases, which by that time were mostly black Creoles, or blacks born in the Americas. Slave women in this area represented a smaller proportion than men throughout the eighteenth century. Slaves were legally introduced through Cartagena and sold directly in the lowlands or in the market of Popayán. There was, however, an illegal trade that reached the region by the Atrato River and the Pacific Ocean, via Panama.

Mining labor was organized into slave gangs called *cuadrillas*, which comprised anywhere from 5 or 6 slaves to more than 100. At the head of each labor gang was a slave captain who mediated the relations between the other slaves and the administrator. He helped organize work, distribute food, and collect the produce. Some of the slaves engaged in agriculture near the mining camps. However, most of the supplies needed to feed the gangs were brought from the highland farms owned by the same people who owned the mines. That landed elite benefited from the colonial economy and enjoyed the wealth produced by black slave labor. Popayán, one of the most important colonial cities of what is now Colombia, achieved its splendor based on a system that treated black people as commodities.

Nevertheless, slaves were a special type of commodity; they had limited rights (*see* Black Codes in Latin America). They could work on Saturdays for themselves, either producing food or mining for gold, and on Sundays they were allowed to rest. With the gold they saved from the weekend some were able to buy their freedom. Once free, many continued to work to liberate their families. Data collected to document how the *libres* (freed slaves) from the Citará and Nóvita mining districts moved into the Baudó River valley indicate that the self-purchase process could have begun to gain momentum as early as 1720. In the south of Colombia, for instance, around the turn of the eighteenth century, more than 40 percent of the black population was free. By the mid-nineteenth century the slave-based colonial gold mining industry had lost its force and importance (*see* also Latin America, Blacks and Indians in: An Interpretation).

Throughout the eighteenth and nineteenth centuries free blacks looked for new places to live. Some stayed in the mining areas in the upper parts of the watersheds. Others went downstream and settled where the narrow alluvial terraces are wider and hence provide more space for agriculture. Plantain, corn, and sugar cane were among the most important crops, although the quantities produced – for subsistence or local markets – were small. Others went farther, to the coasts, both to the flat and marshy southern coastline and to the northern high and mountainous shore. Fishing and coconut groves provided a sustainable lifestyle by the sea. The libres' subsistence economy was complemented, in some localities and for certain periods of time, by the gathering of natural products to supply larger market networks. Small quantities of gold continued to be sold in the mining areas, and the bonanzas of products demanded in the international market, such as black rubber and tagua nuts, provided a source of income and encouraged the colonization of certain areas.

Little by little, through the mid-twentieth century descendants of African slaves came to occupy the region, forming a myriad of villages among the forests. Indians continued to live primarily in the headwaters of some rivers, as they had done since the Spanish arrival. During these years black communities developed their own ways of organizing themselves and of understanding and using their environment. Their productive practices, based in part on those performed by Indians, are specific to local conditions. Communal labor forms reminiscent of the mining *cuadrillas* still exist today. The ways black people in this region classify their environment and illnesses denote their peculiar way of making sense of the world in which they live. The importance of extended family relations is another trait that distinguishes the inhabitants of the Pacific coast of Colombia. Religious practices, such as holding a wake for one week for adults and for one night for *pangels* (babies), are quite unique to this population. Music types, such as the *chirimía* in the north and the *currulao* in the south, are products of the particular histories of the lowland black people.

It would be misleading, however, to portray a single image of the Afro-Colombian groups that inhabit the Pacific coast. There are cultural differences between the north and the south, of which music is one example. Dissimilarities can also be seen between older and younger people, just as between genders and rural and urban people. In recent decades urbanization and migration have altered the region. Some towns have become small chaotic cities, and black young men and women have joined the cane plantation workers of the Cauca Valley, the construction workers of Medellín, and the domestic service of Andean cities. Changes in the lowland economy have also shaped the lives of these people. The development of palm oil plantations near ECUADOR, for example, has transformed many peasants into landless workers.

A significant recent development may prove to have serious consequences for the future of Afro-Colombians. The 1991 constitution and the subsequent Law 70 of 1993 recognized collective land rights to territories occupied by black people and opened the possibility for communal titling. This law was the product of an emerging movement that was reinforced by the law itself, which based its claims on the argument that black people constitute an ethnic group. Community leader Diego Córdoba and the Movimiento Nacional Cimarrón had previously fought for the rights of black people under the idea of equality. Despite these efforts the recent "discovery" of the enormous wealth of natural resources in the region and of its strategic location for international trade has attracted government modernization projects and investors. The many armed groups that seek wealth and territorial control have also reached the area. In the Chocó, for instance, guerrilla groups arrived first, and then the armed forces and paramilitary organizations followed. The traditional inhabitants, both indigenous and black, have been caught in the crossfire and have become victims of summary executions, disappearances, forced displacement, and hunger (*see* HUMAN RIGHTS IN LATIN AMERICA AND THE CARIBBEAN). These pervasive violations were previously unknown in the Chocó, which, though poor, was one of the most peaceful regions of Colombia. Despite such terrible threats by March 1998 the National Land Reform Institute entitled the first 670,000 hectares to community councils throughout the region. However, immediately thereafter the head of one of the councils was gunned down. Hopes for the future of the black communities of the Chocó lie in their continued struggle and resistance to save their culture, lands, and lives.

Claudia Leal

SEE ALSO

Transatlantic Slave Trade; Cartagena de Indias, Colombia; Córdoba, Diego Luis; Colonial Latin America and the Caribbean.

Latin America and the Caribbean

Padmore, George (b. 1902?, Tacarigua, Trinidad; d. September 23, 1959, London, England), anticolonial activist, Communist, and Pan-Africanist whose career spanned the Americas, Europe, the Soviet Union, and Africa.

George Padmore dedicated his life to the black liberation movement in Africa. After Padmore died in 1959, Ghanaian leader KWAME NKRUMAH stated that "one day the whole of Africa will surely be free and united and when the final tale is told the significance of George Padmore's work will be revealed."

Padmore was born Malcolm Ivan Meredith Nurse. He was the son of Anna Susanna Syminster and James Nurse, a senior agricultural instructor and the son of a former slave. After graduating from a Trinidadian private school in 1918 Padmore became a reporter for the *Weekly Guardian* newspaper. In 1924 he emigrated to the United States with the aim of obtaining a university medical education, and a year later he enrolled at FISK UNIVERSITY in Nashville, Tennessee. He did not, however, complete his degree at Fisk, possibly because of Ku Klux Klan threats, and in 1927 he transferred to HOWARD UNIVERSITY Law School, where he became known as an excellent public speaker and student leader. As his professor Metz Lochard recalled, Padmore "was admired immensely by both faculty and student body.... He was our favorite speaker." Padmore also organized protests on campus, including a demonstration against a visit to the university by British ambassador Sir Esme Howard.

By 1928 Padmore had joined the Communist Party, adopting the name he is now known by as a cover for his political work. A year later he took up an invitation from the Moscow-based Communist International (Comintern) to visit the Soviet Union, which many black intellectuals at the time regarded as a haven of racial tolerance and a positive force for black emancipation worldwide. On receiving his tickets he discovered that they provided one-way passage only, and that the Comintern expected him to stay abroad. Such was his enthusiasm for the Communist cause that he withdrew from Howard and emigrated to the Soviet Union. He never returned to the United States.

Once in Moscow Padmore became secretary of the International Trade Union Committee of Negro Workers, the Soviet Union's agency for promoting revolution among black peoples worldwide. After a stint in Moscow, during which he had an office in the Kremlin, he was transferred to Vienna. From there he traveled widely, recruiting leaders for African liberation movements. In 1934 Soviet priorities shifted: wishing to align with GREAT BRITAIN and FRANCE in opposition to Germany, the Soviet Union decided to soften its anticolonialist policies, and Padmore was instructed to discontinue his work. He refused and was expelled from the Comintern and the Communist Party. Padmore became a staunch critic of Stalin's policies but retained his faith in the Soviet Union. In his 1947 book *How Russia Transformed her Colonial Empire: A Challenge to Imperialist Powers,* he wrote that "national and cultural independence and political unity among multi-racial and national groups is possible only along the lines of a socialized planned economy."

In 1935 Padmore moved permanently to London. Over the next 20 years, with the help of his typist and companion Dorothy Pizer, he established himself as a leading spokesman for anticolonialist sentiment in Africa and around the world. His numerous books on Africa's struggle for independence include *How Britain Rules Africa* (1936), *Africa and World Peace* (1937), *Africa: Britain's Third Empire* (1949), and *Pan-Africanism or Communism?* (1956). Shortly before World War II he established the International African Service Bureau, which in 1939 condemned all the European colonial powers, equating the Nazi takeover of Europe with the European colonization of Africa. That same year he wrote an article humorously titled "The British Empire Is the Worst Racket Yet Invented by Man."

During the 1940s Padmore moved closer to Pan-Africanism, advocating the unification of Africa into a single country. He was instrumental in founding the Pan-African Federation (PAF), which in 1945 organized the All-Colonial Peoples' Conference in Manchester, England. Among those attending was Kwame Nkrumah, a radical Pan-Africanist leader from the British Gold Coast (present-day Ghana). Padmore and Nkrumah became close friends. As Nkrumah later recalled, "there existed between us that rare affinity for which one searches for so long but seldom finds in another human being." Nkrumah's Convention People's Party came to power in 1956 and helped GHANA achieve independence the following year, and Padmore became Nkrumah's chief advisor on African affairs. He met with considerable opposition from Ghana's elite, who objected to his special privileges as an outsider. Illness and exhaustion forced Padmore to return to Great Britain in 1959, shortly before his death.

Jonathan Edwards

SEE ALSO

Russia and the Former Soviet Union; Pan-Africanism; Trinidad and Tobago.

Latin America and the Caribbean

Pagode, a type of Brazilian samba music that is played at informal parties and social gatherings. It became commercialized and popularized in the 1980s by artists such as Grupo Fundo de Quintal, Zeca Pagodino, and Beth Carvalho (*see* SAMBA).

North America

Paige, Leroy Robert ("Satchel") (b. July 7, 1906, Mobile, Ala.; d. June 8, 1982), American baseball player, the first African American pitcher in the American League, and the first representative of the NEGRO LEAGUES to be inducted into the Baseball Hall of Fame.

Born in Mobile, Alabama, to gardener John Paige and washerwoman Lulu Paige, Leroy

Paige earned his nickname as a boy, carrying satchels, or suitcases, at the Mobile train station. Accused of stealing toy rings, Paige was sent at a young age to the Mount Meigs, Alabama, reform school. It was here that he began to play baseball, assuming a place on the pitcher's mound that he held for more than 40 years and becoming, according to ballplayer Dizzy Dean, the greatest pitcher of all time.

Paige began his career with the semipro Mobile Tigers in 1924. He played for several teams in the Negro Leagues, including the Birmingham Black Barons. Paige was the most widely known African American baseball player until JACKIE ROBINSON integrated the major leagues in the late 1940s. With a lanky 1.9 m (6 ft 3 in) body and huge feet, Paige had a characteristic stance that was unmistakable on the mound as he uncoiled his long arms and let the ball fly. In the 1930s he drew huge crowds as he was pitted against major leaguers, including Dean. Throughout the 1930s Paige appeared regularly in the East-West "All-Star" games, and due in part to his enormous popular following, this yearly event drew unprecedented numbers of African Americans together. The "barnstorming tours" of the Negro League were exhausting, as the teams traveled sometimes as much as 48,278 km (30,000 mi) a year to play exhibition games. Paige once commented that at times it was only when he put on his uniform that he found the spark to continue. It is little wonder that Paige suffered from exhaustion: he once pitched 29 consecutive games in 29 days.

As a free agent Paige played throughout North and South America, as well as in the Caribbean during winter seasons. He left the Pittsburgh Crawfords in 1937 to accept the invitation of President Rafael Trujillo to play for the DOMINICAN REPUBLIC team Ciudad Trujillo. He returned to the United States several years later and pitched the Kansas Monarchs to victory in the 1942 Negro League World Series (*see* BASEBALL IN LATIN AMERICA AND THE CARIBBEAN).

Paige became the first African American pitcher in the American League when he joined the Cleveland Indians in 1948. With Paige on the pitcher's mound, the Indians won the World Series in his first year on the team. By 1952 he was pitching on the American League All-Star squad. Paige, who kept fans guessing his true age, was in his forties by this time. "Don't look back," the quick-witted Paige once advised, "Something might be gaining on you."

By his own count Paige threw 55 no-hitters and won more than 2000 of the 2500 games he pitched. He pitched his last game for the Indianapolis Clowns in 1967. Four years later, long after the disbanding of the Negro League, he was the first member of that league to be inducted into the Baseball Hall of Fame. Paige continued to work as a pitching coach for the Atlanta Braves of the National League. Appropriately, his autobiography is titled *Maybe I'll Pitch Forever* (1961).

Marian Aguiar

SEE ALSO
Baseball in the United States.

Latin America and the Caribbean

Palacios, Arnoldo

(b. January 20, 1924, Certeguí, Chocó, Colombia), Afro-Colombian novelist, short story writer, and collector of cultural artifacts from the Pacific coast and the department of Chocó, a predominantly black region.

Little is known about the life of Arnoldo Palacios, an intensely private man. He grew up in his native Chocó and moved to Bogota to continue his studies at the Universidad Nacional. Later he left the country and lived in France and Russia. His reputation was established in 1949 with publication of the critically acclaimed novel *Las estrellas son negras* (The Stars Are Black). Set on the riverbank of the Atrato River in the department of Chocó, the book portrays the brutal impact of utter poverty and social marginalization on the region's black communities. In its detached and cold depiction of the cruelest aspects of poverty, the novel recalls other classics in the genre, such as Knut Hamsun's *Hunger* (1890), RICHARD WRIGHT's *American Hunger* (1977), and CAROLINA MARIA DE JESUS' *Quarto de Despejo* (1962, Child of the Dark). As Richard Jackson points out, *Las estrellas son negras* illustrates "how black rage stemming from unemployment and gnawing hunger, two aspects of the black experience in Colombia, can drive a man to drastic acts."

Using a technique reminiscent of James Joyce's stream of consciousness, *Las estrellas son negras* follows the path of a man, Israel, for a whole day and records in their most minute details the hopelessness, terror, and humiliation brought about by constant pangs of hunger. Israel, or Irra (phonetically, "anger" in Spanish), as he is referred to throughout the novel, in the end realizes that his will to survive is greater than his desire for violent retaliation or self-destruction. Despite its fierce depiction of misery, the novel reaches a lyric beauty that has few precedents in black literature in Spanish America.

In 1958 in Moscow Palacios published *La selva y la lluvia* (The Jungle and the Rain). Though it revisits many of the themes in his first novel, this work was not well received by critics, who deemed it too politically charged. More recently it has been hailed by some as a superb synthesis of the region's three cultural influences (African, Indian, and European), especially in its treatment of oral culture. Palacios has also published various books about the region's folklore and a survey of black literature in the Americas.

Francisco Ortega

SEE ALSO
Pacific Coast of Colombia; Literature, Black, in Spanish America.

Latin America and the Caribbean

Palenque de San Basilio,

a Colombian community descended from an encampment of fugitive, African-born slaves who, rebelling against the Spanish colonial system of slavery, fled into swamps, marshes, and shrublands in search of liberty.

The Palenque de San Basilio, a settlement of some 3000 inhabitants in the foothills of the Sierra de María, is 70 km (43.75 mi) from Cartagena de Indias, which was the principal Caribbean port of the TRANSATLANTIC SLAVE TRADE from the sixteenth century to the beginning of the nineteenth century. In Cartagena de Indias resistance to slavery was constant. Those who were able to escape were known as *cimarrones*, a word that in the Americas was applied to insurgent Native Americans, wild plants and fruits, escaped domesticated animals, and later, runaway African slaves (*see* COMPLEXITIES OF ETHNIC AND RACIAL TERMINOLOGY IN LATIN AMERICA AND THE CARIBBEAN). The slaves fled from the galleys of ships, from mining operations, from ranches, and from domestic service; after their escape they often came together to form small bands. Many were able to settle in rough encampments protected by swamps and thick brush. To protect themselves from the weapons and dogs of the Spanish slave-hunting parties, these communities surrounded themselves with fences made of posts, branches, and thorns. Such encampments became known as *palenques*.

Armed with arrows, blunderbusses, and stones, the encamped cimarrón communities fought furiously against colonial domination and often went to battle with their faces painted red and white. They attacked local ranches, burned them, stole cattle, and at times raped indigenous and black women. Some palenques grew to comprise 600 men, organized in squads headed by a *capitán*, or captain, and a warlord. Spanish militias counterattacked by burning cassava, corn, bean, potato, and plantain patches maintained by the palenques, and by capturing indigenous and black women to obtain inside information about the encampments. The inhabitants of the palenque (the *palenqueros*) were often forced to flee deeper into the bush to seek new refuge or other palenques. The history of these rebellions in COLOMBIA has been called the *Guerra de los cimarrones*, or the Cimarrón War.

In 1603 clashes at the palenque of La Matuna between Spanish forces and groups of palenqueros headed by Domingo Benkos Biohó, known in traditional lore as the King of Matuna, brought about a peace settlement signed by the governor of Cartagena, Gerónimo Suazo. On August 23, 1691, the king of Spain issued a decree that granted liberty to palenqueros in the Sierra de María. The decree affirmed the urgency of a "comprehensive and absolute liberty, which unless unconditionally granted would never be accepted [by the palenqueros]."

Palenque de San Basilio is the result of a series of concessions agreed to by Spaniards and palenqueros in the Sierra de María in 1713. It was established as the outcome of a dispute mediated by the bishop of Cartagena, Father Antonio María Casiani, concerning the recognition of land rights and the authority of a palenquero government that was led by a cimarrón capitán. The bishop gave the palenque the name San Basilio. In 1774 San Basilio for the first time figured in the census of the Spanish colonial government.

Palenquero, a Creole language still spoken by the inhabitants of San Basilio, is a living legacy of the Bantu KONGO and MBUNDU languages. Likewise, the day-to-day culture of this and other villages in the Colombian Caribbean bears the stamp of their African past, evident in musical rhythms, the particularity of gestures, funeral rites such as the lumbalú in San Basilio, modes of kinship and social organization, and a strong oral tradition. Representations of an early liberation movement and a history of resistance to colonial slavery in Colombia and the Americas remain in the oral tradition of Benkos Domingo Biohó, the African leader of La Matuna, as well as in the modern-day Palenque de San Basilio, a community directly descending from the days of maroonage in Colombia.

Nina Friedemann

SEE ALSO

Maroonage in the Americas; Slavery in Latin America and the Caribbean; Cartagena de Indias, Colombia; Biohó, Benkos.

Latin America and the Caribbean

Palés Matos, Luis

(b. March 20, 1898, Guayama, PUERTO RICO; d. February 23, 1959, SAN JUAN, PUERTO RICO), Puerto Rican poet and novelist who explored the contributions of African culture to the Americas in his writing.

Neither black nor mulatto, Luis Palés Matos is of the few non-Cuban poets from the Caribbean to have seriously represented blacks in his literary work. The Palés Matos family was very prominent in Puerto Rico, and Luis probably got his first exposure to African culture from the black servants who lived in the family mansion and who took care of him as a boy.

Palés Matos began his career writing modernist poems (his first book, *Azaleas,* was published in 1915) and acquired fame when he started publishing poems with a "Negro" theme, including "Danzarina Africana" (1918) and "Pueblo Negro" (1925). His work picked up on the contemporary cultural interest in primitivism, African arts, and folklore, with the "Negro" in Palés Matos's writing symbolizing a redemptive, primitive, sensual revitalizing force that stands in antithesis to a desiccated Western civilization. The association of African cultural traditions with primitive animal sensuality, a hallmark of modernism, can be glimpsed in Palés Matos's first collection with a black theme, *Tuntún de pasa y grifería* (1937), in which Palés Matos evokes African rhythms, uses nonsense words meant to reference the sound of African languages, and comments on the vitality of African culture in Puerto Rico.

Most critics agree that Palés Matos's interest in African culture represents only one dimension of his idiosyncratic poetry. In the 1920s, while living and working in San Juan, Palés Matos engaged in modernist experiments with sound and onomatopoeia. This interest in sound may have led him to represent African speech in his later poetry. Palés Matos's interest in interpreting African culture in his poems, however, abruptly stopped in the 1950s. He published a collection of his life's work in 1957 titled *Poesías, 1915-1956.*

Bill Johnson-González

Latin America and the Caribbean

Palmares: An African State in Brazil

Without slaves from Africa, reported an early Portuguese source, "it is impossible to do anything in BRAZIL."

Although prior arrivals are suspected, the first known landing of slaves from Africa on Brazilian soil took place in 1552. In 1580, five years after the founding of Loanda (now Luanda) and on the eve of Brazil's sugar boom, there were no fewer than 10,000 Africans in Brazil. Fifty years later Pernambuco alone imported 4400 slaves annually from Africa. It also contained 150 *engenhos,* or a third of the total sugar mill and plantation complex in Brazil. In 1630 the Dutch West India Company captured Pernambuco, and within a decade Portugal had abandoned Brazil to the Dutch. It was ultimately the decision of local settlers, the *moradores,* to fight the West India Company that led to restoration of Portuguese control in 1654. The Dutch retreat from Brazil, however, was secured through a joint Afro-Portuguese effort, which gave the Black Regiment of HENRIQUE DIAS its colonial fame. If early settlement and a sugar-based economy could not have been sustained without the African laborer, neither could the Portuguese continue to hold Brazil without the African soldier. The subsequent evolution of Brazil is no less a story of Euro-African enterprise. Exploitation of gold and diamonds in the eighteenth century, pioneering shifts of population from the coast to the interior, dilution of monoculture, formation of mining states, and the advent of an abolitionist movement in the nineteenth century were all dependent on the same combination. The blend of race, language, and culture in contemporary Brazil confirms this evolution.

Africa's impact on Brazil and, more generally, the role of the Negro in Brazilian history and society are subjects of an extensive literature. Its principal stress is on assimilation rather than divergence, and frequently the early colonial society has been postulated from descriptions left by European and North American travelers who visited Brazil much later. It is hence not surprising that active Negro resistance to slavery in Brazil has not received comparable attention and is consequently less known (*see* MAROONAGE IN THE AMERICAS and SLAVE REBELLIONS IN LATIN AMERICA AND THE CARIBBEAN).

According to one working definition, there were three basic forms of active resistance: fugitive slave settlements called *quilombos*; attempts at seizure of power; and armed insurrections, which sought neither escape nor control but amelioration. The latter two prevailed in the first half of the nineteenth century, a period of political transition in Brazil and of accelerated slave trade with Africa. They encompass, for example, nine Bahian revolts between 1807 and 1835, which involved a number of HAUSA, YORUBA, and Kwa-speaking groups, as well as the Ogboni Society, Muslim *alufas*, and even a back-to-Africa movement (*see* MUSLIM UPRISINGS IN BAHIA, BRAZIL). The quilombos constitute a pre-nineteenth-century phenomenon and are of considerable interest to the African historian. They came closest to the idea of re-creating African societies in a new environment and against consistently heavier odds. The quilombos were regarded as a threat to the Portuguese plantation, an inducement for escape from the slave hut. They were rarely, therefore, allowed to last a long time. Of the ten major quilombos in colonial Brazil, seven were destroyed within two years of being formed. Four fell in the state of BAHIA in 1632, 1636, 1646, and 1796. The other three met the same fate in Rio in 1650, Parahyba (now Paraíba) in 1731, and Piumhy (now Piauí) in 1758. One quilombo, in MINAS GERAIS, lasted from 1712 to 1719. Another, the "Carlota" of Mato Grosso, was wiped out after existing for 25 years, from 1770 to 1795.

Nothing, however, compares in the annals of Brazilian history with the "Negro Republic" of Palmares in Pernambuco. It spanned almost the entire seventeenth century. Between 1672 and 1694 it withstood, on the average, one Portuguese expedition every 15 months. In the last *entrada* (assault) against Palmares a force of 6000 took part in 42 days of siege. The Portuguese Crown sustained a cumulative loss of 400,000 *cruzados*, or roughly three times the total revenue lease of eight Brazilian captaincies in 1612. As Brazil's classic quilombo, Palmares gained two more distinctions. It opened the study of Negro history in modern Brazil. Minutes of the Brazilian Historical Institute reveal that Palmares was the subject of lively discussions in 1840 and that the search for written materials relative to it began in 1851. Important gaps in knowledge persist, but enough primary sources have been found and published to trace the development of Palmares, to examine it as a society and government, and to suggest its significance to both Brazilian and African history.

I

Early writers attributed the birth of Palmares to Portuguese-Dutch struggles for Pernambuco, from which slaves profited by escaping in groups. They made no reference to Palmares as a quilombo. Robert Southey came across the term in a Minas Gerais decree of 1722. An official letter sent from Pernambuco to Lisbon in 1692 contains the first and only definition of Palmares as a quilombo in primary sources. The point is worth stressing. The accepted definition of a quilombo as a fugitive slave settlement has been continuously applied to Palmares since the turn of this century, and the problem of interpretation has been more difficult as a result. An early nineteenth-century historian, for example, could easily classify Palmares as the "unusual exception, a real government of escaped Blacks on Brazilian soil." But subsequent identification of the state, which was a major historical event, with a mere colony of escaped slaves, could not provide a framework to fit the problem. *Ki-lombo*, according to Antonio Cavazzi, was a Jaga war camp, and there is no lack of sources that have translated it correctly as "arrayal." Could a historico-linguistic link between a Palmares in a formative stage and the Jaga *ki-lombo* perhaps be assumed, faute de mieux?

Slaves who freed themselves by escaping into the bush became something of a problem several decades before the Dutch took Pernambuco. In 1597 a Jesuit priest, Pero Rodrigues, was able to write that the "foremost enemies of the colonizer are revolted Negroes from Guiné in some mountain areas, from where they raid and give much trouble, and the time may come when they will dare to attack and destroy farms as their relatives do on the island of São Thomé." Shortly after his arrival from Portugal Governor Diogo Botelho (1602-1608) learned from an Amerindian chief named Zorobabé that there was a "*mocambo*... of Negroes from Guiné... in the *palmares* of river Itapicuru." Zorobabé was asked to destroy the mocambo and return with slaves, but "few were brought back since the Indians killed many and Zorobabé sold some along the way." If the Itapicuru mocambo went almost unnoticed by Portuguese authorities, this was not the case with a similar manifestation farther north. In the captaincy of Pernambuco, reported a high official in 1612, "some 30 leagues inland, there is a site between mountains called Palmares which harbours runaway slaves... whose attacks and raids force the whites into armed pursuits which amount to little for they return to raid again.... This makes it impossible to... end the transgressions which gave Palmares its reputation." Botelho, before he left Brazil, sent a punitive expedition to Palmares.

Clearly, "quilombo" does not appear in the vocabulary of early seventeenth-century Brazil. Instead, the fugitive slave settlement is known as mocambo, an appropriate description since *mu-kambo* in Ambundu means a hideout. Around 1603 "palmares" was simply any area covered by palm trees. There was no connection between the Itapicuru mocambo south of Sergipe and the Palmares of Pernambuco. Palmares was not regarded as an ordinary mocambo. By 1612 it had a considerable reputation. It was an organization with which the moradores could not cope alone. The foundation of Palmares thus appears to have taken place in 1605-1606, possibly earlier, but certainly not later. As the report of 1612 indicates, the first Portuguese expedition against Palmares attained little by way of military victory. Nothing else, however, is heard of Palmares until the mid-1630s. Frei Vicente do Salvador's history of Brazil, written in 1629, and recently published official documents for the years 1607-1633 are equally silent on Palmares. In 1634 a Pernambucan morador described Palmares as a "great calamity." The Dutch viewed it as a "serious danger" in 1640. Increasing palmarista militancy after 1630 can safely be associated with slaves who took advantage of the Dutch presence to escape and who eventually found their way into Palmares. It is also certain that Palmares antedates the Dutch in Brazil by at least a quarter of a century. Given an earlier origin and the absence of "quilombo" from the contemporary vocabulary, it is even less probable that Jagas were the founders of Palmares. It would be tempting to accept a recent claim that the Jagas gave Palmares its ruling dynasty after being sent to Brazil in 1616 by the Angolan governor, Luis Mendes de Vascocellos, who assumed office in August 1617 and fought against the Ngola *with* Jaga auxiliaries. A large contingent of Jagas was sold into slavery after a punitive expedition against Kasanje in 1624 and may have reached Brazil along with other prisoners from the *guerra preta* (black war). But the account of Andrew Battell, who was with the Jagas until 1603, shows nothing to indicate that any of them could have landed in Pernambuco by 1605. There remains the alternative of "Negroes from Guiné."

"Negroes from Guiné" were mentioned long before 1597 in connection with attempted rebellion. Rocha Pitta, a contemporary of Palmares, held that it was founded by "forty Negroes from Guiné" who had abandoned plantations around Porto Calvo. But the "Guiné" of early Portuguese sources is not a precise geographical expression. It stood for nearly anything between a limited section of West Africa and the entire continent. "Slaves from Guiné," according to the 1612 report, "are bought dearly because of the gifts and duties which must be paid for them in Angola." Henrique Dias wrote a letter – most likely in 1648 – which stated that the Black Regiment was composed mainly of "Angolas" and *crioulos* (Brazilian-born slaves) with a sprinkling of "Minas" and "Ardras." With Loanda as the undisputed slave funnel from the 1580s until well into the seventeenth century, it is quite unlikely that more than a handful of palmaristas originated outside the Angola-Congo perimeter. Crioulos in Pernambuco of 1605 could not have been numerous either. All of this leads to the only plausible hypothesis about the founders of Palmares. They must have been Bantu-speaking and could not have belonged exclusively to any subgroup. Palmares was a reaction to a slaveholding society entirely out of step with forms of bondage familiar to Africa. As such, it had to cut across ethnic lines and draw upon all those who managed to escape from various plantations and at different times. The Palmares that emerged out of this amalgam may be glimpsed in a little more detail during the second half of the seventeenth century.

II

Dutch activities concerning Palmares, from 1640 until the Reijmbach expedition of 1645, are known mainly through Caspar Barleus and Johan Nieuhof. They begin with a reconnaissance mission by Bartholomeus Lintz, a Dutch scout who brought back the first rudimentary information about Palmares. Lintz discovered that Palmares was not a single enclave, but a combination of many *kleine* (small) and two *groote* (large) units. The smaller ones were clustered on the left bank of the Gurungumba, 6 leagues from its confluence with the larger Paraiba and 20 leagues from Alagoas. They contained "about 6,000 Negroes living in numerous huts." The two large *palmares* were deeper inland, 30 leagues from Santo Amaro in the mountain region of Barriga, and "harboured some 5,000 Negroes." In January 1643 the West India Company sent its Amerindian interpreter Roelox Baro with a force of Tapuyas and several Dutch regulars to "put the large Palmares through 'fire and sword,' devastate and plunder the small Palmares." Baro seems to have returned without his men to report that "100 Negroes of Palmares were killed as against one killed and four wounded Dutchmen, our force having captured 31 defenders, including 7 Indians and some mulatto children." The four Dutchmen and a handful of Tapuyas were found two months later. There was no one with them.

A second Dutch expedition left Selgado for Palmares on February 26, 1645. It was headed by Jürgens Reijmbach, an army lieutenant who kept a diary for 36 consecutive days. His task was to destroy the two *groote* Palmares. On March 18 Reijmbach reached the first and found that it had been abandoned months earlier. "When we arrived the bush growth was so thick that it took much doing to cut a path through." Three days later his men located the second one. "Our Brasilenses managed to kill two or three Negroes in the bush but most of the people had vanished." Their kin – the few captives told Reijmbach – "knew of the expedition for some time because he had been forewarned from Alagoas." This Palmares, reads the entry of March 21, "is equally half a mile long, its street six feet wide and running along a large swamp, tall trees alongside.... There are 220 *casas* [houses], amid them a church, four smithies and a huge *casa de conselho* [or counsel house]; all kinds of artifacts are to be seen.... (The) king rules... with iron justice, without permitting any *feticeiros* [sorcerers] among the inhabitants; when some Negroes attempt to flee, he sends *crioulos* after them and once retaken their death is swift and of the kind to instill fear, especially among the Angolan Negroes; the king also has another *casa*, some two miles away, with its own rich fields.... We asked the Negroes how many of them live (here) and were told some 500, and from what we saw around us as well we presumed that there were 1500 inhabitants all told.... This is the Palmares *grandes* of which so much is heard in Brazil, with its well-kept lands, all kinds of cereals, beautifully irrigated with streamlets."

In military terms Reijmbach fared no better than his two predecessors, Bartolomeu Bezzerra and Roelox Baro. An undestroyed Palmares, of which "so much is heard in Brazil," remained free of further interference by Pernambucan authorities until 1672. The ensuing two decades can best be described as a period of sustained war, which ended in the complete destruction of Palmares in 1694. As is often the case, warfare and more intimate knowledge of the enemy went together, and the growing information about Palmares in the 1670s threw light on its evolution during the 27 years of relative peace.

"Our campaigns," complained a group of Pernambucan moradores in 1681, "have not had the slightest effect on the Negroes of Palmares... who seem invincible." The claim was not altogether true. Of the eight expeditions between 1672 and 1680, two did hurt Palmares. They were led by *capitão-mor* (captain) Fernão Carrilho, who had distinguished "himself in the destruction of *mocambos* in the Captaincy of Sergipe del Rey." The Carrilho entradas of 1676-1677 produced the most extensive firsthand report ever found. The Palmares of 1677 encompassed more than 60 leagues and included several villages: "In the northeast, *mocambo* of *Zambi*, located 16 leagues from Porto Calvo; north of it, at 5 leagues' distance, mocambo of *Arotirene;* along it two others called *Tabocas;* northeast of these, at 14 leagues, the one of *Dombabanga;* 8 leagues north another, called *Subupuira;* another 6 leagues north, the royal enclave of *Macoco;* west of it, at 5 leagues, the mocambo of *Osenga;* at 9 leagues from our Serinhaem, northwest, the enclave of *Amaro;* at 25 leagues from Alagoas, northwest, the palmar of *Andalaquituche,* brother of *Zambi;* and between all these, which are the largest and most fortified, there are others of lesser importance and with less people in them."

There was no doubt, said the report, that Palmares maintained its "real strength" by providing "food as well as security" for the inhabitants – largely tillers of land who planted "every kind of vegetables" and knew how to store them against "wartime and winter." All the inhabitants of Palmares considered themselves "subjects of king who is called *Ganga-Zumba*, which means Great Lord, and he is recognized as such both by those born in Palmares and by those who join them from outside; he has a palatial residence, *casas* for members of his family, and is assisted by guards and officials who have, by custom, *casas* which approach those of royalty. He is treated with all respect due a Monarch and all the honours due a Lord. Those who are in his presence kneel on the ground and strike palm leaves with their hands as sign of appreciation of His excellence. They address him as Majesty and obey him with reverence. He lives in the royal enclave, called *Macoco*, a name which was begotten from the death of an animal on the site. This is the capital of Palmares; it is fortified with parapets full of caltrops, a big danger even when detected. The enclave itself consists of some 1,500 *casas*. There are keepers of law (and) their office is duplicated elsewhere. And although these barbarians have all but forgotten their subjugation, they have not completely lost allegiance to the Church. There is a *capela* [chapel], to which they flock whenever time allows, and *imagens* [images] to which they direct their worship.... One of the most crafty, whom they venerate as *paroco*, baptizes and marries them. Baptismals are, however, not identical with the form determined by the Church and the marriage is singularly close to laws of nature.... The king has three [women], a *mulata* and two *crioulas*. The first [wife] has given him [the king] many sons, the other two none. All the foregoing applies to the *cidade principal* of Palmares and it is the king who rules it directly; other *cidades* are in the charge of potentates and major chiefs who govern in his name. The second *cidade* in importance is called *Subupuira* and is ruled by king's brother (Ganga) *Zona*.... It has 800 *casas* and occupies a site one square league in size, right along the river *Cachingi*. It is here that Negroes are trained to fight our assaults (and weapons are forged there)."

Nearly three decades of peace had a number of important results in the internal evolution of Palmares. Instead of the two major *palmars* of 1645, there were now ten. There was a very substantial element in the Macaco of those native to Palmares, people unfamiliar with engenho slavery. Afro-Brazilians continued to enjoy preferential status, but the distinction between crioulos and Angolas does not appear to have been as sharp as it was in 1645. There was a greater degree of religious acculturation. The reference to a population composed mainly of those born in Palmares and those who joined from outside suggests that slaves had become less numerous than free commoners. According to Pitta, the only slaves in Palmares were those captured in razzias (raids). But they had the option of going out on raids to secure freedom by returning with a substitute. This is confirmed by Nieuhof, who wrote that the main "business" of palmaristas "is to rob the Portuguese of their slaves, who remain in slavery among them, until they have redeemed themselves by stealing another; but such slaves as run over to them, are as free as the rest."

Although slim and often corrupted, linguistic evidence leads to two unavoidable conclusions. The king and most of the hierarchy at the head of individual mocambos were not crioulos. Macoco/Makoko points to Loango; Tabocas/Taboka to Ambundu; Andalaquituche/Ndala Kafuche to Kisama; Osenga/Osanga/Hosanga to Kwango; Subupuira/Subusupu hara vura and Zumba to Zande; and Dombabanga/Ndombetbanga to a Benguella-Yombe composite. Arotirene appears to be Amerindian. Zambi/Nzambi and Ganga/Nganga, respectively "divinity" and "lord," are too widely used in Central Africa to be traced further. Translated as "brother," Zona may be an extreme corruption of Mona, an equally common term. Amaro/Amargo derives from a very bitter kind of wild-growing tea shrub, chimarrão, which resembles *cimarrones*, the name for runaway slaves in the West Indies. The principle of *cujus regio ejus religio*, slightly bent to accommodate ethnic subgroups, cannot be deduced from this evidence. What it does affirm, however, is that Palmares did not spring from a single social structure. It was, rather, an African political system that came to govern a plural society and thus give continuity to what could have been at best a group of scattered hideouts.

The almost equally long years of peace and war between 1645 and 1694 point to Palmares as a fluctuating "peril." While not necessarily unfair to the merits of a particular event, the Portuguese took it as an article of faith that Palmares was an aggressor state. No written document originating within Palmares has come to light. It probably does not exist. The late Arthur Ramos made a search for oral traditions in the 1930s. It yielded only an annual stage play recalling a history of strife in the township of Pilar: "The sensation of security (in Palmares) diminished after the first attacks of the colonists. The Palmares Negroes reacted by increasing their defences... to maintain their little republic, the Negroes were forced to make sorties to the neighboring Indian villages and the towns of nearby valleys. This brought about (more) reprisals.... " The play recalls this sequence of events as it persists in the memory of the people. However blurred by the passage of time, the play at least allows for aggression on each side. There is no need to depend, in this case, on collective memory to illustrate both the specific and broad nature of the "peril."

Pernambucan authorities did not view Palmares from the perspective of the moradores who were in contact with it. They were too far removed from the general area of Palmares. Reijmbach, for example, had to march at a fast clip for 20 days to reach it from the coast, which the Pernambucan governors – Dutch or Portuguese – seldom left. The governors did, however, respond to morador pressure. "Moradores of this Captaincy, Your Majesty, are not capable of doing much by themselves in this war.... At all hours they complain to me of tyrannies they must suffer from [the Negroes of Palmares]." Among the complaints most frequently heard were loss of field hands and domestic servants, loss of settler lives, and kidnapping and rape of white women. Two of the common grievances do not stand up too well. Women were a rarity in Palmares and were actively sought during razzias. But female relatives of the morador did not constitute the main target, and those occasionally taken were returned unmolested for ransom. Checking the "rape of Sabines" tales, Edison Carneiro discovered one exception to the ransom rule reported by a Pernambucan soldier in 1682. Close examination of documents in the Ennes and Camara de Alagoas collections – 117 in all – failed to reveal a single substantiated case of a morador killed in palmarista raids. Settler lives appear to have been lost in the numerous and forever unrecorded "little" entradas into Palmares. They were carried out by small, private armies of plantation owners who sought to recapture lost hands or to acquire new ones without paying for them. Some of the moradores had secret commercial compacts with Palmares, usually exchanging firearms for gold and silver taken in the razzias. Evidence of this is not lacking. A gubernatorial proclamation of November 26, 1670, bitterly denounced "those who possess firearms" and pass them on to palmaristas "in disregard of God and local laws." In 1687 the state of Pernambuco empowered a Paulista colonel-of-foot to imprison moradores merely suspected of relations with Palmares, "irrespective of their station." Town merchants are also known to have carried on an active trade with Palmares, bartering utensils for agricultural produce. More than that, they "were most useful to the Negroes... by supplying advance information on expeditions prepared against them [and] for which the Negroes paid dearly." And Reijmbach's entry of March 21, 1645, makes it clear that this relationship was an old one.

Loss of plantation slaves, through raids as well as escape, emerges as the one solid reason behind the morador-palmarista conflict. The price of slaves is known to have increased considerably by the late 1660s. The very growth of Palmares served to increase its fame among the plantation slaves. "More and more Negroes from Angola," wrote a governor in 1671, "have now for some years fled on their own from the *rigor de cativeiro* in mills and plantations of this Captaincy." But its growth was not one-sided. Advances into the morador frontier, which had protruded from the littoral by the early 1640s, contracted between 1645 and 1654, a decade of Portuguese-Dutch struggle for Pernambuco. Contacts with Palmares were thus minimized until new bulges began to form. In a painstaking study of territorial expansion in Brazil, Felisbello Freire has shown that this movement away from the coast began in the late 1650s from Bahia, Sergipe, and Espírito Santo. It was retarded by no more than a few years for southern Pernambuco. The northern section merely took a little longer. "The Negroes," writes Carneiro, "had good relations with moradores, as long as the latter kept their slave huts and plantations away from the free lands of Palmares." But what looked like free lands to the Portuguese were not regarded in the same light by rulers of Palmares, and neither party understood the problem. There were, to be sure, no "great frontier" proportions in the inland movement of the concluding seventeenth-century decades. According to Basílio Magalhães, it was an "*expansão pequena*" (small expansion) at 50 or so leagues inland. Palmares was, however, well within it. Toward the end of the seventeenth century its territorial domain was estimated at about 1100 square leagues. "Those who live in a state of constant danger," reads another proclamation, "are people in the vicinity of the mocambos belonging to Palmares."

The hard-hitting Carrilho entradas of 1676-1677 evoked at least one response familiar to Palmares besides warfare. As he had done earlier, whenever a new governor came to Pernambuco, Ganga-Zumba sued for peace. The terms, however, were new and rather surprising. On June 18, 1678, "The junior lieutenants whom don Pedro (de Almeida) had sent to Palmares returned with three of the king's sons and 12 more Negroes who prostrated themselves at the feet of don Pedro.... They brought the king's request for fealty, asking for peace which was desired, stating that only peace could end the difficulties of Palmares, peace which so many governors and leaders had proffered but never stuck to; that they have come to ask for his good offices; that they have never desired war; that they only fought to save their own lives; that they were being left without *cidades*, without supplies, without wives.... The king had sent them to seek peace with no other desires but to trade with moradores, to have a treaty, to serve his Highness in whatever capacity; it is only the liberty of those born in Palmares that is now being sought while those who fled from our people will be returned; Palmares will be no more as long as a site is provided where they will be able to live, at his grace."

Three days after the embassy's arrival, the new governor, Aires de Souza Castro – replacing Almeida – called a council of state. He proposed that a draft treaty be sent to Ganga-Zumba extending peace, the requested liberties, and the release of palmarista women, who seem to have constituted by far the largest group of captives. The council agreed, and a *sargento-mor* who had served in the Black Regiment and knew how to read and write was sent to the Macoco, *"para que lesse e declarasse ao rei e aos mais o tratado de paz"* ("in order to read and to declare to the king and others the peace treaty"). Ganga-Zumba was confirmed as supreme ruler over his people. The question of Palmares's territorial limits was not settled in any precise way. "The solemnity which surrounded all these acts," wrote Nina Rodrigues, "gave a real importance to the Negro State which now the Colony treated as one nation would another, (for) this was no mere pact of a strong party concluded with disorganized bands of fugitive Negroes."

On paper the treaty seemed conclusive. But there were peculiarities in the immediate situation. A strong detachment that had been attacking Palmares since 1677 or early 1678 was not demobilized, and a group of Alagoan moradores led by a spokesman named João da Fonesca made certain that it would remain there. The ink of the treaty was hardly dry when Aires de Souza Castro began to distribute some 192 leagues of land to 16 individuals who had taken part in wars against Palmares, Carrilho alone obtaining a 20-league *sesmaria*. By 1679 a palmarista "captain named Zambi (whose uncle is Gana-Zona) was in revolt (with João Mulato, Canhonga, Gaspar [and] Amaro), having done the person of Ganga-Zumba to death." By March 1680 Zambi was being called upon to surrender, without success. The war was on once more.

Reactions to the treaty, on both sides, are revealing. Ganga-Zumba's peace proposal contained two clauses that could not be fulfilled. To allow a sovereign, if vassal, state to exist in Pernambuco would have meant reversing a 150-year-old policy of exclusive Portuguese claim to Brazil. The Almeida-de Souza move, was, therefore, a tactical one. It was, as Ennes stated after careful study, "an easy way of postponing that question which already had, without any positive accomplishment, consumed infinite time." Conversely, to hand over to the Portuguese half or more of some 15,000 to 20,000 palmaristas – a difficult logistical problem in its own right – would have required the kind of obedience that only a modern totalitarian state can secure.

The native-newcomer ratio was not identical in every mocambo of Palmares. The Macoco, at 45 leagues from Porto Calvo, must have had a far greater number of the native-born than did the mocambos of Zumbi, at 16 leagues from Porto Calvo, and Amaro, at 9 leagues from Serinhaem. Sociocultural differences, moreover, between crioulos and recent arrivals from Africa were not sufficiently great to challenge the unity of Palmares, which stood against the Portuguese economic and political order. The diplomacy of Ganga-Zumba, an elected ruler, might have worked had the promise to return those who found refuge in Palmares been observed. It might have worked if Palmares had been contiguous to other similar states facing an intrusive minority. Again, it might have worked if Palmares had been a homogeneous society with hereditary rulers. None of these conditions was present. In its time and place, Palmares had only two choices. It could continue to hold its ground as an independent state or suffer complete extinction. Zambi's palace revolt finally brought the unyielding palmarista and morador elements to full agreement.

Six expeditions went into Palmares between 1680 and 1686. Their total cost must have been large. In 1694 the Overseas Council in Lisbon was advised that Palmares caused a cumulative loss of not less than one million cruzados to the "people of Pernambuco." The estimate appears exaggerated unless the 400,000 cruzados contributed directly by the Crown were included. A single municipality did, however, spend 3000 cruzados (109,800 *reis*) in the fiscal year 1679-1680 to cover the running cost of Palmares wars, and a tenfold figure for the local and state treasuries would seem modest for the six years. Casualties aside, the results did not justify the cost. Palmares stood undefeated at the end of 1686. It was apparent that the state of Pernambuco could not deal with Palmares out of its own resources. In March 1687 the new governor, Sotto-Maior, informed Lisbon that he had accepted the services of *bandeirantes* (or expedition leaders and slave-raiders) from São Paulo, "at small expense to the treasure of Your Majesty." The Paulistas of the time were Portuguese-Amerindian *metis* and transfrontiersmen, renowned in Brazil for special skills in jungle warfare. Their leader, Domingos Jorge Velho, had written to Sotto-Maior in 1685 asking "for commissions as commander-in-chief and captains in order to subdue... [Palmares]." Largely because Lisbon could not be convinced that their services would come cheap, the Paulistas did not reach Pernambuco until 1692. In crossing so great a distance, 192 lives were lost in the backlands of Brazil, and 200 men deserted the Paulista ranks, unable to face "hunger, thirst, and agony."

The story of Palmares's final destruction has been told in great detail. Two-thirds of the secondary works discuss the Paulistas and the 1690s, some 60 of the 95 documents in the Ernesto Ennes collection refer to little else, and Ennes has published a useful summary in English. The Paulistas had to fight for two years to reduce Palmares to a single fortified site. After 20 days of siege by the Paulistas, the state of Pernambuco had to provide an additional 3000 men to maintain the seige for another 22 days. The breakthrough occurred during the night of February 5-6, 1694. Some 200 palmaristas fell or hurled themselves – the point has been long debated – "from a rock so high that they were broken to pieces." Hand-to-hand combat took another 200 palmarista lives, and more than 500 "of both sexes and all ages" were captured and sold outside Pernambuco. Zambi, taken alive and wounded, was decapitated on November 20, 1695. His head was exhibited in public "to kill the legend of his immortality."

III

The service rendered by the destruction of Palmares, wrote one of Brazil's early Africanists, is beyond discussion. It removed, Nina Rodrigues stated, the "greatest threat to future evolution of the Brazilian people and civilization – a threat which this new Haiti, if victorious, would have planted (forever) in the heart of Brazil." Indeed, Palmares came quite close to altering the subsequent history of Brazil. Had they not experienced the threat of Palmares in the seventeenth century, the Portuguese might well have found themselves hugging the littoral and facing not one but a number of independent African states dominating the backlands of eighteenth-century Brazil. In spite of the fact that hundreds of mocambos tried to come together, Palmares was never duplicated on Brazilian soil. This is ample testimony to its impact on the Portuguese settler and official. They organized special units, under *capitães-do-mato*, or bush captains, to hunt for mocambos and nip them in the bud. And they sought to prevent, at ports of entry, an overconcentration of African slaves from the same ethnic group or ship. This policy was abandoned in the wake of the Napoleonic Wars, and the immediate repercussion came by way of the nine Bahian revolts after 1807. The well-established thesis that uninhibited miscegenation and the corporate nature of the Portuguese society in Brazil produced a successful example of social engineering must also take into account the historical role of Palmares.

Palmares was a centralized kingdom with an elected ruler. Ganga-Zumba delegated territorial power and appointed to office. The most important ones went to his relatives. His nephew, Zambi, was the war chief. Ganga-Zona, the king's brother, was in charge of the arsenal. Interregnum problems do not seem to have troubled Palmares, the history of which spans about five generations of rulers. Zambi's palace revolt did not displace the ruling family. Assuming that Loanda was the main embarkation point for Pernambucan slaves, which is confirmed by linguistic evidence, the model for Palmares could have come from nowhere else but Central Africa. Can it be pinpointed? Internal attitudes toward slavery, prostrations before the king, site initiation with animal blood, the placing of the casa de conselho in the "main square," or the use of a high rock as part of a man-made fortress lead in no particular direction. The names of mocambo chiefs suggest a number of possible candidates. The most likely answer is that the political system did not derive from a particular Central African model, but from several. Only a far more detailed study of Palmares through additional sources in the archives of Angola and Torre do Tombo could refine the answer. Nonetheless, the most apparent significance of Palmares to African history is its demonstration that an African political system could be transferred to a different continent; that it could come to govern not only individuals from a variety of ethnic groups in Africa but also those born in Brazil, pitch black or almost white, Latinized or close to Amerindian roots; and that it could endure for almost a full century against two European powers, Holland and Portugal. And this is no small tribute to the vitality of the traditional African art in governing men.

R.K. Kent

From "Palmares: An African State in Brazil," in *Maroon Societies: Rebel Slave Communities in the Americas*, 3rd edition, ed. Richard Price, 170-188. Johns Hopkins University Press, 1996. Used with permission.

See Also

Angola; São Tomé and Príncipe; Nina Rodrigues, Raimundo; Zumbi; Slavery in Africa.

Latin America and the Caribbean

Palma Sola, Dominican town; site of the massacre of a largely Afro-Dominican religious community by government forces in 1962.

The massacre of a largely black and mulatto group of Dominicans in the Palma Sola township in the province of San Juan de la Maguana in 1962 remains an unresolved historical episode with regard to its specific causes and unfolding. However, the result – the death of hundreds of unarmed human beings – is clear.

Palma Sola was a small, rather isolated religious community near the Haitian-Dominican border. Its border location is significant because of the racist anti-Haitian attitudes held by members of the Dominican elite (*see* Dominican-Haitian Relations).

Palma Sola was considered a threat to the social, economic, and religious status quo, partly because of the community's practice of Vodou, which was regarded as immoral and opposed to Christian values. Other activities were considered antiestablishment as well. For instance, the community did not use money and prohibited the sale of food. While the residents of Palma Sola were never involved in physical attacks on people or property – in fact, they were not allowed to carry weapons – their activities were considered a major form of social protest, a quiet revolution in effect.

The province of San Juan de la Maguana has, in fact, served throughout Dominican history as the home of a people who challenged the system and prevailing ideologies. As early as 1543 it was the home of hundreds of Dominican runaway slaves. Some viewed the community in Palma Sola as a religious peasant movement reviving the cult of Liborio Mateo (Andrés Olivo Mateo), an Afro-Dominican who, at the turn of the century, was a messianic spiritual leader of a group of followers known as Liboristas. In 1922 Liborio was killed with the assistance of the United States military.

The provisional government of President Rafael Filberto Bonnelly (1961-1963), established after the assassination in 1961 of dictator Rafael Trujillo, determined that the religious activities and social protest of the inhabitants of Palma Sola were subverting "Christian values and morals" in the country. It ordered an attack on December 28, 1962. Allegedly, Miguel Rodríguez Reyes, inspector general of the armed forces, arrived at Palma Sola that day in the hope of negotiating a peaceful agreement with the Mellizos. According to accounts, he was extremely surprised to learn that he had been followed to the site by Chief of Police Francisco Camaño Deñó, with about 600 soldiers in tow. Confusion and shooting ensued, and Gen. Rodríguez Reyes was accidentally killed.

What followed was the murder by gas and bullets of hundreds of innocent victims – adults and children. After the massacre officers of the police and army burned the bodies or buried them in common graves. The survivors were taken prisoner and carried off to various jails throughout the region.

James Davis

Cross Cultural

Pan-African Congress of 1919, major international gathering to promote worldwide black unity, held in Paris in 1919.

African American activist and writer W. E. B. Du Bois organized the Pan-African Congress in order to bring together Africans and leaders of nations involved in the African diaspora, and to promote the cause of African independence. Du Bois insisted that the conference be held in Paris in 1919 during the proceedings of the Paris Peace Conference, soon after World War I. He wanted Germany's former colonies in eastern and southern Africa internationalized as the first step in gradual African self-determination (*see* Decolonization in Africa: An Interpretation). The Paris gathering followed a previous conference held in London in 1900, organized by Henry Sylvester Williams, a London barrister born in Trinidad.

The congress received considerable publicity, partly because of the cooperation of French Prime Minister Georges Clemenceau, who accepted its resolutions. The congress delegates did not advocate immediate independence for Africa. Instead they called for greater African participation in the affairs of the colonies and for the newly created League of Nations to undertake the protection and well-being of the African people. Individual resolutions called on the colonial powers to allow Africans to own land and participate in government, to tax and regulate companies operating in Africa in the interests of Africans' welfare, to ban forced labor and corporal punishment, and to safeguard Africans' religious and social freedom.

Blaise Diagne of Senegal, the first African to serve in the French Chamber of Deputies, delivered the keynote speech at the congress, which attracted 57 delegates. Despite the refusal of the United States and Great Britain to issue passports to some potential delegates, Americans constituted the most numerous contingent, with 16 delegates. Other nations represented were the French West Indies (*see* Guadeloupe and Martinique), 13; Haiti, 7; France, 7; Liberia, 3; and the Spanish colonies, 2. There was one delegate each from the Portuguese colonies, Santo Domingo, England, British Africa, French Africa, Algeria, Egypt, the Belgian Congo (now the Democratic Republic of the Congo), and Abyssinia (Ethiopia).

Prominent black Americans at the congress included Dr. Robert R. Moton, principal of the Tuskegee Institute; his secretary Nathan A. Hunt; and Lester A. Walton, managing editor of the *New York Age*, a weekly black newspaper in New York. White support was welcome; liberal activists such as Charles Edward Russell and William English Walling of the National Association for the Advancement of Colored People (NAACP) attended.

To keep African solidarity alive, Du Bois was also instrumental in the convening of several subsequent gatherings. The second Pan-African Congress was held in three sessions in 1921 in London, Brussels, and Paris; a third congress was held in 1923 in London and Lisbon. In 1974 – well after most African countries had achieved independence – the sixth Pan-African Congress was held in Dar es Salaam, Tanzania, and hosted by Tanzanian president Julius Nyerere. Attended by delegates from all over the world, including activists Owusu Sadaukai and Amiri Baraka, the gathering revealed a growing split between revolutionary Marxists and those delegates who supported African governments already in power.

David P. Johnson, Jr.

See Also

Dar es Salaam, Tanzania; Nyerere, Julius Kambarage; Great Britain; Pan-Africanism; Du Bois, William Edward Burghardt (W. E. B.); Moton, Robert Russa; New York, New York; Tuskegee University; Trinidad and Tobago.

Cross Cultural

Pan-Africanism, a wide range of ideologies that are committed to common political or cultural projects for Africans and people of African descent.

In its most straightforward version Pan-Africanism is the political project calling for the unification of all Africans into a single African state to which those in the African diaspora can return. In its vaguer, more cultural forms Pan-Africanism has pursued literary and artistic projects that bring together people in Africa and her diaspora.

Main Trends

The Pan-Africanist Movement began in the nineteenth century among intellectuals of African descent in North America and the Caribbean who thought of themselves as members of a single, "Negro," race. In this they were merely following the mainstream of nineteenth-century thought in North America and Europe, which developed an increasingly strong focus on the idea that human beings were divided into races, each of which had its own distinctive spiritual, physical, and cultural character. As a result the earliest Pan-Africanists often limited their focus to sub-Saharan Africa: to the region, that is, whose population consists mostly of darker-skinned (or, as they would have said, "Negro") peoples. In this way they intentionally left out lighter-skinned North Africans, including the large majority who speak Arabic as their first language.

In the twentieth century this way of thinking of African identity in racial terms has been challenged. In particular, the intellectuals born in Africa who took over the movement's leadership in the period after the World War II developed a more geographical idea of African identity. The founders of the Organization of African Unity (OAU), such as Gamal Abdel Nasser of Egypt and Kwame Nkrumah of Ghana, for example, had a notion of Africa that was more straightforwardly continental. African unity for them was the unity of those who shared the African continent (though it continued to include, in some unspecified way, those whose ancestors had left the continent in the enforced exile of the slave trade).

Nevertheless, the movement's intellectual roots lie firmly in the racial understanding of Africa in the thought of the African American and Afro-Caribbean intellectuals who founded it. Because Pan-Africanism began as a movement in the New World, among the descendants of slave populations, and then spread back to Africa, it aimed to challenge antiblack racism on two fronts. On the one hand, it opposed racial domination in the diaspora; on the other, it challenged colonial domination, which almost always took a racial form, in Africa itself. The stresses and strains that have sometimes divided the movement have largely occurred where these two rather different goals have pulled it in different directions.

Intellectual Origins

The idea of linking together the whole "Negro" race for political purposes was developed by a wide range of nineteenth-century, African American intellectuals. We can still speak of these nineteenth-century thinkers as Pan-Africanist, even though they did not use the term. Like Pan-Slavism in Eastern Europe and the forms of romantic nationalism that created modern Germany and Italy, early Pan-Africanism reflected a philosophical tradition, derived from the German philosopher Johann Gottfried Herder (1744-1803). In Herder's opinion, peoples (or, as they were often called, nations) such as the Slavs, Germans, and Italians, were the central actors of world history. He suggested that their identities were expressed largely in language, in literature, and in folk culture. And he thought that such nations were naturally drawn together by the desire to live together in states, with a shared language, culture, and traditions. The cultural oneness of a nation led naturally, in Herder's view, to political union.

The first black intellectual to apply this theory in a systematic way to people of African descent was W. E. B. Du Bois (1868-1963). In a lecture on "The Conservation of Races," published by the American Negro Academy in 1897, Du Bois used the word "Pan-Negroism." Du Bois was an African American who had studied as an undergraduate at Harvard with the philosopher William James. But in 1892 Du Bois had gone on to do graduate work at the Friedrich Wilhelm University in Berlin, and was, therefore, thoroughly familiar with the intellectual traditions of modern European nationalism, as well as with the philosophical tradition that began with Herder.

In "The Conservation of Races" Du Bois argued that "the history of the world is the history, not of individuals, but of groups, not of nations, but of races." (But he mentions Slavs, Teutons – that is, Germans – and the Romance race, indicating that, like so many other Western intellectuals of his day, he took real nations to *be* races.) He argued, too, that the differences among races were "spiritual, psychical, differences – undoubtedly based on the physical, but infinitely transcending them." And, finally, he insisted (in a manner strongly reminiscent of Herder) that each race was "striving... in its own way, to develop for civilization its particular message."

The problem for Pan-Negroism was how the Negro people were to deliver their message. Du Bois believed that African Americans (whom he called the "advance guard of the Negro people") were to play the leading role in that task. He thought that they were especially well-suited for this task because some of them, like Du Bois himself, had been exposed to the best modern educations and the highest forms of knowledge.

Though Du Bois's formulation had roots in the theorists of European nationalism, he was also strongly influenced by a number of earlier African American thinkers, whose work we can understand most easily in the context of the broad nineteenth-century history of antislavery or "abolitionist" thought. The focus of attention for all the major black thinkers in the New World in the early nineteenth century was the abolition of slavery and of the slave trade. Since most people, both black and white, believed that racial hostility between blacks and whites was inevitable (this view was explicitly held, for example, by United States presidents Jefferson and Lincoln), one major preoccupation of some abolitionists concerned finding territories that could be inhabited by freed blacks. The colony of Sierra Leone was created in the late eighteenth century by British abolitionists, in part as a home for freed blacks and the black poor of England; the American Colonization Society played a similar role in the creation of Liberia in the 1820s. But other schemes were proposed to colonize parts of Latin America, the Caribbean, and the American western frontier.

All of these schemes, of course, presupposed that Africans (and their descendants in the New World) belonged naturally together in a political community, separated from other peoples. There were significant voices raised in protest against this assumption – notably that of the American ex-slave and abolitionist Frederick Douglass – and they were joined by many others after the United States formally recognized the citizenship of people of African descent in the post-Civil War amendments to the U.S. Constitution. But in the first half of the nineteenth century the majority view, among both black and white intellectuals, was that a home was needed for the Negroes if they were to be free.

Perhaps the most important black intellectual forerunners of Pan-Africanism were three men who addressed themselves to this situation: Martin R. Delany (1812-1885), Alexander Crummell (1822-1898), and Edward Wilmot Blyden (1832-1912). Martin R. Delany was born in the southern United States, but his family moved to Pennsylvania during his youth. He began a medical education at Harvard, but was forced to leave because white students would not work alongside him. Delany's contributions to the pre-history of Pan-Africanism begin with his own sense of a profound connection with Africa. He was proud that he was a "full-blooded Negro" and he named his children for – among others – Toussaint L'Ouverture (the black leader of the Haitian Revolution), Ramses II (the pharaoh of Egypt), and Alexander Dumas (the French novelist of African ancestry). But he was also a powerful voice for black emigration from the United States, arguing in his *The Condition, Elevation, Emigration and Destiny of the Colored People of the United States* (1852) that only in a country without white people could black people flourish. In that early work Delany did not make the obvious suggestion that blacks should "return" to Africa. This was not because he was against the idea but because, along with other leaders of the re-emigration movement, he believed that most African Americans (convinced by anti-Negro propaganda) were likely to see Africa as a very unattractive place to live. In his *Official Report of the Niger Valley Exploration Party* (1861), written after he had been to Africa, he wrote of the continent as "our fatherland" and argued that its regeneration required the development of a "national character." And he proposed the formula, "Africa for the African race and black men to rule them," which is one of the earliest formulations of a Pan-Africanist principle.

Alexander Crummell was born in New York and studied at Cambridge University in England. He was the first African American to do so and was an ordained Anglican clergyman. He was also the first African American intellectual to spend a significant amount of time in Liberia. (When Delany visited that country in 1859, he met Crummell, who by then had been there for two decades.) In *The Future of Africa* (1862), a collection of essays and lectures written while he was in Liberia, Crummell developed a vision of Africa as the motherland of the Negro race. In "The English Language in Liberia," based on a lecture given on Liberian independence day in 1860, he argued that African Americans who had been "exiled" in slavery to the New World had been given by divine providence "at least this one item of compensation, namely, the possession of the Anglo-Saxon tongue." Similarly he argued for the providential nature of the transmission of Christianity to Negro slaves, and that it was the duty of "free colored men" in America to convert their ancestral continent to Christianity (*see* Christianity: Missionaries in Africa).

In the essay "The Relations and Duties of Free Colored Men in America to Africa," he also expressed with great clarity the underlying racial basis of his understanding of Negro identity. There he defined a race as "a compact, homogeneous population of one blood ancestry and lineage," and argued that each race had certain "determinate proclivities," which manifested themselves in the behavior of its members. Crummell was, with Blyden, one of the founders of Liberia College (later the University of Liberia). Unlike Blyden, however, he did not become a permanent resident of Liberia, returning rather to the United States, where he continued to argue for the importance of an engagement with Africa on the part of blacks in the African diaspora. Crummell was the leading spirit in the foundation of the American Negro Academy, and was present at the meeting at which Du Bois first read "The Conservation of Races." He was also a significant influence on Du Bois, who included an essay about Crummell in his extremely influential volume *The Souls of Black Folk* (1903).

Edward Blyden was born in the West Indies but traveled to Liberia in 1850 under the auspices of the American Colonization Society and became a citizen of that country for the rest of his life. Like Crummell, he was a priest, and, as we have seen, they worked together in the early days of the University of Liberia. Blyden spoke many languages. His essays include quotations in the original languages from Dante and Virgil, and he studied Arabic in order to teach it at Liberia College. Later he became the Liberian ambassador to Queen Victoria.

In *Christianity, Islam and the Negro Race* (1887) Blyden expressed the conviction that underlies Du Bois's first explicit formulation of Pan-Africanism: "Among the conclusions to which study and research are conducting philosophers, none is clearer than this – that each of the races of mankind has a specific character and specific work." Blyden, like Crummell, had little respect for the traditional cultures of Africa. They shared the view that Christian blacks in the diaspora had a responsibility to convert their African cousins. But Blyden argued explicitly that what he called Africa's current "state of barbarism" did not reflect any innate deficiency in the Negro. "There is not a single mental or moral deficiency now existing among Africans," he said, "... to which we cannot find a parallel in the past history of Europe."

The Pan-African Congresses

Pan-Africanism as an intellectual movement begins, then, in the work of Du Bois, Delany, Crummell, and Blyden. But its institutional history starts with Henry Sylvester Williams, a London barrister born in Trinidad. He planned to bring together people of the "African race" from around the world in 1897; and in July 1900, after a preliminary conference in 1899, such a gathering took place in London. (The actual word "Pan-Africanism" seems to have been coined either at this first Pan-African Congress or at the earlier planning conference.) There were four African representatives – one each from Ethiopia, Sierra Leone, Liberia, and the Gold Coast colony – and a dozen from North America (among them Du Bois); eleven representatives came from the West Indies, five from London. The conference opened with the clearly stated aim of allowing black people to discuss the condition of the black race around the world.

The First Pan-African Congress convened in Paris in February 1919; it was attended by 57 delegates from 15 countries. In 1921 Du Bois and others organized a second Pan-African Congress, which met in three sessions, in London, Brussels, and Paris, this time with representatives from French and Portuguese colonies in Africa as well. They issued a final declaration that insisted on the equality of the races, the diffusion of democracy, and the development of political institutions in the colonies. It also urged the "return" of Negroes to their own countries and urged the League of Nations to pay attention both to race relations in the industrialized world and the condition of workers in the colonies.

A third congress occurred in London in 1923 and continued, according to Du Bois, in Lisbon (though this appears to have been little more than an opportunity for Du Bois to talk to some people from the Portuguese colonies on his way from London to Liberia, where he was the official representative of the United States at the installation of the Liberian president). The Pan-African Congress movement then effectively disappeared until the fifth congress in Manchester in 1945, during which the baton was handed from the diaspora to the continent. Du Bois's contribution now lay in the shadow of that of figures such as Kwame Nkrumah, who was to be Ghana's first prime minister. (And, indeed, Du Bois was the only African American present.) The sixth Congress, held in 1974 in Dar es Salaam, was presided over by Tanzanian president Julius Nyerere.

During the period between World War I and World War II, in the heyday of the Pan-African Congress movement, the sentiment received a substantial practical boost from the growth of the Universal Negro Improvement Association (UNIA). Led by Marcus Garvey, a Jamaican immigrant to the United States, the UNIA became the largest black movement in the African diaspora. While the slogan of the movement was "Back to Africa," and Garvey did indeed plan a shipping line for the purpose, relatively few members of the organization actually left the New World for the Old. Nevertheless, Garvey's commitment to racial pride and to the celebration of black historical achievement, and his concern to link the diaspora to the continent, make him an important figure in the movement's history.

One West-Indian-born intellectual *did* play an important role in planning the 1945 Congress, namely George Padmore (1902-1959). (Padmore was a pseudonym: he was born Malcolm Nurse.) Padmore was a Trinidadian who had spent some time in the United States studying at Columbia University and at Fisk (a university in Nashville, Tennessee, which Du Bois had also attended). He worked as a Communist Party organizer among students at Howard University in Washington, D.C. Later he spent time in Germany and in Russia, where he became in 1930 the head of the Negro Bureau of the Red International of labor unions. In the next few years he worked for communist organizations in Austria and Germany, moving to London in 1935. From then until his death in 1959 he was the leading theorist of Pan-Africanism, and was a close friend and adviser of Kwame Nkrumah. His *Pan-Africanism or Communism* (1956) is probably the most important statement of his position.

Pan-Africanism Today

In the period after World War II African intellectuals were preoccupied with the question of independence. Once independence was attained, Pan-Africanism became an ideology through which relations among the newly independent states could be thought about. Pan-Africanist rhetoric continues to be important in the language of the Organization of African Unity, which was founded in 1963.

In that same period black intellectuals in North America were taken up with questions of civil rights. There were always resonances between these two projects – Du Bois was involved in both throughout his long life, and died a citizen of Ghana; African diplomats sought to have civil rights questions raised in the forum of the United Nations. But Pan-Africanism took philosophical form in the period leading up to Padmore's work, and its major theoretical works are those of Padmore and Du Bois.

Kwame Anthony Appiah

See Also

Christianity, African: An Overview; Dar es Salaam, Tanzania; Egypt, Ancient Kingdom of; Nyerere, Julius Kambarage; Race: An Interpretation; Transatlantic Slave Trade; Dumas, Alexandre, Père; Tanzania; World War I and African Americans; Abolitionism in the United States; American Negro Academy; Civil Rights Movement; Civil War, American; Delany, Martin Robison; Du Bois, William Edward Burghardt (W. E. B.); Fisk University; Garvey, Marcus Mosiah; New York, New York; Jamaica; Trinidad and Tobago; Communist Party USA, African Americans and the; Toussaint L'Ouverture, François Dominique.

Latin America and the Caribbean

Pan-Africanism and Afro-Latin Americans

Darién J. Davis

"No nos vamos a unir por ser personas negras, sino por identificarnos con las obras de personas negras" (We are not going to unite because we are black, but because we identify with legacies of black people) (Juan de Dios Mosquera, Moviemento Nacional Cimarrón, Colombia).

"In cooperation we need to build bridges. We cannot do it alone" (Charles Mohan, employee association delegate, United States).

Between 1900 and 1974 Pan-Africanists organized six international conferences. African Americans from the United States had a crucial role in these forums, and English-speaking black people initially appeared in the forefront. African American W. E. B. Du Bois and Jamaican-born Marcus Garvey were Pan-Africanism's two most important figures in the early twentieth century. While Du Bois toiled for self-reliance and integration, Garvey promoted self-determination and separatism. Both struggled for the promotion of black consciousness and dignity; Du Bois was involved in the organization of the Pan-Africanist conferences for more than 40 years. The first such conference, in Paris in 1919, resulted in the indictment of imperialism and support for self-determination for African nations. At the next three conferences – 1921, 1923, and 1927 – colonialism in Africa remained the central focus.

The fifth Pan-African Congress of 1944 produced a schism between Garveyites and followers of Du Bois, as new voices from Africa and the Caribbean emerged. While colonialism remained an important issue, Caribbean Pan-Africanists such as C. L. R. James stressed the need for class analysis of racial problems. For the first time the conference demanded the outright independence of Africa and the rights of all peoples throughout the African diaspora. Between the fifth and the sixth conferences a host of regional movements, particularly in Africa, the United States, and the Caribbean, attained momentum. By the time of the sixth Pan-African Conference in 1974, regional movements were on the rise in the Americas. Nationalist struggles and civil rights movements had emerged with specific national agendas, not always in step with international Pan-Africanism.

Latin American Pan-Africanists have long recognized Africa as the source of a shared experience and have denounced European and North American imperialism in Africa, condemned racism and prejudice internationally, celebrated heroes of the African diaspora, and forged links with groups and individuals abroad. Yet Afro-Latin American participation in the Pan-Africanist movement has been historically weak. Language barriers have limited the participation of Spanish- and Portuguese-speaking activists, while sociocultural, economic, and political disfranchisement often prohibited Afro-Latin Americans from creating strong national or international voices.

Language, for example, becomes a barrier when individuals throughout the diaspora are prohibited from meaningful discourse. Afro-Americans all over the continent speak and write in many languages, from *patois*, Papiamento, and Garifuna to major European languages (*see* Languages, Creole, in the Caribbean). Thus, international dialogue is often fractured by language groups. In recent years the propagation of English as an unofficial lingua franca has facilitated dialogue among people involved in race consciousness and civil rights movements. But many grassroots organizers do not have access to English classes, and many Latin Americans regard the prevalence of English as a form of cultural imperialism. Adoption of Spanish, however, does not solve the problem entirely, particularly, of course, for Brazilians.

While education and interpretation services slowly erode language barriers among Latin American Pan-Africanists, other factors remain endemic. Political, economic, and cultural underdevelopment greatly affects the ability of would-be Pan-Africanists to participate in global forums. Although Afro-Latin Americans' political participation has never been explicitly restricted by race, slavery, disfranchisement, and economic deprivation have inhibited the growth of a coherent black middle class. Lower-income classes, in general, have less discretionary time to invest in national, much less international, enterprises. Moreover, lack of political access prohibits racial discrimination from becoming an agenda issue in favor of class inequalities.

The politics of racial identity represent the most formidable enemy of Pan-Africanism. In the great majority of countries in Latin America and the Caribbean, *mestizaje*, miscegenation, nationalism, and color codes have inhibited solidarity among people of African descent within individual countries. In many such countries race is seemingly unimportant, while color has a more significant role in the social hierarchy. This color consciousness, combined with fervent patriotism and nationalism, encourages identification with the nation rather than with extranational entities. The apparently fluid color line and theories of whitening thus together prohibit the development of a strong race consciousness. Yet despite such difficulties, many Afro-Latin Americans have opposed national and social constructs that seek to make them "invisible."

Although race consciousness heightened in the post-World War II era, the onslaught of military dictatorships in many Latin American countries further hindered the possible emergence of black movements in the 1960s and 1970s. With the return to liberal democratic governments in the 1980s and 1990s, national movements and organizations have blossomed. As a consequence the Americas have witnessed an increase in international cooperation among people of the African diaspora, most notably the series of Congresses on Black Culture in the Americas.

Congresses on Black Culture in the Americas

The Congresses on Black Culture in the Americas, organized between 1977 and 1984, represented a rare success in Pan-African organization. While participation came overwhelmingly from artists and intellectuals, the spirit of the conferences reflected a strong desire to forge solidarity among people of African descent throughout the diaspora.

Held in Cali, COLOMBIA, in 1977 and sponsored by the Organization of American States in conjunction with the Fundación Colombiana de Investigaciones Folklóricas, the first congress took pride in the fact that it represented the first hemispheric reflection on Afro-Americans by Afro-Americans. After an emotional opening Afro-American delegates divided themselves among several working commissions to discuss political ideas, religions, aesthetics, and morals; socioeconomic structures; art and technologies; and ethnicity, mestizaje, castes, and classes. The commissions were united in their denunciation of all mechanisms of alienation aimed at people of African descent in the Americas. Delegates called for greater unity while pledging to increase investigations of the historical importance of Africans in the creation of Latin American culture and to support struggles of liberation in Africa.

The Second Congress on Black Culture in the Americas, held in Panama City, PANAMA, in 1980, developed the theme of race and class. Delegates discussed issues under the broad theme of "Cultural Identity of Blacks in the Americas." Sponsored by the Instituto Nacional de Cultura de Panama with the aid of the Centro de Estudios Afro-Panameños and the Patrimonio Histórico, four commissions were convened, along with roundtables to discuss future strategies of cooperation. According to Congress president Gerado Maloney, two major achievements of the conference were the integration and incorporation of Afro-Americans from all regions of the Americas, including the English- and French-speaking Caribbean, and the conviction of all members to acknowledge the inseparable relationship between ethnicity and class.

The third congress, held in São Paulo, BRAZIL, in 1982 under the directorship of the Brazilian political activist ABDIAS DO NASCIMENTO in conjunction with the Instituto de Pesquisa e Estudos Afro-Brasileiros, was more defiant in tone. The theme of this congress, "African Diaspora: Political Consciousness and African Culture," reflected the growing political consciousness of Afro-American communities. Increased black consciousness and politicization of black movements led to a more forceful condemnation of racist politics around the globe. Delegates declared solidarity with a number of national liberation movements, particularly in Africa and the Middle East. The conference passed motions of support for, and solidarity with, NAMIBIA'S SOUTH WEST AFRICA PEOPLE'S ORGANIZATION (SWAPO), SOUTH AFRICA'S AFRICAN NATIONAL CONGRESS (ANC), and the Palestine Liberation Organization. The conference also recognized the need to reach out to marginalized Afro-American communities and organizations in countries previously unrepresented in Pan-African work. In particular it was noted that Afro-Uruguayans were in danger of being further isolated from national life.

The fourth congress, initially planned for Paris with the theme "Afro-America and the European Community," instead took place in Quito, ECUADOR, in 1984, focusing on black women in the Americas.

Since 1984 several regional meetings have drawn scholars, intellectuals, and activists from around the hemisphere. The dream of a formal and permanent Pan-African organization, however, is yet to be achieved. Funding and regional and national problems still plague national movements and make international coordination difficult. Besides, such international organizations have historically emphasized scholarship, art, and intellectual concerns, rather than grassroots activities. Nonetheless, pressures of economic and political globalization, and the collapse of Eastern European state socialism make the need for international communication among African Americans ever more urgent.

THE FIRST SEMINAR ON RACISM AND XENOPHOBIA, MONTEVIDEO, DECEMBER 1994

The uneven development of the various Afro-Latin American movements, especially in regions not usually associated with the African diaspora, such as the Southern Cone and the Andes, has made communication among many Afro-Latin American grassroots movements difficult. With these constraints in mind, Mundo Afro of URUGUAY announced its plans to host in December 1994 the First Seminar on Racism and Xenophobia in Montevideo.

The Uruguayan conference reflected, on the one hand, the development of Pan-Africanism in the Americas; on the other hand, it illustrated the long and hard work ahead if the dream of an intercontinental organization is to be brought to fruition. Unlike previous meetings, the one in Uruguay was largely anti-academic. Indeed, its United States coordinator, Michael Franklin of the Organization of Africans in the Americas, stressed the problem-solving focus. While political awareness and activism have heightened over the years, activists and grassroots organizers see the importance of establishing a rapport with international political and economic institutions, particularly in the United States. Partnerships with such institutions may provide valuable future contacts and access to funds as well as information, not to mention the chance to raise visibility internationally and thus nationally. Unfortunately grassroots movements representing poor or disfranchised minority groups often receive national attention only after they have obtained international recognition, particularly from the United States or the European Union.

The Montevideo conference was, however, far more than an exercise in seeking visibility. Organizers and participants searched for a balance between grassroots action and intellectual cooperation, with the long-term goal of educating the public.

For Afro-Uruguayans the conference was a crucial turning point in a long but slow civil rights struggle. Young and old Uruguayans turned out in support of platforms and ideas that would be of central importance to their communities. While participants were expected from all of the cultural and linguistic regions of the Americas, representatives and advocates of Afro-Latin Americans from the United States, Brazil, Uruguay, ARGENTINA, HONDURAS, the Dominican Republic, Colombia, PERU, and CUBA constituted the majority of the participants. The absence of major leaders from past conferences and community activists from many other Latin American communities was an indication of far-reaching structural problems that limit communication among Latin American nations. Many activists from Brazil, Central America, and the Caribbean were not aware of the conference, for example. Indeed, there is no intercontinental database that registers the major movements or activists from each country, nor are there sufficient resources to ensure contact and follow-up.

Structural and political problems notwithstanding, Montevideo symbolized an important watershed in black consciousness within the region as delegates began to define, in the words of the official agenda, a "Program for the Development of Black Latin America." In addition, major networking took place after the official presentations, in the lobbies, bars, cafés, and restaurants. Personal contacts were made, and discussions held, among union leaders, representatives of women's groups, human rights and development workers, local campaigners and organizers, and other participants.

The Montevideo Conference: Commissions and Outcomes

The five commissions at Montevideo provided important frameworks for future cooperation and consideration. A brief description of the activities of each commission follows.

Education, Culture, and Communication. Delegates in this commission debated issues related to the educational reality and cultural rejuvenation of Afro-Americans, focusing particularly on proposals that would permit advances within black communities. The commission arrived at several long term goals, including a commitment to set up an inter-American communications network using fax and electronic mail. It was agreed that the interhemispheric network should be further divided into the three regions of North America, the Caribbean and Central America, and South America. Other resolutions included the creation of an intercontinental pressure group responsible for responding to events affecting black communities throughout the hemisphere and the promotion of educational programs related to Africans.

Women and Society. Afro-Americans clearly understand the extra pressures that women face in their respective communities. This commission set out to develop economic alternatives to improve family income, to generate work, and to improve the standard of living of black women around the hemisphere, while promoting the most efficient forms of social integration. The historical contributions of black women to American societies were discussed. Those contributions, the session unanimously agreed, have been continually minimized and ignored. The illiteracy, pauperization, and hardship that so many Afro-American women experience today is indicative of that neglect. High unemployment and rural-urban migration have led to problems of sexual exploitation, involuntary sterilization, lack of access to education and health services, and a high incidence of acquired immune deficiency syndrome (AIDS). The lack of role models, multiplication of negative stereotypes, and severe underrepresentation of women in the decision-making processes of nongovernmental and governmental organizations and agencies have further compounded the problem. The commission agreed to pursue strategies to increase the visibility of Afro-American women and to guarantee their access to credit, education, and health care.

International Cooperation and Alternative Development. This commission listed its main aim as the generation of collective ideas for a quantitative and qualitative advancement of Afro-American communities in the third millennium. Participants also saw their role as helping to create a continental network of cooperation that would facilitate the sustainable development of Afro-American communities. Representatives from Latin America were particularly concerned to promote cooperative relationships with multinational corporations, nongovernmental organizations, and other international institutions; other delegates warned that relations with international organizations should be approached with caution. Most agreed that grassroots movements should under no circumstances relinquish direction and control of their projects and communities to international financial institutions. Likewise, it was argued that cooperation among Latin American countries should take into account the relative development and potential of each national community. A representative from the international financial community warned that Afro-Americans cannot simply shun international lending institutions because they need to become not just job seekers, but job creators. Two broad goals expressed by this commission, largely in agreement with proposals made by other commissions, were, first, to encourage black organizations to alert financial institutions to their plans for the development of black communities; and, second, to encourage and persuade financial institutions to direct funds toward black communities.

Political Strategies. Mundo Afro's vision of political strategies was decidedly long-term. After centuries of isolation Afro-Latin Americans were looking at ways to consolidate and augment their political power. Delegates began their discussion with an eye toward stimulating initiatives with governments and private institutions that would lead to the further integration of black communities into national life. The development of strategies of cooperation, representation, information, promotion, and technical aid for the interchange of information among the countries of Europe, the Americas, and black Africa became the guiding aim. Many political strategies emerged, ranging from the theoretical and long-term to immediate activities for specific groups and communities. One general project united participants, however: the desire to develop an intercontinental network based on regional commissions with a continental directory comprising delegates from each Afro-Latin American organization. Such a network could serve as a coordinating body for the future.

Population, Human Rights, Youth, and the Elderly. Human rights specialists and activists structured their discussions around two main goals: first, to promote human rights for young people, children, and the elderly through continual action and the implementation of specific programs of assistance and development; second, to formulate proposals for better management of the natural environment that reflect the black community's knowledge, experience, and needs in relation to nature and natural resources. Participants regarded human rights, care for the elderly, and guidance for the young as fundamental to the preservation of their African American identity.

Conclusions and Future Prospects

The plethora of proposals, suggestions, and resolutions from the five commissions at Montevideo reflected the political, economic, and cultural diversity within the Afro-American community. While race was the major factor around which the delegates of these five commissions converged, many Latin American civil rights activists are first and foremost interested in political commitment. However, it is the sense of commitment itself, an awareness of the necessity for collective struggle, that united participants and opposed them to a more individualist and assimilationist outlook. As one delegate put it, "We are interested in conscious people. It doesn't matter if you're black or white. But we want a commitment." While race is the indisputable basis of the shared Pan-African experience, the history of mestizaje and the assimilation of Africans make the issue of levels of commitment an important one among Afro-Latin Americans.

By the end of the four-day encounter the Montevideo conference had arrived at a series of resolutions for the short and the long term. Personal contacts and institutional partnerships had been built. Delegates unanimously supported the creation of an intercontinental network that would first be based on regional integration. On the closing day of the conference South American delegates agreed to hold a second meeting in April 1995 in the southern Brazilian city of Santa Ana do Livramento to elaborate on the network, its goals, parameters, and methods of working. Delegates from the United States, the Caribbean, and Central America were also to be invited to the meeting as observers.

The U.S. delegation also committed itself to establishing future communications among Afro-Latin Americans and African Americans in the United States. Tentatively planned for late 1995 at Howard University, Washington, D.C., the conference "Race, Institutional Development and Human Rights: The Present Status and Condition of Blacks in Latin America," would, it was hoped, examine issues of race relations in Latin America on a country-by-country basis, as well as the role of African Americans in addressing some of those issues.

Since 1995 a number of regional initiatives have brought black Latin Americans together to discuss important issues relevant to local development and international cooperation. In August 1996 Afro-Latin Americans gathered at San José and Limón, Costa Rica, to celebrate what was billed as a "Black Family Reunion." In November of that year, Claire Nelson of the Inter-American Development Bank in Washington, D.C., helped organize an unprecedented meeting on "Alleviating Poverty for Minority Communities in Latin America," which saw the participation of black academics and writers in addition to politicians such as Benedita da Silva, Rio de Janeiro's first black congresswoman. The year 1997 saw similar initiatives, as black Latin Americans continued dialogues among themselves and with blacks in the United States.

Whatever the outcome of the international network, Montevideo arguably represented a turning point for Pan-Africanism in the Americas. Afro-Latin Americans around the continent are increasingly mobilizing and refusing to allow their national governments to ignore them. They are renewing themselves through forms of political and economic organization, building on international links and partnerships. At the end of the conference participants shared a more hopeful and purposeful vision of the future, and there was a strong sense of being involved in a process that promises to help release Afro-Latin Americans from the burdens of centuries of oppression.

Originally published in *No Longer Invisible: Afro-Latin Americans Today* (London, 1995).

See Also

Pan-Africanism; Du Bois, William Edward Burghardt (W. E. B.); Garvey, Marcus Mosiah; James, Cyril Lionel Richard; Dominican Republic; Rio de Janeiro, Brazil; Transculturation, Mestizaje, and the Cosmic Race: An Interpretation; Human Rights in Latin America and the Caribbean.

Africa

Pan-Africanist Congress, South African antiapartheid organization and political party.

Founded in 1959 as an offshoot of the African National Congress (ANC), the Pan-Africanist Congress (PAC) has always been the more radical of the two antiapartheid organizations. Explicitly nationalistic and racialist, less committed to nonviolence than the ANC, the PAC has played an important role in South African history while never achieving the membership or international recognition of its parent organization.

Among the PAC's founders were Robert Sobukwe, Potlako Leballo, A. P. Mda, and other former ANC members. They were disappointed by what they saw as the older organization's excessive caution and willingness to compromise in its campaign to overthrow South Africa's apartheid regime. In particular, PAC leaders opposed the ANC's multiracialism – it welcomed white and Indian members – and what was seen as the ANC's embrace of communism.

Their objections grew following the ANC's 1956 adoption of the Freedom Charter, a document calling for multiracial cooperation and communal economic principles. Arguing for "authentic African nationalism," Sobukwe and others tried to take over the local ANC leadership in the Transvaal, which some felt was the region of strongest Africanist sentiment. Failing that, and after Labello's expulsion from the ANC, Sobukwe and his fellow dissidents announced the formation in April 1959 of the Pan-Africanist Congress.

As the PAC's first president, Sobukwe delineated the differences between his organization and the ANC. While the ANC, he said, viewed the antiapartheid movement as "a class struggle," for the PAC the fight was "a national struggle." Accordingly, rather than seeking a free South Africa for all, as the ANC did, the PAC would fight for "Afrika for Africans." As part of its wish that black South Africans could escape their "slave mentality," the PAC encouraged a "mental revolution" for the country it called "Azania."

Promising complete revolution by 1963, the PAC boasted some 31,000 members soon after its founding. Beyond the Transvaal, however, its organization was weak. The PAC's first major test came in 1960. For years Africans had been subject to arrest, fines, and imprisonment if they failed to produce their passes – sometimes called registration books – which contained identification, tax, and travel documents. Sobukwe called for a national demonstration on March 21, asking that Africans gather at their local police stations, turn in their passes, and invite arrest. The largest demonstration was in Sharpeville, a black township south of Johannesburg. Police opened fire on the unarmed protesters, killing 69, almost all of whom were shot in the back while trying to flee.

The government reacted to the widespread rioting that followed the massacre by banning both the PAC and the ANC. Operating in exile in Basutoland (now Lesotho) and led after 1962 by acting president Labello, the PAC underwent ideological flux and dissension; by the late 1960s the formerly anticommunist organization was avowedly Maoist. In its support for armed resistance, the PAC attracted new followers after the Soweto uprising of 1976, but it also lost members to splinter groups, including the Azanian People's Revolutionary Party. The PAC put forward candidates in South Africa's first free elections in 1994, winning 243,000 votes and five seats in the National Assembly.

Kate Tuttle

See Also

Antiapartheid Movement; Indian Communities in Africa; Johannesburg, South Africa; Nationalism in Africa; Sharpeville, South Africa; Soweto, South Africa; Pan-Africanism; Pass Laws; South Africa.

Latin America and the Caribbean

Panama, republic of Central America and home to a large black minority comprising the descendants of slaves or of West Indian workers brought to the country to build the Panama Canal.

Panama has been inhabited by aborigines, descendants of migrants who crossed from Asia to North America, for at least 10,000 years. Pre-Columbian peoples settled in Panama and the surrounding region, developed agriculture and stone tool making, and eventually produced elaborate gold jewelry, beads, and multicolored pottery, which have been found in their *huacas* (burial mounds). Later peoples flourished, but a single, powerful kingdom comparable to the Mayan, Aztec, or Incan was not in evidence at the time of European arrival (*see* Mexico and Peru). Most early inhabitants farmed, fished, traded goods among villages, and lived in thatched-roof huts like those in which many of their descendants live today.

Spaniards first arrived in Panama in 1501, and among the several hundred who arrived in the century's first decade were many African slaves (*see* Slavery in Latin America and the Caribbean). Most of the earliest settlers – European and African alike – succumbed to tropical disease and other perils. Nonetheless, when the Spanish explorer Vasco Núñez de Balboa mounted a journey across the Panamanian isthmus in 1513, African soldiers and assistants went with him. Thus as Balboa became the first European to see the Pacific Ocean, so too were his black cohorts the first Africans to reach the Pacific. The following year the new royal governor of the colony brought with him to the isthmus a group of *ladino* servants, Africans who had been Christianized and Hispanicized in Spain.

Panama was important to Spain because it offered the narrowest land route from the Atlantic to the Pacific – and thus an ideal place from which to launch military expeditions to Peru and the rest of South America. In short order goods and people were shipped to the Panamanian ports of Nombre de Dios and Portobelo on the Atlantic coast, hauled across Panama, and put aboard ships at the Pacific port of Panama City, from which they sailed to further ports. (Not long thereafter, exports returned in the reverse direction back to Spain.) At first Africans played only a small role in this trade; the Spaniards preferred to rely on readily available Indian labor rather than on expensive imports from Africa. Under Governor Pedro Arias de Ávila (also known as Pedrarias), however, Indians were treated brutally; those not killed by new diseases were subjected to vicious treatment as slaves or were massacred outright. In a matter of years the Indian population – estimated at more than half a million at the time of the Spanish arrival – dwindled to a few thousand, with survivors fleeing to remote parts of the isthmus.

Pedrarias the Cruel, as the governor was called, was denounced by some of the priests in the region, notably Bartolomé de Las Casas. Las Casas returned to Spain, persuaded the Crown to adopt and enforce more humane policies toward the Indians, and urged that Indian slaves in Panama and the rest of the New World be replaced with Africans, whose enslavement he did not question. The suggestion regarding the importation of Africans was one that Las Casas would live to regret. In 1517 King Charles V authorized the shipment of several thousand slaves to the New World, inaugurating an era as cruel as the one it was intended to replace.

The Rapid Rise of Slavery

A large number of the new slaves arrived in the first half of the 1500s, but at first the port of Panama was used more as a distribution center than a final destination. By the mid-1500s, however, transisthmus commerce had increased to the point that more and more slaves were sent to work in Panama. Most of these slaves appear to have originated from Upper Guinea, the area of coastal western Africa stretching from present-day Senegal to present-day Liberia. African slaves built and maintained the warehouses at the trade bazaars on both coasts as well as the ships that sailed to and from the commercial sector. Scores of slaves were also responsible for driving more than a thousand mules laden with goods back and forth across the peninsula. The work of crossing the isthmus could be harsh, plagued as it was by difficult roads, inclement weather, and attacks by Indians (*see* Slavery in Latin America and the Caribbean).

Slaves in Panama often took advantage of their numbers and the mountainous, jungled topography of the trade route to escape. The escapees were known as *cimarrones*, a word that was originally applied to wild plants or animals and later to runaway slaves. Some established villages and some preyed on the transisthmus travel from which they had escaped. In the early 1550s a group of cimarrones led by a former slave called King Bayano wreaked enough havoc on the trade route to prompt a hunt for Bayano. Captured in 1553, he was castrated, pardoned, and released, whereupon he organized another group of raiders. Bayano was again captured in 1558, his fate unknown. Two other prominent cimarrón leaders, Luis de Mozambique and Antón Mandinga, raided until Spain issued a general pardon for all of Panama's cimarrones in the 1570s. The raiders under de Mozambique and Mandinga then established the maroon settlements (*cimarroneras*) named Santiago del Príncipe and Santa Cruz la Real.

Still, there were indications that slave revolts continued for several decades: in the early seventeenth century officials in Panama and other parts of Central America asked the Crown to ban the import of *bozales* (slaves who came directly from Africa). Bozales, claimed the officials, were more prone to disobedience and more able to disrupt colonial life after they escaped than were Hispanicized slaves.

As they did in other parts of the Spanish Empire, slaves also performed routine tasks in Panama. Many served in the houses of their European masters or worked in small enterprises where such goods as textiles and dyes were produced. Some slaves were trained as artisans: as blacksmiths, cobblers, and carpenters. When gold was periodically discovered in Panama, slaves were sent to the mines, an assignment not conducive to a long life. The reliance on forced labor in so many fields fueled the importation of Africans, and in most parts of the colony blacks far outnumbered their white owners by the end of the 1500s (*see* COLONIAL LATIN AMERICA AND THE CARIBBEAN). In 1610 a census of Panama City recorded 548 (European) citizens, 303 (European) women, 156 (European) children, 146 mulattos (persons of African and European descent), 148 West Indian blacks, and 3500 slaves. By 1625 blacks in Panama numbered 12,000, and by 1630 blacks outnumbered whites by ten to one. The vast majority lived in the trade zone between Panama City and Portobelo.

As long as whites and blacks were both outnumbered by Amerindians, slaves received some degree of preference since it was important for Europeans to have reliable allies against the numerous natives. However, as the Indian population declined and the black population grew, Africans and their descendants began to be viewed by whites as the larger threat. Accordingly, racial segregation and restrictions on social mobility grew rigid. As the free black population grew (slaves were emancipated either by their masters or by buying their own freedom) and some blacks were able to acquire education and income, they were banned from many professions as well as most political offices. Free blacks thus were limited to lesser roles as artisans and petty bureaucrats. As trade increased on the isthmus and more blacks were brought to Panama, their sheer numbers, coupled with the scarcity of whites in parts of the country, assured the penetration of free blacks into at least the lower and middle echelons of government and the small shop-owning class. Through the seventeenth and eighteenth centuries the work and lifestyle of Afro-Panamanians changed little. By 1789 nearly 23,000 of the 36,000 residents in Panama were of African descent.

INDEPENDENCE OF A SORT

In the early 1800s, when the wars of liberation erupted in Central America, the *criollos* (settlers of Spanish descent) so outnumbered recent Spanish immigrants that the rule of Spain was cast off with very little fighting. Although Africans in Panama (which was part of COLOMBIA after independence from Spain in 1821 and remained as such until 1903) achieved the abolition of slavery, their social status did not rise automatically. They did not ascend within the caste system by virtue of their military service in the wars of independence as Africans elsewhere in Latin America did (*see* RACIAL QUESTION DURING STRUGGLES OF INDEPENDENCE IN LATIN AMERICA). Realizing their lack of progress, militant blacks made increasingly public demands on the Colombian government, of which they were citizens, in the 1830s. A race war was narrowly averted through skillful negotiation in the Colombian city of Mompóx in 1837 and 1838, but race riots were not so easily avoided in Panama City and Colón around that time. Before officials put down these uprisings, they had approached full-scale warfare. At the end of the fighting, however, whites prevailed and the caste system, both in its formal and informal senses, was preserved. Formal manifestations of the caste system included national prohibitions on

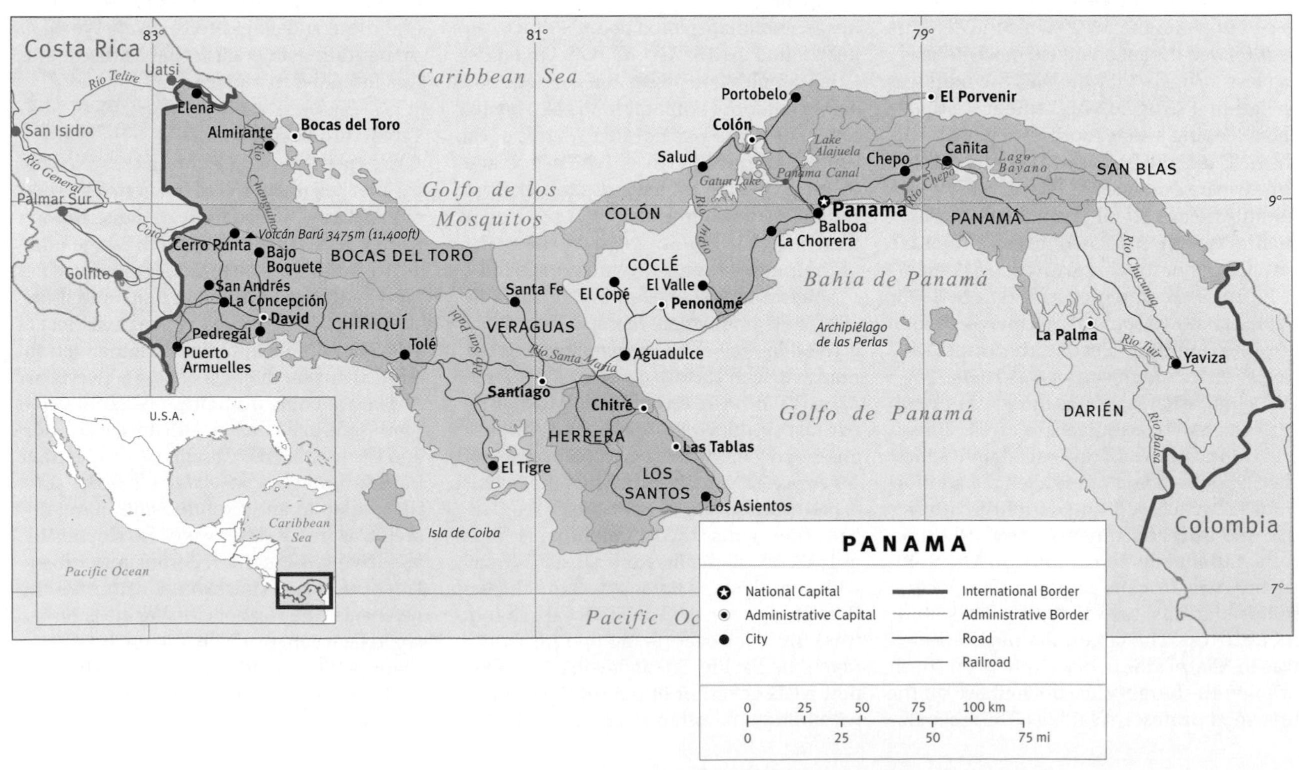

Dos Caras de la misma corazón (Two Faces of the Same Heart), 1992, Bocas de Toro, Panama. *Tony Gleaton*

voting for those who were illiterate or who possessed no property (groups that necessarily included large numbers of blacks). Less formal – but no less rigid – was the refusal by almost all whites to marry darker-skinned people. Any white who crossed the color line risked social and economic ostracism. As a result, black culture in Panama, although it largely mirrored the dominant culture (for example, virtually all Afro-Panamanians were Catholic), was isolated and apart from it.

In November 1903, supported by a United States government eager to build a canal across the isthmus (in order to shorten ship travel between the Atlantic and Pacific oceans), Panama seceded from Colombia. Two weeks later the United States and Panama signed the Hay-Bunau Varilla Treaty, giving the United States the right to build and exercise virtual sovereignty over an 8-km (5-mi) strip on each side of the canal route. For manual labor the United States at first gave incentives to poor migrants from Spain and Italy. Later the government imported black West Indians, particularly from Jamaica, Barbados, and Trinidad. In all some 50,000 blacks were brought in for the ten-year construction project.

West Indian blacks, also known as Antilleans or, derogatorily, *chumbos*, faced routine discrimination from their U.S. supervisors. While the white, mostly North American technicians and engineers working on the canal were paid in gold, Panamanian manual laborers were paid in silver. Blacks and other Panamanians were also paid less than the Spaniards and Italians who performed manual labor alongside them. Moreover, the U.S. government recruited many of its supervisors from the U.S. South, on the theory that Southerners were more accustomed to dealing with black laborers than were Northerners. The Southerners quickly established a system of segregation in housing and public facilities that mirrored the Jim Crow laws of their homeland.

The societal changes caused by the building of the canal had far-reaching effects beyond the Canal Zone. Most *mestizo* (of Indian and European descent) and Creole (of European descent born in America) Panamanians were deeply offended that the U.S. government lumped them together with "inferior" blacks. Whether the blacks were Spanish-speaking Panamian citizens or English-speaking West Indian migrants was largely beside the point, for mestizos had long enjoyed dominance over anyone of darker color. Creoles and mestizos vented their frustration outside the Canal Zone by sharpening discrimination against all blacks, not just West Indians. The completion of the canal in 1914 brought no end to racial tensions, especially since 20,000 West Indians remained in the country despite being offered tickets home. The West Indians – who often lived in separate settlements, sent their children to separate schools, continued to speak English instead of Spanish, and brought their relatives to join them in Panama – stirred a xenophobia that spread beyond the nonblack Panamanian population. Afro-Panamanians who had long lived in Panama were often hostile to the West Indian newcomers, accusing them of making life even harder for all blacks in Panama.

After the Canal

In 1926 Panama's congress responded to racial tensions by sharply curbing West Indian immigration. Six years later Panama asked the United States to help deport the West Indians, and the U.S. Congress authorized $100,000 for the purpose. Many West Indians were forced to return to their native countries. However, when World War II broke out in 1939 the United States again imported West Indians to build fortifications protecting the canal from German and Japanese attack. In response President Arnulfo Arias Madrid proposed a new constitution barring citizenship for "persons of African origin" who did not speak Spanish. The constitution was not put into effect permanently, but its impact was felt for years. A language requirement for citizenship was later passed and Arias Madrid held the presidency on and off until 1968 largely by exploiting the animus against the West Indian community, which ended up affecting all blacks in general.

In 1946 the United States gradually relaxed racial segregation in the Canal Zone. However, when civil rights protests flared up in the early 1950s many militant blacks were expelled from the zone. The rapid expulsions prevented the formation of cohesive opposition groups. Nonetheless, by the late 1950s official segregation had mostly come to a halt (in large part because the U.S. government was bringing an end to segregation at home), and by the 1960s Afro-Panamanians held important positions in the administration of the canal. Partly as a result and partly as a cause of these events, Afro-Panamanians in the 1960s began to organize efficiently and cohesively for the first time in Panama's history. Most of this organization took place under the aegis of the national labor unions, in particular the National Center of Panamanian Workers (CNTP). The CNTP had long been associated with the People's Party, which itself had long enjoyed support among United Fruit farm workers, many of whom were West Indian. By the late 1960s a few blacks had penetrated the upper echelons of government, with a handful of Afro-Panamanians sitting in the national assembly on the People's Party and one serving on the supreme court.

Discrimination persisted, however, in informal and subtle forms. Most light-skinned mulattos preferred to consider themselves white, most people of any color preferred not to marry someone of a darker color, and Afro-Panamanians still found themselves barred (either through lack of opportunities or simple discrimination) from many of the better schools and higher-paying occupations.

Under the government of Omar Torrijos in the 1970s Panamanians became more vocal about evicting the United States from the Canal Zone. This desire culminated in a 1977 treaty providing for an end to U.S. rule by 1999, but the movement was also significant for bringing about an uncommon degree of unity between Afro-Panamanians and other Panamanians. Afro-Panamanians organized several congresses to discuss issues surrounding NÉGRITUDE. At the first such congress in 1981 participants drew attention to the discrimination against Afro-Panamanians in the National Symphony Orchestra; later congresses also drew attention to specific, tangible instances of racial discrimination.

In the mid-1980s Gen. Manuel Antonio Noriega became the first person of African descent to rule Panama since Carlos Mendoza (a light-skinned mulatto who ruled for eight months in 1910 after the death of the former president; he did not attempt reelection). Noriega's authoritarianism was unpopular with many Panamanians, and his African heritage was often cited as an aggravating factor in his disfavor. In December 1989 the United States invaded Panama and overthrew Noriega. Among the 2000 Panamanians who died, the many more who remain unaccounted for, and the 20,000 who lost their homes in the invasion, a disproportionate number lived in poor neighborhoods and were thus Afro-Panamanian (*see* HUMAN RIGHTS IN LATIN AMERICA AND THE CARIBBEAN).

Despite the destruction of 1989, Afro-Panamanians achieved a few modest gains in the 1990s. Another round of congresses was held to address the devastation following the U.S. invasion; the Center for Afro-Panamanian Studies in Panama City gained prominence as a repository of information on blacks; and the University of Panama devoted greater attention and funding to black studies. Many challenges confront Afro-Panamanians as they enter the twenty-first century. They must achieve unity between blacks from the West Indies and blacks who have long lived in Panama (currently, the former group leads most activist organizations), and they must elect political candidates who help blacks receive better education, health care, housing, and economic development. Moreover, as prominent Afro-Panamanian women like GRACIELA DIXON have emphasized, female activists face an extra burden in that they must overcome discrimination not only *against* their race but also *within* their race. Machismo and prejudice against women are prevalent in both the minority and majority cultures, and even fewer inroads have been made to achieve equality for black women than for black men.

SEE ALSO
Transatlantic Slave Trade; Maroonage in the Americas; Trinidad and Tobago; Abolition and Emancipation in Latin America and the Caribbean.

Africa

Pande (also known as Pende), ethnic group of west Central Africa.

The Pande are scattered across western CENTRAL AFRICAN REPUBLIC, western DEMOCRATIC REPUBLIC OF THE CONGO, and northeastern ANGOLA. They speak a Bantu language. Approximately 500,000 people consider themselves Pande.

SEE ALSO
Bantu: Dispersion and Settlement.

Latin America and the Caribbean

Pandeiro, Jackson do (José Gomes Filho) (b. 1919, Alagoa Grande, Paraíba, Brazil; d. 1982, Rio de Janeiro, Brazil), black musician who popularized the Afro-Brazilian folk styles of BRAZIL's urban northeast.

Jackson do Pandeiro grew up in a poor family in the coastal towns of Brazil's Nordeste (northeast). His mother was a professional singer, and Jackson performed with her from an early age. Legend has it that he had wanted to play the accordion like his hero LUIZ GONZAGA, but his family could only afford to buy him a *pandeiro* (tambourine). Besides music, the young Jackson's other great love was American Western films. His nickname, "Jackson," came from his resemblance to the American actor Jack Perry.

At age 18 Jackson became a professional musician and moved to Recife. There he worked for local radio stations, performing northeastern genres such as *coco*, *forró*, and *embolada*. He also recorded his first hit songs, including "Sebastiana" and "Forró em Limoeiro." During this time Jackson met Almira Castilhos de Albuquerque, his first wife and singing partner.

In 1956 Jackson moved to Rio de Janeiro, where he combined SAMBA with traditional folk styles and adopted the stage image of a Rio *malandro* (hustler). His hits included "O Canto da Ema," "Um a Um," and "Xote de Copacabana."

Jackson's music influenced many of Brazil's most popular musicians. Perhaps the most internationally known is GILBERTO GIL, who recorded Jackson's "Chiclete com Banana" (Bubblegum with Banana), a wry critique of North American influence on Brazilian culture. Jackson died in July 1982 from medical complications caused by diabetes.

Ben Penglase

SEE ALSO
Rio de Janeiro, Brazil.

Latin America and the Caribbean

Paraguay, landlocked country of South America. It is bordered to the north by Bolivia; to the northeast and east by Brazil; and to the south and southwest by Argentina.

Paraguay has been described as the most homogeneous society in all of South America. The mixing of Guaraní Indian and Spanish created a largely *mestizo* (of indigenous and European ancestry) society that prides itself on its Guaraní descent. What is often overlooked is that people of African descent were also part of the racial and cultural mix since early colonial times. The country's long history of reenslavement under the *amparo* system and its claim to being the last former Spanish South American territory to emancipate its slaves have gained little notice. Considering their history and their contributions to the country's development, Afro-Paraguayans deserve more than the brief mention they have traditionally received.

STANDARD HISTORY

Long before the Spaniards arrived, semi-nomadic and warlike tribes of Guaraní speakers settled mostly in the southern part of the region that is now Paraguay. Spanish explorers arrived in the area in 1524 and established colonies in 1536. In 1537 the Fort of Nuestra Señora de la Asunción was founded at the site of the present-day capital of Paraguay. A city council, established there in 1541, became the political center for the province of Paraguay. Eventually Paraguay became the center of Spanish power in the southeastern section of the continent, but lost that power and prestige when it became part of the viceroyalty of Río de La Plata, administered from Buenos Aires, in 1776. The leaders of Paraguay increasingly resented their province's loss of status. Argentina declared independence in 1810 and sought to extend its influence over the entire area of the former viceroyalty, sending an army under Gen. Manuel Belgrano to force Paraguayan acceptance of Buenos Aires's declaration. Paraguayan forces repelled Belgrano's army, and Paraguay declared independence on May 14, 1811. The new republic developed under the dictatorship of José Gaspar Rodríguez de Francia, who ruled until his death in 1840.

Francia was succeeded by another dictator, Carlos Antonio López (1844-1862), under whose rule Paraguay developed an impressive military capability. He was succeeded by his son Francisco Solano López (1862-1870), who involved the country in the disastrous War of the Triple Alliance (1864-1870) against URUGUAY, BRAZIL, and ARGENTINA, a territorial conflict that cost Paraguay more than a third of its population. Paraguay later fought BOLIVIA in the Chaco War (1932-1935), motivated by a dispute over the Chaco region. Paraguay suc-

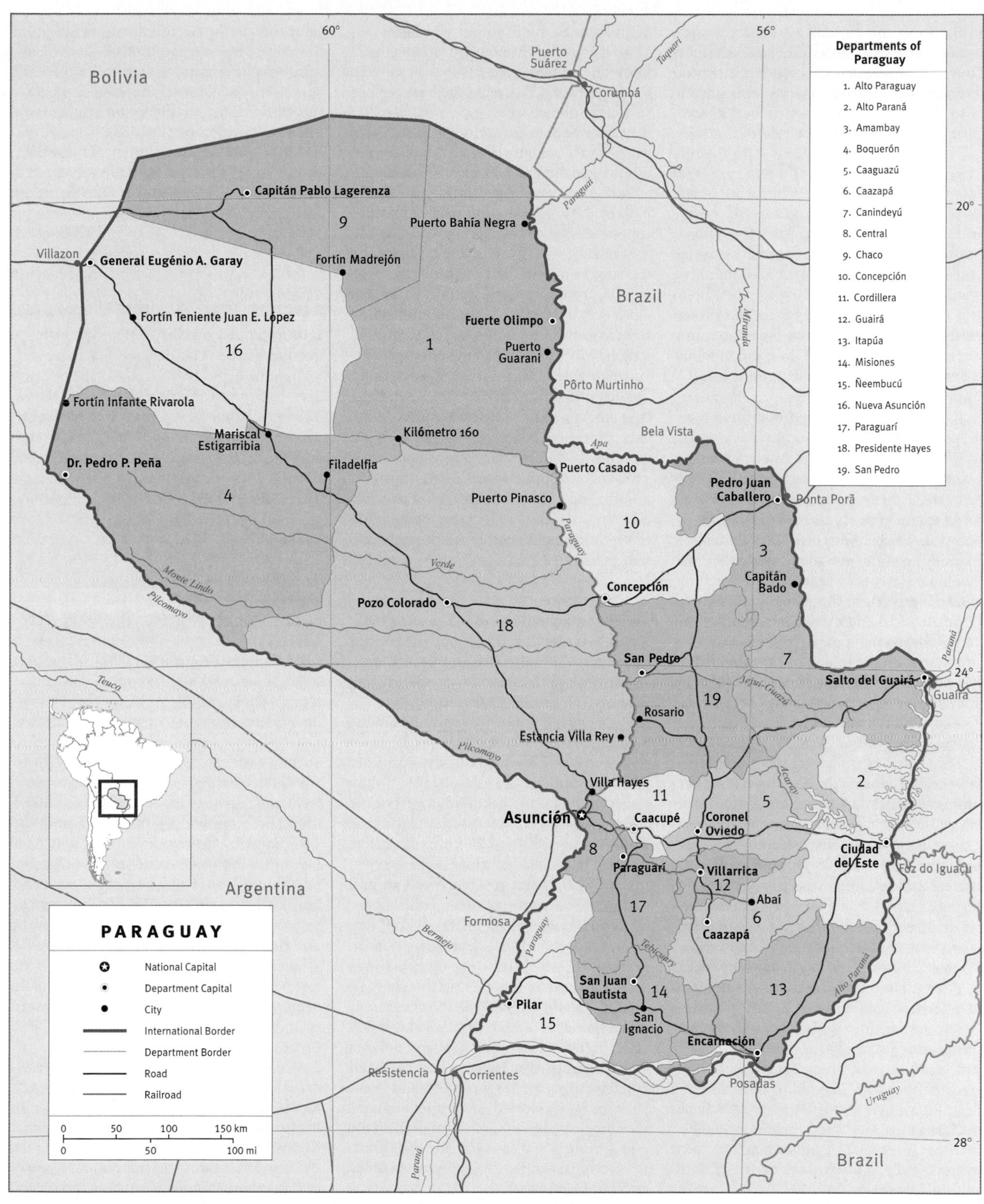

ceeded in winning three-fourths of the territory in dispute, but the Chaco War unleashed new political demands, particularly within the increasingly nationalist and politically dominant military. A period of authoritarian rule ensued, notably marked by the repressive dictatorship of Gen. Alfredo Stroessner, installed by a coup in 1954 and deposed by another one in 1989. Democratic elections were held later that year. After the democratization of Paraguay, its political system, its society, and its economy began to stabilize, although tensions between the popularly elected government and the military continued.

Slavery

A small number of Africans was introduced into the region in the early 1520s, when the first explorers entered Paraguay searching for gold and other riches. Large-scale importation did not occur in Paraguay as compared to other territories in the southern region of South America because the country lacked significant exploitable resources and had a large Indian population to fulfill its labor needs. The labor that black slaves initially performed in Paraguay was no different from that of the Indians: cattle ranching, agricultural tasks, and domestic servitude. Only later would blacks be placed in more specialized fields such as iron smelting and road repair (*see* Latin America, Blacks and Indians in: An Interpretation).

African slaves were imported to the region through the ports of Buenos Aires and Montevideo. Like most Africans who passed through these ports, most of these slaves were from Angola, taken from the Guinea and Congo River Stations on the western coast of Africa. Many slaves in Paraguay were of the same cultural group, but there is no indication that they formed ethnic communities once in Paraguay. The number of blacks in Paraguay increased mainly from racial intermixing, not additional importations of African slaves. Estimates of the Afro-Paraguayan population in the colonial period are incomplete as a result of inconsistent records and the misleading observations of record keepers. In 1570, for example, 3000 mulattos (persons of African and European descent) and mestizos were counted together, with no mention of other black groups. Despite the limitations of the available data, evidence indicates a subsequent growth in the Afro-Paraguayan population. The next available records, from 1650, indicate that people of African descent numbered 15,000 in a total population of 250,000. Another jump to 1782, however, shows a population decline to approximately 10,840, which included both free and enslaved Afro-Paraguayans.

Unique to Paraguay was a system of the late sixteenth century called *amparo* (shelter or protection), in which a manumitted slave who could not pay tribute to the Crown was placed in the protective custody of religious orders or local government officials. In what was essentially a form of *encomienda* (agrarian land grant) for people of African descent, newly "freed" slaves were collected into segregated black towns and forced to work for their custodians in conditions reminiscent of slavery. The amparo system was also used as a form of social control in that it kept blacks under the watchful eye of colonial authorities. Even fugitive slaves from Brazil and Uruguay wanting political asylum became amparos. Instead of returning the fugitives to their owner, Paraguayan officials declared them free upon their entering the territory, then placed them in government custody to become workers on farms or in national factories.

Most Afro-Paraguayan amparos were moved to towns established by religious orders such as the Franciscans, the Jesuits, and the Dominicans (*see* Catholic Church in Latin America and the Caribbean). Areguá (Arequi) and Tabapí (Tobapy) were two such towns controlled by these groups. Other settlements were established by the colonial government as military outposts to protect Paraguayan territory. The town of Emboscada, for example, was formed in 1740 when several hundred Afro-Paraguayans under the amparo system were relocated by the government. These blacks lived free but served as soldiers when they were needed to fight the Mbayá (Albayas) Indians. Emboscada was the first of many towns created on the frontier to maintain the country's boundaries.

Perhaps because of the tight control held by the colonial administration under the amparo system, Paraguayan historical records suggest that there were no *cimarrones* (runaway slaves) or even significant slave revolts. Brief mention is made of an 1838 slave revolt on a farm, but no additional information is available. Considering the long history of slavery in the country, it is surprising that there is no record of major revolts or of a significant number of fugitives. In fact, historical text suggests that it was common practice for a slave to return voluntarily to the owner a few days after escaping. A fugitive's decision to return was influenced by fear of the ire and punishment of the master and the fact that Paraguay's boundaries had become increasingly difficult to escape.

Independence

Paraguay's separation from Spanish power in 1811 was achieved without the need to enlist Afro-Paraguayans in the military. In contrast to the process in other former Spanish American colonies, independence in Paraguay did not bring about the gradual abolition of slavery there. Afro-Paraguayan bondage continued, as did the amparo system, even with the establishment of the Free Womb Law in 1842. This law freed the children of slaves only after they reached age 24 for women and age 25 for men. Articles in the law also ended the external slave trade. The systems of slavery and amparo within the country, however, continued.

When Paraguay entered the War of the Triple Alliance in 1864, slaves were required for battle. A year later slave owners were given the option of selling their slaves to the military as soldiers. By 1867 the government had required that all free blacks and slaves enlist in the army. A third of the population, including most Afro-Paraguayans, had been killed by the time Paraguay lost the war. In 1869 the newly elected government ordered the complete abolition of slavery, which took effect in the 1870 constitution (*see* Abolition and Emancipation in Latin America and the Caribbean).

Contemporary Times

The historical records of Afro-Paraguayans become inconsistent and incomplete in the period after Brazil enacted total emancipation. Some sources report that people of African descent were completely absorbed into the racial mix of the country and as a result lost any distinctiveness. Other sources claim that the Afro-Paraguayan population flourished in the twentieth century. By 1925 there were an estimated 10,000 to 31,500 Afro-Paraguayans in the country. In the 1990s some sources claimed that blacks constituted 3.5 percent of the nation's population, placing their number at 156,000. It is difficult to determine the accuracy of these often contradictory sources, given the very limited amount of research that is available on the Afro-Paraguayan population.

Rob Garrison

Africa

Pare (also known as the Asu), ethnic group of Tanzania.

The Pare primarily inhabit the Pare Mountains of northeastern Tanzania. They speak a Bantu language and are closely related to the Shambaa people. Approximately 300,000 people consider themselves Pare.

See Also

Bantu: Dispersion and Settlement.

North America

Parker, Charles Christopher ("Bird") (b. August 29, 1920, Kansas City, Kans.; d. March 12, 1955, New York, N.Y.), masterful alto saxophonist who, along with Dizzy Gillespie, founded bebop, or modern jazz.

Together with trumpeter John Birks "Dizzy" Gillespie, Charlie Parker was the primary creator of bebop, or modern jazz. His musical innovations profoundly influenced other alto saxophonists, as is evident in the playing of Julian "Cannonball" Adderley, Eric Dolphy, Lou Donaldson, Charles McPherson, and Frank Morgan. Indeed, Parker's influence extended well beyond jazz to popular music and film and television scores. Despite his musical brilliance, however, Parker led a troubled life that included the use of heroin at an early age, an addiction that contributed materially to his death and was deeply intertwined with his musical mystique.

Parker was born in Kansas City, Kansas, across the Kaw River from the much larger Kansas City, Missouri. His father, Charles Parker Sr., was a singer and dancer from Mississippi and Tennessee who abandoned the family when his son was about 11 years old. His mother, Adelaide Bailey Parker, was originally from Oklahoma. Between 1927 and 1931 the family moved to Kansas City, Missouri, the jazz capital of the Southwest.

Under the corrupt reign of Democratic boss Thomas Pendergast, Kansas City was a wide-open town, and its bars, honky-tonks, and nightclubs remained open until dawn, featuring live music and often no-holds-barred jam sessions. Kansas City gave birth to a freewheeling, stripped-down form of swing music that was deeply grounded in THE BLUES and was epitomized by the Count Basie Band. Parker soon developed an interest in music. Lawrence Keyes, a musician and friend of Parker's at Lincoln High School remarked, "If he had been as conscientious about his school work as he was about music, he would have become a professor, but he was a terrible truant."

During 1935 and 1936, when Parker was about 15, his life changed dramatically. He dropped out of school, married Rebecca Ruffin, began playing with the Deans of Swing – a band led by Keyes – and had his first experience with heroin. Within a year he was addicted. Periodically throughout his life Parker would try to limit his heroin use, generally by substituting large quantities of alcohol, which was no less debilitating. In 1938 his first son, Francis Leon Parker, was born. Over the next few years Parker concentrated on his music and learned from older musicians in Kansas City and at resorts in the Ozarks. In 1939 Parker decided to hazard a trip to New York City, the nation's jazz center. There he took part in jam sessions, most notably at two Harlem nightspots, Clark Monroe's Uptown House and Dan Wall's Chili House.

While jamming at the Chili House one night in December 1939, Parker had a profound musical breakthrough. He recalled: "I'd been getting bored with the stereotyped changes that were being used at the time, and I kept thinking there's bound to be something else. I could hear it sometimes, but I couldn't play it. Well, that night I was working over 'Cherokee,' and as I did I found that by using the higher intervals of a chord as a melody line and backing them with appropriately related changes, I could play the thing I heard. I came alive." Although it took Parker several years to consolidate the full implications of this discovery, his achievement heralded a new era in jazz.

In early 1940, however, Parker left New York for Kansas City to join Jay McShann's big band. Parker would stay with McShann about two and a half years. During the swing era big bands provided the majority of job opportunities for jazzmen, but musicians such as Parker and Dizzy Gillespie, then playing in Cab Calloway's orchestra, rankled at their lack of artistic freedom. Parker's job with McShann did bring him back to New York City in late 1941 or 1942. Soon he began collaborating with Gillespie, who had independently achieved comparable harmonic breakthroughs.

The musical sparks Parker and Gillespie struck while playing together created modern jazz, initially known as bebop or simply bop. Parker clearly recognized the musical symbiosis between the two and regarded Gillespie as "the other half of my heartbeat." They worked together during 1943 and 1944 in Earl Hines's big band, an important bop incubator. But they perfected their music in jam sessions, especially at Monroe's Uptown House and Minton's. The new music offered richer harmonic textures with more varied tempos – both much faster and, on ballads, much slower than typical swing-era jazz – and a subtler rhythmic pulse.

Besides his advanced harmonic approach, Parker attained a previously unheard of rhythmic subtlety with his elliptical and fluid melodic lines. His technical mastery allowed him continuously to reinvent melodies, including rapid double-time passages, over the chord sequence of a given song. He was also at ease playing in every key, at a time when many jazz musicians were far more limited.

In 1943, while in WASHINGTON, D.C., with the Hines band, Parker married Geraldine Scott without bothering to divorce his first wife. Parker's heroin habit worsened, and fellow musicians pressured him to quit hard drugs. Instead Parker quit the band and returned to Kansas City, ending his relationship with Geraldine. The Hines band broke up soon after, and a number of its more modernist players regrouped around a new leader, singer Billy Eckstine, with Gillespie as musical director. The Eckstine band was the first bop big band and included, besides Gillespie, drummer ART BLAKEY, vocalist SARAH VAUGHAN, and, soon, Parker. Yet once again Parker quickly left an environment he found stifling. With few exceptions, the rest of his career involved playing in small groups.

Parker's first significant recording sessions came in late 1944 and 1945 for Savoy and, under Gillespie's leadership, for Musicraft. The latter produced a number of particularly fine recordings, including "Salt Peanuts" and "Shaw 'Nuff." Gillespie and Parker also played an extended gig at the Three Deuces, which Gillespie later described as the "height of perfection of our music." But Parker's subsequent career was increasingly erratic. Gillespie asked Parker to join him on a trip to California to play at Billy Berg's, a Los Angeles nightclub. For Parker, the decision to go was a fateful one.

In California Parker made his first classic Dial recordings – including "Moose the Mooche," "Yardbird Suite," and "Ornithology." Yet the arrest of his drug dealer, Emery "Moose the Mooche" Byrd, resulted in Parker's having a nervous breakdown on July 29, 1946, while recording "Lover Man." Parker spent several months in Camarillo State Hospital, and Ross Russell, the owner of Dial Records, released his tortured "Lover Man." Although the record was acclaimed by Parker's many followers, Parker insisted that it was "a horrible thing that should never have been released."

Charlie "Bird" Parker plays saxophone in a club, with Miles Davis on trumpet. *Frank Driggs/Archive Photos*

Beginning in 1947 Parker made New York City his home base. There he formed his great quintet, which included Miles Davis and Max Roach, and recorded a number of sessions for Dial, highlighted by the superb ballads "My Old Flame," "Embraceable You," and "Don't Blame Me." In 1948 Parker began recording with Norman Granz's Verve label, including groundbreaking sessions with strings. However, the greatest moments of his later career took place in concert. Two of these were recorded, a 1949 appearance at Carnegie Hall and a 1953 reunion with Gillespie at Toronto's Massey Hall. During these years Parker regularly won the annual *Downbeat* magazine readers' poll as best alto player, and his fame extended to Europe, taking him to Paris in 1949 and to Scandinavia the following year.

But Parker's personal life became increasingly troubled. In 1948 he married his third wife, Doris Sydnor, but left her two years later to enter a relationship with Chan Richardson, with whom he had a daughter, Pree, and a son, Baird. Due to a drug conviction he lost his "cabaret card," required of all musicians playing in New York City nightclubs from 1951 to 1953, seriously limiting his ability to work.

The physical cost of Parker's heroin and alcohol abuse was also clearly mounting. Besides making his performances increasingly erratic, it gave him stomach ulcers, liver problems, and at least one heart attack. When he died in 1955, the attending physician estimated Parker's age at between 50 and 60 years. In fact, he was only 34. Yet despite his early death, Parker's uncompromising and innovative musicianship have assured his immortality. Indeed soon after his funeral, graffiti began appearing around New York City proclaiming, "Bird Lives!"

James Clyde Sellman

See Also

Adderley, Julian Edwin ("Cannonball"); Basie, William James ("Count"); Calloway, Cabell (Cab); Davis, Miles Dewey, III; Eckstine, William Clarence (Billy); Gillespie, John Birks ("Dizzy"); Harlem, New York; Hines, Earl Kenneth ("Fatha"); New York, New York; Roach, Maxwell Lemuel (Max).

North America

Parks, Gordon, Jr.

(b. December 7, 1934, Minneapolis, Minn.; d. April 3, 1979, Nairobi, Kenya), African American filmmaker who inaugurated the blaxploitation film genre.

The son of Sally Alvis and director, writer, and photographer Gordon Parks Sr., Gordon Parks Jr. worked to define his own creative expression independently of his famous father. He even used the name Gordon Rogers early in his career to forge his own identity. After spending his early years at the American School in Paris, Parks graduated from White Plains High School in 1952, worked in New York City's garment district, and joined the army in 1956. In the 1960s he began his career in entertainment as a café folksinger in New York's Greenwich Village.

Parks entered the field of cinematography as a cameraman on his father's film *The Learning Tree* (1969) and as a still photographer for *Burn* (1969) and *The Godfather* (1972). In 1972 Parks took the director's chair with *Superfly*, which has often been cited as the defining example of a new genre of African American film: blaxploitation. Set in a dense urban landscape, the film chronicles a conflict between a black criminal and the white organized crime establishment, a symbolic representation of African American male self-determination in the face of an oppressive system. Enhancing this new cinematic form was Curtis Mayfield's memorable score. Despite controversy sparked by its uncritical depiction of a "heroic" drug dealer, *Superfly* was remarkably popular among black audiences hungry for powerful black images in film, and grossed more than $24.8 million. Parks quickly followed *Superfly*'s success with three new feature films: *Thomasine and Bushrod* (1974), the action film *Three the Hard Way* (1974), and the teen love story *Aaron Loves Angela* (1975).

Parks moved to Kenya in 1979, where he started the Africa International Productions/Panther Film Company and died in a Nairobi plane crash a short time later.

Marian Aguiar

See Also

Nairobi, Kenya; Blaxploitation Films; Mayfield, Curtis; Parks, Gordon, Sr.; Film, Blacks in American.

North America

Parks, Gordon, Sr.

(b. November 30, 1912, Fort Scott, Kans.), African American photographer famous for his portrait photography; first African American director of a major Hollywood film.

The youngest of 15 children, Gordon Parks, the son of a dirt farmer, left home when he was 16, shortly after his mother's death. After an unhappy attempt to move in with a married sister in Minneapolis, Parks ended up spending a frigid winter homeless, an experience that sensitized him to the plight of the poor and that he would draw on in later photography and films. At the time his hunger and loneliness nearly led him to a life of crime, but he managed to struggle through high school, working odd jobs herding cattle, carrying bricks, and even touring with a semipro basketball team.

Working as a waiter on the Northern Pacific Railroad, Parks saw magazine photos produced by the Farm Security Administration, a federally funded project chronicling the Great Depression in rural and urban America. Later, after watching a World War II newsreel by documentary filmmaker Norman Alley, Parks resolved to become a photographer.

Based in St. Paul, Minnesota, the self-taught Parks immediately showed an original eye for his subjects, even if he lacked the technical training at the time to capture them flawlessly. Once, after finally getting the big break of a fashion shoot, he double-exposed all but one photo. Yet even the results of these mishaps captivated his viewers, and Parks soon had established himself as a much-in-demand fashion photographer in St. Paul. His work eventually was discovered by Marva Louis, the wife of boxer Joe Louis, who helped him set up shop as a fashion photographer in a bigger market, Chicago.

In his spare time Parks turned his camera from the fantasy world of fashion to the destitute streets of the South Side of Chicago. These pictures, exhibited at the South Side Community Art Center, won him a Julius Rosenwald Fellowship in 1941 and an opportunity to work at the Farm Security Administration, where he took on the assignment of showing the "face of America." Under the tutelage of Roy Stryker, the director of the staff photographers, Parks found that he could express himself more powerfully with the camera than with words. "I learned that photography would enable me to show what was right and wrong about America, the world and life," he said.

With the closing of the Farm Security Administration, Parks went to work at the Office of War Information in 1943, and then for the Standard Oil Company of New Jersey as a documentary photographer. Continuing his work in fashion photography, he published two books, *Flash Photography* (1947) and *Camera Portraits: The Techniques and Principles of Documentary Portraiture* (1948). In 1948 Parks was hired by *Life* magazine, then one of America's leading pictorial publications, and spent two years based in Paris. His work in the United States in the 1950s and early 1960s, and a highly acclaimed series on the slums of Rio de Janeiro won Parks international recognition as a photojournalist. His photographs in the United States dealt with many arenas, from politics to entertainment to the daily routines of ordinary men and women. Particularly noteworthy were his chronicles of the political activities of African Americans: the Civil Rights Movement (later collected into the 1971 anthology *Born Black*), the Black Power movement, and the growth of the Nation of Islam.

With photographs driven by a strong sense of narrative, it is no surprise that Parks found another calling in writing. In 1963 he published *The Learning Tree*, the saga of a farm family in the 1920s very much like Parks's own. *The Learning Tree* was the first in a trilogy of autobiographical novels, followed three years later by *A Choice of Weapons* and *To Smile in Autumn, A Memoir* in 1979. Parks combined his literary and visual talents in a 1969 movie version of *The Learning Tree*, becoming the first African American director of a major Hollywood movie (*see* Film, Blacks in American). His hit movie *Shaft*, often cited as a forerunner of the blaxploitation genre, was released in 1971, followed by *Leadbelly* (1976) and *The Odyssey of Solomon Northup* (1984), the story of a free black sold into slavery. Parks, also a poet and composer, wrote the music for a ballet about the life of Dr. Martin Luther King Jr.

Parks received the Spingarn Medal from the National Association for the Advancement of Colored People in 1972, and the National Medal for the Arts in 1986. He is the father of the late filmmaker Gordon Parks Jr., whose credits include *Superfly* (1972).

Marian Aguiar

See Also

Slavery in the United States; World War II and African Americans; Blaxploitation Films; Chicago, Illinois; King, Martin Luther, Jr.; Parks, Gordon, Jr.; Northrup, Solomon; Rio de Janeiro, Brazil.

North America

Parks, Rosa Louise McCauley

(b. February 4, 1913, Tuskegee, Ala.), African American civil rights activist, often called the "Mother of the Civil Rights Movement"; her arrest for refusing to give up her seat on a bus triggered the 1955-1956 Montgomery bus boycott and set in motion the test case for the desegregation of public transportation.

On December 1, 1955, in Montgomery, Alabama, the arrest of a black woman, Rosa Parks, for disregarding an order to surrender her bus seat to a white passenger galvanized a growing movement to desegregate public transportation, and marked a historic turning point in the African American battle for civil rights. Yet Parks was much more than an accidental symbol. It is sometimes overlooked that at the time of her arrest she was no ordinary bus rider, but an experienced activist with strong beliefs.

Parks was the granddaughter of former slaves and the daughter of James McCauley, a carpenter, and Leona McCauley, a rural schoolteacher. The future civil rights leader grew up in Montgomery, Alabama, where she attended the all-black Alabama State College. In 1932 Parks married Raymond Parks, a barber, with whom she became active in Montgomery's chapter of the National Association for the Advancement of Colored People (NAACP).

Raymond Parks's volunteer efforts went toward helping to free the defendants in the famous Scottsboro case, and Rosa Parks worked as the chapter's youth advisor. In 1943, when Rosa Parks actually joined the NAACP, her involvement with the organization became even greater as she worked with the organization's state president E. D. Nixon to mobilize a voter registration drive in Montgomery. That same year Parks also was elected secretary of the Montgomery branch.

In the early 1950s Parks found work as a tailor's assistant at the Montgomery Fair department store. She had a part-time job working as a seamstress for Virginia and Clifford Durr, a white liberal couple who encouraged Parks in her civil rights work. Six months before her famous protest, Parks received a scholarship to attend a workshop on school integration for community leaders at the Highlander Folk School in Monteagle, Tennessee, and spent several weeks there.

The segregated seating policies on public buses had long been a source of resentment within the black community in Montgomery and in other cities throughout the Deep South. African Americans were required to pay their fares at the front of the bus and then reboard through the back door. The white bus drivers, who were invested with police powers, frequently harassed blacks, sometimes driving away before African American passengers were able to get back on the bus. At peak hours the drivers pushed back boundary markers segregating the bus, crowding those in the "colored section" so that whites could be provided with seats.

On December 1, 1955, Parks took her seat in the front of the "colored section" of a Montgomery bus. When the driver asked Parks and three other black riders to relinquish their seats to whites, Parks refused (the others complied). The driver called the police, and Parks was arrested. Later that night she was released, after Nixon and the Durrs posted a $100 bond.

Although three black women had been arrested earlier that year for similar acts of defiance, and Parks herself had been thrown off a bus by the same driver 12 years before, this time the opponents of segregation were prepared to mount a counterattack. The Montgomery chapter of the NAACP had been looking for a test case to challenge the legality of segregated bus seating, and to woo public opinion with a series of protests. The morning after her arrest Parks agreed to let the NAACP take on her case. Another organization, the Women's Political Council (WPC), led by JoAnn Robinson, initiated the idea of a one-day bus boycott. Within 24 hours of Parks's defiance, the WPC had distributed more than 52,000 fliers announcing the bus boycott that was to take place the day of Parks's trial. On December 5, as buses went through their routes virtually empty, Parks was convicted by the local court. She refused to pay the fine of $14, and with the help of her lawyer, Ed D. Gray, appealed to the circuit court.

On the evening of December 5, several thousand protesters crowded into the Holt Street Baptist Church to create the Montgomery Improvement Association (MIA) and to rally behind its new president, Rev. Martin Luther King Jr., who had just moved to Montgomery as the new pastor at the Dexter Avenue Baptist Church. What was planned as a day-long bus boycott swelled to 381 days, during which time 42,000 protesters walked, carpooled, or took taxis, rather than ride the segregated city buses of Montgomery. In a move designed to reverse the segregation laws on public transportation, King and the MIA filed a separate case in United States District Court. The district court ruled for the plaintiffs, declaring segregated seating on buses unconstitutional, a decision later upheld by the U.S. Supreme Court.

Parks was widely known as "the Mother of the Civil Rights Movement," but her iconic stature afforded her little financial security. She lost her job as a seamstress at Montgomery Fair and was unable to find other work in Montgomery. Parks and her husband relocated to Detroit, Michigan, in 1957, where they struggled financially for the next eight years. Parks's fortunes improved somewhat in 1965, when Congressman John Conyers hired her as an administrative assistant, a position she held until 1987.

Parks has remained a committed activist. In the 1980s she worked in support of the South African antiapartheid movement, and in 1987 she founded the Rosa and Raymond Parks Institute for Self-Development in Detroit, a career counseling center for black youth.

A friend once described Parks as someone who, as a rule, did not defy authority, but once determined on a course of action, refused to back down: "She might ignore you, go around you, but never retreat."

Marian Aguiar

See Also

South Africa; Conyers, John F., Jr.; King, Martin Luther, Jr.; Nixon, Edgar Daniel; Robinson, JoAnn Gibson.

North America

Parsons, Lucy

(b. March 1853, Tex.; d. March 7, 1942, Chicago, Ill.), African American socialist and anarchist whose work as a journalist and organizer during the late nineteenth and early twentieth centuries made her a prominent figure in American radical politics.

Lucy Parsons has often been portrayed as merely an assistant to her famous anarchist husband, Albert Parsons. Although the couple worked together on many issues, Lucy Parsons was herself a leading political figure in American radical social movements. A woman whose alliances shifted over the years from socialism to anarchism and finally to communism, Parsons was distinctive as a nineteenth-century woman who called for poor people to seize power – by force if necessary.

Accounts differ as to Parsons's racial origins and the extent to which she passed. At one point she claimed to be the daughter of a Mexican and a Creek Native American, but some historians have pointed to the possibility that she was born a slave in Texas and was partially African American. Certainly, her marriage to Albert Parsons, a former Confederate soldier turned Radical Republican, was viewed as interracial. Later in her life many identified her as black, and her son's race at birth was registered as Negro.

Shortly after their 1871 marriage Lucy and Albert Parsons left Waco, Texas, for Chicago, Illinois, then a center of labor unrest and radical political movements. After Albert was blacklisted from the printing trade, Lucy supported the family as a dressmaker.

The couple became heavily involved in the socialist labor movement, including the Workingmen's Party and the Social Democratic Party. Around 1879 Lucy Parsons began writing for journals such as the *Socialist* and *Scribner's Magazine*, arguing the traditional Marxist view that the interests of labor and capital were inherently at odds. During this time she also actively organized with the Working Women's Union for wageless working women such as housewives.

As her political thought and work became more radical, Parsons joined the Socialist Revolutionary Club, which advocated military organization and the study of revolutionary tactics. In 1883 she helped found an early American anarchist organization, the International Working People's Association. A year later Parsons published her famous article, "To Tramps: The Unemployed, the Disinherited, and Miserable," in the socialist journal *The Alarm*, speaking to the 35,000 unemployed in Chicago, whom she saw as victims of capitalist overproduction, who "received only enough of [their] labor product to furnish [themselves] the bare, course necessaries of life."

But it was her vision of the dispossessed as potential saboteurs and her closing admonition to "Learn the use of explosives!" that earned Parsons her reputation as, in the words of a nineteenth-century journalist, "the goddess of Anarchy and would-be destroyer of all existing forms and institutions of government." Parsons advocated "propaganda by the deed," a stance argued in her article "Dynamite! The Only Voice the Oppressors of the People Can Understand." She led demonstrations of the unemployed, sometimes with her two children, Lulu and Alfred, in tow.

Some critics have accused Parsons of subordinating issues of race to those of class, pointing to her article "The Negro: Let Him Leave Politics to the Politicians and Prayers to the Preacher," published in 1886 in response to lynchings of blacks in Carrollton, Mississippi. Here she claimed that African Americans were victims of injustices because, as a class, they were poor and economically dependent, but she acknowledged the divisions forced by racism and sexism that were exploited by employers to create cheap labor. Despite the fact that Parsons consistently wrote about racial injustices throughout her life, she maintained the traditional Marxist view that economics lay at the root of oppression. In this way her work was a forerunner of many of the socialist black thinkers, such as W. E. B. Du Bois, who would grapple with the intersecting issues of race and class in the American context.

Parsons's commitment to class struggle brought her to the front lines of the 1886 movement for the eight-hour work day. Shortly after a general strike began in Chicago, her husband was arrested following a riot in which protesters threw a bomb at police in Haymarket Square. Albert Parsons and seven other radical organizers were accused of instigating the bombing through political writings and sentenced to death. Lucy Parsons turned her energies to a lecture tour in which she spoke of the Haymarket incident, and attempted, unsuccessfully, to get her husband's sentence commuted. After the execution of her husband Parsons traveled widely, speaking on anarchism and the Haymarket incident. She became an icon of free speech for the radical left after being arrested in March 1887 in Columbus, Ohio, before a lecture.

In 1891 she began to edit *Freedom, A Revolutionary Anarchist-Communist Monthly*. In this journal Parsons denounced racial violence in the South, where "women are stripped to the skin in the presence of leering white-skinned, black-hearted brutes and lashed into insensibility and strangled to death from the limbs of trees."

When the International Workers of the World (IWW) was formed in 1905, Parsons was the second woman (after Mother Jones) to sign up. In 1914 and 1915 she commanded headlines in the mainstream press by leading two mass hunger demonstrations of homeless and unemployed people in San Francisco and Chicago. Parsons, by then in her sixties, was arrested for her role. She also joined the International Labor Defense (ILD) to fight for the release of "class war prisoners," such as Tom Mooney, and incarcerated African Americans, including the Scottsboro Nine and Angelo Herndon. Late in life her political orientation within the radical movement shifted again, this time toward communism. At age 86, she joined the Communist Party.

Following Parsons's death in a fire in Chicago, police seized her books and personal papers, leaving few permanent records of her life and writings.

Marian Aguiar

See Also

American Indians; Du Bois, William Edward Burghardt (W. E. B.); Lynching; Scottsboro Case; Communist Party USA, African Americans and the.

Latin America and the Caribbean

Partido Independiente de Color,

black political party organized in 1908 by Afro-Cuban activists, many of whom were veterans of the War of Independence (1895-1898). Two years after it was founded, the party was banned, accused of being divisive for Cuba, where, its critics alleged, special political organizations for Afro-Cubans were unnecessary. In 1912 members of the outlawed party organized an insurrection – the Guerrita de Mayo (Little War of May) – which was met with harsh state repression against party members and other Afro-Cubans, leaving more than 3000 dead (*see* Cuba).

North America

Passing in the United States,

the phenomenon of African Americans, who in physical appearance approach the "white" racial type, choosing to live and identify themselves, whether temporarily or permanently, as white (*see* Race: An Interpretation).

Africa

Pass Laws,

South African legislation controlling the movements of blacks and Coloureds (people of mixed racial descent) under the system of apartheid, or racial segregation. The earliest pass controls were developed in the eighteenth century by the whites in South Africa in order to control black labor and to keep blacks and Coloureds in inferior positions.

A regulation of 1760 passed in the Cape Colony (what is now western South Africa) required slaves moving between town and country to carry passes signed by their owners authorizing their journeys. When the British purchased the Cape Colony from the Dutch in 1814, a system of passes already existed for Coloureds and blacks. Beginning in 1809 pass laws were introduced and amended frequently across South Africa. The purpose of these laws was to control the movement of blacks and to obtain their labor in both rural and urban areas. The mining industry became a major force behind demands for pass law controls.

Beginning in 1923 pass regulations were constantly tightened and amended. Between 1939 and 1941 as many as 273,790 people were convicted of pass law offenses in the Transvaal alone. Major unrest from 1944 to 1946 in opposition to the pass laws led the government to tighten them still further. By 1948, 265 urban areas had been *proclaimed*, which meant that black movement was rigidly controlled. In 1952, the Natives (Abolition of Passes and Coordination of Documents) Act substituted a single *reference book* for 11 existing pass laws. It was a crime for black men and women over age 16 to be without their books, which gave their personal information and also their employment record. At the same time an amendment to the Natives (Urban Areas) Act applied strict regulations to all urban areas; a black person entering such an area had only 72 hours to find employment before being subject to arrest. Amendments to the laws in 1955, 1957, and 1964 made it increasingly difficult for blacks to qualify for permanent residence in any urban area. The aim was to control the population in such a way that only single male contract laborers could go to work in urban areas, and they could work for no more than a year before returning to the rural areas. What became known as "endorsing out" took place, which meant that Africans without work in an urban area had their passes stamped to show that they had to return to the rural areas.

Many demonstrations, acts of passive resistance, and uprisings were directed at the pass system. In 1930, for example, the Communist Party organized a mass burning of passes on Dingane's Day, a day celebrated in honor of the Zulu chief DINGANE. A major antipass campaign was mounted in 1944. In March 1960 countrywide demonstrations against the pass laws culminated in the Sharpeville Massacre of March 21, when the police fired on a crowd of demonstrators, killing 69 blacks. Between 1952 and 1986 millions of blacks were punished by the courts for failing to carry their passes, and by the early 1970s about 1 million blacks were arrested every year under the pass laws. The pass laws and influx control were finally abolished in 1986 when the process of dismantling the apartheid system began.

SEE ALSO

Sharpeville, South Africa; South African Communist Party.

Africa

Pastoralism, a livelihood based on the care of domesticated livestock, practiced widely in Africa.

Africa's pastoral populations live primarily in arid and semi-arid regions of West, North, East, and southern Africa. Unlike many agrarian societies, which combine cultivation with raising livestock, pastoralists depend critically on their animals' milk, meat, hides, and, in some cases, blood, as well as on the sales of yearling livestock to purchase grain and other necessities.

The breeding of domesticated livestock was practiced in combination with farming as early as 11,000 years ago in the MIDDLE EAST and shortly afterward in North Africa. Pure pastoralism (with no farming) emerged as a livelihood as early as 4000 years ago in the Middle East and 3000 years ago in North Africa. In Africa the principal types of livestock are goats and sheep, dromedaries (single-hump camels), horses, donkeys, and several types of bovine animals, including cattle, zebus, and yaks.

Pastoralists necessarily invest much labor and thought in caring for their herds. They must protect them from predators, help them find pasture, assist in calving and foaling, and attend sick animals. In turn the animals supply milk and meat for nourishment and their hides provide clothing, storage bags

RIGHT: Cows are an important economic resource for a farmer tending his herd in the Ngundu region of Tanzania. *CORBIS/Paul Almasy*

BELOW: A nomad child rides a donkey laden with baskets in Niger. The nomadic way of life remains important in a number of Saharan and sub-Saharan nations. *CORBIS/Tiziana and Gianni B*

for grain and household goods, water buckets, and, in some societies, material to make tents. Additionally, cow dung is used as fuel for kitchen fires. Because pastoral groups are attuned to the biological needs of their herds and faced with the challenges of coping in often marginal environments, they tend to move their herds seasonally. Their division of labor and organization of daily work, their economic customs and political alliances, and their family celebrations and public ritual life reflect their preoccupation with herding.

The work of pastoral life is divided into herding and watering routines usually performed by men, and milking and food-processing tasks done mostly by women. In most pastoral societies even children work, tending young animals and doing household chores. In some societies, such as that of the TUAREG camel herders of the central Sahara in NIGER and MALI, labor is further divided between social classes, with a dependent or vassal class caring for most of the livestock, including the herds of a smaller warrior aristocracy, whose men take responsibility for group defense and leadership.

Pastoralists may be transhumants, part of a basically sedentary group that moves its flocks from summer pastures to winter pastures or from a warm valley in the winter to a cool mountainside in the summer. Other pastoralists, especially those inhabiting the Sahara and other desert areas, are nomadic, following annual migrations in search of pasture in regions where rainfall is erratic and sparse. Pastoral nomads circulate slowly in a "home-well area" during the dry months, relying on a particular well for water and on dried grasses and acacia trees for fodder. They then move through a "transhumance zone" during the wet season, when rainfall creates rich pasture lands in a river basin or watershed area.

Ritual and family celebrations become most important during the season of abundant pastures, when families and larger social groups congregate to take advantage of the rich vegetation in watershed areas and river valleys. There are frequent parties and musical gatherings as well as initiation rituals, and young people engage in courting behavior and celebrate weddings at this time. FULANI cattle herders in Niger, for example, celebrate the rainy season with *gereol* dances, in which the men apply colorful make-up to their faces and dance with movements suggestive of their camels.

Livestock also become the basis for economic exchange and can be used to create and maintain family and political alliances. In wedding ceremonies of the TURKANA of KENYA, for example, camels are an important part of the bride price. Traditionally, riding camels have been used in warfare, a practice that continues today among such groups as the Tuaregs and Tubus of Niger.

Saharan pastoralists such as Tuaregs, Moors, and Bedouin Arabs specialize in camel and goat herding, since these animals are "browsers" able to reach or climb the side of acacia trees to eat the leaves when no other vegetation is available, giving them an adaptive advantage over cows and sheep in a desert climate. The pastoralists of the SAHEL, such as the Fulani, and those of East and South Africa, such as the MAASAI, Turkana, and Barabaig (to name only a few), mainly raise cattle, "grazers" that depend on ground-level vegetation.

Today pure pastoralism is becoming increasingly rare as many young men – traditionally the herders – migrate into cities to seek wage labor. Pastoralism also fits uneasily into national boundaries and politics of contemporary Africa because nomadic herders are remote from government centers and difficult to tax, educate, and control. As they tend to produce only sufficient food to feed themselves, pastoralists are perceived as contributing little to national economic growth. Furthermore, the nomadic existence is generally regarded as primitive and occupies the lowest priority for development funds in many countries. Prevented by national legislation from migrating across administrative borders to distant pastures to save their herds during times of drought, pastoralists in the Sahara, the Sahel, and the Horn of Africa have suffered enormous livestock losses over the past 30 years. Many pastoral groups, particularly those in desert environments or in countries undergoing ethnic conflict, suffer chronically from food shortages and lack of adequate medical care. Some pastoral groups, including the SAHRAWI of WESTERN SAHARA, the Moors of MAURITANIA, the Tubus of CHAD and Niger, and the Fulanis and Tuaregs of Niger and Mali, have initiated separatist movements or participated in insurrections to protest unequal treatment by national governments.

Barbara Worley

SEE ALSO
Camel; Sahara Desert.

Africa

Patassé, Ange-Félix (b. 1937?, Paoua, Central African Republic), president of the Central African Republic (1993-).

Ange-Félix Patassé was born in Paoua, in northwestern CENTRAL AFRICAN REPUBLIC. After studying at the Higher School of Tropical Agriculture in suburban Paris, Patassé worked for the Central African Republic's department of agriculture from 1959 to 1965, and then held numerous agriculture and development ministerial positions for the next ten years. He was appointed prime minister by President JEAN-BÉDEL BOKASSA in September 1976, but two months later Bokassa dissolved the government and declared himself emperor. Patassé was incarcerated briefly in 1979 before Bokassa was overthrown by DAVID DACKO in a coup d'état backed by the French government. The leader of the opposition, Patassé narrowly lost the 1981 presidential election to Dacko. After Dacko was overthrown later that year by André Kolingba, Patassé was accused of leading an unsuccessful coup in March 1982, and fled to TOGO. Exiled for ten years, Patassé returned to the Central African Republic when Kolingba was forced to hold multiparty elections in 1992. The 1992 elections were ruled invalid by the Supreme Court and rescheduled for September 1993. Patassé defeated both Kolingba and Dacko in the presidential elections, which were fraught with problems but certified by a delegation of international observers.

Patassé spent most of 1994 trying to reestablish the Central African Republic's close ties with FRANCE, which had been weakened during Bokassa's erratic presidency. However, relations further deteriorated after a banking scandal in which a French associate of Patassé was arrested and charged with involvement in the disappearance of 75 million francs in African loan guarantees. Although Patassé met with French president François Mitterrand in 1994, his diplomatic efforts were undermined by a string of mutinies and civil servant strikes in the Central African Republic from late 1995 until early in 1997. The groups claimed that Patassé had not kept his campaign promise to pay them current wages and owed back wages. These strikes culminated on April 19, 1996, when a group of renegade soldiers from the Central African Republic army, led by Sgt. Cyriaque Souke, rebelled against Patassé and demanded that he resign from the presidency. The groups, which numbered around 400 in the first attack, looted the capital, Bangui, and freed prisoners. The mutinies were finally quelled by French troops, who intervened on behalf of Patassé. After the mutiny was over, Patassé signed an accord pledging to bring in more members of the opposition into his government. This mutiny, however, was just the first in a series that continued throughout 1996 and into early 1997. In each instance the French army had to intervene to stop the rebel troops. By the middle of 1997 Patassé had lost public confidence, and state officials threatened to overthrow his government and hold new elections.

Elizabeth Heath

SEE ALSO
Bangui, Central African Republic.

Africa

Paton, Alan Stewart

(b. January 11, 1903, Pietermaritzburg, South Africa; d. April 12, 1985, Durban, South Africa), South African writer and founder of the Liberal Party, best known for his novel *Cry the Beloved Country*, which explored the human cost of racial division.

A white South African of British descent, Alan Paton wrote what is considered one of the great African novels in English. His mother was a teacher and his father was a civil servant, and after growing up in Pietermaritzburg he attended the University of Natal. Paton taught school for a decade, then switched careers in 1935 to head Johannesburg's Diepkloof Reformatory, home to 650 black youths who had been labeled "delinquent" by the authorities. As principal he liberalized the reformatory's regulations, giving inmates greater freedom and respect. His interest in social work stemmed in part from his conversion to the Anglican faith and his growing interest in racial justice. When his first novel, *Cry the Beloved Country*, was published in 1948, the reviews hailed it as "beautiful and profoundly moving... steeped in sadness and grief but radiant with hope and compassion."

The book's protagonist is Stephen Kumalo, a ZULU priest who travels to Johannesburg from the countryside in search of his sister and his son. When he arrives, he discovers that his sister has been forced into prostitution and his son has fled after being involved in the murder of a white man. In the book's most famous passage Paton warns of the specter of large-scale racial violence: "Cry, the beloved country, for the unborn child that is the inheritor of our fear." Not a simple political allegory, Paton's novel contains layers of social and spiritual complexity and ends with the hope of reconciliation between black and white South Africans.

Cry the Beloved Country has been translated into 20 languages and has sold 15 million copies. It was adapted into a 1948 play, *Lost in the Stars* (with songs by the composer Kurt Weill), and filmed in 1952 and in 1995, with JAMES EARL JONES as Kumalo. Paton, who eventually left his job to write full time, also became a political activist. In 1953 he helped found the Liberal Party, of which he was the first president. The party, which advocated universal voting rights and nonviolence, was banned in 1968 when the South African government prohibited all multiracial parties. For most of the 1960s Paton was forbidden to leave the country, but he continued to write, producing a second novel, seven works of nonfiction, and a play. None, however, is as well known as *Cry the Beloved Country*, which he said was written "to influence my fellow whites." Toward the end of his life Paton faced significant criticism for opposing economic sanctions against South Africa's APARTHEID regime, which he believed would harm poor blacks.

Kate Tuttle

SEE ALSO

Johannesburg, South Africa; South Africa.

Latin America and the Caribbean

Patrocínio, José Carlos do

(b. October 8, 1853, Campos, Rio de Janeiro, Brazil; d. February 1, 1905, Rio de Janeiro, Brazil), one of Brazil's most influential abolitionists and journalists of African descent.

The son of a white Catholic priest and a free black fruit vendor, José Carlos do Patrocínio grew up on his father's plantation in Campos, Rio de Janeiro, where he was exposed to the brutalities of slavery. In 1868 he left home to begin an apprenticeship at Misericórdia Hospital in Rio de Janeiro. With the financial assistance of his father and a beneficent society, he went on to complete the pharmacy course. Unable to secure work as a pharmacist, he accepted an offer to live with and tutor the children of a wealthy realtor, whose daughter he later married.

Patrocínio first established himself as an opponent of slavery through the press. In 1877 he joined the staff of the *Gazeta de notícias*, Rio's daily newspaper. His editorials and poetry won him recognition as a leading abolitionist. In 1881, with the financial support of his father-in-law, Patrocínio bought and took over the *Gazeta de tarde*, turning it into Brazil's most influential abolitionist newspaper. In 1887 he established the equally authoritative abolitionist journal *A Cidade do Rio*. In his lifetime he published hundreds of articles opposing slavery.

Patrocínio helped coordinate and unite Brazil's abolition movement. In the early 1880s he became the main figure behind the Associação Central Emancipadora (Central Emancipation Association) and helped compose the manifesto of the Confederação Abolicionista (Abolitionist Confederation). Patrocínio promoted local abolition movements in Ceará, Santos, and his hometown of Campos, and traveled to Europe to gather support for the abolitionist movement.

Patrocínio was an inspirational orator, earning the epithet "The Tiger of Abolitionism." In the words of abolitionist Carolina Nabuco, Patrocínio "did not deliver his speeches. He acted them out with extraordinary power.... They possessed a communicative ardor and a vibrant spontaneity." Patrocínio customarily addressed free black and mulatto audiences with fiery rhetoric, hoping to rouse them to participate in the abolition movement. His speeches were sometimes interrupted by whites shouting racial slurs; on one such occasion he retorted: "God gave me the color of Othello so that I would be the envy of my country."

Patrocínio was instrumental in persuading Princess Isabela, who was acting as regent, to sign the Lei Aurea (Golden Law), which on May 13, 1888, freed all of Brazil's slaves. After abolition Patrocínio sought to defend the princess from a growing Republican movement and facilitate her ascension to the throne by forming a black militant association called Guarda Negra (Black Guard). But a military revolt in 1889 established the Republic of Brazil, leading to Patrocínio's exile to Amazonas and the suspension of his newspaper. He eventually resumed his journalistic activities and continued writing until his death in 1905.

Aaron Myers

SEE ALSO

Slavery in Latin America and the Caribbean; Brazil; Rio de Janeiro, Brazil; Abolition and Emancipation in Latin America and the Caribbean.

Latin America and the Caribbean

Patronato,

system of apprenticeship that required freed slaves to continue working for their masters for a determined period of time. This system was often instituted in Latin America and the Caribbean to circumvent laws that freed slaves (*see* ABOLITION AND EMANCIPATION IN LATIN AMERICA AND THE CARIBBEAN).

North America

Patterson, Floyd

(b. January 4, 1935, Waco, N.C.), African American professional boxer, an Olympic gold medalist, and the first to lose and then regain the heavyweight championship title.

Born in Waco, North Carolina, Floyd Patterson moved with his family to Brooklyn, New York, as a young boy and had a difficult childhood. He was sent to the Wiltwyck School, where he learned to box. When he returned to New York City he entered Golden Gloves competitions, winning national titles in 1951 and 1952 as a middleweight. At the 1952 Summer Olympic Games in Helsinki, Finland, he won all of his fights and the gold medal. After the games he turned professional.

In his first 36 professional fights Patterson lost only once, and in 1956 he beat Archie Moore for the heavyweight title. Patterson became the youngest heavyweight champion and the first Olympic gold medalist to hold the title. He made four successful title defenses before losing to Sweden's Ingemar Johansson in 1959. Johansson knocked Patterson down seven times before the fight was stopped. A year later Patterson knocked out Johansson in the fifth round and became the first boxer to regain the heavyweight title. Patterson defended his title successfully until losing to Sonny Liston in 1962. Patterson continued to fight but never won another title. In his last fight, in 1972, he was knocked out by Muhammad Ali. Patterson later became a sports official in the state of New York.

See Also
Boxing; Liston, Charles ("Sonny").

North America

Patterson, William

(b. August 27, 1891, San Francisco, Calif.; d. March 5, 1980, Bronx, N.Y.), African American attorney, civil rights activist, and Communist Party leader who publicly charged the United States with genocide against African Americans.

Born and raised in the San Francisco area, William L. Patterson attended local public schools and later abandoned studies in engineering at the University of California at Berkeley to pursue a J.D. at the Hastings College of Law in San Francisco. At Hastings, Patterson began a lifelong involvement in political issues, protesting racism and arguing against African American participation in the "white man's" World War I. Earning his law degree in 1919, Patterson moved to New York City and established a legal practice in Harlem with two colleagues. His years in New York coincided with the height of the Harlem Renaissance, and Patterson developed relationships with Paul Robeson, W. E. B. Du Bois, and other prominent African American activists. He began to work increasingly with left-wing causes and was active in the ultimately fruitless campaign to free Nicola Sacco and Bartolomeo Vanzetti, immigrant Italian anarchists who were convicted of murder and executed in 1927.

Convinced that African American oppression was caused by capitalism and economic exploitation, Patterson devoted himself to anticapitalist activities, joining the Communist Party USA, in 1927 (one of the few African Americans to do so) and studying for three years at the University of the Toiling People of the Far East in Moscow. After returning from the Soviet Union in 1930 Patterson continued his leftist political activities: in 1932 he was elected to the Central Committee of the Communist Party and was the Communist candidate in the New York City mayoral election. Putting his electoral ambitions on hold after failing to win public office, from 1932 to 1946 Patterson focused on legal work as executive director of the Communist-influenced International Labor Defense, helping to plan the legal strategy for the Scottsboro Case defendants.

After moving to Chicago in 1938 Patterson became a community organizer on Chicago's South Side and a writer and editor for Communist newspapers such as the *Daily Record* and the *Daily Worker.* He also worked to safeguard the rights of African Americans and radical activists as the executive director of the Civil Rights Congress, a post he held from 1946 to 1956.

In 1951 Patterson edited *We Charge Genocide: The Crime of Government Against the Negro People*, and joined Paul Robeson in submitting a petition to the United Nations that accused the United States of genocide against African Americans. A year earlier the United States Congress's House Committee on Un-American Activities (HUAC) had demanded that Patterson testify about his Communist associations, and in 1954 he was found in contempt for his refusal to answer HUAC's questions. After three months in prison he was released upon successful appeal of the contempt citation.

Patterson published his autobiography, *The Man Who Cried Genocide*, in 1971. Though Patterson's political activities had raised the ire of the U.S. government, they earned him the praise of many Communist countries: in 1978 he was awarded the Paul Robeson Memorial Medal by East Germany's Academy of Arts.

Jalane Schmidt

See Also
World War I and African Americans; Chicago, Illinois; Du Bois, William Edward Burghardt (W. E. B.); Harlem, New York; New York, New York; San Francisco and Oakland, California; Communist Party USA, African Americans and the.

North America

Patton, Charley

(b. 1887, Edwards, Miss.; d. April 28, 1934, Indianola, Miss.), African American blues guitarist and vocalist, a key figure in the development of the Mississippi Delta blues style.

Although he possessed a strong, deep voice, Charley Patton was of small stature and too frail to perform the difficult labor on the farms of the Mississippi Delta region, where he lived his entire life. Instead, Patton – whose inability to read, rough personality, and womanizing epitomized the bluesman – learned to play the guitar and compose his own songs. By his early teenage years he began playing local gigs, performing in Jackson and Yazoo City at parties, work camps, jook joints, and picnics.

After his family's 1912 move to Will Dockery's plantation near Cleveland, Mississippi, Patton began performing with Willie Brown, Dick Bangston, and Tommy Johnson. He is considered a creator of the Delta blues, the most primitive blues genre, which is characterized by uneven rhyming, spoken – as opposed to sung – lyrics, including shouts, gutteral groans and haunting moans, and a bottleneck guitar technique in which melodic phrases are often blurred and repeated. Patton's lyrics often recounted the events of his life and those of his friends. His innovative playing style included thumping, and at times talking to, his guitar, which created a musical tension and dynamism often imitated by later blues musicians.

Patton made many recordings between 1929 and 1934, including ragtime, folk songs, white rural music, adaptations of popular tunes, religious songs, and of course, blues. Through these recordings he became one of the first Delta blues performers to emerge from anonymity and achieve broader musical influence.

Jalane Schmidt

See Also
Blues, The.

North America

Payne, Daniel Alexander

(b. February 24, 1811, Charleston, S.C.; d. November 21, 1893, Xenia, Ohio), African American bishop in the African Methodist Episcopal Church (AME) who helped establish Wilberforce University for the education of blacks.

Daniel Alexander Payne was born to London Payne, who was of mixed British and African descent, and Martha Payne, who was of mixed Native American and African descent. Both were free blacks, and they placed great importance on Payne's early education. They died before he was ten years old, leaving him to the care of relatives. He continued his education at a school for free blacks in Charleston, South Carolina, and thereafter on his own while apprenticed to artisans in several different fields. He later received private tutoring in Greek and Latin.

At age 17, Payne opened his own school in Charleston with a handful of students. The school grew quickly, and in addition to the daytime curriculum, he taught slaves at night. But in 1834 South Carolina outlawed the education of African Americans, and Payne was forced to close the school. The next year he moved North, pursuing his own studies at the Lutheran Seminary in Gettysburg, Pennsylvania. His eyesight worsened during his studies, and in 1837 his disability forced him to leave the school.

Payne nonetheless received a license to preach, and in 1839 the Franckean Synod of the Lutheran Church ordained him its first African American minister. After a short tenure at a Presbyterian church in New York, Payne established a school in Philadelphia, Pennsylvania, in 1840. Denied a Lutheran parish, he joined the AME in 1841. At first Payne was reluctant to join the church, wary of the AME's known opposition to educated clergy and its reliance on emotional worship services. Once inside the church, however, Payne worked to institutionalize his formal style and to advance the cause of an educated ministry. Supporters said Payne raised the standards of the AME Church; critics claimed he denigrated African and folk traditions to imitate white respectability.

Payne was soon appointed to the AME's traveling ministry, a role that took him across the Northeast to found schools and build churches. In 1845 he moved to BALTIMORE, MARYLAND, where he ministered at the Bethel Church. After coming into conflict with Baltimore blacks over his liturgical style of worship, Payne sought permission from the AME to write a history of the church, which he hoped would create interest in educated, standardized methods of preaching. The writing of the *History of the African Methodist Episcopal Church* (1891) took more than four decades and proved a valuable resource for later historians.

In 1852 Payne was elected a bishop of the church. His travels now extended throughout the country, for the organization of congregations, the creation of schools, and the promotion of informal education among those, such as women and slaves, who could not attend schools. On several occasions his presence in the South drew threats.

In 1863 Payne secured funds to buy WILBERFORCE UNIVERSITY, a school in Xenia, Ohio, that was then owned by the METHODIST EPISCOPAL CHURCH. Payne turned the school over to the AME and became the first black president of the first black-controlled college in the United States. The work to get the struggling college on its feet was formidable. He raised funds to make the college solvent and then more funds to rebuild after a devastating fire in 1865. He also attracted high-caliber teachers and students through his emphasis on discipline and morality. By the early post-Civil War era, Wilberforce was on solid financial and academic ground. While president Payne continued his AME duties, traveling as far as Europe. In 1876 he resigned from the presidency but remained active in the school as chancellor.

In the last years of his life Payne devoted increasing amounts of time to his writings. In 1885 he published *Treatise on Domestic Education*, in which he summarized his experiences in schooling. He followed in 1888 with a widely read autobiography, *Recollections of Seventy Years*.

SEE ALSO

Slavery in the United States; American Indians; Civil War, American; Free Blacks in the United States, 1619 to 1863.

North America

Payne, Donald (b. July 16, 1934, Newark, N.J.), Democratic member of the United States House of Representatives from New Jersey (1989-).

Donald Payne was the first black member of Congress from New Jersey, and in 1994 he was elected chairman of the CONGRESSIONAL BLACK CAUCUS, a panel dedicated to promoting the legislative interests of black Americans. Payne was born in NEWARK, NEW JERSEY, and received a bachelor's degree from Seton Hall University in 1957. He was a community affairs executive at the Prudential Insurance Company, and he served as national president of the Young Men's Christian Association (YMCA) in 1970. From 1972 to 1978 Payne was a member of the Essex County Board of Freeholders. He became vice president of Urban Data Systems Incorporated in 1975 and served on the Newark Municipal Council from 1982 to 1988.

Payne made two unsuccessful bids for Congress against incumbent Democrat Peter Rodino in 1980 and 1986. When Rodino retired in 1988, Payne easily won the seat representing New Jersey's Tenth Congressional District. He was reelected with more than 75 percent of the district's vote from 1990 to 1996.

Encompassing much of Newark and parts of Jersey City, the Tenth District is 60 percent black and overwhelmingly supports the Democratic Party. Newark's population has declined to half what it was in the 1950s, but the city remains New Jersey's largest. Poverty is a fundamental problem in the district.

In the 105th Congress (1997-1999), Payne served on the Education and the Workforce Committee and was ranking member of its Employer-Employee Relations Subcommittee. He also served on the International Relations Committee.

Africa

P'Bitek, Okot (b. 1931, Gulu, Uganda; d. 1982), Ugandan poet, novelist, and social anthropologist who dedicated his life to preserving his country's traditional literature and culture. He wrote in both English and ACHOLI and is generally regarded as the finest East African poet of the twentieth century.

Born in Gulu, in northern UGANDA, Okot p'Bitek received his early education locally and went on to the prestigious King's College Budo in Uganda. At age 22 he wrote his first book, *Lak tar miyo kinyero wi lobo* (1953; translated as *White Teeth*, 1989). This Acholi-language novel reflected his strong interests in music, song, literature, and traditional culture, concerns that surfaced in all his subsequent writing.

In the mid-1950s p'Bitek went to GREAT BRITAIN as a member of Uganda's national soccer team and stayed on to continue his education. He attended Bristol University, where he earned a diploma in education, and then the University of Oxford, where he earned a B.Litt. (bachelor of letters) in social anthropology. Returning to Uganda, he taught at Makerere University in the mid-1960s, then at the University of Nairobi in KENYA in the late 1960s, and again at Makerere University in the late 1970s. He later served as visiting professor or writer-in-residence at other universities in Africa and the United States.

P'Bitek produced his most important works in the mid- and late 1960s, beginning with *Song of Lawino, A Lament* (1966; published in the original Acholi as *Wer pa Lawino*, 1969), the finest of his narrative poems. Drawing on the form and content of traditional Acholi songs of abuse and praise, the poem is a song sung by an illiterate wife who complains about her relationship with her educated husband. Her persistent questioning of why she is abused simply for being African results in a sharp satire of Africans' superficial acceptance of European culture. The husband then states his case in *Song of Ocul* (1970), but his own words condemn him.

P'Bitek also published several books that directly reflect his Acholi background. They include the poetry volume *The Horn of My Love* (1974), the folktale collection *Hare and the Hornbill* (1978), and such nonfiction works as *Religion of the Central Luo* (1971) and *Africa's Cultural Revolution* (1973). The emphasis in all his work, both scholarly and creative, is on the idea that literature is a living social art that must be understood within the context of the culture in which it is produced and enjoyed.

Africa

Pedi (also known as Bapedi), ethnic group of SOUTH AFRICA.

The Pedi primarily inhabit Northern Province, South Africa. Some live in neighboring SWAZILAND. They speak a Bantu language and are closely related to the SOTHO people. More than 500,000 people consider themselves Pedi.

SEE ALSO

Bantu: Dispersion and Settlement.

Latin America and the Caribbean

Pedroso, Regino (b. 1898, CUBA; d. 1983, Cuba), Afro-Chinese politically committed poet also known for his contribution to Négritude poetry.

Described by some scholars as a NÉGRITUDE poet, Regino Pedroso preferred to be identified as a humanist social poet. The many layers of his identity provided much inspiration for his work. As a Marxist and a member of the working class, he spoke for the exploited worker. As a Cuban growing up in a time when politics and racism in the United States had infiltrated his country after the 1898 SPANISH-CUBAN-AMERICAN WAR, he cried out against imperialism. As a man of Afro-Chinese descent raised in a society in which blackness was deprecated, he condemned racial discrimination and called for revolutionary action. Through his work Pedroso was able to reach a variety of people and discussed issues such as humanism and related themes on which other poets of the time did not focus.

Since Pedroso's heritage was African and Chinese, identity was an issue of central importance to him. Although at one point he declared himself to be predominantly Chinese because of his father's strong influence, Pedroso also acknowledged his African ancestry. Of all his poems, "Hermano Negro" (Black Brother), which addresses the SCOTTSBORO CASE, best illustrates his connection with the plight of people of African descent in Cuba from the late 1920s to the early 1930s. The poem has been interpreted as dealing with basic human struggle instead of a specifically black struggle, yet the imagery is all too revealing. Though Pedroso was well aware of the history of oppression against blacks in Cuba, he was often uninspired by the vision of the Cuban NEGRISTA POETS (such as Zacarías Tallet and Emilio Ballagas), who saw black culture in an exotic, animalistic, and often erotic manner. Like many Afro-Cubans he avoided the stereotypical images embraced by these poets and focused instead on mobilizing blacks for social protest. In his work Pedroso applied a variation of the exotic image of blacks and added concrete examples of social injustice against people of African descent to create poetry that gained international recognition.

Credited by his contemporaries in 1927 with being Cuba's first social poet for his work "Salutación fraterna al taller mecánico" (A Fraternal Salute to the Factory), Regino Pedroso paid homage to the community of which he was a part. The support and financial contributions of fellow artists and the working-class community enabled him to publish his first book of poetry, *Nosotros* (Us), in 1933. Six years later he was awarded the National Literary Prize of Cuba for the poem "Más allá canta el mar" (Beyond There Sings the Sea). His work was praised by famous scholars and contemporaries, like the anthropologist FERNANDO ORTIZ (1881-1969), who appreciated the power of "Hermano Negro," and the poet NICOLÁS GUILLÉN (1902-1989), who understood Pedroso's artistic inspirations. Guillén thought of Pedroso as three distinct beings: the avant-garde poet, the social poet, and the Chinese poet. All three came together to create one lyrically pure, true poet who lived the experiences of which he wrote. As a significant contributor to the world of literature, Pedroso remains relatively unstudied. He died in 1983 in Havana but left behind a legacy ripe for exploration.

SEE ALSO

Literature, Black, in Spanish America; Havana, Cuba.

Latin America and the Caribbean

Pelé (Edson Arantes do Nascimento) (b. October 23, 1940, Tres Corações, BRAZIL), Afro-Brazilian soccer player, considered by many to be the greatest in the history of the game, and one of the most recognized black people in the world.

Born in a small town in the state of MINAS GERAIS with a semiprofessional soccer player as a father, Edson Arantes do Nascimento grew up in the city of Bauru. There he occasionally attended school and performed odd jobs until, while still an adolescent, he began to play for the local youth soccer team. It was at this time that he acquired the nickname "Pelé," by which he is now known throughout the world.

At age 15 Pelé was transferred to Santos, a team in the much larger port city with the same name. Pelé would play for Santos for most of his career, and he would forever become associated with its white Number 10 shirt – along with the yellow shirt of the Brazilian national team.

In the 18 years that Pelé played at Santos, the club team won numerous state and national championships in Brazil and two world club championships, in 1962 and 1963. During what has been called Pelé's reign (in Brazil he is referred to as "King Pelé"), Santos frequently toured throughout the world and enormous crowds gathered wherever the team played.

In Asia, Africa, and Europe fans paid homage to this black Brazilian. Concerned that such devotion might result in offers for Pelé to play for teams in richer countries, in 1962 the Brazilian Congress declared the 22-year-old to be a "non-exportable national treasure." And in a story often recalled, a visit to NIGERIA by Pelé's Santos in 1969 caused the warring factions in a civil war to agree to a temporary truce lasting the duration of the Brazilian's stay.

With the Brazilian national team Pelé played in four World Cups, figuring in Brazil's unprecedented three victories between 1958 and 1970. In 1970 Brazil's military dictatorship claimed the team's victory as its own in an attempt to associate itself with the triumphant soccer team. General Médici hosted the team's players, and his military government used an image of Pelé celebrating a goal as part of its propaganda, fueling years of debate concerning Pelé's possible complicity with the authoritarian regime. The song "Pra frente Brasil" (Forward, Brazil), composed for the 1970 team, was also appropriated by the government for its propaganda.

Pelé retired from his club team, Santos, in 1974, and it is rumored that even the president of Brazil attempted, unsuccessfully, to convince him to continue playing. In 1975, however, a multimillion-dollar offer lured him back into the game to play for the New York Cosmos as a North American league attempted to spread soccer to the United States. His second and final retirement came in October 1977.

Pelé is considered by many to have been the most complete soccer player in the history of soccer and has been repeatedly chosen as the most outstanding athlete of the century. He scored his 1000th goal in 1969 playing for Santos in Rio de Janeiro's

Pelé, *right,* maneuvering around a defender, led the Brazilian national soccer team to three World Cup titles. *Express Newspapers/Archive Photos*

famous Maracana Stadium – a goal he dedicated to the "children of Brazil." Pelé would ultimately score a total of 1279 goals in 1362 games, only 50 fewer than fellow Brazilian Arthur Friedenreich, whose reported 1329 goals were scored in an earlier time when games generally had higher scores.

Pelé's importance in Brazil is of such magnitude that some have claimed that he would be elected president if he ever chose to be a candidate. This is remarkable in a country that has had only light-skinned presidents despite a black and *mestizo* (of indigenous and European descent) majority in the general population. In 1993, in a move widely praised, President Fernando Henrique Cardoso appointed Pelé to the position of minister of sports. Yet Pelé's fame reaches far beyond the confines of Brazil and sports. He was the first black man to be on the cover of *Life* magazine, for instance, and even more than two decades after the end of his professional soccer career he is certainly among the most recognized people of African descent in the world.

Marcos Natalí

SEE ALSO

Rio de Janeiro, Brazil; Soccer in Latin America and the Caribbean.

Latin America and the Caribbean

Peña Gómez, José Francisco

(b. March 3, 1937, Loma de El Flaco, Dominican Republic; d. May 10, 1998, Santo Domingo, DOMINICAN REPUBLIC), Afro-Dominican politician who was the secretary-general of the Dominican Revolutionary Party (Partido Revolucionario Dominicano, PRD), president of the Socialist International's Latin American section, and an eloquent spokesman for and defender of political, social, and racial equality.

José Francisco Peña Gómez was born into a poor black family in March 1937 in the mountains bordering HAITI. On October 3 of that same year, the dictator RAFAEL TRUJILLO, motivated by intense nationalism and racist doctrines, ordered his army to kill all Haitians living within the borders of the Dominican Republic (*see* DOMINICAN-HAITIAN RELATIONS). Fearing that they would be confused with Haitians because the military was killing indiscriminately, Peña Gómez's parents fled to Haiti to avoid the massacre that took the lives of as many as 20,000 black Dominicans and Haitians. The couple left their children behind in hopes that they would survive under the protection of neighbors. Peña Gómez was adopted by Regino Peña and Fermina Gómez, a *mestizo* (of indigenous and European descent) Dominican peasant couple who brought him up as their own child.

From an early age Peña Gómez distinguished himself as a brilliant student. At age 15 he became an instructor in a literacy program for poor children. Later he worked as a teacher in rural and night schools. A wealthy family, whom Peña Gómez had assisted during the literacy campaigns they had sponsored, supported him so that he could continue his studies. He entered law school in 1957 at the Universidad Autónoma de Santo Domingo. During his university studies he worked as a sports announcer and began to participate in politics.

In 1961 Peña Gómez became an important political figure during the presidential campaign of his political mentor, PRD leader Juan Bosch. Bosch became the first democratically elected president of the country in 1962, after many years of dictatorship (Rafael Trujillo, 1930-1960; Joaquín Balaguer, 1960-1962). Seven months later Bosch's government was overthrown by a military coup, forcing Bosch into exile and thrusting Peña Gómez into leadership of the PRD. In 1965 Peña Gómez successfully led a civil-military revolt demanding Bosch's return. Thousands of United States Marines arrived four days later to stop the upheaval. JOAQUÍN BALAGUER, a former president under Trujillo's dictatorship, became president in 1966 after new (and, some critics say, fraudulent) elections were held. Though Peña Gómez was able to complete his law degree during these years, he was forced into exile by Balaguer's repression of political opponents.

During his years abroad Peña Gómez attended courses in political science and law at Harvard, Michigan State University, and the University of Paris. After returning to the Dominican Republic he was credited as the driving force behind PRD victories. In 1978 he was instrumental in the PRD victory that led Antonio Guzmán to the presidency of the Dominican Republic. The PRD won the presidency again in 1982, with Salvador Jorge Blanco as its candidate. Peña Gómez won the election for mayor of Santo Domingo in 1982, and thus became a strong contender for the presidential elections of 1986. However, when the time came to launch his candidacy, leaders of the PRD fought his nomination, arguing that a black man with family links to Haiti would be unable to defeat the opposition candidate Balaguer. Although it presented a white candidate, the PRD lost to Balaguer anyway.

After many years of accepting positions of lesser political importance because of racism, Peña Gómez was nominated for the PRD presidential candidacy in 1990. He and Juan Bosch, now a candidate for the Dominican Liberation Party (Partido de la Liberación Dominicana, PLD), were defeated by the powerful Joaquín Balaguer, whose political campaign employed racist images to evoke the specter of a historically feared Haitian takeover.

In 1994 Peña Gómez lost again to Balaguer in the presidential election, this time by a very narrow margin. The PRD claimed that the elections were fraudulent and marred by yet another racist campaign. After much domestic and international protest, Balaguer was forced to shorten his four-year term to two years and was barred from running for office again.

Peña Gómez ran for president of his country for the last time in 1996 against Leonel Fernández Reyna, a light-skinned mulatto (of African and European descent) candidate who had grown up in New York and was running for the PLD. Peña Gómez won the first round of the presidential elections, receiving 47 percent of the votes compared with Fernández's 39 percent. Fearing a defeat for the second round, in which only the two top candidates from the first round compete, Fernández took advantage of Balaguer's public endorsement in his favor and successfully created yet another racist and xenophobic campaign against his opponent. Peña Gómez was depicted through toy monkeys and gorillas and was charged with being a VODOU practitioner who wanted to annex the Dominican Republic to Haiti. He lost the election by a narrow margin.

Peña Gómez died on May 10, 1998, of pancreatic cancer, less than a week before Santo Domingo mayoral elections in which he figured as the favorite candidate.

Liliana Obregón

Cross Cultural

Pentecostalism,

worldwide charismatic Christian movement originating in America at the beginning of the twentieth century that emphasized the believer's "baptism in the Holy Spirit" and speaking in tongues as central to the Christian experience.

The theological basis for Pentecostalism is found in the New Testament. The Book of Acts, chapter 2, recounts the phenomenon of Christ's disciples being "baptized in the Holy Spirit" while meeting for the Jewish observance of Shavu'ot (Pentecost in Greek), with glossalalia, or speaking in tongues, as the sign of the baptism. The modern focus on spirit-baptism has its origins in two main strains of religious experience in America: the Holiness Movement and African American Christianity.

The first strain is found in the nineteenth-century Holiness Movement that influenced a major segment of American Protestantism, particularly the Methodists, whose belief in perfectionism was probably its origin. Forming the interdenominational National Holiness Association from 1867 to 1887, these Protestants promoted the notion that once a person had accepted Christ or experienced justification, he or she would move toward a second state of perfect love termed sanctification, which was to be brought on by a spiritual baptism.

The Holiness Movement had both black and white adherents and exists today in different forms throughout the United States and elsewhere.

By the 1890s the Holiness Movement had fragmented, and new doctrines were spreading. In 1901 Charles Parham, a white Holiness minister, asserted that instead of sanctification being the final result of spirit-baptism, it was the glossalalia described in Acts 2 that announced the spirit's descent upon the human body. Rife with millennialism, the "announcement" was seen as the harbinger of the Second Coming of Christ.

This "Pentecostal" idea was preached first in the Midwest but soon spread to small circles throughout the South. In 1905 an African American Holiness minister named William J. Seymour attended Parham's Bethel Bible School in Houston, Texas, where he was forced to listen from outside the lecture room because of Parham's policy of segregation. Nonetheless, Seymour assimilated Parham's teachings into what was already a strong foundation for the belief in Pentecostalism. In 1906 Seymour went to Los Angeles, where one of his flock of Evening Light Saints experienced speaking in tongues, an event that sparked the Azusa Street Revival, the seminal movement in what is currently termed Pentecostalism.

The second strain that gave rise to Pentecostalism is the nature of Christianity practiced by Africans enslaved in the New World. Merging the teachings of the Bible and styles of worship with antecedents in traditional African religions, communities of black people produced a new version of Christianity. This synthesis was immediately recognizable in the Azusa Street Revival. Salient features included holy dancing, singing, a trancelike spirit possession, a focus on testimony and testifying, and the immediate experience of the divine presence in the worship service.

Seymour's Azusa Street Revival was characterized by the full participation of people of every race and ethnicity. Native-born and newly immigrated whites, Mexican Americans, Asian Americans, and African Americans gathered to experience the glossalalia spirit-baptism that they had not found in the churches of other denominations. The idea of interracial worship was repugnant, however, to many whites, including the Ku Klux Klan, who harassed the new Pentecostals. Yet from 1906 until 1914, Seymour's movement attracted Christians from all over the United States who, according to one white parishioner, saw "the color line washed away in the blood [of Jesus Christ]."

Seymour published a journal titled *Apostolic Faith* that made explicit his belief that baptism in the Holy Spirit was capable not only of elevating the individual soul, but also of ameliorating the rampant racial hostility of the day. The multitudes in America who adopted Pentecostalism, including a large portion of the Holiness Movement, were joined by believers around the world who were being evangelized by missionaries. By 1908 Pentecostal missionaries were working in 50 countries.

Despite Seymour's early success at holding together a multiracial ensemble of believers in Pentecost, in 1914 the Assemblies of God was established by whites who wished to see their churches segregated. Around the same time black Pentecostals as well removed themselves from such bodies as the Pentecostal Holiness Church. This sparked a pattern of churches separated by race, spawning numerous conferences and associations composed of one racial group or another. Nonetheless, many Pentecostals remained in interracial churches and organizations, including the CHURCH OF GOD IN CHRIST and Pentecostal Assemblies of the World.

The historical structures of Pentecostal churches and denominations have differed from those of other Protestant groups in that doctrine and liturgy have not always been determined by a central governing body. Thus, individual pastors have had a significant role in shaping the character of their own congregations. The malleable structure of Pentecostal churches has allowed for significant adaptability across cultures and regions. Within the past 25 years Pentecostalism has found bases in mainline African American denominations, including several African Methodist Episcopal and Baptist churches in which the emotional exuberance of Pentecostal worship had previously been avoided.

Currently more than 400 million people worldwide – one out of every four Christians – are Pentecostals. According to theologian Harvey Cox, "Pentecostalism is not a denomination or a creed but a movement, a cluster of religious practices and attitudes that transcends ecclesiastical boundaries." Its converts throughout the world have come from all races and classes, yet, as did its original adherents, Pentecostalism finds its greatest reception among women, the poor, and the oppressed groups of the world. Throughout the African diaspora and within Africa itself, millions of people have been drawn to its empowering beliefs and practices. In Latin America, and in BRAZIL in particular, Pentecostals are now competing with the once dominant Roman Catholic Church for adherents. Beginning in 1910 with Luigi Francescon's Christian Congregations of Brazil, Pentecostalism has emerged as a powerful force in Brazil because of its emphasis on exuberant personal religious experience unmediated by authoritarian leadership. This experience is grounded in the well-being of a community of believers whose goal of communion with the Holy Spirit is seen as leading to Christ's Second Coming.

In Africa Pentecostalism is the fastest spreading religious movement on the continent, largely as a result of the compatibility of traditional indigenous religions and the doctrines of Pentecost. Christian churches, independent of non-African rule, have arisen throughout Africa, such as the Church of the Lord Jesus Christ on Earth, founded by the prophet SIMON KIMBANGU in 1921, and the Apostolic Church, founded by the prophet John Maranke in 1932. These thousands of new denominations have assimilated indigenous beliefs and practices, including ancestral veneration, spirit possession, and most important, healing, into the idiom of Christian baptism and salvation. The remarkable growth of Pentecostalism throughout the world bespeaks a common need for both emotional attachment to community and spiritual transcendence.

SEE ALSO

Methodist Episcopal Church; African Methodist Episcopal Church; Apostolic Movement; Baptists; Seymour, William Joseph; Los Angeles, California; Catholic Church in Latin America and the Caribbean.

Latin America and the Caribbean

Péralte, Charlemagne Masséna

(b. October 10, 1885, Hinche, Haiti; d. November 1, 1919, Grande Rivière du Nord, Haiti), leader of the so-called Caco rebellion (*see* CACOS) against the first United States occupation of HAITI (which lasted from 1915 to 1934).

Charlemagne Masséna Péralte was born in the rural town of Hinche in central Haiti and grew up in a prominent middle-class family. While still very young he entered politics and served in a few minor official roles. When his brother-in-law Oreste Zamor became president in 1914, Péralte was made military commander of the town of Port-de-Paix.

In 1915, at the beginning of the U.S. occupation, Péralte was the military commander of the southern town of Léogane, near Port-au-Prince. He refused to surrender his command to the American troops, and as a result was fired by the recently "elected" puppet government of President Sudre Dartiguenave. Péralte then withdrew to his estates near Hinche. On October 11, 1917, he was arrested along with his brother Saul, allegedly for plotting against the American invasion. He was sentenced to five years of hard labor in prison, and shortly thereafter his brother Saul was killed in an alleged escape attempt.

Péralte served a year of his prison sentence at Cap-Haïtien. He escaped in September 1918 and returned to the central plateau to launch a liberation war against the U.S. Army. Péralte founded a local peasant army with several thousand supporters, declared the provisional independence of the north, and appointed himself the head of its government.

Péralte's troops attacked local military establishments and in October 1919 marched on Port-au-Prince itself but were driven back. Since the American troops could not defeat him in an open battle because he was using hit-and-run guerrilla tactics, they decided to get rid of him by whatever means necessary.

Sgt. Herman H. Hanneken of the U.S. Marine Corps soon came up with a plan to reveal Péralte's whereabouts. The Americans hired J. B. Conze, whom they groomed as rebel leader who was supposed to offer his alliance to Péralte. The scheme worked perfectly, and Conze revealed Péralte's plans to the Americans. During an attack on the town of Grande Rivière du Nord, the Americans discovered Péralte's headquarters and shot him dead.

Péralte's body was brought to Cap-Haïtien and exposed in the yard of the military barracks, crucified on a door with the Haitian flag around his head. The body was buried secretly by the Americans at the Chabert internment camp. In October 1934, after the departure of the Americans, Péralte was exhumed and reburied, with great pomp, in a Cap-Haïtien cemetery. Péralte has since become a prime symbol of Haitian nationalism.

Georges Michel

See Also
Cap-Haïtien, Haiti; Port-au-Prince, Haiti.

Africa

Pereira, Aristides (b. 1924, Boa Vista, Cape Verde), the first president of the Republic of Cape Verde.

Aristides Pereira grew up on the Cape Verdean island of Boa Vista. After completing school he trained to become a radio-telegraph technician. By the late 1950s he had moved up to the position of chief of telecommunications in Guinea-Bissau, another Portuguese colony. He was also increasingly involved in the labor movement and was one of the key organizers of the 1959 Pijiguiti strike. The strike, during which Portuguese forces fired on demonstrators, killing at least 50 and wounding more than 100 others, marked a turning point in the growing nationalist movement led by Amílcar Cabral and the Partido Africano da Independencia da Guine e Cabo Verde (PAIGC). Pereira joined the struggle and became a member of the PAIGC's Central Committee.

For the next 14 years Pereira dedicated himself to the fight for Cape Verdean independence and gradually rose through the ranks of the PAIGC leadership. When Cabral was assassinated in January 1973, Pereira assumed leadership of the PAIGC.

Cape Verde won independence on July 5, 1975. Pereira became the new republic's first president, promising that "Our state will be profoundly democratic and will guarantee the participation of all without distinction of color, religion, or sex in the conduct of the affairs of the states." With Pedro Pires as his prime minister, Pereira was part of the PAIGC's successful joint rule over Cape Verde and Guinea-Bissau. A 1980 coup overthrowing Guinea-Bissau president Luís Cabral ended this affiliation, and Pereira responded to perceived threats to his own government by arresting potential opponents. The crackdown on dissent undermined his promise of democratic rule and added to the grievances of a citizenry already struggling with near-chronic food shortages.

At a time when many newly independent African nations were allying themselves with one or the other of the cold war superpowers, Pereira advocated nonalignment as well as economic independence for the Cape Verde islands. Toward the latter goal, he promoted Marxist programs of land reform and nationalization. In foreign relations the administration cultivated controversial relationships with Palestinians as well as with China and Libya, and openly criticized both South African apartheid and foreign intervention in Africa.

From the early 1980s onward the PAIGC's economic programs as well as its single-party rule met with increasing opposition. Finally, in 1991, Pereira agreed to allow multiparty elections. The PAIGC was defeated by the Movimento para a Democracia, and Pereira gave up his presidential seat to António Monteiro. Now in semiretirement, he occasionally comments publicly on African affairs.

Marian Aguiar

See Also
Nationalism in Africa; Pires, Pedro Verona Rodrigues.

Latin America and the Caribbean

Pérez Prado, Dámaso
(b. December 11, 1916, Matanzas, Cuba; d. December 4, 1983, Colonia del Valle, Mexico), Afro-Cuban pianist and bandleader who was one of the foremost popularizers of the mambo.

In the early 1940s Dámaso Pérez Prado played piano with the Cuban orchestra Casino de la Playa, but in 1948 he moved to Mexico, which thereafter became his principal base. In 1948 he began recording instrumental mambos with an ensemble inspired by American jazz big bands, using large trumpet, trombone, and saxophone sections. Cuban music was then typically played by smaller, seven-to-ten-member *septetos* and *conjuntos* (*see* Son). RCA Records marketed these mambos for a Latin audience in the United States. In the late 1940s an American Federation of Musicians' strike and recording ban sharply reduced the number of American record releases, and Pérez Prado's recordings gained considerable success in the United States, although the bandleader did not tour that country until 1951.

Pérez Prado did not play a major role in the Afro-Latin jazz movement epitomized by bandleaders Machito and Tito Puente, but he did feature talented jazz musicians, including such white non-Latinos as trumpeters Pete Candoli (part of Pérez Prado's 1951 United States touring band), Shorty Rogers, Maynard Ferguson, and Rolf Erickson. In hiring musicians without regard to race, Pérez Prado actively challenged the Jim Crow practices that were commonplace in American entertainment.

Over the years Pérez Prado featured numerous Latin American musicians who would later become leaders themselves, including Cuban conga drummer Mongo Santamaría, Cuban singer and guitarist Beny Moré, and future Fania Records founder Johnny Pacheco, who was Dominican. Critics are divided in their assessments of Pérez Prado's musical accomplishments. Latin music scholar John Storm Roberts regarded "Moliendo Café" and other popular Pérez Prado recordings as "among the most awful works of their time," characterizing them as "banal, and worse than banal." On the other hand, Hernando Calvo Ospina credited Pérez Prado with being the "first person to adapt North American jazz bands to Cuban traditions." Most critics, including Roberts, agree that Pérez Prado played a central role in the popularizing of mambo music.

James Clyde Sellman

See Also
Dominican Republic; Matanzas, Cuba; Puente, Ernesto Antonio (Tito); Santamaría, Ramón ("Mongo").

Africa

Perry, Ruth (b. 1939?, Liberia), former transitional president of Liberia; the first woman head of state in modern Africa.

Ruth Perry served as a senator from Grand Cape Mount County in northern Liberia before being named chairwoman of Liberia's transitional Council of State in September 1996. Her appointment came at the hands of the factional leaders whose fighting had thrust Liberia into a seven-year-long civil war, but Perry, a widowed grandmother of 57, dealt firmly with the rival warlords, overseeing a mostly successful disarmament and free elections in July 1997.

Perry, the mother of seven children, first became involved in politics when she finished her husband's term as senator after his death. In the 1980s she attracted attention for her public opposition to then-President Samuel K. Doe's efforts to legalize polygamy. After Charles Taylor's National Patriotic Front of Liberia began to take control of the Liberian countryside in 1989, the country's government collapsed and Perry returned to her home (where she helped shelter refugees). A series of transitional governments was appointed throughout the 1990s, but none held much real power. In 1996 at ABUJA, NIGERIA, the ECONOMIC COMMUNITY OF WEST AFRICAN STATES brought together the most powerful of the factional leaders to draft a disarmament plan and name a new head of state.

Analysts reported surprise at the choice of Perry, but she quickly warned Taylor and the other warlords that she would "treat them like a mother and, if necessary, that means discipline." Lacking money and political power, Perry used her largely symbolic position to try to educate Liberians about their basic political rights. After nearly a year in office Perry oversaw the July 1997 elections, widely considered fair, in which Charles Taylor was elected president.

Kate Tuttle

SEE ALSO
Doe, Samuel Kanyon; Taylor, Charles Ghankay.

Cross Cultural

Persian Gulf War (1991), America's first military confrontation of the post-cold war era, launched in response to Iraq's invasion of Kuwait, in which African Americans made up more than a quarter of all United States forces in the war zone.

On August 2, 1990, a force of 120,000 Iraqi troops spearheaded by 850 tanks invaded and occupied the small nation of Kuwait, sparking an international crisis that culminated in the Persian Gulf War. Although African Americans made up only 12 percent of America's military-age population, they constituted 26 percent of American military manpower in the gulf. This overrepresentation of BLACKS IN THE AMERICAN MILITARY reflected the military's success in addressing racial prejudice as well as the relative lack of employment opportunities for African Americans.

During the gulf crisis two African American officers in particular personified the opportunities available to blacks in the armed services: Gen. Colin L. Powell, chairman of the Joint Chiefs of Staff, and Lt. Gen. Cal Waller, second-in-command over U.S. operations in the gulf. The invasion of Kuwait represented America's first foreign policy crisis in the post-cold war era as well as the nation's greatest overseas commitment of military power since the VIETNAM WAR. Recalling the domestic unrest and opposition created by the Vietnam War, Powell argued against committing American military forces without first clearly informing and securing the support of the American public.

Moreover, unlike past American interventions, such as the invasions of GRENADA and PANAMA and the Vietnam War itself, in the Persian Gulf War the United States did not act unilaterally. President George Bush orchestrated a 38-nation coalition to oppose Iraq's invasion, which included – for the first time – the Soviet Union working alongside the United States in an armed conflict. Moreover, U.S. policy only employed military intervention after diplomatic overtures and economic sanctions failed to affect Iraqi leader Saddam Hussein. Nonetheless, some blacks – such as Mark Harrison, the national organizer of the African-American Network Against U.S. Intervention in the Gulf – opposed the military buildup. In general, however, African Americans were supportive of U.S. policy.

Powell and his military planners made a successful effort to concentrate allied forces in the gulf region well before the start of a military conflict. Two weeks after the Iraqi invasion Bush ordered U.S. forces to the gulf to defend Saudi Arabia, an oil-rich U.S. ally, from a possible Iraqi attack – an operation that the Pentagon designated Desert Shield. By mid-October some 230,000 American troops had arrived in the Persian Gulf, and by January 1991 the troop level reached 580,000, a greater number of troops than the maximum U.S. commitment during the Vietnam War.

When a last-minute United Nations peace mission to the Iraqi government failed to achieve a resolution, Bush announced the start of allied offensive operations, which the Pentagon dubbed Desert Storm, on January 16, 1991. After more than five weeks of intensive bombing, American and allied forces launched a ground offensive on February 24, 1991. The war, which ended just five days later, resulting in the deaths of as many as 100,000 Iraqis. Confounding predictions that African Americans would bear the brunt of American casualties, only 15 percent of the 184 U.S. soldiers killed were black.

James Clyde Sellman

SEE ALSO
Powell, Colin Luther.

Latin America and the Caribbean

Peru, country of South America bordered on the east by the Pacific Ocean, on the south by CHILE, on the west by BRAZIL, on the southwest by BOLIVIA, and on the north by ECUADOR and COLOMBIA.

Peru has long been known for the powerful and sophisticated Incas, who built their cities high in the mineral-rich Andes Mountains; for the Spanish conquistadors who marched into Peru and conquered the enormous Inca Empire in a matter of months; and for the thousands upon thousands of tons of gold and silver that Spain extracted from the region now known as Peru over the next several centuries. It is less well known that the conquest, the extraction, and indeed much of contemporary Peruvian culture were the result of the labor and input of African slaves and their descendants.

BLACKS IN THE CONQUEST AND COLONIAL PERU

Indigenous peoples, originally migrants from North and Central America, have lived in Peru since at least the ninth millennium B.C.E. As early as 1200 C.E., a Quechua-speaking people known as the Inca began subduing their neighbors, eventually controlling the entire region of the Andes, some 3000 km (2000 mi) in length.

In 1524 the Spanish explorer Francisco Pizarro, in the company of Diego de Almagro, entered Ecuador and Peru searching for the Inca Empire, where there were rumored gold and silver deposits. African slaves were among the members of the earliest such expeditions, serving as both sailors and soldiers. When the Spanish established contact with Indian groups, they assigned some of the slaves the duty of interpreting, based on the erroneous belief that Africans, being "primitive," would better understand the Indians.

When Pizarro captured and executed the Inca leader Atahualpa in 1532, and when he defeated and plundered the Inca stronghold of Cuzco in 1533, African soldiers were among his ranks. Perhaps the most notable of the early black conquistadors of Peru was a slave named Juan Valiente. In 1534 Valiente obtained permission from his owner to join Pedro de Alvarado's army on its passage from Guatemala to Peru. Valiente fought fiercely in Peru in 1535 against the remnants of the Incas, then moved on to Chile, where he gained fame for his fighting against the Araucanian Indians. In the mid-1540s he was rewarded with an estate near Santiago and received an *encomienda*, a group of tribute-paying Indians – probably the first instance in which an African was given an encomienda (*see* COLONIAL LATIN AMERICA AND THE CARIBBEAN). Valiente remained, nonetheless, a slave; while negotiations for his freedom were pending with his master (who wanted Valiente returned, along with all the property he had amassed), he was killed by Araucanians at Tucapel.

The wealth of Peru's gold and silver lodes, tucked high in the Andes Mountains, matched the expectations of the Spaniards. In the early years of the colonies, however, the Spaniards used mainly Indians to work the deep-shaft mines. Not only was Indian labor abundant (originally, at least), but the Spaniards believed Africans were ill suited to the cold alpine climate and the dank mines.

Instead, the life of the early Afro-Peruvian slave revolved around the coastal capital of Lima, founded by Pizarro in 1535, and former Inca cities like Cuzco, which were being transformed into Hispanic cities. Afro-Peruvians performed much of the land clearing, road building, and construction to erect these cities. In Lima slaves were also prominent among the dockworkers and mule drivers who greased the gears of the rapidly growing export of gold and silver and import of food and other goods. Female

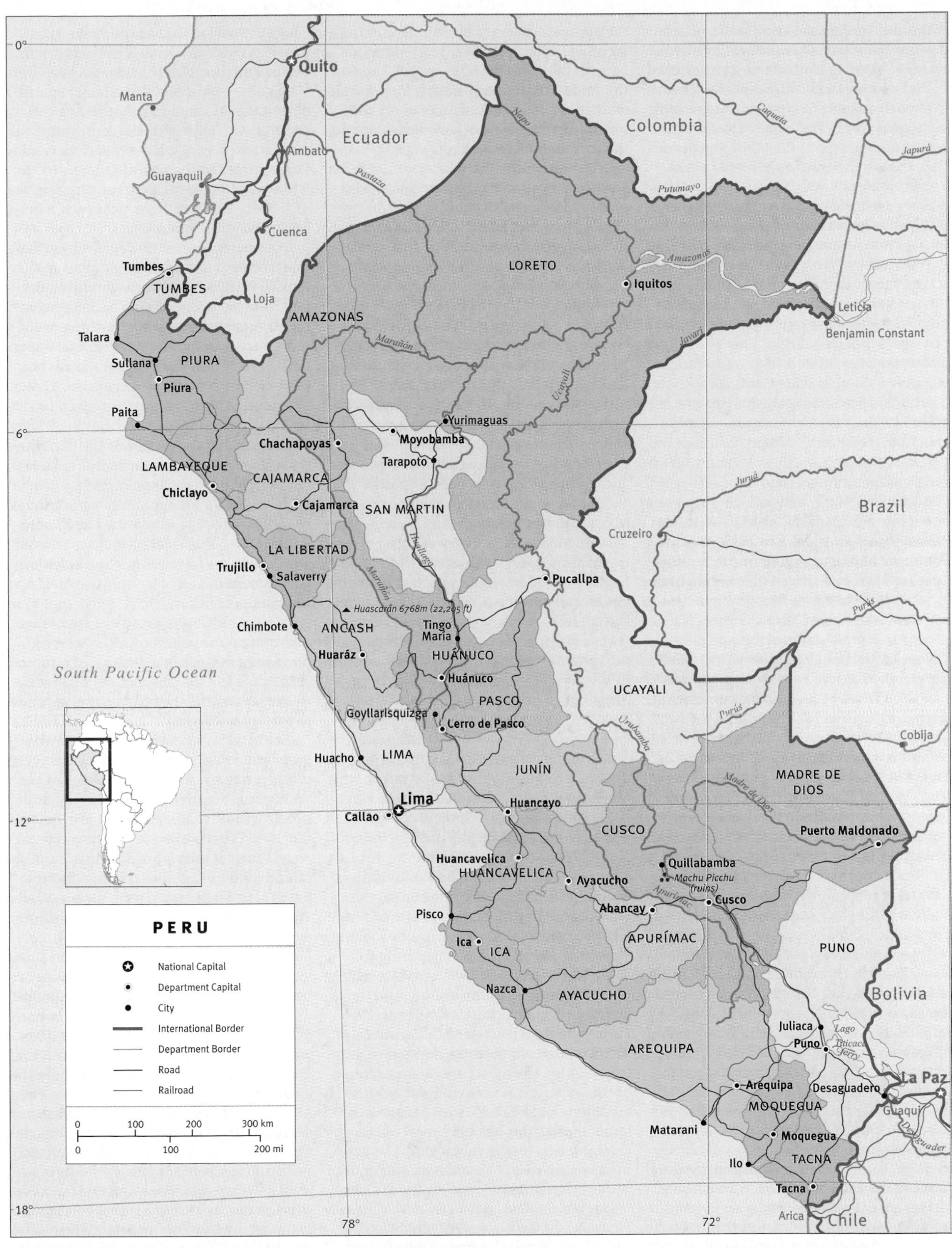

slaves also performed highly valued domestic tasks like cooking and laundering.

The narrow strip of land along the Peruvian coast was (and is) mostly desert, but where mountain streams provided irrigation, it could be made fertile. In order to become less dependent on imported food, Peruvian settlers fanned out across the coastal plain and settled at the few well-watered sites. There they established plantations on land cleared and worked by slaves. (Indians were used initially, but most of the coastal Indians had fled to the mountains or had been killed by disease and warfare.) For the most part the crops grown were for the internal use of the colony; little was exported. In places, however, cotton was grown, creating a viable textile industry in Lima, where slaves worked in the factories. Later SUGAR cane was grown in enough quantity to export to Europe. Most haciendas were small, their size dictated by the sparseness of the land. Thus even the largest of the farms had only a few dozen workers.

The slave trade itself was a costly endeavor since slaves had to journey on a several-month voyage from Africa to the Americas (usually PANAMA); they then traveled overland for several weeks to the Pacific Ocean and were further transported by boat to Lima. Many died en route. Slaves were valued for their physical labor. In addition, many of the arriving slaves had worked farms in African climates not unlike that of Peru. Thus they contributed precious expertise about growing crops in a dry land. Other slaves, skilled in crafts and metalworking before their capture, would continue to work in artisan trades as slaves, in both the city and the country.

By the end of the sixteenth century Peru also had a substantial number of free blacks: perhaps one-fourth to one-third of Afro-Peruvians had bought their freedom under Spanish laws, had arrived free, or had been granted their freedom for fighting in the conquest with Pizarro. Most of the free blacks, known as *libertos*, shunned the agricultural regions for the cities, particularly Lima, where they worked as low- to mid-wage laborers, maids, and the like. Their actions were rigidly circumscribed: in 1577, for example, the viceroy of Peru banned any black person from owning a weapon, and throughout colonial times blacks were barred as a matter of course from many of the skilled trades. Although in word Spanish law allowed any slave to buy his or her freedom, slaves' activities were closely monitored. According to historian Frederick Bowser, the vast majority of slaves who were manumitted between 1580 and 1650 in Lima were women and children, particularly female children – considered the least valuable slaves. Only 4 percent of slaves freed in Lima during that time period were between ages 16 and 25 – for a master, the most profitable years of a slave's life. Apparently slaveholders had informal means of keeping their most valuable slaves closely tethered. It is little wonder, then, that when a male liberto obtained his freedom he often elected to join the comparatively egalitarian Spanish colonial army in Peru, or left Peru altogether to enlist in another colony's military. At the turn of the sixteenth century black slaves and libertos made up perhaps 10 percent of Peru's population. In the Andes African slaves and libertos were probably equal in number to Spaniards until as late as 1640.

Despite the high cost of slaves, demand for imports grew well into the seventeenth century. Occasionally, a few African slaves were bought and/or captured by Indians. With greater frequency Spanish colonists sent incoming African slaves to work alongside Incas in the gold- and silver-mining gangs of the Andes. In the deep-shaft mines, brutal labor, poor ventilation, and cave-ins combined to keep the life of a worker short and the demand for slaves high.

The demand for slave labor prompted colonists to circumvent Spain's rigid control of the lucrative slave trade, which it monitored in order to collect tax. Typically Spain granted the rights to its slave trade to a particular company or companies and forbade Spanish colonists from trading with anyone else. For example, from 1701 to 1713 several French companies held the *asiento* (the right to the slave trade) for Spanish America. During this time France exported several thousand blacks to Peru from their stations along Africa's CONGO RIVER – a long voyage with a high cost. If a buyer was willing to deal with smugglers, slaves could be obtained more cheaply from Portuguese Brazil or the British and French colonies in the Caribbean.

Spain reluctantly acknowledged its lack of control over the trade in 1740, when it allowed privileged Peruvian colonists to buy *licencias* (licenses) with which they could buy as many slaves as they wanted from any nation not at war with Spain. The licencia system lasted half a century but did little to curb smuggling. After 1795 Spain abandoned the system and allowed any Spanish colonist to buy as many slaves as he wanted from any source not at war with Spain.

CULTURAL SURVIVAL AND RESISTANCE

Much of the African slaves' cultural and linguistic heritage was lost as a result of the long distance they were forced to travel and the length of time they sometimes spent in other colonies even before arriving in Peru. Nonetheless, many slaves kept the drum-saturated music of their homelands alive; over the centuries they blended those sounds with the string-influenced music of the Spanish colonists. African forms of cooking were also preserved since preparing food was a task that slaves working as domestics often performed, both en route and upon arrival in Spanish America. As most Afro-Peruvians were converted to Catholicism, African religious customs merged with Christianity. The most prominent example of this syncretism surviving today is the ceremony of El Señor de los Milagros, an annual march through the streets of Lima celebrated by tens of thousands. The ceremony originated in the mid-seventeenth century, when blacks, primarily from Angola, organized in *cofradías*, societies of mutual support (*see* CATHOLIC CHURCH IN LATIN AMERICA AND THE CARIBBEAN). Here they recalled songs of their homeland and applied them to the Catholic reverence for saints and images, as well as to the belief in Christ as a redeemer who would someday free the righteous. Thus the cofradías helped to create a ritual and faith that simultaneously preserved African heritage, upheld Hispanic values, and espoused bold ideas of liberation.

Afro-Peruvians rebelled against Spanish oppression in sporadic outbreaks as early as the 1540s. One of the larger revolts took place when the English buccaneer Sir Francis Drake attacked the city of Lima in 1578. Ultimately Drake released the city, and the Afro-Peruvian revolt, like most such rebellions, was quickly put down.

In some instances, however, slaves fled their masters and established *palenques*, remote villages in which they were relatively free from harassment. One of the longest enduring palenques was Huachipa, which was established in the central coastal region in the early 1700s under the direction of a slave named Francisco Congo, also known as Chavelilla. Few records survive related to Congo's rule of Huachipa, but the leader appears to have steered the settlement through a prosperous period of farming, ranching, and occasional raiding.

In 1763 and 1764 another group of *cimarrones* (escaped slaves) in the Carabayllo Valley near Lima leveled such a series of attacks against travelers that the colonial government mounted a punitive expedition against the fugitives. A large force under the command of Pablo Sáenz de Bustamonte, including 60 soldiers from the viceroy's personal guard, dealt a decisive blow to the cimarrones in 1764. The accused ringleaders were executed, the rest beaten and reduced to slavery once again.

Free blacks also exerted autonomy when their limited rights were threatened. In 1779 the government tried to levy a special tax on libertos in order to replenish the ailing treasury. Most complied, but libertos in the northern coastal town of Lambayeque refused. The colonial government apparently intended to punish the resisting libertos, but at roughly the same time Indians under Tupac Amaru began a massive rebellion against the government's oppression of Indians. It was one of the most far-reaching and influential uprisings in the history of colonial Spanish America, but the rebellion was ultimately crushed and Tupac Amaru executed in 1780. The insurgent Indians were joined in their fight by many blacks, the most powerful of whom were under the leadership of Juan Santos Atahualpa. The Africans added the liberation of slaves to the demands of the Indians, making this the first insurrection to include such a demand. Peru's outnumbered Spaniards, badly frightened and in need of black and mulatto allies, allowed the libertos in Lambayeque their tax revolt and did not retaliate. Even after the defeat of Tupac Amaru, the Spaniards made little attempt to enforce the liberto tax. Eventually the colonial government was forced to enact several of the reforms Tupac Amaru had demanded, though freeing slaves was not among these. Still, Lambayeque remains one of the few instances of Afro-Peruvian triumph over the Spanish colonial regime.

Independent Peru

By the late eighteenth century a reform movement with several factions had evolved in Spanish America generally and in Peru in particular. One such faction advocated an end to black slavery; another, more prominent camp advocated an end to Spanish rule. Eventually the two groups merged, albeit somewhat uncomfortably. At the time that Simón Bolívar began his war of liberation against Spain in Venezuela, Peru had an estimated 90,000 African slaves. In his first two attempts to liberate Venezuela and Colombia, Bolívar rejected the use of black soldiers. However, by 1819, he began to enlist black troops and defeated the Spanish in Venezuela and Colombia. His success sparked similar revolts in South America. In 1821 Argentine José de San Martín followed Bolívar's example, drafting blacks, mulattos, and whites, and seized Lima (*see* Racial Question during Struggles of Independence in Latin America).

In the rebel armies blacks were generally segregated from whites into their own regiments and battalions. Often these troops were among the worst supplied and worst fed of all soldiers yet were required to undertake some of the most dangerous fighting. The South American wars of independence reached a peak in 1824, when rebel forces under Antonio José de Sucre met Loyalists at Ayacucho and Junín in the mineral-rich region of south central Peru. There the Husare del Peru, a battalion of libertos, slaves, and *mestizos* (persons of indigenous and European descent), was largely responsible for the decisive rebel victories that sealed the liberation of Peru from Spain.

In 1821, during San Martín's brief rule of war-torn Peru, the leader emancipated children born to slaves after July 28, 1821. Later that year he freed slaves owned by Loyalists, promised emancipation to slaves who fought honorably in the rebel army, and forbade the importation of slaves in the future. It took several years, however – until 1828 – for these freedoms to be affirmed by a new constitution. Even after 1828 all slaves who were born before July 28, 1821, and belonged to rebel sympathizers were still in bondage.

Matters would worsen before they improved for Peru's remaining slaves, as the country dissolved into civil war in the late 1820s. From then until the mid-1830s a string of short-lived dictators tried to ingratiate themselves to wealthy slaveholders by allowing many abuses against free and enslaved blacks. Consequently many libertos experienced conditions that were little better than the slavery from which they had been freed. Such abuses culminated in 1835, when Gen. Felipe Salavery declared that Peru was once again open to the slave trade, and in 1839, when Agustín Gamarra took over the country and signed a law that reenslaved all libertos for the next half century.

In 1848 slaves on plantations near the northern coastal city of Trujillo staged a widespread revolt. They quickly captured the plantations, retaliated against their masters, and proceeded to march on Trujillo. There, with the help of urban slaves, the insurgents stormed the city, attacked many slaveholders, and held others hostage. As it soon became clear the revolt could not be sustained – Peruvian forces laid siege to and eventually took the city – the slaves killed a good number of the hostages. The revolt unnerved much of Peru, but slavery continued, with between 15,000 to 20,000 in servitude.

Emancipation and Beyond

In 1854 Peru fell into another period of civil war. In order to bolster his muster of troops, President José Rufino Echenique declared that all slaves who joined his army for two years would be freed after the fighting. Not to be outdone, Echenique's rival, Ramón Castilla, declared in December 1854 that all slavery was officially abolished – assuming that he and his army (many of whom he expected would be slaves) could seize power. Many slaves joined Castilla, and by January 1855 he was victorious. True to his word, Castilla ended slavery at last. To mollify Peru's powerful former slaveholders, Castilla's government paid them partial compensation for their loss. Slaves received no compensation for their years of servitude.

After the slaves' emancipation many fled the coastal plantations and Andean mines for the cities. Former slaveholders were thus left with a labor shortage in both the fields and the mines, a problem they solved by importing massive numbers of workers from East Asia. The indentured laborers, mostly Chinese, were treated as slaves in all but name. Some of the former Afro-Peruvian slaves found work overseeing the Asians. The government and others also employed free blacks to quell the not infrequent riots by maltreated Asians. By 1875 Peru's blacks were surpassed in number by perhaps 80,000 Asians. The increased competition from Asians and Indians (many of whom moved from the highlands to the coastal regions in the late 1800s) made it extremely difficult for Afro-Peruvians to find work.

At the turn of the twentieth century and for decades to come, many Afro-Peruvians remained in poverty, and most lived in urban slums, primarily in Lima. By day, those who could find jobs worked as domestic servants, bus drivers, textile laborers, and construction workers; few of these jobs offered hope of advancement. By night, Afro-Peruvians returned home to neighborhoods severely lacking in hygienic facilities. Often several families shared a single water faucet, and houses were extremely overcrowded and poorly built. The situation was little better for the (fewer) Afro-Peruvians who remained in the countryside and mountains and worked the same fields and mines their ancestors had worked as slaves.

Because discrimination was persistent throughout Peru, many Afro-Peruvians denied their African ancestry when they could. Afro-Peruvians commonly aspired for their children to marry lighter-skinned people. Still, the influence of Afro-Peruvian culture extended from music to cooking to sports.

After World War II Peru underwent a gradual but disruptive change from rule by a privileged oligarchy to rule by a more representative democracy, though military leaders still held power. This change yielded new opportunities in schooling and health for the poor and, simultaneously, a massive rural-to-urban migration. These two factors made Peruvian cities vibrant centers of black culture. African dance and theater groups were founded, Afro-Peruvian literature was more widely disseminated, and racial discrimination against blacks and other minorities eased somewhat by the 1950s and 1960s. Influenced by the Civil Rights Movement in the United States during this time, Afro-Peruvians formed several groups to agitate for political reforms to help blacks. Perhaps the most important of these were the Movimiento Negro Francisco Congo (Francisco Congo Black Movement) and the Asociación pro Derechos Humanos del Negro (Association for Black Human Rights).

In the 1970s several private groups supporting Afro-Peruvian advancement came together briefly around the Cultural Association of Black Peruvian Youth. The association taught Afro-Peruvian children about their heritage and encouraged education and political organization of their communities. Although it ultimately splintered, several factions of the movement continued their work in the 1980s and 1990s, contributing to a greater awareness of black history and culture in Peru. For example, Lima's Afro-Peruvian Research Institute continues to serve as a resource for black studies in Peru. As of the late 1990s, however, Afro-Peruvians had yet to coalesce behind one or more political parties that would promote an agenda to help blacks – thus leaving a significant challenge for Afro-Peruvians of the twenty-first century (*see* Human Rights in Latin America and the Caribbean).

See Also

Angola; Transatlantic Slave Trade; Maroonage in the Americas; Slavery in Latin America and the Caribbean; Central America; Abolition and Emancipation in Latin America and the Caribbean; Slave Laws in Colonial Spanish America; Religious Brotherhoods in Latin America.

North America

Peterson, Oscar Emmanuel

(b. August 15, 1925, Montreal, Quebec), renowned Canadian jazz pianist and composer.

One of the shining lights in the history of JAZZ, pianist Oscar Peterson is known both for his technical brilliance as a soloist and for his hard-driving percussive style on the keyboard. Encouraged by his father, a railroad porter who saw music as a refuge from poverty, Peterson began piano lessons at age six. He started recording while still in high school and was soon playing on a weekly Montreal radio show. In 1949, brought to New York by producer Norman Grantz, Peterson played at Carnegie Hall as part of the popular star-studded touring group Jazz at the Philharmonic.

After touring regularly with the ensemble he formed the first incarnation of the Oscar Peterson Trio in 1953 with bassist Ray Brown and guitarist Herb Ellis. After drummer Ed Thigpen replaced Ellis in 1958, the trio remained together until Brown left in 1967. While Peterson also worked as a sideman with a roster of jazz heavyweights including ELLA FITZGERALD, Louis Armstrong, BILLIE HOLIDAY, Lester Young, and Coleman Hawkins, it was the trio that helped him earn his reputation as a dazzling improviser.

Since the 1970s his stellar unaccompanied live performances and recordings have, according to one critic, "proved incontestably that he was one of the greatest solo pianists in the history of jazz." Peterson is a prolific composer and recording artist with more than 80 albums under his belt. His 1965 *Canadiana Suite* was nominated by the National Academy of Arts and Science as best jazz composition. Peterson's lifelong devotion to jazz, as well as his tireless opposition to racism, prompted Toronto's York University to name him in 1991 to a three-year term as chancellor.

Peter Hudson

SEE ALSO

Armstrong, Louis ("Satchmo"); Young, Lester Willis ("Prez"); Hawkins, Coleman Randolph.

Latin America and the Caribbean

Pétion, Alexandre

(b. April 2, 1770, PORT-AU-PRINCE, HAITI; d. March 29, 1818, Port-au-Prince, Haiti), president of HAITI from 1807 to 1818.

Alexander Sabès Pétion was the son of a French colonist and a freeborn mulatto woman. It is unclear why he used the name Pétion instead of his father's surname, Sabès. The name Pétion was derived from the nickname "Pitchoun" (little lad). Pétion's father did not recognize his son as his own because of the boy's dark skin, but did send Pétion to FRANCE to be educated.

At age 18 Pétion joined the colonial militia, and in 1791, with the outbreak of the HAITIAN REVOLUTION, he joined the rebellion sparked by the slave rebel BOUKMAN. Pétion initially fought under the black forces led by Toussaint L'Ouverture, which managed to expel a British invasion of Saint-Domingue (now Haiti) and eventually assume complete control over the island. After this victory, however, discord between the black and mulatto officers in Toussaint's company began to emerge. Pétion's allegiance soon shifted to André Rigaud's mulatto forces, which more closely reflected Pétion's own background and interests. Rigaud was the leader of the *affranchis* party of freeborn mulattos who were fighting to obtain complete equality with the whites of Saint-Domingue. Rigaud's forces opposed Toussaint in the 1799 civil war that came to be known as the "War of the South." Pétion was sent to the key city of Jacmel, which was besieged by Toussaint's lieutenants, JEAN-JACQUES DESSALINES and HENRI CHRISTOPHE.

In 1800, when Rigaud's forces were defeated by Toussaint and the conflict ended, Pétion left Saint-Domingue for exile in France. In 1802, though, he returned to the island with French forces sent by Napoleon to restore French rule under the command of Gen. Charles-Victor Leclerc. The French beat back the rebel forces, imprisoned Toussaint, and Toussaint's generals joined the French. The French forces were weakened by disease after the battle, however, and fears grew that they were intent on reinstituting slavery. Pétion realized that Leclerc's rule would mean a loss of rights for both mulattos and blacks and joined the new rebel group under the leadership of Dessalines.

On January 1, 1804, the French were finally decisively defeated, and the country was declared independent and renamed Haiti. Dessalines became Haiti's new ruler, first as governor general and later as emperor. Together with Dessalines, Pétion is said to have designed the Haitian flag.

Divisions grew between the black forces and the mulattos (now led by Pétion), though, and these tensions sparked a new revolt against Dessalines. On October 17, 1806, Dessalines was ambushed and killed as he attempted to resolve the revolt, and the presidency was offered by the rebels to his principal lieutenant, Henri Christophe. The presidency that Christophe was offered, however, would have lacked real force: Pétion's group sought to retain the most political power in the government they conceived for a mulatto-controlled senate.

Christophe refused the presidency and marched on Port-au-Prince, but Pétion's troops forced him back to his stronghold in the north. Christophe led an independent kingdom in the north while a mulatto-controlled republic ruled the south, and this schism would divide Haiti for 14 years. Pétion was secure within his constituency, though, and he was elected president by the senate in 1807 and again in 1811 and 1815. In 1816 he was declared president for life, with the right to choose his successor.

During his rule Pétion fostered the development of southern Haiti as a republic and was the main force behind its first constitution. He also transformed the new country's agricultural system, organizing a massive land distribution that granted small plots of government land to former soldiers. Although he envisioned a Haiti ruled by a mulatto-controlled oligarchy, with large landholdings mainly in mulatto hands, Pétion implemented policies that had an unforeseen effect on the country's agricultural economy. Originally one of the most prosperous plantation-based export economies in the Caribbean, Haiti's agricultural system came to be characterized by small-scale subsistence production.

Though he held absolute power, Pétion exercised moderation and was genuinely popular among the people, who nicknamed him "Papa bon coeur" (Father good heart). He was influential within the region as well, offering crucial early support to the Pan-American movement in 1816 by assisting Simón Bolívar in his landing at VENEZUELA. Citizens wept openly in the streets when Pétion died at age 48 of what is believed to have been an acute attack of malaria.

Paulette Poujol-Oriol

SEE ALSO

Toussaint L'Ouverture, François Dominique.

North America

Petry, Ann Lane

(b. October 12, 1908, Saybrook, Conn.; d. April 28, 1997, Old Saybrook, Conn.), African American writer of adult novels and children's literature who chronicled the urban black female experience.

Ann Petry was born and raised in the predominantly white, middle-class community of Saybrook, Connecticut. The daughter of a pharmacist, she worked in her father's drugstore as a teenager and went on to major in pharmacology at the University of Connecticut. After graduating she worked at and managed the family drugstore in Old Saybrook. Her pharmacological endeavors notwithstanding, Petry wrote short stories while working, none of which have been published. After marrying George Petry, a mystery writer, in 1939, she moved to New York City and dropped pharmacy altogether, choosing instead to develop her career as a writer.

Her first job in New York was at a Harlem newspaper, the AMSTERDAM NEWS, where she worked for four years. Petry moved on to the *People's Voice*, where she wrote a column on Harlem society in the women's section of the paper. Her first published work of fiction, a short story titled "Marie of the Cabin Club," was a romantic drama that she published under a pseudonym, preferring to save her real name for more serious works. In addition to writing Petry became involved in community issues. Her activities included the formation of a black women's consumer advocacy group and the establishment of a program in a Harlem school to help children living in crime-ridden neighborhoods.

During this period Petry joined writing workshops and creative writing classes at Columbia University. She wrote a few short stories, one of which, "On Saturday Night, the Sirens Sound," foreshadowed her first novel, *The Street*, which was to become her first literary coup. This short story, along with a few more she wrote, ran in the NATIONAL ASSOCIATION FOR THE ADVANCEMENT OF COLORED PEOPLE publication, *Crisis*, where it caught the attention of editors at Houghton Mifflin. Petry was urged to apply for a writer's fellowship awarded by the publishing company. She did, and won a $2400 grant and a book contract in 1945.

The Street (1946) was a resounding success, eventually selling more than 2 million copies, the first book by a black woman to do so. An unsentimental tale of a single mother's fruitless efforts to secure a livelihood and shelter her child from the danger that the street represents, the book launched Petry's career as an author of considerable renown. She went on to publish two more novels, *Country Place* in 1947 and *The Narrows* in 1988. Neither work achieved the level of success that *The Street* had enjoyed, but in later years both were acknowledged as works of great literary merit.

In addition to her novels Petry authored works of adolescent nonfiction chronicling the lives of historical black figures, including *Harriet Tubman: Conductor on the Underground Railroad* (1955) and *Tituba of Salem Village* (1964). She also wrote two children's books, *The Drugstore Cat* (1949) and *Legend of the Saints* (1970), and penned numerous essays on a variety of topics.

Petry received numerous awards and honors in recognition of her contributions to the black literary canon, both juvenile and adult. A visionary and pioneer of multiculturalism and black feminism, Petry died on April 28, 1997, in Old Saybrook, Connecticut.

James Smethurst

SEE ALSO
Literature, African American; Women Writers, Black, in the United States; *Crisis, The*; Harlem, New York.

North America

Pettiford, Oscar

(b. September 30, 1922, Okmulgee, Okla.; d. September 8, 1960), jazz bassist, bandleader, and bebop innovator.

Oscar Pettiford helped to invent and popularize the bass solo in JAZZ, significantly expanding the vocabulary and syntax of the language of the bass. Pettiford drew inspiration from the playing style of Jimmy Blanton, a bassist with Duke Ellington's band. Blanton had emphasized the melodic possibilities of the instrument at a time when the bass was most often relegated to the rhythm section of an ensemble. Pettiford, following Blanton's lead, plucked his strings with the length, rather than the width, of his index finger, thus extending the tonal and temporal possibilities for individual notes. At his best Pettiford produced a melodic clarity and complexity that echoed that of jazz guitar, and this bravura lent itself to a solo playing style. Pettiford was considered one of the top three bassists of his time, rivaling as well as influencing his contemporaries Ray Brown and Charles Mingus.

Born in Okmulgee, Oklahoma, to parents of Chocktaw, Cherokee, and African extraction, Pettiford moved with his family to Minneapolis when he was three years old. Pettiford came from a show-business family, and he contributed to the family's musical act as it toured the Minnesota vaudeville circuit. He demonstrated precocious musicality and by age 14 was devoting almost all of his attention to the string bass.

In 1943 Pettiford joined Charlie Barnet's big band and followed the group to New York, where he began working with other musicians. During his early New York years Pettiford collaborated with Roy Eldridge, Thelonious Monk, and Dizzy Gillespie. Pettiford participated in the legendary jam sessions at Minton's Playhouse, helping to establish the roots of bebop, a frenetic, hard-driving, and heavily improvisational style of jazz that broke away from the sweetness and set arrangements of swing. In 1944 Pettiford and Gillespie headed the first working bebop combo at the Onyx Club on 52nd Street, but the two parted within a year because of personal differences.

After a brief stint with the legendary tenor saxaphonist Coleman Hawkins, Pettiford performed with his childhood idol, Duke Ellington, with whose band he remained for three years. Despite a long-running alcohol problem, Pettiford continued to be active on the club and concert circuit both in the United States and abroad. In the early 1950s he returned to New York full time to lead the Café Bohemia's house band, and in 1958 Pettiford immigrated to Copenhagen, where he remained until his death in 1960.

In addition to helping invent bebop and elevating the status of the bass in jazz, Pettiford won many music industry awards for his recordings and contributed a number of memorable songs to the jazz repertory, including "Tricrotism," "Bohemia After Dark," and "Swingin' Till the Girls Come Home."

Eric Bennett

SEE ALSO
Gillespie, John Birks ("Dizzy"); Hawkins, Coleman Randolph; Mingus, Charles, Jr.; Monk, Thelonious Sphere; New York, New York; Ellington, Edward Kennedy ("Duke").

Africa

Phal, Louis

(b. 1897, French West Africa [now SENEGAL]; d. December 15, 1925, New York, N.Y.), Senegalese boxer known as the Battling Siki.

The first African to win a world boxing title, Louis Phal was a light heavyweight whose 1922 defeat of the French champion Georges Carpentier won him international fame and, later, the status of a legend. He has been the subject of two novels and one documentary, yet very little is known of his early life. According to African American cultural critic Gerald Early, the competing strains of myth and fable about Phal are a portrait in contradiction.

By some accounts an orphan adopted by a French soldier, Phal was depicted as an illiterate primitive by most of the Western press. One obituary in the African American newspaper the *Chicago Defender*, however, claimed he knew seven languages. He certainly spoke French, having moved as a child to FRANCE, where he served with distinction in the French army during World War I. Known as an artless boxer, Phal became an instant celebrity in France following his victory over Carpentier.

After Phal moved to the United States in 1923, his behavior outside the ring – drinking, brawling, and sporting flamboyant clothes and exotic pets – alternately delighted and appalled Americans. Mainstream white newspapers called him a "natural man," or even an animal – labels that white athletes with similar lifestyles never received, as Early points out. Phal's career declined quickly; by 1925 he had lost several bouts and was rumored to be on the brink of deportation. In December of that year Phal was fatally shot in the back.

Kate Tuttle

SEE ALSO
Boxing; *Chicago Defender*.

North America

Philadelphia, Pennsylvania

Africans first arrived in Philadelphia in 1684, when the ship *Isabella* brought 150 slaves. By 1720 around 2500 Africans had been brought to Pennsylvania as slaves.

The growing abolitionist movement of the next few decades led to a 1780 law that began to dismantle slavery. The 1790 census confirmed that Philadelphia's free black community, numbering 2000, was the largest in the United States. The free blacks formed

LEFT: Neighbors enjoy a block party in Philadelphia in 1982. *CORBIS/Ted Spiegel*
BELOW LEFT: Mayor Wilson Goode of Philadelphia waits to make his television speech about the MOVE group shootout on March 3, 1986. *CORBIS*

a burial ground in 1786 and a FREE AFRICAN SOCIETY in 1787. Community members included RICHARD ALLEN and ABSALOM JONES, who together pioneered the independent black church movement in the United States. In a little over a quarter of a century Philadelphia became home to a number of historic black churches. The African Church, founded in about 1787, became the First African Church of St. Thomas in 1794, with Jones as its pastor. Two years later Allen became pastor of the Bethel Methodist Church. The First African Baptist Church was founded in 1809, followed in 1811 by the First African Presbyterian Church. In 1816 Allen and others organized the AFRICAN METHODIST EPISCOPAL CHURCH, the first African American denomination. Over the next 280 years the black churches of Philadelphia became powerful and important institutions, sustaining everyone from a distinctive and large black elite to the Black Panthers. By 1820 slavery had disappeared from Philadelphia, and African Americans flooded into the city. Among the city's 100,622 inhabitants, 12,110 were free blacks.

In the antebellum period, however, African Americans were excluded from the developing industrial economy and grew increasingly poor. As competition for work grew, so did white hostility. Mobs invaded African American homes during numerous race riots in the 1840s. Prohibited from voting by 1838, blacks regained suffrage in 1871, which precipitated more riots and led to the murder of black leader Octavius Catto.

The black community continued to develop. In 1830 it hosted the first National Negro Convention. By the end of the nineteenth century it had founded schools, orphanages, welfare societies, nursing homes, and the renowned Lincoln University in Oxford. The *Philadelphia Tribune* – the oldest black newspaper still publishing – was founded in 1884 and counted Gertrude Bustill Mosell among its contributors. With the development of wealth came a religious, business, and cultural elite that included HENRY OSSAWA TANNER, a leading American painter of the late nineteenth and early twentieth centuries. Octavius Catto and Gilbert "Gil" Ball founded the Equal Rights League in 1864. Novelist Frances E. W. Harper and "Fanny" Jackson Coppin were celebrated orators on behalf of black civil rights. In 1871 Coppin succeeded Catto as principal of the Institute for Colored Youth (later Cheyney State College, now University). After the turn of the century Arthur Huff Fauset fought to improve housing for black Philadelphians, while his sister JESSIE REDMON FAUSET wrote critically acclaimed novels and became literary editor of the *Crisis* in the 1920s.

Until World War I, however, most African Americans in Philadelphia worked as laborers and domestics – "purveyors to the rich," said W. E. B. Du Bois in his pioneering study *The Philadelphia Negro* (1899). Political representation, moreover, was limited.

Nonetheless, blacks fled the South for Philadelphia. By 1900 the black community in Philadelphia – numbering 62,613 – was the largest in the North. That increased size initiated segregation of the black population in north and west Philadelphia and the creation of segregated bars, restaurants, and hotels. A race riot in 1918 followed labor conflicts and increased demands from African Americans for equality. Turning inward, the black community further developed its own business and professional class.

With the devastation of the GREAT DEPRESSION, unemployment reached 46 percent among employable blacks. NEW DEAL work projects for "Negroes" produced a massive political shift to the Democratic Party. In 1938 Democrat Crystal Bird Fauset became the first black woman in the United States to be elected to a state assembly.

The labor demand created by World War II precipitated a second, massive migration to Philadelphia, increasing the African American population to 379,000 – 18 percent of the city's population – by 1950. The Educational Equity League and the NATIONAL ASSOCIATION FOR THE ADVANCEMENT OF COLORED PEOPLE (NAACP) led initiatives against inequality in the schools, but 84.8 percent of black schoolchildren attended black-majority schools in 1950. The NAACP was more successful in its efforts to integrate Girard College in North Philadelphia.

Prominent entertainers and musicians, including BILL COSBY and John Coltrane, emerged from the postwar generation in Philadelphia, but overall conditions in the black community were bleak, given employment discrimination and housing segregation. In the 1960s activism grew, the Black Panthers mobilized chapters, and race riots followed. The first black mayor of Philadelphia, W. Wilson Goode, was elected in 1983, then reelected in 1987. Goode's political career was adversely affected in 1985 when police bombed the headquarters of the separatist organization MOVE, a group of black nationalists in West Philadelphia. The bomb killed 11 MOVE members, including children, and started a fire that destroyed two city blocks.

The overall income of black Philadelphians rose moderately in the 1990s, but unemployment and a deteriorating educational system remain serious problems for now and the foreseeable future.

Jim Mendelsohn

SEE ALSO

Slavery in the United States; World War I and African Americans; World War II and African Americans; Abolitionism in the United States; Black Panther Party; Coltrane, John William; Coppin, Frances (Fanny) Jackson; *Crisis, The*; Du Bois, William Edward Burghardt (W. E. B.); Free Blacks in the United States, 1619 to 1863; Harper, Frances Ellen Watkins; Lincoln University (Pennsylvania); Black Nationalism in the United States.

North America

Philip, Marlene Nourbese

(b. February 3, 1947, Tobago), Canadian poet, novelist, and essayist known for experimentation with literary form and for her commitment to social justice.

"English / is a foreign anguish," writes Marlene Nourbese Philip in her poem "Discourse on the Logic of Language" from *She Tries Her Tongue; Her Silence Softly Breaks* (1989). The poem examines the often brutal encounter of colonial subjects with the English language and its literature. Philips, through exploring what critic Barbara Fister has described as "the conundrum of language in a postcolonial context," works alongside fellow Canadian poets Dionne Brand and Claire Harris, and Caribbean writers EDWARD KAMAU BRATHWAITE and Lorna Goodison.

Scorned for its formal innovation and political engagement by publishers in Philip's adopted home of Canada, *She Tries Her Tongue* received the Cuban Casa de Las Americas prize in 1988 while still in manuscript form. The collection was eventually published in Great Britain. *Salmon Courage* (1983) and *Thorns* (1980) also engage the intersection of politics, language, and literary form, as does *Looking for Livingstone: An Odyssey of Silence* (1991), her narrative of a metaphoric return to Africa.

Philip also writes children's literature and is a prolific essayist. Her novel for young adults, *Harriet's Daughter* (1988), written as a corrective to the absence of black characters in Canadian children's literature, suffered the same fate as *She Tries Her Tongue*. Canadian presses, afraid that a black protagonist would not sell, rejected it before Heinemann published it in England. Philip's articles and essays, collected in *Frontiers* (1992) and *Showing Grit* (1993), demonstrate a persistent critique and an impassioned concern for issues of social justice and equity in the arts, prompting Selwyn R. Cudjoe's assertion that Philip "serves as a lightning rod of black cultural defiance of the Canadian mainstream." More to the point is the epigram in *Frontiers,* in which Philip dedicates the book to Canada, "in the effort of becoming a space of true true be/longing."

Though her writing suggests an in-depth understanding of the canon, Philip's career undoubtedly helped to free her from the constraints of tradition and to nurture her social analysis and criticism. She studied economics at the University of the West Indies before immigrating to Canada in 1968 and completing a master's degree at the University of Western Ontario. In 1973 she became a practicing lawyer and subsequently worked for seven years at a legal clinic. Philips has taught at York University and the University of Toronto. She was a Guggenheim Fellow for poetry in 1990-1991 and in 1995 received the Toronto Arts Award for Writing and Publishing.

Peter Hudson

SEE ALSO

Trinidad and Tobago.

North America

Photography, African American

Deborah Willis

The first known African Americans to practice the art and business of photography were Jules Lion, James Presley Ball, John B. Bailey, Augustus Washington, and the Goodridge Brothers, between 1840 and 1850. They worked as daguerreotypists, documentarians, artists, and studio photographers. The French inventor Nicéphore Niepce (1765-1833) produced the earliest extant photographic image, made by a camera obscura in 1827. After the death of Niepce, Louis Jacques Mandé Daguerre (1787-1851) successfully fixed an image and announced to the Paris press his discovery, which he named after himself, in January 1839.

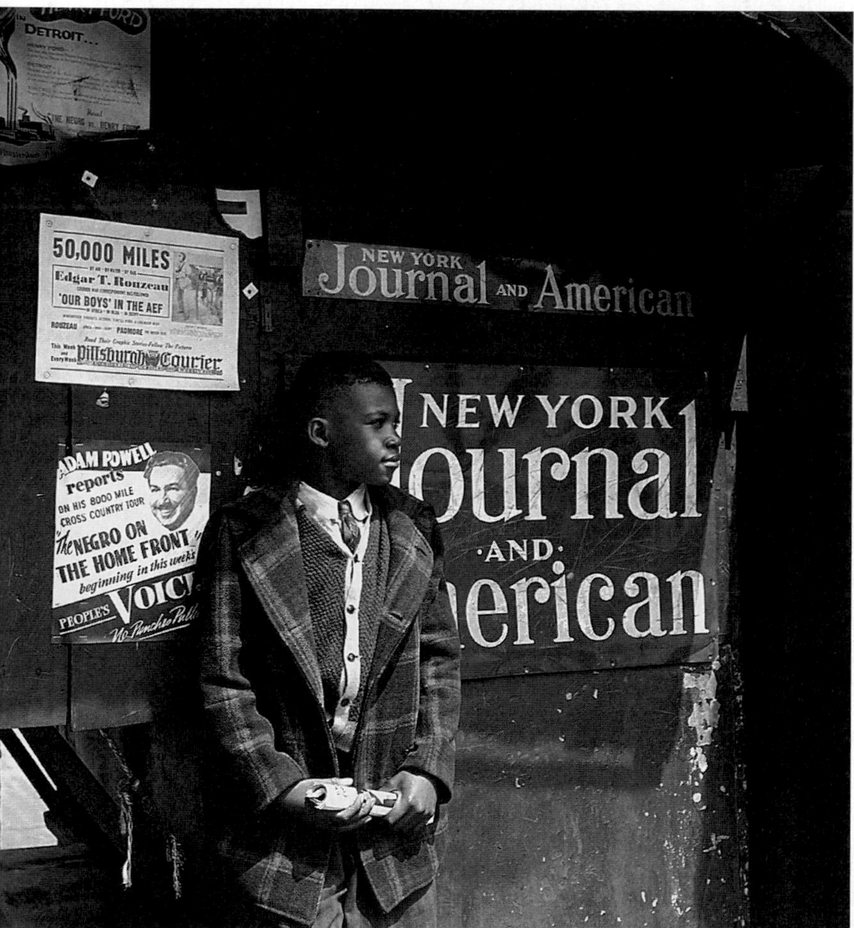

In 1943 Gordon Parks Sr. photographed a young boy before a Harlem newsstand. *CORBIS*

Newspapers in the spring of 1839 published accounts of Americans experimenting with the daguerreotype process. On August 19, 1839, Daguerre publicly explained the process and published an instruction manual. By late August newspapers in Paris and London described Daguerre's process in detail. The *Great Western*, one of the fastest known transatlantic steamers of the period, which arrived in New York on September 10, 1839, is noted for carrying aboard the French and English newspapers with descriptions of the daguerreotype process.

Six months after the process was publicized in Paris, Jules Lion, a free man of color, lithographer, and portrait painter, exhibited the first successful daguerreotype views. This first publicized exhibition of works by a black photographer, organized and sponsored by the artist, occurred on March 15, 1840, at the St. Charles Museum in New Orleans. The exhibition was reported to have drawn a large crowd. Despite the condition of African Americans who were still enslaved, there were numerous free black men and women who had established themselves as daguerreotypers, photographers, inventors, celebrities, artists, and artisans who had gained local and national recognition in their respective cities. Portraits of preachers, soldiers, writers, and prominent and lesser-known African Americans were produced regularly in galleries and studios throughout the country. Portraits of prominent African Americans became popular, and photography increasingly was the medium chosen for creating a likeness. Most of the photographs made in the nineteenth century were not intended for publication or public presentation, except for those made of celebrities, lecturers, and other prominent citizens. Some African American families thought it important to have their likenesses preserved for posterity, however.

During most of photography's early history images produced by African American photographers were idealized glimpses of family members in romanticized or dramatic settings. Many African American photographers sought to integrate elements of romanticism and classicism, modeling their work after the style of many painters in previous centuries. Most photographs taken in the early years commemorated a special occasion in the sitter's life such as courtship, marriage, birth, death, graduation, confirmation, military service, an anniversary, or a social or political success.

A number of the early photographers recorded celebratory as well as dispiriting moments within their communities. They photographed genre scenes and landscapes, and they created elaborate backdrops for studio portraits. Many owned and operated studios in small towns and major cities, while others worked as itinerants. They photographed the prosperous, the laborers, and the poor, and they documented the activities of nineteenth-century abolitionists and twentieth-century civil rights activists.

In photography's first decade, the 1840s, James Presley Ball (1825-1905) and Augustus Washington (1820-?) operated successful galleries in Cincinnati, Ohio, and Hartford, Connecticut. Ball and Washington were active abolitionists who often used their photographic skills to expose the inhumane institution of slavery and to promote the activities of the abolitionist movement. Between 1859 and 1899 photography advanced swiftly with the development of the glass-plate negative and the paper-print processes; images were mounted on cabinet cards, *cartes-de-visite,* and stereographs. With these advances numerous photographers and itinerants flourished in the North, South, and the emerging West. Studios opened for business producing paper prints as well as tintypes, utilizing the newer and faster processes of the period.

At the turn of the century photography expanded in a variety of ways. Newspapers, journals, and books published photographic images. Schools and colleges offered courses in photography, and correspondence courses were available. C. M. Battey (1873-1927) was a noted educator in photography and an accom-

RIGHT: James VanDerZee is best known for the photographs he took in Harlem, where he had a commercial studio. VanDerZee's portraits of Harlemites are alive with aspiration, achievement, energy, and style. *"My Corsage," 1931, James VanDerZee/ © Donna VanDerZee*
BELOW: Prentice H. Polk specialized in portraits at Tuskegee Institute, where he photographed *The Boss* (silver gelatin print) in 1932. *In the collection of The Corcoran Gallery of Art, Washington, D.C. Museum Purchase, Anna E. Clark Fund. 1981.64.2*

plished portraitist and fine-art photographer. Battey founded the photography division at Tuskegee Institute, Alabama, in 1916. In 1917 *Crisis* magazine highlighted Battey in the "Men of the Month" column as "one of the few colored photographers who has gained real artistic success." The greatest number of portraits of African American leaders produced in the nineteenth and early part of the twentieth century were done by Battey. His photographic portraits of John Mercer Langston, FREDERICK DOUGLASS, W. E. B. Du Bois, Booker T. Washington, and PAUL LAURENCE DUNBAR were sold nationally and produced in two formats: postcard and poster. Black Americans were subjugated in practice and representation by the dominant culture. In order to resist labeling, black photographers continually redefined the image of African Americans within their photography studios.

Between 1900 and 1919 African American photographers flourished in the larger cities. They produced photographs of rural and urban experiences as well as architectural prints and images of leisure.

ADDISON SCURLOCK (1883-1964) of WASHINGTON, D.C., HOWARD UNIVERSITY's official photographer, opened his studio in 1911, where he worked with his wife and sons, Robert and George, until 1964. In

New York City, James VanDerZee (1886-1983), undoubtedly the best known of black studio photographers, captured the spirit and life of New York's Harlem for more than 50 years.

During the period defined by Howard University professor and philosopher Alain Locke in 1925 as the era of the "New Negro," photographers lived, recorded, and worked in New York City's Harlem and the rural South. The "New Negro" image replaced the prevailing stereotype of blacks as unintelligent, lazy, and lacking a work ethic. The photographers working during this period made a conscious attempt, as Cheryl Wall notes, to "convert a defensive into an offensive position, a handicap into an incentive." The 1920s and 1930s witnessed the concluding disfranchisement of African Americans, THE GREAT MIGRATION, a literary and an artistic renaissance, the Great Depression, and President Franklin Delano Roosevelt's NEW DEAL programs. Photographers began to exhibit their work widely in their respective communities. The bulk of this work emerged during an era when the overwhelming majority of postcards, lantern slides, and popular cultural artifacts representing African Americans contained crude, degrading racial caricatures. The work and vision of the black photographer can be considered a powerful challenge to the blatantly stereotypical depictions of African Americans sold and produced during this period. The black photographer provided, by contrast, photographs that depicted a sense of self and self-worth. The photographs celebrated achievements within the photographers' communities and in their personal lives. The photographs of the "New Negro" period devised optimistic overviews of both the nineteenth- and early twentieth-century African

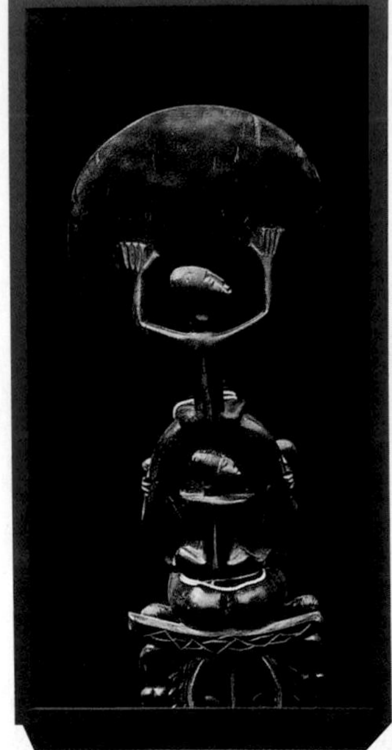

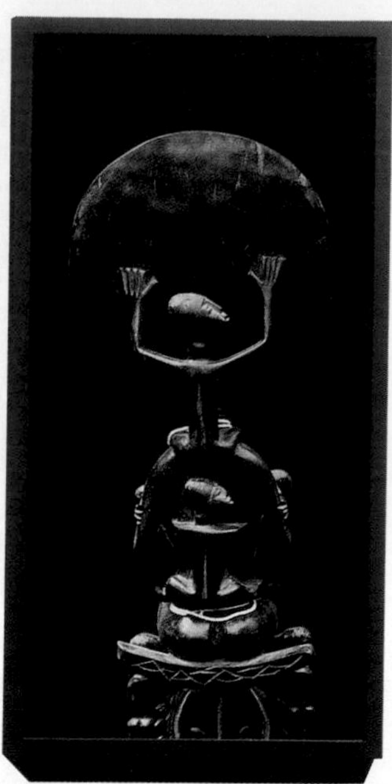

Carrie Mae Weems. *Africa Series: She Had Her Keys to the Kingdom.* 1993. 3 C-prints, etched glass. 76.2 x 152.4 cm (30 x 60 in). *Courtesy of the artist*

American experience. In the 1920s young black photographers who viewed themselves as artists moved to the larger cities seeking education, patronage, and support for their art. Harlem was a cultural mecca for many of these photographers.

James Latimer Allen (1907-1977) produced genre portraits of African American men, women, and children. He published and exhibited his work in art journals and galleries. He also photographed writers of the period such as Alain Locke, LANGSTON HUGHES, COUNTEE CULLEN, and CLAUDE MCKAY. Photographers active between 1920 and 1940 included students of C. M. Battey's such as P. H. Polk (1898-1985) of Tuskegee, Alabama, who opened his first studio in Tuskegee in 1927. The following year he was appointed to the faculty of Tuskegee Institute's photography department, photographed prominent visitors, such as educator MARY MCLEOD BETHUNE and activist-artist Paul Robeson, and made extensive portraits of scientist and inventor GEORGE WASHINGTON CARVER. Richard S. Roberts (1881-1936) of Columbia, South Carolina, opened his studio in the early 1920s. He began studying photography through correspondence courses and specialized journals and advertised that his studio took superior photographs by day or night.

Morgan Smith (1910-1993) and Marvin Smith (1910-), twin brothers, were prolific photographers in Harlem in the 1930s and early 1940s. They photographed members of the community – famous and infamous – and their cameras also captured political rallies, bread lines during the Great Depression, families, and lindy hoppers at the SAVOY BALLROOM. Also working in Harlem was Winifred Hall Allen. She documented the businesses owned and operated by women in that community. Robert H. McNeill (1917-) created a comprehensive documentary record of African American life in Washington during the 1930s and 1940s. Frequently working with the black press, including the *Pittsburgh Courier, Washington Afro-American*, and the *Chicago Defender*, McNeill's photographs documented that African Americans living in a segregated city survived – even thrived – by creating their own social and community organizations.

The Farm Security Administration (FSA) began in 1935 as the Resettlement Administration, an independent coordinating agency that inherited rural relief activities and land-use administration from the Department of the Interior, the Federal Emergency Relief Administration, and the Agricultural Adjustment Administration. The FSA photography project generated 270,000 images of rural, urban, and industrial America between 1935 and 1943 including numerous photographs of black migrant workers in the South. In 1937 Gordon Parks Sr. (1912-) decided that he wanted to be a photographer after viewing the work of the FSA photographers. He was hired by the FSA in 1941 and during World War II worked as an Office of War Information correspondent. After the war he was a photographer for Standard Oil Company. In 1949 he became the first African American photographer to work on the staff of *Life* magazine.

Roy DeCarava (1919-) is the link to contemporary street photography. He studied art at Cooper Union in New York City, the Work Progress Administration's Harlem Art Center, and the George Washington Carver Art School. In 1955 DeCarava collaborated with Langston Hughes on a book titled *The Sweet Flypaper of Life*, which depicted the life of a black family in Harlem. In 1954 he founded a photography gallery that became one of the first galleries in the United States devoted to the exhibition and sale of photography as a fine art. Also noted for his jazz photography, DeCarava in 1963 founded the Kamoinge Workshop, a workshop of concerned black photographers. Members included artists such as Shawn Walker, Lou Draper, Beauford Smith, Anthony Barboza, and Ming Smith.

Photographers in the 1930s through the 1960s began working as photojournalists for local newspapers and such national magazines that marketed to African American audiences as *Our World, Ebony, Jet, Sepia*, and *Flash*. (Only a few African American photojournalists, notably Parks and DeCarava, were employed by the larger picture magazines such as *Life* and *Sports Illustrated.*) Most of them learned photography while in the military and studied photography at schools of journalism.

This period also encompassed the beginning of reportage and the documentation of public and political events. In the 1930s smaller hand-held cameras and faster films aided photographers in expressing their frustration and discontent with social and political conditions within their communities. The modern CIVIL RIGHTS MOVEMENT activities were well documented by photographers such as Moneta Sleet Jr., in New York and Chicago, and Jack T. Franklin, in Philadelphia. During the active years of the Civil Rights and BLACK POWER movements, the early 1960s through the 1970s, a significant number of socially committed men and women became photographers. They set a new standard for the documentation of the struggles, achievements, and tragedies of the freedom movement. Student Nonviolent Coordinating Committee photographers Doug Harris, Elaine Tomlin, and Bob Fletcher were in the forefront of documenting the voter registration drives in the South; Roland Freeman, Robert Sengstacke, Howard Bingham, Jeffrey Scales, and Brent Jones photographed the activities of the BLACK PANTHER PARTY and desegregation rallies in the North and on the West Coast. Between 1969 and 1986 six African American photographers received the coveted Pulitzer Prize in photography. The first to win the award was Moneta Sleet Jr. in 1969, for a photograph of CORETTA SCOTT KING and her daughter at the funeral of Dr. Martin Luther King Jr.

In the 1970s universities and art colleges began to offer undergraduate and graduate degrees in photography. African American photographers began studying photography and creating works for exhibition. Outside the academy, others studied in community centers and workshops. These photographers began to explore and redefine the photographic image. They respected the photograph as a document and simultaneously looked at the photograph as a metaphor. The symbolic and expressive imagery of the works produced in the 1980s and 1990s is concerned with offering sociological and psychological insights into the past. Many of the themes explored in these photographs focused on the photographers' own families and communities. They created symbolic works that referred to social issues such as racism, unemployment, child and sexual abuse, and death and dying. The viewer becomes a participant; the viewer is asked to contextualize his or her own experiences with the visual references offered by the photographer and in doing so create a personal historical perspective, interpretation, or meaning. Clarissa Sligh, Lorna Simpson, Jeffrey Scales, Dawoud Bey, Coreen Simpson, Albert Chong, Fern Logan, CARRIE MAE WEEMS, Pat Ward Williams, Willie Middlebrook, Roland Charles, Chester Higgins, Stephen Marc, Cynthia Wiggins, Carla Williams, Christian Walker, Lynn Marshall-Linnemeier, and Hank Sloane Thomas are just a few of the photographers who began creating works in this genre in the 1980s.

Most African American photographers of the 1980s and the 1990s were engaging storytellers who discovered the intersection of the private and public in art. A number challenged current art practices and, as photographer and writer Rick Bolton stated, created "a new social basis for art." The photobiographers used appropriation, multiple printing, fabric, straight images, and manipulated photographs to make compelling visual statements about modern-day culture and create narratives about our collective history in multiethnic America. They employed themes relating to identity, spirituality, gender, family, race, difference, and stereotyping. Some of the artists examined the implications of historical and contemporary references for women and offered new strategies in incorporating their personal perspectives in the construction of their work.

Many of the photographers mentioned in this essay create provocative and sensitive visual references to their African American cultural experience. Some use text to create tension and paradigms of a sort relating to the transformative nature of the medium. Albert Chong, for example, uses family photographs, religious icons, and animal remains to explore ritual as it is translated into art. He likens his task to that of archaeologists in unearthing the past to explore family history. Chong is strongly conscious of composition and form. The exact placement of cultural objects acts as a signifier and suggests authentication of his cultural roots. Born in JAMAICA of African and Chinese ancestry, Chong imbues his work with references to all the cultures that have informed his identity. His photographs are highly individualized, spiritually oriented images.

Photographed by Addison N. Scurlock (1883-1964) in 1915, a black family prepares for a ride in a rowboat near Great Falls, Virginia. Scurlock had a prominent studio in Washington, D.C., and served for five decades as official photographer of Howard University. *Smithsonian Institution, Washington, DC*

Coreen Simpson makes portraits that speak to us about the experience of young black men and women living in New York City. Many are oversized images that are extremely stylized, as the photographer and her subject create a visually expressive dialogue. Jeffrey Scales records commonplace scenes and occurrences within his community of Harlem (New York City), while simultaneously addressing cultural and sociological issues. His portraits of young and older men depict connections that are embodied in the bonding of male relationships. He is concerned about the stereotyping of black men and how black men are perceived in the culture by their peers and others.

Fern Logan reexamines her family relationships in her art. Using the cyanotype, also known as the blueprint, a printing process based on the light sensitivity of iron salts, Logan critiques memories from her past in a warm voice using old letters and imagined responses. Looking back at old photographs of her son, she raises provocative issues about her son's and her own American childhood and the irony of their fate. Her perspective is written on the print as the photograph is submerged. The issues presented are difficult and are intended to evoke a twentieth-century consciousness of miscegenation. Delving into this consciousness in the context of her own family, Logan stimulates an open discussion about race, racism, denial, and domination.

Lorna Simpson focuses on the construction of meaning and values by juxtaposing text and image. Her style creates a format for her critical examination of race and gender. She focuses specifically on the notion of invisibility, representing black women as survivors, protagonists, and victims. Simpson's work is rooted in the tradition of African American storytelling and incorporates visual narratives that border on biography.

Family experiences form the core of inspiration for Clarissa Sligh's work, which is layered with political, familial, and racially charged messages. Using family photographs and archival references, she directs her audience's gaze into sociological relationships centered on experiences in African American communities in the nineteenth and twentieth centuries. Sligh is the keeper of her family album of photographs and other memorabilia. She places her family history within the larger picture of American

For many African Americans, portrait photography – such as this 1888 image of William C. Irvin, taken in Helena, Montana, by J. P. Ball – was a means to express pride and positive self-image in an era that saw both the birth of a black middle class and the thwarting of many of its dreams. *Montana Historical Society, Helena*

history. In shifting attention away from her personal experiences, she is able to analyze other shared experiences of black children across generations. She is cognizant of the role she plays in preserving her family history. Sligh's work is important not only because she addresses the realities of racism and sexism in a direct yet not confrontational style, but also because she is an accomplished storyteller. Photoartist Sligh looks carefully at her own family relationships and examines the lives of men, women, and children in general. Her images incorporate both historical and social perspectives and her work is provocative and historically introspective.

Christian Walker uses the format of the family photo album to "document" a history of the extended or archetypal African American family. He enlarges this form with paint and pigment as well as vintage rephotographed images, a manipulation that emphasizes the artistic rather than the technical aspects of the medium.

Carla Williams's photographs capture the viewer's and the photographer's imagination and fascination with the human body. Williams's subject is her own body, which she has documented continually for more than ten years. Her self-portraits are consciously posed as iconic references to the photographic tableaux of the nineteenth century. She also allows the viewer to explore the notion of being desired by photographing her body at different stages in her life cycle. She projects the fragmented and whole body; the physical representation of the body can be viewed as a link to her past and her future. Her body is linked to her culture and she is interested in the experience of the female body as subject and object to be desired.

Carrie Mae Weems creates sequential photographs and insightful text that examine the experiences of women in general, and black women specifically. Her work brings to life the overlapping of fantasy and lived experiences, where gesture is seen as metaphor.

Black American photographers of the nineteenth and twentieth centuries respond to their own lives and their communities in similar ways. Some evoke in their work an emotional message that goes beyond the self-representation but connects in the recharacterization of the African American experience. The photographers have coupled the aspirations and dreams of their subjects with their own.

Many of the photographers working today respond to social issues beyond the sometimes insular photographic community. They comment on politics, culture, family, and history from internal and external points of view. The fact that many of these photographers probably have witnessed societal injustice has not clouded their eyes. In interpreting these works the viewer is encouraged to explore multiple readings, including some based in satire, humor, parody, and testimony. The issues addressed in contemporary photography and the interpretations implied coalesce to capture an exhilarating visionary biography of African American life.

See Also
Abolitionism in the United States; Battey, Cornelius M.; *Chicago Defender*; Chicago, Illinois; Du Bois, William Edward Burghardt (W. E. B.); *Ebony*; Harlem, New York; *Jet*; King, Martin Luther, Jr.; Locke, Alain Leroy; New York, New York; Parks, Gordon, Sr.; Philadelphia, Pennsylvania; *Pittsburgh Courier*; Polk, Prentice Herman; Sleet, Moneta J., Jr.; Smith, Marvin and Morgan; Student Nonviolent Coordinating Committee (SNCC); Tuskegee University; VanDerZee, James Augustus; Washington, Booker Taliaferro; Dance in the United States.

Latin America and the Caribbean

Piar, Manuel, a mulatto general in Venezuela in the nineteenth century (*see* Racial Question during Struggles of Independence in Latin America).

North America

Pickett, Bill (b. December 5, 1870?, Williamson County, Tex.; d. April 2, 1932), cowboy and rodeo star.

Bill Pickett invented and popularized "bulldogging," a method of steer wrestling inspired by cattle dogs. To bring a bull to the ground, Pickett would leap atop its back, twist its horns with his hands, and bite its upper lip. Pickett initially adopted bulldogging while working as a ranch hand, but his steer wrestling skills soon launched him into the rodeo show business of the West.

Pickett was born near Austin, Texas. He quit school after the fifth grade and began working full-time as a cowboy, developing his talents in roping and horsemanship. As a teenager he began performing at carnivals, rodeos, and county fairs throughout the southwest. Initially promoters dressed Pickett as a Mexican bullfighter, obscuring his African American descent for commercial reasons. In 1907 Pickett signed on with the Miller Brothers 101 Ranch Wild West Show, based in Oklahoma's Cherokee Strip. Pickett adopted the name "The Dusky Demon" and soon earned top billing. Pickett and the Miller Brothers toured widely throughout the United States, playing Madison Square Garden and other top venues. They also performed in Canada, South America, and Europe, where Pickett unveiled his rodeo tricks for the likes of King George V and Queen Mary of England. Pickett went into partial retirement after 1916, but remained active both as cowboy and performer until 1932 when he died after a kick in the head from a horse.

Pickett was widely admired for his showmanship and bravery. One of his most devoted fans was the comedian Will Rogers, with whom Pickett sometimes performed. In 1971 the National Rodeo Cowboy Hall of Fame inducted Pickett as its first black honoree, and in 1994 he appeared on a commemorative postage stamp.

Eric Bennett

See Also
Black Cowboys; Rodeo.

North America

Pickett, Wilson (b. March 18, 1941, Prattville, Ala.), African American soul singer.

Known for his dynamic stage presence and hard-rocking hits such as "Mustang Sally," "Land of 1,000 Dances," and "In the Midnight Hour," Wilson Pickett was one of the biggest stars of the 1960s. Influenced by the gospel music he sang as a child, along with the rhythm and blues then in vogue, Pickett began singing with a band, the Falcons, in 1959. Pickett, who had moved to Detroit, Michigan, at age 15, also wrote some of the band's songs, one of which, "I Found a Love," became a Top Ten hit in 1962.

In 1964 Atlantic Records signed Pickett, sending him to Memphis, Tennessee, to record his first album. Working with Booker T and the MG's – the house band from the Stax record label – Pickett produced some of his most popular songs during this era, which lasted until 1967. Pickett's screams, growls, and moans punctuated the funky beat and powerful horn section that characterized these recordings, which not only defined the Southern soul sound but became some of the most played dance music ever.

Recording both at Stax and Muscle Shoals (the Atlantic studio famous as the birthplace of Aretha Franklin's most soulful music), Pickett also toured heavily. Billing himself as "Wicked Pickett," he was known as the king of the dance floor, one of soul's most thrilling performers. Throughout the 1970s and 1980s Pickett played concerts worldwide, though he ceased to produce noteworthy hits after leaving Atlantic in the early 1970s. In 1991, the same year he was elected to the Rock and Roll Hall of Fame, Pickett announced his retirement.

Kate Tuttle

See Also
Soul Music; Franklin, Aretha Louise; Stax Records.

Latin America and the Caribbean

Pietri, Pedro Juan (b. March 21, 1943, Ponce, Puerto Rico), Afro-Puerto Rican poet, educator, and playwright who, with authors such as Miguel Algarín, introduced the influential Nuyorican poetry movement.

Pedro Juan Pietri's family moved from Puerto Rico to New York City's Spanish Harlem in 1947 as part of the migration wave following World War II. He attended New York City public schools and, after completing high school, served in the army and fought in the Vietnam War between 1966 and 1968. The war affected him greatly – especially the mistreatment suffered by blacks and Puerto Ricans – and culminated in his renowned collection of poems, *Puerto Rican Obituary* (1971). After returning to the United States he went on to teach creative writing at the State University of New York in Buffalo. He then directed poetry workshops for children between 1970 and 1972.

In 1974 Pietri became a member of a bilingual childhood project directed by the Puerto Rican Association for Community Affairs and also served as a consultant to El Museo del Barrio, New York's museum honoring the contribution of Latinos in the United States. In 1975 he emerged as one of the city's most distinct voices and, together with Miguel Algarín, founded the literary movement known as Nuyorican poetry. In this genre urban Puerto Rican artists affirmed their identities – often through humor and punning simultaneously in Spanish and English – and detailed their lives in verse.

Pietri joined the Cultural Council Foundation as a literary artist in 1978. He has received numerous awards, including a grant from the New York State Council of Creative Arts; a Public Service Grant in 1971, 1974, and 1975; a New York Foundation for the Arts award for poetry in 1986; and a Just Buffalo Inc. award in 1986. His published works include *Traffic Violation* (1973), *Invisible Poetry* (1979), *Out of Order* (1980), *Uptown Train* (1980), and a narrative titled *Lost in the Museum of Natural History* (1981). He has authored 23 plays, including *The Livingroom* (1975), *The Masses Are Asses* (1983), and *Mondo Mambo/A Mambo Rap Sodi* (1990), all of which have been publicly performed in New York. His pieces can also be read in a number of anthologies, among them *Nuyorican Poetry: An Anthology of Puerto Rican Words and Feelings* (1975) and *Herejes y mitificadores: Muestra de poesía puertorriqueña en los Estados Unidos* (1980). His extensive list of published works has established him as one of the best-known Puerto Rican authors of his genre.

See Also
New York, New York.

North America

Pinchback, Pinckney Benton Stewart (b. May 10, 1837, Macon, Ga.; d. December 21, 1921, Washington, D.C.), America's first black governor. He held more major political positions than any other African American during Reconstruction.

P. B. S. Pinchback was the freeborn son of a wealthy white planter, William Pinchback, and his longtime mistress, an emancipated slave named Eliza Steward. William Pinchback's family successfully challenged his will after his death in 1848, leaving Eliza and the couple's five children destitute. Fearing that Pinchback's relatives would attempt to enslave them, Eliza moved the family to Cincinnati, where Pinchback attended Gilmore High School.

In 1862, after working as a steward on a Mississippi riverboat, Pinchback joined the Union Army in New Orleans. He recruited and commanded a company of the Corps d'Afrique, a Louisiana cavalry unit. Initially, all of the Corps d'Afrique's officers were black. The black officers learned, however, that their commissions were subject to qualification examinations. All of the black officers, except Pinchback, were replaced by white officers. When authorities repeatedly ignored Pinchback's demands for equal treatment of black officers and troops, he resigned in protest in September 1863.

Pinchback remained in New Orleans after the Civil War, helping to shape Louisiana's Republican Party and holding public offices. In 1867 he served as a member of the state's Constitutional Convention, and a year later he was elected to Louisiana's state senate. He served as president pro tempore of the senate in 1871, and succeeded Oscar J. Dunn as lieutenant governor after Dunn's death in January 1872. When the Louisiana House of Representatives began impeachment proceedings against Governor Henry Clay Warmoth in December 1872, Pinchback became Louisiana's acting governor, serving until January 1873, when W. P. Kellogg succeeded him.

Pinchback's career suffered several political setbacks. He was elected to the United States House of Representatives in 1872, but both Pinchback and his opponent, George A. Sheridan, claimed victory. They contested the seat until February 4, 1875, when the House Committee on Elections judged Sheridan the winner. Meanwhile, in January 1873, the Louisiana legislature elected Pinchback to the U.S. Senate, but this mandate was also contested by another rival, W. L. McMillen. Though McMillen eventually acknowledged Pinchback's claim to the seat, senators uncovered evidence that Pinchback had paid $10,000 to obtain it. On March 13, 1875, the Senate denied Pinchback his seat by a vote of 32 to 29.

The end of Reconstruction in 1877 and the restoration of white supremacist rule in the South ended Pinchback's career in public office. As a wealthy man with considerable political skills, however, he continued to advocate on behalf of American blacks by attempting to slow the momentum of Southern Democrats who were working to disfranchise blacks and enforce the segregation of the races. He also attempted to sway public opinion by publishing a newspaper, the *Louisianan*. In 1875 he became chairman of the Convention of Colored Newspaper Men, which led to the formation of the Associated Negro Press.

Pinchback succeeded in several business ventures throughout his life. He was a cotton dealer and helped to found the Mississippi River Packet Company. He also profited from his positions in government and the information that they provided. For instance, Pinchback arranged for the New Orleans Park Commission, on which he served, to purchase property he owned for more than its market value. He also profited from bond speculation, stating that "I belonged to the General Assembly, and knew about what it would do.... My investments were made accordingly." In 1897 Pinchback and his wife, Nina Hawthorne, moved to WASHINGTON, D.C., where he became a leading member of the city's black social elite until his death in 1921. Among his grandchildren was JEAN TOOMER, the well-known novelist of the HARLEM RENAISSANCE.

Robert Fay

See Also

Press, Black, in the United States; Civil War, American; New Orleans, Louisiana.

Latin America and the Caribbean

Pindling, Lynden (b. 1930, Bahamas), first prime minister and first black leader of the BAHAMAS.

Sir Lynden O. Pindling has been one of the most influential Bahamian politicians. The son of a local merchant, Pindling was an outstanding student and was accepted at London University in England, where he studied law. After returning to the Bahamas and being admitted to the bar in 1953, Pindling joined the brand-new Progressive Liberal Party (PLP), the Bahamas' first political party, which was dedicated to the goal of black political representation. Pindling was elected to Parliament as a PLP representative in 1956 and served as leader of the opposition in the house from 1964 to 1967.

One of Pindling's earliest political triumphs came during a parliamentary debate on April 27, 1965 – the date now remembered as "Black Tuesday." While the population of the Bahamas was more than 80 percent black, the political districts at the time had been drawn so that white areas were unfairly overrepresented, and the PLP minority was pushing to have the districts redrawn. At the end of that day's debate Pindling gave a passionate speech in which he declared that he did not want to be a part of a government that did not accurately represent its constituents. He then took the ceremonial wooden mace that had been the symbol of parliamentary authority in the Bahamas since 1799 and threw it out of an open window, declaring that its power actually belonged outside with the people.

The mace broke in half in the middle of the black crowd that had gathered outside, and Pindling's actions were met with shock and horror by white members of Parliament and the local newspaper, but the drama had an effect. Two years later, when the districts were finally redrawn, the PLP won a majority, and as the party's leader Pindling became premier of the Bahamas. When the country's constitution was changed in 1969 so that its chief executive would be prime minister instead of simply a premier, Pindling became the first prime minister of the Bahamas.

Pindling was not content to stop with that change, however, and instead led the PLP and the rest of the country in pushing for total independence for the Bahamas from Great Britain. The boldness of this move again shocked many Bahamians, but the campaign was successful; on July 10, 1973, the Bahamas became an independent country, with prime minister Pindling as its first leader. As prime minister, Pindling employed his speaking ability as one of his major strengths; as one observer noted, "Witty, caustic, full of mockery and mimicry... [m]ixing Bahamian English with Standard English at just the right moments, he is a platform master."

Pindling's tremendous popularity allowed him to stay in power until 1992. But his reputation was irrevocably damaged by the charges of drug-trade corruption that were leveled at his administration in the mid-1980s. These accusations and a depressed economy allowed the Free National Movement Party to win election in 1992, making Hubert Ingraham the new prime minister. In 1997 Pindling finally resigned as the leader of the PLP after 41 years at his party's helm. While his public political career has drawn to its close, Pindling remains a bold leader whose willingness to fight for black political equality has forever changed the course of the Bahamas' history.

Lisa Clayton Robinson

See Also

London, Blacks In: An Interpretation.

Latin America and the Caribbean

Piñeiro, Ignacio (b. 1888; d. 1969), Afro-Cuban bass player, composer, and musical director of the legendary Septeto Nacional from 1927 to 1937 and again from 1958 to 1969. Together with Arsenio Rodríguez and Miguel Matamoros, Piñeiro is universally regarded as one of the most influential figures in the development of contemporary Cuban music, particularly of the Afro-Cuban genre SON.

North America

Pippen, Scottie (b. September 25, 1965, Hamburg, Ark.), African American professional BASKETBALL player, considered one of the most skilled and versatile players in the National Basketball Association (NBA).

Scottie Pippen, a forward, earned admiration for the variety of his talents. In the 1990s he consistently ranked among the NBA leaders in scoring, rebounding, assists, and steals.

Pippen was slow to develop as a basketball player and did not win a starting position on a team until his senior year in high school. He enrolled at the University of Central

Arkansas in 1983 and worked initially as manager of the basketball team. His play rapidly improved, however, and by his senior year he was a starting guard and the team's best player.

The Seattle SuperSonics selected Pippen in the first round of the 1987 NBA draft and immediately traded him to the Chicago Bulls. Pippen earned a spot as the starting forward for the Bulls during his second year, the 1988-1989 season. Pippen and acclaimed guard Michael Jordan helped lead the Bulls to six NBA championship titles (1991-1993, 1996, 1997, 1998). In the 1995-1996 season the Bulls also became the first NBA team to win 70 or more games in a season, finishing with 72 victories. Pippen was a member of the United States basketball team known as the Dream Team, which won gold medals at the 1992 Olympic Games in Barcelona, Spain, and the 1996 games in Atlanta, Georgia. Pippen played in the NBA All-Star game in 1990 and from 1992 to 1997. He was elected most valuable player of the 1994 All-Star game.

See Also

Jordan, Michael Jeffrey.

North America

Pippin, Horace

(b. February 22, 1888, West Chester, Pa.; d. July 6, 1946, West Chester, Pa.), African American painter who became famous for his nonacademic approach to art and superimposition of historical events and personal experiences.

Horace Pippin was discovered at a time in art history when such artists as Pablo Picasso were breaking away from academic painting standards to define a modern aesthetic. Art critics and dealers became particularly interested in self-taught artists whose works had not been influenced by traditional approaches to painting. One such artist was Henri Rousseau, a French painter hailed by Picasso for his indifference to perspective, use of strong color, and unorthodox, dreamlike subject matter. Pippin was compared to Rousseau because of his tendency to ignore concepts of realism, such as perspective and shadowing.

Another aspect of Pippin's work that intrigued art critics and dealers was the way in which Pippin interpreted historical events in terms of his own personal experiences. His painting *Abraham Lincoln and His Father Building Their Cabin on Pigeon Creek,* for example, is cast in the mold of his childhood memories from Goshen, New York, as reflected in the structure and fixtures of the house. The personal dimension in *John Brown Going to His Hanging* (1942) stems from Pippin's inclusion of his grandmother, who actually witnessed the event in 1859 (*see* John Brown). These personal details lend to Pippin's depictions of historical events a sense of immediacy and intimacy.

Art critic and historian Christian Brinton discovered Pippin after seeing his *Cabin in the Cotton* on display in a barbershop window in 1936. Brinton sought Pippin out and arranged for ten of his works to be displayed at the West Chester Community Center on June 9, 1937. Within a year four of Pippin's works were included in an exhibition of self-taught French and American painters, "Masters of Popular Painting," at the Museum of Modern Art. In 1940 artist-turned-dealer Robert Carlen mounted Pippin's first gallery show in Philadelphia, Pennsylvania. During the 1940s Pippin's paintings were purchased by several major American museums, and galleries throughout the country mounted exhibitions featuring his works.

Part of the reason Pippin began to paint was to rehabilitate his right arm following a World War I injury. Pippin had taken an interest in drawing at an early age. As a boy he won a box of crayons and a set of watercolors for his entry in an art supply company's advertising contest. Pippin used the crayons and watercolors to decorate doilies, which were sold in a Sunday school festival. During his childhood and early adulthood he spent much of his free time drawing.

When the United States declared war in 1917, he enlisted and served as a corporal in what would become known as the 369th Colored Infantry Regiment of the United States Army. Pippin continued to sketch while in the service. Only six of the drawings documenting Pippin's war experiences survive, since he was made to destroy the others for security reasons. He was honorably discharged in October 1918 after a German sniper's shot seriously wounded his right shoulder. Pippin, who was very proud of his frontline service, was awarded a French Croix de Guerre in 1919 and a retroactive Purple Heart in 1945.

Upon returning to the United States from France, Pippin met Jennie Ora Featherstone, a widow with a young son living in West Chester, Pennsylvania; the couple married on November 21, 1920. Pippin's disability check was not enough to support the two of them, and he did his best with his good left arm to assist his wife at her laundry service. In 1925 he began to make pictures by burning images onto wood panels with a hot poker. This endeavor was intended to serve as therapy for his injured arm, which he rested across his knee. It also allowed him to work out the war memories that continued to trouble him.

Pyrography, burning drawings into wood, was a challenging way for Pippin to resume creating. Pyrography's laborious process allows no erasure and required that he work out the entire composition in his head before beginning. Toward the end of the 1920s, his right arm gaining strength, he attempted his first easel painting, supporting his disabled arm at the wrist with his left hand. He spent three years of his life painting and repainting his first work in oil, *The End of the War: Starting Home* (1930), which ambivalently depicts the surrender of German soldiers against a background of violence and chaos. Although his output was slow and exhausting during the early 1930s, he continued to reconstruct his personal past, particularly childhood and war memories, through painting.

Pippin's growing popularity in the 1940s led to some changes in his work. Collector Albert Barnes, who wrote two catalogue essays on the artist, invited Pippin to see his world-famous collection of paintings, to which he added two of Pippin's works. After seeing Barnes's collection, Pippin brightened his palette (influenced by Renoir's colors) and began creating still-life compositions (meticulously rendered flowers). The impact of other artists is also seen in Pippin's *John Brown* paintings, a narrative group of works inspired by Jacob Lawrence's *Toussaint L'Ouverture* series. In spite of these influences and Barnes's unsuccessful attempt to get Pippin to take art classes at the Barnes Foundation's art school, Pippin maintained his philosophy about art. He said, "My opinion of art is that a man should have a love for it, because it is my idea that he paints from his heart and mind. To me it seems impossible for another to teach one of art."

Pippin worked with increasing productivity until his death on July 6, 1946, creating more than 75 of his 137 known works in the last six years of his life. Unlike other important self-taught artists who tended to repeat themselves, Pippin explored a variety of subjects (American history, biblical themes, winter landscapes, portraits, and scenes of everyday black communal life) on a variety of mediums (fabric, paper, and wood). In attempting to be direct and true to reality as he understood it, Pippin created works with some of modern art's fundamental characteristics – unmodulated, sharply delineated colors and flat, shadowless forms – which makes him one of the twentieth century's most remarkable artists.

Aaron Myers

See Also

World War I and African Americans; Lawrence, Jacob Armstead; Philadelphia, Pennsylvania; Art, African American.

Africa

Pires, Pedro Verona Rodrigues

(b. 1934, Fogo Island, Cape Verde), the first prime minister of the Republic of Cape Verde.

Pedro Pires was born in a small village on Fogo Island, Cape Verde. While studying engineering in Lisbon, Portugal, he encountered a community of Africans hotly debating the issue of Portuguese colonial

RULE. In 1959 Pires joined the underground movement for independence.

Fleeing conscription in the Portuguese army, Pires went to GHANA, where GUINEA-BISSAU nationalist leader AMÍLCAR CABRAL and the Partido Africano da Independencia da Guine e Cabo Verde (PAIGC) were based. From there he went to ALGERIA, where he received military training, and then to CUBA, where in 1966 he helped mastermind a PAIGC invasion of Cape Verde. Although the outlawed party ultimately decided against the invasion, Pires continued to play a key role as both a fighter and an administrator, taking charge of the party's health and education departments.

As Cape Verde and Guinea-Bissau neared independence, Pires acted as PAIGC's chief negotiator. He led a 1974 delegation to talks in London and Algiers and lobbied the United States Congress for support. Following independence in 1975, the Cape Verde Popular National Assembly chose Pires to be the first prime minister.

Pires worked alongside fellow PAIGC member ARISTIDES PEREIRA, who now served as president. Pursuing a policy of nonalignment, the two attempted to position Cape Verde between the cold war superpowers. They also called on African nations to handle their own affairs through the ORGANIZATION OF AFRICAN UNITY, rather than inviting foreign intervention. The outspoken administration also demanded the end of APARTHEID in SOUTH AFRICA and appealed to its own citizens to conserve the natural resources of their drought-stricken islands.

Following the split with the Guinea-Bissau PAIGC in 1980, Pires created a new, one-nation party – the Partido Africano da Independencia da Cabo Verde (PAICV) – as well as a one-party nation. He subsequently undertook agrarian reforms and a campaign to nationalize foreign businesses, raising fears among some Cape Verdeans that Pires was courting support from the Soviet Union and was perhaps planning to allow a Soviet base on the strategically located islands. Fearing a coup, the administration suppressed dissent through arrests and expulsions.

Despite these struggles, during the 1980s Cape Verde received more per capita economic aid than almost any country in the world. Most of it came from European nations and expatriate Cape Verdeans, who by then were nearly twice as numerous as the resident population. Even though the administration promised to invest in industrialization and urban renewal, opposition groups as well as the international community called for the end to its one-party rule. In 1991 Cape Verde held the first multiparty elections of any former Portuguese colony. The Movimento para a Democracia (MpD) carried the day, and Pires was forced to resign. He retained his position as the head of the PIACV and became a member of the "loyal opposition."

Marian Aguiar

SEE ALSO

Algiers, Algeria.

Europe

Pitt, David (b. October 3, 1913, Hampstead, Grenada; d. December 18, 1994, London, England), physician and one of the first black politicians in Great Britain.

At a time when prejudice and even violence against blacks was common in GREAT BRITAIN, David Thomas Pitt spoke out for the unrepresented black immigrant community. In his obituary for Pitt in the *Guardian* in 1994, black British journalist Mike Phillips wrote: "At that point, Dr. Pitt was the only black person who figured in the public and political life of the country; and as such, if only by default, when he spoke, he spoke for us."

Born on the island of GRENADA in the West Indies, David Pitt attended Grenada Boys' Secondary school and was raised a devout Roman Catholic. In 1932 he won Grenada's only overseas scholarship to attend the prestigious medical school at the University of Edinburgh in Scotland. After graduating with honors, he returned to the West Indies in 1938 and practiced medicine in St. Vincent and Trinidad. There he met and married Dorothy Alleyne; they had three children.

In 1943 Pitt helped found the West Indian National Party, and he served as its president until 1947. This party was considered radical in its day because it advocated independence for Trinidad within a West Indian federation. He won election to the borough council in San Fernando, Trinidad, where he also served as deputy mayor. In order to lobby the British government for independence, he traveled to Great Britain in 1947. His efforts were unsuccessful, and he grew disillusioned with West Indian politics. He decided to settle in the London district of Euston, where he established a medical practice that he ran for more than 30 years.

In the 1950s Pitt was one of the few blacks active in defending the growing black population of Great Britain against discrimination and prejudice. In the 1960s and 1970s he organized efforts to help immigrants and improve race relations. Pitt became the first and only chair of the Campaign Against Racial Discrimination, an association founded with the encouragement of Martin Luther King Jr. Pitt believed in fighting racism within the existing power structure. In 1959 Pitt sought to represent London's wealthy Hampstead district in Parliament, becoming the first West Indian black to seek a seat in Parliament. After a campaign plagued by racist insinuations, Pitt lost the election.

In 1961, however, Pitt was elected to represent the ethnically mixed, working-class Hackney district in London's city government, the London County Council. In 1964 this body was absorbed by the Greater London Council (GLC). Pitt served as deputy chair of the GLC from 1969 to 1970 and in 1974 became the first black chair, a post he held until 1975. Pitt paved the way for the multiracial politics for which the GLC became known.

In 1970 Pitt ran for Parliament again, this time as a candidate in London's Clapham district. The post was a secure Labour seat that many believed he would win. He lost by an unusually large margin; race undoubtedly played a large role in his defeat. He was bitterly disappointed and did not attempt to run for Parliament again.

In 1975 Prime Minister Harold Wilson appointed Pitt to the House of Lords as Lord Pitt of Hampstead. According to Pitt himself, however, his most valued honor was his election as president of the British Medical Association from 1985 to 1986, a position few general practitioners achieve. After Pitt's death many lamented that he "should have been the first Labour Member of Parliament."

Leyla Keough

SEE ALSO

King, Martin Luther, Jr.; St. Vincent and the Grenadines; Trinidad and Tobago.

North America

Pittsburgh Courier, one of the most influential African American newspapers of the early twentieth century.

The *Pittsburgh Courier* was founded in the spring of 1910 by Edwin Harleston and a small group of Pittsburgh blacks that included attorney Robert Lee Vann. At the time of the *Courier*'s founding, Pittsburgh's white newspapers either ignored African American news or reported it in a separate section, often focusing on crime and other lurid subjects. By the fall of 1910 Vann had become editor, treasurer, and legal counsel of the newspaper and was the driving force behind its growth. Through its first troubled decade Vann steered the *Courier* to a small circulation among Pittsburgh's blacks and used its pages to further his legal career (in 1918 he won appointment as a Pittsburgh city solicitor).

By the early 1920s the *Courier*'s circulation reached 55,000 and by the mid-1930s it totaled about 150,000. This growth was partly the result of demographics: large numbers of blacks moved from the South to the North as part of the Great Migration of the early 1900s. But it was also the result of shrewd management of the *Courier:* popular journalist George Schuyler was hired to write a widely read column; *Courier* journalists were sent on tours of the South to report on JIM CROW and to attract a national audience; and the *Courier* undertook a well-publicized campaign attacking RACIAL STEREOTYPES in the "Amos 'n' Andy" radio program.

In the 1930s and 1940s the newspaper continued to increase its local and national circulation with coverage of boxer Joe Louis and calls for fair treatment of blacks in the American military during World War II. By 1947 circulation reached a peak of more than 350,000, but in the following years the readership and influence of the *Courier*, like that of many black newspapers, declined steadily as white newspapers began to cover the Civil Rights Movement and other news relating to the black community. In the 1960s the *Courier* was sold and renamed the *New Pittsburgh Courier*, which continued publication into the 1990s.

See Also

World War II and African Americans; Amos 'n' Andy; Press, Black, in the United States; Great Migration, The; Pittsburgh, Pennsylvania; Schuyler, George S.

North America

Pittsburgh, Pennsylvania,

a city whose black population countered its marginal economic position by prospering in civic and cultural spheres.

The historian Roy Lubove describes early industrial Pittsburgh as "the 'Smokey City,' America's classic coketown... frequently compared to hell... an economic rather than civic entity." Indeed, by the turn of the twentieth century belching smoke stacks and polluted waterways encroached on Pittsburgh's river-valley beauty. African Americans, however, had little hand in the desecration. From the founding of Pittsburgh in 1763 until World War II, blacks found few opportunities in the town's industries.

Despite the poverty that plagued African Americans until the Civil War, their numbers grew from 1000 to 20,000 during Reconstruction. Flocks of migrants arrived from Virginia to work in Pittsburgh's factories, but few newcomers found well-paying jobs. White employers excluded blacks from Pittsburgh's thriving iron and glass industries, and most of the blacks settled for unskilled domestic work. Even when World War I occasioned a large demand for industrial labor, foremen hired blacks for only the most grueling and low-paid work. A 1918 sociology study revealed that 95 percent of African American factory workers in Pittsburgh held unskilled positions, regardless of education level. The Great Depression made a bad situation worse, as job opportunities dwindled and unfair hiring practices continued. Although World War II created numerous jobs, black people benefited far less than whites, emerging into the second half of the century with little hope of improvement.

Nevertheless, the richness of black Pittsburgh's cultural history surpassed that of comparably populated cities. Twenty years before the Civil War, the journalist Martin Robinson Delany was editing *Mystery*, one of the earliest black newspapers. His small constituency of poor black readers also supported a large array of churches, clubs, and schools as well as other publications. During Reconstruction, African American civic successes kept pace with the growth in population, and literary societies and philanthropic organizations added to the enduring antebellum network of social groups. Between World War I and 1930 the journalist Robert Lee Vann edited the *Pittsburgh Courier*, helping the paper to become the most widely read black periodical in the nation. In the 1930s Pittsburgh's African American baseball teams often topped the Negro League, boosted by players Satchel Paige and James "Cool Papa" Bell. At the same time the city's jazz scene boasted such names as vocalist Lena Horne and trumpeter Roy Eldridge.

After World War II white citizens of Pittsburgh created urban renewal programs in which old neighborhoods were cleared to make room for new ones. For African Americans in Pittsburgh's lower-hill district, "renewal" often meant unfair eviction. The programs worsened ghetto conditions by pushing more people into fewer homes.

Pittsburgh, however, endured less urban decay than other, similarly constituted industrial towns. Because Pittsburgh blacks faced fewer opportunities to begin with, the decline of industry brought no sudden shock, no sky-rocketing crime or drug use. While economic conditions toward the end of the century worsened, Pittsburgh retained some of its vitality in the jazz music of George Benson, Erroll Garner, and Stanley Turrentine, and the novels and plays of John Edgar Wideman and August Wilson.

Eric Bennett

See Also

World War I and African Americans; World War II and African Americans; Civil War, American; Delany, Martin Robison; Paige, Leroy Robert ("Satchel"); *Pittsburgh Courier*.

Latin America and the Caribbean

Pixinguinha

(b. April 23, 1898, Rio de Janeiro, Brazil; d. February 17, 1973, Rio de Janeiro, Brazil), Brazilian bandleader, *choro* musician, *sambista*, and composer of more than 600 instrumental pieces, including choros, *valsas*, *maxixes*, and sambas.

Pixinguinha grew up in a large family in the working-class district of Catumbi in north Rio de Janeiro. His birth name was Alfredo da Rocha Viana Jr., but his grandparents gave him the nickname "Pizinguim," of African origin, meaning "good child." Eventually it was Brazilianized, becoming Pixinguinha.

The musical genre choro (from the word "cry") emerged in the late nineteenth century. Pixinguinha's father, a telegraph worker by trade, was a flutist and choro musician. At

Pixinguinha's musical innovations in the early twentieth century helped pave the way for the birth of samba and the emergence of *Música Popular Brasileira*. *Tom Rica/Contexto*

night his home was the meeting place for many neighborhood choro musicians. In this setting Pixinguinha became immersed in the choro tradition. He was playing flute professionally at age 15 in Choro Carioca, a group led by his teacher, Irineu de Almeida. Before he was out of his teens, he was well regarded in the music circles of northern Rio de Janeiro.

In 1919, together with Donga, Pixinguinha formed his first group, Oito Batutas (the Eight Lads). The band got its first break playing in the foyer of the Palais cinema; soon after, they began a national tour.

In 1922 Arnaldo Guine, a rich patron, fronted the money for the Oito Batutas to go to Paris, where they played for six months. These appearances met with disapproval from many upper-class *cariocas* (citizens of Rio), who were outraged at the prospect of a black band acting as Brazil's first cultural ambassadors to Europe. Discriminatory protests in their own country notwithstanding, the Oito Batutas received favorable reviews in Europe. The band's unique blend of samba, choro, and maxixe had provided Europe with its first glimpse of Brazil's rich musical culture. Without a doubt it was this tour that opened the doors for the massive worldwide exportation of Brazilian music that was to follow.

During the 1930s Pixinguinha embarked on one of the most successful periods of his career. A few years earlier he had written some arrangements for Carmen Miranda's international debut record, thereby becoming one of the recording industry's most sought-after arrangers. His band, Velha Guarda, provided the instrumental accompaniment for numerous recording projects during this period.

Pixinguinha is often credited with helping to invent the samba. Indeed, it was his colleague, Donga, who recorded the first samba, "Pelo Telefone," in 1917. It has recently been suggested, however, that this composition was likely a group effort in which many musicians, possibly including Pixinguinha, took part. At any rate Pixinguinha is certainly one of samba's most prolific composers, with pieces numbering in the hundreds. Yet during his lifetime Pixinguinha was known more for his arrangements than his compositions. Often his complex harmonic language and elaborate formal experimentation met with severe criticism; such was the case with his 1926 choro "Lamento." Today, however, Pixinguinha's innovations are considered to have laid the foundations for Música Popular Brasileira (MPB), and many eminent composers, such as Antonio Carlos Jobim, Chico Buarque, and Milton Nascimento, have cited him as a major influence on their work. Pixinguinha has often been hailed as the King of Samba and the Father of MPB (*see* Contemporary Afro-Brazilian Music).

Gordon Root

See Also
Samba.

Africa

Plaatje, Solomon Tshekisho

(b. 1876, South Africa; d. 1932, South Africa), South African writer and journalist and one of the founders of the African National Congress (ANC), who served as its first secretary-general.

Although ethnically a Tswana of the Rolong branch, Solomon Tshekisho took the Dutch name Plaatje from a nickname used by his father. Following some schooling in the 1880s, Plaatje took a job as a postal clerk at Kimberley in Northern Cape Province, South Africa. During the Boer War (1899-1902) he reported the siege of Mafeking (now Mafikeng) and kept a diary of the period. In 1904 he launched the first newspaper in the Tswana language, *Koranta ea Bechuana* (Newspaper of the Tswana), and began opposing white violations of black rights.

In 1912 he became the secretary-general of what was at first known as the South African Native National Congress, later the ANC, with John Langalibalele Dube as president. Plaatje was a fine orator and in 1913 went with Dube and a delegation to Great Britain to oppose the 1913 Natives Land Act, which had drastically curtailed the right of blacks to purchase or own land. He remained in Great Britain during World War I (1914-1918), where he wrote and published several books. In *Native Life in South Africa* (1916) he outlined the reasons for black opposition to the Land Act. At the end of the war he was part of another black delegation that attended the Versailles peace conference but that was not allowed to participate. He also attended the Pan-African Congress, which was held in Paris at the same time, and was among the first South African black leaders to make contact with other African black leaders. Plaatje traveled back to Great Britain and went with delegations to see Prime Minister David Lloyd George and the Archbishop of Canterbury, but failed to obtain help for the black cause in South Africa. From there he traveled to Canada and the United States. He wrote poetry and translated five of Shakespeare's plays into Tswana. His novel *Mhudi: An Epic of Native Life 100 Years Ago* (1930) was one of the first novels in English by a black African.

See Also
Pan-Africanism; South Africa; Pan-African Congress of 1919.

North America

Plato, Ann

(b. 1820?; d. ?, Hartford, Conn.), African American poet and essayist who was the second African American woman to publish a book in the United States.

Although little is known about the life of Ann Plato, her legacy holds an important place in African American literature. Plato's sole book, *Essays: Including Biographies and Miscellaneous Pieces in Prose and Poetry*, published in 1841, represents the only book of essays issued by a black American between 1840 and 1865. Following that of Phillis Wheatley, it was also only the second book published by an African American woman.

Based on information garnered primarily from her writings, scholars have determined that Plato probably was born about 1820. Her poem "The Infant Class," for example, suggests that Plato began to teach young children when she herself was only 15 years old. Her poem "The Natives of America" links her to her paternal Native American heritage, and another poem, "I Have No Brother," indicates that she had a brother named Henry, who died when she was very young. Plato probably joined the Congregational Church at age 13. As she was not a slave, her writing provides unusual insight into the life of a mid-nineteenth-century, middle-class, free black woman.

The introduction to Plato's book was written by James W. C. Pennington, minister of the Colored Congregational Church in Hartford. Pennington presents Plato's work by emphasizing first her color, then her age and sex, and finally the literary tradition from which she drew. Pennington was reluctant, but felt obliged to stress that Plato was black: "I am not in the habit of introducing myself or others to notice by the adjective 'colored,'... but it seems proper that I should... say here that my authoress is a colored lady." He also emphasized Plato's "large heart full of chaste and pious affection for those of her own age and sex.... " He compares her to Phillis Wheatley, the eighteenth-century black poet: "She, as Phillis Wheatley was, is passionately fond of reading and delights in searching the Holy Scriptures; and is now rapidly improving her knowledge."

In her book Plato eulogizes four other black women, all of whom died at an early age: Louisa Sebury, Julia Ann Pell, Eliza Loomis Sherman, and Elizabeth Low. Eleven of Plato's twenty published poems have death as their themes, suggesting Plato's concern with the grim lives often led even by free blacks.

Some scholars have criticized Plato's writing, including one who described it as "the pious, moralistic effusions of a Puritan girl." Many of her poems are juvenile, her verse uneven. She almost always wrote in iambic tetrameter, and her language often reflected her puritanical environment. Still, Plato occasionally branches out to topics outside her personal experience, shedding her moral, florid tone in favor of more politically charged themes. Her poem "To the First of August" hailed the end of slavery in the West Indies in 1838.

Most of Plato's works elucidate events and sentiments drawn from her own life. In "Written upon Being Examined in School Studies for the Preparation of a Teacher" she demands, "Learn me the way to teach the word of love / For that's the pure intelligence above." While Plato's contribution to American literature is often regarded as insignificant, the circumstances in which she wrote elevate her achievements and place her at the head of the canon of esteemed African American poets.

See Also
Women Writers, Black, in the United States; Free Blacks in the United States, 1619 to 1863.

North America

Platters, The,

the most successful African American vocal group of the 1950s, who played a key role in popularizing the rhythm-and-blues (R&B) vocal harmony group style that has since become known as doo wop.

The Platters were a popular vocal quintet and a consistent hit-maker for Mercury Records. But at the outset Mercury was more interested in acquiring the Penguins, another West Coast vocal group that had scored a major hit with "Earth Angel," recorded for the small Dootone label. The Platters, on the other hand, had found little success after several early releases on Federal Records. Mercury, one of the six major record companies of the day, wanted the Penguins in order to strengthen its rhythm and blues

(R&B) catalogue and thus gain more of the African American market. But arranger Buck Ram, who served as manager for both groups, insisted that if Mercury wanted the Penguins, it would have to sign the Platters as well.

In late 1954 Mercury reluctantly agreed. Ironically, the Penguins never had another Top Ten hit, whereas the Platters quickly rose to become the most successful vocal group of the decade. Although they recorded numerous up-tempo R&B numbers, the Platters were above all a ballad group. Their most successful recordings featured the smooth and romantic lead of Tony Williams. Williams ranks as one of the greatest lead tenors of the so-called doo wop era and – along with Sonny Til of the Orioles, Willie Winfield of the Harptones, and Nate Nelson of the Flamingos – one of the great ballad interpreters of the 1950s.

The Platters were a product of the new African American culture created by THE GREAT MIGRATION of blacks out of the South – in particular, those who came to Los Angeles, a city with a black community that had tripled in size during the 1940s as a result of the booming wartime economy. Los Angeles was home to the Platters, the Penguins, the Hollywood Flames, the Olympic Games, and many other African American vocal groups whose members had often begun singing together in informal groups while still in high school.

The Platters began as a quartet in 1952, performing at amateur night competitions at Los Angeles's Club Alabam and more informal settings. Herbert Reed, who had sung bass in a gospel group during his stint in the United States Air Force, suggested the name the Platters. "I remember... thinking to myself, on the radio they always say, 'Here's the latest platter by so-and-so,'" Reed recalled. The group experienced several changes in membership over its first two years, including the addition of Williams and Zola Taylor, a 14-year-old alto who became known as "the dish of the Platters." In 1954, not long before signing with Mercury, the group coalesced. Between 1955 and 1960, the years of its greatest success, the Platters consisted of Williams (tenor lead), Taylor (alto), David Lynch (tenor), Paul Robi (baritone), and Reed (bass).

The most demanding fans of African American vocal harmony singing dismissed the Platters for taking a simplistic approach to R&B group harmony singing. The Platters displayed little of the sophisticated voicings or complex harmonies found in the ballads performed by the Flamingos or the Harptones. Yet the Platters attained far greater commercial success, in large part because their singing was direct and emotionally engaging but also because they had the backing of a major record company. The group's first Mercury release, the haunting "Only You," hit the charts and clearly revealed the group's crossover potential, reaching not only Number One on the R&B chart, but a striking Number Five on the white popular music chart.

Six months later Mercury released "The Great Pretender," and the Platters became the first African American group to have a Number One hit on the white pop charts. Over the next six years the group enjoyed phenomenal success. During 1956 the Platters were second only to rock 'n' roller Elvis Presley in popularity. By 1962 the group had given Mercury Records 35 songs on *Billboard* magazine's Pop Hot 100 chart. A number of Platters hits, including the memorable "Smoke Gets in Your Eyes" (1958) and "Harbor Lights" (1959), actually ranked higher on the white pop charts than on R&B listings.

Success swept up the five African American singers in a whirlwind of travel and performances. The Platters were particularly significant for their crossing of racial barriers in popular music. They performed in Las Vegas and at the Olympia Theater in Paris with bandleader Quincy Jones, as well as for Pope Pius XII at the Vatican and for Queen Elizabeth II of England. In 1959 they became the first African American group to appear in the Eastern bloc, serving as goodwill ambassadors and performing in Poland.

The group's fall from success came suddenly. On August 10, 1959, Cincinnati police arrested the four men in the group for allegedly consorting with prostitutes. The case was eventually dismissed, and *Billboard* magazine published a charge that the arrests were a result of racism. But for several months the Platters discovered that their concert dates were canceled and radio disc jockeys refused to give them airplay.

The Platters returned to popularity with "Harbor Lights" (1959), which reached the Pop Top Ten, but their success was short-lived. Tony Williams left the group in 1960 to begin what proved to be a rather unsuccessful solo career. Other personnel changes followed, with Herbert Reed, the last of the original group members, departing in 1969. By the mid-1960s the Platters had become less a group than a franchise. During the 1980s and 1990s as many as ten different groups calling themselves the "Platters" toured and performed throughout the United States, but most had no relationship to the musicians of the original group.

On the other hand, during the years of their greatest successes the Platters had a powerful impact on popular music. Their importance was belatedly acknowledged by the popular music industry in 1990, when the Platters were inducted into the Rock and Roll Hall of Fame. Herbert Reed, one of the original members of the group, eloquently summed up the Platters' significance. "[B]ecause of our music," he declared, "white kids had a sense of fair play about blacks long before the CIVIL RIGHTS MOVEMENT.... It opened a lot of doors to a better understanding. And it gave us, five kids from Watts, a taste of a better life.... "

James Clyde Sellman

SEE ALSO

Jones, Quincy Delight, Jr.; Los Angeles, California; Rhythm and Blues.

Africa

Player, Gary (b. November 1, 1935, Johannesburg, South Africa), top professional golfer from SOUTH AFRICA.

Not only South Africa's greatest golfer, Gary Player may be one of the greatest golfers of all time. He has won more than 100 major international titles and is one of only four men to win each of the game's four major professional tournaments. After a difficult childhood – his mother died when he was eight years old, and his father, a gold miner, barely made enough to live on – he learned to play golf on a local course and turned professional in 1953. Four years later he entered the United States Professional Golfers' Association (PGA) circuit. Player's long roster of victories includes the British Open (1959, 1968, 1974); the U.S. PGA (1962, 1972); the U.S. Open (1965); and the Masters (1961, 1974, 1978). In addition, he won the South Africa Open 13 times and the Australian Open 7 times. Player joined the Senior Tour in 1985 and in 1989 won the U.S. Senior Open.

One of golf's biggest money winners, Player has reputedly traveled more miles than any other athlete in history. Preceded by the career of South African Bobby Locke, Player's success helped bring attention to other African golfers, including Nick Price (South Africa) and Ernie Elys (ZIMBABWE). Like many South African athletes, Player, who is of European descent, competed and lived abroad much of his life due to international athletic sanctions against South Africa's APARTHEID regime.

Kate Tuttle

North America

Pleasant, Mary Ellen ("Mammy") (b. 1814?, near Augusta, Ga.; d. 1903?, San Francisco, Calif.), African American businesswoman and financial backer of abolitionist JOHN BROWN.

One of San Francisco's most colorful and controversial characters in the late nineteenth century was Mary Ellen Pleasant, a former slave who moved to the city in 1849. She began managing a boarding house whose reputation for cards, liquor, and beautiful women – it is likely her services included procuring prostitutes – earned it a devoted following.

No mere businesswoman, Pleasant involved herself in both local and national politics. In 1858 she personally presented abolitionist John Brown a $30,000 United States Treasury Bond, after which she traveled south to promote his upcoming revolt. When Brown was captured at Harpers Ferry, Pleasant returned to California under an assumed name. She raised money for the Union cause in the Civil War and continued her work for civil rights.

Throughout her life Pleasant helped escaped and former slaves find work in San Francisco, mostly as domestic servants. Some historians speculate that Pleasant used her informal employment agency to gather information she used either to advance her business dealings or to blackmail the city's rich whites.

Pleasant lived in an ornate mansion she shared with a white former prostitute, whom she had helped to marry a wealthy financier. Though accounts vary, it seems likely that Pleasant owned the property but posed as its housekeeper. What is certain is that she inspired fear and obedience in what was locally called the "House of Mystery" through her real or implied mastery of VODOU.

Despite her scandalous business and personal affairs, her gravestone emphasizes her political contributions. As she had requested, the epitaph reads, "Mother of Civil Rights in California. Friend of John Brown."

Kate Tuttle

SEE ALSO

Civil War, American; San Francisco and Oakland, California.

Latin America and the Caribbean

Plena and Bomba, two of the most important genres of Afro-Puerto Rican music and dance.

Bomba music is a generic category that includes a variety of rhythms and kinds of dances, such as *calinda, sica, grasima, lero, cuembe, holande, yuba, bambulae,* and *seis bombeao.* By some accounts bomba music and dance arrived in PUERTO RICO in the sixteenth century, brought by the ASANTE, who had come from the African region of GHANA. While its precise origins are unclear, the bomba and its many variants continued to evolve, particularly among slaves on the SUGAR plantations. These slaves would hold bomba dances on Sundays and holidays in places outside the plantations themselves. Many slave rebellions were planned during these gatherings.

The instruments used to accompany bomba music are two drums, *cua* (two sticks), and *maracas,* a Native American instrument originally used by the Taíno Indians. The drums essentially are barrels with heads of goatskin. The *buleador* is a low-pitched drum that is considered the heart of this music. The *primo* is a high-pitched drum that the drummer uses to communicate with the dancer. The primo player needs to be skilled enough to hold the tempo and at the same time improvise over the buleador's strong rhythmic pattern. A third drummer strikes the sides of the buleador with the cua, and a fourth musician plays the maracas. The dancers and vocalists are important elements in bomba. One or more of the dance couples sustain a rhythmical dance conversation with the primo at a specific point. Different variants of bomba can be distinguished by their rhythm, chants, melodic lines, dance forms, and choreographic changes (*see* DANCE IN LATIN AMERICA AND THE CARIBBEAN).

An interesting bomba variant is the *lero,* derived from the French "la rose" because the dancers form a rose pattern in the choreography. The *yuba* is a 6/8-pattern bomba with much energy. The *holande* is a perfect bomba for celebration. Still another variation, the *seis bombeao,* is danced mainly in the town of Loiza on the northeastern coast; the other variants of bomba are danced throughout the island.

The rhythmic pattern of the holande is close to the plena, a highly important genre of Afro-Puerto Rican music that had become widely popular by the 1930s. Sometimes referred to as a "sung newspaper," the plena served both as entertainment and as a sort of chronicle reflecting day-to-day issues. Using the structure of a chorus followed by lines of improvisation by male or female singers, the dance became a means by which the people could illustrate their lives, customs, and circumstances.

The plena was more strongly influenced by Spanish music than the bomba, but its Afro-Caribbean character is still apparent. By various accounts the plena originated in the nineteenth century, though the circumstances of its inception are still obscure. It is closely associated with Ponce, Puerto Rico's second largest city, and in particular with the largely black neighborhood of San Antón. The first great professional singer of plenas was the Afro-Puerto Rican Joselino "Bumbum" Oppenheimer. Many of Oppenheimer's compositions from the early twentieth century remain classics. By the 1930s the plena had become very popular.

The principal instruments used in plenas are *panderos,* rounded wooden drums with a goatskin head on one side. The *pleneros* (musicians who perform the genre) use a combination of three panderos: the *bajo,* or bass drum; the *banao* or *segunda,* the second drum; and the *quinto,* which has a higher pitch. To make these instruments, musicians replaced the rounded covers of wooden boxes with goatskin. Another type of pandero, made from the body of a banjo, was created by Puerto Rican pleneros who had emigrated to New York. Panderos are also made from metal pots and from plastic or fiberglass tubes and pipes. The other instruments used are the *guiro* (of Native American origin), the guitar (of Arab-Spanish origin), the *acordeon* (of German origin), and the *cuatro* (a Puerto Rican guitarlike variant also of Spanish origin).

A number of groups promote and maintain the plena in Puerto Rico. Plena Libre is directed by Gary Nuñez, who is responsible for bringing the plena back to the radio charts. ABC Orchestra is directed by Jesús Cepeda, who borrowed the name from a plena group started by his father in the 1930s. Los Guayacanes from San Antón, directed by Joe Santiago; Atabal, directed by Hector Rodríguez; and Bomplene are among other groups responsible for promoting the plena.

Other plena groups have been established by Puerto Rican immigrants to the United States. Los Pleneros de la 21, from New York (the name refers to bus stop #21 in Santurce, Puerto Rico), is directed by Juan Gutiérrez. Los Pleneros del Batey, from Philadelphia, is directed by Joaquín Rivera. La Familia Ayala, from Boston (an extension of La Familia Ayala from Puerto Rico), is directed by Celia and Sixto Ayala. These and other composers and producers carry forth a tradition established by Don Rafael Cepeda, Don Rafael Cortijo y su Combo, Ismael Rivera, Ramón "Mon" Rivera, Manuel Jímenez (Canario), Toñin Romero, Petra Cepeda, Marcial Reyes, Tomasito Flores, Enrique Soto (Mayaguez), Jacinto Salomón, Toribio Laporte, Vitrín Calderón, Ramón Pedraza, and many others.

Jorge Arce

North America

Plessy v. Ferguson, 1896 United States Supreme Court case that reconciled the equal protection clause of the Fourteenth Amendment with a system of state-imposed racial segregation via the formula "separate but equal."

When 30-year-old shoemaker Homer Plessy refused to leave his seat on a New Orleans train in 1892, he set in motion a battle that traveled all the way to the U.S. Supreme Court. The court's 1896 decision, *Plessy* v. *Ferguson,* permitted states to institute racially separate public accommodations despite the Constitution's Fourteenth Amendment, which guarantees all citizens equal protection under the law. It would take nearly 60 years for the court to reverse itself, in BROWN V. BOARD OF EDUCATION (1954), and overturn the judicial precedent for segregation.

The segregated public transportation system that Plessy challenged in 1892 was relatively new to New Orleans, whose French and Spanish roots, many free blacks, and community of prominent Creole citizens made it one of America's most socially and economically progressive cities. Plessy himself had been born free in 1862, the second year of the Civil War, in which Union forces took control of the city's port. Throughout the war and RECONSTRUCTION, the

Northern army provided a check on the Southern Democrats who sought a restoration of white power at all costs.

Just before the war, in 1860, New Orleans's trains were first segregated. Those adorned with black stars were meant for black passengers only. The rule was difficult to enforce because of the many mixed-race people and mixed marriages in New Orleans. Plessy himself was fair-skinned enough to pass for white. In 1867 the city removed the black stars from its trains, and the system returned to its earlier, integrated state.

But with the declining support of the Republican-controlled U.S. government, Reconstruction faltered. Increasingly, Southern Democrats took back the power they had lost in Louisiana. In 1890 Governor Francis T. Nicholls – elected as part of an 1876 compromise balancing a Republican president with Democratic control of the South – signed the law re-segregating Louisiana's railways. It stated that train companies had to provide "equal but separate" cars for blacks and whites, and that individuals of different races could not ride together without risking a $25 fine or 20 days in jail. The Louisiana Senate passed the law by a vote of 23 to 6.

African Americans and Creoles in New Orleans mobilized to fight the law. Rodolphe Desdunes, columnist for the *Crusader*, a black-owned newspaper, proposed that African Americans boycott the train system, writing that blacks "can withdraw the patronage from these corporations and travel only by necessity." But his idea did not take hold. Fears of violent white reprisals limited black political activism, and noted African American leaders like Booker T. Washington preached patience and accommodation.

A Louisiana group calling itself the Comité des Citoyens (Citizens' Committee) planned to test the law's constitutionality – specifically, to prove that the law violated the Fourteenth Amendment to the U.S. Constitution, which guarantees all citizens "the equal protection of the laws." Made up of prominent New Orleans blacks and whites, including the *Crusader*'s publisher, Louis Martinet, and Desdunes, the committee arranged for Plessy to board a whites-only train. By prearrangement with contacts in the East Louisiana Railroad Company, a conductor asked Plessy, who was of mixed race, if he was a "colored man." When Plessy said he was, and refused to move, the conductor and private detective hired by the Comité accompanied him to the police station, where he was booked and then released on $500 bond posted by a Comité member.

Judge John H. Ferguson, a Massachusetts native, presided over Plessy's arraignment a month later. Ferguson had earlier ruled the Louisiana law unconstitutional when it demanded segregated train cars for travel between states. Martinet had written in the *Crusader* that, with this decision, "Jim Crow is dead as a doornail." But in Plessy's case Ferguson sided with the state, saying that Louisiana, in compelling racial segregation on its in-state train system, had not violated African Americans' constitutional rights.

Louisiana's state supreme court agreed with Ferguson, citing a Massachusetts case, *Roberts* v. *City of Boston*, in which the state's chief justice had written that "prejudice, if it exists, is not created by law and cannot be changed by law." In addition, *Roberts* was the source of the phrase "separate but equal." The opinion also quoted a Pennsylvania case whose ruling rested upon the "natural, legal, and customary difference between the black and white races."

Plessy's lawyer, the white activist and writer Albion Tourgée, brought the case before the U.S. Supreme Court in 1896. Tourgée's brief argued that the Louisiana law "is obnoxious to the spirit of republican institutions, because it is a legalization of caste." He also stated that the law violated both the Thirteenth and Fourteenth Amendments in limiting "the natural rights of man."

The Court ruled seven to one (one justice did not participate) that Plessy's constitutional rights had not been violated. Writing for the majority, Justice Henry B. Brown wrote that while the Fourteenth Amendment had "undoubtedly" been meant to enforce "absolute equality" between the races, it did not "abolish distinction based on color," citing many states' laws mandating separate schools and prohibiting interracial marriages – laws that were themselves ruled unconstitutional later. The opinion went on to say that "legislation is powerless to eradicate racial instincts or to abolish distinctions."

In a lone but strong dissent, Justice John Marshall Harlan, a Southerner, cited cases in which segregated juries had been found unconstitutional, and went on to say in plain language what Plessy's opponents would not admit: that the separate car law not only separated the races but did so to accommodate white racial prejudice. Legal segregation, Harlan wrote, allowed "the seeds of race hate to be planted under the sanctions of law." He went on to say that "the thin disguise of 'equal' accommodations… will not mislead anyone, nor atone for the wrong this day done."

Harlan's words proved prophetic. The "separate but equal" doctrine relegated African American children to inadequate, unsafe schools, while the South's Jim Crow laws forbade black citizens from exercising their rights as citizens on an equal footing with white citizens. Not until the Supreme Court reversed itself in 1954's *Brown* v. *Board of Education* would African Americans be able to claim the rights promised in the U.S. Constitution.

Kate Tuttle

See Also

France; Spain; Civil War, American; Creoles; Fourteenth Amendment to the U.S. Constitution; Free Blacks in the United States, 1619 to 1863; New Orleans, Louisiana; Washington, Booker Taliaferro.

Africa

Pogoro (also known as Chipogolo and Pogolu), ethnic group of Tanzania.

The Pogoro primarily inhabit eastern Tanzania. They speak a Bantu language. More than 200,000 people consider themselves Pogoro.

See Also

Bantu: Dispersion and Settlement.

North America

Pointer Sisters, The, African American singing group.

The Pointer Sisters – Ruth (b. March 19, 1946), Anita (b. January 23, 1948), Bonnie (b. July 11, 1950), and June (b. November 20, 1954) – gained fame in the 1970s and 1980s with catchy pop songs that successfully spanned the country and rhythm and blues genres. Born and raised in Oakland, California, as children the Pointers sang in the choir of the West Oakland Church of God, where their parents were ministers. Although they performed gospel music, they grew up listening to the broad range of secular music that abounded in the Bay Area in the 1960s – jazz, soul, country, and everything in between. The Pointers quickly made contacts in the music industry, and by 1969 they were singing backup for several San Francisco-based musicians, including Elvin Bishop, Taj Mahal, Boz Scaggs, and Tower of Power.

The Pointer Sisters' self-titled debut, issued in 1973 on ABC/Blue Thumb Records, drew from blues and soul and enjoyed popular success: the single "Yes We Can Can" climbed to number 11 on the *Billboard* pop chart. Their sudden popularity led to a number of television appearances in which the sisters were featured wearing their trademark 1940s-style outfits that were reminiscent of the Andrews Sisters.

The Pointers' success continued in 1974 with the release of their second album, *That's a Plenty*, which featured the hit single "Fairytale," a song that garnered the group's first Grammy Award. The quartet was reduced to a trio when Bonnie Pointer embarked on a solo career with Motown Records in 1977, but the group remained popular, earning acclaim for its versatility. The Pointers experimented with rock on 1978's *Energy*, an album that included the hits "Happiness" and "Fire" (a cover of a Bruce Springsteen song), but focused on rhythm and blues in the 1980s, recording such hits as "Slow Hand" (1981), "What a Surprise" (1981), "Excited" (1982), "I Need You" (1983), and the Grammy Award-winning "Jump" (1983) and "Automatic" (1984). The group had its heyday in the mid-1980s, but continued to perform and record into the 1990s, switching to RCA Records in 1985 and to Motown in 1991, and starring in the musical *Ain't Misbehavin'* in 1995.

Though usually regarded as a pop or rhythm and blues group, the Pointer Sisters earned some of their highest accolades for their country performances. In 1974 they performed at the legendary Grand Ole Opry in Nashville, Tennessee, the first African American female group to do so. They were also the first black women to grace the top of *Billboard*'s country and western charts. In honor of their country roots the Pointers collaborated with Clint Black to cover "Chain of Fools" for the *Rhythm, Country and Blues* collection in 1994.

Aaron Myers

See Also
Soul Music; Blues, The; Motown; San Francisco and Oakland, California.

North America

Poitier, Sidney (b. February 20, 1927, Miami, Fla.), African American actor, director, and filmmaker, leading post-World War II African American movie star.

Sidney Poitier was raised in the Bahamas and returned to the United States as a teenager. He served in the United States Army during World War II and moved to New York in 1945 to study acting. At his first audition for the American Negro Theater, Poitier was rejected because of his strong Caribbean accent. After only six months he perfected a mainstream American accent by imitating radio announcers and was accepted on his second audition.

Poitier's first film role was in *No Way Out* (1950). Many leading roles followed, and in 1963 he became the first African American to win the Oscar for Best Actor for his performance in *Lilies of the Field.* Poitier's other films include *Blackboard Jungle* (1955), *The Defiant Ones* (1958), *In the Heat of the Night, To Sir with Love,* and *Guess Who's Coming to Dinner* (all 1967). He also originated the role of Walter Lee Younger in the 1959 Broadway production of Lorraine Hansberry's *A Raisin in the Sun.*

Poitier was the first African American to become a major Hollywood star with mainstream audiences. In the process he was criticized by some members of the black community for portraying stereotypical "noble Negroes." In response, as the 1960s ended, Poitier began to play more diverse roles. He also began to produce and direct films, and directed several hit films in the 1970s and 1980s. In 1993 Poitier won the National Association for the Advancement of Colored People's first Thurgood Marshall Lifetime Achievement Award.

Lisa Clayton Robinson

See Also
World War II and African Americans; American Negro Theatre; New York, New York; Film, Blacks in American.

Africa

Pokot (also known as Suk), ethnic group of Kenya.

The Pokot primarily inhabit the highlands of western Kenya. Some also live in eastern Uganda. They speak a Nilo-Saharan language and are one of the Kalenjin peoples. More than 200,000 people consider themselves Pokot.

See Also
Languages, African: An Overview.

Africa

Polisario (Frente Popular para la Liberación de Saguia El-Hamra y Río de Oro), a politico-military organization that has struggled for more than 20 years to gain national independence for Western Sahara.

The Popular Front for the Liberation of Saguia el-Hamra and Río de Oro, or Polisario, was founded on May 10, 1973, at a secret meeting on the Western Sahara-Mauritania border. Led mainly by some members of the Sahrawi ethnic group who had attended university together in Morocco, Polisario announced a program of violent resistance to Spanish colonialism. Ten days after its formation Polisario launched a guerrilla war against Spanish forces. Although the Spanish initially agreed to hold a referendum on independence for Western Sahara, in late 1975 they decided to allow Morocco and Mauritania to partition and occupy the territory, over the objections of most Sahrawis.

Polisario quickly denounced the new system and declared Western Sahara to be the Sahrawi Arab Democratic Republic (SADR). The organization worked to evacuate as much of the Sahrawi population as possible to a safe haven within Algeria. With support from Algeria, Polisario fought to drive out the two occupying armies. Polisario chose to focus first on Mauritania; in 1979 Mauritania was forced to relinquish its claims in Western Sahara and to recognize the SADR.

Polisario's campaign against Morocco continues today and has been less successful. Though Polisario managed to inflict heavy losses on Moroccan forces during the 1980s, Moroccan military engineers limited Polisario military incursions by encompassing Western Sahara in an earthen wall protected by motion detectors, explosives, and soldiers. Attempts at intervention by the Organization of African Unity and United Nations (UN) failed to bring a withdrawal by Morocco, which still controls nearly the entire territory.

Both Polisario and Morocco faced increasing financial difficulties in the 1990s, and in 1991 the UN brokered a cease-fire agreement, pending a referendum. Disagreements between Polisario and King Hassan II of Morocco over the eligibility of voters caused repeated postponements of the referendum.

Robert Fay

See Also
United Nations in Africa; Spain.

Latin America and the Caribbean

Political Parties and Black Social Movements in Latin America and the Caribbean, struggles for racial equality by African-descended populations during the course of the twentieth century in the Caribbean and Latin America; these have more often taken the shape of social and cultural movements seeking cultural recognition and civil rights than formal political parties.

In the Spanish- and Portuguese-influenced Caribbean and Latin America, myths of racial harmony have served to de-emphasize racial difference and identification. Instead, the stories have emphasized one single national identity despite evidence of racial discrimination in the areas of employment and education and in derogatory stereotypes concerning African and African-descended peoples. As a consequence, people of African descent in many Latin American nation-states rarely organize themselves in terms of racial solidarity or common cultural origin.

Ironically, the first black political parties in the hemisphere were founded by people of African descent in Spanish and Portuguese colonies. These were the Partido Independiente de Color of Cuba and the Frente Negra Brasileira of Brazil, founded in 1908 and 1931 respectively. Both parties were ultimately outlawed via legislation that prohibited political organization according to race and equated black political mobilization for equal rights with racial prejudice and chauvinism. The histories of these parties and their repression by Cuban and Brazilian governments underscore how difficult it was for African-descended populations to organize racially specific political parties in the former Spanish and Portuguese colonies. Often Afro-Latin peoples who have protested and organized against racial discrimination in their countries have been characterized as racist and antinational.

In the English-speaking Caribbean and Latin America, however, differences in ideology, colonial rule, and the racial composition of former colonies have made racial difference and inequality important factors in political mobilization. The first difference between the Anglophone societies and others in the Caribbean and Latin America is the length of time that those in each group were subject to colonial rule. By the mid-nineteenth century most Spanish colonies in the New World had obtained independence, Cuba being a notable exception. By contrast, the move toward national independence in the English-speaking Caribbean would begin in earnest only after World War II. The first attempt at political autonomy in the English-speaking Caribbean was undertaken on the initiative of British colonies of the Greater Antilles. Several colonies attempted to create a West Indian Federation to seek collective independence from Britain. However, Jamaica, a critical member of the federation, abandoned the collective cause after three years. Most commentators suggest that Jamaican nationalist leader Norman Manley, father of future two-time prime minister MICHAEL MANLEY, did not want Jamaica to bear the economic and political cost of the coalition and decided to withdraw his country from the federation (*see* JAMAICA). Jamaica formally abandoned the federation initiative in 1961 and achieved independence from Britain on August 6, 1962. Jamaica's departure from the federation had long-term repercussions for independent political mobilization in the region. It effectively ended the prospects for regional consolidation and alliances against the major powers in the post-World War II period.

The processes of decolonization and the formation of nationalist movements after World War II in the English-speaking Caribbean were two factors that influenced the shape of party politics and political participation. In many colonial societies nationalist politics were deeply intertwined with racial politics, as the quest for political sovereignty was often considered parallel with the struggle for the equal rights for black populations. A key difference between such movements in the English-speaking Caribbean and similar movements in North America and the Spanish-speaking Caribbean was the fact that African Americans constituted the overwhelming majority of the population in places like Jamaica, BERMUDA, BARBADOS, GRENADA, and most Anglophone colonies. This was not always the situation in other Caribbean colonies, where African-descended populations were in the numerical or categorical minority, depending on how they were classified. In the Anglophone societies, where citizenship depended on the racial hierarchies of colonialism, aspirant nationalist parties had to deal directly with matters of race. This was unavoidable because social hierarchies were usually closely correlated to skin color in these societies and the majority of the poor were black. A second difference was that British colonial rule maintained more legally restricted patterns of racial segregation and interaction. (It should be stated that Spanish colonies like Cuba and Nicaragua, with Afro-Latin populations, had a combination of Spanish and United States influences on racial dynamics and patterns due to U.S. occupation of these countries during the first two decades of the twentieth century.) Most English-speaking colonies elected black leaders to presidential and prime ministerial posts soon after the formation of newly independent nation-states. In the Spanish-speaking Caribbean there was *mestizo* (of indigenous and European ancestry) political dominance.

In Caribbean societies with multiple non-white populations (these are often known as plural societies), racial and ethnic tensions have often determined political allegiances. The former British colonies of TRINIDAD AND TOBAGO and GUYANA (the only English-speaking country of continental South America) have East Indian- and African-descended populations that are roughly equal in size. In Guyana Forbes Burnham used politics based on race and the cold war to his advantage to limit support for and prospects for coalition with his chief rival, CHEDDI JAGAN, an East Indian Guyanese, in the 1960s. Burnham also neutralized popular support for more radical political programs offered by black intellectuals such as WALTER RODNEY.

Nationalist sentiment in Trinidad and Tobago in the 1950s led to the formation of the black-dominated People's National Movement (PNM), which won the first federal elections in Trinidad in 1958. ERIC WILLIAMS, the dominant political figure of the Trinidadian independence movement and author of *The Negro in the Caribbean* and *Capitalism and Slavery*, attempted to unify Trinidad under the banner of nonracialism. As chief minister of the PNM he sought to avoid the cold war isolation that plagued Cuba because of the Cuban Revolution's adoption of socialist principles and its incorporation into the Soviet Bloc. Williams dismissed socialism because it would have alienated East Indians and Chinese in the rural areas of Trinidad, who were mainly small landholders. The PNM eventually became embroiled in intense political competition with the East Indian-dominated Democratic Labour Party, led by Radaranth Capildeo. Successive elections and periods of rule were marked with intermittent ethnic and racial conflict. This unrest culminated in a general strike in 1970 and a short-lived black power movement that attempted to unite students and East Indian and black working classes in an assault on what black-power advocates called "Afro-Saxonism," or black neocolonialism in the country. After Williams's death in 1981 the PNM, led by Williams's successor, George Chambers, continued to lead the country until a massive defeat in the 1986 general elections. The PNM was defeated by the National Alliance for Reconstruction (NAF), whose political platform was marked more by a desire to end PNM rule than by a unified coalition of diverse ideological interests. The "One Love" campaign of the NAF sought to replace the ethno-political tenor of Trinidadian party politics with a more ideologically based party competition. This attempt foundered by 1990 as the party's leader, A. N. R. Robinson, a former protege of Eric Williams, was accused of black partisanship by East Indian party members. Abu Bakr, an Afro-Trinidadian Muslim, led a coup attempt in 1990, plunging the nation into a six-day crisis. National dissatisfaction with Robinson did not translate into support for Bakr's coup d'état. Like Williams, the PNM, the black power movement, and the NAF, Bakr tried to unify economically disadvantaged blacks and East Indian Muslims, but to no avail. As in Jamaica and Grenada, two other black-dominated societies with a history of multiparty politics, the association of a specific political party or regime with the state itself led to heightened tensions during electoral campaigns that were manifested in mass demonstrations and violence.

In addition to problems of political participation in multiethnic and multiracial societies after independence, many Caribbean societies experienced the brunt of economic recession by the late 1970s and 1980s. This financial lull limited the ability of dominant political parties to make good on campaign promises of economic revival and political reform. In Jamaica the charismatic, cerebral Michael Manley was prime minister twice in the 1970s (1972-1977; 1977-1980) and led the People's National Party during this period. Manley's regime represented an alternative path of democratic socialist development, an attempt to create an economy combining state intervention and social welfare policies with socioeconomic growth and industrial development.

By the 1970s Jamaica emerged as a pivotal nation-state within the ambit of "Third World" politics. Jamaica's status had a profound impact on Afro-diasporic communities in other parts of the Caribbean and Africa, as Manley attempted to steer his political party and Jamaica away from the geopolitical imperatives of the United States. Recession, inflation, and cold war rhetoric proved to be difficult obstacles for the Manley regime and were used to full political advantage by Edward Seaga of the Jamaican Labour Party (JLP), who was elected prime minister in 1980.

In GRENADA the rise of the popular New Jewel Movement and installation via coup d'état of the charismatic MAURICE BISHOP to the position of president in 1979 further complicated Caribbean politics. By the late 1970s Caribbean nations were often forced to align themselves with the United States or risk economic and political isolation.

Like Manley, Bishop alienated the United States by expressing solidarity with Cuba and the nonaligned movements of Third World peoples, and the Reagan administration was far less tolerant of ideological diversity in the region than the Carter administration had been. Following the triumph of the Nicaraguan Sandinista revolution in March 1979, both the Carter and Reagan administrations perceived the increasing autonomy of Manley and Bishop as a threat to U.S. dominance and a sign of increasing Soviet influence. The "red scare" would be put to good use by Edward Seaga during the Jamaican national elections of 1980. Seaga's close relations with the Reagan administration guaranteed monetary aid from both the United States and international lending sources.

In October 1983 the U.S. Marines invaded the island of Grenada. The invasion was undertaken under the pretext of protecting U.S. citizens, mainly students, against an alleged communist threat. The supposed danger was posed by the presence of Cuban construction workers on the island to assist in the construction of an airport, and by the assassination of Maurice Bishop after an internal power struggle between Bishop supporters and a more sectarian, Marxist-Leninist faction led by cabinet member Bernard Coard. Construction workers as well as Grenadan citizens were killed during the invasion. The U.S. students, whose lives were never endangered during the entire crisis, were unharmed and evacuated from the island without incident.

In relatively new nation-states such as these, political conflict often threatens not only particular regimes but the nation's ability to govern itself. The vulnerability of Trinidadian and Grenadan governments in times of crisis highlights the precarious position of new governments and civil societies during moments of political turmoil. It is important to recognize, however, that these nation-states are quite young in relation to other nation-states in the Americas and even in Europe. When contrasted with the long, often bloody periods of authoritarian rule in Cuba, Salvador, Guatemala, and the Dominican Republic, black social movements and political parties of these regions have undergone rapid transformations as these countries have moved from colonies to independent states and developing nations in a short period of time. In these and other independent societies of the English-speaking Caribbean that gained independence over the past 30 years, however, the political sovereignty of national independence has not been accompanied by economic and geopolitical sovereignty.

Michael Hanchard

See Also
Burnham, Linden Forbes Sampson; Manley, Norman Washington.

North America

Polk, Prentice Herman

(b. November 25, 1898, Bessemar, Ala.; d. December 29, 1984, Tuskegee, Ala.), photographer and documentarian of the Tuskegee Institute community as well as the everyday lives of slaves and sharecroppers.

Prentice Herman Polk became interested in photography at a young age. He began studying through a correspondence course that he paid for with $10 he was mistakenly given as change after buying a candy bar at a local store.

Polk attended Tuskegee Institute from 1916 to 1920 and was appointed to the faculty of the photography department in 1928. He served as department head from 1933 to 1938. Between 1933 and 1982 he was the official school photographer, taking pictures of members of the Tuskegee community and of visitors such as Henry Ford and Eleanor Roosevelt. He also chronicled the experiences of George Washington Carver. Polk retired in 1982.

See Also
Tuskegee University; Photography, African American.

North America

Pollard, Frederick Douglass (Fritz)

(b. January 27, 1894, Chicago, Ill.; d. May 11, 1986, Silver Spring, Md.), pioneer African American football player and the first African American coach in the National Football League (NFL).

Frederick "Fritz" Pollard grew up in Chicago, Illinois, and inherited a love of sports from his father, a former boxer, and his older brothers, who played football. By the time he graduated from Chicago's Albert G. Lane Technical High School, he was an accomplished baseball player, a star running back, and a three-time Cook County track champion. After high school he briefly attended and played football for Northwestern, Harvard, and Dartmouth before receiving a scholarship from the Rockefeller family to attend Brown University in 1915. Though just 1.7 m (5 ft 8 in) and 67.5 kg (150 lb) and initially ostracized by his teammates, Pollard eventually became a star running back and defensive player for the Brown football team, leading the squad to a 1916 Rose Bowl game against Washington State. He was the first African American ever to play in the Rose Bowl, and the second to be named an All-American in college football.

After leaving Brown Pollard briefly pursued a degree in dentistry, worked as director of an army YMCA, and coached football at Lincoln University before being signed to play professionally for the Akron Pros in the American Professional Football League (APFA). Leading the Pros to a championship in 1920, Pollard was named head coach in 1921 and continued to play for the Pros as well. The APFA was renamed the NFL in 1922, making Pollard the first African American coach in NFL history. Pollard remained with the Pros until 1926, and went on to coach NFL teams in Indiana and Milwaukee. He remained the only African American to have coached in the NFL until the 1990s.

In the late 1920s and 1930s Pollard successfully coached African American football teams in Chicago and New York before retiring from football in 1937 to pursue a career in business.

Though he struggled against harassment and racial discrimination throughout his collegiate and professional careers (hostile players and crowds would often hurl insults and objects at him), Pollard brought spectacular talent and admirable dignity to American football and helped to create opportunities for later black players and coaches. He was inducted into the National Football Foundation's collegiate Hall of Fame in 1954, and became the first African American inducted into Brown's Football Hall of Fame in 1971.

Lisa Clayton Robinson

See Also
Baseball in the United States; Boxing; Football, Collegiate; Football, Professional.

North America

Poor People's Washington Campaign,

a demonstration in Washington, D.C., organized in 1968 by the Southern Christian Leadership Conference (SCLC) to demand federal legislation ensuring employment, income, and housing for the poor.

On June 19, 1968, more than 50,000 people assembled in Washington, D.C., to voice their support for the Poor People's Campaign for economic justice in America. The day was the highlight of the Southern Christian Leadership Conference (SCLC) campaign, set in motion by Martin Luther King Jr. to secure federal legislation guaranteeing employment, income, and housing for the poor. Considered only minimally successful by most historians, the Poor People's Campaign has been called the last of the 1960s mass mobilizations of nonviolent resistance.

The Poor People's Campaign marked several important shifts in the orientation of SCLC as a whole, and in the thinking of King, its leader. The SCLC had expanded its operations from a regional base in the South to a national operation by the mid-1960s. In the South rural blacks had faced debilitating poverty and segregation: a National Association for the Advancement of Colored People (NAACP) survey in Mississippi found that blacks there suffered from hunger, malnutrition, and even starvation. In Northern cities such as Chicago the SCLC found an urban crisis of poverty grounded in ingrained racist economic structures. Here, the organization found, the forces of institutionalized racism did not yield to the strategies of resistance used against segregation in the South.

King became increasingly critical of a federal government and capitalist system that left a large population of African Americans, urban and rural, in poverty. He said: "We are called upon to help the discouraged beggars in life's market place. But one day we must come to see that an edifice which produces beggars needs restructuring." King pointed directly at the "edifice" of the federal government, which he had formerly viewed as a benevolent force that needed only to understand the conditions under which blacks lived in order to join the fight for change. Poverty, King now claimed, was to blame for the urban riots that plagued the country, and capitalism was to blame for poverty: "When you begin to ask why are there 40 million poor people in America, you are raising questions about the economic system, about a broader distribution of wealth. When you ask that question, you begin to question the capitalistic economy."

King took up the suggestion of Marian Wright to have the poor demonstrate in Washington, D.C., and if necessary, disrupt the national government. He envisioned a "tent city," with protesters living out of temporary structures on the mall of Capitol Hill. Unlike King's earlier campaigns for African American equality, this movement was to be staged on behalf of a spectrum of peoples, including Native Americans, Mexican Americans, Puerto Ricans, and Appalachian whites.

King began mobilizing the SCLC for a national campaign amid fears of an increasingly violent turn in the struggle for rights. The campaign moved slowly, in part for this reason and in part because of financial and organizational difficulties. Civil rights activists, such as Bayard Rustin and NAACP Executive Secretary Roy Wilkins, questioned the wisdom of a mass march on Washington that might lead to violence, while others, namely President Lyndon B. Johnson and the Federal Bureau of Investigation, waged an outright campaign to derail the organizing process. When a march led by King in Memphis, Tennessee, to support striking sanitation workers turned violent, it seemed to be the end of the campaign to march on Washington.

King's assassination on April 4, 1968, turned the tide of support for the march, and within a month over $500,000 in donations poured in for King's movement. The new SCLC leader, the Rev. Ralph Abernathy, kept the movement going, and former opponents of the march, such as Rustin, now joined in.

On May 13 the first residents of Resurrection City set up house, populating West Potomac Park in tents made from canvas and plywood. By late May, 2500 people were living there, including groups from Tennessee, New Mexico, Chicago, and the Mississippi Delta. Each day Resurrection City residents marched to various federal agencies to present demands. They joined more than 50,000 others on Solidarity Day, June 19, for a mass demonstration organized by Sterling Tucker and led by Abernathy and Coretta Scott King. Five days later 1500 police arrived, arresting hundreds and destroying Resurrection City.

For some who had been active in the early successes of the SCLC, the Poor People's Campaign was a failure. Many found the protest poorly organized despite its ample funding, and some protesters were critical of SCLC leaders who slept at night in a motel. For others, who remembered King's prophecy that organizing around the basic rights of jobs and income would prove even more difficult than opposing the Vietnam War, the Poor People's Campaign was a necessary turn from protests against segregation to a larger demand for economic justice.

Marian Aguiar

See Also

Abernathy, Ralph David; American Indians; Chicago, Illinois; Edelman, Marian Wright; King, Martin Luther, Jr.; Wilkins, Roy Ottoway; Puerto Rico.

Africa

Popular Movement for the Liberation of Angola (Movimento Popular de Libertação de Angola), a leading nationalist organization and a major political party in Angola.

According to the movement's official history, two small nationalist groups created the Popular Movement for the Liberation of Angola (MPLA) in 1956. From the outset the MPLA's support came primarily from urban, educated members of the Ovimbundu ethnic group, Portuguese Marxists, and *mestiços,* or those of mixed African and European parentage. Despite the Portuguese colonial authorities' efforts to suppress nationalist activities, the MPLA succeeded in organizing the 1961 attack on the Luanda prison that the movement came to consider the beginning of the war for independence.

During the war the MPLA competed for international and national support with the National Front for the Liberation of Angola (FNLA) and the National Union for the Total Independence of Angola (UNITA). Although the MPLA had not achieved military dominance, when Portugal withdrew from Angola in 1975, the group was able to capture the capital and thereby proclaim victory. The movement's first leader, Agostinho Neto, became president of independent Angola.

The war did not end at independence, and UNITA fought the MPLA government for the next two decades. In 1977 the MPLA renamed itself the MPLA-Workers Party (MPLA-PT), officially adopted Marxist-Leninism, and began a program to transform radically the Angolan economy. With Soviet assistance and advice, the MPLA-PT nationalized most industries, especially agriculture and mining, and renegotiated contracts with Western oil companies. President José Eduardo dos Santos and the MPLA-PT ran Angola as a one-party state, though the party was not monolithic as it was divided along ideological, ethnic, racial, and urban-rural lines. In 1990, with the war going poorly, the MPLA-PT leadership ceded to international pressure to introduce a new constitution calling for economic and political liberalization, including a multiparty system. Elections in 1992 gave MPLA-PT candidates a majority of seats in parliament, but UNITA refused to recognize the results and resumed the war. In early 1997, as the peace process progressed, the MPLA-PT became the majority party in the government of national reconciliation.

Eric Young

See Also

Luanda, Angola; Nationalism in Africa.

Africa

Population Growth in Sub-Saharan Africa, historical and contemporary trends in fertility, mortality, and population growth rates in Africa.

Up until the past century, Africa's population has grown slowly by world standards. Twentieth-century improvements in hygiene and medical care, however, dramatically reduced mortality rates and contributed to a period of extremely rapid growth between the 1950s and the 1980s. According to a 1997 United Nations estimate, the average woman in Africa has 5.3 children during her lifetime. (In contrast, women in Europe have only 1.6 children on average.) But fertility rates have begun to decline in several African countries due to a combination of urbanization, education, and increased contraceptive use. If current trends continue, the population in Africa may stabilize shortly after 2050 at just over 2 billion people.

African Population Growth in History

For most of human history Africa, like other continents, was inhabited by small groups of foragers who had relatively low rates of population growth. Consequently, in Africa as elsewhere, the total population grew slowly until the advent of agriculture, perhaps around 10,000 years ago. Although increased food supplies supported higher fertility rates, mortality rates remained high in Africa due to the prevalence of tropical disease. Famines brought on by pestilence and periodic droughts also claimed lives. Until relatively recently, then, most of Africa's agrarian societies have lived under conditions of abundant land but scarce labor. These conditions supported cultural norms that valued large families. Having many children ensured an adequate labor supply, even if some children died, and also provided a degree of old-age security for parents.

European contact from the fifteenth century onward brought new diseases to

Africa, including smallpox, syphilis, and gonorrhea. Although these diseases claimed many lives in Africa, they were much less devastating than they had been in the New World. A far more significant demographic consequence of European expansion was the TRANSATLANTIC SLAVE TRADE. Between the sixteenth and nineteenth centuries, perhaps 12 million Africans were taken aboard ships headed for the Americas. Millions more were sold into the INDIAN OCEAN SLAVE TRADE during this period, and countless others died during slave raids or en route to coastal slave forts. In addition, some groups fleeing slave raiders ended up in regions where sleeping sickness and other deadly diseases were endemic.

European colonialism (*see* COLONIAL RULE) had mixed effects on African population growth. In some regions, especially Central Africa, colonization brought devastating epidemics of foreign diseases such as smallpox. In 1913, for example, a doctor in Nyasaland (present-day MALAWI) estimated that 93 percent of all adults and 63 percent of all children had been infected with smallpox. Tens of thousands of Africans were also killed by accidents, brutal discipline, and disease in mining camps and on railroad projects. In addition, some European military actions against regional uprisings took a huge toll: the German crackdown on the HERERO rebellion in southwest Africa (modern-day NAMIBIA) between 1904 and 1907 led to the deaths of 65,000 of the original population of 80,000 Herero. Colonial land and labor policies that compelled Africans to forgo food-crop cultivation for cash cropping or migrant labor also increased vulnerability to famine in some areas, though famine itself was not a new phenomenon. Parts of Upper Volta (present-day BURKINA FASO) experienced famine in 1931, after a combination of drought and plunging world cotton prices left peasants with neither food nor the money to buy it. Nyasaland also experienced a severe famine in 1949. Finally, venereal diseases (which often led to infertility) and tuberculosis plagued both African and European inhabitants of many colonial-era cities and mining towns.

Nevertheless, colonial public health and sanitation campaigns – aimed partly at improving the health and survival rates of European troops and civil servants stationed in Africa – led to a dramatic drop in mortality rates after World War II. Colonial administrations built hospitals and urban water systems, and undertook smallpox vaccination programs. During the late colonial period improved access to clean water significantly reduced the incidence of waterborne diseases such as cholera. The development of effective or at least improved treatments for a variety of killers – tuberculosis, syphilis, measles, polio, and malaria – also affected mortality rates, as did improved education campaigns on the causes of infant diarrhea. These measures may have con-

POPULATION GROWTH IN AFRICA

Country	Annual population growth rate 1998
Algeria	2.14
Angola	2.84
Benin	3.31
Botswana	1.11
Burkina Faso	2.72
Burundi	3.51
Cameroon	2.81
Cape Verde	1.49
Central African Republic	2.02
Chad	2.66
Comoros	3.10
Congo, Democratic Republic of the	2.99
Congo, Republic of the	2.21
Côte d'Ivoire	2.41
Djibouti	1.51
Egypt	1.86
Equatorial Guinea	2.56
Eritrea	3.39
Ethiopia	2.21
Gabon	1.48
Gambia, The	3.42
Ghana	2.13
Guinea	0.83
Guinea-Bissau	2.32
Kenya	1.71
Lesotho	1.91
Liberia	5.76
Libya	3.68
Madagascar	2.81
Malawi	1.66
Mali	3.24
Mauritania	2.52
Mauritius	1.20
Morocco	1.89
Mozambique	2.57
Namibia	1.60
Niger	2.96
Nigeria	2.96
Réunion	1.81
Rwanda	2.50
São Tomé and Príncipe	3.10
Senegal	3.33
Seychelles	0.67
Sierra Leone	4.01
Somalia	4.43
South Africa	1.42
Sudan	2.73
Swaziland	1.96
Tanzania	2.14
Togo	3.52
Tunisia	1.43
Uganda	2.85
Western Sahara	2.40
Zambia	2.13
Zimbabwe	1.12

Source: *U.S. Central Intelligence Agency, World Factbook* 1998

POPULATION LESS THAN 15 YEARS OF AGE IN AFRICA

Country	% of Population Under 15 Years Old
Algeria	38
Angola	45
Benin	48
Botswana	42
Burkina Faso	48
Burundi	47
Cameroon	46
Cape Verde	44
Central African Republic	42
Chad	44
Comoros	43
Congo, Democratic Republic of the	48
Congo, Republic of the	43
Côte d'Ivoire	47
Djibouti	43
Egypt	36
Equatorial Guinea	43
Eritrea	43
Ethiopia	46
Gabon	33
Gambia, The	46
Ghana	43
Guinea	44
Guinea-Bissau	42
Kenya	44
Lesotho	40
Liberia	45
Libya	48
Madagascar	45
Malawi	46
Mali	47
Mauritania	46
Mauritius	26
Morocco	36
Mozambique	45
Namibia	44
Niger	48
Nigeria	45
Réunion	32
Rwanda	46
São Tomé and Príncipe	48
Senegal	48
Seychelles	30
Sierra Leone	45
Somalia	44
South Africa	35
Sudan	45
Swaziland	46
Tanzania	45
Togo	48
Tunisia	32
Uganda	51
Western Sahara	N/A
Zambia	49
Zimbabwe	44

Source: *U.S. Central Intelligence Agency, World Factbook* 1998

INFANT MORTALITY RATE IN AFRICA (Deaths per 1000 live births; 1998 estimate)

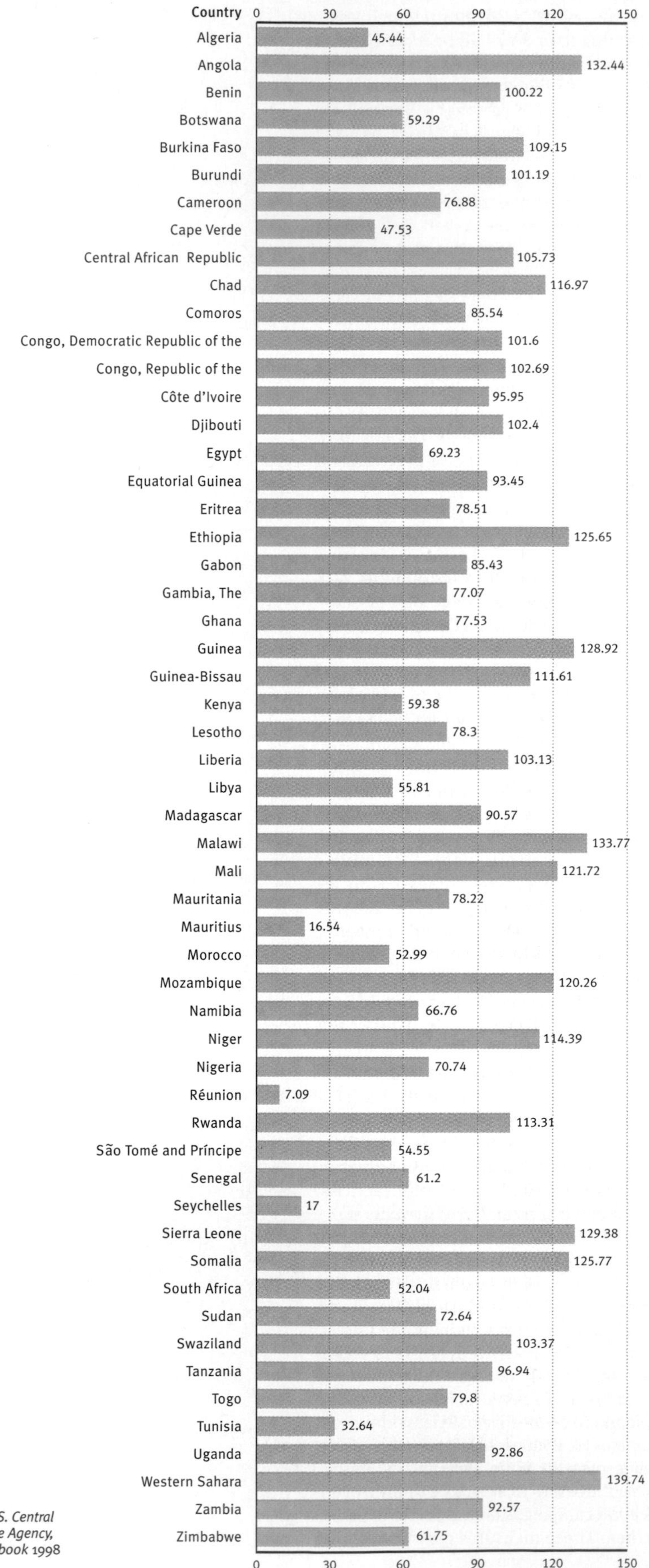

Source: *U.S. Central Intelligence Agency, World Factbook 1998*

tributed to slight increases in fertility rates in some areas, such as the Belgian Congo (present-day DEMOCRATIC REPUBLIC OF THE CONGO). Diseases such as gonorrhea that caused infertility had been more rare, while birth spacing, a practice intended to maximize infant survivability, shortened in response to reduced infant mortality.

As a result of these changes African populations began to increase dramatically in the 1950s. By the 1960s the continent's overall population was growing at approximately 3 percent annually, a rate that remained constant through the 1980s. Many observers in the mid-twentieth century assumed that urbanization and industrialization would lead to a demographic shift toward smaller family size, as had occurred in Europe. But industrialization in Africa has been limited to a few countries, and elsewhere urbanization alone did not, for decades, bring down fertility rates.

POPULATION GROWTH AND ECONOMIC DEVELOPMENT

African national population growth rates continue to rank among the highest in the world. Except in a few small countries, however – RWANDA, BURUNDI, LESOTHO, and MAURITIUS – population densities remain relatively low. Currently, Africa covers 25 percent of the earth's land surface but contains only about 12 percent of the world's population (about 758 million people). However, by 2050 the population, expected to exceed 2.265 billion, would account for 23 percent of the world's population, and NIGERIA, already Africa's most populous nation, would be the fifth most populous in the world.

Scholars disagree about Africa's capacity to support a much larger population in the future. A great deal will depend not only on how much food Africa will be able to grow for itself – a factor contingent on potential climatic shifts and developments in agricultural technology, among other things – but also on Africa's overall economic prosperity. Currently, the majority of the continent's people depend on land-based livelihoods, but industrialization and increased power on world markets would allow African countries to support potentially much higher population densities.

The more immediate problem for many African countries is that neither government nor the private sector can keep up with the rapidly growing need for housing, education and other social services, and employment. Already, large cities such as Johannesburg and Nairobi suffer acute shortages of affordable housing, and primary schools across much of the continent are severely overcrowded and underequipped. Some groups, such as Population Action International, argue that population growth rates must decrease – and with them public expenditures on social services – if Africa is ever to achieve sustained economic development. But others argue that fertility rates and, consequently, population growth rates will fall only if people have access to education, improved medical care, and greater economic security.

Current Demographic Trends

The preference for large families remains widespread in many parts of Africa. Having many children is seen not only as proof of virility, but also as a strategy for increasing the chances that at least some children will be successful and therefore able to provide for the rest of the family. In addition, children's labor is still considered an economic asset, especially in rural areas and among the many families who make their living in small-scale urban trade and artisanal activities.

But according to the United Nations, fertility rates are declining in several African countries. The fertility rate in Kenya dropped from an estimated 7.5 during the period between 1980 and 1985 to 5.4 between 1990 and 1995. Within the same ten-year period, the fertility rate in Côte d'Ivoire decreased from 7.4 to 5.7. The decline is generally linked to family-planning education and families' changing economic demands, among other factors. In North Africa fertility rates have been declining for several decades, due primarily to women's later marriage ages and the increasing use of contraception. But in sub-Saharan Africa it was not until the 1980s, when contraceptives first became widely available, that fertility rates began to drop. Countries such as Madagascar and Tanzania have joined Kenya, Botswana, and others in showing a decline in the fertility rate.

The reduction in fertility found in many African countries is probably also a result of the perceived escalating costs of having a large family. A 1991 study in Kenya showed increasing concern about large families among both men and women. School fees are an especially important consideration. In some densely populated rural areas parents also expressed concern that they would not be able to provide numerous offspring with adequate farmland. Although women in much of Africa have always combined childbearing with work outside the home, at least in some countries there are signs that women are delaying marriage and having fewer children in order to devote more time and energy to their careers.

Demographers and epidemiologists are currently debating how the ongoing acquired immune deficiency syndrome (AIDS) epidemic will affect population growth in Africa. Today perhaps two-thirds of the world's 22 million human immunodeficiency virus (HIV) cases occur in Africa, and it is thought that as much as 15 percent of the adult population of Botswana and Zimbabwe is infected with HIV. Between 1985 and 1995 approximately 4.2 million people in Africa died from AIDS; between 1995 and 2005 the United Nations Development Program predicts that deaths from AIDS in the 24 most severely affected countries will increase mortality rates by 25 percent and reduce the average life expectancy by six years. If current trends continue, therefore, AIDS is expected to reduce the rate of population growth slightly. But the rise in infant mortality brought on by the epidemic may reverse the demographic shift, as people compensate for the disease by having more children. Precisely how AIDS affects Africa's demographic trends will depend at least in part on whether treatments or preventive vaccines become not only available but affordable in poor countries.

Family-Planning Trends

Initially, most newly independent African governments were reluctant to promote family planning, which was widely viewed as a neocolonial attempt by the West to maintain control over African populations. Kenya became the first African country to promote family planning actively when it began subsidizing contraceptives in 1967; Ghana was next, implementing family-planning policies in 1969. Many African countries have since begun their own programs, and after years of relatively slow progress, some have been fairly successful at promoting contraceptive use. In 1977-1978 only 7 percent of Kenyan couples used contraceptives, for example, but by 1993 that number had risen to 33 percent. Similar increases in contraceptive use have occurred in Rwanda and Zimbabwe. Programs geared toward educating women have been credited with the extensive adoption of contraceptives.

Birth control pills are the most widely used method of modern contraception. Depo-Provera injections are commonly used in South Africa, Kenya, and Botswana. While as of 1993 condoms were still only sporadically used as a form of birth control among married couples, countries throughout Africa have for several years promoted their use as an AIDS prophylactic. In Zaire (present-day Democratic Republic of the Congo), for example, condom sales increased from 20,000 units in 1987 to 18.3 million units in 1991.

But effective family-planning programs in Africa still suffer not only from logistical problems, such as inadequate funding and distribution systems, but also from legal and ideological obstacles. For example, in Kenya women under age 18 are unable to obtain contraceptives legally, leading to many teenage pregnancies and subsequent illegal abortions. The Roman Catholic Church, which opposes many current family-planning practices, is a powerful lobbying group in many African countries, making governments reluctant to endorse either contraceptive use or abortion. In response, governments of countries in which the Roman Catholic Church is influential, such as Kenya, have couched family-planning policies in terms of improving women's health rather than limiting population growth.

Ari Nave

LIFE EXPECTANCY AT BIRTH IN AFRICA

Country	Male	Female
Algeria	67.78	70.12
Angola	45.60	50.23
Benin	51.56	55.72
Botswana	39.46	40.75
Burkina Faso	45.38	46.85
Burundi	43.79	47.38
Cameroon	49.90	53.03
Cape Verde	67.21	73.89
Central African Republic	45.02	48.68
Chad	45.81	50.73
Comoros	57.95	62.84
Congo, Democratic Republic of the	47.27	51.40
Congo, Republic of the	45.29	48.89
Côte d'Ivoire	44.73	47.80
Djibouti	49.06	53.15
Egypt	60.09	64.14
Equatorial Guinea	51.61	56.31
Eritrea	53.19	57.51
Ethiopia	39.76	41.97
Gabon	53.55	59.56
Gambia, The	51.59	56.29
Ghana	54.77	58.92
Guinea	43.58	48.52
Guinea-Bissau	47.47	50.85
Kenya	47.02	48.13
Lesotho	52.18	55.81
Liberia	56.81	62.16
Libya	63.21	67.78
Madagascar	51.70	54.10
Malawi	36.64	36.54
Mali	45.67	48.43
Mauritania	46.95	53.11
Mauritius	67.05	74.74
Morocco	66.49	70.64
Mozambique	44.22	46.55
Namibia	41.73	41.24
Niger	41.83	41.21
Nigeria	52.68	54.45
Réunion	72.36	78.60
Rwanda	41.49	42.40
São Tomé and Príncipe	62.87	65.86
Senegal	54.55	60.28
Seychelles	66.13	75.53
Sierra Leone	45.56	51.66
Somalia	44.66	47.85
South Africa	53.56	57.80
Sudan	55.00	56.98
Swaziland	37.31	39.79
Tanzania	44.22	48.59
Togo	56.52	61.12
Tunisia	71.72	74.58
Uganda	41.81	43.41
Western Sahara	47.32	49.83
Zambia	36.81	37.33
Zimbabwe	39.12	39.19

Source: *U.S. Central Intelligence Agency, World Factbook* 1998

See Also
Drought and Desertification; Johannesburg, South Africa; Nairobi, Kenya; United Nations in Africa; Urbanism and Urbanization in Africa; AIDS in Africa: An Interpretation.

Latin America and the Caribbean

Porres, San Martín de

(b. December 9, 1579, Lima, Peru; d. November 3, 1639, Lima, Peru), Afro-Peruvian saint canonized in 1962.

Six officially recognized saints lived in colonial Peru during the sixteenth and seventeenth centuries, four of whom belonged to the Dominican order: Toribio de Mogrovejo (1538-1606), second archbishop of Lima and defender of the Indians; Francisco Solano (1549-1619), a Franciscan missionary, musician, and evangelizer of the south; Rosa de Lima (1586-1617), a tertiary of the Order of Preachers and the first native in the New World to be canonized; Juan Macías (1585-1645), a lay brother of the same order and a servant of the poor; Ana de los Ángeles Monteagudo (1602-1686), a mystic nun of a cloistered convent in Arequipa; and Martín de Porres. In the context of this generation of saints, Martín is distinctive for being the first mulatto (person of African and European descent) ever to be canonized by the Roman Catholic Church.

De Porres was born in Lima on December 9, 1579, the natural son of Juan de Porres, a Spanish nobleman, and Ana Velázquez, a free black woman from Panama. His interracial and illegitimate origins were common in Spanish America during the colonization period (*see* Colonial Latin America and the Caribbean). Although his parents never married, his father assumed responsibility for Martín and his sister, and brought them with him to Guayaquil (Ecuador), where Martín received his elementary schooling. During his childhood and adolescence he showed signs of a fine sensitivity and a unique generosity for the sick and the poor.

Saint Martín de Porres is the patron saint of interracial justice. *Oronoz*

When Martín was 12 years old, his father brought him back to Lima and left him in the care of his mother, who apprenticed him to a barber-surgeon. Given the important social role that a barber-surgeon had at the time, this was a meaningful mentorship for the young Martín, who quickly gained a reputation as a healer. Three years later, at age 15, he received the habit of the Third Order of Saint Dominic and entered the Rosary convent of the Friar Priests in Lima, where he spent the next 45 years.

The Dominican order prohibited black men from receiving the habit. For this reason, Martín de Porres entered the order as a *donate* (servant) for nine years, without being allowed to become a member. However, in 1603, after Martin showed much devotion and dedication to helping the poor and sick, the order made an exception and admitted him as a lay brother. As an official member of the community, he worked as a barber, healer, and farmer, and allegedly performed miraculous cures on sick people and animals.

Martín based his spiritual life on the strictest practices of prayer and penance, according to the ascetic models of his time. His charity reputedly had no limits either in or out of his convent. He disregarded racial remarks belittling him and tried to aid those who called on him. The future saint was instrumental in founding an orphanage and a foundling hospital in the city of Lima. He also ministered among the African slaves who were brought to Peru (*see* Slavery in Latin America and the Caribbean). Even animals received the benefit of his generosity.

Martín died on November 3, 1639, at age 60. His funeral is remembered as one of the most solemn events in Lima at the time. Prelates and nobles were his pallbearers among the multitude of the poor who accompanied their benefactor to his tomb.

Martín de Porres was beatified two centuries later by Pope Gregory XVI in 1837. In 1945 Pope Pius XII proclaimed him the patron of social justice. He was canonized in 1962 by Pope John XXIII in the context of the preparation for the Second Vatican Council. Martín's fame has transcended the boundaries of Peru and South America. For his followers in the five continents, he represents a different paradigm of holiness. As an illegitimate child and a person of color, he was subjected to social and ecclesiastical discrimination, yet he became a symbol of understanding and compassion.

Carlos Parra

See Also
Catholic Church in Latin America and the Caribbean.

Latin America and the Caribbean

Port-au-Prince, Haiti, capital of Haiti and of Ouest Department on the Gonâve Gulf.

Port-au-Prince is the principal seaport and commercial center of Haiti. Major manufactured goods include processed food, beverages, tobacco products, textiles, and building materials. Tourism and construction are also important to the city's economy. Port-au-Prince is the site of the State University of Haiti (founded 1920), the National Library, the National Museum, the Archaeological Museum, the Art Center, a technical institute, and a polytechnic college. Other points of interest include the National Palace, the Basilica of Notre Dame, and the French-built stone quay (1780).

The settlement was laid out by the French in 1749 and served as the capital of the French colony of Saint-Domingue from 1770 to 1804. When Haiti became independent in 1804, the city was chosen as the new nation's capital (*see* Haitian Revolution).

North America

Porter, James Amos

(b. December 22, 1905, Baltimore, Md.; d. February 28, 1970, Washington, D.C.), African American painter and art historian, instrumental in the development of the scholarly study of African American art.

Raised in Baltimore, Maryland, James Porter studied art as an undergraduate at Howard University, graduating in 1927. He joined the Howard faculty that same year as a drawing and painting instructor and remained a professor there until the end of his life.

The first exhibition of one of Porter's paintings was in 1928. Group and solo exhibitions followed in the United States and abroad. In 1937, already an acknowledged teacher and painter, he earned an M.A. in art history from New York University. In 1935 and 1945 he received Rockefeller Foundation grants, and traveled to Europe, Haiti, and Cuba to seek inspiration for his work.

As an artist, Porter was best known for his portraits, including the prize-winning *Woman Holding a Jug* (1933). Several of his paintings are now held by the National Archives in Washington, D.C., and his portrait of his wife, Dorothy Burnett Porter, curator of the Moorland-Spingarn Research Center at Howard University, is in the National Portrait Gallery.

Porter made his most lasting mark, however, as a historian and scholar of African American art. His landmark study, *Modern Negro Art*, published in 1943, remains a foundational text. Porter gave generous attention to his contemporaries in painting and sculpture and helped legitimize their contributions to American art by examining their artistic styles.

See Also
Moorland-Spingarn Research Collection; Wesley, Dorothy Burnett Porter.

Africa

Porto-Novo, Benin, capital and second-largest city of the People's Republic of Benin.

The capital of Benin, Porto-Novo is located on the West African coast, southeast of the port of Cotonou. Originally a village known as Ajase, it was founded during the seventeenth century by an Allada group fleeing conquest by the kingdom of Dahomey. Ajase was conquered by the Yoruba kingdom of Oyo in 1730 and became the kingdom's main port.

During the eighteenth century Ajase served as the Oyo's primary port in the transatlantic slave trade. Portuguese merchants gained extensive influence in the region, and in 1752 they renamed the port Porto-Novo. In the early nineteenth century, however, the Oyo lost control of the region, and the Portuguese ceded the land to the French. The king of Porto-Novo, fearful of a Dahomean invasion, asked the French for protection; the port was subsequently made a French protectorate. Dahomean attacks on Porto-Novo in the 1880s led to the 1890 and 1892 Franco-Dahomean wars, which in turn led to French colonization in 1894. Porto-Novo became the capital of colonial Dahomey in 1900.

Under French colonial rule, Porto-Novo became the colony's main administrative and economic center. After independence, however, most seafaring commerce moved to the deeper and safer port of neighboring Cotonou. Government followed suit, and by the mid-1970s Cotonou had essentially become Benin's capital. Consequently, Porto-Novo has few of the modern amenities found in most African capitals; paved roads and reliable phone lines are scarce. Nevertheless, Porto-Novo remains the official capital of Benin and continues to house important cultural centers, such as the National Archives and the National Library, and national treasures, including the recently restored palace of King Toffa, the last king of Porto-Novo. Today Porto-Novo has a population of more than 180,000.

Elizabeth Heath

See Also
Dahomey, Early Kingdom of; France; Oyo, Early Kingdom of; Portugal; Cotonou, Benin.

North America

Port Royal Experiment, a series of events that took place after the United States Navy occupied South Carolina's Sea Islands in 1861, liberating thousands of slaves. This event has been called a "rehearsal" for Reconstruction because it dealt informally and on a small scale with many of the social, political, and economic questions that would arise in the aftermath of the Civil War, and it underscored some of the differing responses to the issues made by whites and blacks.

The name "Port Royal Experiment" is misleading because it suggests a guiding plan or institution. The reality was quite different. The individuals and groups who participated in the Port Royal Experiment – government agents, soldiers, philanthropists, and land speculators among them – converged on this area of the South Carolina coast independently of each other and with their own intentions for the newly liberated blacks. The Port Royal Experiment began on November 6, 1861, when plantation owners on South Carolina's Sea Islands fled the approaching U.S. Navy and abandoned their plantations – leaving behind nearly 10,000 slaves.

Slaves on the Sea Islands had lived far more independently than their counterparts on the mainland. After completing their daily assigned tasks, for example, blacks on the Sea Islands had the remainder of the day for their own pursuits, such as hunting, fishing, or cultivating their own food. Many blacks had sold their produce and purchased small plots of land for themselves. Freedom for them meant land ownership and subsistence farming, as opposed to working merely to increase someone else's wealth. Soon after the plantation owners fled, blacks on the Sea Islands destroyed the plantation houses and the cotton gins. They claimed the abandoned lands as their own and began their own independent farms.

News of the federal occupation of the Sea Islands soon reached the North, and many people began to see different possibilities in the situation. A group of philanthropists called Gideon's Band traveled south to create schools that would educate the former slaves. Other groups, including U.S. treasury officials, army officers, and speculators, also traveled to the Sea Islands, with less altruistic motives, intending to take advantage of the wartime cotton shortage. They planned to purchase the "vacant" plantation lands and to hire the former slaves as cheap labor. In addition to being attracted by the lure of profits, many whites believed that they could help blacks better adjust to free life by imposing a system of wage labor. While many whites thought that slavery was wrong, they also supposed that slavery had instilled a sense of dependence in blacks. "Giving" blacks the abandoned lands would be equally wrong, they believed, because it would not teach thrift.

Over black protest, treasury agents sold most of the abandoned land at auction in 1863 and 1864, mostly to government officials, army officers, Northern land speculators, and cotton companies. One Boston company purchased 11 entire plantations. Only by pooling their resources could blacks purchase property; even then, they could only acquire a small percentage of that which was available.

In January 1865, in the wake of the Emancipation Proclamation, Gen. William T. Sherman issued Special Order No. 15, which awarded the remaining unclaimed land on the Sea Islands to freedpeople. Shortly after the end of the Civil War, however, President Andrew Johnson rescinded the order, enabling former plantation owners to reclaim their land and forcing blacks either to work as wage laborers or to leave. Only a few blacks retained the land that they had claimed.

The Port Royal Experiment illustrated the differing, sometimes opposing, conceptions that Northern whites and freedpeople had regarding "freedom" and the government's responsibility toward the freedpeople. To former slaves freedom meant economic independence. To whites it meant freedom from ownership only. Many whites viewed blacks as incapable of an independent life – either inherently, or as a result of the debilitations of slavery. The Port Royal Experiment also highlighted how crucial federal support of the freedpeople would be in order for them to make a successful transition from slavery to freedom. And the federal government demonstrated early in the process that it was largely indifferent to the problems inherent in that transition.

Robert Fay

See Also

Slavery in the United States; Civil War, American; Thirteenth Amendment of the United States Constitution and the Emancipation Proclamation.

Europe

Portugal, a country in southwestern Europe in which blacks have had a presence for centuries.

Black Africans and people of African descent almost certainly came to present-day Portugal with the Romans and Carthaginians toward the end of the first millennium B.C.E., but little record remains of their presence. Likewise, the Muslim occupation (711-1250 C.E.) brought many people of African descent to the region. However, Portugal's modern expansion toward Africa dates from the end of the fourteenth century, with the partial occupation of the Canary Islands and the island of Madeira. This expansion had an important sponsor during the fifteenth century in the Infante (Prince) Dom Henrique (Henry the Navigator). He promoted a number of plunder expeditions led by various noblemen along the western coast of the African continent. In 1444 one of these raids up the Senegal River brought a group of black slaves from the area of Senegal to Lisbon. As told in Gomes Eanes de Zurara's *History of the Discovery and Conquest of Guinea*, Portugal established a series of outposts, or *feitorías,* both on the coast and the adjacent islands. The first was São Jorge da Mina, later known as Elmina (1482), in present-day Ghana, followed rapidly by Axim (also in Ghana), the Cape Verde Islands, and São Tomé and Príncipe.

The king of Portugal started using the title Lord of Guinea. Arbitration by the pope in 1493 led to the 1494 Treaty of Tordesillas which divided the world into two spheres of influence: one assigned to Spain – which had conquered the Canary Islands – and the other to Portugal. Portugal received all lands east of a north-south line drawn 370 leagues, or roughly 1790 km (1110 mi), west of the Cape Verde Islands. This demarcation placed part of Brazil and the entire African continent and southern Asia in Portuguese hands. The Portuguese policy of enslavement in Africa was based on the papal bull *Dum diversas* of 1452, which elevated Portuguese raids in West Africa to the equivalent of crusades against infidels and pagans, who could be dispossessed and made perpetual servants of Christian kings. Backed by church policy, the Portuguese exported slaves from Africa, primarily from coastal West Africa but increasingly also from the coasts of present-day Angola and Mozambique (*see* Transatlantic Slave Trade). Although most of these slaves were taken to Portuguese colonies in the Atlantic (such as the Cape Verde Islands, São Tomé, or Madeira) or to Brazil, some were sent to Portugal itself.

All sectors of Portuguese society – clergy, nobles, and commoners – owned slaves, though usually only the more affluent could afford them. The nobility used them primarily as domestic servants and as an external sign of power and prestige, but no group, with the exception of the royal government, possessed large numbers at any point during the fifteenth and sixteenth centuries. On the other side of the spectrum, some black slaves were purchased for employment in undesirable tasks, such as hospital work, then a dangerous occupation due to frequent epidemics.

During the sixteenth century the Portuguese began to bring enslaved Africans to Portugal in larger numbers. By about 1600 blacks constituted almost 10 percent of the population of Lisbon and parts of the Algarve. There is also abundant evidence of the employment of blacks as crew on ships sailing between Portugal and Africa. Ferrymen carrying passengers across the River Tagus in Lisbon were mostly black. These ferrymen were a source of worry to the authorities since their control of ferries enabled them to engage in illegal traffic, including the smuggling of escaped slaves.

In Portuguese cities and towns many black slaves – *negros de ganho* – were hired out by their owners to work in agriculture and other industries. In many cases they belonged to noblemen who did not have any means other than the slave labor they hired out. Black slaves who employed themselves outside their masters' homes entered arrangements with their masters to keep part of their earnings and eventually purchase their own freedom, sometimes in installments. Owners often manumitted slaves, especially when slave women bore children fathered by the owner, although former slaves frequently had to serve their owners' families for a set period of time. Several people in a family sometimes inherited a single slave, and this produced the legal case in which an individual was half-slave and half-free through manumission or self-purchase from one of the owning parties. Clearly, as the Portuguese writer Garcia de Resende put it, a black slave was an excellent investment, since his or her sale in Castile or in the Caribbean Islands could double or triple his or her original purchase value.

In the sixteenth century Portugal was the western European country with the highest percentage of black people, both enslaved and free. Out of a total Portuguese population of slightly over a million, there were around 35,000 blacks by the middle of the sixteenth century, of whom only around 2000 were free. Migration of whites to India, and also Brazil, made the importation of slave workers a necessity in many cases, but the high prices that African slaves commanded in foreign markets limited their importation to Portugal.

Black Africans in Portugal, both free and enslaved, started organizing church confraternities, such as Our Lady of the Rosary (Nossa Senhora do Rosario) in Lisbon, for mutual help and sometimes to maintain social structures from Africa. These confraternities, or guilds, took part in processions during religious festivals. The processions provided blacks, wearing various forms of African dress, an occasion to show their racial and ethnic pride. The authorities both encouraged and tried to control these organizations, which the rest of the population viewed with suspicion. Black confraternities existed in the main cities: Lisbon, Evora, Elvas, and Lagos. Because of the restrictions blacks faced in Portuguese society, black religious guilds were among the only legal forms of association and organizations to defend the interests of their members.

Religion also created a source of conflict due to the Christian duty to rest on Sundays. Authorities normally made an exception for enslaved blacks, whose domestic work inside their masters' homes was not taken into account. Only their work outside, in which many earned a living for themselves, was subject to the official restrictions. Formal religious life for blacks in Portugal was also beset with difficulties. Black men were barred from the priesthood in general, either because they were slaves or because they were born out of wedlock. The pope granted some exceptions to the second rule, but only on the condition that black priests would limit their ministry to other blacks, and mostly outside the Portuguese mainland. Convents accepted black women only as slaves to their mistresses or as lay sisters without the privileges of full vows.

Integration into the larger society was always hampered by legal constraints based on principles of *limpeza de sangue*, or blood purity. Free blacks, for instance, were barred from most trades and professions. The guilds of Lisbon and Oporto started passing bans against the admission of blacks, both free and enslaved, as officers in different trades, which consigned them to the trades' lower levels. Black women, on the other hand, had even fewer possibilities for gainful employment, since trade guilds were exclusively male domains. The most lucrative of all forms of self-employment for women was street vending. Black women sold mostly foodstuffs. They also employed themselves as water sellers, by peddling water in the streets, and as washerwomen, and were considered by the authorities to be more reliable than free and enslaved Moorish women. Trust in blacks was widespread in general because their dark skin made it difficult to escape their social condition by flight, a possibility that lay open to lighter-skinned Muslim slaves from North Africa. Nonetheless, records of escapes by blacks to Spanish cities such as Seville demonstrate that they could find shelter among race brethren in other areas of the Iberian Peninsula. However, the monetary rewards promised by masters for the capture of their escaped slaves made the white population a potential enemy to any escape attempt.

Black slaves fell under court jurisdiction only when their crimes involved people or property outside their masters' household. Punishment for the crime of attempted escape was harsh, including public lashings; the infamous application of the *pingamento* (hot lard poured over the back of the victim), typically reserved for blacks; jail sentences; and sale to a different master or to the king for employment in public works. In most cases the courts commuted the sentence to lashings or jail in exchange for the payment of a fine by the slave's master. After all, they were dealing with the property of a white Portuguese.

Marriage among blacks in Portugal, although legally possible, encountered practical difficulties of all sorts. Interracial marriages were almost impossible, except among free people. More frequent were forced sexual relations between white men and black enslaved women. Most children born to black women in Portugal were extramarital. Few masters owned more than a few slaves, and therefore most slaves lived in separate households belonging to different masters, where they had little opportunity to enter marriages with other slaves. In some cases the priests were unwilling to perform slave marriage ceremonies, or the masters themselves were opposed to the union. In any case, the children born to a slave woman always belonged to her master, regardless of the legal status of her husband.

The condition of free blacks in Portugal was in many ways not very different from that of the enslaved ones. Many, after receiving their manumission, still had contractual obligations to their former masters or their families, which they had to fulfill without pay. Finding gainful employment was difficult because of competition from slave laborers and poor whites. Also, prejudice on the part of prospective white employers and numerous legal prohibitions against blacks working in many trades effectively kept almost all blacks on the lowest rungs of the economic ladder.

Portuguese authors like Gil Vicente were the first in Europe to create a stereotype of blacks, both male and female, on stage and in songs and other literary pieces. A stage language called *fala de negro* (black speech) developed and was even exported as a theatrical fashion to neighboring Spain. The practice of staging *entremezes* – one-act intermission pieces between the acts of larger plays – with black comic figures lasted until the end of the nineteenth century. Collections of Renaissance music found in Spain and Portugal also contained many songs that not only reproduced black speech, but clearly reflected the influence of African musical practices, rhythms, and instrumentation (*see* African Music). Dances like the *fofa*, developed by blacks in Bahia in Brazil (*see* Dance in Latin America and the Caribbean), became extremely popular in high-society circles during the eighteenth century. Afro-Brazilian culture was also responsible for the early stages of the *fado*, the national musical composition of Portugal.

In the nineteenth century Great Britain pressured Portugal into abolishing the slave trade, and the revolutionary government of 1836 decreed the abolition of the trade in its territories south of the equator. This measure gave rise to an increase in the traffic from coastal West Africa toward Brazil, which had declared independence in 1822. Due to pressure from slaveholding landowners from the Alentejo and Algarve provinces in the south, who succeeded in delaying the measure, the final abolition of slavery in Portugal did not occur until 1877.

In the nineteenth century Portugal had the largest population of African descent in all of Europe, and Lisbon saw the development of a black and mulatto urban population characterized by its economic and social marginalization. They lived mostly in the riverside area, where the men found temporary work as stevedores in the port and in other menial occupations. Meanwhile, black and mulatto women found themselves excluded from attending the fruit and produce markets as vendors, and were thereby denied a traditional means of earning their living.

Blacks in Lisbon in the late nineteenth century struggled to preserve traditions of group identity, such as the ritual enthroning of Congo kings and queens, a practice that was still recorded in some white newspapers with a sense of amusement and incomprehension. The revived interest of the Portuguese society and government in the African colonies of Angola and Mozambique relegated the notion of a Portuguese black population to a condition of official nonexistence, especially after the final abolition of slavery on Portuguese territory.

New arrivals of black Africans in Portugal in the twentieth century took place as a result of colonial policies. Immigration of blacks from the African colonies was severely restricted until the 1960s, when international pressure forced the Oliveira Salazar regime to grant the black population of the African colonies equal status with the whites living both in Africa and on the Portuguese mainland. The new African immigrants living in Portuguese cities faced chronic unemployment and substandard living conditions that the economic crisis of Portugal during the 1970s only worsened. Many of them migrated to other European countries, such as France, the Netherlands, and even Spain. After the 1974 revolution, provoked by the unresolved colonial war, Portugal granted independence to its African colonies. Since the 1970s Portugal has emulated the models of France and Great Britain in attempting to create a community of Portuguese-speaking peoples, including Brazil and the five new Luso-African republics. Cultural and economic ties between Portugal and its former colonies remain strong.

Migrants from the ex-colonies to Portuguese cities faced new restrictions with the change in policies after the admission of Portugal to the European Union in 1986. Meanwhile, increasing numbers of Africans from countries other than Portuguese ex-colonies migrated to the Algarve and Setubal regions, mainly seeking work as agricultural laborers under substandard living conditions. However, the Afro-Portuguese population continued to increase, and not only in the main cities such as Lisbon and Porto. The lack of economic opportunity for blacks in Portugal did not impede a high rate of educational achievement, which increased their social status.

Baltasar Fra-Molinero

See Also

Cape Verde; Carthage.

Africa

Portuguese East Africa. Former name of Mozambique.

Africa

Portuguese Guinea. Former name of Guinea-Bissau.

Africa

Portuguese West Africa. Former name of Angola.

Latin America and the Caribbean

Poujol-Oriol, Paulette

(b. May 12, 1926, Port-au-Prince, Haiti), one of the most well-known literary personalities in Haiti, who blends the French language with Creole imagery.

Paulette Poujol-Oriol's writing is a testimony to the aspirations and intellectual resiliency of an elite that is often dismissed for its arrogance and condescension toward Haiti's majority peasant class. Her contribution to literary expression lies in her ability to connect the faintly pulsating white roots of the old aristocracy to the rhythm of the black populace through a language of proverbs, folktales, and music. Poujol-Oriol's writing explores potential means by which to effect a cultural reconciliation within Haitian society, which has historically been divided along racial lines.

Her career started at the École Normale in Port-au-Prince, as a student of literature and business administration. She was the director of studies there for eight years, and taught French literature, history of theater, and dramatic arts. She also founded a theater school for the young. Poujol-Oriol has frequently participated in radio and television projects, while remaining a most active member of the National Society of Dramatic Art. She has contributed to many literary and political magazines. In 1996 she joined the Deschamps Prize jury, and worked for the International Academy for Peace as an advocate for Haitian women's rights.

Poujol-Oriol is active with La Ligue Féminine d'Action Sociale, the first women's organization in Haiti, which has been responsible since 1934 for promoting and defending the rights of women of all social strata. Under Poujol-Oriol's direction the group's members have labored to enhance women's workplace skills in the fields of education, nursing, and child care.

Poujol-Oriol is best known for her creative literary expression, which she adeptly and subtly manipulates to disseminate important social commentary. In her work she has remained an outspoken voice of opposition against successive dictatorial regimes. In her writing she denounces governmental abuses and uses her poetic verve to sanction an assassination or to commemorate a notorious death, as, for example, in the poem "Prières pour deux anges envolés" (Prayers for Two Vanished Angels).

Poujol-Oriol's novels, such as the internationally acclaimed *Le creuset* (The Crucible), for which she received the Henri Deschamps Award in 1980, convey a compassionate and moving portrayal of the Haitian search for an ancestral identity built on the power of myths. *The Crucible* shows a slice of life in Haiti, posing questions in French that are answered in Creole. *Domestiques*, or maids, share their wisdom with the anguished aristocrats, and past history is relived in the present. Poujol-Oriol's originality stems from an ability to consider, from a position of privilege, the crossing of cultures (*métissage*) that creates a diasporic blend of Indian, Spanish, French, and African influences. Though Poujol-Oriol is a member of the bourgeoisie in a country where the vast majority of the population is illiterate, her writing is devoid of the exotic European trappings that characterized many other Haitian writers of her generation who had composed abroad.

Paulette Smith

See Also

Port-au-Prince, Haiti; Languages, Creole, in the Caribbean.

North America

Poussaint, Alvin Francis

(b. May 15, 1934, New York, N. Y.), African American psychiatrist and educator who does pioneering research on African American-related psychological and social issues.

Alvin Poussaint was born in East Harlem, New York City, and attended Stuyvesant High School. He received his B.A. from Columbia College in 1956 and an M.D. from Cornell University Medical School in 1960. From 1964 to 1965 he received postgraduate training at the University of California's Neuropsychiatric Institute.

From 1965 to 1967 Poussaint was employed by the Medical Committee for Human Rights in Jackson, Mississippi, where he provided medical care to civil rights workers and helped desegregate Southern health facilities. He taught at Tufts Medical School from 1965 to 1969 and then at Harvard Medical School. In 1971 he joined Rev. Jesse Jackson's Operation PUSH (People United to Save Humanity); he then served as one of Jackson's advisers in the 1984 presidential campaign. Poussaint was a consultant for *The Cosby Show* from 1984 to 1992 and *A Different World* from 1986 to 1993. He read scripts to ensure that the two television series presented positive images of blacks. Poussaint became a professor of psychiatry and an associate dean at the Harvard Medical School in 1993.

Poussaint has researched and written about such topics as the psychological and social adjustments of children of interracial marriages and the impact of racism on the psychological development of blacks. He is the author of *Why Blacks Kill Blacks* (1972) and the coauthor with James P. Comer of *Raising Black Children* (1992), originally titled *Black Child Care* [1975]).

Aaron Myers

See Also

Civil Rights Movement; Cosby, Bill; Harlem, New York; Jackson, Jesse Louis; Television and African Americans; Interracial Marriage in the United States.

North America

Poverty in the United States,

strongly correlated with race because of a variety of factors (*see* Work, African Americans and the Changing Nature of, in the Post-World War II Era: An Interpretation).

North America

Powell, Adam Clayton, Jr.

(b. November 29, 1908, New Haven, Conn.; d. April 4, 1972, Miami, Fla.), African American congressman and minister, one of the most vocal and flamboyant black campaigners for civil rights.

Adam Clayton Powell Jr. grew up in Harlem, where his father was the minister of Abyssinian Baptist Church, one of the largest congregations in the nation. After a poor academic performance at City College of New York, Powell attended Colgate University in Hamilton, New York. Light-skinned enough to pass as white, he did so. When fellow students learned he was black, both the whites among whom he had tried to live and the blacks whose ethnicity he had rejected were angered. Upon graduation Powell helped in his father's church and went to Union Theological Seminary for studies, which he soon terminated. He instead took a master's degree in religious education from Columbia University and assisted his father until 1937, when Adam Sr. retired and Adam Jr. became pastor of Abyssinian. Throughout this period Powell maintained a high-profile lifestyle noted for luxury and associations with the rich and famous.

Asked by the *New York Post* to comment in the newspaper on the Harlem Riot of 1935, he obliged with a scathing attack on discrimination and on police brutality. These articles led to a regular "Soap Box" column in the New York Amsterdam News and later the *People's Voice*, which Powell cofounded and published from 1942 to 1946. He also used the pulpit to spur political action. Through marches to city hall and Harlem Hospital, he protested discrimination in hiring and services. He also led the "Don't Buy Where You Can't Work" campaign against New York's stores, which succeeded in breaking hiring barriers. His pressure on utility companies and a highly successful strike against New York City buses resulted in quotas for the hiring of blacks.

In 1941 Powell won a city council seat as an independent. He continued to challenge discrimination, particularly in New York's public schools, occasionally irritating even reformist mayor Fiorello LaGuardia. In 1943 a new congressional district was established in Harlem that would almost certainly produce the state's first black congressperson. Powell undertook an ambitious campaign for the seat, winning the support of Democrats (on whose ticket he ran), Republicans, and Communists. In 1945 he became the second of two black members then serving in Congress.

In his first year in WASHINGTON, D.C., Powell denounced First Lady Bess Truman for her affiliation with the Daughters of the American Revolution, which then had racially discriminatory policies. President Harry S. Truman was outraged, and Powell fell out of favor with the White House. Also relegated to a marginal role in the legislature, Powell pressed for changes where he could – personally demanding to be served by discriminatory Washington businesses, ending segregation in congressional service facilities, campaigning to have black journalists admitted to the press galleries, and challenging congresspersons who used the word "nigger" on the House floor. He also repeatedly tried to pass what became known as the Powell Amendment, which would have denied funding to institutions that practiced racial discrimination.

In the 1956 presidential election Powell infuriated his party by supporting Republican Dwight D. Eisenhower, whom he saw as mildly progressive on civil rights. However, in 1960 Powell campaigned ardently for Democrat John F. Kennedy and brought with him many of the black votes that had gone to Eisenhower in 1956. Kennedy's narrow victory coincided with Powell's rise to the chairmanship of the House Committee on Education and Labor; this was the first time an African American had headed such a powerful committee. Powell was highly instrumental in passing much of the progressive legislation enacted in the 1960s, including increases to the minimum wage; the creation of Medicare, Medicaid, and Head Start; and the protection of civil rights. A version of the Powell Amendment was finally codified in the landmark Civil Rights Act of 1964.

At the same time that Powell's power was growing, his support was being drained by accusations and scandals. The most serious of these emerged in the early 1950s when several of his aides were convicted of income tax evasion and rumors circulated that they had also given kickbacks from their salaries to Powell. Powell was also indicted for tax evasion in 1958, but his trial resulted in a hung jury and the Department of Justice declined to retry him. In 1960 Powell was embroiled in controversy again when he accused a constituent of being a "bag woman" – someone who transported payoffs to police from illegal gambling rackets. The woman sued for libel and won a large judgment against Powell, who refused to honor the court's decision and its warrants. The case dragged on for years before Powell agreed to settle. Powell also received negative publicity for his many absences from Congress and for his personal extravagances.

In 1966 a House committee found that Powell had improperly placed his wife on his committee's payroll and traveled at committee expense on vacations to Europe and the Bahamas. Powell maintained he was doing neither more nor less than his colleagues and was being held to a racist double standard. After the November 1966 elections the House voted to deny to seat Powell. He challenged the vote, and in 1969 the United States Supreme Court held that although Congress could expel a member, it could not deny to seat someone duly elected. Powell was finally seated, after an absence of two years, but without his seniority and with his pay docked to pay for financial abuses. In 1970 Charles Rangel emerged from a field of several Democratic challengers to defeat him.

SEE ALSO

Harlem Riots of 1935; Harlem, New York; Rangel, Charles Bernard; Communist Party USA, African Americans and the.

North America

Powell, Adam Clayton, Sr.

(b. May 5, 1865, Soak Creek, Va.; d. June 12, 1953, New York, N.Y.), Baptist minister, father of United States Representative Adam Clayton Powell Jr.

Adam Clayton Powell Sr. worked as a sharecropper and a miner before becoming a Baptist minister in 1892. In 1908 he assumed leadership of the Abyssinian Baptist Church, New York City's oldest black Baptist church. As pastor Powell expanded both the scope of the church's involvement in the community and the size of its membership. By the time of his retirement in 1937, the congregation was the largest of any Protestant church in the United States. Powell's ministry was succeeded by that of his son, Adam Clayton Powell Jr., and Adam Powell Sr. spent the rest of his life writing three books and working for civil rights causes.

Lawrie Balfour

SEE ALSO

Baptists; Powell, Adam Clayton, Jr.

North America

Powell, Colin Luther

(b. April 5, 1937, New York, N.Y.), chair of the United States Joint Chiefs of Staff (1989-1993) whose leadership role in the PERSIAN GULF WAR gained him immense popularity, prompting speculation that he might run for president.

MILITARY LIFE

A first-generation American, Colin Powell was born to Jamaican immigrant parents in HARLEM, NEW YORK. The family relocated and settled in the Bronx early in Powell's childhood. After graduating from Morris High School in 1954, Powell earned a degree from the City College of New York's Kings College, where he joined the Reserve Officers Training Corps (ROTC). His academic career was unremarkable, but his tenure with the ROTC proved fruitful. He rose to the highest rank achievable, cadet colonel, and upon his graduation in 1958 was appointed second lieutenant in the United States Army. Powell received his military training at Fort Benning, Georgia.

His first posting was to West Germany, where he remained for two years, followed by a two-year stint in Massachusetts. He met and married Alma Vivian Johnson, a young speech pathologist, in 1962. The couple subsequently had three children, Michael, Linda, and Anne Marie. Months after the marriage, Powell, now a captain, was stationed in Vietnam. He was injured by a punji-stick booby trap set by the Viet Cong, for which he received the Purple Heart. Upon his 1963 return to the United States, Powell moved back to Fort Benning, where he studied and worked as an instructor at the infantry school.

Moving up the ranks of the military, Powell became a major in 1966. The highlight of the period was his impressive performance at the United States Army Command and General Staff College, where he distinguished himself by graduating second in his class. He was sent back to Vietnam in 1968 to work under Gen. Charles Gettys. Once again Powell was wounded, this time in a helicopter accident; despite his injuries he saved other servicemen from the burning site of the crash. This deed earned him his second Purple Heart and a Soldiers Medal.

POLITICAL APPOINTMENTS

On his return from Vietnam in 1969 Powell was promoted to lieutenant colonel. He earned an M.B.A. from George Washington University in 1971 and received his first political appointment a year later, as a White House fellow assigned to work in the Office of Management and Budget (OMB) under the Nixon administration. His tenure at the OMB afforded him the opportunity to work with Caspar Weinberger and Frank Carlucci, director and deputy director of the OMB respectively. The two held Powell in high esteem, and would both, in later years, figure prominently in his political advancement.

Capitalizing on Powell's reputation as a troubleshooter, the army assigned him to command a troubled infantry battalion in South Korea, where drug abuse and racial tensions threatened to paralyze the unit. The following year he was restationed in the United States, working in the Pentagon. In rapid succession, he enrolled in a nine-month program at the National War College, was made a full colonel, and in 1976 was assigned to lead the 2nd Brigade of the 101st Airborne Division at Fort Campbell, Kentucky. Powell returned to the Pentagon in 1977, although not for long. By 1979 he had been promoted to brigadier general and went on to work briefly as Charles Duncan's aide in his capacity as secretary of the Energy Department.

The National Security Council and Joint Chiefs

Powell's professional ascent continued unchecked through the 1980s. In 1981 he took on a military assignment, taking command of the Fourth Infantry Division at Fort Carson, Colorado. Secretary of Defense Caspar Weinberger, Powell's former superior at the OMB, then appointed him senior military assistant. His job was to act as a bridge between the Pentagon and the White House, a role in which he excelled. By mid-1986 Powell had been promoted to lieutenant general, commanding the Fifth Corps in Frankfurt, Germany. The Iran-Contra debacle and ensuing restructuring in Washington resulted in Frank Carlucci's appointment as national security advisor. Carlucci requested that Powell be recalled to Washington as his deputy and, although initially hesitant, Powell agreed. In 1987, when Carlucci was appointed secretary of defense, Powell received a corresponding promotion to national security advisor. As national security advisor Powell advocated a strong military budget but opposed heavy spending on the space-based Strategic Defense Initiative (nicknamed Star Wars). He served as national security advisor until President Ronald Reagan's term ended in January 1989. In April of that year Powell became a four-star general.

In the late 1980s Powell continued to distinguish himself through diplomatic and military breakthroughs, orchestrating groundbreaking meetings between Reagan and then Soviet leader Mikhail Gorbachev. In recognition of his sterling efforts, President George Bush appointed Colin Powell chairman of the Joint Chiefs of Staff in 1989. His installation was a dual triumph: he was both the youngest person and the first African American ever appointed to the highest rank in the military. Early in his term Powell was confronted with Bush's plan to invade Panama to overthrow and capture Gen. Manuel Noriega. Powell reportedly counseled against the invasion, but Bush chose to proceed and Powell planned the successful assault by 25,000 U.S. troops in December 1989.

After the outbreak of the Gulf War Powell coordinated a successful ground strategy with Gen. Norman Schwarzkopf, gaining popular approval from the American public for his clear thinking and effective military strategy. His capable and comforting demeanor was an added bonus at a time when television was often the public's principal source of information on the state of the war. Bush reappointed Powell chairman of the Joint Chiefs in 1991. During this time Powell faced regional crises in Somalia and the former Yugoslavia but had little success in guiding the administration to a clear policy in either area.

In 1992 Democratic candidate Bill Clinton was elected president. In an effort to fulfill to a campaign promise, Clinton began exploring measures to end the ban on gays in the military. Powell opposed the endeavor and it was largely through his efforts that the "Don't ask, don't tell" policy was established, whereby gays were allowed in the armed forces as long as they did not reveal their sexual orientation. Clinton and Powell also disagreed over Clinton's proposal to cut drastically the military budget.

In September 1993 Powell retired from the military. This move fueled intense national speculation that he intended to run for president against Clinton in 1996. Powell never refuted the rumors, concentrating instead on promoting his 1995 autobiography, *My American Journey*. At the end of the book tour Powell announced that he would not run for the presidency and retired into private life.

See Also
Germany; Vietnam War; Jamaica.

North America

Powell, Earl ("Bud")

(b. September 27, 1924, New York, N.Y.; d. August 1, 1966, New York, N.Y.), African American jazz pianist, often regarded as the most important bebop pianist of the 1940s.

In 1940 Powell began playing at Minton's Playhouse in New York and became a student of Thelonious Monk. From 1942 to 1944 he frequently played with his other mentor, Cootie Williams. Under the guidance of these two masters he developed his distinctive style and made a significant impact on the piano playing of the emerging bebop movement. Mike Baillie has written of Powell that "his total emotional commitment, at times quite ferocious, with an unrelenting sense of urgency... comes through on every recording he ever made." Powell, often in the trio format, has played with such jazz greats as Dizzy Gillespie, Charlie Parker, and Max Roach. Among his better-known jazz compositions are *Hallucinations*, recorded by Miles Davis as *Budo, Dance of the Infidels, Tempus Fugue-it*, and *Bouncing with Bud*.

Powell suffered a head injury in 1945 during a racial incident, after which he experienced several nervous breakdowns. His composition *The Glass Enclosure* is a musical expression of his numerous stays in mental institutions. His playing appearances began to decline in the late 1940s.

In 1959 Powell moved to Paris, where he led a trio with Kenny Clarke until 1962. There he enjoyed a brief renewal of his celebrity status. He returned to America in 1964. After performing a poorly received concert at Carnegie Hall in 1965, he abandoned music altogether.

See Also
Davis, Miles Dewey, III; Gillespie, John Birks ("Dizzy"); Monk, Thelonious Sphere; New York, New York; Parker, Charles Christopher ("Bird"); Roach, Maxwell Lemuel (Max).

Latin America and the Caribbean

Pozo y González, Luciano (Chano)

(b. January 7, 1915, Havana, Cuba; d. December 2, 1948, New York, N.Y.), Afro-Cuban conga drummer who helped create Afro-Latin Jazz during the 1940s.

Luciano "Chano" Pozo y González, better known as Chano Pozo, played a seminal role in the founding of Afro-Latin jazz during the 1940s. Afro-Latin jazz combined Cuban rhythms and song forms with African American jazz improvisation and complex, bop-derived harmonies. Pioneering Afro-Cuban jazz trumpeter Mario Bauza brought Pozo to New York in May 1946 and in the following year recommended him to Dizzy Gillespie, who wanted a conga drummer for his big band. Pozo had learned to play the conga drum in Cuba through his involvement in an Abakuá secret society. One of his first jazz performances took place at New York City's Carnegie Hall on September 17, 1947, shortly after he joined Gillespie's band.

Pozo was featured on the extended composition "Cubana Be, Cubana Bop," also known as the "Afro-Cuban Suite." His percussion work was electrifying, and over the succeeding months Gillespie added more Latin-inspired numbers including "Algo Bueno," also known as "Woody 'n' You" (1947), in order to feature his conga drummer. Although Pozo could not read music, he created or cocomposed several key examples of Afro-Latin jazz, including "Manteca" (1947), recorded by the Gillespie big band, and "Tin Tin Deo" (1948), first recorded by a nine-man group under the leadership of saxophonist James Moody.

Pozo's musical career was cut short by his hot temper. Bassist Al McKibbon, who played alongside him in Gillespie's big band, recalled that "Chano was a hoodlum... a rough character." He was killed just one month short of his 34th birthday in the Rio Café, a bar in Spanish Harlem. Nonetheless, his legacy endured in the playing of such Afro-Latin *congeros* as Louis "Sabu" Martinez, his successor in Gillespie's band; Mongo Santamaría; and Cándido Camero.

James Clyde Sellman

See Also
Gillespie, John Birks ("Dizzy"); New York, New York; Abakuás; Afro-Latino Cultures in the United States; Santamaría, Ramón ("Mongo"); Music, Afro-Caribbean Secular; Havana, Cuba.

Latin America and the Caribbean

Preciado Bedoya, Antonio, (b. 1941, Esmeraldas, Ecuador), Afro-Ecuadorian writer.

Antonio Preciado Bedoya was born in the capital of the province of Esmeraldas, in the northwest region of the Republic of Ecuador. He grew up with his mother, who was a *lavandera* (laundry woman) for other families. Because he applied himself academically, he was able to finish his high school education and later graduate from a local university. In addition to his work as a poet, for many years Preciado has also been the director of the cultural center and the historical archives of the Banco Central del Ecuador in the city of Esmeraldas, where he also served as the director of the Universidad Luis Vargas Torres.

Preciado followed in the footsteps of two other famous Esmeraldian writers, Nelson Estupiñán Bass and Adalberto Ortiz. He was influenced by international literary currents of the time such as Afrocubanismo (*see* Nicolás Guillén) and magical realism (*see* Alejo Carpentier) and composed negrista poems using black people and Afro-Esmeraldian cultural traditions as primary material. Many believe the quality of his poetry has surpassed that of his two celebrated predecessors. Preciado's work has been lauded for its use of subtle rhythms in the production of meaning. In "Matábara del hombre malo" (Matábara of the bad man), he writes:

¡Atabé!
¡Atabé!
¡Ururé!
¡Matábara!

Tengo una hoguera de estrellas,
de las estrellas más altas,
y un lugar en plena luna
para que arda.

La claridad crece y crece
con fuerza de cien mañanas...
Cátala catún balé,
catún balé caté cátala.

(... I have a bonfire of stars, / of the highest stars / and a place in broad moonlight / where it can burn. / The brightness grows and grows / with the strength of one hundred mornings....)

Jean Muteba Rahier

See Also
Negrista Poets.

Africa

Présence Africaine, influential journal produced in Paris after World War II by African intellectuals as part of the movement known as Négritude.

Born amid the intellectual tumult shaking post-World War II Paris, *Présence Africaine* has had greater influence on politics and culture than most intellectual journals. It has revolutionized European thought on African culture and helped launch the literary and political careers of several prominent Africans.

After the war a debate emerged in France over the role of the empire and the fate of the French colonies. In addition, Paris had a sizable population of students and intellectuals from various colonies, including Africans and West Indians, and their opposition to the colonial system had been gaining sympathy among French intellectuals. After the war anticolonial ideas became increasingly mainstream. The wartime experience of Nazi repression had increased the attraction of socialism and liberalism, and allied opposition to Nazi tyranny made it more difficult for many French to justify undemocratic colonial rule.

When it first appeared in Paris in 1947, *Présence Africaine* had the effect of a match lit in a room full of gas. *Présence Africaine* changed forever the French and, later, European perception of African people and culture. It provided intellectual backing for the eventual independence of the former French colonies as well as an influential forum for African writers. It gave a vital boost to French-language African literature (*see* Literature, French Language, in Africa).

Senegalese writer Alioune Diop founded *Présence Africaine* to promote Négritude, an intellectual movement that explored the cultural and political ties connecting Africans and people of African descent in the diaspora. Négritude also sought recognition for the achievements of African civilization. The publication did not attack French or European culture per se, but it did challenge the moral and intellectual bases of colonialism and racism. Diop announced three goals for the journal: to publish studies on African culture; to examine ways to integrate Africans into the Western world; and to review art and other topics relevant to Africans and people of African descent. In 1949 Diop founded Présence Africaine Editions, a publishing house for African authors.

Although *Présence Africaine* would remain true to the Pan-Africanist ideal of uniting Africans and their descendants throughout the world, the publication focused primarily on Africa. This choice was partly a response to the newspaper *L'Etudiant Noir*, founded in Paris in the 1930s by Léopold Sédar Senghor of Senegal and Aimé Césaire from Martinique, which had adopted a Caribbean focus. Senghor, however, gave his enthusiastic blessing to *Présence Africaine*, calling it "the primary instrument of the Négritude movement." Senghor and Césaire contributed to the 196-page first issue, as did many of the leading French intellectuals of the time, including Jean-Paul Sartre and André Gide. Albert Camus, who was born and raised in Algeria, served on the committee supporting *Présence Africaine*.

Although it began as a monthly, *Présence Africaine* later appeared as a quarterly. It has continued to be published quarterly into the late 1990s. Over the years, *Présence Africaine* has tackled topics ranging from France's relationship with its former colonies to the African presence in Haiti and Brazil.

David P. Johnson, Jr.

See Also
Pan-Africanism; Senegal; West Indies.

North America

Press, Black, in the United States, American newspapers and magazines published by African Americans and focused on black political, social, and cultural issues.

The black press has represented the spectrum of African American opinion for nearly 150 years. It has enabled African Americans to (1) define their own identity; (2) create a sense of unity by establishing a communication network among literate blacks and sympathetic whites; (3) present events from a black perspective; (4) highlight black achievement ignored by the mainstream press; and (5) work for black equality.

The first black newspaper in the United States was *Freedom's Journal*, founded March 16, 1827, in New York City by John B. Russwurm and Samuel E. Cornish, who used it as a forum to discuss slavery and its related issues and to enable blacks in various states to exchange ideas on such issues as whether blacks should strive for full citizenship or opt for separation and repatriation in Africa. Cornish, an integrationist, and Russwurm, a separatist, disagreed on that issue, and six months after the paper's founding, Cornish left. Russwurm continued to publish *Freedom's Journal* until March 28, 1829, when he moved to Liberia, living there until his death in 1851.

Cornish began editing Philip A. Bell's *Weekly Advocate* in 1837. Later called the *Colored American*, it was published until 1842 and is noted for its high editorial quality and militant call for black unity and full citizenship for black Americans. It was probably published in New York and Philadelphia, which would make it the first African American newspaper to operate in more than one city with different editions.

More African Americans began to publish in the mid-nineteenth century. Most publications were in New York City, but several others existed, such as Cleveland's *Alienated American,* Pittsburgh's *Mystery,* published by Martin R. Delany, the first African American graduate of Harvard, and Albany's *Elevator,* published by Stephen Myers.

African American newspapers were understandably a Northern phenomenon before the Civil War. However, the *Daily Creole* began publishing in New Orleans in 1856, although its editors were pressured by whites into an anti-abolitionist position. The *Daily Creole* was followed by the *New Orleans Tribune,* which appeared in July of 1864, and is considered the first African American daily.

Most newspapers of this era were similar in that they depended on their publisher's personal resources or contributions from white sympathizers to supplement their small subscription income. Approximately 40 newspapers were published before the Civil War, the most important of which was FREDERICK DOUGLASS's *North Star,* whose goal characterized black publishing: "The object of the *North Star* will be to attack slavery in all its forms and aspects; advocate Universal Emancipation; exact the standard of public morality; promote the moral and intellectual improvement of the colored people; and to hasten the day of freedom to our three million enslaved fellow countrymen."

Black publishing expanded after the Civil War. An estimated 575 black publications began by 1890. Most quickly failed, but many survived, most notably the *Philadelphia Tribune.* Founded in 1884, it continued to be published into the 1990s, making it the oldest continuously published black newspaper in the United States.

The explosion of black newspapers after the Civil War resulted from increasing literacy and greater mobility among African Americans combined with a further need for advocacy in the battles against segregation, disfranchisement, and lynchings. Migrants to the North experienced poor conditions and discrimination that was stifling if not as debilitating as it was in the South. Thus the black press was still a protest organ for African Americans. However, as the century ended, protest had to be disguised because of the nation's conservative political shift.

Booker T. Washington, considered the spokesman for black America during this era, wielded great power among the black press by controlling advertisements, loans, and political subsidies. The journalist most closely associated with Washington was T. Thomas Fortune, considered the dean of black journalism. He learned the newspaper trade beginning as a typesetter and was one of the only African Americans to write for white dailies, the *New York Sun* and the *Evening Sun.*

Fortune was firmly committed to racial equality. However, his newspaper, the *New York Age,* experienced the same monetary problems as other black newspapers. He relied on Washington's financial support and was therefore obligated to write editorials that Washington favored. Some journalists resisted the conservative trend and the muted editorial tones that it demanded from black newspapers. Ida B. Wells-Barnett repeatedly risked her life in the South to report about atrocities suffered by blacks. William Monroe Trotter, who founded the Boston *Guardian* with George Forbes in 1901, formed the first organized resistance to Washington's ideas. Later, with W. E. B. Du Bois, he organized the foundation of the NIAGARA MOVEMENT, a forerunner to the NATIONAL ASSOCIATION FOR THE ADVANCEMENT OF COLORED PEOPLE (NAACP).

Black newspapers did not attain commercial success until Robert S. Abbott founded the *Chicago Defender* in 1905. Capitalizing on the sensationalist techniques developed by William Randolph Hearst, Abbott designed the *Defender* as a paper for the masses. Abbott initially avoided politics, but the paper came into its own when he concentrated on muckraking stories about the black community. By 1920 the *Defender* had a circulation of 283,571.

Another successful paper of the modern era was the *Pittsburgh Courier,* which was founded in 1910 by Robert L. Vann. More editorially staid than the *Defender,* the *Courier* nevertheless advocated for blacks, demanding that large industrial firms hire African Americans and European immigrants in the 1920s. One reason the *Courier* succeeded was its superior writers, such as George Schuyler, a columnist known for his satirical style, and Joel A. Rogers, whose "Your History" column told of black achievements that were largely ignored or denied by white society. By 1937 the *Courier*'s weekly circulation exceeded 250,000. By 1946 the *Courier* produced 14 local and national editions, and had branch offices in 12 cities. It was the most popular black publication even in cities that had their own black publications. By May 1947 the *Courier's* circulation reached 357,212, a record for black newspapers. After 1948, with the death of Vann's successor, Ira Lewis, the *Courier* declined. It was eventually purchased by John Sengstacke, Robert Abbott's nephew, who ran the *Defender* after Abbott's death in 1940.

Another modern black national paper was the *Afro-American.* John H. Murphy, a former slave, created it in Baltimore by merging his Sunday-school publication with two others and expanding coverage to include items of general interest. Murphy died in 1922, and his son, Carl, built the *Afro-American* into a national publication. Featuring solid reportage and a moderate editorial point of view, the *Afro-American* nevertheless defended PAUL ROBESON and W. E. B. Du Bois when they were accused of being Communists during the McCarthy era. In addition to the national papers, several successful local papers developed during this era, including the *Amsterdam News,* established in 1909 in New York City, the *Norfolk Journal-Guide,* in Norfolk, Virginia, and the *Atlanta Daily World.* Established in 1932, the Atlanta newspaper is the oldest surviving black daily in the nation and only one of three black dailies to survive into the 1990s.

From 1900 to the CIVIL RIGHTS MOVEMENT of the late 1950s, black papers thrived in almost every city because the mainstream press still either ignored African Americans or portrayed them stereotypically, often as the perpetrators of crimes. "Black news," if included, appeared in segregated "Afro-American" sections. Even celebrities or sports stars who received mainstream coverage were used to reinforce stereotypes about African Americans.

The discovery by white publications of the drama surrounding the Civil Rights Movement marked a period of decline for the black press. Mainstream newspapers, news magazines, and radio and television networks, which had greater resources than black papers, could cover more stories than the black papers. Though the mainstream press began to cover "black" news, few blacks were writing the stories. By 1955 only 31 African Americans worked on mainstream papers. In television, it was not until 1962, when Mal Goode joined ABC, that a national network hired its first African American correspondent.

Coverage of black issues did not change until the late 1960s, after riots in black ghettos forced mainstream editors to reevaluate the role of blacks in journalism. As a result of this analysis white editors discovered black mistrust for white journalists and quickly realized that they needed black reporters to get accurate stories regarding black communities. In the early 1970s mainstream newspapers and television stations began active recruitment of African American journalists. By the mid-1970s more than 100 African American journalists were working for mainstream publications. By 1990, 4000 African Americans worked for newspapers.

The mainstream press's coverage of traditionally black issues and the recruitment of talented African American journalists devastated the black press. In the 1960s more than 300 black papers were published. By late 1980s only 170 remained. By 1977 circulation for the *Defender* was 34,000 daily and 38,000 for the weekend edition, the *Pittsburgh New Courier's* circulation had declined to 30,000 weekly, and the *Afro-American* was at a 34,000 average for two weekday editions, 18,500 for its Sunday edition. This decline in readership was paralleled by a drop in quality as the more talented African American reporters and editors went to mainstream publications.

While black newspapers declined, magazines thrived. The first black magazine to have a lasting impact was the *Crisis*. Created by W. E. B. Du Bois in 1910, the *Crisis* was the official publication of the NAACP. In it Du Bois criticized policies that prevented black progress, and he offered protest techniques. In 1934, after quarreling with the NAACP, Du Bois resigned as editor, but the NAACP continued to publish the *Crisis* into the 1990s. Other magazines founded on the *Crisis* model included *Opportunity*, the publication of the NATIONAL URBAN LEAGUE, which documented literary and artistic accomplishments of the HARLEM RENAISSANCE, and A. Philip Randolph's and Chandler Owen's *Messenger*.

These magazines paralleled early black newspapers in that they provided mostly commentary and little news coverage, and they depended on subsidies to sustain them. Commercially viable black-owned magazines did not exist until the 1940s when John H. Johnson created *Negro Digest*, which became the cornerstone of his publishing empire. Johnson followed *Negro Digest* with *Ebony* in 1946. By 1992 Johnson Publishing Company's roster included several successful periodicals: *Ebony* had a circulation of 1.9 million, *Jet*, a circulation of 1 million, and *Ebony Man*, a circulation of 225,000. Johnson then expanded into radio and television broadcasting and cosmetics, and amassed holdings reportedly worth over $200 million.

The Civil Rights Movement led to economic improvement for many African Americans, creating a market for magazines aimed at the black middle class, including Essence and *Black Enterprise*. *Essence* targeted modern black women and by 1992 achieved a circulation of 900,000. *Black Enterprise* focused on black entrepreneurs and had a readership of 205,500 by 1992.

African Americans remain underrepresented in journalism. Those who have jobs do not hold decision-making power. A 1985 survey indicated that 95 percent of the journalists at daily newspapers were white, 92 percent of United States newspapers had no African Americans in news executive positions, and 54 percent had no African American employees. In 1985 African Americans constituted more than 11 percent of the U.S. population, but only 4 percent of newsroom staffs.

The industry leader in providing African Americans with opportunity was Gannett, the publisher of *USA Today* and the largest news publisher in the United States. Gannett aggressively recruited and promoted African Americans. One example was Pam Johnson, who, upon becoming the publisher of the *Ithaca Journal* in 1981, was the first African American woman to control a mainstream daily. Similarly, when Robert Maynard became publisher of the *Oakland Tribune*, he was the first African American to head a general-market daily. Maynard eventually purchased the paper.

Still, in the 1990s, many African Americans in journalism experienced racism at work, received less attractive assignments than their white counterparts, and received fewer promotions. Compounding these problems was the conservative political and social movement in the United States that began in the early 1980s, and challenged the AFFIRMATIVE ACTION programs that were designed to encourage African American participation in mainstream professions. African Americans still find themselves largely misrepresented and portrayed negatively by the mainstream media. Thus many of the conditions that prompted African Americans to begin newspapers and magazines in the nineteenth century still exist.

However, the decline of black newspapers means that a countervailing voice is almost nonexistent. Many African American journalists find themselves walking a fine line between the journalistic ideals of objectivity and advocacy. Faced with isolation in newsrooms, fragmentation, and concerns for their overall effectiveness, black journalists in 1975 founded the NATIONAL ASSOCIATION OF BLACK JOURNALISTS (NABJ) to provide guidance and support. By 1992 NABJ had 2000 members in print and broadcast journalism.

Robert Fay

SEE ALSO

Slavery in the United States; Baltimore, Maryland; *Chicago Defender*; Civil War, American; *Crisis, The*; Delany, Martin Robison; Du Bois, William Edward Burghardt (W. E. B.); *Ebony*; *Essence*; *Freedom's Journal*; Great Migration, The; *Jet*; Johnson Publishing Company; *Messenger, The*; Murphy, Carl; New Orleans, Louisiana; New York, New York; *Opportunity: Journal of Negro Life*; Philadelphia, Pennsylvania; *Pittsburgh Courier*; Pittsburgh, Pennsylvania; Racial Stereotypes; Randolph, Asa Philip; Rogers, Joel Augustus; Russwurm, John Brown; Schuyler, George S.; Television and African Americans; Washington, Booker Taliaferro; Wells-Barnett, Ida Bell; Lynching; Abbott, Robert Sengstacke; Communist Party USA, African Americans and the.

Africa

Pretoria, South Africa, administrative capital of SOUTH AFRICA, located in the northeastern part of the country, in Gauteng province on the Apies River.

The Pretoria settlement was established by Marthinus W. Pretorius in 1855 and named in honor of his father, Andries W. J. Pretorius, the AFRIKANER (or Boer) soldier and statesman. It became the capital of the South African Republic in 1860 and was the site of clashes between Afrikaners and British during the Boer War. The Peace of Vereeniging, which ended the war, was signed here in 1902. When the Union of South Africa was organized in 1910, Pretoria was designated the seat of its administration, a status it retained after the Republic of South Africa was formed in 1961. Even in the 1990s Pretoria has been the center for the nation's Afrikaner political activities and organizations. Segregated residential areas that grew during the period of APARTHEID divide the city into distinct black, white, Indian, and Cape Coloured neighborhoods.

The modern city contains large parks and a number of landmarks. Pretoria is the site of the University of South Africa (founded in 1873), the University of Pretoria (founded as Transvaal University College in 1908 and renamed in 1930), Vista University (founded in 1982), a technical college, the state library, and government archives. Points of interest include the home of Paul Kruger, president of the South African Republic from 1883 to 1902; the Transvaal Museum, containing natural history displays; the Municipal Art Gallery, featuring South African art; the Pretoria Art Museum, with a collection of seventeenth-century Dutch art; the National Cultural History and Open Air Museum, with a variety of collections; the Military Museum, which is located in Fort Schanskop (built in 1867); and the National Zoological Gardens.

Pretoria is a major commercial, manufacturing, transportation, and cultural center. Principal products include iron and steel, processed food, ceramics, and chemicals. The population in 1999 was about 1.6 million.

North America

Price, Florence Beatrice Smith (b. April 9, 1887, Little Rock, Ark.; d. June 3, 1953, Chicago, Ill.), composer and pianist who was one of the first African American women to achieve national recognition as a composer.

The third child of Little Rock's first black dentist, Florence Price had already published musical compositions as a high school student. She graduated as an organist and teacher from the New England Conservatory of Music in 1906, and in 1912 she married the attorney Thomas J. Price. Florence Price won the Wanamaker Prize in 1932 for her *Symphony in E minor*, which the Chicago Symphony Orchestra premiered at the 1933 Chicago World's Fair. She thus became the first African American woman to create a score played by a leading American orchestra. Price composed more than 300 works, and her songs and arrangements were performed by some of the most admired voices of her day, including MARIAN ANDERSON. Her symphonies and chamber works were famous for incorporating melodies from Negro spirituals, and her work is considered an important part of the New Negro Arts Movement.

See Also
Spirituals, African American.

Latin America and the Caribbean

Price-Mars, Jean

(b. October 15, 1876, Grande Rivière du Nord, Haiti; d. March 1, 1969?, Pétionville, Haiti), Haitian historian, diplomat, politician, and ethnographer who preceded and influenced the Négritude movement.

After studying medicine, anthropology, and political science in Haiti and Paris, Jean Price-Mars joined the Haitian diplomatic corps. It was through this work that Price-Mars discovered his oratorical skills, giving a great number of lectures on Haitian culture and politics from 1910 to 1930 that were gathered in his first published works, *La Vocation de l'élite* (1919), *Ainsi parla l'Oncle* (1928), and *Une étape de l'évolution haïtienne* (1929). Price-Mars subsequently split his time between active politics and more intellectual pursuits throughout the rest of his life. During the tumultuous middle of the century he remained close to Haiti's ever-changing power elite, running twice for president and being appointed ambassador to Paris by François Duvalier in 1957.

More significant, Price-Mars continued to write about the history of Haiti and on the importance of racial and cultural pride in works such as *De Saint-Domingue à Haïti: Essai sur la culture, les arts et la littérature* (1959) and *Silhouette de nègres et de négrophiles* (1960). During the humiliating period of the United States occupation of Haiti (1934-1957), Price-Mars strove in his lectures to remind Haitians of their rich cultural heritage.

Although Price-Mars's ideas seem tame by comparison to those of Aimé Césaire and Frantz Fanon, they were revolutionary in their time and place. Léopold Sédar Senghor, for one, acknowledged a debt to Price-Mars, a writer who showed him "the treasures of Négritude that he discovered in Haiti.... [He] taught me to discover those same riches – albeit in raw and undiluted form – in Africa."

Richard Watts

See Also
Senghor, Léopold Sédar.

North America

Pride, Charley Frank

(b. March 18, 1938, Sledge, Miss.), first African American country music superstar.

The son of sharecroppers in rural Mississippi, Charley Pride spent his early years surrounded by blues music, but chose to pursue country music professionally. Pride began his bid to be the first black to mount the Grand Ole Opry stage (the apex of country music performance) unconventionally – as a baseball player in the late 1950s. In between innings and on the tour bus as an outfielder for several Negro League teams, Pride displayed his sinewy voice and self-taught mastery of the guitar. Eventually, his nightclub singing was noticed and encouraged by Nashville producers. He gave up baseball for music in 1963. The popularity of his first hits, "Snakes Crawl at Night" (1965) and "Just Between You and Me" (1966), earned him invitations to perform at the Opry, making him the first black country music star to appear there.

Success in music and business followed. He is a superstar singer/composer of more than 50 Top Ten hits, the winner of three Grammy Awards, *Cash Box* magazine's Top Male Country Singer of the Decade (1970s), and the 1971 Country Music Association Entertainer of the Year. He is second only to Elvis Presley in records sold for the RCA label. In addition to owning other businesses whose profits have made him a multimillionaire, Pride owns First Texas Bank in Dallas, Texas.

While Pride's rise to fame was meteoric, he faced criticism from within the black community, which perceived country music to be a white arena. Also, early in his career, the Nashville music industry hid Pride's race by issuing publicity material without his photo. In order to help others avoid such discrimination, Pride has been active in a new Nashville organization, the Minority Country Music Association.

See Also
Baseball in the United States; Blues, The; Negro Leagues.

North America

Primus, Pearl

(b. November 26, 1919, Trinidad; d. October 29, 1994, New Rochelle, N.Y.), pioneer dancer, choreographer, and teacher who performed, taught, and popularized African American, African, and Caribbean dance styles internationally.

Pearl Primus studied to be a doctor, not a dancer. A biology major at Hunter College in New York City (where her family had immigrated from Trinidad in 1921), then a graduate student of psychology and health education, she was prevented from gaining a laboratory job by racial prejudice. Pressed for money, Primus applied to the National Youth Administration and was placed as an understudy in a dance troupe. Primus's superb athletic ability won her a scholarship to the New Dance Group in 1941. The first black to study and perform there, she began a long career that sought to counteract racism with Afrodiasporic performance culture.

Primus's early work evidenced her careful research of traditional African dance styles and her desire to infuse dance with political and social commentary. Her 1943 professional debut, *African Ceremonial,* received such positive reviews that she was able to open on Broadway with her own troupe. Interpreting pieces such as Langston Hughes's poem "The Negro Speaks of Rivers" (1943) and Lewis Allan's "Strange Fruit" (1945), Primus brought African dance styles to bear on African American racial issues. Her work was recognized by a 1948 Julius Rosenwald Fellowship, which she used to study dance in Central and West Africa.

While beginning her career, Primus continued her academic work, studying anthropology and education at universities in New York. She met her husband, dancer/choreographer Percival Borde, in Trinidad, while researching folklore there in 1953. She and Borde collaborated until his death in 1979. The couple and their son, Onwin, spent two years in Liberia (1959-1961), where Primus directed Liberia's performing arts center.

Throughout the 1960s Primus focused on teaching. She held numerous academic appointments in anthropology, dance, and ethnic studies in the 1980s and 1990s, after earning her doctorate in education from New York University in 1978. The recipient of many distinguished awards, Primus's career was capped by the 1991 National Medal of Art, presented to her by George Bush, president of the United States. Although she stopped performing personally in the 1980s, Primus taught dance until her death in 1994.

See Also
Dance in Sub-Saharan Africa; New York, New York; Trinidad and Tobago.

North America

Prince

(⚥, born Prince Rogers Nelson) (b. June 7, 1958, Minneapolis, Minn.), virtuoso pop musician known for his provocative musical and personal style.

Born Prince Rogers Nelson, ⚥ had many transformations on the journey from his childhood nickname, "Skipper," to his current name, ⚥, an unpronounceable glyph that he assumed in 1993 that is representative of male and female principles. Deliberately frustrating efforts to characterize his image and his music, ⚥ announced a new persona with his 1996 album, *Emancipation,* which was a hoped-for return to his commercial and artistic success of the 1980s.

Notoriously private about his personal life, ⚥ is the biracial son of jazz musicians Mattie Shaw Nelson and John Nelson. Self-taught on the guitar, piano, and drums, he received a recording contract at age 20. His first album, 1978's *For You,* blends funk, rock, pop, and jazz; like those albums that follow, it evidences the eclectic musical influences of James Brown, George Clinton, Jimi Hendrix, and the Beatles.

Like his idol, Little Richard, ⚥ is flamboyant in dress and personality. After

For You, his next few albums brought him notoriety as a result of their explicitly sexual lyrics and his own provocative androgyny. Neither black nor white, his music neither rock nor funk, ♀ appealed to all, a fact that helped him crossover onto MTV. He created a virtual cult following with the 1982 album *1999,* which went triple platinum, and with 1984's *Purple Rain,* which won three Grammy Awards. ♀ starred in and produced the semiautobiographical film *Purple Rain,* for which he earned an Oscar for best score. His other films include the modestly successful *Under the Cherry Moon* (1986) and *Graffiti Bridge* (1990).

♀ took a brief retirement in 1993 and was then involved in a court battle with his former record label, Warner Brothers. He reemerged with his own label in 1996, no longer what he referred to as a "slave" to music industry commercialism or his own former reputation. He credits his "emancipation" to the influence of former dancer and backup singer Mayte Garcia, whom he married on Valentine's Day, 1996.

North America

Prince, Lucy Terry (b. 1730?, West Africa; d. August 21, 1821, Sunderland, Vt.), pioneering African American poet known for her extraordinary oratorical skills.

Eulogized as one whose "fluidity of… speech captured all around her," Lucy Terry Prince is probably the first African American poet. Prince's single surviving poem, "Bars Fight," is the chronicle of an Indian raid on Deerfield, Massachusetts, in 1746. It was not published, however, until 1855 by Josiah Gilbert in his *History of Western Massachusetts.*

Born in West Africa, enslaved, and brought to Rhode Island, Prince was sold at age five to a Massachusetts resident, Ebenezer Wells. Baptized soon after, she was taught to read and write, skills that enhanced her poetic ability as well as her later skill at oratorical argument. At age 16, she was witness to an Indian raid in a field outside of Deerfield known as The Bars and chronicled the experience in a poem that was hailed as an accurate description of the event.

While her reputation as a poet rests on a single poem, Prince's standing as an orator follows from two unusual events. She married Abijah Prince, a free black who purchased her freedom, and moved to Vermont in 1756. They were the parents of six children. When one of her sons was ready to go to college, he was rejected by Williams College because of his race. Incensed by this injustice, Lucy Prince reputedly pleaded her case for three hours in front of the college trustees, quoting both the Bible and the law.

Although unsuccessful with the trustees, a few years later Prince won a case in the United States Circuit Court. When a land dispute between the Princes and their neighbors could not be solved in the local judiciary, it went to the circuit court. Dissatisfied with her lawyer, Isaac Ticknor (later governor of Vermont), Prince pleaded her own case, earning the praise that she argued "better than [the judge] had heard from any lawyer at the Vermont bar."

See Also

Free Blacks in the United States, 1619 to 1863.

Europe

Prince, Mary (b. 1788, Bermuda; d. ?, Great Britain), first black woman to publish a slave narrative.

The History of Mary Prince, A West Indian Slave, Related by Herself (1831) was the earliest account that gave a firsthand description of the brutality women suffered under slavery. Prince's autobiography became very popular and stirred debate on slavery and the treatment of slaves in the West Indies. Describing the harsh conditions she faced in the West Indies, Prince countered biased white conclusions that "slaves don't want to get out of slavery." As she explained, "They [whites] put a cloak about the truth. It is not so. All slaves want to be free.… I have been a slave myself – and I know what slaves feel – I can tell by myself what other slaves feel, and by what they have told me." With these words she became the first black woman to challenge whites on behalf of all black people.

Born a slave in Bermuda around 1788, Prince was separated from family members when they were sold to different West Indian plantation owners. Prince herself worked on various estates as a domestic servant and in the fields. Not only did she experience sexual exploitation, but she was left with severe scarring from beatings, and her labor on a salt plantation deformed her feet because of long exposure to the harsh chemicals. Prince married a free black man in 1826, but according to West Indian law she was still the property of her masters, John Wood and his wife, who often beat her in full view of her husband. Rheumatism further disabled Prince, which angered the Woods, who increasingly threatened to evict her. Finally, while traveling in England with the Woods in 1828, Prince escaped.

Having joined the Moravian Church in the West Indies, Prince now sought shelter at the church's branch in London. She obtained financial and legal aid from the British Anti-Slavery Society. One member, Thomas Pringle, hired her, and offered to purchase her freedom from Wood. Wood rebuffed his offer and insisted that she return to the West Indies. Prince refused, even though this meant she would be separated from her husband.

Prince was determined to fight for her freedom in the English courts, Parliament, and press. She recounted her slave narrative to a female member of the Anti-Slavery Society; it was then edited by Thomas Pringle, who took pains to keep to the original wording. Despite the publicity she received from the popularity of her book, she seems to have lost her celebrity status soon after. It is known that she remained legally a slave until 1834, when slavery was abolished in England and its colonies.

Leyla Keough

See Also

Great Britain; Slavery in Latin America and the Caribbean; Slave Narratives; London, Blacks in: An Interpretation; Protestant Church in Latin America and the Caribbean.

North America

Prince, Nancy Gardner (b. September 15, 1799, Newburyport, Mass.; d. 1856?), African American autobiographer, philanthropist, and chronicler of travels to Russia and Jamaica.

Nancy Gardner Prince's 1850 *Narrative of the Life and Travels of Mrs. Nancy Prince, Written by Herself,* chronicles the antebellum economic conditions of free blacks, her experience in the courts of two Russian tsars, and the difficulties of missionary work in politically volatile, newly emancipated Jamaica. Prince's life, as told in this fascinating volume, reveals the opportunities available to and hindrances suffered by nineteenth-century black women.

Prince's early life as a free black in New England was marked by hunger, hard work, and racism. She endured these harsh conditions by clinging to the dignity of her family history, which included the exploits of an African grandfather who fought in the Revolutionary War, a Native American grandmother once enslaved by the British, and an African stepfather who emancipated himself by jumping off a slave ship. Despite her pride in her heritage, her frustration with the social and economic oppression of free blacks in antebellum America led to her expatriation. After marrying Nero Prince in 1824, a former seaman and a servant in the courts of Russian tsars Alexander I and Nicholas I, she spent the next 10 years in Europe and Russia. While living in St. Petersburg, Prince held such diverse positions as director of an orphanage and seamstress to the empress.

Due to illness, Prince returned to America in 1833 and was soon widowed. In Boston she worked for the American Anti-Slavery Society and set up an orphanage for colored children. Deeply religious, she took two missionary trips to Jamaica in 1841 and 1842 to proselytize blacks emancipated by the British in 1834. In danger from black insurrection and extortion of her limited monetary resources, Prince returned to Boston in 1843 and struggled to support herself. She wrote her autobiography to earn money; the preface to the third edition in

1856 records the author as very ill. Nothing more is known about her life or the conditions of her death.

See Also
Literature, African American; American Indians; American Revolution; Women Writers, Black, in the United States; Boston, Massachusetts; Free Blacks in the United States, 1619 to 1863.

North America

Prisons in the United States,

correctional facilities holding a sharply disproportionate number of African Americans; prison experience informed the social criticism of such black writers as Chester Himes, Eldridge Cleaver, and Mumia Abu-Jamal. In 1971 black inmates took part in one of the most controversial incidents in the history of American prisons, the Attica Uprising.

See Also
Cleaver, Eldridge Leroy.

North America

Proctor, Henry Hugh

(b. December 8, 1868, near Fayetteville, Tenn.; d. May 12, 1933, Brooklyn, N.Y.), African American Congregational minister known for establishing community programs within his church.

The child of former slaves Richard and Hannah (Murray) Proctor, Henry Hugh Proctor attended public school in Fayetteville, Tennessee, where, after teaching briefly in Pea Ridge, Tennessee, he became principal. In 1884 Proctor attended Central Tennessee College in Nashville, but soon transferred to nearby Fisk University, where he received a B.A. in 1891.

After graduating from Yale Divinity School in 1894, Proctor was ordained as a minister in the Congregational Church. As pastor of the prestigious First Congregational Church in Atlanta, Georgia, from 1894 until 1920, Proctor was instrumental in establishing multifaceted community activity and service programs within his church, while also working with whites to reduce racial strife. He died in 1933 in Brooklyn, New York, where he was pastor of the Nazarene Congregational Church.

North America

Professor Longhair (Henry Byrd)

(b. December 19, 1918, Bogalusa, La.; d. January 30, 1980, New Orleans, La.), African American rhythm and blues artist, regarded as the progenitor of post-World War II New Orleans R&B sound.

Henry Byrd was born to James L. and Ella Mae Byrd, both musicians, but was reared in New Orleans, Louisiana, solely by his mother. Impoverished, Byrd left school to work on the streets as a musical performer and dancer. At the age of eight he was working for the CJK Medicine Show as a stuntman, while remaining a street performer.

Despite the fact that Byrd could play the guitar and the piano, dancing provided his main source of work even into the 1930s, most notably with singer Champion Jack Dupree at the Cotton Club in New Orleans. From 1937 to 1942 Byrd worked mostly outside of entertainment in the Civilian Conservation Corps and as a cook, in addition to gambling professionally throughout Louisiana.

After World War II Byrd focused on music as his source of livelihood, developing his patented style of "flamboyant... strutting and riffing barrelhouse piano style." Before heading his own band, Professor Longhair and the Four Hairs, in 1949 Byrd played piano with several local bands. Under the names Professor Longhair and his Shuffling Hungarians and Roy Byrd, he recorded several hit records including "Baldhead (a.k.a. 'She Ain't Got No Hair')," "Tipitina," and "Go to the Mardi Gras," known as the "unofficial anthem" of New Orleans. These hits were popular due to Byrd's distinctively hoarse, semi-yodelling singing style, as well as his infectious piano rhythms. From the early 1960s until about 1970 Byrd faded from the musical world, but he regained wide renown after appearing in the 1971 New Orleans Jazz and Heritage Festival.

Professor Longhair's resurgent popularity continued even after his death in 1980; he was posthumously inducted into the Rock and Roll Hall of Fame in 1992. Leaving his mark on pianists from Fats Domino and Allen Toussaint to Harry Connick Jr., Professor Longhair, according to *Downbeat* magazine, "is the most influential pianist to emerge from the New Orleans milieu since Jelly Roll Morton."

See Also
World War II and African Americans; Domino, Antoine ("Fats"), Jr.; Morton, Ferdinand Joseph ("Jelly Roll"); New Orleans, Louisiana.

North America

Prophet, Nancy Elizabeth

(b. March 19, 1890, Warwick, R.I.; d. December 1960, Providence, R.I.), African American sculptor who was active in the Harlem Renaissance and in Paris through the 1930s.

A classically trained sculptor lauded for her sensitive and dignified busts of people of color, Nancy Elizabeth Prophet was born into humble circumstances. At an early age she was recognized as having unusual artistic skill. Earnings from work as a domestic enabled her to take a degree in painting and portraiture from the Rhode Island School of Design (RISD) in 1918.

A teaching job in Harlem brought Prophet to New York during the Harlem Renaissance. The atmosphere ignited her creativity, and she left New York for Paris's Ecole des Beaux Arts, where she studied from 1922 to 1925. Prophet's next 12 years in Paris were marked by a high level of artistic achievement, during which she produced her well-known sculpture *Congolaise* (1930). Even though her work was exhibited at Paris salons between 1924 and 1927 and in the United States (at RISD and in Boston, 1928), Prophet had great difficulty supporting herself as an artist. In fact, her poverty, malnutrition, and near starvation were so obvious to other artists in Paris that Henry O. Tanner nominated her for the Harmon Foundation Prize in 1928, hoping to gain her some financial relief. Prophet won the Harmon's Otto Kahn Prize in 1929 for *Head of a Negro* and later won the 1932 Newport Art Association prize for her portrait *Discontent*.

Prophet moved back to the United States, at the suggestion of her admirer W. E. B. Du Bois, to take a teaching job at Spelman College in 1934. With painter Hale Woodruff, she taught art at Atlanta University and Spelman College (1934-1944). Frustrated by a lack of materials, space, and time in which to produce her own art, as well as the prejudices of Atlanta's art community, she returned to Providence in 1944.

Prophet produced little sculpture in her later years, and she was again forced to support herself as a domestic servant. In the last 20 years of her life she destroyed many of her sculptures and watched her wood and metal artworks rot and rust for lack of money for storage space. Once a producer of "stark, aggressive, naturalistic and non-sentimental" sculpted portraits, she died penniless at age 70.

See Also
Boston, Massachusetts; Du Bois, William Edward Burghardt (W. E. B.); Harlem, New York; New York, New York; Tanner, Henry Ossawa; Woodruff, Hale Aspacio.

Latin America and the Caribbean

Protestant Church in Latin America and the Caribbean,

since the nineteenth century, but especially since World War II, Protestant churches in Latin America and the Caribbean have been magnets for people of African descent. The reasons are complex. First, in contrast to the Roman Catholic Church, these churches do not carry the stigma of many centuries' complicity with slavery; they offer structures of authority and leadership that are relatively open to people of color; and their doctrine of democratic access to the Holy Spirit is undoubtedly attractive to the socially disempowered. This essay examines these and other reasons for Protestantism's

appeal among the religion's four main types in the region: historical Protestantism, nonorthodox Evangelicalism, PENTECOSTALISM, and Neopentecostalism.

HISTORICAL PROTESTANTISM

The first Protestant churches to arrive in the region were noncharismatic BAPTISTS (from the United States) and Methodists (from GREAT BRITAIN). These churches' earliest missionaries strove to attract a mass black audience, but ultimately succeeded only in reaching a small, literate black contingent. In JAMAICA the Baptist mission was led by George Lisle, a manumitted slave from the American South who arrived in 1783. Although the number of Jamaican slaves converted to Baptism grew to nearly 10,000 on the eve of abolition in the 1830s, and may even have contributed to the slave rebellions of the period, interest in the church declined in the years after emancipation (*see* ABOLITION AND EMANCIPATION IN LATIN AMERICA AND THE CARIBBEAN), as it came to be replaced by the indigenously Jamaican religious movements of Native Baptism and Revival Zion. The historical Baptist Church, however, retained the better-educated, urban black elite who did not wish to be mistaken for their proletarian counterparts. Similarly, in BRAZIL, the missionaries of the North American Baptist Church never developed a mass black following. From the start they were associated with the urbanized and educated classes, including better-off mulattos; this remains the Brazilian Baptists' social base to this day.

The story of the Methodists is similar. Upon arriving in Jamaica from England in the 1780s, they sought to form a cadre of slave ministers. Numerous blacks flocked to the church as a result, but their numbers dwindled in the century following abolition, as nonelite ex-slaves turned to Pentecostal and Rastafarian groups. In Brazil the Methodists arrived early, in 1836, but directed their attention from the start to the literate mulatto elite, who were happy to find a religion that, unlike the Roman Catholic Church, would not snub them.

The elite people of color who were attracted to the historical Protestant churches found a degree of respect and opportunities for advancement that did not exist for them in the Roman Catholic Church. In Brazil the Methodists were innovators in addressing the racial issue. Home to many upwardly mobile mulattos, the Methodist Church became an important location from which to identify and criticize obstacles in the socioeconomic path of people of African descent. As early as the 1950s the Methodist José da Silva Oliveira preached against white prejudice and sought to promote among blacks an ideology of hard work, literacy, and social uplift. Later, in the 1980s, the Methodists were leaders in founding the national Ministry to Combat Racism. This ministry now has regular meetings at which members examine the teachings of the Bible on racism. The ministry promotes the inclusion in the Protestant liturgy of black music such as hip hop, REGGAE, RAP, and SAMBA. Despite these efforts, the church, with its emphasis on literacy, cool rationality, and education continues to appeal primarily to the black elite, not the masses.

NONORTHODOX EVANGELICALISM

No discussion of the participation of the African diaspora in Protestantism would be complete without mention of the powerful nonorthodox Protestant traditions in the Caribbean. In the wake of nineteenth-century revivalist awakenings, religious leaders emerged who articulated powerful Bible-centered visions syncretized with elements of non-Christian and traditional African belief. These include the Spiritual Baptists and Shouters of Trinidad, the Shakers of St. Vincent, and the Revival Zionists and Rastafarians of Jamaica.

Until the mid-eighteenth century, Protestantism in Jamaica was limited to the Anglicanism of the planter class. In 1783 George Lisle founded the Baptist Church, which eventually led to the emergence of Native Baptists. This group mingled Protestant theology, a strong preoccupation with dreams and visions, and the slave healing cult known as Myal. By the 1860s more than half the blacks of Kingston were Native Baptists. The 1890s saw the emergence of a major revivalist movement led by Alexander Bedward, whose preaching united biblical theology with the practice of healing using water from sacred springs. His followers, in turn, divided between the two biblical sects of Pocomania and Revival Zion.

Revival Zion is now, in Jamaica, one of the more popular religious groups among the descendants of slaves. Although staunchly committed to the Bible as its source of inspiration, the religion resembles the non-Christian groups of the hemisphere in its acceptance of possession by entities other than the Holy Spirit. Like the Pentecostals, Revival Zionists seek the experience of the Holy Ghost; unlike the Pentecostals, they also seek possession by the great prophets and evangelists of the Bible, from Moses, Joshua, and Ezekiel, to the apostles and archangels, to the spirits of the religion's deceased leaders. All these spirits visit the believer, taking him or her through spiritual, shamanlike journeys, and endowing him or her with the ability to heal. This power is also transmitted through drinking water drawn from a sacred spring, thereby bringing the spirits into the bodies of the believers.

An evangelist missionary prays in Largo-Carioca in Rio de Janeiro, Brazil. *Michael Ende/Aurora*

Revival Zion has strong Ethiopianist and back-to-Africa dimensions. African ancestors sometimes possess the faithful; the colors of the Ethiopian flag are often present in the ritual center; ETHIOPIA is regarded as the promised land to which the descendants of slaves will eventually return; and the color of gold, used in the adornment of the central spiritual pole of the cult center, is said to symbolize the lost riches of Africa. The music played during rituals, in contrast to that used in mainstream Protestantism, is self-consciously "African," as it uses traditional drums and percussive rhythms. The ritual itself is strongly reminiscent of the various African-derived cults and is based on the movement of mediums in a counterclockwise motion around a sacred center.

All these elements contributed in the 1930s to the hiving off from Revival Zion of Rastafarianism. Marcus Garvey was very influential among Revival Zionists because of his Ethiopianist views. When Garvey prophesied in 1929 that the Messiah would appear in the form of the Ethiopian emperor, he tapped into the messianism embedded in the Zionist reading of the Bible. Thus when Haile Selassie I was crowned emperor of Ethiopia in 1930, many Revival Zionists took this to be the fulfillment of Garvey's prophecy. Those who accepted the divinity of Selassie and his power to bring about the long-awaited return of the diaspora to the Zion of Ethiopia began to call themselves by Selassie's pre-imperial name, Ras Tafari. The sect grew quickly in the 1930s, as Ethiopia's Babylonian captivity by the Italian fascists seemed to many to be the realization of biblical prophecy. The religion fused the notions of sacred nature, healing, and Ethiopianism in the crucible of seething resentment against colonialism and white domination. Between the 1940s and 1960s the religion thrived in Kingston among the black underclass. In the 1970s the influence of reggae transformed the religion into a worldwide movement. Its roots in Garveyism's Ethiopianism meant that Rasta would become the spiritual and aesthetic heart of the Pan-Africanist movement from the 1970s to the present. Yet Rastafarianism continues to be a strongly biblical movement, deriving its ideological strength from its reading of the Old Testament.

Pentecostalism

Pentecostalism encompasses the numerous Protestant churches that emphasize the gifts of the Holy Spirit, such as prophecy and speaking in tongues. Pentecostalism is the fastest growing, most popular form of religiosity in Latin America and the Caribbean today, accounting for up to 85 percent of all Protestants. The religion arrived in Brazil and Jamaica in the second decade of the twentieth century, has grown at breakneck speed since the 1950s, and now can boast more than 20 million faithful in Brazil and half a million in Jamaica. Many of these people are black. While no more than 7 percent of Brazilians identify themselves to census takers as "black," fully 15 percent of Pentecostals do so. And in Jamaica, the majority of Pentecostals are black (rather than mulatto).

The causes for the religion's growth among blacks are not difficult to determine. In contrast to historical Protestantism, in which secular hierarchies are transferred to the church, Pentecostalism makes available the explosive experience of the Holy Spirit, which razes social distinctions. Further, in societies in which dark skin tones and nappy hair have low social prestige, people with these features are attracted by Pentecostalism's unequivocal language valuing natural over artificial, and inner over external beauty. Equally important, the building of strong self-esteem offers poor black youth in both societies a powerful alternative to the world of drugs and gangs. And, as is the case for all Pentecostals, irrespective of race, the abandonment of drinking, smoking, adultery, and gambling transforms household relationships, creating greater gender equality and offering couples hope of economic and emotional stability.

Neopentecostalism

Traditional Pentecostal denominations, such as the Assembly of God, have been slow to tap into the new, emerging groups of young people with hopes for upward mobility. In particular, these churches have been reluctant to incorporate young people's commercial music, dance, and the acceptance of "vanity" (stylish clothing and makeup) into their liturgical forms. Into this gap have moved a number of churches that spun off in the 1970s from the mainstream Pentecostal churches, and now are growing at a rapid clip through television, radio, and spectacular showlike revival meetings. These churches, such as the Universal Church of the Kingdom of God or the Church of Rebirth, embrace popular music, including traditionally black music, as well as styles of dance and dress that are rejected as too worldly by the older Pentecostals. The churches have a huge youth following, including young people of African descent. Yet because these are young people who can, in general, afford nicer clothes, and who look to religion primarily as a source of sociability rather than survival, they tend to belong to a relatively better-off class segment. The vast majority of poorer blacks continue to participate in the traditional Pentecostal churches. For them the impact of the Neopentecostals may be felt indirectly, as the older denominations feel obliged to rethink their doctrinal stances on music, dress, and dance. By the end of the century most denominations will no doubt have internalized the influence of Neopentecostalism.

It has become common in Latin America and the Caribbean for intellectuals who espouse some form of Pan-Africanism or Afrocentrism to criticize both Roman Catholic and Protestant Christianity as Eurocentric ideologies imposed on Africans from the outside and as having a deracinating influence on them. Without engaging this debate, the foregoing remarks on the Protestant traditions in the region have suggested that these traditions are not inevitably at odds with the development of a strong black racial identity, and that they have even been known at times to contribute to that identity.

John Burdick

See Also

Pan-Africanism; Garvey, Marcus Mosiah; Hip Hop in the United States; Kingston, Jamaica; Rastafarians; St. Vincent and the Grenadines; Trinidad and Tobago; Catholic Church in Latin America and the Caribbean; Slave Rebellions in Latin America and the Caribbean.

North America

Pryor, Richard Franklin Lenox Thomas (b. December 1, 1940, Peoria, Ill.), African American comedian known for his free-flowing, uncensored brand of humor.

Considered by many to be the most influential comedian since 1970, Richard Pryor was born to Gertrude Thomas and Leroy Pryor, who met in a brothel managed by Marie Carter, Leroy's mother. Raised in the brothel primarily by Carter, Pryor gravitated to humor early on to cope with his chaotic family life. A disruptive student, Pryor left school at age 14 and joined a community drama group, which he quit two years later. After serving in the army for two years Pryor began his stand-up comedy career. He performed successfully in Peoria nightclubs, giving him the confidence to go to the more competitive nightclub scene of New York City. Pryor modeled his first performances in New York closely on the comedy of Bill Cosby and Dick Gregory.

By the late 1960s, however, Pryor had decided to present "the real side" of himself, replacing a more refined persona with a raw, unglossy funkiness. His recognition grew as he recorded stand-up routines and appeared in several films, including *Lady Sings the Blues* and *Uptown Saturday Night*, Pryor's classic explorations of black life. In 1974 Pryor appeared on the cover of *Rolling Stone* magazine because of his gold-selling album, *That Nigger's Crazy*. Despite his overwhelming success Pryor was plagued with financial and drug problems. In 1980, at the time of the release of his first self-produced film, *Bustin' Loose*, he had a near fatal accident while freebasing cocaine. Throughout his turbulent life Pryor retained his sense of humor, as he demonstrated in his autobiographical film *Jo Jo Dancer, Your Life is Calling* (1986). Diagnosed with multiple sclerosis in 1986, Pryor continued to appear in several films, notably in *Harlem Nights* (1989).

See Also

Gregory, Richard Claxton "Dick"; New York, New York; Film, Blacks in American.

North America

Public Enemy, one of the premier African American rap music groups of the 1980s and 1990s. Public Enemy infused a funk- and soul-based sound with sound samples (electronic snippets of prerecorded music) and other sound fragments, such as traffic noise and police sirens. A political consciousness pervaded this multilayered sound, through rap texts and through physical appearance: group members held fake automatic weapons and wore army fatigues and boots, projecting an image of black militancy. Public Enemy's strident

lyrics were highly controversial, striking responsive chords with many people while drawing critical responses from many others.

Public Enemy formed in Long Island, New York, in 1987 out of collaborations among lead rappers Chuck D. (Carlton Ridenhour) and Flavor Flav (William Drayton), disk jockey (DJ) Terminator X (Norman Rogers), and the group's so-called minister of information, Professor Griff (Richard Griffin). The group's producers, Hank Shocklee, Eric "Vietnam" Sadler, and Chuck D., were collectively known as the Bomb Squad. The group took its name from "Public Enemy Number One," a popular rap written by Chuck D. along with DJs Hank and Keith Shocklee.

Public Enemy's first release, *Yo! Bum Rush the Show* (1987), relied upon the rhythms of funk music to create an aggressive sound. The group's second release, *It Takes a Nation of Millions to Hold Us Back* (1988), was layered with additional samples to form a more complex sound. As the group perfected its production and sampling techniques, the content grew more politicized and Public Enemy grew more popular. Chuck D.'s strong vocals were countered by Flavor Flav's rasping voice, with dance steps by the militaristic quartet known as the S1W (Security of the First World). With this combination the group advocated black nationalist activism and opposed what it felt was mindless American consumerism. This world-view in combination with Public Enemy's occasional invectives against whites, women, gays, and Jews elicited strong reactions from listeners – both positive and negative.

In 1989 Public Enemy's song "Fight the Power" was part of the soundtrack for the motion picture *Do the Right Thing,* directed by African American filmmaker Spike Lee. Shortly thereafter Professor Griff made some anti-Semitic statements to the American press, and the group temporarily disbanded. It soon returned, without Griff, and released the commercially successful and critically acclaimed albums *Fear of a Black Planet* (1990) and *Apocalypse 91... The Enemy Strikes Black* (1991). Other albums by Public Enemy include *Greatest Misses* (1992) and *Muse Sick-N-Hour Mess Age* (1994).

See Also
Soul Music; Funk; Lee, Shelton Jackson ("Spike"); Black Nationalism in the United States.

Latin America and the Caribbean

Puello, José Joaquín **(b. 1805?, Santo Domingo [present-day Trujillo], Dominican Republic; d. December 23, 1847, Santo Domingo, Dominican Republic), Afro-Dominican military figure and revolutionary.**

Little is known about José Joaquín Puello's early life. He was born to a family of humble means and at an early age exhibited a keen interest in and talent for handling firearms. His military career began in 1822 when he fought in the Haitian invasion of Santo Domingo under the command of Haitian president Jean-Pierre Boyer. This marked the beginning of a 22-year Haitian occupation of the eastern two-thirds of the island of Hispaniola. For his service in this effort Puello became captain of one of the Haitian regiments. However, Puello and some of his comrades became dismayed with Haitian policies, which included the imposition of high taxes, confiscation of land, and destruction of the educational system. Puello and others who were disillusioned with Boyer initiated a reform movement that in 1843 resulted in Puello's dismissal from his military post. Puello later protested the formation of a Haiti-Colombia confederation, which threatened to reinstate slavery in Hispaniola.

In order to fight for the creation of a self-governing republic, Puello became active in the Dominican Republic's independence movement. Commanding a large battalion against Haitian forces, he helped the Dominican Republic win its independence from Haiti on February 27, 1844. He was named general and commandant of arms in the capitol Santo Domingo and played a significant role in the organization of the Junta Central Gubernativo (Central Independent Government).

When the Haitian militia launched a second military campaign against the Dominican Republic on May 10, 1845, Puello and his troops forced them into retreat. Dominican president Pedro Santana recognized Puello's leadership skills and appointed him to a position in the Ministerios de Hacienda y Comercio (Treasury and Commerce Departments). But two years after his appointment, Puello and his brother Gabino were accused of conspiring to overthrow the government through a black insurrection. Although Puello's military record demonstrated his commitment to liberating all peoples, conservatives had earlier accused him of being "anti-white" and of fighting solely in the interests of persons of color on the island. A 25-man commission drawn from the judiciary, legislature, and military condemned Puello and his brother to death. They were executed on December 23, 1847. Despite Puello's role in establishing and maintaining an independent Dominican Republic, he is now a scarcely remembered military hero.

Aaron Myers

See Also
Haiti; Racial Question during Struggles of Independence in Latin America.

Tito Puente, composer, bandleader, percussionist, outstanding *timbales* player, and an originator of Afro-Latin jazz, performs at the Monterey Jazz Festival. *CORBIS/Craig Lovell*

Latin America and the Caribbean

Puente, Ernesto Antonio (Tito) **(b. April 20, 1923, New York, N.Y.), bandleader, composer, multi-instrumentalist – accomplished on timbales, conga, bongos, vibraphone, piano, and saxophone – and last of the great originators of Afro-Latin jazz.**

With the death of Mario Bauza in 1993, Tito Puente became the last of the early innovators of Afro-Latin jazz who continued to be musically active. Although best known as a bandleader and *timbales* player, Puente is a multi-instrumentalist, performing on a wide range of percussion instruments as well as on piano and saxophone. For over half a century he has been a dynamic entertainer, emerging in the 1980s as a pop-culture celebrity.

Puente was born in New York City's Spanish Harlem. He had hoped to become a dancer, but an ankle injury led him to choose a career of instrumental performance. As a youth he played percussion and piano in the local band Los Happy Boys. He performed with Machito, Fernando Alvarez, and others while a teenager. He served three years in the United States Navy during World War II, and received his first informal lessons in composition and orchestration from white bandleader Charlie Spivak aboard the USS *Santee.* After his discharge in 1945 Puente studied music theory, orchestration, and conducting at the Juilliard School of Music in New York City.

During the late 1940s and early 1950s Puente played a key role in the merging of Latin American rhythms with contemporary jazz that produced Afro-Latin jazz. In the late 1940s he formed the Piccadilly Boys, which became the Tito Puente Orchestra. The group played a major role in promoting the mambo craze of the late 1940s. A decade later Puente helped popularize the chachachá sound. He produced swinging and danceable style by transforming the music of *charanga* bands, which feature violin and flute, and arranging it for a Latin jazz big band with saxes, trumpets, and trombones. In the

1970s, when salsa became popular, he gained a new and younger audience.

Since 1949 Puente has released more than 100 albums as a leader, an accomplishment rivaled by few musicians of any genre. His recording "Abaniquito" (1949) was a hit single and an early crossover success. In the 1970s Carlos Santana covered two of Puente's compositions: "Para los rumberos" (1956) and a hugely popular rendition of "Oye como va" (1963). Puente's various bands have featured many musicians who went on to prominence in Afro-Latin jazz, including percussionists Ray Barreto, Mongo Santamaría, and Willie Bobo; Fania Records founder Johnny Pacheco; and, more recently, saxophonist Mario Rivera, pianist Hilton Ruiz, trumpeter Charlie Sepúlveda, and drummer Ignacio Berroa. Outside of the world of jazz Puente has performed with various Latin music stars, including the Fania All Stars, Celia Cruz, and Carlos "Patato" Valdez.

Since the late 1970s Puente has also gained wider exposure in American popular culture. In the 1980s he appeared on *The Cosby Show* and in a stylish and well-received Coca-Cola commercial. He was in Jeremy Marre's television film *Salsa '79* (1979), and seven years later made his feature film debut with cameos in *Radio Days* (1986) and *Armed and Dangerous* (1986). Puente's most significant film role was in *The Mambo Kings* (1991), playing a Latin jazz bandleader; he also arranged and performed much of the music on the film's soundtrack. He received Grammy Awards for *A Tribute to Benny Moré* (1979), *On Broadway* (1983), *Mambo Diablo* (1985), and *Goza mi timbal* (1989).

James Clyde Sellman

See Also

Cosby, Bill; Harlem, New York; Salsa Music; New York, New York; Santamaría, Ramón ("Mongo").

Latin America and the Caribbean

Puerto Rico, the easternmost island of the Greater Antilles, bounded on the north by the Atlantic Ocean, on the south by the Caribbean Sea, on the east by the Virgin Passage, and on the west by the Mona Passage, which separates it from the Dominican Republic.

Heralded as "the shining star of the Caribbean" in tourism brochures and advertisements, Puerto Rico exemplifies the complexities of race relations and the use of terminology and definitions to describe them. Considered by some as "the whitest of all the Antilles," Puerto Ricans are usually described as mostly Hispanic, a homogeneous race of mixed people. This conception of the Puerto Rican underestimates the African component, one that has had a significant impact on the culture and ethnic composition of Puerto Rico. The African traditions brought to Puerto Rico were syncretized with the Spanish, the Taíno, and, later, the Anglo-American traditions to produce a rich cultural and ethnic amalgam. The racial mixture between blacks and whites has shaped the conception of race in Puerto Rico. There has been a growing scholarly interest in the Creole blacks and their importance in the formation of the Puerto Rican society (*see* José Luis González), in contrast to the traditional history that has focused on the actions of the ruling white Creole elite.

Traditional United States conceptions of blackness (including anyone with some African blood) and whiteness are of limited use in assessing Puerto Rican conceptions of race. The population's seemingly genial attitude toward race relations gives the impression of a society free from racism and prejudice. Yet this idea is proved wrong by the social, political, and economic status of Afro-Puerto Ricans.

Native American Presence

The recorded history of Puerto Rico began with the arrival of Columbus on November 19, 1493. Puerto Rico was inhabited by the aboriginal Indians named Taínos, who called their island Boriquén. Since there is no reliable documentation, estimates regarding the number of Taínos have ranged from the unlikely figure of 8 million to the more realistic 60,000. The colonization of San Juan, the name given to the island by the Spanish, began in 1508 when Juan Ponce de León established the first settlement. The Taíno population decreased dramatically during the first period of colonization as a result of the spread of European diseases, various rebellions, and the *encomiendas* system, the regime of forced labor that distributed Taíno Indians among the settlers. Although the Taínos were legally exempted from slavery by royal decree in 1542, rebel Indians were enslaved and exploited by the colonists. By the end of the sixteenth century the Taínos were virtually extinct.

African Arrival in Puerto Rico

The first Africans arrived with Columbus in 1493. However, the slave trade was not authorized until 1510. Many free blacks, mainly from Seville, emigrated, searching for better opportunities in the New World. They were mainly *ladinos*, or Christianized blacks, who came to serve as domestic servants. In Puerto Rico there were always larger numbers of free blacks than slaves. These free blacks worked in the mines and helped the militia to subjugate the Taínos. They acted individually and moved frequently in search of better work opportunities.

Since the Taíno population was rapidly diminishing, many colonists favored the introduction of black slaves as a substitute for the Indian work force. African slaves were initially used to search for gold. Yet during the first half of the sixteenth century the slave population remained relatively small. Only 1500 enslaved Africans were legally introduced to Puerto Rico from 1536 to 1553. Throughout the seventeenth century the legal trade remained very limited, although an undetermined number of African slaves were introduced as contraband.

Puerto Rico in the Eighteenth and Nineteenth Centuries

In the eighteenth century Puerto Rico's economy remained underdeveloped because Spain refused to see the island as anything other than a military outpost. It was not until 1815 that the economic development of Puerto Rico received official support, when Ferdinand VII issued the Real Cédula de Gracias, which liberalized trade, offered incentives for immigrants, and opened Puerto Rican ports to legal commerce. It was also an attempt to "whiten" the island because, at the time, the population was mainly black and mulatto (of African and European descent).

The Trade of Enslaved Africans

The sugar industry became the most important economic activity of Puerto Rico in the nineteenth century. Spain grew more interested in the economic development of the Antilles as a way of regaining control of the mainland. There was a boom in sugar production in Cuba, Spanish Santo Domingo, and Puerto Rico, leading to increased slave importation from West Africa. While information on the slave trade to Puerto Rico is incomplete, the available records indicate that Senegal, Sudan, and Guinea were major sources. The black population was concentrated in the coastal sugar plantations, in places like Mayagüez, Guayama, and Ponce, in the southern region of the island. The number of black slaves and free *pardos* (mulattos) grew rapidly between 1820 and 1840. For example, from 5037 slaves in 1765, the number grew to 21,730 in 1821. In the 1830s women constituted almost half of the slave population. They were preferred because they could give birth to more slaves as well as work on the plantations. The forced immigration of Africans reached its peak by the 1840s. The 1845 census shows that there were 216,083 whites, 175,000 free coloreds, and 51,265 slaves in Puerto Rico.

Forced immigration rapidly declined primarily because of the inability of Puerto Rican plantation owners, or *hacendados,* to compete against the Cuban slave owners in the international slave market. For example, in 1840 the *bozales,* or African-born slaves, constituted 46 percent of the total slave population in Ponce, the city with the largest number of slaves at the time. By 1872 they represented only 18 percent. The last enslaved Africans who came to the island were relatively young and came from Nigeria, Ghana, and the Democratic Republic of the Congo.

Resistance and the Abolition of Slavery

As they did in the rest of the Americas, members of the enslaved population of Puerto Rico resisted the slave system. The first recorded rebellion against European domination in the hemisphere occurred in 1514 and was jointly planned and executed by Taínos and Africans.

Numerous revolts, conspiracies, and individual escapes occurred in different municipalities throughout the island from 1775 to 1873. For example, between 1795 and 1848, 22 conspiracies were reported. These acts of resistance occurred mostly in the towns of Guayama and Ponce, where in 1821 the slave Marcos Xiorro revolted without success but achieved legendary status among the slaves. For most slaves, running away was the only way to escape from a life of oppressive work and inhumane treatment. For example, slaves were labeled with a red-hot iron called a *carimbo,* used to prevent them from being illegally introduced into the island. They were frequently whipped. Not even pregnant women were exempt; they were forced to lie on the ground with their bellies in a dug-out hole (designed to protect the unborn slave) and then they were whipped (*see* Punishment of Slaves in Colonial Latin America and the Caribbean).

The slaves who successfully escaped to the mountains were called *cimarrones.* In Puerto Rico there were never enough of them to take over the land or proclaim a war against their oppressors. It was common practice for the cimarrones to set fire to the cane fields as a means of attracting the militia's attention in order to steal their weapons. Owners controlled and closely watched any slave gatherings. Sometimes the slaves planned conspiracies and revolts when they got together to play and dance *bomba.* They risked being found out by their master/overseer and being exposed by other slaves. Colonial authorities encouraged antagonistic relations between slaves by granting liberty to those cimarrones who turned in other escaped slaves. They also gave freedom and 500 pesos to blacks who reported any kind of slave conspiracy. Some slaves bought their liberty by paying their owner; however, not many could afford to do this. One slave annually was awarded freedom because of good behavior; some bought their children's freedom when they were baptized. Others escaped bondage by committing suicide. Many of them believed their spirit would return to Africa after they died. Other fugitive slaves escaped to Haiti and Santo Domingo. Given the large free black labor force on the island, some slaves tried to escape their bondage by passing as free workers, moving from town to town until they were discovered.

In 1826 Miguel de la Torre, the governor of Puerto Rico, enacted the first regulation regarding slave treatment, which was inspired by the increasing number of conspiracies. It required the slave owner to feed slaves properly and provide medical aid in the case of acute illness. Domestic slaves had to convert to Roman Catholicism and remain obedient to authorities and respectful of whites. The regulation imposed harsh penalties for rebellious slaves, including slashing and imprisonment.

In May 1848 Governor Juan Prim adopted the infamous Bando contra la Raza Africana (Proclamation Against the African Race). It was an oppressive ordinance directed against all people of African descent, including free blacks. All blacks were subject to court-martial for any offense. The proclamation also imposed the penalty of "hand cutting" to those free persons of African descent who raised a weapon against whites, even if the aggression was justified. Those slaves found guilty were executed. Harsh prison sentences were imposed on any black who insulted or threatened a white man. The succeeding governor, Juan de la Pezuela, abolished Prim's measures in November of the same year, but rebellions and conspiracies continued.

The system of slavery started to erode in Puerto Rico after the 1850s, with the beginning of Puerto Rico's independence movement. At that time independence and abolition went hand in hand with political radicalism. Thus the first goal of the independence movement was to end forced labor. The Sociedad Abolicionista Española (Spanish Abolitionist Society) was founded in 1855 by Ramón Emeterio Betances and a group of white Creoles who secretly worked against the institution of slavery. They promised freedom to their slaves if they participated in the revolution. After being exiled in 1867, Betances helped foment the Grito de Lares in 1868, which was the first independence revolt against Spain. Although the Lares revolt failed, it catalyzed the abolition process. Spain was not willing to grant independence to Puerto Rico after Grito de Lares, but it realized that slavery could no longer be maintained in the island. In 1870 the Spanish government passed the Moret Law, which provided for the liberation of children born between 1868 and 1870 and those slaves over 60 years of age. Under this partial abolition statute, about 10,000 slaves were set free in Puerto Rico. Nevertheless, they had to work under a contract for three years after acquiring their freedom. More than 90 percent of the slaves at this time were *criollos* (Creoles).

On March 22, 1873, slavery was completely abolished, hastened by the economic situation of the plantation owners. The plantation economy in Puerto Rico had declined after 1850. The members of the slave-owning class had neither the infrastructure nor the cash flow of their Cuban counterparts, and most of them were in debt by the 1860s. Therefore, they were not in an economically viable position to oppose abolition effectively. These factors marked the end of the old plantation system of *haciendas,* characterized by small and midsize plantations owned by white Creoles, and marked the beginning of one of Puerto Rico's worst economic crises. For the former slaves this period meant the continuation of harsh conditions under an obligatory contract system in which they were paid but had to rely on their owners to survive.

Importance of Free Coloreds in the Island

People of African descent, predominantly free, constituted the majority of the island's inhabitants. Most lived restricted lives, with no control over where they lived or worked, no freedom to decide whom to marry, and no access to social institutions. Nevertheless, some managed to secure a rudimentary education; rented or owned land, stores, and houses; and attained important positions. For example, in 1845, reports mentioned Manuel Elías, a free colored silversmith who owned three houses and had three slaves. María Francisca Ferrer owned a house and two male slaves, and saved an impressive amount of money. Also, Micaela Pizarro apparently was in the real estate business and owned slaves. Free people of color used their legal position to acquire some wealth even when they had to deal with racial prejudice. Some inherited property from their masters.

As in the rest of Spanish America, the free colored men had to serve in the segregated militia. In Puerto Rico, however, they had the right by royal decree to bear arms, even in times of peace, and to protect the island in the event of a slave revolt, an insurrection, or any kind of attack or invasion. These men played a vital role in the defense of the island, especially in resisting the English attack of 1797. Apparently, whites were not threatened by the fact that colored men were in charge of defense.

The number of free blacks and pardos increased more rapidly than the number of whites between 1820 and 1840. They suffered more than whites from the consequences of the cholera epidemic that claimed thousands of lives in the second half of the century. They also had to cope, more than whites, with the deterioration of the public health system. For these reasons, and the fact that the racial classifications changed, the white population in the second half of the century appeared to grow more rapidly. The increasing numbers of those classified as "white" also reflected the fluidity of racial definitions. In a context in which few could claim "purity of blood" and whiteness was the preferred designation, many simply elected to emphasize European ancestry. Under Spanish law, "whiteness" could be purchased, and those who accumulated sufficient wealth paid for an official change in their records.

Free colored people lived in an elaborate caste system, in which the degree of whiteness determined their position and possibilities in the colonial society. The stratification of the Puerto Rican society resulting from this system granted superiority to whites over the pardos and blacks. The mixing of races was associated with illegitimacy and provided whites with another reason for rejecting blacks. Still, *limpieza de sangre,* or purity (*see* WHITENING) of blood through marrying a lighter-skinned person, was the way to ascend in the social class structure. Light-skinned people had better economic and social possibilities.

The government always wanted to maintain control over the laboring population, white and black, slave and free. Between 1838 and 1868 the government improved the mechanisms of control by implementing mandatory labor laws that affected all laboring sectors, whites as well as blacks and pardos. All men between 16 and 60 years old who did not own or rent land were called *jornaleros,* or workers who earn a salary. In 1849 Juan de la Pezuela instituted what is known as *la libreta* (the notebook), which stated that every jornalero had to carry a notebook in which the owner made notes on the worker's behavior. Authorities revised la libreta and labeled as "lazy" anyone who was not earning a salary, in which case the worker had to move to another town. This practice often tied the workers to their owner's land and promoted complete dependency.

By the end of the nineteenth century the majority of blacks in Puerto Rico were "Creole blacks," born and raised on the Island. Creole blacks were better characterized as black Puerto Ricans rather than Africans living in a foreign Caribbean island. While preserving many African traditions, blacks adopted much of Spanish culture and were instrumental in maintaining aspects of the Taíno culture as well. Although Roman Catholicism was the only recognized religion, the vast majority of the population practiced syncretic forms, combining Christian images and traditions with African beliefs. There was a paucity of Roman Catholic clergy and other resources (doctors, etc.), a reflection of Spain's general neglect of Puerto Rico. Thus, lay forms of religion were often the only option for the populace.

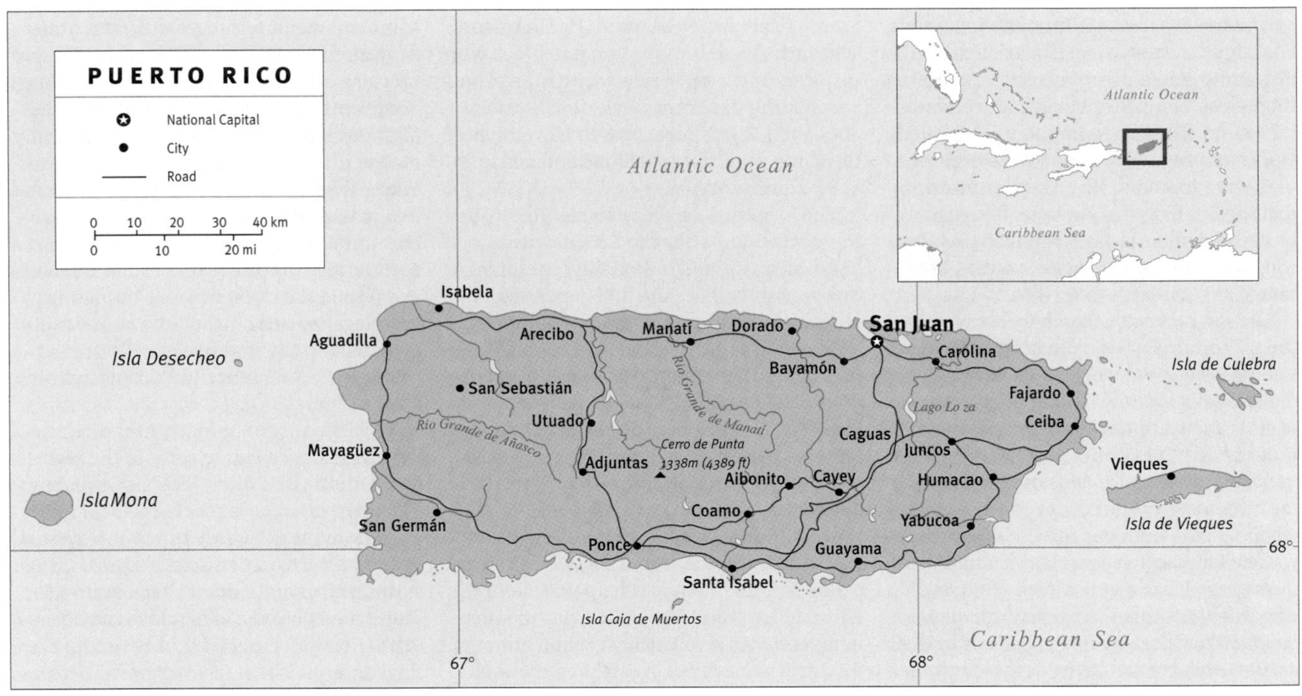

Puerto Rico in the Twentieth Century

In 1898, just as Puerto Rico was making strides toward autonomy, it was ceded to the United States under the Treaty of Paris, after the SPANISH-CUBAN-AMERICAN WAR. The military led the island for a short time, followed by a civil government outlined in the Foraker Act, which was approved in 1900. United States racial attitudes and race issues then began to affect Puerto Rican life, aggravating the already existing racism on the island in which the definition of a national identity privileged the Hispanic heritage over the African. For example, in 1917, with the imminent participation of the United States in World War I, the Jones Act granted American citizenship to Puerto Ricans, many of whom then had to fight in the U.S. military. Since that time, Puerto Ricans have participated in every military conflict in which the United States has been involved. At first, Puerto Rican males were grouped with segregated Negro units. Those Puerto Ricans who considered themselves whites were offended by this grouping.

Puerto Ricans who migrated to the mainland to work from the end of the nineteenth century on, especially after World War I and until the 1940s, underwent a similar experience with racial classifications. They were confronted with the fact that the way they defined themselves was different from how they were defined on the mainland. The complex racial prejudice that came from the times of slavery developed a conception that equated African heritage with a supposed lack of capacity to perform well socially and intellectually. This clearly affected the development and definition of a national identity in and outside the island. Subscribing to a different definition of national and racial identity, Afro-Puerto Ricans were discouraged to learn about their African heritage and its importance historically.

In 1943 Luis Muñoz Marín, who later became the first elected Puerto Rican governor for the Popular Democratic Party when the commonwealth was established in 1952, passed the first Civil Rights Act of Puerto Rico. Before this legislation, it was common practice to turn away people of color at places that were open to the rest of the public, such as casinos and restaurants. The new act imposed criminal penalties for anyone who denied services to people on the basis of race or color in public places, in businesses, or on public transportation, but the law was not enforced.

The Bill of Rights of Puerto Rico's Constitution was approved in 1952 and included a specific provision prohibiting discrimination on the basis of race, color, or social condition. In 1965 a civil rights commission was created for the purpose of investigating and educating the public and proposing legal reforms on issues of civil rights, including racial discrimination. Under the commonwealth status, the United States Constitution

LEFT: Two generations of Puerto Rican women get ready to dance the *bomba* in their folkloric costumes. *Suzanne L. Murphy/D. Donne Bryant Stock Photo*
BELOW LEFT: This photo shows city walls and the governor's mansion, known as "La Fortaleza" (the Fortress), in San Juan. *A.G.E. FotoStock*

and civil rights laws are fully applicable to Puerto Rico, reinforcing the local laws that existed before federal protections became effective.

In spite of these legislative changes, racism has continued to exist in various forms in the island. For example, in the 1950s the Commission for Civil Rights gathered evidence that proved that Afro-Puerto Rican professors and students were victims of discrimination in private schools. There is a correlation between race and social class in Puerto Rico. The economic elite in Puerto Rico continues to be predominantly white, while the Afro-Puerto Rican and mulatto communities are generally associated with poor conditions and crime. Racial prejudice varies from class to class yet tends to be more evident in the upper classes. This prejudice is also directed against the Dominican undocumented immigrants who come to the island through the Mona Passage looking for better economic opportunities.

The problems of racism and marginality in Puerto Rico are far from being solved. Still, there is increasing awareness and discussion of the Afro-Puerto Rican situation in the island and on the mainland as well that have brought many Puerto Ricans of African descent together for the purpose of confronting enduring discrimination. Scholarly works, like ISABELO ZENÓN CRUZ's *Narciso descubre su trasero* and José Luis González's *El país de cuatro pisos*, have been essential in fomenting that awareness. Other important contributions have come from Puerto Rican immigrants in the United States who have been deeply influenced by African American civil rights movements; for example, the Young Lords, who resemble the Black Panthers of the 1960s (*see* AFRO-LATINO CULTURES IN THE UNITED STATES). Other organizations, like the Unión de mujeres negras puertorriqueñas (Union of Afro-Puerto Rican Women) and the Concilio puertorriqueño contra el racismo (Puerto Rican Council Against Racism), have come forward in defense of people of African descent in the island.

African heritage is an essential and undeniable part of Puerto Rican culture. It is evident in musical expressions like salsa; in the vernacular rhythms of PLENA AND BOMBA, which are also dances; in the language; in the cuisine; and in popular traditions of the island. Afro-Puerto Ricans like ROBERTO CLEMENTE have distinguished themselves in sports. Many political leaders of African descent, such as PEDRO ALBIZU CAMPOS, Ernesto Ramos Antonini, and JOSÉ CELSO BARBOSA, have played important roles in history. In the arts, musicians like RAFAEL CORTIJO, Ismael Rivera, Rafael Hernández, and WILLIE COLÓN; painters like JOSÉ CAMPECHE; and writers like JULIA DE BURGOS, LUIS PALÉS MATOS, and Luis Rafel Sánchez serve as examples of the importance of Afro-Puerto Rican culture and ethnicity.

Mayda Grano de Oro

SEE ALSO

Congo, Democratic Republic of the; Transatlantic Slave Trade; Complexities of Ethnic and Racial Terminology in Latin America and the Caribbean; Slavery in Latin America and the Caribbean; Creoles; Salsa Music; Sánchez, Luis Rafael; Abolition and Emancipation in Latin America and the Caribbean; Catholic Church in Latin America and the Caribbean; Ramos Antonini, Ernesto.

Puff Daddy. Please see COMBS, SEAN ("PUFFY")

Latin America and the Caribbean

Punishment of Slaves in Colonial Latin America and the Caribbean, corporal inflictions used as corrective and demoralizing penalties for individual slaves and as exemplary measures to control other blacks in bondage through terror and fear.

Corporal punishment was designed with various goals in mind. Broadly speaking, one could argue that its purpose was fivefold: (1) to deter rebellious behavior; (2) to instill fear in order to prevent defiance from becoming exemplary; (3) to inculcate the Roman Catholic religion and prevent the expression of African spiritual practices and other forms of resistance to the colonizers' culture; (4) to regulate sexual conduct in order to prevent MISCEGENATION and preserve clear-cut socioracial hierarchies; and (5) to sustain the interests of various corporations or elite groups.

Punishment for slaves in colonial Latin America was of two types: de jure (regulated by law) or de facto (according to the custom and will of the slave owners). De jure punishment was established in *cédulas* (legislation issued by the Spanish king), local edicts and orders (issued by the viceroy), and codes. These laws regulated a variety of corporal punishments for slaves according to the types of crimes and their severity. The punishments escalated from whipping to branding to mutilations to death. The normative structure allowed for masters or government authorities to discipline slaves physically for many actions considered defiant or unruly, such as engaging in religious rites that were not Roman Catholic; gathering in groups; stealing; carrying arms; and talking back to or hitting whites. The most extreme punishment, death, was designated for runaway slaves or for leaders of slave revolts if caught.

Orders and cédulas also set forth punishments for a broad variety of actions and were issued as a direct response to a local offense. For example, as scholar Leslie Rout's research shows, cutting down trees or picking fruit or corn merited 100 floggings for the first offense and the mutilation of the slave's genitals if the action was repeated (PERU, 1537). Male slaves who had sexual relations with Indian women were to be whipped 100 times (CHILE, 1550). Changing the course of an irrigation channel could also merit 100 lashes (Peru, 1537). Slaves who were found to have Indians as their servants would receive 100 whippings for the first offense and have their ears cut off if they were found culpable a second time (Peru, 1551). Playing cards merited 50 to 200 lashes (Chile, 1577). Slaves who worked in the printing business without being under direct control of their master would receive 100 to 200 lashes (MEXICO, 1605).

As if these laws did not allow for severe enough punishment, it has been generally recognized that they were ignored as the local authorities and masters interpreted them to fit their specific circumstances and cruel creativity. In colonial Latin America there was a generalized belief that "carelessness, laziness and an aversion to work are natural for the inhabitants of Africa"; therefore slaveholders thought it was necessary to subject enslaved Africans to a harsh regime and to perform exemplifying punishments. Slaves were also believed to be little more than material goods. Because they had ownership rights, masters felt they could dispose of slaves according to their own judgment. Compassion was based on limiting the damage to their economic investment rather than on humanitarian motives. However, rage against runaways and rebels was particularly vicious because of the challenge they presented to the whole system. Historians have found accounts of escaped or rebellious slaves being roasted to death or hung on the island of HISPANIOLA, fitted with iron collars and thrown to hungry dogs in PANAMA, tortured and beheaded in Mexico, boiled to death in Costa Rica, dragged through streets and quartered in URUGUAY, and branded with hot irons in BRAZIL.

Epifanio de Moirans, a Spanish priest, described such punishments in his 1682 testimony: "Other [slave owners] will burn [the slaves'] ribs with red hot irons, or apply a knife to their intimate parts; some will cut off pieces of meat or the testicles with a knife; but all of the slaves are jailed with chains, and are made to work this way or with a type of horn made of iron around their neck. Mules and horses are not so ill treated as are Christian slaves by the Catholics of the Indies.... The [master's] mistake is to believe that they have ownership over [the slaves] as over pigs; and as such some of the masters and mistresses proceed with furious passion and murder their slaves, drowning them and cutting them up into pieces.... Runaways that were captured were beaten until their bones were broken or they were hung by law or they were murdered by their captors.... In other regions fugitives that were caught received two hundred whippings and had their ears cut off. These are excesses that I have seen and been informed of with all certainty, because I have been able to travel through regions of the Portuguese, Spanish and French, to see the good and bad works of men."

Liliana Obregón

SEE ALSO

Slavery in Latin America and the Caribbean; Central America; Panama; Andes, Blacks During Colonial Times in the; Catholic Church in Latin America and the Caribbean; Colonial Latin America and the Caribbean; Religions, African, in Latin America and the Caribbean; Slave Rebellions in Latin America and the Caribbean; Slave Laws in Colonial Spanish America; Colonial Critics of Slavery; Black Codes in Latin America; Biohó, Benkos.

Africa

Punt, a mysterious African land that provided ancient Egypt with luxury goods.

Few things are certain about the land of Punt. Scholars have not confidently identified any Puntite artifacts, and they are uncertain of the country's location. In fact, it seems possible that the Egyptians referred to different regions as "Punt" at different times. Egyptians recorded sea journeys to Punt south down the Red Sea, or river journeys via the Nile. Punt may have been in present-day SUDAN, ETHIOPIA, ERITREA, DJIBOUTI, or SOMALIA – or in more than one of these places at different times. Punt's boundaries could have enclosed coastal areas, inland areas, or both.

Egyptian records document trading expeditions to Punt for more than a thousand years. The Palermo Stone of the Fifth Dynasty first mentions imports from Punt during Sahure's reign (2458-2446 B.C.E.). Most information about Punt comes from reliefs in the temple of Queen Hatshepsut (1472-1458 B.C.E.), which tell not only of trade but also of Puntites and their land. The final Egyptian reference to trade with Punt was during Ramses III's reign (1194-1163 B.C.E.); however, other sources mention Punt as late as the XXVI Dynasty (664-525 B.C.E.). The Greeks also traded with Punt beginning in the fourth century B.C.E., and Greek geographers wrote of Punt as recently as 100 B.C.E.

Egypt exchanged foods, alcohol, and other goods with Puntites for luxury goods such as myrrh, incense, herbs, electrum, gold, staves, cosmetics, ebony, ivory, monkeys, cattle and hounds, leopard skins, and probably slaves. While the evidence clearly illustrates Egyptian expeditions to Punt, it also appears that the Puntites voyaged to Egypt as traders.

The Egyptian reliefs suggest that Punt was a mostly arid land, rich in minerals and animal life, including domestic donkeys, as well as birds, giraffes, ibexes, leopards, elephants, and rhinoceroses. The people are believed to have been pastoralists who lived in round huts on stilts, perhaps to protect the residents from wild animals or to provide shelter for livestock below. The women were mostly slender. The men, clothed in bifurcated kilts, wore their hair both shaved and long, with short, blunt beards, or long beards in the Egyptian style with curled ends.

Robert Fay

SEE ALSO
Elephant; Giraffe; Gold Trade; Ivory Trade; Egypt, Ancient Kingdom of; Nile River; Pastoralism; Rhinoceros.

Europe

Pushkin, Alexander

(b. June 6, 1799, Moscow; d. February 10, 1837, St. Petersburg, Russia), Russian poet and author of plays, novels, and short stories, considered the founder of modern Russian literature; his maternal great-grandfather was African.

This undated illustration by Vasily Tropinin shows the poet Alexander Pushkin (1799-1837), whose work reflected both his love of Russian folktales and his fascination with his partially African heritage. His great-grandfather, Abram Hannibal, was a slave who had become a major general in the Russian army. *CORBIS/Bettmann*

Alexander Pushkin was of high birth: his father came from a long line of Russian aristocracy, and his mother was the granddaughter of ABRAM HANNIBAL, who proclaimed himself to be an African prince. Sold into slavery in the early eighteenth century, Hannibal became an engineer and major general in the Russian army and was a favorite of Tsar Peter I (Peter the Great) (*see* RUSSIA AND THE FORMER SOVIET UNION).

Enchanted with his African ancestry, Pushkin often employed the subject in his poetry, to the point of exaggeration and obsession, according to his critics. In 1830 Faddey Bulgarin berated Pushkin for bragging about a nobility stemming from a "Negro" who had been "acquired" by a skipper in exchange for a bottle of rum. Pushkin replied sharply to "Figliarin" (which translates roughly into "buffoon") in a poem entitled "My Genealogy": "Postscriptum / Figliarin, snug at home, decided / That my black grandsire, Hannibal, / Was for a bottle of rum acquired / And fell into a skipper's hands. / This skipper was the glorious skipper / Through whom our country was advanced / Who to our native vessel's helm / Gave mightily a sovereign course. / This skipper was accessible / To my grandsire: the blackamoor, / Bought at a bargain, grew up stanch and loyal / The emperor's bosom friend, not slave."

Pushkin was deeply influenced by the Russian folklore and stories his maternal grandmother told him as a child, and he searched out similar stories from Russian villagers throughout his life. As were many Russian aristocrats, he was also well versed in French language and literature. Educated at the Imperial Lyceum at Tsarkoye Selo, Pushkin demonstrated an early poetic genius in works such as "To My Friend the Poet" (1820), which demonstrated his allegiance to Romantic literary styles.

Pushkin diverged from this style in later works. In *Ruslan and Liudmila* (1820) he espoused a literary manner characterized by ample use of Russian folklore in the form of a narrative poem. Because this work rejected established rules and genres, he was criticized by the main literary schools of the day, classicism and sentimentalism. Still, *Ruslan and Liudmila* earned him a reputation as one of Russia's most promising poetic talents.

In 1817 Pushkin accepted a position in the Ministry of Foreign Affairs in St. Petersburg. He participated in the city's social life and belonged to an underground branch of the revolutionary group Union of Welfare. The radical fervor he expressed through his verse made him an inspiring spokesman for the revolutionaries who fought in the 1825 Decembrist uprising for a constitutional monarchy. They were violently suppressed. It was during this period that Pushkin wrote "Ode to Liberty" (1820), for which he was exiled to the Caucasus.

Pushkin's works written in exile, called his "southern cycle," were clearly influenced by the English poet Lord Byron. He demonstrates the love for liberty typical of his contemporaries in the romantic narrative poems *The Prisoner of the Caucasus* (1822), *The Fountain of Bakhchisarai* (1824), and *The Gypsies* (1824). In 1823 he began *Eugene Onegin* (1831), known to be the first of the great Russian novels (although in verse). Though a Byronic love story, *Eugene Onegin* treats the Russian historical setting realistically and the characters objectively.

Pushkin was transferred to Odessa in 1823, but after a series of incidents, including an affair with a superior's wife, he was dismissed from government service in 1824. He was banished to his mother's estate near Pskov, where he wrote *Boris Godunov* (1931), a Russian historical tragedy in the Shakespearean tradition. In *Boris Godunov*,

Pushkin emphasizes the moral and political importance of "the judgment of the people" toward their rulers, and proved that he could, as he felt poet-prophets should, "fire the hearts of men with his words."

In 1826 Tsar Nicholas I, recognizing Pushkin's enormous popularity, pardoned him. On his return to the capital Pushkin continued to evoke Russian nationalist themes in two long poems, *Poltava* (1828) and *The Bronze Horseman* (1833), as well as in his novel of the Pugachev rebellion, *The Captain's Daughter* (1836). He also wrote short stories including "The Queen of Spades" (1834) and a fictionalized biography of his great-grandfather, *The Negro of Peter the Great* (unfinished version published in 1837). In this biography Pushkin represented Hannibal in a completely positive manner, making the novel one of the earliest to promote the "Negro as hero" in world literature.

Pushkin died tragically on February 10, 1837, from wounds that he suffered in a duel he fought in St. Petersburg. Allison Blakely, author of *Russia and the Negro* (1986), argues that Pushkin had been experiencing emotional stress regarding his nominal position at the court as "Gentlemen of the Chamber." Pushkin had been given this title, which was usually reserved for aristocratic youths, primarily because it allowed his beautiful – and notoriously flirtatious – wife to attend social functions. Not only was Pushkin humiliated by his position, but he may have been insulted by the presence of colorfully attired African slaves at the court. The fateful duel, Blakely asserts, was fought not only on behalf of the Pushkins, but also to defend the honor of his Hannibal ancestry.

Leyla Keough

Africa

Pygmy, a term loosely applied to people of shorter-than-average height who live in the forest of Central Africa; the ethnic groups generally identified as pygmies are the Binga, the Gelli, the Aka, the Twa, and the Mbuti.

The first recorded encounter between so-called pygmies and foreigners occurred in 2500 B.C.E., when the Egyptian pharaoh Nefrikare sent an expedition to find the source of the Nile River. The group traveled southward into the interior of Africa and encountered people of short stature living in the forests. The Egyptians called the people "pygmies" and spread knowledge of them throughout the Mediterranean region; Homer and Aristotle both mention pygmies in their writings.

By the thirteenth century, however, the pygmies were widely held to be a myth. Illustrations and descriptions of pygmies depicted them as winged, semihuman creatures who lived in treetops, hung from tails, and turned themselves invisible. Strangely, European contact with the pygmies in the sixteenth and seventeenth centuries did little to dispel these myths. In the seventeenth century English anatomist Edward Tyson published his treatise "The Anatomy of the Pygmie Compared with That of a Monkey, an Ape, and a Man," in which he claimed to prove "scientifically" through a comparison of skeletons that pygmies were actually monkeys. Later it was proven that Tyson's pygmy skeleton was, in fact, a chimpanzee skeleton.

Although Europeans finally accepted that pygmies were human, they believed them to be racially inferior to other Africans. This idea was in fact promoted by some neighboring groups whom the European explorers and colonialists encountered. Village dwellers such as the Lese tried to "civilize" the neighboring forest-dwellers, the Efe. The Lese tried to force the Efe to settle in villages, clear land, and cultivate crops. According to the Lese, however, their attempts failed because the pygmies were of inferior intellect, incapable of reason and foresight, and lazy thieves. These perceptions enabled Europeans to justify their display of pygmies as "exotic oddities" in international expositions and fairs such as the Indian and Colonial Exhibition of 1887 and the Franco-British Exhibition of 1908. Although it is now clear that forest peoples such as the Twa, Mbutis, and Aka have distinctive histories and customs, the stereotypes of the pygmy persist to this day.

Elizabeth Heath

q

Africa

Qaddafi, Muammar al- (also spelled Moammar Gadhafi, or Mu'ammar al-Qadhdafi) (b. 1942), head of state in Libya since 1970.

Muammar al-Qaddafi was born to a Bedouin family near the Libyan town of Surt. The strict Islamic Bedouin way of life profoundly influenced Qaddafi's later asceticism as well as his political philosophy. In an interview he once noted that growing up Bedouin helped him discover "the natural laws, natural relationships, life in its true nature, before life knew oppression, coercion and exploitation."

When Qaddafi was a young man, both Gamal Abdel Nasser's nationalist struggle in neighboring Egypt and the Arab struggle for Palestine drew him to Arab populist politics. In 1961 he entered the Libyan military academy in Binghazi, where he helped found a student military group called the Free Officers Movement and met the men who would eventually plot to overthrow the Libyan monarchy.

In September 1969, at a time when anti-Western, Arab nationalist sentiments were running high in Libya, the Free Officers Movement seized power in a two-hour bloodless coup. Some historians have called Qaddafi the engineer of this coup; others have characterized him as simply a participant. Although the new government, known as the Revolutionary Command Council (RCC), was initially headed by former political prisoner Mahmud Sulayman al-Maghrabi, the young Qaddafi rose quickly in the new government's powerful military. At age 27 he had de facto control of Libya. The extent of power-sharing during the early period of Qaddafi's rule remains a subject of debate.

Once in power Qaddafi immediately began to overhaul Libyan government and society. He charged many of the nation's former leaders with treason, outlawed the politically influential Islamic Sanusi sect, and weakened tribal affiliations by reorganizing administrative structures. He denounced communism for its atheism, and promoted Muslim asceticism by banning liquor. In 1973 he instituted People's Committees to give citizens direct control of local and regional government. The General People's Congress took over as the national representative body from the RCC, and Qaddafi became the general secretariat of the Socialist People's Libyan Arab Jamahiriya (state of the masses) – thus remaining the nation's ultimate decision maker and military leader. Several years later he created "revolutionary committees" to guide the People's Committees, and took the title "Leader of the Revolution." He also nationalized the oil and banking industries as well as a large proportion of the retail sector. All these measures were inspired by Qaddafi's vision of populist Arab nationalism, which he described in *The Green Book* (1976).

Not surprisingly, Qaddafi's policies provoked significant opposition. Many of the middle class fled the country. Islamic leaders resented the nationalization of Islamic properties as well as Qaddafi's theological justifications of political policy. Army officers opposed to his reforms staged an unsuccessful coup in 1975; they were subsequently arrested and executed. Qaddafi dealt severely with all his challengers and allegedly sponsored the assassination of exiled opposition leaders.

Qaddafi made equally bold moves in foreign policy throughout the 1970s. Intent on creating a powerful pan-Arab state, he negotiated political mergers with Egypt, Syria, Tunisia, Chad, Morocco, and Algeria. Libya was a founding member – and a militant voice – in the Organization of Petroleum Exporting Countries. Qaddafi offered military aid to Idi Amin's brutal regime in Uganda, and then asylum after the dictator's fall. His public support and alleged assistance of militant rebels in Chad, the Sudan, Ireland, the Philippines, and Japan made him an international pariah. In addition, Qaddafi has long been a prominent supporter of an independent Palestine. Throughout the 1970s and 1980s the United States accused him of supporting anti-Western movements. Following several diplomatic conflicts over the extradition of suspected terrorists, the United States bombed Libya in 1986. Since then tensions between the former trading partners remain high, and the United States has accused Qaddafi of manufacturing chemical weapons.

Despite the United States' and the United Nations' ongoing embargoes on trade with and international flights to the country, Libya under Qaddafi is still one of the richest countries in Africa, enjoying high levels of literacy and social services. Qaddafi has had little trouble finding European investors or trading partners, and in recent years he has stepped up efforts to cultivate political and economic ties with sub-Saharan African nations. Seemingly secure in his seat of power, Qaddafi continues to pursue ambitious projects, such as the $30 billion "Great Man-Made River," billed as the soon-to-be world's largest pipeline, intended to move subterranean water in the southern desert to the heavily populated Mediterranean coast.

Marian Aguiar

See Also
Amin, Idi; Nationalism in Africa; Islam and Tradition: An Interpretation.

North America

Quarles, Benjamin

(b. January 23, 1904, Boston, Mass.; d. November 17, 1996, Cheverly, Md.), African American historian, author, and editor, key figure in the emergence of African American history as an academic discipline.

Benjamin Quarles was the son of a subway porter. He earned a B.A. in 1931 from Shaw University, in Raleigh, North Carolina, an M.A. in 1933, and a Ph.D. in 1940, both from the University of Wisconsin. Quarles taught at Shaw, was the dean of Dillard University in New Orleans, Louisiana, and served as chair of the history department at Morgan State University in Baltimore, Maryland.

One of the focuses of Quarles's historical research and writing was race relations. His first published journal article was "The Breach Between Douglass and Garrison," which appeared in the *Journal of Negro*

History in 1938. Many of his other scholarly articles and monographs developed the same theme. However, Quarles has also focused on the black contribution during two major American crises in *The Negro in the American Revolution* (1961) (*see* AMERICAN REVOLUTION) and *The Negro in the Civil War* (1953) (*see* CIVIL WAR, AMERICAN).

Early in Quarles's career, two popular misconceptions existed regarding African American history. The first was that African Americans could not write objective history. The second was that few documentary sources existed for research and writing in African American history. Quarles's scholarship did much to dispel these notions. He was the first African American to publish essays in the *Mississippi Valley Historical Review* (now the *Journal of American History*), in 1945 and 1959. He served as a contributing editor to the journal *Phylon* and as an associate editor of the *Journal of Negro History*. Quarles also wrote two textbooks, *The Negro in the Making of America* and *The Negro American: A Documentary History*.

Robert Fay

SEE ALSO
Journal of Negro History, The.

North America

Queen Latifah (b. March 18, 1970, Newark, N.J.), African American rap artist, actress, entertainment executive, and entrepreneur.

Queen Latifah, born Dana Owens in NEWARK, NEW JERSEY, was nicknamed "Latifah" (which means "delicate" and "sensitive" in Arabic) at age eight by a black Muslim cousin. Soon afterward her parents separated, and Latifah moved with her mother, Rita, and older brother, Lance Jr., into a housing project in East Newark.

Determined to offer her children a better life, Rita Owens worked two jobs while attending community college. She eventually took a position as an art teacher at Irvington High School and the family moved to Newark.

In the second grade Latifah was found to be intellectually gifted. Her mother stretched the family finances so that she could attend Saint Anne's parochial school, where Latifah first performed as Dorothy in her school's production of *The Wiz*.

In high school Latifah played power forward on the school's BASKETBALL team. During her sophomore year she began rapping with two friends in an all-women's group called Ladies Fresh. Encouraged by her mother, she began recording and performing, and added "Queen" to her nickname.

Latifah was attending the Borough of Manhattan Community College in Manhattan when a demo tape featuring her rap "Princess of the Posse" made its way to Tommy Boy Records, based in New York City. She was quickly signed by the label, and in 1988 she released two singles, "Wrath of My Madness" and "Dance for Me." In 1989 she toured Europe, appeared at the APOLLO THEATER in Harlem, and issued her first album, *All Hail the Queen*, to wide acclaim. The album earned her the Best New Artist Award for 1990 from the New Music Seminar of Manhattan, and subsquently went platinum. Its second single, "Ladies First," celebrated black women's contributions to the struggle for black liberation in America, Africa, and around the world. It became a rap classic, eventually named by the Rock and Roll Hall of Fame as one of the 500 Songs That Shaped Rock 'n' Roll.

By the time her second album *Nature of a Sista'* came out in 1991, Latifah had begun investing in small businesses in her neighborhood and acting both in television and movies (including Spike Lee's *Jungle Fever*, 1992). These successes were marred by contract conflicts that caused her to leave Tommy Boy, and by her brother's tragic death in a motorcycle accident in 1992.

After signing with MOTOWN in 1993, Latifah released her third album, *Black Reign*, and with her newfound clout founded Flavor Unit Records and Management, which primarily handles rap and new-style RHYTHM AND BLUES groups. "U.N.I.T.Y," the album's first single, denounced sexist attitudes and violence against women. Latifah also landed a regular spot on the highly rated television sitcom *Living Single*, which lasted five seasons.

Over the next few years Latifah went on to more film roles, including the critically acclaimed portrayal of Cleo, a lesbian bank robber, in *Set It Off* (1996). She also produced and guest-starred on various musical projects, managed Flavor Unit artists, and worked for numerous causes, including antidrug campaigns.

In 1997 Queen Latifah was awarded the Aretha Franklin Award for Entertainer of the Year at the SOUL TRAIN Lady of Soul Awards. She released her fourth album, *Order in the Court*, in 1998.

Marc Mazique

SEE ALSO
Franklin, Aretha Louise; Harlem, New York; Lee, Shelton Jackson ("Spike"); New York, New York; Television and African Americans; Film, Blacks in American.

In Western European medieval art the Queen of Sheba often symbolizes the pagan world converting to Christianity. Usually she is depicted as a white woman with an African attendant. In this early thirteenth-century statue on the facade of the cathedral in Chartres, France, the Queen of Sheba, *above*, stands on the shoulders of her black servant *(detail below)*. *Image of the Black Project, Harvard University*

Africa

Queen of Sheba, **legendary queen of South Arabia or Ethiopia, credited in Ethiopian tradition with marrying King Solomon of Israel and founding Ethiopia's ruling Dynasty.**

According to the Book of Kings in the Bible, the Queen of Sheba learned of the wisdom of King Solomon and went to Jerusalem to test him "with hard questions." She arrived in a vast caravan, "with camels that bore spices, and very much gold, and precious stones."

Yemenis and Ethiopians both claim that the Queen of Sheba once ruled in their country. While an ancient kingdom of Saba did flourish in South Arabia (present-day Yemen) some centuries after the reign of Solomon, growing rich from the spice trade, ancient inscriptions reveal that there was also a kingdom in Ethiopia known by the dual name Daamat and Saba. The incense, or spice, that grew in South Arabia also grew on the other side of the Red Sea.

The Ethiopian claim to the Queen of Sheba is detailed in the famous epic *Kebra Nagast* (The Glory of Kings). It is based on the visit described in the Bible but adds that the queen bore a son, Menilek, to King Solomon. When Menilek was grown he visited his father, who anointed him to rule in Africa and sent the sons of his own counselors to help Menilek as king. The young men were unhappy to leave the famous temple in Jerusalem, especially as it contained the Ark of the Covenant, in which the presence of God was believed to dwell. In secret they removed the Ark and took it with them to Ethiopia. For centuries Ethiopian tradition has maintained that it is still preserved in the cathedral at Aksum.

The Ethiopian epic seems to have been compiled and recorded in writing during the thirteenth century, but its origin is difficult to determine. It is certainly true that from the restoration of the Solomonic Dynasty around 1270 until the death of the last emperor, Haile Selassie I, in 1974, the emperors of Ethiopia claimed descent from Solomon and the Queen of Sheba. The claim was even part of the constitution proclaimed by Haile Selassie in 1955.

Latin America and the Caribbean

Querino, Manoel Raimundo

(b. July 28, 1851, Santo Amaro, Bahia, Brazil; d. February 14, 1923, Salvador, Bahia, Brazil), the first Afro-Brazilian historian to document African contributions to Brazil.

During a lifetime that spanned the abolition movement, the emancipation of the slaves, and the beginning of modernization in Brazil, Manoel Raimundo Querino distinguished himself as an artist, teacher, social activist, and above all, historian. He was born free one year after the abolition of the slave trade in Brazil. In 1855 a cholera epidemic swept Bahia, claiming the lives of some 30,000 people, including Querino's parents. He was then sent to the state capital, Salvador, where Manoel Correira Garcia, a state deputy and a professor in the state teacher training institute, became his guardian. Garcia provided the orphan Querino with an education, which at that time was a privilege enjoyed by few Brazilians – black or white. At age seventeen Querino enlisted in the army and served from 1868 to 1871, during the latter part of the Paraguayan War.

Querino's career as an artist and teacher began in 1871, when he returned to Salvador. There he continued his studies and began working as a painter and decorator. He became a proponent of the arts in Bahia, helping to found in Salvador a vocational arts school, the Liceu de Artes e Ofícios (1874), and the state's fine arts academy, the Escola de Belas Artes (1877). He studied architecture at the Escola de Belas Artes from 1881 to 1884. In 1885 he began teaching geometric design at the Liceu de Artes e Ofícios; he later taught that course at the Escola de Belas Artes. While in academia he continued his work as a painter and decorator, earning the credentials that led to his appointment as designer for the Provincial Directory of Public Works (1884-1895). In addition, Querino authored *As artes na Bahia*, a definitive work on the art, artists, and artisans of Bahia.

Querino became involved in Brazil's labor movement in the mid-1870s. He helped organize the Sociedade Liga Operária Bahiana (the Bahian Workers Society League) in 1876 and became one of its leading spokespersons. In labor journals such as *A província* and *O trabalho*, Querino published articles defending working-class interests. He argued that the government's restrictions on and abuse of labor thwarted the state's prosperity. Querino garnered enough support to win a seat on Salvador's city council in 1889, the year Brazil became a republic. Since 1878, the year Querino joined the Republican Club of Bahia, he had supported the establishment of the republic in hopes that it would redress working-class grievances, but its leaders largely ignored concerns of the working class.

Querino participated in the abolition movement in Brazil during the 1880s, joining the Bahian Liberation Society (established 1887) and writing a number of articles calling for the "immediate and unconditional freedom" of the slaves. Nevertheless, he did his most important work in connection with Afro-Brazilians after abolition in 1888. While remaining committed to art and the working-class struggle, Querino spent an increasing amount of time researching and writing about Afro-Brazilian culture and history. Up until the early twentieth century books on Brazilian history made little or no mention of the contributions of Africans to the country's development. Querino began documenting and analyzing the history of black Brazilians in order to revise and balance the traditional historiography on Brazil that emphasized European experiences.

Thus Querino was not only the first Afro-Brazilian historian, but also one of the first Brazilian historians of *any* background to research and document the importance of African culture in Brazil. In highlighting the struggles and achievements of Afro-Brazilians, Querino hoped to combat racism and to imbue Afro-Brazilians with a sense of pride in their past. In works such as "O colono prêto como fator da civilação Brasileiro" (The African Contribution to Brazilian Civilization), Querino introduced readers to numerous accomplished Afro-Brazilian figures from the past and asserted that "in truth, it was the black who built Brazil."

Before Querino, no Afro-Brazilian had given his or her perspective on Brazilian history. His perspective was based not only on his own research, but also on his exchanges with the members of the predominantly black neighborhood of Matutú Grande where he lived. For this reason Arthur Ramos, a leading scholar of Afro-Brazilian history, said, "[Querino] remains one of the most solid sources of honest documentation for the Negro in Brazil."

Aaron Myers

See Also

Abolition and Emancipation in Latin America and the Caribbean; Art in Latin America and the Caribbean; Salvador, Brazil.

Latin America and the Caribbean

Quilombhoje, **an organization of black writers in Brazil founded in 1980.**

Quilombhoje is an Afro-Brazilian literary organization founded by the poet Luiz Silva Cuti (*see* Literature, Black, in Brazil). A significant contributor to Brazil's Movimento Negro Unificado (United Black Movement), Quilombhoje publishes *Cadernos Negros*, an anthology of black literature established to provide publication opportunities for black writers who had been denied by the commercial and academic presses.

During the late 1970s the black neighborhood of Beixiga in São Paulo was a center for black cultural activity. Beixiga (also known as the Quilombo de Saracura) became home to the famous Vai Vai samba school, the Center for Negro Culture and Art, and later the Federation of Afro-Brazilian Institutes of São Paulo. As a result, Beixiga became a focal point for a group of black writers and poets, many of whom collaborated on Quilombhoje's literary newspaper, *Jornegro*.

In the late 1970s Cuti and Hugo Ferreira established *Cadernos Negros*. In 1980 Cuti decided to formalize the group, which had been meeting for discussions, poetry readings, and debates, and create an Afro-Brazilian literary organization. Quilombhoje was born, and its original members included Oswaldo de Camargo, Abelardo Rodrigues, and the Argentine Paulo Colina.

The group derived its name from the Afro-Brazilian word *quilombo,* denoting an organized settlement to which blacks escaped from enslavement and assimilation and which thus represented a bastion of black resistance (*see* MAROONAGE IN THE AMERICAS). The neologism Quilombhoje, which combines the word *quilombo* with *hoje* (today) and *bojo* (a surge, swelling), encompasses the notion of the retaking of the quilombo.

In time the group grew and older members left, making way for a new generation of Quilombhoje, which includes Míriam Álves, Oubí Jnaê Kibuko, Esmeralda Ribeiro, Sônia Fátima de Conceição, and Jamu Minka. Today the group continues to publish the annual anthology *Cadernos Negros* and functions as a nonprofit institution.

Nicola Cooney

SEE ALSO
Samba Schools.

North America

Quinn, William Paul (b. 1788?; d. February 21, 1873, Richmond, Ind.), African American bishop in the African Methodist Episcopal (AME) Church.

Little is known of William Paul Quinn's early life. He was born in a British colony and migrated to Pennsylvania while young, at which time he was introduced to organized religion. An official of the AME church for more than 30 years (he spent five years away from the church), by 1844 Quinn as an itinerant preacher had organized over 120 AME congregations and 50 Sunday schools in the Midwest, including the slave states of Kentucky and Missouri. In 1849 Quinn was elected the AME Church's senior bishop. He settled in Richmond, Indiana, and was active as a pastor and in AME affairs until 1872 when illness forced him into retirement.

In addition to preaching, Quinn wrote to promote an antislavery agenda. In 1834 Quinn published *The Origins, Horrors and Results of Slavery,* a pamphlet condemning slavery and the South Carolina laws that prohibited African American education and employment training.

Robert Fay

SEE ALSO
Slavery in the United States; African Methodist Episcopal Church.

r

R & B. Please see RHYTHM AND BLUES

Africa

Rabat, Morocco, capital city of MOROCCO, located on the Atlantic coast in the northwestern part of the country.

Near Rabat, in the contemporary town of Salé, are the ruins of a Roman settlement said to have originated as a small community of traders. Under Islamic influence after the tenth century, Salé was home to a group of Berbers from an heretical sect. In 1150 C.E., an Almohad sultan established a rabat, or citadel, for his army near Salé. The position of the fort along the Atlantic Ocean and the banks of the Sebou River offered a prime location from which to launch his holy war against SPAIN. By the turn of the century his son had finished the construction of the city, which came to be known as Rabat al-Fath (autonomous or victorious citadel). Although Rabat flourished first as an imperial city and then as an important military center under the Almohads, only the citadel was left inhabited after that dynasty fell. In the sixteenth century the historian LEO AFRICANUS described the city as overgrown with vines.

During the early seventeenth century Rabat's economy benefited from the increased trade, exploration, and piracy in the Atlantic. In the same period Rabat also became home to a large number of Muslim and Jewish refugees from Southern Spain following the Christian Reconquest. These refugees were a heterogeneous population from different parts of Spain, and they brought the intellectual and cultural influences of Andalusia (Southern Spain) and built a new quarter near the citadel. Over the years these soldiers, merchants, artisans, and seamen transformed the town from a military base into a prosperous port that exported skins, leather, wool, wax, and copper. The city drew a great deal of income from corsair activities, as pirates based out of Rabat plundered ships on the Atlantic and evaded their pursuers in the tricky river channel. In the late seventeenth century, after the sultan successfully suppressed hostile corsairs, the city became a secondary capital for the Alawite Dynasty.

During the late eighteenth and nineteenth century Rabat lost much of its significance as a port of trade. First the sultan shifted the kingdom's commercial trade to Essaouira, and then Casablanca outstripped the port in the increasingly European-controlled trade. Conditions further deteriorated as the city faced an earthquake in 1755 followed by a series of plagues, the first of which killed some two-thirds of the population in Rabat and Salé.

Despite its economic decline Rabat became an important seat of government; the Sultan assembled his government there as early as 1768. In 1912 the French made Rabat the administrative capital for the protectorate, and built a modern city for the French expatriate community outside the wall of the medina, or old city, where the Muslims lived. Following independence in 1956, the city became the capital of Morocco. The royal residence is located in Rabat as are the government's ministries and embassies. In 1957 the Université Mohammad V was founded as a center for modern education.

The population of Rabat and Salé has grown to approximately 2 million. The city's main industries include textiles, fruit and fish processing, and building materials. Artisans continue to produce traditional handicrafts such as worked leather and copper, as well as the famed Rabat carpets.

Marian Aguiar

SEE ALSO

Berber; Casablanca, Morocco; France; Almohads.

Africa

Rabih (also known as Rabih, Rabih al-Zubayr, and Rabih bin FadlAllah) (b. 1845, Salamat al-Basha, present-day Sudan; d. 1900, Lakhta, present-day Chad), slave raider and adventurer who built a nineteenth-century empire that spanned parts of present-day CHAD, CENTRAL AFRICAN REPUBLIC, CAMEROON, NIGERIA, and NIGER.

Rabih was born in SUDAN, probably near Khartoum, though the details of his early life are uncertain. Some believe that he was originally a slave freed by his master, Zubayr Rahma Mansur, while others think he was born free and joined the Turkic-Egyptian army before working for Zubayr, the largest slave trader in southern Sudan. He joined Zubayr's company in 1850 and had become a competent military leader by 1875, when the British declared slavery illegal.

When the British forcibly shut down Zubayr's operations four years later, Rabih gathered what was left of Zubayr's slave army and established a raiding stronghold in the Azande region to the west. During the 1880s Rabih and his army attacked and pillaged groups such as the Banda and SARA. In the early 1890s Rabih defeated a French expedition and conquered the Bagirmi state in present-day Chad, from which he staged his conquest of the Bornu Empire to the west. Exploiting divisions among the Bornu rulers, Rabih, in alliance with the ruler of Adamawa in present-day Cameroon, attacked the empire in 1894. Within three years he had gained control of the entire Bornu Empire, which stretched from northeastern Nigeria around LAKE CHAD and into adjacent parts of Niger and Cameroon. After securing his new empire Rabih decided to attack the Damagaram Empire, based in Zinder, further west in the area that is now Niger. But the Damagaram resisted his aggression, and French and British efforts to control the region eroded his power. Although he successfully repelled the Europeans for several years, he was killed in battle in 1900, and subsequently his empire was divided between the French and British.

Elizabeth Heath

SEE ALSO

Khartoum, Sudan; Kanuri; Zinder, Niger; Slavery in Africa.

Latin America and the Caribbean

Race and Class in Brazil: An Interpretation

Our understanding of modern-day race relations in BRAZIL rests primarily on research done between 1945 and 1965. To appreciate the context of that work, we need to look at the history of sociology and anthropology in Brazil. Before 1945 both disciplines were in the early stages of development, centered largely in São Paulo with clusters of researchers in Rio de Janeiro and BAHIA. The 1930s had seen an influx of influential foreign scholars, such as Donald Pierson, Roger Bastide, and Emílio Willems. All played important roles in the development of graduate faculties at the University of São Paulo (USP) and the Escola Livre de Sociologia e Política, both in São Paulo. One of the most significant publications of this era was by the United States scholar Donald Pierson, whose *Negroes in Brazil* remains an outstanding research work on Bahia and the Northeast, although its conclusions are now generally rejected.

With the end of World War II there was a renewed surge of foreign interest that reinforced the efforts of the small community of Brazilian researchers. Prominent among the non-Brazilians were North American anthropologists, especially from Columbia University, and French scholars. Most knowledgeable among the latter was Roger Bastide, who had been in Brazil since 1938 and had already won USP support to begin a large-scale survey research project on race relations of São Paulo. Key Brazilian scholars included FLORESTAN FERNANDES (USP) and Thales de Azevedo (Federal University of Bahia). Among those who distinguished themselves in the study of race relations were Charles Wagley, Marvin Harris, Costa Pinto, René Ribeiro, Oracy Nogueira, Fernando Henrique Cardoso, Octávio Ianni, and Arthur Ramos. We largely owe our present knowledge to these researchers and their collaborators.

Several themes have emerged from this body of scholarship. Most relevant for our purposes is the direct, at times explicit, challenge to the long prevailing view of Brazil as a "racial democracy." In its more extreme form, that belief held that race and skin color make virtually no difference in Brazil. Vianna Moog, a prominent Brazilian writer, has stated, "The highest, most significant and most edifying aspect of our culture is racial brotherhood." If there are few dark-skinned Brazilians at the higher levels of society, it simply reflects past disadvantages – poverty and the lack of education that inevitably accompanied slavery. The belief held by the elite was well stated by a former president of the National Congress: "In Brazil, access to society depends upon individual effort, intellectual ability, and merit.... We have all inherited common attributes, and what we are building – socially, economically and politically – proves the correctness of our rejection of the myths of racial superiority." This view holds that if race does play a part in stratification, it is a small part. Brazilians may not give the benefit of the doubt to a darker person, but the frequency of such behavior is not great enough to alter the fact that Brazil is substantially free of racial discrimination.

How did Brazil reach this supposedly harmonious state? The answer, say believers in its "racial democracy," is to be found in Brazilian history. Almost in spite of themselves, the Portuguese created a multiracial, slave-based society with a large, free, colored population. Portuguese colonization seemed somehow immune to racial prejudice. In the words of the congressional president, "In our land the three ethnic groups interacted to produce the union of which we are the expression and synthesis." The Portuguese male was crucial in this process. At home he had known the charms of dark-skinned Moorish women, and thus it is not surprising that in the New World he succumbed to the Indian, and later African, women. This trend was reinforced by the absence of women among the Portuguese explorers and colonists. The inevitable outcome was miscegenation.

Most important for future race relations, according to this view, was the fact that Portuguese men had guilty consciences, as well as strong libidos. As a result, they often manumitted the mixed-blood offspring they had sired by their slave women. Affectionate weakness for the illegitimate progeny of miscegenation led directly to the sharp contrast between the fate of people of color in Brazil and those in the United States. This simplistic idea was well expressed in the 1940s by Waldo Frank, a minor United States literary figure who often traveled to Latin America: "Why is the difference so great between the exploited Negro of Brazil and the exploited Negro of the U.S.? Because the latter have known lust and greed of their masters; the former, lust and greed no less, but tenderness also."

The belief in "racial democracy," whether it fit the historical facts or not, has been the operating racial ideal among the Brazilian elite since at least 1920. It accompanies an equally fervent faith in *branqueamento* or WHITENING, the result of the elite's struggle to reconcile Brazil's actual social relations – the absence of a clear line between white and nonwhite – with the doctrines of scientific racism that had penetrated Brazil from abroad. It also implied that the inexorable process of whitening would produce a white (or light tan?) Brazil. Thus the legacy of the Portuguese libido would "solve" Brazil's race problem. This remained the elite view through World War II – despite the fact that "scientific racism" had become discredited in academic circles by the 1930s.

Elsewhere the 1930s saw the application of one of history's most vicious racist dogmas, anti-Semitism. In the aftermath of 1945 Europeans looked abroad for models of interracial peace. Had not Brazil for years been disproving the racist shibboleths about miscegenation? In 1950 the United Nations Educational, Scientific, and Cultural Organization (UNESCO) decided to study Brazil's harmonious race relations and share Brazil's secret with the world. International teams of scholars, primarily anthropologists, undertook field research around the country, pursuing common research goals. Such international recognition greatly reinforced the Brazilian elite's belief in their "racial democracy." In fact, however, this and succeeding research raised serious questions about, and partially discredited, this image of Brazilian society.

Other factors were also eroding the image. An important element in the definition of Brazil's "racial democracy" had always been the contrast with the United States. The phenomena of segregation and racial violence, such as urban riots and lynchings, were unknown in Brazil. Even if there had once been onerous barriers to black advancement, Brazil had never been infected with the race hatred so evident in the United States. Whatever the precise explanation for the difference, Brazilians could say that their country had the distinction of representing humanity's best future. Had not UNESCO said as much?

But the United States was changing. The United States Supreme Court decision of 1954, BROWN V. BOARD OF EDUCATION, sounded the death knell for racial segregation, and subsequent legislation closed virtually every loophole sought by the die-hard racists. Where once the law had been used to segregate, it was now a force for integration. Both uses assumed a clearly defined biracial society. Both stemmed from the assumption that race is a fundamental, perhaps the most fundamental, characteristic of North Americans.

From the Brazilian viewpoint it might at first appear that the United States, by finally eliminating legal color bars, was merely catching up to Brazil in the early nineteenth century, when its few color bars, remnants of the colonial era, disappeared. The difference in the United States, however, was the militancy and organization of nonwhites. In the nonviolent resistance movement led by Southern clergymen such as Martin Luther King Jr., blacks forcefully claimed their "rights." Brazilian nonwhites had not shown a comparable degree of initiative since final abolition in 1888. U.S. society, the major point of reference for Brazilians when describing their "racial democracy," had changed in a basic way.

Another shift in the Brazilian elite's foreign points of reference occurred in Africa. There, as in Asia, World War II brought in its wake a cry for decolonization. The remaining empires of GREAT BRITAIN, FRANCE, Holland, and Belgium were now an unpleasant reminder of the era when white Europeans, using racist language, had taken control of much of today's "Third World." In Africa the departure of the empires and their ruling whites paved the way for the appearance on the world scene of nations totally governed by blacks. This trend contradicted one of the central assumptions of the Brazilian belief in "whitening": the closer to African origins, the less civilized the person of color. Indeed, faith in "whitening" was based on the assumption that the superior racial element, that is, white, was prevailing. Now Africa had not white, not even mulatto, but black nations. These new peoples wanted no part of "whitening," a doctrine that assumed assimilation, if not extinction, of African identity. As in the case of U.S. desegregation, history was removing the very landmarks that had helped anchor the Brazilian elite in its racial beliefs.

Brazil's relations with Africa were further complicated by the fact that PORTUGAL was the last European power to relinquish its African colonies. It was a Brazilian, GILBERTO FREYRE, who had spelled out the most ambitious doctrine to justify Portuguese colonialism, "Lusotropicalism." He argued that the Portuguese were the only European colonizers to create a new civilization in the tropics, an accomplishment attributable above all to their racial tolerance. The logical conclusion was that the Lusitanian legacy would spare Portugal the anticolonial violence found elsewhere in Africa. Freyre himself remained a staunch defender of Portuguese COLONIAL RULE.

Because of Antonio Salazar's repressive regime and an enormous per capita investment of resources, the Portuguese government prolonged its rule over ANGOLA and Mozambique into the 1970s. By the time the armed struggle began in Africa, Brazil had a military government that was completely committed to the Salazar policy. Freyre, an enthusiastic adherent to the 1964 "revolution" that installed the military, gained increased publicity for his Lusotropical theories. Meanwhile, government censorship prevented an open debate over Brazil's African policy.

As Salazar finally faded from power in the early 1970s, it was his army officers who pushed for withdrawal from Africa. The peoples of Portuguese Africa won independence, and many whites left. After those events were well under way, Brazil also experienced political change. Ernesto Geisel's presidency (1974-1979) brought an "opening" and the possibility for re-thinking Brazil's African interests and policies.

One incident shows how this new relationship with Africa called into question the Brazilian elite's image of their nation's race relations. In 1978 and 1979 Brazil's leading television network, Rede Globo, broadcast a series for children adapted from stories by Monteiro Lobato. Brazilians generally considered it a high-level effort for the children's hour. Angolan television, which is state controlled, decided to take advantage of this Portuguese-language resource by broadcasting the series in early 1979. This set no precedent, as they had shown Globo's version of Jorge Amado's *Gabriela, cravo e canela* with no apparent problems. After seven installments, however, the Angolan television network abruptly canceled the children's series. It was "racist," they charged, because blacks were depicted only in inferior positions. Most offensive was the role of Tia Nastácia, the 60-year-old black cook whom the Angolans thought a caricature. Reaction in Brazil was rapid, and many questions arose. Were the Angolans justified? How should blacks be depicted? Had Lobato's characterization been faithfully rendered in the televised script? What was the true meaning of Tia Nastácia's role in the household? Brazil was undoubtedly in for more such surprises in its cultural relations with Africa. It was not the world Freyre had led the Brazilian elite to expect.

These fundamental changes in Brazil's external points of reference in race relations – the United States and Lusophone Africa – did not produce an immediate rethinking of race relations in Brazil; that began only in the late 1970s. There are several reasons for this.

First, the Brazilian elite tenaciously defended their image of Brazil as a "racial democracy." They did it in a number of ways. One was to attack as "un-Brazilian" anyone who raised serious questions about race relations in Brazil. Such a tactic was common among politicians, cultural luminaries, and media controllers. The usual argument was that "The only racial 'problems' in Brazil result from the agitation of those who claim there are problems." An interesting case is the reaction to a small "black is beautiful" movement, primarily in Rio de Janeiro (*see* BLACK CONSCIOUSNESS IN BRAZIL). In August 1976 the prominent Rio daily *Jornal do Brasil* ran a feature story of "black Rio," with photographs of young black men wearing Afro hairstyles and platform shoes. This publicity ignited an angry reaction from readers, who denounced the movement and its coverage by the press. Critics implied that reporting on such "un-Brazilian" groups was itself divisive and unpatriotic. As for the movement, it was branded by many whites as a foreign import, illustrating little more than the "cultural alienation" into which Brazilian blacks could slip.

Such vigilance by the elite could not suffice to explain the lack of debate. There was a second factor – government repression. After 1965, and especially after 1968, successive military governments closely controlled the media and all public events. They justified repression as necessary to meet the threat of "subversion," which in the early 1970s did include a guerrilla movement. But the military branded as "subversive" not only kidnappers with guns but also social scientists with ideas. That was bound to include academics who had raised questions about Brazil's "racial democracy."

One of the most dramatic cases in point was the purge of the faculty at USP in 1969. Prominent among those social scientists involuntarily retired were Florestan Fernandes and his colleagues Fernando Henrique Cardoso and Octavio Ianni. Given their well-known, although differing, ideological and political views, it is not surprising that they should be targets for a military concerned with "national security." Could it be coincidental, however, that they were also among the handful of Brazil's researchers into race relations? And that, by their research, writing, and teaching they had raised troubling questions about the realities of Brazilian race relations? The military government frequently intervened to suppress news that contradicted the official image of racial harmony. Under full-scale censorship from 1969 until gradual liberalization began in 1975, television and radio were closely scrutinized. Vigilance was especially intense on the popular television soap operas (*telenovelas*), as well as in SAMBA songs. More often than once, television scripts rejected by the censors touched the subject of race relations.

A similar preoccupation appeared in the censorship of the print media. In 1973 a new journal of opinion, *Argumento*, appeared on the newsstands of São Paulo. It was quickly confiscated by the authorities. On the cover was an African-looking boy and the title of an article comparing postabolition race relations in Brazil and the United States. Although the police gave no explanation, many observers thought the article on race relations had, at least in part, provoked their action. Another example of such moves was the Brazilian government's 1978 decision to bar the Inter-American Foundation from further activity in Brazil. Brazilian authorities believed that this foundation, financed by U.S. government-originated funds but operating independently from other U.S. agencies, was supporting "subversive" Brazilian organizations. Among the groups receiving financing at that time were three black organizations whose stated purpose of "consciousness-raising" undoubtedly displeased Brasília.

A third example of government sensitivity to the issue of race relations came in connection with a scholarly conference on blacks in the Americas, scheduled to be held in Bogotá, Colombia, in August 1977. Countries were invited to send delegations, on the usual assumption that each government would finance its delegates' travel. Not so in Brazil. Brasília dragged its feet on the travel authorization until it was too late, and most of the Brazilian delegates missed the meeting.

Another incident that occurred in the late 1960s was the most revealing of all: the decision to omit race from the census of 1970. Opponents of racial identification argued that the language of racial categories, such as *preto*, *negro*, and *moreno*, was applied so inconsistently that meaningful data collection would be impossible. No responsible observer would dispute the fact that there is a problem, yet the census commission's extreme solution of eliminating race altogether precluded the collection of any data by race whatsoever. Undoubtedly, many commission members who voted for this policy genuinely believed that race could not be studied. In eliminating the category, however, they were reflecting the elite consensus that race was not an independent variable in Brazilian society. Without data, of course, discussion would continue being reduced to the anecdotal level. That is where defenders of Brazil's racial myth have always preferred to operate, dwelling on examples of famous Brazilians whose physical features have borne little relation to their station in life.

There has been another factor responsible for muting Brazilian discussion of race relations: the belief by the Left that race is insignificant. Social class is the most fundamental variable, leftists argue, both for studying society and for changing it. Advocates of this view usually have dismissed race as a "false issue." Because the Left has remained very strong in the university faculties that have produced most Brazilian researchers, its negative attitude toward studying race relations has, ironically, helped contribute to the silence on race sought by the authoritarian government.

In the late 1970s this picture began to change. Attention to race increased in a small but perceptible fashion. Brazilians of color began to question publicly the myth of racial democracy. With the gradual political opening pursued by the government of Geisel, debate emerged into the open.

Other writers have described in detail the rapid growth of a black movement that contradicts everything the predominant myth would have led us to expect. Brazil now has militant groups that may come to rival their most ambitious counterparts of the FRENTE NEGRA BRASILEIRA era in the 1930s. The *abertura democrática* (transition to democracy) has allowed many taboo topics to surface, with race relations high on the list. Dramatic confirmation of this change came in the decision to include race in the 1980 census. Initially, the census authorities wanted to follow the 1970 precedent of omitting race. That created a strong reaction among the staff and the public and led to reconsideration and a reversal of the decision. The less repressive atmosphere surrounding the 1980 decision facilitated the collection of data that, even if not wholly reliable, are the sine qua non for any informed discussion of race relations.

Before discussing the renewed attention to race in Brazil, it is worth noting that a more traditional area of interest has never lacked attention: Afro-Brazilian religion, folklore, and art. Interest here centered on African origins and African survivals. Most familiar are the religions of CANDOMBLÉ in Bahia and UMBANDA in Rio de Janeiro, both well-known tourist attractions. Included also are the "exotic" costumes and foods identified with Africa. The (adopted) patron saints of this world are Gilberto Freyre and Jorge Amado, writers who have gained much of their fame by showing the Afro-Brazilian contribution to Brazilian culture and national character. Although undoubtedly important and valuable, the study and preservation of Afro-Brazilian beliefs and customs have been politically very safe. It fits perfectly with the elite view that Brazil's historic links to Africa are now essentially quaint. For this reason the Sociedade de Estudos da Cultura Negra no Brasil (Society for the Study of Black Culture in Brazil) represented no threat to the government or elite figures. Another example was the Semanas Afro-Brasileiras held at the Museum of Modern Art in Rio de Janeiro in 1974. The emphasis of such groups has allowed them to avoid the thorny questions of present-day race relationships among Brazilians.

A significant change that took place in the late 1970s was the promotion of racial consciousness among Brazilians of color. Although some leading activists were researchers, they did not use questionnaires or interview forms. They believed that they knew what the facts were. As people of color, they passionately believed that Brazil's claim to be a racial democracy was a fraud. They wanted Brazilians to know that their country's race relations bore no relation to the idyllic scene praised by the elite and many foreigners. This activist explosion has startled many. Is it possible that a significant "black power" movement is arising Brazil? The militant tone of these activists is more aggressive than that of any group since the Frente Negra of the 1930s. They repudiate whitening – still Brazil's dominant ideology of race relations – and uphold the virtues of blackness. Most important, they want to provoke Afro-Brazilians into racial consciousness. They want to act against what they see as white exploitation – a line of protest that has been forbidden to people of color for the past 40 years.

The new black protest movements can now denounce the conditions that Brazilian scholars have long been documenting. To take one example, Thales de Azevedo, one of the doyens of Brazilian anthropology, has attacked the racial democracy myth by publishing a compilation of cases of racial discrimination as reported in the national press. Carlos A. Hasenbalg's important 1979 monograph used similar sources and carried the analysis of discrimination to the most systematic level possible with the limited data then available.

We seem to be on the threshold of a major debate about the role of race in Brazilian society. Any debate is bounded by the terms by which it is defined. What will be the definitions for the debate on race? What are the questions to be posed? What is the subject to be studied? If it is race relations in the broadest sense, how should we proceed?

Research efforts are needed on all fronts, not least the historical front. Surprising as it might seem, our understanding of the history of Brazilian race relations is extremely uneven. Despite the fame of Gilberto Freyre's writing on Brazil's patriarchal past, and much recent work on slavery by many other scholars, we know all too little about some of the most important features of Brazilian social history. One is the historical experience of free persons of color, both in the colonial era and in the nineteenth century.

In the first half of the 1800s there was a strong mulatto movement, which even published its own newspapers. An important imperial institution, the Guarda Nacional, had become a vehicle for mulatto mobility. By the 1840s the officer corps included many mulattos, as they were elected by the predominately colored ranks. This channel of mobility was abruptly closed in 1850, however, when the Crown made officers appointive. The command soon turned markedly whiter.

The questions are obvious: How extensive was this mulatto movement? What were its relationships to other Brazilians of color, slave and free? Why did the Crown abolish the election of officers? Did the political and social elite see a threat from the mulatto movement? How did they rationalize their actions?

The early decades of the twentieth century provided similar questions. How do we explain the assertion of black and mulatto consciousness in the 1920s and 1930s? Just as they had a century earlier, black newspapers appeared, aggressively promoting the cause of the Brazilian of color. Why did they appear in the 1920s, and not immediately after final abolition in 1888? Were there unusual economic circumstances in the 1920s and 1930s? Were they comparable to those of the early nineteenth century?

This twentieth-century movement was snuffed out by the authoritarian coup of 1937. The disbanding of the black and mulatto organizations was hardly surprising, given the fact that the Estado Nôvo government (1937-1945) was able to repress all opposition groups. But the return of open government in 1945 did not see the reappearance of the movement, and three decades after 1945 it saw nothing comparable to the black and mulatto movements prior to 1937, despite the persistent organizing efforts of a few individuals such as ABDIAS DO NASCIMENTO. Such movements did not come until the late 1970s. Why? Is there a general explanation for the militancy that erupted in the late 1970s, the 1920s to the 1930s, and the 1840s?

Part of the answer lies in a better understanding of the dynamics of Brazilian socioeconomic history. Most important is a deeper understanding of the role of the free person of color before slavery expired in 1888. Some of the most lasting forms of interracial social behavior must have been established in those years. The scholarly consensus has been that Brazil created a multiracial society, as contrasted to the biracial system in the United States. In his extended comparison of the United States and Brazil in *Neither Black nor White* (1971),

Carl Degler suggested that the "mulatto escape hatch" was the key to the difference. Yet Degler's book, the most thoughtful and exhaustive comparative analysis of race relations in Brazil and the United States, gives virtually no hard evidence to support his thesis. The reader searches in vain for historical documentation to show that the person of mixed blood got preferential treatment. How do we know that mulattoes enjoyed mobility? What data such as census records, tax records, and court records confirm such mobility? Degler could not provide such information because the necessary research has only recently begun. The escape hatch is a plausible hypothesis, but we await evidence of what actually happened.

One priority area for investigation is relations between whites and persons of color in the labor force. In the United States' South, for example, there was a period, roughly from 1865 to 1900, when poor whites and newly freed blacks might have made common cause against the old agrarian order. Instead, white politicians successfully got poor whites to focus on the threat of job competition from blacks, rather than on the fundamental questions of economic structure. As a result the Jim Crow system became fixed in the South and the cause of black progress was set back for decades to come.

There are obvious perils in carrying historical comparison too far. It might well be argued that by the time of the Emancipation Proclamation in the United States there was no possibility for the emergence of a multiracial society. Yet some of the explanations given for the U.S. case may suggest questions about Brazil. What were the racial attitudes of Brazilian workers? Were they manipulated by employers who used similar techniques to maximize control over the labor force? We know, for example, that racist sentiments helped divide Rio de Janeiro dockworkers between 1910 and 1930. Did this occur in other sectors? Could such patterns be seen in earlier eras? What effect did these patterns have on subsequent race relations? Such questions are implicit in virtually all our attempts to explain present-day Brazilian race relations.

No amount of subsequent research and documentation, however helpful, will answer all our questions. Just as in the study of race relations in the United States, with its avalanche of monographs, symposia, and syntheses, the questions go too deep and in the end their meaning is too elusive for us to be satisfied with the answers provided by conventional social and economic history. In Brazil, also, we will find ourselves drawn toward examining "mentalities," habits of mind, and social beliefs. What is uniquely Brazilian about Brazilian race relations? Does it have anything to do with the now oft-denigrated idea of Brazilian national character? There has been a long and rich debate over the Brazilian's alleged *cordialidade* (hospitality). Does that idea furnish any clues in our quest to understand how and why Brazil has created its particular form of multiracial society? What about those qualities that anthropologists, sociologists, and political scientists have explored – patrimonialism, paternalism, and clientelism? However slippery these concepts may be for the historian, we must remind ourselves that the most enduring attempt to explain the United States – that of Alexis de Tocqueville – was built around a discussion of precisely these kinds of collective traits.

Our efforts to understand Brazilian race relations will necessarily carry us into the ongoing debate about the nature of Brazilian society. It will thus parallel and perhaps at times coincide with attention to the history of labor relations in Brazil, also inseparably linked to our views about the essence of Brazilian social relations.

We are therefore brought to the elusive relationship between ideas and societies. Seen abstractly, they are socioeconomic structures and ideologies. When viewed historically, they embrace the many realities of human behavior and human thought. We appear to be on the verge of a new burst of inquiry into these realities, and although we may ask new questions and produce new evidence, we will be walking familiar ground.

Thomas Skidmore

From "Race and Class in Brazil: Historical Perspectives," *Luso-Brazilian Review*, 20, no. 1 (Summer 1983). ©1983. Reproduced by permission of the University of Wisconsin Press.

See Also

Decolonization in Africa: An Interpretation; King, Martin Luther, Jr.; Thirteenth Amendment of the United States Constitution and the Emancipation Proclamation; Rio de Janeiro, Brazil; Religions, African, in Brazil; Myth of Racial Democracy in Latin America and the Caribbean: An Interpretation.

North America

Race and Class Issues in the United States, interrelated issues that have had a complex effect on African Americans, as made clear in the research of sociologist William Julius Wilson (*see* Work, African Americans and the Changing Nature of, in the Post-World War II Era: An Interpretation).

North America

Race and the American Presidency

"Our fathers brought forth on this continent," Abraham Lincoln said on a great battlefield of the Civil War, "a new nation, conceived in Liberty, and dedicated to the proposition that all men are created equal." Unfortunately, that proposition remained in doubt for the entire four score and seven years before Gettysburg, and much of the six score and fifteen years since.

Thomas Jefferson's original draft of the nation's founding document, the Declaration of Independence of July 4, 1776, included an assault on slavery that Southerners excised. The founders who wrote the Constitution included nine specific protections for the South's peculiar institution. It ought not be a surprise that 9 of the 15 commanders in chief before Lincoln owned slaves; all five two-term presidents during the years 1789-1861 claimed human property rights; four of the six who did not own slaves were "doughfaces" (Northerners with Southern principles); and the remaining two spoke not a word against slavery during their four-year terms.

A profound ambivalence on questions of race has characterized the 42 men who have held the nation's highest office. There have been spectacular exceptions: Lincoln, obviously, and also Lyndon B. Johnson during the great Southern war on Jim Crow in the time of Martin Luther King Jr. But by and large the presidency has been more committed to preserving the nation's original story of white over black. Whether before or after the Civil War, and whether on the issue of slavery, on the legal racism that ruled for nearly a century after the Reconstruction era (1865-1877), or on what is often referred to in modern times as institutionalized racism, the White House has acted aggressively in a consistent manner on one lone front: the use of race to organize the voting blocs necessary to carry a presidential candidate to office.

The Antebellum White House, 1788-1860

If George Washington fantasized in his private correspondence about freeing the nation's slaves, as president he remained silent when Benjamin Franklin begged his support for a Quaker petition demanding exactly that. The next president, John Adams, questioned the wisdom of emancipation: "Would not the most shiftless among them be in danger of perishing for want… work at horrible jobs, become squatters, incorporate with Indians, commit crimes in bands." Such fears immobilized the nation's third president. Jefferson left behind in his writings dozens of assaults on "the malign twins" (the plantation system and slavery), but he saw enough personal utility in the institution to include "25 negroes little and big" in daughter Martha's dowry. James Madison, the fourth president, left the White House obsessed with the threat that he perceived free Southern blacks posed to white women. This was, to say the least, ironic. After Madison died, Daniel Webster, acting out of charity for the widow, Dolly, bought the freedom of Madison's body servant, Paul Jennings.

This former slave, now in Madison's class of "vicious free blacks," brought food to the penniless Dolly at Webster's direction. On his own, he gave her money from his pocket.

Jefferson and Madison did oppose the TRANSATLANTIC SLAVE TRADE (though not the interstate slave trade). But that opposition represented the entirety of positive presidential action prior to Lincoln. James Monroe helped form the AMERICAN COLONIZATION SOCIETY. Andrew Jackson denied the growing abolitionist movement the use of the mails and concocted stories if discipline crippled or killed one of his own slaves. "You may say to Dr. Hogg," he wrote to a coconspirator, "that her lament was occasioned by a stroke from Betty [another slave], or jumping over a rope, in which her feet became entangled, and she fell." John Quincy Adams emerged as an abolitionist champion only upon leaving the White House, notably by leading the Gag Rule fight. Martin Van Buren, a New Yorker, conspired with Supreme Court justices in hope of a decision in the Amistad case (1841) favorable to slave owners. Another Northerner, James Buchanan, conspired more successfully in DRED SCOTT V. SANFORD (1857), in which the Supreme Court held that Negroes had "no rights which any white man was bound to respect."

Lincoln would debate *Dred Scott* with Stephen Douglas and help people understand that slavery threatened the dreams and freedoms of white America, too. While Lincoln remained infected with the colonization movement's send-them-back-to-Africa panacea, he believed one thing first and foremost: "If slavery is not wrong, nothing is wrong." More to the point, he was the first chief executive to act his conscience on matters of race. A singular man, he became singularly great in the White House. He made a war to bring the South back to the Union into a war on slavery, and he did as much as any American at Gettysburg or elsewhere to make America into a nation in which Jefferson's proposition was truly the fundamental creed.

Jesse Jackson announces his candidacy for president of the United States in 1987. *CORBIS/Bettmann*

From Emancipation to Jim Crow, 1860-1900

Of course, Lincoln's commitment could not last. John Wilkes Booth's shot and leap at Ford's Theater brought an explicit racist, Andrew Johnson, to the presidency. The Reconstruction battles that Johnson fought with the Radical Republicans in Congress led to the Thirteenth, Fourteenth, and Fifteenth Amendments to the Constitution, ending slavery forever. But Reconstruction foundered and died with the Compromise of 1877. At issue were the old questions of using race to organize voting blocs and the fear of race war. The latter proved compelling enough to freeze Ulysses S. Grant in place. Utterly fearless on the Civil War's battlefields, President Grant shook at the thought of sending his armies after the Ku Klux Klan in Mississippi. Republican presidents Hayes, Garfield, Arthur, Harrison, and McKinley left the freedpeople's fate within the states of the former Confederacy in the hands of the great white race. Where disfranchisement and the separate-but-equal doctrine established in the latest Supreme Court case, PLESSY V. FERGUSON (1896), did not suffice, the South relied on lynch-mob terror.

Progressive Era, 1900-1920

Theodore Roosevelt, the first twentieth-century president, also led the Progressive movement (1900-1917), the first of this century's three major periods of liberal reform. Roosevelt's reformist impulse, however, owed a greater debt to *Plessy* than to the timeless proposition of Jefferson and Lincoln. This president looked at Klan hoods and robes in the context of white women raped by Negroes freed too soon. So he supported

ABOVE LEFT: **President Ronald Reagan signs the bill that established a national holiday in honor of Martin Luther King Jr., as dignitaries including Vice President George Bush and King's widow, Coretta Scott King, look on.** *CORBIS/Bettmann-UPI*
ABOVE: **At the end of the 1963 March on Washington, President John F. Kennedy met with leaders of the march, including Whitney Young, Martin Luther King Jr., John Lewis, A. Philip Randolph, and Roy Wilkins.** *AP/Wide World Photos*
LEFT: **President Lyndon B. Johnson shakes hands with Martin Luther King Jr. after signing the Civil Rights Act in 1964.** *CORBIS/Bettmann*

segregation as a scientific response to problems of racial division. If fully capable of making such a dramatic gesture as inviting Booker T. Washington to dine at the White House, Roosevelt always acted with the politician's eye for votes. Concluding that the key to Republican Party electoral success in this century lay in building up what his successor, William Howard Taft, called "a decent white man's party" below the Mason-Dixon line, Roosevelt gradually abandoned such gestures. Stumping again for the presidency in 1912 on the Bull Moose ticket, he ran a self-professed "lily white" campaign.

Woodrow Wilson, the next Progressive after Roosevelt, already had a decent white man's party in place. So he took a different reformist tack – launching a campaign to institutionalize Jim Crow within the civil service. Wilson also gave a private White House screening of THE BIRTH OF A NATION (1915), the D. W. Griffith Reconstruction-era epic film that presented the Ku Klux Klan as a heroic force. "History written with lightning," Wilson said. When asked to condemn Southern LYNCHING, in contrast, he remained silent. The pressures of World War I, accompanied by a wave of race rioting in WASHINGTON, D.C., and elsewhere, did lead him to take a more moderate stance thereafter. But Wilson never abandoned the position he adopted as a young student of history – defending slavery as part of the civilizing process and dismissing Reconstruction as merely "a host of dusky children untimely put out of school."

New Era, 1921-1933

The New Era interlude before the nation's next major reform movement, Franklin D. Roosevelt's NEW DEAL, began with the Warren G. Harding administration's far-ranging search for an indictable offense to hang on Marcus Garvey. J. Edgar Hoover, a young Justice Department official who went on to head the Federal Bureau of Investigation (FBI), led the charge. The next president, Calvin Coolidge, left town on the day the Ku Klux Klan paraded through the streets of the nation's capital. Herbert Hoover, the third and last New Era chief executive, who had the particular misfortune to preside when the GREAT DEPRESSION arrived, emerged as the most bitter White House enemy of the NATIONAL ASSOCIATION FOR THE ADVANCEMENT OF COLORED PEOPLE (NAACP) in that organization's history. This was the result of the president's nomination of a segregationist, John J. Parker, to the Supreme Court. "Hoover's intransigence," as NAACP executive secretary Walter White said, "permanently alienated Negroes" and thus made the coming political revolution that much more likely.

New Deal, 1933-1945

Such intransigence, combined with New Deal economic reforms, caused an African American exodus from the party of Lincoln to the party of Jefferson Davis. The white South, meanwhile, not only continued to vote Democratic but to enforce Jim Crow by any means necessary. If Franklin Roosevelt so feared alienating those voters that he remained silent even on lynching, he did support anti-poll tax legislation. He also made an occasional symbolic gesture. When the Daughters of the American Revolution (DAR) refused to allow singer MARIAN ANDERSON to perform in Constitution Hall, Eleanor Roosevelt resigned her DAR membership in protest, and her husband approved a free public concert at the Lincoln Memorial. More important, the New Deal established something of a "black brain trust" or "black cabinet" that included MARY MCLEOD BETHUNE and Robert Weaver and approached the ideal of equal treatment for all in several alphabet agencies (notably the Public Works Administration.

Roosevelt lacked anything approaching a systematic civil rights program before A. Philip Randolph threatened, in the summer before Pearl Harbor, a massive all-black march on Washington to force an executive order creating a Fair Employment Practice Committee. Paradoxically, the Roosevelt administration pursued a very systematic approach on the surveillance front, sending G-men off to spy on the march on Washington and to gather intelligence on the "mood" of Negro communities from Harlem to Watts. From FDR's election in 1932 to the FBI director's death in 1972 at the end of Richard M. Nixon's first term, J. Edgar Hoover was the first person every chief executive turned to when confronted with any issue along the color line.

COLD WAR, 1945-1961

Harry S. Truman, who came to the oval office at Roosevelt's death in 1945, was an unlikely candidate to make one of the century's most dramatic civil rights gestures. FDR had selected Truman as his vice-presidential running mate in 1944 to appease white Southerners who were alarmed at the left-wing politics of then Vice President Henry Wallace. "Everything is going to be all right," one senator predicted from the funeral train carrying Roosevelt's body. "The new president knows how to handle the niggers." It became clear just how wrong such sentiments were in late 1946 when Truman created a President's Committee on Civil Rights in response to the latest wave of lynching in the Deep South. In 1948 Truman sent civil rights legislation to Congress and issued a stunning executive order ending segregation in the armed forces (*see* MILITARY, BLACKS IN THE AMERICAN). If the president's motives were somewhat suspect and if he failed to push his own program in Congress, he did create a momentum that helped the modern CIVIL RIGHTS MOVEMENT press forward. Truman did more for racial justice than Franklin Roosevelt or any other predecessor (Lincoln aside) – more, too, than most who would follow.

This post-World War II momentum forced Dwight D. Eisenhower, the first Republican president since Herbert Hoover, to confront his own convictions. Eisenhower was a nineteenth-century man comfortable in the world of *Plessy*, a world that the Supreme Court cracked open in BROWN V. BOARD OF EDUCATION (1954). In 1957 the president sent troops into Arkansas to force state compliance with a federal court order to desegregate Little Rock Central High School. Acting in defense of the federal order (not civil rights), he said the decision to commit the 101st Airborne was the hardest of his presidency because it interfered with his dream to bring the white South over to the Republican Party. He also had to confront the post-*Brown* spectacle of black demonstrations and mass protests, notably the MONTGOMERY BUS BOYCOTT, starting in 1955, and the sit-ins of 1960 (*see* CIVIL RIGHTS MOVEMENT). Coinciding with the rise of television, the new movement strategy pioneered by Martin Luther King Jr., and others put an incredible amount of pressure on the White House to choose sides in the integrationist/segregationist struggle.

NEW FRONTIERS AND GREAT SOCIETIES

John F. Kennedy inherited a bewildering array of direct action protest and segregationist violence, from the Freedom Rides to the desegregation crisis at the University of Mississippi; from the marches in Bull Connor's Birmingham to a March on Washington in 1963 that witnessed King's "I Have a Dream" speech; from the turn-the-other-cheek rhetoric of Christian churches to the less accommodating rhetoric of MALCOLM X. Intent on keeping both black votes and white Southern votes, Kennedy hoped to wait out the movement. This was not unlike waiting out a snowstorm, as a White House aide noted. By spring 1963 the president finally realized that the movement was not going away and chose sides in his own particular style – sending civil rights legislation to Congress and acquiescing in the decision to place an FBI wiretap on King's telephone.

By the time Kennedy died in Dallas and Lyndon B. Johnson took the oath of office, a wave of assassinations in fall 1963 had already shaken the nation. A Ku Klux Klan bomb in the basement of Birmingham's Sixteenth Street Baptist Church killed four young girls. In Vietnam, a military coup with at least some Central Intelligence Agency (CIA) assistance toppled and murdered Ngo Dinh Diem. Then Kennedy's own assassin was gunned down while in police custody and in full view of television cameras. By the time Johnson left office in 1969, assassins would kill King, Malcolm X, and Robert Kennedy; and the war in Vietnam had become a televised nightmare rivaled only by racial strife at home that set urban America ablaze.

Initially, President Johnson seemed quite determined to and capable of putting the fall 1963 violence to rest. In 1964 the Klan rose again, killing three civil rights workers in Neshoba County, Mississippi. But Johnson was already moving his Great Society reforms forward, pushing through Congress the sweeping Civil Rights Act of 1964 and implementing a War on Poverty. In 1965 he responded to Bloody Sunday and other segregationist violence in Selma, Alabama, with the final deathblow for Jim Crow – the VOTING RIGHTS ACT OF 1965. Still, this is where things began coming apart. Rather than celebrate these triumphs, the movement turned leftward with "Black Power," "Off the Pig," and "Burn, Baby, Burn" militancy, and the nation's cities exploded. Watts in 1965 and NEWARK, NEW JERSEY, and Detroit, Michigan, in 1967 represented only the largest of several hundred riots. Then, when Johnson appointed a presidential commission to investigate the riots, the so-called Kerner Commission identified white racism as the root cause.

John H. Sengstacke presents President Harry S. Truman with the Robert S. Abbott memorial award, named for his uncle – founding editor of the *Chicago Defender* – for his contributions to democracy. Mary McLeod Bethune, *right*, observes the presentation. *CORBIS/Bettmann*

SOUTHERN STRATEGIES, 1969-1998

Here, the Republican Party saw an opportunity to fulfill Theodore Roosevelt's dream of building a decent white man's party in the South. In contrast to the Kerner Commission, the GOP's presidential candidate in 1968, Richard Nixon, identified the liberal excesses of John Kennedy's New Frontier and Lyndon Johnson's Great Society as the root cause of racial strife. Nixon also had to counter Alabama governor George Wallace's third-party appeal for the racist vote. Everything from the fires in Detroit to the new AFFIRMATIVE ACTION bureaucracies and court-ordered busing of schoolchildren made the white South ripe for revolt, and Nixon did not intend to lose those voters to Wallace. Race, to put it another way, was the ultimate wedge issue, a tool to pit black against white generally and the various segments of the old Roosevelt coalition against one another more specifically (e.g., organized labor versus the organized civil rights community). Nixon called this his "southern strategy," which consisted largely of reminding white voters in the South and white working-class voters in the Midwest that tax-paying white Americans were the victims of a new discrimination created by the Democratic Party.

Southern strategy remained a staple of GOP politics after Watergate. Republican Gerald Ford awkwardly questioned the historic school desegregation case, *Brown* v. *Board of Education*, and crusaded against court-ordered busing. The next Republican, Ronald Reagan, opened his 1980 campaign against Jimmy Carter at the Neshoba County Fair by telling the crowd that he was a states' righter. The Ku Klux Klansmen who murdered civil rights workers Michael Schwerner, James Chaney, and Andrew Goodman in Neshoba 16 years earlier had said they were states' righters, too. Carter's suggestion that the affair demonstrated a racist streak in Reagan merely led to a media debate over whether the charge indicated a mean streak in Jimmy Carter. In 1988 George Bush organized his GOP campaign around the great race taboo, that of a black man who raped a white woman.

Democrat Bill Clinton preempted a repeat of Bush's Willie Horton gambit in the 1992 campaign by baiting Jesse Jackson (the Sister Souljah affair); by posing with a black chain gang as backdrop for a crime control ad; golfing at a segregated Little Rock club; and presiding over the execution of a black man, Rickey Ray Rector, brain damaged enough to ask the men wielding the needle to save his last meal's dessert pie "for later." In the White House President Clinton has been more aggressive on the subject of racial justice. This was particularly true in the second term, when he offered a mend-it-don't-end-it defense of affirmative action and a Civil Rights Initiative intended to spark a national dialogue on race. The latter also included a pledge in the State of the Union Address of 1998 to accelerate enforcement of current civil rights laws affecting employment, education, housing, and health care.

Kenneth O'Reilly

SEE ALSO
Slavery in the United States; World War I and African Americans; World War II and African Americans; Abolitionism in the United States; Amistad Mutiny; Black Cabinet; Chaney, James Earl; Civil War, American; Detroit Riot of 1967; Fair Employment Practices Committee; Fifteenth Amendment to the United States Constitution; Fourteenth Amendment to the United States Constitution; Free Blacks in the United States, 1619 to 1863; Garvey, Marcus Mosiah; Harlem, New York; Jackson, Jesse Louis; Kerner Report; King, Martin Luther, Jr.; Los Angeles Watts Riot of 1965; Randolph, Asa Philip; Sixteenth Street Baptist Church (Birmingham, Ala.); Thirteenth Amendment of the United States Constitution and the Emancipation Proclamation; Vietnam War; Washington, Booker Taliaferro; Weaver, Robert Clifton; Lynching; White, Walter Francis; March on Washington, 1963; Black Power; Little Rock Crisis, 1957; March on Washington, 1941.

Cross Cultural

Race: An Interpretation

Stretch forth! stretch forth! from the south
to the North,
From the east to the west – stretch forth!
stretch forth!
Strengthen thy stakes and lengthen
thy cords –
The world is a tent for the world's true
lords!
Break forth and spread over every place
The world is a world for the Saxon race!
(Martin Tupper, "The Anglo-Saxon Race")

These famous words were published in 1850 in a new journal called *The Anglo-Saxon*. The publication lasted only a year, but the tone of Tupper's lines is emblematic of an important development in the way educated Englishmen and women thought of themselves and of what it was that made them English. This development was itself part of a wider movement of ideas in Europe and North America. As heirs to the culture of the modern world, a culture so crucially shaped by the ideas that Tupper's poem represents, most twentieth-century readers, not merely in Europe and America but throughout the world, are able to take for granted a set of assumptions about what Tupper means by "race." Those assumptions, which amounted to a new theory of race, inform our modern understanding of literature – indeed of most symbolic culture – in fundamental ways, despite the fact that, as we shall see, many of them have been officially discarded.

That the specific form race-theory took was new does not, of course, mean that it had no historical antecedents. Almost as far back as the earliest human writings, we can find more or less well-articulated views about the differences between "our own kind" and the people of other cultures. These doctrines, like modern theories of race, have often placed a central emphasis on physical appearance in defining the "Other," and on common ancestry in explaining why groups of people display differences in their attitudes and aptitudes.

IDEAS ABOUT HUMAN DIFFERENCE

CLASSICAL GREEKS: ENVIRONMENTALISM

If we call any group of human beings of common descent living together in some sort of association, however loosely structured, a "people," we can say that every human culture that was aware of other peoples seems to have had views about what accounted for the differences – in appearance, in customs, in language – between peoples. This is certainly true of the two main ancient traditions to which Western thinkers look back – those of the classical Greeks and the ancient Hebrews. Thus, we find Hippocrates in the fifth century B.C.E. in Greece seeking to explain the (supposed) superiority of his own people to the peoples of (western) Asia by arguing that the barren soils of Greece had forced the Greeks to become tougher and more independent. Such a view attributes the characteristics of a people to their environment, leaving open the possibility that their descendants could change if they moved to new conditions.

While the general opinion in Greece in the few centuries on either side of the beginning of the common era appears to have been that both the black "Ethiopians" to the south and the blond "Scythians" to the north were inferior to the Hellenes, there was no general assumption that this inferiority was incorrigible. Educated Greeks, after all, knew that in the *Iliad* Homer had described Zeus and other Olympians feasting with the "blameless Ethiopians"; and there are arguments in the works of the pre-Socratic Sophists to the effect that it is individual character and not skin color that determines a person's worth.

ANCIENT HEBREWS AND THE OLD TESTAMENT

In the Old Testament, on the other hand, what is thought to be distinctive about peoples is not so much appearance and custom as their relationship, through a common ancestor, to God. Thus, in the book of Genesis, Jehovah says to Abraham: "Go your way out of your country and from your relatives and from the house of your father and to the country that I shall show you; and I shall make a great people of you and I will make your name great" (Genesis 12:1-2). And from this founding moment – this covenant or agreement between Abraham and Jehovah – the descendants of Abraham have a special place in history. It is, of course, Abraham's grandson Jacob who takes the name of Israel: his descendants thus become the "people of Israel."

The Old Testament is full of names of peoples. Some of them are still familiar –

Syrians, Assyrians, and Persians; some of them are less so – Canaanites, Philistines, and Medes. Many of these groups are accounted for in the genealogies of the peoples of the earth and are explicitly seen as descending ultimately not only from the first human couple, Adam and Eve, but more particularly from Noah. Just as the Israelites are "sons of Shem," the children of Ham and of Japheth account for the rest of the human "family."

But while these different peoples are taken to have different specific characteristics and ancestries, the fundamentally theocentric perspective of the Old Testament requires that what *essentially* differentiates them all from the Hebrews is that they do not have the special relationship to Jehovah of the children, the descendants, of Israel. There is very little hint that the early Jewish writers developed any theories about the relative importance of the biological and the cultural inheritances by which God made these different peoples distinct. Indeed, in the theocentric framework it is God's covenant that matters and the very distinction between environmental and inherited characteristics is anachronistic.

"Racialists" and Scientific Conceptions of Biological Heredity

Neither the Greeks' environmentalism nor the Hebrews' theocentric notion of the significance of being one people represents ideas that we should naturally apply in understanding Tupper's use of the idea of race. To the extent that we think of Tupper's doggerel as modern, as involving ideas that *we* understand, we will suppose that he believed that the world was "a world for the Saxon race" because of that race's *inherited* capacities. For by Tupper's day a distinctively modern understanding of what it was to be a people – an understanding in terms of our modern notion of race – was beginning to be forged: that notion had at its heart a new scientific conception of biological heredity, even as it carried on some of the roles played in Greek and Hebraic thought by the idea of a people. But it was, also, as we shall see, interwoven with a new understanding of a people as a nation and of the role of culture – and, crucially for our purposes, of literature – in the life of nations.

In short, Tupper, unlike the Greeks and the Hebrews, was what I shall call a *racialist*. He believed, as did most educated Victorians by the mid-century, that we could divide human beings into a small number of groups, called "races," in such a way that all the members of these races shared certain fundamental, biologically heritable moral and intellectual characteristics with one another that they did not share with members of any other race. The characteristics that each member of a race was supposed to share with every other were sometimes called the *essence* of that race; they were characteristics that were necessary and sufficient, taken together, for someone to be a member of the race.

Unlike the Greeks and the Hebrews, racialists believed that the racial essence accounted for more than the obvious visible characteristics – skin color, hair – on the basis of which we decide whether people are, say, Asian Americans or African Americans. For a racialist, then, to say someone is "Negro" is not just to say that he or she has inherited black skin or curly hair: it is to say that his or her skin color goes along with other important inherited characteristics. By the end of the nineteenth century most Western scientists (indeed, most educated Westerners) believed that racialism was correct, and theorists sought to explain many characteristics – including, for example, literary "genius," intelligence, and honesty – by supposing that they were inherited along with (or were in fact part of) a person's racial essence.

LITERARY REPRESENTATIONS OF RACIAL STEREOTYPES

The twentieth century inherited these conceptions, but it was the nineteenth century that was the heyday of appeals to race in literary study. By our own day the idea that the concept of race should have any place – let alone an important one – in literary studies has been attacked from a good many directions. Perhaps the most surprising has been an attack in the name of "science." In a society like ours, in which most people take their race to be a significant aspect of their identity, it comes as a shock to many to learn that there is a fairly widespread consensus in the sciences of biology and anthropology that the word *race*, at least as it is used in most unscientific discussions, refers to nothing that science should recognize as real.

And it is not just the claim that there is a racial essence that can explain a person's moral, intellectual, or literary aptitudes that scientists have rejected. They also believe that such classifications as *Negro, Caucasian*, and *Mongoloid* are of no importance for biological purposes. First, because there are simply too many people who do not fit into any such category; and second, because, even when you succeed in assigning someone to one of these categories – on the basis of skin pigmentation and hair, say – that implies very little about most of their other biological characteristics. Even those scientists who still have a use for the term *race* agree that a good deal of what is popularly believed about races is false – often wildly false.

But, of course, a discussion of some of the literary ramifications of the idea of race can proceed while accepting the essential unreality of races and the falsehood of most of what is believed about them. For, at least in this respect, races are like, for example, witches: however unreal witches are, *belief* in witches, like belief in races, has had – and in many communities continues to have – profound consequences for human social life.

Elizabethan Theater: "Othello, the Moor of Venice," "The Merchant of Venice," and "The Jew of Malta"

The racialism we see in Tupper and his contemporaries is real enough to make up for the unreality of races. We can see something of the long process of transition from the views of the ancient world to the racialism we find in Tupper, if we ask how we should interpret the handling of questions of difference between peoples in such plays as Shakespeare's *Othello* (c. 1603) and *The Merchant of Venice* (c. 1597) or in Christopher Marlowe's *The Jew of Malta* (c. 1592).

In each of these plays a central figure – Othello, Shylock, Barabas – plays out a role we can only understand in terms of a stereotype of a people, Moors or Jews, a stereotype we are likely, if we are hasty, to conceive of as simply racialist. So it is important to go carefully. We should begin by recognizing that in Shakespearean England both Jews and Moors were barely an empirical reality. And even though there were small numbers of Jews and black people in England in Shakespeare's day, attitudes to "the Moor" and "the Jew" do not seem to have been based on experience of these people. Furthermore, despite the fact that there was an increasing amount of information available about dark-skinned foreigners in this, the first great period of modern Western exploration, actual reports of black or Jewish foreigners did not play an important part in forming these images, either. Rather, it seems that the stereotypes were based on an essentially theological conception of the status of both Moors and Jews as non-Christians; the former were distinguished by their black skin, whose color was associated in Christian iconography with sin and the devil; the latter by their being, as Saint Matthew's account of the crucifixion suggests, "Christ-killers."

There is good reason, then, to interpret these Elizabethan stereotypes, which *we* might naturally think of as what I have called "racialist," as rooted far less in notions of inherited dispositions and far more in the idea of the Moor and the Jew as infidels: unbelievers whose physical differences are signs (but not causes or effects) of their unbelief. Yet in some ways the most revealing of the plays for the purposes of underscoring the distance that was still to be traveled from Shakespeare's Moor of Venice or Marlowe's Maltese Jew to the imperializing race of Tupper's Anglo-Saxonist vision is a play that does not explicitly invoke either of these the most familiar for us of "racial" stereotypes: and that is Shakespeare's *The Tempest*.

"The Tempest" as a Metaphor for British Expansion in the Mid-Seventeenth Century

We are accustomed nowadays to interpretations that cast Caliban as the colonial subject; and that is not anachronistic, given the play's historical context. *The Tempest* was first performed in 1611 for the court of James I, during an era of extensive overseas expansion. From abundant internal evidence we know that Shakespeare's conception of the "savage and deformed slave" was informed by contemporary pamphlets and speculative essays about the nature of the "native," travelogues describing European encounters with the inhabitants of the New World.

Now, Caliban, as Prospero asserts, is "a born devil," (literally, perhaps) "on whose nature/Nurture can never stick" (act 4, scene 1). And if Caliban is the representative colonial, the peculiar brutality of Prospero as colonizer can only be justified by Caliban's incorrigibly devilish nature. For, of course, it is more than just colonialism in general that needs to be justified. What needs to be justified is the especial brutality of the colonization of nonwhite peoples – Africans and Indians. It is only because Caliban is incorrigibly wicked that Prospero can maintain our sympathy while making Caliban's colonization into what is simply a form of slavery. Miranda makes the issue clear the first time she addresses Caliban:

Abhorréd slave,
Which any print of goodness wilt not take,
Being capable of all ill! I pitied thee,
Took pains to make thee speak, taught thee each hour
One thing or other. When thou didst not, savage,
Know thine own meaning, but wouldst gabble like
A thing most brutish, I endowed thy purposes
With words that made them known.
But thy vile race,
Though thou didst learn, had that in't which good natures
Could not abide to be with… (act 1, scene 2)

Echoes here of the later image of the colonized male subject – ungovernable in his lusts, intractable, learning the colonizer's language in order to articulate his own vile purposes – may lead us to read back into this passage the triumphalist racialism of "The Anglo-Saxon Race." Yet if it is clear enough now how this ideology that will develop into racialism could serve already in the seventeenth century to license the domination of subject peoples, it is important to mark its differences.

The word *race* occurs only in this place in *The Tempest* and an unprepared modern reader risks misunderstanding it. For race here in its Elizabethan usage means – as the *Oxford English Dictionary* tells us – "natural or inherited disposition." Miranda's point in speaking of Caliban's "race" is only to restate her earlier insistence on his individual moral incorrigibility: he will not take any "print of goodness" because it is not in his nature. For Tupper, of course, "race" is also a natural or inherited disposition; but it is, by contrast, one that is shared with a whole people.

"The Tempest" as an Allegory of Colonialism in the Nineteenth Century

What is interesting is that the very possibility of reading *The Tempest* as an allegory of colonialism does not appear to occur to theatrical interpreters of the play until the nineteenth century; while from the mid-nineteenth century on – at the pinnacle of British imperial power – productions of *The Tempest* in Britain increasingly reflected ongoing disagreements about the nature of subject peoples and the justice of their colonization. And when a conception of "primitive" peoples became biologized during the later nineteenth century – especially under the influence of Darwin's *Origin of Species* – we find productions of *The Tempest* mirrored current speculation. In the age of social Darwinism, Caliban became quite literally the "missing link" of evolutionary theory (the English actor F. R. Benson, who played the part in a touring company all around Britain in the 1890s, spent time observing various apes in the zoo in order to perfect his movements!). If Caliban is the "missing link," his status as a proper object of the colonizer's control is not in doubt. The very fact that by the end of the nineteenth century the character can move back and forth between interpretations as subhuman and as the colonial human subject shows the tendency of an increasingly biologized idea of race to allow an uneasy oscillation between thinking of the natives as of the same fundamental kind as the ruling race – and thus, both capable of elevation and, at least potentially, *wrongly* subjected – and thinking of them as of a different kind – and thus perpetually its natural subjects.

Victorian Literature: Celebration of the Anglo-Saxon "Race"

The distance from Shakespeare's understanding of the issue of difference between peoples to the ideas that surrounded Tupper is evidenced in these new Victorian readings of Shakespeare's play. For literary purposes, the developments that begin at the turn of the nineteenth century have another immediate consequence: *race* becomes important as the *theme* of a great body of writing in Europe and North America – and, indeed, in the rest of the world under the influence of "Western" cultures – and the concept often plays a crucial role in structuring plot.

"Ivanhoe"

Thus, in *Ivanhoe*, a novel published by the Scottish novelist and poet Sir Walter Scott in 1819, the theme of the story is the hatred between Anglo-Saxons, the "original," inhabitants of Britain, and the Norman rulers imposed upon them by the conquest of England in 1066 by William the Conqueror. The presupposition of the story (which seems to have little historical basis) is that there was a natural antipathy between the Anglo-Saxon race and their French-speaking Norman rulers; our understanding of the plot depends, in part, on our recognition of the struggle between Anglo-Saxons and Normans not simply as a struggle of the poor and oppressed against their rich oppressors, but as a struggle for Anglo-Saxon national (or, equivalently, racial) autonomy. The racial theme of the book is reinforced by the presence of the character "Isaac the Jew" and his daughter Rebecca; as the Norman aristocracy is stereotyped as lawless and corrupt, and the Anglo-Saxons as noble and downtrodden, Isaac is stereotyped as avaricious, torn between love of his daughter and love of money.

Ideas about race could, in principle, have developed without a commitment to the view that some races were superior to others; but they did not. While the Christian tradition insisted on the common ancestry of all human beings, and the Enlightenment, even when it was critical of official Christianity, emphasized the universality of reason, by the middle of the nineteenth century the notion that all races were equal in their capacities was a distinctly minority view. Even those who insisted that all human beings had the same rights largely acknowledged that nonwhite people lacked either the intelligence or the vigor of the white races, among which the highest, it was widely agreed, was the Indo-European stock from which the Germanic peoples emerged. In England and North America there was a further narrowing of focus: the Anglo-Saxons were the favored offshoot of the Germanic stock.

Indeed, one of the central questions for nineteenth century race-science became the question *why* it was that the white races were superior to the others; there was an almost equal interest in how the others should be ranked below them. But though there was, therefore, an inevitable element of moral evaluation in most theories of race, it is important to be clear that the racial theme never required a simple identification of one race with evil and another with good. In *Ivanhoe*, our hero – son of Cedric, an *Anglo-Saxon* "nationalist" who wishes to see the reestablishment of the Saxon monarchy – cooperates as a loyal subject with the *Norman* king, Richard the Lionheart, to overthrow the corruption of the Norman nobility that the king has left behind while taking part in the Crusades; and, at a crucial point in the plot, Rebecca, Isaac's daughter – despite the essentially anti-Semitic presuppositions of Scott's day – nurses Ivanhoe back to life and falls in love with him. Nevertheless, the book depends not only, as we have seen, on an assumption of the naturalness of racial feeling but also on the maintenance of certain racial boundaries: despite Rebecca's more substantial character, it is Rowena, the Anglo-Saxon heiress, whom Ivanhoe marries, and Rebecca, who is, in a sense, ruled out by race as a spouse, disappears from England with her father at the end of the book.

Forty years after *Ivanhoe*, in *Salammbo*, published in 1862, the French novelist Gustave Flaubert created a similar racial romance, set in ancient Carthage. While the central contrast in the work is between civilized and barbarous peoples – the French word *barbares* (which is both noun and adjective) occurs 238 times, more often than any other noun or adjective – the novel is replete with references to Campanians, Garamantes, Gauls, Greeks, Iberians, Lusitanians, Libyans, Negroes, Numidians, Phoenicians, and Syssites; these types are often identified with certain physical and moral characteristics.

Ivanhoe and *Salammbo* depend on projecting nineteenth-century racial concerns back into the past. But in the heyday of the European world empires, as the great European powers divided the world between them (and as Americans of European descent conquered Native Americans through their superiority in military technologies), it was common to offer the racial superiority of the "white man" as an explanation for the contemporary successes of imperialism; these successes became the theme of a substantial body of literature.

James Fenimore Cooper and the American Frontier

In the United States, for example, in James Fenimore Cooper's well-known "Leatherstocking Tales" – from *The Pioneers* (1823) to *The Deerslayer* (1841) – a celebration of the American frontier (itself a substantial literary theme) elicits the overarching theme of the decline of the "red man" and the triumph of the "white man." Cooper's style is in many ways reminiscent of Scott's and, in fact, Cooper could hardly have escaped the influence of Scott's romances: for these were amongst the most widely read and admired works of fiction in the United States in the first half of the nineteenth century. They were adapted over and over again for the American stage and published in numerous editions (something that was easier in an age before copyright). Scott's interest for Americans must have been in part a consequence of the fact that much of his work, unlike *Ivanhoe*, was devoted to establishing not English but Scottish national feeling. In such adventures as *Rob Roy*, Scott celebrates the people and the life of the Scottish borders, a world whose romantically conceived landscape and rough "manly" manners were easily transferred in imagination to the rigors of North American pioneer life.

Like Scott's representation of the Jew, Cooper's image of the Indian, though stereotyped, was ambivalent – Natty Bumppo, Cooper's hero, distinguishes between "Good Indians" – like Chingachgook, Bumppo's Indian companion, who will fight with the white man against other red men – and "Bad Indians" who combine the lack of civilization, common to all Indians, with an absence of the natural nobility that Chingachgook displays. In Cooper's racial scheme (unlike Thomas Jefferson's), the Indian is below the "white man" but above the "Negro": Indians in Cooper are sometimes "Nature's gentlemen"; blacks almost always evoke contempt. We could argue that the Negro in Cooper plays the same sort of role as the Jew in *Ivanhoe:* the main plot in each case pits one race (Anglo-Saxon, red man) against another (Norman, white man) that dominates it, and the third race (Jew, Negro) provides a point of contrast with each of the others; a point of contrast that allows us to understand the sympathies between the members of the first two races, even though their conflict is at the center of the plot. In this case, then, as I suggested, the hierarchy of races becomes an essential element in structuring the plot.

RACE, NATION, AND THE IDEA OF LITERATURE

In a world whose politics were so dominated by racialism, it is hardly surprising that races became a central literary theme. What is, perhaps, more puzzling is the fact that many of those works that have been central to our understanding of what literature is are also thematically preoccupied with racial issues. But the reason for this is not far to seek: it lies in the dual connection made in eighteenth- and nineteenth-century thought between, on the one hand, race and nationality, and, on the other, nationality and literature. In short, the nation is the key middle term in understanding the relations between the concept of race and the idea of literature.

The first of these linkages, between nation and race, will surely be the less puzzling. In the Old World, where people were the hereditary subjects of monarchies, it was natural that the emergent European nations conceived of themselves in terms of descent. Eighteenth-century theorists of the nation had, of course, to make a sharp distinction between nations and states because in eighteenth-century Europe there was not even an approximate correlation between linguistic and political boundaries. (It is important to remember that the correlation remains in most parts of the world quite rough and ready.) The modern European nationalism, which produced, for example, the German and Italian states, involved trying to create states to correspond to nationalities – nationalities conceived of as sharing a civilization, and, more particularly a language and literature. And because political geography did not correspond to nationalities, eighteenth-century theorists were obliged to draw a distinction between the nation as a natural entity and the state as the product of culture, as a human artifice.

But with the increasing influence of the natural sciences in the nineteenth century, what is natural in human beings – human nature – came increasingly to be thought of in terms of the sciences of biology and anthropology. Inevitably, then, the nation comes more and more to be identified as a biological unit, defined by the shared essence that flows from a common descent.

Anglo-Saxon Roots of Constitutional Monarchy

Yet the increasing identification of race and nation in European – and more particularly in English – thought was a complex process. The Anglo-Saxonism of the nineteenth century in Britain has its roots deep in the soil of historical argument about the English constitution; in the fascinating process through which a rising commercial class transformed the monarchy in Britain from its feudal roots into the "constitutional monarchy" that was established at the Restoration of 1660. In the arguments that surround this development, a mythology took hold in the seventeenth century of a free Anglo-Saxon people living under parliamentary government in the period before the Norman Conquest of 1066. Increasingly Anglo-Saxon institutions were seen both to account for the Englishman's natural love of freedom and to underlie the immemorial rights of free men against the Crown.

This mythology was counterposed against the mainstream historiography of the Middle Ages, which traced the *History of the Kings of Britain* – as Geoffrey of Monmouth's influential work of 1136 was called – to Brutus, grandson of Aeneas of Troy. It was Geoffrey who established the story of King Arthur, son of Utherpendragon, as forever part of British mythology; and his work played a significant part in providing a framework within which the different cultural streams – Roman, Saxon, Danish, and Norman – that had come together over the first millennium in Britain could be gathered into a single unifying history.

When Richard Verstegen published his influential *Restitution of Decayed Intelligence* in 1605, he claimed that England's Anglo-Saxon past was the past of a Germanic people who shared their language and institutions with the Germanic tribes, whose great courage and fierce independence Tacitus had described many centuries earlier. Verstegen argued that these tribes were also the ancestors of the Danes and the Normans, whose invasions of Britain had thus not essentially disturbed the unity of the English as a Germanic people. The effect of this argument, of course, was to provide for the seventeenth century what the *History of the Kings of England* had provided in the Middle Ages: a framework within which the peoples of England could be conceived as united.

By the eve of the American Revolution Anglo-Saxon historiography and the study of the Anglo-Saxon law, language, and institutions were established scholarly pursuits; and the notion of a free Anglo-Saxon past, whose reestablishment would be an escape from the monarchy's potential to develop into a tyranny, was one that appealed naturally to such figures as Thomas Jefferson. Anglo-Saxonism spread easily to a United States whose dominant culture imagined itself – even after the Revolution – as British. And when Jefferson, himself no mean Anglo-Saxon scholar, designed a curriculum for the University of Virginia, he included the study of the Anglo-Saxon language, because, as he said, reading the "histories and laws left us in that… dialect," students would "imbibe with the language their free principles of government."

Herder and Modern Nationalism

But the deep-rooted character of the second linkage – between nation and literature – will probably be less naturally intelligible. And our starting point for understanding the role of the idea of a national literature in the development of the concept of a national culture must be in the work of the man who developed its first real theoretical articulation: Johann Gottfried Herder.

In his *On the New German Literature: Fragments* of 1767, Herder – who is, in some ways, the first important philosopher of modern nationalism – put forward the notion that language is not just "a tool of the arts and sciences" but "a part of them." Herder's notion of the *Sprachgeist* – literally the "spirit" of the language – embodies the thought that language is not merely the medium through which speakers communicate, but the sacred essence of a nationality. Herder himself identified the highest point of the nation's language in its poetry, both the popular lyrics of the folk song, which he collected, and the work of great poets. The emergence of nationalism in the eighteenth and early nineteenth centuries depended on the imaginative re-creation of a common cultural past that was, in no small part, crafted into a shared tradition by literary scholars like Herder and – to return to an earlier example – Sir Walter Scott, whose *Minstrelsy of the Scottish Border* was intended, as he said in the preface, to "contribute somewhat to the history of my native country; the peculiar features of whose manners and character are daily melting and dissolving into those of her sister and ally" (i.e., England). From its inception, literary history, like the collection of folk culture, served the ends of nation building.

Racial Understandings of Literature in the Nineteenth Century

Imposing the post-Herderian identification of the core of the nation with its national literature on top of the racial conception of the nation, we arrive at the racial understanding of literature that flourishes from the mid-nineteenth century in the work of the first modern literary historians. Thomas Carlyle, the great British essayist and man-of-letters, wrote in 1831: "The history of a nation's poetry is the essence of its history." It was only a step from here to the identification of that history with the history of the race. Hippolyte Taine's monumental *History of English Literature*, published in France in the 1860s – perhaps the first modern literary history of English – begins with the words "History has been transformed, within a hundred years in Germany, within sixty in France, and that by the study of their literatures." But he is soon telling us that "a race, like the Old Aryans, scattered from the Ganges as far as the Hebrides, settled in every clime, and every stage of civilization, transformed by thirty centuries of revolutions, nevertheless manifests in its languages, religions, literatures, philosophies, the community of blood and of intellect which to this day binds its offshoots together."

What is revealed, in short, by the study of literature that has transformed the discipline of history is the "moral state" of the race whose literature it is. It is because of this conception that Taine finds it proper to start his study of English literature with a chapter on the Saxons; so that chapter 1, book 1 of Taine's *History* begins not in England at all, but in Holland: "As you coast the North Sea from Scheldt to Jutland, you will mark in the first place that the characteristic feature is the want of slope: marsh, waster, shoal; the rivers hardly drag themselves along, swollen and sluggish, with long, blacklooking waves…. " The "Saxons, Angles, Jutes, Frisians… [and] Danes" who occupied this region of Holland at the beginning of the first millennium are, according to Taine, the ancestors of the English; but since they, themselves, are of German descent, Taine also refers, in describing this "race" a few pages later, to some of their traits reported in Tacitus.

Anglo-Saxonism and the Literary "Canon"

It is the conception of the binding core of the English nation as the Anglo-Saxon race that accounts for Taine's decision to identify the origins of English literature not in its antecedents in the Greek and Roman classics that provided the models and themes of so much of the best-known works of English "poesy"; not in the Italian models that influenced the drama of Marlowe and Shakespeare; but in *Beowulf*, a poem in the Anglo-Saxon tongue, a poem that was unknown to Chaucer and Spenser and Shakespeare, the first poets to write in a version of the English language that we can still almost understand.

Yet this decision was quite representative. When the teaching of English literature was institutionalized in the English universities in the nineteenth century, students were required to learn Anglo-Saxon in order to study *Beowulf*. Anglo-Saxonism thus played a major role in the establishment of the canon of literary works that were to be studied in both British and American colleges; and the teachers who came from these colleges to the high schools brought the Anglo-Saxon canon with them.

American Literature in the Twentieth Century

We must examine one final role for questions of race in literary study, a role that is especially visible in much recent writing about American literature. And that is in understanding how American literature and literary study both reflect the existence of ethnic groups, the very contours of which are, in a certain sense, the product of racism. For, however mythical the notion of race seems to be, we cannot deny the obvious fact that having one set of heritable characteristics – dark skin, say – rather than another – blond hair, for example – can have profound psychological, economic, or other social consequences, especially in societies where many people are not only racialists but racists. Indeed, much of what is said about races nowadays in American social life, while literally false if understood as being about biological races, can be interpreted as reporting truths about social groups – African Americans, Asian Americans, Jewish Americans – whose experience of life and whose political relations are strongly determined by the existence of racist stereotypes.

African American Literary Criticism

The most prominent such reflection of racially understood ethnicity in literary studies in recent years is in the development of African American literary criticism. Anyone who has followed the argument so far will anticipate that the persistent stream of African American nationalist argument (whose beginnings we can trace well before Tupper) has been accompanied by appeals to an African cultural heritage expressed in black folk music, poetry, and song. To the extent that African Americans were thought of as a separate people – and with the rise of racialism, this became increasingly inevitable – nineteenth-century thought proposed nationalism as a reflection of that separate status. Once black nationalism takes on this form, it is equally inevitable that a national literature, consisting of the folk art of the race, should be seen as the highest expression of the black national spirit. Such intellectual pioneers as W. E. B. Du Bois from the latter nineteenth century on attempted to articulate a racial tradition of black letters as a natural expression of the Herderian view of the nation as identified above all else with its expression in "poesy."

But there is another reason why the identification of a history of black literary production has been central not merely to African American literary criticism but to the culture of African Americans: namely, that for almost the whole period in which there have been people of African descent in the New World, a powerful European and American intellectual tradition has consistently denied that black people were capable of contributing to "the arts and letters." Starting before the fixing of race as a biological concept, influential figures expressed their doubts about the inherited "capacity of the Negro" to produce literature. Even in the Enlightenment, which emphasized the universality of reason, philosophers such as Voltaire in France, David Hume in Scotland, and Immanuel Kant in Germany, like Jefferson in the New World, denied literary capacity to people of African descent. And, as we have seen, once race was conceptualized in biological terms, such low opinions of black people would lead easily to the belief that these incapacities were part of an inescapable racial essence.

Formation of a "Black" Canon?

In response to this long line of antiblack invective, black writers in the United States since the very first African American poet – Phillis Wheatley, who lived in Boston in the latter part of the eighteenth century – have sought to establish the "capacity of the Negro" by writing and publishing literature. More than this, the major proportion of the published writing of African Americans, even when not directed to countering racist mythology, has been concerned thematically with issues of race, a fact that is hardly surprising in a country where black people were subjected to racial slavery until the mid-nineteenth century and then treated legally as second-class citizens in many places until the 1960s.

The recognition, especially in recent years, of the role of Anglo-Saxonism, in particular, and racism, more generally, in the construction of the canon of literature studied in American university departments of English, has led many scholars to argue for the inclusion of texts by African Americans in that canon, in part because their initial exclusion was an expression of racism. But it has led others to argue for the recognition of an African American tradition of writing, with its own major texts, which can be studied as an independent canon. Some of those who make such claims – the critics of the Black Aesthetic movement, for example – have been motivated largely by a black nationalism that is, in part, a response to racism; others have argued for the recognition of a black canon because they have identified formal features in the writings of black authors that derive from a self-conscious awareness of black literary predecessors and African or African American folk traditions. Though the debates about the African American literary tradition may be couched in terms of the existence of a tradition of aesthetically valuable texts that has been ignored, the issue of an African American canon is inevitably a political one. The politics of Anglo-Saxonist nationalism *ex*cluded African American culture from the official American canon, and the politics of American race relations inevitably structures discussion of their *in*clusion.

Literature and the Politics of Racial Difference

Differences among peoples, like differences among communities within a single society, play a central role in our thinking about who "we" are; in structuring our values and determining the identities through which we live. In the past century and a half racialism and nationalism, often so bound up together that one can hardly tell them apart, have played a central role in our thinking about these differences, and since one of the contributions of modern nationalism has been to see literature as central to national life, race has been central to literature and to thought about literature throughout this period. The racialism of Tupper's verse now seems merely ridiculous, even though such sentiments went with the reprehensible abuses of British imperialism; but racialism in our own century has produced lynchings in the American South, sustained the racist South African state, and led to the still unthinkable horrors of the Nazi Holocaust. The universal revulsion against these moral disasters does not, unfortunately, mean that racism is over. And so long as it continues it is likely that race will continue to be a preoccupation, not only of the literary history of the nineteenth and twentieth centuries but also of future literary production and literary study.

Kwame Anthony Appiah

See Also

South Africa; Literature, African American; Black Aesthetic, The; Boston, Massachusetts; Du Bois, William Edward Burghardt (W. E. B.); Lynching; Black Nationalism in the United States.

Latin America and the Caribbean

Race in Latin America

Millions of Africans of different ethnic groups were shipped halfway across the world to work the sugar, coffee, tobacco, and rice plantations and the mines of the New World. They brought with them their religions, their languages, their dance, their music, and their instruments. European colonial masters did their utmost to strip these Africans of their freedom, their dignity, and their culture; culture was perhaps the easiest of the three for peoples of African descent to maintain.

From the United States South and the Mexico altiplano in the north, to the Peruvian coastal lowlands and the Argentine pampas down south, the rhythms of Africa continued to beat. The samba and Candomblé of Brazil; the son and Santería of Cuba; the street Carnivals of Salvador de Bahia, Rio de Janeiro, and a host of other towns and cities; the merengue of the Dominican Republic and Venezuela; modern-day salsa; the very ingredients of the languages spoken and the foods eaten; family, community, and other organizational forms: in all lie manifestations of the strivings of Afro-Latin Americans to create a viable reality in which life could then, and can now, be lived with dignity.

Colonial and postcolonial society partitioned off people, classifying and categorizing skin pigmentation with a bewildering array of legal codes and linguistic terms (170 such terms exist in Brazil alone). In this context, "whitening" the race denoted upward social mobility, while blackening was equated with backwardness, poverty, and underdevelopment (*see* Whitening). The exceptions to racial hostility and oppression are pitifully thin at the national level and testify to the stigma of a perverse colonial legacy.

In many countries in Latin America and the Caribbean, people of African descent have constituted a majority of the population, and the race issue has been uppermost. But the prevailing currents of the region's history, dominated by a sense of "Europeanness," have repeatedly undermined and denied awareness of the African heritage, forcing Afro-Latin Americans to rediscover their ancestry and culture and renew the struggle for their rights.

Variants in Race Relations

A key variant in race relations in Latin America and the Caribbean occurs between the relatively fluid race relations of, for example, Brazil and Cuba, and the more bipolar situation in the United States and the non-Hispanic Caribbean. This has been explained in two ways: in terms of colonial cultures, and in terms of stages of development. One side of the argument is that the reason for the difference is not economic but cultural. Iberians (or people from Portugal and Spain), it is claimed, instituted a more benign form of slavery than did northern Europeans because of the strong Moorish influences on, and the nature of feudalism and Catholicism in, the Iberian Peninsula. The counterargument is that there are powerful underlying economic explanations for racism tied to the growth of the plantation economy in the Americas. Thus it makes little sense to compare nineteenth-century Cuba, a booming slave-plantation economy, and nineteenth-century Puerto Rico, which was an imperial backwater with no significant development of the plantation of slavery.

Both the "imperial cultures" and the economic materialism approaches tend to focus on power structures and official thinking. A third argument highlights the extent to which people have been active agents in shaping their own history, building and abolishing slavery, erecting and transgressing the intricacies of color and class codes. A distinction has been made between public and private, between the rules of behavior regulating contact between racial groups and actual intimate personal relations. According to this view, Iberian differed from non-Iberian America far more in the public than in the private.

No part of the world, it has been claimed, ever witnessed such a gigantic mixing of races as that which took place in Latin America and the Caribbean. It is useful, however, to think of the region in terms of a threefold division within Afro-Latin America: the Caribbean and northeast Brazil; Euro-Latin America, made up of Argentina, Uruguay, southern Chile, and south Brazil, which received great waves of European immigrants over the past 100 years; and *mestizo* America, where there are scattered enclaves of indigenous populations in locations such as Mexico, Guatemala, the Andes, and the Amazon Basin.

The extent of race mixing in Latin America might have engendered hopes of a new cosmic race, but it also meant that there has been no generally agreed-upon racial classification, and racial distinctions are necessarily vague. What is considered black in one context might be white in another. This depends, to a large extent, on the tensions between prevailing definitions of race – as phenotype, or physical characteristics, and as genotype, or heredity – and on how far there has been cultural as well as biological mixing.

Throughout Latin America, after plantation slavery a general hardening of race prejudice occurred, incorporating nineteenth-century European pseudoscientific eugenicist notions (*see* Eugenics). These ideas sat uneasily with Latin American intellectual thinking, which romanticized indigenism and Africanism, and celebrated *mestizaje* (or race mixture) as the new symbiosis (*see* Négritude and Transculturation, Mestizaje, and the Cosmic Race: An Interpretation). As a result notions of mestizaje were also permeated with ideas about the superiority of whitening. Hence, the contradiction between the myth of racial democracy and the prevalence of discrimination and prejudice against indigenous peoples, blacks, and mulattos.

Africa and the Atlantic World

Essential to a contemporary understanding of the Afro-Latin American reality is the legacy of almost 400 years of plantation slavery and what is today recognized as the largest forced migration in modern history (*see* Slavery in Latin America and the Caribbean and Transatlantic Slave Trade). About 12 million Africans were shipped to Brazil, Cuba, the Caribbean, and the United States. Several countries in the region not usually associated with slave traffic also had a substantial African presence, such as Mexico, which received an estimated 500,000 black captives.

Two aspects of Europe's enslavement of Africans have been much debated. The first is the commodity-driven nature of New World slavery, in contrast to Old World slave-based civilizations. The second is the deculturation of Africans in the trauma of the Middle Passage and what followed. Deculturation, or the loss of African-derived culture by slaves in the Americas, was seen as an inherent consequence of every form of colonial or neocolonial exploitation. It was usual for the dominant class to protect and even stimulate isolated cultural values of the dominated class, but only insofar as those values helped reinforce the desired social structure. The dominated class was forced to seek refuge in its culture as a means of surviving and preserving its identity.

The vast and tortured movement of African peoples across the Atlantic marked a major turning point in world history, facilitating the beginnings of the modern world capitalist economy and the emergence of empires spanning oceans. In the field of Atlantic studies, a key unresolved question is the extent to which both Eurocentric and Afrocentric approaches converge in depicting Africa and Africans as passive victims. How active were Africa's political and economic elite as partners in trade with Europe? How far did African slaves accommodate to or resist slavery in the Americas? How strong was African culture in the re-creation of Afro-Latin American societies?

To understand the Africa of Latin America therefore requires more than a retracing of African footsteps. We must grasp how African, along with European, indigenous, and Asian social groups created new and complex societies that differed from their component parts. After independence and the abolition of slavery a racist idea gained currency in Latin America, whereby the chaotic situation was explained in terms of, among other things, blacks being the obstacle to the development of Latin American societies. Blaming the victim – perhaps the most damning outcome of the denial of the African past – made subsequent reevaluations of the African contribution to the development of Latin America imperative. This has proven no mean task since racial values were constantly being socially reworked and codified, re-created, and reproduced.

The legal end of slavery, which came last to Cuba (1886) and Brazil (1888), did not end its legacy, and in the struggle over land and labor the process of emancipation proved as varied, long, and bloodied as abolition (*see* Abolition and Emancipation in Latin America and the Caribbean). Its impact wrought major changes in the nineteenth-century Latin American and world economy, including the collapse of older production centers. It ushered in waves of indentured Asian and immigrant European labor, and massive outmigrations of Afro-Latin Americans from poor and marginal lands to cities and overseas.

From slavery to the present, the predominant – though far from universal – experience for Afro-Latin Americans has been of oppression and inferiorization. There have, however, been times when they have demonstrated great individual and collective achievement, awareness, and organization in challenging their oppression, eliciting official concern and recognition, gaining in political power, and establishing themselves as an accepted part of the culture and national self-identity.

Black Self-Liberation

An important lesson of history is that political leadership matters. Race and ethnicity hold strategic, not inherent or absolute, value (*see* Race: An Interpretation). Ethnic and racial identity take on different meanings in different contexts, depending on who uses them and for what purposes. They are relative, situational categories. Competition and conflict between racial and ethnic groups may occur but need not necessarily do so, and may or may not be institutionalized in the political system at a societal level. Political systems may generate heightened racial or ethnic sentiments, but they can also channel negotiations and cross-cutting alliances, allowing scope for individual and collective action.

In the context of Latin America we can distinguish three forms of political systems. First are those in which one dominant segment of the population claimed that its racial or ethnic identity was the only legitimate one in the nation. Second are the political systems in which newly empowered elite sought legitimacy by promoting a synthetic national culture, discouraging racial or ethnic thinking that might separate citizens from the nation. Third are those systems in which groups shared more equally in the political life of the nation in proportion to their population, and where the citizenry encompassed different yet compatible ethnic identities that together constituted the nation.

The first political system was more likely to develop when a relatively large settler group from the colonizing power attained independence without a social revolution – the U.S. model but one that, to a lesser degree, might be applied to Puerto Rico, the Dominican Republic, Mexico, and South American Andean countries. The second system has been perhaps the most common, certainly in Brazil, Cuba, Colombia, and Venezuela, with their evidently significant numbers of African-descended peoples. Central and South American countries, with their smaller Afro-Caribbean and Afro-Latin American enclaves, developed systems somewhere between the first two. The third case, harboring what might be the closest approximation to racial democracy in the region, is arguably only attributable in part to Belize.

Any meaningful notion of racial democracy must encompass black self-liberation. Studies of Afro-Latin America continue to reflect the racist denigration of blacks as primitive, backward, anti-intellectual beings. Antislavery continues to be seen more as a transatlantic than a regional phenomenon with its own philosophical and ideological underpinnings, involving localized resistance and awareness. Yet black-led antislavery movements represented a critical element at the core of transatlantic abolitionism and might be seen as the first international political movement of modern times.

In the context of the modern-day black Atlantic, African-descended identities and cultures alternate between asserting an absolutist sense of difference and recognizing an awareness of the double consciousness of trying to face (at least) two ways at once, between closure and openness in what have been called cultures of mediation.

Race and Gender

The gender parameters of cultures of mediation, as well as the Afro-Latin American presence, are still to be explored in full. The slaves brought over from Africa were predominantly male and hence skewed the population. The process by which the model transformed into one that was slave-reproducing rather than slave-importing was also highly gendered. Later Afro-Caribbean migrant workers on the Panama Canal and on Costa Rican and Cuban plantations were also mainly male. Conversely, the more recent Puerto Rican out-migration into the New York garment industry was largely led by Afro-Puerto Rican women.

Moreover, family and kinship patterns and accompanying value systems, linked with pronatalist (or antinatalist) state policies, have all been crucial in shaping the emergent societies. A modern-day example of this principle was Puerto Rico's Operation Bootstrap, which was accompanied by a drastic sterilization program that targeted poor and black women.

Prevailing ideas on gender vary markedly in Latin America and the Caribbean, especially where the family and sexuality are concerned, and largely along race lines. The polarized stereotypes are of the white Ibero-American patriarch (with repressed, controlled female) and the black Afro-Caribbean matriarch (with marginal, emasculated male). These are issues that continue to command attention.

Jean Stubbs and Pedro Pérez-Sarduy

See Also

Middle Passage, The; Merengue: Music, Race and Nation in the Dominican Republic; Colombia; Peru; Salsa Music; Rio de Janeiro, Brazil; Afro-Atlantic Culture: On the Live Dialogue Between Africa and the Americas; Abolition and Emancipation in Latin America and the Caribbean; Carnivals in Latin America and the Caribbean; Myth of Racial Democracy in Latin America and the Caribbean: An Interpretation; Argentina; Salvador, Brazil.

North America

Race Riots in the United States, over the course of the past hundred years a recurring part of American life; incidents include the Wilmington, N.C., Riot of 1898; New Orleans Riot of 1900; Atlanta Riot of 1906; East St. Louis Riot of 1917; Chicago Riots of 1919; Elaine, Arkansas, Race Riot of 1919; Tulsa Riot of 1921; Harlem Riots of 1935; Detroit Riot of 1943; Harlem Riots of 1943; Harlem Riot of 1964; Los Angeles Watts Riot of 1965; Detroit Riot of 1967; Miami Riot of 1980; and Los Angeles Riot of 1992.

See Also

East St. Louis, Illinois, Riot of 1917.

Latin America and the Caribbean

Race War of 1912, also known as the Little War of 1912 or the Little War of May. The conflict arose in Cuba in 1912 when an insurrection was mounted to protest the outlawing of the Partido Independiente de Color, an Afro-Cuban political party. The uprising was met with harsh repression by the government and armed civilians that left more than 3000 Afro-Cubans dead (*see* Cuba).

Latin America and the Caribbean

Racial Question during Struggles of Independence in Latin America

As early as the seventeenth century blacks formed part of the Spanish colonial armed forces throughout the Americas. Many men of African descent commanded or comprised military units whose actions in combat often turned the tide in military conflicts. This trend continued throughout the nineteenth century, a period (1808-1843) characterized by the prevalence of revolutionary and independence movements throughout the continent.

Traditionally, the history of the wars of independence in Latin America has been presented as the struggle of Creoles (American-born colonists) to liberate themselves from Spanish rule. The lesser-known dimension of racial tensions between whites (Spanish and Creoles) and people of African descent has been overlooked despite its significant impact on the development and outcome of the independence wars. Not only were the Creole rebels and the Spanish colonizers' armies composed – and in some cases led – by many blacks and mulattos, but the future status of people of color became one of the leading incentives for supporting or opposing independence from the Spanish Crown. The participation of American-born blacks in the pro-Spanish rule as well as the pro-independence armies made the armed confrontations, in terms of popular participation, into civil wars. American-born blacks and mulattos found themselves on both sides of the battlefield, choosing sides based on who they thought would carry out promises of a better future for people of color.

On one side, at the beginning of the nineteenth century the idea of revolutionary independence sparked hope for broad social changes. Throughout Spanish America black and mulatto leaders interpreted the possibility of forming new and independent nations as an opportunity to change the social order and to abolish slavery. Black and mulatto optimists saw independence as an occasion for bringing about new regimes under the government of the castas (or castes, a term describing the socioracial stratification of racially "mixed" peoples), which they called a *pardocracia*. This hope – or illusion – and the fear that it generated might have been a factor in determining the later development of Spanish America's nations.

On the other hand, many blacks and mulattos thought that it was safer for them to continue under Spanish rule. Despite occupying the lowest strata in the colonizers' society, people of color felt they had more guarantees under the Spanish laws, which imposed some restrictions on Creole abuse, than under the future rule of those who had enslaved and exploited them.

Therefore, both the Spanish and the Creole commanders took advantage of the uncertain future for blacks and encouraged racial animosities as a weapon in the battlefield. For example, in 1815 Simón Bolívar (1783-1830), the greatest figure in the rebellions for independence in Spanish America, complained that "the Spanish commanders of Venezuela... following the example of Saint-Domingue [Haiti], though ignoring the real causes of that revolution, strove to subvert all people of color, even slaves against white Creoles, in order to establish a wasteland under the flags of [Spanish king] Fernando VII."

Venezuela is a case in point. Radical divisions among Indians, Spaniards, *mestizos*, blacks, and *pardos* made it hard to choose which side to be on during the era of independence fervor (1808-1821). Spanish commander José Tomás Boves's promise of freedom and a reluctance to fight with Creole masters caused many blacks, slave and free, to join the Spanish army voluntarily in 1813 and 1814. According to Mr. Robinson, a British tradesman of La Guayra, in 1814 "under Boves'[s] command there were at least seven or eight thousand men, among whom there were no more than 50 whites or European Spaniards and one thousand free pardos; the rest were slaves, blacks and zambos." The black and mulatto officers reached the highest ranks in the Spanish army and carried on a "war until death" against the white patriots. This turned the confrontation into a civil war in which most Creoles hesitated between siding with the Spanish Crown or against it, dreading a later government of the castas.

Despite the strong fear of a racial revolution, Bolívar needed to recruit soldiers of African descent. To do so, he had to follow the strategy of the Spanish commanders: promise freedom for slaves and promote some mulattos and mestizos to positions of command. At one point a few colored leaders gathered enough power to threaten to control the patriot army and were sentenced to death by the white Creoles for allegedly promoting a "race war." The most notorious executions were those of Gen. Manuel Piar in 1817, before total independence from Spain was achieved; Col. Leonardo Infante in 1825; and Adm. José Prudencio Padilla in 1829, when the wars were over and the former *caudillos* (military leaders) were internally defining the allocation of power among them.

Another country in which blacks played a role in the wars of independence is ARGENTINA. Slaves were recruited into defensive forces as early as 1806, when the white Creoles repelled the English invasion and finally defeated the British army of Gen. Whitelocke. Seventy of the Afro-Argentine combatants were emancipated in recognition of their deeds. A decade later, during the struggles for independence, forcibly conscripted slaves composed at least 25 percent of the army. Creoles resorted to using pardo and mestizo regiments, often commanded by mulatto captains. Some captains were even honored with the title of "Don" (Sir) from 1811 on, but none of them ever rose above this rank.

Despite the fact that during the struggles for independence in Argentina the black or mulatto population in Buenos Aires constituted between 25 and 30 percent of the total population, white supremacy in the country was never questioned. The same could be said for other countries of the Southern Cone where no attempts were made to establish a government of the castes. However, in 1814 Chilean rebel leaders established that male slaves able to carry arms would be granted their freedom upon enlisting. When Gen. José de San Martín led his army across the Andes into Chile to liberate the country from Spanish rule, half of his troops were ex-slaves from Buenos Aires and the provinces of western Argentina. These units were organized into the all-black Seventh and Eighth Infantry Battalion and the integrated Eleventh Infantry. In PERU, by virtue of a decree issued by the Argentine liberator San Martín, slave soldiers were declared free in 1821.

In the Spanish Caribbean, the Batallón de los Morenos (Battalion of Mixed/Black Persons) of Santo Domingo is yet another example of the crucial presence of enlisted blacks in the wars for independence. The battalion was active in two critical independence movements that took place in what is now the DOMINICAN REPUBLIC. The first occurred in 1821, when José Núñez de Cáceres led elite white Creole insurgents against Spanish rule. In order to garner military strength Núñez de Cáceres promised freedom to enslaved blacks if they fought on the side of the insurgents. He managed to enlist blacks and gained the support of Dominican commander PABLO ALÍ, who led the Batallón de los Morenos. Haitian general JEAN-PIERRE BOYER subsequently gained control of the entire island (today's HAITI and Dominican Republic) in 1821.

Blacks became increasingly disgruntled as land promised to them by the new Haitian government remained in the hands of white landowners reluctant to release their properties. Eager to escape the conditions on the plantations, Afro-Dominicans enlisted in Batallón 32. Batallón 32 became the primary military unit to protect the eastern section of the island and was an essential part of the independence movement in April 1843. The black battalion opted to side with the revolutionaries led by La Trinitaria, an underground insurgent group that advocated for the declaration of the eastern part of the island as an independent state free from Haitian rule.

In MEXICO, Father Miguel Hidalgo y Costilla led the Batallón de los Morenos, in which mestizo and indigenous individuals also participated in an attempt to abolish Spanish rule in September 1810. The revolt was halted and the insurgents were executed on July 30, 1811.

Besides the obvious participation of men of color in the white-led wars mentioned above, it is still uncertain to what extent the general population of blacks and mulattos was in fact aware of the possibility of a radical sociopolitical change. British pressure for the abolition of slavery was publicly known, and it is conceivable that many blacks knew of it. The ideas of the French Revolution also reached blacks, free and slave alike. At the same time President Pétion's rise to power in Haiti was widely known. Venezuelan black and mulatto leaders knew well that the economic and military support he had given to Bolívar for the cause of independence in 1816 was in exchange for the abolition of slavery. In fact, Manuel Piar was accused, tried, and condemned in part for allegedly intending to follow Haiti's political experience in GUYANA.

One historian claims that the revolutionary ideals did promote a separatist character in VENEZUELA and the area east of the Rio de la Plata. In other areas, however, it is not clear if these outbreaks were isolated and spontaneous or had similar political intentions. For example, racial struggle became a mass mobilizing phenomenon in Peru during the 1780 and 1781 Indian rebellions headed by the mestizo José Gabriel Condorcarqui, known as Túpac Amaru II. Even though it was an Indian revolt, many blacks joined the fight against the Creoles, and Condorcarqui's brother, Diego, issued a decree abolishing slavery in 1781. In Venezuela the bloody riot of the Coro Peninsula was clearly a black insurrection against slavery, rather than an independence movement. In COLOMBIA, the *comunero* revolt against new taxes also had a racial element. There the castas were not revolting against the Spanish Crown, but against the white Creoles controlling the local government. Three decades later this outrage intensified in Venezuela, where the clamor "Kill the whites! Long live the King!" spread in 1813. Such opposition threatened the stability of the new regime even after the Spaniards had been defeated, as in the popular riot in the town of Petaré in 1824.

Accounts tell us that in several other places in South America the racial question reached the level of a social revolution. When the rebels fled from Caracas before the arrival of the Spanish commander Boves and the "Mulato" Machado, a foreign merchant witnessed the fact that "only a few people could embark [in the port of La Guayra]. Those who remained were relentlessly massacred. The African Race carried on every kind of excess, and in La Guayra black people started the massacre [even] before the arrival of the troops."

In sum, for free and enslaved blacks backing the Spanish flag was usually a pretext to wage war against their masters or repressive leaders. Blacks feared further oppression under the Creoles in power, who would certainly wipe out the few legal protections blacks had under the Spanish Crown. On the other side, most of the black or mulatto leaders struggling for independence had little or no education, and the few who did were killed during the internal struggles that followed the wars. This made it extremely difficult for the colored masses to conceive an alternative social order through a strong and vocal leadership. The revolts never went any further than temporary havoc, and the few attempts to set up a government controlled by the castas were severely repressed by the white Creole commanders.

Another aspect of the racial question during this period is to what extent the white Creoles – influenced by the French Revolution's ideas of liberty, equality, and fraternity, as well as by the North American concept of democracy – were willing to accept the sociopolitical ascent of black and mulatto people. For example, the Argentine liberator José Francisco de San Martín (1778-1850) introduced several protections in favor of slaves, such as the free womb laws and the ban of the slave trade, but at the same time he questioned the mental capabilities of the blacks and precluded the ascent of any black or mulatto to the highest military ranks. Gen. Manuel Belgrano, another Argentine leader, shared this view. He said that "the blacks and mulattos are a rabble that is as cowardly as it is bloodthirsty." Creole leaders used blacks and mulattos when they needed them, but they were by no means committed to promoting racial equality.

The same is true for other South American leaders. As the wars in those countries became bloodier, those in charge had to accept a greater participation of the black population in order to defeat the Spaniards, but, again, the supremacy of the whites was never questioned. Bolívar, for example, admired republican institutions, but considered that too many individual rights, especially those concerning representation and equality, were unsuited for nations in which whites were a minority. In Argentina historians attribute the "disappearance" of two-thirds of the black population in the region to the significant number who died, deserted, or otherwise vanished while in the army.

At the end of the period of independence struggles in Spanish America (1808-1843), the vows of general freedom were forgotten and only some of the slaves who fought against Spain as soldiers were freed. The so-called "revolutions" were not such for indigenous people and blacks, whose social and economic situation as members of the castas remained almost unaltered, and in many cases deteriorated, under the new governments of the white Creoles. Abolition and a slight improvement in black socio-political status were to come only 30 years later (*see* individual country entries for further information).

Juan Botero

See Also

Complexities of Ethnic and Racial Terminology in Latin America and the Caribbean; Chile; Spain; Haitian Revolution; Pétion, Alexandre; Abolition and Emancipation in Latin America and the Caribbean; Latin America, Blacks and Indians in: An Interpretation.

North America

Racial Stereotypes

Sticks and stones will break my bones, but names will never hurt me. Our era has moved beyond this proverb, which parents teach vulnerable children. Forget sticks – we worry now about deadly weapons. Forget names – we all have to deal with racial and ethnic stereotypes. Stereotypes are proverbial generalizations broadcast by the powerful media of the modern era. Their racial dimensions are what concern us here, but first let us look at the broad issues stereotypes provoke and the history of the term.

The term "stereotype," now used with reference to our society's old problem with nasty names, was developed when, at the outset of the modern industrial age in 1798, two European printers invented a new way to reproduce images that would fix them permanently. The image-setting process was called stereotyping, and in time the word "stereotype" came to apply to the fixing of intellectual, as opposed to printed, images. One's stereotype of a jet, for instance, wipes away the marks of specific makes in order to stand in for all jets. One's stereotype of a ballet dancer may not be male or female and may not have a realized face; thus the image can represent all ballet dancers. Stereotypes simplify real images in order to make a generalization. All peoples produce stereotyped ideas in order to create a shorthand form of communication among themselves.

All peoples also produce racial stereotypes about themselves and others. That is, people simplify the intellectual images they maintain of specific ethnic groups, including their own, often in cruel or damaging ways. Poor white Southerners ("Crackers") are said to be slow, red-necked, and fat. Immigrant Italians ("Wops") are said to be short, oily, and hot-tempered. Upper-class whites ("Wasps") are said to be greedy, emotionally cold, and haughty. Negroes ("Niggers") are said to be stupid, promiscuous, and happy. These generalizations are not accurate, but they are spread widely – not only by word of mouth but also through images in television, movies, newspapers, music, comic books, talk shows, pseudo-scientific research, and even textbooks. These media make stereotypes, whose dissemination was once confined to oral transmission from one person to another, seem more like factual knowledge than personal opinion.

Perhaps the most chilling aspect of racial stereotyping is that members of groups being characterized sometimes come to believe the generalizations' damaging simplifications. Members of target groups may even try to fulfill the stereotypes. The media regularly depict people of African descent as drug dealers and teen mothers, and so it is not surprising when young black artists also adopt the roles of thugs and "bitches 'n 'ho's." Even stereotypes that include positive human attributes can warp people. For instance, if the dominant culture emphasizes that men of African descent are excellent athletes or entertainers, the glamour associated with these professions may influence the youth of that group. They may try to fulfill a simplified stereotype of their potential rather than develop other traits. That is the force of stereotypes.

Racial stereotypes reflect and are facilitated by power relations in a society. Stereotypes of a demeaned group are frequently accepted as the truth and are not understood as problematic until the group can manifest its fully human condition. As the group's relative power grows, it can sometimes stop the public proliferation of blatant stereotypes about it. That's what happened in the 1950s when the National Association for the Advancement of Colored People (NAACP) made concerted complaints about minstrel shows. The NAACP effectively stopped the practice of white Americans blacking up to represent black people in ragged, ignorant, and grotesque stereotypes. (Isolated examples of whites mounting minstrel shows continued in backwaters of the north and south United States into the 1980s. "Darkie Days" have survived in England, as in Padstow, Cornwall, right through the late 1990s, finally causing a member of Parliament to complain in 1998. Blacks in England remain much less empowered than those in the United States.)

The many paradoxes in stereotypes are analytically useful. When one group creates stereotypes to manage its thoughts about others, dispassionate observers gain access to the compact assumptions controlling that group's thought. Created in moments and locations of stress and anxiety, stereotypes satisfy various functions for their creators. One group will create stereotypes about another group in order to control them (or to fight back against control) or to justify their power over that group (or to strike back against that power). By classifying the target group as subhuman or grotesque, stereotypes are likely to minimize their creators' misgivings about participating in uneven power relations. A stereotype always isolates one perhaps imagined aspect of the target group and substitutes it for the whole. Because it denies the complex humanity of the demeaned target, every racial stereotype says much more about the creators' needs than about the target's nature. Because they always display their creators' dread of the target group, racial stereotypes eventually subvert their makers' cruel intentions. For instance, a cultural group that classifies women of another culture exclusively as mammies displays alarm about its own nurturing capacity. A people that stereotypes others as greedy money-changers betrays its own concern for prosperity.

Studying stereotypes reveals both their present power and their historical flow. Despite their power to disturb us in the present, stereotypes turn in cycles. Their meanings can change dramatically over time. The Jim Crow figure, which rapidly became a stereotype standing for United States racism, began (and persists) as a figure of black folklore. Poor white actors and workers who identified with the suffering of black slaves in the early 1800s copied their gestures to speak out against employers. But their opponents, in turn, used the image of this Jim Crow mimicry to mock the alliance between blacks and their sympathizers. It was a full century before the NAACP could gain some control over the stereotype. The evolutionary nature of stereotypes shows that they are anything but permanent. Indeed, they may help change social attitudes over time. Many sensitive artists of every hue have known how to turn stereotypes inside out. They push them hard enough so that audiences see both the stereotypes' cruelty and their makers' weakness.

W.T. Lhamon, Jr.

See Also
Great Britain; Minstrelsy.

North America

Ragtime, a late nineteenth-century African American musical genre that influenced strongly an emerging American popular music and that provided a major impetus in the development of jazz.

Although *ragtime* has come to connote a particular form of piano music associated with composer Scott Joplin, the term originally applied to a larger body of instrumental music and song. Emerging in the 1890s, ragtime thrived for two decades, as millions of middle-class whites bought sheet music, pianos, and piano rolls. Through its immense commercial success, ragtime gave birth to the American music industry, and through its rhythmic and melodic innovations, it signaled the end of America's dependency on Western European music. Ragtime ushered in a new style of concert music that built upon Afrodiasporic musical traditions.

Because ragtime emerged from African American folk music, its precise origins remain undocumented and obscure. Yet the roots of ragtime undoubtedly lie in the music of itinerant black pianists who played in bordellos and saloons. Ironically, ragtime's quick acceptance was due in part to the minstrel tradition that portrayed African Americans as exotic, lazy, and funny. Primed by these stereotypes as well as bastardized versions of black songs, middle-class audiences readily accepted real African American music.

The origin of the word "ragtime" also remains obscure. Some historians suspect it derives from the "ragged," or syncopated, playing style that characterized black music in the late nineteenth century. Others cite the use of "rag" as a name for a short African American folk tune. Evidence such as an early piece by Joplin, "Original Rags," suggests that ragtime piano originally anthologized folk melodies. Bordello pianists probably collected and blended familiar strains. Nevertheless, "rag" soon came to designate the larger structure instead of the fragments that composed it.

Joplin, along with black composer James Scott and white composer Joseph Lamb, established the conventions of ragtime piano and influenced a generation of black composers that included Arthur Marshall, Louis Chauvin, and Artie Matthews, all of whom, like Joplin and Scott, came from Missouri. Joplin, Scott, and Lamb also influenced white composers such as Paul Pratt and J. Russell Robinson.

Classic ragtime followed a number of formal conventions. First, it combined march-like bass notes with a heavily syncopated melody. Second, it comprised self-contained sections of 16 bars that each repeated once before giving way to a change; a typical pattern was AA BB A CC DD, where each letter represented a separate 16-measure section. Finally, it usually employed Western European harmonies, beginning and ending on a tonic key, while changing in the middle to the subdominant: for instance, a piece that began in C would alternate to F and return to conclude in C.

Joplin and Scott had defined these elements by 1897, just as sales of ragtime sheet music began to boom. Later innovations such as shifted accents and dotted rhythms added to the body of "hot," or syncopated, ragtime sounds, but were not in fact syncopated. Ragtime also influenced other African American styles such as blues and jazz. Jazz, in fact, probably grew out of ragtime, a lineage apparent in the career of the great musician and composer Jelly Roll Morton.

White bandleader William Krell published the first ragtime piano music, a piece called "Mississippi Rag," in 1897. Between 1897 and 1899 more than 150 "rags," written by both blacks and whites, supplied popular demand. Joplin's "Maple Leaf Rag," released in 1899, sold a million copies of sheet music alone. Indeed, ragtime sold so well that New York music companies hurried to mass-produce it, slapping the name "ragtime" on a wide range of music. Hack writers churned out "ragtime" vocal music, which often contained little or no syncopation at all.

Although many listeners considered Irving Berlin's 1911 hit "Alexander's Ragtime Band" the crowning accomplishment of the ragtime era, the majority of innovation and the best composition had occurred ten years before. Nevertheless, public enthusiasm continued until the early 1920s, reflected in high piano and sheet-music sales and the sheer volume of mediocre ragtime-style songs produced by New York's Tin Pan Alley.

The popularity of ragtime provoked much criticism from both musical and moral conservatives. Because ragtime's new rhythms inspired lively dancing, many older people found it threatening, and its syncopation sometimes caused musicians trained in simple European rhythms to find it cacophonous. The controversy reflected ragtime's revolutionary significance. By ushering in the jazz age and establishing African American rhythms as viable roots for classical music, ragtime challenged the old order, socially as well as musically. J. B. Priestly wrote, "Out of this ragtime came the fragmentary outlines of the menace to old Europe, the domination of America, the emergence of Africa, the end of confidence and any feeling of security, the nervous excitement, the feeling of modern times."

Eric Bennett

See Also
Blues, The; Minstrelsy; Morton, Ferdinand Joseph ("Jelly Roll").

North America

Rainey, Gertrude Pridgett ("Ma") (b. April 26, 1886, Columbus, Ga.; d. December 22, 1939, Columbus, Ga.), African American classic blues singer and vaudeville performer.

Born to minstrels Thomas and Ella Pridgett, Gertrude Pridgett entered show business at age 14 as a member of the traveling stage show the "Bunch of Blackberries." In 1904 she married showman William "Pa" Rainey, and the two formed a song and dance act called "Rainey and Rainey: The Assassinators of the Blues" that lasted until 1916. While touring mostly in the South during that period, and subsequently as a soloist with the Rabbit Foot Minstrels on the Theater Owners' Booking Association circuit, Ma Rainey developed her "classic blues" style of rough-edged reality moans and humorous shouts.

In 1923 Ma Rainey began a brief but prolific recording career with Chicago-based Paramount Records with "Moonshine Blues." By 1928 she had recorded 93 songs, many of which she wrote herself. As a result of the wide circulation of these records, Rainey gained enormous popularity with African Americans. Her contract was rescinded by Paramount, however, because it was felt that her style could not compete with the new male acts such as "Big Bill" Broonzy and "Leadbelly," nor with her friend Bessie Smith's growing status and stature. Rainey's once appealing raw style was believed to be out of vogue with the African American record-buying public.

Ma Rainey maintained a loyal fan base, however, and continued to perform throughout the country until 1935, when both her sister Malissa and her mother died. Returning to her home in Columbus, she owned and managed two theaters until her death four years later. Rainey's significance within African American popular culture is exemplified not only by her impact on musical heirs such as singer Koko Taylor, but also by her appearance in the writing of poet Sterling Brown ("Ma Rainey") and playwright August Wilson (*Ma Rainey's Black Bottom*). In 1990 Ma Rainey was inducted into the Rock and Roll Hall of Fame.

See Also
Blues, The; Brown, Sterling Allen; Ledbetter, Hudson William ("Leadbelly"); Minstrelsy; Smith, Bessie.

Africa

Ramgoolam, Seewoosagur (b. September 18, 1900, Bois d'Oiseaux, Mauritius; d. 1985, Mauritius), leader of the Mauritius Labour Party and prime minister of Mauritius from 1968 to 1982.

Seewoosagur Ramgoolam grew up in the small village of Belle Rive. An Anglophile and ardent student even as a boy, he left home to attend the Royal College of Curepipe, a prestigious Mauritian public secondary school, and then traveled to GREAT BRITAIN for medical school. While in England Ramgoolam met with Mohandas Gandhi, joined the Fabian Society (a political group committed to SOCIALISM and nonviolence), and became secretary of the local Indian National Congress chapter. Upon returning to Mauritius in 1935, Ramgoolam joined a vanguard of Indo-Mauritian intellectuals and founded a newspaper, the *Advance*.

In 1940 Ramgoolam was nominated to the Council of Government as a representative of Hindu interests. With the extension of suffrage to all literate adults in 1948, Ramgoolam gained a seat in the Legislative Council. He was reelected in 1953 and joined the Mauritian Labour Party (MLP). As party leader he successfully steered the MLP to victory in the 1959 elections, becoming chief minister in 1961 and premier in 1965. In the interests of political and economic stability, Ramgoolam sought to promote the rights of workers without alienating the island's landed aristocracy. For example, he advocated free market economic policies and abandoned MLP proposals to nationalize SUGAR estates. At the same time he promised working-class Mauritians a welfare state. Despite opposition from groups fearful of a Hindu-dominated government, Ramgoolam was elected prime minister of newly independent Mauritius in 1968.

His early years in office were tumultuous as a weak economy and high rates of unemployment contributed to widespread discontent. Confronted by labor strikes organized by the Marxist Mouvement Militant Mauricien (MMM), Ramgoolam's government postponed the scheduled 1972 election and declared a state of emergency. MMM leaders were imprisoned without charges, strikes were outlawed, and the press was censored, effectively banning political opposition. Fortunately, world sugar prices rose dramatically during the early 1970s, and a newly created Industrial Export Processing Zone brought in foreign investment and created jobs. Although Ramgoolam's oppressive political measures hurt his party's popularity, he managed to retain his position in the 1976 elections.

But the economy remained a liability. In 1979, with unemployment rates running at 21 percent and inflation at 30 percent, Ramgoolam was forced to ask the International Monetary Fund and World Bank for assistance. Understandably, Ramgoolam's popular support waned and he was ousted in the 1982 elections. His sucessor, ANEROOD JUGNAUTH, proposed making Mauritius a republic with Ramgoolam as president. However, the legislation failed to pass. Instead, Ramgoolam was appointed governor-general, an office he held until his death in 1985.

Despite his authoritative actions in the early 1970s and his mixed success in developing the Mauritian economy, Ramgoolam is remembered by Mauritians as a man whose moderation, caution, and vision contributed to a relatively peaceful transition from colony to independent democratic state.

Ari Nave

Latin America and the Caribbean

Ramos Antonini, Ernesto

(b. Mayaguez, Puerto Rico, 1898; d. Santurce, Puerto Rico, 1963), black Puerto Rican labor leader and politician, the first Speaker of the House of Representatives under the Commonwealth of PUERTO RICO.

Ernesto Ramos Antonini started his public career as a labor lawyer defending the rights of Puerto Rican workers. In the early 1940s he successfully represented the General Confederation of Workers of Puerto Rico (GCW) – the union that represented the sugar workers – in important labor cases, and lobbied for the approval of labor-relations laws. He later became secretary of foreign relations of the GCW and established ties with other labor organizations in the United States and abroad. He was a relentless advocate of the unification of the Puerto Rican labor movement, which at the time was badly fragmented.

As a politician, Romos Antonini stood out for his superb public speaking and principled public service. One of the founders and leaders of the Popular Democratic Party, he worked side by side with the first elected governor of Puerto Rico, Luis Muñoz Marín, in the economic development program known as Operation Bootstrap. For 15 years (1948-1963) he was Speaker of the House of Representatives of Puerto Rico. He was also a delegate in the constituent assembly (1951-1952), which drafted the constitution of the Commonwealth of Puerto Rico.

The son of the renowned pianist and composer Federico Ramos Buensont, Ramos Antonini is also remembered for having fostered the formal study of music in Puerto Rico. A talented pianist himself, Ramos Antonini authored legislation that established the first publicly funded schools of music, the first conservatory of music, and the Symphony Orchestra of Puerto Rico.

Carlos Dalmau

Africa

Ramses III (reigned 1182-1151 B.C.E.)

Egyptian king of the Twentieth Dynasty, a great military leader who repeatedly saved the country from invasion.

In the fifth year of his reign Ramses III defeated an attack by the Libyans from the west, and two years later he routed invaders known as the Sea Peoples. In his eleventh year he again repelled an attempted Libyan invasion. Ramses III was also a builder of temples and palaces in the tradition of his Nineteenth Dynasty predecessor, Ramses II. His victories are depicted on the walls of his mortuary temple at Medinet Habu, near Luxor. Egyptian records tell of a strike by workers at Ramses III's burial site and of a plot against the king near the end of his reign. Ramses III was the last of the great rulers of ancient Egypt; his death was followed by centuries of weakness and foreign domination.

SEE ALSO

Egypt, Ancient Kingdom of.

Africa

Ranavalona I, Queen (Ramavo)

(b. 1790?; d. August 16, 1861), queen of the Merina Empire (1828-1861).

Upon the death of her husband and cousin, Radama I, in 1821, Ramavo took the throne as queen of the Merina Empire, a kingdom that extended over most of MADAGASCAR and was recognized by the British as the island's sovereign authority.

During Radama I's tenure the Merina court had incorporated English beliefs and values along with their military and financial support. Missionaries had established schools, printed Bibles, and transcribed the MALAGASY language. Many Merina aristocrats and Hova, middle-caste commoners, resented the imposition of British culture and Christian values. Even before coming to power, Ramavo cultivated their support. Upon the death of her husband, she immediately laid claim to the throne, changed her name to Ranavalona ("the lady who has been folded," a reference to her aristocratic attire), and executed all her potential rivals, including Radama's mother, daughter, and nephew. She then began to retract the pro-European policies of her deceased husband, declaring all previously negotiated treaties null and void in 1828 (although she later renegotiated most of them).

Although Ranavalona associated Christianity with European hegemony, she initially allowed missionaries to remain in Madagascar because they taught her subjects useful skills including literacy, carpentry, and metalworking. In 1831 Ranavalona even agreed to let Malagasy be baptized, but then quickly reversed her decision when she saw the large number of converts undergoing the religious rite. By 1835 missionaries were banned from proselytizing and Christianity was outlawed. Several converted Malagasy were executed for refusing to denounce their Christian beliefs. Unable to preach, most missionaries left the island.

Although Ranavalona was insistent on retaining Malagasy culture and sovereignty, she was not adverse to doing business with Europeans. Notably, Frenchman Napoléon de Lastelle ran coffee and cocoa plantations and became the loci of the island's import-export trade, particularly with France. Likewise, an adventurer named Jean Laborde ran a SUGAR plantation and oversaw a large complex employing more than 1200 workers in the manufacture of arms, ammunition, porcelain, and other products. Although known as "the queen's foreigner," Laborde also influenced Ranavalona's son, Radama II, who ultimately reversed most of her policies.

In 1845 Ranavalona pronounced that European residents of Madagascar would be subject to traditional Malagasy law, which included multiple forms of capital and corporal punishment, such as the use of hot irons and poising ordeals. The resident foreigners appealed to their governments for protection. After boarding French and British ships, the European traders saw their homes looted, and in response, the ships opened fire on the port of Tamatave. Once news of the event reached Ranavalona, she banned all trade with the British and French except for de Lastelle and Laborde. Although trade relations were ultimately restored, Ranavalona's rash actions weakened her support among the Hova families who had profited from the trade.

French and British agents continued to wrestle for influence in the Merina court. For example, Joseph Lambert, a French entrepreneur, convinced Ranavalona's son to sign the Lambert Charter, a document conceding enormous land and mineral rights once he came to the throne. In 1857 Ranavalona discovered a planned coup d'état, authored in part by Laborde, Lambert, and her son. Laborde and Lambert were promptly expelled and thousands of others were enslaved for allegedly colluding with the plotters. She spared her son, however, and he succeeded her to the throne.

On Ranavalona's death in 1861 Madagascar reentered relations with Europe. While often portrayed simply as a cruel and backward leader, Ranavalona was in fact an astute politician interested in preserving Malagasy sovereignty while retaining profitable economic relations with foreign powers. Her name was frequently evoked by nationalists during French COLONIAL RULE as a Malagasy leader who asserted the legitimacy of Malagasy culture.

Ari Nave

See Also

Nationalism in Africa; Great Britain; Christianity: Missionaries in Africa.

North America

Randall, Dudley Felker

(b. January 14, 1914, Washington, D.C.), African American poet and publisher who was instrumental in promoting poetry of the Black Arts Movement.

Dudley Randall was the son of a teacher, Ada Viola Bradley Randall, and a Congregational minister, Arthur George Clyde Randall. In 1923 the family moved from WASHINGTON, D.C., to DETROIT, MICHIGAN, where Randall has since spent most of his life.

After completing high school Randall worked for the Ford Motor Company and served in the army during World War II. He was unable to attend college until his early 30s. In 1949 Randall received a B.A. in English from Wayne University (now Wayne State University). He then earned a master of library science from the University of Michigan in 1951, providing him with credentials to work as a reference librarian at several colleges, including Morgan State College (now University) and the University of Detroit. In addition, he taught poetry at the University of Michigan and was poet-in-residence at the University of Detroit from 1969 to 1977.

In 1965 Randall established Broadside Press. He published his own poems and other important works by such writers as Gwendolyn Brooks, SONIA SANCHEZ, Haki Madhubuti (Don L. Lee), and Audre Lorde. These artists viewed African American creativity as the essence of their culture and contributed to the Black Arts Movement of the late 1960s and early 1970s. Randall's poetry collections include *Cities Burning* (1968), *Love You* (1970), and *A Litany of Friends: New and Selected Poems* (1981).

Randall's major contribution to AFRICAN AMERICAN LITERATURE has been to offer access to a liberating voice in print, where one had not existed on a mass scale since the HARLEM RENAISSANCE. According to poet Addison Gayle, he has "bridged the gap between poets of the 20s and those of the 60s and 70s."

See Also

World War II and African Americans; Brooks, Gwendolyn Elizabeth; Lorde, Audre Geraldine.

North America

Randolph, Asa Philip

(b. April 15, 1889, Crescent City, Fla.; d. May 16, 1979, New York, N.Y.), founder and president of the Brotherhood of Sleeping Car Porters (BSCP); editor of the *Messenger;* and architect of the March on Washington Movement in 1941, which led to the establishment of the Fair Employment Practices Committee (FEPC), and the 1963 March on Washington.

Although many civil rights leaders focused on voting, education, and other governmental functions, A. Philip Randolph spent his long career as a labor leader working to bring more and better jobs to African Americans. After a long, successful battle to win representation for the nation's Pullman porters, Randolph was instrumental in the formation of the FEPC, which protected African Americans against job discrimination in the army and defense industries. In addition, Randolph cofounded and edited the *Messenger,* the socialist black magazine.

The son of a minister, Randolph grew up in Jacksonville, Florida, and graduated from the Cookman Institute in 1907. A lack of economic opportunity for blacks led Randolph, the class valedictorian, into a series of menial jobs until 1911, when he moved to New York City. Working as an elevator operator and living in Harlem, Randolph took classes at the City College of New York and New York University, acted in amateur theatricals, and eventually took a job with a Harlem employment agency.

In 1914 Randolph met CHANDLER OWEN, whose progressive politics and interest in socialism matched his own. In 1917 the two founded the *Messenger,* whose editorials strongly opposed United States entry into World War I, saying that "no intelligent Negro is willing to lay down his life for the United States as it now exists." Though the magazine was never profitable, it was influential, offering a more radical voice than that of W. E. B. Du Bois's *Crisis* or the even more conventional *New York Age.* The *Messenger,* with its advocacy of labor unions, was especially popular among Pullman porters – all of whom were black who served white railroad passengers in luxurious sleeping cars. Founded just after the Civil War, the Pullman company had by the 1920s become the nation's single largest employer of African Americans. Many of the Pullman porters were college graduates who enjoyed great respect within their communities, but at work they were subjected to unfair and discriminatory practices.

In 1925 with Randolph at the helm, the BSCP began organizing the nearly 10,000 porters. For ten years Randolph kept the members unified and inspired, often in the face of intimidation and firings, while he negotiated with the president and Congress to amend the Railway Labor Act. Finally, in a hard-won victory hailed by African Americans and progressives nationwide, the company recognized their union in 1935.

Randolph continued to fight for racial and economic justice in the late 1930s as president of the National Negro Congress before resigning in protest over its increasing domination by Communists. In 1940 he returned to the issue of jobs, joining Walter White, secretary of the NATIONAL ASSOCIATION FOR THE ADVANCEMENT OF COLORED PEOPLE (NAACP), and T. Arnold Hill of the NATIONAL URBAN LEAGUE in urging President Franklin D. Roosevelt to desegregate the military and defense industries before World War II. After an unsatisfactory resolution to a meeting with the president, Randolph began planning a march on WASHINGTON, D.C., by the BSCP and others to demand "the right to work and fight for our country." The date for at least 10,000 African Americans to demonstrate before the Lincoln Memorial

A. Philip Randolph stands before the Lincoln Memorial on August 28, 1963, the day of the March on Washington, an event that was the culmination of Randolph's long career as an advocate of racial and economic justice. *CORBIS/Bettmann*

was set for July 1, 1941. Despite the president's wish to avoid a mass demonstration, Randolph refused to call off the march unless Roosevelt banned discrimination in the burgeoning defense industries. Following another meeting with Randolph and White, the president at last issued Executive Order 8002, which not only outlawed such discrimination but also established the FEPC to investigate breaches of the order.

Though the FEPC operated only from 1941 to 1946, Randolph continued to push for his other goal: desegregation of the U.S. armed forces. When President Harry S. Truman instituted a peacetime draft, Randolph told him "this time Negroes will not take a JIM CROW draft lying down." In July 1948 Truman signed Executive Order 9981, finally ending the historic segregation of African American soldiers.

Throughout the 1950s Randolph worked with the NAACP and other civil rights leaders. He helped plan and spoke at Pilgrimage Day, a 1957 prayer meeting in Washington, D.C. He met with President Dwight D. Eisenhower to push for faster school integration in the wake of BROWN V. BOARD OF EDUCATION and planned a 1958 Youth March for Integrated Schools. He also continued his union work and became vice president of the newly consolidated AFL-CIO from 1955 to 1968.

Randolph's brainchild, the March on Washington Movement, bore new fruit in 1963 with the help of BAYARD RUSTIN and Rev. Martin Luther King Jr., who, along with Randolph, mobilized the largest demonstration of the CIVIL RIGHTS MOVEMENT. Speaking before King did, the 74-year-old Randolph exhorted the crowd of 250,000 to take part in a "revolution for jobs and freedom." The next year President Lyndon B. Johnson signed the Civil Rights Act of 1964 and awarded Randolph the Presidential Medal of Freedom. In his final years Randolph established the A. Philip Randolph Institute, a job skills and training bureau in Harlem. Upon Randolph's death in 1979, Rustin said of his late colleague, "No individual did more to help the poor, the dispossessed and the working class… than A. Philip Randolph."

Kate Tuttle

SEE ALSO

World War I and African Americans; World War II and African Americans; American Federation of Labor and Congress of Industrial Organizations; Military, Blacks in the American; Civil War, American; *Crisis, The*; Du Bois, William Edward Burghardt (W. E. B.); Harlem, New York; King, Martin Luther, Jr.; Labor Unions in the United States; *Messenger, The*; New York, New York; Socialism; White, Walter Francis; Communist Party USA, African Americans and the; March on Washington, 1941.

North America

Rangel, Charles Bernard

(b. June 11, 1930, Harlem, N.Y.), 14-term member of the United States House of Representatives from New York.

Charles Rangel was born in Harlem. Raised by his mother and grandmother after his parents' separation, he dropped out of high school and held several jobs until joining the army in 1948 (*see* MILITARY, BLACKS IN THE AMERICAN). He served until 1952 and saw action in South Korea, for which he was awarded the Bronze Star and the Purple Heart (*see* KOREAN WAR).

Rangel returned to New York and resumed his high school career, obtaining his diploma in 1953. He earned a B.S. from the New York School of Commerce in 1957 and a law degree from St. John's Law School in 1960. Rangel held various positions before entering politics. Directly after graduating from law school he served as an attorney for civil rights activists. In 1961 he was appointed assistant district attorney for the Southern District of New York. Rangel then began to work in politics, serving as legal council for the New York City Housing and Redevelopment Board, as legal assistant to then-speaker of the New York State Assembly, Judge James L. Watson. In addition, with close friend Percy Sutton, Rangel helped to found the John F. Kennedy Democratic Club in Harlem (later named the Rev. Martin Luther King Jr. Democratic Club). Rangel first entered political office locally and was elected in 1966 to the New York State Assembly as representative from central Harlem.

Rangel's congressional career began when he unseated Harlem Democratic political stalwart Adam Clayton Powell Jr. in the closely contested 1970 primary election. Rangel held the seat for 14 terms despite a challenge from Powell's son, Adam Clayton Powell IV, in 1994. During Rangel's lengthy legislative career, he distinguished himself as one of the most liberal members of the House. He consistently supported a woman's right to abortion, voted for busing to desegregate public schools, opposed the VIETNAM WAR, and opposed the illegal drug trade. In 1974 he served on the House Judiciary Committee during its hearings on the impeachment of President Richard Nixon. In 1997 Rangel cosponsored the African Growth and Opportunities Act, which was designed to promote economic investment in Africa. In addition, Rangel helped found and chaired the CONGRESSIONAL BLACK CAUCUS.

Robert Fay

See Also
Harlem, New York; King, Martin Luther, Jr.; Powell, Adam Clayton, Jr.; Sutton, Percy Ellis.

Africa

Rangi (also known as Irangi and Rongo), ethnic group of Tanzania.

The Rangi primarily inhabit central Tanzania around the town of Dodoma. They speak a Bantu language. Approximately 300,000 people consider themselves Rangi.

See Also
Bantu: Dispersion and Settlement.

North America

Rap, an urban music that emerged from the hip hop movement of the South Bronx, New York, in the 1970s and that still thrives today.

Rap music combines rhythmic instrumental tracks created by a disc jockey, or DJ, with the spoken, rhyming bravura of a master of ceremonies, or MC. DJs often "sample" pieces of other recorded music in the creation of songs. MCs frequently rap about politics, sexual exploits, the conditions of daily life, and their own (sometimes exaggerated) personal attributes. MCs and DJs appropriate pop culture through lyrical allusions as well as rhythmic sound bites, leading many critics to consider rap the preeminent example of postmodern music. Writer John Pareles suggests, "In its structure and its content rap is the music of the television age, and the first truly popular music to adapt the fast, fractured rhythms, the bizarre juxtapositions, and the ceaseless self-promotion that are as much a part of television as logos and laugh tracks."

Unlike television, however, rap gives some African Americans a powerful voice. Its esoteric lyrical form provides ample space for political dissent, and the fact that rap music seems recondite and frightening to some white listeners adds to rap's political sting. In a talk-show discussion, rap activist Harry Allen argued that "[b]lack people are attempting to compensate for their lack of power under white supremacy, and it comes out in our art, it comes out in our music. They're trying to make up for what's missing. What's missing is order. What's missing is power." The eager embrace of rap by young whites, however, complicates the dynamic. Rap reflects racial confusion as well as cultural innovation in an age of cable television, digital technology, and marked class stratification.

Forerunners

The thematic content of many rap songs – egoistic self-assertion and playful attack on one's competitor – follows traditions of African and African American "toasting" and "signifying." The value that some African tribes assign to oral humor, confidence, and derision has its analog on North American streets. Writer Khephra Burns compares rap music with the "pattin' juba" of the 1850s, in which African Americans joined in "trading tall tales, handing out verbal abuse in rhymes, and providing [their] own rhythmic, chest-whacking, thigh slapping accompaniment."

More immediately, rap draws from the conventions of urban street jive, a form of speech that developed in the black community in Chicago, Illinois, in the 1920s. Jive speakers subverted standard usage, adopted metaphorical replacements for common words, and valued wit and innovation. Popular substitutions included "cat" for man, "chick" for woman, "crib" for home, "axe" for instrument, and "bad" for good. Henry Louis Gates Jr. suggests that such substitutions "have enabled many blacks to share messages only the initiated understand." This form of linguistic encoding was a ubiquitous survival tool for African Americans in times of slavery.

While derivative of jive in a broad sense, rap lyrics descend directly from a few specific cultural figures of the twentieth century. Black radio DJs from the 1950s (Holmes "Daddy-O" Daylie and Al Benson in Chicago) through the 1970s (DJ Hollywood in New York) spoke witty, jive-based talk. Heavyweight champion boxer Muhammad Ali showcased the craft of clever rhymes and cocky toasts. "H. Rap" Brown, a Black Nationalist who was active in the 1960s, gave both his name and his oratory style to rap music. In the late 1960s the Watts Prophets of Los Angeles and the Last Poets of Harlem pioneered a kind of protorap by setting Brown's speaking style to rhythmic, musical accompaniments.

The musical roots of rap stretch equally far back in history, drawing upon African, Afro-Caribbean, and African American rhythmic styles. In contrast to Western European music, which emphasizes harmonic progression and a sense of linear, forward motion, African music often marks time, emphasizes cycles, incorporates polyrhythmic figures, and includes nonharmonic percussive sounds.

Rap originally took its rhythms from the soul and funk of James Brown, George Clinton, and others who had emerged from the rhythm and blues (R&B) tradition. As rap developed, other kinds of music were sampled and imitated. In the 1990s Wu Tang Clan borrowed orchestral excerpts and Sean "Puff Daddy" Combs achieved popularity by rapping to the rhythm track of "Every Breath You Take," a song by the British rock band The Police.

Origin

Popular lore attributes the birth of rap to Jamaican immigrant Clive Campbell, who performed under the name DJ Kool Herc. In Jamaica Herc had frequented backyard dance parties that were hosted by sound-systems operator King George, powered by booming speakers, and attended by working-class youth. When Herc DJed his first dance party in New York City in 1973, he joined the Bronx tradition of "mobile DJs," mixing up the music of James Brown, Sly Stone, and Rare Earth for kids on the street. In addition, however, Herc introduced the art of Jamaican toasting, in which DJs speak with humor and syncopation over remixed instrumental versions of records. Herc and other Bronx DJs combined old songs into new, danceable collages, which contained "break beats" – the rhythmic figures that gave rise to breakdancing.

Herc's popularity grew rapidly and inspired others to imitate his act. Soon a few popular DJs divided the Bronx into competing territories. Friendly rivalries arose between Herc in the west, Afrika Bambaataa in the east, Breakout in the north, and Grandmaster Flash in the South and Central Bronx. Competition spawned innovation. Grandmaster Flash invented backspinning, in which he played one record while turning a second one backward, repeating phrases and beats in a stuttering, rhythmic manner. Grandwizard Theodore invented scratching, a technique in which he shimmied a record back and forth beneath the needle of a turntable. Other DJs soon adopted these innovations, which became standards of the rap sound.

DJs first gained popularity by providing a soundtrack for other facets of the hip hop movement, namely dance, graffiti art, and fashion. By the late 1970s, however, artful mixing became a spectacle unto itself, and crowds ceased dancing in order to watch DJs spin. To keep people on the move, DJs recruited MCs, who led call-and-response sessions and fired up the crowd with shouts of "get up," and "jam to the beat," in the fashion of James Brown. Such oratory had precedent in gospel music, the covert rituals of slave religion, and the traditions of West Africa. Grandmaster Flash MCs the Furious Five – Melle Mel, Cowboy, Raheim, Kid Creole, and Mr. Ness – completed the genesis of rap when they began speaking to the rhythm of the music, trading rhymes in synch with each other and the DJ.

Rappers often tried to out-rhyme each other, and watching MCs became a major pastime. Independent labels such as Enjoy, Winley, and Sugar Hill Records began to record rap, and the music soon spread to other parts of New York City. In the fall of 1979 a group of rappers from Brooklyn called the Sugarhill Gang released the hit single "Rapper's Delight." Because it came from Brooklyn, many Bronx residents flouted it as derivative. The song, however, catapulted rap into the public eye, topping the R&B charts and reaching Number 36 on *Billboard*'s Top 40.

Commercialization

In 1980 rapper Kurtis Blow scored two hit singles, "Christmas Rappin'" and "The

Breaks," both of which went gold. The same year Blow played Madison Square Garden with Bob Marley and the Commodores. Meanwhile, Bronx hip hop musicians began to perform in Manhattan's downtown clubs, importing rap to the hub of urban white culture.

In 1981 the Funky Four + 1 More appeared on *Saturday Night Live* while the *Village Voice* and *20/20* gave coverage to breakdancing and rap. In 1983 and 1984 *Flashdance* and *Style Wars* took rap to the movies, and a PBS documentary brought it to the attention of suburbanites.

Innovation accompanied acclaim. In the early 1980s Afrika Bambaataa popularized the use of drum machines and synthesizers, creating the new sound of "techno-pop." Techno-pop, in turn, led to the digital manipulation of samples (pieces of other recorded music), placing rap on the cutting edge of music technology. Rappers who preceded Bambaataa's innovations earned the title of "old school" rappers and included the Fat Boys, Whodini, Kool Moe Dee, and Melle Mel. The "new school" included those who incorporated Bambaataa's digital approach. A feud, originating between Kool Moe Dee and new school rapper LL Cool J (short for Ladies Love Cool James), further characterized the split. New school rappers included Queen Latifah, DJ Jazzy Jeff & the Fresh Prince, Tone Loc, Ice-T, and Ice Cube. In addition to New York musicians, Los Angeles-based rappers began developing new styles of their own. Eventually scenes in Houston, Atlanta, and Chicago each produced new hip hop artists.

Despite the depressed economic conditions under which rap developed, early rappers seldom wrote socially conscious lyrics. As rappers attracted larger audiences in the early 1980s, however, they began to address ghetto conditions and economic inequalities of the United States under President Ronald Reagan. "The Message" (1981) by Grandmaster Flash and the Furious Five marked the advent of political rap, inspiring KRS-One (short for Knowledge Reigns Supreme-Over nearly everyone), Sister Souljah, Public Enemy, and Arrested Development.

The Golden Age

When the rap group Run-D.M.C. fused rap and hard rock on their eponymous album in 1984, rap completed its break into the mainstream. The album sold more than 500,000 copies, becoming the first rap LP to go gold. Run-D.M.C.'s label, Def Jam Records, became the most successful independent record company in the business. Def Jam released hit music by rap star LL Cool J and, in 1985, signed a major distribution agreement with Columbia Records. Run-D.M.C.'s success among white audiences as well as their contract with a white-owned label reflected the mainstream appropriation of the new black form.

This appropriation prompted many to speculate about underlying issues of race. To some black critics, white listeners appeared to be seeking thrills from racially motivated fantasies. Writer David Samuels suggests that "the ways in which rap has been consumed and popularized speak not of cross-cultural understanding, musical or otherwise, but of a voyeurism and tolerance of racism in which blacks and whites are both complicit."

Throughout the 1980s and 1990s, however, the popularity of white rappers like Vanilla Ice, the Beastie Boys, Third Bass, and House of Pain demonstrated that more than race was at play. Latino rappers began performing in Spanish (Mellow Man Ace, Kid Frost, and Gerardo), while Cypress Hill, with its mixed black and Hispanic membership, suggested that the integration of rap was happening at all levels.

Although rap began as a predominantly male activity, a number of successful female performers punctuated its history. Hit acts included MC Lyte, the Real Roxanne, Roxanne Shante, and Yo-Yo. In the 1990s women rappers often followed the male model, however, portraying men in the same derogatory way that men portrayed women. Sister Souljah broke this limited mold by addressing drug abuse, black-on-black violence, and national politics, while Queen Latifah and Salt 'n' Pepa both addressed female self-empowerment. The successful rap arranger, writer, and producer Missy "Misdemeanor" Elliott gained fame as a performer with the 1997 release of her solo debut album, *Supa Dupa Fly*.

Gangsta Rap and its Alternatives

In the late 1980s a more brutal brand of rap developed, which described drugs, sex, and violence in detail. Tremendous white consumption of such music made the grim, lurid, and angry lyrics profitable. "Gansta" rap, as performed by the Geto Boys, N.W.A., Ice Cube, Ice-T, and Too Short, supplied this demand. David Samuels writes that "rap's appeal to whites rested in its evocation of an age-old image of blackness: a foreign, sexually charged and criminal underworld against which the norms of white society are defined...."

The glorification of misogyny and violence had ardent critics in both the black and white establishments. In 1990 a Florida district court declared the album *Nasty as They Wanna Be*, recorded by the Miami group 2 Live Crew, to be legally obscene – a ruling that outlawed the sale of the record. When Ice-T released *Cop-Killer* in 1991, policemen organized a boycott against Time Warner, the company that distributed the album. In addition, police started blaming crimes on rap songs, as criminals cited the influence of gansta rap as part of their defense.

Many black critics declared white anger hypocritical, however, by pointing to the uncensored obscenity of popular white comedian Andrew Dice Clay as well as anti-police messages in songs by Eric Clapton, Bob Dylan, and Woody Guthrie. Commenting on *Nasty as They Wanna Be*, Henry Louis Gates Jr. likened the ribaldry of 2 Live Crew to the street tradition of playing the dozens: "In the face of racist stereotypes about black sexuality, you can do two things: you can disavow them or explode them with exaggeration. 2 Live Crew, like many 'hip hop' groups, is engaged in sexual Carnivalesque. Parody reigns supreme.... their off-color nursery rhymes are part of a venerable Western tradition."

Other African American leaders, however, dissented. Although most opposition reflected nothing more than a generation gap – parents scorning rap as their parents had scorned R&B – some of the criticism was grounded in ethical and political concern. On a talk show in 1993 Rev. Jesse Jackson railed against the rhetoric of gangsta rap. In the same year Rev. Calvin O. Butts III held a rally in New York to run over certain rap albums with a steamroller. Both men thought that the hyperbolic language of gansta rappers and groups like 2 Live Crew only hurt African Americans in their struggle against racism. Some events in the 1990s led critics to question the lifestyle of gansta rappers as well as the culpability of the media in celebrity-related crime. These events included the death of rapper Eazy-E from AIDS, and the murders of East Coast-West Coast rivals Chris Wallace, a.k.a. Biggie Smalls (The Notorious B.I.G.), and Tupac Shakur, a.k.a. 2PAC.

Often called "the queen of hip-hop soul," Mary J. Blige blends rhythm and blues, rap, soul, and jazz influences on such hit albums as 1997's *Share My World*. *Russell Einhorn/Liaison Agency*

An increasingly popular and gentrified form of rap developed concurrently with gangsta rap. In the late 1980s lighthearted songs, more in the spirit of early Bronx rap, garnered popularity. Performers such as Young MC, MC Rob Base & DJ EZ Rock, and DJ Jazzy Jeff & the Fresh Prince recorded clean hits filled with playful braggadocio. Rap-based Saturday morning cartoons appeared in the wake of such songs. In 1990 rap reached prime-time television in the form of *The Fresh Prince of Bel-Air,* a situation comedy. Even the more serious rappers often found themselves in the thick of popular culture. LL Cool J landed a sitcom, while Tone Loc, Ice-T, Ice Cube, and Queen Latifah appeared in Hollywood films. Will Smith, a.k.a. the Fresh Prince, went furthest in this direction, starring in two summer block-busters, *Independence Day* (1996) and *Men In Black* (1997).

Meanwhile, however, most rappers neither perpetrated gangsta lyrics nor appeared in cartoons. Rappers who were dubbed "alternative" disavowed rap's violence while trying to preserve its edge. They included Me Phi Me, Disposable Heroes of Hiphoprisy, and Arrested Development. KRS-One of Boogie Down Productions initiated the Stop the Violence movement, and the West Coast Rap All-Stars began the Human Education Against Lies (H.E.A.L.) program, both of which pitted rap's influence against social ills. More bohemian acts, such as A Tribe Called Quest and De La Soul, concentrated on musical innovations, developing the art, rather than the politics, of rap.

In the late 1990s the widespread popularity of the Fugees reflected the new, international direction of rap. The Fugees addressed problems both within and outside the United States, and one of the group's members, Haitian Wyclef Jean, released material performed in Creole. Wu Tang Clan, a group of nine rappers from the East Coast, rejected R&B influences, adhering instead to global sensibilities and trends. At the end of the century rap scenes were burgeoning in most major European cities: MC Solar of France drew an international following while Japanese youth began to emulate the rap culture of the West.

Rap had begun as a homemade music, and its commercialization did not steal it from the streets. In the late 1990s amateurs across the United Sstes and the world continued to create innovative hip hop sounds, generating a culture far larger than that reflected by the recording industry. "Famous" rap became famous by virtue of mainstream listeners and media, while fresher sounds often remained local and undiscovered. Such new rap continues to prosper as a living art, always outdistancing its commercialized, pop-chart predecessors.

Eric Bennett

See Also

AIDS in the United States; Slavery in the United States; Soul Music; KRS-One; Atlanta, Georgia; Brown, Hubert G. ("H. Rap"); Butts, Calvin O., III; Chicago, Illinois; Grandmaster Flash, Melle Mel, and the Furious Five; Harlem, New York; Hip Hop in the United States; Houston, Texas; Jackson, Jesse Louis; Last Poets, The; Los Angeles, California; Campbell, Luther; Niggaz with Attitude; New York, New York; Notorious B.I.G. ("Biggie Smalls"); Rhythm and Blues; Run-DMC; Salt 'n' Pepa; Television and African Americans; Wu-Tang Clan; Sly and the Family Stone; Los Angeles, California; Haiti; Film, Blacks in American; Combs, Sean ("Puffy"); Black Nationalism in the United States.

Africa

Rassemblement Démocratique Africain, an alliance of nationalist political parties in the French colonies of West and Central Africa.

The Rassemblement Démocratique Africain (RDA) was one of the driving forces of decolonization in several of France's African colonies. It was founded by African deputies to the French National Assembly at a congress held in 1946 in Bamako, the colonial capital of French Sudan (now Mali). The RDA's leading spokesperson in the French assembly (*see* France) was Félix Houphouët Boigny, the future president of Côte d'Ivoire. The RDA's initial demand was full French citizenship for Africans in France's colonies. Later the RDA played an important role in debates over the conditions of independence for the French colonies.

In its early years the RDA was allied with the French Communist Party, the only major party in France that supported the RDA's goals. The French government of Charles de Gaulle viewed the RDA as a threat, and the government often arrested RDA activists and banned their meetings. In the early 1950s the RDA broke with the French Communists and formed closer ties with de Gaulle's government. In Africa the RDA drew its membership primarily from urban areas; trade unions were a particularly strong source of support for the RDA branches in Cameroon and Guinea.

By the late 1950s French military defeats in the French colonies of Indochina and Algeria had convinced the French government to accept African demands for decolonization. The RDA favored France's offer to grant its colonies internal self-rule within a "French Community" under the executive control of the French president. For many RDA leaders this proposal appeared to offer the colonies an opportunity to gain greater autonomy without losing the benefits of French citizenship and economic support. Only Sékou Touré of Guinea – the leader of an RDA affiliate, the Parti Démocratique de Guinée – called for complete independence. When a referendum on federation within a French Community was held in all of the French African colonies in 1958, only Guinea voted to reject federation in favor of complete independence. France itself, however, soon abandoned its support for the proposed federation. Within a few years candidates of RDA-affiliated parties were elected to lead some of the first independent governments of French-speaking Africa. Leaders who began their careers with the RDA included Félix Houphouët-Boigny in Côte d'Ivoire (who had long since abandoned the RDA's initial leftist positions), Sékou Touré in Guinea, Modibo Keita in Mali, and Hamani Diori in Niger. After independence the RDA's international influence faded, although many of the leaders it fostered remained in office for years.

Elizabeth Heath

See Also

Bamako, Mali; Decolonization in Africa: An Interpretation; Nationalism in Africa.

Latin America and the Caribbean

Rastafarians, members of a social movement established in Jamaica around 1930 that combines elements of religious prophecy, specifically the idea of a black God and Messiah; the Pan-Africanist philosophy of Marcus Garvey; the ideas of Black Power Movement leader Walter Rodney; and the defiance of reggae music.

Religion has been the principal form of resistance in Jamaica since colonial times. As scholar of Rastafarianism Barry Chevannes affirms: "Whether resistance through the use of force, or resistance through symbolic forms such as language, folk-tales and proverbs... religion was the main driving force among the Jamaican peasants." During the early twentieth century resistance in Jamaica reached its pinnacle with the birth of Rastafarianism – as much an Afrocentric world-view and form of black nationalism as it was a new religion, inspired by the independent, anticolonial Christian tradition of the Ethiopian Orthodox Church. As Horace Campell notes, "Rastafari culture combines the histories of the children of slaves in different societies. Within it are both the negative and the positive – the idealist and the ideological – responses of an exploited and racially humiliated people."

The Rastafari Movement

The roots of Rastafarianism can be traced back to Jamaica's earliest freedom fighters against colonialism. According to Leonard E. Barrett Sr., author of *The Rastafarians,* Jamaica's African population "suffered the most frustrating and oppressive slavery ever experienced in a British colony.... Under such complete domination two reactions were provoked: fight and flight." The Jamaican maroons – African slaves, who, following the British defeat of the Spaniards in 1655, escaped to the mountains – waged guerrilla warfare against the British colonizers. In 1738 the British were compelled to grant them a limited freedom: although the maroons were allowed their own lands and leaders, they were also required to police the plantation slaves, a duty that they accepted. Henceforth, the maroons were loyal to the Crown. The freedom movement was taken up by plantation slaves. Indeed, in 1831, under the leadership of the slave and Baptist religious leader SAMUEL SHARPE, Jamaica's slaves waged a mass rebellion against the planters. Like Sharpe, many Jamaican slaves believed that God was calling on them to fight for their freedom – a messianic vision partly influenced by Baptist and Methodist missionaries, who, during the mid-eighteenth century, established churches in Jamaica and contributed to a syncretism of Christianity and the island's African religions. Although the rebellion was violently repressed by the British, it was one of the main reasons that England emancipated the slaves in 1834.

In 1865 the Morant Bay Rebellion – another large-scale uprising of Jamaica's rural blacks against the colonial elite – forced political and economic reforms that diminished the power and privileges of Jamaica's ruling white planter class. Jamaica became a Crown Colony: the British drew up a new constitution that removed direct rule from the hands of the local elite and gave decision-making power to an appointed British governor, who presided over a legislative council. Yet the reforms only went so far: the overwhelming majority of council members, nominated by the governor himself, were white, and the gulf that existed between Jamaica's poor blacks (a significant majority of the island's population) and middle-class whites and mulattos continued to widen.

Jamaica's black population was systematically repressed until 1962, the year British colonial rule came to an end. Indeed, Jamaican blacks did not have the freedom to assemble or organize trade unions; abysmal working conditions led many to seek employment abroad. In 1914 Jamaican worker Marcus Garvey founded the UNIVERSAL NEGRO IMPROVEMENT ASSOCIATION (UNIA). Garvey's Pan-Africanist philosophy, which established a sense of national identity based on race, instilled in many blacks worldwide the belief that their economic and political liberation could ultimately be found in a strong and unified Africa. After spending a decade in GREAT BRITAIN and the United States, in 1927 Garvey returned to Jamaica, where he spread his political views among black workers and farmers. He told blacks to "look to Africa for the crowning of a king to know that your redemption is nigh."

In 1930 Ras Tafari Makonnen was crowned the new emperor of ETHIOPIA, HAILE SELASSIE I ("Power of the Trinity," his baptismal name) – a monumental event that many blacks in Africa and the Americas saw as the fulfillment of Garvey's prophecy. Since the Middle Ages a part of Ethiopia's nobility, including the Makonnens, had perceived themselves as descendants of King Solomon of Judah and the Queen of Sheba. This was a belief stemming from biblical prophecies, including the Song of Solomon 1:5-6, which states: "I am Black, but comely, O ye daughters of Jersusalem, as the tents of Kedar, as the curtains of Solomon." As Chevannes points out, "if Solomon was Black, so was the Christ. Both were descendants of David. Redemption of the African race was therefore at hand." The prophecy was further reinforced by Emperor Haile Selassie himself, who appropriated the titles "King of Kings" and "Conquering Lion of the Tribe of Judah."

The name Rastafari is taken from *Ras*, meaning "prince" in the Amharic language, and *Tafari*, the name of the emperor of Ethiopia. The earliest preachers of the Rastafarian world-view were the Jamaican workers Leonard Howell, Archibald Dunkley, and Joseph Hibbert. They asserted the idea of a black God, who physically lived on the earth; proclaimed that the African peoples shared in this divinity; and equated the liberation of blacks with their repatriation to Africa. Indeed, on three separate occasions (1934, 1956, and 1959) Jamaica's Rastafarian leaders attempted – unsuccessfully, due to a lack of governmental and organizational support – to repatriate brethren to their homeland. Howell also called for "death to Black and White oppressors," an approach that ignited considerable hostility among Jamaica's elite: both Howell and Dunkley were imprisoned on several occasions, and Howell was branded "insane."

In 1935 the Italian army invaded Ethiopia, an event that drew attention to the incompetence of the Selassie regime, which had left Ethiopia's peasantry impoverished, uneducated, and untrained in military service and thus entirely unprepared for war. Moreover, Jamaica's economic crisis continued to worsen. Black workers, plagued by malnutrition and low wages, turned to practical action instead of religion as a form of resistance. Spurred on by these developments, the Rastafarian movement became increasingly politicized: during the 1940s and 1950s leaders intensified their opposition to the colonial state by defying the police and organizing illegal street marches.

During the late 1950s Claudius Henry, head of a Rastafarian meetinghouse in Kingston, set up a guerrilla training camp and in 1959 unsuccessfully tried to repatriate a group of Jamaican Rastas to Africa. Soon after, the police invaded Henry's headquarters, where they found a supply of arms and a letter inviting the Cuban leader Fidel Castro to take over Jamaica. Henry was arrested and tried on charges of treason. Throughout the 1960s Rastafarian demonstrations against segregation and black poverty were violently repressed by the Jamaican police and military. While several Rastafari were killed in such clashes, hundreds more were arrested and humiliated by being forced to have their dreadlocks cut off.

Philosophically opposed to a culture of violence, many Rastafari soon turned to more peaceful means of resistance – a goal considerably aided by the visit of Haile Selassie to Jamaica in 1966. As Campbell notes, "state officials had to take a back seat while the

RIGHT: With its Afrocentric world view, emphasis on Black Nationalism, and ties to the Ethiopian Orthodox Church, Rastafarian philosophy has had considerable influence in Jamaica, where it originated. Rastafarian males customarily have full beards and grow their hair into dreadlocks. *Durrell McKenna/Hutchison*

OPPOSITE: Jamaican flute player, his dreadlocks wrapped in a colorful scarf, performs in an outdoor concert. *Macintyre/Hutchison*

mass of the black populace thrust forward to pay homage to the Ethiopian monarch. So profound was the popular feeling expressed for Africa that the Jamaican ruling class realized that it could not simply write off Rastafari." Rastafarian culture was explored and promoted in a plethora of academic studies in Jamaica and abroad, while the ETHIOPIAN ORTHODOX CHURCH was recognized as an institution worthy of respect. Rastafarianism also gained a new measure of credibility among Jamaica's middle-class blacks and mulattos who, during the late 1960s, formed their own Rastafarian group, the Twelve Tribes of Israel.

In 1968 WALTER RODNEY, then a lecturer at the University of the West Indies in Kingston, started the Black Power Movement, which significantly influenced the development of Rastafarianism in the Caribbean. Black Power was a call to blacks to overthrow the capitalist order that ensured white dominion and to reconstruct their societies in the image of blacks. In DOMINICA, GRENADA, and Trinidad, Rastafarians played a central role in radical left-wing politics. In Jamaica, Rastafarian resistence was expressed through cultural forms, particularly reggae music. Popular reggae singers, such as BOB MARLEY and PETER TOSH, expressed Rastafarian ideas and social criticism in their song lyrics; during the 1970s they significantly contributed to the growth of the Rastafarian movement throughout the Caribbean, the United States, England, Canada, Europe, Australia, New Zealand, and parts of Latin America.

RASTAFARI RITUALS, PRACTICES, AND RECENT DEVELOPMENTS

The rituals and practices central to Rastafarianism developed during the late 1930s and 1940s. Of particular importance are "reasonings" and "binghi." At reasonings Rastafari members gather informally to offer prayers and smoke ganja, or marijuana, considered a holy weed; it is passed around in a water pipe, which some Rastafari have likened to the Christian communion cup in its symbolic significance. Binghi are all-night celebrations that feature dancing accompanied by the distinctive rhythms of Rasta drums; they are held to mark special occasions throughout the year, such as the coronation of Haile Selassie I, Marcus Garvey's birthday, and the emancipation from slavery. Other significant practices include the wearing of facial hair by adult males (Ras Tafari was pictured with a full beard) and dreadlocks, or long matted hair. According to Chevannes, dreadlocks originated among a group of Rastas known as the Youth Black Faith, who adopted the hairstyle as a symbol of their radically defiant views in a society in which blacks were made to feel ashamed of their skin color and hair texture.

Since the 1980s the Rastafarian movement has become increasingly secular: many of the movement's symbols have lost their religious and ideological significance and the influence of Rastafari ideology on Jamaica's urban youth has considerably declined. The Rasta colors (red, green, and gold), in which all Rasta banners and artifacts are painted, have been largely shorn of their ideological meaning and are now worn by all. Dreadlocks too are sported as a trendy hairstyle by both blacks and whites in Jamaica and abroad. The loosening of Rastafari ideology has also led women to become increasingly outspoken within the movement. Women traditionally had been forbidden to play an important role in rituals; they were also expected to show complete deference to males. During the last decade, however, some women have begun to protest against and defy the movement's patriarchal beliefs and conventions.

The Rastafarian movement in Jamaica remains fragmented and unorganized; brethren adhere to the Rastafarian worldview through inner conviction and generally prefer autonomy to cohesive organizational structures and rules. Nonetheless, two highly organized Rastafari groups exist in Jamaica: the Bobos and the Twelve Tribes of Israel. The Bobos maintain a communal life on the fringes of Kingston, where they earn a living producing and selling brooms. The Twelve Tribes, on the other hand, is a predominantly middle-class group, led by Prophet Gad. Members of the Twelve Tribes accept the authority of designated group members, pay dues, and hold regular meetings and events. In addition, there is the House of Nyabinghi, a loosely organized assembly of Rasta elders, who settle disputes between brethren and organize events. "Beyond the Assembly of Elders," notes Chevannes, "there is no membership, as such. All are free to come or stay away, to participate or remain silent, to contribute or withhold financial dues... the openness of this sort of structure permits a great measure of democracy, in which all are equal, regardless of age, ability or function."

Rastafarianism remains a culture of resistance in many parts of the world. Although the Rastafarian movement has experienced a turbulent social history in Jamaica, it retains significant moral authority there, and its influence is increasingly felt beyond Jamaica. Indeed, it was one of the first full-fledged movements to confront issues of racial identity and prejudice, and to incite Jamaica's middle-class blacks to reflect on the importance of their African heritage.

Roanne Edwards

SEE ALSO

Maroonage in the Americas; Pan-Africanism; Early Rastafarian Leaders; Baptists; Garvey, Marcus Mosiah; Kingston, Jamaica; Trinidad and Tobago; Religions, African, in Latin America and the Caribbean; Black Power; Protestant Church in Latin America and the Caribbean; Howell, Leonard P.

Africa

Ratsiraka, Didier

(b. November 4, 1936, Vato-mandry, Madagascar), president of MADAGASCAR from 1975 to 1993 and again since 1997.

Didier Ratsiraka's father was a founding member of the Parti des Déshérités de Madagascar, a pro-Western political party. Taught by Jesuits as a child, Ratsiraka obtained an engineering degree from the French Naval Academy in Brest. After graduating, he joined the Malagasy navy and was posted to the Embassy of Madagascar in FRANCE until ailing president PHILIBERT TSIRANANA was ousted during the May 1972 revolution, when 100,000 protesters marched on the presidential palace. His successor, army chief of staff Gen. Gabriel Ramanatsoa, asked Ratsiraka to return to Madagascar to serve as minister of foreign affairs. An attempted coup d'état resulted in the removal of Ramanatsoa and a power struggle between Ratsiraka and Richard Ratsimandrava, an army colonel. While Ratsimandrava became president in 1975, he was assassinated only six days later. Ratsiraka served on the military council that took control and subsequently named him president of the "Second Republic." Ratsiraka was defeated by Albert Zafy in presidential elections between 1992 and 1993. However, Ratsiraka remained a strong political force, subsequently beating Zafy in 1996 presidential elections to reclaim the office of president in 1997.

Ari Nave

Africa

Rawlings, Jerry (b. June 22, 1947, Accra, Ghana), military officer who twice overthrew the government, in 1979 and 1981; ruled Ghana after 1981; and won election as president in 1992.

Although he came to power as a Marxist populist, Jerry John Rawlings has since successfully instituted free-market reforms to revive Ghana's faltering economy. However, he is often seen as an enigma because of his shifting rhetoric and changing policies.

Rawlings is the son of a Scottish pharmacist and a woman of the Ewe people, one of Ghana's largest ethnic groups. Politically, Ewe have been among his staunchest supporters. He attended Achimota Secondary School and Ghana Military Academy in Teshie. In 1969 Rawlings became an air force pilot and in 1978 was promoted to flight lieutenant.

Rawlings became politically active in the late 1970s. He blamed food shortages, inflation, and economic stagnation on the corruption and mismanagement of the military government. In 1979, when authorities lifted the ban on political parties, the charismatic Rawlings started speaking out against the government and endorsed measures to help the poor. He quickly won a wide public following. Rawlings and other junior officers were arrested and imprisoned during an attempted coup in May 1979. A second attempt succeeded in June 1979, and coup organizers promptly freed Rawlings.

Rawlings became head of the Armed Forces Revolutionary Council (AFRC), which took charge of government with a goal of bringing the previous military regime to justice. During the 112 days the AFRC held power it tried a number of former officials and military leaders on corruption charges. Akwasi Afrifa, Gen. I. K. Acheampong, and Gen. F. W. K. Akuffo were among the eight former officials who were executed. In July 1979 the AFRC held previously scheduled elections, which resulted in Hilla Limann's victory as president. Rawlings handed over power to Limann in September of that year. Limann retired Rawlings from the air force. However, Limann failed to revitalize Ghana's deteriorating economy. With the country crippled by a staggering foreign debt and an annual inflation rate of over 140 percent, public discontent soared.

In December 1981 Rawlings staged another coup and became head of state as chairman of the Provisional National Defense Council (PNDC). At first the PNDC implemented such Marxist-inspired measures as the creation of worker councils to monitor factory output and Workers' Defense Committees in each neighborhood. Rawlings also sought support from the former Soviet Union and such anti-Western states as Libya.

However, by 1983 these measures had clearly failed to reverse the country's economic decline, and Rawlings turned to free-market reforms. Over the next several years the Rawlings administration devalued Ghana's currency, froze the hiring of public employees, and privatized state-owned enterprises, including a number of potentially lucrative coffee and cocoa plantations. His austerity measures won approval from Western governments and international organizations, such as the International Monetary Fund, but fostered unhappiness at home. Rawlings faced coup attempts each year between 1983 and 1987. He maintained tight control over Ghana's political life; his government jailed opponents and executed at least one person convicted of plotting a coup. Human rights groups such as Amnesty International condemned his regime for human rights abuses.

By the early 1990s the government's reforms had led the country to an economic recovery. Rawlings remained sufficiently popular to win election in 1992 with 58 percent of the vote. He won reelection to another four-year term in 1996. Foreign observers judged the elections reasonably free and fair. Rawlings has said that he will retire in the year 2000.

David P. Johnson, Jr.

See Also
Human Rights in Africa.

North America

Rawls, Louis Allen (Lou) (b. December 1, 1936, Chicago, Ill.), African American fusion singer and a founder of the Lou Rawls Parade of Stars in support of the United Negro College Fund.

Raised by his grandmother on the South Side of Chicago, Lou Rawls began singing in his church choir at age seven. In the mid-1950s Rawls and friend Sam Cooke joined with two other vocalists and formed the Pilgrim Travelers, a gospel group. After the group disbanded in 1959, Rawls sang in blues clubs and cafes around Los Angeles. At one show a producer from Capitol Records asked him to submit an audition tape. His debut album, *Stormy Monday* (1962), was soon released. *Lou Rawls Live* followed in 1966, achieving gold status on the strength of its single, "Love is a Hurtin' Thing," which reached Number One on the rhythm-and-blues charts. In 1967 Rawls won his first Grammy Award for Best Male R&B Vocals for the song "Dead End Street." He won again in 1971 for "A Natural Man." Rawls's success continued with his first platinum album, *All Things in Time* (1977), and the Grammy Award-winning album *Unmistakably Lou* (1977).

In 1979 Rawls and Anheuser-Busch founded the Lou Rawls Parade of Stars, an annual telethon for the United Negro College Fund (UNCF). By 1998 Rawls's telethon had raised an estimated $175 million for the UNCF and had featured such entertainers as Bill Cosby, Whoopi Goldberg, and Stevie Wonder. Rawls released two albums in 1993, *Portrait of the Blues* and *Christmas Is The Time*. He has also acted in television and film, from the late 1950s show *77 Sunset Strip* to the 1995 film *Leaving Las Vegas*.

See Also
Blues, The; Cooke, Samuel (Sam); Gospel Music; Los Angeles, California; Rhythm and Blues; Television and African Americans; Film, Blacks in American.

North America

Razaf, Andy (b. December 15, 1895, Washington, D.C.; d. February 3, 1973, Hollywood, Calif.), African American popular song lyricist.

Andy Razaf had his greatest success writing for Harlem stage shows of the 1920s, collaborating with greats like Willie "The Lion" Smith, Eubie Blake, and James P. Johnson. His most lasting work, however, was with Thomas "Fats" Waller. The two produced many of the era's most popular songs, such as "Honeysuckle Rose," "Ain't Misbehavin'," and "The Joint is Jumpin'." When Harlem stage shows became less popular, Razaf's career declined. He retired after 1940 and died in relative obscurity of kidney failure. He was married four times, once to Jean Blackwell, who was the curator of the Schomburg Center for Research in Black Culture of the New York Public Library.

Robert Fay

See Also
Blake, James Hubert ("Eubie"); Harlem, New York; Hutson, Jean Blackwell; Smith, Willie ("the Lion"); Waller, Thomas Wright ("Fats"); Schomburg Library.

RDA. Please see Rassemblement Démocratique Africain

Latin America and the Caribbean

Rebouças, André

(b. January 13, 1838, Cachoeira, Bahia, Brazil; d. May 9, 1898, Madeira), Afro-Brazilian abolitionist, engineer, and teacher who campaigned for land reform in Brazil's abolitionist movement of the 1880s.

The son of national deputy Antônio Pereira Rebouças, André Rebouças grew up in the northeastern province of Bahia. After studying math and engineering at Rio de Janeiro's military school, he traveled and studied in Europe. Upon returning to Brazil, he became an advisor and strategist during the Paraguayan War (1864-1870). Rebouças then supervised several engineering projects, including the construction of railroads and docks in Rio de Janeiro. Rebouças's engineering achievements won him the respect of the royal family. He later became a professor of botany and math at the city's Polytechnic School, where he established an abolitionist society in 1883.

Rebouças conducted most of his abolitionist work behind the scenes, rarely addressing audiences. He organized abolitionist meetings and associations, and inspired readers with his antislavery literature and propaganda. Rebouças cofounded the Sociedade Brasileira contra a Escravidão (Brazilian Antislavery Society) in Rio de Janeiro in 1880 and became its first treasurer. He was a frequent contributor to the famous abolitionist newspaper *Gazeta da tarde* and cowrote the 1883 manifesto for the Rio de Janeiro-based Confederação Abolicionista (Abolitionist Confederation). In all, Rebouças authored more than 120 antislavery articles as well as numerous essays analyzing Brazil's social and economic problems.

Unlike many other abolitionists, Rebouças realized that emancipation alone, without wider reforms, would likely do little to improve the living standards and opportunities of black Brazilians. For this reason his abolitionist agenda included expanding access to education, which had long been denied to almost all Brazilian slaves. The educational program he envisioned, but never saw realized, called for establishing at least one school in every village in Brazil to educate all segments of the population.

Both during and after the abolition movement Rebouças distinguished himself as an advocate of land reform. He believed that small scale farming was the key to Brazil's agricultural progress, and that given a small plot of land and the necessary equipment, ex-slaves and their families would become productive citizens. In his 1883 treatise *Agricultura nacional,* he proposed a program of "rural democracy" that would subdivide large estates for distribution to ex-slaves, immigrants, and the rural poor. As part of this effort he attempted to set up a government-sponsored Territorial Association to break up plantations that had fallen into debt. Furthermore, Rebouças's abolitionist society proposed that taxes be levied on all uncultivated land located within 20 km (12 mi) of lines of communication.

The Republic of Brazil was established in 1889. Subsequently Rebouças, devoted to the monarchy because it had abolished slavery, accompanied the imperial family into exile. He spent the rest of his life in Europe and Africa, and on the island of Madeira, where he died mysteriously exactly ten years after slavery in Brazil ended. Although Rebouças had greater renown in Brazil as an engineer, abolitionist Joaquim Nabuco affirmed his importance to abolitionism, saying, "Rebouças incarnated like no one else the antislavery spirit."

Aaron Myers

See Also

Rio de Janeiro, Brazil; Abolition and Emancipation in Latin America and the Caribbean.

North America

Reconstruction, **the period immediately following the Civil War during which the United States sought to rebuild the South physically, politically, socially, and economically.**

Reconstruction, also called the "Second American Revolution," is an often misunderstood era of United States history. For decades historians presented Reconstruction as a time when the South was a region besieged by a punitive North. According to this view President Abraham Lincoln initially offered reasonable terms to the rebellious Southern states to speed reunion; but Radical Republicans, the liberal wing of the Republican Party, instituted a period of "Negro rule" in which blacks, incompetent to govern, mismanaged the South. In this interpretation conscientious whites "redeemed" the South by using secret patriotic organizations such as the Ku Klux Klan to depose black rule. Only during the "Second Reconstruction," the Civil Rights Movement, did most historians begin to reevaluate previous conclusions about Reconstruction. Concurring with W. E. B. Du Bois, most scholars now agree that Reconstruction was a period of progressive politics in which newly emancipated blacks, with the help of the federal government and sympathetic whites in the South, helped build a more democratic society.

The Federal Government During Reconstruction

Most historians consider Reconstruction to encompass the years between 1865 and 1877. But the course Reconstruction would take and the questions associated with it were the subjects of national debate even before the end of the Civil War. Who should be punished for inciting secession and the war? How would the Southern states be readmitted to the Union? What penalties would apply? What was the federal government's responsibility to the freed slaves? Should the government extend rights to former slaves, and, if so, which rights? How would the Southern economy replace slave labor with free labor? Finally, and perhaps most important to the federal government, who was responsible for implementing Reconstruction policy – the president or Congress? Although Lincoln had been granted far-reaching powers during the war, Congress could not allow the president such latitude in peacetime.

By issuing the Emancipation Proclamation on January 1, 1863, Lincoln committed the United States to abolishing slavery. Because slavery had been part of the American social fabric from the nation's beginning, its abolition would fundamentally alter the nation. Combined with this drastic social and political change was the need to rebuild the war-torn South. Many Southern cities lay in ruins. In addition, the loss of farmland and animals, as well as human labor – not only black slaves but whites killed or disabled in the war – jeopardized its agrarian economy.

Presidential Reconstruction

In December 1863 Lincoln introduced the first Reconstruction scheme, the Ten Percent Plan, thus beginning the period known as Presidential Reconstruction. The plan decreed that when 10 percent of a state's prewar voters had taken an oath of loyalty to the U.S. Constitution, its citizens could elect a new state government and apply for readmission to the Union. In addition, Lincoln promised to pardon all but a few high-ranking Confederates if they would take this oath and accept the fact of abolition. The plan also required that states amend their constitutions to abolish slavery. Conspicuous in this plan was the stipulation that only whites could vote or hold office. Despite the objections of Northern abolitionists, Lincoln began to implement the plan in Louisiana, which the Union army had occupied since 1862. In a private meeting at the White House a group of highly accomplished free blacks from New Orleans objected to their unequal status. Spurred by this protest, Lincoln unsuccessfully urged Louisiana's governor to allow the state's qualified free blacks to vote.

Congress, believing that Lincoln's Reconstruction plan was too permissive, took a series of steps to counteract it. Congress passed the Wade-Davis Bill in late 1864, which contained more stringent readmission policies. It required that 50 percent of a state's voters declare loyalty to the Constitution before the state could create a new government, and also that these new governments recognize freedpeople as equal before the law. In addition, in January 1865 Congress

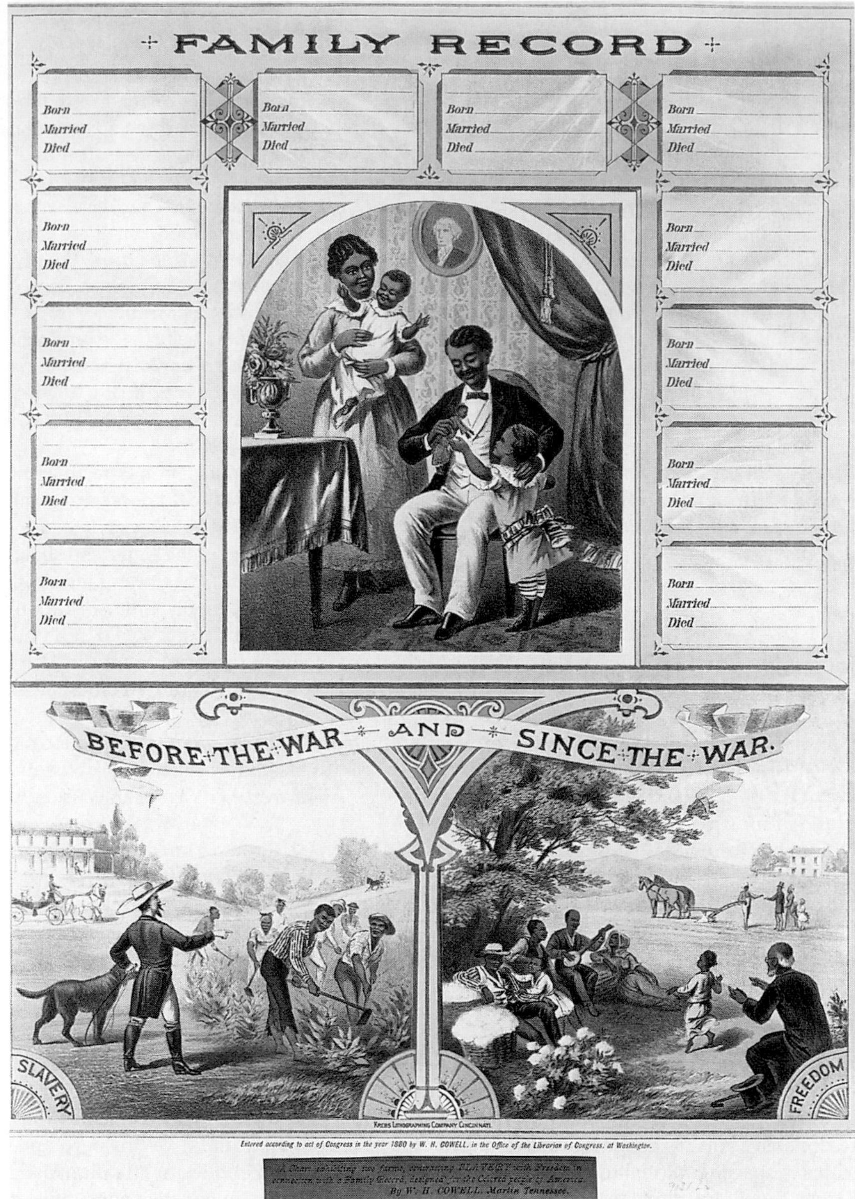

This 1880 Reconstruction-era diagram of a family tree contrasts farm life before and after the Civil War. The slave family on the left works under the watchful eye of a white master. The free family on the right enjoys leisure time together. *CORBIS*

approved the Thirteenth Amendment, which constitutionally ended slavery. It was ratified in December of that year, and in March 1865 Congress established the Bureau of Refugees, Freedmen and Abandoned Lands, or Freedmen's Bureau, a relief agency for needy refugees. Although the agency represented both black and white refugees, it was primarily intended to aid blacks in the transition from slavery to freedom.

Lincoln indirectly vetoed Wade-Davis by leaving it unsigned until Congress adjourned in late March 1865. He considered the Ten Percent Plan experimental, however, and in his final speech indicated that at least some blacks should vote. Because of this, many historians believe he might have adapted his Ten Percent Plan had he not been assassinated. It was obvious, however, that Lincoln and Congress disagreed on the basic nature of Reconstruction policy. When the war ended and Reconstruction began in earnest, the federal government had no solid plan for its direction.

Congress had adjourned by the end of the war and did not reconvene until December. With Lincoln's assassination in early April 1865, Vice President Andrew Johnson became president, controlling Reconstruction policy at its crucial beginning. Johnson, a poor white from Tennessee, harbored disdain for both the Southern planter aristocracy and blacks. In May 1865 he began issuing proclamations that were even more lenient than Lincoln's.

Johnson pardoned all Southern whites except Confederate leaders and persons whose wealth exceeded $20,000. They would have to apply personally for Johnson's pardon. Johnson appointed provisional governors and required that to rejoin the union, the states need only abolish slavery and repudiate both secession and the Confederate war debt. After the rebellious states met these requirements they were considered "reconstructed." In addition, Johnson ordered that abandoned plantations be returned to their former owners. Though representatives from the Freedmen's Bureau initially refused to follow Johnson's directive, he ultimately sent federal troops to force the return of these lands.

Southern states, encouraged by Johnson's leniency, began to return the old elites to power. In addition, Southern state governments issued Black Codes, laws that aimed to limit black mobility and economic options, and virtually to reinstate the plantation system. Under the Black Codes interracial marriages were banned and blacks could be forced to sign yearly contracts. They could also be declared vagrants for not having a certain (typically unreasonable) amount of money on their person and be sentenced to labor on a white-owned plantation. In addition, these laws limited the types of occupations and property blacks could hold. Other laws sought forcibly to apprentice black children. As a result, freedpeople existed somewhere between freedom and slavery.

Congress had observed these events during adjournment and, upon returning to Washington, D.C., in December 1865, sought to alter Johnson's policies. When the newly elected Southern representatives arrived and Northern congressmen discovered that many of them were former Confederate cabinet members, congressmen, and generals who had won congressional seats in the state governments restored under Johnson, Congress refused to seat them. Many congressional Republicans, especially Radical Republicans such as Thaddeus Stevens in the House and Charles Sumner in the Senate, believed that the Johnson state governments should be dissolved and Reconstruction begun again, this time based on equality under law and universal male suffrage. Moderate members of the party, however, attempted to work with Johnson and convince him to modify his policies.

In early 1866 Congress sought to advance Reconstruction by passage of the Freedmen's Bureau Act and the Civil Rights Act. The Freedmen's Bureau Act extended the agency's life for another year. The Civil Rights Act defined people born in the United States as national citizens and stated explicitly the rights to which they were entitled regardless of race. Johnson vetoed both bills, insisting that they violated states' rights. Congress quickly overrode Johnson's vetoes. Shortly thereafter, Congress approved the Fourteenth Amendment, which was ratified in 1868. Designed to protect the rights of freedpeople and to restrict the political power of former

The political cartoon, *Re-Construction, or "A White Man's Government,"* presents a drowning white Southerner refusing the help of a black man, who clings to an allegorical "Tree of Liberty." President Ulysses S. Grant stands onshore, urging the desperate man to accept whatever help he is offered. *CORBIS*

Confederates, the Fourteenth Amendment defined U.S. citizenship in much the same way as the Civil Rights Bill had and prohibited states from abridging the "privileges or immunities" of citizens without due process. Rather than prohibit states from restricting suffrage, it encouraged Southern states to allow black suffrage by reducing representation in states that disfranchised any male citizens.

Johnson's Reconstruction program became the decisive issue in the 1866 congressional elections. Although Johnson had toured the North to win support for candidates sympathetic to his program, his efforts were mostly unsuccessful. His rhetoric was more influential in the South: all of the former confederate states, except Tennessee, rejected the Fourteenth Amendment, which Johnson had publicly disavowed. By 1867 moderate and radical Republicans in Congress, tired of Johnson's obstruction to their more ambitious Reconstruction plan, began to take advantage of the president's waning power to forge an era of Congressional Reconstruction.

Congressional Reconstruction

After a series of compromises Congress decided upon a Reconstruction plan that was far more broad-ranging than Johnson's. In March 1867 Congress began by passing the Reconstruction Acts, which divided the ten unreconstructed states (except Tennessee, which had already ratified the Fourteenth Amendment) into five military districts, each headed by a commander whose responsibilities included overseeing the writing of new constitutions that provided for enfranchisement of all adult males.

Only after ratifying the new state constitution and the Fourteenth Amendment would a state be considered reconstructed and readmitted to the Union. In addition, Congress passed several laws to restrict Johnson's power to undermine congressional policy. In response, Johnson removed military officers who were enforcing the Reconstruction Act and fired his secretary of war. Shortly thereafter Congress began impeachment proceedings against Johnson, ultimately coming within one vote of conviction.

In 1869 Congress passed the Fifteenth Amendment, which broadened the Fourteenth Amendment's protection of black voting rights, stating that no citizen could be denied the vote on the basis of race, color, or "previous condition of servitude." It was ratified in 1870. In addition, Congress passed the Civil Rights Act of 1875, which barred discrimination by hotels, theaters, and railroads. The act, however, was rarely enforced.

The Supreme Court and Reconstruction

The Supreme Court, which had been largely silent during the war years, became active during this period, facilitating a retreat from Reconstruction by overturning many congressional measures. In *Bradwell* v. *Illinois* (1873) the Court ruled against a female attorney who claimed that in prohibiting her from practicing law because of her gender, Illinois had violated the "privileges and immunities" clause of the Fourteenth Amendment.

The following day the Court further narrowed the Fourteenth Amendment's scope in the Slaughterhouse cases (1873), rejecting the argument that the Fourteenth Amendment had transformed citizenship by making it the federal government's responsibility. In *United States* v. *Cruikshank* (1876), it ruled that the duty to protect citizens' rights rested with states. In *United States* v. *Reese* (1876), the Court ruled that the Fifteenth Amendment did not guarantee citizens the right to vote, but listed the grounds impermissible for denying the vote. Southern states now had a clear path toward the disfranchisement of black voters.

Freedpeople During Reconstruction The first decision facing former slaves was often whether to stay on the plantation or to move. In general, the choice depended on the disposition of the former master: if a master had been mean or violent, few of his former slaves were likely to remain; if the master had been fair, however, former slaves did often stay. Southern whites exaggerated the number of black men who refused to work after emancipation as a supporting argument for black inferiority, but these numbers were in fact low. Many freedwomen, however, refused to work in the fields any longer after emancipation, choosing instead to remain at home with their children.

To some freedpeople, emancipation meant the freedom to move about, either because it had been prohibited or because they wished to search for family members who had been sold away during slavery. The Reconstruction era produced many touching stories of ex-slaves who traveled thousands of miles, with very little information about their relatives' whereabouts, to reunite with family members. Others found no success in their searches.

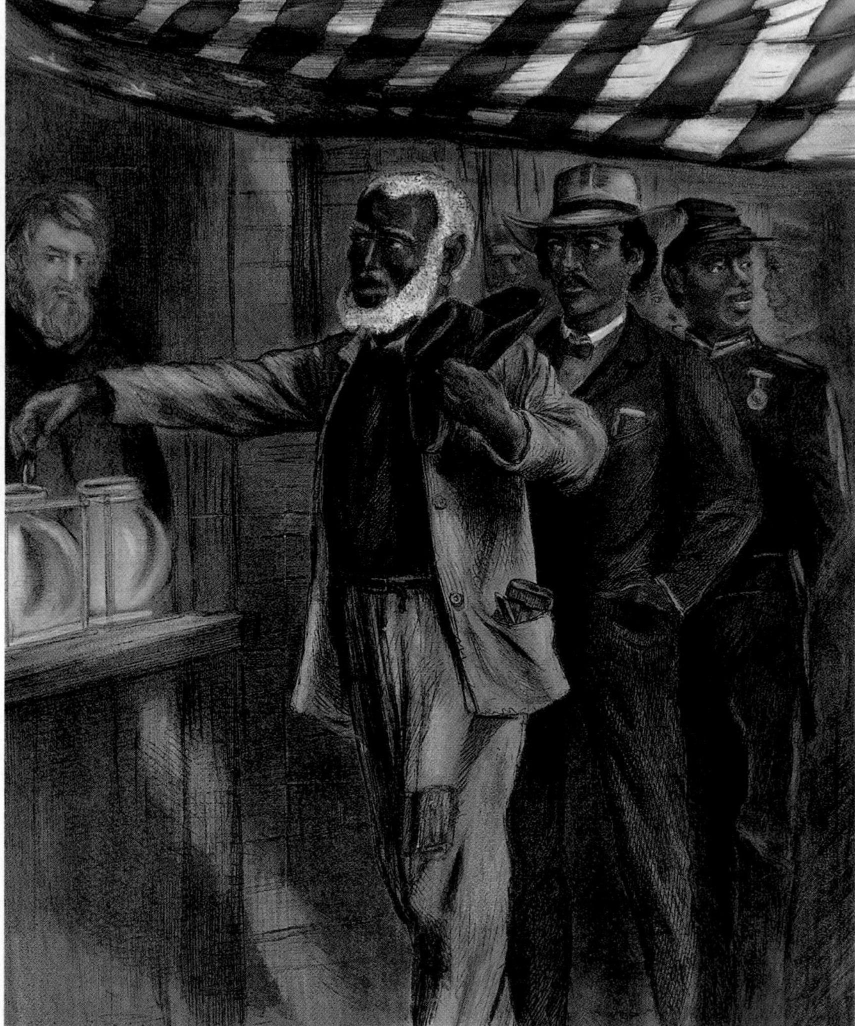

Above: Hiram Rhoades Revels (1822-1901) was the son of former slaves. He became a Methodist minister, an educator, and the first African American in the United States Senate. *CORBIS*
Right: A.R. Waud's 1867 illustration, *The First Vote,* shows recently freed African American men going to the polls for the first time in a state election in the South. *CORBIS/Bettmann*

Blacks, denied literacy during slavery, also sought education, often paying for it themselves. By 1877 more than 600,000 African Americans had enrolled in elementary schools throughout the South. The Freedmen's Bureau founded more than 4000 schools, including Howard University, and many benevolent organizations, black and white, offered education. The American Missionary Association founded seven colleges, including Fisk and Atlanta universities.

Freedpeople established other black institutions, especially churches, that profoundly affected African American history. As slaves, blacks had been forced to worship in their masters' churches. After emancipation freedpeople founded their own churches or moved to black denominations, which served as social and political centers in the black community. Ministers often became community leaders, a practice that continues to this day.

Freedpeople also knew that land meant independence and that they were entitled to some of the lands of their former owners. Early in the war, as the U.S. Navy approached South Carolina, Confederates abandoned their lands on the Sea Islands. Freedpeople immediately lobbied for ownership of the land, insisting that it was rightfully theirs after generations of forced servitude. Instead, the U.S. government implemented the Port Royal Experiment, in which freedpeople labored in the abandoned Sea Island lands as wage workers. Eventually, Gen. William T. Sherman issued Special Order No. 15, which gave the land to the freedpeople. President Johnson, however, rescinded the order, and the land reverted to its original owners. One of Reconstruction's great failings is that the U.S. government did not effectively redistribute land after the Civil War.

Most freedpeople were unable to buy land and instead rented it for farming. Freedmen's Bureau agents, many of whom wanted to change the Southern economy by introducing Northern concepts such as wage labor, needed to retain enough of the old system to ensure stability. To do this efficiently, Freedmen's Bureau agents developed work contracts, which, in the cash-poor South, would promise the slave a certain wage in exchange for crops. Although intended to mediate disputes, bureau agents often sided with the former master. The Freedmen's Bureau grew less active after 1866, leaving tenants and planters to find their own way. Thus, contracts between former slaves and masters were not enforced, and slaves often depended on the good will of their former owners.

Freedpeople also took advantage of the franchise, voting almost unanimously for Republican candidates in the 1866 congressional elections. Freedpeople also joined governments. Largely because of large black turnout and because Congress banned many former Confederates from politics, the Republican Party won control of many Southern constitutional conventions. Of the 1000 Republican delegates to constitutional conventions throughout the South, 265 were black.

Participation in government among blacks was greatest in state and local governments, where many attained high rank. Francis Cardozo was a member of South Carolina's constitutional convention and later served as state secretary of the treasury and as South Carolina's secretary of state. In Louisiana P. B. S. Pinchback became the first black governor in U.S. history. He also served as lieutenant governor and he was elected to both the U.S. Senate and the U.S. House of Representatives. Blanche K. Bruce was a U.S. senator from Mississippi, as was Hiram Revels. In all, 16 blacks served in the U.S. Congress during Reconstruction.

Born in the years following the Civil War, the Ku Klux Klan was a secret terrorist organization that opposed Reconstruction and equal rights for blacks and, eventually, Jews and Catholics. This klansman, photographed in 1868, was from Tennessee; although the Klan started in the South, by the 1920s it had spread as far north as New Jersey. *Tennessee State Museum Collection; copy photography by June Dorman*

Although whites who sought to disfranchise blacks justified their actions by claiming that they had been subjected to incompetent "Negro rule," blacks constituted the majority in only two state conventions, and only in South Carolina's lower house were black representatives a majority. In many ways the biracial coalitions of which most Republican governments were composed made progressive changes, such as creating state-funded public schools and a fairer tax system, outlawing discrimination in public transportation, and ending the death penalty.

Opposition to Reconstruction

As Reconstruction was implemented, a struggle began in the South over the new social order. On one side were the freedpeople and their allies, who wanted to participate in a free society. On the other side were white elites and their followers, who wanted to restore the old order. Many whites – even those who had not owned slaves before the Civil War – found it difficult to imagine a society in which blacks had the same rights as they.

Reconstruction inspired deep resentment among Southern whites. Former Confederates were bitter about losing the war and facing their new prospects. They believed that white Republicans were race traitors, and they objected to the high taxes that Republicans imposed to pay for Reconstruction. Many believed that Reconstruction politics and the politicians who practiced them were corrupt. Though Southerners did not have a defined course, to restore white rule meant white unity. In states with white majorities, convincing white Democrats to vote Democratic was enough to eliminate Republican rule, and by 1871 Democrats had taken back Tennessee, North Carolina, Virginia, and Georgia.

In other states, however, where Republican rule depended on interracial coalitions, white Democrats were determined to convince some people not to vote, often through the violence and intimidation of such terrorist organizations as the Ku Klux Klan, which was founded in late 1865. Often led by the most prominent whites in a community, Klan members concealed themselves in white robes and hoods and often acted at night, beating, LYNCHING, burning, or merely threatening.

Problems existed between the elite planters, who were almost unanimously Democrats, and the Republicans, who represented three main groups: freedpeople, carpetbaggers (as Northern republicans were called, supposedly because they had come South with all their possessions in carpetbags), and scalawags, those white Southerners who supported Reconstruction. Wherever possible, white Southerners reasserted themselves and their control; forcing blacks to stop voting was their primary tool to regain control of the South. In addition, whites still exercised a great deal of economic control over blacks, who usually had to work for whites. During this period many blacks were told explicitly, "If you vote, don't come back to work."

Another method of increasing the dependence of blacks on whites was sharecropping, in which a farmer provided a tenant land and materials in exchange for a share of the crop. Although sharecropping began as a way to maximize land under cultivation and extend credit in a credit-poor region, it relegated many freedpeople and poor whites to a state of virtual peonage. Sometimes the conditions in which peonage and sharecropping put blacks were even worse materially than slavery.

End of Reconstruction

The country had been in an economic depression since around 1873, and white Northern attention turned from the plight of black people in the South to the national economy. State by state, Southern Democrats began to take control of local governments, working to reinstate the conditions of the antebellum South. Southern white supremacists believed, correctly, that Northern whites would no longer enforce Reconstruction policy. They began to subjugate blacks again, reinstating the Black Codes. Many Southern states began to pass segregation or JIM CROW laws.

For many the Compromise of 1877 marks the end of Reconstruction. In the presidential election of 1876, Republican Rutherford B. Hayes and Democrat Samuel J. Tilden were virtually deadlocked. Tilden won the popular vote, but Republicans had control of South Carolina, Florida, and Louisiana, thus giving them control of the electoral college. Because each party in those three states had competing electors, however, Congress needed to decide the election. Hayes, the incumbent, appointed an electoral commission, which, with one more Republican than Democrat, declared him the winner.

The Democrats and the Republicans had worked out a deal, however, in which the Democrats conceded the White House in exchange for "Home Rule" in the critical three states. In a meeting that, ironically, took place in the black-owned Wormly House Hotel, the Republicans agreed. The remaining military presence in the three states departed, and Republican rule crumbled: the Democrats had won back the South. Though it would take until the 1890s for them to finish the job, the white supremacists were well on their way to what Southerners referred to as "Redemption."

Historians have presented differing interpretations of the legacy of Reconstruction. Many historians now argue that Reconstruction fundamentally changed how the United States defined citizenship, as well as the way in which U.S. citizens perceive the power and role of the federal government. The Bill of Rights, for instance, was created to prevent the federal government from infringing on the rights of the people. The Thirteenth, Fourteenth, and Fifteenth Amendments, however, placed the federal government in the role of protector of citizens' rights. This new concept of federal power and responsibility provided a framework for the Civil Rights Movement, which, a century later, finally realized what Reconstruction had begun.

Robert Fay

See Also

Slavery in the United States; Abolitionism in the United States; Black Codes in the United States; Bruce, Blanche Kelso; Cardozo, Francis Louis; Civil War, American; Du Bois, William Edward Burghardt (W. E. B.); Fifteenth Amendment to the United States Constitution; Fisk University; Fourteenth Amendment to the United States Constitution; Free Blacks in the United States, 1619 to 1863; Miscegenation; New Orleans, Louisiana; Pinchback, Pinckney Benton Stewart; Revels, Hiram Rhoades; Thirteenth Amendment of the United States Constitution and the Emancipation Proclamation; Black Church, The.

North America

Redding, Jay Saunders

(b. October 13, 1906, Wilmington, Del.; d. March 2, 1988, Ithaca, N.Y.), African American writer, social critic, and educator.

Jay Saunders Redding grew up in a middle-class family in Wilmington, Delaware. He received his Ph.B. (bachelor of philosophy) in 1928 and his M.A. in 1932 from Brown University. Redding taught English at a number of colleges and universities, including MOREHOUSE COLLEGE (1928-1931), Louisville Municipal College (1934-1936), and Southern University in Louisiana (1936-1938), where he was department chair.

In 1939 Redding published his first book, *To Make a Poet Black*, in which he trained a critical eye on AFRICAN AMERICAN LITERATURE and produced a unique study. As a result of this scholarship he received a fellowship from the Rockefeller Foundation to study the life of blacks in the South. The product of his study was the semiautobiographical book *No Day of Triumph* (1942). After publishing this book Redding gained a reputation as a scholar of and spokesperson for both the accomplishments and tribulations of African Americans. In addition to this landmark work, he wrote several other studies including *They Came in Chains: Americans from Africa* (1950) and *The Negro* (1967).

Redding returned to teaching in 1943, taking a professorship at the Hampton Institute, where he remained until 1966. He also taught at George Washington University (1968-1970) and Cornell University (1975-1988). Besides his scholarly work, Redding wrote for many national publications, including the *Atlantic Monthly* and the *Saturday Review*. He received many awards, including two Guggenheim fellowships and a Ford Foundation fellowship, and numerous honorary degrees.

SEE ALSO
Hampton University.

North America

Redding, Otis

(b. September 9, 1941, Dawson, Ga.; d. December 10, 1967, Madison, Wis.), African American singer and songwriter who played a key role in the rise of SOUL MUSIC during the 1960s, but who attained his greatest success only after his premature death.

Otis Redding's life is the stuff of pop-music tragedy. From an early age he clearly had musical talent, first as a drummer, then as a singer. But his family was poor, and he had to endure a series of odd jobs and struggle to make ends meet before he got his big break in 1963, an opportunity to record for MEMPHIS, TENNESSEE-based STAX RECORDS. His career unfolded in a steep upward arc, culminating with a triumphant performance at the 1967 Monterey Pop Festival. Then – in an instant – it was over. Redding died in December of that year when his chartered plane crashed near Madison, Wisconsin. Since his death Redding has been hailed as perhaps the quintessential male soul singer. But fame proved far more elusive during his lifetime.

Redding was born to a poor Georgia family and learned to play drums in school. On Sundays he played behind the various gospel groups that performed on local radio station WIBB. In 1957 he dropped out of high school in order to support his family, taking a variety of menial jobs and occasional gigs as a musician. He began to concentrate on his singing and entered a number of local amateur contests. Redding's early singing style was in the tradition of such rock 'n' roll shouters as LITTLE RICHARD. In 1961 he made his recording debut, on a small Macon, Georgia, label.

But his big break did not come until two years later, when he was working in the band of guitarist Johnny Jenkins – and serving as the band's chauffeur. During a recording session at Stax Records he had the chance to record a featured vocal, the ballad "These Arms of Mine," which became a RHYTHM AND BLUES (R&B) hit and earned Redding a Stax recording contract. Redding's vocals matured from his earlier shouting style to one that conveyed the emotion behind his lyrics by means of an expressive, hoarse singing voice that was grounded in gospel sonorities.

To black listeners, Redding was one of the definitive examples of the Memphis Soul sound. His live performances were legendary for their intensity and emotional fervor. During 1965 and 1966 Redding scored several R&B hits – including "Mr. Pitiful," "I've Been Loving You Too Long," a version of the Rolling Stones's hit "(I Can't Get No) Satisfaction," and his now-famous rendition of "Try a Little Tenderness" – but none "crossed over" to the white popular-music charts. According to Norm N. Nite's *Rock On Almanac* (1989), Redding only appeared on the American pop charts once in his lifetime – in October 1966, with his now little-remembered recording "Fa-Fa-Fa-Fa-Fa (Sad Song)."

In 1967, however, Redding's incandescent appearance at the Monterey Pop Festival put him on a trajectory for pop-music stardom. His musical promise is evident in many of his compositions – including "Respect," which became a much bigger hit in the hands of Aretha Franklin, and "(Sittin' on) The Dock of the Bay," which he recorded just three days before his death at age 26. Four members of the Bar-Kays, Redding's backup band, also died in the crash. With the posthumous release of "(Sittin' on) The Dock of the Bay," Redding charted his first Number One pop single.

SEE ALSO
Franklin, Aretha Louise; Gospel Music.

North America

Reed, Ishmael

(b. February 22, 1938, Chattanooga, Tenn.), African American novelist, journalist, and poet; satirist of Western culture and critic of Eurocentrism.

Ishmael Reed was raised and educated in Buffalo, New York, where he attended the University of Buffalo from 1956 to 1960. He began his studies in the night school division but was moved to the day school when an English teacher saw talent in his short satirical story "Something Pure."

After moving to the Lower East Side of New York in 1962, Reed began to write professionally. As a journalist he wrote for the *Empire Star Weekly* and later edited the weekly *Advance*. Reed was also involved in the creation of the *East Village Other*, a prototype of modern underground newspapers. In 1967 he published his first novel, *The Free-Lance Pallbearers*, a parody of RALPH ELLISON's bestseller *Invisible Man*. That same year he moved to California's San Francisco Bay Area, whose cultural diversity has greatly influenced his writing. With his 1972 novel *Mumbo Jumbo* he presented a countermythology, dubbed HooDooism, that challenged the myth that Western culture must be glorified at the expense of all other cultures. He used satire and parody to emphasize and advocate multiculturalism, or the importance of all cultures as opposed to the hegemony of one.

Reed has also written poetry and essays, drawing on non-European cultures for his symbolism and further developing his countermythology. His writing and satire form a compelling critique of Eurocentrism, and in his multicultural beliefs he encourages creativity and freedom, not confinement.

SEE ALSO
Literature, African American; San Francisco and Oakland, California.

Latin America and the Caribbean

Reggae,

a style of music that originated in the musically diverse and politically charged climate of JAMAICA during the late 1960s.

Reggae combined the Zionistic beliefs of RASTAFARIANS with loping rhythms and rich melodic textures. Reggae's freshness appealed to both casual listeners and dedicated ideologues worldwide, generating a fan base that included Indonesians and Moroccans,

Parisians and Brazilians, Irish schoolchildren and American teens. Michael Manley, former prime minister of Jamaica, favored a political explanation of reggae's appeal: "Among other things, reggae is the spontaneous sound of a local revolutionary impulse. But revolution is a universal category. It is this, possibly, which sets reggae apart, even to the international ear."

Since the "discovery" of Jamaica by Christopher Columbus in 1494, a range of foreign influences – African, European, and American – have defined the culture and ethnic composition of the island. Reggae's forefathers spoke in numerous musical dialects, including Caribbean calypso, English balladic form, and African rhythms. While Jamaica's history led to reggae's musical synthesis, it also provided reggae with its content: the new music often protested the colonialism and exploitation that characterized the last 500 years of the island's history.

Reggae grew most directly from the rhythm and blues (R&B) music of the United States. In the 1950s Jamaicans often listened to R&B songs that were broadcast from Miami, Florida. Local musicians soon covered songs by acts such as Fats Domino and Louis Jordan and wrote new tunes in a similar style. The fusion of R&B with Jamaican music, or *mento*, yielded a new form called ska. Jamaican promoters such as Duke Reid and Clement Dodd recorded local acts, broadcasting ska over large sound systems at outdoor dance parties. Unlike R&B, which emphasized the first and third beats of a measure, ska hit the second and fourth, or "back" beats. In the early 1960s ska evolved into rocksteady, a slower, more bass-driven form.

Amid a quickly changing Jamaican political climate, rocksteady soon developed into reggae. During the 1950s and 1960s many Jamaicans migrated to the cities – especially Kingston, the capital – in search of better job opportunities. The demographic shift contributed to the proliferation of Rastafarianism. Inspired by the Black Nationalist philosophy of Marcus Garvey, the Rastafarian movement began in Jamaica early in the twentieth century as a way to cope with the oppressive conditions of colonial Jamaica. Rastafarians adopted the Bible as a sacred text but rejected Christ, couching their faith in the divinity of Africa, the homeland. A return to Ethiopia – whether spiritual or actual – became the highest goal, and Rastafarians considered Ethiopian king Haile Selassie I a messiah.

The apocalyptic vision of Rastafarians appealed to disillusioned immigrants, who had not found the bounty they expected in Kingston. Rural newcomers adopted the religion; the religion, in turn, adopted rocksteady as a voice. Since many of the rural immigrants introduced African musical traditions that had survived in the countryside – and since rocksteady, like ska, invited musical experimentation – reggae soon emerged. The importation of new recording technology from England as well as increased overcrowding in the ghettoes of Kingston also contributed to the synthesis of reggae. In 1968 a band called Toots and the Maytals recorded "Do the Reggay," giving name to the emerging style.

Reggae slowed rocksteady as rocksteady had slowed ska. The languorous new form included a more robust and driving bass sound that gave the drummer freedom to "play around the beat." In reggae, pianists and guitarists often emphasized beats in unison, producing sparser melodies but richer tones and rhythms. And in reggae the lyrical message had changed. Rocksteady's romantic lyrics, which often derived from local proverbs, gave way to frontal descriptions of ghetto life and biting indictments of economic and political oppression. Reggae retained some of rocksteady's romance, however. In addition to singing about street toughs or "rude boys," reggae artists described Rastafarian religious rapture and earthly despair in a manner analogous to American blues and spirituals.

Jamaican disc jockeys quickly adopted the new music, blasting local recordings over impressive sound systems at outdoor dances. By separating parts of the recorded mix, adding echo effects, and speaking or "toasting" along with the music, DJs assumed an active role in the development of reggae's sound. Toasting became a reggae convention that pointed toward the advent of rap in the United States.

In the 1970s reggae garnered international attention, largely due to the stirring riffs, powerful lyrics, and riveting performances of Bob Marley and the Wailers. In the eyes of many Marley became emblematic of reggae and its Rastafarian influences. A 1972 film about the reggae lifestyle, *The Harder They Come*, added to reggae's popularity. *The Harder They Come* starred musician Jimmy Cliff as an outlaw and pop star and featured a driving reggae soundtrack. The film became a mainstay of bohemian movie theaters in the United States, adding vibrant visuals to the captivating aural picture that Bob Marley created through his music.

Like rock 'n' roll and rap, reggae was soon appropriated by white musicians and adored by white fans. In the mid-1970s its influence appeared in the songs of Paul Simon and Eric Clapton; in the late 1970s and early 1980s it flavored new wave and punk. Rastafarianism's apocalyptic ideology attracted punk rockers, who adopted the rhythmic emphasis of ska-based music in many of their frenzied compositions.

Meanwhile, African American fans of reggae – many of whom came from the West Indies themselves – took the music in other directions. DJs toasted faster and faster until the resulting "dancehall" reggae seemed an analog of rap. Reggae fans soon globalized a provincial sound, and in the 1980s and 1990s the international music of "world beat" followed the formula of reggae's wide success.

Since the genesis of reggae was grounded so thoroughly in the Rastafarian movement – and since its portrayal of alienation captivated white Americans in the Nixon era – the music's relevance lessened with the passing of time. While reggae continues to influence the vocabulary of other musical styles, its politico-religious aspect, as epitomized by Bob Marley, has become a historical – rather than living – form. Many fans, however, celebrate this history and laud the staying power of reggae's message. Writers Steven Davis and Peter Simon proclaim: "Reggae is a philosophy that heals. The mini-trance produced by good roots reggae is Jamaican psychic hygiene for our apocalyptic era."

Eric Bennett

See Also

Blues, The; Domino, Antoine ("Fats"), Jr.; Garvey, Marcus Mosiah; Kingston, Jamaica; Spirituals, African American; World Music, World Beat, and the Re-Africanization of Latin American Popular Music.

Latin America and the Caribbean

Regla de Palo, a Bantu-derived Cuban religion that was originally practiced by Congo slaves in Cuba's eastern Oriente province and that has gained popularity with many throughout the island.

Along with the Yoruba-derived religion of Regla de Ocha or Lucumí (more commonly known as Santería), Palo is the second most popular African-derived religious system in Cuba (*see* Religions, African, in Latin America and the Caribbean). Unlike Santería, which has been studied much more extensively, Palo does not feature orisha worship, an altar, or characteristic colors, clothing, or stylized dances dedicated to particular spirits. Both religions feature drumming, music, possession trance, and animal sacrifice as well as systems of divination. Palo divination is ordinarily conducted with an *npaca menzo*, an ox horn mounted with a mirror on its blunt end, used in conjunction with white plates and candle wax, or with *chamalongos*, seven pieces of dried coconut shell that are thrown on the ground. (Multiples of seven hold an important place in Palo numerology.)

The word *palo* means "sticks" or "branches of trees," which adherents (known as *Paleros*) believe to hold magical powers.

Bantu Origins

The transatlantic slave trade of the sixteenth through the nineteenth century brought primarily Africans of Yoruba and Bantu origin to Cuba. These major African groups, known respectively in Cuba as the Lucumí and the Congo, have had an enormous influence on Cuban culture as a whole (*see* African Ethnic Groups in Latin America and the Caribbean). The Bantus are not a single ethnic group; this name was applied to a rather extensive grouping of sub-Saharan African peoples. The Bantu who were brought to Cuba are thought to have resided primarily in the areas of present-day Angola, Democratic Republic of the Congo, and Namibia. It is believed that before their enslavement, this particular group of Bantus did not have contact with the Yorubas, who are a linguistically and culturally separate group of people living farther north in present-day Nigeria. At least 27 different ethnic subgroups of Bantu peoples in Cuba have been identified, including the Quicongos, Quimbandeiros, and Nganguleros from the inner area of the Congo basin. During the initial period of Spanish colonization most slaves brought to Cuba, particularly to eastern Cuba, were Bantus. The Yorubas generally came to Cuba later, in the early nineteenth century, after the fall of the city-state Kingdom of Oyo had left them vulnerable to slave traders.

Nzambi and the Muertos

Cuban Paleros believe that the power of Nzambi, a creator god, resides in all natural elements of the world (such as rocks, trees, and people) and within the spirits of the ancestors, the *Nfumbi* and the *Npungo*, who served Nzambi during their earthly lives. The Nfumbi are the spirits of recent generations of deceased ancestors, who, as a result of their more recent lives, are believed to be in closer proximity to their human descendants. The Npungo are ancestors of long ago, who are believed to be unified now with the primordial forces that birthed them: namely, the forces of nature – Nzambi himself.

The spirits of Palo are more closely identified with forces of nature than the orishas of Santería, who for the most part were at one time archetypal human beings and thus have comparatively more stable personalities and characteristics that can be directed. In contrast, the spirits of Palo are perceived to be more chaotic and relatively difficult to control, although a talented Palo priest is able to corral them. During Palo rituals, which include polyrhythmic drumming, music, and dances, adherents can become possessed by natural forces and by the *muertos* (spirits of dead ancestors). Such possession is not considered to be worship of these elements but rather worship of Nzambi, the creator who animates everything and mediates all relationships.

Nganga

The goal of Palo is to control events by corralling the forces of nature. This is accomplished by concentrating the powers of Nzambi within the magical center of the religion's rituals, the *nganga*. The nganga is a clay pot or iron cauldron often placed in the home of the Palero. It contains many things: earth taken from sites of social and natural significance, such as a courthouse, a graveyard, or a volcano; objects of nature, such as sticks and stones; animal and human bones, the latter often acquired from deceased Paleros; and, in the center, a *matari*, or stone. Sometimes a crucifix is included, and such ngangas are termed "Christian." Since Nzambi is believed to animate all elements of the natural order, these objects must be present in the nganga in order for Nzambi to reside there. It is common for Palo ceremonies to begin with a greeting to the nganga, which is considered central to religious ceremonies. The nganga is a Cuban innovation necessitated by the conditions of slavery, which did not allow enslaved Paleros sufficient mobility: in Africa religious practitioners simply visited specific trees or stones believed to be manifestations of Nzambi. It is believed that the nganga must be "fed" with the blood of live animals, which are ritually sacrificed over the nganga by the *tata nganga*, a priest of Palo.

Initiation

Initiation is conducted not on the basis of enthusiasm or desire on the part of the *ngayu* (a potential Palo initiate), but rather because of a need to solve a particular problem in the ngayu's life. During an extensive initiation process the *padrino* (godfather) diagnoses the ngayu through divination and brings the ngayu before the nganga, where promises are made that must be kept. After a time the ceremony of *rayamiento en palo* is performed, in which the ngayu may be marked with three small vertical incisions on the tongue and over each breast or shoulder. At the conclusion of this initiation ceremony, during which the ngayu is said to be "born of the nganga," the tata nganga gives the new Palero his own nganga and reveals to him the secrets of Palo, which are well guarded. The new Palero must then observe certain rules during a period of apprenticeship. When it is determined that the new Palero has kept his promises and grown in the religion, he is considered a full member.

Paleros have a different relationship to their spirits than do the adherents of Santería, who must appeal to the sometimes-fickle orishas, submit to their discretion, and await their appearance and assistance, which may or may not be tendered. By contrast, it is the Paleros who are masters of the nganga, which is sometimes referred to as the Palero's "dog" or "slave." For this reason, it is often said in Cuba that if you don't mind waiting for results, consult with the Roman Catholic Church or with the orishas; if you want immediate results, go to a Palero. During palo rituals, Paleros command spirits, including Nzambi, to manifest themselves in the nganga and to perform requested deeds. A reciprocal bargaining then takes place between the Palero and the nganga: if the spirits are to follow the Palero's wishes, the Palero must "feed" the spirits (through the nganga) according to the pact that has been made between them. Without such a pact, it is believed, the spirit will not act to change events as the Palero requests.

The Palo religious community is not as central to the religion as is the "family" of Santería adherents. Although Palo has an extensive set of *reglas*, or rules, the religion is generally considered to be more flexible regarding the needs of its individual adherents.

Jalane Schmidt

See Also

Oyo, Early Kingdom of; Catholic Church in Latin America and the Caribbean; Orishas.

North America

Reid, Ira De A.

(b. July 2, 1901, Clifton Forge, Va.; d. August 15, 1968, Haverford, Pa.), African American sociologist who contributed to an understanding of race relations, labor, and immigration in America.

As a student, Ira Reid earned degrees from three institutions: a B.A. from Morehouse College (1922), an M.A. at the University of Pittsburgh (1925), and a Ph.D. in sociology from Columbia University (1929).

In his role as a sociologist, Reid contributed to an understanding of race relations, adult education, Southern sharecropping, and immigration. Among his six books are *Negro Membership in American Labor Unions* (1930), *Adult Education Among Negroes* (1936), *Sharecroppers All* (coauthored with Arthur Raper, 1941), and *The Negro Immigrant*, posthumously published in 1969. He lectured and advised the United States government and such social service agencies as the American Friends Service Committee on a range of subjects, including education, human resources, youth services, and social security.

In his academic appointments as a professor of sociology, Reid was a forerunner in the desegregation of the faculties in Northern higher education by scholars from historically black colleges in the South. At Atlanta University Reid served as professor of sociology (1934-1946) and department chair (1944-1946). Working under his mentor, W. E. B. Du Bois, Reid was managing editor (1940-1944) and, later, editor of *Phylon*, the scholarly journal on race and culture published by African American scholars. He also produced adult-education radio programs for working-class listeners in Atlanta. Following a visiting professorship sponsored by the American Friends Service Committee at Haverford College (1946-1947), Reid returned to Haverford as professor and chair of the sociology department (1948-1966), becoming the college's first African American professor.

During the McCarthy era Reid was erroneously labeled a Communist by a

Pennsylvania politician in 1949, leading to the seizure of his passport by the U.S. State Department. Reid joined the Society of Friends (Quakers) in 1950. In honor of his scholarship, teaching, and contributions to peace and justice in the United States and abroad, Reid received honorary doctorates from Haverford and Morehouse. He died from cancer on August 15, 1968.

Harold Weaver

SEE ALSO
Du Bois, William Edward Burghardt (W. E. B.); Morehouse College; Communist Party USA, African Americans and the.

Latin America and the Caribbean

Reid, V. S. **(b. May 1, 1913, Kingston, Jamaica; d. August 25, 1987, Kingston, Jamaica), Jamaican novelist, short story writer, and journalist known for his use of Jamaican history and dialect in his fiction.**

Victor Stafford Reid (often called V. S. or Vic) is one of the pioneering figures in the Anglo-Caribbean literary tradition. Reid was born in Kingston, Jamaica, in 1913. His father was in the shipping business, and Reid was educated by private tutors and at Kingston Technical High School. He worked as a farm overseer, an advertising executive, and a newspaper and magazine reporter and editor all before beginning his career as a writer. Reid worked as a journalist throughout much of his writing career and was widely respected as editor of the newspaper *Daily Gleaner,* the political-cultural journal *Public Opinion,* and the newsmagazine *Spotlight.* But he is still best remembered for his historically based fiction, particularly his influential first novel, *New Day* (1949).

New Day is the story of Johnny Campbell, the oldest member of a Jamaican family that closely resembles the Manleys, prominent Jamaican politicians (*see* MICHAEL MANLEY and Norman Manley). *New Day* is often praised for being the first West Indian novel to attempt to recreate an authentic West Indian dialect, which has since become a major feature of Caribbean literature. But it is also significant for its use of Caribbean history. As Johnny thinks back over events that took place during his long life, the novel becomes a first-person retelling of Jamaican history – from the 1865 Morant Bay rebellion (*see* SLAVE REBELLIONS IN LATIN AMERICA AND THE CARIBBEAN) to a new constitution in 1944. As it explores Jamaican history and culture, the novel celebrates Jamaicans' struggles for independence, and *New Day* is recognized as the first nationalistic Jamaican novel.

Reid's second novel, *The Leopard* (1958), was another historical reconstruction – this time of events in KENYA during the MAU MAU REBELLION. The work portrays the negative consequences of colonialism for one multiracial family. In his later novels Reid returned to Jamaican history for his subjects: *The Jamaicans* (1976) told about the leader of a pre-maroon guerrilla group, and *Nanny-Town* (1983) focused on the famous maroon leader. Reid also wrote a biography of prime minister Norman Manley, *The Horses of Morning,* and a history of Jamaican architecture. In addition to these works, he wrote three historical novels for children: *Sixty-Five* (1960), again about the Morant Bay rebellion; *The Young Warriors* (1967), again about the maroons; and *Peter of Mount Ephraim* (1971), about the 1831 SAMUEL SHARPE slave uprising.

Reid once claimed that his work "is necessarily for the next generation." This belief explains his commitment to creating a Jamaican history and national legacy in all of his writings. While Reid was eventually overshadowed by other Caribbean writers, his accomplishments were well recognized during his lifetime. In 1959 he became the first Jamaican to win a Guggenheim Fellowship. He was also awarded the Institute of Jamaica's Silver and Gold Musgrave Medals (1955, 1978), the Order of Jamaica (1980), and the Norman Manley Award for Excellence in Literature (1981). At the time of his death Reid had just published the first section of a projected three-volume "bio-poem," *The Kingston Chronicles.* Reid's publication legacy stands as a significant contribution to West Indian literature in general and to Jamaican literature in particular.

Lisa Clayton Robinson

SEE ALSO
Literature, English Language, Caribbean; Jamaica; Manley, Norman Washington.

Latin America and the Caribbean

Religions, African, in Brazil, **religions that initially arose and developed during the more than 350 years of official and unofficial intensive importation of what were classified as "Sudanese" and "Bantu" African slaves to BRAZIL. Practiced by millions of Brazilians, these are all spirit possession or mediumistic religions. They are found in the capital cities and ports along Brazil's extensive Atlantic coast as well as throughout the vast interior backcountry, towns, and villages.**

Brazil's Sudanese slaves came from north of the equator, primarily from West Africa. The Bantu came from south of the equator, primarily from ANGOLA, the Congo, and to a lesser degree, MOZAMBIQUE (*see* TRANSATLANTIC SLAVE TRADE and AFRICAN ETHNIC GROUPS IN LATIN AMERICA AND THE CARIBBEAN). Early evidence of their practices in Brazil includes references by the seventeenth-century Bahian poet Gregório de Mattos to *calundus* (a generic term for African ritual dances) in Salvador, the current capital of the state of BAHIA. There are also descriptions in eighteenth-century Inquisition records discovered by anthropologist Luiz Mott of a religious sect of African slaves called *Acotundá,* which flourished in a rural mining district in the state of MINAS GERAIS in the 1740s.

Today Brazil boasts an enormous variety of African-derived or African-influenced religions with literally millions of followers (*see* CANDOMBLÉ and UMBANDA). In each, adepts believe in a pantheon of gods or spirits that are summoned in ritual contexts, very often by drums and chanting, and that possess those who are mediums. The possessing gods or spirits then dance or communicate verbally to the community through the entranced mediums, teaching and resolving individual and community problems. The leader of the religious group may also invoke the gods or spirits for private divination consultations. Here, an adept's or client's spiritual development or problems of health, family, finances, or social relations are diagnosed. This can lead either to initiation and religious involvement or to the performance of healing and sorcery rites. Some of the religions also have complex devotional practices informed by rich African mythologies.

All these religions, having descended from the practices of African slaves in Brazil, reflect varying degrees of fidelity to the original African models. Some are remarkably faithful. But all include varying degrees of syncretism (a mixing, merging, or integrating of elements of more than one religion). It is a syncretism of diverse African but also Native Amerindian tribal sources, as well as popular Roman Catholic beliefs and practices – especially concerning the saints, as in what has been called the "cult of the saints" (*see,* for example, NOSSA SENHORA DO ROSÁRIO).

In addition, in the late nineteenth century another influence on some African-Brazilian religions emerged in the two major Brazilian metropolises of Rio de Janeiro and São Paulo. This was a European form of Spiritualism, a mediumistic religion originating in America, which revolved around seances and communication with the dead. In Brazil it was called *Espiritismo* (Spiritualism) or *Kardecismo* (Kardec-ism) after its French reformer, Allan Kardec (the alias of Hippolyte Léon Rivail). Kardec integrated Spiritualism and spirit-communicated doctrines with Eastern ideas of reincarnation, Swedenborgian philosophy, Christian moral principles, and social-evolutionary dogma. Kardecismo was quickly adopted by Brazil's wealthy and intellectual elite. By the 1920s and 1930s, however, Kardecismo was affecting and being affected by the pariah-class, African-Brazilian sects of *Macumba* in Rio and São Paulo. The result was a new, class-synthesizing or class-mediating continuum of religious forms in these cities, which are referred to under the one umbrella term *Umbanda.*

The Syncretic Character and Geography of African-Brazilian Religions

Viewed broadly in terms of their historical perspective and geographic distribution, three complex syncretic groupings of the African-Brazilian religions can be identified. The first consists of the most African or African-influenced religions, what I will call here the "African religions of Brazil," though they are also shaped by non-African influences. These developed in the coastal port cities. In contrast, the second grouping consists of the most Amerindian or Amerindian-influenced and Indio-Catholic of the mediumistic religions, the so-called "Caboclo religions," though they also manifest African influences to varying degrees. These religions originated in the rural backcountry and villages. The third complex refers to the syncretic wedding of the two, what I call the "African-Caboclo religions." These are centered in urban areas that include both the coastal cities and the larger rural towns. The African-Caboclo religions bridge the ideological and ritual characters of the coastal and rural backcountry traditions, and are the fastest growing of the African-Brazilian religions. All the religions of these three broad groupings have evolved and maintained their areas of influence for centuries, but have also spread to other regions. The emergence and spread of the Umbandas is another important new development. But let us turn first to each of the three groupings.

The African Religions of Brazil

The African religions of Brazil developed in the major urban centers of the African slave trade along the Brazilian coast (e.g., São Luís in the state of Maranhão, Recife in Pernambuco, Salvador in Bahia, Rio in the state of Rio de Janeiro, and Porto Alegre in Rio Grande do Sul). These cities maintained the largest concentrations of African slaves. Originally there were more than 30 different tribal sources for the African religions of Brazil, and as many distinct religions corresponding to each source. Though elements of many of these persist today, the most readily distinguishable influences are those of the Sudanese-speaking Fon and Yoruba of old Dahomey (present-day Benin) and Nigeria, respectively, and the Bantu-speaking Bakongo, Ambundo, and other ethnic groups from Angola, the Republic of the Congo (formerly Zaire), and Mozambique. In Salvador, Bahia, alone there are more than 1000 practicing centers of the *Candomblé* religion, which derives from these African tribal and intertribal sources, and more than 2000 when the syncretic variants of the Candomblés are taken into account. The Candomblés are distinguished according to *nação* (nation, in the sense of ethnic group), such as the *Nagô, Kétu,* and *Ijexá Candomblés* (from the Yoruba); *Jêjê Candomblé* (from the Fon); and the *Angola* and *Congo Candomblés* (from BaKongo, Ambundo, and other Bantu groups of Angola and the Republic of the Congo). The liturgical languages spoken and sung in the Candomblés are called *Nagô* (a Brazilianized Yoruba dialect); *Jêjê* (a Brazilianized dialect of Ewe); and *Angola* (a mixture of Bantu-derived dialects and Portuguese). Their gods are referred to as *orixás* (pronounced *oh-ree-shahs*) in Nagô; *voduns* (pronounced *vo-dunes*) in Jêjê; and *inquices* (or *een-kee-sees*) in Angola. In addition, there is a secret, Yoruba-derived, all-male society devoted to the ancestors called the Culto aos Eguns (Cult to the Ancestors). Its traditional centers are located on the island of Itaparica, near Salvador.

Other African religions in Brazil include the *Tambor de Mina* (Drums of Mina) in the far north (the city of São Luís, Maranhão). This religion takes two forms. The first, a *Mina-Jêjê* form, as in the *Casa das Minas* (House of Minas), is notably of Fon derivation. The second, a *Mina-Nagô* form, as in the *Casa de Nagô* (House of Nagô), syncretizes Fon and Yoruba elements. Also of rich African tradition are the *Xangô* and *Xambá* of the northeast (the city of Recife, Pernambuco), which are of Yoruba derivation. The old *Cabula* (or *Batuque*) of Rio de Janeiro in the southeast was originally of Bantu origin but is now extinct. It was probably the source of the current *Macumba* sects in both Rio and São Paulo. Finally, *Pará* in the far south (the city of Porto Alegre, Rio Grande do Sul) is Yoruba-based, though there are strong Dahomean influences in a variant of Pará (which outsiders call Batuque, a common name for African practices in Brazil).

These religions are all still remarkably very African, emphasizing African languages and deities, possession trance dances, and divination procedures that in many cases are guided by a substantial corpus of African myths. The rituals include complex devotions to the gods and their fetish objects and intensive initiations and animal sacrifices, all accompanied by the intricacies of African drumming. However, again, within the group of African religions and across each group's internal variations, they have maintained their original African source traditions in

ABOVE: Rituals of devotion to the orishas, or deities, incorporate highly stylized costumes and accessories. *Fundação Pierre Verger*

RIGHT: In ceremonies honoring Yemayá, boats transport gifts of flowers, champagne, and perfume to the sea goddess. *Fundação Pierre Verger*

these and other features to varying degrees. The Nagô Candomblé and the Culto aos Eguns of Bahia are considered the most African of the African religions of Brazil.

The Caboclo Religions of Brazil

In contrast, the Caboclo religions of the vast Brazilian hinterland are more predominantly influenced or inspired by Amerindian and Indio-Catholic elements. But it is important to note that in many areas their adherents are not only *mamelucos* (people with white and Indian ancestry), but also black, sometimes predominantly black, African descendants, or *cafusos* (people of black and Indian descent). They are called Caboclo religions because practitioners believe in a pantheon of actual Amerindian spirits or spirits that are stereotypical images of Indians, both of which are called Caboclos. "Caboclo" also refers to the spirits of rural "natives," people born in the Brazilian *sertão* (backcountry), who, like the Indians, are intimately tied to the land, such as the *boiadeiros* (cattle drovers). In some groups "Caboclo" is also applied to a host of other spirits, including rural African "masters" ("experts") of healing and sorcery. Many other features of these religions, such as the healing rites, trance experiences, and music, are also inspired by Amerindian traditions.

At the same time vestiges of African mythology appear in these faiths' conceptualization of the Caboclo spirits and of the folk Catholic saints, which are also foundational to the pantheons of Caboclo religions. Moreover, African terms and principles are often found in the ritual practices of Caboclo religions, as we will see. But again the degree of these Amerindian, Indio-Catholic, and African influences varies across regions and particular religious traditions.

Scanning regionally from north to south, the strongest Amerindian influences in the Caboclo religions are found in *Pajelança*, primarily a healing cult of the northern states of Amazonas, Pará, Maranhão, and northern Piaui. Amerindian elements include, for instance, the extensive ritual use of tobacco smoke and hallucinogenic roots, both considered sacred and therapeutic; the use of gourd rattles (*maracás*) and feathers (of the *arara*, a macaw from the parrot family) to summon familiar spirits, instead of drums; the religious experiences of "trance voyages" (akin to shamanic trance) in addition to spirit possession; and the typical Amerindian healing procedure, in which disease-carrying "objects," such as invisible darts, are sucked out of patients by the leader, or *pajé* (shaman). Finally, the divine pantheons of these religions include not only Caboclos of characteristically Amerindian spirits, but also Amerindian-derived animal and underwater spirits called *companheiros* (companions) or *encantados* (enchanted ones) and the folk Catholic saints.

African influence varies across Pajelança sects, which Mario Andrade distinguishes, broadly, as "Indian" and "Negro" Pajelanças.

LEFT: On the third day of their initiation as *filhos de santo* (sons of the orisha), these novices kneel in prayer, their shaven heads decorated with white chalk. *Fundação Pierre Verger*
ABOVE: Bahia practioner of Candomblé manifests the spirit of Yemayá, orisha of the ocean and mother of many of the Yoruba deities. *Fundação Pierre Verger*

Pantheons of the latter, for instance, in the state of Maranhão, include simplified versions of the Dahomean Fon gods. But even in the Indian Pajelanças there is an African structure to the ritual possession dances, and many adepts may become mediums, as in African traditions, instead of just the shamanic leader alone.

As one moves south through the rural interior of Brazil, the Amerindian influence decreases and manifests in different ways or with different emphases. An example is the *Catimbó* religion, which is widely practiced in the northeastern states of Rio Grande do Norte, Paraiba, Pernambuco, Ceará, and Southern Piaui. Catimbó is composed of some of the Amerindian characteristics of the Pajelança but with a strong measure of European black and white magic. Thus, like Pajelança, Catimbó also emphasizes *curandeirismo* (healing), and leaders draw from a copious Amerindian herbal pharmacopeia. Also, tobacco and hallucinogenic roots such as the *jurema* (*Mimosa hostilis*) are used ritually, as are maracás and arara feathers to invoke spirits. But Catimbó is also dedicated to *feitiçaria* (sorcery), which derives from medieval European spells and rituals. Further, Catimbó practitioners believe in a different kind of pantheon than that of Pajelança. For, in addition to Caboclos and saints, adherents believe in spirits called *mestres* (masters). These are the spirits of deceased Catimbó leaders who are well known for their knowledge of healing and sorcery. They include rural *mestiços* (people of indigenous and European descent) such as *Mestre Carlos* (Master Carlos), *Índios* (Indians) such as *Mestre Itapuã* (the name of the Tupi Indian sun god), and *Africanos* (Africans) such as *Pai Joaquim* (Father Joaquim), a wise old African master. In many Catimbós there is also devotion to and possession by gods with Yoruba names such as Xangó and Ogum. These, too, are called mestres, and adepts refer to them and the spirits who are stereotypical images of Africans as the African line of the Catimbó. Hence, overall, Amerindian influence is smaller in the Catimbó than in the Pajelança, while European and other sources are stronger.

Passing by the state of Bahia, for a moment, we continue south through the *sertão,* or rural backlands, to the southeastern region of Minas Gerais, Espírito Santo, Rio de Janeiro state, and São Paulo state. Here we encounter the Caboclo religions with the least direct Amerindian influences and greatest African-inspired beliefs and practices. These are the *Canjerês, Cabulas,* and rural *Macumbas.* All appear to have derived from very early Bantu religious sects with Angolese and Congolese gods. But today they are Caboclo religions dominated by Caboclo spirits and the saints, though their pantheons also include some of the previous Bantu or Bantu-inspired gods, and there is Bantu influence in their ritual vocabulary and drumming. The Caboclo spirits of these religions also now reflect exclusively stereotypical images of the Indian and rural cowboy heroes, rather than actual Amerindian-derived spirits. One such Caboclo is a chief called by the name of a whole tribe, Tupinambá. And there are also spirits of deceased folkloric figures, including white leaders (Dom Pedro II, the last emperor of Brazil) as well as wise old Africans, such as the *tias Africanas* (African aunts) and Catimbó's Pai Joaquim. Of course, vestiges of Amerindian practices, such as the use of tobacco smoke and the suction of disease-causing objects, are valued in their healing rites. But as in Catimbó, European magic informs other aspects, as it does their sorcery. And adding to the mix, practitioners of these Caboclo religions frequently invoke their own, demonized form of the Yoruba trickster god, Exú, to cause harm and mischief in the lives of others.

Finally, in the state of Bahia, which is sandwiched geographically between the Caboclo religions to the north (the Pajelanças and Catimbós) and to the south (the Canjerês, Cabulas, and rural Macumbas), are Bahia's own *Cultos aos Caboclos* (Caboclo Cults), such as *Piji, Jarê,* and *Bembê.* Like the groups to the north, these religions were influenced by local Amerindian groups, particularly the Kiriri Indians in the case of Piji, and by the regional Cult of the Saints. From the Kiriri Indians, Piji inherited, for example, the ritual use of the hallucinogenic root jurema and added the Kiriri *toré* thump dance used in ceremonies. Also, as elsewhere in the sertão, devotees of Piji make frequent pilgrimages to local shrines of the saints and to charismatic miracle-healers in the region who are believed to be "living saints." Paradoxically, Piji leaders emulate both these virtuous living saints and the powerful sorcerers of their local myths in a fusion that attracts messianic followers.

Yet at the same time Piji is the most African of the Caboclo religions and in that sense resembles the Caboclo sects to the south. Such features as Bantu drumming, African liturgical terms, particular details of animal sacrifices, and initiatory rites that reproduce the preliminary initiatory rites of the African religion of Candomblé characterize many Pijis. Moreover, in addition to the prominent Caboclo spirits, saints, mestres, and encantados of their pantheon, many groups worship serpent spirits. These recall the famous serpent deity *Dã* of the Fon-derived Jêjê Candomblés.

That there is a stronger African influence in the Piji than in the other Caboclo religions is not surprising, since both Sudanese Fon and Bantu slaves were sent to work in the mines of the Chapada Diamantina region of rural Bahia, where Piji and Jarê are prevalent. In fact, today there are still several former *quilombo* communities in the region. The quilombos were hidden enclaves of fugitive African slaves (*see* Maroonage in the Americas). And, though Piji and Jarê are Caboclo religions with prominent Amerindian-inspired and Indio-Catholic features, they are nevertheless devoutly practiced in these *quilombos remanescentes* (remaining quilombos) and were uniquely influenced by them.

The African-Caboclo Religions of Brazil

This third grouping consists of religious forms that directly combine or integrate the beliefs and practices of the coastal African religions and the hinterland Caboclo religions. Some of these religions actually compartmentalize in parallel fashion the foundations of an African tradition in Brazil, on the one hand, and a rural Caboclo religion, on the other. In one moment they appear to be exemplars of the African tradition and in another moment or in a different ritual, of a Caboclo tradition. In such cases the gods of an African religion and its chants and drumming, its ritual devotional requisites, and possession experiences, for instance, are juxtaposed to a pantheon of Caboclo spirits, saints, and Caboclo-related devotions, healing practices, and other ritual attributes of a Caboclo religion. But still other African-Caboclo religions do not so compartmentalize, and rather integrate African and Caboclo beliefs and practices in unique ways. Often, some of each of these patterns occurs in some of the religions.

For example, the Candomblé de Caboclo (Caboclo Candomblé) of Bahia's coastal cities and large rural towns strongly resembles, in part, the regional African religion of Candomblé, and in part the rural Bahian Caboclo religions, such as Piji, though each is simplified and reconciled to the whole. In the Amazonian city of Belém and nearby towns, the religion called Batuque both combines and integrates the Caboclo religion of rural Pajelança, especially its central healing beliefs and practices and pantheon of Caboclos and encantados, with significant features of the regional African religion of Tambor de Mina. Mythologies from each are intertwined, for instance, and gods and spirits manifest as African-Caboclo composites.

These "in between" magico-religious forms, the African-Caboclo religions, are estimated to be the most numerous of the African-Brazilian religions and are rapidly spreading. As a general principle, they occur in urban areas, which include virtually all of the coastal area cities, and are increasingly developing in the large rural towns of their respective states. From north to south and indexed by region and the principal cities in which they are prevalent, they include the Batuque, mentioned above, *Babassuê* (*Batuque-de-Santa Barbara*), and *Encanteria* of the northern coastal cities of Belém and São Luís, and inland, Teresinha, respectively; the *Jurema, Xangô de Caboclo,* and *Toré* cults of the northeastern coastal capitals of Fortaleza, Natal, and João Pessoa (for Jurema), and Recife and Maceió (for both Xangô de Caboclo and Toré); the Candomblé de Caboclo in Salvador, discussed above; and the urban Macumba of Rio de Janeiro and São Paulo. The Umbandas of these same mega-metropolises constitute a special form of the African-Caboclo religions Umbanda. They are variants of the urban Macumbas, in which the African, Caboclo, and folk Catholic elements of the Macumbas syncretize with a strong foundation of Kardecian Spiritualism. Finally, many Umbandas (like most of the Caboclo and African-Caboclo religions) include a negative side, dominated by evil spirits and black magic, which also takes the form of an independent cult called Quimbanda.

Dispersion of the African-Brazilian Religions

In all cases these various African-Brazilian religions have spread to regions outside their originating sites and areas of prevalence, often forming other local syncretic combinations. For instance, the Candomblés of Salvador, Bahia, hold tremendous prestige in southern Brazil in cities like Rio, São Paulo, and Porto Alegre. Their popular representation as more mystical and/or truly African encouraged many hundreds of Bahian practitioners of one or another variant of the Candomblés to take advantage of that fame by relocating to these other major metropolitan urban centers. There they founded new and successful *terreiros* (centers), syncretizing with the local religions to varying degrees. And this is true of the other African religions of the coastal cities, such as the Xangôs of Recife and the Tambor de Mina of São Luís, which with their variants have spread to other cities north, south, and inland of their original centers. Of the other religions, most notable is the spread of the Umbandas.

Though concentrated in Rio and São Paulo, they have also fanned out to the towns in the rural interior and to the metropolitan urban centers of other regions.

In sum, these three loose categories of the African religions, Caboclo religions, and the African-Caboclo religions serve the purpose of providing a general description of the African-derived or African-influenced religions in Brazil. The African religions are best represented in the literature, but the Caboclo and African-Caboclo religions (with the exception of the Umbandas) have been given far less attention, as evidenced in Carlos Moura's periodically updated bibliographies on the African-Brazilian religions. For the student of religion, the study of these traditions is in one breath the study of cultural survival under extraordinarily adverse circumstances. And in another breath, it is the study of cultural change, adaptation, and compromise, resulting in the formation of truly Brazilian religions. The study of the tremendous variation not only between but also within each of these religions has important implications for our understanding of the origins and character of religion, and for our understanding of cultural change, human creativity, and religiosity.

Patric V. Giesler

See Also

Bantu: Dispersion and Settlement; Congo, Democratic Republic of the; Dahomey, Early Kingdom of; Nigeria; Slavery in Latin America and the Caribbean; Rio de Janeiro, Brazil; Catholic Church in Latin America and the Caribbean; Orishas.

Latin America and the Caribbean

Religions, African, in Latin America and the Caribbean

The African-derived religions of Latin American and Caribbean slaves (*see* Slavery in Latin America and the Caribbean) and their descendants are marked by a dual heritage. While deeply rooted in African spiritual traditions, these religions have also been indelibly shaped by the history of New World enslavement, exploitation, and racism. From Shango in Trinidad to Cumina in Jamaica, from Kele in St. Lucia to Batuque in Brazil, the story is similar: molded by and resonant with Old World African world-views, these ritual systems also always express and reflect the wrenching experience of diaspora. This essay explores how three religions – Haitian Vodou, Cuban Santería, and Brazilian Umbanda – illustrate this duality.

Haitian Vodou

In the French colony of Saint-Domingue (present-day Haiti), where a large number of slaves were from the African kingdom of Dahomey, slavery destroyed traditional African priesthoods and secret societies. Still, the great Dahomean deities, known now as *lwa*, came to be worshiped in secret ceremonies administered by religious leaders (*houngans*) who regulated the descent of the lwa into mediums (*ounsis*). The bitter experience of enslavement led to the division of the lwas into *Rada* and *Petro* versions. The Rada version of the lwa is regarded as rooted in Africa and tends to be characterized by tranquillity and generosity ("Rada" derives from Arada, a kingdom in Dahomey during Haiti's colonial period). The Petro version of the lwa, meanwhile, is rooted in the New World and is characterized by impatience and anger. ("Petro" derives from a certain Dom Pedro, who is supposed to have led a rebellion of runaway slaves in the eighteenth century.) Legba, for example, as a Rada spirit, is the guardian of destiny and preserves the West African notion that the place of each person is established at birth. This Legba is a positive force, representing fecundity and the continuity of generations. As a Petro spirit, in contrast, Legba reflects the deep antagonisms of slave society. He arranges unexpected accidents, works at night, and commits acts of sorcery. In a fit of vindictiveness he can unleash people-eating werewolves, who, like slave catchers, roam the countryside at night to steal people or their possessions.

The Petro versions of two other spirits are particularly important for practitioners of Vodou. Gede, while inheriting his name from Dahomey, is a distinctively New World phenomenon, serving the need of slaves and their descendants to find hope in the midst of oppression. Gede embodies the fact that within every episode of destruction there is the promise of a new beginning. Master of cemeteries and night, Gede is also master of the moon, and carefully watches over the rebirth of the dead. When he possesses a medium, his lifeless, petrified arms and feet recall the maiming and chaining of slavery. Yet far from being defeated by these occurrences, he expresses himself through humor and satire. He mocks pretension, parodies Roman Catholic priests (*see* Catholic Church in Latin America and the Caribbean), and sings about the secret foibles of his devotees. He personifies the power of humans to transcend adversity through comic self-awareness.

Another important lwa is Ogou. In Dahomey Ogou was the god of iron and war. In Saint-Domingue Ogou gave spiritual sustenance to runaway slave communities, as well as to the great Haitian Revolution, which led to the overthrow of slavery and the eventual independence of Haiti from France. It is believed that the slaves' trust in the powers of Ogou was important to the slave Macandal, who led a major uprising in the 1750s. Legend also has it that Boukman, one of the early leaders of the Haitian Revolution, was a houngan. When in 1791 he assembled his followers, he declared that Ogou had ordered vengeance and would assist the slaves in their task. To this day Ogou is associated in Vodou with these episodes. Boukman's assembly is reenacted annually in Vodou ceremonies, and Ogou sometimes takes on the persona of Toussaint L'Ouverture, one of the leaders of the Haitian Revolution. The revolutionary phrase *Vive la liberté* occurs regularly in Ogou's rites; in one the lwa appears dressed as a guerrilla warrior and reenacts the victory over the French, played by devotees who come attired in eighteenth-century French military uniforms.

After the revolution the ex-slaves of Haiti had the experience, virtually unique in the hemisphere, of avoiding the return to the plantation; instead, large numbers of them became small landholders. Like their forbears in Africa, but in contrast to others in the diaspora who never became landowners, Haitians strengthened and renewed their spiritual bond with the land by developing an elaborate system of burying the dead. To this day death provides practitioners of Vodou the occasion to close the circle of history and make sense of the diaspora by drawing on the power of Africa to help fulfill and realize life in the New World. Vodou practitioners believe that upon death the soul migrates back to *Ginen* (Guinea, or Africa), imagined to be a watery depth below the surface of the earth. After reaching Africa the soul finally achieves true freedom and becomes able to return to Haiti. A year and a day after the person's death, a special Vodou ritual calls him back, reclaiming the soul from the waters of Ginen so that it might help nurture its New World descendants.

Cuban Santería

In contrast to Haitian Vodou, but like Candomblé in Brazil and Shango in Trinidad, Cuban Santería is based on the Yoruba pantheon of deities, or orishas. A large proportion of the 700,000 Africans brought to Cuba were Yorubas, including numerous priests and priestesses. As in Brazil and Trinidad, enslaved religious leaders in Cuba established followings in Catholic religious brotherhoods, then moved out of them to create a religion that was both a continuation of traditional African practices and an adaptation to the new needs and experiences of the present. Santería is now practiced in the residences of priests or priestesses who act as godfathers or godmothers to families of mediums. These fictive kin groups, which may include as few as 6 or as many as 30 or 40 people, are structured by seniority of initiation into mediumship. Mediums become possessed by one or more of the orishas.

The orishas of Santería are selective reinterpretations of the Yoruba pantheon. Among the Yoruba, Eleguá is an erotic, phallic god invoked in rituals of fertility. In Cuba Eleguá has lost these associations, for slaves had little incentive to encourage their own fertility. He has become more sinister, for he

For detailed map of Religious Practices in Brazil, see "Religions, African, in Brazil"

LEFT: Cuban women carry in procession a statue of the Catholic Saint Barbara, often associated with Shangó (also known as Xangô or Changó), an African deity who represents strength and justice. *Fundação Pierre Verger*

BELOW LEFT: Participating in a procession, a man plays a batá drum. Music, primarily drumming and singing – often in an archaic Yoruba dialect – plays a crucial role in the worship of orishas, or deities. *Fundação Pierre Verger*

may now help to kill and poison enemies and masters. As the gatekeeper to the other gods, he has come to be associated in Cuba with Saint Peter, the Catholic saint who holds the keys to heaven. In Cuba, too, as in Haiti, Ogun is associated with resistance; but unlike his counterpart in Haiti, where resistance became revolution, the Cuban Ogun avoids overt rebellion. Ogun's traditional connection with warfare became transmuted in Cuba into the sentiments of passive resistance and a burning thirst for justice. His rituals include, symbolically, the chains of enslavement and torture, and the machetes and picks of slave labor. His Catholic counterpart became Saint John the Baptist, in part because this figure wished to bring about a revolution without being fully able to do so himself.

There are a number of Yoruba divinities that govern water, whether the ocean or rivers; these goddesses tend to have strongly sexual overtones and to be associated with the celebration of fertility, large families, and many descendants. In Cuba, too, there is Yemayá, the spirit of the ocean and salt water, and Oshún, the spirit of rivers and sweet water. Here, however, these figures are not about creating and celebrating large families. Yemayá exemplifies the sober virtues of motherhood – caretaking, wisdom, nurturance – and is associated with the Virgin Mary. Oshún has become a goddess of youthful beauty and coquetry. Hers is not a sexuality that aims to create large families but rather to remind devotees of the limits of vanity. She too is associated with Mary.

Of special importance in Cuba is the spirit of Babalú-Ayé. In Africa this is a minor, secondary divinity, but in Cuba, where death and disease under slavery became rampant, this healing god became prominent. Not surprisingly, he became identified with Saint Lazarus, the Catholic saint who is the patron of skin diseases. Thus in the end the pantheon of African deities that once existed to express and celebrate the intense joys and hopes of life have become in Santería expressions of the longing to overcome oppression and reminders of the limits of human power, desire, and bodies.

Brazilian Umbanda

Umbanda, fast becoming one of the most widely practiced religions in Brazil, emerged in the 1930s as a syncretism (or fusion) of Yoruba-based Candomblé religion, Catholicism, and European spiritism. It has been suggested that Umbanda reflects the special aptitude for syncretism of the descendants of Bantu and Angolan slaves. Whether or not this is the case, it is clear that in Umbanda, in contrast to the Yoruba-derived religion of Candomblé, the orishas have been relegated to a distant spiritual plane. In their place, three main types of spirits descend to earth and possess mediums. These are the Caboclos, spirits of people who once walked upon Brazilian ground and breathed Brazilian air, and now, in death, perform works of charity through their intermediaries, the mediums who belong to cult centers.

Caboclos are the spirits of deceased indigenous people. They are admired for their skill in hunting and warfare and their knowledge of the forest. Above all, they are respected as proud and courageous for having resisted slavery. When they possess mediums, their demeanor is haughty, even arrogant. They perform magical healing and offer advice and assistance for the unemployed and people battling the bureaucracy. *Pretos velhos* ("old blacks") are old Brazilian men and women who died while still enslaved. They are characterized not by the fearsome might of the orishas, or even the pride of the Caboclos; they are, rather, humble, loving, gentle, and patient. They walk slowly and hunchbacked, sit down in order to consult with their petitioners, speak in soft, stereotyped slave Portuguese, and puff on pipes. Their specialty is offering warm advice to people faced with domestic conflict. The third main category of Umbanda spirits are the *exús*. These are spirits of people – above all, slaves and marginalized blacks – who died unresigned to their lot. They were petty thieves and tricksters who now, in death, make trouble on command and set obstacles in the paths of their petitioners' enemies. They are inherently untrustworthy, often charging handsomely for their knavery. They refuse to conform to the ideal of the subordinate black. As Roger Bastide, a French expert on Afro-Brazilian religion, put it, "This 'bad Negro' is nothing other than the image of the runaway slave."

The Umbanda pantheon has tended to be interpreted by scholars as embodying racist stereotypes of blacks and indigenous people: the good black is the docile, submissive one; the bad black is the rebellious one; the dignified Caboclo Indian is the one who preferred death to enslavement. These may well be the meanings attributed to the Caboclo and preto velho spirits by the religion's lighter-skinned practitioners. There is evidence, however, that black practitioners interpret the pantheon differently. In particular, some black mediums have developed relationships with the spirit of ZUMBI, the great seventeenth-century leader of runaway slaves. For them Zumbi is both an exú and a preto velho. He appears in their cult centers and teaches

the pretos velhos the "true" history of slavery in Brazil: how, for instance, the emancipation of slaves did not occur through the good will of the white ruling class, as is taught in Brazilian grade schools, but rather through the struggles and resistance of slaves themselves (*see* Abolition and Emancipation in Latin America and the Caribbean). These mediums say they know that the pretos velhos suffered under slavery and never felt resigned to it. "They never accepted it," said one medium, "but what could they do? They just nodded and said 'Yes, sir.' But in their hearts they did not accept it." Zumbi's mentorship of the pretos velhos, and his own dual identity as exú and preto velho, reveal that for black adherents of Umbanda, the pretos velhos always retain, just below the surface, the potential to rebel.

The examples of Vodou, Santería, and Umbanda show that the religious traditions of Africa were not transferred to the New World in static form. Rather, slaves and their descendants in Latin America and the Caribbean selected from and reshaped the meanings of the old beliefs to make sense of and to cope with the devastation and exploitation of New World slavery and racism. The spirit of the Old World helped them, in the end, to discover, develop bonds with, and, to a certain extent, be healed by the spirits of the New.

John Burdick

See Also

Dahomey, Early Kingdom of; Racial Stereotypes; Trinidad and Tobago; Toussaint L'Ouverture, François Dominique; Iwa.

Latin America and the Caribbean

Religious Brotherhoods in Latin America (*cofradía* and *cabildo* in Spanish America; *irmandade* in Brazil), secular groups centered on the adoration of particular Catholic saints such as, for example, Nossa Senhora do Rosário. Black religious brotherhoods were often organized along ethnic lines and constituted one of the main types of institutions that preserved African culture in Latin America and the Caribbean (*see* Catholic Church in Latin America and the Caribbean).

North America

Remond, Charles Lenox

(b. 1810?, Salem, Mass.; d. December 22, 1873, Boston, Mass.), African American abolitionist and advocate of integration and equality.

Charles Lenox Remond was born into a family of abolitionists and activists. His mother helped found the Salem Female Anti-Slavery Society, and his father was a lifetime member of the American Anti-Slavery Society (AASS). Both Remond and his younger sister, Sarah Parker Remond, became respected abolitionist speakers.

Charles Remond was involved with the AASS nearly from its beginning. Philosophically, he concurred with William Lloyd Garrison's doctrines of nonresistance and moral persuasion. In 1838 the Massachusetts Anti-Slavery Society named him its first full-time black lecturer. In a tour of the British Isles he pressed the cause of abolition, although this was not the sole focus of his advocacy. When the 1840 World's Anti-Slavery Convention, meeting in London, refused to seat women delegates, he spoke against the policy and left the meeting. After returning to the United States he traveled through the Midwest on a speaking tour with Frederick Douglass.

Remond's sympathies moved away from nonresistance as federal laws and court rulings of the 1850s soured him on the possibility of ending slavery through moral persuasion. By the late 1850s he came to argue in defense of slave revolts and warned of a violent end to Southern slavery. Despite this turn toward more active resistance, Remond always firmly believed in integration. He sought to make racial justice, not simply emancipation, the cause of the AASS. Remond retired from public life in 1867 and during his last years worked as a clerk in the Boston Customs House.

See Also

Abolitionism in the United States.

North America

Remond, Sarah Parker

(b. June 6, 1826, Salem, Mass.; d. December 13, 1894, Rome, Italy), African American abolitionist, rights activist, and physician.

The daughter of a free black immigrant and granddaughter of a black veteran of the American Revolution, Sarah Parker Remond was born into a family that would not tolerate the injustices of slavery and inequality. When Salem's high school would not admit Sarah, the family moved to Newport, Rhode Island, until her graduation. Dedicated to education and political activism for both sexes, her mother, Nancy Remond, was a founder of the Salem Female Anti-Slavery Society.

In July 1842, at age 16, Sarah joined her brother, Charles Lenox Remond, on the antislavery lecture circuit. She not only spoke out against slavery, but also challenged segregation in churches, theaters, and other public places. In 1856 she began touring the Midwest as a lecturer with the American Anti-Slavery Society and won acclaim as a persuasive speaker. Also concerned with the rights of women, Remond was a member of the platform group at the 1858 National Women's Rights Convention. From 1859 to 1861 Remond toured England and Ireland with her brother, continuing to rally support for the American antislavery cause. She stayed on in England during the Civil War, returning to the United States in 1866 to lobby for universal suffrage at the New York Constitutional Convention, an effort that proved unsuccessful.

Remond returned to Europe in 1866. In 1868, having studied in Florence, Italy, Remond received her diploma for "professional medical practice." She married Lorenzo Pintor in 1877 and lived out the rest of her life in Italy.

See Also

Civil War, American; Free Blacks in the United States, 1619 to 1863.

RENAMO. Please see Mozambican National Resistance

Africa

René, Albert (b. November 16, 1935, Farquhar Islands), president of the Seychelles (1977-).

Born in the Farquhar Islands, Albert René spent his youth on a plantation that his father managed before enrolling in Saint Louis College, in Victoria on the island of Mahé, and later Saint Moritz, in Switzerland. After abandoning plans to become a priest he studied law in England at Saint Mary's College, King's College, and the London School of Economics (1962-1964), where he became active in the British Labour Party. Returning home in 1964, he founded the Seychelles People's United Party (SPUP), as well as the nation's first labor union. Elected to the legislative assembly in 1965, René vocally attacked British colonial rule and opposed plans endorsed by James Mancham, leader of the rival Seychelles Democratic Party, to integrate the Seychelles into the British Commonwealth. Upon independence in 1976, René became prime minister in a coalition government headed by Mancham, who became president. In June 1977 SPUP supporters staged an armed coup while Mancham was abroad and installed René, who claimed ignorance of the coup plot, as president.

René initially ruled by decree but, after introducing a new constitution in 1979, the legislative assembly was reinstated. Shortly after the reformulated SPUP, renamed the Seychelles People's Progressive Front (SPPF), became the only legal party in 1979, René, the sole candidate, won election to a five-year term as president. He was reelected in 1984 and 1989. A series of attempted coups involving foreign mercenaries in the late 1970s and 1980s made René's rule increasingly autocratic. However, in the face of pressure from dissenters at home and international donors in the early 1990s, he endorsed a return to multiparty democracy and a shift toward a free-market economy. In 1993, following the adoption of a new constitution, René defeated Mancham in multiparty presidential elections and won reelection to a five-year term. Under René the economy of the Seychelles has grown steadily, and per capita income has increased fivefold.

North America

Reparations, government-administered funding and social programs intended to compensate African Americans for the past injustices of slavery and discrimination.

In 1988 the United States government issued a national apology to Japanese Americans who had been placed in American internment camps during World War II and paid $20,000 to each victim. This prompted many African Americans to press for similar reparations. Cited as grounds for compensation were the unfulfilled Civil War promise that each slave would receive forty acres and a mule; the millions of dollars of German aid to Jews following the Holocaust; and the U.S. Marshall Plan, which rebuilt Europe after World War II.

Advocates of reparations have proposed packages that range from $700 billion to $4 trillion. Most favor investing the money in education and economic development for the African American community. This proposed use of reparations contrasts with that of some earlier reparation movements, which sought to found an independent black state (in Africa or in the southern United States) or secure pensions for ex-slaves and their descendants.

Some opponents of reparations believe that such payments cannot truly make up for past injustices. Jesse Jackson's aide Frank Watkins draws this conclusion through analogy: "If you have two people running in a mile race around a track and one has a ball and chain tied around his leg for three laps, you can't take the ball and chain off for the final lap and still expect him to win." Although the U.S. government has not yet awarded reparations to African Americans or made a formal apology for nearly 250 years of slavery, many African Americans continue to demand that the nation officially confront and redress its past injustices.

Aaron Myers

See Also

Slavery in the United States; World War II and African Americans; Civil War, American; Jackson, Jesse Louis.

North America

Republic of New Africa, African American organization devoted to the establishment of an autonomous black nation in the southern United States.

At the height of the Black Power Movement in the late 1960s members of the Republic of New Africa (RNA) called for the creation of an independent black nation spanning the states of Louisiana, Mississippi, Alabama, Georgia, and South Carolina. They advocated cooperative economics and community self-sufficiency. At the same time members of the RNA aimed to limit political rights and freedom of the press, prohibit unions, make military service mandatory, and legalize polygamy. Their manifesto demanded that the United States government cede the five proposed states to the RNA and pay $400 billion in REPARATIONS to African Americans for the injustices of slavery and segregation.

In 1968 attorney Milton Henry and his brother Richard, former acquaintances of MALCOLM X who renamed themselves Gaidi Obadele and Imari Abubakari Obadele, respectively, convened a group of militant black nationalists in DETROIT, MICHIGAN, to discuss the creation of a black nation within the United States. Conference members established the RNA and declared their allegiance to the provisional government. They elected Imari Obadele as provisional president.

The RNA quickly became a target of the U.S. Federal Bureau of Investigation (FBI), which conducted raids on the group's meetings. These confrontations were violent and led to the repeated imprisonment of RNA leaders for assault and sedition. Following his 1980 release from prison, Imari Obadele attended Temple University and earned a Ph.D. in political science. While teaching at various universities, he published books and articles upholding the RNA's principles of reparations, acquisition of land, and establishment of an autonomous black nation. Based in WASHINGTON, D.C., the RNA continues to promote the formation of a black nation.

Aaron Myers

See Also

Slavery in the United States; Labor Unions in the United States; Black Power; Black Nationalism in the United States.

Africa

Reshewa (also known as Bareshe, Gungawa, Reshawa, Reshiat, and Tsureshe), ethnic group of NIGERIA.

The Reshewa primarily inhabit the banks of the NIGER RIVER in northwestern Nigeria. They speak a Niger-Congo language. More than 100,000 people consider themselves Reshewa.

See Also

Languages, African: An Overview.

Africa

Réunion, an island territory of FRANCE located in the Indian Ocean 760 km (407 mi) east of MADAGASCAR.

Although most of France's overseas possessions are now independent, Réunion has remained a French Département d'Outre Mer, an overseas department intricately tied to the political economy of France. The island's demography reflects its history of colonization, slavery, and indentured labor. Creoles – people of mixed African descent – constitute the largest group, followed by people whose descent can be traced directly to FRANCE. Réunion is also home to a significant Indian population, mostly Hindu Tamils but also some Catholics and Muslims, as well as Chinese and East African communities. French culture has had a strong influence: the majority of the people speak French and/or Kreole and practice Roman Catholicism, and many combine the worship of Catholic saints with popular beliefs in magic and sorcery.

Precolonial History

Most accounts of precolonial Réunion claim that the Portuguese explorer Pedro de Mascarenhas discovered the uninhabited volcanic island on February 9, Saint Apollina's Day, during his 1512-1514 voyage to India, after which he named it Saint Appollina. Other sources suggest that another Portuguese explorer, Tristan da Cunha, discovered the island in 1507. Still others have claimed that the Phoenicians, Indians, and Arabs knew of the island much earlier. The first known inclusion of the island on a map occurred in 1518, on a map of the region by the Portuguese cartographer Pedro Reinel. During the early seventeenth century the French cardinal Armand Jean du Plessis Richelieu sent a ship to take possession of the island under the name Mascarin Island, in honor of its presumed discoverer.

Colonial History

Recognizing the island's strategic location along sea routes to India, France claimed ownership of it in 1638 and renamed it Ile Bourbon. French soldiers expelled from Fort Dauphin, MADAGASCAR, on charges of mutiny moved there in 1662, but it was only formally settled in 1665, by the French East India Company. In 1669 the company's settlement was moved from Saint Paul's Bay to Saint-Denis, a harbor on the northern coast, and France showed little interest in the small colony until Fort Dauphin was attacked by MALAGASY in 1674. After the attack the French survivors relocated to Bourbon. The island then took center stage in the French Campagnie des Indes and as the principal port of call between the Cape of Good Hope and French outposts in Pondicherry, India. The early settlement grew very slowly, with only 316 inhabitants (113 of them slaves) in 1698. By 1710 the population had grown to approximately 1000, but after the French East India Company introduced coffee in 1715, the population grew rapidly, particularly in terms of the number of slaves. The company required that all settlers grow the crop, and by 1744 the colony was exporting more than 1000 tons of coffee each year.

By 1724 the population of the island had grown to 12,500. But France was already turning its attention to nearby MAURITIUS, abandoned by the Dutch in 1715. Attracted by the island's excellent natural harbor, the French quickly claimed and began to settle Mauritius under the name Ile de France. Between 1727 and 1735 Bourbon remained the administrative capital, under the governorship of Pierre-Benoît Dunmas, but when Bertrand Francois Mahé de Labourdonnais took over in 1735, he moved the seat of government to Ile de France. The Bourbon economy stagnated during much of the eighteenth century. Coffee harvests were small, and, due to increasing production from the West Indies, world coffee prices were low. In response the settlers began to cultivate alternative crops, including cotton and tobacco. Although the French East India Company introduced spice crops such as cloves, vanilla, and nutmeg, the island's economy came to be centered on the production of food crops for Ile de France.

Ownership of Bourbon, along with Ile de France, transferred from the French East India Company to the French Crown in 1767. After the French Revolution, Bourbon became known as Ile de la Réunion, and a local, elected assembly began to govern the colony. The settlers gained more local autonomy, but the abolition of slavery within the French Empire threatened to undermine their heavily slave-based economy. In the face of settler opposition in Réunion, Ile de France, and elsewhere, France revoked the ban on slavery in 1802 but also resumed direct control over all the island colonies.

France and GREAT BRITAIN had been competing for hegemony in the Indian Ocean since the War of Austrian Succession (1740-1748). Conflicts continued throughout the eighteenth and nineteenth centuries during the Seven Years' War (1756-1763), the War of American Independence (1775-1783), and finally the Napoleonic Wars (1793-1815). In 1810 the British captured Réunion and Ile de France, renaming them Bourbon and Mauritius, respectively, and firmly establishing British dominance in the Indian Ocean. Because Bourbon's poor harbor minimized its strategic importance and value to Britain, it was returned to France in 1814 under the Treaty of Paris.

The only remaining French possession in the Indian Ocean, Bourbon reoriented agricultural production to prioritize SUGAR, which France had previously imported from Mauritius. Bourbon's annual sugar exports increased from 21 tons in 1815 to 74,000 tons in 1860. Meanwhile, because Bourbon was no longer forced to supply food to Mauritius, production of foodstuffs plummeted, and the island became a net food importer by the 1840s.

The year 1848 saw the creation of the Second Republic in France and brought major social reforms. Universal suffrage was instituted and slavery once again abolished in both France and its possessions, including the again-renamed Ile de la Réunion. Once again an economic crisis loomed, as sugar cultivation required a large labor force. Many freed slaves, no longer wishing to work on the large sugar plantations but unable to grow sugar efficiently on the small plots that remained, moved to towns or to the less densely populated highland areas, where they became subsistence horticulturists.

Large numbers of Indians, primarily from Pondicherry, emigrated to Réunion as indentured laborers. The French were permitted to recruit workers from British-controlled India with the stipulation that workers be repatriated upon the completion of their contract, if they so desired. Many did in fact return to India after a stint in Réunion. But the British officially prohibited Réunion's recruitment of Indian labor in 1885, leaving the island's plantation owners more dependent on labor recruited from Malaysia, China, East Africa, and the Annamite Mountains in Vietnam.

Réunion lost much of its strategic significance after the opening of the SUEZ CANAL in 1869. Although some farmers began to diversify into crops used in the production of perfume oils, such as geraniums, vanilla, and vetiver, the economy remained heavily dependent on sugar, and thus vulnerable to fluctuations in world market prices. Nonetheless, the second half of the nineteenth century saw the construction of an artificial port and a railway that spanned the island. These projects helped Réunion increase sugar exports during World War I, but the resulting economic recovery was short lived. By the end of World War II Réunion's economy had again deteriorated, leaving much of the population desperately poor. Long relegated to the periphery of French concerns, the troubled island became a Département d'Outre-Mer in 1946.

POSTCOLONIAL DEVELOPMENTS

As a Département, Réunion gained representation in the French senate as well as access to government funds for much-needed infrastructural improvements. The island experienced a massive influx of money to improve transportation, communications, and agricultural productivity. Complete political-economic integration with France also meant that Réunionais were eligible for the same government programs – such as social security benefits, free education, and public health care – available to other French citizens. These and other social reforms helped build the island's middle class, while protective trade barriers and the establishment of media ties to the *métropole* (continential France) fostered the dominance of French culture, as did the influx of large numbers of Parisian bureaucrats.

CONTEMPORARY EVENTS

In 1973 the French established a military base on the island with 4000 troops. The following year Réunion became a region of France, similar in status to the 22 other regions of metropolitan France. In the 1980s Réunion's status was once again redefined, this time as a *collectivité territoriale*, a status that granted the island's residents greater autonomy over internal affairs. Although occasionally certain groups, such as the French Communist Party in 1959 and the ORGANIZATION OF AFRICAN UNITY in 1978, have called for the island's independence, the proposals have received little support from a population well aware of the economic security gained through ties to France.

Indeed, Réunion's economic improvements since the 1950s have been fueled more by the steady flow of funds from France than by productivity on the island itself. Sugar still dominates the economy, accounting for 60 percent of export earnings, although the industry employs only 9.7 percent of the population. Approximately three-quarters of all employment is within the service sector, especially tourism. But many people are unemployed and depend on social security; a full three-quarters of the population receives social security benefits. Public opinion in France tends to view Réunion as a financial liability. In turn, many Réunionais resent the obvious disparity in wealth between themselves and tourists, most of whom are French. The average Réunionais earns a gross disposable income equal to only 57 percent of that of the typical person in metropolitan France, despite the recent increase in the minimum wage to a level on par with the *métropole*.

Ari Nave

SEE ALSO

Colonial Rule; Indian Communities in Africa; Portugal; Tourism in Africa; Indian Ocean Slave Trade.

North America

Revels, Hiram Rhoades

(b. September 1, 1822, Fayetteville, N.C.; d. January 16, 1901, Aberdeen, Miss.), American minister and university president, first African American to serve in the United States Senate.

Hiram Revels, the son of former slaves, studied at several seminaries in Indiana and Ohio before becoming a minister in the AFRICAN METHODIST EPISCOPAL CHURCH. During the Civil War Revels helped to organize African American regiments in Maryland and Mississippi. After the Civil War he moved to Mississippi and became active in Republican politics. He was selected to complete Jefferson Davis's unexpired term in the U.S. Senate. After leaving the Senate, Revels served as the president of Alcorn University.

Robert Fay

See Also
Civil War, American.

North America

Reverend Ike

(Frederick Eikerenkoetter) (b. June 1, 1935, Ridgeland, S.C.), African American minister whose teachings emphasize that happiness and fulfillment come from financial prosperity and self-confidence.

Frederick Eikerenkoetter, known familiarly as Reverend Ike, earned a B.A. in theology from the American Bible College in Chicago in 1955. In 1962 he established the United Christian Evangelistic Association (UCEA). In acknowledgement of donations, he sent Blessing Plans, which he claimed would provide the framework for success.

Eminently successful himself, he became the first African American minister with a television show. Reverend Ike claimed over 1 million followers by 1972, and over 7 million by 1982. Critics called him a con artist, and many argued that his belief in personal success undermined African American community advancement and distorted the Christian message. Though less visible today, the UCEA still operates internationally.

Robert Fay

See Also
Television and African Americans.

North America

Revolutionary Action Movement,

an African American nationalist organization, in operation between 1963 and 1968, that advocated violence to achieve black empowerment.

During the 1960s some African Americans, frustrated by the government's lack of responsiveness to problems in the black community such as unemployment, overcrowded housing, and police brutality, formulated and organized radical ways of effecting political and social change. This large-scale effort became known, overall, as the Black Power Movement. The Revolutionary Action Movement (RAM), one of the earliest Black Nationalist organizations of the 1960s, asserted that violence was the only way to alter fundamentally the structure of American society.

Through grassroots organizing that included African American history classes, RAM built up a liberation army in Philadelphia and New York. The organization also published a bimonthly magazine, *Black America,* and a free weekly, *RAM Speaks.* Its several hundred members included teachers, students, and businesspeople. Robert Franklin Williams, a former leader of a North Carolina branch of the National Association for the Advancement of Colored People (NAACP), served as RAM's president while in self-imposed exile, first in Cuba, then in China.

Because of RAM's militant ideology and grassroots activism, the United States Federal Bureau of Investigation (FBI) tried to destroy it. Two 1967 FBI raids of RAM headquarters in New York City led to 24 arrests and the seizure of about 130 weapons. Nine RAM members were convicted and imprisoned for conspiring to poison the police force, blow up city hall, and/or murder local and national leaders, including leaders of the NAACP and the National Urban League. RAM leaders not imprisoned either left the country or were placed under surveillance. This resulted in the collapse of the organization in 1968. In spite of the group's short existence, many former RAM members went on to contribute to the formation of other Black Nationalist organizations, such as the Republic of New Africa.

Aaron Myers

See Also
New York, New York; Philadelphia, Pennsylvania; Black Nationalism in the United States.

Africa

Rhinoceros,

the second-largest land mammal after the elephant, two species of which are found in Africa.

The larger of the African species, the white rhinoceros (*Ceratotherium simum*) grows to 1.8 m (about 6 ft) at the shoulder and weighs up to 2300 kg (about 5000 lb), while the black rhinoceros (*Deceros bicornis*) grows to 1.6 m (5.5 ft) and weighs up to 1100 kg (2500 lb). Both species possess two horns, the longer of which can grow to over 1 m (about 3 ft).

Yet this near-sighted herbivore is generally peaceful, only becoming aggressive when its territory is disturbed. Both African species are endangered and are officially protected, but they are still illegally killed because their horns are highly valued as ingredients in traditional Asian medicine and as dagger handles in Yemen. In 1994 naturalists estimated that a total of 2000 black rhinoceroses and 5000 white rhinoceroses remain scattered throughout sub-Saharan Africa.

Robert Fay

Africa

Rhodes, Cecil

(b. July 5, 1853, Bishop's Stortford, England; d. March 26, 1902, Cape Town, South Africa), British colonial statesman and financier; one of the main promoters of British rule in southern Africa.

At age 17 Cecil Rhodes was sent from his home in England to live with his brother in what is now South Africa. Diamond fields had been discovered at Kimberley in Cape Colony that year, and Rhodes became a diamond prospector. By the time he was 19 years old he had accumulated a large fortune. At age 20 he returned to England to study at the University of Oxford, and for the next eight years he divided his time between the university and the diamond fields. During this period he consolidated the Cape Colony's diamond-mining claims to form De Beers Mining Company.

Rhodes's control over this important industry earned him an audience in the colonial Parliament, where he advocated the use of military might to secure a cheap African labor force and also expressed his views on race. In a speech before Parliament in 1877 he said, "These are my politics on native affairs, and these are the politics of South Africa. Treat the natives as subject people as long as they continue in a state of barbarism and communal tenure; be the lords over them, and let them be a subject race, and keep the liquor from them."

In 1881 he entered the Cape Colony Parliament, where he served for the remainder of his life. Rhodes was largely responsible for the annexation to the British Empire of Bechuanaland (now Botswana) in 1885. In 1888, with the founding of De Beers Consolidated Mines, Ltd., Rhodes monopolized the diamond production of Kimberley. In the same year he wrested exclusive mining rights from Lobengula, the ruler of Matabeleland (now in Zimbabwe). In 1889 Rhodes was granted a charter to incorporate the British South Africa Company. It controlled what are now Zimbabwe and Zambia – the area was named Rhodesia in 1894 in honor of Rhodes – until 1923.

In 1890 Rhodes was made prime minister of Cape Colony. Five years later he supported a conspiracy by British settlers in the South African Republic, in what is now northeastern South Africa, to overthrow the government of the republic, which was dominated by the Afrikaners, or Boers. The revolt was to be backed by a British South Africa Company force led by Sir Leander Starr Jameson, British administrator of the lands comprising present-day Zimbabwe. On December 29, 1895, Jameson prematurely and unsuccessfully invaded the South African Republic. Rhodes was acquitted of responsibility for the invasion, known as Jameson's Raid, but was censured for his role in the plot against the government of the South African Republic and forced to resign his premiership the following month. After his resignation he devoted himself to the development of Rhodesia. During the Boer War he was prominent in the defense of Kimberley, although he died before the war was over. In his will Rhodes left most of his fortune to the establishment of the Rhodes scholarships.

Alonford James Robinson, Jr.

Africa

Rhodesia. **Former name of Zimbabwe.**

Africa

Rhodesia, Northern. **Former name of Zambia.**

Latin America and the Caribbean

Rhys, Jean **(b. August 24, 1890, Roseau, Dominica; d. May 14, 1979, Devon, England), novelist and short-story writer.**

Jean Rhys is best remembered by many readers as the English author of the novel *Wide Sargasso Sea* (1966), whose plot is a "prequel" to Charlotte Brontë's classic English novel *Jane Eyre* (1847). For critics of Caribbean literature, however, Rhys evokes the provocative question of how one defines a Caribbean writer. Rhys was born in Dominica to a Welsh father and a white Dominican Creole mother, but after moving to England at age 16, she never lived in the Caribbean again. Writer and scholar Edward Kamau Brathwaite spoke for many West Indians when he argued that "white Creoles in the English and French West Indies have separated themselves by too wide a gulf and have contributed too little culturally as a group" for Rhys and those like her to be considered Caribbean writers. But the influences and impressions of Rhys's Dominican childhood are woven throughout all of her fiction and are essential to *Wide Sargasso Sea,* which is considered one of the best depictions of West Indian Creole society and an important postcolonial Caribbean novel.

Wide Sargasso Sea was written when Rhys was 76 years old, and it marked a renaissance in her writing career. As a young woman Rhys attended drama school in London and then joined a traveling drama troupe for several years. She lived in cities throughout Europe during the 1920s with the first of her three husbands, and began her writing career while living in Paris. Her friends there included writers James Joyce, Ernest Hemingway, and Ford Madox Ford. With their encouragement she published *Left Bank,* her first collection of short stories, in 1927, and her first novel, *Postures,* in 1928 (re-released the following year as *Quartet*), which was based on Rhys's affair with Ford and his girlfriend. Three more novels followed in the early 1930s, and while these stories and novels all have European settings, several of their characters have West Indian pasts similar to Rhys's own.

After this productive period, however, her writing slowed, and for most of the 1940s and 1950s she lived in England in relative obscurity. But in 1957 a British Broadcasting Corporation (BBC) radio adaptation of her 1934 novel *Good Morning, Midnight* brought Rhys to the attention of critic Francis Wyndham, who encouraged her to rework the old draft that became *Wide Sargasso Sea.* The novel tells the story of *Jane Eyre*'s "madwoman in the attic" – a character Rhys creates as Antoinette Cosway, Mr. Rochester's West Indian first wife. Like Rhys, Antoinette is a white Creole. Through Antoinette's relationship with her black nursemaid Christophine and the other black West Indians around her, Rhys paints a compelling portrait of the complicated – and often incestuous – racial tensions in West Indian society just after emancipation. It is this exploration of race and class that has made *Wide Sargasso Sea* such an important postcolonial Caribbean novel.

Rhys's last collection of stories, *Sleep It Off Lady* (1976), is also set largely in the Caribbean. But it is *Wide Sargasso Sea* that is most often discussed in West Indian journals and included in anthologies of Caribbean literature, and while some critics still question this inclusion, others see it as completely natural. Rhys has been compared to Caribbean writers such as V. S. Naipaul, Paule Marshall, and Michelle Cliff, who also spent most of their lives elsewhere, but whose work nevertheless is identified with the Caribbean literary tradition. She is included in the *Dictionary of Literary Biography* in both volume 36, *British Novelists, 1890-1929: Modernists* and volume 117, *Twentieth-Century Caribbean and Black African Writers.* The entry in volume 117 asserts that "[t]he themes of alienation, exile, and displacement that are central in her work are also central to Caribbean writing as a whole.... No one who knows the Caribbean well could deny that Rhys's work is grounded in a Caribbean consciousness."

Lisa Clayton Robinson

See Also

Literature, English Language, Caribbean.

North America

Rhythm and Blues, **an African American musical style developed after World War II that both reflected the growing confidence of urban African Americans and introduced a greater emotional depth to American popular music.**

Rhythm and blues (R&B) is the general term for African American popular music since World War II. R&B melded earlier musical styles of blues, jazz, boogie woogie, and gospel music. It matured in the late 1940s and between 1954 and 1960 broke through racial barriers and achieved unprecedented visibility in white-oriented popular music. In launching R&B, however, African Americans lost control over their own musical creation as white performers backed by major record companies and playing watered-down versions of R&B effectively hijacked the form.

R&B thus reflects complex relationships between the races, as well as the constraints placed on black cultural expression. Yet despite these constraints, R&B transformed American popular culture. It challenged the vapidity of white pop music, and its propulsive beat and sexual overtones catalyzed rock 'n' roll. Most significant, however, R&B expressed the pride and vitality of a new urban black culture that emerged as a product of the Great Migration out of the rural South.

The Musical Sources of R&B

R&B developed out of various earlier styles of black music, especially blues, jazz, and gospel and harmony singing. Chicago blues, epitomized by the searing electric guitar of Muddy Waters and the raspy, acid-etched singing of Howlin' Wolf, emerged almost simultaneously with R&B and was a major component of the R&B sound. Southwestern blues shouters such as Big Joe Turner were also important. The driving, eight-to-the-bar rhythm of boogie woogie also influenced many piano players, including Amos Milburn and Little Richard, and provided the underlying rhythm that characterized much R&B.

Jazz contributed to R&B through jump bands like Louis Jordan and His Tympany Five. Jordan's rhythmic approach, using a heavy backbeat that placed the stress on the second and fourth beats of each measure, was particularly important. R&B's gruff, blustery tenor saxophones drew inspiration from jazz players Illinois Jacquet and Arnett Cobb. Indeed, many jazz musicians played on R&B recording sessions or toured in R&B bands, as did John Coltrane and Clifford Brown.

Harmony singing contributed the last key ingredient in R&B. African Americans have a tradition of a cappella group singing that reaches back at least to the ragtime quartets of the late nineteenth century. Many R&B vocal groups began by modeling themselves on such popular singing groups of the 1930s as the Mills Brothers and especially the Ink Spots. Even more important was the influence of gospel music. Gospel quartets, from the jazzed-up harmonies of the Golden Gate Quartet to the more soulful approach of the Soul Stirrers and the Dixie Hummingbirds, gained popularity in the 1930s and 1940s and offered encouragement to many later R&B singers.

An equally strong influence came out of the nondenominational, sanctified churches with their fervent and freewheeling vocal approach. This style of singing uses complex improvised embellishment *(melisma),* including dips, slides, and blue notes, as seen in the singing of Clyde McPhatter, Jerry Butler, and Otis Redding. But the greatest exemplar of the secularized gospel sound is the music of pianist and singer Ray Charles.

AFRICAN AMERICANS IN THE ROCK AND ROLL HALL OF FAME

Year	Inductee	Category
1986	Robert Johnson	Early Influences
	Jimmy Yancey	Early Influences
	Chuck Berry	Artists
	James Brown	Artists
	Ray Charles	Artists
	Sam Cooke	Artists
	Fats Domino	Artists
	Little Richard	Artists
1987	Louis Jordan	Early Influences
	T-Bone Walker	Early Influences
	Bo Diddley	Artists
	The Coasters	Artists
	Aretha Franklin	Artists
	Marvin Gaye	Artists
	B.B. King	Artists
	Clyde McPhatter	Artists
	Smokey Robinson	Artists
	Big Joe Turner	Artists
	Muddy Waters	Artists
	Jackie Wilson	Artists
1988	Berry Gordy Jr.	Nonperforming
	Leadbelly	Early Influences
	The Drifters	Artists
	The Supremes	Artists
1989	The Ink Spots	Early Influences
	Bessie Smith	Early Influences
	The Soul Stirrers	Early Influences
	Otis Redding	Artists
	The Temptations	Artists
	Stevie Wonder	Artists
1990	Lamont Dozier, Brian Holland & Eddie Holland	Nonperforming
	Louis Armstrong	Early Influences
	Hank Ballard	Artists
	The Platters	Artists
1991	Dave Bartholomew	Nonperforming
	Howlin' Wolf	Early Influences
	La Vern Baker	Artists
	John Lee Hooker	Artists
	The Impressions	Artists
	Wilson Pickett	Artists
	Jimmy Reed	Artists
	Ike and Tina Turner	Artists
1992	Elmore James	Early Influences
	Professor Longhair	Early Influences
	Bobby "Blue" Bland	Artists
	Booker T. and the MG's	Artists
	The Jimi Hendrix Experience	Artists
	The Isley Brothers	Artists
	Sam and Dave	Artists
1993	Dinah Washington	Early Influences
	Ruth Brown	Artists
	Etta James	Artists
	Frankie Lymon & the Teenagers	Artists
	Sly & the Family Stone	Artists
1994	Willie Dixon	Early Influences
	Bob Marley	Artists

R&B and its Cultural Milieu

R&B was above all an urban music, emerging in various black communities that burgeoned during the Great Migration, including Los Angeles's Central Avenue, Chicago's South Side, and Harlem. R&B performers perfected their music at Harlem's Apollo Theater and in countless nightclubs, cabarets, and after-hours spots that were urban manifestations of the jook (or juke) joints found throughout the South. Singer Jimmy Witherspoon (1923-1997) fondly recalled LA's many after-hours spots, including "Alex Lovejoy's Big Legged Chicken, Brother's, Stuff Crouch's Back Stage, [and] Black Dot McGee's."

This new music voiced the pride of a new generation of African Americans. Numerous songs paid tribute to a lively black conviviality, including Amos Milburn's "Chicken Shack Boogie" (1947), Louis Jordan's "Saturday Night Fish Fry" (1949), and the Robins's "Smokey Joe's Café" (1955). R&B also expressed black pride in its masculine braggadocio, which particularly challenged the white practice of referring to black men as "boys." Songs like Willie Dixon's "Hoochie Coochie Man" (recorded by Muddy Waters in 1954) and Bo Diddley's "I'm a Man" (1955) announced in no uncertain terms that black men's patience was at an end. Initially, however, it remained unclear whether anyone besides African Americans would hear this music, for popular music was as segregated as any other part of American life.

The Legacy of R&B in American Popular Culture

In the years following World War II the major recording studios concentrated on producing bland music for a white market, virtually ignoring black listeners. A few black performers such as Nat King Cole managed to cross over to the white pop music charts. R&B, however, was the domain of small independent record companies, known as indies, that appeared in every American city with a sizable black population. The indies themselves, with the exception of Exclusive/Excelsior in Los Angeles, Vee Jay in Chicago, and Peacock in Houston, were white-owned.

Although initially meant for blacks, R&B ultimately transformed all of American popular culture by delivering vitality in a bland era. Compared with staid white singers like Perry Como and Doris Day, the popular R&B acts of Aaron "T-Bone" Walker, Willie Mae "Big Mama" Thornton, "Screamin'" Jay Hawkins, Clarence "Gatemouth" Brown, and "Bull Moose" Jackson offered raw energy and uninhibited music. R&B lyrics likewise conveyed greater emotional intensity than anything found in white pop music. Where Como crooned lines such as "We can wink at the moon as we hold each other tight," R&B offered earthiness and deep feeling. For example, in "He May Be Your Man" (1945), Helen Humes exclaimed:

Yes, that man rocks me, he rocks me with one steady roll,
And when he rocks me, Lord, he satisfies my soul.

Similarly, in "I Got a Woman" (1954), Ray Charles sang, "She saves her lovin', early in the mornin', just for me." As was often the case in R&B, the singer's delivery was as important as the song's lyrics. With the horns acting as an amen chorus, Charles surged through the verses, stoking the emotional fires and at times letting his voice soar into a transcendent falsetto.

Longtime Apollo Theater emcee Ralph Cooper recalled that – long before Elvis Presley made his appearance – such singing drove young audiences wild: "Singers became idols… [a]nd when they grabbed a mike, cocked their hips, and swaggered to the backbeat, [the fans'] screaming was the sound of uncontrolled excitement. With all that sexuality letting loose, things got downright hysterical."

The growth of R&B also offered young African Americans new avenues for success, symbolized by the dream of winning a major talent contest, such as Amateur Night in Harlem, and finding fame and fortune through music.

Countless vocal groups practiced on street corners and in private homes and schoolyards of black neighborhoods, hoping for a recording contract. Yet in all but a few cases, music industry gatekeepers, the record company owners, booking agents, and disc jockeys (DJs) were white, and black performers discovered that they had little control over their music. Even the phrase R&B was of white origin, introduced by Jerry Wexler, reporter for *Billboard* magazine and future head of Atlantic Records, as a euphemism for "race records," the term then in use. On June 25, 1949, *Billboard* renamed its black music chart, and – in the eyes of the music industry – the R&B era had officially begun.

R&B and Rock 'n' Roll

R&B was a music of transgression, challenging the boundaries of segregation. In the mid-1950s many black R&B performers adopted a harder beat and ascended the pop charts as increasing numbers of white teenagers discovered the more visceral R&B sound. Many first heard this music through the broadcasts of black-format radio stations like Memphis's WDIA or the rare white R&B DJs such as Alan Freed. Historian Robert Pruter noted that package tours of leading R&B acts were also "instrumental in helping break rhythm and blues into the white market as rock 'n' roll music." In 1952 Freed began hosting racially integrated R&B concerts, and in Los Angeles concerts produced by R&B performer Johnny Otis brought together blacks, whites, and Mexican Americans.

Older whites responded by condemning R&B, allegedly on musical grounds, but also because it violated racial boundaries. Some blacks, especially those who identified with middle-class values, criticized the music because it was rough and did not project what they considered to be a suitable image of the race. In 1953 the entertainment magazine *Variety* concluded that "100 percent rhythm and blues platters sell only in the colored market, although diluted interpretations have been seeping into the pop field with increasing frequency."

In 1954, however, Nat King Cole found his crossover success challenged by such rowdy R&B acts as Ruth Brown, Ray Charles, B. B. King, Big Joe Turner, Muddy Waters, the Clovers, and Hank Ballard and the Midnighters. In the following year Chuck Berry, Little Richard, Etta James, and Bo Diddley all made their recording debuts. The mid-1950s were also the golden era of R&B vocal groups. Some, like the Clovers, Hank Ballard and the Midnighters, and the Robins (which gave rise to the Coasters), took a raucous and bluesy approach. Other groups – including the Moonglows, the Harptones, the Orioles, and the Flamingos – emphasized complex voicings and greater interplay between the lead singer and the rest of the group, in a style that the *Chicago Defender*, an African American newspaper, labeled "doo wop."

For the first time, R&B performers began charting songs among the year's Top Ten. Such successful releases including the following:
1956 – The Platters, "My Prayer"
1957 – Sam Cooke, "You Send Me"
1959 – Wilbert Harrison, "Kansas City"; The Platters, "Smoke Gets in Your Eyes"; Lloyd Price, "Stagger Lee"
1960 – The Drifters, "Save the Last Dance for Me"; Chubby Checker, "The Twist"

The major record companies responded by turning to "covers," recordings made by white groups with the intention of pre-empting the hit songs of black performers.

Since the major labels had far greater resources behind their versions, covers often crowded out the black originals. For example, the hit songs of two black groups – "Sh-Boom" (1954), a novelty number by the Chords, and "A Story Untold" (1955), a ballad by the Nutmegs – were successfully covered by Mercury's slick white group, the Crewcuts. On the other hand, the McGuire Sisters' cover of the Moonglows' "Sincerely" (1954) could not keep the original out of the Top Twenty. In the mid-1950s Elvis Presley launched his career through covers of R&B hits like Roy Brown's "Good Rockin' Tonight" (1948) and Big Mama Thornton's "Hound Dog" (1953).

The End of the R&B Era

By the early 1960s the R&B era was over. Indeed, on November 30, 1963, *Billboard* stopped publishing a separate R&B chart because the music had effectively been absorbed into the pop music mainstream. African American performers either adapted to fit prevailing white tastes or else they created new musical forms that were more expressly grounded in black culture. In the 1960s these contrasting approaches were exemplified in Motown's smooth pop stylings versus the harder edge of soul music, and during the 1970s in the wide appeal of disco versus funk music's largely black audience.

Although in later years *Billboard* reintroduced an R&B chart, it has generally served as a residual category for black music that is not rap, reggae, or blues – in a sense, black middle-of-the-road. In its golden age, however, R&B was by no means middle-of-the-road. It broke down racial barriers that had long divided American music, furthering a process of cross-fertilization that reaches from the Fisk Jubilee Singers, through jazz artists like Louis Armstrong, Cab Calloway, and Duke Ellington, up to the present. In its heyday R&B offered a high-spirited affirmation of black life. Most of all, it was the musical voice of a generation of African Americans who would no longer tolerate second-class citizenship or balcony-seat tickets to the American dream.

James Clyde Sellman

See Also

World War II and African Americans; Vee Jay Records; Armstrong, Louis ("Satchmo"); Berry, Charles Edward Anderson, (Chuck); Blues, The; Calloway, Cabell (Cab); *Chicago Defender*; Chicago, Illinois; Cole, Nat ("King"); Coltrane, John William; Cooke, Samuel (Sam); Diddley, Bo; Dixon, Willie; Great Migration, The; Harlem, New York; King, Riley B. ("B. B."); Los Angeles, California; Motown; Thornton, Willie Mae ("Big Mama"); Walker, Aaron ("T-Bone"); Ellington, Edward Kennedy ("Duke").

North America

Richards, Lloyd George

(b. June 29, 1919, Toronto, Ontario), Canadian theater director and educator who directed the award-winning play *A Raisin in the Sun.*

Lloyd Richards was born in Canada to Jamaican immigrants Albert and Rose Richards. His father died when he was young and the family moved to Detroit, Michigan. Richards graduated from Wayne State University in 1943 and went on to serve in the United States Air Force as a pilot during World War II. After the war he returned to Detroit, where he began working in theater and radio drama. Richards moved to New York City in the 1950s and studied with Paul Mann, a teacher of the Stanislavsky acting method.

Richards's first major directorial assignment was Lorraine Hansberry's *A Raisin in the Sun*, which won the 1959 New York Critics Circle Award. After this success he directed four other Broadway productions during the 1960s. Beginning in the mid-1960s Richards held positions at the New York University School of Arts, the Eugene O'Neill Theater Center, Hunter College, and the Yale School of Drama, where he was appointed dean in 1979. He retired from that position in 1991 and continued to write and direct.

Richards is also known for his collaborations with playwright August Wilson, starting with a 1982 production of *Ma Rainey's Black Botton*. Richards directed all of Wilson's plays and received a Tony Award in 1986 for his direction of Wilson's *Fences*. The following year Richards received the Pioneer Award, the Frederick Douglass Award, and the Golden Plate Award for his accomplishments in drama.

Aaron Myers

See Also

World War II and African Americans; Hansberry, Lorraine; New York, New York.

North America

Richardson, Gloria St. Clair Hayes (b. May 6, 1922, Baltimore, Md.), leader of the struggle for desegregation in Cambridge, Maryland.

As cochair of the Cambridge Nonviolent Action Committee, Gloria Richardson initiated a series of demonstrations against segregation and the economic oppression of blacks in Cambridge, Maryland. She was among the 80 protesters arrested and fined one penny apiece in the widely publicized Penny Trials of May 1963. After several weeks of violence and the imposition of martial law, Richardson, along with other black leaders and Cambridge officials, signed the Treaty of Cambridge on June 23, 1963. Although criticized for her direct-action tactics at the time, Richardson has since been credited with making desegregation possible in Cambridge. In 1964 she moved to New York City to work for the Department for the Aging.

Lawrie Balfour

SEE ALSO

New York, New York.

North America

Richmond, Virginia, center of the slave trade, capital of the Confederacy, and cradle of a cohesive African American community.

A short 60 years after its founding in 1607, the tiny James River trading post of Richmond was already doing a brisk business in the sale of slaves. The fertile Virginia soil supported a thriving tobacco trade that created a demand for cheap labor. Despite Virginia's manumission laws, which granted freedom to the children of slaves, and an antislavery organization run by Quakers, Richmond's slave trade prospered before the Revolutionary War.

The central location of Richmond endowed it with political as well as economic significance, leading to its designation as state capital. As Richmond grew in size and importance, slaves, who constituted half the population and a majority of the work force, actually constructed much of the city. During the AMERICAN REVOLUTION slaves worked on public projects, assisted the military, and repaired arms. Two African Americans from Richmond even served in the Colonial Army, and one spied for the Americans in order to win his freedom.

Agriculture expanded and thrived around Richmond until the early nineteenth century when the soil began to show signs of overuse. As tobacco farming declined, so did the demand for slaves. The resulting economic lull led many white citizens of Richmond to talk favorably of abolition. Nat Turner's Rebellion, however, in which a band of fugitive slaves killed 57 whites, caused widespread paranoia among slaveholders and undermined the abolitionist movement in Virginia. Meanwhile, the growth of new industries led to new demands for cheap labor and a revitalized slave trade.

Until the Civil War African Americans supplied the tobacco and iron industries of Richmond with the majority of their work force. Although still legally enslaved, factory workers enjoyed greater freedom than plantation slaves. They often took responsibility for their own housing, earned bonuses and "board" money, and were allowed considerable physical mobility. These freedoms, and the accompanying discretionary income, enabled factory workers to support a separate economy of craftsmen and business owners that served the black community. Slaves now ran their own boarding houses and barbershops, and fixed their own shoes. However, Richmond's slave trade continued to prosper, as surplus slaves left over from the tobacco heyday were sold to regions farther south.

African American Richmonders served both the Union and the Confederacy during the Civil War. After Richmond became the capital of the Confederacy in 1862, some slaves were forced to lay new railroads and help reinforce the city's fortifications. Others served alongside free blacks and Union soldiers in undercover operations against the Confederates. Appropriately, black troops led the Union army into a surrendering Richmond, signaling the end of slavery and the war.

During RECONSTRUCTION the community networks that black factory workers had created became the center of African American economic and social life. "Secret societies" proliferated, and freedpeople met the challenges of emancipation with the help of fraternal orders and churches. This strong social network also enabled the founding of the Richmond Theological Seminary (later Virginia Union University) and newspapers such as the *Richmond Planet*. The experiences of African Americans in earlier mutual-aid organizations facilitated their political involvement, and by the 1880s new movements, such as the Knights of Labor, served working-class blacks as they strove for justice and empowerment. The Knights of Labor included whites as well as blacks, and during the early 1880s class cooperation mitigated the racial divide. Together workers campaigned for better working conditions and higher wages. By 1886, however, the union dissolved, in part from racial tensions. African Americans once again had to work alone.

By 1900 the white establishment of Richmond had instigated an effective counterattack against the gains blacks had won. For the next 50 years the African American community fought the discriminatory practices of the white elite, in both the public and private sectors. The Richmond Theater and local hotels adopted the JIM CROW system, and whites pushed blacks out of housing and jobs. While black people won some voting rights and founded banks upon previous financial networks, whites enforced segregation in an increasing number of spheres.

World War II marked the end of the most pernicious discrimination. In the early postwar years African Americans gained access to the Richmond Public Library, found employment with the police and fire departments, and benefited tangibly from the United States Supreme Court's BROWN V. BOARD OF EDUCATION (1954) ruling, which led to the desegregation of public schools. Richmond's blacks played a significant role in the CIVIL RIGHTS MOVEMENT of the 1950s and 1960s, holding boycotts, fighting poll taxes, and hosting the SOUTHERN CHRISTIAN LEADERSHIP CONFERENCE's convention in 1963.

Like other major U.S. cities in the 1960s and 1970s, Richmond experienced a white evacuation to the suburbs, leaving the city with a black majority. Unfortunately, Richmond also suffered the problems of unemployment and urban decay resulting from a weakened tax base caused by white flight. Furthermore, white politicians aggravated the problems of African Americans with efforts to redraw electoral lines to benefit white suburbanites. After seven years of deadlock and court deliberation the African American community expunged the white-dominated electoral system under the Voting Rights Act, winning control of the local government. Despite the 1977 election of an African American mayor, Henry Marsh III, and the 1989 gubernatorial victory of black candidate L. Douglas Wilder, however, Richmond continued to suffer from crime, violence, drugs, and indigence throughout the last quarter of the twentieth century.

Eric Bennett

SEE ALSO

Slavery in the United States; World War II and African Americans; Abolitionism in the United States; Civil War, American; Free Blacks in the United States, 1619 to 1863; Manumission Societies; Mutual Benefit Societies; Wilder, Lawrence Douglas; Turner, Nat; Voting Rights Act of 1965; Black Church, The.

Africa

Rift Valleys, or Great Rift Valley, one of the world's most impressive physical features; the defining feature of the East African landscape and the site of some of the world's oldest fossil hominids.

The Great Rift Valley was formed about 20 million years ago when two parallel fault lines pulled apart, forcing the land in between to move down. A massive depression resulted, which stretches through East Africa from the Jordan River valley of the Red Sea to central MOZAMBIQUE. The Rift Valley extends over 7000 km (about 4350 mi) and ranges from 40 to 60 km wide (about 25 to

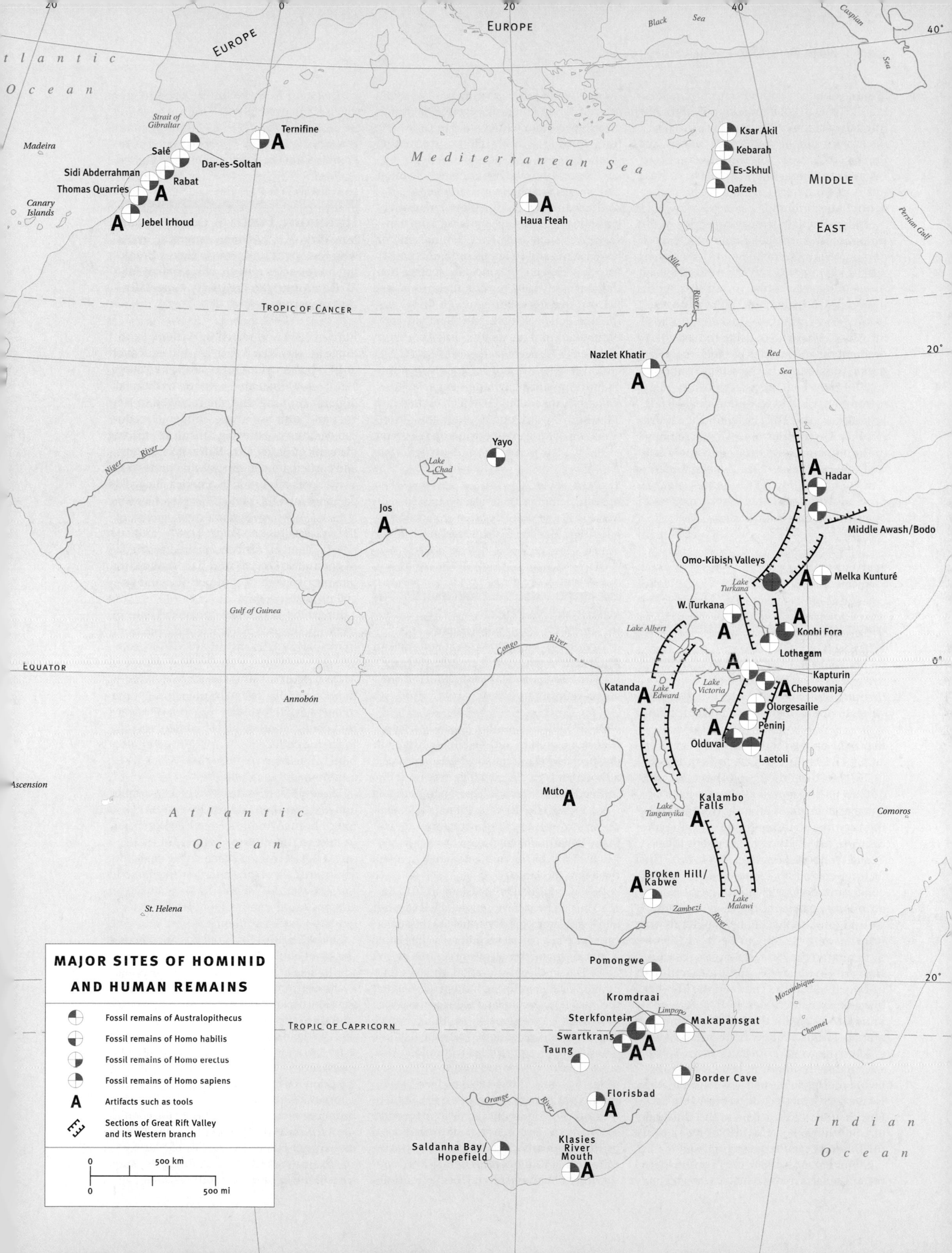

MAJOR SITES OF HOMINID AND HUMAN REMAINS
Fossil remains of Australopithecus
Fossil remains of Homo habilis
Fossil remains of Homo erectus
Fossil remains of Homo sapiens
Artifacts such as tools
Sections of Great Rift Valley and its Western branch
0 500 km
0 500 mi
Europe
Europe
Atlantic Ocean
Mediterranean Sea
Black Sea
Caspian Sea
Persian Gulf
Middle East
Red Sea
Indian Ocean
Tropic of Cancer
Tropic of Capricorn
Equator
Strait of Gibraltar
Madeira
Canary Islands
Ternifine
Dar-es-Soltan
Salé
Rabat
Sidi Abderrahman
Thomas Quarries
Jebel Irhoud
Haua Fteah
Ksar Akil
Kebarah
Es-Skhul
Qafzeh
Nile River
Nazlet Khatir
Yayo
Lake Chad
Niger River
Jos
Gulf of Guinea
Annobón
Congo River
Hadar
Middle Awash/Bodo
Omo-Kibish Valleys
Melka Kunturé
Lake Turkana
W. Turkana
Koobi Fora
Lothagam
Lake Albert
Kapturin
Chesowanja
Katanda
Lake Edward
Lake Victoria
Olorgesailie
Peninj
Olduvai
Laetoli
Ascension
Muto
Lake Tanganyika
Kalambo Falls
Comoros
Broken Hill/Kabwe
Lake Malawi
Zambezi River
St. Helena
Pomongwe
Kromdraai
Limpopo
Sterkfontein
Makapansgat
Swartkrans
Taung
Mozambique Channel
Border Cave
Florisbad
Orange River
Saldanha Bay/Hopefield
Klasies River Mouth

37 mi), varying in depth from a few meters (about 10 ft) to 2000 m (about 6560 ft). The Rift Valley actually consists of two valleys, the Eastern and the Western (or Gregory Rift Zone). The Eastern Rift runs from central Ethiopia to central Kenya, while the Western Rift runs from north of Lake Victoria to central Mozambique.

Volcanic activity along either side of the rift produced spectacular mountains, most notably Mount Kilimanjaro, Africa's highest peak, and Mount Kenya. The Western Rift left a series of depressions that became East Africa's deepest lakes, including Lake Tanganyika, Lake Malawi, and Lake Turkana. Because the rift lakes have no outlet to the sea, their evaporation often results in a higher concentration of minerals in the waters. Although Lake Turkana contains water fresh enough to support fish and wildlife, Lake Magadi, Lake Nakuru, and Lake Elementita are heavily alkaline. Discoveries of fossilized remains of human ancestors, as well as tools and weapons, at sites around Lake Turkana in Kenya and in Olduvai Gorge in Tanzania provide strong evidence that Africa is the cradle of human evolution.

Robert Fay

See Also

Kilimanjaro.

North America

Riggs, Marlon Troy

(b. February 3, 1957, Fort Worth, Tex.; d. April 5, 1994, Oakland, Calif.), documentary filmmaker and educator who used video to oppose racism and homophobia.

Reflecting on the death of Marlon Riggs from acquired immune deficiency syndrome (AIDS), cultural theorist Kobena Mercer observed, "Independent cinema lost the voice and vision of an important artist at the very moment that he was coming into his own." At the time of his death Riggs was at work on *Black Is.... Black Ain't.* This feature-length film, completed by Riggs's collaborators in 1995, chronicled the variety of American identities seen as "black."

Riggs grew up in a military family, moving from Texas to Georgia to Germany before returning to the United States to attend Harvard University. As an undergraduate he began to explore connections between black and gay identities; his research culminated in a senior thesis on the treatment of male homosexuality in literature. After graduating magna cum laude in 1978, Riggs worked briefly at a Texas television station before moving to the San Francisco Bay Area. He received a master's degree from the Graduate School of Journalism at the University of California at Berkeley in 1981 and joined the Berkeley faculty six years later.

Ethnic Notions (1986), the first film Riggs wrote, directed, and produced, won an Emmy Award in 1988 for its investigation of racial stereotypes in American society. That same year Riggs began work on his most famous film, *Tongues Untied* (1989). A work that interweaves poetry, personal reflections, and scenes from the lives of black gay men, *Tongues Untied* challenged the marginalization of gayness in the black community. It also inspired outraged attacks from conservatives such as North Carolina senator Jesse Helms and religious fundamentalist Patrick Buchanan, who included footage from the film in his 1992 presidential campaign.

Despite deteriorating health, Riggs remained active as a lecturer, teacher, and filmmaker until his death. *Anthem* (1990) and *Non, Je Ne Regrette Rien/No Regret* (1991) continued the work of *Tongues Untied* in examining black gay men's experiences. *Color Adjustment* (1991), which earned him a Peabody Award, documented the representation of African Americans on television.

Lawrie Balfour

See Also

AIDS in the United States; San Francisco and Oakland, California; Television and African Americans; Gay and Lesbian Movements in the United States.

North America

Rillieux, Norbert

(b. March 17, 1806, New Orleans, La.; d. October 8, 1894, Paris, France), African American inventor and engineer whose patented inventions revolutionized the sugar-refining industry.

Norbert Rillieux's mother was an African American woman and his father, a French engineer and plantation owner. He was free, although it is not known if he was born free or freed later. After studying engineering at L'Ecole Centrale in Paris, Rillieux became the school's youngest instructor ever to date in the department of applied mechanics. At L'Ecole Centrale he published many papers on steam technology.

Rillieux returned to Louisiana in 1840. In 1843 he patented the multiple-effect vacuum pan evaporator. This device heated the sugar cane juice in a partial vacuum, which reduced its boiling point, thus allowing a much greater fuel efficiency. This innovation, widely adopted in the sugar-refining industry, escalated the rate of production and reduced the price of sugar. It was responsible for transforming sugar, previously an upper-class luxury, into a household item. Similar technology was subsequently developed for the production of soap, gelatin, and glue. Some have called Rillieux's evaporator the greatest invention in the history of American chemical engineering.

When post-Reconstruction conditions proved oppressive in Louisiana for African Americans, Rillieux returned to Paris, serving as headmaster at L'Ecole Centrale. He began to study Egyptology and helped decipher hieroglyphics.

See Also

Free Blacks in the United States, 1619 to 1863.

North America

Ringgold, Faith

(b. October 8, 1934, New York, N.Y.), African American artist who has spent her artistic career breaking boundaries and clearing spaces for African American creativity, especially that of women.

Born in 1934 and raised in Harlem, Faith Ringgold earned a B.A. in art and education in 1955 and an M.F.A. in 1959 at City College, New York. Dissatisfied with the traditional high art training that she received in New York and later in Europe, Ringgold reeducated herself by studying African art, reading the work of Black Arts Movement authors, and participating in the growing protest for a civil rights revolution in America. Ringgold's paintings from this period, *The Flag is Bleeding* (1967), *US Postage Stamp Commemorating the Advent of Black Power* (1967), and *Die* (1967), blend an African-inspired aesthetic of geometric shapes and flat, shadowless perspective with potent political and social protest.

Ringgold has been an outspoken critic of racial and gender prejudice in the art world. In the early 1970s she organized protests against the Whitney Museum of American Art and other major museums for excluding the works of blacks and women. In response to the museum world's exclusionary policies, Ringgold and other black women artists formed a collective and organized an exhibit of their own, whose title, *Where We At,* announced their visibility.

Ringgold's art focuses on black women and black women's issues. Diverse works – a mural in the Women's House of Detention in Riker's Island, New York (1971-1972) and a performance piece using soft cloth sculptures, *The Wake and Resurrection of the Bicentennial Negro* (1976) – focused on women's ability to heal and brought her work to a wider audience.

Since the 1970s Ringgold has documented her local community and national events in life-size soft sculptures, representing everyone from ordinary Harlem denizens to Rev. Martin Luther King Jr. and the young victims of the Atlanta child murders (1979-80). Ringgold's latest chosen medium, fabric, is traditionally associated with women.

Ringgold's expression of black women's experience is perhaps best captured in her "storyquilts." A combination of quilting and narrative text, quilts like *Who's Afraid of Aunt Jemima?* (1982) and the series *Women on a Bridge* (1988) tell stories of pain and survival in a medium that Ringgold finds essentially female and empowering. She transformed one of her quilts into a children's book, *Tar Beach,* that won the 1992 Caldecott Honor Book Award and the Coretta Scott King award.

See Also
Civil Rights Movement; Harlem, New York; King, Martin Luther, Jr.; Art, African American.

Latin America and the Caribbean

Rio de Janeiro, Brazil, city in southeastern Brazil, on the Atlantic Ocean, and the capital of the state of Rio de Janeiro. Its name is Portuguese for "river of January." This refers to its location near the entrance to Guanabara Bay, which appeared to be a large river estuary to early sixteenth-century explorers, and to the date it was discovered – January 1, 1502.

Rio de Janeiro is the second most populous city in Brazil, after São Paulo, and ranks second only to São Paulo in industrial production. Rio also boasts one of the busiest ports and airports in the nation. Internationally, it is still the nation's best-known city, and it was the site of the United Nations Environmental Conference in 1992. The city's inhabitants are called *cariocas* and are characterized within Brazil as fun-loving, sensual, and easygoing.

Rio's climate is tropical and rainfall is common, averaging about 1080 mm (43 in) per year. Temperatures during the humid summer months – December to March – can top 35° C (95° F), but typically drop to between 20° C and 30° C (68° F and 86° F) during the rest of the year. Sea breezes moderate temperatures throughout the year.

Rio and Its Metropolitan Area

In Brazil Rio is known as the Marvelous City, a name that reflects the city's stunning natural setting between the mountains and the sea. Rio is located on the western side of Guanabara Bay on a flat, narrow coastal plain adjacent to the foothills of the Brazilian Highlands. As the city has expanded, it has occupied the spurs of these coastal mountains, often with the homes of the poor.

The municipality of Rio, the city proper, occupies a relatively small area, about 1170 sq km (about 450 sq mi). The metropolitan region outside the city is vast, however. It includes 13 other municipalities, making the total metropolitan region about 6500 sq km (about 2500 sq mi). This urbanized area even spans Guanabara Bay to include the suburban areas of Niterói, Neves, and São Gonçalo located on its eastern shores. These suburbs are connected to the city by the Rio-Niterói Bridge, a 14 km- (9 mi-) span constructed in 1974.

The local topography has been reengineered considerably to expand the city and facilitate transportation within it. The site of the city's original founding, a low hill known as Morro do Castelo, was leveled in the early years of the twentieth century to expand the central business district. In the twentieth century San Antonio Hill was removed, a number of tunnels were constructed to facilitate traffic, and several large landfill projects extended the city into Guanabara Bay and widened its beaches.

The city of Rio can be thought of as being divided into three principal areas: the traditional historical core at the eastern base of the Serra da Carioca, a small coastal mountain range running east to west; the northern zone situated to the northwest of the core; and the southern zone located to the south and southwest of the core. The Serra da Carioca provides a natural physical boundary between the northern and southern zones.

The commercial area of the city is compact, centering on Avenida Rio Branco and Avenida Presidente Vargas. The city's subway system follows these two avenues through the downtown area. The center includes many tall office buildings, and on weekdays its streets are clogged with motor vehicles and pedestrians. Most government offices, banks, financial institutions, major airline offices, and commercial buildings are located in the city's core. Museums, colonial churches, and notable public buildings are also located in this area.

The metropolitan area's industrial districts and extensive lower-income suburbs, like the municipalities of Nova Iguaçu, São João Meriti, and Duque de Caxias, are found in the city's northern zone. The city's southern zone is largely the home of Rio's upper classes. Traditionally these wealthy residents have lived in the coastal neighborhoods of Copacabana, Ipanema, Leblon, and Gávea. While these areas are still popular, upscale locations, Barra da Tijuca, farther west along the coast, has perhaps become Rio's most fashionable neighborhood. Squatter settlements, known in Brazil as favelas, cover the steep slopes of many of the hills throughout the city, often in close proximity to wealthy residential neighborhoods. Rocinha, the city's largest favela, with 150,000 to 300,000 residents, sits in the southern zone adjacent to the wealthy neighborhood of Gávea.

Urban transportation in Rio is dominated by buses, which account for nearly 70 percent of all passenger trips. Automobiles and taxis are used in slightly less than 20 percent of such trips. Suburban trains, the subway, and ferries provide transportation for a limited proportion of passenger trips – about 7 percent, 3 percent, and 2 percent, respectively.

Population

The municipality of Rio, the city proper, had a population of 5,480,768 at the 1991 census. The vast metropolitan region, however, was home to a population of 10,389,441. Although population growth had been rapid during most of the twentieth century, it slowed significantly between 1980 and 1990; during this period the metropolitan region posted the lowest annual population growth rate, only 0.7 percent, since modern census taking began. That growth has been uneven, with the municipality of Rio posting only a 0.4 percent annual gain, while outlying suburban municipalities have averaged about 1.5 percent annually.

Rio's ethnic makeup mirrors its history, which has included people of African, European, and Native American origin. Nearly two-thirds of the population is of African descent, although this group reflects the widespread racial mixing and intermarriage that have characterized Brazilian society. While racial tolerance and acceptance are often heralded as characteristics of Brazilian society, whites typically enjoy more privileged social and economic positions than people of African or native descent (*see* Race and Class in Brazil: An Interpretation).

Education and Culture).

Although Rio is not Brazil's largest city, nor its capital, its historical role as the nation's preeminent urban center makes it the single most important city in the country in terms of education, culture, and the arts. The city is well endowed with both public and private universities. Public universities include the Federal University of Rio de Janeiro (1920), the State University of Rio de Janeiro (1961), and the University of Rio de Janeiro (1969). Cándido Mendes University Conglomerate (1981), Gama Filho University (1972), Pontifical Catholic University of Rio de Janeiro (1941), and University Santa Úrsula (1938) are all private universities.

Rio contains the National Library, housed in an impressive neoclassical building, and the National Archive. Another important part of the city's cultural offerings are its museums, including the National Museum, the Museum of Modern Art, the National Fine Arts Museum, the National Historical Museum, the Museum of the Indian, and the Carmen Miranda Museum. The Municipal Theater, built in 1905 and modeled on the Paris Opera House, is in the core of the city and is home to Rio's ballet troupe and opera company.

Architecture is an important component in the city's landscape. Examples of religious architecture include the Convent of San Antonio, which was built in 1608 and is thought to be the oldest religious structure in the city; the Monastery of Saint Bento, with an impressive Baroque-style chapel; Our Lady of Carmo Church, where both Brazil's emperors were crowned; and Our Lady of Candelária Church, thought by some to be the city's most beautiful church.

Another building of interest is the Imperial Palace, located several blocks west of Santos Dumont Airport. Originally constructed as Brazil's colonial governor's capitol in 1743, it was converted to the royal palace during the city's period as an imperial capital. It has recently been restored and now houses a cultural center. Other impressive nineteenth-century palaces include Itamaraty and Catete, both located in the city center. The latter was occupied by the country's presidents between 1896 and 1954 and now houses the Museum of the Republic. The state legislature meets in the Palacio Tiradentes, formerly the home of the federal assembly when Rio was the nation's capital. The city's architecture from the seventeenth, eighteenth, and nineteenth centuries stands in dramatic contrast with its ultramodern Petrobras building, headquarters of the state petroleum company, and the avant-garde Metropolitan Cathedral. The city's most famous landmarks are Pão de Açúcar (395 m/1296 ft), which is situated on a peninsula jutting into Guanabara Bay and is known as Sugar Loaf Mountain in English, and the massive (40 m/131 ft) Christ the Redeemer statue, which overlooks the city from the top of Corcovado Mountain (704 m/2310 ft) in the Serra da Carioca coastal range.

Recreation

Recreational activities abound in Rio. Extensive sandy beaches along the Atlantic Ocean in the southern margins of the city are used heavily by both residents and tourists. Tijuca National Park is outside the urbanized area, atop the Serra da Carioca range, and contains remnants of the tropical rain forest that once covered the entire region. Urban parks include Quinta da Boa Vista Park (site of the National Museum, which focuses on natural history), the Botanical Gardens, Lage Park, and Flamengo Park. These parks provide opportunities for a range of recreational activities – including hiking, climbing, hang-gliding, jogging, walking, and cycling – for both residents and tourists. Maracaña Stadium, which holds more than 100,000 spectators for soccer games, is located just outside Quinta da Boa Vista Park.

Rio's milestone social event and preeminent tourist attraction each year is Carnival, a major festival held in late February or early March, just prior to the beginning of the Christian season of Lent. During the weeks that precede Carnival the city receives thousands of tourists. Events include spontaneous street dancing behind popular *bandas* (marching bands of brass and percussion instruments), formal Carnival balls for nearly every income level, and several days of Sambodromo parades in which the best SAMBA SCHOOLS compete in marathon musical and dance presentations along a specially designed street where thousands of spectators gather to watch the event unfold.

Economy

Rio ranks second nationally in industrial production and is a major financial and service center. The city's industries produce processed foods, chemicals, petroleum products, pharmaceuticals, metal products, ships, textiles, clothing, and furniture. The service sector dominates the economy, however, and includes banking and the second most active stock market in Brazil, the Bolsa da Valores do Brasil.

Tourism and entertainment are other key aspects of the city's economic life and the city is the nation's top tourist attraction for both Brazilians and foreigners. Revenue from tourism began declining sharply in the late 1980s and early 1990s, due in part to a global recession and the Persian Gulf War (1991), but also because of political turmoil and rampant crime in the city. The annual number of foreign travelers visiting Rio dropped from a high of 750,000 in 1988 to 425,000 in 1990. Local authorities responded by creating a special police unit in 1992 to patrol those areas most frequented by tourists, especially the Copacabana neighborhood – home to many of the city's hotels, tourist facilities, and attractive beaches.

Rio is well connected to the rest of Brazil by land, sea, and air. It is linked to all key points in the nation by an extensive highway system. Most freight moves by truck and a wide range of buses provide direct service to all major Brazilian cities. Two airports serve the city: Santos Dumont Airport, a downtown facility for local shuttle flights between Rio and São Paulo, and Galeão Airport, a major national and international airport located on Governor's Island in Guanabara Bay. The volume of cargo moved through Rio's port ranks second in the nation. Only the port of Santos, which serves as the port for São Paulo, exceeds its volume.

Government

Rio's metropolitan region includes the 14 independent municipal governments that make up the urban area. Municipalities are the foundation of democratic government in Brazil, as laid out in the 1988 constitution. They are governed by elected mayors and municipal councils and have responsibility for primary education, basic health services, solid-waste collection and disposal, and municipal upkeep, including streets and parks. Municipal funding sources include taxes on property and services, as well as revenue from state and federal sources.

There is no metropolitan planning or development authority, although in the 1980s the state-instituted Metropolitan Development Foundation attempted to fulfill such a role. It has since been disbanded.

Contemporary Issues

Although Rio may be Brazil's most beautiful city, it is also one of its most troubled. The favelas, which blanket the slopes of surrounding hillsides, house approximately 20 percent of the city's residents and are often dangerous, unsanitary, and lacking in basic services such as water, sewerage, and, to a lesser extent, electricity. Many of the city's poor have no jobs, no access to schools, and only limited access to medical care. However, literacy rates for Rio are high, nearly 90 percent, and a system of public hospitals and clinics provides at least some medical care to the city's poorest residents. Police corruption is widespread. Environmental pollution is a problem throughout the metropolitan region, and the waters of Guanabara Bay are considered too polluted for safe bathing.

Rio experienced serious crime problems in the early 1990s, when powerful criminal gangs took over entire favela neighborhoods. The murders of homeless children in 1993 by corrupt police officers acting on behalf of commercial interests drew international attention to Rio's social and criminal problems. With a murder rate of 61 per 100,000 people in 1994, Rio was one of the world's most violent cities. This was more than twice the rate of 28 per 100,000 for São Paulo.

History

Portuguese explorers arrived at Guanabara Bay in 1502, and in 1555 French colonists established a Calvinist settlement. Native Americans from the Tupí family occupied the area at the time of European contact. The French were expelled in 1567 by the Portuguese, who maintained a small colony based on subsistence agriculture, fishing, and the export of brazilwood and SUGAR cane until the beginning of the eighteenth century. In 1704 the completion of a road from Rio to the gold mines of Minas Gerais made the city a major center of transportation, commerce, and wealth. Rio was captured by the French in 1710, and the Portuguese paid a substantial ransom for its return. The city's fortunes rose in 1763 when the capital of colonial Brazil was moved to Rio from Salvador, a port city in northeastern Brazil known at the time as Bahia. After Napoleon Bonaparte's armies captured Lisbon, Portugal, in 1808, Rio became the seat of Portugal's exiled royal family. In the decade that followed the city grew dramatically and took on a decidedly European flavor. In 1822 it became the capital of the independent Brazilian Empire. With the overthrow of the monarchy in 1889, Rio was made the capital of the Brazilian republic. Beginning in the late 1800s and continuing well into the middle of the 1900s, coffee cultivation expanded widely in the mountainous terrain surrounding Rio, fueling a commercial boom that enriched the city and its residents. By 1900 Rio's population had grown to about 800,000.

The global economic depression of the 1930s and World War II (1939-1945) drastically reduced the flow of manufactured goods into Brazil, encouraging the development of national industries; many of these were based in Rio. After World War II Rio prospered from increasing commerce and international trade. During this period Rio attracted large numbers of migrants who came from small towns and rural areas of Brazil seeking jobs and better living conditions. In 1960 the capital of the nation was transferred to Brasília, deep in the country's interior. This marked a dramatic change for Rio, resulting in a loss of political status and prestige. In addition, large amounts of federal aid – as well as related investment and jobs – were shifted to the new capital, undermining Rio's economic dominance. Nevertheless, the city's population continued to mushroom until the 1980s, when growth tapered off.

Afro-Brazilian History and Culture in Rio de Janeiro

The city of Rio de Janeiro became an important slave-trading port and commercial center in the eighteenth century, when the mining of gold and diamonds in the interior province of Minas Gerais produced great profits for Brazil. The city's commercial significance increased in the nineteenth century, when the cultivation of coffee in the states of Rio de Janeiro and São Paulo became the country's most important economic activity. At this time the state of Rio de Janeiro absorbed large numbers of African slaves. In 1819 nearly one-quarter of the state's population was enslaved; there were approximately 146,000 slaves. By 1885, three years before the abolition of slavery in Brazil, more than half the city's population was black (comprising about 162,400 slaves and 9500 free blacks).

During the first part of the nineteenth century the majority of these slaves were imported from Africa, but after the end of slave trade to Brazil in 1850 coffee farmers in Rio de Janeiro purchased many slaves from northeast provinces, previously the prosperous sugar-growing region in Brazil. The coffee plantation owners in Rio were the strongest defenders of slavery in Brazil. They were opposed by a small but vocal abolitionist movement that included Afro-Brazilian abolitionists such as José Ferreira de Menezes, André Rebouças, and José do Patrocínio.

Following the abolition of slavery on May 13, 1888, a great number of ex-slaves migrated to Rio de Janeiro's metropolitan area. Many of the Afro-Brazilians settled in the city's downtown area. One of the black neighborhoods that emerged, Estácio, became the birthplace of samba. However, around the turn of the twentieth century the city launched an urbanization program that sought to improve the sanitation and transportation systems and to make the city more attractive to foreign investment. As a result, many Afro-Brazilians were forced out of the downtown area. This displaced Afro-Brazilian population, along with arriving black immigrants, relocated to the hills surrounding the city, forming what are known today as *favelas*. There was no specific policy to compensate or integrate these former slaves, who found themselves squeezed out of jobs by waves of European immigrants arriving in Brazil.

Over the course of the twentieth century Afro-Brazilians in Rio have gained prominence as soccer players and as samba artists, but they continue to confront racial prejudice and discrimination. Rio's Afro-Brazilian population has sought to resolve the social, political, and economic inequalities resulting from these injustices since the 1930s, when the Movimento Negro Unificado (Unified Black Movement) emerged. Only recently have this and similar types of movements produced concrete results, paving the way for the appointment of Afro-Brazilian politician Benedita da Silva to Rio de Janeiro's city council. Silva went on to represent Rio de Janeiro as a federal deputy and senator. In spite of Silva's achievements, there are few black members of the city or state councils, and Rio de Janeiro has never had a black mayor or governor.

Michelle Gueraldi

See Also

Transatlantic Slave Trade; Rebouças, André; Patrocínio, José Carlos do; Abolition and Emancipation in Latin America and the Caribbean; Soccer in Latin America and the Caribbean; Salvador, Brazil.

Europe

Riots in Great Britain, 1985,

a series of race riots, the most intense of which occurred in September and October in Birmingham and the Brixton and Tottenham districts of London.

A sequence of disturbances between white police officers and youths, predominantly black, occurred in London and Birmingham in the summer and autumn of 1985. These riots revealed that race relations in British society were deteriorating and brought to public attention the destitute conditions in which many blacks and whites lived. The worst riots took place in the Handsworth district of Birmingham, the Brixton district of London, and the Tottenham district of London. Although different incidents sparked each riot in 1985, all arose from similar social conditions: pervasive racial discrimination; consequent poverty, unemployment, and dilapidated housing; and poor relations between the police and the community.

Blacks from former British colonies in Africa and the West Indies began coming to Great Britain in large numbers after World War II and have since constituted about 2 percent of the British population. Although white-on-black violence had long existed, as demonstrated in the Notting Hill Riots of 1958, no large-scale race riots had occurred in Britain until the Brixton Riots of 1981. The 1985 riots were similar in some ways to those that had occurred four years earlier.

During the early 1980s good relations had existed between the police and youth in Handsworth. However, in April 1985 a heavy policing approach designed to root out individuals who used or sold marijuana or committed other minor offenses gave the police special powers to raid local cafés; this enhanced police presence strained relations between the police and the community. At around 5:00 PM on September 9 in the Handsworth district of Birmingham, Great Britain's second-largest city, a black driver and white police officer got into an altercation over a parking ticket. The tension exploded when the police officer arrested the black driver. A crowd of young blacks of West Indian descent – some report as many as 100 – gathered and accused the officer of racism. As more police arrived on the scene, a fight ensued, during which the police allegedly assaulted a black woman. Eleven officers were injured and seven police vehicles damaged; two people were arrested.

A few hours later a nearby bingo hall was in flames. When firefighters responded, a group of youths tried to prevent them from putting the fire out by throwing bricks and gasoline bombs. Other fires occurred in the area of Lozells Road. Looting and attacks on the police by as many as 400 rioters continued until about midnight, when more than 800 policemen gained control of the area. However, the violence continued the next day. Newly elected Home Secretary Douglas Hurd attempted to show his concern by cruising the area in his car and talking to local people. However, the rioters showered him with insults and bricks, and his visit spurred further arson and looting. By evening on September 10, order was restored. The police had arrested a total of 437 people of various ethnic backgrounds, most of whom lived in Handsworth. Two Asian men who were stuck in a burning post office died of smoke inhalation; 79 police, 8 fire officers, and 35 civilians were injured; and 83 premises and 23 vehicles were damaged, at an estimated cost of £7.5 million. Later that week, so-called "copycat riots" took place in the West Midlands in places such as Dudley, West Bromwich, and Moseley. The disorder reportedly spread to Coventry and Wolverhampton on September 12 and the St. Paul's district of Bristol on September 13.

Intense policing and raiding also spurred a similar riot in Brixton a few weeks later. On September 28 at 7:00 AM, a group of police raided a house in Brixton searching for Michael Groce, a black man wanted for illegal possession of a shotgun. During the raid Groce's mother was shot and permanently paralyzed. As news of the event spread, tension in the area grew, and a few hours later 300 youths attacked the local police station with gasoline bombs. This attack began eight hours of burning and looting by both blacks and whites that caused £3 million in damages. By midnight the police shed their usual defensive tactics and charged the crowd; the disorder subsided by 2:30 AM. The next day clashes between the police and youths occurred sporadically but dissolved quickly. In all, 43 civilians and 10 police officers were injured, and 55 vehicles and a few properties were burned. The police arrested 230 people, half of whom were white, and recorded 724 serious crimes, including more than 90 burglaries and a number of assaults and robberies. A photographer, David Hodge, died from injuries he sustained during the riot. A few days later riots also occurred in Liverpool and Peckham in South London.

The most severe riot of 1985 occurred at the Broadwater Farm Estate public housing development, where most residents are nonwhites, in the predominantly white Tottenham district of London. As they had in Birmingham in the summer of 1985, the police had instituted a heavy policing approach around Broadwater. The initiative involved extensive stop-and-search procedures. Black youths complained that in the course of such searches they were harassed, abused, and treated unfairly.

As in Birmingham, a dispute between a black driver and a white policeman instigated the rioting in Tottenham, and a woman was killed during the disturbance. On October 5, a white police officer stopped Floyd Jarrett, a 23-year-old black man, and questioned him about why his car was not properly licensed. Although Jarrett explained that he had just returned from a two-month youth exchange trip to Jamaica and had not yet updated his paperwork, the officer arrested him on charges of car theft and, after an alleged altercation, on charges of assaulting a police officer. The driver was later cleared of all charges and received damages in the amount of £350.

However, while the police held Jarrett at the station, other officers proceeded to his home to search for stolen property; during this search his mother, Cynthia Jarrett, collapsed and died. The Jarrett family maintained that the police pushed her purposely and caused her death, but the police insisted that Mrs. Jarrett was unhealthy and had suffered a stroke. As news of the Jarrett incident spread, the next evening blacks and others in the housing development responded with violence. Forty-seven cars and some buildings were burned, and 20 civilians and 223 police officers were injured; policeman Keith Blakelock was stabbed to death.

Blakelock's death drew the condemnation of political figures from all parties, but conservatives and liberals differed on how to cope with the riots. The conservatives wanted law and order to be preserved at all costs, and they supported harsh police strategies. Extreme right-wing figures such as Enoch Powell called for the repatriation of blacks to their "homelands," even though many of these blacks had been born in England and were British citizens.

Liberals saw the social conditions of the affected areas as the root of the problem: many communities suffered from decaying housing, high unemployment rates, especially among young black men, declining populations, and underdevelopment. Some liberals also condemned the policing policies and called for a concerted effort to recruit black police (at the time only 1 percent of the police force was black). In his report on the Brixton Riots of 1981, former judge Lord Leslie George Scarman had recommended better policing policies and an engaged social policy to improve the conditions of blacks in Great Britain and prevent racial conflict; but little had been done in the four years since the report was published.

Riots continued to occur in Great Britain in the 1990s as British society and successive governments continued their uneasy accommodation with the legacy of British colonialism, the realities of a multicultural society, and the persistence of racism and economic injustice.

Leyla Keough

See Also

Colonial Rule; Nottingham and Notting Hill Riots, 1958.

North America

Roach, Maxwell Lemuel (Max)

(b. January 10, 1924, Elizabeth City, N.C.), African American percussionist and an innovative jazz drummer.

Max Roach was born Maxwell Lemuel Roach and grew up in Brooklyn, New York. At age ten he began playing the drums in gospel music groups. He graduated from high school in 1941 and in the early 1950s studied at the Manhattan School of Music.

Roach began performing in 1942 with Charlie Parker and Thelonious Monk at Clark Monroe's Uptown House in Harlem. During the 1940s and 1950s he performed and recorded with other jazz greats, including Duke Ellington, Coleman Hawkins, Dizzy Gillespie, and Clifford Brown. In 1960 Roach recorded *We Insist: Freedom Now Suite*, an album that explores the theme of racial oppression in America and South Africa. In 1970 he created the all-percussion ensemble M'Boom and continued to write, record, and perform music throughout the 1980s.

Roach was a part of a small circle of musicians that helped pioneer a form of jazz called bebop. Along with Kenny Clark, Roach redefined jazz drumming by keeping time on the cymbal and using the drums for rhythmic accents. He received an Obie Award in 1985 and a MacArthur Prize in 1988. Roach set a new standard in jazz music not only in terms of the rhythmic complexity and creativity he engineered, but also in terms of his political emphasis on racial justice.

Aaron Myers

See Also

Clark, Kenneth Bancroft; Gillespie, John Birks ("Dizzy"); Harlem, New York; Hawkins, Coleman Randolph; Monk, Thelonious Sphere; Parker, Charles Christopher ("Bird"); Ellington, Edward Kennedy ("Duke").

Africa

Robben Island, South African island prison notorious for its brutal treatment of political prisoners.

When Nelson Mandela, future president of South Africa, was convicted of treason in 1964 for his work with the African National Congress (ANC), he was sent to Robben Island to serve out his life sentence. In his autobiography Mandela described Robben Island, the place where he spent 18 years before being transferred to other facilities, as "without question the harshest, most iron-fisted outpost in the South African penal system."

Robben Island is situated in the Atlantic Ocean, 8 km (5 mi) off the South African coast and 16 km (10 mi) north of Cape Town. The island was used as a prison as early as the seventeenth century – it also housed an army base, leper colony, and insane asylum – but it was not until the 1960s that Robben Island became the country's primary location for incarcerating political prisoners. Such prisoners, often convicted of treason for their association with such antiapartheid groups as the ANC, Pan-Africanist Congress, or Communist Party, were kept separated from the other prisoners. Robben Island's political prisoners left their cells – which measured just over 2 m sq (about 7 by 7 ft) and lacked heat or plumbing – only to break rocks in the island's limestone quarries. As in everyday South African life, strict racial divisions applied: Indian and "Coloured" (the racial category encompassing people of mixed racial descent) prisoners were allowed to wear long pants, socks, and shoes; Africans like Mandela wore shorts and sandals, even in the wintertime.

Worse, perhaps, than the physical deprivations on Robben Island were the measures designed to isolate political prisoners. The one letter they were allowed to receive each month often arrived cut to pieces by censors. Reading newspapers was strictly forbidden. Yet the prisoners still managed to obtain news from the outside world; they bribed wardens for newspapers, for instance, which they would then copy and share in coded notes. In hushed conversations in the quarry, Mandela, Walter Sisulu, and others transmitted the history of the ANC to new prisoners, leading Robben Island to become known among antiapartheid activists as "the University." Today Robben Island is no longer a prison. Instead, government-chartered boats take tourists there to see the historic site of their former president's long imprisonment.

Kate Tuttle

See Also
Antiapartheid Movement; Cape Town, South Africa; Mandela, Nelson Rolihlahla; South African Communist Party.

North America

Roberts, Charles Luckeyeth (Luckey) (b. August 7, 1887, Philadelphia, Pa.; d. February 5, 1968, New York, N.Y.), African American jazz pianist, composer, bandleader, and stride piano pioneer.

Luckey Roberts's varied career reflected the breadth of his musical talent. As a composer, he authored 14 scores for stage musicals. His popular songs included "Junk Man Rag," "Pork and Beans," and "Mo'lasses," and he composed concert-length works, most notably, *Whistlin' Pete – Miniature Syncopated Rhapsody*. He led his own band from the 1920s through the 1940s. From 1940 to 1954 he owned and operated the Rendezvous Club in Harlem, performing nightly piano solos.

Roberts was considered a gifted stride pianist whose elegance and fluent imagination won him the esteem of colleagues, such as James P. Johnson and Willie "the Lion" Smith.

Robert Fay

See Also
Harlem, New York; Smith, Willie ("the Lion").

North America

Robeson, Eslanda Cardozo Goode (b. December 15, 1896, Washington, D.C.; d. December 13, 1965, New York, N.Y.), African American activist and writer who advocated African independence and managed the singing and acting career of her husband, Paul Robeson.

Eslanda Robeson's father died when she was six years old, and the family moved to New York City. In 1921 she married Paul Robeson. Eslanda ("Essie") Robeson received a B.S. in chemistry from Columbia University and, in 1945, a Ph.D. in anthropology from the Hartford Seminary Foundation. She cofounded the Council for African Affairs in 1941 and participated in many left-wing causes. Robeson was the author of two books: *Paul Robeson, Negro* (1930) and *African Journey* (1945).

Aaron Myers

North America

Robeson, Paul (b. April 9, 1898, Princeton, N. J.; d. January 23, 1976, Philadelphia, Pa.), African American dramatic actor, singer of spirituals, civil rights activist, and political radical.

Paul Robeson was one of the most gifted men of this century. His resonant bass and commanding presence made him a world-renowned singer and actor and proved equally valuable when he spoke out against bigotry and injustice. By the 1930s Robeson was active in a wide range of causes, but his radicalism led to a long period of political harassment that culminated in his blacklisting during the McCarthy era. Although he resumed public performances in the late 1950s, this return to active life was brief. In the 1960s serious health problems sidelined him definitively.

Family Background and Education

Robeson's father, William Drew Robeson, was a North Carolina slave who escaped to freedom at age 15, graduated from college, and entered the ministry. Robeson's mother was Maria Louisa Bustill, a teacher and member of one of Philadelphia's leading black families. The youngest of five children, Robeson was only six years old when his mother died. His father set high expectations for his children and sent them to high school in the neighboring town of Somerville, New Jersey, because Princeton's segregated system offered no secondary education for blacks.

In 1915 Robeson won a scholarship to Rutgers College, where he excelled academically, becoming a junior-year Phi Beta Kappa, a champion debater, and class valedictorian. He was equally triumphant on the athletic field, where his imposing 1.89 m (6 ft 2 in), 86 kg- (190 lb-) frame served him well. Twice named an All-American in football, Robeson also lettered in baseball, basketball, and track. He graduated in 1919. Two years later, while a student at Columbia University Law School, he married Eslanda Goode. Paul and Essie Robeson's relationship would be a rocky one, but her assertiveness and gift for organization proved vital to his career. Their only son, Paul Robeson Jr., was born in 1927. In 1923, after earning his law degree and joining an otherwise all-white firm, Robeson decided to leave the legal profession. He had found his true calling as a performing artist.

Stage, Concert, and Film Career

While in law school Robeson had occasionally taken parts in amateur theatrical productions, leading in 1922 to his first professional roles – a lead in the short-lived Broadway play *Taboo* and as a replacement cast member in Eubie Blake and Noble Sissle's pioneering all-black musical, *Shuffle Along*. Robeson's career-making opportunity came when he was asked to join the Provincetown Players, an influential Greenwich Village theater company that included the playwright Eugene O'Neill among its three associate directors. In 1924 Robeson appeared in a revival of O'Neill's *The Emperor Jones* and premiered in the playwright's *All God's Chillun Got Wings*. In reviewing the latter, the *American Mercury* drama critic George Jean Nathan praised Robeson as "one of the most thoroughly eloquent, impressive, and convincing actors that I have looked at and listened to in almost twenty years of professional theater-going." Soon Robeson was offered other roles, most notably in a 1930 London production of *Othello* opposite Peggy Ashcroft; in a 1932 Broadway revival of Oscar Hammerstein II and Jerome Kern's musical, *Showboat*, which featured Robeson's dramatic rendition of "Ol' Man River"; and in a long-running, critically acclaimed 1943 production of *Othello* on Broadway.

Equally significant were Robeson's musical contributions. Robeson and his longtime pianist and arranger Lawrence Brown played a pivotal role in bringing spirituals into the classical music repertory. Robeson's 1925 recital at the Greenwich Village Theater was the first in which a black soloist sang an entire program of spirituals. The concert garnered superlative reviews, propelling Robeson into a new career as a concert singer and inspiring similar recitals by other black artists. Robeson also signed a recording contract with the Victor Talking Machine Company, which released his first recorded spirituals later that same year. Although Robeson would sing a wide range of material – including sentimental popular tunes, work songs, political ballads, and folk music from many different lands – he made his mark as an interpreter of spirituals.

During the 1930s Robeson also emerged as a film star. His first role was in the black director Oscar Micheaux's *Body and Soul* (1925), but he was most active on the screen between 1933 and 1942, a period in which he was prominently featured in Hollywood versions of *The Emperor Jones* (1933) and *Show Boat* (1936), *Tales of Manhattan* (1942), and several British films. Robeson, however, was dissatisfied with his work in motion pictures. He came to believe that – with the exceptions of his roles in *Song of Freedom* (1936) and *The Proud Valley* (1940) – his characters reflected current racial stereotypes, or what Robeson derided as "Stepin Fetchit comics and savages with leopard skin and spear." Working in films like *Sanders of the River* (1935), which sang the praises of British imperialism, became particularly distasteful as Robeson discovered his African heritage.

His Discovery of Africa

During the 1930s Robeson made London his primary residence, and "it was there," he recalled, "that I 'discovered' Africa." In 1933 he undertook the study of several African languages at the University of London. He also took part in activities sponsored by the West African Students Union and became acquainted with future African leaders Jomo Kenyatta of Kenya and Nnamdi Azikiwe of Nigeria. Robeson began to stress the positive aspects of African life. African culture, he argued, was more spiritual and more

Singer, actor, and activist Paul Robeson played Othello in 1943 on Broadway. Here Robeson rehearses his part. *CORBIS/Hulton-Deutsch Collection*

grounded in community than that of Europe or white America. Long before the Black Power Movement, he stressed the need to be "proud of being black.... For no one respects a man who does not respect himself."

Unlike many American blacks, who saw their role as one of helping to "uplift" and modernize the African people, Robeson thought it imperative that the American-born regain their own African roots. He rejected the assimilationism then prevalent among the black elite, insisting that "in every black man flows the rhythm of Africa." Indeed, he wrote, "I came to consider that I was an African." Yet Robeson clearly saw this "return to Africa" as a spiritual, rather than a literal journey. He rejected separatism no less than assimilationism and never abandoned his vision of an integrated society. Instead he fashioned a world-view that anchored cultural diversity in universal values, among which the most important was a faith in human solidarity that lay at the heart of his encounter with SOCIALISM.

Socialism and Political Activism

During the 1930s Robeson began reading about socialism and taking part in political discussions with various activists and scholars, including C. L. R. James, the radical Caribbean theorist; William L. Patterson, a black Communist and American trade unionist; and the American anarchist Emma Goldman. In 1934 Robeson made the first of many visits to the Soviet Union. He was impressed by the seeming lack of racial prejudice in the USSR and by the Soviet Constitution, which guaranteed citizens equality, "irrespective of their nationality or race." About the same time Robeson became active in various radical causes. In England he took part in labor and peace rallies, Save China assemblies, and meetings to protest British colonialism in JAMAICA. He spoke at a London rally for India's Jawaharlal Nehru, performed at benefit concerts for the Spanish Republic, and in 1938 traveled there to sing for republican troops.

In 1939 Paul and Essie Robeson returned to the United States, where he continued to be politically active. Robeson sang the egalitarian "Ballad for Americans" over national radio late that year and recorded a best-selling version of the song for Victor. He supported the United Auto Workers and other unions of the Congress of Industrial Organizations (CIO); he served on the board of the new Negro Playwrights' Company; and he became chairman of the Council on African Affairs, an American-based organization that provided information on African struggles for freedom and lobbied African concerns. During World War II Robeson committed his prodigious energies in support of the Allied war effort and in protests against the poll tax, the segregation of America's armed forces, and the segregated venues for some of his own concerts. After the war Robeson, W. E. B. Du Bois, and Bartley Crum, a liberal white lawyer, called for a national conference to secure a federal antilynching law. Robeson also protested the antilabor Taft-Hartley Act and campaigned for the Progressive Party in the 1948 election. Robeson highlighted the black struggle for equality in all his campaign speeches, even those he delivered – at considerable risk – in the Deep South.

Difficulties During the Cold War Era

However, as the United States entered the cold war, Robeson found himself increasingly isolated. Although he was not in fact a member of the Communist Party, he had close ties to many in the party's leadership, and he staunchly defended the Soviet Union despite the 1939 Nazi-Soviet Pact and Nikita Khrushchev's 1956 revelations about Joseph Stalin's purges. The Federal Bureau of Investigation (FBI) placed Robeson under surveillance as early as 1941 and compiled a massive dossier on his activities. Yet it seems clear that he was targeted as much for his militancy on civil rights issues as for his alleged Communism. The real turning point for Robeson came in 1949 when the Associated Press, in reporting his criticisms of the United States at a Paris peace conference, quoted him as saying: "It is unthinkable that American Negroes would go to war on behalf of those who have oppressed us for generations against a country [the Soviet Union] which in one generation has raised our people to the full dignity of mankind."

Most Americans were outraged. The House Committee on Un-American Activities (HUAC) announced that it would hold hearings to investigate Robeson and the loyalty of black Americans. White liberals and the black establishment, offended by his growing stridency and fearful of the taint of Communism, distanced themselves from him. Even one-time friends, such as Walter White, executive director of the NATIONAL ASSOCIATION FOR THE ADVANCEMENT OF COLORED PEOPLE, and Max Yergan, former executive director of the Council on African Affairs, denounced his remarks.

Later that year a mob of young white men disrupted an outdoor Robeson concert near Peekskill, New York, attacking concertgoers and sending a dozen to the hospital. Robeson himself narrowly escaped injury. A rescheduled concert, guarded by members of several left-wing CIO unions, came off without incident, but at its conclusion the audience found itself facing a gauntlet of enraged, rock-throwing locals. State and local police did little to restrain the attackers; indeed many joined the mob. But a grand jury investigation wrote off the violence as having been provoked by Robeson's previous unpatriotic remarks.

Ultimately, Robeson was silenced, but doing so required the combined efforts of the black establishment – including leaders of the fledgling CIVIL RIGHTS MOVEMENT – white liberals, the entertainment industry, and the government. In 1950 the State Department rescinded Robeson's passport, preventing him from performing or traveling abroad. At home he found himself blacklisted by Broadway and Hollywood, by concert halls and record companies, radio, and television. His only opportunities to perform were at small affairs organized by a dwindling core of radicals and at a few black churches like Harlem's Mother AFRICAN METHODIST EPISCOPAL ZION CHURCH, whose pastor was Robeson's brother, Rev. Benjamin C. Robeson. Denied a public voice, Robeson struggled mightily to vindicate himself and win back his freedom of travel. In his 1956 testimony before HUAC, Robeson offered a powerful indictment of America's continuing racial injustice, but he steadfastly refused to condemn the Soviet Union, to provide the names of American Communists, or to answer whether he was a party member, a question that he viewed as a violation of his Constitutional rights. In 1957, after a seven-year delay, the State Department finally granted him a hearing on the revocation of his passport. The result was a six-hour grilling, but no change in the government's policy.

THE FINAL YEARS

Robeson fought his lonely battle at great personal cost. In 1955 he began to show the first clear signs of the emotional difficulties – probably bipolar disorder, a condition once known as manic-depression – that would eventually halt his public activities. It is ironic that he should pay so dearly for his alleged Communism. In truth, what lay at the heart of Robeson's political convictions was not Marxism so much as an empathy for African culture and an identification with common people, the poor, and the oppressed.

By the end of the decade the worst years of the cold war had passed, and Robeson's troubles began to ease. In 1958 he gave his first commercial concerts in several years, appearing in Chicago, Portland, and several California cities. He published *Here I Stand*, a trenchant autobiography written with Lloyd Brown. And a Supreme Court decision once again permitted him to travel abroad. The next few years were busy ones, with American concerts and recording sessions for Vanguard; concert tours of Europe, Australia, and New Zealand; visits to the Soviet Union; and in 1959 another London production of *Othello*. But on March 27, 1961, Robeson suffered a nervous breakdown and attempted suicide. For the rest of his life he would struggle with severe depression, and his public appearances would be extremely rare. Robeson dropped out of public awareness and was largely ignored by the leadership of the Civil Rights Movement, except for the militant young leaders of the STUDENT NONVIOLENT COORDINATING COMMITTEE (SNCC). At a gala celebration for his 67th birthday, Robeson was deeply moved when keynote speaker JOHN LEWIS, then the chairman of SNCC, proclaimed, "We of SNCC are Paul Robeson's spiritual children. We too have rejected gradualism and moderation." Yet there was more to Robeson than this. Beneath his militancy – and intertwined with it – was a profound compassion and a deep bond with Africa best seen in a passage he wrote in 1936: "I am a singer and an actor. I am primarily an artist. Had I been born in Africa, I would have belonged, I hope, to that family which sings and chants the glories and legends of the tribe. I would have liked in my mature years to have been a wise elder, for I worship wisdom and knowledge of the ways of men."

Robeson's final public appearance was at a 1966 benefit dinner for SNCC.

James Clyde Sellman

SEE ALSO

Azikiwe, Benjamin Nnamdi; Russia and the Former Soviet Union; Track and Field in the United States; World War II and African Americans; American Federation of Labor and Congress of Industrial Organizations; Antilynching Movement; Baseball in the United States; Blake, James Hubert ("Eubie"); Du Bois, William Edward Burghardt (W. E. B.); Football, Collegiate; James, Cyril Lionel Richard; Labor Unions in the United States; Micheaux, Oscar; Patterson, William; Sissle, Noble; White, Walter Francis; Film, Blacks in American; Communist Party USA, African Americans and the; Spirituals, African American; Black Power.

North America

Robinson, Bill ("Bojangles")

(b. May 25, 1878, Richmond, Va.; d. November 15, 1949, New York, N.Y.), African American vaudeville performer, tap dancer, and movie star, considered the most famous African American entertainer of the early twentieth century.

Bill "Bojangles" Robinson was born Luther Robinson, the son of Maxwell Robinson, a machinist, and Maria Robinson, a singer. Robinson and his brother Bill, whose name he would later appropriate, were orphaned when their parents died in 1885. Following this the brothers lived with their paternal grandmother, Bedilia Robinson, and Robinson worked as a bootblack and danced on street corners for money. He began to use the nickname "Bojangles," which was possibly derived from "jangle," a slang term for fighting, and supposedly invented the expression "Everything's copasetic," which meant "life is great." At age 12 Robinson ran away to WASHINGTON, D.C., where he worked as a street dancer and at a racetrack.

His first professional job came in 1892 as a member of the "pickaninny" chorus – a group of African American children who sang backup for the main performer – in the revue *The South Before the War*. After a two-year stint in the army, Robinson moved to New York in 1900, where he emerged as one of the first black stars of vaudeville. At the time black roles normally were performed by whites in blackface, but from 1902 to 1914 Robinson toured the vaudeville circuit as the partner of the black comedian George W. Cooper. Cooper played the straight man to Robinson's clown. Although theirs was not a dance team, when the duo broke up Robinson persuaded his manager, Marty Forkins, to book him performances as a solo dancer. In 1917 Robinson performed for American serviceman ordered to Europe to fight in World War I, and in 1918 he premiered at New York's legendary Palace Theater, where he first performed his trademark "stair dance," a rapid TAP DANCE up and down a five-step staircase, to a standing ovation. Robinson was one of the first black performers to star at the Palace, where audiences were amazed by his dancing. His footwork was complex, graceful, and often improvised. Often bedecked in tails and a top hat tilted to one side, Robinson charmed audiences with his irresistible smile. His career as a vaudeville star culminated in a European tour in 1926.

Robinson became one of the first black Broadway stars, debuting as the lead in the all-black revue *Blackbirds of 1928*. Newspaper reviews hailed him as the best tap dancer ever. Robinson's other notable Broadway starring appearances include *Brown Buddies* (1930), *Blackbirds of 1933*, *The Hot Mikado* (1939), *All in Fun* (1940), and *Memphis Bound* (1945). Because of his Broadway success, Robinson was crowned the honorary "Mayor of Harlem" in 1933.

Robinson began to make Hollywood films in the 1930s, at a time when the industry offered few opportunities to blacks. His films include *Dixiana* (1930), *Harlem is Heaven* (1933), and *Hooray for Love* (1935). His most popular films, however, were the four he made with white child star Shirley Temple: *The Littlest Colonel* (1935), *The Littlest Rebel* (1935), *Just Around the Corner* (1938), and *Rebecca of Sunnybrook Farm* (1938).

Throughout his career Robinson donated money and benefit performances to many causes and to organizations, including the NATIONAL ASSOCIATION FOR THE ADVANCEMENT OF COLORED PEOPLE. In recognition for his achievements and philanthropy, the Negro Actors Guild named Robinson its honorary president in 1937.

During his lifetime Robinson was married three times. In 1907 he married Lena Chase; that relationship ended in 1922. He next married his business manager Fannie Clay, divorcing her in 1943. He married the dancer Elaine Paines in 1944.

Robinson performed ceaselessly, keeping a hectic dancing schedule well into his 60s. His show business career spanned 50 years. He died of a heart attack backstage, after performing with Milton Berle, a month before his 70th birthday. Robinson is remembered as one of the greatest entertainers of our century. Dance historian Rusty E. Frank wrote of him, "They said that Bill Robinson could do the easiest routine in the world and get away with it because of his charm and charisma. They said that he could drive a dancer crazy with the complexity of a step that looked so easy. But when tap dancers talk about Bill Robinson, they talk about the greatest tap dancer of all time."

See Also

World War I and African Americans; New York, New York; Film, Blacks in American; Dance in the United States.

North America

Robinson, Jackie

(b. January 31, 1919, Cairo, Ga.; d. October 24, 1972, Stamford, Conn.), African American baseball player and civil rights activist; first African American to play major league baseball in modern times.

Born to sharecroppers Jerry and Mallie Robinson, Jackie Robinson was raised in Pasadena, California, primarily by his mother, who worked as a domestic after moving the family from Georgia. Taught by his mother to confront racism by showing his talent, Robinson turned to athletics as a way to compete with the white children who would shout racist epithets at him and his siblings.

At John Muir High School Robinson starred on several of the school's athletic teams. In 1938 he began attending Pasadena Junior College, where he continued to excel in sports. In 1940 Robinson transferred to the University of California-Los Angeles (UCLA), where he became known as one of the best collegiate athletes in the United States. Robinson was the first man in the school's history to earn varsity letters in four sports. An All-America running back in football, he also competed in track and field – breaking his older brother's national record in the broad jump – and led the league in scoring while on the BASKETBALL team. Ironically, baseball was not Robinson's best sport, nor the one he most enjoyed.

Robinson left UCLA in 1941, before graduating, to become the assistant athletic director of the National Youth Administration Camp in Atascadero, California. During that year he also played semiprofessional football for the Honolulu Bears. With the onset of World War II, Robinson was drafted into the United States Army in 1942. His army experience sharpened his sense of racial injustice. Only after boxer JOE LOUIS intervened with officials in Washington on Robinson's behalf did Robinson become an officer at Fort Riley in Kansas. Transferred to Fort Hood in Texas after protesting the mistreatment of his fellow African American soldiers, Robinson was court-martialed for refusing to sit in the back of an army bus. He was soon reinstated but was discharged from the army in 1944.

In 1945 Jackie Robinson began his professional baseball career by joining the Kansas City Monarchs of the Negro American League with a salary of $400 per month. Robinson was not accustomed to the difficult schedule and travel of the Negro League, and he was disturbed by the oppressive treatment of black ball players throughout the country. He excelled, nonetheless, during the 1945 season, batting .345 and proving himself to be an all-around talent.

It was at this time that Branch Rickey, the general manager of the Brooklyn Dodgers, quietly began to search for the best candidate to break the color barrier in major league baseball. The time was right for Rickey's project. In 1944 Commissioner Kenesaw Mountain Landis, who had upheld the "gentlemen's agreement" to keep the major leagues white only, died. African American sacrifices during World War II engendered hope and support for their fuller participation in all facets of American society, thus leading to a burgeoning CIVIL RIGHTS MOVEMENT. In a secret vote held by new Commissioner Albert "Happy" Chandler's office, all of the major league owners rejected the idea of integrating baseball, except for Branch Rickey. On October 23, 1945, he defied the owners' vote and signed the college-educated army officer Robinson to a contract with the minor league Montreal Royals, the top team in the Dodgers' farm system.

After playing in VENEZUELA during the winter, Robinson joined the Royals in Florida for the 1946 spring training season. Robinson's venture into white organized baseball was opposed from the start by coaches, teammates, other teams, and many white fans. Facing racist taunts and segregated living conditions, Robinson managed to lead the Class AAA International League in batting (.349) and runs scored (113), and helped bring his team to the league championship.

In the spring of 1947 Robinson joined the Brooklyn Dodgers in CUBA for spring training. Several Dodgers circulated a petition to exclude Robinson. Dodger manager Leo Durocher told the protesters they could leave if they wanted. Nobody left, and Robinson began "baseball's great experiment" in April 1947, becoming the first African American in the major leagues since Moses Fleetwood Walker had played in 1885. He set the league on fire, earning Rookie of the Year honors with a .297 batting average and a league-leading 29 stolen bases. During his ten seasons with the Dodgers, Robinson batted .311, led the team to six pennants and one World Series Championship, won the 1949 National League Most Valuable Player award, and paved the way for African American players in all professional team sports. Robinson proved himself on and off the field to be an exemplar of character and grace. With the help of his wife Rachel, Robinson heroically upheld his promise to Rickey not to retaliate against

Jackie Robinson began playing first base for the Brooklyn Dodgers in April 1947. In this photograph Robinson poses with other infield players *from left*, third baseman John Jorgensen, shortstop Pee Wee Reese, and second baseman Ed Stanky. *AP/Wide World Photos*

Pictured here in the uniform of his minor-league team, the Montreal Royals, Jackie Robinson went on to join the Brooklyn Dodgers in 1947 as the first African American to play in the modern-day big leagues. He finished his career with a batting average of .311 and in 1962 became the first black player elected to the Baseball Hall of Fame. *CORBIS/Bettmann*

racist insults. In 1962 he was inducted into the Baseball Hall of Fame.

After his baseball career Robinson was vocal in the struggle for integration and black self-improvement, supporting conservative means for improving the conditions of African Americans. He refused to attend games or play in "old-timers" games because of the dearth of blacks in management and coaching positions. By 1972, however, he celebrated the 25th anniversary of his debut, throwing out the first pitch in the World Series. He died nine days later, having proved the equality of African Americans in one sphere that had profound effects on the rest of American society. In posthumous tribute to Robinson's contributions and in celebration of the 50th anniversary of his debut, in April 1997 baseball commissioner Bud Selig retired Robinson's number 42 forever throughout major league baseball.

See Also
Track and Field in the United States; World War II and African Americans; Baseball in the United States; Football, Collegiate; Los Angeles, California; Negro Leagues.

North America

Robinson, JoAnn Gibson

(b. April 17, 1912, Culloden, Ga.), African American civil rights activist; a leader in the Montgomery Bus Boycott.

JoAnn Robinson attended Fort Valley State College and earned an M.A. in English from Atlanta University in 1948, after which she taught at Alabama State College in Montgomery. It was in Montgomery that she became active in the Civil Rights Movement.

Robinson became the president of the Women's Political Council (WPC), an organization composed mainly of middle-class black women and committed to increasing African American participation in civic affairs. The WPC challenged Montgomery's policy of segregated seating on public transportation by organizing a successful bus boycott after Rosa Parks's arrest for violating segregation laws in 1955. Robinson left Alabama State College in 1960 and taught English in Los Angeles until retiring in 1976.

Robinson's 1987 memoir, *The Montgomery Bus Boycott and the Women Who Started It*, was awarded special acclaim by the Southern Association for Women's Historians. Her book emphasized the important role women played in the daily organization and the planned activities of the Civil Rights Movement.

Alonford James Robinson, Jr.

See Also
Parks, Rosa Louise McCauley.

North America

Robinson, Ruby Doris Smith

(b. April 25, 1942, Atlanta, Ga.; d. October 7, 1967, Atlanta, Ga.), American civil rights activist and a founder of the Student Nonviolent Coordinating Committee (SNCC).

Ruby Doris Smith Robinson was inspired as a teenager by media images of the Montgomery Bus Boycott that occurred in 1955-1956. After joining the Civil Rights Movement, Robinson was arrested for the first time as part of a lunch counter desegregation sit-in in 1959 while she was a sophomore at Spelman College in Atlanta. In 1960 she became one of the founding members of the Student Nonviolent Coordinating Committee (SNCC).

Robinson was one of the original Freedom Riders, and she helped create SNCC's "jail, no bail" policy, a strategy to fill Southern jails with protesters and thus keep public attention on the movement. In 1966 Robinson became SNCC's first (and only) female executive secretary. She left SNCC in early 1967, and died of leukemia that October.

Lisa Clayton Robinson

See Also
Sit-Ins.

North America

Robinson, Sugar Ray

(b. May 3, 1921, Detroit, Mich.; d. April 12, 1989, Culver City, Calif.), one of the great boxers of modern history, noted for lightning speed and impressive power.

Sugar Ray Robinson was born Walker Smith Jr. He became interested in Boxing early in life, idolizing heavyweight champion Joe Louis, who also came from Detroit. To compete in tournaments at a young age, Robinson borrowed the amateur certificate of another fighter, whose name, Ray Robinson, stuck. He rode an incredible string of amateur victories in the welterweight division to Golden Gloves titles in 1939 and 1940. His style, combining graceful movement with brute power, was described by one of his handlers as "sweet as sugar."

Robinson turned professional in 1940 and won 40 straight fights – more than 20 by knockout – until Jake LaMotta beat him by decision in 1943. In World War II Robinson entered the United States Army and performed in exhibitions for soldiers on the same bill as his hero Louis. He also protested racial segregation in the armed forces, once even fighting a military policeman who harassed Louis for using a whites-only phone. After the War, in December 1946, Robinson captured the welterweight title by defeating Tommy Bell. Defending the title in 1947, he delivered fatal blows to challenger Jimmy Doyle. A reporter asked if Robinson meant to get Doyle in trouble, and Robinson is said to have replied, "Mister, it's my business to get him into trouble."

Later that year Robinson moved up to the middleweight division. In 1951 he again met LaMotta, now the world middleweight champion, in a fight reporters called the St. Valentine's Day Massacre. Robinson emerged from the savage contest the winner. Losing his title to Englishman Randy Turpin in July 1951, Robinson won it back in a rematch two months later. In 1952 Robinson went after Joey Maxim, the light heavyweight champion, at New York's Yankee Stadium. Although he outboxed Maxim, Robinson was overwhelmed by the heat and forced to call the fight in the 13th round – this marked the only defeat by knockout in his career.

After the fight Robinson surprised the boxing world by retiring and working for two years as a tap dancer. In 1955, however, he returned, taking back his middleweight title with a second-round knockout of Bobo Olson. Twice more Robinson lost and regained the title, holding it a record five times. He permanently lost the title to Paul Pender on January 22, 1960. Although friends encouraged the 38-year-old Robinson to retire, he continued to fight until 1965, in part to maintain his income. In his later years he established the Sugar Ray Robinson Youth Foundation for children in Los Angeles.

See Also
World War II and African Americans; Detroit, Michigan; Tap Dance.

North America

Robinson, William ("Smokey")

(b. 1940?, Detroit, Mich.), popular rhythm and blues (R&B) singer and songwriter known for his romantic lyrics and his passionate, high-reaching voice. A leading member of the MOTOWN vocal group the Miracles from 1958 to 1971, Robinson was one of the most influential singers and songwriters in popular music during the 1960s and 1970s.

William "Smokey" Robinson was born in DETROIT, MICHIGAN. At age 18, he formed a vocal group, which later became known as the Miracles, with high school friends Ronnie White, Pete Moore, Bobby Rogers, and Rogers's sister Claudette, whom Robinson later married. The group so impressed Motown owner Berry Gordy that he signed them to a recording contract in 1960.

The Miracles' first hit record was "Shop Around" (1961), an R&B song recorded for Tamla, one of the Motown Record Company labels. It was a phenomenal success, reaching Number One on the *Billboard* magazine R&B charts and Number Two on the *Billboard* pop music charts, and helping to launch Gordy's fledgling music studio. In the decade that followed the Miracles produced a highly popular body of work, including the song "You Really Got a Hold on Me" (1962); hard-edged dance tunes such as "Mickey's Monkey" (1963) and "Going to Go-Go" (1965); and the dreamy songs "More Love" (1967) and "I Second That Emotion" (1967). Perhaps even more enduring are the ballads "Ooo Baby Baby" (1965), "The Tracks of My Tears" (1965), and "Baby, Baby Don't Cry" (1969). In 1967 the group became known as Smokey Robinson and the Miracles.

During the 1960s Robinson also wrote and produced classics for other Motown artists. "My Girl" was written for the vocal group the Temptations. Robinson's "You Beat Me to the Punch" (1962) and "My Guy" (1964) were written for soul singer Mary Wells, and he wrote "Ain't That Peculiar" (1965) for soul singer MARVIN GAYE. Robinson's songwriting skills were admired by many popular musicians, including folk-rock artist Bob Dylan. Robinson's songs have endured, and many were later recorded by pop artists, including British rock group the Beatles, soul singers Aretha Franklin and Luther Vandross, and popular singers Linda Ronstadt and Kim Carnes.

Robinson left the Miracles in 1972 to pursue a solo music career. He released the highly regarded album *Quiet Storm* in 1975. In the 1980s Robinson continued to release a stream of dreamy romantic songs, including "Cruisin'" (1979), written with longtime collaborator and guitarist Marv Tarplin. Robinson's other notable hits include "Being with You" (1981) and "Just to See Her" (1987; Grammy Award, 1988). Robinson won a 1990 Grammy Legends Award. He was inducted into the Rock and Roll Hall of Fame in 1987.

Robert Fay

SEE ALSO
Franklin, Aretha Louise; Rhythm and Blues; Temptations, The.

North America

Rock, John Sweat

(b. October 13, 1825, Salem, N.J.; d. December 3, 1866, Washington, D.C.), African American abolitionist, doctor, and the first black lawyer allowed to argue before the United States Supreme Court.

John Sweat Rock, the son of free blacks, attended common schools in his hometown until age 19, when he was given the opportunity to study medicine with two white physicians in the area. After being trained by a white dentist, Rock earned his medical degree in 1852 from the American Medical College in Philadelphia.

By 1855 Rock had relocated to Massachusetts, where he became one of the first African American members of the Massachusetts Medical Society. While in Boston, Rock supported the abolitionist movement, providing medical treatment to FUGITIVE SLAVES. He was a participant in the 1855 abolitionist campaign to desegregate the city's public schools and spoke at the 1858 Faneuil Hall commemoration of CRISPUS ATTUCKS Day.

Rock later earned a law degree and was admitted to the Massachusetts Bar on September 14, 1861. As an active leader in the abolitionist movement, Rock recruited black soldiers for the Fifty-fourth and Fifty-fifth Massachusetts Infantry Regiments during the Civil War. He was the first to speak during a celebration of the Emancipation Proclamation at the Tremont Temple meetinghouse in Boston on January 1, 1863.

Rock is perhaps best remembered as the first African American to be allowed to argue before the U.S. Supreme Court. This 1865 victory was largely symbolic, as Rock's health prevented him from actually arguing before the Court. He died of tuberculosis at his mother's home in WASHINGTON, D.C., at age 41.

Alonford James Robinson, Jr.

SEE ALSO
Abolitionism in the United States; Boston, Massachusetts; Civil War, American; Fifty-fourth Regiment of Massachusetts Volunteer Infantry; Free Blacks in the United States, 1619 to 1863; Philadelphia, Pennsylvania; Thirteenth Amendment of the United States Constitution and the Emancipation Proclamation.

Latin America and the Caribbean

Rocksteady,

a musical form that flourished in JAMAICA from 1966 to 1968, providing the transition from SKA to REGGAE.

Although the heyday of rocksteady lasted for only two years, it brought critical and thematic innovations that strongly influenced the course of Jamaican music. By the mid-1960s it was evident to working- and lower-class Jamaicans that Jamaica's 1962 independence from Great Britain brought about no substantial improvement in living conditions. British rule was substituted for economic dependence on the United States, and jobs were equally difficult to find.

The upbeat shuffle of ska, reflective of Jamaican's early optimism, was gradually replaced by a sinister, less hurried, and "cooler" sound. An increase in musical stylization accompanied this decrease in tempo. The characteristic trombone solos of ska gave way to instrumental songs with added emphasis on the bass and drum. Instead of playing the bass guitar on the beat, rocksteady performers incorporated a lagging syncopation. Influential guitarist Lynn Tait began playing bass lines on his guitar in tandem with the bassist, and these changes transformed ska into what became known as rocksteady. The new form further distinguished itself from ska because it took as its target audience the rough-and-tumble streetwise youth known as the "rude boys."

"Rocksteady" originally referred to the dance steps the form inspired, but the name quickly spread to the music as well. In 1966 rocksteady mainstay Alton Ellis released *Rocksteady*, the genre's first full-length album. Ellis was among many top rocksteady performers who worked with producer Duke Reid and his seminal Treasure Isle record label.

Rocksteady developed in tandem with the "rude boy" culture of Kingston. Rude boys were young city men, many of whom had recently emigrated from rural villages and were unable to make a decent living in the impoverished neighborhoods of West Kingston. Rude boys took to the streets, hustling, stealing, and living with consummate "cool" style. Short pants, slim suits, dark sunglasses, and chrome-covered motorcycles became the rage, although these angry young rebels carried German ratchet knives and guns under their veneer of stylish cool. The Wailers' 1966 hit "Rude Boy" sparked widespread romanticization of the rude boy image. That same year Prince Buster released "Judge Dread," the most famous condemnation of the rude boy. Although "Judge Dread" suggested that rude boy crime was self-destructive to the black community, the song was nevertheless met with countless rebuffs in the years to come.

The avalanche of pro-rude boy tunes emphasized its macho vogue with lines such as Prince Buster's "Rudies don't fear / Rougher than rougher / Tougher than tough / Strong like iron...." While Prince Buster was too comic to deliver truly trenchant political messages, the Ethiopian Judge Dread character in his song was meant to appeal to Jamaicans as a strong symbol of authority, in anticipation of the interest in Rastafarianism, which would fuel rocksteady's further slowing down into the "dread" rhythms of roots reggae in the late 1960s.

Alongside lyrics expressing rude boy aggression and cool, elements of Rastafarianism were slowly ushered into rocksteady's repertoire, especially by the Wailers (*see* BOB MARLEY). All of these factors – socially conscious lyrics, emphasis on the newly available electric bass guitar, slower tempos, and syncopated melodic accompaniment – were foundational elements in reggae, the next step in Jamaican musical evolution.

Jace Clayton

SEE ALSO

Kingston, Jamaica; Rastafarians.

North America

Rodeo, American sport that combines cowboy skills with Wild West mythology.

Charles Sampson, national bull-riding champion in 1982, grew up in the Watts section of LOS ANGELES, CALIFORNIA, and he is African American. In a sport built on the overwhelmingly white mythology of the American Wild West, Sampson's success may seem surprising, but as he points out, there is historical precedent for his career. "Some people still don't realize," Sampson told the *New York Times*, "that something like a quarter of all the cowboys back in the old West were black."

Rodeo grew out of the games and competitions devised by cowboys. Whether along the trail during the great cattle drives or during the twice-yearly roundups, whenever cowboys gathered together they would compete. As the ranching industry grew, roundups became festivals at which cowboys could drink, gamble, and show off their riding and roping skills. The word rodeo derives from the Spanish *rodear,* for "encircle" or "surround."

Despite the end of large-scale cattle drives around 1890, rodeo-based Western shows, such as those staged by William "Buffalo Bill" Cody, were popular well into the 1930s. One of the era's most renowned stars was BILL PICKETT, a black cowboy known as "the bulldogger" for chasing a steer on horseback, then jumping down and wrestling the steer to the ground without using his hands. His trick, inspired by watching dogs subdue bulls in his native Texas, was to clench the bull's lip between his teeth. Though later a star performer on the rodeo circuit, Pickett had to dress as a Mexican toreador in his early years to evade rules barring blacks from rodeos. Now called steer-wrestling, Pickett's specialty is the only one of rodeo's seven main events to have been invented by an individual.

Gradually, the big western shows headlined by Pickett and colleagues such as Will Rogers and Tom Mix died out. Today's rodeos, no longer produced by local livestock companies, have become big business, with corporate sponsorship from the tobacco, liquor, and clothing industries. Recently the sport has faced charges of animal cruelty from the Humane Society and other groups. Bulldogging a steer in the way Bill Pickett did is no longer legal.

Although black membership in the Professional Rodeo Cowboys Association remains low, the modern era has seen several successful African American riders. Sampson's mentor, Myrtis Dightman, reached the national finals in bull-riding several times in the late 1960s. Most recently, Texan Fred Whitfield was the first black cowboy to win the world calf-roping title in 1990 and was also selected the Cowboys Association's Rookie of the Year. Events such as the National Black Invitational Rodeo and the Bill Pickett Invitational Rodeo suggest that African American presence in the Wild West sport will continue to grow.

Kate Tuttle

SEE ALSO

Black Cowboys.

Rodney King Case. Please see LOS ANGELES RIOT OF 1992

Latin America and the Caribbean

Rodney, Walter (b. March 23, 1942, Georgetown, Guyana; d. June 13, 1980, Georgetown, Guyana), Afro-Guyanese scholar, activist, and author.

Walter Rodney was an outspoken author, scholar, and activist who championed the rights of the working class around the world. He was born in Georgetown, GUYANA, in 1942. Rodney excelled academically, displaying a strong command of history and social theory. He graduated from the University of the West Indies in JAMAICA and from London University's prestigious School of Oriental and African Studies (SOAS). At age 24 he was awarded a Ph.D. in history by SOAS.

Rodney's voice was powerful and articulate as he spoke out against colonialism and worked to develop a political consciousness among the Caribbean working class. As a professor, Rodney had a profound impact on students and workers at the University of the West Indies. His immense popularity with young radicals and organized labor threatened the Jamaican government, and in 1968 – while he was attending a meeting of the Montreal Congress of Black Writers – he was banished from Jamaica. Among the many influential books that Rodney wrote, perhaps the best known is *How Europe Underdeveloped Africa* (1981). In it he discussed how the colonization of Africa undermined its potential for autonomous development.

Throughout the early 1970s Rodney taught at colleges and universities in Africa, Germany, and Great Britain. In 1973 he returned to his home in Guyana and became a leading figure in Guyanese organized labor. Rodney helped to establish the Working People's Alliance (WPA) in 1973, a multiracial organization that became a vocal opposition political party in 1979. Members of the WPA pushed for economic and political reforms, and they openly criticized Prime Minister Linden Forbes Burnham.

Under Rodney's leadership the WPA became one of the leading opposition parties in post-independence Guyana. His activities caught the attention of Prime Minister Burnham, and when Rodney was appointed chair of the history department at the University of the West Indies, Burnham blocked the appointment.

When a suspicious fire in 1979 destroyed the headquarters of the ruling People's National Congress (PNC), Burnham charged Rodney and two other opposition leaders with arson. Although Rodney was never convicted, he was followed and harassed by government officials. After returning from a trip to Africa, Rodney was killed on June 13, 1980, when a bomb ripped through his car. Much to the outrage of Rodney's family and supporters, his brother, Donald, who was injured in the blast, was implicated in the death when he was charged with the illegal possession of explosive materials.

It is widely believed that Burnham, along with members of the PNC, were participants in a plot to kill Rodney. Burnham died in office in 1985, but Rodney's family continued to call for an official investigation. Rodney's eldest son, Shaka, waged a hunger strike in 1995 to force then prime minister CHEDDI JAGAN to conduct an official investigation. Under the leadership of the Netherlands-based International Court of Justice, Guyana reopened the files on Rodney's death.

In 1996 the government brought formal criminal charges in the death of Rodney against former army sergeant Gregory Smith – also known as Cyril Johnson – who was hiding in French Guiana. The government also posthumously awarded Rodney the country's highest distinction, the Order of Excellence.

Alonford James Robinson, Jr.

SEE ALSO

Colonial Rule; Burnham, Linden Forbes Sampson.

Latin America and the Caribbean

Rodríguez, Arsenio (b. April 30, 1911, Güira de Macurije, Matanzas Province, CUBA; d. December 31, 1970, New York, N.Y.), Afro-Cuban bandleader and *tres* player who created the medium-sized Cuban *conjunto* ensemble and played a key role in popularizing the MAMBO.

Arsenio Rodríguez, also known as the "Ciego maravilloso" (Marvelous Blind Man), was one of Cuba's most important musical innovators. Rather than remaining within the established musical traditions, he experimented with new ensembles and musical forms, most notably the mambo, and in the process laid the foundations for the musical style known as salsa. His greatest contribution was successfully introducing Afro-Cuban elements into mainstream popular music.

Rodríguez was a third-generation descendant of African slaves who were taken from the Congo region. He lost his sight at age seven after being kicked by a horse; he commenced his musical career about a year later. Initially he played an African-derived bass instrument, the conga drum, and other percussion instruments. But street *soneros* – musicians who performed the Cuban song form known as SON – introduced Rodríguez to the tres, a six- or nine-stringed instrument in the guitar family, which he quickly mastered. He began composing music while still a teenager and in his lifetime wrote nearly 200 songs.

In 1940 Rodríguez transformed the typical *septeto* ensemble of trumpet, guitar, tres, maracas, bass, *claves,* and bongo by adding a second (and sometimes a third) trumpet, a piano, and – most significantly – the conga drum. Before Rodríguez formed his conjunto – a nine-to-eleven-member expansion of the traditional Cuban septeto – most Cuban popular musicians avoided the conga drum, due to its strong association with Africa. With a trumpet section and a deep-toned conga drum, Rodríguez's conjunto played rhythmically driving and eminently danceable music. The conjunto format quickly caught on; its lineal descendant is the contemporary salsa conjunto.

During the 1940s Rodríguez introduced a new *son* form known as the *son montuno,* which included an extended passage in which the vocalist – and instrumentalists in AFRO-LATIN JAZZ – improvised while the rest of the group played a repeating vamp figure. In formulating the son montuno, he was influenced by the flute riffs of Antonio Arcaño, leader of Arcaño y sus Maravillas. Along with Damaso Pérez Prado, the brothers Orestes and Israel "Cachao" López, and Arcaño, Rodríguez also played a key role in originating and popularizing the mambo, which not only inspired a worldwide dance fad but also provided the underlying musical form for much Afro-Latin jazz of the 1940s and 1950s. Moreover, the conjunto format, the son montuno, and the mambo rhythm are three of the key elements in the musical style known as salsa, which rose to worldwide popularity in the 1970s.

Rodríguez visited New York City during the 1940s, where he took part in a historic 1947 recording session that brought together several leading figures in Afro-Latin jazz, including Afro-Cuban conga drummer Chano Pozo, Puerto Rican vocalist Tito Rodríguez, and MACHITO's orchestra. In the early 1950s Arsenio Rodríguez left Cuba and settled in New York City, where he organized a band that included his brothers – percussionist and vocalist Raúl "Caesar" Travieso and percussionist Israel Moises "Quinque" Travieso. During the 1960s *típico* revival, a "back to the roots" movement within Latin music, Rodríguez gained new recognition as Latin musicians returned to traditional ensembles and performance styles. Yet he himself was never a musical purist or stylistic conservator.

During the 1960s Rodríguez continued to experiment with new instrumental combinations and approaches. At times he replaced one or more of the conjunto's trumpets with saxophones, and he introduced a musical fusion that he called *quindembo,* which he described as a Congolese word for a mixture of many disparate elements. Since his death Rodríguez has continued to exert a strong influence in Latin music. His compositions – including "Hay fuego en el veinte y tres" and "Bruca manigua" – continue to be mainstays in the repertoires of many salsa bands.

James Clyde Sellman

SEE ALSO

Congo, Republic of the; New York, New York; López, Israel ("Cachao"); Matanzas, Cuba; Pérez Prado, Dámaso; Pozo y González, Luciano (Chano); Salsa Music.

Latin America and the Caribbean

Rodríguez, Evangelina

(b. November 10, 1879, Higüey, DOMINICAN REPUBLIC; d. January 11, 1947, San Pedro de Macorís, Dominican Republic), Afro-Dominican woman who became the first female physician in her country. Though harassed throughout her life because she was a black woman working in a male-dominated profession, Rodríguez bravely used her scientific knowledge and feminist principles to advocate social health care as well as equality and education for poor Dominicans, especially women and children.

Ana Evangelina Rodríguez Perozo was born in 1879 as the illegitimate child of Ramón Rodríguez and Felipa Perozo, a poor, illiterate woman who worked as a servant in the homes of wealthy Dominicans. Ramón Rodríguez abandoned the family, and Evangelina's mother died when Evangelina was six years old. The young girl's maternal grandmother, Tomasina, took over the child's care and moved with her to the city of San Pedro de Macorís.

There the family met the poet Rafael Deligne (1863-1902), who was impressed with Evangelina's intelligence and urged Tomasina to send her granddaughter to school. Deligne thus became a father figure and mentor to Rodríguez. With his support she finished her primary studies at the top of her class and went on to become a schoolteacher.

After teaching for a few years Rodríguez decided that she wanted to become a doctor. In 1903 she became the first woman to be accepted to a school of medicine in the Dominican Republic. Rodríguez finished her studies and dissertation while also working as the headmaster of a girls school. In 1911 she was the first woman to graduate from medical school in her country.

Rodríguez dreamed of pursuing a medical specialization in France. In 1915 she wrote a book, *Granos de polen,* with the main purpose of raising money for her graduate studies. The book, which outlines her views about health care, was so badly edited and published that it produced more losses than gains. However, Rodríguez persisted. By 1921, with savings and donations from friends, she was able to begin her studies at the Sorbonne university in Paris. In 1925 she became the first black Dominican woman to graduate as a specialist in gynecology and pediatrics from the well-known French university.

Upon her return to the Dominican Republic, Rodríguez defied conservative church and government policies by working in areas of health care where no other Dominican doctors dared to venture. With a feminist perspective, she actively promoted family planning and education for prostitutes and poor women in order to combat venereal disease. She also founded a health center for people suffering from leprosy and tuberculosis, opened a night school to educate illiterate peasants, founded a maternity and children's hospital, and did charity work for the poorest in her society. Many of these activities scandalized the Roman Catholic Church and the Dominican upper class, who criticized her work. However, Rodríguez found refuge and support in two other black schoolteachers, Altagracia Domínguez and Petronila Angélica Gómez. Together the three women founded *Fémina,* a magazine advocating women's rights.

Immediately after the dictator Gen. RAFAEL TRUJILLO took power in 1930, Rodríguez became an outspoken opponent of his authoritarian regime. Her political standing not only scared many of her paying middle-class patients away, but also isolated her from the general medical community. As a result, her mental health began to deteriorate. By 1946 Rodríguez's friends and family had deserted her. Poor, abandoned, and sick, Rodríguez would walk aimlessly around the countryside. Her biographer claims that on one of these walks she was brutally hit and tortured by Trujillo's men and left to die on an abandoned road. She partially recovered from this incident, but in January 1947 she was found dying from hunger and thirst when it was too late to save her.

Though Rodríguez was a very prominent Afro-Dominican woman, her name and her struggle are not included in most Dominican history books. Today, however, two Dominican health facilities have been named in her honor: a sexual and reproductive health clinic for the poorest and most populated sectors of Santo Domingo and a health center in San Rafael del Yuma. Both tributes recognize the significance of Rodríguez's contributions to Dominican medicine.

Liliana Obregón

See Also

Dominican Republic; Catholic Church in Latin America and the Caribbean.

North America

Rogers, Joel Augustus

(b. September 6, 1883, Negril, Jamaica; d. March 26, 1965, New York, N.Y.), African American historian who pioneered the popularization of African American history.

Joel Augustus Rogers spent his childhood in Jamaica and served in the British Royal Navy there before migrating to the United States in 1906. He was largely self-educated, and although he had no formal postsecondary education, he taught himself French, German, Portuguese, and Spanish, and conducted his own research in library and museum archives.

As a historian, Rogers was often criticized because he had no formal academic credentials, and because his research focused on black history. Rogers therefore published much of his work himself over his 50-year career. His books were widely read by other African Americans and slowly began to influence mainstream historians. Rogers reached a mainstream audience more quickly through the white press when he became the first African American war correspondent, covering Italy's invasion of Ethiopia for the *Pittsburgh Courier* from 1935 to 1936. His newspaper columns were collected into a book called *The Real Facts About Ethiopia* (1936).

Several of Rogers's works were so popular that they went through multiple editions. *One Hundred Amazing Facts About the Negro* (1934) was printed in at least 19 editions. *Sex and Race* (1941-1944), a comprehensive three-volume work on miscegenation throughout history, went through nine editions. The two-volume *World's Great Men of Color* (1946) was republished in 1972.

Rogers's other books include *Your History from the Beginning of Time to the Present* (1940) and *Africa's Gift to America* (1959). In addition to books, Rogers wrote a series of articles on African American history for the *Pittsburgh Courier* and a weekly series that was carried in African American newspapers throughout the country.

Lisa Clayton Robinson

See Also

Italy; *Pittsburgh Courier.*

Latin America and the Caribbean

Rolando, Gloria

(b. April 4, 1953, Havana, Cuba), Afro-Cuban director of documentary films that focus on Afro-Cuban history and culture.

Gloria Rolando is one of Cuba's leading producers of documentary films on Afro-Cuban culture, which, she believes "contains legends and universal values that explain the world." In a speech at the Black Women Writers and the Future conference in New York City in October 1997, she stated that her motivation for creating documentary films about Cuba's African heritage was to transform "the tears held back by our ancestors" into life-affirming "tears of joy."

After university studies in music, literature, and art history, in 1976 Rolando began working at the Instituto Cubano de Artes e Industrias Cinematograficas (Cuban Institute of Art and Film Industry) in Havana, specializing in documentary films. After many years as a scriptwriter, narrator, and assistant director, she directed three documentaries, all of which have English-language versions. *Oggún: The Eternal Present* (1991) – the first in a projected series on Afro-Cuban traditions – portrays the Yoruba singing tradition, with special focus on Lázaro Ros, a prominent Afro-Cuban *akpwon* (Yoruba singer). *Oggún* also delves into the Santería religion and its primary deity Oggún, the god of metal and warfare. *My Footsteps in Baragua* (1996) studies the cultural effects of the presence in Cuba of immigrants from British Caribbean islands. *Eyes of the Rainbow* (1997) profiles Assata Shakur, the Black Panther and Black Liberation Army leader who fled the United States and settled in Cuba. Rolando's subsequent plans included a documentary on the life of Afro-Cuban film director Sara Gómez, who participated in the Cuban Revolution and died of asthma at age 31.

Roanne Edwards

See Also

Black Panther Party; New York, New York; Havana, Cuba; Ros, Lázaro.

Latin America and the Caribbean

Roldán, Amadeo

(b. July 12, 1900, Paris, France; d. March 2, 1939, Havana, Cuba), Afro-Cuban composer, conductor, and violinist; one of the first composers to combine Afro-Cuban folk music with the stylistic traits and forms of European classical music.

During the 1920s Amadeo Roldán, along with Alejandro Garcia Caturla, was Cuba's leading musical representative of afrocubanismo, an artistic and literary movement that looked to Cuba's urban black culture, folklore, and music as a basis for new art and literary forms. In his compositions Roldán employed Afro-Cuban folklore and ritual music, as well as the rhythms of such Afro-Cuban dances as the rumba, conga, *danzón*, and *son afrocubano*. His African-derived works also became central to Cuba's national identity, inspiring the slogan "Down with the lyre, up with the bongo," allegedly coined by the Cuban writer and ethnomusicologist Alejo Carpentier.

Born in Paris of Cuban parents, Roldán studied music at Spain's Madrid Conservatory, where he pursued a classical European education and won the Sarasate violin prize. In 1919 he settled in Havana. He continued his musical studies with Pedro Sanjuán while playing violin in a local cabaret to support himself. In 1924 he became concertmaster of the Havana Philharmonic Orchestra. Promoted to the position of conductor in 1932, he transformed the orchestra into one of the most distinguished instrumental groups in Latin America and introduced a wealth of contemporary music to the Havana public.

In 1925 Roldán premiered his *Obertura sobre temas cubanos*, the first major symphonic work by a Cuban composer to employ Afro-Cuban elements and musical instruments. His most celebrated work, the ballet *La Rebambaramba*, is based on a story by Alejo Carpentier and endeavors to evoke Kings' Day (January 6) celebrations in Havana. The first of its kind in Cuba, the ballet featured black cooks, *calash* (carriage) drivers, Spanish soldiers, and processional groups – a colorful representation of popular life in Cuba during the colonial era.

During the 1930s the work of two eminent Cubans exerted a decisive influence on Roldán: the Afro-Cuban poet Nicolás Guillén and the Cuban ethnomusicologist Fernando Ortiz. Guillén developed a poetic language based on the son, an Afro-Cuban musical form, which inspired Roldán to further consolidate an African-derived musical language in such compositions as *Tres toques* (1931-1932) and *Motivos de son* (1934). Through the work of Ortiz, Roldán came to appreciate the highly varied rhythmic patterns of African music. He worked with an *abakuá* drummer and had African drums made for use in performances of his works. Indeed, he scored his *Rítmicas* Nos. 5 and 6 for percussion instruments only, including the *quijada del burro* (Donkey's Jawbone), a typical African instrument used in Cuba, Peru, and Mexico.

Although Roldán met an early death in 1939, he gave formal shape to a distinctive Afro-Cuban musical style, thus profoundly influencing both art music and jazz in Cuba up to the present time. Moreover, he mastered prevailing European techniques, employing the most advanced harmony and orchestration. Both Roldán and Caturla, wrote music scholar Gerard Béhague, "raised the level of musical professionalism in Cuba and opened the way to international music circles for the following generation of Cuban composers."

Roanne Edwards

See Also

Cuba; Abakuás; Music, Classical, in Latin America and the Caribbean; Havana, Cuba.

North America

Rollins, Theodore ("Sonny")

(b. September 9, 1930, New York, N.Y.), African American JAZZ tenor saxophonist and composer whose innovations influenced music in the 1950s.

Sonny Rollins began making music at age nine, playing the piano and alto saxophone. Picking up the tenor saxophone in 1948, he led a group that included Jackie McLean, Kenny Drew, and Art Taylor. He made his first recording with pianist Bud Powell in 1949. For the next six years Rollins played professionally alongside famous jazz artists Charlie Parker, Fats Navarro, Bud Powell, Max Roach, ART BLAKEY, and, most frequently, Miles Davis. His compositions "Airegin," "Doxy," and "Oleo," recorded with Davis in 1954, have since taken their place as jazz standards.

Rollins joined the Max Roach-Clifford Brown quintet in 1955, working in the RHYTHM AND BLUES-influenced tradition of "hard bop." He made the landmark recording "Valse Hot" in 1956. With "Saxophone Colossus" and "Tenor Madness," recorded with John Coltrane, Rollins developed his "thematic improvisation" form. He led his own group after 1957, fusing jazz with CALYPSO patterns in works such as "St. Thomas."

By the late 1950s Rollins was well established as a gifted and innovative saxophone player. The 1958 recording *Freedom Suite* marked the beginning of a period of intermittent reclusiveness. During this time he was sometimes spotted practicing on New York's Williamsburg Bridge. Rollins returned to public life in 1961, experimenting with free jazz and later recording the score for the film *Alfie* (1966). He left the music scene again in 1968 to follow a spiritual path to India. After 1971, he continued to record and perform with such works as *G-Man* (1987), and *The Solo Album* (1985).

Marian Aguiar

See Also

Coltrane, John William; Davis, Miles Dewey, III; Navarro, Theodore "Fats"; Parker, Charles Christopher ("Bird"); Powell, Earl ("Bud"); Roach, Maxwell Lemuel (Max).

Africa

Roman Africa: An Interpretation,

a discussion of the Roman presence in North Africa, including the Roman province of Africa, incorporating present-day TUNISIA and eastern ALGERIA.

The Achievement of Caesar Augustus

Roman Africa never constituted a large part of the enormous continent of Africa. Only in EGYPT did Roman control extend deep into the continent along the valley of the Nile; elsewhere it consisted of a narrow strip of land, sometimes only a few miles in width, between the desert and the sea. At Cyrene, in present-day LIBYA, and at New Carthage, the city erected by the Romans in present-day Tunisia to replace the one they had destroyed, the climate permitted intensive agriculture, and Roman control reached farther inland. Those places were the exception.

But if Roman Africa was never an important part of Africa, it was for 500 years an important part of Rome. The history of this region of the world is vastly complex and, in some respects, still relatively unknown. This article deals with only a few isolated events and the influence of a few men, which, however, was very great and continues until the present day.

When Antony and CLEOPATRA lost the naval battle of Actium to the young Octavian, later known as Caesar Augustus, on September 2, 31 B.C.E., their fate was sealed. They escaped and returned to Alexandria, but it was only a matter of time before Octavian would gather his forces and overwhelm them in Egypt. The end came in August of the next year when Cleopatra, recognizing inevitable defeat, sent a false message to Antony that she had killed herself. He committed suicide. Later, she too died by her own hand. Her death ended the 300-year rule of the Greek Ptolemies over Egypt from their capital in Alexandria.

Octavian, now the unchallenged ruler of the Roman world, immediately set about creating a new kind of government that would, first, be (or seem to be) constitutional, and second, be both effective and enduring. The task was daunting, and perhaps no other man could have accomplished it.

The Roman Republic was in ruins, as everyone knew; it could not be revived. Most men had lost the dignified old Roman sense of moral and political responsibility; luxury and corruption had taken its place, together with a despairing fatalism that vitiated all hope for the future. Caesar Augustus gave them hope again. He established rules of conduct and had laws passed that set strict limits on behavior, both public and private; he returned formal control of legal affairs to the Senate, but gave it no real power; and he claimed no title for himself, not even that of consul, accepting no more than the role of first tribune (or representative) of the people. In time he gave up even that, calling himself only "first citizen," or *princeps*, with the result that the government began to be (and was for 200 years) called a principate. These actions won him great popularity among rich and poor alike, but they did not mean that he gave up any power whatsoever. As time went on, it became very evident that he personally controlled everything and made every important decision: political, economic, even cultural. His will was the will of all, and it could almost be said of him what Dante has Piccarda say of God in *The Divine Comedy: "Nella sua voluntade è nostra pace"* (In His will is our peace).

Pax Romana

The peace established by Augustus was enjoyed by all Romans, most Italians, and many prominent citizens of the far-flung provinces of the empire. But not by all. Twice during his reign, Augustus, with great ceremony, opened the doors of the temple of Januarius, symbolizing that the nation was at peace. But on each of those occasions, without ceremony, he closed the doors again, and they remained closed throughout most of the next 500 years. The wars that ensued, however, did not constitute civil strife. They were fought against peoples and tribes on the outskirts of the empire who were either rebelling against Rome or resisting being absorbed by it. Sometimes, of course, these distant conflicts, in Gaul, in Spain, in the East, and in Africa, were accompanied by terrible misery for the conquered victims. The historian Tacitus quotes a Roman officer who, aware of the suffering his men were causing, remarked: *"Faciunt solitudinem et pacem appellant"* (They make a wilderness and call it peace). But it would be merely cynical to affirm that this was always true. In no part of the empire, perhaps, was it less true than along the shore of Africa.

Egypt, in the east, was an ancient civilization that had learned how to govern itself 2000 years before the Romans came. From Cyrene all the way to the Atlantic a narrow strip of fertile land had been inhabited by independent bands of Berbers, the aboriginal peoples of northern Africa. Over many centuries they had learned to live in diverse ways, as nomads, as hunters and gatherers, as agriculturists. But they had not learned to live with one another without the threat, and the practice, of almost constant warfare. The land was rich, or could be with irrigation; the people were energetic and could be hard working; their immemorial contacts with that other Africa south of the desert offered untold possibilities of trade and gain. For a while, two centuries before, the Carthaginians had kept the Berbers' aggression in check, but without any real attempt to create a political society based on law. This, of course, was what the Romans knew how to do better than anybody. It was natural, therefore, that they brought law, and with law peace, and with peace prosperity to the Maghreb (stretching from present-day Libya to MOROCCO) during the five centuries from about 100 B.C.E. to about 400 C.E.

The Romans also founded cities, which had been rarities before their coming. There had been CARTHAGE and a few Phoenician and Greek settlements, but the Romans had obliterated Carthage and paid little attention to the other possibilities of Africa. Now, under the Pax Romana, they paid much attention. A military career, with its promise of steady income and advancement, was a potent attraction for young Berbers. In the area south of Cyrene there was ample water for irrigation, which Roman engineers exploited, thereby helping to found a thriving agriculture; within a few decades Cyrenaica (in present-day eastern Libya) was the main source of grain for southern Italy, including the city of Rome itself. Alexandria, of course, was a world-renowned center of scholarship and literature; but it did not command a monopoly of art and learning, which spread slowly westward along the Mediterranean coastline as new cities were established, as trade and therefore wealth increased, and as perpetual peace came to be an expectation instead of an impossible dream.

Septimius Severus

Two cities of the ancient African coast deserve mention, if only because of their most famous citizens. One of these was Septimius Severus. After the assassination of Emperor Commodus in 192 C.E., a furious power struggle ensued, resulting in the proclamation of four different emperors in the space of a few months. Each was a general with an army faithful to him, and none had any political experience. As much by luck as by skill, Septimius Severus emerged victorious and ruled for 18 years.

The reign of Septimius Severus coincides with the effective end of the empire as a constitutional monarchy and its beginning as a military dictatorship, which lasted until it was destroyed by the barbarians in the fifth century. It was probably not Septimius's fault. It had been a long time since Romans had had any sense whatever of ruling themselves according to law; they had been cared for by an absolute executive bureaucracy that had left no opening for political entrepreneurism or innovation. Perhaps, too, by the

The ancient theatre at Leptis Magna (present-day Tripoli) in Libya, a city believed to have been founded by the Carthaginians as early as 600 B.C.E and the home of Emperor Septimius Severus. *CORBIS/Roger Wood*

time Septimius became emperor there was no longer any other way to rule the enormous, sprawling, and unruly world that was Rome. Romans had shown themselves to be brilliant innovators in law, government, and politics, but they were not up to the challenge of creating a polity like the British Empire, for instance, which endured as a workable constitutional monarchy for centuries. In any event, Septimius inaugurated a rigid, despotic tyranny that was markedly different from what had gone before.

Septimius was also the first Roman emperor to have been born in Africa. His birth occurred in Leptis Magna, the site of which is near present-day Tripoli in Libya. Founded by the Carthaginians as early as 600 B.C.E., it was a major center for trade with the African interior. It later became the capital of Numidia, and after that the seat of government of a Roman province. Already prosperous when Septimius was born there in 146 C.E., Leptis Magna enjoyed a major resurgence as he constructed a series of magnificent buildings to honor his birthplace. Today their ruins are among the outstanding Roman monuments remaining in the Mediterranean world.

AUGUSTINE

Edward Gibbon, in the notorious closing chapters of his great work, *The Decline and Fall of the Roman Empire* (first published in the pregnant year 1776), was so unguarded as to conclude that there were two causes of the decline, not just one: barbarism and religion. The association of the two terms produced much distress in his time, but there is no denying that there is at least some truth in his thesis.

Jesus of Nazareth was born about 6 B.C.E., that is, during the later years of the reign of Augustus. His disciples and followers soon began to create commotions, first in Palestine, then in Rome. The emperors, for both state and private reasons, were resolute pagans. Paganism, after all, was the official religion, and many persons had an interest in keeping it that way. In addition, most of the emperors, including Augustus, were worshiped as gods of the Roman pantheon. As a consequence, for 300 years after Christ's birth Christians experienced either persecution or contempt; but they also endured numerous episodes of internal strife based on differences of belief, many of which occasioned charges of heresy.

Africa, perhaps because of its distance from Rome, fostered a number of Christian cults as well as a striking intensity of religious beliefs. Alexandria, in particular, saw several great heresies rise and fall. Arius, for example, the founder (or instigator) of Arianism, which flourished in the fourth century, was an Alexandrian. The Donatist heresy originated in Carthage, also in the fourth century. And Egyptian Christians, who continued to speak Coptic, the final form of the ancient Egyptian language, formed their own church, which today is one of the Eastern or Orthodox Churches. Even though Africa saw the rise of heresy and schism, however, it was also the source of fanatic Christian piety and asceticism in such persons as (to give just one example) Saint Anthony of Egypt, the founder of Western monasticism, whose temptations by the Devil, in numerous disguises, are the subject of innumerable works of art.

Hippo Regius, another important city of the ancient African littoral that was probably founded by Carthaginians around 400 B.C.E., later became the capital of the Numidian monarchy and was absorbed by Rome after the defeat of Carthage. Today it is the city of Annaba in Algeria. By the time its most famous citizen was born it was officially a Roman *colonia*, which meant that its inhabitants were Roman citizens.

Aurelius Augustinus, whom we know as SAINT AUGUSTINE, was born at Tagaste, near Hippo, on November 13, 354 C.E., to middle-class parents who soon recognized the intellectual promise of their son and devoted all their resources to his education. At age 19 he was sent to Carthage, where he worked for ten years as a freelance tutor. While there he read Cicero, who introduced him to the seductions of philosophy, and he later became a disciple of the Manichaeans, a religious sect popular in the western empire. When Manichaean teachers were unable to answer his hard questions, he went to Rome in search of better pupils as well as better teachers. He found neither, but he did discover the works of Plotinus, the Greek pagan Neoplatonist philosopher who opened his mind, he thought, to the belief he was seeking.

St. Augustine and Youth by the Sea, **by the Italian painter Sandro Botticelli (1445-1510), depicts the North African priest who became one of Christianity's most influential thinkers.** *CORBIS/Arte & Immagini srl*

Augustine's mother, Monica (now Saint Monica in large part because she *was* his mother), was a devout Christian. Her husband was a pagan, and this distressed her; but a greater torture was the fact that her brilliant son, if not a pagan, was not a Christian either. She followed him to Rome and then to Milan, where he had gone to meet the famous Ambrose, bishop of that city. Augustine went to hear Ambrose preach, but, although moved, was not convinced. Monica also visited Saint Ambrose and fell to her knees, pleading for him to help convert her son. Gently he raised her, blessed her, and promised: "The son of these tears shall not perish."

As a young man Augustine had formed a relationship with a woman, said to have been "of low birth," who bore him a son whom he called Adeonatus. (There is apparently no record of the mother's name.) The sexual tie between the man and woman was strong, and as time went on he grew to feel that this more than anything stood between him and his elevation to a higher plane of moral and religious existence. He found it hard to break the tie and prayed, as he tells us in his *Confessions*, "Give me chastity, but not yet." The unforgettable honesty of his plea was rewarded in the late summer of 386 C.E., when, sitting in a garden in Milan, he heard some children crying out, *"tolle lege, tolle lege"* (take up and read). He thought at first that they were playing a game, but he could remember no game with those words; then he looked down at the Bible in his lap and opened it at random to these words from Paul's Epistle to the Romans: "Put on the Lord Jesus Christ, and make no provision for the flesh, to gratify its desires" (Rom. 13:14). From that moment he was a Christian.

Augustine was baptized by Ambrose in the spring of 387 C.E., whereupon he determined to return with his mother to Africa. At Ostia, near Rome, his mother fell ill, and he sat with her as she expressed her joy at his newfound freedom. He helped her as they went to the window, where both he and she had a mystical experience that is described in moving terms in the *Confessions*. She died shortly after, and he returned to Hippo alone. Becoming a priest, he was shortly afterward called to serve as bishop of the place. He died there on August 28, 430 C.E. As he lay near death, he heard a clamor of cries and weeping. Asking what had occurred, he was informed that the barbarians were at the gate.

For 43 years Augustine had served the people of Hippo as pastor, teacher, and judge; but he had served a wider pastorate as well. By the time of his death he was the best-known Christian philosopher and theologian in the world, recognized not only for his writings, including especially *The City of God*, but also for his unremitting struggle against heresies that still afflicted the Roman Catholic Church, despite its adoption as the official state religion by the emperor Constantine a century before. One of his last works was the so-called *Rule of St. Augustine*, a prescription for a Christian life that was adopted by several monastic orders and is still followed today. His influence on the culture and self-image of the West is not now as great as it once was, but for at least 1000 years after his death he, perhaps better than any other man, defined the Western conception of the history and the destiny of mankind.

THE END OF ROMAN AFRICA

The barbarians at Hippo's gate were Vandals, a name that comes down to us as a synonym for willful destructiveness. They were a Germanic tribe that, fleeing the Huns, ranged westward into Spain and then eastward again along the African coast of the Mediterranean. Subduing Hippo and the region around it by 435 C.E., they remained the lords of the region for a century, until they were subdued in turn by the Byzantine general Belisarius, after which they disappear from history.

The Vandals may have been vandals, but they were also Romans and Christians to boot. The problem was, they were Arians and believed that Jesus, the Son of God, was only *like* God and was not *of one substance* with God. This distinction was of great importance in the fifth century. The belief survives even today, however, for example among the Jehovah's Witnesses, who assert that Arius was an ancestor of their founder, Charles Taze Russell.

All such distinctions became moot, at least in Africa, within a century or two after the defeat of the Vandals, when the irresistible force of Islam poured out of Arabia first into Persia and Syria, then into Egypt, then westward across the Maghreb, and then into Spain. By 700 C.E. or a few years afterward, Muslims controlled all of North Africa; the Roman Empire, which by that time had retreated to Byzantium, ceased to exist upon the continent.

Charles Van Doren

SEE ALSO

Berber; Tripoli, Libya; Alexandria and Grecian Africa: An Interpretation.

Africa

Ronga (also known as Baronga, Rhonga, and Rsonga), ethnic group of MOZAMBIQUE.

The Ronga primarily inhabit southern Mozambique in and around Maputo. They speak a Bantu language and are closely related to the TONGA people. Approximately 500,000 people consider themselves Ronga.

SEE ALSO

Bantu: Dispersion and Settlement; Maputo, Mozambique.

Latin America and the Caribbean

Roseau, Dominica (formerly Charlotte Town), capital of DOMINICA, a West Indian island nation.

Roseau is situated at the mouth of the Roseau River in the Caribbean Sea. The town is a port and serves as Dominica's main commercial and transportation center. Tourism is also important to the community's economy. A Roman Catholic cathedral built in the eighteenth century and botanical gardens are in Roseau, and the twin waterfalls at Trafalgar, a popular tourist attraction, are nearby. The population in 1991 was roughly 15,853.

North America

Rosewood Case, one of the worst race riots in American history, in which hundreds of angry whites killed an undetermined number of blacks and burned down their entire Florida community.

In 1922 Rosewood, Florida, was a small, predominantly black town. During the winter of 1922 two events in the vicinity of Rosewood aggravated local race relations: the murder of a white schoolteacher in nearby Perry, which led to the murder of three blacks, and a Ku Klux Klan rally in Gainesville on New Year's Eve.

On New Year's Day of 1923, Fannie Taylor, a young white woman living in Sumner, claimed that a black man sexually assaulted her in her home. A small group of whites began searching for a recently escaped black convict named Jesse Hunter, whom they believed to be responsible. They incarcerated one suspected accomplice, Aaron Carrier, and lynched another, Sam Carter. The men then targeted Aaron's cousin Sylvester Carrier, a fur trapper and private music instructor who was rumored to be harboring Jesse Hunter.

A group of 20 to 30 white men came to Sylvester Carrier's house to confront him. They shot his dog, and when his mother, Sarah, stepped outside to talk with the men, they shot her. Carrier killed two men and wounded four in the shootout that ensued. After the men left, the women and children, who prior to this had gathered in Carrier's house for protection, fled to the swamp where the majority of Rosewood's residents had already sought refuge.

The white men returned to Carrier's house the following evening. After a brief shootout they entered the house, found the bodies of Sarah Carrier and a black man whom they believed to be Sylvester Carrier, and set the residence on fire. The men then proceeded on a rampage through Rosewood, torching other buildings and slaughtering animals. They were joined by a mob of approximately 200 whites who converged on Rosewood after finding out that a black man had killed two whites.

That night two local white train conductors, John and William Bryce, who knew all of Rosewood's residents, picked up the black women and children and took them to Gainesville. John Wright, a white general-store owner who hid a number of black women and children in his home during the riot, planned and helped carry out this evacuation effort. The African Americans who escaped by foot headed for Gainesville or for other cities in the northern United States.

By the end of the weekend all of Rosewood, except the Wright house and general store, was leveled. Although the state of Florida claimed that only eight people died in the Rosewood riot – two whites and six blacks – survivors' testimonies suggest that more

African Americans perished. No one was charged with the Rosewood murders. After the riot the town was deserted, and even blacks living in surrounding communities moved out.

It is unclear what became of Jesse Hunter. Residents of nearby Cedar Key claimed that he was captured and killed after the massacre. The descendants of the Carrier family, however, contend that Jesse Hunter was not the man who had attacked Taylor. Philomena Carrier, who had been working with her grandmother Sarah Carrier at Fannie Taylor's house at the time of the alleged sexual assault, claimed that the man responsible was a white railroad engineer. She said that the man had come to see Taylor the morning of January 1 after her husband left for work. After an argument between them erupted, Philomena witnessed the man exit the back door and jog down the road toward Rosewood.

The Carriers' descendants maintain that the man was a Mason who persuaded Aaron Carrier, a member of Rosewood's black Masonic lodge, to help him escape by appealing to the society's code requiring members to help one another regardless of race. Carrier in turn persuaded another black Mason, Sam Carter, one of the few men in Rosewood with a wagon, to pick up the white man at Carrier's house and drop him off in the swamp, where he disappeared without a trace.

Though the Rosewood riot received national coverage in the *New York Times* and *Washington Post* as it unfolded, it was neglected by historians. Survivors of Rosewood did not come forward to tell their stories because of the shame they felt for having been connected with the riot and their fear of being persecuted or killed. In 1993 the Florida Department of Law Enforcement conducted an investigation into the case, which led to the drafting of a bill to compensate the survivors of the massacre.

After an extended debate and several hearings, the Rosewood Bill, which awarded $150,000 to each of the riot's nine eligible black survivors, was passed in April 1994. In spite of the state's financial compensation, the survivors remained frightened. When asked if he would go back to Rosewood, survivor Wilson Hall said, "No,... They still don't want me down there."

The director John Singleton, best known for his film *Boyz 'N the Hood*, released a fictionalized account of the massacre, called *Rosewood* and based on survivors' testimony, in 1997.

Aaron Myers

See Also
Lynching; Film, Blacks in American.

Latin America and the Caribbean

Ros, Lázaro (b. 1925), legendary Afro-Cuban Akpwon (lead singer) in the Yoruba musical tradition and promoter of Afro-Cuban music and culture. One of Cuba's best-loved artists, Ros has worked with the Conjunto Folklórico Nacional (National Folkloric Ensemble), the Contemporary Afro-Latin Jazz, the Cuban-based band Mezcla, and Carlos Santana. His life and work are presented in the film *Oggun* (1991), directed by Gloria Rolando (see Music, Afro-Caribbean Religious).

North America

Ross-Barnett, Marguerite (b. May 21, 1942, Charlottesville, Va.; d. February 26, 1992, Wailuku, Hawaii), African American educator who wrote about negative black imagery.

Marguerite Ross-Barnett graduated from Antioch College and earned a doctorate in political science from the University of Chicago. She focused her early work on Indian and African American studies. She taught at Princeton University, Howard University, and Columbia University before being appointed vice chancellor for academic affairs at City University of New York (CUNY) in 1983.

In 1985 Ross-Barnett published *Images of Blacks in Popular Culture: 1865-1955*, a controversial study of negative black stereotypes, based in part on her own collection. A year later she was appointed chancellor of the University of Missouri at St. Louis. In 1990 she became president of the University of Houston, where she served until dying of cancer two years later at age 50.

Marian Aguiar

See Also
Racial Stereotypes.

North America

Ross, Diana (b. March 26, 1944, Detroit, Mich.), African American singer and actress; lead vocalist of the Supremes, whose songs topped the *Billboard* charts throughout the 1960s, 1970s, and 1980s.

Diana Ross was born Diane Ross, the second of six children, to Fred and Ernestine Ross. She grew up in a poor district of Detroit, Michigan. As a child Ross sang with her siblings and parents in the choir at the Olivet Baptist Church and collaborated with neighborhood friends on renditions of the most popular songs of the day. She showcased her talent by performing on street corners, in school talent shows, and at dances. In 1959, while still in high school, Ross joined Mary Wilson, Florence Ballard, and Betty McGlown in a vocal group called the Primettes, the "sister act" for a group of male singers that later became the Temptations. In 1961, after both McGlown and her replacement Barbara Martin left the group, the Primettes signed a recording contract with Motown Records as a trio and changed their name to the Supremes.

The Supremes did not enjoy immediate recognition and success. Initially they sang as backup vocalists or served as handclappers for other Motown acts, including Mary Wells, Marvin Gaye, and the Shirelles. After three years as a group, the Supremes achieved their first Number-One hit in July 1964 with "Where Did Our Love Go," their ninth release. A string of Number-One recordings followed: "Baby Love" (1964), "Come See About Me" (1964), "Stop! In the Name of Love" (1965), and "Back in My Arms Again" (1965). In 1967 Cindy Birdsong replaced Florence Ballard, and the group changed its name to Diana Ross and the Supremes. In 1970 Ross left the Supremes to pursue a solo career in singing and acting, but not before issuing one more group hit, "Someday We'll Be Together." A series of female singers assumed the lead vocals of the Supremes before the group's breakup in 1977.

Ross launched her career as a soloist with the Number-One single "Ain't No Mountain High Enough" (1970). She then turned her attention to film. In 1972 Ross's portrayal of Billie Holiday in *Lady Sings the Blues*, in which the actress costarred with Billy Dee Williams, earned her an Academy Award nomination. Ross starred in *Mahogany* (1975), singing the hit theme song, "Do You Know Where You're Going To?," and later in *The Wiz* (1978). After recording two disco sensations, "Love Hangover" (1976) and "Upside Down" (1980), Ross collaborated with Lionel Richie on the ballad "Endless Love" (1981). Ross left Motown Records in 1981 but returned in 1989 to work as a recording artist, an equity partner, and a director of the company.

The Supremes were inducted into the Rock and Roll Hall of Fame in 1988, confirming their status as the most famous black performing group and the most famous female recording group in American music history. As the lead vocalist for the Supremes, Ross had 12 Number-One singles and sold more than 50 million records. Between 1970 and 1984 she recorded 31 albums and more than 50 singles, 6 of which reached the top spot on the *Billboard* chart. Ross is considered to be one of the most influential and versatile recording artists of the twentieth century.

Aaron Myers

See Also
Motown; Supremes, The; Temptations, The; Film, Blacks in American.

Europe

Rouche, Jean (b. May 31, 1917, Paris, France), French ethnographer and cinematographer.

A pioneer of ethnographic filmmaking, Jean Rouche is responsible for stylistic and technical innovations that influenced a generation of African cinematographers. His mother was a painter and his father was a naval explorer. Rouche originally trained to be an engineer. He graduated from a prestigious Parisian engineering college in 1941 and immediately left Nazi-occupied FRANCE for the freer West African colony of NIGER.

Rouche was hired to oversee the construction of the Niamey-Gao road, but the lack of equipment halted the project. During this time he became aware of aspects of Songhai culture, including spirit-possession ceremonies that were being conducted by several African workers he had befriended. Fascinated by the events and curious to learn more, Rouche returned to France, where he enrolled in a doctoral program in anthropology and studied with the famous ethnographer Marcel Griaule. He took a break from his studies in 1946, when he returned to Niger and spent a year exploring the NIGER RIVER. On this voyage Rouche had brought along a camera, and when a group of MANDINKA hunters on Lake Debo encouraged him to film their HIPPOPOTAMUS hunt, his career in cinematography began.

Over the next 50 years Rouche made more than 70 films and wrote almost 20 books about West Africa and the Songhai, an ethnic group on which many people still consider him to be the preeminent authority. His early work focused primarily on Songhai rites and rituals and resulted in several well-known films, such as *Les magiciens de Wanzerbé*, *Les maîtres fous*, *Jaguar*, and *Les tambours d'avant*. During the production of these films Rouche strove to develop cinéma vérité – a style of documentary filmmaking that stresses "unbiased" realism. He also initiated what he called participatory anthropology – forums in which he showed the Songhai the films he had made about them, in order to glean the Songhai's criticism and advice. During the 1960s Rouche decided to concentrate solely on ethnographic film, and he expanded his work to encompass his experiences in West Africa.

During his many travels and film tours Rouche continually sought out promising young filmmakers. For instance, he hired Moustapha Alassane and SAFI FAYE to work on his projects. Rouche's ability to work with minimal equipment and a small film crew earned him a reputation as a versatile and efficient filmmaker. In 1975 the newly independent country of MOZAMBIQUE asked for his help in building a state film industry. Although Mozambique later rejected Rouche's efforts, his style and technique continue to influence the work of many African filmmakers.

Since the early 1980s Rouche has produced only a handful of films, but he continues to teach Saturday morning seminars at the Musée de l'Homme in Paris. His achievements were celebrated in a retrospective of his work in Niamey (1986-1987) titled *Jean Rouche, Seventy Years/Seventy Films*. Despite his popularity, in recent years he has also been the subject of controversy. Some people, like the Senegalese filmmaker Ousmane Sembène, consider the work of Rouche to be a mere continuation of the colonial legacy in African film; others argue that Rouche's films and techniques, regardless of the subjects they develop, inspired a generation of African filmmakers whose work might have otherwise been lost.

Elizabeth Heath

SEE ALSO

Cinema, African; Niamey, Niger; Ousmane Sembène; Senegal; Songhai Empire; Anthropology in Africa; Songhai People.

Latin America and the Caribbean

Roumain, Jacques (b. June 4, 1907, Port-au-Prince, HAITI; d. August 18, 1944, Port-au-Prince, Haiti), writer, ethnographer, and political dissident whose novel *Gouverneurs de la rosée* is a classic of Haitian literature.

Born to upper-middle-class, mixed-race parents, Jacques Roumain attended excellent schools in both HAITI and Europe, where he acquired remarkable language skills (he spoke English, German, and Spanish, in addition to French and Creole) and a profound understanding of European cultures. At a young age, he rejected his parents' cosmopolitanism, and returned to Haiti from Paris in 1927 to help found *La revue indigène*. This journal, which was instrumental in the development of a specifically Haitian literary aesthetic rooted in traditional peasant life, published many of Roumain's early poems. Roumain wrote prodigiously and fearlessly during this period, publishing two collections of novellas in 1931 (*La proie et l'ombre* and *Les fantoches*) that denounced the greed of Haiti's ruling class.

In 1934 Roumain was elected secretary general of the Haitian Communist Party, which he had helped establish. That same year Haitian president Sténio Vincent, alarmed by the forceful criticism in Roumain's political writings, ordered him arrested. As a result of international pressure on the Haitian government, Roumain spent only two years in jail. Following his release, Roumain left for France, where he became involved with the Popular Front, an association that would lead him to fight among the antifascists in the Spanish Civil War (the poem "Madrid," recounting this experience, was published in a French journal in 1937). In 1939 Roumain, who found himself once again in France, published an article titled "Les griefs de l'homme noir" (The Grievances of the Black Man), which attracted both the attention and the ire of the French public.

Roumain published several literary and ethnographic works between 1939 and his death in 1944, but it is *Gouverneurs de la rosée* (1944; *Masters of the Dew*, 1947), published just weeks after he died, that endures as Roumain's most important work. The story of a Haitian peasant who brings two warring factions in a village together in the name of a common cause, the novel is a celebration of the collective potential of the Haitian peasantry. But the lasting appeal of this novel stems from Roumain's ability to express political didacticism in artful language – a lyrical French inflected by Creole words and rhythms. Roumain's successful integration of politics and art is his legacy and will serve as a model for many Francophone writers of the Caribbean.

Richard Watts

SEE ALSO

Literature, French Language, in Caribbean; Languages, Creole, in the Caribbean.

North America

Rowan, Carl Thomas (b. August 11, 1925, Ravenscroft, Tenn.), African American journalist, head of the United States Information Agency (USIA).

A veteran officer of the then segregated U.S. Navy, Carl Rowan entered into his career as a journalist at the white-owned newspaper *Minneapolis Tribune*. One of the first African American reporters for a large urban daily newspaper, Rowan captured the racial struggles of the 1950s with a series on discrimination in the South and articles on the U.S. Supreme Court school desegregation case BROWN V. BOARD OF EDUCATION. He entered government in 1961 as deputy assistant secretary of state to President John F. Kennedy and was appointed ambassador to Finland in 1963, making him one of the first African Americans to serve in a predominantly white nation. As head of the USIA in 1963, he reached the highest executive branch position held thus far by an African American. He has remained visible with a nationally syndicated column, as well as radio and television broadcasts. Rowan's writings tend to espouse mainstream liberal politics, and he has drawn the fire of both conservatives and black nationalists.

Marian Aguiar

SEE ALSO

Black Nationalism in the United States.

Rowlands, John. Please see STANLEY, SIR HENRY MORTON

Africa

Ruanda-Urundi. Former Belgian mandate incorporating present-day Rwanda and Burundi.

North America

Rudd, Daniel A. (b. August 7, 1854, Bardstown, Ky.; d. 1933, Bardstown, Ky.), active Roman Catholic layman who organized the first black Roman Catholic congress.

The child of Roman Catholic slaves, Daniel Rudd founded the first African American Catholic newspaper, the *Ohio State Tribune*, in 1886. The newspaper, later called *American Catholic Tribune*, promoted the Roman Catholic Church as an institution recognizing all people as equals. In 1889 Rudd organized the first National Conference of African American Catholics to address such issues as equal access for African Americans to employment, housing, and Catholic schooling. The conference received Pope Leo XIII's blessing and was followed by a visit to President Grover Cleveland. Rudd continued to participate actively in the church, including the first lay Roman Catholic congress, until his death in 1933.

Marian Aguiar

North America

Rudolph, Wilma Glodean (b. June 23, 1940, Bethlehem, Tenn.; d. November 12, 1994, Detroit, Mich.), African American sprinter and first American woman to win three Olympic Gold Medals.

As a child, Wilma Rudolph had suffered from scarlet fever, double pneumonia, and polio, leaving her without the use of her left leg. She wore a brace until age 9, but by age 12, she was the fastest runner in her school. At Burt High School she starred in both track and Basketball. At a track meet at Tuskegee, Alabama, Rudolph impressed coach Ed Temple, who invited her to a summer track camp in Nashville, Tennessee. This led to a place on the 1956 United States Olympic 4 x 100-meter relay team in Melbourne, Australia, which won the Bronze Medal. In the 1960 Olympic Games in Rome, Rudolph won Gold Medals in the 100- and 200-meter dashes and the 4 x 100-meter relay. She held the world record in all three events when she retired from amateur competition in 1962.

After graduating from Tennessee State University in 1963, Rudolph dedicated her professional life to youth programs and education. She worked with the Job Corps in St. Louis and Boston, and the Watts Community Action Committee in Los Angeles, California. Rudolph was inducted to the Black Sports Hall of Fame in 1973, the Women's Sports Hall of Fame in 1980, and the U.S. Olympic Hall of Fame in 1983. In 1977 she published her autobiography, *Wilma: The Story of Wilma Rudolph*. In 1981 she founded the Wilma Rudolph Foundation, a nonprofit organization focused on developing young athletic talent.

Robert Fay

See Also

Track and Field in the United States; Boston, Massachusetts.

North America

Ruffin, Josephine Saint Pierre (b. 1842, Boston, Mass.; d. March 13, 1924, Boston, Mass.), African American journalist, civic leader, civil rights activist, and suffragist.

Josephine Saint Pierre Ruffin's long career of humanitarian work began during the Civil War, when she and her husband George recruited soldiers for the Fifty-fourth and Fifty-fifth Colored Regiments of Massachusetts. She was active in integrated and African American women's clubs and charitable organizations, including the Associated Charities of Boston and the Massachusetts State Federation of Women's Clubs. In 1893 she founded and was president of the Women's Era Club (WEC) and edited its newspaper, the *Women's Era*, the first newspaper to be owned, managed, and published by African American women.

In 1895, in response to a Missouri editor's assertions that African American women were without virtue, Ruffin organized a national convention of African American women's clubs. Twenty clubs met and formed the National Federation of Afro-American Women. In 1896 they merged with the National Association of Colored Women.

Resistance to integrated clubs led to the "Ruffin Incident" in 1900 at the General Federation of Women's Clubs' biennial meeting in Milwaukee. When the executive board learned that the WEC's members were African Americans, it refused to seat Ruffin, who then refused to leave. Although Northern and Midwestern delegates backed Ruffin, the Southern contingent successfully blocked her participation.

After the WEC disbanded in 1903, Ruffin helped found the Association for the Promotion of Child Training in the South and the first branch of the National Association for the Advancement of Colored People in Boston.

Robert Fay

See Also

Boston, Massachusetts; Civil War, American; Fifty-fourth Regiment of Massachusetts Volunteer Infantry.

Rugaamba. Please see Ntare II

North America

Ruggles, David (b. March 15, 1810, Norwich, Conn.; d. 1849, Northampton, Mass.), orator, journalist, and militant abolitionist who said, "The pleas of crying soft and sparing never answered the purpose of a reform, and never will."

At age 20 David Ruggles, child of free parents in Connecticut, penned a letter to the Marquis de Lafayette asking for his support for the abolition of slavery. It was the beginning of a prominent public life of lectures and letters for the self-educated Ruggles. Three years later, in 1833, Ruggles traveled as an agent for New York's antislavery newspaper the *Emancipator*, inspiring audiences with news of the growing abolitionist movement.

Ruggles used the written word as well as the platform to describe the horrors of slavery. In 1834 he opened in New York City the first known African American bookshop. Such pamphlets as *Extinguisher, Extinguished... or David M. Reese, M.D. "Used Up"* (1834) and *The Abrogation of the Seventh Commandment by the American Churches* (1835) were distributed in contemporary slavery debates taking place around the issues of colonization and the women's movement. Expanding his antislavery forum, Ruggles published the first African American weekly magazine, *Mirror of Liberty*, in 1838.

As founder and head of the New York Vigilance Committee, Ruggles risked his own personal safety to protect endangered African Americans. He confronted slave catchers personally, and published a New York *Slaveholders Directory* (1839) to expose whites thought to own free people. He is remembered for assisting Frederick Douglass and more than a thousand slaves through the Underground Railroad.

By 1842 Ruggles was nearly blind and financially ruined after being imprisoned for helping an accused thief. He found support from Lydia Maria Child in Northampton, Massachusetts, and spent his last seven years there building a successful hydropathy, or "water cure," practice.

Marian Aguiar

See Also

Slavery in the United States; Abolitionism in the United States; New York, New York.

Latin America and the Caribbean

Ruiz Belvis, Segundo (b. 1829; d. 1867, Chile), Puerto Rican abolitionist. Segundo Ruiz Belvis liberated his slaves and founded an abolitionist society with Ramón Emetrio Betances. In 1867 he petitioned Spain to abolish slavery. He died in Chile later that year (*see* Betances, Ramón Emeterio).

Latin America and the Caribbean

Rumba, **a secular Afro-Cuban performance ritual synthesizing dance, song, and music.**

During the eighteenth century large numbers of slaves of YORUBA, Calabar, and KONGO descent were brought to CUBA to work in the sugar-producing region of Matanzas. Following the abolition of slavery in 1886, these and other liberated blacks headed to Cuba's urban centers in search of employment and settled on the outskirts of the cities. The rumba was born out of festive social gatherings in the suburban environment of Matanzas during the late nineteenth and early twentieth centuries. Rumba synthesizes African-derived rhythms, songs, and dances, in particular those of Bantu origin. Rumba soon spread to Havana and other parts of Cuba and, after World War II, was exported to Europe and the United States, where it was modified into a type of ballroom dance. This article focuses on the original form of rumba, as performed in contemporary Afro-Cuban communities.

A number of percussive instruments accompany the rumba. Originally, empty drawers turned upside down, empty bottles, frying pans, and spoons were used to make music for the rumba. Subsequently, rumba musicians replaced these instruments with wooden boxes, in particular those used to package salted cod and candles. Although wooden boxes are still occasionally incorporated, today rumba instrumentation usually features three conga drums, which are collectively referred to as the *tambores.* These include the bass *tumbador,* the middle-range *tres dos,* and the high-pitched *quinto.* Generally, the tumbador and the tres dos play constant rhythms, while the quinto improvises. Other instruments in the rumba repertoire are the *cata* or *guagua* (a wooden tube played with sticks), the *guiro* (a serrated wooden cylinder played with a metal, pick-like object), and either the *maruga* (an iron shaker) or the maracas. The *claves* (two hardwood sticks) are struck together to produce a syncopated beat of the same name (*clave*), which provides a distinctive ground rhythm for the other instruments (*see* SON).

There are three types of rumba: *yambú, guaguanco,* and *columbia,* each with its own unique rhythms, song format, and dance steps. Of these, the guaguanco is the most popular. It is faster than the yambú, but slower than the columbia.

The music for guaguanco has the following structure. After the claves have set the tempo for the song, the drums and the other instruments gradually join in, and the singer enters with the *diana,* a short string of melodic syllables. The singer, who is usually a man, then proceeds to sing an extended, lyrical solo or duet, known in Spanish as the *canto,* which often recalls and comments upon a certain person or event. The singer eventually indicates a phrase in the song that will be used as the chorus. The dancers usually enter after the chorus has started. An animated call-response section begins in which the singer improvises lines, which alternate with the chorus. This exchange may continue for several minutes before the song ends.

In the guaguanco a male dancer tries to attract the female dancer, but she flirtatiously avoids his advances. While circling around her, the male dancer intermittently makes a quick gesture with his hand or leg that symbolizes an attempt to "possess" the female dancer, who responds by quickly covering her pelvic region with her hands or crossed arms. The ultimate possessive gesture is a pelvic thrust by the male called the *vacunao.* The dance ends when the male has successfully caught the female off-guard with the vacunao or when the female dancer proves herself to be impervious to the male dancer's efforts to possess her.

The yambú is a slower dance in which a male and a female performer dance as if they were elderly. The male does not do the vacunao in this dance. The yambú is the least frequently performed type of rumba.

The columbia is the fastest and most acrobatic of the three types of rumba. Its rhythmic patterns are short and sharp, and it is done by a solo male dancer. Some of the steps are closely related to those performed by members of all-male secret societies known as ABAKUÁS. In the columbia, the dancer and the player of the quinto engage in a competitive dialogue in which the dancer attempts to match, through dance steps, the rhythmic improvisations of the quinto. Unlike the other two forms of rumba, columbia's lyrics sometimes include words and phrases in African languages, in particular Yoruba.

Rumba continues to be a vital tradition at the grassroots level, especially in and around Matanzas and Havana. During the course of rumba's development, neighborhood-based rumba groups known as *bandos* and *coros de rumba* emerged, mounting performances and hosting parties. Such ensembles as AfroCuba and Los MUÑEQUITOS DE MATANZAS, whose members span three generations, have achieved international renown.

Aaron Myers

SEE ALSO

Bantu: Dispersion and Settlement; Matanzas, Cuba; Abolition and Emancipation in Latin America and the Caribbean; Havana, Cuba.

North America

Run-DMC, **an early and influential RAP music group from New York City. The group was known during the 1980s for its aggressive "raps" (spoken rhymes) on top of strong beats. Run-DMC further distinguished its sound by incorporating elements of rock music, specifically heavy-metal guitar, which helped popularize black rap among many white listeners. By bringing the hip hop street look to the stage, Run-DMC also changed the image of rap, wearing black leather in winter, athletic warm-up suits in summer, and always wearing their signature Adidas sneakers. The first rap group to be broadcast regularly on Music Television (MTV), Run-DMC in 1985 also became the first rap group to appear on the television program *American Bandstand,* hosted by media personality Dick Clark.**

Run-DMC was formed in 1983 by three friends from New York City's borough of Queens. Rapper Joseph "Run" Simmons recorded as a solo artist in 1982 for his older brother, rap producer Russell "Rush" Simmons, before teaming with rapper Darryl "D.M.C." McDaniels to record two minor singles. The two then brought in disc jockey (DJ) Jason "Jam Master Jay" Mizell, and the trio soon became known as Run-DMC. The group released its first album in 1984, *Run-D.M.C.* On the strength of one song, "Sucker M.C.'s," the album became the best-selling rap album to that time. The album gained attention for its tough-sounding lyrics and its spare, clean sound; the group used only a drum machine and scratchy turntable noises for accompaniment. Another single from the album, "Rock Box," was one of the first rap pieces to include tracks of heavy-metal electric guitar, and was also distributed as a video.

In 1985 Run-DMC released its second album, *King of Rock,* and acted and performed in the motion picture *Krush Groove,* a fictionalized account of Run-DMC and the development of rap-music record label Def Jam. Also in 1985, a number of violent incidents at rap concerts caused the national media to focus on rap as a reflection of violence and drug abuse among young black males. Run-DMC and other rap groups found themselves caught between this negative image and the acceptance of rap by MTV and *American Bandstand.*

The group's third album, *Raising Hell* (1986), featured a remake of "Walk This Way," a song first performed by the hard-rock group Aerosmith in 1976. The remake, which included new performances by Aerosmith members Steven Tyler and Joe Perry, was a popular success and was hailed by critics as a breakthrough that masterfully fused white rock music with black rap. In 1988 the group starred in *Tougher Than Leather,* a film produced by Def Jam's Rick Rubin. Other albums from Run-DMC include *Back from Hell* (1990) and *Down with the King* (1993).

SEE ALSO

Hip Hop in the United States; New York, New York.

North America

RuPaul (RuPaul Andre Charles)

(b. November 17, 1960, New Orleans, La.), African American singer, entertainer, actor, and the first openly gay cross-dresser to become a supermodel and mainstream celebrity.

Since the release of his debut album *Supermodel of the World* in 1992, RuPaul has become a nationally recognized celebrity. Although best known as a drag queen, he also enjoys surprising audiences by appearing as a man. "Drag queens are like the shamans of our society, reminding people of what's funny and what's a stereotype," he told *People Weekly* writer Tim Allis in 1993. "I feel very powerful when I'm in drag, and when I'm out of drag I observe our culture." RuPaul is 2 m (6 ft 7 in) tall (in heels). He is painfully aware of the contradictions of being a black man who wears a platinum wig and platform shoes. "When I'm dressed up as this goddess," he told Allis, "people trip over themselves to give me things. But as an African American male, I can walk into an elevator and have people clutch their handbags."

Born RuPaul Andre Charles, RuPaul grew up in San Diego, California, one of four children of Irving Charles, the operator of a beauty supply store, and Ernestine Charles, a college clerk. His parents divorced when he was 6. At age 15 he moved with his sister Renetta to Atlanta, Georgia, where he studied at the Northside High School of the Performing Arts. "In school I was kind of alien to every group," he told Guy Trebay of the *New Yorker*. "I was perpetually an outsider... until the day I decided to get into drag." Inspired by images of Diana Ross, he began performing at Atlanta cabarets and comedy clubs in wigs and high heels. He also sang in various rock groups, including RuPaul and the U-Hauls.

In 1987 he moved to New York City, where he sang with the band Now Explosion, at the Pyramid, a popular East Village gay club. In 1991 he received a contract with Tommy Boy Records. Three songs from his debut album reached Number One on the *Billboard* chart, propelling RuPaul to national celebrity. Since then he has contributed to Elton John's *Duets* album, released a Christmas single, "The Little Drummer Boy," and recorded a second album, *Foxy Lady* (1996). In 1995 he won a contract with M.A.C. Cosmetics and was made cochair of the company's acquired immune deficiency syndrome (AIDS) fund.

In 1996 RuPaul began hosting a television talk show, whose guests have included Dennis Rodman, Whoopi Goldberg, and Cher. He has appeared in numerous films, including Spike Lee's *Crooklyn* (1994) and Wayne Wang's *Blue in the Face* (1995).

Roanne Edwards

See Also

AIDS in the United States; Lee, Shelton Jackson ("Spike"); New York, New York; Television and African Americans; Racial Stereotypes; Film, Blacks in American.

North America

Rush, Bobby

(b. November 23, 1946, Albany, Ga.), Democratic member of the United States House of Representatives from Illinois since 1993.

Bobby Lee Rush was born in Albany, Georgia, and grew up in Chicago. He joined the army in 1963, and in 1966 he became active in the Civil Rights Movement in the South. Rush was honorably discharged from the army in 1968; the same year he cofounded the Illinois Black Panther Party.

During his time with the Black Panthers, Rush also managed a medical clinic that developed the nation's first mass testing program for sickle cell anemia, a disease that, in the United States, occurs primarily among blacks. Rush received a bachelor's degree from Roosevelt University in 1973 and earned a master's degree from the University of Illinois in 1994. He was elected a city alderman in 1983 and served in that position for nearly ten years.

By a slim margin Rush defeated the incumbent representative, Charles A. Hayes, in the 1992 Democratic primary for the First Congressional District seat in Illinois. He then won the general election with 83 percent of the vote and was returned to office in subsequent elections. The First District is predominantly black and Democratic, covering parts of inner-city Chicago and nearby suburbs. The district includes middle-class communities and crime-ridden housing projects.

In the 105th Congress (1997-1999), Rush served on the Commerce Committee. He is also a member of the Congressional Black Caucus.

See Also

Chicago, Illinois.

North America

Rushing, Jimmy

(b. August 26, 1903, Oklahoma City, Okla.; d. June 8, 1972), African American jazz vocalist.

Jimmy Rushing was reared in a musical family and studied piano, violin, and voice from childhood. In 1927 he began his singing career with Walter Page's Blue Devils, moving to Bennie Moten's Kansas City Orchestra two years later. Rushing's career predated the microphone, and his rich and bellowing tenor voice carried over the sound of the band without mechanical amplification. Rushing performed as a vocalist with the Count Basie Orchestra from 1935 to 1950, producing such songs as "Goin' to Chicago," "How Long, How Long," and the self-descriptive "Mr. Five by Five."

See Also

Basie, William James ("Count"); Moten, Benjamin (Bennie).

North America

Russell, Nipsey

(b. October 13, 1923, Atlanta, Ga.), American comedian who was the first African American to appear as a host of a national television show.

Nipsey Russell began his career in 1948 when he moved to New York City to try his hand at stand-up comedy. Eschewing Black Vernacular English and racial references, Russell moved from Harlem nightclubs, like the Apollo Theater, Smalls Paradise, and the Baby Grand, to mainstream clubs and television appearances. He was one of the first African Americans to appear on talk shows and was a frequent guest of Jack Paar on *The Tonight Show*. He had a serial role on the television show *Car 54 Where Are You?*, and won critical acclaim as the Tin Man in the movie *The Wiz*.

See Also

Television and African Americans.

North America

Russell, William Fenton (Bill)

(b. February 12, 1934), African American basketball player who led the Boston Celtics to 11 National Basketball Association (NBA) championship titles and was voted by sportswriters in 1980 as the Greatest Player in the History of the NBA.

Graduating from McClymonds High School in Oakland, California, in 1952, at his NBA height of 2.1 m (6 ft 10 in), Bill Russell won an athletic scholarship to the University of San Francisco (USF). He led USF to National Collegiate Athletic Association (NCAA) championships in 1955 and 1956. Russell was part of the 1956 United States Olympic Team, which won a Gold Medal in Melbourne, Australia. He then joined the Boston Celtics. Playing from 1957 to 1969, he led the Celtics to 11 championship titles. He was revered as the league's best rebounder and defensive player. He was named the NBA's Most Valuable Player five times, and played in 12 All-Star games. In 1966, while still an active player, Russell began coaching the Celtics, becoming the first African American coach in the NBA. As player-coach he led the Celtics to two NBA championships. From 1973 to 1977 he coached the fledgling Seattle SuperSonics, and briefly the Sacramento Kings. He was inducted into the Basketball Hall of Fame in 1975.

A leader off the court as well, Russell was a vigilant defender of equal rights for African American athletes. In 1966, at the height of his career, Russell voiced a powerful assertion of black pride and protest with his autobiography, *Go Up for Glory*.

See Also
San Francisco and Oakland, California.

Europe

Russia and the Former Soviet Union, **a large country extending from eastern Europe into northern Asia, which has hosted a black population for centuries.**

Blacks in Russia

From the eighteenth century, when Peter the Great first recruited black servants, until the post-Soviet present, black people have been an uncommon sight in the lands that once constituted the Russian Empire and, later, the Soviet Union (or Union of Soviet Socialist Republics, USSR). Except in tiny black enclaves in the Caucasus, blacks have always been outsiders in this part of the world. As early as 1858 the celebrated black Shakespearean actor Ira Aldridge beguiled Russian audiences with the power of his performances, while his presence sparked heated discussions on racial issues in the Russian press. In the decades preceding the 1917 Bolshevik Revolution a number of American blacks went to Russia, where they pursued successful careers as businessmen and diplomats.

The heyday for blacks in Russia occurred between the 1917 revolution and the 1960s. Communist leaders, eager to display their country as a place of racial equality, gave visiting black artists, intellectuals, and political figures privileges that the average Soviet citizen could only dream of – albeit not without motives informed by Soviet ideology and international politics. Although blacks encountered racial prejudice in the former Soviet Union, the general reaction to them was one of curiosity more than hostility. Writer Langston Hughes wrote of his 1932 experience in Russia, "What few Negroes there were in Moscow, of course, were conspicuous wherever they went, attracting friendly curiosity if very dark, and sometimes startling a peasant fresh from the country who had never seen a black face before."

The Black Population of the Caucasus

In 1913 Russian naturalist V. P. Vradii published a report on an unusual discovery he had made while visiting the western Caucasus Mountains. He revealed that several hundred blacks were living in small, isolated farming settlements around two Black Sea towns, Batumi and Sukhumi, in what is now the republic of Georgia. Most of the blacks were Muslims and spoke the Abkhazian language. Vradii's testimony was confirmed in the following decades by several journalists and scholars who traveled to the remote region.

The origins of these black inhabitants are not entirely clear. Many were brought from Africa as slaves for local Turkish and Abkhazian rulers between the sixteenth and nineteenth centuries. It is likely, however, that small communities of blacks have lived in the region for much longer. The ancient Greeks developed slave-trading colonies on the Black Sea coast, as did the Romans, Arabs, Genoese, and Turks in later centuries. Moreover, the region that is now Georgia was called Colchis by the ancient Greeks, and the Greek historian Herodotus, writing in the fifth century B.C.E., stated that the Colchians had black skin and woolly hair, and that they wove linen in the same manner as the Egyptians. Recent scholars have pointed out a likeness between many Abkhazian and Egyptian place names, family names, and names of similar customs.

Little is known about the Caucasus blacks. Two who rose to prominence in the early years of the Soviet Union were Shaaban Abash and Bashir Shambe. After the October 1917 revolution, Abash, a shepherd, joined the forces supporting the Bolsheviks and was subsequently elected to the Central Executive Committee of the Abkhazian *Soviet* (city council), the highest local executive authority. Shambe also enlisted in the Red Army and later joined both the Georgian Communist Party and Tbilisi Soviet.

Opinions differ on the current situation of the Caucasus blacks. It is thought that over the years many have intermarried and assimilated into Abkhazian or wider Soviet society. In 1992, however, the black Russian journalist Yelena Khanga reported that her mother, Lily Golden-Hanga, visited some of the black villages in the 1960s and discovered that the inhabitants were living in poverty, isolated from other local peoples. Golden-Hanga reported her findings to her long-time friend Svetlana Allilueva, Joseph Stalin's daughter, who defected to the West in 1966 and was at the time writing a book on Russia. Allilueva included Golden-Hanga's findings in her book *Only One Year*, published in the United States in 1969. Her account suggests that some of the Abkhazian blacks had been forcibly relocated by the Soviet authorities – a common fate of other Caucasian peoples, such as the Kabardians and the Chechen-Ingush. In the Soviet edition of Allilueva's book, however, censors removed all references to the plight of the Abkhazian blacks.

Black Servants in Imperial Russia

Beginning with the reign of Peter the Great (1682-1725), blacks were brought to Russia to work as slaves or servants. In the eighteenth and early nineteenth century, it was fashionable in Russia, as in the rest of Europe, for wealthy aristocratic families to employ one or two black servants. The tsars also maintained a staff of between 10 and 20 blacks. Until the nineteenth century blacks were acquired as slaves; on arrival in Russia they were given their freedom in exchange for lifelong service. Some are portrayed, with their employers, in paintings by the nineteenth-century artists Karl Briullov and Konstantin Makovskii.

Although most of these blacks came from Africa, some came from the United States. A black man named Nelson accompanied the family of John Quincy Adams to Russia in 1809, when Adams was appointed minister to Russia, and remained after joining the tsar's service. Moreover, most of the ships that sailed to Russia from major United States ports in the nineteenth century contained black crewmen, some of whom stayed.

One who remained was Nero Prince, a cook and prominent freemason from Boston, who first sailed to Russia in 1810 and settled there as a butler for a noble family. When Prince brought his second wife, Nancy, to Russia in 1824, she was presented at court to Tsar Alexander I. Nancy Prince set up a sewing shop, became active in the Russian Bible Society, and helped establish an orphanage in St. Petersburg. She left firsthand accounts of the great flood of St. Petersburg of 1824 and the bloody suppression of the Decembrist Revolt in 1825.

The most famous black servant in Russia was Abram Hannibal, the great-grandfather of Russia's beloved writer, Alexander Pushkin. Hannibal, whose parents were probably from Ethiopia, arrived in Russia around 1700 as a servant to Tsar Peter the Great and ended his life as a military general and prominent landowner. In 1716 Hannibal was sent by Tsar Peter to Paris for higher education in military engineering. At this time Peter was in the midst of his lifelong struggle to build Russia into a major European land power with a large, well-organized army and well-fortified defenses, and many Russians were sent to Western Europe for training in modern military techniques.

Hannibal returned to Russia in 1723 and began working on military engineering projects. After Peter's death he spent three years designing fortifications in Siberia. In 1730 he was promoted to captain and assigned to Pernau, a fortress in western Russia on the shores of the Baltic Sea. Under the Empress Elizabeth, his career flourished further. He was promoted to major general in 1742 and served as commandant of the city of Reval from 1743 to 1751. He retired in 1762 to one of the many estates he had been given by the empress, where he lived until his death in his early 90s. He is considered Russia's first outstanding modern engineer, an expert in canal and fortress construction, and one of the most highly educated Russians of his time.

In the 1820s Alexander Pushkin wrote a fictionalized biography of Hannibal called *The Negro of Peter the Great*, which, according to Russia scholar Allison Blakely, "represented one of the earliest characterizations of the Negro as hero in world literature." Pushkin often referred in his poetry to his African heritage, which he valued highly and considered a mark of distinction. During the twentieth century the Russian poets Vladimir Mayakovsky and Marina Tsvetaeva wrote verse extolling Pushkin's black ancestry.

Black Immigrants and Visitors in Russia Before 1917

During the late nineteenth century a number of blacks immigrated to Russia voluntarily in order to improve their economic lot. Exact numbers and other details are hard to obtain, but studies indicate that most of these immigrants came from the United States. Many of those who became financially successful later left Russia to escape the Bolshevik regime, which considered wealthy people to be enemies of the working class.

George Thomas, an African American, moved to St. Petersburg in 1890 and adopted the Russian name Fyodor. During the next 25 years he became a highly successful businessman, owning a large amusement complex in Moscow called the Aquarium. He is said to have become a close confidant of Tsar Nicholas II. The jockey Jimmy Winkfield, who had won two Kentucky Derbys, moved to Russia in 1904 to ride horses for wealthy noblemen and married an aristocratic Russian woman. At the height of his career in 1916, he is said to have made $100,000 a year. Other black immigrants found jobs as traveling circus performers and singers.

Three notable black visitors to Russia before 1917 were the Shakespearean actor Ira Aldridge, the philanthropist T. Morris Chester, and the diplomat Richard T. Greener. All three were African Americans, and all met with greater acceptance in Russia than they had experienced at home. Of the three, Aldridge had by far the greatest impact on Russian society and culture.

Aldridge, who had left the United States in 1824 to make his career in Europe, first visited Russia in 1858. He made several tours of Russia between 1861 and 1866, giving many Russians a memorable first experience of Shakespeare, even though his performances in English were largely incomprehensible to his audiences. He was made an honorary member of the Imperial Academy of Fine Arts and became a friend of the famous Ukrainian poet Taras Shevchenko.

Because Aldridge was the first black person to make a major impression in Russian intellectual circles, his visits stimulated considerable discussion on racial issues in the Russian press and public. Although some critics were initially outraged that a black actor would perform Shakespeare, they were soon swept away by Aldridge's talent and humanity. The power of his performances brought Russians' experience of Shakespeare to a new level of intensity – a fact illuminated in the following Russian review of Aldridge's performance, as cited in Allison Blakely's *Russia and the Negro* (1986): "Look at Aldridge... an African, with a swarthy face, dark skin, kinky hair, dilated nostrils, guttural speech. He does not attract us with any exquisite form, such as we are accustomed to, but such is the power of his soul, such is the majesty of his art that you... understand everything he says... you seem to hear the beating of his heart, you are following a magician through all the gamut of human emotions."

Aldridge's visits came at a time of intense debate surrounding Tsar Alexander II's emancipation of Russia's huge population of serfs, which occurred in 1861. Aldridge's artistic genius served as an example of what an oppressed people could achieve if given the right opportunities; he was often cited by the liberal intelligentsia who were becoming increasingly critical of the autocratic Russian state. During the 1860s, as Russia became more restrictive of radical opinion, Aldridge was forbidden to perform *Macbeth* or *King Lear*, apparently because the works offended the tsar. In 1864 Aldridge was officially banned from St. Petersburg.

T. Morris Chester, the leader of the Garnet League – a philanthropic society that provided aid to freed slaves in the United States – visited Russia in the winter of 1866 to 1867 and was well received by Tsar Alexander II. He published an appeal for donations in the daily newspaper *Golos* (The Voice). Among the responses he received was a letter from a Russian peasant landholder and former serf, who wrote that he considered America's freed slaves as "brothers, not merely on account of the principle that all men are brethren, but by the force of those feelings which must unite the freedpeople of one land to those of another." After returning to the United States, Chester became an important state and federal official, and frequently gave public speeches and interviews. Through his visit, many American blacks came to see Russia as a racially tolerant land.

Richard T. Greener, a lawyer and diplomat, and the first African American graduate of Harvard College, served from 1898 to 1905 as the U.S. commercial agent in Vladivostok, Russia's major Pacific port. While in Russia he wrote many reports for the U.S. government on the economic potential of Siberia and its importance for the United States. Greener made suggestions to local officials for public improvements, and in return was elected to the Statistical Society of Amur and Primorsky Provinces, an honor reserved for leading officials and businessmen. When the Russo-Japanese War (1904-1905) broke out, Greener was charged by the U.S. government with protecting Japanese interests in Siberia, and he was forced to leave Russia in 1905. Like Chester, Greener returned to the United States, where he spoke widely to both black and white audiences about his experiences in Russia and the economic opportunities there.

Black Immigrants and Visitors to the Soviet Union

The Soviet Union, the new country formed in 1922 out of the Russian Empire, was a highly attractive destination for many black people. It was, after all, the first country founded on the principles of racial equality, world peace, anticolonialism, and economic advancement of the working class. It seemed to offer an ideal society to those suffering under COLONIAL RULE in Africa, or racism and economic depression in the United States. As a result, many blacks traveled to the Soviet Union, and a number settled there.

The Soviet authorities had many reasons for encouraging blacks to come to their country. They believed that blacks, as members of an oppressed social group, would be key participants in the Communist revolution that would topple colonial and capitalist regimes around the world, and they wanted to ensure that potential revolutionary leaders were firmly under the control of Moscow. Giving blacks free education in Soviet universities was a means to that end. Also, by demonstrating the Soviet Union's own racial tolerance and progressive thinking, Soviet leaders were enhancing their country's appeal to liberal-minded white and black intellectuals around the world, thus securing sympathy for the Communist cause.

Black Students in the Soviet Union Before World War II

In 1920, during the Second Congress of the Communist International – the Comintern, the organization formed to spread world revolution – white American Communist John Reed passed a note to Vladimir Lenin asking, "Should I say something about the Negroes in America?" Lenin wrote back, "*Yes*. Absolutely necessary." After a discussion of the situation of American blacks, the Comintern proposed to invite blacks to study in Russia.

Between 1925 and 1938 several dozen African and West Indian blacks and between 60 and 90 American blacks were invited to study at the Comintern-controlled Stalin Communist University of the Toilers of the East (KUTV) in Moscow. Most completed a 14-month program, which principally dealt with Marxist-Leninist theory, although training was also provided in espionage, guerrilla warfare, secret codes, and techniques of underground political work.

The blacks, like all foreign students, were treated as honored guests, receiving free room and board, clothing and travel allowances, special tutors, paid vacations in the Soviet Union and at home, and access to high officials. At that time no other country offered blacks such opportunities. Yet some blacks encountered racism from both local people and Communist party workers. In his study on blacks in Comintern schools, Woodford McClellan noted that "The Russian-Ukrainian national experiences did not embrace racism... on the British, Spanish, or American model, but discrimination directed against minority peoples – Tartars and other Orientals, Turkic peoples, Jews – stained the record of the East Slavs, and black visitors inevitably felt its blows." Indeed, one black student, Pierre Kalmek, reported that he encountered "greater chauvinism here than in capitalist countries... People have spat on me three or four times."

Because the Soviet authorities often suppressed news of racial incidents, it is unclear to what extent black students experienced racism at KUTV. Like the general public, university teachers were expected to adhere to Communist principles and to suppress all racial prejudices. According to McClellan, it was foreign whites, in particular the Americans, British, and Canadians, who were usually responsible for racial provocations in the Comintern schools. In 1932 black students formally complained about racism to the Comintern, which eventually set up an investigative commission: as a result, two whites and one black were expelled from KUTV.

KUTV students also voiced outrage at the abandonment of the film *Black and White*, which was to have depicted racial and labor conflicts in Birmingham, Alabama. In 1932, 21 African Americans, including the writer Langston Hughes, were invited to the Soviet Union to participate in the film project. The Soviets apparently canceled the film, already in progress, at the insistence of Col. Hugh L. Cooper, the white American supervising the construction of the Dneprostroi hydroelectric power station. Cooper threatened construction delays if the film went ahead. Many black students saw the film's cancellation as a sacrifice of Communist ideals to economic expediency.

Political, Literary, and Artistic Visitors

Many famous black political activists as well as literary and artistic figures visited the Soviet Union, drawn by its reputed racial tolerance and by its attempt to put Marxist ideas into practice. While some were committed Communists, others were artists or writers who upheld the aims of the Russian Revolution but had no formal ties to any Communist party.

One of the most important black visitors in the interwar period was Jamaican-born poet Claude McKay, who stayed from 1922 to 1923 and wrote about his trip for the American press. Received warmly by such Soviet leaders as Trotsky, Zinoviev, and Bukharin, McKay and Otto Huiswood were the first blacks to discuss the American race problem before a Russian audience, at the Fourth Congress of the Comintern (1922). He also became a literary celebrity and was handsomely paid for the publication in the USSR of poems, articles, and a Soviet-commissioned book titled *The Negroes in America* (1923) – a propagandistic discussion of the plight of blacks in America as a key component of the class struggle.

Although McKay was interested in Communist Party politics, he saw himself as an independent-minded poet, devoted first and foremost to his art. Reflecting on his experience in Russia, he wrote: "The fact is that I spent most of my leisure time in non-partisan and anti-Bolshevist circles.... I grew tired to death of meeting the proletarian ambassadors from foreign lands, some of whom bore themselves as if they were the holy messengers of Jesus, Prince of Heaven, instead of working-class representatives." He did, however, enjoy the respect he received in Russia, saying that "never in my life did I feel prouder of being an African, a black, and no mistake about it."

The African American lawyer and Communist William L. Patterson lived in Russia from 1927 to 1930 and married a Russian, with whom he later had two daughters. In Russia he experienced an exhilarating lack of racism: "It is as if one had suffered with a painful affliction for many years and had suddenly awakened to discover that the pain had gone."

The African American brothers Otto and Haywood Hall, who became Communists after the 1917 revolution, went to the Soviet Union in the mid-1920s. Like Patterson, Haywood Hall married a Russian. He visited Stalin at the Kremlin in 1927 and became vice-chairman of the Negro subcommittee of the Comintern. He returned to the United States in 1930 to continue his Communist organizational work. Both Patterson and the Hall brothers studied at KUTV.

In 1929 George Padmore, a Trinidadian Communist, abandoned his wife and university studies in the United States to go to Russia. He became an important figure in Profintern, the Comintern's trade union organization. He also lectured at KUTV, had an office in the Kremlin, and was given a special place on the reviewing stand in Red Square for the 1930 May Day parade. In 1930 he was transferred to Vienna to continue his work in the black labor movement. He and fellow African American James Ford were crucial in establishing the International Trade Union Committee of Negro Workers, which was the most important organization in promoting black revolutions around the world. Like many Communist Party Loyalists, Padmore was discredited and expelled from the party in 1934 during Stalin's purges, but he remained devoted to the Soviet system.

Langston Hughes, who traveled to Moscow in 1932 as a consultant on the doomed *Black and White* film project, provided a humorous account of his Soviet experience in his autobiography, *I Wonder As I Wander*. In one lively passage he described how Sylvia, one of the actors in the film, also sang African American spirituals on Radio Moscow. Since all mention of God or Jesus was forbidden, Sylvia chose to spell "God" backward, and sang, "Rise, shine, and give Dog the glory!" He also wrote of Emma Harris, a 60-year-old African American woman originally from the American South, who had been living in Moscow since before the 1917 revolution. According to Hughes, "Everybody in Moscow knew Emma, and Emma knew everybody. Stalin, I am sure, was aware of her presence in the capital." Formerly an actress, Harris joked frequently about the Soviet dictator, saying "anything she wanted to say" in an era when freedom of speech was nonexistent.

The great African American intellectual W. E. B. Du Bois visited the Soviet Union four times, in 1926, 1936, 1949, and 1958 to 1959. In his autobiography, published in 1968, he said that he felt more comfortable and inconspicuous in Russia than in any other country. During his 1958 visit, Du Bois, accompanied by his wife, Shirley Graham Du Bois, attended a New Year's banquet at the Kremlin. The two were joined by the African American singer and actor Paul Robeson, who sang "The Song of the Plains" to the accompaniment of a Russian chorus.

The following January the Du Boises met with Soviet leader Nikita Khrushchev. They proposed the creation of an Institute of African Studies, which was founded that same year under the directorship of a friend, Ivan Potekhin, one of the coeditors of the 1954 ethnographic survey *Narody Afriki* (Peoples of Africa). In 1959 W. E. B. Du Bois was awarded the International Lenin Peace Prize.

Robeson, the black artist who has arguably had the greatest influence on Soviet culture, first visited the USSR in 1934 at the invitation of the Soviet filmmaker Sergei Eisenstein, who would become a close friend. Robeson and his wife Eslanda traveled to Moscow by train and endured a one-day layover in Berlin, where Hitler's Nazi Party had come to power the previous year. The contrast between the Berlin train station, where fascist storm troopers and passers-by alike glared at the black couple like "wolves waiting to spring," and the welcoming attitude of Soviet officials, who were impressed with Robeson's fluent Russian, left an indelible impression on the American singer. For the next two weeks the Robesons were treated like visiting dignitaries.

Robeson returned to the Soviet Union at least seven times between 1936 and 1961. His concerts included performances of African American spirituals, American labor songs such as "Joe Hill," and especially Russian folk and patriotic songs, which endeared him to his Russian audiences. He was given the highest honors: he received the Stalin Peace Prize in 1952, which carried a $25,000 award; a mountain in Central Asia was named after him; he appeared on television; and his songs were played repeatedly on Soviet radio.

Although not a registered Communist, Robeson remained committed to the socialist ideal throughout his life. Long after most American blacks had distanced themselves from Soviet Communism, he continued to feel immense gratitude for the warm welcome he had received in the USSR. In a 1957 interview with a Soviet newspaper, he explained, "In the Soviet Union I felt like a person for the first time.... I visited many schools, watched the pupils and saw in their eyes that the children... are taught a very important thing: that it is necessary to treat people equally, regardless of their skin color."

JAZZ has been a major vehicle for black cultural influence in Russia. Russians were first introduced to black music by the African American dancer Ida Forsyne, who performed THE CAKEWALK in Moscow in 1911. Beginning in the 1920s numerous black jazz musicians visited the Soviet Union, including the Leland and Drayton revue, Benny Peyton's New Orleans jazz band (with saxophonist Sidney Bechet), Earl "Fatha" Hines, the Charles Lloyd Quartet, Duke Ellington, and B.B. King.

The Cotton Farmers

One of the most striking examples of African American emigration to the Soviet Union is the story of the cotton farmers. In 1931 Oliver Golden, an agricultural specialist who had studied at Tuskegee Institute, organized a group of 16 black Americans of various professional backgrounds to travel to Uzbekistan in Soviet Central Asia to develop an experimental cotton plantation. The men were paid the equivalent of several hundred dollars a month, a fortune by the standards of the GREAT DEPRESSION. They also enjoyed a month's free vacation every year in elite Crimean resorts. The group spent three years crossing Uzbek seeds with American seeds and finally produced a new strain of cotton that took 25 percent less time to mature than cotton in the American South.

At this time even the Uzbek capital, Tashkent, was economically primitive, with few cars, telephones, or other conveniences. Donkeys were the chief mode of transportation. In the village of Yangiyul, where the group was sent, women wore veils, polygamy and harems were common, and few, if any, people spoke English.

The farmers encountered very little racism during their stay and, being from the rural South, were delighted at the absence of segregation. Joseph Roane, who spent six years in the USSR, recalled only one racist incident. When he and another black man entered a hotel barber's shop in Moscow and asked for a haircut, two white Americans who were having their hair cut said, "What are you niggers doing here? Get out." When Roane explained the situation to the Russian barbers, they expelled the white men from the shop with lather still on their faces.

The Yangiyul group's initial contract expired in 1934. All the farmers signed up for another three years, but many were sent away from Yangiyul because their skills were in demand elsewhere. Roane was sent to Georgia to help operate a tomato-canning plant. George "Whirlwind" Tynes, formerly a Pittsburgh football star, worked as a poultry breeder, and John Sutton developed a new type of rope, using a fiber derived from rice as a substitute for jute. Both Sutton and Tynes married Russian women.

By 1937 Stalin's purges were in full swing. Anyone suspected of being remotely hostile to Stalin was arrested and interned in labor and death camps, and suspicion of foreigners became intense. All the members of the group were ordered to adopt Soviet citizenship immediately. Those who did not were expelled from the Soviet Union.

Golden stayed, becoming a popular and innovative professor at the Institute of Irrigation and Mechanization in Tashkent, where he taught until his death in 1940. Thousands of people came to his funeral. He had brought his Polish Jewish wife Bertha with him to Uzbekistan, and they had a daughter, Lily, who later married the Zanzibari leader Abdullah Hanga. In 1988 Lily's daughter Yelena Khanga, who was raised as a black Russian, became the first black commentator on Soviet television – a result of Mikhail Gorbachev's *glasnost* policy that encouraged Soviets to openly voice their opinions on controversial topics.

Other Black Immigrants

Many other blacks came individually as immigrants to the Soviet Union in the 1930s. Robert Robinson, an engineer from Detroit, went to the Soviet Union in 1930. He became a leading inventor and senior engineer at the state ball-bearing plant in Moscow. The only racism that Robinson, like Roane, is known to have experienced in the Soviet Union was from American visitors. In the early 1930s he was assigned to a tractor plant at Stalingrad where 300 American engineers worked. When two white Americans ordered him out of the mess hall because of his color, they were arrested, convicted of "white chauvinism," and expelled from the Soviet Union.

In 1932 Homer Smith, a postal worker from Minneapolis, came to work for the Moscow Post Office for a salary higher than his previous wage. He also became the Moscow correspondent for the African American press. He reported that he and other blacks were well treated by the Russians and were often allowed to go to the front of lengthy lines of people waiting to buy food. He married a Russian woman and remained in the country until after World War II.

The African American actor Wayland Rudd emigrated to Moscow in 1932 after realizing that in the United States his race would restrict him to minor acting roles. He remained in the Soviet Union until his death in 1952, participating in the experimental movements in Russian theater and becoming the first black actor to play the role of Othello in Russian. He stated that the liberated atmosphere of the Russian stage was the most thrilling experience of his life.

Lloyd Patterson, an African American artist, came to the Soviet Union with the 1932 film project and stayed, marrying a Russian and working first in the Meyerhold Theatre, then as a journalist, and finally serving in World War II, in which he was killed. His son James Patterson became a well-known poet, drawing extensively on his dual Russian and African American identity.

Soviet Policy Regarding American Blacks

As has been discussed, the Soviet Union was eager to encourage blacks in the United States to rise up against capitalist society. The Comintern struggled with the issue of how best to motivate the black masses. Marxist-Leninist theory subordinated all differences among people, including racial differences, to the struggle between the ruling class and the workers. Correspondingly, early Soviet doctrine held that racism was an artificial distraction created by the ruling classes in order to divide the workers and distract them from revolution. Feelings of racial or national pride were considered harmful.

By the Sixth Congress of the Comintern in 1928, it was recognized that the issue of racial feeling was far more important than had at first been thought. James Ford, an African American delegate, criticized the official position and argued that it must be altered if the Communist movement were to attract discontented blacks. As a result, the Comintern redefined the status of American blacks as an oppressed people, much like an African colony, and advocated the creation of an independent black republic in the Southern United States. This remained the official Communist Party stance until 1959, despite the fact that it was highly unsatisfactory to many African American leaders (the NATIONAL ASSOCIATION FOR THE ADVANCEMENT OF COLORED PEOPLE characterized it as "Red segregation"). The policy was abandoned in an effort to improve relations with the United States.

Although the Soviets were able to offer few solutions for American blacks, they succeeded in drawing international attention to the plight of African Americans. From the 1950s onward Soviet propaganda drew heavily on the sufferings of African Americans. In one of countless such Soviet cartoons, two images of the Statue of Liberty are juxtaposed: a conventional view from New York Harbor and a close-up of the statue's terror-stricken face, with the rays emanating from her head shown to be hooded Klansmen brandishing clubs and guns. Such propaganda disappeared during the Gorbachev era of the late 1980s.

Russian and Soviet Relations with Black Africa

Unlike the European colonial powers, Russia was never significantly involved in the TRANSATLANTIC SLAVE TRADE. Russia laid claim to an enormous portion of land in the American far North, yet most of this land was unexplored and unsuitable for the development of a plantation economy. Moreover, Russia had a long history of enslaving its own people: serf populations, made up of Russian peasants, provided an abundant supply of indigenous labor until their emancipation in 1861. Although the Russian government did acquire a small number of black slaves, they were viewed less as an important labor source than as exotic embellishments to aristocratic households. In 1818 representatives of the tsar called for the abolition of the African slave trade, though their motivation for doing so remains unclear, given that Russia maintained the institution of serfdom for an additional 43 years.

Before the 1917 revolution the main area of Russian interest in Africa was the ancient, independent kingdom of Ethiopia. Like Russia, Ethiopia was an Orthodox Christian nation. It was also of key geopolitical importance, given its location at the mouth of the Red Sea (the SUEZ CANAL had been opened in 1869) and its potential as a base for Russia to control the western Indian Ocean, a goal dear to Russian leaders past and present. Beginning in the mid-nineteenth century, contacts with Ethiopia were developed. Explorers visited, and Russian diplomats sought to forge a military alliance with Ethiopia against the Turkish Ottoman Empire.

The Soviet leaders had specific aims in Africa, goals similar to those for black America. They hoped to train revolutionaries and to exploit African nationalist feelings in order to encourage anticolonialism and to weaken the capitalist powers. But Soviet policy toward Africa changed dramatically during the 1930s, when the Soviet Union chose to ally with GREAT BRITAIN and FRANCE against the growing power of Nazi Germany. This required the Soviets to moderate their anticolonialist stance. In an act that deeply disappointed many blacks, the Soviet Union sold fuel to fascist Italy despite Italy's invasion of Ethiopia. Moreover, the Soviets were secretly discussing with Nazi Germany a partitioning of Africa into colonial-style "spheres of influence," in which Germany would control Central Africa, Italy the north and northeast, and the Soviet Union the eastern coast.

During the 1940s the Soviet Union was engaged in World War II and the mass repression of dissenters within its borders. It was not until the 1950s that the Soviet government once again turned its attention to Africa. Nation-building was now in full swing, and new African countries were emerging from COLONIAL RULE every year. The Soviet Union eagerly provided technical, economic, and military assistance to these new states in order to secure them as allies.

In 1960 Soviet leader Nikita Khrushchev and his advisers strongly believed that the new states of Africa, many of them headed by strong, socialist-oriented leaders such as KWAME NKRUMAH in GHANA, Sékou Touré in GUINEA, and MODIBO KEITA in MALI, would bypass capitalism and develop a specifically African version of socialism (*see* AFRICAN SOCIALISM). Moreover, the Soviets were hoping that not only these three countries, but many more would become strong Soviet allies. From the perspective of many African nations, however, the USSR was just another northern industrial power seeking to dominate and exploit them.

By the end of the 1960s, after the break with Guinea and the collapse of Nkrumah's and Keita's regimes, the USSR had tempered its aspirations in Africa to the provision of limited technical and military advice to many of its governments and the training in the Soviet Union of civil servants and administrators. The Patrice Lumumba University, founded in Moscow in 1961, offered a four-year program with courses in a wide range of topics, and tuition, housing, medical care, and travel were free. This and similar programs became extremely popular, and by 1966 there were approximately 4000 African students in the Soviet Union.

Given the larger number of black students than in the 1920s and 1930s, racial incidents surfaced more frequently during this period. Of particular importance was the demonstration held by 500 African students in Red Square in the winter of 1963 to protest the death of a Ghanaian student. Soviet authorities claimed that he had been drinking and had frozen to death. The students argued that he had been murdered by Russians because of his plans to marry a Russian woman.

Some African students felt they were being manipulated by the Soviets for propaganda purposes. As Everest Mulekezi, a Ugandan who came to Moscow University in the late 1950s, described, at one gathering of Ugandans: "In our name a stranger called for a vote on a resolution demanding immediate independence for UGANDA ... Before we could open our mouths, a roar of approval went up. Cameras snapped as the Russian actors gathered around to congratulate us on our 'action.' Tape recordings were made for broadcasts to be beamed back home. Suddenly it was over, and we Ugandans were left dumbfounded and angry."

In the early 1970s, as the USSR focused on improving relations with the United States, Soviet involvement in Africa became a lower priority. Beginning in 1975, however, the USSR began its most intense period ever of involvement in Africa, intervening militarily in ANGOLA and in the Horn of Africa. The Soviets were able to accomplish this partly due to the unwillingness of the United States to involve itself in foreign conflicts following the defeat in Vietnam.

In 1974 Portugal decided to grant independence to Angola, and a bloody civil war broke out among the three principal factions of the Angolan independence movement. By the time Angola became independent in November 1975, the Soviet-backed POPULAR MOVEMENT FOR THE LIBERATION OF ANGOLA (MPLA) was strong enough to form a government. In response, SOUTH AFRICA and the United States began to ship arms to MPLA's opponents, especially to Jonas Savimbi's NATIONAL UNION FOR THE TOTAL INDEPENDENCE OF ANGOLA (UNITA) movement. The USSR now began massive shipments of arms and of Cuban military personnel to the Angolan government. This support from both superpowers fueled a conflict that would devastate Angola for years to come.

Until 1974 Ethiopia had been aligned militarily and economically with the West. The Soviets had supported Ethiopia's longtime enemy SOMALIA, which had embraced socialism with the 1969 arrival in power of Gen. MUHAMMAD SIAD BARRE, who had been trained in the Soviet army. During the early 1970s the USSR built Somalia's army into one of the strongest in the region. However, by 1974 Siad Barre was moving openly toward alignment with the Arab world, specifically the anti-Soviet regime of Saudi Arabia.

In the same year the regime of HAILE SELASSIE I in Ethiopia was overthrown by a Marxist-oriented military council. Over the next few years the USSR provided large-scale military assistance to Ethiopia, enabling it to win against Somalia in the Ogaden War in 1978. Ethiopia, the largest country in the Horn of Africa, became a Soviet bridgehead in the key strategic region of the Red Sea, a major triumph of Soviet foreign policy.

With the Soviet invasion of Afghanistan in 1979 and the escalation of Soviet-American rivalry in CENTRAL AMERICA during the 1980s, Soviet attentions again turned away from Africa. The arrival of Gorbachev in 1985 caused a gradual withdrawal of the USSR from involvement in the Third World, as relations with the West improved and Soviet policymakers focused attention on internal economic and social problems.

Blacks in Russia: Overview

Since the publication of Blakely's comprehensive book *Russia and the Negro* in 1986, few scholarly accounts have been issued on the contemporary experiences of blacks in Russia or Central Asia. Since the 1991 breakup of the Soviet Union, however, journalists and human rights activists have observed a sharpening of ethnic and racial strife throughout the region. With the collapse of communism as a unifying ideology, a variety of ethnic and nationalist movements have gained momentum. Moreover, the former Soviet republics have faced continuing economic hardships. Such developments have incited deep-seated racial prejudices and hostilities. Indeed, the majority of nationalist agendas offer a stark contrast to the racial idealism that the Soviet government espoused for so many decades.

Roanne Edwards

See Also

Decolonization in Africa: An Interpretation; Savimbi, Jonas Malheiro; Touré, Sékou; Bechet, Sidney Joseph; Du Bois, William Edward Burghardt (W. E. B.); Ford, James W.; Hines, Earl Kenneth ("Fatha"); Tuskegee University; Vietnam War; Ellington, Edward Kennedy ("Duke"); King, Riley B. ("B. B."); Patterson, William; Prince, Nancy Gardner.

North America

Russwurm, John Brown

(b. October 1, 1799, Port Antonio, Jamaica; d. June 9, 1851, Harper, Liberia), African American publisher of the first black newspaper in the United States, emigrationist, and Liberian government official.

Born John Brown to a Jamaican slave mother and a white American merchant father, he became John Russwurm when his stepmother demanded that his father acknowledge paternity by name. Sent to Quebec for schooling, Russwurm was taken by his father to Portland, Maine, in 1812. He attended Hebron Academy in Hebron, Maine, and graduated in 1826 from Bowdoin College, making Russwurm one of the first black graduates of an American college. In his graduation speech he advocated the resettlement of American blacks to Haiti.

Moving to New York City in 1827, Russwurm helped found *Freedom's Journal* with Samuel E. Cornish. It was the first black-owned and black-printed newspaper in the United States. The paper employed itinerant black abolitionists and urged an end to Southern slavery and Northern inequality. In February 1829 he stopped publishing the paper and accepted a position as the superintendent of education in Liberia. He left for Liberia having given up hope that African Americans would have any future equality or prosperity in the United States.

In Liberia, in addition to his government position, he edited the *Liberia Herald* and served as a Liberian agent, recruiting American blacks to return to Africa. Russwurm became the first black governor of the Maryland area of Liberia in 1836 and worked to enhance the country's economic and diplomatic position.

See Also

Slavery in the United States; Abolitionism in the United States; Press, Black, in the United States; *Freedom's Journal*; New York, New York; Jamaica.

North America

Rustin, Bayard

(b. March 17, 1910, West Chester, Pa.; d. August 24, 1987, New York, N.Y.), African American civil rights leader and political organizer.

Bayard Rustin was born into a Quaker family, and the pacifism he learned from the Society of Friends remained with him his entire life. After a comfortable childhood in West Chester, Pennsylvania, he studied at West Chester State College. Before graduating, he moved to Harlem during the 1930s and began studying at City College, while singing in local clubs with African American folk artists Josh White and Huddie Ledbetter. Attracted to the Young Communist League's stance on race issues, Rustin joined the group in 1936 and worked as an organizer until 1941, when he quit the party.

However, his resistance to the American government continued throughout 1941. Rustin was asked by A. Philip Randolph to help plan a 1941 march on Washington, D.C., to protest discrimination in defense industries. The march was called off when President Roosevelt made concessions. During World War II Rustin traveled to California to help interned Japanese Americans protect their property. As a pacifist Rustin spent two and a half years in prison for refusing to serve in the military.

Rustin's involvement in the Fellowship of Reconciliation, a radical pacifist movement, connected him to the establishment of the New York branch of the Congress of Racial Equality. Throughout the 1940s and 1950s he led weekend seminars on nonviolent action for both groups. Rustin helped organize the Montgomery Bus Boycott in 1955, and he was also involved in the formation of the Southern Christian Leadership Conference. In August 1963 he served as the coordinator of the March on Washington, an event attended by 200,000 people. Rustin was arrested 23 times in his lifetime, but he continued to believe that racial equality should be pursued through nonviolent means.

See Also

World War II and African Americans; Harlem, New York; Ledbetter, Hudson William ("Leadbelly"); Randolph, Asa Philip; March on Washington, 1963; March on Washington, 1941.

Africa

Rwanda,

a small Central African country bordered by Uganda, Tanzania, Burundi, and the Democratic Republic of the Congo (formerly Zaire).

Known as "the land of a thousand hills," Rwanda is one of Africa's smallest and most densely populated countries. Located in a region of fertile land and ample rainfall, precolonial Rwandan society was – according to early European visitors – prosperous and orderly; but it was also extremely hierarchical. A centuries-old Tutsi monarchy ruled over a bureaucracy of chiefs, who in turn collected tribute from Hutu commoners. Under German and then Belgian colonial rule, stratification in Rwanda grew wider and more rigid, with disastrous consequences.

Even before independence in 1962 the Tutsi monarchy was overthrown by a Hutu revolution. In 1963 and 1973 civil conflict emerged, the latter episode leading to a coup d'état bringing to power Maj. Gen. Juvénal Habyarimana. In 1994, when Rwanda was coping with an invasion from Uganda, a collapsed economy, and an active democratization movement, a hard-line government seized power on the death of President Habyarimana, and proceeded to organize the calculated destruction of its Hutu opponents and all Tutsi. More than 500,000 people were killed, and over 2 million fled.

The government that took power in July 1994 pledged to bring about justice and reconciliation, but progress has been slow. Government troops under the leadership of Gen. Paul Kagame, Rwanda's most powerful political and military leader, have clashed repeatedly with Hutu militia groups, fostering ongoing insecurity in the countryside. Conflict within Rwanda has fueled – and been fueled by – conflicts elsewhere in the Great Lake Region, which also includes Burundi, Uganda, and the Democratic Republic of the Congo. Meanwhile, Rwanda faces severe land shortages, poverty, and public health problems.

Early Rwandan Society

The earliest inhabitants of the Great Lakes Region were the ancestors of today's Twa people (once referred to as "pygmies" by Europeans), who now account for about 1 percent of Rwanda's population. Probably around 1000 b.c.e., Bantu-speaking people from Central Africa began to settle in the fertile highlands that define the landscape of Rwanda and Burundi. Slowly in the course of a long process of political centralization, these people became identified as Hutu; this identity group now constitutes cultivators (although they also raised cattle) as well as the majority of Rwanda's population.

Around the end of the fourteenth century the region's existing population was joined by new cultural groups who sometimes became identified as Tutsi. Contemporary events have made this period of Rwandan history a subject of great dispute, but at least a few sources indicate that the Tutsi pastoralists coexisted peacefully with the cultivators, at least initially. Members of the two groups intermarried, and came to share the same language – Kinyarwanda – and many of the same social and religious customs, including participation in the Kubandwa possession cult (*see* Ethnicity in Rwanda: An Interpretation).

Over the course of several centuries a kingdom gradually emerged in the area of Lake Muhazi. Through a process of conquest and assimilation, this kingdom eventually encompassed about half the area of present-day Rwanda by the end of the nineteenth century.

The king, or *mwami*, was considered the physical personification of the land itself. He presided over a large court – many Twa served as court storytellers, dancers, and guards – and an elaborate bureaucracy of chiefs. Each province was administered by chiefs with three types of responsibilities: administration of agricultural lands, supervision of grazing lands and cattle, and recruitment of soldiers for the king's army. In some areas these administrative responsibilities were divided and carried out by separate individuals, particularly in the central regions of the kingdom. Elsewhere the roles were often combined under the authority of a single chief. Where separate chiefs existed for the administration of agricultural lands, these were sometimes Hutu; but Tutsi typically occupied most positions of high political authority.

As the monarchy expanded, it promoted a series of so-called clientship relations, which bound people of different social status in relations of mutual obligation. Under the form of clientship known as *ubuhake*, for example, clients received cattle and protection from a patron, and in return owed the patron their loyalty and service. The patron was also supposed to provide land (though ironically, this land might actually have been expropriated from the client's family or neighbors). From the early nineteenth century, ubuhake spread in association with increased control over land by political authorities; a patron (*shebuja*) was typically Tutsi, but the client (*umugaragu*) could be a Tutsi or a Hutu. A Hutu who gained significant wealth and married a Tutsi woman might, over time, come to be regarded as Tutsi – a process (popularly referred to as *kwiihutura*) that might take a couple of generations and was not available to most people. Conversely, a Tutsi family that fell on hard times and lost its cattle might come to be regarded as "Hutu" over time. Thus, Hutu and Tutsi identity was not defined only by birth; nor were all Tutsi wealthy and powerful. However, high status and political power remained firmly associated with Tutsi identity.

Rwanda Under Colonial Rule

As European powers moved to colonize Africa in the late nineteenth century (*see* Scramble for Africa), the Great Lakes Region became one of the most contested parts of the continent, in part because the European powers – Great Britain especially – sought control over the source of the Nile River. At the 1884-1885 Berlin Conference, Great Britain and Germany agreed to split the region. Great Britain took the kingdom of Buganda and surrounding areas (now known as Uganda), while Germany took Rwanda and the neighboring kingdom of Burundi. The territory of "Ruanda-Urundi," along with the vast territory now known as mainland Tanzania, together became part of German East Africa.

Over the next several years the Berlin agreement meant little in Rwanda, except that a few German explorers passed through. In 1895, however, the death of King Kigeli Rwabugiri led to a violent struggle over succession, the Coup of Rucunshu. This important event pitted members of the powerful Abega clan (one of four clans that provided queen mothers for successive Rwandan monarchs) against members of

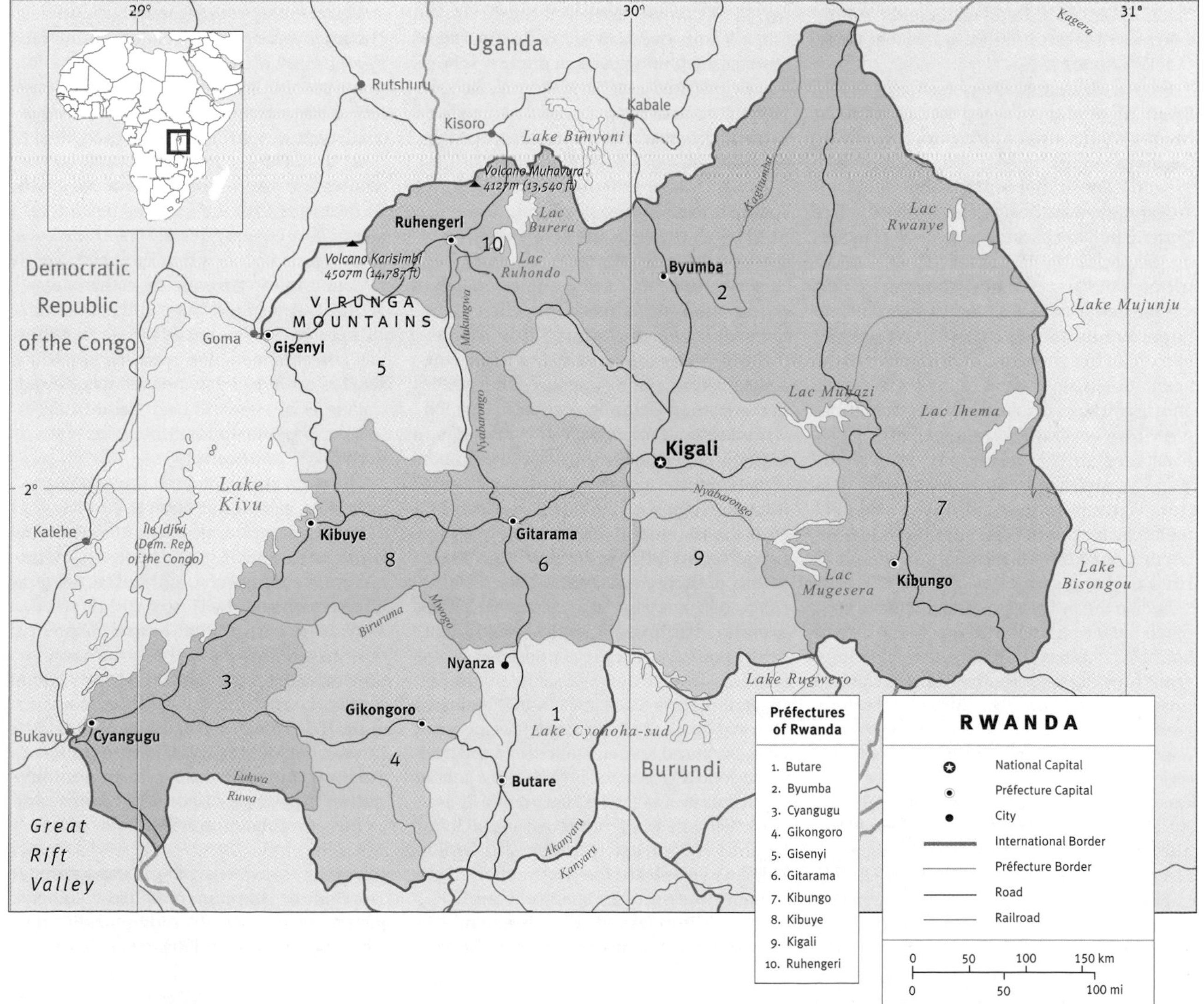

the royal Abanyiginya clan. Kanjogera, an Abega clan member and one of Rwabugiri's wives, had been appointed adoptive queen mother of Rutarindwa, the son of Rwabugiri and legitimate heir to the throne. But after Rwabugiri's death, Kanjogera plotted with her brothers to overthrow Rutarindwa. After several bloody battles the Abega emerged victorious; Rutarindwa and his key supporters and ritual specialists were killed, and the Abega proceeded to purge Abanyiginya political authorities and their associates. Kanjogera and her brothers then enthroned Kanjogera's own son Musinga. He was a young boy at the time, so during the early years of German rule it was Musinga's mother and maternal uncles who wielded power at court. They developed a modus vivendi with German-led troops who, they hoped, would help them extend and consolidate the kingdom.

French as well as German Roman Catholic missionaries also arrived around the turn of the century. Like the colonial administrators, they took the Tutsi's political dominance – as well as their typically tall, thin stature – as an indication of Tutsi racial superiority. Missionaries, in fact, were among the proponents of the now-discredited Hamitic theory, which held that the Tutsi were "caucasoids" from a faraway land (though it was never clear exactly where).

For the Germans, the presence of the Rwandan monarchy eased their own task of COLONIAL RULE, even as the presence of the Germans helped the Rwandan royal court to expand its territorial control. In some areas Tutsi political authorities took advantage of German military backing to increase demands on the population for labor, services, and tributes of various kinds. These demands fell particularly heavily on Hutu, creating intense resentment among the rural population. In the north, a region that had never been under firm control of the royal court, efforts by the court to impose Tutsi authorities from central Rwanda met with stiff resistance. In 1911 a Hutu revolt in the region was quashed by Tutsi troops, with help from German military force. This defeat fueled lasting anti-Tutsi sentiment in the north, which later became a stronghold of Hutu nationalism.

Unlike the intense exploitation that took place in German colonies such as German South West Africa (now NAMIBIA) and Kamerun (now CAMEROON), the German colonial presence in Ruanda-Burundi was hardly visible, except for the experimental attempts at growing export crops undertaken on the region's sloping farmlands. Germany's presence was also short-lived: Germany lost all its African colonies after World War I. Belgium, already the ruler of the massive Belgian Congo, took over control of Ruanda-Urundi.

Like Germany, Belgium adopted a policy of indirect rule, which meant it relied heavily on the monarchy to collect taxes, recruit labor, and maintain social order. For these purposes, the ubuhake system was preserved, but the demands made on the Hutu peasants were greatly intensified. They were required to perform forced labor and pay steep taxes, and if they failed to do so they risked losing their land. In addition, the system of provincial administration with competing authorities, which had traditionally helped to prevent abuses of power in some areas, was replaced by a system in which a single Tutsi chief, according to scholar René Lemarchand, exercised "unfettered control over his people." The resulting exploitation left much of the Hutu population dangerously vulnerable to famine during poor harvest years. Irregular rainfall also hurt yields of coffee – the colony's main export crop, and one that Hutu farmers were required to cultivate.

The rigid ethnic categories implicit in the colonial era hierarchy became official in 1933, when the Belgian administration began requiring all colonial subjects to carry passes identifying themselves as either Tutsi, Hutu, or Twa. No longer could wealthy Hutu become Tutsified – now ethnic identity became absolute and permanent. It also became a means of defining access to education, which for much of the colonial period was provided primarily by the Roman Catholic missions. Children of the Tutsi elite more easily found places in primary schools and were offered a separate, more challenging curriculum than Hutu children. Although few Rwandans had access to secondary schools, of those who did, a larger proportion of Tutsi than Hutu were able to complete primary school and continue beyond it. Indeed, until the early 1950s the elite government-sponsored secondary school in Butare (then called Astrida) retained a minimum height requirement for admission, which effectively excluded students shorter than the prototypically tall Tutsi. Hutu boys were generally only able to pursue further studies in the Roman Catholic seminaries, which were designed to encourage young men to enter the priesthood. The favored treatment of Tutsi in the school system was in part intended to ensure that the elite associated with the monarchy and the colonial civil service shared the values and Christian beliefs of their colonizers.

The Belgians went to considerable lengths to ensure that Tutsi authorities would adopt Christianity. In 1931 they deposed Musinga for recalcitrance and refusal to abandon "pagan" practices. Musinga's son Rudahigwa, who was installed by the Belgians as the new king, embraced Roman Catholicism and cultivated good relations with the Roman Catholic Church as well as the Belgian administration.

In 1945 Ruanda-Urundi became a United Nations (UN) Trust Territory, still under Belgian control. But the postwar period saw dramatic pressures for change. From 1947, regular visits to Rwanda by a visiting mission of the United Nations Trusteeship Council subjected Belgian policies to outside scrutiny and provided a forum for the expression of discontent by Rwandans. For the first time, in the early 1950s the glaring inequalities in Rwandan society began to receive public attention. Rural dwellers were restive, chafing under heavy labor demands, burdensome rules associated with coffee cultivation (often enforced in abusive fashion), insecure access to land, and the exploitative practices of Tutsi authorities and their henchmen. A new generation of European missionaries showed sympathy for the plight of the Hutu and provided encouragement to a small core of Hutu leaders who had been educated in Roman Catholic seminaries. During the 1950s a Kinyarwanda-language newspaper, *Kinyamateka*, began to serve as a forum for political debate. Critiques by Hutu activists drew attention to inequalities between Hutu and Tutsi and deplored indignities experienced by Hutu at the hands of Tutsi political authorities. These critics also identified conflicts over land as a key issue.

Aware of pressures for change, the Belgian administration introduced indirect elections for local councils, held in 1953 and 1957. These elections provoked anxiety among Tutsi authorities, as the implications of potential ethnic voting blocks became clear. The final years of the decade were marked by a complicated contest over how and when decolonization should occur. In the 1957 *Bahutu Manifesto*, a Hutu counterelite challenged the monopoly of power held by Tutsi authorities, and called for reforms to remove the discrimination experienced by Hutu throughout the colonial period. In response, conservative elders at the royal court asserted publicly that Hutu had no right to claim a role in governance. In this charged political atmosphere, hard-liners associated with the royal court began to demand immediate independence from Belgium; Hutu activists countered that independence should wait until the state had been democratized, so as to provide opportunities for Hutu to participate politically.

These positions divided the two main political parties that emerged in Rwanda during this period: the Rwandan National Union, a monarchist party with its main following among Tutsi, and the Party for the Emancipation of the Hutu (PARMEHUTU), a pro-Hutu party militating for the interests of Hutu. Another party, the Association for the Social Promotion of the Masses, aimed initially to mobilize all poor people, but appealed mainly to Hutu. The Democratic Rwandan Assembly was a party of moderate Tutsi, supported by the Belgian administration, who favored political reforms and a constitutional monarchy.

REVOLUTION, INDEPENDENCE, AND REPUBLIC The *Bahutu Manifesto* provided ideological justification for the Rwandan Revolution, which began in central Rwanda in November

1959 as a rural revolt. Triggered by an assault on a Hutu subchief by a group of Tutsi youths, the violence quickly spread to the northwest areas of the country, and, later, to other regions as well. Gangs of Hutu moved from hill to hill, attacking Tutsi authorities and wealthy Tutsi, forcing them to flee and burning their homes. Belgium attempted to reestablish order by bringing in troops from the Belgian Congo, and appointing Col. Guy Logiest as military head of the administration in Rwanda. Finding it impossible to continue relying on Tutsi chiefs because of rural resistance, Logiest openly supported PARMEHUTU and assisted in ousting Tutsi authorities, replacing them with Hutu. In September 1961 Rwandans voted in UN-supervised elections to abolish the monarchy and elect Grégoire Kayibanda as president. Meanwhile, more than 100,000 Rwandans, most of them Tutsi, had fled into neighboring countries by the time Rwanda became independent on July 1, 1962.

Under President Kayibanda, the First Republic (1962-1973) was led by Hutu, mostly from southern and central Rwanda. It began and ended with violence. In 1963 a group of armed Rwandan Tutsi exiles invaded Rwanda from Burundi; though the attack was repulsed, the invaders came within about 8 km (5 mi) of Kigali. Frightened by this threat, Kayibanda's government allowed (or ordered) the massacre of an estimated 10,000 Tutsi living within the country, thus making the internal population scapegoats for the activities of Tutsi exiles. Ten years later, after Burundi's Tutsi-dominated government and military massacred an estimated 250,000 Hutu, Kayibanda's regime retaliated against Rwandan Tutsi. As the violence increased, a group of northern Hutu led by Gen. Juvénal Habyarimana seized power and proclaimed the Second Republic in July 1973.

Calling for national unity while executing ministers from the First Republic, President Habyarimana surrounded himself with a close-knit group of supporters, many of whom were his relatives. A new constitution, instituted in 1975, established the National Revolutionary Movement for Development as the only legal political party, and Habyarimana was easily reelected three times over the next 14 years. Reinforcing a regime that was actually more authoritarian than was the case under Kayibanda, Habyarimana significantly extended the reach of the central government into local communities. His stance toward the Tutsi, however, was more moderate than Kayibanda's. Until the late 1980s the main axes of conflict in Rwanda under Habyarimana were less ethnicity than region and class. Higher status jobs, scholarships, and funds for development went disproportionately to the president's home region in the north, and the gap between a tiny wealthy minority (connected to the government) and the majority of the population became ever wider.

In 1976 Rwanda joined with Burundi and Zaire to form the Economic Community of the Great Lakes Countries. But efforts to coordinate economic development in the region were undermined by ongoing civil conflicts. Refugees from these conflicts were often resented abroad, and many joined their host countries' rebel movements. Many Tutsi refugees in Uganda, for example, helped that country's rebels (among them future Ugandan president Yoweri Museveni) overthrow first Idi Amin in 1979 and then Milton Obote in 1985. These Tutsi fighters formed the core of the Rwandan Patriotic Front (RPF), a group determined to win the right to return to their country. In addition, they claimed to want democratic reforms in Rwanda, including the end of one-party rule.

Refugees returning to Rwanda after the 1994 genocide pass piles of machetes used in the slayings. *CORBIS/David Turnley*

Turmoil and Genocide

Armed and supported financially by Museveni, the RPF's 6000 troops entered Rwanda from the north in October 1990. They were met by not only the relatively small Rwandan army, but also forces sent by Zaire's President Mobutu Sese Seko and paratroopers provided by France, all of whom preferred to maintain Rwanda's

Women chat as they make wedding and baptismal dresses in Kigali, the capital and largest city in Rwanda. *Betty Press*

status quo. The Habyarimana regime's immediate response to the RPF threat was to jail thousands of suspected sympathizers.

By June 1991, however, in response to growing pressures for reform from internal groups and foreign donors, Habyarimana had agreed to end one-party rule and allow opposition parties to form. Months later, representatives from the former ruling party and the four main opposition parties were included in a coalition government with Habyarimana. Several new parties sprang up, including the multiethnic Liberal Party. Habyarimana also agreed to negotiate with the RPF and the opposition parties. At the same time, however, hard-line Hutu nationalists in Habyarimana's party and the equally hard-line Coalition for the Defense of the Republic (CDR) were recruiting militia troops. The year-long negotiations, held in Arusha, Tanzania, from 1992 to 1993, led to a cease-fire between the government and the CDR, as well as an agreement to form a power-sharing transitional government. The hard-line groups, who were left out of the talks and adamantly opposed the results, retaliated by killing Tutsi civilians, including some 300 in one attack in Gisenyi.

Into this already turbulent atmosphere came the voice of an increasingly virulent media. The monthly magazine *Kangura* had in 1990 published its "Call to the Conscience of the Bahutu Peoples," which proclaimed that "Hutu should stop feeling pity for the Tutsi," and that they should "regard as a traitor every Hutu" who did not join in the anti-Tutsi movement. By 1993 the independent radio station Mille Collines (Thousand Hills) – owned by close associates of Habyarimana – urged Hutu to kill the *inyenzi,* or "cockroaches," as it called Uganda-born Tutsi. "The grave is only half full," Mille Collines broadcasts blared, asking, "Who will help us fill it?" Such propaganda cast all Tutsi, not just the RPF, as the enemy.

The "enemy" in these broadcasts was presented as an economic as well as political threat – in particular, as a potential thief of Hutu land. Given that the land was already scarce in Rwanda, this was an incendiary charge. Rwanda's economy was in particularly poor shape due to declining world coffee prices, and the Tutsi became a convenient scapegoat for all the country's ills.

In October 1993 the assassination of Burundi's Hutu president Melchior Ndadaye by Tutsi elements in the Burundi army further inflamed tensions in Rwanda. These finally exploded after a plane carrying both Habyarimana and Burundi's new president, Cyprien Ntariyamira, was shot down over Kigali on April 6, 1994. Although responsibility for the fatal crash remained unclear years later, Hutu hard-liners in the late president's party immediately blamed the RPF.

Just hours after the crash the Hutu militia (known as *interahamwe,* or "those who stand together") began killing both Hutu and Tutsi leaders of the moderate political parties, including members of the transitional government. All of the victims had been identified on a list circulated even before the plane's downing. In the following weeks and months the killing escalated at a horrific rate. The militias set up roadblocks and killed all those with Tutsi identity cards. Some people whose cards identified them as Hutu were also killed, if they were suspected of Tutsi sympathies or if they appeared more Tutsi than Hutu. In addition, militia members searched each hillside to meet the deadline set by Mille Collines radio broadcasts, which stated that "by 5 May, the country must be completely cleansed of Tutsi." The churches offered no sanctuary; some were forcibly invaded, and others were run by priests and nuns who collaborated with the militia. These churches became the sites of some of the worst massacres in the genocide.

According to the medical aid group Médecins Sans Frontières, by the end of April about 100,000 people had been killed, mostly by weapons such as machetes and spiked wooden clubs. Rapes were also common. By July the genocide had claimed more than 500,000 victims, and an estimated 2 million refugees had fled into Burundi, Tanzania, and Zaire. The killers included not only interahamwe troops, but also villagers who had received orders to kill. Although some Hutu families sheltered Tutsi friends and relatives, they did so at risk to their own lives.

International Response and Aftermath

Although the UN had established an assistance mission to Rwanda (UNAMIR) in October 1993, it did virtually nothing to stop the killings. In fact, the UN Security Council reduced the mission's troops from 2500 to 270 soon after the genocide started. According to many observers, the UN's hands were tied in part by the United States, which, after its highly unpopular participation in an earlier UN "peacekeeping" mission in Somalia, refused to support another intervention in a dangerous and strategically insignificant African country.

Among non-African countries, France alone responded to the Rwandan crisis, securing a large portion of southwestern Rwanda in its Operation Turquoise. The security zone undoubtedly saved some lives, but it also allowed leaders of the hard-line Hutu groups an escape route to the west. Later, in the postgenocide period, elements from the former Rwandan army and from militia groups used refugee camps in neighboring eastern Zaire as a base for incursions into western Rwanda. This created a dilemma for international humanitarian agencies; in providing food, shelter, and medical care to the refugees, most of whom were women and children, they were also aiding militia members, who were visibly indistinguishable from other camp residents.

Throughout the genocide, RPF troops had been advancing on Kigali. They finally took control of the capital on July 4, 1994, and proclaimed a new multiparty government. Both the appointed president, Pasteur Bizimungu, and the prime minister, Faustin Twagiramungu, were Hutu, but most observers agree that from the beginning the government's real leader was Vice President and Defense Minister Kagame, a long-time RPF member. Many of the cabinet and military posts were held by fellow Tutsi from Uganda or other neighboring countries.

The government promised that the genocide's perpetrators would receive swift justice, and by late 1995 an estimated 80,000 Hutu suspects had been arrested. Many died of disease in desperately overcrowded jails while awaiting trial. Rwanda's barely functioning justice system was incapable of trying so many people, and has since proven unable to protect Rwandans in their own villages, where not only the militia but also the army have killed suspected foes. The return of hundreds of thousands of exiled Tutsi after the RPF took power also led to local-level conflicts over property; many Hutu were removed from their homes by force. In addition, clashes between the militia and the army have continued.

In November 1994 the UN Security Council established the International Criminal Tribunal for Rwanda in Arusha, Tanzania. Charged with "prosecuting persons responsible for genocide and other serious violations of international humanitarian law," the tribunal initially moved extremely slowly, due to delays caused by everything from frequent power outages to difficulty in bringing to trial the leading suspects, many of whom had fled abroad. Rwanda itself, which lacked trained personnel and had rejected offers from other countries to provide judges and lawyers, began trials only in 1997; in early 1998 the Rwandan government began carrying out death sentences against convicted *genocidaires*.

In the late 1990s Rwanda was plagued not only by internal violence but also by severe economic and public health problems, and by the destabilizing effect of conflict elsewhere in the Great Lakes Region. The production of coffee – still the country's main export – had suffered from years of rural dislocation and insecurity, as had food crop production. A $600 million aid package from the European Union in the mid-1990s was expected to help restore the nation's economy, but, in the face of a serious shortage of arable land, farming remained an impoverished livelihood for most of Rwanda's overwhelmingly rural population. In addition, much of the Kagera National Park, home to some of the greatest diversity of animal life in Africa, has reportedly been taken over by cattle herders, displaced by war.

With an average fertility rate of 5.86 children per woman, Rwanda has one of the highest population growth rates in Africa. Close ties between the Roman Catholic Church and health services have traditionally helped keep family planning programs to a minimum, and some reports suggest birth rates actually rose after the genocide, as many woman tried to rebuild destroyed families. Rwanda also has one of the highest rates of acquired immune deficiency syndrome (AIDS) infection in Africa, as well as high rates of malnutrition, malaria, and tuberculosis.

Even after reported human rights abuses, Rwanda's government in the late 1990s continued to enjoy strong support from the United States and Europe, where Kagame was seen to belong to a "new generation" of pragmatic, competent African leaders. Regional instability, however, continued to threaten Rwanda's recovery, as demonstrated by the renewed fighting along the Democratic Republic of the Congo border in mid-1998. Many Tutsi on both sides of the border helped Laurent-Désiré Kabila topple Zaire's President Mobutu. But Kabila, facing pressure within his own country, purged his military of Rwandan and Congolese Tutsi in 1997. This breach of trust, combined with the continuing agitation of Hutu refugees in Congo, led Rwanda's government to back an armed rebellion against Kabila's government in the Democratic Republic of the Congo during 1998 and 1999.

Kate Tuttle

See Also

Bantu: Dispersion and Settlement; Buganda, Early Kingdom of; Decolonization in Africa: An Interpretation; Education in Africa; Explorers in Africa Since 1800; Habyarimana, Juvénal; Hutu and Tutsi; Kigali, Rwanda; Languages, African: An Overview; Museveni, Yoweri; Nile River; United Nations in Africa; Population Growth in Sub-Saharan Africa; Pygmy; African Religions: An Interpretation; AIDS in Africa: An Interpretation; Christianity: Missionaries in Africa; Human Rights in Africa; Berlin Conference of 1884-1885.

Africa

Rwanda (Ready Reference)

Official Name: Rwandan Republic
Area: 26,338 sq km (10,169 sq mi)
Location: Central Africa; borders Burundi, Tanzania, Uganda, the Democratic Republic of the Congo (formerly Zaire)
Capital: Kigali (population 219,000 [1990 estimate])
Other Major Cities: Butare (population 21,961 [1978 estimate])
Population: 7,956,172 (1998 estimate); genocide and civil war in 1994 killed more than 1 million Rwandans and forced more than 2 million to flee to neighboring countries.
Population Density: 316 persons per sq km (about 819 persons per sq mi [1995 estimate])
Population Below Age 15: Total population: 45 percent (male 1,785,650; female 1,772,609 [1998 estimate])
Population Growth Rate: 2.5 percent (1998 estimate)
Total Fertility Rate: 5.86 children born per woman (1998 estimate)
Life Expectancy at Birth: Total population: 44.93 years (male 41.49 years; female 42.4 years [1998 estimate])
Infant Mortality Rate: 118.8 deaths per 1000 live births (1996 estimate)
Literacy Rate (age 15 and over can read and write): Total population: 60.5 percent (male 69.8 percent; female 51.6 percent [1995 estimate])
Education: Compulsory in principle for children aged 7 through 15. In the early 1990s primary school enrollment in Rwanda was about 1.1 million, and secondary and technical schools had about 70,000 students.
Languages: The official languages are Kinyarwanda (a Bantu language) and French.
Ethnic Groups: Rwanda is composed of three principle ethnic groups. The Hutu

constitute about 90 percent of the total population; the Tutsi, about 9 percent; and the Twa, 1 percent. The Twa are thought to be the original inhabitants of the region.
Religions: About 65 percent of the population is Catholic, about 9 percent is Muslim, and some 9 percent is Protestant. Approximately 17 percent of the people follow traditional religions.
Climate: Rwanda is temperate. It has two rainy seasons (from February to April and November to January). Weather is mild in the mountains with frost and snow possible. The average yearly rainfall is 787 mm (31 in) and is heaviest in the western and northwestern mountain regions. Wide temperature variations occur because of elevation differences. The average daily temperature in the Lake Kivu area is 22.8° C (73° F). In the mountains in the northwest, frost occurs at night.
Land, Plants, and Animals: The central portion of Rwanda is dominated by a hilly plateau averaging about 1700 m (about 5600 ft) in elevation. On the western side of the plateau is a mountain system averaging about 2740 m (about 9000 ft), forming the watershed between the Nile and Congo river systems. The Virunga Mountains, a volcanic range that forms the northern reaches of this system, include Volcan Karisimbi (4507 m/14,787 ft), Rwanda's highest peak. Forests containing eucalyptus, acacia, and oil palms are concentrated in the western mountains and the Lake Kivu area. Wildlife includes includes elephants, hippopotamuses, crocodiles, wild boars, leopards, antelope, and lemurs. The Virunga Mountains in northern Rwanda are home to what is estimated to be half of the world's remaining mountain gorillas.
Natural Resources: Gold, cassiterite (tin ore), wolframite (tungsten ore), natural gas, hydropower
Currency: The Rwandan *franc*
Gross Domestic Product (GDP): $3 billion (1996 estimate)
GDP per Capita: $440 (1996 estimate)
GDP Real Growth Rate: 13.3 percent (1996 estimate)
Primary Economic Activities: Agriculture (52 percent of GDP, 93 percent of work force), industry (13 percent of GDP), services (35 percent of GDP) (1994 estimate)
Primary crops: Coffee, tea, pyrethrum (insecticide made from chrysanthemums), bananas, beans, sorghum, potatoes, livestock
Industries: Mining of cassiterite (tin ore) and wolframite (tungsten ore), tin, cement, agricultural processing, beverages, light consumer goods
Primary Exports: Coffee, tea, cassiterite, wolframite, pyrethrum
Primary Imports: Textiles, foodstuffs, machines and equipment, capital goods, steel, petroleum products, cement, construction material
Primary Trade Partners: Germany, Belgium, Italy, Uganda, United Kingdom, France, United States, Kenya, Japan
Government: Under a constitution approved in 1978, the sole political party in Rwanda was the National Revolutionary Movement for Development. Executive power was vested in a president, assisted by an appointed council of ministers; legislative power was exercised by an elected National Development Council. A new constitution, promulgated in 1991, provides for a multiparty democracy with a limited presidential term and independent executive, legislative, and judicial branches. In August 1994 the Tutsi-dominated Rwandan Patriotic Front placed Rwanda under martial law and suspended the 1991 constitution. Pasteur Bizimungu is president of Rwanda, but Vice President and Minister of Defense Paul Kagame is widely recognized as the most powerful government figure.

Robert Fay

See Also

Bantu: Dispersion and Settlement; Crocodile; Elephant; Gorilla; Hippopotamus; Hutu and Tutsi; Kigali, Rwanda; Nile River.

S

North America

Saar, Betye Irene (b. July 30, 1926, Los Angeles, Calif.), African American artist best known for three-dimensional explorations of history, memory, cultural identity, and spirituality.

Born Betye Brown, Betye Saar (pronounced Say-er) is the daughter of Jefferson and Beatrice Brown. She married artist Richard Saar shortly after earning a B.A. in design from the University of California at Los Angeles (UCLA) in 1949. Saar pursued graduate studies at California State University at Long Beach, the University of Southern California, the Pasadena School of Fine Arts Filmmaking, and the American Film Institute. She has taught at UCLA and at the Parsons-Otis Institute in Los Angeles, California.

Although Saar began as a printmaker, she has made a transition to three-dimensional work. The work marking this turn is *Black Girl's Window*, in which Saar placed a print of an African American girl into a segmented window frame with existing objects. She gradually replaced prints in her assemblages with existing objects. She has increased the scale of her work to include room-sized installations, through which she explores ritual and mysticism. In *Mojotech*, an installation created for the Massachusetts Institute of Technology, Saar explores technology and magic by creating altars that juxtapose high-tech objects such as circuit boards with traditional religious items.

Saar has had solo shows at California State University at Los Angeles, the Whitney Museum of American Art, and the Museum of Contemporary Art, Los Angeles. She was one of two artists who represented the United States in the 1994 São Paulo Biennial in Brazil.

Robert Fay

See Also

Art, African American.

Africa

Sab, ethnic group of Somalia.

The Sab primarily inhabit southern Somalia. They speak Somali, an Afro-Asiatic language, although they are believed to be partly of Bantu origin. They are sometimes considered a low-status subgroup of the Somali people, and some people called Sab find the label derogatory. The so-called Sab number roughly 500,000.

See Also

Bantu: Dispersion and Settlement; Languages, African: An Overview.

Latin America and the Caribbean

Saco, José Antonio (b. May 7, 1797, Bayamo, Cuba; d. September 26, 1879, Barcelona, Spain), white Cuban intellectual of the colonial period who wrote one of the first extensive histories of slavery in Spanish America and promoted abolition in order to decrease the number of blacks in Cuba.

José Antonio Saco received what was a typical education for Catholic boys in early nineteenth-century Cuba. He first studied in a small schoolhouse next to his home and later transferred to a Catholic school in Santiago de Cuba. Saco continued higher-level education in modern philosophy at the San Carlos seminary in Havana. Under the tutelage of Father Félix Varela y Morales, one of the most influential professors and prominent intellectuals of his time, Saco studied with a group of young men who were to become representatives of the urban bourgeoisie that promoted the independence of Cuba from Spain. In his autobiography Saco claims that these early years with Varela, who provided guidance and friendship and whom Saco considered the "most virtuous man" he ever met, were definitive in the formation of his thinking and ideology.

In 1821 Varela asked Saco to take over his seminar in philosophy. This initiated Saco's academic work as a lecturer in philosophy, physics, and chemistry. Later in his life Saco promoted education as a political tool that should adapt to the needs of the country. He felt that without education there would be no progress and advocated that schooling be both free and mandatory. Saco was in favor of education for women, as was his mentor Varela. However, as we shall see further on, this seemingly progressive perspective did not incorporate black Cubans as equal members of the society (*see* Education in Latin America and the Caribbean).

In 1828 Saco traveled to New York and founded *El mensajero quincenal* (The Quarterly Messenger), a liberal publication that discussed the problems of continuing with the illegal slave trade to Cuba. In 1830 Saco wrote *Memoria sobre la vagancia* (Memoir on Vagrancy), in which he describes the causes of Cuban's backwardness and gives possible solutions. One of the chapters, titled "People of Color in the Arts," suggests that certain trades were no longer honorable in Cuba because blacks had become highly involved in them. In 1834 Saco was forced into exile to Trinidad for writing an article that identified him as a significant political critic and leader.

Toward the end of the nineteenth century a massive number of black slaves was imported to Cuba to support the growing sugar industry. This increase in the black population and the potential for uprisings (real and imagined) was a cause of great concern among members of the white privileged class of Cuba, who were beginning to conceive a Cuban identity that did not include blacks (*see* Conspiración de la Escalera). Saco became a spokesman for the white middle classes, promoting abolition with the goal of diminishing the role and influence of black people in Cuba. He thought that by encouraging white immigration and miscegenation the island could counterbalance the demographic effects of the slave trade and become a modern and democratic society.

Saco lived almost half of his life – from 1834 to 1879 – in exile and wrote prolifically while abroad. It was in exile that Saco wrote his greatest work: the five-volume *Historia de la esclavitud* (1875-1879, History of Slavery). The introduction to *History of Slavery* calls for the immigration of workers "white and free, from all parts of the world, all races, provided they have a white face and can do honest labor." Saco explicitly expressed his purpose in advocating abolition as well, stating: "I can not deny… that I ardently wish, not through violent means, but through pacific ones, the decrease, and if possible, the total extinction of the black race; and I wish it because at our current political state, they can be the most powerful instrument to destroy our island."

As a militant nationalist, Saco clashed with Spanish authorities and opposed the annexation of Cuba to the United States. His works were influential in the independence movement of the time and in the formation of a national identity based on a segregationist idea of society.

Liliana Obregón

See Also
Slavery in Latin America and the Caribbean; New York, New York; Trinidad and Tobago; Abolition and Emancipation in Latin America and the Caribbean; Catholic Church in Latin America and the Caribbean; Colonial Latin America and the Caribbean; Havana, Cuba.

Africa

Sadat, Anwar al-

(b. December 25, 1918, Mit Abu al-Kum, al-Minufiyah Governate, Egypt; d. October 6, 1981, Cairo, Egypt), president of Egypt from 1970 to 1981 and the first Arab leader to recognize the state of Israel.

The son of a hospital clerk, Anwar Sadat was born in the Nile delta. Graduated from Cairo Military Academy in 1938, he was part of the first generation of Egyptian soldiers recruited from the middle class rather than the elite. During World War II, Sadat was twice arrested for conspiring with the Germans' campaign to drive the British from Egypt. In 1950 he joined the Free Officers Committee Organization, chaired by Gamal Abdel Nasser. In 1952 he participated in Nasser's overthrow of the Egyptian monarchy.

After Nasser was elected president of Egypt in 1956, Sadat held various offices in the government, including two terms as vice president (1964-1966 and 1969-1970). With Nasser's death in September 1970, Sadat became president. Although his political opponents considered him an interim leader, he was elected president less than a month later. Sadat moved quickly to consolidate his support, loosening state control over the economy and relaxing restrictions on political activity. In addition, shortly after taking office, Sadat began to strengthen the Egyptian military, which had been soundly defeated by Israel in the 1967 Six-Day War.

Sadat's tenure was marked by an emphasis on foreign policy. In 1972 he expelled Soviet military advisors, signaling an end to Egypt's close ties with the Eastern Bloc. On October 6, 1973, Egypt and Syria attacked Israel, launching the Yom Kippur War. After Egypt's initial successes, Israel took the offensive. Although Egypt did not win the war, it did achieve his primary goal – to improve Egypt's negotiating position with Israel. In addition, as the first Arab military leader to reclaim land from Israel, Sadat earned enhanced prestige in the Arab world.

Sadat's lasting legacy was his peace settlement with Israel. In November 1977 he visited Jerusalem and presented his peace plan to the Israeli Knesset (Parliament). Despite widespread criticism from the Arab world, Sadat held a series of diplomatic meetings with Israel, culminating in the Camp David Accords in 1979, in which Egypt normalized relations with Israel. The fallout from the Arab world was quick and severe, however, as Egypt was soon expelled from the Arab League and denied economic support from fellow Arab nations.

On October 6, 1981, the anniversary of the Yom Kippur War, Sadat presided over a military parade in Cairo. During the parade a military vehicle stopped abruptly, and five soldiers who were later linked to an Islamic protest group leapt out and began firing machine guns and throwing hand grenades at the president. Sadat and six others were killed. The leader was succeeded by his vice president, Hosni Mubarak.

Robert Fay

See Also
Nile River; Russia and the Former Soviet Union; Great Britain; Cairo, Egypt.

Europe

Sade

(b. 1959, Ibadan, Nigeria), British singer and songwriter known for her smooth and sultry voice.

Sade (pronounced Shar-day) was born Helen Folasade Adu in Nigeria to a British nurse and a Nigerian economist. In 1963 her parents divorced, and she, her brother, and mother moved to Great Britain. In her youth Sade frequented dance clubs and developed a passion for jazz, funk, and soul music.

Sade did not at first consider a musical career. She studied fashion in London and for a few years ran her own design business and supplemented her income by modeling. The manager of Pride, a London funk group, noticed her sensuous good looks and encouraged her to audition as a backup singer for the band, which she joined during the early 1980s.

London clubgoers loved Sade's subtle, restrained style. She developed a substantial following when she and Pride saxophonist, Stuart Mathewman, began writing songs and playing them between Pride sets. She soon left Pride and signed with Epic, which released her first album, *Diamond Life*, in 1984.

With the popularity of songs such as "Your Love Is King" and "Smooth Operator," *Diamond Life* soared to the top of the music charts in Great Britain and received rave reviews in America. It became the best-selling album by a British woman singer in history and won Sade the Grammy Award for best new artist. In 1985 Epic released the follow-up album, *Promise*, featuring the hit "Sweetest Taboo." *Stronger than Pride* (1988) went platinum within just two weeks of being on the music charts. And the song "No Ordinary Love" from the *Love Deluxe* LP, released in 1992, won a Grammy for best rhythm and blues duo or group performance.

Sade values her privacy and seldom gives interviews. She was married briefly to filmmaker Carlos Scola from 1989 to 1990. In 1995 she moved to Jamaica to have a child with her partner, Bob Morgan, a record producer.

Leyla Keough

Africa

Safwa, ethnic group of Tanzania.

The Safwa primarily inhabit southwestern Tanzania. They speak a Bantu language. Approximately 300,000 people consider themselves Safwa.

See Also
Bantu: Dispersion and Settlement.

Africa

Sahara Desert, the world's largest desert.

The Sahara Desert covers the area between the Atlas Mountains in the north, the semiarid Sahel region in the south, the Red Sea in the east, and the Atlantic Ocean in the west. Although its boundaries have always been unstable, the desert currently stretches about 5150 km (about 3200 mi) from east to west and about 1610 km (about 1000 mi) from north to south, covering a total land area of about 9,065,000 sq km (about 3,500,000 sq mi). It comprises three distinct areas, the western Sahara (or Sahara Proper), the Libyan Desert, and the central Ahaggar Mountains and the Tibesti massif, a plateau. In total the Sahara covers part or all of 11 countries: Western Sahara, Libya, Egypt, Morocco, Algeria, Tunisia, Mauritania, Mali, Niger, Chad, and the Sudan.

Because of ongoing climatic change, the Sahara has not always been a desert (*see* Climate of Africa). Ten thousand years ago relatively humid conditions supported a wide variety of savanna flora and fauna, as well as human activities such as agriculture, hunting, and fishing. Much evidence of this activity remains in the forms of rock paintings and tools. Since approximately 5000 years ago, however, the Sahara's climate has been much less hospitable. Twenty percent of the desert is sand; the rest is predominantly rock and gravel. Average daily temperatures range from 0° C (32° F) to 54.4° C (130° F). Rainfall is minimal and erratic, but at times intense, creating occasional flash floods. In addition, several underground rivers originating in the mountains support lush, tree-lined oases, and the NILE RIVER runs through a portion of the eastern Sahara, leaving the surrounding valley fertile and habitable.

Despite the desert's extreme environment, it is home to nearly 2.5 million humans and many animal species, including gazelles, antelopes, jackals, foxes, badgers, and hyenas. Most of the permanent human settlements are clustered in oases, the mountain highlands, or at the desert's edges. Three main groups inhabit the desert, but after centuries of interaction, the most clear-cut distinctions among them are linguistic. Arab-speaking groups, such as the Bedouins and the CHAMBA, live on the northern edge. Berbers live on the northern and western edge and include the Shluh or Tashelhayt, and the TUAREG. The Teda (Tubu) people live mostly in the eastern part of the desert.

PASTORALISM and trade have long provided the economic basis for survival as well as state-building in the Sahara. The introduction of the CAMEL to the Sahara from Egypt in the early centuries B.C.E. enabled merchant caravans to reach the trading capitals of the early sub-Saharan kingdoms, such as ancient Ghana, which built its wealth partly through control of Saharan salt mines. In addition to salt, many other goods were exchanged: gold, slaves, spices, and leather traveled north, while weapons, horses, textiles, and paper traveled south. Desert peoples not only participated in this trade but also collected tolls and protection money from the caravans. Although trans-Saharan trade diminished as West African trade with Europeans increased, nomadic peoples such as the Tuareg continue to trade Saharan salt for food and other supplies with the communities who live on the desert edges or around the oases. Oases settlements also support themselves through date production and garden agriculture.

There are petroleum deposits in Algeria and Libya, and the discovery of minerals such as uranium, iron, bauxite, and phosphate has once again made mining one of the most important sources of revenue for Africa's Saharan states. Most of the desert's nomadic peoples, however, have benefited little from the region's subterranean wealth. With their customary migratory routes and grazing grounds now crossed by national boundaries, many nomadic groups are either neglected or viewed with suspicion by national governments, and the loss of traditional sources of income has made them more vulnerable to the ravages of the desert's recurring droughts.

Robert Fay

SEE ALSO

Berber; Ghana, Early Kingdom of; Gold Trade; Salt Trade; Bedouin; Trans-Saharan and Red Sea Slave Trade.

Africa

Sahel, a transition zone between the Sahara and the southern subtropical zone in West Africa.

Derived from the Arabic word for shore or border, *sahil*, the Sahel is a hot, semi-arid region characterized by sparse savanna vegetation and shrubbery. It covers an area south of the SAHARA DESERT approximately 200 to 400 km (about 125 to 250 mi) wide, extending across the African continent from the Atlantic Ocean to the Red Sea and covering at least part of ten countries – SENEGAL, THE GAMBIA, MAURITANIA, MALI, BURKINA FASO, NIGERIA, NIGER, CHAD, CAMEROON, and SUDAN.

A land of extreme conditions, the Sahel experiences two hot seasons – from approximately February to April and September to October – punctuated by a short rainy season between May and August. During December and January the Harmattan, a wind from the desert, brings cooler weather and thick dust. Annual rainfall in the Sahel is notoriously variable and unpredictable, but in recent years it has averaged between 102 and 203 mm (4 to 8 in) a year (*see* CLIMATE OF AFRICA). Since the late 1960s rainfall has been gradually declining, but whether this trend indicates that the Sahel is undergoing desertification remains a subject of scientific debate.

Despite its harsh climate, the Sahel has long been home to nomadic pastoralists such as the Tuaregs and the FULANI as well as to cities established by the precolonial states of the Songhai, the HAUSA, and the SOKOTO CALIPHATE. Food supplies for Sahelian cities such as Bamako, Ouagadougou, Niamey, and Kano have depended historically on a combination of rainy-season agriculture, irrigation from year-round water sources such as the NIGER RIVER and LAKE CHAD, and trade. Recent experiences of severe drought, however, have caused many to wonder how long the Sahel can continue to support its inhabitants, the majority of whom still rely on land-based livelihoods.

Although periodic droughts have long afflicted the Sahel, environmental, economic, and political changes have recently combined to make many of the region's inhabitants more vulnerable to drought-related deprivation. Severe droughts from 1968 to 1973 and from 1984 to 1985, for example, led to famine in rural areas of the Sahel, afflicting millions of people. Many of the victims were pastoralists who, restricted by international borders from migrating to their traditional watering holes, lost or were forced to sell most of their livestock. Others were small farmers too poor to buy food when their own crops failed, and too remotely located to have access to urban-based food aid. Rural poverty was compounded in many areas by the interrelated problems of soil erosion and deforestation, which reduced the already fragile land's food-producing capacity.

Since the 1980s numerous local, regional, and international organizations have launched environmental restoration campaigns in the Sahel. Several Sahelian nations have formed the Interstate Committee for Drought Control in the Sahel (CILSS), which coordinates many of the region's research and aid projects. Although much of the funding for forestry and land conservation projects comes from abroad, some of the most successful efforts have been planned and carried out at the village level. But most observers agree that over the long term, reducing vulnerability to drought will depend on improving the region's national economies, which remain some of the poorest and least industrialized in the world.

Elizabeth Heath

SEE ALSO

Bamako, Mali; Drought and Desertification; Kano, Nigeria; Niamey, Niger; Ouagadougou, Burkina Faso; Pastoralism; Songhai Empire; Tuareg.

Africa

Sahrawi, an ethnic group in WESTERN SAHARA, MOROCCO, and ALGERIA.

Berbers initially settled in Western Sahara by the first millennium B.C.E. By the sixth century B.C.E. the Berbers separated into several groups, the most prominent of which were the Sanhadja, Zenata, Lemtuna, and Messoufa.

Bedouin Arabs known as the Beni Hassan, originally from Yemen, began settling in the area around the thirteenth century C.E. The Beni Hassan slowly came to dominate the Berber tribes. They intermarried with Sanhadja leaders or subdued them militarily. The conquering Beni Hassan forced the Berbers to pay tribute. Some Berber tribes, therefore, fell into an inferior status that did not change until well into the twentieth century. Other Sanhadja, however, declared themselves "people of the book," that is, dedicated themselves to religious life, and their status rose to just below that of the Beni Hassan.

Composed of 20 autonomous tribal groups, the Sahrawi did not form an especially cohesive ethnic group in precolonial times. They did, however, share common mores and customs, a similar social organization, the same religion (Islam), and the same language (Hassaniya Arabic), as well as intermarriage and alliances. Traditionally, the Sahrawi practiced a mixed economy, one suited to the extreme conditions of the desert. The majority were pastoralists who kept camels, sheep, and goats and migrated seasonally with their animals in search of water and grazing. Camels had multiple purposes:

they served as pack animals, an instrument of war, and a form of exchange, and their milk formed the foundation of the Sahrawi diet. Other Sahrawi practiced agriculture, while some of the poorer tribes fished. In addition, the Sahrawi engaged in trading of animals, wool, skin, salt (their main export), tea, sugar, firearms, rugs, and pots.

By 1884 the SCRAMBLE FOR AFRICA was in full swing and the Spanish declared Western Sahara a protectorate. Spain exerted control only over an extremely limited area, and its hold on the Sahrawi was tenuous at best. The Sahrawi repeatedly attacked Spanish holdings. It was not until 1934 that a combined French and Spanish military effort finally subdued the Sahrawi.

Nevertheless, the Sahrawi continued to practice their traditional way of life. Starting in 1959 the region underwent a prolonged drought, which roughly coincided with the Spanish discovery of phosphate deposits. During this period many Sahrawis gave up their nomadic existence to move to the major population centers in Western Sahara. The Sahrawi formed the Polisario Front to take up armed struggle against Spanish colonial rule. Upon Spain's pullout from Western Sahara in 1975, the land was occupied by Morocco and MAURITANIA. The Sahrawi declared Western Sahara an independent country, and many evacuated to the Tindouf region in Algeria. The armed struggle continued, now directed at Mauritania (which recognized the Sahrawi Arab Democratic Republic [SADR] and Western Sahara in 1984) and Morocco.

The United Nations (UN) became involved in the conflict beginning in late 1985. A UN-brokered agreement between the Polisario and the government of Morocco was to have resulted in a referendum among the citizens of Western Sahara to determine their future – either as an independent Western Sahara or as part of Morocco. Disagreements between the two governments, however, regarding who should be allowed to vote, continued to delay the referendum as of 1998. In the meantime, many Sahrawi remained in exile in the Tindouf region in Algeria.

Robert Fay

SEE ALSO

Berber; Camel; United Nations in Africa; Salt Trade; Pastoralism; Polisario.

Africa

Sa'id Sayyid ibn Sultan (b. 1791, Oman; d. 1856, Zanzibar), sultan of Oman and founder of the Busaidi Dynasty who ruled his empire from the East African island of ZANZIBAR.

The first Omani sultan to formalize control of the East Africa coastal islands, Sa'id Sayyid ibn Sultan began traveling to Zanzibar in the early eighteenth century. Recognizing Zanzibar's strategic location for commerce between African, European, and American merchants, Sa'id took control of the island and surrounding trade routes, including the INDIAN OCEAN SLAVE TRADE. Sa'id hired traders to bring caravans of goods from the interior, such as ivory, cloth, and slaves, which he then sold to merchants from Europe. The wealth he accumulated enabled Sa'id to extend his empire over the coastal region of present-day TANZANIA. There, he allocated part of the revenue from the customs duties and taxes imposed on local traders to local Swahili chiefs.

During the 1820s, however, European powers, particularly the British and Germans, stepped up efforts to abolish the profitable Indian Ocean slave trade. Under threat of military force, Britain coerced Sa'id to sign several international treaties, such as the Morseby Treaty, which made it illegal for Sa'id to sell slaves to Christian merchants, and the Hamerton Treaty, which made the sale of slaves north of Mogadishu illegal. These treaties effectively destroyed the Zanzibari slave market, forcing Sa'id to find new uses for the slaves who were still arriving from the African interior. He soon put them to work on the many clove plantations he established around the island. By the time he moved the capital of his empire to Zanzibar in 1840, Zanzibar had become the world's leading exporter of cloves, a title it still claims today.

Upon Sa'id's death in 1856, the Busaidi Dynasty split into two factions – the Omani sultans and the Zanzibari sultans. This split was formalized in 1861, when the Sultanate of Zanzibar became a political entity separate from the Omani. Sa'id's majid succeeded his rule in Zanzibar, and the Busaidi family continued to rule the island until Zanzibar's independence in 1963.

Elizabeth Heath

SEE ALSO

Mogadishu, Somalia; Swahili People.

Saint Augustine. Please see AUGUSTINE, SAINT

Latin America and the Caribbean

Saint-Domingue, colonial name of present-day Haiti, on the western third of the island of Hispaniola. It was named Saint-Domingue after the Spanish ceded this territory to the French in 1697, under the Treaty of Ryswick (*see* HAITI).

Europe

Saint-Georges, Chevalier de (b. December 25, 1745, near Basse Terre, Guadeloupe, West Indies; d. June 10?, 1799, Paris, France), Afro-French composer, violinist, and conductor; one of the first black composers to make a notable contribution to the European classical music tradition.

A singular figure on the musical landscape of prerevolutionary FRANCE, the Chevalier de Saint-Georges gained renown as a composer and violinist. Influenced by the French classical tradition, he wrote in a variety of forms: concertos for violin and orchestra; symphonies; string quartets; operas; sonatas for keyboard and violin; and *simphonies concertantes*, the popular French form of concerto that featured two or more soloists and an orchestra. He was also recognized throughout Europe as one of the outstanding swordsmen of his time, and in 1792 he became colonel of his own regiment in France's National Guard. In 1838 he was the subject of a four-volume adventure novel by Roger de Beauvoir.

The Chevalier de Saint-Georges, born Joseph de Boulogne, was the son of an African slave woman from GUADELOUPE and an aristocratic French plantation owner, from whom he inherited his name and title. At age ten he moved with his father to Paris. A student of the great fencing master La Boessière, Saint-Georges revealed remarkable strength and speed with the sword, inspiring La Boessière's son to call him "perhaps the most extraordinary man to appear in the history of fencing." In 1787 Saint-Georges took part in a London fencing exhibition with the notorious cross-dresser Chevalier d'Eon – a fight immortalized in a painting by Robineau that depicts d'Éon, in full silk dress and lace bonnet, opposite the dashing figure of Saint-Georges.

Although little is known about his early musical studies, as a young man he studied composition with French composer François Joseph Gossec, who in 1773 appointed him director of the Concert des Amateurs, a newly established public concert series in Paris. Saint-Georges also performed his own violin concertos, which, according to music editor Gabriel Banat, became "a bridge, connecting the violin technique of the violinist-composers of the late baroque... to the technique of the nineteenth-century romantics." In 1776 Saint-Georges was invited to become director of the Paris Opéra, but this offer was withdrawn when political intrigue and racial prejudice caused company members to protest his appointment. He continued to compose and perform and in 1779 was appointed musical director of the distinguished private orchestra of Madame de Montesson.

In the early 1780s Saint-Georges became affiliated with the Freemasons after the Loge Olympique, a Masonic Lodge in Paris, rescued the Concert des Amateurs from bankruptcy and relocated his orchestra to the Palais Royal. In 1785 the Palais Royal's owner, Duke Philippe Egalité, turned the grounds into a safe enclave for artists and revolutionaries, where class and social distinctions were disregarded. Saint-Georges became a regular performer at the Palais Royal. In addition to his orchestral concerts, he composed and produced several operas. He also developed a close friendship with the duke that involved him in revolutionary politics and led to his arrest and imprisonment in 1793 by the French Revolutionary Tribunal, presided over by Robespierre.

Released from prison in July 1794, Saint-Georges spent two years in Saint-Domingue, the French Caribbean colony where black slaves were in revolt against France. Music historian Eileen Southern wrote that "he fought in the uprisings there against Spain and the slaveholding colonists." Upon his return to Paris in 1797, Saint-Georges resumed his musical career but died of a gangrenous leg ulcer two years later, at age 54.

Roanne Edwards

See Also
Opera; Music, Classical, in Latin America and the Caribbean.

Africa

Sakalava, ethnic group of Madagascar.

The Sakalava primarily inhabit western Madagascar. They speak Malagasy, a Malayo-Polynesian language (*see* Ethnicity in Madagascar). More than 1 million people consider themselves Sakalava.

Latin America and the Caribbean

Saldaña, Excilia (b. August 7, 1946, Havana, Cuba), Cuban poet, essayist, translator, writer, and editor of children's stories whose works integrate her Hispanic poetic heritage with the religious and cultural heritage of the African diaspora.

Born into a middle-class family, Excilia Saldaña responded with fervor as a young girl to the social and political changes that took place in Cuba after the triumph of the 1959 revolution led by Fidel Castro. During college she became fully acquainted with Afro-Cuban culture through the ethnographic work of Lydia Cabrera and Fernando Ortiz.

Saldaña, like her poetic mentor and Cuba's poet laureate Nicolás Guillén, celebrates her African ancestry by populating her poems with gods and goddesses and flora and fauna symbolically drawn from the Afro-Cuban Santería religion. Saldaña is indebted to Guillén's integration of Hispanic and African cultural traditions in poetry, but she brings to the forefront the strength of the feminine heritage in the Caribbean.

Saldaña's lengthy elegy, *My Name (A Family Anti-Elegy)*, published in 1991 by Ediciones Unión, bears a dedication to both Guillén and to her grandmother, Ana Excilia Bregante. While establishing a direct link with Guillén's "The Last Name: A Family Elegy" (1951), Saldaña's poem constitutes a rejection of the male tradition and posits a female tradition the poet inherited from her grandmother in an act of poetic self-definition. Saldaña repeatedly appeals to the domestic yet mythical figure of her grandmother. Under the guise of rescuing her grandmother's forgotten and unusual name, Excilia, Saldaña establishes her name as the ultimate source of life for her poetry. Like Walt Whitman in "Song of Myself," the poet sets out to create the world of the Caribbean basin by the persistent invocation of her name.

Recreating the grandmother's voice and silences in the written poetic word, Saldaña has published a series of children's books that have been awarded literary prizes in Cuba. The two that have received the most acclaim are *Kele Kele* (1987) and *La Noche* (1989, Night). The first, a book of prose poems dedicated to young adults, recreates five *patakín* (Yoruba legends) based on the rhythm of the "romance," the traditional Spanish verse composed of eight syllables rhyming on every even line on the accented vowels. The second consists of poetic conversations between an inquiring child-self and the grandmother, whose wise aphorisms instruct the granddaughter. In her own poetic terms, Saldaña defines for all Cubans their European and African heritage within the context of a feminine voice.

Saldaña has written more than 20 books, including children's poems and legends, a feminist rewriting of the classics from the Greeks on, two autobiographical epic poems, erotic letters, and a poetic novel. She is a visiting professor at the Félix Varela Teaching Institute in Santa Clara and works as an editor at the children's press Gente Nueva in Havana.

Flora González

Latin America and the Caribbean

Saldanha, José da Natividade (b. September 8, 1795, Santo Amaro de Jaboatão, Pernambuco, Brazil; d. March 30, 1830, Bogotá, Colombia), Afro-Brazilian poet, lawyer, fervent nationalist, and political revolutionary.

The illegitimate son of a Portuguese priest and a mulatto woman, José da Natividade Saldanha went to Portugal to study law at Coimbra University. While in law school Saldanha wrote and published his first collection of poems, *Poemas dedicadas aos amigos e amantes do Brasil* (1822, Poems Dedicated to the Friends and Lovers of Brazil).

As a poet marked by Arcadianism, the influential neoclassical movement prevailing in some circles in Portugal and Brazil, Saldanha emphasized national and liberal ideologies that included the idea of a Brazilian republic and the abolition of slavery. Upon returning to Brazil the poet joined the secessionist movements brewing in Pernambuco and became a member of the junta that declared the independence of the Republic of Equador from Portugal in 1824. Condemned to death after the failure of this movement, Saldanha fled to the United States and from there to England, France, Venezuela, and finally Colombia, where he would live out the rest of his days in poverty. Saldanha died in Bogotá in 1830. During the course of his exile much of his work was lost, and that which remained was collected posthumously in *Poesia de Natividade Saldanha* (1875, Natividade Saldanha's Poetry).

Nicola Cooney

See Also
Great Britain; Slavery in Latin America and the Caribbean; Abolition and Emancipation in Latin America and the Caribbean.

North America

Salem, Peter (b. 1750, Framingham, Mass.; d. August 16, 1816, Framingham, Mass.), Revolutionary War soldier who played a decisive role in the Battle of Bunker Hill.

Freed from slavery by his owner in order to fight in the Continental Army, Peter Salem was one of about 500 African Americans who served in the Revolutionary War. Along with Salem Poor, Peter Salem fought bravely in early pivotal battles, including Concord in April 1775 and Bunker (Breed's) Hill in June 1775. Some contemporary eyewitnesses credited Salem with firing the decisive shot that killed British major John Pitcairn at Bunker Hill. Artist John Trumbull is said to have depicted Salem in his 1786 painting *The Battle of Bunker's Hill*, which shows a black soldier holding a musket. Serving bravely until the end of the war, Salem died in poverty in his hometown of Framingham, Massachusetts, after a career as a cane weaver. In 1882 a monument was erected to his memory in Framingham.

See Also
Slavery in the United States; American Revolution; Military, Blacks in the American.

Africa

Salisbury. Former name of Harare, Zimbabwe.

Latin America and the Caribbean

Salomon, Lysius Félicité (b. 1815, Les Cayes, Haiti; d. 1888, Paris, France), a black Haitian politician who challenged the racial aristocracy imposed by Haiti's mulatto bourgeoisie, eventually becoming president from 1879 to 1888.

Born to a black family of southern Haitian landowners, Lysius Félicité Salomon was involved at an early age in social and political activities. In 1843 he became a spokesperson for black peasants of Les Cayes who were rebelling against the mulatto-led Liberal Party. Salomon's participation in the cause, which began after the government suppressed the formation of small landholdings in the interest of larger estates, made him a legendary figure. A senator in his early 30s, he went on to hold the influential post of minister of finance for 11 years under Faustin Soulouque (1847-1859), a national president who later declared himself emperor.

After a coup overthrew Soulouque, Salomon lived in exile in JAMAICA and EUROPE for more than 20 years. During Salomon's period of exile the Haitian elite were divided into various competing groups, and Salomon's family was deeply involved in the ensuing political struggle. Salomon's two brothers, two uncles, a brother-in-law, and his adoptive son all died in the strife.

Salomon tried to return to his homeland in 1876 and 1878, but it was only during the 1879 elections that he returned as a presidential candidate for the black-dominated National Party and defeated the Liberals by a landslide. As president, Salomon instituted numerous economic and educational reforms, including the creation of the National Bank, the selling off of public lands to poor peasants, and the development of rural schools.

In 1886 Salomon had the 1879 Constitution revised so that he could be reelected president for seven more years. His opponents, fearing that Salomon would establish himself as president for life, conducted a successful insurrection two years later, in 1888. Forced to retire and ailing, Salomon left for France, where he died that same year.

Martine Fernández

SEE ALSO

Soulouque, Faustin Elie.

Cross Cultural

Salsa Music

It is hard to define exactly what salsa music is or what music falls into the category, or, indeed, if there is a significant difference between the salsa of the 1970s and older Cuban music. What nobody denies is that the commercial labeling of "salsa" had much to do with the boom in musical production by Cubans, Puerto Ricans, Newyoricans (Puerto Rican immigrants in New York), and members of other Caribbean communities in the late 1960s and early 1970s. Literally, *salsa* means "sauce," a semiliquid combination of ingredients and spices; some critics affirm that this definition accurately describes the particular spicy taste (*sabor*) of this music and its free combination of Afro-Caribbean rhythms. But others state that salsa is only an adulterated form of the Cuban SON and maintain that the music's short period of innovation and experimentation can ultimately be attributed to its continuity with Cuban music. Nevertheless, almost everyone recognizes that salsa is the commercial label that names the Afro-Cuban music produced by Spanish-speaking Caribbean communities both in New York and in their homelands since the late 1960s.

Salsa comes from the Afro-Cuban religious and secular music of the slaves. Like the Cuban *son*, the heart of salsa is the clave, a 3-2 or 2-3 beat spanning two measures that creates the syncopated foundation sustaining the lyrics and instrumentation. Salsa groups generally contain drums, bass, piano, a brass section, and vocals. Like the music of the Cuban *son*, the structure of a salsa composition contains an instrumental introduction followed by short and simple lyrics, another instrumental section, and the chorus, which includes some lyrical improvisations by the lead singer; there are exceptions to this general form. The call-and-response section between singer and chorus as well as the syncopated beat of the clave are among the musical elements traceable to African musical styles.

The word "salsa" came into use in the late 1960s as a label principally for the music produced by FANIA RECORDS, by then emerging as the strongest "Latin" music category in New York City. Some scholars argue that this commercial label underscores the differences between the new groups promoted by Fania and the music of the Latin big bands that were extremely popular in New York during the 1950s. They maintain that salsa expresses the "soul" of the Latin (mainly Puerto Rican and Caribbean) neighborhoods of New York, drawing on Cuban music for its rhythmic core but also incorporating some influences from other Afro-Caribbean musical genres as well as from African American music. For this audience salsa is an expression of the multicultural experience of the New York ghettos, which combines Cuban and other Afro-Caribbean rhythms with the influence of rock 'n' roll, soul, and JAZZ. Salsa is thus not so much a rhythm as a musical style distinguished by its free combination of rhythms, innovation, and experimentation. Critics of this argument state that whatever the innovation and experimentation, what is called salsa is in fact strongly rooted in such Cuban rhythms as *son*, *guaracha*, and RUMBA, not to mention MAMBO, which already drew heavily on American jazz.

Whether a new musical phenomenon or an adulteration of Cuban *son*, salsa is strongly linked to the history of the Puerto Rican and Cuban immigration to New York. The resulting immigrant communities have affected the music of their homelands as well as that of the United States. During the 1940s and 1950s Cuban big bands were very popular in New York and other big cities, as well as in Hollywood films. Key among these was the Afro-Cuban band started by Frank Grillo (MACHITO) and his brother-in-law MARIO BAUZA. In the 1950s Machito's band was a featured attraction at the Palladium Ballroom, the epicenter of the New York Latin scene, along with two bands led by Puerto Rican musicians Ernesto "Tito" Puente and Pablo "Tito" Rodriguez.

Puerto Rican immigration to the United States increased dramatically during these years, forming what is today an immigrant population of 2.7 million, more than 1 million of whom are in New York City. Not only was this community the main market for the Cuban big bands, but almost all of these bands contained Puerto Rican musicians.

The 1960s were years of change and commotion. For Puerto Rican and Cuban musicians in New York and PUERTO RICO, the Cuban revolution and subsequent United States blockade marked a rupture in communication with CUBA. It was also becoming difficult economically to sustain a big band; new, smaller groups emerged, requiring changes in the instrumentation, particularly reductions in the brass section and the number of singers. The big dance halls were also closing, replaced by smaller venues. The new bands needed not only to be smaller but also to have instruments that were easier to carry, requiring the introduction of the electric bass and electric piano.

It is not difficult to trace the evolution of salsa music in the United States from this point. First, one should note that these groups contained second- rather than first-generation immigrants. For them, New York represented their life experience. This meant that their musical inspiration not only came from their Afro-Cuban and Puerto Rican heritage but from greater contact with other American communities, particularly with African Americans. While there was clearly a cross-pollination between jazz and the MAMBO big bands of the 1940s and 1950s, these second-generation musicians drew even more upon African American music. Second, the closing of the big dancing halls put the musicians literally on the streets. Playing on the street and in smaller and cheaper clubs, these musicians formed a somewhat closer tie with the community than had the big bands. Third, the introduction of the electric bass and electric piano was for convenience but marked a change in how music was played, producing a louder sound, closer to that of rock 'n' roll groups. Fourth, many of the new songs presented a sort of new chronicle of the Newyorican everyday life, immediately appealing to this community. All these factors were expressed in an aggressive, loud, and daring sound, which strongly emphasized improvisations and the free combination of rhythms.

This new genre or style was represented by Fania Records, which effectively and aggressively recruited well-known musicians and bands. JOHNNY PACHECO, the founder of Fania, CELIA CRUZ, and Ray Barreto, as well as the newer bands of Larry Harlow, Bobby

Valentín, and Willie Colón, were among the talents working with Fania.

Marked by the New York experience, these young musicians experimented with many rhythms and musical genres. Before salsa, they created the *boogaloo*, a genre closer to soul. The boogaloo in part represented an attempt by Latin musicians to cross over into a non-Latin audience. Boogaloos were often in English and fused elements not only of soul but of rhythm and blues. Joe Cuba, Joe Bataan, the Lebron Brothers, and Johnny Colon were among the noted contributors to this genre. Fania, at the beginning, recorded almost equal amounts of Cuban music and boogaloo, the latter gaining popularity among the Spanish-speaking community as well as among non-Latin audiences. There is no answer that completely explains the boogaloo's demise by the early 1970s. A number of its creators attribute its demise to the politics of the Latin music industry, suggesting that they were shut out of radio and recording after a group of them sought a more independent path for the genre. Perhaps salsa, more strongly rooted in its Afro-Cuban heritage, signified stronger community identity and resistance.

Fania Records continued promoting the new salsa groups, whose sounds and Spanish lyrics made it easier to corner the market in Puerto Rico and other Spanish-speaking Caribbean countries. Indeed, during the 1970s the popularity of salsa spread throughout Latin America but particularly to Caribbean countries. In Colombia, for instance, groups such as Fruko y Los Tesos sowed the seeds for what is now a national industry, producing some of the world's most well-known salsa bands (Grupo Niche and Orquesta Guayacán, for example). Venezuela's Oscar d'Leon and Panamanian singer Rubén Blades also became giants on the international stage.

For Newyoricans, however, salsa is their music. It expresses their experience, their identity with Afro- and Spanish-Caribbean roots and culture, and the free combination of these with African American musical genres. The term *salsa* is said by some to have originated with the Venezuelan radio program *Echale Salsita* (Put on the Sauce), widely broadcast throughout the Caribbean. But the term *salsa* is also linked with Fania Records, which commercially promoted the genre under the new name.

The commercial promotion of salsa reflects the tensions between community expression and commercial appropriation. This relation can be seen in the two movies produced by Fania. The first, *Our Latin Thing*, relates salsa to the everyday life of the Newyorican community; the second, *Salsa*, erases these community signs, replacing them with more homogeneous and ambiguous signs common to a broader Afro-Caribbean tradition.

This process of the homogenization of salsa developed what in the 1980s became known as romantic or erotic salsa, which simplified salsa lyrics in almost exclusively love songs, many of which were modeled on old romantic ballads. Other musicians, however, continue the innovative lyrics and instrumental experimentation that characterized the genre in the 1970s. In particular, a new generation of Cuban talent has emerged on the international stage. Groups such as Los Van Van and NG La Banda continue to create new musical hybrids, drawing not only on Cuban music but on other musical expressions of the diaspora.

Juan Otero-Garabis

See Also

Soul Music; Puente, Ernesto Antonio (Tito).

North America

Salt 'n' Pepa, the first female rap group to produce a platinum album.

Cheryl "Salt" James, Sandi "Pepa" Denton, and Dee Dee "Spinderella" Roper make up the female rap trio Salt 'n' Pepa. Since 1985 the group has released five award-winning albums (one gold, two platinum, and one triple platinum), and earned the honor of being the first female rap group to produce an album that sold more than 1 million copies. After more than 12 years in the male-dominated rap music industry, Salt 'n' Pepa have sold more than 4 million records and released eight singles that ranked in *Billboard*'s Top 40, two of which climbed to the Number Three and Four positions on *Billboard*'s Top Ten. In their fifth album, *Brand New*, Salt 'n' Pepa continue to blend thought-provoking lyrics with upbeat hip hop tempos.

Cheryl James and Sandi Denton first met in the mid-1980s when both were attending nursing school in Queens, New York. While working part-time at a department store, James and Denton met Hurby Azor, who had just finished composing a song titled "The Showstopper." Azor's song was a lyrical response to the 1985 hit "The Show," released by rappers Doug E. Fresh and Slick Rick. James and Denton performed "Showstopper" later that year.

Taking the name "Super Nature," James and Denton caught the eye of Next Plateau Records, which quickly signed them. After fans picked up on a line in "Showstopper" in which James and Denton refer to themselves as "the salt and pepa MCs," the duo became known as Salt 'n' Pepa. In 1986 the group's name was officially changed, just in time for the release of its second single, "I'll Take Your Man." That year the group also released its first album, *Hot, Cool, and Vicious*. Featuring such hits as "Tramp," "Beauty and the Beat," and "Push It," *Hot, Cool, and Vicious* was an instant success and sold more than 1 million copies, making Salt 'n' Pepa the first female rap group with a platinum album.

In 1987 the group replaced DJ Latoya Hanson with Dee Dee "Spinderella" Roper. With Hurby Azor as its producer, Salt 'n' Pepa released its second album, *A Salt with a Deadly Pepa*. Filled with contemporary remixes of Isley Brothers classics, including "Twist and Shout" and "It's Your Thang," the album received a mixed reaction. It sold 500,000 copies before the group announced plans for another album.

In 1990 members of Salt 'n' Pepa took more control of the writing, composing, and production of their work and released *Blacks' Magic*. Hits such as "Independent" and "Expression" encouraged listeners not to follow the crowd and reminded young women to stand tall with pride. Their message and hard work were rewarded when the album went platinum. A single from the album, "Let's Talk About Sex," captured the attention of ABC News journalist Peter Jennings, who asked Salt 'n' Pepa to rewrite the song for a public service announcement about acquired immune deficiency syndrome (AIDS). The new song, titled "Let's Talk About AIDS," was released in 1992 and earned the group national acclaim.

A year later Salt 'n' Pepa delivered their fourth album, *Very Necessary*. With Top-Ten hits such as "Shoop" and "Whatta Man," the album went triple platinum. The single "None of Your Business" earned the group a Grammy Award in 1994 for Best Rap Vocal by a Group or Duo. At the height of their career, Salt 'n' Pepa have toured the world promoting female pride and social consciousness. They have won three MTV Video Music Awards, produced an all-female charity album called *Ain't Nuthin' But A She Thang*, and performed the song "Freedom" for the movie *Panther*. In 1995 Salt 'n' Pepa signed a multi-million-dollar contract with MCA Records and in 1997 they released their fifth album, *Brand New*. As leaders and innovators in the hip hop generation, they remain at the forefront of rap music.

Alonford James Robinson, Jr.

See Also

AIDS in the United States; Hip Hop in the United States.

Africa

Salt Trade, exchange of salt for commodities such as gold and slaves, particularly in West Africa.

Salt was probably one of the earliest goods traded over long distances in Africa. While the vital mineral was scarce in the savanna and forest regions of Africa, large deposits of salt occurred in the Sahara Desert. Those who controlled these deposits traded salt for slaves, gold, ivory, craft goods, malaguetta pepper, cola nuts, and foodstuffs from the forest and savanna zones. In turn, trans-Saharan traders purchased some of these goods, especially gold, ivory, slaves, and cola nuts, and carried them to North Africa.

In exchange for these goods, caravans transported horses and Mediterranean craft goods, such as glass, south across the Sahara. Some sources even suggest that gold-producing peoples exchanged salt in equal weight for gold. Thus the value of gold depended, to an extent, on the value of salt in the markets of West Africa.

The accumulation of goods exchanged for salt, including slaves and gold, promoted social stratification in the SAHEL. The trade thus contributed to the rise of empires such as Ghana, Mali, and Songhai, though these empires also arose due to internal developments. However, horses obtained in North Africa increased the military strength of these expansionist kingdoms.

Salt mines in the Sahara produced large slabs of salt, weighing as much as 100 kg (220 lb), that porters transported by camel to central markets in cities such as Tombouctou. Slaves working in the enormous salt mines at Taghaza lived in houses and prayed in mosques constructed out of salt slabs. Another source of salt was the Songhai Empire, in present-day MALI, where salt functioned as currency. The kingdom's rulers kept the location of salt deposits secret and heavily guarded. Canoes carried large quantities of cake salt from Gao up and down the NIGER RIVER and from river ports throughout West Africa. The mines of the Sahara were not the only source of salt. Kisama in Luanda, ANGOLA, also produced significant amounts of salt. The IJAW evaporated the seawater of the Niger Delta to produce salt in significant quantities. But other coastal peoples, who could evaporate sea salt, apparently preferred the taste of pure rock salt from the desert. The kingdom of Bornu (*see* KANURI) also exported salt that was produced by evaporating the saline waters of LAKE CHAD. Customers apparently preferred the taste of the lake salt, heavy in sodium carbonate, to pure rock salt for their MILLET porridge.

The salt trade helped to promote the spread of Islam (*see* ISLAM AND TRADITION: AN INTERPRETATION). Muslim traders carrying salt also brought their religion to the people of the south. For example, while the ancient kingdom of Ghana dominated the gold trade during the second half of the first millennium B.C.E., the kingdom depended on the salt of Aoudaghost to the north. By the twelfth century the rulers of Ghana had converted to Islam.

Ari Nave

SEE ALSO

Ghana, Early Kingdom of; Gold Trade; Ivory Trade; Luanda, Angola; Songhai Empire; Tombouctou, Mali; Slavery in Africa; Trans-Saharan and Red Sea Slave Trade; Mali Empire.

Latin America and the Caribbean

Salvador, Brazil. A city in the state of BAHIA.

Latin America and the Caribbean

Samba, Brazil's most famous musical genre and dance, created by Brazilians of African descent living in Rio de Janeiro during the early twentieth century.

To Brazilians, samba is many different things: abandon and solace, celebration and exuberance, national identity and pride. Though samba is most closely associated with the pre-Lent festivities known as Carnival, there are several forms of samba that are played year-round in various contexts. Percussive instruments dominate samba and give it a highly syncopated, layered sound. Technically, a 2/4 meter with the heaviest accent on the second beat and a stanza-and-refrain structure characterize samba.

Samba is rooted in the music and dance traditions of ANGOLA, the African country from which many of the slaves brought to Brazil had come. The term *samba* is believed to have derived from the Kimbundu term *semba*, a reference to the *umbigada* navel-touching dance step found in many African circle dances. Musically, many historians trace samba to the *lundu* music tradition brought to Brazil by slaves from Angola. This African dance and form of music are two of the numerous elements that were fused to create samba in Rio de Janeiro during the early twentieth century.

Following the abolition of slavery in 1888 and the subsequent decline of the plantation economy, a large number of ex-slaves living in the northern region of Brazil migrated south to Rio de Janeiro in search of opportunity. Some settled on the steep hillsides surrounding the city, the *morros*, while others settled in a central part of the city in the neighborhood of Estácio near Praça Onze (Plaza Eleven). Praça Onze and the houses of prominent black female figures known as *Tias* (aunts), who sold African food and led services for the worship of African gods, became meeting places for black musicians. The music they played – lundu, polka, and *habanera* as well as *marcha* and *maxixe*, two popular types of Brazilian music – factored in the creation of samba music.

Pioneering musicians such as Ismael Silva distinguished samba from marcha and maxixe by slowing the tempo and adding longer notes and two-bar phrasing. In 1917 a musician named Donga recorded "Pelo Telefone" (On the Telephone), a song widely regarded as the first samba composition. The traditional form of samba – played on a four-stringed, ukulele-like instrument called *cavaquinho*; a shallow, covered drumhead with jingling disks called the *pandeiro*; and its smaller, cymbal-less counterpart the *tamborim*, which is played with a stick – later became known as the *samba de morro*.

Numerous forms of samba developed out of the traditional samba de morro. One of the earliest variations was *samba de breque*, a style developed during the 1930s by singer Moreira da Silva. In songs such as "Acertei no milhar" (1938, I Hit Upon Thousands), Silva would periodically stop the song in order to dramatize the situation about which he was singing through improvised dialogues. It was also during the 1930s that numerous white Brazilians began to compose samba songs that popularized samba with the light-skinned middle class. According to historians Chris McGowan and Ricardo Pessanha, these musicians and singers downplayed the rhythm in favor of melody and wrote more complex and often sentimental lyrics.

This form of samba became known as *samba-canção* and is associated with composers such as Noel Rosa and Ary Barosso. Barosso spawned yet another form of samba in 1939 when he recorded one of the most famous Brazilian songs of all time, "Aquarela do Brasil" (Watercolor of Brazil). This song launched a new category of samba called *samba-exaltação* (samba of praise) that celebrated the natural wonders of Brazil.

The national and international popularity of these emerging forms of samba endured through the 1940s and overshadowed the traditional samba de morro. Despite this trend – and the growing tendency of some musicians to fuse samba with other popular styles of music – black Brazilians living on the outskirts of Rio and around Praça Onze preserved and embellished the rhythm of samba de morro. In the 1950s they reasserted the importance of samba de morro during their Carnival celebrations.

In the 1970s several musicians living in Ramos, a suburb of Rio, espoused a form of samba known as *samba-pagode*. They incorporated a type of drum called the *tan-tan*, exchanged the cavaquinho for a banjo, and sang about daily life in a colloquial language that endowed their music with an unpolished, down-to-earth quality. While samba-pagode was initially limited to informal settings such as parties, singer Beth Carvalho popularized the genre through her 1983 album *Beth Carvalho no Pagode*. Numerous other forms of samba thrive in Brazil today, including *samba de gafieira*, *samba de roda*, and *samba-reggae*.

Aaron Myers

SEE ALSO

Abolition and Emancipation in Latin America and the Caribbean; Rio de Janeiro, Brazil; Carnivals in Latin America and the Caribbean.

Africa

Samba, Martin-Paul (b. 1875, Metoutou-Engong, present-day CAMEROON; d. August 8, 1914, Douala, German Kamerun [present-day Cameroon]), German military officer and nationalist leader in Cameroon.

Like many early African nationalists, Martin-Paul Samba had a relationship with colonial authorities that progressed from initial cooperation to determined resistance. Born Mebenga-M'Ebono, Samba became familiar with German settlers during his childhood in what would soon become the German colony of Kamerun. After serving on an expedition led by German explorer Kurt von Morgan, Samba was taken to Berlin by von Morgan for education and military training. He ultimately reached the rank of captain in the German Imperial Army. In 1895 Samba returned home, and throughout the next 15 years participated in several expeditions into the hinterland to further German colonial ambitions.

By 1910 Samba had grown acquainted with early nationalists such as Rudolph Douala Manga Bell, and had begun to share their grievances. Two years later Samba became chief of the Ebolowa and the leader and strategist of the local anticolonial resistance movement. Pretending to be a businessman, Samba clandestinely stockpiled weapons. He convinced local chiefs to support a future uprising against the Germans. When World War I broke out, Samba notified the French in Brazzaville (now capital of the REPUBLIC OF THE CONGO) that he would assist them in military action against the Germans. But his letter was intercepted, and Samba was arrested, charged, and convicted of high treason. He was killed by a German firing squad in 1914.

Eric Young

SEE ALSO

Brazzaville, Republic of the Congo; Nationalism in Africa; Douala, Cameroon.

Latin America and the Caribbean

Samba Schools, organizations that annually mount elaborate musical parades for the pre-Lent Carnival celebration in BRAZIL.

In 1928 several musicians from the Estácio neighborhood in Rio de Janeiro formed the first SAMBA school, Deixa Falar (Let Them Speak). One of the reasons they created this organization was to parade during Carnival, a celebration from which they had historically been denied participation. Other black musicians followed their lead and came together to found their own samba schools, including Mangueira in 1929 and Portela in 1935. Although Afro-Brazilians had informally paraded through their own neighborhoods during Carnival festivities since the early nineteenth century, the samba schools lent a degree of formality to the Afro-Brazilians' street revelry and allowed them to assert their presence during Carnival. When Getúlio Vargas came into political power in 1935, he put an end to the repression of Afro-Brazilians and their samba schools and gave official recognition to their parades.

The Vargas administration changed Carnival by requiring participating samba schools to have a theme (*enredo*) related to Brazilian culture, history, or politics, and by making it into a competition. This fostered the emergence of new samba schools and increasingly elaborate presentations, including spectacular costumes and magnificent floats. It also led to the creation of a new category of samba music, *samba-enredo*, which features a lead singer whose lyrics illustrate the group's theme and a booming percussion section, the *bateria*, which may include more than 300 members playing more than a dozen different types of percussion instruments.

Over time, many samba schools have become internally diversified – as reflected in the different *alas*, or wings, of each parade, each with distinct costumes – and larger. Today Rio de Janeiro's Carnival features some 60 samba schools, each averaging 5000 members and 60 wings. Members of each school invest an enormous amount of time, year-round, and money – as much as $1 million – in preparing for Carnival, in hopes of being named the best samba school, a title that carries great prestige as well as a sizable financial award. Some of the more famous samba schools include the aforementioned Portela and Mangueira as well as Império Serrano, Beija-Flor, and Mocidade Independente.

Although many light-skinned Brazilians have joined these and other samba schools, most samba schools are composed of Afro-Brazilians. For these people samba schools continue to be, as they have been in the past, important sources of identity and pride. They have also provided Afro-Brazilians, who historically have not had a strong political voice, with a means of protest. This is especially true in Salvador, where *afoxés* and *blocos Afros* – Carnival organizations that also offer social services – have become a major feature of that city's Carnival.

In 1988 on the 100th anniversary of the abolition of slavery in Brazil, Mangueira's theme was *100 Anos de Liberdade: Realidade ou Illusão* (100 Years of Freedom: Reality or Illusion), which was in part a protest of the enduring poverty of blacks in Brazil. While the samba school tradition began in Rio in conjunction with Carnival, samba schools and large-scale Carnival celebrations can be found today throughout Brazil, especially in the northeastern seaboard cities of Recife and Salvador.

Aaron Myers

SEE ALSO

Afoxés/Blocos Afros; Carnivals in Latin America and the Caribbean; Abolition and Emancipation in Latin America and the Caribbean; Rio de Janeiro, Brazil.

Africa

Samburu, an ethnic group of KENYA.

The Samburu share the eastern Nilotic language and many of the cultural practices of the MAASAI. The name Samburu is thought to be a derivation of the Maasai word *samburr*, used to describe a leather pouch for carrying meat and honey, and suggests to some that this was once a hunting and gathering society. The Samburu generally refer to themselves as *L'oikop*, another word of Maasai origin. They are believed to have migrated up the Nile from the SUDAN beginning in the fifteenth century C.E. They now reside in the northern highlands of Kenya's Samburu district.

Like the Maasai, the Samburu have traditionally practiced pastoralism; they measure wealth by the size of their cattle herds. Each of the eight Samburu clans has a special brand for its cattle, and each Samburu family slits the ears of its cattle according to a particular pattern to identify the animals to other clan members. The Samburu typically do not settle in one place for very long, but rather move with their herds in search of water and pasturage. They survive largely on a diet of milk, drunk fresh or curdled as ghee or yogurt, and blood. Blood is obtained by opening a wound in a cow's jugular vein, extracting two or three liters, and closing the wound.

Similar to the Maasai, traditional Samburu society recognizes a series of age-sets. Both female and male youth are circumcised (*see* FEMALE CIRCUMCISION IN AFRICA), after which they pass into "adulthood." Females have two significant life stages, girlhood and womanhood. Males have several life stages. After circumcision (roughly between ages 14 and 25), a boy becomes a junior *moran* or "warrior." After a period of approximately 15 years the junior moran becomes a senior moran, then a junior elder, and finally a senior elder.

The Samburu, after the imposition of British COLONIAL RULE, were considered residents of the Northern Frontier District (NFD), which was closed to Europeans and Africans who were not citizens of colonial Kenya. In addition, Kenyan citizens needed special permission to enter the NFD. Although this isolation freed the Samburu from the more burdensome demands of the colonial government, independence brought an end to the NFD and an abrupt introduction to the politics and market economy of modern Kenya. While some Samburu have settled in towns in northern Kenya, most continue to live with their herds in rural areas.

Robert Fay

SEE ALSO

Nile River; Great Britain; Pastoralism.

Africa

Samo, ethnic group of Burkina Faso.

The Samo primarily inhabit northwestern Burkina Faso. Others live in southern Mali. They speak a Mande language. Approximately 300,000 people consider themselves Samo.

See Also
Languages, African: An Overview.

Africa

Samory Touré (b. 1830?, present-day Guinea; d. 1900?, Gabon), West African empire builder and fighter against French colonialism.

Born into the Touré clan in the Beyla region of present-day Guinea, Samory Touré became a soldier in the local conflicts that ravaged the area around the middle of the nineteenth century and soon began to exploit the situation to his own ends. By 1870 he had forged a large private army, with which he eventually conquered an area reaching from the Fouta Djallon in the west to the Asante country of present-day Ghana in the east. Establishing his capital at Bissandougou in what is now the Côte d'Ivoire, Touré tried at first to hold off the encroaching French through diplomacy and negotiations but later waged a brilliant, although ultimately unsuccessful, guerrilla war against them. Captured by the French in 1898, Samory Touré died two years later in exile in Gabon. He was the great-grandfather of Sékou Touré, first president of modern Guinea.

Samory Ture. Please see Samory Touré

Africa

San, southern African Khoisan-speaking societies, historically known as nomadic foragers.

The term *San* encompasses several societies in southern Africa. Among the best known are the Kung, who live in eastern Namibia and western Botswana; the Xo and the Gwi, who live in the central region of the Kalahari Desert, and the Naron of Botswana.

Khoisan-speaking societies have inhabited some parts of southern Africa for at least 2000 years. Although the region's earliest inhabitants probably lived primarily from gathering and hunting, archaeological evidence indicates that they came into contact with pastoral societies earlier than was once believed. Much of this evidence comes from rock paintings in South Africa's mountain ranges. The San's ancestors traded and engaged in tribute relations with the pastoralists (now usually referred to as the Khoikhoi or Kxoe) and at least some kept livestock themselves. After the arrival of Bantu-speaking cultivators sometime after 200 C.E., many Khoisan speakers were incorporated into their village communities (*see* Nguni).

The Dutch settlers who arrived on the Cape of Good Hope in 1652 proved less tolerant of San groups' nomadic ways than had earlier immigrants to the region. Although initial meetings between the San and Europeans were amiable, the settlers' demands for land and supplies soon caused tensions. As more Europeans arrived and began settling the Cape interior, they came to see the foraging societies (whom they called *Bosjieman*, or Bushmen) as "bandits" and "outlaws." The Dutch government subsequently authorized the extermination of the San, subjecting generations of "wild Bushmen" to intentional killings. In the 1770s, for example, Afrikaner migrants (also known as Boers) traveling across the Sneeuwberg Mountains nearly destroyed the adult San population and enslaved the children. In the mid-nineteenth century Boer communities near the border of present-day Namibia commonly hired "hunting parties" to track and kill San. During this period some San groups, such as the Xam in the Cape Colony, disappeared completely. Other groups fled into remote areas, and many who had previously lived elsewhere migrated into the Kalahari Desert.

Even while they faced persecution from European settlers, San groups became increasingly integrated into the market economy. During the nineteenth century some groups, such as the Western Kweneng, supplied fur, ostrich feathers, skins, and ivory to Goba and Tswana traders. Others, such as the Kung San, hired their services out to European hunters. By the end of the century, however, ivory and animal skins had become scarce. Many San sought work as field laborers or cattle herders on Tswana farms, often taking the place of men who had left to work in the South African mines. More recently the San have accepted positions as trackers for European hunting groups; during the 1970s and 1980s some were even recruited by the South African Defense Force (SADF). Although the San are still commonly stereotyped as foragers, few contemporary San live solely from foraging.

Elizabeth Heath

See Also
Bantu: Dispersion and Settlement; Ivory Trade; Pastoralism.

Latin America and the Caribbean

Sánchez, Luis Rafael (b. 1936, Puerto Rico), one of Puerto Rico's major writers, he has explored different genres including the short story, novel, play, and essay with equal success.

When the stories of Luis Rafael Sánchez were first published, in *En cuerpo de camisa* (1966), they constituted a departure from the more canonical models in Puerto Rican narrative. While sharing with previous writers the desire to explore the social and cultural alienation that Puerto Rico's dependent relation to the United States has created, Sánchez's stories are characterized by a corrosive sense of humor that incorporates the urban vernacular into the texture of the prose.

Sánchez is also an important playwright, and in this genre he has used different forms that range from traditional realism to the incorporation of Brechtian and absurdist elements. His early plays include *Cuento de la cucarachita viudita* (1960), *Los ángeles se han fatigado* (1961), *La hiel nuestra de cada día* (1961), and *O casi el alma* (1964). His extremely successful *La pasión según Antígona Pérez* (1968) is a rewriting of the classical Greek tragedy set in the context of a modern-day Latin American dictatorship. *Quíntuples* (1985) is a highly satirical exploration of grotesque characters who illustrate different degrees and styles of sociocultural alienation in modern Puerto Rican society.

Sánchez achieved international acclaim with the publication of his highly praised novel *La guaracha del Macho Camacho* (1976), his only work to be translated into English, by Gregory Rabassa in 1980, as *Macho Camacho's Beat*. Influenced by the narrative experiments of the Latin American Boom, this novel offers a devastating, albeit humorous, portrayal of Puerto Rican society suffering from the stagnation of colonial domination, social inequalities, and corruption. *La importancia de llamarse Daniel Santos* (1988) is a more optimistic book in which a legendary bolero singer becomes a symbol of popular culture's constant renewal and self-affirmation, and of the people's resistance to cultural alienation. In these books Sánchez displays a highly elaborate style, musical and baroque, which is also close to the inflections of everyday orality.

He has written essays that have appeared mostly in magazines and newspapers, often exploring the effects of Puerto Rico's political status, cultural life, and national identity (for example, "La generación o sea," 1972; "El debut en Viena," 1975). In 1994 he published *La guagua aérea*, in which he explores the diasporic migrations of Puerto Ricans between the island and the continental United States.

Still writing and skillfully exploring a variety of genres, Sánchez remains one of the most significant voices in contemporary Caribbean writing.

Victor Figueroa

See Also
Puerto Rico; Literature, Black, in Spanish America.

North America

Sanchez, Sonia

(b. September 9, 1934, Birmingham, Ala.), African American writer, activist, and educator who focuses on black women's struggle with racism.

Born Wilsonia Driver, Sonia Sanchez moved with her family to Harlem when she was a young girl. She received a B.A. in 1955 from Hunter College in New York City and spent the next year studying poetry at New York University.

An activist associated first with the CONGRESS OF RACIAL EQUALITY, Sanchez was further radicalized by MALCOLM X and the NATION OF ISLAM in the early 1970s. Her first volume of poetry, *Homecoming*, appeared in 1969, after several years of publishing in journals with other Black Nationalist poets such as LARRY NEAL and LeRoi Jones (AMIRI BARAKA). Sanchez's poems from this period were experimental and irreverent in style, content, and presentation. She became famous for bravura spoken-word performances that captured the cadences of African American speech. From 1965 to 1969 she taught in San Francisco and was actively involved in the founding of a controversial black studies program at San Francisco State University.

Sanchez left the Nation of Islam in the early 1970s to protest the organization's treatment of women. Her poetry and activism since have highlighted black women's struggle with racism from the dominant culture and within the black community. Her best-known collections of poetry are *A Blues Book for Blue Black Magical Women* (1973), a spiritual autobiography, and *homegirls and handgrenades* (1984), for which she earned an American Book Award in 1985. In addition to being a poet, Sanchez is an accomplished playwright, the author of children's books, and the mother of three. More recently, Sanchez has taught creative writing and black literature at Temple University in Philadelphia.

SEE ALSO

Literature, African American; Women Writers, Black, in the United States; Harlem, New York; New York, New York; Black Nationalism in the United States.

Europe

Sancho, Ignatius

(b. 1729, slave ship; d. December 14, 1780, England), an educated African ex-slave in Britain whose published letters formed an early and important slave narrative.

Ignatius Sancho was born on a slave ship en route to the West Indies; both of his parents died during the journey, casualties of THE MIDDLE PASSAGE. Never having lived in Africa, Sancho was in many ways a product of Western civilization. His letters, written between 1768 and 1780, and published posthumously in 1782, proved to the English public that an African could not only master the language and literature of England but become a discriminating reader and a discerning critic.

Upon arriving in Britain, Sancho was bought by three sisters in Greenwich who treated him poorly and denied him education. But the sisters' neighbors, the duke and duchess of Montague, were impressed by Sancho's curiosity about books and his quick mind and secretly lent him materials to read. In 1749, when the sisters threatened to sell him into American slavery, Sancho fled to the Montague household.

The duke and duchess died a few years later, leaving an inheritance to Sancho, who soon left Greenwich for the literary and artistic circles of London. There he wrote music and befriended musicians and artists, including the famous actor David Garrick. After a brief period of reckless living and gambling, Sancho returned to serve the new duke of Montague. But gout and a weight problem led him to retire in 1773, and he subsequently opened his own London grocery store, which became popular less for Sancho's produce than for his counsel. The duchess of Queensbury sought his help with her favored but troublemaking servant Julius Soubise. Other patrons included the artist Joseph Nollekens and the painter John Hamilton Mortimer, who consulted Sancho for his artistic sensibilities.

Sancho proved skillful in cultivating friendship and came to have many correspondents, including English novelist Laurence Sterne. Though Sancho praised Sterne's words against slavery, he wrote little on the subject himself, except to place it within the wider context of the greed for money and lust for power of the Christian East Indian traders. Sancho held a deep faith that the conditions blacks and the poor faced in this life would be resolved in "our next habitation," where, "there will be no care – love will possess our souls – and praise and harmony – and ever fresh rays of knowledge, wonder, and mutual communication will be our employ." He advocated patience to one black correspondent, and advised him to "tread as cautiously as the strictest rectitude can guide ye – yet must you suffer from this – but armed with truth –

In 1768 English portraitist Thomas Gainsborough painted Ignatius Sancho who, having been freed from slavery, became known for his letters and music in English society. *National Gallery of Canada, Ottawa*

honesty – and conscious integrity – you will be sure of the plaudit and countenance of the good." In this conviction, and in his words of affection for his West Indian wife, Anne, and their six children, Sancho's writing displays the sentimentalism of this era.

Although Sancho supported such liberal causes as a more equitable distribution of wealth, as a businessman, his interests lay in the proliferation of commerce, and, as a patriot, he denounced radicalism. Unlike black radicals such as Ottobah Cugoano or Robert Wedderburn, he preferred to use moral persuasion and his own example to convince the English people that Africans deserve equal treatment. Scholar Lloyd Brown explains that Sancho's background as a culturally assimilated outsider "subvert[ed] the standard images of the uncivilized Negro." Although he did not write antislavery appeals, Sancho's published letters testified to the humanity of Africans, thus strengthening the arguments of English abolitionists.

Leyla Keough

See Also

Slavery in the United States; Great Britain; Slave Narratives.

Latin America and the Caribbean

Sandoval, Alonso de, a missionary Jesuit priest who devised a system for the classification of African slaves being brought to Cartagena de Indias, Colombia, in the seventeenth century.

Latin America and the Caribbean

Sandoval, Arturo

(b. November 6, 1949, Artemis, Cuba), classically trained Cuban jazz trumpeter and flugelhorn player; a founder of the Afro-Cuban jazz ensemble Irakere.

Trumpeter Arturo Sandoval is one of the most dynamic Cuban jazz musicians. Along with pianists Gonzalo Rubalcaba and Chucho Valdés, and saxophonist Paquito D'Rivera, he is part of a younger generation that demonstrates the continuing vitality and creativity of Cuban jazz. Sandoval plays superb bravura trumpet, making particularly effective use of a powerful upper register and excellent articulation. His musical approach places him comfortably within the modern jazz mainstream that grew out of bebop or bop in the 1940s. In addition, as jazz critic Leonard Feather observed in the *Los Angeles Times*, Sandoval reveals "exceptional talent as a pianist and could easily make his living at the keyboard." He also performs on timbales with his working jazz group.

Sandoval, the son of an auto mechanic, was born in 1949 in a small village in the province of Havana, Cuba. At age 13 he started playing in the village band, and after trying various instruments, he settled on the trumpet and its mellow-toned relative, the flugelhorn. Initially, he had little awareness of jazz; a United States embargo on Cuba since 1960 had made American jazz recordings all but unavailable. As Sandoval explained in a 1993 interview in *Downbeat* magazine, "The only thing I used to hear was traditional Cuban music, what we call son, which was played by a septet with a trumpet and bongos."

In 1964 Sandoval entered the Cuban National School of Arts and studied classical trumpet for three years. After being drafted in 1971, he played in the Orquesta Cubana de Musica Moderna. He also discovered that his interest in jazz involved personal risk. "While I was in the army," he told Feather, "they caught me listening to Willis Conover's Voice of America jazz show, accused me of being pro-American, and threw me in jail for 3½ months.... "

Upon completing his military service in 1973, Sandoval – along with D'Rivera and Valdés – founded the groundbreaking Afro-Cuban jazz-rock band Irakere. Irakere quickly became Cuba's most popular musical group. Sandoval met and played with trumpeter Dizzy Gillespie – whom he regards as a primary influence – when the American jazz innovator visited Cuba in 1977. Sandoval later recorded the album *To Finland Station* (1982) with Gillespie and in the late 1980s toured widely with Gillespie's United Nation Orchestra, which also included D'Rivera. In July 1990 while appearing with the group in Rome, Sandoval entered the U.S. Embassy and requested political asylum for himself, his wife, and their 15-year-old son, who had accompanied him on the tour.

Sandoval's music expresses the stylistic diversity that has characterized Afro-Latin jazz from its inception. His recordings cross many musical boundaries, including jazz, Cuban dance music, and classical or art music. *I Remember Clifford* (1992), Sandoval's tribute to hard bop trumpeter Clifford Brown (1930-1956), is a straight-ahead jazz album, featuring pieces closely identified with the influential American trumpeter, including a fiery, up-tempo rendition of "Cherokee." Sandoval also regularly returns to his roots in Afro-Cuban music, as in *Danzon* (1993).

Like American jazz trumpeter Wynton Marsalis, Sandoval has performed classical music. He has appeared with symphony orchestras in London and St. Petersburg. He premiered his first classical composition, *Concerto for Trumpet and Orchestra*, with the National Symphony Orchestra under the direction of Luis Haza in 1994 . Writing in the *Washington Post*, critic Mike Joyce described the three-movement, 19-minute-long concerto as being "full of sharp and sometimes sudden contrasts, juxtaposing fiery trumpet flourishes with tender flugelhorn balladry, jazz and folk dance rhythms with orchestral rhapsodies, playful exchanges with bravura solos." He has thus emerged as more than just a trumpeter of superb range and technical mastery. Equally at home in American jazz or in traditional Cuban music, he exemplifies the richness and excitement of the Afro-Latin fusion.

James Clyde Sellman

See Also

Gillespie, John Birks ("Dizzy"); Valdés, Jesús (Chucho); Music, Classical, in Latin America and the Caribbean.

North America

San Francisco and Oakland, California

Although Mexican and Spanish blacks were in the De Anza expedition that settled San Francisco in 1776, until the California gold rush there were only a few Africans and African Americans in the San Francisco/Oakland area. Notable among them was William Leidesdorff, a merchant in Mexican San Francisco and later United States vice consul to Mexico.

After 1848 a small African American community developed on San Francisco's Telegraph Hill and on the waterfront. Blacks could not testify in court cases until 1863 nor vote until 1869, but the black community included well-educated, prosperous people and immigrants from the Caribbean and Cape Verde, making the group an unusually diverse one in the United States. After 1900 African Americans occupied the Western Addition neighborhood.

In West Oakland a black community developed when the Western Pacific Railroad established its terminus there in 1869. Attracted by railroad and port jobs, blacks came to Oakland and the city's black population increased sixfold – to 6000 – between 1900 and 1920. Under the guidance of C. V. Dellums, a well-organized chapter of the Brotherhood of Sleeping Car Porters formed in the 1920s.

From 1940 to 1950 the black population in the Bay Area increased from 16,500 to 147,000, the result of labor demand in the Oakland and San Francisco shipyards. Under political and legal pressure, unions began accepting African Americans. But discrimination was present, especially during the Port Chicago Mutiny incident. An explosion at the Port Chicago naval ammunition base shipyards killed 320 people, including 202 black ammunition leaders. After the incident many black sailors refused to return to work out of concern for their safety. Subsequently, 258 black sailors were arrested, and 50 were court-martialed. Housing discrimination was also rampant. In San Francisco it forced almost all African Americans into the Fillmore and Bayview-Hunter's Point areas. The West Oakland black community nonetheless expanded into North and East Oakland as well as Richmond. In 1946, protest against housing discrimination led to the appointment of African American William McKinley Thomas as commissioner of the San Francisco Housing Authority and the election of William Byron Rumsford as the first black state legislator from northern California.

By the 1960s, however, most Bay Area African Americans still lived in substandard housing in virtually segregated communities. The black community organized, and in 1964 Terry Francois was elected to the San Francisco Board of Supervisors and Willie Brown to the state assembly. Brown became speaker of the California House of Representatives and, most recently, mayor of San Francisco. In the early 1960s the Congress of Racial Equality (CORE) led opposition to police brutality and advocated for better job opportunities for African Americans and more effective integration of public schools. The Berkeley Free Speech Movement inspired large-scale civil rights protests in 1964. But de facto segregation continued.

The year 1966 was a banner one in the history of the Bay Area black community. Oakland residents Bobby Seale and Huey Newton formed the radical Black Panther Party, whose platform was to defend local black communities nationwide against relentless racism and capitalist exploitation. Direct, sometimes armed, opposition to police brutality, the provision of free breakfast for black schoolchildren, and the construction of a housing center for homeless blacks and a community school are among the actions that made the Panthers nationally prominent. By the end of the 1970s, however, internal fighting as well as intense police and Federal Bureau of Investigation (FBI) opposition led to the dissolution of the party – though not before the Panthers helped Lionel Wilson become the first black mayor of Oakland in 1977.

In 1968 the Oakland Black Caucus was formed, and in 1971 Oakland's Ronald Dellums became the first African American from northern California elected to the U.S. Congress. In 1991 Elihu Harris was the second black elected mayor of Oakland. Beginning in the late 1960s a gay and lesbian community developed in San Francisco, supporting celebrated filmmaker Marlon Riggs, among others, but encountering opposition for gentrifying black neighborhoods. Beset by urban problems and poverty, the black community is now concentrated in the Fillmore and Bayview neighborhoods of San Francisco and East Oakland.

Jim Mendelsohn

See Also

Brown, Willie Lewis, Jr.; Civil Rights Movement; Dellums, Ronald V. (Ron); Newton, Huey P.; Riggs, Marlon Troy; Gay and Lesbian Movements in the United States.

Africa

Sangaré, Oumou, (b. 1968?, Mali), Malian singer.

Known as Mali's songbird, Oumou Sangaré uses a mix of traditional and modern instruments, along with her powerful voice, to update Mali's renowned Wassoulou sound. Based on music made by hunters, these old songs asked for protection and good fortune in the densely forested Wassoulou region. Sangaré, who says she sings "for the women," retains much of the original sound – using *kamelen ngoni* (a small, harplike, stringed instrument), guitar, and a variety of percussion instruments – but adds lyrics dealing with the changing status of women in Africa.

"In Africa it's still men who make all the decisions," Sangaré says. "It's time for women to be heard." Accordingly, one song on her third album, *Worotan* (1997), describes the outcast status of childless women, while others deal with domestic abuse and polygamy. Although little is known about the singer's personal life, Sangaré, who sings in her native language, Bambara, has spoken of her mother as her first musical teacher, and of a childhood in which she sang often at parties and family gatherings.

Formal training with the Mali National Ensemble led to work with Djolive Percussions, the musical group with whom Sangaré first toured Europe in 1986. While singing in Paris, Sangaré first heard the legendary South African singer Miriam Makeba, to whom some critics have compared her rich, passionate vocal style. Sangaré's first album, *Moussolou*, became West Africa's best-selling recording in 1991. Two years later she followed with *Ko Sira*, which won an award as Europe's favorite world-music album.

Kate Tuttle

See Also

Makeba, Miriam Zenzi; South Africa; World Music, World Beat, and the Re-Africanization of Latin American Popular Music.

Latin America and the Caribbean

San Juan, Puerto Rico, capital of the Commonwealth of Puerto Rico on the Atlantic Ocean, in the northeastern part of the commonwealth. It is Puerto Rico's largest city and principal seaport, as well as its main manufacturing, financial, cultural, and tourist center.

Economy

Since World War II San Juan's economy has grown rapidly. Major manufactures include chemicals, pharmaceuticals, rum and other beverages, fertilizer, machine tools, electronic equipment, plastic goods, textiles, clothing, and food products. San Juan has excellent transportation facilities. A network of highways connects the city to the rest of the island, and a busy airport in nearby Isla Verde and San Juan's modern port facilities provide connections to international points.

Points of Interest

The historical heart of the city, referred to as Old San Juan, lies on a small island connected to the mainland by bridges and a causeway. It is characterized by narrow, crooked streets and a number of buildings dating from the sixteenth and seventeenth century (*see* Colonial Latin America and the Caribbean). The oldest part remains partly enclosed by massive walls and contains several notable forts, such as El Morro (begun in 1539) and San Cristóbal (built in the seventeenth century), both part of the San Juan National Historic Site, and La Fortaleza (begun in 1533), which now serves as the governor's mansion. Also on the island is the Cathedral of San Juan Bautista (begun in the 1520s), a Gothic structure that contains the tomb of the Spanish explorer Juan Ponce de León.

On the mainland just east of Old San Juan is the section known as Condado Beach. High rise luxury hotels and condominiums prevail in this area, which is the main focus of tourist activity in the city. To the south are two separate business districts, Santurce and Hato Rey, both encompassing tall office buildings. Farther south is the residential area of Río Piedras, which contains the main campus of the University of Puerto Rico, founded in 1903. Also in the San Juan area are the Inter-American University of Puerto Rico (1912), the Sacred Heart University (1976), the Museum of Puerto Rican Art, and the Ponce de León Museum.

History

The region's first European settlement, called Caparra and located west of the present-day city of San Juan, was begun in 1508 under the direction of Ponce de León. Taíno indigenous peoples lived in the area at the time. In 1521 the original settlement was moved to the site of what is now called Old San Juan. Interestingly, this settlement was originally known as Puerto Rico (rich port), whereas the island had been named San Juan Bautista (Saint John the Baptist) by Christopher Columbus in 1492; later the names were reversed. The community was subjected to frequent attacks by Europeans (including Sir Francis Drake in 1595), and several imposing fortifications were built. The city of San Juan remained under Spanish control until 1898, when the island was ceded to the United States at the conclusion of the Spanish-Cuban-American War. The large-scale expansion of the city limits outward from Old San Juan to the mainland has occurred during the twentieth century.

See Also

World War II and African Americans; Spanish-Cuban-American War, African Americans in the.

Africa

Sankara, Thomas

(b. December 21, 1949, Yako, Upper Volta; d. October 15, 1987, Ouagadougou, Burkina Faso), revolutionary leader and former president of Burkina Faso.

On October 15, 1987, Thomas Sankara was assassinated in a coup led by troops loyal to Capt. Blaise Compaoré. The Compaoré regime later denounced Sankara, calling him a "traitor" to his own revolution that was begun four years earlier. Yet Sankara, who came to power at age 33, was widely credited with initiating reforms that benefited the country's most oppressed groups, namely women and the rural poor. Sankara's radical policies and defiant attitude toward the West proved costly, but his integrity – and the changing of the country's name from Upper Volta to Burkina Faso, "land of upright people" – instilled in many Burkinabè a lasting sense of national pride.

Sankara was the third of ten children of a Mossi mother and a Peul (Fulani) father who worked for the colonial administration's postal service. Sankara's political views took shape during his military schooling in the early 1970s. While attending the Antsirabe military academy in Madagascar, he witnessed the 1972 Communist-led revolution, and he had further exposure to Marxist thought while training as a parachutist in France. After returning to Upper Volta in 1974, he fought in the border war against Mali, which he called a "pointless and unjust battle." He later joined the National Parachute Regiment, trade unions, and underground revolutionary groups.

In 1978 Sankara met Compaoré during military training in Rabat, Morocco. The two officers, later stationed together in Upper Volta, became inseparable friends and set up a small "popular republic" at their base to discuss their revolutionary ideas. In 1981 Sankara became minister of information under the Zerbo government, but soon resigned in protest over government censorship of the radio. This stance won widespread support, and when Zerbo was overthrown in 1982, the new military council appointed Sankara prime minister. He used his position to denounce Western imperialism, a stance that particularly appealed to workers and students.

Sankara's radicalism, however, did not endear him to more conservative members of the council, who had him placed under house arrest in May 1983. Students protested in Ouagadougou, and Compaoré led a military coup in August 1983 that brought Sankara to power as president of the new Conseil National de la Révolution.

During his tenure as president, Sankara initiated a series of reforms, many of them for the benefit of the rural poor. These included irrigation projects, literacy drives, and mass rural vaccination campaigns. He also set out to cut government spending, setting an example as the president: he paid himself a clerk's salary, turned off the presidential palace air conditioning, and drove a used car. A staunch advocate of sexual equality, he called for "the abolition of the system of slavery to which [Burkinabè women] have been subjected for millennia," and started a national campaign encouraging Burkinabè men to partake in household chores and other family responsibilities. He also appointed five women to ministerial posts and hired a team of women motorcycle guards to escort him in public. On the international level, Sankara raised funds and supported national liberation movements worldwide.

Not everybody welcomed the president's reforms. Sankara's efforts to undermine the power of rural chiefs and other traditional authorities by installing "revolutionary defense committees" in villages and neighborhoods, for example, proved especially unpopular among the Mossi, Burkina Faso's largest ethnic group. While the radical wing of his government felt Sankara's reforms had not gone far enough, many members of the business community resented his government's restrictions on trade. Sankara's tendency to dismiss his political opponents from office also cost him support.

The circumstances surrounding Sankara's death remain unclear. Compaoré has denied any involvement in the assassination, but the mysterious disappearances in 1996 of some alleged members of the hit squad have renewed suspicions that the current president still seeks to silence potential informants. In Ouagadougou, meanwhile, the commoner's grave of Sankara still receives daily visitors. Indeed, as *New York Times* writer Howard W. French noted in March 1997, "Few African leaders have been mourned so deeply at home or as widely on this continent since... Africa's early independence days."

Roanne Edwards

See Also

Colonial Rule; Ouagadougou, Burkina Faso; Nationalism in Africa.

Latin America and the Caribbean

Santa Cruz, Nicomedes

(b. June 4, 1925, Lima, Peru; d. February 4, 1992, Madrid, Spain), Afro-Peruvian poet, folklorist, essayist, and one of the most important Afro-Latin American intellectuals of the twentieth century.

Nicomedes Santa Cruz is the author of three major collections of poetry: *Cumanana* (1964); *Décimas* (first edition, 1960, second edition, 1969); and *Canto a mi Perú* (1966, Song to My Peru). Two anthologies of his work appeared in 1971: *Ritmos negros de Perú* (Black Rhythms of Peru) and *Décimas y poemas: Antología* (Décimas and Poems: An Anthology). He also wrote a book of literary history and criticism titled *La décima en el Perú* (1982, The Décima in Peru). Santa Cruz recited and sang his poetry and shared his knowledge of Peruvian folklore on television and radio, as well as in live performances. He also made three sound recordings: *Canto negro* (1968, Black Song), *Cumanana, Antología Afro-peruana* (1970, Cumanana: Afro-Peruvian Anthology), and *Socabón* (1975). An English translation of his works is yet to be published.

Although he employed various poetic forms, he is best known for his cultivation of the traditional popular form called the Décima, a stanza of ten octosyllabic lines with a particular rhyme scheme. It is often improvised and sung to musical accompaniment and is sometimes used for poetic duels.

Throughout his youth, Santa Cruz was exposed to classical poetry from Spain and the popular poetry of his native land of the Peruvian coast. He soon began to create his own verses, and with the coaching of an older gentleman, he mastered the art of composing décimas. In his late 20s he abandoned the profession of iron working in order to pursue a literary career.

As a young man Santa Cruz became aware of the racism that permeated Peruvian society. His father had been a writer, but because he was black, he received no attention from leading Peruvian literary critics. Santa Cruz's own family discouraged him from marrying a woman because they wanted him to "improve the race," that is, marry someone of lighter skin. During the 1950s Santa Cruz noticed that the religious authorities were slow to make sixteenth-century Afro-Peruvian friar Martín de Porres into a saint. Santa Cruz used poetry to speak out against such discrimination and to heighten awareness of the contributions of black people.

Santa Cruz composed poems on a wide range of topics, but he is most noted for his works about the experience of people of African descent in Peru, the Americas, and the world. In the collection *Décimas*, for example, one finds poems about how the enslaved Africans resisted oppression through their language, religion, music, and dance, and created enduring cultural forms. Santa Cruz also recorded the achievements and struggles of blacks in areas as diverse as Christianity and sports. One poem, for example, pays homage to great soccer players from the poet's home neighborhood of La Victoria in the Peruvian capital of Lima. The well-known poem "Muerte en el ring" ("Death in the Ring," in *Cumanana*) describes the death of Cuban boxer Benny "Kid" Paret as an example of the exploitation of poor blacks in violent sports. "Formigas pretas" ("Black Ants") is another poem about exploitation; in this case Santa Cruz describes the toil of blacks in Brazil, where he lived in 1963. Three poems in *Cumanana* express solidarity with the struggles of African peoples against colonialism and racism in the Republic of the Congo and SOUTH AFRICA. Throughout his poetic career, Santa Cruz affirmed the positive value of African heritage and denounced racial and ethnic prejudice.

Santa Cruz was committed to improving the political, social, and economic situations of all oppressed peoples. For example, in "Talara" he urged Peru to resist foreign control of Peruvian natural resources. In another poem he calls for an end to conflicts and exploitation in large cities. Although Santa Cruz was most familiar with the African-influenced coastal region around Lima, he also reached out to the indigenous peoples of the mountainous regions of Peru: poems like "Indio" and "Agro" show that Santa Cruz sympathized with the struggles of Native American tribes and peasants. Santa Cruz's desire for a more equitable society led him to support the Cuban Revolution and to join a Peruvian political party. However, he became disenchanted with Peruvian politics and society, and in the 1970s he moved to Spain, where he resided until his death.

Santa Cruz is known as the foremost Afro-Peruvian poet. While he did much to expose others to the cultural richness of his people and his region, his work spoke to the whole of human experience.

Marveta Ryan

SEE ALSO
Music, African; Congo, Republic of the; Cuba; Porres, San Martín de; Literature, Black, in Spanish America; Religions, African, in Latin America and the Caribbean; Dance in Latin America and the Caribbean; Soccer in Latin America and the Caribbean; Influence of African Languages and Cultures on Colonial Languages in Latin America and the Caribbean;.

Latin America and the Caribbean

Santamaría, Ramón ("Mongo")

(b. April 7, 1922, Havana, CUBA), Afro-Cuban conga and bongo drummer and bandleader who found popular success during the 1960s by incorporating elements of RHYTHM AND BLUES (R&B) into AFRO-LATIN JAZZ.

For more than 30 years Mongo Santamaría has led one of the top-rated bands in Afro-Latin jazz, yet he remains far less well-known than bandleaders MACHITO and Tito Puente, who rose to prominence during the 1940s and 1950s. Many scholars and musicians rank Santamaría as the most influential Cuban percussionist since Chano Pozo. He has continued – well into his 70s – to play with remarkable speed and authority, employing complex polyrhythms that invariably swing. During the 1960s he created a distinctive fusion of Latin jazz and SOUL MUSIC, anticipating the funky *bugalú* fad.

Although he began by studying violin, Santamaría soon switched to drums, dropping out of school to become a professional conga drummer. In 1948, after having established himself as a performer in Cuba, Santamaría went to Mexico City with his cousin Armando Peraza, who would be the long-time percussionist in Carlos Santana's Latin rock band during the 1970s. In the late 1940s Santamaría traveled to New York City, where he performed with the city's first *charanga* – an ensemble featuring flute, violins, a percussion section, and vocals. After a short stint in the big band of Damaso Pérez Prado, he joined Tito Puente from 1951 to 1957. In concert and on records, Santamaría and timbales player Puente played fiery percussion duels that remain legendary among Afro-Latin jazz musicians.

In 1957 Santamaría and fellow percussionist Willie Bobo left Puente's band after having roused the bandleader's ire by appearing on an album by Latin jazz vibraphone player Cal Tjader. Tjader quickly hired both musicians, who remained with Tjader's sextet for four years, adding fire and drive to the leader's otherwise cool music. During the 1950s Santamaría began recording as a leader. His early albums generally feature Afro-Latin jazz, but his first, the notable *Changó* (1955) – reissued under the title *Drums and Chants* – explores the roots of Afro-Cuban music and includes Santamaría and fellow Cuban percussionists Silvestre Méndez, Carlos "Patato" Valdez, and Julito Collazo.

In 1960 Santamaría and Bobo traveled to Cuba, where they recorded together with a number of outstanding Cuban musicians – including *tres* player Niño Rivera, pianist Paquito Echavarria, and vocalists Mercedita Valdés and Carlos Embales. The resulting album, *Our Man in Havana* (1960), was a direct precursor of the *típico* revival movement that emerged in the 1960s as a predominant force in Latin music. In 1961 Santamaría took over Armando Sánchez's Orquesta Nuevo Ritmo and consistently infused the group's flute and strings charanga format with a jazz feeling.

After 1962 Santamaría largely abandoned traditional Cuban ensembles and the típico movement in favor of Afro-Latin jazz fusion. The infectious soul jazz tune "Watermelon Man" (1962) – written by Herbie Hancock, Santamaría's pianist at the time – emerged as a Top Ten hit with virtually no record company promotion, and resulted in Santamaría signing with Columbia Records for a series of highly commercial albums produced between 1964 and 1969. "Watermelon Man" effectively defined Santamaría's approach for most of the following 30 years, resulting in Latin soul versions of such hits as "Proud Mary," made famous by Ike and Tina Turner; STEVIE WONDER'S "My Cherie Amour"; THE SUPREMES' "Love Child"; and even – rather improbably – the country-pop confection "Little Green Apples."

Santamaría has helped develop some leading talents in jazz and Latin music, including Hancock, pianist Chick Corea, tenor saxophonist José "Chombo" Silva, and flutist Hubert Laws. He also composed "Afro-Blue" (1958-1959), which became a jazz standard through tenor saxophonist John Coltrane's influential 1963 rendition. Santamaría's notable albums include *Changó*, *Afro-Roots* (1958-1959), *Our Man in Havana* (1960), *Skins* (1962), *Soy Yo* (1987), and *Live at Jazz Alley* (1990).

James Clyde Sellman

SEE ALSO
Coltrane, John William; New York, New York; Turner, Tina; Pérez Prado, Dámaso; Pozo y González, Luciano (Chano); Puente, Ernesto Antonio (Tito); Valdés, Merceditas.

Latin America and the Caribbean

Santería,

a syncretized religion derived from African and Roman Catholic religious practices and beliefs that developed in CUBA and later spread to other countries.

Santería came into being between the sixteenth and nineteenth centuries, when the Spanish colonizers of Cuba imported hundreds of thousands of slaves from Africa to work on the island's sugar and coffee plantations. The Spanish, who established Roman Catholicism in Cuba, baptized these slaves and forbade them to practice African religions. In these circumstances slaves preserved elements of their religions by identifying their deities, known as ORISHAS, with Roman Catholic saints. This syncretism allowed slaves to worship the orishas secretly while externally paying homage to the Catholic saints. For this reason, the religion that emerged is known as Santería, "the way of the saints."

Historians have identified slaves from the YORUBA ethnic group of southwestern NIGERIA as the most influential group in the forging of Santería. Yoruba slaves believed in one supreme being, Olodumare, who in Cuba became equated with the Christian concept of God, and numerous orishas, the children and servants of Olodumare, who in Cuba became correlated with the Christian saints. While the Yoruba religion includes some 400 to 500 orishas, each of which protects and is worshiped by the inhabitants of a different city, the practitioners of Santería only recognize some 16 orishas. In Cuba this smaller set of intermediary deities is sometimes termed *Lucumí*, the name originally used by the Spanish to refer to Yoruban slaves, in order to distinguish it from the Yoruban pantheon from which it derives.

Because practitioners of Santería regard Olodumare as a distant, inaccessible God, they focus their religious activities on the intermediary orishas. To those who worship them, the orishas are divine ancestors, immaterial in form, who control some aspect of nature and some domain of human activity. Ogun, for example, is regarded as the deity

only by a *santero* or *santera*, a standard Santería priest or priestess. The obi may be used by both types of priests. Divination is used in the early stages of initiation to determine an individual's personal orisha and thereafter to determine the will of the orisha for that person. According to one scholar, divination is the process through which the orishas diagnose people's problems and recommend solutions.

Practitioners of Santería hold elaborate ceremonies called *bembés* to invoke their orishas. Each orisha has its own drum rhythm, song, and dance step. In performing the music and choreography of a particular orisha, a worshiper tries to persuade the orisha to descend upon the ceremony and possess him or her. An orisha that temporarily takes over the body of a worshiper, an act often described as "mounting," is able to participate in the festivities, accepting food offerings and giving advice. The orisha eventually takes leave of his or her human medium, who then regains consciousness without recalling the possession.

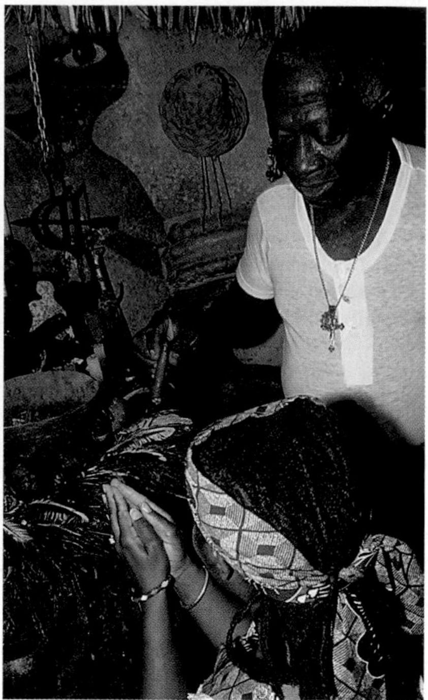

TOP: Drummers play during a Santería ceremony. Each orisha, or Santería deity, has its own drum rhythm, song, and dance step. *CORBIS/Françoise de Mulder*
ABOVE: Santería, a faith that combines elements of African and Roman Catholic religious practices, developed in Cuba and spread to other countries. This photo shows a Santería altar in Havana. *CORBIS/Robert van der Hilst*
RIGHT: A Santería high priest, or *babalao*, guides a devotee in a prayer before an altar. *CORBIS/Françoise de Mulder*

of iron and minerals, and he oversees blacksmiths and those who drive vehicles with metal parts.

In Santería an individual develops a reciprocal relationship with one of the orishas. In exchange for guidance and protection, the worshiper makes offerings (*ebó*) to his or her orisha. Communication with the orishas is established through various forms of divination performed by a Santería priest or priestess and through spirit possession, which takes place during drum and dance ceremonies.

Santería employs three types of divination: *obi, dilloggún,* and a combination of the *opelé* and *tablero de ifá.* In each type, a priest or priestess tosses and interprets the fall of certain objects – a quartered coconut for obi, 16 cowry shells for dilloggún, and a necklace with 8 evenly spaced disks for opelé. The tablero de ifá is a wooden tray upon which a priest sprinkles powder and draws configurations based on the heads-or-tails patterns resulting from several throwings of the opelé.

The three divination types correspond to various individuals in the Santería priesthood. The opelé and the tablero de ifá are used exclusively by *babalawos,* the male high priests of Santería. The dilloggún is used

Santería has taken root beyond Cuba, especially in the United States. Hundreds of thousands of Cuban exiles have arrived in the United States since the 1959 revolution in Cuba, bringing Santería with them. Many of these Cubans settled in New York City and southern Florida. Over time the number of non-Cubans practicing Santería has increased, and the religion has become more public, but not without some resistance. Santería's use of animal sacrifice to feed symbolically the orishas triggered a controversial national debate. In 1987 the city of Hialeah, Florida, responded to this practice by banning animal sacrifice. However, a 1993 Supreme Court ruling stating that the ban represented unconstitutional infringement on freedom of religion has enabled Santería to continue to thrive in the United States.

Aaron Myers

Africa

São Tomé and Príncipe, Africa's smallest country, comprising two islands off the coast of GABON in the Gulf of Guinea.

The tiny island nation of São Tomé and Príncipe has had a different history than most other African countries. São Tomé and Príncipe – often referred to simply as São Tomé – comprises two separate islands. Uninhabited before Portuguese exploration in the fifteenth century, the islands were settled by both Africans and Europeans – most brought against their will. In time, a Creole people, known as the FORROS, emerged. Subsequent waves of involuntary migrants passed through the islands, including hundreds of thousands of African slaves on their way across the Atlantic to the markets in BRAZIL and Latin America. Originally a SUGAR-growing economy, São Tomé later produced a large share of the world's coffee and COCOA. It has never escaped the limitations of a plantation economy. Its size and a shortage of skilled workers force it to rely on imported goods and services. It achieved political independence in 1975 from PORTUGAL, its former colonial master. Its abundant natural beauty has begun to attract tourism. However, São Tomé remains heavily dependent on foreign aid and a single plantation crop, cocoa.

GEOGRAPHY AND ECOLOGY

São Tomé, the larger of the two islands, lies 290 km (180 mi) off the African coast, due west of Gabon. Príncipe is 260 km (160 mi) west of the coast of EQUATORIAL GUINEA and 150 km (95 mi) northeast of São Tomé. São Tomé and Príncipe are part of an archipelago of four islands. The other two, Annobón (or Pagalu) and Bioko (formerly known as Fernando Po) are part of Equatorial Guinea. Together they are known as the Guinea Islands and form part of a volcanic mountain chain that also includes MOUNT CAMEROON on the mainland.

Despite their size – São Tomé is 855 sq km (330 sq mi) and Príncipe just 109 sq km (42 sq mi) – the islands' steep and rugged terrain creates several microclimates, each suited to different economic activities. The islands receive abundant rainfall on their windward (southwestern) sides – interrupted by dry seasons from January to February, and May to September – but there are arid and semi-arid regions on the eastern and northern sides of both islands, where the islands' steep volcanic mountains create rain shadows. Tropical rainforests originally covered the islands; today they remain on the steeper slopes and the wetter sides of the islands, while the remainder of the land has been cleared for agriculture. The country's highest point, known as Pico de São Tomé, towers 2024 m (6639 ft) above the coastline; four other peaks on São Tomé exceed 1524 m (5000 ft). Príncipe's mountains do not reach such heights, but an early visitor described it as "a most beautiful romantic looking island," with its cliffs, ravines, and thick forest.

SUGAR AND SLAVES

Portuguese explorers probably first sighted the Guinea Islands in 1478. After several years of planning, in 1486 João de Paiva founded the first settlement on São Tomé, but the settlement failed shortly thereafter. Álvaro da Caminha, a Portuguese nobleman, was given control over the island in 1493. He quickly sent hundreds of settlers to his town on the bay of Ana de Chaves. The colonies' first inhabitants included a mixture of African slaves, Jewish children taken from their parents as part of Portugal's religious persecution, and Portuguese criminals. Caminha had a hand in creating the subsequent Creole population by enforcing marriage between slave women and male Portuguese convicts. Following Caminha's lead, other Portuguese aristocratic families acquired land on the islands.

During their first two centuries as Portuguese colonies, the islands specialized in the cultivation of SUGAR cane. During the very early sixteenth century, in fact, the islands were the leading source of sugar for the European market. The islands' plantation economy provided a model for European sugar-producing colonies in BRAZIL and the Caribbean. Together with timber exports and trade with the peoples along the Gulf of Guinea Coast, sugar production provided the colony with an early prosperity.

During the early sixteenth century vast sugar plantations covered São Tomé and Príncipe. The Portuguese brought thousands of African slaves to the island to carry out the backbreaking work of cultivating and harvesting the cane on the plantations, or *roças*. Known for their harsh and unhealthy living conditions, the roças were owned and run by Portuguese landowners; the workers, called *serviçais* or *tongas*, were slaves imported from the African mainland. A growing mixed population, known as *forros* or *filhos da terra*, mostly avoided the roça work that some of their ancestors had done and instead farmed small plots of land and worked as tradesmen.

Sãotoméan sugar, never as high in quality as that exported by Madeira, had difficulty competing with the expanding volume of sugar produced in the Americas. In addition, plant disease and soil exhaustion caused by primitive agricultural practices soon led to lower yields. From a height of 2800 tons of sugar exported in 1570, by 1600 São Tomé's production had dropped to 857 tons. At the same time a series of slave uprisings cost the roças a portion of their labor force when slaves and *Angolares*, supposedly survivors of a wrecked slave ship from ANGOLA, fled to the rainforest. By 1615 the Portuguese had abandoned more than three-quarters of the sugar plantations.

With the collapse of its sugar industry, São Tomé's economy went into a decline. By the late seventeenth century, however, the islands played an increasingly important role in supporting the TRANSATLANTIC SLAVE TRADE. In fact, the strategic position of the islands in this trade attracted the interest of the Dutch, who seized them for a few years in the 1740s before Portugal managed to reassert control. The islands supported the slave trade in a number of ways. Plantations on the two islands used slave labor to produce food and other supplies for the slave ships. Also, the islands served as a marketplace for slaves brought from the African coast in small vessels. In São Tomé and Príncipe these slaves were sold to traders who loaded them (along with food and supplies) onto larger oceangoing ships for transport to the Americas.

Between 1809 and 1815 about 33,000 slaves entered São Tomé, most of them bound for CUBA or Brazil (then a Portuguese colony). As an important way station between the mainland and the Brazilian slave markets, São Tomé also became a trading center for Brazilian tobacco that was destined for African markets. Because of this, and because of its historic dependence on plantation agriculture, many historians consider São Tomé's history more typical of the West Indies than of Africa.

COFFEE AND COCOA

The decline of the slave trade during the early nineteenth century forced São Tomé and Príncipe once again to shift their economic focus. Growing demand for African products, such as ivory and palm oil, allowed São Tomé, with its favorable location and infrastructure, to serve as a market for commodities other than slaves. Meanwhile, the islands' plantations began to cultivate cash crops that were in demand on European markets. Coffee, probably introduced into Príncipe in 1800, became a major cash crop by the 1830s. Cocoa, brought to Príncipe in 1822, was being produced in large amounts by the 1850s. Both industries benefited from a reduction in the export duties charged by Portugal and, more important, from the large tracts of land left fallow when the sugar plantations were abandoned. Unlike the earlier sugar boom, the coffee and cocoa boom – at least initially – benefited the forros, São Tomé's local Creole population, many of whom rushed to claim plots of land and farmed them successfully.

It was not long, however, before Portuguese landowners, aided by the Banco Nacional Ultramarino, moved in and foreclosed on many of the Creole small farmers. By the late nineteenth century the old roça system, first

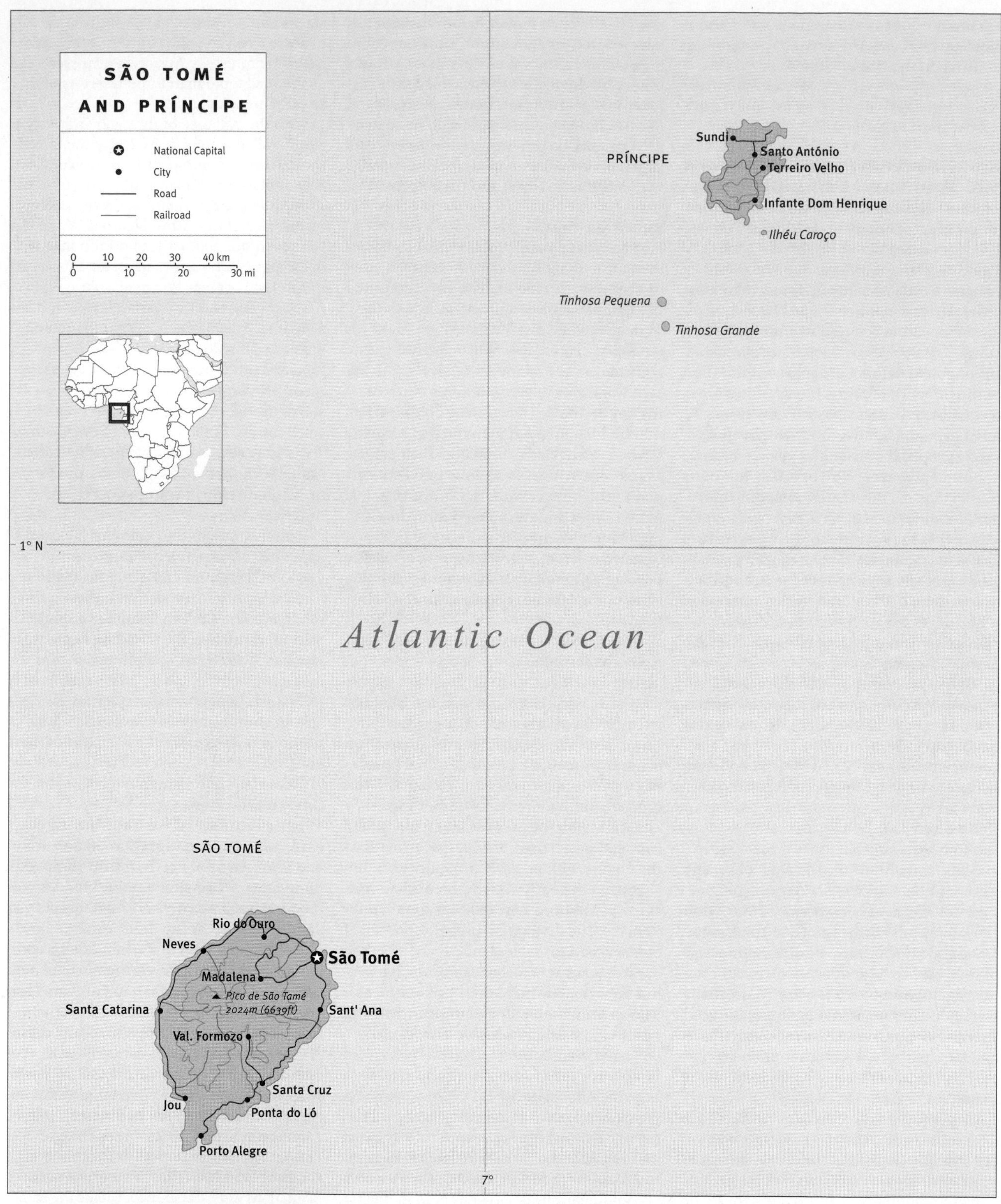

employed in the production of sugar, had been revived, this time to produce cocoa. But much had changed. Slavery, which had been made illegal in the Portuguese colonies in 1858, continued under another name. Plantation owners still effectively owned the roça workers, now called *libertos* (freedpeople). Cocoa production boomed, and during the first years of the twentieth century São Tomé and Príncipe were the world's leading producers of cocoa. While the islands continued to produce small amounts of coffee and other cash crops, cocoa came to dominate the islands' economy, as it does to this day.

However, press coverage of the importation of slaves from Angola and the bleak conditions of the liberto workers on the roças led to a boycott of São Tomé cocoa by the world's chocolate producers in 1909. Portugal responded by pledging to revamp its recruitment practices. Portugal replaced imported Angolan workers with Mozambican and especially Cape Verdean laborers. Despite new laws against conscripted labor, it is now clear that Africans were forced to work on the roças until at least World War I. The 1920s saw legislation designed to help workers limit their contracts with the roças and provided for their repatriation. During subsequent decades plantation owners' exploitation of their lands led to a gradual loss of soil fertility and a decline in cocoa yields.

Independence and Uncertainty

The cocoa plantation economy left a lasting imprint on Sãotoméan society, which to this day remains divided along caste and, to a lesser extent, racial lines. The white European planters who owned and ran the roça system depended on imported African labor. These African laborers, or serviçais, had an abysmally low quality of life, with almost no educational opportunities, no political representation, hard physical labor, and dangerous public health conditions. The Angolares escaped roça work and lived in small fishing villages on the southern coasts. The large Creole population, known as forros, occupied a middle position. A few forros went abroad, mostly to Portugal, and received a higher education; the majority stayed in São Tomé, where they worked as small farmers or tradesmen. Their culture – in particular, the *tchilolí*, a ritual theatrical dance, along with celebrations of Catholic feast days – has been adopted to some extent by other islanders and provides a basis for a national Sãotoméan identity.

It was the forros who initiated the first protests against the Portuguese since the slave uprisings of the seventeenth century. The forros resented coercive measures, including increased taxes and vagrancy laws, which the Portuguese introduced during the 1930s to force them into roça work. These concerns combined with frustration over the forros' lack of a voice in the islands' government at a time when nationalist movements were taking hold in Africa. In 1953 the tensions erupted. Following a series of demonstrations by the forros, the roça owners responded with small-scale vigilantism and mobilized armed gangs of serviçais to put down the protest. In doing so the plantation owners successfully marshaled the historic antipathy between forros and serviçais. About 1000 forros were killed in the resulting violence.

The event spurred Sãotoméan intellectuals in Portugal and elsewhere to organize a movement to end Portuguese colonial rule and the oppressive roça system. In 1960 a group of exiled Sãotoméan students formed the Comité de Libertação de São Tomé e Príncipe (CLSTP), which hoped to fight colonial rule by uniting the middle-class forros and the largely disfranchised serviçais. Among its founders was Manuel Pinto da Costa, who would become the independent country's first president. Taking the group's message to the world community, the CLSTP won international support, including support at the United Nations. But Portuguese repression, including a ban on nationalist literature, kept the budding independence movement from making inroads within São Tomé in the 1960s. Meanwhile, the CLSTP succumbed to internal rivalries and disbanded in the mid-1960s.

Palm trees line a beach on São Tomé and Príncipe. The islands' beauty has started to attract international tourism. © *Geopress/Explorer*

The organization that grew in the CLSTP's wake, the Movimento de Libertação de São Tomé e Príncipe (MLSTP) finally won the country's independence. Working with independence armies in Mozambique and Guinea-Bissau, the MLSTP forced the Portuguese into a series of concessions, including the right to local self-rule (although they remained subject to colonial authority) in 1974. Pushing for more, the MLSTP – still mostly in exile – inspired local groups to stage massive demonstrations and armed raids against the government. Later that year, at talks in Algiers, the Portuguese agreed to grant full independence to São Tomé and Príncipe in July 1975.

At independence the new government of President Pinto da Costa wrote a constitution establishing São Tomé as a single-party state, led by the Marxist-influenced MLSTP. The party, which demanded of its members a year's training before they could be named "militants" or full members, exerted increasingly centralized control over the country's political and economic life. Immediately after independence, the government nationalized the cocoa plantations that still formed the basis of the country's economy. This put more than 80 percent of the available cropland under central government control.

São Tomé initially cultivated close ties with eastern European communist countries and Cuba. Starting in the mid-1980s, however, economic instability and the need for foreign aid led São Tomé to seek closer ties with the West. In 1987 the country accepted a structural adjustment plan sponsored by the International Monetary Fund and the World Bank. A combination of currency devaluation and government budget cuts led to worsening economic conditions initially, and the populace reacted with a series of riots protesting high food costs. Politically, however, the government moved to promote democracy: a new constitution in 1990 allowed for a multiparty system.

Elections in 1991 removed President Pinta da Costa from office. Miguel Trovoada, like Pinto da Costa a prominent forro, assumed the presidency. Cocoa production continues to be São Tomé's principal economic activity, though state ownership has failed to increase yields. Many believe that tourism will soon become a major income source as well. The country boasts a relatively high literacy rate. However, it continues to depend heavily on foreign aid, and its citizens remain poor. The islands have yet to find a way to move beyond the limits of their plantation economy.

Kate Tuttle

See Also

Algiers, Algeria; Cape Verde; Explorers in Africa Before 1500; Ivory Trade; Mozambique; Creoles; Nationalism in Africa; Transatlantic Slave Trade; Structural Adjustment in Africa; Tourism in Africa.

Africa

São Tomé and Príncipe (Ready Reference)

Official Name: Democratic Republic of São Tomé and Príncipe
Area: 960 sq km (371 sq mi)
Location: In the Gulf of Guinea, along the equator off the western coast of Central Africa
Capital: São Tomé (population 35,000 [1984 estimate])
Other Major Cities: Santo Antonio (population 1000; [1984 estimate])
Population: 150,128 (1998 estimate)
Population Density: 154 persons per sq km (about 399 persons per sq mi)
Population Below Age 15: 48 percent (male 36,127; female: 35,253 [1998 estimate])
Population Growth Rate: 3.1 percent (1998 estimate)
Total Fertility Rate: 6.19 children born per woman (1998 estimate)
Life Expectancy at Birth: Total population: 64.34 years (male 62.87 years; female 65.86 years [1998 estimate])
Infant Mortality Rate: 54.55 deaths per 1000 live births (1998 estimate)
Literacy Rate (age 15 and over who can read and write): Total population: 73 percent (male 85 percent; female 62 percent [1991 estimate])
Education: No information available
Languages: Portuguese is the official language, but most people speak Crioulo, a language combining Portuguese and African elements.
Ethnic Groups: Because it was uninhabited before European colonization in the fifteenth century, much of São Tomé's population consists of the racially mixed descendants of Portuguese settlers and African slaves. Such *mestiços* are also known as *forros*, or *filhos da terra* (children of the earth). In addition, the islands are inhabited by *serviçais* (contract laborers, mostly from the CAPE VERDE Islands, ANGOLA, and MOZAMBIQUE), *tongas* (descendants of earlier generations of serviçais), *Angolares* (who take their name from shipwrecked Angolan slaves, though the name now refers to all people of African descent whose livelihood depends not on the plantation economy but on fishing), and Europeans (mostly Portuguese).
Religions: Roman Catholic (about 80 percent), Evangelical Protestant, Seventh-day Adventist
Climate: Both of the islands that comprise São Tomé and Príncipe share a hot, humid, tropical climate. Temperatures range from an average of 25° C (77° F) in the lower, coastal areas to 18° C (65° F) in the higher elevations. Although there is virtually no seasonal variation in temperature, there is a rainy season from October to May. In addition, rainfall varies greatly, from 5100 mm (about 200 in) in the southwestern mountains to 1020 mm (about 40 in) in the lowlands to the northeast.
Land, Plants, and Animals: São Tomé, the larger of the two islands that make up the Democratic Republic of São Tomé and Príncipe, is home to the country's highest mountain, Pico de São Tomé, with an elevation of 2024 m (6640 ft). Both islands are volcanic in origin, with rugged, mountainous interiors. Coastal areas, particularly on the southwestern and northeastern sides, are fertile lowlands. The interior mountains are forested. The islands have few native species of mammals but are home to a great variety of birds.
Natural Resources: São Tomé's most important natural resource is its rich soil, which is the basis for its plantation economy.
Currency: The dobra
Gross Domestic Product (GDP): $154 million (1996 estimate)
GDP per Capita: $1000 (1996 estimate)
GDP Real Growth Rate: 1.5 percent (1996 estimate)
Primary Economic Activities: São Tomé's economy is almost completely dependent on its production and export of cocoa, responsible for about 60 percent of export earnings. Other crops raised include coffee, copra, oil palms, coconuts, bananas, and papayas. A small fishing industry also exists. In recent years the country has attempted to build a tourist industry capitalizing on its great natural beauty.
Primary Crops: Cocoa, coffee, palm kernels, copra, coconuts, bananas, and papayas
Industries: Food processing
Primary Exports: Cocoa, coffee, copra, and palm oil
Primary Imports: Because of its island location and agricultural specialization, São Tomé imports about 90 percent of its food and nearly all of its consumer goods.
Primary Trade Partners: Portugal, France, Netherlands, and Germany
Government: São Tomé and Príncipe has been a parliamentary republic since 1990. The country consists of two administrative districts: São Tomé and Príncipe. As of 1999, it was governed by President Miguel Trovoada and Prime Minister Raul Bragança Neto. Voters elect a unicameral National Assembly consisting of 55 legislators, which chooses the prime minister and cabinet and appoints justices to the Supreme Court. The dominant party from independence in 1975 into the late 1990s was the Movement for the Liberation of São Tomé and Príncipe (MLSTP); other parties include the Party for Democratic Reconvergence-Reflection Group (PCD-GR) and Independent Democratic Action (ADI). São Tomé has universal suffrage for those aged 18 and over.

Robert Fay

Africa

Sara (also known as Kaba, Ngambai, and Sar), ethnic group of CHAD.

The Sara primarily inhabit southern Chad. Others live in the northern CENTRAL AFRICAN REPUBLIC. They speak a Nilo-Saharan language. More than 1 million people consider themselves Sara.

SEE ALSO
Languages, African: An Overview.

Africa

Saro-Wiwa, Kenule Beeson

(b. October 10, 1941, Bori, Rivers State, Nigeria; d. November 10, 1995, Port Harcourt, Nigeria), writer and Ogoni political activist whose campaign against Shell Oil led to his execution by the military government of NIGERIA.

Kenule Beeson Saro-Wiwa grew up in a large, polygamous Anglican household. A good student, he won a scholarship to study English at Government College in Umauhia. He finished his studies at Ibadan University in 1965, and then worked as a teaching assistant at the University of Nigeria at Nsukka and lectured at Lagos University. Cultivating a taste for pipe smoking and fine Scotch, he soon assumed his place among the Nigerian elite, which had assumed power after the British pulled out of Nigeria in 1960.

During the Biafran Civil War (1967-1970) Saro-Wiwa expressed strong support of the federal government while serving first as administrator of Bonny and then as a cabinet member in the newly created Rivers State. But political differences with associates caused him to leave the public sector in 1973. Thereafter he devoted himself to his writing career, dabbling in numerous genres and producing many books. By the end of his life he had written four novels, two books of short stories, three books of essays, two volumes of drama, one volume of folklore, and nine children's books. His most famous novel, *Sozaboy: A Novel in Rotten English*, lampooned corruption and power mongering in the military government of Nigeria. Saro-Wiwa also wrote for Nigeria's favorite soap opera and contributed columns to Nigerian as well as English newspapers.

Saro-Wiwa reentered politics in 1987 when President Ibrahim Babangida appointed him to assist in the proclaimed transition from military to civilian rule. Saro-Wiwa quit within the year, however, convinced that Babangida's efforts were insincere. Thereafter Saro-Wiwa turned his political energies to human rights and environmental issues in Ogoniland.

The Royal Dutch Shell Company, known as Shell Oil, had been extracting oil from the fertile, swampy lowlands of the Ogoni's

The Nigerian writer Ken Saro-Wiwa publicized the plight of the Ogoni people, whose land had been seized and polluted by multinational oil companies. His activism on behalf of environmental and human rights led to conflict with the Nigerian government of Sani Abacha, which had Saro-Wiwa executed in 1995. *Reuters/Archive Photos*

1036 sq km (400 sq mi) homeland in southeastern Nigeria since 1958. The company offered few benefits to local communities, and its sloppy practices contaminated the water and land, reducing fish and crop yields. In 1990 a group of Ogoni traditional leaders formed the Movement for the Survival of the Ogoni People (*see* ENVIRONMENTAL MOVEMENTS IN AFRICA). Listing among their primary goals not only better environmental protection but also Ogoni statehood, the group appointed Saro-Wiwa as spokesman.

Saro-Wiwa joined the movement convinced that success depended on both high-profile protest actions and international support. To the disapproval of the more conservative Ogoni leadership, he supported the sabotage of Shell Oil facilities, carried out by the movement's younger members. Hoping to win the favor of environmentalists in England and the United States, Saro-Wiwa filmed the degradation of Ogoniland and distributed the footage abroad. His efforts caught the attention of environmental groups such as Greenpeace as well as the international media, which further publicized Shell Oil's activities. In 1992 Saro-Wiwa traveled to Geneva, where he addressed the United Nations (UN) Working Group on Indigenous Populations; later that year he spoke before a committee of delegates at the UN in New York.

Meanwhile, Shell Oil ordered the military government of Gen. SANI ABACHA to "protect" its operations. Government officials, who profited financially from the company's presence, complied readily by sending troops to Ogoniland. These police efforts were extraordinarily harsh, however, involving the massacre of villages and murder of innocent Ogoni. Shell Oil withdrew from the area in 1993, but the conflict persisted as the federal government maintained operation of the lucrative wells.

On May 21, 1994, Saro-Wiwa was arrested along with 14 colleagues, allegedly for involvement in the murder of four progovernment Ogoni chiefs. In 1995 the imprisoned Saro-Wiwa won a Goldman Environmental Prize, a prestigious award given annually to one environmental activist on each continent. Despite such publicity and lobbying efforts by numerous foreign parties, however, Saro-Wiwa was hanged on November 10, 1995.

Many Ogoni devotees and foreign activists consider Saro-Wiwa a martyr. Some observers, however, noting his political ambitions and his followers' violent vigilantism, have questioned the purity of his motives. Nonetheless, his imprisonment and execution reflected the injustice and intransigence of the Nigerian military dictatorship.

Eric Bennett

SEE ALSO

Babangida, Ibrahim Gbadamosi.

Africa

Sasala (also known as Isala, Pisala, and Sissala), ethnic group of West Africa.

The Sasala primarily inhabit the Upper West Province of northwestern GHANA and neighboring southern BURKINA FASO. They speak a Niger-Congo language and belong to the GRUSI cultural and linguistic group. Approximately 100,000 people consider themselves Sasala.

SEE ALSO

Languages, African: An Overview.

Africa

Sassou-Nguesso, Denis (b. 1943, Edou, Moyen-Congo [present-day REPUBLIC OF THE CONGO]), an army general who served as president of the Congo (1979-1992, 1997-).

Denis Sassou-Nguesso, a MBOCHI from the north of the Republic of the Congo, began his political career as a soldier. After school he joined the military and trained in FRANCE. In 1963 he returned to the Republic of the Congo to assume command of the airborne infantry, and later took charge of the important Brazzaville military zone. When the northern military officer MARIEN NGOUABI came to power in 1968, Sassou-Nguesso became a member of the central committee of the ruling party, the Congolese Workers

Party (PCT), and later the minister of defense. Although the accusation has never been proven, Sassou-Nguesso was suspected of helping plot Ngouabi's 1977 assassination. Following the assassination Sassou-Nguesso became vice president of the new PCT military committee.

Two years later Sassou-Nguesso organized the bloodless overthrow of President Yhombi-Opango, and the PCT elected him as the country's next leader. During the oil boom of the early 1980s Sassou-Nguesso's government dramatically increased spending on public-sector employment and development projects; both were gestures that helped weaken opposition groups. Sassou-Nguesso targeted his hometown for military recruitment, and brought loyal friends and Mbochi kin into the government. While espousing Marxist-Leninism, Sassou-Nguesso lavishly entertained Western dignitaries and was known to wear a bulletproof vest under his expensive designer suits. When revenues from oil began to dry up in the mid-1980s, he tried to cut the bloated state bureaucracy, but ran into stiff opposition. Economic decline and widespread protests eventually forced Sassou-Nguesso to make democratic reforms. In national elections in 1992 he placed a distant third.

In 1997 Sassou-Nguesso reappeared on the national political scene along with his private militia, the Cobras, and was quickly suspected of planning to disrupt the upcoming presidential elections. Government troops' attempts to arrest Cobra members led to a five-month civil war. The war ended when Sassou-Nguesso took the capital of Brazzaville with considerable help from Angolan troops and reclaimed the presidency. He has since promised national reconciliation, a return to civilian rule in two years, and a professional military.

Eric Young

See Also
Angola.

North America

Savage, Augusta Christine Fells

(b. February 29, 1892, Green Cove Springs, Fla.; d. March 26, 1962, Saugerties, N.Y.), African American sculptor and arts educator who specialized in portrait sculptures of African American leaders.

The 7th of 14 children, Augusta Savage began to mold human figures out of clay at age six. She commenced professional art training after moving to New York City in 1921. Though Savage had briefly studied to be a teacher at the Tallahassee State Normal School (now Florida A&M), she enrolled at Cooper Union to study sculpture.

During the same period Savage received a commission to sculpt a bust of W. E. B. Du Bois. Following the success of this work, she sculpted likenesses of other African American heroes and leaders, including Frederick Douglass and Marcus Garvey.

Savage continued to create and exhibit portrait sculptures for the next two decades. Many depicted African or African American themes. In 1929 she traveled to Paris to work and study. Returning to America in 1932, she opened the Savage School of Arts and Crafts in Harlem, where she taught art classes and where her students included Jacob Lawrence and Norman Lewis.

In the 1930s Savage organized black artists to benefit from the New Deal's Works Progress Administration commissions. She opened New York's first gallery devoted to African American art, the short-lived Salon of Contemporary Art, in 1939. Savage also contributed a grand public sculpture, *Lift Every Voice and Sing*, to that year's World's Fair. The plaster sculpture was ultimately demolished when she could not raise the necessary funds to cast it in bronze.

Savage retired to Saugerties, New York, in the mid-1940s and died there in 1962.

See Also
Du Bois, William Edward Burghardt (W. E. B.); Garvey, Marcus Mosiah; Harlem, New York; New York, New York;Lawrence, Jacob Armstead; New Deal; Art, African American.

Africa

Savimbi, Jonas Malheiro

(b. August 3, 1934, Munhango, Angola), Angolan nationalist politician and leader of the insurgent group National Union for the Total Independence of Angola (UNITA).

Jonas Savimbi, often denounced as "Africa's enemy number one" and a stooge of the West, is a controversial figure. The son of a railway worker, Savimbi attended Protestant mission schools until he won a scholarship to study in Portugal. Already involved in Angolan nationalist politics, Savimbi was detained by Portuguese police three times before he fled to Switzerland, where, in 1965, he graduated from Lausanne University with honors in political and juridical sciences (although he would often refer to himself as a doctor). While a university student Savimbi contacted the Popular Movement for the Liberation of Angola (MPLA), but ultimately decided to join the nationalist Union of Angolan People (UPA), in 1961. As secretary general of the UPA, Savimbi worked to gain recognition for the movement and to unite the movement with others, ultimately helping to form the National Front for the Liberation of Angola (FNLA).

Savimbi, from the Ovimbundu ethnic group, soon became disenchanted with the FNLA's Kongo-dominated leadership and exclusively politico-military strategy. He broke from the party in 1964 to form UNITA two years later. With its base in the south among the Ovimbundu people and with military assistance from China, UNITA joined the war for independence, launching assaults while also fighting other nationalist groups. Employing Maoist strategies, Savimbi's movement attacked economic targets and sought to politicize the peasantry. After a coup d'état in Portugal in 1974 made Angolan independence inevitable, UNITA struggled to prevail over the other nationalist movements. Despite South African assistance UNITA failed to gain ascendancy, and the MPLA became the dominant political and military force in Angola.

In 1976 Savimbi returned to his base at Huambo, in southern Angola, to fight an insurgency war against the MPLA government that would last more than two decades. In public Savimbi espoused an ideology that vaguely resembled Négritude, and he claimed to be fighting for a political system in which local ethnic identities and customs would be respected. But it has been through charisma and force that Savimbi has maintained control of UNITA, and his conservative ideology is probably a product of his sources of international military support. Throughout the 1980s South Africa, the United States, and western European countries supported Savimbi against the Soviet- and Cuban-backed MPLA government, and it was not until the end of the cold war that the two sides ended the civil war. After a peace accord in 1992, UNITA and the MPLA contested elections in 1994. When it appeared that Angolan president José Eduardo dos Santos would win, Savimbi restarted the war. Two years later Savimbi took his place at the negotiating table, but peace in Angola remains tentative, sustained only through sanctions on UNITA and an international peacekeeping contingent.

Eric Young

See Also
Angola; Nationalism in Africa; South Africa; Popular Movement for the Liberation of Angola.

North America

Savoy Ballroom, **"Home of the Happy Feet," the most famous dance hall in Harlem, New York; birthplace of the dance style called the Lindy hop.**

Inspired by the success of the segregated Roseland and Arcadia Ballrooms downtown on Broadway, white businessmen Moe Gale and Jay Faggen opened a dance hall for African Americans on Lenox Avenue in Harlem. The two white entrepreneurs bought an entire block of property and oversaw the construction of the palatial ballroom, which boasted marble staircases, thick carpets, two bandstands, a soda fountain, and room for 7000 patrons. Gale and Faggen hired Charles Buchanan, an African American, to manage the Savoy, which he did for the ballroom's

30 years of operation. Opening on Friday, March 12, 1926, to the music of Fletcher Henderson's Orchestra, the venture achieved instant success. The Savoy was the first elegant and spacious ballroom in a neighborhood of cramped and poorly ventilated clubs.

During the 1920s and 1930s the Savoy attracted crowds of Harlem residents – as well as white celebrities – to hear the biggest names in big-band music, including Duke Ellington and Louis Armstrong. Bennie Moten's band introduced Kansas City swing to New York at the Savoy in 1932, and the dance hall featured Chick Webb's Orchestra, backing ELLA FITZGERALD, from 1932 to 1939. The Savoy also showcased its own house bands, like Fess Williams and his Royal Flush Orchestra, the Charleston Bearcats, and Al Cooper's Savoy Sultans. Arranger and saxophonist Edgar Sampson composed "Stompin' at the Savoy," in 1934, which became the ballroom's anthem.

White as well as black dancers at the Savoy pioneered the Lindy hop, a fast and free style of swing dancing that broke from conventions of popular dance. Since the crowd at the Savoy placed an unspoken premium on innovative dancing, every dancer tried something new. Each generation of Lindy hoppers kept hopping upward, and airborne movements in the 1930s superseded the "floor steps" of the 1920s.

While the harmonious integration of the Savoy was one of its exceptional qualities – black and white bands played, black and white dancers danced – the mingling also caused trouble. Provoked by the written testimony of a white police officer who claimed he had contracted syphilis from an African American prostitute, city officials harassed the Savoy's management and revoked its operating license in April 1943. The ballroom was closed until the following October, a suspension that reflected the heightened racial tension of Harlem during World War II.

After its reopening, the ballroom flourished once more, but when rock 'n' roll displaced big-band jazz as America's favorite music, the management found it difficult to book bands. The ballroom closed in 1958 and was demolished to make room for a housing project.

In its 32 years of operation, the Savoy Ballroom featured more than 250 bands and many of the biggest names in JAZZ. During those years the mixed audiences of working-class blacks and white celebrities danced together, peacefully if acrobatically.

Eric Bennett

SEE ALSO

World War II and African Americans; Armstrong, Louis ("Satchmo"); Moten, Benjamin (Bennie); Henderson, Fletcher Hamilton, Jr.; Ellington, Edward Kennedy ("Duke"); Dance in the United States.

Europe

Schoelcher, Victor

(b. July 21, 1804, Paris, France; d. December 26, 1893, Houilles, France), famous French abolitionist who played a crucial role in the definitive abolition of slavery in the French colonies in 1848 and fought tirelessly for the rights of slaves and former slaves throughout his long public career.

Victor Schoelcher was born into a wealthy bourgeois Parisian family, allowing him to undertake many voyages on which he observed firsthand the terrors of slavery, facilitating his decision to pursue political office.

Schoelcher affirmed his liberal political leanings in the period of the restoration of the French monarchy (1815-1830), and his ideological awakening occurred during a voyage he made in 1829 to MEXICO, the United States, and CUBA, when he was exposed to the harsh reality of slavery. He returned from this trip a fervent abolitionist and joined the Society for the Abolition of Slavery in Paris. In 1833 Schoelcher published his first important work: *De l'esclavage des noirs et de la législation coloniale* (On the Enslavement of Blacks and Colonial Legislation).

Abolitionist activism in FRANCE increased markedly during the liberal July Monarchy (1830-1848). The example of Britain, which outlawed slavery in 1834, strengthened the cause of French abolitionists. During this period Schoelcher traveled widely and published influential polemics calling for the immediate suppression of slavery, in opposition to more moderate reformers who argued for the institution's gradual disappearance in order to avoid upsetting colonialist economic productivity. In 1839 Schoelcher visited the French and Danish Antilles, including HAITI, GUADELOUPE, and MARTINIQUE, and after this he published what was perhaps his most influential work: *Des colonies françaises: Abolition immédiate de l'esclavage* (1842, On the French Colonies: Immediate Abolition of Slavery). In 1845 Schoelcher traveled throughout the Middle East, observing slavery as it existed in this region. In 1847 he went to SENEGAL to witness the capture of African slaves (*see* TRANSATLANTIC SLAVE TRADE).

In 1848, as undersecretary for the navy, Schoelcher prepared the decree that abolished slavery in France's colonies. That same year the French republican revolutionary government of February 1848 named him undersecretary of state and president of the commission for the abolition of slavery. He remained highly active within the radical left until Napoleon III's coup d'état of December 2, 1851, after which Schoelcher was sent into exile along with other outspoken opponents of the Second Empire (1851-1870) such as Victor Hugo. From Belgium and later England, Schoelcher continued to attack Louis Napoleon's government. With the formation of the Third Republic in 1870 Schoelcher returned to France, where he was elected representative of Martinique and Guiana in the French National Assembly. In 1875 he was named senator for life. During this period Schoelcher fought for obligatory schooling and, as a publicly committed atheist, for the separation of church and state in France. In 1889 Schoelcher published *Vie de Toussaint-Louverture* (Life of Toussaint L'Ouverture), in which he argues for the contradictory status of Toussaint L'Ouverture as both liberator and tyrant of the Haitian people.

From 1848 until well into the twentieth century Schoelcher remained the emblematic figure of liberal thought and practice in the French Antillean colonies. Only after World War II did Antilleans search for defenders of Antillean autonomy from their own history, such as LOUIS DELGRÈS and JEAN IGNACE. The French government placed Schoelcher's ashes in the Pantheon in 1949, recognizing and affirming his historical preeminence in the struggle to put into practice and generalize the revolutionary ideals of liberty, equality, and fraternity.

Nick Nesbitt

SEE ALSO

France; French Guiana; Slavery in Latin America and the Caribbean; Toussaint L'Ouverture, François Dominique; Abolition and Emancipation in Latin America and the Caribbean.

North America

Schomburg, Arthur Alfonso

(b. January 24, 1874, San Juan, Puerto Rico; d. June 10, 1938, New York, N.Y.), Afro-Puerto Rican bibliophile and librarian who collected the literature and art of the African diaspora.

The son of a German father and a West Indian mother, Arthur Schomburg spent his childhood in PUERTO RICO. After briefly attending St. Thomas College in the Virgin Islands, he came to the United States in 1891 and began working in a New York City law office. In New York Schomburg began to collect literary works and visual art by and about people of African descent. In 1906 Schomburg began working in the mailroom at Bankers Trust Company, where he remained until 1929. He became an active Prince Hall Mason, serving as grand secretary of the Grand Lodge from 1918 to 1926.

In 1911 Schomburg and John E. Bruce founded the Negro Society for Historical Research as a base from which to publish articles on black history. In 1922 Schomburg was elected president of the AMERICAN NEGRO ACADEMY. Three years later his important essay "The Negro Digs Up His Past" appeared in Alain Locke's *The New Negro*. Schomburg and his collection of books, manuscripts, and artifacts was an invaluable resource and an inspiration to both historians and HARLEM RENAISSANCE artists. Through his collection of literature and art by people of African descent, Schomburg sought to disprove the pseudo-scientific racism of the day.

In 1926 the Carnegie Corporation purchased Schomburg's collection and donated it to the Negro Division of the New York Public Library, the 135th Street branch in Harlem. Schomburg was hired as curator in 1932, holding the position until his death in 1938. Two years later the library was named the Schomburg Collection of Negro Literature and History, and it has since been moved and renamed the Schomburg Center for Research in Black Culture. It is the largest, most important collection of African and African American cultural materials in the world.

SEE ALSO
Harlem, New York; Locke, Alain Leroy; New York, New York; Virgin Islands (United States and British).

North America

Schomburg Library, **the largest collection in the world of materials by and about people of African descent.**

In 1925 the New York Public Library opened a Negro Division at its 135th Street branch, off Lenox Avenue in Harlem. The following year the Carnegie Corporation purchased Arthur Schomburg's vast collection of African American books, manuscripts, and art, and donated it to the library. Schomburg, an Afro-Puerto Rican bibliophile who had amassed these works in an effort to prove the depth and richness of black history and culture, became the collection's curator in 1932, a post he held until his death in 1938. The collection has borne his name since 1940.

The collection grew rapidly, and today it houses more than 5 million items relating to the history and culture of the people of Africa and the African diaspora. In 1972 the New York Public Library transferred the collection from the neighborhood branch system to make it part of its research libraries. Now officially called the Schomburg Center for Research in Black Culture, the collection encompasses five divisions. The art and artifacts division collects objects from the seventeenth century to the present, including masks, weapons, statues, and rare items from such places as the Gold Coast of Africa (present-day GHANA). The general research and reference division possesses flyers, newspapers, magazine clippings, pamphlets, and monographs in English, French, Spanish, Portuguese, German, Russian, and all African languages, as well as indigenous languages such as Creole. The manuscripts, archives, and rare books division houses materials relating to history, literature, politics, and culture. The moving image and recorded sound division features the center's oral history and video documentation programs. The photographs and prints division holds the works of many famous photographers, including Gordon Parks Sr., Coreen Simpson, Aaron Siskind, James VanDerZee, and Carl Van Vechten.

Robert Fay

SEE ALSO
Languages, African: An Overview; Harlem, New York; VanDerZee, James Augustus; Schomburg, Arthur Alfonso; Parks, Gordon, Sr.

Africa

Schreiner, Olive **(b. 1855, Wittebergen, South Africa; d. 1920, South Africa), South African novelist and political activist most famous for her book *The Story of an African Farm* (1883). Schreiner was a pioneer in her treatment of women in fiction and made many perceptive observations on the political future of South Africa, particularly the situation of blacks under APARTHEID.**

Born Olive Emilie Albertina Schreiner in Wittebergen, South Africa (then Cape Colony), Schreiner had no formal education but was taught at home by her mother. She began writing two of her novels while supporting herself as a governess from 1874 to 1881, after which she went to England, hoping to study. *The Story of an African Farm* was published under the pseudonym Ralph Iron while Schreiner was in England. The story of a young girl growing up on a farm in the grasslands of southern Africa, trying to attain her independence in the face of a rigid, repressive society, the book met with immediate success. In England Schreiner came to be accepted in literary and political circles and became a supporter of women's rights. She was a friend of CECIL RHODES, a British statesman and major proponent for British rule in southern Africa, but parted company with him for political reasons. Schreiner caused controversy in relation to Rhodes's activities with her book *Trooper Halkett of Mashonaland* (1897), which criticized the way Rhodesia (which became ZIMBABWE in 1980) was colonized. She returned to South Africa in 1899 and worked on behalf of the Boers, a local, white AFRIKANER group that refused to live under British rule, during the Boer War (1899-1902). Schreiner also met and married a politician, Samuel Cronwright – he changed his name to Cronwright-Schreiner – and the two worked for a variety of political causes. In 1911 Schreiner wrote *Women and Labour,* a feminist novel criticizing the relations between men and women. Schreiner spent her last years in England, separated from her husband, but returned to South Africa in 1920 shortly before she died. Her other novels, both with feminist themes, are *From Man to Man* (1927) and *Undine* (1929). They were published posthumously.

North America

Schuyler, George S. **(b. 1895, Providence, R.I.; d. 1977, New York, N.Y.), African American journalist and novelist known for his conservative political views who was the first African American to be recognized primarily as a satirist.**

George S. Schuyler was raised in Syracuse, New York. He had what he considered an ideal childhood in which he grew up believing that the United States, even with its considerable racial problems, was the best place for African Americans to live. He dropped out of high school to enlist in the United States Army and spent seven years in the service. During World War I he saw action in FRANCE and attained the rank of first lieutenant.

After returning to the United States after the war, Schuyler worked in menial jobs and lived with hobos in New York's Bowery before becoming a staff writer for A. Philip Randolph's the *Messenger* in 1923. Soon after joining the paper, he had his own column, "Shafts and Darts: A Page of Calumny and Satire." Later he became the paper's managing editor. Under Schuyler, the publication was considered so inflammatory that Southern members of the U.S. House of Representatives investigated it.

Schuyler's satire focused on the obsession in the United States with race, a subject he addressed in *Black No More* (1931). In this novel African Americans are able to become white by means of a surgical process. After treatment they disappear from Harlem and appear as whites in other places. Americans initially believe the race problem is solved. However, the blacks who have received the treatment are discovered to be three shades lighter than the original whites, who then begin adding pigmentation to their skin to differentiate themselves from the new whites. The race problem begins anew.

Black No More was critically well received. However, critics soon began to pay more attention to African American protest novels, and *Black No More* was eventually forgotten. Adding to this problem was Schuyler's conservatism, which often put him in opposition to his more liberal colleagues and left him alienated from the mainstream African American intelligentsia.

Schuyler continued to publish columns and fiction. In addition to *Black No More,* he wrote *Slaves Today: A Story of Liberia* (1931), which exposed the slavelike conditions many laborers experienced in LIBERIA. A third novel, *Black Empire,* which Schuyler wrote under the pen name Samuel I. Brooks, was published posthumously in 1991 and is a compilation of a serial that was published in the *Pittsburgh Courier* from 1936 to 1937.

Schuyler's journalistic contributions were considerable. From 1927 to 1931 Schuyler contributed nine essays to H. L. Mencken's *American Mercury.* In addition to maintaining a 40-year association with the *Courier*, where he was a columnist and a special correspondent in Latin America, the West Indies, and West Africa, he contributed to several white-owned journals, the *Nation*, *Plain Talk*, and *Common Ground* among them.

Schuyler also published nonfiction, including *Racial Intermarriage in the United States* (1929) and his autobiography, *Black and Conservative: The Autobiography of George S. Schuyler*, which was published in 1966.

Schuyler was married to Josephine Cogdell, a white artist who, like Schuyler, believed that the children of interracial marriages would be genetically superior by virtue of "hybrid vigor" and would thus end racial problems in the United States. The couple had one daughter, Phillipa Duke Schuyler, who became a concert pianist.

Robert Fay

See Also
World War I and African Americans; New York, New York; Harlem, New York; *Messenger, The*; *Pittsburgh Courier*; Randolph, Asa Philip.

North America

Schuyler, Phillipa Duke

(b. August 2, 1931, New York, N.Y.; d. May 9, 1967, Da Nang, Vietnam), African American concert pianist and writer; interracial daughter of author George Schuyler.

Phillipa Schuyler was the only child of the most celebrated interracial marriage of the Harlem Renaissance – that between African American author and journalist George Schuyler and white Texan artist and journalist Josephine Cogdell. As a consequence of Cogdell's family farming background, she and Schuyler applied to their daughter the agricultural theory that crossing different genetic strains produced superior offspring known as "hybrid vigor." The Schuylers were firmly convinced that racial disharmony in the United States could be rectified through creating interracial children, and they invested all of their hopes for this in their daughter.

Fulfilling her parents' unusual expectations, Phillipa Schuyler was in fact a child prodigy whose extraordinary talents were developed by tutors in isolation from her peers. With an IQ of 185, she could read and write at age two-and-a-half, and began playing the piano at age 3. At age 4 Schuyler was composing, and she performed at age 5 on the radio. By age 11 she was touring, with over 100 piano compositions to her credit by age 13. She scored "Manhattan Nocturne" for 100 instruments and performed it with the New York Philharmonic in 1944. At the New York World's Fair, New York Mayor Fiorello LaGuardia declared June 19, 1940, "Phillipa Duke Schuyler Day."

Despite their daughter's abilities, Schuyler's parents shunned the word "prodigy" and attributed Phillipa's talent to "hybrid genetics, proper nutrition, and intensive education." Her diet consisted exclusively of raw foods as a result of her mother's steadfast belief that cooking destroyed vitamin content. Raised on wheat germ, unpasteurized milk, cod liver oil, mother's milk, fruit, and daily doses of vitamin C, Schuyler also avoided alcohol, tobacco, and sugar – all forbidden in the Schuyler home – for her entire life.

While the country was awed by Schuyler's genius, her visibility and fame were greatly heightened by her father's media connections as well as his own regular coverage of her exemplary progress in the *Pittsburgh Courier*. Moreover, Cogdell's multiple roles as impresario, business manager, confidante, and best friend guided Schuyler well into adulthood.

For the better part of Schuyler's youth, her father was away on national and international assignments. A great admirer of her father, she inherited his conservative beliefs in educational advancement, self-help, and introspection. But despite her proximity to the black intelligentsia, "her precocity was fed on notions and conceits of the white milieu; and her passion for classical music would essentially reflect the same bias."

As a young adult, when white America lost interest in her, Schuyler encountered the race prejudice from which she had previously been shielded as a child curiosity and the daughter of well-to-do parents. Forced to play piano concerts overseas, she traveled to more than 80 countries, giving command performances for Ethiopia's Emperor Haile Selassie I, Queen Elizabeth of Belgium, and many other international leaders. In spite of her worldwide fame, she was never invited to perform in the United States for comparable leaders.

Spending more than half of the last ten years of her life abroad, Schuyler sought an alternative home where she could find comfort and acceptance: "I had 30 miserable years in the U.S.A. because of having the taint of being a 'strange curiosity' applied to me."

In the late 1950s Schuyler traveled with a visa from Rome and performed to white audiences in apartheid-era South Africa. Shortly after, she briefly toured in Europe as Felipa Monterro, a gifted musician and writer who was no longer identifiable as the daughter of a Negro journalist. Between 1960 and 1969 she published five books about her life and travels, including one in collaboration with her mother.

In 1963, along with Leontyne Price and Lena Horne, Schuyler was honored at the Delta Sigma Theta "We Salute Women of Achievement" awards.

Just before her death Schuyler had begun a career as a news correspondent, publishing articles in several languages, including French and German. She died at age 35 in a helicopter crash during the Vietnam War while attempting to rescue Catholic schoolchildren from a war zone in Hue and bring them to the shelter of a school in Da Nang.

See Also
Pittsburgh Courier; Schuyler, George S.

Latin America and the Caribbean

Schwartz-Bart, Simone

(b. January 8, 1938, Charente-Maritime, France), Afro-Guadeloupean writer best known for her characterization of strong Caribbean women and incorporation of stylish Creole cadence into French.

Simone Schwartz-Bart's family returned to Guadeloupe when she was three. She spent her childhood on the island and then left to study in France, where she met and married writer André Schwartz-Bart. After traveling widely the couple settled in Guadeloupe.

Schwartz-Bart cowrote her first novel, *Un plat de porc aux bananes vertes* (1967), with her husband. It tells the story of an old Martinican woman who is spending her last days in an institution for the aged in Paris.

In 1972 Schwartz-Bart published *Pluie et vent sur Télumée Miracle* (translated as *The Bridge of Beyond*, 1982), a fictional narrative of an old woman recounting the events of her life in a remote, rural region of Guadeloupe. This novel, praised for its portrayal of the black Caribbean experience from a feminine perspective (it engages several generations of women in the narrator's family) and for its masterful use of language, incorporates the rhythms and inflections of the Creole language into French.

Schwartz-Bart's third book, *Ti-Jean L'horizon* (1979; translated as *Between Two Worlds: A Novel*, 1981) follows young Ti-Jean, a popular hero of Creole folktales, from the Caribbean to Africa and back, in a mythical trip that tries to capture the different elements that have contributed to the formation of an Afro-Caribbean identity. This novel also deploys skillful narration and an adept use of language. In addition to her novels, Schwartz- Bart also published a play, *Ton beau capitain*, in 1987.

Despite wide praise for Schwartz-Bart's lyrical use of Creole and for her portrayal of Afro-Caribbean identity, some critics have attacked the author for what they say is an excessive use of exoticism.

Victor Figueroa

See Also
Martinique; Literature, French Language, in Caribbean; Languages, Creole, in the Caribbean.

Latin America and the Caribbean

Science, Chico

(Francisco de Assis França) (b. 1967, Recife, Pernambuco, Brazil; d. February 2, 1997, Olinda, Pernambuco, Brazil), the leader, vocalist, and composer of Chico Science e Nação Zumbi, an innovative multiracial band from Recife that mixes funky bass lines, heavy-metal guitars, acid jazz ambiance,

and northeast Brazilian rhythms such as the *maracatú* and the *embolada;* the group's name, Zumbi Nation, refers to the leader of a seventeenth-century settlement called Palmares, the largest and longest-lasting community of fugitive slaves in Brazilian history.

Chico Science e Nação Zumbi's 1994 debut album, *Da lama ao caos* (From Mud to Chaos), launched *mangue* beat, a musical movement that includes other bands from Recife like Mundo Livre S/A and Mestre Ambrósio. The debut album included a manifesto that explains that the mangue (the muddy mangrove swamplands that form where rivers meet the ocean) is an ecosystem of enormous fertility and variety that had deteriorated into a site of abject poverty and misery in metropolitan Recife. According to the manifesto, it was necessary to "inject a little energy into the mud and stimulate the fertile potential of the veins of Recife." The symbol of the mangue beat movement was a parabolic antenna stuck in the mud – an image combining a local perspective of urban underdevelopment with global postmodern sensibilities. Chico Science's lyrics mix the poetics of traditional *cordel* literature of the Brazilian northeast (*see* LITERATURE, BLACK, IN BRAZIL) with images of urban-industrial society. The group's second album, *Afrociberdélia,* further develops this musical and poetic strategy with more sophisticated production values and extensive sampling of other Brazilian artists. The band has continued to perform despite Science's untimely death in a car accident.

Christopher Dunn

SEE ALSO
Palmares: An African State in Brazil.

SCLC. Please see SOUTHERN CHRISTIAN LEADERSHIP CONFERENCE

North America

Scott, Emmett J.

(b. February 13, 1873, Houston, Tex.; d. December 12, 1957, Washington, D.C.), secretary of Tuskegee Institute and co-founder of the National Negro Business League.

After working as a journalist for the *Houston Post,* in 1894 Emmett J. Scott founded and edited the weekly *Houston Freeman.* The views therein largely agreed with those of Booker T. Washington, who hired Scott as his personal secretary at the Tuskegee Institute. In 1912 Scott became Tuskegee's secretary; as part of the "Tuskegee Machine," he spread Washington's self-help and accommodationist political and social message, which he expounded on in *Tuskegee and Its People* (1910) and *Builder of a Civilization* (1916), a biography of Washington. Scott left Tuskegee after Washington's death in 1915 and was special assistant to the United States secretary of war during World War I. From 1919 to 1939 Scott held various positions at HOWARD UNIVERSITY. Active in WASHINGTON, D.C.'s business community, Scott became the chief organizer of the National Negro Business League.

Robert Fay

SEE ALSO
World War I and African Americans; Tuskegee University; Washington, Booker Taliaferro.

North America

Scott, Hazel

(b. June 11, 1920, Port of Spain, Trinidad; d. October 2, 1981, New York, N.Y.), Caribbean-American jazz musician and political activist; the first black woman to host her own television show.

Hazel Scott made her debut as a pianist in Trinidad at age three. By her eighth birthday she had performed in New York City and won a scholarship to the Juilliard School of Music. Scott became a star of radio and Broadway in the 1930s and appeared in several movies in the 1940s. Her marriage in 1945 to Harlem minister and congressman Adam Clayton Powell Jr. was one of the year's major social events; the two divorced in 1956.

In the late 1940s Scott became the first black woman to host her own television show. She lost this job in 1950 when she was accused of being a Communist sympathizer. She refused to perform in segregated theaters and became an outspoken critic of both McCarthyism and racial injustice. After living abroad for five years in the 1960s, she returned to the United States and to her television and nightclub career. Called a "musical chameleon" for her ability to shift from JAZZ to classical to blues, Scott continued to perform until her death.

Lawrie Balfour

SEE ALSO
Blues, The; Harlem, New York; New York, New York; Powell, Adam Clayton, Jr.; Television and African Americans; Communist Party USA, African Americans and the; Trinidad and Tobago.

North America

Scott, Robert

(b. 1947, Washington, D.C.), Democratic member of the United States House of Representatives from Virginia (1993-).

Robert Scott was born in WASHINGTON, D.C., and received a bachelor's degree from Harvard University in 1969. He served in the U.S. Army Reserves from 1970 to 1974, and in the National Guard from 1974 to 1976. He received a law degree from Boston College in 1973 and practiced law from 1973 to 1991. In 1977 Scott was elected to the Virginia House of Delegates, where he served until 1983. He held a seat in the state Senate for the next nine years, until his election in 1992 to the U.S. House from Virginia's Third Congressional District. He was reelected with more than 75 percent of the vote in 1994 and 1996.

Scott was the beneficiary of a Democratic-led redistricting in 1991 that set the boundaries of the Third District so as to include a majority of black voters. The district's largest employer is the Newport News Shipbuilding and Drydock Company, which employs up to 25,000 workers building aircraft carriers and submarines for the U.S. Navy. The district also includes much of the state capital of Richmond, making government employment another important part of the local economy.

In the 105th Congress (1997-1999) Scott sat on the Education and the Workforce Committee and the Judiciary Committee. He was also a member of the CONGRESSIONAL BLACK CAUCUS.

North America

Scottsboro Case

an international cause célèbre during the 1930s in which nine young black men were accused of raping two white women in Alabama.

The Scottsboro case began in 1931 when two white women falsely accused nine young African Americans of rape. Throughout the world of the 1930s the Scottsboro defendants came to symbolize the racism and injustice of the American South. In their initial trials the defendants received what critics described as a "legal lynching." But the assistance of the Communist Party of the United States of America (CPUSA) gave the young men a second chance, and the ensuing struggle became one of the great civil rights cases of the twentieth century.

After several retrials, worldwide protests, massive publicity, and two landmark rulings by the Supreme Court of the United States, only four of the men gained their freedom, after having spent six years in jail. Full vindication did not come until 1976, when Alabama governor George Wallace pardoned all nine "Scottsboro boys." At that time only one of the defendants, Clarence Norris, was still alive to hear the news.

On March 25, 1931, after several young white men complained that a "bunch of Negroes" had thrown them off a freight train, a posse in Paint Rock, Alabama, searched the train and arrested nine black males. The posse also discovered two white females wearing men's caps and overalls. Within an hour the young blacks and both women were taken to Scottsboro, the seat of Jackson County. The women were examined by two physicians, who found evidence of sexual activity, though probably not within the previous twelve hours, and no signs of rape. The young men – Norris, Olen Montgomery, Haywood Patterson, Ozie Powell, Willie Roberson, Charlie Weems, Eugene Williams, and Andrew and Leroy Wright – were jailed. At 20 years of age, Weems was the oldest; the youngest, Leroy Wright, was 13.

Although the women initially denied that any assault had taken place, under the pressure of a lynch mob that filled the streets that evening and after repeated goading by a local prosecutor, they conceded that they had been raped by the black youths. Although later investigation revealed that the women were "notorious prostitutes" with prior arrest records on a variety of charges, nothing could shake the Southern ethos that made them symbols of endangered "white Southern womanhood."

During their trials the nine men received inadequate legal counsel. They were given no witness preparation before entering the courtroom, and in none of the cases did their court-appointed attorneys make closing arguments to the jury. As was customary, each jury was composed only of white men. The trials were concluded in four days with eight guilty verdicts and eight sentences of death. In the case of Leroy Wright, the youngest defendant, the jury could not reach agreement. Jurors had no doubt as to his guilt, but 11 insisted on nothing less than death, although the state had asked only for life imprisonment. The judge reluctantly declared a mistrial.

Sentencing eight men to death on a single day for the same crime was "without parallel in the history of the nation," the Birmingham *Age-Herald* observed in concluding its trial coverage. But the Scottsboro case was far from over. Even as the trials were under way, the judge received a telegram from the International Labor Defense (ILD), a Communist-front legal organization, demanding a change of venue. The Communist Party decided to take up the young men's defense on the basis of reports from two party representatives, one black and one white, who had been sent to observe the trials. The party's enthusiastic involvement transformed what had essentially been a local matter into a cause of national importance.

In contrast, the National Association for the Advancement of Colored People (NAACP) remained aloof. Protective of its reputation, the NAACP was unwilling to aid a group of poor black hoboes unless it was certain of their innocence. Only after the case reached international proportions did the organization offer financial assistance to the ILD. Initially, NAACP representatives had warned the defendants that the Communists were only interested in them for propaganda purposes.

Communist organizing efforts made the Scottsboro case an international cause célèbre, as well as one of the decade's top news stories. The effectiveness of the party's response significantly increased its stature among Depression-era African Americans. Communist-sponsored protests took place in many Northern cities as well as in London, Moscow, and elsewhere around the world. These protests garnered invaluable publicity for CPUSA itself, but in the main its efforts drew attention to the plight of the defendants. In so doing, the party challenged the deeper symbolism of the Scottsboro case, particularly by confronting the virtual equation of "black man" and "rapist."

At the outset public understanding of the case had been tainted by white visions of black sexual depravity and by a presumption of the defendants' guilt. The party worked to humanize the image of the nine men, especially through rallies and marches that featured their mothers. It inspired sympathetic news stories about the defendants during their lengthy incarceration. As a result of this dogged publicity work, the Scottsboro case came to be seen as a great miscarriage of justice, and its defendants were increasingly regarded as innocent victims of Southern racism. At the same time the party refused to limit itself to symbolic action; it also mounted an aggressive legal defense.

The ILD provided experienced attorneys to aid in the young men's defense, the most important of whom was the distinguished lawyer Samuel Leibowitz. Over the next five years Leibowitz defended the Scottsboro Nine a total of five times. The ILD won the defendants retrials as a result of its successful appeal to the United States Supreme Court. The Court ruled, in *Powell* v. *Alabama* (1932), that defendants being tried for capital crimes must receive more than a perfunctory or pro forma defense. Following a change of venue, the trials opened in Decatur, Alabama, before Judge James E. Horton.

In Decatur, Ruby Bates renounced her previous testimony against the nine defendants. Indeed, during 1933 and 1934 she appeared at Communist-organized Scottsboro rallies, posed in photographs with the Scottsboro mothers, and joined 3000 protesters in a march to the White House seeking the defendants' release from prison. Nonetheless, the first jury, in the trial of Patterson, again returned a verdict of guilty. Convinced that Patterson and the other defendants were innocent, Judge Horton set the verdict aside and ordered new trials. As a result, however, Horton was defeated in the May 1934 primary election and replaced by a man far more friendly to the prosecution.

The ILD once more made a successful appeal to the Supreme Court, this time challenging the systematic exclusion of blacks from Alabama jury rolls. In *Norris* v. *Alabama* (1935), Chief Justice Charles Evans Hughes ruled that the exclusion of African Americans from jury service did in fact deprive black defendants of equal protection under the law, as guaranteed by the Fourteenth Amendment. In essence, the Court remanded the case back to the state for retrial. Thus the Scottsboro Nine returned to the courtroom yet again. By this point a vast amount of testimony had revealed much more than a reasonable doubt as to the young men's guilt.

In 1936, as part of the CPUSA's coalition-oriented Popular Front strategy, the ILD relinquished its primary role in the case to a broader group that included the NAACP, the Socialist Party's League for Industrial Democracy, the American Civil Liberties Union, and the Methodist Federation for Social Service. Although Leibowitz continued as the defendants' counsel, the state of Alabama used the seeming displacement of the Communists as a pretext for seeking a legal compromise.

In the final set of trials that began in 1937, the state dropped all charges against the four youngest defendants – Leroy Wright, Montgomery, Roberson, and Williams. The others were duly convicted, but rather than the death penalty they received sentences ranging from 20 years to life. Norris, Powell, Patterson, Weems, and Andrew Wright gained their freedom piecemeal between 1943 and 1950. All told, the nine men spent more than 100 years in the jails and penitentiaries of Alabama.

James Clyde Sellman

See Also

Fourteenth Amendment to the U.S. Constitution; Communist Party USA, African Americans and the.

Scottsboro Nine. Please see Scottsboro Case

Africa

Scramble for Africa, phrase often used to describe the European partition and conquest of Africa in the late nineteenth century.

The Scramble for Africa, a British term coined in 1884, describes the period of 20-odd years when European powers explored, partitioned, and conquered nearly 90 percent of the African continent. An observer at the time described it as "one of the most remarkable episodes in the history of the world."

Scholars disagree on the scramble's exact origins. Most date its beginning to the 1870s and its conclusion to 1902, with the British defeat of the Boers (now Afrikaners) in South Africa. Explanations for what provoked such rapid conquest fall into two broad categories. The "Eurocentric" explanation contends that European competition for new markets and investments drove imperialist expansion, while the "Afrocentric theory" focuses on the conflicts between African states and peoples. Others contend that it was a combination of the two.

The historical progression of the scramble is clearer. In the mid-1800s European pres-

COLONIALISM: THE EUROPEAN PARTITION OF AFRICA, 1902

In 1912 the European partition was completed by:
1. The Italian annexation of Tripoli (Libya)
2. The definitive partition of Morocco between France and Spain

ence on the continent was limited to coastal regions and a few interior areas in the south and east. In 1876, however, Belgium's King Leopold II announced his intent to explore the Republic of the Congo region, and in 1879 Leopold sent Henry Morton Stanley to the Republic of the Congo. In the same year the French began building a railway east from Dakar, hoping to tap potentially huge Sahelian markets. That year FRANCE also joined GREAT BRITAIN in taking financial control of EGYPT.

Tensions between the European powers seeking African spheres of influence increased. In response, Chancellor Otto von Bismarck of Germany convened the BERLIN CONFERENCE OF 1884-1885. The European participants at the conference recognized King Leopold as the legitimate authority in the Congo basin, but more important, it was decided that a European power could only claim an area of Africa that it "effectively occupied." The first phase of the scramble was largely a paper conquest, conducted in the drawing rooms of European capitals. On the continent, explorers and soldiers such as Henry Morton Stanley, Pierre de Brazza, Frederick Lugard, and CECIL RHODES acted as the agents of European power, conquering weak African chiefs and signing treaties with the powerful ones.

In the early 1890s treaty making gave way to conquest. Advances in military technology and medicine (especially the discovery of the antimalarial agent quinine) enabled Europeans to send troops into the heart of the continent, where the persistence of inter-African wars facilitated European conquest. Although European firepower crushed most African resistance movements, other offensives, such as those waged by the Boers, NDEBELE, and ZULU in southern Africa, the BAULE in CÔTE D'IVOIRE, and the Mahdi in SUDAN, fought off colonial armies for several years. In ETHIOPIA the Emperor MENILEK II defeated Italian colonization efforts altogether.

In half a generation France, GERMANY, Great Britain, ITALY, PORTUGAL, SPAIN, and King Leopold II of Belgium had acquired 30 new African colonies or protectorates, covering 16 million sq km (10 million sq mi). They had divided a population of approximately 110 million Africans into 40 new political units, with some 30 percent of the borders drawn as straight lines, cutting through villages, ethnic groups, and African kingdoms.

Eric Young

SEE ALSO

Congo, Democratic Republic of the; Afrikaner; Dakar, Senegal; Brazza, Pierre Savorgnan de; Explorers in Africa Since 1800; Leopold II; Lugard, Frederick John Dealtry; Mahdist State; Sahel; Stanley, Sir Henry Morton.

North America

Scurlock, Addison (b. June 19, 1883, Fayetteville, N.C.; d. 1964, Washington, D.C.), African American photographer known for his portraits of African American leaders and of Washington, D.C., luminaries.

The son of George Clay Scurlock, a WASHINGTON, D.C., lawyer who had moved his family from Fayetteville in 1900, Addison Scurlock began his career in photography as an assistant to Moses P. Rice in the same year. After four years of apprenticeship, Scurlock started his first studio at home, and in 1911 he opened the Scurlock Studio.

While employed as the official HOWARD UNIVERSITY photographer, Scurlock produced newsreels in Washington, in addition to a portrait series sponsored by Carter G. Woodson for United States schools. He died at age 81, after passing the management of his business on to his son.

SEE ALSO

Woodson, Carter Godwin; Photography, African American.

Europe

Seacole, Mary (b. 1805, Jamaica; d. 1881, England), nurse famous for her courage and honor in serving the British Army during the Crimean War.

Unlike her well-known contemporary, Florence Nightingale, Mary Seacole has been all but forgotten. In 1857, however, one *London Times* reporter noted, "Few names were more familiar to the public during the late [Crimean] war than that of Mrs. Seacole."

The daughter of a Scottish army officer and a free black woman in JAMAICA, Seacole was celebrated in GREAT BRITAIN for her work as a nurse in the Crimean War (1853-1856), during which Great Britain and FRANCE aided the Ottoman Empire against Russia. Seacole, who learned FOLK MEDICINE from her mother and became skilled at treating tropical diseases in PANAMA, Jamaica, and COLOMBIA, moved to London in 1854 to enlist in the war effort. Because of racial discrimination, her attempts to join the British army were frustrated. Determined, she made her own way to the Crimea and ran an institution called the British Hotel, which served as a combination of store, dispensary, and hospital for British officers. She also volunteered her services to various military hospitals and nursed the wounded and dying soldiers on the battlefield.

Seacole recounted her impressions of the war in her autobiography, *The Wonderful Adventures of Mary Seacole in Many Lands* (1857). Her descriptions of the soldiers' injuries and the war are criticized now for their flowery language and excessive sentimentality, but the book was popular at the time for its fervent expression of British patriotism and religiosity. Seacole was the second black woman to publish a book in Great Britain; MARY PRINCE had published her autobiography in 1831.

After the conclusion of the war the British demonstrated their appreciation of Seacole's service with a four-day benefit festival in her honor at the Royal Surrey Gardens, which was attended by more than 40,000 supporters. Until her death in 1881, she subsisted on the funds that were raised at this event; she left a substantial estate valued at £2615.

Leyla Keough

North America

Seale, Bobby (b. October 22, 1936, Dallas, Tex.), political and social activist of the 1960s; cofounder of the militant BLACK PANTHER PARTY.

Bobby Seale, the son of George and Thelma Seale, moved to California with his family at age ten. He entered the United States Air Force at age 18 and served as an aircraft-sheet mechanic. Three years later he was dishonorably discharged for insubordination and absence without leave. In 1961 he was admitted to Merritt College in Oakland, California.

While at Merritt, Seale became a member of the Afro-American Association in Oakland. Through this militant organization, Seale met and befriended fellow student Huey Newton. Together, Newton and Seale formed the Soul Students Advisory Committee at Merritt. In 1966 the two created the BLACK PANTHER PARTY, whose political platform called for equality of opportunity for African Americans and an end to police brutality against black people.

Seale was arrested in 1968 for his participation in anti-VIETNAM WAR demonstrations at the Democratic National Convention in Chicago, and spent two years in jail. He was arrested a second time in 1972 for the murder of suspected Black Panther informer Alex Rackley, but the charges against him were dropped. In 1973 he made an unsuccessful bid for the office of mayor of Oakland, and in 1974 he resigned as chairman of the Black Panther Party. In the 1980s Seale became involved in an organization called Youth Employment Strategies. He published two autobiographies, *Seize the Time: The Story of the Black Panther Party and Huey P. Newton* in 1970 and *A Lonely Rage* in 1978.

Aaron Myers

SEE ALSO

Chicago, Illinois; Newton, Huey P.; San Francisco and Oakland, California.

North America

Seattle, Washington, American city whose black population long endured mixed messages of racial tolerance in public and private life.

Very few blacks lived in Seattle during the city's first 80 years. African Americans did not arrive in Seattle until 1858, and in 1900 fewer than 400 African Americans lived there. Even by World War II, the population remained below 4000. As a result, Seattle whites often took unwarranted pride in their city's racial climate. In an era when other American cities faced massive immigration, racial tension, and ghettoization, Seattle seemed a stable and racially reconciled town.

Although African Americans in Seattle lived where they pleased, voted freely, and shared public transit with whites, they faced persistent economic discrimination. White people cornered blacks into unskilled labor and domestic servitude, often presuming that African Americans accepted such work because of inbred servility. In truth, the small size of the black community left it powerless to voice dissent, and this silence perpetuated the oppressive stereotypes of white employers.

World War II transformed Seattle. In 1942 the War Manpower Commission and the Civil Service Commission began recruiting African Americans from across the nation to work in the industries of the northwest coast. During the war the black population of Seattle grew from about 4000 to 16,000. Seattle's shipyards, the Boeing Aircraft Company, and numerous nonmilitary government jobs readily employed newcomers.

Unlike companies that faltered after the wartime boom, Boeing's success continued throughout the century. While Boeing's demand for labor remained high, however, mass immigration exceeded the company's needs, causing poverty, overcrowding, and residential segregation. Seattle's predominantly black Central District grew, schools began to reflect the segregated composition of neighborhoods, and whites elbowed blacks out of white neighborhoods. As a result, African Americans in Seattle embraced the Civil Rights Movement in the 1960s. Though violence never erupted from protests in Seattle as it did in other cities, minor skirmishes between activists and police disrupted many businesses in 1967 and 1968.

In the 1970s and 1980s Seattle's growing financial services and budding computer industry joined Boeing as major employers of blacks. The prospering economy and growing African American population helped to support black politicians. In 1989 Norman Rice was elected the city's first black mayor with significant support from Seattle whites. In the 1990s Seattle began to reflect the kind of tolerance and equality that had falsely characterized the first half of its history.

Eric Bennett

See Also
World War II and African Americans.

Africa

Sebei (also known as the Sabaot), ethnic group of Uganda.

The Sebei primarily inhabit the area near Mount Elgon in eastern Uganda. Others live in western Kenya. They speak a Nilo-Saharan language and are one of the Kalenjin peoples. Approximately 100,000 people consider themselves Sebei.

See Also
Languages, African: An Overview.

Africa

Segogela, Johannes (b. 1936, Sekhukhuneland, South Africa), South African sculptor who uses traditional woodcarving methods.

Johannes Segogela was born and educated in South Africa's northern Transvaal region. As a young man he worked as a boilermaker and sculpted small wooden figures in his spare time. In 1985 an exhibition of work by little-known contemporary South African artists was organized in Johannesburg, and Segogela's figures were included. The show, called *Tributaries*, helped launch the careers of several participants, among them Segogela.

Segogela's early pieces featured small figures or groups of figures carved from indigenous wood and decorated with bright enamel paint. Some depicted biblical themes, such as *Samson and the Lion* (1986), while others portrayed scenes from contemporary urban life. Because these works, which include many elements, are meant to be rearranged, they are never fixed to a base.

Segogela's more recent pieces are highly stylized and somewhat satirical. Biblical lessons remain a common theme, reflecting his interest in questions of good and evil. *Satan's Fresh Meat Market* (1993), for example, depicts Satan as a butcher surrounded by human body parts. Other sculptures represent current events in South Africa, such as *President Mandela Voting* (1994). Segogela continues to live and work in the Transvaal. In addition to being featured in exhibits in South Africa, his work has been shown in galleries and museums throughout Europe, as well as at the 1994 Havana Biennale in Cuba.

Christopher Tiné

See Also
Johannesburg, South Africa; Art and Architecture, African.

North America

Segregation in the United States, systematic separation of blacks and whites that circumscribed African American life in much of the country. The most thorough-going system of racial segregation and disfranchisement was that found in the South and known as Jim Crow.

Africa

Sekhukhune (b. 1814; d. 1882), chief of the Pedi people (1861-1879) and the last major African ruler to hold out against European power in the Transvaal, in northern South Africa.

On the death of his father Sekwati in 1861, Sekhukhune assumed command, although his succession was disputed by his half-brother Mampura. Alarmed by increasing European encroachment in his territory, Sekhukhune became deeply suspicious of the German Lutheran missionaries of the Berlin Missionary Society whom his father had allowed into the kingdom in 1861. He believed that by converting his subjects to Christianity, the missionaries were undermining his authority and conspiring against him with the local Afrikaners, or Boers. As a result, in 1866 Sekhukhune expelled the missionaries and prohibited Christianity. Aware that the Afrikaners would eventually invade his kingdom, he began stockpiling arms. In 1876 the president of the Transvaal Republic, Thomas François Burgers, attacked the Pedi in alliance with Mampura, but Sekhukhune successfully defended his kingdom. In 1877, however, the Transvaal was annexed by Sir Theophilus Shepstone to Great Britain, which in 1879 launched its own war against the Pedi. In an uneven struggle, with the Pedi facing two British regiments and 6000 Swazi under commander Sir Garnett Wolseley, about 1000 Pedi were killed and Sekhukhune was captured. He was held prisoner in Pretoria while Mampura was installed as chief in his place. In 1881, after the British returned the sovereignty of the Transvaal to the Afrikaners, Sekhukhune was allowed to return to his home. The following year he was assassinated by Mampura, whom the Afrikaners subsequently hanged. This effectively ended the independence of the Pedi.

See Also
Afrikaner; Christianity: Missionaries in Africa.

Latin America and the Caribbean

Selvon, Samuel (b. May 20, 1923, Trinidad; d. April 16, 1994, Trinidad), Trinidadian novelist, journalist, and dramatist.

Samuel Selvon is often compared to V. S. NAIPAUL; both writers were born in Trinidad and are considered canonical writers of the WEST INDIES. In addition, both spent much of their careers abroad, and both share the outsider's perspective of having grown up East Indians in predominantly black West Indian society (*see* EAST INDIAN COMMUNITIES IN THE CARIBBEAN). Despite being an outsider, Selvon strongly identified with his West Indian heritage, and his novels and plays focus on aspects of the West Indian struggle for self-improvement that cut across racial lines. His works often include black characters, and he has been especially praised for his skillful use of Caribbean folk tradition and dialect (*see* LANGUAGES, CREOLE, IN THE CARIBBEAN).

Selvon graduated from Trinidad's Naparima College in 1938 and began writing fiction while serving in the Royal Naval Reserve during World War II. After working as a fiction editor for the *Trinidad Guardian*, in 1950 Selvon emigrated to England, where his first novel, *A Brighter Sun*, was published in 1952. The story of a young Trinidadian Indian trying to establish his identity as he watches his country doing the same, *A Brighter Sun* immediately won Selvon recognition as part of a rising generation of West Indian writers. The book has been described as having "introduced the great period of Trinidadian novels which continues to this day."

Two years later Selvon won the first of two Guggenheim Fellowships. The prolific career that followed produced more than a dozen more novels, a collection of prose essays, and an anthology of plays that included dramatic works produced on British Broadcasting Corporation (BBC) radio (*see* THEATER IN THE CARIBBEAN). In 1978 Selvon moved from England to CANADA, and many of his later novels focus on the West Indian immigrant experience. Once again Selvon's work featured issues he shared with black West Indians, such as cultural alienation and color prejudice.

Selvon's other honors included a 1969 Hummingbird Medal from the Trinidad and Tobago government. In 1994 Selvon died of a heart attack during a visit home to Trinidad. He continues to be remembered as a leading figure in the West Indian literary tradition (*see* LITERATURE, ENGLISH LANGUAGE, CARIBBEAN).

Lisa Clayton Robinson

SEE ALSO

Great Britain; Trinidad and Tobago.

North America

Seminole Wars, nineteenth-century conflict that pitted blacks and Native Americans against the United States Army in Florida.

While some African Americans would later fight against Native Americans on the Western frontier, an amalgam of the two groups battled the U.S. Army during the decades-long conflict known as the Seminole Wars. Few Americans realize that the Seminole tribe grew to include blacks as well as Indians, and that most Seminoles were forced to leave Florida for the West.

THE SEMINOLES

About 1750 a group of Creek Indians left Georgia and established their own community in Florida. They were known as the Seminoles after the Creek word for "runaway." Like some other Indian groups, the Seminoles kept African American slaves. Contemporary accounts show that, unlike white slaveowners, Seminoles allowed their slaves to live freely with their families in exchange for a percentage of their harvests.

At the beginning of the nineteenth century Florida belonged to SPAIN, which did not recognize the type of slavery practiced by white colonists. Many slaves escaped and fled south to Florida, where the Spanish Crown freed them and gave them land to cultivate. Before long, intermarriage between escaped African American slaves – called "maroons" from the Spanish word for runaways – and the Seminoles and their black slaves became common, and the groups developed kinship bonds.

THE FIRST SEMINOLE WAR, 1816-1818

Whites in neighboring states, enraged at the loss of their valuable slaves in Florida, pressed the U.S. government for action. Following a series of failed negotiations, in 1816 Congress authorized the use of force. Many black and Indian allies had sought protection in Fort Nichols, an abandoned stronghold on the Apalachicola River in Florida that remained from the War of 1812. The army, coming from both land and sea, attacked the fort in the summer of 1816, killing 270 blacks and 30 Indians.

Those who survived began preparing for war. They harvested and stored their crops, sent the women, children, and livestock deep into the woods, and bought arms and ammunition from Spanish and British traders. On April 19, 1817, Gen. Andrew Jackson – later to become U.S. president – led a charge against the allied black and Indian soldiers.

In May 1818, after taking the cities of Pensacola and Sewanee, General Jackson wrote to President Monroe and won permission to end the war. Nearly half his soldiers had died, either from battle wounds or from the indigenous diseases of malaria and yellow fever. Many of the exiles died as well, but none was captured or re-enslaved.

THE SECOND SEMINOLE WAR, 1835-1842

After the first war came an uneasy peace, interrupted often by white slaveholders and Creek Indians raiding to capture escaped slaves. The existence of free blacks – in what was at last, following Florida's cessation from Spain in 1819, part of the United States – threatened the institution of slavery, and the Seminoles held valuable land. Once again the government intervened, adopting a policy that relocated the Seminoles, black and Indian, west of the Mississippi, to the Indian Territory in present-day Oklahoma.

While a scouting group traveled west in 1833, government officials broke their agreement and informed the Seminoles they had no choice but to migrate. Angered by yet another broken promise, the Seminoles and maroons again prepared for war. Led by a young, charismatic chief named Osceola, a group of Seminoles waylaid and murdered a local army colonel in 1835. Some accounts suggest that the colonel had earlier jailed Osceola for attempting to protect his wife from being captured as an escaped slave. The army responded with a surprise attack on the Seminoles but was foiled by an advance warning from one of the officer's black slaves.

Fighting continued through 1836 and 1837, with government forces often pinned down and forced to eat their own horses to survive. Meanwhile, the Seminoles refused to sign the treaties the United States offered because they failed to provide for the freedom of their black allies. Negotiations broke down irretrievably when the army seized the allies' representatives, including Osceola, and had them jailed as prisoners of war. Osceola died in captivity in 1838, the same year nearly 2000 of his fellow Seminoles were sent to the West.

By 1842, when the army finally stopped hunting the few remaining Seminoles in Florida, the war had cost the U.S. government more than 1500 men and $40 million. Experts estimate that about 500 escaped slaves were returned to captivity. It is not known how many blacks and Indians died in their fight to remain free.

THE SEMINOLES AFTER THE WARS

Finding their new home – with its sparse game, arid soil, and proximity to both the slave-holding Creeks and the slave state of Arkansas – inhospitable, many Seminoles, black and Indian, moved yet again. Led by an Indian named Wild Cat and a black man named JOHN HORSE, a group of about 300 fled to northern MEXICO, where they tried to resume their peaceful farming life.

Now renowned as great fighters, the Seminoles attracted the attention of Mexico's president, who offered them land in exchange for driving out the Kickapoo Indians. Led by John Kibbits, they did so. In 1870 the U.S. Army, just 30 years after attempting to exterminate the Seminoles, asked for their help in defeating the Plains Indians. In exchange for a promise of land and food, Chief John Horse moved an entire Seminole village to Texas. The outfit, known as the Seminole Negro Indian Scouts, became one of the most decorated U.S. Army units in history. The unit never lost a man in battle. In a move that would not have surprised the previous generation, the government failed to keep its promises of land and food to the Scouts, leaving them to fend for themselves in often violently racist south Texas. Many black Seminoles, even those who had won Medals of Honor, were denied army pensions.

By the 1960s only about 1000 Seminoles still lived in Florida, and perhaps twice that number lived in Oklahoma, in addition to communities in Mexico. Nearly all Seminoles can claim both Indian and black ancestors.

Kate Tuttle

See Also

Slavery in the United States; Maroonage in the Americas; American Indians; Military, Blacks in the American; Free Blacks in the United States, 1619 to 1863; Miscegenation.

Africa

Sena, ethnic group of southern Africa.

The Sena primarily inhabit far southern Malawi and central Mozambique. They speak a Bantu language. More than 1.5 million people consider themselves Sena.

See Also

Bantu: Dispersion and Settlement.

Africa

Senegal, a coastal West African country bordered by Mauritania, Mali, Guinea, Guinea-Bissau, and the Atlantic Ocean and nearly surrounding The Gambia, which forms a virtual enclave within Senegal's borders.

Located in the Sahel region, where kingdoms prospered from trans-Saharan trade in premodern times, Senegal came to serve as the beachhead for France's conquest of a colonial empire in Africa. Senegal's coastal cities were France's first colonial outposts; the country's largest city and capital, Dakar, served as the capital and the commercial center of colonial French West Africa. Citizens of Senegal were the first Africans to gain French citizenship rights, and the African nation has maintained close ties to France since independence. French-speaking Senegalese elite occupied administrative posts throughout France's African empire and contributed to the anticolonial struggles of the 1950s. Senegal's precolonial past, dating back to the eleventh century when the area served as point of entry for Islam south of the Sahara, is not as well known as its history under French rule. The Tukulor and Fulani peoples of interior Senegal helped spread Islam across large areas of West Africa, from Mali to Nigeria. During the 1990s the Muridiyah, an Islamic brotherhood, remained a powerful force in Senegalese society. Today Senegal faces challenges common to many African countries, including economic stagnation, large income disparities, and persistent rebellion by regional separatists in the southern Casamance region. However, Senegal's continued role as an intellectual and cultural center in French-speaking Africa, its relative stability, and its political openness offer the hope that Senegal might once again lead Africa in building a democratic and economically secure society.

Early History

Archaeologists have found stone tools indicating a human presence dating back more than 10,000 years in Senegambia, a region comprising present-day Senegal and the Gambia. They have also found clusters of stone circles, some nearly 2000 years old, that probably had religious significance. Archaeologists have also found iron-smelting sites dating to the fourth century C.E., indicating the development of metalworking skills among the region's people. By this time speakers of West Atlantic languages (which belong to the larger Niger-Congo family of languages had probably settled in Senegal. Their descendants include the Fulani, Jola, Tukulor, Serer, and Wolof peoples of present-day Senegal.

Scholars disagree on exactly when the ethnic groups living in Senegal today arrived in the region and where they came from. The late Senegalese scholar Cheikh Anta Diop claimed that linguistic and cultural similarities with ancient Egypt indicated that most of Senegal's people had migrated from the Nile River valley. Most linguists and archaeologists, however, doubt the likelihood of such an origin. Mande-speaking groups such as the Mandinka doubtless migrated from the Niger River valley to the east.

The development of metalworking technology by the fourth century C.E. may have contributed to the rise of the region's first centralized state, the Tekrur kingdom in the Senegal River valley. This kingdom stretched across the central savanna into the Sahara to the north. Tekrur drew wealth from the lucrative trans-Saharan trade, exchanging gold and slaves from the south for weapons, salt, and luxury goods from the north. Tekrur, dominated by the ancestors of the Tukulor, had extensive contact with peoples from North Africa, including the Zenaga Berbers. It is from "Zenaga" that the name "Senegal" probably derives.

After their conversion to Islam beginning in the eighth century C.E., Berbers brought Islam to Senegambia. The Zenaga founded a monastery, probably along the Senegal River, around 1040. This hermitage housed an ascetic Islamic sect known as the Almoravids who swept north and, over the course of the century, conquered Morocco and established a Muslim kingdom in Spain. The sect's leader, 'Abd Allah ibn Yasin, converted the Tekrur king, War Jabi, and many of the Tukulor people to Islam.

During the thirteenth century, as Tekrur fell under the dominance of the Mali Empire to the east, the Jolof Kingdom arose on the northwestern savanna, conquering the Wolof people. By the end of the century the Jolof had conquered most of the Wolof region, and during the fourteenth century came to dominate the Serer kingdoms of Sine and Saloum as well. Unlike the Tukulor to their east, the Wolof and Serer resisted Islam initially.

Senegal's early history accounts for much of its present cultural diversity. The peoples of the northern grasslands and central savannas, such as the Wolof, Serer, Tukulor, and Fulani, share a tradition of centralized states and social hierarchies based on hereditary castes. They engaged in millet and sorghum cultivation and in long-distance trade. The Jola, Bañun (Bainounk), and Manjaco people of the forested southern Casamance region lacked such hierarchical traditions. For most of their history they lived in semi-autonomous, relatively egalitarian villages organized by extended family units. They cultivated rice and traded in local markets. These peoples of the forest have generally resisted Islam and maintain their traditional religions to this day.

The Coming of Europeans and the Shift to the Atlantic Trade

With their exploration of the lower Senegal River in 1444, Portuguese navigators became the first Europeans known to visit Senegambia. The Portuguese soon began to export slaves, and the Wolof and Serer states imported horses, guns, brass, and iron bars. Until the end of the sixteenth century the Senegambian region was the most important source of slaves for the transatlantic slave trade. During the seventeenth century other European states challenged Portuguese commercial dominance in the region. The Dutch built a series of coastal forts, the most famous of which on Gorée Island quickly developed into a major slave-trading station.

By the late 1600s the strongest European powers on the coast were France and Great Britain, neither of which was strong enough to drive out the other or penetrate the interior, which remained under the control of the indigenous population. In 1659 the French established a slave-trading post on the island of Saint-Louis at the mouth of the Senegal River; they later established a fort there. From Saint-Louis the French moved south. They occupied or destroyed Dutch forts and captured Gorée around 1677. During the eighteenth century Saint-Louis and Gorée developed a French-speaking black and mulatto population of merchants and workers who relied for their livelihoods on the Atlantic trade. The British, meanwhile, established themselves at the mouth of the Gambia River in strongholds they would retain for more than 200 years. This division of British

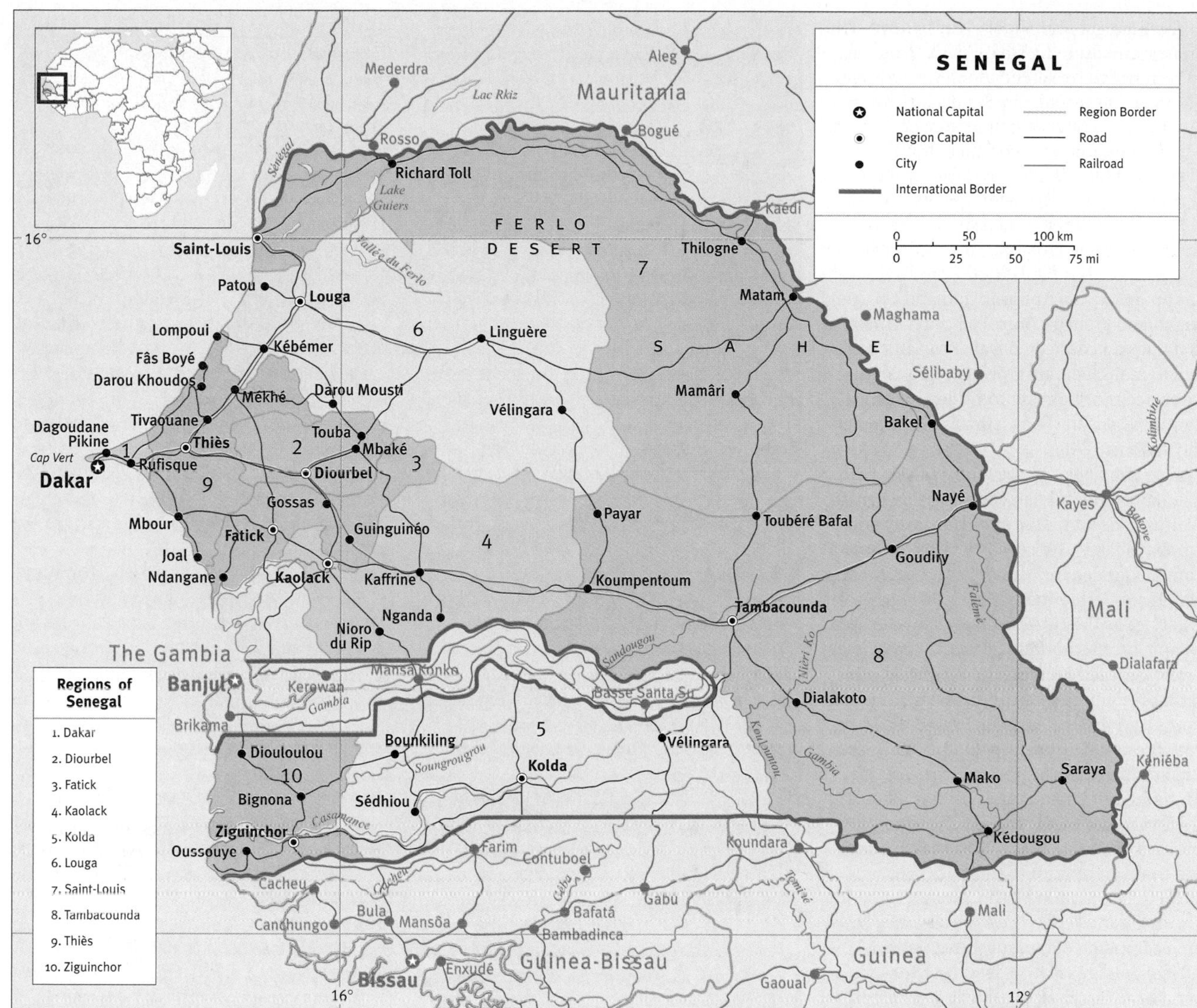

and French territory would eventually result in the independent nations of the English-speaking Gambia and French-speaking Senegal.

Slaves were the most profitable commodity in the eighteenth century, and Senegambia exported an average of 2000 to 3500 slaves each year. The largest market for slaves in the French Empire was the colony of Saint-Domingue (present-day HAITI). In addition to slaves, major exports included gum arabic, leather, ivory, wax, and gold.

The slave trade and the introduction of modern weaponry disrupted traditional social and political patterns and indirectly fostered the spread of Islam. During the late sixteenth century the Jolof kingdom disintegrated into the rival kingdoms of Jolof, Walo, Cayor, Baol, Sine, and Saloum. Meanwhile, the Tukulor kingdom of Futa Toro in the northeast and the Mandinka-dominated kingdom of Kaabu in the southeast asserted their independence from the crumbling Mali Empire. The competition to supply slaves gave rise to continuous fighting among these states. The emphasis on war reduced food production and caused famine in some areas. Around 1673 to 1677 Muslim clerics, or marabouts, led an antislavery revolt and tried to topple the slave-trading African aristocracies of the Senegambian states. With French armaments brought from Saint-Louis, the aristocrats were able to crush the revolt. However, the episode doubtless helped spread Islam among the peasantry, who were the main victims of slavery.

The French Colony

The spread of Islam and French expansionism occurred simultaneously during the late eighteenth and nineteenth centuries; these two forces shaped modern Senegal. Around 1776 Tukulor marabouts overthrew the Deniankè Dynasty that had ruled the state of Fouta Toro for nearly 300 years. The Islamic theocracy they set up in its place sent missionaries throughout the region.

After the slave revolt in Saint-Domingue, which began in 1791 and resulted in the independent nation of Haiti, the French slave trade declined until, in 1848, France outlawed slavery. The French made several failed attempts to find alternative sources of profit. During the 1830s the French extended their network of trading posts to the southern Casamance region. Finally, during the 1840s, peanuts grown in the central region proved a lucrative export crop.

The lure of the peanut trade spurred the imperialistic government of the French emperor Napoleon III to expand its control over Senegal after 1850. The French wanted to end the economic autonomy of the African states, which controlled inland trading routes and charged tariffs on products crossing their territory. Dakar, which had been a trading post since 1750, was developed as a planned town in 1862 and its port was equipped to handle exports from nearby peanut-growing regions. During the 1850s and 1860s Governor Louis Faidherbe conquered the Wolof and Serer states. These were the first African states to come under direct French control, and their conquest marked the beginning of France's colonial empire in Africa. Faidherbe built a series of forts along the Senegal River and stopped a Muslim advance from the east. About the same time a Tukulor religious leader named AL-HAJJ UMAR TAL began to attract numerous followers. Starting in 1854 he waged a series of *jihads*, or "holy wars," in the Senegal and Niger river valleys. The French concluded a treaty with Umar in 1857 in which he agreed to tolerate a French presence in present-day Senegal. However, during the 1860s African leader Lat Jor Jop began to mount a successful campaign to end French domination in Cayor. In 1871 the French were forced to withdraw from Cayor.

In 1879 the French launched a second campaign of expansion. They built a series of rail lines that facilitated French domination by moving troops inland and bringing peanuts to French-controlled ports. Africa's first railroad connected Dakar to Saint-Louis and to major peanut-growing regions. After three years of fighting to build the railroad through Cayor, the French finally reconquered the state in 1886.

After the defeat of the Wolof rulers, who maintained traditional religious beliefs, many Wolof turned for leadership to Ahmadu Bamba Mbake, a Wolof Muslim cleric. Ahmadu Bamba founded the Muridiyah brotherhood, which converted many Senegalese to Islam and is today the largest and most important Islamic brotherhood in Senegal. Though the French initially feared the authority of Ahmadu Bamba and other powerful marabouts, they eventually sought to cooperate with these leaders, whose doctrines furthered the commercial interests of the French. Ahmadu Bamba and other marabouts urged their rural followers to work hard raising peanuts and to show their devotion by donating their income to the Muridiyah, who steadily gained influence in Senegal's interior.

During the 1890s the French embarked on a campaign of conquest throughout West Africa. Senegal served as a base for this conquest. The campaign included the brutal so-called pacification of the Casamance, which was not fully subjugated until the 1920s. In 1895 the French established the colony of French West Africa, with its capital at Dakar after 1902. Dakar thus became the administrative center for a huge region. Completion of a rail line to Bamako in 1923 made Dakar the main port for the vast Niger Valley as well.

Senegal was unique among African colonies before World War II in that some of its African residents enjoyed rights as French citizens. In 1890 France extended full citizenship rights to African males living in the Four Communes: Saint-Louis, Dakar, Gorée, and Rufisque. These men had access to a French education and could vote and hold office, provided they were familiar with French language and culture. Dakar, Gorée, and Saint-Louis were France's oldest African possessions, with solid French-speaking

TOP: A man walks through the doorway of a house on Gorée Island, Senegal. The island was a major port of departure in the transatlantic slave trade. *CORBIS/Hans Georg Roth*

RIGHT: Abandoned cannons guard the entrance to the former Portuguese fort on Gorée Island, which later became a major French slave trading center. The fort is now a prison. *M & E Bernheim*

African populations. Although these areas contained no more than 5 percent of Senegal's population, the elite society located there would become very influential. Senegalese from these towns served as administrators throughout France's African colonies. Senegal thus acquired a leadership role in Francophone Africa far out of proportion to its size.

Peanut production increased from 45,000 to 300,000 tons between 1885 and 1914. The peanut trade made Senegal the richest colony in French West Africa, but mainly benefited the French trading companies and the principal marabouts. Farmers operating on credit often found it hard to pay off debt when peanut prices fell. Farmers often cultivated peanuts at the expense of other food crops, and this increased their dependence on the market for survival.

Recognizing the contribution of the marabouts to Senegal's commerce and its stability as a colony, the French granted them vast tracts of land beginning in the second decade of the twentieth century. The French thus won the marabouts' support for colonial rule, especially in the interior. In return some Muslim leaders enlisted troops for the French army in World War I to demonstrate their loyalty.

During the mid-twentieth century Senegal assumed a leadership role in French West African politics. In 1914 a French customs officer, Blaise Diagne, became the first African deputy to the French National Assembly. In 1919 he founded the Republican Socialist Party, the first Western-style political party in the region. His leading opponent, Lamine Guèye, Senegal's first black lawyer, took a different path. In 1929 Guèye founded the Senegalese Socialist Party, linked to the French Socialist Party. From 1936 to 1938 the Popular Front, led by the French Socialists, governed France. The Popular Front government eased harsh colonial policies in Africa, restricting the use of forced labor in the colonies, allowing Africans to form trade unions, and making it easier for Africans to become French citizens. Guèye organized Socialist Party chapters around Senegal, and encouraged educated Africans to become politically involved.

A decline in global demand for peanuts in the 1930s caused hardship in Senegal. Living standards declined, and debt increased. France provided some relief by ensuring a guaranteed, protected market for Senegal's products. However, French banks and export firms gained increased influence over Senegal's economy.

After World War II the French government extended the vote to rural Senegal, which gained a seat in the French assembly alongside that of the communes. Guèye won the election for the urban seat while his protégé, Léopold Sédar Senghor, won the rural seat. Senghor later broke with the Socialists and founded his own party, the Senegalese Democratic Bloc (BDS). The Socialists attracted support from the Four Communes and among workers and students, who were becoming increasingly radical. The BDS, on the other hand, received strong support from the newly enfranchised countryside, where the party formed ties with influential marabouts. The BDS gradually became the leading political party in Senegal. In 1956 France permitted limited self-government within its African colonies. In 1958 the BDS and the Socialists merged to form the Senegalese Progressive Union (UPS), which won a strong majority in the 1959 national elections. As demands for independence grew, the UPS negotiated with the French government for independence as part of a Mali Federation, combining present-day Mali and Senegal. On April 4, 1960, the federation became independent. However, rivalry between Senegal and Mali broke up the federation in August, and Senegal became an independent state with Senghor as president.

Independence

From 1960 until 1981 President Senghor dominated Senegalese politics, dispensing patronage with a generous hand to urban elites and rural leaders alike. Under Senghor, Senegal maintained a close relationship to France: Senegal supported the former colonial power's international policies in exchange for economic aid, military support, and a favored position for Senegalese products on the French market.

During the 1960s Senghor advocated African socialism and instituted a series of Four Year plans. He increased the government's role in the economy by establishing several state-owned firms, including one that controlled peanut prices paid to farmers and handled all peanut exports. The government maintained its alliance with the principal marabouts, who received higher prices for their harvests than others. Some sources have estimated that at independence, peanuts and their byproducts constituted more than 80 percent of Senegal's exports. Peanut processing and exporting represented nearly half of Senegal's industrial activity. Through 1967 France bought virtually all of Senegal's peanut production, providing price supports.

At first Senegal was a multiparty state with competitive elections. However, during a 1962 power struggle with Prime Minister Mamadou Dia, Senghor had Dia arrested, tried, and imprisoned. Senghor's government banned opposition parties and ran unopposed in subsequent elections. The lack of political debate generated considerable unrest. The government sent in the army to crush student and union strikes in 1968.

The end of French price supports for peanuts in 1967 exposed Senegal to the fluctuations of the global market. In the early 1970s a devastating drought in the Sahel and a rapid rise in the cost of imported oil caused an economic crisis. The World Bank estimated that between 1964 and 1974, Senegal's per capita income had dropped 21 percent in the cities and 3 percent in the countryside. Widespread hardship generated popular discontent.

At the root of the combined economic and political crisis was the fact that Senghor's socialism had failed to address profound structural problems in Senegal's economy. State control over the economy had simply replaced the French colonialists with an African bureaucratic elite rife with nepotism and corruption. During the mid-1970s Senghor and the ruling elite responded to popular discontent, instituting reforms that have been called the "passive revolution," which opened avenues for political opposition. By permitting limited opposition, the elite did not truly give up power; it simply switched tactics, replacing repression and authoritarianism with strategic alliances. In 1976 the government released Dia from prison, and a new constitution permitted three political parties. In 1978 Senghor easily won the first contested presidential election since 1963.

In response to the economic crisis of the 1970s the government promoted other industries, such as fishing and tourism, to reduce reliance on peanuts and phosphates. To fund these programs and pay for oil imports, Senghor's government had to borrow from foreign lenders, who gained increasing control over the Senegalese economy. The economy continued to stagnate, however, and as his popularity declined, Senghor resigned in 1980.

Senghor's protégé, Abdou Diouf, took office in 1981 and has won every election since then. Diouf has increased economic and political liberalism. Under pressure from the World Bank, International Monetary Fund, and other aid donors to implement structural adjustment, he announced a program in 1985 to privatize state-owned firms, but few firms had actually been sold by the late 1990s. Lower inflation and reduced government spending improved Senegal's financial status in the eyes of the world, but Senegal's rural majority reaped little benefit from these apparent improvements. Meanwhile, the devaluation of Senegal's currency in 1994 by 50 percent caused a substantial jump in the cost of living. Diouf legalized all political parties, regardless of ideology. He has included opposition leaders in the government and stressed national reconciliation. Economist Mamadou Lamine Loum became the new prime minister in July 1998 and the government appears likely to continue on its present free-market course.

Since Diouf came to power Senegal has had disputes with several of its neighbors. Senegalese troops entered the Gambia in 1981 to put down a coup, and the two governments proclaimed a regional alliance, the Senegambian Confederation. The confederation disbanded in 1989 over Gambian fears of absorption into Senegal. Since then Senegal has accused its neighbor of tolerating massive smuggling. Senegal cut diplomatic relations with Mauritania in the late 1980s when a border dispute over grazing rights broke out along the two countries' common border. Bloody massacres occurred in both countries and resulted in the large-scale flight of Senegal's Moorish population to Mauritania, while Mauritania expelled thousands of black farmers to Senegal. Diplomatic relations and communications resumed following the 1991 Islamic Conference.

Around 1984 discontent in the rural Casamance region of Senegal, south of the Gambia, led to the beginning of an internal rebellion by the Movement of Democratic Forces of the Casamance (MFDC). The conflict has several causes. Many Casamance residents blame the region's economic stagnation on neglect by the central government. Although the rebellion is a regional rather than a purely ethnic conflict, religious and cultural differences also foster opposition to the Senegalese government within the region. Unlike other Senegalese, who are overwhelmingly Muslim, residents of the Casamance are largely Christian or adherents of traditional religions. The Roman Catholic priest Diamacoune Senghor, along with Paris-based intellectuals, leads the rebels. Political objections accompany religious ones in this conflict: the Jola and other Casamance peoples resent the Wolof-dominated national government. The discontented region's geographic isolation from the rest of Senegal – it is sandwiched between Guinea-Bissau and the Gambia – has facilitated the rebellion, since it is easy for rebels to withdraw strategically across one of the neighboring borders. Groups such as Amnesty International have accused both the Senegalese government and the MFDC of torture and other human rights violations. The government and rebels have agreed to sporadic truces and negotiations, and France has attempted to mediate, but the rebellion continued in 1998.

The Casamance rebellion has contributed to uneasy relations between Senegal and its southern neighbor, Guinea-Bissau, which Senegal accused of aiding Casamance rebels during the late 1980s. The two countries also disputed offshore fishing and oil-mining rights. In a 1993 agreement Senegal agreed to share fishing and mineral rights with Guinea-Bissau, which in turn agreed to stop providing sanctuary for Casamance fighters. In 1998 forces with purported links to the MFDC mounted an armed rebellion against Guinea-Bissau's government.

Although France remained Senegal's most important trading partner and provided about 20 percent of its foreign aid in the late 1990s, the French military and commercial presence in Senegal has diminished in recent decades. United States president Bill Clinton's 1998 visit to Senegal signaled a greater American interest in the country.

David P. Johnson, Jr.

SEE ALSO
Bamako, Mali; Berber; Dakar, Senegal; Explorers in Africa Before 1500; Gold Trade; France; Gorée Island, Senegal; Ivory Trade; Languages, African: An Overview; Salt Trade; Structural Adjustment in Africa; Tourism in Africa; Marabout; Islam and Tradition: An Interpretation; Afro-Atlantic Culture: On the Live Dialogue Between Africa and the Americas; Trans-Saharan and Red Sea Slave Trade.

Africa

Senegal (Ready Reference)

Official Name: Republic of Senegal
Area: 196,190 sq km (about 74,552 sq mi)
Location: Western Africa; borders the North Atlantic Ocean, GUINEA-BISSAU, and MAURITANIA
Capital: Dakar (population 1,729,823 [1992 estimate])
Other Major Cities: Thiès (population 216,381), Kaolack (193,115), Ziguinchor (161,680), and Saint-Louis (132,499) (1994 estimates)
Population: 9,723,149 (1998 estimate)
Population Density: 46 persons per sq km (about 121 persons per sq mi)
Population Below Age 15: 48 percent (male 2,331,388; female 2,343,654 [1998 estimate])
Population Growth Rate: 3.3 percent (1998 estimate)
Total Fertility Rate: 6.1 children born per woman (1998 estimate)
Life Expectancy at Birth: Total population: 57.37 years (male 54.55 years; female 60.28 years [1998 estimate])
Infant Mortality Rate: 61.2 deaths per 1000 live births (1998 estimate)
Literacy Rate (age 15 and over who can read and write): Total population: 33.1 percent (male 43 percent; female 23.2 percent [1995 estimate])
Education: Education is officially compulsory for all children between the ages of 6 and 12, but only 48 percent of primary-school-age children attended school in the late 1980s, and only 13 percent of secondary-school-age children attended school.
Languages: French is the official language. Almost half the population also speaks Wolof, the most widely understood of the African languages, but Pulaar, Jola, and Mandingo are also spoken.
Ethnic Groups: 44 percent of the population are WOLOF. Other principal ethnic groups are the FULANI, TUKULOR, Serer, Jola, and Malinke.
Religions: About 92 percent of the population are Sunni Muslim. About 2 percent are Christian (mostly Roman Catholic), and 6 percent follow indigenous beliefs.
Climate: Senegal is arid desert in the north and tropical in the south. It has a transitional climate from the dry desert zone in the north to the moist tropical zone in the south. The rainy season lasts from July to October in the north. Average rainfall in the north averages about 350 mm (14 in). In the south the rainy season lasts from June to October, with an average rainfall of about 1525 mm (about 60 in). Average temperatures on the coast are 22° C (72° F) in January and 28° C (82° F) in July.
Land, Plants, and Animals: The northern part of Senegal is part of the SAHEL, a transition zone between the SAHARA DESERT on the north and the wetter regions to the south. Vegetation toward the south consists mainly of savanna grass with scattered clumps of trees and spiny shrubs. Farther south, near the GAMBIA RIVER, trees are more common; in the extreme south there are mangrove swamps and dense forests of oil palms, mahogany, teak, and bamboo. Animals include elephants, lions, cheetahs, and ANTELOPE in the less populated eastern half of the country. In the rivers there are hippopotamuses and crocodiles. Senegal also has cobras and boa constrictors.
Natural Resources: Mineral resources include phosphates and iron ore. The deposits of iron ore, however, have not been exploited because of their remoteness. Senegal also has reserves of petroleum and natural gas offshore.
Currency: The Communauté Financière Africaine franc
Gross Domestic Product (GDP): $15.6 billion (1997 estimate)
GDP per Capita: $1850 (1997 estimate)
GDP Real Growth Rate: 4.7 percent (1997 estimate)
Primary Economic Activities: Agriculture (employing 78 percent of the labor force), roundwood production, fishing, phosphate mining, and manufacturing
Primary Crops: Peanuts, millet, corn, sorghum, rice, cotton, tomatoes, green vegetables, and livestock
Industries: Agricultural and fish processing, phosphate mining, petroleum refining, and construction materials
Primary Exports: Fish, peanuts, petroleum products, phosphates, and cotton
Primary Imports: Foods and beverages, consumer goods, capital goods, and petroleum
Primary Trade Partners: European Union (France especially), Nigeria, Côte d'Ivoire, Algeria, China, and Japan
Government: Senegal is a constitutional republic under a multiparty democracy. The executive branch is led by President ABDOU DIOUF, who appointed Prime Minister Habib Thiam. The prime minister appoints the cabinet, called the Council of Ministers. The legislative branch is the elected, 120-member National Assembly, currently dominated by President Diouf's party, the Socialist Party.

Elizabeth Heath

SEE ALSO
Cheetah; Crocodile; Dakar, Senegal; Elephant; Hippopotamus; Lion.

Africa

Senegal River, one of West Africa's longest and most important rivers.

The Senegal River flows for more than 1600 km (1000 mi) through the countries of MALI, SENEGAL, and MAURITANIA, forming the border between the latter two countries. Its headwaters are located in the FOUTA DJALLON mountains in GUINEA; they meet to form the Senegal River in Bafoulabé, Mali. The river flows northwest, west, and then southwest in a sweeping arc and empties into the Atlantic Ocean near Saint-Louis, Senegal. Boats can navigate the Senegal year-round as far upstream as Podor, Senegal. During the rainy season (roughly July-November), boats reach Kayes, Mali, more than 800 km (500 mi) upstream from the Atlantic.

The Senegal differs from the region's other major rivers in that it flows year-round. In September the river floods, leaving fertile silt as the floodwaters recede. Rice, sorghum, MILLET, maize, tobacco, and sweet potatoes are grown along the Senegal's banks. Local fishermen catch carp, catfish, eel, and bass.

In the early 1970s the governments of Mali, Senegal, and Mauritania formed an international authority to provide for irrigation and hydroelectric power through the construction of the Diama and Manantali dams on the river. The results have been disappointing. Because the dams regulate the river's flow, the annual floods have diminished. This has necessitated the introduction of irrigated agriculture in place of the traditional flood-watered agriculture. Agricultural output decreased after the construction of the dams. The creation of freshwater reservoirs and canals for irrigation agriculture has led to an increase of waterborne diseases, such as malaria and schistosomiasis. In addition, the dams' electricity production was disappointing.

Robert Fay

Africa

Senegambia and Niger Territories. Former name of MALI.

Africa

Senegambia, Confederation of. Former federation incorporating both SENEGAL and the Gambia.

SEE ALSO

Gambia, The.

Africa

Senga (also known as Nsenga), ethnic group of ZAMBIA.

The Senga primarily inhabit eastern Zambia. Others live in ZIMBABWE and MOZAMBIQUE. They speak a Bantu language related to that of the neighboring TONGA people. More than 300,000 people consider themselves Senga.

SEE ALSO

Bantu: Dispersion and Settlement.

Sengbe. Please see CINQUE, JOSEPH

Africa

Senghor, Léopold Sédar

(b. August 15, 1906, Ndjitor, Senegal), scholar, poet, philosopher, and statesman; founder of the cultural and political movement known as NÉGRITUDE, and president of SENEGAL (1960-1980).

Demonstrating a rare combination of intellectual, artistic, and political talent, Léopold Sédar Senghor has towered over modern Senegal unlike any other figure in that country's history. Senghor's lifelong quest to find a synthesis, artistically and politically, between two seemingly opposing ways of life – African and European – inspired his lifelong record of creative achievement. Although as a youth he immersed himself in French culture, his ultimate inability to become "a black-skinned Frenchman" led him to cultivate his "Africanness." He helped to define two of the key political and intellectual movements of twentieth-century Africa: AFRICAN SOCIALISM and Négritude.

Born to a SERER father and a FULANI mother, Senghor has striven to represent all of Senegal's peoples in his writing and politics. He attended Roman Catholic mission schools in what was then French West Africa and, in 1922, entered the Collège Libermann, a seminary in Dakar, where he intended to study for the priesthood. He was forced to leave the seminary after participating in a protest against racism. After graduating from secondary school in 1928, Senghor won a scholarship to study in FRANCE.

While at the prestigious Ecole Normale Supérieure in Paris, Senghor studied contemporary French literature, including the work of Charles Baudelaire, on whom Senghor wrote his thesis. Senghor also studied the intellectual underpinnings of French political thought between the two world wars. Georges Pompidou, who later became the French president, was a classmate and a friend. Senghor was drafted into the French army at the start of World War II, after teaching classics at schools in Tours and Paris.

Outside class Senghor absorbed the intellectual ferment of Paris in the 1930s. Black students, writers, and artists from Africa, North America, and the Caribbean were discovering their common roots and defining their identities in opposition to colonial rule. The Pan-African Congress and the writings of W. E. B. Du Bois and the HARLEM RENAISSANCE all recognized and celebrated a growing black confidence and self-awareness, and this intellectual awakening deeply influenced Senghor and his contemporaries. In 1932 Senghor met AIMÉ CÉSAIRE, a writer from MARTINIQUE who would become an influential literary figure. Césaire and Senghor cofounded a newspaper, *L'Etudiant noir* (The Black Student), and founded a new artistic and intellectual movement, Négritude. The movement went beyond opposition to colonialism to attack white racism. Négritude sought to explore the common experience of peoples of African descent and to formulate a new black identity. Senghor would later say that the philosophy embodies the "sum total of African values of civilization."

The years after World War II were the high point of Senghor's political career. In 1945 and 1946 Senghor, along with his political mentor, LAMINE GUÈYE, was elected to represent Senegal in the French Constituent Assembly (later the National Assembly). He won reelection and served in the National Assembly until 1958. Meanwhile, in 1948, he became a professor at the Ecole Nationale de la France d'Outre mer. Senghor became president of the parliament of the Mali Federation, comprising present-day Senegal and MALI, when it became independent in April 1960. Several months later the federation collapsed, and Senghor was elected the first president of Senegal. As a Serer Christian leading a predominantly Muslim and WOLOF country, Senghor's political career can itself be considered an expression of Négritude, in that his African cultural background enabled him to serve and lead his people despite these differences.

Senghor also launched his literary career in earnest in 1945 with the publication of his first book of poetry, *Songs of the Shadow*. Two years later, in collaboration with fellow Senegalese ALIOUNE DIOP, he helped launch the journal *Présence Africaine*, which showcased African literature, including Senghor's writing. Torn between two very different worlds, Senghor dramatized the identity crisis of the Westernized African. He pushed French poetry past its preoccupation with the exotic, implying a detachment from the "other." Instead, Senghor's poetry presents a personal confrontation with the African past and present. "Black Woman," one of his most famous poems, uses classical Western themes to describe the figure of an African woman and, by extension, black humanity.

Throughout the next two decades a number of other poetry volumes followed and received critical acclaim both for their vivid language and imagery and for their broader themes. While he was president (1960-1980) Senghor published less. However, he won the Apollinaire Prize for Poetry in 1974, and he published volumes of poetry in 1979 and 1980.

As Senegalese president during the 1960s and 1970s, Senghor implemented a moderate (pro-Western) form of African socialism, in which the state played a major role in the economy in alliance with the established indigenous elite. He also replaced Senegal's multiparty democracy in the early 1960s with a one-party authoritarian state. However, in the so-called passive revolution of 1976, Senghor responded to economic and political stagnation by introducing greater political and economic freedom. However, Senegal's economic crisis persisted and, bowing to popular discontent, Senghor retired from office in 1980, one of the few African rulers to relinquish power voluntarily. He left a legacy of relative stability and freedom of expression in Senegal. However, Senghor had also monopolized power and discouraged debate and opposition, and thus contributed to the stagnation of Senegalese politics.

Since his retirement Senghor has resettled in Verson, France, the hometown of his wife. In 1988 he published a philosophical memoir titled *Ce que je crois* (What I Believe). During the 1990s he published poetry and cultivated a quiet seclusion.

David P. Johnson, Jr.

SEE ALSO

Présence Africaine; Dakar, Senegal; Pan-Africanism; Du Bois, William Edward Burghardt (W. E. B.).

Africa

Senufo (also known as Siena and Sene), ethnic group of CÔTE D'IVOIRE, MALI, and BURKINA FASO.

There are more than 3 million ethnic Senufo. Many of them live in the Middle Volta valley, between the Bagoe, Bani, and Mouhoun (formerly Black Volta) rivers in West Africa. The Senufo ancestry is not entirely known. Some, at least, are believed to have migrated north from the area around Odienne (in present-day Côte d'Ivoire) sometime prior to the seventeenth century C.E. As farmers, they adapted techniques for growing corn and MILLET on the region's poor soil.

The peoples now known as the northern, central, and southern Senufo had distinct histories. In the early seventeenth century DYULA traders migrated from the collapsing SONGHAI EMPIRE into the Middle Volta valley and settled among the southern groups. The merchants called their peasant neighbors Senufo, a MANDE term for "those who speak Senari." The Dyula also converted many Senufo chiefs to Islam, and in the eighteenth century the Dyula traders took control of the KONG Empire.

Islam made relatively few inroads among the northern Senufo (also known as the Supide or the Kenedougou) and central Senufo until the increased urban migration after World War II; traditional Senufo religion has always emphasized the worship of ancestors and earth spirits. The Senufo's secret societies – Lo for men, Sandogo for women – provide for the transmission of ritual knowledge from one generation to the next. Elder Lo members also serve as consultants to village chiefs.

During the colonial era many Senufo migrated to work on cash-cropping schemes in more fertile areas to the south and west; today many Senufo youth still seek wage employment outside their rural homelands. Senufo farmers grow a variety of cash crops, depending on the local ecology. Certain towns in Senufo regions, such as Sikasso, Mali, have become important commercial centers.

While the Senufo play relatively minor roles in the national governments of the countries in which they live, they have won international renown for their art. The most spectacular pieces are the sculptures of hornbill birds, which feature long beaks and outstretched wings, and stand more than 1.2 m (4 ft) high. In recent years many Senufo artisans have begun producing for tourist markets.

Elizabeth Heath

SEE ALSO

Islam and Tradition: An Interpretation; Colonial Rule.

Africa

Serengeti National Park, nature preserve in northern TANZANIA. Established in 1941, the park covers about 14,760 sq km (about 5700 sq mi) and consists mainly of flat, open grassland, with a few rocky *kopjes* (small hills) and some areas of woodland and bushy savanna in the western part of the park. The Serengeti is the only national park in Africa in which seasonal migrations of plains animals take place.

Serengeti National Park is inhabited by more than 200 species of birds and 35 species of plains mammals, including cheetahs, leopards, lions, and giraffes. Zebras, gnus (large African antelopes also called wildebeests), gazelles, and elephants did not exist in large numbers in the park until the 1960s, when the rising human population in the region caused a shortage of natural resources and forced many of these animals into the protected area. About 200,000 zebras, 2 million gnus, 1 million gazelles, and thousands of elephants now live in the park. The plains of Serengeti National Park are also home to black rhinoceroses. During the rainy season, from November to May, millions of animals graze on the park's southeastern plains. This area has few rivers and becomes excessively dry once the rainy season ends, so gnus, gazelles, and zebras migrate to the western savanna and as far north as the grasslands of Maasai Mara Game Park, across the KENYA-Tanzania border, where they spend the dry season.

The park was declared a World Heritage Site by the United Nations Educational, Scientific and Cultural Organization (UNESCO) in 1981. Illegal hunting in the park is a serious problem, posing a particular threat to the survival of elephants and rhinoceroses.

SEE ALSO

Cheetah; Elephant; Giraffe; Gnu; Lion; Rhinoceros; Wildebeest; Zebra.

Africa

Serer (also known as Sarer, Ser, and Serre), ethnic group of SENEGAL.

The Serer primarily inhabit western Senegal, where they constitute the second largest ethnic group. Others live in THE GAMBIA and GUINEA-BISSAU. They speak a Niger-Congo language closely related to that of the neighboring WOLOF. Approximately 1 million people consider themselves Serer.

SEE ALSO

Languages, African: An Overview.

Latin America and the Caribbean

Serra y Montalvo, Rafael

(b. March 24, 1858, Havana, Cuba; d. October 24, 1909, Havana, Cuba), Cuban poet, journalist, exile, independence leader, and close friend and collaborator of JOSÉ MARTÍ.

At age 13, after finishing primary school, Rafael Serra y Montalvo became a tobacco apprentice. *Tabaqueros* (tobacco workers) were known as the aristocrats of the working class, in part because they were generally well paid but also because of their expensive tastes. Serra was largely self-educated and developed a special affinity for literature. As a young man, he founded primary schools in CUBA that were free of charge both in Havana and Matanzas. In 1879 he also established La Armonía (Harmony), a hybrid social welfare and political organization, and began to publish a proindependence political weekly by the same name. He gradually established himself as a young firebrand, gaining popularity and political prestige.

In 1880, under pressure from a high-ranking colonel to join the military – perhaps to silence his journalistic voice – Serra instead accompanied MARTÍN MORÚA DELGADO, an Afro-Cuban who had been organizing workers at the time, to Key West, Florida, where the two lived in exile. There they reignited cries for Cuban independence that had been squelched by the Zanjón Pact of 1878 (the treaty that ended the TEN YEARS' WAR, a failed war to win independence). He continued to lead and organize political and welfare organizations, and integrated his literary and political interests through poetry readings and through directing the San Carlos Center, where Cuban exiles met for cultural expression and political organization.

Yet Serra's stay in Key West was relatively brief. He soon joined other exiles in New York who organized resistance to the colonial regime and published Spanish-language newspapers stateside. In 1885 he published his first book, in JAMAICA, *Ecos del alma* (Echoes of the Soul). In the same year he helped plan and participated in the Cuban invasion masterminded by Máximo Gómez and Antonio Maceo. When the attempt to secure independence failed, its organizers scattered across the continent. Serra fled to PANAMA and then to KINGSTON, JAMAICA, where he compiled poetry and published *Ideas y pensamientos, album poético, político y literario* (Ideas and Thoughts, Poetic Album, Political and Literary) in 1886.

In 1887 Serra returned once again to New York, where he submitted letters and articles to periodicals in Havana, Matanzas, and New York in support of the independence movement. Active in a number of political and social organizations, he served as secretary for the club Los Independientes and participated in the Cuerpo de Consejo de New York. In 1892 Serra published his first prose book, *Ensayos políticos* (Political Essays) and, in 1894, a short-lived illustrated political and literary journal called *La verdad* (Truth). With José Martí, Cuba's most famous poet-patriot, Serra was a founder of the Partido Revolucionario Cubano, the political party organized to fight for Cuban independence, and its newspaper, *Patria* (Fatherland). In 1890 he established La Liga, a school for Afro-Cubans and Afro-Puerto Ricans living in New York, whose aim was to spread the anti-colonial message. La Liga opened branches in Tampa, Florida; Havana; and Santiago de Cuba. These two organizations, the party and the school, influenced many to take up the cause of independence. On February 24, 1895, Cuba's war of independence began (*see* SPANISH-CUBAN-AMERICAN WAR).

In the same year Martí was killed in battle. In 1896 Serra and the Revolutionary Party published a key illustrated periodical titled *La dóctrina de Martí* (Martí's Doctrine). This newspaper repeatedly highlighted the need to address racial discrimination and social reform after independence, neither of which could be taken for granted with the end of colonialism. Also in 1896 Serra published the second volume of *Ensayos políticos*. It included further articles and letters to him from eminent patriots, including Pedro Betancourt, Juan Gualberto Gómez, Martí, and others. These documents acknowledged the important role Serra played in the independence movement, from organizing exiles in the United States to laying some of the intellectual foundation for the rebellion. In 1902 Serra returned to Cuba, where he published another journal, *El nuevo Criollo* (The New Creole). The journal criticized the continued discrimination that Afro-Cubans faced in employment and in social venues as well as government efforts to encourage European immigration so as to "whiten" the country (*see* WHITENING). Serra published two more books before his death: *Para blancos y negros* (For Blacks and Whites) in 1907 and *La república posible* (The Possible Republic) in 1909, which further developed some of his ideas about a multiracial Cuba and the ideological contours of an independent Cuba, first put forth in *El nuevo Criollo*. Martí best summed up Serra's contributions when he characterized him as an "indefatigable worker for our independence."

Joy Elizondo

SEE ALSO

New York, New York; Maceo y Grajales, Antonio; Matanzas, Cuba; Havana, Cuba.

Africa

Serval, long-legged wildcat native to the grasslands and brush country of ALGERIA, MOROCCO, and sub-Saharan Africa.

The serval is buff colored with black spots in rows sometimes merging into stripes down its back and legs. It has a slender body 0.67 to 1 m (2.2 to 3 ft) long and 54 to 62 cm (21 to 24 in) high at the shoulder, and a small head with long, rounded ears; it weighs 8.7 to 18 kg (19 to 40 lb). The serval feeds mostly on small mammals, lizards, and birds, although it is powerful enough to kill young ANTELOPE. It hunts by speed and climbs trees well. When captured young, servals can be tamed, but they are difficult to raise. **Scientific classification:** The serval belongs to the family Felidae. It is classified as *Felis serval.*

Africa

Seven-Seven, Twins (b. 1944, Ogidi, Nigeria), Nigerian painter, musician, politician, and businessman.

The only survivor in a line of seven sets of twins, Twins Seven-Seven, who was born Taiwo Olaniyi Salan, named himself to honor this unusual lineage. He began his career as a musician and dancer, and has several records and tours to his credit. Twins Seven-Seven first encountered painting and the graphic arts by chance, when he came upon the Mbari Mbayo Club in 1964. This group eventually developed into the Oshobgo School, a well-known community of Nigerian artists.

Initially, Twins Seven-Seven was most interested in drawing. His early drawings demonstrate a strong attention to fine detail, and he filled the entire visual field with lines and patterns. When Twins Seven-Seven began to paint, he worked on flat sheets of plywood that he pieced together and layered to create a collage effect. His images are drawn from Yoruba religion and folklore, and his paintings' themes explore connections between the spiritual and earthly worlds.

Christopher Tiné

Africa

Seychelles, an African archipelago country located in the Indian Ocean.

Strung out along 115 islands and coral atolls in the Indian Ocean, the Seychelles is one of the smallest countries in the world, 444 sq km (171 sq mi) of land scattered across 1.35 million sq km (500,000 sq mi) of ocean. Most of its estimated 77,575 inhabitants live on the largest islands, Mahé, Praslin, and La Digue. Unlike other Indian Ocean island nations such as MAURITIUS, the Seychelles is marked by a relatively homogenous population of mixed African and European descent, except for small Indian, European and Chinese communities. Despite nearly 200 years of British rule, French cultural influences such as the Roman Catholic Church are still evident in the Seychelles, as are African religious practices. Because of the island's small size and poor soil, the inhabitants of the Seychelles have long depended on passers-by to sustain their economy. Once a base for pirates and then a supply post for Indian Ocean merchant ships, the Seychelles now draws large numbers of beach-loving tourists as well as entrepreneurs attracted to its relatively open investment policies.

PRECOLONIAL HISTORY

Located 1600 km (994 mi) from the nearest mainland shore, the scattered archipelago was uninhabited by humans until relatively recently. The Seychelles broke away from the African continental plate about 50 million years ago, carrying away fauna and flora that would evolve in isolation into unique endemic species found nowhere else. The large double coconuts of the coco-de-mer, for example, would wash up along the shores of the Maldives, another archipelago located south of India. The once rare and mysterious fruit, thought to be an aphrodisiac, was highly prized until specimens were discovered growing in the Seychelles and subsequently exported en masse.

Evidence suggests that early Arab and Swahili explorers knew about the Seychelles. An Arabic manuscript written in 810 C.E. describes a place that is probably the Seychelles, as do accounts written by the Arab geographer al-Husayn al-Mas'udi in 915 C.E. Maps associated with these texts denote the Rukh Islands, the word "Rukh" probably being derived from the Divehi word for palm

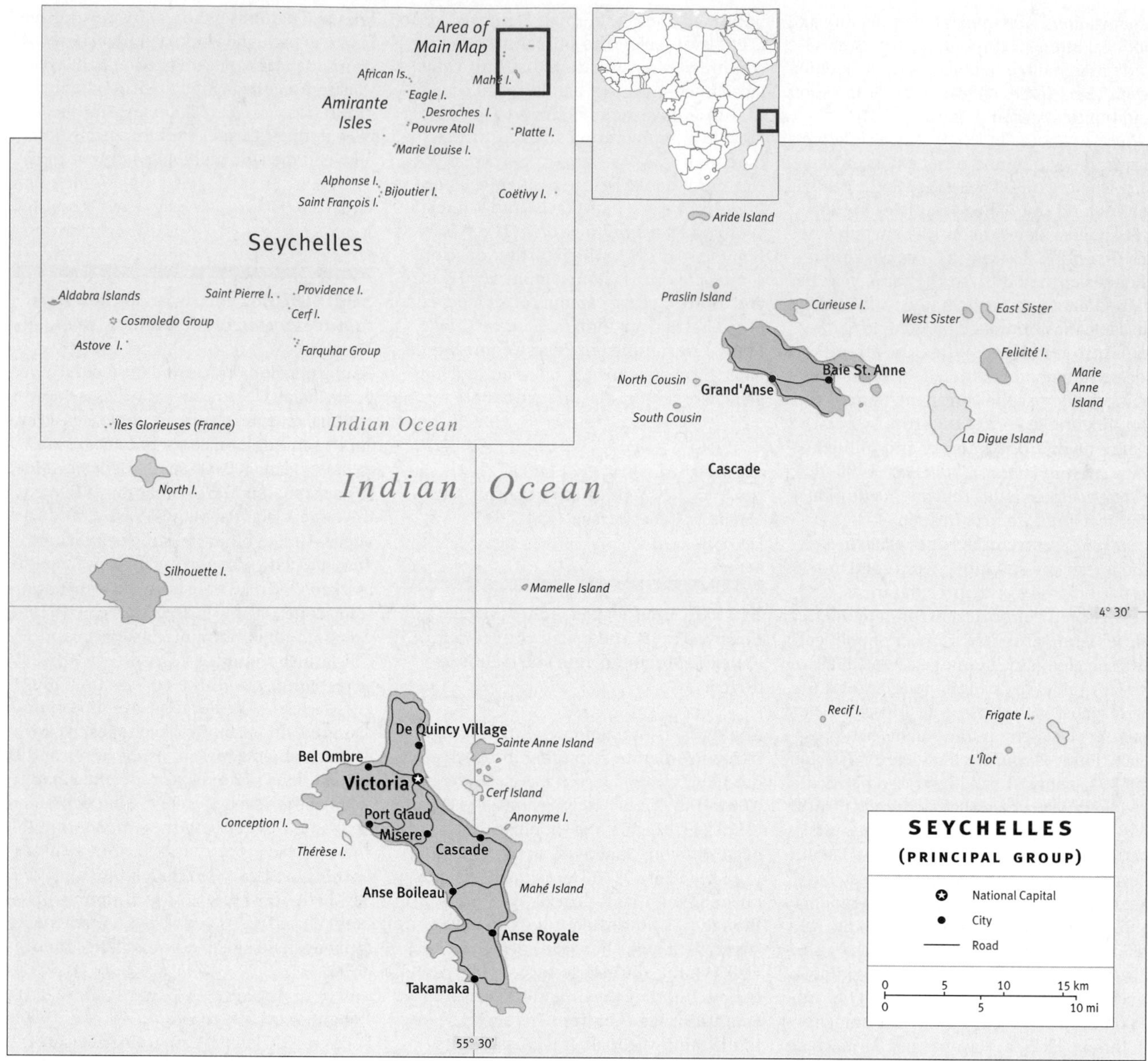

tree, *ruka*, suggesting that inhabitants of the Maldives had knowledge of the "palm tree islands." En route to India, Portuguese explorers spotted the islands in 1501 and named the largest of them the Seven Sisters. For several decades the Portuguese, most notably Vasco da Gama, explored the many small islets and reportedly established a small and ultimately unsuccessful settlement in 1598. Employees of the British East India Company explored the islands in 1609. During 1742 and 1743 a French expedition from Mauritius mapped the islands, naming them Ile de la Bourdonnais (after Mauritian governor Mahé de la Bourdonnais). By the time the French crown laid claim to the islands in 1756, they were again uninhabited with the exception of transient pirates. The French explorer Mahé Morphy renamed the islands Séchelles, honoring the French controller general of finance Vicomte Morceau des Séchelles. The first settlement was established in 1771 when Captain Lécore of the French ship *Thélémaque* dropped off 15 French, 7 slaves, 5 South Indians, and a black woman. The islands were considered a dependency of the larger colony Ile de France (Mauritius), from which most settlers originated. Although they introduced spices such as nutmeg, cloves, and cinnamon, the colonists primarily provided supplies and maintenance for passing ships. Settlers were quick to exploit the existing natural resources, stripping the forests to build and repair ships, and harvesting more than 13,000 giant tortoises by 1789. By this time the population had grown to 591, of which 487 were slaves. Hearing of the French Revolution, the colonists claimed independence the following year, although France quickly reestablished sovereignty.

Colonial History

One of the primary reasons the French laid claim to the Seychelles was to maintain secure sea lanes. United States merchant ships had been purchasing stolen goods from pirates such as the American Captain Nemesis, who commanded a fleet of 15 vessels with which he raided British and French ships. The infamous French pirate Oliver le Vasseur, "the Buzzard," also operated from the Seychelles. Legend holds that le Vasseur threw his treasure map to the crowd just before being hung from the gallows in France. Based upon this map, a large expedition exhaustively searched what appeared to be manmade tunnels on Mahé from 1948 until 1970 but failed to turn up any valuables.

Tired of pirates preying on its ships, Britain took control of the Seychelles in 1794, although possession of the islands alternated between the British and the French in the late eighteenth and early nineteenth centuries. In this period of British-French hostility in the Indian Ocean, the Seychelles governor, Chevalier Queau de Quinssay, hoisted a different flag depending on which nation's ships were sailing into the harbor, a practice that kept the Seychelles out of the

TOP: **Famous for the islands' double coconuts, known as *cocos de mer,* and their beautiful beaches, the Seychelles have stimulated their economy by developing tourism.** *CORBIS/Christine Osborne*
ABOVE: **A Seychelles baker takes freshly baked bread from the oven.** *CORBIS/Zen Icknow*

conflict. In the 1814 Treaty of Paris, France formally ceded Mauritius and the Seychelles, with the latter remaining a dependency of the former. The British abolished slavery in 1834, but the colony's 9000 ex-slaves (constituting 90 percent of the population) had to endure an additional five years of forced labor "apprenticeship" in the colony's cotton and sugar fields. Upon gaining their freedom, most abandoned the plantations, and harvests dropped dramatically. Plantation owners were able to temporarily replace a portion of the lost labor force by taking on Africans "rescued" from Arab dhow sailing ships engaged in the newly illegal Indian Ocean slave trade. These "liberated Africans" were likewise forced to work five-year "apprenticeships," but afterward also quit the plantation fields to work as artisans, fishermen, and independent farmers.

Strapped for labor, colonists shifted to less labor-intensive crops such as coconuts, and they introduced sharecropping. Since the 1840s coconuts have been the country's dominant export product, in the form of oil and later as copra (the white meat of the seed), though for a short time during the late nineteenth century exports of vanilla were also important.

During the twentieth century the Seychelles gradually gained autonomy. A governor was assigned in 1897, and suffrage slightly extended. In 1903 the Seychelles became a separate Crown Colony despite the protest of prominent Seychellois, who preferred the more protected status as a dependency of Mauritius. By 1948, 4 of the 24 seats on the Legislative Council were allocated to elected officials, all of whom represented the Seychelles Taxpayers and Producers Association. The number of political parties and trade unions grew in the 1950s and 1960s. Among the most prominent were the liberal Seychelles Democratic Party (SDP), led by James Mancham, who preferred to maintain ties to Great Britain; and the socialist Seychelles People's United Party (SPUP), headed by Albert René, who called for complete independence. In 1967 Great Britain declared universal suffrage in the Seychelles and doubled the number of elected seats in the Legislative Council. The SDP won four seats and the SPUP won three. Recognizing that independence was inevitable, the British detached several islands from the Seychelles and Mauritius, including Diego Garcia, creating the British Indian Ocean Territory (BIOT) in order to retain a military presence in the area. In return, they built an international airport on Mahé, enabling tourism to become a major industry.

Postcolonial Development and Nationhood

A constitutional conference was held in London, England, in 1970, after which the Legislative Council became a fully elected Legislative Assembly, dominated by the SDP with Mancham as chief minister. On June 29, 1976, the islands became the independent Republic of Seychelles, with Mancham as president and René as prime minister. The BIOT islands were returned to Seychelles, although the Mauritian island of Diego Garcia remained under British control.

Less than one year later, on June 5, 1977, René led a coup d'état, ousting Mancham while he was away at a commonwealth conference in London. SPUP supporters resented Mancham's extravagant lifestyle and economic policies that prioritized tourism and banking over agriculture and fishing. René created a one-party state, declared himself president, party chief, and leader of the armed forces, and renamed the SPUP the Seychelles People's Progressive Front (SPPF). René's socialist policies, such as the formation of state-run farms and the elimination of elite private schools, won little support among the middle and upper classes.

Several times during his first years in office René claimed to have uncovered coup plots, temporarily detaining individuals under the Public Security Regulations and authorizing his government to detain and monitor the mail of suspect individuals under the Post Office Act. In 1981 the then-62-year-old Irishman "Mad" Mike Hoare flew into Seychelles along with fellow mercenaries from South Africa in an attempt to overthrow René. After a confrontation at the airport, all but six of the mercenaries hijacked an Air India plane and flew back to South Africa, only to be arrested there. At René's request, Tanzania sent 400 troops to ensure stability; a year later they helped defeat an army mutiny. Some implicated the United States and South Africa, citing those countries' interest in removing a socialist political leader who had pursued a nonaligned foreign policy and advocated a nuclear-free Indian Ocean. René blamed the political unrest on Mancham, who was leading the Mouvement pour la Résistance while exiled in London. Mancham denied any involvement.

The political intrigue continued when Mancham's successor as head of the Mouvement pour la Résistance, Gerard Hoareau, was assassinated in London, and it was subsequently discovered that his telephone had been tapped. Hoareau allegedly had been supported by businessmen interested in creating an off-shore banking system to launder money procured through drug trafficking. In 1986 a second reported coup attempt failed, this time led by defense minister Ogilvy Berlouis, who had secretly visited the United States Department of Defense in 1985.

Contemporary Events

Despite recurrent coup plots, René was elected to a third term in 1989. In 1991 five of the exiled opposition parties established a coalition, the United Democratic Movement, led by Dr. Maxime Ferrari. Pressured by the international community and aid donors, particularly France and England, René began to institute democratic reforms, including the reintroduction of a multiparty political system. Opposition leaders, including Ferrari, returned to Seychelles, as did Mancham, who headed the newly formed National Democratic Party. The SPPF dominated the 1992 elections, which were held to form an assembly and draw up a new constitution. Disagreements over proposed constitutional reforms eventually led Mancham's party to withdraw its representatives in protest. A second assembly was formed in January 1993, producing a constitution that was ratified by a popular referendum in June. In the elections that soon followed, René and his party once again triumphed.

Since the 1993 election René has begun to implement a number of free-market reforms, promoting the islands as a center for offshore banking. Several national industries, including the port, were privatized. In 1995 the Seychelles raised international concern by announcing the Economic Development Act, which assured any individual who invested a minimum of $10 million in the country against extradition or having assets seized. Under pressure from the United States and other countries, René later amended the act to include provisions to prevent money laundering.

Today most Seychellois work in the service sector, especially the tourist industry. Hopes of finding exploitable petroleum resources have faded. Heavily dependent on imported food, fuel, and other commodities, the economy faces a near-chronic foreign exchange crisis. In response the government has redoubled efforts to attract foreign investors, creating a tax-free business park in the early 1990s known as the Seychelles International Trade Zone.

Ari Nave

See Also

African Socialism; Explorers in Africa, 1500 to 1800; Indian Communities in Africa; France; Portugal; Swahili People; Tourism in Africa; African Religions: An Interpretation.

Africa

Seychelles (Ready Reference)

Official Name: Republic of Seychelles
Area: 455 sq km (about 174 sq mi)
Location: Eastern Africa; a group of 115 islands scattered across the western Indian Ocean, northeast of the island of Madagascar
Capital: Victoria (population 24,324 [1987 estimate])
Population: 78,641 (1998 estimate)
Population Density: 168.2 persons per sq km (about 434 persons per sq mi); concentrated on Mahe Island
Population Below Age 15: 30 percent (male 11,787; female 11,694 [1998 estimate])
Population Growth Rate: 0.67 percent (1998 estimate)
Total Fertility Rate: 1.98 children born per woman (1998 estimate)
Life Expectancy at Birth: Total population: 70 years (male 66.13 years; female 75.5 years [1998 estimate])
Infant Mortality Rate: 17 deaths per 1000 live births (1998 estimate)
Literacy Rate (age 15 and over who can read and write): Total population: 58 percent (1996 estimate)
Education: Education is officially compulsory for children aged 6 to 15. In 1993 there were 9873 primary school students, and 763 enrolled in secondary education. One year of National Youth Service is mandatory for higher education.
Languages: Creole, English, and French are all official languages.
Ethnic Groups: Most Seychellois are of mixed African and French descent; Indian and Chinese minorities are also present.
Religions: About 90 percent of the population are Roman Catholic, about 8 percent are Anglican, and about 2 percent belong to other religions.
Climate: The climate is tropical and humid, with a slighty cooler season during southeast monsoon (late May to September) and a slightly warmer season during northwest monsoon (March to May). For the most part, however, temperatures are roughly constant throughout the year, with average temperatures of 25° C (78° F) in both January and July. Average rainfall is 400 mm (16 in) in January and 50 mm (2 in) in July.
Land, Plants, and Animals: Of the 115 islands, the 32 in the Mahe Group are rocky and hilly. All of the country's principal islands belong to this group; they include Mahe Island (the largest), Praslin, Silhouette, and La Digue. The 83 coral islands are largely without water resources, and most are uninhabited. Only 18 percent of the islands' land is used for permanent crops.
Natural Resources: Guano is the only mineral product; other resources include fish, copra, and cinnamon trees.
Currency: The Seychelles rupee
Gross Domestic Product (GDP): $550 million (1997 estimate)
GDP per Capita: $7000 (1997 estimate)
GDP Real Growth Rate: NA
Primary Economic Activities: Tourism, farming, fishing, and small-scale manufacturing
Primary Crops: Coconuts, cinnamon, vanilla, sweet potatoes, cassava (tapioca), and bananas
Industries: Tourism, coconut and vanilla processing, fishing, coir (coconut fiber) rope processing, boat building, printing, furniture, and beverage production
Primary Exports: Fish, cinnamon bark, copra, petroleum products (re-exports)
Primary Imports: Manufactured goods, food, petroleum products, tobacco, beverages, machinery, and transportation equipment
Primary Trade Partners: France, the United Kingdom, Singapore, Bahrain, and South Africa
Government: The Seychelles is a constitutional republic that gained its independence from the United Kingdom in 1976. It is divided into 23 administrative districts. The executive branch has been led by President Albert René and his appointed Council of Ministers since 1977. The legislative branch is the elected, 11-member People's Assembly (Assemblée du Peuple), currently dominated by President René's party, the Seychelles People's Progressive Front. Other political parties include the Democratic Party and United Opposition.

Lisa Clayton Robinson

North America

Seymour, William Joseph

(b. May 2, 1870, Centersville, La.; d. September 28, 1922, Los Angeles, Calif.), African American minister and leader of the 1906 Azusa Street Revival, the birthplace of the modern Pentecostal movement.

The self-taught son of former slaves, William Joseph Seymour was the first leader of Pentecostalism, a religious movement that has swept the United States, Africa, Latin America, and the rest of the world, acquiring millions of adherents and often described as the religious phenomenon of the twentieth century.

Seymour's religious journey to the Azusa Street Pentecostal Mission in Los Angeles,

California, began in his experiences growing up as a Baptist, and in a young adulthood spent in Methodist churches. A follower of the Holiness Movement, a perfectionist group growing out of Methodism, Seymour believed that the achievement of grace was a two-step process. After conversion God "sanctified" the believer with a "sign." Seymour saw his sign after a bout of smallpox in Cincinnati, Ohio, the result of which was the loss of the use of his left eye.

Having become an evangelist, Seymour went to Houston, Texas, in 1903 and attended classes offered by Charles F. Parham, a leading white Holiness minister. Since segregation laws prohibited him from sitting with the white students, Seymour listened to lectures in the hallway. Parham taught that speaking in tongues, or glossolalia, was further proof of God's grace. Seymour came to believe that glossalalia was a third and final step in the achievement of purity.

Arriving in Los Angeles, California, in 1906, Seymour preached the doctrine of speaking in tongues, igniting an international religious revival known as Pentecostalism, named for the religious enthusiasm experienced by Jesus' disciples and described in the Book of Acts. In its early years the Pentecostal movement under Seymour was unique; despite the racism and sexism of American society at large, the church was integrated and men and women were church officers and preachers. As the movement spread nationally and internationally, much a result of Seymour's newsletter, *The Apostolic Faith*, it was unable to maintain such policies. The church split into white and black groups by 1915, and Seymour preached to a largely black Azusa Street congregation until his death in 1922.

See Also
Baptists.

North America

Shabazz, Hajj Bahiyah Betty

(1936-1997), American educator and widow of black leader Malcolm X who became an international black cultural icon symbolizing the growing influence of Malcolm's name and nationalist message.

There is some uncertainty about Betty Shabazz's origins and early life. Reportedly the daughter of Shelman Sandlin and a woman named Sanders, she was born Betty Sanders and grew up as a foster child in the Detroit, Michigan, home of a black family named Malloy. As a youth she was active in her local African Methodist Episcopal Church. She briefly attended Tuskegee Institute in Alabama, but moved to New York City to escape Southern racism and to study at the Brooklyn States Hospital School of Nursing. During her junior year she attended the Nation of Islam's Temple No. 7 in Harlem. There she taught a women's health and hygiene class and was noticed by Malcolm X, who was a minister at the temple. He proposed by telephone from Detroit, and they eloped and were married in 1958.

Shabazz converted to Islam and became a dutiful Muslim wife. She left Malcolm temporarily on several occasions, however, presumably over disagreements caused by his extensive travel schedule as a spokesman for the Nation of Islam. They became the parents of six daughters, Attallah, Qubilah, Ilyasah, Gamilah, Malaak, and Malikah. Shabazz was pregnant with the twins Malaak and Malikah when Malcolm was assassinated in the Audubon Ballroom in New York City on February 21, 1965, an event she and her other children witnessed.

After Malcolm's death Shabazz raised her children and continued her education, which culminated in a Ph.D. in educational administration from the University of Massachusetts in 1975. She taught health sciences and then became head of public relations at Medgar Evers College in Brooklyn. She left the Nation of Islam at Malcolm's death, but took the *hajj*, the sacred Islamic pilgrimage to Mecca, in Saudi Arabia, and considered herself a Sunni Muslim. She believed that Malcolm had been murdered by the Nation and said so in interviews until a public reconciliation in 1995 with Louis Farrakhan, the head of the Nation of Islam and a rival of Malcolm's at the time of his assassination.

Her reconciliation with Farrakhan helped to establish his legitimacy in the black community, but Shabazz's presence aided even more in the rehabilitation of Malcolm X himself. During the Civil Rights Movement Malcolm was considered by many blacks and whites to be a nationalist, a separatist, even a racist. After his death, however, Malcolm's ideas took on increasing authority as integration failed to solve the crisis of the black urban underclass. Betty Shabazz's existence helped keep Malcolm's name and message fresh, although she personally espoused the more accommodationist self-help doctrine of Booker T. Washington, founder of Tuskegee Institute. She was also active in black social organizations such as the Links, Delta Sigma Theta, and Jack and Jill of America.

On June 1, 1997, Betty Shabazz's only grandson, 12-year-old Malcolm Shabazz, set fire to her apartment in Yonkers, New York. A troubled child, he was staying with his grandmother because his mother, Qubilah, had problems of her own, including substance abuse and involvement in a plot to kill Farrakhan. In the fire Shabazz received third-degree burns over 95 percent of her body, and she died three weeks later. Shabazz was widely honored at her death, especially by black women, in part because the once-reviled Malcolm X had now become a cultural hero, but primarily because her own life had come to exemplify extraordinary courage and perseverance in the face of great difficulties.

Richard Newman

See Also
Farrakhan, Louis Abdul; Harlem, New York; Tuskegee University; Washington, Booker Taliaferro; Black Nationalism in the United States.

Africa

Shaka

(b. 1787?, present-day KwaZulu-Natal, South Africa; d. September 22, 1828, present-day KwaZulu-Natal, South Africa), warrior chief who set in motion the far-reaching changes of the Mfecane, a period of warfare and forced migrations among southern African peoples.

The son of the Zulu chieftain but born of a repudiated wife, Shaka spent his childhood and youth in exile, stigmatized and humiliated. In his 20s he distinguished himself for six years as a warrior in the service of Chief Dingiswayo of the Mthethwa. When Shaka's father died in 1816, Dingiswayo sent Shaka to rule the Zulu. He immediately reorganized the Zulu fighting force and, with innovations in tactics and weaponry, shaped it into a formidable military machine geared to total warfare. Within a year Shaka had quadrupled the number of his subjects and army members by absorbing conquered groups into his Zulu nation.

By the time his overlord, Dingiswayo, was killed in 1817, Shaka was ready to take on all other groups in the area. This he did in annual campaigns during the next ten years. The result was a wave of migrations of uprooted peoples as far north as modern Tanzania and as far south as the Cape Colony (later Cape Province). At the same time the Zulu grew by the addition of other groups, all of which were politically integrated and culturally assimilated. A decade of warfare, however, had taken a heavy toll on the Zulu. Psychologically disturbed throughout his life and obsessively fearful of being supplanted by an heir, Shaka became clearly deranged by the death of his mother in 1828. Later that year he was killed by his half-brother, Dingane, who succeeded him as ruler.

North America

Shakur, Assata

(b. 1947, New York, N.Y.), advocate of black revolution in America who was convicted of murdering a New Jersey state trooper in 1973. In 1979 Shakur escaped from prison and fled to Cuba.

Born Joanne Deborah Byron in Queens, New York, Assata Shakur spent her early years living alternately with her mother in New York and her grandparents in Wilmington, North Carolina. As an adolescent she ran away from home and lived among strangers until taken in by her aunt, Evelyn Williams, a lawyer who later represented her in court. With her aunt's help, she earned her general equivalency diploma (GED) and attended college, first at Manhattan Community College, then at the City College of New York.

In college Shakur became active in student politics, taking part in protests and SIT-INS. She was married briefly, becoming Joanne Chesimard, then changed her name to one that reflected her African heritage: Assata ("she who struggles") Olugbala ("love for the people") Shakur ("the thankful"). During a stay in Oakland, California, around 1970 she met several members of the BLACK PANTHER PARTY and on her return to New York became a leading member of the party's Harlem branch. There she coordinated a breakfast program for schoolchildren. Later in 1970 she left the party for the Black Liberation Army (BLA), a small, loosely organized national group that sought to create an armed uprising among blacks.

Between 1971 and 1973 the BLA is believed to have robbed several banks, kidnapped enemies, and attempted to murder several police officers in different cities. Shakur was personally charged with several crimes, including bank robbery, the murder of a drug dealer, and the attempted murder of policemen. She was also targeted by the Counterintelligence Program (COINTELPRO) of the Federal Bureau of Investigation (FBI), which believed she was a leader of the BLA. In fact, the group likely had little formal hierarchy. It is unclear whether COINTELPRO began to track Shakur before or after she joined the BLA.

On May 2, 1973, state troopers stopped Shakur and two other activists on the New Jersey Turnpike for a minor traffic violation. A shootout followed, leaving one state trooper and one activist dead and Shakur severely wounded; the details of the exchange have never been settled. Shakur was treated for her wounds, but there is evidence that her medical care during her pretrial detention was substandard. She was also subjected to long periods of solitary confinement, and she claimed she was beaten. While awaiting trial for murder Shakur faced the other charges pending against her. She was acquitted of one bank robbery and one kidnapping, while the remaining charges were dropped for lack of evidence and, in one case, due to a hung jury. During this time Shakur gave birth to a daughter, Kakuya, who was conceived with a codefendant.

At the murder trial Shakur proclaimed her innocence, argued that she was being prosecuted for her politics, and offered medical experts who testified that her wounds would have kept her from firing the fatal bullet. In March 1977 she was found guilty of murder and assault and sentenced to life plus 26 to 33 years in prison. Many American leftists and black activists viewed her as a political prisoner. On November 2, 1979, three visitors to the Correctional Facility for Women in Clinton, New Jersey, pulled guns on guards and forced them to release Shakur. The group fled, and Shakur was not heard from again until 1984, when she was granted political asylum in Cuba. In 1987 she published her autobiography, *Assata*.

SEE ALSO

Harlem, New York; San Francisco and Oakland, California; New York, New York.

North America

Shakur, Tupac (2Pac)

(b. June 16, 1971, New York, N.Y.; d. September 13, 1996, Las Vegas, Nev.), African American RAP star praised for his thought-provoking lyrics and criticized for his violent lifestyle; one of the most popular rap artists in the world when he was shot and killed at age 25.

Tupac Shakur was one of the most influential and controversial voices to emerge from hip hop's much maligned club of so-called gangster rappers. Criticized for their violent lyrics and misogynistic claims, gangster rappers became symbols of the best and worst of American musical creativity. Over a six-year period in the early 1990s Shakur became the voice for a generation of young, often frustrated, African Americans.

Through his music and his life Shakur embodied many of the harsh realities of "ghetto life." His raps addressed the difficulties of being young, black, and poor in the United States, and as a promising actor he captured those realities on the screen. True to the thuggish lifestyle that he rapped about, Shakur was arrested and served time in jail on more than one occasion, and often foreshadowed his own death in his songs and videos. Shakur's predictions of his violent death came true on September 13, 1996, when he was murdered shortly after attending a professional boxing match in Las Vegas, Nevada.

Shakur was born in New York City on June 16, 1971, to black activists Afeni Shakur and Billy Garland. Garland interacted infrequently with Tupac, but Shakur exposed her son to many of the activities and philosophies of the BLACK PANTHER PARTY. At times destitute, Shakur and his mother moved often between apartments in New York City. As a young teenager in Harlem, he explored his desire to act by joining the 127th Street Ensemble theater group and was cast as Travis in Lorraine Hansberry's play *A Raisin in the Sun*.

By 1988 the Shakurs had moved several times, finally settling in Marin, California. While in Marin Shakur pursued his interest in music, leaving home in 1988 to join the rap group Strictly Dope. Three years later he left Strictly Dope and joined forces with friends from Oakland, California, who had formed the successful rap group Digital Underground. Shakur initially served as a background dancer for the group, but he was given an opportunity to rap on the group's 1991 single, "Same Song." His powerful delivery and stage charisma made an immediate impression, and friends were soon urging him to go solo.

In late 1991 Shakur released his first solo album, *2Pacalypse Now*, which sold more than 500,000 copies and featured the acclaimed hit "Brenda's Got a Baby." Heralded for its compelling portrayals of the hardships faced by single black mothers and rebuked for its vivid depictions of violence, *2Pacalypse Now* marked powerful contradictions within Shakur's music and life. These contradictions would also be manifest on the silver screen.

Shakur's portrayal of the aggressive, unbalanced character Bishop in the movie *Juice* (1992) and his role as Lucky in the film *Poetic Justice* (1993) mirrored many of the problems in his private life. In 1993 Shakur was arrested for using drugs, and he was later sentenced to ten days in jail for brutally beating another rapper with a baseball bat. In October 1993 Shakur was once again arrested, for allegedly shooting two off-duty Atlanta police officers. Although the charges were later dropped, Shakur's failure to draw a distinction between his public and private personas earned him public criticism.

Among those to criticize Shakur's music and behavior was C. Delores Tucker, chair of the National Political Congress of Black Women. Tucker objected to Shakur's glorification of what he referred to as "thug life" and urged him to use his podium in more positive ways. Shakur's response to Tucker and other critics was often hostile and bitter. Shakur claimed that in his music he was reflecting a lifestyle inspired by a poverty and despair that many Americans wished to ignore. He argued that his music represented the voices of those in America's most marginalized communities, and that to vilify his music simply vilified the realities facing those communities.

By 1994 Shakur's life was a blurred reflection of his art. In March Shakur lost his temper when he was cut from a film and was arrested when he assaulted the film's director, Allen Hughes. After Shakur spent 15 days in jail, his career received a boost when his third film, *Above the Rim*, was released. But eight months later Shakur was back in court defending himself against charges by a 19-year-old woman of sexual assault.

Shakur's troubles climaxed in 1995 when he was robbed and shot five times in the lobby of a recording studio in New York City. Like many of the characters in his movies and songs, Shakur managed to defy death. Although it is unclear who was involved in the attempt on Shakur's life, he blamed the shooting on rival rappers from New York, the Notorious B.I.G. and Sean "Puffy" Combs. At the time Shakur and B.I.G. were leading figures in a fierce rivalry between West Coast and East Coast rappers. When Shakur emerged from the hospital, a jury convicted him of sexual abuse and sentenced him to four and a half years in prison.

While in prison Shakur released his third album, *Me Against the World*, which debuted at Number One on the *Billboard* charts and earned him a Grammy Award nomination for Best Rap Album. *Me Against the World* went on to sell more than 2 million copies in seven months. On the album Shakur talked about his own mortality in the songs "If I Die 2Nite" and "Death Around the Corner," two of many songs that foreshadowed his violent death. Also featured on the album is the song "Dear Mama," which earned Shakur a second Grammy nomination for Best Rap Solo Performance.

After eight months in prison Shakur was released when Suge Knight, head of Death Row Records, paid his $1 million bail. Shakur joined Knight's recording label, and in 1996 he released the double album *All Eyez on Me*. The album has sold 5 million copies and contains Shakur's biggest hit to date, "California Love." While at Death Row Shakur was part of a team that featured many of the most prominent rappers/producers on the West Coast, including Dr. Dre and SNOOP DOGGY DOGG. By all accounts, Shakur's future seemed very promising.

But that promise ended on September 13, 1996, when Shakur was cut down in a barrage of bullets. Shakur and Knight were in Las Vegas, Nevada, attending the championship fight of boxer MIKE TYSON. After the fight Shakur and Knight were driving along the Las Vegas strip when a car pulled up next to theirs and unloaded several rounds. While attempting to flee into the car's back seat, Shakur was shot several times. Knight sustained minor injuries, but Shakur was placed in intensive care. After six days in the hospital he was pronounced dead.

Since the rapper's death Shakur's estate has been plagued by lawsuits, including one by C. Delores Tucker. Tucker claims that Shakur's derogatory references to her in several of his songs caused damage to her marriage. Lawsuits by Shakur's biological father and by a fan injured during a rap concert in which Shakur allegedly taunted the crowd into rioting have been filed. Also, Shakur's mother has filed a lawsuit against Death Row Records for control of her son's unreleased songs.

Shakur's final video, filmed a month before his death, depicts his violent demise. Titled "I Aint Mad At Cha,'" the video and its song aired publicly just a few days after his death. Altogether, Shakur starred in six movies (three of which – *Bullet, Gridlock'd,* and *Gang-Related* – were released in 1997, after Shakur's death) and released six albums, two posthumously. He earned two Grammy Award nominations and sold millions of albums around the world. Shakur's voice echoed the concerns and the rage of many young African Americans who are left to face the challenges of the ghetto alone. But his music also spoke to young adults – many of them middle-class blacks and whites – who understood and valued Shakur's ability to bring the hardships of the marginalized to the surface of American culture.

Alonford James Robinson, Jr.

SEE ALSO

Hansberry, Lorraine; Harlem, New York; Hip Hop in the United States; New York, New York; Notorious B.I.G. ("Biggie Smalls"); San Francisco and Oakland, California; Film, Blacks in American; Combs, Sean ("Puffy").

Shakur, 2PAC. Please see SHAKUR, TUPAC

Africa

Shambaa (also known as Shamba, Sambaa, and Shambala), ethnic group of TANZANIA.

The Shambaa primarily inhabit the coastal plains of northeastern Tanzania. They speak a Bantu language and form a cultural and linguistic cluster together with the BONDEI and PARE. Approximately 500,000 people consider themselves Shambaa.

SEE ALSO

Bantu: Dispersion and Settlement.

Africa

Shangaan (also known as Changane, Shangana, and Shangane), ethnic group of MOZAMBIQUE.

The Shangaan primarily inhabit southern Mozambique. Others live in SOUTH AFRICA and SWAZILAND. They speak a Bantu language and are closely related to the TONGA people. Approximately 1.5 million people identify themselves as Shangaan.

SEE ALSO

Bantu: Dispersion and Settlement.

North America

Shange, Ntozake

(b. October 18, 1948, Trenton, N.J.), African American writer known for innovative, experimental drama, poetry, and fiction.

As prolific as she is provocative, Ntozake Shange pushes the limits of literary form as she questions the social and political limitations imposed on people of color, especially women and children. Inventing her own dramatic medium, Shange created the choreopoem, a combination of narrative text, dance, and music. Her music opens up as many avenues as possible to the exploration of the diverse experiences of the oppressed.

Born Paulette Williams, the daughter of a surgeon and psychiatric social worker, Shange spent her early years in Trenton, New Jersey, in privileged circumstances. Her parents' friends, including JOSEPHINE BAKER, Miles Davis, and W. E. B. Du Bois, provided a culturally affirming black atmosphere. The family moved to St. Louis, Missouri, when Shange was eight. There she was one of the first students to integrate a school.

Depressed by a failed teenage marriage and the limitations she encountered as a talented black woman, Shange attempted suicide several times during her years at Barnard College (1966-1970). She began a new chapter of her life during graduate study at the University of Southern California (USC) in 1973, when she changed her name to the ZULU words Ntozake, "she who comes with her own things," and Shange, "who walks like a lion." After taking an M.A. from USC, Shange moved to the San Francisco Bay Area, where she taught women's studies and writing at area colleges and universities while performing her own poetry and dance. Her best-known work, *for colored girls who have considered suicide, when the rainbow is enuf,* originated in poems from this period.

In 1975 a move to New York saw the performance of *for colored girls* and the beginning of Shange's success. The Broadway production earned a 1977 Obie Award, and Tony, Emmy, and Grammy nominations. Her other plays include *Three Pieces* (1981), *Mother Courage and Her Children* (1980), and a collaboration with South African musicians LADYSMITH BLACK MAMBAZO, *Nomathemba* (1996). Her other work includes poetry collections such as *Nappy Edges* (1978) and the novels *Sassafras, Cypress and Indigo* (1982), the autobiographical *Betsy Brown* (1985), and *Liliane: Resurrection of the Daughter* (1994).

Married to JAZZ musician David Murray in 1977, Shange lives with the couple's daughter Savannah in PHILADELPHIA, PENNSYLVANIA, where Shange teaches at Villanova University.

SEE ALSO

Women Writers, Black, in the United States; Davis, Miles Dewey, III; Du Bois, William Edward Burghardt (W. E. B.); San Francisco and Oakland, California.

Latin America and the Caribbean

Shango, an African-derived religion practiced in Trinidad that developed during the nineteenth century; Shango is also the name of a Yoruba deity worshiped in African-derived religions such as Candomblé and Santería.

There are several dozen Shango centers in Trinidad with thousands of regular devotees and an additional number of less consistent participants and clients. Reflecting the religion's origins among the YORUBA, who were brought to Trinidad as slaves or who arrived there from other islands in the West Indies, the people who practice Shango call themselves "Yoruba people" and call the religion "Yoruba work." Practitioners of Shango often attend Roman Catholic, Protestant, and Shouter (also known as Spiritual Baptist) churches as well.

Shango, CUBA's SANTERÍA, and BRAZIL's CANDOMBLÉ share many elements because of their common Yoruba origins. All of these religions feature the worship of a pantheon of deities (called *"*ORISHAS*"* in Santería, *"orixás"* in Candomblé, *"orisas"* in Yoruba, and "powers" in Shango) and the ritual use of drumming, dance, and singing. In all cases, these Yoruba deities manifest themselves when they possess their devotees during specific rituals, and they are appeased and worshiped through dance, song, and sacrifice. (Though Shango takes its name from one particular deity – Shango, the god of thunder – the religion involves the worship of several other deities.) In the Yoruba religion from which the Shango, Candomblé, and Santería religions derive, each orisha was worshiped in a distinct temple and was associated with particular geographical features and historically specific lineages. The deities of the three derived religions, however, are worshiped in one common center and are seen as the embodiment of less specific forces of nature. Practitioners of these three religions are also believed to "belong" to particular "powers," who control their fate and who must be appeased through worship and the observance of particular ritual requirements and proscriptions. All three religions are also largely devoted to invoking the blessing and assistance of the orishas in order to solve the problems faced by their devotees in this life, and are less concerned with the issues of sin and absolution, and life after death, that are such central features of Christian religions.

Shango, Candomblé, and Santería have all incorporated elements of Roman Catholicism. Most prominently, the symbols, statues, and iconography of particular Roman Catholic saints have been used to stand for Yoruba deities with whom they share similarities. For example, in Shango, the deity Shango himself is often represented by statues of Saint John the Baptist, while Abatala is symbolized by Saint Benedict, and Ogun by Saint Michael (these correspondences vary within particular Shango temples and are not consistent across Candomblé, Santería, and Shango).

Because its history differs, Shango differs from Candomblé and Santería in other essential respects as well. Reflecting its development in Trinidad, a former British colony, Shango has been more deeply influenced by Protestant Christian religions, not just by Roman Catholicism. According to the scholar George Eaton Simpson, Shango has thus become a more "syncretized," or hybrid, religion. For example, in contrast with practices in VODOU shrines in HAITI and Candomblé centers in Brazil, the African symbols used in Shango are not kept in a separate room from the Christian ones. Recently Shango has been increasingly influenced by the Shouter religion, with which it shares certain similarities, such as the high value placed on the direct experience of the divine.

Each Shango center holds one big annual meeting in addition to the smaller rituals held for particular powers, which are performed three or four times a year. The Shango cult center consists of a shrine area with five or more shrines for the most important powers; a *chapelle*, or small cult house; and a *palais*, where healing ceremonies are held. Shango involves the worship of some non-Yoruba powers as well, like Mama Latay and Gabriel. Each power has certain characteristics that define its personality and the objects and colors it uses. For example, the colors of the deity Shango are red or yellow and red; he dances in the fire and carries a whip (i.e., when his devotees are possessed by him they carry his iconic whip). He receives bulls, rams, red or white cocks, and white pigeons as sacrifices, and is said to be quiet, peaceful, and charitable. Other powers are Ogun (Saint Michael), Oshun (Saint Philomena or Saint Anne), Shakpana (Saint Francis, Moses, or Saint Jerome), and Emanja (Saint Anne or Saint Catherine).

In Trinidad someone becomes a devotee of a certain deity when he or she is possessed by it in a ceremony; when that power assists someone with an illness or a problem; or when it is a family tradition to worship that power. Nevertheless, there is no direct relationship between the deity's personality and the devotee's character. The same deity can even provoke different reactions in the same devotee. The powers punish their followers for behavior they do not like, and they reveal their will in dreams or through the interpretations of Shango priests and priestesses.

The Shango center's large annual ceremony begins on Tuesday night with a prayer meeting. Eshu, the trickster, who is the divine messenger among the deities, is always invoked first and appeased, then dismissed lest he cause too much trouble. Then other male and female powers are invited to appear at the ritual in turn, beginning with Ogun. From time to time rum or water is poured in the four corners of the palais by a ceremonial assistant or a possessed person. Each person who is possessed by a particular power gets the ritual paraphernalia associated with the deity from the chapelle and comes back to dance near the shrine of the deity. Drumming, dancing, and possessions last all night. People identify the powers through the rhythms played by the drums and from the songs the possessed people sing, the objects they bring back from the chapelle, and the way they behave. The most important stimuli for the possessions are the different beats played on the drums.

In addition to Shango worship in Trinidad, there is also a religion in Grenada called Shango that features the worship of Yoruba deities. The Xangô religion in northeastern Brazil is also Yoruba-derived and broadly similar (*see* RELIGIONS, AFRICAN, IN BRAZIL). Overall, the worship of Shango in Trinidad, as well as in other parts of Latin America and the Caribbean, is one of the more lasting religious legacies of Africa in the New World, and is testament to the deep religious conviction and perseverance of generations of Afro-Caribbeans and Latin Americans.

Mayda Grano de Oro

SEE ALSO

Trinidad and Tobago; Catholic Church in Latin America and the Caribbean; Protestant Church in Latin America and the Caribbean; Exú.

Shari. Please see CHARI

Latin America and the Caribbean

Sharpe, Samuel, a freed slave who led the Baptist War in Montego Bay, Jamaica, in 1831 (*see* JAMAICA).

Africa

Sharpeville, South Africa, a black township in SOUTH AFRICA in which protesting residents were massacred by police in 1960.

On March 21, 1960, South African police fired upon a group of demonstrators in the black township of Sharpeville, killing at least 69 and injuring nearly 200. The incident sparked both internal turmoil and international outrage against South Africa's oppressive APARTHEID regime.

Sharpeville, situated south of Johannesburg in South Africa's Transvaal region, was created in 1942. Like other black, "Coloured," and Asian townships, Sharpeville was home to people forced to move there in accordance with South Africa's racial segregation laws. Early laws, such as the 1913 Natives Land Act, aimed to keep Africans in rural areas, but rapid industrialization in the 1940s increased demand for cheap labor in the cities. The Urban Areas Acts of the 1940s allowed for greater numbers of "non-whites" to live legally in urban areas, but only in designated townships.

When the AFRIKANER-dominated NATIONAL PARTY came to power in 1948, the government imposed a new and more drastic system of racial control, known as apartheid. In addition to imposing urban residential segregation, the national government assigned Africans to rural "Bantu Homelands" according to the "tribe" to which they belonged. The government also increased enforcement of the PASS LAWS, which forced blacks to carry with them at all times documents – work permits, tax receipts, and identification information stating name and "tribe" – and produce them whenever asked. Anyone who refused could be fined or imprisoned.

By 1960 pass-law protests already had a long history in South Africa, but the protest on March 21 of that year marked a tragic turning point. Robert Sobukwe, leader of the Pan-Africanist Congress (PAC), called for all black South Africans to defy the pass laws by staying home from work so that they could hand in their passes (now called "reference books") at their local police stations.

At about eight in the morning, many gathered at the Sharpeville police station; a similar demonstration unfolded in Langa, a township near Cape Town. Photographic evidence shows that the crowd in Sharpeville was unarmed, peaceful, and significantly smaller than the police report claimed (there were about 5000 people, including numerous children). At the scene, the police – whose ranks soon swelled to 300 officers – neither asked the demonstrators to disperse, nor warned them of any consequences if they did not. Sometime after half past one, the police opened fire. Of the 69 killed, 10 were children; another 19 children were wounded.

Despite the medical examiner's report, which confirmed witness testimony that most victims were shot in the back while trying to escape the gunfire, the police were never sanctioned for their actions. The massacre, which was widely reported in the international press, led to worldwide criticism and continuing demonstrations throughout South Africa. The South African government subsequently banned the African National Congress and the PAC (many of the leaders of these two antiapartheid groups had already fled or been imprisoned). Although the declaration of a state of emergency eventually stifled the protests, Sharpeville was again the site of violence in 1984, when demonstrators against rent increases allegedly killed one of the township's councilors.

Kate Tuttle

See Also
Cape Town, South Africa.

Europe

Sharp, Granville

(b. November 10, 1735, Durham, England; d. July 6, 1813, London, England), white English abolitionist.

Granville Sharp was a leader of the abolitionist legal battle in Great Britain. He assisted lawyers in their efforts to prove that existing British court decisions that condoned slavery and the slave trade were not only inhumane, but illegal, according to British law. A contemporary of his once suggested that it was obvious that Sharp was not trained as a lawyer because he was less interested in the law as it was than in the law as it should be.

Described by scholar Gretchen Gerzina as a man with an "unflinching moral sense,"

"A toleration of Slavery," wrote English abolitionist Granville Sharp, "is, in effect, a toleration of inhumanity." Beginning with the case of Jonathan Strong in 1765, Sharp spent decades working to free escaped slaves and to end the institution of slavery in England. *Archive Photos*

Sharp came from a religious Durham family. His formal education ended when he was 14 years old. After several apprenticeships, Sharp became a clerk at the ordinance office in London at age 22. He drew most of his satisfaction in life, however, by gathering with his numerous brothers and sisters, all of whom lived in England, to play music together.

In 1765 Sharp had an encounter in his brother's medical office with a severely wounded runaway slave named Jonathan Strong. This was Sharp's introduction to the horrifying conditions of slavery. The Sharp brothers helped Strong until he was healed, and then they found him employment. Three years later Strong's former owner kidnapped him in order to sell him back into slavery, and Strong asked Sharp for legal assistance. Sharp argued Strong's case successfully, and Strong was freed. However, Strong's former owner threatened to sue Sharp for damages. As a result, and in an attempt to intimidate the former owner, Sharp wrote his famous abolitionist tract, *A Representation of the Injustice and Dangerous Tendency of Tolerating Slavery; or of Admitting the Least Claim of Private Property in the Persons of Men, in England.*

In the memorandum Sharp reiterated Justice John Holt's 1706 comments that English air was "too pure" for slaves to breathe and that England was not, and should not be, a setting conducive to slavery. He showed that several English cases upheld this precedent, despite the 1729 Yorke and Talbot opinion that slaves could be held by West Indian masters while in England. Sharp claimed that only with a pre-existing written contract could a master legally keep a person in slavery when traveling to England. Furthermore, he argued, nobody could obtain such a document because no person would freely enter into a contract that submitted him or her to slavery. Sharp rejected the notion that a person could be considered private property, and he claimed that when anyone – black or white – entered England, he or she became a subject of the king. The tract warned Strong's former owners that they could be penalized for defying the 1679 Habeas Corpus Act, which protected the liberty and human rights of British subjects from unjust imprisonment and expatriation. He ended by claiming that "A toleration of Slavery, is, in effect, a toleration of inhumanity." Sharp sent the tract to several British judges, including William Blackstone, who had mentioned Holt's comments in his famous *Commentaries on the Laws of England.* Blackstone warned Sharp of the difficulties ahead, saying that "it would be uphill work in the Court of King's Bench" to bring forth such abolitionist claims.

Despite the difficulties Sharp did not waiver from the task. He continued to help kidnapped slaves gain legal rights. He assisted the defense for John and Mary Hylas in late 1768, a case in which John Hylas sued his wife's former master for forcibly selling her back into West Indian slavery. Mary Hylas was allowed to return to her husband, but the case did not determine rights of slaves in Britain; according to the court, she was only entitled to her freedom because her husband was free. Then in 1771 Sharp defended Thomas Lewis, who had been kidnapped and held by his former owner Robert Stapylton. Justice William Mansfield presided over the case. Wanting to avoid ruling on the issue of whether a master had such a right over a slave, Mansfield freed Lewis on the technicality that there was no evidence of Stapylton ever having purchased Lewis. The judge stated that he hoped the issue of slavery would never be finally discussed. This angered Sharp, who accused Mansfield of "open contempt of the principle of the constitution."

In the case of James Somerset a year later, Mansfield could no longer avoid the issue. He ruled that the forcible repatriation of blacks into slavery was illegal. Though Sharp did not attend the Somerset hearings, his support of the defense was invaluable. His active publicizing of the issues surrounding the case greatly influenced the outcome.

After the Somerset case Sharp continued to be called on to help former slaves and others who constituted the black poor community in London. Several years before the government funded a plan to resettle the black population in Sierra Leone for profit, Sharp had proposed a similar scheme, although his intentions were humanitarian. He envisioned the blacks living in an idealized moral community with a consensual government (*see* London's Black Poor and the Sierra Leone Settlement Plan).

"Granville Town," as this proposed settlement was called, was never fully realized, but Sharp continued as a valued member of the Society for the Abolition of the Slave Trade until his death in 1818. Although he did not live to see the results of his work, his tireless efforts on behalf of abolition in Great Britain helped to outlaw the slave trade there in 1808, and to emancipate British slaves in 1834.

Leyla Keough

See Also

Transatlantic Slave Trade; London's Black Poor and the Sierra Leone Settlement Plan; Abolitionism in the United States; Fugitive Slaves; Holt Decision.

North America

Sharpton, Alfred (Al), Jr.

(b. October 3, 1954, Brooklyn, N.Y.), African American Pentecostal minister, controversial civil rights activist, and first African American candidate for New York State Senate.

Rev. Al Sharpton made a reputation as a leader who who does not shy away from controversy. Some observers have criticized him as an attention-seeking self-promoter, but none can discount his long career of activism and protest on behalf of African Americans and especially of the poor. In the pulpit at age 4, Sharpton – known as "the Wonderboy" – spent his early years as a sensation on the Pentecostal preaching circuit. For years he traveled to various Pentecostal churches, including a tour with famed Gospel Music performer Mahalia Jackson.

In 1969 Rev. Jesse Jackson chose Sharpton as youth director of Operation Breadbasket, during which Sharpton organized protest demonstrations and boycotts to pressure businesses to hire more minority employees. At around the same time, Sharpton began his own organization, the National Youth Movement, and met longtime friend and mentor, musician James Brown. From 1973 to the early 1980s, in addition to his civil rights activism, Sharpton served as one of Brown's tour managers. Sharpton's wife, Kathy Jordan-Sharpton, is a gospel singer and former back-up vocalist for Brown. The couple have two daughters, Dominique and Ashley.

Although he had entered politics in 1978 with an unsuccessful run for the new York state senate, Rev. Sharpton did not gain wide recognition until 1985, with his public statements in the case of Bernard Goetz, a white man who shot four young black men on the New York subway, permanently disabling one of them. Sharpton continued to speak out in 1986, when he called for a special prosecutor in the aftermath of the Howard Beach racial incident, in which a crowd of whites chased a black man named Michael Griffiths onto a highway where he was struck and killed by a passing car. Two years later Sharpton served as adviser to Tawana Brawley, a black teenager who claimed that she had been abducted and raped by three white police officers. Although a grand jury ultimately concluded that her accusations were a hoax, Sharpton continues to maintain that the officers are guilty. In 1989 Rev. Sharpton played a prominent role in the protests that followed the shooting death of Yusef Hawkins, a black youth who encountered a white mob in the Bensonhurst section of New York City.

Sharpton garnered both praise and criticism for his unceasing activism. His National Youth Movement faced charges of fraud and Sharpton was stung by allegations that he was an informant for the Federal Bureau of Investigation (FBI). Still, Sharpton's mastery at organizing demonstrations and delivering newsworthy sound bites quickly made him a fixture in New York City's tumultuous local politics. During the 1990s he began attempting to refine and tone down his public image, although he remained a controversial figure. As he prepared to lead a demonstration in 1991, Sharpton was attacked and stabbed by Michael Riccardi, a white resident of Bensonhurst.

In 1990 Sharpton served a 15-day sentence for disorderly conduct, and on March 9, 1993, he was remanded to Rikers Island to begin a 45-day sentence incurred as a result of a demonstration that took place in the late 1980s. Sharpton took his difficulties in stride. "This is the first time since I was 17," he told the *New York Post,* "that James Brown will play New York without me there."

After failed bids for the United States Senate in 1992 and 1994, in 1997 Sharpton made an impressive showing in the city's Democratic Mayoral primary, winning 32 percent of the vote. While recasting his public persona, Sharpton insisted that fundamentally he had not changed. "I don't think that I've changed in terms of basics," he explained to the *New York Times*. "I think I've changed in terms of style.... In the 1980s I was... concerned about getting my issues straight in the newspapers. In the 1990s, I'm far more concerned about getting our message straight in history."

Kate Tuttle

See Also

Jackson, Jesse Louis; Pentecostalism.

Africa

Shashi, ethnic group of Tanzania.

The Shashi primarily inhabit Tanzania just southeast of Lake Victoria. They speak a Bantu language and are closely related to the neighboring Sukuma people. More than 100,000 people consider themselves Shashi.

See Also

Bantu: Dispersion and Settlement.

North America

Shell, Arthur

(b. November 26, 1946, Charleston, S.C.), a member of the Professional Football Hall of Fame; the second African American (the first since Fritz Pollard retired in 1937) to be named head coach in the National Football League.

Arthur Shell, the eldest of five, was born in 1946 in the Daniel Jenkins Housing Project in Charleston, South Carolina. He lost his mother to a fatal heart attack when he was just 15 years old and helped his father, who worked in a paper mill, raise his siblings. Shell was a star athlete in high school, excelling in both football and basketball at Bonds-Wilson High in North Charleston. Shell's size (1.9 m [6 ft 5 in]) and athletic talent earned him a scholarship in 1963 to attend Maryland State (now Maryland-Eastern Shore), where he played both offense and defense on the school's football team (*see* Football, Collegiate).

In 1968 Shell was drafted in the third round by the Oakland Raiders. In 15 seasons with the Raiders Shell played in 207 regular season and 24 postseason games. He was an eight-time All-Pro and a member of the Raiders' champion Super Bowl XI and XV teams. After the 1982 season Shell retired from professional football, and a year later he became an assistant coach with the newly relocated Los Angeles Raiders. In 1989 Shell was inducted into the Professional Football Hall of Fame and was named head coach of the Raiders, the first of only a handful of African American coaches to be afforded that opportunity in the 1990s. Shell left the Raiders in 1994, becoming an assistant coach of the Kansas City Chiefs (1995-1996). He joined the Atlanta Falcons in 1997 as an assistant coach.

See Also

Atlanta, Georgia; Football, Professional; Kansas City, Missouri; Los Angeles, California; Pollard, Frederick Douglass (Fritz).

Africa

Sherbro, ethnic group of Sierra Leone.

The Sherbro primarily inhabit coastal southern Sierra Leone, including Sherbro Island. They speak a Niger-Congo language and are related to the Temne people. In recent years they have increasingly assimilated to the neighboring Mende people. Approximately 200,000 people consider themselves Sherbro.

See Also

Languages, African: An Overview.

North America

Sherrod, Charles (b. January 2, 1937, St. Petersburg, Va.), African American civil rights activist and field secretary of the Student Nonviolent Coordinating Committee (SNCC) (1961-1966).

After putting himself through Virginia Union University, where he received a B.A. in 1958 and a B.D. in 1961, Charles Sherrod took part in the struggle against racial discrimination in the United States by joining SNCC. With the two-pronged aim of desegregation and voter registration, Sherrod settled in Georgia, where he and other SNCC members united with local leaders of the African American community to defeat racist laws and practices. Sherrod broke with SNCC in 1966, largely because of his support of white inclusion in the organization. Subsequently, he organized the Southwest Georgia Independent Voters Project, which he directed until 1987, and he worked toward creating agricultural co-operatives in the area. In 1976 he was elected city commissioner in Albany, Georgia, the site of his early work with SNCC.

Africa

Shilluk (also known as Collo), ethnic group of Sudan.

The Shilluk primarily inhabit the basin of the White Nile in south central Sudan. They speak a Nilo-Saharan language. More than 150,000 people consider themselves Shilluk.

See Also
Languages, African: An Overview.

Africa

Shirazi (also known as Mbwera), ethnic group of East Africa and the Indian Ocean islands.

According to oral tradition, beginning in the tenth century immigrants from the Shiraz region of Persia (now Iran) settled the islands and mainland ports of coastal East Africa, from Mogadishu, Somalia, in the north to the Sofala coast of Mozambique in the south. Many scholars, however, believe that the Shirazi actually began their settlement of the East African coast in the twelfth century and that they originated in Somalia. Shirazi settlers established themselves on the following islands: Lamu, Kenya; Pemba, Zanzibar, Mafia, and Kilwa Kisiwani, all in Tanzania; and the Comoros. Most likely the Shirazi combined African, Arab, and Persian elements to form a unique ethnic identity. They contributed to the development of the Swahili language and the spread of this language and Islam in East Africa.

Known for their mercantile prowess, the Shirazi asserted themselves as ruling elites as early as the twelfth century on the islands that were their base. Trade in gold, ivory, and slaves brought prosperity to the Shirazi, who probably commissioned the Husuni Kubwa palace of Kilwa during the thirteenth and fourteenth centuries. Shirazi traders regularly traveled as far as Persia, the Arabian Peninsula, and the Indian subcontinent. The Shirazi never created a single, centralized empire. Several sultanates competed for power as political and economic fortunes waxed and waned. For example, the Shirazi sultanate of Kilwa declined in importance after the fifteenth century, while the Shirazi of coastal Kenya prospered, particularly at Malindi.

Today the Shirazi number more than 300,000 and comprise three major subgroups: the Hadimu, the Tumbatu, and the Pemba. The Shirazi distinguish themselves from other Swahili-speaking peoples. They are particularly concentrated on the island of Zanzibar.

Ari Nave

See Also
Gold Trade; Ivory Trade; Swahili Language; Indian Ocean Slave Trade; Mogadishu, Somalia; Swahili People; Lamu, Kenya; Islam and Tradition: An Interpretation.

Africa

Shona, an ethno-linguistic group of southeastern Africa.

The history and culture of the Shona people is contested and complex. Those who call themselves Shona and speak a Shona dialect inhabit present-day Zimbabwe, southern Zambia, and west central Mozambique. The exact origin of the Shona is unknown: linguists generally contend that the diversity of dialects indicates a first millennium arrival, while historians usually date the arrival of Shona speakers to the Iron Age. It is agreed that the Shona were most likely the first Bantu-speaking people in the area, displacing the Khoikhoi and possibly some central Sudanic inhabitants. By the tenth century Shona speakers had become the most numerous people between the Zambezi and Limpopo rivers, though they were by no means the only inhabitants. The Shona comprised a mosaic of disparate chieftainships, similar in their languages and livelihoods – based on a combination of agriculture and animal husbandry – but with a diversity of religious beliefs and customs. Although all were patrilineal, their political organization and means of succession varied considerably. Familial and dynastic competition was common, though there were no standing armies and major conflicts were few.

After 1000 C.E. centralized states began to emerge among the Shona. It was not until the fourteenth century, however, that these empires became distinguishable, as they competed for trade in gold and ivory with Arab and, later, Portuguese merchants. The first major empire was based at Great Zimbabwe between approximately 1250 and 1550, to be succeeded by the Torwa Empire based at Khame to the west. At about the same time came the emergence of the Mhonomotapa and the Mutapa state to the northeast, an expansionist gold-producing and trading state. The last great Shona empire was that of Changamire, and those who became known as the Rozvi, a confederation of tribute-paying chieftainships in the southwest. This empire also disintegrated in the mid-1800s, due to the Nguni invasion resulting from the Mfecane, or violent upheavals in South Africa.

Nineteenth-century Ndebele invasions and British intrusions led disparate groups, concerned to protect their own interests, to take on Shona as a common identity. Unlike many ethnic groups in Africa, the Shona retain strong beliefs in totems and have never had a myth of the origin of humanity. They believe in a high god, the most prominent and powerful being the Mwari of the Changamire, and ancestral spirits, or *mudzimu*. Despite the similarities among them, the diverse clusters of dialects that roughly correspond to ethnic groups have become increasingly politicized. These include the Korekore in the north of Zimbabwe, Zezuru in the center, Karanga in the south, Kalanga farther west, Manyika in the east, and the Ndau in the southeast and in west central Mozambique. In modern Zimbabwean politics the Shona hold most important political positions and are, after whites, the captains of industry. Among the Shona the Zezuru are the predominant group. In Mozambique the Ndau, a Shona-speaking group, were prominent as the leadership of the opposition Mozambican National Resistance (RENAMO). In addition, the Shona, with their contested history and varied past, have also adapted to popular culture; Shona stone sculpture produced by contemporary Shona artists, for example, has gained international recognition as a fine art form.

Eric Young

See Also
Bantu: Dispersion and Settlement; Gold Trade; Ivory Trade; Pastoralism; Portugal; Zambezi River.

Africa

Shope (also known as Chope, Chopi, and Vachopi), ethnic group of Mozambique.

The Shope primarily inhabit southern Mozambique. Others live in South Africa. They speak a Bantu language. Approximately 400,000 people consider themselves Shope.

See Also
Bantu: Dispersion and Settlement.

North America

Short, Bobby (b. September 15, 1924, Danville, Ill.), African American cabaret singer and pianist known for suave nightclub performances.

Bobby Short became a recognized talent in the New York cabaret world as early as 1937, the year he was acclaimed in *Variety* magazine. During the 1940s and 1950s he toured the United States, establishing himself as a premier nightclub act with his elegant stage personality and singing style. Short then settled in New York City, where he played in several Broadway shows and at well-known "café society" nightclubs. Dividing his time between France and the United States, Short performed four months out of the year at Cafe Carlyle in New York City beginning in 1968.

See Also
New York, New York.

North America

Shuttlesworth, Fred L.
(b. March 18, 1922, Mugler, Ala.), African American Baptist minister and civil rights leader who was a founding member and secretary of the Southern Christian Leadership Conference (SCLC).

After receiving a B.A. from Selma University in Alabama in 1951 and a B.S. from Alabama State Teachers College in 1952, Fred Shuttlesworth became pastor first of Bethel Baptist Church, and then of the First Baptist Church in Birmingham, Alabama.

Shuttlesworth formed the Alabama Christian Movement for Human Rights (ACMHR) in 1956. As president from its inception until 1969, Shuttlesworth led Birmingham's integration movement. He became secretary of the SCLC, founded in 1958. With Martin Luther King Jr., Shuttlesworth was instrumental in uniting the two organizations in an antisegregation campaign; the joining of forces led to the Birmingham demonstration of the spring of 1963. Shuttlesworth continued to organize demonstrations and marches, and finished his term as secretary of the SCLC in 1970. As a minister in Cincinnati, Ohio, Shuttlesworth has remained committed to issues of social justice.

See Also
King, Martin Luther, Jr.

Africa

Sia (also known as Sya), ethnic group of West Africa.

The Sia primarily inhabit western Burkina Faso and neighboring Mali. They speak a Mande language. More than 100,000 people consider themselves Sia.

See Also
Languages, African: An Overview.

Africa

Siad Barre, Muhammad
(b. 1916, Ganane, Italian Somaliland; d. January 2, 1995, Lagos, Nigeria), president and military dictator of Somalia from 1969 to 1991.

Muhammad Siad Barre was born into a family of nomadic herders in what was then Italian Somaliland. He belonged to the Marehan, a subgroup of the large Somali Daarood clan. In 1941, after part of Somalia fell under British control, Siad Barre joined the police force. In 1950 he attended a military academy in Italy, returning home when Somalia achieved independence in 1960.

Siad Barre rose quickly through the ranks of the Somali National Army, reaching the position of major general and commander in chief by 1966. After the assassination of President Abdel-Rashid Ali Shermarke and a military coup d'état in October 1969, Siad Barre took power as head of the Supreme Revolutionary Council.

Siad Barre's promise to end tribalism and forge a modern socialist (*see* African Socialism) state won him early support from urban intellectuals and professionals as well as the military. Although he officially banned clan loyalties, he himself depended on clan elders to keep order in rural areas. At the same time he increased the power of the Supreme Revolutionary Council, censored the press, and banned labor unions. In keeping with his official ideology of "scientific socialism," he also placed a large part of the economy under state control. Some historians have argued that this centralization of power and money in the traditionally dispersed nomadic economy was one of the leading causes of later violence. His successful literacy campaign in the early 1970s included the controversial decision to institutionalize Latin rather than Arabic characters in the long-planned written Somali language.

Known as a chain-smoking insomniac who called journalists for interviews in the middle of the night, Siad Barre's main preoccupation was security. He spared no expense to make the Somali military one of the most powerful armies in Sub-Saharan Africa: by the early 1980s approximately three-quarters of the state budget went to the military. He bought weapons from both the East and the West during the cold war, as well as from Libya, South Africa, China, and several Middle Eastern countries.

In 1977 Siad Barre used the army to seize the long-disputed territory of Ogaden from Ethiopia. When the Soviet-backed Ethiopians reclaimed the territory the following year, Siad Barre appealed to the United States for military and economic aid. He received $100 million a year in exchange for the United States' use of formerly Soviet-occupied Red Sea military facilities.

Siad Barre also used the armed forces against his own people. In addition to many individual cases of torture and assassination, whole clans were subject to mass execution, systematic rape, and village bombardment by military aircraft. The army also destroyed the grazing lands and water reservoirs of rural clans, leading to mass starvation and death by thirst. Between 1978 and 1988 Siad Barre's regime is thought to have killed at least 20,000 Somalis.

Siad Barre was the sole candidate in the 1986 presidential election, assuring him another seven years in office. By 1990, however, international as well as internal pressure had forced him to promise reforms allowing for a multiparty system, legalizing the narcotic Qaat, revoking equal inheritance for women, and liberalizing the economy. By January 1991 it was clear that reforms would not suffice. The paramilitary United Somali Congress took Mogadishu, and Siad Barre fled to Kenya. After the Kenyan parliament denied him refuge, he went to Nigeria. He died in Lagos in 1995.

Marian Aguiar

See Also
Lagos, Nigeria; Mogadishu, Somalia.

Cross Cultural

Sickle Cell Anemia, a genetically inherited condition of the red blood cells that causes chronic anemia, episodes of pain, and eventually death, mainly affecting people of African descent.

In 1997 there were approximately 72,000 individuals affected by sickle cell anemia, mostly African Americans, including 1 out of every 500 African Americans born each year. Some 2 million Americans – 1 out of every 12 African Americans – carry the genetic trait. The disease has produced a call, both federally and locally, for the development of appropriate testing of individuals at risk, effective treatments to reduce the debilitating symptoms and irreversible damage to major body systems, genetic screening of fetuses, and remedies for the psychosocial well-being of affected individuals and their families.

Sickle cell anemia is caused by a genetic error that causes the body to produce abnormal red blood cells. This cell mutation originated in West Africa thousands of years ago, where it served as a survival advantage to West African populations plagued by a deadly form of malaria. Individuals who inherited the sickle cell gene did not contract malaria. In fact, today in areas where malaria is prevalent, such as equatorial Africa, more deaths result from malaria than from sickle cell disease.

The sickle cell gene tells the body to produce an abnormal form of the chemical compound in hemoglobin responsible for bringing oxygen into the red blood cells. Low levels of blood oxygen cause blood cells to polymerize, or become jagged and tough, taking on a sickle shape instead of assuming their usual soft, round shape. The red blood cells, because of their irregular, hard edges, get caught in narrow blood vessels and collect there, causing restricted blood flow. The result of this restriction is the so-called "pain episode," which can occur unpredictably and for a period of several hours to several days. With a much shorter life span than ordinary cells, the sickled cells cause the blood to be chronically short of red blood cells, which also causes anemia in affected individuals. The complications of sickle cell anemia include stroke, osteomyelitis (an inflammatory disease of the bone leading to destruction of bone tissue), priapism (painful and persistent penile erection), and dactylitis (swollen fingers and toes, usually in babies). As the affected individual ages, other complications may arise, including blindness, heart and lung conditions, kidney failure, and damage to the spleen and liver.

Individuals who carry the sickle cell genetic *trait* do not have sickle cell *disease*. The sickle cell trait (which has no symptoms) results when an individual inherits the sickle cell gene from only one parent (a heterozygous form). Such a person can transmit the sickle cell gene to future generations but will not contract the illness himself. Sickle cell *disease*, often referred to as sickle cell anemia, results when an individual inherits the gene from both parents (a homozygous form).

Contrary to popular conception, sickle cell disease does not affect only Africans or African Americans. In fact, sickle cell disease can be genetically transmitted across populations to the offspring of any two parents who bear the sickle cell gene. While a large percentage of the cases in the United States have been among African Americans, the disease has also been found in Burma, Greece, India, Turkey, and Yemen and is not limited to any one ethnic group. The highest incidence of the disease, affecting 20 percent of the population, has been found in Central Africa near the equator, where malaria is prevalent.

Testing for sickle cell disease has improved greatly over the past two decades. In the 1970s the solubility test that was used was not capable of distinguishing between people who merely had the heterozygous genetic trait (not diseased) and those who were homozygous for sickled blood cells (diseased). The results indicated that a large number of African Americans had the disease. In the black community, a number of concerned leaders and organizations, including the Black Panthers, pressed for increased testing of African Americans, unaware of the deficiency in the testing procedures and the difficulties the results could pose for their constituents.

In Chicago alone, the exaggerated test results of 5000 black public school children led to the incorrect statistic that 1 out of every 10 children had sickle cell disease. The resulting overstated claims by the Heart and Lung Institute, an otherwise reputable source, that a significant percentage of the African American population was affected by sickle cell disease had negative effects on the entire community, which was then subject to routine screening for jobs and dramatic increases in insurance rates.

Pressure from the black community and local politicians has led to legislation in 12 states concerning mandatory screening for sickle cell anemia. In 1972 Congress passed the National Sickle Cell Anemia Control Act, which was expanded in 1976 and amended in 1978. The misinformation from the 1970s testing and other popular misunderstandings informed such legislation, and led to the government's desire to control the disease, even though it had been demonstrated to be genetically transmitted, not contagious (for a more sinister example of the United States government's intervention in disease "control" among blacks, *see* TUSKEGEE SYPHILIS EXPERIMENT). Finally, federal support of community sickle cell programs led to the establishment of Comprehensive Sickle Cell Centers, which offered testing, education, and counseling, and which continued research to develop more sophisticated and more reliable testing procedures, including electrophoresis techniques.

At present sickle cell treatment is aimed at the early detection of the disease so that affected individuals may begin treatment before they manifest debilitating symptoms. Babies who are homozygous for sickle cell disease can be protected against infections by being given penicillin orally at about four months of age. Patients who have begun to display advanced symptoms are provided with various forms of supportive management, including psychological counseling for the pain and discomfort associated with the disease.

The death rate from sickle cell disease is steadily decreasing due to improved therapies. Exchange transfusion therapy, which temporarily reduces the number of sickled cells in the blood, is used to manage advanced chronic pain and acute conditions such as stroke. Two experimental drugs developed in the late 1980s are erythropoietin, a hormone that helps increase the production of red blood cells, and hydroxyurea. Both of these medications, when given to sickle cell disease patients, help promote the synthesis of normal fetal hemoglobin, which replaces some of the sickled blood in the individual. Bone marrow transplants have been used to cure children with sickle cell disease, but the risk of death is as great as 50 percent, and the cost is prohibitive for most families. Gene therapy is possibly the cure of the future for sickle cell disease, but it is still at an experimental stage.

Barbara Worley

SEE ALSO

Black Panther Party; Chicago, Illinois.

Africa

Sidamo (also known as Sidama and Sadama), ethnic group of ETHIOPIA.

The Sidamo primarily inhabit southwestern Ethiopia. They speak an Afro-Asiatic language in the Cushitic group. More than 3 million people consider themselves Sidamo.

SEE ALSO

Languages, African: An Overview.

Africa

Sierra Leone, a country on the Atlantic coast of West Africa bordered by LIBERIA and GUINEA.

Today war-torn and impoverished, Sierra Leone played a role in Africa's colonial history far out of proportion to its size. (It is one of the smallest West African countries and has a population of just over 4 million.) Abolitionists founded the Sierra Leone Colony at the end of the eighteenth century as a refuge for freed slaves (*see* LONDON'S BLACK POOR AND THE SIERRA LEONE SETTLEMENT PLAN). As Great Britain's first real colony on African soil, Sierra Leone served as a testing ground for subsequent colonial efforts elsewhere on the continent. The colony's mixed population of freed slaves, Europeans, and indigenous Africans gave rise to the unique KRIO culture, which blends Western and indigenous features. As the first group of Africans exposed to British cultural and administrative practices, Sierra Leoneans served in the British colonial administration throughout West Africa. During most of the twentieth century Sierra Leone provided leaders for West African nationalism. Although Sierra Leone is rich in valuable mineral deposits and agricultural potential, regional resentments and governmental corruption steadily undermined the country's economy in the years after independence and left it vulnerable to military adventurers. Intermittent warfare and civil strife since 1991 exposed Sierra Leoneans to a nightmare of violence and economic devastation. Partly as a consequence, Sierra Leone is today one of the five poorest nations on earth. However, with the return of a civilian government to power in 1998, came some hope that Sierra Leone's fortunes will improve.

EARLY HISTORY

Archaeologists have shown that human beings have inhabited the area now called Sierra Leone since at least 2500 B.C.E. The region's inhabitants were working iron by 600 C.E. During the fifteenth and sixteenth centuries MANDE-speaking peoples migrated or invaded from the east. They intermarried with the ancestors of the modern Bullom, Kissi, and

Krim peoples, who had occupied the country for centuries. The mixture produced such present-day peoples as the MENDE, Loko, and Vai.

In precolonial times people reared cattle in the northern grasslands and savanna, and cultivated plants across the region including rice, MILLET, yams, and vegetables. Women collected and extracted palm oil, which they used for food and soap production. Coastal peoples relied on fish as a major source of protein, and they traded sea salt with interior peoples. In the northeast part of the region inhabitants mined iron. Yalunka and Koranko blacksmiths controlled the iron trade and were known as skilled workers. The region's people collected gold, mostly by panning, for trade, religious rituals, and to manufacture ornaments and jewelry. Cotton grown and woven in Mendeland and the northeast was an important trade item often used as a currency.

No single state dominated Sierra Leone in the precolonial period. Even the large ethnic groups like the MENDE and TEMNE remained divided among smaller chieftaincies that traded and fought with their neighbors. Secret societies such as Poro and Sande, however, crosscut these political and ethnic divisions and united men and women throughout the region in networks of trade, mutual assistance, education, and spiritual practice.

Portuguese explorers first anchored off the mountainous Sierra Leone Peninsula in the fifteenth century. They gave the peninsula its name, which means "lion mountain," and has come to refer to the entire country.

The region's small, militarized political formations profited from the slave trade, which was well established in the region by the sixteenth century. Chiefs along the coast leased land to European slave traders without relinquishing their sovereignty. Local groups exported slaves both directly to Europeans on the coast and, by the eighteenth century, to the FULANI, who led them to FOUTA DJALLON and even Hausaland to the east.

THE COLONIAL ERA

While British slave traders had traded on the coast for more than a century, it was the movement for the abolition of slavery that spurred the initial colonization of Sierra Leone. British abolitionists founded the colony to create a community of free blacks. They intended the colony as a new home for ex-slaves in London, many of whom were legally free but unemployed, poor, and ineligible for the relief provided to white Englishmen. The Sierra Leone Peninsula was then inhabited by Temne people. The first attempt at colonization in 1787 failed primarily because of poor weather; poor relations with the local Temne; and the attractive work that nearby African and Afro-European slave traders offered to the literate, English-speaking free black settlers. A second, more successful attempt to settle ex-slaves from Nova Scotia followed in 1792. The settlement was named Freetown. Eight years later the British settled another contingent, composed of escaped slaves from JAMAICA. However, the colony soon faced resistance from the local Temne. Although the British had secured treaties from the Temne, transferring much of the peninsula to the new colony, the Temne assumed that the treaties, like those they had concluded with Europeans for generations, merely involved a lease. When the British rejected Temne claims of territorial sovereignty, the Temne declared war and attacked the colony. In response the British expelled the Temne from the peninsula.

The British declared Freetown, the peninsula, and its environs a Crown Colony in 1808. They established a naval base at Freetown, from which they policed the African coast in an effort to enforce the 1807 British law banning the slave trade. British authorities freed thousands of Africans from slave traders and settled them in the colony between 1808 and 1860. The colony became a magnet for Africans in the region looking for work, trade opportunities, or an escape from their own leaders or owners. Freetown became a major center for the external trade of the entire region, including the hinterlands that at first remained outside British rule. These waves of settlement gave rise to Freetown's distinctive Krio culture.

However, the colony encompassed only Freetown and its immediate environs on the peninsula. Most of present-day Sierra Leone remained in the hands of its indigenous peoples through most of the nineteenth century. Although abolitionists had founded the colony and enforced a ban on the coastal slave trade throughout the region, FULANI traders continued to export slaves to the interior, and the Mende, Temne, and other peoples of the area continued to hold slaves. With the abolition of the coastal slave trade, inhabitants focused on the production of other goods for trade with the British. The most important of these was palm oil, although local people traded lumber, ivory, gold, and other products for Western manufactures.

During the course of the nineteenth century the British sought to control the lucrative trade routes emanating from the colony to its hinterlands. A series of wars in the interior, then called "tribal wars" but now more accurately styled "trade wars," frustrated British attempts to assert control. Toward the end of the century, during the SCRAMBLE FOR AFRICA, the British authorities entered a four-sided

Regional wars and political chaos have displaced thousands of Sierra Leone natives, including these children, pictured in a displaced persons camp near Freetown in 1996. *CORBIS/Jon Spaull*

RIGHT: Textiles have great importance in African societies as objects of utility and beauty, as gifts, and as emblems of rank. In Gbonokobana, Sierra Leone, members of a women's cooperative make *garas*, a traditional tie-dyed cloth. *CORBIS/Caroline Penn*

BELOW: Citizens celebrate the opening of the Sierra Leone parliament in 1996. *CORBIS/Jon Spaull*

contest with SAMORY TOURÉ, the French, and Touré's Sikasso enemies (in present-day CÔTE D'IVOIRE) for Touré's extensive commercial empire, including parts of modern Côte d'Ivoire, GUINEA, and Sierra Leone.

However, the frontier police posted by the British to guard trade routes after 1890 were insufficient for the task. Following a skirmish with the French in 1893, the British abandoned their effort to take control of Touré's eastern holdings, which now fell into French hands. The British declared a protectorate in 1896 over the more immediate hinterland of the Sierra Leone Colony. While the British ruled the colony directly, with a governor and legislative council based in Freetown, in the much larger protectorate they introduced a policy of indirect rule, relying on indigenous chiefs to carry out local administration. The peoples of the protectorate resisted British attempts to assert control, and particularly their imposition of a hut tax, in the Hut Tax War and Mende Rising of 1898.

Ironically, while the British founded the Sierra Leone Colony as a focal point of their campaign against slavery, in the protectorate official British collusion with slavery lasted longer than in any other African territory. In the protectorate COLONIAL RULE served to strengthen the chiefs allied with the British, many of whom relied on slaves to grow and harvest palm oil and other agricultural products. The British allowed this slave economy to persist until 1928, when they finally banned slavery in the protectorate.

The different administrative statuses of the colony and protectorate paralleled differences in wealth, educational resources, and political power. The colony, and especially Freetown, continued to be an important trading center. Syrian traders and large European companies ended Krio domination of the export trade after the late nineteenth century. With their gradual displacement from commerce, however, members of this group, who enjoyed privileged access to Western education, took up important roles as civil servants, not only in Sierra Leone, but in other British colonies as well. Meanwhile, colonial authorities established the protectorate as a source of cash crops and minerals for export. One of the main purposes of the hut tax was to force the region's inhabitants to participate in the cash economy as wage laborers or producers of cash crops. In 1916 the British completed a rail line to the rich agricultural lands of the southeast, where, after the 1920s, COCOA and coffee became important cash crops.

After 1930 diamond and iron mining became an important part of the country's economy. By 1961 more than 80 percent of export income came from mining. The movement of workers to mining areas promoted urbanization within the protectorate. A mining boom in the 1950s attracted increasing numbers of peasants away from food production. This aggravated inflation; the price of food rose, and the miners spent more on imported goods. Inflation sparked political discontent, expressed most sharply in riots in 1955 and 1956.

Sierra Leoneans were among the earliest modern nationalists in Africa, and many played prominent roles in the National Congress of British West Africa in the 1920s. The process of democratic reforms, which led to independence far more quickly than the British had intended, began after World War II with the establishment of an assembly for the protectorate. Chiefs dominated this body, which met for the first time in 1946.

The new constitution in 1947 provided for ten elected representatives from the protectorate and did not require that these representatives be literate. The members of the Krio elite feared poor government and a loss of authority if "tribal Africans" gained power. Therefore, they formed an alliance with conservative chiefs in the Sierra Leone People's Party (SLPP), led by Sir Milton A. S. Margai, a former medical officer and member of the Mende ethnic group. The SLPP won the 1951 election, and the process of constitutional change continued. In 1957 Siaka Stevens led a group that broke away from the SLPP to form the People's National Party, and, in 1960, he founded the All People's Congress (APC). The SLPP drew most of its support from the Mende south, while the APC dominated the primarily Temne north. In 1958 the SLPP won an electoral victory under a constitution that gave them greater powers. The popular Margai was able to withstand allegations that his administration was tribalist and to fend off demands for another general election before independence in 1961.

Independence

Sierra Leone gained independence on April 27, 1961. In 1964 Albert Margai (who was knighted the following year) succeeded his brother, Sir Milton Margai. Albert Margai unsuccessfully proposed a one-party government in 1966. He did adopt measures to replace Krio officials in the government's administration. The Krio voters largely shifted their allegiance to the northern-based APC in the 1967 election, and the APC won. The military intervened, ruled for one year, and handed over power to Stevens in 1968.

Sierra Leone has continued to concentrate on the pattern of exporting primary products that was established during the colonial period after independence. The country was nonaligned during the cold war but remained one of the more conservative West African countries, allied with the capitalist West. A development policy passed in 1960 aimed to encourage domestic industrial production.

Stevens's government adopted a more left-wing orientation in the early 1970s. His administration acquired a 52 percent stake in the diamond industry, and he developed a closer relationship with the countries of Eastern Europe. However, all of these measures had more to do with an assertive nationalism than communism, and his government retained its close connections with the West. In 1971 a new constitution mandated a strong presidency.

The 1973-1974 oil crisis precipitated a serious economic decline from which Sierra Leone has not yet recovered. The increase in oil prices coincided with a decrease in export earnings. The country's iron ore reserves were depleted, and smugglers increasingly commandeered the country's diamond production and thus deprived the government of vital revenue. Meanwhile, government corruption became pervasive. Beginning in the mid-1970s the Stevens government faced growing opposition, notably from professionals and the trade unions. Stevens adopted an increasingly autocratic stance, and in 1978 he declared the country a one-party state. However, popular opposition forced Stevens to resign in 1985. His hand-picked successor, Maj. Gen. Joseph Momoh, went on to win the presidential election that year as the sole legal candidate. Beginning in 1986 Momoh accepted a structural adjustment program supported by the International Monetary Fund (IMF), but this collapsed because of debt repayment difficulties in 1988. The government accepted a new structural adjustment program in 1989 that involved a range of neoliberal measures, including large cuts in government staffing levels and extensive privatization. Momoh moved to reinstate multiparty democracy. Voters approved a new, more liberal constitution in 1991, and elections were scheduled for later that year.

In the same year, however, the civil war in Liberia spilled over into Sierra Leone. Supporters of Liberian rebel leader Charles Taylor invaded Sierra Leone, and fighting quickly engulfed about one-third of the country. Warfare ravaged the country's already faltering economy. Invaders seized control of diamond mines and disrupted agricultural activity. Dissatisfaction in the military with Momoh's response to the invasion prompted the 1992 coup led by Capt. Valentine Strasser. Strasser continued with the structural adjustment program and attempted to reduce government spending. By 1994 a rebel army, the Revolutionary United Front (RUF), a growing number of predatory "warlords," and Taylor's forces together had reduced much of the countryside to a state of violence and chaos. The economy was in a shambles.

Attempts to find a peace included elections in March 1996, in which Alhaji Ahmad Tejan Kabbah of the SLPP won the presidency. Kabbah continued efforts toward peace until junior army officers within the so-called Armed Forces Revolutionary Council, supported by many RUF soldiers, overthrew him in 1997. This coup returned Sierra Leone to a state of violence, political chaos, and economic ruin. Nigerian forces, acting as part of the Economic Community of West African States' Military Observer Group (ECOMOG), occupied Freetown in early 1998, deposed the military junta, and continued to fight the RUF. The Kamajors, armies of young men who take inspiration from traditional religion and are proud of their hunting prowess, have remained loyal to Kabbah but are still armed and represent a disruptive influence in parts of the countryside.

The war devastated the country's agriculture and rural areas and drove thousands of refugees into Freetown and other urban areas. In 1997 government revenues collapsed almost completely. The economy was ruined, and only a limited, informal, and black-market economy remained. People in southern Sierra Leone were reported to be suffering from food shortages and malnutrition in early 1998. In July 1999 President Kabbah and Revolutionary United Front leader Foday Sankoh signed a plan that called for an end to warfare and granted Sankoh's group greater governmental power, but the plan faced opposition from human rights groups who protested the granting of amnesty in the wake of mutilations carried out by rebel forces.

Alistair Chisholm

See Also

Krio; Colonial Rule; Freetown, Sierra Leone; Gold Trade; Ivory Trade; Taylor, Charles Ghankay; Nationalism in Africa; Transatlantic Slave Trade; Structural Adjustment in Africa; Abolitionism in the United States.

Africa

Sierra Leone (Ready Reference)

Official Name: Sierra Leone
Area: 71,740 sq km (27,699 sq mi)
Location: Western Africa; borders the North Atlantic Ocean, Guinea, and Liberia
Capital: Freetown (population 470,000 [1994 estimate])
Other Major Cities: Kenema (population 337,000) and Bo (269,000) (1994 estimates)
Population: 5,080,004 (1998 estimate)
Population Density: 66 persons per sq km (about 173 persons per sq mi)
Population Below Age 15: 45 percent (male 1,130,728; female 1,167,084 [1998 estimate])
Population Growth Rate: 4.01 percent (1998 estimate)
Total Fertility Rate: 6.23 children born per woman (1998 estimate)
Life Expectancy at Birth: Total population: 48.57 years (male 45.56 years; female 51.66 years [1998 estimate])
Infant Mortality Rate: 129.38 deaths per

1000 live births (1998 estimate)
Literacy Rate (age 15 and over who can read and write): Total population: 31.4 percent (male 45.4 percent; female 18.2 percent [1995 estimate])
Education: In the early 1990s annual enrollment for primary schools was about 315,000. About 79,400 were enrolled in secondary, vocational, and teacher-training schools.
Languages: English is the official language, although its regular use is limited to a literate minority (less than 20 percent of the adult population is literate). About 20 African languages are spoken in Sierra Leone. MENDE is the principal language of the south, and Temne is the principal language of the north. Another common language is KRIO, a Creole language derived from English and various African languages.
Ethnic Groups: There are 13 different ethnic groups in the Sierra Leone population. The largest groups are the Mende in the south, who account for nearly 30 percent of the population, and the TEMNE in the north, who account for nearly 30 percent of the population. Creoles, descendants of freed slaves returned from the Americas, are an important minority in the Freetown area, where small numbers of Lebanese, Indians, and Europeans also reside.
Religions: About 60 percent of the population is Muslim. About 30 percent adheres to indigenous beliefs, and 10 percent is Christian.
Climate: Tropical. Hot and humid with a rainy season between May and October. The mean temperature in Freetown is 27° C (about 80° F) in January and 26° C (78° F) in July. Annual rainfall averages more than 3800 mm (150 in) along the coast and 2030 mm (about 80 in) in the northern interior.
Land, Plants, and Animals: Sierra Leone's geography ranges from coastal mangrove swamps, grassy savanna in the north, and mountains in the east. There are dense forests in the southeast that contain varieties of palm, mahogany, and teak trees. Animals include bush pigs, chimpanzees, monkeys, and porcupines. Crocodiles and hippopotamuses are found in the rivers.
Natural Resources: Mineral resources include diamonds, bauxite, and rutile. Diamonds, however, are being produced at much lower levels than in the past due to the near exhaustion of mines, persistent smuggling, and civil insurrection in some areas.
Currency: Leones issued by the Bank of Sierra Leone.
Gross Domestic Product (GDP): $2.65 billion (1997 estimate)
GDP Real Growth Rate: -27 percent (1997 estimate)
GDP Per Capita: $540 (1997 estimate)
External Debt: $1.4 billion (year-end, 1993)
Primary Economic Activities: Agriculture (employing 65 percent of the population), industry, and services
Primary Crops: Rice, coffee, cocoa, palm kernels, palm oil, peanuts, and livestock
Industries: Mining (diamonds, bauxite, and rutile), small-scale manufacturing (textiles, beverages, cigarettes, and footwear), petroleum refining
Primary Exports: Rutile, bauxite, diamonds, coffee, cocoa, and fish
Primary Imports: Foodstuffs, machinery and equipment, fuels, and lubricants
Primary Trade Partners: United States, United Kingdom, Belgium, and Germany
Government: Constitutional multiparty democracy. The executive branch is led by President Ahmad Tejan Kabbah and the Ministers of State. The legislative branch is the elected, 105-member House of Representatives.

Elizabeth Heath

SEE ALSO
Freetown, Sierra Leone.

Africa

Sihanaka (also known as Antisihanaka), ethnic group of MADAGASCAR.

The Sihanaka primarily inhabit eastern Madagascar. They speak MALAGASY, a Malayo-Polynesian language (*see* ETHNICITY IN MADAGASCAR). Over 200,000 people consider themselves Sihanaka.

Latin America and the Caribbean

Silva, Benedita da

(b. March 11, 1943, Rio de Janeiro, Brazil), Afro-Brazilian senator and social activist; the first black woman to enter the Brazilian Congress and the first woman from the FAVELAS to become a major political figure in BRAZIL.

Known affectionately as Bené, Benedita da Silva is one of Brazil's foremost political figures. Born and raised in Brazil's favelas, or squatter settlements, she became a leading community organizer. In 1980 she helped found the leftist Partido dos Trabalhadores (the Workers' Party, or PT), a broad-based coalition of workers, grassroots organizers, and intellectuals. Six years later she became the first black woman to enter the Brazilian Congress, where she was one of only 26 women and 7 blacks among 559 deputies. Silva has consistently fought to prioritize racial, class, and gender issues within both the PT and Brazil's political institutions, and has strongly opposed discrimination against women and blacks. Indeed, in her opening speech before Congress in 1986, she stated: "If our opinion is not taken into account and we women are not guaranteed equality, we won't feel obligated to respect your laws. We are going to start a rebellion and hundreds of us will occupy the space now taken by insensitive people like you."

The youngest of 13 children, Silva grew up in Rio de Janiero, in the favela of Chapéu Mangueira. Her father was a construction worker, and her mother earned a living as a washerwoman and midwife. At age seven Silva began supplementing the family income by selling candy and fruit on the street. "My experience growing up on the streets was difficult but it was also a... school of life where you learn everything," she noted in her autobiography. Unlike most favelas, Chapéu Mangueira had an elementary school, and at an early age Silva learned to read and write. After the death of her mother in 1957 she began working with the progressive wing of the Roman Catholic Church (*see* CATHOLIC CHURCH IN LATIN AMERICA AND THE CARIBBEAN), which organized literacy and health programs in the favelas.

At age 16 Silva married a handyman, and during the next four years she gave birth to four children – two of whom died shortly after they were born. "I saw my first child buried like a pauper," she wrote in her autobiography. "The image of my baby inside that little box will always be etched in my memory." Silva worked as a housemaid and street vendor, but her family nevertheless lived in poverty and often had to eat from restaurant trash cans to survive. Moreover, during the late 1950s the government attempted to control the favelas by establishing government-run neighborhood associations that undermined the organizing work of community leaders. In 1964, after the Brazilian military assumed power in a coup, repression of independent organizations increased as did pressures to eradicate and relocate the favelas. Residents of favelas who opposed eviction were often targeted: "We were exiled in our own country," wrote Silva. "We weren't allowed to sing our religious hymns or celebrate our festivals. We dug holes in our houses to hide our books and notepads. We couldn't keep minutes of our meetings because it was considered subversive to demand better living conditions like electricity, plumbing or paved roads."

In 1969 Silva joined the Assembly of God, an Evangelical Protestant Church (*see* PROTESTANT CHURCH IN LATIN AMERICA AND THE CARIBBEAN). "I was going through an extremely difficult period in my life," she said. "I was feeling overwhelmed by poverty and hunger." Silva found emotional and spiritual support in the predominantly conservative Evangelical community – a development that baffled many of her political colleagues, who perceived her religious affiliation to be incompatible with her radical political views. Indeed, Latin American Evangelicals have often aligned themselves with repressive governments. Yet Silva has always maintained her political independence and sees the church as a place where she can reaffirm and strengthen her faith.

Despite prolonged government repression, Silva played a central role in building the local women's movement. In 1978, with the

The first black woman elected to Brazil's congress, Benedita da Silva has been an advocate for Afro-Brazilians, women, and the poor since entering politics in the 1970s. *Kit Miller*

support of women activists, she was elected president of the Chapéu Mangueira neighborhood association. She continued to work while preparing for the high school equivalency exam. After receiving her high school diploma in 1980, she enrolled in college to study social work and in 1982 successfully campaigned for the city council. She became the first PT representative in Rio de Janeiro and the first black city councilwoman in Brazil. In 1986 she was elected a federal deputy for the National Assembly; four years later she was reelected.

In 1992 Silva ran for mayor of Rio de Janeiro. Although she was ahead of her opponent in the polls, the conservative elite launched a bitter campaign in the media to discredit her, and she lost the election by a narrow margin. Two years later, however, she became the first black woman elected to the Brazilian Senate.

Silva's support base consists of the people she most often represented during her political career: women, blacks, the poor, churchgoers, workers, and social activists. Still, according to Medea Benjamin and Maisa Mendonça, social activists who have followed Silva's career, "Bené moves in and out of the most diverse circles imaginable. In a gathering of blacks or whites, men or women, rich or poor, Bené holds her ground with great dignity. In the Senate, she is mostly surrounded by rich, white men. Although she fights them tooth and nail on economic policies, she greets them with a broad smile."

Silva's political position differs from those of many Brazilian leftist politicians, who typically prioritize class issues over racial ones. As an Afro-Brazilian, she has been subjected to humiliating racial slurs all her life, from both the Brazilian public and the conservative political elite. "Blacks suffer because they are poor, but they are poor precisely because they are black," she argues. "And when blacks do manage to move up the social and economic ladder, they still can't escape racism." At the same time she believes that the reluctance of Brazilian blacks to embrace their own identity has precluded a "strong, cohesive national movement that can really influence policy." She advocates "a version of socialism that is not imported or top-down, but [one] that respects our culture and works from the bottom up." Central to her vision is agrarian reform. Silva has proposed that land be distributed to the landless, so that they will not have to migrate to the cities to find sustenance, and that people living in the favelas receive legal title to the land on which they already live. "My aim," notes Silva, "is to help gain access to power for groups that have traditionally been locked out." In this vein she successfully campaigned for an affirmative action policy within the PT that guarantees that at least 30 percent of the party's deputies are women.

Although Silva has had to move to Brasília, the capital, to pursue her political career, she remains an active participant in the community affairs of Chapéu Mangueira, which she still considers her home. Her many years of community work have helped to transform her neighborhood into a model favela – a strong, well-organized community that maintains its own health and educational facilities.

Roanne Edwards

See Also

Rio de Janeiro, Brazil.

Latin America and the Caribbean

Silva, Xica da (b. 1734?, Minas Gerais, Brazil; d. ?), a legendary eighteenth-century Afro-Brazilian woman who freed herself from slavery and challenged the aristocracy of colonial Brazil.

In every version of her life story, Francisca "Xica" da Silva is described as a slave who was freed by João Fernandes de Oliveira around 1760. Fernandes was a *contratador*, or a vassal of the Portuguese Crown, sent to the province of Minas Gerais in colonial Brazil to explore the soil for diamonds and gold. Da Silva lived and worked as a slave until she was purchased by Oliveira, who lived with da Silva as her husband despite the racial prejudice that existed at that time in Brazil.

Instead of sending the mineral riches he discovered to Portugal, Oliveira kept them for himself and became a very rich man. He and da Silva lived a luxurious life in Arraial do Tijuco, a small village in Minas Gerais. He built a palace; imported gifts for da Silva from all over the world, including gold and diamonds; and built her a ship to sail on a nearby river. Da Silva came to be known as the unofficial empress of Brazil.

The story of da Silva's life was filmed by the noted Brazilian director Carlos Diegues, who called her the Brazilian Joan of Arc (*see* Cinema Novo). In Diegues's 1976 movie, the Portuguese Crown sends an officer to investigate complaints of irregularities concerning Oliveira's activities. Oliveira ends up returning to Portugal, leaving da Silva and his fortune behind. Without Oliveira's protection and facing the contempt of the local society, da Silva supposedly rescued herself by retreating to a monastery for blacks built under Oliveira's command. Other versions of da Silva's life state that Oliveira never went back to Portugal, and that they married, raised a large family, and lived together until their death.

The details of Xica da Silva's biography remain unclear. For example, her origin is uncertain. It is possible that she was a daughter of the slave Silvana Oliveira da Silva and that she was born a slave in 1734 on the farm of the priest José da Silva e Oliveira Rolim in Minas Gerais. She is also described as being the daughter of a Portuguese father or of an indigenous Brazilian and an Afro-Brazilian slave. Plays, romances, and other sources that tell the story of Xica da Silva repeatedly show signs of white society's hostility to her, including her exclusion from the local Roman Catholic church. Da Silva, however, is generally shown as an astute woman who struggled to overcome the racial and social prejudices of her time.

In 1962 Xica da Silva was the Carnival theme of the Salgueiro samba school in Rio de Janeiro, and in 1997 a soap opera based on her life was broadcast on Brazil's TV Manchete.

Michelle Gueraldi

See Also
Slavery in Latin America and the Caribbean; Samba Schools; Rio de Janeiro, Brazil; Carnivals in Latin America and the Caribbean; Catholic Church in Latin America and the Caribbean.

Latin America and the Caribbean

Silvera, Makeda (b. 1955?, Kingston, Jamaica), Jamaican-Canadian editor and writer.

Born in Kingston, Jamaica, Makeda Silvera immigrated to Toronto, Canada, in the late 1960s. A lesbian with working-class immigrant roots, Silvera cofounded Sister Vision Press in 1985. Under her editorial direction, Sister Vision has brought discussions of class, gender, and sexuality to the fore of Canadian literature and redressed the absence of writing by lesbians and women of color in mainstream presses. Silvera has written two collections of short fiction, *Remembering G* (1991) and *Her Head a Village* (1993), as well as a collection of oral testimonies by West Indian domestic workers, *Silenced* (1983).

Peter Hudson

North America

Simkins, Mary Modjeska Monteith (b. December 5, 1899, Columbia, S.C.; d. May 15, 1992, Columbia, S.C.), African American civil rights activist known for her lifetime commitment to progressive causes.

The child of prosperous parents Henry Clarence Monteith and Rachel Evelyn Hull Monteith, Mary Modjeska Monteith Simkins was instilled early on with a sense of both gentility and the duty to fight for equality. After graduating from Benedict College in 1921 with a B.A., she remained at the school until she was hired by the Booker T. Washington School in Columbia, South Carolina, a year later. When she married Andrew Whitfield Simkins in 1929, Modjeska was required to leave her job due to the city policy that married women could not teach in public schools.

In 1931 Simkins began working for the South Carolina Tuberculosis Association as director of Negro Work, establishing clinics and educating the population about the disease. In addition to organizing for several alternative political parties, she was one of the founding members of the South Carolina Conference of Branches of the National Association for the Advancement of Colored People (NAACP). In 1942, due to her civil rights activities she was fired from her job with the South Carolina Tuberculosis Association.

Elected state secretary of the NAACP the same year, Simkins led victorious fights for equalizing wages for African American public school teachers and countermanding the segregated primary elections in South Carolina. Simkins and the NAACP helped to desegregate the South Carolina public schools by filing *Briggs* v. *Elliot* in 1951, paving the way for Brown v. Board of Education in 1954, which ended legal segregation in public schools. Despite her many successful projects, she was not re-elected to her post as state secretary due to her affiliation with the Communist Party. Turning her focus to issues of community development, Simkins worked for African American-owned Victory Savings Bank in Columbia until her retirement.

See Also
Communist Party USA, African Americans and the.

North America

Simone, Nina (b. February 21, 1933, Tryon, N.C.), African American vocalist known for her musical versatility and emotionally charged singing.

Nina Simone is widely known as "the high priestess of soul" – less for her interpretation of soul music than for the soulful intensity she brings to her highly eclectic repertoire. Since the late 1950s Simone has recorded extensively in the jazz, blues, soul, gospel, and pop idioms, interpreting both standard and original songs. During the 1960s her vocal career took on a powerfully political dimension. Indeed, "more than any other popular performer of the day, she has captured the essence of the black revolution and sings of it without biting her tongue," noted *Ebony* magazine in 1969.

The *All Music Guide to Jazz* (1996) has described Simone's voice as "moody-yet-elegant… presenting a fiercely independent soul who harbors enormous (if somewhat hard-bitten) tenderness." The quotation also reflects her struggle to succeed as a black female musician. She had originally dreamed of becoming a classical pianist and, during the 1950s, studied at New York's prestigious Juilliard School of Music. Yet black musicians met with considerable discrimination in the mostly white and exclusive realm of classical music, and Simone soon found herself performing at an Atlantic City nightclub. Asked to sing in addition to play piano, she began her career as a jazz vocalist. In 1959 she achieved a Top Twenty hit single with her recording of George Gershwin's "I Love You Porgy."

Simone has since recorded more than 40 albums. Her songs range from ballad interpretations of Billie Holiday and Jacques Brel to her own fiercely political pieces, "Old Jim Crow" and "Mississippi Goddam" – responses to the burgeoning violence committed against American blacks during the early 1960s. During the 1970s and 1980s she recorded rarely but experienced a career comeback in the United States with her 1993 album, *A Single Woman*.

Roanne Edwards

See Also
Soul Music; Blues, The; Gospel Music.

North America

Simpson, O.J. (b. July 9, 1947, San Francisco, Calif.), African American athlete; one of the greatest running backs in the history of American football and the defendant in two sensational trials concerning the brutal murder of his ex-wife and her friend.

Football Career

Orenthal James ("O.J.") Simpson was born in a poor neighborhood of San Francisco, the third of four children. His father separated from the family when Simpson was a child. At a young age Simpson wore braces to correct weakness in his legs, but as a teenager at Galileo High School he was a star in baseball, track, and football. Simpson also received several suspensions from school for misbehavior. He graduated from Galileo in 1965, but his grades kept him from attending a major university. Instead, he enrolled at City College in San Francisco, where he had a fantastic first season of football and was offered many scholarships. He remained one more year at City College before meeting the admissions standards for the University of Southern California (USC), which he entered in 1967. In 1967 he also married his first wife, Marguerite.

At 1.85 m (6 ft 1 in) and 92.9 kg (205 lb),

Simpson was big for a running back, but he had tremendous speed – a combination that made him one of the best runners in collegiate history. Over two seasons he ran for 3295 yards, leading USC to a Rose Bowl victory and a national championship in 1967, and earning consensus All-American status for himself both years. In 1968 he won the Heisman Trophy as college football's best player. Simpson also ran track for USC and was a member of a world-record-setting 440-yard-relay team.

In the 1969 American Football League (AFL) draft, the Buffalo Bills chose Simpson first overall. He was used sparingly his first three seasons and rushed for less than 2000 total yards, but in 1972 the Bills built their offense around him. The "Juice," as he was called, produced a league-leading 1251 yards. (By this time the AFL had merged with the National Football League [NFL]). In 1973 Simpson became the first NFL player to rush for more than 2000 yards, gaining 2003. He led the league in rushing again in 1975 and 1976 and was a member of the Pro Bowl team each year from 1972 to 1976. Although the Bills never reached the Super Bowl, Simpson drew large crowds for his exciting play. After suffering knee injuries in the mid-1970s, he was traded to the San Francisco 49ers in 1978. At the time of his retirement in 1979, his 11,236 total yards gained was second only to Jim Brown's 12,312 career yards. In 1985 Simpson was elected to the Professional Football Hall of Fame.

Simpson parlayed his fame and attractiveness into a film and television acting career, including appearances in *The Towering Inferno* (1974), *Roots* (1977), and three *Naked Gun* films (1988, 1991, and 1994). He also endorsed products in television advertisements and was a commentator for televised sports. Having divorced his first wife, he married Nicole Brown in 1985. The couple had two children before she filed for and received a divorce in 1992. She accused him of physical abuse and womanizing, which he denied.

The Simpson Trials

On June 12, 1994, Nicole Brown Simpson and a friend, Ronald Goldman, were found murdered in front of her townhouse in Brentwood, California. She had been stabbed about 10 times and her throat was slashed; he had been stabbed 17 times. Both were white. Five days later Simpson was charged with the killings. Simpson resisted arrest and, with a friend driving his car, led police on an orderly, slow-speed chase through greater Los Angeles for several hours. As airborne television crews broadcast the pursuit around the world, Simpson held a gun to his head, threatening to kill himself. He eventually surrendered to police.

Simpson hired a team of prominent defense lawyers and pleaded "100 percent not guilty." By the time a protracted jury selection process began in late September, the case had attracted the attention of millions. Opening arguments began on January 24, 1995, and several television stations and networks broadcast the entire proceedings. Lacking a witness to the crime, the prosecution introduced experts who testified that DNA in blood gathered as evidence at the crime scene matched Simpson's, and that DNA in blood found in Simpson's truck and home matched the victims'. Other items such as shoe prints and bloody gloves – one of each at the crime scene and at Simpson's home – were introduced. A limousine driver testified that Simpson was not home on the night of the killings at the time he claimed to be. The prosecution also revealed Simpson's history of abusing his former wife, including a 1989 conviction for spousal battery.

The defense argued that the police had illegally obtained and sloppily handled much of the evidence. Experts testified that the laboratory of the Los Angeles Police Department was incompetent and that the blood samples might have been contaminated. The defense also revealed that Detective Mark Fuhrman, a leading investigator of the murders, once told a writer he had previously planted evidence against black defendants. Fuhrman had also used derogatory terms for blacks, contradicting testimony he had given the court. Prosecutors also inadvertently helped the defense team when they asked Simpson to try on one of the bloody gloves: it appeared to be too small for him. In one of the climactic moments of the trial, defense attorney Johnnie Cochran urged the jury's nine blacks, two whites, and one Latino to send a message about racism and incompetence to the police by acquitting Simpson.

On October 3, 1995, after less than four hours of deliberation, the jury acquitted Simpson of all charges as hundreds of millions of people watched on television. According to several public opinion polls, most blacks agreed with the verdict, while a large majority of whites opposed it. This striking disparity drew attention to the different ways blacks and whites viewed the police, courts, and the prevalence of racism.

After the criminal proceedings Simpson faced a civil suit by the Goldman family and the estate of Nicole Simpson for the wrongful deaths of the murder victims. In a civil suit less proof is needed to find a defendant guilty, and the jury need not reach a unanimous verdict. The trial began on October 23, 1996, and, like the criminal trial, it attracted international attention. On February 4, 1997, a jury of nine whites, one black, one Latino, and one person of mixed black and Asian ancestry found Simpson responsible for the deaths of both Goldman and Nicole Simpson. Simpson was ordered to pay $8.5 million in damages to the plaintiffs. Simpson filed an appeal of the verdict on May 28. Again, opinion polls showed large numbers of whites agreeing with the jury's finding, while large numbers of blacks believed he was not guilty. Simpson is the author of *I Want to Tell You* (1995), which he wrote while detained during the criminal trial.

See Also

Track and Field in the United States; Baseball in the United States; Football, Collegiate; Football, Professional; Television and African Americans; Film, Blacks in American.

North America

Singleton, Arthur James ("Zutty") **(b. May 14, 1898, Bunkie, La.; d. July 14, 1975, New York, N.Y.), African American musician and bandleader responsible for innovations in jazz percussion accompaniment.**

Raised in New Orleans, Louisiana, Arthur James "Zutty" Singleton began his professional musical career at age 15 as a drummer for silent film theater orchestras. He served in the United States Navy during World War I. Returning to New Orleans, he worked as a freelance drummer with several popular local bands, including Papa Celestin's, Louis "Big Eye" Nelson's, and Luis Russell's, in addition to forming his own band around 1920.

In 1924 Singleton recorded his first song, "Frankie and Johnny," with the Fate Marable riverboat band, with which he had performed since 1921. After playing in St. Louis, Missouri, with Charlie Creath in 1925, Singleton became an integral part of the burgeoning Chicago School of jazz, which placed soloists such as Louis Armstrong in the spotlight. However, he continued to play long stints in other cities, including New York and Los Angeles from the 1930s to the 1950s.

It was Singleton's introduction of sock cymbals and wire brushes, along with new accenting techniques, that secured his place as an accompanist for such musical giants as Louis Armstrong, "Jelly Roll" Morton, "Fats" Waller, "Dizzy" Gillespie, and Charlie Parker, as well as appearances on television and in films. Spanning several decades, Singleton's career was marked by an ability to play flexibly with all types of jazz. In 1953 he settled in New York. He continued to tour internationally until he accepted a permanent position at Jimmy Ryan's, the jazz club on West 57th Street, in 1963. A stroke forced Singleton to retire in 1970, and he died in New York City five years later.

See Also

World War I and African Americans; Armstrong, Louis ("Satchmo"); Chicago, Illinois; Gillespie, John Birks ("Dizzy"); Morton, Ferdinand Joseph ("Jelly Roll"); Parker, Charles Christopher ("Bird"); Waller, Thomas Wright ("Fats"); Los Angeles, California; New York, New York.

North America

Singleton, Benjamin ("Pap")

(b. 1809, Nashville, Tenn.; d. 1892, St. Louis, Mo.), early advocate of American western migration and Black Nationalism.

As a young man, Benjamin "Pap" Singleton escaped from enslavement in Nashville, where he had been born and raised. Originally fleeing to Canada, he settled in Detroit, Michigan, where he harbored fugitive slaves until the Civil War ended. Believing himself divinely chosen, he returned to Tennessee to begin his lifetime work of establishing an independent black society comprising the new freedpeople.

Singleton counseled ex-slaves to buy land in rural sections of Tennessee. Rebuffed by white landowners and officials, Singleton worked with W. A. Sizemore and Columbus Johnson, both former slaves, to promote migration west to Kansas. Beginning in the early 1870s several African American families, led by Singleton, settled there. Historian John Hope Franklin has noted that when Singleton circulated such fliers as "The Advantage of Living in a Free State" throughout the American South, whites enacted laws and practices to restrict African American movement.

From 1877 to 1879 several hundred Tennessee families migrated to Singleton's new black colonies. In 1879, two years after Reconstruction ended, more than 20,000 African Americans migrated from Southern states to Kansas, earning the name "Exodusters." In 1880 the United States Senate held an inquiry into this unprecedented movement. Singleton's direct influence remains unclear, yet in his testimony before the Senate he took sole responsibility for the migration, calling himself "the Moses of the colored exodus." Later that year Singleton, the "Father of the Exodus," attempted to ally with the white Greenbacker political party to form a cooperative economy, but by 1883 he organized the Chief League (later Trans-Atlantic Society) to promote black emigration first to Cyprus, then to Africa.

See Also
Civil War, American; Black Nationalism in the United States.

Latin America and the Caribbean

Sinhô

(José Barbosa da Silva) (b. 1888; d. 1930), the most popular of the early samba composers in Rio de Janeiro, Brazil. His string of Carnival hits during the 1920s earned him the title "King of the Samba" (*see* Samba).

North America

Sissle, Noble

(b. July 10, 1889, Indianapolis, Ind.; d. December 17, 1975, Tampa, Fla.), African American musician and composer who participated in *Shuffle Along*, the most successful musical comedy created by African Americans.

Noble Sissle first sang in his father's Methodist church, and he was a soloist at his Cleveland, Ohio, high school's glee club. After serving in World War I as a drum major, Sissle had enormous success in the vaudeville theater, teaming up with "Eubie" Blake as the Dixie Duo. In 1921 the two created *Shuffle Along*, starring Florence Mills. *Shuffle Along* changed Broadway musical theater by introducing a jazz dancing chorus line and the vitality and style of African American music to a more "refined" mainstream theater. Sissle and Blake wrote songs, including the well-known "I'm Just Wild About Harry." They also produced *Runnin' Wild* (1924) and *Chocolate Dandies* (1924). In 1937 Sissle was the co-founder and first president of the Negro Actors' Guild. In 1945 and 1946 Sissle toured Europe with a United Service Organizations (USO) show, performing a restaged *Shuffle Along*.

See Also
World War I and African Americans; Blake, James Hubert ("Eubie").

Latin America and the Caribbean

Sistren Collective

women's theater collective founded in Jamaica in 1977 by Honor Ford-Smith. The Sistren Collective creates plays representing Caribbean women's issues and uses workshops and improvisation to address community concerns (*see* Theater in the Caribbean).

Africa

Sisulu, Walter

(b. May 18, 1912, the Transkei, South Africa), former deputy president of the African National Congress and a key figure in South Africa's anti-apartheid movement.

Walter Sisulu, known for his commitment to studying and teaching while imprisoned on Robben Island with Nelson Mandela, was called by one of his African National Congress (ANC) colleagues "the organization's encyclopedia in prison." A mentor to younger members such as Mandela and Oliver Tambo, Sisulu joined the ANC in 1940, after his impoverished Johannesburg childhood and work in the country's gold mines had introduced him to the injustices facing South African blacks.

In addition to helping Mandela and Tambo complete their law studies, Sisulu also joined the two in the newly formed ANC Youth League, planning strategy and serving as its treasurer. Elected ANC secretary general in 1949, Sisulu played a key role in coordinating activities with other antiapartheid groups, including the South African Communist Party (SACP) and the South African Indian Congress. This work, he said, influenced his commitment to a multiracial antiapartheid movement. The South African government convicted Sisulu under its Suppression of Communism Act in 1952. Although his sentence was suspended, he was banned from participating in political activity and forced to resign from his ANC position (like other banned leaders, Sisulu continued to work covertly).

Along with Mandela, Sisulu was one of 156 antiapartheid activists charged with treason in 1956. After their 1961 acquittal, Sisulu was among the founders of Umkhonto we Sizwe (Spear of the Nation), the armed paramilitary wing jointly supported by the ANC and the SACP. In 1964, after fleeing house arrest and working underground, Sisulu, Mandela, and six others were captured, convicted of treason, and sentenced to life in prison on Robben Island, South Africa's notoriously brutal penitentiary for political prisoners. While there Sisulu read widely and wrote a history of the ANC. After his 1989 release (which came as South Africa began to loosen its apartheid system in the face of international pressure) he told reporters that "it was not possible to despair" while in prison, "because the spirit of the people outside was too great." Elected ANC deputy president in 1991, Sisulu resigned from that position in 1994 at age 82.

Kate Tuttle

See Also
Johannesburg, South Africa; Mandela, Nelson Rolihlahla.

North America

Sit-Ins

series of African American student protests in 1960 in which black students occupied "white-only" lunch counters and other segregated public institutions throughout the South to protest segregated seating.

On February 5, 1960, four black college students sat down at a "white-only" department store lunch counter in Greensboro, North Carolina. This Woolworth's counter was but one of the many segregated public facilities in the American South where African Americans were prohibited from such activities as eating, swimming, and drinking by whites who not only opposed equal treatment of the races, but feared any possibility of bodily contact. When the restaurant refused these students service, they remained seated until the store closed for the evening. The students returned each morning for the next five days to occupy the lunch counter, joined by a group of protesters that grew to the hundreds. Faced by a mob of angry white residents and management that refused to serve them a cup of coffee, the students maintained their protest until they forced the store to close its doors.

The protest by Joseph McNeil, Franklin McCain, Ezell Blair Jr., and David Richmand marked the beginning of a grassroots sit-in movement led by African American students against the segregated public spaces of the South. Black or racially integrated groups of students would sit down in white-only spaces and refuse to move until they were served or forcibly removed. By the end of 1960 about 70,000 black students had participated in a sit-in or marched in support of the demonstrators.

Although there had been a few sit-in protests before 1960, including two in 1943, the mass mobilization of 1960 was new. Few in the economically struggling black community of the South had been willing to undertake these types of direct-action protests, since they would be in danger of losing their jobs after an arrest. Black students generally had fewer financial responsibilities than their older counterparts, and they were interested in forcing change more immediate than that promised by the legal reform advocated by the NATIONAL ASSOCIATION FOR THE ADVANCEMENT OF COLORED PEOPLE (NAACP).

In 1960, as African American students entered the political arena in large numbers for the first time, the character of the civil rights protesting began to change. Influenced by the successful protests led by Mohandas K. Gandhi in India's Independence Movement, black students saw the potential for using nonviolent resistance to undermine the segregationist system and ideologies that supported it. Nonviolence was not just a strategy, although it did garner sympathy from many whites and the national press; it was a moral and revolutionary philosophy. Proponents such as James Lawson Jr. felt that nonviolence was an "invincible instrument of war," imbued with "soul force" and moral integrity, which would use the mass organization of bodies to strike at the heart of the morally unsound system of segregationism.

The pivotal demonstration was the Greensboro sit-in. But students had already begun organizing elsewhere. Shortly after the Greensboro protest Lawson and the Nashville Student Movement launched a well-organized and orchestrated campaign to integrate the lunch counters of Nashville, Tennessee. In less than a month Nashville yielded to the pressure of the protests. The success of these original protests inspired other black students throughout the South, who organized sit-ins to force the desegregation of public places.

During 1960 sit-ins began to break down the segregation of the upper South, and lunch counters were integrated in cities in Texas, North Carolina, and Tennessee. The reasons for integration were economic as well as moral. Boycotters, both black and white, supported the protesters, and many merchants did not want to lose the revenue of customers.

In the Deep South, however, including Louisiana, Mississippi, Alabama, Georgia, and South Carolina, white supremacy was more entrenched in the community and local government. Cities such as Montgomery, Alabama, outlawed the demonstrations, and white store owners refused to serve blacks under the rationale that they could make the rules on their own private property.

Throughout the South protesters faced not only arrest but vigilante violence as police and the Ku Klux Klan worked hand-in-hand to suppress the protests. By the end of 1960, 36,000 students had been arrested, and thousands expelled from college.

With support from ELLA J. BAKER of the SOUTHERN CHRISTIAN LEADERSHIP CONFERENCE, students formed a permanent organization in April 1960: the STUDENT NONVIOLENT COORDINATING COMMITTEE (SNCC). SNCC maintained the autonomy of the grassroots students' movement and facilitated training in nonviolent resistance. The strategy of occupying a place as a means of nonviolent protest gained currency in the CIVIL RIGHTS MOVEMENT. Sit-ins at lunch counters inspired similar forms of protest at other types of segregated facilities, such as wade-ins at swimming places.

The efficacy of nonviolent resistance was one of the most important legacies of the 1960 sit-in protests. Segregation was seen to be a moral, as well as a legal issue, and the dignity of blacks in the face of white supremacist rage went far to win white and black support for the movement. In the words of SNCC's founding members, "By appealing to conscience and standing on the moral nature of human existence, non-violence nurtures the atmosphere in which reconciliation and justice become actual possibilities."

Marian Aguiar

SEE ALSO
Lawson, James Morris.

North America

Sixteenth Street Baptist Church (Birmingham, Ala.),

center for civil rights in Birmingham, Alabama; site of the 1963 bombing that killed four African American girls.

On September 15, 1963, 4 young black girls were killed and 20 other people wounded when a bomb planted by Ku Klux Klan member Robert Edward Chambliss exploded at the 16th Street Baptist Church in Birmingham, Alabama. The terrorist attack revealed the growing hostility of segregationists toward the CIVIL RIGHTS MOVEMENT as it was making inroads in the Deep South. At the time of the bombing Birmingham was in a battle over the desegregation of schools; only weeks before, the National Guard had been called in to protect black students. For civil rights leaders the bombing, which followed less than three weeks after the euphoria of the 1963 MARCH ON WASHINGTON, was a reminder of the long struggle that remained.

The 16th Street Baptist Church was a center for the Civil Rights Movement in Birmingham. Martin Luther King Jr., ANDREW YOUNG, FRED L. SHUTTLESWORTH, James Bevel, Dick Gregory, and Ralph Abernathy all regularly took the pulpit at mass rallies of Birmingham's black community, such as the one following King's April 1963 arrest. The church had been the headquarters for a number of desegregation protests, including the May 1963 SOUTHERN CHRISTIAN LEADERSHIP CONFERENCE (SCLC) rally in which more than 2000 black youth marched from the church through Birmingham.

The Ku Klux Klan targeted the church on the annual Youth Sunday. Eleven-year-old Denise McNair was with Cynthia Wesley, Carole Robertson, and Addie Mae Collins, all age 14, in the basement of the church. They were preparing to take their special roles as ushers when the bomb exploded, killing them and burying them in rubble. Twenty others, many children, were injured by the blast. In the day of increased tension that followed, two other black youths were killed. A black 13-year-old was shot by two Eagle Scouts who were on the way home from a white supremacist rally. That evening a 16-year-old black boy was shot by one of 300 state troopers ordered into the city by Gov. George C. Wallace to preserve the peace in Birmingham.

As black and white youths battled in the streets of Birmingham the night of the bombing, many white residents wavered between fear of antiwhite violence and feelings of guilt. In the words of white lawyer Charles Morgan the next day, "We all did it… every person in this community who has in any way contributed… to the popularity of hatred is at least as guilty… as the demented fool who threw that bomb." Many in the community, and indeed in the nation, struggled with a new awareness of the brutal underside of what had been characterized as simply the Southern way of life.

Connie Lynch articulated the white supremacist reaction. Rallying the Klan shortly after the bombing, Lynch said the victims "weren't children. Children are little people, little human beings, and that means white people… They're just little niggers, and if there's four less niggers tonight, then I say, 'Good for whoever planted the bomb!'"

Eight thousand people attended a joint funeral for three of the girls. Martin Luther King Jr. gave the eulogy to a community that, having witnessed seven bombings within the previous six months, was torn between exhaustion and rage.

An eyewitness reported seeing four men

plant the bomb. Police arrested Chambliss after the bombing, but let him go shortly after. In 1977 Alabama Attorney General William Baxley reopened the case, and Chambliss was tried and convicted of first-degree murder.

Marian Aguiar

See Also

Abernathy, Ralph David; Gregory, Richard Claxton "Dick"; King, Martin Luther, Jr.

Cross Cultural

Ska, a form of Jamaican music that fuses elements of black American music, especially rhythm and blues, with *mento*, the island's folk music.

Ska is the product of the encounter of two different black musical traditions, one indigenous to Jamaica and the other transmitted from the United States to Jamaica via radio in the 1950s. Ska's unique sound derives from its emphasis on the second and fourth beats, a rhythmic characteristic found in other forms of Jamaican music that developed out of ska – rocksteady, reggae, dub, and dancehall – and, less prominently, in rhythm and blues. In ska the offbeat, or "drop" as it is sometimes called, is created by the guitar and drums and is sometimes accentuated by the brass section.

During the World War II era technological advances made radio broadcasting more extensive and radios more receptive to distant signals, enabling Jamaica to tune in to radio stations based in the southern United States. Many Jamaicans became infatuated with the sounds of jazz and rhythm and blues (R&B). Since radios were not readily available or affordable in Jamaica at that time, musical entrepreneurs such as Clement "Sir Coxsone Downbeat" Dodd and Duke "The Trojan" Reid assembled sound systems, mobile audio units consisting of a radio, turntable(s), and speakers, in order to bring black American music to Jamaican audiences.

In the late 1950s, however, rock 'n' roll emerged as the new popular American music, and R&B was less often heard on the airwaves. Jamaicans largely rejected rock 'n' roll, which they found less danceable. In response to this predicament, Dodd began to advocate the creation of a new form of popular music in Jamaica based on swing, R&B, and boogie woogie as well as mento, which previously had been the most popular Jamaican music. One of the first groups to rise to the challenge was Clue J and the Blues Blasters. Although bassist Clue J, who often greeted friends with the buzzword "Skavoovie," inspired the name of this new form of music, "ska," it was a band by the name of the Skatalites that defined its sound.

In 1967 a heat wave came over the West Indies, which many historians have cited as the cause for ska's transformation into rocksteady. Compared to ska, rocksteady has a slower tempo, lighter horns, and a heavier bass. Desmond Dekker was one of the early popular rocksteady artists. In 1967 his "007 Shanty Town" reached Number Eleven on the British pop charts, and in 1969 his "Israelites" climbed to the Number One spot. The advent of rocksteady in the late 1960s marked the end of ska's first phase in Jamaica.

Though ska had largely faded from the Jamaican music scene, British youth who had become infatuated with the music of Jamaican artists such as Desmond Dekker revived ska a decade later, around 1979. That same year Jerry Dammers, a member of what would become one of Great Britain's premier ska bands, the Specials (originally the Special A.K.A.), founded the 2 Tone record label, whose name became synonymous with the ska movement in Britain. At a time when police brutality against Jamaican immigrants was on the rise and race riots broke out with increasing frequency, 2 Tone sought to promote racial harmony and unity in Great Britian. This was reflected in the composition of ska bands, the majority of which were racially integrated, and in their aesthetic, which featured black-and-white clothing combinations and black-and-white checkered accessories. They adopted as their icon Walt Jabsco, a man in a black suit, white shirt, black tie, white socks, black loafers, sunglasses, and a pork-pie hat. This was essentially a British rehashing of the Jamaican rude boy often referred to in Jamaican ska, a transformation in which the menacing gangster became a happy, dancing figure.

After affiliating itself with Chrysalis Records around 1980, the 2 Tone label issued a string of hits. Each of the seven singles pressed by 2 Tone at this time sold at least 250,000 copies. The label's primary group, the Specials, repeatedly topped the British pop charts with such songs as "Too Much Too Young," "A Message to Rudy," and "Ghost Town." Other groups that enjoyed success recording on the 2 Tone label included the Selecter, Madness, and the (English) Beat. Encouraged by the success of 2 Tone Records, several other ska bands and ska record labels emerged. At ska shows, however, violence frequently erupted between the neatly dressed rude boys and the poorer skinheads. This made British music venues reluctant to book ska bands and ultimately contributed to the demise of ska in the United Kingdom. The dissolution of the 2 Tone label around 1985 signaled the end of the British ska craze.

In spite of ska's short-lived popularity in Britain, such British artists as Elvis Costello and Madness, who had launched their careers on the 2 Tone label, preserved elements of ska in their music and became well known in the United States, where ska's third wave began in 1983. That year ska bands by the name of Not Bob Marley, which later became known as the Toasters, and Bim Skala Bim formed in New York City and Boston, respectively. In the mid-1980s each of these groups established its own record label for the production and distribution of ska music: Moon Records in New York City and Fonograff Records in Boston. As had been the case in Jamaica with Dodd's Studio One and in Britain with Dammers's 2 Tone label, these independent record labels enabled ska to flourish.

Unlike the 2 Tone movement, which attempted to recapture the classic 1960s style of Jamaican ska and its accompanying dress code, the new ska in the United States blended the original form with several different music styles, including hardcore punk, funk, and Latin. In the mid- to late 1980s groups such as the Mighty Mighty Bosstones and Operation Ivy incorporated ska into their hardcore songs. At about the same time a band called Fishbone created a style of music based on ska and funk. More recently, such groups as Jump With Joey and Babaloo have successfully merged ska with Latin rhythms. Acts such as the Allstonians and Skavoovie and the Epitones, however, have attempted to preserve the late 1960s Jamaican ska sound. Almost all of these bands continue to play today and draw large audiences. The undisputed kings of the ska scene are the Skatalites, who reunited in 1983 and continue to tour worldwide.

Aaron Myers

See Also

Great Britain; Boston, Massachusetts; New York, New York.

Latin America and the Caribbean

Slave Laws in Colonial Spanish America, laws that until the late seventeenth century were issued to control the slave population in Spain's New World colonies.

Slaves were a source of labor to peoples worldwide for thousands of years before the conquest and colonization of the Americas (*see* Slavery in Africa). Justifications for the enslavement of human beings, in either moral or legal terms, have varied. In some societies individuals were enslaved when they committed crimes; when they were born into a social class of slaves; or when out of poverty or extreme indebtedness they had to sell themselves, or were sold by their creditors, into slavery. Other groups enslaved those captured in "just" (properly declared) wars when they considered the enemy inferior or "barbarian" for expressing a different culture, language, or religion. In many cases slaves could not be differentiated in physical appearance from their masters.

During the middle ages the greatest proportion of slaves in Western Europe came from the non-Christian, light-skinned central and east European people known as the Saqaliba (or Slavs). As early as the twelfth century the word for "slave" in all Western

European languages derived from the word "Slav" (e.g., *esclave, esclavo, escravo, schiavo, sklave*). From the eleventh to the late thirteenth century Western Europeans embarked on the CRUSADES, which led to an expansion of commercial activity and the capturing of slaves who were Jews, Moors, "Turks" (Syrians, Egyptians, and Lebanese), white Christians (Sardinians, Greeks, and Russians), and *Guanches* (Canary Islanders). During this period the use of ancient Roman law spread and was assimilated throughout legal systems in Europe.

In the kingdom of Castile and León, King Alfonso X the Wise (1221-1284) commissioned a group of jurists to unify and universalize the norms and legal dispositions of the lands over which he was sovereign. The Siete Partidas (Seven Part Code) was issued as comprehensive legislation to replace the diverse, confusing, and often contradictory local laws (known as *fueros*), which carried the influence of Roman law. The Roman civil code known as Justinian's Corpus Juris Civilis was used as a main source for the Partidas.

In 1493, after Columbus's first trip to America, Pope Alexander VI issued four papal bulls that granted "to the present and future sovereigns of Castile the lands discovered and to be discovered by their envoys and not previously possessed by any Christian owner." The New World, or what Spain called the "Indies," became part of the Crown of Castile. Castile enjoyed exclusive rights to the New World and reserved the privilege of immigration for Castilian subjects or those authorized by Castile. In theory, the laws and institutions of Castile became the basis of government in Spanish America.

Because the slave population was not characterized by one predominant race before the conquest of the Americas, the laws derived from the Romans that were used to control the small number of domestic slaves in what today is Spain were not racially defined. Hence, the norms expressed in the Siete Partidas, which addressed slavery and manumission in Spain at the time of the conquest, were largely the same as those rules that regulated the ancient political and social institution of slavery in Rome. Spanish slave laws, like those in Rome, allowed for various forms of manumission and limitations to punishments. They did not, however, permit slaves to have legal representation, be party to a civil legal action, or to act as witnesses in matters of great importance. Slavery, and thus the laws regulating the institution, took on a specifically racial character only in the sixteenth century, when the demand for slaves increased with the conquest and colonization of the Americas and when Africa became the largest source of forced labor.

In 1517 Charles I, the king who united the thrones of Castile and Aragón into the Spanish state, issued a decree allowing the direct shipment of blacks from Africa to the Spanish colonies. Hispanicized slaves (who were called *ladinos*) and others brought from Europe were not only more expensive and scarce than Africans, but they were also thought to be responsible for inciting slaves in the Americas to rebel, as happened in HISPANIOLA (in the present-day DOMINICAN REPUBLIC and HAITI) in 1522. Therefore, two final decrees in 1530 and 1532 prohibited the dispatch of any white Moorish, Jewish, or ladino slave to the Indies. From then on, only African-born slaves, who were considered "peaceful and obedient," could be legally shipped to the Indies. *Cédulas* (or royal laws) and slave contracts for the next 60 years continued to insist on the Africanness of slaves, as indicated by their darker skin color, so that they would not be replaced with the sometimes lighter-skinned ladinos, or white pagan slaves. The economic incentives of the African slave trade further contributed to changes in the imagery of slavery, so that the term *esclavos* (slaves) came to be synonymous with *negros* (blacks).

Strict implementation of many of the principles and norms offered by the Siete Partidas was inapplicable in the New World for a variety of reasons. These included the racial factor; the economic and religious motives that informed the colonizing enterprise; the slave trade; the relation with the indigenous people; and the administrative challenges. From as early as 1526 royal cédulas were created in order to justify and regulate circumstances that were not foreseen by or could not be managed by the Siete Partidas. For example, many of the first slaves brought to the New World from Spain took advantage of the Partidas norm that allowed a slave to marry a free person and thus become free himself. Cédulas in 1526 and 1538 prohibited further manumission through marriage.

In 1680 the Spanish king issued a compilation summarizing the local legislation in order for the laws to be applied in all of the colonies (known as the *Recopilación de leyes de los Reynos de las Indias*). Colonial officials (such as viceroys and town councilors) issued additional legislation in the form of local ordinances (*ordenanzas*) that regulated slave relations in a particular location. With the need to subjugate the increasing number of slaves and free blacks, the language of the local statutes became racially principled, and the statutes themselves became far more brutal and less permissive than those found in the Siete Partidas or the royal cédulas. The ordinances could be raised to the status of royal cédula by a royal confirmation (*real confirmación*), though this approval could take decades. In the meantime the local orders regulated punishment and all aspects of social, economic, religious, sexual, and labor relations of slaves. By doing so, they equated "blacks" with the characteristics given generally to slaves since antiquity in order to justify human bondage. Cruel and demeaning punishment could be justified if slaves were objectified as property or chattel in the law. The local laws also constructed a sociocultural idea of blacks as inferior humans. Many norms referred to slaves and free blacks as being lazy, sexually deviant, heretic, rebellious, festive, childlike, and intellectually inferior, among other traits considered negative by the ruling elite.

By 1685 the slave population in the American colonies had become so large that the French king issued the first comprehensive black code (or *Code Noir*) for France's Caribbean colonies. The Spanish Crown followed with its codification almost a century later by taking into account the French Code Noir, the Siete Partidas, and the legislation that had been produced specifically for the colonies in the past 250 years (*see* BLACK CODES IN LATIN AMERICA).

In sum, the treatment of slaves during the colonial era in Spanish America was regulated by several legal sources, often contradictory in nature and purpose and seldom respected. Today, however, we can still view these written laws as embodiments of the ideas then held about black people in the Americas, and can see their persistence in current manifestations of racism, discrimination, and general human rights violations.

Liliana Obregón

SEE ALSO

Transatlantic Slave Trade; Slavery in Latin America and the Caribbean; Spain; Human Rights in Latin America and the Caribbean; Punishment of Slaves in Colonial Latin America and the Caribbean.

North America

Slave Narratives, written autobiographies and oral testimonies by escaped or freed slaves.

At the conclusion of her Pulitzer-Prize-winning novel *Beloved*, TONI MORRISON sums up her retelling of one slave family's experience: "It was not a story to pass on." There are certainly logical reasons why the story of slavery might never have been passed on. One, the reason Morrison suggests, was its sheer horror and trauma – those who lived through slavery may not have wanted to remember their experiences. A second is more practical: it was illegal to teach slaves to read and write, which meant that the act of putting a story on paper was generally denied them. But neither of these reasons kept former slaves from passing on their stories and leaving a record about what living as a piece of property had been like. Slave narratives set the standard for a tradition of African American autobiography that continues today.

Although slave narratives were written in several parts of the diaspora and in a variety of languages, the majority of published narratives by African slaves and their descendants were written in English in what is now the United States. Black literary scholar Henry Louis Gates Jr. argues that African American slaves were unique in the history of world slavery because they were the only enslaved people to produce a body of writing that testified to their experiences.

For many of these authors, writing narratives served a dual purpose: it was a way of publicizing the horrors they had gone through and it was also a method of proving their humanity. One of the common arguments in support of race-based slavery was that blacks were simply an inferior species, incapable of thinking and feeling in the ways whites did. Through their narratives slave authors were able to display their emotions and their intellects.

Historians estimate that there are approximately 6000 published narratives by African American slaves. This number includes both book-length autobiographies and shorter accounts published in newspapers or transcribed from interviews, and it spans 170 years' worth of testimonies from ex-slaves. Most of these narratives were published or collected after slavery was abolished in 1865, as slaves who had been emancipated looked back on their experiences. The most famous slave narratives are autobiographies by FUGITIVE SLAVES that were published before 1865.

During this period ex-slaves' narratives were a powerful tool in the fight against slavery. Many abolitionist groups correctly guessed that first-person accounts of the horrors of slavery would be the most effective means of explaining slavery's evils to a wide audience, and they often helped black authors to find publishers and audiences for their work. Approximately 70 slave narratives were published in the United States in book or pamphlet form before the end of the Civil War, and hundreds more appeared in American and British periodicals. Slave narratives often went through multiple editions and sometimes sold thousands of copies in the United States and throughout Europe. Such was the case with OLAUDAH EQUIANO's *The Interesting Narrative of the Life of Olaudah Equiano,* published in London in 1789. Equiano's narrative, which recounts his life in Africa, his capture, and the Middle Passage, is one of the rare autobiographies in English by a slave who was born in Africa.

The best-known slave narrative is Frederick Douglass's *Narrative of the Life of Frederick Douglass, an American Slave, Written by Himself* (1845). In it Douglass describes his childhood separation from his mother, his struggle to teach himself to read and write, the brutal whippings he witnessed and received, and his determination to be free – all the while stressing his own humanity and the inhumanity of the system that kept him a slave. Douglass's autobiography was an international bestseller. After its publication Douglass traveled the world as a lecturer, implicitly providing a model for just how "civilized" blacks could be, and went on to become the most famous and respected black individual of the nineteenth century. His narrative's patterns and images were repeated not only in many later slave narratives, but also in such diverse works of AFRICAN AMERICAN LITERATURE as Zora Neale Hurston's *Their Eyes Were Watching God* (1937) and Ralph Ellison's *Invisible Man* (1952).

Other famous slave narrators from this period include WILLIAM WELLS BROWN and Harriet Jacobs. Brown was one of the earliest African American novelists. Jacobs, whose *Incidents in the Life of a Slave Girl* is the best example of a woman's slave narrative, discusses the sexual intimidation and abuse and the agony of being a slave mother that made slavery a different experience for women than for men.

Frederick Douglass

NARRATIVE

OF THE

LIFE

OF

FREDERICK DOUGLASS,

AN

AMERICAN SLAVE.

WRITTEN BY HIMSELF.

BOSTON:

PUBLISHED AT THE ANTI-SLAVERY OFFICE,

No. 25 CORNHILL.

1845.

The portrait of Frederick Douglass shown here appeared facing the title page of *Narrative of the Life of Frederick Douglass, an American Slave, Written by Himself,* which was published in Boston in 1845. *CORBIS/Bettmann*

Authors such as Henry "Box" Brown and William and Ellen Craft were memorable for their novel methods of escape from slavery: Brown was packed into a crate and shipped to the free North as freight; the Crafts traveled disguised as a dark-skinned Spanish gentleman and his black servant. Throughout this period narrators worked both to give credible accounts of their own individual experiences in slavery and to argue that their experiences were representative, and that thousands of others still suffered just as they had. They strove to convince readers that all of the slaves must be freed, and indeed, the narratives did help to make the end of American slavery a reality.

After Emancipation the tone of many slave narratives changed. Authors continued to portray their experiences as slaves, but for many the new purpose in writing was to prove that slavery had been a testing ground from which African Americans had successfully emerged, ready to participate in the larger American society. Booker T. Washington's 1901 autobiography *Up From Slavery* is the best-known example of this new type of slave narrative. Washington uses many of the same conventions found in Douglass's slave narrative, but he turns them around so that in his autobiography slavery becomes the foundation for a classic rags-to-riches American success story.

The last documents classified as slave narratives are the transcriptions of interviews with ex-slaves conducted in the first several decades of the twentieth century. The largest collection of these was compiled by interviewers with the federally funded FEDERAL WRITERS' PROJECT in the 1930s, which gathered testimonies from 2500 ex-slaves in 17 states.

In the late twentieth century the slave narratives' presence is still felt throughout African American literature in both form and function. Many authors have written contemporary retellings of slave narratives, in books as varied as Morrison's lyrical *Beloved* (1987), Octavia Butler's science fiction novel *Kindred* (1979), and ISHMAEL REED's parody *Flight to Canada* (1976). Other novels, such as *Invisible Man*, use the narratives' themes and structure with very different subject matter. And throughout the history of African American literature, autobiography has remained a dominant genre. Many African Americans still identify with the need to write about themselves as a means of sharing their common humanity. LANGSTON HUGHES, ZORA NEALE HURSTON, RICHARD WRIGHT, MALCOLM X, and MAYA ANGELOU are among recent black writers who continued this tradition of using the written word to pass their stories on.

Lisa Clayton Robinson

SEE ALSO

Middle Passage, The; Slavery in the United States; Abolitionism in the United States; Brown, Henry ("Box"); Butler, Octavia Estelle; Civil War, American; Craft, Ellen and William; Douglass, Frederick; Ellison, Ralph; Hurston, Zora Neale; Jacobs, Harriet Ann; Washington, Booker Taliaferro.

Latin America and the Caribbean

Slave Rebellions in Latin America and the Caribbean

Enslaved Africans living in the Americas actively fought for their freedom in many different ways. The most vivid examples of resistance are slave revolts, which often grew out of other acts of rebellion. Expressions of slave protest included work slowdowns, sabotage of plantation production, and, in some instances, suicide. Often, escape was a form of resistance. Slaves who were able to avoid capture formed or joined maroon communities with other escaped slaves (*see* MAROONAGE IN THE AMERICAS). These black communities served as bases for large-scale slave revolts in the Caribbean and Latin America. Often, African leaders such as BENKOS BIOHÓ used maroon communities as safe havens from which to strategize and mobilize supporters to participate in ensuing battles against slavery.

The Caribbean is the site of the most successful slave rebellion. In the French colony of Saint-Domingue (present-day HAITI), a Jamaican-born slave named BOUKMAN led a mass rebellion. On August 22, 1791, after a heated labor dispute, Boukman, a strong military strategist, made his attack on the slave regime with two favorable conditions on his side. First, there were 14 enslaved Africans for every one white person in Saint-Domingue. Second, Boukman received considerable support from thousands of war-hardened civil war revolutionaries from the Congo who had recently been sold into slavery. Toussaint L'Ouverture, a great Caribbean freedom fighter, also gained prominence in this revolution. The 1791 rebellion, which became a revolution, stunned slave owners throughout the Americas (*see* HAITIAN REVOLUTION). Many whites suppressed news of the revolution for fear that their own slaves would be inspired to revolt as well. Ultimately, the rebellion led to heightened concern over slavery in the hemisphere, leading some slave owners to adopt greater leniency and others greater cruelty so as to thwart revolutionary tendencies among black populations. Despite slave owners' attempts to suppress news of the rebellion, Africans did use the successful movement as a model for future revolts. Louisiana's Point Coupé Conspiracy of 1795 and Virginia's GABRIEL PROSSER CONSPIRACY of 1800, for instance, found inspiration in the Haitian Revolution.

It is perhaps not surprising that Boukman's birthplace was JAMAICA, which itself had a long history of slave rebellions. The first revolt in Jamaica took place in 1522. In the 1670s rebellions became more frequent and more violent. Revolts, in fact, became a constant in Jamaican history from the mid-seventeenth century until 1740, culminating in the Maroon War, after which the British were forced to concede the rebel slaves' freedom, establishing some free maroon towns. On December 25, 1831, 20,000 slaves engaged in a massive uprising. The success of this revolution fueled the creation of the British Emancipation Act of 1833. The act called for a gradual freeing of slaves, which liberated about 500,000 Africans throughout the British colonies.

In BARBADOS the history of insurrection is different. Long military oppression in Barbados generally tempered slave rebellions, but in April 1816, the Easter Rebellion, also known as Bussa's Insurrection, flared. This three-day rebellion led to the death of more than 1000 blacks and about 50 whites.

The Brazilian city of Salvador, BAHIA, was the stage for a number of slave revolts between 1807 and 1835. Known as Malê Uprisings, the revolts were led by Muslim slaves. In 1835 hundreds fought in the streets of Bahia for several hours. The 1830s were also characterized by revolts throughout the region, in Belém, Rio Grande do Sul, Bahia, and Maranhão. Afro-Brazilian maroon communities, called *quilombos* or *mocambos*, engaged in battles against the *capitães do mato*, violent bounty hunters who frequently attacked the settlements looking to resell slaves or return slaves to their owners.

In the Spanish-speaking Americas slaves demonstrated their courage in a historic uprising in ESMERALDAS, in present-day ECUADOR. In 1553 a boat carrying 17 men and 6 women slaves shipwrecked on the Ecuadorian coast. The slaves revolted against their surviving captors and escaped to create a *palenque* (a maroon community), which, after several generations, blended with the neighboring region's population. Slave revolts are a significant part of the history of Africans in the Americas; they serve as a powerful reminder of the resistance with which black communities confronted conditions of oppression throughout the Americas and the Caribbean.

Judith Morrison

SEE ALSO

Muslim Uprisings in Bahia, Brazil; Toussaint L'Ouverture, François Dominique.

North America

Slave Religion, the religious beliefs and practices of African American slaves in North America.

In a system in which mobility, marriage, employment, housing, food, and clothing were all regulated by slave owners, religion was the only form of slave expression not totally under white control. As a result religion played a central role in the lives of slaves. Slave congregations became new versions of the African village, with the slave preacher serving as chief, griot, and even doctor.

Religious meetings provided important ritual communal opportunities for African American slaves to worship in ways that connected them to African traditions, while also creating, over time, a new belief system adapted to their lives in the New World. Religion gave individual slaves a sense of their place in the world, a sense of their worth, and a life-sustaining faith in a better future.

Some masters organized mandatory Christian church services, in the hope that Christian slaves would be more docile. Some allowed slaves to hold their own services. Many others, however, did not allow their slaves to attend church at all, either because they felt threatened by any such communal gatherings or because they disliked the suggestion that slaves might have souls to be saved. But even on plantations where religious gatherings were forbidden, secret meetings were held at night in secluded outdoor sanctuaries – often bush arbors that slaves nicknamed "hush harbors."

Many facts about slaves' religious practices went unrecorded, but it is known that slave religion combined elements of traditional African religions and American evangelical Protestant Christianity. African influences were present in many of the slaves' ceremonies. For example, in the ring shout, a common form of worship, believers formed a circle and moved counterclockwise, shouting and professing their faith, while others stood outside the circle and sang. The call-and-response worship pattern, in which the preacher's sermon was interspersed with responses from members of the audience, also had African roots and is still a common characteristic of African American preaching and music.

Slave theology was predominantly Christian, but slaves appropriated from the Christian Bible only what they found most useful. A common complaint about the sermons preached by white ministers in the slave quarters was that nearly all relied on only one verse: "Slaves, obey your masters." But as slaves learned more about the Bible, they were able to decide what other messages it held for them. Consequently, they identified with the God who favored the poor and meek over the wealthy and strong, the God who praised the little David over the mighty Goliath, and, above all, the God who freed the Hebrew slaves from their Egyptian captors. In this way slaves were able to see themselves not as property but as people created in God's image, important in his eyes, and people who would have deliverance and justice in the days to come.

Religious meetings offered benefits that were not only spiritual. Regarded as a democratic space where all were welcome to speak if they felt the spirit, meetings provided what was essentially the only opportunity slaves had for public speaking. As a result they also provided a rare forum for leadership to emerge, and slave preachers were generally respected as the speakers and leaders of the entire community. NAT TURNER and Gabriel Prosser, two famous slave rebellion leaders, both began as religious leaders.

One of the most common forms of religious expression was spirituals, songs with a rich double purpose. Slave masters often encouraged this music because they saw the spirituals as simple hymns and thought that singing kept slaves content as they worked. Spirituals also played a key role in teaching the Bible to slaves who were not literate, because the lyrics of common spirituals retell the biblical narrative from Creation to Revelation. But many of these lyrics also had secret meanings. It was common knowledge among the slaves who sang spirituals that "Steal Away" did not mean only to Jesus, and "I Am Bound for the Promised Land" did not refer only to Heaven. Spirituals offered a method of secretly communicating plans and directions for escape from the plantation.

For all these reasons, slave religion played a crucial part in slave life. It provided the basis for a cohesive community in which slaves were able to communicate more openly and express themselves more freely than in any other context. Through this community, with its shared rituals, beliefs, and songs, slaves could find the spiritual validation and hope for the future that many relied upon to sustain them through their trials. An enslaved woman named Polly summed up one view of the slaves' religious faith: "We poor creatures have need to believe in God, for if God Almighty will not be good to us some day, why were we born? When I heard of his delivering his people from bondage I know it means the poor African."

Lisa Clayton Robinson

SEE ALSO

Slavery in the United States; Gabriel Prosser Conspiracy; Spirituals, African American; African Religions: An Interpretation.

Africa

Slavery in Africa

Too often, observers have treated Africa as a region in isolation. The history of slavery, in contrast, shows the significance of Africa's socioeconomic connections to other world regions. The very distinctiveness of African society and African slavery results in large part from local responses to global connections.

This essay focuses on three historical points. First, slavery existed and sometimes flourished in Africa before the TRANSATLANTIC SLAVE TRADE, but neither the African continent nor persons of African origin were as prominent in the world of slaveholding as they would later become. Second, the capture and sale of slaves across the Atlantic between 1450 and 1850 encouraged expansion and repeated transformation of slavery within Africa, to the point that systems of slavery became central to societies all across the continent. Third, even after the abolition of the transatlantic slave trade (largely accomplished by 1850) and the European conquest of Africa (mostly by 1900), millions of persons remained in slavery in Africa as late as 1930.

The three sections of this essay address each of these points, giving particular attention to the last two. While the argument reviews the rise and decline of export slave trades – across the Atlantic, the Sahara, the Red Sea, and the Indian Ocean – it focuses on the nature and extent of slavery within sub-Saharan Africa.

BEFORE THE TRANSATLANTIC SLAVE TRADE

In ancient Egypt and Nubia slavery existed but not as a dominant institution. The enslavement of the Hebrews in Babylonia and Egypt was a significant exception. In classical times the commercial North African state of CARTHAGE as well as the Greek states and Rome all relied on slave labor in galleys and in agriculture, and acquired some of their slaves through trade with sub-Saharan Africa.

The rise of Islam in the seventh century C.E. brought a set of rules that provided protection for those in slave status, but in so doing reinforced the institution of slavery. In Africa Islam took root first in North Africa, then later in West Africa and along the eastern coast. A large proportion of slaves in Islamic society served as domestics, but slaves also worked as farm laborers and porters. Elite corps of slaves entered the military and government.

Among pre-1500 sub-Saharan states, traces of slavery are only occasionally clear. Evidence of slavery in AKSUM and the Christian kingdoms of Nubia, for example, is scarce. For the ancient West African empires of Ghana and Mali, the written record makes only an occasional reference to slave status. For the Islamic empire of Songhai, on the other hand, there are clearer indications of significant numbers of persons held in slave status by the monarchy and by lords of the realm. To the east of Songhai the kingdom of Kanem-Bornu may also have had substantial numbers of slaves. In East Africa slaves were important to the labor of the Islamic Swahili states along the coast as well as to the greater Indian Ocean regional economy. In the states of Ife, Oyo, and Benin in West Africa, KONGO in Central Africa, and Munhumutapa in what is now ZIMBABWE, slave populations took form around powerful monarchs.

It is difficult to assess the extent of slavery outside of these major states prior to 1500 because of the lack of data. But the earliest written reports by visitors from Europe and North Africa and the later anthropological records suggest that various kinds of slavery existed in smaller as in larger polities.

It is also difficult to assess the *nature* of servility during this era, and to know whether it was equivalent to chattel slavery. By the beginning of the twentieth century, according to the descriptions of European writers,

African societies had developed many different types of servitude. But some of this variation may have developed over time, in response to the imposition of chattel slavery in the plantations and mines of the Americas (*see* Slavery in Latin America and the Caribbean).

During the Transatlantic Slave Trade, 1450-1850

Portuguese and Spanish holdings of African slaves expanded with the maritime voyages of the fifteenth century, then grew moderately until, after 1650, the transatlantic trade exceeded the slave trade across the Sahara and Red Sea. Portuguese and then Dutch purchasers focused in Senegambia, Kongo, Angola, and Sierra Leone. Africans' willingness to participate in the export of slaves varied. The kingdom of Benin, for example, eventually withdrew from the slave trade, but in Kongo and Senegambia those willing to profit from capture and export of slaves became dominant. These and then other African societies developed the means to capture, feed, finance, and transport captives for sale to European buyers.

As the trade expanded, Europeans developed a preference for males and were willing to pay more for them. Africans, in contrast, paid higher prices for female slaves, who were preferred because they could be used as domestic and agricultural laborers, as concubines, and as bearers of children. They were also considered easier to control than men. As prices diverged, the European and African markets for slaves grew in tandem. Their parallel expansion meant that, from the seventeenth century, the number of persons in slavery in Africa roughly equaled the number in the Americas.

Between 1700 and 1800, for the western coast of Africa from Senegal to Angola, the export of massive numbers of primarily male slaves led to both overall population decline and the dramatic increase in female slavery. Thus the transatlantic slave trade had not only demographic consequences for African societies but also economic and social ones.

At the turn of the eighteenth century the Bight of Benin was the principal region of slave supply. Wars among competing coastal states supplied as many as 15,000 slaves per year for export. Many of these slaves spoke the Gbe language and practiced the religion of Vodun (a predecessor of Haitian Vodou). But as 5 percent of the population were exported each year in chains, the population declined and captives became more expensive to collect and deliver. As a result prices of slaves in the Bight of Benin rose dramatically between 1690 and 1730. As population declined and prices rose in one area, other areas were drawn into the slave trade: the Bight of Biafra (southern Nigeria), Sierra Leone, the Gold Coast (now Ghana), Angola, and the Republic of the Congo. As traders all along Africa's west coast began to deliver captives, the excess of males delivered across the Atlantic led to a changed population structure in the homeland. Women exceeded men by a substantial proportion in West and Central Africa, with an average of 100 adult females for every 70 adult males. In areas such as Angola and the Bight of Benin, the ratio reached two adult women for every man.

Most captive women were sold into slavery and kept by families. A huge system of female-dominated family slavery arose all along the African coast during the eighteenth century. It expanded as long as demand for slaves in the Americas expanded – that is, until the end of the eighteenth century. Women worked as servants or in the fields. They were without family except for their owners and their children, and the children were property of their owners. This century of numerical dominance but social inferiority for women had a lasting influence on the institution of marriage and on the sexual division of labor in societies along Africa's west coast.

A soldier guards a group of slaves linked together by chains in 1896. *Hulton Getty/Liaison Agency*

Between 1800 and 1850 two distinct but related developments led to an increase in the number of persons held in slavery in Africa and to the overall transformation of African systems of slavery. The first development was the growing demand for slaves in the Muslim Mediterranean and the lands bordering the Indian Ocean, beginning in

LEFT: Slaves of the Pasha of Taoundenni, in Mali, stack blocks of salt in the 1950s. *CORBIS/Hulton-Deutsch Collection*

BELOW LEFT: Two African slave boys in a nineteenth-century photograph. *CORBIS/Hulton-Deutsch Collection*

the late eighteenth century. Perhaps this demand reflected the general growth in commercial activity; perhaps it reflected simply the spread of the system of slave labor from the Atlantic Basin. It remained primarily a demand for female slaves, who served largely as domestics. Societies of the northern savanna and the Horn of Africa, therefore, had populations with an excess of males, in contrast to the excess of females in societies along the Atlantic.

The second development occurred along the west coast of Africa, where the decline of slave exports after the gradual abolition of the transatlantic trade led to expansion and transformation of the African system of slavery. African sex ratios tended to equalize as the proportion of exiled males declined. Slaves were now both male and female, and they lived not in the households of their masters but in separate villages. For the continent as a whole the expansion of this new system of slavery coincided with ongoing population decline. The number of captives exported from West Africa declined, but exports remained high in the Republic of the Congo and Angola, and exports actually rose along the Sahara fringe as well as along the Horn and the east coast of Africa. As population declined and levels of enslavement rose, plantation slavery and slave villages became more common in many areas in Africa. In southern Africa slavery declined under British COLONIAL RULE in the west but expanded in the east, where slaves were captured for export to lands around the Indian Ocean.

AFRICAN SLAVERY AFTER THE ABOLITION OF THE TRANSATLANTIC SLAVE TRADE

Slave trade across the Atlantic had virtually halted by 1850. But the various regions of the African continent continued to feel heavily the impact of enslavement and slavery for most of the next century. The result was that Africa in the late nineteenth century had more people in slavery than at any previous time. The final great emancipations of the Americas – the United States in 1865, Cuba in 1886, and Brazil in 1888 – left Africa, and especially the SOKOTO CALIPHATE in northern Nigeria, holding the world's principal enslaved populations.

Slave exports across the Indian Ocean, the Sahara, and the Red Sea reached their peak in about 1850, then declined at varying rates until the end of the century. During this time some enslaved Africans were carried across the Red Sea to build an expanded pilgrimage site at Mecca, in Saudi Arabia; others were carried on steamers through the SUEZ CANAL, bound for Istanbul and Izmir.

In coastal West Africa slavery expanded on plantations producing export commodities such as palm oil. The result was social turmoil, as slaves revolted in several regions from Calabar to Dahomey during the 1850s. Although the revolts were suppressed, they also set new limits on the exploitation of slaves. In the Republic of the Congo and Angola exports finally halted around 1850, though enslavement for local purposes continued. In the northern savanna exports of slaves peaked in the mid-nineteenth century, but the number of captives exceeded what could be explained as a by-product of export trade. In regions of the upper Niger Valley there were repeated reports that the majority of the region's population was in slavery, and that the slaves were principally female: they produced grains and textiles for the domestic market and leather goods for export. Captive workers in the Sahara mined salt and produced dates and grains in oases. Slave labor forces in Senegal produced peanuts for export.

In the Horn of Africa the continued export of slaves to Arabia left large holdings of slaves within Africa. Exports of slaves and a population decline also continued in East Africa, where European purchasers, based in MADAGASCAR and the Mascarene Islands, maintained a high demand for slaves into the 1880s.

In short, the world markets for slave labor and for the goods produced by slaves remained strong in the middle and late nineteenth century, and these markets supported slavery and slave trading in Africa. The European powers poised to invade the continent pointed to the persistence of African slavery to justify colonization. Thus the BERLIN CONFERENCE OF 1884-1885, convened as an antislavery meeting, in fact set the rules for the European conquest of Africa (*see* SCRAMBLE FOR AFRICA).

Between 1890 and 1940 the European colonial powers strengthened their grip on African lands and African societies and preached a doctrine of antislavery. The result was not, however, immediate emancipation. Large-scale slave raiding came to an end because the European powers had monopolized the use of armed force. But slavery itself continued for millions of Africans until the eve of World War II.

The European conquest of Africa took place, in large measure, between 1880 and 1900. By 1900 African armies had been routed and European hegemony was established nearly everywhere except ETHIOPIA, LIBERIA, MOROCCO, and parts of the Sahara. Great numbers of slaves took their liberty with the change in power, and European authorities decreed, for the most part, that slave raiding was henceforth prohibited. Yet only infrequently were African slaves emancipated. The slaves of Madagascar were liberated after the 1897-1898 French conquest, but British conquests during those same years did not lead to the emancipation of slaves in either SUDAN or the Sokoto Caliphate.

With the establishment of COLONIAL RULE, slavery was reformed but not abolished. Slave owners, no longer able to hope for new captives, put higher value on infant and child slaves; both the prices and the level of nourishment of children increased. Workloads for adult slaves decreased accordingly, as their survival now became more important. In Ethiopia, for instance, the abolition of the slave trade during World War I (when Ethiopia sought European approbation of its regime in order to avoid conquest) brought a rapid rise in prices of child slaves. The accounts of colonial ethnographers who visited African societies after 1900 describe systems that protected the rights of slaves; these rights had been expanded just as slave raiding had ended. The colonial-era African system of slavery without slave raiding corresponded in many ways to SLAVERY IN THE UNITED STATES.

Instead of emancipation, European rulers in Africa resorted to gradual and indirect means to end slavery. One was through the courts: slaves who claimed mistreatment could appeal for redress or emancipation in colonial courts. Slaves could purchase their own freedom. In British colonies the administration tended to declare that the state no longer recognized the institution of slavery. This approach, first implemented in British India in 1843, prevented slave owners from appealing to the state to retrieve escaped slaves; it also prevented slaves from challenging their condition, since the state argued that slavery no longer existed. Still another device was the legislation of the emancipation of infants born after a given date; in Sierra Leone, for example, the date was 1928. Further, as Paul Lovejoy and Jan Hogendorn have shown in *Slow Death for Slavery: The Course of Abolition in Northern Nigeria, 1897-1936* (1993), the institution of concubinage continued beyond the era of slavery. Northern Nigerian landowners continued to pressure poor families to provide young women for their harems.

The distinction between slave and master in Africa was not, as in the Americas, typically based on a distinction in race. But indicators such as name, language, scarification, dress, and manners all distinguished the identity and social status of slaves from those of their masters. Thus, while the heritage of slavery was kept alive in the Americas through discrimination by race, the heritage of slavery remained alive in Africa through discrimination by class. African countries, though millions of their inhabitants are descendants of slaves, have no holiday to celebrate the emancipation of slaves. The lack of a clear act of emancipation helped to propagate relations of servility into the mid- and late twentieth century.

Patrick Manning

SEE ALSO

Benin, Early Kingdom of; Explorers in Africa Before 1500; Dahomey, Early Kingdom of; Ghana, Early Kingdom of; Kanuri; Egypt, Ancient Kingdom of; Nubian; Oyo, Early Kingdom of; Sahara Desert; Songhai Empire; Swahili People; Indian Ocean Slave Trade; Abolition and Emancipation in Latin America and the Caribbean; Islam and Tradition: An Interpretation; Trans-Saharan and Red Sea Slave Trade; Mali Empire.

Latin America and the Caribbean

Slavery in Latin America and the Caribbean

Slaves have existed on every populated continent since well before the opening of the Western Hemisphere to European colonization. In fact the modern word "slave" comes from the identification of slaves with Slavic peoples in the Muslim societies of the MIDDLE EAST. There were still Muslim, Jewish, and Christian slaves in Europe and the Middle East in 1492. Most of these slaves were tied to their masters' households and did not produce the basic food or manufactured products in these societies. This work was usually done by free urban and peasant labor. In a few societies, however, slaves did make up the primary labor force in agriculture and industry. This type of slavery, sometimes referred to as "industrial slavery," was developed in classical Greece and Rome, and it would become the type of slavery adopted in most of the American colonies.

WHY AFRICANS WERE IMPORTED INTO LATIN AMERICA

The Spanish and Portuguese conquest of the Americas created a new demand for African slave labor. America was abundant in land but not in labor. Despite the availability of at least 20 to 25 million American Indians in 1500, labor was still a high-cost item for the Spanish and the Portuguese. With more opportunities and wealth available through Spanish and Portuguese expansion in Europe, Asia, and Africa, the small populations of the Iberian Peninsula were reluctant to migrate to the New World. Wages necessary to entice European workers to America were too high to make colonization profitable. Moreover, the use of Muslim slaves from North Africa and the Middle East was coming to an end, and the Roman Catholic Church pushed hard to end European enslavement of any Christian peoples. Thus by 1500 most slaves held in Europe were Africans.

Queen Isabel rejected Columbus's proposal that Indians be enslaved. It was held that American Indians were free subjects and should be enslaved only if they waged war against the Spaniards. Even this "just war" reasoning for enslaving some of the frontier Indians was finally rejected by the Crown in the middle of the sixteenth century. Portuguese colonizers, on the other hand, enslaved Indians from the beginning of their settlement of BRAZIL well into the eighteenth century. But even though Indian slaves in Brazil or Indian peasants in MEXICO and PERU were quickly mobilized for the labor needs of the European colonists, there still existed a labor shortage in America due to the decimation of American Indian populations by new European diseases. Indian populations declined in the fifteenth and sixteenth centuries, often to 20 percent or less of their preconquest levels.

In this context importing labor became a necessity. Given the reluctance of poor Europeans to migrate, Africans were seen as an unlimited labor supply that could be brought to America. The institution of slavery, moreover, offered additional advantages to European colonizers. As slaves Africans were completely mobile and could be put to any labor that their masters demanded, without restrictions. Furthermore, because enslavement was usually for life, slaves could not compete with their masters, whereas contract or indentured servants could do so after completing their term of service.

For centuries prior to European penetration, slaves had been exported via the East African ports and by caravans overland to North Africa. Africa was opened to direct European seaborne trade by Portuguese explorers in the early fifteenth century. In 1444 Europeans first shipped African slaves, along with gold and ivory, off the Senegambian coast in West Africa. Thereafter a steady trade developed with Africa. A small number of African slaves were thus diverted into the TRANSATLANTIC SLAVE TRADE even before Columbus's first voyage. They soon became the most numerous of the slaves in SPAIN and PORTUGAL. Also Portugal began to use African slaves for sugar production in the African coastal islands of CAPE VERDE and São Tomé. Thus when the New World was finally opened to European settlement, a steady supply of West African slaves was available to the Europeans, who were accustomed to using them in commercial export agriculture – especially to produce SUGAR.

SLAVERY IN MEXICO AND PERU

The Spanish conquistadors, enriched by mining in the Caribbean Islands, Mexico, and the Andes, were the first colonists able to pay for the importation of African slaves. By 1650 some 200,000 Africans had been imported to these mainland and island regions of Spain. Spaniards found their need for slaves constantly increasing, especially in those lowland regions where European disease had decimated the Indian population. Peru took the most African slaves because it was initially richer and had a smaller Indian population base than Mexico. There were 3000 African slaves in the viceroyalty of Peru by the 1550s, half of whom lived in the capital city of Lima. This pattern of slave settlement, with approximately half of the African slaves residing in the cities and working at skilled and unskilled urban occupations, became the norm in the Spanish American colonies. Some slaves were used on small farms to produce fruits and vegetables for city markets; others produced sugar on plantations, though primarily for local rather than European consumption. But most agricultural goods were produced by Indian peasants either working on their own lands in communal villages or as landless workers on the estates of the Spaniards, and all mining was done with free Indian wage laborers or forced Indian contract workers.

But in the cities of Spanish America, African slaves and their descendants played a vital role in the economy. Urban slavery involved both skilled and unskilled labor, and African and Indian artisans were the dominant labor force throughout urban Spanish America. Though they were underrepresented in the elite group of skilled master craftsworkers, African and African American (or Creole) slaves and freedpeople were well represented in the beginning apprenticeship and journeyman levels of the skilled crafts by the middle of the seventeenth century. Sometimes white and even Indian opposition to blacks in the professions was quite bitter, but the lack of a powerful American guild organization permitted blacks, both free and slave, to exercise most crafts, even at the master level. So important were these slave and free colored skilled, semiskilled, and unskilled workers in the continental and island colonies of Spain and Portugal that in all the major ports and cities of Latin America, they made up close to half of the population by the eighteenth century. Both Portuguese and Spanish America were far more urbanized than any other American zones in this period, with 21 cities having a population of 50,000 to 100,000 persons.

It was common for urban slaves to live on their own and to rent themselves out, or make contracts for work as semiautonomous artisans and pay their masters a given weekly or monthly sum. Others lived in their masters' houses and were fed and controlled by their owners. Relative to rural slaves, therefore, those residing in urban centers had more options available in their economic and social activities. It was also among these slaves that the common-law practice of self-purchase (called *coartación* in Spanish and *coartação* in Portuguese) developed. This practice allowed slaves to take their masters to court and force them to sell the slaves to themselves in installments over a fixed period of time. During the period in which the slaves were purchasing their freedom, the masters could not sell them to a third party. The whole process was a very expensive undertaking and was used mostly by a minority of skilled slaves who had the ability to accumulate savings.

After Peru, the viceroyalty of New Spain (or Mexico) imported the largest number of slaves into Spanish America. By the seventeenth century slaves numbered close to the total white colonist population in most of Mexico's cities and were as heavily urban as in Spanish South America. As they were in Peru, Afro-American (used here to refer

During the 1770s artist Agostino Brunias painted a number of pictures of slaves and mulattoes in the English-owned Caribbean islands of Dominica and St. Vincent. Rarely, however, did he depict slaves at work, as in this painting. *Simon Dickinson Ltd., London*

to people of African descent in the Americas) slaves in this region were used on relatively small estates with no more than 40 slaves per unit in sugar production for the local and regional markets. As they did elsewhere in continental Spanish America, the Afro-American slaves in the rural areas of Mexico worked primarily in mixed farming enterprises rather than on the type of commercial plantations that exported to Europe and were prevalent in BRAZIL and the West Indies. African slaves could also be found alongside free Indian workers weaving and doing other tasks in the local textile factories (*obrajes*). In northern Mexico there was even an early attempt to use slaves in silver mining, though they were quickly replaced by free Indian workers. Ultimately urban slavery was less important in Mexico due to the larger presence of Indians in all the leading towns.

Given its much larger Indian population, Mexico ended up with a smaller African slave population than Peru. By 1646 Mexico's slave population peaked at 35,000, while by this time Peru had some 100,000 Afro-Americans. Moreover, Mexico progressively freed most of its slave population and stopped importing Africans on a major scale. By the 1790s it had only 6000 Afro-American slaves left, while Peru still had some 90,000.

SLAVERY IN COLONIAL BRAZIL

In the 1530s Portugal finally began the systematic exploitation of Brazil. Although both Indian and Afro-American slaves were initially used on the plantations (*fazendas*), by 1600 Africans and their descendants dominated the slave labor force, producing sugar for the European market. BRAZIL provided the model for all other major slave plantations in the Caribbean and North America. Although Brazil exploited American Indian slave labor with an intensity and profitability that no other European power developed in America, Brazilian Indians, like their counterparts throughout the Americas, suffered terrible devastation from previously unknown diseases. Thus after 1600 Africans replaced Indians on the Brazilian sugar estate, and only when African slave markets were closed to them in the middle decades of the seventeenth century did the Brazilians temporarily return to Indian labor.

The revolt of the Dutch provinces of Spain in 1584 would set the stage for the expansion of the sugar plantation model to the Caribbean. In 1621 the Dutch West Indies Company was established to compete with the Portuguese in Africa and America. Eventually the Dutch took Pernambuco, Brazil's premier sugar province. The company then denied Portuguese access to its sources of African slaves.

It seized both the Gold Coast (El Mina) and most of ANGOLA in the late 1630s and early 1640s. The impact of this Dutch colonization in Brazil was profound. For the Portuguese it meant that Bahia replaced Pernambuco as the leading sugar province, and it encouraged the temporary reemergence of Indian slavery until the Portuguese African ports could be recaptured. The ensuing interior Indian slave trade led by the residents of São Paulo opened up additional regions to Portuguese settlement and ultimately to a major new use of slave labor in the newly discovered interior gold and diamond fields of MINAS GERAIS and Matto Grosso in the 1700s.

ABOVE: In his *Voyage pittoresque dans le Brésil* (1835), Johann Moritz Rugendas represented some of the urban slaves who earned money carrying water or selling prepared foods in such Brazilian cities as Rio de Janeiro and Salvador, Bahia. *Oronoz*
RIGHT: In his *Voyage pittoresque dans le Brésil* (1835), Johann Moritz Rugendas depicted several Afro-Brazilian couples, including this pair of plantation slaves. *By permission of the Houghton Library, Harvard University*
OPPOSITE: The cultivation and harvesting of both sugar cane and coffee beans required large labor forces, which Brazilian plantation owners filled by importing enslaved Africans. Johann Moritz Rugendas's 1835 lithograph illustrates Afro-Brazilian slaves harvesting coffee beans. *Ricardo Funari/Contexto*

The Caribbean Colonies

For the rest of America, Dutch Brazil would become the source for the tools, techniques, credit, and slaves that would carry the sugar revolution into the West Indies. Because fighting between the Dutch and Portuguese in the interior reduced Pernambuco's role as the region's leading sugar producer, the Dutch began to bring slaves and the latest milling equipment to the British and French settlers in the Caribbean, whose sugar they transported and sold on the European market. It was thus the Dutch from Brazil who brought the sugar technology, machinery, and even slaves to the struggling English island of Barbados and the French islands of Martinique and Guadeloupe.

These islands of the Lesser Antilles were first settled by the English and French in the 1620s. Indentured European workers composed the labor force until an export crop was developed that could pay for the importation of African slaves. After experimenting with tobacco, indigo, and other crops, colonizers finally settled on sugar, and it was the Dutch from Brazil who were crucial in opening up the sugar industries. The success of sugar transformed these islands. At first largely white populations lived on small farms with relatively few slaves, but by the 1680s and 1690s island populations were dominated by African slaves, and most of the land was owned by a few whites controlling very large estates. In the 1650s the English seized Jamaica from the Spanish; then came the French settlement of Saint-Domingue on the western half of the island of Hispaniola in the 1660s. These two colonies by the late eighteenth century would constitute the premier sugar-producing zone in the Americas. Thus by the end of the seventeenth century the French and English had established thriving sugar colonies in both the Greater and Lesser Antilles, and these islands had already absorbed more than 450,000 African slaves. This figure compares to the 500,000 to 1 million African slaves who arrived in Brazil and to the 350,000 to 400,000 who arrived in Spanish America before 1700. The French and English colonies on the North American continent were primarily small free farmer agricultural colonies except in the region from the Chesapeake Bay to the south, and those colonies that used slaves brought in less than 30,000 Africans in this same period.

The West Indian sugar plantation colonies of France and England were unique by American standards. Whereas in Brazil and eventually in the United States slaves represented only about a third of the population, in the West Indies African slaves made up three-quarters or more of the population. In contrast to the continental slave plantation, the typical plantation on these islands employed double the number of slaves (usually around 200 slaves per unit). In most of the British and French islands blacks dominated the population by a ratio of ten to one. Moreover, 95 percent of the slaves were found in the rural areas, and 75 percent were involved in sugar production. Urban slavery of the kind developed in Spanish and Portuguese America was of minor importance in a society whose leading towns held less than 15,000 persons. Also, the production of diversified commercial foodstuffs for local consumption, which was a major occupation of Peruvian blacks, hardly existed in societies that were so dependent on foreign imports, or slave subsistence plot production, for all their basic food supplies.

The Haitian Revolution and Slavery in the Nineteenth Century

The dominant West Indian colony was Saint-Domingue. By the 1780s it had 460,000 slaves, though, unlike the British islands, it also had an important free colored class of some 13,000 persons, many of whom were slave and plantation owners, a group unique in the Americas. In fact it was the conflict between the white and mulatto plantation owners on this wealthiest of West Indian colonies that opened the way for a successful slave rebellion in 1791. After years of bitter fighting and the defeat of several invading

armies, the end result was the liberation of the slaves and the creation of the independent government of HAITI in 1804. The fighting and the abolition of slave labor combined to destroy first the sugar production in this, the world's leading sugar producer, and then its major coffee output as well.

The result of the HAITIAN REVOLUTION was a profound change in the relative importance of American slave plantation agriculture. The elimination of sugar exports and the progressive decline of coffee production in this French island permitted all the competing plantation areas to expand production. By the fourth and fifth decades of the nineteenth century CUBA would emerge as the world's leading sugar cane producer, and Brazil would become the leading producer of coffee. But everywhere in the New World slave plantation agriculture surged both because of the elimination of Saint-Domingue's production and because of a rapid expansion of the sugar, coffee, and cotton market in Europe.

The Haitian slave revolution also had an impact on the treatment of slaves and free colored people in all the major slave societies of America. Fearful of a possible slave rebellion in their own societies, other colonies and republics repressed free blacks, made manumission more difficult, and passed harsher slave codes. In the case of PUERTO RICO, Cuba, and Brazil the Haitian Revolution led to the reluctance of the planter and master class to support independence movements or regional rebellions. Although manumission and full rights were restored in most Latin American areas, in the United States the role of free blacks only worsened in the course of the nineteenth century.

NINETEENTH-CENTURY CUBA

The leading slave society in the West Indies in the nineteenth century was the Spanish-controlled island of Cuba. Neglected for most of the colonial period by the Spanish Crown, the island exported free labor and produced tobacco. It was also used as a provisioning center for the colonial fleets. But the Crown finally promoted sugar plantations and slavery on the island just before the Haitian rebellion and in 1789 permitted the free importation of slaves by any foreign merchants. The result was a spectacular growth in sugar production. By the 1830s Cuba's sugar output equaled that of Jamaica, and a decade later Cuba became the world's leading producer of sugar. Coffee, brought by migrating French planters, also became a major plantation crop, and by the late 1830s the island's coffee plantations numbered just over 2000 units and employed some 50,000 slaves, a number equal to those employed in sugar production. Nineteenth-century Cuba followed the eighteenth-century Caribbean model in the basic organization of plantations and slaves. But it resembled more the rest of Latin America in the size and growth of both its free colored and white populations and in the relative importance of its urban centers. Cuban towns (defined as settlements of more than 1000 persons) contained more than 500,000 persons by the 1860s, only 76,000 of whom were slaves. Though the number of slaves increased to 370,000 by the 1860s, there were then 233,000 free colored people, and whites still accounted for well over half the island's population of 1.4 million persons.

Given the dynamism of the expanding sugar economy and the dependence on slaves, the Cuban planters and the Spanish government fought against the abolition of the transatlantic slave trade. But in the early 1860s the trade ended for Cuba, the last slave-importing region in America, and the Cuban planters decided to experiment with the forced labor of Mayan Indians brought from Yucatan and indentured Chinese servants, all of whom worked alongside the African and American-born black slaves. By the early 1860s more than 100,000 Chinese were working in the Cuban sugar fields. There was also a major revival of sugar production after the Napoleonic Wars (1799-1815) in the remaining French West Indian colonies of Martinique and Guadeloupe. By the early decades of the nineteenth century these two islands held 160,000 slaves and were also beginning to supplement this sugar plantation labor force with indentured workers from Africa and other regions.

EIGHTEENTH- AND NINETEENTH-CENTURY BRAZIL

The discovery of gold in central Brazil in the late 1690s opened up an entirely new activity for slave usage. The gold mines of Minas Gerais were the wealthiest in the world in the eighteenth century, and they were exclusively worked by African slave labor. Later diamond deposits were discovered in the same region, and the two industries together employed some 225,000 slaves by the late eighteenth century. This expansion of slave labor in the interior provinces was matched by the growth of traditional and new plantation agriculture along the coast.

The Haitian collapse revived the sugar industry in the older northeastern plantations and the sugar fields in Rio de Janeiro. But even more important was the expansion of Brazilian coffee production. Although as early as the eighteenth century coffee was grown in Brazil, the introduction of the latest West Indian technology created a new opportunity for expansion. By 1831 the value of coffee exports surpassed the value of sugar exports, and by the middle of the decade Brazil was the world's largest producer of coffee, shipping double the combined output of Cuba and Puerto Rico, previously the major coffee producers in the Americas. Coffee was a slave crop. It was produced primarily in three states in central Brazil: Rio de Janeiro, São Paulo, and the old mining state of Minas Gerais. Slaves were imported into Brazil until the 1860s when the British finally forced the Brazilians to end their slave trade. Thereafter an internal slave trade developed that moved Brazilian slaves in ever larger numbers into coffee.

Nevertheless, although the coffee plantations increased the number of slave workers to 284,000, by 1883 the majority of Brazil's slaves did not work in the coffee fields of the central-south zone. By 1872 some 563,000 rural slaves worked both in other plantation crops, such as sugar, and in a host of other rural occupations, including cattle raising. The remaining 690,000 of the economically active slaves in 1872 not directly engaged in agriculture were often closely allied with plantation life. Some 95,000 slaves were listed as day laborers, and many of these were employed in the fazendas alongside the resident slave forces. Some of the 7000 artisans listed as working in wood and metal crafts, especially carpenters and blacksmiths, may also have been employed on plantations. But as the example of Minas Gerais reveals, there was also within the vast slave labor force of 1.5 million slaves a significant proportion who were not directly related to export agriculture yet still played a significant role in the economy. Many of Brazil's 1.5 million slaves also lived in the cities, composing 15 percent of the urban population in towns of 20,000 or more. But it was the recently freed slaves and their descendants, some 4.2 million persons, who made up most of the country's urban population and were a major presence in all the rural areas.

Freedpeople Under Slavery

The process and rate of manumission in Latin America varied widely from region to region. Unlike the United States, Latin American governments recognized the right to manumission of all slaves. Manumission in Latin America was both voluntary and involuntary on the part of the master class and involved a complex pattern of passive and active intervention of the slaves themselves. Close to half of the manumitted slaves purchased their freedom; about two-thirds were women; and most were manumitted at less than 45 years of age. These demographic factors help explain the very rapid growth of free black populations through both new manumissions and children born to free black women. More urban slaves had access to manumission than did rural ones, but in no area was manumission ever stopped.

Although manumission had occurred from the beginning of colonization, its pace increased in the eighteenth and nineteenth centuries. This led to a major growth of free colored populations everywhere in the Latin American world. By 1800 there were more free colored persons than slaves in continental Spanish America. In the region of northeastern South America known as the viceroyalty of New Granada and encompassing the future republics of Colombia and Ecuador, there were 420,000 free colored people as compared to 80,000 slaves. In Venezuela there were 198,000 free colored persons and about 64,000 slaves despite a thriving slave plantation zone producing cacao beans. The Mexican viceroyalty had about 70,000 free colored people and 10,000 slaves by 1810. In all the colonies of Spain on the continent, there were a total of 650,000 free persons of color and 271,000 slaves. With the exception of Cuba, Spain's island possessions were little different. Puerto Rico in 1820 had 104,000 free persons of color and 22,000 slaves, whereas Cuba by 1861 contained 232,000 free colored people and 371,000 African slaves. Brazil saw an ever more dynamic growth of the free colored population in the nineteenth century, well before final abolition of slavery occurred in 1888. At the time of the first imperial census of 1872 there were 4.2 million free colored people in Brazil compared to 1.5 million slaves and 3.8 million whites.

In contrast to the rest of Latin America and relative to the number of slaves, the population of free blacks remained small in both the French West Indies and the English colonies. In the 1780s, just prior to the French Revolution, the major French colonies had 30,000 free colored persons and 575,000 slaves. Unlike those in the British islands, however, these free blacks played a far more important role in their local economies; many were major slave holders and plantation owners in their own right.

This difference in the importance of the free colored classes in each of the major regions of the Americas was due to many factors. The most important was the willingness of the Spanish and Portuguese colonies and republics to accept normal market and religious forces that produced a large number of manumitted ex-slaves. Though all slave societies in the Americas began with a fairly steady process of manumission, most of the Anglo-Saxon and French colonies slowly closed down this process. In the Latin American context, this process was never stopped, and in fact increased in intensity over time. Thus the free colored, even before the end of slavery, played a major economic role within their local societies. This does not mean they faced any less opposition from whites or that racism and exclusion did not operate. All slave societies in the Americas eventually became intensely racist over time. It does mean, however, that whites were unable or unwilling to use these beliefs to deny the free colored access to some measure of social and economic mobility. The creation of active and large free colored populations in all these societies also helped prepare all slaves for their future roles as citizens and economically participatory members of the postabolition societies.

Freedpeople, whatever their relative economic position in the colonial societies, all played a crucial role in the development of postcolonial polities. They formed their own important militia companies in both Spanish and Portuguese America and were a crucial element in the defense establishments of these colonies well into the nineteenth century. Moreover, there was not a major social or political movement in the nineteenth century in which these free persons did not participate, from the wars of independence to the establishment of revolutionary regimes. They also had their own religious confraternities or brotherhoods in the Roman Catholic Church, which were important social institutions that often helped maintain the survival of African religious practices and ideas. These fraternal organizations, which often built their own churches and acted as burial societies as well, helped people to maintain friendships and create group identities. They were found in every city in Latin America that had a substantial free black population.

Conclusion

The end of slavery in Latin America was accomplished by a variety of means. In the continental colonies the wars of independence from 1808 to 1825 led to the freeing of large numbers of slaves by both republicans and royalists, so that even before final emancipation slaves were a reduced element among the colored population. Chile was the first to free its 4000 slaves unconditionally in 1823, and Mexico freed the 3000 slaves remaining there in the 1830s. Most of the other new republics did not finally liberate all remaining slaves until the 1850s, though most adopted early laws declaring freedom for all children born of slaves. In the French colonies of America some 177,500 slaves were finally liberated in 1848, but slavery continued on the islands of Cuba and Puerto Rico and in Brazil until the late 1880s. In 1871 Brazil finally adopted a law of free birth, as did Spain for Cuba and Puerto Rico in 1868. Final emancipation for all slaves came to the Spanish Caribbean islands in 1886 and to Brazil in 1888.

See Also

Explorers in Africa, 1500 to 1800; Middle East; Mexico; Netherlands, The; Portugal; São Tomé and Príncipe; Rio de Janeiro, Brazil; Islam and Tradition: An Interpretation; Catholic Church in Latin America and the Caribbean;Abolition and Emancipation in Latin America and the Caribbean; Slave Laws in Colonial Spanish America; Trans-Saharan and Red Sea Slave Trade; Religious Brotherhoods in Latin America.

North America

Slavery in the United States

Slavery has appeared in many forms throughout its long history. Slaves have served in capacities as diverse as concubines, warriors, servants, craftsmen, tutors, and victims of ritual sacrifice. In the New World (the Americas), however, slavery emerged as a system of forced labor designed to facilitate the production of staple crops. Depending on location, these crops included sugar, coffee, tobacco, and cotton; in the southern United States, by far the most important staples were tobacco and cotton. A stark racial component distinguished this modern Western slavery from the slavery that existed in many other times and places: the vast majority of slaves consisted of Africans and their descendants, whereas the vast majority of masters consisted of Europeans and their descendants.

Slavery has played a central role in the history of the United States. It existed in all the English mainland colonies and came to dominate productive relations from Maryland south. Most of the Founding Fathers were large-scale slaveholders, as were 8 of the first 12 presidents of the United States. Debate over slavery increasingly dominated American politics, leading eventually to the nation's only civil war, which in turn finally brought slavery to an end. After emancipation, overcoming slavery's legacy remained a crucial issue in American history, from Reconstruction following the Civil War to the Civil Rights Movement a century later.

The Introduction of Slavery

There was nothing inevitable about the use of black slaves. Although Dutch traders brought 20 Africans to Jamestown, Virginia, as early as 1619, throughout most of the seventeenth century the number of Africans in the English mainland colonies grew very slowly. During those years colonists experimented with two other sources of unfree labor: Native American slaves and European indentured servants.

Although some Native American slaves existed in every colony, the number was limited. Indian men balked at performing agricultural labor, which they regarded as women's work, and colonists complained that they were "haughty" and made poor slaves. Even more important, the settlers found it more convenient to sell Native Americans captured in war to planters in the Caribbean than to turn them into slaves on their own terrain, where escape was relatively easy and violent resistance a constant threat. Ultimately, the policy of killing Indians or driving them away from white settlements proved incompatible with their widespread employment as slaves.

Far more important as a form of labor than Indian slavery was white indentured servitude. Most indentured servants were poor Europeans who, desiring to escape harsh conditions and take advantage of fabled opportunities in America, traded four to seven years of their labor in exchange for the transatlantic passage. At first predominantly English but later increasingly Irish, Welsh, and German, servants consisted primarily (although not exclusively) of young males. Once in the colonies, they were essentially temporary slaves; most served as agricultural workers although some, especially in the North, were taught skilled trades. During the seventeenth century they performed most of the heavy labor in the Southern colonies and also provided the bulk of immigrants to those colonies.

For a variety of reasons, foremost among them improved conditions in England, the number of persons willing to sell themselves into indentured servitude declined sharply toward the end of the seventeenth century. Since the labor needs of the rapidly growing colonies were increasing, this decline in servant migration produced a labor crisis. To meet their needs, landowners turned to African slaves, who from the 1680s began to supplant indentured servants; in Virginia, for example, blacks (the great majority of whom were slaves) increased from about 7 percent of the population in 1680 to more than 40 percent by the middle of the eighteenth century. During the first two-thirds of the seventeenth century Holland and Portugal had dominated the African slave trade, and the number of Africans available to English colonists was limited. During the late seventeenth and eighteenth centuries, by contrast, naval superiority gave England a dominant position in the slave trade, and English traders (some of whom lived in English America) transported millions of Africans across the Atlantic.

The transatlantic slave trade produced one of the largest forced migrations in history. From the early sixteenth century to the mid-nineteenth century about 12 million Africans were torn from their homes, herded onto ships where they were sometimes so tightly packed that they could barely move, and deposited in a strange new land. (Since others died in transit, Africa's population loss was greater still.) By far the largest importers of slaves were Brazil and the Caribbean sugar colonies; together they received well over three-quarters of all Africans brought to the New World. About 6 percent of the total (600,000 to 650,000 persons) came to the area of the present United States.

Slavery in the Colonial Era

Slavery spread quickly in the American colonies. At first the legal status of Africans in America was poorly defined, and some – like European indentured servants – managed to become free after several years of service. From the 1660s, however, the colonies began enacting laws that defined and regulated slave relations; central to these laws was the provision that black slaves, and the children of slave women, would serve for life. By the eve of the American Revolution slaves constituted about 40 percent of the population of the southern mainland colonies, with the highest concentration in South Carolina, where well over half the population were slaves.

Slaves performed numerous tasks, from clearing the forest to serving as craftsmen, guides, trappers, nurses, and house servants, but they were most essential as agricultural laborers and most numerous where landowners sought to grow staple crops for market. The most important of these crops were tobacco in the upper South (Maryland, Virginia, and North Carolina) and rice in the lower South (South Carolina and Georgia); farther south still, on Caribbean islands such as Barbados, Jamaica, and Saint-Domingue (present-day Haiti), sugar was an even more valuable slave-grown commodity. Slaves also worked on large wheat-producing estates in New York and on horse-breeding farms in Rhode Island, but climate and soil restricted the development of commercial agriculture in the Northern colonies, and slavery never became as economically central there as it was in the South. Slaves in the North were typically held in small numbers, and most served as domestic servants; only in New York, with its Dutch legacy, did they form more than 10 percent of the population. In the North as a whole, less than 5 percent of the inhabitants were slaves.

By the mid-eighteenth century American slavery had acquired a number of distinctive features. Well over 90 percent of American slaves lived in the South, where demographic conditions contrasted sharply with those to both the south and the north. In Caribbean colonies such as Jamaica and Saint-Domingue, blacks outnumbered whites by more than ten to one, and slaves often lived on huge estates whose inhabitants numbered in the hundreds. In the Northern colonies blacks were few, and slaves were typically held in small groups of less than five. The South, by contrast, was neither overwhelmingly white nor overwhelmingly black: slaves formed a large minority of the population (in some areas, of course, they formed the majority), and despite regional variations, most slaves lived on small and medium-sized holdings containing between 5 and 50 slaves.

A second distinctive feature was the rapid "Americanization" of both masters and slaves. English colonists quickly came to feel "at home" on their American holdings. Few sought to make quick killings on their planting ventures and then retire to a life of leisure in England, and the kind of absentee ownership common in much of the Caribbean was relatively rare in the American South; instead, masters typically took an active role in running their farms and plantations. Equally significant was the shift from an African to an African American slave population. By the eve of the American Revolution only about 20 percent of American slaves were African-born (although the concentration of Africans remained higher in South Carolina and Georgia), and after the outlawing of new slave imports beginning in 1808, the proportion of African-born slaves became tiny. The emergence of a native-born slave population had numerous important consequences. To take one example, among African-born slaves (imported primarily for their ability to perform physical labor) there were few children, and men outnumbered women by about two to one; American-born slaves, by contrast, began their slave careers as children, and there were approximately even numbers of males and females in their ranks.

This shift from African to African American was closely related to a third distinctive characteristic of American slavery that was in many ways the most important of all: in contrast to most other slaves in the New World, those in the United States experienced what demographers refer to as "natural population growth." Elsewhere, in regions as diverse as Brazil, Jamaica, Saint-Domingue, and Cuba, slave mortality rates exceeded birth rates, and growth of the slave population depended on the importation of new slaves from Africa; as soon as that importation ended, the slave population began to decline.

A plaque identifies the block on a Fredericksburg, Virginia, street where slaves were sold at auction. *CORBIS/Bettmann*

At first, deaths among slaves also exceeded births in the American colonies, but in the eighteenth century those colonies experienced a demographic transition as birth rates rose, mortality rates fell, and the slave population became self-reproducing. This transition, which occurred earlier in the upper than in the lower South, meant that even after the outlawing of slave imports, the number of slaves would continue to grow rapidly; during the next half century the slave population of the United States more than tripled, from about 1.2 million to almost 4 million in 1860. The natural growth of the slave population shaped a distinctive slavery in the American South and hastened the transition among slaves from African to African American.

The Revolutionary Challenge

Throughout most of the colonial period opposition to slavery among white Americans was virtually nonexistent. Settlers in the seventeenth and early eighteenth centuries came from a sharply stratified society in which the upper classes savagely exploited members of the "lower orders"; lacking a later generation's belief in natural human equality, they saw little reason to question the enslavement of Africans. As they sought to mold a docile labor force, these planters resorted to harshly repressive measures that included whippings and brandings.

Gradually, as slavery became more entrenched, changes occurred in the way masters looked on their slaves (and themselves). Many second-generation masters, who unlike their parents had grown up with slaves, came to regard slaves as inferior members of their extended families, and to look upon themselves as kindly patriarchs who, like benevolent despots, ruled their "people" firmly but fairly and looked after their needs. Such slave owners continued to rely heavily on the lash (and other forms of punishment) for discipline, and few slaves saw their owners as the kindly guardians that they proclaimed themselves to be. Still, the most extreme forms of physical abuse became less common over the course of the eighteenth century, at the same time that many slave owners accepted the idea that they should treat their slaves humanely.

Some slave owners went further. The last third of the eighteenth century saw the first widespread questioning of slavery by white Americans. This questioning was boosted by the American Revolution, which sparked a sharp increase in egalitarian thinking. Many of the Founding Fathers, including George Washington and Thomas Jefferson, while slaveholders, were profoundly troubled by slavery; leery of rash actions, they initiated a series of cautious acts that they thought would lead to slavery's gradual abolition.

These acts included measures in all states north of Delaware to abolish slavery. A few states did away with slavery immediately. More typical were gradual emancipation acts such as that passed by Pennsylvania in 1780, whereby all children born to slaves in the future would be freed at age 28. Two significant measures dating from 1787 were the Northwest Ordinance, which barred slavery from the Northwest Territory (including much of what is now the upper Midwest), and a compromise reached at the Constitutional Convention that would allow Congress to outlaw the importation of slaves in 1808. Meanwhile, a number of states passed acts to ease the freeing of slaves by slave owners, hundreds of whom – especially in the upper South – set some or all of their slaves free. In addition, tens of thousands of slaves acted on their own, taking advantage of wartime disruption to escape bondage. As a result the number of free blacks, which had been tiny before the Revolution, surged during the last quarter of the eighteenth century.

Nevertheless, the Revolutionary-era challenge to slavery proved successful only in the North, where the investment in slaves was small. The antislavery movement never made much headway in Georgia and South Carolina, where labor-hungry planters rushed to import tens of thousands of Africans before the 1808 cutoff. In the upper South, Revolution-inspired egalitarianism withered in the 1790s and 1800s. And because the American slave population was self-reproducing, the end of slave imports in the United States did not undermine slavery as it did elsewhere, or as many of the Founding Fathers expected. Ultimately the first antislavery movement rendered slavery a newly sectional institution that was on the road to abolition throughout the North but largely unscathed in the South.

Slavery in the Antebellum Era

During the antebellum (pre-Civil War) years slavery expanded aggressively along with the United States. Fueled by a surging world demand for cotton, slavery spread quickly into the new states of the Southwest; by the 1830s Alabama, Mississippi, and Louisiana formed the heart of a new "cotton kingdom," together producing more than half of the nation's supply of the crop. The great bulk of this cotton was cultivated by slaves. Between 1790 and 1860 about 1 million slaves (almost twice the number of Africans shipped to the United States during the whole period of the transatlantic slave trade) moved west, some together with their masters and others as part of a new domestic trade in which owners from the seaboard states provided "surplus" slaves to planters in the Southwest.

As slavery grew, so too did its diversity. Slavery varied according to region, crops, and size of holdings. On farms and small plantations most slaves came in frequent contact with their owners, but on very large plantations, where slave owners often employed overseers, slaves might rarely see their masters. Some owners left their holdings entirely in the care of subordinates, usually hired white overseers but sometimes slaves. A few slave owners were even black themselves: a small percentage of free blacks owned slaves, in some cases essentially as a fiction so that they could protect family members, but more often to profit, like other slaveholders, from unfree labor. Most slaves on large holdings worked in gangs, under the supervision of overseers and (slave) drivers. Some, however, especially in the coastal region of South Carolina and Georgia, labored under the "task" system: assigned a certain amount of work to complete in a day, they received less supervision than gang laborers and were free to use their time as they wished once they had completed their daily assignments. In addition to performing fieldwork, slaves served as house servants, nurses, midwives, carpenters, blacksmiths, drivers, preachers, gardeners, and handymen.

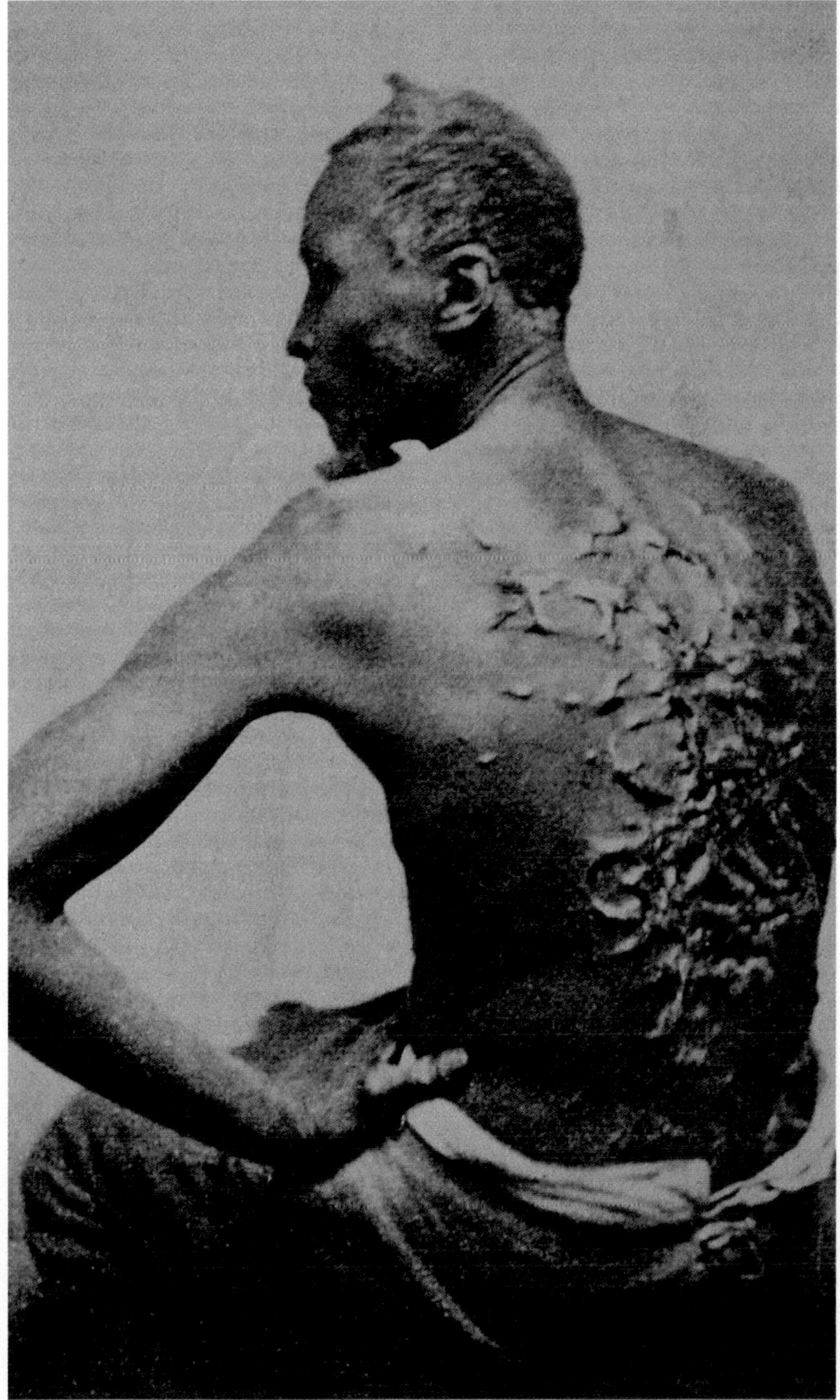

Despite such variations there were a number of dominant trends. First, slavery was overwhelmingly rural: in 1860 only about 5 percent of all slaves lived in towns of at least 2500 persons. Second, although some slaves lived on giant estates and others on small farms, the norm was in between: in 1860 about one-half of all slaves lived on plantations with 10 to 49 other slaves, about one-quarter on smaller and one-quarter on larger units. (Holdings tended to be bigger in the Deep South than in the upper South.) Third, most slaves lived with resident masters; owner absenteeism was most prevalent in the South Carolina and Georgia low country, but in the South as a whole it was less common than in the Caribbean. Fourth, most able-bodied adult slaves engaged in field work. Owners relied heavily on children, the elderly, and the infirm for "nonproductive" work (such as house service); only the largest plantations could spare healthy adults for exclusive assignment to specialized occupations. The main business of Southern farms and plantations – and of the slaves who supported them – was to grow cotton, tobacco, rice, corn, wheat, hemp, and sugar.

Southern slaveholders took an active role in managing their human property. Viewing themselves as the slaves' guardians, they stressed the degree to which they cared for their "people." The character of such care varied, but in purely material terms – food, clothing, housing, medical attention – it was generally better in the antebellum than in the colonial period and (judging by measurable criteria such as slave height and life expectancy) better in the American South than in the Caribbean or Brazil. Although young children were often malnourished, most working slaves received a steady supply of pork and corn which, if lacking in nutritional balance (about which antebellum Americans knew nothing), provided sufficient calories to fuel their labor, especially when supplemented with produce that slaves raised on the garden plots that they were often allotted. Clothing and housing were crude but functional: slaves typically received four coarse "suits" per year (pants and shirts for men, dresses for women, long shirts for children) and lived in small wooden cabins, one to a family. Wealthy slave owners often sent for physicians to treat slaves who became ill; given the state of medical knowledge,

A freed slave displays his whip-scarred back in Baton Rouge, Louisiana, in 1863. The man, named Gordon, later became a corporal in the Union army. ***CORBIS***

however, such treatment – which could range from providing various concoctions to "bleeding" a patient – often did as much harm as good.

Masters intervened continuously in the lives of their slaves, from directing their labor to approving (and disapproving) marriages. Some masters made elaborate written "rules" and most engaged in constant meddling – directing, nagging, threatening, and punishing. Many took advantage of their position to exploit slave women sexually. What slaves hated most about slavery was not the hard work to which they were subjected (most people in the rural United States expected to engage in hard physical labor), but the lack of control over their lives – their lack of freedom. Masters may have prided themselves on the care they provided for their "people"; the slaves, however, had a different idea of that care. They resented the constant interference in their lives and struggled to achieve whatever autonomy they could.

Slave Life and Slave Resistance

Such autonomy was not totally lacking. In the quarters – the collection of slave cabins that on large plantations resembled a miniature village – slaves developed their own way of life. The degree of social independence available to slaves was not constant: throughout the South a continuing power struggle raged in which slaves strove to increase and masters strove to limit this independence. The character and resolution of this struggle in turn depended on a host of factors, from size of holdings and organization of production to residence and disposition of masters. Masters rarely were able, however, to shape the lives of their slaves as fully as they wanted.

Away from the view of owners and overseers, slaves lived their own lives. They made friends and made love, played and prayed, sang, told stories, cooked, joked, quarreled, and engaged in the necessary chores of day-to-day living, from cleaning house, cooking, and sewing to working on their garden plots. Especially important as anchors of the slaves' lives were their families and their religion.

Throughout the South the family defined the actual living arrangements of slaves: most slaves lived together in nuclear families – mother, father, children. The security and stability of these families faced severe challenges: no state law recognized marriage among slaves, masters rather than parents had legal authority over slave children, and the possibility of forced separation through sale hung over every family. (Such separations were especially frequent in the slave-exporting states of the upper South.) Still, despite their tenuous status, families served as the slaves' most basic refuge, the center of private lives that owners could never fully control.

Religion served as a second refuge. Although African slaves usually clung to their native religions, and many slave owners in the early colonial period were leery of those who sought to convert their slaves to Christianity (in part because of fears that converted slaves would have to be freed), during the antebellum years Christianity was increasingly central to the slaves' cultural life. Many slaves were converted during the religious revivals that swept the South in the late eighteenth and early nineteenth centuries. Slaves typically belonged to the same denominations as white Southerners – Baptists and Methodists were the largest groups – and some masters encouraged their "people" to come to the white church, where they usually sat in a special "slave gallery" and received advice about being obedient to their masters. In the quarters, however, there developed a parallel ("invisible") church controlled by the slaves themselves, who listened to sermons delivered by their own preachers. Not all slaves had access to these preachers and not all accepted their message, but for many, religion served as a great comfort in a hostile world.

If their families and religion helped slaves to avoid total control by their owners, slaves also more directly challenged that control through active resistance. The limits of such resistance must be kept in mind. Unlike slaves in Saint-Domingue, who rose up against their French masters in bloody rebellion and established the black republic of Haiti in 1804, American slaves faced a balance of power that discouraged armed resistance. When it occurred, such resistance was always quickly suppressed and followed by harsh repression designed to discourage repetition. Aside from "conspiracies" aborted before any actual outbreak of violence in New York (1741), Virginia (1800), and South Carolina (1822), the most noted uprisings included the Stono Rebellion near Charleston, South Carolina (1739), an attempted attack on New Orleans (1811), and the Nat Turner insurrection that rocked Southampton County, Virginia, in 1831. The Turner insurrection, which at its peak included 60 to 80 rebels, resulted in the deaths of about 60 whites; the number of blacks killed during the uprising and executed or lynched afterward may have reached 100. But the rebellion lasted less than two days and was easily suppressed by local residents. Like other slave uprisings in the United States, it caused enormous fear among whites but did not seriously threaten the slave regime.

Lower-level resistance was both more widespread and more successful. This included "silent sabotage," or foot dragging, by slaves who pretended to be sick, feigned difficulty understanding instructions, and "accidentally" misused tools and animals. It also included small-scale resistance by individuals who fought back physically – at times successfully – against what they regarded as unjust treatment. But the most common form of resistance was flight. About 1000 slaves per year managed to escape to the North during the late antebellum period (most from the upper South), but this represented only the tip of the iceberg, since for every slave who made it to freedom, several more tried. Other fugitives remained within the South, heading for cities or swamps, or hiding out near their plantations for days or weeks before either returning voluntarily or being tracked down and captured. On a continuing basis, slaves "voted with their feet" against slavery.

Like all people, slaves felt diverse, overlapping attachments. They identified themselves as members of families, parishioners of churches, residents of particular farms and plantations, and members of an exploited class, the fruits of whose labor were appropriated by their owners. They also identified themselves as African Americans and saw themselves as an oppressed people. Because most blacks in the antebellum South were slaves, the line separating black from white approximated that separating slave from free, and the class exploitation of slave by master often appeared indistinguishable from the racial oppression of black by white. Racial identification drew support not only from common African origins and the close ties that often existed between slaves and free blacks but also from the virulent racism

LEFT: An anonymous daguerrotype taken in about 1850 shows Caesar, a house servant to the Van R. Nicoll family, who was purportedly the last slave liberated in New York State. *Collection of the New-York Historical Society*

OPPOSITE: A group of slaves stands outside their quarters on a plantation on Cockspur Island, Georgia, one of the barrier reef Sea Islands that stretch along the coasts of Florida, Georgia, and South Carolina. *CORBIS*

of many nonslaveholding whites that made it easy for slaves to look upon whites in general as their oppressors. Early African American cultural identity was forged in the crucible of slavery.

Sectional Tensions over Slavery

Slavery was an increasingly Southern institution. Abolition of slavery in the North, begun in the Revolutionary era and largely complete by the 1830s, divided the United States into the "slave" South and the "free" North. As this happened, slavery came – both to Northerners and Southerners – to define the essence of the South: to defend slavery was to be "pro-Southern," whereas opposition to slavery was "anti-Southern." Although *most* Southern whites did not own slaves (the proportion of white families that owned slaves declined from 35 percent to 26 percent between 1830 and 1860), slavery more and more set the South off from the rest of the country – and the Western world. If at one time slavery had been common in much of the New World, by the middle of the nineteenth century it remained only in Brazil, Cuba, Puerto Rico, and the southern United States. In an era that celebrated liberty and equality, the slave South came to seem backward and repressive, associated in many people's minds with that other bastion of reaction, serfholding Russia.

In fact, the slave economy grew rapidly, enriched by the spectacular increase in cotton cultivation to meet the burgeoning demand of Northern and European textile manufacturers. But Southern economic growth was based largely on putting more acreage under cultivation; the South did not undergo the kind of industrial revolution that was beginning to transform the North, and the South remained almost entirely rural. In 1860 there were only five Southern cities with more than 50,000 inhabitants (only one of which, New Orleans, was in the Deep South); less than 10 percent of Southerners lived in towns of at least 2500 persons, compared to more than 25 percent of Northerners. The South also increasingly lagged in other indices of modernization, from railroad construction to literacy and public education.

But the biggest gap between North and South was ideological. As Northern states abolished slavery and then saw the growth of a small but articulate abolitionist movement, Southern white spokesmen – from politicians to ministers, newspaper editors, and authors – rallied around slavery as the bedrock of Southern society. Defenders of slavery developed a wide range of arguments to buttress their cause, from those that stressed the institution's "practical" necessity to those that depicted it as a "positive good." They made heavy use of religious themes, pointing to the biblical "curse of Ham" to explain the origins of black bondage and portraying slavery as part of God's plan for civilizing a primitive, heathen people.

Racial justifications were especially prevalent in proslavery arguments, in part because of the widespread racism that united most white Americans and in part because such arguments were especially effective in appealing to the majority of Southern whites who did *not* own slaves. The extreme – "scientific" – version of these arguments purported to prove that blacks were so physiologically different from whites that they amounted to a different species (or, in the reformulation of some theoreticians, were the products of a separate creation). Such an approach violated the Christian sensibilities of too many Southern whites, however, to become a central staple of proslavery propaganda. Far more common were brief, unscientific, and vaguely supported assertions that blacks were by nature different, inferior, and therefore unsuited for freedom. Hardworking, loyal, and productive under loving but firm direction (i.e., slavery), blacks supposedly lacked the intellectual capacity for independent existence and in freedom would quickly degenerate, perhaps even fall into extinction.

During the 1840s and 1850s Southern spokesmen increasingly based their case for slavery on social arguments that contrasted the harmonious, orderly, religious, and conservative society that supposedly existed in the South with the tumultuous, heretical, and mercenary ways of a North torn apart by radical reform, individualism, class conflict, and – worst of all – abolitionism. Insisting that Southern slaves were treated far better than Northern wage laborers, proslavery ideologues developed a biting critique of free-labor capitalism ("wage-slavery") as cruel, exploitative, and selfish, and pointed to the degraded condition of supposedly free British paupers and Irish peasants. This defense in many ways represented the mirror image of the "free-labor" argument increasingly prevalent in the North: as free-labor spokesmen argued that slavery kept the South backward, poor, inefficient, and degraded, proslavery advocates retorted that only slavery could save the South (and the world) from the evils of modernity run wild.

From the mid-1840s the struggle over slavery became more and more central to American politics. Northerners committed to the concept of "free soil" (the idea that new, western territories should be reserved exclusively for free white settlers) clashed repeatedly with Southern spokesmen who insisted that any limitation on slavery's expansion represented unconstitutional meddling with the Southern order and a grave affront to Southern honor. In 1860 the election of Abraham Lincoln as president on a free-soil platform set off a major political and constitutional crisis, as seven states in the Deep South seceded from the United States and formed the Confederate States of America; the start of hostilities between the United States and the rebel Confederates in April 1861 led to the additional secession of four states in the upper South. (Four other slave states – Maryland, Delaware, Kentucky, and Missouri – remained in the Union, as did the new state of West Virginia, which split off from Virginia.)

Emancipation – and After

Ironically, although Southern politicians supported secession in order to preserve slavery, their action led instead to slavery's death. As the war dragged on, Northern war aims gradually shifted from preserving the Union to abolishing slavery and *remaking* the Union. Two especially important catalysts of this shift were the following: (1) the wartime behavior of Southern blacks, who under conditions of weakened authority at home increasingly refused to behave like slaves; and (2) the changing views of Northern whites, a growing number of whom accepted the Radical Republican position that the war provided an ideal opportunity to overthrow slavery and institute a sweeping transformation of the Southern social order.

Slavery ended for hundreds of thousands of Southern blacks well before the Confederate surrender, as Union troops occupied larger and larger areas of the South and as increasing numbers of slaves fled from their owners and sought refuge within Union lines. In Union-occupied areas of the South, blacks experienced a rehearsal for Reconstruction, as federal officials experimented with various forms of free and semifree labor and as Northern missionaries established schools to help turn slaves into citizens. The freedpeople's enthusiasm for education, in turn, created a powerful impression among Northern whites and contributed to their growing determination that the war must yield what President Lincoln termed "a new birth of freedom."

This goal received symbolic recognition with the Emancipation Proclamation that Lincoln issued on January 1, 1863. Although the proclamation applied only to areas under rebel control and did not end slavery in the United States, it marked a clear turning point in the struggle against the "peculiar institution": a war for union had become a war for freedom, and henceforth everyone recognized that a federal victory would mean the death of slavery. During the second half of the war, as slavery crumbled in much of the South, more than 188,000 African Americans, both Southern and Northern, served in the Union's armed forces, fighting to hasten that death. The Thirteenth Amendment to the Constitution, passed by Congress in January and ratified by the states in December 1865, completed the process, outlawing slavery everywhere in the United States.

Despite the overthrow of slavery, at war's end the future status of the former slaves remained unclear, and resolving that status remained at the center of the nation's political agenda. An intense struggle ensued, as freedpeople strove for economic security, social autonomy, and civil rights; former slave owners sought to preserve their old prerogatives; and Northern politicians became divided over the proper course of Reconstruction. The compromise that resulted from this struggle yielded an unprecedented – although temporary – national commitment to turn former slaves into citizens, anchored by the Fourteenth and Fifteenth Amendments to the United States Constitution and the Reconstruction Acts of 1867. Together these measures provided basic civil rights to former slaves, enfranchised black males, and imposed a largely self-administered democratization process on the former Confederate states, under federal supervision.

Emancipation brought many tangible rewards. Among the most obvious was the significant increase in personal freedom that came with no longer being someone else's property: whatever hardships they faced, free blacks could not be forcibly sold away from their loved ones. But emancipation did not bring full equality, and many of the most striking gains of Reconstruction – including the substantial political power that African Americans were briefly able to exercise – were soon lost. In the decades after Reconstruction African Americans experienced continued poverty and exploitation and a rising tide of violence at the hands of whites determined to reimpose black subordination. They also experienced new forms of discrimination, spearheaded by a variety of state laws that instituted rigid racial segregation in virtually all areas of life and that (in violation of the Fourteenth and Fifteenth Amendments) effectively disfranchised black voters. The struggle to overcome the bitter legacy of slavery would be long and arduous.

Peter Kolchin

See Also

Abolitionism in the United States; Civil War, American; Fifteenth Amendment to the United States Constitution; Fourteenth Amendment to the United States Constitution; Fugitive Slaves; New Orleans, Louisiana; Slave Religion; Race and the American Presidency; Thirteenth Amendment of the United States Constitution and the Emancipation Proclamation.

Cross Cultural

Slaves, African, in Iraq

Western historians have long presumed that the great natural expanses of the Indian Ocean and the Sahara Desert proved to be insurmountable barriers to the Africans who lived in proximity to them. They assumed incorrectly that Africans, unlike all other human beings, would not see these natural wonders as conduits, as highways through which to connect to other civilizations and other human beings. Trade is the enemy of distance. It is also the godfather of movements among peoples that result in captivity and enslavement.

Eleven centuries ago slaves from East Africa – the "Zanj" – at Basra engaged in a war against their masters in Baghdad. Between 869 and 883 C.E. these slaves struck their blows for freedom against the Abbasid Empire (762-1258 C.E.). For 14 years they succeeded, achieving remarkable military victories and even building their own capital. Their achievement is all the more impressive considering that at its height the Abbasid Empire was one of the world's most powerful states, presiding directly over Iraq, Mesopotamia, and western Persia, and indirectly over territories from North Africa to Central Asia, and from the Caspian Sea to the Red Sea.

The Zanj were commonly found as slaves in Muslim countries. Like all slaves they were stereotyped as thieves and rapists who were devoid of reason and lacking memory. Nevertheless, these brutally oppressed slaves – forcibly packed into camps by the hundreds and thousands, without family or hope, and given meager rations of food – under Ali B. Muhammad's leadership rose up against their masters, and fought to the death for their freedom. Their uprising brings to mind the revolts of Eunus (140 B.C.E.) and of Spartacus (73-71 B.C.E.) against Rome, as well as those of Toussaint L'Ouverture in Haiti and the strikes of the Indian laborers in Natal led by Mohandas Gandhi against European colonialism (1906-1913).

Henry Louis Gates, Jr.

See Also

Toussaint L'Ouverture, François Dominique; Indian Ocean Slave Trade; Slavery in Africa.

North America

Sleet, Moneta J., Jr.

(b. February 14, 1926, Owensboro, Ky.; d. September 30, 1996, New York, N.Y.), photojournalist and the first African American man to win a Pulitzer Prize, his photographs chronicled pivotal moments in contemporary black history, such as Martin Luther King Jr.'s 1968 funeral and Ghana's independence in 1957.

Aspiring to become a photographer since early childhood, Moneta Sleet Jr. studied photography and business at Kentucky State College. In 1955 he became a staff photographer for *Ebony* magazine. On assignment he met Martin Luther King Jr. in 1956, and the two remained friends until King's assassination. During this period Sleet photographed the marches and rallies of the CIVIL RIGHTS MOVEMENT, and won critical acclaim for his sensitive and vivid photos of both famous and ordinary people.

SEE ALSO
Ghana; *Ebony*; Photography, African American; King, Martin Luther, Jr.

Africa

Slovo, Joe

(b. 1926, Lithuania; d. January 6, 1995, Johannesburg, South Africa), lawyer, antiapartheid activist, and general secretary of the South Africa Communist Party.

Joe Slovo moved to SOUTH AFRICA at age nine and grew up in a working-class Jewish neighborhood in Johannesburg. In 1942 he joined the Communist Party and, shortly thereafter, the South African army, with which he fought in World War II. After the war he studied law at the University of Witwatersrand, where he befriended Nelson Mandela, who was then the university's only black student. When Mandela and others formed the AFRICAN NATIONAL CONGRESS (ANC) Youth League in 1943, Slovo argued for the multiracial cooperation that became an ANC trademark.

Slovo acted as Mandela's lawyer in his first trial for treason in 1956, a trial in which Slovo was also a defendant. In the early 1960s Slovo helped found Umkhonto we Sizwe, the ANC's covert military wing, and served for a time as its commander in chief. After the government raided Umkhonto's headquarters Slovo was forced into 27 years of exile – years that Slovo spent working against apartheid from London, ZAMBIA, and MOZAMBIQUE. In 1982 his wife RUTH FIRST, also an antiapartheid activist, was assassinated.

Known for his quick wit and gentle humor (in his first public speech after the ANC ban was lifted in 1990, Slovo began, "As I was saying before I was so rudely interrupted… "), Slovo helped negotiate the transition to democratic government that culminated in South Africa's first free elections in 1994. He served in the administration of President Mandela, allocating $500 million in government loans for black township residents to buy their own homes. Ten years after becoming the first white person elected to the ANC Executive Committee, Slovo died in 1995 after a long battle with cancer.

Kate Tuttle

SEE ALSO
Antiapartheid Movement; Mandela, Nelson Rolihlahla; South African Communist Party.

North America

Sly and the Family Stone,

an interracial musical group formed in the late 1960s by African American singer Sly Stone (Sylvester Stewart); Sly and the Family Stone, together with singer JAMES BROWN, helped create the FUNK music style.

Sly and the Family Stone played a key role in the genesis of funk, a musical fusion combining gospel-inspired SOUL MUSIC with the guitar-driven sound and performance style of 1960s psychedelic rock. Sly Stone was born Sylvester Stewart in 1944 and moved in the 1950s with his family from Texas to San Francisco.

After playing in several area bands, Stone became a RHYTHM AND BLUES (R&B) disc jockey for stations KSOL and later KDIA. As a record producer for Autumn Records, he recorded with such local bands as the Beau Brummels and the Mojo Men. In 1967 he organized Sly and the Family Stone, which was unique among 1960s rock or funk bands in including both blacks and whites, and women as well as men.

The group featured punchy horn riffs and wild guitar solos played over a deep funk rhythm. It soon had two hits, "Everyday People" (1968) and "Hot Fun in the Summertime" (1969), and appeared at the 1969 Woodstock Festival. The group's songs often displayed a racial militancy reminiscent of the BLACK POWER movement, as in "Don't Call Me Nigger, Whitey" (1969). The album *There's a Riot Going On* (1971) combined social commentary with highly danceable music, setting the pattern for funk music in the 1970s.

By the early 1970s Sly and the Family Stone's music had turned darkly pessimistic as Stone began to fall apart. He became addicted to narcotics and acquired a reputation for unreliability after repeated no-shows at concerts. Sly and the Family Stone produced one more exceptional album, *Fresh* (1973), but changing musical tastes and Stone's mounting personal problems ended the group's national visibility.

In the early 1980s Stone joined GEORGE CLINTON on Funkadelic's *The Electric Spanking of War Babies* (1981) and toured with the P-Funk All-Stars. During the 1980s Stone was repeatedly in trouble with the law and spent time in prison for cocaine possession.

In 1993, the year that he was inducted into the Rock and Roll Hall of Fame, Stone was reportedly living in a sheltered-housing complex. Yet despite his difficulties, Stone made a lasting contribution. In the 1990s urban soul, funk, and RAP all reveal a debt to the music of Sly and the Family Stone.

James Clyde Sellman

SEE ALSO
Gospel Music; San Francisco and Oakland, California.

North America

Smalls, Robert

(b. 1839, Beaufort, S.C.; d. 1915), Civil War steamboat pilot and United States congressman; he achieved fame by sailing the Confederate steamship *Planter* to the Union side.

As a slave Robert Smalls was permitted to hire himself out in Charleston, South Carolina, as a boatman. Because of his familiarity with local waterways, he was made a wheelman (the title "pilot" being reserved for whites) of the steamboat *Planter*. On May 12, 1862, with the white crew members on the shore, Smalls stowed his family and several other slaves on board, and piloted the ship across Union lines. The *Planter* was a 300-ton armed vessel, which Smalls presented to the United States Army; he also provided useful intelligence about Confederate operations. The story of the incident was wildly popular throughout the North, and Smalls was awarded $1500 and made a second lieutenant in the Union's Colored Troops.

During RECONSTRUCTION Smalls became a state official in South Carolina, and later a U.S. Congressman. A loyal Republican, he helped write the state's 1868 constitution. In office he fought for free compulsory public education, health care, and the enforcement of the Civil Rights Act. Smalls was also influential in the business community, investing in South Carolina real estate and companies. He remained a congressman until 1886, when the influence of Reconstruction and its reforms subsided.

SEE ALSO
Civil War, American.

North America

Smith, Ada "Bricktop"

(b. August 14, 1894, Alderson, W. Va.; d. January 31, 1984, New York, N.Y.), African American singer and nightclub owner whose Parisian café attracted a wealthy and famous international clientele in the 1920s and 1930s.

A performer throughout her childhood, Ada Smith left school at age 16 to begin her career as a singer and dancer in minstrel and vaudeville shows. Her bright red hair earned her the nickname "Bricktop." She performed extensively in New York, Los Angeles, and Chicago. In 1924 she began singing at Paris's Le Grand Duc, a nightclub favored by the Parisian elite and community of black expatriates, where she became acquainted with Cole Porter, Josephine Baker, and Pablo Picasso among others. In 1927 she bought the club and renamed it Bricktop's. It became one of Paris's most popular nightclubs in the 1930s. Smith left Paris in 1939 because of World War II. A string of nightclubs she opened in the 1940s and 1950s failed, and Smith retired from the business in 1964. She had occasional singing engagements in the 1970s.

See Also

Chicago, Illinois; Minstrelsy; New York, New York.

North America

Smith, Albert Alexander

(b. 1896, New York, N.Y.; d. 1940, Haute-Savoie, France), African American painter, illustrator, and jazz musician whose work emphasized African American daily life.

Albert Smith was trained in piano and guitar at the Ethical Culture High School in New York, and later studied at the National Academy of Design in Belgium, where he twice won the Suyden Bronze Medal. After serving in a military band during World War I, in the 1920s he settled in Paris, where his art was frequently exhibited. He gained international fame as an artist after exhibitions in Brussels and New York. He worked often as an illustrator for the magazines *Crisis* and *Opportunity*. Creating daily scenes from African American life, Smith wanted to enforce positive images of black folk through art. He supported himself playing banjo in Paris cabarets.

See Also

World War I and African Americans; *Crisis, The*; Jazz; *Opportunity: Journal of Negro Life*.

North America

Smith, Anna Deveare

(b. September 18, 1950, Baltimore, Md.), African American actor, playwright, and educator.

Born in Baltimore, Maryland, Anna Deveare Smith was the oldest of Deveare and Anna Smith's five children. Her father owned a coffee and tea business, while her mother was an elementary school principal. In 1971, after receiving a bachelor's degree in linguistics from Beaver College, Smith left for San Francisco, California, where her acting talent earned her a place at the American Conservatory Theater and enabled her to work as an actor and director. She received a master of fine arts degree in 1976, and left for New York City in the same year. There, Smith played minor roles in soap operas and worked for KLM Airlines before becoming a drama teacher at Carnegie-Mellon University in Pittsburgh, Pennsylvania.

Though a casting agent had once told her she was too pale to convincingly portray black characters, Smith launched a one-woman performance, *On the Road: A Search for American Character* (1983), beginning a quest to represent dramatically America's multiple voices and identities. In 1992 Smith produced the 26-character, one-woman performance, *Fires in the Mirror*, which dealt with the riots that erupted in Crown Heights, Brooklyn, after an African American child was accidentally killed by a Jewish motorist, and a Jewish scholar was stabbed in apparent retaliation. Based on interviews with more than 50 people connected to the riots, the performance was described by Smith as an exploration of the incident's causes and impact, and of "the place where language fails, where people have to struggle to find words."

Fires in the Mirror received an Obie Award, a Drama Desk Award, the Lucille Lortel Award, the $10,000 Kesselring Prize, and the George and Elizabeth Marton Award. It was a runner-up for a Pulitzer Prize. This success led directly to a commission that resulted in *Twilight: Los Angeles 1992*, a performance that examined the five days of rioting in L.A. that followed the acquittal of four policeman accused of severely beating a black motorist, Rodney King. *Twilight* opened in 1993 in Los Angeles and then moved to New York City, where it was the first nonmusical show by a black woman to open on Broadway in ten years. *Twilight* won two Tony Award nominations, an Obie Award, a Drama Desk Award, and an Outer Circle Critics Special Achievement Award. Because *Twilight*, like *Fires*, was dependent on Smith's verbatim portrayals of the people she interviewed (a "documentary" work rather than a "theater" work), the Pulitzer board decided to withdraw her nomination for the Pulitzer Prize.

Other works by Smith include the plays *A Birthday Card and Aunt Julia's Shoes* (1983) and *Aye, Aye, Aye, I'm Integrated* (1984). She appeared in minor roles in the motion pictures *Dave* (1993) and *Philadelphia* (1993). Smith has taught at New York University, Yale University, and the University of Southern California at Los Angeles, and is now a tenured professor at Stanford University.

See Also

Los Angeles Riot of 1992; Los Angeles, California; New York, New York; San Francisco and Oakland, California.

North America

Smith, Bessie

(b. April 15, 1894?, Chattanooga, Tenn.; d. September 26, 1937, Clarksdale, Miss.), greatest blues vocalist of the 1920s, known as the Empress of the Blues.

Bessie Smith was the greatest of the classic blues singers of the 1920s; she laid the foundation for all subsequent women's blues and jazz singing. Her singing combined an array of vocal embellishments, including scoops, slides, and blue notes, and a rhythmic freedom that heightened the emotional effect of her lyrics. African American audiences loved her, especially those in the South and those in the North made up of recent southern migrants, who appreciated her rough, down-home style. "She could bring about mass hypnotism," New Orleans guitarist Danny Barker recalled. "When she was performing you could hear a pin drop." In part, this was due to her musical artistry and showmanship; in part, it was because many identified with her success. Smith had risen from poverty to comparative wealth on her own terms and by her own talent. Many African Americans also admired her attitude toward white people – Smith made no effort to befriend whites and never altered her performing style to appeal to them.

Smith was born around 1894 in a poor section of Chattanooga, Tennessee. One of seven children and orphaned young, she was singing on street corners by age nine. Smith grew to be a large-boned woman with a powerful and expressive voice. In 1912, while still a teenager, she joined a traveling vaudeville show. Surprisingly, she was hired as a dancer rather than as a singer, joining her dancer and comedian brother Clarence, who was already in the show. The troupe also included blues singer Gertrude "Ma" Rainey, who reportedly took Smith under her wing.

Smith settled in Atlanta, Georgia, where she performed regularly at the 81 Theater, part of the black nationwide Theater Owners Booking Association (TOBA) circuit. She began touring on the TOBA circuit, performing in the North as well as in the Southeast, and by the end of World War I she was TOBA's star attraction. During these years Smith also had a brief marriage to Jack Gee and began a lifetime of hard drinking. She did not enter a recording studio until she was nearly 30 years old and fully formed as an artist.

With the phenomenal success of "Crazy Blues," recorded in 1920 by Mamie Smith (no relation), record companies began to make "race records" for African American listeners, and began seeking black talent. At least two companies turned down Bessie Smith before Columbia Record Company brought her to its New York studios in 1923. Unlike many classic blues vocalists whose singing backgrounds were in vaudeville or popular music, Smith was primarily grounded in the blues. Consequently, as pianist Clarence Williams later explained, a number of record companies "said that her voice was too rough."

African American listeners did not agree. In less than six months her first record, "Downhearted Blues," sold an astonishing 780,000 copies. In fact, Smith played a direct role in rescuing Columbia, then nearly in receivership, and putting it on a firm financial basis. Columbia proclaimed its new star the Empress of the Blues, but Smith received no royalties, only a flat fee for each recording. During the 1920s she recorded prolifically with a wide range of accompanists, including cornetist Louis Armstrong, clarinet player Sidney Bechet, pianist Fletcher Henderson, and her two favorite muscians, trumpeter Joe Smith and trombone player Charlie Green.

In addressing what made Smith "such a superior singer," musicologist Gunther Schuller stressed the importance of her "remarkable ear for and control of intonation... [her] perfectly centered, naturally produced voice... [her] extreme sensitivity to word meaning and the sensory, almost physical, feeling of a word; and related to this, superb diction and what singers call projection."

Among Smith's important recordings are "Jailhouse Blues" (1923); "Cold in Hand Blues," "J. C. Holmes Blues," "You've Been a Good Old Wagon" (all 1925); "Gin House Blues," "Young Woman's Blues" (both 1926); and "Nobody Knows You When You're Down and Out" (1929). Throughout her career she also recorded popular songs and standards that were not blues based, including "After You've Gone" (1927) and "Gimme a Pigfoot" (1933).

Smith toured extensively. During the winter she appeared at black theaters and at occasional whites-only venues such as Nashville's Orpheum Theater. In warm weather she headlined her own big-tent variety show, with the entire cast traveling from performance to performance in her private Pullman car. In 1924 she made her first radio broadcast on WMC in MEMPHIS, TENNESSEE, singing a set that included "Mistreatin' Papa" and "Chicago Bound." Five years later she starred in a black-and-white short, *St. Louis Blues*, singing the title song; this short provides the only film footage of Smith performing. Although her Northern audiences declined when the blues craze passed in the late 1920s, Smith remained popular throughout the South, where the blues was indigenous. After the Depression put an end to her recording career in 1931, she continued performing before appreciative Southern audiences.

During the 1930s Smith made the transition from a heavier blues style to the more lightly swinging jazz of the Swing Era. She was featured at Harlem's renowned APOLLO THEATER during 1935 and a short time later substituted for BILLIE HOLIDAY in the Broadway show *Stars over Broadway*. Smith appeared to be on the verge of a comeback when she was killed in a 1937 automobile accident. Record producer John Hammond, writing in *Downbeat* magazine five years after her death, and playwright Edward Albee, in *The Death of Bessie Smith* (1960), popularized the idea that the singer died because a whites-only hospital refused to admit her. However, her biographer Chris Albertson concluded that Smith died at the scene of the accident, and, given the extent of her injuries, she could not have been saved.

James Clyde Sellman

SEE ALSO

World War I and African Americans; Armstrong, Louis ("Satchmo"); Bechet, Sidney Joseph; Blues, The; Great Depression; Harlem, New York; Rainey, Gertrude Pridgett ("Ma")Henderson; Fletcher Hamilton, Jr.

North America

Smith, Clara (b. 1894?, Spartanburg, S.C.; d. February 2, 1935, Detroit, Mich.), African American blues singer and pianist during the 1920s, known as the Queen of the Moaners.

Clara Smith began performing around 1910, working the Southern black vaudeville circuit. By 1918 she was a star in the Theater Owners Booking Association (TOBA), which managed acts for black theater. Smith settled in Harlem in 1923, where she played in cellar clubs, speakeasies, and revues.

One of Smith's biggest recorded hits was "Every Woman's Blues" (1923). On her recordings Smith performed with Louis Armstrong, Fletcher Henderson, and Don Redman, and sang duets with BESSIE SMITH (no relation). Her style was dramatic and comic, and she is best remembered for expressive performances of songs like "Whip It to a Jelly" that played with sexual double entendres. Smith also managed her own revues, including the Clara Smith Theatrical Club.

Marian Aguiar

SEE ALSO

Armstrong, Louis ("Satchmo"); Blues, The; Harlem, New York; Henderson, Fletcher Hamilton, Jr.

North America

Smith, Clarence ("Pine Top") (b. June 11, 1904, Troy, Ala.; d. March 15, 1929, Chicago, Ill.), African American jazz pianist who originated the boogie-woogie style.

Clarence "Pine Top" Smith began to play piano professionally in 1918, working at clubs in Birmingham, Alabama, before touring on the vaudeville and black Theater Owners Booking Association circuit. He was discovered by Charles "Cow Cow" Davenport in the mid-1920s, and began recording in 1928. With "Pine Top's Boogie Woogie" (1928) he coined the term "BOOGIE WOOGIE." The boogie-woogie style, marked by lively, improvised melodies on the right hand and rolling eight-to-the-bar figures on the left, developed as one of the most important strains of JAZZ piano. Smith recorded 20 songs in all, including "Pine Top's Blues." He died at 25 during a brawl in a Chicago dance hall.

Marian Aguiar

SEE ALSO

Chicago, Illinois.

Africa

Smith, Ian Douglas (b. April 8, 1919, Selukwe, Southern Rhodesia [now Zimbabwe]), prime minister of Southern Rhodesia and leading politician in ZIMBABWE.

Throughout his life Ian Smith has been a conservative rebel. For years he was one of the most ardent proponents of white settler society in southern Africa, and he has since become one of the most vociferous critics of independent rule in Zimbabwe.

Born and raised in colonial Southern Rhodesia, in 1939 Smith joined the British Royal Air Force. After serving as a combat pilot in World War II, Smith attended Rhodes University in SOUTH AFRICA and upon graduation returned to Southern Rhodesia to work on his large cattle ranch. Smith was elected to the Legislative Assembly of the British colony as a member of the Liberal Party in 1948, only to switch five years later to the more conservative United (Federal) Party. He later became chief whip but left the party in 1961 to help form the Rhodesian Front, a party opposed to making concessions to Africans. There he served as deputy prime minister until a right-wing revolt propelled him into the leadership position.

Smith became prime minister in April 1964, vowing to proclaim white-ruled Rhodesia's independence from Britain. He called for an all-white referendum, and with overwhelming support Smith made his Unilateral Declaration of Independence in November 1965, putting Southern Rhodesia on a collision course with rising African nationalism. Despite the imposition of severe international sanctions, for several years Smith remained intransigent, promising the white community that the government would fight "communist terrorism" (i.e., African nationalists of the Zimbabwe African National Union [ZANU] and the Zimbabwe African People's Union [ZAPU]) to the end, and that Rhodesia would remain a settler state as long as he lived. Meanwhile he remained a centrist in Rhodesian politics, purging the leadership of right-wing elements. Representing whites of the small town and farm communities, Smith and his "cowboy cabinet" were not well liked by the Rhodesian business community, but it was ultimately the financial strength of this community that sustained the economy throughout 15 years of war.

As the war expanded and South African pressure increased, Smith gradually became more amenable to African demands and four years later recognized the possibility of independence. A long series of negotiations culminated in the "internal settlement" with conservative nationalists, wherein Smith would be a member of a rotating chairmanship. Most African Zimbabweans, the main nationalist groups, and the international community, however, did not recognize the internal settlement, and Smith was forced to sue for peace.

At Zimbabwean independence in 1980, Smith remained in the parliament as head of the opposition, all-white Republican Front (the new Rhodesian Front), later known as the Conservative Alliance of Zimbabwe. As one of the government's most vocal critics, in 1987 Smith was suspended from parliament because of his outspoken moral support for South Africa. Soon thereafter he formally retired from politics after serving four decades in parliament. In retirement Smith continued to lambaste Zimbabwe's economic policies, even as other whites disavowed him and sought to work with the government. He has retained a significant following throughout Zimbabwe, among both whites and blacks, who see him as a symbol of the country's lost prosperity.

Eric Young

See Also
Nationalism in Africa; Great Britain; World War II and African Americans; Zimbabwe.

North America

Smith, Mamie

(b. May 26, 1883, Cincinnati, Ohio; d. September 16, 1946, New York, N.Y.), singer who was the first African American woman to record the blues.

Mamie Smith began performing in vaudeville shows at age ten and came to New York in 1913 with the Smart Set Revue. After Smith appeared in Perry Bradford's musical *Made in Harlem*, Bradford helped her get a recording contract at OKeh Records for "That Thing Called Love" (1920) and "You Can't Keep a Good Man Down" (1920). That same year she recorded "Crazy Blues" with a backup band including Willie "the Lion" Smith. "Crazy Blues" sold close to a million copies. Its success energized the "race music" industry, which marketed blues and jazz recordings specifically to an African American audience. Smith continued to tour as a singer and actress throughout the 1930s and 1940s, appearing in films such as *Paradise in Harlem* (1939), and on stage with Billie Holiday.

Marian Aguiar

See Also
Blues, The; New York, New York; Smith, Willie ("the Lion").

North America

Smith, Marvin and Morgan

(Marvin: b. February 16, 1910, Nicholsville, Ky. / Morgan: b. February 16, 1910, Nicholsville, Ky.; d. February 17, 1993?), African American photographers who depicted Harlem in the 1930s.

The twin sons of tenant farmers, Marvin and Morgan Smith grew up in Lexington, Kentucky, where they began painting and drawing. After moving to New York, they studied art under Augusta Savage and painted murals with the Works Progress Administration (WPA), a federal employment assistance program during the Depression. The Smiths realistically captured Harlem in the 1930s on film with photographs of Savoy Ballroom Lindy hoppers, street-corner preachers, and bread lines. In 1937 they were hired by New York's *Amsterdam News* as staff photographers. After a brief period in France the Smiths opened their M&M studio near the Apollo Theater. Their photographs continued to appear in prominent African American newspapers and magazines such as *Ebony*, *Crisis*, and the *Pittsburgh Courier*.

Marian Aguiar

See Also
Crisis, The; *Ebony*; Great Depression; Harlem, New York; New York, New York; *Pittsburgh Courier*; Savage, Augusta Christine Fells; Photography, African American; Dance in the United States.

North America

Smith, William Gardner

(b. February 6, 1927, Philadelphia, Pa.; d. November 6, 1974, France), African American novelist whose work posits a uniquely black artistry as part of the larger community.

William Gardner Smith spent much of his adult life as an exile, living in Paris and, for a time, Ghana. While writing for black periodicals in the United States and France, he wrote four novels, *Last of the Conquerors* (1948); *Anger at Innocence* (1950); *South Street* (1954); *The Stone Face* (1963); and one African American work, *Return to Black America* (1970), all of which attempt to resolve African Americans' tensions with the hostile larger society. Smith's project for himself and other black writers was two-fold: to harness deep empathy for suffering in the service of expressing profound truth and to resist a persistent artistic victimization of blacks that ended only in artistic ineffectiveness. Smith's work resembles that of other black writers of the 1940s and 1950s, including Richard Wright, James Baldwin, and Ann Petry, who depicted the conflicts between the artist and his society, and specifically between the black artist trying to establish a name in a largely white society hostile to recognizing black artistic achievements. Although Smith's own work found only a relatively small audience, his concerns anticipate more recent developments in African American literature.

Robert Fay

See Also
Petry, Ann Lane.

North America

Smith, Willie Mae Ford

(b. 1906?, Rolling Fort, Miss.; d. February 2, 1994, St. Louis, Mo.), African American gospel singer and preacher who contributed to the organized growth and development of gospel music.

Willie Mae Ford Smith's involvement with the world of gospel music started early; the daughter of the deacon of a Baptist church, she sang in church as a child. As a teen she was the lead vocalist in a gospel quartet she formed with her sisters. The group performed to great acclaim at the National Baptist Convention of 1922.

Smith was ordained as a minister in 1926, but as a woman was forbidden to preach in the Baptist church. This edict prompted her departure from that church in later years. In 1932, along with Thomas A. Dorsey and Sallie Martin, Smith formed the National Convention of Gospel Choirs and Choruses, an establishment credited with the nationwide popularization and development of gospel music. She then became the director of the National Convention Soloists Bureau where she was charged with teaching and mentoring young gospel singers.

Departing from the Baptist Church in 1939, Smith joined the Holiness Church of God Apostolic and began to make fewer stage performances, focusing instead on singing principally at religious gatherings. It was at these performances that Smith's trademark "sermonnette," a short spoken statement preceding the song, gained fame.

In spite of the fact that she never focused on developing a professional recording career, Smith had an impact on the world of gospel music that remains unparalleled. Her protégés include Mahalia Jackson, the O'Neal twins, Martha Bass, and Delois Barret Campbell. The documentary *Say Amen, Somebody* celebrated Smith's life and contributions to gospel music. Willie Mae Ford Smith died in St. Louis in 1994.

Aaron Myers

See Also
Baptists; Dorsey, Thomas Andrew.

North America

Smith, Willie ("the Lion")

(b. November 25, 1897, Goshen, N.Y.; d. April 18, 1973, New York, N.Y.), African American jazz pianist and composer who was an innovator in the "stride" style of jazz piano.

Willie "the Lion" Smith was raised in NEWARK, NEW JERSEY, by his mother and his stepfather. By age 15 he was playing the piano professionally in local clubs and parties. Smith was a innovator in the "stride" style of JAZZ piano, which features a strong pumping line in the left hand. As early as 1921 Smith was making records, having performed in the backup band for Mamie Smith's "Crazy Blues." Although less well known than his contemporaries James P. Johnson and Fats Waller, Smith influenced musicians, most notably Duke Ellington. Smith's career surged in the 1950s and 1960s, and he recorded extensively. He published his autobiography, *Music on My Mind*, in 1964.

Robert Fay

SEE ALSO

Smith, Mamie; Waller, Thomas Wright ("Fats"); Ellington, Edward Kennedy ("Duke").

North America

Snoop Doggy Dogg

(Calvin Broadus) (b. 1972, Los Angeles, Calif.), the best-known figure in gangsta RAP, a genre that chronicles in explicit detail life in and around the gangs of urban America.

Snoop Doggy Dogg's career began suddenly, when Dr. Dre, recently retired from NWA, asked Snoop to rap on the title song from the soundtrack to the film *Deep Cover*. The track, which described the murder of an undercover cop, was an underground hit, and Snoop joined the roster of Dre's Death Row Records.

In 1992 Dr. Dre released his solo debut, *The Chronic*, which featured Snoop's slow, nasal drawl on tracks like "Nuthin' but a 'G' Thang." *The Chronic* album achieved multi-platinum success, and Snoop capitalized on his sudden fame with *Doggystyle* (1993) – the most highly anticipated debut in hip hop history. Tracks like "Doggy Dogg World" and "Gin and Juice" exemplified the feel-good side of Snoop's Long Beach Sound, while "Murder Was the Case" prefigured Snoop's subsequent trial (and acquittal) in a murder case.

In 1996 Dr. Dre quit Death Row, leaving Marion "Suge" Knight to run the label. Snoop appeared on tracks by label mates Tha Dogg Pound and TUPAC SHAKUR, but the absence of his mentor, Dre, was sorely felt: *Tha Doggfather* (1996), Snoop's sophomore effort, garnered respectable sales but lousy reviews. On the eve of the album's release Shakur was murdered; a few months later Knight was indicted for probation violations. With Death Row in disarray, Snoop made an acrimonious public split; he currently records with the New Orleans-based No Limit Records.

Andrew Du Bois

SEE ALSO

Hip Hop in the United States; Niggaz with Attitude.

SNYC. Please see SOUTHERN NEGRO YOUTH CONGRESS

Africa

Sobhuza II

(b. 1899; d. 1982, Swaziland), *ngwenyama* (paramount chief or king) of SWAZILAND (1921-1982).

Following the death in 1899 of his father, King Bhunu, Sobhuza II was named heir to the throne when only six months old. Labotsibeni, his grandmother, ruled on his behalf until he was 22. Studying first under a South African tutor, Sobhuza completed secondary education at the National School at Zombodze, which was built by his grandmother so that Sobhuza would not be forced to attend missionary schools. Shortly after his formal induction as ngwenyama in December 1921, Sobhuza petitioned King George V of Britain for the return of Swazi lands that had been allocated to British settlers in the 1907 Partitions Proclamation. When diplomatic efforts failed, he initiated legal proceedings, which were also unsuccessful. During World War II (1939-1945) he managed to gain some land concessions from the British in exchange for Swazi support for the British war effort. When negotiations with the British for independence began in 1964, Sobhuza founded the Imbokodvo National Movement (INM), a traditionalist political party that swept parliamentary elections in 1964. The INM convinced the British to redraft a Swazi constitution vesting executive power in the ngwenyama. Following independence in September 1968, the INM continued to dominate the legislature. Sobhuza suspended the constitution in 1973, replacing it, in 1978, with a new constitution. The new constitution consolidated his powers and replaced the legislative council with the Libandla, an advisory body without legislative powers and composed of members nominated by local councils. An economic modernizer, Sobhuza exploited Swaziland's mineral and forest resources, encouraged tourism, and established the nation as an important regional power. Resisting democracy as "un-Swazi," he was an extremely popular autocrat. Sobhuza died in 1982 after ruling for 61 years, making him the longest-reigning monarch in the world. He left more than 100 wives and 200 children, and was succeeded by his second-youngest son, MSWATI III.

SEE ALSO

Great Britain; Tourism in Africa.

Latin America and the Caribbean

Soca,

a dance-oriented variety of CALYPSO music that first appeared in Trinidad in 1977 and has predominated in the country's local music since that time.

During the 1970s Trinidad's calypso music appeared to be in decline; trapped by its own narrow stylistic conventions, it faced stiff competition from rock 'n' roll and REGGAE music. Moreover, during the 1960s and 1970s the island experienced transforming political and economic changes. A significant Black Power Movement became a political force to be reckoned with, inspired by the unfolding CIVIL RIGHTS MOVEMENT in the United States and nationalistic movements in Africa and Latin America. Trinidad's economic prospects improved markedly due to its membership in the Organization of Petroleum Exporting Countries (OPEC), which vastly increased the value of the island's petroleum resources. An increase in the price of SUGAR made that export crop more valuable as well.

As the people of Trinidad experienced new forms of empowerment, calypso music seemed increasingly out of touch. The calypso musician Lord Shorty – who is about 2 m (6 ft 4 in) tall – took the lead in making calypso music more compelling. In 1977 Lord Shorty and arranger Ed Watson developed a new and danceable rhythm, which they termed *soca*. It features a steady bass drum beat set against intricate syncopated patterns played on the cymbals and snare drum. Besides employing a new rhythm, soca makes use of a wider range of instruments, including electric bass, electric guitar, and synthesizers.

The word "soca" often is used to refer to all calypso music performed since the late 1970s, but there is a difference between calypso, in which the lyrics are of primary importance, and soca, which is primarily dance music (*see* DANCE IN LATIN AMERICA AND THE CARIBBEAN). The lyrics of soca are slight; most are replete with references to "jam and wine," Trinidadian Creole terms for "dance and drink." Although such socially oriented calypso singers as Chalkdust (Hollis Liverpool) lament soca as "mindless" music, the genre has regained some of the audience that calypso had lost. Given the current interest in world music, some observers regard soca as the style most likely to win Trinidad an international music audience.

James Clyde Sellman

SEE ALSO

Trinidad and Tobago; World Music, World Beat, and the Re-Africanization of Latin American Popular Music.

Latin America and the Caribbean

Soccer in Latin America and the Caribbean, a British athletic export at first practiced only by local elites, the sport was appropriated by blacks who through it achieved prominence and participated in the construction of national identities.

Although a number of ancient societies practiced games that involved moving a ball to a goal, the game of soccer in its modern form arose from an agreement between British gentlemen in 1863, when the sport was effectively unified. The sport was soon exported by the British along with other products, so that in turn-of-the-century Latin America, for instance, soccer as well as a variety of industries were dominated by British companies. The introduction of soccer in different Latin American countries thus followed similar patterns, with Englishmen founding the first clubs in ARGENTINA (Buenos Aires Football Club), CHILE (Valparaíso F.C.), and URUGUAY (Albion F.C.) in the last decades of the nineteenth century. Charles Miller, the man credited with introducing soccer to BRAZIL, was Brazilian-born, of British parents.

Although at first the practice of soccer was limited to privileged European expatriates, gradually local elites joined the Europeans in the restricted spaces where soccer was played, and the sport became a ritual uniting national and foreign elites. Tradition claims that nonelite locals began to imitate the game upon seeing British sailors playing at docks, but it is certain that soccer was seized rapidly by the lower classes and that soon many working-class players attracted the attention of elite soccer clubs. This process was aided by the nature of soccer itself, a game that has been described as ideally suited for the poor: the space in which it is practiced can be easily improvised on practically any surface, with two objects of any kind serving as goal posts; the only equipment necessary is a ball, and this too has often been improvised; furthermore, the game does not excessively privilege particular physical characteristics.

The spread of soccer to the popular classes allowed for the participation of disfranchised blacks, yet the history of their inclusion in the formal settings where the sport was practiced is filled with conflicts. According to historian Eduardo Galeano, Uruguay was the first country in the world to include black players on its national team. When Uruguay beat Chile in the first South American championship in 1916 with a team that included two black players, Isabelino Gradín and Juan Delgado, Chile asked that the game be annulled, claiming its opponent had used "two Africans." Both men were, of course, Uruguayan, great-grandchildren of slaves.

Early soccer in Brazil was also contaminated by the racism of the society at large. It is believed that early idol Arthur Friedenreich straightened his hair, while Carlos Alberto, the only mulatto playing for Fluminense, whitened his face with rice powder. When a black player was signed by the América team in Rio de Janeiro, nine members left in protest. Most disturbing, however, was governmental racism: in 1921 Brazilian president Epitácio Pessoa prohibited blacks from playing on the team that was to represent Brazil in the South American championship in Buenos Aires.

The competitive pressure that followed professionalization in the 1930s made it increasingly difficult to limit the choice of players to elite whites. Soon many of the most admired players in Brazil, like Leonidas da Silva and Domingos da Guia, were black and played in the World Cup of 1938. National and international admiration of black Brazilian players, however, was not enough to dispel the racist ideology that claimed that Brazil would never be successful when facing European teams or "whiter" South American teams such as Uruguay. After Brazilian defeats in the World Cup of 1950 and of 1954 (to Uruguay and Hungary, respectively), racist explanations were quickly given for Brazil's ineptness, and old theories condemning miscegenation as degeneration were recycled.

The manner in which ethnic and class conflicts were played out symbolically on soccer fields can be demonstrated with the example of a team from PERU. Alianza Lima was founded in 1901 by working-class players and soon developed a fierce rivalry with the upper-class Universitario de Deportes. As early as the 1920s Alianza's teams included significant numbers of nonwhite players, while Universitario fielded mostly light-skinned players. Alejandro Villanueva and José María Lavalle, both black, played for Alianza Lima and were among the earliest sports idols in Peru. Games between Universitario and Alianza played out the ethnic and class conflicts present in the larger Peruvian society. Many players from Alianza were finally chosen to play in the national selection, yet later resigned in protest over preferential treatment given to the team's nonblack players in 1929. Alianza Lima continued its association with the historically working-class Rímac neighborhood, even as, to the dismay of Peruvian elites, it won numerous national championships.

Throughout much of Latin America soccer became a privileged milieu for the construction of a positive national identity. The unique ways in which soccer developed allowed people to imagine a larger community of which all could be proud, and made it impossible to ignore the physical presence of blacks or black cultural practices. The process through which soccer was localized may be compared with the evolution of Latin American Carnivals, in which an elite diversion with European traditions was gradually appropriated by the lower classes and then profoundly transformed. As José Sergio Leite Lopes has argued, "The Brazilian style of football is associated with bodily techniques... which resemble those physical activities which have ethnic Afro-Brazilian origins. One can look, for instance, to those occasioning features of Afro-Brazilian dances of different kinds (like SAMBA) or of those manifest in Afro-religions, or in martial arts such as CAPOEIRA. These footballing bodily techniques, largely subconscious as most bodily hexis and bodily habitus appear to be, were probably developed after the massive influx of blacks and mulattos into the first division."

Of the countless black, mulatto, and *mestizo* (of indigenous and European descent) soccer players in Latin America who have enchanted the world with their skill, a few may be highlighted: Obdulio Varela from Uruguay; Villanueva and Lavalle from the 1920s and Teofilo Cubillas from the 1970s in Peru; Friedenreich, Domingos da Guia, Leonidas da Silva, Garrincha, Didi, and PELÉ from Brazil; and Faustino Asprilla, Carlos Valderrama, and Freddy Rincón, the Colombian trio that delighted the world in the 1990 World Cup.

Marcos Natalí

SEE ALSO

Garrincha, Mané; Carnivals in Latin America and the Caribbean.

North America

Socialism, the economic and social doctrine that critiques capitalist production and advocates state control over vital industries, income distribution, and private property.

AMERICAN SOCIALISM

The roots of American socialism can be found in antebellum communitarian settlements, such as the Shakers, and other utopian experiments that sought to establish cooperative societies within the emerging nation. Although some of these settlements were officially abolitionist, few offered refuge to African Americans. With the industrial boom that followed the Civil War, however, immigrant socialists lay the groundwork for a well-defined socialist doctrine and political party that – at least in theory – represented working people of all races against the growing might of American capitalism.

German immigrants brought Marxist socialist ideals to American organizations and in 1877 helped form the Socialist Labor Party. Meanwhile, American utopian reformers such as Edward Bellamy and Laurence Gronlund sought to achieve a classless society through peaceful means. From these two strands emerged a socialist doctrine reflecting the labor conditions particular to post-Civil War industrialization in the United States.

African Americans in American Socialism

Prior to World War I the socialist movement in the United States devoted little attention to racial inequality. Formed in 1901 from socialist parties in several states, the Socialist Party of America urged African Americans to join the party and participate in the "world movement for economic emancipation." The party did not, however, establish a policy of race issues. As a result socialist positions on race differed from member to member and reflected particular attitudes and beliefs.

Socialist leader and presidential candidate Eugene V. Debs, for example, refused to address racial inequality as an issue separate from the issue of class. Instead, he maintained that there was "no Negro question outside the labor question" and believed that the overthrow of the capitalist system would free both whites and blacks. Debs claimed that African Americans, as a group that suffered keenly from capitalism and the wage labor system, would reap great benefits from the work of the socialist party and the eventual overthrow of capitalism. As a result Debs recruited African Americans and refused to address segregated audiences.

Other members of the Socialist Party of America took a more active position on race; William English Walling and Mary White Ovington, for example, worked against racial inequality and helped found the National Association for the Advancement of Colored People in 1909. On the other hand, some members, such as Victor L. Berger and William Noyes, refused to address black audiences due to their belief that "negroes and mulattos constitute a lower race."

As a result of these divergent attitudes, state socialist parties varied greatly in the extent to which they challenged the economic, social, and political inequalities faced by blacks. Socialists in Louisiana actively recruited African Americans, but insisted on segregated chapters of the state party; Oklahoma socialists promoted black voting rights and economic equality but, like other socialist parties in the South and southwest, refused to support social equality for blacks for fear that it would promote miscegenation. In contrast, some Northern Socialist parties advocated complete equality for blacks and made concerted efforts toward those goals. The New York party, for example, nominated African American candidates such as A. Philip Randolph for municipal and state public offices. Regardless of state policies, however, the national Socialist Party of America remained conspicuously silent on the issue of race and did little to recruit black members at the national level.

Nevertheless, some African Americans did join the Socialist Party. George Washington Woodbey, a Baptist minister, was the first black to join; he later actively recruited other African Americans. Like Debs, Woodbey did not consider racial inequality to be an issue separate from class. Other African American socialists, however, criticized those in the party who marginalized the issue of race. Hubert H. Harrison, for example, chastised the Socialist Party of America for its failure to understand that blacks suffered more acutely than white workers the indignities of capitalism. Harrison argued against the party's ineffectual efforts to counter African American political disfranchisement and eventually formed his own party, the Liberty League of Negro-Americans.

Two of the most notable African American socialists were A. Philip Randolph and Chandler Owen. Randolph and Owen worked together to transgress racial boundaries in the labor force and in unions. Beginning in 1917 they published the *Messenger*, a radical magazine promoting desegregated labor unions. During the 1920s Randolph used the *Messenger* to denounce the Pullman company and its union and to issue support for the nascent Brotherhood of Sleeping Car Porters, an independent black union.

By this time, however, the Socialist Party of America had splintered into factions and lost political credibility, due in part to the party's split during World War I. Ironically, the party had just started to establish a consistent policy on race and had begun working to eradicate racial inequality. Apart from a short resurgence prior to World War II, American socialism all but disappeared after World War II and the McCarthy era, when cold-war politics prompted government intimidation and discrimination against socialists. The socialist organizations that do exist today, however, tend to be closely involved with antiracist and anti-imperialist politics.

Elizabeth Heath

See Also

World War I and African Americans; World War II and African Americans; Abolitionism in the United States; Civil War, American; Labor Unions in the United States; *Messenger, The*; Randolph, Asa Philip.

Cross Cultural

Sociedad Abolicionista Española

(Spanish Abolitionist Society; SAE), organization founded in 1865 with the objective of abolishing slavery in the Spanish colonies of Cuba and Puerto Rico. The SAE and Spanish abolitionism, while sharing characteristics of abolitionism elsewhere, were also specific to the history of Spain and its colonies. Indeed, Spanish abolitionism – the last European abolitionist movement – stands as one of the most remarkable and original movements of its type.

The slave trade was nominally abolished in Spain in 1817, but subsequently the Cuban and Puerto Rican slave economies boomed, fed by an illegal slave trade largely based in the United States. British diplomatic pressure to end the trade had limited effect in Cuba, though Puerto Rican slave imports virtually ended in the 1850s. During the United States Civil War the Union navy joined Britain in blockading the slave trade to Cuba, a trade that soon became extinct (*see* Transatlantic Slave Trade). However, slavery itself could have endured in the Spanish colonies far longer. Slavery had powerful defenders in Spain, including dynamic (and protectionist) bourgeois groups such as the Catalan textile industrialists.

The SAE sprang from the free-trade Sociedad Libre de Economía Política (Free Society of Political Economy). Julio Vizcarrondo, a Puerto Rican, was the driving force and perennial secretary of the SAE, which attracted rising liberals and radicals and Cuban and Puerto Rican reformers. All four of the future presidents of the Spanish Republic belonged to the SAE, as did leading figures in the Spanish Cortes (the national parliament) after 1868. Colonial slavery was the strategic nexus between economic protectionism, military government in the colonies, and oligarchic rule in Spain, and presented Spanish liberals and radicals with a powerful and concrete metaphor for limited freedom in Spain. Secret abolitionist societies were formed in Cuba and Puerto Rico, and their impetus made itself felt in the SAE through Vizcarrondo and the other Antillian members.

The SAE was banned from public activity in 1866 but returned with the September Revolution, which overthrew Queen Isabella II of Spain in 1868, and the start of Cuba's Ten Years' War, an unsuccessful war for independence from Spain. The organization engaged in petitioning, lobbying, poetry contests, parades, and public meetings that featured members of Madrid's small black community. The SAE also published a newspaper, *El Abolicionista* (issued thrice monthly from 1872 to 1873). These activities were combined with strategies akin to British abolitionism. In general the SAE appealed to humanitarian sentiment.

After 1868 abolition became a commonplace theme. Several SAE members were catapulted to the Spanish Cortes and the ministries. The SAE became very active in parliamentary politics, as well as in the press and among republican groupings throughout Spain. A special parliamentary commission was created to address slave emancipation. With SAE support projects for immediate abolition were presented, but only emancipation for newborn children and slaves over 60 was enacted.

Proslavery groups, too, were quick to mobilize. Beginning in 1871 they created Centros Hispano-Ultramarinos (Hispano-Overseas Centers) in Madrid and major port cities. In 1872 these forces launched the broader Liga Nacional contra las Reformas (National League Against Reforms) throughout Spain. Like the SAE, the Liga was active on the extraparliamentary front, especially through the press and in meetings.

Unlike those in the U.S. South, Spanish proslavery forces offered no moral defense of slavery but claimed instead that abolition entailed economic and political catastrophe. The religiosity, disciplinarian bent, and dourness of British abolitionism also contrasted with the libertarian and expressive strains of Spanish abolitionism and its numerous anticlerical republicans (Vizcarrondo, however, was a devout Protestant). Faced with an impervious Roman Catholic Church, Spanish abolitionism relied on poetry in theaters rather than on lectures in churches.

Between 1868 and 1872 the contending forces on both sides of the slavery issue gained unprecedented breadth and cohesion. Their major confrontation was over a proposal for immediate abolition in Puerto Rico, presented in December 1872. In Puerto Rico slavery had never been as important as it had been in Cuba, and the slave population in the former island was down to 7 percent: a total of 29,000 slaves as compared to Cuba's 350,000 (constituting 40 percent of the population). However, Puerto Rican emancipation was perceived on all sides as the threshold to Cuban emancipation. The controversy over Puerto Rican emancipation was perhaps the most representative episode of the abolition controversy in Spain; the political context allowed the SAE a margin of expression it would not have during the Restoration, which brought back the Spanish monarchy in 1876.

In mid-December 1872 the Liga provoked an unsuccessful military mutiny in Madrid and a small riot in a working-class neighborhood. They also forced the resignation of the colonial minister and demanded the abdication of Amadeus of Savoy, the invited monarch (who eventually did abdicate in February 1873). Immediately after the project for Puerto Rican abolition was filed, 300 of the most powerful rightist figures in Spain (including virtually all the Grandes de España) held an emergency meeting and agreed to support the Liga's opposition to the project.

In response, from December 1872 to January 1873 the SAE held public meetings in theaters and streets of Madrid, Barcelona, and Seville. Republican societies throughout Spain held parades, poured petitions on Madrid, and printed abolitionist manifestos, making slave abolition their paramount issue for the first time. In Madrid the SAE and its republican allies organized a street demonstration in January 1873 with more than 15,000 participants.

The Puerto Rican abolition law was finally enacted in March 1873, though with full compensation to the slaveholders and a three-year "apprenticeship" that continued to tie slaves to their masters – both of which the SAE had originally opposed. The Republic faltered through 1873 and collapsed in 1874; the SAE was again banned between 1875 and 1879. In the midst of the Restoration and the Cuban war, there was little discussion of further abolition. When Cuban emancipation was finally broached (1879), the SAE renewed its efforts. Abolition was decreed on the island in 1880, though an eight-year apprenticeship period was also introduced. The SAE criticized the law's harsh regulations and lobbied successfully for ending the apprenticeship period in 1886.

The SAE developed in a context in which the overseas slave trade was ending, but a vigorous plantation system fueled by slave labor was enmeshed in relatively advanced capitalist relations and sheltered by protectionist walls. From the start the SAE contended with slavery and the wider Spanish polity. Perhaps for this reason, Spanish abolitionism sparked a relatively broad-based movement.

Anarchists and Marxists, as well as separatists in Puerto Rico and (especially) Cuba, viewed SAE efforts as distractions from larger struggles. Yet the SAE weakened proslavery forces in the metropolis and deepened Spanish republicanism. The strength of the Spanish proslavery forces suggests that the demise of Spanish colonial slavery may have been "inevitable" only in the long run.

Spain demonstrates forcefully the interplay between colonial antislavery and metropolitan radicalism that C. L. R. James sketched for Saint-Domingue (present-day Haiti) and France in *The Black Jacobins* (1963). In Madrid from 1872 to 1873 as in Paris in 1791, the "aristocrats of the skin" suddenly exemplified all that was contemptuous about the metropolitan state.

Juan Giusti Cordero

See Also

Slavery in Latin America and the Caribbean; Civil War, American; James, Cyril Lionel Richard; Abolition and Emancipation in Latin America and the Caribbean; Catholic Church in Latin America and the Caribbean; Colonial Latin America and the Caribbean.

Europe

Société des Amis des Noirs, a French antislavery organization founded in 1788.

The Société des Amis des Noirs (Society of Friends of Blacks), founded during the French revolutionary era, condemned the institution of slavery (*see* Colonial Critics of Slavery). However, it reflected contradictions in Enlightenment thinking on France's plantation colonies and on the status of Africans and people of African descent.

A branch of the English Society for the Abolition of the Slave Trade, the French Société was founded by the publicist Jacques-Pierre Brissot in Paris in 1788. He became engaged in the antislavery movement following a trip to London, where he met some of England's leading abolitionists. The Société, which attracted more than 100 members, consisted mainly of aristocrats and professionals with moderate political views, including such notables as the Marquis de Lafayette, the Comte de Mirabeau, and Charles-Maurice de Talleyrand. The abolitionists depicted in vivid detail the devastating effects of the slave trade on African societies and sought to counter the negative images of Africans perpetuated by the slave traders. Yet some abolitionists retained the belief that Europeans were superior to Africans. One Société member, the academician Marquis de Condorcet, went so far as to argue that blacks, due to their longtime enslavement, could achieve equality with whites only through intermarriage.

The Société arose at a time when onerous racial policies aimed at blacks prevailed not only in the colonies but also in France. The French authorities feared that France's growing number of black slaves and freedpeople, inspired by egalitarian ideas, would return to the colonies and incite revolt. Thus in 1738 the French government established laws aimed at eradicating interracial marriage in France. By the late 1770s slaves and free blacks were forbidden entry into France, and authorities deported many resident slaves back to the colonies. According to scholar William B. Cohen, "racist fears of being 'contaminated' by blacks also played a role. For it was not just the entry of slaves but of any person of color that the metropolitan authorities opposed." Indeed, in 1789 even the Revolutionary Assemblies refused to grant equal rights, such as full citizenship, to people of color.

The Société's title reflects Enlightenment thinking on the subject of people of color. During the seventeenth and early eighteenth century, the French usually equated the term *nègre* with black slaves in the colonies. After Enlightenment thinkers such as the Baron de Montesquieu began to attack slavery and defend the slaves' humanity, "nègre" acquired a pejorative meaning and writers began to use the word "noir" to refer to blacks. Nonetheless, many French Enlightenment thinkers, such as Denis Diderot and Voltaire, had contradictory and ambiguous views on the institution of slavery; while they openly condemned it, they also recognized the importance of the plantation colonies to the French economy and their own personal and economic interests. As Cohen notes, "the abolitionists were usually practical men who were not willing to sacrifice national advantage to humanity." Instead of building a large and socially diverse membership, the Société focused on attracting members of the French elite, many of whom had a vested interest in maintaining slavery for economic reasons despite their condemnation of human bondage and their appeals to "the rights of man."

Moreover, some abolitionists believed that blacks had become too degraded and morally desensitized by slavery to be emancipated immediately. They thought that sudden emancipation would result in collective chaos and violence against the slave masters. Thus they promoted a gradual program of emancipation and compensation of the slave masters for their losses – an approach that reflected their lingering conception of slaves as "property." Indeed, Société member Abbé Grégoire considered the Revolutionary Assembly's 1794 decision to emancipate the slaves "a disastrous measure." Abolitionists also espoused the idea of supplanting the slave colonies with plantations based on free labor in West Africa. In this way, they believed, France would fulfill both its economic needs and human rights ideals – a viewpoint that helped to pave the way for European expansion into Africa.

The fact that the Société was a branch of an English organization raised questions in the minds of many about its loyalty to France. The Société called for an international agreement to abolish slavery, which French authorities reckoned would give the English a commercial and political advantage, since, it was thought, England was less dependent on slavery than France. Thus the Société hesitated to wage a full-scale attack on slavery and, as Cohen asserts, "was but a pale imitation of its British counterpart." As a consequence the slave trade reached a record high in the French colonies during the period from 1783 to 1791.

In 1791 a large-scale slave rebellion broke out in the French colony of Saint-Domingue (present-day HAITI) – a development that French authorities blamed on the abolitionist movement (*see* HAITIAN REVOLUTION). As the revolution became more repressive, many Société members were forced to flee France. Abolitionism lost favor among French intellectuals, who, stunned by the events in Saint-Domingue, began to reassess their views of people of African descent. Although Grégoire founded a new abolitionist society in 1796, abolitionism as a concerted movement did not resurface in France until the 1830s.

Roanne Edwards

SEE ALSO

Transatlantic Slave Trade; Abolitionism in the United States.

Africa

Soga (also known as Basoga and Lusoga), ethnic group of UGANDA.

The Soga primarily inhabit southeastern Uganda, just north of LAKE VICTORIA. They speak a Bantu language. Approximately 1.5 million people consider themselves Soga.

SEE ALSO

Bantu: Dispersion and Settlement.

Africa

Soglo, Nicéphore (b. 1934?, Togo), president of BENIN (1991-1996).

Born in Togo, Nicéphore Soglo received degrees in public and private law and in economics from the University of Paris and the Ecole Nationale d'Administration in Paris. After returning from France, he served as inspector of finance (1965-1967) in Benin (then called Dahomey) until appointed minister of finance and economic affairs by his cousin, Col. Christophe Soglo, after the latter overthrew President Sourou Apithy.

In 1972, in the wake of the coup by MATHIEU KÉRÉKOU, Soglo left Benin, serving first as a governor at the International Monetary Fund (IMF) and then as director for Africa at the International Bank for Reconstruction and Development (1979-1986). In February 1990 Soglo was appointed interim prime minister by delegates at a national conference responsible for implementing Benin's transition to civilian rule. In March 1991 Soglo defeated Kérékou in Benin's first multiparty elections in 20 years, drawing 67 percent of the vote.

Following a period of ill health and widespread rumors that exaggerated the extent of his illness and attributed it to witchcraft, Soglo began efforts to refurbish Benin's devastated economy. Harsh economic measures, including currency devaluation and the decision not to pay overdue salaries, inspired civil unrest and undermined Soglo's popular support. Soglo had entered office with the backing of a parliamentary alliance that constituted a majority, but by 1995 his opponents in parliament occupied 50 of 83 seats. In March 1996 presidential elections Soglo was defeated by former dictator Kérékou.

Soils, African. Please see GEOMORPHOLOGY, AFRICAN

Latin America and the Caribbean

Sojo, Juan Pablo
(b. December 25, 1908, Curiepe, VENEZUELA; d. October 8, 1948, Caracas, Venezuela), Afro-Venezuelan novelist, poet, journalist, scholar, dramatist, and musician.

Juan Pablo Sojo was one of the first intellectuals to study the African influences on contemporary Venezuelan culture and society. His father, Juan Pablo B. Sojo *el Viejo* (the Elder) (1865-1929), a distinguished musician, composer, dramatist, professor, and folklorist, was the first to teach him about African heritage in Venezuela and the Caribbean region. As a result of this early exposure, Sojo's interest was manifested in a wealth of scholarly articles about the diverse cultural manifestations of African people in Venezuela during colonial times as well as in a number of important literary texts.

Sojo's work ranges from a collection of his early articles, *Tierras del Estado de Miranda, sobre la ruta de los cacahuales* (1938, Lands of the State of Miranda, on the Path of the Cacao Plantations), to his critically acclaimed 1943 novel *Nochebuena Negra* (Black St. John's Eve). He also published a collection of interpretive essays on the role of Afro-Venezuelans in *mestizaje* (the cultural mixing characteristic of Latin America) titled *Temas y apuntes afro-venezolanos* (1943, Afro-Venezuelan Themes and Notes). His unpublished work includes poetry, *Cantos Negros* (Black Songs); short stories collected in *Zambo;* essays of *Los abuelos de color* (The Colored Grandparents); and three novels *La historia de un novelista* (The Story of a Novelist, finished in 1938), *La luz misteriosa* (The Mysterious Light), and *La tía Benedicta* (Aunt Benedicta). A more complete reading of his entire work is still necessary in order to make a definite assessment of Sojo's contribution to the black literature of Spanish America.

Sojo's anthropological, historical, and literary works attempted to rewrite the social history of Venezuela, especially in reference to the participation of the diverse ethnic groups, and within this context the protagonist role of the African. Sojo was strongly influenced by the legacies of the 1930s NÉGRITUDE and AFROCUBANISMO movements. The ideas of transculturation (which, unlike acculturation, implies a substantial retention of culture despite the pressure to assimilate), elaborated by Cuban ethnographer and cultural historian FERNANDO ORTIZ (1881-1969), as well as the *cultural mulatez* (mulatto culture) espoused by the Cuban poet NICOLÁS GUILLÉN (1902-1989), played central roles in Sojo's intellectual perspective. He applied these concepts and methodologies to the analysis of Venezuelan history and culture in his book *Temas y apuntes afro-venezolanos.*

Sojo's novel *Nochebuena Negra* was – along with *Juyungo* (1943), the novel by the Ecuadorian ADALBERTO ORTIZ (b. 1914) – one of the earliest black novels published in Spanish America. It has been praised because it perfectly combines the author's understanding of the problems faced by Afro-Venezuelans, his extraordinary linguistic knowledge of Venezuelan Spanish (strongly influenced by the diaspora's oral culture) (*see* INFLUENCE OF AFRICAN LANGUAGES AND CULTURES ON COLONIAL LANGUAGES IN LATIN AMERICA AND THE CARIBBEAN), and the use of popular myths and legends. All of these elements contribute to a work that literary critic Marvín Lewis said "demonstrates clearly an attempt to escape intolerable social and economical circumstances through the creation of Afro-Venezuelan spiritual and psychological alternatives."

Carlos L. Orihuela

SEE ALSO

Transculturation, Mestizaje, and the Cosmic Race: An Interpretation; Literature, Black, in Spanish America.

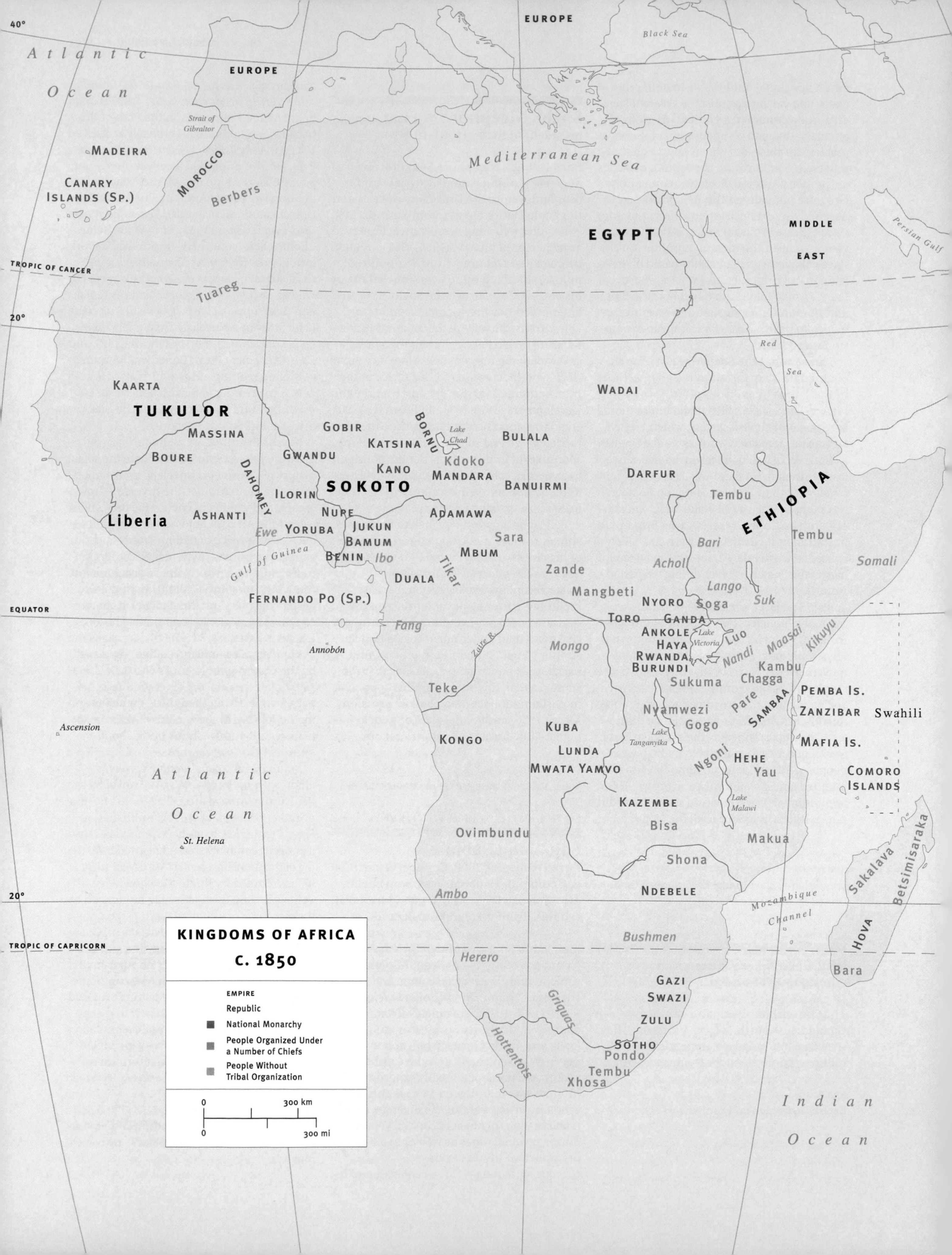

KINGDOMS OF AFRICA
C. 1850
EMPIRE
Republic
National Monarchy
People Organized Under a Number of Chiefs
People Without Tribal Organization
0
300 km
0
300 mi
40°
20°
EQUATOR
20°
TROPIC OF CANCER
TROPIC OF CAPRICORN
EUROPE
EUROPE
Black Sea
Atlantic Ocean
Strait of Gibraltor
Mediterranean Sea
MADEIRA
CANARY ISLANDS (SP.)
MOROCCO
Berbers
EGYPT
MIDDLE EAST
Persian Gulf
Tuareg
Red Sea
KAARTA
TUKULOR
MASSINA
BOURE
Liberia
ASHANTI
DAHOMEY
Ewe
GOBIR
GWANDU
KATSINA
KANO
SOKOTO
ILORIN
NUPE
YORUBA
JUKUN
BAMUM
BENIN
Ibo
Gulf of Guinea
BORNU
Lake Chad
Kdoko
MANDARA
ADAMAWA
Tikar
DUALA
FERNANDO PO (SP.)
Fang
Annobón
WADAI
BULALA
DARFUR
BANUIRMI
Sara
MBUM
Zande
Mangbeti
ETHIOPIA
Tembu
Tembu
Somali
Bari
Acholi
Lango
Suk
NYORO
Soga
TORO
GANDA
ANKOLE
Lake Victoria
Luo
HAYA
RWANDA
BURUNDI
Nandi
Maasai
Kikuyu
Kambu
Chagga
Sukuma
Mongo
Zaire R.
Teke
Nyamwezi
Pare
SAMBAA
PEMBA IS.
ZANZIBAR
Swahili
Gogo
Lake Tanganyika
KUBA
KONGO
LUNDA
MWATA YAMVO
Ngoni
HEHE
Yau
MAFIA IS.
COMORO ISLANDS
KAZEMBE
Bisa
Lake Malawi
Makua
Ascension
Atlantic Ocean
St. Helena
Ovimbundu
Shona
NDEBELE
Ambo
Mozambique Channel
Sakalava
Betsimisaraka
HOVA
Bara
Bushmen
Herero
GAZI
SWAZI
Griquas
ZULU
Hottentots
SOTHO
Pondo
Tembu
Xhosa
Indian Ocean

Africa

Sokoto Caliphate (1804-1903), an Islamic empire that united much of nineteenth-century Hausaland.

The Sokoto Caliphate conquered and united for the first time the HAUSA states of present-day northern NIGERIA, under the leadership of a mostly FULANI aristocracy. The empire also incorporated neighboring non-Hausa territories. The caliphate was the largest independent state in Africa during the nineteenth century.

Muslim Fulani pastoralists migrated into Hausaland as early as the twelfth century. They played an important part in spreading Islam to the Hausa, and over the centuries many Fulani took up settled life in the rich Hausa city-states as Islamic scholars. One such scholar, USMAN DAN FODIO of the Qadiriyya Sufi order, initiated a reform movement in Hausaland during the late eighteenth century. This movement promoted an ascetic and purist version of Islam and advocated a society based on the *Shari'a* (Islamic law). It united Hausa and Fulani communities of devout Muslims in a populist campaign to reform the wealthy Hausa states, which Usman's followers considered corrupt.

Usman's movement posed a growing threat to the existing Hausa elites. When the rulers of Gobir, Usman's home state, repressed the reform movement, Usman, following the model of the prophet Mohammed, fled Gobir and launched a *jihad* (holy war) in 1804 to overthrow the Hausa states. Usman made conquered territories emirates and placed them under the control of leaders acknowledging his authority. In 1808 Usman defeated the rulers of Gobir, renamed the city Sokoto, and made it the capital of an Islamic caliphate ruling over the subject emirates.

A ruling class composed chiefly of Fulani clan chiefs ruled over the emirates. They enjoyed a degree of autonomy but acknowledged the leadership of the caliph, or sheikh, in Sokoto, to whom they paid tribute. Sokoto engaged in periodic warfare against neighboring non-Muslim peoples, taking many captives to use as slaves, as well as against other Muslim kingdoms, such as Kanem-Bornu to the east. The Damagaram Kingdom, based at Zinder to the north, successfully resisted conquest by Sokoto until it fell to the French.

Under the rule of Sokoto, Hausaland prospered. The austere style of Sokoto's Islamic aristocrats enabled them to reduce the tax burden that supported conspicuous consumption by the preceding rulers of the Hausa states. At the same time the caliphate economically unified a vast and rich area, stretching from the NIGER RIVER nearly to LAKE CHAD. The creation of a large and secure economic unit facilitated a boom in trade and artisanal production. Hausa traders assumed a dominant position in much of West Africa, and Sokoto's cowrie shell currency was widely accepted beyond its boundaries. Around Sokoto and other cities slave villages produced much of the urban food supply; large numbers of slaves also worked as soldiers, porters, domestics, and concubines.

Unity under Sokoto also promoted a sense of Hausa nationhood among the caliphate's rich and powerful merchant class. Together with the Hausa merchants, a largely Fulani class of Islamic scholars enjoyed an authority that tempered the power of the emirate chiefs. The prominence of Islamic scholarship also encouraged an increase in literacy.

However, the caliphate's loose federal structure eventually undermined its strength. Sokoto experienced civil wars in the 1840s and 1850s and again in the 1890s. This disunity reduced the ability of the caliphate to withstand British imperialism at the turn of the twentieth century. Until 1900 the relationship between Europeans and the caliphate was tense but peaceful. Europeans were allowed to trade in the region but had no political power in the caliphate. In 1900, however, F. D. Lugard, a British colonial official, declared Northern Nigeria a British protectorate. His campaign of military conquest put an end to peaceful British attempts to establish informal political control over the caliphate. The British occupied Sokoto in 1903. The caliph attempted to flee but lost his life in a battle the same year that ended military resistance to British COLONIAL RULE.

Lugard inaugurated the classic British policy of indirect rule in the conquered caliphate when he appointed a new caliph, Attahiru II, in 1903. British rule retained the administrative organization of the caliphate and tolerated the practice of Islam throughout the colonial period. This helped to preserve many administrative elements of the caliphate, which remain an important part of NIGERIA's political structure down to the present day.

Esperanza Brizvela-Garcia

SEE ALSO

Lugard, Frederick John Dealtry; Pastoralism; Sufism; Zinder, Niger; Slavery in Africa.

Africa

Somali, a major ethnic group in the Horn of Africa.

The Somali are one of the largest ethnic groups in Africa; more than 8 million live in a territory that stretches north from northern KENYA to DJIBOUTI, and west from the Indian Ocean to the Ogaden in ETHIOPIA. They are often cited as one of the few ethnic groups that define a nation, though the country of SOMALIA contains some small pockets of other groups. They share the language of Somali and the Sunni Muslim religion.

Genealogy is of great importance among the Somali. Some histories based on early Arab sources and northern oral traditions trace the origins of the Somali to the region of the Red Sea. According to this history the Somali migrated during the tenth century into the OROMO-populated region and later moved farther south, into the Bantu-speaking area. Somali oral history traces descent from a single family, with the father Aquil Abuu Ta'alib begetting the two major lines of descent through his sons Sab and Samaale. Other historians have challenged the idea of the migration of a southern Arab people, arguing that Islamic identification has prompted a revision of ethnic history. These historians cite early documents that link contemporary Somali clans to earlier inhabitants. The six clans of present-day Somalia carry the following family lines: the Dir, Issaq, Darod, and Hawiye of the Samaale family, and the Digil and Rahanweyne (Digil-Mirifle) of the Sab family. Some of these clans claim relation to the Arab elite who settled along the coast, though such claims are also debated.

Kinship formed the basis of traditional political units in Somali society. The unit closest to the individual is the *diya*-paying group, a group within a clan that is responsible for paying and receiving diya, or blood compensation, for infractions of one group against another. The traditional Somali legal system integrated Islamic law with a type of verbal social contract known as *xeer* that set out obligations and rights. Councils of elders negotiate these contracts, which delineate such economic considerations as rights to water and pasture. This political system continued in the rural areas through the colonial period and even into the 1980s in the military regime of President MUHAMMAD SIAD BARRE, who attempted to use tribal leadership to secure his control of the rural areas. Following the onset of drought and civil war in the early 1990s, many of the organized political structures disintegrated.

Poetry plays an unusually important role in Somali society, serving as both a form of artistic expression and a political tool. Its highly stylized forms have been compared to Western legal rhetoric, and it is used in diplomatic situations to promote animosities as well as counsel peace.

Most rural Somali, such as the Samaale clans, practice nomadic PASTORALISM and migrate seasonally with their herds to grazing fields. The Digil and Rahanweyn clans, who live in the fertile region between the Jubba and Shabeelle rivers, combine livestock raising with agriculture. Others, such as the Hawiye in Mogadishu, historically have lived in coastal towns, where they have been influenced by the language and culture of Swahili traders. In the 1990s many rural Somali moved to Mogadishu and other cities, both to search for wage labor and to escape drought.

Marian Aguiar

SEE ALSO

Bantu: Dispersion and Settlement; Mogadishu, Somalia; Swahili Coast.

Africa

Somalia, country on the northeastern Horn of Africa, along the Red Sea coast.

Introduction

On the surface Somalia is perhaps the most homogenous country in Africa – most of its citizens share the same language, ethnic identity, religion, and culture. Yet it has never achieved lasting stability as a nation; since the early 1990s its civil war has been one of the most devastating in modern African history. Some scholars attribute this political instability to the Somali clan system, in which retaliation for offenses committed by members of rival clans can easily escalate into warfare. Others argue that Somalia's recent turmoil reflects efforts by the powerful elite to manipulate clan loyalties in the hope of increasing their own wealth. Still others contend that Somalia's homogeneity is in fact a myth that obscures long-standing tensions between nomadic groups and the descendants of Bantu-speaking slaves. Finally, some trace the roots of conflict to the colonial period, when access to power and pastoral resources – long regulated by Somalia's many widely dispersed clan leaders – came under the control of the centralized colonial (and then postcolonial) state.

Whatever the precise reasons for violence during and since the military dictatorship of Maj. Gen. Muhammad Siad Barre, the upheaval has clearly taken its toll. The collapse of the state in the early 1990s not only undermined Somalia's ability to cope with the immediate crisis of famine, it also left the country without the government structures needed to provide education, health care, and other basic social services for the general population.

Early History

Linguists trace Somali to the Cushitic language group. According to Arab historical sources, the ancestors of the Somali people migrated south from the shores of the Red Sea into the Cushitic-speaking Oromo regions beginning around the tenth century, with the Oromos later displacing Bantu speakers farther south. According to another source based in northern oral history, the Somali are a hybrid group originating in the marriages of two Arab patriarchs to local Dir women, the descendants of whom migrated from the Gulf of Aden toward northern Kenya in the tenth century. Some contemporary scholars, however, argue that the ancestors of the Somali came not from Arabia but from an area between southern Ethiopia and northern Kenya. The uncertainty stems in part from the history of the term *Somali,* the first known written appearance of which is in a fifteenth-century Ethiopian song.

It is known, however, that coastal settlements of non-Somali people existed well before the tenth century. The coastal culture was a hybrid one, incorporating the influences of the Egyptians, Phoenicians, Persians, Greeks, and Romans who came to trade and to tap frankincense and myrrh along the Gulf of Aden, and sometimes to settle. The market town of Zelia, or Seylac, on the coast of northern Somalia, dates back to the sixth century C.E. Merchants there traded goods from the African interior, such as hides, leopard and giraffe skins, ostrich feathers, ivory, rhinoceros horns, and slaves. Coffee was also brought from the Abyssinian highlands to supply the large local market. Zelia would later become the northern region's center of Islamic culture.

On the whole, however, both urban commerce and Islamic institutions were more highly developed in the south, where coastal towns came in contact with Swahili trading settlements and vessels sailing from the Indian subcontinent, China, and southwest Asia. By the ninth century Mogadishu was the most prosperous of these towns, due in part to exports of gold transported from Central Africa.

Between the eleventh and thirteenth century many Somali converted to Islam. Along the coast, generations of intermarriage created communities of Islamic Arab-Somali elite, who dominated trade and local politics in cities such as Mogadishu and Merka. During this period trade in livestock, leather, ivory, and slaves also strengthened ties between the south's coastal towns and its inland nomadic pastoralists. Such commercial linkages were relatively weak in the north. By the late thirteenth century the Arab-influenced Hawiye Somali clan, which had expanded from the Shebelle region toward the coast, assumed political leadership in the coastal region between Itala and Merka. A related clan, the Ajuran, established a sultanate in the fertile Shebelle basin, trading with the coastal cities.

The political unit that developed in the interior from the thirteenth century onward – and that forms a prototype for contemporary political structures – was the *diya*-paying group. In this system groups belonging to the same clan have a contractual alliance that joins them together in the payment and receipt of damages to or from another group. These groups were governed by the *Heer,* a type of social contract that incorporated elements of the *Shari'a,* or Islamic law, and common laws determined by consensus among the males of the community. In addition, Somali songs and poetry took on the social and political importance they retain today, preserving oral histories of the clan as well as expressing political ideas and military ambitions.

Beginning in the thirteenth century rulers of emirates based in Zelia and other coastal towns sought to extend their control over the interior's nomads, partly in an effort to strengthen their defenses against the powerful Christian Abyssinia (later Ethiopia) to the west. In the early fourteenth century skirmishes gave way to a large holy war as Haq al-Din, sultan of Ifat, seized the Christian territory that the dynasty held until his successor Sad al-Din was defeated in 1415. A century later the legendary Ahmed ibn Ibrahim al-Ghazi, "Ahmed the Left-Handed," solicited the help of the Ottomans to fight alongside his Somali troops and conquered a large portion of Abyssinia, establishing his capital at Harer. The Abyssinians, allied with the Portuguese – who had captured Zelia in 1516 – overthrew and killed Ahmed. Fighting between the Abyssinians and the Somali was interrupted in the 1570s, at least temporarily, by Oromo migration into the contested territory. The Turkish presence along the coast of the Horn, however, continued long after Ahmed's death. The Ottomans occupied Massawa and Arkikio in present-day Eritrea in 1557, and maintained claims along the coast well into the nineteenth century.

From the late fifteenth century until the early seventeenth century a series of migrations brought clans more or less into the regions they now occupy. The Rahanweyn, for example, migrated south to the Juba and Shebelle river basins, where they displaced the ruling Ajuran confederation. By the mid-seventeenth century the Rahanweyn clan had settled in the rich agricultural region and established its own confederations.

From the sixteenth century through the eighteenth century trade between the interior and the coast increased and clans struggled to establish control over caravan routes to the Benadir Coast. Eventually, the Somali clans were able to dislodge the Arab-dominated merchant oligarchies in the coastal towns, though in the early nineteenth century these towns fell under the nominal control of the Omani Sultanate, then based in Zanzibar.

One of the most important trades during this period was in slaves. The Indian Ocean slave trade was booming at this time, and many captives passed through port towns such as Bimal, Merka, Mogadishu, and Baraawe. Landholding Somali had long used slaves, since farming was considered a lowly occupation. Bantu-speaking slaves captured from the interior in present-day Tanzania and Malawi harvested grain and cotton along the Shabelle and Jubba rivers for the Digil and Rahanweyn clans. Oromo women and children were also captured for use as domestic slaves and concubines. During the nineteenth century some 50,000 agricultural slaves escaped into the wooded areas of the Shabeelle Valley, where they established permanent settlements; others settled in the Jubba Valley. After abolition in 1900 both these areas would become destinations for freed slaves.

Colonization

As the European powers' "scramble for Africa" gained momentum during the latter half of the nineteenth century, the strategic

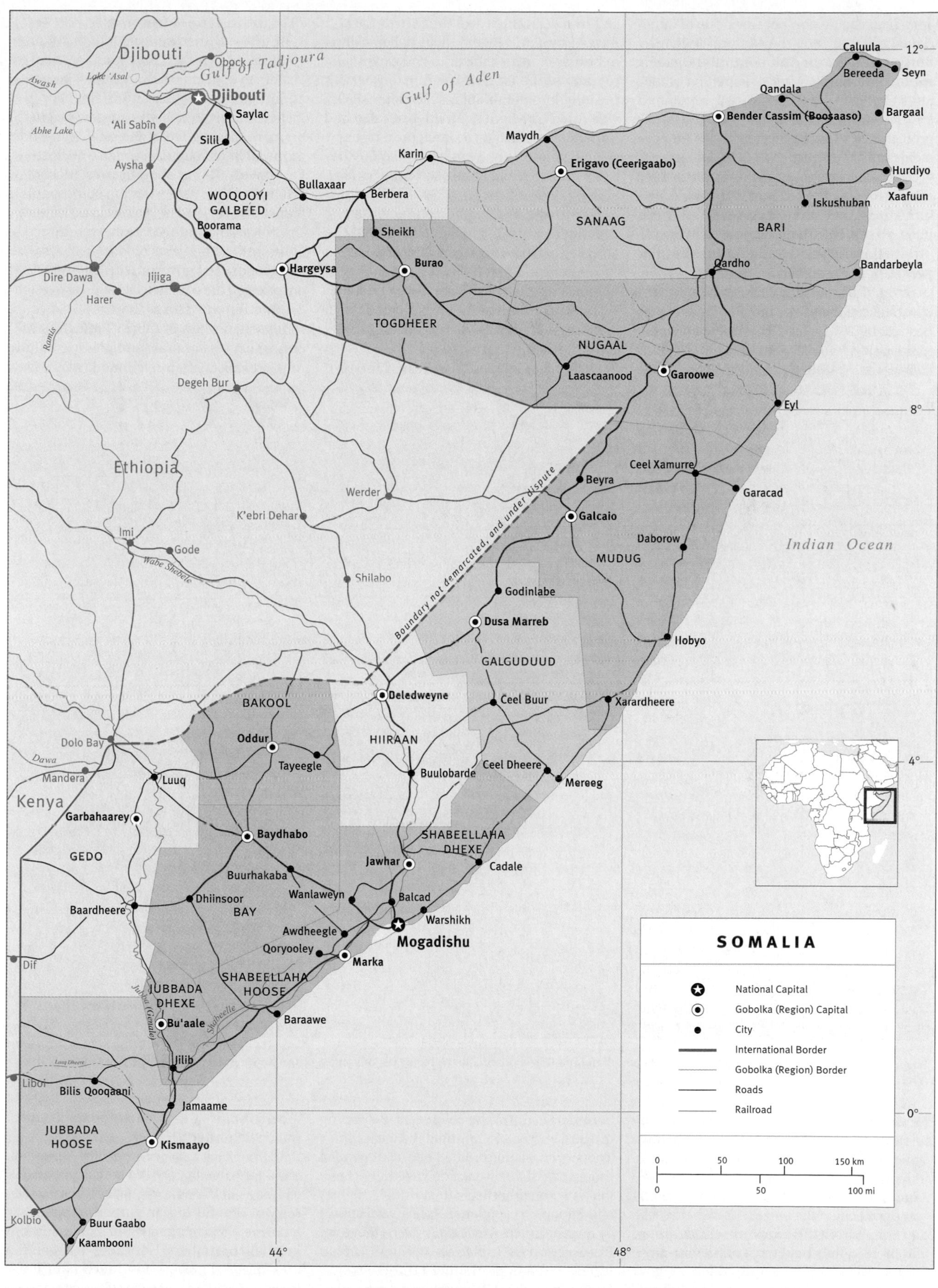
SOMALIA
National Capital
Gobolka (Region) Capital
City
International Border
Gobolka (Region) Border
Roads
Railroad
Djibouti
Gulf of Tadjoura
Gulf of Aden
Indian Ocean
Ethiopia
Kenya
Boundary not demarcated, and under dispute
WOQOOYI GALBEED
TOGDHEER
SANAAG
BARI
NUGAAL
MUDUG
GALGUDUUD
HIIRAAN
BAKOOL
GEDO
BAY
SHABEELLAHA DHEXE
SHABEELLAHA HOOSE
JUBBADA DHEXE
JUBBADA HOOSE
Mogadishu
Hargeysa
Berbera
Burao
Bender Cassim (Boosaaso)
Erigavo (Ceerigaabo)
Garoowe
Galcaio
Dusa Marreb
Deledweyne
Baydhabo
Kismaayo
Caluula
Seyn
Bargaal
Hurdiyo
Xaafuun
Eyl
Garacad
Hobyo
Xarardheere
Merca
Marka
Baraawe
Jilib
Jamaame
Buur Gaabo
Kaambooni
44°
48°
12°
8°
4°
0°
0 50 100 150 km
0 50 100 mi

Somali coastal region became a site of imperial contest. In 1855 the explorer Richard Burton led an expedition into the Ogaden region of Ethiopia. After the opening of the SUEZ CANAL in 1869, the British negotiated treaties with coastal clans to establish a protectorate over the coast in return for payments from the British Crown. GREAT BRITAIN was particularly interested in securing a meat supply for its base at Aden, which was in turn important to the defense of British-ruled India. To this end, they encouraged livestock production, as they would during the later period of colonial occupation.

EGYPT also asserted a claim to the northern coast, taking the towns of Zelia, Bulhar, and Berbera by 1874. France negotiated claims to the port of Obock, near the French colony of DJIBOUTI, in 1859. It became the home base for the Franco-Ethiopian trading company in 1881, and later served as a coal-fueling station for French ships traveling to Indochina. Italy, meanwhile, scrambled for the Horn of Africa's leftovers. In 1870 an Italian shipping company bought the port of Assab in present-day Eritrea from the local AFAR ethnic group, and by 1885 Italy held most of present-day Eritrea. In 1889 Italy acquired lease rights to the southern Benadir Coast, including Mogadishu, as a result of treaties with the sultan of ZANZIBAR and the British East Africa Company. By the 1890s Italian claims in both the north and south had expanded to parts of the interior, leading to war with the kingdom of Ethiopia, which after 1889 was ruled by MENILEK II. Ethiopia also had imperial claims to territory in present-day Somalia and Eritrea, but an 1898 treaty between Ethiopia and Italy secured the border, at least temporarily.

By the end of the nineteenth century years of treaty making had partitioned the Somali homeland into the British Somaliland Protectorate, French Somaliland, Italian Somalia, northern KENYA, and the Ogaden in Ethiopia. These divisions traversed traditional clan boundaries and disrupted centuries-old seasonal migrations.

Early Somali resistance crossed the boundaries drawn by colonizers. Beginning in 1899 Sayyid Mohammad A. Hasan, the leader of an Islamic brotherhood, commanded thousands of followers, known as dervishes, in a sustained battle against British, Italian, and Ethiopian occupation. Heavy retaliation by imperial forces – including several thousand British regulars, Indian units, King's African Rifles, AFRIKANER mounted troops, and Somali irregulars – brought heavy casualties. The British defeated Sayyid Mohammad in 1920 with a series of air raids.

Both the British and the Italian colonial governments relied on Somali regional leaders to collect taxes and Somali judges to administer customary and Islamic law. In Italian Somalia the colonial economy centered on plantation agriculture, producing export crops such as bananas, sugar, and cotton. Faced with a labor shortage – relatively few Italian farmers settled in the colony, and Somali nomads had no interest in agriculture – the colonial administration used forced labor from settlements of former slaves. The British colonial government, meanwhile, encouraged the commercialization of livestock production. It was a policy that, according to historian Mark Bradbury, "affected the entire social, economic and political culture of pastoralists, their livelihood, security of food supplies and their relationship with the environment."

Two boys study the Koran from a printed text. Behind them are Koran boards, on which *suras*, or verses, of the Koran are written for the teaching of children. *CORBIS/Kevin Fleming*

In the 1930s Italy, then ruled by Mussolini, recruited more than 40,000 Somali to pursue its claims in Ethiopia, particularly the Ogaden region. The Ethiopian emperor HAILE SELASSIE I also recruited Somali nomads, but in smaller numbers. Hostilities between the two imperial powers continued after Italy took the Ogaden, and were still ongoing when Italy entered World War II in 1940. That year

Somali troops helped Italy take the British Somaliland Protectorate, but seven months later the Allied army retook both Somalia and the Ogaden. For the next ten years Great Britain held all Somali areas except French Somaliland. This period of unity, in a region that had originally been under the control of separate groups and then divided under different imperial rulers, helped create a pan-Somali identity that would become stronger during the independence struggle.

Independence

By the end of World War II the rapidly growing Somali coastal cities had become centers of labor organizing, as well as home to an emerging anticolonial movement. War veterans were prominent in early political organizations, as were Somali civil servants. The Somali Youth League (SYL), founded in 1943 in Mogadishu, called for the unification of all Somali territories and opposed the return of any form of Italian rule in Somalia. In 1950 the United Nations (UN) did, in fact, grant Italy trusteeship over Somalia, but only under close supervision and on the condition – first proposed by the SYL and other Somali political organizations – that Somalia achieve independence within ten years.

Great Britain, meanwhile, had begun withdrawing from some of its Horn territories. It ceded the Ogaden region to Ethiopia in 1948, and after a gradual withdrawal culminating in a 1954 treaty, it relinquished the adjacent Haud region. Both areas were home to grazing lands frequented annually by more than 300,000 nomadic Somali pastoralists, who strongly opposed the transfer. Although they were still allowed some seasonal access, the nomads viewed the treaty as a betrayal; it became a rallying point for anti-British sentiment and a pan-Somali movement that lasted well after independence.

In a negotiated settlement in 1960, the British Somaliland Protectorate and Italian Somalia were united to form the independent Somali Republic. The southern-based SYL dominated the parliament, and its leader, Abdirashid Ali Sharmarke, became the first prime minister; Aadan Abdulle Osmaan Daar, of the northern Somali National League, was elected president. Both leaders served until 1964. Afterward, the SYL controlled the parliament entirely, creating some tensions between political parties in the north and south, both of which had fought for independence.

During the 1960s and 1970s the SYL-dominated government expanded and grew increasingly centralized. Government economic policy focused on developing the country's fisheries and its manufacturing, mining, and oil-refining industries, but most Somali remained in rural areas, and more than half the population continued to practice nomadic pastoralism.

Somalia's economic growth during the 1960s and 1970s was undermined by heavy spending in an ongoing campaign to reunite the Somali homeland. The five points of the Somali flag symbolized the territory's colonial-era division into five parts; the Somali republic sought to retrieve the missing pieces – Ethiopia's Ogaden and a portion of northern Kenya. As Kenya neared independence, the Somali government provided support for Somali guerrilla campaigns in Kenya's Northern Frontier District as well as in the Ogaden, and fought a brief, inconclusive war against Ethiopia in 1964.

Hopes of greater unity between the north and south were raised when Sharmarke, a southerner, became president in 1967 and appointed as his prime minister Mohamed Ibrahim Egal, a northerner. Egal attempted to move the country away from the goal of reclaiming Somali-occupied territories. Some saw this as a betrayal of the pan-Somali dream that had propelled the nationalist struggle; others, particularly outside the country, saw his regime as one that would bring peace to the Horn. But these hopes were dashed with the military-sponsored assassination of Sharmarke in October 1969. Six days later the army seized power, disbanded the National Assembly, and suspended the constitution. It placed Maj. Gen. Muhammad Siad Barre at the head of the Supreme Revolutionary Council (SRC). Siad Barre's main support outside of the military came from urban intellectuals and technocrats, who wished to diminish the power of clan identification and establish Somalia as a modern nation.

A proponent of scientific socialism, Siad Barre nationalized manufacturing and agricultural trade, accelerated infrastructure development, and built an oil refinery in Mogadishu. The government went deeply into debt as a result of this spending, which coincided with a decline in agricultural production. When a 1974-1975 drought destroyed approximately 30 percent of Somalia's livestock, many Somali were faced with famine. In 1984 the Somali economy went into a tailspin after Saudi Arabia, Somalia's major trade partner, banned the importation of meat because of an alleged outbreak of rinderpest.

Yet even as Somalia became increasingly dependent on international food aid, the Siad Barre regime stepped up military spending, which by the early 1980s consumed approximately three-quarters of the national budget. Although the government granted the Soviet Union (now Russia) rights to naval and air installments in return for military aid, it also acquired weapons from China, the Middle East, and the United States and other Western powers. These military resources were used in 1977 in another war against Ethiopia, which resulted in Somalia taking the Ogaden. A year later the Soviet Union switched sides, transferring more than two billion dollars' worth of arms to Ethiopia. The United States, under President Jimmy Carter, initially offered aid, but soon withdrew the offer, and Somalia lost the territory.

Siad Barre continued to receive international aid, however, claiming the burden of 1.5 million refugees fleeing the Ethiopian-ruled Ogaden. Western relief organizations provided large amounts of food aid, which some claim was consistently stolen to be used or resold by Siad Barre's military. The refugee camps, which disrupted the traditional economy by attracting nomads who historically had sought sustenance from the land, were filled with both disease and bureaucratic corruption. Italy and the United States continued other types of aid to Siad Barre. Italy poured more than a billion dollars into large infrastructure development projects in its former colony, and showed support of Siad Barre by publicly congratulating the dictator on his victory in a 1987 reelection in which he was the only legal candidate. Later, under United States presidents Ronald Reagan and George Bush, Siad Barre received more than $100 million a year in military and economic aid, becoming the third-largest recipient of U.S. foreign aid at the time.

Increasingly, Siad Barre used this money and his military to quash real or suspected internal dissent. Although Siad Barre came to power with the avowed mission to stamp out tribalism, he in fact manipulated clan loyalties and antagonisms to secure his own power. He also targeted whole clans in reprisals for the actions of clan members against his regime. In 1978, after an attempted coup organized by members of the Majeerteen clan, Siad Barre sent soldiers on a scorched-earth mission aimed at the clan's grazing land and reservoirs, which were crucial to both human and livestock survival. Between May and June 1979 more than 2000 people died of thirst and sun exposure; many livestock were lost as well. Siad Barre also sponsored an urban terrorist militia, commonly called the Victory Pioneers, which systematically raped women associated with the clan.

Later challenges to Siad Barre's power met with similarly severe reprisals. The Somali National Movement (SNM) was organized in London in 1980 by intellectuals, businessmen, and religious leaders, most of whom belonged to the Isaaq clan. This clan, which had constituted a majority in the north under Great Britain and later held key political positions in the post-independence civilian governments, also played an important part in the lucrative livestock and *qaat* trades. By the 1980s the clan faced trade restrictions and feared genocide by the military government. After the SNM soldiers took the northern cities of Burco and Hargeisa in 1988, Siad Barre's soldiers retaliated against the Isaaq population, killing more than 5000 Isaaqs in eight months. Other rebel militias formed in Ethiopia, as well as in the northern and southern regions of Somalia. Several clandestine militias operated from different regions: the SNM, in the northwest; the United Somali Congress (USC), in the south, and the Somali Salvation Democratic Front, operating out of Ethiopia. The latter group, organized in

1988 by Rome-based exiles of the large southern-based Hawiye clan, would ultimately overthrow Siad Barre. The price, however, was high: bodies of executed Hawiye lay in Somalia's riverbeds and in half-covered mass graves.

In Mogadishu demonstrators protested the government's use of censorship and other repressive measures, as well as its mismanagement of the economy. In 1989, following the assassination of a Roman Catholic bishop and the subsequent arrest of religious leaders, riots broke out and mass arrests followed. The Manifesto Group, comprising more than 100 prominent citizens, published an open letter of condemnation that called for the government to begin discussion with opposition groups. The arrest of 45 of those who signed the letter led to internal riots and international criticism. Under pressure, Siad Barre agreed to their release, and later to a multiparty system and a new constitution. These reforms came too late. Forces of the USC, backed by other organizations, drove the dictator out of Mogadishu in January 1991.

As faction leaders played on clan rivalries, the resulting power vacuum gave way to civil war. The USC's interim president, Ali Mahdi Mohamed, was opposed first by other factions and then by the USC's own Gen. Mohammad Farrah Aidid; the resulting war in Mogadishu left more than 30,000 dead and effectively destroyed the central state. That same year the northern-based SNM, led by the Isaaq clan, declared an independent Republic of Somaliland in the former British protectorate and set up a new government, disbanding all existing militias and beginning negotiations among clans. This state has yet to be recognized by the UN community.

The war's disruption of farming and food marketing, combined with ongoing drought, plunged southern Somalia into severe famine. Battles over the allocation of relief aid led, after considerable debate, to the UN's Operation Restore Hope. For the intervention the United States authorized 30,000 troops, the first of whom arrived in 1992. Although the mission's stated purpose was to support humanitarian relief operations, it was widely criticized for coming too late, and for legitimating the "warlords" by negotiating with them. The UN expanded its operations in 1993, bringing in "peacekeeping" forces from 27 countries. Violence continued in Mogadishu, however, and clashes between UN troops and various Somali factions led to the deaths of an estimated 6000 Somali and 83 UN soldiers. After media coverage of dead U.S. soldiers being dragged through the streets of Mogadishu outraged the American public, the United States withdrew in March 1994. Pakistani forces took over the leadership of the UN mission, which finally retreated in March 1995.

In 1996 Gen. Aidid was killed and replaced by his son Hussein Mohammed – a former U.S. marine – whose clan controls one section of Mogadishu. In 1996 the flooding of the Jubba River destroyed the crops of more than 20,000 families and ushered in another wave of famine; the shortages hit particularly hard because few international aid organizations were operating out of Somalia. Ironically, the private sector has flourished amid the chaos, offering formerly government-provided services such as health care, telephone connections, and education at premium prices. As of mid-1999 Somalia still lacked a functioning government, though several regional powers have proposed holding peace talks for national reconciliation.

Marian Aguiar

See Also

African Socialism; Egypt; Bantu: Dispersion and Settlement; Explorers in Africa Since 1800; Gold Trade; Ivory Trade; Law in Africa: Colonial and Contemporary; Languages, African: An Overview; Massawa, Eritrea; Mogadishu, Somalia; United Nations in Africa; Nationalism in Africa; Portugal; Swahili People; Burton, Sir Richard.

Africa

Somalia (Ready Reference)

Official Name: Somalia
Area: 637,657 sq km (246,200 sq mi)
Location: Eastern Africa; borders the Gulf of Aden, the Indian Ocean, Kenya, Ethiopia, and Djibouti
Capital: Mogadishu (population 700,000 [1985 estimate])
Other Major Cities: Hargeysa, Kismayu, and Marka
Population: 6,841,695 (July 1998 estimate)
Population Density: 15 persons per sq km (39 persons per sq mi)
Population Below Age 15: 44 percent (male 1,512,014; female 1,511,858 [1998 estimate])
Population Growth Rate: 4.43 percent (1998 estimate)
Total Fertility Rate: 7.01 children born per woman (1998 estimate)
Life Expectancy at Birth: Total population: 46.2 years (male 44.6 years; female 47.8 years [1998 estimate])
Infant Mortality Rate: 125.8 deaths per 1000 live births (1998 estimate)
Literacy Rate (age 15 and over who can read and write): Total population: 24 percent (male 36 percent; female 14 percent [1990 estimate])
Education: Before Somalia's government collapsed in 1991, education was free and compulsory for children between ages 6 and 14. As a result of Somalia's civil war, most schools have closed, including the Somali National University (1954-1991) in Mogadishu. In 1993 a primary school opened in Mogadishu; the only other primary schools are being operated by fundamentalist Islamic groups.
Languages: Somali is the official language. Arabic, Italian, and English are also spoken.
Ethnic Groups: Most of the population consists of Somali, a Cushitic people. A small minority of Bantu-speaking people live in the southern part of the country. Other minority groups include Arabs, Indians, Italians, and Pakistanis.
Religion: Sunni Muslim
Climate: The climate of Somalia ranges from tropical to subtropical and from arid to semi-arid. Temperatures usually average 28° C (82° F), but may be as low as 0° C (32° F) in the mountain areas and as high as 47° C (116° F) along the coast. The monsoon winds bring a dry season from September to December and a rainy season from March to May. The average annual rainfall is only about 280 mm (11 in).
Land, Plants, and Animals: Somalia has a long coastline, but it has few natural harbors. A sandy coastal plain borders on the Gulf of Aden in the north, and a series of mountain ranges dominates the northern part of the country. To the south the interior consists of a rugged plateau. In the south a wide coastal plain, which has many sand dunes, borders on the Indian Ocean. The country's two major rivers are found on the southern plateau, the Genale (Jubba) in the southern part and the Shabeelle in the south central section.

Vegetation in Somalia consists chiefly of coarse grass and stunted thorn and acacia trees, but flora producing frankincense and myrrh are indigenous to the mountain slopes. In the south eucalyptus, euphorbia, and mahogany trees are found. Wildlife includes crocodiles, elephants, giraffes, leopards, lions, zebras, and many poisonous snakes.
Natural Resources: Livestock, agricultural crops, petroleum, copper, manganese, iron, gypsum, marble, salt, tin, and uranium
Currency: The Somali shilling
Gross Domestic Product (GDP): $8 billion (1996 estimate)
GDP per Capita: $600 (1996 estimate)
GDP Real Growth Rate: 4 percent (1996 estimate)
Primary Economic Activities: Until the civil war intensified, the economy of Somalia was based primarily on livestock raising and small-scale commerce. Crop farming was of importance only in the south.
Primary Crops: Maize, sorghum, bananas, sugar cane, cassava, and mangoes
Industries: Some small industries, including sugar refining, textiles, and petroleum refining
Primary Exports: Bananas, live animals, fish, hides
Primary Imports: Petroleum products, foodstuffs, and construction materials
Primary Trade Partners: Saudi Arabia, Germany, Italy, United States, Kenya, United Kingdom, and other gulf states
Government: Somalia has been in a state of civil war with no clear central governmental authority since the January 1991 ouster of President Muhammad Siad Barre.

Marian Aguiar

See Also
Bantu: Dispersion and Settlement; Crocodile; Elephant; Giraffe; Indian Communities in Africa; Lion; Mogadishu, Somalia; Zebra.

Africa

Somba (also known as Bataba and Temberma), ethnic group of West Africa.

The Somba primarily inhabit northwestern Benin and northern Togo. They speak a Niger-Congo language. Approximately 300,000 people consider themselves Somba.

See Also
Languages, African: An Overview.

Latin America and the Caribbean

Son, an Afro-Cuban dance music that became a defining element in the Cuban national consciousness and served as the foundation for much twentieth-century Latin American popular music, including mambo and salsa music.

The *son* is a strongly syncopated style of Cuban dance music that coalesced in the early twentieth century. The term *son* refers both to the dance and to the music that accompanies it. A distinctly Afro-Cuban musical style, *son* is closely tied to the creation of a Cuban cultural and national identity during a period in which the island was economically and politically dominated by the United States (*see* Cuba).

The first *sones* appeared near the end of the twentieth century, not long after the 1886 abolition of slavery in Cuba. The new music first emerged in the rural province of Oriente in eastern Cuba, where the African influence was particularly strong. *Son* is a product of the musical heritages of Cuba's black and white forebears, but it was mainly developed by poor and working-class Cubans who were either black or of mixed racial backgrounds. *Son* combined African percussion and rhythmic patterns (especially those of Bantu origins) with Spanish stringed instruments and lyrical styles (*see* Décima).

As musicologist John Storm Roberts pointed out, scholars regard the *clave* beat, the basic rhythm of *son* (and other forms of Cuban music), as "the first rhythm *invented* by Cubans." The clave beat is named for the claves, two hand-held hardwood cylinders, approximately 12 to 18 cm (5 to 7 in) long. The musician plays the claves by cupping one in one hand and striking it with the other clave, producing a high-pitched, resonant sound. Typically, the claves player sets the clave beat. It is played in common time, with four beats to the measure, and involves a two-measure repeating rhythm. In the first measure the musician strikes the claves on the first downbeat, on the second upbeat, and on the fourth downbeat. In the second measure the rhythm is played on the second and third downbeats. The result is a loping, off-balance beat that defies American rhythmic conventions, which emphasize the downbeats, accenting either one and three, or two and four, in a four-beat measure.

The *son*, with its three-two clave – which in some songs is reversed to produce a two-three clave – eventually became the key musical form in Cuba and throughout the Spanish-speaking Caribbean and beyond. Indeed, its musical descendants – popularized as the modern rumba, the mambo, and salsa music – also shaped the musical culture of the United States and Europe.

Son began as vocal music, with lyrics that addressed a wide range of topics. The most influential lyrical traditions were the décima and *punto guajiro*, two popular Spanish poetic forms in which improvisation plays a major role. Ethnomusicologist Peter Manuel observed that often *soneros'* "song texts were rooted in Afro-Cuban street life." For example, the lyrics of perhaps the most famous *son*, Moises Simons's "El manisero," (The Peanut Vendor), evoke the flavor of the streets of Havana by invoking the cries of a peanut seller: "Peanuts, peanuts, peanuts, peanuts, / Little maid, don't go to sleep, / Without eating a little bunch of my peanuts." Other popular topics for *sones* are love, nostalgia for the past, patriotic themes, or social and political issues.

At first *soneros* were individual musicians, mostly from the rural eastern portion of the country. They were in some ways analogous to rural blues musicians of the southern United States, singing to the accompaniment of their own guitar, playing in the rural eastern portion of the country. Apart from the guitar, soneros often played two other Spanish-derived stringed instruments, the *tres*, a six-stringed instrument with three sets of doubled strings, and the *laúd* (*see* Creolized Musical Instruments of the Caribbean).

In the early twentieth century Cuban musicians began to organize *son* groups – larger ensembles that included a *marímbula* (derived from the African thumb piano and later replaced by the double bass) and percussion instruments, in particular the *güiro* (gourd), bongos, maracas, and claves. From the outset soneros emphasized improvisation in their playing, and when urban musical styles, such as the popular late nineteenth-century *danzón*, made their appearance in rural areas, soneros incorporated them into their repertoire.

The rise of *son* groups, particularly those with multiple vocalists, permitted greater complexity in the *montuno* call-and-response patterns. During the early 1920s, when the style appeared in Havana, *son* groups added one or two trumpets to create the ensemble styles known as *septeto* and *conjunto*, exemplified by the legendary Ignacio Piñeiro's Septeto Nacional, the Conjunto Casino, and, above all, Arsenio Rodríguez's pathbreaking conjunto. The styles of trumpet playing common in these groups can still be heard in the performances of Afro-Cuban trumpeter Alfredo "Chocolate" Armenteros.

As Manuel noted, *son* helped create a sense of Cuban national identity, serving to "unite the entire population – white, black, and mulatto." *Son*, which Cuban musicologist Ordilio Urfé considered the most perfect synthesis of the Caribbean's Afro-Hispanic heritage, provided a poetic meter for many Cuban poets. During the early 1930s Nicolás Guillén used the *son*'s syncopated rhythms in his poetry, for example, in his collections *Motivos de Son* (1930) and *Sóngoro Cosongo* (1931). The *son* was more than Cuba's leading dance music; it came to be seen as an intrinsic part of what it was to be Cuban.

For many years Cubans of the middle and upper classes remained aloof from the music – in particular, because of its association with lower-class black life. Yet despite its lower-class origins, *son* grew increasingly popular. As middle-class Cubans embraced *son* as a distinctive national music, it became less spontaneous and more formalized. It also attracted the attention of well-established composers of popular and classical music, such as Moises Simons, whose "El manisero" became a huge hit in the United States, Ernesto Lecuona, and Amadeo Roldán.

Son retained its musical significance through subsequent decades. Beyond Cuba and Latin America, it had a direct impact on American popular music. In the United States the popularity of Latin music coincided with a series of dance crazes – the rumba in the 1930s, the mambo in the 1940s, and the chachachá in the 1950s (*see* Afro-Latino Cultures in the United States). In *The Latin Tinge*, Roberts noted that most of the songs that Americans labeled rumbas during the rumba craze were actually *sones*. Mambos were also generally based on up-tempo versions of the *son* – or the *guaracha*, another Cuban dance genre. Likewise, since the 1960s a majority of the pieces identified as salsa music have been *sones* in form.

American music also effected changes in the *son*. Prior to the Cuban Revolution the political dominance of the United States in the Caribbean basin encouraged this process of cross-fertilization. When *son* – and its descendants rumba and mambo – intersected with American jazz, one result was the appearance of large Latin music bands – including those of Xavier Cugat, Dámaso Pérez Prado, Machito, and Tito Puente – which combined the trumpet, trombone, and saxophone sections of American swing-era big bands with Afro-Cuban rhythms and repertoire. More significant, the Cuban-American musical synthesis produced a new style or genre, Afro-Latin jazz.

Bandleaders such as Benny Moré of Cuba; Puente of Puerto Rico; Pérez Prado, a Cuban who settled in Mexico City; and the Cuban expatriate Machito in New York City helped popularize the new genre. From the 1930s to the 1990s Cuban jazz musicians – including MARIO BAUZA, Chico O'Farrill, Israel "Cachao" López, Armenteros, Rubén González, and Chucho Valdés – have repeatedly turned to the traditional *son* as the foundation for further musical innovations.

James Clyde Sellman

SEE ALSO

Bantu: Dispersion and Settlement; Blues, The; New York, New York; López, Israel ("Cachao"); Armenteros, Alfredo "Chocolate; Mambo; Moré, Beny; Puente, Ernesto Antonio (Tito); Valdés, Jesús (Chucho); Abolition and Emancipation in Latin America and the Caribbean; Havana, Cuba; Music, Classical, in Latin America and the Caribbean.

Africa

Songhai Empire, West African empire.

As early as the seventh century C.E., a polity known as Songhai existed in the area of the great northward bend of the NIGER RIVER. In the thirteenth century it was part of the empire of ancient Mali, but in 1335 the Songhai people broke away from Mali and began to conquer the surrounding area with a well-trained army and cavalry. Like that of the empires before it, the wealth of Songhai came largely from the Saharan trade in salt and gold, mostly through the great trading cities of Gao, Djenné, and Tombouctou.

In the late fifteenth century the empire was led by SUNNI ALI (1462-1492), a military commander who defeated armies of the MOSSI to the south and the TUAREG to the north. Soon after the death of Sunni Ali control of the empire was taken by Muhammad I Askia, who was from a Mande-speaking family. The new rulers, whose ancestors had governed ancient Mali, were Muslims who opposed the pagan Songhai rulers. Under Muhammad I Askia, the Songhai Empire reached its greatest expanse. It stretched from the borders of Kanem-Bornu and the Hausa states in the east to the upper Senegal River in the west and included the salt-mining area of Teghaza in the desert to the north. The capital was Gao, a town in modern Mali that still contains part of the mosque where Muhammad I Askia was buried in 1538.

Late in the sixteenth century the empire began to decline because its area was too large to control effectively. Other states began to compete for the rich Saharan trade. Around 1585 Songhai was attacked by an army from MOROCCO, which captured the salt-mining areas of Teghaza and Taodeni and defeated the Songhai at the Battle of Tondibi. The Songhai rulers retreated southward to the region of Dendi on the Niger, to the northwest of the present border of NIGERIA. There they continued to rule over their own people, although their economic and military power in the SUDAN was broken.

Meanwhile the Moroccans could not control the many different peoples of the Sudan and the desert, and in the seventeenth century a number of smaller states took the place of the empire. But none of them was powerful enough to bring peace and prosperity to the Sudan region.

Today there are still several hundreds of thousands of Songhai who claim descent from the people of the historic empire. They are mainly farmers and fishermen who live along the north bend of the Niger in Mali.

SEE ALSO

Gold Trade; Djenné-Djeno, Mali; Sahara Desert; Salt Trade; Askia Muhammad; Tombouctou, Mali; Mali Empire; Songhai People.

Africa

Songhai People (also known as Songhay, Songhoi, Songrai, Sonhrai, and Sonhray), ethnic group of West Africa.

The Songhai primarily inhabit southeastern MALI, along the bend of the NIGER RIVER, and western NIGER. Others live in BENIN, BURKINA FASO, and NIGERIA. Some have migrated to GHANA, where they are known as the Zabrama or Gao, as well as to Togo and CÔTE D'IVOIRE. They speak a unique Nilo-Saharan language, also called Songhai. The ancestors of the Songhai established a kingdom on the Niger bend as early as the seventh century C.E. Its ruling dynasty would last until 1492. The Songhai trace descent patrilineally, or along the father's line. Traditionally, they inherited a distinct position as noble, griot (professional bard) (*see* MUSIC, AFRICAN), commoner, or slave.

Today the Songhai are mostly subsistence farmers. They grow rice along riverbanks, as well as MILLET, sorghum, peanuts, black-eyed peas, sorrel, and other crops. Many Songhai also live in cities such as Tombouctou (Timbuktu), Niamey, and Bamako, where they engage in a wide range of trades and professions. Paramount chiefs from noble lines hold office and continue to exert at least symbolic authority in rural regions. The Songhai include a number of regional subgroups, including the Fono, the Gabibi, the Gow, the Kado, the Kortey, the Sorko, and the ZERMA (also known as the Djerma or Zaberma). More than 2 million people consider themselves Songhai.

Ari Nave

SEE ALSO

Bamako, Mali; Languages, African: An Overview; Niamey, Niger; Tombouctou, Mali.

Songhay Empire. Please see SONGHAI EMPIRE

Africa

Songye (also known as Songe), ethnic group of the DEMOCRATIC REPUBLIC OF THE CONGO.

The Songye primarily inhabit the Kasai-Oriental region of the Democratic Republic of the Congo. They speak a Bantu language and are closely related to the LUBA people. Approximately 1 million people consider themselves Songye.

SEE ALSO

Bantu: Dispersion and Settlement.

Africa

Soninké (known by a variety of names, including Sarakole, Diankanke, and Wangarawa), ethnic group originating in MALI, SENEGAL, and MAURITANIA that has dispersed to other West African countries.

Soninké oral history traces the group's descent from Berbers, but both the Soninké's traditional MANDE language and archaeological evidence suggest that their ancestors lived in present-day Mali and Mauritania for thousands of years. They were the founders and rulers of ancient Ghana, centered in Koumbi Saleh. Straddling the desert and the Sahel, Ghana developed into a center of trans-Saharan exchange, and the Soninké became famous merchants. In 1076 Almoravid Berbers briefly conquered ancient Ghana and forcibly converted some Soninké to Islam. Although the kingdom regained independence for more than a century, Muslim Berbers remained influential, and increasing numbers of Soninké adopted Islam. Some of the most prominent and devoted Muslim scholars in West Africa since have been Soninké. Today approximately half of all Soninké are Muslims, the majority of whom follow a form of Sufi mysticism known as Tijaniyya. However, except for the members of clerical clans, most Soninké Muslims also retain traditional religious beliefs.

During the thirteenth century the MALI EMPIRE absorbed the remnants of ancient Ghana, including most of the Soninké homeland. Some Soninké were absorbed into the DYULA ethnic group, which was also known for its trading activities. Still others dispersed from their homeland and settled throughout West Africa, where they maintained a distinct identity. The Marka of Mali and BURKINA FASO claim Soninké ancestry, as do the Yarsé of Burkino Faso and the Dyankanké of the Gambia and Senegal. Each of these groups is known for its mercantile traditions and adherence to Islam.

Traditional Soninké society is highly stratified, with status determined by an individual's patrilineal descent group. Wealthy Islamic clerical lineages are distinguished from secular ruling families; together these groups form the Soninké elite. However, most Soninké lineages belong to the class of commoners, the caste-defined artisan groups, or a poor and disfranchised underclass largely descended from slaves. During precolonial times one-third to one-half of the Soninké population was composed of chattel slaves, who labored at farming, and crown slaves, who collected taxes. Many Soninké villages continue to have distinct quarters that segregate slaves' descendants, known as "serfs," whose status has changed little since slavery.

Today the majority of Soninké proper continue to live in the Kayes, Yelimane, Nioro, and Nara districts of northwestern Mali, and adjacent parts of Senegal and Mauritania. However, Burkina Faso, Côte d'Ivoire, the Gambia, Guinea-Bissau, and Guinea all have significant Soninké populations. Today the Soninké number more than 2.6 million people. Except in Mauritania and Senegal, most Soninké have abandoned their native tongue, Azer, for the languages of surrounding peoples. Many adult males travel to France, where they work as laborers and send home remittances.

The Soninké continue to have a reputation throughout West Africa as itinerant traders of diamonds and other goods. Those living in coastal communities have become skilled sailors, and some have even enlisted in the French merchant marines. In the Soninké homeland most are small-scale farmers who cultivate millet, sorghum, fonio (a crabgrass cereal), maize, and other grain crops.

Ari Nave

See Also

Berber; Gambia, The; Ghana, Early Kingdom of; Almoravids; Koumbi Saleh, Mauritania.

Africa

Sophiatown, South Africa,

South African township that was a center for artistic and political activity in the 1940s and 1950s.

Sophiatown, located on the outskirts of Johannesburg, was founded in 1897 by Herman Tobiansky, a white developer who named the settlement after his wife. His grand plans for a white suburb were thwarted by the construction of a sewage disposal facility nearby. By World War I, however, booming industrialization had created a huge demand for workers' housing near Johannesburg, so Tobiansky began selling plots of land to blacks, "Coloureds," and Indians, as well as whites. As the township expanded, it earned a reputation as a place where gangsters with nicknames like "King Kong" reigned, and where informal pubs and wild parties drew white bohemians like the young Nadine Gordimer. Writers, artists, and journalists of different races came to share both creative and political ideas, and later the township became an early stronghold for opposition to apartheid.

Considered one of the most intellectually and creatively vibrant communities in the history of South Africa, Sophiatown in the 1940s and early 1950s has been compared to Harlem during the 1920s Harlem Renaissance. Writers such as Can Themba, Lewis Nkosi, Es'kia Mphahlele, Nat Nakasa, Bloke Modisane, and Arthur Maimane had their creative beginnings in the cultural milieu of Sophiatown. The prominent South African magazine *Drum*, founded in 1951 by Jim Bailey and later under the editorship of Anthony Sampson, brought these writers' works to the larger nation and to interested readers abroad. The magazine served an important historical role in South Africa, spreading and legitimating the work of black authors, poets, and journalists. Anglican Father Trevor Huddleston, who operated a school and ministry out of the township, became a key figure in the community and later led a fight against the early apartheid Bantu Education Act.

As one of the few areas near Johannesburg where blacks could own property alongside whites, Coloureds, and Asians, Sophiatown became a target for the forced relocation campaigns undertaken by the National Party's apartheid government, which came to power in 1948. By 1953 the government had drawn up a plan to evict all of Sophiatown's residents and relocate blacks to the newly built Meadowlands housing project, 24 km (15 mi) outside Johannesburg. The threat of relocation turned Sophiatown into a center for antiapartheid resistance. Residents met in the large Odin Cinema to discuss tactics for opposing the relocation. National organizations such as the African National Congress (ANC) and the Indian Congress also drew many members from Sophiatown. Leaders of the antiapartheid struggle, such as Nelson Mandela and Lillian Ngoyi, addressed giant protest rallies in Sophiatown during the early 1950s.

The government scheduled the Sophiatown relocation for February 10, 1955. The ANC planned a nonviolent demonstration in Sophiatown for that day, but the minister of justice, wishing to justify the use of force against the protesters, told Parliament the ANC was planning armed resistance. Police arrived two days early, in the middle of the night. Many black residents were moved immediately to the Meadowlands; those who remained faced the immediate bulldozing of their property. Over the new few years Sophiatown was demolished entirely, and an all-white suburb, named Triomf, replaced it.

Marian Aguiar

See Also

Antiapartheid Movement; Indian Communities in Africa; Johannesburg, South Africa; Mandela, Nelson Rolihlahla; South Africa; National Party; Harlem, New York.

Latin America and the Caribbean

Soriano, Florinda Muñoz

(b. 1914?, Villa Mella, Dominican Republic; d. November 1, 1974, Dominican Republic), Afro-Dominican peasant organizer who fought and died defending peasant lands and fighting for social justice.

An illiterate, hard-working farmer, Florinda Muñoz Soriano gained recognition for advocating the causes of poor landowners and tenant farmers in Hato Viejo, Yamasá, in the Dominican province of Monte Plata. In the 1930s Soriano married Felipe Soriano, who inherited from his father a parcel of land in Hato Viejo. There Soriano reared her ten children. With her husband she raised cattle and pigs and harvested vegetables and fruit to provide for the family. Several years after the death of her first husband, she married Jesús María de Paula, also a poor farmer from Hato Viejo.

Because of her strong will and tenacity, Soriano became known as Mamá Tingó, or Doña Tingó, throughout her region and later throughout the country. "Tingó" is a Dominican word that refers to someone or something that brings happiness. Constantly concerned with the rights of poor landowners, Mamá Tingó became a local leader on behalf of the Federación de las Ligas Agrarias Cristianas (Federation of the Christian Agrarian Leagues). The ruthless and powerful landowner Pedro Díaz Hernández claimed that he had bought the land of her fellow farmers in the region. To protect their rights as landowners, she helped launch a legal defense against him. In retaliation Díaz enclosed the farmers' land with wire and posted armed guards around it. Subsequently he plowed up their crops to demonstrate his alleged ownership of the land.

According to accounts, Mamá Tingó was shot to death on November 1, 1974, at age 60, on her way home from a court hearing on Díaz's claim. She had been informed that one of Díaz's employees had released her hogs. While she was searching for them, she was ambushed and shot in the head by the same man who had released them.

Scholar Silvio Torres-Saillant summed up the importance of Soriano's legacy for social justice, and for the role of blacks in Dominican cultural history, in this way: "The social indignation caused by the brutal murder of Mamá Tingó led the Balaguer government, if not to side with peasants against the landowning class, at least to declare the disputed lands state property with the declared purpose of employing them in the implementation of land reforms." Mamá Tingó became a martyr for her people because of a tenacity she shared with the Dominican peasantry.

At least two published works have been dedicated to the life of Mamá Tingó. Ramon Alberto Ferrarras, in *Negros,* offered a revealing and suitable dedication: "To Florinda Soriano

(Mamá Tingó) and to other black women who have known throughout our history how to defend – even with their lives – the sacred land on which they were born and the land which gave them a means of survival." Celsa Albert Batista, in *Mujer y esclavitud en Santo Domingo* (Women and Slavery in Santo Domingo), lauded her martyrdom thus: "To the Dominican woman in the person of Florinda Soriano 'Mamá Tingó,' a woman who struggled and sacrificed for the right to work and for social justice." Finally, Dominican poet Blas Jiménez immortalized Soriano in his poem "Mamá Tingó." The final verses read: "How black you were / Mamá Tingó / with your machete / and with your pride / how brave and beautiful / Mamá Tingó / Mamá Tingó."

Latin America and the Caribbean

Sosa, Domingo (b. 1788, Buenos Aires, Argentina; d. October 8, 1866, Buenos Aires, Argentina), Afro-Argentine military figure; founding member of the Artisans Club (an Afro-Argentine social club) and national representative to the legislature of the province of Buenos Aires from 1856 to 1862.

Domingo Sosa joined ARGENTINA's military in 1808 and remained in the military for his entire career. After returning from service in the Sixth Infantry, he was assigned to duty as a drill instructor in the Argentine Auxiliaries, an all-black regiment (*see* RACIAL QUESTION DURING STRUGGLES OF INDEPENDENCE IN LATIN AMERICA). In 1828 Sosa was called up to serve in the all-black Fourth Militia Battalion, where he would remain for 17 years, fighting in both the Indian wars of the 1820s and civil wars of the 1830s.

The next stage in Sosa's career came in 1845, when Juan Manuel Rosas, Argentine dictator in the 1830s and 1840s, named Sosa colonel and granted him command of the Provisional Battalion. After the demise of Rosas's federalist regime, Sosa remained in Argentina's subsequent Unitarian government, maintaining both his rank and command of his troops. During the post-Rosas period Casildo Thompson Sr. served under Sosa in the Fourth Battalion of the National Guard. Later Sosa was appointed national representative to the legislature of the province of Buenos Aires and remained in this post from 1856 to 1862. By the end of his career Sosa had served Buenos Aires for more than 40 years. The colonel died quietly at home of natural causes in 1866. The provincial army was renamed the Sosa Battalion in his honor.

Joy Elizondo

Africa

Soso (also called Susu, Sosso, or Sousou), a coastal West African ethnic group living primarily in GUINEA.

Among Guinea's major ethnic groups – including the MANDINKA, FULANI, and various forest peoples of southeast Guinea – the Soso are the third largest. Some Soso also live in SENEGAL and SIERRA LEONE. The most recent estimates place the total Soso population at more than 1 million. Guinean Soso mostly inhabit the coastal regions known as Lower Guinea. On the coast itself, many Soso earn their livelihood from fishing or salt production; other Soso are traders or farmers, cultivating a mix of subsistence and cash crops such as rice, MILLET, coconuts, pineapples, bananas, and palm kernels.

Although the exact history of the Soso people is unclear, most anthropologists now believe that they arrived in Guinea around 900 C.E. However, they carry the name of a powerful kingdom that dominated parts of present-day MALI and MAURITANIA from the early twelfth century until its defeat by the MALI EMPIRE in the thirteenth century. Refugees from the defeated kingdom may have settled among the people who then became known as the Soso. One theory argues that the Soso later split off from the YALUNKA (or Djallonka) people who once inhabited the Middle Guinea empire of FOUTA DJALLON, because the two groups speak similar MANDE languages. According to this theory, when the Muslim Fulani took over that region, the Soso migrated to the coast, probably around the eighteenth century, joining the Konangi, BAGA, and Nalou peoples.

The majority of the Soso are now Muslims, but some still observe traditional religious practices. Soso society is organized into patrilineal clans; polygamy and marriage between cousins are common. The Soso are also known for their crafts, such as basketry, cabinetry, and leatherwork.

Kate Tuttle

Africa

Sotho (also known as Suthu or Suto), southern African ethnic groups that speak the seSotho language.

More than 7 million people who inhabit southern Africa speak seSotho, a Bantu language. These people are known collectively as the Sotho. Scholars believe that the ancestors of the present-day Sotho migrated around a millennium ago into the region near the Caledon River, where they cultivated sorghum and raised cattle. The large number of KHOISAN loan words found in seSotho suggests that Sotho farmers traded their agricultural produce for game that was hunted by the neighboring foraging communities. The Sotho themselves lived in densely populated villages; archaeological remains indicate that as many as 1500 people clustered together in a single settlement, perhaps as a defense against neighboring cattle-raiding groups. Hereditary chiefs are believed to have ruled over these large villages.

The Sotho are commonly seen as three distinct groups – the Basotho (also known as the baSotho or Basuto) of LESOTHO, the TSWANA of BOTSWANA, and the Sotho of Transvaal. The Basotho recognized no collective identity or centralized state until the 1820s, when the ZULU campaign of conquest and expansion, known as the MFECANE, provoked a wave of NGUNI migrations into areas inhabited by Sotho clans. In the face of Nguni invasions the young chief of the Sotho Kwena clan, MOSHOESHOE, led his people onto the Thaba Bosiu plateau, where they were later joined by other seSotho-speaking clans. Mosheshoe united these clans into the Basotho kingdom (also known as Basutoland). He established a royal hierarchy that was maintained during British COLONIAL RULE – a hierarchy that is still recognized by the constitution of contemporary Lesotho.

The Tswana are thought to have migrated from southwestern Transvaal along the edge of the KALAHARI DESERT, where they intermingled with KHOIKHOI pastoralists. They are believed to have settled in their current location in Botswana after 1700. The groups known as Transvaal Sotho, including the PEDI, are believed to have migrated from the area around Pretoria to their present locations in northern Transvaal and SWAZILAND during the seventeenth century.

Christianity is widespread, especially among the Basotho, in part due to Moshoeshoe's friendly relations with European missionaries. Polygamy is still widely practiced. Virtually all Sotho groups trace descent and inheritance through the male line. These patrilineal lineages are divided into age grades. Members of each age grade undergo initiation rites around the age of puberty.

Farming remains an important source of livelihood for rural Sotho communities. Many rural Sotho keep goats and cattle, the latter being an important currency of bride wealth. Horses are also raised on the highlands of Lesotho. In addition, large numbers of men from Lesotho and Botswana migrate to jobs in the gold and diamond mines of SOUTH AFRICA, leaving women to tend the farms. In recent years, however, fewer and fewer migrant Sotho laborers have been able to find employment in South African mines, as a drop in gold prices has forced mining companies to cut production.

SEE ALSO
Bantu: Dispersion and Settlement; Christianity, African: An Overview; Gold Trade; Languages, African: An Overview; Pastoralism; Pretoria, South Africa; Christianity: Missionaries in Africa.

North America

Soul Music, a style of African American popular music, heavily influenced by GOSPEL MUSIC, that emerged in the 1960s from RHYTHM AND BLUES (R&B) and had a powerful impact on American vernacular culture.

During the soul music era of the 1960s African American music – for the first time in American history – gained popularity in an undiluted and culturally black form. Black music has long exerted a significant influence on American popular culture. Turn-of-the-century RAGTIME, classic JAZZ in the 1920s, 1930s big-band swing, and 1950s doo wop vocal groups each served to shape the musical tastes of mainstream America. But in the 1960s white Americans heard a genre of black music performed almost exclusively by African American artists, rather than a watered-down imitation sung by white performers. The new genre became known as soul music.

The soul music style was rooted in earlier forms of African American popular music. It was a direct extension of R&B but drew its primary influences from gospel music rather than from the blues. Important precursors to the soul style appeared during the 1950s, including RAY CHARLES's sanctified sound introduced on "I've Got a Woman" (1955); JAMES BROWN's "Please, Please, Please" (1956); Sam Cooke's "You Send Me" (1957); and the rich gospel sonorities heard in Arlene Smith and the Chantels' "Maybe" (1957) and Jerry Butler and the Impressions' "For Your Precious Love" (1958).

The soul aesthetic crystallized in the 1960s. Many elements of the new style are evident in GLADYS KNIGHT and the Pips' recording of "Every Beat of My Heart" (1960), especially in Knight's emotional lead singing, the prominent churchlike organ, and the emphasis on the back beats, two and four – in this case by percussive guitar chords. There were a number of distinct styles or approaches to soul. Most significant were the harder-edged "Memphis sound," associated with STAX RECORDS (1960-1975) of MEMPHIS, TENNESSEE, and the slicker, more pop-oriented "Motown sound," of Berry Gordy's Detroit-based Motown Records (founded in 1959). In addition, James Brown had a rhythmic and danceable style all his own.

The hard soul of Stax – and of New York City's Atlantic Records – featured stripped-down production values and gritty small ensembles, such as Stax's Booker T. and the MGs or the Bar-Kays, that provided a powerful rhythmic drive and tightly riffing horns behind the gospel- and blues-tinged vocals of such singers as OTIS REDDING, Sam and Dave (Sam Moore and David Prater), Carla Thomas, the STAPLE SINGERS, WILSON PICKETT, and Aretha Franklin. Gordy's Motown recordings employed more lavish production values, including the use of string sections, and achieved a sweeter sound that appealed to whites as well as blacks. Among Motown's most influential artists were DIANA Ross and THE SUPREMES, Smokey Robinson and the Miracles, STEVIE WONDER, the Jackson Five, and the Temptations.

In the 1960s, during the height of the CIVIL RIGHTS MOVEMENT, a historic process of racial integration began in the previously segregated realm of American popular music. Black artists achieved significant crossover success, producing hit records that sold in significant numbers to both whites and blacks. During the 1950s the popularity of black performers such as Nat "King" Cole, DINAH WASHINGTON, Chuck Berry, and the Platters revealed the beginnings of integration in American pop music. But prior to the soul music era black musicians had gained success primarily by appealing to the musical tastes of white listeners. During the 1960s an unparalleled number of black artists scored hits that made few concessions to white tastes, including Booker T. and the MGs' "Green Onions" (1962), Brown's "Papa's Got a Brand New Bag" (1965) and "I Got You (I Feel Good)" (1966), Pickett's "In the Midnight Hour" (1965), Sam and Dave's "Hold On! I'm Comin'" (1966), Percy Sledge's "When a Man Loves a Woman" (1966), and Franklin's "R-E-S-P-E-C-T" (1967). Soul music also inspired a "white soul" counterpart, exemplified in the early 1970s by such white pop singers as Carole King and Van Morrison.

Unlike R&B artists of the 1940s and 1950s who emphasized good-time music and made little effort to confront social issues, soul musicians engaged in cultural politics. Soul music – like R&B – concentrated mainly on themes of love and its discontents. But in the hands of a soul singer like Franklin, the frustrated lover's complaint in "R-E-S-P-E-C-T" became a sweeping anthem to freedom and empowerment. By the late 1960s a number of soul musicians gained popularity with songs that addressed a wide range of social issues and expressed black pride, exemplified by Brown's Top Ten hit "Say It Loud, I'm Black and I'm Proud" (1969). At the height of the Vietnam conflict Edwin Starr's "War" (1970) delivered an impassioned antiwar message. MARVIN GAYE's "Mercy Mercy Me" (1971) was a gentler but no less earnest form of protest music, informed by ecological concerns.

CURTIS MAYFIELD and Stevie Wonder in particular invested their music with a strong social conscience. As part of the Impressions in the 1960s and as a solo artist in the 1970s, Mayfield wrote many examples of soul music with a message, including "If There's a Hell Below We're All Going to Go" (1970) and "We People Who Are Darker Than Blue" (1970). Wonder proved equally adept at addressing issues of social injustice or spiritual uplift in songs such as "Living for the City" and "Higher Ground," from his album *Innervisions* (1973). Along with Isaac Hayes and Gaye, Mayfield and Wonder experimented with ambitious musical forms, for example the artistically unified "concept album," examples of which include Wonder's *Music of My Mind* (1972) and Mayfield's *There's No Place Like America Today* (1975).

Soul music retained an undiminished vigor into the 1970s and remained popular with black listeners. But by the late 1960s the larger white public had become less receptive. This change in musical tastes was part of a larger shift in white attitudes that was reflected in the waning of white support for the Civil Rights Movement, in the nation's growing political conservatism, and in a general heightening of racial tensions. In popular culture white and black musical styles seemed once more to retreat from each other. White pop music returned to the spotlight through the "British invasion" of such hit-making rock 'n' roll bands as the Beatles and the Rolling Stones, and black musicians found fewer opportunities. Although some African American artists, such as Donna Summer and the Commodores, had hits during the 1970s disco craze, black listeners preferred the contemporaneous but harder-edged FUNK style. As soul music became increasingly marginal and record sales dropped, Stax Records folded in the mid-1970s.

Both Motown and Atlantic have continued to be major forces in American popular music, as have Franklin, Mayfield, and Wonder. But the distinctive sound and aesthetic of soul music appears to have been lost. Subsequent developments in black popular music – most notably RAP – reflect a general distancing from the gospel overtones and broad, quasi-religious themes of affirmation that lay at the heart of soul music.

James Clyde Sellman

SEE ALSO

Berry, Charles Edward Anderson (Chuck); Blues, The; Cole, Nat ("King"); Cooke, Samuel (Sam); Detroit, Michigan; Franklin, Aretha Louise; New York, New York; Jackson, Michael, and the Jackson Family; Vietnam War; Motown; Platters, The; Robinson, William ("Smokey"); Temptations, The.

Latin America and the Caribbean

Soulouque, Faustin Elie (1788-1873), president of Haiti (1847-1849); then emperor of Haiti (1849-1859). Soulouque was elected president of Haiti by the National Assembly under the belief that he could be easily manipulated. On the contrary, Soulouque established a strong and repressive regime. In 1849 he unsuccessfully attempted an invasion of the neighboring DOMINICAN REPUBLIC, which had won its independence from Haiti five years earlier. Later that year Soulouque declared himself Emperor Faustin I. He was forced into exile in 1859, defeated by the forces of Gen. Nicolas Fabre Géffard (*see* HAITI).

North America

Soul Stirrers, gospel quartet that created the modern male gospel quartet style.

Founded in Trinity, Texas, by Roy Crain in 1926, the Soul Stirrers were the first gospel quartet to add a second lead to solo over the usual four-part harmony. Further innovations by this group include the use of guitar accompaniment and the performance of concerts consisting solely of gospel compositions. Alan Lomax recorded the Soul Stirrers for the Library of Congress because it was "the most polyrhythmic music you ever heard." According to scholar Tony Heilbut, Robert H. Harris, the Soul Stirrers' lead singer, "created the entire gospel quartet tradition."

Harris's style of singing is often said to have influenced every male vocalist in gospel, soul, pop, and rock 'n' roll. Some of his techniques that have become standard are solo improvisation over the background repetition of key phrases, rising into falsetto at climactic moments, and singing off-time to create polyrhythms with the backup singers. Harris himself claims that "I was the first to sing delayed time. I'd be in and out, front and behind, all across there." Harris and the Soul Stirrers' rendition of "By and By," a hymn by C. A. Tindley, is considered a gospel classic.

In 1950 Harris quit the group after tiring of touring. At this time Sam Cooke replaced Harris and developed a smoother, more modern pop sound. With the addition of instrumental accompaniment and Cooke's stylistic changes, the group attracted a younger audience. While Cooke was with the Soul Stirrers, the group's most well-known recordings were "Wonderful" and "Jesus Wash Away My Troubles." Cooke left the ensemble in 1957 and became an internationally popular soul singer until his death in 1964. Other members of the group, including Jesse Farley, James Medlock, Leroy Taylor, Paul Foster, Willie Rogers, and Jimmy Outler, continued to perform as two groups, the Original Soul Stirrers and the Soul Stirrers.

See Also

Soul Music; Cooke, Samuel (Sam); Gospel Music; Gospel Quartets.

North America

Soul Train, one of the first nationally successful television shows conceived and produced by African Americans.

Don Cornelius, *Soul Train*'s creator, envisioned the show as a black analogue to *American Bandstand*, a popular dance and music show. After gaining popularity in the early 1970s on a local channel in Chicago, *Soul Train* was adopted by stations nationwide. The show appealed to a far broader audience than the black teenagers for whom Cornelius had designed it. *Soul Train* returned season after season in the 1980s and 1990s, charting the evolving trends of pop music by showcasing RHYTHM AND BLUES, soul, and eventually RAP.

Soul Train was among the few major television programs of the 1970s that did not portray blacks by drawing on formulas and stereotypes. After the major civil rights victories of the 1960s – which redressed overt legal injustices – African Americans faced the equally formidable obstacle of ingrained cultural discrimination, expressed both on and off screen. The National Black Media Coalition, an organization that protested such racism, criticized the larger broadcasting networks, while some African Americans fought racial prejudice on the local level. *Soul Train* was the most successful among regional programs whose content was engineered by African Americans for African Americans.

Eric Bennett

See Also

Soul Music; Chicago, Illinois; Racial Stereotypes; Television and African Americans.

Africa

South Africa, country in Africa bordering NAMIBIA, BOTSWANA, ZIMBABWE, MOZAMBIQUE, Lesotho, and SWAZILAND.

Introduction

On May 9, 1994, Nelson Mandela marked his election as president of South Africa with a speech from the balcony of Cape Town's city hall, overlooking the Cape of Good Hope. Originally named by European merchant sailors, the Cape became the site of one of the earliest European colonies in sub-Saharan Africa, which would later grow to become the continent's wealthiest but also most racially oppressive independent nation. Mandela's speech, however, reclaimed the Cape as a symbol of hope for a new South Africa, one in which decades of struggle against the apartheid regime had finally triumphed and made possible the country's peaceful transition to a nonracial democracy. In his speech Mandela challenged South Africa's citizens to "heal the wounds of the past," a goal that later became the defining project of the TRUTH AND RECONCILIATION COMMISSION (TRC).

But upon taking office Mandela faced enormous challenges, among them high unemployment, escalating crime, and continued political violence. Militant resistance from the country's conservative white community also posed an ominous threat. Since 1994 South Africa's efforts to alleviate poverty while winning back foreign investors have made some progress, but hardly enough to satisfy the country's highly politicized citizenry. At the same time South Africa has become an increasingly influential economic and political power, both on the African continent and beyond it.

Indigenous Communities in Southern Africa

The earliest known human societies in southern Africa were KHOISAN-speaking hunter-gatherers, often referred to today as the SAN. Living in small, nomadic communities, they inhabited the region's richest ecosystems, hunting game in the grasslands and collecting shellfish along the coast. Around 2000 years ago the San were joined by the KHOIKHOI, pastoralists who migrated south from the Middle ZAMBEZI RIVER valley.

Humans' relationship with their environment in this fertile, temperate, but sparsely populated land began to change dramatically with the arrival of Bantu-speaking migrants in the first centuries C.E. These settlers came with livestock, but even more important, they introduced iron tools, weapons, and agriculture to the region. The Bantu speakers' numbers grew rapidly, and they established southern Africa's first large settled communities. Ancestors of the SOTHO people, for example, lived in towns of up to 20,000 people. Some San and Khoikhoi were incorporated into these communities; others were pushed onto more marginal lands. Although cattle raiding between Bantu-speaking societies was common, political power in the region of present-day South Africa remained relatively decentralized, compared to the kingdoms established by the SHONA to the north (*see* GREAT ZIMBABWE).

The Cape Colony

The first Europeans to come ashore in southern Africa were Portuguese explorers looking for a sea route to Asia. In February 1488 Bartolomeu Dias landed at what is now known as Mossell Bay. In 1497 VASCO DA GAMA sailed around the Cape of Good Hope and went on to become the first European explorer to reach India. For the next 150 years European sailors stopped periodically along the Cape to collect fresh water and repair battered ships. Given that it took a year to travel between Europe and India, the Cape was a logical site for the establishment of a more permanent provisioning post. In 1647 a group of some 60 men were left at Table Bay to salvage the cargo of the grounded Dutch ship *Haarlem* and await the arrival of the following year's trading fleet. Upon their return to Amsterdam, they recommended the area around Cape Peninsula as a suitable site for a provisioning post. Three years later the Dutch East India Company sent Jan van Riebeeck and 80 others to establish a supply station at the Cape. They arrived at Table Bay on April 6, 1652.

The primary purpose of the settlement, later known as Cape Town, was to provide services and supplies for passing ships, including wheat, vegetables, and livestock. From the beginning the settlers supplemented

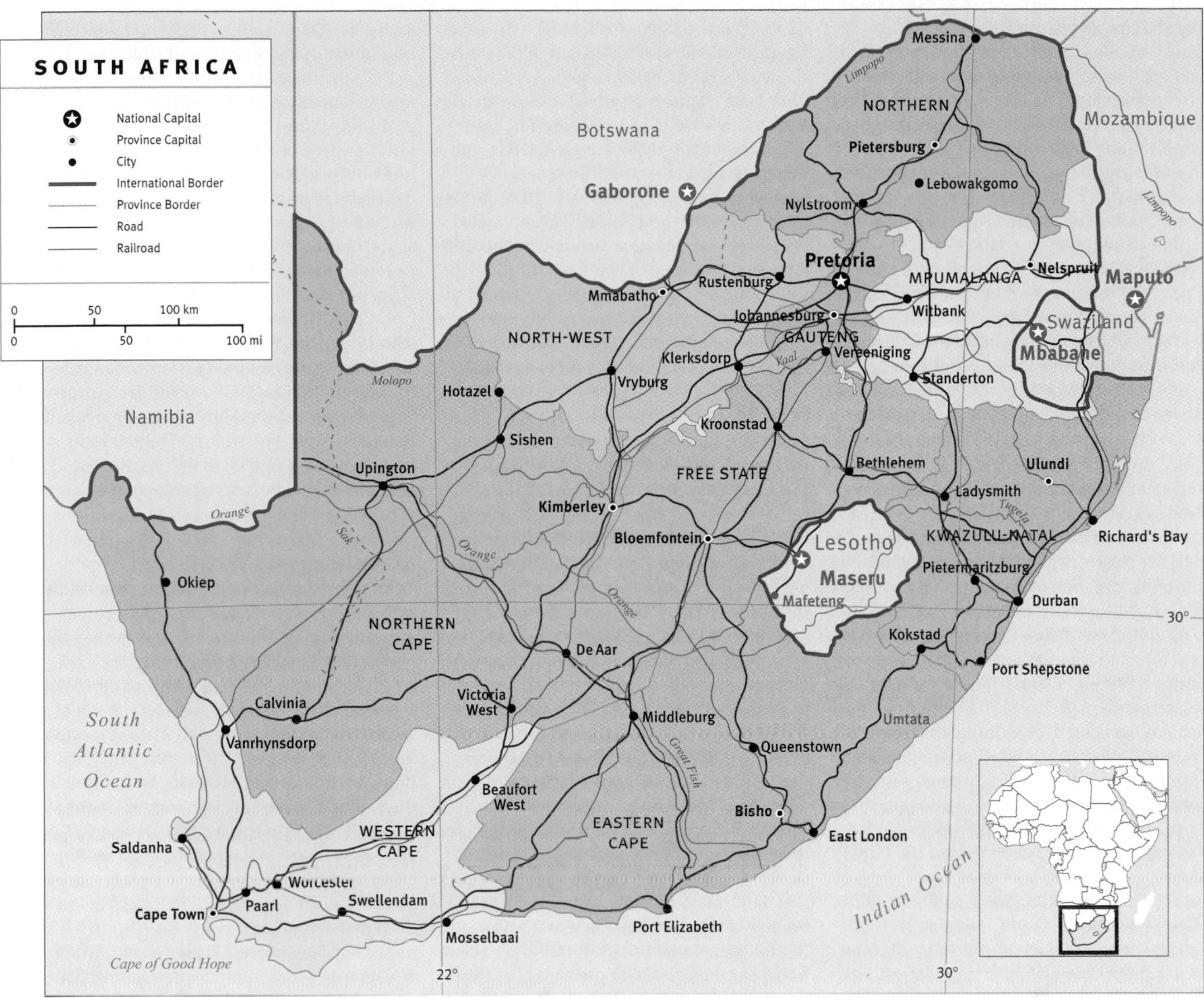

their own production with livestock bartered by local Khoikhoi in exchange for metal goods, tobacco, and alcohol. Although the settlers arrived on the Dutch East India Company payroll, a small number of them were released from their contracts in 1657 (to save the company money), and were granted land to cultivate independently. These "free burghers," and the others who soon joined them, gradually moved northward, out of the company's direct oversight.

Both the original settlement of Cape Town and the farms farther afield faced a labor shortage. Beginning in 1657 the company began to import slaves from throughout the Dutch East Indian Empire, as well as from MADAGASCAR, Angola, and Mozambique. Slavery lasted nearly 180 years in South Africa, during which time racial distinctions became both more complicated (the descendants of Asian slaves were among the people who later became known as "Coloured") and more stratified, as slaveholding became a mark of wealth within the white community.

Peaceful relations between the settlers and the Khoikhoi did not last long, once free burghers began encroaching on Khoikhoi-occupied land, and the company began trading directly with African kingdoms in the interior, thereby circumventing the Khoikhoi role as middlemen. Open conflict between the Khoikhoi and the settlers first broke out in 1659; it abated, but then erupted again in 1673, this time lasting four years. During this confrontation tens of thousands of Khoikhoi were killed or imprisoned; in addition more than 14,000 cattle and 32,000 sheep were confiscated by the settlers from the Khoikhoi between 1660 and 1675, according to colonial records. By 1677 the Khoikhoi population had been reduced to several thousand. By 1713 the group was virtually extinct after a smallpox epidemic swept through the Cape.

By the middle of the eighteenth century military forts throughout the Cape attested to the substantial amount of territory under Dutch control. European immigrants – mostly Dutch, German, and French Huguenot families, some quite poor – arrived steadily, driving up the white population from around 2000 in 1717 to more than 10,000 by 1780. Those who moved into and around the northern reaches of the colony became known as *Trekboers,* due to their livelihoods as semi-nomadic farmers and ranchers (the name was later shorted to *Boer,* Dutch for "farmer"). Encouraged by the Dutch East India Company to settle new lands, they eventually pushed into territories occupied by Bantu-speaking groups such as the XHOSA, where competition for pasture and water led to increasingly hostile relations.

The threat of war with an unknown number of Bantu-speaking groups frightened officials in the Cape. They reacted to Trekboer expansion and its destabilizing effects by establishing a colonial border around the Great Fish River. The 1780 border was initially designed to separate Bantu-speaking groups (the Xhosa in particular) from the burghers, but it was established without the consent of the several Xhosa clans who already occupied the land. In addition, colonial officials forcibly removed Xhosa who lived west of the Great Fish River, destroying villages, seizing livestock, and killing Xhosa elders in the process. Sporadic fighting between colonial militias and outgunned Xhosa warriors stretched into the last decade of the eighteenth century.

Expansion and Conquest

At the turn of the nineteenth century at least three major developments altered the course of history in southern Africa. The first was the arrival of the British on the Cape, which many of the burghers viewed as a threat to their way of life, both economically and culturally. The second was the acceleration of the Industrial Revolution in Europe, which brought to the Cape Colony both increased trade and the abolition of slavery. The third major event was the Zulu king Shaka's campaign of expansion and conquest known as the mfecane, which provoked wars and migrations throughout southern Africa.

By 1800 the white settler population had divided into two distinct groups. In rural areas slave-owning burghers, many of them poor and illiterate, had come to see themselves as a separate community, known as Boers or Afrikaners. They spoke a variant of Dutch known as Afrikaans and cultivated a defiant relationship with town-dwelling counterparts, even though many of them sold their produce in urban markets. Although large numbers of slaves worked in Cape Town and other coastal settlements, urban-based white merchants or artisans were typically less dependent on slave labor. Over time the schism between the two white communities widened, even as their combined populations represented an increasingly small minority in the colony. For example, in 1800, slaves outnumbered whites by two to one.

Great Britain seized control of the Cape Colony during the Napoleonic Wars, initially to protect its maritime trade with Asia. But the establishment of British rule in 1806 quickly brought dramatic political, economic, and cultural changes within the colony itself. A wave of European immigration boosted the colony's white population to nearly 47,000 (from approximately 10,500 in 1780), narrowing what the British administration had viewed as a disturbingly high black-to-white ratio. Although more than 80 percent of the colony's settlers were Dutch, British lawmakers replaced the Dutch legislature in Cape Town; a British-style educational system replaced Dutch traditions of schooling; and English became the official language.

Many Boers did not welcome the increasing influence of British culture – visible in such traditional English activities as cricket, tea drinking, and debating societies – nor the British colonial court system's efforts to regulate relations between Boers and Africans. But perhaps the most crippling blow to the Afrikaner way of life came in 1834 when the British abolished slavery in all of their territories, including the Cape Colony. The abolition of slavery eliminated the primary source of labor for rural white farmers.

Afrikaners responded with a mass northern exodus out of established colonial territory, known as the Great Trek. Traveling by ox-drawn covered wagons, several thousand *voortrekkers* moved into lands that had only recently witnessed the mfecane. Led by Afrikaner separatists Andries Pretorius and Piet Retief, the well-armed trekkers crushed Ndebele and, later, Zulu resistance en route, but suffered a serious setback when Retief was killed in February 1838 during a meeting with the Zulu chief, Dingane. The exact circumstances surrounding his death are disputed, but whatever the truth, the Afrikaners exacted brutal revenge later that year in what became known as the Battle of Blood River. Although vastly outnumbered, they defeated the Zulu army through sheer firepower, and afterward established an independent government on the site, naming it the Republic of Natal.

War and Reunification

The Republic of Natal lasted only five years before it was annexed by the British. But the Afrikaners continued efforts to establish independent Afrikaner republics, forming the Orange Free State in 1854 and merging three smaller states into the South African Republic (in the area of present-day Transvaal) in 1860.

The Cape Colony administration's tolerant attitude toward Afrikaner statehood changed dramatically with the discovery of diamonds in Kimberley (1867) and then gold in Witwatersrand (1886), both Afrikaner-held areas. At a time of growing competition between the world's industrial powers, Great Britain deemed it imperative that British South Africa control the region's abundant mineral resources, even if it took military action to claim them. By 1899 Anglo-Boer tensions had reached the point where war appeared inevitable, and in October that year the Afrikaner republics invaded British-held Natal. The four-year Boer War took the lives of approximately 22,000 British and 14,000 Boer soldiers, as well as some 20,000 Afrikaner civilians who died in concentration camps. But the war between whites also took a huge toll on black Africans: 100,000 blacks were interned in such camps, and tens of thousands died in them. The British emerged victorious. The Treaty of Vereeniging, signed in 1902 after the Boers sued for peace, extended British rule over the predominantly Afrikaner Transvaal and Orange Free State.

In 1910 the Afrikaner states joined with the British states (Natal and the Cape) to form the Union of South Africa. The new government moved quickly to mend Anglo-Afrikaner differences by institutionalizing white hegemony. It provided abundant loans and capital to Afrikaner farmers and British miners, and granted white women the right to vote. It made both Afrikaans and English the country's official languages, and allowed for the formation of the Afrikaner National Party. Africans were excluded from voting in three of the four colonies and granted only limited franchise in the Cape. But as the colony's mineral wealth fueled an industrial revolution, the government's biggest challenges were to manage rapid urbanization while assuring supplies of cheap labor for both the mining industry and white farmers.

By 1904 more than 1 million people had migrated to urban areas, making Johannesburg and Kimberley two of the colony's largest cities. More than half of those people were nonwhites seeking employment in the gold fields and diamond mines. The government's response to urbanization, and the increased social contact that it inevitably brought between whites and Africans, was to impose strict policies of racial segregation. Africans, Coloureds (mixed-race people, usually of blended African, European, and Asian descent), and Asians were confined to nonwhite slums, including Sophiatown, Alexandria, and Orlando (present-day Soweto). In a particularly humiliating gesture, whites in Johannesburg requested the removal of Indian merchants, claiming they were "a filthy group" who contributed to the city's unsanitary conditions.

Early Resistance

The South African government's discriminatory policies soon spurred a range of protest groups. In 1902 Coloured activists formed the African Political Organization (APO), led by Abdullah Abdurahman. Originally focused on advancing Coloureds' interests, the APO increasingly forged ties with African groups, and by 1910 boasted more than 100 local branches and nearly 20,000 members. Within the Indian community, Mohandas Gandhi led a passive resistance campaign against the 1906 Pass Laws – which restricted freedom of movement by requiring people to carry extensive documentation of their identity and employment at all times – for Asians. This movement later became known as *satyagraha*, and it propelled Gandhi to international fame when he led India to independence from the British.

It was black African political groups, however, that mobilized the largest protests. The South African Native Congress was the first black political organization, founded in 1898 in the eastern Cape by members of the first generation of missionary-trained Africans, many of whom had been educated in Europe and America. In 1912 more than 100 black activists assembled in Bloemfontein to create an even larger civil rights organization, the South African Native National Congress (SANNC), which became the African National Congress (ANC) in 1923. Pixley Ka Isaka Seme, John Tengo Jabavu, Walter Rubusana, Sol Plaatje, and John Dube were just a few of the black leaders during these formative years of South Africa's civil rights movement.

As SANNC pushed to attain civil rights for blacks, African labor unions multiplied and grew increasingly vocal. "Color bars" excluded most nonwhites from occupying skilled positions within the country's largest mines, and many blacks in particular worked under extremely dangerous conditions, even while receiving only a fraction of the pay of white laborers. By 1918 black railway workers, municipal sanitary workers, and gold and diamond miners had begun waging a series of strikes, setting a precedent for labor protests that spread to rural areas in the 1920s. The Communist Party of South Africa, founded in 1921 as a mostly white organization, was also supporting black labor movements by the late 1920s.

Booming industrialization in the 1940s spurred a new wave of urban migration and with it a new round of political protest. In addition to widespread protests against the pass laws, the ANC and community groups organized boycotts of government-run beer halls and bus lines, and thousands protested urban housing shortages by squatting on vacant land. By the end of the 1940s uncontrollable urbanization and increasingly militant black resistance had convinced the colonial government that it needed more than racial segregation if it was to maintain both white rule and economic growth.

The Apartheid Era

In 1948 the election of the Afrikaner-led National Party heralded a much more extreme policy, known as apartheid. Under apartheid the government recognized three distinct racial groups: white, Bantu or black African, and Coloured. Asians were later recognized as a distinct racial group, as well. Apartheid sought to control and divide South African society through an elaborate set of race-based laws, restricting not only where people could live or work but also with whom they could marry or even associate.

In addition to racial categories, apartheid recognized ten black African "tribes" or "Bantu nations," each of which was assigned a rural Bantustan, or "Bantu homeland." Although the National Party claimed that these homelands allowed blacks to maintain their "tribal" customs and political structures, the primary objective of the homelands was to prevent formation of class-based resistance movements among black workers. In fact, intense poverty in the rural areas forced continued labor migration, which in turn led to growing tensions in the cities. In response the government passed increasingly restrictive policies: it banned interracial marriage in 1949 and declared black trade unions illegal in 1953.

Apartheid provided an ideological justification for massive, ongoing population relocations. As black townships situated on the outskirts of major white urban cities became too large, the government tore them down and moved them farther out. The township of Sophiatown, for years the home of a thriving community of writers and artists, was torn down, beginning in 1955. In Cape Town the African neighborhood known as District Six was razed during the 1970s and relocated. During apartheid's 44-year existence more than 3 million Africans, 150,000 Asians, and 300,000 Coloureds were forcibly relocated to areas with dwindling businesses and inefficient public services. By 1985 more than 60 percent of the country's African population were restricted to one of ten homelands. But the growth of apartheid renewed resistance.

In 1952 the ANC united with several Coloured political groups to wage a nonviolent campaign of boycotts, strikes, and marches. These activities quickly revitalized ANC membership, which by 1953 numbered nearly 100,000. The antiapartheid movement gained momentum on June 26, 1955, when several organizations, including the ANC, the South African Indian Congress, and the South African Coloured People's Organization gathered outside Johannesburg at a meeting known as the Congress of the People. Here a Freedom Charter outlining demands for a nonracial South Africa was adopted.

Police walk among the bodies of some of the people killed when police opened fire on demonstrators in Sharpeville, South Africa, in 1960. Of the approximately 5000 people gathered to protest pass laws, at least 69 were killed and 200 injured in the incident. *CORBIS/Bettmann*

Although one of the tenets of the charter called for nonviolent protest, the South African police responded to nonviolent demonstrators by beating, torturing, and, in some cases, killing them. In 1958, when it was clear that nonviolent action would be met consistently with government-sanctioned violence, the youth wing of the ANC broke away and formed the more militant Pan-Africanist Congress (PAC).

Tragic affirmation of the PAC view that

nonviolence was ineffective came in 1960, when police shot and killed 69 unarmed demonstrators in a PAC-sponsored antipass protest in the township of Sharpeville. Shortly afterward the government banned the ANC and other antiapartheid organizations, and over the next several years it continued to rely on pass laws, relocations, and other apartheid mechanisms to suppress resistance efforts. In response, the banned ANC and the Communist Party, then led by Joe Slovo, together formed the guerrilla army Umkhonto we Sizwe (MK), "the Spear of the Nation." The National Party government responded by jailing many black political leaders and embarking on a campaign of severe repression that squelched most organized resistance during the 1960s. Meanwhile the South African economy enjoyed unparalleled growth, contributing to the already vast disparity in wealth between whites and blacks.

In the 1970s political protest once again intensified, as even younger students participated. Student activists, among them the charismatic Steve Biko, promoted Black Consciousness, a philosophy of black pride and unity influenced by the ideas of both Malcolm X and African Négritude thinkers. In June 1976 elementary and secondary school students marched in protest of apartheid educational policies, and police fired into the crowd. Several children were killed and many more injured; riots subsequently erupted in Soweto and throughout the country. The event provoked international condemnation and economic boycotts against South Africa, and fueled the spread of the antiapartheid movement at home. A year later the "accidental" death of Steve Biko in prison further galvanized protest. It was not until 1997 that members of the South African police, testifying at the TRC, described how Biko had been beaten to death.

Fearing complete administrative collapse, P. W. Botha and his government undertook their "Total Strategy" to maintain the economic and political viability of apartheid. In 1981, aiming to weaken antiapartheid coalitions, the government approved a new constitution granting Asians and Coloureds – but not Africans – seats in the country's new tricameral parliament. The government also made modest reforms (aimed mainly at co-opting the middle-class blacks) in education, housing, and labor laws, at the same time that it increased the size and presence of the police, army, and intelligence forces.

LEFT: A father and daughter play guitars early in the morning before he leaves for his job as a field hand on a farm. *CORBIS/David Turnley*
ABOVE: Albertina Sisulu, a founder of the African National Congress Women's League, member of South Africa's Parliament, and wife of Walter Sisulu, gives her young son a hug in the kitchen of their Soweto home. *CORBIS/David Turnley*
OPPOSITE: Black residents of Katishong, a township east of Johannesburg, line up to vote in the first all-race elections in South African history in April 1994. *CORBIS/Juda Ngwenya*

Total Strategy failed to prevent either coalition building – as demonstrated by the 1983 birth of the United Democratic Front (UDF), which combined the efforts of numerous nonwhite churches, student groups, civic organizations, women's groups, and trade unions – or a proliferation of strikes, protests, and MK-organized guerrilla attacks. In a 1986 state of emergency, the government detained thousands of dissidents, harassed civic leaders, and censored the press. But the sheer cost of maintaining order, combined with international sanctions, was beginning to take its toll on the South African economy, and some members of the government began to realize that change was inevitable. In 1989 the National Party signaled its desire for a new approach when it replaced President Botha with the more moderate F. W. De Klerk.

For both sides, geopolitical events added to the pressure for change. Western superpowers' policies of "constructive engagement" with the apartheid regime had long been justified in terms of cold-war realpolitik. But the collapse of the Soviet Union not only diminished the South African government's strategic importance to the West, but also cut off one of the ANC's primary sources of overseas support. In 1990 the ANC, led by the imprisoned Mandela, offered to negotiate; De Klerk responded by lifting the ban on the ANC and 17 other organizations, and releasing Mandela, who had by then spent 27 years behind bars.

Negotiations to end apartheid took nearly four years and proceeded against a backdrop of ongoing violence. Thousands died, both in terrorist attacks waged by groups that opposed the anticipated changes (such as the far-right Afrikaner Resistance Movement) and in conflicts between members of the ANC and the Inkatha Freedom Party (IFP), led by Zulu chief Mangosutho Gatsha Buthelezi. In late 1993 the ANC, the National Party, and the numerous other parties involved in the negotiations completed an interim constitution, providing for a postapartheid state based on multiparty elections, a two-house legislature, provincial assemblies, and a bill of rights. The IFP and the far-right Afrikaners both initially threatened to boycott forthcoming elections in April 1994, but at the last minute Buthelezi joined De Klerk and Mandela in the presidential race.

To no one's surprise, the African National Congress and Mandela won an overwhelming victory. Since then the Government of National Unity – which includes representatives of the National Party and the IFP, in addition to the ANC – has faced the challenge of meeting the high expectations of its more than 40 million citizens.

The New South Africa

The results of the 1994 elections did not complete the transition to democratic rule in South Africa. For the next two years negotiators representing all the members of the Government of National Unity worked to craft a new constitution. Largely attributed to ANC leader Cyril Ramaphosa and trade unionist Jayendra Naidoo, the 1996 constitution provided for shared rights and responsibilities among the central government, nine provinces, and local cities and towns. Buthelezi's IFP and the former ruling National Party were given control over the provinces in which they received a majority of the vote (KwaZulu/Natal and the Western Cape, respectively). Leadership by chiefs and other traditional authorities would be recognized but could be overruled by federal courts.

The first rupture of the Government of National Unity came just after the constitution's ratification – not, as many had feared, from the Zulu-dominated IFP, but rather from De Klerk's National Party. Much of the tension between Mandela and De Klerk centered on the work of the TRC, established in 1996 to investigate apartheid-era crimes. Headed by former archbishop Desmond Tutu, the TRC ultimately had to determine which of its more

than 10,000 applicants would receive amnesty for their crimes. De Klerk, under whose presidency some acts of kidnapping, torture, and murder of antiapartheid activists had taken place, continued to defend his police force as "good and honorable men," an assertion Mandela called "a joke." For its part, the ANC reported its own apartheid-era crimes, including the execution of suspected spies. Not surprisingly, the TRC's work generated considerable controversy. Many felt that by granting amnesty to the criminals, it denied justice to the victims and their families. Even after it began compensating victims, the TRC seemed to many an exercise in erasing the past and forgiving the unforgivable.

Race relations in the new South Africa remain complicated. Although the school system is officially integrated, white families have boycotted some formerly all-white schools, claiming that educational standards have declined since integration. Black and white families have faced harassment and even violence from some of the boycotters. Despite their still-dominant role in corporate culture, some whites have opposed affirmative action laws and have labeled the hiring of black government officials as "cronyism" or even "reverse apartheid."

By the late 1990s South Africa's murder rate was estimated to be seven times higher than that of the United States. Concerns about violent crime sparked a dramatic rise in white emigration from South Africa in the first few years after the 1994 elections, but poor and predominantly black urban neighborhoods remain some of the hardest-hit areas. One reason for the rising crime rate is that postapartheid South Africa has become attractive to international drug traders.

Along with crime rate problems, the new government has had to grapple with an unstable and sometimes sluggish economy. Once hailed as the continent's new economic superpower, South Africa since 1994 has seen slower than expected growth, despite the privatization and deregulation measures undertaken as part of the government's Growth, Employment, and Redistribution program (GEAR). In mid-1998 the value of the South African currency (the rand) fell to a record low, raising fears of a long-term economic crisis. However, by mid-1999 the rand had recovered some of its lost value.

Still, South Africa's economy remains the largest and most industrialized in sub-Saharan Africa, and it is now providing for more of its citizens. The country still faces an acute housing shortage, for example, but the government has been able to provide millions of homes with water and electrical service, and in 1997 it appropriated $500 million for new housing loans. In addition, there are hopes that South African industry and capital will help drive economic growth across the continent, or at least within the Southern African Development Community (SADC), a regional economic bloc. By the late 1990s South African firms were investing in West and Central African mining operations, as well as in hotels and other tourist facilities across East and southern Africa.

Several developments in 1998, however, threatened South Africa's role as a regional leader. South Africa sent 800 troops into nearby Lesotho in September 1998 at the request of Lesotho's government as part of an SADC action to quell public unrest and prevent a possible military coup. The South African troops met unexpectedly stiff resistance, however, and the botched military intervention threatened to mire South Africa in a guerrilla war in Lesotho and drew public criticism in both countries.

Two years before the scheduled 1999 elections, Mandela handed over the ANC leadership to his deputy, Thabo Mbeki, whom he said was "already de facto president of the country." Most observers believed that Mbeki, who is considered less conciliatory toward whites than Mandela, would face his biggest challenge from other blacks, including those within the ANC who oppose the free-market orientation of the party's GEAR program. In addition, the ANC has continued to face opposition. Violence in the late 1990s in KwaZulu/Natal was caused by rivalry between the ANC and the United Democratic

Cape Town is one of South Africa's most popular tourist destinations and the country's legislative capital. Its location has made it an important port city since the seventeenth century. *CORBIS/Amos Nachoum*

Movement, a new party drawing from both the ANC and National Party. This prompted some to speak again of a "third force," a term used in the late 1970s and 1980s to refer to clandestine destabilization efforts directed against the ANC. Other political parties vying for power will likely include the white-dominated Democratic Party (which has attracted many voters from the dwindling ranks of the National Party), the right-wing Conservative Party, and the Freedom Front. In 1999 the ANC once again won the presidency. Despite receiving a landslide vote, the ANC did not garner the two-thirds majority necessary to amend the constitution.

Alonford James Robinson, Jr. and Kate Tuttle

See Also

Afrikaner; Antiapartheid Movement; Bantu: Dispersion and Settlement; Biko, Stephen; Cape Coloured; Cape Town, South Africa; Dube, John Langalibalele; Explorers in Africa Before 1500; Sophiatown, South Africa; Sophiatown, South Africa; Indian Communities in Africa; Johannesburg, South Africa; Lesotho; Mandela, Nelson Rolihlahla; Sharpeville, South Africa; Soweto, South Africa; Pastoralism; Plaatje, Solomon Tshekisho; Black Consciousness in Africa; Tourism in Africa; Buthelezi, Mangosutho Gatsha; Botha, Pieter Willem; Tutu, Desmond Mpilo; Southern African Development Community; De Klerk, Frederik Willem; Christianity: Missionaries in Africa; South African Communist Party.

Africa

South Africa (Ready Reference)

Official Name: The Republic of South Africa
Area: 1,223,201 sq km (about 472,281 sq mi)
Location: Southern Africa, at the southern tip of the continent of Africa. Includes the Prince Edward Islands (Marion Island and Prince Edward Island). South Africa borders Botswana, Namibia, Zimbabwe, and Mozambique; Lesotho and Swaziland lie within its borders.
Capitals: Pretoria (population 525,583 [administrative]); Cape Town (population 854,616 [legislative]); and Bloemfontein (population 126,867 [judicial]) (1991 estimates)
Other Major Cities: Johannesburg (712,507), Port Elizabeth (303,353), Germiston (134,005), Soweto (596,632; some estimate the number is closer to 2 million), and Durban (715,669)
Population: 42,834,520 (1998 estimate)
Population Density: 35 persons per sq km (about 90 persons per sq mi)
Population Below Age 15: Total population: 35 percent (male 7,502,396; female 7,366,144 [1998 estimate])
Population Growth Rate: 1.42 percent (1998 estimate)
Total Fertility Rate: 3.16 children born per woman (1998 estimate)
Life Expectancy at Birth: Total population: 55.65 years (male 53.56 years; female 57.8 years [1998 estimate])
Infant Mortality Rate: 52.04 deaths per 1000 live births (1998 estimate)
Literacy Rate (age 15 and over who can read and write): Total population: 81.8 percent (male 81.9 percent; female 81.7 percent [1995 estimate])
Education: The legacy of apartheid in South Africa manifests itself most clearly in education. Although government spending on black education has increased significantly since the mid-1980s, at the end of the apartheid era expenditures for white pupils were about four times higher than those for black pupils. The teacher-to-student ratio for blacks was 1 to 60 in urban areas and 1 to 90 in rural areas. By comparison, the teacher-to-student ratio for whites averaged 1 to 30 or even lower. In the early 1990s South Africa's primary, secondary, and special schools annually enrolled about 5,794,100 blacks, 1,021,400 whites, 874,300 Coloureds, and 255,500 Asians. South Africa has numerous universities, with the following enrollment levels: 281,800 whites, 184,600 blacks, 42,100 Coloureds, and 34,800 Asians.
Languages: South Africa has 11 official languages: Afrikaans, English, Ndebele, Sesotho

sa Leboa, Sesotho, siSwati, Tsonga, Tswana, Venda, Xhosa, and Zulu. Afrikaans, a variant of the Dutch language, is the first language of almost all Afrikaners and many Coloured people. English is used as the primary language by many whites and is also spoken by some Asians and blacks. Most blacks, however, primarily use one of the Bantu languages such as Xhosa, Sesotho, or Zulu.
Ethnic Groups: South Africa has a multiracial and multiethnic population. Blacks constitute 75.2 percent of the population, whites make up 13.6 percent of the population while Coloreds and Asians compose 8.6 and 2.6 percent of the population respectively. Blacks belong to nine ethnic groups: Zulu, Xhosa, Pedi, Sotho, Tswana, Tsonga, Swazi, Ndebele, and Venda. The Zulu are the largest of these groups, making up about 22 percent of the total black population. Whites are descended primarily from British, Dutch, German, and French Huguenot (Protestant) settlers. South Africans of Dutch ancestry, who often have German and French heritage as well, are known as Afrikaners or Boers and form about three-fifths of the white population. Those of mixed racial origin, mainly black and Afrikaner and known as Coloured in South Africa, live chiefly in the Cape provinces. The Asians are mainly of Indian ancestry and are most numerous in the province of KwaZulu-Natal. A small number of people of Malay origin are also included in the Asian population. They reside mostly in the Cape provinces.
Religions: Christianity (followed by most whites and Coloureds and about 60 percent of blacks), Hindu (embraced by 60 percent of Indians), and Muslim (2 percent)
Climate: Nearly all of South Africa enjoys a mild, temperate climate. The High Veld receives about 380 to 760 mm (15 to 30 in) of precipitation annually, the amount diminishing rapidly toward the west, where rainfall is often as low as 50 mm (2 in) annually. Rainfall is deposited by the trade winds mainly between October and April. In the drier regions of the plateaus the amount of rainfall and the beginning of the rainy season vary greatly from year to year. The extreme southwest receives about 560 mm (22 in) of rainfall, mostly between June and September.

The average January temperature range in Durban is 21° to 27° C (69° to 81° F). The corresponding temperature range in Johannesburg is 14° to 26° C (58° to 78° F); in Cape Town it is 16° to 26° C (60° to 78° F); the winter temperature ranges follow the same regional pattern. The average July temperature range is 11° to 22° C (52° to 72° F) in Durban, 4° to 17° C (39° to 63° F) in Johannesburg, and 7° to 17° C (45° to 63° F) in Cape Town. Snow is rare in South Africa, although winter frosts occur in the higher areas of the plateau.
Land, Plants, and Animals: The topography of South Africa consists primarily of a great plateau region, which occupies about two-thirds of the country, bordered by the Drakensberg Mountains. The chief rivers of South Africa are the Orange, Limpopo, and Vaal. Numerous large mammals, including lions, elephants, zebras, leopards, monkeys, baboons, hippopotamuses, and antelope, are indigenous to South Africa. For the most part such animals are found only on game reserves. One of the most notable national game reserves is Kruger National Park in the northeast along the border with Mozambique.
Natural Resources: Gold, chromium, antimony, coal, iron ore, manganese, nickel, phosphates, tin, uranium, gem diamonds, platinum, copper, vanadium, salt, and natural gas
Currency: The rand
Gross Domestic Product (GDP): $270 billion (1997 estimate)
GDP per Capita: $6200 (1997 estimate)
GDP Real Growth Rate: 3 percent (1997 estimate)
Primary Economic Activities: Gold, platinum, chromium, diamonds, agriculture, timber, and fishing
Primary Crops: Corn, wheat, sugar cane, fruits, and vegetables; dairy and beef cattle, poultry, and sheep
Industries: Mining, automobile assembly, metalworking, machinery, textile, iron, steel, chemical, fertilizer, and foodstuffs
Primary Exports: Gold, other minerals and metals, foodstuffs, and chemicals
Primary Imports: Machinery, transport equipment, chemicals, oil, textiles, and scientific instruments
Primary Trade Partners: European Union, the United States, Japan, and Switzerland
Government: South Africa is a republic. It is divided into nine provinces or administrative divisions: Eastern Cape, Free State, Gauteng, KwaZulu-Natal, Mpumalanga, North-West, Northern Cape, Northern Province, and Western Cape. President Thabo Mbeki presides over a bicameral legislature that comprises the National Assembly (400 seats) and the Senate (90 seats). Currently, any political party that wins 20 percent or more of the National Assembly votes in a general election is entitled to name a deputy executive president, and to become a member of the governing coalition, currently made up of the African National Congress, the Inkatha Freedom Party, and the National Party. Together they constitute a Government of National Unity.

The legislature adopted a constitution on April 27, 1994 (this interim constitution replaced the constitution of September 3, 1984). On May 8, 1996, the Constitutional Assembly voted 421 to 2 to pass a new constitution that, after certification by the Constitutional Court, gradually went into effect over a three-year period and came into full force with the national elections in May 1999. South Africa has universal suffrage for those age 18 and over.

Alonford James Robinson, Jr.

See Also
Afrikaner; Baboon; Bantu: Dispersion and Settlement; Cape Town, South Africa; Elephant; Gold Trade; Hippopotamus; Johannesburg, South Africa; Salt Trade; Zebra; Cameroon Lions.

Africa

South African Communist Party, political party important in the overthrow of apartheid.

An influential force in the antiapartheid movement, the South African Communist Party has long cooperated with other organizations, especially the African National Congress (ANC). Although its ultimate goal remains the creation of a socialist society in South Africa, during the apartheid era the SACP worked for another goal as well. Calling for an end to the white supremacist state, the party sought the formation of a democratic government in which all South Africans would be equally represented.

Founded in 1921 as the Communist Party of South Africa (CPSA), the party was initially concerned more with overthrowing capitalism than with achieving racial justice and an independent African nation. Its early membership was overwhelmingly white, but within a decade, the majority of its 1750 members were black. Debate over the direction of the party led to a 1928 proclamation that the CPSA was a "nationalist revolutionary organisation" dedicated to fighting "the white bourgeoisie and British imperialists."

At the time the ANC was the leading anti-segregationist group in South Africa, but after it fell under conservative leadership in 1930, it spurned cooperation with the CPSA. A combination of internal conflict and a weakened labor movement during the Great Depression led to a dramatic decline in the CPSA's membership during the 1930s. During World War II, however, the revival of the organized labor movement in turn helped revive the party. Together the ANC and the CPSA organized the African Mine Workers' Union, and the 1946 strike of 100,000 mine-workers brought the party new energy, attention, and members.

In 1948 South Africa's conservative National Party was voted into power, and began implementing apartheid policies. Two years it later passed the Suppression of Communism Act, effectively banning the CPSA. But the party's renewed mission – which emphasized "the unity of interests that exist between workers of all races" – was not crushed. In 1953 the party re-formed as an underground movement, renamed the South African Communist Party (SACP). Operating illegally but relatively openly, SACP members such as Joe Slovo worked with the ANC on the 1952 Defiance of Unjust Laws campaign. SACP members also participated in the 1955 Congress of the People (the meeting that drafted the Freedom Charter, a document adopted by both the ANC and the SACP).

The party's participation in the antiapartheid campaign, however, made its members targets for government harassment. Many SAPC members, for example, were among the 156 activists charged with treason in 1956. Slovo, a defendant in the trial, also acted as defense attorney; no convictions resulted. After the government banned the ANC in 1960, Slovo, Nelson Mandela, and others formed Umkhonto we Sizwe (Spear of the Nation, also known as MK), an armed resistance body that carried out acts of sabotage. A raid on Umkhonto's headquarters at Rivonia in 1963 led to the arrest and conviction of many in the party, along with ANC leaders such as Mandela and Walter Sisulu. Slovo, out of the country at the time, remained in exile for the next 27 years.

Operating mostly out of London and Mozambique, the SACP contributed to the antiapartheid movement mostly by its role as a conduit for foreign aid, particularly from the Soviet Union and other communist countries, to support Umkhonto. Since its unbanning in 1990, the SACP has played an important role in South African political life. Joe Slovo, its secretary general, helped negotiate the peaceful transition that led to multiracial, democratic elections in 1994.

Kate Tuttle

See Also

Mandela, Nelson Rolihlahla.

Cross Cultural

South Asia, Africans in, people of African descent who live in the present-day countries of Bangladesh, Bhutan, India, Nepal, Pakistan, and Sri Lanka.

For centuries African slaves were part of an African-Asian trade, and today many of their descendants remain in South Asia. In a few areas African Asians actively maintain aspects of their cultural heritage, some living in separate communities. However, many African Asians have completely assimilated into the local cultures. Anthropologists and historians have conducted few studies of African slaves and their descendants in South Asia, so much of the history of African Asians is poorly known. Some African traders may have settled voluntarily in South Asia, but historians know even less about them.

The African-South Asian Slave Trade

Archaeological evidence of contact between South Asia and Africa dates as far back as the second millennium B.C.E., but it seems that the slave trade did not begin until the sixth century C.E. The trade remained relatively small until the eighteenth century, when, according to estimates, the number of slaves brought to South Asia reached more than 3000 per year. Britain – the colonial ruler of much of South Asia – abolished the slave trade in India in 1811 and outlawed slavery itself in 1843. However, these laws were not fully enforced until decades later.

The East African slave trade resembled the transatlantic slave trade, except that it was smaller. Most slaves were captured in raids inland and marched to the coast bound in chains. In the early years Indian bankers usually financed the raids, and Arabs conducted them, supported by the African rulers. Local Africans were subdued by threats from nearby Arab populations, but some local rulers also received part of the profits for their cooperation. On arriving at the coast the raiders sold their captives in open slave markets. Those chosen for Asia were packed into the holds of ships, lying side by side, several platforms deep, with only a few centimeters between platforms. If a slave died, there was no way to remove him or her until after the voyage. Food and water were scarce, if even provided, and many slaves died before arrival. During the height of the trade Portuguese, Dutch, French, and British shippers all participated.

Africans in South Asian History

Most of the slaves, known as Siddis or Habshis, served as soldiers, though some became plantation and domestic workers. Most slaves converted to Islam. Sometimes they became free under various circumstances, and a few became military and social leaders. Jalaluddin Yakut, the earliest well-known Siddi figure, was the favorite slave of thirteenth-century Sultana Raziya of Delhi. She appointed Yakut the royal stable master; however, her father and the kingdom's nobles disapproved and eventually killed Yakut.

Other notables of the early period included Siddi Maula, a religious figure who attracted many followers, and Malik Sarvar, who in 1389 became deputy of the sultan Muhammad of Delhi. He was later appointed governor of the eastern province of Jaunpur. Later another Siddi, Ibrahim, ruled Jaunpur during a time of great prosperity and learning. In fifteenth-century Bengal, King Rukn-ud-din Barbak promoted large numbers of African slaves to high posts. Barbak had about 8000 slave soldiers, and in 1486, after Barbak's death, Sultan Shahzada led the Siddis in a takeover of the kingdom. They ruled until 1493. In 1573 Sheik Sayeed al-Habshi Sultani, a well-known Siddi ruler of Ahmadabad, constructed a mosque still noted for its superior floral tracery. In the province of Sindh, currently in Pakistan, Hosh Mohammed became famous as a leader of eighteenth-century battles against the British. Also in Sindh, Zahur Shah Hasmi, Murad Sahir, and Mohammad Siddiq Mussafar gained fame as writers, while Mohammad Jharak excelled as a singer.

Malik Ambar

The best-known Siddi leader of South Asia was Malik Ambar, born about 1550 in Ethiopia. Malik Ambar was brought to central India as a slave. He became a Muslim and received some education from various owners before being promoted to the position of military commander of a group of Arab troops in central India. He later built a mercenary army of more than 1500 and was invited by the king of Ahmadnagar to join him in a fight against the powerful Mughal invaders of the time. Following his success in this endeavor, Malik Ambar founded his own capital at Kirkee and again kept the Mughals at bay. He maintained a 60,000-horse army, obtained artillery from the British, and received naval support from the Siddis who controlled the island of Janjira (discussed below). By the 1620s, however, after 20 years of war, strife beset Malik Ambar's community. Upon his death in 1626, his son could not keep the kingdom together. The civic achievements of Malik Ambar were many: a postal service, educational support for all ethnic groups, communal ownership of land for the poor, graduated taxes, and support of the courtly arts. He also built many public buildings, some using black stone, which, it is said, was a reference to his heritage.

Janjira

The island of Janjira, a critical trading locale about 70 km (about 45 mi) southwest of Bombay, was under Siddi control for a long period of time. According to some accounts, Malik Ahmad Siddi, founder of a dynasty at Ahmadnagar, installed Abyssinians as the captains of the island fort of Janjira in about 1500. By 1636 the Mughal armies had defeated the Marathas at Ahmadnagar and were conquering everyone in the area, yet they maintained an alliance with the Siddis of Janjira. These Siddis were also a powerful force in the later struggles between the Dutch, English, and Portuguese, as the colonial powers vied for control. In 1759 the British finally overpowered the Siddis in Janjira.

Siddi Risala

Once Britain outlawed the slave trade, British forces confiscated and freed many slaves en route to South Asia. The British made some attempt to find employment for the freed slaves or to return them to Africa. During this period the trade was especially large in the province of Hyderabad, which soon became home to many freed African captives from other parts of India. In addition, many freed slaves migrated there. The local king organized many of them as the African Cavalry Guard in 1863. Siddi Risala, or "African regiment" refers, after the guard, to the area in Hyderabad, still in existence, in which they lived.

In Siddi Risala, the Siddis built their own mosque and established a community for their families. But there were few Siddi women, so many Siddi men had to marry outside the group. Because the Siddis themselves were from many different African regions and spoke many different languages, it was difficult to maintain African culture. But some musical instruments and ceremonial dances were kept alive, and some can be seen today. In 1882 the British restricted movements in Hyderabad out of fear that the sizable Siddi population would organize against them. The Siddis of Hyderabad today number about 2000. They are aware of their ancestry, but largely identify with the Muslim community. They occasionally perform African-style dances and songs for the public.

Other Siddis Today

The performances of the Siddi Risala have occasionally been called "barbaric" by Indian critics. Siddis are still associated with the disadvantages of slavery. In addition, Indians have a long history, perhaps dating back several thousand years, of associating light skin with high castes. Moreover, many South Asian societies were most likely influenced by British derogatory attitudes toward the Africans during the colonial period. As most Siddis today are Muslims, they also sometimes confront the difficulties of being a religious minority in mostly Hindu India. Many Siddis, of course, have intermarried and moved away from their communities, although distinct Siddi communities exist in Bombay, North Karnataka, Junagarh, Broach, Sindh, and Baluchistan, as well as in other places outside India. Possibly because these communities are small and lack financial power, they have been largely ignored by Africans in other countries; perhaps as a consequence, the Siddis have shown little interest in Pan Africanism.

See Also

Indian Ocean Slave Trade; Abyssinia.

Africa

Southern African Development Community,

a group of southern African nations promoting economic growth and development and economic interdependence.

During the 1960s a sense of common purpose developed among the countries in southern Africa that were involved in struggles for political independence from colonial and white-minority governments. After years of informally coordinating resources and strategies, several nations agreed to meet with donor governments and development organizations in Gaborone, Botswana, in May 1979 and again in July in Arusha, Tanzania. The purpose of the meetings was to discuss the possibility of forming an organized coalition. In 1980 nine countries met in Lusaka, Zambia, to form the Southern African Development Coordination Conference (SADCC), including Angola, Botswana, Lesotho, Malawi, Zambia, Mozambique, Swaziland, Tanzania, and Zimbabwe. (Namibia, South Africa, and Mauritius joined in the early 1990s.) In their mission statement, known as the Lusaka Declaration, SADCC members pledged to "pursue policies aimed at economic liberation and integrated development of our national economies."

SADCC members initially focused on coordinating and pooling resources around communications, energy issues, and agricultural research. The end of the cold war followed by the end of Apartheid in South Africa, however, brought the necessity and the possibility for closer ties among these nations. In 1992 SADCC changed its name to the Southern African Development Community (SADC) and expanded its mission. In addition to aiming for regional economic integration, SADC had goals that included the evolution of common political values and institutions, environmental protection, and the preservation of the social and cultural affinities in the region. Most recently, SADC developed a defense and security branch for the purpose of peacefully resolving both civil and cross-border conflicts.

SADC has sponsored projects ranging in scope from environmental protection to tourism in conjunction with regional and foreign nongovernmental organizations, but the group has been criticized by the regional press for failing to address human rights concerns, such as police brutality. Additionally, SADC has not effectively tackled the massive debts that plague most southern African nations. Despite these shortcomings, SADC continues to attract new members beyond the region; Seychelles and the Democratic Republic of the Congo were the most recent to join.

Jessica Hochman

See Also

Botswana (Ready Reference); Tourism in Africa; Human Rights in Africa.

North America

Southern Christian Leadership Conference,

civil rights organization led by Martin Luther King Jr. and a coalition of other Southern black ministers that organized protests in the 1950s and 1960s against segregation and barriers to voting.

The civil rights activist Bayard Rustin once described the Southern Christian Leadership Conference (SCLC) as the "dynamic center" of the cluster of organizations that made up the Civil Rights Movement. It differed from such organizations as the Student Nonviolent Coordinating Committee (SNCC) and the National Association for the Advancement of Colored People (NAACP), which functioned nationwide and sought to recruit individual members. SCLC served as an umbrella group for affiliates and initially concentrated its energies on America's segregated South. With prominent black ministers on its executive board and Rev. Martin Luther King Jr. at its helm, SCLC proved to be a guiding force and inspiration to the organizations and protesters engaged in the struggle for civil rights. In the words of one activist, "Southern Christian Leadership Conference is not an organization – it's a church."

In January 1957, 60 activists responded to a call for an Atlanta conference on nonviolent integration. Among the leaders were Northern activists Rustin, Ella J. Baker, and Stanley Levison, and Southern civil rights veterans King, Fred L. Shuttlesworth, Ralph Abernathy, C. K. Steele, Joseph Lowery, and William Holmes Borders. Shortly after this meeting the group established a permanent organization, the Southern Christian Leadership Conference, and elected King as president. The goal was to "to redeem the soul of America" through nonviolent resistance based on the teachings of Mohandas Gandhi. The organization drew its strength from the black churches of the South, whose ministers were said to mirror the spirit of the community.

John Tilley and, later, Baker took the job of running the Atlanta headquarters. Despite the increasingly contentious climate in the South, where black students led sit-ins and Freedom Rides to protest segregation, SCLC's early activities were fairly mild, focusing on education programs and on bringing rural blacks to the voting booth.

A SNCC-led protest against segregation in Albany, Georgia, was already under way in late November 1961, when King and executive director Wyatt T. Walker brought the SCLC into its first major nonviolent campaign. In some ways it was unsuccessful; demonstrations and arrests provoked few changes and garnered little national attention. The federal courts, which had acted in support of earlier desegregation disputes, refused to back up the protesters. After a failed attempt to raise national support by calling attention to the imprisonment of King and Abernathy, SCLC retreated from Albany.

The SCLC's 1963 campaign in Birmingham, Alabama, succeeded in every way the Albany campaign had not. In a city where white supremacist Eugene "Bull" Connor controlled the police, SCLC launched Project C ("C" for confrontation). The movement drew criticism from white liberals like Robert Kennedy, as well as some blacks, who suggested that the protesters await the reforms promised by the recently elected mayor. But as King pointed out: "Justice too long delayed is justice denied." Without its usual supporters, the demonstration limped on, and black protesters who sat-in at white-only counters soon crowded the city jails.

A brilliant strategic move turned the tide of the faltering demonstration. On May 2, 1963, 700 black children marched from the 16th Street Baptist Church in through town. After police wagons were filled, the children were carted to jail in school buses. When 2500 more young protesters marched the next day, the police turned fire hoses on them, and the international press turned its lenses on Birmingham's police. The world saw pictures of black children knocked down by a force of water so powerful that it tore the bark off nearby trees. Now under international pressure and the growing threat of a riot, Birmingham's officials returned to the bargaining table more willing to deal with SCLC.

As a result of the Birmingham protest, SCLC won a desegregation settlement. More important, the protest laid the groundwork for the nation's 1964 Civil Rights Act. After its Birmingham triumph, SCLC organized other desegregation campaigns in Savannah, Georgia, and St. Augustine, Florida, and played a pivotal role in the 1963 MARCH ON WASHINGTON. During FREEDOM SUMMER of 1964, it joined the CONGRESS OF RACIAL EQUALITY (CORE) for a massive voter registration campaign.

In its 1965 campaign in Selma, Alabama, SCLC took aim at unjust registration tests designed to keep blacks from voting. In some Southern counties less than 5 percent of the eligible black population was registered; in other counties no blacks could vote. When 400 prospective black voters, led by King and JOHN LEWIS, staged a "stand-in" at the Dallas County Courthouse, they were harassed and arrested. As King wrote in the *New York Times*, more blacks were in Selma jails than were registered to vote.

Galvanized by a surge of police brutality in neighboring Marion County, SCLC organized a 50-mile march from Selma to Montgomery. As 600 marchers began the walk, state troopers, under orders from Governor George Wallace, attacked them with clubs and tear gas. The day was dubbed Bloody Sunday.

More protesters came to Selma to undertake the march again, but tension between the two organizers, SCLC and SNCC, delayed the protest. King led a second march just over the Pettus Bridge. SNCC members accused King of mapping this partial march after negotiating a compromise with Wallace, and the rift between the organizations widened. By the time the full march led by both organizations took place in March, the landmark Voting Rights Act banning unfair voting tests had already been passed. The march took place anyway as a symbolic gesture of the solidarity needed for the long journey ahead.

Some observers criticized the SCLC for being too dependent on white liberal support and, as compared to the rising BLACK POWER movement, too moderate. SCLC responded to the criticism by expanding its operations north to CHICAGO, ILLINOIS, where, according to one historian, "SCLC discovered... that discrimination was a far more insidious and tenacious enemy than segregation." The organization shifted its attention to economic inequality.

OPERATION BREADBASKET, organized in July 1967 as a national program to put "bread, money, and income into the baskets of black and poor people," became the economic arm of SCLC, organizing black consumers to press for jobs and to encourage black-owned businesses. Seeing poverty as the root of inner-city violence, SCLC began planning the Poor People's Campaign that would push for federal legislation to guarantee employment, income, and housing for the nation's economically disadvantaged blacks.

The assassination of King on April 4, 1968, interrupted plans for the Poor People's Campaign. The SCLC resumed planning the Washington demonstration. Under its newly elected leader, Ralph Abernathy, the SCLC brought between 50,000 and 100,000 people to Washington to rally support for economic justice for African Americans.

After King's death the organization went into a tailspin, beset by a decline in contributions and internal dissension over Abernathy's leadership. Lowery revived the SCLC in the late 1970s by expanding the organization's operations beyond traditional civil rights programs, but the organization never regained its original stature.

Marian Aguiar

SEE ALSO

Abernathy, Ralph David; King, Martin Luther, Jr.; Lowery, Joseph Echols; Poor People's Washington Campaign; Sixteenth Street Baptist Church (Birmingham, Ala.); Voting Rights Act of 1965; Walker, Wyatt Tee.

North America

Southern Negro Youth Congress, **organization established in RICHMOND, VIRGINIA, in February 1937; until its demise in 1949 the Southern Negro Youth Congress (SNYC) played a critical role in the struggle of black Americans for full citizenship and for social, political, and economic justice.**

In the spring of 1937 black tobacco stemmers spontaneously walked out of Richmond-area tobacco plants protesting poor wages and hazardous working conditions. With the American Federation of Labor refusing assistance, C. Columbus Alston, Francis Grandison, and James E. Jackson Jr. helped the stemmers organize a Congress of Industrial Organizations (CIO)-affiliated union, which successfully struck Richmond's Export Leaf Tobacco Company. The victory had the effect of raising wages throughout the tobacco industry, and it inaugurated the SNYC's work in the South. By 1939 the organization had established a headquarters in Birmingham, Alabama, from which it coordinated organizing efforts across the South.

The SNYC's initial membership drew from the 1930s student movement, the Communist Party, and the CIO. Early leaders included Edward Strong, William Richardson, Louis Burnham, and Jackson. These men worked to connect the ongoing black struggle for civil rights to the industrial union movement of the late 1930s. But from the inception of the SNYC women played key roles in the organization, and by the early 1940s they assumed formal leadership positions. Esther Cooper Jackson served as SNYC's executive secretary during the 1940s. Jackson, Sallye Davis, Dorothy Burnham, and Augusta Jackson Strong agitated for gender equity within the organization. At the same time they worked to establish ties between the SNYC and preexisting networks of protest and resistance within Southern black communities.

The SNYC's connection with the Communist Party provided important links to an international arena of struggle and to a cadre of aggressive grassroots organizers. The SNYC was, however, firmly rooted in the institutional and intellectual life of black communities across the South. Its members and constituencies came to the organization from the black Baptist church, the NATIONAL ASSOCIATION FOR THE ADVANCEMENT OF COLORED PEOPLE (NAACP), women's clubs, and fraternal and benevolent associations. Members of the SNYC worked hard to build coalitions, drawing on organizations, institutions, and individuals across lines of class, gender, and generation. They also attempted to reach out to white Southerners interested in economic and political transformation.

During its 12-year existence the SNYC organized eight youth legislatures in cities like Richmond; Birmingham; Chattanooga, Tennessee; and Columbia, South Carolina. The youth legislatures were living laboratories of the SNYC's vision of life and struggle. The meetings brought together various individuals and organizations active in struggles for justice in the South and the nation. Local advisory boards were formed, and older leaders from respective host cities filled positions in them. Federal government officials, national labor leaders, and icons of the black struggle for freedom, like W. E. B. Du Bois and PAUL ROBESON, attended and addressed meetings of the youth leglisature. Through small working groups, legislature participants developed plans of action and drew up resolutions for federal government legislation. The legislatures invigorated local struggles and helped garner support for the SNYC's agenda of political and economic transformation. They also provided important venues for connecting local struggles to broader international ones. At the 1946 Columbia, South Carolina, meeting Du Bois explained, "This is the firing line not simply for the emancipation of the American Negro but for the emancipation of the African Negro and the Negroes of the West Indies... and for the emancipation of the white slaves of modern capitalist monopoly."

In 1940 the House Un-American Activities Committee listed the SNYC as a Communist Party front and agent of foreign powers. The Federal Bureau of Investigation placed the organization and its leaders under surveillance over the next 12 years. Although the SNYC's affiliation with the Communist Party did little to hamper its support in black communities through the World War II years, by 1947 and the advent of the cold war, the organization encountered increased opposition along many fronts. In 1948 the Internal Revenue Service withdrew the group's tax-exempt status. Liberal organizations stopped providing financial and public support. The SNYC's final youth legislature, held in Birmingham, was disrupted by local vigilantes and the city's chief of police, Eugene "Bull" Connor. By 1949 the organization ceased operations, and its members were forced to pursue new avenues of struggle. The SNYC, however, anticipated the student movement of the 1960s and left a lasting imprint on African Americans' struggle for freedom.

Peter Lau

See Also

World War II and African Americans; Baptists; Civil Rights Movement; Du Bois, William Edward Burghardt (W. E. B.); Labor Unions in the United States; Richmond, Virginia; Communist Party USA, African Americans and the.

Africa

Southern Rhodesia. Former name of Zimbabwe.

Africa

South West Africa. Former name of Namibia.

Africa

South West Africa People's Organization, nationalist organization that became the governing party of independent Namibia.

In the late 1950s Andimba Toivo ja Toivo and other nationalists formed the Ovambo People's Congress, later named the Ovambo People's Organization (OPO), to protest South Africa's occupation and its discriminatory labor and land policies. In April 1960, seeking to broaden the group's appeal and thwart rival nationalist groups, the OPO changed its name to the South West African People's Organization (SWAPO), and redefined its goal as "the liberation of the Namibian people from colonial oppression and exploitation." It defined its struggle in terms of class warfare and colonial racial discrimination. Supported by workers and educated youth, SWAPO was dominated by ethnic Ovambos, including its president, Sam Nujoma. The other major nationalist group at the time was the ethnic Herero-dominated South West African National Union, which sought support among the rural youth. By 1961 SWAPO claimed 50,000 members, though much of its leadership was either in prison or exile.

Around 1962 SWAPO began sending members overseas for military training, and in 1966 it launched a guerrilla war for independence that lasted for 23 years. In addition to its armed wing, the People's Liberation Army of Namibia, the party expanded its support base, forming a Women's Council as well as a radical Youth League. It also publicized its campaign internationally through the party paper, the *Namibian News*, and nine overseas offices. In 1973 SWAPO won international recognition as the sole representative of the Namibian people. But in 1976 disagreement about how the party should approach South Africa's offers for an "internal settlement" led to a serious rift in the party, as did the killing and torture of many dissident members throughout the struggle. Still, SWAPO emerged from this crisis the unchallenged leader of the nationalist cause. From the late 1970s onward Nujoma led SWAPO in both the war effort and international negotiations for Namibian independence, which was achieved in 1990. The organization's majority position in the country's first parliament increased to 72 percent in 1994 elections. Since independence SWAPO has opted for a mixed economy and has done little to challenge the white minority population's hold over much of the country's land and industry.

Eric Young

See Also

Nationalism in Africa; Nujoma, Samuel.

Africa

Soweto, South Africa, South African township near Johannesburg.

Situated 24 km (about 15 mi) to the southwest of Johannesburg in the Gauteng Province, Soweto is one of the largest urban areas in southern Africa, with an estimated population of at least 2 million people. It has also become one of South Africa's most famous townships, mostly due to a massive uprising there in 1976, in which police killed hundreds of protesters. Once a squatters' camp, Soweto became not only a center of the fight against apartheid, but also one of the most visible symbols of its brutality.

Between World War I and World War II rapid industrialization in South Africa sparked a massive migration of rural Africans to Johannesburg, which was the center of the country's mining industry. Many of the migrant workers lived in camps outside town. In part due to white fears of black self-rule in the squatters' camps, the South African government in 1948 set aside 65 sq km (25 sq mi) of land to accommodate the workers. They built thousands of two-room houses and named the new township Soweto, an abbreviation for "South-Western Townships." Soweto's population grew quickly as the result of continued voluntary migration and the new policies of the Afrikaner-dominated National Party government, which forcibly resettled blacks into townships.

Poverty, overcrowding, and oppression characterized life in Soweto under apartheid. The former archbishop Desmond Tutu, who lived in Soweto in the mid-1970s, recalled that at the time more than a million residents shared a single swimming pool. The schools were ill-equipped and underfunded – and increasingly staffed by teachers who had not completed university degrees. The typical house, which served as home for 12 to 15 people, lacked both internal plumbing and, until the 1980s, electricity.

By 1976, the year of the uprising, political protest had become an established part of township life, and students were among the most active participants (*see* Black Consciousness in Africa). That year the government's ruling that half the classes in the nation's secondary schools were to be taught in Afrikaans – which many Africans considered the language of the oppressor – led student groups to organize a protest march on June 16, 1976. An estimated 15,000 schoolchildren attended. Most observers now agree that the demonstration was peaceful until police fired a tear gas canister into the crowd, and the children retaliated by throwing rocks. The police opened fire, killing and wounding hundreds of Soweto residents, including many children. The incident set off rioting throughout the country, leading to more than 575 deaths.

Soweto, home to Tutu, Winnie Madikizela-Mandela, and, after his release from prison, Nelson Mandela, continued to be the epicenter of antiapartheid action. Protests continued even after P. W. Botha cracked down on opposition groups in the 1980s. The political atmosphere became so tense that some Soweto residents suspected of working as informants for the South African government were assaulted or killed, a situation decried by Mandela and others. Since the end of apartheid and Mandela's election as South Africa's president in 1994, conditions in Soweto have improved somewhat, although poverty and crime are still pressing problems. One of the most dramatic signs of change is that Soweto is now a popular tourist destination, with local entrepreneurs guiding visitors through a postapartheid Soweto.

Kate Tuttle

See Also

Antiapartheid Movement; Johannesburg, South Africa; Mandela, Nelson Rolihlahla; Tourism in Africa; Botha, Pieter Willem; Tutu, Desmond Mpilo.

Africa

Soyinka, Wole (b. July 13, 1934, Abeokuta, Nigeria), internationally acclaimed Nigerian writer.

In 1986 Wole Soyinka (pronounced Sho-yin-ka), born Akinwande Oluwole Soyinka, was the first African writer to receive the Nobel Prize for Literature. The committee conferring the prize described the creator of more than 20 major works as "one of the finest poetical playwrights that have written in English," and also remarked that his writing was "full of life and urgency." Soyinka is the recipient of numerous other prestigious awards, including several honorary doctorates from universities all over the world. Apart from his stature as a pioneer in African drama written in English, Soyinka has produced a vast body of work – as poet, dramatist, theater director, novelist, essayist, autobiographer, political commentator, critic, and theorist of art and culture. Above all, he has remained a responsible citizen committed to the values of human freedom, truth, and justice. "Social commitment," he remarks, "is a citizen's commitment and embraces equally the carpenter, the mason, the banker, the farmer, the customs officer, etc., not forgetting the critic. I accept a general citizen's commitment which only happens to express itself through art and words." Through his entire career spanning more than 40 years, Soyinka has retained a remarkable consistency of vision in his dedication as an artist and as a socially responsible citizen.

Soyinka's vast creative talent is expressed in some 16 published plays – comedies, tragedies, and satires. His early play, *A Dance of the Forests* (1960), was written on the occasion of Nigeria's independence and includes his characteristic watchful irony and a warning to the Nigerian people and leaders not to romanticize the past as they forge a future for the new nation. *Death and the King's Horseman* (1975) typifies his imaginative engagement with tradition. *Priority Projects* (1982) are satirical agitprop sketches, written and performed with the Unife Guerrilla Theatre. Soyinka's recent play, *The Beatification of Area Boy: A Lagosian Kaleidoscope* (1996), is about the survival of the underclass in a deteriorating urban landscape around Lagos. Soyinka has created dramatic and memorable characters, including Elesin Oba, Iyaloja, Eman, Kongi, Sidi, and Sadiku, as well as the autobiographically inspired figures of his mother (The Wild Christian) and his father (Essay) in *Ake: The Years of Childhood* (1981). He has published four volumes of poetry, the most recent titled *Mandela's Earth and Other Poems* (1988). That collection begins with the striking opening lines, "Your logic frightens me, Mandela.... Your bounty... that taut / Drumskin on your heart on which our millions / dance." Soyinka's three collections of essays include *Myth, Literature and the African World* (1976); *Art, Dialogue and Outrage: Essays on Literature and Culture* (1988); and most recently, *The Open Sore of a Continent: Personal Narrative of the Nigerian Crisis* (1996). Soyinka has also written lyrics and musical compositions for a record album, *Unlimited Liability Company*. Songs such as "Ethike Revolution" and "I Love My Country" are, like his newspaper articles, topical, hard-hitting, and responsive to particular situations.

An artist to the core – indeed, a cultural worker in the best tradition – Soyinka is deeply rooted in the African tradition of an artist who functions as the voice of vision of his times. He is not afraid to take action when necessary; he is never merely a commentator from the sidelines and never untrue to the demands of his craft, whether his work is in the form of a poem, an essay, or a play. Indeed, in Soyinka we discover the remarkable fusing of the creative and the political; he invents new ways (often misunderstood by his critics) of linking the mythic and political, of forging imaginative links between harsh political realities and cosmological, spiritual realms.

A biographical overview of this manifold artist must emphasize his YORUBA heritage and his roots in the Yoruba culture and world-view. (The Yoruba are among the three largest ethnic groups in Nigeria, along with the IGBO and the HAUSA.) Although his parents, Ayo and Eniola, had converted to Christianity (*see* CHRISTIANITY, AFRICAN: AN OVERVIEW), Soyinka himself never embraced the Christian religion; he feels more at home with traditional Yoruba religion and is a personal devotee of the Yoruba god Ogun, who also figures prominently in his writings. Soyinka describes Ogun as "god of creativity, guardian of the road, god of metallic lore and artistry. Explorer, hunter, god of war... custodian of the sacred oath." Changing historical times enable creative redefinitions of roles played by anthropomorphized deities like Ogun; today Ogun, as god of metal and of the road, is worshiped not only by blacksmiths, but also by truck drivers and airline pilots – all workers in metal.

In addition to his Yoruba-Christian upbringing, Soyinka received a Western academic education. Born in Abeokuta, Soyinka began his Western schooling in the Nigeria of the 1930s and 1940s, when it was still ruled by British colonizers. Next he spent two years (1952-1954) at the newly established University College in Ibadan, where his classmates included CHINUA ACHEBE, CHRISTOPHER OKIGBO, and JOHN PEPPER CLARK, all of whom made their marks later in Nigerian literature. Soyinka then earned a B.A. from the University of Leeds (1954-1957) in GREAT BRITAIN. He spent a year as play reader at the Royal Court Theatre in London (1958-1959) and returned to Nigeria in 1960 on a Rockefeller Fellowship for the study of Nigerian traditions and culture.

Through his education Soyinka imbibed the Western intellectual tradition, but in his writing he comes across first and foremost as a Yoruba, and it is from a base in Yoruba culture – his inspiration – that he responds to other literary and cultural traditions. His art is eclectic, a successful blend of African themes with Western forms and techniques. In his hands African traditions assume meanings that are much wider than the ones accepted within their geographical location. "We must not think that traditionalism means raffia skirts," Soyinka has remarked. "It's no longer possible for a purist literature for the simple reason that even our most traditional literature has never been purist."

Just as he confronts African "traditionalism" in the narrow sense, Soyinka also recognizes the irony of using the English language – a lingering legacy of colonialism. However, he is never apologetic about this matter; rather, he proudly accepts the challenge of making the English language "carry the weight," as Achebe puts it, "of [his] African experience. But it will have to be a new English, still in full communion with its ancestral home, but altered to suit its new African surroundings.... The price a world language must be prepared to pay is submission to many different kinds of use." The role of English as a link language among people with various indigenous languages is certainly a historical reality in postcolonial societies (*see* DECOLONIZATION IN AFRICA: AN INTERPRETATION). Language itself becomes a weapon for writers like Achebe, Soyinka, and others from the Third World to confront the disruptive remnants of colonialism and the negative continuities of neocolonialism in contemporary times.

Along with adapting the English language to his African experience, Soyinka optimally uses his education to transform literary forms from their European origins – often problematically considered universal – to suit his own cultural reality. In dramas such as *The Road* (1965) and *Death and the King's Horseman*, Soyinka presents a new form: Yoruba tragedy that departs in significant ways from Western dramatic forms, such as Shakespearean or Greek tragedy. In this form ritual, masquerade, dance, music, and mythopoeic language all work toward the very purpose of Yoruba tragedy, which is communal benefit.

Soyinka's contribution to Nigerian drama has gone beyond his considerable achievement as a playwright to his key role in professionalizing the English-language theater in Nigeria, forming companies such as the 1960 Masks and the Orisun Theater. The history of English-language professional theater in Nigeria is related integrally to Soyinka's dramatic career. There is a clear correspondence between the timing of his plays and the prevalent political climate. Biting satirical plays such as *The Trials of Brother Jero* (1963), *Opera Wonyosi* (1981), *Kongi's Harvest* (1967), and *A Play of Giants: A Fantasia on the Aminian Theme* (1984) indict African presidents-for-life (such as IDI AMIN) as a "parade of monsters." Most recently, *The Beatification of Area Boy: A Lagosian Kaleidoscope* theatrically enacts the survival of the urban underclass under SANI ABACHA's military regime.

Soyinka has the unique capacity not simply to write about social injustice in his creative work, but to meet the challenge and

In 1986 Wole Soyinka became the first African writer and the first black person to receive the Nobel Prize for Literature. Here the author displays the prize to the audience. *AP/Wide World Photos*

be an activist whenever necessary. There is no contradiction between Soyinka the artist, imaginatively exploring metaphysical matters in his creative work, and Soyinka the engaged citizen, commenting on Nigerian sociopolitical issues. He is concerned with the quality of public life and speaks openly as the conscience of his nation. (An example of Soyinka's civic activism and his attempt to improve the safety of road travel in Nigeria was his establishment of the Oyo Road Safety Corps in 1980.) His incarceration for nearly two years (although he was never formally charged or tried) during the Nigerian civil war was a painful result of his attempt to redress "the colossal moral failure" in the nation. "The man dies in all who keep silent in the face of tyranny," he remarks in his prison notes, titled *The Man Died* (1972). Soyinka considers "justice... the first condition of humanity" and recognizes that "books and all forms of writing have always been objects of terror to those who seek to suppress truth."

Soyinka's deep and energetic concern for his country has remained unflagging over the past 40 years of his literary career. He has always been a stern and uncompromising critic of social injustice, regardless of its source. He roundly criticized Yakubu Gowon's military government in *The Man Died*, just as he criticized Shehu Shagari's "civilian" government in *Priority Projects* and Abacha's military rule in *The Open Sore of a Continent*.

Soyinka's artistic vision, even as it engages with Nigeria, encompasses a universal scope. "A historic vision is of necessity universal," Soyinka remarked in "The Writer in an African State," a 1967 essay. In *The Open Sore of a Continent*, even as he explores the troubled notion of the nation in Nigeria (*see* NATIONALISM IN AFRICA), he makes links to similar crises of nationhood in Yugoslavia and the Soviet Union. He asks directly and poignantly, "What price a nation?" especially when atrocities are committed in the name of "national protection, sovereignty, [and] development." His personal voice – bitter, angry, anguished – recognizes the traps of nationhood when the state acts as a repressive force crushing those who dissent.

Like Ogun, god of the road, Soyinka's creativity and courage blaze paths toward democratic ideals and social justice in Nigeria. "I have one abiding religion, human liberty," he has remarked. With his passion for freedom, with his deep concern for the quality of human life, Soyinka's work has profound significance in contemporary world literature.

Ketu Katrak

SEE ALSO

Abeokuta, Nigeria; Colonial Rule; Gowon, Yakubu; Ibadan, Nigeria; Lagos, Nigeria; Nigeria; Ogun.

Europe

Spain, a country in southwestern Europe in which blacks have had a presence for centuries.

Black Africans have inhabited the Iberian Peninsula since the beginnings of recorded history. Blacks accompanied the Carthaginians when they colonized the Iberian Peninsula in the fifth century B.C.E. and blacks, both free and enslaved, were present in the social life of the Roman province of Spain.

Throughout the Middle Ages both Christian and Muslim states on the peninsula enslaved black Africans. Moors, a people from northern Africa, provided most of the troops for the Muslim conquest of the Iberian Peninsula (711-718). Although the Arab ruling minority claimed political power under the caliphate of Cordoba (850-1033), the Moorish majority pushed for most of the changes in the emerging new society. The cultural life of al-Andalus, as Muslim Spain was known, helped shape modern Spanish society. Black African slaves, as well as gold transported across the Sahara, contributed to the wealth of Muslim Spain (*see* TRANS-SAHARAN AND RED SEA SLAVE TRADE). Records indicate that Christian bishops in Catalonia purchased black slaves as early as the tenth century. In the eleventh century King Alfonso VI of Castile and León sponsored the arrival of the French clergy of Cluny to his kingdom with donations of gold from West Africa.

In Muslim Spain, after the fall of the Córdoba caliphate, a series of invasions and immigrations from northwestern Africa – led by the ALMORAVIDS and ALMOHADS – brought significant numbers of blacks to Iberian soil. Black troops in the Almoravid army of Yusuf helped deal a serious defeat to Alfonso VI in the battle of Sagrejas. The Moorish political ascendancy in the Iberian Peninsula would not fade until the final defeat in 1492 of the kingdom of Granada by the Roman Catholic monarchs Isabella and Ferdinand.

The Atlantic expansion of the kingdom of Castile in the fifteenth century would shift the practice of enslaving black Africans in a dramatic way. PORTUGAL and Spain established modern slavery in the West through the forced importation of an almost exclusively black African work force first to the Iberian Peninsula, then to the African Atlantic islands (*see* CAPE VERDE), and finally to the Americas after 1492. Christopher Columbus, in his diaries, established an early connection between the enslavement of Africans and the possible enslavement of the indigenous inhabitants of the New World.

The forced relocation of black Africans to Renaissance Spain provoked changes in Spanish society. Discriminatory policies alternated with measures for the Africans' welfare. In 1478 Ferdinand and Isabella appointed Juan de Valladolid, "black of high birth in his nation," as judge of blacks in Seville – a position similar to the ones existing in Portugal to police the increasing urban black population. Black religious guilds and confraternities (*cofradías de negros*) also appeared in the major cities such as Valencia, Barcelona, Seville, and Jaén. These confraternities followed the model of the trade guilds that then existed throughout Europe. Confraternities were among the most popular forms of civil association in Spanish society. They provided the only means of acquiring social recognition for the black population. These groups provided mutual help and religious association like other confraternities of the day, but because of the nature of slavery as an institution, black confraternities were always under suspicion and faced staunch opposition and rejection from their white counterparts.

In Seville, the city with the largest black population in Spain during the Renaissance, blacks were frequently denied proper burial. Recent archaeological excavations have unearthed literal dumping grounds outside the old city walls for people who were of African descent. The Cofradía de los negritos fought for space in churches allotted to their members for proper religious burial. The religious education of enslaved blacks was the responsibility of their owners, who often favored or discriminated against slaves according to their show of religious devotion. The Inquisition also persecuted black slaves; most were accused of blasphemy. In many cases abused black slaves resorted to uttering blasphemous statements in the belief that Inquisition authorities would then seize them and treat them more mercifully than their masters.

The discovery and conquest of America by the Spaniards propelled the demographic revolution of modern slavery. Portugal, through its African colonies and *feitorias* (trading posts), provided slaves to private individuals to whom the king of Spain granted special licenses – *licencias* and later *asientos* – to import slaves to America and the Spanish mainland. SUGAR plantations in the Canary Islands were the forerunners of the Caribbean system of labor, relying on contingents of African slaves. Seville, as the center of commerce in the new American colonies, became one of Europe's foremost slave ports, second only to Lisbon. Sub-Saharan Africans were not the only slave populations living in Spain in the sixteenth and seventeenth centuries. Muslim prisoners and victims of slaving raids from North Africa – present-day ALGERIA and TUNISIA – were also living in captivity on Spanish soil.

However, the West African slave trade (*see* TRANSATLANTIC SLAVE TRADE) soon became the main source of a captive labor force in Spanish society, to such a point that the

OPPOSITE: A prime example of Moorish architecture is the Court of Lions at the Alhambra, once the palace of the Moorish monarchy in Granada, Spain. Built in the thirteenth and fourteenth centuries, the Alhambra was partially destroyed by Spain's King Charles I in the sixteenth century. *CORBIS/Adam Woolfitt*

LEFT: The renowned seventeenth-century Spanish artist Diego Rodríguez de Silva y Velázquez painted fellow artist and assistant Juan de Pareja (c. 1610-1670) in 1650. *The Metropolitan Museum of Art, Fletcher Fund, Rogers Fund, and Bequest of Miss Adelaide Milton de Groot (1876-1967), by exchange, supplemented by gifts from friends of the Museum, 1971. (1971.86) Photograph by Malcolm Varon, © 1989 The Metropolitan Museum of Art*

BELOW LEFT: Between 1252 and 1284 Alfonso X the Wise directed the compilation of a book of songs in honor of Our Lady, titled ***Las Cántigas de Santa Maria.*** In this illuminated manuscript one painting illustrates Muslim armies invading Christian lands and taking booty. *Image of the Black Project, Harvard University*

Spanish word *"negro"* (meaning "black") became synonymous with "slave." Slave owners belonged to all sectors of society, from the aristocracy to the clergy, businessmen, artisans, and wealthy peasants. At the end of the sixteenth century in Seville and its surrounding area, more than 14,000 slaves were counted out of a total population of 150,000. Estimates for that period suggest that 100,000 slaves lived in Spain, of whom the majority were black. African slaves were generally employed to perform unsafe and difficult tasks. Women, for instance, were hired out by their owners to make soap or to sell produce in the streets. Their masters forced many female slaves into prostitution, although it was illegal. Male slaves typically worked in taverns and gambling houses, where violence erupted frequently. Black slaves were on the staff of the printing houses in Seville that sent the first books to the Americas. But most slaves, male and female, were employed both as agricultural workers and domestic servants.

Life for black Africans was harder than for any other group in Spanish society. Malnutrition, physical exhaustion, and punishment constituted their common lot. In larger cities special quarters existed for blacks, both free and in bondage, since some masters did not allow slaves to live with them, and officials sought to keep blacks separate from the white population. Escape was very difficult in a hostile society, and punishment for it very harsh, in the form of lashes, branding, and amputations.

Free blacks had little opportunity to advance in society because they were excluded from almost every trade and profession. Laws and local ordinances limited the access of blacks to professional ranks, the church hierarchy, convents for women, universities, and practically all legitimate trade guilds. Various cities enacted laws limiting the movement of blacks, both free and enslaved. Laws prohibited blacks in most cases from carrying weapons either in cities or in the countryside at a time when violent crime was rampant, especially in cities like Madrid or Seville. Laws of *limpieza de sangre*, or "purity of blood" (*see* RACE IN LATIN AMERICA) permitted legal discrimination against anyone of black African descent.

Many free blacks decided to immigrate to America early in the conquest. One of them, Juan de Grijalba, introduced wheat to

Mexico when Hernán Cortés conquered the country (1519-1521). Other blacks who achieved fame in their time were the sixteenth-century scholar and humanist Juan Latino, author of the *Austriad*, an epic poem written in Latin, and the seventeenth-century painter Juan de Pareja.

Blacks made a major impact on Spanish culture during the Golden Age (c. 1500-1681). Contemporary writers portrayed the presence of blacks in a variety of ways. The playwright Lope de Vega created the first full dramatic roles for black men and women, both as comic-relief characters and as protagonists. Imported from Portugal, black speech – *lengua de negro* – was used as a typical form of characterization. Blacks were also hired as dancers and entertainers in religious pageants and celebrations. The influence of African music and dance in Spain during the Renaissance was formidable, and it crossed the Atlantic to Mexico, Peru, the Caribbean, and elsewhere (*see* Dance in Latin America and the Caribbean). The *zarabanda* (saraband) was blamed for the decay in morals, and the *chacona* (chaconne), *mozambique*, *guineo*, *zamba*, and dozens of other dancing rhythms influenced popular music on both sides of the ocean.

The flood of slaves that had arrived in Spain during this period came to a slow end in the early seventeenth century, when Portugal lost its control of the coast of Guinea to the Dutch, and the Spanish economy began to decline. Seville's commercial monopoly in the colonies eroded, and it lost its position as a slave trade center. The price of black slaves became too expensive in relation to that of free labor. The remaining population of African descent ceased to be a distinct group within a few generations. The Spanish Crown tried to establish diplomatic ties with the kingdom of Allada (in present-day Benin), and Capuchin missionaries were sent there in the 1660s. The mission failed when the king of Allada realized that he would not obtain commercial benefits from the alliance in the short term.

By the eighteenth century the West African slave trade supplied markets in the Americas almost exclusively. The only regular supply of slaves to Spain during the eighteenth century came from North Africa – Morocco, Algeria, Tunisia – in the course of the continuous wars between Spain and North African states. Combatants on both sides of the Mediterranean enslaved prisoners of war well into the late eighteenth century, when warfare began to give way to diplomatic missions between King Carlos III of Spain and the sultan of Morocco.

Intermarriage after manumission and merger within a few generations with the nonblack population led to the disappearance of a significant black population in Spain by the mid-eighteenth century. The absence of large plantations for the cultivation of sugar, cotton, coffee, and tobacco, or even extensive mining, limited the demand for slave labor in Spain. The local supply of free labor also competed successfully with slaves (whose purchase and maintenance could be expensive). In cities like Seville, Madrid, Jaen, or Valladolid, religious confraternities of blacks – both free and enslaved – saw the numbers of their brothers dwindle. As among the descendants of Spanish Jews, the descendants of black Spaniards had little incentive to preserve the memory of their African origins. Black African ancestry had been a severe social handicap in Spain for centuries.

The only new group of Africans to arrive in Spain in the eighteenth century were escapees from the southern Portuguese region of Alentejo. They crossed the Spanish border and established themselves in the towns of Gibraleón and Niebla, in western Andalusia. As it did in the American colonies, the Spanish government established special military companies composed entirely of black soldiers. These companies were employed in defending and patrolling the border with Portugal along the Guadiana River. The descendants of these eighteenth-century blacks who fled slavery in Portugal still constitute the only group of Spaniards who trace their ancestry back to sub-Saharan Africa.

Spain never officially abolished slavery. Although the government signed treaties with Great Britain to abolish the slave trade, Spain did not free slaves when they entered the European part of the empire, a practice followed in other European countries. Thus slave owners from Cuba and Puerto Rico who traveled back to Spain with black slaves did not lose them when they touched Spanish soil. The 1870 Moret Law, which proclaimed the gradual abolition of slavery in the Caribbean colonies, was the first document to suppress the institution legally. Restrictions imposed by the Spanish government successfully blocked any massive immigration of black colonial subjects to Spain. After the loss of Cuba and Puerto Rico in 1898, this possibility became even more remote.

During the Spanish Civil War (1936-1939), Gen. Francisco Franco's Nationalists employed Moroccan troops. These soldiers, however, were purposely isolated from the rest of society and were seen as a sort of occupying force – ironically, from one of Spain's few remaining colonies. Spain's other remaining colony in Africa was the territory known as Spanish Guinea. After 1959 the black population of Spanish Guinea gained equal legal standing with Spanish whites. This facilitated the migration of many to Spain seeking work and higher education. The Roman Catholic Church aided many Guineans in obtaining grants to study in Spain. Profound political and economic instability followed the independence of the new republic of Equatorial Guinea in 1968, partly caused by the actions of different factions in the Spanish government of General Franco. Large numbers of Equatorial Guineans chose exile in Spain, many as dual citizens. They still compose the largest single national group of African descent in Spain today. Their acceptance by Spanish society is lukewarm at best, even though they share language, religion, and culture with the Spanish white majority.

Spanish society underwent a remarkable transformation during the 1970s. After General Franco's death in 1975 and the installation of a democratic regime in 1977, the Spanish

In the *Chessbook* of Alfonso X of Castile, dating from 1283, a Muslim nobleman plays chess with a black servant. *Image of the Black Project, Harvard University* economy, once so weak that its surplus work force had to emigrate to northern Europe, now required immigrants to fill low-wage jobs. The agricultural sectors of eastern Andalusia and Catalonia employed many undocumented African immigrants. This led to a cycle of legal persecution and economic dependence typical of affluent countries in Western Europe. African immigrants in Spain, both "legal" and "illegal," originate mostly from the Maghreb countries – Morocco, Algeria, Tunisia, and MAURITANIA – and from the West African states of SENEGAL, GHANA, SIERRA LEONE, and NIGERIA. The 1984 Spanish film *Las cartas de Alou* (Letters from Alou), by Montxo Armendáriz, was one of the first attempts by a Spanish artist to address the new issues of African immigration to Spain.

In addition to African immigrants, Dominican citizens of African descent, mostly women, have traveled to Spain seeking domestic employment in the houses of the Spanish urban middle class. They form a growing group of workers, together with Equatorial Guinean women, who are employed in domestic work because of their Spanish-language ability. Their lack of legal rights and vulnerability to deportation, common to immigrants in many more affluent countries, make them victims of abuses, physical and sexual, and of sheer economic exploitation.

The substantial presence of black African and Maghrebi citizens in Spain has challenged certain monolithic cultural and religious traditions. There are more practicing Muslims in Spain today than at any other point in its history since 1492. With Spain's integration into the European Union in 1986 the government adopted measures to stop the arrival of mostly undocumented immigrants, and bouts of xenophobic attacks against Africans and people of African descent have taken place on different occasions. Nongovernmental organizations and immigrant associations continually challenge discriminatory practices and forced repatriations of so-called illegal workers, mostly African. A new generation of Afro-Spaniards is growing in numbers: the Spanish Constitution of 1978 confers automatic citizenship to all born on Spanish soil. The present population of African descent in Spain was estimated in 1998 at more than 500,000 – as a proportion of the Spanish population, it is the highest since the Middle Ages.

Baltasar Fra-Molinero

SEE ALSO

Dance in Sub-Saharan Africa; Gold Trade; Sahara Desert; Christianity: Missionaries in Africa; Dominican Republic; Carthage; Trans-Saharan and Red Sea Slave Trade.

Spanish-American War. Please see SPANISH-CUBAN-AMERICAN WAR, AFRICAN AMERICANS IN THE

Latin America and the Caribbean

Spanish-Cuban-American War

(1895-1898), war for Cuban independence.

CUBA's second major war of independence began in earnest in April 1895, but it was the product of many years of planning. Its political leader was JOSÉ MARTÍ, who founded the Cuban Revolutionary Party; its military leaders were Máximo Gómez and ANTONIO MACEO Y GRAJALES. Tomás Estrada Palma was its emissary in the United States.

Martí was killed in May 1895, but his martyrdom gave the cause new impetus. Unlike their failed attempt in the TEN YEARS' WAR (1868-1878), rebel forces successfully moved into the western provinces quickly, as part of a three-month campaign that swept the entire island. By early 1896 the Cuban rebel forces were active in every region of the country. Martínez de Campos, the Spanish captain general and veteran of the Ten Years' War, was replaced by Gen. Valeriano Weyler. Weyler waged a total war, but Maceo eluded his grasp for months. Spain sent huge reinforcements to Cuba: more than 200,000 Spanish troops during the course of the war. Malaria and yellow fever also decimated the Spanish ranks, proving as formidable as the Cuban rebels.

The Cuban insurrectionists continued to score victories, but in December 1896 Maceo was killed. The Spanish thought this loss would destroy the revolution, but subsequent rebel victories quickly dispelled the notion. The Spanish army eventually did successfully counterattack, driving the Cubans away from the westernmost province and cutting off contact among Cuban forces on several fronts. The Spanish treasury, however, was bleeding, since Spain was also waging a costly colonial war in the Philippines. The United States government was pressuring Spain to bring the war to an end. When the Liberal Party leader Práxedes Mateo Sagasta became prime minister, Spain offered PUERTO RICO and Cuba autonomy, giving the islands the power to legislate on matters such as justice, the treasury, economic development, commerce, and banking. This frustrated Weyler's plans for total military victory; he was replaced by another general. There was conservative opposition to autonomy among Spaniards and procolonial Cubans on the island, but when the United States sent warships to Cuban waters, the situation calmed.

Then, on February 15, 1898, the U.S. battleship *Maine* blew up in Havana harbor, killing 266 men. Both the United States and Spain conducted investigations, but the United States believed that Spain was responsible. It now appears that incorrect storage of fuel caused the blast.

The role of the United States in the war was decisive in its aftermath. Cuba had long been the object of the imperial ambitions of some within the U.S. government. In addition, Cuban landowners had appealed to the U.S. to intervene in Cuba and thus restrain the more radical elements of the independence movement. The sinking of the USS *Maine* provided the needed excuse. Trying to avoid war, the United States offered Spain $300 million for Cuba. Spain rejected the offer and tensions increased between the two countries. On April 25 the United States officially declared war on Spain and two days later imposed a naval blockade on the island. Congress, overall more restrained in its expansionist aspirations than President William McKinley, added the Teller Amendment to its approval to send U.S. troops, blocking any future U.S. claims on Cuban sovereignty. The U.S. intervention in June occurred when Cuban independence forces were already close to victory. By July 16 the Spanish and the Americans were signing a peace treaty; the Cubans were not part of that signing.

The signing of the Paris Treaty on December 10, 1898 – again, the Cubans were not present – officially ceded Puerto Rico, Cuba, Guam, and the Philippines to the United States. The United States occupied Cuba until May 1902, when Tomás Estrada Palma was elected president. To circumvent the Teller Amendment's restrictions against formally incorporating Cuba as part of its empire, the United States pressured the Cuban constituent assembly into adopting the Platt Amendment into the constitution of 1901. The amendment permitted the United States to intervene unilaterally in Cuba if it felt its interests were threatened. This amendment was not abrogated until 1934. The end of Spain's empire led to the rise of the U.S. empire in the Caribbean, a danger of which Martí and Maceo had been aware in their analysis of the U.S. role vis-à-vis the Cuban independence movement. U.S. economic interests in Cuba were huge: by the beginning of the war, about 80 percent of the island's SUGAR industry was controlled by the United States.

Many Cuban combatants were black or mulatto: estimates range between 50 and 80 percent. In 1899 roughly a third of the Cuban population was black or mulatto. After their brave deeds on the battlefield, blacks and mulattos faced discrimination on a large scale. The literacy rate was half that of whites (about 28 percent, compared to over 50 percent for whites). While many Afro-Cubans were part of the workforce, they were grossly underrepresented in some professions: 6 percent of merchants; less than 1 percent of doctors and lawyers; 5 percent of teachers; 10 percent of journalists; 5 percent of architects. These frustrations led to a rise in black political mobilization, the establishment of the PARTIDO INDEPENDIENTE DE COLOR, an Afro-Cuban political party, and an uprising in 1912 that was violently repressed. These developments were a reminder that Cuba, as a new nation, still had a racial legacy with unresolved issues that ran deep.

Alan West

North America

Spanish-Cuban-American War, African Americans in the,

military action from April 20 to December 10, 1898, in which the United States Army's four black regiments played a prominent role.

In the Spanish-Cuban-American War, as in the American Civil War, World War I, and World War II, the involvement of African Americans from the very start served to challenge the American racial status quo. When the U.S. battleship *Maine* exploded in Havana harbor on February 15, 1898, there were 22 blacks among the 266 fatalities. Although a 1976 navy inquiry headed by Adm. Hyman Rickover concluded that the sinking of the *Maine* was most likely due to sparking of coal dust in one of the ship's holds, Americans in 1898 viewed it as an act of Spanish sabotage. As the army mobilized, its four black regiments, the Ninth and Tenth Cavalry and the Twenty-fourth and Twenty-fifth Infantry, stood at the forefront.

In March the army transferred the Twenty-fifth Infantry from Montana to Dry Tortugas Island, located between Key West, Florida, and Cuba. On April 14 the Ninth and Tenth Cavalry and the Twenty-fourth Infantry left their stations in the West for southern staging areas. Their leading role was a product of the widely held but ill-grounded belief that African Americans were immune to tropical diseases. Aware of the health hazards that its men would face in Cuba, the army turned to its black regiments. There was, in any case, no shortage of manpower, black or white. The war was popular, and hundreds of thousands volunteered.

Since African Americans were generally barred from existing state militias, several states, among them Alabama, Illinois, Indiana, Kansas, North Carolina, Ohio, and Virginia, hastily organized all-black regiments. In addition, Congress authorized the army to raise ten new regiments, four of which were for black recruits. However, the volunteers never completed their training in time to see action in the ten-week war. The regular army bore the brunt of the fighting, with the nation's four black regiments playing a key role.

Many blacks hoped that loyal service might win their race better treatment. As the *Boston Evening Transcript* reported, blacks thought that "willingness to die on an equality with white men gives them the claim to live on something like an equality with them." Some African American soldiers took the opportunity to act on this principle. In Macon, Georgia, black soldiers cut down a tree well known as a site for lynchings and destroyed a sign that declared "No Dogs and Niggers Allowed." In Tampa, Florida, members of the Twenty-fourth and Twenty-fifth regiments attacked soldiers from an Ohio unit who were using a two-year-old black boy for target practice by competing to see who could come closest without harming the child.

In Cuba black soldiers distinguished themselves in combat. The Twenty-fourth played a key role in the charge up San Juan Hill (July 1, 1898). The Tenth and Twenty-fifth fought well in the Battle of El Caney (July 1, 1898). Most significantly, in the war's first battle at Las Guâsimas (June 23, 1898), the Tenth was conspicuous in relieving the First Volunteer Cavalry Regiment, better known as the Rough Riders, when it was pinned down by enemy fire. Theodore Roosevelt, one of the beleaguered Rough Riders, later declared, "I don't think any Rough Rider will ever forget the tie that binds us to the... Tenth Cavalry." The Tenth's regimental quartermaster, Capt. John J. Pershing, future American commander in World War I, acquired his nickname, "Black Jack," through his service with African American troops.

Ironically, one byproduct of victory was the gradual exclusion of African Americans from the U.S. Navy. Throughout the nineteenth century blacks had accounted for 10 to 15 percent of naval manpower. Although since the 1870s they had increasingly been relegated to menial roles in galleys and boiler rooms, blacks nonetheless served on racially integrated ships. After the Spanish-Cuban-American War, however, the Navy began recruiting its messmen in the newly acquired Philippines, and by the early twentieth century blacks only accounted for about 5 percent of naval manpower.

James Clyde Sellman

See Also

World War I and African Americans; World War II and African Americans; Lynching.

Africa

Spanish Guinea.

Former name of Equatorial Guinea.

Africa

Spanish Sahara.

Former name of Western Sahara.

North America

Spasm Bands,

ensembles of black children who improvised music on the streets of New Orleans, Louisiana.

At the turn of the twentieth century spasm bands roamed the Storyville district of New Orleans, adding to the hodgepodge of musical styles that filled the city's air. Adolescent boys brandished kitchen utensils, whistles, fiddles, harmonicas, cowbells, brass, gourds, kazoos, ukuleles, guitars, drums, and crude, jerry-built instruments. Some musicians punctuated their performances with yells of "hi-de-ho, ho-de-ho," while others danced and did head-stands as part of the act.

Often spasm bands played in front of brothels and gambling joints, mischievously drowning out the music from within. Although the sound of these spontaneous groups reflected more novelty than skill, spasm bands contributed to the synthetic milieu of New Orleans, from which jazz emerged.

Eric Bennett

North America

Spaulding, Charles Clinton

(b. August 1, 1874, Columbus County, N.C.; d. August 1, 1952, Durham, N.C.), American entrepreneur, leader of the North Carolina Mutual Life Insurance Company.

In 1923 C.C. Spaulding became president of North Carolina Mutual Life Insurance Company, which became the largest insurer of African Americans in the United States. His reorganization plan for the company allowed it to survive the Great Depression, during which Spaulding served on state and federal relief committees, attempting to ensure equitable distribution of relief services for African Americans. In his home city of Durham he worked to register black voters and convinced the city to hire African American police officers. Spaulding served as a trustee for Shaw University, Howard University, and North Carolina College.

Robert Fay

North America

Spelman College,

a prestigious, historically black college located in Atlanta, Georgia; the oldest black women's college in the United States.

Spelman College asserts that "since 1881, Spelman has sought to develop the total woman; to help our students discover their own power – and to prepare them to wield that power in a positive way." Spelman was founded by two white New England missionaries, Sophia Packard and Harriet Giles, who were concerned about the lack of educational opportunities for Southern black women. In 1881 they raised enough money from a Massachusetts church and the Women's American Baptist Home Missionary Society to open their new school, and the first classes of the Atlanta Baptist Female Seminary, as it was first called, met in a church basement with 11 students. Three months later the enrollment had grown to 80, and within a year 200 women ranging in age from 15 to 52 attended the school.

On an 1882 fundraising trip Giles and Packard received a donation from John D. Rockefeller that helped finance the school's move into a building of its own. Two years later Rockefeller made another contribution that helped stop a proposed merger with a nearby men's institution, the Atlanta Baptist Seminary (later MOREHOUSE COLLEGE). The school was renamed Spelman Seminary after Rockefeller's wife, Laura Spelman Rockefeller. The school now included normal, industrial, and college preparatory departments. A nurse training department opened in 1886, a missionary training department in 1891, and a college department in 1897. In 1901 Spelman granted its first two college degrees.

In 1924 the school officially changed its name to Spelman College. In the mid-1920s enough college-level courses were offered and enough students were enrolled in the college program that Spelman began phasing out other departments. By 1930 its focus was solely on liberal arts education. In 1929 Spelman chose to affiliate its financial and administrative sources with Morehouse College and Atlanta University, making those three schools the founding members of what became Atlanta University Center, the consortium of Atlanta's black colleges and universities.

Spelman's first four presidents were white women, as were the majority of its instructors during its first four decades. Beginning in the 1920s larger numbers of black women, including many Spelman graduates, were hired as faculty; by 1937 they outnumbered white teachers by two to one, and eventually the faculty became predominantly African American, women and men. The college's first black president, Alfred E. Manley, took office in 1953.

During the CIVIL RIGHTS MOVEMENT of the 1950s and 1960s Spelman students were among the cofounders of the STUDENT NONVIOLENT COORDINATING COMMITTEE (SNCC), and many participated in Atlanta-area SIT-INS and boycotts. In 1976 students locked Spelman's board of trustees in their boardroom for 20 hours to protest the appointment of Donald Steward as the college's next president, arguing that it was time for Spelman to be led by a black woman. Eleven years later that hope finally came to pass when Johnetta Betsch Cole, the popular "Sister President," became the college's seventh president.

In 1988 entertainer BILL COSBY and his wife Camille gave Spelman a widely publicized $20 million gift. In the 1990s Spelman received national attention for its role as a site of the 1996 Olympic Games in Atlanta, and for its recognition as the best liberal arts college in the South by a leading poll of American colleges and universities. Spelman alumnae include Pulitzer Prize-winning author ALICE WALKER, attorney and children's rights advocate MARIAN WRIGHT EDELMAN, former Acting Surgeon General Audrey Manley, and many physicians, attorneys, educators, and other professionals. Nearly 2000 women are currently enrolled at Spelman.

Lisa Clayton Robinson

SEE ALSO

Women and the Black Baptist Church.

North America

Spencer, Anne **(b. February 6, 1882, Henry County, Va.; d. July 12, 1975, Lynchburg, Va.), African American writer, HARLEM RENAISSANCE poet whose work combined nineteenth-century and modernist literary traditions.**

Anne Bethel Bannister spent her early years with a foster family while her mother Sarah Scales, separated from her husband Joel Bannister, worked nearby as a cook. At age 11 she began formal schooling in the Virginia Seminary in Lynchburg under the name Annie Scales. With her first poem, "The Skeptic" (1896), Scales revealed the independent thinking that would characterize her life and work. She graduated in 1899, taught for two years in West Virginia, and then returned to Lynchburg to marry Edward Spencer and raise their children, Bethel Calloway, Alroy Sarah, and Chauncey Edward.

During this time Spencer cultivated her poetry as well as her famous garden. When NATIONAL ASSOCIATION FOR THE ADVANCEMENT OF COLORED PEOPLE (NAACP) activist JAMES WELDON JOHNSON visited her in 1917, he convinced her that she ought to publish, and "Before the Feast of Shushan" appeared in the February 1920 issue of *Crisis*. For the next 20 years her voice was heard in every collection of African American poetry.

Spencer's poetry invokes biblical and mythological allusions to speak of beauty in a decaying world. Her writing has been described as depicting a private vision, and she often employed images of the natural world. Despite the apparent influences of literary romanticism, Spencer has often been characterized as modernist, both for her complex style and her contemporary feminist concerns. She worked powerfully with detailed, focused images: a woman's hand, "Twisted, awry, like crumpled roots,/ bleached poor white in a sudsy tub," portrays the condition of women in "Lady, Lady."

Spencer's political activism in Lynchburg attested to her commitment to African American equality. She agitated for the hiring of African American teachers at the local segregated high school, she refused to ride segregated public transportation, and she initiated an African American library, where she worked from 1923 to 1945. Her garden home became a Southern locus for prominent African Americans that was visited regularly by such guests as W. E. B. Du Bois, PAUL ROBESON, and LANGSTON HUGHES. In the mid-1930s Spencer moved out of public life and lived as a recluse until her death in 1975.

Marian Aguiar

SEE ALSO

Literature, African American; Women Writers, Black, in the United States; *Crisis, The*; Du Bois, William Edward Burghardt (W. E. B.).

North America

Spinks, Leon **(b. July 11, 1953, St. Louis, Mo.), African American boxer and heavyweight gold medalist in the 1976 Summer Olympic Games.**

Leon Spinks served in the Marines before winning a spot on the Olympic BOXING team. He won the heavyweight Gold Medal in the 1976 Summer Olympic Games in Montreal, an accomplishment matched by his younger brother, Michael, in the middleweight division.

After turning professional in 1977, Spinks won his first nine bouts, including a 15-round fight with MUHAMMAD ALI. After losing to Ali in a rematch in September 1978, Spinks was not able to duplicate his earlier success. By 1986 Spinks was forced to file for bankruptcy, after which he worked at a bar in DETROIT, MICHIGAN.

Aaron Myers

North America

Spirituals, African American

Over the years immigrant groups from across the world have brought their national music to America, but aside from Native Americans, African Americans were the first to create an indigenous American music. The African experience was unique: stolen from their homes, transported involuntarily in chains, and sentenced to lifetimes of slavery, Africans were cut off from their various ethnic cultures and their languages. Their first challenge in America, therefore, was to transcend their different traditions and come together as a single people. During that process an astonishing and still little recognized cultural interchange and transformation took place.

CULTURAL SYNTHESIS

As Africans were themselves uniting, they were at the same time thrown into constant contact with Europeans. The first Africans were brought to British North America at Jamestown, Virginia, in early August 1619. Before the Pilgrims landed at Plymouth Rock, the cultures of the two continents and the two races had begun the process of interaction and synthesis. It was a long time before white Americans believed that African American history is fundamental to an understanding American history. Now, however, as we come to understand just how intermingled African and European cultures really were, we can see that American history is actually African American history as well.

This melding is the basis and background for the emergence of the spirituals as a new and distinct musical form. As Benjamin Mays, longtime president of MOREHOUSE COLLEGE, explained, "The creation of the spirituals was no accident. It was a creation born of necessity, so that the slave might more adequately adjust himself to the conditions of the new world."

Music and dance were vital dimensions of daily African life, and if slaves could not carry physical cultural artifacts with them to North America, they could, and did, bring their extensive and complex expressive cultures. It has been suggested that the earliest synthesis of Europe and Africa and the first manifestation of African American culture took place on the slave ships during the horrendous Middle Passage between Africa and America. On the upper decks slaves were forced under the lash to dance for exercise. The rhythms, patterns, music, and lyrics have been lost, but it was here that Africa and Europe met, that the process of creative interaction began, and that a vital new people and culture suffered the pains of birth.

The emergence of the spirituals is rooted in the encounter between African traditional life and the evangelical Protestant Christianity of the white American South. In that encounter the African village became the slave quarters and the slave congregation; the root doctor and griot, or storyteller, became the preacher-healer-song leader; spirit possession became the ecstasy of emotional revivalism; the circle dance became the ring shout; community participation became call-and-response; and the history of the ancestors became the narratives of the King James Bible. Theologian James Cone writes: "Through song they built new structures for existence in an alien land. The spirituals enabled blacks to retain a measure of African identity while living in the midst of American slavery, providing both the substance and the rhythm to cope with human servitude."

People's Music

The Library of Congress identifies more than 6,000 spirituals, but some exist only in fragments. Many spirituals have been lost forever – especially, we can assume, the earliest ones, as well as earlier versions of spirituals that have survived. The creation of the spirituals was organic, coming up from below, coming up from the people. Spirituals constituted a living folk art – with no authors, no composers, no dates, no lyricists, nothing written down, no fixed or authoritative texts – belonging to the community. The same phrases might appear in different songs, the same words might be sung to different tunes, and every set of lyrics had its variants across the plantation South.

Like the blues and jazz, for which they are the foundation, spirituals are improvisational. Usually a lead singer, although it could be anyone, would sing one line, and the others present would repeat it or reply with a familiar chorus in a call-and-response antiphony. Anyone could add new verses, and the best of these survived through a kind of natural selection. In singing the spirituals there was no separation between artist and audience, no distinction between creator and performer, and this style continued in later African American music. "The singer is found by the song," the writer James Baldwin once commented. Spirituals were never meant to be performed on a concert stage. As folklorist Zora Neale Hurston points out, "these songs are authentic only when they are sung by and for the people themselves, expressing feelings of the moment and of the situation. They are spontaneous songs," Hurston says, whose "truth dies under training like flowers under hot water."

With some exceptions African American slaves were a nonliterate people with a strong and sophisticated oral tradition of songs, stories, historical accounts, proverbs, and tales. Facility with speech, cleverness with words, verbal wit, and dramatic oratory were – and remain – highly admired qualities within the African American community. The spirituals are poems, expressing emotions; they are full of symbols, tropes, and metaphors, often containing layers of meaning. Their use of vernacular language is sometimes striking. Deceptively simple, spirituals can rise to piercing directness and immediacy. Many have lines of poetic power and a provocative turn of phrase:

I sweep my house with the gospel broom

I'm a-rolling in Jesus' arms

I'm going to sit down at the welcome table

Fix me, Jesus, fix me right

If anybody asks you what's the matter with me / just tell him I say / I'm running for my life

Mary set her table / 'Spite of all her foes

Sometimes entire lyrics are startlingly innovative in their use of words:

When the preacher, the preacher done give me over,
King Jesus is my only friend.
When my house, my house become a public hall,
King Jesus is my only friend.
When my face, my face become a looking glass,
King Jesus is my, only friend.

Religious Songs

The spirituals are essentially religious songs. Early white American Protestants sang the Psalms in meter along with the traditional stately hymns of the church. But on the rural frontier religion was more informal, more individualistic and personal, more emotional, and a new kind of vernacular music emerged to reflect the new religious democracy. Called "spiritual songs," the new music was religious in nature but lacked the reserve of conventional hymns. The African American slave songs influenced spiritual songs, so it is not surprising that the name "spirituals" was given to these religious slave songs when, following the Civil War, they were first recognized as a discrete African American creation.

The earliest known mention of a distinctive black religious music, according to scholar Dena J. Epstein, was published in 1819 by John F. Watson, a white man who was criticizing black "excesses" at Methodist camp meeting revivals. Watson's words are revealing: "We have, too, a growing evil in the practice of singing in our places of public and societal worship, merry airs, adapted from old songs, to hymns... most frequently composed and first sung by the illiterate blacks of the society.... [At camp meetings] in the blacks' quarter, the colored people get together, and sing for hours together, short scraps of disjointed affirmations, pledges, or prayers, lengthened out with long repetitive choruses. These are all sung in the merry-chorus manner of the southern harvest field, or husking frolic method of the slave blacks; and also very like the Indian dances. With every word so sung, they have a sinking on one or other leg of the body alternately, producing an audible sound of the feet at every step and as manifest as the steps of actual Negro dancing in Virginia, etc. If some in the meantime sit, they strike the sounds alternately on each thigh."

Despite its critical stance Watson's description is full of relevant and important information. African Americans may have been segregated at camp meetings, but they were present and participating. We can see the process of cultural interaction and blending taking place: as Watson's words "first sung by" suggest, whites picked up both songs and styles from blacks. Whatever the meldings, however, spirituals remained distinctly different from white spiritual songs, and the African retentions and influences are clear: the "long repetitive choruses," the "merry airs," and, most clearly, the elements of African dance in the rhythmic body movements.

Watson's comparison of the religious music to harvest and husking songs shows the relationship of spirituals to other slave musical creations such as work songs, love songs, shouts, songs for dancing, and railroad songs. And the reference to "actual Negro dancing" reveals that black dance, with its strong African character, was perceived as distinct from European forms of dance. In a fascinating aside Watson even touches on the possibility of Native American influences. Overall, Watson's account tells us that spirituals were well formed by 1819. Of course, we do not know what the black community sang by and for itself when it was not in the presence of whites, but we can assume it was less, rather than more, European.

Experiencing the Bible

What was the content of these slave songs? "The clue to the meaning of the spirituals," writes theologian Howard Thurman, "is to be found in religious experience and spiritual discernment." As religious songs the spirituals reflect many of the characteristics of evangelical Protestantism of the day: the centrality of the Bible, the sovereignty of a God of justice, personal accountability for one's life on earth, trust in Jesus, and hope for eternal life in heaven. Spirituality accompanied theology, and the spirituals reveal the slaves' deep personal and collective faith. Tied to this was a surprisingly hopeful optimism, which transcended the wretchedness of the slave experience. The anguished cry of despair in one version of "Nobody Knows the Trouble I See" ends with an affirmation as positive as it is unexpected:

Nobody knows the trouble I see,
Nobody knows my sorrow.
Nobody knows the trouble I see.
Glory, Hallelujah!

Some slave owners permitted white ministers and missionaries to preach to their slaves. The ministers' usual text was Colossians 3:22, "Servants, obey in all things your masters." But as they accepted the Protestant principle of scriptural authority, African Americans would hear or read the rest of the Bible, and they would encounter there another message altogether. In the words of James Cone they discovered that "faith, as trust in God's Word of liberation stands at the heart of biblical revelation" and that "God's liberation is at work in the world."

The biblical narrative that resonated most strongly with the slaves' bitter experiences, while at the same time promising hope for deliverance, was the story of the Israelites' bondage in Egypt. Moses is one of the most often mentioned persons in the spirituals. African Americans also identified with Noah, Daniel, Jonah, and others of God's faithful people who were rescued by a just God from a sinful world of unfaithfulness and oppression. The nonliterate slaves told the biblical stories by turning them into songs, which, when stitched together, recount the Scriptures from beginning to end – from Adam in the garden to John the revelator. The Bible is whole: personalities from both Testaments are indiscriminately lumped together. Jesus appears in several forms: as the innocent child, the victim of whipping, the king on a milk-white horse who protects his subjects. In Cone's potent words Jesus is even "God's black slave who has come to put an end to human bondage."

"Go Down, Moses" is perhaps the best-known spiritual. The song's direct and powerful appeal for human liberation exemplifies the theme and thread of freedom that runs through all spirituals. "Go Down, Moses" has even been associated with Nat Turner, the leader of a slave revolt in Southampton County, Virginia, in 1831, the bloodiest of the 250 North American slave revolts. Turner is thought to have been either the author or subject of the song. The message of "Go Down, Moses" was so clear that some slaveholders forbade its singing on their plantations. The song's great popularity and widespread use not only demonstrate the inspiration the slaves got from the Bible and their identification with the chosen Israelites but also show that slaves sought freedom as a physical reality in this world and not merely an otherworldly aspiration.

Double Meaning

The metaphorical nature of the spirituals has been greatly debated and disputed. Most white critics have thought that the spirituals are essentially concerned with life in heaven, undoubtedly because they believed black slaves were docile folks, content with their lives of servitude. But African Americans have always known that the spirituals are full of coded words and secret signals, messages between and among only themselves, communications that could be concealed from the white master class. The testimonies of Frederick Douglass – and other self-liberated slaves who recounted their experiences – confirm that the spirituals were full of symbolic language (*see* Slave Narratives). The slaves themselves were God's people: Israel. Moses was a leader and deliverer. Egypt or Babylon represented the South, and hell the Deep South. Pharaoh was a slave owner. The River Jordan was the Ohio River or a similar body of water between the North and the South. The Red Sea was the Atlantic Ocean. Home, Canaan, camp meeting, or the Promised Land were Africa, the free states, Canada, or Liberia. Any agency of travel or movement – trains, shoes, chariots, wheels – spoke of escape.

This political aspect of the spirituals is perhaps their most important legacy, both historically and now; it cannot be overemphasized. A few lyrics obviously convey political statements: "Master going to sell us tomorrow" or "No more hundred lash for me / Many thousand gone." Numerous verses mention family members, remembering those sold away in slave owners' cruel disregard for human relationships. Other songs are more subtle. Frederick Douglass said that the words "Run to Jesus / Shun the danger" first gave him the idea of escaping from bondage. Still other songs are also about running away, the Underground Railroad, and God's promised destruction of a sinful social order: "I don't intend to die in Egypt land"; "When the train comes along / I'll meet you at the station"; "God's going to set the world on fire." There are songs of the liberation that is to come: "You can hinder me here, but you can't hinder me there" are lines from "Free at Last," the spiritual Martin Luther King Jr. recited in his 1963 March on Washington speech, "I Have a Dream." A profoundly radical, even revolutionary, thrust to these songs came as the slaves expanded their struggle for freedom to encompass all the disinherited: "Didn't my Lord deliver Daniel / And why not every man?"

A New Poetics

The anonymous slave poets, those "black and unknown bards," as the poet James Weldon Johnson called them, were the progenitors of a great new Afropoetics. The first African American to publish a book was Phillis Wheatley, a slave whose book of poetry was published in London in 1773. Despite making unappreciated references to Africa and liberty, Wheatley nonetheless followed the European and classical literary tradition. It is the vibrant vernacular language of the spirituals, their marriage of Africa and Europe, and their grand obsession with freedom that makes them unique. Antonin Dvorák, the Czech composer, recognized this early on and incorporated African American themes into his *New World Symphony* of 1893. He writes, "The so-called plantation songs are among the most striking and appealing melodies that have been found this side of the water."

African American spirituals have not been particularly well documented, either historically or musically. African music, especially its complex polyrhythms, is not easily comprehended by Western-trained ears, and whites of the slavocracy did not take the slaves' music seriously or treat it with respect. There are surprisingly few references to spirituals in antebellum diaries and letters. The first sympathetic interest on the part of whites came during the Civil War from abolitionists in and out of the United States Army who heard the singing of so-called contrabands, self-liberated slaves who had escaped to the protection of Union lines.

One of the earliest white reports of spirituals came from the Rev. Lewis Lockwood, an agent of the American Missionary Association sent to do educational and relief work among contrabands at Fortress Monroe on Chesapeake Bay. Lockwood first heard black singing on September 3, 1861, and soon provided the *New York Tribune* with the text of "Go Down, Moses," facilitating the song's first appearance in print. The discussion over the accurate representation of both African American words and music began then and has not yet been resolved. Curiously, little attention has been paid to the use of spirituals in the writing of African Americans. Martin Delany's novel *Blake, or The Huts of America,* issued serially in 1881 and 1882, includes what the scholar Allen Austin calls "the largest compendium of black-created or black-adapted verses and songs in the antebellum period." Pauline E. Hopkins also utilizes spirituals significantly in her novel *Of One Blood, or The Hidden Self,* serialized in the *Colored American Magazine* in 1902 and 1903.

One achievement of the spirituals was to offer the nation its first compendium of authentic African American music and lyrics. White America had been so fascinated with black life that throughout the nineteenth century the country's most popular entertainment came in the form of minstrel shows. MINSTRELSY was a grotesque white parody of black singing, dancing, humor, and style, even though it was based, as blues composer W. C. Handy and others have pointed out, on real African American expressive culture. A less demeaning form of white imitation of blacks can be recognized in the sentimental ballads of Stephen Foster. Foster had heard black songs and adapted them for white audiences, combining theft with homogenization – a practice that continued with RAGTIME and jazz.

SAVING THE SPIRITUALS

Despite the fact that the spirituals were, in the scholar W E. B. Du Bois's words, "the slaves' one articulate message to the world," the truth is that they were nearly lost. Beyond the flutter of abolitionist interest during the Civil War there were few white people who had heard spirituals, and the freedpeople were eager to forget the songs as a relic of the slavery they were trying to put behind them. In particular, members of the small but influential African American middle class were anxious to embrace European culture in order to prove that they were as capable and deserving as white people were. A similar attitude would develop later in response to blues, jazz, RAP, and Ebonics – all expressions that have bubbled up from the underclass to challenge and even subvert the dominant cultural establishment.

The spirituals were actually saved for posterity by a small group of African American men and women at FISK UNIVERSITY, a school for freedpeople established just after the Civil War in Nashville, Tennessee, by the American Missionary Association. The school was so overcrowded and so poor that students and faculty sold the iron from Nashville's former slave pens to buy spelling books. George White, Fisk's music teacher, organized a small choir called the FISK JUBILEE SINGERS and then hit upon the idea of taking the group on a concert tour to raise money for the floundering college. Leaving Nashville in 1871 on borrowed money, the choir was markedly unsuccessful until they began singing spirituals to white church groups in the North, which included former abolitionists sympathetic to African Americans, their struggle for freedom, and their culture. Suddenly the singers became a smashing success: they sang in Henry Ward Beecher's Brooklyn church, for President Ulysses Grant, and for Queen Victoria in England. (At the request of the British prime minister's wife the Fisk Jubilee Singers sang "John Brown's Body" for the Grand Duchess Maria Fyodorovna, whose father-in-law, Tsar Alexander II, had just liberated the Russian serfs.) The Fisk Jubilee Singers rescued the spirituals and made it respectable to sing them. As the music scholar Mary Jo Sanna points out, "Negro spirituals" became commonplace in American popular culture, marking "the only way whites knowingly and willingly participated in the contributions of blacks to American culture."

The lasting power of the spirituals lies in their message. Calling the spirituals "sorrow songs," Du Bois wrote, "They are the music of an unhappy people, of the children of disappointment; they tell of death and suffering and unvoiced longing toward a truer world." There is a little-noted parallel between the spirituals and their secular offspring, the blues – a body of music that also deals with the sadness and melancholy of men and women struggling with the "blue devils" of despair. The twentieth-century writer RALPH ELLISON describes the redemptive function of blues: "The blues is an impulse to keep the painful details and episodes of a brutal experience alive in one's aching consciousness, to finger its jagged edge, and to transcend it, not by the consolation of philosophy, but by squeezing from it a near-tragic, near-comic lyricism." The same holds true for the spirituals. These songs reflect the slaves' sorrows, but the pain is transformed by the act of expression, by fingering the "jagged edge." They are metamorphosed, like the blues, into songs of resilience and overcoming, and even into affirmations of divine redemption and human triumph.

Richard Newman

SEE ALSO

Middle Passage, The; Slavery in the United States; American Indians; Black Vernacular English; Blues, The; Civil War, American; Cone, James Hal; Delany, Martin Robison; Du Bois, William Edward Burghardt (W. E. B.); Handy, William Christopher (W.C.); Hopkins, Pauline Elizabeth; King, Martin Luther, Jr.; Mays, Benjamin Elijah; Turner, Nat; Dance in the United States.

North America

Spivey, Victoria Regina

(b. October 6, 1906, Houston, Tex.; d. October 3, 1976, New York, N.Y.), urban blues singer and the first African American woman to found a record label.

Known to many as "Queen Victoria," Spivey learned the piano while singing with her father's band in Dallas, Texas. After her father died, she performed wherever she could find work. In 1926 Spivey moved to St. Louis, Missouri, where she wrote and recorded songs, including her best-known, "T.B. Blues," for the St. Louis Music Company and for Okeh Records. Leaving Okeh but continuing to record, between 1929 and 1952 she also appeared in several stage shows, including *Hellzapoppin'* and in an all-black movie, *Hallelujah*. Her signature vocal sound was a nasal type of evocative moan that she termed her "tiger squall."

After a brief retirement Spivey returned to music with the revival of the blues in the 1960s. In 1961 she formed Queen Vee Records, changing the name to Spivey Records the following year. She died in 1976, the same year she released her last album, *The Blues Is Life*.

Gabriel Mendes

SEE ALSO

Blues, The.

Africa

Stanley, Sir Henry Morton

(born John Rowlands) (b. January 28, 1841, Denbeigh, Wales; d. May 10, 1904, London, England), Anglo-American journalist and explorer, the first European to map the Congo Basin.

Beginning his career as a journalist, Henry Morton Stanley first traveled to Africa in 1869 on assignment for the *New York Herald*. The newspaper dispatched Stanley to find DAVID LIVINGSTONE, a Scottish missionary who had gone to explore Africa and subsequently disappeared from the public eye. Traveling from ZANZIBAR into the interior of East Africa, Stanley finally met the ailing Livingstone at Ujiji, a town on LAKE TANGANYIKA, on November 10, 1871. He is said to have greeted him with the famous remark, "Dr. Livingstone, I presume?" After Livingstone was nursed back to health, the two men explored the northern end of Lake Tanganyika. Stanley returned to Europe in 1872, but was sent back to West Africa the following year to report on the British campaign against the ASANTE.

In 1874 the *New York Herald* and *London Daily Telegraph* sent Stanley back to Africa to continue Livingstone's work. Stanley first visited King Mutesa of Buganda and then circumnavigated LAKE VICTORIA and LAKE TANGANYIKA. Finally, he traveled down the Lualaba and Congo rivers. Amazed by the enormous navigability of the CONGO RIVER, Stanley returned to Europe in 1878 to share his "discoveries."

The following year, under the sponsorship of King LEOPOLD II of Belgium, Stanley returned to the Congo for yet another expedition. Taking with him hundreds of laborers, he laid the foundations for the Congo Free State by constructing a road from the lower Congo to Pool Malebo and making contracts with local tribes. This expedition helped Leopold II establish control over the Congo basin.

Stanley returned to Africa briefly in 1887 and 1897. After his 1897 trip he retired to London, where he served in Parliament.

Elizabeth Heath

SEE ALSO

Buganda, Early Kingdom of; Explorers in Africa Since 1800; Mutesa I; Christianity: Missionaries in Africa.

North America

Staple Singers, a well-known African American family music group that has performed and recorded gospel, folk, and SOUL MUSIC since the early 1950s.

The Staple Singers, composed of various members of the Staples family of CHICAGO, ILLINOIS, made significant contributions to gospel and soul music as well as to the folk music revival. Even after leaving the realm of religious music, the group has continued to perform songs with an inspirational or uplifting message. At the heart of the four-person group was Roebuck "Pop" Staples, whose lead vocals and Delta blues-influenced guitar playing helped give the Staple Singers their distinctive sound. His youngest daughter, Mavis Staples, added an exhilarating contralto. Over time as various family members joined or left the group, the Staple Singers gradually altered its style. During the group's first decade the Staple Singers performed gospel music, but in the early 1960s the group took its increasingly secular repertoire on the folk music circuit. In 1968 the Staple Singers signed with STAX RECORDS, perhaps the most important soul music record company, and soon emerged as one of the country's top soul groups.

Pop Staples was born in 1915 in Winona, Mississippi, where he came under the influence of the guitar style of such legendary Delta bluesmen as Robert Johnson, Bukka White, and "Big Bill" Broonzy. In 1935 Staples moved to Chicago with his wife Oceola and two children, Pervis and Cleotha. In Chicago the family grew with the addition of Yvonne and Mavis. The elder Staples sang in GOSPEL QUARTETS during the 1930s and began teaching his children music when they were quite young in the hope of forming a group. In the early 1950s Pervis, Cleotha, and Mavis joined him in performances at local churches.

Although the Staple Singers first recorded in 1953, the group did not gain recognition until it moved in 1955 to Chicago's black-owned Vee Jay Records, which released five notable gospel albums by the group over the next five years. But the Staple Singers achieved their greatest popularity with a series of more elaborately produced recordings for Stax, that featured a fuller instrumentation, including horn sections and synthesizers, exemplified by the hits "Respect Yourself" (1971), "I'll Take You There" (1972), and "If You're Ready (Come Go with Me)" (1973), as well as by their 1975 album for Curtis Mayfield's Custom label, *Let's Do It Again*, the group's all-time bestseller. The Staple Singers became less visible as soul music lost its popular appeal in the late 1970s, although the group briefly returned to prominence in the mid-1980s when it backed actor Bruce Willis's cover of "Respect Yourself," which gained considerable airplay on MTV.

James Clyde Sellman

SEE ALSO

Gospel Music; Johnson, Robert Leroy; Mayfield, Curtis.

North America

Stax Records, an American recording studio based in MEMPHIS, TENNESSEE, that played a key role in defining SOUL MUSIC and in popularizing the horn-driven "Memphis sound" during the 1960s.

Stax Record Company of Memphis, Tennessee, helped define the SOUL MUSIC era of the mid-1960s with what came to be known as its "Memphis sound," which combined gospel and blues-tinged vocals, tightly riffing horn sections, and a powerful rhythmic drive. Important Stax performers included OTIS REDDING, Booker T. and the MGs, Carla and Rufus Thomas, Sam and Dave (Sam Moore and David Prater), and the STAPLE SINGERS. Stax recordings also benefited from talented songwriters, especially the team of Isaac Hayes and David Porter, responsible for such hits as Sam and Dave's "Hold On, I'm Comin'" and Carla Thomas's "B-A-B-Y."

White siblings Jim Stewart and Estelle Axton opened the recording studio that would become Stax in 1960. They named their company Satellite Records, but in order to avoid confusion with another record company of the same name, they changed their label to Stax, derived from the first two letters of their last names. The Stax studio was located in a former movie theater whose marquee soon proclaimed: "SOULSVILLE USA." After a regional RHYTHM AND BLUES hit in 1960 – a Rufus and Carla Thomas duet titled "'Cause I Love You" – the fledgling company reached a long-term agreement with Atlantic Records to distribute that and future Stax recordings.

In search of the Memphis magic, Atlantic executive Jerry Wexler also began to bring his own artists to Stax, most notably WILSON PICKETT. After several unsuccessful Atlantic recordings with large orchestras and elaborate arrangements, Pickett found his key to success in the leaner Stax approach, utilizing a small R&B band and simple riff-based accompaniments. His career-making Stax sessions of May and December 1965 yielded the hits "In the Midnight Hour," "634-5789," and "Ninety-Nine and One-Half Won't Do" and introduced what would be Pickett's signature sound.

One of the keys to Stax's success was the hiring in 1965 of Al Bell, a black disc jockey who had previously founded his own record label, to manage national promotion and sales. Bell was the first African American in the otherwise all-white Stax management. In 1968 he bought out Axton's share of the company and became a co-owner. The combination of Bell's vision and energy and the company's compelling music propelled Stax into a period of rapid growth and expansion. Stax – its management and musicians alike – began to view their studio as an alternative to Detroit's far larger Motown Records.

In contrast to Motown – which took a sweeter and slicker approach, often using lush string sections and producing music that seemed to emulate white pop songs – Stax brought an earthier, more hard-driving sound to American popular music. Al Jackson Jr., drummer for Booker T. and the MGs as well as for many other Stax recording sessions, dismissed Motown recordings as being "made from the switchboard." Daily operations at Stax were marked by a closeness and informality that cut across racial barriers and seemed to draw everyone – musicians, engineers, and principal partners – together. Regular Stax session players included both blacks, such as Jackson, keyboards player Booker T. Jones, and sax player Andrew Love, and whites, including guitarist Steve Cropper, bass player Donald "Duck" Dunn, and trumpeter Wayne Jackson.

Yet despite numerous hits in the 1960s and early 1970s the company's success was short-lived. A combination of economic and political factors – including the consequences of the company's own sudden success and a deteriorating racial climate, particularly following the assassination of Martin Luther King Jr. in 1968 – resulted in growing internal frictions that contributed to the bankruptcy that put Stax out of business in 1975.

James Clyde Sellman

SEE ALSO

Blues, The; Gospel Music; King, Martin Luther, Jr.; Motown.

Africa

Stevens, Siaka (b. 1905; d. May 1988), prime minister and president of SIERRA LEONE (1971-1985), a major force in Sierra Leone politics for almost 40 years.

Siaka Stevens was educated at Albert Academy at Freetown and went on to study trade-union operation and industrial relations at Ruskin College, Oxford, England (1947-1948). He first gained national recognition through his work in trade-union organization. In 1943 he cofounded the United Mine Workers' Union, after becoming a mine worker at the Marampa Mines with the Sierra Leone Development Company (DELCO). His energetic prominence in the labor movement resulted in his appointment to the Sierra Leone Protectorate Assembly in 1946.

In 1951 Siaka Stevens, Milton Margai, and several others formed the Sierra Leone People's Party. The SLPP became a powerful force in national politics. In the same year Stevens was also elected to the Legislative Council, and in 1952 went on to become minister of Lands, Mines, and Labour.

Stevens's growing disillusionment with the SLPP culminated in his leaving it in 1958, after which he cofounded, with Albert Margai, the People's National Party (PNP). From 1958 to 1960 Stevens was a deputy leader of PNP. In 1960 all the national parties, including the PNP, formed a United Front to negotiate independence from Great Britain, and Stevens was chosen as a member of the delegation to be sent to the Constitutional Conference in London. He objected to the decisions taken there and argued that the SLPP government was unrepresentative, demanding new elections before independence. His agitation in the Elections Before Independence Movement, which was later to become the All People's Party (APC), resulted in his being imprisoned on independence day, April 27, 1961, although the charges of conspiracy and libel brought against him were soon quashed.

Stevens became the major opposition leader. He was also mayor of Freetown (1964-1965). In elections on March 17, 1967, the APC won a majority and Stevens became prime minister, although not for long because the commander of the Sierra Leone Military Force, Brigadier Lansana intervened and military officers seized power. This coup government only lasted until April 1968, when an inquiry into the elections showed that Stevens and the APC had fairly won the election and Stevens was reinstated as prime minister. After another unsuccessful coup attempt in 1971, Stevens's government introduced a Republican Constitution, and on April 21, 1971, Stevens was sworn in as the country's first executive president. Stevens became increasingly concerned with consolidating his authority, and in 1978 Sierra Leone became a one-party state under the APC and Stevens's presidency. Despite Steven's authoritarianism, his rule never degenerated into total repression since he preferred a policy of coopting his opponents. He enjoyed a sound level of popular support, which earned him the affectionate nickname of "Pa" among large numbers of the population.

In October 1985 Stevens retired and was succeeded by Brig. Joseph Momoh. He died in May 1988, and was given a state funeral, accompanied by a great expression of public grief.

Chloe Campbell

See Also
Freetown, Sierra Leone.

North America

Steward, Theophilus Gould

(b. April 17, 1843, Gouldtown [Bridgetown], N.J.; d. January 11, 1924, Wilberforce, Ohio), African American preacher and author.

Although Theophilus Steward had only a grammar school education, his interest in history and literature was nurtured by his family's home instruction. His mother, Rebecca Steward, encouraged him to question ideas commonly accepted as the truth. With this background he began preaching in 1862 and the following year received a license from the African Methodist Episcopal (AME) Church. Steward was one of the three people who accompanied Bishop Daniel Payne to South Carolina in 1865 to reestablish the AME church that had been banned there in 1822 as a result of the Denmark Vesey conspiracy.

Steward continued to build churches and schools in South Carolina and Georgia through 1870, although his outspoken criticism of all-white juries in 1870 made him a controversial figure among his peers in the clergy. From 1870 to 1891 Steward served as the pastor of several churches along the east coast. He joined the Twenty-fifth United States Colored Infantry as a chaplain at the end of this period of church service. Finally, in 1907 Steward became a faculty member at the AME's Wilberforce University, where he taught for the last 17 years of his life.

In 1873 he made a brief missionary trip to Haiti, during which he produced two books on theology: *Genesis Re-read* (1885) and *The End of the World* (1888). Steward revisited Haiti and its history in his 1914 book *The Haitian Revolution*. He was a prolific author, even while serving in the military, where he wrote a novel, *Charleston Love Story* (1899), and a highly acclaimed non-fiction book titled *The Colored Regulars*.

Aaron Myers

See Also
African Methodist Episcopal Church; Payne, Daniel Alexander.

North America

Stewart, Maria Miller

(b. 1803?, Hartford, Conn.; d. December 17, 1879, Washington, D.C.), African American women's rights activist, orator, writer, educator, first United States-born woman to speak publicly on political issues before a mixed-gender audience.

Born to a free family but orphaned at age 5, Maria Stewart lived with the family of a clergyman until age 15. She acquired literacy and a religious education at Sabbath schools. Stewart married James Stewart on August 10, 1826, in Boston, Massachusetts. After her husband's death in 1829 and through the 1860s, Stewart worked as a teacher in the public school systems of New York City, Baltimore, Maryland, and Washington, D.C. In Washington she established a Sunday school for children in 1871 and worked and lived at the Howard University-affiliated Freedmen's Hospital for the last nine years of her life.

Stewart's two-year speaking career began in 1832 and included four lectures, all published in William Lloyd Garrison's abolitionist newspaper, the *Liberator*. Her lecture to the New England Anti-Slavery Society on September 21, 1832, was the first public lecture by an American-born woman before an audience of men and women. Stewart's speeches and subsequent writings emphasized women's ability and activism: "Daughters of Africa, awake! arise! distinguish yourselves." Her words were imbued with religious significance and delivered with a militancy also inherent in the writings of her contemporary David Walker. Stewart criticized racism and sexism in an era in which it was deemed inappropriate for women to participate publicly in political debates. She is the author of *Religion and the Pure Principles of Morality, the Sure Foundation on Which We Must Build* (1831), *Productions of Mrs. Maria W. Stewart* (1835), and *Meditations From the Pen of Mrs. Maria W. Stewart* (1879).

Aaron Myers

See Also
Liberator, The; New York, New York.

North America

Still, William

(b. 1821, Burlington County, N.J.; d. July 14, 1902, Philadelphia, Pa.), African American abolitionist and author who documented the experience of fugitive slaves in the book *The Underground Railroad.*

The last of 18 children born to former slaves Levin and Charity Still, William Still spent most of his life in Philadelphia, Pennsylvania, where he had moved in 1844. By 1847 Still began his involvement in the antislavery movement while working for the Pennsylvania Society for the Abolition of Slavery. Until the Civil War he headed the Society's Philadelphia Vigilance Committee harboring fugitive slaves and directing them to Canada. Still would later compile the first detailed account of the Underground Railroad, as told by its participants. Published in 1872, *The Underground Railroad* remains an important text.

Leaving the Society in 1861, Still advocated for the economic development of the Philadelphia African American community, exemplified by the founding of his own coal business during the Civil War. Still remained attached to civil rights organizations as a researcher, writer, and activist until his death in 1902.

See Also
Abolitionism in the United States; Civil War, American.

North America

Still, William Grant

(b. May 11, 1895, Woodville, Miss.; d. December 3, 1978, Los Angeles, Calif.), African American composer whose musical works included African American themes and spanned JAZZ, popular, OPERA, and classical genres.

William Grant Still grew up in Little Rock, Arkansas where, as a boy, he played the violin. He dropped out of WILBERFORCE UNIVERSITY, where he had been studying to become a medical doctor, in order to pursue music. He studied music for two years at Oberlin Conservatory, and in 1921 he became a student of George Chadwick at the New England Conservatory in Boston. Still received a scholarship to study composition with Edgar Varese in New York as well as a Guggenheim and a Rosenwald fellowship.

Early in his career Still gained experience playing the oboe, violin, and cello for dance and theater orchestras. He toured the South with W.C. Handy's band, then went to New York, where he worked as a songwriter, arranger, and director of the black-owned recording company BLACK SWAN RECORDS. In 1921 Still performed in NOBLE SISSLE and Eubie Blake's path-breaking show *Shuffle Along*, playing oboe in the pit orchestra. In the late 1920s Still turned to composing classical music. He created more than 150 musical works, including a series of five symphonies, four ballets, and nine operas. Two of his best-known compositions are *Afro-American Symphony* (1930) and *A Bayou Legend* (1941).

After studying the works of European masters, Still developed his own compositional style that incorporated African American folk and Native American songs. He was the first black composer to have a work performed by a major orchestra, to have an opera performed by a major company, and to conduct a major orchestra.

Aaron Myers

SEE ALSO

Blake, James Hubert ("Eubie"); Handy, William Christopher (W.C.);Boston, Massachusetts; New York, New York.

Latin America and the Caribbean

St. Kitts and Nevis, a country in the Lesser Antilles, 113 km (70 mi) south of Anguilla and 300 km (186 mi) southeast of PUERTO RICO in the Caribbean Sea.

Few of the nearly 100,000 tourists who flock to the beaches of St. Kitts and Nevis each year probably know that the country has been at the forefront of so many different trends in Caribbean history. For example, St. Kitts was the first settled British colony; Nevis was once universally regarded as the "Queen of the Caribbees" for its success at SUGAR cultivation; and St. Kitts's workers helped begin the labor movements that eventually brought self-government to the black majorities across the Caribbean. Although it is a small state, St. Kitts and Nevis has taken the lead in some of the most important movements in the region.

As with most of the Caribbean, St. Kitts and Nevis's original inhabitants were Arawak and later Carib Indians, who migrated from South America to settle in the islands between 5000 and 7000 years ago. The Caribs named St. Kitts *Liamuiga*, or "fertile land," because its volcanic soil was so fruitful for agriculture. On November 12, 1493, Christopher Columbus "discovered" the islands during his second exploratory trip to the Caribbean, an encounter that changed the islands' names and histories forever.

The name St. Kitts comes from English sailors' slang for St. Christopher, St. Kitts's full legal name. While there is a persistent myth that Columbus himself chose the name San Cristobal in his own honor, the name was actually given to the island by Spanish sailors, who also named Nevis. Columbus had intended to call that island St. Martin, because he first sighted it on St. Martin's feast day. But the sailors began calling it *Nuestra Señora del las Nieves*, or "Our Lady of the Snows," because of the white clouds that permanently surround the island's central peak. The Spanish chose not to establish a permanent settlement on either island, and so the islands of St. Kitts and Nevis were granted a reprieve from colonization for another hundred years. But by the end of the sixteenth century both the English and the French used St. Kitts as a source for salt and building timber. In 1623 England established its first permanent settlement in the West Indies when Thomas Warner led a group of 16 settlers to what is now Old Road Bay off St. Kitts.

Two years later they were joined by the first French settlers, when a group led by Pierre Belain d'Esnambue was forced to seek refuge on St. Kitts after losing a fight to a Spanish galleon. The two colonies' first cooperative effort was to join forces to attack the islands' indigenous inhabitants: most of the remaining Carib Indians were killed during the 1626 massacre at Bloody Point. But as the colonies grew, their coexistence grew more uneasy, and the English and French fought over St. Kitts and Nevis several times over the next 150 years before the islands finally became one British colony in 1783.

Both the English and French initially used St. Kitts as a strategic base for colonizing nearby islands – for the English, Antigua, Barbuda, Tortola, and MONTSERRAT; for the French, MARTINIQUE, GUADELOUPE, St. Martin, St. Barts, La Désirade, and Les Saintes. It was from this colonization that St. Kitts became known as the "mother colony of the West Indies." Nevis, on the other hand, was used primarily for agriculture. The first planters grew tobacco, cotton, ginger, and indigo. But when sugar was first introduced to Nevis in 1640, it was immediately apparent that the planters had found the crop that was going to make Nevis the "Queen of the Caribbee." It was also apparent that sugar plantations would require an enormous amount of inexpensive labor to reach their maximum profit potential – and so began the widespread importation of African slaves to St. Kitts and Nevis.

By the 1660s St. Kitts had approximately 6000 inhabitants, and roughly one-half of them were black. One hundred years later blacks outnumbered whites on the island by ten to one – with 20,000 blacks (most of them still slaves) and 2000 whites. For white residents of St. Kitts and Nevis, the eighteenth century was a time of unparalleled prosperity. On St. Kitts sugar production rose from 1000 tons in 1710 to 10,000 tons by 1770, and the figures were even better in Nevis. Nevis's natural hot springs also enabled that island to become the Caribbean's first spa resort. For much of the 1700s European tourists flocked to the lavish Bath Hotel and the other estates that had been built on the island. But these enormous profits and pleasures came at a cost that was borne by the people who were forced to do the labor.

The *Prince of Orange* tragedy is just one example of the horror that accompanied slavery in the islands. In March 1737 the ship *Prince of Orange* docked at Basseterre, St. Kitts, with several hundred slaves from Africa's Guinea Coast on board. As was typical, the slaves were kept on the ship for several days to recuperate from the crossing in order that they might look healthy enough to get a better price at auction. The ship's captain noted in his log that during that time he noticed "a great deal of discontent among the slaves." But the slave traders on board and those waiting on land were unprepared for the afternoon of March 16, 1737, when more than a hundred slaves jumped overboard in an attempted mass suicide.

Thirty-three of the slaves drowned, and many more were forcibly rescued but died onshore within the next few days. For those who survived, life on the St. Kitts and Nevis sugar plantations was arduous, with harsh treatment compounded by difficult work. Many of the plantation owners were absentee landlords, and estates were run by agents or managers whose only concern was making the highest profit possible. Life expectancy for slaves in St. Kitts and Nevis barely reached double digits. In 1834 slavery was finally abolished in all English colonies. At the end of the four-year "apprenticeship" program, during which former slaves had to work for their former masters in exchange for a small salary, the blacks of St. Kitts and Nevis were finally free. But for all practical purposes, freedom brought the same economic and employment constraints that slavery had.

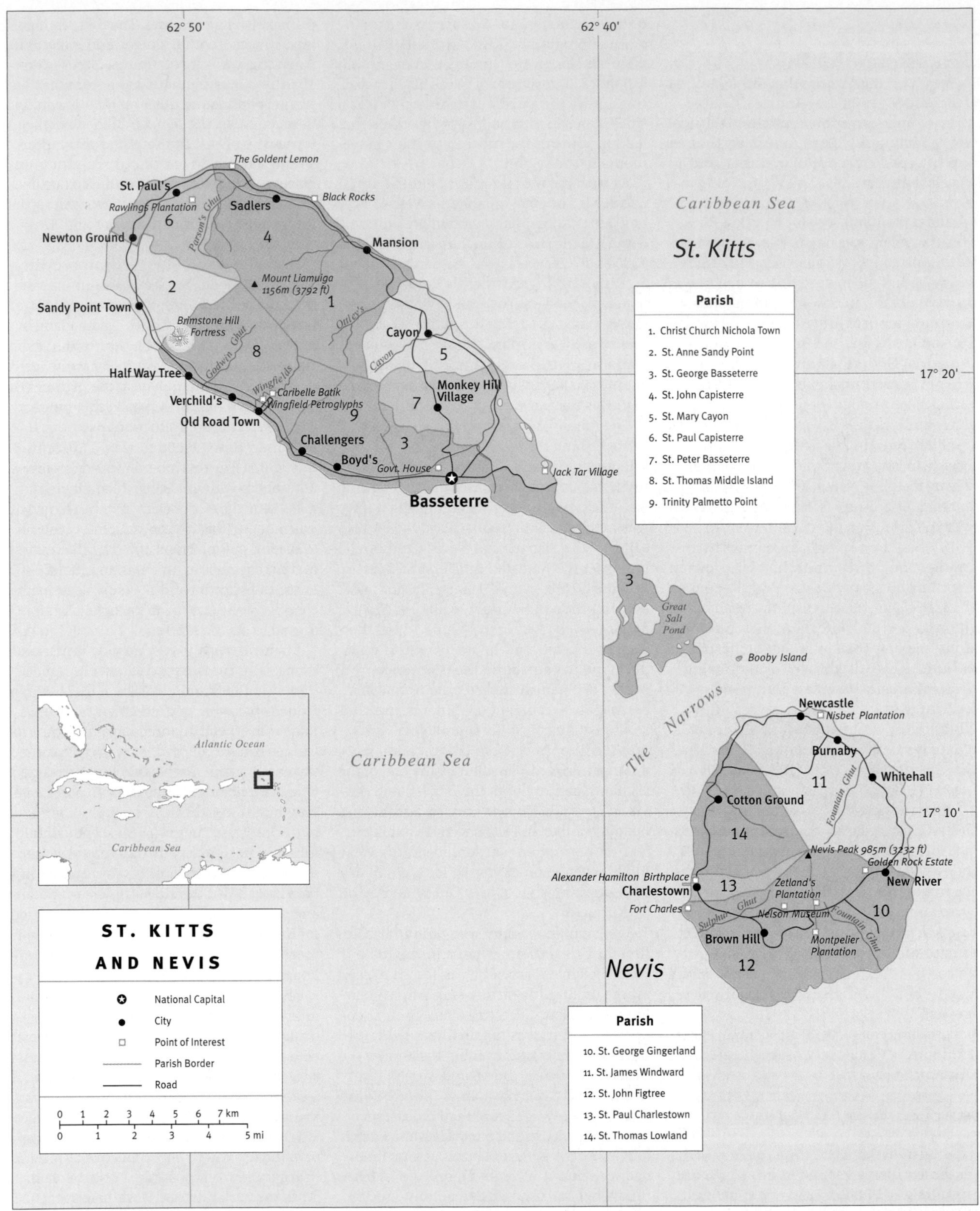

Sugar remained the only real industry on the islands, and most of the viable land already belonged to planters who were not interested in redistributing it among the former slaves. As a result many black Kittitians and Nevisians continued to work in the sugar fields for much of the twentieth century, often now forced to rent land and housing on the same estates where they had once been slaves. White planters also continued to regulate strictly their employees' working hours, sick days, and physical mobility. A series of natural disasters in the second half of the nineteenth century – the great earthquake of 1843, the cholera epidemic of 1854, the great fire of 1867, and the great flood of 1880 – compounded the already miserable living and working conditions on the islands. By the turn of the twentieth century the black majority on St. Kitts and Nevis was ready for real change.

One way they found it was through emigration. Between 1900 and 1930, approximately 10,000 Kittitians and Nevisians moved to the United States, CUBA, the DOMINICAN REPUBLIC,

TOP: Residents buy produce at the port of Nevis. Sugar production is a principal industry in St. Kitts and Nevis, as it has been since the eighteenth century. *Hutchison Library*
ABOVE: A woman stands behind the counter of her shop on Nevis. *CORBIS/Kit Kittle*

PANAMA, or neighboring islands in search of better jobs – or at the very least, better treatment. For those who chose to stay, change came through unionizing and fighting for political power. After the collapse of sugar prices during the Great Depression hurt the islands' economy yet again, many planters announced that they would be attempting to salvage their losses by cutting workers' wages and bonuses. This time the workers decided to fight.

St. Kitts was at the forefront of the labor movements that swept across the Caribbean in the 1930s. As one historian put it, it was the "St. Kitts human chain [that] link[ed] the West Indian working class." In 1932 Robert Bradshaw organized the Workers League, St. Kitts's first union. Black workers also turned to supplementary methods of protest against unfair conditions, most notably the general strikes and riots that occurred in 1935 and 1936. In each case laborers wanted to create better workplaces. But they were also determined to create a better and fairer political system. The traditional government, which consisted solely of political appointees who were all members of the wealthy white "plantocracy," was long outmoded.

In 1937 the British governor in St. Kitts and Nevis finally allowed five seats on the legislature to be chosen by popular election. Voting rights were still limited by property and income qualifications, so most of the black majority were still ineligible, but they strategized together to take advantage of the small influence they did have. In 1940 the Workers League became the St. Kitts and Nevis Trades and Labour Union. It soon established a new political wing, the St. Kitts and Nevis Labour Party, led by Bradshaw. He was elected to the Legislative Council in 1946, marking the beginning of the Labour Party's 30-year reign in St. Kitts and Nevis politics.

Universal suffrage was finally granted to all citizens in 1952, along with a legislature with a majority of elected members. The Labour Party easily won all of the available seats in the next elections, and for the first time in its 330-year history as a British Crown Colony, St. Kitts and Nevis was ruled by the majority of its people. In 1967 the country took an important step toward full independence when St. Kitts, Nevis, and the island of ANGUILLA became a single British state instead of a colony. Anguilla, which had been administered jointly with St. Kitts and Nevis, opposed the new arrangement, and in 1971 it returned to being a Crown Colony. Some Nevisians considered following Anguilla's lead, because they were also apprehensive that permanent affiliation with St. Kitts would threaten Nevis's autonomy. But the British government strongly encouraged St. Kitts and Nevis to remain together. Despite Nevisian dissent, on September 19, 1983, St. Kitts and Nevis became independent as a single nation.

The Labour Party continued to control the government until 1980, with Bradshaw, who had become the country's first premier in 1967, leading the country until his death in 1978. But by the 1970s there were two common complaints about the government: it had assumed too much state control and it had done too little to diversify the economy, which remained one of the Caribbean's last sugar monocultures. The People's Action Movement (PAM), led by Kennedy Simmonds, came to power in 1980 and stayed there until 1995. Under the PAM government St. Kitts and Nevis successfully increased tourism, providing much-needed new industries for the country. But a 1994 drug trafficking scandal led to the resignation of the deputy prime minister, the arrest of two of his sons, the murder of a third, and the call for new elections three years ahead of schedule. The elections were marred by protests and violence. In July 1995 the Labour Party was returned to power, with Denzil Douglass as the new prime minister.

Today St. Kitts and Nevis has returned to the task of setting the country's course for the twenty-first century. In several areas the islands are at a crossroads. There is still disagreement as to whether or not St. Kitts and Nevis should remain a single country. In both islands tourism continues to increase rapidly, but sugar production remains a key part of the economy. Some of the country's culture remains undeniably British – for example, the government system, the language, and the national passion for cricket – but many more traditions reflect the population's African and Caribbean heritage. Carnival is celebrated grandly every year between Christmas and New Year's, as it is across the Caribbean. The new annual St. Kitts Music Festival, which began in 1996, gives another indication of the country's diasporic heritage: the five-day festival features salsa, soul, SOCA, SAMBA, REGGAE, and JAZZ and concludes with a gospel revival. These apparent contradictions are characteristic of the entire Caribbean, however, and they are part of what makes St. Kitts and Nevis a vibrant and vital modern nation.

Lisa Clayton Robinson

See Also

Middle Passage, The; Soul Music; Transatlantic Slave Trade; Slavery in Latin America and the Caribbean; Gospel Music; Salsa Music; Antigua and Barbuda; Apprenticeship in the British Caribbean; Abolition and Emancipation in Latin America and the Caribbean; Carnivals in Latin America and the Caribbean.

Latin America and the Caribbean

St. Lucia, country in the Caribbean Sea, approximately 42 km (25 mi) south of Martinique and 33 km (20 mi) north of St. Vincent.

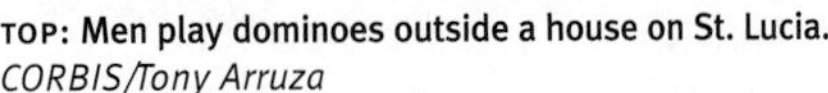

TOP: Men play dominoes outside a house on St. Lucia. *CORBIS/Tony Arruza*

ABOVE: The sun sets behind the drying sails of boats in the harbor of Soufrière, on the west coast of St. Lucia. *CORBIS/Tony Arruza*

ABOVE RIGHT: The intense concentration of a soccer match shows in the play of these two men on St. Lucia. *CORBIS/Tony Arruza*

RIGHT: Construction workers take a break from building a home in Anse la Raye, St. Lucia. *Horner/Hutchison*

As its nickname, "The Helen of the West Indies" suggests, St. Lucia is considered one of the most beautiful islands in the Caribbean. Its beauty is in large measure due to the fact that it has more forests and more indigenous flora and fauna than many Caribbean islands.

St. Lucia was inhabited first by the Arawak Indians, who migrated to the island around 200 C.E., and then by the Carib Indians, who replaced the Arawaks by about 800 C.E. The original Amerindian name for the island was *Iouanalao*, or "the place where the iguana is found." There has been some debate over when Europeans first sighted St. Lucia, though tradition holds that Christopher Columbus himself discovered the island on St. Lucy's feast day, December 13, 1502. What is certain, however, is that Carib resistance to European settlement on the island was fierce, and St. Lucian Caribs were able to resist European colonization until the mid-seventeenth century.

Once colonization began, there was competition over which European colonial power would control St. Lucia. Although Spanish explorers had claimed the island first, Spanish colonists never made a serious attempt to settle it, and the real battle for St. Lucia was fought between the French and the British. Both held other islands close to St. Lucia, and both coveted the excellent natural harbor at Castries, which is considered the best harbor in the West Indies. The British and French continued fighting over the island until 1814, with the island changing hands seven times. The constant political instability meant that neither country was able to develop the permanent plantation economy on St. Lucia that they had created on other islands.

This was a fortunate development that left much of St. Lucia's land untouched – land that might otherwise have been covered in Sugar or coffee plantations by the end of the eighteenth century. But some colonists were able to establish plantations on St. Lucia, and like plantation owners across the Americas, they turned to Africa for the cheap labor they needed to run their estates. The first African slaves arrived in St. Lucia around 1763, brought by French planters who had purchased them from the slave traders who abducted them from their West African homes. It was during slavery that the patois still spoken today developed, a combination of French and several African languages.

The fact that most St. Lucian blacks spoke French patois put them at a disadvantage when the country permanently became a British territory in 1814; this linguistic difference is one of the factors that continues to contribute to the island's high illiteracy rate. In 1834 slavery was abolished in all British territories, making the 13,291 St. Lucian slaves free. At the time of emancipation St. Lucia already had more small estates than any of the other Windward Islands, and this number grew as newly emancipated slaves

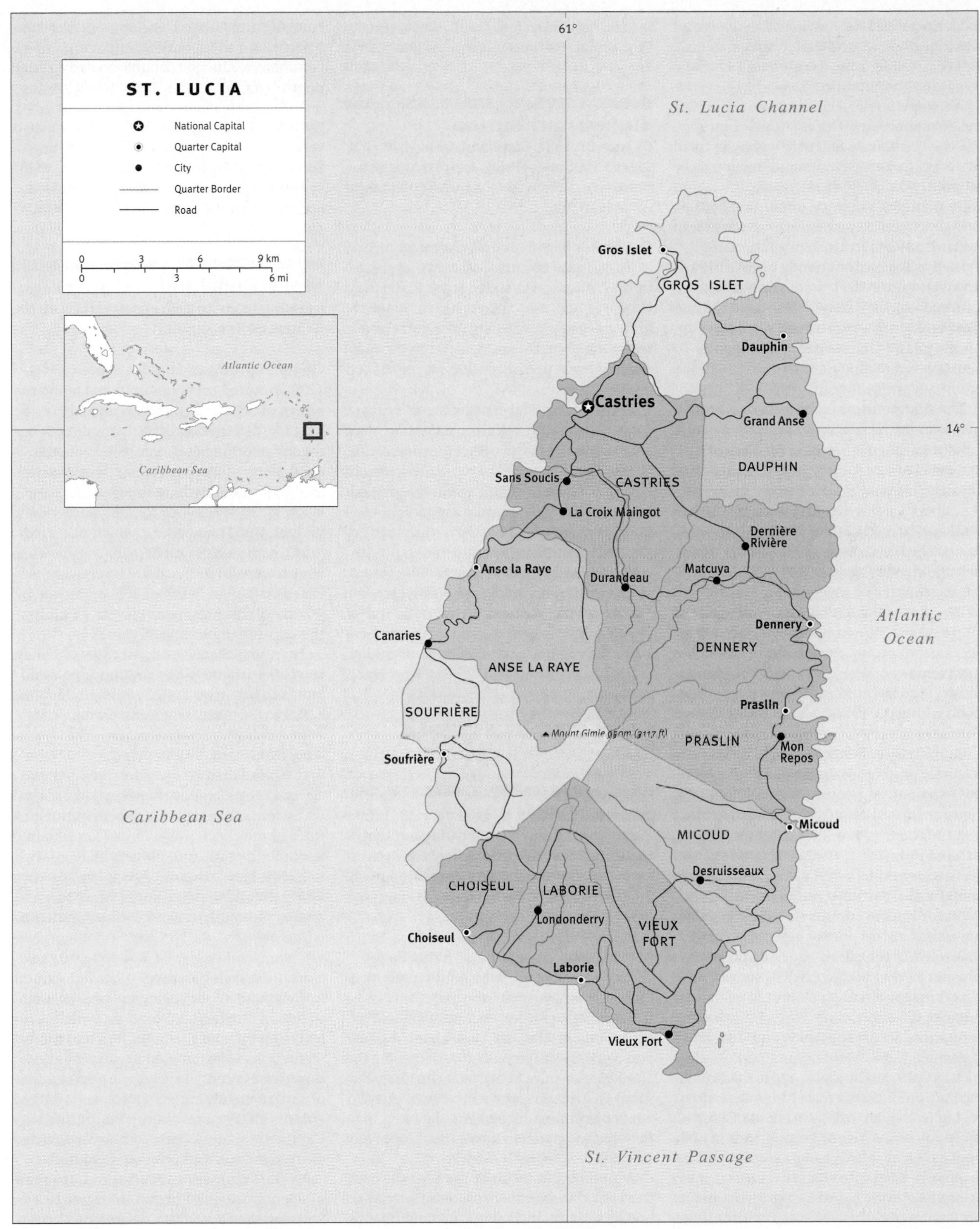

fled their former owners and established their own farms. This left white planters with a labor shortage, and in response they introduced a sharecropping system in 1838. But this system left much to be desired for its black workers, and poverty, smallpox and yellow fever, and other ills plagued both black and white St. Lucians for much of the nineteenth century.

The introduction of the coal industry in 1883 brought relief for a short time, as did the transfer of a British military base to St. Lucia from BARBADOS during the same period. But for the most part St. Lucia was regarded as a poor, undeveloped nation, even by its Caribbean neighbors. By the middle of the twentieth century even the sugar industry that had been the backbone of much of the Caribbean economy was in decline. The growth of the banana industry in the 1950s finally brought a period of relative prosperity to St. Lucia, and for the first time the island was able to concentrate on bringing roads, electricity, and a fresh water supply to its large rural population.

Welcome political changes soon followed the economic ones. During its first century of British authority St. Lucia had been ruled by Crown Colony government, under which all political decisions regarding the island were made by a council appointed by the British Crown. Representative government was introduced in 1924, but it remained limited to the predominantly white elite, and it was not until 1951 that universal adult suffrage was established. For the first time black St. Lucians – who had been the majority on the island since the late eighteenth century – were able to have their say in the country's government.

The first political party to rise to prominence under the new system was the St. Lucia Labour Party, which was an offshoot of the St. Lucia Workers Union. In 1961 a faction of younger, university-educated members of the Labour Party broke off to found the United Workers Party (UWP). When the UWP won its first election in 1964, leader John Compton became chief minister of St. Lucia. Compton led the country's government from 1964 to 1979. After being voted out of office in the 1979 elections, he returned in 1982 for another six years. Compton presided over one of the most important developments in the island's history – its transition to independent statehood within the British Commonwealth on February 22, 1979.

Since independence the country has been relatively prosperous, particularly as tourism has experienced strong growth in the 1990s. However, droughts and changes in the European market, which have threatened the banana industry in the last several years, serve as reminders of the country's need to continue diversifying its economic base. The need for improvements in education also remains a national priority, especially changes that will help the patois-speaking population prosper in the official English society.

St. Lucia is already celebrated as the home of the Caribbean's two Nobel laureates, economist Sir Arthur Lewis and poet and playwright Derek Walcott. Prominent novelists such as Garth St. Omer also add to the island's reputation. Finally, tourist literature about St. Lucia is quick to celebrate the island's multicultural African, French, and British heritage as one of its greatest assets. St. Lucia is already a favorite site for visitors from around the world, and St. Lucians remain optimistic that their country will continue prospering into the next century.

Lisa Clayton Robinson

See Also

Transatlantic Slave Trade; Literature, English Language, Caribbean; Slavery in Latin America and the Caribbean; Walcott, Derek Alton; St. Vincent and the Grenadines; Abolition and Emancipation in Latin America and the Caribbean; Languages, Creole, in the Caribbean; Lewis, Arthur.

North America

Stokes, Carl Burton

(b. June 21, 1927, Cleveland, Ohio; d. April 3, 1996, Cleveland, Ohio), African American politician, the first black mayor of a major American city.

Carl Stokes began his political career in 1958 as an assistant city prosecutor in Cleveland. In 1967, after serving three terms in the Ohio House of Representatives, he was elected mayor of Cleveland, Ohio, the eighth-largest city in the United States. Stokes thus became the first black person elected mayor of such a large American city.

Initially successful at negotiating between conservative white interests and urban black concerns, Stokes faced a decline in popularity after an armed conflict between black nationalists and Cleveland police officers sparked rioting in an African American neighborhood. Stokes served two terms as mayor of Cleveland, until 1971, but decided not to run for a third term when this conflict overshadowed the improvements his administration had made in city streets, welfare, and water purification. He later worked as a reporter, a labor lawyer, and a municipal court judge.

Paul Foster

See Also

Black Nationalism in the United States.

North America

Stokes, Louis

(b. February 23, 1925, Cleveland, Ohio), Democratic member of the United States House of Representatives from Ohio (1969-); his 1968 election made Stokes the first black member of Congress from Ohio.

Louis Stokes served in the United States Army from 1943 to 1946 and then attended Case Western Reserve University from 1946 to 1948. Stokes received a law degree from the Cleveland-Marshall Law School in 1953 and worked as a lawyer before becoming the U.S. Representative from Ohio's 11th Congressional District. He was reelected every two years beginning in 1970 and defeated his Republican opponent by nearly 125,000 votes in 1996.

A predominantly black, Democratic area, the 11th District covers eastern Cleveland and its suburbs, including Cleveland Heights, Shaker Heights, and University Heights. Redistricting during the 1990s added more white and middle-class voters to the district. Case Western Reserve University and many of Cleveland's prominent cultural institutions are located here.

In 1993, as a member of the Appropriations Committee, Stokes became the chair of the Housing and Urban Development, Veterans Affairs, and Independent Agencies subcommittees. After the Republican Party gained control of Congress in 1995, Stokes lost his chairmanship and became ranking member. In the 105th Congress (1997-1999), he also served on the Labor, Health and Human Services, and Education Subcommittee of the Appropriations committees. He was also a member of the Congressional Black Caucus.

North America

Stono Rebellion,

the largest slave uprising in an American colony before the American Revolution.

On the morning of Sunday, September 9, 1739, hundreds of slaves gathered along the banks of South Carolina's Stono River to fight for their freedom. The rhythmic cadence of African drum beats, combined with cries for "Liberty," followed a small army of slaves as they marched along the river, freeing fellow slaves, killing their masters, and torching plantations. The uprising, which occurred near Charleston, South Carolina, began while whites were attending church services and lasted until nightfall when it was crushed by state militias. Sixty people were killed in the fighting, including 35 slaves.

There are 250 documented cases of violent slave disturbances on the American mainland and 250 more at sea. While subtle forms of slave resistance – such as working slowly or pretending to misunderstand orders – were daily features of life, the potential for overt and violent disturbances terrified whites. Those in colonial South Carolina had a special cause for fear because by the beginning of the eighteenth century, South Carolina had become the first, and only, British colony to have a black majority. A Swiss visitor once wrote that the colony "looks more like a negro country than like a country settled by white people."

Colonial officials tried desperately to deal with the growing number of slaves. Armed militias patrolled the colony and were allowed to detain "suspicious" blacks at will. Slaves traveling beyond the boundaries of their plantations were required to carry identification passes, and all slaves were forced to observe a nightly curfew. Those who violated colonial laws were whipped in public. Captured runaways were routinely convicted of insurrection and publicly executed.

By the summer of 1739 South Carolina's black majority had begun to organize a massive rebellion. A black slave named Jemmy emerged as the leader of the uprising. Little is known about Jemmy. His age, slave occupation, and education are a mystery, but historians believe that he was captured in Africa and forced into slavery. In fact, most of South Carolina's 32,000 slaves came from the same region of Africa, Angola, and their kinship and linguistic ties made secrecy and communicating plans about the insurrection easier. Although information about how the uprising was planned is not known, eyewitness accounts provide vivid details of its execution.

Early on the morning of September 9, around 20 slaves assembled in St. Paul's Parish, located near the western edge of the Stono River. At daybreak the group marched to Stono Bridge, broke into a white-owned firearms store and seized boxes of guns and ammunition. The white storeowners stumbled upon the burglary and were killed in a brief struggle. Their severed heads were placed on the store's front porch.

Twenty-five whites were murdered, including women and children, as the slaves traveled along the plantations lining the Stono River. Many of Charleston's most valuable estates were set on fire and white-owned stores were destroyed. By midday more than 50 slaves had gathered on a site 17 km (10 mi) outside town. Drumming and shouts of "Liberty" drew more slaves to the battlefield. (Henry Louis Gates Jr. sees the beating of African drums as a form of literacy, arguing that, "both forms of literacy – of English letters and of the black vernacular – had been pivotal to the slave's capacity to rebel.")

Late that evening an army of 20 to 100 white soldiers arrived upstream of the celebrating slaves. A battle followed, but the slaves were badly outgunned. Many slaves who attempted to fight were shot and killed. Some tried to return to their plantations, hoping they could avoid being implicated in the uprising. But most of them were captured, convicted, and executed. The heads of those executed were posted on fences throughout the Charleston area. A small group of slaves actually managed to escape and hide for several weeks. But an armed white militia eventually caught and killed them all after a brief gunfight.

In response to the Stono Uprising, South Carolina officials tried to reduce the provocation for insurrection, imposing penalties on masters who overworked their slaves or beat them excessively. Colonial officials established a Negro school in Charleston, largely to teach slaves selected Christian values like obedience and submissiveness. But the benevolence of colonial officials was overshadowed by the legal attacks on the mobility and limited personal liberties of South Carolina slaves.

One of the most definitive measures of the Negro Act of 1740 led to the abolition of the "talking drum," the beating of African drums during slave gatherings. According to historian Peter H. Wood, "freedom of movement and freedom of assembly, freedom to raise food, to earn money, to learn to read English" were also restricted in some cases and abolished in most. Strict laws were passed that closely monitored the ratio of blacks to whites.

The Stono Rebellion did not succeed, but it persuaded many whites to leave South Carolina. Hundreds packed their bags and fled to neighboring colonies. Armed white patrols were increased in and around Charleston, and after the uprising slaves were routinely beaten and harassed. But despite the consequences, as Wood explains, "the troubled waters of resistance did not subside any more abruptly than they had risen." The Gabriel Prosser Rebellion in 1800, and the Denmark Vesey Conspiracy in 1822 are two noteworthy examples of later acts of resistance.

Alonford James Robinson, Jr.

See Also
Slavery in the United States; Black Codes in the United States; Gabriel Prosser Conspiracy.

North America

Strayhorn, Billy

(b. November 29, 1915, Dayton, Ohio; d. May 31, 1967, New York, N.Y.), African American jazz composer, arranger, pianist; associate of the Duke Ellington Orchestra from 1939 to 1967.

Billy Strayhorn was born into a family that relocated from his birthplace in Dayton, Ohio, to Hillsborough, North Carolina, and finally to Pittsburgh, Pennsylvania. In Pittsburgh Strayhorn received private piano instruction in the classics. A technically accomplished student, he coupled his classical music training with an inventive approach to his playing, working out his own chromatic harmonies.

In December 1938 Strayhorn showed some of his own compositions to Duke Ellington, hoping to impress him enough to be taken on as a lyricist. Three months later Ellington recorded Strayhorn's "Something to Live For." As Ellington later recounted in his memoir, "Billy Strayhorn successfully married melody, words, and harmony, equating the fitting with happiness." "Something to Live For" was followed by four more recordings with Ellington's orchestra in 1939.

For the next 30 years Strayhorn worked with Ellington as an associate arranger and second pianist. The two collaborated so closely that it is difficult to assess the contribution of each on such arrangements as "Lush Life," "Satin Drill," and the orchestra's theme song, "Take the A Train," which Strayhorn composed. Ellington recalled that he and Strayhorn were so like-minded that once, when composing separately on a given mood, they chose the same first and last notes.

Strayhorn produced an album in his own name, the 1950 *Billy Strayhorn Trio*, and also participated in small group recordings with Ellington sidemen. His main work continued to be collaborative, creating such compositions as "Such Sweet Thunder," "Suite Thursday, and "Far East Suite" for Ellington's orchestra, before his death in 1967.

Marian Aguiar

See Also
Ellington, Edward Kennedy ("Duke").

Africa

Structural Adjustment in Africa, **national economic reform programs undertaken by countries in return for assistance from the World Bank and other international donor institutions.**

Numerous countries in Africa began to experience difficulty meeting their financial obligations during the 1970s. By the early 1980s most African countries were receiving loans from international financial institutions that were subject to conditions on borrowers' national economic policies. The conditions that accompanied these loans were known collectively as structural adjustment policies (SAPs). The lending agencies responsible for devising SAPs included the World Bank, the International Monetary Fund (IMF), and bilateral agencies such as the United States Agency for International Development and European aid agencies.

The history of SAPs is controversial in Africa, possibly more so than elsewhere. The results have been disappointing. Critics portray SAPs as a failure, foisted on Africa by heartless outsiders. Other critics have complained that theorists unfamiliar with African problems designed policies that are poorly suited to African realities. Defenders claim that incomplete and incoherent implementation of SAPs often accounted for their disappointing results. They emphasize the benefits of these policies, not the failings.

Background
The increase in oil prices of the mid-1970s caused problems for African oil importers in their balance of payments (in a given country, total money received in export earnings and financial assistance, less total money spent on imports and external debt). When oil prices increased, many countries found that the money they received (in export earnings and aid funding) failed to cover the cost of oil imports. Many countries met their increased need for foreign exchange by borrowing funds, rather than by curtailing other imports or increasing exports. Thus they failed to adjust to the new scarcity of foreign exchange.

Meanwhile, they increased their foreign debts and only worsened their long-term balance of payments problems, since in the future they would have to pay not only for oil imports but also for debt service. There were a number of commodity booms in the mid-1970s that temporarily generated increased foreign exchange earnings for some African countries. Prices of coffee, cocoa, tea, and phosphates were all high, and the boom encouraged even more borrowing. Banks were willing to loan to African countries because of the countries' high export earnings at the time and because of the banks' need to find ways to invest the petrodollars on deposit from the oil exporters. However, the recession in the early 1980s caused commodity prices to collapse, as global demand dropped. High interest rates imposed by the Federal Reserve Bank to fight inflation in the United States caused real interest rates to rise to highs that were unforeseen when African countries negotiated their external loans. By the early 1980s many African countries, facing potential bankruptcy, turned to the World Bank, IMF, and bilateral agencies for assistance.

Structural Adjustment Programs

Assistance included additional lending, some grants, and some debt forgiveness. Lenders required acceptance of conditions intended to promote short-term stabilization, generally combining devaluation of the local currency with government financial austerity. They also required policy changes aimed to increase growth over the medium to long term. Currency devaluation was expected to improve the balance of payments because it would make imports more expensive and hence reduce demand for them, while it would make exports more attractive on the global market and hence increase the supply of foreign exchange. Financial austerity required governments to reduce expenditures or increase taxes, or both. This was supposed to reduce monetary growth and, hence, inflation. Inflation contributed to currency overvaluation by making domestic prices rise faster than international prices, so inflation increased demand for imports and reduced supply of exports. Reducing inflation was essential to regaining balance of payments equilibrium. Since devaluation itself spurred inflation by increasing the prices of imported goods, it needed to be combined with austerity to keep overvaluation from recurring.

SAPs also compelled countries to implement longer-term policy reforms, including the privatization of public enterprises, the deregulation of prices and interest rates, and financial liberalization, including free trade in all sorts of commodities and financial instruments, among them foreign exchange. Foreign trade was also supposed to be liberalized and trade barriers of all types reduced. These measures were expected to attract foreign investment and improve the efficiency of resource use.

The World Bank published a major study of structural adjustment in Africa in 1994. They found evidence that countries that adhered to SAPs improved their economic performance, and that they had better performance than countries that flouted SAP requirements. They cited increased growth in gross domestic product (GDP, a measure of the volume of economic activity), industrial output, and exports in countries that followed SAPs. However, the improvements were extremely modest and would be considered poor in other developing regions. Economic growth rates remain too low to expect much reduction in poverty in the next 20 or 30 years. SAPs, which included additional loans, have left the adjusting countries still deeply indebted, and hence vulnerable to economic downturns in the future.

Assessment

Why has the record of structural adjustment been so disappointing in Africa? There has been little political support from within Africa for SAPs, which has made their implementation difficult. Policymakers are especially sensitive to the interests of urban populations, because of the danger of rioting in countries' capitals. Devaluation makes locally produced goods relatively less expensive and imports more expensive. The income of many urban residents comes from selling services locally, while they consume many imported goods. Hence devaluation hurts the standard of living of many urban residents. Likewise, government austerity hurts many urban dwellers via lower expenditures or higher taxes, especially if there are layoffs of public employees. Thus governments have often implemented SAPs reluctantly, partially, and only under duress.

The logic behind SAPs includes many assumptions about the ways in which markets allocate resources. In Africa markets have often not worked according to the assumptions of neoclassical models. African governments have often had a much bigger economic role than is presumed in such models. Also, much of the economy may still be focused on subsistence production, which does not pass through markets and may not respond to market incentives, especially if farmers lack the physical or institutional infrastructure that would permit marketing. For example, government bodies, rather than market forces, have often set commodity prices in Africa. Partial implementation of SAPs in such an environment can have perverse consequences. In one such example, when government bodies set prices, devaluation does not automatically translate into higher producer prices for exported goods. Paying producers higher prices – in line with the increased export earnings that result from devaluation – would mean higher costs for government marketing boards. Thus higher producer prices contradicted the logic of austerity, and governments sometimes failed to implement them fully. The result of devaluation without passing through price increases to producers was to increase farmers' costs (for imported inputs), and to make it less rather than more profitable to produce export crops. Thus partial implementation of SAPs can be ineffective or even harmful.

Critics of SAPs have often claimed that SAPs harm the welfare of the poor because they result in higher prices for basic goods and cutbacks in government services. Supporters of SAP counter that countries needing balance of payments support are already experiencing economic problems; for example, per capita GDP in Ghana had declined for nearly a decade before Ghana began structural adjustment. There is no doubt that the poor in Ghana suffered mightily during structural adjustment, but supporters claim that structural adjustment stopped the shrinkage of the economy and helped most people, including the poor. Ghana is often cited as the country with the best adjustment record in Africa. In theory, those employed in exporting sectors should gain from SAPs, and to the extent that this includes large numbers of peasant farmers, SAPs in Africa may raise incomes and improve the welfare of the poor.

The countries of West Africa that share the CFA franc as their currency (comprising most of the countries of former French West Africa) have had the most difficult time with structural adjustment. Since they could not devalue their currency without a unanimous vote of all of the countries using it, they had to adjust without devaluation. This left austerity as the only real tool to achieve adjustment: they needed to slow their own price increases below those of trading partners to achieve real devaluation, in order to improve their balance of payments. The degree of austerity necessary to achieve such deflation proved politically unacceptable, so that these countries floundered with less austerity than necessary to be effective, but enough to ensure prolonged recession. Finally, they devalued their currency in 1994 for the first time since the 1940s.

Western donors compounded the controversy over SAPs in the 1990s by adding a whole new set of political conditions. Following the end of the cold war and the collapse of communist regimes in the former Soviet bloc, Western donors had less need to secure third-world allies and a simultaneous desire to distribute aid to the former Soviet-bloc countries. In this context donors became less willing to offer support to African regimes that they viewed as corrupt and undemocratic. They added conditions requiring less corruption and greater democracy to the long list of conditions already required under SAP lending. Some believe that these requirements helped the emerging democratic opposition, but incumbent rulers deeply resented the intrusive nature of these conditions. The effectiveness of these political conditions is questionable. They probably worked best in Kenya, where President Daniel Arap Moi responded to a moratorium on balance of payments assistance by restoring multiparty elections. The case of the former Zaire (today the Democratic Republic of the Congo) is more troubling: there President Mobutu Sese Seko refused to accept a democratic transition, clinging to office as the state decayed and collapsed.

Barbara Grosh

Africa

St. Thomas and Prince Islands.

Former name of São Tomé and Príncipe.

North America

Student Nonviolent Coordinating Committee (SNCC)

(pronounced "snick"), civil rights group that played a major role in the 1960s campaign to end segregation in the southern United States.

Founding and Early Protest

On February 1, 1960, four black college students attracted widespread attention when they refused to leave a whites-only lunch counter in an F. W. Woolworth store in Greensboro, North Carolina (*see* Jim Crow). The sit-in continued for several weeks and inspired dozens of similar sit-ins across the South. Although not the first time students had taken part in civil rights protests, the sit-in movement was among the largest and most spontaneous. Reacting to the protests, Ella J. Baker, executive director of the Southern Christian Leadership Conference (SCLC), held a conference for student activists in April at Shaw University in Raleigh, North Carolina. Baker believed that larger, more cautious civil rights groups such as the SCLC might have failed to serve students who were impatient for racial equality. She urged the 200 attendees to establish a new student group that would harness its energy and frustration to challenge white racism as well as the larger and more conventional civil rights groups.

Other civil rights leaders, such as SCLC's Martin Luther King Jr., argued that a united movement would be stronger than a divided one and invited the students to create a wing within SCLC. Representatives of the National Association for the Advancement of Colored People (NAACP) and the National Urban League made similar invitations. The students created a Temporary Coordinating Committee to debate the issue; in May the committee embraced the mainstream's practice of nonviolence but created an independent group, the Temporary Student Nonviolent Coordinating Committee. ("Temporary" was dropped from the name in October.) Made up of both black and white members, the group elected Marion Barry, a student at Nashville's Fisk University who would later become mayor of Washington, D.C., SNCC's first chairman and set up its headquarters in Atlanta, Georgia. When Barry returned to graduate studies a few months later, he was replaced by Charles McDew, a student at South Carolina State College.

In its first months SNCC served mostly as a channel for student groups to communicate and coordinate the sit-in campaign. The images on national television of well-groomed, peaceful protesters being refused a cup of coffee and, in some instances, being hauled off to jail, generated sympathy among many whites across the country. Several SNCC and other protesters capitalized on the publicity with a "jail-no-bail" campaign. Refusing to pay fines or bail, the students served jail sentences, thereby filling Southern jails and continuing media coverage. By the end of 1960 several chain stores in the upper South and Texas responded to the movement by ending segregation at their lunch counters. Several cities also agreed to desegregate public restaurants.

Freedom Rides

From the end of 1960 through the fall of 1961 SNCC underwent a critical internal debate that it never completely resolved. One faction wanted to continue generating white sympathy through sit-ins and demonstrations, while another faction wanted to give Southern blacks power more directly by helping them register to vote. SNCC's James Forman, a schoolteacher-turned-coordinator who was well respected among students, urged the group in late 1961 to pursue both goals. Forman reasoned that helping blacks register to vote was a form of nonviolent protest that would stir up Southern hostility, generate white sympathy, and give blacks more power. SNCC's membership agreed.

As the debate over SNCC's direction was taking place, the Congress of Racial Equality (CORE) was undertaking the Freedom Ride of 1961. On May 4 seven blacks and six whites left Washington, D.C., on two public buses bound for the Deep South. They intended to test the Supreme Court's ruling in *Boynton* v. *Virginia* (1960), which declared segregation in interstate bus and rail stations unconstitutional. In the first few days the riders encountered only minor hostility, but in the second week the riders were severely beaten. Outside Anniston, Alabama, one of their buses was burned, and in Birmingham several dozen whites attacked the riders only two blocks from the sheriff's office. With the intervention of the United States Justice Department, most of CORE's Freedom Riders were evacuated from Birmingham, Alabama to New Orleans. John Lewis, a former seminary student who would later lead SNCC and become a U.S. Congressman, stayed in Birmingham, as did another rider.

SNCC leaders hurriedly decided that letting violence end the trip would send the wrong signal to the country. They reinforced the pair of remaining riders with volunteers, and under SNCC leadership the trip continued. The group traveled from Birmingham to Montgomery without incident, but on their arrival in Montgomery they were savagely attacked by a mob of more than 1000 whites. The extreme violence and the indifference of local police prompted a national outcry of support for the riders, putting pressure on President John F. Kennedy to end the violence. The riders continued to Mississippi, where they endured further brutality and jail terms but generated more publicity and inspired dozens more Freedom Rides. By the end of the summer the protests had spread to train stations and airports across the South, and in November the Interstate Commerce Commission issued rules prohibiting segregated transportation facilities.

Winning the Vote

Following the sit-in and Freedom Ride victories, SNCC joined with CORE, the NAACP, SCLC, and the Urban League in the Voter Education Project (VEP). Funded by large private grants, VEP sought to increase the number of Southern blacks registered to vote. SNCC had failed at a similar voter-registration effort in rural Georgia in 1961 and 1962. When VEP funds became available in 1962, SNCC shifted its focus to Mississippi and Louisiana, where it also met stern resistance and succeeded in registering only a few blacks.

In 1963, however, several highly publicized conflicts changed the course of the movement. In May police in Birmingham brutally beat black and white protesters, prompting another wave of public sympathy. The next month Kennedy introduced a strong civil rights bill to Congress, which was passed during the administration of Lyndon Johnson as the Civil Rights Act of 1964. (The act prohibited segregation in several types of public facilities.) Liberal contributors responded to the violence by pouring large donations into virtually all of the civil rights groups, whose staffs and programs grew accordingly. In late 1963, when VEP decided to abandon Mississippi for lack of progress, SNCC, now led by John Lewis, could afford to stay.

Many SNCC activists were critical of the way larger civil rights groups "invaded" towns for a protest, then left after the protest ended. SNCC's field workers in Mississippi believed they could best help blacks by living in their communities and working with them over the long term. In late 1963, with help from CORE and, nominally, other civil rights groups, SNCC revitalized the Council of Federated Organizations (COFO); COFO had been created in 1961 to help free jailed Freedom Riders. It would now oversee voter registration in Mississippi. Bob Moses, a Harvard graduate student, veteran SNCC field worker, and leading advocate of commitment to communities, was placed in charge of COFO. COFO functioned largely as an arm of SNCC.

Despite COFO's efforts whites effectively used intimidation and discriminatory tactics to keep blacks from registering to vote in Mississippi. To Northern reporters, Mississippi officials argued that the state's blacks did not vote because they were too apathetic. COFO countered the claim by holding a Freedom Vote at the same time as the November 1963 elections. In mock elections 80,000 blacks cast ballots in their own communities, where they did not have to face hostile whites.

Amid the success many of COFO's black workers were angered by the role whites were playing in the organization. White students often came to the South for a few months (typically a summer), assumed high-profile leadership positions while there, then returned to safe campuses in the North while blacks continued the hard work. Many black activists were also tired of accepting beatings and jail sentences in order to win sympathy from white federal officials, white liberal donors, and the white public. They were weary as well of having to tone down their militancy and rhetoric at the request of whites in power. SNCC's Lewis voiced many of these frustrations during a speech in the March on Washington of August 1963; that Lewis was made to tone down his remarks by mainstream civil rights groups and white officials only further angered blacks in SNCC. For these reasons many COFO activists argued it was important for blacks to succeed on their own, without the help of white volunteers. Some even wondered if it would be possible to continue working with mainstream civil rights groups.

Moses was forced to address this debate when he proposed the FREEDOM SUMMER of 1964, a registration and education project that would build on the Freedom Vote. Moses argued forcefully that if COFO excluded whites, blacks had no moral standing to demand integration. Moreover, the movement would not receive as much publicity since national news groups would pay more attention to violence against whites than blacks. Moses's words were borne out when COFO's Michael Schwerner, James Chaney, and Andrew Goodman were murdered in June (Schwerner and Goodman were white) and the press and public responded with shock and outrage.

For years murders of blacks by whites in the South had gone unnoticed in the national media. President Johnson ordered a large FBI presence in Mississippi, and many whites became aware of the obstacles blacks faced when trying to vote in the Deep South. Still, COFO's 1000 volunteers managed to register only 1200 blacks statewide. Within COFO many student workers were convinced after the Schwerner, Chaney, and Goodman murders that nonviolence would not win blacks the vote. By the end of the summer SNCC officially defended the right of its Mississippi field secretaries to carry weapons.

Moses was able to exploit COFO's failure to register voters by creating a new party, the Mississippi Freedom Democratic Party (MFDP). Some 60,000 blacks joined the MFDP, which served as an alternative to Mississippi's all-white Democratic Party. With the presidential election of 1964 approaching, the MFDP sent 44 delegates to the national Democratic convention in Atlantic City, New Jersey. The delegation demanded to be seated at the convention in place of the regular Mississippi delegation. They were pledged to Johnson, while the white Democratic delegates were not. Although several Northern states supported seating the MFDP, Southern states threatened to walk out of the convention if the MFDP delegates were seated. Johnson, wary of losing the conservative South in the general election that fall, offered the MFDP a compromise: two of its black delegates would be seated along with the white delegates. The MFDP rejected the offer and, in a move largely coordinated by SNCC, walked out of the convention. In the aftermath, many whites across the country saw SNCC as an extremist group unwilling to bend, while many blacks became even more convinced that they could not work with whites.

SELMA AND BEYOND

In early 1965 King and SCLC attempted to register voters in Selma, Alabama. Learning from past mistakes, state and local officials denied the SCLC the brutal attacks that had created sympathy for blacks elsewhere. Instead, officials simply jailed blacks who tried to register. In March King called for a march from Selma to the capitol in Montgomery to protest black exclusion from the polls; however, he abruptly called off the protest on the eve of the march, probably to avoid antagonizing Johnson. After King left Selma, SNCC field workers and other activists urged local SCLC leaders to go ahead with the march. On March 7, 500 protesters headed by the SCLC's Hosea Williams and SNCC's Lewis began the march. In a matter of minutes a large deputized posse and dozens of state troopers attacked the marchers. The gruesome reports and photographs prompted one of the nation's largest outcries in support of the CIVIL RIGHTS MOVEMENT. Largely as a result, Congress passed the VOTING RIGHTS ACT OF 1965, which provided federal protections and guarantees for black voters.

Though many SNCC members were pleased the events in Selma had generated white sympathy, many others were again weary of taking abuse. They were also angered that a second Selma march, led by King a week later, was cut short after federal officials cautioned against it. When riots broke out in the black Watts neighborhood of Los Angeles in the summer of 1965, many SNCC members argued that the time had come for blacks to seize power rather than seek accommodation with whites. In May 1966 SNCC formalized its shift in this direction by electing STOKELY CARMICHAEL (later Kwame Turé), a recent graduate of HOWARD UNIVERSITY, to the chairmanship over John Lewis. Rejecting nonviolence, Carmichael argued at first that violence should be used in self-defense; later he called for offensive violence to overthrow oppression. Carmichael also denounced Johnson's civil rights bills, which were supported by the SCLC and the NAACP.

In June 1966, in Greenwood, Mississippi, Carmichael advocated BLACK POWER in a well-publicized speech. Although "Black Power" had been used before as a shorthand for black pride and political equality, Carmichael popularized the term through repeated speeches. Many whites were offended by Carmichael's views, which they saw as racist or separatist, and most of the mainstream civil rights groups severed their few remaining ties with SNCC. SNCC's white staff and volunteers, who had already begun to drift away from the group, soon left. Eventually Carmichael expelled the remaining white staff and denounced SNCC's white donors. By early 1967 SNCC was near bankruptcy, and both its staff and membership had dwindled.

In June 1967, when Carmichael left SNCC to help lead the BLACK PANTHER PARTY, he was replaced by 23-year-old H. Rap Brown. In his first months Brown removed the word "Nonviolent" from SNCC (renaming the group the Student National Coordinating Committee) and made urgent calls for violence. When Detroit rioted in the summer of 1967, Brown urged an audience in Cambridge, Massachusetts, to do the same. When a Cambridge school was set aflame hours later, Brown was charged with inciting a riot, one of several charges he would face in the following years. In May 1968 his legal problems forced him to resign SNCC's chairmanship. SNCC continued to operate into the early 1970s, but its impact on politics was minimal.

SEE ALSO

Barry, Marion Shepilov, Jr.; Brown, Hubert G. ("H. Rap"); Chaney, James Earl; Detroit Riot of 1967; King, Martin Luther, Jr.; Los Angeles Watts Riot of 1965; Moses, Robert Parris; New Orleans, Louisiana; Sit-Ins; March on Washington, 1963.

Latin America and the Caribbean

St. Vincent and the Grenadines,

country consisting of a chain of islands in the Caribbean Sea, with GRENADA to the south and ST. LUCIA to the north (the southern end of the Grenadine Islands chain is administered with Grenada).

The Carib Indians who inhabited St. Vincent at the time of Christopher Columbus's 1498 arrival called their island *Youlou* or *Hairoun*, meaning "home of the blessed." Indeed, for centuries before the European invasion of the Caribbean, the hilly, dramatic islands now known as St. Vincent and the Grenadines were home to several indigenous groups, who fought to preserve their islands after the colonists arrived. The first inhabitants of these islands were probably Ciboney Indians who arrived around 4300 B.C.E., followed by the Arawaks and then the Caribs. Although Columbus landed on St. Vincent on the feast day of St. Vincent, January 22, 1498, the Caribs successfully resisted any permanent European colonization on the island until the early 1700s (*see* COLONIAL LATIN AMERICA AND THE CARIBBEAN).

The first outsiders that the Caribs allowed to settle in St. Vincent were not Europeans but Africans. In 1675 a Dutch slave ship sank off the coast of Bequia, one of the nearby Grenadine Islands. None of the whites on board survived, but a group of Africans made it to shore. They subsequently migrated to St. Vincent, where they were assimilated into the Carib community. These Africans and their descendants were called Black Caribs, distinguishing them from the indigenous Yellow Caribs. St. Vincent's reputation as a Carib stronghold quickly spread; escaped slaves from nearby St. Lucia and Barbados soon joined St. Vincent's black community.

When the Caribs signed a treaty with the Europeans in the early 1700s, allowing European settlement, St. Vincent's transition to a slave society began (*see* Slavery in Latin America and the Caribbean). The first European settlers were French, and because they initially held only small farms that could be worked by small numbers of slaves, they coexisted with the Caribs for several years. But as the British also began to occupy the island, and both the British and the French grew interested in spreading out and establishing larger plantations, conflicts arose.

The French took advantage of their better relationship with the Caribs by encouraging them to attack British settlements. After a 1795 revolt, however, in which the Black Caribs seized much of St. Vincent, the British captured 5080 Caribs and deported them to British Honduras (present-day Belize). With much of the island's free black leadership now gone, most blacks remaining in St. Vincent and the Grenadines were slaves.

TOP: The market in the capital city of Kingstown, St. Vincent, bustles with activity. *Henderson/Hutchison*

ABOVE: Two fishermen repair their nets in Kingstown, St. Vincent, which is located on the southern tip of the island. *Gary A. Conner/D. Donne Bryant Stock Photo*

In 1812 a volcanic eruption on St. Vincent destroyed many of the island's coffee plants and cacao trees, making conditions even worse for all of the island's residents. Only the sugar plantations were left, and they could not support the population. In 1834 slavery was abolished (*see* Abolition and Emancipation in Latin America and the Caribbean) in all British territories, and many former slaves chose to leave the plantations and try to make their own living through subsistence farming. British landowners were forced to turn to East Indian and Portuguese indentured servants to help supply their labor. These workers on the large estates in the nineteenth century generally grew sugar cane. The sugar industry became less profitable as the century went on; an 1877 report found that St. Vincent was already among the poorest territories in the Caribbean.

The government's solution was to turn over more land to small farmers. But even blacks who owned their own farms found that they were still largely engaged in subsistence farming and were not able to produce crops for profit. An 1898 hurricane and another volcanic eruption in 1902 destroyed farms throughout the islands, making the precarious economic situation in St. Vincent and the Grenadines even worse. By the turn of the century some new crops had been introduced, such as cotton, arrowroot, and coconuts, and by the 1950s bananas would become the most successful crop. But the fact that the islands' economy has always been dependent on agriculture has made it very vulnerable to natural disasters and diseases, and has meant that most of the population are employed as agricultural laborers.

It was the demand for better working conditions for these laborers that brought political changes to St. Vincent and the Grenadines. Throughout the nineteenth and much of the twentieth century, the government of St. Vincent and the Grenadines was controlled by the islands' elite white minority. In the 1930s George McIntosh organized the Workingmen's Association, the first organization to push for both better working conditions and increased political power for the island's working-class black majority. Similar organizations soon followed, and in the face of these increasingly vocal demands, the first elections that allowed universal adult suffrage were held in 1952.

Ebenezer Joshua was one of the labor leaders elected to the legislature that year, and he became the founder of the People's Political Party (PPP), St. Vincent and the Grenadines' first political party. When ministerial government was established in 1957, Joshua became the country's first chief minister and remained in control of the government until 1967. In 1969, under new chief minister James Mitchell, St. Vincent and the Grenadines was granted associated statehood, bringing it even more internal autonomy. But the largest political change

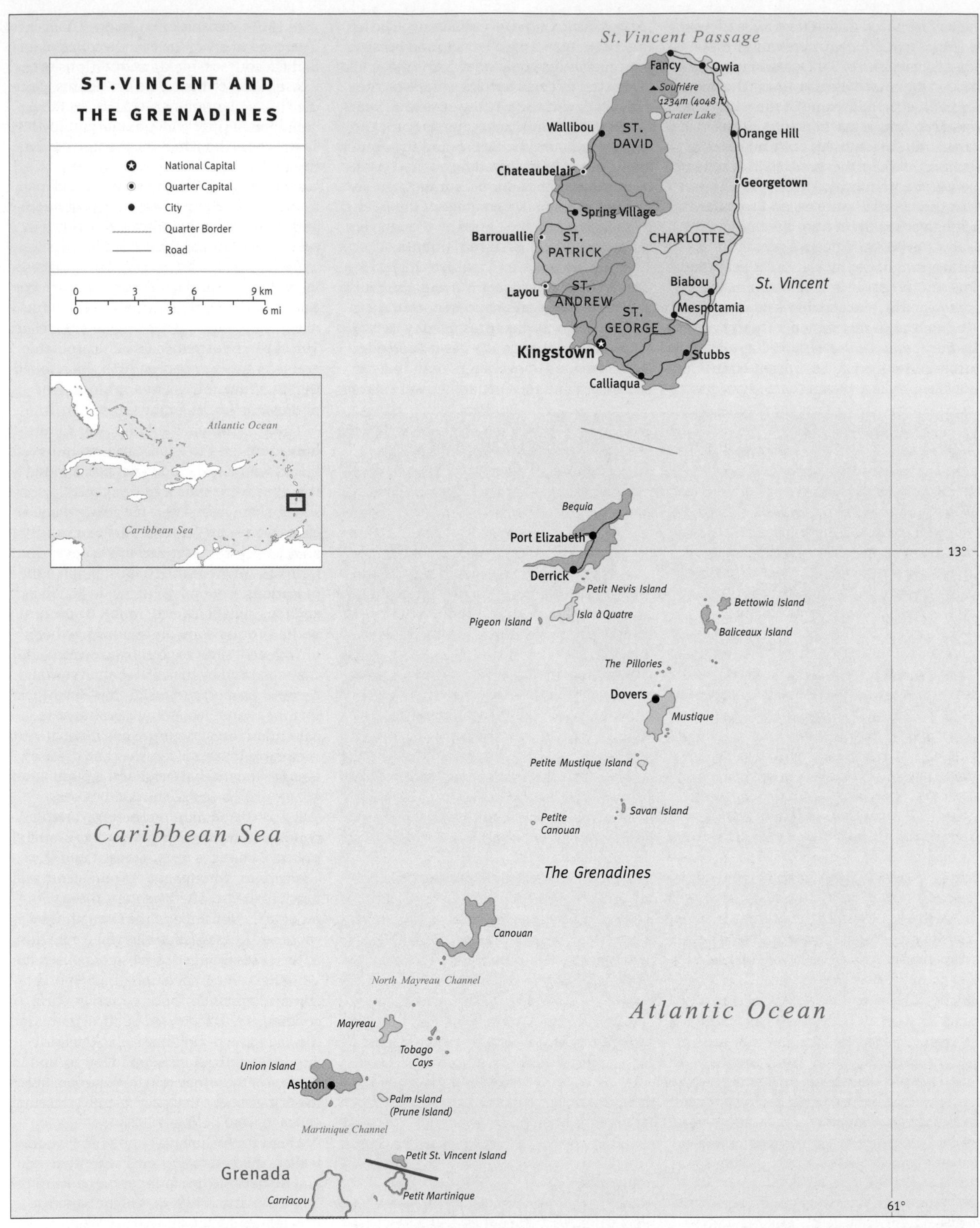

came when St. Vincent and the Grenadines achieved independence on October 27, 1979, becoming an independent state within the British Commonwealth.

Aside from a brief 1980 uprising in which student leaders from Union Island tried to secede from the rest of the state, St. Vincent and the Grenadines has enjoyed political stability. "Son" Mitchell, the prime minister since 1984, followed his father James Mitchell into politics. The 1980 uprising called attention to the fact that residents of the Grenadines often felt unfairly treated by St. Vincent, which accounts for 90 percent of the country's land and population, and there have been attempts to address these inequities. In recent years tourism has become an important source of revenue for the country, and St. Vincent and the Grenadines is often regarded as a playground for the rich and famous.

But for most of the population, the standard of living remains tied to the unpredictable agricultural industry, and, as a result, unemployment in the 1990s was as high as 40 percent. The country is often considered the second poorest in the Caribbean, after HAITI. In recent years Prime Minister Mitchell has supported discussions about the possibility of unifying St. Vincent and the Grenadines with St. Lucia, Grenada, and DOMINICA into a single state. This would undoubtedly alleviate the economic pressures on any single member of that group, but it remains unclear whether this state will ever become a reality. In the meantime new industries are needed to allow the residents of St. Vincent and the Grenadines more economic stability and prosperity in the new century.

Lisa Clayton Robinson

SEE ALSO
Maroonage in the Americas.

Latin America and the Caribbean

Suárez y Romero, Anselmo

(b. April 20, 1818, HAVANA, CUBA; d. January 7, 1878, Havana, CUBA), novelist, university professor, and journalist. Suárez y Romero was an important member of a literary coterie that gathered at the home of Domingo del Monte (1804-1853), a white Creole intellectual and patron to the principal antislavery writers of the period.

Although Anselmo Suárez y Romero was born into the ruling plantation class – his father, José Ildefonso Suárez, was the legal adviser to the despotic Capt. Gen. Miguel Tacón, the Spanish Crown's principal administrator in Cuba – his life was marked by periods of economic impoverishment. Suárez y Romero's father died in SPAIN in 1843, leaving the family in economic ruin. In 1842 Suárez y Romero began a sporadic career in teaching as a substitute for a friend, José Zacarías González del Valle. The writer received a law degree in 1866, but he never practiced as an attorney.

Suárez y Romero is recognized today primarily in connection with two events: (1) the copying and correction between 1835 and 1839 of the slave and poet JUAN FRANCISCO MANZANO's *Autobiografía de un esclavo* (Autobiography of a Slave, only published in Spanish a century later in 1937); and (2) the 1839 writing of one of the earliest antislavery novels, *Francisco* (published in New York in 1880). The latter was, in fact, commissioned by Domingo del Monte as part of a portfolio of writings about slavery for the Irish abolitionist Richard Robert Madden. Madden, who translated Manzano's autobiography into English in 1840, was eager to collect texts that highlighted the abuses of slavery. Del Monte, in order to heighten the sense of what was peculiarly Cuban in the text, added the subtitle *El ingenio, o las delicias del campo* (The Sugar Mill, or the Delights of the Countryside). The book describes the tragic love between two slaves, Francisco and Dorotea, which ends with the suicide of the latter. Although the novel has been criticized for presenting a highly sentimental and idealized portrait of Afro-Cubans (*see* SERGIO GIRAL), its value in registering the tensions of the time is beyond question.

Edward Mullen

SEE ALSO
Slavery in Latin America and the Caribbean; Creoles; New York, New York.

Africa

Sudan,

a country in northeastern Africa; with a coastline along the Red Sea, Sudan borders ERITREA, ETHIOPIA, KENYA, UGANDA, the DEMOCRATIC REPUBLIC OF THE CONGO, the CENTRAL AFRICAN REPUBLIC, CHAD, LIBYA, and EGYPT.

Covering a territory of close to a million square miles, the Republic of the Sudan is the largest nation in Africa. Stretching from the Nubian and Libyan deserts along the Egyptian border to the rain forests of the Nile-Congo divide, Sudan is a bridge between the Arabic-speaking peoples of northern Africa and the peoples of sub-Saharan Africa. The NILE RIVER flows the length of the country, providing a common focus for the diverse peoples of Sudan. Its waters have transformed a narrow stretch of desert along the banks of the lower Nile into a fertile valley capable of supporting large urban centers.

With the exception of a narrow strip of arable land along the Nile, the area north of Khartoum is desert, sparsely populated by nomadic Arab or Nubian communities. Cultivation is possible only with the aid of irrigation. At Wadi Halfa, a riverine community along the Egyptian border, rainfall averages less than 7 cm (3 in) per year. As one moves southward rainfall increases. The southern quarter of the country is well watered, averaging 90 cm (35 in) per annum at Malakal and more than 127 cm (50 in) along the Congo border. With the exception of the western portion, southern Sudan has been isolated from the north by a variety of natural obstacles. A 800-km (500-mi) stretch of floating masses of vegetation, known as the Sudd (Arabic for "barrier"), clogged the White Nile and its tributaries over an area of roughly 100,000 sq km (40,000 sq mi), thereby preventing all significant water transportation until the 1840s.

EARLY HISTORY

Archaeological evidence indicates that people have inhabited the area known today as Sudan for at least 30,000 years. By about 3000 B.C.E. the descendants of these early hunter-gatherers had domesticated animals and begun to practice agriculture.

The inhabitants of the region known as NUBIA, located along the Nile in the northern part of present-day Sudan, had extensive contact with Egypt just to the north and the more agrarian cultures to the south and west (*see* ANCIENT AFRICAN CIVILIZATIONS). Early Egyptian chronicles report numerous military expeditions up the Nile and periodic conquests of Nubia before 2000 B.C.E. During times of peace the Nubians and neighboring pastoral peoples, such as the Blemmyes (BEJA) of the Red Sea Hills, traded gold, cattle, ivory, and slaves to Egypt. They also served as intermediaries in the Egyptian trade with PUNT, a kingdom that may have been located in present-day SOMALIA.

By about 2000 B.C.E. a Kushitic culture, drawing on African traditions of the upper Nile and the eastern savannas as well as those of Egypt, became the dominant culture of Nubia. In the sixteenth century B.C.E. Ahmose, an Egyptian pharaoh, conquered Nubia and increased slave-trading activities. Kush regained its independence under the Kingdom of Napata, which in the eighth century B.C.E. conquered and ruled most of Egypt for more than 100 years. By the fourth century B.C.E. Meroe had replaced Napata as the capital of the Kushitic kingdom, while Napata remained a religious center. Kush successfully resisted conquest by Egypt, but its power gradually declined. By the fourth century C.E., when the Ethiopian kingdom of AKSUM invaded the area, it is unclear if the Kushitic state based at Meroe still existed.

Beginning in the sixth century missionaries from Egypt converted the ruling classes of the small Nubian states to Coptic Christianity, which gradually spread to the rest of the population. Christianity apparently spread as far as the present-day region of DARFUR to the southwest. Two kingdoms, Makuria and Alwa, emerged as the most powerful states in Nubia. Twelve years after the Arab conquest of Egypt in 639, Arab armies tried unsuccessfully to conquer Nubia. Instead, Egypt and Makuria signed a treaty pledging to respect each other's political and cultural integrity. The king of Makuria agreed to permit the construction of a mosque at his capital, Dunqulah, to return runaway slaves who entered his territory, and to pay an annual tribute of 360 slaves to the governor of Aswan in Egypt. Outside the terms of the treaty, Makuria received goods that often exceeded the strictly commercial value of the exported slaves. The treaty governed Egyptian-Nubian relations for almost 600 years.

In subsequent years Egyptian Arabs, seeking greater freedom and opportunity, settled in Nubia. Arab men married into matrilineal families of the Nubians and the Beja and attained powerful positions in Nubian society. While they received Nubian inheritances from their mothers, they bestowed their inheritances patrilineally, thus bringing these newly acquired properties and titles under Arab control. Arab settlers also brought Islam to Nubia, where it gradually spread. In time an Arabized Nubian society emerged as the dominant cultural form in the region. Beginning in the thirteenth cen-

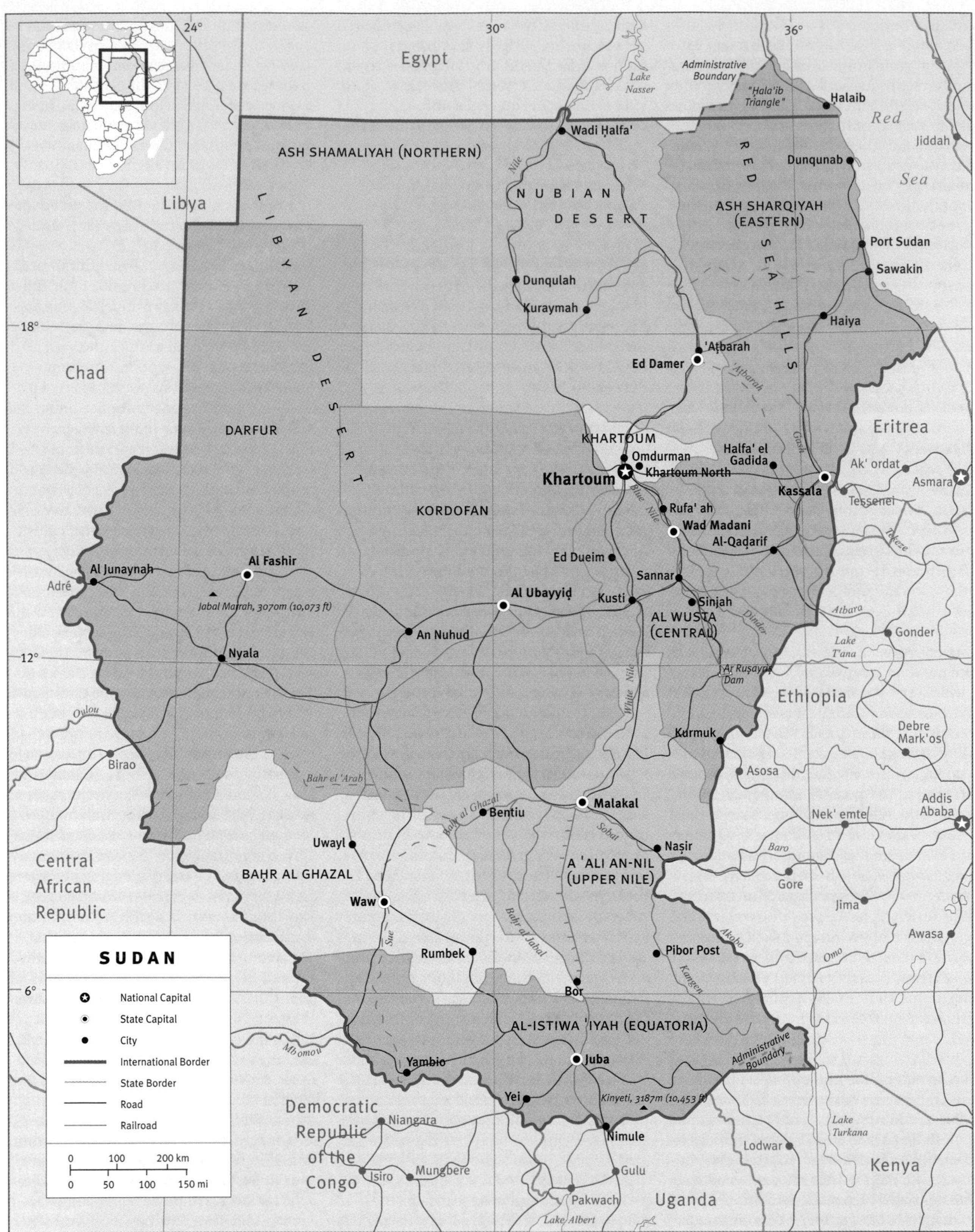

tury the Mamluk state in Egypt carried out a series of devastating military campaigns that weakened the Christian kingdom of Makuria. By the fifteenth century Makuria could no longer resist conquest by a powerful confederacy of Arab nomads allied with Egypt. By the end of the fifteenth century Alwa, the last Christian kingdom of Nubia, had fallen to the Arab confederacy.

An Era of Muslim Hegemony

While the Egyptian Mamluk state occupied Nubia, Amara Dunqas founded the Funj Kingdom in the area just to the south, the Gezira, between the White and Blue Niles, where he ruled from 1504 until 1534. Dunqas converted to Islam during his reign and promoted Islam throughout present-day central Sudan. At its peak in the seventeenth century the Funj Kingdom, with its capital at Sennar, incorporated most of Nubia and extended to the Ethiopian border in the southeast and the semi-arid steppes of Kordofan in the west. The Funj Kingdom's control of important trade routes from West Africa and Ethiopia to Egypt assured it prosperity into the eighteenth century. By the seventeenth century an independent Islamic sultanate, Darfur, was able to exert control over trade routes to Kanem-Bornu, thereby becoming the major state in the western portion of present-day Sudan.

In the early nineteenth century two Turkish-Egyptian armies, sent by Muhammad Ali, moved to conquer the Funj Kingdom and Darfur. Muhammad Ali valued the area because of its high potential for slave raiding and saw little risk in attacking either kingdom. As Muhammad Ali wrote to his son-in-law, commander of one of the armies: "You are aware that the end of all our efforts and this expense is to procure Negroes." Many of these captives were conscripted into a modernized, standing Egyptian army. The technological superiority of the Turkish-Egyptian forces, called the Turkiyya in Sudan, allowed the small army to conquer the Nile valley without major difficulties. During the 1820s the Turkiyya established a colonial administration in northern and central Sudan and encouraged the production of cotton and indigo for market. Northern Sudanese increasingly raided southern Sudan for slaves.

However, the Sudd, the vast swamp to the south of the Shilluk Kingdom, hindered northerners from asserting control over the peoples of the far south, such as the DINKA. Moreover, the Shilluk army was able to repel external threats. In 1831 the Shilluk Kingdom defeated a Turkiyya slaving expedition of more than 2000 troops. The transhumant Dinka retreated into the swamps, where their greater mobility protected them from northern slave raiders. Thus the main supply of ivory and slaves came from the present-day Bahr al Ghazal province to the west, which was subject to raids by the BAGGARA and FUR peoples of the Darfur region. In the south in the eighteenth century, the AZANDE and the Dinka slowly expanded their control over neighboring peoples. The expansion of the Azande and Dinka propelled a NUER expansion into areas surrounding the Sudd and an Anuak expansion into the foothills of the Ethiopian escarpment.

Meanwhile, the Turkiyya aimed to extend its control south of the Sudd. In 1841 a Turkiyya-sponsored expedition found a river channel through the Sudd to the present-day Equatoria province. Once a route to the upper Nile was opened, the Turkiyya government promoted the ivory, gold, and slave trades. Northern Sudanese came to control the slave trade by organizing private armies of up to 2500 men, supported by as many as 500 porters. Some slave traders became virtual rulers of vast tracts of southern Sudan. In exchange for exclusive territorial concessions, traders paid substantial sums to the Turkiyya treasury. The most powerful of these slave traders was al-Zubayr Rahman, who exported approximately 1800 slaves a year in the 1850s and 1860s. The infamous slave trader and empire builder RABIH started his career as an aide to al-Zubayr Rahman.

While the slave trade and interethnic warfare had existed before the opening of the river route to southern Sudan, the level of violence escalated in the last half of the nineteenth century. What had previously been intermittent warfare and raiding became nearly constant, with heavy casualties and widespread seizures of slaves. Preferring a subservient position in a traditional antagonist's community to slavery in a raider's army or a foreign land, many of the smaller ethnic groups of southern Sudan sought refuge among the Dinka or Azande.

Although the Turkiyya administration in Egypt signed various agreements with European powers abolishing the slave trade, it made little effort to enforce them. After issuing several edicts outlawing the slave trade, in 1872 Khedive Ismail appointed Zubayr governor of the Bahr al Ghazal, an area where Zubayr had recently dominated the slave trade. In the late 1870s the khedive appointed an Englishman, Gen. Charles Gordon, as governor of Equatoria. Gordon banished Zubayr and attempted to eliminate the slave trade. His abolitionist campaign, however, disrupted the Sudanese economy and alienated traders and northern Sudanese alike.

Northern Sudanese discontent with the Turkiyya administration had other causes besides the suppression of the slave trade. The lavishness of the Egyptian court, its neglect of Islamic obligations, government corruption, and heavy taxation all contributed to the growing discontent. In 1879 the British deposed Khedive Ismail and replaced him with a puppet ruler, Muhammad Tawfiq. Armed resistance to this new government erupted in Egypt and Sudan. In 1881 a man named Muhammad Ahmad announced that he was the Mahdi, "the guided one," who had been sent by Allah to cleanse the Islamic community of corruption and to establish a truly Islamic state. From his base in the Kordofan region he called for a *jihad* (holy war) against the Turkiyya, which had surrendered to a foe of Islam, the British. The initial followers of the Mahdi were Baggara pastoralists, but he quickly expanded his support among ascetic religious communities, traders who resented government interference, and nomadic Arabs. By 1885 his followers had defeated the Turkiyya and established a Muslim state controlling most of present-day Sudan (*see* MAHDIST STATE). However, the Mahdi died shortly thereafter, and his successors failed to eliminate the corruption that had plagued the Turkiyya administration.

THE ANGLO-EGYPTIAN CONDOMINIUM

Determined to prevent French expansion into the Nile valley, the British organized an Anglo-Egyptian force that reoccupied Sudan and overthrew the Mahdist state in 1898. In 1899 the British and Egyptian governments signed what became known as the Condominium Agreement, which provided for joint rule over Sudan. While the agreement dictated joint and equal rule by the two partners, during the early stages of Condominium rule Egypt was a virtual British protectorate and could not act autonomously. The Condominium government sought to appease Muslims and discourage the nationalistic Islam of the Mahdists by confining Christian missionaries to southern Sudan, where there were few Muslims. The Condominium government did establish secular schools in the north, however, primarily in order to train indigenous Sudanese civil servants.

In southern Sudan the British reopened the Nile channel and began to consolidate their control of the region. Freed from all but sporadic interference during the Mahdist era, southerners sought to retain their independence from the British. The British faced armed resistance from the Azande, Nuer, and Dinka. The Nuer and Dinka, led by prophets claiming direct revelation from powerful spirits of the sky, resisted British rule into the 1930s. Hoping to create a Christian and "civilized" region in the south, the Condominium decided to separate the two regions of Sudan. The 1906 Closed Districts Ordinance and subsequent legislation required northern Sudanese and non-Sudanese to have visas in order to enter southern Sudan. Expatriates replaced northern administrators, and the British introduced indirect rule, in which "traditional" rulers, appointed by British provincial governors for their loyalty, exercised local government. Among the Nuer and Dinka, who lacked a tradition of community rulers, the government arbitrarily endowed members of the priestly class with civil powers, including the power to adjudicate minor offenses and to impose punishments. The government left the educational development of the south to Christian missionaries. It specifically prohibited instruction in Arabic and encouraged the use of English.

During the first half of the twentieth century the Condominium developed the economy and infrastructure of Sudan, including a railroad connecting most northern Sudanese cities. The Condominium absorbed many former slaves into its military and police forces. Their children were some of the first students at the new government schools and eventually found their way into the civil service. In 1925 workers completed the Sennar Dam, which provided the essential water for the Gezira Scheme, a vast cotton-farming project that began a year later. The Gezira Scheme involved an unusual partnership among the Condominium government, the private Sudan Plantations Syndicate, and tenant farmers who actually grew the cotton. Profits were divided among the three parties.

Other agricultural schemes in Kassala and Gash also centered on cotton. Apart from a limited trade in ivory and tropical foodstuffs, southern Sudan saw little economic development under the Condominium. The Great Depression of the 1930s, however, devastated Sudan's economy and revealed the dangers of overreliance on a single cash crop.

Meanwhile, anticolonial organizations began to emerge in Sudan. In 1921 Ali Abd al-Latif, a Dinka Muslim, founded the Sudanese United Tribes Society. Drawing on support in both regions of Sudan, he demanded complete independence for Sudan and a federal government that would provide autonomy for the various Sudanese peoples. His arrest generated a wave of nationalist sentiment, not only in Sudan but in Egypt as well. In 1938 alumni of Sudan's Gordon College established the Graduates General Congress. Under Ismail al-Azhari's leadership in the 1940s, the congress broadened its membership and demanded the right to self-determination through a representative legislature as well as the abolition of the Closed Districts Ordinance, which separated the northern and southern parts of the country. In 1944 two political parties organized to contest the first elections to the Advisory Council for northern Sudan. The Shaqqa party, led by Azhari, advocated independence with close ties to Egypt, while the Umma party favored complete independence.

During the 1940s administrators of southern Sudan debated whether to integrate the region into a unified Sudan, join it to a possible East African federation, or allow it to progress toward independence on its own. However, British East African states showed little interest in integrating their poorer neighbor into a federation. An independent south would lack an economic base, a transportation and communications infrastructure, and a basis for regional unity. Integration with the north seemed to be the only viable alternative, yet considerable expenditures would be required to raise the south's education, its infrastructure, and its political institutions to levels comparable to the north's. In order to accomplish this, the government implemented the Zande Scheme in 1948 to encourage cotton and other cash crops in southern Sudan, increase government expenditures for schools, and reintegrate the two halves of the country.

In 1949 Sudanese, Egyptian, and British representatives drafted a new constitution providing limited self-rule for an integrated Sudan. Southern Sudanese preferred to postpone unification with the north until, through economic and educational development, they could enter into an equal partnership; however, the new constitution took effect in a unified Sudan in 1950. Sudanization of the civil service replaced British expatriates with northern Sudanese; southerners occupied less than 1 percent of administrative posts. In 1955 southern politicians called for a new constitutional assembly to consider a federal system for Sudan.However, this request was ignored. In 1956 a unitary Sudan became a sovereign nation.

Independent Sudan

As Sudanese independence approached, rumors began to circulate that the new government was going to disarm the Equatoria Corps, the southern regiments in the Sudanese army. Rather than leave the south defenseless, the Equatoria Corps refused orders to leave for the capital at Khartoum. Southerners looted northern Sudanese shops and killed many northerners. The Sudanese government responded with a reign of terror, including mass arrests and summary executions. Thousands of refugees fled to the bush or to neighboring countries. Remnants of the Equatoria Corps continued a guerrilla war.

A Dinka boy stands in front of a wall painted with pictures of the civil war that displaced him from his home in southern Sudan. *CORBIS/Adrian Arbib*

Ismail al-Azhari was the first prime minister of an independent Sudan. In the 1956 elections, however, the Umma Party and the Peoples Democratic Party, which opposed formal ties with Egypt, defeated Azhari's pro-Egyptian Union Party. When the new Southern Bloc began to forge an alliance with northern groups like the Beja and ethnic minorities in Kordofan and Darfur in support of a federal structure, the military decided to seize power. It dissolved the legislature and banned all political parties. In the south the military regime encouraged the spread of Islam and the Arabic language and suppressed all forms of resistance. Southern exile organizations estimate that the military government arrested 5000 political prisoners in the south. Several hundred thousand refugees fled to neighboring countries.

In 1963 southern Sudanese refugees formed the nonviolent Sudan African National Union (SANU) to advocate an independent Southern Sudan. They charged the government of Sudan with genocide and petitioned the United Nations to intervene. Sudan's military government rejected offers by the ORGANIZATION OF AFRICAN UNITY (OAU) to mediate the dispute. During the same period remnants of the Equatoria Corps and other military groups formed a coalition called Anya-Nya (meaning, literally, "snake poison") in Dinka to fight for independence.

Northerners also lost patience with the conflict in the south and the continued ban on political activity throughout the country. In 1964 student riots and labor strikes in the Khartoum area toppled the military regime. Sir al-Khatim al-Khalifa, the new prime minister, granted a general amnesty and assured all Sudanese of the right to free political expression and freedom of religion. He held a conference on the future of the south at Khartoum and included representatives from the OAU as outside observers. Opposing the government of Khalifa, conference-appointed mediators called for a federal system of government, with strong regional governments.

Despite rising tensions, Khalifa held parliamentary elections. The elections brought to office a new prime minister, Muhammad Ahmad Mahjub, who promptly rejected the mediators' recommendations. Mahjub opted for a military solution. In 1965 Sudanese soldiers targeted southern leaders for execution and killed many other southerners. Refugees fled the cities and Anya-Nya regained a central role in southern resistance. In 1967 Anya-Nya proclaimed the independence of the Southern Sudan and set up a shadow government. Warfare intensified and the Sudanese economy collapsed.

Once again the government's inability to resolve problems in the south provoked a military coup. In 1969 Col. Gaafar Muhammad al-Nimeiri and a group of junior officers overthrew the government of Prime Minister Mahjub, and in 1971 Nimeiri assumed the presidency. The Nimeiri government nationalized foreign businesses and private banks and implemented land reform in the north. Nimeiri invited southern leaders to the conference table and declared his acceptance of cultural pluralism in Sudan. He blamed the civil war on the legacy of British colonialism and stressed that neocolonialism, which was "oppressing and exploiting the African and Arab peoples," was the common enemy of both north and south. He appointed a minister for southern affairs and supported a general amnesty for all civil war activity. Despite his offer, the civil war continued.

In 1972, however, negotiations between the Sudan government and the Anya-Nya resulted in a cease-fire and peace agreement. A southern regional government assumed full control of economic development and the preservation of public order. A governor, appointed by the president, held executive power within the south. Arabic remained the official language of Sudan, but the government permitted the use of English and southern Sudanese languages. An amnesty protected participants in the civil war. The accords also provided for the reabsorption of refugees and the integration of Anya-Nya soldiers into the military.

However, Islamic groups and the urban poor opposed Nimeiri's regime. A coup attempt by Islamic groups associated with Sadiq al-Mahdi led Nimeiri to forge an alliance with the Muslim Brotherhood. In 1983, attempting to accommodate Muslim opposition, Nimeiri imposed *Shari'a* (Islamic law) in Sudan. This provoked widespread opposition in the

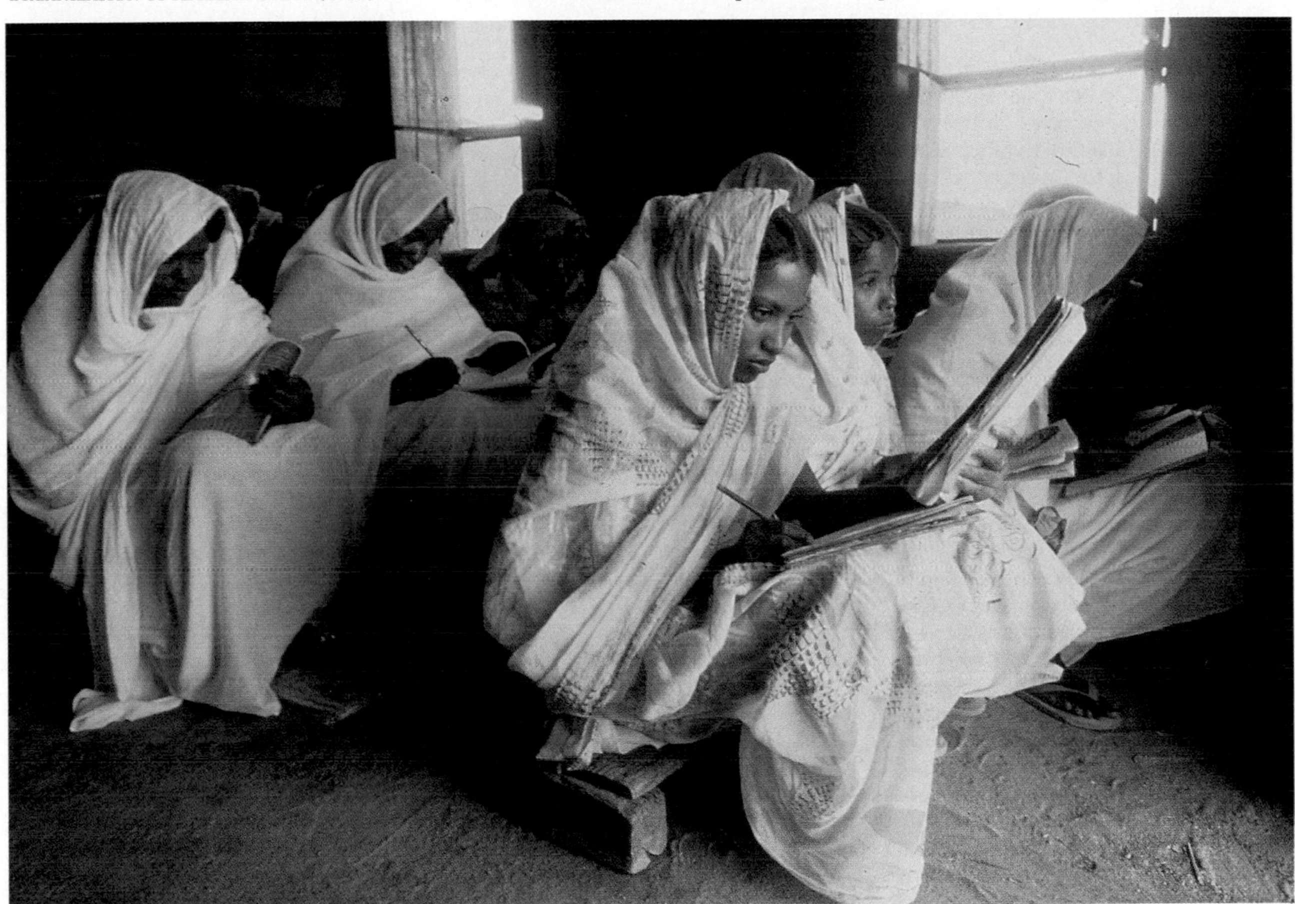

Muslim girls attend school in Sudan, where 34.6 percent of the females, as opposed to 57.7 percent of the males, are literate. *Mike Yamashita*

RIGHT: A nomad leads his camel to a watering hole in Darfur, Sudan. *CORBIS/Liba Taylor*
BELOW RIGHT: A Dinka woman pounds millet with a wooden pole in southern Sudan, which has been devastated by civil war and famine since the 1960s. *CORBIS/Adrian Arbib*

south, where there were few Muslims. The government decided to divide the three southern provinces and to transfer former Anya-Nya soldiers to the north. Southern troops mutinied in 1983, and southern politicians created the Sudan People's Liberation Movement, led by Col. John Garang de Mabior. The civil war resumed. Meanwhile, Nimeiri's accommodation failed to appease Islamic groups. In 1985 military officers supported by the National Islamic Front overthrew the Nimeiri government and established an Islamic state under the leadership of Nimeiri's former chief of staff, Gen. 'Abd ar-Rahman Siwar ad-Dahab.

Elections in 1986 brought Nimeiri's longtime foe, Sadiq al-Mahdi, to office, but he was unable to gain effective control of the government. In 1989 the Revolutionary Command Council for National Salvation (RCCNS), led by Lieut. Gen. Umar Hasan Ahmad al-Bashir, overthrew Mahdi. The RCCNS followed the agenda of the National Islamic Front and sought the arrest of its opponents.The RCCNS escalated the military conflict in the south and established an Islamic police force in the north. The imposition of Islamic law, support for Iraq in the Persian Gulf War, and accusations that the Bashir regime supported terrorism meant increased isolation for Sudan.

The intensification of the civil war and the loss of investments and international credits from the imposition of economic sanctions crippled the Sudanese economy. A drought-related famine from 1984 to 1986 and a war-related famine from 1988 to 1992 cost several million lives, mostly in the south, and devastated the national economy. As warfare escalated, it became increasingly difficult to grow food or to transport famine relief. Observers charged that the Sudanese government and the Sudan People's Liberation Army were impeding food shipments for short-term political gains. The politicization of famine relief left thousands of southern Sudanese dead of hunger and disease, while refugees poured into neighboring countries and to the secure areas of northern Sudan.

Colonel Garang expanded the nature of the conflict by seeking the support of northern ethnic minorities for a genuine federal system. By 1997 the forces of Garang were able to threaten the major cities of the south. In 1998, despite growing dissatisfaction with the government's failure to resolve the southern crisis or to reverse the decline of the economy, Bashir scheduled parliamentary elections. Most opposition leaders were excluded from participation, leading many Sudanese to question the elections' legitimacy.

Robert Baum

See Also
Christianity, African: An Overview; Colonial Rule; Gold Trade; Ivory Trade; Khartoum, Sudan; Egypt, Ancient Kingdom of; Kush, Early Kingdom of; Nationalism in Africa; Pastoralism; Nimeiri, Gaafar Muhammad al-; Christianity: Missionaries in Africa; Trans-Saharan and Red Sea Slave Trade.

Africa

Sudan (Ready Reference)

Official Name: The Republic of the Sudan
Former Name: Anglo-Egyptian Sudan
Area: 2,505,813 sq km (about 967,495 sq mi)
Location: North Africa, on the Red Sea, bordered by Ethiopia, Kenya, Uganda, Democratic Republic of the Congo, Central African Republic, Chad, Libya, and Egypt
Capital: Khartoum (population 473,597 [1983 estimate])
Other Major Cities: Omdurman, Khartoum North, and Port Sudan (data on population unavailable)
Population: 33,550,552 (1998 estimate)
Population Density: 8 persons per sq km (about 21 persons per sq mi)
Population Below Age 15: 45 percent (male 7,769,266; female 7,499,510 [1998 estimate])
Population Growth Rate: 2.73 percent (1998 estimate)
Total Fertility Rate: 5.68 children born per woman (1998 estimate)
Life Expectancy at Birth: Total population: 55.97 years (male 55 years; female 56.98 years [1998 estimate])
Infant Mortality: 72.64 deaths per 1000 live births (1998 estimate)
Literacy Rate (age 15 and over who can read and write): Total population: 46.1 percent (male 57.7 percent; female 34.6 percent [1995 estimate])
Education: Some 2.3 million elementary school students in the early 1990s, and about 696,000 students in secondary schools. Some 3600 students attended vocational and teacher-training institutions, and more than 60,000 attended institutions of higher education, including the University of Khartoum, Omdurman Islamic University, the University of Juba, and the College of Fine and Applied Art.
Languages: Arabic is the official language. English is widely spoken, and African languages, used mainly in the south, include Nubian, Ta Bedawie, numerous dialects of Nilotic, Nilo-Hamitic, and Sudanic languages, and English.
Ethnic Groups: 39 percent of the Sudanese population is Arab, inhabiting the north of the country. Also in the north are the Beja, Jamala, and Nubian peoples. The Azande, Dinka, Nuer, and Shilluk inhabit the south.
Religions: The majority (70 percent) of Sudan's citizens are Sunni Muslim; indigenous beliefs account for about 20 percent of the population, and 5 percent of the Sudanese are Christian.
Climate: Arid desert in north, tropical in south. In the desert temperatures vary from 4.4° C (about 40° F) in the winter to 43.3° C (about 110° F) in the summer. Around Khartoum the average annual temperature is about 26.7° C (80° F); and annual rainfall, most of which occurs between mid-June and September, is about 254 mm (10 in). In southern Sudan the average annual temperature is about 29.4° C (85° F), and annual rainfall is more than 1015 mm (40 in).
Land, Plants, and Animals: The northern third of Sudan is desert; central Sudan is characterized by steppes and low mountains; and the south has vast swamps and rain forests. Numerous species of acacia tree can be found along the Nile valley in the north, and central Sudan has forests that include hashab, talh, heglig, and acacia. Ebony, silag, and baobab trees are common in the Blue Nile valley, and ebony and mahogany trees grow in the White Nile basin. Other species of indigenous vegetation include cotton, papyrus, castor-oil plants, and rubber plants. Animal life includes elephants, crocodiles, hippopotamuses, giraffes, leopards, lions, monkeys, tropical birds, and snakes.
Natural Resources: Petroleum, iron ore, copper, chromium ore, zinc, tungsten, mica, silver, and gold
Currency: The Sudanese pound
Gross Domestic Product (GDP): $26.6 billion (1997 estimate)
GDP per Capita: $875 (1997 estimate)
GDP Real Growth Rate: 5 percent (1997 estimate)
Primary Economic Activities: Agriculture, industry, and services
Primary Crops: Cotton, oilseed, sorghum, millet, wheat, gum arabic, and sheep
Industries: Cotton ginning, textiles, cement, edible oils, sugar, soap distilling, shoes, and petroleum refining
Primary Exports: Cotton, livestock, and gum arabic
Primary Imports: Foodstuffs, petroleum products, manufactured goods, machinery and equipment, medicines, chemicals, and textiles
Primary Trade Partners: European Union, Libya, Egypt, Saudi Arabia, Japan, and United States
Government: The Sudan, previously ruled by a military junta, currently has a transitional government, following presidential and National Assembly elections held in 1996, when Lt. Gen. Umar Hasan Ahmad al-Bashir and his supporters swept presidential and legislative elections, and won a five-year term. Hassan al Turabi was elected president of the National Assembly. The cabinet, consisting of 20 federal ministers, is appointed by the president.

Barbara Worley

See Also
Chimpanzee; Khartoum, Sudan; Nile River.

Africa

Suez Canal, a constructed waterway across the Isthmus of Suez in northeastern Egypt that connects the Mediterranean Sea and the Red Sea.

The Suez Canal is approximately 163 km long (about 101 mi), and approximately 60 m wide (about 200 ft), and permits direct passage from Europe and the Mediterranean Sea to the Indian Ocean instead of the long voyage around the Cape of Good Hope in South Africa. The canal links the Mediterranean Sea at Port Said to the Red Sea at Suez by connecting a series of lakes: Lake Manzilah, Lake Timsah, and the Bitter Lakes. It has no locks, since these lakes lie nearly at sea level. In most places the canal has only one shipping lane although passing lanes exist at several points.

The canal was constructed by the French- and Egyptian-owned Compagnie Universelle du Canal Maritime de Suez (Universal Company of the Suez Ocean Canal), which had obtained a 99-year lease from the Egyptian viceroy, Said Pasha. After the expiration of the lease, control would revert to Egypt. Construction began in 1859, performed mostly by Egyptian workers under poor conditions, and it was completed in 1867. The canal opened to sea traffic on November 17, 1869.

In 1875 the British government bought Egypt's shares in the company. In 1936 Great Britain negotiated an agreement with the Egyptian government that granted Great Britain the right to defend the Suez Canal Zone, including the canal's approaches. The canal became a symbol of Third World emergence from colonialism when Egypt contested British control in the years after World War II. Egyptian nationalism compelled the British in 1955 to agree to withdraw its troops by 1962.

In July 1956, however, after the United States withdrew monetary support for construction of the Aswan High Dam, Egyptian president Gamal Abdel Nasser seized the canal, despite the claims of British and French shareholders. He earmarked its revenues for dam construction costs. Nasser did promise, however, to reimburse shareholders and to keep the canal open to ships from all nations.

The British and French governments, citing the strategic importance of the canal, demanded that Nasser relinquish control. On October 29, 1956, Israeli forces, under an agreement with Great Britain and France, invaded Egypt across the Sinai Peninsula. They took control of most of the peninsula in less than a week, and advanced to within a few miles of the Suez Canal. On October 30 the British and French, with the public intent of maintaining free passage through the canal, issued an ultimatum demanding that both Israeli and Egyptian forces evacuate the canal zone. After Nasser's refusal the following day, combined British and French forces conducted an air strike, which crippled the Egyptian air force before it could leave the ground. In response, Nasser ordered the sinking of 40 vessels, rendering the canal impassable.

The United States, the Union of Soviet Socialist Republics, and the United Nations then intervened, demanding a withdrawal of British, French, and Israeli forces. The withdrawal was completed by the end of 1956. Control of the canal, as well as the Sinai, returned to Egypt, and the canal reopened in March 1957.

Robert Fay

See Also

Nationalism in Africa; Great Britain; France.

Africa

Sufism, a mystical form of Islam that has been found in Africa since the twelfth century C.E.

Derived from the Arabic *suf*, meaning wool, the term "sufi" was originally used to describe a type of ascetic Muslim who wore coarse woolen garb. Unlike Islamic law and theology, which emphasize the severity of God and the strict codes of conduct described in the Koran and Hadiths, Sufism – often referred to as Islamic mysticism – emphasizes the beneficence of God and the spirit of faith and submission. Sufism developed in the seventh century alongside the emergence of formal Islam in the Middle East and spread to Africa in the twelfth century C.E. Beginning in the nineteenth century Sufi orders proliferated in Africa, and in the twentieth century they became a venue for political and economic organization.

Sufis emphasize a personal and direct experience of God, which they believe is possible through disciplined renunciation, humility and love toward God, and a yearning for paradise. Scholars claim that the Koran's call for *ihsan*, or "doing what is beautiful," is ritually translated for Sufis into *dhikr*, honoring God through the methodical repetition of phrases from the Koran and through various ways of saying God's name. Ibn al-Arabi (d. 1240), the great theoretician of Sufism, asserted that the ultimate goal of these rituals is "assuming the character traits of God." By imagining the face of God, a Sufi attempts to "unveil" this image and perceive God's unifying presence in the world and within the self. In this state a Sufi can mediate between the divine and material worlds, allowing Sufi *shaykhs* (masters) to perform magic and miracles.

Sufic knowledge is passed down through masters, and initiation rights promote disciples from one "station" of knowledge to another. Thus the lineage of a Sufi is important and determines the order (in Arabic, *tariqah*, meaning "path" or "way") to which he or she belongs. The Qadiriya and Shadhiliya orders are the two most widespread Sufi lineages in Africa.

The loosely structured Qadiriya order, inspired by the teachings of the Baghdad scholar 'Abd al-Qadir al-Jilani (d. 1166), proved easily adaptable to existing religious beliefs and local authority structures in the Sudan, allowing it to spread quickly to other parts of Africa. The Qadiriya order and its suborders are now present throughout West Africa and the Nile valley.

Like the Qadiriya, the Shadhiliya order is a large and inclusive tradition based on a core devotional literature and organized around one influential master. The Shadhiliya order was established by Abu al-Hasan al-Shadhili (d. 1258) in Egypt and, influenced by the teachings of Abu 'Abdallah Muhammad ibn Sulaiman al-Jazuli (d. 1465?) and other Sufi masters, extended throughout North Africa in the fifteenth century. As frequently happened with Sufi orders, this order branched into suborders, such as the Hamidiya Shadhiliya, founded in 1867 by Salama al-Radi (d. 1939) in Cairo. This order's members celebrated its founder at his shrine every year, a ritual called the *mawlid*. Such Sufi shrines have often become places of pilgrimage.

Like the Hamidiya Shadhiliya, other Sufi orders in the nineteenth century branched into new orders that sought to replace mysticism with a more structured and "pure" form of Sufism. The best-known leader of such a revivalist movement was the Fulani scholar and Qadiriya Usman dan Fodio (1754-1817). Beginning in 1804 he led a *jihad* (holy war) against the emirs of Hausaland, eventually forging the Sokoto Caliphate, the largest state in nineteenth-century West Africa.

Another example of the Sufi mission for a purist Islam was the Tijanya, founded by the North African Ahmad Tijani (d. 1815). Al-Hajj 'Umar (d. 1864) extended this order's influence to the far reaches of West Africa, where he led a holy war against impending French colonization. The Tijanya remained a political force in West Africa well into the twentieth century.

These new Sufi orders often helped African Muslims respond to the tumultuous changes brought by colonialism. While the West African Tijanya resisted European conquest, other orders willingly collaborated with colonial authorities, who in turn appreciated the Sufi leaders' capacity to discipline and recruit labor from among their followers. In colonial Senegal, for example, the French came to depend on the spiritual authority of Amadou Bamba (1850-1927), the founder of the highly popular Mourides (or Muridiyah) order. The Mourides recruited tens of thousands of peasants and young male "apprentices" to clear land and cultivate export crops such as peanuts, providing the colony with valuable revenue.

In North Africa Sufi orders' relations with foreign powers also varied considerably. The order best known for its resistance to colonial rule was the Sanusi, or Sanusiya, founded by Muhammad ibn Ali al-Sanusi (d. 1859) in Libya. This order drew followers from among the Bedouin of the Cyrenaica region of Libya, where lodges provided shelter and meeting places for trans-Saharan trade caravans. Sanusi resistance began when the Italians invaded Cyrenaica in 1911, and continued intermittently for decades. The order was granted considerable autonomy as the colony moved toward independence, and the Sanusi leader, Idris I, eventually became the king of independent Libya.

In Sudan in the 1880s the Sammaniya order, led by Ahmad al-Mahdi, launched the Mahdist revolt against Egyptian rule and helped to oppose British intervention. Another order in Sudan, the Khatmiya, founded upon the teachings of Muhammad 'Uthman al-Mirghani (1793-1853), opposed the Mahdist state, and cooperated with the British in this conflict. Eventually the Khatmiya order became the basis for the nationalist Union Party of the early twentieth century. Sufism was also an important discipline for Hasan al-Banna (d. 1949), who organized the Muslim Brotherhood in Egypt.

Some secular governments claimed that Sufism could not coexist with twentieth-century modernity, rationality, and science. But in fact Sufism has found a place in contemporary Africa, where it serves as a popular alternative to formal Islamic traditions of religious expression as well as a basis for modern political and economic organization.

Leyla Keough

See Also

Mahdist State; Nationalism in Africa; Great Britain; France; Al-Hajj Umar Tal; Cairo, Egypt; Islam and Tradition: An Interpretation.

Cross Cultural

Sugar

Almost a thousand years ago an obscure German monk named Albert of Aachen wrote: "In that place the people sucked little honeyed reeds, found in plenty throughout the plains, which they called 'zucra'; they enjoyed this reed's wholesome sap, and because of its sweetness once they had tasted it they could scarcely get enough of it. This kind of grass is cultivated every year by extremely hard work on the part of the farmers. Then at harvest time the natives crush the ripe crop in little mortars, putting the filtered sap into their utensils until it curdles and hardens with the appearance of snow or white salt. They shave pieces off and it seems to those who taste it sweeter and more wholesome even than a comb of honey. Some say that it is a sort of that honey which Jonathan, son of King Saul, found on the face of the earth and disobediently dared to taste. The people, who were troubled by a dreadful hunger, were greatly refreshed by these little honey-flavored reeds during the sieges of Albara, Ma'arra and Arga."

These words explain how the Crusaders discovered the use of sugar in the Holy Land in the Middle Ages, and indicate the reasons that sugar would later fuel the rise of the TRANSATLANTIC SLAVE TRADE.

Slavery in Europe was over by the year 1000, except for a few areas around the Mediterranean. But slaves were used in sugar production, and as the consumption of sugar spread around the world, so did slavery. Along with precious metals, the sugar-slave trade provided the first enduring economic links between the Old World and the New. The Atlantic trade based on slave-grown sugar was key to the economic development of Europe, North and South America, the Caribbean, and (perversely) Africa.

The Spread of Sugar and Slavery

The Venetian Crusaders introduced sugar to Europe after they found Muslims cultivating it in the Holy Land – Palestine and Syria – in the late Middle Ages, as Albert of Aachen described. The Muslims finally expelled the Europeans from the Holy Land at the end of the thirteenth century. To sustain the lucrative sugar industry, the Venetians transplanted it to islands in the eastern Mediterranean: first Cyprus, then Crete and Sicily. Islamic conquest introduced sugar plantations to SPAIN and PORTUGAL, but soon this production was overshadowed by the output on the islands off Africa's Atlantic coast.

The uninhabited island of Madeira was rediscovered by Portuguese sailors in the service of Prince Henry the Navigator in 1425. To make their new colony profitable, the Portuguese introduced sugar production. By 1500 Madeira was the world's largest sugar producer. The Spanish conquered the Canary Islands, off the coast of Africa, in the middle of the fifteenth century. They easily overcame the islands' inhabitants, the Guanches, and initiated sugar cultivation in parts of the islands where growing conditions were favorable. Eventually the Canaries came to rival Madeira as Europe's primary source of sugar.

From the Canaries sugar production moved down the African coast to the island of São Tomé, colonized by the Portuguese. Sugar production methods were transported from there across the Atlantic to BRAZIL, from Brazil to the Caribbean, and from the Caribbean to the British North American colonies. Modern slavery followed this path.

From the start of the sugar industry, slaves were an essential part of the labor force. As sugar production moved west, slavery became increasingly important. Some scholars believe that slaves were already in use for sugar production in Mesopotamia in the late Sassanid period and in Palestine before the CRUSADES. The Venetians had slave markets on Crete and used slaves there for sugar production. Venetians and Genoese had slave markets on Cyprus, where slaves from Arabia and Syria worked alongside indigenous serfs and immigrants from Palestine. Slaves were apparently not used to produce sugar in Sicily.

The slave labor force for sugar production on Madeira and the Canaries included Berbers, Arabs, Spanish Moors, and Africans, all of whom alongside nonslave labor. After the discovery of São Tomé the Portuguese used Jews kidnapped in Portugal and black slaves from Africa to convert the island into an important exporter of sugar to Europe.

Brazil was not planned as a sugar colony but became one. Portugal sought gold in Brazil, but in the meantime it needed an economic base to pay for the colony and fend off rivals. Among the ten early Portuguese settlements, only those associated with sugar survived. Amerindians provided the first labor force, but as the sugar industry expanded they were supplanted by African slaves.

The first European settlers in the West Indies struggled to survive by growing tobacco, indigo, and cotton, using white indentured labor as well as slaves. They did not succeed. Once sugar was introduced to the West Indies, the small-scale farms were transformed into large sugar plantations, worked by African slaves.

In both Europe and the Americas, besides working on plantations, slaves labored in workshops, as craftsmen, and as servants. But these slave occupations either dwindled away or were overwhelmed by the number of slaves in plantation agriculture.

Why Is Slavery Associated with Sugar?

Why is it that sugar (and to a lesser extent cotton, rice, indigo, and tobacco) used slave labor? Albert of Aachen understood why in the year 1100. Wherever the work was difficult, and free laborers would shrink from performing it unless offered very high wages, slavery was a likely outcome. Slaves would presumably dislike the work as well, and be motivated to do it badly, commit sabotage, or in the extreme case run away. So a crop that required onerous labor – and was thus a likely candidate for slave labor – would have to be produced under conditions conducive to the supervision and control of the labor force. Moreover, the crop would have to be important enough in the world economy to induce European countries to adopt slavery and the legal, social, and political ideas attendant upon it – ideas with which they had had little familiarity for half a millennium.

Albert of Aachen saw in sugar the characteristics that made it a likely candidate for slave labor: (1) the difficulty of growing it and (2) the great demand it was likely to engender. From the time he wrote about sugar until the emancipations of the nineteenth century, sugar and slavery were inextricably bound together. Sugar was grown with slave or coerced labor in North and South America, the Caribbean, Britain's Natal Colony (part of present-day SOUTH AFRICA), Australia (Queensland), and the South Seas (Fiji).

Sugar production indeed requires hard labor. The plantation fields must first be cleared. The next task, also physically demanding, is to plant the sugar by burying sections of old cane in deep holes. As the plants grow, they must be weeded and cultivated. Unwanted shoots must be cut back, and sometimes fertilizer must be applied. When the growing season is over, the cane must be cut – an extremely difficult job in tropical climates. After it is cut, the cane must be rushed to the mill immediately to prevent the sucrose in the cane from turning to starch.

The cane is ground in a mill by three vertical rollers, powered at one time by wind or animals and later by steam. The juice is pressed out and the crushed cane is removed for fuel. Then the juice is transferred to a large copper receptacle, where it is boiled to just the right temperature, a task that requires skill and judgment. The liquid mass is then ladled into a series of copper pans, skimmed of impurities, and finally poured into containers with holes in the bottom. The syrup eventually crystallizes and the molasses drips through.

Consider this production system. First, the onerous fieldwork requires tremendous strength; death rates on sugar plantations exceed those for other crops. Second, harvesting cannot be done gradually; the demand for labor peaks at certain times. Third, there are economies of scale in milling; it costs as much to build a mill for 100 hogsheads of sugar as for 300, so small-scale mills cannot compete. The optimal plantation size in the Caribbean in the eighteenth century was about a hundred acres. This required the labor of a hundred slaves who worked in unison as gangs, holing, planting, cultivating, and cutting cane.

Free labor would avoid this difficult and dangerous work, with its concomitant regimentation and discipline. Workers were reluctant to submit to the rigors of factory work in the early days of the Industrial Revolution; in the sugar-producing colonies, the rigidities of the industrialized world had yet to be introduced into economic life. Using slaves to mobilize for peak labor requirements was much easier than depending on hired free labor.

At the same time the cost of monitoring slave labor was low. One overseer with a whip could control a large gang of field hands, especially for the strenuous but uncomplicated work of sugar production. On a small mixed farm, where the work involved a variety of tasks, each requiring skill and judgment, slaves could easily have expressed their resentment, and it would have been very costly to monitor them; in the extreme case it might have taken one overseer to watch one slave. This is one of the chief reasons that most agriculture is poorly suited to collectivization. The sugar plantation, however, is well suited. It has rightly been called a factory in a field.

Of all agricultural crops sugar offers the greatest cost advantages in the use of slave labor rather than free labor. Gang labor is also economical in the production of cotton, rice, and indigo. Slave labor is not necessarily cheaper than free labor for the production of tobacco and coffee.

No insignificant crop could have justified the reintroduction of slavery. Albert of Aachen thought that sugar was addictive: "because of its sweetness once [people] tasted it they could scarcely get enough of it." Since it was introduced in Europe, sugar has played a major role in international trade. It was England's dominant import from the middle of the eighteenth century until the middle of the nineteenth. The combination of sugar and its complements, tea and coffee, captured a large proportion of international trade before 1850.

The Atlantic System Before Columbus

Just as the methods of sugar production explain why sugar was the vehicle for the rise of modern slavery, so does the organization of the sugar industry as a whole explain why sugar and slavery were so important in the development of the Atlantic world. When most of Europe was slowly emerging from feudalism, the slave-based sugar industry was organized along capitalistic lines. It required large investments, capital and credit markets, imported labor, disciplined production, and a marketing system involving shipping and insurance. It was a long-distance trade, requiring facilities for ships and harbors.

Even before Columbus sailed for America, the slave-based sugar economy was established on the Atlantic islands. Genoa, Germany, and Portugal sent capital to the islands; Africa and the Iberian Peninsula sent labor; England and the Netherlands sent textiles and other supplies; and the sugar was sent to northern Europe to be marketed. The slave-based sugar industry of the Atlantic islands drew together Italy, Germany, Portugal, Spain, the Netherlands, and Africa in an interdependent economic network that could not have emerged without the labor of slaves on sugar plantations.

The New World Before Sugar and Slavery

For two centuries after Columbus discovered America, the economic impact of the New World on the Old was barely felt, aside from Spain's trade in precious metals. Only Brazil, Virginia, and Barbados were built on a firm economic foundation, and further economic growth would require slaves.

All new colonies require an export crop to pay for what they cannot yet produce and to sustain themselves while they build up their societies. The Spanish found nothing to develop in the Caribbean islands. Long before the end of the sixteenth century, the Spanish abandoned the West Indies. The indigenous peoples had been killed off by disease and social dislocation, and the islands themselves, inhabited by a small number of mostly transient Spaniards and some slaves, served as nothing more than a support area for the mining interests of mainland South America. When mining waned, the Spanish Empire fell into a state of decline.

The British and French occupied the islands the Spanish abandoned, but they too were initially unable to build viable economies. The white population of the British West Indies peaked in the 1640s. It consisted of small farmers trying to make a living from tobacco and other crops with the labor of white indentured servants and a few slaves. The early history of the British West Indies is one of corruption, famine, disease, and

TOP: Between 1636 and 1644 Dutch artist Frans Post participated in a scientific/artistic expedition to Brazil and depicted African slaves cultivating sugar cane and processing it in an *engenho* or sugar mill. This nineteenth-century colored lithograph is a copy by Johann Moritz Rugendas after Post. *Oronoz*
ABOVE: Photographed in 1901, this woman was one of the many field hands needed to cultivate sugar cane in Louisiana. *CORBIS*

failure, with the greatest concentration of poverty-stricken free people in any part of Britain's colonial dominions.

The French fared no better. Their earliest colonists also tried tobacco; when it failed to yield the necessary profits, they tried cotton, indigo, and other, lesser crops. Like the early English colonies in the West Indies, the French colonies remained outposts of impoverished farmers. The future greatness of British North America – the United States and Canada – was nowhere apparent in the early colonial period, and Europe's links with the New World were frail and unimportant.

The New World After the Introduction of Sugar and Slavery

Portugal's transfer of the slave-based sugar plantation economy across the Atlantic to Brazil was one of the most momentous events of modern times. It initiated the forced removal of some 11 to 12 million slaves from Africa to the Western Hemisphere, and the inclusion of the Western Hemisphere in the world economy. With an assured labor supply and a dependable staple crop, Europe began to send capital to the New World and organize production there. The introduction of the sugar plantation with slave labor solved the problem of economic development in the colonies, and turned them into valuable assets.

With sugar production 20-fold higher in Brazil than in the Atlantic islands at the close of the seventeenth century, the per capita income of white settlers in Brazil far exceeded the prevailing per capita income in Europe. In the late seventeenth and early eighteenth century the sugar industry spread from Brazil to the British and French islands of the Lesser Antilles: Barbados, St. Kitts and Nevis, Montserrat, Guadeloupe and Martinique. By the middle of the eighteenth century sugar production had reached its peak in Jamaica and Saint-Domingue (now Haiti) in the Greater Antilles, making the latter the most successful colony in the New World. Also, by this time the Atlantic was crisscrossed by ships laden with human and economic cargoes to support the sugar industry: slaves, the products of slave labor, supplies and capital bound for slave colonies, and European goods purchased with the profits of the slave colonies. Not much else of human origin moved in the Atlantic at this time.

In 1650 the British mainland colonies in North America were 97 percent white and the British West Indies were 80 percent white. By 1750 the mainland was 80 percent white and the islands only 16 percent white. Nineteen out of 20 slaves shipped to the mainland colonies were sent below the Mason-Dixon Line to work in crops suited to slave labor.

By the third quarter of the eighteenth century the exports of the Upper and Lower South attributable to slave labor amounted to 50 and 75 percent of their total exports, respectively. Forty-two percent of the exports of the Middle Colonies went to slave colonies, and 78 percent of New England's exports went there. The colonies with the greatest wealth per (white) person were those with the closest links to slavery. The West Indies and the American South were the wealthiest colonies, the Middle States and New England the least wealthy. The transformation of these latter colonies from simple agricultural economies into mercantile societies was due in large measure to trade with the West Indies slave colonies. To a great extent the development of the United States in the colonial era depended on the sugar of the West Indies, and on the slavery there and in the American South.

Europe After the Introduction of Slavery and Sugar

Once the Atlantic system was in place, European trade shifted accordingly. Europe realized great economic benefits by combining European investment, technology, and organizational skills with labor stolen from Africa and land stolen from Amerindians. Saving and investment increased; commercial services – banking, shipping, and insurance – developed; and above all, industrialization accelerated. The most dynamic sectors in Europe at the end of the eighteenth century were exporting simple manufactures and other industrial products to the Americas.

In particular, the notable increase in the growth of the British economy in the last quarter of the eighteenth century was fueled in large part by American demand for goods. Without this demand, ultimately generated by slave production, England would have been less commercial, less industrial, and poorer, and it would have grown more slowly.

Conclusion

The Renaissance marked the start of the modern era. Until then the civilizations of classical Greece and Rome were considered unsurpassed in the Western world. As long as this view persisted, the idea of progress could not take hold. With the Renaissance it became apparent that the ancients had lacked many important inventions. A famous series of prints made at the end of the sixteenth century portrays these discoveries: printing, gunpowder, the mariner's compass, windmills, several others – and sugar.

Barbara Solow

See Also

Berber; São Tomé and Príncipe; Crusades.

North America

Sugarhill Gang, African American musical group whose "Rapper's Delight" was the first rap song to achieve commercial success.

With the phenomenal success of their 1979 single "Rapper's Delight," the Sugarhill Gang became the first rap group to break out of the dance clubs of New York and Los Angeles and achieve international fame. Ironically, the group did not originate in the post-disco DJ scene of other rap innovators, like Afrika Bambaataa and Grandmaster Flash. Instead, the Sugarhill Gang was the creation of Sugar Hill Records, a black-owned label that was the first to bring rap to a commercial audience.

The Sugarhill Gang consisted of three relatively unknown rappers – Big Bank Hank (Henry Jackson), Master Gee (Guy O'Brien), and Wonder Mike (Michael Wright) – whom Sylvia Robinson of Sugar Hill Records approached in early 1979. Backed by a track sampled from the disco group Chic's hit song "Good Times," the group's hit single exemplified the playful, positive, dance-oriented feel of early rap (which later fans have dubbed "old school"). Accused by veteran rappers of appropriating their trademark lyrics, the Sugarhill Gang popularized, rather than created, the sound for which they became famous. Despite the issues surrounding the group's authenticity, their work spawned a host of imitators and brought rap music into the American mainstream.

After the success of "Rapper's Delight," which was the first rap record to break into Top Forty radio play, the group dropped out of the public eye, though they continue to play (with manager Joey Robinson Jr. replacing Master Gee). In 1997 Rhino Records re-released the Sugarhill Gang's first record, now considered a classic of old school rap.

Kate Tuttle

See Also

Grandmaster Flash, Melle Mel, and the Furious Five; Los Angeles, California; New York, New York.

Africa

Sukuma, ethnic group of northwestern Tanzania.

Ancestors of the Sukuma are believed to have first settled near Lake Victoria in the Mwanza region of present-day Tanzania during the period of Bantu expansion. They were long thought to be a subgroup of the Nyamwezi, who speak a similar language and share many customs, and they derive their name, which means "people from the north," from their geographical relation to the larger ethnic group. But although the Sukuma may originally have been a group that broke off from Nyamwezi, they have since developed a distinctive culture based on farming and raising livestock (or pastoralism).

Prior to European colonial rule the Sukuma lived in farming villages scattered throughout the Mwanza region and organized into loosely affiliated chiefdoms. They cultivated crops such as sorghum, millet, and maize and also kept cattle, which continue to be an important symbol of wealth. Unlike the Nyamwezi, who participated actively in the East African ivory and slave trades and thus interacted with coastal Arab/Swahili traders and Europeans, the Sukuma sought to isolate themselves from such influences. They avoided missionaries and other Europeans until the German East African Company took control of the area in 1891. At that time the Germans relocated the Sukuma onto commercial farms, where they were expected to grow export crops such as tea and coffee. At first resentful, the Sukuma later excelled at commercial farming under British colonial rule and grew prosperous from sales of cotton, tobacco, and grain crops such as millet, sorghum, and maize. Today Sukumaland, which covers more than 52,000 sq km (20,077 sq mi), continues to be one of the most important farming areas in Tanzania.

Elizabeth Heath

See Also
Bantu: Dispersion and Settlement; Ivory Trade; Swahili People; Indian Ocean Slave Trade.

North America

Sullivan, Leon Howard

(b. October 16, 1922, Charleston, W.Va.), African American minister; author of the "Sullivan Principles," guidelines for American companies doing business in South Africa.

Raised by his grandmother, who encouraged him to help the disadvantaged, Leon Sullivan pursued this goal by entering the ministry. He was pastor of Philadelphia's Zion Baptist Church from 1950 to 1988. In 1964 he founded the Opportunities Industrialization Centers of America (OIC), which provided educational and vocational training for unskilled African American workers. For this work Sullivan was awarded the National Association for the Advancement of Colored People's prestigious Spingarn Medal in 1971. By 1980 the OIC had grown into a national force and, by 1993, despite funding cuts, the OIC's programs had been instituted in several sub-Saharan African countries.

In 1977 Sullivan enumerated six principles that were guidelines for American corporations doing business in South Africa. Known as the Sullivan Principles, these guidelines were designed to use American corporate power to promote fair treatment for black workers. The principles concerned equal pay, equal working conditions, integration of blacks and whites in work facilities, training programs, supervisory positions for blacks, and improvements in living conditions outside the workplace. Sullivan declared the principles a failure in 1987 because apartheid continued. In 1991 he received two honors for his work with the American and African poor: the Presidential Medal of Freedom in the United States, and the Distinguished Service Award, the highest honor awarded in the Côte d'Ivoire.

Africa

Sumbwa, ethnic group of Tanzania.

The Sumbwa primarily inhabit the region south of Lake Victoria in northwestern Tanzania. They speak a Bantu language and are closely related to the Nyamwezi and Sukuma peoples. Approximately 200,000 people consider themselves Sumbwa.

See Also
Bantu: Dispersion and Settlement.

Africa

Sundi (also known as the Basundi and the Kongo-Sundi), ethnic group of west Central Africa.

The Sundi primarily inhabit Angola, the Republic of the Congo (Congo-Brazzaville), and the Democratic Republic of the Congo (Congo-Kinshasa). They speak a Bantu language and are one of the Kongo peoples. Approximately 200,000 people consider themselves Sundi.

See Also
Bantu: Dispersion and Settlement.

Africa

Sundiata Keita (1210?-1260?), founder and ruler of the Mali Empire in West Africa.

Sundiata was the son of Nare Maghan, the ruler of Kangaba, a small state located on a tributary of the upper Niger River. Sundiata left Kangaba, but the reason is unknown: he may have gone into voluntary exile to avoid a jealous half-brother, or he may have been exiled by Sumanguru Kante, king of the Soso, who killed Sundiata's father and took over his kingdom. Sundiata responded to the requests of his people to return to Kangaba to help them regain independence. He assembled a coalition of Malinké chiefdoms and in 1235 led them to victory in the Battle of Kirina. According to popular tradition, Sundiata triumphed because he was a stronger magician than his opponent. This victory marked the beginning of the Mali Empire.

After defeating the Soso, Sundiata consolidated his authority among the Malinké people and established a strong centralized monarchy. According to Ibn Khaldun, a fourteenth century North African historian, Sundiata ruled Mali for 25 years. He expanded the state by incorporating the Ghana Empire and the West African gold fields. Sundiata built his capital at Niani, which was in his home region. Mali gained economic strength by controlling the region's trade routes and gold fields. Although he was Muslim, Sundiata allowed the people to practice their own religions. When Sundiata died, his son Uli became the *mansa,* or king, of Mali. The Malinké people of West Africa continue to regard Sundiata as a national hero.

See Also
Ghana, Early Kingdom of; Gold Trade; Malinké.

Africa

Sunni Ali (also known as Sunni Ali Ber and Si) (b. ?; d. 1492), founder of the Songhai Empire.

At a time when the collapse of the once powerful Mali Empire left a power vacuum in western and central Sudan, Sunni Ali undertook a series of military campaigns that united the area under a new power, the Songhai Empire. Through military acumen and skillful leadership he amassed an empire that, by the time of his death in 1492, spanned most of present-day Mali and parts of present-day Niger, Nigeria, and Benin. He conquered important trading centers such as Djenné and Tombouctou (Timbuktu). Sunni Ali's empire continued to control the area until the late sixteenth century, when it was destroyed by Moroccan invaders.

A Songhai state had existed since the seventh century, and in 1335 it declared independence from the enfeebled Mali Empire. Its rulers, however, had done little to strengthen and expand the state before Sunni Ali ascended the throne in 1464. He immediately launched a campaign against Tuareg raiders, who had seized the important trading center of Tombouctou and were attacking the valuable trans-Saharan trade caravans that traveled through the area. In 1468 Sunni Ali wrested Tombouctou from the Tuareg. He immediately set out to defeat other neighboring groups, such as the Mossi, Dogon, and Fulbe. These campaigns earned Sunni Ali a reputation as a shrewd military ruler and brilliant strategist. Relying on the strength of his Niger River navy, Sunni Ali was able to push the Mossi and other groups out of the rich river ports. Sunni Ali was also a skilled ruler who established a centralized structure to ensure control over the cities and outlying regions of his empire.

Highly skilled at warfare, Sunni Ali is also reputed to have used sorcery to undermine his enemies and guarantee victory. Legend tells that he not only transformed himself and his horse into a vulture before battle, but also gave his troops amulets that enabled them to become invisible and fly. His failure to renounce sorcery eventually led to conflicts with Islamic leaders and scholars. Although Sunni Ali claimed to be a Muslim, his decision to restrict religious practices in the empire and to continue practicing magic earned him a reputation as a heathen. His status among Muslims declined further after he ordered the massacre of the Tombouctou scribes. Although his motives were political, not religious, many believe that this act united some of his Muslim subjects behind his nephew, Askia Muhammad. According to legend, Askia Muhammad, a devout Muslim, murdered his uncle and seized the throne to avenge the death of the scribes. According to another legend, however, Sunni Ali drowned in a flash flood after a military expedition. Some believe that Sunni Ali's head is buried in Wanzerbe, purportedly the center of Songhai magical power.

Elizabeth Heath

See Also
Fulani; Djenné-Djeno, Mali; Morocco; Tombouctou, Mali.

North America

Sun Ra (b. May 22, 1914, Birmingham, Ala.; d. May 30, 1993, Birmingham, Ala.), African American jazz bandleader, arranger, and pianist, pioneer of collective improvisation and electric instruments who mounted multimedia, futuristic concerts from the 1950s through the early 1990s.

Sun Ra was born Herman "Sonny" Blount and grew up in Birmingham, Alabama, before moving to Chicago, Illinois during his teenage years. He played the piano as a boy, led his own band while in high school, and studied music education at Alabama A&M (now Alabama University). After touring with John "Fess" Whatley's band during the mid-1930s, Blount played piano and arranged songs for Fletcher Henderson in Chicago.

In the late 1940s Blount adopted the name Sun Ra, began calling Saturn his birthplace, and sported the motto "Space is the Place." His characteristic flowing Egyptian clothes reflected his new spiritual outlook. In 1953 Ra formed a musical ensemble called the Arkestra, which fused Afro-Cuban, avant-garde jazz, big-band, and hard bop styles. At the same time Ra founded Saturn Records, which released the Arkestra's albums during the following four decades. In the late 1970s the group moved its base from New York City to Philadelphia. Over the course of the Arkestra's 40 years, they recorded numerous albums, toured the United States, Europe, and Asia, and won international acclaim.

Sun Ra's music is characterized by a cosmic consciousness and outer space overtones. His performances incorporated dance, film, lighting effects, and music and featured many notable soloists, including John Coltrane's mentor, tenor saxophone player John Gilmore. Three documentaries were produced about Sun Ra: *The Cry of Jazz* (1959), *Space is the Place* (1971), and *Sun Ra: A Joyful Noise* (1980).

Aaron Myers

See Also
Coltrane, John William; Henderson, Fletcher Hamilton, Jr.; Philadelphia, Pennsylvania; New York, New York.

North America

Supremes, The, African American female Motown popular music group that achieved commercial success in the 1960s by bringing African American singing style to a national audience.

From their first number one hit, "Where Did Our Love Go?" (1964) to later chart-toppers such as "Reflections" (1968) and "Someday We Will Be Together" (1969), the Supremes stand as the most commercially successful female group in 1960s popular music. They emerged as the top "model" in Berry Gordy Jr.'s "fleet" of acts at the Motown Record Company in Detroit, Michigan. Gordy, who worked briefly at Ford Motor Company, sought to produce and market his artists with an assembly-line technique. He wanted Motown music to appeal to audiences across racial boundaries. The Supremes achieved this goal and transformed American popular music.

The group's original members, Diana Ross, Florence Ballard, and Mary Wilson first began singing together in the late 1950s. They called themselves the Primettes – the sister group to the Primes, who eventually became known as The Temptations. After they won a local talent show the women secured an audition at Motown Records. They signed a contract in January 1961 and changed their name to The Supremes. Their first few records – "I Want A Guy" and "Buttered Popcorn" – were only modest successes and by 1963 the group earned the nickname, the "no-hit" Supremes. In 1964, however, the group's fate changed dramatically when "Where Did Our Love Go?" raced to the top of the charts. "Baby Love" and "Come See About Me" quickly followed and the Supremes were a national sensation.

The Supremes' success exemplified Motown's ability to market African American music to the baby boomer teenagers of the 1960s. The skillful songwriting team of Eddie Holland, Lamont Dozier, and Brian Holland – also known as Holland-Dozier-Holland – was responsible for the group's unique sound. The company's in-house charm school groomed the young women for the public spotlight. They learned choreography, manners, and fashion tips from entertainment veterans. As the group's fame grew, they became regulars on top television shows and toured around the world. For many, the Supremes epitomized elegance and glamour – a refreshingly new public image of black womanhood.

By the late 1960s the Supremes faced several professional and political challenges. In 1967 Cindy Birdsong replaced Florence Ballard, who struggled with the pressures of

The Supremes, *left to right*, Florence Ballard, Diana Ross, and Mary Wilson, were the most commercially successful female group in 1960s pop music. *The Everett Collection*

celebrity life, and Motown changed the group's name to Diana Ross and the Supremes. The group's music began to reflect the social turmoil of the times. Songs including "Love Child" (1968) and "I'm Living in Shame" (1969) spoke of the trials of life in an urban ghetto.

In January 1970 Diana Ross performed her last show as a Supreme at the Frontier Hotel in Las Vegas. She went on to pursue a solo singing and film career and received an Academy Award nomination for her portrayal of BILLIE HOLIDAY in *Lady Sings the Blues* (1972). Jean Terrell replaced Diana Ross and the new Supremes were successful with songs such as "Stoned Love" (1970). The group never regained the popularity it attained throughout the 1960s, however, and disbanded in the late 1970s. In 1981 the musical *Dreamgirls*, which was largely based on the Supremes' story, became a hit on Broadway.

SEE ALSO
Motown.

Latin America and the Caribbean

Suriname, a country located on the northeastern coast of South America; Suriname is bordered on the west by GUYANA, on the east by FRENCH GUIANA, and on the south by BRAZIL.

Suriname is a former Dutch colony located on the northeast corner of South America. Although Dutch is the official language, English, Hindi, Javanese, Sranana and Papiamento (both Creole languages), and numerous Amerindian languages are spoken widely. Suriname's 437,000 inhabitants come from diverse backgrounds, giving the country a unique mix of ethnicities: its population includes people of Javanese, so-called Hindustani (or East Indian), and Chinese origin, in addition to the region's original indigenous inhabitants. But Suriname is perhaps best known for its Creole and maroon (sometimes also called *bosnegers*, or "Bush Negroes" by outsiders) communities. CREOLES are Afro-Surinames, the descendants of former slaves, freed blacks, and people of mixed African and European ancestry. Maroons are descendants of runaway slaves who are now organized into six distinct groups and live in semi-autonomous villages. The maroon population in Suriname was the largest community of escaped slaves in South America, and (with the notable exception of HAITI) long constituted one of the most highly developed and autonomous communities of African descendants in the Americas. Both the maroon and Creole communities retain elements of African culture, including traditional African languages, oral histories, and religious ceremonies. In 1998 Creoles and maroons composed nearly 41 percent of Suriname's total population.

AMERINDIAN PRESENCE

The earliest inhabitants of Suriname were Amerindian migrants from South America and the Caribbean, who arrived in waves beginning in the fifteenth century. They are often referred to as Arawak, Carib, and Warrau, and lived primarily in small subsistence communities. Suriname's indigenous population cultivated crops such as cassava and separated into residential communities often based on linguistic patterns. Those who spoke the Arawakan language tended to reside along the coast, while those who spoke Cariban lived in the area's hilly interior.

EUROPEAN SETTLEMENT

European explorers from England, France, and Holland began investigating the coastline of Suriname in the sixteenth century. Most were looking for gold, but some were following tales of a wealthy indigenous community called El Dorado that was supposedly located in the region's interior. Although El Dorado was never discovered, European explorers established trading posts all along the coastline to provide supplies for European vessels traveling between the Caribbean and South America.

In 1650 England established the first permanent settlement on Suriname – a plantation colony on the Suriname River. However, in 1667 England traded the territory of Suriname to Holland in exchange for the Dutch colony of New Amsterdam (now New York). The Dutch West India Company controlled Suriname until 1794, when it became an official Dutch colony.

SLAVERY

Like Brazil, its South American neighbor to the south, Suriname's colonial economy was driven by slavery. SUGAR, coffee, cotton, and cocoa plantations were supported by more than 325,000 African slaves transported to Suriname between 1667 and 1863, the year that Holland abolished slavery (*see* SLAVERY IN LATIN AMERICA AND THE CARIBBEAN). Scholars believe that by 1800 there were more than 600 plantations in Suriname, operated by Dutch, German, French, and English landowners. Indeed, Suriname was so well known at this period that in the mid-1700s the French philosopher Voltaire cited it in his novel *Candide* as an example of the cruelty of slavery. During the seventeenth and eighteenth centuries almost one-third of these plantation owners were Jews, many of whom had originally fled Europe for Dutch-controlled northeastern Brazil during the Inquisition, and later left Brazil for Suriname. Overall, these plantation owners occupied the highest social strata in colonial Suriname, and reserved many of the most powerful government positions for themselves.

Chattel slavery allowed Suriname's wealthy European elite to earn enormous profits from agricultural plantations throughout the seventeenth, eighteenth, and nineteenth centuries. The African provenance of the slaves who were brought to Suriname is not entirely clear. The areas from which Africans were taken varied over time and according to the arrangements made by the DUTCH WEST INDIA COMPANY, which was responsible for bringing most African slaves to Suriname in the TRANSATLANTIC SLAVE TRADE. Nonetheless, the Dutch planters in Suriname – as with the English, Spanish, and Portuguese elsewhere in the New World – were often highly interested in what they thought were the "national characteristics" of slaves from different ethnic groups, and did compile some records on the origins of slaves (*see* AFRICAN ETHNIC GROUPS IN LATIN AMERICA AND THE CARIBBEAN).

In broad terms, according to statistics compiled by anthropologist Richard Price, from the 1640s to 1725, the majority of slaves were brought from the "Slave Coast" (more or less present-day TOGO and BENIN), with significant numbers also coming from the ANGOLA region in southwestern Africa. In the second and third decades of the eighteenth century slaves were also imported, in equal proportions, from the Gold Coast (the area of present-day GHANA), and the trade shifted. By the late eighteenth century almost half of the slaves sold in Suriname came from the "Windward Coast" (the coastal area of West Africa stretching from present-day GUINEA-BISSAU to CÔTE D'IVOIRE) and the Angola region, and fewer from the "Slave Coast." In Suriname these groups of slaves were called Gangu, Kormantines, and Loangu, respectively, though their precise ethnic origins are unclear. Overall, studies have argued that Bantu-speaking Africans from the Loango-Angola region of southwestern Africa composed perhaps the single largest group of Africans sent to Suriname.

The rapid expansion of slavery, and the high mortality rates, meant that Suriname witnessed the tremendous infusion of Africans, constituting what Richard Price has characterized as an unusually high proportion of slaves born in Africa to slaves born in the New World, and a high ratio of recently arrived slaves to ones who had been in the colonies for longer periods of time. Indeed, according to Price, during the first 100 years of Suriname's colonial history, more than 90 percent of the slave population was African-born, and well into the eighteenth century more than one-third of Suriname's blacks had left Africa within the previous five years. (In comparison, in North America as early as 1680, native-born blacks already outnumbered Africans, who after that time never came to constitute a majority.) The linguistic and cultural ties of these displaced Africans meant that Suriname was deeply marked by African cultures and languages, and also allowed Suriname's slaves to organize numerous acts of resistance, both overt and hidden.

Although violent slave insurrections were a common feature of slave resistance in the Caribbean and South America, the most common form of slave resistance in Suriname was self-emancipation – running away (*see* MAROONAGE IN THE AMERICAS). Beginning in the 1690s, groups of Africans, the descendants of today's maroon communities, began to engage in large-scale flight from the plantations where they were held captive. This did not imply a peaceful situation, though, as deserting slaves often set fire to plantations; by the mid-eighteenth century wars between organized bands of maroons and settlers led one traveler at that time to call Suriname a "theater of perpetual war."

MAROONS

The escape of slaves from plantations plagued Suriname since the early days of slavery. Runaway slaves, or maroons, were a major problem for European slave owners throughout the region. But the intense heat and hilly interior made it much more difficult for slave owners in Suriname to recapture runaways, and after large-scale escapes in the late seventeenth century, major maroon communities were established along the Marowijne and Saramacca rivers. Some of the most famous maroon villages were located along major rivers, such as the Claes and Pedro villages in the area surrounding the Saramacca River. Although legend and the fears of the colonists has inflated the number of maroons, scholars believe that there may have been nearly 1500 runaway slaves living in hidden villages throughout Suriname by the mid-eighteenth century. Most lived autonomously, finding their own food and establishing their own communities.

Stories about their history and origins are treated with great respect by Suriname's maroons and are seen as spiritually powerful. Some of these stories, collected by Richard Price, reveal the origins of some of the oldest maroon communities. For example, the Matjáu subgroup of the Saramaka trace their origins to a small core group of Africans who escaped from slavery sometime around 1685. They lived for a time along a small creek just beyond the area colonized and settled by plantation owners. Around 1690 they returned to conduct a large raid on a plantation (which historical records indicate was owned by Imanuel Machado), freeing slaves who came to constitute the core of their communty.

MAROON WARS

The existence of communities of self-emancipated former slaves was seen by colonial officials as a serious threat. They feared maroon-inspired insurrections, although few actually formed, and they created colonial militias with the sole purpose of recapturing maroons. Those who were recaptured were often publicly tortured and executed, to serve as an example to other slaves – a practice that continued into the late eighteenth century. Several of the larger maroon groups also fought intermittent wars with colonial militias.

Between 1760 and 1762 two of the largest maroon communities, the Ndjuka and Saramaka, ended a century-long war with the colonists, and won their independence by signing peace treaties with the Dutch colonial government. But the desire to escape continued, and new maroon communities were formed in the nineteenth century as more slaves escaped. This led to further wars between the colonists and other maroon communities, especially the Aluku (or Boni) during the eighteenth century.

The peace treaties signed between the Ndjuka, Saramaka, and Matawai maroons and the Dutch gave these maroon communities wide freedom in regulating their internal affairs. In return they pledged to turn over to the colonists any newly escaped slaves or other maroons that they might encounter. The Dutch authorities, for their part, pledged to provide the maroon communities with periodic "tribute," and allowed them to conduct trading trips from their homes in the rain forest to the coastal cities. Other maroon "tribes" probably developed from new escapes and from groups that split off the older communities. After the peace treaties with the Ndjuka, Saramaka and Matawai, the main leaders of warfare against the colonists were the Aluku (or Boni). During the late 1700s warfare was so intense that the colonists established a 60-meter-wide "protective cordon," manned by soldiers posted at short intervals, all along the outer edges of the forested southern plantation region. Overall, the combination of treaties between the maroons and the colonial authorities and stiff maroon resistance meant that, unlike many other maroon communities in Latin America and the Caribbean, Suriname's maroons were not defeated by colonial armies, nor gradually assimilated into the general population, but have constituted flourishing, semiautonomous societies.

The maroon communities have survived over the years; in the mid-1980s the maroon population was about 45,000. There are six maroon groups in Suriname: the two largest maroon communities are the Ndjuka and the Saramaka, and others are the Paramaka, Aluki, Kwinti, and Matawai. Many of these communities have managed to retain traditional African-derived customs, including a matrilineal kinship structure, local political leadership forms, spiritual practices such as Obeah and the Winti religion, and agricultural techniques such as shifting cultivation or "slash and burn."

Today maroons also engage heavily in logging, and the men often work as wage laborers on the coast, away from their home communities. Though the communities retain their pride in their own culture – for example, the Saramaka keep memories of the dark days of war alive in oral history known as "first time" stories – they also face a series of threats to their survival. They face strong pressure to assimilate, as well as discrimination and harassment. In addition, during the 1960s almost half of the Saramaka's territory was flooded when a dam was built on the Saramacca River to provide electricity to a massive bauxite smelter. Periodic "development plans" have also called for the consolidation of scattered maroon villages into large, new planned towns as a precondition to their "integration" into the nation. Finally, a war between the military government of Dési Bouterse, and a guerrilla group known as the Surinamese Liberation Army (SLA), also known as the Jungle Commando (led by Ronnie Brunswijk, and composed largely of Ndjuka maroons) has also had a devastating impact on Suriname's maroons. In the 1980s some 10,000 fled to French Guiana to escape bombings, massacres, and other attacks on their communities by the Surinamese military.

EMANCIPATION

The maroons were not the only ones who resisted slavery. In perhaps the most dramatic act of resistance, rebellious slaves burned much of the capital in 1832, and as late as 1860 the entire slave population of a plantation escaped to the forest. Responding to these and other pressures, in 1863 Holland abolished slavery in all of its colonial territories, freeing close to 33,000 slaves (*see* ABOLITION AND EMANCIPATION IN LATIN AMERICA AND THE CARIBBEAN). Even before this period the collapse of the plantation economy in the late 1700s had significantly altered Surinamese society. Many of the Dutch plantation owners and overseers left the colony to return to Europe. Jewish plantation owners remained, though, and intermarriage between white plantation owners and slave women became increasingly legitimate during this period. Some scholars argue that the offspring of these semi-accepted unions were manumitted and received better education and a higher social status. It also seems to be true that the majority of free blacks and coloreds (people of mixed race) in the cities of colonial Suriname were female.

However, abolition brought even more challenges, as free blacks and Creoles struggled to make a living in the new wage-based economy. A large number of Creoles emerged as the non-white elite, securing coveted positions as miners, industrial workers, and merchants. Those blacks who were not Creoles found few opportunities outside the plantation. Many migrated to the country's capital, Paramaribo, in search of employment.

Throughout the latter half of the nineteenth century black workers routinely searched for employment in urban areas. In an effort to replace these workers, colonial officials began importing indentured servants from Asia in 1873. More than 60,000 Javanese, Indian, and Chinese indentured servants immigrated to Suriname between 1873 and 1939. In 1916 large bauxite deposits were discovered, and mines were established by the Alcoa mining company. Most of the workers who came to Suriname at this time thus worked on colonial plantations, and some joined black and Creole workers in the country's bauxite and gold mines. This has given Suriname an ethnically diverse population: by the mid-1980s the population was 37 percent East Indian, 31 percent Creole, 15.3 percent Javanese, 10.3 percent maroon, 2.6 percent Amerindian, 1.7 percent Chinese, and 2.1 percent European and others.

Independence

In 1954 Suriname became an autonomous state within the kingdom of the Netherlands. This allowed all of the residents of Suriname to elect a Parliament which formed the government, along with a governor appointed by colonial officials. Between 1954 and 1972 several political parties were established in Suriname, and most represented the interests of a specific ethnic group. In 1973 a Creole-Javanese political coalition won a majority of the parliamentary seats and exercised its constitutional right to appoint Creole politician Henck Arron as prime minister. Arron initiated the negotiations with the Dutch government that culminated two years later on November 25, 1975, in independence for Suriname. Victory was bittersweet, when in the months preceding independence more than 40,000 Asians immigrated to the Netherlands, citing concerns over the stability of the new nation.

Political Instability

In 1977 Arron was reelected as prime minister of Suriname, but was overthrown three years later by a coup led by then-sergeant Bouterse. Army officers under Bouterse's command dissolved the parliament, suspended the constitution, declared a state of emergency, and violently repressed all opposition. Bouterse's government ruled through force, stifling opposition. In the notorious murders perpetrated on December 8, 1982, the security forces arrested, tortured, and summarily executed 15 prominent Surinamese, including former government ministers, a professor, a prominent trade unionist, and others. Distrusted by the urban population, Bouterse came to surround himself with young military officers from maroon communities. The Bouterse regime was also unable to manage the country's economy, and the stagnation that hit the country in the early 1980s left military dictators vulnerable to challengers.

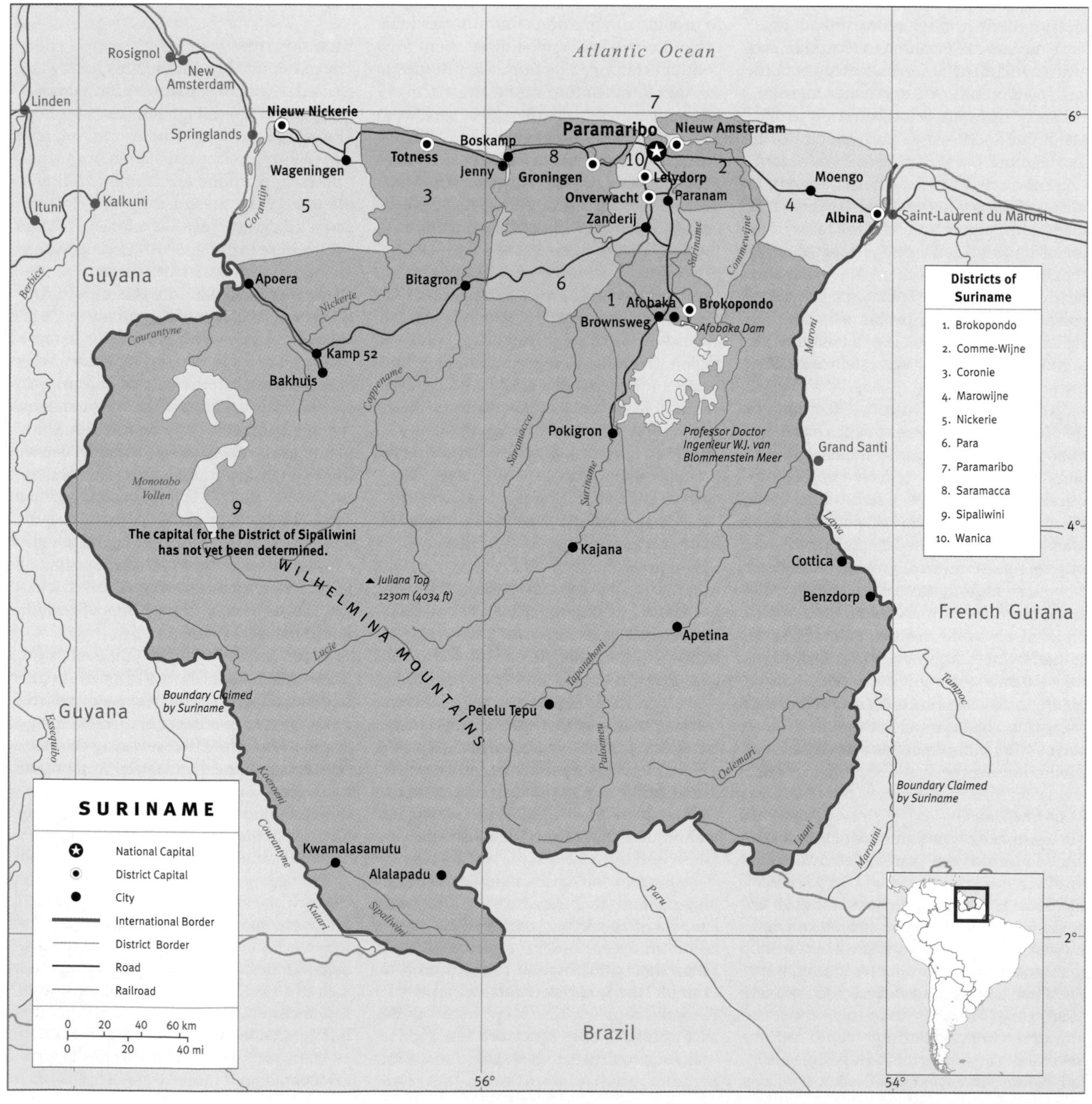

In 1986 Bouterse's reliance on maroon supporters would backfire. A small guerrilla group, drawn mainly from the Ndjuka group of maroons, joined former presidential bodyguard Ronnie Brunswijk, himself a Ndjuka maroon, to form the Surinamese Liberation Army (SLA). The SLA waged a guerrilla war against the Bouterse regime, demanding a full restoration of the country's constitution. During the war maroon communities were often singled out for harsh reprisals for their alleged support of the SLA. Following massacres carried out against maroon civilians by the military in 1986, as many as 10,000 maroons became refugees in French Guiana (*see* Human Rights in Latin America and the Caribbean). The country endured civil war and political instability until 1992, when the SLA signed a peace treaty with former education minister Ronald Venetiaan, who was chosen president of Suriname by the national assembly. In 1993 Bouterse was removed as commander in chief of the military.

Present Situation

The deteriorating economic situation, international and local pressures, and raids by the Jungle Commando led Bouterse and the military to relinquish control of the government, and in 1985 a national assembly was formed. After a new constitution was drafted in 1987, elections were held in November of that year, and the military's political wing was defeated. Though many observers doubted the independence of the new civilian government, it opened peace talks with Brunswijk's Jungle Commando in 1989. But on December 24, 1990, the military once again seized control of the government in a coup engineered by Bouterse.

This Ndjuka man, pictured painting his canoe paddle in a traditional style, descends from the founders of one of Suriname's largest communities of maroons, or escaped slaves. *CORBIS/Adam Woolfitt*

In response to pressure from the United States, the Netherlands, France, and the Organization of American States, new elections were held in May 1991. The New Front for Democracy and Development, a group that combined several pre-coup political parties, won a majority of seats in the assembly. Despite its position of power, the New Front was not able to control the requisite two-thirds of parliament needed to select a president until September 1991, when Ronald Venetiaan was chosen. The New Front government eventually officially deprived the military of much of its prior power, opened peace negotiations with the Jungle Commando and dissident Amerindian groups, and continued negotiations on the repatriation of maroon refugees in French Guiana. In new elections held in 1996 which proved to be the closest in Suriname's independent history, Jules Wijdenbosch, a former chief member of the military government, defeated Venetiaan and began a five-year term. Nevertheless, since 1996 Wijdenbosch's administration has been criticized for its inability to control increasing inflation and steady rates of unemployment. The country continues to rely on its bauxite industry, leaving it susceptible to international fluctuations in price.

The economic and political challenges have posed particular difficulties for Suriname's maroon communities. Most continue to live in the country's hilly interior and struggle to keep pace with the country's transition from a military dictatorship to an open democracy. More than half of Suriname's population live in rural areas, and 90 percent of those who live in urban areas are concentrated along the country's narrow coastal plain. Although these political and economic challenges pose formidable obstacles, Suriname is working to provide a stable environment for the future.

Alonford James Robinson, Jr.

See Also

Bantu: Dispersion and Settlement; New York, New York; Languages, Creole, in the Caribbean.

North America

Sutton, Percy Ellis

(b. November 24, 1920, San Antonio, Texas), African American attorney, politician, and media businessman.

In the 1950s, after completing his education under the G.I. Bill, Percy Sutton opened a law firm in Harlem that specialized in civil rights cases. Sutton's political career began when he was elected to the New York State

Assembly in 1964. He became president of the Manhattan Borough in 1966, a position he held through 1977. After an unsuccessful mayoral bid he retired from public office, but continued to be an advisor to New York politicians, including United States Representative Charles Rangel and Mayor David Dinkins.

In 1971 Sutton began purchasing black-owned media businesses, becoming the owner and chairman of the Inner-City Broadcasting Company in 1977. Through this corporation he purchased and restored the APOLLO THEATER. Sutton was awarded the NATIONAL ASSOCIATION FOR THE ADVANCEMENT OF COLORED PEOPLE's Spingarn Medal for his work in 1987. In 1997, along with Dinkins, Sutton served as the attorney for Malcolm Shabazz, the 12-year-old grandson of MALCOLM X who admitted to setting a fire that led to the death of Betty Shabazz, Malcolm X's widow.

SEE ALSO

Dinkins, David Norman; Rangel, Charles Bernard; Harlem, New York; Shabazz, Hajj Bahiyah Betty.

Africa

Suzman, Helen (b. November 7, 1917, Germinston, South Africa), South African politician and outspoken opponent of APARTHEID, South Africa's former system of racial separation.

Born Helen Gavronsky in Germiston, in what is now Gauteng province, northeastern SOUTH AFRICA, of Jewish immigrant parents, she was educated at the Parktown Convent until 1933 and then attended the University of the Witwatersrand in Johannesburg. In 1937 she married Moses Meyer Suzman, and they settled in Johannesburg. During World War II (1939-1945) she worked for the War Supplies Board. She joined the United Party (UP) in 1949 and became a well-known speaker as honorary information officer, before being elected as the party's member of parliament (MP) for the Johannesburg suburb of Houghton in April 1953.

In 1959 the party was split between conservatives and progressives following the party's decision to oppose further land allocations for blacks. Eleven of its progressive members resigned, including Suzman. In August 1959 they formed the new Progressive Party (PP), but in the general election of 1961 only Suzman was returned to Parliament where she was the sole PP representative for the next 13 years. She was a staunch opponent of the NATIONAL PARTY government's racially biased policies, sometimes hers was the only voice in Parliament raised against new oppressive legislation (*see* VERWOERD, HENDRIK FRENSCH; VORSTER, BALTHAZAR JOHANNES). She retained her seat in the elections of 1966 and 1970, and only in 1974 was she joined by seven more Progressive Party MPs. The PP continued to increase its strength in Parliament, and the new members took much of the burden of opposition from Suzman. During the 1970s, with the terminal decline of the UP, the PP and the Reform Party merged in 1977 to become the Progressive Federal Party (PFP). As the party with the second-largest representation in Parliament the PFP was the official opposition party.

Suzman traveled extensively in the United States and Europe, and in 1971, with PP leader Colin Eglin, she visited SENEGAL, THE GAMBIA, SIERRA LEONE, and TANZANIA, an almost unheard of event for a white South African MP. She has received many awards from universities in Great Britain, the United States, and South Africa. In 1985 and 1986 she lost considerable support inside and outside South Africa for opposing international sanctions against South Africa on the grounds that these would encourage a siege mentality; she argued instead for internal black boycotts. Suzman retired from Parliament in 1989, just before the dismantling of apartheid began. She was one of 11 veteran South African figures of all races chosen to sit on the Independent Electoral Commission, which was appointed by the Transitional Executive Council that was set up in December 1993 to oversee the transition to majority rule.

SEE ALSO

Johannesburg, South Africa.

Africa

Swahili Coast, a 3000 km (about 1865 mi) stretch of East African coastline between southern SOMALIA in the north and northern MOZAMBIQUE in the south, home to more than 400 settlements.

The Swahili Coast has been the site of cultural and commercial exchanges between East Africa and the outside world – particularly the Middle East, Asia, and Europe – since at least the second century C.E. The earliest coastal communities practiced ironworking and were mainly subsistence farmers and riverine fishers, who supplemented their economy with hunting, keeping livestock, fishing in the ocean, and trading with outsiders. Between 500 and 800 C.E. they shifted to a sea-based trading economy and began to migrate south by ship. In the following centuries trade in goods from the African interior, such as gold, ivory, and slaves (*see* SLAVERY IN AFRICA and INDIAN OCEAN SLAVE TRADE) stimulated the development of market towns such as Mogadishu, Shanga, Kilwa, and Mombasa. By around the ninth century C.E. Africans, Arabs, and Persians who lived and traded on the coast had developed a lingua franca, Kiswahili, a language based on the Bantu language Sabaki that uses Arab and Persian loan words. They had also developed the distinctive Swahili culture, characterized by the almost universal practice of Islam, as well as by Arabic and Asian-influenced art and architectural styles.

The arrival of the Portuguese explorer VASCO DA GAMA in 1498 signaled a new era of foreign rule on the Swahili Coast. By this time Mombasa was the dominant Swahili power, so control over this city meant control over the coastal region. PORTUGAL, seeking to monopolize trade throughout the Indian Ocean trade, built Fort Jesus in Mombasa, and also set up a customs house on Pate Island. The Portuguese were finally pushed out of power on the Swahili Coast in 1698 by combined forces from Oman and Pate, though the Portuguese remained in Mozambique until the late twentieth century.

The imam (religious leader) of Oman then sought control of the coast, but matters closer to home drew his attention. It was instead the Mazrui clan of Mombasa (whose ancestors came from Omani long before) who gained predominance in the region. They were in turn driven out of the city in 1837 by Omani forces. The sultan of Oman then moved his capital to ZANZIBAR and established a commercial empire, bringing renewed prosperity to the coast.

The sultan then expanded his trading empire, sending caravans into the African interior to trade firearms for gold, ivory, and slaves. The slave trade on the East African coast had persisted for centuries, but it intensified during the early nineteenth century in order to meet the labor demands on French plantations on RÉUNION and MAURITIUS, as well as on the sultan's plantations on Zanzibar. By the late nineteenth century pressure from the British had forced an end to the trade, and the Swahili Coast was exporting a variety of spices and other tropical crops.

Following the SCRAMBLE FOR AFRICA of the late nineteenth century, during which the European powers divided Africa among themselves, the hegemony of the sultan in Zanzibar gave way to European overrule. The colonial powers began to control trade in the interior, bypassing the Swahili middlemen.

Today Dar es Salaam and Mombasa are the biggest port cities on the Swahili Coast; both have been significantly transformed by industrial development as well as by the migration of upcountry Africans. Smaller Swahili towns, however, such as Pate in KENYA, retain much of their traditional culture. For these towns, beachfront tourism has become an important economic component.

Robert Fay

SEE ALSO

Dar es Salaam, Tanzania; Explorers in Africa Before 1500; Gold Trade; Ivory Trade; Swahili Language; Mogadishu, Somalia; Mombasa, Kenya; Swahili People; Tourism in Africa; Islam and Tradition: An Interpretation; Slavery in Africa.

Africa

Swahili Language, Bantu language and one of the most widely spoken African languages.

Swahili is the official language of Tanzania and Kenya and is spoken as a lingua franca throughout most of East Africa, as well as parts of Central Africa. The language is heavily influenced by Arabic – a result of the long-standing trading relationships in the region – while many contemporary words are adapted from English. The main dialects of Swahili, or Kiswahili, as it is also called, are Kiunguja, Kimvita, and Kiamu.

Swahili has a long tradition of literary production, and poetry has been written in Swahili since at least the middle of the seventeenth century. It draws on Arabic, Urdu, and Persian literary sources. Though Swahili was originally only written in Arabic script, Latin script became more popular in the mid-nineteenth century and has since become standard. The oldest survivng Swahili epic is the *Hamziya*, which was written by Sayyid Aidarusi in Arabic script in the old Kingozi dialect in 1749. Bwana Muku II, the ruler of the island of Pate, off the coast of present-day Kenya, commissioned the poem. Mwana Kupona binti Msham was a well-known poet of the nineteenth century who wrote *tenzi*, didactic poems that were traditionally concerned with Islamic religious subjects and public commentary. This form is still used by contemporary poets such as Abdilatif Abdalla. Muyaka bin Haji al-Ghassaniy (1776-1840) wrote poetic commentaries on urban life in the form of mashairi. Perhaps the most famous contemporary Swahili author is Shaaban Robert, a Tanzanian known for his poetry, children's literature, essays and novels. Many works of Western authors have been translated into Swahili, such as the well-known renderings of William Shakespeare's plays by Julius Nyerere.

See Also

Languages, African: An Overview; Nyerere, Julius Kambarage.

Africa

Swahili People, an ethnic group occupying coastal areas in parts of Somalia, Kenya, and Tanzania.

The Swahili people number approximately half a million, inhabiting a string of small settlements along the East African coast, from Mogadishu in the north to Mozambique in the south, spanning approximately 1800 km (about 1118 mi). They are believed to have descended from Bantu-speaking agriculturalists who lived in an area reaching roughly from Kenya's Tana River in present-day Kenya to the Webi Shabelle region of Somalia. Although the Swahili people had long supplemented their farming with fishing, it is believed that around 500 c.e. they began to trade and migrate along the coast. Over the next three centuries migrant groups moved south by ship, establishing settlements both on the coast and on adjacent islands. These independent polities were linked by trade as well as by a common culture and language, Swahili (*see* Swahili Coast). From an early date merchants from the Arab peninsula, Persia, and India (*see* Indian Communities in Africa) settled among and intermarried with the Swahili towns' African founders.

By the twelfth century Swahili culture exhibited Arab and Asian cultural influences. A distinctive Swahili architecture had emerged, which reflected these influences. Houses made of coral rag and coral stone had replaced the circular mud-and-wattle buildings found in parts of inland East Africa. The ruins at Gedi in Kenya provide one example of early Swahili architecture. Islam was also well established along the Swahili Coast by the twelfth century, though elements of indigenous African religions remained (*see* African Religions: An Interpretation).

For centuries Swahili merchants served as middlemen, exporting products from the East African interior in exchange for goods purchased from Indian Ocean merchant ships. Especially during the nineteenth century, Swahili caravans traveled far into the interior in search of slaves and ivory, and some of these traders established inland trading posts. One of the most renowned nineteenth-century Swahili traders was the Zanzibari Tippu Tip (*see* Zanzibar), whose trading empire stretched from the East African coast to the western bank of the Lualaba River in the modern Democratic Republic of the Congo (formerly Zaire).

The Swahili were never unified politically, and their towns and states varied considerably in size and structure. Royal dynasties ruled some Swahili polities, such as those on Pate Island, while local oligarchies, known as *waungwana*, ruled others. Most Swahili towns were divided into wards, each dominated by a few families. In addition, Swahili towns were divided into northern and southern halves, with the wealthier and older families occupying the northern half, and the less well-off, including Swahili migrants and foreigners, occupying the southern half.

In smaller and less prosperous Swahili towns most of the townspeople engaged in agriculture and supplemented their own production with trade. The most powerful families in the larger and more prosperous Swahili towns typically oversaw agricultural production in the surrounding countryside, where crops were tended by slaves or hired labor. In the larger towns Swahili society became highly hierarchical. The waungwana attempted to consolidate their power through family alliances forged through marriage. Women were prohibited from marrying people who were considered below their social level in this hierarchy. Married women were to retain ritual purity and remain indoors during daylight hours. When traveling outside, married women were veiled. They often traveled in a tentlike cover, called a *shirra*, until the British outlawed the practice. In addition, wives were to be observant Muslims; they were to pray and read sacred texts in the home, as well as to practice works of charity. The less wealthy, the poor women, and the women in smaller towns had fewer restrictions, out of economic necessity.

The arrival of the Portuguese in the late fifteenth century began a long era of foreign rule on the Swahili Coast, but not all foreign powers left equally lasting influences. The Portuguese, for example, established only a limited presence on the Swahili Coast, compared to the size of their colonies in southern Africa (*see* Portugal). They left few traces, except the ruin of Fort Jesus in Mombasa.

The imam (religious leader) of Oman drove the Portuguese from the coast in 1698, and gradually established his hegemony over the coast. Omani influences on Swahili culture proved much more significant. In addition to introducing many Arabic loan words into the Swahili language, the Omani cultivated the belief that the way they practiced Islam and their social status were superior to that of the Swahili. Arab ancestry thus became a marker of status.

Beginning in the late nineteenth century European colonial rule brought further changes to Swahili society. Although parts of the Swahili Coast remained under Omani control, European colonialism eventually brought an end to slave trading, and more generally undermined the Swahili's traditional role as East African middlemen. Modern shipping has taken over the long-distance ocean trade routes once traveled by *dhows*, the Swahili's wooden sailing vessels. Cities such as Mogadishu and Mombasa, now major industrial ports, have attracted many migrants from the East African interior. Kiswahili now contains many loan words from English and has become the lingua franca (a means of communication among peoples of different languages) of much of East Africa, spoken by more than 130 million people.

Robert Fay

See Also

Ivory Trade; Languages, African: An Overview; Swahili Language; Mogadishu, Somalia; Mombasa, Kenya; Indian Ocean Slave Trade; Islam and Tradition: An Interpretation.

SWAPO. Please see South West Africa People's Organization

Africa

Swazi, the founding ethnic group of the kingdom of Swaziland.

The name Swazi derives from that of a nineteenth-century ruler, Mswati II, under whom Swaziland expanded into an empire that incorporated numerous peoples and covered an area roughly twice its present-day size. Prior to the reign of Mswati II, the Swazi people were a group of Nguni clans known either as the Dlamini, after their ruling clan, or collectively as the Ngwane. The Ngwane arrived in southern Africa as part of the great Bantu migrations, and by the fifteenth century had established small, pastoral communities along the coast of Delagoa Bay in southern Mozambique. The heavily forested terrain proved unsuitable for agriculture, and the Ngwane clans eventually migrated farther into southern Africa.

In the early nineteenth century the military conquests of the Zulu king Shaka pushed the Ngwane clans, under the leadership of Sobhuza I, into the grasslands that constitute present-day Swaziland's "middleveld" region. There, Sobhuza I, and later his son Mswati II, conquered and incorporated the Tsonga, Nguni, and Sotho clans, by the 1840s forging one of southern Africa's largest kingdoms.

Although the Ngwane had encountered Portuguese explorers and traders as early as the sixteenth century, Swazi-European relationships did not begin in earnest until the 1840s. At that time Boer settlers began trading cloth, beads, and guns in exchange for cattle-grazing privileges in Swazi territory, and English missionaries began converting the Swazi to Methodism (nearly 60 percent of Swazi today profess Christianity). When gold was discovered in the Lembombo Mountains in 1882, European mining concessions began pouring into Swaziland, and in 1894 the kingdom was officially annexed by the South African Boer Republic. Following the Boer War (1899-1902), Swaziland reverted to British rule and its boundaries were redrawn, leaving many Swazi involuntary residents of South Africa.

Today more than a million Swazi live in Swaziland, and an additional 700,000 reside in South Africa, where until 1990 they were confined to Swazi homelands called the KaNgwane. After Swaziland gained independence in 1968, King Sobhuza II launched a diplomatic campaign to annex the KaNgwane homelands, but the South African government refused. Even in the postapartheid era, most South African Swazi have chosen to remain in South Africa, where many work in the mining industry.

Swaziland survived colonial rule with much of its political structure and many of its customs intact. The nation is still ruled by a king, known as the *ngwenyama* (lion), and a queen mother, called the *ndlovuzaki* (female elephant), both of whom trace their ancestry back to the Nkosi Dlamini, the royal line of the ruling Dlamini clan. Despite the prominent presence of Christian churches in Swaziland, ancestor worship and other elements of traditional Swazi religion remain part of everyday life for many Swazi.

Andrew Hermann

See Also

Bantu: Dispersion and Settlement; Christianity, African: An Overview; Christianity: Missionaries in Africa.

Africa

Swaziland, a small landlocked southern African kingdom bordering South Africa to the north, west, and south, and Mozambique to the east.

Swaziland's beautiful, mountainous topography and unusually peaceful transition from colonialism to independence have earned it the nickname "the Switzerland of Africa." Swaziland is a kingdom, ruled jointly by a king and a queen mother, who trace their royal lineage back to the fifteenth century, making Swaziland one of only a handful of African nations to have survived the colonial period with most of its precolonial political system intact. This is due largely to the efforts of one man, King Sobhuza II, who managed to maintain his position and popularity during nearly half a century of British control. However, since Swaziland became independent in 1968, and particularly since Sobhuza's death in 1983, the nation's urban intellectuals and businesspeople have become increasingly dissatisfied with the old system of hereditary, autocratic rule. As mounting foreign debt and natural resource depletion have weakened Swaziland's once relatively prosperous economy, general strikes and civil unrest have jeopardized the fragile political stability that the current ruler, Mswati III, inherited from his revered predecessor. Bowing to domestic and international pressure, Mswati declared his support for democratic reforms and a new constitution in 1996, but so far he has failed to deliver on his promises.

Precolonial History

Swaziland's earliest inhabitants were Khoisan-speaking hunter-gatherers, who lived in small, scattered nomadic communities throughout southern Africa. Many lived solely by foraging and hunting, but the people who came to be known as the Khoikhoi also raised cattle and sheep. Around the third century C.E. Bantu-speaking groups began migrating to southern Africa, bringing with them iron tools to clear and cultivate the land as well as more livestock. Centuries of population growth, periodic migrations, and gradual assimilation between indigenous and migrant groups gave rise to a number of distinct Bantu-speaking societies, practicing different combinations of agriculture and pastoralism. One of these societies, the Dlamini, are believed to be the ancestors of present-day Swazis.

According to Swazi oral traditions, the Dlamini chief Ngwane III founded the kingdom around 1750, when he led his people out of the mountains of southern Mozambique and founded a permanent settlement at Lobamba, which remains the royal capital of present-day Swaziland. The fertile, temperate valleys of this region, which had long served as an important migratory route for many Bantu-speaking groups, were conducive to agriculture and cattle grazing, and the Dlamini quickly grew from a small nomadic clan into one of the region's most prosperous kingdoms.

The early nineteenth century was a period of increased militarization for all southern African kingdoms, as they resisted the encroachment of both Afrikaner (or Boer) settlers from the Cape and African groups fleeing the Portuguese colonies to the north. The Swazi Kingdom expanded dramatically during this violent period, led by two aggressive kings, Sobhuza I (r. 1816-1836) and Mswati II (r. 1839-1865). By mid-century the kingdom was roughly twice its present size, stretching from the coastline of what is now Mozambique into the interior bushlands as far north as Zimbabwe. The victims of this expansion, mostly Nguni, Sotho, and Tonga clans, were allowed to maintain their traditional leaders and customs if they submitted peacefully to Swazi rule, and were brutally assimilated if they did not. The resulting polyglot kingdom came to be known, after Mswati, as Swaziland, although to this day Swazi citizens who can trace their clan name back to the original Lobamba settlement refer to themselves as "true Swazi."

In 1846 the Swazis had their first direct contact with Europeans, in the form of Boer settlers and English missionaries. About 69% of Swaziland's population is Christian; the remaining population still practices traditional indigenous beliefs. Early Swazi-European relations were cordial, and the Boers and Swazis even aided one another in skirmishes against rival kingdoms, particularly the powerful Zulus to the west. In 1860 Mswati signed the first of several concessions allowing for Boer and English settlements in Swazi territory. Although these agreements did nothing to contravene Swazi independence, they laid the groundwork for the coming period of colonial rule.

The Period of Concessions

Swazi laws of royal succession are complex and often involve a protracted period of infighting and bloodshed before a new king and queen mother can assume control. Such a period ensued following the death of Mswati II in 1865, and the Boers seized the opportunity to gain further influence in the region. By providing military backing to Mbandzeni, one of several potential monarchs, the Boers won the young king's favor and

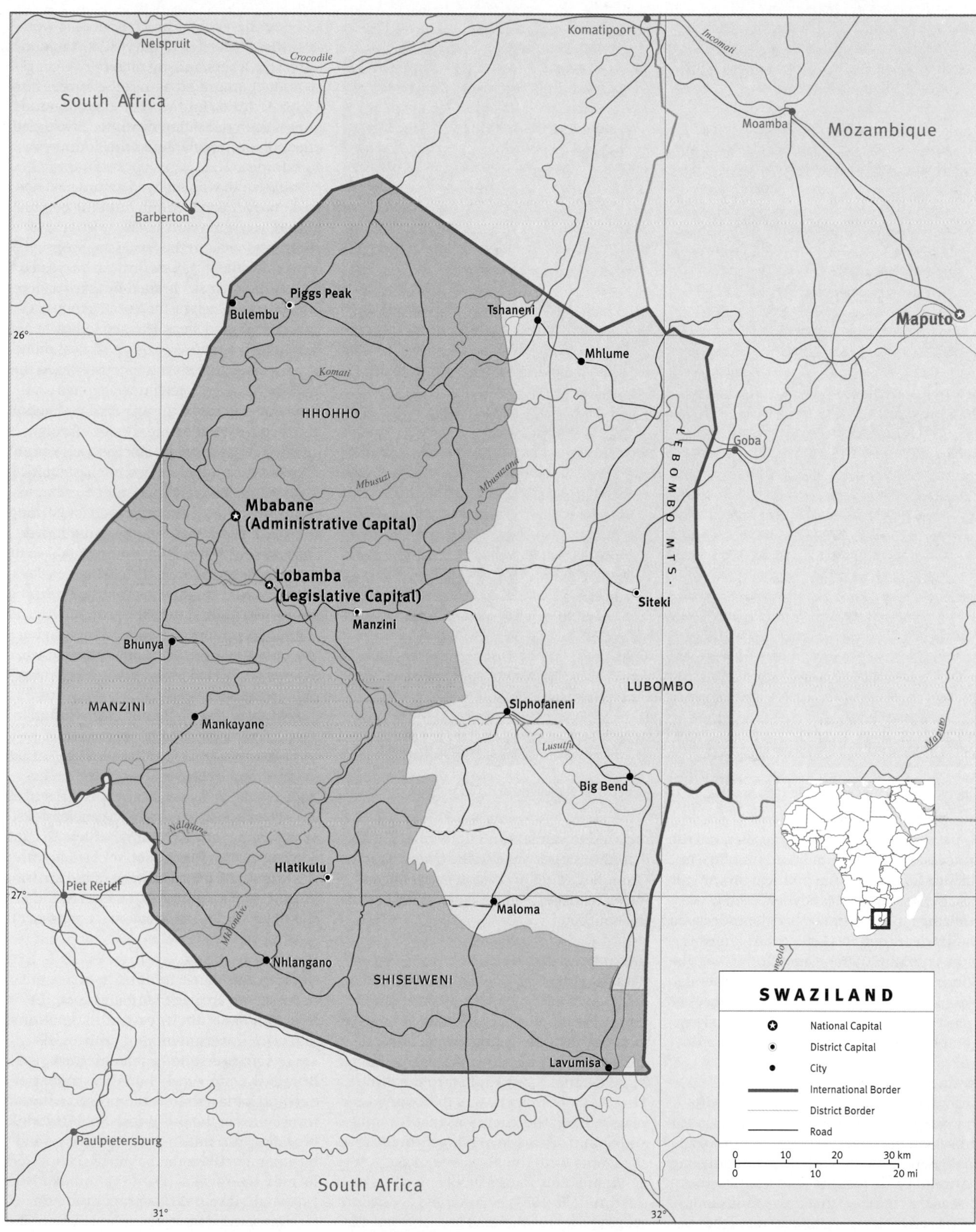

were rewarded with further territorial concessions.

In the 1880s conventions between Great Britain and the Boers over the disputed Transvaal territory reaffirmed Swazi sovereignty, but the discovery of gold in the Lembombo Range in 1882 spoke more loudly than any treaty. Soon hundreds of European prospectors from around southern Africa were making the trek to Lobamba to buy Mbandzeni's permission to mine the Lebombo Range. Called "concessionaires," these Boer and English fortuneseekers had soon overrun the western half of Swaziland and had virtually taken control of the kingdom's economy.

Confused and overwhelmed, Mbandzeni turned to an English ally, a former colonial administrator named Theophilus Shepstone, whose past diplomatic dealings with Swaziland had earned him the king's trust. On Shepstone's advice Mbandzeni appointed Shepstone's son "Offy" to the position of "resident advisor and agent." It was the king's last and greatest mistake. Over the next

King Sobhuza II, shown here in 1964 opening the railway between Swaziland and Mozambique, ruled the tiny nation from 1921 to 1982. *CORBIS/Hulton-Deutsch Collection*

three years Offy Shepstone accelerated the concessions process and used his office to dismantle most of the political power still held by the king and his advisers. Mbandzeni, realizing too late what he had done, declared on his deathbed in 1889, "Swazi kingship ends with me." When Great Britain and the South African Boer Republics together declared Swaziland a "political dependency" of Transvaal in 1894, it appeared that Mbandzeni had been right.

Boer Swaziland

Swaziland remained a dependency of Transvaal only until 1899, when the Boer War broke out. But it was an incredibly turbulent five-year period. Swaziland's economy and national pride were ravaged by livestock disease, a "hut tax" that drove thousands of Swazis off their farms to seek wage labor in the mines and on white-owned ranches, and the absconding of Mbandzeni's successor, Bhunu, who decided in 1898 to flee to Zululand rather than stand trial in a Boer court for the murder of a political rival.

Ironically, the Boer War brought to Swaziland a brief period of peace, as the Boer government fell into disarray and the kingdom reverted to semiautonomous rule. Bhunu died that same year and the Queen Mother, Gwamile Mdluli, who took over as regent, maintained Swaziland's neutrality throughout the conflict.

British Swaziland

With the end of the Boer War in 1902, Britain assumed control of Swaziland. At about the same time the Swazi royal family, in an effort to reestablish the legitimacy and stability of the Dlamini line, chose the son of Bhunu's highest-ranking wife as heir to the throne. That son, Sobhuza II, was then only three years old, but the intent was that Gwamile and Sobhuza's uncle Malunge would serve as regents until the boy came of age.

When Sobhuza was finally installed on the throne in 1921, he inherited a kingdom splintered by colonial land and labor policies. Britain's 1907 Partition Proclamation had used an elaborate tally of Mbandzeni's and Mswati II's concessions as a pretext for awarding roughly two-thirds of their protectorate's lands to white settlers. The remaining "Native Areas" were largely unsuitable for agriculture or cattle-grazing, and so many Swazis stayed on their former lands – now owned by Boer and English ranchers and farmers – to work as cattle herders or to harvest cotton and tobacco. Others, mostly men between ages 18 and 40, migrated across the border into South Africa to find work in the diamond mines. Such relocation disrupted Swazi clan life and severely depleted the country's workforce.

Sobhuza II, who enjoyed an unusual degree of sovereignty throughout the colonial period, went to court in Great Britain to attempt to reclaim the Swazi's appropriated land, but without success. Instead he created a royal "land trust," funded by taxes paid by his subjects, which he then used to buy back the appropriated areas. He then redistributed most of this land to Swazis – a tactical show of patronage that simultaneously eased the land shortage crisis, reaffirmed his own royal authority, and paved the way for a new period of prosperity. Following the war, foreign firms, impressed by the colony's rich natural resources and apparent economic stability, invested extensively in Swaziland's manufacturing, mining, and commercial farming and forestry sectors, transforming it over the next decade from "the least reputable and most neglected of the British dependencies" into a small regional powerhouse, exporting SUGAR, citrus, and forestry products.

Rapid economic growth was followed in the early 1960s by the proliferation of Swazi nationalist and labor movements. The most influential of the early political parties was the Ngwane National Liberatory Congress (NNLC), which called for universal adult suffrage and complete independence, leaving the monarch relatively few powers. The NNLC organized a series of industrial strikes in 1962 and 1963, followed by a general strike in the capital city, Mbabane, which was put down by British troops. Sobhuza sided with the British, taking advantage of the crisis to improve his standing in the eyes of the increasingly disillusioned colonial government.

Independent Swaziland

Great Britain had intended to phase out dependency in Swaziland and cede the kingdom to South Africa, but that nation's maverick government and policies of APARTHEID precluded such a route. Great Britain therefore switched to a strategy of decolonization that would preserve the royal status of the pro-British Sobhuza while providing for a British-style constitution and bicameral parliament. Sobhuza's supporters formed the royalist party, the Imbokodvo National Movement, in preparation for elections, while the constitution allowed the king to nominate half the senate. But when Swaziland was finally awarded independence in 1968, Sobhuza acted quickly to consolidate his power even further. Within five years he had abolished the constitution, banned all political parties, and effectively marginalized the role of the parliament.

Despite his autocratic style Sobhuza was

LEFT: A worker shapes blown glass in a factory in Swaziland. *CORBIS/Lindsay Hebberd*
MIDDLE LEFT: Women in Swaziland attend an agricultural extension class. *R. Lord*
BELOW LEFT: Swaziland's team enters the Olympic stadium in Atlanta, Georgia, in 1996. *CORBIS/Frank Seguin; TempSport*

revered by the people. He was seen as their deliverer from colonial subjugation, and he took much credit for restoring traditional Swazi culture and sustaining the kingdom's prosperity, which was largely fed by foreign investment in manufacturing and agro-processing, and close economic ties to South Africa. Although the king was sharply critical of the latter country's regime under apartheid, postcolonial Swaziland drew not only trade, investment capital, and labor remittances from South Africa, but also increasing numbers of tourists, who came to enjoy the kingdom's wildlife, scenery, and casinos.

Sobhuza's death in 1982 left the country devoid of strong leadership and led to a period of political turmoil that continues to the present day. Sobhuza's successor, MSWATI III, did not assume the throne until 1986, and in the intervening years pro-democratic forces in Swaziland, particularly trade unions, did much to undermine the royal power base. Mswati III's extreme youth (18 at the start of his reign) has further goaded on reformists, who see their king as too inexperienced to contend with the many challenges posed by the dramatic political, economic, and social changes sweeping southern Africa.

The end of apartheid in South Africa, for example, has already proved a mixed blessing. During the 1980s Swaziland became a refuge for South African as well as Western firms, including Coca-Cola, seeking to avoid the international sanctions and boycotts imposed on the regime of apartheid. To this day Swaziland maintains one of Africa's largest per capita manufacturing sectors and boasts an extensive modern infrastructure. Unlike almost every other country on the continent, Swaziland has never confronted an economic crisis so severe that it had to undertake the difficult austerity measures required as part of World Bank structural adjustment loan programs. But with sanctions now lifted from its nearest neighbor, Swaziland's ability to compete for foreign capital and tourists has suffered.

Natural resource depletion and growing foreign debt have also hurt the national economy. Swaziland's once-profitable mining industry is now almost completely nonexistent. The country relies on agriculture (mainly sugar and citrus products) and forestry for its exports, while subsistence farming and cattle ranching account for most of its domestic economic base. Swaziland's other major, hidden export continues to be labor – it is estimated that remittance from Swazi mineworkers in South Africa adds as much as 20 percent to Swaziland's gross domestic product (GDP). The spread of acquired immune deficiency syndrome (AIDS) represents another major domestic crisis, with some rural areas reporting an infection rate as high as 50 percent.

In 1993 Mswati III called for Swaziland's first general election in 20 years, and 55 of the 65 seats in the general assembly were included in the voting. The king, however, retained power to appoint the prime minister, cabinet, and a majority in the senate; pro-democratic forces viewed the elections as inadequate. More recently Swaziland has been rocked by waves of general strikes, most of them organized by the Swazi Federation of Trade Unions (SFTU). The last major strike, in early 1996, led to the formation of a Constitutional Review Commission, which Mswati promised would deliver several democratic reforms. But Mswati has restricted membership on the commission to his own appointees, prompting the SFTU and its allies to reject the commission and call for further strikes. So far Mswati has refused to recognize the SFTU or any of the nation's democratic and socialist political parties, but international pressure from various sources – particularly South Africa, on which Swaziland depends for 90 percent of its imports – may ultimately force him to relinquish Swaziland's monarchic system of government.

Andrew Hermann

See Also
African Socialism; Gold Trade; Iron in Africa; Bantu: Dispersion and Settlement; Nationalism in Africa; Structural Adjustment in Africa; Tourism in Africa; Zulu; AIDS in Africa: An Interpretation; Christianity: Missionaries in Africa.

Surrounded by completed works, this Swaziland artist sculpts in soapstone. *CORBIS/Nik Wheeler*

Africa

Swaziland (Ready Reference)

Official Name: Kingdom of Swaziland
Area: 17,360 sq km (6,704 sq mi)
Location: Southern Africa, between Mozambique and South Africa (landlocked; almost completely surrounded by South Africa)
Capital: Mbabane (administrative; population 46,000 [1990 estimate]); Lobamba (royal and legislative; [data on population unavailable])
Population: 966,462 (1998 estimate)
Population Below Age 15: 46 percent (male 223,648; female 224,782 [1998 estimate])
Population Growth Rate: 1.96 percent (1998 estimate)
Total Fertility Rate: 6 children born per woman (1998 estimate)
Life Expectancy at Birth: Total population: 38.53 years (male 37.31 years; female 39.79 years [1998 estimate])
Infant Mortality Rate: 103.37 deaths per 1000 live births (1998 estimate)
Literacy Rate (age 15 and over who can read and write): Total population: 76.7 percent (male 78 percent; female 75.6 percent [1995 estimate])
Education: In the early 1990s about 180,300 children attended primary schools annually, and some 51,500 were enrolled in secondary schools. There is one major university, the University of Swaziland, located in Kwaluseni.
Languages: English and siSwati are the official languages; government business is conducted in English.
Ethnic Groups: Roughly 97 percent of the people in Swaziland are ethnic Swazi, although there are small populations of Zulu, Tsonga, Asians, and Europeans. Europeans constitute 3 percent of the population.
Religions: Christianity is the professed religion of 60% of the population: 40% practice indigenous beliefs
Climate: The climate is mostly temperate, with cool temperatures at higher elevations and more tropical weather in the low veld. Precipitation, which is heavier toward the west, is concentrated in the warmer months of October through April; the rest of the year is characterized by sunny, clear weather. The temperature in Mbabane, located in the western highlands, ranges from 15° to 25° C (59° to 77° F) in January and 6° to 19° C (42° to 67° F) in July.
Land, Plants, and Animals: Swaziland has mostly mountains and hills, as well as some

moderately sloping plains. Some 62 percent of the land comprises meadows and pastures. About 57 percent of the country's land has been set aside by the monarchy for exclusive use by the Swazi people. The principal rivers are the Komati, Lusutfu, and Umbuluzi. The steady flow of the rivers, fed by abundant rain in the mountains, supports irrigation and hydroelectric power projects in the lowlands.

Natural Resources: Asbestos, coal, clay, cassiterite, hydropower, forests, small gold and diamond deposits, quarry stone, and talc

Currency: The lilangeni

Gross Domestic Product (GDP): $3.9 billion (1997 estimate)

GDP per Capita: $3800 (1997 estimate)

GDP Real Growth Rate: 3 percent (1997 estimate)

Primary Economic Activities: Subsistence agriculture, and mining

Primary Crops: Sugar cane, cotton, maize, tobacco, rice, citrus, pineapples, corn, sorghum, and peanuts; cattle, goats, and sheep

Industries: Mining (coal and asbestos), wood pulp, and sugar

Primary Exports: Sugar, wood pulp, cotton yarn, asbestos, and fresh and canned fruit

Primary Imports: Motor vehicles, machinery, transport equipment, petroleum products, foodstuffs, and chemicals

Primary Trade Partners: South Africa, European Union (EU) countries, and Canada

Government: Swaziland is a monarchy and an independent member of the Commonwealth. National executive power in Swaziland is vested in a king, Mswati III, who appoints a prime minister and council of ministers. One house of parliament is the National Assembly, which has 65 members, 55 of whom are elected from a list of candidates nominated by traditional local councils or directly elected, and 10 of whom are appointed by the king. The 30-member Senate includes 10 members who are elected by the National Assembly and 20 who are appointed by the king. Judicial authority is vested in a high court and subordinate courts. Civil matters among Swazi are handled by traditional leaders, subject to appeals to the High Court.

Alonford James Robinson, Jr.

North America

Sweatt v. Painter, 1950 United States Supreme Court case that outlawed segregation in graduate education, providing a legal basis for Brown v. Board of Education (1954).

After decades of challenging state-imposed segregation, the National Association for the Advancement of Colored People (NAACP) in 1946 joined in a lawsuit that paved the way for its eventual victory in *Brown* v. *Board of Education* (1954). The case, *Sweatt* v. *Painter*, originated when Heman Sweatt, an African American letter carrier, was rejected on racial grounds for admission to the University of Texas law school. Following his protest a district court ordered Texas to provide a law school for black students. Rather than accept the state's attempts at compliance – first by appending law classes to a black vocational school, then by renting rooms in an office building and hiring three part-time law professors – Sweatt chose to pursue his case.

Sweatt was represented by Thurgood Marshall of the NAACP Legal Defense Fund. The NAACP's longstanding strategy – paradoxically based on Plessy v. Ferguson, an earlier case that defended segregation – was to force states into choosing between providing expensive "equal" graduate schools and admitting black students to existing schools. In *Sweatt* and a related case, *McLaurin* v. *Oklahoma*, Marshall went further. Using sociological and psychological testimony, he argued that a segregated education, however comparable the physical facilities, was inherently unequal in that it denied black students interaction with classmates, access to extracurricular activities, and the status and alumni network of established white schools.

In a sign of the case's significance, several groups filed amicus curiae (friend of the court) briefs when it reached the Supreme Court. Eleven southern states argued in support of Texas's segregation, while nearly 200 law professors signed a brief backing the NAACP. Perhaps the most influential amicus brief was presented by the U.S. Justice Department. For the first time the U.S. government said it was time to overturn *Plessy*.

The justices, however, were not prepared to go that far. Writing for a unanimous court, Chief Justice Fred Vinson declared that Heman Sweatt was denied an equal legal education in the segregated school. But the cautious opinion declined to comment on the constitutionality of "separate but equal." Despite this shortcoming, *Sweatt* and its companion cases helped prepare the court for its most significant civil rights case of the twentieth century, *Brown* v. *Board of Education* (1954).

Kate Tuttle

See Also

NAACP Legal Defense and Educational Fund.

North America

Sweet Honey in the Rock (est. 1973), African American female a cappella group that addresses global issues of social injustice through its music.

Sweet Honey in the Rock draws upon a wide range of styles, including the blues, spirituals, gospel, jazz, rap, and African traditional songs. Though an a cappella group, hand clapping, foot stomping, and light percussive African instruments such as *shekeres* sometimes accompany their harmonious vocal arrangements.

Struggle is a major theme in the music of Sweet Honey in the Rock, and their songs have consistently aimed to raise social consciousness. The group's founder and vocal director, Bernice Johnson Reagon, was a civil rights activist during the 1960s with the Student Nonviolent Coordinating Committee (SNCC) and a member of the SNCC Freedom Singers. Reagon has preserved a socially and politically responsible vision in her ongoing work with Sweet Honey in the Rock. Acquired immune deficiency syndrome (AIDS), worker and environmental exploitation, and racism are just a few of the issues addressed by the group.

Sweet Honey in the Rock refers to a land described in a religious parable as being so rich that if you crack open a rock, honey will flow. Bernice Johnson Reagon also relates the name to the legacy of African American women in the United States: "So, too, we, black women, have had to have the standing power of rocks and of mountains – cold and hard, strong and stationary. That quality has often obscured the fact that inside the strength, partnering the sturdiness, we are as honey." The group has witnessed some 20 personnel changes during the past 25 years and currently includes Ysaye Maria Barnwell, Nitanju Bolade Casel, Shirley Childress Johnson (a sign language interpreter), Aisha Kahlil, Carol Maillard, and Bernice Johnson Reagon. Sweet Honey in the Rock has recorded some ten albums, toured extensively within and beyond the United States, and won a Grammy Award in 1988 for their album *A Vision Shared: A Tribute to Woody Guthrie and Leadbelly.*

Aaron Myers

See Also

Civil Rights Movement; Gospel Music; Spirituals, African American.

North America

Swoopes, Sheryl

(b. 1971, Brownfield, Texas), African American basketball player, a forward who scored 47 points in the final game of the 1993 National Collegiate Athletic Association (NCAA) tournament, breaking the NCAA Championship Game record of 44 points set by Bill Walton in 1973.

Known for her speed and shooting ability, Sheryl Denise Swoopes was a starter on the Gold-Medal-winning 1996 United States women's Olympic basketball team. She was also one of the first players signed to the Women's National Basketball Association (WNBA) in 1997.

Swoopes was a leading scorer for her high school team and earned the Texas high school player of the year award in 1988. During her career at Texas Tech University in Lubbock,

Texas, she averaged 25.1 points and 10 rebounds per game. In 1993 she led Texas Tech to a national championship, averaging 28.1 points per game in the NCAA tournament. For her performance Swoopes won the Naismith Award as the nation's outstanding female basketball player.

Swoopes played for a professional team in Italy during the 1994 season but returned to the United States to train for the 1996 Olympic Games in Atlanta, Georgia. During Olympic play she was the third-leading scorer on the U.S. team, averaging 13 points per game and helping the United States win the Gold Medal. Swoopes signed with the Houston Comets of the WNBA for 1997, the league's inaugural season.

Latin America and the Caribbean

Sylvain, Georges (b. April 2, 1866, Puerto-Plata, Dominican Republic; d. August 2, 1925, Port-au-Prince, Haiti), Haitian politician, writer, staunch promoter of literature, arts, and education in Haiti; best remembered as a symbol of Haitian resistance to the United States military occupation from 1915 to 1934.

Trained as a lawyer in Paris, Sylvain founded a law school in Haiti in 1888, and worked in the Department of Public Education in 1894. As a great defender of culture he originated several writing and theatrical venues, including the influential, L'Oeuvre des écrivains haïtiens (an organization for Haitian writers), and participated in the cultural events that celebrated the hundredth anniversary of the Haitian Revolution in 1904. Among his literary incursions, his collection of poems *Confidences et mélancolies* (Confidences and Melancholia) and his fables in Créole, *Cric? Crac!,* stand out for their beauty and passion.

He received the distinguished title of "Chevalier de la légion d'honneur" from the French government after he opened a branch of the "Alliance Française" in Haiti – an organization that sought to expand the influence of France abroad through the propagation of the French language and culture. From 1909 to 1912 he held several posts in France as a Haitian official.

After the American occupation in 1915, he fought fiercely for his country's independence. He founded the newspaper *La Patrie* (Homeland) and a political organization *L'Union patriotique* (The Patriotic Union) that served to restore patriotism and educate the Haitian population. When he died in 1925, the whole of Port-au-Prince mourned him, and a magnificent funeral was organized to pay a last tribute to his courage and patriotism.

Martine Fernández

See Also

Haitian Art; Port-au-Prince, Haiti; Literature, French Language, in Caribbean; Education in Latin America and the Caribbean.

t

Africa

Tabwa, ethnic group of south Central Africa.

The Tabwa primarily inhabit the Marungu highlands of the southeastern Democratic Republic of the Congo. Others live in southwestern Tanzania and northernmost Zambia. They speak a dialect of Bemba, a Bantu language, and are closely related to the Bemba people. More than 200,000 people consider themselves Tabwa.

See Also
Bantu: Dispersion and Settlement.

Africa

Taita (also known as the Teita), ethnic group of Kenya.

The Taita primarily inhabit the Taita Hills in the Coast Province of southern Kenya. They speak a Bantu language. Approximately 300,000 people consider themselves Taita.

See Also
Bantu: Dispersion and Settlement.

Africa

Talensi (also known as Tale, Talen, and Tallensi), ethnic group of Ghana.

The Talensi primarily inhabit northeastern Ghana. Others live across the border in southern Burkina Faso. They speak a Niger-Congo language. Approximately 300,000 people consider themselves Talensi.

See Also
Languages, African: An Overview.

Africa

Tama, ethnic group of north Central Africa.

The Tama primarily inhabit eastern Chad and western Sudan. They speak a Nilo-Saharan language. Approximately 200,000 people consider themselves Tama.

See Also
Languages, African: An Overview.

Africa

Tambo, Oliver (b. October 27, 1917, Bizania, South Africa; d. April 24, 1993, Johannesburg, South Africa), former president of the African National Congress, law partner of Nelson Mandela, and important South African antiapartheid leader.

Oliver Tambo was eulogized at his funeral by longtime friend and partner Nelson Mandela as the man who had made the African National Congress (ANC) "the strongest political force in the country." Raised in a devout Anglican farming family in the Transkei region of South Africa, he described his childhood as politically sheltered. While a student at Fort Hare University, however, Tambo led protests against the administration, resulting in his expulsion in 1942. At Fort Hare Tambo also met Mandela, then a fellow student.

Tambo was teaching science and mathematics at Saint Peter's University (he had received a bachelor's degree in science before his expulsion) when he and Mandela helped form the ANC's Youth League in 1944. The Youth League energized the historically conservative ANC and facilitated the elections of Tambo and Mandela to the ANC's executive body in 1949. In the 1950s Tambo, Mandela, and other ANC leaders led a bold new protest effort, which included mass demonstrations, strikes, boycotts, and acts of civil disobedience. In 1952 Tambo and Mandela combined their experiences as apprentices at a Johannesburg law firm (both positions were arranged by fellow Youth League member Walter Sisulu) and formed South Africa's first black law practice.

In 1956 they and 154 other antiapartheid activists were charged with treason. They were acquitted in 1960, but the government banned the ANC later that year. While Mandela went underground and founded the ANC paramilitary wing Umkhonto we Sizwe, the "Spear of the Nation," Tambo left the country, partly to escape increasingly frequent threats on his life but mostly to recruit international support in the fight against apartheid. After Mandela was captured in 1962 and sentenced to life in prison, it was Tambo who held the ANC together. He was elected ANC president in 1967.

Leading the banned organization from Lusaka, Zambia, Tambo oversaw growing resistance to apartheid, both within and beyond South Africa's borders. By 1981 Umkhonto we Sizwe was carrying out frequent sabotage attacks on police and military bases, government records offices, and other strategic sites. By the mid-1980s international economic sanctions and internal violence had placed enormous strain on the South African government, and Tambo's meetings with leaders in the West helped convince the regime that, in order to avert full-scale civil war, negotiations with the ANC were needed. Tambo suffered a disabling stroke in 1989 but continued as ANC president. In 1990 Mandela was released from prison, and a year later took over the ANC presidency. Tambo's 1993 death came just a year before Mandela was elected president of a newly democratic South Africa.

Kate Tuttle

See Also
Antiapartheid Movement; Mandela, Nelson Rolihlahla.

Latin America and the Caribbean

Tambor de Mina, also called Casa de Mina, an African-derived religion of Brazil, practiced mainly in the northeastern state of Maranhão (*see* Religions, African, in Brazil).

North America

Tampa Red (Hudson Whittaker) (b. December 25, 1900, Smithville, Ga.; d. December 19, 1981, Chicago, Ill.), African American blues guitarist and singer who helped define the urban blues sound in Chicago.

Hudson Whittaker, born Hudson Woodbridge, took the last name of the grandmother who raised him. He adopted the stage name Tampa Red after moving to Chicago in the 1920s. Initially, he played bottleneck slide guitar on recordings for Ma Rainey and Memphis Minnie. Whittaker wrote and performed his first hit, "It's Tight Like That" (1928), with gospel composer and impresario Thomas Dorsey. He formed a quintet in 1932 and continued to perform and record until 1953 when his wife died. In the early 1960s, he made an unsuccessful comeback attempt.

Aaron Myers

See Also
Blues, The; Chicago, Illinois; Dorsey, Thomas Andrew; Gospel Music; Rainey, Gertrude Pridgett ("Ma").

Africa

Tanala, ethnic group of Madagascar.

The Tanala primarily inhabit the highlands of southeastern Madagascar. They speak Malagasy, a Malayo-Polynesian language (*see* Ethnicity in Madagascar). Approximately 400,000 people consider themselves Tanala.

Tananarive, Madagascar. Please see Antananarivo, Madagascar

Africa

Tangale (also known as Biliri and Tangle), ethnic group of Nigeria.

The Tangale primarily inhabit eastern Bauchi State in northeastern Nigeria. They speak an Afro-Asiatic language in the Chadic group. Approximately 200,000 people consider themselves Tangale.

See Also
Languages, African: An Overview.

Africa

Tanganyika. Former name for the mainland of present-day Tanzania.

Africa

Tanganyika, Lake, lake in east Central Africa, in the Great Rift Valley, bordered on the north by Burundi, on the east by Tanzania, on the south by Zambia, and on the west by the Democratic Republic of the Congo. The lake is 676 km (420 mi) long and about 72 km (45 mi) wide at the widest point and covers about 32,900 sq km (12,700 sq mi). The greatest depth is over 1370 m (4500 ft), making it the second-deepest freshwater lake in the world. The only outlet is the Lukuga River, which flows into the Congo River. The lake is noted for its many varieties of fish; crocodiles and hippopotamuses are found on its shores, and the surrounding area is very fertile. The lake was first seen by Europeans in 1858, when the British explorers John Speke and Sir Richard Burton arrived here.

See Also
Explorers in Africa Since 1800; Rift Valleys.

Latin America and the Caribbean

Tango, Argentine dance and musical genre, rooted in a combination of African, European, and native Argentine music and dance traditions.

Often referred to by Argentines as "a sad feeling that can be danced," the tango has become one of the most popular dance and musical forms worldwide. As a dance, the tango requires a couple to be chest-to-chest, in a tight embrace. "As the couple sways and pauses, bodies locked, feet twining in intricate *ochos* (figure eights) and *cortes* (short, rapid steps), it's as if they're carrying on an intensely intimate exchange," writes Chiori Santiago in *Smithsonian* magazine. As a musical form, tango has evolved from improvised dance pieces of the mid- to late nineteenth century – often performed by black and mulatto instrumentalists – to the modern *nuevo tango* compositions of the late Argentine musician Astor Piazzolla (*see* Argentina).

The black community of Buenos Aires played an indirect but significant role in the creation of the tango. By the mid-nineteenth century nearly a quarter of Buenos Aires's inhabitants were black, owing to the city's role as a port of entry for the slave trade in the previous century. Argentine blacks, who resided in poor neighborhoods, succeeded in preserving their culture through community events such as dance and music festivals. The most popular Afro-Argentine dance was the *candombe*, which fused syncopated rhythms and improvised steps from various African traditions. According to the early Argentine scholar of tango, José Gobello, the candombe was the precursor of the tango.

Gobello suggests that contact between Afro-Argentines and the *compadritos* – poor urban street roughs, who recalled in their behavior and dress the nineteenth-century gaucho, or Argentine cowboy – gave rise to the tango at a late 1870s dance venue. In an article published in 1913, Gobello wrote that the Afro-Argentines of Mondongo improvised a dance they called tango, based on the candombe. Some compadritos from Corrales Viejos, the slaughterhouse district of Buenos Aires, saw the dance, and soon after introduced it into their own community. Here the style and movements of the Afro-Argentine tango became fused with the *milonga* – a popular Argentine dance inspired by the European polka and the Cuban *habanera.* As scholar Simon Collier confirms, "The distinctive features of the new dance-form came entirely from the *compadritos* parodistic borrowings from the African-Argentine tradition.... [Yet in the new dance] partners danced *together*, not, as in the African-Argentine 'tango', apart." Many of the early tango musicians were Afro-Argentine: the noted pianist Rosendo Mendizábal played a central role in the development of tango music, while Sebastián Ramos Mejía became the first notable player of the bandoneon – an accordion-like instrument of German origin that later became fundamental to tango music.

The Argentine historian Ricardo Rodríguez Molas contends that the word "tango," which in certain African languages means "closed place" or "reserved ground," is likely to be of African origin. Other scholars have traced the word back to the Latin verb *tangere*, meaning to touch; they believe that African slaves might have picked up the word "tango" from their European captors. In many parts of Latin America "tango" came to connote a place where blacks, both free and enslaved, gathered together to dance; while in Argentina, "tango" came to be associated with black dances in general. "It was in this sense," notes Collier, "that the word eventually reached Spain, as a name for African-American or African-influenced dances of transatlantic provenance."

Before World War II the tango was developed in dance halls, cafés, and brothels in the working-class *barrios* (districts) of Argentina's major cities. By 1913 the tango had become popular among the Argentine middle classes, who contributed to the development of a tango craze in Europe and Russia. By the 1920s Argentina had become one of the world's wealthiest nations. As the focal point of economic and demographic growth, Buenos Aires attracted a massive influx of predominantly Italian and Spanish immigrants. These immigrants introduced new instruments, such as the accordion and mandolin, and contributed to the development of *tango liso,* a style of tango that toned down some of the rougher movements. As Collier affirms, "This early division of dancing styles was fraught with significance for the future: the 'smooth' tango was undoubtedly the forerunner of the ballroom tango of the twentieth century, while the fierce, lubricious aggressiveness favoured in the outer barrios eventually faded away." Since the golden age of tango in the 1920s, tango music and dance have continued to gain popularity worldwide (*see* Dance in Latin America and the Caribbean).

Roanne Edwards

North America

Tanner, Benjamin Tucker

(b. December 25, 1835, Pittsburgh, Pa.; d. January 14, 1923), African American bishop of the African Methodist Episcopal (AME) Church, editor, and writer.

Benjamin Tucker Tanner studied at Avery College from 1852 to 1857 and at Western Theological Seminary from 1857 to 1860. In 1858 he married Sarah Miller. One of their seven children was the painter Henry Ossawa Tanner.

Tanner edited the *Christian Recorder*, an AME publication, from 1868 to 1884, and founded the *A.M.E. Church Review*, a journal devoted to African American concerns, in 1884. After serving as a deacon and then an elder in the AME church, he was consecrated a bishop in 1888 and retired in 1908. He is the author of *An Apology for African Methodism* (1867).

Aaron Myers

See Also

African Methodist Episcopal Church.

North America

Tanner, Henry Ossawa

(b. June 21, 1859, Pittsburgh, Pa; d. May 25, 1937, Paris, France), African American painter who was called "the first genius among Negro artists" by art historian James A. Porter.

The son of a bishop of the African Methodist Episcopal Church, Henry Ossawa Tanner was named after Osawatomie, the site of John Brown's antislavery raid in Kansas. Tanner began painting at age 13, and beginning in 1880 was a student at the Philadelphia Academy of Fine Arts, where he studied with Thomas Eakins. Tanner taught at Clark College in Atlanta, Georgia, from 1889 to 1891, when he relocated to Paris, largely to escape racial prejudice in America. In Paris Tanner took courses at the Académie Julien and, with the exception of two brief visits home in 1893 and 1896, continued to live and paint there until his death in 1937.

While at the Pennsylvania Academy of Design and through 1890, Tanner painted traditional European subjects such as landscapes and animals. In the 1890s, however, Tanner began painting genre scenes of African American life, including his well-known works *The Banjo Lesson* (1893) and *The Thankful Poor* (1894). He is best known, though, for his paintings of biblical subjects, a theme Tanner began exploring in the mid-1890s, most famously in his 1896 painting *The Raising of Lazarus*. From 1894 to 1914 Tanner regularly exhibited his work at the Salon de la Société des Artistes Français in Paris, and after 1900 he also exhibited widely in the United States as well. In 1923 the French government named Tanner a chevalier of the French Legion of Honor.

Aaron Myers

Africa

Tansi, Sony Labou

(b. July 5, 1947, Kimwanza, Belgian Congo; d. June 14, 1995, Foufoundou, Republic of the Congo), renowned Central African novelist, playwright, and poet.

Born Marcel Sony, Tansi moved from his home in what was then the Belgian Congo to independent Congo (now Congo-Brazzaville) in 1959 to attend French schools. Starting in 1971 he worked as a schoolteacher in Brazzaville, and in 1979 he was appointed both to a position with the ministry of culture and to the directorship of the Rocado Zulu Theatre. That same year Tansi published his first novel, *La vie et demie* (Life and a Half), as well as his first play, *Conscience de tracteur* (Tractor Awareness). In the latter Tansi used some of the conventions of science fiction to tell a political parable; the play won second place in a theater competition sponsored by Radio France.

Tansi wrote three more novels in the 1980s – *L'Etat honteux* (1981), *L'Anté-Peuple* (1983), and *Les yeux du volcan* (1988) – and four plays, becoming well known not only throughout Francophone Africa but also in France and elsewhere. Critics hailed his work for its social conscience and rich verbal playfulness. Tansi's fiction is liberally infused with puns, literary allusions, and allegory; he said that he wanted his writing "to contain madness, humor, and tragedy, mixing everything up in the same way life does." Deeply committed to a literature of and for Africa, Tansi wrote about colonialism's "rape" of Africa and the resulting obsession with power in the postcolonial era. Especially in his plays, Tansi explored both the brutality and the dramatic absurdity of dictatorships and dictators.

In 1992 and 1993 Tansi was elected to the national assembly, but never attended. He published his first works of poetry in the 1990s, along with two novels and two plays. He told friends he wanted to write nonfiction, and planned a manifesto arguing for an African Marshall Plan, saying that "Africa is the only continent left that has not found its way." He never finished that work, but his last novel, *The Seven Solitudes of Lorsa Lopez*, was published posthumously in the fall of 1995.

Tansi and his wife, Pierrette, both suffering from acquired immune deficiency syndrome (AIDS), were hospitalized in Paris in the spring of 1995. Returning to Republic of the Congo, they secluded themselves in a small village not far from Brazzaville, where they placed their faith in traditional healing and Christian mysticism. Although he told newspaper reporters that he felt he was getting better under this regimen, Tansi and his wife died in June, only four days apart.

Kate Tuttle

See Also

Brazzaville, Republic of the Congo; Christianity, African: An Overview; Literature, French Language, in Africa; AIDS in Africa: An Interpretation.

Africa

Tanzania,

a country in southeastern Africa comprising former Tanganyika and the island of Zanzibar; bordered by eight countries and the Indian Ocean.

Tanzania defies most perceptions of poor, nonindustrialized nations. The first East African country to achieve independence, Tanzania immediately developed a stable, popularly supported, and democratically elected government that has successfully weathered both its political unification with the historically separate island of Zanzibar and the turmoil of neighbors afflicted with civil conflict, ethnic stratification, and autocratic regimes. Tanzania's economic path has also been different from most. Under the guidance of the country's first president, Julius K. Nyerere, Tanzania attempted to avoid the traps of neocolonialism and foreign dependency, instead embarking on a socialist experiment that sought to achieve local as well as national self-sufficiency. Although the experiment proved an economic disaster – not helped by the fact that much of rural Tanzania is resource-poor – it did raise Tanzania's standards of social welfare above those of most of its wealthier neighbors. Today Tanzania continues to struggle with widespread poverty, but progressive leaders have enabled the nation to seize new economic opportunities, and some observers note promising signs of recovery.

Precolonial History

Early human history in Tanzania centers on the Great Rift Valley, which served as home and highway for the region's first inhabitants. Among them were two of the world's oldest known hominids – *Zinjanthropus boisei* and *Homo habilis* – whose remains were discovered by archaeologist Mary Leakey at Olduvai Gorge in the 1960s. Although evidence is inconclusive, it appears that many of the early stages of human evolution may have occurred in Tanzanian sections of the Rift Valley several million years ago. It was not until 10,000 years ago, however, that human societies began to settle in Tanzania. The first were Khoisan-speaking foragers who established residence in small villages throughout the eastern Rift Valley. Around the first millennium B.C.E. they were joined by Cushitic-speaking people who migrated along the Rift Valley from Ethiopia. Finally, Bantu speakers emigrated to Tanzania and settled in the western mountainous region around the first millennium C.E.

For several hundred years these groups lived in small communities with relatively little interaction. In the tenth century seminomadic Nilotic-speaking groups, which had been gradually migrating from the north and northwest, settled in East Africa. Although some, such as the Maasai, retained their

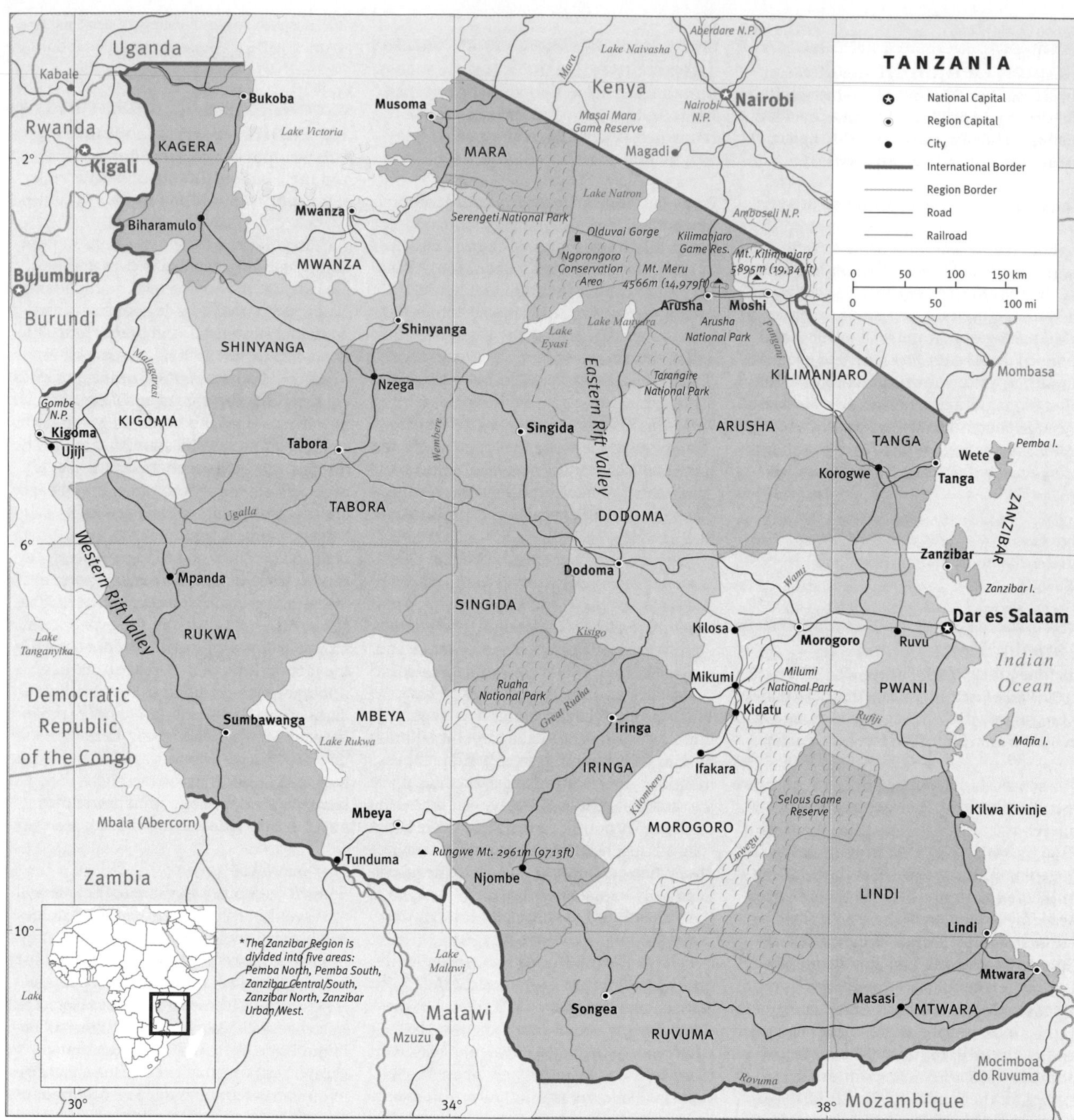

seminomadic lifestyle, most Nilotics settled in permanent villages, and in some cases assimilated with Bantu speakers.

Even after centuries of migration, human settlements in the East African interior remained small, scattered, and self-governing. Consequently, few foreign travelers or traders ventured through the interior's thick bush until the eighteenth century, when traders employed by the sultan of Zanzibar and financed by Indian merchants (*see* Indian Communities in Africa) began leading caravans inland, seeking slaves and ivory. Although a few interior groups – such as the Nyamwezi – began participating in the trade around 1800, their control over routes was limited by the well-armed and well-organized coastal traders. By 1830 Arab-Swahili traders had established routes from the coast to Lake Tanganyika and the kingdom of Buganda and built trading posts in Tabora and Ujiji. Despite these advances, the sultan's power remained weak in the interior, a fact that would later facilitate German colonialism in East Africa.

Scramble for Africa

By the mid-nineteenth century the sultan of Zanzibar had established amicable relations with most European powers, who saw the island as an ideal launching point for European forays into mainland Africa. On the understanding that land was easily attainable on the East African coast, the Society for German Colonization sent Dr. Carl Peters on an exploratory mission in November 1884. Within two months Peters acquired roughly 6500 sq km (2500 sq mi) through treaties with mainland chiefs. Peters subsequently used these treaties to persuade the ambivalent German government that African colonization was an easy way to acquire land and to divert the attention of their European rivals away from Europe. In February 1885 German emperor Wilhelm I and Chancellor Otto von Bismarck acquiesced and granted a government charter to Peters's German East Africa Company.

The company immediately tried to consolidate power in the region. Feeling threatened by Barghash ibn Sa'id, the sultan of Zanzibar, the Germans met secretly with the British in 1886 and created a German protectorate north of the Ruvuma River and south of the present-day border between Kenya and

Tanzania. Although the Europeans permitted the sultanate to maintain control over the coastal islands and a small strip of coast, two years later the Germans forced the sultan to cede the mainland strip. All of these actions were facilitated by the British, who exercised tremendous influence on Barghash.

German East Africa

The German East Africa Company's attempts to establish colonial rule in East Africa met immediate resistance. The sultan is widely believed to have encouraged revolt among the Swahili peoples on the coast who resented the Germans' tax policies and considered Germans to be unpleasant drunkards with little respect for Islam. In the interior, resistance came from both Arab merchants who feared losing their trading routes and village chiefs who resented the German requisition of their village labor. United by their discontent, people throughout the region formed small military bands in the coastal towns from which they initiated attacks on the Germans in August 1888. After two years of fighting the German colonialists appeared to be near defeat. In March 1891, however, they brought in battleship mercenaries from Mozambique and Sudan, and their sheer firepower quickly overwhelmed resistance forces.

Once the company established control, it began building a colonial economy based on the production of export crops, especially coffee and tea. The administration seized land for plantations, conscripted African laborers, and forced Africans to grow export crops on their own land. It also confiscated land to give to newly arrived German settlers.

This *dhow*, sailing before a mangrove swamp on the edge of the Indian Ocean, differs little from the vessels that aided early Swahili traders in their role as East Africa's primary middlemen in the Indian Ocean economy. *M & E Bernheim*

In 1902 German governor Count Adolf von Götzen added to the list of obligatory crops cotton, which was difficult to cultivate and hard on the soil. Already strained by colonial taxes and labor policies, Africans soon rebelled against the mandate. On July 31, 1905, the Matumbi people, led by Abdullah Mapanda, initiated an attack, later called the Maji-Maji Rebellion, which forced German colonists in the southern coastal area out of their homes. The Germans retaliated with a scorched earth campaign that killed between 75,000 and 120,000 Africans – out of a population of 2 million – and provoked international outrage.

Shortly thereafter, the German government took control of the colony, instituted reforms, and began providing basic services, such as public education for Africans. Only a few years later World War I began, and Great Britain soon occupied most of German East Africa. After the defeat of the Axis powers the League of Nations gave Great Britain control of the territory, and it was renamed Tanganyika.

Tanganyika

Although Tanganyika was technically an internationally mandated territory, Great Britain treated it as a new colony. In 1925 Sir Donald Cameron was appointed governor and created a government based on indirect rule, a British colonial policy that attempted to use "native authority" as the foundation for colonial administration. Although this policy worked relatively well in areas historically governed by hierarchical states, most ethnic groups in Tanganyika had no tradition of centralized political authority. Consequently, the British imposed an invented hierarchy on many ethnic groups and nominated chiefs to collect taxes, recruit labor, and enforce other colonial mandates. Thus many appointed chiefs commanded little respect among their "subjects," and often proved either unable or unwilling to carry out their duties.

Like the Germans, the British based the colonial economy on export crops that were produced both on plantations and peasant farms. To ensure an adequate supply of plantation labor, the British encouraged village families to move to the plantations by building educational and health facilities nearby, and by offering technical support and price incentives for crops grown on the family's land. Although the "plant-more-crops" campaign did increase cash crop production considerably, it also led to the dangerous neglect of food crops. With the majority of fertile land devoted exclusively to export crops, Tanganyika was affected by several serious food shortages during the interwar years.

Although plantation communities may have disrupted precolonial social systems, they did foster the formation of African associations and community collectives that would later provide the foundation for political organizing. Some groups, including Bahaya Union, the Haya civic association, began in agricultural communities such as Bukoba. Others, such as the Tanganyika African Association, a multiethnic welfare agency and social club formed in 1927, originated in Dar es Salaam and then spread to the rural communities, where it ultimately merged with the extremely popular Tanganyika African National Union (TANU). These groups were among the first to contest British post-World War II agricultural policies and political reforms and to initiate the independence movement.

After World War II two competing requirements were imposed on Tanganyika: increased agricultural export production, in order to help rebuild Great Britain's postwar economy, and demonstrable progress toward self-government, as mandated by new United Nations regulations. To comply with the latter, the colonial administration made "native" authorities responsible for devising and implementing development plans with funds available from government agencies. In addition Governor Sir Edward Twining tried to implement self-rule by creating local councils, for which he required equal representation for the unequal populations of Europeans, Asians, and Africans, even in areas with small or nonexistent European or Asian populations. These plans were at best ineffective, but more often they provoked serious and even violent opposition, which soon found a collective voice in one organization: TANU.

Created in 1954, TANU was led by a dynamic schoolteacher, JULIUS KAMBARAGE NYERERE, who immediately announced the organization's goal to be nothing less than self-governance without ethnic or racial divisions. Nyerere launched a massive recruitment campaign, and within a year TANU had become the largest political organization in Tanganyika. Emboldened by popular support, it entered candidates in the 1958-1959 elections for the Tanganyika Legislative Council, an advisory group that had always been dominated by non-Africans. Governor Twining managed to keep TANU members largely out of the Council by reserving two-thirds of the seats for Europeans and Asians, and by restricting voter registration.

With tensions clearly mounting in the colony, the British government replaced Twining with a new governor, Sir Richard Turnbull, who was instructed to guide Tanganyika toward gradual decolonization. In subsequent elections for the Legislative Council and for a new government of internal affairs, TANU candidates easily triumphed and Nyerere was named chief minister. In this position Nyerere guided Tanganyika toward self-rule and on December 9, 1961, became prime minister of an independent Tanganyika.

UNITED REPUBLIC OF TANZANIA

After independence Nyerere immediately instituted a number of major changes to complete the process of decolonization. Casting off the British model, he hired Tanganyikan citizens to fill civil servant positions and restructured the government into a one-party republic of which he was elected president. Soon afterward he offered assistance to the troubled island of Zanzibar, and on April 26, 1964, the two formed a union later called the United Republic of Tanzania. In this new arrangement Nyerere was named president and Zanzibari president Sheikh Abeid Amani Karume became one of two vice presidents, but the mainland and the island retained mostly autonomous control of internal affairs.

In addition to building a government, Nyerere sought to forge a sense of national identity. His first step was to facilitate dialogue among Tanzania's 120 different ethnic groups, such as the Ha, SUKUMA, CHAGGA, MAKONDE, and IRAQW. He achieved this goal in part by making Swahili the official national language and mandating that it be universally taught. Soon Swahili became the lingua franca even in areas where it had not been widely used before.

Upon election to a second term in 1965, Nyerere articulated the goals that would guide his policies for the next 20 years: to bring a moral order to international affairs and to build Tanzania into a self-sufficient nation free of neocolonial dependencies. Both goals quickly defined Tanzania as one of the "radical" post-colonial African states and distinguished it from its pro-Western neighbor, Kenya.

Of the two goals Nyerere had greater success with the first. Within months of his reelection Nyerere began asserting his views on international affairs, particularly the events of southern Africa. In December 1965 Tanzania broke diplomatic relations with Great Britain over its support for the white-ruled government of colonial Rhodesia (now ZIMBABWE). Shortly afterward Nyerere launched an anti-apartheid campaign and urged neighboring nations to boycott South African goods and divest from South African companies. In subsequent years Nyerere supported independence causes in the Portuguese colonies of ANGOLA and Mozambique and denounced South Africa's occupation of NAMIBIA. In addition, he ordered the 1978 Tanzanian military invasion of Uganda in opposition to its dictator, IDI AMIN. By the time he stepped down from office in 1985, Nyerere's statesmanship had won international respect, and he has continued to play an active diplomatic role in African affairs.

The setting sun gilds the facades of houses in Zanzibar Old Town, Tanzania, which is the capital of the Zanzibar region. *© P. Maille/Explorer*

Nyerere's attempt to build a debt-free and self-sufficient national economy was less successful. In 1967 he announced the Arusha Declaration, in which he described his vision of AFRICAN SOCIALISM, which drew on Maoist principles of rural mobilization but incorporated what he called "traditional" African values and social organization. He also outlined the specific measures needed to realize this vision. The engine of economic and social development would be large, collectivized villages; the driving ideology would be *ujamaa*, "familyhood." The government ordered millions of peasants into the communal villages and by 1977 more than 13 million people (about 80 percent of the population) had been resettled into more than 8000 ujamaa villages.

Although rural collectivization did improve access to clean water, health care, and schools – helping Tanzanians become one of the most literate populations in sub-Saharan Africa – it failed to increase agricultural productivity and in fact did the opposite. The villages tended to be overcrowded, and the surrounding lands were usually incapable of supporting dense populations. Many people continued to depend on farmland they had left behind for food, and women, in particular, commonly worked daily both on communal fields and on their family's farms several kilometers away. By the late 1970s it was evident that ujamaa had failed to create a sustainable economy, and Tanzania was forced to take out loans from donor countries and the International Monetary Fund (IMF).

As Tanzania sank further into debt, international donors threatened to stop assistance until the government undertook major economic reforms, including liberalization and privatization. Unwilling to enact these reforms himself, Nyerere offered to step down from office, although he remained president of the Tanzanian socialist party, Charma Cha Mapinduzi (CCM, formerly TANU). In 1985 ALI HASSAN MWINYI was elected president. During the next ten years Mwinyi attempted to revive the national economy. Despite Nyerere's protests of his successor's willingness to "starve the children to pay the debts," Mwinyi accepted and implemented stiff IMF austerity measures. In addition, Mwinyi privatized businesses, authorized the country's first private bank, and led a campaign against government corruption. Although he failed to eradicate either debt or corruption, Mwinyi did initiate the transition to a multiparty state and promoted free speech. He completed his term in 1995 after the election of CCM member Benjamin Mkapa.

As president, Mkapa has been forced to address a number of difficult problems, of which the most visible is the country's lagging and debt-saddled economy. In an effort to balance the budget and increase government revenue, he has downsized the civil service and enacted stringent new laws against tax evasion. He has also cracked down on gold and gemstone smuggling in Dar es Salaam and Magauzo, which, like other black markets, has long diverted a significant amount of potential government revenue. Much more than his predecessors, Mkapa has tried to attract international investment and revive trade relations in the East African Community (which includes Uganda and Kenya). Finally, Mkapa has taken steps to promote the country's tourist industry, particularly along Zanzibar and the mainland coast, and in the many national parks around Arusha, including the Serengeti, Taragnire, Arusha national parks, Mount Kilimanjaro, and Olduvai Gorge.

The Tanzanian government's scarce resources have limited its capacity to confront a number of noneconomic problems. One of the most difficult is an epidemic of acquired immune deficiency syndrome (AIDS) – estimated to affect more than 1 million people in Tanzania – for which adequate care and medication are not available. In addition, Mkapa has had to address environmental concerns, such as urban pollution and wildlife and forest conservation, on a budget that makes it difficult to catch and punish industrial polluters and poachers. Finally, Mkapa has played a relatively active role in regional affairs, particularly in the civil conflicts with neighboring Rwanda and Burundi. He has recently come under attack for his decision to close the border with Burundi in order to prevent the entrance of new refugees, whom the Tanzanian government is financially unable to support.

Elizabeth Heath

See Also

Antiapartheid Movement; Bantu: Dispersion and Settlement; Buganda, Early Kingdom of; Dar es Salaam, Tanzania; Barghash ibn Said; Decolonization in Africa: An Interpretation; Explorers in Africa Since 1800; Kilimanjaro; Ivory Trade; Languages, African: An Overview; Swahili Language; Leakey, Mary Douglas Nicol; United Nations in Africa; Rift Valleys; Serengeti National Park; South Africa; Swahili People; AIDS in Africa: An Interpretation; Indian Ocean Slave Trade.

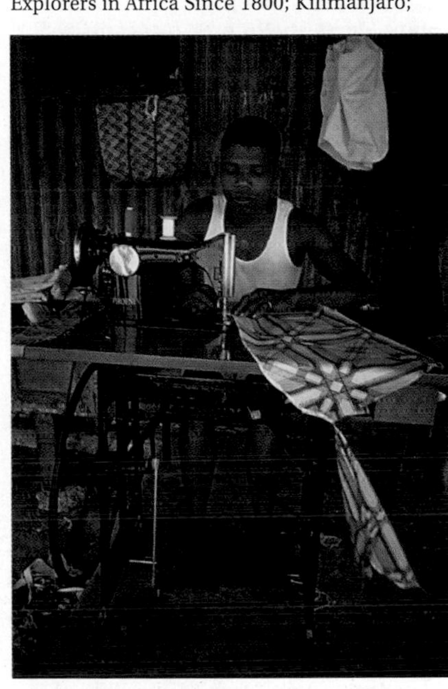

LEFT: Only ruins remain of the mosque at what was once Kilwa Kisiwani, an Islamic city-state that flourished from the eleventh to the fifteenth century. *M & E Bernheim*
ABOVE: A Tanzanian man stitches up garments on a treadle-powered sewing machine. *CORBIS/Jack Fields*

Africa

Tanzania (Ready Reference)

Official Name: United Republic of Tanzania
Former Names: United Republic of Tanganyika and Zanzibar
Area: 945,087 sq km (364,898 sq mi)
Location: Eastern Africa, on the Indian Ocean, bordered by Burundi, Kenya, Malawi, Mozambique, Rwanda, Uganda, the Democratic Republic of the Congo, Zambia

Capital: Dar es Salaam (population 1,651,534 [1995 estimate])
Other Major Cities: Mwanza (population 2,280,206); Tanga (population 1,590,381); Zanzibar (population 456,934); Dodoma (population 1,502,344) (1995 estimates)
Population: 30,608,769 (1998 estimate)
Population Density: 55 persons per sq km (about 88 persons per sq mi [1998 estimate])
Population Below Age 15: 45 percent (male 6,804,194; female 6,844,815 [1998 estimate])
Population Growth Rate: 2.14 percent (1998 estimate)
Total Fertility Rate: 5.5 children born per woman (1998 estimate)
Life Expectancy at Birth: Total population: 46.37 years (male 44.22 years; female 48.59 years [1998 estimate])
Infant Mortality Rate: 96.94 deaths per 1000 live births (1998 estimate)
Literacy Rate (age 15 and over who can read and write): Total population: 67.8 percent (male 79.4 percent; female 56.8 percent [1995 estimate])
Education: Primary education in Tanzania is compulsory, but only 50 percent of eligible children are enrolled because not enough schools are available. Adult education campaigns have contributed to relatively high literacy rates. In the early 1990s government schools were attended annually by some 3.5 million elementary pupils and about 167,000 secondary students. In addition, many children attended private schools, which were mostly run by religious groups.
Languages: Tanzania's official languages are English and Swahili, and the latter is almost universally understood. Many people, however, continue to use the language of their ethnic group.
Ethnic groups: The SUKUMA and the NYAMWEZI represent about one-fifth of the population. Other significant groups include the HAYA, Ngonde, CHAGGA, Gogo, Ha, Hehe, Nyakyusa, Nyika, NGONI, YAO, and MAASAI. The population also includes people of Indian, Pakistani, and Goan origin, and small Arab and European communities.
Religions: About one-third of the population follow traditional religions. About one-third practice Islam. Catholicism is the largest Christian denomination of Tanzania, with some 6 million adherents.
Climate: On the mainland coastal strip along the Indian Ocean the climate is warm and tropical, with temperatures averaging 27° C (80° F) and annual rainfall varying from 750 to 1400 mm (30 to 55 in). The inland plateau is hot and dry, with annual rainfall averaging as little as 500 mm (20 in). The climate on the islands is generally tropical, but the heat is tempered by a sea breeze throughout the year. The annual mean temperature for the city of Zanzibar is 29° C (85° F) maximum, and 25° C (77° F) minimum; for Wete in Pemba, 30° C (86° F) maximum and 24° C (76° F) minimum.
Land, Plants, and Animals: Mainland Tanzania is generally flat and low along the coast, but a plateau at an average altitude of about 1200 m (about 4000 ft) constitutes the greater part of the country. Isolated mountain groups rise in the northeast and southwest. The volcanic KILIMANJARO (5895 m/19,340 ft), the highest mountain in Africa, is located near the northeastern border. Three of the great lakes of Africa lie on the borders of the country and partially within it. LAKE TANGANYIKA is located on the western border, LAKE VICTORIA on the northwest, and LAKE MALAWI (Nyasa) on the southwest. Lakes Nyasa and Tanganyika lie in the Great Rift Valley, a tremendous geological fault system extending from the Middle East to Mozambique. Zanzibar, separated from the mainland by a 40-km (25-mi) channel, is about 90 km (55 mi) long and covers an area of 1658 sq km (640 sq mi). It is the largest coral island off the coast of Africa. Pemba, some 40 km (25 mi) northwest of Zanzibar, is about 68 km (42 mi) long and has an area of approximately 984 sq km (380 sq mi). Wildlife includes ANTELOPE, ZEBRA, ELEPHANT, HIPPOPOTAMUS, RHINOCEROS, GIRAFFE, LION, leopard, CHEETAH, and monkey. Tanzania's national parks, among them SERENGETI NATIONAL PARK, are home to many of these species.
Natural Resources: Diamonds, coal and iron ore, and hardwood forests
Currency: The Tanzanian shilling
Gross National Product (GDP): $21.1 billion (1997 estimate)
GDP per Capita: $700 (1997 estimate)
GDP Real Growth Rate: 4.3 percent (1997 estimate)
Primary Economic Activities: Agriculture, industry, services, and mining
Primary Crops: Coffee, sisal, tea, cotton, pyrethrum (insecticide made from chrysanthemums), cashews, tobacco, cloves (Zanzibar), corn, wheat, cassava (tapioca), bananas, fruits, and vegetables; cattle, sheep, and goats
Industries: Agricultural processing (sugar, beer, cigarettes, sisal twine), diamond and gold mining, oil refining, shoes, cement, textiles, wood products, and fertilizer
Primary Exports: Coffee, cotton, tobacco, tea, cashew nuts, and sisal
Primary Imports: Manufactured goods, machinery and transportation equipment, cotton piece goods, crude oil, and foodstuffs
Primary Trade Partners: Germany, United Kingdom, United States, Japan, Italy, Denmark, Netherlands, Kenya, and China
Government: Tanzania is governed under a constitution of 1977, as amended. The internal affairs of Zanzibar are administered under a constitution of 1985. Tanzania's chief executive is a popularly elected president, who serves a five-year term. The president (Benjamin Mkapa since November 22, 1995) appoints a vice president, prime minister (Fredrick Sumaye since November 27, 1995), and cabinet. Tanzania's legislature is the multiparty unicameral National Assembly. Of its 244 members, 169 (119 from the mainland and 50 from Zanzibar) are popularly elected to terms of up to five years. Most of the rest of the members are either elected by the National Assembly, appointed by the president, or sit by virtue of being commissioners of the country's regions.

Robert Fay

SEE ALSO

Dar es Salaam, Tanzania; Chimpanzee; Indian Communities in Africa; Swahili Language; Rift Valleys.

North America

Tap Dance, art form indigenous to the United States that combines African and European dance with a complicated JAZZ-based percussive sensibility created by elaborate footwork.

Tap dance originated in the cross-fertilization of African and Anglo-European cultures in the New World. During the 1600s the social dances of Irish and Scottish indentured laborers were fused with African Juba and ring dances. Slaves in the southern United States imitated the rapid toe and heel action of the Irish jig and the percussive sensibility of the Lancashire clog, danced in wooden shoes. Combined with West African body movements and rhythms, these new dances were the forerunners of the buck-and-wing dancing and clogging of the southern United States and of modern-day tap dancing.

The names of the innovators from the early slave community went unrecorded. When the slave dances were adapted theatrically for minstrel shows in the late 1820s, individual artists began to be recognized, though the first of these performers were black-faced white minstrels. William Henry Lane was the first African American to rise to prominence on the minstrel stage. Described by music historian Eileen Southern as "a link between the white world and authentic black source materials; [whose] dancing contributed to the preservation of artistic integrity in the performance of black dances on the minstrel stage," Lane is a legendary figure in the history of tap. Known as Master Juba, Lane was born free in Rhode Island in the 1820s and began his career in the dance halls of Manhattan's notorious "Five Points" district. Mastering the moves of the slave dances and the routines of white minstrels, Lane's agility and grace made him the only African American to perform on the whites-only minstrel stages of the antebellum era.

When the ban on black performers on the minstrel stage was lifted after the Civil War, these venues became the site of numerous innovations in steps and choreography. Alongside the increasingly popular vaudeville performance of the late 1800s, the exposure that the minstrel stage offered helped launch the Broadway careers of performers such as Williams and Walker (BERT WILLIAMS and George Walker), Ulysses "Slow Kid" Thompson, and Bill Bailey while also forging the aesthetics of Broadway jazz dance and the Broadway musical. Behind them were many master tap dancers, including King Rastus Brown, who were born too soon to be accepted on the white stages.

Broadway ushered in a golden age for tap. The combination of sharply choreographed chorus lines performing to RAGTIME and early jazz with tap and other vernacular dances proved a hit with audiences and critics. During this period the marquee performers popularly associated with the genre – such as Bill "Bojangles" Robinson – rose to prominence. Robinson combined an irresistible onstage persona with his impeccably timed routines, becoming the best-known hoofer of his generation.

John "Bubbles" Sublett is widely acknowledged as the most innovative dancer of the era. Part of the popular duo "Buck and Bubbles" (with Ford Lee "Buck" Washington), Sublett played the original Sportin' Life in *Porgy and Bess*. He was also the inventor of rhythm tap. While most tap dancers performed on their toes before launching into a flashy routine of kicks and splits, Sublett reemphasized the percussive aspect of tap and reintroduced it to a jazz idiom. He switched its accenting and dropped his heel to give his performances a more syncopated sound. By slowing his tempo, he was able to add more steps. In addition, Sublett extended his combinations over a previously unheard-of number of bars, aligning himself with the polyrhythmic movements of jazz.

If Broadway and, later, Hollywood cinema, gave tap its greatest exposure, the Hoofer's Club provided its unofficial academy. Both rookies and veterans gathered at this small venue next to Harlem's LAFAYETTE THEATRE, whose fiercely competitive atmosphere produced a stunning array of fresh routines. Dancers would watch, imitate, and steal each other's moves in an effort to gain prominence among their peers.

By the 1930s tap had become an integral part of Hollywood musicals. Prominent African American dancers, including Robinson, Sublett, the NICHOLAS BROTHERS, and the Berry Brothers, were often featured, but Hollywood best served the careers of whites such as Shirley Temple and Fred Astaire. Their success further popularized tap, making it the premier form of theatrical dance in the United States. Yet some critics have suggested that as whites became more closely aligned with tap, its integrity was compromised as its meter became regimented and its percussive and improvisational aspects were deemphasized.

By the 1950s tap dance had fallen out of vogue with American audiences, and many preeminent dancers were unable to find work. Many dancers link tap's decline to a number of phenomena including Agnes de Mille's ballet-influenced choreography for the 1943 production of *Oklahoma!* and the rise of modern jazz dance – both of which created new paradigms for popular dance – and also the demise of the big bands, night clubs, and theaters that provided the performance culture in which tap was embedded.

In the 1970s tap underwent a resurgence. Buoyed by a series of documentaries, films, television specials, and live performances – and the emergence of ambassadors such as Gregory and Rupert Hines – tap began a popular revival. By the 1990s, as the long run of the young, dreadlocked virtuoso Savion Glover's highly acclaimed Broadway show *Bring In da Noise, Bring In da Funk* attests, tap has regained its place as one of the most important American dance forms.

Peter Hudson

SEE ALSO

Buck and Bubbles; Civil War, American; Harlem, New York; Hines, Gregory; Minstrelsy; Robinson, Bill ("Bojangles").

North America

Tatum, Art (b. October 13, 1909, Toledo, Ohio; d. November 5, 1956, Los Angeles, Calif.), African American jazz pianist whose harmonic and technical innovations set new standards in JAZZ music during the 1930s, 1940s, and 1950s.

Art Tatum was born partially blind, his vision impaired by cataracts in both eyes. He began playing the piano as a child, using his keen ear to imitate songs he heard on the radio. Encouraged by his musically inclined parents, Tatum also learned to play accordion, guitar, and violin at a young age. He further developed himself as a musician at the Cousino School for the Blind in Columbus, Ohio, and at the Toledo School of Music.

Tatum's career took off in 1929 when he began to play regularly for a Toledo radio station. After being hired by singer Adelaide Hall in 1932, Tatum went to New York City, where he performed at 52nd Street nightclubs. Over the course of the following decade he toured the United States and England, electrifying audiences with his virtuosity. As a member of a jazz trio featuring guitarist Tiny Grimes and bassist Slam Stewart, he enjoyed continued success from 1944 until his death in 1956. Tatum's bold exploration of extended harmonies deeply influenced the birth of bebop.

Tatum first recorded in 1933, after his arrival in New York City. While he intermittently collaborated with other jazz musicians on recordings, he is best known for his solo performances, of which he recorded more than 100 between 1953 and 1955. Two of his outstanding renditions of popular songs are "Tea for Two" (1933) and "Rosetta" (1944). Tatum's dexterity was so refined that he could play the piano just as effectively with the backs of his fingers, palms up, as with the tips of his fingers, palms down.

Aaron Myers

SEE ALSO

New York, New York.

Africa

Taya, Maaouya Ould Sidi Ahmed (b. 1943), president of MAURITANIA (1984-).

Born in Atar, in western Mauritania, Maaouya Ould Sidi Taya received advanced military training after joining the Mauritanian army. He served as aide-de-camp (military assistant) to MOKTAR OULD DADDAH, Mauritania's first president and deputy chief of operations and commander in the northern region during the war against POLISARIO Front, the nationalist movement in adjacent WESTERN SAHARA. Taya was appointed deputy chief of staff in 1978 and, after Daddah was deposed later that year, minister of defense. In July 1980, after another coup, Taya became army chief of staff and in April 1981 prime minister, but was demoted back to army chief of staff in early 1984 by President Mohamed Ould Haidalla, who considered Taya a threatening political rival. Taya responded, in December 1984, by leading a bloodless coup.

In one of his first acts as president, Taya formally recognized the independence of Polisario's Sahrawi Arab Democratic Republic in Western Sahara, initially heightening tensions with neighboring MOROCCO (which occupies Western Sahara); diplomatic relations with Morocco were restored in April 1985. Domestically, he appointed civilians to government posts and drafted a new constitution in 1991 that both consolidated his power and allowed for the registration of opposition parties. In January 1992 Taya, backed by the newly formed Democratic and Social Republican Party, was elected to a six-year term as president amidst protests of fraudulent election practices. Taya included an opposition member in his new, civilian-dominated cabinet. Taya's economic reforms, including currency devaluation and other austerity measures, provoked violent protests. Ethnic clashes, between those of sub-Saharan descent and those of North African descent, have also produced tension both within Mauritania – with government purges of dark-skinned army officers and violent repression of protests against the institution of Islam as the state religion – and with neighboring SENEGAL, where nearly 200,000 Mauritanian refugees reside.

SEE ALSO

Islamic Fundamentalism: An Interpretation.

Africa

Taylor, Charles Ghankay

(b. January 28, 1948, Liberia), rebel leader and president of Liberia, elected in 1997.

By the time Charles Taylor won election on July 19, 1997, he had already considered himself Liberia's president for nearly seven years. Little is known about the former rebel leader's early life. The son of an American father and an Americo-Liberian mother, Taylor was born in Liberia but left for the United States in the early 1970s and attended Bentley College in Massachusetts, from which he graduated in 1977.

Although a member of Liberia's elite, in the United States Taylor joined with fellow Liberian expatriates in denouncing the Americo-Liberian domination of his country's government, then headed by President William Tolbert. Soon after Samuel K. Doe led a military overthrow of Tolbert in 1980, Taylor returned to Liberia and became one of Doe's advisers, as well as the director of the government's General Services Agency. Three years later he was accused of embezzling $900,000. Taylor fled to Boston, Massachusetts, where he was soon arrested on the Liberian warrant. Rather than return to face charges, Taylor escaped from prison and made his way back to Africa, where he spent the next several years traveling and building support for an anti-Doe movement.

Along with other exiled Liberians, Taylor became involved in the National Patriotic Front of Liberia (NPFL), and by the late 1980s had become its leader. On Christmas Day, 1989, he led NPFL forces in an attack on Liberia's northern Nimba County. Within months Taylor's rebels had taken control of most of the countryside, and Doe was effectively trapped in Monrovia, the capital. Prince Yormie Johnson, leader of a rival rebel group, assassinated Doe in September 1990, leading to a transitional government headed by Dr. Amos Sawyer, a moderate professor.

Over the next seven years Taylor, who had declared himself president in October 1990, consolidated his power over the Liberian population. The NPFL controlled the interior's transportation, commerce, and banking systems, and won over supporters from the ethnic groups historically at odds with the Krahn, who had dominated the Doe government. But Taylor's bid to elicit United States support faltered as he was charged with repeated human rights abuses (*see* Human Rights in Africa), including the military conscription of children and the assassination of rivals. His increasing use of foreign soldiers also put him in conflict with neighboring governments, which feared the NPFL would set off a broader regional conflict.

After years of fighting among the NPFL, other dissident factions, and ECOMOG (the monitoring group of the Economic Union of West African States, a multinational peace-keeping force whose proclaimed neutrality Taylor repeatedly attacked), Liberia held elections in July 1997. Unlike the previous election in 1985, which Doe was widely believed to have won through fraud, most international observers believe the 1997 voting was legitimate. Taylor, representing the newly formed National Patriotic Party, won about 75 percent of the vote. In the months following the election, questions remained about Taylor's pledge to lead Liberia as a modern, progressive president. The silencing of independent media and the unsolved murder of a former rival generated fears that Taylor had returned to his warlord past, but Taylor has also brought in respected financial advisors and made efforts to fight corruption.

Kate Tuttle

See Also

Americo-Liberians; Doe, Samuel Kanyon; Tolbert, William Richard, Jr.; Monrovia, Liberia.

North America

Taylor, Gardner Calvin

(b. June 8, 1918, Baton Rouge, La.), African American Baptist minister known as the "Dean of Black Preachers" who led church support for the civil rights struggle.

With a bachelor's degree from Leland College, Gardner C. Taylor began his theological training at Oberlin Theological Seminary in 1937. He was ordained a Baptist minister in 1939, and he followed his theological degree (1940) with pastorates in New Orleans and Baton Rouge.

In 1948 Taylor moved to New York City to preach at the Concord Baptist Church of Christ in the Bedford-Stuyvesant section of Brooklyn. He was a dynamic leader, establishing social service programs such as a nursing home and clothing exchange. In 1962, with 12,000 members, the church became the largest Protestant congregation in the United States. Taylor was known internationally for the brilliance of his preaching, and was called the best preacher in America.

An active proponent of educational reform, Taylor risked his position on the New York City Board of Education in 1958 to support the demand for better school conditions for African American children. He served on the Citywide Committee for Integrated Schools, and in 1961 he and his wife, Laura, founded the Concord Elementary Day School.

During the 1960s Taylor rose to prominence as a civil rights leader through his involvement in the Congress of Racial Equality (CORE). During this time he worked closely with a group of Baptist ministers that included the Reverend Martin Luther King Jr. In 1961, dissatisfied with the leadership of Joseph H. Jackson, the group split from the National Baptist Convention, USA, Inc. The newly formed Progressive National Baptist Convention (PNBC) publicly supported civil rights struggles of CORE and the Southern Christian Leadership Conference (SCLC).

Renowned for his mastery of the spoken word, Taylor continued to serve as a visiting and guest preacher after his retirement in 1990 from Concord Baptist Church of Christ.

Marian Aguiar

See Also

Baptists; Civil Rights Movement; King, Martin Luther, Jr.; New York, New York; New Orleans, Louisiana.

North America

Taylor, Koko (Cora Walton)

(b. September 28, 1935, Memphis, Tenn.), African American blues singer and a master of the electric Chicago blues style, known as the "Queen of the Blues."

The youngest of six children, Koko Taylor – whose name was originally Cora Walton – was born in Memphis, Tennessee. Her sharecropper father brought the children up after their mother's death in 1939. Taylor's father raised cotton, and she and her siblings worked in the fields. Taylor began singing gospel music in church, but she listened to the blues and rhythm and blues (R&B) broadcasts of B. B. King and Rufus Thomas (b. 1917) on Memphis's black radio station, WDIA. "The first blues record I ever heard," she recalled, "was 'Me and My Memphis Blues,' by Memphis Minnie [Douglas (1897-1973)]. I was 12 or 13, and just loved it."

At age 18 Taylor met truck driver Robert "Pops" Taylor. When he decided to leave Tennessee to work in a Chicago slaughterhouse, Taylor married him and moved north. In 1953 Taylor arrived in Chicago, part of a vast migration of African Americans leaving the South for greater opportunities in the urban North and West. She arrived in Chicago at the height of the new Chicago blues style, which featured electric guitars in small combos and used heavier, more driving rhythms than traditional rural blues. During the week she worked cleaning suburban homes, but she spent her weekends in Chicago's South Side blues bars.

During the mid-1950s Chicago's South Side nightspots featured such blues musicians as guitarist and singer Muddy Waters, the person most responsible for creating the Chicago blues style; harmonica player and vocalist Howlin' Wolf; guitarist and vocalist Buddy Guy (b. 1936); and guitarist, harmonica player, and vocalist Jimmy Reed (1925-1976). Taylor began sitting in with various performers, joining them on the stand to sing. Her powerful and rough-edged singing – in particular, her use of growling, raspy effects – quickly attracted attention. Taylor's singing reflected the influence not only of female blues singers Big Mama Thornton and Bessie Smith, but also bluesmen Muddy Waters and Howlin' Wolf, but she quickly forged her own distinctive style.

One evening in 1962, bass player and composer Willie Dixon, a prominent figure in the Chicago blues community, heard Taylor perform. Dixon took Taylor under his wing, and her career took off. In 1963 she made her recording debut, recording her own "Honky Tonky" for the small record label USA, but she soon signed a contract with Chess Records, Chicago's leading blues recording company. Taylor's 1966 rendition of Dixon's "Wang Dang Doodle" became a million-selling recording and gave Chess Records its last Top Ten R&B hit.

During the early 1970s interest in blues music waned, and Taylor dropped from sight until signing with Alligator Records in 1974. The first of her six albums for Alligator, *I Got What It Takes* (1975), was nominated for a Grammy Award. There were many more Grammy nominations in the following years. During the 1980s Taylor gained widespread recognition, including a Grammy Award for the album *Blues Explosion* (1984) and, between 1983 and 1992, a total of ten Handy Awards, the blues music equivalent of the Grammy, which is named for blues composer W.C. Handy.

While on tour in 1988 Taylor experienced a profound personal tragedy when her tour van was involved in an accident. Two band members and her husband, Pops Taylor, were seriously injured; six months later Taylor died of his injuries. Koko Taylor suffered a fractured shoulder, collarbone and ribs, which kept her from performing for several months. But she resolved to return to music, and soon resumed an active touring schedule, including appearances at many blues and folk music festivals.

James Clyde Sellman

See Also

Blues, The; Chicago, Illinois; Great Migration, The; Handy, William Christopher (W.C.); King, Riley B. ("B. B."); Thornton, Willie Mae ("Big Mama").

North America

Taylor, Susie Baker King

(b. August 6, 1848, Liberty County, Ga.; d. 1912), African American teacher, nurse, and writer; the only black woman to write of her experiences in the Civil War.

Born a Georgia slave, Susie Baker was quite young when an arrangement was made to send her to live with her grandmother in Savannah. She learned to read and write from two white children, even though this was illegal prior to the Civil War. When war broke out she moved with her uncle's family to the Sea Islands of South Carolina. The Union army, fighting for these islands, pressed her into service as a teacher of freed slave children and adults. Soon after, the men in her family joined the Union's First South Carolina Infantry, and she traveled with them as a nurse and laundress. In 1862 she married one of the regiment's sergeants, Edward King who died in 1866. In her memoir, *A Black Woman's Civil War Memoirs*, she recounted the events of her life in camp with the regiment. She is the only black woman known to have written of her life during the war.

After the war she remained in Georgia. At different times she began and ran schools for black children and adults. In 1879 she married Russell Taylor and moved to Boston, Massachusetts. She returned south in 1898 to care for her dying son in Louisiana; en route she rode in a segregated rail car and witnessed a lynching. Her memoir, published in 1902, not only spoke of the war, but of life after the war, ending with hopeful memories of the "wonderful revolution" that had taken place in 1861.

See Also

Civil War, American.

Africa

Tayyib, Salih al-

(b. 1929, al-Dabba, Sudan), contemporary Sudanese writer.

Al-Tayyib Salih was born in a large village in the northern province of the Sudan, where as a young man he received an Islamic schooling and worked on the family's farm. Salih continued his education at Khartoum University and then left the Sudan to study in England. After completing degrees at the University of London and the University of Exeter, he returned to his home country to teach. Salih joined the British Broadcasting Corporation, working his way up from scriptwriter to head of the Arabic language service. He has since continued working in the fields of broadcast and print journalism. Salih, who considers himself a socialist, has also occupied various advisory government positions.

Salih started writing stories in the 1950s, but did not publish until 1964, when his friend the poet Tawfiq Sayigh began printing Salih's work in the Beirut journal *Hiwar*. His stories, based on his childhood village life, were infused with the mystical vision of Sufi Islam. In these stories his writing style, often compared to magical realism, shows the influence of traditional Arabic storytelling. He depicts a troubled marriage between a European woman and a Sudanese man. (Salih himself had married a British woman.) Many critics interpret his portrayal of personal relations as representing the fraught relations between the First and Third World. In 1966 he published the stories as *Urs al-Zayn: Riwaya wa-sab qusas* (The Wedding of Zein and Other Stories). The title novella *Urs al-Zayn* was made into a play in Libya, and in 1976 it was made into an award-winning Kuwaiti film.

Mawsim al-hijrah ila al-shamal (Season of Migration to the North) is Salih's best-known novel; it is credited with transforming modern Arabic writing. Taking up what would become a common theme in postcolonial writing, the novel represented the alienation of an Islamic African man returning from the West. It went beyond the issue of exile to consider what it means to belong to a community, and traversed conventional norms in its use of graphic sex and violence as metaphors for the penetrating, often brutal, ways that cultures intersect. According to critic Kamal Abu-Deeb, the novel also breaks with regional traditions of writing, "[focusing on] African rather than Arab identity, social, cultural, and artistic issues rather than political and ideological ones, the community rather than the State, ordinary people rather than intellectuals, popular culture rather than official culture, religious and mystical belief rather than secularism, the Sudanese dialect rather than Standard Arabic, and the small village rather than the great metropolis."

In 1971 Salih published *Bandar Shah, Daw al-bayt*, which explores the nature of leadership in a contemporary village. He continued the story in *Bandar Shah, Maryud* (1977). In 1976 he published "Al-Rajul al-qubrusi" (translated as "The Cypriot Man"; 1980). In this story Salih took on one of the most difficult subjects: the meaning of death. "Al-Rajul al-qubrusi" was his last story before a 20-year literary silence, which continues to the present.

Marian Aguiar

See Also

African Socialism; Khartoum, Sudan; Sudan; Sufism.

Latin America and the Caribbean

Teatro Experimental do Negro

(TEN), also known as the Black Experimental Theater, a company of actors, actresses, artists, and playwrights created in Rio de Janeiro, Brazil, in order to redefine the roles of Afro-Brazilians in Brazilian theater; active from 1944 to 1968.

In 1941 black Brazilian activist Abdias do Nascimento saw a performance of Eugene O'Neill's *The Emperor Jones* in Lima, Peru. He was disturbed to see the black hero of this drama being played by a white actor in blackface. Nascimento could find no justification for this, since there was a sizable Afro-Peruvian population in Lima. He then contemplated the fact that people of African descent constituted the majority in his homeland, Brazil, yet they had been almost completely excluded from the stage. As a result, he created the Teatro Experimental do Negro (TEN) in 1944.

Until then Afro-Brazilians were allowed on stage only in roles as servants and folklore figures – or, after the show, as janitors. TEN's principal objectives were to affirm the values of African culture, to eliminate the use of white actors in blackface and the use of black actors in debased roles, and to act out Afro-Brazilian problems in a white racist society. TEN's first production was the play that had inspired its creation, *The Emperor Jones*. The play opened on May 8, 1945, in Rio de Janeiro's Municipal Theater with Afro-Brazilian actor Aguinaldo Camargo in the lead role of Brutus Jones. The play was lauded in reviews.

In spite of TEN's successful debut, in subsequent years the group repeatedly clashed with the government's Censorship Bureau. For example, the police prevented Nascimento's *Sortilégio* (Black Mystery) from being performed on the grounds that it contained pornographic language. Nascimento argued that the show was banned because of its subject matter, which depicts the transformation of an assimilated black character, Emanuel, into an Afro-Brazilian who asserts his African heritage. When the play was finally presented in 1957, it was labeled a racist play that had been designed to foment Afro-Brazilians' hate for whites.

TEN launched the careers of the first generation of Afro-Brazilian actors and actresses, including José Maria Monteiro, Arinda Serafim, and Marina Gonçalves. In order to train the hundreds of men and women eager to join the company, TEN set up a literacy course, a "general culture" course, and a course in the fundamentals of acting. TEN also generated numerous Afro-Brazilian playwrights, including Joaquim Ribeiro (author of *Aruanda*), José de Morais Pinto (author of *Filhos de Santo* [Children of the Saint]), and, of course, Abdias do Nascimento (author of *Sortilégio* and *Rapsódia Negra* [Black Rhapsody]). Their scripts were among the first exploring Afro-Brazilian themes without reducing them to folklore. Instead, Afro-Brazilians were portrayed as complex human beings and as heroes, transcending the traditional stereotypes.

TEN made unique use of drama to redeem African identity and aesthetics, and to defend the human rights of Afro-Brazilians. After TEN's emergence, one-dimensional caricatures of Afro-Brazilians could no longer be easily accepted. Although the group was dissolved with Nascimento's exile to the United States in 1968, TEN inspired many other similar theatrical companies that preserved its legacy, including the *Teatro Negro Experimental* of São Paulo, the *Grupo dos Novos* in Rio de Janeiro, and the Brazilian Popular Theater.

Aaron Myers

See Also

Brazil's Relationship with Africa: An Interpretation; Rio de Janeiro, Brazil.

Tebu. Please see Toubou

Latin America and the Caribbean

Teixeira e Souza, Antônio Gonçalves (b. 1812, Cabo Frio, State of Rio de Janeiro, Brazil; d. 1861, Rio de Janeiro, Brazil), Afro-Brazilian poet and novelist; one of Brazil's most popular authors of fiction in the nineteenth century.

Antônio Gonçalves Teixeira e Souza was born of humble parents and orphaned at a young age. He worked as a carpenter during his early years of study. Teixeira e Souza moved to the city of Rio de Janeiro and worked in the printing office of the well-known intellectual Paula Brito, and it was there that he met the literary figures of his time and began to write his first poetry and prose.

Teixeira e Souza later taught and worked as a registrar, and these jobs allowed time for his writing. In 1843 he wrote *O filho do pescador* (The Fisherman's Son). This work was marked by Brazilian nationalistic tendencies of the sort that would later be taken up by José de Alencar, the late nineteenth-century Brazilian nationalist novelist, and others. Teixeira e Souza is considered one of the first Romantics to espouse the historical novel, a genre that allowed him to explore issues of racial and national identity. The epic narrative *A independência do Brasil* (1847-1857, Brazil's Independence) is an example of one work that explores these themes. Other important novels by Teixeira e Souza are *O três dias de um noivado* (The Three Days of a Betrothal), *Contos lyricos* (Lyric Stories), and *O Cavaleiro teutônico* (1855, The Teutonic Knight).

Nicola Cooney

Africa

Téké, ethnic group in central Republic of the Congo.

Since Congolese independence in 1960, the Téké of central Congo have often acted as a swing group between the politically dominant northern Mbochi and the more numerous southern Kongo. However, few Téké have held senior government, military, or economic positions, although they constitute 14 percent of the population, or approximately 2.5 million people.

The Téké's political marginalization was a gradual process. Historians believe that the Téké probably migrated to the central plateau in the late fifteenth century and became part of the decentralized Kongo Kingdom. With the disintegration of the Kongo Kingdom in the seventeenth century, the viceroyalty of the Anzika, by which name the Téké are also known, established his own decentralized kingdom, known as Tio. The *makoko*, or king, ruled from his capital at Mbé through appointed subchiefs. But the kingdom's commercial hub developed in the Pool region farther south, where the Téké exchanged slaves captured in the interior for goods brought by European merchant ships. The Mbochis and other northern groups' efforts to circumvent the Téké control of trade contributed to the slow disintegration of the kingdom. In 1880 the Téké makoko signed a treaty with Pierre Savorgnan de Brazza to gain protection from France. This agreement effectively gave up the northern bank of the Congo to France. By the time the last makoko died in 1918, the kingdom had been in serious decline for several decades. Under French colonial rule many Téké migrated south to the capital, Brazzaville for employment. Today they make up a large proportion of the city's population; many are engaged in carving masks and fetishes.

Eric Young

See Also

Brazzaville, Republic of the Congo; Transatlantic Slave Trade.

North America

Television and African Americans, the history of African American depiction on and involvement in the medium of television.

From the negative stereotypes in Beulah and *Amos 'n' Andy* to the "white Negroes" in *Julia* and *I Spy* to the arguably too-perfect Huxtable family on *The Cosby Show*, the majority of portrayals of African Americans on television have been one-dimensional, distorted, insulting, or sugarcoated. For many viewers, though, even unsatisfactory images seemed preferable to the general absence of black television characters during television's early days. The history of the depiction of blacks on television has evolved from near invisibility broken by a parade of stereotypes to greater diversity and realism, but most critics agree that the medium has far to go.

The Early Years

Commercial television was born in 1948 as each of the three major networks, ABC, CBS, and NBC, began broadcasting. This was also a significant year in African American history, with the desegregation of the United States armed forces (see Blacks in the American Military) and an endorsement of civil rights in the presidential platform of the Democratic Party, headed by President Harry S. Truman.

But black presence in the early years of television followed the pattern earlier set by radio. In fact, the first two series starring African Americans both came to television after decades of popularity on radio – and each replaced white radio actors with black actors. *Beulah*, which showcased a supporting character on the popular *Fibber McGee and Molly* show, debuted in 1950. As played by Ethel Waters, Hattie McDaniel, and Louise Beavers on television, Beulah was cast in the stereotypical mold of the happy, overweight, black female "mammy." Cheerfully caring for the white family who employed her as housekeeper, Beulah had little discernible life of her own (although the cultural critic Donald Bogle points out that the interaction between Beulah and her long-time boyfriend provided some of the show's best moments). Beulah ran until 1953, when protests by the NATIONAL ASSOCIATION FOR THE ADVANCEMENT OF COLORED PEOPLE (NAACP) and other groups forced the network to cancel the series.

Amos 'n' Andy, which ran from 1951 to 1953, was based on the most listened-to radio show of the 1930s and 1940s. Unlike *Beulah, Amos 'n' Andy* portrayed an all-black world in which the shiftless, joking Andy (played by Spencer Williams) and the passive, long-suffering Amos (Alvin Childress) interacted with characters depicting the entire range of stereotypical black images. Its roots in the tradition of MINSTRELSY caused the NAACP to launch lawsuits and boycott threats that were instrumental in causing the show's cancellation. Speaking in the documentary *Color Adjustment,* written and directed by Marlon Riggs, the actress DIAHANN CARROLL remembers being forbidden to watch *Amos 'n' Andy,* which her parents felt was demeaning to blacks. But some modern critics have praised the show's intricate and sophisticated comedy and lauded the actors, many of whom came from the black vaudeville tradition. After the series was canceled, it continued to appear in syndication until 1966.

Other black images in 1950s television included variety shows, which occasionally featured African American entertainers. Duke Ellington, Cab Calloway, PAUL ROBESON, ELLA FITZGERALD, SARAH VAUGHAN, and others appeared on shows hosted by veteran white entertainers such as Ed Sullivan, Milton Berle, and Steve Allen. But no African American had his own national variety show until 1956, when *The Nat "King" Cole Show* premiered. Cole, who had hosted a radio program in the 1940s, was urbane, elegant, and considered nonthreatening by white viewers. His show featured both white and black entertainers, including PEARL BAILEY, Count Basie, and MAHALIA JACKSON, and was a great source of pride for black viewers starved for positive African American television images. But with the deepening racial tensions of the 1950s, Cole had difficulty attracting corporate sponsors, especially after some white viewers became outraged when Cole touched the arm of a white female guest. The show was canceled after one season.

CIVIL RIGHTS AND THE "WHITE NEGRO"

One arena in which African Americans appeared on television beginning in the 1950s – and reaching a peak in the 1960s – was in the serious documentaries about rural poverty, segregation, and the growing CIVIL RIGHTS MOVEMENT. In addition, as the white segregationist backlash exploded into violence throughout the American South, "images of black people dominated the news," according to the writer and scholar Henry Louis Gates Jr. Seen as a noble, almost saintly figure, Rev. Martin Luther King Jr., whose marches in Selma, Birmingham, and Montgomery, Alabama, heightened white America's awareness of the Civil Rights Movement, became black America's spokesperson on television in the eyes of many newly sympathetic white viewers. By contrast, some black leaders were treated harshly on television. MALCOLM X was the subject of a documentary titled *The Hate that Hate Produced* (1959), which did little to dispel white fears of the NATION OF ISLAM leader.

Even as television news shows began to report seriously on racism and the fight for civil rights, television's entertainment programs became even more overwhelmingly white. Since its birth the medium had avoided controversy possibly offensive to viewers (and advertisers). During the 1960s, as protests rose against both racism and the VIETNAM WAR, programming became less and less realistic. (For example, some of the most popular shows on television at that time featured witches, genies, and other escapist fantasies). As the cultural critic J. Fred McDonald pointed out, comedies such as *Petticoat Junction* and *The Andy Griffith Show,* both set in the South, portrayed all-white worlds in which prejudice seemingly did not exist.

When black characters did appear, network executives crafted the most inoffensive, blandly perfect images possible. *I Spy* (1965-1968), which starred BILL COSBY and Robert Culp as an interracial team of secret agents, presented Cosby's character, Alexander Scott, as a Rhodes scholar, an elegant sophisticate whose education was superior not only to most African Americans but also to nearly all whites. *Julia* (1968-1971) featured Diahann Carroll as a widowed nurse and single mother. Carroll's character was bland, bleached of all evidence of black culture. Derided as a "white Negro" by critics – and suspected of being played by a white actress in darkening makeup – Carroll's Julia never encountered poverty or racism. Still, Julia was, according to African American actress Esther Rolle, "a step above the grinning domestic."

Designed to overcome negative stereotypes, such series presented "fully assimilable black people," according to Gates. In an era that featured so few black representations in the mass media, even positive images were heavily scrutinized by African Americans and usually found wanting. Shows like *I Spy, Julia,* and the action series *Mod Squad* and *Mission Impossible* (each of which featured black co-stars) clashed with the reality of most African Americans' lives. But attempts to present a more balanced picture, such as the short-lived dramatic series *East Side, West Side* (1963-1964), usually failed quickly. Starring JAMES EARL JONES and CICELY TYSON, *East Side, West Side* featured sophisticated writing and provocative situations depicting both ghetto life and the pain of integration. The show lasted only one season.

RELEVANCE AND ROOTS

By the late 1960s television began to emerge from its fantasy world to present programming more in touch with the reality of the tumultuous times. The first comedy series to deal with race was *All in the Family* (1971-1979), a show with a mostly white cast. At its head was Archie Bunker (played by Carroll O'Connor), an unrepentant racist, bigot, and homophobe. While some felt that Archie's use of racial slurs amounted to condoning prejudice, most saw the series as an important move toward realism, particularly in terms of race relations, on television. (The Bunkers's next door neighbors were a black family whose characters were later featured in a popular spinoff series, *The Jeffersons,* which aired from 1975 to 1985.)

One of the most dramatic changes came in children's television, which had been a wasteland in terms of black images. Starting in 1969, the public television series *Sesame Street* showed children and adults of a variety of racial and ethnic backgrounds interacting and learning. *Fat Albert and the Cosby Kids* (1972-1989) was an animated version of children and events from producer Bill Cosby's own Philadelphia childhood. More shows followed, including cartoons based on the adventures of the Jackson Five and the HARLEM GLOBETROTTERS.

Produced by the *All in the Family* team, *Good Times* (1974-1979) was the first television comedy to focus on a poor black family – one including both father and mother – living in the midst of a vibrant, diverse black community. But social relevance gave way to echoes of the minstrel character STEPIN FETCHIT, as the show increasingly revolved around the buffoonish character of JJ, the elder son. According to Esther Rolle, the actress who played JJ's mother, "negative images have been quietly slipped in on us" through the clowning, wide-eyed JJ.

Although the 1970s saw a dramatic rise in the number of television shows built around black characters, most made no pretense of seriousness or realism. *Sanford and Son* (1972-1977) starred the veteran comedian REDD FOXX as an irascible junk dealer and Demond Wilson as his long-suffering son. Despite the implied social relevance of its ghetto setting, the show was vintage 1970s escapism. Its wide popularity derived in part from its self-aware use of stereotypical aspects of black humor – elaborate insults, shrill women, scheming men – and it inspired a succession of inferior shows, including *Grady* (1975-1976), *Baby I'm Back* (1978), and *What's Happenin'* (1976-1979), which critics dubbed "the new minstrelsy."

No dramatic series starring a black actor aired until the 1980s. But it was in drama – made-for-television movies and miniseries – that some of the most significant television images of African Americans emerged in the 1970s. *The Autobiography of Miss Jane Pittman* (1974), starring CICELY TYSON, was hailed as "possibly the finest movie ever made for television." The movie, a series of flashbacks, is set in 1962 and traces Pittman's life from her childhood in slavery to the civil rights era she lived to see (the character is 110 years old). Its climactic scene features

Pittman bending to take a sip from a whites-only water fountain.

Roots, which aired over eight nights in 1977, was a television event not only for African Americans but for all Americans. The highest-rated miniseries ever, *Roots*, based on Alex Haley's book about his family's history, from freedom in Africa to slavery in the American South, attracted an estimated 130 million viewers. According to the cultural critic Marlon Riggs, *Roots* was presented as an immigrant tale that white audiences could relate to, "transforming a national disgrace into an epic triumph of the family and the American dream." Although carefully crafted to appeal to the white audience (it was reported that the actor LeVar Burton, who played Kunta Kinte, was nearly dropped from the project because producers thought his lips were too large),

ABOVE: As co-anchor of NBC's popular *Today* show from 1981 to 1997, Bryant Gumbel became one of America's most recognizable black journalists. *Yvonne Hemsey/Gamma-Liaison*

RIGHT: Known for her empathy and compassion, television talk show host Oprah Winfrey is also a successful businesswoman whose influence extends into film and book publishing. *Scott McKiernan/Gamma-Liaison*

FAR RIGHT: A veteran of both silent and talking films, actor Louise Beavers portrayed family maid Beulah in the 1950s television series of the same name. *The Everett Collection*

Roots was nonetheless a stirring and powerful drama. It was also a showcase for many black actors, including Burton, Louis Gossett Jr., and Cicely Tyson.

Material Success

By the late 1970s no obvious color line remained in television. Black actors appeared in soap operas, as costars in dramatic series, and as the focus of comedies. In the wake of *Roots*, several television movies, including *King* (1978), *Roots: The Next Generations* (1979), and *Attica* (1980), featured African American historical themes. But most depictions of blacks in television continued to follow the pattern of either high-minded history lesson or low-rent stereotypic comedy. Rarely allowed to exist as fully realized human beings, some of the most popular black characters of the early 1980s were wisecracking black children adopted into white families – the situation in both *Diff'rent Strokes* (1978-1986) and *Webster* (1983-1987) – or, as in earlier television history, loyal sidekicks to white heroes.

When *The Cosby Show* debuted in 1984, it won enthusiastic reviews and a loyal audience, both black and white. Focusing on a loving, intact, successful African American family, *The Cosby Show* starred Bill Cosby and Phylicia Rashad as the upper-middle-class parents of five children. Like the white families in 1950s television, theirs was a caring, supportive unit that blended humor with wisdom. Cosby, who had long criticized the negative portrayals of African Americans in television, consulted psychiatrist Dr. Alvin Poussaint in writing and producing the program, resulting in a positive, almost educational tone. The top-rated series for many of its nine seasons, *Cosby*, according to critic Patricia Turner, reinforced "the notion that the Civil Rights Movement took care of all the racial inequities of society."

One series that attempted a more balanced depiction was the short-lived *Frank's Place* (1987-1988), about a black professor who inherits a New Orleans restaurant. Tim Reid, who had previously costarred in *WKRP in Cincinnati*, produced and starred in *Frank's Place*, a program he said reflected his desire to see blacks portrayed not monolithically but with the full range of humanity. Although the well-written show won an Emmy Award, it was canceled after one season.

Like Cosby and Reid, a rising number of African Americans began working behind the television camera in the late 1980s, resulting in a flowering of black-themed shows. *A Different World*, which spun off from *Cosby* and was produced by Debbie Allen, depicted life at a historically black university. Others included Quincy Jones's *Fresh Prince of Bel Air*, starring Will Smith, and *In Living Color*, produced by Keenan Ivory Wayans. *In Living Color*, one of the then-new Fox network's first hits, brought freshness and irreverence to its humor, much of which was based on racial stereotypes (the show's outrageousness reminded some critics of *The Flip Wilson Show*, which ran from 1970 to 1974).

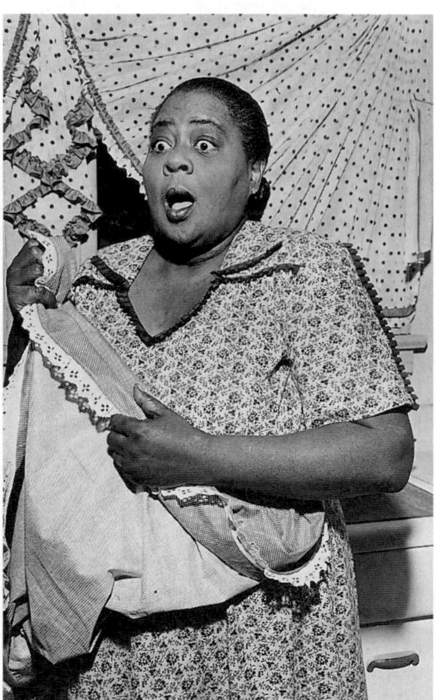

Fox, which also produced *Living Single*, *Martin*, and *South Central*, was the first network to focus so much energy on attracting black audiences with shows featuring African American actors. Some critics, among them Frank Reid, charged that the Fox shows merely perpetuated the old, negative stereotypes, this time in the lingo of the hip hop generation. (One Fox series, *Roc*, with a brilliant ensemble cast culled mostly from August Wilson's stage play *Fences*, escaped this criticism.) But with the increasing fragmentation of the television audience – caused in part by the growth of cable television – black viewers responded eagerly to the new black shows. Another venue for television geared exclusively to the African American community came of age in the early 1990s. Black Entertainment Television (BET) capitalized on music videos, sports, and reruns of black-focused series to attract a nationwide audience.

Black programming was lucrative because it appealed not only to the black audience but

AFRICAN AMERICAN EMMY AWARD WINNERS

Year	Performer	Category	Performance
1959	Harry Belafonte	Outstanding Performer in a Variety or Musical Program	"Tonight with Belafonte," Revlon Revue
1966	Bill Cosby	Outstanding Continued Performance by an Actor in a Leading Role of a Dramatic Series	I Spy
1967	Bill Cosby	Outstanding Continued Performance by an Actor in a Leading Role of a Dramatic Series	I Spy
1968	Bill Cosby	Outstanding Variety or Musical Program	The Bill Cosby Special
1970	Flip Wilson	Outstanding Writing Achievement in a Variety or Musical Series	The Flip Wilson Show
1973	Cicely Tyson	Best Lead Actress in a Drama – Special Program	The Autobiography of Miss Jane Pittman
	Cicely Tyson	Actress of the Year – Special Program	The Autobiography of Miss Jane Pittman
1976	Olivia Cole	Outstanding Single Performance by a Supporting Actress in a Drama or Comedy Series	Roots Part 8
	Louis Gossett Jr.	Outstanding Lead Actor for a Single Appearance in a Drama or Comedy Series	Roots Part 1
	Quincy Jones	Outstanding Music Series Composition	Roots Part 1
1978	Robert Guillaume	Outstanding Supporting Actor in a Comedy Series or Music Series	Soap
	Esther Rolle	Outstanding Supporting Actress in a Limited Series	Summer of My German Soldier
1980	Isabel Sanford	Outstanding Lead Actress in a Comedy Series	The Jeffersons
1981	Debbie Allen	Outstanding Choreography	"Come One, Come All," Fame
	Nell Carter	Outstanding Individual Achievement – Special Class	"Ain't Misbehavin'"
1982	Debbie Allen	Outstanding Choreography	"Class Act," Fame
	Leontyne Price	Outsanding Individual Performance in a Variety or Music Program	From Lincoln Center
	Leslie Uggams	Outstanding Host/Hostess in a Variety Series	Fantasy
1983	Suzanne de Passe	Outstanding Producing	Motown 25: Yesterday, Today and Forever
1984	Robert Guillaume	Outstanding Lead Actor in a Comedy Series	Benson
1985	Alfre Woodard	Outstanding Supporting Actress in a Drama Series	"Doris in Wonderland," Hill Street Blues
	George Stanford Brown	Outstanding Direction in a Drama Series	"Parting Shots," Cagney & Lacey
	Roscoe Lee Brown	Oustanding Guest Performer in a Comedy Series	The Cosby Show
	Suzanne de Passe	Outstanding Producing	Motown at the Apollo
	Whitney Houston	Outstanding Individual Performance in a Variety or Music Series	The 28th Annual Grammy Awards
1986	Alfre Woodard	Outstanding Guest Performer in a Drama Series	L.A. Law
1987	Jackée (Harry)	Outstanding Supporting Actress in a Comedy Series	227
1988	Beah Richards	Outstanding Guest Performer in a Comedy Series	Frank's Place
1989	Suzanne de Passe	Outstanding Producing	Lonesome Dove
1991	Debbie Allen	Outstanding Choreography	Motown 30: What's Goin' On!
	Ruby Dee	Outstanding Supporting Actress in a Miniseries or Special	"Decoration Day," Hallmark Hall of Fame
	James Earl Jones	Outstanding Lead Actor in a Drama Series	Gabriel's Fire
	James Earl Jones	Outstanding Supporting Actor in a Miniseries or Special	Heat Wave
	Madge Sinclair	Outstanding Supporting Actress in a Drama Series	Gabriel's Fire
	Lynn Whitfield	Outstanding Lead Actress in a Miniseries or Special	The Josephine Baker Story
1992	Eric Laneuville	Outstanding Individual Achievement in Directing in a Drama Series	"All God's Children"
1993	Mary Alice	Outstanding Supporting Actress in a Drama Series	I'll Fly Away
	Laurence Fishburne	Outstanding Guest Actor in a Drama Series	"The Box," Tribeca

also to whites, especially white youth, increasingly enamored of black culture. Michael Jordan and other basketball stars became some of corporate America's favorite spokespersons, and white teenagers took their fashion and language cues from RAP musicians. The success of African Americans ARSENIO HALL and Oprah Winfrey in late-night and daytime talk shows led to dozens of imitators, both black and white. In addition, Winfrey produced and acted in *The Women of Brewster Place*, a 1988 miniseries based on GLORIA NAYLOR's novel, and in 1998 produced the television adaptation of DOROTHY WEST's *The Wedding*, among other made-for-television projects. A cultural phenomenon and one of the richest people in America, Winfrey's naturalness, warmth, and pride in her African American culture have found favor with both blacks and whites.

Beginning with his co-starring role on the television series *I Spy* in the 1960s, Bill Cosby has been one of television's most popular performers, black or white. With *The Cosby Show* (1984-1992), Cosby countered what he saw as negative racial stereotyping on television by depicting a well-educated, upper-middle-class African American family. In addition to his work as an actor, Cosby – who holds a doctorate in education – is also a producer, writer, and philanthropist. *The Everett Collection*

By the late 1990s more African Americans than ever were involved in the television industry, some in executive and production roles. Taboos against interracial sex and other forms of social equality had eroded. But there were still no prime-time dramatic series devoted to telling the stories of black Americans, and many of the images seen by black children (who are estimated to watch television at a rate 64 percent higher than the national average) continued to perpetuate stereotypes.

Kate Tuttle

SEE ALSO

Slavery in the United States; Amos 'n' Andy; Basie, William James ("Count"); Calloway, Cabell (Cab); Cole, Nat ("King"); Gossett, Louis, Jr.; Haley, Alexander Palmer (Alex); Hip Hop in the United States; Jackson, Michael, and the Jackson Family; Jones, Quincy Delight, Jr.; Jordan, Michael Jeffrey; King, Martin Luther, Jr.; New Orleans, Louisiana; Poussaint, Alvin Francis; Racial Stereotypes; Riggs, Marlon Troy; Williams, Spencer, Jr.; Winfrey, Oprah Gail; Ellington, Edward Kennedy ("Duke").

Africa

Temne (also known as Timne), ethnic group of SIERRA LEONE.

The Temne primarily inhabit northern Sierra Leone; they represent about a third of the country's population. Others live in GUINEA. They speak a Niger-Congo language that is related to JOLA and other languages to the north. Approximately 1.5 million people consider themselves Temne.

SEE ALSO

Languages, African: An Overview.

North America

Temptations, The, an African American vocal group that enjoyed its greatest successes during the 1960s and 1970s with a repertoire encompassing romantic ballads and hard-edged SOUL MUSIC.

The Temptations was one of the most successful groups in the history of black music. Over the course of 25 years the group had 43 Top Ten singles and by the early 1980s had sold more than 20 million records. The vocal quintet, initially called the Elgins, was founded in Detroit in 1961 by members of two local RHYTHM AND BLUES (R&B) groups: Eddie Kendricks and Paul Williams sang with the Primes; Melvin Franklin, Eldridge Bryant, and Otis Williams came from the Distants. In that year Berry Gordy signed them to his Detroit-based Motown Records and renamed them the Temptations. The group attained its classic lineup in 1963, when Bryant was replaced by David Ruffin. Many of the group's hits featured the contrasting leads of Ruffin's gritty baritone and Kendricks's crystalline high tenor and falsetto.

In conjunction with two gifted Motown producers – Smokey Robinson, 1962-1966, and Norman Whitfield, 1966-1975 – the Temptations created memorable pop music. Robinson, a songwriter as well as a record producer, provided the group with several hits during 1965-1966. He co-wrote the group's first Number-One pop hit, "My Girl" (1965), an irresistible confection that set the Temptations' shimmering harmonies against a pungent electric-guitar line, with lush orchestral accompaniment that suggested classical music.

Whitfield continued the Temptations' success, encouraging performances of raw urgency that made it the only Motown group to match the harder soul music produced by Stax and Atlantic Records. The group also recorded "psychedelic soul music" – such as "Cloud Nine" (1968) – that reflected the influence of SLY AND THE FAMILY STONE. On occasion the Temptations even performed protest music such as "Stop the War Now" (1970). The group's most significant hit with Whitfield was the soulful and funky "Papa Was a Rolling Stone" (1972), which won Motown its first Grammy Award.

By the mid-1970s, however, the Temptations had fallen from prominence. Between 1976 and 1980 the group left Motown for an unsuccessful stint with Atlantic Records before returning to Berry Gordy's label. Personnel changes undermined the group's identity. Ruffin left in 1968; Kendricks and Paul Williams followed three years later. Although Otis Williams and Franklin continued with the group for more than 30 years, the Temptations became less a band and more a brand name.

By the late 1990s all of the original, hit-making Temptations had died, except for Otis Williams. Paul Williams shot himself in 1973. Ruffin died of a drug overdose in 1991. In the following year Kendricks succumbed to lung cancer. Franklin died in 1995 of a heart attack. Following Franklin's death, Otis Williams told the *Chicago Tribune*, "I almost see us like a football franchise or a baseball franchise. People come and go, but [the group] still goes on."

James Clyde Sellman

SEE ALSO

Detroit, Michigan; Motown; Robinson, William ("Smokey"); Stax Records.

Latin America and the Caribbean

Ten Years' War (1868-1878), war waged unsuccessfully to gain Cuba's independence from Spain.

In 1865, when efforts by a reform commission to the Spanish Cortes (National Parliament) concerning greater autonomy for CUBA and PUERTO RICO failed, the groundwork was laid for the first major war for Cuban independence in the nineteenth century. Then in 1867, without consulting the colonies, the Spanish Crown increased taxes on real estate, incomes, and all types of businesses. Coupled with an economic downturn, this aggravated the already widespread discontent.

On October 10, 1868, Carlos Manuel de Céspedes, a wealthy landowner from Oriente province, freed his 30 slaves and issued a call for an uprising to overthrow Spanish colonialism, known as El Grito de Yara. Céspedes began fighting with a group of 147 men, but by the end of the month the insurrectionists had a force of 12,000. Ignacio Agramonte and his rebels took Puerto Príncipe. Soon Perucho Figueredo wrote the verses "La Bayamesa," later to become Cuba's national anthem. The Spanish had an army of 7000 regular soldiers and 30,000 volunteers, a kind of civilian paramilitary force known for its brutality and anti-Cuban sentiments. By 1869 Spain had sent about 35,000 more troops as reinforcements.

The Cuban insurrectionists, despite popular support, soon faced two major political obstacles: the question of abolition and the disunity of forces fighting for independence. To obtain the backing of wealthy landowners in the western provinces (some of whom were living in New York), Céspedes, despite his freeing his own slaves, did not immediately put forth abolition as a demand. This, of course, cost the rebels popular support. Nonetheless, some of the revolutionary generals, like Máximo Gómez and Antonio Maceo, despite their overall loyalty to the government-in-arms, would on their own initiative free slaves in territory they captured from the Spanish. The crisis led to the Constitutional Convention of Guaimaro in April 1869. Article 24 of the document that emerged states, "All citizens of the Republic are completely free." Conservative elements of the movement, however, remained entrenched on this issue. The convention also favored United States annexation, but the United States continued to favor Spanish control over the island.

The tension between conservatives and radicals cost the revolution dearly. The radicals reasoned, for example, that if the war did not extend to all of Cuba, the landed elite in the western provinces would continue to back antirebel forces financially. The conservatives, themselves constituted in part by members of the elite, claimed that Maceo, an Afro-Cuban, favored blacks in his ranks and ultimately wanted to set up a black republic. The Spanish often used this argument to discredit and divide the revolutionary forces. Agramonte was killed in 1873; in the same year Céspedes was thrown out as president of the rebel forces, and was killed the following year in an ambush by the Spanish. Gómez and Maceo eventually attempted an invasion of the western provinces. They waged a successful but costly campaign in Camagüey that would ultimately force them to turn back. The conservative factions kept the western provinces free from combat for the duration of the war.

More internal strife between conservatives and radicals in 1875 and 1876 weakened the rebel cause, as did the hope, ultimately dashed, that the United States would recognize the Cubans as a legitimate political force. Dissension within the ranks, along with Spanish counterattacks, further weakened rebel efforts. Spanish offers of amnesty followed, which encouraged defection and the laying down of arms. Ultimately, in February 1878, the war ended with the signing of the Pact of Zanjón. Some leaders, particularly Maceo, rejected the terms of the pact, since abolition and independence were both denied, and instead issued the Protest of Baraguá in March 1878. A year later, on August 26, 1879, Maceo, Calixto García, and others attempted to revive the insurrection with what became known as La Guerra Chiquita (the Little War), which lasted only a year. As with its predecessor, lack of unity and equipment, racism, indifference and even hostility to the cause of independence on the part of the landowners, and confusion among the popular classes brought defeat.

Despite its immediate outcome, the Ten Years' War marked an important chapter in Cuba's struggle for independence. It made crucial political inroads in the consciousness of the nation. Slavery would be abolished six years later. The costs of the war were huge: 208,000 Spanish and 50,000 Cuban dead, and economic damage of $300 million.

Alan West

See Also

New York, New York; Maceo y Grajales, Antonio; Abolition and Emancipation in Latin America and the Caribbean.

North America

Terrell, Mary Eliza Church

(b. September 23, 1863, Memphis, Tenn.; d. July 24, 1954, Washington, D.C.), African American educator and a prominent advocate for African American civil rights and women's rights, and for nineteenth-century black women's club organizations.

Mary Church Terrell was born to Louisa and Robert Church, who had emerged from slavery to become prosperous business owners. Although the couple separated, Robert Church financially supported his daughter as she completed a classical education at Oberlin College. When she received her bachelor's degree in 1884, her father wanted her to assume the role of hostess, a refined position he felt appropriate for the daughter of the wealthiest black man in the South. She refused the conventional role, however, and entered the professional world of education instead.

Mary Church put her energy and training to work as a teacher at Ohio's black Wilberforce College in 1885. Two years later she moved to the M Street High School in Washington D.C., where she met her future husband, Robert Heberton Terrell. She completed a master's degree at Oberlin, followed, in 1888, by a two-year European tour. For an African American woman, this American rite of passage, usually reserved for the white elite, provided more than the opportunity to see diverse cultures: it was also a chance for her to experience a different racial environment than that of the United States. Church also used the trip to develop the language skills she would later use in Europe to promote the cause of African American equality.

When Church returned to the United States in 1890, she married Terrell, retired from teaching, and focused on managing her household. That quiet life ended in 1892, when a lifelong friend, Tom Moss, was lynched in Memphis. Mary Church Terrell, along with her friend Frederick Douglass, demanded a meeting with President Benjamin Harrison. Although they did receive a hearing, Harrison made no public statement opposing the violence. The event galvanized Terrell into activism, a vocation which lasted for more than 60 years.

Terrell became an active participant in the women's club movement, leading the Colored Women's League in 1892. When this group merged with several others to form the National Association of Colored Women (NACW) in 1896, she became the president of this first American national black organization. Under Terrell's leadership NACW organized around issues of health, housing, employment, and child care, as these matters specifically applied to the lives of African American women.

As a member of the National American Woman Suffrage Association, Terrell took the podium for the cause of women's voting rights, often speaking before all-white audiences. She was striking in her learning and political savvy: at the 1904 International Council of Women conference in Berlin, for instance, she delivered her speech in German, and then translated into French and English.

Terrell worked alongside many of the prominent African American activists of the era on issues of racial equity. She supported the work of Booker T. Washington, despite others' criticism of his vocational educational programs. In 1909 she joined W. E. B. Du Bois as a founding member of the National Association for the Advancement of Colored People (NAACP).

An active supporter of the Republican Party until 1952 and the wife of a federal judge, Terrell used her political clout in the upper echelons of American politics to fight for social justice for African Americans. Yet she often risked this position to speak what she saw to be the truth. In 1906, when three companies of black soldiers were dismissed from the United States Army without a hearing after a racial incident in Brownsville, Texas, Terrell publicly attacked President Theodore Roosevelt's decision. After her meeting with Secretary of War William Howard Taft, the soldiers were granted a hearing, although the dismissal ultimately remained in place.

During World War I and World War II, Terrell positioned herself as an advocate for the black women and girls who were entering the employment arena. Following World War II she became even more militant in her activism, as she saw the discrimination and economic hardship that continued in the nation even after black soldiers had given their lives abroad.

Despite the privileges afforded her by her social status and fair skin, Terrell encountered the same discrimination faced by other African Americans. In her autobiography, *A Colored Woman in a White World* (1940), she wrote of the difficulty of being black and female: "A White woman has only one handicap to overcome – that of sex. I have two – both sex and race."

In 1950 Terrell entered a segregated Washington, D.C., restaurant with an interracial group. After the blacks were refused service, they filed affidavits against the restaurant. Three years of protest and legal battles ended in the protesters' favor, in *District of Columbia* v. *John Thompson*, and at 90 years of age, Terrell saw the desegregation of eating facilities in Washington, D.C.

Marian Aguiar

See Also

Slavery in the United States; World War II and African Americans; Black Women's Club Movement; Military, Blacks in the American; Du Bois, William Edward Burghardt (W. E. B.); Lynching; Washington, Booker Taliaferro; Wilberforce University.

Africa

Tetela, ethnic group of the Democratic Republic of the Congo.

The Tetela primarily inhabit east central Congo-Kinshasa. They speak a Bantu language. Approximately 800,000 people consider themselves Tetela.

See Also

Bantu: Dispersion and Settlement.

Africa

Tharaka, ethnic group of Kenya.

The Tharaka primarily inhabit the highlands of central Kenya. They speak a Bantu language and are closely related to the Meru people. More than 100,000 people consider themselves Tharaka.

See Also

Bantu: Dispersion and Settlement.

North America

Tharpe, "Sister" Rosetta

(b. March 20, 1915, Cotton Plant, Ark.; d. October 9, 1973, Philadelphia, Pa.), gospel singer who paved the way for gospel's golden age in the 1940s and 1950s.

Born to Katie (Bell) Nubin, a singing and mandolin-playing evangelist for the Church of God in Christ (COGIC), the leading Pentecostal denomination, Sister Rosetta Tharpe (born Rosetta Nubin) made her gospel debut at age five, singing "I Looked Down the Line and I Wondered," in front of an audience of 1000 people. She became known as "Little Sister" as she traveled with her mother between 1923 and 1934, and she gained a reputation among Pentecostal Holiness people as a singer and guitar player. Tharpe's style was influenced by the sanctified blind pianist, Arizona Dranes, also a member of COGIC. Both Tharpe and Dranes traveled with Rev. F. W. McGee on the tent-meeting revival circuit.

In 1938 Thorne made national headlines, including a feature in *Life* magazine, when she performed her sacred music with Cab Calloway at the Cotton Club in New York City. That same year Tharpe became the first gospel performer to sign with a major record label when Decca Records offered her a recording contract. Her subsequent recording of Thomas A. Dorsey's composition "Hide Me in Thy Bosom" under the title "Rock Me," became a hit. Also in 1938 Tharpe performed in John Hammond's legendary Carnegie Hall concert, "Spirituals to Swing."

By 1940 Tharpe had become very popular and toured America and Europe, performing in nightclubs, concert halls, and jazz festivals. Her success in these secular spaces created a controversy among the Holiness Churches. In spite of the controversey, Tharpe teamed with Marie Knight and the two made the *Billboard* charts with their song "Up Above My Head." She and Knight later recorded and performed the blues. This action caused a rift between Tharpe and the Holiness people that never completely healed. Tharpe continued to perform in secular venues throughout the 1940s, 1950s, and 1960s. She toured with secular performers such as Roy Acuff, Mary Lou Williams and Lucky Millender, as well as with gospel groups like the James Cleveland Singers, the Golden Gate Quartet, and the Dixie Hummingbirds.

Tharpe generally sang solo while accompanying herself on the guitar. Her style of playing placed her in a category with bluesmen Big Bill Broonzy and Lonnie Johnson. She used the guitar to respond to her vocal melodies, playing single note lines that were improvised variations of the vocal melody. Her biggest hits came from her upbeat and syncopated renditions of songs like "I Looked Down the Line," "That's All," and "This Train."

By the late 1960s Tharpe's popularity had waned, but she continued to tour the country on the "chitlin circuit," playing in backwoods bars and small-town theaters. She suffered a stroke in 1973 and died in Philadelphia, Pennsylvania, one day before an anticipated recording session.

See Also

Broonzy, William Lee Conley ("Big Bill"); Calloway, Cabell (Cab); Church of God in Christ; Cleveland, James Edward; Dorsey, Thomas Andrew; Gospel Music; New York, New York; Pentecostalism.

Africa

Theater, African overview of theatrical traditions in Africa.

Africa is home to several traditions of theater. Some of these traditions are of ancient origin, while others emerged with formal European colonization of the continent in the nineteenth century and the subsequent imposition of Western education, religion, and culture.

The older traditions are mostly nonscripted, improvisatory, and performed in indigenous African languages. Their conceptions of theater space and stage-audience relations are fluid and informal: any space can be turned into a performance stage, and the audience is free to interact with the performance in a variety of ways and even move in and out of the theater space during the performance. This type of performance is often public and the audience does not pay a fee, although performers could be rewarded in cash or kind for their artistry.

Many of the newer theater traditions are text based, written in European languages or indigenous African languages with Latin script. The plays are designed to be performed in more or less formal theater buildings with fixed relations between performers and audience. The audience usually pays a fee, although the theater may not be expressly commercial.

In all cases, as indeed in all societies, the functions of the theater traditions are broadly similar in their mixing of the pleasing and the pedagogical: their representations provide the audience with pleasurable entertainment while simultaneously channeling passions and sentiments in certain directions.

Theater in Africa could be categorized into four distinct traditions: festival theater, popular theater, development theater, and art theater.

Festival Theater

In many African communities the foremost indigenous cultural and artistic institution is the festival. These might be organized around certain deities or spirits (*see* African Religions: An Interpretation), to celebrate rites of passage, or to mark the passage of seasons. Festivals incorporate diverse forms, such as singing, chanting, drama, drumming, masking, miming, costuming, and puppetry (*see* Music, African). The accompanying theatrical enactments – from the sacred and secretive to the secular and public – can last from a few hours to several days, weeks, or months. Each festival dramatizes a story or myth (or sometimes related sets of stories or myths) connecting the particular subject of the festival, for example a deity or a season, to the life of the community. Artistically, the performances also serve to showcase the community's new artistic forms as well as changes in existing ones.

Festival theater is performed in an open space in the town square or a similarly appointed location. The audience members sit or stand in layers of circles around the performers, and are able to drift in and out of the performance. They close in or fan out depending on perceptions of the volume of space needed by the performers at particular moments of the action. There is a close relationship between the performers and the audience, with the latter sometimes even serving as chorus, but there are also distinctions, and it is treasured cultural knowledge to know when to and when not to interject in the performance. Aesthetically, the performance may take a full range of styles from realism to surrealism and spirit possession. This is partly why an empty space, with little prop or theatrical pretensions, is all that is needed for the communion between performer and audience on one hand, and the performance and society on the other.

There are two ways in which scholars have tried to understand African festivals. Some scholars label the festival as "pre-drama" or "traditional ritual" or "ritual drama," because of its expansive multimedia format, its firm integration of the dramatic amidst the other arts, and the presence of both religious and secular reenactments. The assumption of these scholars, whether acknowledged or not, is that the twentieth-century Western theater, with its packaged three hours, strict compartmentalization of the arts, and the virtual absence of the sacred, constitutes the norm of "theater."

Other scholars have argued that the festival is in fact the fully fledged theater and that contemporary Western theater could in fact be seen as nothing more than severely abbreviated festival. The argument of Wole Soyinka, Africa's leading dramatist and winner of the Nobel Prize for Literature, best exemplifies this view. He insists that festivals be seen as constituting "in themselves pure theater at its most prodigal and resourceful… the most stirring expressions of man's instinct and need for drama at its most comprehensive and community-involving." In one sweeping move, he turns a colonialist interpretation of the festival on its head: "Instead of considering festivals from one point of view only – that of providing, in a primitive form, the ingredients of drama – we may even begin examining the opposite point of view: that contemporary drama, as we experience it today, is a contraction of drama, necessitated by the productive order of society in other directions."

Popular Theater

"Popular" theater – those theater forms that have large followings at the point of reception – cuts across class or status boundaries. Early forms have their roots in sacred ceremonies and involve elaborate masking, such as the Alarinjo and Apidan theaters of Nigeria.

Today the recurring themes in African popular theater are those with broad appeal, and are intimately linked to genre. Particularly common in comedies and melodramas are themes such as unrequited love; marital infidelity; unemployment; pretensions to wealth, status, or sophistication; the conundrums of modern city life; and dreams of travel abroad. Satires have targeted egotistical chiefs; the rich but miserly; the strange manners of Europeans (explorers, missionaries, or colonial administrators and their spouses); corrupt politicians; overly Westernized African men and women; prostitutes; and the rural village teacher. Matters of fate and predestination and the mythological lives of deities, legends, and powerful historical figures have been explored in tragedies and other serious dramas.

One reason for the wide appeal of popular theater is that it is most often performed in the indigenous language or hybrids of them designed to be understood across linguistic borders. Increasingly many subtraditions are being produced in forms of the European languages that came with colonization, or in "pidgin" – a distinctive mixture of one such foreign language and an indigenous language.

Early forms, and even more recent forms such as the Ghanaian Concert Party, have traditionally been composed only of male performers. Generally, more recent forms such as the Yoruba Popular Travelling Theater, the Chikwakwa Theater of Zambia, and the South African Township Theater, include both male and female performers. The performers are in most cases organized as traveling troupes that perform in a variety of available spaces, including open squares, enclosed courtyards of kings and chiefs, school classrooms, concert or cinema halls, bars or nightclubs, and well-equipped theaters. Most popular theater forms are not scripted but are based on improvisations, giving the performers much leeway but also demanding an unusual dexterity in speech, movement, and gesture.

Development Theater

In certain radical or leftist traditions of African theater scholarship, "development theater" is also known as popular theater, but the conception of the "popular" in this case is vastly different from that mentioned above. While in popular theater the "popular" is marked at the point of consumption or reception, in development theater, the "popular" is read at the point of production. In other words, "popular" here means produced by an alliance of intellectuals, workers, and peasants and expressly constructed to advance the interests of the oppressed classes in society. This conception of the popular is inspired by the radical Marxist German dramatist Bertolt Brecht.

This form of theater is geared to raising the consciousness of the exploited classes so they can struggle for their liberation. To liberate themselves, in the Marxist understanding, is also to liberate the productive forces of the society from private appropriation and so ensure genuine development. It is in this sense that this tradition of theater is called "development theater." In addition to Brecht, other significant conceptual supports for development theater come from Augusto Boal and Paulo Freire.

Not all forms of development theater are obviously or tendentiously ideologically charged. Many are designed as adult education programs to teach literacy or explain the political process so people can better know their rights and responsibilities. Others communicate better agricultural techniques, teach ways of treating or preventing certain diseases, or encourage community mobilization for self-help projects and general rural development. Workshops are held regularly to teach the people how to organize themselves to use the theater both as an expression of culture and as a tool for fostering social, political, and economic development.

Development theater practitioners are mostly professional intellectuals, often affiliated with a university, working with a variety of groups in mostly rural areas. In much of Africa rural areas receive fewer of the benefits of "modernity" and are therefore the target of development schemes (*see* Development in Africa: An Interpretation and Development).

Given the direct, instrumentalist goal of the theater, the performances are often didactic and exhortatory, though the more skilled adult educators go to great lengths to emphasize aesthetics and even incorporate popular forms from the people's indigenous performance traditions. A minor form of development theater practice is the "guerrilla theater," in which committed groups emerge unannounced at carefully chosen public locations and stage provocative performances, usually against particular government policies, and disappear before the agents of law and order appear.

An important example of development theater practice includes the Laedza Batanani of Botswana in the mid-1970s, which subsequently served as a model and inspiration for similar experiments in Lesotho, Zambia, Malawi, Sierra Leone, and Nigeria. Perhaps the most oppositional of the experiments was the Kamiriithu Education and Cultural Center, led by Ngugi wa Thiong'o, the leading Kenyan writer. The center was so successful in mobilizing the community to explore their history and culture and contemporary situation critically through theater that Ngugi was imprisoned for a year without trial in 1977. By 1982 the Kenyan government had razed the center and banned all theater activities in the area.

Art Theater

Art theater is the tradition of African theater most familiar to the outside world through the published works of the continent's notable playwrights such as Wole Soyinka, Athol Fugard, Femi Osofisan, Ama Ata Aidoo, Zulu Sofola, Efua Sutherland, Ola Rotimi, J. P. Clark-Bekederemo, Sony Labou Tansi, Guillaume Oyono-Mbia, Werewere Liking, and Tess Onwueme, among others. Art theater in Africa is of colonial origin; it emerged with the training of Africans in European languages and literatures and dramatic traditions, and it is most often written in the colonial languages. The label "art theater" signifies the tradition's relationship to, and investment in, notions of "high art" or "great works" characteristic of Western bourgeois cultural discourse since the nineteenth century.

The practitioners of art theater are usually professional intellectuals affiliated with universities or other institutions of higher education. Although the best dramas of this tradition borrow richly from indigenous performance forms, the overall "mold" of drama into which those borrowings are poured, as well as the languages in which they are written and performed, are European and greatly circumscribe their popularity with the majority of Africans who are not schooled in those aesthetics or languages. The Nigerian dramatist J. P. Clark-Bekederemo, comparing the YORUBA Popular Travelling Theater with the art theater, once observed that "[s]ome would say that the latter has its head deep in the wings of American and European theater!" It was for this reason that Ngugi wa Thiong'o, after a distinguished career of writing several novels and plays in English, switched to creating plays in his KIKUYU language.

Some have questioned whether art theater could really be original and authentically African as long as it borrows aesthetic structures from and speaks the languages of Europe. Such a charge and its purist conceptions of transcultural relations have never been a serious handicap for the truly creative minds of African art theater. They continue to confront the colonial inheritance and revise it from a variety of perspectives, without any surrender of initiative. For them, the centuries of African unequal contact with Europe are undeniable, and cultural purism, absolutism, and insularity are not necessarily worthy coordinates of "originality." The Mexican writer Octavio Paz speaks for the writers of the ex-colonial world when he argues that the literatures they write "did not passively accept the changing fortunes of their transplanted languages: they participated in the process and even accelerated it. Soon they ceased to be mere transatlantic reflections. At times they have been the negation of the literatures of Europe; more often, they have been a reply."

The hub of art theater activity in Africa is mostly the urban areas – cities and universities. This is also where most of the audience, those schooled in Western languages, is located. Performance takes place in formal theater buildings, frequently with the proscenium stage, which is hegemonic in Europe and America. Art theater is primarily state-subsidized and rarely self-sustaining as a commercial enterprise. Indeed, art theater is consumed more as dramatic literature – read widely in schools and colleges – than as theater.

Many practitioners of art theater have attempted to ameliorate the obvious elitism of the tradition by establishing community theaters or traveling theaters run by university resident professionals or drama students. These projects designed to take the art theater to the masses of the people are often very expensive and have existed only intermittently. Some of the famous examples are the University of Ibadan traveling theater (Nigeria, in the 1960s), the Makerere Free Travelling Theater (Uganda, 1960s and 1970s), the University of Malawi Travelling Theater (1970s), and the University of Zambia Chikwakwa Theater (1970s and 1980s). There is the particularly unique case of the South African Athol Fugard, who broke for some time from his normal routine of formal playwriting in the 1970s to collaborate with the actors Winston Ntshona and John Kani. Their improvisations led to many well-received plays against the APARTHEID state and inaugurated a genre of popular theater labeled South African protest theater. The most frequently performed of such plays is *Sizwe Bansi Is Dead* (1973). These efforts, in less formal surroundings, make art theater performances – sometimes of plays in translations or in pidgin, or of text-based improvisations – available to audiences that would otherwise not have access to them.

Tejumola Olaniyan

SEE ALSO
Antiapartheid Movement; South Africa.

Latin America and the Caribbean

Theater in the Caribbean,

the history of theater in the Spanish-, French-, and English-speaking Caribbean, particularly as it pertains to people of African descent.

Contemporary theater in the Caribbean has been shaped by the different cultures – Native American, European, African, East Indian, Madeiran, and Chinese – that have brought forms of performance from around the world to the Caribbean basin. Throughout the nineteenth and twentieth centuries in the Caribbean, the elements of stage and street performance, including written plays, storytelling, festivals, music and dance, combined to create new types of theater. During colonial times stage performance was often sponsored by the wealthy and evolved separately from African culture. More recently, however, performers and directors have begun to explore the African roots of a Caribbean theater through the incorporation of Afro-Caribbean religious practices and social rituals (such as dance, storytelling, and singing), which date to the period of slavery or earlier.

EARLY INFLUENCES

Performance was a critical part of the early colonial history of the islands, mediating the contacts between natives and European missionaries. The native Carib and Arawak peoples of the Antilles enacted *areítos*, which, according to scholar Sandra Cypess, were "complex theatre-dance forms that incorporated music with full-dress costume to recount the historical, religious, and cultural repertoire of the society." When missionaries arrived, they appropriated the *areítos* dramatic form to teach the tenets of Christianity (*see* CATHOLIC CHURCH IN LATIN AMERICA AND THE CARIBBEAN).

Later, European colonizers, as well as elite mulattos (people of African and European descent) in the French and Spanish territories such as present-day CUBA, PUERTO RICO, DOMINICAN REPUBLIC, and HAITI, enjoyed imported theatrical performances on stage. From the seventeenth century onward and during the course of the TRANSATLANTIC SLAVE TRADE, landholders and the small commercial elite watched professional companies from Europe, and later North America, perform plays written abroad. The audience of mostly white Creole (offspring of Europeans born in the Americas) plantation owners and wealthy merchants attended performances in newly built playhouses and public halls. By 1800 strolling players from North America were entertaining those who could not afford the expensive theater tickets.

On the plantations slaves kept alive African performance traditions (*see* THEATER, AFRICAN), developing these into new forms that were both modes of resistance and expressions of celebration. Gifted storytellers integrated tales and performance, often incorporating music and dance. ASANTE slaves from the African Gold Coast (now GHANA) brought one narrative tradition, the Anancy (Anansi) story, that developed as a form throughout the Afro-Caribbean. Originally centered on the trickster character of a spider who was a master of wit and cunning, the Anancy stories evolved to include African beast fables and sometimes even European fairy tales, but maintained the element of song. Frequently these stories centered on survival strategies to maintain the spirit in the face of slavery. Festivals such as the Christmas celebration *Jonkonnu* in JAMAICA incorporated the sounds of drums, horns, flutes, rattles and fiddles – instruments that later made their way into the music of contemporary Caribbean theater. Some of these festivals also brought elements of closed stage to the streets: often a performer reproduced stage drama scenes and costumes for audiences outside the theater.

Starting in the mid-nineteenth century another group added its dramatic traditions to the mix. Indentured laborers came from India, bringing their own festivals to Trinidad, GUYANA, SURINAME and JAMAICA. The Caribbean transformed these performances: for example, the Muslim celebration of *Muharram*, a reenactment of a mythical story staged the first month of the Muslim year, came to incorporate influences from Hindus and Afro-Caribbean participants as well (*see* EAST INDIAN COMMUNITIES IN THE CARIBBEAN).

Over the years Afro-Caribbean performance grew from an art form barely tolerated by plantation owners, to an underground movement after abolition, and finally to an expression of national culture in the twentieth century. Yet even as traditions of storytelling, music, dance and festival maintained their presence in their homes and on the streets, Afro-Caribbeans themselves also sought to enter the world of stage theater. It was not until well into the twentieth century that plays by Afro-Caribbeans began to be produced in considerable numbers. The same was true in BRAZIL, where the TEATRO EXPERIMENTAL DO NEGRO (Black Experimental Theater, TEN) brought Afro-Brazilian plays to the stage beginning in 1944. When blacks finally made their way onto the stage, they transformed the Caribbean theater world by incorporating their performance traditions and by emphasizing community building through theater.

THEATER IN THE HISPANIC CARIBBEAN

In 1588 the first white *criollo* (American born of Spanish descent) playwright, Cristóbal de Llerena de Rueda, from HISPANIOLA (now DOMINICAN REPUBLIC), began the Caribbean theatrical traditions of parody and social commentary that would continue to characterize Spanish-speaking Caribbean theater well into the twentieth century. Although it was some time before Afro-Caribbeans themselves made it into the exclusive ranks of art theater, their presence was felt on the stage long before that. In PUERTO RICO Alejandro Tapia y Rivera (1826-1882), for example, wrote plays such as *La cuarterona* (1867, The Quadroon), that underscored the racially mixed milieu of the colony (see COLONIAL LATIN AMERICA AND THE CARIBBEAN). Sometimes the awareness of an African presence took the form of anxious ridicule: Francisco Covarrubias, considered the "father of Cuban national theater," used the trope of *"el negrito,"* or blackface. This *teatro bufo*, as it came to be known, became increasingly popular in mid to late nineteenth-century Cuba, demonstrating the centrality of the African presence in Cuba. Performed by white actors who parodied the looks and manners of blacks, el negrito revealed more about the racism of white society than it presented an accurate portrayal of Afro-Cubans. As scholar Jill Lane points out, teatro bufo used stereotypical portrayals of Africans to define a distinct white *criollo* identity: "Blackface performance catered to the anxieties of a white social class deeply concerned with their own racial definition in an unstable matrix of race, class, and power." In other words, in a racial milieu that was increasingly mixed, the Caribbean-born whites forged their own identity in uneasy opposition to the Afro-Caribbeans.

By the 1930s theater in Puerto Rico had become an important vehicle to represent and define national identity. In 1938 playwright and director Emilio Belaval (b. 1903) developed the short-lived national theater in San Juan, producing plays with national themes such as the need for social reform. The theater used drama to advocate the cause of the *jíbaro* (peasant), a figure that was increasingly becoming a rallying point for national identity. Belaval's theater also explored such politicized issues as the immigrant experience in the United States (*see* AFRO-LATINO CULTURES IN THE UNITED STATES). From 1944 the presentation of Puerto Rican plays at the University of Puerto Rico was banned following the adoption of commonwealth status in 1952, possibly because of the genre's potential for political commentary. After 1956 Puerto Rican theater found its renewal under the direction of Francisco Arriví, Manuel Méndez Ballester, and René Marqués. This trio dominated the theater scene, producing plays that explored a range of social, political, philosophic, and psychological quandaries. These directors were responding to the political and economic situation after the United States-sponsored plan for accelerated development known as Operation Bootstrap. Like many Puerto Rican writers and intellectuals of the time, they reacted to U.S. imperialism by defending the Hispanic culture: Marqués's *La carreta* (1952, The Ox-Cart), for example, underscored the economic difficulties faced by Puerto Ricans in the island and focused on the need to preserve Hispanic culture. As a result, within nationalist narratives of Puerto Rico, the history of Hispanic culture was frequently emphasized over that of Africans.

Early twentieth-century theater in CUBA, particularly Luis A. Baralt's (1892-1969) *Teatro la Cueva* (1928, Cave Theatre), drew on avant-garde movements of Latin American and European theater more closely than other places. Since the 1959 Cuban Revolution theater has enjoyed a privileged position in the island. Seeing theater as a critical tool of education to reach working classes, the Cuban leader Fidel Castro encouraged the movement of the theater into public spaces and the development of community-based theater. This was the theater of collective creation. According to scholar Martin Banham: "Community based, this movement adopts the method of research into problems of a given geographic area in which the theater is located with attempts to solve these problems in a dramatic presentation with community involvement." For example, Grupo Teatro Escambray, founded in 1968, used regional interviews to create local performances incorporating the concerns of a particular community. Cuban theater has explored Cuba's vibrant African traditions. For example, Eugenio Hernández Espinosa, with his plays *María Antonia* (1976), *Oba y Shangó* (1980, King and Shangó), and *Odebí el cazador* (1980, Odebí the Hunter), has focused on issues of ethnic marginality and African mythic traditions. However, given the administration's official position that class conflict is the main factor underlying racial tensions, plays that emphasize class issues have frequently been supported over those that accentuate the African racial and cultural heritage of Cuba.

THEATER IN HAITI AND THE FRANCOPHONE CARIBBEAN

Early Haitian theater can be divided into two linguistic groups: French-speaking and Creole-speaking. The first type was the most popular within elite classes, even after the HAITIAN REVOLUTION (1791-1804). Early Francophone stage theater in HAITI was mostly confined to imported performances, or theater focused on the themes dominant in France. The second theatrical form developed around Creole, the everyday language of most Haitians. The *Indigéniste* (Autochthonous) movement, was an early Haitian movement which asserted folk culture in response to the 1915-1934 United States occupation. It has only been recently, however, as Creole gains official recognition within Haiti, that art theater has expanded to include Creole performances.

In French-speaking MARTINIQUE and GUADELOUPE theater underwent a transformation during the 1930s, shifting from themes that emphasized French cultural heritage to a celebration of African identity. The NÉGRITUDE movement that shaped Francophone theater in the twentieth century was initiated by AIMÉ CÉSAIRE (b. 1913) from Martinique, LÉON-GONTRAN DAMAS (1912-1978) from FRENCH GUIANA, and Léopold Sédar Senghor (b. 1906) from SENEGAL. According to scholar Juris Silenieks, the 1960-1975 period of the Négritude movement and its followers "feature a spirit of confrontational combativeness and a commitment to intervene in the burning sociopolitical issues of the day." Those issues were most often colonization and African identity. Three of Césaire's plays from that period, *La Tragédie du Roi Christophe* (1963, The Tragedy of King Christophe), *Une saison au Congo* (1966, A Season in Congo), and *Une tempête* (1969, A Tempest, an adaptation of William Shakespeare's *The Tempest*), focus on the impact of colonialism and the need for a decolonization that is cultural as well as political. In both historical and contemporary plays Césaire integrated African, Caribbean, and French themes to engage with the black liberation movements of the 1960s.

Despite their Afrocentric outlooks, for the most part Négritude playwrights chose French as their mode of expression over the Creole spoken by many of African descent. They also looked more toward a pure African identity rather than the hybrid culture of the Caribbean. Haitians Félix Morisseau-Leroy (*b.* 1912) and Gérard Chenet (*b.* 1929), despite their dissimilar politics and styles, continued to turn to Africa as a source of inspiration for their work.

As interest in Afro-Caribbean identity widened, more writers became interested in theatrical works incorporating Creole language. As early as 1954 Morriseau-Leroy had published the play *Antigone en Creole*, in part as a response to elite notions that French was the only language for intellectual works in Haitian theater. EDOUARD GLISSANT (*b.* 1928), a student of Césaire, began using Creole words and phrases as well as syntax in his work. More recent playwrights, such as Martiniquan writers Ina Césaire and PATRICK CHAMOISEAU, have integrated Creole as well as other elements of oral culture and folklore into their theatrical works.

Many contemporary playwrights have concerned themselves with exploring the many cultural, as well as linguistic, influences in the French-speaking Caribbean. Maryse Condé's plays *Dieu nous l'a donné* (1972, God Gave it to Us) and *Mort d'Oluwémi d'Ajumako* (1973, The Death of Oluwémi of Ajumako), examined the impact of new values upon traditional communities in the Caribbean. Franck Fouché integrated elements from Catholic and Vodou rituals to produce *Général Baron-la-Croix ou le silence masqué* (1971, General Baron of the Cross or Masked Silence), a play performed in Creole.

Theater in the Anglophone Caribbean
The 1930s were a turning point in Anglophone Caribbean theater, as cultural leaders, spurred by the Négritude movement, turned to drama with the end goal of validating African identity and retelling Caribbean history. This was accompanied by a movement to take art theater outside the confines of the stage, begun as early as 1869, when Henry G. Murray toured Jamaica with oral performances representing Jamaican society. In 1931 Guyanese writer Norman Cameron (b. 1903), for example, wrote plays based on African history and performed them in Guyanese schools. By integrating political drama with the vibrant cultural forms of storytelling and festival, producers and playwrights sought to promote political causes such as decolonization and nationalism. In Jamaica the Pan-Africanist Marcus Garvey (1887-1940) created a "theater for the masses" in 1930 on an open-air stage in Kingston. Along with three of his own productions, the stage hosted the popular comedy work of Ranny Williams. In 1939, as labor unrest increased in Jamaica, Frank Hill produced *Upheaval*, using the stage to promote social revolution.

In London Trinidadian C.L.R. James (1901-1989) brought the experience and aftermath of the Haitian Revolution to the world with his production of *Toussaint L'Overture* (1936). The play was groundbreaking, not only because it represented the little-known history of the Haitian Revolution, but also because it turned the attention of the Caribbean theater as a whole toward the relatively unexplored subject of Caribbean history. Other authors, such as Una Marson (1905-1965), considered by some to be the most successful playwright in 1930s Jamaica, explored the social milieu of the Caribbean with plays such as *Pocomania* (1938).

The expansion of national theater in the Anglophone Caribbean during the 1930s was followed by an increased interest in both folk tradition and the production of local plays. The opening of the University of the West Indies in 1947 was a critical factor in the increase in writing and publication of plays by Anglophone West Indians. The production of local plays expanded exponentially during the 1950s: writers included Cicely Waite-Smith (b. 1913), Barry Reckord (b. 1930), and Samuel Hillary (b. 1936) in Jamaica; Douglas Archibald (b. 1919), Errol Hill (b. 1921), and Errol John (b. 1918) in Trinidad; Derek Walcott (b. 1930) and twin brother Roddy Walcott (b. 1930) in St. Lucia; Frank Pilgrim and Sheik Sadeek (1921-) in Guyana. The most internationally successful of this group was Nobel Prize winner Derek Walcott, whose early plays such as *Dream on Monkey Mountain* (1967) and *Pantomime* (1980) merged the language of poetry with a condemnation of colonialism and racism. Walcott also founded the Trinidad Theatre Workshop in 1959, a group that was instrumental in bringing to the stage *patois* – a dialect mixing European and African languages that was, for many, the everyday language in this part of the Caribbean.

Also during the 1950s Louise Bennett (b. 1919) of Jamaica was fundamental in the development of a style that came to be known as "speech theater." Integrating storytelling techniques with stage theater, she helped validate traditional Afro-Caribbean cultural forms such as the already-mentioned Anancy Story. Later dramatists such as Paul Keens-Douglas (b. 1942) were influenced by her groundbreaking work.

Bennett combined drama with social organizing by working with villages to help identify their needs and solve them. This kind of work was taken up by the Sistren Collective, founded in 1977. Led by director Honor Ford-Smith, the theater's first major production was "Bellywoman Bangarang" in 1978, which used experiences drawn from working-class women's lives, as well as games, songs, and dances. Sistren Collective has been instrumental in recuperating the history of women's contributions to Afro-Caribbean struggles: the play *Nana Yah* was about the seventeenth century slave maroon leader Nanny. The Sistren Collective, which published *Lionheart Gal: Life Stories of Jamaican Women* in 1986, has been an important role model in a Caribbean theater world that remains dominated by male playwrights.

Marian Aguiar

See Also
Condé, Maryse; Senghor, Léopold Sédar; Maroonage in the Americas; Pan-Africanism; Slavery in Latin America and the Caribbean; Creoles; Garvey, Marcus Mosiah; James, Cyril Lionel Richard; Racial Stereotypes; Walcott, Derek Alton; Kingston, Jamaica; Trinidad and Tobago; East Indian Communities in the Caribbean; Abolition and Emancipation in Latin America and the Caribbean; Catholic Church in Latin America and the Caribbean; Languages, Creole, in the Caribbean; Afrocentrism; San Juan, Puerto Rico; Anancy Story.

Africa

Thebes, Egypt, capital city and ceremonial center of the ancient Egyptian empire.

The ancient city of Thebes was situated on both sides of the Nile in upper Egypt. It comprised a residential town on the eastern bank, whose ruins extend into present-day Luxor and Karnak, and a more famous western side, which contained the pharaonic cemetery and the Valley of the Kings. It is in this location that the graves of the New Kingdom pharaohs lie (also called the Theban necropolis and the "city of the dead").

The history of the city of Thebes can be traced back approximately 4500 years to the twenty-fifth century B.C.E. The city began as an obscure village called *Waset*, named after *Wast*, the village's local goddess. During a period of political instability in Egypt referred to as the First Intermediate Period (2130-1938 B.C.E.), however, powerful Theban *nomarchs* (governors) emerged, and the city grew in importance with them. Eventually, these nomarchs successfully challenged the Heracleopolitan pharaohs of the north. Mentuhotep II of Thebes, who reigned 2008-1957 B.C.E., reunited Egypt. He established Thebes as his capital as well as the center of worship of the national god, Amon, which was brought to the city at that time. Though during the Twelfth Dynasty (1938-1756 B.C.E.) the descendants of Mentuhotep moved their capital to Memphis to the north (*see* Cairo, Egypt), they continued to bestow riches on the temples and tombs of the city of Amon.

Hyksos invaders from Asia took control of Egypt during the Second Intermediate Period (1630-1540 B.C.E.). However, powerful ruling families from Thebes succeeded in driving the Hyksos out of Egypt in about 1540 B.C.E. They reunited the kingdom and made Thebes the center of Egyptian political and religious life. As Egypt expanded to encompass an empire that spanned from Syria to Nubia, vast wealth from every corner of the empire funneled into Thebes. During the early fourteenth century B.C.E. Thebes reached the height of its power and prosperity.

After a brief eclipse when Akhenaton, who ruled from 1353 to 1336 B.C.E., moved the capital to Memphis, Thebes enjoyed renewed prosperity. Pharaohs such as Ramses II, who ruled from 1279 to 1213 B.C.E., resided in Thebes for only part of each year but generously funded the maintenance and expansion of the temple complex. From the twelfth century B.C.E. onward, however, Thebes began a slow and irreversible decline. The Assyrians sacked the city in 663 B.C.E., and the Romans destroyed it in the first century B.C.E.

Under Roman rule a provincial center rose among the southernmost ruins of Thebes. This town, the forerunner of modern Luxor, was home to a substantial community of Coptic Christians, who built churches among the ruins. To this day many of Luxor's inhabitants are Christian.

Modern visitors can explore the town of Karnak, located among the northern ruins of Thebes. Situated in Karnak are the ruins of the precinct of Amon, a complex of buildings commissioned by a succession of pharaohs. In addition, Karnak features ruins of the precinct of Amon's wife Mut, the war god Montu, and an avenue of sphinxes. In Luxor to the south, one can visit the ruins of the old and new winter palaces, and the Luxor temple.

Robert Fay

See Also

Roman Africa: An Interpretation; Christianity, African: An Overview; Egypt, Ancient Kingdom of; Nile River.

Africa

Theiler, Max (b. 1899; d. 1972), South African virologist and Nobel Prize winner who made major contributions to research on the viral disease known as yellow fever.

Born in Pretoria, Max Theiler studied medicine at the University of Cape Town, leaving for England in 1919 for Saint Thomas's Hospital Medical School, London, where he completed his medical training in 1922. That year he moved to the United States and joined the Department of Tropical Medicine at the Harvard Medical School. In 1930 he accepted a post with the Rockefeller Foundation in New York City. He remained with the foundation until 1964, when he became professor of epidemiology at Yale University, New Haven, Connecticut.

At Harvard, Theiler's early research interest was in amoebic dysentery, but he soon switched his efforts to yellow fever. An important finding during the 1920s was that monkeys could be infected with the virus and then used for experimentation. Theiler, in a major advance, demonstrated that mice could serve as a much more convenient and inexpensive experimental model.

Using mice, he developed highly efficient methods for breeding the yellow fever virus as he pursued various strategies for vaccines. In 1934 Theiler developed a vaccine based on an "attenuated," or weakened, form of the virus cultivated in mice. Scratched into the skin, the virus would not cause yellow fever, but would provoke the body's immune system to protect against any subsequent infections. Because this vaccine sometimes caused encephalitis, an inflammation of the brain, Theiler continued to refine his vaccine experiments. In 1937 he introduced another vaccine, designated 17D, based on another strain of the virus that was grown in chicken embryos. Between 1940 and 1947 the 17D vaccine was used to protect more than 28 million people in Africa and the Americas. Today, although still a problem in remote areas, yellow fever has been vastly reduced as a health threat.

In addition to his Nobel Prize, Theiler received the Albert Lasher Award in 1945. Theiler remained in the United States for the rest of his life although he never became a United States citizen.

Barbara Worley

See Also

New York, New York.

North America

Theology, Black, an African American theological movement founded in the 1960s whose biblical interpretations supported black liberation.

When the nonviolent tactics of the Civil Rights Movement gave way to Black Power in the mid-1960s, African American ministers considered the compatibility of the new militancy with Christianity. Many of them had participated in Civil Rights protests. They were jailed and attacked by police dogs, often finding themselves performing funeral services for fellow activists slain by Southern racists. The lagging pace of social change and the noble stoicism advocated by white liberals in the face of the increasing entrenchment of white supremacy frustrated them as much as it did the insurgent generation of black nationalists. Realizing the urgent need to adopt new political tactics and calling themselves the National Council of Black Churchmen, these ministers published on July 26, 1966, an opinion piece in the *New York Times* endorsing Black Power and set about finding a way to reconcile it with Christian theology.

Black Power, according to James H. Cone, a theologian who contributed to the *Times* article, was "Christ's central message to twentieth-century America." Cone soon emerged as the outstanding figure in what became known as Black Theology. His *Black Theology and Black Power* (1969) was the first book to use the term and, alongside Cone's *A Black Theology of Liberation* (1970), provided its most articulate explanations.

Black Theology little resembled dominant theological beliefs in North America and Europe. Where the traditional discipline of theology responded to the crisis of spirituality that originated in the rationalism of the European Enlightenment, Black Theology's focus was less abstract. It was more concerned with the material deprivation and suffering of people in the real world. The theoretical methods of the social sciences were used to discern the causes of the oppression of African Americans, and interpretations of Christ's teachings provided a justification for black emancipation. "Black Theology seeks to analyze the Satanic nature of Whiteness," Cone wrote, "and by doing so to prepare all Non-Whites for revolutionary action."

In part, Black Theology emerged in response to claims that the black church lacked the theological acumen of the white church. "Negro congregations are not churches but religious societies," wrote theologian Joseph Washington in *Black Religion* (1964). "Religion can choose to worship God as it so pleases. But a church without a theology... is a contradiction in terms." Washington argued that the African American church was a unique institution, deeply rooted in New World interpretations of African traditions, but that its development was arrested because of its separation from mainstream denominations. To remedy its primitive nature, he advocated the full-scale absorption of the black church by mainstream Protestantism.

Black Religion was praised by whites, but denounced by blacks. Albert Cleage's heated response in *The Black Messiah* and *Black Christian Nationalism* attempted to refute Washington's claims and in so doing provided an early articulation of Black Theology. Pastor of Detroit's Shrine of the Black Madonna, Cleage argued that African Americans should liberate themselves from the oppressive religious doctrines of white Christianity. He posited that Christ was a black revolutionary leader sent by God to help liberate black people and build a black nation. Cone's *The Spirituals and the Blues* (1972), on the other hand, asserted that the long history of popular manifestations of black culture – sermons, sayings, songs, and stories – provided the theological grounding that Washington suggested was missing.

By championing the oppressed populations of black America, Black Theology displayed an affinity with the radical, socially committed Liberation Theology concurrently developing in Latin America. However, while Black Theology focused on the primacy of race and white supremacy in the oppression of African Americans, Liberation Theology's understanding of exploitation was based on analyses of class and capitalism. Latin American Liberation Theology applied Marxist social theory to understand the political economy of dependency, underdevelopment, neocolonialism, and imperialism in the region. It was not until Black Theologians had contact with their Third World brethren in the late 1970s that the effects of capitalism were understood alongside those of racism.

Despite its strong endorsement of Black Power and its appropriation of many of its methods and aims, Black Theology had a paradoxical relationship to that movement. It found a large audience within clerical circles, but remained distant from much of the secular politicking of Black Power. Although part of its aim was to reclaim and revive Christianity in black-centered terms, many Black Nationalist leaders, including Malcolm X and Stokely Carmichael, denounced Christianity as the white man's religion. Often, the Church was seen only in terms of its role in abetting the oppression of black people. Furthermore, critics have charged that by the demise of the Black Power Movement in the 1970s, Black Theology had lost its insurgent edge. As Black Theology became ensconced in academia, it grew disconnected from the black community and church. "With its growing establishment as an academic discipline," writes Diana L. Hayes in her primer of Black Theology, *And Still We Rise* (1996), "its discussions became increasingly abstract and lifeless; they, to a certain extent, established Black Theology's academic credentials but at the risk of losing its contextual relevance and liberative force."

The challenges that Black Theology posed to traditional theology and black and white churches, however, cannot be overlooked. In addition, the impact of Black Theology goes beyond the borders of the United States. The dialogues on the theory and practice of theology generated through the Theologies in the Americas Project and the Ecumenical Association of Third World Theologians have fostered a sense of solidarity among an international contingent of theologians. In SOUTH AFRICA the struggle that led to the downfall of APARTHEID and the rise of a nonracial democracy benefited from Black Theology, especially the work of James Cone. Steve Biko, the father of South Africa's Black Consciousness Movement, read *Black Theology and Black Power* alongside the work of Malcolm X and other African American activists. Its effects can also be seen in Rev. Allan Boesak's *Black Theology, Black Power* (1978) and *Black and Reformed* (1984), as well as in the political work of such churchmen as former archbishop Desmond Tutu and Bishop Manas Buthelezi.

Peter Hudson

SEE ALSO
Biko, Stephen; Race: An Interpretation; Black Consciousness in Africa; Buthelezi, Mangosutho Gatsha; Tutu, Desmond Mpilo; Black Church, The; Black Nationalism in the United States.

Cross Cultural

Third Cinema, also called Third World cinema; a type of film and film theory prevalent in Africa, Latin America, and Asia that aims to transform society by educating and radicalizing the film audience through "subversive" cinema.

In the early 1960s a series of events paved the way for a new and distinctive type of Third World film. In Africa decolonization freed film directors such as Ousmane Sembène, Med Hondo, and HAILE GERIMA to make films for and about Africans. In Latin America and Asia revolutionary movements, combined with the development of Marxist film theory and Italian neorealism, inspired film directors such as Bolivian Jorge Sanjines and Indian Satyajit Ray to make politically charged films. Guided by the assumption that all film is ideological, they experimented with film as a weapon against the cultural imperialism of Hollywood.

During the next decade film directors from Africa, Asia, and Latin America met and discussed their work at meetings and international film festivals. They called their cinema "Third Cinema" to identify it with the Third World and to differentiate it from the "first," or traditional, cinema (characterized by commercial films produced by Hollywood) and the "second," or counter, cinema (characterized by art film movements such as French New Wave). By the late 1960s Third Cinema had established itself as an influential theory, especially in Africa.

Inspired by Marxist film criticism and the writings of FRANTZ FANON, Third Cinema theory radically reinterprets the relationship between film, audience, and film director. It characterizes traditional film directors as agents of capitalism who "sell" to their passive audiences movies that promote colonial stereotypes and consumer society values. According to African American filmmaker Charles Taylor, traditional Hollywood cinema "concocts an artificial mental landscape harmonious with [capitalism's] need to depersonalize its audiences into zombies of its economy and addicts of its industrial culture, and to trash, trivialize, and erase the human culture that supply its victims."

By contrast Third Cinema must, in the words of Latin American directors Fernando Solanas and Octavio Gettino, produce "films that directly and explicitly set out to fight the System." Said director Jorges Sanjines, "the work of revolutionary cinema must not limit itself to denouncing, or to the appeal for reflection; it must be a summons for action." In fact, films such as *La hora de los hornos* (1968) and *Me gustan los estudiantes* (1969) provoked student riots in URUGUAY and VENEZUELA during the late 1960s. Since the mid-1970s, however, the goal of most Third Cinema directors has been to inspire political and social change rather than complete revolution.

In sub-Saharan Africa most filmmakers subscribe to the ideas of Third Cinema and make films that are often quite critical of the postcolonial bourgeoisie. The films of Ousmane Sembène, Med Hondo, and SOULEYMANE CISSÉ fuse documentary and fiction, and use ambiguous and unresolved endings to invite discussion from the audience. In Latin America and Asia, Third Cinema filmmakers now constitute only a small minority, but they continue to denounce capitalism and cultural imperialism as well as the persistent problem of racism.

Elizabeth Heath

SEE ALSO
Hondo, Abid Mohamed Medoun (Med); Ousmane Sembène.

North America

Thirteenth Amendment of the United States Constitution and the Emancipation Proclamation, document that signaled the government's commitment to ending slavery, which was followed by the constitutional amendment that officially abolished slavery in the United States.

The Thirteenth Amendment is best understood against the background of the AMERICAN CIVIL WAR. Although President Abraham Lincoln personally opposed slavery, ending slavery was not one of his administration's initial war aims. Instead he sought to "save the Union, and not either to save or destroy slavery." As president, Lincoln had sworn to uphold the Constitution; the Supreme Court had affirmed the constitutionality of slavery in its 1857 Dred Scott decision. As Southern states seceded, Lincoln had serious concerns about keeping the four border states – Delaware, Maryland, Kentucky, and Missouri – in the Union and about the loyalty of Northern Democrats. Also, he had promised slaveholders who were loyal to the federal government that they would be able to keep their slaves. Lincoln had first attempted to convince slaveholders in the border states gradually to eliminate slavery in return for compensation, but the slaveholders refused.

Lincoln's commitment to winning the war led him by 1862 to see emancipation as a necessity because he realized that slaves were a vital component of the Southern economy and that freeing slaves would destabilize the South. Thus in July 1862 Congress passed two laws regarding slaves. The first was a confiscation act that freed slaves from owners who had rebelled against the United States. The second was a militia act that enabled the president to use freed slaves in the army. In this context Lincoln was prepared to use presidential war powers to emancipate slaves in the rebel states.

Lincoln issued the Emancipation Proclamation on January 1, 1863, declaring that slaves in all states still at war with the federal government were free and would remain so. While taking care to exempt border slave states and the three Confederate states that the Union controlled, Lincoln nevertheless endorsed the idea of recruiting freed slaves and free blacks for service in the armed forces. The Emancipation Proclamation, however, technically freed no one, because Lincoln's authority was not recognized in the Confederacy.

Many Republican Party members recognized that the proclamation was only a war measure that might have no lasting impact on the institution of slavery. Still, its effect was to signal the federal government's opposition to slavery and to bolster the abolitionist cause. The war ceased to be one aimed only at saving the Union and became a war to end slavery as well. An initial stream of escaping slaves slowly expanded to become a flood of runaways. In response to the proclamation's endorsement of black military enlistment, more than 180,000 blacks enrolled in the army and 10,000 in the navy by the end of the war (*see* MILITARY, BLACKS IN THE AMERICAN).

A variety of forces began to press for a constitutional amendment to abolish slavery permanently. Women's groups were in the forefront in this battle, particularly the National Women's Loyal League, a predominantly white organization led by suffragists Susan B. Anthony and Elizabeth Cady Stanton. They believed that chattel slavery as practiced in the United States was closely linked to women's inferior place in society, and that progress in one area could result in progress in another. The Republican Party outlined support for such an amendment in its 1864 platform. Lincoln, after winning the 1864 presidential election, began pushing Congress to pass an amendment, using both his electoral mandate and his political skills to overcome Democratic opposition.

Early in 1865, shortly before the end of the Civil War and Lincoln's assassination, Congress approved the amendment. Its simplicity and brevity belies the fundamental changes it made to American society. Section 1 states that, "Neither slavery nor involuntary servitude, except as a punishment for crime whereof the party shall have been duly convicted, shall exist within the United States, or any place subject to their jurisdiction." Section 2 gives Congress the "power to enforce this article by appropriate legislation."

Although it was approved by Congress, the amendment had to be ratified by three-fourths of the states before becoming part of the Constitution. Most Northern states had ratified it, but it was up to President Andrew Johnson, who assumed the presidency after Lincoln's assassination in April 1865, to secure the necessary approval from Southern states. Johnson set very lenient terms for Southern reentry into American political society (*see* RECONSTRUCTION), but he required that Southern states ratify the amendment as a condition of readmission. Many state constitutional conventions, including those of Delaware and Kentucky, which had never outlawed slavery, opposed this requirement. Southern states especially disliked the second section, which provided for federal intervention if slavery were practiced. Johnson's tactics gained cooperation of enough states and the amendment was ratified on December 18, 1865, finally abolishing legalized slavery throughout the United States.

Robert Fay

SEE ALSO

Slavery in the United States; Abolitionism in the United States; *Dred Scott* v. *Sanford*.

In 1867 Louis Prang & Co., lithographers in Boston, issued *The American Declaration of Independence Illustrated*, in which the American Eagle lifts a recently freed black man and a white to freedom. Above their heads is the line: "Break every yoke; let the oppressed go free." *CORBIS/Bettmann*

North America

Thomas, Clarence (b. June 23, 1948, Pin Point, Ga.), African American associate justice of the United States Supreme Court known for his conservative views and judicial record.

Clarence Thomas was raised by his grandparents in Savannah, Georgia. He attended Roman Catholic schools, and in 1967 enrolled in Immaculate Conception Seminary in Conception, Missouri, to study to become a priest. Subjected to overt racism at the school, however, he transferred to Holy Cross College in Worcester, Massachusetts, where he became active in the Black Power Movement.

After graduating cum laude with an A.B. in English literature in 1971, Thomas entered Yale University Law School later that year. At Yale Thomas developed the view that the Democratic Party had failed and was failing African Americans. By the time of his graduation in 1974, Thomas had become staunchly conservative and decided to work for John Danforth, Missouri's Republican attorney general, whom he followed to WASHINGTON, D.C., when Danforth became a U.S. Senator.

Known within the Republican Party as a consistently conservative critic of governmental civil rights activity and of AFFIRMATIVE ACTION, Thomas was appointed assistant secretary for civil rights in the Department of Education. In 1982 President Ronald Reagan named Thomas chair of the Equal Employment Opportunity Commission (EEOC), a post to which he was re-appointed in 1986, passing both confirmation processes with little difficulty despite opposition from civil rights groups.

In 1989 President George Bush nominated Thomas for the U.S. Circuit Court of Appeals, and he was confirmed by the Senate Judiciary Committee on March 6, 1990 by a vote of 13 to 1. When THURGOOD MARSHALL announced his retirement from the Supreme Court in July 1991, Bush nominated Thomas for the opening, despite his brief judicial record. The committee reached an impasse regarding Thomas's nomination and, for the first time in U.S. history, a Supreme Court nominee was sent to the Senate floor without recommendation. Soon after, Anita Hill, a University of Oklahoma law professor, went public with allegations that Thomas had sexually harassed her during the time she worked with him as an EEOC staff attorney. Hearings held in October to examine Hill's claims were given extraordinary popular media coverage. Despite heated sentiment against Thomas from many groups, the Senate voted 52 to 48 to confirm Thomas by the second closest margin ever for a Supreme Court nominee. Thomas was sworn in on October 19, 1991, and has not only amassed one of the Court's most conserative records, but has also attracted public criticism from many prominent African Americans.

See Also

Hill, Anita Faye; Hill-Thomas Hearings; Black Power.

North America

Thomas, Franklin Augustine

(b. May 27, 1934, Brooklyn, N.Y.), African American lawyer, community developer, and the first African American president of the Ford Foundation.

Franklin Thomas grew up in the Bedford-Stuyvesant area of New York City and graduated with a B.A. in 1956 and a law degree in 1963, both from Columbia University. He worked stints as an attorney with the Federal Housing and Home Finance Agency, with the district attorney's office, and with the New York City Police Department. From 1967 to 1977 he was president of the Bedford-Stuyvesant Restoration Corporation, working on business, job, and housing development in his home neighborhood. He was named president of the Ford Foundation in 1979, the first African American to hold this position, and he remained in this post until 1994.

See Also

New York, New York.

North America

Thomas, Isiah

(b. 1961, Chicago, Ill.), African American professional basketball player who was one of the top point guards in the National Basketball Association (NBA) during the 1980s and early 1990s.

Isiah Thomas, adept at dribbling, passing, and shooting, was a quick and dazzling player. At only 1.85 m (6 ft 1 in) – small when compared to most NBA players – he was one of only a few players of his size who could dominate a professional BASKETBALL game.

Born Isiah Lord Thomas, he attended Indiana University. After his first college season (1979-1980) he won a place on the 1980 United States Olympic basketball team, although the United States boycotted the Olympic Games, held in Moscow that year, for political reasons. As a sophomore Thomas led the Indiana University team to the 1981 National Collegiate Athletic Association (NCAA) basketball championship. He left Indiana University after two seasons and was selected by the Detroit Pistons as the second pick (after Mark Aguirre) in the 1981 NBA draft.

The Pistons earned the nickname Bad Boys in the 1980s for their physical style of play, but Thomas, who often used a variety of fancy moves, was a popular and charismatic player, emerging as the leader of the team. Beginning in his rookie season (1981-1982), he was named to the NBA All-Star team 12 consecutive times. He led the league in assists in the 1984-1985 season, averaging 13.9 per game, and over his 13-season career he recorded averages of 19.2 points per game and 9.3 assists per game. Thomas led the Pistons to the NBA Finals three consecutive times (1988-1990). In 1988 the Pistons lost in the finals to the Los Angeles Lakers, but they won the championship in 1989 and 1990. In 1990 Thomas was named Most Valuable Player of the championship finals. After his retirement in 1994 he became an executive with the Toronto Raptors, an NBA expansion team that began playing in the 1995-1996 season. In 1997 Thomas left his position in the Raptors franchise to work as a basketball analyst for the National Broadcasting Company (NBC).

North America

Thomas, Piri

(b. September 20, 1928, New York, N.Y.), Afro-Puerto Rican writer known for his innovative autobiographical works.

Piri Thomas was raised in the *barrios* (ghettos) of Spanish Harlem in New York City. His parents had immigrated to the United States from PUERTO RICO. He attended public schools, where he was first introduced to institutionalized assimilation and racism. In 1952 he was incarcerated on charges of attempted armed robbery, and in prison he began writing his first book, the autobiography *Down These Mean Streets* (1967).

Down These Mean Streets gained critical acclaim for its portrayal of Spanish Harlem and its bold new literary style, which mixed Spanish Harlem dialect with slang Thomas had learned in prison. Thomas is known for his use of authentic Afro-Puerto Rican settings and dialect. Thomas went on to publish two more autobiographical works, *Saviour, Saviour, Hold My Hand* (1972) and *Seven Long Times* (1974). He also established himself as a playwright, authoring *Las calles de oro* (1970, The Golden Streets), and published a young adult book, *Stories of El Barrio* (1978). Thomas's works are included in the anthology *Boricuas: Influential Puerto Rican Work* (1995).

In addition to his writing, Thomas has been a community activist since his release from prison. He has volunteered in prison and drug rehabilitation programs in New York City since 1956, and received the Louis M. Rabinowitz Foundation Grant in 1962. In 1964 Time-Life Associates produced a documentary, *Petey and Johnny,* on his work with youth in street gangs. He was awarded a Lever Brothers Community Service Award in 1967, and since that year has been a staff associate for the Center for Urban Education in New York.

Thomas moved to San Francisco in 1983, where he has expanded his work to explore musical mediums of expression, continuing to channel a voice from marginalized populations in the United States into the larger public consciousness.

See Also

New York, New York; San Francisco and Oakland, California.

North America

Thompson, Bennie

(b. 1948), Democratic member of the United States House of Representatives from Mississippi (1993-).

Born in Bolton, Mississippi, Bennie Gordon Thompson earned a bachelor's degree from Tougaloo College in 1968 and a master's degree from Jackson State University in 1972. He ran for alderman of Bolton when he was 20. Although victorious at the polls, Thompson, who is black, was initially denied the seat by white officials. A court order secured his position, and he served from 1969 to 1973. He was mayor of Bolton from 1973 to 1979 and a member of the Hinds County Board of Supervisors from 1980 to 1993.

When Congressman Mike Espy was selected by President Bill Clinton to serve as secretary of agriculture in 1993, Thompson moved to fill Espy's vacant seat in Mississippi's Second Congressional District. Thompson placed second in an open primary and won the runoff election in April 1993. He was returned to office in subsequent elections.

The Second District covers the great Mississippi Delta region in the western part of the state. It is Mississippi's only black-majority district and is the most heavily Democratic district in the state. Although it has some of the best farmland in the United States, the region itself is impoverished. In the 105th Congress (1997-1999), Thompson served on the Agriculture and Budget committees and was a member of the CONGRESSIONAL BLACK CAUCUS.

Latin America and the Caribbean

Thompson, Casildo

(b. 1856, Buenos Aires, ARGENTINA; d. 1928, Buenos Aires, Argentina), Afro-Argentine poet, musician, and composer.

Casildo Thompson grew up in a family that was active in the vibrant and creative Afro-Argentine community of nineteenth-century Buenos Aires. His father, Capitán Casildo Thompson, a veteran of the Paraguayan war (among others), founded the most successful and the longest lasting Afro-Argentine mutual aid society of his time, La Sociedad Fraternal (The Fraternal Society). According to historian George Reid Andrews, Capitán Thompson was also a respected vocalist and composer who enjoyed a large following and wrote some of the most popular songs of his era. These included "La locomotiva" (The Locomotive) and

"Recuerdo del campamento" (Memory of the Encampment), commemorating the anniversary of Argentina's first railroads and memorializing the Paraguayan campaign, respectively.

Thus Casildo Thompson had a powerful family legacy to equal. Following his father's example he, too, became an accomplished musician and composer, attending the conservatory in Buenos Aires and winning a series of national awards for his religious compositions (*see* MUSIC, CLASSICAL, IN LATIN AMERICA AND THE CARIBBEAN). Like his father, he rose to the rank of captain by participating in a series of wars between 1870 and 1890.

A talented pianist and composer, Thompson also played guitar. Estrada, a biographer of nineteenth-century Afro-Argentines, even contends that Thompson's "inseparable friend," GABINO EZEIZA, the most famous Afro-Argentine *payador*, learned a lot from him. (*Payadores* were guitar-playing singers who swapped witty digs in a kind of poetic competition.) Thompson's works ranged from popular music to literature and included poetry published in local black newspapers like *La juventud*, where his most famous poem, *Canto al África* (Song to Africa) first appeared in 1877. Ironically, it is one of few Afro-Argentine poems to invoke black pride thematically by constructing mythical images of precolonial Africa in an indictment of slavery and colonialism (*see* COLONIAL LATIN AMERICA AND THE CARIBBEAN).

Argentine blacks, considered by many other Argentines as social pariahs at the time, have until recently been consistently written out of national history. Indeed, Thompson's poetry, whether because of its quality, quantity, or Thompson's lack of a wide audience, was never published in book form. Still, this poem, like some by his contemporary HORACIO MENDIZÁBAL, stands as a testament to the existence of a bustling black community in nineteenth-century Buenos Aires.

Joy Elizondo

North America

Thornton, Willie Mae ("Big Mama") (b. December 11, 1926, Montgomery, Ala.; d. July 25, 1984, Los Angeles, Calif.), African American blues singer, songwriter, and musician known for boisterous stage performances, shouting vocals, outspoken lyrics, and an eccentric lifestyle that influenced a later generation of popular musicians.

Willie Mae Thornton sang GOSPEL MUSIC as a child in her minister father's church. Shortly after her mother's death, when Thornton was age 14, she joined Sammy Green's *Hot Harlem Revue*, traveling throughout the South's "chitlin circuit," singing and teaching herself the harmonica, guitar, and drums.

In 1948 Thornton moved to Houston, Texas, and signed an exclusive contract with Peacock Records. Thornton's 1.83 m (6 ft) tall and 114-kg (250-lb) frame earned her the nickname Big Mama, which she celebrated in "They Call Me Big Mama." Her recording sessions with the Johnny Otis rhythm-and-blues Caravan yielded "Hound Dog," which reached Number One on the rhythm-and-blues charts and was made famous in the 1950s by Elvis Presley, and "Ball and Chain," which became Janis Joplin's signature song in the late 1960s. Though both songs earned Thornton enough fame to tour nationally, she had signed away her royalty rights and saw little of the money that Presley and Joplin later did.

In the early 1960s, her career declining, Thornton moved to San Francisco in an attempt to revitalize her career. Because of the blues revival occurring in the late 1960s, Thornton's career rebounded. Through the 1960s and 1970s she played JAZZ and blues festivals in the United States and Europe, and recorded several albums.

Thornton suffered from alcohol-related problems, and she died of a heart attack poor and little known. A benefit concert was given to raise burial money. Though popular acclaim eluded Thornton, she influenced many later musicians, including Joplin, Aretha Franklin, Grace Slick, Stevie Nicks, and Angela Strehli.

Robert Fay

SEE ALSO

Blues, The; Franklin, Aretha Louise; Rhythm and Blues; San Francisco and Oakland, California.

North America

Thrash, Dox (b. March 22, 1893, Griffin, Ga.; d. 1965, Philadelphia, Pa.), African American artist and printer; also coinventor of the carborundum print-process.

Having studied for several years at the school at the Art Institute of Chicago, Dox Thrash settled in PHILADELPHIA, PENNSYLVANIA. Once there he painted signs and worked on the Federal Arts Project (FAP) to earn a living. Working with the FAP in the Graphic Division, he helped invent a new lithographic process, called the carborundum print-process. This method of printing created prints with more expressive tones and variation. His carbographs explored the portraits of African Americans, landscapes, and scenes of slum life. *My Neighbor* (1937) and the landscape *Deserted Cabin* (1939) are examples of Thrash's carbographs. In the late 1930s and through the 1940s Thrash's work was shown in many prominent places, including a 1942 solo exhibition at the Philadelphia Museum of Art.

SEE ALSO

Art, African American.

Africa

Thuku, Harry (b. 1895, Mbari ya-Gathirimu, Kenya; d. June 14, 1970, Kenya), Kenyan nationalist and first president of the East African Association.

Harry Thuku was among KENYA's first nationalists, known for his opposition to British colonial land and labor policies. Born in northern Kenya, he attended a Gospel Mission Society school, and at age 16 moved to Nairobi. He held several jobs and even served a prison term for fraud before he began working as a typesetter at the publication *Leader of British East Africa*, a job that awakened his political consciousness.

In 1921 Thuku became president of the newly founded Young KIKUYU Association, later named the East African Association (EAA), a group devoted to fighting colonial policies that forced Africans off Kenya's most fertile farmland and into menial employment. The EAA's early demands were moderate, asking only for an end to the appropriation of Kikuyu lands, not for a return of what had been taken. Their methods of protest included writing letters to the colonial secretary in London and organizing protest meetings. But colonial officials considered Thuku a radical and arrested him in 1922. When the EAA demonstrated to protest Thuku's arrest, the British responded with force, killing 20 Africans. The colonial government subsequently sent Thuku away from Nairobi, and he spent almost nine years in detention in coastal and northern Kenya. During this time other Kenyan nationalists, including future president JOMO KENYATTA, stepped up the EAA's activities.

Thuku was released in 1930 and spent the rest of his life working on his farm, which earned him considerable wealth. He published *Harry Thuku: An Autobiography* in 1970, the same year he died.

Kate Tuttle

SEE ALSO

Colonial Rule; Nationalism in Africa; Nairobi, Kenya.

North America

Thurman, Howard (b. November 18, 1900, Daytona Beach, Fla.; d. April 10, 1981, San Francisco, Calif.), African American minister, educator, author, and mystic who advocated the cooperation and kinship of humankind.

Howard Thurman, a grandson of slaves, grew up in the black section of segregated Daytona Beach, Florida. His ability to achieve despite obstacles became obvious when he was the first African American to finish the eighth grade in the local public school. After studying at Florida Baptist Academy, one of three black high schools in the state, Thurman earned a B.A. at MOREHOUSE COLLEGE. Turning his interest to religious studies, he was awarded a M.Div. degree at Colgate Rochester Divinity School. After serving as pastor of a Baptist church in Oberlin, Ohio, between 1926 and 1928, he pursued his quest for enhanced religious experience by studying under Quaker mystic Rufus Jones as a Kent Fellow at Haverford College.

Thurman's lifelong career as a spiritual teacher began when he became director of religious life and professor of religion at Morehouse and Spelman colleges (1929-1930). He then served as dean of Rankin Chapel and professor of religion at HOWARD UNIVERSITY from 1932 to 1944. In 1944 Thurman's ministry expanded as cofounder of the interracial and interfaith Fellowship Church for All Peoples. This radical, experimental church, located in San Francisco, employed Thurman as pastor until 1953 and emphasized an inclusive religious community. Thurman became professor of spiritual resources and disciplines and dean of Marsh Chapel at Boston University, the first African American appointed dean of a Northern university. He stayed until his retirement in 1965.

Within his creative religious beliefs Howard Thurman accentuated the common ground and kinship of all people. He authored many journal articles and 20 books, and his eloquence in preaching and lecturing was celebrated at many institutions internationally. Thurman's major emphasis – that Christianity teaches cooperation among humankind – was incorporated into the CIVIL RIGHTS MOVEMENT. Further, his religious mysticism drew lines to India including the notion of the sacredness of life and Mohandas Ghandi's technique of passive resistance. Through Thurman many of these ideas were communicated to Martin Luther King Jr., and influenced the American Civil Rights Movement.

SEE ALSO

King, Martin Luther, Jr.; Morehouse College; Spelman College; San Francisco and Oakland, California.

North America

Thurman, Wallace

(b. August 16, 1902, Salt Lake City, Utah; d. December 22, 1934, New York, N.Y.), African American writer of the Harlem Renaissance who espoused a frank and sometimes stark assessment of African American life in America.

In 1925 Wallace Thurman began his writing career at the University of Southern California, where he started and edited the short-lived *Outlet*, a literary magazine that discussed many ideas of the HARLEM RENAISSANCE. Leaving school for Harlem that same year, Thurman became a part of the cultural outpouring that he had been observing. He began working in New York as an editorial assistant at a small magazine called *Looking Glass*, followed by positions at other publications, such as the white magazine *The World Tomorrow*. At the left-wing *Messenger*, where he was temporary editor, Thurman became associated with other writers in Harlem, including LANGSTON HUGHES and ZORA NEALE HURSTON.

In 1926 Thurman helped found *Fire!!*, a journal intended to expose the new thinking of the Harlem Renaissance and publish writing about African Americans who broke free from mainstream American culture. Unfortunately, the journal, which Thurman edited, was plagued with financial problems, and an actual fire in a basement where many issues of *Fire!!* were stored secured the downfall of the publication after only one issue. Thurman started a similar magazine in 1928, *Harlem, a Forum of Negro Life*, which failed after one issue.

Despite his failures as a publisher, Thurman wrote three books, a play, and several articles and editorials for numerous magazines. His writing often satirized African American life and the Harlem Renaissance, depicting the contradictions within black thought of the time, especially in his novels *The Blacker the Berry* (1929) and *Infants of the Spring* (1932). His play *Harlem* was originally produced at the APOLLO THEATER in 1929 and may have been his largest success. His final novel, *The Interne* (1932), exposed the injustices at City Hospital on Welfare Island (now Roosevelt Island). He died at that hospital in 1934, of tuberculosis and consumption, related to chronic alcoholism.

SEE ALSO

Harlem, New York; *Messenger, The*; New York, New York.

Latin America and the Caribbean

Tia Ciata

(Hilária Batista de Almeida) (b. 1854, Salvador, Bahia, Brazil; d. 1924, Rio de Janeiro, Brazil), one of several legendary black Brazilian women known as *"tias"* or aunts, who hosted social gatherings at which Afro-Brazilian culture was celebrated and SAMBA music was developed.

At the end of the nineteenth century, just at the time of the abolition of slavery in BRAZIL, Rio de Janeiro's Praça Onze was the center of a neighborhood composed largely of Afro-Brazilians. Many of these people were recent migrants from the state of BAHIA, and the Praça Onze neighborhood became known as "*Pequena África*" (or small Africa). Tia Ciata moved to Rio from Bahia at age 22, and during the day worked selling home-cooked food at a food stall. Tia Ciata was also deeply involved in the Afro-Brazilian religion of CANDOMBLÉ. At night and on the weekends she hosted gatherings at her home in Praça Onze that brought together some of the most famous black Brazilian musicians and composers and probably served as one of the birthplaces of samba music.

Ben Penglase

SEE ALSO

Rio de Janeiro, Brazil; Abolition and Emancipation in Latin America and the Caribbean.

Africa

Tigre

(sometimes erroneously known as Tigray), ethnic group of the Horn of Africa who live in ERITREA and neighboring parts of SUDAN.

The Tigre are a loose grouping of predominantly Muslim people who speak a Semitic language of the Afro-Asiatic linguistic family. The Tigre language is closely related to TIGRINYA, a main language of Eritrea, and Amharic, the leading language of Ethiopia. The Tigre should not be confused with the predominantly Christian Tigrinya people of Eritrea and Ethiopia's Tigray Province. Europeans have repeatedly confused the two related but distinct groups.

The Tigre and Tigrinya probably share a common ancestry dating back to the arrival of Semitic-speaking peoples in the region more than 2000 years ago. Coptic Christianity (*see* ETHIOPIAN ORTHODOX CHURCH) spread from Egypt throughout the Horn of Africa during the fourth and fifth centuries C.E. The ancient sacred language of the Ethiopian church is Ge'ez (*see* ETHIOPIC SCRIPT AND LANGUAGE), a language from which both Tigre and Tigrinya later evolved. However, Islam, which Arabian traders brought to the Dahlak Islands around the year 700, gradually spread along the coast and across the western plains. The pastoral nomads of these dry plains, who migrated periodically in search of water and pastures for livestock, were organized into clans based on extended family ties. Gradually these nomads, the ancestors of the Tigre, converted to Islam (*see* ISLAM AND TRADITION: AN INTERPRETATION). By the nineteenth century the Tigre were solidly Muslim. Arabic was the language of scholarship. This worked to prevent the growth of literature in the Tigrean language. Ironically, it was Christian missionaries (*see* CHRISTIANITY: MISSIONARIES IN AFRICA) and European scholars who began compiling the Tigre's rich tradition of oral stories and poetry in the 1970s and who spurred a Tigre literary flowering.

The Tigre were long subject to the control of neighboring peoples. Many Tigre are serfs owing obligations to aristocratic clans, especially the BENI AMER people. In fact, the word "Tigre" is sometimes taken to mean "serf." The Tigre have also clashed periodically with the dominant Christian Tigrinya farmers of the highlands. Religious and cultural differences have heightened the inevitable competition for scarce water and desirable land. Following World War II, bloody clashes broke out between Muslim Tigre, who overwhelmingly favored an independent nation of Eritrea, and Christians, supporting union with Ethiopia. Fearing domination by a primarily Christian Ethiopia, Tigreans helped found the Eritrean

Liberation Front (ELF) and got early support from Muslim states.

In an effort to counter Tigrean independence sympathies, the Ethiopian government began Tigre-language radio broadcasts in the 1960s. This did little to rally the Tigre to Ethiopia's cause, but it promoted a widespread awareness of Tigre music and culture. The Eritrean People's Liberation Front (EPLF) also promoted the use Tigre for political purposes and employed it as a language of instruction in areas it controlled. The rival ELF generally favored Arabic as the language of instruction.

Today Eritrea has one of the most nomadic populations in the world. But the Tigre also farm when possible and raise an indigenous cereal called *teff* as well as corn, wheat, barley, sorghum, and MILLET. Numbering close to 2 million, the Tigre compose about 40 percent of Eritrea's population.

SEE ALSO
Amhara; Languages, African: An Overview; Pastoralism.

Africa

Tigrinya, major language and ethnic group in the Horn of Africa.

The Tigrinya language belongs to the Semitic family of the Afro-Asiatic linguistic grouping. It is closely related to AMHARA, the main language of ETHIOPIA, and to TIGRE, the second most common language in ERITREA. Tigrinya speakers live primarily in the central highlands of Eritrea and in northern Ethiopia. Their ancestors – descendants of indigenous Cushitic peoples and Semitic peoples from the Arabian Peninsula – probably settled this region more than 2000 years ago. The Tigrinya language most likely evolved from Ge'ez, the language spoken in the ancient kingdom of AKSUM. Unlike Ge'ez, however, early Tingrinya appears to have been primarily a spoken language (*see* ETHIOPIC SCRIPT AND LANGUAGE). The oldest existing document in Tigrinya is a law code from the nineteenth century.

The Tigrinya people have long been settled agriculturalists, though many also keep livestock. Their staple crops include the indigenous grain *teff*, wheat, barley, MILLET, sorghum, and pulses. Along with the Amhara, the Tigrinya consider themselves descendants of the people of Aksum, and until the twentieth century they have historically accepted as legitimate the rule of Ethiopia's Amharic emperors. Both Tigrinya and Amharic speakers are adherents of Coptic Christianity, which became the religion of Aksum in the mid-fourth-century C.E. (*see* ETHIOPIAN ORTHODOX CHURCH and CHRISTIANITY, AFRICAN: AN OVERVIEW). Relatively few Tigrinya speakers converted to Islam, which was brought by Arab traders beginning in the eighth century C.E.

When the Italians began their colonial conquest of the Horn in the 1880s, the highland regions were suffering through a period of poor harvests and food shortages, and the Tigrinya people initially put up relatively little resistance. Shortly after Italy declared rule over Eritrea in 1890, however, the colonial administration began a massive land expropriation campaign in the highlands, intending to create an Italian settler colony. An 1894 uprising in Tigrinya-speaking areas forced the administration to scale back these plans, but many Tigrinya remained landless and became laborers either on Italian settler farms or in the industrializing cities of Asmara and Massawa. Tigrinya peasants participated in the colonial economy as producers of export crops such as coffee.

After World War II the Tigrinya, along with other Christians, fought bloody street battles with Muslims over Eritrea's proposed unification with Ethiopia. Generally, Christians supported unification and Muslims opposed it. However, the Tigrinya became increasingly disenchanted with Emperor HAILE SELASSIE I's autocratic rule and with the imposition of Amharic language and culture. The Tigrinya also had economic reasons for joining their Muslim neighbors in the battle for independence. The Ethiopian government discriminated against non-Amharic when hiring for civil service positions, and it relocated much of the industry from Asmara, the main city in the Tigrinya highlands, to Addis Ababa, the Ethiopian capital.

By the late 1960s many Tigrinya, including the future Eritrean president ISAIAS AFWERKI, had joined the Eritrean Liberation Front (ELF). Afwerki and a number of other Christians later split from the ELF and formed the Eritrean People's Liberation Front (EPLF), which subsequently became the larger of the two rebel forces and increasingly multiethnic. By the late 1980s the EPLF was cooperating with rebel groups within Ethiopia, such as the Ethiopian People's Revolutionary Democratic Front, led by MELES ZENAWI, a Tigrinya.

Since Eritrea attained independence in 1991, Eritrea and Ethiopia have been led by Afwerki and Zenawi, respectively – both Tigrinya heads of state. Afwerki has his critics but remains overwhelmingly popular with the Eritrean people. Zenawi, on the other hand, has been accused of favoring Tigrinya-speaking regions in Ethiopia at the expense of the once-dominant Amhara. About 2 million Tigrinya speakers live in Eritrea and 3 million in Ethiopia.

SEE ALSO
Addis Ababa, Ethiopia; Asmara, Eritrea; Colonial Rule; Languages, African: An Overview; Massawa, Eritrea; Islam and Tradition: An Interpretation.

Africa

Tikar, ethnic group of CAMEROON.

The Tikar primarily inhabit the North West Province of Cameroon. They speak a Niger-Congo language and are closely related to the BAMILÉKÉ people. Approximately 100,000 people consider themselves Tikar.

SEE ALSO
Languages, African: An Overview.

North America

Till, Emmett Louis (b. July 25, 1941, Chicago, Ill.; d. August 28, 1955, LeFlore County, Miss.), African American teenager who was an early victim of civil rights-era violence.

Emmett Till was born and raised in CHICAGO, ILLINOIS. When he was 14 years of age, he was sent to Mississippi to spend the summer with his uncle. Because of his Northern upbringing, Till was not accustomed to the racial taboos of the segregated South; he bragged to his Southern black friends that in Chicago he even had a white girlfriend. These unbelieving friends dared him to enter a store and ask a white woman for a date. Inside, Till hugged Carol Bryant's waist and squeezed her hand, then whistled at her as his friends rushed him away.

On August 28, 1955, Carol Bryant's husband, Roy, and his half-brother, J.W. Milam, abducted Till from his uncle's home. Three days later his naked, beaten, decomposed body was found in the Tallahatchie River; he had been shot in the head. The two white men were tried one month later by an all-white jury, and despite the fact that they admitted abducting Till, they were acquitted because the body was too mangled to be positively identified.

Till's murder became a rallying point for the CIVIL RIGHTS MOVEMENT. Photographs of his open casket were reprinted across the country, and protests were organized by the NATIONAL ASSOCIATION FOR THE ADVANCEMENT OF COLORED PEOPLE (NAACP), the BROTHERHOOD OF SLEEPING CAR PORTERS, and such leaders as W. E. B. Du Bois. The public outrage over the injustice of the trial helped ensure that Congress included a provision for federal investigations of civil rights violations in the Civil Rights Act of 1957.

Lisa Clayton Robinson

SEE ALSO
Du Bois, William Edward Burghardt (W. E. B.).

Timbuktu. Please see TOMBOUCTOU, MALI

North America

Tindley, Charles Albert (b. July 7, 1851, Berlin, Md.; d. July 26, 1933, Philadelphia, Pa.), African American minister and gospel musician whose hymns became a basis of twentieth-century African American church music.

In 1916 Tindley published *New Songs of Paradise*, a collection of 37 gospel songs. By

1941 the collection had run to its seventh edition. Among his best-known songs are "A Better Home," "Stand by Me," "What Are They Doing in Heaven Tonight?," "We'll Understand it Better By and By," and "I'll Overcome Some Day." Many of them and others of his works are now standards in African American churches. His work inspired the gospel songs of Thomas A. Dorsey and Rev. Herbert Brewster.

Robert Fay

See Also

Dorsey, Thomas Andrew; Gospel Music.

Africa

Tinné, Alexandrine-Pieternella-Françoise

(b. 1835?, The Hague, The Netherlands; d. 1869, Libya), Dutch explorer of the Nile River and North Africa. Tinné was born in The Hague, The Netherlands, to a wealthy family. An unhappy love affair may have prompted her to leave home and embark on a voyage up the Nile in search of the river's source.

In 1862 Alexandrine-Pieternella-Françoise Tinné hired a small fleet of boats in Cairo, Egypt, and left on her first expedition up the Nile. Accompanying her were her mother, her aunt, several scientists, and a number of assistants and servants. Tinné ascended the Nile as far as Gondokoro, in present-day southern Sudan, above which the river became unnavigable. She planned to meet British explorer John Hanning Speke, who was exploring the upper reaches of the Nile to the south. When Speke's expedition failed to arrive when expected, Tinné set off on her own to determine the source of the Nile. Traveling overland, she ventured into the watershed region between the Zaire (Congo) and Nile rivers, in the northeastern part of present-day Democratic Republic of the Congo. Tinné's explorations took her into regions of Central Africa that were not yet mapped and seldom visited by Europeans. She returned to Gondokoro in September 1862, and after again failing to meet up with Speke, she headed downriver and back to Cairo. Both her mother and her aunt, as well as two of the scientists, died of fever during the trip.

Tinné lived in Cairo until she moved to Algiers, Algeria, in 1867. She resumed her African explorations in 1869, intending to become the first European woman to cross the Sahara Desert. From Tripoli, on the Mediterranean Sea coast of Libya, she headed south to the oasis city of Murzuk. While waiting there for an Arab caravan with which she planned to continue her journey southward, Tinné took a side trip to visit the nomadic Tuareg tribes. On the way to a Tuareg encampment Tinné was robbed and murdered by her guides.

See Also

Congo River; Explorers in Africa Since 1800; Tripoli, Libya.

Africa

Tippu Tip

(real name Hamid bin Muhammad; b. 1830, Zanzibar; d. 1905, Zanzibar), one of the most powerful traders in Central and East Africa in the late nineteenth century.

Tippu Tip began his career at age 12, when he accompanied his father on short trading trips. In 1850 he set out on his own and within a span of 15 years had built one of the most extensive trade empires in Central Africa.

Trading slaves and ivory for firearms, Tippu Tip's large caravans also served as his personal armies and hunting bands. Tippu Tip accumulated incredible wealth and power, expanding his territorial control through raids as well as deals with regional chiefs and other traders. By the early 1880s he was the most powerful trader in Central and East Africa.

Tippu Tip's caravans carried goods between Zanzibar on the east coast of Africa and Kasongo on the west coast of the Lualaba River, and his bands of followers hunted elephants and raided villages for slaves in Central African forests. Many of the captives were put to work cultivating sugar cane, rice, and maize on plantations near the towns of Kasongo and Nyangwe. Tippu Tip's power, however, was short-lived. In 1885 Leopold II of Belgium claimed control over the Congo Free State, which included Tippu Tip's empire. Tippu Tip resisted the European presence at first, but after negotiations with Henry Morton Stanley, Leopold's agent in the Congo, he forfeited his empire in return for the governorship of what is now the eastern Democratic Republic of the Congo. Although this deal kept Tippu Tip in power, it angered his traders, who resented the ban on the slave trade. After numerous revolts, Tippu Tip stepped down and retired to Zanzibar, where he wrote his biography in Swahili.

Elizabeth Heath

See Also

Ivory Trade; Swahili Language; Stanley, Sir Henry Morton; Slavery in Africa.

Africa

Tiv

(also known as Munchi and Munshi), ethnic group of Nigeria.

The Tiv primarily inhabit the valley of the Benue River in central Nigeria, particularly in Benue State, where they largely farm yams, sorghum, and millet for subsistence. Prior to European contact, the Tiv lived in defensive villages of 500 to 600 people. After British occupation of the area in 1911, however, village sizes decreased dramatically. Under the policy of indirect rule (*see* Colonial Rule), in 1948 the British assigned the Tiv a paramount chief. Previously the Tiv were organized into numerous independent lineages that traced descent to a single mythical male ancestor. Lineage elders resolved disputes and handled lineage-wide political issues. Despite British efforts to create a strict hierarchical political system, elders continue to have substantial influence in Tiv society. The Tiv, who number approximately 2.5 million, speak a Niger-Congo language.

See Also

Languages, African: An Overview.

Africa

Tlali, Miriam

(b. 1933, Johannesburg, South Africa), South African writer, many of whose works were banned under apartheid.

Born to educated parents, as a child Miriam Tlali was encouraged to study and write. But as a black South African she found her educational opportunities limited. After attending local elementary schools and studying art in high school, she won a scholarship to the University of Witwatersrand, but her hopes of studying medicine were dashed by the university's quotas for black students, which would allow her to study only administration. Tlali later pursued pre-medical training at Roma University in Lesotho but ran out of money after a year and never finished her medical training.

Back in Johannesburg, Tlali drew on her experiences working as a furniture store bookkeeper to write her autobiographical first novel, *Muriel at Metropolitan*. Written in 1969, the book was not published in South Africa until 1975, partly because of its subtle but scathing portrayal of white insensitivity and everyday cruelty toward black people. In the 1970s Tlali also began writing articles and stories that appeared in South African magazines such as the *Rand Daily Mail* and *Staffrider*.

Leaving Africa for the first time, Tlali attended the International Writers Program at the University of Iowa in 1978-1979. Her second novel, *Amandla* (1980), told the story of a black family living in Soweto during the 1976 uprising and was, like Tlali's first novel, banned in South Africa. (Tlali herself was banned from political activity for many years.) In the 1980s Tlali, by then a wife and mother, wrote an interview series for *Staffrider* called *Soweto Speaking*. She also published three books in 1989 alone: *Mihloti* and *Soweto Stories*, both collections of Tlali's journalism, and *Footprints in the Quag: Stories and Dialogues from Soweto*. Declining to describe herself as a feminist in "the narrow, Western" sense, Tlali has become an important proponent of womanism, the theory that black women living in a racially oppressive society must empower their community's men while at the same time supporting their sisters. As one of Tlali's female characters says to another in one of her short stories, "We're all alike; we're women. We need each other when things are difficult."

Kate Tuttle

See Also

Johannesburg, South Africa; Women Writers in English-Speaking Africa; Soweto, South Africa; South Africa; Feminism in Africa: An Interpretation.

North America

Tobias, Channing Heggie

(b. February 1, 1882, Augusta, Ga.; d. November 5, 1961?), African American public official, Young Men's Christian Association (YMCA), and National Association for the Advancement of Colored People (NAACP) leader, domestic and international emissary for improved race relations.

Channing Tobias received bachelors' degrees from Paine College (then Paine Institute) and Drew University. In 1911 he became secretary of the National Council of the YMCA in Washington, D.C. Tobias remained with the YMCA for the next three decades, and was a strong advocate for the organization's desegregation.

In 1946 he left the YMCA to become the first black director of the Phelps-Stokes Fund, which supported black education. Tobias won the NAACP's Spingarn Medal in 1948, and was chairman of the board of the NAACP from 1953 to 1959.

Lisa Clayton Robinson

Togbo. Please see Banda

Africa

Togo, a small coastal West African country located between Benin, Ghana, and Burkina Faso.

Despite its small size, Togo encompasses considerable geographic, ethnic, and economic diversity, which has haunted the country's political development. The German and French colonial administrations concentrated economic development in the mostly Ewe coastal region south of the Togo Mountains, while the more ethnically diverse north remained impoverished. Since independence Ewe prosperity and separatism have aroused northern resentment and fear. Togo has been called "the Jurassic Park of Africa," because of the persistence of its military dictatorship, led by a northerner, Gen. Gnassingbé Eyadéma, since 1967. Eyadéma's patronage has solidified his base of support in the north and among the powerful market women of the capital but alienated many in the more urbanized, mostly Ewe south. Although since 1989 Eyadéma has been promising a transition to more democratic rule, his government and military have repeatedly harassed opposition figures, disrupted elections, and blocked the formation of an independent electoral commission. After a long decline from the late 1970s through the early 1990s, the country's economy has showed signs of renewed strength. Harassment of opposition leaders and other irregularities tarnished Eyadéma's reelection in 1998, and Eyadéma's military regime seems determined to deflect the winds of democratic change.

Precolonial History

Archaeological finds demonstrate a human presence in the area extending back at least 50,000 years. A gradual shift from hunting and gathering to agriculture began about 5000 years ago with the cultivation of yams in the forest zone surrounding the Togo Mountains and millet in the savanna to the north and south. On the country's northern plateaus, livestock herding has supplemented agriculture since prehistoric times, as has fishing along the Atlantic coast.

The area of present-day Togo never developed the strong state structures characteristic of Asante to the west or Dahomey to the east. Although some of its peoples repeatedly fell under the domination of neighboring kingdoms, the southern Ewe region as well as the territories of the Gurma, Kabré, and other groups in the north remained divided among numerous small chiefdoms. While the neighboring kingdoms participated in the export of gold and slaves, the Togolese peoples retained a subsistence economy.

The Portuguese first visited the Togo coast during the late fifteenth century. Other Europeans, including the Dutch, English, French, and Danish, arrived by the seventeenth century, when the demand for slaves in the Americas began to dominate commercial relations. Local rulers exchanged slaves for firearms, which they used to maintain power and conduct more raids. Soon, the southern and central parts of Togo fell prey to slave raiders from the neighboring Asante and Dahomey states, and northern regions fell under the domination of the kingdoms of Mamprusi and Dagomba, centered in what is today northern Ghana. Much of the trade in Ewe slaves operated through ports just outside present-day Togo, such as Whydah to the east and Keta to the west, but some of the trade flowed through Petit Popo, now known as Aného – the only significant port on the Togolese coast until the colonial period. By the eighteenth century Denmark dominated the trade along the Togolese coast. The Danes prohibited the slave trade in 1802 and withdrew from the area in 1850.

Meanwhile, the region attracted missionaries. From the eighteenth century onward Danes sponsored Protestant missionaries in the region, many of them German-speaking. During the 1850s the North German Mission Society, based in Bremen, became the dominant Christian organization in Togolese territory, and during the 1860s a number of German merchants, also based in Bremen, set up operations on the Togolese coast.

German Togoland

By the 1880s the scramble for Africa was in full swing, and the neighboring French and British colonial establishments' efforts, supported by some local elites, to secure a dominant position on the Togolese coast alarmed the German merchants of Aného. They appealed to the imperial government in Berlin to intervene, and in 1884 Gustav Nachtigal, one of Germany's foremost African strategists, concluded a treaty with the chief of a small coastal village called Togo. The treaty granted Germany an exclusive protectorate over the entire coast of Togoland, which derived its name from this tiny chiefdom. The Germans quickly assumed control of the mostly Ewe region near the coast, but began their conquest of the interior only after 1893. They successfully subdued the north by 1897, although they confronted minor rebellions during the next few years. In 1897 they chose Lomé, until then a small fishing village, as the colonial capital.

Exports of Ewe-produced palm oil, along with a harsh system of taxation, resulted in a positive financial balance for the colony by 1907. For this reason, the Germans referred to Togo as their *Musterkolonie*, or "showcase colony." The Germans required 12 days of forced labor yearly from every able-bodied male in the colony, or a cash payment calculated on the basis of an individual's (often non-cash) income. Forced labor was deployed primarily on public works projects, such as the pier at Lomé, completed in 1904, and a series of railroads radiating out from the capital to the major cash-crop production zones in the south.

The possibility of substituting a cash payment for forced labor encouraged many Togolese to cultivate cash crops or accept wage labor. Germans enlisted researchers, including several from the Tuskegee Institute of Alabama, in finding a variety of cotton suited to the climate, and cotton became one of the colony's major exports. Though a few German settlers managed plantations, the colonial administration left production of both subsistence and cash crops mostly in the hands of Togolese, while German firms on the coast handled processing and export. Ownership of cocoa plantations in the mountainous interior provided the basis for an indigenous, mostly Ewe, bourgeoisie. Together these developments yielded steadily increasing export earnings as well as the growth of a class of wage laborers, particularly in the south, no longer tied to subsistence agriculture. The Germans also recruited Togolese, especially Ewe educated in mission schools, for positions in the local administration.

When World War I broke out in 1914, France and Great Britain invaded Togo from neighboring Dahomey and the Gold Coast, and within a month had seized the entire colony. In 1919 the two countries agreed to partition German Togoland into two League of Nations mandates. France received the

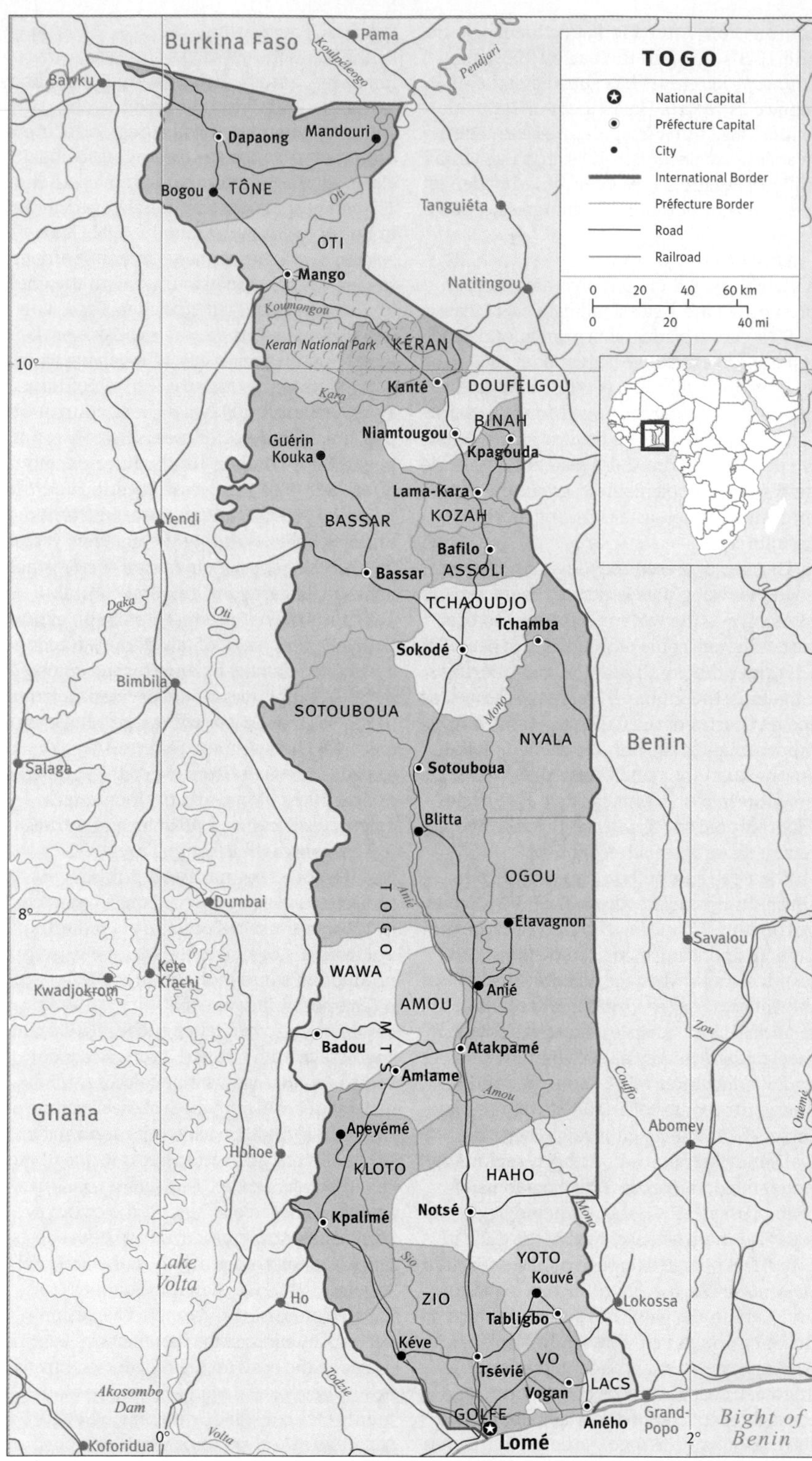

eastern two-thirds, including Lomé and the entire coastline and rail network, and Britain received a strip of land bordering its Gold Coast colony (present-day Ghana).

French Togo

Though the two parts of Togoland were to be held in "trust" with the implicit goal of future reunification, the French and British incorporated the mandates into their respective colonial spheres. The French administered Togo jointly with Dahomey from 1934 to 1936 and as a subunit of French West Africa from 1936 to 1946. In 1946 Togo became a United Nations trust territory, separate from the rest of French West Africa, with representation in the French parliament and an eventual goal of independence.

The French built on foundations laid by the Germans. They introduced coffee cultivation in the Togo Mountains, extended the railway network, and improved the Lomé port. They also replaced the German requirement of forced labor with a system of taxation that more effectively compelled cultivation of cash crops or wage labor. Like the Germans, the French focused most of their investments on the country's more developed south. An international consortium to exploit Togo's rich phosphate deposits formed in 1954 but would not begin extensive production until the country had achieved independence.

Beginning in 1947, the All-Ewe Conference, based in the Gold Coast, and the Comité de l'Unité Togolaise (CUT) argued before the UN Trusteeship Council for reunification of the French and British portions of Togoland, or alternatively for the unification of all Ewe territories, including those in the Gold Coast. The French viewed this Ewe unification movement with alarm because it played into the hands of Kwame Nkrumah's campaign to unify Togo with Ghana, which would have eliminated French influence in the region. Meanwhile, in 1956 a plebiscite in British Togoland approved a merger with the Gold Coast, although a majority in the southern Ewe districts opposed the merger. British Togoland merged with the Gold Coast and in 1957 gained independence under Nkrumah as Ghana.

The French held a referendum in 1956 approving the creation of an autonomous republic of French Togo, despite Ewe opposition. Nicolas Grunitzky, a northerner, was appointed premier. After a protest by the mostly Ewe CUT to the United Nations, an election held in 1958 approved complete independence for Togo and replaced Grunitzky with a government led by CUT's Sylvanus Olympio. Togo proclaimed full independence on April 27, 1960.

Independent Togo

Olympio's Ewe-based government maintained economic and political ties with France and Francophone Africa. But Olympio moved ruthlessly to suppress opposition, and his program of austerity alienated not only northerners but much of his Ewe constituency. He resisted Nkrumah's desire for integration of Togo with Ghana, and the subsequent border closings alienated Lomé's market women, who have been called the "principal socioeconomic force in the country." Meanwhile, the end of French colonialism meant layoffs for Togolese soldiers (mostly Kabré from the impoverished north) who had served in the French military. In 1963, when the widely unpopular Olympio refused to offer a group of unemployed Kabré soldiers positions in the country's army, they staged West Africa's first military coup. Though little blood was actually shed, Etienne Gnassingbé (later Gnassingbé Eyadéma) murdered Olympio as he sought refuge at the gates of the U.S. embassy.

During a four-year interlude, Nicolas Grunitzky served as "provisional president" with the backing of the expanded, mostly Kabré military. But Grunitzky's indecisive leadership alienated a number of constituen-

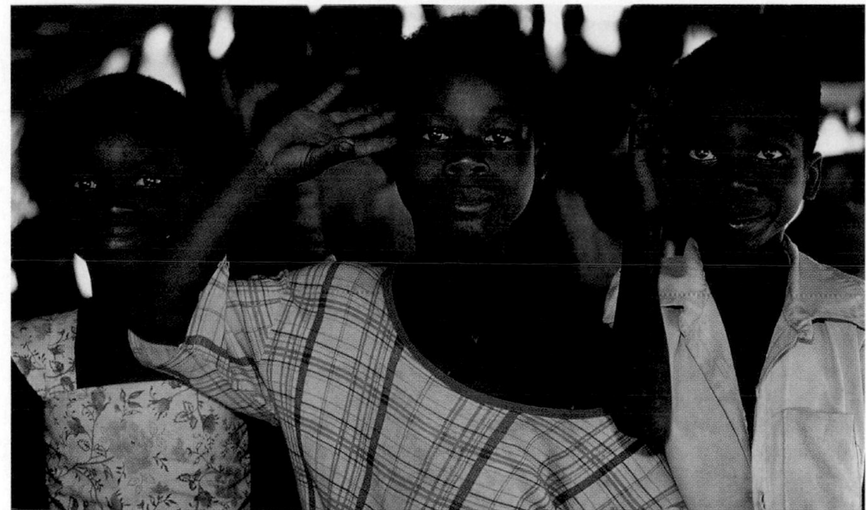

LEFT: Children raise their hands in a classroom in Togo, where about 76 percent of school-age children attend school. *CORBIS/Brian Vikander*
BELOW LEFT: In the capital city of Lomé, a Togolese woman runs a stall selling cloth dyed using a local batik process. The Lomé market women have been called the "principal socioeconomic force" in Togo. *Betty Press*

cies, including the crucial market women, and his subjection to the military made him unable to appease Ewe leaders, who demanded that Eyadéma and other participants in the 1963 coup be brought to justice. When Ewe unrest threatened the survival of Grunitzky's regime, Eyadéma and his military colleagues acted to ward off their certain doom at the hands of Olympio's political heirs. In 1967 the military demanded Grunitzky's resignation, and Eyadéma declared himself president and banned all political parties.

Eyadéma's ascent to power coincided with the onset of unprecedented prosperity in Togo, which helped him win popular support. Togo's growing phosphate-export earnings bankrolled a lavish program of patronage, and civil servants and other employees received generous pay increases. Eyadéma's government, freed from reliance on customs duties, enacted a free trade policy that opened up a profitable smuggling trade with neighboring Ghana. This ingratiated him with Togo's market women, as did his construction of a network of regional markets across the country. Meanwhile, Eyadéma carried out an extensive building program in Lomé and development projects benefiting the hitherto neglected north, including the completion of a paved road linking Lomé to Burkina Faso.

Eyadéma followed the pattern of his idol, former Zaire's General Mobutu Sese Seko, in institutionalizing his military rule. In 1969 he created the Rassemblement du peuple togolais (RPT) as the country's sole legal party. Legislative elections in 1979 and 1985 confirmed a single slate of candidates prepared by the RPT. In response to his call for "authenticity," the government abandoned colonial place names and required civil servants to follow his example in dropping his European name (Etienne) for an "indigenous" one (Gnassingbé). With the assistance of North Korean advisors, he built a personality cult around himself. Massive photographs and statues of the general, referred to as "The Savior of the Common Man" or simply "Le Guide," were installed throughout Togo.

When phosphate prices soared briefly in the mid-1970s, Togo nationalized the phosphate sector and based an "industrialization drive" on the construction of massive state enterprises with international borrowing. By the late 1970s, however, phosphate prices had plummeted, and when newly built facilities such as a petroleum refinery and a steel mill began operation, they proved economically unviable. Meanwhile, Togo had accumulated a massive external debt that it could not repay.

During the 1980s the government, under pressure from the French government and the International Monetary Fund (IMF), was forced to privatize state enterprises, eliminate widespread mismanagement and cronyism, and implement an austerity plan. This put an end to Eyadéma's patronage system and precipitated a severe economic decline, which in turn led to growing popular dissatisfaction with the regime, particularly in the more commercial south. Eyadéma responded by staging elections in 1986 that showed virtually unanimous support for his continued leadership, while the military, led by Eyadéma's relatives and neighbors, mounted a campaign of imprisonment, torture, and murder in an attempt to suppress dissent. But the regime's rigorous adherence to the IMF austerity plan earned it international support, and in 1986 French troops helped repress an attempted coup, reportedly organized by the exiled sons of Olympio.

Revelations of the regime's human rights abuses, however, put Eyadéma under international pressure to allow a more open political process. After demonstrations calling for Eyadéma's resignation met with bloody military responses in 1990 and 1991, Eyadéma agreed to the formation of political parties and a National Conference on political reforms. Opposition leaders attempted to use the National Conference as a vehicle to replace Eyadéma's government, but ongoing military harassment and attempted assassinations of opposition leaders confirmed the general's hold on power. The pattern of harassment and the government's delay in scheduling national elections sparked a wave of general strikes in 1992 and 1993 that crippled Togo's ailing economy.

When elections finally took place in 1993, government-sponsored violence and electoral manipulation led to the withdrawal of an international monitoring team and a boycott by opposition leaders. With a turnout of about 36 percent, Eyadéma was reelected to a five-year term. Despite continued military harassment, legislative elections in 1994 yielded a slim majority for the opposition. However, government manipulation led to the disqualification of several opposition legislators and the formation of a government favorable to General Eyadéma.

Since 1994 the Togolese economy has seen a partial recovery, based on strong export earnings, from the preceding 15-year decline. Funding has been approved for an improvement of the port of Lomé and the highway to Burkina Faso. But the current political scene is less encouraging: in 1997 Eyadéma's government blocked the creation of an independent electoral commission, and after military harassment of opposition leaders marred the 1998 presidential campaign, Eyadéma's claim to have won reelection for another five years sparked opposition protests and rioting in the streets of the capital.

Mark O'Malley

See Also

Colonial Rule; Dahomey, Early Kingdom of; Gold Trade; Lomé, Togo; Transatlantic Slave Trade; United Nations in Africa; Great Britain; France; Germany; Netherlands, The; Pastoralism; Portugal; Tuskegee University; Christianity: Missionaries in Africa; Human Rights in Africa; Slavery in Africa.

Africa

Togo (Ready Reference)

Official Name: Togolese Republic
Former Name: French Togo
Area: 56,790 sq km (21,925 sq mi)
Location: Western Africa, bordered by Burkina Faso, Benin, Ghana, and the Atlantic Ocean
Capital: Lomé (population 600,000 [1994 estimate])
Other Major Cities: Sokodé (population 55,000 [1987 estimate]) and Kpalimé (population 31,000 [1987 estimate])
Population: 4,905,827 (1998 estimate)
Population Density: 128 persons per sq km (about 207 persons per sq mi [1998 estimate])
Population Below Age 15: 48 percent (male 1,190,812; female 1,180,739 [1998 estimate])
Population Growth Rate: 3.52 percent (1998 estimate)
Total Fertility Rate: 6.6 children born per woman (1998 estimate)
Life Expectancy at Birth: Total population: 58.7 years (male 56.5 years; female 61.1 years [1998 estimate])
Infant Mortality Rate: 79.8 deaths per 1000 live births (1998 estimate)
Literacy Rate (age 15 and over who can read and write): Total population: 51.7 percent (male 67 percent; female 37 percent [1995 estimate])
Education: In the early 1970s the Togolese government undertook a campaign to provide free education to all children between ages 2 and 15. By the early 1990s nearly 76 percent of all school-age children attended school. Missionary schools are also important and educate roughly half of all students.
Languages: French is the official language; it is used for administration, commerce, and in schools. Ewe, Mina, Dagomba, and Kabye (sometimes spelled Kabiye) are the four major African languages spoken in Togo.
Ethnic Groups: There are 37 different ethnic groups in Togo. The largest of these are the Ewe in the south, the Mina and the Kabré in the north.
Religions: About 70 percent of the population adhere to indigenous beliefs. About 20 percent are Christian; 10 percent are Muslim.
Climate: Tropical in the south and semi-arid in the north. Average annual temperatures range from 27° C (about 80° F) at the coast to 30° C (86° F) in the north. The south has two rainy seasons, from March to July and October to November. The annual rainfall in the south averages 875 mm (35 in) and doubles in the mountains, a few kilometers in from the coast. In the north, where is there is one rainy season between April and July, the average rainfall is 1145 mm (45 in).
Land, Plants, and Animals: Togo's geography varies from tropical forest at the coast to savanna in the rest of the country. There are buffalo, antelopes, lions, and deer in the northern regions. In the forests there are snakes and monkeys. Hippopotamuses and crocodiles live in the rivers.
Natural Resources: Phosphates, limestone, and marble
Currency: The CFA franc
Gross Domestic Product (GDP): $6.2 billion (1997 estimate)
GDP per Capita: $1300 (1997 estimate)
GDP Real Growth Rate: 4.8 percent (1997 estimate)
Primary Economic Activities: Agriculture, industry, and services
Primary Crops: Coffee, cocoa, cotton, yams, cassava (tapioca), corn, beans, rice, millet, sorghum, meat, and fish
Industries: Phosphate mining, agricultural processing, cement, handicrafts, textiles, and beverages
Primary Exports: Phosphates, cotton, cocoa, and coffee
Primary Imports: Machinery and equipment, consumer goods, food, and chemical products
Primary Trade Partners: European Union, Africa, United States, and Japan
Government: Togo is a republic under transition to multiparty democratic rule. The executive branch is led by President Gen. Gnassingbé Eyadéma and Prime Minister Edem Kodjo. The legislative branch is the elected 81-member National Assembly.

Elizabeth Heath

See Also

Antelope; Crocodile; Eyadéma, Gnassingbé; Hippopotamus; Kabré; Lion; Lomé, Togo.

Africa

Toivo ja Toivo, Andimba

(b. August 22, 1924, Umungundu, South West Africa [present-day Namibia]), leading Namibian nationalist and senior government minister.

The founding father of Namibian nationalism, Andimba Toivo ja Toivo remains one of Namibia's most venerated public figures. Toivo ja Toivo received a mission school education in South West Africa, which was then occupied by South Africa. During World War II he served as a corporal in the Native Military Corps. After the war he worked in South Africa, first in a mine on the Witwatersand and then in a Cape Town grocery. In a Cape Town barbershop Toivo ja Toivo organized South West Africa contract laborers into what became the Ovambo People's Organization, or OPO, in 1958. When he returned home in 1961 to help organize the successor to the OPO, the South West Africa People's Organization, or SWAPO, the South African government placed him under house arrest.

Despite the arrest, Toivo ja Toivo continued his organizing activities, and consequently was tried and convicted at the Terrorism Trial in 1966. Sentenced to 20 years of imprisonment on Robben Island, Toivo ja Toivo became a close associate of Nelson Mandela. In 1984 he was released from prison early in what some considered an attempt by South Africa to divide the SWAPO leadership. Instead, Toivo ja Toivo, then 69 years old, returned to Windhoek a hero, and became secretary general of the party. In the 1989 elections Toivo ja Toivo was elected to the National Assembly, and a year later became minister of mines and energy in independent Namibia. In 1991 he stepped down from his party post to devote more time to his ministerial position. Toivo ja Toivo has repeatedly demanded an investigation into torture and disappearances at SWAPO camps during the war for independence.

Eric Young

See Also

Cape Town, South Africa; Mandela, Nelson Rolihlahla; Nationalism in Africa; Windhoek, Namibia; World War II and African Americans.

Toivo ya Toivo, Herman. Please see Toivo ja Toivo, Andimba

Africa

Tolbert, William Richard, Jr.

(b. May 13, 1913, Bensonville, Liberia; d. April 12, 1980, Monrovia, Liberia), president of Liberia from 1971 until his assassination in 1980.

When William R. Tolbert took office as Liberia's twentieth president in 1971, he seemed poised to continue the dominance of the True Whig

Party (TWP), which had ruled Liberian politics for more than a century. Instead, Tolbert's administration was plagued by indecision and confusion, and his 1980 assassination marked the beginning of 17 years of political, economic, and social chaos.

A member of the Americo-Liberian elite, Tolbert attended a private Episcopal high school and the University of Liberia, from which he graduated in 1934. He worked in various government jobs before his 1943 election to the House of Representatives. In 1951 Tolbert became William V. S. Tubman's vice president, a position he maintained through five elections until Tubman's death in 1971, at which time Tolbert became president.

Long under Tubman's shadow, Tolbert took immediate steps to distinguish himself from his predecessor. Wearing casual dress to his inauguration, the KPELLE-speaking president promised greater openness to opposition groups as well as economic growth that would aid the country's poor. But while Tolbert's vague pronouncements were intended to appeal to both populist Liberians and the more conservative business community, his actual policies pleased few on either side. In 1979 the deregulation of food prices sparked protests and, after Tolbert sent in the army to break them up, widespread rioting. On April 12, 1980, an army master sergeant, Samuel K. Doe, led a small group of soldiers into Tolbert's presidential palace and assassinated him. Doe subsequently proclaimed himself Liberia's new head of state.

Kate Tuttle

SEE ALSO
Americo-Liberians; Doe, Samuel Kanyon; Tubman, William Vacanarat Shadrach.

North America

Tolson, Melvin Beaunorus

(b. February 6, 1898, Moberly, Mo.; d. August 29, 1966, Guthrie, Okla.), African American poet, chronicler of the cultural scene in Harlem.

Melvin Tolson attended FISK UNIVERSITY before transferring to Lincoln University, where he received his bachelor's degree in 1922. He took positions teaching English literature and coaching the debate team at Wiley College in Marshall, Texas, but was inspired to develop his talent for poetry after attending Columbia University on a Rockefeller Foundation scholarship from 1931 to 1932. Tolson's year at Columbia put him in Harlem at the end of the HARLEM RENAISSANCE, and he became friendly with many writers associated with it, most notably LANGSTON HUGHES. In several poems over the next two decades, Tolson would revisit the atmosphere of 1930s Harlem.

Tolson's first major work, *Rendezvous with America,* was published in 1944. Throughout the 1940s, his poems, characterized by their allusive, complex, modernist style and their long poetic sequences, were published in such magazines and journals as the *Atlantic Monthly,* the *Modern Quarterly,* the *Arts Quarterly,* and *Poetry.* In 1947 the government of LIBERIA named Tolson its poet laureate and commissioned him to write a piece for the country's centennial; the result was *Libretto for the Republic of Liberia* (1953). Tolson's best-known piece, the poetic sequence *Harlem Gallery,* was published in 1965. In 1966 he won the Arts and Letters Award in literature from the American Academy and Institute of Arts and Letters. *A Gallery of Harlem Portraits,* an extended work Tolson had begun with a single sonnet in 1932, was published posthumously in 1979.

Lisa Clayton Robinson

SEE ALSO
Literature, African American; Harlem, New York.

North America

Tolton, Augustus

(b. 1854?, Brush Creek, Mo.; d. July 9, 1897, CHICAGO, ILLINOIS), African American Catholic priest who served a Chicago African American congregation.

Augustus Tolton was raised in Quincy, Illinois. He began studying for the priesthood in 1873, and though initially refused admission at local seminaries, was eventually able to attend Quincy College and complete his studies in Rome, Italy.

Tolton was ordained in Rome in 1886 and returned to the United States to serve as one of the first African American Catholic priests. His first congregation was in a racially mixed parish in Quincy; after pressure from local priests, he took over a black congregation in Chicago. Tolton was a leader in the black Catholic congresses between 1889 and 1894.

Lisa Clayton Robinson

Africa

Tombalbaye, François

(b. 1918, Chad; d. 1975, Chad), prime minister of French-governed CHAD (1959-1960) and first president of independent Chad (1960-1975).

Raised in southern Chad, François Tombalbaye was educated in Brazzaville, Congo, and was one of the few Chadians to have obtained a secondary education by the end of World War II (1939-1945). While working as a teacher in 1947, Tombalbaye helped organize the Parti Progressiste Tchadien (PPT or Chadian Progressive Party), the Chadian branch of the African Democratic Rally, an interterritorial political party across French West Africa. Tombalbaye's political career prospered after 1952. He was elected to the regional legislature and also began to climb the ranks of the PPT leadership. Tombalbaye represented Chad in the 1957 General Council for French Equatorial Africa, and in 1959 he became leader of the PPT and Chad's prime minister.

Tombalbaye led Chad to independence in 1960 and became its first president. In his first years in power he worked to isolate and eliminate all political rivals, and in 1962 banned all opposition parties. Tombalbaye ruled in authoritarian fashion, surviving uprisings in southern and eastern Chad, a full-scale rebellion in northern Chad in 1965, border conflicts with LIBYA, and coup attempts in 1971 and 1972. Tombalbaye's presidency was associated with turning opposition groups against each other, an attempt to promote African cultural practices, and overambitious development projects that achieved less than promised. In a 1975 military coup he was killed in the crossfire between rebels and palace guards.

SEE ALSO
Brazzaville, Republic of the Congo; World War II and African Americans.

Africa

Tombouctou, Mali,

the principal southern terminus of trans-Saharan trade and former center of Islamic studies, famous for its university in medieval times.

Founded by Tuaregs nine miles from the northwest bend of the NIGER RIVER in MALI, Tombouctou (Timbuktu) is known for its prominence as a commercial, religious, and educational center in the Middle Ages, especially during the 1500s. At present Tombouctou, with an estimated population of 20,500, is a town of mostly adobe buildings, with a prominent cone-shaped great mosque on its western skirts. Two other mosques, Sidi Yahia, at the town's center, and Sankoré, located northeast of the town, punctuate its skyline. The majority of the town's inhabitants are Songhai. Tombouctou is connected with the Niger River by canals, and the town of Kabara serves as its port. Between March and June caravan traders and nomadic herders camp out around town to sell their goods at the market, increasing the population significantly. Tombouctou has a variety of resident artisans, including weavers, potters, leather-workers, and smiths. Most of the town's permanent residents are merchants and traders. Salt brought by camel caravan from salt mines at Taodeni 625 km (375 mi) to the north and livestock from Tuareg herders inhabiting sparse pasture lands in the southern Saharan regions of Mali are two of the major commodities sold at the market, along with dates from oasis gardens.

In ancient times the region around Tombouctou is said to have been populated by the Songhai, who reputedly migrated to the bend of the Niger from the valley of the Nile in EGYPT. Rock inscriptions showing horse-drawn chariots west of Tombouctou place it along the pre-Roman trade routes of the Sahara, linking it with MOROCCO. Early Songhai settlers first established Gao along the northeastern bend of the Niger, directly east of Tombouctou, and Djenné-Djeno to the south, both commercial centers along the trans-Saharan caravan routes. In the eleventh century a market center was founded at Tombouctou by Tuareg pastoralists. From the twelfth century onward, caravans carrying West African gold passed through Tombouctou en route to the Barbary Coast.

When the Moroccan Berber historian IBN BATTUTAH visited Tombouctou in 1353, he noted that most of its inhabitants were "wearers of the face-veil," a style used by Tuareg men to wind their turbans so that they drape across the face, creating a mask or "veil." Battutah describes a fourteenth-century "turbaning ritual" at Tombouctou very similar to those performed among some Tuareg groups today, in which the ruling governor presents an ascending Tuareg confederation chief with a new robe, a turban, and trousers of indigo-dyed cloth. In the ceremony the governor wrapped the new turban around the Tuareg ruler's head and face, "bade him sit upon a shield, and the chiefs of his tribe raised him on their heads."

The Songhai captured Tombouctou in 1468. Between 1494 and 1529 Tombouctou reached what was perhaps its greatest height under Askia Muhammad's rule. During this period a center of higher learning, the "university" of Tombouctou, was established at the mosque of Sankoré; it became a renowned center of Islamic studies, with scholars educated in leading Islamic academies of the MIDDLE EAST. Tombouctou is still the repository of a number of valuable manuscripts in Arabic, including the *Tarik es-Sudan*, a history of the SUDAN written by the religious scholar Abderrahman Sadi in the 1600s.

In 1591 the sultan of Morocco sent an army to Tombouctou to capture the city and take control of the gold trade. This invasion brought the SONGHAI EMPIRE to an end. The Moorish conquerors from Morocco who controlled the city began feuding among themselves, however, and the town was almost in ruins by the time the Tuaregs took over again in 1800. The city was subsequently captured by FULANI tribesmen in 1813 and by the TUKULOR in 1840.

By the time British and French explorers began arriving at Tombouctou in the 1800s, Tombouctou had fallen into decay. Maj. Gordon Laing traveled across the Sahara from Tripoli, arriving at Tombouctou in 1826, but he was murdered by the Fulani. René Caillié visited Tombouctou for two weeks, traveling from the coast in 1828; he noted that, although its commercial significance had diminished, many Tombouctou merchants were still receiving commodities from North Africa, and certain European goods – in particular, double-barreled French guns – were much sought. The marketplace also sold gold and slaves from the West Africa savanna and forest regions.

The explorer HEINRICH BARTH spent six months in Tombouctou from 1853 to 1854, traveling across the Sahara to represent the British government and establish British influence there. He noted the decreasing trade in slaves and the volume of trade in Moroccan tobacco, cloth from Europe, and Saharan oasis-grown dates, as well as sword blades from Germany. Explorer Oskar Lenz traveled to Tombouctou from Morocco in 1880. The following year French troops began the conquest of the regions along the Niger bend, arriving at Tombouctou in 1893 just after Tuaregs had again taken control of the town, and capturing the city in 1894.

Tombouctou remains a crossroads of Saharan and Sahelian peoples, including Tuareg camel nomads and caravaneers, Fulani cattle herders, Hassaniya-speaking Arabized BERBER nomads, Songhai traders and gardeners, and Mandingo and BAMBARA farmers and traders. The city can be reached by boat from Bamako and Gao on the Niger River.

Barbara Worley

SEE ALSO

Bamako, Mali; Explorers in Africa Since 1800; Gold Trade; Djenné-Djeno, Mali; Askia Muhammad; Nile River; Pastoralism; Sahara Desert; Salt Trade; Tuareg; Tripoli, Libya; Caillié, René-Auguste; Slavery in Africa; Songhai People.

Ton. Please see BAULE

Africa

Tonga (also known as Batonga), linguistic and ethnic group of the Zambezi basin.

The Tonga include approximately 12 percent of Zambia's 10 million inhabitants. While the majority live in southern ZAMBIA along Lake Kariba and the ZAMBEZI RIVER, some Tonga also live in northern ZIMBABWE, BOTSWANA, MALAWI, and MOZAMBIQUE. Other ethnic groups also speak the Tonga language, including the Lenje, Soli, Ila, Toka, Leya, Sala, and Gowa. Altogether, about one-fifth of Zambians speak Tonga. Archaeological evidence (namely, stylistic continuity in pottery) shows that the Tonga have occupied Sebanzi Hill in Zambia since about 1100 C.E. Some sources suggest that the Tonga migrated from an area south of the Zambezi River, though their Bantu language suggests an ancient migration from the north.

The Tonga fall into two broad groups: the Plateau Tonga and the Valley (or Gwembe) Tonga. Traditionally, each group inhabited a distinct ecological niche. Since the soils are not particularly fertile, the Plateau Tonga raise cattle, although they also cultivate maize and peanuts. The Plateau Tonga are also known for their ironworking. The Valley Tonga traditionally practiced floodplain cultivation, primarily of maize, MILLET, and sorghum. During the dry season the Valley Tonga lived near the river to protect their crop against invading pests. However, after the crops were harvested and the water levels rose, they abandoned these garden settlements for higher ground until the following year.

The Tonga traditionally lacked chiefs and political hierarchies. They remained divided into numerous matrilineages. These lineages traditionally provided the basic structure for the Tonga's small, widely dispersed, permanent hamlets, consisting of related women and their husbands and sons. Daily politics, such as land-tenure disputes, fell under the purview of the lineage. The loosely organized Tonga suffered heavily from the actions of more hierarchical neighboring groups such as the LOZI, who periodically raided for slaves.

When the British took control of the region, they identified Native Authorities to administer local government under their policy of indirect rule. Among groups such as the Tonga who did not have such political leaders, the British appointed them. Thus over the course of the twentieth century, Tonga political organization has become more centralized and hierarchical. In 1913 many Tonga were forced off their lands, particularly those adjacent to the railroad, to make way for European settlers. Deprived of land and forced to pay taxes, some young men traveled to the mines of Southern Rhodesia (today Zimbabwe) in search of employment. The majority of the Tonga remained, and shifted from the cultivation of finger millet to maize, which they sold for consumption in the burgeoning mining towns. Thus the Tonga have remained less urban than other ethnic groups.

The Tonga have faced a number of setbacks in recent years. Relatively affluent Tonga farmers helped found the nationalist movement after World War II, and supported the (Zambian) African National Congress, led by the Tonga-speaking Harry Nkumbula. In the late 1950s, however, the colonial government dammed the Zambezi River. This action created Lake Kariba, which submerged the farms of many of the Valley Tonga. Some 60,000 farmers, forcibly relocated around the lake, continued to depend on agriculture on the sandier soils of the lakeshore. Some took up fishing. However, the lifestyle of the Valley Tonga, previously revolving around the seasonal floods, had radically changed. The group became increasingly marginalized after its forcible relocation to more marginal areas. In the early 1960s the United National Independence Party, dominated by BEMBA-speakers, eclipsed the Tonga-led African National Congress. Recent constitutional amendments have barred traditional chiefs, including the Tonga leader Chief Munyumbwe, from politics in a ploy to increase the disfranchisement of already marginal groups.

Ari Nave

SEE ALSO

Bantu: Dispersion and Settlement; Colonial Rule; Nkumbula, Harry Mwaanga; Iron in Africa; Nationalism in Africa; Djebar, Assia; Slavery in Africa.

Latin America and the Caribbean

Tonton Macoutes (also known as Tonton Makout), a fearsome paramilitary group established in Haiti under the dictatorship of François Duvalier.

The name Tonton Macoute was originally attached to a haunting character in Haitian folk literature. Translating roughly as "bogeyman with a basket," the name referred to an old bearded man who carried a bag of woven straw (a *macoute* in Creole) and appeared at night to carry away naughty children. Haitian mothers invoked the image of Tonton Macoute to encourage obedience among their children, saying: "If you do not behave, I'll call Tonton Macoute and he will drag you away."

When François Duvalier took power in Haiti on October 22, 1957, he soon inaugurated a regime of terror against his opponents. He desired a source of power parallel to, but independent from, the armed forces; in order to serve Duvalier's needs the new group would have to attach its loyalty exclusively to the Haitian leader. By July 1958 Duvalier had established his personal militia, the Tonton Macoutes. Duvalier's henchmen attacked, beat, raped, and harassed the opponents of his regime, initially wearing hoods to mask their features. (As a hood is called a *cagoule* in French, these forces were initially called *Cagoulards*; eventually the more popular Tonton Macoutes took hold.) Early in Duvalier's rule this force targeted academics and other intellectuals who might oppose Duvalier, provoking one of many waves of migration from Haiti to the United States and elsewhere. Though there are no solid estimates, it is believed that during the early Duvalier years the Tonton Macoutes killed tens of thousands of people. The militia's abuses were generally documented in urban Haiti, but less is known about the actions of the Tonton Macoutes in rural areas, where their presence was stronger and where the vast majority of the Haitian population resides.

The Tonton Macoutes, which was not officially acknowledged by the Haitian government, soon evolved into a pervasive secret police force in Haiti. In 1962 the Duvalier regime created a militia called the Volontaires de la Sécurité Nationale (VSN), whose connection to the Tonton Macoutes was suspected if not explicit. The true status of the VSN is unclear: some believe it served as a virtual cover for the Tonton Macoutes, but others hold that it was a second official military force designed to neutralize the army. Supporters of the latter belief point out that the VSN was created shortly after a coup attempt against Duvalier.

Regardless of its official affiliation, the Tonton Macoutes was an ominous presence, particularly in rural Haiti. Notorious for their blue uniforms, straw hats, and red sashes – calculated to appear like the traditional dress of the Haitian peasantry – the Macoutes not only carried out violence but exercised overwhelming power in government administration; most rural section chiefs and other local officials were Macoutes. As the militia's power increased, so did its numbers: the Tonton Macoutes eventually became twice as large as the army (estimates of the militia's full membership range from 9000 to as high as 300,000). This led not only to serious rivalry between the Tonton Macoutes and other political and military forces, but also to rivalry within the Macoutes ranks.

When François Duvalier's rule passed on to his son, Jean-Claude Duvalier, the links between the police, the army, and the VSN/Tonton Macoutes became stronger, and many feel that the head of the Macoutes, Minister of the Interior Roger Lafontant, became the real power behind Jean-Claude Duvalier's rule. But some observers also argue that the Tonton Macoutes came to be increasingly critical of "Baby Doc" Duvalier, whom they saw as betraying the "ideals" of his father. These divisions within the VSN/Tonton Macoutes were partially responsible for the collapse of Jean-Claude Duvalier's spectacularly corrupt regime, which finally fell on February 7, 1986. Nevertheless, at the end of his rule, "Baby Doc" Duvalier declared a state of siege and called the Tonton Macoutes and the army into the streets, where they killed hundreds. The end of the Duvaliers's sovereignty thus provoked Carnivals and street celebrations. It also incited the *dechoukaj*, or "uprooting," a strong backlash against the Tonton Macoutes in which citizens killed scores of the organization's more visible members.

Though the Tonton Macoutes was not the first or the last paramilitary organization in Haiti, their use by Duvalier established a legacy of fear and violence that poses powerful dilemmas. Particularly urgent in a post-Duvalier and incipiently democratic Haiti is the issue of how to deal with past abuses, whether or not to bring past abusers to justice while seeking to create a unified, just, and democratic Haiti.

Paulette Poujol-Oriol

Tony Williams. Please see Platters, The

North America

Toomer, Jean (b. December 26, 1894, Washington, D.C.; d. March 30, 1967), African American writer whose experimental novel of Southern life, *Cane*, profoundly influenced twentieth-century black writers.

Jean Toomer's position in the canon of African American literature rests on his haunting narrative of Southern life, *Cane*. Since its original publication in 1923, the novel has been rediscovered by successive generations of black writers, despite Toomer's later ambivalence toward his racial identity. Toomer, racially mixed but able to pass for white, sought a unifying thesis that would resolve the conflicts of his identity. He spent his life trying to evade the categories of American racial and ethnic identification, which he felt constricted the complexity of a lineage like his.

As a writer Toomer was nurtured in the 1910s and 1920s by Greenwich Village progressive aesthetes like Waldo Frank and Hart Crane, but *Cane* was inspired by his two-month stint as a substitute principal at the black Sparta Agricultural and Industrial Institute in Georgia in 1921. Entranced by Georgia's rural geography and its black folk traditions, he saw in Southern life the harmony that escaped him, although he believed the culture to be disappearing through migration to the North and its encounter with modernity.

Cane is a series of vignettes whose narrative structure moves from the South to the North

Author Jean Toomer's 1923 novel, *Cane*, influenced generations of African American writers. The author is shown here in 1934. *CORBIS/Bettmann*

and back to the South, forming a troubled synthesis of the two regions. The book was a commercial failure on its first publication, but critics initiated a chorus of praise that has spanned the generations. Members of the Harlem Renaissance and the Black Arts Movement, as well as later African American women writers like Toni Morrison and Alice Walker, have cited its influence and acclaimed the author's sensitive treatment of black folk life, his formal elegance, and his progressive, uninhibited approach to sexuality and gender.

Cane was Toomer's only work that explicitly treated the lives of African Americans; after its publication he disappeared from literary circles. In 1924 the restless author made the first of several pilgrimages to Fontainebleau, France, to study with the mystic and psychologist Georges Ivanovich Gurdjieff at the Institute for the Harmonious Development of Man. Gurdjieff believed that a transcendent "essence," obscured by a socially determined "personality," could be recovered through his teachings. Through Gurdjieff, Toomer found a way to express his attempts at defining a holistic identity. He taught Gurdjieff's philosophy in Harlem and Chicago until his break with the mystic in the mid-1930s.

Toomer wrote voluminously until his death, and although much of his writing received occasional praise for its experimentation, it was largely dismissed by African American critics, who saw it not only as propaganda for Gurdjieff's teachings, but as being white-identified. Indeed, in 1930 Toomer declined to be included in JAMES WELDON JOHNSON's *Book of American Negro Poetry,* on the grounds that he was not a Negro. Toomer continued to strive for a sense of wholeness, however, and for a definition of what Henry Louis Gates Jr. has described as a "remarkably fluid notion of race." He found this in the potential of an "American" race, described in the 1936 long poem *Blue Meridian* – the last work published while he was alive – as a hybrid, "blue," comprising the black, the white, and the red races.

Peter Hudson

SEE ALSO
Pass Laws; Women Writers, Black, in the United States; Chicago, Illinois; Great Migration, The; Harlem, New York.

Africa

Toposa (also known as Topotha), ethnic group of SUDAN.

The Toposa primarily inhabit far southern Sudan. They speak a Nilo-Saharan language. Approximately 100,000 people consider themselves Toposa.

SEE ALSO
Languages, African: An Overview.

Africa

Toro (also known as Rutoro), ethnic group of UGANDA.

The Toro primarily inhabit western Uganda. They speak a Bantu language and are closely related to the NYANKORE people. More than 700,000 people consider themselves Toro.

SEE ALSO
Bantu: Dispersion and Settlement.

Latin America and the Caribbean

Tosh, Peter (Peter McIntosh) (b. 1944; d. 1987, Westmoreland, Jamaica), Jamaican singer and songwriter, best known as an original member of the Wailers, the singing trio that also included BOB MARLEY and Bunny Wailer (Neville O'Riley Livingston), and as an internationally popular solo artist with an emphatic political and prophetic bent.

Peter Tosh's entrance into music began during his teenage years in the Trenchtown ghetto of Kingston, where he and his friends Bob Marley and Bunny Wailer imitated the vocal harmonies of CURTIS MAYFIELD. Tosh's early recordings as part of a SKA/REGGAE trio with Marley and Wailer (who became known as the Wailers) made clear that his singing and songwriting talents were strongly flavored by rage against hypocritical individuals and institutions. Songs like "400 Years" and "Downpressor" are prime examples of his mastery of political protest songwriting. His first recordings as a solo artist in the early 1960s include a wry commentary on sexual mores ("Shame and Scandal") and a boastful declaration of Rastafarian identity ("Rasta Shook Them Up").

After quitting the Wailers in 1972, Tosh pursued a performing and recording career as a solo artist, marked by the cultivation of a persona of supreme toughness and righteous wrath, sentiments encapsulated in the song that became his anthem, "I'm the Toughest." This stance was reinforced during a Jamaican concert when Tosh lectured JAMAICA's prime minister, sitting in the audience, about the errors of the minister's ways. An overview of his recording career is available on CD as *Peter Tosh: Honorary Citizen* (Columbia). His murder by armed robbers silenced reggae's most politically inspired artist.

Norman Weinstein

SEE ALSO
Kingston, Jamaica; Rastafarians.

Latin America and the Caribbean

Totó la Momposina (b. 1946, Mompox, COLOMBIA), Afro-Colombian singer, dancer, and performer of traditional rhythms from Colombia's Atlantic and Pacific coasts.

Totó la Momposina, as she is known, was born Sonia Bazanta in the town of Talaigua, on the river island of Mompox, from which she took her stage name. The small towns on the Magdalena River (on Mompox and in surrounding areas, including Soplaviento, PALENQUE DE SAN BASILIO, Botón de Leyva, and Altos del Rosario) are heirs to a rich Afro-Indian musical tradition. Originally inhabited by indigenous peoples, during the colonial period these areas became a safe haven for fugitive slaves, who built fortified villages known as *palenques.*

Totó is a third-generation musician – her grandfather was an accordionist, her father is a traditional drummer (*tambolero*), and her mother was a traditional singer (*cantadora*). Totó's parents and family sought to preserve secular and sacred musical forms played at religious festivals, funerals, ritual ceremonies, and local Carnivals. From an early age Totó learned the Afro-Colombian rhythms of *chandé, mapalé, fandango, currulao, porro, puya,* and CUMBIA. Totó was also raised in the tradition of the cantadoras, female singers who improvise verses (*coplas*). She learned about music from the many musicians and cantadoras who visited the family home, and by taking part in fiestas and ceremonies in neighboring villages.

In the late 1960s Totó traveled to Paris to study dance history at the Sorbonne. In France she began her musical career by singing in train stations and on street corners. She was "discovered" in Europe and it was there that she released her first two albums, *Totó la Momposina* and *Colombia: Musique de la Cité Atlantique.* She later traveled to CUBA to learn more about BOLERO, SON, *guaracha,* RUMBA, and other Afro-Cuban rhythms, and went on to include these sounds in her repertoire.

In 1982 Totó and her group – Totó la Momposina y Sus Tambores – accompanied Colombian writer Gabriel García Márquez to receive the Nobel Prize for Literature in Stockholm. In the 1990s British singer and producer Peter Gabriel invited the group to record for his Real World label and to be part of the annual World of Music, Arts, and Dance (WOMAD) tour.

Totó has since gained much popularity in Europe performing the traditional rhythms she began learning in childhood. Her success is attributable not only to her music but to her lively performances, which feature traditional dress and authentic Afro-Colombian instruments.

In one interview Totó stated that she disliked having the term "folklore" applied to her music, because it connotes a "stiff and archaic form of expression." Totó prefers to describe these Afro-Colombian rhythms as vibrant, living "traditional music." "At home," she says, "the rural people have always composed music based on nature, and when music comes from the land, its language knows no frontiers. When I listen to drummers from SENEGAL or Congo, I can hear affinities with Cuban, Brazilian and Colombian drummers."

Liliana Obregón

SEE ALSO
Congo, Democratic Republic of the; Maroonage in the Americas; Music, Afro-Caribbean Secular.

Touareg. Please see TUAREG

Africa

Toubou, ethnic group of CHAD, NIGER, and LIBYA, in the southern Sahara.

A nomadic group numbering about 250,000 people, the Toubou were once the dominant pastoralists of the central Sudan. Their early origins are unknown; they are believed to be related to the Berbers, but their Nilo-Saharan language is closely related to that of the KANEMBU to the south.

According to legend the Toubou originally migrated to their present location from the

Nile valley during the seventh century C.E. Upon their arrival, they joined with the Kanembu to help form the Kanem Kingdom and took control of the valuable salt mines of Bilma, in present-day Niger. After a series of succession disputes in the thirteenth century, the group lost the protection of the Kanem Kingdom and came into conflict with such neighboring groups as the Mobeur and the Tuareg. During subsequent centuries the Toubou practiced pastoralism and oasis agriculture, though some smaller groups broke off and settled in sedentary agricultural communities. Many supplemented their incomes with the tariffs imposed on trade caravans. By the nineteenth century the Toubou had split into two main subgroups – the Teda and the Daza – each made up of smaller clans and dispersed throughout northern Chad and Niger and southern Libya.

Both Toubou groups fiercely resisted French colonialism until 1920, when they were defeated and forced to accept colonial rule. The brutal French conquest devastated the fragile economy of these desert people, and taxes imposed by the colonial administration thwarted the trans-Saharan trade that had once underlain their prosperity. Their resistance to external rule reemerged after Chadian independence in 1960, and they were integral to the defeat of the southern N'Djamena government. Since the 1970s droughts and famines have impoverished the Toubou, especially the Teda. Some have joined with Nigerien Tuareg rebel groups in advocating a secessionist state, and in Niger the Teda have formed their own liberation front.

Elizabeth Heath

See Also

Colonial Rule; Berber; Drought and Desertification; Languages, African: An Overview; N'Djamena, Chad; Nile River; France; Sahara Desert; Salt Trade.

Africa

Touré, Ali Farka **(b. 1939, Kanau, Mali), African blues musician.**

With a Grammy Award to his name and years of worldwide touring, Ali Farka Touré is one of the best-known African musicians outside Africa. As Touré, who is particularly popular in America, told the *New York Times*, "Where you are, you may call it the blues." But he says that his guitar style, which reminds listeners of John Lee Hooker, Lightnin' Hopkins, and other blues legends, is really in the "African tradition."

Growing up amid poverty in Mali, Touré was his parents' tenth child, but the first to reach adolescence. Nicknamed "the donkey" (Farka) by his family because of his stubbornness, Touré made music despite his parents' objections. By age 17 he had learned the traditional Malian instruments, including the single-stringed *njarka* and the harplike *ngoni*. During the 1960s he directed a group specializing in traditional music. They toured Europe, where he acquired his first guitar and began to learn about Western music.

In 1970 Touré joined the house band of Mali's national radio station as its guitarist, and spent the next ten years recording six albums, which were released in France and West Africa. By the 1980s Touré had begun to build a reputation outside Mali, which culminated in worldwide fame after the 1988 release of his self-titled album, *Ali Farka Touré*. Collaborations with Western artists such as Ry Cooder, Clarence "Gatemouth" Brown, the Chieftains, and Taj Mahal have expanded Touré's popularity as a guitarist and singer. His 1994 album *Talking Timbuktu* won a Grammy for best world music album. Despite that record's success, Touré had to cancel concert plans, in part to help defend his family's farming community during Mali's war with the Tuaregs.

Kate Tuttle

See Also

Tuareg; Blues, The; Hopkins, ("Lightnin'") Sam; World Music, World Beat, and the Re-Africanization of Latin American Popular Music.

Africa

Touré, Sékou **(b. January 9, 1922, Faranah, French Guinea [now Guinea]; d. March 26, 1984, Cleveland, Ohio), Guinea's first president and a well-known political figure throughout Africa.**

Many in the former French colonies of West Africa consider Sékou Touré an independence movement hero. In his own country, however, where his 26-year-long presidency was characterized by increasing violence and suppression of civil liberties, his legacy is more complex.

Raised in a poor Muslim farming household, Touré claimed to be descended from the renowned nineteenth-century military leader Samory Touré. His parents sent Touré to the Georges Poiret technical school in Conakry when he was 14 years old. Expelled for unruly behavior one year later, he nevertheless continued to read and to educate himself, particularly in the works of Karl Marx. After holding several different jobs, Touré went to work for the Post and Telecommunications Service in 1941; he became the secretary general of PTT Workers' Union in 1945. As a union leader Touré organized labor strikes in the late 1940s and, according to some historians, began to use the strong-arm tactics that characterized his presidency. In 1946 Touré joined with nationalist leaders such as Félix Houphouët-Boigny of the Côte d'Ivoire to found the Rassemblement Démocratique Africain (RDA), which became a powerful engine of opposition to French colonialism.

For Touré, membership in RDA meant that, although he was elected twice to the French National Assembly (in 1951 and 1954), he was kept from taking his seat until 1956, when he was elected mayor of Conakry. In the meantime he became secretary general of the Parti Démocratique de Guinée, the national wing of the RDA. He went on to become vice president of the Executive Council of Guinea, and founder of the Union Générale des Travailleurs d'Afrique Noire (UGTAN), a French West African labor union. An eloquent speaker who reached out not only to Guinea's workers but to peasants and women, Touré became one of Africa's strongest voices for independence.

In 1958 France offered the colonies internal self-government within a new international "French Community." Declaring "We prefer poverty in freedom to opulence in slavery," Touré and other Guineans rejected the offer, voting overwhelmingly instead for total independence in the September 28, 1958, referendum. Guinea was the only French colony to choose autonomy, and France responded by repatriating most of its skilled workers as well as all the infrastructural equipment it could transport. Touré, who was elected Guinea's first president shortly after the independence vote, sought help for his stripped-bare country from both the West and the Eastern bloc.

Touré soon steered Guinea down a socialist path and into a closer alliance with the Eastern bloc. But as agricultural collectivization and state-run industries failed to alleviate poverty, the president resorted to increasingly authoritarian means of suppressing dissent. Although at least initially he remained sensitive to the appeals of certain groups – Guinea's politically active market women, in particular – it is estimated that as many as a million Guineans fled Touré's police state, and many thousand others were killed under his leadership. Still, he was considered an influential diplomat, especially within the Islamic world. Like his friend Ghanaian president Kwame Nkrumah, he was also an outspoken proponent of Pan-African unity, and published dozens of books and pamphlets (including one book of poetry) calling for an "African Africa." Touré, who had visited the United States many times, died in a hospital in Cleveland, Ohio, in 1984.

Kate Tuttle

See Also

African Socialism; Colonial Rule; Decolonization in Africa: An Interpretation; Conakry, Guinea; Nationalism in Africa; France; Pan-Africanism; Human Rights in Africa; Islam and Tradition: An Interpretation.

Africa

Tourism in Africa, **recreational travel in Africa.**

In 1997, 23 million tourists (a number researchers predicted would increase to 75 million by 2020) traveled to Africa's game parks, natural wonders, historic sites, markets, and beaches. Tourism in 1997 accounted for approximately 12.6 percent of the average gross domestic product for African countries and employed 13 million people. The World

Travel and Tourism Council predicted that tourism in Africa would grow by 80 percent by 2008. Africa's share in the global tourism market is low, however. In 1996 only about 3.5 percent of the 594 million tourists worldwide chose Africa as a destination. And of the approximately $425 billion that tourists spent worldwide, tourists in Africa spent only about $5.1 billion (about 1.8 percent).

In many African countries tourism is a major source of jobs and foreign currency. Tourism gives African governments an incentive to protect endangered species and historic monuments, and it can provide foreign visitors with a deeper appreciation of Africa's history and cultures than they could ever obtain from movies and textbooks.

Still, how much Africa's economies, ecosystems, and citizens really benefit from tourism remains open to debate. Tourism is typically a low-wage and often highly seasonal industry, and the popularity of a particular region or site can shift according to the promotional campaigns of foreign travel agencies. In addition, much of the revenue generated by tourism does not remain in the host country. The amount that goes to foreign airlines, hotel chains, and tour operators, known as "leakage," is very high in countries where many visitors come as part of organized package tours. For example, in KENYA, leakage has been estimated to consume about 70 percent of tourism revenue; in the Gambia, the figure is 60 percent.

Also, the development of the infrastructure necessary to house, transport, and entertain tourists can harm the environment, even where the tourist attractions themselves – be they animals, beaches, or monuments – are carefully protected. The creation of wildlife parks and other tourist facilities has displaced some African peoples, such as the MAASAI of East Africa, from their pastures and farmlands. Finally, some African countries have found that tourism has generated negative side industries, such as prostitution and the smuggling of art objects. Regardless of its drawbacks, however, many African countries look to tourism as a source of future economic growth.

Early Tourism

Some of the activities associated with tourism in Africa date back centuries. As far back as the Roman occupation of EGYPT beginning around 30 B.C.E., Romans explored the ruins of Thebes and tombs in the VALLEY OF THE KINGS. For centuries Arab, Asian, and later European explorers trekked across portions of the continent, often keeping records of the sites and peoples they encountered.

It was not until the early colonial period, however, that modern tourism emerged in Africa. Inspired by the published accounts of nineteenth-century European explorers, well-to-do Europeans and Americans began to travel to Africa, to glimpse first the wonders of Egypt and the Nile, then other scenic wonders, such as MOUNT KENYA and KILIMANJARO. By the turn of the century wealthy sportsmen were traveling to East and southern Africa to hunt big game, eager to return with trophies of LIONS, elephants, or RHINOCEROS.

Even though the numbers of foreign travelers in Africa increased during the colonial period, the tourism infrastructure – transportation systems, hotels, guide services – remained minimal. After World War II this changed: the development of fast, easy, and relatively inexpensive transoceanic travel and the construction of luxury accommodations around Africa's prime attractions set the stage for mass tourism. By the late twentieth century tourism in Africa took many forms.

Cultural Tourism

Cultural tourism has been popular for many years in Africa. Egypt, which boasts some of the continent's most ancient and spectacular monuments and artifacts, has for decades received a steady stream of tourists, most of whom come to see the Valley of the Kings, Thebes, the Nile, and the museums in Cairo. Together with cities such as Casablanca, Marrakech, and Fès, Egypt has helped make North Africa the continent's most visited region. For European tourists, North Africa's proximity makes it a viable destination even for short trips.

Since the late 1970s cultural tourism has expanded to encompass a broader range of activities. West African countries, for example, are now attracting African Americans and other tourists interested in learning more about the TRANSATLANTIC SLAVE TRADE. Such tourists typically visit Gorée Island, a major slave port off the coast of SENEGAL, as well as sites in BENIN and GHANA. Three former slave forts in Ghana were declared World Heritage sites by the United Nations: Cape Coast Castle, Elmina Castle, and Fort Saint Jago. In THE GAMBIA, the village of Jufurre became a pilgrimage site for many African Americans after the television series based on Alex Haley's 1977 book *Roots* made it famous. Now the Gambia holds an annual Roots Homecoming Festival, which highlights the cultural ties between diasporic Africans and Africa. In addition to historic sites related to the slave trade, visitors can attend demonstrations of dance and wrestling, purchase traditional African crafts, and arrange to stay with local families.

Cultural tourism is also a growing business in southern Africa. Visitors to SOUTH AFRICA, for example, can spend a night in the home of a XHOSA, SOTHO, PEDI, or ZULU family in the Lesedi Cultural Village outside Johannesburg. Residents of the village wear the traditional dress of their own people – cotton wraps for the Xhosa, fur loincloths for the Zulu – and perform dances and storytelling for the visitors. In ZIMBABWE members of the SHANGAAN ethnic group began construction on a similar model village, where small numbers of visitors will be able to stay overnight and participate in village activities. Its organizers estimated that the venture had the capacity to generate $1 million annually, helping fund such social services as schools and hospitals for Shangaan communities. Proponents of this kind of cultural tourism maintain that it helps keep traditional cultural practices alive. Critics insist that tourists witness nothing more than "staged authenticity" in model villages, and in the process intrude on the privacy of village residents.

Wildlife Tourism

Africa's wildlife has long fascinated foreigners. Wildlife safaris remain one of the most popular forms of tourism in Africa and an important source of revenue for countries such as Kenya, TANZANIA, UGANDA, NAMIBIA, BOTSWANA, ZIMBABWE, ZAMBIA, MALAWI, and South Africa. In these countries private companies drive visitors through wildlife parks or game reserves and provide lodging in lodges or luxury tent camps nearby. Tours in game reserves are aimed at hunters, who pay for the trophies they take, but most safari tourists visit national parks and take only photographs. Many companies in South Africa guarantee a sighting of the Big Five, that is, lions, elephants, rhinoceros, leopards, and buffalo.

The revenue generated from safari tourism has made the survival of endangered species a high priority for African governments (*see* WILDLIFE MANAGEMENT IN AFRICA). In Kenya, for example, a single lion is worth an estimated $7000 per year in tourist income, while an elephant herd is worth $610,000 annually. Hunting of both species in Kenya is legal only with a permit. On the other hand, citizens of wildlife-rich countries – some of whom have been displaced from their traditional lands to make way for wildlife parks, and many of whom face the chronic threat of crop destruction and even attack by wild animals – have often claimed that their governments protect animals at the expense of people.

Some wildlife management programs are trying to win local communities' support for conservation by giving them a voice in the planning processes and awarding them a share of the profits from safari tourism. In Zimbabwe, for example, the Communal Areas Management Programme for Indigenous Resources (CAMPFIRE) gives farming communities in elephant-hunting areas a portion of the trophy fees paid by foreign hunters (each area sets an annual limit on the number of animals that can be legally killed). Among other things the communities can use the money to fence their fields, thus protecting them from elephant damage. In return the communities look out for the local elephant populations by maintaining watering holes during the dry season and discouraging poaching.

Coastal Resort Tourism

Sunbathing, snorkeling, and sailing on Africa's balmy coastlines are favorite pastimes for European and South African tourists. The beaches of Kenya, TOGO, MAURITIUS, the SEYCHELLES, and the Gambia are all popular winter vacation spots for Europeans. Like other tourist destinations in Africa, coastal resorts have generated problems along with profits. In the Gambia, for example, resorts have created strong local markets for crafts and fresh produce, but the behavior and skimpy clothing of the tourists themselves offend many of the Gambia's conservative Muslims. Both female and male prostitution is widespread in coastal areas, as is drug addiction among Gambian youth.

Ecotourism and Beyond

In response to the many criticisms leveled at conventional forms of tourism, many national and local governments and private companies are now promoting ecotourism. In principle ecotourism is environmentally and culturally sensitive, educational, and locally controlled – or at least locally beneficial. Thus host communities would see the economic value of preserving resources and biodiversity.

Some ecotourism organizations focus on the preservation of a particular culture or historic site. In Tunisia, for example, an ancient, abandoned agricultural community in the Matmata Mountains, Doiret, has been undergoing restoration since 1986. The nongovernmental organization behind the project sought to rebuild the economy as well as the physical structure of the town, but erratic rainfall makes agriculture alone an insufficient source of revenue. So now the restoration effort is focused on developing educational, "low-impact" tourist facilities in and around Doiret: an old primary school has become a youth hostel; the town's distinctive troglodyte (cave) houses will be turned into additional tourist lodging; and volunteers are building a museum and a model Roman theater.

Another variation on the ecotourism theme is the research holiday. The nonprofit organization Earthwatch funds its scientific research projects partly with the fees paid by the projects' volunteer participants. In Africa Earthwatch volunteers in recent years have taken part in archaeological digs in Namibia; gathered data on ecological change around Kenya's Lake Naivasha; and investigated the feasibility of wind and solar power in Kenya.

In the 1990s more and more tourist enterprises have adopted the prefix "eco" to appeal to tourists seeking environmentally friendly recreation. In some cases these enterprises bear little resemblance to ecotourism as it is normally understood. For example, the South African-based Conservation Corporation (Conscorp) has been building an international chain of luxury "eco-tourist" resorts since 1990. By 1997 the corporation had completed 52 lodges in South Africa, Kenya, Zimbabwe, and Tanzania. Room costs average $350 per night. Conscorp claims that its lodges benefit local people by providing not only jobs but also tax revenues that have paid for schools and health clinics. Conscorp also claims that its resorts stimulate local entrepreneurialism. For example, much of the food served at the resort restaurants is grown locally, and on the South African resorts Zulu people own the safari vehicles.

On the other hand, resorts like Conscorp's do not allow local communities much, if any, say over how local resources are used. Nor are their facilities remotely affordable for most Africans. But for some of Africa's poorest countries, high-end tourism ("eco" or otherwise) appears to offer the quickest possible source of much-needed foreign investment and jobs. In 1996 Mozambique granted American entrepreneur James Blanchard a long-term lease to an extensive tract of land south of the capital of Maputo, which included dune forests, lakes, 200 elephants, coral reefs, marine turtles, and approximately 100 km (about 70 mi) of undeveloped coastline. Blanchard planned to construct 4 "Club Med-style" resorts, 9 "beach resorts," 2 vacation villages, 350 private lodges, 2 casinos, a yacht marina, and a railway. The complex would offer all the activities associated with both coastal resorts and wildlife parks, which some have labeled "surf and turf" tourism.

Critics feared that Blanchard's mega-resort would not only damage the environment but also result in the "Disneyfication" of the region. But Mozambique is one of the world's poorest countries, and it badly needs capital to rebuild its economy after a long civil war. Blanchard alone promised to invest $800 million and claimed that his project would create 12,000 jobs.

Robert Fay

See Also

Casablanca, Morocco; Elephant; Explorers in Africa Before 1500; Explorers in Africa Since 1800; Fès, Morocco; Gambia, The; Gorée Island, Senegal; Johannesburg, South Africa; Thebes, Egypt; Maputo, Mozambique; Marrakech, Morocco; Nile River; United Nations in Africa; Haley, Alexander Palmer (Alex); Cairo, Egypt.

Latin America and the Caribbean

Toussaint L'Ouverture, François Dominique

(b. May 1743?, Haut du Cap, Haiti; d. April 6, 1803, Fort de Joux [Jura], France), leader of the slave revolution that brought Haiti independence from France in 1804; a man who, in the words of Aimé Césaire, took "a population and turned it into a people."

There is little documentation regarding the life of François Dominique Toussaint L'Ouverture before the first slave uprising in 1791 in Saint-Domingue (as Haiti was known before independence; *see* Haitian Revolution). According to contemporary oral accounts, his parents were from Dahomey (present-day Benin) and his father was a powerful chief in that country before his enslavement (*see* Slavery in Africa). Toussaint was the first of eight children born on the Bréda plantation near the northern coast of Saint-Domingue. Born in the French colony and familiar with its culture, Toussaint was considered a Creole rather than an African, which – according to the logic of European colonialism – guaranteed him a more elevated social status. This status, and the plantation owner's affection for him, freed Toussaint from ever having to toil in the sugar cane fields. Instead he worked as a domestic servant in the plantation house (*see* Slavery in Latin America and the Caribbean). Toussaint was emancipated in 1776 at the young age of 33. In 1779 he rented a plot of land with 13 slaves attached to it and enjoyed the prerogatives of a colonizer, which included the amassing of a small fortune. From 1791, when he became politically active, until his death in 1803, he never publicly referred to this part of his life, choosing for political reasons to focus on his once having been a slave. Yet, in keeping with his complex history, his status as slave owner allowed him to gain the confidence of the French after the first slave revolts, even though he had actively participated in them. This confidence would prove decisive in his drive to bring independence to Saint-Domingue.

On the evening of August 22, 1791, the first slave revolt began under the leadership of the Jamaican Boukman. Toussaint, the only literate officer in the revolt, was named secretary of the movement. As Toussaint and others noted, those who rose up were reacting to a chasm between the ideals, on the one hand, of liberty, equality, and fraternity for all – which French political and intellectual leaders had been spreading throughout the world during and after the French Revolution of 1789 – and, on the other hand, their lived experience as blacks, mulattos, and free men of color on Saint-Domingue. If all men were created equal, asked Saint-Domingues's people of color, how could slavery exist? The French responded to these questions and to the revolts they inspired by abolishing slavery in all the colonies on September 4, 1793. The first slave revolt had been successful. (Slavery, however, would be reinstated a few years later in all the French colonies and would remain in place until 1848.)

With the (temporary) abolition of slavery by the French and with the western part of the island under siege by the British and the Spanish in 1794, Toussaint offered his services to the French army. His valor and shrewdness in repelling the invaders allowed him to rise quickly through the ranks and become lieutenant governor of Saint-Domingue. But Toussaint was not satisfied with being second in command of the colony. As commander in chief of the military he did not hide his ambition to become the sole leader of Saint-Domingue. His considerable influence over the black population worried the French so much that in 1798 the French general Hédouville was sent to the colony with the secret mission of undermining Toussaint's authority. But Toussaint outmaneuvered Hédouville and others sent to unseat him diplomatically. Having gained control of the entire island of Hispaniola (present-day Haiti and the Dominican Republic), Toussaint formed a commission of ten called the Central Assembly, which drafted a constitution in 1801. While affirming that Saint-Domingue was still a French colony, the constitution rendered it administratively independent and named Toussaint L'Ouverture governor general of Saint-Domingue for life. Thereafter relations with France disintegrated completely. Napoleon Bonaparte, now first consul of France, sent forces led by his brother-in-law, Gen. Charles Leclerc, to reclaim control of the colony. Leclerc and his 22,000 troops surrounded Toussaint in his stronghold in Crête-à-Pierrot, and on May 5, 1802, forced him to surrender. Toussaint was shipped to the Fort de Joux prison in France, where he died on April 6, 1803, from malnutrition and tuberculosis. Though the Haitian Revolution had lost its mastermind and leader, those who had served under him continued to fight for what he had envisioned and nearly achieved. On January 1, 1804, Jean-Jacques Dessalines, a protégé of Toussaint, was able to declare that the French colony of Saint-Domingue was now the independent republic of Haiti.

Toussaint's heroism and martyrdom have been memorialized by some of the Caribbean's most significant writers, including Martinican authors Edouard Glissant (*Monsieur Toussaint*, 1961) and Aimé Césaire (*Toussaint L'Ouverture*, 1961), and C. L. R. James (*The Black Jacobins*, 1938) of Trinidad and Tobago. While not discounting the complexities and paradoxes that shaped his character, these writers and others have pointed to Toussaint's singular importance in the formation of modern Caribbean identity and to the inspiration he continues to provide in the struggles of Caribbean people for cultural and political independence.

Richard Watts

In 1805 Marcus Rainford published *An Historical Account of the Black Empire of Hayti* in which he included an imaginary portrait of Toussaint L'Ouverture, leader of the Haitian Revolution. *Image of the Black Project, Harvard University*

See Also
James, Cyril Lionel Richard; Abolition and Emancipation in Latin America and the Caribbean.

North America

Toussaint, Pierre **(b. 1766, Haiti; d. 1853, New York, N.Y.), Haitian American businessman and philanthropist whose support for nineteenth-century orphans is recognized in his candidacy for sainthood a century and a half later.**

Pierre Toussaint was a slave until 1809. After his owners moved from Haiti to New York City in 1787, he was apprenticed to a New York hairdresser. Toussaint eventually developed his own thriving career and supported his widowed mistress and her daughter with his earnings.

Toussaint and his wife Juliette, both devout Catholics, also used their money to raise African American orphans, support the Catholic Orphan Asylum in New York City, and help fund the building of St. Vincent de Paul's. In recognition of his piety and charity, John Cardinal O'Connor of New York and other Catholics began seeking Toussaint's canonization in the 1990s.

Lisa Clayton Robinson

See Also
New York, New York.

North America

Towns, Edolphus **(b. July 21, 1934, Chadbourn, N.C.), Democratic member of the United States House of Representatives from New York (1983-).**

Towns received a bachelor's degree from North Carolina Agricultural and Technical State University in 1956 and entered the U.S. Army the same year. He served until 1958 and then moved to New York, where he worked as a hospital administrator and a professor at Medgar Evers College. In 1973 he earned a master's degree in social work from Adelphi University. In 1976 Towns began his political career, serving for six years, until 1982, as Brooklyn Borough deputy president. In 1982 Towns was elected to the U.S. House from New York's Eleventh Congressional District.

Following redistricting in 1992, Towns won election from the new Tenth District, which included much of his old district. He had no Democratic opponent in 1994, and he won the general election with 89 percent of the vote. He received 91 percent of the vote in 1996. Stretching from the neat brownstones of upper-middle-class Brooklyn Heights to the ruined buildings and stark depression of east New York, the Tenth Congressional District was home to a large contingency of Democrats, most of them black, but some Hispanic, Italian, and Jewish.

In the 105th Congress (1997-1999), Towns served on the Government Reform and Oversight Committee and the Commerce Committee. He was ranking member of the Human Resources and Intergovernmental Relations Subcommittee of the Government Reform and Oversight Committee. He was also a member of the CONGRESSIONAL BLACK CAUCUS.

SEE ALSO
New York, New York.

North America

Track and Field in the United States,

one of the oldest sports in the world, track and field (or athletics, as it is called in many countries) consists of more than two dozen events that usually include running, jumping, walking, and throwing

EARLY AMERICAN SOCIETY

Foot racing was a common feature of early American slave society. In the narratives of former slaves foot racing is recounted as a popular sport on Southern plantations. In one such narrative, former slave FREDERICK DOUGLASS described the popularity of sports such as boxing, wrestling, and foot racing in his autobiography, *The Life and Times of Frederick Douglass* (1881).

Since most sporting competitions during slavery were segregated, the opportunities for blacks to compete against whites in foot races were limited. Exceptionally, in the 1830s the Highland Games – organized by Scottish American civic groups – and colored branches of the Young Men's Christian Association (YMCA) featured interracial and interethnic competition. Foot racing and fast walking (pedestrianism) were among the events in which African American athletes excelled.

In the latter half of the nineteenth century the performance of African American short- and long-distance runners was celebrated. Francis Smith and Frank Hart were among the most notable of these athletes. Both were legendary walkers who dominated the sport in the 1830s and 1870s, respectively.

RACIAL SEGREGATION

In 1871 the all-white New York Athletic Club held what some scholars believe to be the first formally organized track and field meet in America. Five years later the club sponsored America's first National Amateur Track Meet. African Americans were not allowed to participate in either meet. In 1888 white athletic clubs united to form the Amateur Athletic Union (AAU), an organizing body responsible for promoting athletic competition throughout the country. However, like the New York Athletic Club, it too excluded blacks from participating.

NINETEENTH-CENTURY BLACK STARS

Despite these obstacles a small number of black athletes did participate and did excel in track and field during the late nineteenth century. Most were students at predominantly white colleges and universities in the North. One of the earliest such stars was William Tecumseh Sherman Jackson, who attended Amherst College in Massachusetts (1890-1892). In addition to Jackson, Napoleon Bonaparte Marshall (Harvard College, 1895-1897), Spencer Dickerson (University of Chicago, 1896-1897), G.C.H. Burleigh (University of Illinois), and John Baxter "Doc" Taylor (University of Pennsylvania, 1904, 1907-1908) were also major stars at predominantly white schools.

Contrary to contemporary stereotypes, most of these early black stars were long-distance runners. Long-distance events were the most prestigious and those who excelled at longer distances were held in great esteem by other athletes. It was not until the first half of the twentieth century that speed and power in the shorter distances became a celebrated talent.

EARLY BLACK TRACK AND FIELD ORGANIZATIONS

In the face of racial segregation and discrimination African Americans established their own athletic organizations and programs. In 1893 Tuskegee Institute (now TUSKEGEE UNIVERSITY) in Alabama held the first major black track and field meet in the country. The meet consisted of events such as running, jumping, tug-of-war, and a new event called the relay race. The relay race was one of the most popular events at black track and field meets and soon became a regular feature at white track and field meets.

In 1906 the Interscholastic Athletic Association (ISAA) held the first inter-city track and field meet for African American boys in WASHINGTON, D.C. Schools throughout the city sent athletes to the meet, including HOWARD UNIVERSITY, "M" Street High School (now Dunbar High School), and the Colored Young Men's Christian Association (YMCA). One year later African American runner Matthew Bullock created the first black intercollegiate track and field meet for southeastern colleges.

EARLY BLACK OLYMPIANS

After making a mark at the collegiate level, several black stars went on to enjoy successful careers. At the turn of the twentieth century the most important post-collegiate event in the career of a track and field athlete was undoubtedly the Olympic Games. The Olympic Games, held every four years, showcased some of the best athletes in the world.

Since women were not allowed to participate in the Olympic Games until 1928, black men represented the country and their race as they competed against athletes from around the world. At the 1904 Olympic Games George Poage captured a Bronze Medal in the 400-meter hurdles. Four years later at the Olympic Games in London, England, black sprinters "Doc" Taylor and J.C. Carpenter both competed in the 400-meter race. Taylor became the first African American in Olympic history to earn a Gold Medal after running the third leg on the 4-by-400-meter relay team.

AFRICAN AMERICANS IN THE TRACK AND FIELD HALL OF FAME

Year of Induction	Member	Born/Died
1974	Ralph Boston	1939
1974	Lee Calhoun	1933
1974	Harrison Dillard	1923
1974	Rafer Johnson	1935
1974	Jesse Owens	1913-1980
1974	Wilma Rudolph	1940
1974	Mal Whitfield	1924
1975	Alice Coachman (David)	1932
1975	Edward Hurt	1900-1989
1975	Ralph Metcalf	1910-1978
1976	Mae Faggs (Starrs)	1932
1976	Bob Hayes	1942
1976	Hayes Jones	1938
1977	Bob Beamon	1946
1977	Andy Stanfield	1927-1985
1978	Tommie Smith	1944
1978	John Woodruff	1915
1979	Jim Hines	1946
1979	Dehart Hubbard	1903-1976
1979	Edith McGuire (DuVall)	1944
1980	Dave Albritton	1913-1994
1980	Wyomia Tyus Tillman	1945
1981	Willye White	1939
1982	Willie Davenport	1943
1982	Eddie Tolan	1908-1967
1983	Lee Evans	1947
1983	Mildred McDaniel (Singleton)	1933
1983	Leroy Walker	1918
1984	Madeline Manning (Mims)	1948
1984	Joseph Yancey	1910-1991
1985	John Thomas	1941
1986	Barney Ewell	1918
1987	Eulace Peacock	1914
1987	Martha Watson	1946
1988	Greg Bell	1928
1988	Barbara Ferrell (Edmonson)	1947
1989	Milt Campbell	1933
1989	Nell Jackson	1929-1988
1989	Ed Temple	1927
1990	Charles Dumas	1937
1992	Charles Greene	1944
1992	Charlie Jenkins	1934
1992	Archie Williams	1915-1993
1995	Florence Griffith-Joyner	1959-1998

Early Twentieth Century (to World War I)

The first African American to emerge victorious in a field event was Theodore "Ted" Cable, an athlete at Harvard University in Cambridge, Massachusetts. Cable won the broad jump (22 feet 10¼ inches) and hammer throw (154 feet and 11¼ inches) at the 1912 Harvard-Yale meet. Later that year at the Intercollegiate Track & Field Meet, Cable became the first African American in the meet's history to win the hammer throw competition. Although Cable proved that African American athletes could win at field events, it was still in the sprinting events that African Americans captured international attention.

African American sprinters were so dominant in the period immediately preceding World War I that some states barred them from competing in more than two events. One of the most successful was Howard Porter Drew, a sprinter from Springfield, Massachusetts. Drew held world records in the 100-yard dash (1913, 9.6 seconds), 220-yard dash (1914, 21.2 seconds), and the 100-meter dash (1912, 10.2 seconds). In 1916 World War I prevented him from participating in the Olympic Games, and he failed to qualify for the games in 1920. Despite these setbacks Drew ended his career as one of the most talented sprinters in American history.

Between the Wars (1920s-1930s)

Participation in track and field declined briefly in the years between World War I and World War II. Black club and college programs suffered from a lack of financial support as track and field was forced to compete with other sports, such as football and baseball. Track and field coaches at black colleges and universities in the 1920s had a difficult time convincing young athletes to pursue a sport that had few professional organizations or leagues.

The Colored Intercollegiate Athletic Association (CIAA), founded in 1924, was the exception. For nearly 20 years the CIAA was the only major collegiate conference to hold regular track and field meets for athletes at predominantly black colleges and universities. During this period Hampton Institute in Virginia (now Hampton University) dominated black track and field. Between 1924 and 1931 Morgan State University and Lincoln University (Philadelphia, Pennsylvania) were the only schools to defeat Hampton.

The only other major track and field meet open to blacks at the time was the Tuskegee Relay Carnival, created in 1927. Modeled after the Penn Relays – the only major white track and field meet open to black athletes in the 1920s – the Tuskegee Relay Carnival sponsored competition between some of the best black sprinters, long jumpers, and distance runners in the country.

Black collegiate track and field received a boost in 1933 when the Midwest Athletic Association (MWAA) was formed. Six years later the Southwestern Athletic Association (SWAC) joined the list of black collegiate athletic conferences. All three conferences – the CIAA, MWAA, and SWAC – made great strides in the development of track and field programs at predominantly black schools. However, most of these strides benefited black men, expanding their opportunities to participate on a competitive level.

Black Women in Track and Field

In the 1920s and early 1930s black women were excluded by almost every major track and field program in the country. The New York Mercury Club, the Illinois Women's Athletic Club, and Tennessee State University were among the exceptions. However, the institution most committed to developing black female track and field athletes was Tuskegee Institute. Under the leadership of Athletic Director Cleveland Abbott the Tuskegee female track and field team became one of the leading programs of its kind. In 1936 the team finished second in the Amateur Athletic Union (AAU) national competition. At the time it was the highest finish ever by a black team competing at the AAU. They captured the AAU title the following year and remained champions from 1938 to 1942 and again between 1944 and 1948. Tuskegee's success was due to a long list of exceptional athletes and coaches, such as Amelia C. Roberts, Christine Evans Petty, and Jessie Abbott. Other black female standouts include three-time AAU 80-meter hurdles champion Lillie Purifoy, and Hattie Turner, the first African American crowned champion in the discus and baseball throw.

Black men also excelled in the interwar years. Two of the best sprinters at the 1932 Olympic Games were black Americans Ralph Metcalfe and Thomas "Eddie" Tolan Jr. Tolan became the first African American to win two Gold Medals when he defeated Metcalfe in the 100- and 200-meter races. The growing success of black American track and field superstars set the stage for an international drama at the 1936 Olympic Games in Berlin, Germany.

Jesse Owens

German leader Adolf Hitler planned to use the Olympic Games in 1936 to showcase what he thought was German athletic superiority. Hitler believed that if German athletes could dominate the games, particularly those events in track and field, they would convince the world of the superiority of the Aryan "race." But Jesse Owens, a black sprinter from Oakville, Alabama, proved Hitler wrong.

Owens won an unprecedented four Gold Medals at the 1936 Olympic Games and was reportedly snubbed by Hitler during the award ceremonies. His success was a symbolic victory for America, and it was a proud moment for black America. In a matter of days Jesse Owens challenged every notion of black inferiority.

Ironically, Jesse Owens in victory inspired a whole new set of equally disturbing racial stereotypes. Previous explanations concluded that blacks were successful in athletics because they lacked the mental aptitude for other endeavors. White athletes now suggested that blacks somehow had an unfair advantage because they were genetically predisposed to athletic competition. After the performance by Jesse Owens, critics attributed black success in athletics to the size of their thighs and length of their feet. Athletic accomplishment was seen as a genetic gift, not the result of hard work and unwavering commitment.

Era After World War II

Track and field experienced dramatic changes after the war ended. The success of black sprinters such as Jesse Owens, Ralph Metcalfe, and Thomas Tolan Jr. opened doors for other young black athletes. The competition for coveted athletic scholarships to predominantly white colleges and universities was fierce. Those blacks who did not earn scholarships were forced to pursue track and field with black club teams.

But the Olympic Games continued to occupy center stage for the black athlete. One did not need to attend a wealthy school or wear the newest shoes to earn a spot on the national Olympic team. Track and field was considered the great equalizer because it gave black athletes from some of the most impoverished backgrounds the opportunity to shine. One of the most famous success stories is that of Wilma Goldean Rudolph, a black female sprinter from St. Bethlehem, Tennessee. Rudolph overcame a leg injury that she suffered at birth to become a dominant athlete at the 1960 Olympic Games. She brought home Gold Medals in the 100-, 200-, and 400-meter dashes. Rudolph was the first African American woman to win three Gold Medals during a single Olympic competition.

Civil Rights and Black Power

By the mid-1960s black athletes were regular participants at track and field events around the world. However, their celebrity status did not make them immune to the political and economic challenges facing African Americans at home. The Civil Rights and Black Power movements of the 1960s had a tremendous impact on black track and field stars. With the help of organizations such as the black-led Olympic Project for Human Rights, African American athletes used their status as stars to call attention to the pernicious effects of American racism.

One of the most famous examples of the political activism of black athletes came during the 1968 Olympic Games in Mexico City, Mexico. Wearing black socks and no shoes, African American sprinters Tommie Smith and John Carlos each wore a black glove on his hand and stepped up to the victory podium. As the American anthem played, Smith and Carlos gave a salute to the Black Power Movement by raising their fists defiantly in the air.

In an interview given to sports commentator Howard Cosell (and quoted in the comprehensive volume, *A Hard Road to Glory*), Tommie Smith explained his actions. "I wore a black right-hand glove and Carlos wore the left-hand glove of the same pair. My raised right hand stood for the power in black America. Carlos's raised left hand stood for the unity of black America. Together they formed an arch of unity and power. The black scarf around my neck stood for black pride. The black sock with no shoes stood for black poverty in racist America. The totality of our effort was the regaining of black dignity." Both athletes were ejected from the Olympic village by the International Olympic Committee (IOC).

Black sprinters continued to dominate track and field throughout the 1970s and 1980s. Between 1972 and 1980 blacks won more than 75 Olympic medals in track and field events. New superstars emerged, including hurdler Edwin Moses and sprinters CARL LEWIS, EVELYN ASHFORD, Michael Johnson, Florence Griffith-Joyner ("Flo-Jo"), and Jackie Joyner-Kersee. Carl Lewis holds 9 Gold Medals, more than any other American track and field athlete.

New Competition

In the late 1980s black runners from Africa, Great Britain, and the Caribbean began to challenge the reign of African American speedsters. Sprinters from England, JAMAICA, TRINIDAD AND TOBAGO, CUBA, and CANADA have set or tied world records once held by American men and women. Donovan Bailey (Canada), Merlene Ottey (Jamaica), Daniel Komen (KENYA), Noureddine Morceli (ALGERIA), and HAILE GEBRSELASSIE (ETHIOPIA) are just a few of the blacks outside America who have dominated track and field. African runners from Kenya, SOUTH AFRICA, and Ethiopia routinely win major long distance events, including many of the most prominent competitions in the world, such as the Boston Marathon.

Black athletes from around the world have made a lasting impression on the sport of track and field. They have pushed the limits of human ability, shattering old records and setting new ones that were unimaginable just a few years ago. In the process black athletes have defied racial stereotypes and, with hard work and dedication, have set new standards of excellence for athletes around the world.

Alonford James Robinson, Jr.

See Also

Race: An Interpretation; Baseball in the United States; Civil Rights Movement; Football, Collegiate; Griffith-Joyner, Florence Delorez; Joyner-Kersee, Jacqueline; Lincoln University (Pennsylvania); Owens, James Cleveland ("Jesse"); Rudolph, Wilma Glodean.

Latin America and the Caribbean

Traditional Healing in Latin America and the Caribbean

Illness is a constant part of the life of any community, and communities develop ways of responding to illness: through prevention, avoidance of disease, and ultimately the treatment and healing of illness when it attacks. African peoples in Latin America and the Caribbean brought with them complex beliefs about illness and its healing, and adapted these to the new and often brutal circumstances of the New World (*see* RELIGIONS, AFRICAN, IN LATIN AMERICA AND THE CARIBBEAN). In the new lands to which they were brought against their will, unknown diseases killed thousands, and malnutrition claimed the lives of many children. The partial immunity to West African diseases developed over thousands of years of adaptation was of little benefit in protecting Africans from the new assaults on their health.

African peoples arriving in the Caribbean and Latin America encountered infectious diseases such as leprosy, yellow fever, smallpox, and measles. Some of these were familiar; West Africans had developed partial immunity to some, such as malaria. Others were new and deadly, including diseases native to the New World as well as those introduced by Europeans. The conditions of slavery exacerbated the effects of infectious disease, producing high rates of illness and frequent resort to healing rituals and the use of curative substances.

Healing practices derive from beliefs about the nature of persons as well as about illness. For Africans arriving in Latin America and the Caribbean, persons were composed of bodies and spirits, and thus illness was thought to afflict either or both of these components. Illnesses caused or affected by supernatural forces were the domain of religious practitioners. In some parts of South America for example, Obeah men and other ritual practitioners interacted with the supernatural forces that controlled human fortune, whether in the form of luck, fertility, crop success, or health. As in major West African religious systems, common diseases such as smallpox were thought to be controlled by specific gods, who could be addressed in ritual. In the sixteenth and seventeenth centuries the Roman Catholicism of Latin America's European conquerors also incorporated beliefs in a variety of supernatural beings active in human affairs, from angels and saints to demonic spirits. The religious healing practices of Africans (and New World Indians) were thus highly valued by whites and blacks alike, and flourished in the "enchanted" cosmological world of the time.

In contemporary South America, African-based religious systems retain many of these healing functions. In modern BRAZIL, especially, Afro-Brazilian religions (*see* RELIGIONS, AFRICAN, IN BRAZIL) such as CANDOMBLÉ and Macumba have been adapted to the treatment of a wide variety of health problems, from psychiatric illness to acquired immune deficiency syndrome (AIDS). Indigenous religious beliefs have also been incorporated into Amazonian Afro-Brazilian religious movements such as Santo Daime, which uses the hallucinogenic drug *ayahuasca* to contact the spirit world, often for healing purposes. Similarly, Afro-Caribbean religions such as SANTERÍA have adapted themselves to contemporary social and medical conditions, and have emerged as important features of contemporary folk healing practices.

For the illnesses of bodies, the tropical and semitropical environments of Latin America and the Caribbean provided numerous plant medications – more than 5000 have been identified in MEXICO alone. Many of these plants were familiar from related West African plants; others were borrowed from local Indians. Still others were discovered through experimentation or from presumed similarities to African curative plants. Phytotherapy is the technical term for the use of curative plants; phytotherapies are among the most ancient forms of illness treatment, and have a long history among the African peoples in the Caribbean and throughout Latin America.

The traditional use of plant medications in Latin America has not been widely studied, but recent interest in the curative potential of disappearing rain-forest plants has stimulated new research into the subject. A recent comprehensive study of folk medical practices in VENEZUELA, for instance, found that the descendants of African slaves retain numerous beliefs and practices regarding medicinal plants. In each case the plants used in Venezuela were identical, or closely related, to plants used for similar medical purposes in West Africa. In some cases the associations are very specific: for example, the use of tobacco juice in the treatment of snake bite. In other cases, broad curative powers are attributed to the same plants: heliotrope, for example, is used to make an infusion in the treatment of dysentery, fever, and convulsions; *Annonia senegalensis* is used on both sides of the Atlantic to treat arthritis, leprosy, and indigestion and is used as a laxative and during pregnancy. African phytotherapy was so popular in the history of Venezuela that slave curers were often able to purchase their freedom with the proceeds of their medical practices.

The distinction between spiritual practitioners and phytotherapists was not always rigid. A recent study of folk medicine in GUYANA, for instance, notes that Obeah men were not only priest-healers who could contact the spirit world; they also had extensive knowledge of both poisonous and curative plants. In an era before scientific medicine their influence was considerable, even among plantation owners.

Among African peoples enslaved in Latin America and the Caribbean, the power of traditional healers was not only important in curing illness, it was a unifying force for the preservation of culture and even a form of resistance to oppression. As in West African cultures, healing was often directed at curing social ills – the illness of an individual might be only the symptom of tensions and disruption in a community. The effectiveness of this power has to be measured not only in the rates of curing disease, but in the persistence and even spread of such belief systems throughout Latin America and the Caribbean. In the modern forms of these belief systems, such as Candomblé and Santería, and in the renewed interest in research into the possible pharmacological effects of traditional plant medications, this deep legacy continues to affect us.

Donald Pollock

See Also

Slavery in Latin America and the Caribbean; Catholic Church in Latin America and the Caribbean.

North America

TransAfrica, an African American lobby that focuses on United States policy toward Africa and the Caribbean.

TransAfrica was created in 1977 after a Black Leadership Conference convened by the Congressional Black Caucus declared that "the conspicuous absence of African Americans in high-level international affairs positions and the general subordination, if not neglect, of African and Caribbean priorities could only be corrected by the establishment of a private advocacy organization." According to its executive director, Randall Robinson, "TransAfrica is a foreign-policy education advocacy organization… interested in all aspects of American policy that have consequences for Africa and the Caribbean."

TransAfrica lobbies the U.S. Congress and the national administration with funding from various corporations, corporate grants, and individual donations. In 1981 Robinson created the TransAfrica Forum to collect, analyze, and disseminate information about U.S. foreign policy concerning Africa and the Caribbean. The Forum publishes two quarterly journals (*TransAfrica Forum* and *TransAfrica News*), hosts an annual foreign policy conference, and helps prepare black students for the Foreign Service exam. TransAfrica and its educational affiliate, TransAfrica Forum, are based in Washington, D.C.

One of TransAfrica's principal concerns has been to ensure that countries in Africa and the Caribbean that are shifting toward democracy receive an equal amount of financial aid from the U.S. government as democracy-bound countries in Europe and Asia. It has also concerned itself with human rights issues, refugee questions, and the drug war. TransAfrica has successfully lobbied the U.S. government in foreign policies concerning South Africa and Haiti, and is currently working to influence U.S. foreign policy toward Nigeria.

From its inception in 1977 TransAfrica worked to end apartheid in South Africa, the policy of racial segregation intended to promote and maintain white supremacy. The organization's demonstrations against apartheid at the South African Embassy in 1985 led to the 1986 Anti-Apartheid Act by the U.S. Congress that imposed sanctions over President Ronald Regan's veto. As a result, the United States placed a political and economic embargo against South Africa that contributed to the demise of apartheid.

On April 11, 1994, Robinson began a hunger strike to protest the U.S. policy that denied entrance to the country by Haitian refugees. After 27 days the United States agreed to ease its admission policy. Later in the year TransAfrica lobbyists persuaded the government to help restore Haitian president Jean-Bertand Aristide to power.

In 1995 TransAfrica launched a campaign to force Nigeria's 11-year-old military government to return to civilian rule. In a March 1995 letter endorsed by a host of black politicians, educators, and celebrities, Robinson accused Gen. Sani Abacha, the military leader who took control of Nigeria's government in 1993 following a military coup, of killing political opponents and shutting down the press. Robinson urged him "to expedite the restoration of democracy" to Nigeria's 100 million people or face "incalculable damage" and "eventual economic and political isolation of your regime." Robinson followed up with advertisements, speeches, and protests meant to direct negative attention to Nigeria's military rule, which relinquised to civilian hands in May 1999.

Robinson contends that, "African Americans ought to care about Africa and the Caribbean because we are much stronger together than separate. Our potential as black people is to harness our power globally. Then our [African American] business communities will trade with those [African and Caribbean] communities, invest in those communities, and we will all be healthier for it."

Aaron Myers

See Also

Washington, D.C.; Aristide, Jean-Bertrand.

Cross Cultural

Transatlantic Slave Trade

Stephen Behrendt

From the 1520s to the 1860s an estimated 11 to 12 million African men, women, and children were forcibly embarked on European vessels for a life of slavery in the Western Hemisphere. Many more Africans were captured or purchased in the interior of the continent, but a large number died before reaching the coast. About 9 to 10 million Africans survived the Atlantic crossing to be purchased by planters and traders in the New World, where they worked principally as slave laborers in plantation economies requiring a large work force. African peoples were transported from numerous coastal outlets from the SENEGAL RIVER in West Africa and hundreds of trading sites along the coast as far south as Benguela (ANGOLA), and from ports in MOZAMBIQUE in southeast Africa. In the New World slaves were sold in markets as far north as New England and as far south as present-day ARGENTINA.

THE EARLY HISTORY OF EUROPEAN TRADE WITH AFRICA

The marketing of people in the interior of Africa predates European contact with West Africa. A trans-Saharan slave trade developed from the tenth to fourteenth century that featured the buying and selling of African captives in Islamic markets such as the area around present-day SUDAN. A majority of those enslaved were females, who were purchased to work as servants, agricultural laborers, or concubines. Some captives were also shipped north across the deserts of northwest Africa to the Mediterranean coast. There, in slave markets such as Ceuta (MOROCCO), Africans were purchased to work as servants or laborers in SPAIN, PORTUGAL, and other countries.

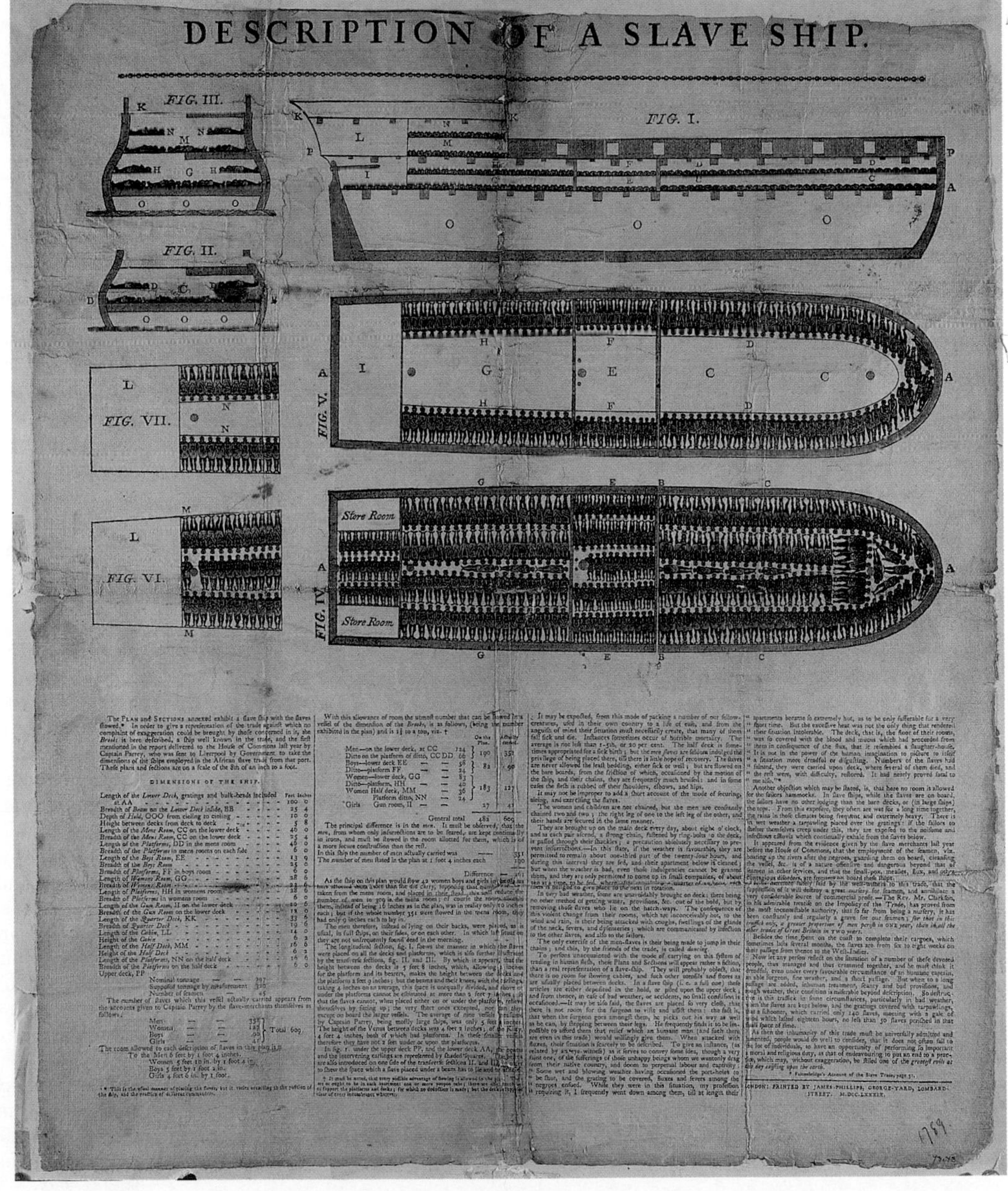

Published in 1789, this engraving shows the cross section of the slave ship *Brookes*, based in Liverpool. British parliamentarian William Wilberforce used the diagram in arguments on the floor of the House of Commons for abolition of the slave trade. *Hickey & Robertson, Houston/Image of the Black Project, Harvard University*

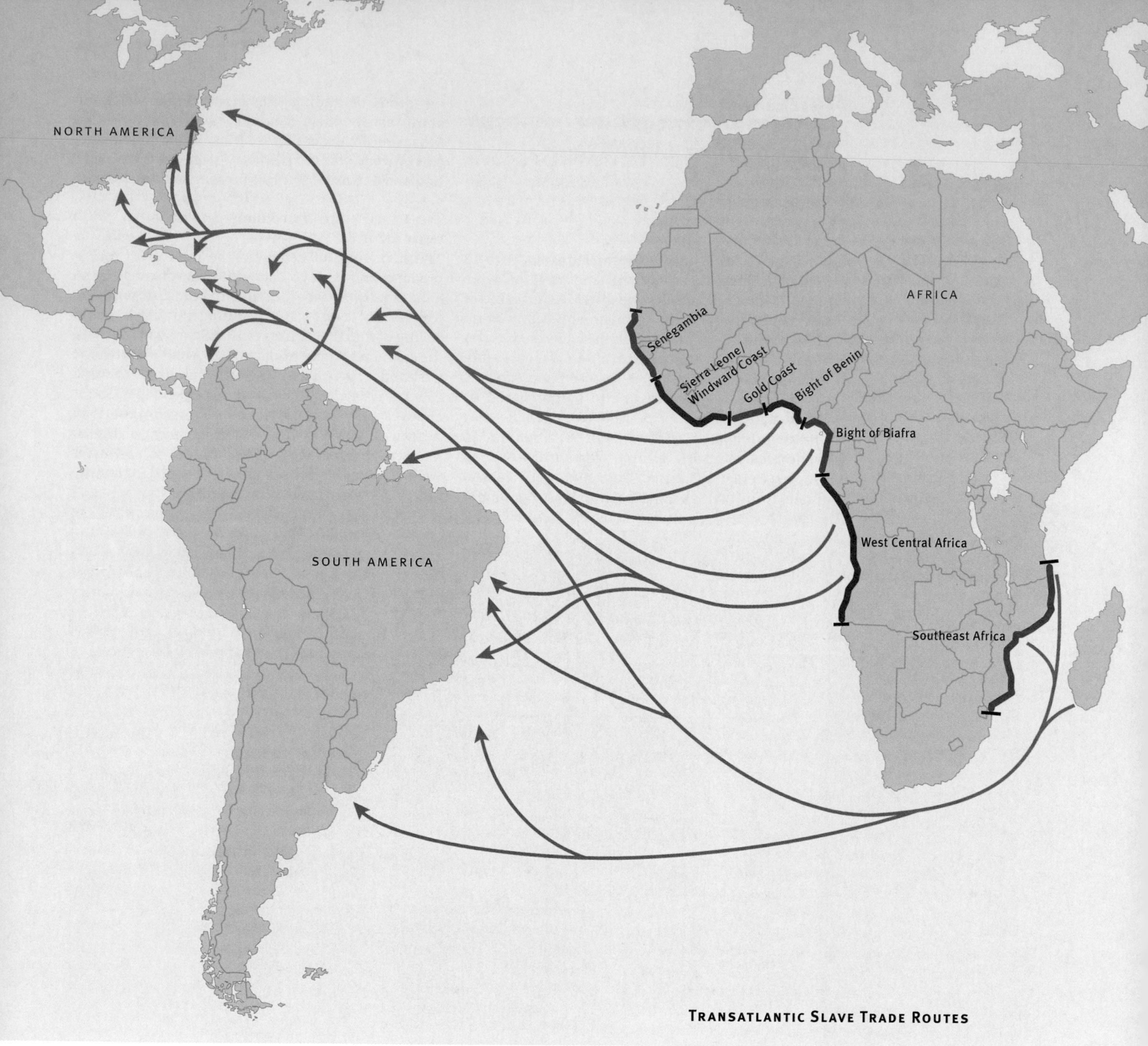

Transatlantic Slave Trade Routes

By the mid-1400s Portuguese ship captains had learned how to navigate the waters along the west coast of Africa and had begun to trade directly with slave suppliers who built small trading posts, or "factories," on the coast. European shippers were thus able to circumvent the trans-Saharan caravan slave trade. The slave trade to Europe began to decrease in the late 1400s with the development of SUGAR plantations in the Atlantic islands of Madeira and São Tomé. These two islands, located off West Africa and in the Gulf of Guinea, became leading centers of world sugar production and plantation slavery from the mid-1400s to the mid-1500s. Portuguese merchants dominated this early trade.

Much of the earliest European trade with West Africa, however, was in gold, not people. Europeans did not have the power to overcome African states before the late nineteenth century, and gold production, centered in Akan gold fields in the backcountry of present-day GHANA, remained in African hands. Europeans called this region the Gold Coast. Agreements between African and European elites and rivalries for the African gold trade resulted in the construction of dozens of trading forts, or stone castles, along a 161 km (100 mi) coastal stretch of Ghana. (Several of these forts survive, have been repaired by the government of Ghana, and are tourist attractions today.) It was not until the late seventeenth century that the value of European goods traded for African people surpassed the value of goods exchanged for gold. Over time these gold forts became slave forts, where hundreds of Africans were confined in prisons awaiting sale and shipment.

The Slave Trade and Development of Plantations in the Americas

Christopher Columbus's "discovery" of the New World in 1492 marked the beginning of a transatlantic trading system. Via the slave trade, Africans played a leading role in the creation and evolution of this large and long-lasting "Atlantic system." Spanish adventurers arrived in the Americas hoping to trade for riches but soon enslaved the Native American peoples in their search for gold and silver. Disease, malnutrition, and Spanish atrocities led to the deaths of millions of the Indians of the Americas. By the 1520s the depopulation of the region prompted the Spanish government to look for alternative sources of labor. Officials contracted with Portuguese merchants to deliver Africans to Spanish territories in the New World. The first transatlantic slave voyages from Africa to the Americas occurred in the early 1520s on Portuguese vessels sailing from West Africa to the large Caribbean island of Hispaniola, the earliest European name for present-day HAITI and the DOMINICAN REPUBLIC.

The transatlantic slave trade increased in the mid-1500s when the Spanish began to use African slave labor alongside Native Americans to mine silver in PERU. Slave ships sailed from Africa to COLOMBIA and PANAMA, and African captives then were transported overland to the Pacific coast of South America. Until the early 1600s most Africans enslaved in the Americas worked in Peruvian or Mexican mines. The 1570s marked the development of sugar plantations in BRAZIL, a Portuguese colony, where merchants adopted production techniques pioneered in Madeira and São Tomé. By the 1620s African labor had replaced Indian labor on Brazilian sugar plantations.

The development of an export-based plantation complex in North America and the Caribbean, areas neglected by the Spanish and Portuguese, awaited the arrival of the British, French, and Dutch in the early 1600s. In the initial development of the British colonies Virginia and BARBADOS (1630s-1640s), JAMAICA (1660s), and South Carolina (1690s) and the French colonies Saint-Domingue (present-day Haiti), MARTINIQUE, and GUADELOUPE (1660s-1680s), most laborers on the plantations were young European males who agreed to work for three to five years in return for free oceanic passage and food and housing in the Americas. These workers were called indentured laborers. By the late seventeenth and early eighteenth centuries tobacco, sugar, indigo (used to make blue dye), and rice plantations switched from European indentured labor to African slave labor. By the mid-1700s Brazil, Saint-Domingue, and Jamaica were the three largest slave colonies in the Americas. By the 1830s CUBA emerged as the principal Caribbean plantation colony. Throughout the history of the transatlantic slave trade, however, more Africans arrived as slaves in Brazil than in any other colony.

Dutch merchants did not develop extensive plantation colonies in the New World but they became

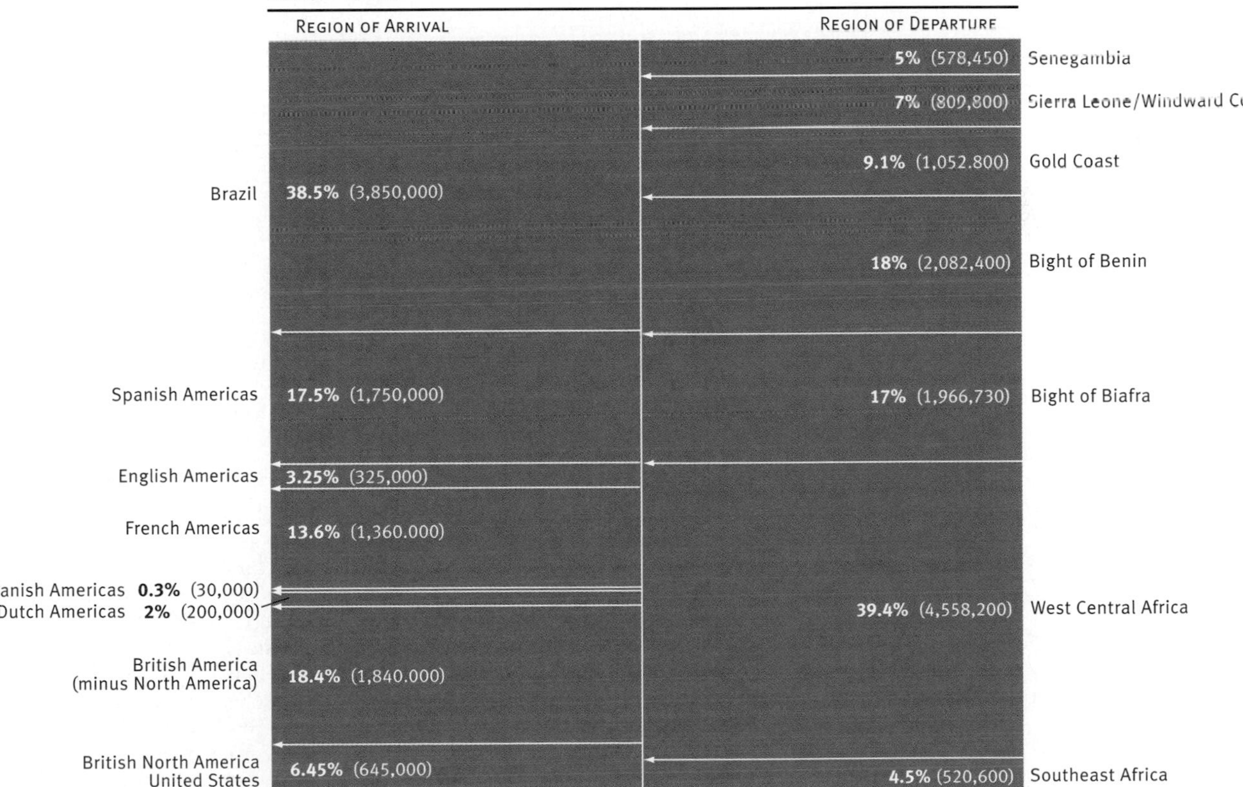

The data presented in the transatlantic slave trade diagrams were prepared by Stephen D. Behrendt, David Richardson, and David Eltis and drawn from the database they created at the W. E. B. Du Bois Institute for Afro-American Research, Harvard University. This database contains records for 27,233 voyages that set out to obtain slaves for the Americas. Based on these records, the estimated total number of Africans transported to the Americas during the transatlantic slave trade is 11,569,000.

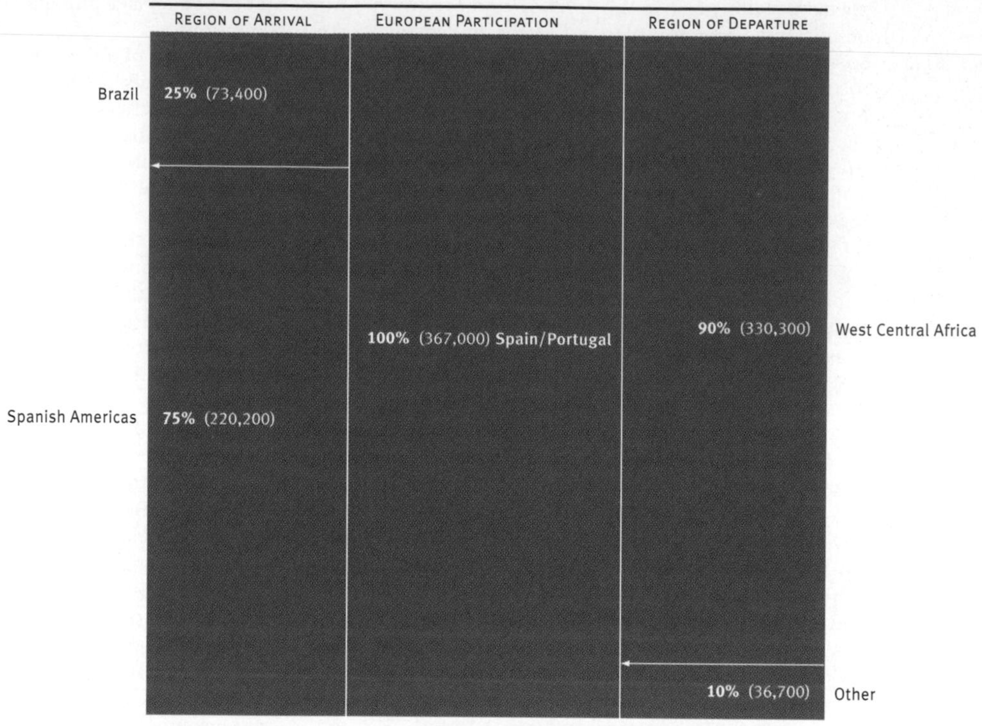
1519 - 1600
Region of Arrival
European Participation
Region of Departure
Brazil
25% (73,400)
Spanish Americas
75% (220,200)
100% (367,000) Spain/Portugal
90% (330,300)
West Central Africa
10% (36,700)
Other

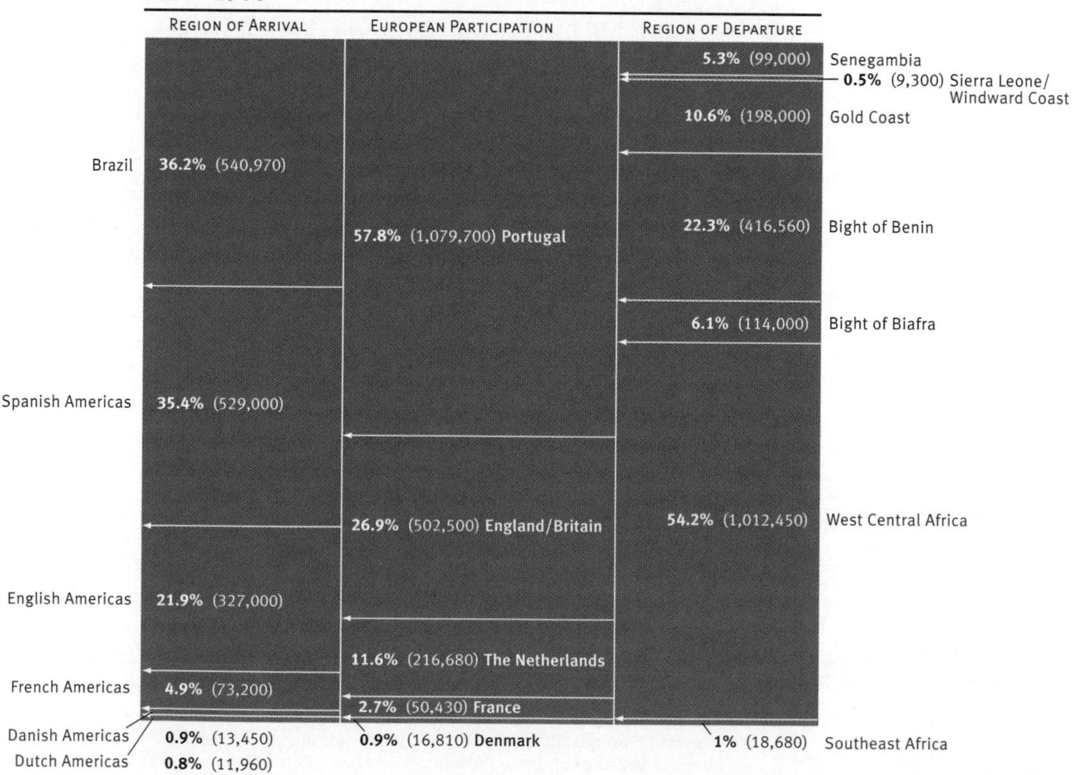
1601 - 1700
Region of Arrival
European Participation
Region of Departure
Brazil
36.2% (540,970)
Spanish Americas
35.4% (529,000)
English Americas
21.9% (327,000)
French Americas
4.9% (73,200)
Danish Americas
0.9% (13,450)
Dutch Americas
0.8% (11,960)
57.8% (1,079,700) Portugal
26.9% (502,500) England/Britain
11.6% (216,680) The Netherlands
2.7% (50,430) France
0.9% (16,810) Denmark
5.3% (99,000)
Senegambia
0.5% (9,300) Sierra Leone/
Windward Coast
10.6% (198,000)
Gold Coast
22.3% (416,560)
Bight of Benin
6.1% (114,000)
Bight of Biafra
54.2% (1,012,450)
West Central Africa
1% (18,680)
Southeast Africa

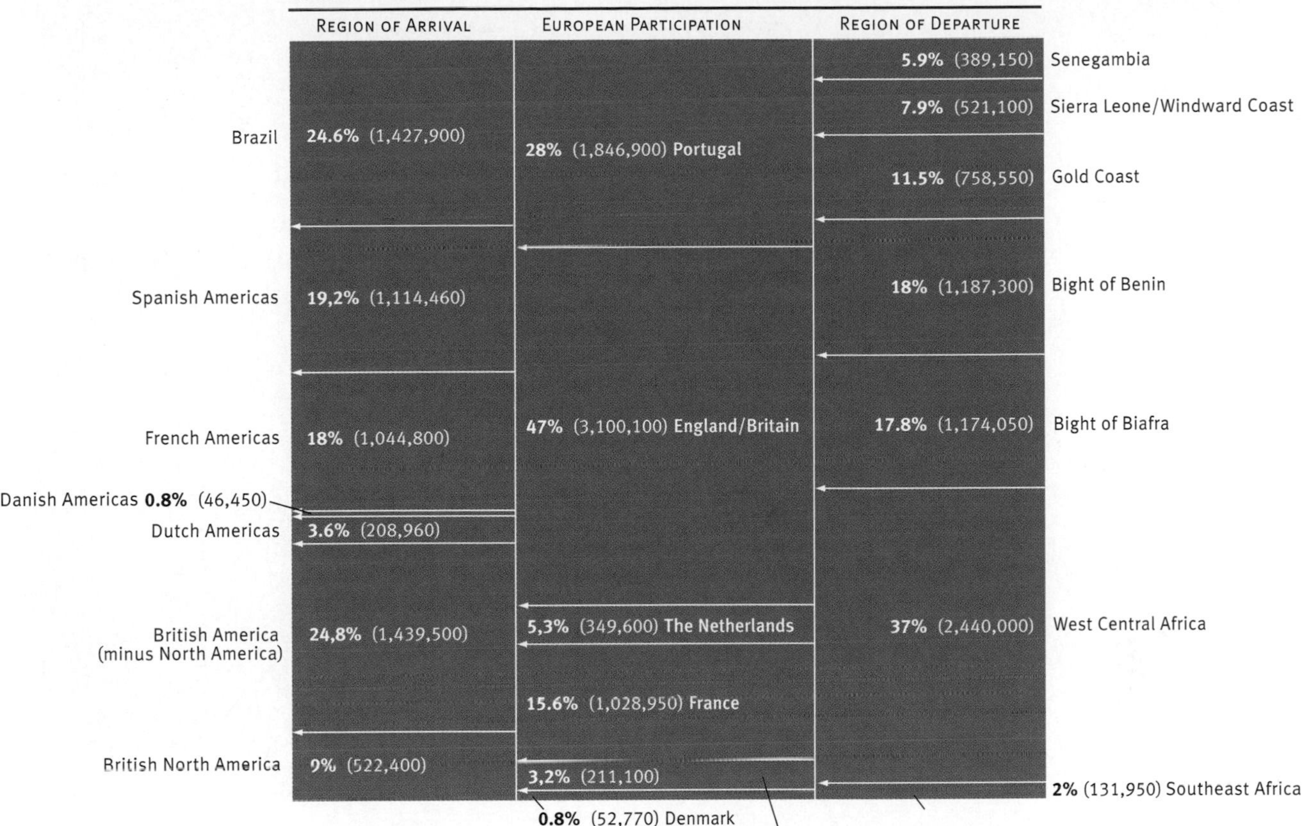
1701 - 1800
Region of Arrival
European Participation
Region of Departure
Brazil 24.6% (1,427,900)
Spanish Americas 19,2% (1,114,460)
French Americas 18% (1,044,800)
Danish Americas 0.8% (46,450)
Dutch Americas 3.6% (208,960)
British America (minus North America) 24,8% (1,439,500)
British North America 9% (522,400)
28% (1,846,900) Portugal
47% (3,100,100) England/Britain
5,3% (349,600) The Netherlands
15.6% (1,028,950) France
3,2% (211,100)
0.8% (52,770) Denmark
British Colonies (and North America)
5.9% (389,150) Senegambia
7.9% (521,100) Sierra Leone/Windward Coast
11.5% (758,550) Gold Coast
18% (1,187,300) Bight of Benin
17.8% (1,174,050) Bight of Biafra
37% (2,440,000) West Central Africa
2% (131,950) Southeast Africa

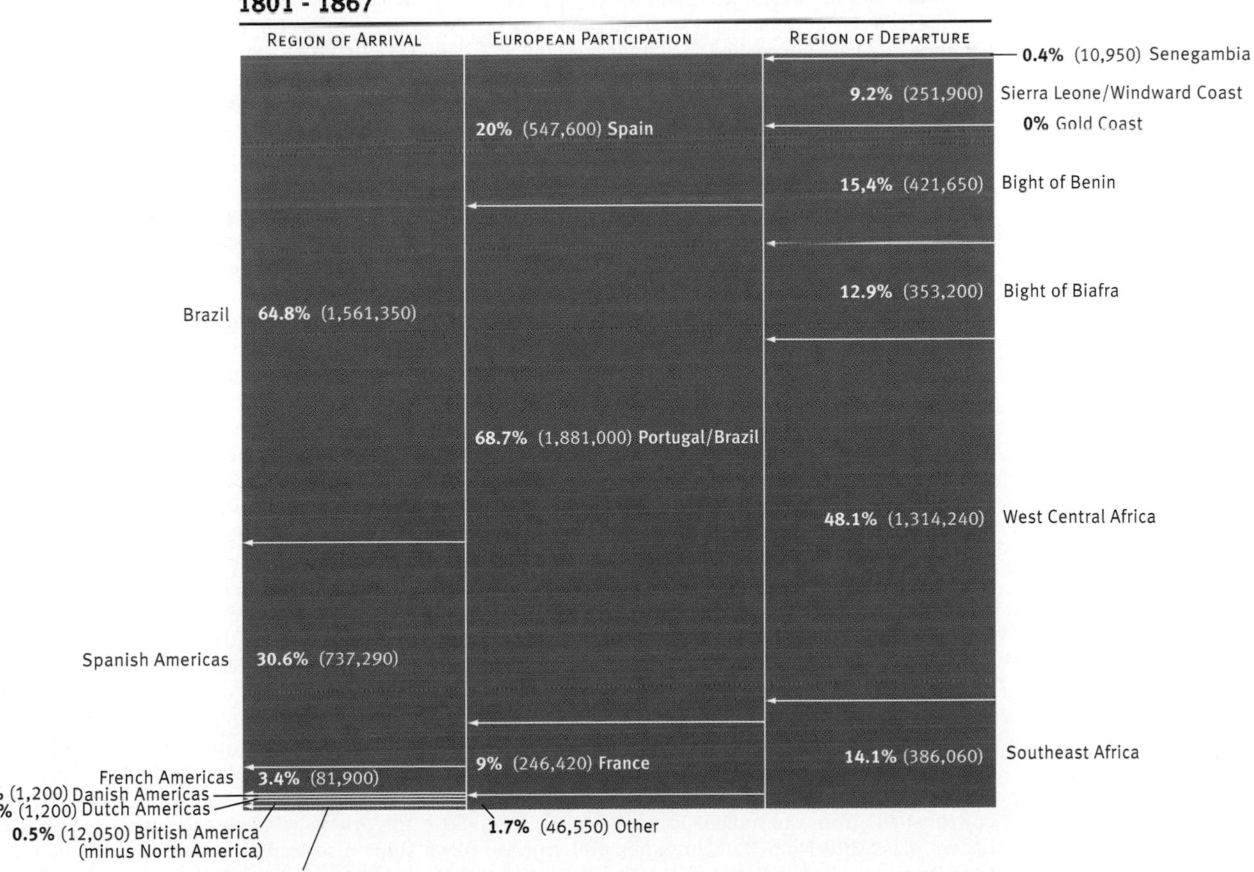
1801 - 1867
Region of Arrival
European Participation
Region of Departure
Brazil 64.8% (1,561,350)
Spanish Americas 30.6% (737,290)
French Americas 3.4% (81,900)
0.05% (1,200) Danish Americas
0.05% (1,200) Dutch Americas
0.5% (12,050) British America (minus North America)
0.6% (14,450) United States
20% (547,600) Spain
68.7% (1,881,000) Portugal/Brazil
9% (246,420) France
1.7% (46,550) Other
0.4% (10,950) Senegambia
9.2% (251,900) Sierra Leone/Windward Coast
0% Gold Coast
15,4% (421,650) Bight of Benin
12.9% (353,200) Bight of Biafra
48.1% (1,314,240) West Central Africa
14.1% (386,060) Southeast Africa

German artist Johann Moritz Rugendas included this illustration of slaves in the hold of a ship as part of his *Voyage pittoresque dans le Brésil*, published in 1827. *Oronoz*

large slave traders in the mid-seventeenth century. The small Dutch Republic was among the first European nations to develop modern commerce, and merchants there had access to shipping, port facilities, and banking credit. Dutch traders occupied several trading castles on the African coast, the most important of which was Elmina (in Ghana), a fort they captured from the Portuguese and rebuilt. The Dutch wrested control of the transatlantic slave trade from the Portuguese in the 1630s, but by the 1640s they faced increasing competition from French and British traders. By the 1680s a variety of nations, private trading companies, and merchant-adventurers sent slave ships to Africa: merchants from Denmark, Sweden, and the German states also organized slave voyages. Throughout the eighteenth century – the height of the transatlantic slave trade – the largest traders were the British, Portuguese, and French.

The Organization of Slave Voyages

Transatlantic slave voyages were complex commercial endeavors. Voyages based in Europe sailed a route linking Europe, Africa, and the Americas. Contemporaries saw this as a profitable "triangular trade." European goods were exchanged for slaves in Africa; slaves were sold in the Americas for plantation produce, such as sugar, which was transported back to Europe in the holds of slave vessels. Trade cargoes organized in Europe cost several millions of dollars in today's money, and the average value of outward cargoes was greater than most overseas trades. Cargoes typically included Indian cotton textiles, cowrie shells from the Indian Ocean, Brazilian tobacco, glassware from Italy, brandies and spirits from France, Spain, and Portugal, Irish linen and beef, and a range of British and European manufactures. At one time historians argued that cheap trinkets were sold for African slaves, but recent research shows that African traders demanded a large variety of goods – in particular, textiles – and that over time more and more European goods were exchanged for African captives as slave prices increased.

Slave vessels sailed from Europe with large crews, including surgeons, carpenters, coopers (barrel-workers), cooks (some of whom were of African descent), sailors (who apprenticed to sea at a young age), and others hired to guard slaves on the African coast and on the Middle Passage, where threats of rebellion and insurrection were constant. Slave vessels ranged in size from small sloops and schooners to larger ships measuring hundreds of tons. Some of these larger three-masted ships had three decks and were more than 30 m (100 ft) in length and 12 m (40 ft) in breadth. Few slave vessels were constructed specifically for the trade. By the mid-1800s some slave vessels were built of wood and iron and powered by steam; these vessels sailed up rivers such as the Congo and sometimes held more than 1000 African slaves. Smaller, shallower-built slave vessels traded in the Gambia, Senegal, and Sierra Leone rivers in West Africa and along the Windward Coast (present-day Liberia). Because the Gold Coast lacks large river outlets or safe anchorages, slave vessels anchored several miles offshore, where they were met by large trading canoes. In the major slave-trading sites of Whydah (in present-day Republic of Benin), Bonny, and Old Calabar (in present-day Nigeria), slave vessels anchored in lagoons or bays close to African villages and small towns. Large slave ships also traded in rivers and bays on the Angolan coast and in Mozambique in southeast

Africa. In comparison with other Atlantic traders, however, most slave vessels were small, relatively inexpensive vessels rigged for speed. Most slave vessels made only a few voyages to Africa and transported between 250 and 300 slaves.

When a slave vessel arrived on the African coast, trade was "broken" by a variety of customs payments to local African rulers or merchants. Captains also paid fees to African sailors who piloted slave vessels across sandbars to anchorages. The captains' first tasks included purchasing (or gathering) wood, water, and other provisions from shore. The wood was brought on board for fuel and for the carpenter to build a large box-shaped barricade placed above the upper deck. Slaves were led through a small door on the barricade to the hatches and decks below. The barricade was a security precaution and it kept Africans from seeing their homeland, according to the testimony of some slave traders. In many parts of Africa a "trust trade" developed as European captains advanced trading goods to African slave dealers with the promise of future slave deliveries. These dealers often were small-scale traders who built factories with connecting warehouses to store goods and outdoor, fenced "pens" or enclosed "barracoons" to confine slaves. Sometimes sons or daughters of the local chiefs were given temporarily to the slave-ship captains as a form of credit known as pawnship. When a captain kidnapped "pawns" (which occurred infrequently), the local African ruler would cut off all slave trading from the region. Often the captain and crew of the next vessel from that port would be killed or taken hostage as retribution.

There was a complex system of exchange between European, Afro-European, and African agents. Bundles, or "assortments," of European trading goods were traded for a specified number of African units of exchange, which then were exchanged for a specified number of slaves. The units of exchange varied regionally in Africa and included European iron bars, cowrie shells from the Indian Ocean, Italian beads, blue-dyed Indian textiles, or Brazilian gold. In the late eighteenth century an assortment of European textiles, firearms, and alcohol would, for example, be equivalent to 12 ounces of gold along the Gold Coast; 12 ounces of gold would be the "price" of an adult male African slave. The profitability of a slave voyage often depended on the ability of a merchant or captain to "assort" his trading goods to meet short-term African demand. There were many coastal agents who traded with slave-ship captains who did not have a properly "assorted" cargo. Many of these agents, particularly those who lived on the coast from present-day Guinea-Bissau southeast to Liberia, were of Afro-European descent.

Slave vessels remained on the coast of Africa usually from four to six months, depending on the trading location, availability of slaves and provisions, and the health of slaves and crew. Some provisions for the coastal stay and Middle Passage were loaded in Europe, but often captains purchased rice, beans, fish, and yams on the coast of Africa. Some small vessels loaded slave cargoes in a few weeks from small wooden factories or the larger stone trading forts. At some trading sites, such as late-eighteenth-century Bonny (in Nigeria), African merchants created sophisticated slave-trading road and river networks from the interior to the coast. Slave supplies were regular, and sometimes 10 to 20 slaves would be purchased and loaded on board ship per day. The supply of slaves from the interior depended largely on political warfare (since many male slaves were war prisoners) and ecological conditions. During times of drought or famine slave supplies increased as people who could not be supported by villages were sold for money or provisions. Slave raiding also occurred, though it is likely that a smaller percentage of Africans entered slavery through village raids. Often, however, the distinction between wars and slave raids was blurred. Within a few weeks of departure from the coast, captains purchased final supplies of food, water, and wood for the Middle Passage.

In 1855 Belgian sculptor Victor van Hove dramatized the horrors of slavery in two plaster statues, *Negro Slave after a Flogging* and *Revenge* (pictured here). *Hickey & Robertson, Houston/Image of the Black Project, Harvard University*

The Middle Passage

From a European geographic perspective, the Middle Passage was the second, or middle, leg of the triangular voyage between Europe, Africa, and the Americas. This was the notorious cross-Atlantic journey during which hundreds of slaves were confined in irons below deck in crowded, hot, unsanitary, and inhumane conditions. The chance of insurrection was greatest during the first few weeks of the Middle Passage. During this time most slaves were kept below deck, naked or only partially clothed with a loincloth, shackled in pairs, right leg to left leg. Nonetheless, slaves sometimes broke free of their chains and attacked the crew with a variety of tools and small weapons. Slave vessels were equipped with guns and cannons which were placed on the raised quarterdeck to fire down upon slaves escaping through the hatches. Occasionally, Africans in war canoes attacked slave vessels from shore. Researchers have documented more than 450 slave insurrections or shore-based attacks, and there were undoubtedly many more that went unrecorded. Occasionally, some captives would regain the shores of Africa. More often the crew regained control of the ship or Africans were reenslaved upon reaching shore. Uprisings were extremely violent, and sometimes many slaves and most crew were killed. When African captives gained control of the ship, they kept a few crew alive to navigate the vessel.

Ships' officers confined the men, women, boys, and girls in separate compartments. Slave vessels were fitted with numerous wooden platforms between decks to allow captains to pack in greater numbers of captives. As the between-deck space was generally from 1.2 m (4 ft) to 1.8 m (6 ft), platforms reduced the head room for captives to only a few feet. All slaves suffered from numerous scrapes

and bruises from lying on these bare planks. Captains claimed that when safely away from shore, slaves were given greater freedom of movement. Women and children, some claimed, were never shackled and were allowed to roam above deck with minimal supervision. Recently, however, archaeologists discovered many small-sized leg irons from the wreck of the slave ship *Henrietta Marie* (c. 1700) off Florida. Women may have been separated from male slaves and given greater freedom of movement to increase the crews' sexual exploitation of them.

Cooks prepared meals of fish, beans, or yams in large copper vats below deck. Surgeons sometimes assisted in the preparation and distribution of food. Slaves were given food at mid-morning and late afternoon in small bowls (or "pannikins"). Weather permitting, groups of African captives were exercised above deck (in their leg irons) in an attempt to offset the debilitating effects of the Middle Passage. Officers, usually boatswains, mates, and surgeons, were armed with whips such as the cat-o'-nine-tails and forced the African captives to dance. The crew's power was enforced through such torture devices as

thumbscrews and iron collars. There were several tubs in each compartment below deck in which slaves could relieve themselves, though hindered by being shackled in pairs. Mates generally had the job of cleaning the slave compartments below deck, which each day would be covered with excrement, blood, and filth. Some captains frequently ordered the rooms washed and dried with fire pans, though sometimes the filth was simply scraped off the decks. To counteract the stench, which was thought to promote sickness, slave vessels were fumigated with vinegars, berries, limes, tars, and turpentines.

By any measurement, mortality rates of both slaves and crew were extraordinarily high on the Atlantic crossing. The crowded, unsanitary conditions below deck were an ideal disease environment for outbreaks of dysentery, the disease from which many slaves died. In addition to gastrointestinal diseases, Africans also died from dehydration, smallpox, or measles. Slaves who resisted captivity sometimes died from flogging or other forms of punishment. Some slaves committed suicide by jumping overboard or by starving or hanging themselves. The resistance to eating was so common that vessels carried metal devices to force-feed slaves.

The Slave Trade, **painted in 1840 by French artist Auguste-François Biard as a catalogue of the miseries suffered by slaves, was exhibited at the Royal Academy in London. Britain had abolished slavery in 1834, but slavery remained legal in France until 1848.** *Wilberforce House: Kingston upon Hull City Museums and Art Galleries, UK*

Africans sold into slavery in the Americas often received brutal punishments, even for minor infractions. Hanging by the ribs, as depicted by William Blake (1757-1827) in Captain John Gabriel Stedman's account of the 1772-1777 maroon wars in Suriname, was reserved for slaves who tried repeatedly to escape. *Image of the Black Project, Harvard University*

Sailors died mostly from malarial and yellow fevers, to which African-born peoples had some acquired immunities. Early in transatlantic slave trade about 15 to 20 percent of African captives died on the Passage. By the later eighteenth century about 5 to 10 percent died, a reduction perhaps caused by improvements in hygiene and sanitation. Slave mortality rose in the nineteenth century during years when the British navy tried to enforce an international ban on the slave trade. About 15 to 20 percent of the crew died on the triangular voyage and sailors died at rates often greater than for all other overseas trades combined. Slave mortality usually increased during the last stages of a particularly long passage when there were shortages of food and water.

The Atlantic crossing lasted three to five weeks from West African trading sites such as the Gambia, Senegal, and Sierra Leone rivers. Near the equator, in regions such as the BIGHT OF BENIN and the Bight of Biafra (near present-day Nigeria), the voyage to the Americas took several months. A few French ships transported slaves from Mozambique or MADAGASCAR to the Mascarene Islands in the Indian Ocean and then returned to France via Saint-Domingue in the West Indies, where additional cargoes of captives from southeast Africa were disembarked. These voyages – via the Indian Ocean – were the most complex in the transatlantic slave trade and took several years to complete. In the nineteenth century passage time in the trade fell dramatically due to advances in shipbuilding and speed.

THE MARKETING OF ENSLAVED AFRICANS IN THE AMERICAS

Upon arriving in the Americas, African captives who survived the Atlantic crossing were "refreshed" with water and colonial provisions (such as citrus fruit) and were shaved and cleaned. Ointments (to hide scars from diseases such as yaws) and oils were applied on their skin in preparation for sale. Agents placed advertisements in colonial gazettes and in taverns for the sale of African labor, which usually occurred a few weeks after arrival. Many sales occurred on ship deck; other sales took place on wharves or in agents' houses or slave pens. Some planters contracted with merchants to purchase a preset number of slaves. Many slaves were sold by "scramble" or by auction. During the scramble planters or their representatives placed ropes or handkerchiefs around groups of slaves whom they wanted to purchase. During auctions the highest-valued slaves, often adult men, were sold first; then, over several weeks or even months, less-valued slaves were sold. The last slaves sold were often old, sick, or debilitated Africans. Termed "refuse slaves," they usually were purchased by doctors or poor colonists. In some sales "prime" slaves were sold by scramble and "refuse" slaves were sold at public auction. Occasionally slave cargoes included family members or relatives, but separation during sale was almost inevitable. Cargoes also usually comprised Africans from different ethnic groups, as can be noted through ethnic scarification. Some planters purchased slaves from a variety of ethnic backgrounds as part of labor control; other planters purchased Africans from the same areas of Africa to maintain work force unity.

Ship captains and colonial agents sold slave cargoes to planters for bills of exchange, which often were resold for return cargoes of plantation produce. Slave vessels were not specialist "West Indiamen" (large produce vessels built for storage capacity), however, and transported only a fraction of the produce of the Americas back to Europe. By the mid-eighteenth century many slave vessels began returning to Europe with the planters' bills of exchange and only small cargoes of plantation produce. Thus though many slave vessels sailed on triangular voyages over the course of about a year, some did not carry on a triangular trade. An important exception to the concept of a triangular trade was the large Brazil-to-Angola shuttle trade, which dates from the 1680s. By the nineteenth century small Brazilian vessels, built for speed, sometimes made three or four slave voyages per year in this direct trade.

Abolition of the Transatlantic Slave Trade

After centuries of broad acceptance, in the mid-eighteenth century some religious leaders began to question the morality of enslaving and owning humans. They began a campaign, termed the abolition movement, to end slavery. Faced with overwhelming opposition of colonial and business groups, the "abolitionists" realized that the first step toward ending slavery would be to end the transatlantic slave trade. Attacking the British slave trade was vital: the British were the largest slave traders by the mid-1700s. The abolition of the British trade was a 20-year process: Parliament first regulated the trade, limiting the number of slaves British vessels could carry from Africa, then closed a number of colonies to slave imports, and then in 1807 passed legislation to abolish the trade itself in 1808. The size of the British trade highlights the important abolitionist triumph: during the previous decade 150 British slave vessels had sailed per year for the African coast to purchase more than 40,000 African men, women, and children.

Five years earlier, in 1802 the small Danish slave trade ended by a government order enacted in 1792. The United States slave trade – centered in Rhode Island – was outlawed in 1807, the first year Congress could address the question of abolition, as agreed to by the compromise between Northern and Southern states writing the Constitution in 1787. (Abolition of the U.S. slave trade went into effect in 1808.) The French slave trade ended temporarily in the early 1790s after the slave revolution in the largest French colony, Saint-Domingue, removed the principal French slave market, and then the French government abolished slavery throughout French colonies in 1793-1794. With the ending of the Napoleonic Wars in 1814-1815, British diplomats attempted to end the international slave trade. The Dutch trade, which largely ended during the late eighteenth-century warfare with France, was abolished by decree in 1814. The restored, conservative French monarchy, however, did not agree to end French participation in the slave trade. French vessels continued to ship slaves to Martinique, Guadeloupe, and Cayenne (in present-day French Guiana), and the French government did not abolish slavery in French colonies until 1848. The French trade, however, had effectively ended by 1831 after a political revolution in the country.

After 1815 the transatlantic slave trade centered on the expanding sugar and coffee colonies of Brazil and Cuba. British diplomats continued to negotiate for a total ban on the slave trade, and British naval ships cruised the African coast to capture illegal slave ships. By the 1820s most slave voyages originated in the West Indies or Brazil. To avoid British confiscation, "flags of convenience" were carried on board. Many European- or American-owned slave vessels sailed under Spanish-Cuban registration. British naval pressure and changing Brazilian attitudes about the slave trade led to government measures that effectively ended the trade by the early 1850s. The remaining market of Cuba experienced a short-term increase in slave imports from 1853 to 1860 as slave and sugar prices rose. Prices fell in the 1860s, and by 1867 British, Spanish, and U.S. authorities were able to end the direct slave trade from Africa to Cuba.

Long-term Trends and Impacts of the Transatlantic Slave Trade

The transatlantic slave trade first centered on West Africa, the Gold Coast, Hispaniola, Mexico, and Peru. Most of the slaves shipped from Africa during the period from 1520 to 1570 were male and worked in Spanish American mines. Over time an increasing number of Africans transported across the Atlantic left from outlets in Nigeria or Angola, and more and more would work in Brazil and the British and French Caribbean colonies. Two of every five Africans arrived in Brazil; in the nineteenth century perhaps four of every five African slaves were destined for Brazilian plantations. The British and French Caribbean colonies each accounted for about one-fifth of the total trade. In the eighteenth century Saint-Domingue and Jamaica were the largest plantation economies in the West Indies and the principal destinations for most African captives on French and British slave vessels. Slave imports, sometimes numbering 20,000 men, women, and children per year, replaced populations that did not increase by natural rates. The slave trade to what is now the United States constituted only about 7 percent of the total trade. This number may seem surprising, given the fact that the United States South developed one of the largest slave societies in the nineteenth century. But the development of a cotton plantation economy in the first half of the 1800s occurred after the abolition of the slave trade. In contrast to many plantation regimes, slave populations increased markedly within the United States. Most African captives arrived in British North America and the United States from the Congo River area, Senegambia, the Bight of Biafra, the Gold Coast, and the Sierra Leone region. In the four years prior to abolition, 5000 to 7000 slaves landed annually in Charleston. This was the height of the transatlantic slave trade to the United States.

During the history of the transatlantic slave trade, conditions of slave supply in Africa, the demand of planters for slaves of certain gender, ages, or broadly understood African "ethnicities," and European commercial rivalries shaped the movement of slaves from African to American markets. Brazil received perhaps two-thirds of African captives from Angola (with principal ports of Luanda and Benguela, under Portuguese control), one-quarter from the Bight of Benin, called also the Slave Coast (near present-day Benin), and smaller numbers from Mozambique and the region around the Bijagós Islands off West Africa. French slave vessels delivered African labor to Saint-Domingue mostly from Angola, the Bight of Benin, the Senegal River area, Calabar, and Gabon. French merchants had few slaving contacts on the Windward Coast (near Liberia) or the Gold Coast. Most African captives arrived in British North America and the United States from the Congo River area, Senegambia, the Bight of Biafra, the Gold Coast, and the Sierra Leone region. The British Caribbean drew laborers from a wide range of African coastal outlets, though by the later eighteenth century the Bight of Biafra (Nigeria) and Angola began to predominate. Jamaica had particularly close commercial links with the Bight of Biafra and the Gold Coast. The Cuban plantation economy developed from the 1760s to 1860s with the most "diversified" African slave labor force. Cuba contracted slave shipments from various European merchants, who had their own African trading contacts. By the late eighteenth century the Spanish government opened the Havana market to flags of all nations. No single African region supplied more than one-third of Cuban slave imports.

Over time there were changes in the stream of men, women, and children who entered transatlantic slaving networks. Throughout most years of the trade the Bight of Biafra supplied the most women captives to coastal traders. Disproportionate numbers of adult male slaves were shipped from the Gambia and Senegal rivers. Often more than one in five Africans transported from the Windward Coast were children. By the nineteenth century greater numbers of children were forced into the trade from almost all regions in Africa. The proportion of men also increased. Scholars have yet to explain fully these age and gender variations between African regions and over time.

Why was African labor forcibly transported thousands of miles to the Americas to work in the economies of the New World? In the past historians have argued that Africans were a low-cost labor alternative to scarce Indian labor (scarce, because most Indian populations were destroyed by disease) or expensive European labor. African skin color also identified plantation slaves from other colonial workers, which facilitated planter control. Further, there were declining numbers of European men who were willing to work as plantation laborers because job opportunities increased in Europe; there was greater competition among European slave shippers, which increased the regularity and lowered the price of Africans in the Americas; and there were entrenched racist attitudes that justified European dominance over peoples from Africa. Others have argued that African peoples had a biological advantage over European laborers in the Americas. With some acquired immunities to tropical diseases such as yellow fever and malaria, Africans proved better able to survive the disease environments of the South Atlantic and Caribbean. Recent scholarship has pointed out that the organization of the European slave trade to Africa was a costly endeavor and that it would in fact have been less expensive to ship European convicts to work the plantations of the Americas. In this view the organization of a European slave trade to the African coast has less to do with economics and more to do with developing European imperial ambitions to enslave and dominate those people defined as outsiders.

Scholars have also disagreed over the size of this forced Atlantic migration. To many the size of the transatlantic slave trade represents the scale of European destructive impact on Africa. We may never know the extent of the slave trade in the interior of Africa, or the numbers of slaves who died en route to the coastal barracoons. As an Atlantic maritime enterprise, however, the transatlantic slave trade is well documented: European governments taxed vessels clearing and entering customs, and many newspapers and colonial gazettes survive, as do general shipping documents such as muster rolls and ship registers. Moreover, slave vessels often were at sea for more than a year and were on the coast of Africa and harbors in the Americas for several months. These vessels were noticed. The large British trade is particularly well documented, and British navy officials kept extensive records of the illegal slave trade of the nineteenth century. Studies based on these numerous shipping and government documents, including Harvard University's W. E. B. Du Bois Institute's database of 27,500 slave voyages, compiled in 1993-1997, have supported an estimate of about 11 to 12 million slave exports and 9 to 10 million slave imports into the Americas. It is important to note that these totals represent more than 60 percent of all Atlantic migrants before the nineteenth century. By the 1820s after the abolition of the British, U.S., and Dutch slave trades, African migrants crossing the Atlantic still outnumbered all other European migrant groups. Also, African women outnumbered European female migrants by a ratio of more than five to one. Only by the 1840s would the number of migrants voluntarily leaving Europe for the Americas exceed the number of enslaved migrants from Africa.

What was the impact of this massive population shift? Scholars have argued that the transatlantic slave trade was an extremely profitable business that created pools of investment capital linked to industrialization in areas of Europe and North America. Extraordinary profits were achieved, however, on only a handful of voyages per year. Slave trading was extremely competitive and risky. In a broader view the transatlantic slave trade provided African labor necessary to develop the plantation economies of the Americas. Most colonies specialized in single crops, such as sugar, and were dependent largely on Europe or North America for supplies and provisions. Thus within the Atlantic system regional, specialized economics, linked through maritime trade, developed. Such trade specialization likely stimulated economic growth and increased prosperity for those living in Europe and the Americas.

By the eighteenth century standards of living had increased among many of the middle and lower classes in Europe and British North America. This in turn increased consumer demand for plantation luxuries such as sugar, tobacco, coffee, and spices. In response to this increased demand, planters in the Americas enlarged their estates, purchasing more labor from Africa to increase production. This expansion of the transatlantic slave trade in the eighteenth century, therefore, is a function of the income of European consumers and their demand for plantation goods. Without the forced labor of peoples of African descent, European consumers would have paid much higher prices for a wide range of subtropical produce. Economic growth in the North Atlantic thus stimulated the slave trade and the latter in turn encouraged economic growth.

The demand for African labor on plantations transformed a few African societies into slave-export economies. Slave-distribution networks developed in the interior to ensure a regular flow of African captives to coastal outlets, which in turn became slave-export centers with facilities to provision and confine Africans for several months. As prices rose over time, African traders gained a greater share of slaving profits. Some argue that the increasing influx of European goods limited African social and economic development. Access to inexpensive Indian- or European-produced textiles, for example, retarded the growth of African textile industries. Also, guns and alcohol are viewed as "socially disruptive" trading goods, and there was a "slave-gun cycle" whereby Africans sold slaves to acquire more firearms for slave raiding. It is likely, however, that the strength of indigenous African domestic economies meant that the major African impact of the slave trade was social rather than economic. Foreign trade constituted a small percentage of African gross domestic product, and ordinary African peoples would have never seen goods produced outside Africa.

The slave trade undoubtedly increased the incidence of warfare and slave raiding among many African societies. Moreover, as about two-thirds of the captive Africans were men between ages 18 and 30, the slave trade likely removed essential workers and soldiers. In response to renewed external threats, villages may have been abandoned as they consolidated with other communities for protection. In certain areas the slave trade altered the ratio of men to women and adults to children, thus prompting further social changes, particularly in kinship structure and marriage patterns. The incidence of slavery increased in Africa during the slave trade era and increased again in the immediate aftermath of abolition, when external demand for slaves ended rather suddenly.

In the Americas the slave trade ensured that, for three centuries, the subtropical areas remained the focal point of New World economic activity. It also ensured a much more complex social milieu and cultural environment than would have been possible without contacts with Africa. With all of its horrors and inhumanity, the transatlantic slave trade was critical in the formation of the modern world.

See Also

Congo River; Gold Trade; Luanda, Angola; Middle Passage, The; Slavery in the United States; São Tomé and Príncipe; Abolitionism in the United States; American Indians; Haitian Revolution; Trans-Saharan and Red Sea Slave Trade; Havana, Cuba.

Latin America and the Caribbean

Transculturation, Mestizaje, and the Cosmic Race: An Interpretation

In 1940 Cuban scholar FERNANDO ORTIZ (1881-1969) coined the term *transculturation* (*transculturación*) to replace the concept of "acculturation," defined as the modification of one culture that adopts traits from another, dominant culture. Ortiz offered the term in order to acknowledge the ongoing history of conflict and difference in which cultural adaptation was above all a process of creative resistance – not just assimilation. Ortiz came to this acknowledgement after having pathologized African culture in CUBA. During his career as a lawyer Ortiz studied the late nineteenth-century theories of Cesare Lombroso, the Italian criminologist who claimed that delinquents were born with certain identifiable physical traits. Like other Latin Americans of this period Ortiz adapted this theory to a local setting and concluded that blacks were congenitally non-conformist. But the attention he was paying to black non-conformism soon made Ortiz take stock of Cuba's cultural debts to Africa (*see* LATIN AMERICA, BLACKS IN). It became clearer to him that the process by which Hispanics and Africans were first uprooted from their soil and later orphaned in the Americas was so complex that it could not have melded in the harmony evident in such friendly words as "syncretism," "hybridism," or even *"mestizaje,"* all of which were widely used to describe the mixing of cultures that has taken place in the Caribbean since the late fifteenth century. These existing words described the results but ignored the 500-year-long tortuous process.

Whereas acculturation seems to indicate a smooth transition of a sub-cultural group into the mainstream of national culture, the most promising feature of transculturation is its admission of conflict. Though crediting it with the power to recognize violence may almost appear to be a perverse thing to say about a word that describes creativity in a national culture, to Ortiz it was more perverse to deny the conflict. It is true that transculturated practices – such as Caribbean dances, for instance – can be used to create the sense of a happy resolution to the antagonisms at the origins of Latin American history. National governments, for example, often celebrate musical, culinary, religious, visual, and other forms of transculturation as signs of an existing racial democracy that accepts a country's mixed heritage, as if to say that more democratic change and tolerance for difference were superfluous or anachronistic. Two such prominent and recent cases are the showcasing of SANTERÍA religious practices as official tourist attractions in Cuba and the use of the slogan "PUERTO RICO is Salsa" as the island's official theme for its participation in the 1992 quincentennial celebration of the Spanish in America held in Seville, SPAIN (*see* COLONIAL LATIN AMERICA AND THE CARIBBEAN). In both cases transcultured forms (Santería and SALSA MUSIC) have gained emblematic status of everything that is national (Cuban or Puerto Rican). But it would be a mistake to dismiss transculturation as merely a mechanism for social control as that would miss its measure of novelty and resistance. Before nation states co-opt its results, transculturation is the exhilarating moment of creating new cultural forms from parent cultures in collision. Before the results are stable and usable for state policies, transculturation plays with dangerous mixes in unpredictable ways.

Ortiz appreciated the dangers and the tragic necessity of compensating for losses in the Americas. What joins Caribbean peoples, he wrote in his classic study of the Caribbean, *Contrapunteo cubano del tabaco y el azúcar* (1940; Cuban Counterpoint of Tobacco and Sugar, 1995), is the fact that none of us really belongs there. Nevertheless, Africans suffered far more losses than did Europeans: "Men, economies, cultures, ambitions were all foreigners here, provisional, changing, 'birds of passage' over the country, at its cost, against its wishes, and without its approval.... All those above and those below, living together in the same atmosphere of terror and oppression, the oppressed in terror of punishment, the oppressor in terror of reprisals, all beside justice, beside themselves. And all in the painful process of transculturation."

Ortiz's significant improvement over the existing concepts (*mestizaje*, syncretism) was to make pain and loss the background for a heightened pleasure of cultural coherence. In such case, the value of a national culture derived, in part, from the enormous cost of forging the nation.

Taken as a process that produces cultural harmony, transculturation may be as heavy with conservative assumptions as the words that it hoped to replace (mestizaje, syncretism). The problem is precisely the univocalism it shares with competing concepts, the presumption that a single word should describe heterogeneous patterns, as if they boiled down to a process of simplification. Therefore, debate over political implications of the word leads to predictable and justified objections. Critics of programs to homogenize national cultures are surely right to object to the depuration of difference in the processes of transculturation, along with the more benign names for the reduction of antagonisms that it would dislodge, names like mestizaje, syncretism, hybridity, or "the cosmic race."

JOSÉ VASCONCELOS (1882-1959), the Mexican philosopher and politician, wrote a book with that title (*The Cosmic Race*) in 1925, when he was MEXICO's minister of education, right after the Mexican Revolution (1910-1920). Vasconcelos's utopian vision of Mexico, in which the existing four races in the world would meld into one "cosmic," postracialized race, was meant to counter the hypocrisy of Latin American "democracies" that excluded their populations of color from active citizenry. Though his "cosmic race" is a shorthand for white, black, indigenous, and Asian characteristics, it shows familiar elitist biases such as the emphasis on the need for black and indigenous communities to assimilate into a white dominated culture. Nevertheless, Vasconcelos was imagining a future in which that hierarchy would no longer exist, and the transformative project that he advocated gives his own prejudices an obsolescent quality. As Vasconcelos imagined it, Mexico, at the vanguard of truly democratic change, would lead a global movement into a racially harmonious future. This is evident from the book's full title, *The Cosmic Race: The Mission of the Ibero American Race*. In that book "Mestizaje" is the first and most important chapter. In English the translation is "miscegenation," and the clumsy word is a sign of the bad fit between the Anglo-American and the Latin American linguistic and social codes. Miscegenation has often been pronounced with mistrust or revulsion by North American white intellectuals, while Latin American racial mixing has often been an official slogan in Spanish and Portuguese. Even GONZALO AGUIRRE BELTRÁN, Mexico's foremost student of black culture, perceived mestizaje as the necessary entryway by Afro-Mexicans into their modern nation.

Mestizaje endorses the particularity of New World peoples through a rhetoric of national brotherhood that is meant to ease racial tensions, not necessarily to address material equity (*see* BLACKNESS IN LATIN AMERICA AND THE CARIBBEAN: AN INTERPRETATION). Vasconcelos's manifesto for merging already had a long tradition, and had become a conventional banner of cultural pride. It was, for example, the standard of the independence movements throughout the continent (1810-1830), when white CREOLES such as Simón Bolívar (1783-1830) proclaimed that Spanish Americans have many fathers, but only one mother, that they are neither Spanish, nor Indian, nor black, but all of these. Bolívar's pronouncement, however, did not resolve racial tensions; it merely acknowledged them (*see* RACIAL QUESTION DURING STRUGGLES OF INDEPENDENCE IN LATIN AMERICA).

A century later, after many variations on the theme, Vasconcelos proposed mestizaje as the way in which Mexico reaffirmed itself as a modern country with a mission to the world. For a hundred years the republic had been torn between indigenist liberals like President Benito Juárez (1806-1872), and the Europeanizing monarchists who replaced him with Maximilian (1832-1867). Both sides would contribute, said the minister of education during the Mexican Revolution, to making "the new man" (a goal that Fidel Castro would take up much later in the 1959 Cuban Revolution). Whites and Indians would be joined by blacks and Asians in the unprecedented culmination of one "cosmic race."

This would happen in Mexico, José Vasconcelos wrote in 1925, because no other country was as free from the racial prejudice that obstructs human progress. The United States had been claiming leadership in the march of freedom, but Vasconcelos disputed this lead. United States writers and politicians were celebrating more than ideals, they also celebrated their Anglo-Saxon selves in racial terms. And they seemed to prosper by divine will, but, Vasconcelos underlined, "they committed the sin of destroying those races, while we assimilated them, and this gives us new rights and hopes for admission without precedent in History."

Ortiz's innovation was to admit to the violence in that self-congratulatory process of assimilation. His *Cuban Counterpoint of Tobacco and Sugar* replaced the emphasis on racial inheritance implied in mestizaje with one on cultural process active in his concept of transculturation. In the case of assimilationists in the United States, a word like "acculturation" missed the novelty altogether by reducing New World clashes of culture into – as Ortiz wrote – a one-way "process of transition from one culture to another, and its manifold social repercussions."

Ortiz was a cultural anthropologist not an ideologue. Unlike institution-builder Vasconcelos, Ortiz was describing an already existing cosmic culture. Cubans were not all equally flattered by the black-and-white boldness of the picture, to be sure. An indigenous culture that owed as much to Africa as to Europe could not have appealed to the white elitism that official Cuba had cultivated since the conquest. To the extent that *Cuban Counterpoint* affirms a more complicated culture, the book is political. It requires acknowledgment of the difference within, the admission, for example, that the religion of the ORISHAS plays in counterpoint to the cult of Roman Catholic saints. That is, one cult comes to depend on the other for its sacred and social power. To the extent that this counterpoint and mutuality are now publicly recognized, transculturation has apparently provided state governments with "resolutions" to racial and cultural conflicts, so that any politics of change seems superfluous and distracting. The only sensible response is to celebrate a complex (rather than a simply coherent) New World self. Understandably, transculturation (along with mestizaje and the cosmic race) has come under criticism during the 1990s as an ideology of social affirmation that amounts to control. If difference is already part of the self, neutralized and melted down to merge with its agonist, how – critics ask – can transculturation promote political vitality? How can it focus on the unequal histories of participants?

Nevertheless, for the purpose of appreciating cultural performances that might otherwise remain incomprehensible, Ortiz's neologism offers a decided advantage: it admits conflict, pain, and loss as constitutive of American cultures. To stretch his point, transculturation can even admit the enduring melancholia of banished cultural forms that haunt new national constitutions. For example, the poem *Sóngoro Cosongo* (1931), by the Cuban NICOLÁS GUILLÉN, can recreate an African ritual to the point of including some non-Spanish words, but the mostly Spanish poem is a record of having displaced the original language of the ritual. In other words, a contemporary reading of transculturation that insists on respecting difference should hesitate at the point before differences would merge and make, for example, a seamless poem; it lingers on the tension between ill-fitting partners. Displaced people will defend their freedom of speech and continue to live in normally double (or multiple) codes, sometimes for generations.

This slightly willful reading of transculturation follows from Ortiz's historically inflected improvement on effortlessly friendly words. But it also departs from Ortiz along the very fault line that he described between cultural partners trapped in a forced marriage, an apt image for transculturation as creativity demanded by unbearable antagonism. But before the coerced marriage, and perhaps surviving it, there is an implied scorn for the requirement to relinquish one's identity, to "bleach one's soul," in the words of W. E. B. Du Bois, for the sake of amalgamation. That scorn is an expression of pride in one's difference, and the energy that keeps one cultural particularity in productive tension with others. Thanks to this tension, to the fact that the pieces of history and culture fit badly and that the bad fits produce internal differences in "national cultures," there are troubled or unsettled spaces that demand the continued creativity of transculturation. This should be our contemporary response to the eagerness of modernization that insists on privileging assimilation over difference: to appreciate the emphasis on movement that does not necessarily lead to rational improvements, and also to value cultural variety (that demands tolerance and flexibility) over modernity's taste for normalization. Does the Ortiz who would modernize through merging convince contemporary readers? Perhaps, one would want to hope, we no longer believe in an incrementally truer and more coherent national consciousness, along with the eugenic arguments for mestizaje as an improvement over dark races by melding them with whites in a single cosmic race.

Doris Sommer

SEE ALSO

Race: An Interpretation; Du Bois, William Edward Burghardt (W. E. B.); Eugenics; Cuba; Salsa Music; Catholic Church in Latin America and the Caribbean; Dance in Latin America and the Caribbean; Myth of Racial Democracy in Latin America and the Caribbean: An Interpretation.

Cross Cultural

Trans-Saharan and Red Sea Slave Trade, traffic in African slaves across the Sahara and the Red Sea for export, mainly to Arabia and South Asia.

The trans-Saharan and Red Sea slave trades both date back several millennia. Ancient Egyptians, as well as Romans, Arabs, Turks, and Europeans, all drew slaves from the Nile valley, particularly Nubia. But little is known about slave trades in and from Africa prior to the spread of Islam across North Africa beginning in the seventh century C.E.

Because many of the Arab, and later BERBER, slave traffickers in North Africa were Muslim, and because they were supplying slaves primarily to Islamic societies in Arabia and South Asia, scholars often refer to the trans-Saharan and Red Sea commerce as the "Islamic Slave Trade." This is a misnomer, however, because the demand for slave labor and the role of slaves in the host societies pre-date the rise of Islam.

Compared to the TRANSATLANTIC SLAVE TRADE, slaving in the Sahara and North Africa was always far less institutionalized, and most of the traders operated on a relatively small scale. The lack of written records combined with the huge time span of the commerce make it extremely difficult to estimate how many slaves were exported from the continent via these trade networks or how many died en route. Some scholars suggest that since about 1500 C.E., approximately 4 million slaves traveled along trans-Saharan routes while another 2 million people were sold into slavery by way of the Red Sea.

The trans-Saharan and Red Sea slave trades were also distinctive because approximately two-thirds of the slaves exported on these routes were female, destined to serve as concubines and domestic servants in Arabia and South Asia. In contrast, demand for cheap plantation labor in the Americas created the need for the high proportion of male slaves who were shipped across the Atlantic.

Along with items such as salt, gold, and ivory, slaves were among the few commodities considered valuable enough to merit risky, long-distance journeys by CAMEL caravan across the Sahara, or on foot in the Horn of Africa. Trans-Saharan traders procured slaves taken primarily from the savanna and forest zones of West Africa, while slaves bound for the Red Sea came mostly from the Nile valley, the Horn of Africa, and, to a lesser extent, the East African coast (*see* INDIAN OCEAN SLAVE TRADE). Traders exchanged luxury items such as Indian cotton, perfumes, spices, and horses for slaves sold either by other merchants, based in market towns such as Tombouctou (Timbuktu) (in present-day MALI) or DARFUR (in present-day SUDAN), or by local rulers, who acquired slaves through raids, warfare, or tribute.

Once purchased, slaves typically traveled on foot, and many had to assist with daily chores en route. The routes they took shifted over time, partly due to the rise and fall of medieval savanna empires such as ancient Mali and Songhai. From Darfur one of the main routes was the Darb al-Arbain (Forty Day Road) to Asyut in Egypt. Mortality rates, not surprisingly, were high.

Upon their arrival in Mediterranean port cities such as Tunis and Tripoli, or Red Sea towns such as Sawakan, slaves were sold in marketplaces where overseers monitored exchanges between brokers and buyers. After the eighth century Islamic principles defined many of the rules of commerce: children under the age of seven could not be separated from their mothers, for example, and Muslim slaves could not be sold to non-Muslims. Buyers were also allowed a three-day trial period to inspect the constitution and health of the slave they had purchased. Women sold as concubines or into harems were often held in escrow by a third party until menstruation proved that they were not pregnant.

Although many slaves stayed on the African continent – especially men used in the armies of North Africa and Egypt – most boarded ships bound for the eastern Mediterranean, the Arabian Peninsula, the Persian Gulf, or India. Africa became an increasingly important source for slaves in Arabia and South Asia as more traditional sources from northern and central Europe were depleted during the twelfth century. Beginning in about the fourteenth century, slaves were also shipped to Italy and other European destinations. In addition to using female slaves for concubinage or domestic service, these buyers used male slaves as low-ranking soldiers or manual laborers on plantations or in cities. A relatively small number of male slaves were castrated; they served as eunuchs, often rising to positions of wealth and power because they were entrusted with important financial and political transactions.

Many scholars have noted the absence of a distinct African population in contemporary southwest Asia, suggesting that the majority of slaves, particularly women who served as concubines, became integrated into the host societies, most often under Muslim law. Male slaves were also circumcised and given Muslim names. Upon bearing a son to their owner, concubines could not be sold or given away. Furthermore, concubines were liberated upon their owner's death, and the child was considered a free individual. Many other slaves were probably manumitted after working a nine-year period, after which many pious Muslims felt that the slaves had worked sufficiently to have earned their freedom.

The trans-Saharan and Red Sea slave trades began to taper off as the abolitionist movement, particularly in England, gained momentum. The abolitionists imposed their political will on slavers through the administrations of newly established European colonies in North and West Africa, beginning with French-controlled ALGERIA in 1830. As late as 1910, however, slaves were secretly being moved from Tibesti (northern CHAD) to the Libyan port city of Benghazi. Demand for African slaves in the MIDDLE EAST has still not disappeared, particularly as the region has grown wealthy from its oil resources. Although Middle Eastern countries abolished slavery when they entered the League of Nations in the 1920s, a minor underground trade in slaves probably still exists.

Ari Nave

SEE ALSO

Gold Trade; Ivory Trade; Egypt, Ancient Kingdom of; Nile River; Nubian; Great Britain; France; Sahara Desert; Salt Trade; Songhai Empire; Tunis, Tunisia; Tripoli, Libya; Slavery in Africa; Mali Empire.

Africa

Traoré, Moussa **(b. 1936, Kayes, French Sudan [present-day Mali]), president of MALI (1969-1991).**

The son of peasant farmers, Moussa Traoré was born in the Kayes region of the French Sudan (present-day Mali). He joined the French army in his early twenties and attended Fréjus Military College in France. When Mali became independent in 1960, Traoré returned to the country and joined the Malian army. In 1967 Mali's first president, MODIBO KEITA, established a militant youth organization, the Popular Militia, which began to threaten the power of the military.

Traoré led a military coup that ousted Keita in 1968 and established the Comité Militaire pour la Libération Nationale (CMLN). Traoré assumed the presidency in early 1969 and promised to return the country to civilian rule as soon as his transitional government had improved the Malian economy. Although Traoré fulfilled this promise in 1979, he maintained political control by establishing a one-party state under his Union Démocratique du Peuple Malien, which assured him successive wins at the ballot box – and millions of dollars in his secret bank accounts.

As president Traoré did not immediately reverse the popular Keita's socialist (*see* AFRICAN SOCIALISM) policies for fear of alienating Keita's supporters. Instead, Traoré supplemented existing programs with renewed financial aid from France and other Western donors. Throughout the 1970s Traoré devoted most of his effort toward consolidating his political power. In the early 1970s and again in the mid-1980s, however, Mali suffered from debilitating droughts that increased economic hardship throughout the country.

In order to acquire new aid during the 1980s, Traoré was forced to comply with the economic programs of the International Monetary Fund (IMF) and World Bank. Under structural adjustment policies, Traoré cut government spending, liberalized the economy, and privatized state businesses throughout the 1980s. The reforms caused rampant unemployment and prompted massive protests by students, workers, and civil servants. At first Traoré attempted to deflect public unrest by making minor economic concessions and dismissing officials accused of corruption. However, public discontent continued to mount, and by 1990 a pro-democracy movement had mobilized. When Traoré sent troops to quell pro-democracy demonstrations in Bamako in 1991, his troops killed at least 106 people and injured hundreds more.

Lieut. Col. Amadou Toumani Touré led a military coup to remove Traoré and arrested him for corruption and murder. A court sentenced Traoré to death in 1993, but President ALPHA OUMAR KONARÉ later commuted his sentence to life in prison.

Elizabeth Heath

SEE ALSO

Bamako, Mali; Drought and Desertification; Structural Adjustment in Africa.

Africa

Tribe. *See* ETHNICITY AND IDENTITY IN AFRICA: AN INTERPRETATION.

North America

Tribe Called Quest, A, **an African American RAP group whose innovative sound helped stretch the sonic parameters of hip hop.**

The members of A Tribe Called Quest – DJ Ali Shaheed Muhammad and MCs Phife (or Malik Taylor) and Q-Tip (or Jonathan Davis) – were friends from high school in New York City. The group came together in 1988 and released its debut album, *People's Instinctive Travels and the Paths of Rhythm*, in 1990. It was a wild critical success, a playfully Afrocentric album full of wit ("I Left My Wallet in El Segundo") and verve ("Bonita Applebum"), and it garnered a rare five-microphone review from the hip hop magazine of record, *The Source*. *People's Instinctive Travels and the Paths of Rhythm* also helped define the "Native Tongues" posse, an informal group of like-minded rap bands that also included DE LA SOUL, Jungle Brothers, and Black Sheep.

On their second album, *The Low End Theory* (1991), A Tribe Called Quest further pared down their already sparse sound. Tribe set its casual rhymes against deceptively simple JAZZ samples on tracks ranging from the thumping, kinetic "Scenario," with future rap star Busta Rhymes, to the more contemplative "Verses from the Abstract," featuring an original groove by renowned jazz bassist Ron Carter. Perhaps more important, *The Low End Theory* marked the creative peak of the jazz-rap movement that also included Guru's *Jazzmatazz* (1993) and Digable Planets' *Reachin' (A New Refutation of Time and Space)* (1993).

Midnight Marauders (1993) confirmed A Tribe Called Quest's reputation as consistently original performers, although after *Beats, Rhymes, and Life* (1996) some critics complained that the band was running low on inspiration. Q-Tip, the highest-profile member of the group, has made memorable guest appearances on Deee-Lite's "Groove is in the Heart," the Beastie Boys' "Get it Together," and Janet Jackson's "Got 'Til It's Gone" (*see* JACKSON, MICHAEL, AND THE JACKSON FAMILY). A Tribe Called Quest released *The Love Movement* in 1998 and disbanded the same year.

Andrew Du Bois

SEE ALSO
Hip Hop in the United States; New York, New York.

Latin America and the Caribbean

Trindade, Solano (b. July 24, 1908, Recife, Pernambuco, Brazil; d. February 20, 1974, Rio de Janeiro, Brazil), Afro-Brazilian poet, filmmaker, stage director, and folklorist known especially for his contribution to and preservation of black popular arts in BRAZIL.

Solano Trindade was born in 1908 in Recife, a town in northeastern Brazil, the son of a mulatto cobbler and a *mestizo* (of indigenous and European descent) woman. His interest in folklore and popular arts was instilled at an early age, as he would routinely accompany his father to local folk dances and read aloud to his illiterate mother.

After some advanced schooling, Trindade became a Presbyterian deacon and began to write poetry. His early works were mystical writings, and his black poetry would evolve soon thereafter. In 1936 Trindade published his first book, *Poemas Negros*, and founded the Frente Negra Pernambucana (Black Front of Pernambuco) and the Centro Cultural Afro-Brasileiro (Afro-Brazilian Cultural Center). These groups united a group of contemporary black writers with a view to collecting and disseminating the work of fellow Afro-Brazilian poets and painters. In 1959 Trindade founded the Teatro Popular Brasileiro (Brazilian Popular Theater), which he would later take to Europe with its eclectic cast of business people, laborers, and students.

In his poetry Trindade cultivated Afro-Brazilian rhythms with extraordinary musicality, exalting the uniqueness of black culture while promoting social awareness of the black experience. A proponent of Marxist ideology, Trindade identified in his work with all oppressed peoples, be they black or white, and condemned all forms of social injustice.

In his time Trindade mingled with both black militants and the literary and artistic elite. He published four books of poetry, including *Poemas de uma Vida Simples* (1944, Poems of a Simple Life) and *Cantares ao meu Povo* (1962, Songs to my People). In addition to being a poet, painter, and stage director, Trindade was also an accomplished filmmaker and folklorist.

Nicola Cooney

SEE ALSO
Blackness in Latin America and the Caribbean: An Interpretation.

Latin America and the Caribbean

Trinidad and Tobago, a country consisting of two islands roughly 35 km (22 mi) apart; the southernmost of the Windward Caribbean islands, Trinidad and Tobago lie just northeast of VENEZUELA.

Trinidad and Tobago is often celebrated as the birthplace of CALYPSO, the famous Caribbean musical form that has spread across the world. The words to one popular calypso song praise another of the country's distinctive legacies: its ethnic diversity.

It is fantastic yes it is
The way how we live as one.
The integration of the nation
Is second to none.
Where the negro, the whiteman, the
Chinee, the Indian
We all live together in this land.
In this wonderful land of calypso
In this wonderful land of steelpan.

While these lyrics may idealize the country's racial harmony, the fact remains that Trinidad and Tobago is one of the most diverse Caribbean nations. Some of this diversity can be traced to the country's colonial origins. Tobago changed hands 22 times between 1626 and 1814. Trinidad place names in English, Spanish, French, Hindi, and native Carib Indian reflect the shifts in the island's population. Today more than 80 percent of Trinidadians and Tobagians are the descendants of either African slaves or East Indian indentured servants; this large segment of the population comprises nearly equal numbers of blacks and East Indians (*see* EAST INDIAN COMMUNITIES IN THE CARIBBEAN). While the two groups share a common history of colonial oppression, the country's greatest challenge for the next century is uniting them in a common vision for a shared future.

Trinidad and Tobago are the southernmost islands in the Lesser Antilles chain and are only 16 km (10 mi) off the northern coast of South America. Trinidad lies within sight of the Venezuelan coast. Because the island was originally part of the South American subcontinent, its flora, fauna, and natural resources resemble those of South America much more than they do those of other Caribbean islands. As a result of the country's affinity to South America, settlement patterns, agriculture, and industry all developed differently in Trinidad and Tobago than they did in many other Caribbean countries. Like those of most other Caribbean islands, however, Trinidad and Tobago's earliest populations were South American indigenous groups gradually migrating north from the South American continent.

Trinidad and Tobago's first inhabitants were Ienian Arawaks. Like the Taínan Arawaks who flourished on other Caribbean islands, the Ienian Arawaks were primarily fishers and farmers. They named Trinidad Lere, or "land of the hummingbirds." The next arrivals on Trinidad and Tobago were the Carib, who quickly outnumbered the Arawaks on Tobago. On Trinidad the Arawaks and the Caribs were able to coexist for a longer period of time. These groups occupied the islands when they were invaded by Christopher Columbus's crew, which first sighted the islands on their third voyage to the New World in 1498.

In his journal Columbus renamed Lere La Trinidad, or "the Holy Trinity," for the three mountain summits that surrounded the southern bay where he landed. While Columbus almost certainly passed by Tobago on the same trip, he did not mention the smaller island in his log. Its name came from the indigenous word *tabaco*, referring to one of its earliest crops. Although Columbus claimed Trinidad for Spain in 1498, over the next 300 years Spanish colonists generally only returned to the island long enough to capture many of the indigenous Arawaks and Caribs and sell them into slavery in other Spanish Caribbean colonies. As European powers throughout the region focused on islands with richer mineral resources, Trinidad was largely ignored.

In 1702 a small number of black slaves who had been taken from their homes in West Africa were imported to Trinidad to work on cacao plantations. This trend would become more important by the end of the century, but for most of the 1700s the numbers of blacks and whites on Trinidad remained relatively small. Tobago, on the other hand, was identified early in the sixteenth century as a valuable strategic harbor and a source of unusually fertile soil. As a result it was hotly contested by the British, Spanish, French, and Dutch. As each group established or reestablished itself on the island, it brought new white colonists who soon brought African slaves. By 1791, 94 percent of Tobago's 15,102 residents were African slaves, most of whom worked on the many SUGAR plantations that had sprung up on the island.

In an attempt to replicate Tobago's agricultural success, in 1776 the Spanish government relaxed immigration restrictions and allowed any Roman Catholic, regardless of nationality, to establish a plantation on Trinidad. As French Catholic planters began creating new SUGAR, coffee, and cotton plantations on the island, there was a new demand for African slaves to perform the plantations' labor. While there were only 310 Trinidadian slaves in 1783, by 1797 there were nearly 10,000. That same year there were also 4,476 free nonwhites in Trinidad, mostly the mixed-race offspring of white planters and slaves or immigrants from other Caribbean islands. Trinidad had the largest free Afro-Creole population in the Caribbean. Many of these free blacks were landowners, and some were even slaveholders. Under Spanish government and French influence, free blacks enjoyed a legal status almost equivalent to that of whites.

But that year (1797) brought political change to the island. British colonial forces had begun to covet Trinidad's growing wealth. After attacking the harbor at Port of Spain in February 1797, the British were granted control of the island. After several more attacks they also won control of Tobago in 1814. The free black population on Tobago was not significant, and so the British did not interfere with its legal status. On Trinidad, however, the British government quickly began stripping away the rights held by free blacks. In the 1820s a coalition of Trinidadian free blacks, led by wealthy doctors and lawyers who had been educated in Europe, began organizing to protest the changes. By that time free blacks made up nearly a third of Trinidad's population. In 1823 Dr. John Baptiste Philip led a delegation to England to air the community's grievances. The delegation was successful in reinstating civil and political rights for free black

Trinidadians, but it did not even attempt to address the injustices faced by the island's enslaved black majority.

The abolition of the British slave trade in 1808 and growing British support for the abolition of slavery in all British possessions soon brought some positive change for all slaves in Trinidad and Tobago and other British islands (*see* Abolition and Emancipation in Latin America and the Caribbean). On August 1, 1834, slavery was legally abolished throughout the British West Indies. Official abolition was to be followed by a six-year period of legal apprenticeship, in which all slaves were to remain on their owners' estates and continue to work there in return for small salaries. But when apprenticeship proved too difficult to administer, it was ended two years before the designated period had elapsed. By 1838 Trinidad and Tobago, like the rest of the British Caribbean, suddenly had substantial newly freed black majorities.

When the slaves were emancipated, fertile Tobago ranked as one of the Caribbean's most important sugar producers. The sugar plantations continued to require a large labor force, and since they represented the island's dominant industry, many black Tobagians were forced to accept low-paying jobs on the same estates where they had been slaves in order to make a living. But on Trinidad, where there was considerably more land for squatting and cultivation, larger numbers of ex-slaves were able to leave their estates and establish their own small farms. By 1840 only 4,000 ex-slaves still worked on Trinidadian plantations, and this left the plantations with the same tremendous demand for labor that had first led them to imprison African slaves. This time Trinidadian planters turned to indentured workers from India as a new solution.

In 1846 the first shipment of 226 Indians arrived, most of them Hindu workers from Calcutta. Two years later the number of Trinidadian East Indians (as distinguished from West Indians) had risen to 5,000. Over the next 20 years nearly 45,000 more were brought to the island to work on the sugar plantations for a minimum of five years each. Portuguese and Chinese laborers were also imported, but in smaller numbers. Employers often made it difficult for the indentured workers to leave when the five-year period had ended, and of the first 45,000 East Indian immigrants only 4,000 returned to India. The numbers of new East Indian immigrants and their descendants continued to grow over the next several decades. As they did, East Indian and black Trinidadians found themselves fighting against one another to wrest political and financial gains from the white minority that continued to control the island's power and wealth.

The competition between blacks and East Indians was made even worse toward the end of the nineteenth century by the decline of the sugar industry, which instigated a recession in the working-class economy of Trinidad and Tobago. In 1888 the British government decided to administer the two islands as a single political unit in an effort to secure more financial stability for Tobago. But one of the main complaints of residents of Trinidad and Tobago concerned precisely their British colonial rule. Trinidad and Tobago's local government consisted of an all-white legislative council whose members were appointed by British representatives in the colony. There was no universal suffrage for the black and East Indian majority, and as Trinidad and Tobago approached the twentieth century, it was clear that change was needed.

The first push for this change came from Trinidad's Afro-Creoles. As Afro-Creoles began to secure even more education and many professional civil service positions, the class division between them and the black working class grew larger, and middle-class Afro-Creoles sometimes emphasized that division. For example, Afro-Creoles were initially hesitant to celebrate Carnival, the African-derived black cultural festival that has since become one of Trinidad and Tobago's trademarks, because they saw the event as too unrefined. They were also opposed to state-sponsored East Indian immigration and had no desire to form a coalition with East Indians. But at the same time Afro-Creoles were vocal opponents of white supremacy and segregation and strong supporters of equal rights for black people, causes that unified them with the black working class.

The emergence of the Pan-African movement in 1897 further solidified this solidarity along color lines. Suddenly, Trinidadian intellectuals such as H. S. Williams and George Padmore were among the black scholars across the diaspora who were celebrating the culture and accomplishments of sub-Saharan Africa and emphasizing the common experience shared by people of African descent in Africa, South America, and the Caribbean. That year the Trinidadian Workingmen's Association (TWA) became the first organization in the country to attempt to unify the black middle and working classes. The TWA's goal was to push for better working and living conditions and for constitutional reform.

In the midst of this political activity major economic changes came to the country with the rise of the oil industry after 1909. Trinidad is the only Caribbean island to have substantial petroleum reserves, and in a period when the agricultural economies of many other islands were in decline, Trinidad beckoned workers from Tobago and across the Caribbean to work in its oil fields. But the arrival of the oil industry only underscored the fact that Trinidad and Tobago's economy continued to be based on the hard labor of the majority of its population. After several internal disputes the TWA had almost disappeared as a strong force by the outbreak of World War I, but in the postwar period it returned to prominence.

Trinidad's spectacular Carnival in Port of Spain includes the Hasay Festival, part of the broader celebration of Muharram, the first month of the Muslim year. *Henderson/Hutchison*

The TWA's new leader after the war was Capt. Andrew Arthur Cipriani, a Corsican Trinidadian who had served as commander of the West India regiment during World War I. As a white Trinidadian, Cipriani was the first leader able to unify the black and East Indian factions in the working class, since he belonged to neither group. When limited elections for the Legislative Council were allowed for the first time in 1925, Cipriani became one of the body's first elected members. By 1934 the TWA was renamed the Trinidad Labour Party (TLP), signifying the organization's goal of becoming more involved in the larger political process. But as the worldwide depression of the 1930s worsened living conditions in the islands, workers wanted more radical leadership than Cipriani provided.

One of the new leaders to emerge was Tubal Uriah Butler, a black Grenadian who worked in Trinidad's oil fields. Butler led oil workers in several island-wide strikes during the 1930s. In 1937 several of these strikes turned violent, leading to 12 deaths and more than 50 injuries. The British commission that investigated the causes of those strikes eventually recommended more representative government. The 1946 election in Trinidad and Tobago was the first held under universal adult suffrage, but there was no cohesive workers' vote. Instead, in the months leading up to the election labor unions split their support along the old black/East Indian racial divides, and for the next ten years Portuguese trade unionist Albert Gomes presided over a fragmented legislative council.

The rise of Eric Williams and the People's National Movement (PNM) in 1956 marked a new era in Trinidadian and Tobagian government. Williams, the son of a Trinidadian postal official, had received a Ph.D. in history from the University of Oxford in 1938. Over the next ten years he rose to prominence as a well-respected scholar and a professor of social and political science at Howard University in Washington, D.C. Williams returned to Trinidad in 1948 as deputy chairman of the Caribbean Research Council of the Caribbean Commission, but he disliked the organization's conservative politics and in 1955 left the commission to found the PNM.

Although the PNM declared itself a multiracial party, its supporters were primarily black. Adherents did include members of both the middle and working classes, however, for while Williams was clearly an educated, articulate member of the middle-class elite, he was also a proponent of Trinidadian and Tobagian nationalism and self-government for the islands' people. The PNM won the national elections in 1956, making Williams chief minister of Trinidad and Tobago. He remained in charge of the country's government until his death in 1981.

Williams's views on self-government were being echoed across the British Caribbean, and British leaders realized that change was probably inevitable. On August 31, 1962, Trinidad and Tobago achieved independence from Britain, becoming an independent country within the British Commonwealth. Trinidad and Tobago was only the second British Caribbean colony to become an independent state – Jamaica had become the first just weeks earlier – but the transition in national status was handled with relative ease. Even white citizens felt a grudging respect for Williams, and this helped to unify the new country. At independence Williams's title changed to prime minister, making him the first in the country to hold that title. He was often called the "Father of the Nation" and had become one of the most popular leaders in the Caribbean.

But Williams eventually came under criticism. His standing as a member of the educated, middle-class elite was a particular liability during the Black Power movement that flourished in Trinidad starting in 1970. Students and activists accused Williams of having Anglo-Saxon values and being complicit in oppressing "black" African and East Indian workers. Williams responded to these and other criticisms during the 1970s by moving further to the right and taking more power into his own hands, and this led to even more dissatisfaction with his government. A poll taken a month before his March 1981 death showed that 50 percent of voters felt he should resign.

The two decades after Williams's death brought even more political challenges, as racial animosities again divided the country in the 1980s and 1990s. More East Indians were able to rise into the highest ranks of government in these years, but their leadership was met with resistance from some black Trinidadians. After the multiracial National Alliance for Reconstruction Party was elected

Trinidad and Tobago have the most diverse populations of all the Caribbean islands, including people of African, East Indian, English, Spanish, Hindi, French, and native Carib Indian descent. That diversity is reflected in the faces of these children in a Trinidadian nursery school. *Hutchison Library*

in 1986 under the campaign slogan "One Love," a radical black Muslim sect staged a brief government coup in 1990. Tensions arose again after East Indian leader Basdeo Panday became prime minister of the country in 1995. Trinidad and Tobago is also becoming one of the most overpopulated countries in the region, and there is suspicion among some that the unusually high birthrates among both blacks and East Indians represent a subtle form of competition, one that has prevented either group from gaining a clear majority in the population.

But the country does have sources of strength. Trinidadians and Tobagians are fortunate in that the oil industry has afforded them the highest standard of living in the Caribbean, and while that industry is not immune to recessions and downswings, it still promises to be a reliable backbone for the country for years to come. Like many Commonwealth Caribbean nations, Trinidad and Tobago has a national passion for cricket, and Trinidad and Tobago's contributions to literature, drama, and music are a crucial part of the country's cultural heritage.

Many of the Caribbean's most celebrated writers, such as C. L. R. James, V. S. Naipaul, and Samuel Selvon, are from Trinidad. Nobel Laureate Derek Walcott lived in Trinidad for years, and while there he founded the Trinidad Theatre Workshop. The country is also well known for its popular music and cultural celebrations. Calypso and steelpan both originated in Trinidad, and the annual Carnival festival is one of the largest such celebrations in the world and attracts thousands of visitors from outside the country each year. These cultural resources help unify all Trinidadians and Tobagians; common celebrations and traditions in the "land of steelpan" strengthen the cherished brotherhood and sisterhood that are idealized in the calypso song.

Lisa Clayton Robinson

See Also

Cocoa; Slavery in Latin America and the Caribbean; World War I and African Americans; James, Cyril Lionel Richard; Walcott, Derek Alton; Apprenticeship in the British Caribbean; Pan-Africanism and Afro-Latin Americans; Theater in the Caribbean; Carnivals in Latin America and the Caribbean.

Africa

Tripoli, Libya, the capital city of Libya.

Until the twentieth century the city of Tripoli seemed destined to share the fate of whatever empire held it – alternately built up, captured, bombarded, and leveled, it rose and fell with these empires. Berber-speaking people were the original inhabitants of the North African peninsula where the city of Tripoli now stands, but Phoenician traders created the settlement. A Carthaginian state controlled the colony as an eastern outpost until Carthage fell to Roman rule. The Roman presence in Tripoli lasted for more than 500 years, with a short interim government by the Garamants from the south. Three cities grew up under the Roman name Tripolitanos, including Ouia, the site of the present-day city, Sabrata, and Libtes. When the Vandals took the three cities in the fifth century C.E., they broke down the walls between them, and the single city Tripoli grew over the old boundaries. The subsequent Byzantine Empire held this city in the sixth century.

The conquest of Tripoli by the Arab Tarablus in the seventh century brought Islam to the city as well as an Arab elite. They rebuilt the city's infrastructure, which had crumbled under Byzantium's rule. Between 1146 and 1158 Sicilian Normans briefly held the city, by then a busy port. But Arabic culture became dominant in Tripoli and the surrounding regions, especially after the migration of the Banu Sulaim from the central Arabian plateau through Egypt to Libya beginning in the eleventh century.

In the sixteenth century the Christian-Islamic rivalry that had dominated the Mediterranean region for centuries came to Tripoli. Spain captured the port and built the castle that still dominates the modern city. But in 1551 the Turkish Ottoman Empire took the city they called Tarablus al-Gharb (Tripoli West), to distinguish it from the other Tripoli in Lebanon. The Ottoman presence would be the longest and in some ways the most influential. Despite the support of Muslim residents for an Islamic ruler, the citizens of Tripoli periodically broke from direct Ottoman rule. The city's rulers came from the ranks of the janissaries, men who arrived in the region as members of the Ottoman military but later adopted a distinct North African identity and claimed power for themselves. Other inhabitants included Berber speakers, *kulughlis* (the children of Turkish men and local women), Jews, and Greeks.

Under nominal Ottoman rule, Tripoli was connected to several important trans-Saharan trade routes as well as to the east-west pilgrimage path to Mecca. But most of the city's wealth came from the corsairs, who gleaned "protection money" from passing European ships. The corsairs' financial backers as well as the captains and sailors exercised considerable influence over Tripoli's economic and political affairs. European travel narratives record the presence of Christian slaves and the European representatives who negotiated on their behalf.

From 1801 to 1805 the United States bombarded Tripoli to end the corsairs' attacks on American ships that would not pay "protection money." In the following years local power weakened from the decline in corsair profits, and in 1835 the Ottoman Empire stepped in to reassert direct control of the city. It subsequently undertook modernization projects, installing water lines and sewers, and improving the port.

When the Turkish-Italian war broke out, however, the port offered little protection to the city, which fell to the Italians in 1911. Italian colonization brought to Libya the mass immigration of unemployed Italians, many of whom settled in Tripoli. During World War II the city suffered from its association with the fascist government; Allied forces bombed it ten times in one year.

Although limited organized anticolonial resistance took place within Tripoli itself, the city hosted negotiations for Libyan independence and, after 1952, became one of the new nation's two royal capitals (the other being Benghazi). In 1970 Libya became a republic, and Tripoli its capital. Industrialization fueled by the 1959 discovery of oil in turn fueled urban migration, drawing job-seeking migrants from the Libyan countryside as well as from neighboring countries. During the late 1970s Tripoli was the site of large demonstrations, including various anti-Qaddafi student demonstrations and a large anti-American demonstration, during which the embassy was burned down. Now with a population that surpasses 1.2 million, the city thrives as an oil depot and a center for the trade of such regional products as olives, tobacco, fish, and grains as well as fresh vegetables and citrus fruits.

Marian Aguiar

See Also

Qaddafi, Muammar al-; Banu Hilal and Banu Sulaim.

Latin America and the Caribbean

Tropicália, an extraordinary flourish of cultural production in Brazil during the late 1960s that coalesced as a controversial movement in popular music.

The Tropicália movement helped to open Brazilian music to international influences, including music of Africa and the diaspora. In the 1970s the leaders of the tropicalist movement, Gilberto Gil and Caetano Veloso, encouraged and defended the emergence of Afro-Brazilian musical movements, particularly in Salvador, Bahia.

Participants in the Tropicália movement included composer-performers Caetano Veloso, Gilberto Gil, Gal Costa, and Tom Zé; poets José Carlos Capinam and Torquato Neto; and intellectual provocateur Rogério Duarte. Except for Torquato Neto, the group hailed from Bahia, the northeastern state noted for its vibrant Afro-Brazilian culture. After migrating to São Paulo, the industrial capital of Brazil, the so-called "Bahian group" joined vanguard composer-arranger Rogério Duprat, and the psychedelic rock group Os Mutantes. Concrete poet and cultural critic Augusto de Campos provided theoretical orientation and defended the group's activities in São Paulo's local press. Journalists Luiz Carlos Maciel and Nelson Motta also helped to define and disseminate the group's project in Rio de Janeiro.

The tropicalist movement emerged at the height of political tensions between an increasingly repressive military regime, which took power in 1964, and the left-wing opposition, led primarily by students, artists, and labor activists. At that time, the field of urban popular music was divided between cultural nationalists, who defended "authentic" Brazilian popular music (known as Música Popular Brasileira, or MPB) and the massively popular Jovem Guarda (Young Guard), a homegrown rock movement led by Roberto Carlos. Key proponents of cultural nationalism, such as Geraldo Vandré, Sérgio Ricardo, and Carlos Lyra, were engaged in creating protest music based on northeastern folk themes and styles. Much of this music promised future redemption for the "people," who were oppressed by a right-wing regime allied with multinational capital interests. The populist left regarded the Jovem Guarda as culturally and politically alienated for singing about everyday desires and using electric instruments.

The most visible sites of cultural struggle in popular music were the immensely popular televised music festivals of São Paulo and Rio de Janeiro. While the Jovem Guarda and international pop dominated the Brazilian music market, defenders of MPB, like Elis Regina, Chico Buarque, Edu Lobo, and Geraldo Vandré, dominated the festivals. The Bahian group identified with MPB but was also fascinated with the pop appeal of Roberto Carlos and globally famous pop luminaries such as the Beatles, Janis Joplin, Jimi Hendrix, and James Brown. In an interview, Veloso explained the group's eclectic vision: "We took the example of *antropofagia*, or cultural cannibalism, a notion put forward by the modernist movement in the 1920s, especially by the poet Oswald de Andrade. You take in anything and everything, coming from anywhere and everywhere, and then you do whatever you like with it, you digest it as you wish. You eat everything there is and then produce something new."

In September 1967 Gil and Veloso introduced their "universal sound" at the Third Festival of Brazilian Popular Music aired by TV Record in São Paulo. The live audience was initially hostile to their experiments, which combined electric instrumentation with Brazilian rhythms and themes. By the end of the festival Gil and Veloso had won second and fourth prizes, respectively, for "Domingo no Parque" and "Alegria, Alegria." By early 1968 their "universal sound" was dubbed *tropicalismo* by the local press and located within a broad range of artistic production.

Key influences on the tropicalists included Glauber Rocha's film *Terra em Transe* (Land in Anguish), a bitter allegory of the collapse of populist politics and the ascension of authoritarianism in Brazil. The play *O rei da vela* (The Candle King), written by Oswald de Andrade in 1933 and staged by the Oficina Theater Group in 1967 under the direction of José Celso Martinez Corrêa, was another famed "happening" of the period. This expressionist farce reveled in the aesthetics of kitsch while cruelly exposing economic dependency, foreign imperialism, and the cynical preservation of class interests. The tropicalist musicians also found allies in two currents of visual arts, *Neorealismo Carioca*, a Brazilian variation of pop art, and *Nova Objetividade*, led by Hélio Oiticica, a radical conceptual artist. His 1967 installation, *Tropicália*, provided the namesake for a song by Caetano Veloso and for the movement.

Each of the tropicalist musicians released solo albums in 1968 and 1969 and the entire group released an acclaimed concept album, *Tropicália: Panis et Circensis*, which was hailed as Brazil's response to the Beatles' *Sgt. Pepper's Lonely Hearts Club Band*. Veloso and Gil did not perform in the televised festivals of 1968, yet staged important alternative "happenings" in nightclubs and on television. At one event, the emerging reggae star, Jimmy Cliff, who was representing Jamaica at Rio's International Song Festival, joined Gil on stage while he performed "Batmacumba." The tropicalists also had a short-lived television program, "Divino Maravilhoso," named after a hit recorded by Costa. The tropicalists' irreverent activities attracted the scrutiny of military authorities. In late 1968 Gil and Veloso were arrested, jailed for several months, and then exiled to London for two years. The tropicalist movement came to a close, but its impact continued to reverberate in Brazilian popular music.

Tropicália was arguably the most important cultural movement in Brazil since *modernismo* of the 1920s. The 1990s saw a new wave of artistic and critical interest in the movement in Brazil and abroad. In 1993 Veloso and Gil commemorated the 25th anniversary with the album *Tropicália II*, which updates many of their original concerns. In 1997 Veloso published a highly acclaimed memoir, *A Verdade Tropical* (Tropical Truth), which relates his personal experience in the tropicalist movement and its painful aftermath. The city of Salvador, Bahia, where the original Bahian group converged in the early 1960s, chose *Tropicália* as its Carnival theme in 1998. During the Carnival contemporary pop bands and percussion troupes performed updated versions of tropicalist classics, and Caetano Veloso was publicly awarded an honorary doctorate degree from the local university.

Christopher Dunn

See Also

Rio de Janeiro, Brazil; Carnivals in Latin America and the Caribbean.

Latin America and the Caribbean

Tropiques, literary journal published in Martinique from 1941 to 1945, edited by Aimé Césaire, his wife Suzanne Césaire, and René Ménil.

Tropiques represents one of the first attempts to identify and promote Afro-Caribbean culture in the French overseas departments.

The editors of *Tropiques*, who at the time of its inception in 1941 were all teachers at the Lycée Schoelcher in Fort-de-France, Martinique, conceived of the journal as a way of filling what Aimé Césaire saw as the "cultural void" that existed on their island. In the view of Césaire and his collaborators, Martinicans of African descent were essentially consumers of culture – notably, of culture imposed on them by the French colonizer – rather than producers of it. *Tropiques* would address this problem by showcasing the poetry, prose fiction, and essays of the three editors (one of whom, Aimé Césaire, was on his way to becoming one of the best-known poets, playwrights, and essayists writing in French during the mid-twentieth century) as well as the work of other Martinicans.

The journal has often been identified with Négritude, a movement that sought to put colonized Africans and people of African descent in touch with the rich cultural heritage that French colonialism had attempted to replace with French culture. For the editors at *Tropiques*, black Martinicans were the descendants of African slaves, but those Africans had not always been slaves. As Suzanne Césaire wrote in the first issue, it was essential that black West Indians reconnect with the glorious precolonial past of Africa. The process of rediscovering their African personality would allow Martinicans to produce authentic works of art, as opposed to the bland imitations of European models the island produced at the time. It was precisely Césaire's poetry that the journal offered as an example of the successful integration of a forgotten African heritage. *Tropiques* also looked beyond the horizons of Martinique for writers who shared a similar set of concerns. Cuban writers such as Alejo Carpentier and Lydia Cabrera contributed essays and works of fiction, and several essays were devoted to the Afro-Cuban painter Wifredo Lam. With these contributions, the editors at *Tropiques* sought to present African diasporic culture as it existed not just in Martinique but throughout the Caribbean. In so doing they anticipated Créolité, a recent literary and cultural movement that emphasizes a multifaceted Caribbean identity, drawing on African, Asian, and European influences. But the Césaires and Ménil also acknowledged the particular status of the Caribbean as cultural nexus and warned that the focus on African heritage should not obscure the importance of other cultural influences. As they wrote, "We stand at the crossroads. The meeting point of races and cultures." This implied the acknowledgment of European influences; the editors paid homage to André Breton and the surrealists in essays as well as in poems written in a style inspired by surrealism.

The dense, sometimes obscure style of writing in the journal was also partly a response to the context in which it was published. When the first issue of *Tropiques* appeared in April 1941, Martinique was under the control of the Vichy government in France, which was collaborating with the Nazis. Paper was hard to come by, and all writing on the island was subjected to vigorous censorship by the Vichy authorities in Martinique. *Tropiques* was allowed to appear only because its editors had presented it as a nonpolitical journal that concerned itself with Martinican folklore. The allusive style of the essays and poems in *Tropiques* allowed it to pass unnoticed initially, but the journal was eventually deemed subversive and forced to cease operations from May 1943 until the end of Vichy control of Martinique in October 1943. Given these difficult conditions, that the journal ever appeared is a testament to the commitment of the Césaires and Ménil to subverting the Vichy regime and, more significantly, to presenting Afro-Caribbean culture in a positive light.

Richard Watts

See Also
France; Slavery in Latin America and the Caribbean; Literature, French Language, in Caribbean.

Latin America and the Caribbean

Trujillo, Rafael (b. October 24, 1891, San Cristóbal, Dominican Republic; d. May 30, 1961, Santo Domingo, Dominican Republic), military dictator of the Dominican Republic.

Rafael Leonidas Trujillo Molina was born in the town of San Cristóbal, located some 30 km (18 mi) from the capital, Santo Domingo, Dominican Republic, on October 24, 1891. The period from 1930 to 1961 has been called the Era of Trujillo. During this time Trujillo exercised power as an absolute dictator, though he occupied the presidency only from 1930 to 1938 and from 1942 to 1952. In the intervening years he ruled through puppet presidents and maintained his position as commander of the armed forces. From 1953 until his death in 1961 he occupied the position of foreign minister.

In 1918, during the United States occupation of the Dominican Republic (1916-1924), Trujillo joined the National Guard established by the United States and quickly rose in its ranks. In 1927, after the Guard was renamed the National Army, he became commander in chief and brigadier general. Trujillo used strong-arm tactics, intimidating and imprisoning many of his opponents, to win the presidential election of 1930. For the next three decades he would dominate political life in the country.

Trujillo is remembered as one of the most brutal dictators of the Dominican Republic and perhaps in all of Latin America. His reign was characterized by state terror, censorship, the omnipresence of the secret police and military corruption, and nepotism. Immediately following the 1930 election he organized a terrorist group known as "La 42," whose job was to assassinate and persecute his political opposition. Trujillo used his power to amass wealth for himself, his family, and his political cronies, establishing monopolies on salt, meat, and other basic goods. According to historian Frank Moya Pons, by 1961 Trujillo controlled approximately 80 percent of the nation's industrial production. According to Robert Alexander, "A 'cult of personality' was established according to which the dictator had to be credited as the ultimate authority in all fields of human knowledge, and numerous things and places, including the capital city, were renamed in his honor."

Among the atrocities that occurred during the Trujillo dictatorship is the massacre of approximately 20,000 Haitians (*see* Haiti and Dominican-Haitian Relations) and Dominican-Haitians in 1937. Haitian peasants had long settled in the Dominican Republic, along the border, a fact that Dominican elites had seen as threatening to Dominican territorial integrity and culture (despite a treaty that finally settled the border dispute between the two countries in 1929). Beyond the cultural, political, and economic reasons for the 1937 massacre was Trujillo's personal conflict with race and ethnicity. While Trujillo cannot be credited with developing anti-Haitianism and antiblackness in the Dominican Republic, his actions demonstrated that he was one of the greatest proponents of what Silvio Torres-Saillant called "the negrophobia of the elite." Trujillo's disdain for blacks and Haitians is perplexing, for he was a mulatto himself who had Haitian blood through his maternal grandmother. This fact was consistently omitted in biographies sanctioned by Trujillo and his family.

After the 1937 massacre Trujillo continued his efforts to Dominicanize and "whiten" (*"blanquear"*) a country that he saw as too phenotypically black (*see* Whitening). He initiated a plan to "import" persons of European, Asian, and Middle Eastern lineage. Trujillo's attitude and policy regarding the new immigration are reflected in his statement: "A great quantity of immigrants of the White race is needed. The immigrants should be Spanish, Italian, and also of French origin. Immigrants of Caucasian stock shall pay a fee of six pesos for the residency permit and those not of such origin shall pay 500 pesos." In addition, Trujillo built a number of towns and military installations along the border with Haiti to ensure that this territory would become Dominicanized and to prevent renewed Haitian penetration.

In the late 1950s economic crisis shook the Trujillo regime. The situation worsened after the Organization of American States imposed economic sanctions on the country following Trujillo's attempt to assassinate Venezuelan president Rómulo Betancourt in 1959. The Venezuelan leader's car was bombed in an act of retaliation for his support of a Dominican exile group that attempted to topple the Dominican dictator earlier that year. In the context of economic and political instability, Trujillo was shot to death by opposing military leaders on May 30, 1961, on a highway between his native San Cristóbal and Santo Domingo. His death by no means meant the death of *Trujillismo*, for he left an indelible imprint on the psyche of the Dominican nation.

James Davis

See Also
Venezuela.

Latin America and the Caribbean

Truque, Carlos Arturo (1927-1970), Afro-Colombian playwright and master of the short story form. He is best known for his collection of stories *Granizada y otros cuentos* (1953, Hailstorm and Other Stories) and the posthumous *El día que terminó el verano y otros cuentos* (1973, The Day Summer Ended and Other Stories) (*see* Literature, Black, in Spanish America).

Africa

Truth and Reconciliation Commission, the body charged with investigating crimes committed during the apartheid era in South Africa.

On April 15, 1996, South Africa's Truth and Reconciliation Commission (TRC) began its hearings. The TRC was a compromise solution to the problem of dealing with the thousands of assaults, kidnappings, and murders that were carried out during the heyday of apartheid. The commission received amnesty applications from more than 8000 people who participated in apartheid-era crimes, which were defined as those having taken place between 1960 and 1993. Nearly 20,000 witnesses gave testimony, either written or verbal. Despite persistent doubts about both its impartiality and its effectiveness, most observers agree that the TRC – which continued to work past its original 18-month deadline – helped reconcile the new South Africa with its past.

Led by former archbishop Desmond Tutu, the TRC had a multiracial staff of more than 60 and consisted of three committees. Each committee was charged with one of the TRC's three separate mandates: to gather evidence, to make decisions regarding amnesty, and to determine what, if any, reparations would be granted to victims. The TRC grew out of negotiations between Nelson Mandela, the African National Congress leader elected president of South Africa in 1994, and the Afrikaner-dominated National Party government. It was modeled after truth commissions in other countries in which citizens had suffered years of violent injustices, such as Argentina, Chile, and Guatemala.

These tribunals operated on the assumption that the only way to discover the truth about large-scale, politically motivated crimes was to offer amnesty to those who committed them. In exchange for their truthful testimony, perpetrators were shielded from criminal prosecution and civil lawsuits – unless the commission determined that their crimes were either nonpolitical or disproportionately brutal. For victims and their families, the TRC hearings provided previously unavailable information about the torture and death of relatives, often including the location of bodies, which families could then re-bury according to their religious traditions. Perhaps the most important goal, however, came from the theory that only by acknowledging the crimes of the past could South Africans begin to heal from them.

Even before it convened, the TRC faced criticism from suspected perpetrators as well as victims' groups. Survivors and the families of victims brought two separate lawsuits in hopes of retaining the right to bring criminal or civil charges against those who had tortured or murdered their relatives. Another legal challenge came from police and security officials fearful of being named in the proceedings. In addition, many white South Africans believed that the TRC would be biased toward the ANC and its supporters, and would end up a "witch hunt," seeking only to humiliate and destroy the reputations of those who had served in the former government.

In fact, Tutu and his associates questioned both former police officers and former ANC officials, although many were suspicious of the controversial blanket amnesty that the TRC granted to 37 ANC leaders. The TRC heard testimony that at last confirmed the details of the torture and murder of Steve Biko, an antiapartheid leader and important figure in the Black Consciousness movement. It also called on Winnie Madikizela-Mandela, Nelson Mandela's former wife, to explain her role in the deaths of Soweto youths accused of being government informants. Beyond such high-profile cases, the TRC heard from thousands of ordinary South Africans. Their tales of beatings, torture, rape, murder, and burial in unmarked graves have left many, including Tutu – who often broke down and cried from the bench – stunned at the extent of apartheid's brutality.

The degree of cooperation by former government officials varied. Dirk Coetzee, a white police officer who was sheltered by the ANC after threatening to expose high-level orders to murder antiapartheid activists, was among the first to testify. Coetzee said that he did not expect forgiveness for his crimes. Others, such as former president F. W. De Klerk, denied that torture and murder were the result of official government orders. Tutu later apologized to De Klerk for implying, during the latter's appearance before him, that this was a lie. De Klerk's predecessor, P. W. Botha, faced contempt of court charges in 1998 for refusing to appear before the TRC, which he characterized as "a circus."

As the TRC's work progressed, some of its initial plans changed. While early guidelines called for symbolic memorials in the name of victims, by the fall of 1997 the TRC had recommended that financial reparation be offered as well. The move came in response to criticism that the TRC, while granting amnesty to criminals, was slighting apartheid's victims, many of whom had been left disabled or impoverished. It was estimated that the government would spend between 500 million and a billion dollars compensating more than 10,000 victims, an action that, Tutu says, "will be an acknowledgment that something happened and [that] the nation is saying sorry."

Despite pressure from both sides, the TRC has shown unflinching independence in its pursuit of the truth. When reports came that witnesses were prepared to offer testimony about secret weapons' research and development, President Mandela, fearing international publicity, asked Tutu to hold private hearings on the matter. Tutu ruled that, while the government was entitled to legal representation, such hearings would go forward in public. On the eve of its report, in October 1998, the TRC faced lawsuits from both former president De Klerk and the ANC leadership. De Klerk objected to being implicated in a series of bombings in the 1980s, while the ANC opposed one section of the report, leaked before its publication, that charged the liberation movement with human rights abuses.

In the end, the report criticized both the apartheid-era government, the ANC, and the other opposition movements, but reserved its strongest condemnation for the state, calling it "the primary perpetrator of gross violations of human rights in South Africa and, from 1974, in southern Africa." While Tutu said he had been "appalled at the evil" revealed before the commission, he also professed gratitude at being able to help "heal a traumatized and wounded people." The TRC was expected to continue investigating individual amnesty requests in 1999.

Kate Tuttle

See Also

Antiapartheid Movement; Biko, Stephen; Mandela, Nelson Rolihlahla; Soweto, South Africa; Black Consciousness in Africa; Botha, Pieter Willem; Tutu, Desmond Mpilo; De Klerk, Frederik Willem; Human Rights in Africa.

North America

Truth, Sojourner (b. 1797?, Ulster County, N.Y.; d. November 26, 1883, Battle Creek, Mich.), African American abolitionist, women's rights advocate, and religious visionary.

Sojourner Truth was one of the best-known black women of her time, rivaled only by Harriet Tubman, yet her life remains surrounded by mystery. Truth, who was illiterate, left no written record apart from her autobiographical *Narrative of Sojourner Truth*, dictated to Olive Gilbert in the late 1840s. Much of what we know about her was reported or perhaps invented by others. More so than Frederick Douglass, her prolifically autobiographical contemporary, Truth has been transformed into myth. Feminists emphasize her challenge to restrictive Victorian codes of femininity; Marxist historians proclaim her solidarity with the working class. Her spirit has been invoked on American college campuses in struggles to create African American and women's studies programs. Yet most interpretations of Truth fail to understand the centrality of her evangelical religious faith.

In their writings both Harriet Beecher Stowe and Douglass recount a central illustration of Truth's faith, which occurred at a protest gathering in Boston's Faneuil Hall after the passage of the Fugitive Slave Act of 1850. Truth sat in the front row, listening to Douglass speak. Events had led him to abandon the nonviolent approach of moral suasion, and he exhorted Southern slaves to take up arms and free themselves. Truth accepted his frustration, but not his loss of faith in God's justice. In a voice that carried throughout the hall, she asked a single question: "Frederick, is God dead?"

By Truth's own account this empowering faith came to her in a moment of divine inspiration after long and traumatic experiences under slavery, which included beatings by her master, John Dumont, and, according to Truth's biographer, Nell Irvin Painter, sexual abuse by his wife. Religion lay at the heart of Truth's transformation from victimized slave to powerful and charismatic leader. Her decision to take the name Sojourner Truth was, in fact, the culmination of a long process of self-remaking.

Born around 1797 in Ulster County, New York, 133 km (80 mi) north of New York City, she was the next to youngest of 10 or 12 children, and her parents, James and Elizabeth Baumfree, named her Isabella. Her slave parents were Dutch speaking, and Isabella first spoke Dutch. Isabella belonged to a series of slave owners, including, from 1810 to 1827, Dumont. When Isabella was about 14, she married Thomas, an older slave owned by Dumont. Between about 1815 and 1826 they had four children, Diana, Peter, Elizabeth, and Sophia, and perhaps a fifth who died.

During 1826 and 1827 Isabella had a series of life-changing experiences. After her son Peter was illegally sold and taken to Alabama, she successfully sued for his return with the help of local Quakers. She also joined the Methodist church after a profound conversion experience recounted in her *Narrative:* "God revealed himself..." with all the suddenness of a flash of lightning, showing her that he pervaded the universe – "and that there was no place where God was not." Her conversion led her to a lifelong involvement in predominantly white communes and fringe religions as well as to the reform activism for which she is better known. When New York abolished slavery in 1827, Isabella gained her freedom and traveled to New York City, taking Peter and leaving her daughters with their father.

In the city Isabella did housework for a living and attended both the African Methodist

During the 1840s and 1850s Sojourner Truth (1797?-1883) was a prominent abolitionist speaker and an outspoken advocate of women's rights. This photograph, dating from between 1864 and 1870, shows Truth in her preferred garb of Quaker plain dress. *National Portrait Gallery, Smithsonian Institution/Art Resource, NY*

Episcopal Zion Church and a white Methodist church. She also began preaching at camp meetings, honing her oratorical skills and learning how to hold an audience. She became a follower of the self-proclaimed white prophet Matthias (Robert Matthews), joining his messianic commune from 1832 until its dissolution in scandal three years later. Little is known of the next several years of her life, although she evidently came under the influence of the Millerites, followers of William Miller, who calculated from biblical prophecies that the world would end in 1843.

In that year Isabella made a complete break with her past, took the name she believed that God had given her – Sojourner Truth – and preached at Millerite gatherings in New York, Connecticut, and Massachusetts. By December, however, with the Millerite prophecy unfulfilled, she joined the Northampton Association, a white utopian community in Florence, Massachusetts. This community, embracing the most advanced ideas of social reform, opened new vistas for Truth. It was there that she first met Douglass and William Lloyd Garrison, and began speaking on social reform as well as religious salvation. Although the Northampton Association broke up in 1846, Truth remained in Florence until she moved ten years later to live among spiritualist Progressive Friends in Battle Creek, Michigan, a Seventh-Day Adventist community.

Truth insisted on the need to include black and working women in any vision of social reform, grounding her speeches in her own experience as a black woman and former slave. She earned a reputation for oratorical power and a ready wit, as seen in the best-known speech of her career, delivered at an 1851 women's rights convention in Akron, Ohio. As reported at the time by Marius Robinson, editor of the Salem, Ohio, *Anti-Slavery Bugle*, Truth spoke proudly of her own strength and accomplishments, and by implication those of all women: "I have plowed and reaped and husked and chopped and mowed, and can any man do more than that?.... And how came Jesus into the world? Through God who created him and woman who bore him. Man, where is your part?"

However, Robinson's contemporary report of this speech is far less widely known than a later account by white reformer Frances Dana Gage (1808-1884). In Gage's memorable retelling, Truth punctuated her speech again and again with the emphatic question, "And ain't I a woman?" Scholars have come to doubt the accuracy of Gage's account, which was published 12 years after the event in question. Gage portrayed Truth facing down a hostile crowd dominated by male skeptics of women's rights and female advocates of sharply distinct gender roles. American scholar Nell Painter argues that this verbal confrontation was Gage's own dramatic invention. In rendering Truth's words, Gage employed a nearly unreadable dialect that reflected contemporary literary conventions about black speech far more than it did Truth's own voice. And Painter believes that Truth probably never uttered the line that has become central to her historical image.

Although her subsequent career is less widely known, Truth continued her reform activism. During the Civil War she journeyed to Washington, D.C., and met President Abraham Lincoln. From 1864 to 1868 she worked with the private National Freedmen's Relief Association and the federal Freedmen's Bureau, assisting freed slaves. In the 1870s Truth participated in the American Woman Suffrage Association. She also championed a proposal to allot Kansas lands to destitute former slaves, making her last major speaking tour in a fruitless effort to rally support. When thousands of Southern blacks, known as the Exodusters, actually moved to Kansas in 1879, Truth applauded them and offered her assistance. She returned from Kansas in 1880 and lived with her daughters in Battle Creek until her death.

James Clyde Sellman

See Also
Slavery in the United States; Boston, Massachusetts; Bureau of Refugees, Freedmen and Abandoned Lands; Civil War, American; Fugitive Slave Laws; New York, New York; Tubman, Harriet Ross.

Africa

Tsetse Fly, any of several species of bloodsucking flies that feed on humans and animals and transmit *Trypanosomiasis,* which causes sleeping sickness in humans and nagana in cattle. This fly has had great influence on population and farming practices in Africa.

Tsetse flies make up the family Muscidae in the order Diptera. The South African tsetse fly is classified as *Glossina palpalis*. The tsetse fly that transmits Rhodesian sleeping sickness and nagana is classified as *Glossina morsitans.* Tsetses are found abundantly in forests and along the edges of lakes and rivers in central and coastal West Africa. The adult flies, which are about 2.5 cm (1 in) long, are brown above and brown with yellow stripes or spots below. The female periodically produces one full-size larva and buries it in the ground or among decayed leaves, where it metamorphoses into an adult fly.

Tsetse flies transmit the parasitic protozoan known to produce the often fatal disease *Trypanosomiasis*, or sleeping sickness. The parasites are drawn into the body of the fly with the blood sucked from an infected person and, after a period of development, can be conveyed to the bloodstream of healthy victims. African sleeping sickness gradually attacks the nervous system, starting with an accelerated heartbeat, enlarged spleen, and fever, followed during the next several months by mood changes, lack of appetite, sleepiness, coma, and often death. Sleeping sickness has had a profound effect on population distribution in Africa. Between 1902 and 1930 sleeping sickness struck an area of Uganda near Lake Victoria, killing 30,000 people and leaving the area sparsely settled.

The tsetse fly also shaped the history of African agriculture and pastoralism. Because cattle and horses are both vulnerable to sleeping sickness (known as "nagana" in animals), agrarian societies in vast areas of the continent have been unable to depend on the use of livestock for draught power or fertilizer, and have had to rely instead on labor-intensive hoe cultivation. The range of nomadic pastoral societies has also been circumscribed by tsetse fly prevalence. Not surprisingly, the elimination of nagana is a high priority for veterinary researchers in Africa.

Robert Fay

See Also
Population Growth in Sub-Saharan Africa.

Africa

Tshombe, Moise-Kapenda (b. 1919; d. 1969, Algeria), Republic of the Congolese politician, president of the secessionist state of Katanga (1960-1963) and prime minister of the Congo (former Zaire) (1964-1965).

Born in Musumba, the son of a wealthy businessman and descendant of Lunda rulers, Moise-Kapenda Tshombe was trained as an accountant under Belgian rule. When the Congo attained independence in 1960, he turned to politics, emerging as a spokesman for decentralization. In July 1960, supported by Belgian mining interests, he declared Katanga independent. The secession was crushed by early 1963, and Tshombe went into exile, having previously displayed to the world his formidable political shrewdness. Recalled by President Joseph Kasavubu in 1964, Tshombe served as prime minister until exiled following a military coup in November 1965. The victim of a plane hijacking in 1967, he landed in Algeria, where he was held under arrest until his death.

See Also
Congo, Democratic Republic of the.

Africa

Tsimihety, ethnic group of Madagascar.

The Tsimihety primarily inhabit northern Madagascar. They speak Malagasy, a Malayo-Polynesian language (*see* Ethnicity in Madagascar). More than 700,000 people consider themselves Tsimihety.

Africa

Tsiranana, Philibert (b. 1910; d. 1978), president of the First Republic of Madagascar.

While attending the University of Montpellier in France, Philibert Tsiranana, an ethnic Tsimihety, formed the Union des Etudiants Malgaches in reaction to the Merina-dominated Association des Etudiants d'Origine Malgache. The Merina had historically dominated precolonial Madagascar and the non-Merina population, also known collectively as *côtiers* or *déshérités,* feared continued subjugation at the hands of Merina rulers. These ethnic and political divisions would shape Tsiranana's political career.

When Tsiranana returned to Madagascar in 1950, he became a schoolteacher in Majuna and took up local politics, joining the Parti des Deshérités de Madagascar. In 1956 he returned to France to represent his district in the French National Assembly, where he also joined the French Socialist Party. Later that year Tsiranana returned to Madagascar and formed the Parti Social Démocrate (PSD), an anti-Merina political party favoring close ties to France over immediate independence. In 1957 he was elected vice president of the Loi-Carde Government Council, created to provide French colonies in Africa greater autonomy.

Tsiranana was elected president of a semi-autonomous Madagascar within the French Union in May 1959. Full independence was granted in 1960. For the ten years that followed, Tsiranana embraced market economic principles and took a staunch anticommunist stance. Although his political rivals labeled him a puppet of French interests, he was credited with an ability to compromise and a sensitivity to ethnic concerns. At first Tsiranana's administration generally abided by democratic principles, allowing a free press, permitting political opposition, and maintaining an autonomous judicial system. While Madagascar remained one of the poorest nations in the world, from 1960 to 1965 the Malagasy economy performed relatively well: unemployment fell, inflation stabilized at reasonable levels, and budget deficits were tolerable. A popular vote confirmed Tsiranana's position as president in 1965.

By the late 1960s, however, the economy had deteriorated significantly and Tsiranana faced opposition on several fronts. In 1970 Tsiranana suffered from a stroke and subsequently spent several months hospitalized in Paris. Following rebellions in the south, Tsiranana attempted to reestablish control by holding elections in which he was the only candidate. Despite receiving 99 percent of the vote, his political legitimacy was undermined. Civil unrest continued to intensify, culminating in the May 1972 Revolution, when student strikes escalated into a full civil revolt. Lacking popular or military support, Tsiranana was forced to relinquish power to Gen. Gabriel Ramanantsoa.

Although he remained involved in Malagasy politics, Tsirnana never again held office. He died in 1978.

Ari Nave

See Also
African Socialism.

Africa

Tsonga (also known as the Thonga), ethnic group of southern Africa.

The Tsonga primarily inhabit southern Mozambique and northern South Africa. Some also live in Zimbabwe. They speak a Bantu language and are related to the Shona people. Approximately 4 million people consider themselves Tsonga.

See Also
Bantu: Dispersion and Settlement.

Africa

Tswana, ethnic group of Botswana, Namibia, and South Africa numbering around 5 million people.

During the eleventh or twelfth century the ancestors of the Tswana settled on the rolling plains around the Vaal River in what is now the South African province of Transvaal. They tended livestock, mostly cattle, and grew crops such as MILLET and sorghum. They were seminomadic and did not privately own land, but measured wealth in terms of cattle. Clan chiefs maintained their wealth and authority by collecting tribute, and in turn loaned parts of their vast royal herds to peasant farmers for milk and breeding purposes.

By 1800 Tswana territory extended into parts of present-day eastern Botswana but still lay mostly to the south. That changed in the 1820s, during the time of warfare known as the MFECANE, when the NDEBELE, fleeing ZULU aggression, invaded the Transvaal region and began raiding Tswana and SOTHO settlements. Many Tswana fled into the KALAHARI DESERT, where the inhospitable climate of sparse rainfall and extreme temperature changes deterred the Ndebele from pursuing them further. By the mid-1830s the Ndebele had continued northward into what is now ZIMBABWE, and the refugee Tswana clans resettled in the more arable lands near the Limpopo, one of the region's only perennial rivers. Nineteenth-century European explorers and missionaries were surprised to encounter the Tswana's large settlements, where up to 20,000 people lived in villages composed primarily of cylindrical mud dwellings with conical thatched roofs.

Although the Tswana language is closely related to other Sotho languages, most Tswana do not identify themselves as Sotho. Today the Tswana are the largest ethnic group in Botswana and dominate that country politically. The Tswana of Botswana are divided into more than 50 "tribes," defined by membership in a lineage traced through the male line. The Tswana are also divided into numerous animal-totem groups that cut across tribal lines. Particularly in Botswana, Tswana groups may include members of non-Tswana ethnic origin. South Africa's APARTHEID regime created a separate "homeland," called Bophuthatswana, for that country's Tswana. However, this state never achieved international recognition. During the 1990s South Africa's majority government dissolved the homeland, and its Tswana residents are now South African citizens.

Traditionally, Tswana women farm maize, sorghum, and millet for subsistence, and men spend much of their time herding livestock. Many men now also migrate to industrial areas, where they are often employed as wage laborers in mines. As the cash economies of Botswana and South Africa have grown, increasing numbers of Tswana have given up traditional rural life for wage labor in towns. Likewise, most Tswana have abandoned traditional religious beliefs for Christianity, though some elements of ancestral worship remain.

Ari Nave

SEE ALSO
Christianity: Missionaries in Africa.

Africa

Tuareg, ethnic group of NIGER, MALI, BURKINA FASO, ALGERIA, and LIBYA.

Often called "the blue people" because of the color that the indigo dye of their clothing leaves on their skin, the Tuareg are a seminomadic people who live in the western and southwestern regions of the Sahara and in the SAHEL. Known to Greek and Roman scholars as the "veiled Sanhadja," the Tuareg claim descent from the Berbers of North Africa and are believed to have migrated southward during Arab invasions of North Africa in the seventh century C.E. These migrants eventually developed several political confederations, called *kels,* all of them affected by caste hierarchies and clan membership, but sharing an adherence to Islam and the use of the Tamacheq language.

Some Tuareg confederations, particularly the Kel Eway and Kel Gress, migrated into the savanna zones of the Sahel. There they combined their traditional pastoralist livelihoods with trans-Saharan trade and sedentary agriculture, allowing them to guard against drought. Beginning around the eleventh century, to assure an adequate agricultural labor supply while the Tuareg nobles traveled on long-distance trade journeys, these confederations conducted raids on communities to the south, acquiring slaves, serfs, and tribute states, which made payments in crops such as MILLET.

By the fifteenth century Tuareg society recognized numerous categories of status and caste. These included *iklan* (slaves), the *irewelen* (descendants of *iklan*), and the *imrad* (tribute-paying clients), as well as the Tuareg nobles – fair-skinned nomads who called themselves the *imageren* (Arabic for "the proud and free"). Most slaves, once captured, were traded to another federation to reduce the chances of escape. The slaves were then assimilated into Tuareg society, cultivating palms, vegetables, and grains on their owner's land and sometimes accompanying trade caravans. Although subordinate to the nobles, the iklan were generally considered part of the family, and both loyalty and marriage offered opportunities for social mobility.

At this time Tuareg confederations had established control over several important trans-Saharan trade routes. In the face of increasing external pressure from the HAUSA, FULANI, and SOKOTO CALIPHATE, Tuareg nobles attempted to forge a more centralized kingdom. The leaders of several kels established a sultanate based in Agadez, a city in present-day Niger. Although the Tuareg were then able to dominate much of the southern Sahara, acquiring control of important trade centers such as Gao and Tombouctou (Timbuktu), they never established the kind of enduring centralized authority structures that were forged by neighboring groups such as the Kanuri-Bornu and HAUSA. This was in part due to their preference for nomadic rather than sedentary living, a preference that later put the Tuareg in direct opposition to both colonial and postcolonial governments.

Beginning in 1900 the colonial governments of French West Africa began a relentless campaign to relocate the Tuareg and other nomads into agricultural villages. They also imposed taxes on the trans-Saharan trade caravans and confiscated camels from the Tuareg to use for their own desert military campaigns. In addition, the prohibition of slavery deprived many Tuareg communities of vital sources of labor and food. The resulting economic decline, coupled with a series of devastating droughts in the 1910s, rallied the Tuareg into rebellion. Throughout the next 12 years the French and Tuareg attempted to undermine each other by filling in wells, destroying crops, and stealing animals and supplies from sedentary farmers, actions that ultimately destroyed much of Tuareg farmland. By 1922 many Tuareg groups sought refuge in non-French colonies, such as NIGERIA and Libya, though most returned home after the French West African colonies became independent in the early 1960s.

In recent years the Tuareg have been involved in a series of conflicts with national governments. Beginning in the 1970s, Niger and Mali both started mining for uranium in territory that had traditionally been claimed by the Tuareg. Displaced and suffering from ongoing drought, Tuareg groups began attacking towns for supplies. In Mali these attacks were met with violent military repression. Many groups attempted to flee the area, but were turned back from Niger, and forced to settle in refugee camps until the drought subsided.

In the early 1990s Tuareg in Niger rebelled after the government failed to fund promised Tuareg relocation projects. Conflict spread across the Sahel into Mali, as Tuareg separatist groups demanded the creation of an all-Tuareg Saharan Republic. Although fighting subsided after peace pacts in the mid-1990s, many wonder how long the Tuareg's customary nomadic ways can survive. Economic necessity has already made many Tuareg permanent fixtures in cities such as Ouagadougou, Niamey, and Bamako, where they make a living selling leather goods to tourists.

Elizabeth Heath

SEE ALSO
Bamako, Mali; Berber; Colonial Rule; Drought and Desertification; Kanuri; Languages, African: An Overview; Niamey, Niger; Ouagadougou, Burkina Faso; Pastoralism; Sahara Desert; Tombouctou, Mali; Islam and Tradition: An Interpretation; Slavery in Africa.

Latin America and the Caribbean

Tubby, King (b. Osbourne Ruddock, Kingston, Jamaica, 1941; d. Kingston, Jamaica, 1989), a skilled sound engineer who pioneered DUB reggae in JAMAICA.

King Tubby gained prominence in 1968 for playing his instrumental mixes accompanied by the crowd-pleasing "talk-over" deejaying of U-Roy (Ewart Beckford). The duo was known as Tubby's Hi-Fi and became highly popular in the impoverished Watertown section of Kingston where Tubby lived. U-Roy's verbal wordplay provided a perfect compliment to Tubby's increasingly experimental song versions. Using homemade and modified studio equipment, Tubby started dropping in vocal snippets, adding ghostly layers of echo and reverberation, soloing various instruments, inserting sudden silences, and employing unusual equalization and other studio effects. Crowds loved the soulful roots REGGAE mutated by technical wizardry and avant-garde mixing approaches. Following Tubby's lead, many musicians and engineers began dubbing.

By 1972 dub fever had arrived. Fierce competition between sound systems kept creative pressures high, although King Tubby remained on top. In 1976 police attempted to shut down a dance at Tubby's Hi-Fi by shooting and axing his speakers on claims that his music attracted a hostile crowd. Dub's largest buying audience was the urban poor, and middle- and upper-class Jamaicans sought to suppress the form for being "rough" and "uncouth."

King Tubby turned to training studio apprentices in the 1980s as dub's popularity waned. Tubby's ideas and techniques have influenced a new generation of electronic musicians who value dub's aggressive re-invention and studio science. Dozens of dub albums feature King Tubby's mixing skills, and contemporary interest has fueled a steady stream of rereleases, such as the superlative *Glen Brown and King Tubby: Termination Dub* and *King Tubby and Soul Syndicate: Freedom Sounds in Dub.*

Jace Clayton

See Also

Kingston, Jamaica.

North America

Tubman, Harriet Ross (b. 1820?, Dorchester County, Md.; d. March 10, 1913, Auburn, N.Y.), African American abolitionist who escaped from slavery and returned repeatedly to the South to lead other slaves to freedom.

Slave Life

Harriet Tubman was born on Maryland's eastern shore, one of 11 children of Harriet Greene and Benjamin Ross, both slaves. As a child she was called Araminta but later defiantly took her mother's first name. (Slaves were often forbidden to form such public attachments.) At a young age Tubman worked in her owner's house as well as in other households to which she was rented. As a teenager she worked in the fields, gaining strength and endurance. Still in her teens, she shielded a slave who was fleeing his owner. The owner hurled a two-pound weight at the runaway that missed and struck Tubman on the head, nearly killing her. For the rest of her life she was prone to sudden sleeping spells, dizziness, and headaches, and bore a deep gash.

In 1844 she married John Tubman, a free black man. Shortly after their marriage, she hired a lawyer to trace her mother's history as a slave. The lawyer discovered records showing that her mother had been briefly free because an earlier owner had died without making provision for her. Apparently, nobody told Harriet Greene that she was free, and a short while later she was returned to slavery. This discovery haunted Tubman. When Tubman's owner died in 1849, she feared that she and members of her family would be sold to the horrible conditions of the Deep South. Resolved to escape, she tried to convince her husband to join her, but he refused. She fled without him, traveling at night and hiding by day until she came to Pennsylvania, a free state.

The Underground Railroad

Tubman went to Philadelphia, where she cleaned and cooked for a living, saving her earnings for a return trip South to bring out other members of her family. In 1850 she made her first covert trip to Baltimore, where she rescued her enslaved sister and two children. Tubman soon became allied with black leader WILLIAM STILL of Philadelphia, white Quaker Thomas Garrett of Wilmington, Delaware, and other activists of the UNDERGROUND RAILROAD. The Railroad was a loose network of abolitionists who arranged for the safe travel from South to North of fugitive slaves, and Tubman became its most successful conductor. In at least 15 trips to the South between 1850 and 1860, she guided more than 200 men, women, and children to freedom, including her own entire family. In 1857 she made perhaps her most remarkable journey, returning to the North with her aging parents.

In her work Tubman carried a gun, not to fend off potential enemies, but to goad fugitives who grew fainthearted or weary and wanted to return. "Live North, or die here," she is said to have told them. She also used drugs to quiet crying babies and employed several disguises. It is believed that all of the slaves in Tubman's care made it safely to the North, despite large bounties offered for her and her charges' capture. After Congress passed the Fugitive Slave Act of 1850, which required Northern states to return escaped slaves, Tubman settled runaways in CANADA, in what is now Ontario. She lived intermittently in Canada, settling with her parents in Auburn, New York, in the late 1850s.

After the Railroad

As Tubman's reputation grew (she was known among blacks and Northern whites as "Moses"), she gained the support and friendship of the day's leading progressives, including Ralph Waldo Emerson, SOJOURNER TRUTH, and Susan B. Anthony. Another supporter, William Seward, the New York senator and United States secretary of state, sold Tubman the land for her Auburn home on generous terms. Among abolitionists Tubman most admired JOHN BROWN, with whom she helped plan the raid on Harpers Ferry in 1859. She failed to join Brown in the raid only because of illness, and she grieved deeply at his hanging. In 1860 she undertook her most public rescue when she led a crowd in Troy, New York, to free a fugitive slave who was being returned to the South.

During the Civil War Northern officials asked Tubman to help the Union Army. She traveled to South Carolina, where she served as liaison between the army and newly freed blacks, whom she schooled in self-sufficiency. Tubman also nursed wounded soldiers, organized and trained scouts, and helped lead a raid against Confederate troops. Although she received commendation from officers, she received no pay. After the war Tubman returned to Auburn to care for her parents. Though poor and illiterate herself, she devoted her time to raising money for the education of former slaves, gathering clothes for poor children, and helping former slaves who were too old for manual labor. Eventually, she converted her house to a home for the old and poor. (With the help of Auburn's AFRICAN METHODIST EPISCOPAL ZION CHURCH, the Harriet Tubman Home for Aged and Indigent Colored People was formally opened in 1908.)

In 1869 Tubman married a former slave and Union army veteran, Nelson Davis. Also in 1869 Tubman's friend Sarah Bradford published a brief biography of her (later expanded), some of the proceeds of which supported Tubman and her causes. Prominent friends tried for two decades to convince the government to give Tubman a pension for her wartime services; failing this, they succeeded in 1890 in gaining her a small veteran's pension as Davis's widow. Tubman spent many of her later years working on behalf of women's suffrage.

See Also

Slavery in the United States; Abolitionism in the United States; Baltimore, Maryland; Civil War, American; Free Blacks in the United States, 1619 to 1863; Fugitive Slave Laws; Fugitive Slaves;

Africa

Tubman, William Vacanarat Shadrach (b. Nov. 29, 1895, Harper, Liberia; d. July 23, 1971, London, England), president of LIBERIA (1944-1971), often called the maker of modern Liberia.

Born in Harper, Liberia of Americo-Liberian descent, Tubman was trained as a preacher and lawyer. Having served as a county attorney and trial judge, he was elected to the Liberian Senate (1923), where he remained (though not uninterruptedly) until 1937; he then became associate justice of the Liberian Supreme Court. The candidate of the ruling True Whig Party, he was elected president in 1943 and assumed office in 1944. During his 27 years as president he made some attempts to bring African men into government and give them, as well as women, a legal status equal to that of the Americo-Liberian elite. To improve the living standard in Liberia, he followed an open-door economic policy, which opened the country to extensive foreign investment, while externally acting as a United States ally and moderate. Tubman sponsored the 1961 conference of African heads of state to promote continental cooperation. He was also an outspoken opponent of white rule in Africa (*see* Colonial Rule).

See Also
Americo-Liberians.

Africa

Tugen (also known as Kamasya), ethnic group of Kenya.

The Tugen primarily inhabit Rift Valley Province in west central Kenya. They speak a Nilo-Saharan language and are one of the Kalenjin peoples. More than 200,000 people consider themselves Tugen.

See Also
Languages, African: An Overview.

Africa

Tukulor, Fulani-speaking ethnic group of Senegal, Mali, Guinea, and Mauritania.

The Tukulor are a Fulani-speaking ethnic group who, traditionally, are sedentary agricultural farmers of the Futa Toro region in Senegal. Historically they have a special commitment to Islam: the partly Tukulor ruling classes of the kingdom of Tekrur converted to Islam in the eleventh century, and the Tukulor claim with pride to be the first black Africans to embrace Islam.

Despite their conversion, Tukulor traditional religious beliefs in spirits, witches, and ghosts (*see* African Religions: An Interpretation) remain powerful. There are five castes in traditional Tukulor society. In descending order by status they are the *Torobe,* or aristocratic Islamic scholars and leaders; the *Rimbe,* or farmers, traders, and administrators who also act as warriors; the *Nyenbe,* or craftsworkers; the *Gallunkobe,* meaning freedpeople or descendants of slaves; and the *Matyube,* or slaves.

In the nineteenth century many Tukulor, inspired by the dynamic religious leader Al-Hajj Umar Tal joined the purist Islamic Sufi order, the Tijaniyah. Al-Hajj Umar Tal mobilized his mostly Tukulor followers in a *jihad* (Islamic holy war) in 1854 against the Bambara states of Ségu and Kaarta. After conquering these states, Umar founded the vast Tukulor Empire in 1864, centered at Ségu and encompassing most of present-day Mali. The Bambara of Ségu never completely surrendered to Tukulor rule; Tukulor power was weak and confined mostly to the towns and major villages. Umar died in 1864, leaving his empire to his sons. Mustafa ruled from 1864 to 1870, when Ahmadu took over, but under the reign of both sons the empire slowly disintegrated as local leaders rebelled against the ruling dynasty. Invading French colonial troops forced Ahmadu to flee, and in 1891 the empire fell to the French.

Because the Torobe control disproportionate amounts of land, and because the lower castes own very little, during the twentieth century many lower-caste Tukulor have given up agriculture for wage labor in the cities. In 1990 there were roughly 750,000 Tukulor spread across West Africa.

Leyla Keough

See Also
Sufism; Islam and Tradition: An Interpretation.

North America

Tulsa Riot of 1921, white riot that devastated some 40 city blocks in the mostly black Greenwood district of Tulsa, Oklahoma.

The growth of the oil industry made Tulsa, Oklahoma, a rich town by 1921. Its predominantly black section, Greenwood, achieved a level of wealth that earned it a reputation as the "Negro Wall Street of America." African Americans constituted about 12 percent of the overall population. Whites reacted violently to the success of African Americans – forming "whipping parties" that randomly assaulted blacks on a daily basis. There had also been several lynchings in the vicinity of Tulsa, a major Ku Klux Klan center, and blacks armed themselves for protection. The riot of 1921 was the culmination of these racial tensions.

In 1921 a 19-year-old black man named Dick Rowland took a break from his downtown job as a shoe shiner to use the restroom at the top of a nearby building. Sarah Page, a 17-year-old white girl who was operating the elevator there, claimed that Rowland assaulted her. Rowland was arrested the following day and incarcerated at the local courthouse.

Before the incident had been investigated, the May 31 Tulsa *Tribune* reported that Rowland, who was identified only by his color, "attacked [Page], scratching her hands and face, and tearing her clothes off." That evening a crowd of whites began to gather outside the courthouse in response to the paper's assertion that Rowland was going to be lynched.

The sheriff tried unsuccessfully to disperse the crowd, which by 10:30 pm had grown to nearly 2000. A group of 50 to 75 armed black men, who previously had been turned away, returned to the courthouse to help the sheriff defend Rowland. One of the white men tried to disarm one of the blacks, a shot was fired, and the two groups opened fire. Vastly outnumbered, the blacks retreated to Greenwood. Whites who did not have arms stole them from hardware stores and pawnshops and headed for the Frisco Railroad tracks, the boundary line that separated the black and white communities. Around 1:00 am on June 1st, warfare resumed.

After several drive-by shootings, whites invaded the Greenwood district in force around 6:00 am and began to burn houses and businesses. They shot at the fleeing blacks, whom they sometimes threw back into the flames. Blacks were largely outnumbered and, during the rioting, police worked continuously to disarm them. When the National Guard arrived at 9:15 am the gunfire had diminished, and the Guard began to help the police round up and place African Americans in holding areas, which were manned by armed guards. Approximately 6000 blacks – half of Tulsa's African American population – were reported to have been incarcerated during the riot.

By 11:30 am violence had ceased, and the Red Cross had arrived to provide medical treatment to the injured blacks. In the following week the Red Cross treated 531 persons and operated on an additional 163. They also erected 350 tents for African Americans whose homes had been destroyed, and they continued to administer aid through the late fall of 1921. Records kept by the Red Cross estimate that 1115 houses and businesses belonging to black people had been burned down, and that another 314 had been looted; that 715 families left Tulsa, some of whom returned after the riot; and that 300 people died, of whom only a small percentage were white. Historical sources disagree about these statistics.

In the midst of Red Cross relief efforts Tulsa's white authorities announced to the nation that they would assume the responsibility of rebuilding Greenwood, and that additional external assistance would not be accepted. The white community, however, abandoned the reconstruction project and tried unsuccessfully to prevent African Americans from rebuilding on their own land. Because the city's white officials delayed their reconstruction efforts, 1000 black Tulsans spent the winter of 1921-1922 in tents.

In the end blacks were blamed for inciting the riot by showing up at the courthouse with firearms. No white Tulsans were arrested or jailed. Page refused to prosecute Rowland: follow-up investigation found that Rowland had stumbled into the girl as he was getting off the elevator, and all charges were dropped. Little discussion of the riot occurred before its 75th anniversary on June 1, 1996, when, at a ceremony in Tulsa, African American survivors of the riot addressed the public. Both whites and blacks in Tulsa had avoided serious discussion of the riot until that event.

Aaron Myers

See Also
Lynching.

Africa

Tumbuka (also known as Batumbuka, Matumbuka, and Tumbukwa), ethnic group of southern Africa.

The Tumbuka primarily inhabit northern Malawi and northeastern Zambia. They speak a Bantu language related to that of the Tonga. Approximately two million people consider themselves Tumbuka.

See Also
Bantu: Dispersion and Settlement.

Africa

Tunisia, country in the northwest of Africa.

Tunisia has often been described as an oasis in the desert. The metaphor refers both to the country's natural beauty, which attracts thousands of tourists, and to its political and social climate. Tunisia has promoted itself as a secular, progressive oasis in North Africa, a haven from the troubles of the rest of the Arab world. Indeed, the country has been on the vanguard of Western-inspired reform since the nineteenth century. Yet with growing populist support within the nation for an Islamic party, it is worth noting that Tunisia has never really been isolated from its North African neighbors – neighbors with whom it shares the religion of Islam, and the legacy of Phoenician, Roman, Arab, and European conquest.

From Ancient Metropolis to French Protectorate

The Berber people have maintained a continual presence since the earliest time in the region that is now Tunisia. They were joined, in the first millennium B.C.E., by traders from the Phoenician Empire who established centers along the Mediterranean coast. During the seventh century B.C.E. the city of Carthage developed as an important maritime trade metropolis in an empire that stretched from North Africa to the Iberian Peninsula, Sardinia, and Sicily. The city's diverse population reached about 500,000, including a number of Jews, who first brought monotheism to the region.

During the reign of the Phoenicians many of the formerly pastoral Berber people began to cultivate the plains around Carthage, transforming them into rich farmlands. The leaders

ABOVE RIGHT: A woman weaves a traditional rug in a factory in Tunis. *© J. Brun/Explorer*
RIGHT: A Berber woman looks out from behind a richly colored shawl in Takruna, Tunisia. *CORBIS/ Fulvio Roiter*

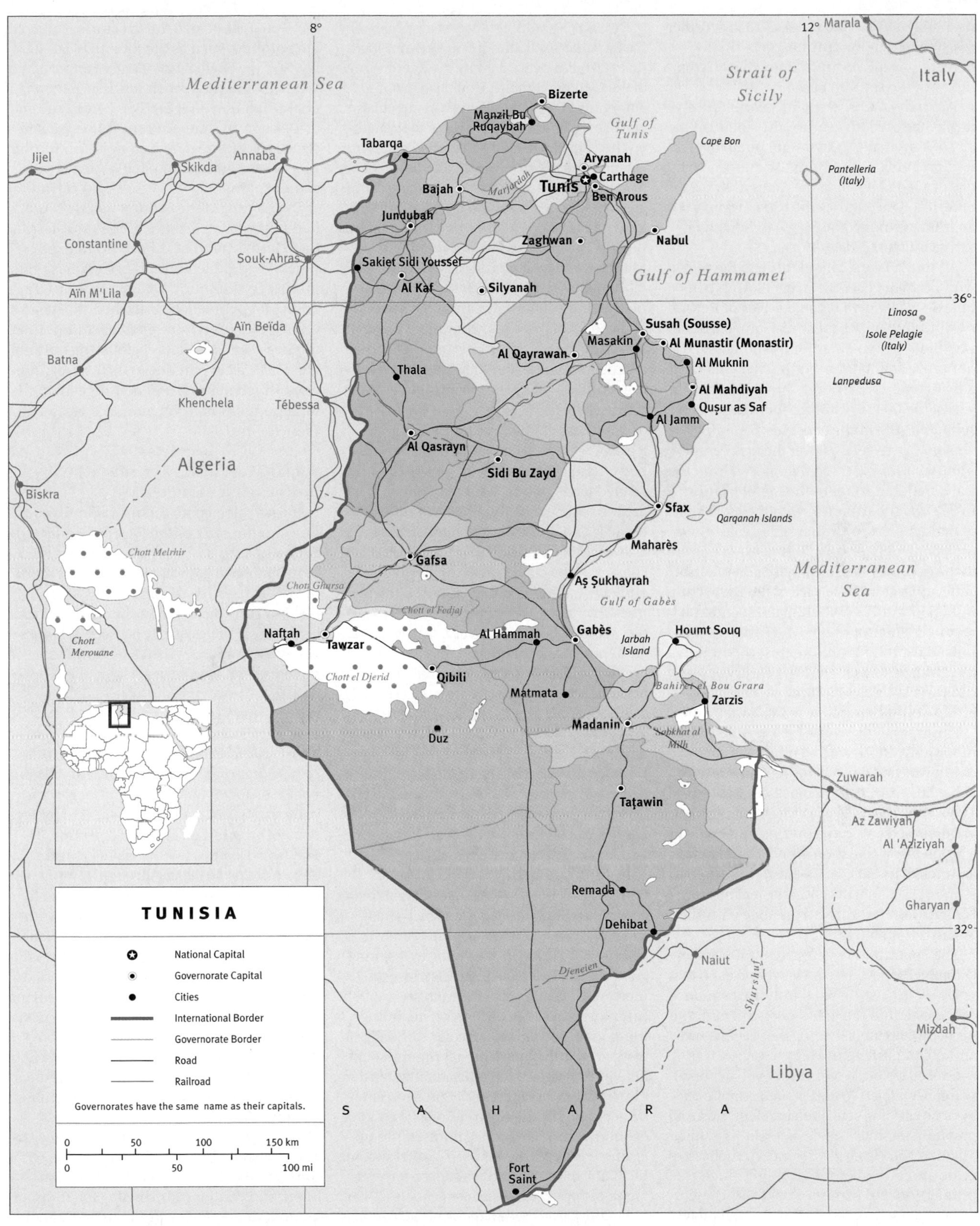

of the Roman Empire saw the advantage of acquiring the fertile region, and beginning in the third century B.C.E. they launched the Punic Wars, finally overcoming the Phoenicians in northern Africa in 146 B.C.E. The victors tore down the conquered city of Carthage, but maintained the region's agriculture to produce wheat, wool, and olive oil for the empire. Once rebuilt Carthage became a center for Christian scholarship and the home of Berber philosopher SAINT AUGUSTINE. Some of the Berber inhabitants converted to Christianity, for the most part joining the Donatist sect.

In general the Berbers resented Roman rule, for the empire had appropriated much of the best land. In the fifth century C.E. disgruntled Berbers assisted the Germanic Vandals as they took Carthage, by then the third most important city of the Roman Empire. A century later the Byzantine army under Emperor Justinian attempted to reestablish Roman rule, but was mostly limited to coastal areas by active Berber resistance. The Byzantines were finally defeated by a BEDOUIN raiding party from EGYPT in the seventh century.

When the Arabs swept into North Africa during the seventh century, they founded the city of Kairouan (Al Qayrawan), south of present-day Tunis, as the cultural center and holy city of a land known to the Arabs as Ifriqiya, or Africa. For centuries the region was part of an Islamic empire, the Maghreb, stretching across much of North Africa.

Although Islam spread through the region with relative ease, the original Arab conquerors in Ifriqiya faced a series of Berber revolts. One of the great resistance leaders was the KAHINA, a Berber queen who led her army against the Arabs, checking their advancement in Ifriqiya for more than ten years. In 800 C.E. Ibrahim ibn Aghlab consolidated rule in the province, founding the Aghlabid Dynasty that over the next century profited from the trade that passed from the trans-Saharan route to the Mediterranean. In 909 C.E. the Fatimids, with the assistance of Berber forces, overthrew this dynasty and took control of Ifriqiya. Basing their empire to the east, they relegated the region to vassal state and left it in the care of the Berber ally Buluggin ibn Ziri. When his descendants revolted a century later, the Fatimids mobilized Arab Bedouins against them. Yet as the Zirids fell in the twelfth century, it was not the Fatimids who took power, but the al-Muwahhid kingdom of the west.

During the thirteenth century the Hafsid monarchy, Berber descendants of the al-Muwahhid Dynasty, rose to power. They shifted the capital from the interior to coastal Tunis, near the ruins of Carthage, signifying an increased emphasis on maritime trade in a region that would soon after become known as Tunisia. In 1534, as the powerful Ottoman Empire cast its shadow over the region, the Hafsids entered into an alliance with the Spanish Hapsburgs.

The Spanish were defeated in 1574 by the Ottoman Empire, assisted by a population that resented Christian rule. Junior Ottoman officers settled the area, mixing in with the Berber inhabitants. During the seventeenth and eighteenth centuries the region was controlled by local governors, deys (later beys), nominally subject to the Ottoman Empire but in fact operating semi-independently. Like all previous regimes the deys, including the Muradid and Husaynid dynasties, emphasized trade and enriched the region through the production and export of olive oil. These dynasties also profited from piracy and protection money extracted from nations trading in the Mediterranean.

In the mid-eighteenth century a series of plagues swept through North Africa, killing Tunisians by the thousands. This population loss, combined with a simultaneous prolonged drought, sent the agricultural economy into crisis.

By the 1830s North Africa was destabilized by the imperial ambitions of FRANCE, which had just seized ALGERIA, and by the death throes of the Ottoman Empire. Hoping to maintain autonomy in the face of European imperialism, Tunisian ruler Ahmad Bey set out to strengthen the Tunisian state through modernization. He modeled his government after European bureaucracies, conscripted peasants for his greatly expanded army and navy, and imposed heavy taxes to pay for both. Under Ahmad Bey Tunisia became the first country in the Islamic world to abolish slavery. His successor, Mohamed Bey, continued reform efforts, instituting the Fundamental Pact, which allowed foreigners to own property, and adopting a civil rights charter. During his regime Mamluk leader Khayr al-Din oversaw the writing of the first constitution in the Islamic world. The document included a declaration of rights, and provisions for a legislative body called the Supreme Council and a secular supreme court. Khair al-Din was elected leader of the Supreme Council.

Some Tunisians opposed the reforms because they saw them as representative of excessive European influence, and pushed for changes more compatible with Islamic law and culture. Many others opposed the high taxes. Provincial leaders and tribal chiefs saw the national constitution as a threat to their autonomy. Although Ahmad Bey hoped that loans from European banks would help build a new nation, the Tunisian economy stagnated as it fell deeper into debt. The situation was exacerbated by erratic spending and massive embezzlement by Prime Minister Mustafa Khaznader. While civil unrest mounted, Tunisia declared bankruptcy in 1869, and an international financial commission consisting of France, GREAT BRITAIN, and ITALY was formed to oversee the monarchy's finances.

In 1873 Khair al-Din, then Tunisian representative to the international financial commission, was elected prime minister. In a last effort to delay foreign intervention, he attempted to boost the economy by restoring guild control in artisan industries, investing more in education, and eradicating corruption from the ranks of government, including the allies of Mustafa Khaznader. Although he worked with the international commission, his efforts to reform the agricultural system led him into direct conflict with European landowners, and his attempt to secure the national economy through grain export set him up against a European-controlled market system. Khair al-Din was unable to avoid the impending catastrophe of foreign intervention.

Enemies from within the Tunisian court who supported Mustafa Khaznader plotted with European consuls to oust Khair al-Din. The French, who vied against Italy and Great Britain for control in the region, occupied the country, using the pretext that some Tunisians had crossed the border into French-controlled Algeria. In 1881 France declared a protectorate over Tunisia with the Bardo Treaty. The protectorate maintained the structures of the old government, such as the monarchical title figure of the bey, but gave France control of the finances and the French resident general final arbitration of all decisions. After crushing an uprising in southern Tunisia, the French signed another treaty tightening its control over the protectorate, and paving the way for settler colonies.

By the turn of the century French settlers had appropriated some of the most fertile farm land, much of it devoted to export vegetable production, and began phosphate mining in the south. Yet compared to the European population in neighboring Algeria, the settlers exercised relatively minor influence over Tunisian religious and cultural life. This was in part due to their small numbers, which never exceeded 7 percent of the total population throughout the period of French control.

SOCIAL MOVEMENTS AND THE INDEPENDENCE STRUGGLE

In the late nineteenth century reformist social movements such as the Western-educated Young Tunisians lobbied for greater Tunisian participation in government and better access to Western-style education. In 1920 the Destour Party demanded a constitutional government ensuring equality between Tunisians and French settlers. When the bey took up the party's cause two years later, the French used the threat of military force to shut down the movement.

In 1934 Habib Bourguiba formed the Neo-Destour Party, an organization that became extraordinarily successful at mobilizing populist support for nationalism. By 1937 the party had 28,000 activists and 49,000 supporters working out of 400 village branches. The Neo-Destour led the way for future decolonizing struggles through acts of civil disobedience, including a general strike in solidarity with nationalist movements in other North African countries. In 1938 the Neo-Destour Party was outlawed, and Bourguiba and other leaders were arrested and deported to France. Four years later, when the Germans occupied both France and Tunisia, Bourguiba was released. Despite his refusal to support the Axis powers, he was allowed to return to Tunis, where he took a leading role in the nationalist struggle emerging in German-occupied Tunisia.

After the war the French returned to power and arrested the bey for collaborating with the Nazis. Bourguiba fled and began an international tour campaigning for Tunisian independence. Following a brief period of liberalism, during which time Bourguiba returned to Tunisia, the nationalist movement gathered militant momentum, and revolutionaries based in the mountains waged a two-year guerrilla campaign. France gradually capitulated, first with the promise for internal autonomy, and later full sovereignty. During this time many French citizens fled the country.

In 1956 Tunisia became an independent constitutional monarchy headed by the last Husainid bey with Bourguiba as president of the National Assembly. The next year the bey was deposed and Bourguiba was elected president of a new republic.

Post-Independence Tunisia

During the first years of the new republic the war for independence in neighboring Algeria strained relations between Tunisia and its former colonial power. France accused Tunisia of siding with Algerian pronationalist forces, and in 1958 bombed the Tunisian village of Saqiyat Sidi Yusuf. A United Nations-mandated cease-fire eventually eased military tension, but France subsequently withdrew all financial aid. In turn Tunisia forged alliances with other Arab countries, especially Saudi Arabia, but maintained its Western orientation.

The 1960s and 1970s were a dynamic period, as the nation followed a path of moderate socialism and campaigns for social justice, women's rights, and education transformed the small country into one of the most literate and progressive in Africa. Bourguiba limited military spending, and allocated most of the national budget to education, agriculture, and health.

Yet popular opinion of Bourguiba and his policies was mixed, and many saw the legal and social reforms as an affront to traditional Islamic law and custom. He put formerly religious schools under secular control, abolished Islamic courts, and even advised workers to break the religious Ramadan fast in order to increase productivity – a suggestion that generated considerable public outrage. Some dissidents also noted that Bourguiba used extreme measures to consolidate his own power and that his tolerance for political opposition faded over the years. After driving his opponents from the Socialist Destour Party, the only legal political party, Bourguiba was named president for life in 1975, at age 72.

The country remained in economic flux during this time. Bourguiba's early emphasis on state intervention gave way to economic liberalization. As the prices of consumer goods rose sharply while wages remained constant, workers organized mass strikes in 1978. Popular discontent, combined with growing support for Islamic parties, generated fears on the part of the administration of a fate similar to that of the rise of Islamic fundamentalism in Algeria. Bourguiba authorized mass arrests of union-based leftists and Islamic fundamentalists.

In 1987 Prime Minister Zine el-Abidine Ben Ali deposed Bourguiba, declaring him mentally unfit. The new president continued efforts to halt the rise of Islam, outlawing the main Islamic party, Al Nahda, in 1991, and arresting or exiling its leaders. Under Ben Ali some 8000 students and activists have been arrested, and human rights observers have accused the government of using detention and torture to quash dissent. At the same time Ben Ali has spearheaded social and economic modernization reforms such as the provision of electricity, running water, and health facilities to impoverished parts of the country. Some have accused Ben Ali of using reforms to undermine popular support for the Islamic movement: women, for example, have been encouraged to take more public roles, but then warned not to observe Islamic tradition by wearing headscarves. The conflicts are familiar ones for Tunisia, a nation that for more than a century has negotiated a path between Western-inspired reform and the religious and cultural legacy of Islam.

Marian Aguiar

See Also

African Socialism; Bourguiba, Habib ibn Ali; Decolonization in Africa: An Interpretation; Jewish Communities in North Africa; Nationalism in Africa; Human Rights in Africa; Islam and Tradition: An Interpretation; Islamic Fundamentalism: An Interpretation.

Africa

Tunisia (Ready Reference)

Official Name: Republic of Tunisia
Area: 163,610 sq km (63,170 sq mi)
Location: Northern Africa, bordering the Mediterranean Sea, Algeria, and Libya
Capital: Tunis (population 674,100 [1994 estimate])
Other Major Cities: Safaqis (Sfax) (population 230,900), Susah (Sousse) (125,000), Bizerte (Bizerta) (98,900) (1994 estimates)
Population: 9,378,000 (1998 estimate)
Population Density: 92 persons per sq km (about 148 persons per sq mi); about 75 percent of the population live in the coastal region
Population Below Age 15: 32 percent (male 1,541,853; female 1,451,035 [1997 estimate])
Population Growth Rate: 1.4 percent (1998 estimate)
Life Expectancy at Birth: Total population: 73.1 years (male 71.72 years; female 74.58 years [1998 estimate])
Infant Mortality Rate: 32.64 deaths per 1000 live births (1998 estimate)
Literacy Rate (age 15 and over who can read and write): Total population: 66.7 percent (male 78.6 percent; female 54.6 percent [1995 estimate])
Education: Education in Tunisia is free, and virtually all eligible children attend primary school. In the early 1990s primary schools had a total enrollment of about 1.4 million pupils, and secondary, technical, and vocational schools, about 567,000.
Languages: Arabic is the official language of Tunisia, but French is used widely, particularly by the educated.
Ethnic groups: Arab-Berber 98 percent, European 1 percent, Jewish 1 percent
Religions: Muslim 98 percent, Christian 1 percent, Jewish 1 percent
Climate: A mild Mediterranean climate prevails in the north of Tunisia, with temperatures averaging 8.9° C (48° F) in January and 25.6° C (78° F) in July; the northern regions have a rainy season that lasts from October to May, with an average annual rainfall of 610 mm (about 24 in). Toward the south the climate becomes progressively hotter and drier, with an annual rainfall of about 200 mm (about 8 in) in the Sahara.
Land, Plants, and Animals: In the north low-lying spurs of the Maritime Atlas Mountains traverse the country, interspersed with fertile valleys and plains. The country's only major river, the Majardah, crosses the region from west to east, emptying into the Gulf of Tunis. To the south a plateau descends gradually to a chain of low-lying salt lakes, known as *shatts,* or *chotts.* On the south the shatts adjoin the Sahara, which constitutes about 40 percent of Tunisia's land area. The regions of the north are characterized by flourishing vineyards and by dense forests of cork oak, pine, and juniper trees. In the extreme south date palms flourish in oases. Among the wildlife are hyena, wild boar, jackal, gazelle, and hare, as well as several varieties of poisonous snakes, including cobras and horned vipers.
Natural Resources: Petroleum, phosphates, iron ore, lead, zinc, and salt
Currency: The Tunisian dinar
Gross Domestic Product (GDP): $56.5 billion (1997 estimate)
GDP per Capita: $6100 (1997 estimate)
GDP Real Growth Rate: 5.6 percent (1997 estimate)
Primary Economic Activities: The Tunisian economy is dominated by agriculture and mining. Tourism is also important, and manufacturing is expanding.
Primary Crops: Wheat, barley, tomatoes, vegetables, melons, grapes, oranges, olives, and dates; sheep, goats, cattle, camels, horses, and poultry; sardines, pilchards, tuna, and whitefish
Industries: Petroleum, mining, tourism, textiles, footwear, food, and beverages
Primary Exports: Hydrocarbons, agricultural products, phosphates, and chemicals
Primary Imports: Industrial goods and equipment, hydrocarbons, food, and consumer goods
Primary Trade Partners: European Union countries, Middle East, Algeria, India, United States, Japan, and Switzerland
Government: According to the constitution of 1959 Tunisia is a free, independent, and sovereign republic. National executive power in Tunisia is exercised by the president, currently Zine El Abidine Ben Ali, who appoints a council of ministers headed by a prime minister, currently Hamed Karoui. Legislative power in Tunisia is vested in the unicameral National Assembly, with 163 members popularly elected to five-year terms. The National Assembly is currently dominated by the Constitutional Democratic Rally Party (RCD; formerly the Destour

Socialist Party). Tunisia is divided into 23 governorates, each headed by a governor who is appointed by the president.

Marian Aguiar

See Also

Sahara Desert; Tunis, Tunisia.

Africa

Tunis, Tunisia, capital city of the North African country of Tunisia.

With a population of more than 1.8 million, the city of Tunis is now the most important political, commercial, and industrial center in Tunisia. This was not always the case, however, for although some historians claim the ancient city was founded by Phoenicians as early as the ninth century B.C.E., for centuries Tunis was overshadowed by other Tunisian cities.

Tunis grew up along the shore of Lake Tunis, about 17 km (10 mi) from the metropolis of Carthage. When the Romans waged war on the Phoenicians during the second century, they made Tunis their base for their attack on Carthage. Victorious, the Romans destroyed both cities in 146 B.C.E.

Although the Romans rebuilt Tunis, the city remained obscured by the importance of Carthage, which by this time was a Christian center. When the Arabs arrived in North Africa in the seventh century, they valued Tunis as a strategic location able to withstand potential naval attacks. Arab leader Hassan ibn Numan also used Tunis as a base for his land-based military campaigns in the region the Arabs called Ifriqiya, including the struggle against the Berber resistance leader the Kahina. Most of the subsequent Arab dynasties ruled from the city of Kairouan, but Tunis also attracted immigrants from the Arab world. An urban elite of government officials, merchants, and scholars flocked to Tunis, including a sizable population of Jews.

When the Berber Hafsids came to power in the thirteenth century, they revived Tunis as a royal city as well as a market town for handling goods passing along the trans-Sahara trade route to the Mediterranean Sea. Accumulating wealth through trade and piracy, the Hafsids built schools, mosques, and fortresses.

During the sixteenth century control of Tunis passed back and forth between the competing powers of Spain and the ultimately victorious Ottoman Empire. Ottoman direct rule was short-lived, however: in 1591 a group of officers in the Ottoman military staged a coup and set up an independent monarchy. The subsequent rulers of Tunis, known as beys, continued maritime raiding until 1816, when the British ended the practice by bombarding the city.

In the nineteenth century European investors financed railways, a telegraph system, and other projects in Tunis. Europeans also settled in the city and along the lake, especially after Tunisia became a French protectorate in 1881.

In 1956 Tunis became the capital of independent Tunisia. Internationally, the city gained prominence when the Arab League moved its headquarters there in 1979; the Palestinian Liberation Organization (PLO), along with several thousand PLO leaders and their families, relocated there in 1982.

Today the city is home to about a fifth of the country's total population. Tunisians have migrated to the city for its schools, hospitals, and employment opportunities. Industrial plants in Tunis produce chemicals – especially superphosphates – processed foods, and textiles, and a shipping channel carries exports of olives, olive oil, carpets, fruit, and iron ore to the Mediterranean Sea. Overall, Tunis produces about one-half of the national industrial output. Amid the new city vestiges of the past remain – including the ruins of a Roman aqueduct, Roman baths, and the eighth-century Mosque of the Olive Tree – making Tunis an increasingly popular tourist destination.

Marian Aguiar

See Also

Sahara Desert; Tourism in Africa.

Africa

Tunjur (or Tungur), ethnic group of eastern Chad and western Sudan.

Although the Tunjur have dwindled in number to around 10,000, they once ruled over a powerful kingdom, Darfur. The excavated palaces and citadels of the Tunjur dot the region today.

The origins of the Tunjur are unclear. Some scholarly sources maintain that they are an indigenous Nilotic group, and not of Arabic origin. Tunjur oral history, in contrast, traces their ancestry to Arabs from Tunisia. During the thirteenth century they apparently peacefully replaced the Daju, a neighboring ethnic group, as rulers of a large kingdom centered around the cities of Uri and Ayn Farah in northern Darfur. The kingdom stretched from Darfur in present-day Sudan to Wadai (Ouaddai) in present-day Chad. During the sixteenth century the Tunjur were themselves overthrown at Darfur by the Keira, a chiefly clan claiming Arab origin who later merged with the region's predominant ethnic group, the Fur. The Tunjur remained in power, however, at Wadai. In the early seventeenth century the Maba expelled the Tunjur from Wadai and installed an Islamic government. Many Tunjur subsequently migrated west to settle in the city of Mao in the Kanem Kingdom. The rise of the Bornu Kingdom frustrated the Tunjurs' renewed attempts at empire building.

Today most Tunjur, who are devout Sunni Muslims, continue to live in Darfur Province, Sudan, and in the Kanem and Wadai prefectures of Chad. Small numbers of Tunjur also live in Nigeria. The Tunjur language is now extinct; most Tunjur speak Fur, Arabic, or Beri. Most cultivate cereal crops, such as millet and sorghum, and dates. Some Tunjur also grow fruits and vegetables in irrigated gardens, while others keep cattle, sheep, and goats.

Ari Nave

See Also

Kanuri; Languages, African: An Overview.

Africa

Tupur (also known as Toupouri, Tuburi, and Tupuri), ethnic group of West Africa.

The Tupur primarily inhabit northern Cameroon, southwestern Chad, and northeastern Nigeria. They speak an Afro-Asiatic language. More than 400,000 people consider themselves Tupur.

See Also

Languages, African: An Overview.

Africa

Turkana, ethnic group of Kenya.

The Turkana inhabit the arid region west of Lake Turkana in northwestern Kenya and regions in neighboring parts of northeastern Uganda. They speak an Eastern Nilotic language. Scholars remain uncertain about the group's origin, but Turkana legend is more colorful: it claims that the people moved to their present homeland by following a lost ox. It is likely that they moved to their present location at least 200 years ago from Uganda, where they separated from the Jie and the Karimojon, who still live there. The Turkana descended the Dodoth escarpment into the Lake Turkana area.

The Turkana have historically been a pastoral society, raising cattle, camels, sheep, goats, and donkeys, all of which provide the majority of their livelihood. The traditional diet of the people comprises meat, milk, butter, ghee, yogurt, and blood – all gotten from their herds. In addition their herds provide bones, skins, and horns for tools and clothing, and serve as bride wealth. To supplement their diet, the Turkana engage in small-scale cultivation (millet and vegetables), fishing, hunting, and gathering.

Traditionally the Turkana establish no permanent settlements and, because they live in areas that regularly receive less than 15 inches of rain per year, they migrate seasonally with their herds in search of water and pasturage. The Turkana, therefore, establish temporary homesteads, including cattle pens and huts constructed of tree branches and palm fronds, in a thorn-fenced enclosure called a *kraal*. A traditional Turkana "camp" contains three or four such enclosures grouped loosely around a common amenity, such as a watering hole.

The basic social unit among the Turkana is an elementary family: a husband, a wife or wives, and their unmarried children. Though traditional Turkana society is based on clans – cattle are given an identifying clan brand – and based loosely on age sets, they do not strictly observe these social conventions. Age-sets have historically functioned only as a method of organizing raiding parties.

Though they number only about 300,000, many Turkana have clung to their traditional way of life in the face of mounting pressures. The British struggled to impose colonial authority in their territory long after establishing their rule in other parts of Kenya. Even as late as 1918, the British military was still trying to subdue the Turkana in a campaign that, while damaging to the people and their herds, did not bring an end to the group's independence. Since the 1950s the Turkana population has tripled. In addition many Turkana have become agriculturists cultivating marginal lands that were historically used for pasture, straining the remaining resources. These changes, combined with a series of droughts in the 1990s and cattle-raiding by rival nomadic groups from Uganda, ETHIOPIA, and the SUDAN, have devastated Turkana herds and made the Turkana dependent on food aid from relief organizations. In addition Kenya's president, DANIEL ARAP MOI, has given oil-drilling concessions in the region to a close associate, Nicholas Biwott. This has exacerbated problems based on the Turkana's land shortage.

A Turkana woman carries a gourd of water on her head in Lokichar, in northern Kenya. *© David Keith Jones/Images of Africa Photobank*

Many observers predict that these factors will ultimately undermine the Turkana's way of life.

Robert Fay

SEE ALSO

Camel; Colonial Rule; Languages, African: An Overview; Great Britain; Pastoralism.

Latin America and the Caribbean

Turks and Caicos Islands, two groups of islands in the North Atlantic Ocean, southeast of the BAHAMAS.

In *The History of Mary Prince, A West Indian Slave* (1831), the first female slave narrative from the Americas, MARY PRINCE writes of her experience in the salt mines off Grand Turk Island, where slaves were forced to stand in the water and rake salt from the ocean beds from four in the morning until nightfall every day: "We... worked through the heat of the day; the sun flaming upon our hands like fire, and raising salt blisters in those parts which were not completely covered. Our feet and legs, from standing in the salt water for so many hours, soon became full of dreadful boils, which eat down in some cases to the very bone, afflicting the sufferers with great torment.... Oh that Turk's Island was a horrible place! The people in England, I am sure, have never found out what is carried on there. Cruel, horrible place!"

The sad irony was that the horrible conditions under which Prince labored were enforced by English slaveholders, and their Spanish and French counterparts, for thousands of slaves in the Turks and Caicos Islands throughout the sixteenth and seventeenth centuries. The lucrative salt trade was the mainstay of these islands for several hundred years, and the cost to workers in the salt mines was tremendous.

The Turks and Caicos Islands' indigenous inhabitants were probably Taíno Indians. They were gradually replaced by Lucayan Arawak Indians around 500 C.E., and the Arawaks lived there peacefully for almost 900 years. The islands were changed forever with their "discovery" by European colonists at the turn of the sixteenth century. There is still discussion over who first sighted the islands; some scholars believe it was Ponce de Leon in 1512, while others claim the Turks were actually the site of Christopher Columbus's first landing in the New World in 1492. It is clear, however, that during the next 150 years the Spanish returned to the islands just long enough to capture the Lucayans who lived there and sell them into slavery in other Spanish holdings in the Caribbean. The name "Caicos" is one of the Lucayans' lasting legacies, since it comes from their word *caya hico*, or "string of islands." The name "Turks" refers to an indigenous cactus that the colonists thought resembled a Turkish fez.

In 1678 English settlers from BERMUDA began mining the salt flats in the Turks and Caicos Islands, bringing African slaves with them to do the miserable work. Salt immediately proved extremely profitable, and soon the British, Spanish, and French were fighting over the right to control the islands. Each group primarily used black slaves to carry out the mining. Cotton and sisal plantations were also established in the islands, but when the soil proved too thin to support them for very long, the focus returned to the salt flats.

By 1776 the Turks and Caicos Islands were officially declared part of the British Bahamian colony. The scene Mary Prince describes is from the beginning of the nineteenth century, when British rule had been firmly established. In 1834 slaves in the Turks and Caicos Islands finally became free when slavery was abolished in all British territories. But life in the islands remained dependent on the salt industry, and very difficult for workers for decades to come.

As with many other territories in the Caribbean, the black majority in the Turks and Caicos Islands was prevented from holding any real political power until well into the twentieth century. The British themselves seemed unsure about how the Turks and Caicos Islands should be administered. From 1799 to 1848 they were governed as part of the Bahamas; from 1848 to 1873 they were granted their own internal government, controlled by the island's white elite; and from 1873 to 1959 they were considered a dependency of JAMAICA

Throughout this period the population in the islands remained relatively small and scattered, which influenced the British decision to administer the islands together with larger territories. By 1959 the push for more self-government was growing throughout the Caribbean. That year, when Jamaica was granted its own governor for the first time, the governor of Jamaica also became governor of the Turks and Caicos Islands. But when Jamaica won full independence three years later, the Turks and Caicos Islands were declared a separate British dependency. In 1969 the constitution was changed so that the governor, who was nominated by the British monarch, shared power with a state council, whose members were largely elected.

In 1976 the constitution was changed once more to establish ministerial government, giving the position of chief minister to the leader of the legislature's ruling party. The People's Democratic Movement party won the 1976 elections, and supported independence for the Turks and Caicos Islands. They promised to push for independence if they were reelected in 1980, essentially making the 1980 elections a referendum on independence. However, they subsequently lost their reelection campaign.

Many Turks and Caicos Islands voters remain hesitant about independence for their tiny country. For much of the twentieth century there was a serious push by many islanders to have their country annexed to Canada; in the mid-1970s the question was considered in the Canadian Parliament.

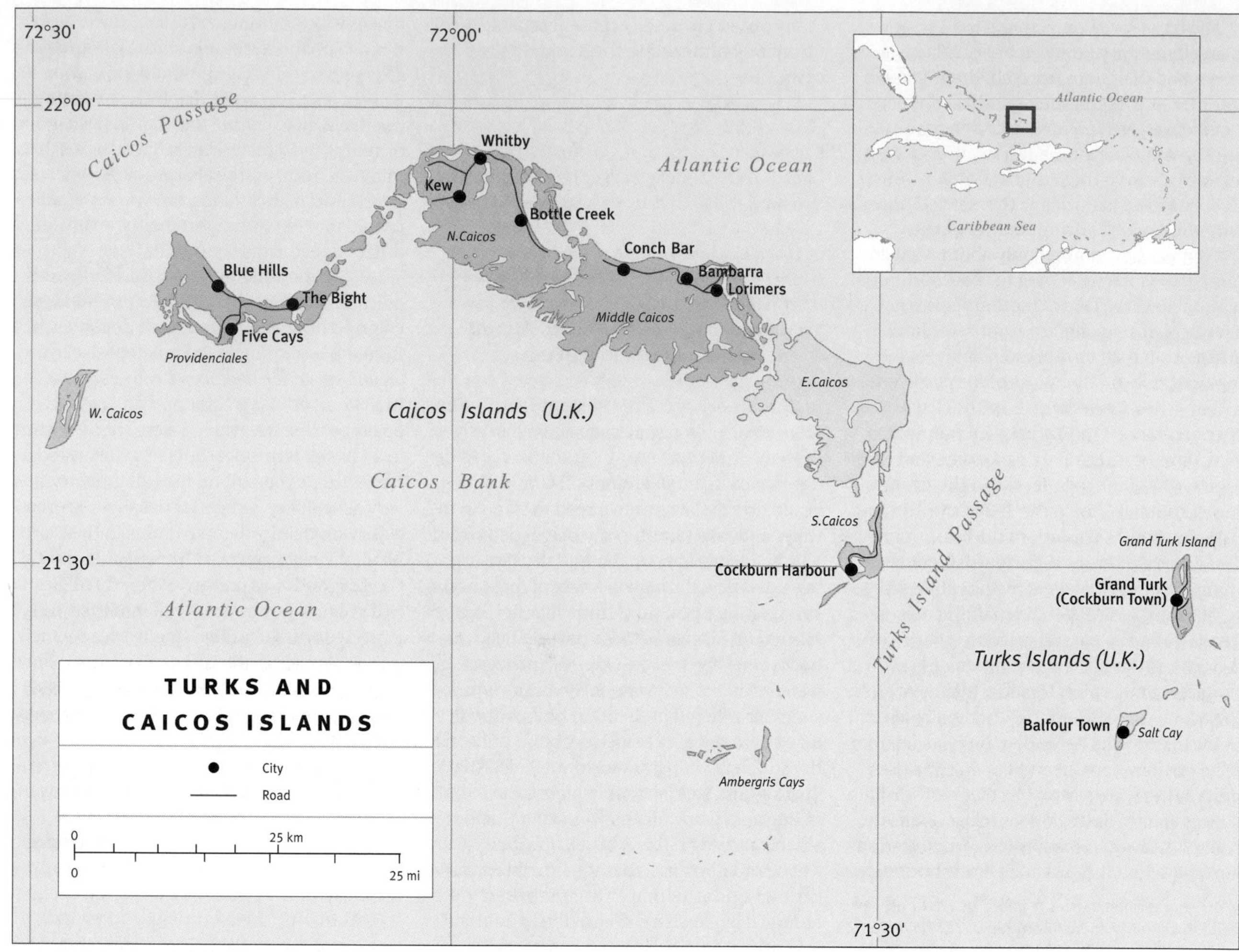

Canada ultimately declined because of fears of racial tensions between black islanders and the white Canadian majority, but in the mid-1980s 90 percent of Turks and Caicos residents continued to support association with Canada. In 1985 a major corruption scandal hit the islands when the chief minister, the minister of commerce and development, and another member of the Legislative Council were all arrested in the United States for drug trafficking. This did little to instill confidence in the Turks and Caicos Islands' own government.

But in the 1990s economic conditions were slowly improving, and helping to stabilize the country. It was not until the 1960s that the salt industry, formerly the mainstay of the economy, finally collapsed, after international competition proved too much for the islands' unprofitable production techniques. Like many other Caribbean countries, the Turks and Caicos Islands then turned to tourism. Many Turks and Caicos Islanders have left the island seeking higher education or employment. But as tourism develops, poor immigrants from neighboring islands have begun coming to the Turks and Caicos Islands in search of jobs. Offshore banking has also brought new jobs to the islands. As a result of these developments the population has fluctuated several times over the last few decades as the ratio of immigrants to emigrants continues to shift. These changes are still in progress, and they will shape the course of the Turks and Caicos Islands for the next century.

Lisa Clayton Robinson

See Also

Slavery in Latin America and the Caribbean; Slave Narratives; Slave Rebellions in Latin America and the Caribbean.

North America

Turner, Henry McNeal

(b. February 1, 1834, Newberry Courthouse, S.C.; d. May 8, 1915, Windsor, Ontario, Canada), African Methodist Episcopal (AME) Church leader, Reconstruction-era Georgia politician, outspoken defender of African American rights, prominent leader of back-to-Africa movements, and supporter of the American Colonization Society.

Henry McNeal Turner was, along with Frederick Douglass and Rev. Henry Highland Garnet, one of the preeminent African American leaders of the late nineteenth century. Turner was born free to a teenaged mother, Sarah Turner. His maternal grandmother, Hannah Greer – who voiced great pride in her African heritage – had a powerful influence on young Henry. From an early age he envisioned becoming a leader of his people. While he was a teenager, Turner experienced a powerful religious conversion during a Methodist camp meeting at Sharon Camp Ground and soon decided to pursue a career in the ministry. In 1853 the 19-year-old Turner became a traveling evangelist for the Methodist Episcopal Church-South.

In 1858 Turner joined the African Methodist Episcopal (AME) Church and during the next five years served as a minister to three different congregations in Baltimore, Maryland, and Washington, D.C. In 1863, when the Union army began accepting African American enlistments, Turner raised the first black regiment of the Civil War and was commissioned as its chaplain. Following the war he traveled to Georgia and, after serving briefly as an agent of the Freedmen's Bureau, became responsible for all of Georgia's AME missions.

Turner's energetic efforts led to a rapid expansion of AME membership throughout the state. In 1876 he was made manager of the Church's publishing department. In taking up this new challenge, he declared, "[A] race that cannot produce its own literature hardly amounts to a cypher." In 1880 he was elevated to bishop, one of the first Southern-born bishops in the history of the denomination.

Between 1867 and 1871, however, Turner devoted most of his prodigious energy to politics. In 1867 he helped organize the Republican Party in Georgia and was elected as a delegate to the state constitutional convention. In the following year he won a seat in the state legislature, but in 1869 all 23 black legislators were illegally unseated by their white Democratic and Republican colleagues. Turner then served briefly as postmaster in Macon, Georgia, and in 1870 he was again elected to the state legislature.

During the immediate postwar years Turner's political outlook was quite conservative. When he arrived in Georgia, for example, he opposed the distribution of land to former slaves and instead encouraged freed blacks to welcome their newly won "freedom of labor." While serving as a state legislator, he supported a petition of clemency for Jefferson Davis, former leader of the Confederate rebellion, and opposed the forced sale of plantations for nonpayment of taxes. He was, however, an active supporter of public education, which had been virtually nonexistent in Georgia and most of the South prior to Reconstruction.

But as Turner encountered the pervasive and vitriolic antiblack hostility of many white Southerners, he became more politically militant. In particular, he revised his earlier sanguine assessment of the opportunities available to his people. He was a staunch defender of the Civil Rights Act of 1875 and harshly condemned the United States Supreme Court for an 1882 decision that largely vitiated that legislation.

During the 1870s Turner grew disenchanted with the prospects for African Americans in the United States. In 1871 he argued for black migration out of the South and suggested Haiti as a possible destination. Three years later he proposed that the federal government reserve New Mexico Territory for African American settlement. From the early 1870s he also advocated immigration to Africa. He saw a twofold purpose in this move to Africa: African Americans would be able to win credit for their accomplishments, and they would fulfill God's purpose by Christianizing the Africans.

Throughout his life Turner remained passionately devoted to the interests of African Americans, but his black nationalism also at times led him into suspect alliances with antiblack whites. In 1876, for example, he became vice president of the white-dominated American Colonization Society, which many blacks regarded as a racist organization. In speeches, pamphlets, and conferences, Turner pressed his point that emigration offered African Americans their best opportunity to prosper and advance. He also argued that the federal government should underwrite the enterprise in partial reparation for slavery.

During the 1890s Turner made four trips to Africa, visiting Liberia, Sierra Leone, British South Africa, and the Transvaal. Yet he never limited himself to a single issue, including colonization. During the 1890s he vehemently opposed America's imperialist ventures in Hawaii, Cuba, and the Philippines. In 1892 he became editor of the AME magazine *Voice of Missions* and, in the years that followed, published articles on African American history, civil rights issues, racial discrimination, and other topics.

During the 1890s more African Americans were the victims of lynching than at any other time in American history (*see* Antilynching Movement). In the *Voice of Missions* for March 1897, Turner advised every black man to acquire firearms and "to keep them loaded and prepared for immediate use." Should their homes be "invaded by bloody lynchers or any mob day or night," Turner proclaimed, they should "blow the fiendish wretches into a thousand giblets."

Turner's outspoken stand against lynching was the subject of widespread discussion, noted his biographer Stephen Ward Angell, and it extended as far away as South Africa. Yet during the early twentieth century Turner once again made a conservative shift, siding with the conciliatory Booker T. Washington rather than the more militant W. E. B. Du Bois. Turner died of a stroke while attending an AME gathering in Windsor, Canada; he was 81 years old.

James Clyde Sellman

See Also

Slavery in the United States; African Methodist Episcopal Church; Bureau of Refugees, Freedmen and Abandoned Lands; Civil War, American; Du Bois, William Edward Burghardt (W. E. B.); Washington, Booker Taliaferro; Black Nationalism in the United States.

North America

Turner, Lorenzo Dow (b. January 1895, Elizabeth City, N.C.; d. February 10, 1972, Chicago, Ill.), African American linguist and ethnologist who identified and analyzed African survivals in African American language.

Lorenzo Dow Turner received a bachelor's degree from Howard University in 1914, a master's degree from Harvard University in 1917, and a doctoral degree from the University of Chicago in 1926. He taught English at several black colleges, and initially became interested in linguistics after hearing the black Gullah language.

In 1931 Turner became the first African-American member of the Linguistics Society. His research on Gullah, Creole, and the Niger-Kordofanian language family established connections between African languages and African American dialects, and helped rebut the common Western belief that African culture had not influenced the New World.

Lisa Clayton Robinson

See Also

Creoles.

North America

Turner, Nat (b. October 2, 1800 Southampton, Va.; d. November 11, 1831 Southampton, Va.), African American slave who led the largest and most significant slave revolt in United States history.

Nat Turner was born on Benjamin Turner's plantation in Southampton County five days before the execution of the African American revolutionary Gabriel Prosser in Richmond, Virginia. Turner's father, whose name is unknown but who was also a Benjamin Turner slave, successfully escaped and is believed to have spent his life in the Great Dismal Swamp, which lies in southern Virginia and in North Carolina, with other escaped African Americans, as maroons.

Turner's mother, a slave named Nancy who was kidnapped from Africa in 1793, believed that he was destined for great things in his life, and she instilled this sense in him. That he acquired literacy in his boyhood added weight to his mother's convictions. Turner also accepted Christianity in his youth, became a preacher, and identified religion with freedom. He claimed to receive religious visions throughout his life.

Turner sought his own freedom, running away in 1821 after he had become the property of Benjamin Turner's son, Samuel. When Samuel Turner hired a harsh overseer, Nat Turner escaped, remaining free for approximately a month. During that time he experienced a vision indicating that he would lead a slave rebellion, and he returned to the plantation to await his signal to begin.

Between 1825 and 1830 Turner became a popular preacher to African American congregations throughout Southampton County. His sermons focused on conflict and liberation, and gained him many followers, some of whom believed he was a prophet. Traveling from church to church allowed Turner to gather the knowledge he needed to organize his revolt, such as road locations and hiding places.

In February 1831, Turner, who was now at the home of Joseph Travis, believed that an eclipse of the sun signaled that the time had come for him to launch his rebellion. He recruited four other slaves, and they developed several plans before accepting one and deciding to begin on the symbolic date of July 4. However, Turner fell ill and the revolt was delayed. On August 13 Turner interpreted a bluish green sky as a positive signal. The group agreed to strike after midnight on August 22. The uprising began at the Travis home, where the rebels killed everyone in the household. Turner initially intended to move from house to house killing whites regardless of age and sex. He hoped that the show of force would intimidate neighboring whites and encourage other slaves to join the rebellion. After they had obtained a foothold, they agreed that the wholesale slaughter would cease.

Turner's destination was Jerusalem, Virginia, the Southampton County seat and home of an arsenal that would allow the insurgents to arm themselves adequately. As the band moved from house to house, more slaves joined the rebellion until they eventually numbered 60 or 70. With this growth the rebels were weakened because they became less organized, and they lost the element of surprise that had worked so effectively. The militia that met the insurrectionists on Monday afternoon retreated soon after, but it intended to reorganize and return.

When the slave army stopped at James Parker's farm for fresh recruits and supplies, the militia, which had regrouped, struck again. Turner's army was dispersed and, though Turner attempted to rally his troops, white reinforcements arrived and began a brutal counterattack in which they killed more than 100 blacks. Turner survived and fled, eluding his captors until October 30. He was quickly tried, sentenced to death, and hanged in Jerusalem, Virginia, on November 11, 1831. While awaiting execution, he told his story to his court-appointed attorney, Thomas Gray. The result was an extraordinary account of his life and of the rebellion, which Gray published as *Nat Turner's Confessions*.

Turner's rebellion lasted almost three days, killed 57 people, and resulted in the executions of more than 100 African American rebels. Some call this rebellion the First War, the Civil War being the second. Turner's rebellion was significant in that it was more violent than any other slave uprising and reshaped the debate over slavery in ways that led to the Civil War a generation later. The uprising intensified both the antislavery movement and the corresponding proslavery forces. It reinforced the notion held by some abolitionists that slaves would be willing to fight if outside forces organized and armed them. Proslavery forces began to endorse reducing the number of free blacks through colonization. Turner's rebellion also disproved the myth of the contented slave, and proved that African Americans would die to end slavery.

Robert Fay

See Also

Slavery in the United States; Maroonage in the Americas; Abolitionism in the United States; American Colonization Society; Civil War, American; Free Blacks in the United States, 1619 to 1863; Gabriel Prosser Conspiracy.

North America

Turner, Tina (b. November 26, 1939, Brownsville, Tenn.), African American pop singer and actress who made one of the biggest comebacks in recording history.

Tina Turner was born Anna Mae Bullock. As a child she sang and danced with a local trombonist named Bootsie Whitelaw. After her parents separated in 1950, she lived with her maternal grandmother. Six years later Turner moved to St. Louis, Missouri, to live with her mother and older sister. The same year she met guitarist Ike Turner after spontaneously performing a song with his group, the Kings of Rhythm, in an East St. Louis nightclub. Turner joined the group in 1957 and changed her name to Tina in 1960, at which time the Kings of Rhythm became the Ike and Tina Turner Revue. Ike and Tina Turner married in 1962, and they toured throughout the United States and Europe. Their biggest hit, "Proud Mary," won a Grammy in 1971. Driven away by Ike's emotional and physical abuse, Tina Turner left the group in 1976.

After finalizing her divorce from Ike in 1978, Turner embarked on a solo career in Europe with the help of David Bowie, Mick Jagger, and Rod Stewart. She secured a recording contract with Capitol Records in 1983 and released the successful single "Let's Stay Together," originally recorded by Al Green in 1971. Turner's 1984 album *Private Dancer*, featuring the hit single "What's Love Got to Do with It," won three Grammy Awards and sold over 25 million copies worldwide. Both of Turner's next two albums, *Break Every Rule* (1986) and *Tina Live in Europe* (1988), received a Grammy. She played leading roles in *Tommy* (1975) and *Mad Max: Beyond the Thunderdome* (1985), and was the subject of the film *What's Love Got to Do with It* (1993). Turner was inducted into the Rock and Roll Hall of Fame in January 1991.

Aaron Myers

Africa

Turu (also known as Nyatura and Rimi), ethnic group of Tanzania.

The Turu primarily inhabit central Tanzania. They speak a Bantu language. More than 500,000 people consider themselves Turu.

See Also

Bantu: Dispersion and Settlement.

North America

Tuskegee Airmen, the segregated United States Army air forces in World War II that broke barriers in the U.S. military and fought successfully as fighter pilots in Europe.

African Americans fought in every American war in racially segregated units, and with the generally unrealized expectation that patriotism and courage would demonstrate their right to first-class citizenship at home (*see* Military, Blacks in the American). As planes and flying developed following World War I, blacks pressured for admission to the air force, but a 1925 study commissioned by the Army War College claimed to have found scientific proof that Negroes were innately unable to operate aircraft because of their limited cranial capacity. Not until April 3, 1939, as Europe prepared for war, did Congress pass Public Law 18, which called for a major expansion of American air forces. The bill provided for the establishment of training programs for Negroes, but for support services only, at several black colleges.

One program was authorized to train black pilots. The 66th Air Force Flying School was to be established at Tuskegee, Alabama, site of Tuskegee Institute, partly because the weather there permitted year-round training, partly because the South was already heavily segregated. Under considerable pressure from the National Association for the Advancement of Colored People (NAACP) and the black press, the War Department authorized the creation of an all-black flying unit, the 99th Pursuit Squadron, later called the 99th Fighter Squadron. African Americans wanted to be eligible for the regular air force, but most white civilians and military personnel did not want them in the service at all. The compromise was a segregated unit.

Nearly 500 black soldiers, all male, entered the Tuskegee program, which was run by white officers. Since those in charge both expected and wanted African Americans to fail, the black trainees were expelled for the slightest reason, resulting in a high drop-out rate from the program. The first class preparing to be pilots began training on August 25, 1941. The class consisted of 13 men, 5 of whom graduated in June 1942. The class included Benjamin O. Davis Jr., who later rose to become the country's first black three-star general. Because the officers at Tuskegee considered the African American pilots unfit for combat and thus insisted on prolonging their practice time, the Tuskegee pilots emerged from the program especially well trained. The men who survived the rigorous training programs were an elite group, largely college educated, and highly motivated.

Eventually, nearly 1000 men won their wings as trained pilots, and another 1000 graduated from the program with various support skills. When finally allowed to fight, some 450 pilots flew combat missions. The segregated black 332nd Fighter Group was formed, comprising four fighter squadrons, the 99th, 100th, 301st, and 302nd. Assigned largely to Italy, their record was impressive. Their fighter planes escorted bombers on their way to Europe, and in 1578 missions and 15,552 sorties, they never lost a bomber. They destroyed or damaged 409 enemy planes. In Trieste harbor they actually sank a German destroyer, marking the first time a ship of that size and offensive capability had ever been sunk simply by machine-gun fire. By war's end the Fighter Group had lost 66 men and been awarded 100 Distinguished Flying Crosses.

On September 5, 1946, the government disbanded the fighter units and closed the Tuskegee base. The outstanding success and courage of the Tuskegee Airmen was a contributory factor in President Harry S. Truman's decision to sign Executive Order 9981 in 1948. The order officially ended racial segregation in the U.S. armed forces, which went on to become a model of racial integration. In addition to their extraordinary war record and their role in the integration of the U.S. military, many graduates of the Tuskegee program went on to become leaders in other fields: Coleman Young, mayor of Detroit; Albert Murray, literary and music scholar; Roscoe Brown, president of Bronx Community College; and Percy Sutton, president of Manhattan Borough.

See Also

World War II and African Americans; Press, Black, in the United States; Davis, Benjamin O., Jr.; Murray, Albert L.; Sutton, Percy Ellis; Tuskegee University; Young, Coleman Alexander.

North America

Tuskegee Syphilis Experiment, a widely condemned study of the natural course of syphilis in which United States public health officials withheld treatment from 600 African American males, two-thirds of whom were infected with syphilis.

The Tuskegee syphilis experiment, conducted by the U.S. Public Health Service (PHS) and the Tuskegee Institute, began in 1932 and was originally planned to last one year. Its founders intended to document the degenerative effects of syphilis, with the ultimate goal of appropriating state funding to treat Southern rural blacks. The study involved 399 syphilitic black males, all in the final stage of the disease, and a control group of 201 noninfected black males. PHS officials based the investigation in and around Tuskegee, in Macon County, Alabama, where severe poverty and insufficient medical care contributed to the highest incidence of syphilis in the South. Most PHS doctors ascribed high syphilis rates among blacks to sexual promiscuity and ignorance. That African Americans were systematically denied medical services was never considered, nor were the overt moral and racial implications that overshadowed the experiment from the beginning.

In order to secure participants, PHS officials offered a series of incentives: free medical treatment for minor illnesses; occasional hot meals; travel to and from the study site; and burial stipends paid out to the deceased person's family. For men whose daily existence was harsh, such inducements were attractive, especially since the burial fee often represented their only life insurance. Not once did PHS doctors inform participants of their real diagnosis, or of the true purpose of the study or the dangers to which it exposed them. The sick men were led to believe they were being treated for rheumatism, stomach disorders, or "bad blood," an umbrella phrase used by rural blacks to describe a range of maladies, including syphilis. They were subjected to an array of tests and medical examinations over the years, while the syphilis was deliberately left untreated.

In the 1940s, when the use of penicillin as an antibiotic for syphilis became widespread, Tuskegee participants did not receive it. Indeed, PHS officials threatened to cut off the benefits of those who attempted to be treated elsewhere, and advised local black doctors not to see them. By 1969 approximately 100 men had died from untreated syphilis, while numerous others suffered painful disease-related complications. Many unknowingly spread syphilis, which is highly contagious, to their wives and children.

A black nurse and Tuskegee resident, Eunice Rivers, facilitated interactions between the researchers and their black subjects. Fully aware of what the study involved, she kept track of the men and often chauffeured them back and forth between their homes and the experiment site. The men trusted her because she was African American and understood the men's cultural background. As *Bad Blood* author James H. Jones points out, the men came to see themselves as "members of a social club and burial society called 'Miss Rivers's Lodge."

The study was never a secret. Between 1932 and 1972 PHS officials published numerous scientific papers on the experiment in leading U.S. medical journals and gave presentations at medical conventions. At the same time the Civil Rights Movement was changing white society's perceptions of blacks, culminating in significantly improved ethical standards regarding the medical treatment of nonwhite patients. It was only when a PHS worker informed the Associated Press of the study that the U.S. Department of Health, Education, and Welfare (HEW) abruptly ended it in 1972. Some leading white doctors continued publicly to defend the study. What Jones refers to as the nineteenth-century legacy of "racial medicine," in which black study participants were seen as subjects to be experimented on rather than as human beings, remained strong in many public health circles.

Compensation for victims of the Tuskegee experiment has come slowly. After the study became widely publicized in 1972, HEW, along with leading U.S. newspapers, decried the study as "ethically unjustified." Commentators condemned the fact that public health officials had failed to get formal consent from the men and had denied them penicillin. An out-of-court settlement guaranteed treatment and modest cash payments for the survivors and families of the deceased, while Congress enacted laws to protect people who participated in medical experiments. It was not until May 1997, however, that the government fully acknowledged its role in the Tuskegee experiment. In a public apology, President Bill Clinton admitted that the study was "racist" and "profoundly, morally wrong," and that "what the United States government did was shameful." He also announced government plans to found a memorial to the study's legacy: the Center for Bioethics in Research and Health Care. Yet the Tuskegee experiment cultivated a mistrust of the public medical establishment among many African Americans, and little has been done since 1972 to remedy the problem of high syphilis rates among rural Southern blacks.

Roanne Edwards

See Also

Tuskegee University.

North America

Tuskegee University, a historically black college in Tuskegee, Alabama, that was organized by Booker T. Washington to emphasize industrial education.

Although Tuskegee University was technically chartered by the Alabama state legislature to repay black voters for their support, its early history is almost synonymous with the name of its first administrator, nineteenth-century African American leader Booker T. Washington. Tuskegee's roots were in the post-Reconstruction era in the South, when higher educational opportunities for African Americans were still severely limited.

In February 1881 the Alabama legislature voted to set aside $2000 a year to fund a state and normal school for blacks in Tuskegee. The trustees asked officials at several other black institutions to recommend someone to head the new school, and although they were implicitly asking for white candidates, Hampton Institute's president Samuel Chapman Armstrong suggested his black protégé, Washington. The trustees agreed to hire Washington as principal. He arrived in Tuskegee on June 24, 1881, and opened the Tuskegee Normal School in a shack adjacent to the black Methodist church on July 4. The first 30 students ranged in age from 16 to 40, and most were teachers hoping to further their own education.

Washington's most significant contribution was his strong belief in industrial education and training as the key to success for African Americans. Students were required to learn a trade and perform manual labor at the school, including making and laying the bricks for the buildings that became the first campus. Tuskegee's charter had mandated that tuition would be free for students who committed to teaching in Alabama public schools. The students' labor helped with financial costs, and Washington solicited much of the remaining funding from Northern white philanthropists.

Tuskegee was incorporated as a private institution in 1892. Because social conventions would have prohibited white instructors from serving under a black principal, Tuskegee became the first black institution of higher learning with a black faculty. In 1896 the school hired a young teacher who would become famous – George Washington Carver, whose groundbreaking agricultural research received

Students at Tuskegee Institute in Tuskegee, Alabama, listen to a history lecture in 1902. In 1986, five years after its centennial, the school renamed itself Tuskegee University. *Library of Congress*

international recognition. Washington also became nationally accepted as a black leader during the 1890s, because many whites appreciated his accomodationist approach to race relations, and Tuskegee gained wide recognition and substantial funding.

Changes to the original industrial training approach came gradually after Washington's death in 1915. Tuskegee awarded its first baccalaureate degree in 1925 and began its first college curriculum in 1927, with departments for business and teachers' and nurses' training. During World War II the United States Air Force established a flying school at Tuskegee that trained more than 900 black pilots known as the Tuskegee Airmen. Graduate programs in veterinary medicine, nursing, business, architecture, agriculture and home economics, education, and arts and sciences were eventually added. In the 1960s and 1970s Tuskegee became the first black college to be designated a Registered National Historic Landmark and a National Historic Site.

By the school's centennial in 1981, Tuskegee's campus included 150 buildings on 20.2 sq km (5000 acres), and its endowment was approximately $22 million. Five years later the school changed its name to Tuskegee University. Today there are approximately 3200 undergraduates enrolled at Tuskegee, and an additional 200 graduate students; the school offers 70 different degrees and has an especially strong engineering program.

Notable Tuskegee graduates include writer Ralph Ellison, who portrays a fictionalized version of the school and its "Founder" in his novel *Invisible Man;* Arthur W. Mitchell, the first black Democratic congressman; and actor/comedian Keenen Ivory Wayans. Tuskegee's 30,000 living alumni are professionals in communities across the country and across the world.

Lisa Clayton Robinson

See Also

World War II and African Americans; Hampton University; Washington, Booker Taliaferro; Accommodationism in the United States.

Africa

Tutu, Desmond Mpilo (b. October 7, 1931, Klerksdorp, South Africa), former archbishop of the Anglican Church in South Africa, winner of the 1984 Nobel Peace Prize, and head of the Truth and Reconciliation Commission.

An outspoken critic of South Africa's apartheid system, Desmond Tutu became one of his country's most prominent symbols of resistance and hope, along with Nelson Mandela.

Tutu was raised in the Transvaal region. The son of a schoolteacher father, he walked miles each day to overcrowded and underequipped schools. The family was better off than most, however, and Tutu has described his childhood as happy. An attack of tuberculosis at age 14 kept Tutu out of school for nearly two years. While recuperating, he met Father Trevor Huddleston, a white Anglican priest known for his opposition to apartheid. Under Huddleston's influence, Tutu first became interested in the church, an interest that coexisted with his plans to become a teacher. In 1954 he graduated from Bantu Normal College outside Pretoria and was certified as a teacher.

Tutu cut short his teaching career after the apartheid government passed the 1955 Bantu Education Act. The act effectively imposed a segregated and inferior educational system on black children. Tutu stayed at his position at Munsieville High School until his last class had graduated; then he resigned in 1958.

Now a family man – Tutu had married Leah Nomalizo Shenxane in 1955 – he entered the seminary at Saint Peter's College in Rosettenville. In 1960 he graduated summa cum laude. He credited the Community of the Resurrection, the order that ran Saint Peter's, with his view that religious study "is authenticated and expressed in our dealings with our neighbor." It was a lesson he would take to his first posts as parish priest in two government-created townships. Tutu became known as a man of the people, treating his flock with warmth, humor, and love; he later wrote that "a good shepherd knows his sheep by name."

Advanced theological study at the University of London took Tutu away from South Africa in 1962, a time of increasing antiapartheid activism. While Tutu was then still relatively apolitical, it is clear that his time in England impressed upon him the depth of the injustices he and his countrymen faced at home. Along with his wife and the couple's four children, Tutu returned to South Africa in 1968 and became a lecturer at his alma mater, Saint Peter's College, which had recently become part of the Federal Theological Seminary. He witnessed the violent reprisals against black student protesters at nearby Fort Hare University, which at the time was the center of the Black Consciousness Movement led by Steve Biko.

Tutu spent another two years as a university lecturer in Lesotho, then returned with his family to England, where he became associate director of the Theological Educational Fund in London. His role as a leader in the antiapartheid struggle began in 1975, when he was elected to the position of dean of Johannesburg. Refusing to occupy the dean's residence, Tutu instead settled in the sprawling black township of Soweto, where a year later police massacred black schoolchildren who were protesting peacefully.

From 1976 to 1978 Tutu served as bishop of Lesotho. During this time Biko died in police custody, and Tutu gave the eulogy. He compared the martyred leader to Jesus Christ and prayed for black South Africans to find "a place in the sun in our own beloved country." In 1978 he returned to his own country to stay. For seven years he served as the general secretary of the South African Council of Churches, an organization known for its outspoken opposition to apartheid (*see* Antiapartheid Movement). The whole country was now Tutu's parish. At home, he worked tirelessly to free the country's many political prisoners; abroad, he called on the international community to use diplomatic and economic sanctions to pressure the apartheid regime.

In 1984 Tutu won the Nobel Peace Prize, and shortly thereafter he was named bishop of Johannesburg. Two years later Tutu became archbishop of Cape Town, where he continued to speak out against apartheid from a Christian perspective. He once said, "If Christ returned to South Africa today he would almost certainly be detained under the present security laws, because of his concern for the poor, the hungry and the oppressed." In the decade after Tutu's appointment he saw most of his goals achieved; Mandela was released from prison in 1990 and in 1994 won the presidency in the country's first-ever democratic vote. In 1996 Tutu became chairman of the Truth and Reconciliation Commission (TRC), the body charged with investigating crimes committed during the apartheid era. During his three years as the TRC's chair, Tutu heard testmony from hundreds of perpetrators and victims – a duty that at times severely tested his skills as a peacemaker.

Kate Tuttle

See Also

Biko, Stephen; Cape Town, South Africa; Johannesburg, South Africa; Mandela, Nelson Rolihlahla; Soweto, South Africa; Pretoria, South Africa; Black Consciousness in Africa; Nobel Prize.

Africa

Tutuola, Amos (b. 1920, Abeokuta, Nigeria; d. June 10, 1997, Ibadan, Nigeria), Nigerian novelist known for his use of Yoruba folktales.

The son of a Yoruba cocoa farmer, Amos Tutuola built his literary career retelling and expanding the stories he heard as a child, listening to elders in the evenings. His ten books, all drawing on Yoruba folklore, have since become classics of African literature.

Tutuola, whose family struggled financially, entered the Salvation Army School in Abeokuta, Nigeria, at age ten, his tuition paid by an uncle. Two years later financial need led Tutuola to seek work as a houseboy for F. O. Mornu, a local civil servant. In 1934 Tutuola, by then a promising student, moved to Lagos with his employer and enrolled in Lagos High School. But Tutuola suffered hunger and abuse while living in Lagos with Mornu, and he returned to Abeokuta in 1936. His father's death in 1939 effectively ended his formal education.

After a failed attempt at farming, Tutuola learned blacksmithing and plied his trade in the British Royal Air Force. Upon his discharge in 1945 he attempted to launch his own business, but this failed too. In 1946, while working as a messenger in Lagos, Tutuola wrote his first novel, *The Palm-Wine Drinkard and His Dead Palm-Wine Tapster in the Deads' Town,* in just two days. After three months of intensive revision – a creative pattern he would repeat in subsequent books – Tutuola sought a publisher. Finally in 1952 the London firm Faber & Faber published the novel. It was one of the first Nigerian works of fiction to reach an international audience.

Reviews in Europe and America were enthusiastic; some in the Nigerian literary community, however, criticized the book for its use of traditional folklore and Yoruba-influenced English. Tutuola's popularity among Western readers – *The Palm-Wine Drinkard* was translated into 11 languages – led some educated Nigerians to suggest that his work merely confirmed the exotic image of Africa held by non-Africans. Tutuola's second book, *My Life in the Bush of Ghosts,* which was published in 1954, also blended myth, magic, and coming-of-age themes, and also received international acclaim.

Tutuola went to work for the Nigerian Broadcasting Company in 1956 and was transferred from Lagos to Ibadan the following year. Although the notably shy and quiet Tutuola was never a part of the then-thriving Nigerian literary scene – in fact, his friends were mostly illiterate tradesmen – he continued to write and helped adapt his first two books for the stage in 1958 (*see* Theater, African). Praise from critics abroad dwindled, however; reviewers saw as "deliberately childish" what they had found "pleasingly childlike" a few years earlier. Some Nigerian critics charged that Tutuola imitated too heavily an earlier Yoruban writer, D. O. Fagunwa. Yet Tutuola credited the Christian novel *Pilgrim's Progress* as well as Greek mythology as influences, and Gerald Moore, writing in the literary magazine *Black Orpheus,* identified universal storytelling patterns in Tutuola's work. Later books such as *The Witch-Herbalist of the Remote Town* (1981) confirmed the critical reappraisal of Tutuola as Africa's premier storyteller.

Kate Tuttle

See Also

Abeokuta, Nigeria; Ibadan, Nigeria; Lagos, Nigeria; Fiction, English-Language, in Africa.

Africa

Twa, a mostly forest-dwelling people sharing an ethnic identity and commonly referred to as "pygmies," who live in Burundi, Rwanda, and eastern parts of the Democratic Republic of the Congo (formerly Zaire).

The seminomadic Twa were the first inhabitants of present-day Burundi and Rwanda, though their exact origins are debated. Archaeological evidence places Twa hunter-gatherers in the area beginning around 70,000 B.C.E., but some ethnographers contend that they migrated to the region from West Africa around 5000 years ago. Some ethnographic evidence supports the argument that the Twa are closely related to the Ituri forest people of Central Africa, while still other evidence suggests that the Twa entered the region from the northeast.

When the HUTU AND TUTSI migrated into the region in the eleventh and mid-sixteenth centuries, respectively, they believed that the short-statured Twa, as the region's original inhabitants, held spiritual and magical powers. As the Twa were gradually incorporated into Hutu and Tutsi society, they lost their own language and became dependents of the Tutsi royal court, particularly the king, whom they served as storytellers, dancers, musicians, spies, executioners, and guardians of the royal court's sacred fire. The king gave the Twa cattle, and they legitimized his rule through their purported spiritual powers. But because of the Twa's physical characteristics and their eating of mutton, a taboo food, the Hutu and Tutsi considered them impure, and they were socially segregated. German and Belgian COLONIAL RULE further marginalized the Twa by destroying the monarchy on which they depended and by favoring the Tutsi in colonial education and employment. Except for pottery making, neither the forest-dwelling Twa nor the "court" Twa acquired skills applicable to a cash economy.

Today there are approximately 25,000 Twa in Rwanda and about 60,000 in Burundi, constituting less than 1 percent of the total national populations. Largely neglected by development programs and hurt by ongoing strife in both countries, they make their livelihood as day laborers, potters, basket makers, and trackers for the military and wildlife safaris.

Eric Young

SEE ALSO
Pygmy.

North America

Twilight, Alexander Lucius (b. 1795?, Bradford, Vt.; d. 1857, Brownington, Vt.), educator and probably the first African American college graduate.

Alexander Lucius Twilight, born to a free black family in Vermont, graduated from Middlebury College in 1823, making him, so far as is known, the first African American to receive a degree from an American college. He was licensed to preach by the Presbyterian Church and served several Congregational churches.

Twilight became principal of the Orleans County Grammar School in Brownington, Vermont, and in 1836 built a massive, three-story granite building, Athenian Hall, which became Brownington Academy. Twilight served in the Vermont state legislature (1836-1837), the first African American to do so.

Richard Newman

SEE ALSO
Free Blacks in the United States, 1619 to 1863.

North America

Tyson, Cicely (b. December 19, 1933, New York City, N.Y.), African American stage, motion-picture, and television actor known for portraying strong female characters.

Cicely Tyson was educated at New York University and at the Actors Studio. After working as a successful fashion model, Tyson acted in Harlem and in off-Broadway productions in New York City in the late 1950s. She had a small role in the motion picture *Odds Against Tomorrow* (1959) and later became widely known as a regular cast member on the critically praised television drama series *East Side, West Side* (1963-1964). After appearing in supporting parts in the motion pictures *A Man Called Adam* (1966), *The Comedians* (1967), and *The Heart Is a Lonely Hunter* (1968), she costarred in *Sounder* (1972), about a black American sharecropper family in the 1930s. Tyson received a 1972 Academy Award nomination for best actress for her performance in *Sounder*. She is best known for her role in the television movie *The Autobiography of Miss Jane Pittman* (1974), for which she won an Emmy Award for best actress, and for her work in the television miniseries *Roots* (1977), which was adapted from the book of the same title by African American author Alex Haley. Her other motion-picture performances include roles in *The River Niger* (1976), *A Hero Ain't Nothin' but a Sandwich* (1978), *Fried Green Tomatoes* (1991), *Riot* (1996), and *Hoodlum* (1997). In 1994 she returned to television drama as a costar in the series *Equal Justice*.

SEE ALSO
Haley, Alexander Palmer (Alex); Harlem, New York; New York, New York; Television and African Americans; Film, Blacks in American.

North America

Tyson, Mike (b. June 30, 1966, Brooklyn, N.Y.), African American professional boxer, 1980s heavyweight champion imprisoned for rape, known as "Iron Mike."

Mike Tyson grew up in a single-parent home in the Brownsville section of Brooklyn, New York. Throughout his youth Tyson was frequently involved in minor criminal offenses. At age 13 he was sent to a juvenile detention center called the Tyron School in Johnstown, New York. There Tyson met the legendary trainer Cus D'Amato and discovered the sport of BOXING. D'Amato recognized Tyson's potential and became the young boy's mentor, acting as both his coach and legal guardian.

Tyson turned professional in 1985 after winning the 1984 Golden Gloves amateur heavyweight championship. Known as "Iron Mike," Tyson enjoyed several years of major victories, amassing both titles and wealth. His personal life was less successful as his brief marriage to actress Robin Givens ended in 1988 with allegations of domestic abuse. Following a 1990 unanticipated championship loss to challenger Buster Douglas, Tyson's career began to decline. In 1991 he was charged with rape, leading to conviction and a three-year imprisonment.

After his release from prison, Tyson returned to the ring in poor condition and lost a 1996 fight to EVANDER HOLYFIELD. Tyson's career met with further adversity in his July 1997 rematch against Holyfield. Tyson was disqualified after biting Holyfield's ear, actually severing a piece of it. Fined and suspended from boxing, Tyson was forced to reevaluate his career after this professional nadir. In 1999 Tyson was imprisoned again, this time for assaulting two motorists after a traffic accident and for violating parole. The 33-year-old boxer was expected to resume boxing later that year.

North America

Tyus, Wyomia (b. August 29, 1945, Griffin, Ga.), African American track and field athlete who won the 100-meter dash at both the 1964 and 1968 Olympic Games; Tyus was the first woman to win the event twice at the games.

Born in Griffin, Georgia, Wyomia Tyus attended Tennessee State University. In 1964 she won the 100-meter dash at the United States outdoor national track championships. She was not expected to win the event at the 1964 Olympic Games in Tokyo because her teammate Edith McGuire had dominated the event over the previous few years. Tyus did win, however, setting a world record of 11.2 seconds in a preliminary race. She was also a member of the second-place 4 x 100-meter relay team.

At the U.S. outdoor national championships Tyus won the 100-yard dash in 1965 and 1966 and the 220-yard dash in 1966. In addition, at the U.S. indoor championships she won the 60-yard dash in three consecutive years (1965-1967). In 1967 she won the 200-meter dash at the Pan American Games in Winnipeg, Manitoba, Canada.

At the 1968 Olympic Games in Mexico City, Tyus repeated her victory in the 100-meter race, setting a new world record of 11.08 seconds. She also earned her third Olympic Gold Medal by anchoring (running the last leg for) the winning 4 x 100-meter relay team. She retired from amateur track competition after the 1968 Olympic Games. In 1974, with tennis player Billie Jean King, swimmer Donna de Varona, diver Micki King, and speed skater and cyclist Sheila Young, Tyus helped found the Women's Sports Foundation, an organization to enhance women's sports experiences. She was inducted into the National Track & Field Hall of Fame in 1980 and into the U.S. Olympic Hall of Fame in 1985.

SEE ALSO
Track and Field in the United States.

U

Africa

Uganda, **landlocked, equatorial East African country bordered by the Democratic Republic of the Congo, Rwanda, Tanzania, Kenya, and Sudan.**

Uganda is a country of varied landscapes and extraordinary ethnic and linguistic diversity. Nilotic and central Sudanic speakers originally made their homes in the savannas of the north, while Bantu speakers settled the fertile lands in the south. While the British colonial administration used ethnic antagonisms to keep the population divided, the animosities between kingdoms and regions existed well before European intervention. The political, economic, and social significance of ethnic identities has changed over time, but ethnic antagonisms remain a formidable obstacle to the development of a national identity and a nonethnic political culture in independent Uganda.

The country has also played host to large numbers of immigrants and refugees. In addition to the colonial-era arrival of Asians, initially brought to build the railroads and later expelled by Idi Amin in 1972, large numbers of Kenyan Luo moved to Uganda in the last century, many of whom were also expelled by another Ugandan dictator, Milton Obote. Long torn by state-sponsored violence, Uganda enjoyed relative peace during the term of President Yoweri Museveni although it did receive thousands of Rwandan, Congolese, and Sudanese refugees fleeing violent conflicts in their own countries. Uganda's recent economic growth has drawn praise from the international community, though the future of this growth will depend at least partly on political events in what remains a highly unstable region.

Early History

Uganda lies at the heart of the Great Lakes region of East Africa, a fertile, humid area with a long history of human habitation. During the first millennium B.C.E. Bantu speakers migrated to the region from the east, displacing the existing populations of foragers, possibly Khoisan speakers. Archaeological evidence indicates that the Bantu immigrants were using sophisticated draft furnaces for iron smelting as early as the fourth century B.C.E. They were also practicing so-called shifting cultivation, a form of agriculture that requires the regular clearing of forests. As the Bantu-speaking populations moved east into the savanna zones of the Great Lakes region, they encountered Nilo-Saharan-speaking pastoralists. From these populations they added new crops to their repertoire of tubers, primarily arid-climate grains such as sorghum and millet.

These Bantu-speaking immigrants settled primarily in the lower half of present-day Uganda, while the Nilo-Saharan speakers continued to dominate the northern arid regions that were more suitable to pastoralism. Over generations increasingly centralized political systems evolved, giving rise to a number of kingdoms during the first half of the second millennium C.E. Some scholars attribute the rise of kingdoms to the adoption of the banana plant, an extremely high-yield crop from Southeast Asia that freed labor and provided the surplus prerequisite to the development of stratified societies. Others trace the rise of centralized politics to the development of patron-client relationships between sedentary Bantu-speaking agriculturalists and more militant Nilotic-speaking pastoralists. In this scenario pastoralists are believed to have offered protection in exchange for the agriculturalists' tending of cattle, which provided milk as well as manure, a valuable fertilizer.

The first of these kingdoms, Bunyoro-Kitara, developed after pastoralists known as the Tembuzi began establishing cattle-clientship over the region's agriculturists around 1200 C.E. Over several centuries a series of royal dynasties took power in Bunyoro-Kitara. The kingdoms' borders expanded when pastoral Binto rulers in the sixteenth century established control over numerous smaller agricultural polities, including Buganda, Ankole, and Toro. These, in turn, developed into full-fledged kingdoms when Bunyoro-Kitara began to collapse in the nineteenth century.

Buganda played a central role in the history of present-day Uganda. Its rulers traded ivory and slaves for cloth and firearms brought by merchants from Egypt and Zanzibar. The trade transformed Buganda into a wealthy and well-armed kingdom by the time European explorers such as John Hanning Speke, Samuel Baker, and Henry Morton Stanley passed through the region in the mid-nineteenth century, in search of the source of the Nile. The explorers' descriptions of Kabaka (or King) Mutesa I's grand, efficiently run court on the northern shores of Lake Victoria raised the interest of Europe's missionary societies – who later established a number of missions in the region. British authorities also began to see great strategic advantage to controlling an area where it might be possible to divert or even dam the waters upon which Egypt relied. When Great Britain took control of Egypt in 1882, its determination to control Buganda grew. Both Great Britain and Germany claimed possession of Buganda until the signing of the Anglo-German Agreement of 1886, in which Germany ceded control over the area of present-day Uganda (which includes Buganda) in exchange for British concessions elsewhere in East Africa.

In 1891 the king of Buganda signed a treaty with agents of the British East Africa Company, permitting Great Britain to dictate internal policies in return for recognition of the king's legitimacy. Using Buganda as a base, Great Britain began to bring surrounding areas under its control, in some places through collaborators and in some places through force. This larger area was declared the Uganda Protectorate on June 18, 1894, creating a political entity where none had previously existed. While in this sense Uganda is a colonial creation, Buganda and other kingdoms of the Great Lakes region were themselves products of conquest, and had become diverse and stratified societies long before the Europeans arrived.

Colonial Rule

Beginning with Buganda colonial rule was imposed quickly in Uganda, though not without resistance. After 1877 missionaries began to arrive in Buganda, where Mutesa I and many of his court members had recently converted to Islam. A series of conflicts between Muslims and Christians as well as

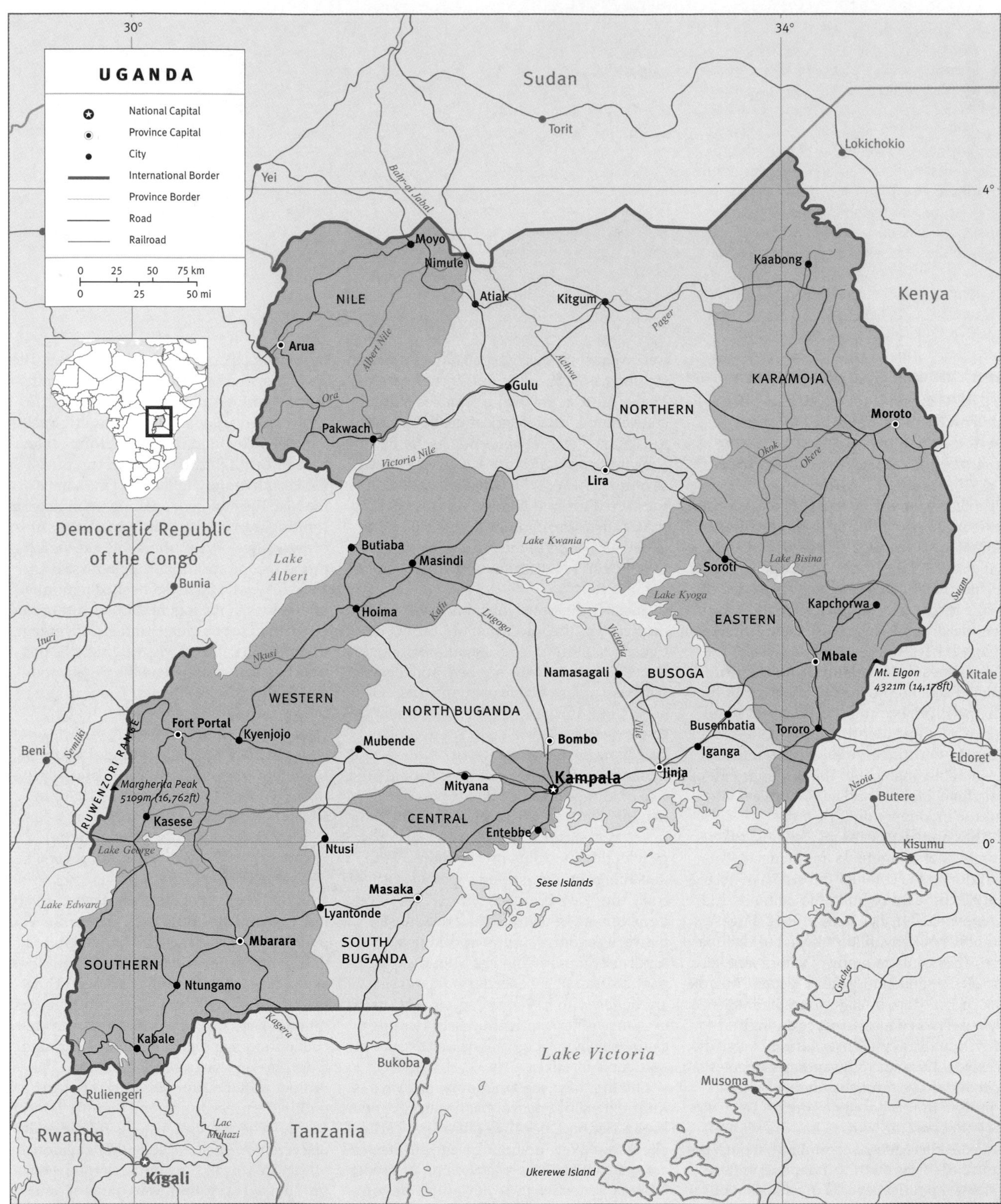

between Protestants and Catholics resulted, with religion becoming associated with particular political agendas. In addition, British efforts to circumvent the authority of the Bugandan king by colluding with recently converted Christian chiefs led the king (then Kabaka Mwanga) to join in an 1897 rebellion with Mukama Kaberga II of neighboring Bunyoro. Mwanga was deposed, and his infant son crowned the new kabaka. Both Mwanga and Kaberga were ultimately exiled to the SEYCHELLES. Also in 1897 the NUBIAN mercenary soldiers that were originally hired by the Egyptian khedive and later used by Capt. Frederick Lugard, rebelled, leading to a bitter two-year battle. The Baganda Christians allied with the British and were ultimately rewarded with a treaty.

The 1900 Uganda Agreement solidified the position of Buganda as a privileged kingdom within Uganda and became the hallmark of British indirect rule. The kabaka would be subject to British authority, but the internal political structure of Buganda would be preserved. The king's own sovereignty was further undermined by the division of the kingdom's land among some 4000 chiefs as private holdings. In a conscious effort to institute a policy of divide-and-rule, the British appointed Bagandans (the inhabitants of the

Buganda kingdom) as local administrators and tax collectors throughout the protectorate. Resentment toward Bagandan dominance sparked a number of early twentieth-century rebellions by the Banyoro and other groups, but the British, playing off animosities between these groups, were able to suppress them relatively quickly. Over the longer term these conflicts, combined with the Bunyoro's persistent demand for the return of their "lost countries" (land the British reallocated to Baganda collaborators), helped stymie the rise of nationalist movements.

Unlike neighboring KENYA, colonial Uganda pursued an "African agriculture" policy in which Africans – rather than white settlers – grew the bulk of the commercial crops. Yields of cotton and coffee, the main export crops, were much higher in the more fertile south. The longstanding cultural differences between northern and southern Uganda were increasingly reinforced by economic and political stratification, as Buganda, already home to the colonial capital Kampala, grew wealthy from agriculture and trade. Bugandan chiefs, many of them owners of large cotton estates, often spent their income on their children's education, leading to the rise of a literate elite who created the Young Baganda Association.

Such associations, as well as more overtly nationalist political parties, began to proliferate in the 1950s. They were primarily defined by ethnicity; even the Uganda National Congress (UNC), formed in 1952 as a pan-Ugandan political party, appealed primarily to Baganda. By the latter part of the decade, following the British withdrawal from India and the emergence of nationalist movements throughout Africa, the parties were maneuvering in anticipation of an inevitable independence.

The UNC split in 1959. The wing led by Milton Obote, who had been elected to the Ugandan Legislative Council a year earlier, eventually became the Uganda People's Congress (UPC). In opposition stood the Democratic Party (DP). It was formed by Roman Catholic Baganda who were intent on preventing the Buganda king, Kabaka Freddie, who was Protestant, from dominating post-colonial Uganda. The DP's concerns were based on the fact that the British had recently granted the kabaka real political power – in particular, the right to appoint and fire chiefs – in return for his agreement to put aside demands for Bugandan sovereignty. Despite this significant concession, the kabaka's supporters, who called themselves the King's Friends, called for a boycott of the pre-independence "self-rule" elections in 1961. As a result most Baganda did not vote, and the DP won 20 of 21 seats reserved for Buganda, giving it a majority of seats in the national assembly.

INDEPENDENCE

Uganda was granted independence on October 9, 1962. In subsequent elections Obote's UPC allied with the Bugandan separatist party,

TOP: Made homeless by the threat of violence from rebel terrorist groups, this family lives in a displaced person's camp in northern Uganda. *CORBIS/Liba Taylor*

ABOVE: Pictured here in 1975, Idi Amin declared himself president for life when he overthrew Uganda's civilian government in 1971. His rule, characterized by corruption and brutality, ended in 1979 when Tanzanian troops and Ugandan rebels combined to force him into exile. *CORBIS/Bettmann*

TOP: A billboard outside Kampala urges sensitivity toward people with acquired immune deficiency syndrome (AIDS). It is estimated that two-thirds of those infected with AIDS worldwide live in Africa. *CORBIS/Staffan Widstrand*

ABOVE: A Ugandan copper miner rests. Rich in copper and other minerals, Uganda's natural resources were part of its appeal for such colonizers as Great Britain and Germany. *CORBIS/Hulton-Deutsch Collection*

Kabaka Yekka (KY). The UPC-KY alliance won, and Obote became prime minister, while the Bugandan kabaka became president. The following year Uganda became a republic of four semiautonomous regions: Buganda, Bunyoro, Ankole, and Toro. Shortly afterward relations between Obote and the kabaka began to deteriorate, as the prime minister sought to dissolve the special status of Buganda and return the long sought-after "lost countries" to the Bunyoro.

In 1966 Obote, together with his general Amin, came under investigation by the legislative council for allegedly smuggling gold and ivory out of the Democratic Republic of the Congo. Faced with the potential demise of his government, Obote quickly moved to centralize his authority and to eliminate his opposition. In addition to arresting five ministers, he abolished the office of the presidency and ordered General Amin to attack the kabaka's palace. He next suspended the constitution, replacing it with a new charter that radically reduced regional autonomy, dissolved the Buganda monarchy, and created an executive presidency, which Obote then claimed for himself.

Obote, an advocate of AFRICAN SOCIALISM, further consolidated his power by nationalizing businesses, as well as by using armed force to maintain order. Meanwhile, however, the loyalty of General Amin was becoming increasingly suspect. Obote survived an assassination attempt in 1969 but then, while out of the country, was deposed by Amin in 1971. Obote lived in exile in Tanzania until Amin himself was overthrown.

Although Ugandans initially welcomed the charismatic Amin as a change from Obote's authoritarianism, the brutality, corruption, and volatility of the Amin regime quickly won international infamy. Amin is best remembered for abruptly expelling Uganda's 50,000 Asians in 1972, and seizing their property. Although Amin referred to the Asians as "parasites," his handing over of the expropriated farms and businesses to army officers – who promptly ruined many of them – contributed to the rapid decline of the Ugandan economy. Amin was also known for his collaboration with the Palestine Liberation Organization in the hijacking of an Air France plane, and above all for his use of state terrorism on his own citizens.

In October 1978 Amin, perhaps to deflect attention away from his troubled economy, invaded Tanzania's Kagera salient. When President Julius Nyerere of Tanzania deployed troops to the area, they found Amin's forces weak. Soon afterward Tanzanian troops, together with exiled Ugandan opposition forces, invaded Uganda and deposed Amin, who fled initially to LIBYA and then ultimately to Saudi Arabia.

In the aftermath of the Tanzanian invasion, Yusuf Kironde Lule, a former vice chancellor of Makerere University, first headed the transitional government. The former attorney general, Godfrey Binaisa, replaced Lule several months later and suspended multiparty politics. Binaisa immediately faced challenges from military officers, including an Obote supporter, Paulo Muwanga, who arrested the president in May 1980 and became the head of a military government. Obote was returned to power six months later after allegedly rigging multiparty elections, much to the dismay of his political opponents.

Initially Obote made some headway in rebuilding the economy and government institutions, both devastated by the Amin years. But formidable guerrilla forces, including the National Resistance Army (NRA) led by Yoweri Museveni, continually challenged the legitimacy of the Obote regime. Obote responded with a brutal campaign to suppress NRA support, particularly in the Luwero Triangle of Buganda, where entire villages were destroyed during Operation Bonanza. The International Committee of the Red Cross estimated that approximately 300,000 people died during the operation, while a similar number fled to the Sudan and then Zaire (present-day Democratic Republic of the Congo).

As the president became increasingly preoccupied with maintaining control, the economic reconstruction floundered. Austerity measures imposed under a World Bank structural adjustment program brought skyrocketing inflation and shortages of staple goods. Obote was further distracted by violent conflicts between Acholi and Lango members of the military. Soon after the appointment of a Lango to a top army post, Acholi soldiers led by Gen. Tito Okello and Lt. Gen. Bazilio Okello ousted Obote in July 1985. In January 1986 Tito Okello was in turn pushed from power by the NRA, led by Museveni.

After his swearing in as president Museveni began a "ten-point program" to ensure basic human rights, cultivate a sense of national unity, and redress the past abuses of Amin and Obote. Believing that a return to multiparty politics would invite the reemergence of ethnic and religious conflicts, Museveni banned all political parties. All candidates have since been required to run under the umbrella of the National Resistance Movement. Although he postponed elections for several years, Museveni created a well-functioning system of resistance councils to govern at the national, regional, and village levels. Formerly an avowed socialist, Museveni also cooperated fully with the World Bank and other donors, winning him praise – as well as generous economic support – from abroad, despite evidence that his regime's human rights record was, in fact, considerably less impressive.

After single-party national elections in February 1989 Museveni's government announced it would extend its term until 1995 to provide adequate time to develop a new constitution, ensure free elections, and develop the country's social services. Museveni also took several steps to reconcile long-term grievances, including the reinstating of the Bugandan and other traditional monarchies, albeit only for ceremonial purposes. Museveni also invited Uganda's expelled Asians to return and reclaim assets that had been confiscated from them. He radically reduced the size of the army, while an amnesty program allowed former guerrillas to rejoin society, so long as they were not guilty of rape or murder.

Despite these measures several rebel groups have remained active in the northern part of the country. The Holy Spirit Movement led by Alice Lakwena, an Acholi priestess who claimed she could protect her followers with magic, met with a "scorched-earth" military campaign that was approved by Museveni but widely criticized by the international community. The government also faces ongoing resistance from the northern-based Lord's Resistance Army.

Museveni, most recently reelected in 1996, remains a firm advocate of his "no-party" electoral system, arguing that Western-style multiparty systems, transferred to the African context, too easily divide the country along ethnic lines. Instead, Uganda's constitution allows candidates to campaign as individuals. Meanwhile the president has had success in rebuilding the economy – one of the fastest growing in Africa in the mid-1990s – and restoring relative domestic peace and stability. These accomplishments have boosted his standing among foreign donors and investors, as well as Africans. Indeed, Uganda is becoming an increasingly influential player in the regional politics of East and Central Africa.

Uganda supported Laurent-Désiré Kabila in his successful 1997 campaign to oust President Mobutu Sese Seko of Zaire (since renamed the Democratic Republic of the Congo). In 1998, however, Uganda's government became frustrated that Kabila had been unable to prevent attacks from within Congolese territory by Ugandan rebels. In mid-1998 Ugandan troops intervened in support of a Tutsi-led rebellion against Kabila's regime. This intervention threatened to engulf Uganda in a broader Central African war when forces from Angola, Zimbabwe, and Namibia intervened in support of Kabila. The Sudanese government moved to cooperate with Kabila's alliance against Uganda because of Ugandan support for John Garang de Mabior's People's Liberation Army in southern Sudan. These military entanglements darken the prospects that Uganda will overcome ethnic strife, widespread acquired immune deficiency syndrome (AIDS) infection, and enduring rural poverty to achieve lasting peace and prosperity.

Ari Nave

See Also

Bantu: Dispersion and Settlement; Buganda, Early Kingdom of; Ethnicity and Identity in Africa: An Interpretation; Explorers in Africa Since 1800; Ivory Trade; Kampala, Uganda; Indian Communities in Africa; Languages, African: An Overview; Lugard, Frederick John Dealtry; Iron in Africa; Nationalism in Africa; Nile River; Nyerere, Julius Kambarage; Stanley, Sir Henry Morton; Structural Adjustment in Africa; Millet; AIDS in Africa: An Interpretation; Christianity: Missionaries in Africa; Human Rights in Africa; Indian Ocean Slave Trade.

Africa

Uganda (Ready Reference)

Official Name: Republic of Uganda
Area: 241,139 sq km (93,104 sq mi)
Location: Eastern Africa, borders Kenya, Rwanda, Sudan, Tanzania, Democratic Republic of the Congo
Capital: Kampala (population 773, 463 [1991 estimates])
Other Major Cities: Jinja (population 60,979), Mbale (53,634), Gulu (42,841), Entebbe (41,638), Soroti (40,602), Mbarara (40,383) (1991 estimates)
Population: 22,167,195 (1998 estimate)
Population Density: 155 persons per sq km (about 250 persons per sq mi)
Population Below Age 15: 51 percent (male 5,157,818; female 5,199,080 [1998 estimate])
Population Growth Rate: 2.85 percent (1998 estimate)
Total Fertility Rate: 7.09 children born per woman (1998 estimate)
Life Expectancy at Birth: Total population: 42.6 years (male 41.81 years; female 43.41 years [1998 estimate])
Infant Mortality Rate: 92.86 deaths per 1000 live births (1998 estimate)
Literacy Rate (age 15 and over who can read and write): Total population: 61.8 percent (male 73.7 percent; female 50.2 percent [1995 estimate])
Education: The British educational system has been influential in Uganda, and missionary schools have played an important role in educating the people. In the late 1980s about 2.6 million pupils attended some 7900 primary schools in Uganda, and some 240,000 students were enrolled in more than 900 secondary, technical, and teacher-training schools. Makerere University in Kampala has historically been one of the top universities in sub-Saharan Africa.
Languages: English, the official language, and Swahili, the language of commerce, are both widely spoken. About two-thirds of the people also speak one of several Bantu or Nilotic languages.
Ethnic Groups: About two-thirds of the people are included in the Ganda, Soga, Nyoro, Nkole, and Toro ethnic groups. The Acholi, Lango, and Karimojon ethnic groups predominate in the north.
Religions: About 60 percent of Uganda's inhabitants are Christian; approximately 5 percent are Muslim; others follow traditional religions.
Climate: Uganda's climate is mild and equable, mainly because of relatively high altitude. Temperature ranges from about 16° to 29° C (60° to 85° F). The average annual

rainfall varies from some 760 mm (30 in) in the northeast to about 1520 mm (60 in) near Lake Victoria.

Land, Plants, and Animals: The area of Uganda includes Lake George and Lake Kyoga; parts of LAKE VICTORIA, LAKE EDWARD, and Lake Albert; and the NILE RIVER from its outlet at Lake Victoria to Nimule on the Sudan frontier. The landscape is varied, with elevated plains, vast forests, low swamps, arid depressions, and snowcapped peaks, the highest of which is Margherita Peak (5109 m/ 16,762 ft) in the Ruwenzori Range. Much of the south is forested, and most of the north is covered with savanna. Plant life includes mvuli tree and elephant grass of the Uganda plateau to the dry thorn scrub, acacia, and euphorbia of the southwest. Animals include CHIMPANZEES, ANTELOPE (including the ELAND and HARTEBEEST), ELEPHANTS, RHINOCEROSES, LIONS, and leopard.

Natural Resources: Soil, gold, copper, tin, tungsten, and hydroelectricity potential

Currency: Ugandan shilling (USh)

Gross Domestic Product (GDP): $34.6 billion (1997 estimate)

GDP per Capita: $1700 (1997 estimate)

GDP Real Growth Rate: 5 percent (1997 estimate)

Primary Economic Activities: Agriculture, industry, and services

Primary Exports: Coffee, cotton, and tea

Primary Imports: Petroleum products, machinery, textiles, metals, transportation equipment, and food

Primary Trading Partners: United States, European Union, and Kenya

Government: Uganda is a republic with a modified parliamentary system. The 1995 constitution officially prohibited political parties until the year 2000, but allowed for non-party presidential and legislative elections in 1996. Lieut. Gen. YOWERI MUSEVENI, in power since a coup in 1985, won that presidential election by a wide margin; his appointed prime minister is Kintu Musoke.

Robert Fay

SEE ALSO

Bantu: Dispersion and Settlement; Kampala, Uganda; Swahili Language.

Latin America and the Caribbean

Umbanda, a religion practiced by millions of Brazilians that combines elements of African religious traditions with Roman Catholicism and European Spiritism.

BRAZIL is known for the vitality and diversity of its African-based religions, and of these Umbanda is the most widely practiced, with an estimated 20 million followers. Unlike CANDOMBLÉ, whose fame is linked to the efforts of its leaders to reproduce faithfully the rituals and practices of its West African forbears, Umbanda represents a tendency toward eclecticism: diverse African traditions have blended with one another, with Roman Catholicism, and with Spiritism, a form of Spiritualism known in Brazil as *Espiritismo* or *Kardecismo.*

Like its rituals, whose roots lie in religions practiced by African slaves and overlain with other religious influences encountered in its Brazilian environment, Umbanda's popularity has moved far beyond the Afro-Brazilian population from which it derives. Its followers today are racially and ethnically diverse, ranging from Afro-Brazilian to Portuguese, Spanish, Italian, German, Lebanese, and Japanese, and are drawn from every economic level, from the wealthy elite to the poorest residents of shantytowns. Umbanda's membership has come to reflect the diversity of Brazil's population, and the faith is often viewed as a "Brazilian" rather than an "African" religion. Characteristically, many (though not all) practitioners also consider themselves Catholics. While some emphasize Umbanda's Spiritist dimensions, others defend its African identity and practices. Before examining how Umbanda's "Brazilianization" came about and the dynamics of its internal differences, it is useful to lay out the central features of Umbanda ritual and its pantheon of deities and spirits.

UMBANDA RITUALS

Umbanda shares with other Afro-Brazilian religions and Spiritism the understanding that a wide variety of deities and spirits may intervene in the daily lives of humans to help or to harm them. Through Umbanda rituals, followers pay homage to these entities, seek their protection, and solicit their help in resolving individual illnesses and personal problems. Umbanda is understood as a pragmatic and instrumental problem-solving religion.

At public ceremonies held each week in thousands of Umbanda churches (known as *centros* or *terreiros*), initiates and members of the congregation gather to celebrate Umbanda deities and spirits. They praise them with hymns, dancing, drumming, and hand clapping and call them to descend from the spirit world, take over or "possess" the bodies of trained initiates and, acting through them, conduct healing rituals and give advice. Members of the congregation then have individual consultations with the spirit counselors, receive ritual cleansings, and may discuss their problems. People confide in the spirits about their health, employment, finances, and family and romantic problems; the spirits may recommend further ritual treatments, give practical advice, or inform clients that they can recover only by undergoing initiation into Umbanda. This is a particularly common diagnosis when clients experience spontaneous spirit possession while watching the ceremony or during their consultation, and it is the most common route through which clients become initiated into ritual roles. New initiates undergo stages of initiation as well as training sessions in mastering spirit possession. But this process is less time consuming and less costly than in Candomblé, and new initiates may rise rapidly within the ritual hierarchy. Within a few years they may gain sufficient knowledge, prestige, and authority to found their own centro.

UMBANDA DEITIES AND SPIRITS

The most powerful spiritual personages of Umbanda are African deities known by the Yoruban term *orixá* (the same deities found in Candomblé). Each orixá is syncretized, or strongly identified with, a particular Roman Catholic saint or member of the Holy Family, and is often represented in its Roman Catholic form on Umbanda altars. Thus Ogun, Yoruban god of ironworking and of war, is identified with Saint George, and his representation on Umbanda altars is often in the form of a Roman Catholic statue of Saint George slaying the dragon. The orixás' histories are recounted in the Yoruba origin myth and each orixá has a distinctive personality and is identified with certain colors, foods, and healing herbs.

While the orixás are often petitioned for aid, the major spiritual entities in Umbanda are the *caboclos* (spirits of Brazilian Indians) and *pretos velhos* ("old blacks," or spirits of Africans enslaved in Brazil). Discarnate spirits of women and men who once lived on earth, they are less powerful than the orixás but more central because they conduct the healing activities in Umbanda ceremonies. Caboclo spirits are proud forest dwellers and warriors; they can be male or female. The caboclo spirits have individual names and hymns that detail their exploits, and they can often be identified in the ceremonies by their feather headdresses and large cigars. Pretos velhos are elderly, humble, and wise; they bear tales of enslavement. They are addressed familiarly as Father *(Pai)* or Aunt *(Tia)* and hobble about on canes puffing on their pipes. Both of these categories of spirits are considered expert in providing healing and advice.

Various other spiritual personages also appear on their appointed days in the centros: child spirits called Cosme and Damião, the twins, who cause great commotion as they crawl about the floor demanding pacifiers and candy; cowboy spirits, a branch of the caboclos whose hymns recount their exploits in the northeastern backlands, or *sertão*; gypsy spirits; and *exús*. Exús are complicated and controversial figures in Umbanda. Properly African orixás, messengers to the other orixás and trickster figures, doing good or evil according to whim and payment, exús under the influence of Roman Catholicism and Spiritism have become syncretized with the Christian Devil and associated with evil and ignorance. Exú and his female counterpart, Pomba Gira, a prostitute, are depicted in Umbanda as devils, with red bodies, often scantily dressed.

In fact, the place of Exú in the pantheon is a good diagnostic and provides a point of

LEFT: This Umbanda altar (photographed in Recife, Brazil, in 1988) celebrates Father Joaquim and Mother Conga, Preto Velho spirits. Once enslaved, Pretos Velhos are now major Umbanda healers. A background mural depicts Brazilian slave scenes. *Photo by Peter Kloehn*

BELOW LEFT: A typical Umbanda altar (photographed in Recife, Brazil, in 1988) combines Catholic images, Spiritist purifying water, and representations of Indian and African deities and spirits, and highlights this religion's syncretic nature. *Photo by Peter Kloehn*

departure for discussing internal differences within Umbanda. More Spiritist forms of Umbanda consider the exús to be amoral and minimize their role, while emphasizing Spiritist and Christian doctrine. These groups conduct very restrained ceremonies that feature initiates in white uniforms, often eliminating dancing and drumming. More Afro-Brazilian forms give Exú, and the orixás in general, a more important ritual role and the ceremonies are far livelier, with drumming and dancing and initiates dressed in brightly colored outfits. Healing often occurs outside the public ceremonies. Another African ritual element emphasized more in these forms of Umbanda is the sacrifice of animals to the deities.

HISTORY AND POLITICS

Before discussing Umbanda's beginnings in Rio de Janeiro in the 1920s, a word must be said about its parent traditions.

Umbanda's African Roots

To appreciate fully the vitality of African religions and culture in Brazil, one must understand that from the beginning of the slave period in 1530 through the end of the trade in the 1850s, Brazilian slave owners continued to rely on slaves imported directly from Africa, rather than on a native-born slave labor force. This phenomenon resulted in continuing infusions of African cultures into Brazil over a period of more than 300 years. At abolition in 1888 many of the newly freed slaves were still African born.

In Bahia the intensity of trade with West Africa resulted in a great numerical predominance of Yoruban and Dahomean slaves, reflected in the dominance of these traditions in Bahian Candomblé. But the slaves imported to Rio de Janeiro were of much more diverse origins. This diversity was compounded by the southward migration of many northern slaves and free blacks to Rio during the nineteenth century. By the 1920s the resultant blending of African religious traditions loosely referred to as Macumba showed some similarities to the Umbanda rituals described above and clearly formed a substratum for the development of Umbanda.

Roman Catholic Influences

The brutal incorporation of slaves into the economic and political system of the colony led to the forced destruction of many aspects of African culture, but religious practices were not as closely controlled. Roger Bastide and others have argued that the Roman Catholic brotherhoods that exercised social control over urban slave populations actually contributed to the preservation of African religious practices. These brotherhoods were a major source of Afro-Catholic syncretism, as slaves worshiped African deities in the guise of

Roman Catholic saints. As the brotherhoods declined in the nineteenth century, Afro-Brazilian religious practices emerged in Rio as in many urban areas of Brazil. Although they were declared illegal and their practitioners were frequently persecuted by the police, their clandestine practice continued, as Afro-Brazilians refused to give up this major part of their heritage.

Spiritist Influences

Rio was also the center of Spiritism, which originated in France in the mid-nineteenth century and quickly became popular among affluent Brazilians. Spiritists summoned discarnate spirits, practiced healing, and through their charitable activities spread their practices to the popular classes.

LEFT: A medium possessed by Exu, an African deity, advises a client in Rio de Janeiro, Brazil, 1970. Portrayed in Umbanda as devil-like and amoral, Exus are considered specialists in resolving problems concerning love and money. *Photo by Diana DeG. Brown*

ABOVE: More experienced mediums help a new Umbanda initiate to receive her spirit in Campinas, São Paulo, Brazil, 1979. *Photo by Diana DeG. Brown*

The Founding of Umbanda

In the 1920s a group of middle-class Spiritists came together to create a "new" religion called Umbanda. At the time Brazil was involved in a period of intense nationalism, its leaders defining a national identity and struggling to unify the country and control its rapidly expanding urban lower classes. In grappling with how to make Brazil a modern nation, the leaders were influenced by European racist ideas. Further, they were worried about how Brazil's large African-descended population could become a part of this modernity, and how its African cultural practices could be symbolically redefined as Brazilian. For many members of the dominant classes, including Umbanda's founders, Afro-Brazilian religions became, and have remained, a key element in this redefinition.

The founders of Umbanda drew upon existing Afro-Brazilian practices but sought to reorganize and transform them, to present a form of Umbanda whitened and purified from many of its African practices. They emphasized the fact that its pantheon of Roman Catholic saints, Brazilian Indian spirits, orixás, and pretos velhos provided a symbolic expression of Brazil's unique blend of Portuguese, Native Brazilian, and African peoples and cultures, following the theme developed in Gilberto Freyre's famous work *The Masters and the Slaves*. In short, the leaders' reorganization of Umbanda represented an effort by members of the dominant classes to appropriate and transform Afro-Brazilian religious culture into national Brazilian culture. Many of the older, more African-oriented centros recognized the racism and the appropriation implicit in this form of Umbanda, and ignored or resisted it. Within Umbanda's history and practice, efforts to appropriate the African religious heritage and resistance to this appropriation are each linked to particular forms of ritual and practice in Umbanda centros.

Given this history it would be easy to imagine that divisions within Umbanda today would break down along class and racial lines, with more affluent white adherents preferring more Spiritist rituals, and the less empowered, especially Afro-Brazilians, identifying far more closely with the more African type of Umbanda. Although such identifications do occur, the overall situation is far more complicated. First, while continuing racial discrimination has greatly limited social mobility for Afro-Brazilians, most of whom remain among the poor, racial identities and solidarities in Brazil are not as clearly delineated as they are in the United States. Thus there are few exclusively Afro-Brazilian constituencies that might form around Afro-Brazilian religions, though certainly there is a middle-class-based white constituency for the more Spiritist type of Umbanda. Moreover, as Michael Hanchard argues, the Afro-Brazilian religious heritage itself has been so successfully appropriated into Brazilian national culture that it may have lost its power to symbolize a distinct Afro-Brazilian identity.

Finally, the prospects of legitimacy, protection from police persecution, possible political favors, and Umbanda's influence in electoral politics have influenced many of the older, more Afro-Brazilian terreiros to join new Umbanda organizations and reshape their rituals in accord with the new mode of practice. Thus it is very hard to draw clear linkages between particular forms of ritual practice and particular sectors of the population.

Nevertheless, recent research suggests that many new forms of opposition are developing to the "whitening" and blending of Afro-Brazilian religions represented in Umbanda, with some centros turning to more African forms of ritual and others rejecting the term *Umbanda* and returning to the older term *Macumba*. Even within those centros that continue to practice Umbanda in the form described here, the pretos velho spirits appear in recent years to have become far more ambivalent figures than the humble spirits of the past. Lindsay Hale and John Burdick argue that these spirits serve as cultural heroes for many people of African descent. The accounts of their lives that the pretos velhos now give to their followers place more emphasis on their acts of resistance to slavery, while some now claim they were never enslaved and served in African revolutionary movements. Umbanda, then, like other Afro-Brazilian religions, is always changing, responsive to the changing ways in which Brazilians relate to and identify with Brazil's African heritage. Its continuing vitality is also reflected in its spread to ARGENTINA, URUGUAY, and to the United States.

Diana DeG. Brown

SEE ALSO

Yoruba; Favelas; Rio de Janeiro, Brazil; Abolition and Emancipation in Latin America and the Caribbean; Religions, African, in Brazil; Orishas.

North America

Uncle Tom's Cabin, best-selling but controversial 1852 American novel that increased worldwide sentiment against slavery.

When Harriet Beecher Stowe's antislavery novel *Uncle Tom's Cabin* was published in 1852, it was an immediate bestseller and became the most sensational and best-selling book of the nineteenth century. French writer George Sand described the international phenomenon: "This book is in all hands and in all journals. It has, and will have, editions in every form; people devour it, they cover it with tears." Today the novel has been criticized for its stereotypical depictions of black characters, as well as for its sentimentalism and moralism. But as problematic as some of the book's language and descriptions are, in the 1850s *Uncle Tom's Cabin* evoked international sympathy for African American slaves.

Harriet Beecher Stowe was born in Connecticut in 1811, the daughter of Lyman Beecher, a prominent Congregational minister. The Beechers, who were white, had never owned slaves, but in 1832 they moved to Cincinnati, just across the Ohio River from slaveholding Kentucky. There Stowe taught at a school for ex-slave children and saw firsthand race riots, terrified runaway slaves, bounty hunters, and suffering freedpeople. Upon returning to New England in 1850, she decided to write a book about her insights, one of the only forms of protest available to her: "My heart was bursting with the anguish excited by the cruelty and injustice our nation was showing to the slave, and praying God to let me do a little and cause my cry for them to be heard."

Uncle Tom's Cabin's strong religious overtones appealed to its largely Christian, white, nineteenth-century audience. Its plot follows the story of Uncle Tom, a pious and faithful slave, as he is sold to several owners. His last owner beats him to death, but even as the Christ-like Uncle Tom is dying, he prays that his master will repent and be saved. A favorite character among readers was Little Eva, a white child who treats her slaves with angelic love and kindness and dies in the middle of the book surrounded by weeping servants. Stowe complements these melodramatic deathbed scenes with equally dramatic descriptions of beatings, sexual abuse, and family separations, all of which added to the novel's powerful effect on its readers.

This 1899 theater poster advertises a stage version of Harriet Beecher Stowe's *Uncle Tom's Cabin*, the antislavery novel first published in 1852. *CORBIS/Bettmann*

Uncle Tom's Cabin has had its critics. The first were Southern slaveholders, who argued that the book was horribly exaggerated fiction; ownership of the book was made illegal in the South. In response Stowe published in 1853 *A Key to Uncle Tom's Cabin*, a collection of SLAVE NARRATIVES, newspaper clippings, and other facts that verified the details in her novel. In more recent years many readers have criticized the condescending racist descriptions of the appearance, speech, and behavior of many of the book's black characters, and the excessive pietism of Uncle Tom.

Uncle Tom's Cabin was so widely read that its characters helped spread common stereotypes of African Americans. These included lazy, carefree Sam, an example of the "happy darky"; Eliza, Cassy, and Emmeline, beautiful light-skinned women who are the products and victims of sexual abuse and stereotypes of the tragic mulatto; and several affectionate, dark-skinned women house servants who are examples of the Mammy figure (including a character named Mammy, the cook at the St. Clare plantation).

The name "Uncle Tom" has itself become a stereotype for an African American who is too eager to please whites. Soon after the book was published, traveling "Tom shows" became popular throughout the United States. These were essentially minstrel shows loosely based on *Uncle Tom's Cabin*, and their grossly exaggerated caricatures further perpetuated some of the stereotypes that Stowe used.

These negative associations now sometimes overshadow Stowe's original intentions, as well as the historical impact of *Uncle Tom's Cabin* as a vital antislavery tool. At the time of its publication, though, the novel's impact was without question. Some have claimed that it so affected British readers that it kept England from joining the AMERICAN CIVIL WAR on the side of the Confederacy, and when President Abraham Lincoln met Stowe in 1862, he reportedly called her "the little woman who wrote the book that started this great war!" The cry that Stowe had hoped to sound about African Americans was indeed heard, and while *Uncle Tom's Cabin* did perpetuate cultural stereotypes of African Americans, it also turned the tide of public opinion against slavery in the United States.

Lisa Clayton Robinson

SEE ALSO

Abolitionism in the United States; Free Blacks in the United States, 1619 to 1863; Fugitive Slaves; Minstrelsy; Racial Stereotypes.

North America

Underground Railroad, beginning in the early nineteenth century and continuing well up to the Civil War, the so-called freedom train was a secret and extensive network of people, places, and modes of transportation that led runaway slaves from the southern United States to freedom in the North and Canada.

Well I don't know how and I don't know when,
But we're gonna be free one day.
That the freedom train's comin' round the bend
And we're gonna be free one day.
But it's comin' sure and its comin' fast
That we're gonna be free one day.
We're gonna step on board and be free at last!

Freedom was never a luxury for African American slaves; it was a destiny that became epitomized in many Negro spirituals (including the one excerpted above). The "freedom train" came infrequently and was often not on time. But when it did arrive, it was big enough and strong enough to carry the souls of the weary and to lighten the burdens of the downtrodden. The freedom train even brought hope and inspiration to those who could not physically make it on board. For years slaveholders mistakenly attributed the imagery of the freedom train in Negro spirituals to fanciful illusions in the minds of slaves about dying and going to heaven. It is now generally known, as the slaveholders learned, that the freedom train was real and powerful.

Known officially as the Underground Railroad, the freedom train was an extensive network of people, places, and modes of transportation – all working in the deepest secrecy to help transport slaves to freedom in the North and CANADA. Many slaves made the journey with the help of guides, who were often free blacks committed to the cause of abolition. White abolitionists also made significant contributions, but the freedom train was a powerful political statement made by African Americans who chose to "vote for freedom with their feet."

Historians have traditionally underestimated and understated the role of blacks, and overestimated the role of sympathetic whites in the Underground Railroad. White abolitionists did provide safe houses, money, boats, and other material resources that were sometimes vital to successful escapes. But free blacks often risked much more – their own freedom and lives – in order to travel South, to help lead others to safety. Among the more prominent "conductors" of the freedom train was Harriet Tubman. A former slave who had escaped to the North, Tubman traveled to the South at least 15 times and guided more than 200 slaves to freedom. She epitomized the success and daring of the freedom train. Through her stories and those of others, there exists a rich legacy detailing the network that is said to have helped more than 1000 slaves each year to free themselves from bondage.

Few details of the Underground Railroad are known because of the extreme secrecy required in its operation, but there are reports of its existence as early as 1837. The exact number of slaves who were freed by the railroad is also not known because, in the interests of security, the conductors of the railroad could not keep records. Although this number was never high enough to threaten the institution of slavery itself, the legends and metaphor of the freedom train worried slaveholders. Tales that were often repeated throughout the nation included, for example, the story of Henry "Box" Brown, a black man who packed himself in a wooden crate and shipped himself to freedom in Philadelphia, and the story of William and Ellen Craft, a married couple whose escape was based on their disguise – she as a "Spanish gentleman" and he as her black slave. The accounts of runaway slaves instilled fear in the hearts of Southern slave owners, and inspired Northern abolitionists to form larger and stronger antislavery organizations.

As the Underground Railroad gained notoriety, its operations became even more secret. A virtually undetected escape route ran from Texas to MEXICO, but almost no information exists about how it functioned or how many African Americans quietly blended into the Mexican populace. It became difficult to distinguish between fact and fiction in accounts of the escapes. But researchers have been able to uncover many details, especially from the accounts of free blacks who wrote memoirs or autobiographies. Free blacks such as WILLIAM STILL, DAVID RUGGLES, WILLIAM WELLS BROWN, FREDERICK DOUGLASS, and HENRY HIGHLAND GARNET joined Tubman in the struggle for self-emancipation. Most worked in silence and sometimes even in disguise.

Runaway slaves waded through swamps, concealed themselves in the hulls of ships, hid on the backs of carriages, and navigated circuitous routes by using the North Star at night – always with the understanding that they might be caught or betrayed at any time. Many were pursued by professional slave catchers (some with dogs), who had the

American artist C. T. Webber's 1893 painting shows fugitives arriving at Levi Coffin's farm in Wayne County, Indiana, a busy station on the Underground Railroad. *CORBIS*

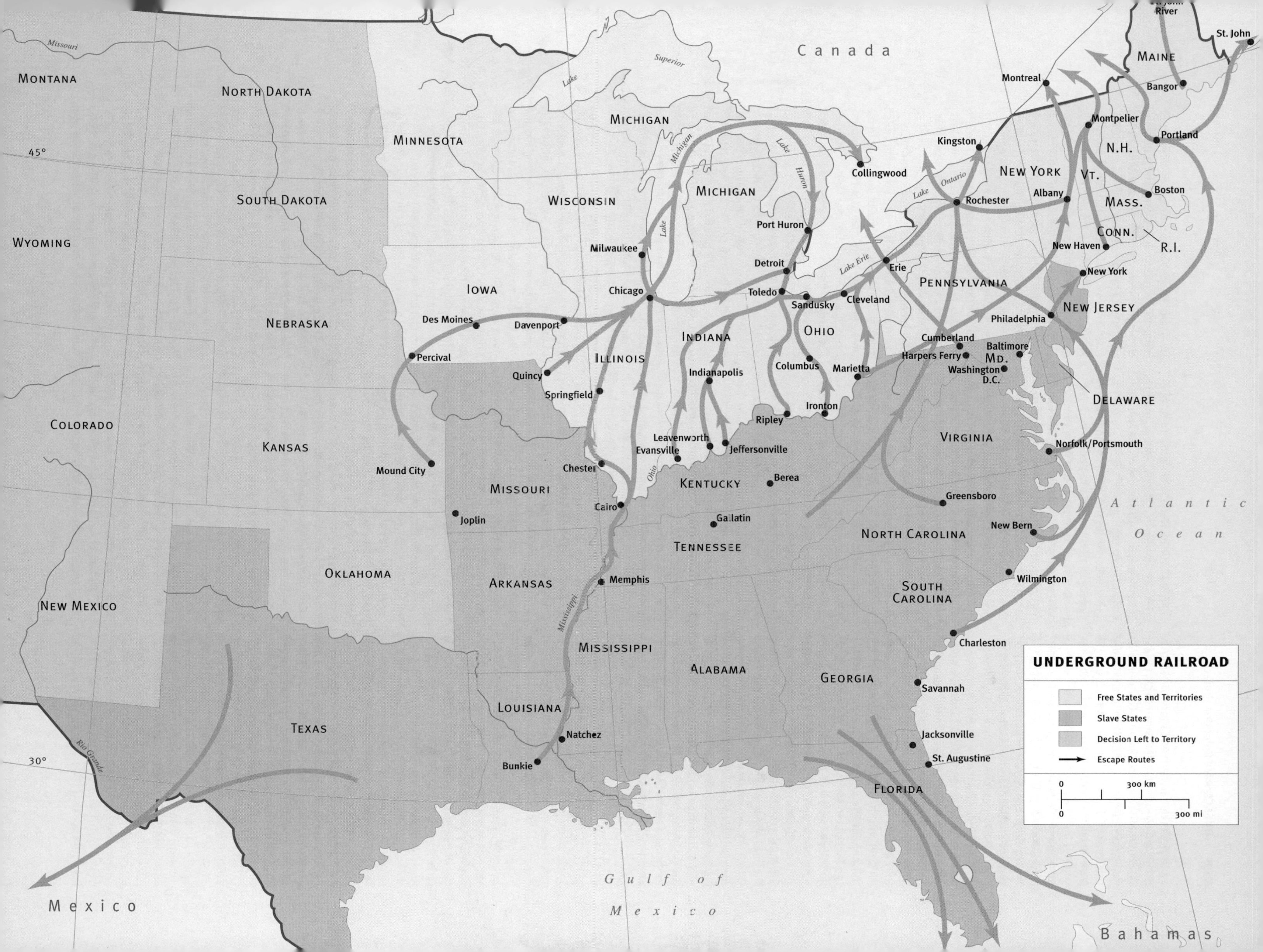
UNDERGROUND RAILROAD
Free States and Territories
Slave States
Decision Left to Territory
Escape Routes
0
300 km
0
300 mi
Canada
Mexico
Bahamas
Atlantic Ocean
Gulf of Mexico
Montana
North Dakota
South Dakota
Wyoming
Minnesota
Wisconsin
Michigan
Iowa
Nebraska
Colorado
Kansas
Oklahoma
New Mexico
Texas
Missouri
Arkansas
Louisiana
Mississippi
Illinois
Indiana
Ohio
Kentucky
Tennessee
Alabama
Georgia
Florida
South Carolina
North Carolina
Virginia
Md.
D.C.
Delaware
Pennsylvania
New Jersey
New York
Conn.
R.I.
Mass.
Vt.
N.H.
Maine
St. John River
St. John
Bangor
Portland
Montpelier
Boston
Montreal
Kingston
Albany
New Haven
New York
Rochester
Collingwood
Port Huron
Detroit
Erie
Toledo
Sandusky
Cleveland
Chicago
Milwaukee
Des Moines
Davenport
Percival
Quincy
Springfield
Indianapolis
Columbus
Marietta
Philadelphia
Cumberland
Harpers Ferry
Baltimore
Washington
Ironton
Ripley
Leavenworth
Jeffersonville
Evansville
Chester
Mound City
Berea
Cairo
Joplin
Gallatin
Memphis
Natchez
Bunkie
Norfolk/Portsmouth
Greensboro
New Bern
Wilmington
Charleston
Savannah
Jacksonville
St. Augustine
Lake Superior
Lake Michigan
Lake Huron
Lake Erie
Lake Ontario
Missouri
Ohio
Mississippi
Rio Grande
45°
30°

authority to detain and hold itinerant African Americans south of the Mason-Dixon Line. The Southern press was full of advertisements for escaped slaves. These descriptions constitute one of the few sources of accurate personal details about individuals in the slave community. The advertisements, in the slaveholders' own words, often mentioned maimed limbs and scars from whipping – vivid descriptions that Northern abolitionists used verbatim in their condemnation of slavery.

On the way to freedom slaves and their guides often found it difficult to obtain food, clothing, and shelter. Free blacks in cities such as Philadelphia and Boston formed "vigilance committees" to meet these and other needs. The committees cared for runaways after they arrived on free soil, hid them to prevent their recapture, and aided them on their way to Canada. The Philadelphia Association for the Moral and Mental Improvement of the People of Color was one of the most prominent black vigilance committees.

With the aid of black vigilance committees the Underground Railroad continued to guide slaves to freedom up until the time of the Civil War itself, when thousands of slaves freed themselves by leaving the plantations and escaping behind Union Army lines. For those who still labored as slaves at the beginning of the Civil War, the legend of the Underground Railroad held out hope. In the words of another Negro spiritual:

I know my Lord is a man of war;
He fought my battle at Hell's dark door.
Satan thought he had me fast;
I broke his chain and got free at last.

Alonford James Robinson, Jr.

See Also

Abolitionism in the United States; Boston, Massachusetts; Brown, Henry ("Box"); Civil War, American; Craft, Ellen and William; Free Blacks in the United States, 1619 to 1863; Fugitive Slaves; Philadelphia, Pennsylvania; Tubman, Harriet Ross; Spirituals, African American.

Latin America and the Caribbean

UNESCO Race Relations Project,

a series of research projects on race relations in Brazil from 1951 to 1952 sponsored by the United Nations Educational, Scientific and Cultural Organization (UNESCO); the studies were aimed at revealing the country's history of race relations, which at the time was deemed unique and positive.

After World War II one of UNESCO's major missions was to understand the conflict and its most perverse consequence, the Holocaust. With the persistence of racism in the United States and South Africa, the emergence of the cold war, and the process of decolonization in Africa and Asia, the issue of race continued to attract attention. UNESCO stimulated the development of scientific knowledge about racism, looking at motivations, consequences, and possible ways of overcoming it.

In the late 1940s two events highlighted the agency's efforts against racial intolerance. First, at a meeting of experts from the social and natural sciences, participants discussed the scientific standing of the concept of race. The resulting "Statement on Race," published in May 1950 at UNESCO's Fifth General Conference in Florence, was the first document published with the support of a supranational agency that denied any deterministic association between physical characteristics, social behaviors, and moral attributes, notions that were still in fashion during the 1930s and 1940s. Second, at the same conference Brazil was selected as the object of a comprehensive investigation of the economic, social, political, cultural, and psychological factors that influenced, or did not influence, the emergence of cooperative relations between races and ethnic groups. In choosing Brazil the purpose was to focus on potentially positive experiences and thus offer the world a new political consciousness based on the possibility of harmony among the races.

Since the nineteenth century travelers to Brazil from Europe and the United States recorded with surprise the apparently peaceful coexistence of races and ethnic groups there. This image of a "racial paradise," in contrast with the persistently turbulent North American experience, also connected with the fears of Brazilian elites. Especially after the belated abolition of slavery and adoption of a republican form of government, Brazil's elites saw the large proportion of blacks in the population, and the frequency of miscegenation, as obstacles to the country's progress toward modernity. However, during the first decades of the twentieth century, particularly between the 1920s and 1940s, this view began to change. Due to Brazil's economic, social, and political transformations, and because of the importance given by intellectual circles to the precise identification of the country's national identity, the pessimistic view about the contributions of the founding races was preempted by a positive perspective. In this view Brazil's racial mix was seen as an indicator of tolerance and harmony, and as a positive and unique feature of the country's national identity. The most sophisticated analysis of the controversial belief in Brazilian racial democracy was developed by Brazilian sociologist Gilberto Freyre. The belief became one of the major ideological components of Brazilian nationalism and was substantial enough to gain an international audience.

It was in the wake of Nazi genocide that Brazil's seemingly harmonious racial and ethnic relations gained increased notoriety, attracting UNESCO's attention. In 1949 the Brazilian anthropologist Arthur Ramos, a specialist in Afro-Brazilian cults, became the head of UNESCO's department of social sciences. He proceeded to draw the outlines of a research project to be developed in Brazil. His concerns merged with those of several social scientists involved in research about Brazilian issues. These scholars were aware that certain demands – such as industrialization and literacy programs – had been included in the agenda of the international agency on account of pressures generated specifically by underdeveloped countries. It was the combination of this belief in the positive nature of Brazilian sociability and of the idea that certain sectors of the population – such as blacks – needed to be incorporated into modernity that gave rise to the UNESCO project.

Research for the project was conducted during the early 1950s in both the traditional north and northeast regions of Brazil and in the more modernized southeast. Social scientists from Brazil, France, and the United States, such as Florestan Fernandes, Roger Bastide, and Charles Wagley, participated in the project. The UNESCO project findings showed not only an enormous social distance between whites and blacks but also little social mobility among nonwhites. In the north and northeast racial prejudice was deemed to be subtle but nonetheless existent. Research in southeastern areas looked at racial relations in Brazil's major development centers, Rio de Janeiro and São Paulo, where economic and social changes had been intense. In these centers during the last years of slavery, black and mulattos had to contend with large numbers of European immigrants, and racial tensions were deemed more visible. Although findings differed from one region to another, there was a consensus about the higher congeniality of the relations between blacks and whites in Brazil as compared to those in the United States and South Africa. The project also found that racial classification in Brazil combined phenotypic definitions with nonbiological attributes such as class, status, and education. Thus a complex system of racial classification was revealed.

Research under UNESCO's auspices in the 1950s brought, first, a reinforcement of the Brazilian sociological tradition of investigating relations between whites and blacks, which had gained earlier prominence in the 1930s with the writings of Freyre and Donald Pierson. Second, social sciences in Brazil, which were then being institutionalized, expanded their scope and have since systematically studied the issue of race relations. The project produced a vast documentation of the existence of prejudice and discrimination against Brazilian blacks. Focusing on these issues, the UNESCO projects prompted new questions about Brazil and helped identify difficulties, deadlocks, and conflicts in a society in the process of urbanization and industrialization. However, the recognition that there was a "Brazilian style of racism" did not preclude the participating social scientists from noticing, nonetheless, the existence of a set of social relations that could contribute to an authentic racial democracy in Brazil.

Marcos Chor Maio

See Also

Decolonization in Africa: An Interpretation; Race: An Interpretation; Rio de Janeiro, Brazil; Abolition and Emancipation in Latin America and the Caribbean; Myth of Racial Democracy in Latin America and the Caribbean: An Interpretation.

United Kingdom. Please see Great Britain

Africa

United Nations in Africa, the

United Nations (UN) agencies and programs in Africa, which have been involved in decolonization, peacekeeping, famine relief, human rights, and economic development.

Africa has been the site of some of the United Nations' greatest achievements as well as its biggest failures. The UN played an important role in assuring many African colonies' peaceful transition to independence, and has since mobilized successful international campaigns for children's health and the eradication of diseases. UN-sponsored diplomacy has helped resolve a number of long-running conflicts, especially in southern Africa. However, long-term solutions to chronic poverty, social inequality, and political instability in Africa have eluded the UN, and the questionable effectiveness of UN peacekeeping troops in Somalia and Rwanda in the early 1990s provoked widespread criticism, both in Africa and abroad.

When the UN was created in 1945, only Ethiopia, Liberia, and South Africa were independent nations in Africa. But for Europe's colonial powers, the costs of maintaining colonial rule were growing unsustainably high, due in part to burgeoning nationalist movements throughout much of Africa. Decolonization was thus one of the UN's first concerns in Africa, and the transition to independence was a principal concern during the early postwar period. In accordance with one of the four guiding UN principles – the development of friendly international relations based on equality and self-determination – the UN General Assembly created a special committee to oversee conditions in colonial territories in 1947. The committee gathered information on the territories and supported their right to self-determination.

In addition, after World War II the UN took over from the League of Nations trusteeships of six former German and Italian colonies in Africa, among them Tanganyika (now Tanzania) and Togo. Like most French, British, and Belgian colonies in Africa, these trusteeships were all independent by the early 1960s. White minority rule persisted in much of southern Africa, however. In 1965 the UN imposed sanctions on Southern Rhodesia, but only after a long liberation war did Ian Smith's regime step down, leading to independence for the renamed Zimbabwe in 1980.

The UN also supported independence for Portuguese-ruled Angola and Mozambique and opposed South Africa's occupation of South West Africa, now Namibia. There a UN program to lead Namibia to independence was established in 1968. After years of resistance South Africa agreed to relinquish Namibia provided that Cuban troops left nearby Angola. The UN-supervised elections took place in 1989, and full Namibian independence was declared the following year. Finally, the UN General Assembly repeatedly condemned apartheid in South Africa itself. When apartheid was finally dismantled in the early 1990s, UN monitors observed the 1994 elections that swept to victory Nelson Mandela, South Africa's first black president.

Soon after the first wave of African decolonization in the early 1960s, UN diplomacy on the continent turned to conflict resolution and peacekeeping. The results have been mixed. The UN operation in the Republic of the Congo (1960-1964) became the first of many such endeavors. UN troops, mostly African, were called to the Republic of the Congo after a secession attempt by Katanga Province led to intervention by Belgian troops, purportedly to protect Belgian citizens. Dag Hammerskjöld, then UN secretary general, died in a plane crash en route to the Republic of the Congo. The UN troops left after the rebels surrendered, but ongoing civil conflict led to a coup in 1965 by Mobutu Sese Seko, whose dictatorship contributed to political instability in Central Africa for decades.

UN peacekeeping troops and observers have since served in many African countries, but two of their most controversial interventions occurred in the early 1990s. In Somalia the UN's Operation Restore Hope (1993-1995) was intended to secure the distribution of famine relief aid under conditions of civil war. The operation was widely criticized for strengthening the hand of Somali warlords in the capital of Mogadishu, and for causing the deaths of 83 UN soldiers. Televised images of the bodies of dead American soldiers being dragged through the streets provoked outrage in the United States. In the wake of the 1994 genocide in Rwanda, many both in Rwanda and abroad blamed the UN peacekeeping force in the country for failing to prevent it. The UN has since defended its role, attributing the force's inaction to opposition from the United States.

The Rwandan genocide and other civil conflicts made refugee crises one of the UN's chief concerns in Africa in the 1990s. In 1995 the UN high commissioner for refugees estimated that some 4.5 million refugees from 30 African countries were in need of assistance.

The UN has been extensively involved in food security in Africa. The Food and Agriculture Organization (FAO) runs many programs to improve agriculture and nutrition. For example, a program was introduced in Zimbabwe in 1996 to reduce pesticide use through the introduction of natural predators, crop rotation, and disease-resistant plant varieties; and a 1993 erosion control plan in Burundi encouraged tree, shrub, and grass planting. The United Nations Development Program also devotes about 25 percent of its aid to food-related projects in Africa. Yet warfare and drought, among other factors, have led to repeated regional food shortages since the 1960s, including famines in the Sahel and the Horn of Africa in the 1970s and mid-1980s and in Sudan in the late 1990s. By the 1970s the FAO was heavily involved in distributing food aid, including emergency relief aid, through its World Food Program. The proportion of FAO resources devoted to disaster relief rather than long-term food security rose even higher in the early 1990s, but the organization is also engaged in crop research and development projects and in programs to improve food distribution systems in African countries.

Since the early 1980s the UN's International Bank for Reconstruction and Development, commonly known as the World Bank, has engaged most countries in Africa in multi-year programs to reduce high national debts and promote economic growth. Known as structural adjustment programs, these initiatives tie multilateral loans to economic reforms, such as price and currency deregulation and the privatization of state-run enterprises. The World Bank also provides funds for many development projects in Africa as well as technical assistance and project evaluation. In the 1990s the World Bank became Africa's largest source of loan funds.

Another major player in the African arena is the UN's World Health Organization (WHO). WHO's most outstanding achievement may have been the eradication of smallpox. Starting in 1958, WHO mounted a massive international vaccination campaign. The last smallpox case was reported in 1977, and in 1980 the disease was declared eradicated worldwide. WHO has also made great progress against onchocerciasis (or river blindness), a debilitating disease that had made large regions of Sahelian West Africa uninhabitable. WHO's Onchocerciasis Control Programme, begun in 1974, has nearly eliminated the disease. WHO also hopes to eradicate both poliomyelitis and iodine deficiency disorders by the year 2000. WHO's Global Programme on Acquired Immune Deficiency Syndrome (AIDS) was launched in 1985. With some 21 million Africans infected with human immunodeficiency virus (HIV)/AIDS – about 80 percent of the world's total number of cases – AIDS prevention and treatment have become major WHO priorities. The agency is also involved in stopping the spread of other diseases, especially malaria, the world's number-one infectious disease in terms of fatalities.

Other UN entities active in Africa include the United Nations Children's Fund (UNICEF);

the United Nations Educational, Scientific and Cultural Organization (UNESCO); and the United Nations Environment Programme (UNEP). Both the present UN secretary general, KOFI ANNAN of Ghana, and his predecessor, the Egyptian BOUTROS BOUTROS-GHALI, are African, indicating the increasing presence of Africans in high-ranking UN positions and helping to focus UN priorities on Africa and other Third World regions. Secretary General Annan has urged member nations to devote more attention to the needs of the poor and to pay their UN dues (many countries, especially the United States, are far behind in payments) so that the organization can more effectively address Africa's problems and conflicts.

David P. Johnson, Jr.

SEE ALSO

Decolonization in Africa: An Interpretation; Mandela, Nelson Rolihlahla; Nationalism in Africa; AIDS in Africa: An Interpretation; Human Rights in Africa.

North America

United Negro College Fund, an American organization founded on April 25, 1944, to provide financial support to students at historically black colleges and universities.

At its inception the United Negro College Fund (UNCF) was a consortium of 27 institutions with 14,000 students. Today there are 39 member colleges, and the UNCF has financially helped more than 300,000 African Americans to graduate. The current president is William Gray III, a Baptist minister from Philadelphia who is a former congressperson. The UNCF headquarters is in Fairfax, Virginia, and there are 20 regional offices.

With the motto "A mind is a terrible thing to waste," the UNCF's programs help provide low-cost, quality education for deserving students and include premedical summer enrichment seminars, international exchange, and technical assistance to faculty and administration at historically black colleges and universities. Many alumni of historically black schools who received UNCF support have gone on to become leaders in the legal and medical fields, academia, politics, and government

The UNCF's largest gift was a $42 million grant from the Lilly Endowment, the country's biggest foundation, in 1998. According to the UNCF, the grant will contribute to the fund's capital projects by providing money for new construction, building renovation, laboratory equipment, and information technology upgrades. This is in addition to need-based as well as merit scholarships, and faculty support via endowed chairs and curriculum development.

ADMISSIONS TO 4-YEAR COLLEGES AND UNIVERSITIES 1972-1991 (in thousands)

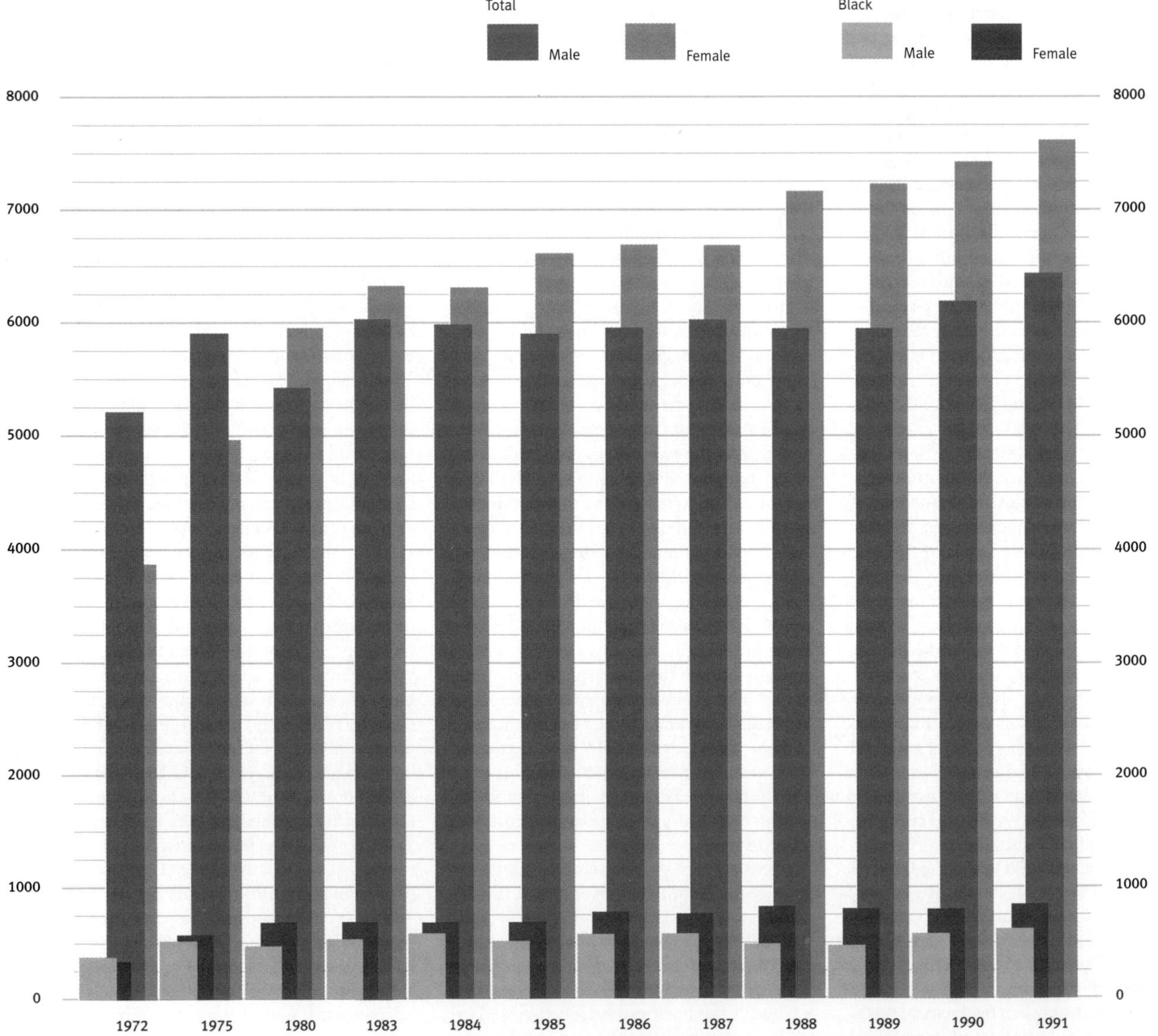

Source: *Encyclopedia of African-American Culture and History* (1996): "College Enrollment, 1972-1991" (Table 6.12); *Statistical Abstracts*, 1993.

HISTORICALLY BLACK COLLEGES AND UNIVERSITIES

State	City	Institution	Founding Date
Alabama	Birmingham	Miles College	1905
	Huntsville	Oakwood College	1896
	Montgomery	Alabama State University	1866
	Normal	Alabama A&M University	1875
	Talladega	Talladega College	1867
	Tuscaloosa	Stillman College	1876
	Tuskegee	Tuskegee University	1881
Arkansas	Little Rock	Arkansas Baptist College	1884
	Little Rock	Philander-Smith College	1877
	Pine Bluff	University of Arkansas at Pine Bluff	1873
Delaware	Dover	Delaware State University	1891
District of Columbia	Washington	Howard University	1867
	Washington	University of the District of Columbia	1851
Florida	Daytona Beach	Bethune-Cookman College	1904
	Jacksonville	Edward Waters College	1866
	Miami	Florida Memorial College	1879
	Tallahassee	Florida A&M University	1887
Georgia	Albany	Albany State College	1903
	Atlanta	Atlanta University	1865
	Atlanta	Charles H. Mason Theological Seminary	1970
	Atlanta	Clark College	1869
	Atlanta	Gammon Theological Seminary	1883
	Atlanta	Johnson C. Smith Theological Seminary	1867
	Atlanta	Morehouse College	1867
	Atlanta	Morehouse School of Medicine	1974
	Atlanta	Morehouse School of Religion	1867
	Atlanta	Morris Brown College	1881
	Atlanta	Phillips School of Theology	1945
	Atlanta	Spelman College	1881
	Atlanta	Turner Theological Seminary	1894
	Augusta	Paine College	1882
	Fort Valley	Fort Valley State College	1895
	Savannah	Savannah State College	1890
Kentucky	Berea	Berea College	1855
	Frankfort	Kentucky State University	1886
Louisiana	Baton Rouge	Southern University and A&M College, Baton Rouge	1880
	Grambling	Grambling State University	1901
	New Orleans	Dillard University	1869
	New Orleans	Southern University at New Orleans	1956
	New Orleans	Xavier University of Louisiana	1915
	Shreveport	Southern University at Shreveport	1964
Maryland	Baltimore	Coppin State College	1900
	Baltimore	Morgan State University	1867
	Bowie	Bowie State College	1865
	Princess Anne	University of Maryland, Eastern Shore	1886
Mississippi	Holly Springs	Rust College	1866
	Itta Bena	Mississippi Valley State University	1946
	Jackson	Jackson State University	1877
	Lorman	Alcorn State University	1871
	Tougaloo	Tougaloo College	1869
Missouri	Jefferson City	Lincoln University	1866
	St. Louis	Harris-Stowe State University	1857
North Carolina	Charlotte	Johnson C. Smith University	1867
	Concord	Barber-Scotia College	1867
	Durham	North Carolina Central University	1909
	Elizabeth City	Elizabeth City State University	1891
	Fayetteville	Fayetteville State University	1867
	Greensboro	Bennett College	1873
	Greensboro	North Carolina A&T State University	1891
	Raleigh	Shaw University	1865
	Raleigh	Saint Augustine's College	1867
	Salisbury	Livingstone College	1879
	Winston-Salem	Winston-Salem State University	1892
Ohio	Wilberforce	Central State University	1887
	Wilberforce	Wilberforce University	1856
Oklahoma	Langston	Langston University	1897
Pennsylvania	Cheyney	Cheyney University	1837
	Lincoln	Lincoln University	1853
South Carolina	Columbia	Allen University	1870
	Columbia	Benedict College	1870
	Denmark	Vorhees College	1897
	Orangeburg	Claflin College	1869
	Orangeburg	South Carolina State University	1872
	Sumter	Morris College	1908
Tennessee	Jackson	Lane College	1882
	Knoxville	Knoxville College	1863
	Memphis	LeMoyne-Owen College	1862
	Nashville	Fisk University	1866
	Nashville	Meharry Medical College	1876
	Nashville	Tennessee State University	1912
Texas	Austin	Huston-Tillotson College	1875
	Hawkins	Jarvis Christian College	1912
	Houston	Texas Southern University	1927
	Marshall	Wiley College	1873
	Prairie View	Prairie View A&M University	1876
	Tyler	Texas College	1894
	Waco	Paul Quinn College	1872
Virginia	Hampton	Hampton University	1868
	Lawrenceville	Saint Paul's College	1883
	Norfolk	Norfolk State University	1935
	Petersburg	Virginia State University	1882
	Richmond	Virginia Union University	1865
West Virginia	Bluefield	Bluefield State College	1895
	Institute	West Virginia State College	1891

Source: *Encyclopedia of African-American Culture and History* (1996): "Historically Black Colleges and Universities" (Table 6.13).

See Also
Gray, William Herbert, III; Philadelphia, Pennsylvania; Congress, African Americans in.

North America

United States Judiciary, Blacks in the

The nominee for the newly created position on the United States Court of Appeals for the Third Circuit approached confirmation hearings with impressive credentials. He was a graduate of Amherst College (Phi Beta Kappa and magna cum laude) and Harvard Law School (J.D., S.J.D.; law review editor) as well as a member of the faculty, and later dean, of Howard University School of Law. He served as assistant solicitor in the U.S. Department of the Interior, civilian aide to the secretary of war in World War II, and was a personal adviser to President Truman. He was a former governor and U.S. District Court judge. The nominee in question was William Henry Hastie, the first African American appointed to the federal bench. His nomination was roundly endorsed by the attorney general and the American Bar Association. Moreover, the sitting judges on the third circuit – his colleagues by virtue of his recess appointment to the new judgeship – actively lobbied their U.S. senators on his behalf. Yet his unprecedented appointment was engulfed in often vicious political controversy – this at one point even degenerated to Hastie's being branded by some as a Communist, which, in the climate of the times, was a deadly accusation. Between his nomination and eventual confirmation fully ten months later, hearings were postponed, a special subcommittee was impaneled to consider his nomination, and the political nerves of those both on and off the bench were rubbed raw.

Federal judges are important not only because they decide conflicts (cases) between individuals and groups in society, but also because they interpret the Constitution. In the process they determine how broad statements like "equal protection under the laws" in the Fourteenth Amendment apply to specific situations such as the legality of segregation or affirmative action. Federal judges are nominated by the president and must be confirmed by the U.S. Senate. They "hold their Offices during good Behavior," which means they serve for life unless removed from office (a truly extraordinary event). Consequently, the mark that presidents make on the courts with their appointments is evident for years or even decades after they leave office. For example, 23 years after Lyndon Johnson left the White House, Thurgood Marshall was still on the Supreme Court.

At the dawn of the twenty-first century some are proclaiming the start of an almost revolutionary diversification of the federal courts. This process was spearheaded by the efforts of President Bill Clinton, who promised to use his appointment power to create a bench that "looks like America." Even though almost 20 percent of President Clinton's appointments went to African Americans, the overall percentage of African Americans on the bench at the end of 1996 stood at only 9.2 percent, fully 25 percent lower than the percentage of African Americans in the general population (12.7 percent). Additionally, the preponderance of Clinton's appointments were to certain states or regions. Indeed, almost half (23) of the states in this country never have had an African American federal judge. The general trend toward diversification is diluted further because most appointments have been to the district courts, rather than to the more prestigious and powerful appeals courts, where the number of sitting African American judges amounts to only 5.8 percent.

Research on federal judicial selection tells us that minority appointments are likely to come from areas where there are higher concentrations of African American voters and economic power, often in the form of business ownership. The African American community in those areas is a force to be recognized and reckoned with, which leads to representation on the bench. Given the structure of the judicial selection process, however, the role of the president is central, and the degree to which diversification is achieved is, in large measure, a product of how important that goal is to a president.

The First Inroads: 1937-1976

The federal judiciary – by nature of a shared institutional appointment process – is inextricably bound to the president and Congress, which in turn interact with the larger society. Genuine progress is rarely made until all the elements in this complex mix are prepared to support change. This principle is demonstrated in the chain of events that started with the Supreme Court's decision in Brown v. Board of Education in 1954, which, among other things, set the stage for congressional approval of the Civil Rights Act of 1964 and the Voting Rights Act of 1965. These two acts were in turn enforced vigorously by President Johnson's attorney general, Ramsey Clark.

No African American was appointed to the federal judiciary until 1937. Even after that, the first two – William Hastie and his successor, Herman Moore – were named as district judges to the Virgin Islands. Unlike judicial appointments from states, territorial appointments are set for a fixed term rather than for life. Additionally, even though territorial appointees must be confirmed by the Senate, they do not serve an area that is represented by a senator. Accordingly, they elide the "not in my backyard" mentality of elected politicians serving in a pervasively racist political climate. Hastie's appointment, in other words, was part of no grand effort to diversify the judiciary. Prior to his nomination he served with distinction as the Interior Department's assistant solicitor in charge of the Virgin Islands; he was subsequently the governor of this territory. Interior Secretary Harold Ickes recommended him to President Roosevelt when a vacancy occurred on the Virgin Islands court.

For his time Roosevelt's successor, Harry Truman, was progressive with regard to issues of race; he ordered the desegregation of the armed forces and an end to discrimination in the civil service. Although he commissioned only three African American judges, two of the three are of special significance. Irvin Mollison was the first African American lifetime appointee, albeit one to the Customs Court, which has a specialized rather than a general jurisdiction. Hastie reemerged as another first – this time as the first African American appointed to the prestigious Circuit Court of Appeals, where he served with distinction until his retirement in 1971.

The election of Dwight Eisenhower in 1952 stalled the process of bench diversification. Eisenhower's opposition to racial justice in general and to the decision in *Brown* v. *Board of Education* in particular are well documented. Both are illustrated in his judicial appointees: in his eight years as president Eisenhower allowed only 1 of his 173 appointments to go to an African American candidate – Walter Gordon, who was posted to the Virgin Islands.

To some John F. Kennedy symbolized a commitment to racial justice, and his election in 1960 heralded to many a new dawn in securing minority appointments to the federal courts. The fact remains, however, that throughout his abbreviated presidency Kennedy was very careful not to antagonize powerful Southerners in the Congress. While it is impossible to know what might have transpired had he served two full terms, Kennedy's timidity in this regard is reflected in his judicial appointments: only 3 percent (4 of 128) went to African Americans. Judge Spottswood Robinson's appointment to the District of Columbia notwithstanding, all of Kennedy's African American appointments were to federal courts in Northern states.

Judicial diversity was fundamentally advanced under Lyndon Johnson. Johnson, for one thing, appointed more than twice as many African Americans (9) as did his predecessor. Further, in 1966 he nominated Constance Baker Motley, the first female African American jurist, to the Southern District of New York. He followed that appointment in 1967 with the stunning announcement that Thurgood Marshall was his choice for a seat on the Supreme Court.

Judge Motley was born in New Haven, Connecticut, in 1921 and graduated from New York University and Columbia Law School. Prior to her appointment to the bench she was an attorney for the National Association for the Advancement of Colored People (NAACP) Legal Defense Fund, a New York state senator, and borough president of Manhattan. She retired from the court in 1986. Justice Marshall was born in Baltimore, Maryland, in 1908 and graduated from Lincoln

University and Howard University Law School. He was solicitor general of the United States (the government's chief lawyer) and prior to his elevation to the Supreme Court he served on the Second Circuit Court of Appeals. He received national prominence when, as director of the NAACP Legal Defense Fund, he argued *Brown* v. *Board of Education* before the Supreme Court. He retired from the bench in 1991.

Richard Nixon, in his 1968 presidential campaign, complained often and vehemently about the liberal decisions made by the Supreme Court in the 1950s and 1960s and pledged that he would appoint only "strict constructionists" to the federal bench. Then and again in his reelection effort in 1972 he pursued a "Southern strategy" designed to attract voters from the nation's Southland who otherwise might be inclined to vote for segregationist George Wallace. Once Nixon was elected, the consequences for the federal bench were predictable. Nixon and his caretaker successor, Gerald Ford, appointed only ten African Americans to the federal bench, and six of those were Republicans; none was appointed to either the more prestigious circuit courts or the Supreme Court. In one case Whitney Young, executive director of the National Urban League, lobbied the president to replace the retired Hastie with Clarence Ferguson. The latter was a lifelong Republican, former dean of Howard University Law School, and professor at Rutgers Law School. Despite Young's contention that Hastie's replacement was a matter of grave concern to the black community, Ferguson was rejected as being too liberal, and Hastie's seat went to a white male.

Jimmy Carter: 1977-1980

Carter was the first president elected from the Deep South in more than a century, and he brought to the Oval Office a personal commitment to racial progress. African Americans were a crucial element of his electoral coalition, especially in the Southern states that ended up leading his margin of victory. During the 1976 campaign he pledged to appoint judges on the basis of merit rather than traditional political considerations, and once in office he worked with Congress to establish merit selection commissions in the states and circuits. Throughout its term the Carter administration promoted racial and gender diversification. Compared to those of his predecessors, Carter's results were stunning. Thirty-eight (14 percent) of his appointments went to African Americans. In contrast to that of other presidents, Carter's appointment rate for African Americans was higher in the circuit courts than in the district courts (he made no appointments to the Supreme Court). Carter made the first African American judicial appointment to a Deep South state – Robert Collins to the Eastern District of Louisiana. Moreover, by the time he left office he had made the first African American appointments to 14 states, including 11 Southern and border states, as well as the first such appointment on 3 circuits. So, in just four years Carter made considerable strides in diversifying the bench in two respects – numerically and geographically.

The Republican Reversal: 1981-1992

Ronald Reagan entered office armed with a conservative political agenda and an avowed hostility to affirmative action. The consequences for racial diversification of the federal bench followed suit: only 7 of Reagan's 369 appointees (1.9 percent) were African American. Only one African American was placed on the circuit courts, and none went to the Supreme Court. Perhaps the only saving grace of Reagan's appointments was that they completed the task – spearheaded by Carter – of integrating the Deep South bench by assigning African American district judges to Virginia and Mississippi.

As Reagan's administration wore on, the level of criticism by the Democrat-controlled Senate rose over the president's apparent inattention to racial and gender diversity on the federal courts. George Bush experienced pressure from the same criticism when he entered office. Additionally, postelection analyses revealed that Bush faced a "gender gap" with female voters (a considerably lower percentage of his supporters were women), and minority voters held the balance of power in several states that would be critical to his reelection efforts. Accordingly, Bush was more attentive to appointing women and Latinos than African Americans, yet he nonetheless improved on Reagan's record by awarding 13 of his 187 appointments to African Americans. Bush also appreciated that minority candidates could be nominated without conceding political or legal agendas contrary to his own: only 2 of Bush's 13 appointees were Democrats. Judge Clarence Thomas was appointed to the Supreme Court in 1991, and he is now one of the staunchest conservatives on the high court.

Justice Thomas was born in Savannah, Georgia, and was educated at Holy Cross College and Yale Law School. He was assistant attorney general for the State of Missouri, legislative assistant to Senator John Danforth (MO), assistant secretary for civil rights in the U.S. Department of Education, and chair of the Equal Employment Opportunity Commission. Prior to his elevation to the Supreme Court he was appointed to the U.S. Court of Appeals for the District of Columbia Circuit by President Bush in 1990.

A Bench That Looks Like America: 1993-

Clinton entered office without wanting to recast the ideological profile of the federal judiciary; he did not base his selection of appointees on litmus tests on issues such as abortion, as had the Reagan administration. While Clinton did have perhaps the most ambitious domestic policy agenda in a generation, he sought to implement it in ways other than a judicial selection strategy. Reluctant to have heated confirmation battles jeopardize his policy aspirations in other areas, he consistently nominated moderate candidates with sound credentials. Nevertheless, during his campaign and once in office Clinton was unambiguous in his intention to broaden representation both in the executive branch and on the federal courts. He made good on his promise by appointing the largest percentage of African Americans in history (19.6); these were by and large moderates, to be sure.

The pace of diversification slowed somewhat once the Republicans wrested control of the Congress from the Democrats in 1994, so Clinton's place in the history of bench diversification remains to be seen. African Americans currently are represented on only 5 of the 12 circuit courts and on the district courts of 25 states. Even so, Carter or Clinton alone had a hand in all but one of the circuit appointments, and in 17 of those to the states.

Gerard Gryski and Gary Zuk

See Also

Military, Blacks in the American; Fourteenth Amendment to the United States Constitution; NAACP Legal Defense and Educational Fund; Young, Whitney Moore, Jr.

Cross Cultural

Universal Negro Improvement Association, an influential international organization advocating African repatriation, self-government, and economic autonomy that thrived during the 1920s under the leadership of founder Marcus Garvey.

Founded in Kingston, Jamaica, in 1914 by black nationalist Marcus Garvey, the Universal Negro Improvement Association (UNIA) is widely recognized as the largest international organization in history of people of African descent. Its full name, the Universal Negro Improvement Association and Conservation and African Communities (Imperial) League, reflects its dual purpose: to promote black social mobility through racial uplift and economic prosperity, and to aid black repatriation and the creation of an autonomous black state in Africa.

It was as a charitable organization that the UNIA first emerged. Garvey envisioned an organization modeled after Masonic and Greek-letter societies that would provide Jamaican blacks with the kind of industrial education offered in the United States by Booker T. Washington's Tuskegee Institute. Yet Garvey was unable to find sufficient support for the UNIA in Jamaica. Attributing this disinterest to a lack of a racial consciousness among black Jamaicans, Garvey moved the UNIA to Harlem, New York, in 1918.

Adopting a strident black nationalist posture in response to the antiblack violence of the

Red Summer of 1919, the UNIA provided a vehicle for the political aspirations of the "New Negro" (*see* Harlem Renaissance). The organization flourished, aided by the brisk sale of shares in the Black Star Line, Inc., a shipping company intended to forge economic ties between the United States and Africa and to support repatriation.

The UNIA saw itself as Africa's government in exile – replete with a national flag and uniformed officers spectacularly displayed at its conventions and parades – with Garvey as its provisional president. Its journal, the *Negro World,* was cited as an instrument of anticolonial insurrection and banned in several African countries. By the early 1920s the UNIA's slogan, "One God, One Aim, One Destiny," had become the rallying cry for an estimated 1 million members distributed among thousands of local branches throughout the African diaspora.

The decline of the UNIA was as quick as its ascent. In 1923, in the wake of the collapse of the Black Star Line, the organization was thrown into disarray when Garvey was imprisoned on charges of mail fraud – charges that were in fact orchestrated by integrationist African Americans. After Garvey's release and deportation to Jamaica, the UNIA was splintered by competing claims to its leadership. Garvey tried to resurrect the UNIA in Jamaica in 1929, but the stock market crash of that year depleted the organization's resources. In 1935 Garvey tried again to launch the organization, this time in London, England, but lost support when he was openly critical of the Ethiopian emperor Haile Selassie I's policies during the Italo-Ethiopian War.

Although membership had dwindled by the time of Garvey's death in London in 1940, a number of UNIA branches have tenaciously survived until the present day, preserving the legacy of the most powerful movement of black self-determination in the twentieth century.

Peter Hudson

See Also

Garvey, Marcus Mosiah; Tuskegee University; Washington, Booker Taliaferro; Black Nationalism in the United States.

Africa

Upper Senegal and Niger.

Former name of Mali.

Africa

Upper Volta.

Former name of Burkina Faso.

Africa

Urbanism and Urbanization in Africa, the process of urban population growth and expansion in Africa, occurring especially rapidly since 1945.

Cities in Precolonial Africa

Historically only a small proportion of Africa's population has lived in cities, yet cities have long played an important role as centers of empire, long-distance trade, and scholarship, particularly in West and North Africa.

North Africa has the longest recorded history of urban dwelling. One of the earliest cities in this region was Carthage, a port on the coast of present-day Tunisia founded by the Phoenicians around 800 b.c.e. At its peak in the fourth century b.c.e. Carthage served as the center of a vast empire that stretched from Libya and Sicily to the Balearic Islands in the western Mediterranean Sea. Carthage was purported to be the wealthiest city in the ancient Mediterranean world; historians believe that it may have had as many as 500,000 inhabitants. Another old North African city is Cairo, the capital of modern Egypt. Cairo was founded in 969 c.e. but is located only 25 km (15 mi) from the site of the capital of ancient Egypt, Memphis, which was established in the fourth millennium b.c.e. Cairo reached the peak of its prosperity in the thirteenth century, under the rule of the Mamluks. In addition to its role in regional and long-distance trade, the city also housed one of the world's most famous institutions of Islamic scholarship, al-Azhar University. Although devastated by the bubonic plague in 1348, Cairo remained a political capital under Turkish and then British rule, and has since become one of the continent's largest cities.

West Africa also has a long history of urbanization. Djenné-Jeno, located about 3 km (2 mi) from contemporary Djenné in Mali, is the earliest known city in this region, dating back to the second century b.c.e. or earlier. Between 700 and 900 c.e. the town had a population of at least 10,000. Other early cities in the West African savanna included Koumbi Saleh (the capital of ancient Ghana), Tombouctou (Timbuktu), and Kano in northern Nigeria, all of which served as important markets for caravan traders traveling between North Africa and coastal West Africa. Early explorers remarked on the gold and other wealth apparent in these savanna cities, but many inhabitants were ordinary farmers. At their peak both Kano and Tombouctou also had sizable populations of scholars, who came from parts of North and West Africa to study Islam.

In coastal West Africa the Yoruba peoples of southwestern Nigeria have lived in towns since around the eighth century c.e. Ile-Ife is the oldest Yoruba town and is the spiritual capital of the Yoruba religion. As in the savanna cities, many residents of Yoruba towns farmed in the surrounding countryside. Living in dense settlements gave them regular opportunities to trade their goods and provided protection from enemy invasions (a consideration that became particularly important in the nineteenth century).

In East Africa precolonial urbanization was concentrated along the coastline, where vessels from the Arabian Peninsula began landing by around 600 c.e. The coastal region between southern Somalia and northern Mozambique became the birthplace of the town-centered Swahili culture, which attracted traders and other settlers from the Arabian Peninsula and from the East African interior. Some of the largest precolonial cities along the Swahili Coast – such as Somalia's capital, Mogadishu, Mombasa in Kenya, and Zanzibar in Tanzania – are still important ports, while others, such as Lamu in Kenya and Kilwa in Tanzania, have lost much of their former commercial and political clout.

Trade was clearly a driving force in precolonial urbanization; the fortunes of a particular city might rise and fall as traders of important commodities, such as gold, ivory, and slaves, shifted their routes to avoid raiders or to take advantage of new supplies. The populations and activity levels of precolonial cities also shifted seasonally, because many residents moved to rural areas during the cultivating season.

Colonial-Era Urbanization

With European colonization, new cities were established and many existing ones were transformed. The colonial powers built some of their administrative capitals in preexisting cities, such as Lagos in Nigeria, Mogadishu in Somalia, and Ouagadougou in Upper Volta (now Burkina Faso). Other colonial capitals were built in locations chosen for their port access, such as Dakar in Senegal, or for their temperate climate, such as Nairobi in Kenya. In colonies with sizable populations of European settlers, such as Kenya and Rhodesia (now Zimbabwe), the newly built cities became settler enclaves, with strict laws limiting which Africans could live in them and where.

Other colonial-era cities grew up around mining operations. In the Belgian Congo (present-day Democratic Republic of the Congo), for example, Elisabethville (present-day Lubumbashi) was built up after copper and diamonds were discovered nearby. In South Africa the discovery of gold deposits in the Witswatersrand hills in 1886 attracted huge numbers of both African and European migrants; within ten years the mining camp of Johannesburg had become a city with a population exceeding 100,000. This rate of growth was exceptional; most cities, whether or not they existed before the colonial era, grew relatively slowly during the late nineteenth and early twentieth century.

Following World War II rates of urbanization increased dramatically throughout much of Africa. Several factors contributed to the urban boom. First, some of the colonial governments that had previously limited African migration to urban areas now loosened these restrictions. Second, expanding civil-service bureaucracies and new industries increased opportunities for urban employment. Third, many people migrated to the cities seeking not only jobs but also access to education and other social services. Finally, natural population growth, which was on the rise, coupled with falling mortality rates, aided urban expansion.

Urbanization in Contemporary Africa

Today Africa is still the least urbanized continent in the world. According to United Nations (UN) figures for 1994, only 34 percent of Africa's population lives in urban areas, compared to the world average of 44.8 percent. The actual percentages, however, vary significantly between regions. The most urbanized regions are southern Africa (48 percent) and North Africa (46 percent), followed by West Africa (36 percent) and Central Africa (33 percent). East Africa is the least urbanized part of the continent, at 21 percent. The percentage of population living in cities also varies dramatically between countries. In Libya, for example, almost 86 percent of the population is urban based, while less than 10 percent of the population of Burundi and Rwanda lives in cities.

At the same time Africa's urban population growth rates are among the highest in the world – 4.3 percent annually, compared to the world average of 2.5 percent. These rates also vary between regions and countries: cities in East Africa and West Africa are growing most rapidly (at average rates of 5.4 and 5.2 percent per annum, respectively), followed by Central Africa (4.5 percent), North Africa (3.2 percent), and southern Africa (3.1 percent). Burkina Faso's urban growth rate averaged 11.2 percent between 1990 and 1995 (a figure reflecting the fact that its cities were small to begin with), while Mauritius had only a 1.2 percent urban growth rate during the same period.

Since decolonization much of the urban growth in Africa has been concentrated in national capitals, due in large part to the typical concentration of employment opportunities, government services, and schools in those cities. Among the few exceptions are those political capitals that have been established relatively recently; these invariably have much smaller populations and economies than the capitals established during the colonial era. Since 1983 Yamoussoukro has been the capital of Côte d'Ivoire, for example, but with a population of only about 150,000 it hardly compares to the former capital, Abidjan (population 2 million), which is still home to most of the country's industries, many of its schools, and its most important port.

Similiarly, Nigeria's political capital was moved from Lagos to the more centrally located Abuja in 1991, but even with nearly a million people the new capital is considered small and sleepy compared to Lagos, which has a population considerably larger than its official census of around 1.3 million. For large cities such as Lagos and Cairo, official figures can vastly understate the actual population by excluding people living outside the city limits and those who inhabit squatter communities, which may be considered illegal by the municipal authorities. Those estimates of Lagos's population that take into account both the city's unofficial residents and people living outside the city's political boundaries range from 6 to nearly 10 million inhabitants, making it sub-Saharan Africa's largest city. Because of the age structure of this population (about half of Lagos's inhabitants are under 15), as well as the continued migration into the city, some predict it will reach 26 million by 2030. If such predictions are accurate, Lagos will then be one of the world's largest cities.

Since the 1970s many organizations and scholars have viewed Africa's high rates of urban growth as indicative of "overurbanization" and failed development policies. Well into the 1980s African governments (as well as the international agencies that supported them financially) were accused of "urban bias," meaning that their budgetary priorities and monetary policies were blamed for the impoverishment of the countryside and the resulting rural exodus. It is certainly true that politicians in the 1960s and 1970s were especially sensitive to the demands of their urban constituents, and some leaders, such as Félix Houphouët-Boigny of Côte d'Ivoire, spent lavishly on projects to turn their capitals into "showcase" cities. But the relationship between "urban-biased" government policies and rural economic conditions is not a simple one, primarily because many urban dwellers in contemporary Africa, as in the past, maintain ties to the countryside. One urban wage earner may support a dozen people in his or her home village.

Cities also offer noneconomic attractions, of course. For women especially, urban life in Africa can offer freedom from the restrictive social norms of village life. Women living in cities have better access to education than their rural counterparts, and except in the relatively few urban communities that enforce Islamic norms of female seclusion, even women with little or no education can make a living – occasionally a fortune – in marketplace trading. In cities such as Lomé and Accra in West Africa, market women have traditionally been a powerful political as well as economic force. In addition, African women in cities tend to have more control over marriage and family-planning decisions than they would in rural areas.

Urban Problems

In the 1990s alarm about the proliferation of mega-cities in Africa has been mixed with the realization, expressed in forums such as the 1996 UN Habitat II conference in Istanbul, that urbanization is not only inevitable but in some ways advantageous. Cities everywhere have historically served as centers of creativity and innovation; they are also places where, in principle, it is easier and cheaper for governments to provide services such as clean water, electricity, and medical care. Greater population density, in other words, allows for economies of scale.

LARGEST CITIES IN AFRICA

City	Country	Population in thousands
Cairo	Egypt	6,663
Kinshasa	Congo, Democratic Republic of the	3,800
Alexandria	Egypt	3,380
Casablanca	Morocco	2,541
Addis Ababa	Ethiopia	2,316
Al Jizah	Egypt	2,144
Abidjan	Côte d'Ivoire	1,929
Algiers	Algeria	1,688
Dar es Salaam	Tanzania	1,651
Dakar	Senegal	1,641
Nairobi	Kenya	1,504
Lagos	Nigeria	1,347
Ibadan	Nigeria	1,295
Harare	Zimbabwe	1,189
Douala	Cameroon	1,030
Maputo	Mozambique	1,007
Lusaka	Zambia	982
Accra	Ghana	954
Conakry	Guinea	950
Brazzaville	Congo, Republic of the	938
Khartoum	Sudan	925

In reality neither urban economies nor urban public services in Africa have been able to keep up with the demands of rapidly growing populations. Especially after economic crisis hit many African countries in the early 1980s, public investment in urban services declined significantly. The Nairobi City Commission's per capita expenditures on water and sewerage, for example, declined from nearly $28 in 1981 to $2.47 in 1987. As a result the infrastructures in many cities are inadequate and poorly maintained, and urban unemployment and underemployment rates are high.

Housing, for example, is a serious problem in most African cities. Public housing estates are too expensive for many urban dwellers, and city center rents tend to be high. Although the absence of high-rise apartment buildings in most African cities (with the exception of larger cities in North Africa and South Africa) means that urban population densities are not very high compared to those in Asia and Latin America, single-story dwellings are often extremely crowded. In Lagos and Johannesburg, for example, it is common for five or six people to share a single room.

The lack of affordable "legal" housing has given rise to the development of "spontaneous," or squatter, settlements (called *bidonvilles* in Francophone countries) on the outskirts of many African cities. Whether this kind of settlement is legal depends on a

The skyscrapers and highways of Cape Town, South Africa, begin to glow under the evening sky. Located on the site of the first European settlement in southern Africa, Cape Town is the legislative capital of South Africa and its largest city. *© David Keith Jones/Images of Africa Photobank*

municipality's property laws. Squatter shelters are often built from insubstantial materials such as cardboard or corrugated iron, though over time their owners may build more solid dwellings. Although the governments of some cities, such as Nairobi and Harare, have in the past periodically bulldozed squatter settlements, since the 1980s it has become more common for municipalities to tolerate or even encourage "self-help" housing.

The provision of services such as clean water, sewerage, waste disposal, and electricity is often nonexistent in settlements on urban peripheries, and such services tend to be poorly maintained even in city centers. Piped water to individual houses is a rarity in the poorer neighborhoods of many cities, so many residents rely on wells, public taps (which are often turned on only a few hours each day), or purchased water. Consequently, poor city dwellers routinely pay more for water than their wealthy counterparts. Even treated, piped water supplies in many cities are of dubious quality, due to old and leaky pipes. Combined with inadequate sanitation services, the poor quality of urban water supplies contributes to the spread of cholera and other waterborne diseases.

Finally, the growth of Africa's urban populations is outpacing the growth of urban labor markets, leading to high rates of unemployment and underemployment. This is not a new problem – the International Labor Organization began to express concern about urban unemployment in Africa in the 1970s – but it has been exacerbated by the economic crisis and subsequent World Bank-designed structural adjustment programs most African countries have undergone since the early 1980s. Among other things, structural adjustment has required African governments to cut back on their own personnel and to downsize and privatize state-run industries. The bulk of the lost jobs have been urban based.

It is nearly impossible to provide accurate estimates of urban unemployment rates in Africa, because in many cities most working-age people earn at least part of their livelihood from employment in the so-called informal sector. This term describes a wide range of economic activities that are relatively unregulated by the state, though they are not necessarily illegal. Common informal-sector activities in African cities include the vending of "street foods" (*see* FOOD IN AFRICA) and other consumer goods, small-scale crafts industries, and a multitude of services ranging from message delivery to bicycle repair to open-air haircutting.

Informal-sector enterprises often depend on family labor and operate on shoestring budgets, and many are relatively short-lived. The numbers of people attempting to earn money by selling goods on the streets of cities such as Lagos and Dakar are so large that it is difficult for individual vendors to break even, much less to make a profit. On the other hand, the informal sector provides low-cost goods and services to a large proportion of the urban population (not just the poor), and income earned in this sector helps support many families – many of them headed by women – who might otherwise be destitute. This is one reason that African governments and institutions such as the World Bank, which in the past viewed the informal sector as evidence of economic backwardness, now encourage certain kinds of informal-sector enterprises through training and credit programs. The hope is that such support will help informal-sector enterprises grow and thus generate more jobs. Clearly, easing the problem of unemployment in African cities will also require the sustained growth of Africa's national economies.

Elizabeth Heath

SEE ALSO

Abidjan, Côte d'Ivoire; Abuja, Nigeria; Accra, Ghana; Dakar, Senegal; Decolonization in Africa: An Interpretation; Development in Africa: An Interpretation; Education in Africa; Explorers in Africa Before 1500; Ghana, Early Kingdom of; Gold Trade; Harare, Zimbabwe; Ivory Trade; Djenné-Djeno, Mali; Johannesburg, South Africa; Kano, Nigeria; Lagos, Nigeria; Egypt, Ancient Kingdom of; Lomé, Togo; Mogadishu, Somalia; Mombasa, Kenya; Ouagadougou, Burkina Faso; Population Growth in Sub-Saharan Africa; Somalia; Structural Adjustment in Africa; Swahili People; Tombouctou, Mali; Mamluk State; Yamoussoukro, Côte d'Ivoire; Djenné, Mali; Koumbi Saleh, Mauritania; Cairo, Egypt; Lamu, Kenya; African Religions: An Interpretation; Islam and Tradition: An Interpretation; Trans-Saharan and Red Sea Slave Trade.

Latin America and the Caribbean

Urbano Gilbert, Gregorio

(b. May 25, 1899, Puerto Plata, Dominican Republic; d. November 29, 1970, Santo Domingo, Dominican Republic), Afro-Dominican guerrilla fighter who resisted the United States occupation of the Dominican Republic in 1916 and left one of the few written testimonies of the events.

Since 1906 the United States administered and controlled the Dominican Republic's customs department and undertook the adjustment of the Dominican government's foreign debt. Increasing debts, internal disorder, and international pressures prompted President Woodrow Wilson of the United States to order the deployment and intervention of the U.S. Navy in the Dominican Republic. The troops arrived on November 29, 1916, and remained in control of the country until 1924.

The U.S. Marines invaded the Dominican Republic, easily occupying the town of San Pedro de Macorís to the passive acceptance of its inhabitants. However, Gregorio Urbano Gilbert decided to confront the marines on his own with only the support of his .32-caliber revolver. In self-defense he killed U.S. Marine Corps Col. C. H. Button and then fled to join the nationalist guerrillas and their anti-imperialist struggle. After being tracked down and captured by the Dominican Army, he went to trial and was sentenced to death. However, in 1922 he was pardoned. When Urbano Gilbert came out of prison, he tried to join Haitian forces struggling against the U.S. occupation of that neighboring country (1915-1934), but this attempt was not successful (*see* Cacos).

He went into exile in Curaçao and Cuba, where he worked as a sugar cane cutter. But he came back to the Dominican Republic in 1927, he rallied in favor of Puerto Rican independence along with Pedro Albizu Campos. In 1928 he went to Nicaragua and joined Augusto César Sandino's Ejercito Libertador in its struggle against U.S. imperialism. He then went back to the Dominican Republic in 1929, a year before Rafael Leonidas Trujillo's dictatorship of more than 30 years began. He worked as a street vendor while he studied in what is now the Autonomous University and completed his doctorate in philosophy in 1956.

Urbano Gilbert wrote one of the few historical testimonies about the 1916 invasion – published after his death in 1975 – under the title *Mi lucha contra el invasor yanqui de 1916* (My Struggle Against the Yankee Invader). It includes his personal experiences with the guerrilla leaders who fought against the United States. He also wrote another testimonial narrative titled *Junto a Sandino* (1979, Beside Sandino), about his years with the Nicaraguan rebels and his struggle against imperialism. While in his 60s Urbano also joined the Dominican military forces that faced the second U.S. invasion in April 1965. He died in poverty five years later. In his writings Urbano Gilbert left his testimony of struggle against imperialism and for popular causes, and his experiences with Dominican guerrilla fighters about whom there is limited information.

Mayda Grano de Oro

See Also

Trujillo, Rafael.

Latin America and the Caribbean

Uruguay,

republic of southeastern South America bordered on the northeast and north by Brazil, on the west by Argentina, and on the east by the Atlantic Ocean. With an area of 176,215 sq km (68,037 sq mi), it is the second-smallest country in South America after Suriname. Its capital is Montevideo.

Uruguay has long enjoyed a reputation as the Switzerland of the Americas, due in part to its small size, its dominant population of European descent, and a perception that it is a country free of racial tensions or other conflicts. The true racial history of Uruguay is much more complicated than this image suggests. Blacks constitute a tiny minority of present-day Uruguayans (about 6 percent of the population), but this was not always the case. In fact, throughout Uruguay's history blacks played an integral role in the nation's development. Afro-Uruguayans today are the inheritors of this legacy, though in standard histories they are sometimes reviled and more often than not forgotten.

The Official History

Before Spaniards arrived in the area now known as Uruguay, a number of seminomadic indigenous groups inhabited the region. The largest of these groups were the Charrúa and the Chaná, who survived principally by hunting and fishing. In 1516 the Spanish explorer Juan Díaz de Solís sailed into the Río de la Plata (the estuary that separates western Uruguay from eastern Argentina) and established a small, short-lived settlement on the riverbank. Before the year was out, the Charrúa killed Díaz and his party. The region was of little interest to Spanish colonizers, as it seemed of minimal economic value. The first permanent Spanish settlement would not be established in Uruguay until 1624, when a small party encamped at the Río Negro at Soriano.

This area came to be known as the Banda Oriental (Eastern Bank), and from the late seventeenth through much of the eighteenth century, it was a zone of contention between Spanish colonists and Portuguese colonists from Brazil. In 1680 the Portuguese founded Colônia do Sacramento on the bank of the Río de la Plata, opposite Buenos Aires. The Spanish made little effort to displace this settlement until the 1720s, when they constructed the fortified city of San Felipe de Montevideo, from which they launched attacks on the Portuguese. The Portuguese finally ceded in 1777, and the region came under the administrative control of the viceroyalty of La Plata.

In the second decade of the nineteenth century Uruguayans fought successfully for their independence, but the country was occupied by and finally annexed to Brazil in 1821. An insurgent group known as the Immortal 33, led by Juan Antonio Lavalleja and aided by Argentina, fought the occupation. A treaty signed in 1828, with British mediation, established Uruguay as an independent buffer zone between Argentina and the Brazilian Empire, and a provisional assembly was established. On July 18, 1830, the assembly ratified a constitution that officially founded the República Oriental del Uruguay (Eastern Republic of Uruguay).

During most of the nineteenth century the new republic was plagued by fighting between two contending political factions comprising supporters of the nation's first two presidents: Fructuoso Rivera (1830-1834; 1838-1842) and Manuel Oribe (1835-1838). The factions were named for the colors adopted by each: the Colorado Party (red), supporting Rivera, and the Blanco Party (white), for Oribe. Both survive today as the dominant political parties. Between 1865 and 1868 Uruguay allied itself with Brazil and Argentina against Paraguay in the War of the Triple Alliance. The Colorado Party became dominant during the course of the century; after 1865 the Blanco Party would remain out of power until 1958.

Uruguay in the twentieth century gained its reputation as a progressive, democratic republic. President José Batlle y Ordóñez (1903-1907; 1911-1915) initiated a period of social reforms that included concessions to labor as well as provisions for social security. Democratic rule was disrupted by a period of authoritarian rule in the 1930s and by a repressive military government between 1973 and 1984. Uruguay's transition to democracy since 1984 has been regarded as one of the most successful in Latin America, as the traditional Blanco and Colorado parties reemerged in what appears to be a remarkably stable regime.

Africans in Colonial Uruguay

Spaniards brought Africans to the region as early as 1534. These *ladinos* (slaves who had been Hispanicized in Spain rather than being brought directly from Africa) took part in early explorations of the Río de la Plata, although nearly all of them settled with their masters in what is now Argentina.

The Uruguayan slave trade was born from a quirk of conquest and geography. By the end of the sixteenth century Spain had extended its slave-capture and trading operations to the ANGOLA region of southern Africa. As they were in the slave trade in northern Africa, captives were shipped by sea to bustling colonies such as MEXICO and the Audiencia de Cartagena (in present-day COLOMBIA), all in the northern half of the Americas. The sea voyage from Angola, however, was even more brutal than that from northern Africa, and many more slaves died en route. Spanish slave traders realized by the end of the sixteenth century that if slaves were transported across a shorter sea route – say, to the Río de la Plata – and then transferred overland to distant points, fewer of them would die. As a result Buenos Aires (in what would later become ARGENTINA) soon became a major point of disembarkation for slaves from southern Africa. By the end of the seventeenth century the Spaniards had discovered that Montevideo, 200 km (120 mi) east of Buenos Aires on the Río de la Plata, had a remarkable natural harbor, and in 1724 they began a settlement there. In no time the bulk of the slave trade had moved from Buenos Aires to Montevideo, the future capital of Uruguay (*see* TRANSATLANTIC SLAVE TRADE).

From the earliest days the Spanish government tried to exercise strict control over the arrival of slaves in the Río de la Plata region, mostly in order to tax the lucrative trade. Only a few authorized traders were allowed to bring slaves to a region. However, as in other parts of Spanish America, slave traders in the Río de la Plata often succeeded in smuggling contraband slaves past officials. In *La trata de negroa en Río de la Plata durante el siglo XVIII* (1958), historian Elena Fanny Scheüss de Studer calculates that only 288 of nearly 13,000 slaves who came to the Río de la Plata region between 1606 and 1655 arrived legally. She estimates that between 1680 and 1806 – an era of mostly tighter Spanish control – perhaps 50 percent of all arrivals from Africa were still smuggled into Río de la Plata. In addition to these contrabands, it appears likely that many slaves were shipped to Montevideo from Rio de Janeiro in Portuguese BRAZIL – in violation of both Spanish and Portuguese law (*see* COLONIAL LATIN AMERICA AND THE CARIBBEAN).

Beginning in 1740 Spain bowed to the reality of its ineffectual control of the slave trade and allowed any colonist with the means to buy a *licencia* (license) to purchase as many Africans as he wanted from any slave trader of any nation not warring against Spain. The licencias were costly, so only a few could afford them; nonetheless, the introduction of licencias opened the door to a much larger legal slave trade. Colonial records show that in one brief period – from 1780 to 1783 – 17 licencias were granted in the Río de la Plata region, allowing the importation of 3400 blacks to Montevideo and Buenos Aires. From 1783 to 1792, 10 more licencias allowed the importation of 4600 more slaves. Most of these slaves were presumably shipped to distant points, like PERU and New Granada (present-day Colombia, ECUADOR, VENEZUELA, and PANAMA), since by 1803 Montevideo had only 899 slaves.

During roughly the same era, in 1776, Spain recognized the increasing importance of the Río de la Plata region by establishing the viceroyalty of La Plata, which included what is today Uruguay, Argentina, BOLIVIA, and Paraguay. The viceregal seat of La Plata was in Buenos Aires. Two decades later Spain acknowledged that even its efforts under the licencia system to control the slave trade were futile; in 1795 the viceroyalty of La Plata abandoned the system altogether. Any Spanish citizen was allowed to buy slaves from any source not at war with Spain.

SLAVE LABOR, LIFE, AND REBELLION

The conditions under which slaves labored in Uruguay are "difficult to analyze," according to historian Leslie Rout in *The African Experience in Spanish America*. Aside, perhaps, from domestic service, slaves did not dominate any industry or occupation in Uruguay; moreover, the plantations or mines that were the province of slaves in much of the rest of Spanish America were virtually nonexistent in Uruguay (*see* SLAVERY IN LATIN AMERICA AND THE CARIBBEAN). Montevideo, a commercial port and practically the only settlement of importance in Uruguay, was indisputably the home of most Uruguayan slaves. Female slaves dominated the domestic industries of cooking, cleaning, laundering, and child rearing, while male slaves worked as manual laborers on docks and in the ranching operations around Montevideo.

The burden of Africans in Uruguay was worsened by the sharp distinctions that Spanish colonists drew between dark-skinned and light-skinned blacks. The latter were in all things favored (if only slightly), and the former disparaged. In May 1760 the *cabildo* (council) of Montevideo passed a series of acts governing *pardos* (mulattos, usually lighter skinned) and *morenos* ("full-blood" blacks, usually darker skinned). Under the acts pardos were allowed to become certain types of tradesmen, including tailors and cobblers, while morenos were forbidden to do anything but physical and domestic labor.

Such racial distinctions persisted despite a few efforts by the Spanish government to diminish them. In 1795, for example, the Spanish Crown allowed blacks to buy writs of *gracias al sacar*, meaning literally "thanks for the exclusion." The writs were a royal dispensation that freed a person from certain caste restrictions. However, in the viceroyalty of La Plata writs were rarely issued, and only those issued to very light-skinned blacks were honored. Darker-skinned blacks who bought them often found them unredeemable. Because of these and similar caste barriers, intermarriage of blacks and whites in La Plata was quite rare; however, as in the rest of Spanish America, the prohibition against white men taking female slaves as concubines was less strict.

Avenues to freedom that were open to slaves in other parts of the Spanish Empire were relatively less accessible to Afro-Uruguayans. In *Negro uruguayo hasta abolición* (1965, The Uruguayan Black Until Abolition), historian Paulo de Carvalho Neto holds that, with the exception of some illegitimate mulatto children with white fathers, the only way for blacks to escape slavery was through death. Historian Carlos Rama agrees, for the most part, adding that a very few slaves were freed as a result of being treated with extreme cruelty, and a few more were allowed to buy their freedom.

Rebellion, then, was one of the very small number of paths to freedom, but even this method was less successful in Uruguay than elsewhere. In 1803, 20 black men, most but not all slaves, gathered in secret to devise a plot for fleeing Montevideo and soon thereafter fled with their wives and children. After several days of travel they established a settlement on a small island in the River Yi, some 200 km (120 mi) north of Montevideo. Their freedom, however, was short-lived; a militia from the town of Villa de la Concepción de Minas attacked them soon after they had settled. In the skirmish that followed, all of the blacks were either captured and reenslaved or killed in the fighting.

WAR AGAINST SPAIN AND EMANCIPATION

The first hint of change in the life of the Uruguayan slave came during the wars of liberation against Spain in the second decade of the nineteenth century. Afro-Uruguayans quickly learned that they could better their social standing by serving in the rebel armies. The rebels, for their part, were not typically possessed of a liberal attitude toward blacks; they were simply desperate enough for troops to enlist anyone who could fight. At first this meant allowing free blacks to fight; later it meant giving guns to slaves.

José Artigas, who would later be considered the father of Uruguay, put together the most formidable army of blacks and mulattos, most of them freedpeople but many of them slaves, to serve alongside white rebels. In 1812 the Sixth Regiment, composed almost entirely of blacks, gained enduring fame through its part in a daring bayonet charge at El Cerrito. Another battalion, Los Libertos Orientales (The Freedmen of the East), fought almost continuously between 1816 and 1820.

Although their fighting earned blacks a measure of respect, the limitations of caste did not fall away. Indeed, black soldiers were usually assigned to the most dangerous fighting yet received the worst food and equipment. Their lot had changed little enough that when a Brazilian force took advantage of the wars against Spain and invaded Uruguay in 1817, more than a hundred of Artigas's black troops switched sides for the flimsy promise that "someday" Brazil would make them free. Many blacks nonetheless remained loyal to the rebel forces, and as the target of rebel attacks shifted from Spanish to Brazilian troops, blacks continued to play a crucial role.

Brazil completed its conquest and annexation of Uruguay by 1821, under the name Cisplantine Province. A small group of insurgents, known as the Immortal 33, reasserted the independence of Uruguay in 1825. Little acknowledged among modern Uruguayans is that a handful of the Immortal 33 were black. Black rebels are not completely forgotten, however. Col. Lorenzo Barcala, an Argentinian known as "the black caballero," played a major role from 1825 to 1828 in the eviction of the Brazilians from Uruguay. Manuel Antonio Ledesma ("Ansina") is known as the aide who faithfully accompanied Artigas to his death in PARAGUAY. Barcala and Ansina were among the few blacks, however, to attain high-ranking positions.

On September 7, 1825, the rebel forces established a congress at which they passed a free-womb law: anyone born to a slave from that date forward was born free. They then opened the ranks of their army to blacks and mulattos – both free and slave. In May 1829 another provisional legislature, established after the 1828 peace agreement recognizing Uruguayan independence, freed all slaves who fought in the struggle for liberation, and in 1830 it ratified the republic's first constitution.

The constitution of the new country included several positive changes for slaves. It reaffirmed the acts of the earlier congresses, asserting that all newborn children of slaves were born free. The overseas slave trade was banned, and any slave whose master had fled to Brazil during or after the fighting was declared free. Still, the old caste distinctions remained. Former slaves found it extremely difficult to find work or decent housing, and many slaves who had fought in the war were denied their freedom because they had no proof of their enlistment.

In 1832 a group of slaves and freedpeople prepared for revolt behind an Afro-Uruguayan named Santa Colombo, who had been a military aide to President Fructuoso Rivera. The government uncovered the plot in May 1832, sentenced the freedpeople to death or long jail terms, and sentenced slaves to 200 lashes. Because several of the plotters had fought against Spain and Brazil in the liberation, many Uruguayans pleaded for leniency on behalf of the prisoners. Eventually the death sentences were commuted.

The constitution's promises to end the slave trade notwithstanding, between 1829 and 1841 some 4000 slaves were brought illegally from Brazil to Uruguay. President Rivera apparently abetted much of the illegal trade. In 1837 a law was passed declaring that all blacks thenceforth brought into the country would be free (with some exceptions, such as runaway slaves from other countries, who were to be returned). The law also established a system of *patronato*, which effectively extended the period of servitude by placing blacks under the "tutelage" of their masters for a determined period of time. Abolition in Uruguay was given impetus by the conflicts in the country and the need for soldiers. Fighting between Blanco and Colorado factions flared following Rivera's 1838 coup against President Manuel Oribe. In 1841, when Blanco rebels, supported by Argentina, threatened Rivera, he freed his many slaves and drafted them into the army. In December 1842 his successor, Joaquín Suárez, abolished slavery throughout the country and drafted all former male slaves into the army. In the hope of winning compliance from slave owners, he promised compensation for the freed slaves. But most slave owners flouted the law, and many sold their slaves in neighboring Brazil.

In 1843 Suárez's troops were backed into Montevideo. The rebels, led by deposed president Oribe, laid siege to the city until 1851, when a signed truce declared that there were no victors or vanquished. Like the besieged, the attacking army also relied heavily on black forces. In October 1846, the third year of the siege, Oribe too declared slavery in Uruguay abolished. Following the truce, a law passed in 1853 abolished the patronato system, freeing all blacks in the country (*see* ABOLITION AND EMANCIPATION IN LATIN AMERICA AND THE CARIBBEAN).

In addition to prompting some Uruguayan slave owners to sell their slaves in Brazil, abolition produced a substantial immigration of escaped Brazilian slaves to Uruguay. Given the extent of this migration, the 1851 peace agreement, in which Brazilian intervention was decisive, included an agreement to return escaped slaves to Brazil, but this provision was largely ignored.

BEYOND EMANCIPATION

Despite abolition many former slaves had no choice but to continue working for their former masters, and slavelike conditions and racial discrimination persisted. In 1860, for example, the Montevideo police force prohibited blacks from being hired as night watchmen. In 1878 a furor erupted when supporters of civil rights tried to gain admittance for blacks to public schools alongside whites.

Afro-Uruguayans, however, were also confronted with a flood of white immigrant labor, which reduced their economic opportunities. In 1842 nearly 20 percent of Montevideo's residents were black. After emancipation Uruguay faced two problems that could be addressed with one solution: it needed a larger labor base to fuel its economic growth, and it "needed" to preserve its white character. Hence between 1850 and 1930 more than a million Europeans, almost all of them white, immigrated to Uruguay. A few blacks also found their way to Uruguay during the early part of this period, but in 1886 the Uruguayan government made clear its preference for white immigrants: people of African origin were barred from settling in Uruguay (*see* WHITENING). A study conducted by Uruguay's National Statistics Institute in 1996-1997 found that approximately 6 percent of Uruguayans identify themselves as black.

In the context of the new European competition for jobs in Uruguay, the stigma of being black persisted. Afro-Uruguayans were clustered in low-paying positions and typically lived in the slums of Montevideo well into the twentieth century. In May 1956 the magazine *Marcha* studied nearly 15,000 barbers, hotel porters, bus drivers, conductors, guards, and store clerks; only 11 of them were black or mulatto, indicating that Afro-Uruguayans had not achieved even the faintest hold on the middle class. *Marcha* also reported that from 1900 to 1956 the National University of Uruguay graduated just two lawyers and one doctor of African heritage. In a separate study in the same year, 700 white Uruguayan students were asked whether they would marry a black; 77 percent said no. When asked whether they would invite a black person to a birthday party, 62 percent said no.

Under such conditions, Afro-Uruguayans created political and cultural organizations of their own. In the early twentieth century they formed groups for socializing and other kinds of support, such as the Black Race Cultural Association and the Colonia Sport and Social Club, both headquartered in Montevideo. In 1917 the magazine *Nuestra Raza* (Our Race) began reporting on issues of concern among the black community. Before going out of business in 1948, *Nuestra Raza* helped introduce Afro-Uruguayans to the music of Julián García Rondeau, the art of Ramón Preya, and the poetry of its editor, PILAR BARRIOS. Barrios was also the secretary of the Black Autochthonous Party. Organized in 1937 and comprising mainly black intellectuals, many of whom were connected with *Nuestra Raza*, the Black Autochthonous Party took a stand for social justice while seeking to appeal broadly to all Afro-Uruguayans. Nonetheless, after the party's poor showing in the 1938 elections, its activities declined, and it finally disbanded in 1944 (*see* POLITICAL PARTIES AND BLACK SOCIAL MOVEMENTS IN LATIN AMERICA AND THE CARIBBEAN).

After World War II the Uruguayan government extended free education to all classes, allowing all blacks for the first time to enter school with whites. Black culture, however, was not studied, a fact that recent historians have attributed to the broader ideal of "whitening" the country, which emphasizes its European influences while erasing its African ones. Most Afro-Uruguayan ethnic societies disappeared; the few that existed in the 1990s were generally weak and often dependent on overseas donations. In its 1996-1997 study the National Statistics Institute found that the average income of blacks was about 65 percent that of whites. Historian Alejandrina da Luz wrote in 1995, "Thus 'invisibility' became official policy. As they grow up, young Afro-Uruguayans today will find that their nation's history records only one black person: the loyal soldier Ansina. There are no black writers in Uruguayan literature; only in the United States are there black musicians; and in painting, black people appear only on canvas. Dozens of Afro-Uruguayan writers, dramatists, painters, musicians, and so on, seem to have faded away."

See Also

Blackness in Latin America and the Caribbean: an Interpretation; Cartagena de Indias, Colombia; Rio de Janeiro, Brazil; Abolition and Emancipation in Latin America and the Caribbean.

Africa

Usman dan Fodio (b. 1750?; d. 1817?), Muslim religious leader and founder of the Sokoto Caliphate in what is now northern Nigeria.

A Fulani born in the Hausa state of Gobir, Usman dan Fodio studied the Koran with his father, an eminent scholar, then moved from place to place to study with other religious scholars. When he was 25 years old, he began teaching and preaching, and from this time his reputation as a holy man grew. He taught Islam in Gobir, and he was probably engaged as tutor to the future sultan Yunfa because of his learned reputation.

Usman criticized the Hausa ruling elite for their heavy taxation and other practices that he claimed violated Islamic law. His call for Islamic reform (and tax reduction) earned him a wide following in the 1780s and 1790s, when he became a political threat to Gobir sultan Nafata. When Yunfa assumed power as sultan in 1802, he ordered the repression of Usman's followers. Following the example of the prophet Muhammad, Usman went on a *hijrah* (spiritual migration), was elected *imam* (leader) of the reformist Muslims, and launched the *jihad* (holy war) that would bring down the Hausa royalty. In the conquered areas Usman set up emirates whose leaders acknowledged his religious sovereignty, and in October 1808 the Gobir capital, Alkalawa, fell. In former Gobir, Usman established a new capital, Sokoto, from which he ruled virtually all of Hausaland. After 1812 Usman withdrew into private life, writing many works on the proper conduct of the pious Islamic community. After his death in 1817, his son Muhammad Bello succeeded him as the ruler of the Sokoto Caliphate, then the largest state in Africa south of the Sahara.

See Also

Sahara Desert; Islam and Tradition: An Interpretation.

V

Africa

Vai (also known as Vei and Vey), ethnic group of West Africa.

The Vai primarily inhabit LIBERIA and SIERRA LEONE. They speak a MANDE language and are related to the MENDE people. Approximately 200,000 people consider themselves Vai.

SEE ALSO

Languages, African: An Overview.

Latin America and the Caribbean

Valdés, Gabriel de la Concepción ("Plácido")

(b. March 18, 1809, Matanzas, CUBA; d. June 26, 1844, Matanzas, Cuba), Cuban poet, journalist, patriot, and martyr best known for his protest poems and his alleged involvement in the CONSPIRACIÓN DE LA ESCALERA.

Gabriel de la Concepción Valdés, more generally known by his pseudonym "Plácido," was born in Matanzas to a white mother, the Spanish dancer Concepción Vásquez, and a black father, Diego Ferrer Matoso, who was prohibited, like all Cuban blacks, from placing "Don" before his name. Plácido was abandoned as an infant, left at an orphanage on April 6, 1809; a note found with him was inscribed with the name "Gabriel de la Concepción." He was given a last name, Valdés, and the phrase "al parecer, blanco" ("appears white") was inscribed on his baptism certificate. In his *Biografías Americanas* (1906), Enrique Piñeyro laments the fact that Plácido's remorseful father retrieved him soon after abandoning him; if he had not reclaimed his son, Plácido would have "lost any trace of his previous servile condition." As it was, Piñeyro says, his father's retrieval of him "condemned the poor thing to a perpetual inferior situation, to an irredeemable fortune." Even free blacks in 1840s Cuba enjoyed little economic and social mobility; however, Plácido's paternal grandmother taught him to read and write.

At age 14 Plácido began working as a cashier in a publishing house. The pay was meager, and the few books and periodicals the business managed to publish were strictly regulated by colonial censorship. Plácido abandoned the press to become a *peinetero* apprentice, crafting women's hair-combs from tortoiseshell. Known for his improvisational skills as a poet, in 1837 he started contributing a daily poem to the newspaper *La aurora de Matanzas*. His "poetry of occasion" – laudatory poems commissioned for distinguished members of society – supplemented his income.

In 1838 Plácido published *Poesías*, followed in 1842 by a collection of *letrillas* and *epigramas* titled *El veguero*. In that same year a promotion at *La aurora* enabled him to dedicate his professional efforts to literary pursuits and his personal ones to married life with a new wife. The "nearly white" poet clearly established his political and ethnic affiliations when he married a woman "de pura sangre africana" (of pure African blood). Many Spanish epic poems compared Spain's empire to that of Rome. In this vein, poems like "Death of Caesar," or the following verses from "Juramento" – which challenged imperial rule and which many Cubans knew by heart – set the stage for Plácido's impending demise:

Ser enemigo eterno del tirano...
Y morir a las manos de un verdugo
Si es necesario por romper el yugo.

(to be an eternal enemy of the tyrant...
and to die at the hands of an executioner
if necessary to break the yoke.)

In 1844 Plácido was executed by colonial troops, accused of participating in a plot to organize a slave revolt in the state of Matanzas and ultimately to win independence for Cuba. Many blacks, slaves and free alike, were brought in for questioning, tortured, and executed. The purge nearly wiped out the leaders of Cuba's free black population, and in the aftermath of the CONSPIRACIÓN DE LA ESCALERA prominent mulattos like journalists Rafael Serra y Montalvo ("the Cuban Booker T. Washington"), politician and activist Juan Gualberto Gómez, and Antonio Maceo, a general in the independence forces, would continue to be the focus of white fears of blacks. Plácido himself was tried partly on the basis of his verse. Three of his most famous poems, "Adiós a mi lira" (Goodbye to My Lyre), "Despedida a mi madre" (Farewell to My Mother), and "Plegaria a Dios" (Prayer to God), are said to have been written in prison only a few days before his death.

Though Plácido's fame increased after his death, he was renowned during his lifetime. His work has received a varied reception. One Spanish critic compared him to Luis de Góngora y Argote, a pillar of seventeenth-century baroque poetry. Some honor Plácido simply for the heroic circumstances of his death; others deem his verse "inferior," citing the poet's lack of education. Most critics remark on his versatility both in style and form. His themes ranged from love to religion to liberty, and his styles included the didactic, elegiac, patriotic, improvised, and satiric. Nor did he limit his choice of form; he composed ballads, letrillas, *redondillas, octavas,* and *décimas* in the "popular" styles and "learned" verse in odes and sonnets. Some critics, like Richard Jackson, argue that Plácido should be celebrated both as a poet and a national hero.

Joy Elizondo

SEE ALSO

Washington, Booker Taliaferro; Maceo y Grajales, Antonio; Matanzas, Cuba.

Latin America and the Caribbean

Valdés, Jesús (Chucho)

(b. October 9, 1941, Quivican, Cuba), an Afro-Latin jazz pianist and one of the foremost JAZZ musicians in CUBA; the founder in 1973 of IRAKERE, Cuba's most significant jazz orchestra.

The jazz pianist Jesús "Chucho" Valdés is one of Cuba's most prominent musicians. He is the son of the Cuban pianist and bandleader Bebo Valdés, who was for many years musical director at Havana's famed Tropicana night-club. In 1960, when his father defected from Cuba following Fidel Castro's revolution, Chucho Valdés remained behind. Because of the United States commercial and political embargo on Cuba, decreed on October 20, 1960, Valdés remained virtually unknown to the American jazz public for many years. But during the 1990s he has found greater opportunities to perform and record in the United States, and has begun to reach a wider American audience despite the continued political intransigence between the United States and Cuba.

Valdés began playing piano at age 3, and by the time he was 16 was leading his own group. He was particularly inspired by American jazz trumpeter John Birks "Dizzy" Gillespie, the cocreator – along with alto saxophonist Charlie "Bird" Parker – of bop or modern jazz. During the 1940s and 1950s Gillespie also participated in some of the formative experiments in Afro-Cuban jazz, including a recording of Chico O'Farrill's arrangement of "Manteca" (1948). Following the U.S. embargo on Cuba, Valdés and other Cuban jazz players were effectively cut off from the musical developments taking place in the United States, except via Willis Conover's *Music U.S.A.* program on the Voice of America. Valdés went on to study at the Havana Conservatory, and in 1967 founded the Orquestra Cubana de Música Moderna (OCMM).

Around 1972 Valdés and several other prominent Cuban jazz musicians left the OCMM and formed a new group that ultimately took the name Irakere, the Yoruba word for forest or woods. Valdés served both as the group's leader and as its principal composer and arranger. Irakere played an infectious Afro-Cuban jazz-rock that, in part, reflected the musical influence of trumpeter Miles Davis, who was instrumental in popularizing the use of rock-style rhythms and electric instruments in jazz. Irakere gained a wide following in Cuba and in the many other parts of the world where the band toured. Because of lingering cold war hostilities, however, it has had few opportunities to play in the United States.

During the 1970s word of Valdés and his superb ensemble gradually reached the United States, particularly through the reports of the few American jazz musicians who performed in Cuba. When Gillespie and his quintet first appeared in Cuba in 1977, they played a memorable concert with Irakere, and Gillespie befriended two of Irakere's founding members: trumpeter Arturo Sandoval and saxophonist Paquito D'Rivera. Sandoval and D'Rivera subsequently left Cuba and commenced successful jazz careers in the United States, including stints during the 1980s with Gillespie's United Nation Orchestra. Valdés, however, by again choosing to stay in Cuba, remained unknown to the wider American jazz public.

In the 1990s, however, Valdés found new opportunities to bring together the two nations as well as the African American and Cuban musical heritages. In 1992 he became president of the Havana Jazz Festival, at which he has presented a number of prominent jazz musicians, including trumpeter Roy Hargrove and saxophonist David Sanchez. In 1996 Valdés joined Crisol, a Cuban American big band under the leadership of Hargrove, which on a number of occasions brought him to New York City. On one of those visits he played for several nights at Bradley's, the New York nightclub. More recently Valdés signed a recording contract with EMI Canada – as *New York Times* music critic Ben Ratliff observed, to do so "with the company's American office would constitute trading with the enemy."

Early in 1998 Valdés played two well-received solo concerts at New York City's Lincoln Center for the Performing Arts, as part of an extended program celebrating Cuban music. Ratliff vividly depicted Valdés's playing in one of those concerts, particularly emphasizing his rhythmic artistry: "[H]e opened with big, sonorous chords, then attenuated his playing into a waltz rhythm, then dived into swirling atonality. In serpentine legato runs, he never missed a note; dozens of tiny dots whizzed by each second, steely and well-defined.... One of Mr. Valdés's best conceits was to bring wild abstractions into *montuno* sections: as the right hand pumped out a two-three clavé, the left hand sketched a torrid storm that hewed to no rhythmic cycle."

In his Lincoln Center debut Valdés not only performed such jazz standards as "Yesterdays" and "Autumn Leaves," but also "La Comparsa," composed by Cuban classical music composer Ernesto Lecuona.

During his years as director of Irakere, Valdés often found himself playing electric keyboards rather than the piano. But recently he has cut back his involvement in that group – turning over its leadership to his son Chuchito – in order to concentrate on his piano playing.

James Clyde Sellman

See Also

Jazz, Afro-Latin; Davis, Miles Dewey, III; Gillespie, John Birks ("Dizzy"); New York, New York; Parker, Charles Christopher ("Bird"); Music, Classical, in Latin America and the Caribbean.

Latin America and the Caribbean

Valdés, José Manuel

(b. July 29, 1767, Lima, Peru; d. 1843?, Lima, Peru), Peruvian of African and indigenous descent; a famed doctor, poet, professor, and philosopher, a member of parliament, and a prominent figure in Lima society.

The natural child of a washerwoman and a musician, José Manuel Valdés was born in Lima, Peru's capital city, when nearly half its population was black. Though his parents could not afford to educate him, his godparents and mother's employers stepped in, seeing to his early education at a prominent religious school. He would later become the first black writer to publish in Peru, both as a doctor and as a poet, as early as 1791.

After completing school Valdés yearned to become a priest, but during the colonial period blacks were denied access to the priesthood by the Roman Catholic Church, and he turned instead to medicine. He could have prospered as a *romancista*, a type of medical practitioner whose training was limited and whose practice was restricted to "external remedies." Rather, in 1788 he took the more challenging route and pursued the title of *latinista* surgeon, for which he studied anatomy and surgical techniques. As a latinista surgeon he was allowed to perform emergency surgeries and administer purgatives.

As his finances continued to improve, he threw himself wholeheartedly into his work, importing the latest surgical instruments and books on surgery from Europe while learning French, English, and Italian. The fruits of his labor appeared in a published dissertation on methods for curing dysentery. During these years another hypothesis of his, namely that uterine cancer was not contagious, was sharply criticized by some of his contemporaries, but was proven correct not long after by European researchers.

The 1790s witnessed the heyday of French philosophers and encyclopedists, spreading liberalism and expounding on the universality of political rights. Yet Valdés, a free black, was denied access to the priesthood, the military, and the university. It took a *dispensa*, an official dispensation from King Carlos VI, to "pardon" his color and allow him to attend the University of Lima in 1807. Later on he was issued a similar document from the pope granting him access to the priesthood, but the Cabildo Metropolitano, upset by his petition, discouraged him from following through. As a practicing physician he became well known in Europe for his medical theories, and as a university professor in Lima he continued to publish medical papers. In 1815, before Peru achieved independence from Spain, he was welcomed into the Royal Academy of Medicine in Madrid.

His literary career developed later in life. Valdés is one of a handful of well-known early republican writers of African descent, such as Candelario Obeso (1849-1884) in Colombia. Valdés wrote mainly mystical poetry, in addition to a biography of Fray Martín de Porres (1579-1639), the black Peruvian saint canonized by the Roman Catholic Church. Valdés also wrote *Poesías espirituales* (1818, Spiritual Poetry) and *Salterio Peruano* (1833), a poetic translation of the Psalms. Not all of his work was strictly religious in nature. He contributed articles to *El Mercurio Peruano*, a progressive and republican newspaper, and composed odes to independence-era generals José de San Martín ("Oda a San Martín") and Simón Bolívar ("Lima libre y pacificada"), well known for their pro-abolition stance.

With the advent of the Peruvian Republic, Valdés was elected to Congress to represent Lima in 1831. He became a member of the illustrious Patriotic Society and was appointed Médico de Cámara del Gobierno, a position similar to United States surgeon general. He received an important Peruvian award, the Order of the Sun of Peru, before attaining a succession of important medical and university titles, among them director of Lima's Medical College of Independence.

Joy Elizondo

See Also

Porres, San Martín de; Abolition and Emancipation in Latin America and the Caribbean; Literature, Black, in Spanish America; Catholic Church in Latin America and the Caribbean; Colonial Latin America and the Caribbean.

Latin America and the Caribbean

Valdés, Merceditas

(b. October 14, 1928, Havana, Cuba; d. June 13, 1996, Havana, Cuba), Afro-Cuban singer, interpreter, and arranger of religious and secular Afro-Caribbean music; a well-known *santera* (a practitioner of Santería, the traditional Yoruba religion, as practiced throughout Cuba).

Mercedes Valdés, or Merceditas, as she was widely known, began her distinguished artistic career in the 1940s, studying at Havana's Supreme Art Institute under José Alonso. As a student, she received awards for several works, including "Babalú," "La Negra merece," and "El chureo."

During the late 1940s Valdés began to display her interpretive talents over the airwaves on Radio Cadena Suaritas. These appearances established the young artist's position as one of Cuba's most prominent interpreters of traditional Yoruban religious music (*see* Music, Afro-Caribbean Religious). In the late 1950s Valdés's Santería recordings for the Panart label helped to secure her importance in the Afro-Cuban movement.

Throughout her career Valdés gained the recognition of Cuba's most acclaimed musicologists and critics, including the anthropologist Fernando Ortiz and the musicologist Argeliers León. In addition, she performed with many notable Cuban artists such as the composer Ernesto Lecuona, the *tres* player and maestro Arsenio Rodríguez, the great *sonero* singer Benny Moré, Zún-Zún Babaé, the percussionist Mongo Santamaría, and the jazz pianist Charlie Palmieri (*see* Afro-Latin Jazz). In 1995 Valdés performed as a member of the Cuban All Stars, and her recordings have been featured on several Cuban compilations, including *Messidor's Finest* and *Cuba: I Am Time* (1997).

By the time of her death in 1996 Valdés had succeeded in bringing Afro-Cuban culture to the world through her acclaimed live appearances and recordings. She also proved her versatility, performing dance-hall boleros, rumbas, and *sones* alongside traditional Santería music.

Valdés consistently received the highest recognition for her work, including a national recognition medal from the Cuban Cultural Ministry. Musicologist Angeliers León aptly characterized Valdés's importance to Cuban culture, and the preservation of Yoruban tradition: "Merceditas Valdés is one of the best exponents of the Yoruban language and its rites, transmitting them through their ancestors and contributing towards a greater knowledge of this African heritage."

Gordon Root

See Also

Rumba; Yoruba; Bolero; Moré, Beny; Son; Santamaría, Ramón ("Mongo"); Music, Afro-Caribbean Secular; Music, Afro-Caribbean Religious.

Latin America and the Caribbean

Valentim, Rubem **(b. 1922), contemporary Brazilian sculptor and painter whose work uses geometric symbols associated with orixás, Afro-Brazilian deities (see Art in Latin America and the Caribbean).**

Latin America and the Caribbean

Valiente, Juan **(b. ?; d. 1553), slave who fought with Spanish colonial armies first in Central America and then in the Southern Cone. He received an encomienda, a land grant, from the Spanish Crown in 1550, and he is thought to be the first black to have received one. He died in battle in 1553 (see Chile).**

Latin America and the Caribbean

Vallenato, **accordion music from Colombia's Caribbean coastal region; it has become commercially successful and since the 1970s has been the best-selling Colombian musical style in the country.**

The origins of Vallenato lie in a pan-Latin American tradition of versification that included *romances* (ballads), *coplas* and *trovas* (rhyming verses), *décimas* (ten-line stanzas), *cantos* (songs), and different forms of oral poetry, sung unaccompanied or perhaps with a guitar. European influences were important, but many singers were of African descent. In Colombia's Caribbean coastal region, African influence is evident in twentieth-century work songs and some funerary songs, as well as in the *bailes cantados* (sung dances), the dancing to drums and singing that forms a parallel tradition (*see* Music, Afro-Caribbean Secular). In the late nineteenth century accordions and harmonicas began to appear in the region, imported from Germany, and were used in this corpus of songs, probably as something of a rarity; they were also used in other local styles played by traditional lineups of African and indigenous drums, flutes, maracas, and so on, and by wind bands. The accordion has usually been described as being in the hands of the troubadour or wandering minstrel, perhaps accompanied by a small hand drum (now known as a *caja*) and a scraper (*guacharaca*).

Accordion music from this region began to be labeled *vallenato* in about the 1940s, shortly after the appearance of the type of accordion that produced the distinctive sound of the genre. The term *vallenato* means "born in the valley" and usually refers to Valledupar, a town in the eastern part of the region, and its surrounding areas. In the early 1900s the term was used locally to refer not to music but to local lower-class people. However, similar sorts of accordion music could be found all over the Colombian Caribbean coastal region at the time. The Valledupar zone produced a number of important accordionists, including Chico Bolaños (b. 1903), Pacho Rada (b. 1907), Emiliano Zuleta (b. 1912), Alejandro Durán (b. 1919), and Leandro Díaz (b. 1928). But the locality also became known as the primary birthplace of this music when local elites (including songwriters Rafael Escalona, Tobías Enrique Pumarejo, Freddy Molina, and Gustavo Gutiérrez) began to write songs for the accordion and claim the music as a tradition special to their area. This development occurred at a time when the area itself was becoming increasingly integrated into the rapidly modernizing nation-state. At this time, too, accordionists were making early recordings in Colombia's fledgling record industry, based in nearby Cartagena and Barranquilla, and were performing on the new radio stations. Claims by the local elite about the unique character of their region were reinforced in the 1960s with political campaigns – which used vallenato music – for a new *departamento* (administrative province) status for the region. In 1968 an annual vallenato festival was established, which insisted on "traditional" three-piece lineups featuring an accordion, a drum, and a scraper).

Accordion music was seen as very plebeian for most of the twentieth century. Vallenato subgenres (particularly *paseo*, merengue, and *son*) became popular nationwide in the 1940s and 1950s, but the tunes were played on the guitar by, for example, Guillermo Buitrago. Accordion vallenato started to become popular nationally in the 1970s, but it was still associated with the lower classes, even as the lineups became larger, more professional, more standardized musically, and less parochial in lyrical content, emphasizing generally the romantic themes that gave it, for some listeners, an air of schmaltz. By the 1980s it had become Colombia's best-selling single national genre, with stars such as Diomedes Díaz, Julio Oñate, and El Binomio de Oro. In the 1990s vallenato of the 1950s and 1960s gained a new popularity and status as a national symbol, after the broadcast of a television dramatization of the life of songwriter Rafael Escalona and albums of "modernized" versions of the music by singer Carlos Vives. These albums broke sales records, appealed to middle-class youth (who generally disparaged vallenato), and also sold well abroad.

Peter Wade

See Also
Cartagena de Indias, Colombia; Durán, Alejo.

Africa

Valley of the Kings, an ancient Egyptian Pharaonic cemetery.

During the Old and Middle Kingdoms of ancient Egypt (2980-1580 B.C.E.), the pharaohs commissioned pyramid tombs and temples in anticipation of their journeys to the afterlife. They filled these tombs with the goods considered necessary for the next life, including jewels, precious metals, food, tools, furniture, and even royal servants and pets. These riches lured grave robbers, who stripped most of the known tombs virtually bare. Beginning with Amenhotep I (r. 1514-1493 B.C.E.), however, the pharaohs located their burial complexes on the west bank of the Nile, across the river from Thebes, in a valley hidden by cliffs and a narrow entrance. Amenhotep I had his temple and tomb built into the side of the limestone cliffs in the valley, with deep corridors stretching as far as 100 m (328 ft) below the earth. Traditionally, work on a pharaoh's tomb began the day he ascended the throne and ended the day he died.

More than 60 such tombs have been rediscovered since the eighteenth century. Over time desert sand had covered the entrances to most of the tombs, and their locations had been forgotten. In 1799, however, army engineers accompanying France's Napoleon I rediscovered several of them, and Europeans proceeded to excavate the tombs and remove their precious contents to museums in their home countries. Perhaps the most extraordinary discovery was of the tomb of the boy king Tutankhamen in 1922. Located on the valley floor, it was robbed twice but escaped large-scale looting because the construction of a later tomb covered its entrance with sand and rubble. Although it is by far the smallest tomb in the valley, it yielded archaeologists more than 5000 artifacts, many of which now reside in the Cairo Museum. During the 1980s archaeologists discovered a tomb that they believe contains 52 sons of Ramses II (r. 1279?-1212? B.C.E.). Scientists have been excavating this tomb ever since. In late 1997 they commissioned the DNA testing of four mummies to determine if they were in fact Ramses' offspring. The Valley of the Kings is also the final resting place for Hatshepsut (r. 1503-1482 B.C.E.), one of the few women who ever ruled Egypt.

Archaeologists worry that these ancient monuments, which have faced centuries of humidity, pollution, and flash floods, are deteriorating. Some say that it is only a matter of time before they are lost forever. In addition, thieves and vandals have been plundering the monuments for thousands of years. Yet the walls of these tombs still contain elaborate bas-relief artwork that provides information and insight into the beliefs and practices of one of the world's oldest and greatest civilizations. As a result Egyptologists have declared the valley the richest archaeological site in the world. Archaeologists are currently developing preservation plans, creating detailed topographic maps of the tombs they have already discovered, and outlining possibilities for further excavations.

The Valley of the Kings is among Egypt's greatest tourist attractions, and has been for millennia, as graffiti from ancient Greek and Roman visitors testify. The continuing fascination with ancient Egypt lures as many as 3000 visitors per day to the valley sites and generates more than $3 billion (US) nationwide each year. But in November 1997 Muslim fundamentalist rebels attacked tourists visiting the Hatshepsut Temple in the Valley of the Kings; gunmen killed 58 visitors. The attack devastated the tourism industry, on which Egypt depends economically. Despite the government's heightened security measures, the attack left many foreigners unwilling to travel to Egypt, especially to vulnerable areas such as the Valley of the Kings.

Robert Fay

See Also
Egypt; Egypt, Ancient Kingdom of; Thebes, Egypt; Nile River; Tourism in Africa; Islamic Fundamentalism: An Interpretation.

Africa

Van der Post, Sir Laurens Jan (b. December 13, 1906, Philippolis, South Africa; d. December 15, 1996, London, England), South African writer best known for his books of personal reflection on travel and anthropology, and whose prose is noted for its striking imagery and minute observation.

Born in Philippolis, Sir Laurens Jan van der Post was raised on a working ranch and educated at Grey College in Bloemfontein, South Africa. In 1925, with two other South African writers, Roy Campbell and William Plomer, he helped start the magazine *Voorslag,* which was strongly opposed to the South African apartheid government. Due to his involvement with the periodical, van der Post was forced to leave South Africa and so traveled to Japan, where he wrote his first novel, *In a Province* (1934), an early indictment of South African racism. From 1939 to 1946 van der Post served with the British Army during World War II (1939-1945); he spent three years (1943-1946) in a Japanese prisoner-of-war camp, an experience on which he based his books *The Seed and the Sower* (1963; filmed as *Merry Christmas, Mr. Lawrence* in 1983), *The Night of the New Moon* (1970), and *Portrait of Japan* (1968).

Van der Post's early exposure to San myths led to a lifelong fascination with this ethnic group of the Kalahari Desert of northern South Africa, whose traditional way of life van der Post has idealized in his writings as an intuitively spiritual state of perfect harmony with the natural environment. His works on San culture, *The Lost World of the Kalahari* (1958), *The Heart of the Hunter* (1961), *A Mantis Carol* (1975), and *Testament to the Bushman* (with Jane Taylor, 1984), are probably his best-known books.

Other books by van der Post include *Venture to the Interior* (1952), *Flamingo Feather* (1955), *Jung and the Story of Our Time* (1976), *Yet Being Someone Other* (1982), *A Walk with a White Bushman* (with Jean-Marc Pottiez, 1986), *About Blady* (1991), and *Feather Fall: An Anthology* (edited by Jean-Marc Pottiez, 1994). Van der Post was knighted by the British government in 1981.

North America

VanDerZee, James Augustus (b. June 29, 1886, Lenox, Mass.; d. May 15, 1983, Washington, D.C.), African American photographer whose work recorded and contributed to the Harlem Renaissance.

James VanDerZee was born in Lenox, Massachussetts, and made his earliest photographs there in 1900, after he won a camera for peddling large amounts of sachet powder. He immediately embraced photography and by the time he moved to New York City in 1906 had mastered the rudiments of the craft. After a job as a waiter, a short stay in Virginia, and a job snapping portraits in a New Jersey department store, VanDerZee opened his own studio in Harlem. From 1916 to 1931 he kept shop at 135th Street and Lenox Avenue, serving as the neighborhood's preeminent photographer.

VanDerZee documented faces and facets of the Harlem Renaissance, as well as numerous weddings, funerals, business clubs, and sports teams. In 1924 Marcus Garvey contracted with him to be the official photographer of the Universal Negro Improvement Association (UNIA). In addition to making documentary photographs that were realistic in style, VanDerZee experimented with photographic techniques – such as doctoring negatives and creating double exposures – demonstrating his artistic as well as technical ability.

Although VanDerZee's business survived the GREAT DEPRESSION and World War II, it began to wane during the early 1950s. For a time he supported himself by running a mail-order restoration service, but in 1969 he was evicted from his studio. At the same time, however, he caught the public eye through his contributions to *Harlem on My Mind*, an exhibition at New York's Metropolitan Museum of Art. Soon afterward a group of young photographers, including *Harlem* curator Reginald McGhee, founded the James VanDerZee Institute (now defunct), which organized exhibitions of his work.

As public recognition of VanDerZee's work grew, the photographer regained the prosperity of his early career. The return to success was strengthened by his marriage to Donna Mussenden in 1978. Mussenden, 60 years his junior, took charge of him and his estate, helped win back copyrights, and transformed the VanDerZee legacy into a business. She also helped VanDerZee with his final project, a series of celebrity portraits shot in the early 1980s.

James VanDerZee died on May 15, 1983, at age 96. Over the course of his long career he photographed numerous African American celebrities, including MUHAMMAD ALI, BILL COSBY, Miles Davis, Eubie Blake, ROMARE BEARDEN, CICELY TYSON, JEAN-MICHEL BASQUIAT, OSSIE DAVIS,and RUBY DEE. He received awards from many institutions, including an honorary doctorate from HOWARD UNIVERSITY.

Eric Bennett

SEE ALSO

World War II and African Americans; Blake, James Hubert ("Eubie"); Davis, Miles Dewey, III; Garvey, Marcus Mosiah; Harlem, New York; New York, New York; Universal Negro Improvement Association; Photography, African American.

North America

Van Peebles, Melvin

(b. August 21, 1932, Chicago, Ill.), author, filmmaker, and playwright, perhaps best known for his groundbreaking 1971 independent film, *Sweet Sweetback's Baadasssss Song.*

Melvin Van Peebles has traded stocks on the floor of the American Stock Exchange, published numerous novels, and directed, produced, composed, and starred in American films and plays. He is an innovative and successful entrepreneur who has worked for more than four decades to offer new, and sometimes controversial, images of African Americans.

Van Peebles was born in 1932 on the South Side of Chicago, but spent most of his adolescent years with his father, a tailor in Phoenix, Illinois. After graduating from high school in 1949 and from Ohio Wesleyan University in 1953, Van Peebles served as a flight navigator for three and a half years in the United States Air Force. After leaving the military he spent brief periods in Mexico and San Francisco – where he was married – before moving to Europe. He studied at the Dutch National Theatre in the Netherlands, then moved to France in the early 1960s. During nearly a decade in Paris Van Peebles wrote and published several novels in French, including *La permission,* which he filmed under the title of *The Story of the Three-Day Pass* and which concerns a black U.S. serviceman. The film won critical acclaim and helped Van Peebles earn a studio contract with Columbia Pictures.

Van Peebles returned to the United States and in 1969 directed *Watermelon Man*, a comedy about a racist white insurance salesman who wakes up one day to find that he has become black. Van Peebles took the proceeds from the film and made *Sweet Sweetback's Baadasssss Song* (1971), one of the most successful and controversial independent films of the era. *Sweetback* pushed the limits of cinematic decorum, combining sex and violence in its depiction of a black sex worker who witnesses the murder of a young black revolutionary by two white police officers. It was one of the first "blaxpoitation" films of the 1970s and its success opened doors for African American directors, camera operators, designers, and editors.

In the early 1970s Van Peebles staged two plays on Broadway: the musical *Ain't Supposed to Die a Natural Death,* and *Don't Play Us Cheap,* based on his novel *Don't Play Us Cheap: A Harlem Party.* Later in the decade he wrote scripts for two television productions, *Just an Old Sweet Song* and *Sophisticated Gents.* Van Peebles turned his attention to business in the early 1980s and became an options trader on the floor of the American Stock Exchange. Drawing on his success, he published two books on the options market. Since then he has written a novel and appeared in the 1993 movie *Posse,* an all-black Western by his son, Mario Van Peebles.

Alonford James Robinson, Jr.

Africa

Van Riebeeck, Jan

(b. April 21, 1619, Culemborg, Netherlands; d. January 18, 1677, Batavia, Dutch East Indies [Jakarta, Indonesia]), founder and first Dutch commander of the European settlement at the Cape of Good Hope in what is now SOUTH AFRICA.

The Dutch East India Company commissioned Jan Van Riebeeck to establish a rest and resupply station at the Cape of Good Hope for Dutch ships en route to the East Indies. He landed at Table Bay on April 6, 1652, with about 90 men, and there he built a fort and hospital. He also established farms in the area around the bay.

Unsuccessful in securing the labor of the indigenous KHOIKHOI and SAN peoples, he advocated the importation of slaves to work the farms well before they were actually brought into the colony. Riebeeck tackled the problem in 1657 by releasing men from their company employment to farm as free burghers, while still maintaining the interests of the company. This practice created the class of independent farmers who became known as Afrikaners, or Boers. The station was not meant to be expanded beyond the area of the bay, and Van Riebeeck's instructions were to keep the Cape establishment as confined and small as possible. Despite this he actively encouraged exploration in the interior, ultimately leading to colonial expansion (*see* EXPLORERS IN AFRICA, 1500 TO 1800). In 1659 he waged a year-long war on the Khoikhoi. In 1662 Riebeeck was transferred to Malacca, after repeated requests to be moved. By then the Cape settlement was well established.

SEE ALSO

Afrikaner; Netherlands, The.

North America

Varick, James

(b. 1750, Orange County, New York; d. July 22, 1827, New York, New York), founder of the African Methodist Episcopal Zion Church.

James Varick was a widely influential free black in New York City at the turn of the nineteenth century. Although both of his parents had Dutch Reformed Church connections, he joined the white John Street Methodist Church. Later he and other blacks withdrew to create the first African American congregation in New York. A shoemaker by trade, he also taught school; participated in black Masonic, mutual aid, and anticolonization societies; petitioned for the right to vote; and was one of the founders of *Freedom's Journal*, the first black American newspaper.

The congregation Varick established grew into a denomination, the AFRICAN METHODIST EPISCOPAL ZION CHURCH (AME Zion), and on July 30, 1822, Varick was elected its first bishop. The denomination, like the AFRICAN METHODIST EPISCOPAL CHURCH founded by RICHARD ALLEN, kept Methodist theology, polity, and worship, but practiced its faith in a black organization under black control. Largely middle class in makeup, the AME Zion Church has been a major institution in African American history. Varick's ashes are preserved in Mother Zion AMEZ Church on 137th Street in Harlem.

Richard Newman

SEE ALSO

Freedom's Journal; Harlem, New York; New York, New York.

Latin America and the Caribbean

Vasconcelos, José

(1722?-1760?), Afro-Mexican poet famous for his wit and humor about whom very little information is known. His improvised verses were published by Nicolás León in 1912 under the title *El negrito poeta mexicano y sus populares versos* (The Little Black Mexican Poet and His Popular Verses) (*see* Literature, Black, in Spanish America).

Latin America and the Caribbean

Vasconcelos, Naná

(Juvenal de Hollanda Vasconcelos) (b. August 2, 1944, Recife, Brazil), Afro-Brazilian percussionist and master of the traditional Brazilian *berimbau.*

Naná Vasconcelos is one of the most significant and influential percussionists of the last 30 years. At age 12 he began playing percussion – bongos and maracas – in the band led by his guitarist father. Later he took up drums and played in a bossa nova band. He is a master of the odd-numbered rhythms, such as 5/4 and 7/4, that are common in northeastern Brazil. In the mid-1960s Vasconcelos joined the band of Afro-Brazilian singer Milton Nascimento and moved to Rio de Janeiro. There he learned to play the berimbau, a traditional Afro-Brazilian percussion instrument shaped like an archer's bow with an attached gourd resonator. The berimbau produces a distinctive buzzing tone when the instrument's single wire string is struck with a thin wooden stick. Its tonal quality can be altered depending on the position of the gourd resonator, and its pitch depends on whether the musician places a coin against the wire.

In 1971 Vasconcelos joined the band of Argentinian tenor saxophonist Gato Barbieri and toured Argentina, the United States, and Europe. After the end of the tour he stayed in Paris for two years, performing and working with handicapped children. In Europe he played with American avant-garde jazz trumpeter Don Cherry and with Brazilian jazz musician Egberto Gismonti. Together with Cherry and Collin Walcott, Vasconcelos formed Codona, an influential trio that combined the musical traditions of several continents. In 1976 Vasconcelos moved to New York City, where, as a multitalented percussionist, he was soon in demand.

Vasconcelos has recorded with such diverse musicians as blues legend B. B. King, jazz pianist Keith Jarrett, fusion guitarist Pat Metheny, and the rock group Talking Heads. He has played with a wide variety of Brazilian musicians, including guitartist and political activist Caetano Veloso, pianist and singer Ivan Lins, and vocalist Marisa Monte. In addition, Vasconcelos has released several albums under his own name, among them *Bush Dance* (1986) and *Storytelling* (1995), both featuring his unique and complex multi-instrumental sound.

James Clyde Sellman

See Also

King, Riley B. ("B. B."); New York, New York; Rio de Janeiro, Brazil.

North America

Vaughan, Sarah

(b. March 27, 1924, Newark, N.J.; d. April 3, 1990, Hidden Hills, Calif.), African American jazz singer and pianist lauded for her ability to command pitch and dynamics across three vocal octaves, Vaughan's singing style was informed by the harmony and improvisation of jazz horn sections.

Sarah Vaughan's parents, both of whom were musicians, cultivated and nurtured her early interest in music. She began taking piano lessons at age 7 and organ lessons at 8. By age 12 she was playing the organ for the Mount Zion Baptist Church and singing in its choir. She later attended Arts High School in Newark, New Jersey.

In 1942 Vaughan entered and won an amateur-night contest in which she sang "Body and Soul." Her award was $10 and a week of performances at the Apollo Theater, an engagement that led to her being hired as a vocalist and second pianist in Earl "Fatha" Hines's big band. In 1944 she joined singer Billy Eckstine's band. She recorded the hit "Lover Man" (1945) with Charlie Parker and Dizzy Gillespie, also members of Eckstine's ensemble, before launching her solo career in 1946 at the New York Cafe Society. In 1949 she landed a five-year recording contract with Columbia Records. Vaughan sustained her success as a singer through the early 1980s, recording on numerous labels, performing with a variety of jazz artists, and touring several countries.

Nicknamed "Sassy" and the "Divine One," Vaughan repeatedly was voted the top female vocalist by *Down Beat* and *Metronome* jazz magazines between 1947 and 1952. Her 1982 album *Gershwin Live!* won a Grammy Award, and in 1989 she received the Grammy Lifetime Achievement Award. Vaughan was inducted into the Jazz Hall of Fame in 1990.

Aaron Myers

See Also

Eckstine, William Clarence (Billy); Gillespie, John Birks ("Dizzy"); Hines, Earl Kenneth ("Fatha"); Parker, Charles Christopher ("Bird").

North America

Vee Jay Records

the most influential and successful African American-owned record company before the appearance of Motown Records.

Vee Jay Records was founded in Chicago in 1952-1953, and it quickly emerged as America's most successful black-owned record company. Vee Jay recorded gospel music, jazz, blues, rhythm and blues, and early soul, but it was unique in concentrating on vocal harmony groups. Like many small record companies, Vee Jay was a family affair, involving Vivian Carter Bracken, her husband James Bracken, and her brother Calvin Carter. Vivian was a disc jockey in Gary, Indiana, where she and James owned a record store. Carter suggested the name Vee Jay, based on the first initials of his sister's and his brother-in-law's first names.

Vee Jay's first vocal group was the Spaniels, which featured the cool lead of James "Pookie" Hudson and which had a major hit with "Goodnight Sweetheart Goodnight" (1954). Other important Vee Jay vocal group hits included the El Dorados' "At My Front" (1955); the Dells' "Oh What a Nite" (1957); a memorable "For Your Precious Love" (1958) by the original Impressions, featuring Jerry Butler and Curtis Mayfield; and "Duke of Earl" by the Dukays, credited solely to the group's lead singer, Gene Chandler.

Within two years of releasing its first Spaniels' single, Vee Jay owned a building on Chicago's Michigan Avenue directly across from the offices of Chess Records, which was a major producer of music for the African American market, featuring such best-selling artists as Muddy Waters, Chuck Berry, and the Moonglows. Besides vocal groups, Vee Jay recorded a number of other significant talents in the late 1950s and early 1960s, including bluesmen John Lee Hooker and Jimmy Reed, solo vocalists Jerry Butler, Dee Clark, and Betty Everett, and gospel singers such as the Staple Singers and Alex Bradford. The company also recorded jazz, including tenor saxophonist Wardell Gray's last recording session, in 1955.

During the early 1960s Vee Jay stood on a par not only with Berry Gordy's fast-growing Motown Records, but also with the independents that focused on the audience for African American R&B and soul music: Chess, Atlantic, and Stax Records. But rapid expansion, sloppy finances, and internal bickering forced the company to declare bankruptcy in 1965.

James Clyde Sellman

See Also

Soul Music; Berry, Charles Edward Anderson (Chuck); Blues, The; Chicago, Illinois; Motown.

Latin America and the Caribbean

Vega, Ana Lydia

(b. December 6, 1946, Santurce, Puerto Rico), writer, feminist critic, and professor of French and Caribbean literature at the University of Puerto Rico at Rio Piedras who regards Afro-Puerto Rican themes and popular language as central to her intellectual production.

Notable among the works of Ana Lydia Vega are *Vírgenes y mártires* (1981), the author's first book, which was coauthored with Carmen Lugo Filipp; *Encancaranublado y otros cuentos de naufragio* (1982), which won Vega the 1982 Casa de Las Americas Prize; *La gran fiesta* (1986), a screenplay that was made into a movie; *Pasión de historia y otras historias de pasión* (1987); and *Falsas crónicas del sur* (1991). Various Vega stories and a novella were translated into English by Andrew Hurley and appeared under the title *True and False Romances* (1994).Vega has received numerous awards for her work, including the PEN (International Association of Poets, Playwrights, Editors, Essayists, and Novelists) Club of Puerto Rico National Literature Prize on several occasions, the prestigious Casa de Las Americas Prize of CUBA (1982), the Juan Rulfo International Short Story Prize (1984), the Premio Casa del Autor Puertorriqueño (1985), and the Guggenheim Fellowship for Literary Creation (1989).

Vega's profound knowledge of Spanish and African oral tradition has been an important influence on her writing. The author wrote her 1978 doctoral thesis on HAITI's King Cristophe in Antillean theater and in black theater in the United States (*see* THEATER IN THE CARIBBEAN), and her narratives often include tales and thematic elements from African folklore. Vega received early exposure to oral tradition through her father, who was an expert in *décimas*, an oral form of poetic improvisation typical of black troubadours (*see* LITERATURE, BLACK, IN SPANISH AMERICA). She has a superb ear for popular language that informs her skillful use of various types of verbal play such as jokes, puns, and riddles to underscore her biting humor. Vega's writing is also characterized by an alternation between formal and vernacular speech, an incisive examination of machismo in Caribbean societies, and vivid depictions of socially motivated violence. All of this serves her well and contributes to the powerful, distinctive quality of her writing. Vega has gained a wide following, and her works engender much discussion in a variety of publications.

Martha Swearington Davis

SEE ALSO

Literature, English Language, Caribbean; Décima; Christophe, Henri.

Africa

Venda (also known as Bavenda), ethnic group of southern Africa.

The Venda primarily inhabit northeastern SOUTH AFRICA and southern ZIMBABWE. They speak a Bantu language related to both SOTHO and SHONA. Approximately 700,000 people consider themselves Venda.

SEE ALSO

Bantu: Dispersion and Settlement.

Latin America and the Caribbean

Venezuela, country of South America bordered on the east by GUYANA, on the south by BRAZIL, on the west and southwest by COLOMBIA, and bounded on the north by the Caribbean Sea and Atlantic Ocean.

Venezuela is often described as the country of *café con leche* (coffee and milk), a "racial democracy" with little or no racism where blacks, whites, and Native Americans intermingle freely, both physically and culturally. As in other Latin American countries that also make this claim, in Venezuela the reputation is sustained by the country's history of miscegenation and the "celebration" (read, "folklorization") of Afro-Venezuelan cultural manifestations. Much is hidden behind the label racial democracy. For although there may be few formal barriers to social mobility for Afro-Venezuelans, they nonetheless face discrimination and racism that place them at the bottom of the economic and political hierarchy.

THE OFFICIAL HISTORY

Christopher Columbus sighted the coast of present-day Venezuela in 1498 during his third voyage to the New World, but the first Spanish settlements were not established until the 1520s. The city of Caracas was established in 1567. Administratively, the region was divided between the viceroyalty of Peru, in southwestern South America, and the Audiencia of Santo Domingo, in the West Indies, until 1717, when the viceroyalty of New Granada was created, encompassing present-day Venezuela, Colombia, ECUADOR, and PANAMA.

Caracas was the birthplace of Simón Bolívar, hero of Latin America's wars of independence. Independence was formally declared in 1811, and Bolívar led the forces in Venezuela. In 1819 the republic of Gran Colombia was established, with its capital in Bogotá. In 1829 Venezuela split to form an independent republic. Until 1935 Venezuelan history was marked by internal political struggles and authoritarian dictators. Its economy was based largely on agriculture and cattle ranching, but the discovery of oil in 1917 gave rise to an important new economic sector. The death of strongman Juan Vicente Gómez (1908-1935) was followed by a protracted and difficult transition to democracy. In 1945 a military coup initiated a three-year period that saw tremendous social reforms. The coup led to the prominence of the political party Acción Democrática (AD). AD leader Rómulo Betancourt headed the ruling junta for two years, and Rómulo Gallegos, a prominent novelist and AD member, was elected president in 1947. The reforms passed by the AD government sparked a backlash from conservative sectors. Another coup in 1948 led to ten years of authoritarian rule under dictator Marcos Pérez Jiménez (1948-1952, as part of a junta; 1952-1958, as sole ruler). Since 1958 the country has maintained a democratic regime. AD and the Christian Democratic party (COPEI) have dominated Venezuelan politics during this time.

EARLY CONTACT WITH EUROPEANS

Before the arrival of Europeans the area now known as Venezuela was inhabited by several native groups who lived mostly in farming and fishing communities. They offered resistance to the first Spanish settlers in the 1520s, but their uncoordinated efforts quickly gave way to the advancing Europeans.

Accompanying the first of the Spanish conquistadors were *ladinos*. Ladinos were black slaves who had been Hispanicized in SPAIN before coming to America, as opposed to *bozales*, slaves who later came directly from Africa. On occasion ladinos fought against the native populations; more often they cleared land for the roads, small settlements, and farm plots of the Spaniards. For their role in the conquest, some ladinos were given their freedom and exempted from taxes.

The area of Venezuela did not immediately yield the riches that were found elsewhere in Spanish America. Its economic life consisted largely of subsistence farming, performed by slaves. There was also some mining of pearls near the eastern islands of Cubagua and Margarita. As in neighboring Colombia, in Venezuela the divers who retrieved the pearls were almost always slaves, who were required to dive among sharks and were constantly at risk of drowning. Moreover, slave masters often believed that sexual gratification would make the divers more buoyant and therefore unable to reach the pearl beds. These slaves were thus forbidden to have sexual partners.

The earliest divers were probably ladinos, but they were soon replaced by bozales, brought directly to Venezuela from GUINEA and CAPE VERDE. Between 1500 and 1550 at least 5000 such slaves arrived in Venezuela. Only a few of them – those who distinguished themselves by bringing up the largest pearls – were able to buy their freedom.

SLAVE LIFE AND LABOR IN THE GROWING ECONOMY

As Spanish colonists grew rich from the pearl beds, a few of them established larger farms and ranches and began exploring for mineral deposits. After the founding in 1567 of Caracas, which would become the capital of Venezuela, masters and slaves fanned gradually south across the country, pressing inland among the surviving Indians. Late in the sixteenth century gold was discovered in several locations, and slaves were sent to the dank, subterranean mines to dig the gold. They were worked routinely to the point of exhaustion and, not infrequently, death – thus requiring the importation of more slaves. By 1600 Venezuela had a black slave population of about 13,000.

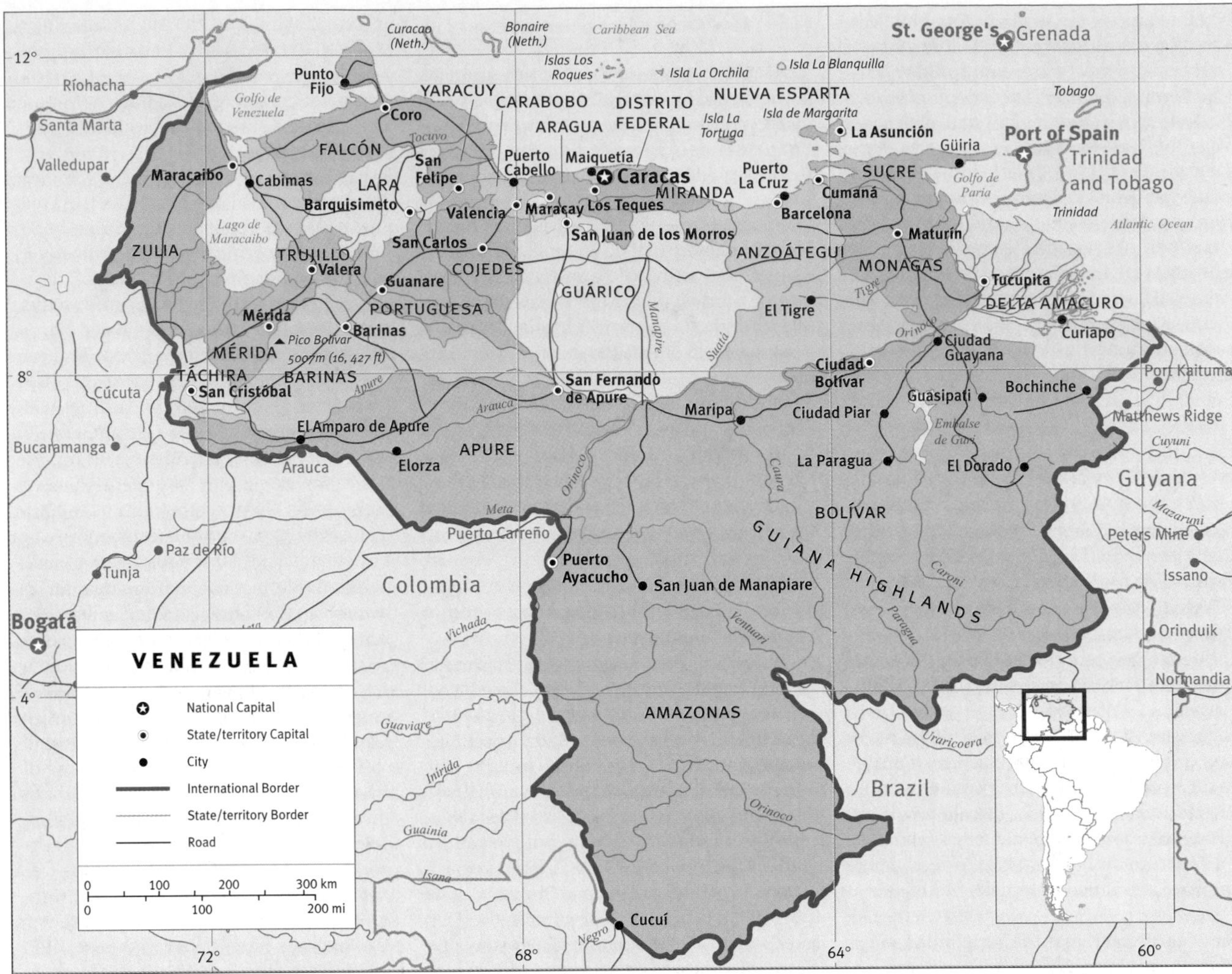

The mines of Venezuela, however, were never to become the primary basis of the colonial economy, and in the seventeenth century mining gave way to plantation farming. Wheat, tobacco, and cotton were grown, but the largest crops were cacao, the tropical evergreen tree prized for its cocoa (and thus chocolate), and the dye indigo. Slaves were, of course, the primary laborers. Early in the seventeenth century the Roman Catholic Church, which the Spanish Crown had entrusted with governing Venezuela, held most of Venezuela's land (*see* Catholic Church in Latin America and the Caribbean). During this period much of a slave's life on a plantation was typical of slave-plantation life elsewhere in the New World: work began under the supervision of a master at 5:00 AM and ended at about 9:00 PM. During harvest season work often continued until midnight.

However throughout the seventeenth century more and more private landholders gained access to the fertile cacao valleys of central Venezuela. With this expansion the influence of the Church eroded, with important implications for slaves. First, because the private landholders were so few, slaves so numerous, and central Venezuela bereft of white settlements, the slave owners relied heavily upon slave foremen to oversee the farming. Eventually both the need for labor and the expanse of cultivated land were great enough that most slave owners allowed slaves to establish *conucos*, or small homesteads where slaves built houses, grew their own food, and could intermingle more or less freely with other slaves.

The conucos were beneficial to both slave and slaveholder. Because the slaves grew their own food and made their own goods, slaveholders did not have to provide these items. The slaves, meanwhile, were spared the rigorous and often harsh enforcement of white masters, as well as the cultural and religious imperialism of living among whites. Moreover, black field bosses and crew chiefs gained rudimentary experience in management and accounting.

Another important effect of the shift from Church control to private control was that by the end of the seventeenth century the Church had lost so much of its land base that it was desperate for tax money. As a result it offered Venezuela's many slaves the right to establish their own religious brotherhoods. The Church stood to benefit from granting this right since it had the power to tax assemblies.

Cocoa production climbed steadily to a peak in the early eighteenth century. By this time (and probably long before), plantation owners in Venezuela were tiring of the high cost of importing slaves from Africa. They thus turned to Spain's Caribbean colonies for imports. After importing thousands of these slaves, Venezuelan landlords smuggled in large numbers from the Caribbean colonies of Spain's rivals, Great Britain and France.

For decades Spain tried to put a stop to the illegal trade, but in 1780 the government bowed to reality and allowed any Spaniard in Venezuela to purchase slaves from the French Caribbean colonies of Guadeloupe, Martinique, and Saint-Domingue (*see* Haiti). In 1783, after Spain and Great Britain agreed to the Peace of Paris, imports were also allowed from British colonies. Between 1784 and 1786 Great Britain brought 4000 slaves to Venezuela and Trinidad, while another contract signed in 1786 allowed the delivery of 5000 to 6000 slaves to Venezuela and Cuba. The last known contract with a British company for importing slaves to Venezuela was for 4000 slaves between 1795 and 1805. Over the whole of the eighteenth century an estimated 70,000 slaves arrived from the Caribbean – a good portion of them illegally. Although most of these slaves were farm laborers, a small but important minority were artisans and trained tradespeople. After 1800 only 2500 slaves were brought from Africa.

Venezuelans lounge in front of a mural portraying the seacoast. *Molins/Hutchison*

The demand for slaves disrupted conuco life. If it was cheaper to buy slaves from the Caribbean than from Africa, it was cheaper still to buy slaves from Venezuelans. A thriving internal trade thus grew in the late eighteenth and early nineteenth century, concentrated on the plantations of the central states and in Caracas. The Black Code – under which Venezuelan slaves (like other Spanish American slaves) were governed after 1785, and which regulated the buying, selling, and punishing of slaves and the rights and obligations of slaveholders – provided few means for keeping families together. Further, it is unclear to what degree the code was followed in practice.

By the turn of the nineteenth century most slaves were no longer of strictly African descent. Due to the remote nature of many of the cacao haciendas, Africans often married and bore children with Indians, creating a mixed race known as *zambos*. Moreover, in part because early colonial Venezuela had few white women, Spanish colonists often had sexual relations with black women, producing another racial category, called mulattos or *pardos* ("browns," referring to people of mixed blood). By the time of the wars of independence in the second decade of the nineteenth century, a large portion of Venezuelans could not be certain of their racial ancestry, and a significant portion of "white" Venezuelans had at least a trace of African or native blood, or both.

Independence from Spain and Emancipation

The early nineteenth century was a time of great economic change for Venezuela. Plantation owners, having grown wealthy, continued to place more acres under cultivation. However, as the reserve of unfarmed land dwindled in the late eighteenth and early nineteenth century, landowners cast their eyes on the conucos that slaves had worked for decades or centuries. Many slaves were evicted from what they regarded as their homelands and placed under more direct supervision by whites, while their former holdings were planted with cacao or indigo. Furthermore, as slaves became more costly to import, slave labor was often supplemented with hired labor, thus putting slaves in a more competitive labor pool.

As a result numerous small rebellions broke out in the late eighteenth and early nineteenth century. Many of the rebels took advantage of the lax oversight to escape and form communities known as *cumbes*. Often located in rugged mountains or jungles, the cumbes served as bases for occasional raids on white settlements. More often slaves simply farmed and raised livestock in the cumbes (*see* Maroonage in the Americas).

The rebellions, which continued into the second decade of the nineteenth century, eventually played into the hands of Simón Bolívar. Initially, however, Bolívar wanted nothing to do with Afro-Venezuelans. He undertook major assaults in 1810 and again in 1813 to overthrow Spanish rule in Venezuela, but in both attempts he banned blacks from enlisting with his troops. In 1813 he even condemned Venezuelan Loyalists to the Spanish Crown for their treachery in using blacks against his "white patriots," but it was the successful fighting of these blacks against him that convinced Bolívar he would need their aid to overthrow Spain.

By 1817, the year of his third major assault on Venezuela, Bolívar realized he would need the aid of blacks, mulattos, and zambos to defeat the Loyalists. He admitted them to his ranks, and with their aid Venezuela was largely liberated of Spanish rule by 1821. For many Afro-Venezuelans fighting with the rebel army, independence represented a hope for reforming the social order and subverting their political marginalization. When several Afro-Venezuelan officers gained what was seen by white officers as too much power within the rebel army, however, they were accused of attempting to incite a race war and were executed. The execution of Gen. Manuel Piar, a mulatto, in October 1817 is the most noted example. Still, the mere presence of black troops in the rebel army was decisive for the future of Afro-Venezuelans. As historian Winthrop Wright has written, "The inclusion of colored and black troops in the independence movement shattered the old colonial social order. Pardos literally came of age as a result of their involvement in the hierarchy of Bolívar's military organization. Slavery also began to disintegrate."

In 1819 Bolívar shifted the focus of his rebellion to Colombia, which at the time controlled Venezuela. Rebel leaders in Colombia questioned his use of black troops, but he argued convincingly that only by using slave fighters would the rebels overthrow Spanish rule. He also argued that if only whites fought, only whites would die and blacks would be left to inherit the revolution. Blacks, he said, should be used to the point of extermination if need be so that there would be fewer of them surviving after the revolution. Afro-Venezuelans appear to have been generally aware that they were wanted only as long as they were needed. Nonetheless, the spoils of fighting and the chance to escape one's master were often reward enough to make becoming a rebel soldier worthwhile (*see* Racial Question during Struggles of Independence in Latin America).

Although Bolívar regarded Afro-Latin Americans as children, his republican ideals were at odds with the institution of slavery. Thus for reasons probably both idealistic and practical, he proposed the total abolition of slavery as early as 1819, though a congress of rebel leaders overruled him. Nevertheless, on July 21, 1821, an assembly of delegates ruling Colombia and Venezuela passed a law stating that the newly born children of slaves were to be set free when they turned 18. These children were thus known as *manumisos* (freedpeople). Older slaves were to be freed as taxes were raised to pay for them. The taxes were collected by a board of collectors in each legislative district, but the boards were dominated by slaveholders. Thus the law was little enforced and slavery continued as before.

Venezuela asserted its independence from Colombia in January 1830 and later that year reaffirmed its commitment to freeing slaves. To pacify slaveowners, however, the age of emancipation for manumisos was changed from 18 to 21. As 1842 approached – 21 years after the 1821 manumission law was enacted – the age was raised again, this time to 25, under the guise of an apprenticeship program.

Afro-Venezuelans, as it happened, would need another war before they became important (or feared) enough to be set free. For the first decades after independence, the Venezuelan government had a weak claim to legitimacy and a tenuous hold on power; coups were often discussed and civil war lurked beneath the surface. In 1845 Gen. José Tadeo Monagas was elected president

Untitled photograph of four men playing dominos in Barlovento, Venezuela, 1994. *Tony Gleaton*

with the Conservative Party, but three years later he switched to the Liberal Party and expelled many Conservatives from Congress. To shore up his power and head off a possible revolt, he declared all manumisos free at age 21. Monagas later ceded power to his brother, José Gregorio Monagas, who conscripted blacks into the army when a revolt broke out against him in May 1853. The rebel troops, which were quickly put down, also used black soldiers.

In order to shore up his support and stave off further revolt, Monagas declared all slaves free in March 1854. He promised slaveholders that they would receive payments in compensation for their lost property, but his regime collapsed shortly thereafter and no payments were made. The emancipation, however, survived the regime. Some 30,000 remaining slaves were at last finally freed (*see* Abolition and Emancipation in Latin America and the Caribbean).

Beyond Emancipation

After emancipation most Afro-Venezuelans continued to work on the farms where they had been enslaved. A few, however, were able to achieve economic or political success. For example, José Rafael Revenga, a mulatto, became a member of Congress in the late 1840s and was secretary of internal affairs in the Monagas government.

From 1858 to 1863 Venezuela descended into a civil war, known as the Federal War, which pitted people from rural areas (federalists) against people in urban areas (centralists). Ex-slaves generally joined with the federalists and for the most part sought assurances that slavery would remain abolished. A few Afro-Venezuelans also struggled to establish autonomous republics for blacks, mulattos, and zambos; such efforts met with only temporary success. An important outcome of the fighting was the ratification of a postwar amendment to the constitution declaring that slavery was indeed abolished and that all former slaves would remain free. Some years later, in 1881, an antidiscrimination law passed.

In 1860 a French company began exploiting gold mines in the southern state of Bolívar. Seeking English-speaking workers, with whom they were more comfortable, the French imported blacks from the nearby English Caribbean islands of Trinidad, St. Thomas, and ARUBA. For the next four decades blacks streamed into southern Venezuela from the Caribbean. By the turn of the twentieth century the larger mines were tapped out, but many of the Afro-Caribbean workers, known as Antilleans, remained. Some continued to work small mines of their own; others farmed. Most retained some connection with their families, cultures, and Anglican religion from their home islands.

The presence of the Antilleans stirred racial tensions. In 1924, when it was rumored that more Antilleans might be imported to help with fall harvests, many Venezuelans called for a ban on black immigration. This was largely due to a fear that black immigrants would "darken" the country and a desire rather to "lighten" it. Thus in 1929 people of African origin were banned from immigrating to Venezuela. From the 1930s to the 1950s the government actively sought white immigrants from Europe, largely in the hope of "whitening" the country, a project pursued in a number of countries in the region (*see* WHITENING).

In the 1930s companies from the United States began oil exploration in Venezuela. Since (English-speaking) Antilleans could no longer be imported, the Antilleans already in the country were in high demand in the oil fields. Many found their way into well-paying jobs.

At roughly the same time that the oil industry was being developed, farm holdings throughout Venezuela were being consolidated. A major result of these twin occurrences was that Venezuela rapidly shifted from a mostly rural to a mostly urban society. Like their fellow citizens, many Afro-Venezuelans from the countryside migrated to cities in search of work; but when they could find it, it was low paying and unskilled. Afro-Venezuelans typically lived in slums, their children received poor education, and a cycle of poverty and powerlessness set in.

The so-called *Trienio* (the three-year period between 1945 and 1948) marked a time of radical distributive change in Venezuela. Under the leadership of the political party Acción Democrática, a series of dramatic reforms was instituted to address the country's considerable economic disparities. These measures included support for education and health care, official encouragement of unionization, and land reform. Much of the party's base consisted of poor farmers and workers, many of whom were black or of mixed race. The populist measures enacted under the Trienio sparked a backlash that led to a military coup. Between 1948 and 1958 Venezuela was ruled by dictator Pérez Jiménez. Pérez Jiménez stifled all dissent, Afro-Venezuelan or otherwise. Many of Acción Democrática's leaders were forced into exile or hiding, though it remained the largest clandestine opposition organization. In January 1958 a general strike in Caracas crippled the government. On January 23 a popularly backed military coup toppled Jiménez and established a democratic regime.

Under the dictatorship Acción Democrática moved to the center, seeking to conciliate groups it had alienated during the Trienio. This culminated with the Pact of Punto Fijo in 1958, a power-sharing agreement signed by leaders of the three major parties. Retaining much of its popular base, the party returned to power in the 1960s, though it was considerably more moderate than it had been under the Trienio. During this time it nonetheless passed a number of reforms, including an agrarian reform law in 1960. Blacks gained increasing power in state farm societies, trade unions, and the oil industry. Many Afro-Venezuelans gained political offices in rural areas and in the central government. In July 1966 the ban on black immigration was officially dropped.

In 1968 the government provided a host of subsidies and scholarships promoting the study and practice of Afro-Venezuelan arts, especially music, dance, and theater. During the 1970s and 1980s most of Venezuela's universities received funding for curricula in Afro-Venezuelan arts and culture. As elsewhere in Latin America, African culture and beliefs in Venezuela have become inextricably intertwined with the fabric of the larger society. In religion, for example, African spiritual beliefs melded with Roman Catholicism to form a Creole religion in which Roman Catholic saints are worshiped alongside black and native deities. Mass in the Creole religion is held to the beat of African drums, and the roles of traditional healer and priest often merge. On the day of Corpus Christi, a traditional Roman Catholic holiday, religious brotherhoods in Afro-Venezuelan towns typically perform dances with masks and movements that have been traced to the Congo (*see* VENEZUELAN RELIGION, AFRICAN ELEMENTS IN).

In the 1990s most blacks in Venezuela still lived in poverty and held little political power. In 1993, however, Acción Democrática placed its first black presidential candidate on the ballot. Also, Afro-Venezuelan Aristúbolo Isturiz, a member of Causa R, a recently created party with roots in the labor movement, was elected mayor of Caracas.

SEE ALSO

Congo, Democratic Republic of the; Trinidad and Tobago; Catholic Church in Latin America and the Caribbean; Racial Question during Struggles of Independence in Latin America; Myth of Racial Democracy in Latin America and the Caribbean: An Interpretation; Black Codes in Latin America; São Tomé and Príncipe; Religious Brotherhoods in Latin America.

Latin America and the Caribbean

Venezuelan Religion, African Elements in

Because slaves first arrived in VENEZUELA before 1800 and were immediately converted, at least superficially, to Roman Catholicism, African religious elements in Venezuela have survived only in fragmentary form in popular rituals for saints and in a few beliefs and practices.

African elements in Venezuelan folk-Catholic practices are found in rural regions with a predominantly black population, such as the Barlovento, the central coast, the southern coast of Lake Maracaibo, and some areas of Yaracuy, Lara, and Carabobo. African elements in the folk Catholicism of these areas are incorporated into the festivals held for particular saints by local brotherhoods. In Carabobo, Yaracuy, Miranda, and Aragua, for example, Saint John is the patron of black peasants and fishermen. On the eve of his feast, *erum* dances are held, while old women sing *sirenas* for the saint, similar to African praise songs. Early the next morning Saint John's icon is bathed in the river and then carried from house to house by drummers, singers, and dancers who are offered food and drinks. The participants use special homemade drums, which are used only during rituals. The faithful thank the saint for having answered their prayers. A similar ceremony is held in Lara in honor of Saint Anthony: celebrants engage in ritual stick fights during a procession with his statue – a custom also widely seen in West Africa.

In the region of Zulia, San Benito of Palermo is the patron of black peasants. His feast is celebrated with drum dances and processions held between Christmas and January 6 in different black villages. The rhythms and drumbeats used in this ceremony have kept their original African flavor. In recent years many traditional customs have disappeared, and the dances for the patron saints, once considered a solemn obligation, are now becoming tourist attractions.

"Devil Dances" are another type of Venezuelan festival that exhibits African elements. These dances are held annually on the Catholic festival of Corpus Christi Day in eight or nine different villages with predominantly black inhabitants. The most traditional dances take place in the isolated village of Chuao, in Aragua, where the male-only fraternity of Diablos (or devils) is responsible for the celebration, while the dances in honor of Saint John are organized by a female-dominated group. The "devils" wear colorful gowns and masks made of papier-mâché that are reminiscent of masks used in similar rituals in the Bapende, in the Congo area of Africa; their dances are similar to masked dances held in Central Africa. During these dances, which are considered a solemn obligation, the gender dichotomy also exists: one man wears a female mask, representing the "wife of the devil." It is important to note that the "devils" are not evil. On the contrary, the dancers dressed as devils visit the homes of the fraternity members in order to chase evil away. The dancers can also be compared to the *egunguns* in BENIN and NIGERIA, who represent the departed ancestors, visiting their living kin in order to bring good luck and chase evil away. Although in San Francisco de Yare the annual devil dances are watched by thousands of tourists, the members of the fraternity have preserved their original solemn ritual.

Some African elements are also found in the funeral rites in the Yaracuy and Barlovento regions. During the nightly wake held in the home of the departed, the women wail for the deceased while the men play cards. Mourners place a glass of water next to the coffin, as it is believed that the soul of the dead is still present and may be thirsty. They also place some personal objects, such as a comb, a toothbrush, and a cap, into the coffin for the spirit's journey to the other world; then they take the coffin out of the house through a hole made in the wall, which is carefully covered up again, so that the spirit cannot find its way back. After praying for nine nights in front of an improvised altar in the house of the departed, the people smash a table upon which flowers, candles, and photos of the dead have been placed. They make noise to indicate to the dead soul that the ritual is over and that it may now depart in peace and not disturb the living. On the night before All Souls' Day, celebrated annually on November 2, black peasants visit the graves of their departed relatives and sometimes spend the whole night in the cemetery. They leave food and libations there for the dead.

In addition to rituals and festivals that historically developed in Venezuela, other Afro-Latin religions are increasingly popular. During the past 40 years, for example, SANTERÍA has been introduced to Venezuela by Cubans and Venezuelans who have traveled to Miami and PUERTO RICO. The majority of converts to this religion belong to the middle class, because initiation ceremonies are expensive. However, Venezuelans of all classes consult *babalawos*, or priests of the Santería religion, to help solve personal problems. Santería beliefs and practices have also been introduced into the native cult of Maria Lionza, which has its roots in both Amerindian beliefs and the teachings of Allan Kardec, a European spiritist. In this cult spirits of different origins are summoned to take possession of mediums in trance, and the spirits can then be consulted by the faithful. This cult is utilitarian in nature: the spirits prescribe cleansing rituals to get rid of evil influences and give advice on how to heal illnesses.

Until about 30 years ago most spiritual entities consulted in the cult of Maria Lionza were spirits of nature or of departed persons of importance, such as Amerindian chiefs who fought the Spanish conquerors or Simón Bolívar, the hero of Latin American independence. In recent years the *siete potencias africanas* – the seven most important ORISHAS of the Cuban-Yoruba pantheon – have been consulted through the mediums. Animal sacrifices are offered to them, drums are used to call the spirits, and colors have a symbolic value, just as in Santería.

Venezuelan cultists often ignore the true African origin of these entities, although today they speak about the "African court," to which, incidentally, the Viking spirits also belong, although they are depicted as bearded white savages. Recently Venezuelan folk healers have begun to mention specific countries in their divination practices, and they may invoke the African spirits to help them in their spiritual work.

In addition to Santería, the Brazilian religion of UMBANDA was introduced to Venezuela about 15 years ago by a white Uruguayan *pai de santo*, or priest. He presides over a center, frequented by members of the middle class, where Afro-Brazilian *caboclo* and *preto velho* spirits manifest themselves in initiated mediums who are consulted by adherents.

Overall, the globalization of Afro-American religion and the influence of religions such as Santería and Umbanda in Venezuela stem from media coverage, the expansion of esoteric literature, and frequent reunions of cultists and esoterics. The prospects for historically Venezuelan religions, though, are quite different. While the cult of Maria Lionza is subject to a re-Africanization process, in which spirits are increasingly identified as being of African origin, traditional folk religiosity is vanishing as the population of Venezuela is becoming more urbanized.

Angelina Pollak-Eltz

SEE ALSO

Benedict of Palermo, Saint; Slavery in Latin America and the Caribbean; Cuba; Catholic Church in Latin America and the Caribbean; Religious Brotherhoods in Latin America.

Latin America and the Caribbean

Ventura, Johnny

(b. March 8, 1940, Santo Domingo, DOMINICAN REPUBLIC), Afro-Dominican politician and merengue musician who incorporates the issues of race, politics, and social change in his music.

Johnny Ventura, affectionately called "El Caballo" (The Horse), has been praised as one of the few artists to blend politics and music successfully. His achievements are facilitated by a strong sense of national identity and a connection with the masses. Ventura made merengue the country's main musical form and a symbol of national identity accessible to all social classes. Unlike most other politicians, Ventura expresses pride in his African heritage within a society that emphasizes its Spanish and indigenous ancestry. Ventura has used music not only as a source of entertainment but also as a medium through which meaningful issues like Dominican identity and concepts of race can be expressed.

Ventura began his musical career under his birth name, Juan de Dios Ventura Soriano. After winning a 1956 radio station singing competition that drew attention to his powerful, smoky voice, the singer changed his name to the stylish Johnny Ventura for artistic as well as political reasons. Ventura's singing career took off soon after his debut. He was well received by Dominican society because his lyrics criticized the country's political system and its denial of an African heritage. Ventura entered the music scene at a time when Dominicans were eager for a new beginning after experiencing the oppressive rule of dictator RAFAEL TRUJILLO.

Between 1930 and 1961 the Trujillo government chose merengue to symbolize national culture and identity. The music was used as a political tool, and its lyrics praised the dictator. Only upon Trujillo's death in 1961 was merengue able to regain the vitality it once had and to develop through foreign musical influences forbidden by the Trujillo government. Ventura led others in revolutionizing merengue, changing the musical instruments merengue artists used and incorporating elements inspired by salsa and rock music. These changes resulted in Ventura's first hit – "La agarradera" (The Handle) – which gained both national and international notice.

In 1964 the young artist formed a band called Johnny Ventura y su Combo-Show and became a model for other *merengueros* (merengue performers). Breaking traditional form, the band's music was livelier and less inhibited than previous forms of merengue. Johnny Ventura y su Combo-Show – the top merengue band of the 1960s – traveled throughout the Dominican Republic, taking merengue out of the ballrooms of the elite and performing it for the rest of society.

Inspired by Elvis Presley and JAMES BROWN, to whom he was later compared, Ventura choreographed dance moves for his band. The artist also created a flashy wardrobe and provocative stage presence for himself. Although Ventura's music and style were influenced by foreign cultures, his political views remained grounded in Dominican thought. During the civil war of 1965 he allied himself with the nationalist party, which once again used merengue as a political tool to promote patriotism and assert Dominican national identity against the invading United States forces.

As a social activist Ventura joined with friends and colleagues to create El Club de Los Monos (The Monkeys' Club), a group whose objective was to eliminate the concept of black racial inferiority in Dominican society. According to Ventura, the group wanted to "demonstrate the brilliance of men and women of our [black] race... strengthening the idea of a re-encounter with [Afro-Dominican] cultural values." Appropriating *monos*, a derogatory name for blacks, the club gathered celebrities from various professions to demonstrate the contributions Afro-Dominicans made to their nation. Ventura's overall purpose in establishing the club reflected his personal goal of promoting awareness among a people who often disavow their African heritage.

Ventura's involvement in politics was not limited to his musical lyrics and social activism. His energy and drive carried over into a political career as a congressman, deputy mayor, and finally mayor of Santo Domingo, the nation's capital. This accomplishment in May 1998 followed the release of Ventura's autobiography, titled *Un poco de mí* (A Little of Me). In his new position Ventura hopes to take the Dominican Republic into a prosperous era, effecting social change and promoting an all-inclusive concept of Dominican identity. His contributions to music and politics in the Dominican Republic continue to gain him international notice.

Rob Garrison

See Also

Merengue: Music, Race and Nation in the Dominican Republic; Salsa Music.

Latin America and the Caribbean

Verger, Pierre Fatumbi

(b. November 4, 1902, Paris, France; d. February 11, 1996, Bahia, Brazil), French ethnographer and photographer.

The holder of a Ph.D in African Studies from the University of Paris, Verger traveled through various countries between 1932 and 1945 as a researcher for the Musée Ethnographique du Trocadéro (Ethnographic Museum of Trocadéro; today the Musée de l'Homme) and as a professional photographer. He eventually settled in Salvador, Bahia in 1946, where he explored in depth the black culture of Africa and Brazil, writing several books on the subject. Verger's pioneering work traced strong links between the religion and culture of Dahomey (now Benin) and Brazil. In 1952, while in Dahomey, he was initiated into the Yoruba religion, given the name Fatumbi, and made a *babalawo*, or priest, of the Ifa divination system. Some of Verger's publications include *Trade Relations Between the Bight of Benin and Bahia from the Seventeenth to Nineteenth Century* (1976), *Retratos da Bahia* (1980), and *50 Anos de Fotographia* (1982). His last publication, *Ewe: The Use of Plants in African Society* (1995), compiled the results of many years of documenting the medicinal and religious use of plants in Yoruba society. Since 1989 the Fundação Pierre Verger (Pierre Verger Foundation) has conserved 62,000 photographic negatives, his vast library, his personal archives, and has promoted the diffusion of his anthropological and photographic contributions.

See Also

Dahomey, Early Kingdom of.

Africa

Verwoerd, Hendrik Frensch

(b. September 8, 1901, Amsterdam, Netherlands; d. September 6, 1966, Cape Town, South Africa), prime minister of South Africa (1958-1966) who promoted a policy of apartheid.

Hendrik Frensch Verwoerd was a professor of sociology and editor of an Afrikaans nationalist newspaper before he was appointed senator in 1948. Rising to cabinet posts, he was made minister of native affairs in 1950 and was responsible for engineering much of the Nationalists' social and political policy of apartheid, legalizing racial segregation and discrimination. He was elected to the House of Assembly in 1958 and became prime minister shortly afterward. In 1959 he initiated the Bantustans policy for resettling South Africa's blacks into eight reservations. In 1961 he withdrew the country from the Commonwealth of Nations after criticism of South Africa's racial policies. Verwoerd was assassinated in 1966.

See Also

Afrikaner.

Africa

Victoria Falls, a waterfall in south Central Africa and the largest waterfall in the world.

Called *Mosi-oa-Tunya* ("the smoke that thunders") by the Makololo people, Victoria Falls is located on the Zambezi River on the border between Zimbabwe and Zambia. The river, here more than 1.6 km (1 mi) wide, plunges about 108 m (354 ft) down basalt gorges, producing a vast mist (or "smoke") that is visible from more than 45 km (about 25 mi) away. A railroad bridge, completed in 1905, spans the gorge below the falls. Since the completion of the bridge Victoria Falls has become a popular tourist destination, providing both the Zimbabwean and Zambian governments with much-needed tourism revenue. The falls are now part of the 23,399,654-sq m (5782-acre) Victoria Falls National Park, which offers canoeing, kayaking, white-water rafting away from the falls, and wildlife safaris.

Scottish missionary and explorer David Livingstone, who in 1855 became the first European to visit the falls, named them after Queen Victoria and believed that the falls were created by a cataclysmic event and not by erosion. In addition to the falls themselves, Livingstone encountered and came to work with the Makololo, who dominated the area at that time.

Robert Fay

See Also

Tourism in Africa.

Africa

Victoria, Lake, or Lake Nyanza, the world's second-largest freshwater lake and primary source of the Nile River.

Lake Victoria is located in East Africa, where it is bordered by Uganda, Kenya, and Tanzania. Occupying an area of 69,482 sq km (26,828 sq mi), it lies approximately 1151 m (3775 ft) above sea level. The lake is about 337 km (210 mi) long and in places stretches about 240 km (150 mi) wide. It is drained by the Nile River and its chief affluent is the Kagera River.

An estimated 30 million people in the Great Lakes region of East Africa, one of the most densely populated parts of the continent, depend on Lake Victoria for their livelihood. Fishing and boat building are the most significant economic activities. In addition, the Owen Falls Dam at Jinja, Uganda, where the Victoria Nile flows out of the lake, produces the hydroelectricity that fuels the surrounding industries and urban areas.

In recent years, however, the ecological deterioration of Lake Victoria has begun to undermine the economic as well as physical health of local communities. For years the lake has been polluted by raw sewage, industrial waste, and agricultural chemicals. The more recent and perhaps the most serious dangers are the depletion of native fish stocks by overfishing, the introduction of the predacious Nile perch (scientists believe that only 200 of the 400 species of fish formerly found in the lake remain), and the proliferation of the water hyacinth. Although the Nile perch is profitable for commercial fisheries, which sell its meat, hide, and bladder, it feeds on cichlids, shallow-water fish that provide both a revenue and protein source for the traditional fishing communities. These communities cannot fish for Nile perch because they have neither the boats nor the equipment necessary to catch the large (up to 1.8 m [6 ft] long and 90 kg [200 lb]), deep-water species.

Another threat to Lake Victoria's ecosystem is the water hyacinth, a floating weed native to the Amazon region of South America. First brought to Africa and introduced into the Nile River in the late nineteenth century, the water hyacinth has spread throughout the continent, reaching Lake Victoria in 1989. The plants grow in thick mats that begin at the shore and spread toward the lake center, inhibiting navigation. The density of this vegetation slows down fishing trips and makes some parts of the lake completely inaccessible to ordinary boats. Local communities have lost access to the livelihood and sustenance once provided by fishing in these areas, resulting in widespread malnutrition. In some cases the weed has prevented villagers from obtaining lake water for domestic use. In addition, water hyacinth provide a habitat for snails that cause bilharzia or schistosomiasis. The weed also blocks sunlight, reduces the amount of oxygen in the water, and alters the water's chemical composition, all changes with possibly detrimental consequences for the lake's remaining plants and animals.

In 1992 the governments of Kenya, Tanzania, and Uganda created the Lake Victoria Organization, aimed at restoring the ecosystem. One of its projects is to rebuild the cichlid population by breeding 40 new species in aquariums, and educating local people about the benefits of fish farming. In addition, several scientific groups are experimenting with possible solutions to the water hyacinth problem, the most promising of which is biological pest control through the introduction of a hyacinth-eating species of beetle.

Robert Fay

Africa

Vieira, João Bernardo (b. 1939, Guinea-Bissau), president of Guinea-Bissau (1980-).

João Bernardo Vieira was born in Guinea-Bissau and trained first as an electrician and later as a military commander. He joined the socialist, revolutionary African Party for the Independence of Guinea and Cape Verde (PAIGC) in 1960 and studied under founder Amílcar Cabral at the PAIGC school in Conakry, Guinea. After serving as a regional military commander and political commissioner (1961-1964) and receiving military training in China, Vieira was given military command of the southern front of the war of independence in 1964 and later of the entire war theater in 1970, while also serving as a ranking member of the council of war (1965-1967; 1971-1973). A member of the PAIGC political bureau, the party's policy-making body, since 1964, Vieira was named deputy secretary-general of the party in 1973. Following independence in 1974 he was elected president of the National People's Assembly, remaining in his position as commander of the armed forces and serving as the minister for the armed forces as well. He was appointed prime minister by President Luís de Almeida Cabral, a Cape Verdean, in August 1978.

By the late 1970s the PAIGC's goal of uniting Guinea-Bissau and Cape Verde became unlikely. Realizing that mainland Guineans resented the predominance of Cape Verdean *mestiços* (persons of indigenous and European descent) within the PAIGC leadership, Vieira overthrew Cabral in November 1980. Dissolving the National Assembly, Vieira installed a National Revolutionary Council, staffed entirely by mainland Guinean military officers. Having initially criticized the former regime for its betrayal of the socialist revolution, Vieira, attempting to attract foreign investment and International Monetary Fund and World Bank support, soon began encouraging private enterprise and limiting government control of trade. After surviving a series of coup attempts and consolidating his power through constitutional revisions, Vieira reinstated the National Assembly and began, in 1990, the transition toward a multiparty state. In July 1994 multiparty elections PAIGC retained a majority in the National People's Assembly, and Vieira was reelected by a narrow margin.

See Also

Conakry, Guinea; Cabral, Luís.

North America

Vietnam War, an American war that divided American society and had profound social and political consequences for African Americans.

The United States government had opposed the insurgency in Vietnam since the early 1950s, but few Americans, black or white, knew of the conflict prior to the commitment of U.S. ground troops in 1965. On August 7, 1964, Congress passed the Tonkin Gulf Resolution, granting President Lyndon B. Johnson broad discretion in Southeast Asia. By December 1965 there were nearly 200,000 American troops in Vietnam.

Although integration of the U.S. armed forces began in 1948 and integrated troops fought in the Korean War, Vietnam was the first war the United States entered with racially integrated armed forces (*see* Military, Blacks in the American). Black soldiers quickly proved their bravery: two of the war's earliest Congressional Medal of Honor recipients, Private Milton Olive and medic Lawrence Joel, were African Americans. Yet, as a black *New York Times* reporter noted, for the first time in American history, "national Negro figures are not urging black youths to take up arms [in order to]... improve the lot of the black man in the United States."

Despite the military's overall success with racial integration, there were still striking imbalances in the Vietnam era. From 1965 to 1967 the black casualty rate of 20 percent was roughly twice that of whites. From 1969 to 1970 the army reduced the imbalance by assigning more blacks to support roles, but African Americans realized that for years their young men had borne the brunt of the casualties.

Discrimination began with predominantly white local draft boards that preferred to conscript young black men. During 1967, 64 percent of eligible blacks were drafted, compared with only 31 percent of whites. Blacks – who were less likely to meet the higher educational requirements of the navy and air force – overwhelmingly entered the army. They were also underrepresented in the officer corps. In 1968 blacks made up nearly 10 percent of total American military personnel, but only 2 percent of all officers.

Black servicemen in Vietnam referred to themselves as "bloods." They fought a bitter jungle war in which there were no decisive engagements and the threat of ambush and booby traps was ever present. Vietnam's dangers also included potent marijuana, hashish, and heroin. Many soldiers, white and black, became dependent on drugs, with devastating consequences.

As military expenditures escalated, Congress forced Johnson to curtail his domestic War on Poverty. The Vietnam War helped split the civil rights coalition. White liberals once active in civil rights became preoccupied with the war, and white student activists, part of the civil rights struggle since the 1961 Freedom Rides, were overwhelmingly drawn to antiwar protests.

The war also divided the black leadership. Moderates such as Rev. Martin Luther King Jr., Bayard Rustin, and Whitney Young were reluctant to speak out against the war. The earliest protests came from radicals such as Malcolm X, who in 1964 linked the war to racial discrimination at home.

In January 1966 the leadership of the Student Nonviolent Coordinating Committee (SNCC) condemned the draft; a year later heavyweight boxing champion Muhammad Ali refused to be drafted. Ali insisted that he would not "murder and kill and burn other people simply to help continue the domination of the white slave masters over the dark people of the world."

The war also had a profound effect on King. Speaking on April 4, 1967, at New York City's Riverside Church, he denounced the war, lamenting that "the Great Society has been shot down on the battlefields of Vietnam." The war revolutionized King's thinking, helping him place the Civil Rights Movement in a world context.

Black opinion turned steadily against the war. A 1971 Gallup poll found a higher level of dissatisfaction with the war among blacks (83 percent) than among whites (67 percent). Yet Vietnam remained a place of much interracial cooperation. Combat troops realized that they had to count on one another regardless of race. In 1968, however, the morale of American troops collapsed due to the Communist Tet Offensive, and racial hostilities sharpened considerably following King's assassination.

After the 1968 election newly elected President Richard Nixon implemented "Vietnamization," shifting the war to the South Vietnamese. The U.S. troop level peaked at 540,000 during 1969, but that June Nixon announced the first withdrawal of 25,000 men. The last units came home in the spring of 1973. The war ended two years later with the fall of South Vietnam.

James Clyde Sellman

See Also

King, Martin Luther, Jr.; Young, Whitney Moore, Jr.

Latin America and the Caribbean

Vincent, Sténio J. (b. 1874; d. 1959), president of Haiti (1930-1941).

Sténio J. Vincent was a member of Haiti's mulatto elite who came to the presidency during the United States occupation of the country (1915-1934). In 1934 he persuaded President Franklin D. Roosevelt to withdraw U.S. troops from the island. In 1935 Vincent's tenure in office was extended by five years. Vincent was widely regarded as being antiblack, and he created a presidential guard to counterbalance the troops left behind by the United States, which was dominated by black officers (*see* Haiti).

Latin America and the Caribbean

Virgin Islands (United States and British), a group of more than 100 Caribbean islands (of which approximately 20 are inhabited) located between the Caribbean Sea and the North Atlantic Ocean, east of Puerto Rico. The group is divided politically into two dependent territories: the British Virgin Islands and the United States Virgin Islands. The main inhabited islands are St. Croix, St. Thomas, and St. John (all U.S. territories), and Tortola, Anegada, Virgin Gorda, and Jost Van Dyke (all British possessions).

When Christopher Columbus first sighted this archipelago of islands in November 1493, he named them Las Once Mil Virgenes (The Eleven Thousand Virgins) both to commemorate the legend of Saint Ursula and her 11,000 martyred virgins and to exaggerate the magnitude of his find to his patron, Queen Isabella of Spain. In reality the total number of Virgin Islands is much closer to 110 than to 11,000. Many of the islands are small and uninhabited, and to outsiders the Virgin Islands are often synonymous with the five large islands that have become immensely popular tourist destinations: St. Croix, St. John, and St. Thomas in the United States group, and Tortola and Virgin Gorda in the British group. The fact that the islands are split into United States and British territories is the end result of the region's complex history of slavery, colonization, and resistance – the story that lies behind today's resorts and restaurants.

The first inhabitants of the Virgin Islands were probably the Ciboney Amerindians, who appear to have migrated from South America to what is now St. Thomas in approximately 300 B.C.E. Within 500 years they were replaced by the Arawaks, who were mainly farmers and who eventually spread out to Tortola and several other Virgin Islands. Beginning at the end of the fourteenth century the Arawaks were overtaken by the more aggressive Caribs, who named St. Croix "Ay Ay" and established themselves on many other islands as well. But it was Columbus's intrusion that would have the most lasting effects.

Columbus and his crew were the first Europeans to "discover" the Caribbean Islands, and in their journeys they nominally claimed each island they saw for the Spanish flag. But because the Virgin Islands were smaller than many of the other Caribbean Islands and were not as rich in minerals and other natural resources, the Spanish chose not to settle them, and the islands were largely ignored during the first century of Caribbean colonization. By the 1600s, however, Europeans were pursuing expansion in the region in earnest.

The struggle for domination inevitably resulted in some conflicts. St. Croix was first shared by the English and Dutch, then held solely by the English, overtaken by the Spanish, then the French, then given to the Knights of Malta and returned to the French before it was sold to the Danish West India and Guinea Company in 1733. St. Thomas was occupied by the Danish, attacked by the Dutch, and captured and then abandoned by the English before being reclaimed by Denmark in 1671. Tortola was settled by Dutch buccaneers before being attacked and captured by the English in 1665. It was not until the beginning of the eighteenth century that the Virgin Islands had reached a more or less stable political configuration, with the islands grouped into Danish and English holdings. By then it was clear just what was at stake for each of these colonial powers: the Virgin Islands were developing into flourishing slave economies.

Once it was discovered that the islands' soil would support both cotton and sugar, settlers were eager to cultivate these crops. The white population at the time was an unpredictable assortment that included Quaker religious dissenters, then-infamous buccaneers, and ex-convicts who were sent to the West Indies as part of their jail sentences. It was clear that these white settlers would not provide all of the labor the new plantations would require. In 1673 the first consignment of 103 African slaves, probably taken from homes in Guinea, landed in St. Thomas. By 1715 the island had 160 plantations and 3042 slaves.

Similarly drastic gains were made across the region by the mid-1700s, and in response to the new demand, Charlotte Amalie in St. Thomas became one of the world's largest slave markets in the eighteenth century (*see* Transatlantic Slave Trade). In both sets of islands working conditions were arduous, the clothing and food given in compensation were minimal, and punishments were harsh. As one historian said, "It is difficult to characterize any slave system as more repressive than that of the Virgin Islands."

One drought in 1725-1726 resulted in a scarcity of food, and many planters chose simply to let their slaves starve to death. In all cases slaves were left with virtually no avenues of formal redress. In the British islands a slave who resisted a white owner could have his nose split, any member amputated, or "as many number of stripes" as the master chose to inflict. In the Danish islands a slave

Two women test rum in a bar in the Virgin Islands. *W. Lynn Seldon, Jr./D. Donne Bryant Stock Photo*

who struck a white person or even threatened to strike one "should be pinched and hung" – or, if the person chose to pardon him, "should lose his right hand." Death by various means of torture was permitted for a wide range of crimes, and especially for being suspected of making any plans to run away. But it was little surprise that many slaves still took the opportunity to escape when they could, and also little surprise that slaves in the Virgin Islands led two of the most dramatic revolts in the Caribbean.

The first was the St. John revolt in 1733. In the months leading up to the uprising, a drought, two hurricanes, and an insect plague had made the slaves' already desperate situation intolerable. The passage of a new, brutally restrictive slave code in September 1733 proved to be the last straw. The leaders of the revolt – allegedly African-born slaves of royal, West African origin – captured St. John's only fort and gave the signal for an islandwide uprising. At that time St. John had 1087 slaves and only 208 whites; the slaves were able to control the island for six months.

It was not until August 1734 that the last rebels finally surrendered; although they had been promised a free pardon, they were instead publicly executed by torture. Many other rebels had committed suicide rather than be recaptured. While their daring effort ultimately ended in tragedy, it provided a powerful signal of the Africans' uncompromising commitment to freedom.

In 1790 British slaves led an uprising on Tortola after a rumor spread that England had granted them their freedom and their masters were holding it back. The rumors had some basis in reality, because by the end of the eighteenth century Britain was already calling for abolition. Several planters on the British islands had already begun manumitting groups of slaves, leading to a growing class of free blacks whose numbers grew even larger after Britain abolished the slave trade in 1808. From that time on illegal cargoes of slaves found on British ships were seized and "liberated"; but instead of being returned to their African homes, they were brought to the West Indies and set free there. Not surprisingly, as the number of free blacks in the islands increased, blacks who remained enslaved grew even more convinced of their own right to be free. British Virgin Islands slave insurrections flared up in 1823, 1827, 1830, and 1831. Full emancipation of all English slaves was finally established on August 1, 1834.

The apprenticeship period that followed emancipation mandated that all slaves remain with their former owners for another four years, and so essentially extended slavery until 1838. But black British Virgin Islanders were still relieved, above all, to be finally free.

In the Danish West Indies, although the slave trade had been abolished in 1792, slavery itself remained legal until 1848. That year, on July 3, Moses Gottlieb, also known as Buddhoe, led fellow St. Croix slaves in another dramatic uprising – arguably among the most successful in history. In this action slaves sacked the houses of the police assistant, the town bailiff, and a wealthy merchant and then took over the fort, threatening to burn the entire town if they were not emancipated within the hour. Most of the whites had already taken refuge on ships docked in the harbor. Sensing just how serious the threat was, within the hour the governor general read the Proclamation of Emancipation, which declared that "all unfree in the Danish West India Islands are from to-day free." Thus these St. Croix slaves became one of the few groups of enslaved people to succeed in liberating themselves.

Girls play outside a colorfully painted house in Road Town, Tortola. *A.G.E. Fotostock*

Across the Caribbean, however, true economic and social freedom came slowly for black Virgin Islanders. In the Danish West Indies the 1849 Labor Act made working conditions for newly emancipated blacks nearly as restrictive as they had been under slavery. In the British West Indies the 1867 reversion to an appointed governing council – and the abolition of free elections – ensured that the colonies would be governed by their white minorities. In both sets of colonies prevailing social traditions continued to

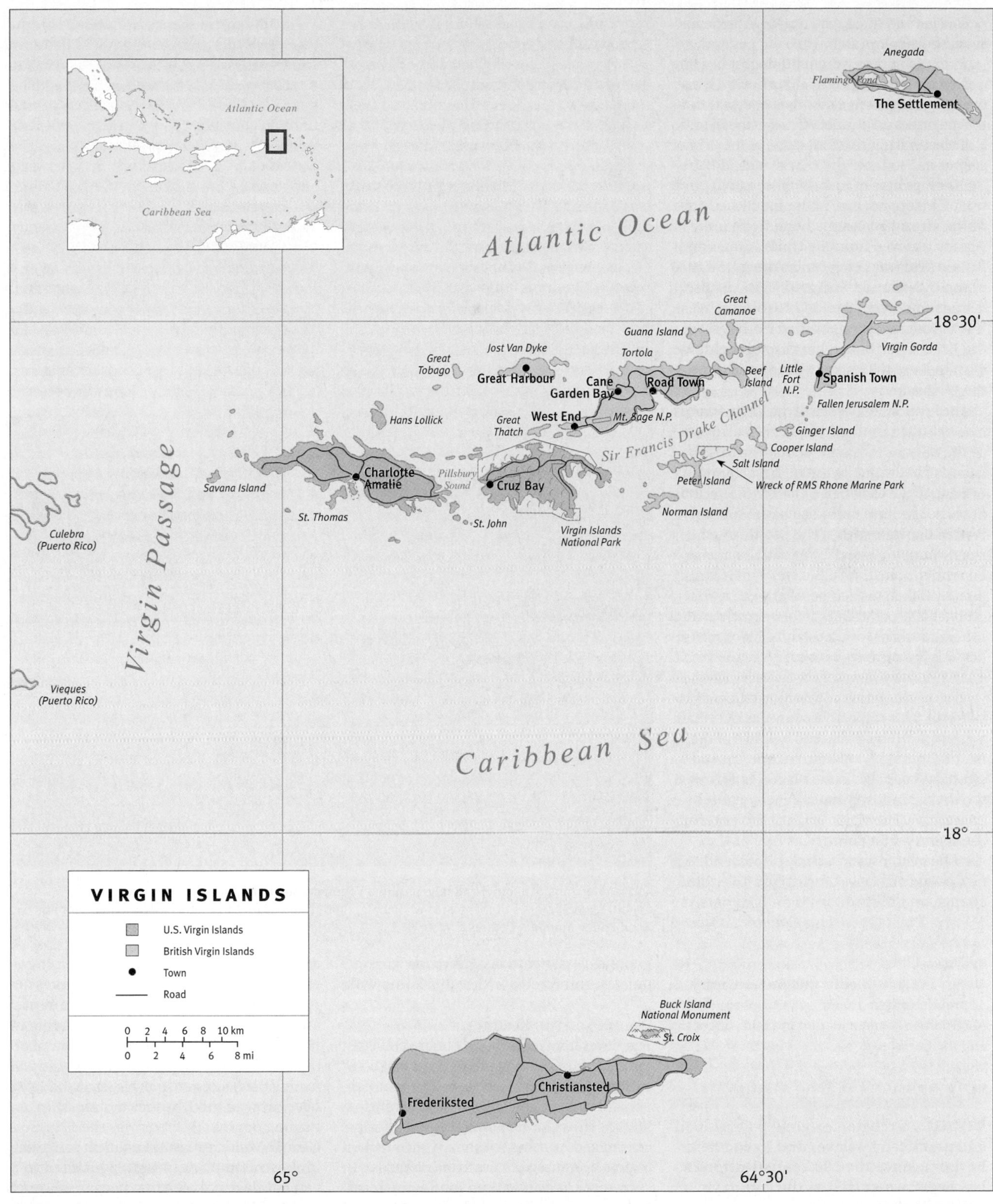

enforce racism and racial separation, on the theory that free blacks were still different from and inferior to free whites. In the Virgin Islands and across the Caribbean, the abolition of slavery also led to a decline in economic productivity. In a tight economy it was the black workers who suffered most.

It was this economic decline that first led Denmark to contemplate selling its colonies to the United States in 1866. After talks that extended over the next 50 years, the transfer became a reality on March 31, 1917. The twentieth century had already brought some small improvements to the Virgin Islands, as both the Danish and British governments had begun establishing schools and banks. Events in 1915 in St. Croix marked the beginning of changes that eventually spread throughout the Caribbean. That year D. Hamilton Jackson formed the first labor union in the West Indies. Within decades the labor movement became the basis not only for a dramatic improvement in working conditions across the region but also for the push for increased self-government. In islands across the Caribbean the black workers who joined labor unions eventually became the black politicians and voters who won independence from their colonial powers.

Virgin Islanders were no different in their desire for greater political authority, and over time legislative changes ensured that the majorities would indeed rule in the islands. Full electoral government came to the British islands in 1967, and the U.S. islands in 1970. But both groups of islands chose not to push for full independence, undoubtedly because of the strong economic benefits that the islands received from the United States and Britain. This was especially true in the case of the U.S. islands, and in 1958 the British islands had even declined to join the West Indies Federation established by the rest of the British Caribbean because of their own wish to keep their strong economic ties to the U.S. islands.

The economies of each of the Virgin Islands also changed dramatically with the advent of the tourist industry. Today the Virgin Islands have some of the highest standards of living in the Caribbean, and the U.S. islands in particular have become a haven for other West Indian immigrants. This prosperity comes largely from the islands' continuing status as dependent territories. But much of it is also directly linked to their popularity as tourist destinations, particularly among American and British tourists. For the islands' black majorities, this has meant jobs in every sector of the tourist industry, from service to construction.

Virgin Islanders today enjoy citizenship status in their respective countries but retain the Afro-Caribbean cultural heritage of their island homes. A 1995 hurricane caused significant damage in the islands, but by 1998 the tourist industry had already begun its comeback. The Virgin Islands are entering the twenty-first century as one of the Caribbean's most successful regions, and this new period of relative prosperity is a welcome change and reward for Virgin Islanders.

Lisa Clayton Robinson

See Also

Slavery in Latin America and the Caribbean; Apprenticeship in the British Caribbean; Abolition and Emancipation in Latin America and the Caribbean.

ABOVE: Members of a Rara band take part in a Vodou parade in Haiti. *Errington/Hutchison*
OPPOSITE: Major joncs from the area of Archaie, Haiti, dressed for the culminating sortie of Rara on Good Friday Morning. *Dolores Yonker, Ph.D.*

Latin America and the Caribbean

Vodou, a religion originally developed and practiced by slaves and freed blacks in Haiti; since the 1987 constitution it has been recognized as the country's national religion.

The slave trade displaced millions of Africans from their native lands. Uprooted from their societies, the Africans brought with them their family values, beliefs, traditions, and religious practices. Although Haiti's culture derives from three sources – African, Amerindian, and European – Haiti emerged as a nation whose African contributions form its principal cultural traits. The Vodou religion must be interpreted within this framework.

Origins of the Religion

The slaves from more than a hundred different ethnic groups who came to Haiti lacked a common language. They were able to unite only through their recreated African religion, Vodou. The colonial powers systematically intermixed Africans so that any recollection of language, lineage, or ties to the motherland, known as *Ginen*, the term for the mythical African homeland, would be permanently lost. Colonialists imposed European values and Roman Catholicism upon the slave population. In an attempt to stop the practice of Vodou, slave gatherings were forbidden. Thus slaves were forced to worship their African deities secretly and to hide their allegiance to their ancestral religion. These interdictions, repressive measures, and the clandestine nature of Vodou ceremonies led to the revalorization of the very African cultural values that Europeans tried to suppress.

This regrouping around a common past and ideal has consistently played a role in Haitian political life and has fueled a number of mass movements, culminating in the war for independence and, much later, in the 1986 overthrow of the Duvalier dictatorship. A turning point in this saga was the 1791 Bois Caiman Vodou ritual and political congress, orchestrated by Boukman, which led to a general slave uprising that became a war of national liberation. Vodou's close ties to its African origins are also a result of Haiti's isolation from the rest of the world following its 1804 successful slave revolution (*see* Haitian Revolution).

The history of persecution of Vodou practitioners continued with the 1896, 1913, and 1941 antisuperstition campaigns, which destroyed shrines and led to the massacre of hundreds of people who admitted their

NY

ABOVE: **Vodou's adherents have become more open about their practices in recent years. Urged on by drummers, these men dance in an expression of Vodou religion.** *© 1996 Michael Ende/Aurora*
RIGHT: ***The Adoration of the Vodou God*, 1949, is an oil on masonite painting by Rigaud Benoit, considered to be Haiti's most famous painter.** *Christie's Images*

adherence to Vodou. The period of the American occupation (1915-1934) as well as the post-Duvalier era were also times of severe persecution of Vodouists. Roman Catholicism, headed exclusively by Westerners until the 1960s, had the political and financial support of the state and remained the country's sole official religion until the constitution of 1987 recognized freedom of religion.

Meaning and Significance

Popular labeling of Vodou as "witchcraft" and "magic" has been a historical tradition perpetuated in Hollywood films and supermarket tabloids, which sustain these same popular myths. Vodou, the preferred term used to designate the Haitian religion, is of Dahomean origin and derives from the Fon word for "God" or "Spirit." Other accurate spellings include *Vodun, Vodoun,* or the French *Vaudou,* but never *voodoo,* the sensationalist and derogatory Western creation. Vodou is a comprehensive system of knowledge that has nothing to do with simplistic and erroneous images of sticking pins into dolls, putting a hex on an adversary, or turning innocents into zombies. It is an organized form of communal support that provides meaning to the human experience in relation to the natural and supernatural forces of the universe.

Despite media portrayals, Vodou shares many elements with other religions. Like members of other persuasions, Vodouists believe in creating harmony, in keeping a balance, and in cultivating virtues and positive values. With its reverence for the ancestors, Vodou is the cement that binds family and community life in Haiti.

Vodou is essentially a monotheistic religion that recognizes a single and supreme spiritual entity or God, known as Mawu-Lisa among the Fon, Olorun among the Yoruba, and

Bondye or Gran Met in Haiti. The Haitian religion originated from the fusion of rituals of a range of African ethnic groups – in particular, the Fon, Yoruba, IGBO, HAUSA, EWE, and KONGO. Scholars have called African culture "additive," in the sense that it often adapted foreign elements into its structure. Following the same pattern, Vodou absorbed many aspects of Roman Catholicism into its ritual. Vodouists use Roman Catholic prayers and hymns at the beginning of ceremonies and use the Gregorian calendar to mark the celebrations of the *lwas*, the spirit intermediaries between humans and God who have been linked to the iconography and stories about Roman Catholic saints. For the *servitors* of the spirits, as Vodouists typically refer to themselves, there is no conflict between Vodou and Roman Catholicism. This syncretism is the subject of debates among scholars: some hold that Roman Catholic practices were actually absorbed into Vodou; others contend that the Haitians never accepted the European elements and instead simply used the saints and Christian rituals as a cover to continue their own practices. Whichever interpretation one accepts, syncretism remains a basic part of Haitian Vodou.

In addition to its visible cultural and ritual dimensions, expressed through the arts, especially in Haitian music and dance, Vodou's teaching and belief system include social, economic, political, and practical components. Today, for example, Vodou's teachings are concerned with what can be done to overcome the limiting social conditions in Haiti, a country that has been strenuously challenged from within and outside its borders. Vodou addresses such questions as what to do in case of illness in a country that counts only one physician for 23,000 people, and what to do before embarking upon major undertakings, such as marriage, business transactions, or traveling abroad. Vodou gives its adherents positive means to address these issues and provides support in times of challenging economic moments and difficult political transitions.

Most Vodou ceremonies conform to one of two major rites. The Rada rite retained from the Old Kingdom of Dahomey (present-day NIGERIA, BENIN, and TOGO) is generally agreed to be most faithful to West African tradition. The Petwo rite is a newer development that arose out of the crucible of the New World plantation system and encompasses elements of the Kongo culture as well as the practices of many other groups from Central Africa to ANGOLA in the southwest. The Rada rite is Vodou's most elaborate rite and includes the great communal spirits, or lwa, such as Atibon Legba, Marasa Dosou Dosa, Danbala and Ayida Wedo, Azaka Mede, Ogou Feray, Agwe Tawoyo, Ezili Freda Daome, Lasirenn and Labalenn, and Gede Nimbo. It is generally assumed by Vodou practitioners and researchers alike that the Rada lwa are *dous* or "sweet." These *fle Ginen*, or true spirits of Africa, are the first lwas to be saluted in ceremonies. Many maintain that the Petwo lwa are *anme*, or "bitter." Associated with fire, they are said to be *lwa cho*, or "hot lwa," engaging in forceful behavior. The Petwo rite includes major lwa such as Met Kalfou, Simbi Andezo, Ezili Danto, and Bawon Samdi. Some of the lwa exist *andezo*, or in two cosmic substances, and are served in both Rada and Petwo rituals. Contrary to popular conception, the line between Rada and Petwo is not as rigid as it appears: much of what is described as Rada goes for Petwo.

Possession, an important dimension of Vodou worship, is among the least understood aspects of the religion. Through possession both the lwa and the community are affirmed. The participants (in particular, the priests and priestesses, the *houngans* and *manbos*, and the other initiates, the *ounsis*) transcend their materiality by becoming spirits, and the spirits renew their vigor by dancing and feasting with the *chwal*, or horses, for it is said that during possession the lwa rides a person like a cavalier rides a horse. Equally important, possession is a time when the lwa communicate in a tangible way with the people, who during such times receive answers to pressing questions.

THE FUTURE OF VODOU

Though Vodou continues to be viewed with ambivalence, increasingly people have been practicing it more openly in Haiti and abroad. Today scholars, patriots, and grassroots organizers continue a crusade for greater respect for Haiti's ancestral religion. Reputable artists, scholars, and writers are affirming their involvement with Vodou. In the past ten years, with the advent of the "root culture" movement driven by the progressive wing of culturalists, Vodou-inspired musical groups such as BOUKMAN EKSPERYANS, Boukan Ginen, RAM, and the Fugees, and organizations such as Zantray, Bode Nasyonal, and New Rada Community have emerged. The touring *Sacred Arts of Haitian Vodou* exhibition constituted one more effort in a series of activities aimed at fostering a better understanding of Vodou. Finally, a 1997 conference held at the University of California, Santa Barbara, in which Haitian scholars and Vodou practitioners met to discuss the role of Vodou in the development of Haiti, led to the creation of the Congress of Santa Barbara, an international scholarly association for the study of Haitian Vodou. However, no single person or organization has the final word on Vodou, which remains a complex but decentralized system of universal knowledge, cultural practices, and communal support.

Claudine Michel and Gerdes Fleurant

SEE ALSO

Dahomey, Early Kingdom of; Transatlantic Slave Trade; Duvalier, Jean-Claude; Duvalier, François; Religions, African, in Latin America and the Caribbean.

Africa

Vorster, Balthazar Johannes

(b. 1915, Jamestown, South Africa; d. 1983), prime minister (1966-1978) and president (1978-1979) of SOUTH AFRICA.

Born in Jamestown the son of an AFRIKANER sheep farmer, Balthazar Johannes Vorster was trained as a lawyer. A founder of an anti-British, extremist group opposed to participation in World War II, he was interned from 1942 to 1944. He subsequently entered politics but did not gain a parliamentary seat until 1953. Having previously held a minor government post, he was made minister of justice in 1961, when his mentor, Prime Minister HENDRIK FRENSCH VERWOERD, needed to restore order in the aftermath of the Sharpeville shootings (1960). Vorster did not fail; he imposed drastic detention and security measures on black dissidents. As prime minister after Verwoerd's assassination, Vorster further tightened security and continued the APARTHEID policy, but also attempted to open a dialogue with black African states. He relinquished the prime minister's office for that of president in 1978 as a result of a government scandal and cover-up; ultimately, the same affair forced him into retirement the following year.

SEE ALSO

Sharpeville, South Africa; World War II and African Americans.

North America

Voting Rights Act of 1965,

legislation that charged the federal government of the United States with helping disfranchised African Americans regain the right to vote in the South.

In the century following RECONSTRUCTION, African Americans in the South faced overwhelming obstacles to voting. Despite the Fifteenth and Nineteenth Amendments to the United States Constitution, which had enfranchised black men and all women respectively, Southern voter registration boards used poll taxes, literacy tests, and other bureaucratic impediments to deny African Americans their legal rights. Southern blacks also risked harassment, intimidation, economic reprisals, and physical violence when they tried to register or vote. As a result African Americans had little if any political power, either locally or nationally. In Mississippi, for instance, only 5 percent of eligible blacks were registered to vote in 1960.

The Voting Rights Act of 1965, meant to reverse this disfranchisement, grew out of both public protest and private political negotiation. Starting in 1961, the SOUTHERN CHRISTIAN LEADERSHIP CONFERENCE (SCLC), led by Rev. Martin Luther King Jr., staged nonviolent demonstrations in Albany, Georgia, and Birmingham, Alabama. King and the

BLACK VOTER REGISTRATION IN THE SOUTH 1940-1984
Estimated percentage of voting-age blacks registered

State	1940	1947	1952	1960	1962	1964	1968	1976	1980	1982	1984
Alabama	0.4	1.2	5.0	13.7	13.4	23.0	56.7	58.4	55.8	69.7	74.0
Arkansas	1.5	17.3	27.0	37.3	34.0	49.3	67.5	94.0	57.2	63.9	67.2
Florida	5.7	15.4	33.0	38.9	36.8	63.8	62.1	61.1	58.3	59.7	63.4
Georgia	3.0	18.8	23.0	29.3	26.7	44.0	56.1	74.8	48.6	50.4	57.9
Louisiana	0.5	2.6	25.0	30.9	27.8	32.0	59.3	63.0	60.7	61.1	65.7
Mississippi	0.4	0.9	4.0	5.2	5.3	6.7	54.4	60.7	62.3	64.2	77.1
North Carolina	7.1	15.2	18.0	38.1	35.8	46.8	55.3	54.8	51.3	50.9	65.4
South Carolina	0.8	13.0	20.0	15.6	22.9	38.7	50.8	56.5	53.7	53.9	58.5
Tennessee	6.5	25.8	27.0	58.9	49.8	69.4	72.8	66.4	64.0	66.1	69.9
Texas	5.6	18.5	31.0	34.9	37.3	57.7	83.1	65.0	56.0	49.5	71.5
Virginia	4.1	13.2	16.0	22.8	24.0	45.7	58.4	54.7	53.2	49.5	62.3
Average	**3.0**	**12.0**	**20.0**	**29.1**	**29.4**	**43.1**	**62.0**	**63.1**	**55.8**	**56.5**	**66.2**

Sources: David Garrow, *Protest at Selma* (1978); U.S. Department of Commerce, Bureau of Census, *Statistical Abstract* (1976, 1981, 1982-1983, 1986).

SOUTHERN AFRICAN AMERICAN VOTERS, POTENTIAL AND ELIGIBLE, 1976-1990

Year	Population (in millions)		% Registered				% Voted			
			Presidential Election Years		Congressional Election Years		Presidential Election Years		Congressional Election Years	
	Total	Black	Total	Black	Total	Black	Total	Black	Total	Black
1976	146.5	14.9	66.7	58.5	–	–	59.2	48.7	–	–
1978	151.6	15.6	–	–	62.6	57.1	–	–	45.9	37.2
1980	157.1	16.4	66.9	60.0	–	–	59.2	50.5	–	–
1982	165.5	17.6	–	–	64.1	59.1	–	–	48.8	43.0
1984	170.0	18.4	68.3	66.3	–	–	59.9	55.8	–	–
1986	173.9	19.0	–	–	64.3	64.0	–	–	46.0	43.2
1988	178.1	19.7	66.6	64.5	–	–	57.4	51.5	–	–
1990	182.1	20.4	–	–	62.2	58.8	–	–	45.0	39.2

Sources: U.S. Bureau of the Census, *Current Population Reports*, Series P-20, no. 453, and earlier reports; *Encyclopedia of African-American Culture and History* (1996): "Voting-Age Population, Percentage Reporting Registered, 1976-1990" (Table 11.7).

SCLC hoped to attract national media attention and pressure the U.S. government to protect African Americans' constitutional rights. The strategy worked. Newspaper photos and television broadcasts of Birmingham's notoriously racist police commissioner, Eugene "Bull" Connor, and his men violently attacking the SCLC's peaceful protesters with water hoses, police dogs, and nightsticks awakened the consciences of white Americans.

Selma, Alabama, was the site of the next campaign. In the first three months of 1965 the SCLC led local residents and visiting volunteers in a series of marches demanding an equal right to vote. As they did in Birmingham, protesters met with violence and imprisonment in Selma. King himself wrote a letter from the Selma jail, published in the *New York Times*, in which he said, "There are more Negroes in jail with me than there are on the voting rolls" in Selma. In the worst attack yet, on Sunday, March 7, a group of Alabama state troopers, local sheriff's officers, and unofficial possemen used tear gas and clubs against 600 peaceful marchers. By now, as King had predicted, the nation was watching.

President Lyndon B. Johnson, who succeeded to the presidency after the 1963 assassination of John F. Kennedy, made civil rights one of his administration's top priorities, using his formidable political skills to pass the Twenty-Fourth Amendment, which outlawed poll taxes, in 1964. Now, a week after "Bloody Sunday" in Selma, Johnson gave a televised speech before Congress in which he not only denounced the assault but called it "wrong – deadly wrong" that African Americans were being denied their constitutional rights. Johnson went on to dramatically quote the movement's motto, "we shall overcome."

Two days later the president sent the voting rights bill to Congress. The resolution, signed into law on August 6, 1965, empowered the federal government to oversee voter registration and elections in counties that had used tests to determine voter eligibility or where registration or turnout had been less than 50 percent in the 1964 presidential election. It also banned discriminatory literacy tests and expanded voting rights for non-English-speaking Americans.

The law's effects were wide and powerful. By 1968 nearly 60 percent of eligible African Americans were registered to vote in Mississippi, and other Southern states showed similar improvement. Between 1965 and 1990 the number of black state legislators and members of Congress rose from 2 to 160. Despite finally reclaiming their constitutional voting rights, however, many African Americans in the South and elsewhere saw little progress on other fronts. They still faced illegal job discrimination, substandard schools, and unequal health care. Following its major victories – the Civil Rights Act of 1964 and the Voting Rights Act of 1965 – the liberal, integrationist Civil Rights Movement began to be eclipsed by the more radical Black Power Movement.

The Voting Rights Act was extended in 1970, 1975, and 1982 – the last time despite vigorous resistance from the Reagan administration. Fearing a largely Democratic black vote, the Republican Party adopted various means to minimize it, including at-large elections and redistricting to dilute black representation. The party also attacked as racial gerrymandering the new "majority-minority" congressional districts drawn by the U.S. Justice Department. In 1996 the Supreme Court agreed, outlawing the use of racial factors in deciding district lines. Some prominent African Americans, like Harvard University law professor Lani Guinier, argued that minority votes would be more effective in a system of proportional representation.

Despite these setbacks and debates, the Voting Rights Act had an enormous impact. It re-enfranchised black Southerners and helped elect African Americans at the local, state, and national levels. By 1989 there were an estimated 7200 black officeholders, of whom 67 percent were in the South.

Kate Tuttle

See Also

Fifteenth Amendment to the United States Constitution; King, Martin Luther, Jr.

W

Africa

Wala (also known as Oule, Walba, Walo, and Wilé), ethnic group of West Africa.

The Wala primarily inhabit northwestern GHANA and neighboring BURKINA FASO. They speak a Niger-Congo language related to MOSSI. More than 100,000 people consider themselves Wala.

SEE ALSO
Languages, African: An Overview.

Latin America and the Caribbean

Walcott, Derek Alton

(b. January 23, 1930, Castries, St. Lucia), poet, playwright, and Nobel laureate who developed a distinctly Caribbean literary style rooted in a mastery of the classical European tradition.

Derek Alton Walcott, winner of the 1992 Nobel Prize for Literature, is widely regarded as one of the most important writers ever to emerge from the English-speaking Caribbean. While other Caribbean writers have responded to what Patricia Ismond has called the West Indian "crisis of historylessness" brought about by the devastation of slavery and colonialism through a search for roots, Walcott celebrates the possibilities of the "newness" of the region. The figure of Robinson Crusoe recurs in his poetry and plays, exemplifying both the predicament of Caribbean isolation and the potential that isolation offers to West Indians for creating a vocabulary uniquely suited to the complexity and richness of their world.

For Walcott, the artistic legacy of classical Western civilization is integral to this creative process. At an early age he "fell madly in love with English." He became familiar with the Western canon through his colonial education in ST. LUCIA and the influence of his mother, a schoolteacher who staged productions of Shakespeare. "In the manner of Joyce and Yeats," wrote critic Stephen Breslow soon after Walcott was awarded the Nobel Prize, "Walcott has merged a profound, rhapsodic reverie upon his remote birthplace – its people, its landscape, and its history – with the central, classical tradition of Western civilization."

Many postcolonial critics have charged, however, that Walcott is out of touch with the very West Indians who are his subject matter. His embrace of Europe, combined with his disavowal of the Africanist aesthetic advocated by black nationalists of the 1960s and 1970s, have led to accusations of elitism. Walcott's writing is often unfavorably compared with that of fellow West Indian author EDWARD KAMAU BRATHWAITE, whose work is deemed more populist. Walcott, in turn, dismisses this criticism as reactionary and bristles at the suggestion that art should be subservient to politics.

Walcott's belief in the universal potential of art and its ability to transcend the particularities of local political issues is manifest in a cosmopolitanism that moves beyond a simple valorization of the European canon. He admires the work of German dramatist and composer Bertolt Brecht, whose interest in Oriental theater introduced Walcott to Asian cultural traditions. Japanese film director Akira Kurosawa's *Rashomon* (1950) helped inspire the development of Walcott's Obie Award-winning masterpiece, *Dream on Monkey Mountain* (1967).

Nonetheless, Walcott makes extensive use of Caribbean vernaculars. The dialogue in *The Sea at Daughin* (1954), for example, utilizes the Creole spoken by ST. LUCIA's fishermen. These fishermen are also the subject of his celebrated epic poem, *Omeros* (1990). *Drums and Colour* (1958), the retelling of Caribbean history that was commissioned for the opening of the inaugural Federal Parliament of the West Indies, has the energy and flavor of Carnival. Masquerade, mime, and CALYPSO were incorporated into the play, and revelers danced and sang during intermissions, creating the atmosphere of West Indian bacchanal. Additionally, during his 17-year relationship with the Trinidad Theater Workshop, which he founded in 1959, Walcott combined regional art, music, language, and dance to create almost ritualistic performances.

Walcott describes the cultural synthesis within his work as a "mulatto" aesthetic that reflects the Caribbean's "illegitimate, rootless, mongrelized" nature in a tradition that is unequivocally Caribbean.

Peter Hudson

SEE ALSO
Literature, English Language, Caribbean; Slavery in Latin America and the Caribbean; Theater in the Caribbean; Trinidad and Tobago; Carnivals in Latin America and the Caribbean.

North America

Walcott, Jersey Joe

(b. January 31, 1914, Merchantville, N.J.; d. February 25, 1994, Camden, N.J.), African American boxer; heavyweight champion of the world during the early 1950s.

Jersey Joe Walcott was born Arnold Raymond Cream to immigrant parents from BARBADOS. His father died when Walcott was 14 years old; as one of 12 children who needed support, the teenager started working at a soup factory and at odd jobs. In 1930 he launched his professional career as a lightweight and took the name of the well-known Barbadian welterweight champion, Joe Walcott. Walcott's earnings from BOXING were not enough to cover the family's living expenses, so from the mid-1930s to the mid-1940s he spent the majority of his time working and boxed only intermittently.

Walcott returned to boxing full-time in 1945, and over the course of the next two years won 11 of 14 bouts, 7 by knockout. JOE LOUIS first defeated Walcott in a 1947 title bout and again in 1948 before Louis retired in 1949. Walcott lost two more title bouts to Ezzard Charles, one in 1949 and another in 1951. On June 15, 1952, in their third match, Walcott knocked Charles out in the seventh round. At age 37 Walcott became the oldest man up to that point to win a heavyweight championship. He lost his heavyweight title to Rocky Marciano on September 23, 1952. Walcott attempted to reclaim the championship the following year, but was knocked out in the first round and retired. He went on to serve as a Camden County (New Jersey) sheriff, New Jersey state athletic commissioner, and then as a coordinator of youth programs.

Aaron Myers

North America

Walker, Aaron ("T-Bone")

(b. May 28, 1910, Linden, Tex.; d. March 16, 1975, Los Angeles, Calif.), African American blues guitarist, pioneer of the electric guitar, and key creator of modern blues.

As a boy growing up in Dallas, Aaron Thibeaux "T-Bone" Walker befriended blues legend Blind Lemon Jefferson by holding his tin can and collecting his tips. In return Jefferson taught Walker the basics of blues. In 1929 Walker recorded "Wichita Falls Blues" and "Trinity River Blues" under the name Oak Cliff T-Bone. (The nickname "T-Bone" is a corruption of "Thibeaux.") In the 1930s in Los Angeles, California, Walker introduced an early form of the electric guitar into his music. His innovative rhythmic playing influenced almost every major blues and rock 'n' roll guitarist after him, including B.B. King, Jimi Hendrix, and Otis Rush. Walker said that "You've got to feel the blues to make them right.... It's played from the heart and if the person listening, understands and is in the right mood, why, man, I've seen them bust out and cry like a baby." His signature songs include "T-Bone Shuffle" and "Call It Stormy Monday," which many consider to be the best blues song of all time.

Walker was also a first-rate singer and master showman, often playing the guitar behind his back or between his legs. His career continued until the 1970s, when he suffered a stroke. Walker died of bronchial pneumonia in 1975.

See Also

Blues, The; Jefferson, ("Blind") Lemon; King, Riley B. ("B. B.").

North America

Walker, Aida Overton

(b. February 14, 1880, New York, N.Y.; d. October 1, 1914, New York, N.Y.), singer, dancer, actress, and choreographer regarded as the leading African American female performing artist at the turn of the century.

Aida Overton began her career as a teenage chorus member of Black Patti's Troubadours. While performing in *Senegambian Carnival* (1899) she met George Walker, and the two were married on June 22, 1899. After the marriage Aida Walker worked as a choreographer for Williams and Walker, her husband's vaudevillian comedy duo. By presenting ragtime musicals with all-black casts, Williams and Walker helped bring authentic black songs and dances to a form of entertainment that had been dominated by demeaning minstrel shows. Walker played the female lead in *The Policy Players* (1899), *Sons of Ham* (1900), *In Dahomey* (1902), *In Abyssinia* (1906), and *Bandanna Land* (1908). A command performance at Buckingham Palace in 1903 transformed Walker into an international star.

In 1908 George Walker became ill and could not continue in the run of *Bandanna Land*. Wearing her husband's male costumes, Aida Walker performed both his role and her own. After her husband's death in 1911, Walker saw her own career fall into decline, although she was celebrated for her part in the spectacular *Salome* at Oscar Hammerstein's Victoria Theater in New York City. This was the last major performance of her career.

As one of the first international black stars, Aida Walker brought versatility to her performances and authenticity to ragtime songs and cakewalk dances. Her dancing and singing abilities have been compared to and sometimes applauded over that of her successors, Florence Mills and Josephine Baker.

Aaron Myers

See Also

Cakewalk, The; Minstrelsy.

North America

Walker, Alice

(b. February 9, 1944, Eatonton, Ga.), African American writer, essayist, and poet, and Pulitzer Prize-winning author of *The Color Purple*.

In a passage from her 1983 essay collection *In Search of Our Mothers' Gardens: Womanist Prose,* Alice Walker reflects that "one thing I try to have in my life and in my fiction is an awareness of and openness to mystery, which, to me, is deeper than any politics, race, or geographical location." Walker was the youngest of eight children of sharecropping parents Willie Lee Walker and Minnie Tallulah (Grant) Walker. Her childhood was colored by an accident at age eight: she lost sight in one eye when an older brother shot her with a BB gun. Socially outcast as a result of her disfigured appearance, Walker became absorbed in books and began to write poetry while young.

Walker has said that while she was in high school, her mother gave her three important gifts: a sewing machine, which gave her the independence to make her own clothes; a suitcase, which gave her permission to leave home and travel; and a typewriter, which gave her permission to write. Walker graduated from high school as class valedictorian, and from 1961 to 1963 attended Spelman College in Atlanta on a scholarship. But when the "puritanical atmosphere" at Spelman became oppressive, Walker transferred to Sarah Lawrence College, where she completed a B.A. in 1965.

Walker then spent time in Georgia and Mississippi, where she registered voters, and in New York City, where she worked at the welfare department. She also married white human rights lawyer and activist Mel Leventhal in 1967, and in 1969 she gave birth to their daughter, Rebecca. She was divorced in 1977. Through all this activity Walker continued to write.

Walker published her first novel, *The Third Life of Grange Copeland,* in 1970 at age 26. Two years later she published *In Love and Trouble,* a short story collection, and the poetry collection *Revolutionary Petunias and Other Poems.* In 1976 she published her second novel, *Meridian.* By this point Walker was well established among the rising generation of black women writers. Her work is often praised for its portrayals of individuals and individual relationships, but it is also known for its depictions of the ways in which individuals can rely on their collective culture and cultural heritage to sustain them.

As Walker continued publishing her essays and poetry, she developed a second career as an educator. She has taught black studies and creative writing at Jackson State College, Tougaloo College, Wellesley College, and the University of Massachusetts at Boston; has served as a distinguished writer in African American studies at the University of California at Berkeley; and was named the Fannie Hurst Professor of Literature at Brandeis University. In 1983, however, she became internationally known with the publication of her third novel, *The Color Purple.*

The Color Purple portrays Celie, a rural black woman in an abusive marriage, as she struggles to find her self-worth. Told entirely in the form of letters – Celie's simple letters to God, her letters to her lost sister Nettie, and Nettie's letters to Celie – the powerful narrative won the 1983 Pulitzer Prize and established Walker as a major American novelist. In 1985 *The Color Purple* was made into a popular movie that was both praised for its portrayal of African American heroines and condemned for its portrayal of black men. Walker reflected on the complicated issues surrounding the film's production in her essay collection *The Same River Twice: Honoring the Difficult* (1996).

One year after *The Color Purple* Walker published *In Search of Our Mothers' Gardens,* an influential essay collection that introduced the new term womanism as a way of defining black women's feminism. In 1984 she cofounded Wild Tree Press in Novarro, California. Since then Walker's publications have included the novels *The Temple of My Familiar* (1989) and *Possessing the Secret of Joy* (1992), another essay collection, several volumes of poetry, and a children's book.

Walker's numerous honors and awards include a National Endowment for the Arts grant and fellowship, a Radcliffe Institute fellowship, an honorary Ph.D. from Russell Sage College, a National Book Award nomination, a Guggenheim Award, and an O'Henry Award. She is highly in demand as a lecturer, and is not only a writer but also an outspoken liberal political activist. Walker's *Anything We Love Can Be Saved: A Writer's Activism* was published in 1997.

Michelle Hunter

See Also
Atlanta, Georgia; Women Writers, Black, in the United States; New York, New York.

North America

Walker, David (b. 1785?, Wilmington, N.C.; d. June 28, 1830, Boston, Mass.), African American abolitionist, civil rights activist, and advocate of African independence best known for his fiery pamphlet *Walker's Appeal... to the Colored Citizens of the World* (1829).

During the antebellum years David Walker was prominent among a generation of politically outspoken free blacks that included Frederick Douglass, Martin Robison Delany, and the Reverend Henry Highland Garnet. Walker, according to historian Sterling Stuckey, deserves recognition as "the father of black nationalist theory in America." His most lasting achievement was his essay, *Walker's Appeal... to the Colored Citizens of the World*, which in part called on African American slaves to revolt against their masters to gain their freedom.

The son of a white mother and a slave father, Walker was born free, taking the status of his mother as stipulated by North Carolina law. Little is known of his life before he moved to Boston in the late 1820s. In particular, it is not known how he learned to read and write. The antebellum South made scant provision for educating African Americans, whether slave or free. Yet before moving to the North, Walker had acquired an education that included a familiarity with Thomas Jefferson's *Notes on the State of Virginia* (1785). He also had ample opportunity to observe the evils of slavery firsthand.

In Boston Walker commenced a used clothes business and quickly gained recognition in the local black community. Walker was evidently a natural leader. He was physically impressive: his wife Eliza described him as "prepossessing, being six feet in height, slender and well-proportioned. His hair was loose, and his complexion was dark." Walker played an active role in the Massachusetts General Colored Association, established in 1826, and was an agent for the first African American newspaper, *Freedom's Journal* (1827-1829).

In an 1828 address to the Massachusetts General Colored Association, Walker exhorted free blacks to improve their lot through mutual aid and self-help organizations. He roundly condemned the passivity of those who acquiesced in racial injustice. In September of the following year Walker published his *Appeal*, which further extended his argument for black activism and solidarity. Rejecting Jefferson's contention in *Notes on the State of Virginia* that blacks were inherently inferior, Walker called on African Americans to acquire copies of the book, in order to study and refute it. "[L]et no one of us suppose," he wrote, "that the refutations which have been written by our white friends are enough – they are *whites* – we are *blacks*."

Besides advocating the violent overthrow of slavery and the formation of black civil rights and self-help organizations, the *Appeal* called for racial equality in the United States and independence for the peoples of Africa. As Stuckey observed, Walker was "the precursor of a long line of advocates of African freedom, extending all the way to Paul Robeson and Malcolm X in our time."

To distribute his pamphlet, Walker relied on the mails and on seamen traveling to Southern ports. Alarmed Southern leaders responded by passing stricter laws against such "seditious" literature and against teaching free blacks to read or write. The Georgia state legislature went so far as to place a price on Walker's head: $10,000, if he were delivered alive, or $1000, if dead. Walker encountered sharp criticism in the North as well, even from such white abolitionists as William Lloyd Garrison and Benjamin Lundy. In 1830, nine months after publishing his *Appeal*, Walker died under mysterious circumstances. Rumor held that he had been poisoned, but the charge was never verified.

James Clyde Sellman

See Also
Slavery in the United States; Abolitionism in the United States; Boston, Massachusetts; *Freedom's Journal*; Black Nationalism in the United States.

North America

Walker, Kara (b. 1969, Stockton, Calif.), African American artist who questions stereotypical images of race and identity through the use of a nineteenth-century method of portraiture.

Kara Walker studied at the Atlanta College of Art, where she received a B.F.A. She continued her studies at the Rhode Island School of Design in Providence, where in 1994 she received an M.F.A. Walker works primarily in figurative, cut-out silhouettes, a cheap, rapid method of portraiture popular in the nineteenth century. Her work features figures, black and white, engaged in a variety of activities of a sexual or violent nature. Framing these images in the "theater" of the Civil War, she creates narratives of the disturbing sides of themes such as romance, and the pleasurable or powerful sides of themes such as war, genocide, and shame. "The nigger wench," she said of a recurring caricature in her work, "is the body that I sort of inhabited accidentally... that somebody else placed over me at some point." In exposing stereotypical images of the past in an ironic and playful way Walker deals with issues of race and identity by confounding traditional dichotomies of black and white, male and female, dominant and submissive, young and old, and North and South.

Walker's work has been exhibited throughout the United States and Europe in both group and solo exhibitions. In 1997 she had solo exhibitions at both the San Francisco Museum of Modern Art and the Renaissance Society in Chicago. She has participated in several group shows, including *New Histories* at the Institute of Contemporary Art in Boston (1996), *La belle et la bête* at the Musée d'Art Moderne de la Ville de Paris (1995), and the Whitney Museum of American Art Biennial (1997). In 1997 she was named the recipient of a prestigious "genius grant" from the MacArthur Foundation.

See Also
Race: An Interpretation; Civil War, American; Racial Stereotypes; Art, African American.

North America

Walker, Maggie Lena (b. July 15, 1867, Richmond, Va.; d. December 15, 1934, Richmond, Va.), American businesswoman, club woman, newspaper founder, lecturer, feminist, first African American female bank president.

For Maggie Lena Walker, who rose from humble beginnings to become the first black woman bank president, the future of the race was dependent on the education and advancement of black women. In her words she was "not born with a silver spoon in mouth: but, instead, with a clothes basket almost upon my head." Former slaves, Walker's mother, Elizabeth (Draper), was a cook's helper and her father, William Mitchell, was the family butler in the Van Lew mansion in Richmond, Virginia. After her father was found floating in the James River, apparently murdered, Walker assumed multiple responsibilities as delivery person and babysitter while she kept up with her studies, church attendance, and public service.

Educated in segregated public schools in Richmond, Walker finished at the head of her class in 1883. After graduation she taught for three years at the Lancaster school while she took classes in accounting and business management. In 1886 she married Arstead Walker, an active member of her church, with whom she had two children, Russell and Melvin DeWitt. She then turned from teaching to community organizing.

In ten years Walker moved from executive secretary to grand secretary-treasurer of the Independent Order of St. Luke, a mutual benefit society, a position she held for 35 years. In 1903 she founded the St. Luke Penny Savings Bank, which became the St. Luke Bank and Trust Company. During the Great Depression the institution absorbed other black banks to become the Consolidated Bank and Trust Company, with Walker as the board chair. In the 1990s it is the oldest continually black-owned and black-run bank in the nation.

North America

Walker, Margaret (b. July 7, 1915, Birmingham, Ala.; d. September 15, 1998, Jackson, Miss.), poet, novelist, and university teacher; the first African American woman to win a prestigious literary prize.

Margaret Walker began writing poems at age 11. Langston Hughes read her poetry when she was 16 and persuaded her parents to take her out of the South so she could "develop into a writer." She matriculated at Northwestern University, where she was influenced by W. E. B. Du Bois, and graduated in 1935. She left Chicago in 1939 to enter the creative writing M.A. program at the University of Iowa. There she published in 1942 a collection of poems, *For My People,* which won the prestigious Yale Young Poets Award. The book's poems, like her work as a whole, display a pride in her African American heritage and interweave autobiographical elements with larger themes of black history. She also wrote a historical novel, *Jubilee*, not completed until 1966, which was based on the life of her grandmother, who lived during the Civil War. It is one of the first modern novels about slavery told from an African American perspective.

Walker published more than ten books, including poems, essays, and short stories. Among these are her *Ballad of the Free* (1966), *Prophets for a New Day* (1970), and *October Journey* (1973). In the 1960s she received her Ph.D. from the University of Iowa and began teaching creative writing at Jackson State College in Mississippi, where she retired in 1979. The books she published since then include a biography of Richard Wright, a volume of poetry that includes old and new works, and a collection of essays.

See Also

Slavery in the United States; Women Writers, Black, in the United States; Civil War, American; Du Bois, William Edward Burghardt (W. E. B.).

North America

Walker, Sarah ("Madam C. J.") (b. December 23, 1867, Delta, La.; d. May 25, 1919, New York, N.Y.), African American entrepreneur who developed special hair care products and styling techniques for black women.

Born to indigent former slaves Owen and Minerva Breedlove, Sarah Walker grew up in poverty on the Burney plantation in Delta, Louisiana, working in the cotton fields from sunrise to sunset. Uneducated in her youth, she learned as an adult to read and write. At age 14 she married Moses McWilliams, who was reportedly killed by a white lynch mob two years after their daughter A'Lelia's birth in 1885.

Walker worked as a domestic until she took several risks as an entrepreneur in black women's hair care products. To meet the needs of women who did not have running water, supplies, or equipment, Walker created a hot comb with specially spaced teeth to soften or straighten black hair. She also created the Wonderful Hair Grower for women who had experienced hair loss through improper care. Business differences ended her marriage to C. J. Walker, a newspaperman whose advertising and mail order knowledge contributed to the business.

Walker was the first woman to sell products via mail order, to organize a nationwide membership of door-to-door agents, the Madam C. J. Walker Hair Culturists Union of America, and to open her own beauty school, the Walker College of Hair Culture. Walker and her daughter A'Lelia established a chain of beauty parlors throughout the United States, the Caribbean, and South America.

By 1914 company earnings grossed more than a million dollars. In addition to making substantial contributions to black women's education, Walker owned a house in Harlem, dubbed the "Dark Tower," and Villa Lewaro, a neo-Palladian-style, 34-room mansion designed by Vetner Woodson Tandy, the first registered black architect. Walker's homes were frequented by Harlem Renaissance notables after her death in 1919 when her daughter took over the helm. Walker's empire, in keeping with her wishes, has since been exclusively managed by her female descendants. In 1976 Villa Lewaro was listed on the National Register of Historic Places.

See Also

Hair and Beauty Culture; Harlem, New York; Lynching.

North America

Walker, Wyatt Tee (b. August 16, 1929, Brockton, Mass.), African American minister, chief strategist for the Southern Christian Leadership Conference during the Civil Rights Movement.

Wyatt Tee Walker left a ministerial post in Petersburg, Virginia, in 1960 to become executive director of the Southern Christian Leadership Conference (SCLC). He proved an excellent tactician, authoring protest strategies that included the Birmingham campaign of April 1963.

Walker left the SCLC in 1964, settled in New York City, and continued to work for social justice. An expert on gospel music, he wrote *Somebody's Calling My Name: Black Sacred Music and Social Change* (1979). He has been the pastor of Canaan Baptist Church of Christ in Harlem since 1967.

Robert Fay

See Also

Harlem, New York; New York, New York.

North America

Wallace, Sippie (b. November 1, 1898, Houston, Tex.; d. November 1, 1986, Detroit, Mich.), African American blues singer who was famous in Chicago during the 1920s for her spirited, hard-edged singing.

Born Beulah Belle Thomas, one of 13 children, Sippie Wallace was first exposed to music through her father's Shiloh Baptist Church. As a child she received the nickname "Sippie" either because of her habit of sipping or a lisp. After singing for several years in Texas and New Orleans, Wallace moved with her brothers in 1923 to Chicago, where she quickly became a blues star with songs like "Up the Country Blues" and "Shorty George." Her singing was a combination of the Chicago blues tradition and her Texas-style blues background, which had a rougher singing style and often racier lyrics. Other well-known songs she recorded include "Special Delivery Blues" (1926), "I'm a Mighty Tight Woman" (1920), and, with Louis Armstrong, "Dead Drunk Blues" (1927).

Wallace moved to Detroit in 1929, and her reputation as a recording star began to wane. Until the 1970s she was the organist at the Leland Baptist Church in Detroit. Long-time friend and blues singer Victoria Spivey persuaded her in 1966 to come out of retirement. Although she suffered a stroke in 1970, she continued her new recording career. Musician Bonnie Raitt, whom Wallace heavily influenced, helped sign Wallace to a contract with Atlantic Records in 1982. Wallace's 1983 album, *Sippie*, featuring Raitt on guitar, won the W. C. Handy Award for the best blues album of the year.

See Also

Armstrong, Louis ("Satchmo"); Blues, The; Detroit, Michigan; Handy, William Christopher (W.C.); New Orleans, Louisiana; Spivey, Victoria Regina.

North America

Waller, Odell, (b. March 6, 1917?, Pittsylvania, Va.; d. July 2, 1942, Richmond, Va.), African American sharecropper whose conviction on murder charges highlighted the need to integrate Southern juries.

In July 1940 Odell Waller, a sharecropper, shot and killed his white landlord in a dispute over the shares owed to him. Waller claimed self-defense, but the all-white jury found him guilty of first-degree murder and sentenced him to death. Waller's defense attorneys argued that Waller did not receive a fair trial because sharecroppers did not pay the poll tax and were thus excluded from jury service. Though several civil rights organizations appealed Waller's conviction for more than two years, he was executed on July 2, 1942.

Robert Fay

North America

Waller, Thomas Wright ("Fats")

(b. May 21, 1904, New York, N.Y.; d. December 15, 1943, Kansas City, Mo.), African American JAZZ pianist, vocalist, organist, and composer whose combination of musical sophistication and lyrical humor made him one of the most popular entertainers of his day.

Fats Waller, born Thomas Wright Waller, was born and raised in New York City, where his father was a Baptist minister. As a boy he charmed his classmates with animated facial gestures while playing piano at school talent shows. During his teenage years he played the organ at various Harlem theaters to accompany silent films. In 1920, the year he left home, he married Edith Hatchett. They divorced three years later, and in 1926 Waller married Anita Rutherford.

Having learned the fundamentals of piano in his childhood, Waller later studied stride piano under Russell Brooks and James P. Johnson. In the 1920s Waller played at Harlem rent parties and nightclubs and composed music for shows and revues. He collaborated with songwriter Andy Razaf to produce some of his best-known numbers: "Honeysuckle Rose" (1928), "(What Did I Do to Be So) Black and Blue" (1929), and "Ain't Misbehavin'" (1929). During the 1930s Waller toured the United States and Europe with his own band, appeared on radio broadcasts and in Hollywood films, and recorded hundreds of songs on the Victor label.

On April 27, 1928, Waller became the first jazz soloist to perform at Carnegie Hall. He is also credited with being the first musician to record jazz music on a pipe organ. *Ain't Misbehavin'*, a tribute to Waller, was voted best Broadway musical in 1978.

Aaron Myers

SEE ALSO
Baptists; Harlem, New York; New York, New York.

North America

Wall of Respect, The,

a street mural on the South Side of CHICAGO, ILLINOIS, depicting numerous black heroes; considered the founding work of the black mural movement.

In 1967, at the beginning of the BLACK POWER Movement, painter William Walker assembled a group of some 20 African American artists to execute a mural celebrating prominent figures in black history. Most of these artists were members of a Chicago-based organization called the Visual Arts Workshop of OBAC (Organization of Black American Culture). Together these artists planned the mural's design and raised the money needed to finance the project. They decided to paint the mural on the side of a two-story, boarded-up tenement building at the intersection of 43rd Street and Langley Avenue. Once a thriving part of the city, this predominantly black area of Chicago had deteriorated into a slum. The mural is a patchwork of famous African Americans, including Charlie "Bird" Parker, MUHAMMAD ALI, and Gwendolyn Brooks.

The artists' objective in painting the *Wall of Respect* was to lift the local black community's morale through highly visible, dignified images of famous black Americans. The response was overwhelmingly positive. People arrived from miles around to view the mural, and the publicity it generated led to the construction of a human resources center in the impoverished neighborhood. Furthermore, the *Wall of Respect* sparked a national black mural movement in which inner-city African American artists began to embellish their neighborhoods with positive black imagery. This movement was ideologically linked to the contemporary Black Power Movement in that it sought to challenge the white-supremacist social order, and aesthetically linked to the mural traditions of postrevolutionary Mexico and Depression-era America in that its artists portrayed historical figures in a social realist vein.

Shortly after the *Wall of Respect* was finished, the Visual Arts Workshop of OBAC broke up. Many of the artists went on to found AfriCOBRA (African Commune of Bad Relevant Artists) in 1968. Although a fire destroyed the *Wall of Respect* in 1971, AfriCOBRA has continued to produce public works of art meant to liberate and uplift the African American community.

Aaron Myers

SEE ALSO
Brooks, Gwendolyn Elizabeth; Great Depression; Parker, Charles Christopher ("Bird"); Art, African American.

North America

Walrond, Eric Derwent

(b. 1898, Georgetown, British Guiana; d. 1966, London, England), a writer who was hailed in the 1920s as one of the most promising young novelists of the Harlem Renaissance.

Abandoned by his father, Eric Walrond was taken by his mother to the Panama Canal Zone to search for him. Though unsuccessful, mother and son settled there in 1910. After reporting for the *Panama Star* for two years, Walrond immigrated to New York in 1918. He attended the College of the City of New York and became an associate editor of Marcus Garvey's *The Negro World*. He eventually broke with Garvey, critical of the latter's "fondness for pageantry," and became one of Garvey's leading African American critics. After leaving Garvey he became business manager for the magazine *Opportunity*.

While with *Opportunity*, Walrond published his only book, *Tropic Death* (1926). It did not sell well but was acclaimed by such critics as W. E. B. Du Bois and LANGSTON HUGHES. *Tropic Death* is a collection of ten stories that take place in Barbados, the Canal Zone, and British Guiana. The work was praised for its impressionistic depiction of the physical suffering and racism African Americans encounter in the imperial setting of the tropics. It vividly recreates the day-to-day reality of African Americans in part by incorporating native dialects.

Walrond received a Guggenheim Fellowship in 1928 and became a Zona Gale Scholar at the University of Wisconsin. Later that year he moved to Europe, where he eventually reconciled with and wrote for Garvey. After garnering much attention during the HARLEM RENAISSANCE, his literary output diminished in the 1930s and stopped in the 1940s.

SEE ALSO
Du Bois, William Edward Burghardt (W. E. B.); Garvey, Marcus Mosiah; *Opportunity: Journal of Negro Life*.

North America

Walters, Alexander

(b. August 1, 1858, Bardstown, Ky.; d. February 2, 1917, Brooklyn, N.Y.), African Methodist Episcopal Zion Church leader and early twentieth-century civil rights advocate.

Alexander Walters was born into a slave family, the sixth of eight children. Displaying academic promise, he was awarded a scholarship by the AFRICAN METHODIST EPISCOPAL ZION CHURCH (AMEZ) to attend private school in 1868. Receiving his license to preach in 1877, he began his pastoral duties in Indianapolis, Indiana. He went on to serve as pastor in Louisville; San Francisco; Portland, Oregon; and Chattanooga and Knoxville, Tennessee. After taking a church in New York City, he continued as a minister until he was consecrated in 1892 as bishop at the seventh district of the AMEZ Church.

Walters's contribution to civil rights activism began in 1898, when he and T. Thomas Fortune, the editor of the *New York Age*, founded the National Afro-American Council. As president of this council, Walters focused on several issues at the heart of current politics: battling the PLESSY V. FERGUSON "separate but equal" Supreme Court ruling of 1896, opposing Bishop Henry McNeal Turner's call for blacks to return to Africa, and challenging Booker T. Washington's ideas of accommodation to segregation and discrimination. A conflict in 1902 with Fortune over Washington's views resulted in Walters's removal as president of the council.

In 1908 Walters joined activist W. E. B. Du Bois's NIAGARA MOVEMENT, and he helped organize the founding conference of the

National Association for the Advancement of Colored People (NAACP). He became vice president of this organization in 1911. After leading AMEZ churches and education programs in West Africa, Walters felt compelled to encourage the American government to increase economic support in Africa. In 1915 President Woodrow Wilson offered Walters a post as minister to Liberia, which he declined in order to continue organizing AMEZ Church education programs in the United States and internationally. Walters maintained this involvement in AMEZ Church affairs until his death in 1917.

See Also
Du Bois, William Edward Burghardt (W. E. B.); New York, New York; Turner, Henry McNeal; Washington, Booker Taliaferro.

Africa

Wanga, ethnic group of East Africa.

The Wanga primarily inhabit western Kenya and southeastern Uganda just north of Lake Victoria. They speak a Bantu language and are one of the Luhya peoples. Approximately 100,000 people consider themselves Wanga.

See Also
Bantu: Dispersion and Settlement.

War Between the States. Please see Civil War, American

North America

Warwick, Dionne

(b. December 12, 1940, East Orange, N.J.), African American popular and soul singer; one of the top non-Motown artists to emerge from the 1960s.

Born Marie Dionne Warwick, this enduring vocalist got her start singing in a Methodist church. In 1960 she met songwriters Burt Bacharach and Hal David, who asked her to start making demonstration records with them; in 1962 the threesome was offered a contract with Scepter Records.

Bacharach and David wrote songs for Warwick that highlighted her diction and mellow alto voice. She remained with Scepter until 1971 and had numerous hits, including the Number-One hit “Anyone Who Had a Heart” (1964). In the mid-1970s her career faltered amidst family troubles and the breakup of Bacharach and David. In 1979 she again achieved popularity with the Number-Five hit “I'll Never Love This Way Again.” Other hits after her comeback include “Deja Vu” (1979) and “That's What Friends Are For” (1986).

Warwick has given her money and talent to support hunger relief and acquired immune deficiency syndrome (AIDS) research. In 1986 she was named Entertainer of the Year by the National Association for the Advancement of Colored People (NAACP) at the Image Awards.

See Also
AIDS in the United States; Soul Music.

North America

Washington, Booker Taliaferro

(b. April 5, 1856, Franklin County, Va.; d. November 14, 1915, Tuskegee, Ala.), African American founder of the Tuskegee Institute, who urged blacks to accommodate themselves to the white South and concentrate on economic self-advancement; supported by influential whites, he became the most prominent black American of the late nineteenth and early twentieth century.

Discipline and Efficiency

Booker T. Washington was born Booker Taliaferro, a slave, in rural Virginia. His mother, Jane, was the plantation's cook; his father was a white man whose identity he never knew. Washington worked as a servant in the plantation house until he was liberated by Union troops near the end of the Civil War. After the war his family moved to Malden, West Virginia, where they joined Washington Ferguson, also a former slave, whom Jane had married during the war.

To help support the family Washington worked first in a salt furnace, then in a coal mine, and later as a houseboy in the home of Gen. Lewis Ruffner, who owned the mines. Here he came under the influence of Viola Ruffner, the general's wife, who taught him a respect for cleanliness, efficiency, and order. During this time, and despite opposition from his stepfather, Booker attended a school for blacks while continuing to work. At school he gave himself the last name Washington for reasons still debated by historians.

In 1872 Washington left Malden, traveling on foot to Virginia's Hampton Institute, which had opened only a few years earlier as a school for blacks. Its white principal, Gen. Samuel Chapman Armstrong, was the son of missionaries to Hawaii and a commander of black Union troops during the war. The South's freed blacks, Armstrong believed, needed a practical, work-based education that would also teach character and morality. Hampton offered not only agricultural and mechanical classes but training in cleanliness, efficiency, discipline, and the dignity of manual labor as well.

Washington arrived at the school dirty and penniless. He was given work as a janitor, which paid for his room and board, and Armstrong secured a white benefactor to pay his tuition. Washington was a diligent student, adopting Armstrong's credo so thoroughly that many historians have concluded that the rest of Washington's public life was a manifestation of Armstrong's philosophy.

Graduating with honors in 1875, Washington returned to West Virginia to teach. In 1878 he attended Wayland Seminary in Washington, D.C., a school offering a decidedly conventional training in the liberal arts. Washington's experience at Wayland – where the black students knew little of manual labor, and, moreover, seemed uninterested in returning South to help rural blacks – further convinced him of the rightness of Armstrong's methods. After a year at Wayland, Washington returned to Hampton, this time as a member of the faculty. He grew closer to Armstrong, and in 1881, when Armstrong was asked by the state of Alabama to name a white principal to head a new school for blacks, he instead suggested Washington.

Tuskegee

The Tuskegee Institute in Macon County, Alabama, had been apportioned $2000 by the state legislature for salaries, but nothing for land or buildings. Washington began classes with a handful of students in a shanty owned by a black church. Intending Tuskegee to be a replica of Hampton, he established a vocational curriculum for both boys and girls that included such courses as carpentry, printing, tinsmithing, and shoemaking. Girls also took classes in cooking and sewing, and boys learned farming and dairying.

Manners, hygiene, and character also received heavy emphasis, and each day was framed by a rigid schedule that included daily chapel. The earliest students were set to work building a kiln, then making bricks, then erecting buildings. The school sold additional bricks to pay part of its expenses, and Washington secured the rest of the funds from philanthropists, mostly white and mostly Northern, to whom Armstrong had introduced him.

A good deal of Washington's work took place beyond the school's walls. He placated the hostile whites of Tuskegee with assurances that he was counseling his students to set aside political activism in favor of economic gains. He also assured skeptical legislators that his students would not flee the South after their education but instead would be productive contributors to the rural economy. These messages resonated with whites not just in the South but also in the North among Tuskegee's benefactors.

Steel magnate Andrew Carnegie, who became the most generous donor to Tuskegee during Washington's lifetime, said Washington was “one of the most wonderful men... who has ever lived.” Blacks also praised the man who built a school from the dirt of the Deep South that had succeeded, by 1890, in training 500 African Americans a year on 500 acres of land.

These triumphs, however, were underscored by pockets of tragedy in Washington's personal life. His first wife, Fanny Smith Washington, a graduate of Hampton and

Booker T. Washington established the Tuskegee Institute (now University) in 1881 and shaped it as an institution that emphasized industrial education. Tuskegee was the first black institution of higher learning to have a black faculty. *Photo by Elmer Chickering; National Portrait Gallery, Smithsonian Institution/Art Resource, NY*

Washington's girlfriend since Malden, died from a fall in 1884, just two years after their marriage. His second wife, Olivia Davidson Washington, also a graduate of Hampton and in chronically poor health, died in 1889. Washington's third wife, MARGARET MURRAY WASHINGTON, was a graduate of FISK UNIVERSITY and, like Olivia Washington, held the title of lady principal of Tuskegee. Margaret Washington helped her husband for the rest of his life and also led regional and national federations of black women.

National Prominence

Although Tuskegee earned him a measure of popularity, Washington did not become a national leader until he spoke, in September 1895, at the Cotton States and International Exposition in ATLANTA, GEORGIA. Over the previous several years relations between the races had steadily deteriorated. The South had codified its discriminatory JIM CROW laws, and violence, especially LYNCHING, was common. Earlier in the year FREDERICK DOUGLASS, the acknowledged leader of blacks North and South, died, and no clear successor had yet emerged. Washington was the only black speaker chosen to address the mixed-race crowd in Atlanta.

He urged Southern blacks to "cast down your bucket where you are" – that is, to remain in the South – and to accept discrimination as unchangeable for the time being. "In all things that are purely social," he said, "we can be as separate as the fingers, yet one as the hand in all things essential to mutual progress." Blacks should first commit themselves to economic improvement, Washington stated; once they had achieved that, he assured his listeners, improvement in civil rights would follow.

The speech, which critics called the Atlanta Compromise, won nearly unanimous acclaim from both blacks and whites. Even the black intellectual W. E. B. Du Bois, who later broke sharply with Washington's accommodating position, praised Washington's message at the time. Donations from white Americans flowed in larger amounts to Tuskegee, and soon white journalists, politicians, and philanthropists sought Washington's word on all things racial.

In 1898 President William McKinley visited Tuskegee, offering praise that further elevated Washington's stature. Although in public Washington disdained politics, in private he assiduously cultivated his own power. He secretly owned stock in several black newspapers, which he influenced to provide favorable reports about him and Tuskegee. Other black newspapers he quietly cajoled, persuaded, and occasionally coerced into giving him positive coverage. At his heavily attended lectures around the country, he endeared himself to whites by telling stories about "darkies" – blacks who fit racist stereotypes – portraying them as lovable, gullible, and shiftless. These stories alienated black intellectuals.

In 1901 Washington published his ghost-written autobiography, *Up From Slavery*. Told simply but movingly, it is a classic American tale of success through hard work. Almost instantly it became a bestseller and was translated into several languages. Theodore Roosevelt, who had become president the same year, invited Washington to the White House for lunch, prompting a flurry of angry editorials in the white South but further increasing Washington's power and appeal elsewhere. Roosevelt (as did President William Howard Taft after him) sought Washington's advice on racial and Southern issues.

In a short time Washington became a dispenser of Republican Party patronage throughout the South and parts of the North. Blacks soon learned that Washington's endorsement was essential for any political appointment or, for that matter, for funding by white philanthropic groups, who readily deferred to Washington's opinions. He, in turn, used his wealth and power secretly to finance some court cases and other activities challenging JIM CROW laws. He also provided the main impetus for founding the National Negro Business League, which served to advocate his Tuskegee philosophy throughout the country. Some observers referred to the powerful Washington as the Wizard of Tuskegee, and to his operation as the Tuskegee Machine.

"Of Mr. Booker T. Washington and Others"

In 1903 W. E. B. Du Bois published *The Souls of Black Folk*. In one of its essays, "Of Mr. Booker T. Washington and Others," he criticized Washington for failing to realize that economic power could not be had without political power, because political power was needed to protect economic gains. Moreover, Du Bois believed that Washington's disparagement of liberal arts education would rob the race of well-trained leaders.

Du Bois insisted that in a time of increasing segregation and discrimination, blacks must struggle for their civil rights rather than accommodate inequality. Washington, then at the peak of his power, was stung by Du Bois's criticisms, and "Of Mr. Booker T. Washington and Others" allowed critics to be more open over the next several years.

The greatest threat to Washington's conservatism and power came in 1909 with the founding of the National Association for the Advancement of Colored People (NAACP). The NAACP, which sought to address the neglected civil rights of blacks, was a direct challenge to Washington, as was its predecessor, Du Bois's Niagara Movement. Washington tried at first to stifle the group; failing that, he sought a rapprochement. As that, too, failed, increasing numbers of blacks gravitated to the NAACP, and Washington's base of power began to weaken.

The election in 1913 of Democrat Woodrow Wilson to the presidency dealt Washington another blow, as his duties as dispenser of Republican patronage came to an end. Washington nonetheless remained personally prominent until his death in 1915. At that time the Tuskegee Institute had a faculty of 200, an enrollment of 2000, and an endowment of $2 million.

See Also

Press, Black, in the United States; Civil War, American; Davidson, Olivia America; Du Bois, William Edward Burghardt (W. E. B.); Hampton University; Racial Stereotypes; Tuskegee University.

North America

Washington, D.C., capital city of the United States and the only major city whose citizens – the majority of whom are black – lack the authority to govern fully their own affairs.

Established under the direction of President George Washington and named in his honor, Washington, D.C., was created to meet the constitutional mandate for the establishment of a federal district. (Washington originally intended the city's name to be the "District of Columbia" in honor of Christopher Columbus.) Established as a unique entity, separate from the states, Washington, D.C., has been hampered by its ambiguous position, both in terms of racial issues and voting rights. Located between a free and a slave state – Maryland and Virginia, respectively – Washington, D.C., has struggled throughout much of its existence to be both a city for the nation and for its residents.

At the time of its founding in 1800, Washington's population of 14,103 persons comprised 10,066 whites, 793 free blacks, and 3244 slaves. Designed principally by the French architect Pierre L'Enfant, the survey for the city was completed in part by the self-taught African American scientist and mathematician Benjamin Banneker. Arranged in a grid format with four quadrants, Washington, D.C., is some 175.5 sq km (63 sq mi) in size and includes both the Potomac and Anacostia rivers.

During its first 50 years Washington, D.C., became a center for both abolitionist activity as well as the establishment of businesses and institutions led by free blacks, including the several schools organized by and for African American women (the most notable being the Miner Normal School, which later evolved into the University of the District of Columbia). Due in part to the federal government's growing uneasiness with the slave trade, this activity increased the city's attractiveness to free blacks, who began to migrate there in significant numbers after 1820. However, the increase in the number of free blacks coming to the nation's capital led to unease among the leaders of the city itself. The District's city council and other local city councils responded by passing laws that attempted to restrict blacks' movement and activities – including preaching and business ownership. Tensions erupted in the Washington Navy Yard and Georgetown during 1835 and 1836 when whites rioted against abolitionists and free blacks.

With the Civil War under way, Congress moved to redress these problems by abolishing slavery in the capital in 1862, several months before the Emancipation Proclamation. More than 3000 black residents of the district volunteered in the Union army, and the city itself became an important stop for runaway slaves. The war also encouraged the formation of several black charitable organizations,

This turn-of-the-century street scene of Washington, D.C., shows the east front of the United States Capitol in the background. *Archive Photos*

POPULATION OF THE DISTRICT OF COLUMBIA 1800-1990

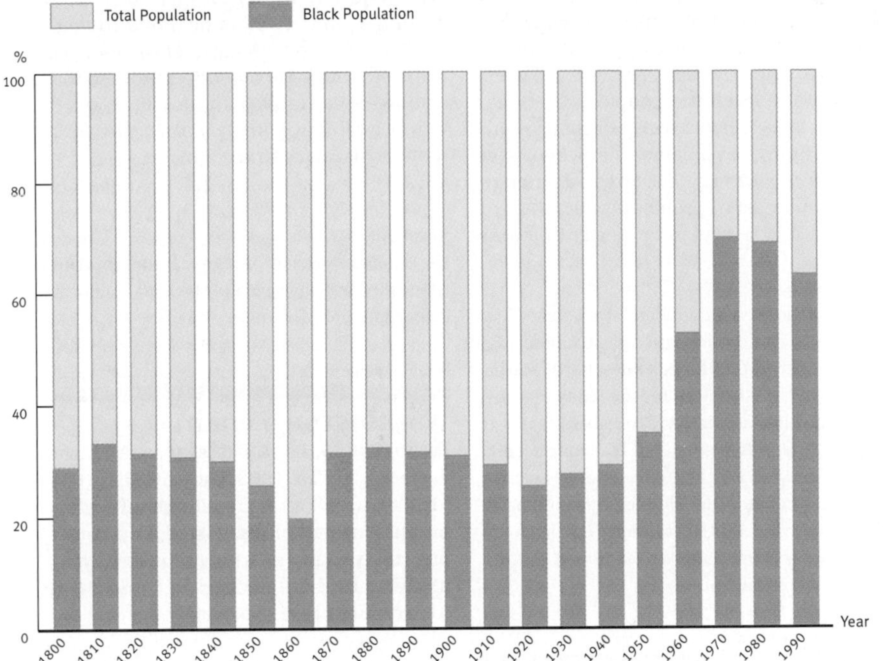

Year	Total Population	Black Population	% Black
1800	14,093	4,027	28.57
1810	24,023	7,944	33.07
1820	33,039	10,425	31.55
1830	39,834	12,271	30.81
1840	43,712	13,055	29.87
1850	51,687	13,746	26.59
1860	75,080	14,316	19.07
1870	131,700	43,404	32.96
1880	177,624	59,596	33.55
1890	230,392	75,572	32.80
1900	278,718	86,702	31.11
1910	331,069	94,446	28.53
1920	437,571	109,966	25.13
1930	486,869	132,068	27.13
1940	663,091	187,226	28.24
1950	802,178	280,803	35.01
1960	763,956	411,737	53.90
1970	756,510	537,712	71.08
1980	638,333	448,370	70.24
1990	606,900	399,604	65.84

including the Contraband Relief Organization and Freedman's Hospital. With Reconstruction, many notable African Americans settled in Washington, D.C., including Frederick Douglass, Alexander Crummell, and Senator Blanche K. Bruce of Mississippi. By 1880 more than 175,000 people lived in Washington, of whom one-third were African Americans.

Although home rule had been a part of the city's political charter since its beginning, suffrage for black voters was repeatedly denied by popular election in the city from 1856 until 1864. It was only after the Civil War that voting rights were conferred on black males by virtue of an act of Congress (the Sumner Civil Rights Amendment). Shortly thereafter, in 1868, the first black mayor of Washington – Sayles Jenks Bowen – was elected. Defeated two years later in his re-election bid by antisuffrage forces, Bowen and other members of Washington's new black political establishment suffered a grievous defeat in 1871 when Congress reversed itself and established a governing body for the city that was appointed by the president and Congress. For the next 100 years African American efforts to assume control of the city would be for naught as the city's political activities were dictated by Congress through a three-member commission whose members would remain exclusively white until 1961.

From Reconstruction until World War I black life in Washington, D.C., advanced most importantly with the establishment of learning organizations such as the American Negro Academy (established by Crummell) and the Association for the Study of Negro Life and History (founded by Carter G. Woodson), and fraternities and sororities such as Omega Psi Phi and Alpha Kappa Alpha, and the founding of Howard University in 1867. Newspapers such as the *Washington Bee* and *Washington Afro-American* also contributed to the city's black life. In addition, Washington continued to attract a large number of black migrants from the South; by 1910 nearly 100,000 African Americans lived in the city, with poor blacks often living in hastily constructed alleys and elite members of the African American community living in neighborhoods such as Le Detroit Park.

Despite the distinct class differences that appeared within the black community in Washington, D.C., the continued growth of the black population in Washington remained a tense issue with its white leaders and their followers. Two days of riots in 1919 confirmed the impression that racial tensions were an indelible part of the city's character. Fueled by newspaper accounts of alleged crimes against white women by black men, the city endured one of its worst race riots. In a city populated with soldiers returning from World War I, whites attacked black citizens in many downtown locations, and black citizens retaliated with attacks in white neighborhoods. Four people died as a result of the riot, including two African Americans, and federal troops were called in to restore calm.

Marion S. Barry celebrates after winning the Democratic mayoral primary in Washington, D.C., in 1994. Barry went on to win his fourth term as mayor. *CORBIS*

With the establishment of the New Deal in 1932 and the rise of Howard University as a center for some of the leading black activists and writers of the day – including Charles Hamilton Houston, Ralph Bunche, and E. Franklin Frazier – organized protests within the district's black community became more common. For instance, the New Negro Alliance, whose members included Houston, Robert C. Weaver, and Mary McLeod Bethune, successfully led protests against employment discrimination. Organized black protest in Washington, D.C., achieved national recognition when the accomplished opera singer and contralto Marian Anderson was denied use of Constitution Hall by the Daughters of the American Revolution in 1939, and instead sang at the Lincoln Memorial before an audience of 75,000 people. (Ironically, the dedication of the Lincoln Memorial itself in 1922 occurred under segregated conditions.) Despite these successes, primary control of Washington remained firmly in the hands of the three-member commission appointed by Congress, and inevitably in the hands of individual Congress members, some of whom – such as Mississippi Democrats Senator Theodore Bilbo and Congressman Ross Collins – were avowed racists.

While congressional oversight of district matters continued, organized efforts to remove Jim Crow laws, coupled with strong migration to the city, meant that the district's black population grew significantly after World War II. By 1960 the black population of Washington, D.C., exceeded 411,000 and represented more than half of the city's citizens. In 1961 ratification of the Twenty-third Amendment to the Constitution occurred, giving residents of Washington, D.C., the right to vote in presidential elections for the first time. The growth of the CIVIL RIGHTS MOVEMENT, and the use of Washington, D.C., as a site for protests by other activist movements brought additional political reforms to the district, including the appointment of African Americans to the newly established office of mayor and the three-member commission. Political reform was hastened by the riots of 1968, which occurred shortly after the assassination of Martin Luther King Jr. Reaction to King's assassination began peacefully when BLACK POWER advocate STOKELY CARMICHAEL (Kwame Turé) asked downtown businesses to close their doors out of respect to the slain civil rights leader. The reaction grew violent as large crowds gathered and reacted to the news of King's death. For three days rioting and looting occurred at a cost of 12 lives, 7600 arrests, and $27 million in property damage, before federal troops were able to restore order.

The 1968 riots, despite the economic devastation they caused, sped the reestablishment of home rule in the city. In 1974, for the first time in nearly 100 years, all citizens of Washington, D.C., were permitted to elect a city council and a mayor. The previously appointed mayor, Walter Washington, was elected mayor in 1974. Marion Barry – a former leader of the STUDENT NONVIOLENT COORDINATING COMMITTEE (SNCC), who moved to Washington, D.C., after working in Mississippi – was elected to the post in 1978 to serve the first of three consecutive terms as mayor. A populist leader whose first-term coalition of poor blacks and white downtown real estate developers would undergo substantial changes in subsequent years, Barry was initially an effective leader who revitalized the downtown and energized long-neglected citizens with his pledges of inclusion. However, Barry's own struggles with drug use, coupled with his desire to expand the city bureaucracy significantly, severely limited his effectiveness as a mayor. In the 1991 election the voters chose to replace Barry with a newcomer, Sharon Pratt Kelly.

The first black woman elected mayor of a major city, Kelly directed reform efforts that failed largely as a result of her inexperience, leaving the city with mounting financial deficits and increasingly frustrated citizens. When Barry was returned to the office of mayor in 1994, the Congress and President Bill Clinton responded to his election and the continued fiscal crisis by establishing the D.C. Control Board, another congressionally appointed body with the power to manage most of the fiscal and administrative affairs of the district until such time as its fiscal condition is stabilized. Despite some successes, the control board has struggled to convince the city's residents that meaningful reform is possible without a self-representative governing body. Its efforts, coupled with Barry's decision in 1998 not to seek reelection, mean that Anthony A. Williams, who was elected mayor in November 1998, faces a daunting but familiar set of problems.

Peter Glenshaw

SEE ALSO

Transatlantic Slave Trade; World War I and African Americans; World War II and African Americans; Abolitionism in the United States; Barry, Marion Shepilov, Jr.; Association for the Study of Afro-American Life and History; Bruce, Blanche Kelso; Bunche, Ralph Johnson; Civil War, American; Frazier, Edward Franklin; Freedmen's Hospital; King, Martin Luther, Jr.; Thirteenth Amendment of the United States Constitution and the Emancipation Proclamation; Weaver, Robert Clifton; Woodson, Carter Godwin.

North America

Washington, Denzel

(b. December 28, 1954, Mount Vernon, N.Y.), Academy Award-winning African American actor.

Denzel Washington grew up in the middle-class family of a Pentecostal minister and a beauty shop owner. Washington won a small role in the 1977 television movie *Wilma*, a film about Olympic star Wilma Rudolph, before he graduated from Fordham University in 1977 with a B.A. in journalism. After graduating, he pursued acting professionally, studying drama at the American Conservatory in San Francisco, California.

Washington first achieved recognition for his stage performances. His portrayals of MALCOLM X in *Chickens Coming Home to Roost* and Private Peterson in the Obie Award-winning *A Soldier's Play* won Washington critical acclaim for carefully chosen roles that resisted Hollywood's stereotypical options for blacks (*see* RACIAL STEREOTYPES). Washington's stage performances led to a role in the popular television drama *St. Elsewhere* from 1982 to 1988, in which he played the dedicated Dr. Philip Chandler. In 1984 he began his successful transition from television to film (*see* FILM, BLACKS IN AMERICAN) when critics praised his reprise of the Private Peterson role in *A Soldier's Story*, the screen adaptation of *A Soldier's Play*.

By the end of the 1980s Washington had become one of Hollywood's most critically and commercially successful actors. He has received three Academy Award nominations, two for Best Supporting Actor (*Cry Freedom*, 1987, and *Glory*, 1990, which he won) and one for Best Actor as Malcolm X in Spike Lee's film of the same name. In addition to collaborating with Lee (in *Malcolm X*, 1992, and *Mo' Better Blues*, 1990), Washington has worked with some of film's most respected directors, including Jonathan Demme (*Philadelphia*, 1993) and Kenneth Branagh (*Much Ado About Nothing*, 1993). He recently solidified his leading-man status with his role opposite WHITNEY HOUSTON in *The Preacher's Wife*, a remake of a Cary Grant film.

Robert Fay

SEE ALSO

Lee, Shelton Jackson ("Spike"); Rudolph, Wilma Glodean; San Francisco and Oakland, California; Television and African Americans.

North America

Washington, Dinah

(b. August 29, 1924, Tuscaloosa, Ala.; d. December 14, 1963, Detroit, Mich.), African American singer and pianist whose music spanned blues, gospel, pop, and RHYTHM AND BLUES, known for her clear diction, uninhibited character, and efforts to promote other musicians.

Dinah Washington was born Ruth Lee Jones to Alice Williams and Ollie Jones. With her parents and three siblings, in 1928 she moved to Chicago, where she attended the city's public schools, including Wendell Phillips High School.

Taught piano by her mother, Washington sang and played solos at St. Luke's Baptist Church while still in elementary school, and gave gospel recitals with her mother at various black churches. At age 15, she won an amateur contest at Chicago's Regal Theater with her rendition of "I Can't Face the Music." Washington then began to sing without her mother's knowledge at local nightclubs.

In 1940 Washington was discovered by gospel singer SALLIE MARTIN, who hired her as an accompanist and singer for the Sallie Martin Colored Ladies Quartet. Washington performed for two years with Martin's ensemble. It was with Martin's group that she took her professional name, before being hired by bandleader Lionel Hampton in 1943.

Washington's career as a soloist was boosted in 1946 when she secured a 16-year recording contract with Mercury Records. During this time she toured extensively and placed 45 songs on *Billboard* magazine's rhythm-and-blues charts. Her biggest hit was "Baby, You've Got What It Takes" (1960). Nicknamed the "Queen of the Blues," she died of an accidental overdose of sleeping pills.

Aaron Myers

SEE ALSO

Blues, The; Chicago, Illinois; Gospel Music; Gospel Quartets; Hampton, Lionel Leo.

North America

Washington, Fredi

(b. December 23, 1903, Savannah, Ga.; d. June 28, 1994, Stamford, Conn.), African American actor who worked for equal opportunity for African American performers.

A gifted performer, Fredi Washington's most famous role typified her Hollywood experience. In *Imitation of Life* (1934) she played a woman who passes for white. Although she won critical acclaim, she was typecast after that as the light-skinned "tragic mulatto." Her performance was so convincing that many African American journalists believed that she carried racial self-hatred. In fact, however, Washington was positive about her heritage and worked on behalf of African American performers by cofounding the Negro Actors Guild in 1937 and serving as its first executive secretary. In 1975 she was inducted into the Black Filmmakers Hall of Fame.

Robert Fay

See Also
Film, Blacks in American.

North America

Washington, Harold

(b. April 15, 1922, Chicago, Ill.; d. November 25, 1987, Chicago, Ill.), African American politician, the first African American mayor of Chicago, Illinois (1983-1987).

Harold Washington was born to Bertha and Roy Lee Washington, who separated when their son was young, and Washington was raised by his father. After dropping out of high school during his junior year, Washington earned a high school equivalency certificate in the army, after he was drafted during World War II. He graduated from Roosevelt University in 1949 with a degree in political science and earned a degree in law from Northwestern University in 1952.

Washington began his political career when he succeeded his deceased father in 1953 as a Democratic Party precinct captain. After holding positions as a city attorney (1954-1958) and a state labor arbitrator (1960-1964), he served in the Illinois House of Representatives (1965-1976). He then advanced to seats in the Illinois State Senate (1976-1980) and the United States House of Representatives (1980-1983). He was active in the 1982 effort to extend the 1965 Voting Rights Act.

In 1977 Washington made an unsuccessful bid to become the mayor of Chicago. In 1983 he again entered the mayoral race and defeated Jane Byrne and Richard M. Daley in the primaries. He edged out Republican Bernard Epton in the general election on April 12, 1983, to become the city's first African American mayor.

Washington increased racial diversity in city administration, assuring equal opportunities for women and minorities seeking employment, and ended city patronage. He had difficulty implementing his initiatives since the majority of the 50 city council seats were held by his political opponents. In 1986, after a federal court called for new elections in certain wards that were deemed racially biased, however, Washington achieved more legislative success. He unexpectedly died of a heart attack shortly after his re-election in 1987, ending hope for a popular, progressive, multiracial city government.

Aaron Myers

See Also
World War II and African Americans; Voting Rights Act of 1965.

North America

Washington, James Melvin

(b. April 24, 1948, Knoxville, Tenn.; d. May 3, 1997, New York, N.Y.), African American historian and minister whose work on the African American religious experience has changed the shape of American church history.

James M. Washington was born on April 24, 1948, in Knoxville, Tennessee, the son of Annie and James W. Washington. He was ordained in 1967 by his home church, Mount Olive Baptist, for the pastorate of the Riverview Missionary Baptist Church. He earned degrees from the University of Tennessee, Harvard Divinity School, and Yale University, from which he received a doctorate in 1979.

Washington taught at Union Theological Seminary in New York from 1975 until his death, being promoted to full professor in 1986. He was the author of *Frustrated Fellowship: The Black Baptist Quest for Social Power* (1986), *A Testament of Hope: The Essential Writings of Martin Luther King Jr.* (1986), and *Conversations with God: Two Centuries of Prayers by African Americans* (1994). He held dual membership at Concord Baptist Church in Brooklyn and the Riverside Church in Manhattan, where he served as chair of the church council.

Washington's scholarly work had three major emphases: the development of African American spirituality, the Christian response to human existence, and the modes of human accommodation and resistance to oppressive social structures. American church history began to be reconsidered and rewritten in light of Washington's investigation of the African American religious experience. He died in New York from hypertension and a massive stroke on May 3, 1997, survived by his wife, Patricia, and their daughter, Ayanna Washington.

Richard Newman

See Also
New York, New York.

North America

Washington, Margaret Murray

(b. 1861, Macon, Miss.; d. June 4, 1925, Tuskegee, Ala.), African American educator and president of the National Association of Colored Women's Clubs.

After graduating in 1889 from Fisk University's preparatory school in Nashville, Tennessee, Margaret Murray Washington joined the faculty at Tuskegee Institute (later Tuskegee University), becoming dean of the women's department in 1890. In 1891 she married Tuskegee's president and founder, Booker T. Washington.

In addition to teaching and helping her husband administer Tuskegee, Washington participated in women's clubs, becoming the president of the National Association of Colored Women's Clubs in 1914. She was also involved in the temperance movement and coordinated self-improvement programs for women in the Tuskegee area. After Booker T. Washington's death in 1915, she continued to work at Tuskegee.

Robert Fay

See Also
Washington, Booker Taliaferro.

North America

Waters, Ethel

(b. October 31, 1896?, Chester, Pa.; d. September 1, 1977, Chatsworth, Calif.), African American singer and actress who brought black urban blues into the mainstream.

Ethel Waters was born to a 12-year-old mother, Louise Anderson, who had been raped by a white man, John Waters. Although she was raised by her maternal grandmother, she took her father's surname. Reared in poverty, she left school at age 13 in order to support herself through domestic housework.

Waters performed for the first time at age five in a children's church program. She was called Baby Star and later, performing on the black vaudeville circuit, became known as Sweet Mama Stringbean. After moving to New York City in 1919, at the start of the Harlem Renaissance, Waters recorded songs for Black Swan Records and then Colombia Records while playing in revues and performing on the white vaudeville circuit during the 1920s. Two of her more popular songs were "Dinah" (1925) and "Stormy Weather" (1933). By refining the genre's lyrics and performance, Waters introduced urban blues to a white audience. Her stylistic alterations created a niche for the black nightclub singers who gained popularity from the 1930s through the 1950s.

In 1927 Waters's career as an actress began with the musical *Africana*. She played singing roles in other Broadway productions: *Blackbirds* (1930), *Rhapsody in Black* (1931),

As Thousands Cheer (1933), *At Home Abroad* (1936), and *Cabin in the Sky* (1940). Waters played more dramatic roles in *Mamba's Daughters* (1939) and *The Member of the Wedding* (1950). Appearing in nine films between 1929 and 1959, she received an Academy Award nomination as Best Supporting Actress in *Pinky* (1949). Through these roles Waters transformed the image of the older black woman from that of the servile "Mammy" to the self-sufficient Earth Mother. She toured with evangelist Billy Graham from 1957 to 1976. Waters is the author of two autobiographies: *His Eye Is on the Sparrow* (1951) and *To Me It's Wonderful* (1972).

Aaron Myers

See Also

Blues, The; New York, New York; Film, Blacks in American.

North America

Waters, Maxine Moore

(b. August 15, 1938, St. Louis, Mo.), African American state assemblywoman and United States Democratic Congresswoman from California known for her commitment to urban renewal.

Maxine Moore Waters gained national recognition during the 1992 Los Angeles riots, when she emerged as one of the black community's principal voices in Congress. She assailed the long-term neglect of America's inner cities, an issue that had propelled her political career from its beginning.

The 5th of 13 children born to Remus and Velma Lee Carr Moore, Waters grew up in a housing project in St. Louis, Missouri. Inspired by a fifth-grade math teacher who took a special interest in her, Waters set high expectations for herself and assumed leadership roles in school. In the late 1960s she became a spokesperson for the Los Angeles-based Head Start program, in which she taught after working as a factory worker and telephone operator. Meanwhile, Waters attended California State University, majoring in sociology, and brought up her two children with her husband, Edward Waters.

In 1973 Waters was appointed chief deputy to city council member David Cunningham; she later campaigned for U.S. senator Alan Cranston and Los Angeles mayor Tom Bradley. She launched her own political career in 1976, when she was elected to the California State Assembly. During her 14-year tenure as an assemblyperson, her legislative successes were numerous and diverse, ranging from a law that curbed California's business investment in South Africa to a training program for child abuse prevention. She prioritized women's rights and helped to found the National Political Congress of Black Women in 1984. In 1990 Waters was elected to the U.S. Congress, where she advocated for minorities and urban renewal. In 1993 she introduced and won passage of a bill that provided $50 million for an innovative training program for disadvantaged youth nationwide. In 1997 she became the third woman to chair the Congressional Black Caucus.

Roanne Edwards

See Also

Bradley, Thomas (Tom); Los Angeles Riot of 1992.

North America

Waters, Muddy

(b. April 4, 1915, Rolling Fork, Miss.; d. April 30, 1983, Chicago, Ill.), African American musician, pioneer of postwar electric blues.

Muddy Waters's long life in music essentially encompasses the story of the blues in the twentieth century. He grew up as McKinley Morganfield in the Mississippi Delta, immersed in the rural blues tradition and particularly fond of Son House and Robert Johnson. He got his nickname from his hobby of fishing in a nearby creek. He was musically active, first playing harmonica and then guitar in small bands around the Delta, and briefly in St. Louis, Missouri.

In 1941 and 1942 the traveling folklorist Alan Lomax recorded Waters, revealing a talented but still imitative singer. In 1943 Waters moved to Chicago, Illinois, and got a job in a paper mill. A year later he bought his first electric guitar, and the impact of the instrument on his music was profound. This new musical technology effectively complemented his powerful voice, and he was soon a popular singer at house parties and clubs on the South Side. He also began recording in 1946, although none of the songs from this period became hits, and he remained a local phenomenon.

In 1948 Waters signed with Chess Records and released his first single, "Rollin' Stone," from which the British rock band the Rolling Stones took its name in the 1960s. It was a hit, and many more followed, including "I Can't Be Satisfied" and "I Feel Like Going Home." These recordings from the late 1940s, with their primitive electric sound and Waters's barely controlled musical and vocal energy, helped to form the foundation of modern rock music.

Waters continued his pioneering work through the 1950s, enlarging his band to include piano and working with such talent as Otis Spann, Little Walter, Willie Dixon, and Buddy Guy. Waters helped to define an exciting new urban blues sound associated with Chicago music in the 1950s, reminiscent of the Delta blues but different from it. This was a mix that appealed strongly to the large population of blacks who had relocated from Mississippi to Chicago. Songs from this period include "I'm Your Hoochie Coochie Man," "I Just Want to Make Love to You," and "Mannish Boy." Though his records did little on the pop charts, Waters was consistently near the top of the rhythm-and-blues charts.

Although he failed to achieve mainstream success in the United States and was largely unknown to white Americans, Waters influenced later musicians, particularly the rising generation of English rock 'n' rollers in the 1960s who experienced Waters firsthand when he toured England in 1958, the first of many successful visits. Waters was honored late in his career with several Grammys and a role in the Band's film, *The Last Waltz*.

See Also

Blues, The; Johnson, Robert Leroy; Rhythm and Blues.

North America

Wattleton, Faye

(b. July 8, 1943, St. Louis, Mo.), former president of the Planned Parenthood Federation of America (PPFA) and the person most responsible for the group's advocacy of abortion rights.

Alyce Faye Wattleton was born the only child of Ozie Walton, a seamstress and minister, and George Wattleton, a factory worker, in St. Louis, Missouri. She graduated from high school at age 16 and attended Ohio State University, from which she received a degree in nursing in 1964. She later entered Columbia University to pursue a master's degree in maternal and infant care. At Columbia – during a time when almost all abortions were illegal – her patients included many girls and women who had attempted abortions with dreadful results. Wattleton soon became active in Planned Parenthood. In the late 1960s she headed a local chapter in Dayton, Ohio, dramatically expanding its services to women and children as well as its donor base. In 1978 she was named president of the PPFA.

At the time Planned Parenthood was known mainly for its several hundred United States clinics offering services such as birth control, prenatal care, and abortions. Although most types of abortions became legal after the Supreme Court confirmed their constitutionality in the 1973 case *Roe* v. *Wade*, abortion opponents were fighting back: the 1977 congressional Hyde Amendment restricted federal funding for abortions, and in 1980 Ronald Reagan became president promising to support the "pro-life" cause.

Eloquent and poised, Wattleton used her position in Planned Parenthood to advocate reproductive rights. Along with other abortion-rights groups, she fought to secure federal funding for birth control and prenatal programs; to forbid states from restricting abortions; and to legalize the sale in the United States of RU-486, the French-made pill that induces abortions. The efforts of Wattleton and others encountered a number of setbacks, including the Supreme Court's 1989 decision in *Webster* v. *Reproductive Health Services* to allow states to restrict abortions.

Wattleton used such defeats to mobilize activists and donors further. In 1992 she resigned from Planned Parenthood to host a talk show based in Chicago. She has one daughter, Felicia, from a marriage in the 1970s.

North America

Watt, Melvin (b. August 26, 1945, Steele Creek, N.C.), Democratic member of the United States House of Representatives from North Carolina (1993-).

Melvin Watt was born in Steele Creek, North Carolina. He received a bachelor's degree from the University of North Carolina at Chapel Hill in 1967 and a law degree from Yale University in 1970. He pursued a career as a civil rights attorney in Charlotte, North Carolina, between 1971 and 1992. Watt served one term in the North Carolina Senate from 1985 to 1987. In 1992 Watt ran successfully for a seat in the U.S. House representing North Carolina's 12th Congressional District. He was easily reelected in 1994 and 1996.

The 12th Congressional District's boundary connects predominately black areas from ten counties in a narrow strip. The district was created in 1992 as one of two North Carolina minority districts mandated by the U.S. Justice Department. However, in June 1996 the U.S. Supreme Court declared the district illegally drawn. In March 1997 the North Carolina Legislature reshaped the district and reduced its number of minority voters. The district's economy relies on tobacco production, furniture manufacture, and textile production. Duke University in Durham is a major employer.

In the 105th Congress (1997-1999), Watt served on the Judiciary Committee and the Banking and Financial Services Committee. He was ranking member of the Immigration and Claims Subcommittee of the Judiciary Committee. He was also a member of the CONGRESSIONAL BLACK CAUCUS.

North America

Watts, André (b. June 20, 1946, Nuremberg, Germany), African American concert pianist, the first black American instrumental superstar.

Since his rise to prominence in 1963, André Watts has been one of the world's leading classical pianists. At age 16, he became the first black instrumental soloist in more than 60 years to perform with the New York Philharmonic Orchestra, under conductor Leonard Bernstein. Within a decade he was renowned worldwide for his poetic style, technical brilliance, and fiery temperament. According to music critic Elyse Mach, "Watts is to a concert stage as lightning is to thunder. Explosive. More than any other pianist, his performances are reminiscent of what a Liszt concert must have been like: mesmerizing, theatrical, charged with energy."

Watts ascribes his career success largely to luck and what he calls "a combination of those funny, indefinable qualities that are in a person at birth." He also cites his mother as a critical influence: "I wouldn't be a pianist today if my mother hadn't made me practice." He was born in a United States Army camp in Nuremberg, Germany, the only child of Herman Watts, an African American career soldier, and Maria Alexandra Gusmits, a Hungarian who had been displaced in Germany following World War II. When he was four he began playing a miniature violin and at age seven studied piano with his mother, an accomplished pianist. In 1954 his family moved to PHILADELPHIA, PENNSYLVANIA, where he received a private school education and studied at the Philadelphia Academy of Music.

Watts first performed publicly at age 9, playing the Haydn Concerto in D Major in a children's concert sponsored by the Philadelphia Orchestra. Several performances with other orchestras followed, and at age 16 he won an audition to perform in a nationally televised Young People's Concert with the New York Philharmonic, playing Liszt's Piano Concerto no. 1. His performance stunned audiences and music critics alike.

In late January 1963, a few weeks after the Liszt performance, Leonard Bernstein, who predicted "gianthood" for the young pianist, invited Watts to substitute as a soloist for ailing pianist Glenn Gould. Bernstein proved instrumental in Watts's success: the young artist's second New York Philharmonic performance won him a ten-minute standing ovation and invitations to perform with the world's major orchestras, which were usually closed to black instrumentalists without the backing of an eminent conductor or music manager. Spared the ordeals of competitive life, he focused on his artistry and academic education.

In 1969 Watts enrolled at Baltimore's Peabody Conservatory of Music, where he studied with pianist Leon Fleisher and, in 1972, obtained his Artist's Diploma. That same year he became the youngest person ever to receive an honorary doctorate from Yale University. Meanwhile, his international career flourished. In 1966 he made his European debut with the London Symphony Orchestra and also performed his first solo recital in New York. He recorded extensively and continued to tour throughout Europe, Asia, and the United States. During the late 1960s and 1970s he was often chosen to perform at important political occasions: he became the first American pianist to play in the People's Republic of China, as a soloist with the Philadelphia Orchestra. In 1973 he toured Russia.

Although the quality of Watts's playing has not been consistent throughout his career, his recent recordings and concerts have reaffirmed his musical brilliance. In 1995 he recorded Tchaikovsky's Piano Concerto no. 1 and Saint-Saens's Piano Concerto no. 2 with the Atlanta Symphony – his first concerto recording in more than ten years. "His playing is technically superb, fluent and melodious," wrote music critic Alexander Morin. "A concert always is an incredible exposition of one's daring and insides," said Watts of his own playing. "If you're not willing to do that... then there's a limit to what you can offer the people."

Roanne Edwards

Africa

Weah, George (b. October 1, 1966, Monrovia, Liberia), Liberian international soccer player.

In the 1990s George Weah emerged as one of the best soccer players in the world and the unofficial leader of the approximately 350 Africans who play soccer in EUROPE. After a difficult childhood in Monrovia, Weah became a devout Muslim and a talented athlete who, at the time, used his African name, Oppong. Weah began his career playing for teams in Monrovia and YAOUNDÉ, CAMEROON. In 1988 he moved to Europe, where he played for AS Monaco (1988-1992), Paris St. Germain (1992-1995), and Italian champion AC Milan (1995-). In 1995 soccer's international governing body, Fédération Internationale de Football Association (FIFA), named Weah the top player of the year, marking the first time the award had gone to an African. A striker, the 1.8-m (6-ft) tall Weah is known for his ball control and ferocious shooting.

Weah is usually soft-spoken, but he criticized groups that were fighting in Liberia's civil war. Afterward, his relatives were attacked, and his house and property were destroyed. In 1996 Weah spent more than $50,000 of his own money to help finance Liberia's ultimately unsuccessful bid to play in the 1998 World Cup, an act that won him the FIFA Fair Play Award. Weah injured his back in 1997; this put his contract with Milan through the year 2000 into question. In interviews Weah has stated that he would like to end his soccer career in New York, where he owns a restaurant and has many friends and family members. He routinely donates money to the SOS Children's Villages in Liberia; he says that he would like to work for the United Nations Children's Fund (UNICEF) after his retirement.

Kate Tuttle

SEE ALSO
Liberia; Monrovia, Liberia; New York, New York.

North America

Weaver, Robert Clifton

(b. December 29, 1907, Washington, D.C.; d. July 17, 1997, New York, N.Y.), first African American United States cabinet member; secretary of housing and urban development (1966-1968).

The son of Mortimer and Florence Weaver, Robert Clifton Weaver grew up attending segregated schools in WASHINGTON, D.C. After graduating from high school, he attended Harvard, where his older brother, Mortimer, was pursuing graduate studies in English. Weaver was refused dormitory accommodations because he was black, so he moved off campus to become his brother's roommate. He graduated cum laude with a degree in economics in 1929, the same year Mortimer died unexpectedly. Weaver remained at Harvard, taking an M.A. in 1931 and a Ph.D. in economics in 1934.

Weaver began his government career in 1933 when Secretary of the Interior Harold Ickes hired him as a race relations advisor in the housing division. By 1937 Weaver had become special assistant to the administrator of the U.S. Housing Authority, a post he held until 1940. As a high-ranking African American in President Franklin D. Roosevelt's administration, Weaver was a member of the "BLACK CABINET," an informal network of African Americans who worked to end racial discrimination in the federal government and the programs it administered.

In 1944, after serving on the National Defense Advisory Committee, the Manpower Commission, and the War Production Board, Weaver was appointed the director of the Mayor's Committee on Race Relations in CHICAGO, ILLINOIS, and then of the American Council on Race Relations. During this time he published two critical studies of discrimination in the United States, *Negro Labor: A National Problem* (1946) and *The Negro Ghetto* (1948).

In 1955 New York governor Averell Harriman made Weaver the first African American to hold a state cabinet-level position by naming him state rent commissioner. Weaver held this post until 1960, when President John F. Kennedy named him director of the U.S. Housing and Home Finance Agency, making him the highest-ranking African American in government.

Kennedy intended to establish a cabinet-level agency to address urban affairs with Weaver as its head. However, Southern members of Congress who opposed an African American cabinet member in general and Weaver's strong support of integrated housing in particular blocked Kennedy's plan. The agency, the Department of Housing and Urban Development (HUD), was not established until President Lyndon B. Johnson was elected in 1965. In 1966, with Johnson better able to exercise power in the Congress, Weaver became the first HUD secretary and the first African American cabinet member.

President Lyndon Johnson congratulates Robert C. Weaver at his swearing in as secretary of the Department of Housing and Urban Development in 1966. *CORBIS*

Weaver effectively administered HUD, but his more ambitious and imaginative plans, such as Demonstration Cities and the Metropolitan Development Act, were unsupported because of the precedence given by the federal government to the VIETNAM WAR and because of conservative reaction to ghetto rioting from 1965 to 1968. In 1969 Weaver ended his career in government, becoming president of City College of New York's (CCNY's) Baruch College. In 1971 he became distinguished professor of urban affairs at CCNY's Hunter College, and he became professor emeritus in 1978.

Weaver's public service extended beyond his careers in government and education. He chaired the board of directors of the NATIONAL ASSOCIATION FOR THE ADVANCEMENT OF COLORED PEOPLE (NAACP) in 1960, and was president of the National Committee against Discrimination in Housing from 1973 to 1987. In addition, Weaver received the Spingarn Medal in 1962, the New York City Urban League's Frederick Douglass Award in 1977, the Schomburg Collection Award in 1978, and the Equal Opportunity Day Award from the NATIONAL URBAN LEAGUE in 1987.

Robert Fay

North America

Webb, Frank J.

(b. 1828, Philadelphia, Pa.; d. 1894?, Galveston, Tex.), African American author who wrote about interracial marriage and passing.

Little is known about Frank Webb's life. Raised in PHILADELPHIA, PENNSYLVANIA, he lived in England, FRANCE, and KINGSTON, JAMAICA. Webb returned to the United States in 1870, publishing two novellas that year, *Two Wolves and a Lamb* and *Marvin Hayle.* Following this he moved to Galveston, Texas, where he edited a radical newspaper before running a school until his death. His one novel, *The Garies and Their Friends*, published in 1857, was the second of only four African American novels published before the Civil War. The first novel about free African Americans in the North, Webb's book explored interracial marriage and passing.

Robert Fay

SEE ALSO
Great Britain; Civil War, American; Interracial Marriage in the United States; Passing in the United States.

North America

W. E. B. Du Bois: An Interpretation

Cornel West

W. E. B. Du Bois is the towering black scholar of the twentieth century. The scope of his interests, the depth of his insights, and the sheer majesty of his prolific writings bespeak a level of genius unequaled among modern black intellectuals. Yet, like all of us, Du Bois was a child of his age. He was shaped by the prevailing presuppositions and prejudices of modern Euro-American civilization. And despite his lifelong struggle – marked by great courage and sacrifice – against white supremacy and for the advancement of Africans around the world, he was, in style and substance, a proud black man of letters primarily influenced by nineteenth-century, Euro-American traditions.

For those of us interested in the relation of white supremacy to modernity (African slavery in the New World and European imperial domination of most of the rest of the world) or the consequences of the construct of "race" during the Age of Europe (1492-1945), the scholarly and literary works of Du Bois are indispensable. For those of us obsessed with alleviating black social misery, the political texts of Du Bois are insightful and inspiring. In this sense, Du Bois is the brook of fire through which we all must pass in order to gain access to the intellectual and political weaponry needed to sustain the radical democratic tradition in our time.

Yet even this great titan of black emancipation falls short of the mark. This is not to deny the remarkable subtlety of his mind or the undeniable sincerity of his heart. The grand example of Du Bois remains problematic principally owing to his inadequate interpretation of the human condition and his inability to immerse himself fully in the rich cultural currents of black everyday life. His famous notion of the Talented Tenth reveals this philosophic inadequacy and personal inability.

What does it mean to claim that Du Bois put forward an inadequate interpretation of the human condition or that he failed to immerse himself fully in the cultural depths of black everyday life? Are these simply rhetorical claims devoid of content – too abstract to yield conclusions and too general to evaluate? Are some interpretations of the human condition and cultural ways of life really better than others? If so, why? These crucial questions sit at the center of my critique of Du Bois because they take us to the heart of black life in the profoundly decadent American civilization at the end of the twentieth century – a ghastly century whose levels of barbarity, bestiality, and brutality are unparalleled in human history.

My assessment of Du Bois primarily concerns his response to the problem of evil – to undeserved harm, unjustified suffering, and unmerited pain. Do his evolving world-view, social analysis, and moral vision enable us to understand and endure this "first century of world wars" (Muriel Rukeyser's apt phrase) in which nearly 200 million fellow human beings have been murdered in the name of some pernicious ideology? Does his work contain the necessary intellectual and existential resources to enable us to confront the indescribable agony and unnameable anguish likely to be unleashed in the twenty-first century – the first century involving a systemic gangsterization of everyday life, shot through with revitalized tribalisms – under the aegis of an uncontested, fast-paced global capitalism? As with any great figure, to grapple with Du Bois is to wrestle with who we are, why we are what we are, and what we are to do about it.

Du Bois was first and foremost a black New England Victorian seduced by the Enlightenment ethos and enchanted with the American Dream. His interpretation of the human condition – that is, in part, his idea of who he was and could be – was based on his experiences and, most important, on his understanding of those experiences through the medium of an Enlightenment world-view that promoted Victorian strategies in order to realize an American optimism; throughout this essay, I shall probe these three basic foundations of his perspective. Like many of the brilliant and ambitious young men of his time, he breathed the intoxicating fumes of "advanced" intellectual and political culture. Yet in the face of entrenched evil and demonic power, Du Bois often found himself either shipwrecked in the depths of his soul or barely afloat with less and less wind in his existential sails.

My fundamental problem with Du Bois is his inadequate grasp of the tragicomic sense of life – a refusal candidly to confront the sheer absurdity of the human condition. This tragicomic sense – tragicomic rather than simply "tragic," because even ultimate purpose and objective order are called into question – propels us toward suicide or madness unless we are buffered by ritual, cushioned by community, or sustained by art. Du Bois's inability to immerse himself in black everyday life precluded his access to the distinctive black tragicomic sense and black encounter with the absurd. He certainly saw, analyzed, and empathized with black sadness, sorrow, and suffering. But he didn't feel it in his bones deeply enough, nor was he intellectually open enough to position himself alongside the sorrowful, suffering, yet striving ordinary black folk. Instead, his own personal and intellectual distance lifted him above them even as he addressed their plight in his progressive writings. Du Bois was never alienated by black people: he lived in black communities where he received great respect and admiration. But there seemed to be something in him that alienated ordinary black people. In short, he was reluctant to learn fundamental lessons about life – and about himself – from them. Such lessons would have required that he, at least momentarily, believe that they were or might be as wise, insightful, and "advanced" as he; and this he could not do.

Du Bois's Enlightenment world-view – his first foundation – prohibited this kind of understanding. Instead, he adopted a mild elitism that underestimated the capacity of everyday people to "know" about life. In "The Talented Tenth," he claims, "knowledge of life and its wider meaning, has been the point of the Negro's deepest ignorance." In his classic book *The Souls of Black Folk* (1903), there are 18 references to "black, backward, and ungraceful" folk, including a statement of his intent "to scatter civilization among a people whose ignorance was not simply of letters, but of life itself."

My aim is not to romanticize those whom Sly Stone calls "everyday people" or to cast them as the sole source of wisdom. The myths of the noble savage and the wise commoner are simply the flip sides of the Enlightenment attempts to degrade and devalue everyday people. Yet Du Bois, owing to his Puritan New England origins and Enlightenment values, found it difficult not to view common black folk as some degraded "other" or "alien" no matter how hard he resisted. His honest response to a church service in the backwoods of Tennessee at a "Southern Negro Revival" bears this out. "A sort of suppressed terror hung in the air and seemed to seize us, – a pythian madness, a demoniac possession, that lent terrible reality to song and word. The black and massive form of the preacher swayed and quivered as the words crowded to his lips and flew at us in singular eloquence. The people moaned and fluttered, and then the gaunt-cheeked brown woman beside me suddenly leaped straight into the air and shrieked like a lost soul, while round about came wail and groan and outcry, and a scene of human passion such as I had never conceived before. Those who have not thus witnessed the frenzy of a Negro revival in the untouched backwoods of the South can but dimly realize the religious feeling of the slave; as described, such scenes appear grotesque and funny, but as seen they are awful."

Du Bois's intriguing description reminds one of an anthropologist visiting some strange and exotic people whose rituals suggest not only the sublime but also the satanic. The "awfulness" of this black church service, similar to that of my own black Baptist tradition, signifies for him both dread and fear, anxiety and disgust. In short, a black ritualistic explosion of energy frightened this black rationalist. It did so not simply because the folk seem so coarse and uncouth, but also because they are out of control, overpowered by something bigger than themselves. This clearly posed a threat to him.

Like a good Enlightenment philosophe, Du Bois pits autonomy against authority, self-mastery against tradition. Autonomy and self-mastery connote self-consciousness and self-criticism; authority and tradition suggest blind deference and subordination. Self-consciousness and self-criticism yield cosmopolitanism and highbrow culture. Authority and tradition reinforce provincialism and lowbrow culture. The educated and chattering class – the Talented Tenth – are the agents of sophistication and mastery, while the uneducated and moaning class – the backward masses – remain locked in tradition; the basic role of the Talented Tenth is to civilize and refine, uplift and elevate the benighted masses.

For Du Bois education was the key. Ignorance was the major obstacle – black ignorance and white ignorance. If the black masses were educated – in order to acquire skills and culture – black America would thrive. If white elites and masses were enlightened, they would not hate and fear black folk. Hence America – black and white – could be true to its democratic ideals. "The Negro Problem was in my mind a matter of systematic investigation and intelligent understanding. The world was thinking wrong about race, because it did not know. The ultimate evil was stupidity. The cure for it was knowledge based on scientific investigation."

This Enlightenment naiveté – not only in regard to white supremacy but with respect to any form of personal and institutional evil – was momentarily shaken by a particular case involving that most peculiar American institution – LYNCHING.

"At the very time when my studies were most successful, there cut across this plan which I had as a scientist, a red ray which could not be ignored. I remember when it first, as it were, startled me to my feet: a poor Negro in central Georgia, Sam Hose, had killed his landlord's wife. I wrote out a careful and reasoned statement concerning the evident facts and started down to the *Atlanta Constitution* office.... I did not get there. On the way news met me: Sam Hose had been lynched, and they said that his knuckles were on exhibition at a grocery store farther down on Mitchell Street, along which I was walking. I turned back to the university. I began to turn aside from my work.... "

"Two considerations thereafter broke in upon my work and eventually disrupted it: first, one could not be a calm, cool, and detached scientist while Negroes were lynched, murdered and starved; and secondly, there was no such definite demand for scientific work of the sort that I was doing.... "

Then, in the very next month, Du Bois lost his 18-month-old son, Burghardt, to diphtheria. If ever Du Bois was forced to confront the tragedy of life and the absurdity of existence, it was in the aftermath of this loss, which he describes in his most moving piece of writing, "Of the Passing of the First-Born," in *The Souls of Black Folk*. In this powerful elegiac essay Du Bois not only mourns his son but speaks directly to death itself – as Prometheus to Zeus or Jesus to his Heavenly Father. "But hearken, O Death! Is not this my life hard enough, is not that dull land that stretches its sneering web about me cold enough, – is not all the world beyond these four little walls pitiless enough, but that thou must needs enter here, – thou, O Death? About my head the thundering storm beat like a heartless voice, and the crazy forest pulsed with the curses of the weak; but what cared I, within my home beside my wife and baby boy? Wast thou so jealous of one little coign of happiness that thou must needs enter there, – thou, O Death?"

This existential gall to go face-to-face and toe-to-toe with death in order to muster some hope against hope is echoed in his most tragic characterization of the black sojourn in white supremacist America. "Within the Veil was he born, said I; and there within shall he live, – a Negro and a Negro's son. Holding in that little head – ah, bitterly! – the unbowed pride of a hunted race, clinging with that tiny dimpled hand – ah, wearily! – to a hope not hopeless but unhopeful, and seeing with those bright wondering eyes that peer into my soul a land whose freedom is to us a mockery and whose liberty a lie."

What is most revealing in this most poignant of moments is Du Bois's refusal to linger with the sheer tragedy of his son's death (a natural, not a social, evil) – without casting his son as an emblem of the race or a symbol of a black deliverance to come. Despite the deep sadness in this beautiful piece of writing, Du Bois sidesteps Dostoyevsky's challenge to wrestle in a sustained way with the irrevocable fact of an innocent child's death. Du Bois's rationalism prevents him from wading in such frightening existential waters. Instead, Du Bois rushes to glib theodicy, weak allegory, and superficial symbolism. In other words his Enlightenment world-view falters in the face of death – the deaths of Sam Hose and Burghardt. The deep despair that lurks around the corner is held at arm's length by rational attempts to boost his flagging spirit.

Du Bois's principal intellectual response to the limits of his Enlightenment world-view was to incorporate certain insights of Marx and Freud. Yet Marx's powerful critique of the unequal relations of power between capitalists and the proletariat in the workplace and Freud's penetrating attempt to exercise rational control over the irrational forces at work in self and society only deepened Du Bois's commitment to the Enlightenment ethos. And though particular features of this ethos are essential to any kind of intellectual integrity and democratic vision – features such as self-criticism and self-development, suspicion of illegitimate authority and suffocating tradition – the Enlightenment world-view held by Du Bois is ultimately inadequate, and, in many ways, antiquated, for our time. The tragic plight and absurd predicament of Africans here and abroad requires a more profound interpretation of the human condition – one that goes far beyond the false dichotomies of expert knowledge versus mass ignorance, individual autonomy versus dogmatic authority, and self-mastery versus intolerant tradition. Our tragicomic times require more democratic concepts of knowledge and leadership which highlight human fallibility and mutual accountability; notions of individuality and contested authority which stress dynamic traditions; and ideals of self-realization within participatory communities.

The second fundamental pillar of Du Bois's intellectual project is his Victorian strategies – namely, the ways in which his Enlightenment world-view can be translated

"One ever feels his two-ness – " W. E. B. Du Bois wrote in an 1897 article, "an American; a Negro; two souls, two thoughts, two unreconciled strivings; two warring ideals in one dark body, whose dogged strength alone keeps it from being torn asunder." *CORBIS*

into action. They rest upon three basic assumptions. First, that the self-appointed agents of Enlightenment constitute a sacrificial cultural elite engaged in service on behalf of the impulsive and irrational masses. Second, that this service consists of shaping and molding the values and viewpoints of the masses by managing educational and political bureaucracies (e.g., schools and political parties). Third, that the effective management of these bureaucracies by the educated few for the benefit of the pathetic many promotes material and spiritual progress. These assumptions form the terrain upon which the Talented Tenth are to operate.

In fact, Du Bois's notion of the Talented Tenth is a descendant of those cultural and political elites conceived by the major Victorian critics during the heyday of the British Empire in its industrial phase. S. T. Coleridge's secular clerisy, Thomas Carlyle's strong heroes, and Matthew Arnold's disinterested aliens all shun the superficial vulgarity of materialism and the cheap thrills of hedonism in order to preserve and promote highbrow culture and to civilize and contain the lowbrow masses. The resounding first and last sentences of Du Bois's essay "The Talented Tenth" not only echo the "truths" of Victorian social criticism, they also bestow upon the educated few a salvific role. "The Negro race, like all races, is going to be saved by its exceptional men." This bold statement is descriptive, prescriptive, and predictive. It assumes that the exceptional men of other races have saved their "race" (Gladstone in Britain, Menilek in Ethiopia, Bismarck in Germany, Napoleon in France, Peter in Russia). Here Du Bois claims that exceptional black men ought to save their "race" and asserts that if any "race" – especially black people – is to be saved, exceptional men will do it. The patriarchal sensibilities speak for themselves.

Like a good Victorian critic, Du Bois argues on rational grounds for the legitimacy of his cultural elite. They are worthy of leadership because they are educated and trained, refined and civilized, disciplined and determined. Most important, they have "honesty of heart" and "Purity of motive." Contrast Matthew Arnold's disinterested aliens, "who are mainly led, not by their class spirit, but by a general humane spirit, by the love of human perfection," in *Culture and Anarchy* (1869) with Du Bois's Talented Tenth.

"The men of culture are the true apostles of equality. The great men of culture are those who have had a passion for diffusing, for making prevail, for carrying from one end of society to the other, the best knowledge, the best ideas of their time, who have laboured to divest knowledge of all that was harsh, uncouth, difficult, abstract, professional, exclusive; to humanize it, to make it efficient outside the clique of the cultivated and learned, yet still remaining the best knowledge and thought of the time, and a true source, therefore, of sweetness and light. Who are today guiding the work of the Negro people? The "exceptions" of course.... A saving remnant continually survives and persists, continually aspires, continually shows itself in thrift and ability and character.... Can the masses of the Negro people be in any possible way more quickly raised than by the effort and example of this aristocracy of talent and character? Was there ever a nation on God's fair earth civilized from the bottom upward? Never; it is, ever was and ever will be from the top downward that culture filters. The Talented Tenth rises and pulls all that are worth the saving up to their vantage ground. This is the history of human progress; and the two historic mistakes which have hindered that progress were the thinking first that no more could ever rise save the few already risen; or second, that it would better the unrisen to pull the risen down."

Just as Arnold seeks to carve out discursive space and a political mission for the educated elite in the British Empire somewhere between the arrogance and complacency of the aristocracy and the vulgarity and anarchy of the working classes, Du Bois wants to create a new vocabulary and social vocation for the black educated elite in America somewhere between the hatred and scorn of the white supremacist majority and the crudity and illiteracy of the black agrarian masses. Yet his gallant efforts suffer from intellectual defects and historical misconceptions.

Let us begin with the latter. Is it true that in 1903 the educated elite were guiding the work of the Negro people? Yes and no. Certainly the most visible national black leaders tended to be educated black men, such as the ubiquitous Booker T. Washington and, of course, Du Bois himself. Yet the two most effective political forms of organizing and mobilizing among black people were the black women's club movement led by Ida B. Wells and the migration movement guided by Benjamin "Pap" Singleton, A. A. Bradley, and Richard H. Cain. Both movements were based in black civil society – that is, black civic associations like churches, lodges, fraternal orders, and sororities. Their fundamental goals were neither civil rights nor social equality but rather respect and dignity, land and self-determination. How astonishing – and limiting – that Du Bois fails to mention and analyze these movements that will result in the great MARY MCLEOD BETHUNE's educational crusade and the inimitable Marcus Garvey's Back-to-Africa Movement in a decade or so!

Regarding the intellectual defects of Du Bois's noble endeavor: first, he assumes that highbrow culture is inherently humanizing, and that exposure to and immersion in great works produce good people. Yet we have little reason to believe that people who delight in the works of geniuses like Mozart and Beethoven or Goethe and Wordsworth are any more or less humane than those who dance in the barnyards to the banjo plucking of nameless rural folk in Tennessee. Certainly those fervent white supremacists who worship the Greek and Roman classics and revel in the plays of the incomparable Shakespeare weaken his case. Second, Du Bois holds that the educated elite can more easily transcend their individual and class interests and more readily act on behalf of the common good than the uneducated masses. But is this so? Are they not just as prone to corruption and graft, envy and jealousy, self-destructive passion and ruthless ambition as everyone else? Were not Carlyle's great heroes, Cromwell and Napoleon, tyrants? Was it not Arnold's disinterested aliens who promoted and implemented the inhumane policies of the imperial British bureaucracies in India and Africa? Was not Du Bois himself both villain and victim in petty political games as well as in the all-too-familiar social exclusions of the educated elite?

Du Bois wisely acknowledges this problem in his 1948 revision of "The Talented Tenth": "When I came out of college into the world of work, I realized that it was quite possible that my plan of training a talented tenth might put in control and power, a group of selfish, self-indulgent, well-to-do men, whose basic interest in solving the Negro Problem was personal; personal freedom and unhampered enjoyment and use of the world, without any real care, or certainly no arousing care, as to what became of the mass of American Negroes, or of the mass of any people. My Talented Tenth, I could see, might result in a sort of interracial free-for-all, with the devil taking the hindmost and the foremost taking anything they could lay hands on."

He then notes the influence of Marx on his thinking and adds that the Talented Tenth must not only be talented but have "expert knowledge" of modern economics, be willing to sacrifice and plan effectively to institute socialist measures. Yet there is still no emphatic call for accountability from below, nor any grappling with the evil that lurks in the hearts of all of us. He recognizes human selfishness as a problem without putting forward adequate philosophical responses to it or institutional mechanisms to alleviate it. In the end he throws up his hands and gives us a grand either/or option. "But we must have honest men or we die. We must have unselfish, far-seeing leadership or we fail."

Victorian social criticism contains elements indispensable to future critical thought about freedom and democracy in the twenty-first century. Most important, it elevates the role of public intellectuals who put forward overarching visions and broad analyses based on a keen sense of history and a subtle grasp of the way the world is going in the present. The rich tradition of Victorian critics – Thomas Carlyle, John Ruskin, Matthew Arnold, John Morley, William Morris, and, in our own century, L. T. Hobhouse, J.A. Hobson, C. E. G. Masterman, R. H. Tawney, Raymond Williams, E. P. Thompson, and others – stands shoulders above the parochial professionalism of much of the academy today. In our era scholarship is often divorced from public engagement, and shoddy journalism often settles for the sensational and superficial aspects of prevailing crises. As the distinguished European man of letters George Steiner notes in regard to the academy, "Specialization has reached moronic vehemence. Learned lives are expended on reiterative minutiae. Academic rewards go to the narrow scholiast, to the blinkered. Men and women in the learned professions proclaim themselves experts on one author, in one brief historical period, in one aesthetic medium. They look with contempt (and dank worry) on the 'Generalist.'... It may be that cows have fields. The geography of consciousness should be that of unfenced errance, Montaigne's comely word."

Yet the Victorian strategies of Du Bois require not piecemeal revision but wholesale reconstruction. A fuller understanding of the human condition should lead us far beyond any notions of free-floating elites, suspicious of the tainted masses – elites who worship at the altar of highbrow culture while ignoring the barbarity and bestiality in their own ranks. The fundamental role of the public intellectual – distinct from, yet building on, the indispensable work of academics, experts, analysts, and pundits – is to create and sustain high-quality public discourse addressing urgent public problems which enlightens and energizes fellow citizens, prompting them to take public action. This role requires a deep commitment to the life of the mind – a perennial attempt to clear our minds of cant (to use Samuel Johnson's famous formulation) – which serves to shape the public destiny of a people. Intellectual and political leadership is neither elitist nor populist; rather it is democratic, in that each of us stands in public space, without humiliation, to put forward our best visions and views for the sake of the public interest. And these arguments are presented in an atmosphere of mutual respect and civic trust.

The last pillar of Du Bois's project is his American optimism. Like most intellectuals of the New World, he was preoccupied with progress. And given his genuine commitment to black advancement, this preoccupation is understandable. Yet, writing as he was in the early stages of the consolidation of the American Empire (some 8 million people of color had been incorporated after the Spanish-American War), when the United States itself was undergoing geographical and economic expansion and millions of "new" Americans were being admitted from eastern Europe, Du Bois tended to assume that United States expansionism was a sign of probable American progress. In this sense, in his early and middle years he was not only a progressivist but also a kind of American exceptionalist. It must be said, to be sure, that unlike most American exceptionalists of his day, he considered the color line the major litmus test for the country. Yet he remained optimistic about a multiracial democratic America.

Du Bois never fully grasped the deeply pessimistic view of American democracy behind the Garvey movement. In fact, he never fully understood or appreciated the strong – though not central – black nationalist strain in the Black Freedom Movement. As much as he hated white supremacy in America, he could never bring himself to identify intimately with the harsh words of the great performing artist JOSEPHINE BAKER, who noted in response to the East St. Louis Riot of July 1917 that left more than 200 black people dead and more than 6000 homeless, "The very idea of America makes me shake and tremble and gives me nightmares." Baker lived most of her life in exile in FRANCE. Even when Du Bois left for Africa in 1961 – as a member of a moribund Communist Party – his attitude toward America was not that of an ELIJAH MUHAMMAD or a MALCOLM X. He was still, in a significant sense, disappointed with America, and there is no disappointment without some dream deferred. Elijah Muhammad and Malcolm X were not disappointed with America. As bona fide black nationalists, they had no expectations of a white supremacist civilization; they adhered neither to American optimism nor to exceptionalism.

Black Nationalism is a complex tradition of thought and action, a tradition best expressed in the numerous insightful texts of black public intellectuals like Maulana Karenga, Imamu Amiri Baraka, Haki R. Madhubuti, Marimba Ani, and Molefi Asante. Black nationalists usually call upon black people to close ranks, to distrust most whites (since the reliable whites are few and relatively powerless in the face of white supremacy), and to promote forms of black self-love, self-defense, and self-determination. Black Nationalism views white supremacy as the definitive systemic constraint on black cultural, political, and economic development. More pointedly, black nationalists claim that American democracy is a modern form of tyranny on the part of the white majority over the black minority. For them, black sanity and freedom require that America not serve as the major framework in which to understand the future of black people. Instead, American civilization – like all civilizations – rises and falls, ebbs and flows. And owing to its deep-seated racism, this society does not warrant black allegiance or loyalty. White supremacy dictates the limits of the operation of American democracy – with black folk the indispensable sacrificial lamb vital to its sustenance. Hence black subordination constitutes the necessary condition for the flourishing of American democracy, the tragic prerequisite for America itself. This is, in part, what RICHARD WRIGHT meant when he noted, "The Negro is America's metaphor."

The most courageous and consistent of twentieth-century black nationalists – Marcus Garvey and Elijah Muhammad – adamantly rejected any form of American optimism or exceptionalism. Du Bois feared that if they were right, he would be left in a state of paralyzing despair. A kind of despair that results not only when all credible options for black freedom in America are closed, but also when the very framework needed to understand and cope with that despair is shattered. The black nationalist challenge to Du Bois cuts much deeper than the rational and political possibilities for change; it resides at the visceral and existential levels of what to do about "what is" or when "what ought to be done" seems undoable. This frightening sense of foreboding pervades much of black America today – a sense that fans and fuels Black Nationalism.

By the 1950s, W. E. B. Du Bois's increasingly radical politics had led to his dismissal from the NAACP, indictment by the United States government as an agent of a foreign government, and, beginning in 1952, a six-year ban on foreign travel. Finally granted a passport in 1958, Du Bois traveled to England, the Soviet Union, and Africa, settling in Ghana in 1960 and living there until his death in 1963. *Photo by Morgan and Marvin P. Smith; Photographs and Prints Division, Schomburg Center for Research in Black Culture, The New York Public Library, Astor, Lenox and Tilden Foundation*

Du Bois's American optimism screened him from this dark night of the soul. His American exceptionalism guarded him from that gray twilight between "nothing to be done" and "I can't go on like this" – a Beckett-like dilemma in which the wait and search for Godot, or for freedom, seem endless. This militant despair about the black condition is expressed in that most arresting of black nationalist speeches by Rev. HENRY HIGHLAND GARNET in 1843: "If we must bleed, let it come all at once – rather die freemen than live to be slaves. It is impossible like the children of Israel, to make a grand Exodus from the land of bondage. The pharaoh's on both sides of the blood-red waters!"

Du Bois's response to such despair is to say, "we surely must do something" – for such rebellion is suicidal and the notion of a separate black nation quixotic. So, he seems to say, let us continue to wait and search for Godot in America – even if it seems, with our luck, that all we get is "Pozzo" (new forms of disrespect, disregard, degradation, and defamation). American optimism couched within the ideals of the American experiment contains crucial components for any desirable form of black self-determination or modern nationhood: precious standards of constitutional democracy, the rule of law, individual liberties, and the dignity of common folk. Yet American optimism – in the ugly face of American white supremacist practices – warrants, if not outright rejection, at least vast attenuation. The twenty-first century will almost certainly not be a time in which American exceptionalism will flower in the world or American optimism will flourish among people of African descent.

If there are any historical parallels between black Americans at the end of the twentieth century and other peoples in earlier times, two candidates loom large: Tolstoy's Russia and Kafka's Prague – soul-starved Russians a generation after the emancipation of the serfs in 1861 and anxiety-ridden Central European Jews a generation before the European Holocaust in the 1940s. Indeed, my major intellectual disappointment with the great Du Bois lies in the fact that there are hardly any traces in his work of any serious grappling with the profound thinkers and spiritual wrestlers in the modern West from these two groups – major figures obsessed with the problem of evil in their time.

We see in Du Bois no engagement with Leo Tolstoy, Fyodor Dostoyevsky, Ivan Turgenev, Alexander Herzen, Lev Shestov, Anton Chekhov, or Franz Kafka, Max Brod, Kurt Tucholsky, Hermann Broch, Hugo Bergmann, or Karl Kraus. These omissions are glaring because the towering figures in both groups were struggling with political and existential issues similar to those facing black people in America. For example, the Russian situation involved the humanity of degraded, impoverished peasants, the fragile stability of an identity-seeking empire, and the alienation of superfluous intellectuals; the Central European Jewish circumstance, the humanity of devalued middle-class Jews, the imminent collapse of a decadent empire, and the militant despair of self-hating intellectuals. The intellectual response on the part of the Russian authors was what Hegel would call "world-historical": they wrote many of the world's greatest novels, short stories, essays, and plays. The writers I cite put forward profound interpretations of the human condition that rejected any Enlightenment world-view, Victorian strategy, or worldly optimism. And although the Central European Jewish authors are often overlooked by contemporary intellectuals – owing to a tendency to focus on Western Europe – their intellectual response was monumental. They composed many of this century's most probing and penetrating novels, short stories, autobiographies, and letters.

Both Russian and Central European Jewish writers share deep elective affinities that underlie their distinctive voices: the "wind of the wing of madness" (to use Baudelaire's phrase) beats incessantly on their souls. The fear of impending social doom and dread of inevitable death haunt them, and they search for a precious individuality in the face of a terror-ridden society and a seductive (yet doubtful) nationalist option. In short, fruitful comparisons may be made between the Russian sense of the tragic and the Central European Jewish sense of the absurd and the black intellectual response to the African American predicament. Tolstoy's *War and Peace* (1869), *The Death of Ivan Ilych* (1886), and "How Much Land Does a Man Need?" (1886), Chekhov's *The Three Sisters* (1901) – the greatest novel, short story, brief tale, and play in modern Europe – and Kafka's "The Judgment" (1913), "The Metamorphosis" (1915), "In the Penal Colony" (1919), and "The Burrow" (1923) – some of the grandest fictive portraits of twentieth-century Europe – constitute the highest moments and most ominous murmurings in Europe before it entered the ugly and fiery inferno of totalitarianism. Similarly, the intellectual response of highbrow black artists – most of whom are musicians and often of plebeian origins – probes the depths of a black sense of the tragic and absurd that yields a subversive joy and sublime melancholia unknown to most in the New World. The form and content of Louis Armstrong's "West End Blues," Duke Ellington's "Mood Indigo," John Coltrane's "Alabama," and Sarah Vaughan's "Send in the Clowns" are a few of the peaks of the black cultural iceberg – towering examples of soul-making and spiritual wrestling that crystallize the most powerful interpretations of the human condition in black life. This is why the best of the black musical tradition in the twentieth century is the most profound and poignant body of artistic works in our time.

Like their Russian and Central European Jewish counterparts, the black artists grapple with madness and melancholia, doom and death, terror and horror, individuality and identity. Unlike them, the black artists do so against the background of an African heritage that puts a premium on voice and body, sound and silence, and the foreground is occupied by an American tradition that highlights mobility and novelty, individuality and democracy. The explosive products of this multilayered cultural hybridity – with its new diasporic notions of time and space, place and face – take us far beyond Du Bois's enlightened optimism. Instead, the profound black cultural efforts to express the truth of modern tragic existence and build on the ruins of modern absurd experiences at the core of American culture take us to the end of this dreadful century. These black artistic endeavors prefigure and pose the most fundamental and formidable challenges to a twilight civilization – an American Empire adrift on turbulent seas in a dark fog. William Faulkner, Mark Twain, Thomas Pynchon, and, above all, the incomparable Herman Melville – the only great Euro-American novelists to be spoken of in the same breath as Tolstoy and Kafka, Armstrong and Coltrane – grasp crucial aspects of this black condition. Just as Richard Wright, RALPH ELLISON, JAMES BALDWIN, and, preeminently, TONI MORRISON guide us through the tragedies and absurdities within the Veil (or behind the color curtain) to disclose on the page what is best revealed in black song, speech, sermon, bodily performance, and the eloquence of black silence. Yet despite his shortcomings, the great Du Bois remains the springboard for any examination of black strivings in American civilization.

On Black Strivings

Black strivings are the creative and complex products of the terrifying African encounter with the absurd in America – and the absurd as America. Like any other group of human beings, black people forged ways of life and ways of struggle under circumstances not of their own choosing. They constructed structures of meaning and structures of feeling in the face of the fundamental facts of human existence – death, dread, despair, disease, and disappointment. Yet the specificity of black culture – namely, those features that distinguish black culture from other cultures – lies in both the African and American character of black people's attempts to sustain their mental sanity and spiritual health, social life and political struggle in the midst of a slaveholding, white supremacist civilization that viewed itself as the most enlightened, free, tolerant, and democratic experiment in human history.

Any serious examination of black culture should begin with what Du Bois dubbed, in Faustian terms, the "spiritual strivings" of black people – the dogged determination to survive and subsist, the tenacious will to persevere, persist, and maybe even prevail. These "strivings" occur within the whirlwind of white supremacy – that is, as responses to the vicious attacks on black beauty, black intelligence, black moral character, black capability, and black possibility. To put it bluntly, every major institution in American society – churches, universities, courts, academies of science, governments, economies, newspapers, magazines, television, film, and others – attempted to exclude black people from the human family in the name of white supremacist ideology. This unrelenting assault on black humanity produced the fundamental condition of black culture – that of black invisibility and namelessness.

This basic predicament exists on at least four levels: existential, social, political, and economic. The existential level is the most relevant here because it has to do with what it means to be a person and live a life under the horrifying realities of racist assault. To be a black human being under circumstances in which one's humanity is questioned is not only to face a difficult challenge but also to exercise a demanding discipline.

The sheer absurdity of being a black human being whose black body is viewed as an abomination, whose black thoughts and ideas are perceived as debased, and whose black pain and grief are rendered invisible on the human and moral scale is the New World context in which black culture emerged. Black people are first and foremost an African people, in that the cultural baggage they brought with them to the New World was grounded in their earlier responses to African conditions. Yet the rich African traditions – including the kinetic orality, passionate physicality, improvisational intellectuality, and combative spirituality – would undergo creative transformation when brought into contact with European languages and rituals in the context of the New World. For example, there would be no JAZZ without New World Africans with European languages and instruments.

On the crucial existential level relating to black invisibility and namelessness, the first difficult challenge and demanding discipline are to ward off madness and discredit suicide as a desirable option. A central preoccupation of black culture is that of confronting candidly the ontological wounds, psychic scars, and existential bruises of black people while fending off insanity and self-annihilation. Black culture consists of black modes of being-in-the-world obsessed with black sadness and sorrow, black agony and anguish, black heartache and heartbreak without fully succumbing to the numbing effects of such misery – to never allow such misery to have the last word. This is why the "urtext" of black culture is neither a word nor a book, not an architectural monument or a legal brief. Instead, it is a guttural cry and a wrenching moan – a cry not so much for help as for home, a moan less out of complaint than for recognition. The most profound black cultural products – John Coltrane's saxophone solos, James Cleveland's gut gospels, Billie Holiday's vocal leaps, Rev. Gardner Taylor's rhapsodic sermons, James Baldwin's poignant essays, Alvin Ailey's graceful dances, Toni Morrison's dissonant novels – transform and transfigure in artistic form this cry and moan. The deep black meaning of this cry and moan goes back to the indescribable cries of Africans on the slave ships during the cruel transatlantic voyages to America and the indecipherable moans of enslaved Afro-Americans on Wednesday nights or Sunday mornings near god-forsaken creeks or on wooden benches at prayer meetings in makeshift black churches. This fragile existential arsenal – rooted in silent tears and weary lament – supports black endurance against madness and suicide. The primal black cries and moans lay bare the profoundly tragicomic character of black life. Ironically, they also embody the life-preserving content of black styles – creative ways of fashioning power and strength through the body and language that yield black joy and ecstasy.

Du Bois captures one such primal scene of black culture at the beginning of *The Souls of Black Folk,* in chapter 1, "Of Our Spiritual Strivings." He starts with 13 lines from the poem "The Crying of Water" by Arthur Symons, the English symbolist critic and decadent poet who went mad a few years after writing the poem. The hearts of human beings in a heartless slave trade cry out like the sea: "All life long crying without avail, / As the water all night long is crying to me."

This metaphorical association of black hearts, black people, and black culture with water (the sea or a river) runs deep in black artistic expression – as in Langston Hughes's recurring refrain "My soul has grown deep like the rivers" in "The Negro Speaks of Rivers." Black striving resides primarily in movement and motion, resilience and resistance against the paralysis of madness and the stillness of death. As it is for Jim in Mark Twain's *The Adventures of Huckleberry Finn* (1885), the river – a road that moves – is the means by which black people can flee from a menacing racist society. Du Bois continues with the musical bars of the Negro spiritual "Nobody Knows the Trouble I've Seen." This spiritual is known not simply for its plaintive melody but also for its inexplicable lyrical reversal.

Nobody knows the trouble I've seen
Nobody knows but Jesus
Nobody knows the trouble I've seen
Glory hallelujah!

This exemplary shift from a mournful brooding to a joyful praising is the product of courageous efforts to look life's abyss in the face and keep "keepin' on." This struggle is sustained primarily by the integrity of style, song, and spirituality in a beloved community (e.g., Jesus' proclamation of the Kingdom). It is rather like Ishmael's tragicomic "free and easy sort of genial, desperado philosophy" in *Moby Dick*, but it is intensified by the fiery art of Aretha Franklin's majestic shouts for joy.

The first of Du Bois's own words in the text completes the primal scene of black culture: "Between me and the other world there is ever an unasked question: unasked by some through feelings of delicacy; by others through the difficulty of rightly framing it. All, nevertheless, flutter round it. They approach me in a half-hesitant sort of way, eye me curiously or compassionately, and then, instead of saying directly, How does it feel to be a problem? they say, I know an excellent colored man in my town; or, I fought at Mechanicsville; or, Do not these Southern outrages make our blood boil? At these I smile, or am interested, or reduce the boiling to a simmer, as the occasion may require. To the real question, How does it feel to be a problem? I answer seldom a word. And yet, being a problem is a strange experience, – peculiar even for one who has never been anything else, save perhaps in babyhood.... "

This seminal passage spells out the basic components of black invisibility and namelessness: black people as a problem-people rather than people with problems; black people as abstractions and objects rather than as individuals and persons; black and white worlds divided by a thick wall (or a Veil) that requires role-playing and mask-wearing rather than genuine humane interaction; black rage, anger, and fury concealed in order to assuage white fear and anxiety; and black people rootless and homeless on a perennial journey to discover who they are in a society content to see blacks remain the permanent underdog.

To view black people as a problem-people is to view them as an undifferentiated blob, a homogeneous bloc, or a monolithic conglomerate. Each black person is interchangeable, indistinguishable, or substitutable since all black people are believed to have the same views and values, sentiments and sensibilities. Hence one set of negative stereotypes holds for all of them, no matter how high certain blacks may ascend in the white world (e.g., "savages in a suit or suite"). And the mere presence of black bodies in a white context generates white unease and discomfort, even among whites of goodwill.

This problematizing of black humanity deprives black people of individuality, diversity, and heterogeneity. It reduces black folk to abstractions and objects born of white fantasies and insecurities – as exotic or transgressive entities, as hypersexual or criminal animals. The celebrated opening passage of Ralph Ellison's classic novel, *Invisible Man* (1952), highlights this reduction. "I am an invisible man. No, I am not a spook like those who haunted Edgar Allan Poe; nor am I one of your Hollywood-movie ectoplasms. I am a man of substance, of flesh and bone, fiber and liquids – and I might even be said to possess a mind. I am invisible, understand, simply because people refuse to see me. Like the bodiless heads you see sometimes in circus sideshows, it is as though I have been surrounded by mirrors of hard, distorting glass. When they approach me they see only my surroundings, themselves, or figments of their imagination – indeed, everything and anything except me."

This distorted perception – the failure to see the humanity and individuality of black people – has its source in the historic "Veil" (slavery, JIM CROW, and segregation) that separates the black and white worlds. Ironically, this refusal to see a people whose epidermis is most visible exists alongside a need to keep tight surveillance over these people. This Veil not only precludes honest communication between blacks and whites, it also forces blacks to live in two worlds in order to survive. Whites need not understand or live in the black world in order to thrive. But blacks must grapple with the painful "doubleconsciousness" that may result in "an almost morbid sense of personality and a moral hesitancy which is fatal to self-confidence." Du Bois notes, "The worlds within and without the Veil of Color are changing, and changing rapidly, but not at the same rate, not in the same way; and this must produce a peculiar wrenching of the soul, a peculiar sense of doubt and bewilderment. Such a double life, with double thoughts, double duties, and double social classes, must give rise to double words and double ideals, and tempt the mind to pretence or to revolt, to hypocrisy or to radicalism."

Echoing PAUL LAURENCE DUNBAR's famous poem "We Wear the Mask," Du Bois proclaims that "the price of culture is a Lie." Why? Because black people will not succeed in American society if they are fully and freely themselves. Instead, they must "endure petty insults with a smile, shut [their] eyes to wrong." They must not be too frank and outspoken and must never fail to flatter and be pleasant in order to lessen white unease and discomfort. Needless to say, this is not the raw stuff for healthy relations between black people and white people.

Yet this suppression of black rage – the reducing "the boiling to a simmer" – backfires in the end. It reinforces a black obsession with the psychic scars, ontological wounds, and existential bruises that tend to reduce the tragic to the pathetic. Instead of exercising agency or engaging in action against the odds, one may wallow in self-pity, acknowledging the sheer absurdity of it all. After playing the role and wearing the mask in the white world, one may accept the white world's view of one's self. As Du Bois writes, "It is a peculiar sensation, this double-consciousness, this sense of always looking at one's self through the eyes of others, of measuring one's soul by the tape of a world that looks on in amused contempt and pity."

Toni Morrison explores this dilemma of black culture through her moving portrayal of the character of Sweet Home in her profound novel *Beloved* (1987), similar to JEAN TOOMER's Karintha and Fern in his marvelous and magical text *Cane* (1923). "For the sadness was at her center, the desolated center where the self that was no self made its home."

This theme of black rootlessness and homelessness is inseparable from black namelessness. When James Baldwin writes about these issues in *Nobody Knows My Name* (1961) and *No Name in the Street* (1972), he is trying to explore effective ways to resist the white supremacist imposition of subordinate roles, stations, and identities on blacks. He is attempting to devise some set of existential strategies against the overwhelming onslaught of white dehumanization, devaluation, and degradation. The search for black space (home), black place (roots), and black face (name) is a flight from the visceral effects of white supremacy. Toni Morrison characterizes these efforts as products of a process of "dirtying you." "That anybody white could take your whole self for anything that came to mind. Not just work, kill, or maim you, but dirty you. Dirty you so bad you couldn't like yourself anymore. Dirty you so bad you forgot who you were and couldn't think it Up."

Toni Morrison's monumental novel holds a privileged place in black culture and modernity precisely because she takes this dilemma to its logical conclusion – that black flight from white supremacy (a chamber of horrors for black people) may lead to the murder of those loved ones who are candidates for the "dirtying" process. The black mother, Sethe, kills her daughter, Beloved, because she loved her so, "to out-hurt the hurter," as an act of resistance against the "dirtying" process. "And though she and others lived through and got over it, she could never let it happen to her own. The best thing she was, was her children. Whites might dirty her all right, but not her best thing, her beautiful, magical best thing – the part of her that was clean. No undreamable dreams about whether the headless, feetless torso hanging in the tree with a sign on it was her husband or Paul A; whether the bubbling-hot girls in the colored-school fire set by patriots included her daughter; whether a gang of whites invaded her daughter's private parts, soiled her daughter's thighs and threw her daughter out of the wagon. She might have to work the slaughterhouse yard, but not her daughter. And no one, nobody on this earth, would list her daughter's characteristics on the animal side of the paper. No. Oh no.... Sethe had refused – and refused still.... [W]hat she had done was right because it came from true love."

Is death the only black space (home), place (roots), and face (name) safe from a pervasive white supremacy? Toni Morrison's Sethe echoes Du Bois's own voice upon the painful passing of his first-born. For Sethe, as for Tolstoy's Ivan, Chekhov's Bishop Pyotr, Kafka's Josephine, Hawthorne's Goodman Brown, Hardy's Jude, Bilchner's Woyzeck, Drelser's Hurstwood, and Shakespeare's Lear, death is the great liberator from suffering and evil.

"But Love sat beside his cradle, and in his ear Wisdom waited to speak. Perhaps now he knows the All-love, and needs not to be wise. Sleep, then, child, – sleep till I sleep and waken to a baby voice and the ceaseless patter of little feet – above the Veil." The most effective and enduring black responses to invisibility and namelessness are those forms of individual and collective black resistance predicated on a deep and abiding black love. These responses take the shape of prophetic thought and action: bold, fearless, courageous attempts to tell the truth about and bear witness to black suffering and to keep faith with a vision of black redemption. Like the "urtexts" of the guttural cry and wrenching moan – enacted in Charlie Parker's bebop sound, Dinah Washington's cool voice, Richard Pryor's comic performances, and James Brown's inimitable funk – the prophetic utterance that focuses on black suffering and sustains a hope-against-hope for black freedom constitutes the heights of black culture. The spiritual depths (the how and what) of Martin Luther King's visionary orations, Nat King Cole's silky soul, August Wilson's probing plays, Martin Puryear's unique sculpture, Harold and Fayard Nicholas's existential acrobatics, Jacob Lawrence's powerful paintings, Marvin Gaye's risky falsettos, Fannie Lou Hamer's fighting songs, and, above all, John Coltrane's *A Love Supreme* exemplify such heights. Two of the greatest moments in black literature also enact such high-quality performances. First, James Baldwin's great self-descriptive visionary passage in *Go Tell It on the Mountain* (1953): "Yes, their parts were all cut off, they were dishonored, their very names were nothing more than dust blown disdainfully across the field of time – to fall where, to blossom where, bringing forth what fruit hereafter, where? – their very names were not their own. Behind them was the darkness, nothing but the darkness, and all around them destruction, and before them nothing but the fire – a bastard people, far from God, singing and crying in the wilderness! Yet, most strangely, and from deeps not before discovered, his faith looked up; before the wickedness that he saw, the wickedness from which he fled, he yet beheld, like a flaming standard in the middle of the air, that power of redemption to which he must, till death, bear witness; which, though it crush him utterly, he could not deny; though none among the living might ever behold it, he had beheld it, and must keep the faith."

For Baldwin the seemingly impossible flight from white supremacy takes the form of a Chekhovian effort to endure lovingly and compassionately, guided by a vision of freedom and empowered by a tradition of black love and faith. To be a bastard people – wrenched from Africa and in, but never fully of, America – is to be a people of highly limited options, if any at all. To bear witness is to make and remake, invent and reinvent oneself as a person and people by keeping faith with the best of such earlier efforts, yet also to acknowledge that the very new selves and peoples to emerge will never fully find a space, place, or face in American society – or Africa. This perennial process of self-making and self-inventing is propelled by a self-loving and self-trusting made possible by overcoming a colonized mind, body, and soul.

This is precisely what Morrison describes in the great litany of black love in Baby Suggs's prayer and sermon of laughter, dance, tears, and silence in "a wide-open place cut deep in the woods nobody knew for what at the end of a path known only to deer and whoever cleared the land in the first place." On those hot Saturday afternoons, Baby Suggs "offered up to them her great big heart." "She told them that the only grace they could have was the grace they could imagine. That if they could not see it, they would not have it. 'Here,' she said, 'in this here place, we flesh; flesh that weeps, laughs; flesh that dances on bare feet in grass. Love it. Love it hard. Yonder they do not love your flesh. They despise it. They don't love your eyes; they'd just as soon pick em out. No more do they love the skin on your back. Yonder they flay it. And O my people they do not love your hands. Those they only use, tie, bind, chopoff and leave empty. Love your hands! Love them. Raise them up and kiss them. Touch others with them, pat them together, stroke them on your face 'cause they don't love that either. You got to love it, you! And no, they ain't in love with your mouth. Yonder, out there, they will see it broken and break it again. What you say out of it they will not heed. What you scream from it they do not hear. What you put into it to nourish your body they will snatch away and give you leavins instead. No, they don't love your mouth. You got to love it. This is flesh I'm talking about here. Flesh that needs to be loved. Feet that need to rest and to dance; backs that need support; shoulders that need arms, strong arms I'm telling you. And O my people, out yonder, hear me, they do not love your neck unnoosed and straight. So love your neck; put a hand on it, grace it, stroke it and hold it up. And all your inside parts that they'd just as soon slop for hogs, you got to love them. The dark, dark liver – love it, love it, and the beat and beating heart, love that too. More than eyes or feet. More than lungs that have yet to draw free air. More than your life-holding womb and your life-giving private parts, hear me now, love your heart. For this is the prize.' Saying no more, she stood up then and danced with her twisted hip the rest of what her heart had to say while the others opened their mouths and gave her the music. Long notes held until the four-part harmony was perfect enough for their deeply loved flesh."

In this powerful passage Toni Morrison depicts in a concrete and graphic way the enactment and expression of black love, black joy, black community, and black faith that bears witness to black suffering and keeps alive a vision of black hope. Black bonds of affection, black networks of support, black ties of empathy, and black harmonies of spiritual camaraderie provide the grounds for the fragile existential weaponry with which to combat black invisibility and namelessness.

Yet these forceful strategies in black culture still have not successfully come to terms with the problem. The black collective quest for a name that designates black people in the United States continues – from colored, Negro, black, Afro-American, Abyssinian, Ethiopian, Nubian, Bilalian, American African, American, African to African American. The black individual quest for names goes on, with unique new ones for children – e.g., Tarsell, Signithia, Jewayne – designed to set them apart from all others for the purpose of accenting their individuality and offsetting their invisibility. And most important, black rage proliferates – sometimes unabated.

Of all the hidden injuries of blackness in American civilization, black rage is the most deadly, the most lethal. Although black culture is in no way reducible

W. E. B. Du Bois congratulates Paul Robeson after Robeson, in a speech delivered in Paris in 1949, denounced United States president Harry S. Truman's program for African development and called for black solidarity with the Soviet Union. *UPI/CORBIS*

to or identical with black rage, it is inseparable from black rage. Du Bois's renowned eulogy for ALEXANDER CRUMMELL, the greatest nineteenth-century black intellectual, is one of the most penetrating analyses of black rage. Du Bois begins his treatment with a virtually generic description of black childhoods – a description that would hold for Arthur Ashe or ICE CUBE, KATHLEEN BATTLE or QUEEN LATIFAH. "This is the history of a human heart, – the tale of a black boy who many long years ago began to struggle with life that he might know the world and know himself. Three temptations he met on those dark dunes that lay gray and dismal before the wonder-eyes of the child: the Temptation of Hate, that stood out against the red dawn; the Temptation of Despair, that darkened noonday; and the Temptation of Doubt, that ever steals along with twilight. Above all, you must hear of the vales he crossed, – the Valley of Humiliation and the Valley of the Shadow of Death."

Black self-hatred and hatred of others parallels that of all human beings, who must gain some sense of themselves and the world. But the tremendous weight of white supremacy makes this human struggle for mature black selfhood even more difficult. As black children come to view themselves more and more as the degraded other, the temptation of hate grows, "gliding stealthily into [their] laughter, fading into [their] play, and seizing [their] dreams by day and night with rough, rude turbulence. So [they ask] of sky and sun and flower the never-answered Why? and love, as [they grow], neither the world nor the world's rough ways."

The two major choices in black culture (or any culture) facing those who succumb to the temptation of hate are a self-hatred that leads to self-destruction or a hatred of others – degraded others – that leads to vengeance of some sort. These options often represent two sides of the same coin. The case of Bigger Thomas, portrayed by Richard Wright in his great novel *Native Son* (1940), is exemplary in this regard. "Bigger's face was metallically black in the strong sunlight. There was in his eyes a pensive, brooding amusement, as of a man who had been long confronted and tantalized by a riddle whose answer seemed always just on the verge of escaping him, but prodding him irresistibly on to seek its solution. The silence irked Bigger; he was anxious to do something to evade looking so squarely at this problem."

The riddle to which Bigger seeks an answer is the riddle of his black existence in America – and he evades it in part because the pain, fear, silence, and hatred cut so deep. Like the "huge black rat" that appears at the beginning of the novel, Bigger reacts to his circumstances instinctually. Yet his instinct to survive is intertwined with his cognitive perception that white supremacy is out to get him. To make himself and invent himself as a black person in America is to strike out against white supremacy – out of pain, fear, silence, and hatred. The result is psychic terror and physical violence – committed against black Bessie and white Mary. "Bigger rose and went to the window. His hands caught the cold steel bars in a hard grip. He knew as he stood there that he could never tell why he had killed. It was not that he did not really want to tell, but the telling of it would have involved an explanation of his entire life. The actual killing of Mary and Bessie was not what concerned him most; it was knowing and feeling that he could never make anybody know what had driven him to it. His crimes were known, but what he had felt before he committed them would never be known. He would have gladly admitted his guilt if he had thought that in doing so he could have also given in the same breath a sense of the deep, choking hate that had been his life, a hate that he had not wanted to have, but could not help having. How could he do that? The impulsion to try to tell was as deep as had been the urge to kill."

The temptation to hate is a double-edged sword. Bigger's own self-hatred not only leads him to hate other blacks but also to deny the humanity of whites. Yet he can overcome this self-hatred only when he views himself as a self-determining agent who is willing to take responsibility for his actions and acknowledge his connection with others. Although Wright has often been criticized for casting Bigger as a pitiful victim, subhuman monster, and isolated individualist – as in James Baldwin's "Everybody's Protest Novel" and "Many Thousands Gone" in *Notes of a Native Son* (1955) – Wright presents brief moments in which Bigger sees the need to transcend his victim status and rapacious individualism. When his family visits him in jail, Bigger responds to their tears and anger. "Bigger wanted to comfort them in the presence of the white folks, but did not know how. Desperately, he cast about for something to say. Hate and shame boiled in him against the people behind his back; he tried to think of words that would defy them, words that would let them know that he had a world and life of his own in spite of them."

Wright does not disclose the internal dynamics of this black world of Bigger's own, but Bigger does acknowledge that he is part of this world. For example, his actions had dire consequences for his sister, Vera. "'Bigger,' his mother sobbed, trying to talk through her tears. 'Bigger, honey, she won't go to school no more. She says the other girls look at her and make her 'shamed.... ' He had lived and acted on the assumption that he was alone, and now he saw that he had not been. What he had done made others suffer. No matter how much he would long for them to forget him, they would not be able to. His family was a part of him, not only in blood, but in spirit. He sat on the cot and his mother knelt at his feet. Her face was lifted to his; her eyes were empty, eyes that looked upward when the last hope of earth had failed."

Yet even this family connection fails to undercut the layers of hate Bigger feels for himself and them. It is only when Bigger receives unconditional support and affirmation across racial lines that his self-hatred and hatred of others subsides – for a moment, from white Jan, the boyfriend of the slain Mary. "He looked at Jan and saw a white face, but an honest face. This white man believed in him, and the moment he felt that belief he felt guilty again; but in a different sense now. Suddenly, this white man had come up to him, flung aside the curtain and walked into the room of his life. Jan had spoken a declaration of friendship that would make other white men hate him: a particle of white rock had detached itself from that looming mountain of white hate and had rolled down the slope, stopping still at his feet. The word had become flesh. For the first time in his life a white man became a human being to him; and the reality of Jan's humanity came in a stab of remorse: he had killed what this man loved and had hurt him. He saw Jan as though someone had performed an operation upon his eyes, or as though someone had snatched a deforming mask from Jan's face."

In both instances Bigger lurches slightly beyond the temptation of hate when he perceives himself as an agent and subject accountable for the consequences of his actions – such as the victimization of his own black sister and a white person. Yet the depths of his self-hatred – his deep-seated colonized mind – permit only a glimpse of self-transformation when the friendship of a white fellow victim is offered to him.

Similar to Bigger Thomas, Alexander Crummell was inspired by a white significant other – Beriah Green. This sort of sympathetic connection makes the temptation of hate grow "fainter and less sinister. It did not wholly fade away, but diffused itself and lingered thick at the edges." Through both Bigger Thomas and Alexander Crummell we see the tremendous pull of the white world and the tragic need for white recognition and affirmation among so many black people.

The temptation of despair is the second element of black rage in Du Bois's analysis. This temptation looms large when black folk conclude that "the way of the world is closed to me." This conclusion yields two options – nihilism and hedonism. Again, two sides of the same coin. This sense of feeling imprisoned, bound, constrained, and circumscribed is a dominant motif in black cultural expressions. Again, Wright captures this predicament well with Bigger Thomas. "'Goddammit!' 'What's the matter?' 'They don't let us do nothing.' 'Who?' 'The white folks.' 'You talk like you just now finding that out,' Gus said. 'Naw. But I just can't get used to it,' Bigger said. 'I swear to God I can't. I know I oughtn't think about it, but I can't help it. Every time I think about it I feel like somebody's poking a red-hot iron down my throat. Goddammit, look! We live here and they live there. We black and they white. They got things and we ain't. They do things and we can't. It's just like living in jail. Half the time I feel like I'm on the outside of the world peeping in through a knot-hole in the fence.'"

The temptation of despair is predicated on a world with no room for black space, place, or face. It feeds on a black futurelessness and black hopelessness – a situation in which visions and dreams of possibility have dried up like raisins in the sun. This nihilism leads to lives of drift, lives in which any pleasure, especially instant gratification, is the primary means of feeling alive. Anger and aggression usually surface in such lives. Bigger says, "I hurt folks 'cause I felt I had to; that's all. They was crowding me too close; they wouldn't give me no room.... I thought they was hard and I acted hard.... I'll be feeling and thinking that they didn't see me and I didn't see them."

The major black cultural response to the temptation of despair has been the black Christian tradition, dominated by music in song, prayer, and sermon. The unique role of this tradition is often noted. Du Bois writes "that the Negro church antedates the Negro home, leads to an explanation of much that is paradoxical in this communistic institution and in the morals of its members. But especially it leads us to regard this institution as peculiarly the expression of the inner ethical life of a people in a sense seldom true elsewhere."

Even Bigger Thomas – the most cynical and secular of rebels in the black literary tradition – is captivated by the power of black church music, the major caressing artistic flow in the black *Sittlichkeit* (ethical life). "The singing from the church vibrated through him, suffusing him with a mood of sensitive sorrow. He tried not to listen, but it seeped into his feelings, whispering of another way of life and death.... The singing filled his ears; it was complete, self-contained, and it mocked his fear and loneliness, his deep yearning for a sense of wholeness. Its fullness contrasted so sharply with his hunger, its richness with his emptiness, that he recoiled from it while answering it."

The black church tradition, along with the rich musical tradition it spawned, generates a sense of movement, motion, and momentum that keeps despair at bay. As with any collective project or performance that puts a premium on change, transformation, conversion, and future possibility, the temptation of despair is not eliminated but attenuated. In this sense, the black church tradition has made ritual art and communal bonds out of black invisibility and namelessness. Ralph Ellison updates and secularizes this endeavor when he writes, "Perhaps I like Louis Armstrong because he's made poetry out of being invisible. I think it must be because he's unaware that he is invisible. And my own grasp of invisibility aids me to understand his music.... Invisibility, let me explain, gives one a slightly different sense of time, you're never quite on the beat. Sometimes you're ahead and sometimes behind. Instead of the swift and imperceptible flowing of time, you are aware of its nodes, those points where time stands still or from which it leaps ahead. And you slip into the breaks and look around. That's what you hear vaguely in Louis' music."

The temptation of doubt is the most persistent of the three temptations. White supremacy drums deeply into the hearts, minds, and souls of black people, causing them to expect little of one another and themselves. This black insecurity and self-doubt produces a debilitating black jealousy in the face of black "success" – a black jealousy that often takes the form of what Eldridge Cleaver called "nigger rituals" – namely, a vicious trashing of black "success" or a black "battle royal" for white spectators. Understandably, under conditions of invisibility and namelessness, most of those blacks with "visibility" and a "name" in the white world are often the object of black scorn and contempt. Such sad, self-fulfilling prophecies of black cowardice make the temptation of doubt especially seductive – one that fans and fuels the flames of black rage. Du Bois states, "Of all the three temptations, this one struck the deepest. Hate? He had outgrown so childish a thing. Despair? He had steeled his right arm against it, and fought it with the vigor of determination. But to doubt the worth of his life-work, – to doubt the destiny and capability of the race his soul loved because it was his; to find listless squalor instead of eager endeavor; to hear his own lips whispering, 'They do not care; they cannot know; they are dumb driven cattle, – why cast your pearls before swine?' – this, this seemed more than man could bear; and he closed the door, and sank upon the steps of the chancel, and cast his robe upon the floor and writhed."

The two principal options for action after one yields to the temptation of doubt in black culture are authoritarian subordination of the "ignorant" masses or individual escape from these masses into the white mainstream. These two options are not two sides of the same coin, though they often flow from a common source: an elitist vision that shuns democratic accountability. And although this elitist vision – that of the Exceptional Negro or Talented Tenth who is "better than those other blacks" – is found more readily among the black educated and middle class, some of the black

OPPOSITE : W. E. B. Du Bois is considered the greatest African American intellectual figure of the twentieth century. *CORBIS*

working poor and very poor subscribe to it too. Even Bigger Thomas. "As he rode, looking at the black people on the sidewalks, he felt that one way to end fear and shame was to make all those black people act together, rule them, tell them what to do, and make them do it.... But he felt that such would never happen to him and his black people, and he hated them and wanted to wave his hand and blot them out. Yet, he still hoped, vaguely. Of late he had liked to hear tell of men who could rule others, for in actions such as these he felt that there was a way to escape from this tight morass of fear and shame that sapped at the base of his life. He liked to hear of how Japan was conquering China; of how Hitler was running Jews to the ground; of how Mussolini was invading Spain. He was not concerned with whether these acts were right or wrong; they simply appealed to him as possible avenues of escape. He felt that some day there would be a black man who would whip the black people into a tight band and together they would act and end fear and shame. He never thought of this in precise mental images; he felt it; he would feel it for a while and then forget. But hope was always waiting somewhere deep down in him."

This hope for black unity and action was based on a profound doubt concerning the ability of black people to think for themselves and act on principles they had examined, scrutinized, and deliberately chosen. Ironically, this same elitist logic is at work among those who uncritically enter the white mainstream and accuse black people of lacking discipline and determination. Alexander Crummell overcame the difficult challenge of self-doubt and the doubt of other black folk by moving to Africa and later returning to America to fight for and "among his own, the low, the grasping, and the wicked, and with that unbending righteousness which is the sword of the just."

In the end, for Du Bois, Alexander Crummell triumphed over hate, despair, and doubt owing to "that full power within, that mighty inspiration" within the Veil. He was able to direct his black rage through moral channels sustained primarily by black bonds of affection, black networks of support, and black ties of empathy. Yet few today know his name and work, principally due to the thick Veil of color then and now: "His name today, in this broad land, means little, and comes to fifty million ears laden with no incense of memory or emulation. And herein lies the tragedy of the age: not that men are poor, – all men know something of poverty; not that men are wicked, – who is good? not that men are ignorant, – what is Truth? Nay, but that men know so little of men."

For Du Bois "the problem of the twentieth century is the problem of the color-line" largely because of the relative lack of communication across the Veil of color. For Du Bois the vicious legacy of white supremacy contributes to the arrested development of democracy. And since communication is the lifeblood of a democracy – the very measure of the vitality of its public life – we either come to terms with race and hang together, or ignore it and hang separately. This is why every examination of black strivings is an important part of understanding the prevailing crisis in American society.

A Twilight Civilization in Our Time

In our time – at the end of the twentieth century – the crisis of race in America is still raging. The problem of black invisibility and namelessness, however, remains marginal to the dominant accounts of our past and present and is relatively absent from our pictures of the future. In this age of globalization, with its impressive scientific and technological innovations in information, communication, and applied biology, a focus on the lingering effects of racism seems outdated and antiquated. The global cultural bazaar of entertainment and enjoyment, the global shopping mall of advertising and marketing, the global workplace of blue-collar and white-collar employment, and the global financial network of computerized transactions and megacorporate mergers appear to render any talk about race irrelevant.

Yet with the collapse of the Soviet Empire, the end of the cold war, and the rise of Japan, corrupt and top-heavy nation-states are being eclipsed by imperial corporations as public life deteriorates owing to class polarization, racial balkanization, and especially a predatory market culture. With the vast erosion of civic networks that nurture and care for citizens – such as families, neighborhoods, and schools – and with what might be called the gangsterization of everyday life, characterized by the escalating fear of violent attack, vicious assault, or cruel insult, we are witnessing a pervasive cultural decay in American civilization. Even public discourse has degenerated into petty name calling and finger pointing, with little room for mutual respect and empathetic exchange. Increasing suicides and homicides, alcoholism and drug addiction, distrust and disloyalty, cold-heartedness and mean-spiritedness, isolation and loneliness, cheap sexual thrills and cowardly patriarchal violence are still other symptoms of this decay. Yet race – in the coded language of welfare reform, immigration policy, criminal punishment, affirmative action, and suburban privatization – remains a central signifier in the political debate.

As in late nineteenth-century Russia and early twentieth-century Central Europe, the ruling political right hides and conceals the privilege and wealth of the few (the 1 percent who own 48 percent of the net financial wealth, the top 10 percent who own 86 percent, the top 20 percent who have 94 percent!) and pits the downwardly mobile middlers against the downtrodden poor. This age-old strategy of scapegoating the most vulnerable, frightening the most insecure, and supporting the most comfortable constitutes a kind of iron law signaling the decline of modern civilizations, as in Tolstoy's Russia and Kafka's Central Europe: chaotic and inchoate rebellion from below, withdrawal and retreat from public life from above, and a desperate search for authoritarian law and order, at any cost, from the middle. In America this suggests not so much a European style of fascism but rather a homespun brand of authoritarian democracy – the systemic stigmatizing, regulating, and policing of the degraded others – women, gays, lesbians, Latinos, Jews, Asians, Indians, and especially black people. As Sinclair Lewis warned over a half century ago, fascism, American-style, can happen here.

Welfare reform means, on the ground, poor people (disproportionately black) with no means of support. Criminal punishment means hundreds of thousands of black men in crowded prisons – many in there forever. And suburban privatization means black urban poor citizens locked into decrepit public schools, dilapidated housing, inadequate health care, and unavailable child care. Furthermore, the lowest priorities on the global corporate agenda of the political right – the low quantity of jobs with a living wage and the low quality

of life for children – have the greatest consequences for the survival of any civilization. Instead, we have generational layers of unemployed and underemployed people (often uncounted in our national statistics) and increasing numbers of hedonistic and nihilistic young people (of all classes, races, genders, and regions) with little interest in public life and with little sense of moral purpose.

This is the classic portrait of a twilight civilization whose dangerous rumblings – now intermittent in much of America but rampant in most of black urban America – will more than likely explode in the twenty-first century if we stay on the present conservative course. In such a bleak scenario, given the dominant tendencies of our day, Du Bois's heralded Talented Tenth will by and large procure a stronger foothold in the well-paid professional managerial sectors of the global economy, and more and more will become intoxicated with the felicities of a parvenu bourgeois existence. The heroic few will attempt to tell unpleasant truths about our plight and bear prophetic witness to our predicament as well as try to organize and mobilize (and be organized and mobilized by) the economically devastated, culturally degraded, and politically marginalized black working poor and very poor. Since a multiracial alliance of progressive meddlers, liberal slices of the corporate elite, and subversive energy from below is the only vehicle by which some form of radical democratic accountability can redistribute resources and wealth and restructure the economy and government so that all benefit, the significant secondary efforts of the black Talented Tenth alone in the twenty-first century will be woefully inadequate and thoroughly frustrating. Yet even progressive social change, though desirable and necessary, may not turn back the deeper and deadly processes of cultural decay in late twentieth-century America.

As this Talented Tenth comes to be viewed more and more with disdain and disgust by the black working poor and very poor, not only class envy but class hatred in black America will escalate in the midst of a more isolated and insulated black America. This will deepen the identity crisis of the black Talented Tenth – a crisis of survivor's guilt and cultural rootlessness. As the glass ceilings (limited promotions) and golden cuffs (big position and good pay with little or no power) remain in place for most, though not all, blacks in corporate America, we will see anguish and hedonism intensify among much of the Talented Tenth. The conservative wing of black elites will climb on the bandwagon of the political right – some for sincere reasons, most for opportunistic ones – as the black working poor and very poor try to cope with the realities of death, disease, and destruction. The progressive wing of the black elite will split into a vociferous (primarily male-led) black nationalist camp that opts for self-help at the lower and middle levels of the entrepreneurial sectors of the global economy and a visionary (disproportionately woman-led) radical democratic camp that works assiduously to keep alive a hope – maybe the last hope – for a twilight civilization that once saw itself as the "last best hope of earth."

After 95 years of the most courageous and unflagging devotion to black freedom witnessed in the twentieth century, W E. B. Du Bois not only left America for Africa but concluded, "I just cannot take any more of this country's treatment. We leave for Ghana October 5th and I set no date for return.... Chin up, and fight on, but realize that American Negroes can't win."

In the end Du Bois's Enlightenment world-view, Victorian strategies, and American optimism failed him. He left America in militant despair – the very despair he had avoided earlier – and mistakenly hoped for the rise of a strong postcolonial and united Africa. Echoing Tolstoy's claim that "it's intolerable to live in Russia.... I've decided to emigrate to England forever" (though he never followed through) and Kafka's dream to leave Prague and live in Palestine (though he died before he could do so), Du Bois concluded that black strivings in a twilight civilization were unbearable for him yet still imperative for others – even if he could not envision black freedom in America as realizable.

For those of us who stand on his broad shoulders, let us begin where he ended – with his militant despair; let us look candidly at the tragicomic and absurd character of black life in America in the spirit of John Coltrane and Toni Morrison; let us continue to strive with genuine compassion, personal integrity, and human decency to fight for radical democracy in the face of the frightening abyss – or terrifying inferno – of the twenty-first century, clinging to "a hope not hopeless but unhopeful."

See Also

Decolonization in Africa: An Interpretation; Middle Passage, The; Slavery in the United States; Transatlantic Slave Trade; Slavery in Latin America and the Caribbean; Ailey, Alvin; Armstrong, Louis ("Satchmo"); Ashe, Arthur Robert, Jr.; Baraka, Amiri; Civil Rights Movement; Cleaver, Eldridge Leroy; Cleveland, James Edward; Cole, Nat ("King"); Coltrane, John William; Du Bois, William Edward Burghardt (W. E. B.); East St. Louis, Illinois, Riot of 1917; Franklin, Aretha Louise; Garvey, Marcus Mosiah; Gaye, Marvin; Hamer, Fannie Lou; Holiday, Billie; Hughes, Langston; King, Martin Luther, Jr.; Lawrence, Jacob Armstead; Nicholas Brothers; Pryor, Richard Franklin Lenox Thomas; Singleton, Benjamin ("Pap"); Spanish-Cuban-American War, African Americans in the; Taylor, Gardner Calvin; Vaughan, Sarah; Washington, Booker Taliaferro; Washington, Dinah; Wells-Barnett, Ida Bell; Wilson, August; Sly and the Family Stone; Ellington, Edward Kennedy ("Duke"); Spirituals, African American; Black Church, The; Black Nationalism in the United States.

North America

Weems, Carrie Mae

(b. April 20, 1953, Portland, Ore.), African American photographer, folklorist, and self-proclaimed "image-maker" whose provocative images depict gender and RACIAL STEREOTYPES.

Carrie Mae Weems grew up in a working-class family in the western United States. After studying at Cal Arts, she earned a master of fine arts degree in photography from the University of California, San Diego, in 1984. A self-proclaimed "image-maker," Weems deals with issues of history, gender, and class by combining photographic images and narrative text. Often achingly personal, Weems's images explore bigotry, self-presentation, and relationships by incorporating African American folklore and bigoted or stereotypical narratives into her work. Her early work focused on the themes of family and class and quite often featured Weems and members of her own family. As in portraits such as *Honey Coloured Boy, Chocolate Coloured Man, Golden Yella Girl,* and *Blue Black Boy,* taken with a Polaroid camera and then hand tinted, many of her photographs illustrate both real and unreal varieties of "black" skin, calling into question the category "black" itself.

Weems's *Sea Islands Series* explores aspects of African American folklore and history from the Georgia Sea Islands, featured in Julie Dash's film *Daughters of the Dust.* Weems's *Untitled (Kitchen Table Series)* features a sequence of posed photographs exploring relationships between black men and women. In her photographs of degrading and stereotypical bric-a-brac and her portraits and self-portraits exploring stereotypes of black people, Weems uses cultural symbols such as watermelons, fried chicken, jump rope, rhymes, folklore, and proverbs to interrogate existing stereotypes.

Weems has received numerous grants and awards and has been published extensively. Her first retrospective was held in 1993 at the National Museum of Women in the Arts in Washington, D.C., and featured her works from 1978 to 1992. She has participated in group exhibitions around the country, including the 1991 Biennial at the Whitney Museum of American Art in New York.

SEE ALSO
Photography, African American; Dash, Julie.

North America

Wells-Barnett, Ida Bell

(b. July 16, 1862, Holly Springs, Miss.; d. March 25, 1931, Chicago, Ill.), African American journalist, advocate of civil rights, women's rights, and economic rights, and antilynching crusader.

Ida B. Wells-Barnett, the first of Jim and Elizabeth Wells's eight children, was born six months before the Emancipation Proclamation went into effect. She attended Shaw University (now Rust College) in her hometown of Holly Springs, Mississippi, until she was forced to drop out when her parents died of yellow fever in 1878. Following their deaths, Wells-Barnett supported herself and her siblings by working as a schoolteacher in rural Mississippi and Tennessee. She took summer courses at FISK UNIVERSITY and continued to teach through 1891, when she was fired for writing an editorial that accused the Memphis school board of providing inadequate resources to black schools.

In May 1884 Wells-Barnett filed suit against a railroad company after she was forced off a train for refusing to sit in the JIM CROW car designated for blacks. She was awarded $500 by a circuit court, but the decision was overruled by the Tennessee Supreme Court in 1887, a rejection that only strengthened her resolve to devote her life to upholding justice.

Wells-Barnett embarked on a career in journalism when she was elected editor of *The Evening Star* and then *The Living Way,* weekly church newspapers in Memphis. She became the editor of *Free Speech,* also in Memphis, in 1889. Her articles, written under the alias "Iola," were direct and confrontational, and two editorials she wrote in 1892 in response to the persecution and eventual LYNCHING of three black businessmen were particularly controversial. The first, published on March 9, encouraged blacks to leave Memphis for Oklahoma and to boycott segregated transportation. The second, which appeared on May 21, suggested that white women were often the willing initiators in interracial relationships. Whites who were angered by her work responded by wrecking the offices and press of *Free Speech.*

Wells-Barnett took refuge in the North, reporting in the black newspapers the *New York Age* and the *Chicago Conservator* on the violence and injustices being perpetrated against African Americans. Through a lecture tour of England, Scotland, and Wales in 1893 and 1894, Wells-Barnett inspired international organizations to apply pressure on America to end segregation and lynching. In 1895 she published an analysis of lynching titled *A Red Record: Tabulated Statistics and Alleged Causes of Lynching in the United States,* which argued that the impetus behind lynching was economic.

Marrying Ferdinand Barnett, a Chicago lawyer and editor, in 1895, Wells-Barnett put

The journalist and activist Ida B. Wells-Barnett wrote and spoke against lynching and other injustices suffered by black people in the United States. *Photographs and Prints Division, Schomburg Center for Research in Black Culture, The New York Public Library, Astor, Lenox and Tilden Foundation*

her writing on hold to focus on her family (the couple had four children), but she remained politically active. She helped to found the NATIONAL ASSOCIATION OF COLORED WOMEN in 1896, the Negro Fellowship League and the NATIONAL ASSOCIATION FOR THE ADVANCEMENT OF COLORED PEOPLE in 1910, and the Alpha Suffrage Club in 1913. In 1916 she became involved with Marcus Garvey's UNIVERSAL NEGRO IMPROVEMENT ASSOCIATION.

During the last 15 years of her life Wells-Barnett wrote extensively on the race riots in East St. Louis (1917), Chicago (1919), and Arkansas (1922), and continued to promote civil rights and justice for African Americans. A low-income housing project in Chicago was named in her honor in 1941, and in 1990 the United States Postal Service issued an Ida B. Wells-Barnett stamp.

Aaron Myers

SEE ALSO
Antilynching Movement; Chicago Riots of 1919; Chicago, Illinois; East St. Louis, Illinois, Riot of 1917; Garvey, Marcus Mosiah; Memphis, Tennessee; Thirteenth Amendment of the United States Constitution and the Emancipation Proclamation.

North America

Wells, Willie

(b. October 10, 1908, Austin, Tex.; d. January 24, 1989, Austin, Tex.), star of the Negro Baseball Leagues who was posthumously elected to the Baseball Hall of Fame.

Willie Wells grew up playing baseball in the sandlots of San Antonio, Texas. In 1924, at age 16, he signed to play with the St. Louis

Stars of the Negro National League (NNL). A gifted shortstop, Wells worked hard to develop his hitting and won batting titles in the 1929 and 1930 seasons. A fierce competitor (fans nicknamed him "El Diablo" when he played in Mexico), Wells led the Stars to NNL championships in 1928, 1930, and 1931.

The NNL folded after the 1931 season, and Wells signed with the Chicago American Giants. The Giants won the 1932 championship as part of the Negro Southern League, and the 1933 championship as part of revamped NNL. In 1936 Wells joined the Newark Eagles of the NNL, where he was part of what was called the "million dollar infield." He spent the late 1930s starring in the Latin American leagues in Cuba and Mexico. In 1942 he became Newark's player-manager, batted .361, was chosen for Cum Posey's All-American Dream Team, and was considered one of the top five players in baseball.

Wells retired in 1949 with a career batting average of .334 in the Negro Leagues (.392 in exhibition games against major leaguers) and played in eight All-Star games. He later managed the Winnipeg Buffaloes in Canada and the Birmingham Black Barons in the United States. In 1997 he was posthumously voted into the Baseball Hall of Fame.

Robert Fay

See Also
Baseball in the United States; Negro Leagues.

North America

Wesley, Charles Harris

(b. December 2, 1891, Louisville, Ky.; d. August 16, 1987, Washington, D.C.), African American historian, educator, and minister who was an early proponent of African American studies.

Charles Harris Wesley attended public schools in his hometown of Louisville, Kentucky, and then went on to receive a B.A. at Fisk University in 1911, an M.A. in economics at Yale University in 1913, and a Ph.D. from Harvard University in 1925. Wesley's doctorate in history was the third awarded by Harvard to an African American. Wesley served on the Howard University faculty from 1913 to 1942. In 1916 Wesley began a long association with Carter G. Woodson's Association for the Study of Negro Life and History, serving as president from 1950 to 1965 and as executive director until 1972. In 1942 Wesley became president of Wilberforce University in Ohio, a school supported by the African Methodist Episcopal Church. As president until 1965, Wesley improved the faculty, founded new programs (such as African studies), and integrated the student body. Wesley served as director of the Afro-American Historical and Cultural Museum in Philadelphia from its opening in 1974 to 1976.

In addition to his work as an educator, Wesley was an AME Church minister and elder from 1914 to 1937. Awarded a Guggenheim Fellowship in 1930, Wesley went to England to study slave emancipation in the British Empire. From 1931 to 1946 he was president of Alpha Phi Alpha, a black fraternity about which he wrote *The History of Alpha Phi Alpha* (1953). Wesley also wrote many other articles and books on African American history, leaders, and organizations, including *Negro Labor in the United States, 1850-1925* (1927), *Collapse of the Confederacy* (1937), and his last book, *The History of the National Association of Colored Women's Clubs: A Legacy of Service* (1984).

See Also
Association for the Study of Afro-American Life and History; Woodson, Carter Godwin.

North America

Wesley, Dorothy Burnett Porter

(b. May 25, 1905, Warrenton, Va.; d. 1995, Washington, D.C.), librarian and bibliographer responsible for building Howard University's Moorland-Spingarn Research Center into one of the world's largest collections of material by and about people of African descent.

Historian and author of several hundred articles and books, Dorothy Porter Wesley is best known for her work as a librarian. At age 25 she was the first to consolidate Howard University's materials by and about African Americans toward building the renowned Moorland-Spingarn Research Center. Wesley spent the rest of her life organizing and making accessible the major archive of black history and culture.

Dorothy Burnett was born in Warrenton, Virginia, and educated in New Jersey, Washington, D.C., and later at Howard University. She married James A. Porter, the painter and historian, in 1929, and in 1932 she became the first African American woman to receive a master's in library sciences from Columbia University. She returned to Howard to serve as curator of the collection, a position she held until 1973. Following her retirement and the death of her first husband, Porter married Charles H. Wesley, the historian, in 1979.

In her career as curator, Wesley contributed to the library's collection in the capacity of scholar, writing articles about topics ranging from Afro-Brazilian poet Caldas Barbosa to the abolitionist movement. More important, though, Wesley produced valuable bibliographies about people of African descent, such as *The Negro in the United States: A Selected Bibliography* (1967) and *Afro-Braziliana: A Working Bibliography* (1978). Her scholarship and development of the Moorland-Spingarn collection opened the door to a new wave of African American scholarship. She earned several honorary degrees, including doctorates of humane letters from Syracuse University and Radcliffe College.

See Also
Abolitionism in the United States; Moorland-Spingarn Research Collection; Porter, James Amos.

North America

West, Cornel

(b. June 2, 1953, Tulsa, Okla.), African American philosopher, theologian, and activist.

Cornel West was born in Oklahoma – a place once envisioned as a homeland for Native Americans displaced by European colonization, and for African Americans acting on the idea of freedom promised by emancipation. The grandson of a Baptist minister, he was reared in the Baptist Church, and the church has remained a profound presence in his life. Even as a child, West was articulate, outspoken, and politically engaged – in elementary school he convinced a group of his classmates to stop saluting the flag to protest the second-class citizenship afforded to African Americans.

West encountered the activities of the Black Panther Party while growing up in Sacramento, California. The Panthers informed his early thinking about democratic socialism and acquainted him with an internationalist vision for black enfranchisement. He was also inspired by the teachings of Martin Luther King Jr. and Malcolm X, as well as by the music of John Coltrane and James Brown. By the time he won a scholarship to Harvard University in 1970, West was already well on his way to becoming an activist-scholar. "Owing to my family, church, and the black social movements of the 1960s," he recalled, "I arrived at Harvard unashamed of my African, Christian, and militant decolonized outlooks." While in Cambridge he worked with the Black Panther Party, volunteering at their children's breakfast program.

West thrived at Harvard, consuming the work of the black intellectual tradition, including that of W. E. B. Du Bois and St. Clair Drake, as well as European philosophers such as Max Weber, Karl Marx, and Friedrich Nietzsche. At the core of West's development as a scholar lay the belief in integrating a religious faith with both political engagement and an intellectually rigorous course of study. "For me there was always a vital spiritual dimension to politics," West has explained. "Issues of death, disease, and despair have always been the fundamental issues of being human, and you didn't get too much talk about these issues in political circles."

After three years at Harvard, West graduated magna cum laude in 1973 and chose to pursue graduate studies in philosophy at Princeton. In 1977 he began teaching at Union Theological Seminary in New York. His doctoral dissertation, completed in 1980, was later revised and republished as the

Ethical Dimensions of Marxist Thought (1991).

A center of liberation theology and black theological education, Union was an ideal place for West's commitment to what he calls a prophetic criticism: "a self-critical and self-corrective enterprise of human 'sense-making' for the preserving and expanding of human empathy and compassion." It is through this philosophic and spiritual enterprise that West understands the experience of race in America, a point made clear by *Prophesy Deliverance! An Afro-American Revolutionary Christianity*, published in 1982.

In 1984 West left Union for Yale Divinity School, where he was granted a full professorship in religion and philosophy. He returned to Union in 1987, but shortly after was recruited to direct Princeton University's program in Afro-American studies. In 1988 West joined Princeton as professor of religion and, working with a community of scholars that included novelist Toni Morrison, he helped revitalize the Afro-American Studies Department.

Other universities were also eager to have West join their faculty. When Henry Louis Gates Jr. took leadership of Harvard University's Department of Afro-American Studies in 1991, he immediately began trying to lure to Harvard the man he called "the preëminent African-American intellectual of our generation." Excited by the possibilities of a group of scholars working across disciplines in the field of African American studies, West joined Harvard in 1993. In 1998 he was appointed the prestigious university professorship, becoming the first Alphonse Fletcher Jr. University Professor.

West's scholarly writing pursues philosophical inquiry into the realm of the political, exploring the existential dimension within the moral, spiritual, and political space. Moreover, he traces this relationship in the work of his philosophic forbears. In *The American Evasion of Philosophy* (1989) West explores the history of American pragmatism, reading the American philosophic tradition, from Ralph Waldo Emerson to Richard Rorty, as an ongoing cultural commentary that responds to American society itself. In *Keeping Faith: Philosophy and Race in America* (1993) he continues to engage with philosophy, spiritual tradition, and history.

A mesmerizing speaker, West draws upon an African American tradition of rhetoric and improvisational public speaking. He has collected some of his many talks and essays in a four-volume work, *Beyond Eurocentrism and Multiculturalism* (1993). After publishing several books and articles addressed primarily to an academic audience, West turned to a broader readership with *Race Matters* (1993). His best-known work, *Race Matters* reads like a sermon and unflinchingly confronts one of the most sensitive issues at the heart of American society: race. Yet West does not offer a specific program in this book. Rather, as he explained in an interview with Jervis Anderson, "I'm just trying to establish a framework within which we can come together for dialogue, and open-ended conversation within which other constructive voices might emerge."

Indeed, West has consistently placed a heavy emphasis on the conversational form as intellectual inquiry. The issues he takes up – sexism, anti-Semitism, homophobia, affirmative action – are timely ones for both the black community and the community at large. In 1991 West engaged in a lively conversation on race and gender with the feminist scholar bell hooks in *breaking bread: insurgent black intellectual life* (1991). He has also taken a particular interest in black-Jewish relations, publishing in 1995 a conversation with Jewish intellectual Michel Lerner titled *Jews and Blacks: Let the Healing Begin*. West has also participated in several discussions on the relationship between African Americans and Hispanics, including a conversation with scholar Jorge Klor de Alva and author Earl Shorris in "Our Next Race Question," published in *Harper's Magazine* in 1996. He and Gates copublished *The Future of the Race* in 1996; in 1998 he coauthored a book on parenting and family policy with Sylvia Ann Hewlett.

Marian Aguiar

See Also

Baptists; Theology, Black; Coltrane, John William; Du Bois, William Edward Burghardt (W. E. B.); King, Martin Luther, Jr.

North America

West, Dorothy (b. June 2, 1907; d. August 16, 1998, Boston, Mass.), African American author and journalist, literary figure of the Harlem Renaissance who specialized in short stories.

The only child of Rachel Pease Benson and Isaac Christopher West, Dorothy West started her education at age two under the tutelage of Bessie Trotter, sister of the *Boston Guardian*'s militant editor, William Monroe Trotter. After attending Farragut and Martin schools, she went to Girl's Latin High School, from which she graduated in 1923. West continued her education at Boston University and the Columbia University School of Journalism.

West's career as a writer began at age seven when the *Boston Globe* published her first short story, "Promise and Fulfillment." In 1926 West, then living in New York among the luminaries of the Harlem Renaissance, shared second-place honors with Zora Neale Hurston in a national writing competition organized by the National Urban League's *Opportunity*. Her interest in the arts was not only literary, and in 1927 she traveled to London as a cast member of the play *Porgy*. In the early 1930s she went to the Soviet Union to participate in the film *Black and White* and remained there for a year after the project was abandoned.

Returning to New York, West founded two short-lived literary journals: *Challenge* in 1934 (six issues) and *New Challenge* in 1937 (one issue). After working as a welfare investigator for a year and a half, West found employment with the federal government's Works Progress Administration's Federal Writers' Project through the early 1940s. She moved to Martha's Vineyard in Massachusetts in 1945 and wrote regularly for *Martha's Vineyard Gazette*. She published *The Living Is Easy* (1948) and *The Wedding* (1995), and more than 60 short stories. In 1997 television producer Oprah Winfrey made *The Wedding* into a popular television miniseries.

Aaron Myers

See Also

Guardian, The; *Opportunity: Journal of Negro Life*; Winfrey, Oprah Gail.

Africa

Western Sahara, a former Spanish province bordering Morocco to the north, Mauritania to the south, the Atlantic Ocean to the west, and Algeria to the east.

Western Sahara is a former Spanish colony. Today it is the site of a conflict between the Polisario Front (a political and military organization of the Sahrawi people) and the kingdom of Morocco. The Polisario Front wants independence for Western Sahara while Morocco wants to annex the province, which it claims on the basis of historical events. Although the area's environment is largely desert, vast phosphate deposits make it economically attractive.

Early History

The area now known as Western Sahara has been populated for thousands of years. What is now the Sahara Desert was once a plentifully watered grassland with a great deal of wildlife. During prehistoric times it supported a small population of hunters and gatherers. The transformation from grassland to desert, beginning around 2500 b.c.e., drove this population south into what is now sub-Saharan Africa. Berber people from the Mediterranean coastal region eventually moved into the area. They were nomadic pastoralists who could manage to exist in the austere environment. Around the first century c.e. the introduction of the camel from the Middle East, a beast of burden that excels in the harsh conditions of the Sahara, improved Berber living standards and increased their military capacity.

The Berber tribes of the western Sahara region have faced many challenges for control of the area. The first major challenge came in 1039 c.e. with the invasion of Almoravids who were for the most part Moroccan, and who followed a militant Islamic leadership. By 1110 the Almoravids had subdued the western Sahara, as well as parts of present-day Algeria, Mauritania, Morocco, and Spain. After the Almoravids came the Bani Hassan (or Maqil) Arabs, who arrived during the fifteenth century. The descendants of the Bani Hassan came to dominate the resident Berbers. The leadership of the modern Polisario Front claims descent from the Bani Hassan.

The European powers of Spain and Portugal also made brief attempts during the fifteenth century to establish fortified trading posts on the coast, but they were vulnerable to raids, either from European rivals or from the indigenous nomads. By 1476 the Spanish had established only one post of note, but the Spanish had abandoned it by 1496. Following the Spanish withdrawal, the Moroccan sultans attempted to subdue the area in a series of raids from the mid-seventeenth century until the early 1880s. Although the Moroccans failed to achieve firm control over the vast and sparsely populated region, they did establish lasting ties with some of the local tribes, such as the Tekna.

Colonization

In 1884 Spain declared the coastal areas of Western Sahara a protectorate, including the settlements of Boujdour and Dakhla. Spanish colonization of the area was minimal. At first Spaniards settled only at Dakhla, which they renamed Villa Cisneros. The Spanish had to contend not only with the French, who occupied Morocco and Mauritania, but also with the Sahrawi leader Shaikh Ma al-Ainin, who offered fierce resistance to European occupation until his defeat in 1910 at the hands of the French. Still, the Sahrawi tribes of the interior proved hard to subdue. The Spanish did not gain full control of Western Sahara until 1934. The colony was reorganized as Spanish Sahara in 1958.

In 1957 the newly independent nation of Morocco claimed Western Sahara as its own. Spain was forced to repel a series of Moroccan military incursions. In 1960 Mauritania achieved independence and it, too, claimed a share of Spanish Sahara. The colony of Spanish Sahara lacked profitable resources, and the Spanish saw it as a financial drain. Thus the Spanish government was unwilling to invest in its possession, and the Spanish presence remained minimal. The indigenous Sahrawi people of the interior continued their centuries-long tradition of nomadic existence. In 1963 scientists discovered phosphate reserves in the northern part of the colony, and Spanish interest in the area revived. Mining activities began in the late 1960s.

In the mid-1960s, however, the United Nations (UN) General Assembly, after appeals from Sahrawi representatives, passed a resolution calling for Spain's withdrawal from the colony. Muhammad Sidi Ibrahim Bassiri led Sahrawi anti-Spanish protests in 1970 in the capital of Al-Ayun. The Spanish responded brutally. Spanish troops crushed the demonstrations and captured Bassiri, who died in prison under suspicious circumstances. Spanish repression, however, fostered increased Sahrawi nationalism.

In 1973 a group of Sahrawis formed the Polisario Front (whose full name in Spanish is Frente Popular para la Liberación de Saguia el-Hamra y Río de Oro) and began armed guerrilla activities against the Spanish. These guerrilla attacks persuaded Spanish leader Gen. Francisco Franco to offer limited Sahrawi autonomy, in the form of a handpicked council, the *Djemaa*, composed mainly of "acceptable" Sahrawi who held political views sympathetic to Spain. Polisario demanded Sahrawi self-determination and continued its war. In August 1974 Spain agreed to a referendum on self-determination.

Sahrawi calls for self-determination met with stiff resistance from the governments of Morocco and Mauritania, which continued to claim the territory. Both governments requested that the International Court of Justice at the Hague rule on their historical claims to Western Sahara. The court ruled in October 1975 that the two countries had no claim to Western Sahara and that the Sahrawi had a right to self-determination.

The ruling proved moot; by 1975 Spain, whose leader Franco was seriously ill, had become unwilling to risk any conflict over Western Sahara. Moroccan troops were poised at the border of the territory, and if Spain had attempted to hold a referendum, there was a risk that Morocco might launch attacks on Spain itself. Spain agreed, as did Morocco and Mauritania, to partition the territory without a referendum, with the northern two-thirds going to Morocco and the southern one-third to Mauritania. Spain withdrew from Western Sahara on February 26, 1976; Moroccan and Mauritanian forces surged across the border and occupied the area.

An Unresolved Conflict

Within 24 hours of Spain's withdrawal, Polisario declared independence as the Saharan Arab Democratic Republic (SADR) and vowed to continue the fight. It began to evacuate as many Sahrawis as possible from Western Sahara and to relocate them across the border in Algeria, its most significant patron. Algeria, alarmed at perceived Moroccan expansionism, supplied weapons to the guerrillas and provided Polisario forces and Western Saharan refugees with a safe haven in its southwestern Tindouf region.

After the evacuation Polisario went on the offensive. At first Polisario focused on the weaker Mauritanian army and attacked Mauritanian targets in Western Sahara as well as in Mauritania. With their superior knowledge of the desert, Polisario forces penetrated the Mauritanian border and attacked deep inside the country. In June 1976 Polisario forces attacked the Mauritanian capital, Nouakchott, and fired artillery shells at the presidential palace before beating a hasty retreat. Military expenditures and losses due to Polisario's campaign drove Mauritania's government into bankruptcy and wrecked the country's economy. Mauritanian public opinion turned against President Ould Daddah. A small band of Mauritanian military officers led an almost bloodless coup d'état against Daddah in 1979, and agreed to an armistice with Polisario and a quick pullout from its Western Saharan holdings.

Shortly after the Mauritanian withdrawal Moroccan forces began to occupy the remaining one-third of Western Sahara. However, Polisario inflicted heavy losses on Morocco. Morocco managed to hold the territory only at great expense. Its military presence of 100,000 troops consumed up to half the national budget. But the military campaign had political benefits for Morocco's King Hassan: it defused political opposition by uniting Moroccans behind a patriotic cause, and it kept the military occupied, well-supplied, and disinclined to stage a coup.

The Organization of African Unity (OAU), whose members were divided on the issue of supporting Morocco or Polisario, attempted to broker a peace deal in the early 1980s. In 1982 the OAU officially recognized SADR as the rightful government of Western Sahara and admitted it to the organization. As a result Morocco later withdrew from the organization, and the OAU abandoned attempts to mediate the dispute. Diplomatic activity halted almost completely between 1984 and 1986.

The military conflict moved toward a stalemate as Morocco consolidated its control over the territory. During the mid-1980s Polisario resumed its attacks. Polisario continued to receive support from Algeria. However, Moroccans built an earthen wall that was armed with mines and motion detectors to defend the major economic and population centers of Western Sahara. This wall severely limited Polisario's military options. Any attempt to breach the barrier would now cost dearly in resources and casualties, although Polisario could still drain Moroccan resources by attacking the wall itself and the soldiers who defended it.

UN Secretary General Javier Pérez de Cuéllar began indirect negotiations. By 1991 negotiators tentatively agreed to a cease-fire agreement and a plan for a referendum on independence. Both Morocco and Polisario agreed to yield to UN forces, which would mediate the agreement's main sticking point: who would be eligible to vote. For years Morocco had been settling Western Sahara with Moroccan citizens. Meanwhile, many Sahrawi who had been living in Western Sahara under the Spanish had fled to refugee camps outside the territory. Polisario argued that only those people (and their descendants) who had been in Western Sahara at the time of the final Spanish census in 1974 should vote, while Morocco favored allowing any person living there at the time of the referendum to vote.

By the mid-1990s both parties had some

interest in reaching a peaceful agreement. Morocco had come under pressure from international lenders to cut its military budget, while Algerian support for Polisario had diminished. The UN suggested a compromise solution to determine voter eligibility, to which Polisario finally agreed in 1997. The arduous process of registering and authenticating eligible voters began again.

The referendum to determine whether Western Sahara will become independent or integrate with Morocco was tentatively scheduled for late 1998; once again it was postponed due to disagreements regarding voter eligibility. If the referendum is held, the outcome may depend on Morocco's success in winning the support of the Sahrawis who remained under Moroccan control after 1974. Those who have benefited from phosphate earnings and Moroccan government spending may choose to cast their lot with Morocco, while those who have faced Moroccan repression, as well as the many Sahrawis who have spent decades in Polisario's refugee camps, will almost certainly side with Polisario.

Robert Fay

See Also

Sahrawi; Daddah, Moktar Ould; Nationalism in Africa; United Nations in Africa; France; Polisario; Pastoralism; Nouakchott, Mauritania.

Africa

Western Sahara (Ready Reference)

Official Name: Western Sahara
Former Name: Spanish Sahara
Area: 267,000 sq km (about 103,000 sq mi)
Location: North Africa, on the North Atlantic Ocean; borders Morocco, Algeria, and Mauritania
Capital: None (under de facto control of Morocco)
Other Major Cities: El Aaiún and Ad Dakhla (Villa Cisneros) (population data unavailable)
Population: 233,730 (1998 estimate)
Population Density: Data unavailable
Population Below Age 15: Data unavailable
Population Growth Rate: 2.4 percent (1998 estimate)
Total Fertility Rate: 6.75 children born per woman (1998 estimate)
Life Expectancy at Birth: Total population: 48.41 years (male 47.32 years; female 49.83 years [1998 estimate])
Infant Mortality Rate: 139.74 deaths per 1000 live births (1998 estimate)
Literacy Rate (age 15 and over who can read and write): Data unavailable
Education: Data unavailable
Languages: Hassaniya Arabic and Moroccan Arabic
Ethnic Groups: Arab and Berber
Religion: Muslim
Climate: Hot, minimal rainfall inland, moist winds offshore; harmattan haze predominates inland, fog along the shore
Land, Plants, and Animals: Almost entirely desert, interrupted by occasional rocky or sandy areas, with low mountains in the south and northeast. Vegetation is sparse, but occasional rainfall permits some nomadic animal husbandry (of sheep, goats, and camels).
Natural Resources: Phosphates and iron ore
Currency: The Moroccan dirham
Gross Domestic Product (GDP): Data unavailable
GDP per Capita: Data unavailable
GDP Real Growth Rate: Data unavailable
Primary Economic Activities: Pastoral nomadism, fishing, oasis gardening, and phosphate mining
Primary Crops: Various fruits and vegetables; camels, sheep, and goats
Industries: Animal husbandry and subsistence farming are practiced by half the labor force.
Primary Export: Phosphates
Primary Imports: Fuel for fishing fleets, and foodstuffs
Primary Trade Partners: Morocco claims and administers Western Sahara, so trade partners are included in overall Moroccan accounts.
Government: Territory administratively controlled by Morocco. The territory's legal status and sovereignty have not been resolved. Both Morocco and the Polisario Front (Popular Front for the Liberation of the Saguia el-Hamra and Rio de Oro) have contested the territory. In February 1976 the Polisario declared a government-in-exile of the Sahrawi Arab Democratic Republic (SADR), and thousands of Sahrawis were displaced by political turmoil and relocated to a settlement in southwest Algeria. In April 1976 Morocco and Mauritania divided the territory between the two countries. Polisario guerrillas forced Mauritania to surrender its claims in 1979; Morocco has had administrative control since then. The Polisario's government-in-exile became a member of the Organization of African Unity in 1984. United Nations forces have been monitoring the territory since a 1991 cease-fire on guerrilla activities. In late 1997 Polisario and Moroccan representatives had tentatively agreed to allow a referendum on Western Sahara self-determination to be held sometime in 1998. The referendum was postponed repeatedly due to disagreements over voter eligibility.

Barbara Worley

See Also

Pastoralism.

Latin America and the Caribbean

West Indies, archipelago in the northern part of the Western Hemisphere that separates the Caribbean Sea from the Atlantic Ocean. Visited and called the Indies by Christopher Columbus, it was subsequently designated the West Indies to distinguish it from the East Indies archipelago.

The West Indies comprises three main island chains that extend in a roughly crescent shape from the eastern tip of the Yucatán Peninsula in Mexico and southeastern Florida in the United States to the Venezuelan coast of South America. The Bahamas, in the north, form a southeasterly line. The Greater Antilles, comprising the islands of Cuba, Hispaniola, Jamaica, and Puerto Rico, lie in the center. To the southeast, arching southward from Puerto Rico and then westward along the Venezuelan coast, are the Lesser Antilles, comprising the Leeward Islands and Windward Islands. Barbados, Trinidad and Tobago, and the Netherlands Antilles are often considered part of this third chain. The land area of the West Indies totals about 235,700 sq km (91,000 sq mi), and the total population (according to a 1990 estimate) is about 34 million.

Most of the noncoral islands of the West Indies are mountainous, projecting remnants of submerged ranges related to Central and South American mountain systems. Elevations of about 2130 to 2440 m (7000 to 8000 ft) are common in the Greater Antilles; the highest point (3175 m/10,417 ft) is Pico Duarte in the Cordillera Central of the Dominican Republic. The inner chain of the Lesser Antilles, part of a submerged volcanic ridge, consists mainly of volcanic cones, a number of which are still active. The outer chain is composed largely of coral and uplifted limestone. Elevations in the Lesser Antilles rarely exceed 1524 m (5000 ft). The southernmost part of the archipelago, from Trinidad to Aruba, is geologically related to South American rock and mountain formations. The Bahamas and northern central Cuba, relatively flat limestone and coral formations, are geologically related to formations in Florida and the Yucatán Peninsula. Several deep ocean trenches lie close offshore and parallel to the islands of the Greater and Lesser Antilles, marking unstable crustal zones in which earthquakes may occur.

Climate

Except for part of the Bahamas chain, all the West Indies islands lie within the Tropic Zone, but temperate climatic conditions exist in many mountainous regions; weather conditions at lower elevations are modified by such oceanic influences as the trade winds. Two seasons are distinguishable: a relatively dry season, from November through May; and a wet season, from June through October.

Hurricanes, formed in the Atlantic, may occur between July and October, destroying much life and property when they sweep onshore.

Political Divisions

Politically, the West Indies comprises 13 independent nations and a number of colonial dependencies, territories, and possessions. The Republic of Cuba, consisting of the island of Cuba and several off-lying islands, is the largest West Indies nation. Haiti and the Dominican Republic, two other independent nations, occupy Hispaniola, the second-largest island of the archipelago. Jamaica, Barbados, the Bahamas, Trinidad and Tobago, Dominica, Grenada, St. Kitts and Nevis, St. Lucia, St. Vincent and the Grenadines, and Antigua and Barbuda are the other sovereign nations.

Sovereignty over nearly all the other West Indies islands is distributed among the United States, France, the Netherlands, and Great Britain. Puerto Rico, the fourth-largest island of the archipelago, is a commonwealth of the United States, and several of the Virgin Islands are United States territories. The French West Indies includes Martinique, Guadeloupe, and a number of small island dependencies of Guadeloupe. The Dutch possessions consist of Curaçao, Bonaire, Aruba, and smaller Lesser Antilles islands. Venezuela holds about 70 Lesser Antilles islands. Dependencies of Great Britain are the Cayman Islands, Turks and Caicos Islands, and some of the Virgin Islands.

See Also

Venezuela; Virgin Islands (United States and British).

North America

Wharton, Clifton Reginald, Sr.

(b. May 11, 1899, Baltimore, Md.; d. April 28, 1990, Phoenix, Ariz.), American lawyer and ambassador who was the first African American to enter the Foreign Service and the first African American diplomat to head a United States delegation to a European country.

Clifton Reginald Wharton Sr. was raised in Boston, Massachusetts, where he graduated from English High School and in 1920 received a law degree from Boston University. He received an advanced law degree from the same institution after practicing law in Boston from 1920 to 1923. He then left Boston and worked in Washington, D.C., as an examiner in the Veteran's Bureau and as a law clerk in the State Department. In Washington Wharton embarked on his career in international diplomacy. From 1925 to 1945 he served as a diplomat in Liberia (1925-1929), Spain (1930-1941), and Madagascar (1942-1945). Following these assignments, he was consul general at the U.S. Embassy in Portugal from 1949 to 1950.

Wharton practiced diplomacy under both Democratic and Republican administrations. In 1953 he became the consul general in France. Five years later President Dwight D. Eisenhower re-appointed him as U.S. minister to Romania, and in 1961 President John F. Kennedy appointed him U.S. Ambassador to Norway. Wharton retired from the Foreign Service in 1964, one year after having received an honorary doctorate of law degree from Boston University.

Aaron Myers

North America

Wheatley, Phillis

(b.1753?, the Gambia, West Africa; d. December 5, 1784, Boston, Mass.), poet, the first African American to publish a book; considered the founder of the African American literary tradition.

Some view our sable race with scornful eye,
"Their colour is a diabolic dye."
Remember, Christians, Negroes, black as Cain,
May be refined, and join the angelic train.

So ends Phillis Wheatley's 1773 poem, "On Being Brought From Africa to America." The poem is remarkable not only for the honest way it speaks about color prejudice among white Christians – never a polite subject, and certainly not one in 1773 – but for the singular achievements of the author. Wheatley wrote the original version of this poem in 1768, seven years after she had come to America as a seven-year-old child and as an African slave. At the time of its publication in 1773, she was just 19 years old, yet already an internationally celebrated poet whose admirers included Benjamin Franklin and George Washington. She had also become the first African American – and the second American woman – to publish a book.

Wheatley was born, probably in 1753, in the Gambia, West Africa, but in 1761 she was stolen from her parents and transported on a slave ship to Boston, Massachusetts. There she was sold to John and Susanna Wheatley, who named her after the ship that had transported her to slavery. They purchased her to be a domestic servant, but when Susanna realized that Phillis had a talent for learning, she allowed her daughter Mary to tutor Phillis in Latin, English, and the Bible. Wheatley soon began composing her own poetry, and her first published poem appeared in the *Newport Mercury* newspaper on December 21, 1767.

Over the next five years several more of Wheatley's poems were published in local papers. In October 1770 she wrote an elegy for the English evangelical minister George Whitefield that was so popular that it was also reprinted in England (*see* London, Blacks in: An Interpretation), bringing her international recognition. But when Wheatley tried in 1772 to publish her first volume of poetry, publishers still felt they needed to guarantee to skeptical readers that a black slave could have written the poems she said were hers. She underwent an oral examination by 18 of "the most respectable Characters in Boston," including the governor of Massachusetts, to prove that she was indeed literate and articulate enough to have composed the poems. Wheatley passed the exam but still could not secure a Boston publisher.

Wheatley found an ally across the Atlantic in Selina, countess of Huntingdon, an evangelical Englishwoman with ties to Whitefield who had read her poetry and who arranged for her book to be published in London. In 1773 *Poems on Various Subjects, Religious and Moral* appeared. The frontispiece of the original edition, requested by the countess, makes the author's identity – and ability – very clear: under the caption "Phillis Wheatley, Negro Servant to Mr. John Wheatley of Boston," there is an engraving of the young black woman at her desk, with a piece of paper in front of her, a book at one hand, and a pen in the other. The image is thought to be the work of Scipio Moorhead, a young African American slave artist.

Wheatley traveled to England to oversee the book's publication, but the trip served other purposes as well. She met many British dignitaries and intellectuals, all of whom celebrated her literary ability, and American diplomat Benjamin Franklin came to call on her in London. Shortly after her trip her owners decided to free her – according to Wheatley, "at the desire of my friends in England." The trip brought Wheatley fame as an author, and pressure from English abolitionists led to her freedom.

Wheatley's poetic subjects were often the people and places that made news around her. She wrote numerous elegies for friends and acquaintances and also several popular poems supporting the colonists in the Revolutionary War, even though the white Wheatleys were Tories. A poem she wrote in October 1775 in honor of George Washington so impressed him that he invited her to a private visit with him in his Cambridge, Massachusetts, military headquarters. Washington was himself a slaveholder, but some scholars have speculated that his conversation with Wheatley may have influenced his later discomfort with slavery.

Some readers have criticized Wheatley because her subject matter is not more distinctly African American, and especially because some of her poetry even appears to condone slavery. For example, in "To the University of Cambridge, in New-England," Wheatley refers to Africa as "the land of errors, and *Egyptian* gloom," and goes on to say that it was God's "gracious hand" that "brought [her] in safety from those dark abodes." But while this poem does reflect Wheatley's evangelical Christianity (she believed that

Just 19 when her first collection of poetry was published in 1773, Phillis Wheatley is pictured here in the frontispiece of that volume. This portrait of the poet is attributed to African American artist Scipio Moorhead. *CORBIS/Bettmann*

the hidden blessing in her capture was that it allowed her to be exposed to the Bible and be saved), it does not capture the complexities of Wheatley's feelings about her enslavement, or her identification with other blacks.

In other poems Wheatley does affirm that her separation from her home was indeed traumatic. For example, in "To the Right Honourable William Legge, Earl of Dartmouth," Wheatley explains that she empathizes with the American colonists because of her own experience with oppression:

when seeming cruel Fate
Me snatched from Afric's fancied happy seat,
... Ah! What bitter pangs molest,
What sorrows laboured in the parent's breast?

And Wheatley's letters, recently recovered, show clearly that she was aware of racial prejudice and injustice, and that she identified with other people of African descent. Recent scholars agree with Wheatley's implication that her poems supporting the American colonists are part of a larger discourse on freedom from tyranny, a discourse that was inextricably linked to the question of slavery–but that she chose to couch in terms her immediate audience would receive best.

In 1778 Wheatley married a free black Bostonian, John Peters. The next year she circulated a proposal for a new collection of poetry, indicating she had written dozens of new poems since 1773. But in a country now at war, the interest that had attended the publication of her first book had waned. Wheatley could not find a publisher and retreated from the public eye. Her short marriage was unhappy, marred by the deaths in infancy of her first two children. On December 5, 1784, Wheatley died in childbirth along with her third child.

At the time of her death Wheatley was living in poverty and obscurity on the outskirts of Boston, but the memory of the famed "Ethiopian muse" was strong enough that her obituary was printed in the Boston papers. Since the early nineteenth century other African American writers have continually acknowledged their debt to her accomplishments. Wheatley is celebrated as the founder of the African American literary tradition, and contemporary readers continue to learn more about the complexities she brought to that role.

Lisa Clayton Robinson

See Also

Slavery in the United States; Abolitionism in the United States; Literature, African American; Women Writers, Black, in the United States; American Revolution.

North America

Whipper, William

(b. February 22, 1804, Little Britain Township, Pa.; d. March 9, 1876, Philadelphia, Pa.), African American moral reformer and businessman.

Little is known about William Whipper's early life. By 1830 he had moved to Philadelphia, Pennsylvania, where he worked as a clothes cleaner and grocery manager.

In the 1820s and 1830s Whipper worked as a moral reformer in literary circles. He delivered an "Address Before the Colored Reading Society of Philadelphia" in 1828, and in 1833 he was one of the nine founders of the Philadelphia Library of Colored Persons. In 1834 he spoke about the centrality of moral reform to racial uplift before the Colored Temperance Society of Philadelphia. At the 1835 annual National Negro Convention (NNC), an event he had attended every year since 1830, Whipper led the movement to create the short-lived American Moral Reform Society (AMRS) and went on to serve as the editor of its journal, the *National Reformer*. He drafted the constitutions of both the NNC and AMRS.

In the mid-1830s Whipper forged a partnership with local lumber merchant Stephen Smith to form a business that served the Philadelphia and Columbia communities. In 1835 Whipper moved to Columbia, Pennsylvania, where his house became one of the stops on the Underground Railroad. Although the AMRS collapsed in 1841, Whipper remained politically active, attending the NNC in 1848, 1853, and 1855. He purchased property in Dresden, Canada (1853), and New Brunswick, New Jersey (1868), before returning to Philadelphia.

Aaron Myers

Latin America and the Caribbean

White Abolitionists in Brazil,

a group of Brazilians of European descent who, beginning in the 1870s, worked to abolish slavery in that nation.

Slaves in Brazil had persistently fought against their own enslavement as well as slavery itself, most notably by revolting and forming escaped slave communities known as *quilombos*. Nevertheless, the movement to abolish slavery in BRAZIL is generally associated with the activities of a group of mainly white abolitionists during the nine years leading up to emancipation in 1888. That year Brazil became the last country in the New World to abolish slavery. Brazil's overwhelming economic dependence on agriculture and mining, and thus on slavery, meant that the abolitionist movement came late to Brazil, in comparison with other Latin American countries and the United States. Furthermore, until the last few years before abolition, the antislavery movement was limited in terms of its participants and the reforms it was able to realize.

Some of Brazil's leading abolitionists, such as Luís Gama, José do Patrocínio, and ANDRÉ REBOUÇAS, were Afro-Brazilians. As a group, however, they cannot be characterized as easily as the movement's white advocates, the most prominent of whom included JOAQUIM NABUCO, RUI BARBOSA, and Antônio de Castro Alves. Although they were not a homogeneous group, white abolitionists in Brazil shared similar backgrounds and views about slaves, and sought similar reforms. In general this group opposed slavery not out of empathy with the slaves, but because they felt that the reliance on slave labor and the presence of slaves in Brazil had a negative impact on the country's society and culture.

Although a few women, such as Luciana de Abreu and Maria Firmina dos Reis, contributed to the abolitionist cause, most white abolitionists in Brazil were male and members of the elite class. They typically grew up on slaveholding plantations in the northeast and attended Brazilian academies or European institutions of higher learning, where they joined or formed abolitionist societies and adopted more critical views of slavery. The liberal ideals of the French Enlightenment and the success of the abolition movement in the United States also fueled their antislavery efforts. White abolitionists usually pursued their fight in the political sphere and/or through the press. They almost always affiliated themselves with the Republican Party and considered themselves liberals, if not radicals. White abolitionists generally sought legal means of abolition, though toward the end of the 1880s many sanctioned more radical activities, such as helping slaves escape.

An important shared characteristic of many whites involved in the abolition movement was a northeastern background. In the late eighteenth century the once-thriving SUGAR industry of the northeast declined, resulting in a demographic shift in the slave population to the southern provinces of Rio de Janeiro, São Paulo, and MINAS GERAIS, where the coffee industry was expanding. Thus by the 1880s whites from the northeast could more easily challenge slavery because they did not have the economic stake in preserving it that planters in the south had.

White abolitionists in Brazil often shared with slaveholders negative views about slaves. Like many Brazilians, they saw slaves as domestic enemies, irrational beasts without morals. Nabuco, for example, contended that slaves did not have the mental capacity to advocate their own freedom. Unlike abolitionists of African descent, he discouraged slaves' involvement in the abolition movement. White abolitionists also excluded free and enslaved blacks from the antislavery struggle because they feared setting off a large-scale, violent revolt.

Because there was little communication or interaction between white abolitionists and black slaves, white abolitionists lacked empathy toward slaves and their plight. At the same time white abolitionists tended to regard slaveholders as humane and capable of being persuaded by reason. They praised Brazilian slaveholders for their supposedly mild treatment of slaves and for their desire to switch to free labor.

White abolitionists appealed primarily to the economic sensibilities of the elite, arguing that Brazil's lack of industrial progress resulted from slavery and that the only way to advance agriculture and industry was to abolish slavery and encourage European immigration. The presence of European immigrants, it was believed, would purify the Brazilian population, offsetting the allegedly corrupt influence of the slaves. Nabuco, for example, stated that through MISCEGENATION, "the vices of the African blood ended up making their way into the general circulation of the country." Thus, white abolitionists were often more concerned with slavery's detrimental impact on the white population than with the suffering of slaves.

Both white and black abolitionists pursued abolition through emancipation funds. In order to raise money to liberate slaves, they organized conferences in city theaters that featured musical and dramatic performances in addition to speeches by the abolitionists. White abolitionists often contended that slaveholders deserved financial compensation for the loss of their slaves. In addition, they generally advocated that slaves should be freed gradually, after a period of compulsory service to be determined by the owner.

Nevertheless, by the late 1880s the small and elite abolitionist movement quickly gained popular support. When, under strong British pressure, Brazil effectively ended the international slave trade in 1850, it seemed that the end of slavery was inevitable: Brazil's slave population had never domestically reproduced itself, and plantations relied on importation to renew their slave labor force. With a slave population that invariably grew older, slavery's days were numbered. This, combined with the declining sugar economy in the northeast, stimulated a late popular abolition movement. In the years immediately before abolition, antislavery movements in several states purchased the freedom of slaves, or convinced slaveholders to manumit their servants. In 1884 Ceará became the first state to declare itself completely emancipated.

During and after abolition few white antislavery proponents concerned themselves with facilitating the slaves' transition to citizenship. They expected ex-slaves and their offspring to integrate into society and, with increased European immigration, eventually disappear. Nevertheless, Nabuco called for expanding the education of former slaves. The most common postemancipation reform, pursued by white and black abolitionists alike, was land reform, which sought to break up large agricultural estates and distribute them to the emancipated population.

Because its aim was to replace slavery with a free-labor system rather than to transform ex-slaves into citizens, Brazil's abolition movement has been labeled a white revolution by some historians. Having educational and political opportunities denied to black abolitionists, white elites were more likely to direct antislavery organizations. Yet numerous Afro-Brazilian freedom fighters, including generations of anonymous slaves – the most enduring opponents of slavery – were instrumental in realizing abolition. Still, abolition in Brazil was not a simple matter of black or white, enslaved or elite. As scholar Robert Conrad points out, Brazilians from every ethnicity, class, and profession eventually became involved in abolitionism.

Aaron Myers

SEE ALSO

Transatlantic Slave Trade; Maroonage in the Americas; Slavery in Latin America and the Caribbean; Abolitionism in the United States; Gama, Luís Gonzaga Pinto da; Patrocínio, José Carlos do; Rio de Janeiro, Brazil; Abolition and Emancipation in Latin America and the Caribbean; Slave Rebellions in Latin America and the Caribbean.

North America

White, Charles (b. April 2, 1918, Chicago, Ill.; d. October 3, 1979, Los Angeles, Calif.), African American artist specializing in black-and-white graphic work whose oeuvre celebrates the courage and dignity of historic black leaders and common African Americans.

Charles White was born to unmarried parents, Ethel Gary and Charles White Sr., who separated when White was three years old. He was raised by his mother in Chicago. After winning a national pencil sketch contest in 1937, White attended the Art Institute of Chicago for a year, then worked as an artist in the WORKS PROGRESS ADMINISTRATION during the late 1930s. In 1941 White traveled through the South on a Rosenwald Fellowship. He moved to New York City in 1942 and studied at the Art Students League.

In 1944, while serving in the army, White was diagnosed with tuberculosis and was hospitalized for three years. In 1947 he had his first one-man show at the ACA Gallery in New York City, after which he went to MEXICO, where he worked for nearly a year at the printmaking workshop Taller de Graphica. During this time White divorced his wife, the sculptor ELIZABETH CATLETT, whom he had married in 1941, and married Frances Barrett in 1950. The couple moved in the mid-1950s to Los Angeles, where White became a teacher at the Otis Art Institute in 1965. White also served as a distinguished professor at Howard University's School of Art before his death in 1979.

Among White's better-known works are the mural *Contribution of the Negro to American Democracy* (1943), executed at Hampton Institute in Virginia, and his series of works based on Civil War posters announcing slave auctions or awards for runaway slaves. One of White's most prestigious honors came in 1972 when he became the second African American to be elected a member of the National Academy of Design since the 1927 election of HENRY OSSAWA TANNER. President Jimmy Carter honored White posthumously at the 22nd annual meeting of the National Conference of Artists.

Aaron Myers

SEE ALSO

Chicago, Illinois; Civil War, American; Hampton University; Howard University; Los Angeles, California; New York, New York.

Latin America and the Caribbean

White, José (b. January 1, 1836, MATANZAS, CUBA; d. March 12, 1918, Paris, FRANCE), Afro-Cuban violinist and professor of classical music, author of the famous "La bella Cubana" (The Beautiful Cuban Maid), a nationalistic composition popular during the nineteenth-century Cuban struggles for independence (*see* CUBA).

José White grew up in Matanzas, an important city east of Havana and a major center of African culture, where he began studying violin, first with his father and later with another Afro-Cuban violinist, J. M. Roman. During this period White developed a reputation as a virtuoso performer and made the acquaintance of North American romantic composer Louis Gottschalk. Gottschalk was so impressed by White's talent that he offered to accompany him in a concert, which took place in Matanzas on March 21, 1855.

A year later, at age 19, White moved to Paris, where he studied classical composition with the famous French violinist Jean Delphin Alard at the Paris Conservatory. By this time he could play 18 other instruments in addition to the violin. While studying at the conservatory, White met Italian opera composer Rossini, whose salon attracted such names as Frédéric Chopin and Franz Liszt. Soon after, Rossini organized several private concerts featuring the Cuban violinist. French composers Charles Gounod, Daniel Auber, and Charles Ambroise began writing music for White.

In 1864, after the death of Alard, White was offered his mentor's teaching position at the Paris Conservatory. He later served briefly as the director of the Rio Conservatory in BRAZIL. Mounting political tensions, however, soon prompted him to leave his post and return to FRANCE.

Though he was principally known as a performer, White also made a name for himself as a composer (*see* MUSIC, CLASSICAL, IN LATIN AMERICA AND THE CARIBBEAN). Many of his works still survive, including a concerto, a string quartet, a collection of studies for violin, several nationalistic pieces, such as "Marcha cubana," and perhaps his most famous composition, the *habanera* (a Cuban dance in slow duple time) "La bella Cubana." Indeed, because of such overtly patriotic pieces he was forced to flee the wrath of Spanish authorities, as Cuba would not gain its independence until 1898.

By the time of his death in 1918 José White had given concerts throughout Europe and Latin America. In addition, he had performed with orchestras in the United States during a time when few North American blacks were afforded such an opportunity.

Gordon Root

SEE ALSO

Havana, Cuba; Spanish-Cuban-American War.

Latin America and the Caribbean

Whitening, a term that has been used over the past century in Latin America that refers to both a process and a concept. As a process it is simply one value-laden way of referring to the combining of gene pools that human populations have always experienced. This process has carried many labels, some of them now of dubious respectability, such as "interbreeding" and miscegenation. The value added in the term *branqueamento* is the alleged superiority of the "white" component. The emergence of the term is a late nineteenth-century addition to the popular interpretation of reproductive mixture among humans. It is based on the concept of race, a term with at least two meanings in the history of the Americas (*see* RACE IN LATIN AMERICA).

When the Portuguese and Spanish first colonized South America, the Iberians were using race (*raça* or *raza*) to distinguish between, on the one hand, the Iberian Christians and, on the other hand, the non-Christians, such as the Jews and the Moors. When an individual's racial status was in dispute, church and secular authorities often demanded church records and/or genealogical evidence of the individual's descent from forbears of the proper religion. This meaning of race was transferred to both Spanish and Portuguese America. The Inquisition was the most infamous institution charged with enforcing this system of racial classification. The second meaning of race, which became rooted in social practice, defined race by physical appearance and by what twentieth-century scientists would call a racial phenotype. The stimulus for the development of this new concept was the growing number of African slaves arriving in the Americas, especially throughout the Caribbean, in the early sixteenth century.

In BRAZIL, for example, sexual contact between Portuguese and Africans produced the new physical phenotype of the mulatto. Since the nonwhite population, that is, black and mulatto, outnumbered the white population from the early seventeenth to the late nineteenth century, some of the mixed-race contingent were likely to rise socially because there was no consistent color line established in colonial Brazil. Instead, a de facto threefold racial stratification emerged: white (European), mulatto, and black – with notoriously blurred lines between the first and second and second and third strata.

Within this hierarchy whiteness had the highest social and therefore political value. The predominance of this white ideal penetrated the entire society, including the nonwhites. This helps to explain how an explicitly racist society managed to maintain (and still maintains) a surprising degree of legitimacy. The lesson for the nonwhite population was to strive to become whiter, whether by producing whiter offspring (by their choice of mate) or by "behaving" white. Thus the entire society could look to the redemption of the nonwhite, even if on a distant timetable. This rationale was reinforced by the widespread acceptance after about 1870 in Latin America of "scientific racist" doctrine, which employed a scientific discourse to ascribe various qualities and capabilities to different races, seen as superior and inferior (*see* EUGENICS).

Between 1880 and 1930 the Brazilian government (controlled by whites) sponsored massive European immigration to accelerate the whitening of the population as well as to create a new work force. During this period whiteness was explicitly proclaimed, even by nonwhite intellectuals, as having the highest moral and aesthetic value. Brazilian scientists lectured abroad, proclaiming that their society would be entirely white in less than a century. This pattern of stratification and elevation of whiteness appeared in other Latin American countries, such as CUBA and the DOMINICAN REPUBLIC, where there was a heavy influx of African slaves.

The discussion of whitening has been made more difficult for its advocates by the inconsistency of census definitions in countries such as Brazil and Cuba. In Brazil, scholars have detected a clear tendency for mulattos to reclassify themselves as white in successive censuses. This renders suspect any attempt to analyze trends in the racial composition of populations. VENEZUELA has solved this problem by eliminating race and color from the census. This has not, of course, eliminated the discussion of race in Venezuela. Rather it has made it possible for the elite to claim that Venezuela is already a "white" society. In Cuba the government under Fidel Castro long delayed the inclusion of race in its censuses, while at the same time claiming that the revolution had eradicated racial discrimination. The Brazilian military government eliminated race from the 1970 census in an effort to undercut discussions of race relations in that country. After vigorous protest by demographers and by the nonwhite community, race was restored in the Brazilian censuses of 1980 and 1990. "Blackness" has sometimes emerged as a rival to white hegemony, but primarily in cultural forms (music, dance, and religion). Its greatest influence is undoubtedly in the West Indies (*see* REGGAE). But nowhere, except HAITI, has it seriously challenged the concept of white superiority inherent in the doctrine of branqueamento.

The concept of whitening is still alive in present-day multiethnic Latin America. It can be found in folklore, popular humor, and popular culture. At the same time it has lost all intellectual respectability in the wake of the death (since the 1940s) of scientific racism. Whitening is now a kind of contraband idea surviving in popular thought but long since repudiated by scientific inquiry.

Thomas Skidmore

North America

White, Walter Francis

(b. July 1, 1893, Atlanta, Ga.; d. March 21, 1955, New York, N.Y.), African American civil rights leader who built the foundations of the CIVIL RIGHTS MOVEMENT as an official of the National Association for the Advancement of Colored People (NAACP), and influential author of the HARLEM RENAISSANCE.

Walter White grew up in a racially mixed neighborhood and, as a light-skinned, blue-eyed man, was able to pass for white. He credited a 1906 race riot in Atlanta, during which he defended his family's home from fire, as the incident that ignited his race consciousness as a black man. From that point on, he chose to live as an African American fighting for political and social justice.

After graduating from Atlanta University in 1916, White's activism with the Atlanta branch of the NATIONAL ASSOCIATION FOR THE ADVANCEMENT OF COLORED PEOPLE (NAACP) became his career. In 1918 he moved to New York to serve as assistant to NAACP executive secretary JAMES WELDON JOHNSON. He was an invaluable researcher for the NAACP's antilynching efforts; passing for white, he investigated lynchings and other racially motivated crimes without hindrance. White's reports for the NAACP were fodder for his fiction; his two novels, *The Fire in the Flint* (1924) and *Flight* (1926), both concern the responses of educated blacks, or "New Negroes," to racial injustice. Although the novels sometimes sacrifice plot and characterization to political message, they earned White a Guggenheim Fellowship in 1926. White used money from the fellowship for support while writing a seminal investigation of lynching, *Rope and Faggot: A Biography of Judge Lynch* (1929).

As executive secretary of the NAACP from 1931 to 1955, White worked with A. Philip Randolph to secure the establishment of the FAIR EMPLOYMENT PRACTICES COMMITTEE in 1941; his efforts also helped produce the executive orders banning discrimination in war-related industries that same year and in the entire United States military in 1948 (*see* MILITARY, BLACKS IN THE AMERICAN). A delegate with W. E. B. Du Bois and MARY MCLEOD BETHUNE to the founding of the United Nations in 1945, White also became involved with seeking justice for the African diaspora. One of White's most lasting achievements as NAACP executive secretary was the recruitment of CHARLES HAMILTON HOUSTON to serve as the NAACP's first full-time chief counsel. Under Houston's leadership and fueled by White's tireless fundraising efforts, the NAACP undertook a series of legal challenges to segregation, culminating in the 1954 United States Supreme Court's historic BROWN V. BOARD OF EDUCATION decision, which finally toppled segregated education in the United States.

SEE ALSO

Antilynching Movement; Atlanta Riot of 1906; Du Bois, William Edward Burghardt (W. E. B.); Lynching; Randolph, Asa Philip; Passing in the United States.

Africa

Widekum, ethnic group of Cameroon.

The Widekum primarily inhabit the North West Province of CAMEROON. Others live in eastern NIGERIA. They speak a Niger-Congo language and are closely related to the BAMILÉKÉ people. More than 200,000 people consider themselves Widekum.

SEE ALSO

Languages, African: An Overview.

North America

Wideman, John Edgar

(b. June 14, 1941, Washington, D.C.), African American author and scholar hailed as one of the most gifted writers of his generation.

According to the title of one of John Edgar Wideman's collections of short stories, "all stories are true." Guided by that principle, Wideman has spent a career as a scholar and author in pursuit of a more truthful history or chronicle of his own experience and that of other African Americans.

The oldest of five children born to Edgar and Betty French Wideman, Wideman spent the first ten years of his life in the predominantly black, middle-class Homewood section of PITTSBURGH, PENNSYLVANIA. Founded by his great-great-great-grandmother, escaped slave Sybela Owens, with help from her former owner's son, Charles Bell (later her husband), Homewood is the setting for Wideman's most acclaimed series of books, *The Homewood Trilogy* (1981-1983). The Wideman family moved to Shadyside, an upper-middle-class, white neighborhood, where Wideman attended high school. A basketball star, class president, and valedictorian, Wideman went to the University of Pennsylvania on a Benjamin Franklin Scholarship in 1959. There Wideman, who majored in English, was a celebrated scholar-athlete. Named to the Big Five Basketball Hall of Fame and inducted into Phi Beta Kappa upon his graduation in 1963, Wideman became the second African American (the first was Alain Locke) to receive a Rhodes Scholarship to Oxford University. He took a degree in eighteenth-century literature from Oxford in 1966.

Wideman went to the famed Iowa Writers' Workshop as a Kent Fellow in 1966-1967. There he wrote his first novel, *A Glance Away* (1967). This and his second novel, *Hurry Home* (1970), received critical accolades for their experimental language, form, and style. Although the novels focus on black characters, both black and white critics found them more akin to works by great American or European modernists such as James Joyce, T. S. Eliot, and William Faulkner than to a black literary tradition.

While teaching at the University of Pennsylvania in the early 1970s, Wideman had a transformative experience when he was asked by black students to teach a course on AFRICAN AMERICAN LITERATURE. Giving them at first what he called "the jive reply that it wasn't [his] field," he eventually accepted the challenge and re-educated himself. The discovery of an alternative literary tradition spurred Wideman to establish and direct the University of Pennsylvania's first Afro-American studies department from 1971 to 1973. After writing a more "black" novel, *The Lynchers*, in 1973, Wideman took a break from writing fiction and left Pennsylvania for a teaching position at the University of Wyoming, which he held until 1986.

In 1981 the first two installments of Wideman's *Homewood Trilogy, Hiding Place* and a short-story collection, *Damballah*, were published. These two books mark the maturation of Wideman's aesthetic philosophy. Deeply concerned with the importance of memory, history, and the interweaving of multiple cultural and historical traditions, the *Homewood* books explore Wideman's own African American roots. *Sent for You Yesterday* (1983), the third book in the trilogy, won the 1984 PEN/Faulkner Award for fiction.

Wideman's next book, *Brothers and Keepers* (1984), continued this autobiographical impulse. A series of letters or essays to his brother Robbie, who was serving a life sentence for murder, the book explored the two very different lives of the two brothers. *Brothers and Keepers* was nominated for the 1985 National Book Award. In 1986 Wideman's son Jacob, then 18, was convicted of murdering a camping companion and was also sentenced to life in prison. After this personal tragedy, Wideman returned to the East Coast and accepted a full professorship at the University of Massachusetts at Amherst. (Wideman has two other children: daughter Jamila, who followed her father's footsteps as an outstanding basketball player in high school and college; and son Danny, who is also a writer.)

Wideman's literary reputation has been secured with the publication of *Fever* (1989), a novel about the yellow fever epidemic in nineteenth-century Philadelphia; *Philadelphia Fire* (1990), a novel about the incidents surrounding the black radical group MOVE for which he won a PEN/Faulkner Award in 1991; the acclaimed memoir *Fatheralong: A Meditation on Fathers and Sons* (1994); and the novel *Cattle Killing* (1996). In 1993 Wideman received a MacArthur Foundation "genius grant."

See Also
Locke, Alain Leroy; Philadelphia, Pennsylvania.

North America

Wilberforce University, the first black institution of higher learning established in the United States.

Wilberforce University's stated goals for its students include helping them "to think logically and act creatively in all areas of human experience, to develop social awareness and a sense of responsibility to self and others, [and] to acquire an acquaintance with the various areas of human knowledge." Wilberforce was founded as Ohio African University by the Methodist Episcopal Church in 1843. Within a few years the college changed its name to honor eighteenth-century British abolitionist William Wilberforce.

The school's first students were slaves and free blacks; the college offered its first post-secondary instruction in 1856, and its first baccalaureate degree in 1857. In 1863 the African Methodist Episcopal (AME) Church bought the property and merged it with the AME Union Seminary, which had been established in Columbus, Ohio. AME Bishop Daniel Alexander Payne took over the combined institution, making him the first black college president in the United States.

Prominent members of Wilberforce's faculty have included Black Women's Club Movement leader Hallie Quinn Brown, who graduated from Wilberforce in 1873 and returned 20 years later to teach English and elocution; intellectual W. E. B. Du Bois, who taught there from 1894 to 1896; and historian Charles H. Wesley, who served as president from 1942 to 1947. Four-year degree programs were first offered in 1922, and in 1947 the university's normal and industrial department became a separate institution, now named Central State University. A mandatory cooperative education program instituted in 1964, which places students in career-oriented work assignments, remains one of Wilberforce University's strongest features. Today Wilberforce offers bachelors of arts and science degrees in 20 areas of concentration to approximately 800 enrolled students.

Lisa Clayton Robinson

See Also
African Methodist Episcopal Church; Du Bois, William Edward Burghardt (W. E. B.); Free Blacks in the United States, 1619 to 1863; Wesley, Charles Harris.

Africa

Wildebeest, or gnu, one of two species of African antelope.

The classification of the black wildebeest is *Connochaetes gnou*, and the blue wildebeest is classified as *Connochaetes taurinus*. The animals can range in height from 1.3 m to 3.2 m (about 8.5 to 10.5 ft) and can weigh from 100 to 180 kg (about 220 to 395 lb). Each species has an oxlike head, horns that grow out and then up, short tufts of hair on the face and chest, and a horselike tail. The black wildebeest, which lives exclusively in the grassy plains of interior South Africa, has been hunted for its meat and hide, and because it competed with livestock for food. Scientists estimate that only 4000 remain, all confined to national parks. Although 1.5 million blue wildebeest live in the wild from northern South Africa to Kenya, habitat encroachment may threaten their survival.

Robert Fay

North America

Wilder, Lawrence Douglas (b. January 17, 1931, Richmond, Va.), American politician and the first African American to be elected governor in the United States.

L. Douglas Wilder has served his home state of Virginia as state senator, lieutenant governor, and governor. A native of Richmond, the son of an insurance agent and a domestic worker, Wilder has made a career of conciliating tensions between the races.

Educated at the historically black Virginia Union University (1947-1951) and a graduate of Howard University Law School in Washington, D.C., in 1959, Wilder was always aware of the political possibilities of his own success. A recipient of the Bronze Star for bravery in the Korean War, he used his recognition as a platform to fight successfully for the promotion of passed-over African American military commanders. A self-made millionaire in his law practice, he parlayed his money and influence into a campaign for state senator in 1969. Wilder's success as a Democrat in a largely white, Republican state flows from his position as a "healer" of racial strife, his moderate views on social policy, his fiscal conservatism, and his ability to remake himself to suit the national political climate.

In the Virginia state legislature from 1969 to 1985, Wilder worked continually to end discrimination in the areas of employment and housing opportunities. In 1985 he ran successfully for lieutenant governor, and four years later he became governor of Virginia. Wilder was the first African American to be elected governor in the United States. (Prior to Wilder only one other black person had served as governor. P. B. S. Pinchback briefly became governor of Louisiana in 1872 after the sitting governor was impeached.)

Wilder's record as governor was mixed. Some claim that too much of Virginia's economic success came at the expense of social programs; others cite Wilder's flip-flopping on issues like capital punishment as evidence of his pandering to white, conservative voters. Nevertheless, Wilder's political ticket was still hot in 1991, when he made an unsuccessful bid for the Democratic nomination for president. Although he withdrew, he emerged as a major spokesperson for the Democratic Party nationally when he delivered the nominating speech for Vice President Al Gore at the Democratic National Convention. Wilder's gubernatorial term ended in 1994. He currently teaches politics at Virginia Commonwealth University and is actively pursuing the establishment of a slavery museum, an idea he first proposed in 1993.

See Also
Richmond, Virginia; Pinchback, Pinckney Benton Stewart.

Africa

Wildlife Management in Africa,

policies and practices aimed at protecting Africa's wild animal species without adversely affecting the welfare of its human population.

Africa is the world's second-largest continent, with a total land area of more than 19 million sq km (about 11.8 million sq mi). It is home to more mammal species than any other land region in the world. But these animals share the continent with approximately 800 million people – whose numbers are increasing at a rate of about 2.8 percent annually – as well as with growing populations of domestic livestock. While humans and wildlife have long coexisted in Africa, unprecedented human population growth over the past century has brought with it an increase in wild habitat destruction and certain forms of hunting. These trends have already driven many animal species to extinction and left many others threatened. But they have also given rise to a wide range of national, regional, and local wildlife management programs, and to ongoing debates about the most appropriate means of preserving Africa's biodiversity while meeting human needs.

Early Conservationism in Africa

Wildlife management, as the term is currently understood, began in Africa in 1900, when European colonial administrators met at the Convention for the Preservation of Animals, Birds, and Fish in Africa. Their wildlife management plans were intended to ensure the continued survival of animals that they considered either useful or harmless to people. Elephants and rhinoceroses were highly valued, for example, for their tusks and horns (*see* Ivory Trade). These and other big-game species, such as hippopotamuses, zebras, and lions, were also considered prize trophy animals by wealthy European and American safari hunters. To ensure conservation of these species, the convention limited rhino and elephant hunting, and prohibited the hunting of infant and adolescent elephants as well as adult female elephants with calves. A few species defined as "harmless," that is, those that did little or no damage to human beings or their property – including gorillas, chimpanzees, pygmy hippopotamuses, white bearded gnus, giraffes, and mountain zebras – were also fully protected. Some of these species, especially the primates, were also considered of scientific interest. Lions, leopards, hyenas, and wild dogs, all of which attacked domestic animals, were defined as vermin and therefore considered open game.

Approaches to wildlife management shifted in the 1920s with the widespread introduction of national parks to Africa. National parks were modeled on those in the United States, such as Yellowstone National Park, which were themselves modeled on hunting parks in medieval Britain. At a time of rapid industrialization and urbanization in the United States, national parks were seen to preserve "unspoiled" scenic areas for tourists. Colonial governments adopted this model for Africa, but their priority was not so much scenery as wildlife. It was to be preserved, observed, and studied, but in a way that would not threaten humans or their property. Thus a central tenet of wildlife management that developed during this period was to *contain* animals in a "wild" but bordered setting. The land set aside for parks, however, was often already inhabited by people, many of whom had long depended on both the land and the wild animals for survival.

In both colonial and independent Africa, the creation of national parks often resulted in the eviction of farming communities and nomadic herders from their traditional lands. During the 1950s the British colonial government evicted the Maasai people from Serengeti National Park. As recently as 1988 in Tanzania more than 5000 pastoral people were relocated to create parkland. Inside park borders, activities such as hunting, cutting timber, gathering wild foods, grazing, and watering domestic livestock are generally officially prohibited. In practice, the prohibitions have proven difficult to enforce. People in local communities who have historically depended on access to the parklands' natural resources for subsistence often sorely resent the restrictions. Poaching is a particularly serious concern to wildlife managers, but it is believed that at least some of the poachers – especially those who target rare species like the black rhino – are not local people killing for meat but rather "professionals" hired by smugglers of rhino horn and other animal products banned from international trade. The governments of Kenya and Zimbabwe have responded to the poaching problem by authorizing park rangers to shoot suspected poachers on sight.

Changing Views on Wildlife Management

For many reasons, wildlife management experts in recent years have begun to look beyond the standard strategies of creating national parks and banning hunting to ensure wildlife conservation. One reason is the difficulty that authorities have controlling poaching. In addition, groups who have been threatened with eviction from their traditional lands have become increasingly vocal in defense of their property rights. Tanzanian Maasai, for example, organized the group Korongoro Integrated Peoples Oriented to Conservation (the acronym KIPOC means "we shall recover" in Maasai) in the early 1990s to lobby for the rights of "indigenous minority peoples." At the same time, however, international conservation groups such as the World Wildlife Fund continue to call for stronger measures to protect certain African wildlife species.

These international groups have launched letter-writing and fundraising campaigns that have made African wildlife conservation an issue of global concern. Yet their stance on certain issues has not always won support in Africa. In the past they have been criticized for ignoring regional variations in wildlife populations and their significance to people, and in some cases for ignoring the counsel of wildlife biologists. These conflicts were especially apparent in the debate leading up to the 1989 global ban on ivory trading, agreed to by the 130 member nations of the Convention on International Trade in Endangered Species of Wild Fauna and Flora (CITES). American and European conservation and animal rights groups led the call for the ban and based their arguments on the endangered status of elephant populations in East Africa. In fact, the elephant populations had declined drastically just in the years since independence: in Kenya, for example, poachers had reduced the elephant population from 167,000 in 1973 to a mere 19,000 by 1989. In southern Africa, on the other hand, elephants had become so numerous that they were regularly damaging not only farmers' crops but also wild vegetation. Some parks in this region cull their elephant populations simply to prevent them from eating all their food supply. Not surprisingly, governments in southern African countries such as South Africa, Botswana, and Zimbabwe, along with many wildlife biologists, all opposed the proposed universal ivory trade ban, which would deprive the countries of millions of dollars of revenue. Nevertheless, the ban was initiated because of the pressure that conservationist groups put on CITES member nations.

It took eight years before the southern African nations convinced other CITES members to agree to a partial lifting of the ivory trade ban. The agreement that passed in June 1997 permitted Botswana, Namibia, and Zimbabwe to sell their excess ivory stocks to Japan. Animal rights groups, such as the United States Humane Society (USHS), which are also against wildlife culling, opposed the agreement. Instead, they promote contraception and park expansion to handle wildlife population growth: in 1996, for example, the USHS gave South Africa's Kruger National Park $5 million to fund both research on hormonal birth control for elephants and additional land purchases.

Contemporary Approaches to Wildlife Management

Despite the controversies surrounding certain species, wildlife managers have agreed on a few basic strategies needed for effective conservation. Many experts endorsed the notion of reserves that will be able to provide for the largest number of species with the largest range. In areas where large amounts of land cannot be set aside, several small reserves can be linked to one another to allow migration. The need for such links became clear in the 1990s in Botswana where, although the country had reserved approximately 40 percent of its total land area for wildlife habitat, the WILDEBEEST population fell by 94 percent between 1979 and 1994, and the hartebeest population by 83 percent. Scientists discovered that these animals' migratory routes had been cut off by farm fencing, and huge numbers had died of thirst or hunger.

Managers must also attempt to keep the genetic diversity alive within the species. Inbreeding can be dangerous. An increase of only 10 percent in inbreeding can lower reproductive performance by 10 to 25 percent, which could explain much of the cheetah's declining numbers. Scientists have determined that cheetahs are heavily inbred. If species numbers drop too low, then captive breeding in zoos or special reserves can help restore genetic diversity. Animals born in captivity, however, then have to be reintroduced into the wild, which raises another set of risks.

Another principle of contemporary wildlife management is to minimize the harm wildlife can inflict on nearby human settlements. One approach is to set aside buffer zones between game reserves and farmland, so wildlife straying off a reserve are less likely to trample crops or attack domestic livestock. The idea of the buffer zone assumes that park authorities are responsible for patrolling the park boundaries, and that once animals cross the buffer zone into human habitat, people should be able to kill them in self-defense.

Perhaps the most difficult task facing wildlife managers is to make conservation worthwhile for local people. One well-known example of an attempt to make conservation profitable for communities is Zimbabwe's Communal Areas Management Programme for Indigenous Resources (CAMPFIRE). Initiated in the mid-1980s, this program seeks to promote economic development in the impoverished communal lands (roughly 42 percent of Zimbabwe's land area) through the sustainable use of natural resources – including elephants. Zimbabwean farmers have traditionally had an adversarial relationship with elephants, because the animals do so much damage to their fields. A single animal can easily eat or trample a family's entire food crop. To make conservation more attractive to farming communities, the Zimbabwean government gave them a voice in determining how many elephants could be hunted each year within their own districts, and then planned to turn over to these communities a portion of the profits generated by hunting tours.

The benefits to local communities from controlled elephant hunting are significant. The mostly foreign hunters who come to shoot elephant and other game in Zimbabwe pay as much as $12,000 for one trophy, in addition to a daily hunting fee of $1000. In 1993, 12 districts with a total population of 400,000 earned more than $1.5 million through trophy fees. Some of this money has gone into village projects such as schools and granaries, but some has also gone into building fences to protect crops from elephants. The revenue has also helped discourage poaching and encouraged communities actively to promote wildlife survival in their districts.

Another approach to reconciling the needs of people and wildlife is the creation of luxury resorts that provide both protected space for animals and abundant employment and entrepreneurial opportunities for local communities. This approach is controversial but increasingly popular with cash-poor African governments. In 1996, for example, MOZAMBIQUE granted American entrepreneur James Blanchard a long-term lease to an extensive tract of land south of the capital of Maputo. He planned to construct an $800 million, 10,360 sq km (4000 sq mi) tourist park and game reserve. It included part of the Atlantic coastline as well as such amenities as golf courses, a floating casino, and a steam train that carried visitors through the areas containing herds of elephant and antelope. Developers anticipated that once the animal populations grew sufficiently, controlled hunting would be introduced as a way to cull herds and attract high-end, big-game hunters. The plan did not please everybody, in part because it would displace an estimated 10,000 people in farming and fishing communities. The park's supporters argued, however, that employment opportunities, ranging from game trackers to construction workers to domestic jobs in the hotels, would mitigate the hardship.

Other reserves in Namibia and Botswana offer basically the same kinds of luxury wildlife tourism, but with one important modification. The parks' developers attempted to win the acceptance of nearby communities by building clinics and schools and by employing as many local people as possible. They offered jobs not only for cooks and chambermaids but also in ironworking and construction. In addition, some of these parks encouraged local farmers to grow produce that could be purchased and used by their hotel restaurants and catering facilities.

Tourism alone offers no definitive solution to the challenges of preserving wildlife and its habitat, and in any case it is only feasible in countries that boast the big-game species and scenic landscapes that attract visitors from overseas. Moreover, foreign tourist companies still receive the lion's share of the profits generated from "safari" tourism in the game-rich countries of East and southern Africa. Still, wildlife management strategies in Africa are now more sensitive than they once were to the needs of both animals and people.

Robert Fay

SEE ALSO

African Hunting Dog; Cheetah; Chimpanzee; Colonial Rule; Elephant; Gnu; Hippopotamus; Hyena; Lion; Gorilla; Maputo, Mozambique; Rhinoceros; Tourism in Africa; Zebra.

North America

Wilkerson, Doxey Alphonso

(b. April 25, 1905, Excelsior Springs, Mo.; d. June 17, 1993, Norwalk, Conn.), African American educator and Communist Party spokesperson on the "Negro question" during the 1940s and 1950s.

In 1944 Doxey Wilkerson published an essay in the anthology *What the Negro Wants*, drawing parallels between the struggle for African American civil rights and the Allied struggle in World War II. In addition to teaching at HOWARD UNIVERSITY in WASHINGTON, D.C., and Yeshiva University in New York, Wilkerson worked to further the African American struggle through his work with the Communist Party, which resulted in repeated investigations by the United States House Un-American Activities Committee. He resigned from the party in 1957 and was active in the CIVIL RIGHTS MOVEMENT through the 1960s. He continued civil rights and educational work until retiring in 1984.

Robert Fay

SEE ALSO

World War II and African Americans; New York, New York; Communist Party USA, African Americans and the.

North America

Wilkins, Roy Ottoway

(b. August 30, 1901, St. Louis, Mo.; d. September 8, 1981, New York, N.Y.), African American journalist, civil rights leader, and director of the National Association for the Advancement of Colored People (NAACP).

Before Roy Wilkins was born, his father had been forced to flee St. Louis to avoid being lynched for refusing to follow a white man's order to get out of the road. Wilkins grew up in St. Paul, Minnesota, where he attended racially integrated schools. He became urgently aware of racial matters at age 18, when three Minnesotan black men were lynched by a mob of 5000 whites. Upon enrolling in the University of Minnesota, Wilkins became active in the NATIONAL ASSOCIATION FOR THE ADVANCEMENT OF COLORED PEOPLE (NAACP), as well as on the campus newspaper. He would pursue both interests in Kansas City following graduation. Wilkins worked for the *Kansas City Call*, an African American newspaper, until 1931. He then became assistant executive secretary for the NAACP, a position he held while editing the organization's newspaper, the *Crisis*, until 1949.

In 1955 Wilkins was appointed to serve as the NAACP's executive director, the organization's highest administrative post. He steered the NAACP through the Civil Rights Movement's most turbulent era, and with Martin Luther King Jr. helped to organize the March on Washington in 1963. Throughout his career Wilkins upheld the principle of nonviolent, legal forms of redress, which tended to alienate him from more radical black groups. Wilkins's struggles for equality and civil rights brought him many awards and earned him the nickname "Mr. Civil Rights."

See Also

Press, Black, in the United States; *Crisis, The*; Kansas City, Missouri; King, Martin Luther, Jr.; Lynching; March on Washington, 1963.

North America

Williams, Bert

(b. December 12, 1874?, Antigua, West Indies?; d. March 4, 1922, New York, N.Y.), actor and comedian of the vaudeville team of Williams and Walker who elevated Negro caricature to an art form.

Bert Williams's exact date and place of birth in the Caribbean is unknown. It is known that he moved to Riverside, California, in 1885 with his parents, Fred and Julia Williams. After high school he lived in San Francisco, where he entertained audiences in saloons and restaurants before touring with a small minstrel company.

In 1893 Williams met George Walker. The two developed an act that soon brought them national recognition. They combined Negro comedy with ragtime music and cakewalk dancing. Williams played the unkempt, fumbling "darky" while Walker was the dapper, smooth-stepping "dandy." Williams's hit songs included "I'm a Jonah Man" and "Nobody." Before Walker fell ill and retired in 1909, they performed several of their ragtime musicals on Broadway: *Son of Ham* (1900), *In Dahomey* (1902), *Abyssinia* (1906), and *Bandanna Land* (1907). *In Dahomey* was performed for the British royal family on Buckingham Palace lawn. They also recorded a number of skits for the Victor Company.

Williams continued to perform, becoming in 1910 the first African American to appear in the Ziegfeld Follies, the leading variety extravaganza of the time. After leaving the Follies in 1919, Williams performed his own shows until his death in 1922 during a run of *Under the Bamboo Tree*. Wearing blackface and using a "darky" dialect, Williams played a racially stereotyped caricature throughout his entire career. Williams's friends reported that despite the actor's stage success, the discrimination and rejection he faced in everyday life drove him to deep depression.

Aaron Myers

See Also

Cakewalk, The; Minstrelsy; Racial Stereotypes.

North America

Williams, Billy Dee

(b. April 6, 1937, New York, N.Y.), African American actor known for his suave character in stage productions, movies, and television shows during the 1960s, 1970s, and 1980s.

Billy Dee Williams was born William December to a Texan father and a West Indian mother in Harlem. His parents juggled several jobs while his maternal grandmother helped raise Williams and his twin sister, Loretta. With aspirations of becoming a painter, Williams attended New York's High School of Music and Art and the National Academy of Fine Arts and Design. While pursuing his art studies, Williams learned about the Stanislavsky method of natural acting through his acquaintance with Sidney Poitier and Paul Mann at the Actors Workshop in Harlem. He initially viewed acting as a way to earn money for art supplies, but by the early 1960s Williams had begun to devote all of his energy to acting.

Williams first appeared on stage at age seven in *The Firebrand of Florence* (1945). His first screen appearance was in *The Last Angry Man* (1959). *A Taste of Honey* (1960), which won the New York Drama Critic's 1961 award for best foreign play, featured him in one of his earliest stage performances. After the failure of two marriages, the first to Audrey Sellers and the second to Marlene Clark, Williams fell into a depression in 1964.

Williams made a triumphant return to acting in 1970 with his Emmy-nominated portrayal of Chicago Bears football player Gale Sayers in *Brian's Song*. His success earned him a seven-year film contract with Motown's Berry Gordy, and he co-starred with Diana Ross in *Lady Sings the Blues* (1972) and *Mahogany* (1975). In the 1980s he was featured in the movies *The Empire Strikes Back* (1980) and *Return of the Jedi* (1983), as well as in the television programs *Dynasty* and *Star Trek*. In 1984 Williams was inducted into the Black Filmmakers Hall of Fame, and in 1985 he was awarded a star on the Hollywood Walk of Fame.

Aaron Myers

See Also

Harlem, New York; Motown; Film, Blacks in American.

North America

Williams, Daniel Hale

(b. January 18, 1856, Hollidaysburg, Pa.; d. August 4, 1931, Idlewild, Mich.), African American surgeon who performed the first successful open-heart surgery.

The son of a barber, Daniel Hale Williams lived on his own after age 12. As a youth he worked as a shoemaker, a roustabout on a lake steamer, and a barber. Moving with his sister to Wisconsin, he met Henry Palmer, a prominent physician, the surgeon general of Wisconsin for ten years. Williams was apprenticed by Palmer, who became his mentor and helped pay his tuition at the Chicago Medical School.

Graduating with an M.D. in 1883, Williams opened a medical practice on the South Side of Chicago, Illinois. An adept doctor, he served as an attending physician at the Protestant Orphan Asylum and as a surgeon at the South Side Dispensary. Williams also worked as a clinical instructor at the Chicago Medical College and as a physician with the city railway company. He was appointed in 1889 to the Illinois Board of Health, on which he served for four years, enforcing medical standards in handling infectious diseases.

Williams pursued a career in medicine at a time when African Americans were not permitted hospital staff positions or allowed the use of equipment at area hospitals. African American women were also barred from the nurses' training programs at these hospitals. In response to these circumstances, Williams founded Provident Hospital in 1891. It was the first black-owned hospital and boasted an interracial staff and a nurses' training school. In 1894 Williams was named the chief surgeon at Freedmen's Hospital in Washington, D.C. This hospital was funded by the federal government and affiliated with Howard University's medical school, although when Williams arrived it was in need of reorganization and leadership.

Reorganizing the hospital into departments, reestablishing a nurses' training school, and developing an internship program, Williams brought new life to the hospital. He returned to Chicago in 1898 to rejoin Provident Hospital and reopen his private practice. Widely published in prominent medical journals, in 1913 he was appointed associate attending surgeon at Chicago's St. Luke's Hospital. He was also the only black charter member of the American College of Surgeons. In 1924 Williams retired to Michigan and died there seven years later.

The feat for which Williams is most known is the successful surgery he performed on James Cornish in 1893. Cornish, a street tough, had been stabbed in the chest. After the external wounds were sewn up, Cornish's condition continued to deteriorate. Concluding that Cornish was bleeding internally, Williams decided to open his chest cavity and try to stop the bleeding. Finding the knife had slashed an artery and tissue around the heart, Williams used catgut thread to sew up these internal wounds. The operation was a success and Cornish lived another 20 years, making Williams the first physician to perform successful open-heart surgery.

See Also
Howard University.

Latin America and the Caribbean

Williams, Eric

(b. September 25, 1911, Port of Spain, Trinidad; d. March 29, 1981, Port of Spain, Trinidad), one of the most distinguished Afro-Caribbean historians and politicians. Williams helped found Trinidad's People's National Movement (PNM) Party and held several different high-ranking political offices, including prime minister.

Eric Williams was the eldest of 12 children, born into a family of modest means. His education was funded by a series of competitive scholarships awarded to those who excelled academically. He attended Queen's Royal College, a preparatory school for boys, and in 1931 won a scholarship to study at a British university. At Oxford University Williams earned a bachelor's degree and in 1938 a doctorate in history. His dissertation, "Economic Aspects of the Abolition of the West Indies Slave Trade," would later be published as *Capitalism and Slavery*.

In 1939 Williams moved to the United States to establish an academic career, teaching social sciences at Howard University. Rising through the academic ranks, he was offered a tenured position in 1946.

Williams returned to Trinidad in 1948 and worked as deputy chairman of the Caribbean Research Council of the Caribbean Commission. The commission was designed to encourage the United Kingdom and the United States to cooperate in the Caribbean. Williams was defiantly unwilling to adhere to the commission's strict requirement of absolute neutrality in political affairs, and his contract was not renewed in 1955.

Shortly after, Williams declared his intention to remain in Trinidad. It is unclear to what extent this decision was influenced by a dispassionate assessment of the limited career prospects available to a colonial abroad. Williams soon began to deliver a series of public lectures in forums throughout the island, but most often in Port of Spain's Woodford Square. The lectures addressed a number of issues, ranging from the need for constitutional and economic reform to race relations in the Caribbean.

The enthusiastic public response to the lectures, coupled with the emergence under Williams's influence of a group of political strategists intent on both shaping and promulgating a nationalist, political vision, led to the founding in January 1956 of a new political party, the People's National Movement (PNM). The multiracial PNM championed a political agenda that mirrored the concerns of its target constituency, the rapidly emerging middle class.

By virtue of his international reputation and experience, Williams was the most authoritative figure in the development of the new party. He proved to be a shrewd political entrepreneur and an inspiring public speaker. Under Williams's leadership the PNM championed colonial nationalism and economic decolonization; the need for territorial integrity; the expansion of the voting franchise; educational and curricular reform, with a heightened emphasis on Caribbean history; and the necessity of Caribbean economic integration.

In Trinidad's 1956 general election, the PNM won a majority of seats. Williams was elected representative to the legislative council for his district of South Port of Spain. The trajectory of his political career, with its increasingly sophisticated administrative responsibilities – Williams was chief minister from 1956 to 1959, premier from 1959 to 1962, and prime minister from 1962 until his death in office on March 29, 1981 – paralleled the country's eventual transformation from a British colony into an independent republic.

Lorraine Anastasia Lezama

See Also
Trinidad and Tobago.

North America

Williams, Franklin Hall

(b. October 22, 1917, Flushing, N.Y.), African American lawyer who was the head of the African division of the Peace Corps and United States ambassador to Ghana.

After graduating from the New York public school system, Franklin Williams acquired an A.B. from Lincoln University and a J.D. from Fordham Law School. Following service in World War II he worked as an assistant to Thurgood Marshall, then assistant counsel to the National Association for the Advancement of Colored People (NAACP), until 1950. Williams served as West Coast director of the NAACP until 1959.

After conducting voter registration dinners that helped elect John F. Kennedy president, Williams was selected to head the African branch of the newly created Peace Corps. Part of his job entailed traveling throughout Africa with Peace Corps director Sargent Shriver to plan the organization's future. His experiences in a wide range of foreign nations primed him for a diplomatic post. In 1964 President Lyndon B. Johnson appointed Williams to serve on a delegation to the Economic and Social Council in Geneva, and one year later named him the U.S. ambassador to Ghana, a position he held until 1968.

Williams returned to the United States to serve as director of Columbia University's Urban Center, and then became president of the Phelps-Stokes Fund, which provides financial support for the education of Africans and African Americans.

See Also
World War II and African Americans.

North America

Williams, George Washington

(b. October 16, 1849, Bedford Springs, Pa.; d. August 2, 1891, Blackpool, England), scholar and minister; considered the first major American historian of African descent.

George Washington Williams left school at age 14 and lied about his age in order to enlist in the Union army during the Civil War. He later enlisted in the Mexican Army, in which he quickly rose to the rank of lieutenant colonel, and then joined the United States Cavalry in 1867, through which he served in the Indian campaigns.

In 1868 he enrolled at Newton Theological Seminary in Cambridge, Massachusetts. Graduating in 1874, he became the school's first African American alumnus. Immediately upon graduation, Williams was ordained as pastor of the Twelfth Baptist Church in Boston. Fascinated with the church, he wrote an 80-page study of its history. He left, however, after one year, and in Washington, D.C., started an unsuccessful academic journal about African Americans. Williams became pastor of Union Baptist Church in Cincinnati, Ohio, where he became a regular contributor to the *Cincinnati Commercial* under the pen name "Aristides." He also passed the bar exam to practice law in Ohio (and he would later practice in Boston), and in 1879 he became the first African American elected to the Ohio legislature.

At this time Williams also began to make his mark as an historian. He was a staunch supporter of the view, current at that time, that history was an objective science, and he was determined to apply this approach to African American history. In Ohio he began the research for his comprehensive, two-volume *History of the Negro Race in America, 1619-1880* (1882), which was the first full-length study of African American history by a person of African descent. He dedicated himself to African American history because of his opinion that African Americans had "been the most vexatious problem in North America from the time of its discovery down to the present day… [and writing] such a history would give the world more correct ideas of the Colored people, and incite the latter to greater effort in the struggle of citizenship and manhood." Williams also later wrote a *History of Negro Troops in the War of Rebellion* (1887), which argued that African Americans were among the most gallant soldiers in the Civil War.

Williams's scholarship brought him renown as an African American historian and advocate. In 1885 he was appointed minister to Haiti by outgoing President Chester A. Arthur. However, the presidency was assumed by Grover Cleveland, who refused to give Williams his post.

Williams became frustrated with Washington politics and turned his attention to international affairs, particularly the colonization and exploitation of Africa. He attended a major antislavery conference in Brussels in 1889. Belgium then sent him to Congo to study conditions there. The country's abysmal poverty so distressed him that, along with his official report, he wrote for wider circulation *An Open Letter to His Serene Majesty, Leopold II, King of Belgium*. This was the first public critique of King Leopold for his savage oppression of the people of the Congo. After his survey Williams traveled widely throughout Africa, and apparently contracted a disease that killed him upon his return to England.

See Also

Congo, Democratic Republic of the; Leopold II; Boston, Massachusetts; Civil War, American.

North America

Williams, John Alfred

(b. December 5, 1925, Hinds County, Miss.), African American writer and educator whose works explore racial and social injustices from an African American perspective.

John Alfred Williams grew up in Syracuse, New York, to which he returned after navy service in World War II to finish high school and graduate from Syracuse University with a degree in English and journalism in 1950. Williams's writing career developed in the late 1950s and early 1960s, when he began serving as a correspondent for numerous magazines, including *Jet*, *Ebony*, *Newsweek*, and *Holiday*. His first novel, *The Angry Ones*, was published in 1960. It has been followed by more than 20 other novels and nonfiction works (including a book on the comedian Richard Pryor titled *If I Stop I'll Die: The Comedy and Tragedy of Richard Pryor*), as well as numerous articles, essays, anthologies, and a play.

Williams's writings examine African American personal and communal struggles. His tone ranges from the romantic to the brutally apocalyptic. Williams's uncompromising calls for social justice and stylistic innovations have strongly influenced the African American literary tradition and contemporary African American aesthetics. His major work, *The Man Who Cried I Am* (1967), fictionalized the events surrounding the retraction of the 1962 Prix de Rome Award by the Academy of American Arts and Letters for his novel *Night Song*, presumably because of academy members' disapproval of Williams's engagement to a white woman. Other works, such as *!Click Song!* (1982) and *The Berhama Account* (1987), deal with love's healing power in the midst of adversity.

Williams has taught at various colleges and universities, most recently at Rutgers University in Newark, New Jersey, as Paul Robeson Distinguished Professor of English. He has received various awards, including the Before Columbus Foundation's American Book Award in 1983, and the John A. Williams Archive was founded at the University of Rochester in New York in 1987.

Marc Mazique

See Also

World War II and African Americans; Literature, African American; *Ebony*; *Jet*; Pryor, Richard Franklin Lenox Thomas.

North America

Williams, Lacey Kirk

(b. July 11, 1871, Eufala, Ala.; d. October 27, 1940), African American minister and denomination leader.

Lacey Kirk Williams was converted and baptized in 1884 at the Thankful Baptist Church, which his parents helped found in Brazos Bottom, Texas. From the start of his career as a Baptist minister he was involved in the government of the Baptist church. In 1916 Williams was named pastor of Chicago's 4000-member Olivet Church. During his pastorship the church's membership increased to 12,000, and the church became a positive force in the life of Chicago's black community, providing it numerous social services. He achieved national prominence as president of the General Baptist Convention of Illinois (1917-1922), as president of the National Baptist Convention (1922-1940), and as vice president of the Baptist World Alliance (1928-1940). He was killed in a plane crash in 1940.

See Also

Baptists; Chicago, Illinois.

North America

Williams, Mary Lou

(b. May 8, 1910, Atlanta, Ga.; d. May 28, 1981, Durham, N.C.), African American pianist,

Pianist and arranger Mary Lou Williams was the most influential woman instrumentalist in the history of jazz, influencing both Kansas City swing and bebop. *CORBIS/Bettmann*

composer, arranger, and educator known as the "First Lady of Jazz" and considered the most significant female instrumentalist in JAZZ history for contributing to the development of both the Kansas City swing style of the 1930s and the bebop style of the early 1940s.

Born Mary Elfrieda Scruggs, Mary Lou Williams began playing piano professionally at age six in PITTSBURGH, PENNSYLVANIA. Her early influences included Earl Hines, Jelly Roll Morton, and Lovie Austin. As an adolescent, Williams performed in the Theater Owners Booking Association (TOBA) black vaudeville circuit alongside such figures as Fats Waller, Duke Ellington, and Willie "The Lion" Smith. In 1926 she married John Williams, a saxophonist and bandleader.

Williams began arranging in 1929 after she joined the Andy Kirk Band, first based in Oklahoma City and later in Kansas City, composing blues-based works that influenced the development of 1930s swing. During the 1930s she performed and arranged for Louis Armstrong, Cab Calloway, Ellington, and others. Williams moved to New York in 1942 and joined Ellington's band as principal arranger and pianist, composing such notable works as "Trumpet No End" (1942). In the 1940s she mentored and jammed with many of the young beboppers, including Charlie Parker, Thelonious Monk, Bud Powell, and Dizzy Gillespie. Her famous *Zodiac Suite*, written in 1945, was adapted and performed by the New York Philharmonic in Carnegie Hall the following year.

In the 1950s Williams converted to Roman Catholicism and began concentrating on charitable activities and composing religious pieces. In 1957 she resumed performing and also formed Mary Records, the first record company established by a woman. Her major religious work, *Mary Lou's Mass* (1969), was commissioned by the Vatican and adapted for ballet by ALVIN AILEY two years later. Williams went on to receive numerous honorary doctorates and two Guggenheim Fellowships. She taught courses on jazz at a number of colleges and universities, including Duke University in Durham, North Carolina, where she died in 1981.

Marc Mazique

SEE ALSO
Armstrong, Louis ("Satchmo"); Calloway, Cabell (Cab); Gillespie, John Birks ("Dizzy"); Hines, Earl Kenneth ("Fatha"); Monk, Thelonious Sphere; Morton, Ferdinand Joseph ("Jelly Roll"); Parker, Charles Christopher ("Bird"); Powell, Earl ("Bud"); Smith, Willie ("the Lion"); Waller, Thomas Wright ("Fats"); Ellington, Edward Kennedy ("Duke"); Blues, The.

North America

Williamson, Johnny Lee ("Sonny Boy")

(b. March 30, 1914, Jackson, Tenn.; d. June 1, 1948, Chicago, Ill.), African American musician revered for transforming the blues harmonica from a novelty instrument to an integral component of Chicago-style blues.

Johnny Lee Williamson taught himself to play the harmonica as a child. In his teens he left home and traveled, hobo-style, throughout the South with mandolin player Yank Rachel and guitarist Sleepy John Estes. He moved to Chicago in 1937 and quickly became one of the city's most popular bluesmen, recording such hits as "Good Morning Little School Girl" and "Sugar Man Blues."

Williamson's imaginative style and stunning virtuosity brought the harmonica to the forefront of blues, and they have influenced virtually every major blues harmonicist after him. Williamson pioneered numerous playing techniques that are now considered standard. Among them are manipulating the sound of the harmonica by cupping the hands, and "crossed key" playing, in which one tunes the harmonica a fourth below the key of the song. This allows the musician to play in the right key by inhaling rather than exhaling, affording him a greater ability to "bend" the notes.

Williamson was known for his distinctive "mumbling" singing style. One sign of his renown is that harmonicist Aleck "Rice" Miller began recording under the name Sonny Boy Williamson and came to be known as Sonny Boy #2.

Williamson was murdered on the steps of his home at the height of his popularity. In 1980 he was inducted into the Blues Foundation's Hall of Fame.

SEE ALSO
Blues, The; Chicago, Illinois.

North America

Williams, Peter, Jr.

(b. 1780, New Brunswick, N.J.; d. October 10, 1840), African American minister, abolitionist, and church founder.

Peter Williams Jr. was raised in the Methodist church under the tutelage of the white minister Thomas Lyell. In 1818, with the blessing of the white congregation of Lyell's St. John Methodist Episcopal Church, Williams organized a separate black congregation. St. Philip's African Church was consecrated in Harlem on July 3, 1819, and in 1826 Williams was ordained, making him the first black Episcopalian priest. An ardent abolitionist, he helped found *Freedom's Journal* in 1827, a black-owned newspaper that demanded an end to slavery and the inception of racial equality. For two years he served as a manager of the AMERICAN ANTI-SLAVERY SOCIETY. Rumors that he had performed an interracial marriage ended his public career, but he continued to be active in his church until his death in 1840.

SEE ALSO
Abolitionism in the United States; *Freedom's Journal*; African Methodist Episcopal Church; Harlem, New York.

North America

Williams, Peter, Sr.

(b. 1749, New York, N.Y.; d. February 1823), African American founder of the African Methodist Episcopal Zion denomination.

Born a slave in the New York City area, Peter Williams Sr. joined a Methodist church and became sexton in 1778. When his master, a Loyalist, returned to England in 1783, the church's trustees bought Williams. Williams firmly believed in equality and was upset when black members of the church were required to sit in segregated pews at the rear of the sanctuary. In 1795 Williams led a group of black members in founding their own church, which was chartered six years later as the African Methodist Episcopal Zion Church. It was the mother church for the denomination of the same name and it was the first black church in New York.

SEE ALSO
African Methodist Episcopal Zion Church; New York, New York.

North America

Williams, Robert Franklin

(b. February 26, 1925, Monroe, N.C.; d. October 15, 1996, Grand Rapids, Mich.), civil rights activist and prominent advocate of black self-defense and revolutionary nationalism.

Robert Franklin Williams grew up in a tradition of resistance to white supremacy. His grandfather, born a slave, had been a Republican Party activist during RECONSTRUCTION after the Civil War, when former slaves sought to establish themselves as equal citizens but found their efforts dashed by white terrorists. His grandfather edited a newspaper called *The People's Voice*. His grandmother, who lived through these struggles, was a daily presence in his life as he grew to manhood. She told young Williams stories of the crusading editor's political exploits and before she died gave him his grandfather's gun.

World War II transformed Williams's life; he moved to Detroit to work in the defense industries, fought white mobs in the DETROIT RIOT OF 1943, and marched for freedom in a segregated United States Army (*see* MILITARY, BLACKS IN THE AMERICAN). Military training "instilled in us what a virtue it was to fight for democracy," he said, "but most of all they taught us to use arms."

When he returned to his birthplace, Monroe, North Carolina, in 1955 Williams served as president of the Monroe chapter of the National Association for the Advancement of Colored People (NAACP). Confronted by Ku Klux Klan terrorism, Williams organized the local chapter into a black militia that repelled armed Klan attacks. In 1959, after an all-white jury acquitted a white man charged with the attempted rape of a pregnant black woman, Williams called for blacks "to meet violence with violence," invoking "the right of armed self-defense against attack." The NAACP suspended Williams for his remarks in a struggle over the meaning of nonviolence for the African American freedom struggle. The following year Williams debated prominent pacifists, including Martin Luther King Jr., the leading spokesperson of the black freedom struggle.

In 1961 followers of King came to Monroe, many of them intent on proving that nonviolence could work. Armed racial conflict broke out, forcing Williams to flee to Cuba under federal indictment on trumped-up kidnapping charges. From Havana, Williams broadcast "Radio Free Dixie," which spread his gospel of "armed self-reliance." He also published his newsletter *The Crusader,* whose readership was about 40,000. His 1962 book *Negroes with Guns* was a decisive influence on the Black Panther Party for Self-Defense, founded in Oakland, California, in 1966, and on a generation of increasingly defiant black activists.

Moving to North Vietnam and then China in 1966, Williams wrote antiwar propaganda aimed at African American soldiers fighting in Vietnam and called for revolution in the United States. In China Williams moved in the upper circles of the Chinese government. The Revolutionary Action Movement and the Republic of New Africa, two important revolutionary black nationalist groups in the United States, both chose him as their president-in-exile. In 1969, as the U.S. government moved to open diplomatic relations with China, Williams traded his knowledge of China for safe passage home and a post at the University of Michigan's Center for Chinese Studies. Just before he died in 1996, Williams completed his autobiography, *While God Lay Sleeping*. Above the desk where he wrote hung the ancient rifle his grandmother had given him.

Williams was typical of the generation of black Southerners who launched the African American freedom movement. His evolution from local NAACP leader to international revolutionary underlines both the growing radicalism of the movement and its origins in traditions of militant African American self-assertion.

Timothy Tyson

See Also
World War II and African Americans; Black Panther Party; Detroit, Michigan; San Francisco and Oakland, California; King, Martin Luther, Jr.; Vietnam War; Havana, Cuba; Black Nationalism in the United States.

North America

Williams, Sherley

(b. August 25, 1944, Bakersfield, Calif.), African American poet, novelist, and scholar who emphasized the importance of history and folklore in shaping black identity.

In an introduction to her first novel, *Dessa Rose,* Sherley Anne Williams writes, "Afro-Americans, having survived by word of mouth – and made of that process a high art – remain at the mercy of literature and writing; often, these have betrayed us." Williams's awareness of skewed histories shaped her own writing. Her consistent ability to tell black stories truthfully through poetry and fiction has brought her prominence among contemporary black American writers.

Born and raised in low-income housing projects, Williams earned an A.B. in history at California State University. After a lengthy absence from school, she received a master's degree from Brown University. Subsequently, Williams returned to California to join the faculty of the University of California, San Diego, in 1975.

Although Williams began writing in 1967, it was not until 1972, following the publication of *Give Birth to Brightness: A Thematic Study in Neo-Black Literature,* that her theories about the value of black folklore in shaping racial identity were fully articulated. These principles took artistic form when her book, *The Peacock Poems,* was published in 1975 to critical and popular acclaim, ultimately winning a nomination for the National Book Award in poetry. Among her other writings were *Some One Sweet Angel Chile* (1982) and *Dessa Rose* (1986), which was named a notable book by the *New York Times.*

North America

Williams, Spencer, Jr.

(b. 1893, Vidalia, La.; d. December 13, 1969, Los Angeles, Calif.), African American television and movie director, actor, and writer best known for his role on the *Amos 'n' Andy* television show.

Born in Louisiana, Spencer Williams attended the University of Minnesota, dropping out to join the army. Returning South after his 1923 discharge, he got his start in movies by writing for a series of short black films based on stories by Octavus Roy Cohen. These films were made by an affiliate of Paramount Pictures, and Williams soon moved to an office on Paramount's lot in Hollywood.

A talented actor, Williams appeared in some of the first African American talking movies of the 1920s, including *The Lady Fare, Oft in the Silly Night,* and *Music Has Charms.* His work as a producer included silent films such as *Hot Biscuits* (1929) and the earliest black Westerns, *Bronze Buckaroo* (1938) and *Harlem Rides the Range* (1939). Films that Williams wrote, directed, and starred in range from the comedy *Juke Joint* (1947) to the allegory *The Blood of Jesus* (1941).

In 1951 Williams accepted the role for which he is most famous, Andy Brown on the television version of *Amos 'n' Andy.* The show used exaggeration and stereotypes as a comic motif, but, airing in a changing and turbulent political climate, it was denounced by the National Association for the Advancement of Colored People (NAACP). Suffering from lack of support, the show lasted three years. After its cancellation Williams supported himself on a veteran's pension and social security until his death from a kidney disorder in 1969.

See Also
Racial Stereotypes; Film, Blacks in American.

North America

Williams, Vanessa L.

(b. March 18, 1963, Tarrytown, N.Y.), African American singer and actress, the first black woman to be crowned Miss America.

Vanessa Williams has enjoyed a successful and diverse career as a singer and actress. Since the release of her debut album in 1988, she has produced six albums and won lead roles in stage and film productions, including the critically acclaimed movie *Soul Food* in 1997.

Williams grew up in predominantly white Millwood, New York. Encouraged by her parents, both music teachers, she learned to play the piano, French horn, and violin, and pursued intensive dance training. While in high school she starred in plays and musicals, and received numerous scholastic and theatrical awards.

Aspiring to become a stage actress, in 1981 Williams enrolled at Syracuse University as a musical theater major. Prompted by a talent scout, she entered and won the Miss Syracuse beauty pageant, a victory that propelled her to the 1983 Miss America pageant, in which she made history as the first black woman ever to be crowned Miss America. While some black leaders attributed her victory to her "light skin" and "middle-class background," others compared her breakthrough to that of Jackie Robinson, who in 1947 became the first black since the 1890s to play major league baseball.

In July 1984 Williams again made history – this time as the first woman forced to resign her Miss America title – after *Penthouse* magazine published explicit photos of her, taken when she was 19 years old. For many observers, Williams's predicament revealed the tension between the pageant's moral code and its business of judging scantily dressed women. Prominent feminists such as Gloria Steinem and Susan Brownmiller rallied to her defense, as did black leaders Benjamin Hooks and Jesse Jackson.

Although Williams lost her crown and a $900,000 advertising contract with the Gillette Company, the setback only steeled her resolve; in 1987 she launched a singing career with Mercury Records. Her debut album, *The Right Stuff*, released in 1988, received three Grammy nominations and the Best New Female Artist Award from the NATIONAL ASSOCIATION FOR THE ADVANCEMENT OF COLORED PEOPLE (NAACP). Her second album, *The Comfort Zone* (1991), which featured the hit singles "Save the Best for Last" and "Work to Do," sold more than 2 million copies. In 1994 she won rave reviews for her lead role in the Broadway musical *Kiss of the Spider Woman*, and performed "Colors of the Wind" on the Academy Award-winning soundtrack to the Disney film *Pocahontas*.

Williams has also appeared in numerous television shows and Hollywood films; in 1996 she starred with Arnold Schwarzenegger in the action film *Eraser*. Divorced, Williams has three children: Melanie, Jillian, and Devin.

Roanne Edwards

SEE ALSO

Baseball in the United States; Hooks, Benjamin Lawrence; Jackson, Jesse Louis; Television and African Americans; Film, Blacks in American.

North America

Wills, Harry (b. January 20, 1889, New Orleans, La.; d. December 21, 1958, New York, N.Y.), African American boxer who won the "colored" heavyweight title in 1920.

Harry Wills, known as the "Brown Panther," began his boxing career in 1911. Discrimination forced him to fight in PANAMA and CUBA for several years. He returned to the United States in 1920 and won the "colored" heavyweight title. Boxing promoter George Lewis "Tex" Richard then booked Wills to fight the white heavyweight champion Jack Dempsey in 1922. Richard later squelched the deal, claiming pressure from politicians, thus depriving the highly qualified Wills of a shot at the title. Wills retired in 1932 with an official record of 94 wins and 8 losses.

SEE ALSO

Boxing.

North America

Wilmington, N.C., Riot of 1898, white supremacist campaign of violence and murder directed at black political officials in Wilmington, North Carolina.

In 1898 Wilmington, with a population of approximately 20,000, was the major city in the eastern region of North Carolina. It was one of the most integrated cities of the South, with blacks and whites living in each of the five wards. African Americans constituted a majority of the city's residents and successfully competed with whites for jobs. A significant number of blacks were successful businessmen and professionals, and many also held important municipal positions such as police chief, deputy sheriff, and federal collector of customs. Wilmington was part of the Second Congressional District, often called the "Black Second" on account of its large number of black political officials.

Part of what had allowed black Republicans to assume important political posts was their alliance with Populists. These two parties controlled the local government until 1898 and, to ensure black representation, had passed a resolution in 1897 to appoint African Americans to five of the ten alderman positions. Blacks were approaching a level of political and social equality that many whites found unacceptable. As a result white Democrats, determined to oust the black officials from office, began campaigning well before the 1898 election. They claimed that the presence of blacks in the local government "emboldens bad Negroes to display their evil, impudent, and mean natures." White Democrats misrepresented black speakers by exaggerating their arguments and threatened to kill them if they did not withdraw from the election. Wilmington's white leaders issued a "Declaration of White Independence" calling for the expulsion of black politicians and businessmen, and organized a "secret nine" committee to facilitate this task.

As part of their attack on black Republicans, white Democrats printed and distributed 300,000 copies of an article that had been written in August 1898 by Alex Manly, editor of the *Wilmington Record* who was of mixed African descent. It read, "Our experience among poor white people in the country teaches us that the women of that race are not any more particular in the matter of clandestine meetings with colored men, than are the white men with the colored women." This assertion against white womanhood fueled anger within the white community and emboldened them to vote black officials out of office. As a result the white Democrats swept the 1898 elections.

On the morning of November 10, the day after the election, a group of approximately 500 men who had been summoned by the white Democrats took up firearms, formed a mob, and marched into Brooklyn, a predominantly black section of town. They burned down the office of Manly, who had reportedly left town 11 days earlier, and local Africans Americans began to fear that the mob would turn on them next. Upon receiving news of what had happened, African American officials resigned and many black employees at the local cotton compress left work to find and defend their families. The mob disbanded and headed home in small groups.

One of these groups of white men encountered a group of armed black men at the intersection of Fourth and Harnett streets and advised them to return to their homes. The blacks crossed the street and refused to move any farther. A shot was fired and one of the white mob, William Mayo, was injured. The two groups opened fire at each other and a shootout ensued. Whites quickly received notice of the incident and flooded the city's black neighborhoods, where they indiscriminately shot at blacks. Whites not participating in the riot sought refuge in churches and schools while blacks fled to the forest to save their lives.

The governor sent in the state militia to aid whites in disarming the blacks, who were regarded as the antagonists. Up-to-the-minute telegraph coverage was wired across the country. By 3:00 PM, gunfire ceased. It is estimated that 7 to 30 blacks were killed. The few remaining blacks that ventured into the open to return home were stopped and searched by white soldiers and pedestrians. In the days following the riot, a large number of blacks and some whites left Wilmington. The white Democrats quickly disfranchised the remaining black community by instituting literacy tests at the polls. By the turn of the century the town had a white majority.

Aaron Myers

North America

Wilson, August (b. April 27, 1945, Pittsburgh, Pa.), playwright and poet; two-time winner of the Pulitzer Prize for drama.

August Wilson was born Frederick August Kittel in a poor, mixed-race neighborhood of PITTSBURGH, PENNSYLVANIA, known as the Hill. His father, a white German baker, was rarely around; his mother held cleaning jobs and received welfare payments to support her six children. When Wilson was a young teenager, his mother remarried and the family moved to a mostly white neighborhood. Wilson's encounters with racism in his new home were more direct, including a pivotal incident in which a teacher wrongly accused him of plagiarizing a paper.

In 1960 Wilson dropped out of school but continued his education in the libraries of Pittsburgh, where he read black writers such as RICHARD WRIGHT and RALPH ELLISON. He received another sort of education in

August Wilson won a Pulitzer Prize for his play, *The Piano Lesson.* Pictured is a scene from that play. *The Everett Collection*

the barber shops, cafés, and street corners that were frequented by a wide range of blacks. In 1965 Wilson began to write poetry. He was heavily influenced by the lyricism of Welsh poet Dylan Thomas and, later, by the Black Nationalism of African American poet and playwright AMIRI BARAKA. Baraka and other activists of the late 1960s argued that blacks, especially black artists, needed to be more race-conscious. Wilson agreed and spent many of the following years bringing life to black history and culture. In 1968, with little previous experience in the theater, he and a friend founded the Black Horizon Theatre Company in his old neighborhood, the Hill. The company featured minor plays by and about blacks. Around this time he also discovered and immersed himself in the blues – the genre's pained, harmonic realism gave him the inspiration for many of his later plays. In a culminating act of symbolism, he rejected his last name, the name of his white father, and took his mother's maiden name, Wilson, in recognition of her black heritage.

Wilson still believed himself to be a poet, but in the early 1970s he began writing plays. In 1977 he wrote *Black Bart and the Sacred Hills*, a musical satire about an outlaw of the Old West that was produced four years later in St. Paul, Minnesota. He finished two more plays (one of which, *Jitney*, about jitney drivers in Pittsburgh, was produced regionally) before Lloyd Richards, dean of the Yale Drama School, noticed his play *Ma Rainey's Black Bottom* in 1982.

Set in Chicago in the 1920s, *Ma Rainey* presents a fictional day in the real life of blues legend Gertrude "Ma" Rainey. Using realistic dialogue, the play depicts black musicians being exploited by white record companies and directing their rage at other blacks instead of their white oppressors. Richards produced the play first at the Yale Repertory Theatre, then on Broadway, establishing a pattern that he and Wilson, working collaboratively, used in Wilson's future plays. Although a few reviewers criticized *Ma Rainey* for over-emphasizing politics, others praised it for presenting a poignant account of the effect of racism.

Shortly after writing *Ma Rainey*, Wilson wrote *Fences*, which focuses on the frustrations and responsibilities of a former Negro League baseball player, now a garbage man, barred from playing in the major leagues. *Fences*, winner of the 1987 Pulitzer Prize for drama, strengthened the playwright's reputation for deft presentation of the consequences of racism. His next play, *Joe Turner's Come and Gone* (1986), further distinguished Wilson by debuting on Broadway while *Fences* was still running there. Set in a Pittsburgh boarding house in 1911, *Joe Turner* chronicles the life of a black freedman who comes North to find his wife, who fled while he was enslaved. Mystical and metaphorical, the play explores assimilation by African Americans into American society and is at once bitter and optimistic.

The Piano Lesson, immensely popular with both critics and audiences, followed in 1987. Set in 1936, its main characters are descendants of a slave family whose father and grandmother were traded for a piano. The grieving grandfather carved likenesses of his wife and son in the piano, which is now in the family's possession. The family is divided between those who want to sell the piano to buy the land where their ancestors were slaves and those who want to preserve the piano as an heirloom. *The Piano Lesson* won both a Pulitzer Prize and a Tony Award for best play.

In 1990 Wilson wrote *Two Trains Running*, a portrayal of friendships and conflicts during the late 1960s; in 1995 he wrote *Seven Guitars*, a portrayal of relationships among a group of musicians set in Pittsburgh in 1948. Wilson has declared that he will write a drama about black American life in each decade of the twentieth century.

SEE ALSO
Slavery in the United States; Blues, The; Chicago, Illinois; Negro Leagues; Rainey, Gertrude Pridgett ("Ma"); Black Nationalism in the United States.

Latin America and the Caribbean

Wilson, Carlos Guillermo

(b. 1941, Panama City, Panama), Afro-Panamanian novelist, poet, and scholar best known for his portrayals of West Indians in PANAMA.

"Cubena," Carlos Guillermo Wilson's pen name, is a Hispanicized version of "Kwabena," which means "Tuesday" in the ASANTE culture of GHANA. Wilson lived through an era of transition marked by profound changes and racial awareness for thousands of West Indian laborers employed in the excavation, construction, and administration of the Panama Canal.

Wilson's grandparents migrated to Panama from the West Indies for the construction of the waterway. Adopted and raised by James Duglin from BARBADOS and Lena MacZeno from JAMAICA, he spent his childhood and most of his adolescence in Panama City. During this period he had extensive contact with West Indians and, through the immigrants' conversations and recapitulations, Wilson developed an in-depth understanding of what their life was like. As a result Wilson's poetry, short stories, and novels reflect his knowledge of West Indians and their descendants in Panama.

In 1959 Wilson relocated to the United States and lived in Mississippi. In 1964 he moved to LOS ANGELES, CALIFORNIA, where he received his first master's degree from the University of California, Los Angeles, in 1970, and a doctoral degree in Latin American literature from the same institution in 1975. He also holds a master's in urban education (1982) and a master's in counseling (1983) from Loyola Marymount University in Los Angeles, California. He is currently a professor of Spanish at San Diego State University in California.

Wilson launched a literary career in 1977 when he published a collection of 12 short stories titled *Cuentos del negro Cubena*. The stories emphasize the day-to-day life and experiences of discrimination and hardship that blacks endured in Panama. The same year he wrote a volume of poems called *Pensamiento del negro Cubena: Pensamiento afro-panameño*, which contains 51 poems examining a variety of subjects, including slavery, love, racial consciousness, and socio-political protest.

Wilson has published two novels: *Chombo* (1981) and *Los nietos de Felicidad Dolores* (1991). Through Lito, the main character in *Chombo*, the narrative goes beyond fiction to examine the lives of West Indians and their descendants during and after the construction of the Panama Canal. *Los nietos de Felicidad Dolores* is rooted in the experiences of people of African descent in the Americas from slavery to the 1990s.

In addition to his literary work Wilson has contributed a number of critical articles to scholarly journals. Also, he is a founder of the *Afro-Hispanic Review* and a contributing editor to the *Publication of the Afro-Latin/America Research Association*.

Wilson's poetry volume and collection of short stories have been translated into English. He has been the subject of a few critical articles and a book titled *Denouncement and Reaffirmation of the Afro-Hispanic Identity in Carlos Guillermo Wilson's Works*, edited by Elba D. Birmingham-Pokorny.

LaVerne M. Seales-Soley

See Also
Slavery in Latin America and the Caribbean.

North America

Wilson, Cassandra

(b. December ?, 1955, Jackson, Miss.), African American jazz vocalist and songwriter acclaimed for her smoky contralto and musical versatility.

Hailed by *Time* magazine as "the most accomplished jazz vocalist of her generation," Cassandra Wilson has enjoyed a success and visibility usually reserved for pop singers. Her singing is eclectic and innovative: she performs both original and standard songs, drawing upon many musical influences, including JAZZ, blues, folk, hip hop, FUNK, and rock. According to critic Gene Santoro, "she is the direct descendant of BILLIE HOLIDAY and DINAH WASHINGTON, with their bluesy pop tunes and wicked jazz feel for the unexpected twist, and can rivet audiences with her languid, curling voice while lighting a room with simmering sexual energy."

Wilson grew up in Jackson, Mississippi, where her mother was an elementary school teacher and her father was a jazz bassist. Her father nurtured her passion for music, and as a child she studied classical piano and taught herself to play the acoustic guitar. Her mother and grandmother, both women of spirit and energy, were her role models: while Wilson admired her mother's strength of character, she found inspiration in her grandmother's religiosity and powerful, uninhibited singing in church. "I come from a long line of women who, against all odds, did what they wanted to do," she told *Ms.* magazine in 1997.

After graduating with a degree in communications from Jackson State University, Wilson worked at a New Orleans television station. She also performed as a singer in local nightclubs. Set on a musical career, in 1982 she moved to New York City. There she met avant-garde saxophonist Steve Coleman, who introduced her to M-BASE, a Brooklyn-based collective of musicians who fused rock, hip hop, funk, and jazz. Wilson became the group's main vocalist, and in collaboration with Coleman and M-BASE musician Jean-Paul Bourelly, she recorded her first album, *Point of View* (1985), on the German label JMT. Subsequent albums won her comparisons to jazz vocalist BETTY CARTER, and in 1989 her *Blue Skies* became the top-selling jazz album of the year.

In 1993 Wilson took a new direction when she signed with Blue Note Records, one of the world's greatest jazz labels. "Once a daredevil of the avant-garde, Wilson is drawing on the very fundamentals of black-music expression, which is in itself a classic avant-garde gesture," said *New York* magazine writer Chris Norris. Collaborating with producer Craig Street, she recorded the widely acclaimed, top-selling album *Blue Light 'til Dawn*, which featured fresh renditions of vintage blues and folk songs as well as songs written by Wilson.

Wilson's Grammy-nominated album *New Moon Daughter* (1996) was praised by the *New York Times* as one of the best albums of the decade. It appealed to a wide audience, from jazz aficionados to mainstream listeners, and propelled her into the limelight as the jazz diva of the 1990s. She has since recorded *Rendezvous* (1997), with jazz pianist Jacky Terrasson, and is the featured vocalist on *Blood on the Fields* (1997), an epic oratorio about SLAVERY IN THE UNITED STATES, composed by WYNTON MARSALIS.

Roanne Edwards

See Also
Blues, The; Hip Hop in the United States; New Orleans, Louisiana; New York, New York.

North America

Wilson, Eric Arthur ("Dooley")

(b. April 3, 1894, Tyler, Tex.; d. May 30, 1953, Los Angeles, Calif.), African American jazz drummer popular in America and Europe who also achieved renown as an actor.

Eric Arthur Wilson began playing bit parts in vaudeville while in his early teens. In 1910 he moved to New York to work as a musician, where he helped popularize RAGTIME. He formed a JAZZ quintet, the Red Devils, with whom he toured Europe from 1919 to 1934. Upon his return to the United States, Wilson worked on Broadway and in Hollywood, most notably as the pianist Sam in the motion picture *Casablanca* (1942). He also appeared in the all-black musicals *Night in New Orleans* (1942) and *Stormy Weather* (1943).

See Also
Film, Blacks in American.

North America

Wilson, Fred

(b. 1954, New York, N.Y.), African American sculptor, mixed media and installation artist.

The son of parents of mixed descent, Fred Wilson received a bachelor of fine arts degree from the State University of New York at Purchase in 1976. After completing his degree, Wilson worked as an administrator in various New York museums, including the Museum of Natural History and the Metropolitan Museum of Art. Between 1978 and 1980 he worked as an artist in East Harlem and was funded by the Comprehensive Employment Training Act (CETA).

Wilson began an association with the Just Above MidTown Gallery in 1981, a space known for its congeniality to African American artists. In 1987 Wilson was the director of the Longwood Art Gallery of the Bronx Council of the Arts, for which he curated the show *Rooms with a View: The Struggle Between Culture and Content and the Context of Art.* The show employed three spaces in the gallery. One was appointed like a "turn of the century salon" museum space, another like a contemporary gallery, and a third like an ethnographic museum. The exhibition questioned issues of insitutional space and history, challenging viewers to radical interrogation of their conception of a museum and museums' relationship to African Americans.

In 1992 Wilson created the award-winning installation *Mining the Museum,* sponsored by the Museum for the Contemporary Arts in Baltimore. The installation used artifacts found at the Maryland Historical Society to explore the ways in which the historical society defined itself and Maryland's history by excluding the experience of African Americans in the state. Wilson juxtaposed seemingly unrelated objects to reinforce his point. For example, in a vitrine displaying nineteenth-century silver work from the state of Maryland, he included a set of slave shackles crafted at the same time.

Wilson's most recent work has involved installations featuring racially stereotypical bric-a-brac, such as Aunt Jemima dolls, that raise questions about stereotypes and racial prejudice. He has had solo exhibitions at the Indianapolis Museum of Art, the Seattle Art Museum, the Museum for Contemporary Art in Baltimore, and the Museum of Contemporary Art in Chicago. In 1994 Wilson represented the United States in the Fourth International Cairo Biennial in Egypt. He has also participated in numerous group shows across the country and around the world, including the 1996 *New Histories* exhibition at the Institute for Contemporary Art in Boston. In addition to receiving numerous awards and grants in recognition of his work, Wilson has lectured at universities and art colleges across the United States.

See Also
Baltimore, Maryland; Black Collectibles; Harlem, New York; Racial Stereotypes; Art, African American.

North America

Wilson, Harriet E. Adams

(b. 1828?, Milford, N.H.; d. 1870?), American writer whose book, *Our Nig,* published in 1859, is considered the first novel published by an African American woman and the first novel published by an African American in the United States.

Little is known about the life of Harriet E. Adams Wilson. The 1850 federal census lists a 22-year-old "Black" woman named Harriet Adams living with the Samuel Boyles family in the town of Milford, which suggests that she was born around 1828. In 1851 she married Thomas Wilson, a free man who pretended to be a fugitive slave from Virginia so he could lecture on the horrors of slavery. Shortly after the birth of the couple's son, George Mason Wilson, in May or June 1852, Thomas Wilson abandoned the family. Wilson, who was unable to work because of the physical and emotional abuse inflicted by her employers, lost custody of her son. She began writing to earn enough money to reclaim him. He died five and one-half months after her book's Boston publication in 1859. Neither the date nor the location of Wilson's death is known.

Our Nig; or, Sketches from the Life of a Free Black, in a Two-Story White House, North. Showing That Slavery's Shadows Fall Even There, is a largely autobiographical novel that explicitly compares the racist conditions suffered by a black indentured servant to slavery in the South. Using the slave narrative as a model, Wilson indicts Northern treatment of blacks. Possibly because of its controversial stand, the book was published at the author's own expense and sold poorly.

The story is told mostly through the eyes of a young girl, the novel's protagonist, Alfrado, a mulatto who is abandoned by her white mother after her black father dies. Left with a white family, she is severely mistreated by the mother and one of the daughters. Although the men of the family are absentmindedly fond of her, they are unable to protect her from the hunger, beatings, and scolding that she constantly endures. Misfortune continues into Alfrado's adulthood when the husband, who she thought would save her, leaves her and her young child. The novel ends with Alfrado, broken in body but not in spirit, expressing her contempt for a society that allowed her virtual slavery.

Robert Fay

See Also

Slavery in the United States; Free Blacks in the United States, 1619 to 1863; Fugitive Slaves; Slave Narratives.

North America

Wilson, William Julius

(b. December 20, 1935, Derry Township, Pa.), one of the most influential sociologists in the twentieth century.

As a sociologist William Julius Wilson has had an impact as wide outside the academy as within. His work has been critical in shaping the international discourse on the relationships among race, poverty, and the economy in the United States in the post-World War II era.

Wilson attended Wilberforce University in Ohio, from which he received a B.A. in 1958. After earning an M.A. from Bowling Green University in 1961, he was recruited to the doctoral program in sociology at Washington State University by a department chair who had committed himself to training minority sociologists. Wilson has commented that he was the beneficiary of affirmative action before the concept was invented. He received his Ph.D. in 1966.

Wilson published *Power, Racism and Privilege: Race Relations in Theoretical and Sociohistorical Perspective* (1973) while he was a faculty member at the University of Massachusetts. Five years later he won national recognition with the publication of *The Declining Significance of Race: Blacks and Changing American Institutions* (1978) while he was a member of the faculty at the University of Chicago, where he taught from 1972 until 1996. The book called attention to factors related to social class, such as lack of education, in the continuing plight of African Americans in a world where racial prejudice, though still clearly important, had eased somewhat for those with salable middle-class skills. Misread by many of his colleagues, who thought he was suggesting that racism had disappeared from United States society, Wilson was censured in 1978 by the Black Caucus of the American Sociological Association.

The Declining Significance of Race exhibited several characteristics that mark Wilson's subsequent scholarship. First, it underscored the importance of economic and macrostructural forces in understanding the position of African Americans. Second, it showed how the economy harmed low-income whites and blacks, as both fought for scarce resources. Wilson would elaborate this argument in subsequent books in which he emphasized the importance of deindustrialization, the movement of manufacturing industries out of U.S. cities – indeed out of the country – in reducing opportunities for the uneducated and unskilled. He argued for "race neutral" policies that sought to overcome backlash and garner political support for programs that would primarily help African Americans.

In *The Truly Disadvantaged* (1987) Wilson described the plight of poor African Americans and the consequences of social isolation they faced as blacks with greater opportunities moved out of the inner city. That book also introduced and explicated the concept of "underclass" to the educated public. *When Work Disappears: The World of the New Urban Poor* (1996) carried these themes further. Exploring the noneconomic as well as the economic costs of deindustrialization, Wilson indicated policy initiatives that could help all of the disadvantaged. Wilson opened the possibility of discourse about problems in the black community. This discourse had been essentially shut down in the 1960s following the publication of the Moynihan Report (1965), which discussed the problems of female-headed households in low-income minority communities. Sometimes incorrectly characterized as a conservative, Wilson is actually a social democrat who favors government involvement in the economy through industrial policy, enforcement of antidiscrimination legislation, and affirmative action.

Wilson has been showered with honors. He was chairman of the sociology department at the University of Chicago from 1984 to 1987, president of the American Sociological Association in 1989, and a MacArthur Foundation "genius award" prize fellow. He is the recipient of 27 honorary degrees. Wilson has been a policy advisor to both President Bill Clinton and Vice President Al Gore. In 1996 Wilson joined Harvard University as a professor of social policy at the John F. Kennedy School of Government. He was appointed Lewis P. and Linda L. Geyser University Professor in 1998.

Richard Taub

See Also

World War II and African Americans.

Africa

Windhoek, Namibia, the capital of Namibia.

Windhoek, with a population of approximately 200,000, is by far the largest town in Namibia, as well as the capital and meeting point of Namibia's major road and rail networks. Situated between several mountain ranges in the center of the country, it was founded in 1840 by the Nama leader Jonker Afrikander, who initially named it Winterhoek, after a South African region where he once had a farm. Only later did it become known as Windhoek, which means "windy corner."

The Herero people had probably inhabited the area for some time, attracted to the nearby natural hot springs. The arrival of Afrikander and other Nama settlers occurred during a time of increasing conflict between the two groups, as the Herero moved south in search of better pastures and the Nama, led by Afrikander, pushed them back north. The Nama settled in the valley, and in 1842 the German Rhenish Mission Society established a mission. But the wars between the Nama and Herero continued until 1885, when Germany intervened. Five years later the Germans built a fort at the abandoned mission site. They also built churches, schools, seven hotels, three breweries, and several "castles" overlooking the main street, Kaiserstrasse. Although the completion of a railway in 1904 linked Windhoek to the coast, ongoing Herero and Nama rebellions discouraged many Germans from settling there.

In 1915 South Africa took control of the city and five years later set up a municipal government. Thereafter, the population increased rapidly, from 716 in 1920 to 10,000 in 1949, and to 36,000 in 1959. White residents, numbering around 20,000, lived in exclusive suburbs, while approximately 16,000 black and Coloured residents lived in the shantytown suburb called the Old Location, and worked as menial laborers and domestic servants. In 1959 Namibia's nationalist struggle began in the streets of Windhoek when Africans protested their forced removal from the Old Location to a desolate new suburb known as Katutura, or "the place where no one lives."

Just prior to independence in 1990, Windhoek experienced another great building boom, as job-seeking Namibians as well as foreign embassies, companies, and nongovernmental agencies all moved to the city. Today there is a mixture of old German and modern architecture in the city center, which houses most of the white population. Light manufacturing, mainly food and wool processing, is located in the suburbs.

Eric Young

See Also

Nationalism in Africa; South Africa; Christianity: Missionaries in Africa.

North America

Winfrey, Oprah Gail

(b. January 29, 1954, Kosciusko, Miss.), African American talk show host, Academy Award-nominated actress, and producer whose syndicated television show, *The Oprah Winfrey Show*, is the most popular talk show ever.

Oprah Winfrey was born on a Mississippi farm and raised by her paternal grandmother until she was six years old, when she moved to Milwaukee to live with her mother, Vernita Lee. Though Winfrey did well in school, she was allegedly sexually abused by male relatives and became increasingly troubled as a teenager. Her mother, a maid who was busy raising two other children, eventually sent Winfrey to live with her disciplinarian father, a barber and businessman in Nashville, Tennessee. Winfrey flowered under Vernon Winfrey's strict supervision, excelling academically and as a public speaker. At age 16 she won a partial scholarship to the Tennessee State University in a public speaking contest sponsored by the Elks Club.

As a freshman at Tennessee State University, Winfrey worked briefly as a radio newscaster before victories in two local beauty pageants helped land her a news anchor position at WTVF-TV in Nashville. In 1976, only a few months shy of her bachelor's degree at Tennessee State University, Winfrey landed a job as a reporter and evening news co-anchor at WJZ-TV in Baltimore. Although she did not succeed in that position, the station management realized that Winfrey, who had no formal journalistic training, was better suited to cohosting WJZ's morning talk show, *People Are Talking*. Winfrey helped turn the show into a ratings success with her personable interviewing style and charismatic presence.

After eight years as the cohost of *People Are Talking*, Winfrey was offered a job as the host of *A.M. Chicago*, a Chicago talk show that aired opposite Phil Donahue's popular morning show and lagged behind it in the ratings. In one month Winfrey's ratings equaled Donahue's, and in three, surpassed them. Donahue acknowledged Winfrey's ratings supremacy by moving his show to New York in 1985. In 1985 *A.M. Chicago* was renamed *The Oprah Winfrey Show*, and it was syndicated in 1986. It eventually became the highest-rated talk show in television history. By 1997, 15 to 20 million viewers watched it daily in the United States, and it was seen in more than 132 countries. The show has received 25 Emmy Awards, 6 of them for best host. In 1996 *Time* magazine named Winfrey one of the 25 most influential people in the world.

Also a talented actress, in 1985 Winfrey earned Golden Globe and Academy Award nominations for her portrayal of Sofia in the film *The Color Purple*, based on Alice Walker's book of the same name. In 1986 Winfrey founded HARPO Productions, becoming only the third woman to own her own television and film studios. Based in Chicago, HARPO (Oprah spelled backwards) owns and produces *The Oprah Winfrey Show* as well as such dramatic miniseries as *The Women of Brewster Place* (1988), based on the book by Gloria Naylor, and *The Wedding* (1998), based on the book by Dorothy West. In addition to supporting African American literature through her television movies, Winfrey presents an on-air book club that has brought new readers to such writers as Toni Morrison.

A political activist as well as an entertainer, Winfrey testified before the United States Senate Judiciary Committee, describing the sexual abuse she suffered as a child, and worked for the passage of the National Child Protection Act in 1991, which provides for the establishment of a nationwide database of convicted child abusers. In December 1993 President Bill Clinton signed "Oprah's Bill" into law. Her many philanthropic ventures include donations of time and money to efforts aimed at protecting children and to the establishment of educational scholarships.

Robert Fay

See Also

Baltimore, Maryland; Chicago, Illinois; New York, New York; Television and African Americans; Walker, Alice; Film, Blacks in American.

North America

Wings Over Jordan, African American choir and radio program popular in the 1930s and 1940s for its performances of traditional black choral music.

The choir Wings Over Jordan debuted in 1937 in Cleveland, Ohio, on a radio show called "The National Negro Hour." The group was formed by Rev. Glenn T. Settle of the Gethsemane Church. Aired every Sunday morning on Cleveland's WGAR station, the choir swiftly gained popularity and, in 1939, attracted a national audience when "Wings Over Jordan" – now a national radio program – was broadcast weekly on Sunday mornings on the CBS national radio network.

During the next 15 years Wings Over Jordan gained fame throughout the United States and abroad. Under the direction of various conductors, including Thomas King, the choir toured nationally and recorded on major labels. In 1945 it toured with the United Services Organization throughout Europe, performing powerfully rendered gospel songs and spirituals for military personnel during World War II.

Wings Over Jordan paved the way for other black college choirs to appear on radio, and by 1950 the ABC network hosted a regular Sunday morning program called "Negro College Choirs." After concluding its own radio program in 1949, Wings Over Jordan continued to perform publicly until 1965.

Roanne Edwards

See Also

World War II and African Americans; Gospel Music; Spirituals, African American.

Africa

Wobé (also known as Ouobe and Wé), ethnic group of West Africa.

The Wobé primarily inhabit western Côte d'Ivoire. Others live in northeastern Liberia. They speak a Niger-Congo language in the Kru group and are closely related to the Guéré people. Approximately 100,000 people consider themselves Wobé.

See Also

Languages, African: An Overview.

Africa

Wolof, ethnic group of Senegal, the Gambia, and Mauritania.

The Wolof, numbering approximately 3 million people, are the largest ethnic group in Senegal and form a minority in the Gambia and in Mauritania. The Wolof language is part of the Atlantic subgroup of the Niger-Congo family of languages. Though the Senegalese scholar Cheikh Anta Diop argues that the Wolof language bears a strong resemblance to ancient Egyptian and that the Wolof are descendants of the ancient Egyptians (*see* Egypt, Ancient Kingdom of), oral traditions and linguistic evidence suggest that the people known as Wolof originated in the Senegal River valley area and gradually moved south into their present territory. The ancestors of the Wolof were dominated by the kingdom of Ghana and the Mali Empire until the fourteenth century, when the Djolof Kingdom asserted its independence.

It was in Djolof that the Wolof developed their characteristic social structure, focused on a small nobility, a large free peasant caste, and smaller artisan castes, including griots, metalworkers, and leatherworkers. Slaves were also a part of Wolof society. Caste determined one's occupation and limited one's choice of spouse. Marriage between castes was strictly forbidden. Oral traditions include some mention of women rulers, and maternal descent was of comparable importance to patrilineage (or extended family based on paternal descent). During this period Wolof farmers eked out a difficult living from growing MILLET and sorghum in the drought-ridden but fertile soils of present-day central and north central Senegal. They also participated in the commercial networks that fed into the trans-Saharan trade. When European traders expanded their regional presence in the sixteenth century, Wolof traded gum arabic, ivory, gold, and slaves for a variety of European goods (*see* TRANSATLANTIC SLAVE TRADE).

By the sixteenth century five predominantly Wolof kingdoms had emerged, though they paid tribute to the Djolof state. These included Walo, Cayor, Baol, Sine, and Saloum. As the transatlantic slave trade became increasingly important in the seventeenth century, the balance of power in the region shifted from the interior states like Djolof, toward coastal ones like Baol, Cayor, Sine, and Saloum. Their proximity to French trading posts at Gorée and Saint-Louis gave the newer coastal kingdoms privileged access to French trade goods, especially gunpowder, muskets, and iron. Some Wolof women at Saint-Louis and Gorée, known as *signare*, married French traders and used their family connections to develop trade routes into the various Wolof states. With easy access to new strategic weapons, the coastal states freed themselves from Djolof dominance. It was during this period that the *tyeddo*, or warrior caste, became central to Wolof political life. Islam became the dominant religious tradition among the Wolof during this period as well.

In the mid-nineteenth century the French expanded their control into the interior of Senegal and conquered the Wolof kingdoms. Lat Dior, the ruler of Cayor, was the leader of Wolof resistance. His conversion to Islam and alliance with the Islamic leader Ma Ba Diakhou failed to prevent French expansion. As the French expanded their control, they encouraged the production of peanuts as a cash crop, and many Wolof migrated into eastern Senegal, where soils were more favorable for peanut production. Members of the Wolof elite, discredited by the colonial conquest, joined an Islamic brotherhood called the Mourides, which was led by an Islamic Sufi mystic named Amadou Bamba. Bamba's rapid success won him the enmity of the French and he was exiled, first to GABON and then to Mauritania. When he was allowed to return to Senegal, he encouraged people to work as a way to honor God. Leaders of this new religious movement became active in the production of peanuts, and encouraged peasants to grow the new cash crop as a way of honoring Allah and supporting the Mouride order. By the 1920s the Mourides dominated Senegalese peanut production and were sending colonies of settlers eastward to plant peanut fields on land that was previously occupied by FULANI herders. Other Wolof became active in the Senegalese division of the French army, the Tirailleurs Sénégalais, which played an important role in the conquest of French West Africa and Equatorial Africa. Still others took advantage of their proximity to the major French ports for all of West Africa, Dakar and Saint-Louis, to receive a French education and enter the civil service.

Because they were located near the French colonial centers of power, the Wolof became the most integrated into the French colonial system. As migrant laborers from other ethnic groups went to work in the cities and along the railroad lines, Wolof became the most commonly used language of the Senegalese, facilitating communication among groups speaking different languages, and Wolof culture became the region's dominant culture. Wolof dominance of Senegal's economy and culture has increased since independence. Most Senegalese speak Wolof, though most cannot speak the official language of the country, which is French. Wolof music, food, clothing styles, and social styles have become the norm in postcolonial Senegal. The Wolof are the most urbanized Senegalese people and they dominate the country's cities, including Saint-Louis and Dakar. They are also a major presence in the capital of the Gambia, Banjul. While the Wolof dominate Senegalese social life, this power has not been translated directly into the political arena. Both of Senegal's presidents have belonged to the SERER ethnic group. Despite the failure of the Wolof to control the presidency, they have exercised considerable political influence, particularly through the leaders of the Mouride Islamic brotherhood and from major power bases in the former kingdoms of Sine and Saloum. More than any other Senegalese group, the Wolof have developed a significant written literature in their own language, including several newspapers and political magazines. In recent years Wolof traders have become active in European and North American cities.

Robert Baum

SEE ALSO

Banjul, the Gambia; Colonial Rule; Dakar, Senegal; Ghana, Early Kingdom of; Gorée Island, Senegal; Ivory Trade; Sufism; Slavery in Africa.

North America

Womanism, a term to encompass the variety of ways that African American women support each other and relate to the world.

The term *womanism* was coined by the African American writer ALICE WALKER in her 1983 book *In Search of Our Mothers' Gardens*. Walker defined a womanist as a black feminist who continues the legacy of "outrageous, audacious, courageous, and willful, responsible, in charge, serious" African American women – women who are agents for social change for the wholeness and liberation of black people, and, by extension, the rest of humanity. A womanist can be a lesbian, a heterosexual, or a bisexual woman. She celebrates and affirms African American women's culture and beauty. She loves herself.

Although the words "Christianity" and "religion" do not appear in Walker's definition, the word womanism has religious as well as secular usage. Because Walker emphasizes African American women's love for the spiritual, black Christian women have used the womanist concept to articulate their participation in, and witness to, divine power and presence in the world. Womanist Christian thought and practices began to flourish in the mid-1980s as a way to challenge racist, sexist, and white feminists' religious discourse and practice, all of which ignored the black experience in church and society.

The secular use of the word "womanist" identifies a culturally specific form of women-centered politics and theory. It finds the term *feminist* inappropriate because of its identification with a predominantly white movement, and because "feminist" has often been used to label a woman as a lesbian, regardless of her actual sexual orientation. Because of this, some women have challenged the term *womanist* as homophobic.

Irene Monroe

North America

Women and the Black Baptist Church

Evelyn Brooks Higginbotham

Black women (and women whose grandmothers were black) are... the main pillars of those social settlements which we call churches; and they have with small doubt raised three-fourths of our church property

(W. E. B. Du Bois, 1918).

Although he does not refer to a specific denomination, W. E. B. Du Bois aptly describes women in the black Baptist church, for today, as well as in 1918, women represent a preponderance of its membership, its financial strength, and its missionary force. Indeed, these three characteristics form the basis for understanding how black Baptist women, in the face of racial and gender discrimination, contributed to the advancement of the black church and the black community during the nineteenth and early twentieth centuries.

Baptist women constitute the largest group of black Christians in America. It is the very presence of women that explains the magnitude of the black Baptist church. Census data for the early twentieth century reveal that the black Baptist church formed a microcosm of the black population in America and included men and women from all social classes and geographic regions. In 1906 black Baptists made up 61.4 percent of all black churchgoers. With a membership of 2,261,607, the black Baptist church had more than four times the members of the second-largest denominational body, the African Methodist Episcopal (AME) Church, with its 494,777 members. By 1916 black Baptists constituted not only the largest black religious group but the third-largest of all religious groups, black or white, in America; trailing only the Roman Catholic and the Methodist Episcopal churches, black Baptists numbered 2,938,579 that year. In 1936 black Baptists continued to constitute the third-largest denomination regardless of race. Equally important, census data consistently have shown that black women make up more than 60 percent of black Baptist membership. From a numerical standpoint, then, the high proportion of female members underscores their vital presence in empowering the Baptist church.

Women's contributions to the church did not begin in the twentieth century but rather took root in the efforts of black Baptists to establish congregations independent of white control during the late eighteenth and early nineteenth centuries. Although little is recorded about the black women who participated in this early freedom movement, women certainly were members and financial supporters of those churches founded from the 1750s to 1810 in such places as Mecklenberg, Virginia; Savannah, Georgia; Boston, Massachusetts; and New York City. Mechal Sobel's 1988 study of African-Baptist Christianity during the era of slavery notes instances of women being deaconesses, members of separate women's committees, delegates to associational meetings of both men and women, and active participants in revivals. Yet the autonomous polity of each Baptist church precluded a consistent participation by women. Ample evidence exists to indicate that there were gender proscriptions: women were categorically denied the right to preach; they were excluded from the business meetings of most black Baptist churches; and in many instances women could not sit beside male members during worship, organize into separate women's societies, or even pray publicly.

The black Baptist church grew tremendously in the years following the Civil War. With the abolition of slavery, black Baptist women and men expressed their newly won freedom by abandoning the white-controlled churches in which they had been forced to worship. Coming together in black-controlled churches, black Baptist women found a spiritual haven for individual communion with God and a public space for schooling, recreation, and organizational meetings. Indeed, women, much more than men, attended church not only for Sunday worship but for a variety of activities that took place throughout the week. For many poor black women who worked in domestic service, sharecropping, and other forms of menial employment, the church offered the only form of social and organizational life outside the family. In choirs, deaconess boards, and missionary societies, women with little income found personal dignity, developed leadership and organizational skills, and forged programs for their people's advancement. At the level of the individual church as well as at the level of the regional association of churches, commonly called conventions, the black Baptist church conflated its private, eschatological witness and its public, political stand, thus becoming a catalyst for the transmission of both spiritual and secular ideas to a broad spectrum of black people.

By means of statewide and other regional conventions, black Baptist churches allied their efforts, embarking upon programs of racial self-help and self-determination. The ministerial-led movement to unite black Baptists into conventions was unique, for, unlike the structured network and hierarchy of other denominations, it emerged only because otherwise independent black Baptist churches voluntarily and freely worked together as race-conscious collectives. Beginning at the local and state levels, the convention movement grew in momentum between the 1860s and 1890s and culminated with the formation of the National Baptist Convention (NBC) in 1895. However, the restricted participation of women in the ministerial-led conventions led Baptist women to form their own, separate local and state organizations in the 1880s and 1890s and, in 1900, a national auxiliary of the NBC, which by 1903 boasted a million members.

State and national women's conventions offered greater opportunity for effective religious proselytism at home and abroad as well as an arena in which women freely discussed and implemented strategies for racial and gender empowerment. The minutes of black Baptist women's state conventions attest to the extensive and sacrificial efforts of overwhelmingly low-income women to meet the spiritual, social, and economic needs of black people, efforts that would have been impossible without the women's capacity to raise funds. These efforts included visiting homes and reading the Bible, donating clothes and food to the needy, counseling prisoners, caring for the sick, training women in household and parental responsibilities, establishing and supporting orphanages and old folks' homes, crusading for temperance, publishing newspapers, establishing day nurseries and kindergartens, instituting vocational training programs, and establishing and/or financing educational institutions.

At a time when Southern states had no public facilities at the high school or college level for black students, late nineteenth- and early twentieth-century women's state conventions worked fervently for the higher education of black men and women. For this reason black Baptist women's conventions often carried the title "educational" as part and parcel of their missionary identity, for example, the Baptist Women's Educational Convention of Kentucky, the Women's Baptist Educational and Missionary Convention of South Carolina, and the Woman's Baptist Missionary and Educational Association of Virginia. Unquestionably, the black church was the most important institution in the black community, and it was largely through the organized fundraising of churchwomen that this claim came to be actualized. In the racist climate of segregation, disfranchisement, and LYNCHING, women's missionary and financial efforts were decisive factors in the black Baptist church's ability to rally the impoverished masses for the staggering task of building and sustaining self-help institutions.

Women's conventions, notwithstanding their auxiliary relationship to the ministerial-dominated conventions, generated their own distinct dynamism and assertiveness. Women's conventions controlled their own budgets and determined the allocation of funds, and they explicitly denied male participation in any role other than as honorary members. Black women found enormous satisfaction in accomplishing the goals of their conventions and in developing their own individual skills and abilities. In 1888 the president of the Kentucky Baptist group told a predominantly male Baptist audience that the women had learned to delegate authority, to raise points of order, and to transact business as well as men. In 1904 the president of a Baptist women's organization in Arkansas credited her state association with building the self-confidence of ordinary women regarding their skills and abilities. She explicitly mentioned women's financial contributions and informed black Baptist ministers: "From a financial standpoint we are prepared to prove that we have given thousands that you would not have, had it not been for the untiring and loyal women in the State." Emboldened by the successes of their separate conventions, black women also were cognizant of their crucial role in building the denomination as a whole.

An educator, religious leader, and civil rights activist, Nannie Helen Burroughs (1879-1961) founded the National Training School for Girls and Women along with the Women's Convention, the powerful female branch of the National Baptist Convention. *Photographs and Prints Division, Schomburg Center for Research in Black Culture, The New York Public Library, Astor, Lenox and Tilden Foundation*

The founding and growth of black Baptist women's societies during the 1880s and 1890s did not occur without gender conflict, however. Ironically, the black Baptist convention movement that united men and women in the struggle against racial inequality betrayed a masculine bias in its institutional structures and discourses. Tensions arose when male ministers expected women to be silent helpmates. Yet the rising prominence of black churchwomen and their growing demand for a separate organizational voice during the last two decades of the nineteenth century reflected a heightened gender consciousness on the part of women who were no longer content to operate merely within the boundaries of individual churches or silently within ministerial-led state conventions.

Throughout the 1880s and 1890s black Baptist women challenged gender proscriptions that thwarted the full utilization of their talents. The debate over women's rights in Arkansas typified that in other states. Ministers argued that separate organizations under the control of women would elicit a desire to rule the men. Some Arkansas ministers contended that women's financial contributions would cease to be under the men's control, whereas others demanded that male officers preside over women's societies – if they were permitted to form. The women of Arkansas responded by stressing their critical importance as a missionary force, insisting that they could better accomplish the work of religiously training the world by uniting as a separate organization. The women claimed their right to be an independent voice in the church on the assumption that they were equally responsible, in proportion to their abilities, as men.

Outstanding leaders such as Virginia W. Broughton of Tennessee and Mary V. Cook of Kentucky turned to the Bible to defend women's rights in the church and the larger society. Broughton, a schoolteacher and zealous missionary, published *Women's Work, as Gleaned from the Women of the Bible* (1904) in order to disclose biblical precedents for gender equality. Her feminist interpretation of the Bible shaped her understanding of women's roles in her own day, and the book summed up the ideas that had marked her public lectures, correspondence, and house-to-house visitations since the 1880s. Broughton led the women of her state in forming Bible bands for the study and interpretation of the Scriptures, and her gender consciousness united

The Missionary Training Department of Spelman Seminary prepared its graduates to offer religious and moral instruction to black communities. The class of 1893, shown here, included such legendary women as Emma De Lamotta, *front row, center,* who was born a slave in 1836 and went on to lead the department until her death in 1903. *Courtesy Spelman College Archives, Atlanta, Georgia*

black Baptist women in other states as well, emboldening them to develop their own societies. Traveling throughout the urban and rural areas of Tennessee, Broughton was instrumental in organizing a statewide association of black Baptist women. She advocated training schools for mothers in order to better the home life of black people, and she ardently promoted higher education for women.

Mary Cook of Kentucky also appropriated biblical images to prove that God used women in every capacity. During the late 1880s Cook, a professor at the black Baptist-owned State University at Louisville (later renamed Simmons University), was the most prominent woman in the ministerial-led convention movement that ultimately led to the founding of the NBC. She urged women to spread their influence in every cause, place, and institution. In newspaper articles and speeches she emphasized woman's suffrage as well as full equality for women in employment, education, social reform, and church work. In a speech given in 1887, Cook praised female teachers, journalists, linguists, and physicians, and she insisted that women must "come from all the professions, from the humble Christian to the expounder of His work; from the obedient citizen to the ruler of the land." Both Cook and Broughton noted male resistance to the formation of women's societies; for example, they claimed that ministers and laymen had locked the doors of their churches, refusing to accommodate women's societies. In her autobiography, *Twenty Years as a Missionary* (1907), Broughton even recalled potentially fatal confrontations and physical threats made against women.

Although the black Baptist convention movement had served the critical role of uniting women and men in the struggle for racial self-determination, it had simultaneously created a separate, gender-based community that reflected and supported women's equality.

In 1900 at the annual meeting of the NBC held in Richmond, Virginia, Nannie Burroughs delivered a speech titled "How the Sisters Are Hindered from

Helping," based on the biblical text, "Ye entered not in yourselves, and them that were entering in ye hindered" (Luke 11:52). Burroughs expressed the discontent and burning zeal of black Baptist women to work unrestricted as a missionary force for the betterment of society. Burroughs's eloquence triumphed. In response to the motion of the influential NBC officer Lewis G. Jordan, and a second from Charles H. Parrish, the male-led convention approved the establishment of the Women's Convention (WC), auxiliary to the NBC. It is interesting to note that Burroughs worked as Jordan's secretary at the time, and Parrish was married to the aforementioned Mary V. Cook of Kentucky.

By the close of the Richmond meeting the women had elected the following officers: S. Willie Layten of Philadelphia, president; Sylvia C. J. Bryant of Atlanta, vice president at large; Virginia Broughton of Nashville, recording secretary; Nannie H. Burroughs of Washington, D.C., corresponding secretary; and Susie C. Foster of Montgomery, Alabama, treasurer. The minutes for 1900 listed 26 state vice presidents, including one each from Indian Territory, Oklahoma Territory, and Washington, D.C. The women described their mission as coming to the rescue of the world, and they adopted the motto "The World for Christ. Women Arise. He Calleth for Thee." The formation of the WC signaled not only a national identity for black Baptist women but also a black women's congress, so to speak, where women as delegates from local churches, district associations, and state conventions assembled annually as a national body to discuss and debate issues of common concern, disseminate information to broader female constituencies, and implement nationally supported programs.

In her first open letter to the black Baptist women of America, S. Willie Layten urged all existing societies to affiliate with the WC, to work closely with the state vice presidents, and to welcome the formation of new societies where none existed at the state and local level. Layten had a long familiarity with the organized work of black Baptists. Her youth was spent in Memphis, where she acquired her early education and probably her first knowledge of women's missionary activities. After living in California during the late 1880s and early 1890s, Layten moved to Philadelphia in 1894 and became active in religious work and secular social reform. During the first decade of the twentieth century Layten was a member of the National Association of Colored Women (NACW) and was a leader in the National Urban League and the Association for the Protection of Colored Women.

By the second decade of the twentieth century

Students at Spelman College, a historically black women's college in Atlanta, Georgia, attend classes in Union Hall in 1883. *Courtesy Spelman College Archives, Atlanta, Georgia*

Students at the National Training School for Women and Girls were taught to see cooking as a "profession." *Smithsonian Institution, Washington, DC*

WC programs reflected the influence of both Progressive-era reform and black urbanization. The changing circumstances of employment, housing, and social problems related to the massive migration of black people from the rural South to the urban North prompted the WC to adopt new methods of mission work. The Baptist women's national organization played an important mediating role in connecting local church and state activities throughout the nation with more sophisticated and changing reform trends. Their organizational networks at the state and national levels facilitated a wide dissemination of ideas and expertise for utilization at the local level. Officers of the WC alluded to the educational role of their annual meetings when they referred to them as "institutes" and "schools of methods" for local communities. Through the convention a national network of communication and cooperation identified women with a particular expertise, collected data, and introduced new methods. The annual meetings of the WC featured papers delivered by physicians, social workers, and civic-improvement activists. Convinced that society and not merely the individual soul was at stake, women in the black Baptist church involved themselves in the practical work of social salvation – establishing settlement houses, holding forums to discuss industrial problems and public health, creating social service commissions, and working to improve the conditions in city slums. Generating support for foreign missions constituted another important aspect of the work of the convention. In 1901 the WC contributed money to support Spelman graduate Emma Delaney, who worked as a missionary to Chiradzulu in British Central Africa (now Malawi). In 1902 the women supplied funds to build a brick mission house for her. Through their support of Delaney, the women learned of the harsh consequences of European colonialism on African people. In a visit to America in 1905 Delaney spoke of the need for black Americans to redeem Africa from colonial rule. In her speech before the WC's annual meeting she poignantly described the suffering of African people "who were compelled to secure rubber for the Belgium Government at any cost, even the loss of their limbs, if the required quantity of rubber was not brought." During the early decades of the twentieth century the WC shipped boxes of food and clothing to missionaries in foreign fields, underwrote the educational expenses of African students in the United States, contributed to mission stations in various parts of Africa, and built a hospital in Liberia.

The role of black Baptist women as a force for missions also entailed the effort to rid American society of the sins of racial and gender discrimination. In this regard the WC went on record against segregation, lynching, injustice in the courts, the inequitable division of school funds, and barriers to voting rights and equal employment. It supported the civil rights agenda of the National Association for the Advancement of Colored People (NAACP) and invited representatives from that organization to appear at the Baptist women's annual meetings. In 1914 the WC joined forces with the NAACP in a national campaign to end negative stereotyping of black people in literature, film, textbooks, newspapers, and on the stage. According to minutes, the groups also advocated boycotts and written protests to publishers and others who use racial slurs.

Thus the WC afforded black women an arena in which to transcend narrow social and intellectual confines and become exposed to new places, personalities, and ideas that negated both racist and sexist stereotypes and limitations. At the very time when Booker T. Washington refused to use his influential voice publicly to criticize the black disfranchisement in the South, the leadership of the WC loudly called for suffrage for black women and men. In 1909 these Baptist women specified that their political input in state legislatures and the federal government would help improve the living and working conditions of black people in general and black women in particular.

Understanding the historic role of black Baptist women ultimately must evoke recognition of the multivalent character of the black church itself. The church was not the exclusive voice of a male ministry but the inclusive voice of men and women in dialogue. As the majority of church members, the mainstay of financial support, and the missionary impetus for social change, black Baptist women were never silent. In the struggle to come into their own voice, they empowered their church, their community, and, not least of all, themselves.

See Also

Colonial Rule; Liberia (Ready Reference); African Methodist Episcopal Church; Baptists; Burroughs, Nannie Helen; Civil War, American; Great Migration, The; Du Bois, William Edward Burghardt (W. E. B.); Memphis, Tennessee; New York, New York; Racial Stereotypes; Spelman College; Washington, Booker Taliaferro; Christianity: Missionaries in Africa.

Latin America and the Caribbean

Women, Black, in the Colonial Hispanic Caribbean, arrivals, along with the Spanish expansionists, who moved to CUBA, the DOMINICAN REPUBLIC, and PUERTO RICO in the late fifteenth and early sixteenth centuries.

Black slaves and freedpeople were common in Spanish and Portuguese urban centers like Seville, Lisbon, and Valencia. Female slaves performed mostly domestic duties in these cities. The ownership of domestic slaves was a status symbol for residents of the Spanish peninsula. Thus as Spanish fortune seekers moved into the newly occupied islands in the Caribbean, some of them brought along their domestic slaves.

Early attempts to establish a slave-based work force to replace the dwindling native Taíno population brought even more black women into the Hispanic Caribbean. As Spain experimented with SUGAR plantations in the sixteenth century, black female slaves worked in the estates, performing both agricultural and domestic tasks. When sugar proved to be unprofitable for the Spanish expansionists, many plantations were abandoned. Black women, slave or free, moved into rural areas to engage in subsistence agriculture or followed other Spanish immigrants who left for MEXICO or PERU to fulfill their dreams of social and economic mobility. Also, some slaves were able to purchase or to receive their freedom, and remained in towns.

The historical record has ignored the presence of slave and free black women in the early stages of Spanish colonial expansion in HISPANIOLA, Puerto Rico, and Cuba; nevertheless, these women were participants in the early difficulties experienced in the new colonies. Many women were employed as domestics or worked in food-related artisan trades. Still, black women were considered a problematic influence in the islands, and many were victims of the accusations and punishments of the Inquisition. A sexually unbalanced population, in which men outnumbered women, also made black women the targets of physical abuse and rape. This situation, alongside marriage and concubinage, made for the spread of *mestizaje*, or interracial mixing among Africans, Spanish, and Taíno people in the island colonies.

Female slaves were coveted not only for their labor, but also for their reproductive potential. It was the mother who passed down the slave status in the Hispanic Caribbean. Planters wanted female slaves in order to multiply their slave holdings and avoid purchasing "new" slaves from Africa. This strategy intensified during the nineteenth century when British pressure to eradicate the slave trade made the direct importation of Africans more expensive and cumbersome. The masters' wishes aside, the slave populations in the Hispanic Caribbean did not reproduce sufficiently to meet the demand for slaves, thus requiring the continuous importation of bonded people from Africa.

Although Spanish law made it clear that marriages among slaves ought to be respected, planters made it very difficult for slave families to exist. Nevertheless, slaves formed families that withstood the difficulties of physical separation. Also, black women challenged traditional Spanish religious marital practices by living in common-law marriages. This practice angered Spanish Catholic Church and colonial officials and was persecuted at various times throughout the colonial period and in the nineteenth century. The tendency of black women and other women of color to live in common-law marriages reflected not only distinct cultural practices, but also skewed sexual demographics in the colonies and the high fees charged by the clergy to provide the sacrament of marriage. In addition, the institutional presence of the Roman Catholic Church was traditionally weak in rural areas and plantations.

During the seventeenth and eighteenth centuries slavery was a feeble institution in the Hispanic Caribbean, in contrast to the plantation societies in other Caribbean islands such as BARBADOS, JAMAICA, and St. Kitts. The Hispanic Caribbean colonies received many runaway slaves from the British and French colonies during these two centuries. Slaves who left a non-Spanish colony became free after one year in the Hispanic Caribbean. The only condition for their freedom was converting to Catholicism and going through catechism. As a result a small but ever-increasing class of free blacks – *libertos*, as they were called in Spanish – emerged in the Hispanic Caribbean. These black freedpeople proved to be a problematic group for Spanish officials once sugar-based plantation societies began to flourish in Cuba and Puerto Rico starting in the second half of the eighteenth century.

Black women played an important role in the urban economies of the Hispanic Caribbean during the eighteenth and nineteenth centuries. Many black women roamed the city streets selling foodstuffs door-to-door. Others sold their goods near the marketplaces or had small shops. Still other black women operated small food-selling shacks, like the *mondonguerías*, where tripe stew was sold to the lower classes within the city. Most of the domestics, slave or free, were black women. They labored alongside other women of color as laundresses, cooks, maids, wet nurses, midwives, and servants. Many black women served as domestics not only to middle- and upper-class families but also to the governmental, military, and religious bureaucracies housed in cities like Havana and San Juan. Some female slaves performed domestic services for a fee, and shared a percentage of the fee with their masters. This practice seems to have been widespread in the cities of Havana, San Juan, and Santo Domingo and seems to have been among the strategies used by planters to supplement their income in times of economic difficulty. Life in urban areas also provided female slaves with more personal freedom than their counterparts working in plantations. Black women also found work in artisan trades such as cigar making. Although the actual job of rolling and finishing cigars was done by men, many black women worked in small tobacco shops classifying, stemming, and stacking tobacco leaves.

The access that female slaves had to additional earnings through domestic work, charging fees for their services, or street selling allowed them to secure the funds to pay for their freedom or that of other family members. One special feature of urban life for black women in the Hispanic Caribbean was the high rate of manumission. Outright manumission and gradual self-purchase (known as *coartación*) were much more common in urban areas than in rural plantations. Female slaves were manumitted, or purchased their freedom, more often than male slaves.

Plantation life was as difficult for female slaves as it was for male slaves. Black women were involved in the arduous agricultural tasks associated with sugar cane cultivation, including field clearing, planting, weeding, and cane cutting. Only from the industrial side of sugar producing – working in the boiling and curing houses, where the sugar cane was crushed and its juice turned into crystals – were female slaves usually excluded. Other black women worked as domestics in the master's family quarters. This strenuous work included tending the plantation's gardens, preparing and cooking meals, repairing, washing, and ironing clothes, supervising children, cleaning, nursing the ill and aged, and tending to the personal requests of the master and his family.

The advent of plantations in the Hispanic Caribbean changed the ideological, legal, and economic perception of black women in the region. As racial purity and separation became more important, churches began to keep different books dividing baptisms, marriages, and deaths by race. Whereas Cuba and Puerto Rico had provided havens for runaway British, Danish, and French slaves in the seventeenth and eighteenth centuries, punitive laws were passed by the Spanish government limiting and policing the entry of non-Spanish freedpeople after slavery was abolished in other Caribbean colonies. Colonial officials feared the potential rebellious and agitating influence of blacks coming from colonies where slavery had ended. The ghost of the Haitian slave rebellion also haunted the Hispanic Caribbean planters and Spanish colonial and military authorities.

Black women were always active in struggles to eradicate slavery in the Hispanic Caribbean. Either through daily resistance or by involving themselves in larger uprisings, black women attempted to undermine slavery.

In Cuba, for example, the slave Fermina was sentenced to death by a war council for her participation in and leadership of an 1843 revolt. Many black domestics were accused of attempting to poison their masters or employers. Female slaves often went to court to defend their rights, whether for violations of coartación agreements or of promises of manumission upon the death of the master. Black women joined bands of *cimarrones* (maroons), slaves who had escaped to the countryside to avoid the indignities of plantation bondage.

Few black women of the colonial period have had their contributions recognized by historians of the Hispanic Caribbean. A notable exception is Mariana Grajales, mother of the famous Cuban nineteenth-century, pro-independence leader Antonio Maceo. Grajales, the mother of 13 children (9 of whom died in the independence wars against Spain), has been canonized as a secular symbol of protest and rebellion against colonialism in Cuba. She ran a hospital for wounded rebels during the TEN YEARS' WAR (1868-1878), the first major war fought by Cubans for independence from Spain. Grajales also became famous for compelling one of her younger sons to go into the battlefield upon seeing her son Antonio arrive at the hospital seriously wounded. Grajales was exiled from Cuba at the end of the war and lived in KINGSTON, JAMAICA, until her death at age 85 in 1893.

Felix V. Matos Rodriguez

SEE ALSO
Transatlantic Slave Trade; Slavery in Latin America and the Caribbean; Maroonage in the Americas; Haitian Revolution; Maceo y Grajales, Antonio; St. Kitts and Nevis; Catholic Church in Latin America and the Caribbean; Abolition and Emancipation in Latin America and the Caribbean; San Juan, Puerto Rico; Slave Rebellions in Latin America and the Caribbean; Havana, Cuba.

North America

Women's Organizations, Early African American, **the mutual relief associations, benevolent societies, literary societies, and antislavery organizations formed by African American women in the first half of the nineteenth century.**

"Visited Mrs. Jones with the Committee and gave her 50 cts worth of groceries. She had been confined 10 days." This 1821 note – recording the delivery of provisions to a shut-in neighbor – documents one of the basic functions of many of the earliest African American women's organizations. Throughout the nineteenth century the reality of life for many black families, even those who were not slaves, included constant economic pressure. Because women and children were especially vulnerable to poverty, women quickly realized that they needed to be at the forefront of efforts to create mutual aid and benevolent societies to help support neighbors in need. The first black women's mutual aid society, the Female Benevolent Society of St. Thomas, was founded in PHILADELPHIA, PENNSYLVANIA, in 1793.

Similar societies quickly sprang up elsewhere in Philadelphia, as well as in Newport, Rhode Island, and Salem, Massachusetts, and soon they existed in towns and cities across the Northeast. In some, members contributed regular dues that were pooled together when an individual member had an emergency; in others, members simply worked together to give help wherever it was needed. Both models made use of their members' commitment to serving their communities – as the Salem Colored Female Religious and Moral Society stated in 1818, "to be charitably watchful over each other."

Black women also began organizing to share their talents for other causes: says one scholar, "'mutual relief' became 'mutual improvement.'" Literary societies, such as the Female Literary Association and Minerva Literary Association in Philadelphia and the Colored Ladies' Literary Society in New York, gave women the chance to express their recommendations for racial uplift as they wrote essays and poetry to be discussed. For example, activist SARAH MAPPS DOUGLASS, who cofounded the Philadelphia Female Society in 1831, argued in her essay "Family Worship" that moral and scholarly instruction would allow blacks to fill their place in American society: "Yes, religion and education would raise us to an equality with the fairest in our land."

These literary societies also gave black women a rare chance to express their political views, which helped galvanize the antislavery movement. Many women included condemnations of slavery in the writings they shared at literary meetings. In 1832 African American women in Salem, Massachusetts, founded the first Female Anti-Slavery Society. Similar organizations quickly followed, and from then on women such as Douglass, the Forten sisters, and FRANCES ELLEN WATKINS HARPER were active in both literary and antislavery societies.

As the century drew to a close these societies and associations were joined by similar clubs in the South and West. Even after slavery ended, black women's organizations were still needed to provide social services in their communities and to continue fighting for black women's economic and political rights. Eventually these societies became the foundation of the national BLACK WOMEN'S CLUB MOVEMENT, which continues today as a major source of assistance in the African American community.

Lisa Clayton Robinson

SEE ALSO
Abolitionism in the United States; Mutual Benefit Societies.

Latin America and the Caribbean

Women Writers, Black, in Brazil, **literature written by women of African descent in BRAZIL.**

Despite a literary history that extends back to the eighteenth century and a veritable explosion of productivity during the 1980s and 1990s, the literary tradition of black Brazilian women has been marginalized. From its beginning black Brazilian women's literature transgressed boundaries, challenged authority, and subverted institutional power.

The writing of Rosa Maria Egipcíaca da Vera Cruz (1725-1767) was the cause of her trial persecution by the Portuguese Inquisition. At age 6 she was kidnapped, enslaved, and brought to Rio de Janeiro. When she was 14 years old, she was sold and brought to the state of MINAS GERAIS, where she suffered public beatings and exorcism after claiming she had mystical visions. She became a nun and learned to read and write. Her organizational acumen led her to establish a shelter for women in Rio de Janeiro. Her autobiographical writing, *A sagrada teologia do amor de Deus, luz brilhante das almas peregrinas* (1752, The Sacred Theology of God's Love, Bright Light of the Pilgrim Souls), a text of more than 200 pages, described her religious experiences and mystic visions. The book caused such a furor that she was seized, taken to PORTUGAL, and tried for false religious claims and heresy. According to her biographer, the Brazilian historian Luiz Mott, a portrait of Rosa Maria Egipcíaca da Vera Cruz that hung in the shelter she established pictured her with a pen in hand. This image of an influential black woman who dared to write in a context that denied literacy to slaves and women must have been a powerful, subversive message for other black women.

A century later Maria Fermina dos Reis (1825-1917), from Maranhão, became the first Brazilian woman novelist. Her book *Ursula* was ahead of its time as Brazil's first abolitionist novel. It was published in 1859, long before the actual abolition of slavery in 1888.

Auta de Souza (1876-1901), from Rio Grande do Norte, wrote romantic poetry. She came from a prosperous family, was well educated, and wrote in both Portuguese and French. Her volume *O Horto* (1901, The Garden) does not have themes dealing with race or racial heritage.

CAROLINA MARIA DE JESUS (1914-1977) wrote about life in the FAVELAS (squatter settlements) of São Paulo in her autobiographical work *Quarto do despejo* (Child of the Dark) in 1960. The book caused a sensation in Brazil and was later published in 20 countries and translated into 13 languages. Her other books were *Casa de Alvernaria* (1961; published as *I'm Going to Have a Little House,* 1997), *Pedaços de fome* (1963, Pieces of Hunger), *Proverbios* (1969, Proverbs), and *Diario de*

Bitita, published posthumously in 1986 (Bitita's Diary, 1998). Carolina Maria de Jesus revealed the hypocrisy of society and anticipated themes such as racial identity, reclaiming the black female body, and quality of life that would gain popularity with subsequent black women writers. Black women writers of the postdictatorship generation regard Carolina Maria de Jesus as their literary forerunner.

The retreat of the military dictatorship in Brazil in 1978, the emergence of the Movimento Negro Unificado, a political black consciousness movement, and increased freedom of expression ended more than 40 years of repression and prohibitions against an authentic discussion of race and ethnic heritage. Consequently, a generation of Afro-Brazilian writers gradually emerged, providing a variety of black voices, including those of black women, to depict aspects of African-Brazilian life. When Brazilian feminists emerged in the 1980s addressing matters such as equal pay for equal work, reproductive rights, and access to higher education, their ranks were dominated by middle-class white women who did not represent the concerns of black women. Black women formed their own organizations to discuss the problems that affected their quality of life, such as illiteracy, hunger, substandard housing, health care, and lack of modern conveniences such as electricity and sewerage. Literary works by black women paralleled the themes of the African-Brazilian women's organizations.

The most frequent site of publication for black women has been *Cadernos Negros* (Black Notebooks), a refereed anthology produced by the literary organization Quilombhoje, established to provide publication opportunities for black authors who were marginalized by the commercial and academic presses. *Cadernos Negros* publishes poems and short stories in alternate years. Because of the lack of receptivity in academic and commercial presses to literature dealing with racial questions, only a handful of women have published extended genres such as the novel.

In 1988, after years of discussion about the role of black women writers, a group of 30 women writers contributed their poetry to a publication project under the leadership of poet Miriam Alves (1952-). It was designed to commemorate the 100th anniversary of the abolition of slavery in 1888 by presenting a comprehensive collection of writing by black Brazilian women for the first time. The project was to be funded by the government, but for some reason funding became unavailable and the project was postponed. Later, segments of the work were published in the United States as a bilingual anthology, *Finally Us: Contemporary Black Brazilian Women Writers* (1995).

Women in Brazilian literature traditionally have been presented as either spiritual or carnal. This division, according to Roberto Reis, has tended to follow racial lines. Stereotypes of the docile mammy and the lascivious mulatto woman (*see* Image of the Mulatta in Latin America and the Caribbean) have existed for centuries in Brazilian literature and would go unchallenged were it not for the writing of black Brazilian women writers like Alves, who called for a broadening of perspectives by "writing our vision of the world." The author Esmeralda Ribeiro (1958-), stating that black women writers are the best equipped to remedy the lack of authentic images of black women in Brazilian literature, suggested that women writers have a responsibility to create an array of credible images by "telling our stories and experiences." Such literature can be used as a tool for intervention in the political process. The author Sônia Fátima da Conceição maintained that the three afflictions of Afro-Brazilian communities – poverty, illiteracy, and racism – can be addressed by using literature as a strategy for survival. She further suggested that the aesthetics of such work should have a basis in the Afro-Brazilian artistic and oral literary tradition.

The desire to reflect a positive identity resulted in an expanded, dynamic portrayal of black women and the pressures that affect them. Conceição Evaristo (1946-) replaced the docile mammy with the assertive, unrelenting mother who cultivates influence because of her many abilities: "I rape the eardrums of the world / I foresee /... I the female matrix / I, the motive power / I-woman shelter of the seed / continual motion / of the world." Lourdes Teodoro asked for opportunity in life: "I ask only for a road / that doesn't have unripe fruit / or illusions / or an end." Alzira Rufino expressed the sense of peril and hardship felt by many women when she declared, "I am the knot on wood / Something that the blade insists on."

The quality of life, poverty, and conditions in the favelas appear frequently in black women's writing. In "Navega coração" (Sail Heart) by Andrea Cristina Rio Branco (1965-), the words wind across the page like a favela ascending the hillside. The poem ends with the words "If I live on the hillside, if I die reaching...," a play on words in Portuguese in which the words "I live, I die" and "the hillside" are pronounced so similarly that they are almost interchangeable. The device suggests that living and dying are the same in the favela. Teodoro writes of a life that consists of subsisting in "Litania" (Litany), a poem that reiterates, "We just hold on." Terezinha Malaquias (1959-) writes of "human cadavers that roll through the gutters of life."

The reconstitution of identity required writing about the psychological effects of discrimination. In much of her prose and poetry, Geni Mariano Guimarães (1947-) describes how rejection of the Eurocentric standard of beauty and the struggle to affirm one's physical characteristics, such as hair, color, and body build, facilitate a process of self-affirmation for black women. In *A cor de ternura* (The Color of Tenderness), her award-winning book, she chronicles the life of a black family. Guimarães states that one of the merits of the book is the theme of the stages of racial prejudice. Her early volumes of poetry, *Terceiro filho* (1979, Third Son) and *Da flor o afeto, da pedra o protesto* (1981, Of the Flower the Affection, Of the Stone the Protest), were written before she began to address the theme of racial identity. In 1995 she published *Balé das emoções* (Ballet of Emotions).

The omission of black women from the historical record is an oversight that Alves seeks to correct with her poetry. She writes a type of epic poetry that deals with the important events of the black community. "Mahin, amanaha" (Mahin, Tomorrow) tells of the role of Luiza Mahín, the woman who was a leader of the Great Revolt of the Males of 1835, the last great slave rebellion in Salvador, Bahia. It provides a portrayal of a heroic, assertive, black woman whose word alone unites the various enslaved African ethnic groups and mobilizes them to strike a blow for freedom. This image is in contrast to the popular belief that black Brazilians are passive and nonconfrontational. "Passo a praça" (Passageway to the Plaza) describes the Plaza of Paissandu in São Paulo, where slaves constructed a church in 1711. The poem reminds the reader that the church has been a site of political resistance and the quest for justice across the centuries. It alludes to the maintenance of African religious tradition and the continuity of African social organization despite the imposition of the Portuguese regime. Alves's poem "Vudu" recalls the Law of the Free Womb, a deceitful law that caused further disorganization of the black family because it encouraged slave mothers to abandon their babies so that the babies could be granted freedom. The law began a cycle of abandonment that persists to the present day. In "Noticiario" (News Report) Alves writes of intolerable contemporary living conditions that have continued from the time of slavery; the poem links the quality of life in the slave shacks to life in the shacks of today's favelas.

Alves also writes poetry with a highly personal tone that speaks of the effects of oppression on the individual. With the publication of *Momentos de busca* (Moments of Search) in 1983, Alves conveyed her personal vision of a world that oppressed her yet failed to bridle her creative imagination. *Estrelas no dedo* (1985, Stars on the Finger) describes her dreams deferred, disillusionment, unfulfilled ambitions, and potential waiting to unfold. The anthropologist and literary critic Abelardo Rodrigues wrote that Alves's poetry shows how the "unresolved crisis of the forced labor and sexual violence of slavery continues to affect the descendants of slaves today."

When Ribeiro called for the expansion of the portrayal of black women, she remembered the women of previous generations who made sacrifices so that their daughters could make educational and professional progress and showed her gratitude by portraying them respectfully in her work. She invents authentic characters by writing about her observations of the African-Brazilian people whom she knows. The grandmother is a key figure in her works because Ribeiro says that the grandmother's role in the family as a caregiver for the children is essential for the economic advancement of many African-Brazilian families. Ribeiro subverts the image of the tragic, sexually exploited mulatto woman in her short story "Keep a Secret." Rather than dying of love, the protagonist turns the table on her unfaithful white lover and seeks revenge. The story is a black, feminist revision of a novel, *Clara dos anjos* (1948) by Afonso Henriques Lima Barreto (1881-1922). At the end of the story Ribeiro slyly indicates the power of authorship when the revengeful character tells the ghost of Lima Barreto that she, the wronged mulatto woman, wrote a better ending than he did, and that we all have the choice to write our own stories. Ribeiro examines the nature of the family in her stories using prose loaded with irony and humor. She believes that Brazilian literature has failed to include representations of black families, often depicting black characters as isolated and merely ornaments in a white world. She concentrates on showing the roles that each member plays in sustaining the family in an adverse world. This is particularly clear in *Malungos e milongas* (1988), a novella describing the disputes among four siblings. It is an allegory about the struggle among blacks since the time of slavery that results when some are given favor and access while others are denied a viable role.

The portrayal of the lascivious mulatto in the past is a cause of sensitivity for black women, and for this reason there are few portrayals by women of romantic love. An exception is the poetry of Ruth Souza, who affirms her love for the black man. Nevertheless, the romantic love that she writes about is reserved, discreet, and understated.

Conceição's straightforward prose fiction treats complicated social issues. Her novel *Sonhos, marcos e raízes* (1992, Dreams, Marks, and Roots) examines the Movimento Negro Unificado (Black Unified Movement), one of Brazil's most influential contemporary social movements. Conceição, who is a social worker in the state orphanage in São Paulo, provides insight into the struggles of black women and abandoned children in her short stories. As a result of her professional experience and training as a social scientist she describes numerous true-to-life situations such as the struggles of the working poor, intergenerational poverty, domestic violence, substance abuse, and the living conditions in the favelas. Conceição's black female characters often represent the 85 percent of black Brazilian women who have less than a fourth-grade education and are functionally illiterate. In one of her short stories she shows that for this segment of the population, middle-class feminism is a joke. The remedy for many of the problems that she analyzes is education and literacy. Conceição's poetry shows her compassion and concern. She touches on the sensitive topics of reproductive health, teen motherhood, and child abuse. In "If Only I Could" she laments that, because of the loss of knowledge of the healing arts traditionally passed from mother to daughter in African societies, she is unable to cure illnesses that cause the high mortality rates among poor Brazilian children. In "Beija Flor Show" (Hummingbird's Show) she deplores the commercialization of African religious values and the degradation of women in *mulata* shows for tourist consumption. The constant theme throughout her work is the need for a return to African family values so that the African-Brazilian community can continue to live.

Black women writers in Brazil for more than 200 years have kept a tradition of using the pen to empower themselves. They have spoken of the unspeakable in order to bring about change. They have seized the word in order to lay claim to themselves and their future. They have inscribed themselves as an irrefutable part of a history that would otherwise exclude them.

Carolyn Richardson Durham

See Also

Muslim Uprisings in Bahia, Brazil; Slavery in Latin America and the Caribbean; Lima Barreto, Afonso Henriques de; Rio de Janeiro, Brazil; Abolition and Emancipation in Latin America and the Caribbean; African Ethnic Groups in Latin America and the Caribbean; Religions, African, in Brazil; Cultural and Political Organizations in Latin America.

North America

Women Writers, Black, in the United States, black American women who have written poetry, fiction, and drama.

In his introduction to the Schomburg's series of books by nineteenth-century black women, scholar Henry Louis Gates Jr. points out that with the publication of her 1773 collection of poetry, Phillis Wheatley "launched two traditions at once – the black American literary tradition *and* the black woman's literary tradition." Gates continues: "That the progenitor of the black literary tradition was a woman means, in the most strictly literal sense, that all subsequent black writers have evolved in a matrilinear line of descent, and that each, consciously or unconsciously, has extended and revised a canon whose foundation was the poetry of a black woman."

Black women writers have been pioneers in several literary genres throughout the last three centuries. They have also been among the most beloved and celebrated American authors for a wide range of readers – black and white, male and female. Writers such as Toni Morrison, Alice Walker, Zora Neale Hurston, and Terry McMillan often represent "black literature" to contemporary audiences; and Morrison, the recipient of the 1993 Nobel Prize for Literature – and the first African American to receive that literary honor – is internationally recognized as one of the most significant living American writers.

Academic courses exclusively devoted to black women writers have become the norm. Within the black literary tradition women writers are often celebrated for their gift of conveying the fullness of the African American experience. As essayist and activist Anna Julia Cooper said in her 1892 book, *A Voice from the South from a Black Woman of the South:* "Only the Black Woman can say 'when and where I enter, in the quiet, undisputed dignity of my womanhood, without violence and without suing or special patronage, then and there the whole *Negro race enters with me.*'"

The first milestone in African American Literature was reached in 1746 by a woman named Lucy Terry. Terry's poem "Bars Fight," which commemorated several residents of her Massachusetts town who had been killed during a clash with Native Americans, is the first known piece of literature by an African American. Three decades later Wheatley published her *Poems on Miscellaneous Subjects* (1773), the first book to be published by an African American writer. Wheatley remained the only African American woman to publish a book of creative literature through the first half of the nineteenth century, although black women continued writing, often in other genres. Ann Plato wrote a collection of essays and poetry, Charlotte Forten Grimké kept a diary, Maria Stewart collected her speeches, Jarena Lee wrote a spiritual autobiography, and Harriet Jacobs wrote an autobiographical slave narrative.

Two new milestones came in 1859, when Harriet Wilson published *Our Nig,* the first known novel written by an African American, and Frances Ellen Watkins Harper published "The Two Offers," the first short story by an African American. Harper, who had already published her first volume of poetry, went on to become the most prominent nineteenth-century black woman writer, publishing several more collections and editions of poetry and short stories, three serialized short novels, and the landmark novel *Iola Leroy* (1892). Other black women novelists of the 1880s and 1890s included Katherine Chapman Tillman, Amelia E. Johnson, and Emma Dunham Kelly-Hawkins. So many black women became known for their literary ability and political activism in the 1890s alone that the decade is called the "Women's Era" in African American literary history.

Popular turn-of-the-century women writers included novelist Pauline E. Hopkins and poet Alice Dunbar-Nelson. In 1916 poet and playwright Angelina Weld Grimké's play *Rachel* became the first staged play by an African American. Grimké's poetry was also widely anthologized during the Harlem Renaissance, the movement of black writers and artists centered in New York City during the 1920s that included novelists Jessie Fauset and Nella Larsen, poet Georgia Douglas Johnson, and novelist, folklorist, and essayist Zora Neale Hurston. Hurston, in particular, has become one of the most beloved and widely read African American writers, now best known for her novel *Their Eyes Were Watching God* (1937).

The 1940s and 1950s saw the publication of such novels as Ann Petry's *The Street* (1946), Dorothy West's *The Living Is Easy* (1948), and Gwendolyn Brooks's *Maud Martha* (1953). Brooks had already become the first African American to win a Pulitzer Prize for the poetry collection *Annie Allen* (1949). Lorraine Hansberry published her award-winning play *A Raisin in the Sun* in 1955. In the 1960s Paule Marshall and Rosa Guy wrote novels that incorporated their West Indian heritage; Margaret Walker published her historical novel *Jubilee;* and poets Nikki Giovanni and Sonia Sanchez were among the integral voices of the Black Arts Movement. But the second "Women's Era" in black literary history – one that continues today – began with a series of publications in 1970.

That year Toni Morrison and Alice Walker published their first novels, and Maya Angelou published her first autobiography. These three writers have since established themselves as key figures in African American and American literary history. Morrison, a novelist and essayist, has written a series of landmark novels, of which the most acclaimed remains her 1988 Pulitzer Prize-winning *Beloved.* Walker has written novels, poetry, essays, autobiography, and children's books, and is best known for her 1982 Pulitzer Prize-winning novel *The Color Purple,* which was made into a successful film. Angelou is widely acclaimed for her poetry and her essays, and was selected to compose and read the poem "On the Pulse of Morning" for the 1993 inauguration of President Bill Clinton.

The literary emergence of these writers coincided with both the emergence of other black women writers, such as poets Audre Lorde and Mari Evans and novelists Gayl Jones and Toni Cade Bambara, and the rise of the women's movement, when audiences became especially receptive to women authors. A strong interest in black women writers in particular increased at this time. Novelists Gloria Naylor and Terry McMillan and American poet laureate Rita Dove are among the many other women writers who have achieved critical and commercial success in the 1980s and 1990s.

Each of these writers appears poised to ensure that this women's era will continue. With their powerful, eloquent voices, contemporary black women writers extend a literary tradition that has been handed down for 200 years. In the process they continue to create new milestones and enter new doors, still ensuring that "when and where they enter," they carry with them the fullness of African American experience.

Lisa Clayton Robinson

See Also

American Indians; Brooks, Gwendolyn Elizabeth; Cooper, Anna Julia Hayward; Evans, Mari E.; Fauset, Jessie Redmon; Giovanni, Yolande Cornelia ("Nikki"); Grimké, Angelina Weld; Jacobs, Harriet Ann; Grimké, Charlotte L. Forten; Guy, Rosa Cuthbert; Hopkins, Pauline Elizabeth; Lorde, Audre Geraldine; Petry, Ann Lane; Prince, Lucy Terry; Slave Narratives; Stewart, Maria Miller; Wilson, Harriet E. Adams; Schomburg Library; New York, New York.

Africa

Women Writers in English-Speaking Africa

In many parts of Africa women have long held primary roles as storytellers, teachers, poets, and oral historians. Yet only since the 1980s has writing by African women garnered significant national and international attention. Schools opened by missionaries during the early colonial period were based on a Western model, prioritizing boys' education over that of girls. These schools in turn became the model for the colonial system of education throughout Africa. Fewer girls than boys have learned to read and write, and the number of women who have been able to study literature at the university level is even lower. Even among educated women, relatively few have had opportunities to pursue careers in writing.

Still, several women were publishing early on in both English and local languages. Early role models, such as Ghanaian playwright Efua Theodora Sutherland, were already publishing in the 1930s. Ghana's Ama Ata Aidoo and South Africa's Bessie Head authored numerous short stories and plays during the 1960s, the "boom" period that propelled male writers like Chinua Achebe and Ngugi wa Thiong'o to the fore. Nigerian author Flora Nwapa wrote *Efuru* in 1966, believed to be the first novel published by an African woman in English. In East Africa by 1960, writers Grace Ogot and Rebeka Njau were already among the first graduates of Makerere College in Uganda, a center for early East African writing in English. In 1967 Head followed with *When Rain Clouds Gather* (1967), a novel set in her adopted home of Botswana. If one includes white South African women's writing, the history stretches back much further to Olive Schreiner's early feminist writing in the late nineteenth century.

Despite the contributions of these early writers, African women's writing still received little attention. Head was the only woman published in the important literary journal *Drum* when it flourished in the 1960s. In fact, as Aidoo put it in one lecture, this obscurity "had nothing to do with anything that African women did or failed to do. It had to do with the politics of sex and the politics of the wealthy of this earth who grabbed it and who held it." In the words of Kenyan novelist Asenath Odaga, "The male has always been dominant in Africa; this is their world, the society is theirs." Whether one agrees or disagrees with this statement, it is fairly clear that men's writing has defined the dominant vision of what issues are central to African life.

When African women writers finally began to gain a wide audience, one of their main tasks was to revise literary portrayals of African womanhood. Influential poets of the Négritude movement in the 1930s, such as Léopold Sédar Senghor, often portrayed the African woman symbolically, as the essence of the earth and of the physical, and above all, as the great mother. Male writers of the next generation, such as Ngugi wa Thiong'o, used the female characters in their work to symbolize the nation, or "motherland."

African women writers have presented a very different picture of their societies than men have. Like their male counterparts, African women authors have written about their societies' traditions and the upheaval caused by colonialism and urbanization. But they have also shown the problems that traditions posed for women. For example, in the novel *Efuru* (1966), Nwapa portrayed a small Igbo village much like the one represented by her contemporary Achebe in *Things Fall Apart.* Yet, as critic Jane Bryce points out, while Achebe centered his plot on the conflicts caused by British colonization, Nwapa focused on conflicts within the community itself, particularly on the difficulties faced by a childless woman. Several of Nwapa's novels explore similar themes. *The Promised Land* (1966), by Kenyan author Ogot, examines how Luo society places moral pressures on women to make personal sacrifices in order to preserve their families. The novels of Nigerian author Buchi Emecheta portray the oppression of women through traditional practices, such as the demand for a bride price and the practice of keeping women as domestic slaves (*see* Slavery in Africa). Her best-known work, *The Joys of Motherhood* (1979), shows women trapped in a society that values them primarily as bearers of children, then forces them to deny their own needs once they become mothers. Funmilayo Fakunle examines the oppressiveness of polygamous marriages in novels such as *Chasing the Shadow* (1980).

While African women writers have shared an awareness of patriarchal oppression, their voices and political views have varied widely. For example, as critic Phyllis Pollard has pointed out, Njau took a clear stand against the practice of female circumcision in her 1965 novel *The Scar*. Kenyan writers Muthoni Likimani and Charity Waciuma, on the other hand, have portrayed the practice in a negative but more morally ambiguous light. In *They Shall Be Chastised* (1974) Likimani portrays a woman caught between the strictures of traditional practices on the one hand and equally oppressive Christian practices on the other. In *Daughter of Mumbi* (1969) Waciuma places the discussion against the backdrop of the clash of cultures during a period of uprising declared a state of emergency by the colonial government (*see* Mau Mau Rebellion).

African women writers whose works criticize traditional practices have often been accused of buying into Western value systems. Responding to this charge, Aidoo argued in a lecture that African women have, in fact, long been outspoken: "So, when we say that we are refusing to be overlooked, we are only acting today as daughters and granddaughters of women who always refused to keep quiet. We haven't learned this from anybody abroad." At the same time some African women writers have acknowledged the need to defend the values of their own societies against Western cultural imperialism. This is one reason that many prominent African women writers have avoided the feminist label, including Aidoo, Head, and Emecheta. In an interview Emecheta said: "I do believe in the African kind of feminism. They call it womanism, because, you see, you Europeans don't worry about water, you don't worry about schooling, you are so well off. Now, I buy land, and I say, 'OK, I can't build on it, I have no money, so I give it to some women to start planting.' That is my brand of feminism." For these women, an African form of feminism is one that takes into account the cultural and material realities of women's lives in Africa.

African women writers have also taken on contemporary political and social issues. The work of poet and playwright Elvania Namukwaya Zirimu, for example, portrayed Uganda, revealing the political and social crises in the 1960s that ultimately led to the ascension of Idi Amin. One of the main themes of writing has been the changing face of countries like Ghana and Nigeria following independence. In novels such as *Changes* (1991) Aidoo portrays the difficulties of women in an increasingly Westernized and urbanized Ghana, as they face the responsibilities of maintaining traditional ways as well as the new possibilities of employment and marriage.

In South Africa both black and white women writers have portrayed life under apartheid. Black women began publishing their writing relatively late in South Africa, and even then they faced many obstacles. Miriam Tlali's novel *Muriel at Metropolitan*, the first novel published in South Africa by a black woman writer, was written in 1969 but not published for another five years. Even then, this book about a young black working woman's life was first censored and then banned. In *Amandla* (1980) Tlali went on to portray the politicization of women and children during the 1976 civil unrest in South African townships that culminated in the Soweto massacre and uprising. Others have contributed to the corpus of South African literature from exile, such as Lauretta Ngcobo, author of *Cross of Gold* (1981), whose work about the events in Sharpeville in 1960 was also banned shortly after publication.

As a white South African who has enjoyed greater freedom than many of her country's writers, Nobel Prize-winner Nadine Gordimer has reached a large international audience with her novels and essays. Chronicling political events from the 1940s to the present, her works paint a vivid picture of "a society whirling, stamping, swaying with the force of revolutionary change." More recently, with novels such as *The House Gun* (1998), she has continued to illumine the challenges South Africa faces in the continued violence of the postapartheid context.

South Africa's newest generation of women writers is setting its stories against the backdrop of a rapidly changing society. The impact of education forms an important theme in several new works. Tsitsi Dangarengba's *Nervous Conditions* (1989) portrays a young woman who leaves her rural home to live with her uncle in the city and finds herself both alienated from her new world and ultimately unable to return home. South African writers of Indian origin, such as Farida Karodia (*Daughters of the Twilight* [1986]), Jayapraga Reddy (*On the Fringe of Dreamtime* [1987]), Beverley Naidoo (*Chain of Fire* [1989]), and Agnes Sam (*Jesus Is Indian* [1989]), have portrayed life in the Indian community in South Africa.

For the most part African Anglophone women authors have written in a realist tradition, and their novels are often highly autobiographical and politically engaged in issues of gender and race. Yet more and more African women writers are turning to experimental styles and subjects. Head's work exploring the nature of madness has provided an early model for nonlinear narratives. South African Zoe Wicomb's *You Can't Get Lost in Cape Town* (1987) has been cited as a multifaceted work that breaks from the single ideological stance that characterized earlier literature committed to mobilization and social change. Women's recent poetic and dramatic contributions have demonstrated the continuing integration and transformation of old and new traditions.

Marian Aguiar

See Also

Colonial Rule; Education in Africa; Ghana; Indian Communities in Africa; Nigeria; Senghor, Léopold Sédar; Soweto, South Africa; Feminism in Africa: An Interpretation; Urbanism and Urbanization in Africa; Christianity: Missionaries in Africa; Female Circumcision in Africa.

Africa

Women Writers in French-Speaking Africa

The beginning of the Francophone novel in Africa (works written in French by African authors) is usually associated with the late 1950s to the early 1960s, when African countries gained their independence from France (*see* Literature, French Language, in Africa). The first female voices, however, did not emerge until the early 1970s.

Until then African women appeared either as peripheral, misrepresented, or nonexistent under men's pens. Ousmane Sembène and Mongo Béti did grant prominent roles to female characters, giving them a certain complexity. But for the most part African women were literally and literarily silenced in public. There was thus a definite need for women to speak out.

Still, the 1970s saw only a handful of titles, mostly from Senegal: Nafissatou Diallo's *De tilène au plateau: Une enfance dakaroise* (1975; translated as *A Dakar Childhood*, 1982); Aoua Keita's *Femme d'Afrique: La vie d'Aoua Keita racontée par elle-même* (1975, Woman of Africa: The Life of Aoua Keita as Told by Herself); *Le revenant* (1976, The Ghost) and *La grève des battù* (1979, The Beggars' Strike, 1982) by Aminata Sow Fall; and Mariama Bâ's *Une si longue lettre* (1979, translated as *So Long a Letter*, 1981). With the exceptions of Sow Fall and the Malian Keita, whose narratives carry more overt sociopolitical overtones and reflect women's interest in the construction of a nation, the writers emphasize the notion of intimate voices and personal testimony, often adopting the autobiographical form or first-person narrative. Typically these earlier works depict a female protagonist in the process of speaking out, not out of an artistic impulse but because she must vent her frustration, suffering, and loneliness. Usually set in a middle-class urban environment, these earlier writings feature a central character who is described as trapped in a deteriorating marital relationship, unable to develop professionally, and burdened by the demands of family and in-laws. The narrator's daily experience in her triple role as daughter, wife, and mother characterizes her oppression. The early goal of these pioneer women writers was to portray African women from within, correcting the stereotypical metaphors in male writing of women merely as symbols of mother Africa or the postcolonial state.

Bâ's *Une si longue lettre* constitutes a landmark in Francophone literary production. Awarded the Japanese Noma Prize in 1980, the novel catapulted Bâ and the other women novelists into the limelight. For the first time Francophone African women writers were becoming visible on the literary stage. The novel addresses most of the issues approached in Francophone female writing in the early 1980s: marital difficulties within a polygamous family, tensions between modernity and tradition, and the search for personal happiness. Other aspects of women's experience that were explored during that period were questions of mandatory motherhood and barrenness. Works such as Ken Bugul's *Le baobab fou* (1983; translated as *The Abandoned Baobab*, 1991) dealt with women's sense of hybridity and estrangement in a changing environment, particularly after a Western education in Europe.

Using the personal has gradually enabled Francophone women writers in Africa to touch on larger issues. No African woman's history can be written without taking the community into consideration: each and all of a woman's key moments (from birth to childhood to puberty to womanhood to marriage to motherhood to death) are defined by the society she lives in. Writers went from unveiling themselves to disclosing family life to a more public role as social critics.

Initially, literary critics, mostly male, saw the choice of the autobiography as a sign of lack of mastery of literary techniques. In the mid-1980s, with the birth of a body of feminist African criticism, critics began to acknowledge that autobiographical emphasis was a chosen form, for such a narrative style enabled the authors to create an empathic tie with the reader. Still, unlike the African male writer, whose words are often seen as representing both self and his country, the female writer was not yet seen as synonymous with her society.

Starting in the mid-1980s, a second generation of female voices has appeared, showing a more aggressive and overtly rebellious tone. While well-established authors like Sow Fall have continued to examine sociopolitical issues in their countries, rising writers are gaining new recognition: for example, Werewere Liking, Calixthe Beyala (who published eight novels in about ten years), Evelyne Mpoudi Ngolle, and Philomène Bassek, all from CAMEROON; the Ivorians Véronique Tadjo and Tanella Boni; and the Gabonese Angèle Rawiri.

Systematic oppression is at the core of these new narratives. Female characters are often from the margins of society: the foreign spouse, the prostitute, or the madwoman. The works explore areas hitherto branded as culturally trivial or taboo, such as mother-daughter relationships, the female body, pain and desire, and the search for new sexual ethics. Fusing the genres of poetry, oral forms, legends, and myths, these writers renew the quality of writing, creating polyphonic narratives. A number of them are in fact poets and playwrights as well as novelists.

Using their female characters' position of marginality, these writers have been able to address openly a number of sociopolitical aspects facing postcolonial Africa. As part of a process of catharsis, they paint the violence and horror that Africans have experienced. Unlike the works of their male counterparts, whose novels often strike the reader as sharply accusatory, the women's works show a visionary quality and an attempt to search for alternative solutions for a healthier Africa. For example, Beyala's early works try to delineate a program for women that would remedy today's hardships. These works suggest a fundamental rethinking of African societies, from the meaning of womanhood and motherhood to the corruption of governments to the relationships that form the basis of societies. The works of Liking, such as *Elle sera de jaspe et de corail: Journal d'une mysovire* (1983, She Will Be of Jasper and Coral: Diary of a Manhater) and Tadjo's *Le royaume aveugle* (1990, The Kingdom of the Blind) best represent this kind of comprehensive rethinking of life and society. Throughout these very diverse and personal voices a common notion recurs: one cannot expect to change a society until one changes one's own expectations and dreams of success. Thus these writers reexamine basic philosophical concepts: philosophy and religion (Liking), education, traditions, and government (Sow Fall), history (Boni), and love (Liking and Tadjo). Today many of the works considered African literature are written from abroad. Writers such as Beyala, who resides in France, give a different voice to African literature.

This second generation of female writers has created a new form of political novel, moving away from a certain status quo in postcolonial African societies to offer a promising vision. Far from constituting a minor literature, Francophone African women writers have created a voice that is central to the Francophone African novel. Accessing areas of language and themes that were until recently regarded as men's prerogative, in particular politics, they have gained equal authority and contributed to reshape the canon.

Odile Cazenave

SEE ALSO

Gabon; Bâ, Mariama; Béti, Mongo; Côte d'Ivoire; Ousmane Sembène.

North America

Wonder, Stevie (b. May 13, 1950, Saginaw, Mich.), African American singer, songwriter, and musician.

Stevie Wonder, born Steveland Morris, is one of the most prolific and inventive artists in American popular music and RHYTHM AND BLUES. Blind from birth, Wonder was first introduced to music as a young child and quickly developed musical skills beyond his years. At age 12 he was discovered by Ronnie White of the Miracles and won an audition at the Motown Record Company in Detroit, Michigan. When Motown's founder, Berry Gordy, witnessed the young boy's startling talents, he dubbed him "Little Stevie Wonder." Wonder was quickly adopted into the Motown "family" at Hitsville Studios. He charmed everyone with his prodigious musical range and lively sense of humor. Although Wonder played the drums, piano, and organ, his first Number-One hit, "Fingertips, Part 2" (1963), featured his exceptional skill on the harmonica, which became a trademark of his early career. More hits followed, including "Workout Stevie, Workout" (1963), "Hey Harmonica Man" (1964), and "Uptight (Everything's Alright)" (1966).

In 1966 Wonder recorded a cover of Bob Dylan's antiwar song, "Blowin' in the Wind." Wonder's interpretation of the song became an anthem of the struggling CIVIL RIGHTS MOVEMENT and foreshadowed his future involvement in political causes. Always an independent spirit, Wonder sought more creative control over his music as he grew into adulthood. He began producing his own albums in 1970, and in 1971 renegotiated his Motown contract to get complete artistic control over his recordings.

The new artistic freedom resulted in one of the most productive phases of Wonder's career, which included hits such as "My Cherie Amour" (1969), "Signed, Sealed, Delivered I'm Yours" (1970), "Superstition" (1972), and "You Are the Sunshine of My Life" (1973). A musical visionary, Wonder combined poetic lyrics with experimental electronic music that he developed through his mastery of the synthesizer. He also took the idea of a "concept" album – an album based on a central theme – to new heights. Albums including *Talking Book* (1972), *Innervisions* (1973), *Fulfillingness' First Finale* (1974), and *Songs in the Key of Life* (1976) reflected Wonder's spiritual style and won him more Grammy Awards than any other Motown artist.

Wonder's music and life have always engaged with social issues and political causes. Songs such as "Living for the City" (1973) offered commentary on urban poverty, and one of his later hits, "Happy Birthday" (1980), was instrumental in the campaign to recognize Martin Luther King Jr.'s birthday as a national holiday. Wonder also performed in the United States for Africa's fundraising song, "We are the World," and was a leader in the antiapartheid movement in the United States. Wonder's recent work includes the soundtrack for Spike Lee's film *Jungle Fever* (1991), and *Conversation Peace* (1995). Wonder has received many awards in recognition of his musical achievements. He was inducted into the Songwriter's Hall of Fame in 1982 and the Rock and Roll Hall of Fame in 1989, and in 1996, at age 46, Wonder received the Grammy's Lifetime Achievement Award.

Robert Fay

See Also
Antiapartheid Movement; Detroit, Michigan; King, Martin Luther, Jr.; Lee, Shelton Jackson ("Spike"); Motown.

North America

Woodbey, George Washington

(b. October 5, 1854, Johnson County, Tenn.; d. 1937), African American Baptist minister and the first black man to join the Socialist Party of America.

George Washington Woodbey was born a slave. He was ordained a Baptist minister in Emporia, Kansas, in 1874 and soon became the pastor of the African Church in Omaha, Nebraska. During his tenure as pastor he became active in politics and joined both the Prohibition Party and the Republican Party. In 1896 he unsuccessfully ran for lieutenant governor on the Nebraska Prohibition ticket. Later that year, however, after reading Edward Bellamy's *Looking Backward 2000-1887* and upon hearing a speech by the socialist labor leader Eugene V. Debs, Woodbey embraced the tenets of SOCIALISM. He resigned his pastorship and dedicated the rest of his life to the socialist movement.

Woodbey joined the Socialist Party of America in 1902 and moved to San Diego, California. In San Diego he lectured widely and appeared often as a soap-box orator around town on behalf of the socialist movement; he was soon known as "The Great Negro Socialist Orator." In addition, Woodbey served as minister of the Mount Zion Baptist Church in San Diego and used his pulpit to convert members of his African American congregation to socialism. In 1904 he published *What to Do and How to Do It or Socialism vs. Capitalism* and *The Bible and Socialism*, two booklets intended to illustrate the compatibility of socialism and Christianity.

Woodbey's writings, like his lectures, were highly valued by members of the Socialist Party not only because they clearly enunciated the socialist position, but because they were widely read by the African American community. Woodbey was elected to the state executive board of the California Socialist Party and served as the only African American delegate to the 1904 and the 1908 Socialist Party conventions. Despite the lack of black representation in the Socialist Party, Woodbey never questioned the organization's position on race. Instead, Woodbey supported the socialist contention that racial inequality, like class stratification, was the direct result of the capitalist system, and he argued that racial equality could only be attained through the institution of a socialist system. "And then the men of all races will share in the results of production according to their services in the process of production. This is Socialism and the only solution to the race problem."

After the 1908 convention Woodbey embarked on a speaking tour of Northern cities to promote the Socialist Party in African American communities and published a booklet titled *Why the Negro Should Vote the Socialist Ticket.* He served as editor of the *New Idea*, a black socialist newspaper in San Diego, from 1921 to 1927.

Elizabeth Heath

See Also
Slavery in the United States; Baptists.

North America

Woodruff, Hale Aspacio

(b. August 26, 1900, Cairo, Ill.; d. September 6, 1980, New York, N.Y.), African American painter and teacher who is best known for his *Amistad Murals*.

Hale Woodruff attended public schools in Nashville, Tennessee, where he was raised by his mother. In 1920 he moved to Indianapolis to study art at the John Herron Art Institute, supporting himself with part-time work as a political cartoonist. During this period he developed an interest in African art, which influenced his later work. In 1926 Woodruff won a Harmon Foundation Award to study at the Académie Moderne de la Grande Chaumière in Paris from 1927 to 1931.

Woodruff returned to the United States in 1931 and founded the art department at Atlanta University, where he helped to develop a cohesive national African American arts community. In addition to teaching, Woodruff brought exhibitions to Atlanta University that featured a wide range of African American artists who were often excluded from mainstream art exhibitions. To promote African American art and artists further, Woodruff organized the Atlanta University Annuals in 1942, a national juried exhibition that continued until 1970. Woodruff used the Annuals to promote the interests of his students, including Frederick Flemister, Eugene Grigsby, Wilmer Jennings, and Hayward Oubré, and independent artists such as Charles Alston, ELIZABETH CATLETT, LOIS MAILOU JONES, and William H. Johnson.

A gifted artist as well as teacher, Woodruff achieved his greatest fame with the *Amistad Murals*, painted for Talladega College's Savery Library. The work reflects the influence of Mexican muralist Diego Rivera, with whom Woodruff studied briefly in 1934, and depicts moments of "the Amistad Incident," the 1839 mutiny by kidnapped Africans aboard a slave ship against their captors. The first panel, *The Mutiny Aboard the Amistad, 1839*, shows the violent struggle that occurred when the enslaved Africans sought to capture the ship. The second panel, *The Amistad Slaves on Trial at New Haven, Connecticut, 1840*, depicts a scene from the trial, as a white sailor who survived the attack accuses the African Cinque of leading the mutiny. The third panel, *The Return to Africa, 1842*, portrays the mutineers after winning their court case and returning home.

Woodruff moved to New York in 1946 and began teaching at New York University (NYU). During this period he abandoned figurative painting and shifted to an abstract expressionist style. He adopted abstract expressionism's spontaneity but also included design components of the African art he became interested in as a student, including ASANTE gold weights, DOGON masks, and YORUBA Shango implements. Woodruff also continued to support other African American artists. In 1963 Woodruff cofounded Spiral, a group whose members sought to represent the CIVIL RIGHTS MOVEMENT in the visual arts. Woodruff was awarded a Great Teacher Award by NYU in 1966, and in 1968 he became professor emeritus at NYU. In April 1980, shortly before his death, he was one of ten African American artists honored by President Jimmy Carter at a White House reception for the National Conference of Artists.

Robert Fay

See Also
Art and Architecture, African; Alston, Charles Henry; Amistad Mutiny; Johnson, William Henry; New York, New York; Cinque, Joseph; Art, African American.

North America

Woodson, Carter Godwin

(b. December 19, 1875, New Canton, Va.; d. April 3, 1950, Washington, D.C.), African American historian and educator who pioneered the research and dissemination of African American history.

One of nine children, Carter G. Woodson grew up on his family's farm in rural Virginia. His mother, a former slave who had secretly learned to read and write as a child, and two of his uncles, who received training at Freedmen's Bureau schools, tutored him and cultivated his interest in learning. In 1892 Woodson moved to Huntington, West Virginia, where he worked in coal mines.

At age 20 Woodson enrolled at Frederick Douglass High School, the only all-black school in the area. He completed the four-year curriculum in two years even though he was working to pay his tuition. Following his graduation he obtained a teaching position in Winona, West Virginia. But in 1901 Woodson returned to his former high school to teach and later to serve as principal. Meanwhile, he intermittently attended Berea College in Kentucky, an integrated school established by abolitionists, from which he graduated in 1903.

Woodson was then hired by the United States War Department to teach English to Spanish-speaking students in the Philippines. While abroad he studied Spanish and other Romance languages through University of Chicago correspondence courses. Returning to the United States following travel in Europe, he matriculated at the University of Chicago in 1907 and received both bachelor's and master's degrees in European history in 1908. Woodson then entered the doctoral program in history at Harvard University and the next year initiated a ten-year teaching career at Dunbar High School in Washington, D.C. He received the Ph.D. in 1912, making him only the second African American to earn a Harvard doctorate degree.

In 1915 Woodson established the Association for the Study of Negro Life and History (ASNLH, later the ASSOCIATION FOR THE STUDY OF AFRO-AMERICAN LIFE AND HISTORY). The organization's aim was to encourage research and writing about the black experience, to publish this writing, and to raise funds to support researchers and writers. As extensions of the ASNLH, Woodson founded the *Journal of Negro History* (1916), the Associated Publishers (1921), and the *Negro History Bulletin* (1937). The *Journal of Negro History* was for the general reader. The Associated Publishers generated revenue to "make possible the publication and circulation of valuable books on colored people not acceptable to most publishers." The *Negro History Bulletin* provided elementary and secondary teachers lessons in African American history.

Woodson always had difficulty securing funds for the ASNLH. He solicited numerous foundations without much success. Although he could have alleviated the ASNLH's financial problems by affiliating it with a university, he rejected this solution in order to maintain his own independence and control over the organization. Money came from Woodson's own meager teaching salary, the income generated by his numerous publications, and the contributions of the African American community.

One of Woodson's enduring achievements is his initiation of Black History Month. In 1926 he launched Negro History Week, a commemoration of black achievement held the second week of February, which marked the birthdays of FREDERICK DOUGLASS and Abraham Lincoln. To encourage African Americans to celebrate Negro History Week, Woodson distributed kits containing pictures of and stories about notable African Americans. Negro History Week was changed to Black History Month in the 1960s.

Woodson was a prodigious writer, authoring or coauthoring 19 books on various aspects of African American history. He was one of the first scholars to consider slavery from the slaves' perspective, to compare SLAVERY IN THE UNITED STATES to slavery in Latin America, and to note the African cultural influences in New World slave culture.

Woodson's mission was to dispel the racist myths about African Americans and their past that the historical writings of white scholars promulgated. He asserted, "If a race has no history, if it has no worthwhile tradition, it becomes a negligible factor in the thought of the world, and it stands in danger of being exterminated."

Perhaps more than any other person, Woodson helped African American history develop into a widely recognized and respected academic discipline. He believed that "the achievements of the Negro properly set forth will crown him as a factor in early human progress and a maker of modern civilization."

Aaron Myers

SEE ALSO

Slavery in Latin America and the Caribbean; Abolitionism in the United States; Black History Month/Negro History Week; Bureau of Refugees, Freedmen and Abandoned Lands; *Journal of Negro History, The.*

North America

Woods, Tiger (b. December 30, 1975, Cypress, Calif.), the first African American and Asian American, and the youngest golfer, to win a major golf tournament.

When Eldrick "Tiger" Woods decided to leave Stanford University in August 1996 to play professional golf, the expectations placed on him were high. A golf prodigy whose father, Earl Woods, taught his son to play golf before the boy could even read, Woods had recorded two holes-in-one by age six. By 1996 he possessed a complete and polished game with the power to hit 300-yard drives routinely, and the touch necessary for a solid "short game" (shots from within 60 yards of the hole, including putting).

Experts lauded Woods's great physical skills, as well as his competitive desire and mental composure, for which Woods credited his father, a former Green Beret in the VIETNAM WAR. Woods had also amassed many amateur titles, including six United States Golf Association national championships, a record-setting three consecutive U.S. Amateur championships, a National College Athletic Association championship.

Woods successfully joined the professional ranks by winning two of the first seven tournaments he entered. In April 1997 Woods won the Masters Tournament, golf's most prestigious tournament, shooting a record-setting 270 and winning by the largest margin in Masters history, 12 strokes. He also set a handful of unofficial records, including the first African American *and* Asian American (his mother, Kutilda [Punsawad] Woods, comes from Thailand) to win a major golf tournament, as well as being the youngest Masters winner. Woods ended 1997 with four tournament wins and nine top-ten finishes.

Woods has had a great impact on the social aspects of golf. When Woods won the Masters, many credited him with breaking RACIAL STEREOTYPES that had labeled athletes of color as poor golfers. Woods himself cited black golfers who paved the way for him, such as Lee Elder, the first African American to play in the Masters, and Ted Rhodes, the first African American to play in the U.S. Open. In addition to winning the respect and admiration of his colleagues on the tour, Woods has increased golf's popularity among African Americans and other minorities.

Robert Fay

North America

Work, African Americans and the Changing Nature of, in the Post-World War II Era: An Interpretation

THE LIMITS OF THE RACE RELATIONS VISION

Despite African Americans' strong focus on racial discrimination in employment, their economic fate is inextricably connected with the structure and functioning of the modern economy, including the global economy. Racial bias continues to be an important factor that aggravates black employment problems. Nonetheless, to overemphasize the racial factor would obscure the nonracial economic forces that have sharply increased joblessness and declining real wages among many African Americans in the last several decades. As the late black economist Sir Vivian Henderson (1975) argued several years ago, racism put blacks in their economic place and stepped aside to watch changes in the modern economy disrupt that place.

In the following sections of this essay I underline the importance of understanding race-neutral economic forces that impact heavily on the African American community, forces that represent changes in the new economy.

THE TWIST IN THE DEMAND FOR LABOR

A "twist" in the demand for different types of labor has occurred in recent years. Today's close interaction between technology and international competition has eroded the basic institutions of the mass production system. In the past several decades almost all of the improvements in productivity have been associated with technology and human capital, thereby drastically reducing the importance of physical capital and natural resources. At the same time that changes in technology are producing new jobs, they are making many others obsolete.

The workplace has been revolutionized by technological changes that range from the development of robotics to information highways. While educated workers are benefiting from the pace of technological change, involving the increased use of computer-based technologies and microcomputers, more routine workers face the growing threat of job displacement in certain industries. In the new global economy highly educated and thoroughly trained men and women are in demand. This may be seen most dramatically in the sharp differences in employment experiences among men. Unlike men with lower education, college-educated men are working more, not less.

The shift in demand has been especially devastating for those low-skilled workers whose incorporation into the mainstream economy has been marginal or recent. Even before the economic restructuring of the nation's economy, low-skilled African Americans were at the end of the employment queue. Their economic situation has been further weakened because they tend to reside in communities that not only have higher jobless rates and lower employment growth but lack access to areas of higher employment and employment growth as well.

Of the changes in the economy that have adversely affected low-skilled African American workers, perhaps the most significant have been those in the manufacturing sector. One study revealed that in the 1970s "up to half of the huge employment declines for less-educated blacks might be explained by industrial shifts away from manufacturing toward other sectors." The manufacturing losses in some Northern cities have been staggering. In the 20-year period from 1967 to 1987 Philadelphia lost 64 percent of its manufacturing jobs; Chicago lost 60 percent; New York City, 58 percent; and Detroit, 51 percent. In absolute numbers these percentages represent the loss of 160,000 jobs in Philadelphia, 326,000 in Chicago, 520,000 – over half a million – in New York, and 108,000 in Detroit.

Another study examined the effects of economic restructuring in the 1980s by highlighting the changes in both the variety and the quality (which was measured in terms of earnings, benefits, union protection, and involuntary part-time employment) of blue-collar employment in general. The authors found that both the relative earnings and employment rates among unskilled black workers were lower. Two reasons were given: traditional jobs that provide a living wage (high-wage blue-collar cluster, of which roughly 50 percent were manufacturing jobs) declined, as did the quality of secondary jobs on which workers increasingly had to rely. The result was lower relative earnings for the remaining workers in the labor market. As employment prospects worsened, rising proportions of low-skilled black workers dropped out of the legitimate labor market.

Industrial restructuring has had serious consequences for African Americans across the nation. John Kasarda states, "As late as the 1968-1970 period, more than 70 percent of all blacks working in metropolitan areas held blue-collar jobs at the same time that more than 50 percent of all metropolitan workers held white-collar jobs. Moreover, of the large numbers of urban blacks classified as blue-collar workers during the late 1960s, more than half were employed in goods-producing industries."

The number of employed black males ages 20 to 29 working in manufacturing industries fell dramatically between 1973 and 1987 (from three of every eight to one in five). Meanwhile, the share of employed young black men in the retail trade and service jobs rose sharply during that period (from 17 to almost 27 percent and from 10 to nearly 21 percent, respectively). And this shift in opportunities was not without economic consequences: in 1987 the average annual earnings of 20- to 29-year-old males who held jobs in the retail trade and service sectors were 25 to 30 percent less than those of males employed in manufacturing.

The structural shifts in the distribution of industrial job opportunities are not the only reason for the declining earnings among young black male workers. There have also been important changes in the patterns of occupational staffing within firms and industries, including those in manufacturing. These changes have primarily benefited those with more formal education. Substantial numbers of new professional, technical, and managerial positions have been created. However, such jobs require at least some years of postsecondary education. According to a study by Andrew Sum and Neal Fogg, young high school dropouts and even high school graduates "have faced a dwindling supply of career jobs offering the real earnings opportunities available to them in the 1960s and early 1970s."

Most of the new jobs for workers with limited training and education are in the service sector and are disproportionately held by women. This is even more true for those who work in social services, which include the industries of health, education, and welfare. Within central cities the number of jobs for less-educated workers has declined precipitously. However, many workers stayed afloat thanks to jobs in the expanding social service sector, especially black women with less than a high school degree. Among all women workers, the proportion employed in social services climbed between 1979 and 1993 (from 28 to 33 percent). The health and education industries absorbed nearly all of this increase. Of the 54 million female workers in 1993, almost one-third were employed in social service industries. Social services tend to feature a more highly educated work force. Only 20 percent of all female workers with less than a high school degree were employed in social services in 1993. (The figure for comparable males is even lower. Only 4 percent of employed, less-educated men held social service jobs in 1993.) Nonetheless, the proportion of less-educated female workers in social services is up notably from 1989.

Indeed, despite the relatively higher educational level of social service workers, 37 percent of employed, less-educated black women in central cities worked in social services in 1993, largely in jobs in hospitals, elementary schools, nursing care, and child care. In central cities in the largest metropolitan areas the percentage of low-educated, African American female workers in social services sharply increased from 30.5 percent in 1979 to 40.5 percent in 1993. Given the overall decline in jobs for less-educated, central-city workers, the opportunity for employment in the social service industries prevented many inner-city workers from joining the growing ranks of the jobless. Less-educated, black female workers depend heavily on social service employment. Even a small number of less-educated black males were able to find jobs in social services.

HOUSEHOLD INCOME GROWTH 1960-1990

	1960	1970	1980	1990
Total (in current dollars)				
All Families	5,620	9,867	21,023	35,353
Married-couple families	5,688	10,169	23,141	39,895
Female householder, no spouse	2,983	4,797	10,408	16,932
Black				
All Families	3,233	6,516	12,674	21,423
Married-couple families	N/A	7,816	18,593	33,784
Female householder, no spouse	N/A	3,576	7,425	12,125
Total (in 1990 dollars)				
All Families	N/A	33,268	33,346	35,353
Married-couple families	N/A	34,268	36,706	39,895
Female householder, no spouse	N/A	16,174	16,509	16,932
Black				
All Families	N/A	21,151	20,103	21,423
Married-couple families	N/A	25,371	29,491	33,784
Female householder, no spouse	N/A	11,608	11,777	12,125

Although only 4 percent of less-educated, employed males worked in social services in 1993, 12 percent of less-educated, employed black men in the central cities of large metropolitan areas held social service jobs.

The Computer Revolution and the Changing Demand for Labor

The computer revolution is a major reason for the shift in demand for skilled workers. Whereas only one-fourth of workers directly used a computer on their jobs in 1983 in the United States, by 1993 that figure had risen to almost half the work force. According to the economist Alan Krueger, "the expansion of computer use can account for one-third to two-thirds of the increase in the payoff to education between 1984 and 1993 [in the United States]." Two reasons are cited: first, even after a number of background factors such as experience and education are controlled, those who use computers at work tend to be paid more than those who do not; second, the industries with the greatest shift in employment toward more highly skilled workers are those in which computer technology is more intensively used. The share of workers with college degrees increased most sharply in the industries with the most rapid expansion of computer use.

Early studies of the diffusion of computer technology revealed strong positive relationships among computer ownership and income and education. And although systematic research is lacking, it is clear that in jobless ghetto areas and depressed rural areas, computerization and telecommunications are severely underrepresented.

A recent study revealed that the problems of lack of access to key resources attributed to race and class may be even more clear-cut with respect to access to and use of the Internet than in other areas. Whereas 73 percent of white students had access to home computers, only 32 percent of black students did. However, African Americans with income above $40,000 were as likely as comparable whites to own home computers. Thus, it is bad enough if you are a low-income family; it is even worse if you are a low-income black family. And since this study was based on a nationwide telephone survey, as opposed to face-to-face, in-home interviews, it probably understates the actual use and access to computers among disadvantaged segments of the population, many of whose members do not have telephones.

This study not only reveals how class intersects with race at the lower income levels, but it also shows that the disparity in computer access according to income is greater among blacks than among whites. The study found a sharp divide in the use of the computer network according to race among households below the median income of $40,000. However, home computer ownership among African Americans with incomes over $40,000 is roughly equal to that of comparable whites. Moreover, these higher-income African Americans were even more likely than their white counterparts to have access to the Internet at work. Nonetheless, since the proportion of higher-income blacks (that is, those with incomes above $40,000) is considerably lower than the proportion of higher-income whites, the problem of computer access for blacks as a group is more serious. The telephone survey revealed that whereas 44.3 percent of whites owned a home computer, only 29 percent of blacks did.

Rising demands for computer workers has compensated for declining demands for workers in other sectors of the economy. Since an overwhelming majority of all new jobs will require the use of computers, the have-not population, especially the minority have-nots, will be in danger of becoming permanent economic proletarians. Let us consider this problem in central-city areas.

Effects on Black Central-City Residents

As urban economies have transformed from goods processing to information processing, black central-city residents with no education beyond high school have become increasingly

HOUSEHOLD INCOME GROWTH 1960-1990

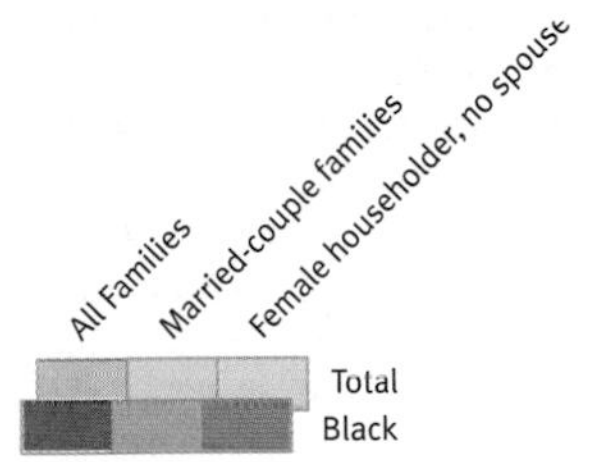

IN CURRENT DOLLARS

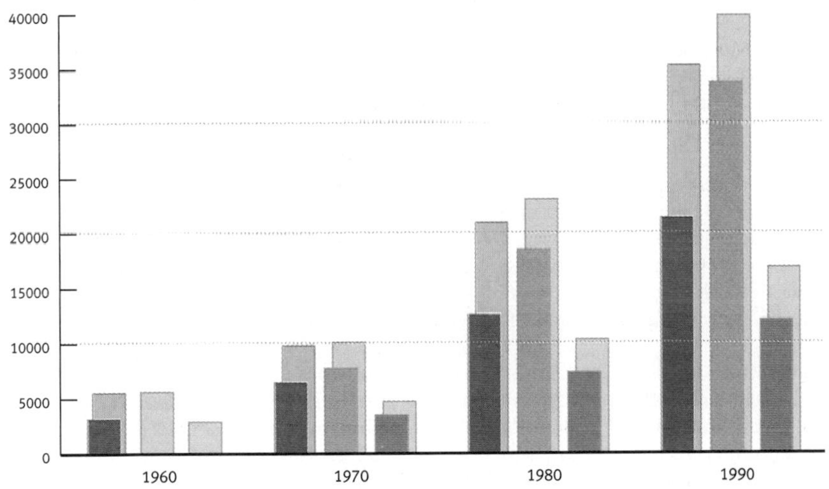

IN 1990 DOLLARS

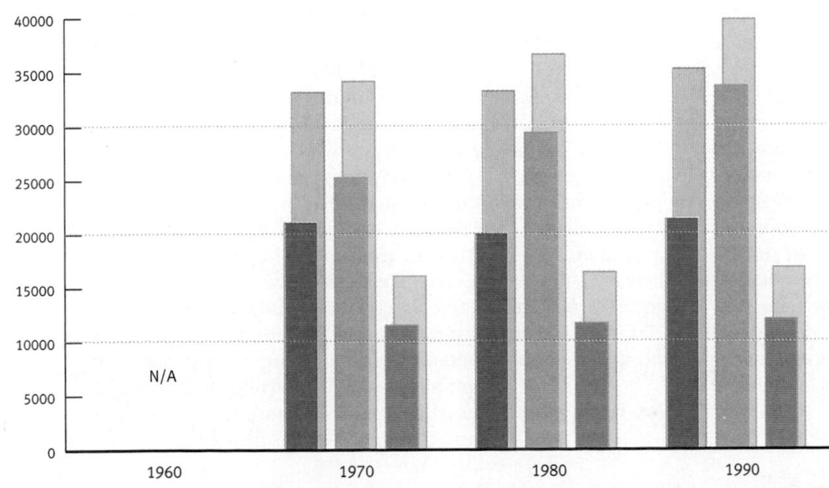

LEFT AND OPPOSITE PAGE: N/A: Not Available
Sources: *Encyclopedia of African-American Culture and History* (1996): "Median Money Income of Families, 1960-1990" (Table 5.4); *Statistical Abstract*, 1992, 1982-83; *Historical Statistics of the United States*; *Current Population Reports.*

displaced. Indeed, with the transition from manufacturing to services, cognitive and interpersonal skills have become prerequisites even for many low-paying jobs.

Surveying 3000 employers in Los Angeles, Atlanta, and Boston, the economist Harry Holzer of Michigan State University found that only 5 to 10 percent of the jobs in central-city areas for non-college graduates require very few work credentials or cognitive skills. This means that most inner-city workers today not only need to have the basic skills of reading, writing, and performing arithmetic calculations but also need to know how to operate a computer as well.

Moreover, the growing suburbanization of jobs, particularly in manufacturing and services, has isolated inner-city minorities from many job opportunities. Most ghetto residents cannot afford an automobile and therefore have to rely on public transit systems, which makes the connection between inner-city neighborhoods and suburban job locations difficult and time consuming.

Increasing the skills of inner-city workers is not the only problem. Many central-city job applicants are physically isolated from places of employment and socially isolated from the informal job networks that have become a major source of job placement. Unlike the markets in previous years, labor markets today are mainly regional. A disproportionate number of metropolitan jobs are in the suburbs. Many inner-city residents lack information or knowledge about job opportunities in the suburbs and/or have difficulty commuting to them. In the inner-city ghettos the breakdown of the informal job information network aggravates the problems of job spatial mismatch.

The Effects of Changes in the Global Economy

The shift in demand for skilled versus low-skilled workers can also be related to changes in the global economy. Two developments facilitated the growth in global economic activity: (1) advances in information and communications technologies, which significantly lowered communications and transportation costs and thereby encouraged companies to shift work to low-wage areas; and (2) the expansion of free trade, which reduced the price of imports and raised the output of export industries.

Whereas the increased output of export industries aids skilled workers, simply because skilled workers are heavily represented in export industries, increasing imports that compete with labor-intensive industries (for example, apparel, textile, toy, footwear, and some manufacturing industries) hurt unskilled labor. According to economic theory, the expansion of trade with countries that have a large proportion of relatively unskilled labor will not only increase competition with unskilled workers in the United States and result in downward pressure on their wages but lower the price of goods produced by unskilled labor in the United States as well. Because of the concentration of low-skilled black workers in vulnerable, labor-intensive industries (e.g., 40 percent of the work force in the apparel industry is African American), developments in international trade may further exacerbate their labor market experiences.

Conclusion

The above analysis reveals that many of the economic woes in the African American community (job displacement – including changes in the variety and quality of jobs – declining real wages, unemployment, and non-labor-force participation) can be traced to fundamental shifts in the demand for labor in the global economy. While the more educated and highly trained African Americans, like their counterparts among other ethnic groups, have benefited from the shifts in labor demand, those with lesser skills have suffered.

The sharp decline in the relative demand for low-skilled labor has had a more adverse effect on blacks than on whites in the United States because a substantially larger proportion of African Americans are unskilled. Although the number of skilled African Americans (including managers, professionals, and technicians) increased sharply in the mid- to late 1990s, the proportion of those who are unskilled remains large, because the black population, burdened by cumulative experiences of racial restrictions, was overwhelmingly unskilled just several decades ago.

Although racial discrimination and segregation exacerbate the labor-market problems of low-skilled African Americans – that is, render them more severe – we should not lose sight of the fact that these problems derive from and are driven by fundamental changes in the new global economy.

Nonetheless, there is a tendency among policymakers, scholars, and black leaders alike to separate the economic problems in the black community from the national and international trends affecting American families and neighborhoods. If the economic problems of the African American community are defined solely in racial terms, they can be isolated and viewed as only requiring race-based solutions. Economist Henderson warned the nation against this short-sighted vision: "The economic future of blacks in the United States is bound up with that of the rest of the nation," he argued. "Politics designed in the future to cope with the problems of the poor and victimized will also yield benefits to blacks. In contrast, any efforts to treat blacks separately from the rest of the nation are likely to lead to frustration, heightened racial animosities, and a waste of the country's resources and the precious resources of black people."

William Julius Wilson

See Also

Boston, Massachusetts; Chicago, Illinois; Detroit, Michigan; Los Angeles, California; New York, New York; Philadelphia, Pennsylvania.

North America

Works Progress Administration,

a program implemented during the Great Depression as part of President Franklin D. Roosevelt's New Deal that provided jobs for many unemployed African Americans.

During the 1930s, as the United States struggled through the Great Depression, millions of people were left unemployed or underemployed. The Works Progress Administration (WPA) – established in 1935 and four years later renamed the Work Projects Administration – was a massive program to provide jobs for the unemployed. It was part of President Franklin D. Roosevelt's New Deal, a set of initiatives designed to revive the American economy. In March 1936, a year after its creation, the WPA had 3.6 million people on its rolls.

Between 1935 and the program's demise in 1943 the WPA constructed more than 1,046,025 km (650,000 mi) of streets and highways. It built or worked on more than 850 airports, 8000 parks, 120,000 bridges, and 125,000 public buildings. African Americans, who accounted for less than 10 percent of the American population, particularly benefited from the WPA, making up 15 to 20 percent of its 8.5 million employees. Moreover, in 1935 Roosevelt signed an executive order forbidding discrimination in WPA projects, one of his strongest actions in support of equality for African Americans and other minorities.

Although mainly employing people to perform manual labor, the WPA also established a variety of educational and arts projects. Ella J. Baker, later instrumental in founding the Student Nonviolent Coordinating Committee (SNCC), taught literacy and consumer education classes – and learned about grassroots political organizing – under the auspices of the WPA. Similarly, future lawyer and civil rights activist Pauli Murray worked in the New York City public schools with the WPA's Remedial Reading Project as well as in the WPA Workers' Education Project. For Baker, Murray, and others, experience in the WPA played a role in their subsequent activism in the Civil Rights Movement.

The WPA supported the arts and sponsored cultural activities through the Federal Writers' Project (FWP), the WPA Dance Theater, the Federal Music Project, and the Federal Theater Project. The Federal Theater Project, which Congress abolished in 1939, supported touring theatrical companies and circuses that brought inexpensive entertainment, including an all-black production of William Shakespeare's *Macbeth*, to towns and cities across the country.

The FWP employed such noted black writers as Ralph Ellison, Claude McKay, Richard Wright, Zora Neale Hurston, and Arna Bontemps. Among its various activities the FWP undertook a large-scale oral history project to interview former African American slaves and collect narratives of their experiences under slavery. In most states the interviewers were white, but Virginia's FWP was notable for its extensive use of black interviewers.

In response to an apparent economic recovery in 1936, Roosevelt and Congress made sharp cuts in the WPA budget. The cutbacks resulted in many workers – including many African Americans – being dismissed from WPA projects and helped trigger an economic downturn between 1937 and 1939, known as the "Roosevelt Recession." WPA policies were the subject of controversy, as evidenced by such topical blues as Casey Bill Weldon's "WPA Blues" (1936) and Porter Grainger's "Pink Slip Blues," recorded by singer Ida Cox in 1939. But the main opponents of the WPA were Republicans and white Southern Democrats, who constituted a conservative anti-New Deal coalition that in 1943 succeeded in abolishing the agency.

James Clyde Sellman

See Also

Slavery in the United States; Blues, The; Slave Narratives.

Cross Cultural

World Music, World Beat, and the Re-Africanization of Latin American Popular Music

The term *world music* has long been used by ethnomusicologists and folklorists for everything that is not Western art music – that is, tribal music, folk music, and non-Western classical music. Typically recorded in situ by scholars, world music records were released by museums or other cultural institutions in austere record jackets with extensive liner notes, and were clearly considered to be serious educational documents for specialists rather than entertainment for mass audiences. This pattern of dissemination changed dramatically in the wake of immigration from so-called Third World countries to postcolonial cities such as Paris, London, and New York, when (mostly imported) recordings of a variety of non-Western musics, both traditional and contemporary popular, began to circulate within immigrant communities with little if any mediation by scholars. However, as immigrant musicians – especially those whose music was intended for dancing – took advantage of the sophisticated recording and broadcast technologies available in northern cities, their potential for appealing to audiences beyond their own ethnic communities greatly increased.

In the early 1980s entrepreneurs from the United States and Europe who recognized the commercial possibilities of these non-Western musics began establishing small, independent record labels specifically designed to market to general United States and European audiences. Since the musics did not fit into existing marketing categories, the term *world music* was appropriated from ethnomusicology.

This "new" category of world music quickly differentiated itself from its highly specialized scholarly antecedent by the nature of its production and distribution: an extensive, interlocking commercial infrastructure comprising specialty record companies, retail and mail order outlets, radio shows, dance clubs, magazines, music festivals, and the like, all dedicated to promoting exotic sounds from developing countries to consumers in the industrialized world, who on the whole were urban, affluent, well educated – and in Europe and the United States, mostly white. Some of the musics promoted via this new infrastructure were the sort of traditional and folk-oriented music that had formerly been categorized by music specialists as world music, but others were technologically sophisticated, stylistically hybridized, and commercially oriented products that fell well beyond the traditional purview of ethnomusicologists.

The marketing term *world beat*, which emerged about the same time as *world music*, referred to a subset of world music that included commercially oriented dance musics. Since the single most important element of dance music is rhythm, it is no accident that most of the musics initially categorized as world beat originated in areas where percussion has been most consistently and successfully cultivated over time – in Africa and its diaspora. Indeed, even a partial listing of musics marketed as world beat confirms the importance of Africa and the diaspora: juju from Nigeria, *soukous* from Congo-Brazzaville/Congo-Kinshasa/Senegal, *chimurenga* from Zimbabwe, *vodou-jazz* and misik raisin from Haiti, samba from Brazil, zouk from Martinique and Guadeloupe, and soca from Trinidad.

Taking advantage of these new musical sources as well as of the growing demand for non-Western popular music, rock musicians such as Paul Simon, Peter Gabriel, and David Byrne began creating pop cross-fertilizations between First and Third World styles – especially those from the diaspora. As interest in Third World popular music grew, styles from places as disparate as Yemen, Pakistan, and Australia began to be marketed as world beat as well. The ever-increasing range of styles and nationalities falling under the world beat umbrella challenged scholars trying to define it; as Andrew Goodwin and Joe Gore wrote: "World Beat might be identified as Western pop stars appropriating non-Western sounds, as third world musicians using Western rock and pop, or as the Western consumption of non-Western folk music." Even such a comprehensive definition, however, did not account for the multilateral stylistic exchanges that began taking place among Third World regions themselves.

In order to assist fans in negotiating the potentially confusing array of new musical offerings, guides and directories to world music began to appear, each arbitrarily dividing up the world into geostylistic regions (e.g., "The Nile and the Gulf" or "The Middle East and the Indian Subcontinent") to facilitate consumer sampling and selecting. As the number of new or previously "unknown" musical genres and styles from around the world has burgeoned, it has become increasingly difficult to distinguish between world music and world beat, and, indeed, the terms are often used interchangeably; the above-mentioned guides, for example, do not distinguish between the two.

While most world beat musics originated in Third World contexts, they were far from the pristine traditional folk musics that had been studied by ethnomusicologists as world music; on the contrary, they were highly hybridized products of cross-fertilization between Third World aesthetics and First World technologies and styles, primarily rock. World beat entrepreneurs, however, tried to distinguish themselves from their pop music counterparts by employing the discourses of education and cultural exchange in order to market their products. For example, detailed liner notes accompanied recordings, mail order catalogues were extensively annotated, and world music magazines and radio programming provided consumers with in-depth information on the origins and cultural contexts of the diverse musical styles. A handful of scholars specializing in non-Western popular musics collaborated with world beat record companies, assisting with content selection as well as preparation of liner notes, while others began writing for industry-related magazines such as *Beat*. Such scholarly participation clearly lent credibility and authority to industry efforts to mark products as genuine and to avoid the taint of crass commercialism.

As world beat became a more visible feature of the international popular musical landscape in the late 1980s and early 1990s, popular music scholars began to analyze its economic and cultural implications. Most analyses focused on the inequalities characterizing the bilateral relationships between north and south and accused the industry of exploiting Third World cultural resources. Others were concerned about the potentially disastrous consequences of homogenization and Westernization upon folk cultures being swept up in and transformed by what have been called global culture flows. The most trenchant critics also charged the world music industry with racism, for ignoring the harsh realities of economic and political subordination experienced by Third World peoples of color, and instead constructing images of cultural authenticity in order to satisfy the desires of northern whites safely to consume exotic otherness. Musicologist Paul Gilroy, for example, denounced the world music industry for using festive images of diasporan people and culture to suggest that the essence of diasporan musics is a good time rather than endorsing their implicit ideological consciousness.

While these concerns are certainly justified, the cultural repercussions of world beat have not been entirely negative. More optimistic observers, for example, have suggested that the powerful forces of cultural and economic hegemony are being resisted by culturally and technologically savvy Third World musicians who are taking control of the production of their own music, revitalizing local musical traditions by modernizing them. Furthermore, the international popular musical landscape, so long dominated by U.S. and European pop and rock, has unquestionably been diversified and enriched by the increased circulation of musics from multiple locations around the globe.

The Spanish Caribbean region serves as a useful case study for examining the impact of world music – world beat in particular – on a particular locality. Prior to the emergence of the world music phenomenon, musical exchanges within the Spanish Caribbean seldom extended beyond linguistic boundaries; for example, Colombian musicians would borrow from Cuban, Dominican, or Puerto Rican music – but not from Haitian or Jamaican music, and certainly not from contemporary African music. Indeed, the Spanish Caribbean was not a propitious region in which the sort of musics under the world beat umbrella would take root: in spite of its racially mixed population, the region had historically ignored or downplayed its African heritage in favor of a more Iberocentric identity, and (except in Cuba) there was little interest, in either the music industry or government cultural agencies, in promoting distinctively Afro-Caribbean expressive culture. In the wake of the world beat-stimulated circulation of diasporan dance musics, however, local Afro-Caribbean genres were revitalized and revalidated, and cross-fertilizations with musical styles from non-Hispanic regions of the diaspora became more frequent, thereby significantly "re-Africanizing" the region's popular music landscape.

The city of Cartagena de Indias, located on Colombia's Caribbean north coast, has the distinction of being the vanguard of this "re-Africanization" process, thanks to the successful local development of mechanisms for importing and circulating recordings of diasporan dance musics originating outside the Spanish Caribbean. These musics were first introduced to Cartagena via locally constructed mobile sound systems called *picós* – resembling but not identical to Jamaican sound systems – which provided music for dance parties attended by the city's predominantly black and poor populace, excluded by poverty and racism from other recreational venues such as discotheques and clubs. Initially these sound systems relied on records of Spanish Caribbean dance music (primarily salsa), but by the mid-1970s – even before the northern emergence of world beat in the 1980s – recordings of various diasporan popular musics had been taken to Cartagena by merchant marine sailors, who had purchased them in immigrant music shops in U.S. or European port cities, and given or sold them to picó owners, who included them in an evening's repertoire as novelties. While stylistically unfamiliar and sung in unintelligible languages, these highly danceable musics – especially West African soukous – eventually became extremely popular among black Cartagena dancers, who began referring to them generically as *música africana* (whether they originated in Africa or other Afro-Caribbean countries) because the people knew – from record jacket photographs – that the musicians were black. Since neither the Colombian music industry nor the international record companies doing business in Colombia was interested in promoting such musics, picó owners turned the local unavailability of recordings into an opportunity, constructing a complex and highly effective system of acquiring and disseminating these musics built upon the concept of "exclusivity," wherein they could profit by attracting fans to their dances because they possessed a scarce but highly desirable product – diasporan dance musics.

Cartagena's middle classes, on the other hand, never attended picó parties, which were considered disreputable, so they were not exposed to non-Spanish Caribbean dance musics until the early 1980s, when a major multicultural popular music festival was established by two Cartagena-based entrepreneurs who had noticed the development of world beat in the north and astutely recognized its economic potential within Colombia. With backing from prestigious private and public institutions and the media, the Festival de Música del Caribe was a high-profile event scheduled during Easter week, when Cartagena is inundated with middle- and upper-class tourists from throughout the country and from neighboring countries such as VENEZUELA, to maximize exposure. Unlike other pan-Caribbean festivals focusing on folk traditions (e.g., Cuba's now defunct Carifesta) or popular music festivals featuring only one genre of music (e.g., Reggae Sunsplash) and sung in one language (e.g., Trinidadian Carnival), Cartagena's festival was explicitly designed to feature the range and diversity of contemporary popular musics from throughout the region. In this regard the festival was identical to the sort of world music festivals (e.g., World of Music, Arts, and Dance [WOMAD] festivals) that were simultaneously emerging in the north – except for the important distinction that it was locally organized and financed. Year after year major performers of French Caribbean zouk, English Caribbean soca and REGGAE, and Haitian *compas* and vodou-jazz were invited to Cartagena, where they alternated with Spanish Caribbean dance bands playing long-popular genres such as Cuban SON, Dominican merengue, Puerto Rican *plena*, and, of course, salsa; beginning in 1986 popular West African soukous bands such as Loketo were invited to perform as well. The back-to-back appearance of these diverse Afro-Caribbean and African popular musics dramatically highlighted the region's shared diasporan roots.

In the early 1990s, stimulated by the festival's success, Colombian music industry entrepreneurs began releasing compilation recordings of popular diasporan musics (many of them unlicensed) targeted at mainstream Colombian audiences, for whom the music was identified as *terapia* (therapy), a marketing term intended to suggest the music's feel-good quality. Additionally, world beat recordings released by U.S. and European labels began to be imported into Colombia. In a region that has long looked upon the United States and Europe as models of cultural progressiveness, these recordings, especially those associated with rock superstars such as Paul Simon and David Byrne, gave a further stamp of approval to diasporan musics.

By the late 1980s the circulation of non-Spanish Caribbean – mostly diasporan – dance musics within Colombia had begun to influence local musical production in a variety of ways. A handful of Colombian musicians was experimenting with non-Colombian genres such as soca and soukous, and also modernizing older, often African-derived Colombian genres such as CUMBIA and *porro* that had been swept aside by the salsa craze in the early 1970s. An example is the Cartagena-born musician Joe Arroyo, who began his career as a salsa singer in the 1970s, but who, in the 1980s, began producing the sort of African and Afro-Caribbean-influenced music that in the north would have been classified as world beat. (He called his zouk- and soca-influenced songs *caribeños*, and his soukous-influenced salsas *joesons*.) But more important, he resuscitated the traditional coastal cumbia by reintroducing the hot, syncopated rhythms that had been eliminated in the late 1960s, when rhythmically simpler variants of cumbia appeared, specially tailored for export to Mexico, Central America, and the Andean region. Subsequently, other Colombian musicians began experimenting with traditional coastal genres as well; these experiments produced Carlos Vives's tremendously successful reinterpretations of the VALLENATO and Moises Angulo's more rock-influenced versions of the porro. In Colombia, then, world beat expanded rather than narrowed the musical horizon, by revalidating the country's own African-derived musical heritage, introducing others from the non-Spanish Caribbean and Africa, and reclaiming all of them as sources for musical experimentation. These changes directly challenge assertions that the hegemonic northern-based culture industry always controls the flow of products, profits, and meaning, and that folk cultures are inevitably destroyed by the introduction of mass-mediated musics.

While other Spanish Caribbean countries have not been as directly and extensively involved with diasporan musics as Colombia, musical cross-fertilizations clearly stimulated by world beat began emerging elsewhere in the region as well. In the 1980s the most influential non-Spanish Caribbean music in the region (other than rock) was *reggae en español*, inspired by Jamaican reggae and its successor, DANCEHALL. PANAMA – which, not coincidentally, has a significant black population of Jamaican origin – has produced the most successful Spanish reggae musicians, Nando Boom and El General, but reggae and dancehall have become extremely popular in other countries as well, especially Puerto Rico. By the early 1990s the degree of cross-fertilization among the various Caribbean linguistic/cultural areas as well as with Africa increased even further. For example, the *punta*, a combination of West Indian soca and Dominican merengue, originated simultaneously in Spanish-speaking Honduras and its English-speaking neighbor, BELIZE. In Cuba groups such as Sintesis combined traditional Afro-Cuban music with rock, while others, such as Mezcla, introduced stylistic elements from contemporary Afropop as well as from French and English Caribbean popular styles. The Dominican Republic's most prestigious merengue musician, Juan Luis Guerra, released a Grammy-winning recording in 1991 (*Bachata Rosa*) that included a Spanish-language, merengue version of "Dede Priscilla," a hit song from the CENTRAL AFRICAN REPUBLIC; his subsequent recording (*Fogaraté*) also included a soukous-inflected merengue called "Mangos Bajitos," with Congolese Diblo Dibala performing on guitar. Even Miami's pop-oriented Gloria Estefan, on her aptly titled recording *Abriendo Puertas* (Opening Doors), mixed salsa, merengue, cumbia, and vallenato with Afro-Latin genres such as Colombian *currulao* and *chandé* and Venezuelan *tamborito*. This new eagerness on the part of Spanish Caribbean musicians to experiment with traditional Afro-Latin genres and to incorporate non-Spanish Caribbean resources surely reflects an interest in gaining access to world beat consumers, but above all it speaks to the increased legitimacy of African-derived music within a region that had long rejected cultural expressions too visibly invoking its African heritage.

This new interest in diasporan musical resources spread to the rest of Spanish Latin America as well as BRAZIL, resulting, for example, in SUSANA BACA's efforts to recover, reinterpret, and disseminate Afro-Peruvian traditions (*see* PERU). Brazilian musicians in BAHIA have drawn heavily on Jamaican and other diasporan influences in developing *axé* and other musical hybrids. Interestingly, much of the experimentation has been done by musicians whose primary identification was with rock: for example, ARGENTINA's Fabulosos Cadillacs and Venezuela's Desorden Público, who have produced Spanish-language hybrids of reggae, SKA (reggae's stylistic predecessor), and RAP. Other rock bands, such as MEXICO's Cafe Tacuba, have taken an even more experimental approach, making unlikely combinations of rock with traditional national styles as well as with other Latin American and diasporan sources.

This is not to say that world beat-influenced musics have swept aside long-popular Spanish Caribbean genres such as salsa, cumbia, and merengue; on the contrary, these styles are alive and well not only throughout the Spanish Caribbean and Latin America but also among U.S. Latinos. Even salsa, merengue, and cumbia, however, have been transformed by a new generation of young musicians eager to reinvent these traditions by hybridizing them with other diasporan sources. For example, a recent recording by the New York-based Dominican merengue band Fulanito includes a *meren-rap* version of a classic 1950s-era Colombian cumbia; another cut is a lively cross-fertilization of accordion-based merengue *típico* and rap. In sum, world beat has stimulated new forms of local musical production and encouraged transnational and transcultural musical exchanges, both of which have served to re-Africanize the region's popular music landscape. Clearly, world beat can be more than just a marketing category for certain cultural artifacts (recordings); it can indicate participation in an ongoing process in which Latin Americans are rediscovering and revalidating the African sources underpinning so many of the region's diverse musical traditions.

Deborah Pacini Hernandez

SEE ALSO

Congo, Republic of the; Merengue: Music, Race and Nation in the Dominican Republic; Colombia; Cuba; Puerto Rico; Salsa Music; New York, New York; Chimurenga Music; Cartagena de Indias, Colombia; Contemporary Afro-Brazilian Music; Dominica; Jamaica; Trinidad and Tobago; Haiti; Plena and Bomba; Carnivals in Latin America and the Caribbean.

North America

World War I and African Americans,

a European conflict (1914-1918) that involved the overseas service of 200,000 African American soldiers but that – despite the initial optimism of black leaders – produced not improved racial conditions, but a racial backlash.

For most African Americans the United States' entry into World War I in the spring of 1917 held the promise that patriotic service could improve their opportunities and treatment in postwar America. W. E. B. Du Bois, a prominent African American leader and intellectual, called on fellow blacks to "close our ranks shoulder to shoulder with our white fellow citizens." Unstinting patriotism, he wrote, would result in "the right to vote and the right to work and the right to live without insult."

Before they could fight the Germans in Europe, however, blacks had to face the opposition of many white Americans. Sen. James K. Vardaman (D-Miss.) condemned any mobilization plan that would result in "arrogant, strutting representatives of black soldiery in every community." Black leaders had to overcome considerable resistance, especially from Southern Democrats, to their insistence that African Americans be included in any wartime draft. Ultimately, their efforts were successful, and 367,710 African Americans were drafted during the war. By this time, however, BLACKS IN THE AMERICAN MILITARY had come to expect little in the way of recognition for their service in any branch of the armed forces. Few African Americans served in the United States Navy and none in the U.S. Marine Corps. The army was strictly segregated, maintaining four black units, the Twenty-fourth and Twenty-fifth Infantry and the Ninth and Tenth Cavalry Regiments – all under the command of white officers.

When posted in the western and southern United States, African American soldiers faced harsh treatment, intimidation, and LYNCHING – yet no white citizen was ever punished for engaging in such assaults. On the other hand, in the 1906 Brownsville Affair, 167 black enlisted men were discharged without honor after a Texas shooting incident in which the men quite likely had no part. President Theodore Roosevelt ordered the discharges despite the regiment's recent and courageous service in CUBA and the Philippines during the SPANISH-CUBAN-AMERICAN WAR.

As the nation mobilized for war, African American leaders faced great difficulties in furthering the opportunities for blacks within the armed services. In light of the service academies' longstanding hostility to black cadets, the NATIONAL ASSOCIATION FOR THE ADVANCEMENT OF COLORED PEOPLE (NAACP) pressed for the establishment of a training school for black officers. NAACP efforts resulted in the establishment of a Colored

Officers' Training Camp (COTC) at Fort Dodge in Des Moines, Iowa. During the war Fort Dodge trained and commissioned 639 African American officers. Although symbolically important, the existence of these black officers did little to alter the great racial imbalance: African Americans comprised 13 percent of active-duty military manpower during the war, but only seven-tenths of 1 percent of the officers.

Black aspirations were dealt a further setback when members of the Third Battalion of the Twenty-fourth Infantry took part in the Houston Mutiny of August 23, 1917 – the first race riot in American history in which more whites than blacks died. The violence left 16 whites and 4 black soldiers dead. After hasty courts-martial, 19 more African American soldiers were executed for their part in the mutiny, and numerous others received lengthy jail sentences. Lt. Col. (Ret.) Michael Lee Lanning, author of *The African-American Soldier*, concluded that a key factor in the riot was, ironically, the previous transfer of 25 of the battalion's most senior sergeants to Des Moines to attend COTC, leaving only one experienced company first sergeant and seriously undermining battalion discipline. In the years to come this incident effectively undermined any proposal to increase the role of black troops.

African Americans did find greater opportunities once the nation entered the war, which had been ongoing in Europe since August 1914. Many Southern blacks moved to the North to take industrial jobs created by the wartime economy. Their numbers added to what would later be known as the Great Migration, a population movement that created or greatly augmented black communities in many Northern cities. In addition, 200,000 black soldiers were deployed to Europe, some serving with the American Expeditionary Force and others detailed to the French Army. But the vast majority of these troops were relegated to Services of Supplies (SOS) units and labor battalions. The War Department did not order its four black regiments to Europe, evidently in response to the Brownsville Affair and the Houston Mutiny. Rather than taking part in World War I, the army's most experienced soldiers remained at their posts along the Mexican border.

Instead the army organized two new black combat divisions, the Ninety-second and Ninety-third Divisions, through which some 40,000 soldiers saw combat in Europe. But Gen. John J. "Black Jack" Pershing, the supreme commander of the American Expeditionary Force (AEF), evidently had misgivings about using African American combat troops. When the Ninety-third Division arrived in France, General Pershing turned the unit over to the French army.

Both the Ninety-third Division and the French inadvertently benefited from white Americans' unwillingness to serve alongside blacks. The 369th Regiment of the Ninety-third Division included Lt. James Reese Europe, the black society musician from New York City who organized the regimental band. Lieutenant Europe was the first black officer to lead troops into combat in World War I, and he and his band introduced the French to African American music, preparing the way for a lasting French fascination with JAZZ.

With the French the Ninety-third experienced far greater acceptance and more equal treatment than that provided by the U.S. Army. The unit served heroically throughout the remainder of the war, suffering a casualty rate of 35 percent. The 369th Infantry Regiment spent more than six months on the front lines – longer than any other American unit – during which it neither surrendered an inch of Allied territory nor lost a single soldier through capture. In the 369th alone 171 officers and men received either Croix de Guerre or Legions of Merit from the French government.

During the war no black soldier received the Congressional Medal of Honor, America's highest award for military heroism. In 1991, however, President George Bush presented relatives of Cpl. Freddie Stowers with what he termed a "long overdue" Medal of Honor in recognition of Stowers's heroism on September 28, 1918, while serving in France with the 371st Infantry Regiment, Ninety-third Infantry Division. Stowers rallied his company after it encountered withering machine-gun and mortar fire that exacted 50 percent casualties and killed or wounded all of the company's more senior officers. After capturing a German machine-gun position in the first trench, Stowers was leading his men against a second trench line when he was mortally wounded by machine-gun fire. Even after being hit he continued to crawl forward, and when he could crawl no farther, he continued to shout encouragement to his men. Inspired by Stowers's heroism, the company overran the remaining German positions.

Yet despite their record of wartime service, black soldiers faced a hostile and often violent reception on their return from France. The Ku Klux Klan, reborn in 1915, spread for the first time into the North as well as throughout the South. Between 1914 and 1920 a total of 382 African Americans were lynched – in some cases, the victims were newly discharged soldiers still wearing their uniforms. A city official in New Orleans reportedly told a group of returning World War I veterans, "You niggers were wondering how you are going to be treated after the war. Well, I'll tell you, you are going to be treated exactly like you were before the war; this is a white man's country, and we expect to rule it."

There were serious race riots during and after the war, especially in Northern cities that had growing black populations – the 1917 riot in East St. Louis, Illinois, for example. In the Red Summer of 1919 riots broke out in more than two dozen cities. Of these, the deadliest by far was the Chicago Riot of 1919, which resulted in the deaths of 23 African Americans and 15 whites, with a total of 520 whites and blacks injured. This wave of violence effectively quashed black hopes for social advance until President Franklin D. Roosevelt's NEW DEAL and, especially, World War II. Yet the war and its aftermath had profound consequences for black culture, setting the stage for the Black Nationalism of Marcus Garvey and the UNIVERSAL NEGRO IMPROVEMENT ASSOCIATION and leading to the emergence of the self-assured and politically militant "New Negro," the Chicago jazz and blues scene, and the HARLEM RENAISSANCE.

James Clyde Sellman

SEE ALSO

World War II and African Americans; Chicago Riots of 1919; Chicago, Illinois; Du Bois, William Edward Burghardt (W. E. B.); East St. Louis, Illinois, Riot of 1917; Garvey, Marcus Mosiah; Great Migration, The; New Orleans, Louisiana; New York, New York; Black Nationalism in the United States.

North America

World War II and African Americans

(December 7, 1941-August 15, 1945), the most destructive military conflict in history, but which gave America renewed prosperity and established its postwar dominance in world affairs. For African Americans the war provided new economic opportunities, accelerated the black migration from the South to Northern urban areas, and prepared the way for the CIVIL RIGHTS MOVEMENT.

World War II had a transforming effect on African Americans. Despite white reluctance and hostility, the black community took pride in its contributions to the war effort at home and overseas. African Americans served in every branch of the military and in every theater of conflict. The war provided new opportunities on the home front and vastly increased the movement of blacks out of the South. It also encouraged civil rights activism, as African Americans broadened their efforts to secure full citizenship rights.

During the war the NATIONAL ASSOCIATION FOR THE ADVANCEMENT OF COLORED PEOPLE (NAACP), along with the black press and other organizations, mounted a "Double-V campaign" intended to achieve victory over fascism abroad and over racism at home. The war contributed to a complex process of change that would transform the whole of African American life. In confronting the nation with a grave crisis, it swept away much of the rationale for segregation.

Hitler's racist doctrines – and, to a lesser extent, the chauvinism of his Japanese and Italian allies – came to the attention of African

Americans long before fighting actually broke out. During the 1930s international sports provided an important surrogate to war, and blacks exulted in boxer Joe Louis's victories over Italian Primo Carnera and German Max Schmeling, and in the Gold Medals won by sprinter Jesse Owens and other black athletes at the 1936 Munich Olympic Games. Nazi racism forced some Americans to consider the blemishes on their own democratic principles – above all, America's subordination of blacks and other racial minorities.

American Mobilization and the First March on Washington

War broke out in Europe after Hitler invaded Poland in September 1939, and the United States began to mobilize for war. But the nation was still struggling through the Great Depression, and Americans were little concerned with events in Europe and Asia. They welcomed the defense buildup mainly because it provided much-needed jobs. Indeed, World War II – far more than President Franklin D. Roosevelt's New Deal economic programs – was responsible for ending the decade-long depression and returning the nation to full prosperity.

But there were few opportunities for African Americans in the booming defense industry. In 1941 black labor leader and civil rights activist A. Philip Randolph took a dramatic step in protesting blacks' exclusion. He began organizing a massive march on Washington, and President Roosevelt, who was eager to head off the protest, signed Executive Order 8802, banning racial discrimination in defense industry and federal government hiring. Executive Order 8802 also established the Fair Employment Practices Committee to implement and oversee the new policy.

Randolph's victory would be the first of many during the war years. The NAACP launched its Double-V campaign in the belief that the war offered an opportunity to "persuade, embarrass, compel, and shame our government and our nation into a more enlightened attitude toward a tenth of its people." The wartime years indeed yielded a great number of firsts, advancements, and breakthroughs.

Blacks on the Home Front

On the home front African Americans faced difficulties and great opportunities. The war spurred a renewal of black migration to the North, which had been slowed by the Great Depression. The resulting population movement did not subside for some 30 years. Between the 1940s and late 1960s about 4.5 million blacks would leave the South for the urban North and West. Upon arrival they faced severe housing shortages and overt hostility from white residents.

There was considerable wartime friction between whites and blacks. In 1943, with the nation in its second year of war, the racial hostilities erupted into violence. During the summer of that year there were more than 250 racial conflicts in 47 American cities, including Mobile, Alabama, and Harlem. The worst race riot of the war took place in Detroit, when a controversy over the employment of blacks escalated into 30 hours of violence that left 25 blacks and 9 whites dead. The federal government did little to address the causes of such confrontations or to prevent their recurrence.

In the aftermath of that violent summer black poet Langston Hughes posed trenchant questions for American society:

Looky here, America
What you done done –
Let things drift
Until the riots come –
Yet you say we're fightin
For democracy.
Then why don't democracy
Include me?
I ask you this question
Cause I want to know
How long I got to fight
BOTH HITLER – AND JIM CROW?

Blacks rankled at other forms of racial segregation. For example, during the war the Red Cross segregated the blood in its blood banks, as if there were any real difference between "white" blood and "black" blood.

Yet the war also had undeniably positive effects. The wartime migration northward had major political and economic consequences. Escaping the poll taxes and literacy tests of the South, Southern migrants found themselves able to vote freely, in many cases, for the first time in their lives. In many Northern cities black voters came to be a significant factor in electoral politics. Migration from the South also brought a large number of African Americans into industrial manufacturing. More than 500,000 blacks, including many former Southerners, joined Congress of Industrial Organizations (CIO) unions such as the United Automobile Workers or the United Steelworkers (*see* American Federation of Labor and Congress of Industrial Organizations). The war thus helped establish a relatively prosperous black working class.

Blacks in a Segregated Military

The war also commenced a process of change that in 1948 would begin the formal integration of the American armed services. But initially, as in past American wars, African Americans encountered resistance from the white majority (*see* Military, Blacks in the American). Throughout the war it was American policy "not to intermingle colored and white enlisted personnel in the same regimental organizations." Moreover, the army's mobilization plan on the eve of World War II would have allowed African Americans to contribute only 6 percent of total army manpower, considerably less than their proportion in the overall population.

In 1940 President Roosevelt promoted Col. Benjamin O. Davis Sr. to brigadier general, making him America's first black general. Roosevelt also committed the nation to establishing combatant and noncombatant black units in each branch of the armed forces. But the military command resisted giving African American soldiers combat assignments. The United States Navy remained the most obdurate on racial issues. Secretary of the Navy Frank Knox and senior naval officers resisted assigning African American sailors to any but the most menial shipboard duties, as servants to officers, in construction battalions, or as messmen or stewards in ships' galleys.

For example, in the heat of the Japanese attack on Pearl Harbor, Dorie Miller manned a machine gun and shot down two, possibly four, enemy aircraft. Miller was a messman, like virtually every other African American in the U.S. Navy, and was ineligible for military training. Moreover, he was ignored for months following the battle. Only after concerted protests in the African American press did he receive a Navy Cross and an invitation to speak to the 1942 graduating class at the Great Lakes Naval Training Center. Miller was then assigned to the aircraft carrier USS *Liscome Bay;* but a year later, when a Japanese submarine sank the ship, the black hero of Pearl Harbor died as a messman.

In 1942 the U.S. Marine Corps admitted African Americans for the first time in its 144-year history, taking George Thompson, a former dogcatcher in Nashville, Tennessee, as its first recruit. But the navy did not commission its first group of black officers, known as the "Golden Thirteen," until March 17, 1944. Three days later it commissioned the USS *Mason*, an antisubmarine ship that was the first navy vessel manned by black sailors. Although it sailed under the command of white officers, the *Mason* at least provided African Americans with an official opportunity for naval combat. But the navy would not desegregate its shore facilities until after the end of the Korean War (1950–1953). Understandably, during World War II African Americans accounted for just 5 percent of the total navy manpower.

Blacks in the U.S. Army

The U.S. Army was more forthcoming; yet African Americans never accounted for more than 8.7 percent of army manpower, and only 15 percent of that number received combat assignments. In 1941 the army activated its first black tank unit, the 758th Tank Battalion, and established a segregated Army Air Force pilot-training facility in Tuskegee, Alabama (*see* Tuskegee University). The NAACP opposed the idea of segregated training but believed that the decision was a step in the right direction. On the other hand, the black National Airmen's Association condemned the plan, insisting that they would rather be "excluded than segregated."

In 1942 the U.S. Army Air Force commissioned its first black pilots, part of the all-black Ninety-ninth Pursuit Squadron – the famed TUSKEGEE AIRMEN – that Col. Benjamin O. Davis Jr., son of General Davis, would command. By 1944 there were 145,242 blacks in the air force, but only 1 in 90 was an officer; for white personnel, the proportion was 1 in 6.

Most blacks in the army served in support roles. In 1942 the army accepted the first black women for the Women's Auxiliary Army Corps, later simplified to the Women's Army Corps. Black men also found themselves treated as wartime auxiliaries, as in the famed Red Ball Express, an overwhelmingly black unit that drove supplies by truck to advancing American forces following the D-Day invasion and performed yeoman service during the Battle of the Bulge late in 1944.

Red Ball Express drivers were not combat troops, but their jobs involved great danger. One driver recalled that they drove "with those slits… at night [which dimmed the headlights to minimize the danger of attack by enemy aircraft], loaded with high-octane gas and all kinds of ammunition and explosives [at speeds of] 30 to 40 mi an hour no matter what the weather."

CHALLENGES TO JIM CROW

White Americans were wholly unprepared for black servicemen's militant protests against racial segregation. The protesters were in many cases Northern blacks unable to abide the Jim Crow policies enforced on U.S. military bases, which were often located in the South. U.S. Air Force historian Alan M. Osur concluded that the story of black airmen in World War II is "a history of attacks on discrimination and segregation."

The army, which had the largest number of black servicemen, first experienced problems in 1941. In 1942 there were protests within the other military branches. The disturbances peaked in 1943 but continued through the final two years of the war. In 1944, for example, 16 black officers entered a whites-only restaurant in Fairfax, South Carolina. Upon being refused service, they shouted "Go to hell" and "Heil, Hitler!" Such protests were by no means restricted to the South. In 1943 four black soldiers damaged a California restaurant after being refused service. In addition, whites instigated race riots on a number of military bases, and white civilians repeatedly assaulted individual black servicemen.

During the war the U.S. Army itself took its first tentative steps against Jim Crow. In 1941 it began integrating its officers' candidate schools. In 1944 the War Department prohibited discrimination in transportation and recreational facilities on all army bases. On a Texas military base not long after this directive was issued, Lt. JACKIE ROBINSON – soon to become the first African American to integrate the whites-only world of major league baseball – refused to go to the back of a bus, resulting in his court-martial and vindication.

Robinson's refusal to abide Southern Jim Crow practices was by no means an isolated example. Indeed, in the postwar years the pride and confidence of African American military veterans and their unwillingness to endure further discrimination would help provide the impetus for the Civil Rights Movement.

On December 26, 1944, during the worst days of the Battle of the Bulge, the army issued a directive requesting African American volunteers for racially integrated combat units, a request that marked the beginning of the end for the Jim Crow army. The army found many volunteers among its black cooks, engineers, quartermaster personnel, and truckers. Black veteran Chester Jones recalled, "Those blacks who did volunteer did a creditable job, which shows all they ever needed was an honest-to-goodness chance."

CONCLUSION

In the postwar years no branch of the American military welcomed the prospect of integration. The persistent delaying tactics of the various service heads outraged African Americans, whose pressure in 1948 moved President Harry S. Truman to sign Executive Order 9981, ordering the integration of America's armed forces and establishing the President's Committee on Equality of Treatment and Opportunity in the Armed Services.

In civilian life African Americans were no less committed to achieving full social and political equality. Membership in the NAACP burgeoned from 50,000 in 1940 to 450,000 six years later. In 1942 James Farmer and other civil rights activists founded the CONGRESS OF RACIAL EQUALITY (CORE). CORE advocated the Gandhian approach of nonviolent direct action and staged SIT-INS at theaters and restaurants in several Northern cities, presaging the sit-in movement begun in 1960 in Greensboro, North Carolina. Thus, in a number of vital respects, World War II prepared the way for the civil rights struggles of the 1950s and 1960s.

James Clyde Sellman

SEE ALSO

Press, Black, in the United States; Detroit Riot of 1943; Davis, Benjamin O., Jr.; Davis, Benjamin O., Sr.; Great Migration, The; Harlem Riots of 1943; Jim Crow; Owens, James Cleveland ("Jesse"); Randolph, Asa Philip; March on Washington, 1941.

WPA. Please see WORKS PROGRESS ADMINISTRATION

WPA Narratives. Please see FEDERAL WRITERS' PROJECT

North America

Wright, Louis Tompkins

(b. July 23, 1891, La Grange, Ga.; d. October 8, 1952, New York, N.Y.), African American surgeon, hospital administrator, and chairman of the board of the NATIONAL ASSOCIATION FOR THE ADVANCEMENT OF COLORED PEOPLE (NAACP).

In a career combining medical and political achievements, Louis T. Wright was one of the most respected black professionals of his time. A doctor's son (and later a doctor's stepson), Wright graduated from Clark University in ATLANTA, GEORGIA, in 1911 and went on to medical school at Harvard University. While at Harvard, Wright voiced strong objection to being treated differently when a professor tried to prevent him from delivering babies at a white teaching hospital. This became an early example of his lifelong insistence upon equal rights.

Unable to win an internship at any of Boston's many hospitals despite graduating fourth in his class at Harvard, Wright did his postgraduate internship at FREEDMEN'S HOSPITAL, an affiliate of HOWARD UNIVERSITY in WASHINGTON, D.C. In 1916 he returned to Atlanta, went into practice with his stepfather, and joined the NAACP. When the United States entered World War I the next year, Wright served as a lieutenant in the Army Medical Corps, ran a field hospital in FRANCE, and was awarded the Purple Heart.

After the war Wright started a small, general practice in Harlem in 1919 and became affiliated with Harlem Hospital. Meanwhile he continued his NAACP work toward racial equality. As he became more prominent, Wright occasionally encountered opposition to his advocacy of more stringent educational standards; especially upset were those members of the black medical establishment who had grown used to separate and at times unequal, less rigorous schools. The New York Police Department appointed Wright police surgeon in 1929; in 1935 the NAACP made him the chairman of its board; eight years later Harlem Hospital made him its chief of surgery. None of these positions had been held before by an African American.

Wright never completely recovered from the lung damage he had suffered in the war; from 1939 to 1942 he was hospitalized for tuberculosis. In 1952 he died following a heart attack. Despite its brevity and interruptions, his medical career was impressive. Wright published 89 scientific papers, including several influential works on the treatment of bone fractures. He helped develop new antibiotics and did pioneering cancer research. In 1940 he was awarded the NAACP's Spingarn Medal. Harlem Hospital renamed its library after Louis Tompkins Wright shortly before his death.

Kate Tuttle

See Also
World War I and African Americans; Harlem, New York.

North America

Wright, Richard

(b. September 4, 1908, Roxie, Miss.; d. November 28, 1960, Paris, France), African American novelist, among the first to show the destructive effects of white racism on both blacks and whites.

Richard Wright was born in rural Mississippi near Natchez, where white hostility was all-pervasive. His mother was a former schoolteacher; his father was a farmer who drank heavily and abandoned the family in 1914. In the absence of her husband Wright's mother took a series of low-wage, unskilled jobs to support her two boys. Moving from town to town, the family settled in Memphis, then in rural Arkansas, often going hungry. After his mother suffered a debilitating stroke, Wright returned to Mississippi in the care of his stern religious grandmother, who disapproved of his literary inclinations. The experience left Wright eager to leave the area and disdainful of religion.

Upon completing the ninth grade, Wright went North, first to Memphis, then to Chicago. He discovered and read H. L. Mencken, whose journalism inspired Wright's later writing, as well as Fyodor Dostoyevsky, Sinclair Lewis, Sherwood Anderson, and Theodore Dreiser. In Chicago in the late 1920s and early 1930s he held odd jobs, eventually settling in the United States post office, which was nicknamed "the University" for its high density of radical intellectuals.

Wright attended meetings of the John Reed Club, an organization of leftist writers, and soon became active in the Communist Party. Encouraged by party members, Wright published poetry, short stories, and articles in Communist newspapers and other left-wing journals. He later said that he had hoped his writings would bridge the gap between party leaders and common people. Beginning in 1935, for several years he wrote travel guides for the Depression-era Federal Writers' Project, first in Chicago, then in Harlem. He also produced fiction – a collection of forceful short stories about racial oppression and a humorous novel about working-class blacks in Chicago. Some of these stories were published in leftist periodicals; the novel was published in 1963, after his death, as *Lawd Today*.

Wright's debut in mainstream publishing came in 1938 with the publication of *Uncle Tom's Children*, a collection of cruel novellas based on his Southern childhood. The book was widely read, and its accounts of the pernicious effects of racism moved and impressed reviewers. Still, Wright was disappointed. He had intended readers to see and feel the devastation of racism on all of society, not just on African Americans.

His next novel, *Native Son* (1940), was merciless. In the story, Bigger Thomas, a young black man hardened by racism and ignorance, accidentally kills a white woman and is condemned to death. Although Bigger's Communist lawyer argues that guilt belongs to the society that would not accept him and drove him to brutality, Bigger, in fact, has tasted his first freedom in the act of murder: for once in his alienated life he has brought about an event to which others must respond. Editors toned down the original manuscript (the restored original version was published only in 1992), but *Native Son* was still the most militant protest novel about American race relations of its time. It became a huge bestseller, a Book-of-the-Month Club selection, and was dramatized on Broadway in a production by Orson Welles. Many reviewers marveled that Wright could make Bigger Thomas an unsympathetic character yet nonetheless force white readers to see their own guilt in Bigger's crime. Other reviewers, while appreciative of the novel's power, criticized Wright for presenting a stereotype and a victim in Bigger Thomas.

In 1944 Wright wrote an essay for the *Atlantic Monthly* titled "I Tried to Be a Communist" in which he expressed his long disenchantment with the dogma of the Communist Party as well as its refusal to speak and act on black civil rights. Shortly thereafter he published *Black Boy* (1945), the autobiography of his youth in the South. Like his previous works, *Black Boy* was unrelenting in its depiction of the scarring effects of racism and poverty. A few critics complained that it gave a one-sided picture of the South, but most heralded it as searing and precise, even a masterpiece.

In the late 1940s Wright traveled to France at the invitation of American expatriate writer Gertrude Stein. He was warmly received in Paris, where he met many of the country's leading intellectuals, including Jean-Paul Sartre and Simone de Beauvoir. Feeling the tensions of racism on his return to New York and annoyed at being acclaimed only as a great *black* writer, he emigrated to France with his second wife – he had been briefly married at the beginning of the 1940s – and young daughter.

In France Wright was deeply influenced by existentialism, a philosophy emphasizing the isolation of the individual in a hostile or indifferent universe. He wrote three more novels, none of which was well received in America, partly because they overintellectualized the question of race, partly because they were perceived as out of touch with recent developments in American race relations, and partly because many critics were upset with him for leaving the United States. Wright also wrote extensively about colonialism in Africa; in his last years he became an international spokesman for Pan-Africanism. He died in Paris.

Among Wright's other works are the novels *The Outsider* (1953), *Savage Holiday* (1954), and *The Long Dream* (1958); the collection of stories *Eight Men* (1961); the nonfiction works *Black Power* (1954), *The Color Curtain* (1956), *Pagan Spain* (1957), and *White Man, Listen!* (1957); and the expanded autobiography, *American Hunger* (1977).

See Also
Colonial Rule; Chicago, Illinois; Great Depression; Harlem, New York; Memphis, Tennessee; New York, New York; Racial Stereotypes; Communist Party USA, African Americans and the.

North America

Wu-Tang Clan, **an avant-garde rap collective whose musical innovation and business acumen made it one of the most influential groups of the late 1990s.**

When the Wu-Tang Clan released its debut album – *Enter the Wu-Tang (36 Chambers)* (1993) – the rap world had to confront eight new MCs at once: RZA, Genius/GZA, Ol' Dirty Bastard, Method Man, U-God, Raekwon, Ghostface Killah, and Rebel INS (a.k.a. Inspectah Deck). Although The Genius had released a pre-Wu-Tang solo album, and RZA (formerly Prince Rakeem) had released two pre-Wu-Tang singles, *Enter the Wu-Tang* was completely unexpected: a rap record that owed nothing to the slow, heavy production style of rap's then-regnant superstar, Dr. Dre, formerly of NWA. The Wu-Tang Clan layered kung-fu mythology (hence the name) over RZA's involved beats, delivering boasts of street violence in impossibly complex narratives. Hardcore rap classics like "Protect Ya Neck" and "Clan in da Front" balanced the album's successful single, "C.R.E.A.M." – a reminder that "Cash Rules Everything Around Me."

The Wu-Tang Clan's revolutionary record contract permitted its individual members to sign solo deals with other record labels. And following the success of *Enter the Wu-Tang*, the Clan members released a dizzying series of solo albums, including Method Man's commercially successful ode to marijuana (*Tical* [1994]); Raekwon's labyrinthine gangster narratives (*Only Built for Cuban Linx* [1995]); Ol' Dirty Bastard's bizarre, Rabelaisian ramblings (*Return to the 36 Chambers (The Dirty Version)* [1995]); the tongue-in-cheek horror stories of RZA's side project, the Gravediggaz (*Six Feet Deep* [1994]); and many other affiliated records, all yoked together by endless intra-Clan guest appearances and by the weird, icily organic soundscapes created by RZA. The Wu-Tang Clan capitalized on its collaborative and solo successes with Wu-Wear, a profitable line of hip hop clothes advertised in a radio-friendly single called "Wu-Wear: The Garment Renaissance."

In 1997 the highly anticipated *Wu-Tang Forever* continued the group's remarkable run of critical and commercial success. The album hawked everything from Wu-Wear to phone lines to Internet access, alongside the group's increasingly cryptic lyrics ("Grow like a fetus / With no hands and feet to complete us") and RZA's experimental beats.

Andrew Du Bois

See Also

Hip Hop in the United States; Niggaz with Attitude.

North America

Wynn, Albert R. (b. 1951, Philadelphia, Pa.), Democratic member of the United States House of Representatives from Maryland (1993-). Wynn was the first black candidate elected to the House from the suburbs of Washington, D.C.

Albert Russell Wynn was born in Philadelphia, Pennsylvania, and received a bachelor's degree from the University of Pittsburgh in 1973. After graduate studies in political science at Howard University (1973-1974), he received a law degree at Georgetown University in 1977. Wynn was executive director of the Consumer Protection Commission in Prince George's County, Maryland, from 1977 to 1981, and then became a practicing attorney.

Wynn served in the Maryland House of Delegates for five years from 1982 to 1987, and then served five years in the Maryland Senate from 1987 to 1992. He was known as a staunch Democrat and a friend of labor unions. In 1992 Wynn ran in a tightly contested Democratic primary for a U.S. House seat from Maryland's Fourth Congressional District, where, in the wake of redistricting, blacks had become the majority of voters. He won 75 percent of the vote in the 1992 general election and was returned to office in subsequent elections.

Maryland's Fourth District is made up of suburbs on the east side of Washington, D.C. The district covers parts of Prince George's and Montgomery counties. Many residents work for the federal government, either in Washington or in federal offices in the fourth district. Wynn consistently addressed concerns of federal workers as well as those of his poorer constituents. In the 105th Congress (1997-1999) Wynn was a member of the Commerce Committee. He was also a member of the Congressional Black Caucus.

x y

Latin America and the Caribbean

Xangô, orisha, or Yoruba deity, of thunder and lightning and masculine virility. He is known as Xangô in Brazil, Chang6 or Shangó in Cuba and the United States, and Shango in Trinidad. Xangô wears red and carries a double-headed ax, the symbol of justice, which he represents (*see* Orishas; Religions, African, in Latin America and the Caribbean; Santería; and Candomblé).

See Also
Trinidad and Tobago.

Africa

Xhosa, ethnic group of South Africa.

The Xhosa are one of several peoples belonging to the broader Nguni linguistic group. They number about 6 million; the majority live in South Africa's Cape Province and belong to one of three subgroups – the Xesibe, Gcaleka, and the Rharhabe. Although a number of other groups in this region speak Xhosa, such as the Thembu, the Mfengu, and the Mpondo, they have historically maintained a distinct identity from the Xhosa.

Like other Nguni groups, the Xhosa are descendants of Bantu speakers who migrated into southeastern Africa from East Africa around 200 C.E. and established village communities based on grain farming and pastoralism. According to oral tradition, the Xhosa nation was founded by a king named Cirha. Cirha was later accused of stinginess and overthrown by his younger brother, Tshawe. Tshawe founded the royal amaXhosa Dynasty to which all Xhosa chiefs trace their ancestry.

For most of their history the Xhosa people have been governed by loosely connected autonomous chiefdoms. Xhosa custom required a chief's sons to leave their father's home and found new settlements, and as the Xhosa dispersed they moved into land occupied by Khoisan-speaking pastoralists. Over time the Xhosa incorporated Khoikhoi communities and adopted aspects of their language and religion; today nearly one-sixth of the Xhosa language consists of Khoi "clicks."

During the late eighteenth century Afrikaner settlers (also known as Boers) began encroaching on Xhosa grazing land, setting off a series of nine wars – the Frontier or "Kaffir" wars – which lasted from 1779 to 1878. The first conflict was prompted by Boer attempts to settle the lush Zuurfeld region, which Xhosa herders used as a summer pasture. Although the Xhosa initially fought off the Boers, they suffered serious losses in battles with the British, who took control of the Cape in 1806. Continual warfare, livestock losses, and social upheaval gradually weakened the Xhosa. In 1856 thousands of Xhosa followed the prophecy of a young girl named Nongquwuse and killed more than 400,000 of their own cattle, resulting in severe famine. By the 1870s the Xhosa had lost much of their land to white settlers.

During the late nineteenth and early twentieth century many Xhosa migrated in search of wage work in South Africa's gold and diamond mines. They also converted to Christianity in large numbers, though ancestor worship is still practiced by many Xhosa even today. After the National Party government began imposing apartheid policies in the early 1950s, the Xhosa as well as other Xhosa-speaking groups were forcibly relocated onto *Bantustans* – Transkei and Ciskei. Many Xhosa subsequently became staunch supporters of the African National Congress (ANC) and of one of its most prominent Xhosa members, former South African president Nelson Mandela. In the 1980s violent conflicts between Xhosa and Zulu migrant workers in urban areas were attributed to rivalries between the ANC and the Zulu-dominated Inkatha movement. Today most rural Xhosa depend on a combination of farming and remittances from migrant laborers. The Xhosa also account for a large number of South Africa's urban professionals and craftspeople.

Elizabeth Heath

See Also
Bantu: Dispersion and Settlement; Christianity, African: An Overview; Gold Trade; Mandela, Nelson Rolihlahla; Inkatha Freedom Party.

Africa

Yaka, ethnic group of west Central Africa.

The Yaka primarily inhabit southern Bandundu Province of southwestern Democratic Republic of the Congo and neighboring northeastern Angola. They speak a Bantu language and are related to the Kongo people. More than 1 million people consider themselves Yaka.

See Also
Bantu: Dispersion and Settlement.

Africa

Yalunka (also known as Dialonke, Djalonke, Dyalonké, Jalonké, Jalonca, and Jalunka), ethnic group of West Africa.

The Yalunka primarily inhabit northeastern Sierra Leone and central Guinea. Other Yalunka also live in eastern Guinea-Bissau. They speak a Mande language and are closely related to the Soso people. Approximately 200,000 people consider themselves Yalunka.

See Also
Languages, African: An Overview.

Africa

Yamoussoukro, Côte d'Ivoire, the capital of Côte d'Ivoire and birthplace of former president Félix Houphouët-Boigny.

Located 250 km (155 mi) inland from the former capital of Abidjan, Yamoussoukro became the official capital of the Côte d'Ivoire in 1983. Little is known about the early history of Yamoussoukro, except that it was originally a village inhabited by the Baule ethnic group, who still account for the majority of the town's population. The town received little attention until Félix Houphouët-Boigny became president of the newly independent nation in 1960. During his 30-year rule Houphouët-Boigny directed vast amounts of federal funds to his hometown, encouraging developers to mold it into his vision of an "African Versailles."

As a result Yamoussoukro, with a population of only 150,000, is full of amenities considered luxuries in most of Côte d'Ivoire – vast parks, well-maintained, multilane highways, reliable utilities, and a regional airport.

Yamoussoukro's most extravagant constructions followed the National Assembly's decision to move the national capital there in 1983, to honor Houphouët-Boigny. One of these is a huge, marble presidential palace surrounded by a lake of crocodiles, the totem animals of Houphouët-Boigny's family. The daily feeding of live chickens to the crocodiles has since become one of the town's few tourist attractions. The other extravaganza is the Our Lady of Peace of Yamoussoukro Basilica. Estimated to have cost between $150 million and $800 million, at least some of which came from government coffers, it is the world's largest church, surpassing even St. Peter's Basilica in Rome. Although the pope once visited the basilica, most Ivoirian Roman Catholics live nowhere near Yamoussoukro and thus do not attend services there.

The decision to move the capital to Yamoussoukro has been widely criticized as a waste of money, given that Abidjan remains the country's economic and cultural center, and that Yamoussoukro's remote location holds little appeal to foreign diplomats or businesspeople. One group to benefit from this move was Houphouët-Boigny's own family, who at the time of the decision owned vast tracts of land in the town and surrounding region.

Elizabeth Heath

See Also
Crocodile; Abidjan, Côte d'Ivoire.

Africa

Yams, an edible root, belonging to any of several hundred species of the genus *Dioscorea,* that has long been a staple of African agriculture.

Many species of yam are indigenous to Africa. People began to recognize and domesticate the naturally occuring tubers roughly 3500 to 4500 years ago in a region known as the "yam zone," where the forest and savanna zones meet in West Africa. The plants were probably among the earliest and easiest to be domesticated, as yams can regenerate once the tuber is removed, if the vine and roots are not damaged. Domestication of yams permitted the spread of agriculture in Africa's forest zones, which are not suited to grain cultivation. Approximately 90 percent of all African-grown yams continue to be cultivated within the yam zone, where the tuber has special cultural significance.

This was particularly true among proto-Kwa speakers, including ancestors of the Akan and the Yoruba, who developed social sanctions to prevent yam-eating during certain stages in its growth cycle. Some scholars suggest that yam cultivation played a role in the spread of Bantu speakers across Central, East, and Southern Africa. The descendants of African slaves continue to respect the importance of yams in many Afro-Latin and Afro-Caribbean cultures.

Yams are well-suited to the tropics, as they can be stored in a humid environment for long periods. Although they are rich in carbohydrates, yams are low in fats, proteins, and minerals.

Ari Nave

See Also
Bantu: Dispersion and Settlement.

Latin America and the Caribbean

Yanga (alive during the late sixteenth and early seventeenth century), leader of a group of maroons, or runaway slaves, in early seventeenth-century Mexico that became the only group of blacks in colonial Mexico to secure their freedom through rebellion and to have that freedom guaranteed by law; Yanga was also known as Ñaga or Ñanga.

Beginning in the 1560s the lowlands and foothills around the port of Veracruz on Mexico's Caribbean coast were the sites of numerous slave revolts and sporadic attacks on settlements by maroons, or escaped slaves (*see* Maroonage in the Americas). It is likely but not certain that Yanga participated in or even led many of these attacks. The inaccessible, jungle-covered mountains lying inland from Veracruz favored the maroons, who established small settlements there called *palenques.* From the palenques the maroons stepped up their attacks on nearby plantations and towns, destroying property and freeing slaves.

Local officials were sent out from time to time to destroy the palenques, but the maroons had situated them in such rugged locations that they were not easily overcome, and often the communities could not even be found. Reports indicate that by 1606 the maroons had made travel between Veracruz and Mexico City unsafe and costly – a troublesome development, since Veracruz was the main port of entry for goods and people to Mexico. That year the viceroy of New Spain (as colonial Mexico was called at that time) sent a force from Mexico City to quell the maroons, but this force also failed to overcome the fugitives.

In 1609 the viceroy sent another force under the command of Capt. Pedro Gonzalo de Herrera. A Jesuit who accompanied Herrera and his 350 troops recorded one of the first detailed accounts of Yanga, told to the Jesuit by a Spaniard whom Yanga had captured and released. "This Yanga was a Negro of the Bron nation," he related, "of whom it is said that if they had not captured him, he would have been king in his own land.... He had been the first maroon to flee his master and for thirty years had gone free in the mountains, and he has united others who held him as chief, who are called Yanguicos." The "Bron nation" was probably a reference to the Brong, or Abron, an Akan group from what is today the African nation of Ghana. Yanga's village was said to have 60 huts, 80 men, more than 20 women (both African and Indian), and several children. The Yanguicos apparently moved their village often, but not so often that they could not cultivate cotton, sweet potato, sugar cane, chile, corn, squash, and other crops. They also maintained a small herd of cattle.

Yanga divided his people into farmers and warriors. The farmers stayed near the village, while the warriors roamed the jungle scouting for advancing Spaniards and raiding the countryside. Most military matters were apparently delegated by Yanga to an Angolan commander, while Yanga himself oversaw the affairs of civil government.

In late February 1609 Herrera's troops surprised Yanga's forces while they were raiding a Spanish settlement. The maroons fled and warned the palenque of the approaching Spaniards. Two days later Herrera arrived to find the village deserted. He pursued the fleeing villagers, caught up with them, and waged a bloody battle in the jungle. Both sides suffered heavy casualties, prompting a cease-fire by Herrera, who sought to negotiate a truce. Yanga and his followers used the opportunity to flee farther into the jungle, eluding Herrera's troops.

Although it is not known exactly how it came about, some time later Herrera and Yanga agreed to terms for a truce. Herrera sought a pledge from Yanga that his people would no longer raid Spanish settlements or help slaves escape from their masters. Yanga agreed, stipulating several demands: all of the Yanguicos who had fled before September 1608 were to be granted their freedom (those who had fled thereafter would be returned to their masters); the palenque was to be chartered as a free town, of which Yanga would be governor; and Spaniards could visit the town only on market days. The viceroy in Mexico City, deciding it would be less costly to accommodate Yanga than to fight him, agreed to the terms, with one further stipulation: Yanga and his followers would help New Spain capture escaped slaves, a service for which they would be paid. After Yanga agreed, he and his people settled in the new town of San Lorenzo de los Negros, a short distance from their destroyed palenque.

See Also
Slavery in Latin America and the Caribbean.

Africa

Yao, ethnic group numbering approximately 1.6 million people, living primarily in southern Malawi; in small numbers in southern Tanzania; and in Mozambique, principally between the Rovuma and Lugenda rivers.

The Yao migrated from northeastern Mozambique to Malawi in the mid-nineteenth century, when Alolo and Makwangala people began to infringe upon Yao lands. There the Yao became middlemen between the slave and ivory suppliers and the Arab traders from the coast. A large percentage of Yao adopted Islam as a consequence of their close association with Arab and Swahili traders. While the Yao sold many slaves to Arab caravans, they also integrated many of the slaves into their own communities in order to increase the size, power, and prestige of their particular villages. Yao men were permitted to marry slave women. Unlike children born to Yao women who remained within their mother's lineage, children from unions between Yao men and slave women remained tied to the man, thus increasing the size of his lineage and the number of his allies. Thus by acquiring slaves, villages could grow in size and military strength. European efforts to abolish slavery in the late nineteenth century, therefore, met with strong resistance from the Yao men.

The Yao have historically lived in settlements of 75 to 100 people. Clusters of Yao villages, each with a headman, are grouped under the political authority of a hereditary chief. Among the chief's responsibilities is the resolution of disputes, with the help of assemblies of village elders and headmen. The matrilineal Yao are also matrilocal: men, upon marriage, move to the village of their wives. When girls are about five years of age, they move in with their maternal grandmothers; boys move to communal huts.

Most Yao have historically practiced swidden (or "slash-and-burn") agriculture, whereby fields are cleared of vegetation through burning, and the ash is worked into the soil as a natural fertilizer. Maize and sorghum are among their staple foods. Since the colonial era the Yao have also produced tobacco as a cash crop. Fishing is an important economic activity among other Yao who live along rivers and lakes.

Ari Nave

SEE ALSO
Ivory Trade; Swahili People; Indian Ocean Slave Trade; Slavery in Africa.

Africa

Yaoundé, Cameroon, the capital of CAMEROON.

In 1888 German explorer and scientist Georg Zenker founded the settlement of Yaoundé in the hilly Ewondo region between the Nyong and Sanaga rivers. Although dense forests separated it from the coast, in 1909 Yaoundé was made the capital of German Kamerun. After a brief Belgian occupation, Yaoundé became the capital of French Cameroun and, later, of independent Cameroon. During the colonial period road and rail projects established links to the port city of Douala, as well as to the northern regions of Cameroon.

Yaoundé's population has grown rapidly, from 100,000 at independence in 1960 to nearly 1 million today. Its population is diverse; especially after the 1972 centralization of government functions, it has come to include many FULANI and BAMILÉKÉ employed in the large civil service. The cost of living is high, and many public services are not able to meet demand. Perennially under construction, the city has seen many of its historic buildings replaced by modern architecture.

After Douala, Yaoundé is Cameroon's second-largest city. Although not highly industrialized, Yaoundé does have a cigarette factory, a plywood-manufacturing plant, a quarry, and a sugar refinery. It is also home to the national university, established in 1962, and several research centers, and serves as the center of a rich agricultural region.

Eric Young

SEE ALSO
Colonial Rule; Douala, Cameroon.

Africa

Yombe (also known as the Mayombe), ethnic group of west Central Africa.

The Yombe primarily inhabit the southwestern highlands of the REPUBLIC OF THE CONGO. Others live in neighboring western Congo-Kinshasa and northwestern ANGOLA, particularly the Cabinda region. They speak a Bantu language and are closely related to the KONGO people. Approximately 200,000 people consider themselves Yombe.

SEE ALSO
Bantu: Dispersion and Settlement; Congo, Democratic Republic of the.

Europe

Yorke and Talbot Opinion, a 1729 legal opinion that established that African slaves did not become free upon entering Great Britain.

In the early eighteenth century West Indian plantation owners traveling with their slaves were alarmed by persistent rumors that in England, their slaves could become legally freed through escape or baptism. Indeed, slaves traveling to England with their owners often tried to run away, seeking freedom in that reputedly free land. But the Yorke and Talbot Opinion of 1729 provided slaveholders with a legal justification for holding slaves while in England, as well as a means of forcing their escaped slaves back into slavery.

The legal status of escaped slaves in England had been wavering for decades. More often than not, English courts ruled in favor of slaveholders, at least in part because West Indian plantation slavery brought great wealth to the British Empire. Nevertheless, the notion that a slave became free the moment he or she stepped on English soil had been upheld in several legal cases, as well as by comments made at the HOLT DECISION of 1706.

Tired of the uncertainty they faced when bringing slaves into Great Britain, in London in 1729 an influential group of West Indian planters and merchants approached Attorney General Philip Yorke and Solicitor General Charles Talbot for a legal opinion. After consideration Yorke and Talbot stated that a slave brought by his or her master from the West Indies to England did not become free on English soil and could be forcibly returned to West Indian slavery. In addition, they asserted that baptism did not confer freedom. This declaration, which became known as the Yorke and Talbot Opinion, was welcomed by the English merchants on both sides of the Atlantic who profited from the fruits of plantation slavery; these people publicized the opinion widely.

Although the Yorke and Talbot Opinion was neither a formal legal decision nor, as was the HOLT DECISION, a set of comments made in court, it reflected the most popular interpretation of English common law and was generally accepted as the "law of the land." To buttress the opinion, when Yorke became Lord Chancellor Hardwick he spelled out his view on the bench in the 1749 case of *Pearne* v. *Lisle*, declaring that blacks were property and that a runaway slave could be recovered legally. The Yorke and Talbot Opinion stood undisputed until the abolitionist GRANVILLE SHARP contested the issue in his legal battles of the late 1760s and early 1770s. It was finally overruled in the James Somerset Case of 1772.

Leyla Keough

Africa

Yoruba, a group of peoples sharing the Yoruba language and a range of cultural traditions, concentrated in NIGERIA but forming smaller communities in BENIN and TOGO.

Today more than 20 million people speak some dialect of Yoruba, which belongs to the Kwa group of the Niger-Congo languages. Most Yoruba speakers live in southwestern Nigeria. They form a majority in Lagos, Africa's second most populous city.

Yoruba speakers are traditionally among the most urbanized African people. For centuries before British colonization, most Yoruba speakers inhabited a complex, urbanized society organized around powerful city-states. These densely populated cities centered on the residence of the king, or *oba*. The basic social units were patrilineages in which inheritance, descent, and political position passed through the male line. Though they lived in cities, traditionally most Yoruba men farmed crops such as YAMS, maize, plantains, peanuts, MILLET, and beans in the surrounding countryside. Many men also engaged in crafts such as blacksmithing, manufacturing textiles, and woodworking. Traditionally Yoruba women specialized in marketing and trade, and could gain considerable independence, status, and wealth through their commercial activity. While many Yoruba speakers continue to farm and trade today, they generally also grow and sell cash crops such as COCOA. Meanwhile, the millions of Yoruba in modern cities such as Lagos pursue a diverse array of manufacturing and service occupations.

Originally Hausa speakers used the name Yoruba for the people of the Oyo Kingdom. Europeans appropriated the term to refer to all speakers of the Yoruba language. Yoruba speakers identify themselves as members of several different groups, including the IFE, Isa, and Ketu. Some of these Yoruba-speaking groups identify with the larger community of Yoruba speakers. Others, such as the Sabe, Idaisa, and Ketu, consider themselves separate ethnic groups and do not feel a sense of community with other Yoruba speakers, though they share Yoruba origin myths. All of these groups, however, share a similar material culture, mythology, and artistic tradition.

Art historians consider thirteenth- and fourteenth-century Yoruba bronzes and terracotta sculptures among Africa's greatest artistic achievements. Yoruba oral histories, folklore, and proverbs have also won international acclaim. Traditional Yoruba religious beliefs recognize a supreme god presiding over a complex pantheon of hundreds of lesser gods. Over the past several centuries Islam and Christianity have spread to Yorubaland. Many Yoruba take a pluralistic approach to religion that integrates traditional religious elements with Christian and Muslim beliefs, as in the Aladura spiritualist movement.

According to folklore, the Yoruba originated from the mythical Olorun, god of the sky, whose son, Oduduwa, founded the ancient holy city of Ile-Ife around the eighth century C.E. Linguistic and archaeological evidence suggest that, in fact, speakers of a distinct Yoruba language emerged near the Niger-Benue confluence some 3000 to 4000 years ago. From there they migrated west to Yorubaland between the eighth and eleventh century. Strategically located on the fertile borderland between the savanna and the forest zones, Ile-Ife was the center of a powerful kingdom by the eleventh century, one of the earliest in Africa south of the SAHEL. Its rulers taxed both food surpluses and trade. While the institution of kingship probably predates the emergence of Ile-Ife, the holy city became the preeminent Yoruba spiritual and cultural center.

In time other Yoruba cities rose to prominence. Oyo probably originated in the eleventh century and became a substantial city by the fourteenth century. Other Yoruba city-states emerged around the same time. During the fifteenth and sixteenth century the nearby non-Yoruba kingdom of Benin conquered parts of eastern and southern Yorubaland.

Oyo, however, became a powerful military state by the seventeenth century. The rulers of Oyo acquired horses by selling slaves to Europeans and reselling European manufactured goods to HAUSA traders. The Oyo cavalry invaded neighboring Yoruba and non-Yoruba kingdoms alike, including Dahomey. By the late eighteenth century, however, Oyo, suffering from internal rivalries, began to disintegrate. During the early nineteenth century Dahomey won its independence in a war that further weakened Oyo. During the 1830s Muslim FULANI from the SOKOTO CALIPHATE conquered northern regions of Oyo and cut off its access to trade with the Hausa. By 1840 the Oyo Kingdom had completely collapsed.

Wars among Yoruba groups and city-states raged for much of the rest of the nineteenth century. The protracted warfare left many Yoruba vulnerable to enslavement. Large numbers were sold to traders who transported them to Latin America. To this day Yoruba culture remains influential in BRAZIL and CUBA, where SANTERÍA religious practice carries on Yoruba traditions.

Aiming to repress the slave trade, encourage the production of raw materials, and open markets for British manufactures, GREAT BRITAIN sought a foothold in the region. In 1851 the British navy seized Lagos, allegedly to shut down the slave market there. In 1888 most of Yorubaland became a protectorate of Great Britain. The colonial administration imposed peace among warring groups after 1892 in an effort to promote its commercial interests. Under the British policy known as indirect rule, Yoruba kings lost their sovereignty but retained a role in local government.

As the capital of British Nigeria, Lagos, dominated by Yoruba, became the center of Nigerian political and economic life. Colonial authorities introduced COCOA as a cash crop in Yorubaland and developed a modern infrastructure of railroads, highways, and schools in the region. As a result large numbers of Yoruba earned substantial cash incomes, became literate in English, and gained positions in the colonial civil service. By the time of independence Yoruba speakers occupied a dominant position in Nigeria's economy and government. Since independence, however, the more numerous northern Hausa have dominated the elected and military governments that have ruled Nigeria, and the relatively prosperous Yoruba have tended to remain political outsiders, often subject to repression.

Ari Nave

SEE ALSO

Hausa; Art and Architecture, African; Benin, Early Kingdom of; Christianity, African: An Overview; Colonial Rule; Dahomey, Early Kingdom of; Lagos, Nigeria; Languages, African: An Overview; Transatlantic Slave Trade; Oyo, Early Kingdom of; Urbanism and Urbanization in Africa; Islam and Tradition: An Interpretation.

Africa

Youlou, Fulbert (b. June 17, 1917, Madibou, Moyen-Congo [REPUBLIC OF THE CONGO]; d. May 6, 1972, Madrid, Spain), Roman Catholic priest, nationalist leader, and president of the Republic of the Congo (1960-1963).

The son of a Lari merchant, Fulbert Youlou, whose last name means "heaven" in Lari, was baptized at age nine and entered the seminary three years later. While attending mission schools in GABON and CAMEROON, he befriended Barthélemy Boganda, the future president-emperor of the CENTRAL AFRICAN REPUBLIC. Youlou later taught in mission schools in what was then French Moyen-Congo, and was ordained in 1946. When Youlou began campaigning for public office, however, he was defrocked. Ignoring the censure, he insisted on wearing his ecclesiastical robes. He also claimed the mantle of Andre Matsou, the dead leader of an anti-French, quasi-religious Lari self-help organization. In 1956 Youlou was elected mayor of Brazzaville and founded the Lari-dominated Democratic Union for the Defense of African Interests (UDDIA), a party supporting close ties with FRANCE. A year later he was elected vice president of the government council, and in 1960 he became president of the newly independent Republic of the Congo.

Youlou's rule was short lived. A political conservative, he sought close ties with France and its former colonies, and attempted to create a single-party state. But he faced ongoing pressure from labor unions, and after three days of labor unrest in 1963, Youlou resigned. After Youlou spent two years in prison, supporters aided his escape, first to Zaire (present-day DEMOCRATIC REPUBLIC OF THE CONGO), then Europe, where he finally settled in SPAIN. In 1972 he died in exile.

Eric Young

SEE ALSO

Brazzaville, Republic of the Congo; Matsoua, André; Boganda, Barthélemy; Christianity: Missionaries in Africa.

Young Adult Literature, African American. Please see CHILDREN'S LITERATURE, AFRICAN AMERICAN

North America

Young, Andrew (b. October 23, 1932, New Orleans, La.), African American civil rights activist and politician who was the first black United States ambassador to the United Nations.

Raised in an affluent African American family in New Orleans, Andrew Young as a child had opportunities available to few blacks in the American South. Among these was an exceptional education: he attended HOWARD

UNIVERSITY and Hartford Theological Seminary. He was ordained a Congregational minister in 1955 and soon after accepted a position in a diocese in rural Georgia and Alabama. This experience made him keenly aware of the poverty African Americans suffered in the rural South and inspired his work as a civil rights activist.

In 1959 Young moved to New York City to be the assistant director of the National Council of Churches and to raise financial support for civil rights activities in the South. He returned to Georgia two years later and joined the SOUTHERN CHRISTIAN LEADERSHIP CONFERENCE (SCLC). His energetic work as funding coordinator and administrator of the SCLC's Citizenship Education Programs soon won him the admiration of Martin Luther King Jr. The two men became close associates, and Young helped King organize SCLC marches in the South.

Young became executive director of the SCLC in 1964 and executive vice president in 1967. After King's death Young helped to guide the SCLC toward activities promoting social and economic improvements for African Americans. He retired from these positions in 1970, but remained on the board of directors until 1972.

In 1972 Young became the first African American to be elected to the U.S. House of Representatives from Georgia since RECONSTRUCTION. While a representative, Young played an instrumental role in winning for the presidential candidate Jimmy Carter the vital backing of those members of the African American community who questioned Carter's commitment to civil rights.

Young resigned from the House of Representatives in 1977 when Carter appointed him U.S. ambassador to the United Nations. As ambassador Young improved communications between the United States and African nations. He was instrumental in focusing American foreign policy on sub-Saharan Africa and bringing American attention to the conditions of APARTHEID in South Africa. Young resigned from the position in 1979 after he was criticized for his contacts with the Palestine Liberation Organization (PLO).

In 1982 Young was elected mayor of Atlanta, an office which he held until 1989. In 1990 he made an unsuccessful bid in the Georgia gubernatorial race and retired from politics. In 1994 he published his memoir, *A Way Out of No Way,* and returned to public life to cochair the Atlanta Committee for the 1996 Summer Olympic Games.

Elizabeth Heath

SEE ALSO

Atlanta, Georgia; King, Martin Luther, Jr.; New Orleans, Louisiana; New York, New York.

North America

Young, Coleman Alexander

(b. May 18, 1919, Tuscaloosa, Ala.; d. November 29, 1997, Detroit, Mich.), five-term mayor of DETROIT, MICHIGAN, former auto worker, member of the TUSKEGEE AIRMEN, and founder of the NATIONAL NEGRO LABOR COUNCIL.

Coleman Young, Detroit's first black mayor, presided for nearly 20 years over America's eighth-largest city – and one of its most troubled. By 1973, when Young first ran for mayor, the auto industry that had been Detroit's economic base was in serious decline. Most whites had fled to the nearby suburbs, leaving the city with a population that was approximately 70 percent African American. Poverty sent the crime rate soaring, and the city's infrastructure fell into a state of decay. Young, a state senator at the time, received 92 percent of the black vote when he defeated police chief John Nicholls in the mayoral election.

Over his 20 years in office Young launched a series of revitalization projects, including a new rail system and General Motors automobile plant as well as construction of the Joe Louis Arena and multi-use Renaissance Center on Detroit's waterfront. He worked to integrate the police department, which he had dubbed "an army of occupation" during his first campaign. In addition, Young dramatically increased city contracts with minority-owned businesses, winning lasting popularity among the city's working-class African Americans. Despite his often abrasive style, which drew criticism from many white suburbanites and the local media, he was elected to an unprecedented five terms, stepping down in 1993 at age 75. Young died of respiratory failure in Detroit four years later.

Kate Tuttle

North America

Young, Lester Willis ("Prez")

(b. August 27, 1909, Woodville, Miss.; d. March 15, 1959, New York, N.Y.), African American tenor saxophonist whose distinctive approach and tone inspired many musicians during the 1940s and 1950s.

Singer BILLIE HOLIDAY gave Lester Young his nickname "Prez," short for president, during the 1930s: it was an era of dukes, counts, and kings of swing, and she insisted that Young should hold the highest office in the land. Today he is most widely heard through his musical collaborations with Holiday. During and after the swing era he and Coleman Hawkins offered the major alternative approaches to the tenor saxophone in JAZZ.

As an improviser Hawkins relied upon arpeggios built over the harmonies of each chord in a song. Young's improvisations were linear – melodies stretched across the chord sequence. Hawkins aggressively pushed the beat; Young's playing was gentle, and consistently behind the beat. Hawkins's tone was full, even harsh; Young's was light.

Young came from a musical family that moved during his childhood from Mississippi to New Orleans to Minneapolis. He learned several instruments and played in the successful Young family band. In 1927, while playing with another group, he took up the tenor saxophone. Eventually he settled in Kansas City, then a booming jazz center. He joined Bennie Moten's band in 1933, then left for New York City to fill the saxophone chair recently vacated by Hawkins in Fletcher Henderson's band. The Henderson band, accustomed to Hawkins's style, ridiculed Young, and he soon returned to Kansas City. But while he was in New York City, a chance encounter in a Harlem jam session introduced him to Billie Holiday, with whom he would collaborate in a classic series of recordings in the late 1930s and early 1940s.

Young influenced few saxophonists during the 1930s. However, the musician upon whom he had the greatest impact – alto saxophonist Charlie Parker – became the key jazz soloist to arise between Louis Armstrong in the 1920s and John Coltrane in the 1960s. Parker, a creator of bop during the 1940s, extended Young's style and made it his own. Parker's early recordings reveal his deep debt to Young.

Young rejoined the Count Basie band in 1935, and in 1936 he made his recording debut with a quintet drawn from that band. Producer John Hammond later recalled it as "one of the only perfect sessions I ever had." Musicologist Gunther Schuller described Young's solo on "Oh, Lady Be Good" as "quintessential Lester Young: economical and lean... and masterful in its control of form." Young remained with Basie between 1935 and 1940, and returned in 1943 for a stint that ended when he was drafted. During the late 1930s he also recorded regularly with Holiday. His improvised fills and counter melodies behind her vocals define the interplay that is the essence of jazz.

After World War II Young did not fare well, although his musical star was clearly ascendant. A large number of saxophonists – including Wardell Gray, Paul Quinichette (nicknamed the Vice President), and numerous white saxophonists such as Stan Getz and Zoot Sims – modeled their playing on Young's. On the other hand, his recordings suggest his unhappiness, which some attributed to his traumatic military experience, and others to his heavy drinking.

Even in the 1950s Young occasionally recaptured the fragile beauty of his early playing. In a 1956 series of recordings – including *The Jazz Giants* and three albums recorded at a nightclub in WASHINGTON, D.C. – Young was in prime form. But when he performed with Holiday in the 1957 television special "The Sound of Jazz," their performance had an aura of tragic finality. Young and Holiday died in 1959 within four months of each other.

James Clyde Sellman

See Also
World War II and African Americans; Basie, William James ("Count"); Armstrong, Louis ("Satchmo"); Coltrane, John William; Harlem, New York; Hawkins, Coleman Randolph; Henderson, Fletcher Hamilton, Jr.; New Orleans, Louisiana; Parker, Charles Christopher ("Bird"); Moten, Benjamin (Bennie); New York, New York.

North America

Young, Plummer Bernard

(b. 1884?, Littleton, N.C.; d. October 9, 1962, Norfolk, Va.), editor of the *Norfolk Journal and Guide,* one of the most influential African American newspapers.

P. B. Young was the son of Sally and Winfield Young, the founders and publishers of the *True Reformer*, an independent newspaper in Littleton, North Carolina. Having learned the trade from his father, Young served as a printing instructor from 1903 to 1905 at St. Augustine's College in Raleigh, North Carolina. He was simultaneously a student but did not graduate.

Young moved to Norfolk, Virginia, to pursue his career as a journalist and by 1910 had bought *The Lodge Journal and Guide*, the organ of the fraternal Knights of the Gideon. He rechristened his paper the *Norfolk Journal and Guide* and nurtured it over the next several years from a small, irregularly published paper with a circulation of 500 to a large, weekly paper with a circulation of more than 30,000. In addition to being one of the largest black newspapers in the country, the *Journal and Guide* was the largest weekly newspaper in the South.

Young, a moderate by nature, refused to indulge in the sensationalist reporting then favored by many other newspapers. Instead the *Journal and Guide* gained a reputation for quiet, well-researched articles and solid, constructive editorials. Young's views that blacks could do much to help themselves were similar to those of Booker T. Washington, although Young was quicker to advocate an end to statutory discrimination than was Washington.

In the 1930s the *Journal and Guide* supported the New Deal and condemned the high rate of black unemployment and poverty. In 1943 Young was appointed to the president's Fair Employment Practices Committee, which investigated workplace discrimination. From the end of World War I to the end of World War II Young was generally considered to be the most powerful African American in Virginia. In his later years he turned over much of the publishing and editing of the *Journal and Guide* to his two sons.

See Also
World War I and African Americans; World War II and African Americans; Washington, Booker Taliaferro.

North America

Young, Whitney Moore, Jr.

(b. July 31, 1921, Lincoln Ridge, Ky.; d. March 11, 1971, Lagos, Nigeria), former executive director of the National Urban League (NUL) who shaped the organization's policy and lobbied industry to provide employment opportunities for African Americans.

When he was named executive director of the National Urban League (NUL) in October 1961, many observers believed that Whitney Young Jr. was not qualified to hold the position. He had served as industrial relations secretary for the St. Paul, Minnesota, branch of the NUL from 1947 to 1949; as executive secretary of the Omaha, Nebraska, branch from 1949 to 1954; and as dean of the Atlanta University School of Social Work from 1954 to 1961. Still, by traditional NUL standards he was young and inexperienced. As executive director during the 1960s, however, Young guided the organization through one of the most socially and politically tumultuous decades in United States history.

The NUL was much less militant than many other organizations involved in the Civil Rights Movement. Since its inception in 1910 it had sought to promote African American participation in the U.S. political system, rather than to change the system itself. In the 1960s though the NUL did not embrace the direct action of other civil rights organizations – it did not sponsor sit-ins, protest marches, bus boycotts (*see* Montgomery Bus Boycott), or voter registration drives (*see* Freedom Summer) – under Young's leadership it took a more active stance that better aligned it with black political and social thought of the day. The NUL provided support for civil rights activists, including cosponsorship of the March on Washington for Jobs and Freedom in 1963.

Young, who had grown up on the campus of the Lincoln Institute, a vocational high school for blacks at which his father was the principal and the faculty was integrated, was accustomed to interracial cooperation. He used his considerable social and political skills to become an unofficial advisor to presidents John F. Kennedy, Lyndon B. Johnson, and Richard Nixon. Johnson drew on some of Young's ideas for his War on Poverty. Young's relationships with white business leaders brought increased employment to blacks and increased funding to the NUL.

Young, who held a master's degree in social work from the University of Minnesota, also called for a "Domestic Marshall Plan" for blacks. In 1968 he introduced the NUL's New Thrust, a program designed to help eliminate ghettos and to increase affordable housing, health care, and educational opportunities for the poor. In addition, Young wrote a weekly column, "To Be Equal," for the New York Amsterdam News. In 1964 a collection of those columns was published as *To Be Equal*. Young died in 1971 while swimming during a visit to Nigeria.

Robert Fay

See Also
March on Washington, 1963.

Africa

Youssou N'Dour

(b. 1959?, Dakar, Senegal), Senegalese singer of world beat music best known for blending traditional Senegalese musical techniques with Cuban and jazz inflections.

Youssou N'Dour was born in Dakar. His mother was a griot (a traditional Senegalese musician), and she taught him the basics of local music, including *tasso* (a kind of rap) and *bakou* (a traditional chant).

Youssou N'Dour began singing with local music and theater groups at age 12. At age 15 he joined the Senegalese band Super Diamono, and toured West Africa in 1975. The following year he began his singing career with the Star Band No. 1, and in 1977 he formed his own band, the Etoile de Dakar, renaming it Super Etoile de Dakar in 1981. Super Etoile de Dakar toured Europe in 1984, playing a modern version of *mbalax* (a traditional rhythm throughout Wolof-speaking Senegal). The band made its North American debut in 1985.

After recording the songs "Immigrés" and "Nelson Mandela," Youssou N'Dour gained the attention of British rock singer and songwriter Peter Gabriel. The Senegalese musician played on Gabriel's best-selling album *So* (1986), and in 1987 he went on tour with Gabriel in the United States, Japan, and Europe. Youssou N'Dour also sang on *Graceland* (1986), the highly successful album by American singer and songwriter Paul Simon, and in 1988 he played at the London birthday concert held for South African activist (and future president) Mandela. In 1989 Youssou N'Dour toured in support of Amnesty International, a human rights organization.

By the time Youssou N'Dour recorded *The Lion* (1989), which was sung partly in English and partly in Wolof, his music had become an intricate blend of Western pop instrumentation (distorted guitars and synthesizers) and traditional Senegalese instruments such as the *tama* (talking drum). Youssou N'Dour's 1994 album *Wommat* (Wolof for the guide) included "Seven Seconds," his hit duet with Swedish-born pop singer Neneh Cherry.

See Also
Mandela, Nelson Rolihlahla; World Music, World Beat, and the Re-Africanization of Latin American Popular Music.

Z

Africa

Zafy, Albert (b. 1931, Antsiranana, Madagascar), president of Madagascar (1993-1996).

Albert Zafy was born in Antsiranana in northern Madagascar. He traveled to France in 1954 to attend medical school in Montpellier and remained in France until 1971. Upon his return to Madagascar he joined Gen. Gabriel Ramanantsoa's regime as minister of public health. When Lt. Com. Didier Ratsiraka assumed power in 1975, Zafy resigned from his post and took a position at the University of Madagascar. In 1989 he returned to politics and created the National Union of Democrats for Development (UNDD). The following year Zafy became the leader of a coalition of opposition parties, the Comité des Forces Vives (CFV). Never having served under Ratsiraka's Democratic Republic of Madagascar, Zafy was seen as an ideal candidate to spearhead opposition to Ratsiraka.

The CFV unilaterally announced the formation of a new government with Zafy as prime minister on July 16, 1991. The 16-member CFV shadow cabinet began to occupy Ratsiraka's ministries until the president declared a state of emergency, arresting and detaining several key players, including Zafy. After his release Zafy was wounded during a mass protest march to the presidential palace, when Ratsiraka's forces fired mortar shells at the 400,000 demonstrators.

The event destroyed Ratsiraka's legitimacy and soon after, facing pressure from France and continued CFV strikes, he agreed to relinquish power while remaining the symbolic head of state. In October 1991 Zafy was appointed chairman of a transitional government, marking a return of civilian rule and multiparty elections, and the birth of the Third Republic.

Zafy enjoyed overwhelming support in the 1992-1993 elections, but his administration soon faced an economic quagmire. Handed an economy weakened by years of mismanagement, Zafy was unwilling to impose unpopular austerity measures required as a condition for aid from the International Monetary Fund and World Bank. Instead he turned to private investors to raise funds for economic development, a strategy he termed "parallel financing." The World Bank traced one such source of funds to a money laundering racket run by drug cartels.

By 1995 the Malagasy economy was facing skyrocketing inflation and crippling international debt. In desperation, Francisque Ravony, the prime minister dismissed the governor of the central bank and negotiated new, less difficult conditions for assistance. Angered by Ravony's insubordination, Zafy successfully pressured for his resignation.

In September 1996 Zafy's own National Assembly impeached him on the grounds that he had violated elements of the constitution and had failed to institute democratic reforms, a decision upheld by the high constitutional court. Despite his poor economic track record, Zafy ran again for president in 1997, but lost by a slight margin to Ratsiraka.

Ari Nave

Africa

Zaghawa, ethnic group of north Central Africa.

The Zaghawa primarily inhabit east central Chad and western Sudan. They speak a Nilo-Saharan language and are closely related to the Beri people. More than 200,000 people consider themselves Zaghawa.

See Also

Languages, African: An Overview.

Africa

Zaire. Former name of the Democratic Republic of the Congo.

Africa

Zambezi River, river in southern Africa, fourth-longest of the continent, about 3540 km (2200 mi) long and draining an area of some 1,300,000 sq km (502,000 sq mi).

The Zambezi River rises in northwestern Zambia and flows southeast to the Indian Ocean. From its headwaters, about 1524 m (5000 ft) above sea level, it flows through eastern Angola, traverses western Zambia, and forms the border of northeastern Botswana; it forms the boundary between Zambia and Zimbabwe, and flowing through Lake Kariba, created by the hydro-electric Kariba Dam, it crosses central Mozambique (where it forms a lake behind the Cabora Bassa Dam) and empties into the Mozambique Channel through many mouths.

In its upper course, totaling about 800 km (500 mi), the Zambezi falls only about 180 m (600 ft). About 100 km (60 mi) below its confluence with the Linyanti River, it forms the great cataract known as Victoria Falls (*Mosi-oa-Tunya*), and for the next 72 km (45 mi) it rushes through a narrow gorge 122 m (400 ft) deep. It then enters its middle course and flows through hilly country for about 1300 km (800 mi) to Quebrabasa Rapids, the last great natural barrier to navigation, in Mozambique. In its lower course it flows through a broad valley to the sea. Besides the Linyanti River, the chief tributaries of the upper river are the Kabompo and the Lungwebungu. The Zambezi receives no important tributaries in its middle course; the chief affluent of the lower river is the Shire.

Despite such barriers as cataracts, rapids, and sandbars, the Zambezi is navigable for long distances. The navigable reaches of the river and its tributaries total about 645 km (400 mi). The Scottish missionary David Livingstone was the first European to explore the Zambezi.

See Also

Explorers in Africa Since 1800.

Africa

Zambia, a landlocked country in Central Africa that borders Angola, the Democratic Republic of the Congo, Tanzania, Malawi, Mozambique, Zimbabwe, Botswana, and Namibia.

An unbalanced economy, the legacy of colonialism, has stunted Zambia's economic and political development. For years foreign firms shipped mineral wealth from the region that is today Zambia. In an era of declining world market prices, however, Zambia's continued reliance on mining, particularly of copper, has thwarted the ambitions of nationalist leaders to harness the country's mineral wealth for the good of its people. Poor soils have aggravated Zambia's economic stagnation by impeding successful cash crop production and agricultural self-sufficiency. Rural villagers fleeing the impoverished countryside have contributed to an unusually high rate of urbanization. However, as earnings from copper exports have declined since the 1970s, and as international donors have forced Zambia's government to introduce painful austerity measures, the nation's city dwellers have experienced hardship as well. Popular unrest and urban rioting compelled Zambia's nationalist leader, KENNETH KAUNDA, to abandon authoritarian rule in 1991 and to accept multiparty elections that resulted in his defeat. Ironically, the freely elected government, led by FREDERICK CHILUBA, has faced allegations of corruption and has taken questionable steps to exclude opponents, including Kaunda, from power. Yet again Zambia's people have had to defer hopes for economic and political renewal.

Water pours over Rainbow Falls and Knife Edge at the eastern cataract of Victoria Falls, on the border between Zimbabwe and Zambia. The local name for the falls is *Mosi-oa-Tunya*, which means "the smoke that thunders." *CORBIS/Charles & Josette Lenars*

EARLY ZAMBIAN SOCIETIES

Traces of human occupation date back over a million years in Zambia, as in other parts of East and Central Africa. Human remains dating from 30,000 to 100,000 years ago have been uncovered at Kabwe. Early rock art in Zambia shows animals, people, and objects dwarfed by abstract designs. Difficult to date, this art may be as much as 6000 years old. Anthropologists believe that the region's earliest inhabitants – hunters and gatherers – may have been the ancestors of present-day KHOISAN speakers or PYGMY populations.

Bantu-speaking settlers displaced or absorbed this early population beginning around 3000 years ago. Contemporary Khoisan speakers in the southwest may be the descendants of foragers who chose to move to more marginal lands rather than lose their way of life to the Bantu expansion. The Bantu speakers brought a new way of life to the region, including ironworking, domestication of sheep and goats, and cultivation of cereal grains. Of the contemporary ethnic groups of Zambia, at least one group, the TONGA, can trace direct descent through material culture to these early immigrants. From an early date the inhabitants participated in extensive trade networks. They smelted and traded copper for glass beads and seashells from outside the area as early as the seventh century C.E. From at least the eleventh century Arab and Indian traders ventured into the region along the ZAMBEZI RIVER to exchange cloth, guns, and Chinese porcelain for products from the interior, such as ivory, gold, and copper ingots, which they then shipped across the Indian Ocean.

A second major wave of migration occurred between the sixteenth and eighteenth century, when Bantu speakers from present-day Angola and the Democratic Republic of Congo moved into north and central Zambia and established control over the local population. These later immigrants, including the LUBA, LUNDA, CHEWA, and BEMBA, established centralized chiefdoms, which enabled them to overpower earlier inhabitants, who were divided into small, lineage-based communities. Other groups migrated into the region to flee the ZULU expansion in SOUTH AFRICA in the early 1800s. They include the NGONI, who conquered the Chewa of southeastern Zambia, and a SOTHO group (the Kololo), who absorbed the Luyama-speakers of the south to form the present-day Lozi people.

Explorer Antonio Fernandes visited the area in 1514; his account of the Zambezi trade sparked Portuguese interest in the region. Portuguese merchants competed with Arab and Swahili traders, and the volume of trade in the region increased. Foreign traders exchanged guns and other exotic products, particularly glass beads and European manufactured goods, for ivory, precious metals, and slaves. The demand for slaves and the

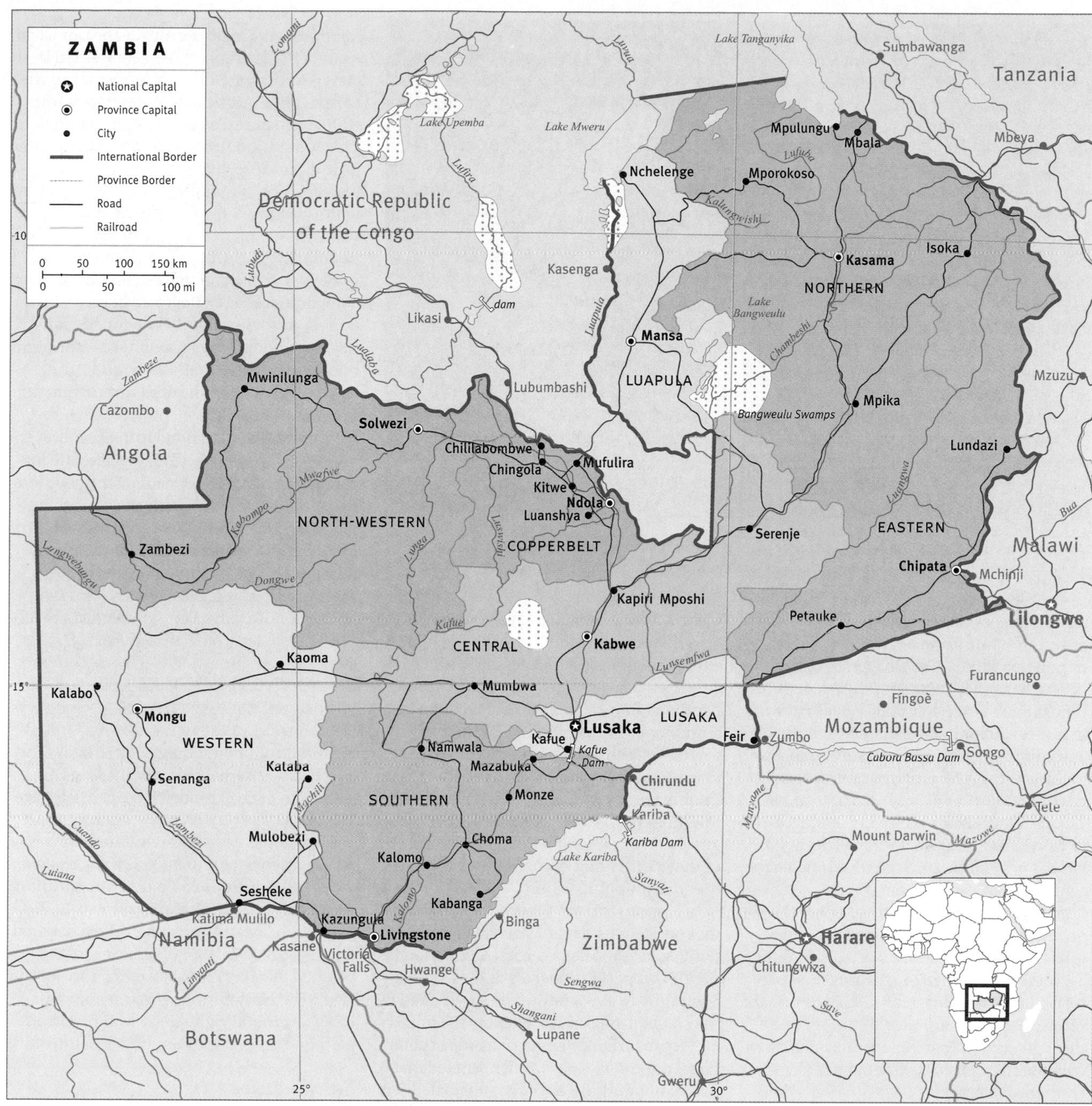

supply of firearms provoked increased warfare and slave raiding, which caused suffering and depopulation in the region well into the nineteenth century. Though the Portuguese established Christian missions along the Zambezi during the eighteenth century, they never effectively occupied the region.

Colonial Rule

In 1851 the missionary David Livingstone explored the Zambezi River basin and surrounding areas. Other missionaries followed. They succeeded in converting large numbers of people to Christianity. Today more than half the population professes Christianity, although many Christians also maintain indigenous beliefs. Livingstone hoped to stimulate the export of cotton and metals as an alternative to the slave trade. His *Missionary Travels and Research in South Africa* received wide attention in Great Britain, particularly among industrialists and colonialists who sought to open new markets for British industry. There were several obstacles to British political-economic control over the area, however. The primary rival to British influence, the Portuguese, had become entrenched over the centuries. In addition, many of the chiefdoms, including the Bemba, had successfully resisted Portuguese control of important trade routes, and would likely do the same with the British.

With the "scramble for Africa" occurring among the European powers, the British used chartered companies as a tool to achieve control over regions, such as the Zambezi Basin, which was believed to be rich in natural resources. Cecil Rhodes's British South Africa Company (BSAC) received a mandate in 1889 to take possession of the region, to exploit it economically, and to prevent further Portuguese infiltration into the interior. Agents of Rhodes had already secured the agreement of several chiefs to treaties surrendering mineral rights in exchange for arms. While the Ngoni temporarily resisted British rule, they faced military conquest in 1898. Divisions among other groups limited their ability to resist British domination.

The British gradually extended their control over the region. Deposits of copper were discovered, and in 1902 a zinc and lead mine was opened at Kabwe. By 1909 the BSAC completed a rail line through the region linking the copper mines of Katanga, in the present-day Democratic Republic of Congo, to the South African coast. In order to force

A miner is hard at work at Consolidated Copper mine in Zambia. Despite the country's mineral wealth, little of the economic benefit realized from mining returns to the miners themselves. *Jason Lauré*

the African population into the colonial economy, the BSAC imposed hut taxes (a kind of poll tax) after 1900. Desperate to acquire the currency needed to pay the tax, tens of thousands of men left their villages to work in mines, including the diamond mines of Southern Rhodesia (present-day Zimbabwe) to the south, leaving many areas practically devoid of adult males.

After World War I European settlers came to Northern Rhodesia, as the territory was named in 1911; by 1924 the white population totaled 4000. These settlers challenged the legitimacy of the BSAC's jurisdiction. Consequently the British government assumed jurisdiction and declared Northern Rhodesia a Protectorate in 1924, a status it would retain until independence in 1964. The colonial office instituted a policy of indirect rule through compliant chiefs, or through other collaborators when they could not identify cooperative chiefs.

While the colonial office now controlled the region politically, the BSAC retained mineral rights until 1960. In the 1920s and 1930s the BSAC opened mines to exploit the vast copper deposits of the north central region, since then known as the Copperbelt. Mining there attracted working-class immigrants from England who organized unions that excluded Africans. This exacerbated the already tense race relations. The European settlers lobbied for the formation of a single colony, joining Northern Rhodesia with Southern Rhodesia, where the larger white settler population controlled the colonial government. World War II, however, interrupted the formation of a Central African Federation (CAF). In the 1920s and 1930s conditions only worsened for Africans as large companies, such as the Anglo-American Corporation, formed a cartel controlling an overwhelming majority of mining interests. This effective monopoly hurt both small entrepreneurs and African miners, who faced an entrenched system of segregation, lower pay than European miners, and limits on their ability to organize. Mining companies invested little in urban amenities in order to discourage permanent settlement in the mining belt by African workers, who mostly migrated from other parts of the country. The colony's mineral wealth thus flowed out of the country and brought little benefit to the African population.

In response to the inhumane conditions, the conspicuous color bar, and the privileged position of European colonists, African laborers organized periodic strikes and uprisings beginning in 1935, only to be suppressed by the colonial authorities. Blaming the unrest on "detribalization" rather than unjust conditions, the colonial government argued that urban life and the absence of tribal chiefs caused African insubordination, a view that was consistent with their advocacy of indirect rule. The colonial administration feared the development of African nationalism in Northern Rhodesia. Since the turn of the century the religious group that is now known as Jehovah's Witnesses had gathered increasing support among Africans and become a forum for political resistance. Wary colonial authorities carefully monitored the organization and banned publications and events considered too provocative.

Meanwhile Africans formed more explicitly political organizations. The Lusaka and Luanshya Welfare Association formed in 1932 to voice African discontent. Likewise, the Northern Rhodesia Congress (renamed the Northern Rhodesia African Congress in 1951) emerged in 1937 to lobby against the formation of the CAF. In 1948 the African Mineworkers' Union organized. The campaign against the creation of the CAF was led by Harry Nkumbula of the Congress, but the conservative British government sided with white settlers and established the federation. This federation united Southern Rhodesia, Nyasaland (present-day Malawi), and Northern Rhodesia, in 1953 under a single, white-dominated government, although whites made up less than two percent of the population of Northern Rhodesia. African workers continued to strike against the mining companies of the Copperbelt, but remained unable to secure significant concessions. A rise in copper prices brought an economic boom during the mid-1950s, and African workers won some limited improvements in their status.

When the boom ended in 1956, however, many Africans were laid off, and resentment over the continued diversion of the country's wealth grew. In 1958 disillusioned young nationalists, including Kaunda, advocating more aggressive tactics, split off to form the Zambia African National Congress (ZANC). That year Kaunda, along with Nyasaland nationalist Hastings Banda, attended the All-African Peoples' Conference in Accra. Shortly after Kaunda's return to Northern Rhodesia, the ZANC was banned and Kaunda was imprisoned. Released in 1960, Kaunda was elected to head the newly formed United National Independence Party (UNIP). The UNIP soon thereafter embarked upon a campaign of civil disobedience and sabotage. The British government recognized that control could only be maintained by force, but it was reluctant to impose rule through violence. It introduced a new constitution, giving Africans the majority of seats in the federation legislature in 1962. The federation was dissolved in 1963. Elections in 1964 resulted in a large legislative majority for the UNIP. The newly formed government acquired BSAC's mineral rights for £4 million, half paid by Zambia, half paid by Great Britain.

Independence

On October 24, 1964, the country assumed independence as the Republic of Zambia, with Kaunda as president. Kaunda faced the need for an improved infrastructure and social services to support the African majority, and not only the 43,000 whites who resided predominately in the Copperbelt. The government built numerous schools and mandated significant wage increases for mine workers. Revenues from rising world copper prices financed large infrastructure investments. However, the government failed to invest in economic diversification, ultimately to the detriment of the country's growth.

In 1965 the white government of Southern Rhodesia (known as Rhodesia until it became Zimbabwe in 1980) unilaterally declared independence. The consequential United Nations sanctions against Rhodesia, including an economic embargo, eliminated one of Zambia's chief outlets to world markets. The Zambian government invested heavily to develop alternative sources of energy (previously imported from the south) and new export routes. China contracted to build a railroad from Zambia to the port of Dar es Salaam in Tanzania in exchange for trading concessions. The Zambian government also commissioned construction of an oil pipeline and a paved road to Dar es Salaam.

Despite these difficulties, Zambia, unlike other newly independent African countries, initially earned nearly enough foreign exchange through the export of copper in order to pay for necessary development projects. In 1969 the government nationalized both the mines and mining firms to increase government revenues. Zambia required relatively little foreign aid, mostly in the form of low-interest loans from the World Bank and the International Monetary Fund (IMF), until the economy faltered in the mid-1970s. Wage increases among miners in the 1960s eased racial tensions but failed to address the needs of subsistence farmers. Though rich in copper ore, Zambia's poor soils prevented the widespread cultivation of cash crops for export. The weak rural economy exacerbated the migration from rural areas to urban areas. A survey in 1980 estimated that 2 million of Zambia's 5.7 million inhabitants lived in cities.

During the post-independence years Kaunda steadily consolidated his power. He reshuffled his cabinet to ensure balanced ethnic representation, but he continued to suppress political opposition and to detain his rivals. Finally, in 1972 Kaunda declared Zambia a one-party state under the umbrella of the UNIP. Because of Zambia's linguistic and ethnic diversity, Kaunda asserted that multiparty democracy would lead to tribalism and ethnic discord. With no limit on his term in office, and with no real political opposition, Kaunda was guaranteed a prolonged political career. Beginning in 1973 he won elections as the sole candidate every five years through 1988. Kaunda further solidified his control when the UNIP took command of Zambia's leading newspaper in 1975.

During the 1970s economic hardships sparked popular discontent. The economy's heavy dependence on copper exports made it vulnerable to fluctuations in market prices. Zambia's import bill climbed when oil prices skyrocketed after 1973, while its export earnings fell when the price of copper collapsed after 1975. Civil war then erupted in Angola and shut down the Benguela railway, one of the few remaining conduits for Zambia's trade. In 1976 Kaunda declared a state of emergency before instituting IMF austerity measures the following year. As the population faced increased hardship, widespread discontent mounted.

Kaunda's increasingly authoritarian government responded to discontent with repression. In 1978 the government introduced constitutional amendments further limiting the ability of opposition groups to voice dissent. Later that year Rhodesia began to bomb Lusaka to retaliate for Zambia's role in harboring rebel forces; this further disrupted the Zambian economy and destabilized Kaunda's regime. Following a failed coup attempt in 1980 and strikes and riots in 1981, Kaunda arrested several prominent trade union leaders. Food shortages, riots, and strikes continued into 1985. Invoking emergency powers, Kaunda banned industrial actions against vital services. He closed the universities in response to student demonstrations in 1986. Further IMF austerity measures, particularly the elimination of the maize subsidy, sparked several riots later that same year. Finally in 1987 Kaunda was forced to abandon the IMF program and restore the subsidies. (IMF structural adjustment programs resumed in 1992.) Kaunda became increasingly fearful of being ousted from power, and he accused various soldiers, politicians, and businessmen of colluding with South Africa and its allies to orchestrate his overthrow. Accusations, arrests, and deportations followed. Price hikes for maize again instigated riots in 1989 and 1990.

In 1990 Kaunda announced a popular referendum to determine whether multiparty politics should be reintroduced. Proponents of such a move formed the Movement for

ABOVE LEFT: A tailor sews in his stall at Bamba Market in Lusaka, capital of Zambia. *CORBIS/Caroline Penn*

LEFT: Neighbors watch as Auntie Lucy dresses a client's hair in her front porch salon in rural Zambia. *Christine Osborne Pictures*

Multiparty Democracy (MMD). Bowing to political pressure, Kaunda abandoned his opposition and suggested that the constitution be modified, without holding a referendum, to legalize multiparty politics. The MMD and 11 other opposition parties were recognized when the constitutional amendments were signed into law. International observers were invited to ensure that the 1991 elections were free and fair. The elections resulted in the UNIP's defeat and Kaunda's removal from power. Frederick T. J. Chiluba, a union activist leading the MMD, assumed office as president.

Despite the relatively peaceful return to multiparty politics, the Zambian government remains authoritarian and corrupt. Political opposition remains stifled, preventing the development of democracy. Chiluba's government has frustrated Zambian hopes for a transition to real democracy. In March 1993 Chiluba declared a state of emergency when documents were allegedly discovered implicating the UNIP in a plot to destabilize the government. Several of Kaunda's sons, members of the UNIP, were arrested. Kaunda ended a brief retirement and won reelection as president of the UNIP with the intention of running against Chiluba in the forthcoming elections. However, a new constitution adopted in 1996 effectively prevented Kaunda from running, as it introduced a provision that a candidate's parents must be Zambian-born (Kaunda's parents were Malawian). Consequently, the UNIP and other opposition parties boycotted the elections and embarked on a program of civil disobedience. Amid student riots and widespread popular dissent, Chiluba was reelected, though much of the electorate refrained from voting. The results were immediately challenged. Civil disturbances continued, and international monitoring agencies denounced police brutality. Later Kaunda was shot during a rally; he accused the government of trying to assassinate him. After an aborted coup attempt by drunken soldiers in October 1997, Chiluba's government declared martial law and detained Kaunda, despite little evidence of Kaunda's involvement in the attempted coup. Sadly, Zambia seems little closer to democracy today than it was in 1972, when Kaunda instituted a one-party state.

Ari Nave

See Also

Accra, Ghana; Bantu: Dispersion and Settlement; Banda, Ngwazi Hastings Kamuzu; Chiluba, Frederick; Colonial Rule; Dar es Salaam, Tanzania; Explorers in Africa, 1500 to 1800; Kabwe, Zambia; Gold Trade; Ivory Trade; Nationalism in Africa; Nkumbula, Harry Mwaanga; Lusaka, Zambia; Iron in Africa; United Nations in Africa; Portugal; Rhodes, Cecil; Structural Adjustment in Africa; Swahili People; Urbanism and Urbanization in Africa; Christianity: Missionaries in Africa; Indian Ocean Slave Trade.

Africa

Zambia (Ready Reference)

Official Name: Republic of Zambia
Former Name: Northern Rhodesia
Area: 752,610 sq km (290,586 sq mi)
Location: Southern Africa; borders Angola, Democratic Republic of the Congo (formerly Zaire), Tanzania, Malawi, Mozambique, Zimbabwe, and Namibia
Capital: Lusaka (population 952,000 [1993 estimate])
Other Major Cities: Ndola (population 589,000), Kitwe (605,000) (1993 estimate); Kabwe (population 381,000), Chingola (161,000), Mufulira (146,999) (1992 estimate)
Population: 9,460,736 (1998 estimate)
Population Density: Data unavailable
Population Below Age 15: 49 percent (male 2,342,043; female 2,316,357 [1998 estimate])
Population Growth Rate: 2.1 percent (1998 estimate)
Total Fertility Rate: 6.41 children born per woman (1998 estimate)
Life Expectancy at Birth: Total population: 37.07 years (male 36.81 years; female 37.33 years [1998 estimate])
Infant Mortality Rate: 92.57 deaths per 1000 live births (1998 estimate)
Literacy Rate (age 15 and over who can read and write in English): Total population: 78.2 percent (male 85.6 percent; female 71.3 percent [1995 estimate])
Education: School attendance has increased substantially since Zambia's independence in 1964. In the early 1990s about 1.5 million pupils were enrolled in primary schools. In the late 1980s about 161,300 pupils were enrolled in secondary schools; vocational and teacher-training schools had 8000 pupils; and the University of Zambia (founded in 1965), at Lusaka, had about 7400 students.
Languages: The official language is English. More than 70 African languages are spoken, including Bemba, Lozi, Luvale, Tonga, and Nyanja.
Ethnic Groups: 98.7 percent of the population belong to 1 of 70 Bantu-speaking ethnic groups, including the Bemba, the Nyanja, and the Tonga. Europeans make up less than 2 percent of the population.
Religions: Christian (50 percent to 75 percent), Muslim and Hindu (24 percent to 49 percent), indigenous beliefs (1 percent)
Climate: Zambia enjoys a pleasant subtropical climate because of its high altitude. The average temperature in Lusaka during July, the coldest month of the year, is 16° C (61° F); the hottest month, January, has an average temperature of 21° C (70° F). Annual rainfall ranges from 750 mm (30 in) in the south to 1300 mm (51 in) in the north. Nearly all of the rain falls between November and April.
Land, Plants, and Animals: Most of Zambia is high plateau with a flat or gently undulating terrain. Elevations average between about 1100 and 1400 m (3500 and 4500 ft). Mountains in the northeast reach 2164 m (7100 ft). Major rivers are the Zambezi in the west and south and its tributaries, the Kafue in the west and the Luangwa in the east; and the Luapula and Chambeshi in the north. Lake Bangweulu, in the north, is surrounded by a vast swampy region. Lake Kariba is a large reservoir formed by Kariba Dam on the Zambezi River. Animals include elephants, lions, rhinoceroses, and several varieties of antelope.
Natural Resources: Copper, cobalt, zinc, lead, coal, emeralds, gold, silver, uranium, and hydropower potential
Currency: The Zambian kwacha
Gross Domestic Product (GDP): $8.8 billion (1997 estimate)
GDP per Capita: $950 (1997 estimate)
GDP Real Annual Growth Rate: 3.5 percent (1997 estimate)
Primary Economic Activities: Zambia's copper mining sector accounts for more than 80 percent of the nation's foreign currency intake. More than 85 percent of Zambia's population are employed in agriculture.
Primary Crops: Corn, sorghum, rice, peanuts, sunflower seeds, tobacco, cotton, sugar cane, cassava (tapioca), livestock, and poultry
Industries: Copper mining and processing, construction, foodstuffs, beverages, textiles, chemicals, and fertilizer
Primary Exports: Copper, zinc, cobalt, lead, and tobacco
Primary Imports: Machinery, transportation equipment, foodstuffs, fuels, and manufactures
Primary Trade Partners: Japan, South Africa, the United States, India, Thailand, and Malaysia
Government: Zambia won independence from the United Kingdom on October 24, 1964. It is a constitutional republic and a multiparty democracy with a president elected to a five-year term by direct universal suffrage. The president appoints a cabinet from among the members of the unicameral legislative body, the National Assembly. The 150 members of this body are likewise directly elected for five-year terms. The dominant political party is the Movement for Multiparty Democracy; others include the National Party and the Zambian Democratic Congress.

Alonford James Robinson, Jr.

See Also

Elephant; Lion; Lusaka, Zambia; Rhinoceros; Zambezi River.

Latin America and the Caribbean

Zambo, term used in Spanish America to refer to people of mixed African and Indian descent (*see* Latin America, Blacks and Indians in: An Interpretation).

Africa

Zanzibar, island off the east coast of Africa; it is part of the United Republic of Tanzania.

An island often overshadowed by its larger partner in the United Republic of Tanzania, Zanzibar nevertheless maintains a history and culture different and separate from that of the mainland. Once a key port on the thriving Indian Ocean trade routes, Zanzibar's history has been shaped by the people who sought to participate in and control these trades. Consequently, Zanzibar's population and culture reflect not only its proximity to the East Africa coast, but the influences of Asians, Arabs, and Europeans. During the colonial era European powers took advantage of Arab hegemony to assume economic control of this thriving city-state and, in an effort to increase its prosperity, turned Zanzibar into a mono-crop export economy. Since independence Zanzibar, with the aid of its mainland TANZANIA, has tried to overcome this colonial legacy and prepare to compete in a global market in which one-crop economies are becoming obsolete.

PRECOLONIAL HISTORY

Although little is known about the island's early history, it is believed that Zanzibar was first inhabited by fisherpeople who traveled to the island from mainland Africa around 4000 B.C.E. By 1000 B.C.E. Zanzibar and the islands off the coast of East Africa were familiar to the Egyptians, Phoenicians, Greeks, and Romans. As these Mediterranean empires extended their trade routes to the south and east, Zanzibar became one of several major commercial ports along the East African coast. Around the third century the trade in goods attracted the attention of merchants from southwestern Arabia, who also began trading with the island residents, bringing weapons, wine, and wheat to barter for ivory and other luxury goods.

By the eighth century the Arabs controlled the trade routes that passed through the coastal islands. Their preeminence was further strengthened by the SHIRAZI, a twelfth-century Arab trading empire based on the nearby island of Kilwa Kisiwani. As the Arabs settled among the island's Bantu-speaking residents, a new culture developed, characterized by its hybridized language, Swahili. The Swahili culture soon spread to the coastal regions of mainland Africa, including Tanzania.

Arab control lasted until the late fifteenth century, when the Portuguese arrived via the Indian Ocean. Within eight years of Portuguese explorer VASCO DA GAMA's first visit in 1498, the Portuguese took control of the trade routes and islands and imposed taxes on the residents. In 1729, however, the forces of the sultan of Oman successfully mobilized popular support and forced the Portuguese off the islands.

THE SULTAN OF ZANZIBAR

Although Zanzibar was now under the authority of the sultanate of Oman, life there changed little until the accession of SA'ID SAYYID IBN SULTAN in 1791. During the first years of his reign Sa'id increased Zanzibar's role in the INDIAN OCEAN SLAVE TRADE by hiring traders, such as TIPPU TIP, to bring slaves from the African interior to be sold to American and European merchants at the Zanzibari market. Within 20 years, however, European naval forces were attempting to shut down the Indian Ocean slave trade, and Sa'id was forced to sign agreements that not only forbade him to sell slaves to non-Muslims but to North Africans as well. Seeking to diversify his interests, the sultan built clove plantations and soon turned Zanzibar into the world's leading exporter of cloves. In addition, Sa'id extended his empire to the mainland coast, where he increased his fortune by collecting export duties. By the time Sa'id moved his capital to Zanzibar in 1840, the island's economy had recovered the prosperity it enjoyed at the peak of the slave trade and had reestablished its power over the neighboring coastal towns and nearby islands, facts that did not go unnoticed by European powers.

COLONIALISM

The British forged close relations with Sa'id and his successors Barghash and Hamoud bin Muhammad by acting as international advisors and confidantes. In 1890 they took advantage of this relationship to establish their own protectorate over the coastal islands of Zanzibar and Pemba. They installed an Anglophone sultan on the throne, but exercised their influence over him only rarely, on issues such as the internal slave trade. Otherwise, the sultan and Arabs assumed control of the economy, island government, and schools.

For almost 100 years Britain supported the sultan's rule and sanctioned the minority Arab population's economic dominance over Zanzibar's African and Asian (mostly Indian) inhabitants. These policies met with little resistance until 1948, when the mainland independence movement inspired African dockworkers and trade unionists to protest British colonialism and Arab domination.

As ethnic divisions deepened, Arabs, Asians, and Africans began to create their own civic and political associations, such as the Zanzibar Nationalist Party, the Afro-Shirazi Party, and the Zanzibar and Pemba People's Party. The British tried to channel these organizations into a parliamentary government under the sultan, and held elections for a Legislative Council in 1957. In the first election the Africans won five of six available seats. The results, which were far from satisfactory to the British, further strained ethnic relations and led to new divisions among the political groups. The British attempted to appease the Arab minority by holding another election for a newly enlarged council, but when this and a third election failed to promote Arab interests, riots erupted throughout the island. Fearful of the spread of violence, the British once again enlarged the council and planned one last election. Although the Afro-Shirazi Party won more than 54 percent of the popular vote, the Arab alliance between the Zanzibar Nationalist Party and the Zanzibar and Pemba People's Party claimed the plurality and took control of the government. Despite obvious inconsistencies, Britain accepted the results and declared Zanzibar an independent nation on December 10, 1963.

INDEPENDENCE

Within a month of independence violent revolution took hold of the island. The Arab coalition was overthrown, and the sultan was forced to flee after riots incited by Ugandan John Okello. Okello, however, lacked the support to create his own government and was overpowered by the Afro-Shirazi Party and the radical party, Umma. They soon formed a coalition government headed by Sheikh Abeid Armani Karume. As the worldwide drop in clove prices began to devastate the vulnerable Zanzibari economy, however, hardship deepened and popular discontent increased. Aware of his increasingly precarious position, Karume appealed to mainland Tanzania for help. After a series of talks and negotiations with mainland president Julius K. Nyerere, the two agreed on a union between the two countries, and on April 26, 1964, the United Republic of Tanzania and Zanzibar – later shortened to the United Republic of Tanzania – was formed. Under this new arrangement Zanzibar retained a great deal of economic and internal independence. The Zanzibaris elected their own president, who controlled Zanzibar internal affairs and served in the national government as one of two vice presidents under the Tanzanian president. In addition, Tanzania gave the much smaller Zanzibar overrepresentation in the National Assembly (50 of 169 seats) and control over its own judicial system. Despite these concessions, however, some Zanzibaris, such as Karume himself, viewed the union with hostility, and as a mainland plot to take over the island.

ZANZIBAR UNDER THE UNITED REPUBLIC OF TANZANIA

Although Karume had initiated and agreed to the union, he did much to prevent real economic and political unity between the countries and consequently guided Zanzibar on a course separate from the mainland. Dismissing Nyerere's socialist program as ineffectual, Karume attempted to institute "hard-line" communism in Zanzibar. He nationalized private businesses and deported Asian noncitizens, who he said were plotting to take over the economy. He also sought to boost export revenues by building new, state-run clove plantations (the profits of which he did not share with mainland Tanzania) with funding from CUBA, China, and the Union of Soviet Socialist Republics. But persistent economic stagnation combined with unpopular social laws, such as a mandate for interracial marriages between Africans and Arabs, cost Karume public support. In 1972 he was assassinated.

Karume was succeeded by Aboud Jumbe, a moderate who desired closer relations with mainland Tanzania. In 1977 he united Zanzibar's Afro-Shirazi Party with Nyerere's Tanzania African National Union and formed the Chama Cha Mapinduzi (Party of the Revolution). This unification proved to be the first step toward a more cohesive political unity in the government and paved the way for Jumbe's successor and CCM member, ALI HASSAN MWINYI, to win the Tanzanian presidential election in 1985. Both Jumbe and Mwinyi presided over a period of relative political stability and economic growth. Faced with volatile clove prices during the 1970s and early 1980s, the Zanzibari government enacted economic reforms to encourage diversification and foreign investment. In addition, Mwinyi promoted the island's nascent tourist industry, helping the industry grow almost 18.5 percent each year between 1982 and 1992. By the end of Mwinyi's term in 1985 it seemed that Zanzibar had overcome the economic stagnation and ethnic and political divisions that had plagued it since the colonial era.

Mwinyi's successor, Idris Abdul Wakil, was elected president and immediately adopted a political style similar to that of Karume. Intolerant of political opposition and hostile toward the union with the mainland, Wakil was preoccupied with maintaining power, which caused him to neglect the political and economic progress made by Jumbe and Mwinyi. In January 1988 Wakil seized control of the military and dismissed his council and ministers, accusing them of planning a coup d'état. When mainland Tanzania then began investigations into government corruption and deployed soldiers to the island, Wakil claimed it was merely a front to enable Tanzania to take over the island. Such rhetoric, combined with Wakil's blatant disregard for civil liberties, eventually turned public support against him, and in October 1990, under pressure from the Tanzanian government, he resigned from the presidency.

Dr. Salmin Amour won the subsequent election, and during his tenure he has strengthened relations between the island and the mainland. Working closely with Tanzanian presidents Mwinyi and BENJAMIN MKAPA, Amour has tried to attract legitimate foreign investors willing to invest in and support the island's local economy. In addition, he has instituted reforms to stop the island's notorious money-laundering businesses, tax evasion, and a thriving black market in electronics. Amour has also promoted tourism with the hopes of capitalizing on the island's "exotic" history. The government has begun to promote "spice tours" of the island's clove plantations, which now produce nutmeg, ginger, cinnamon, and cardamom as well as cloves. In addition, the government has funded a number of restoration projects, hoping to end the common use in travel guides of words such as "decaying" and "crumbling" to describe the island. One of the most ambitious projects is the renovation of the capital's Stone Town, the former Arab and European quarters. Once renowned for its Saracenic architecture and beautiful, hand-carved teak doors, the quarter was basically abandoned for new buildings in the African section, Ngambo, after independence, and most buildings are now unusable. The government has also begun a project to restore part of the Marahubi palace, the former center of the Zanzibari sultanate. Amour hopes that these projects will bolster the island's tourism industry, which he believes will play an integral part in stabilizing the Zanzibar economy by the year 2000.

Elizabeth Heath

SEE ALSO

Bantu: Dispersion and Settlement; Egypt; Barghash ibn Said; Ivory Trade; Swahili Language; Nyerere, Julius Kambarage; Great Britain; Russia and the Former Soviet Union; Portugal; Tourism in Africa.

Latin America and the Caribbean

Zapata Olivella, Manuel

(b. March 17, 1920, Lorica, COLOMBIA), Afro-Colombian writer, essayist, physician, anthropologist, diplomat, and leading intellectual and artist of twentieth-century Latin America. Zapata Olivella is one of the most intriguing voices to emanate from the diaspora and, together with NANCY MOREJÓN and QUINCE DUNCAN, among its most admired Afro-Hispanic writers.

Manuel Zapata Olivella's frequent use of the word "mulatto" (a person of both African and European descent) to describe his background suggests a biological union as much as a cultural mixture. Focusing less on phenotype and more on what the Afro-Cuban poet NICOLÁS GUILLÉN would term cultural *mulatez,* or the mixing of cultures that characterizes the Caribbean, Zapata Olivella has sought to uncover what unites peoples rather than what separates them. Both his parents are of African descent, and he frequently reflects on the constant racial and cultural dynamics that define Latin America (*see* LATIN AMERICA, BLACKS IN). However, from the naming of one of his daughters Harlem to the writing of one of the most artistically accomplished novels about the diaspora, the 1983 *Changó, el gran putas* (Shango: The Greatest S.O.B.), Zapata Olivella is a strong voice in the dialogue on the contribution of African culture to the world. He provides a telling case study for a cultivated sense of an African connection in Latin America (*see* LITERATURE, BLACK, IN SPANISH AMERICA).

Born in the small town of Lorica on the western Caribbean coast of Colombia, Zapata Olivella used the area's rich folklore in his first novel, *Tierra mojada* (1947, Wetlands), to explore the conflicting social relations of the region. The novel recounts in accessible language and a straightforward narrative the struggles between a soon-to-be landless, rice-growing community and a large landowner and political boss. Other central characters are the parish priest, with whom the boss works in cahoots, and the local schoolteacher, a communist sympathizer and a civil rights leader who tries to defend the peasant community. Though simplistic in its approach to issues of good and evil and social disparity, *Tierra mojada* contains many of the thematic characteristics that Zapata Olivella's works would share over the decades: concern for the downtrodden, a sense of history from the viewpoint of the dispossessed, and issues of racial and cultural identity.

Zapata Olivella worked on *Tierra mojada* while traveling from Colombia up through CENTRAL AMERICA to MEXICO and then to the United States. His adventures throughout the Americas are delightfully retold in a series of travel narratives. Most noteworthy is *He visto la noche: Las raíces de la furia negra* (1949, I Have Seen the Night: The Roots of Black Fury), in which the impressionable young man seeks out his African American brothers in the United States in the aftermath of the HARLEM RIOTS OF 1943. It was at this time that Zapata Olivella developed a friendship with LANGSTON HUGHES that would last until Hughes's death in 1967.

Clearly, Olivella's experiences in the United States helped shape a black world-view that grew sharper with each decade. While several of his later works militantly pursue the theme of blackness, three works in particular stand out: the novel *Chambacú: Corral de negros* (1963; translated as *Chambacú: Black Slum,* 1989); the short story "Un extraño bajo mi piel" (1967, A Stranger Under My Skin); and the critically acclaimed *Changó, el gran putas.*

Chambacú: Corral de negros, awarded the prestigious Cuban Casa de las Américas literary prize in 1963, highlights the mistreatment of Afro-Colombians in the coastal city of Cartagena, Colombia. Set against the backdrop of the KOREAN WAR (1950-1953), a war many felt Colombians fought because of U.S. pressure, the action of the novel charts out the path of a black community in the small black town of Chambacú. As the war breaks out, the town is surrounded and occupied by the local military forces who try forcefully to recruit soldiers to man the battle lines. The move is resisted by the population, led by Máximo, a local political activist who is captured and tortured by the army. Translated by Jonathan Tittler in 1989, *Chambacú* has been cited as exemplary of Zapata Olivella's aesthetic of protest against the degradation and oppression of Afro-Colombians.

The story "A Stranger Under My Skin," published in the collection of short stories *¿Quién dió el fusil a Oswaldo?* (1967, Who Passed the Gun to Oswald?), is a humorous probe of one black man's self-loathing. A half-black, half-white mulatto, Leroy Elder, the main character in the story, regrets his black side so much that his life is forever altered. Translated by Brenda Frazier and published in the *Afro-Hispanic Review* in 1983, the story takes its cue from the Martinican political philosopher and revolutionary FRANTZ FANON's *White Mask, Black Skin* (1952), and is one of the most powerful psychological explorations of pain and suffering available in fiction.

When *Changó, el gran putas* was first published in 1983, it constituted a significant breakthrough in Spanish American literature. For the first time the African cultural component was successfully integrated on its own terms as Spanish American and black history in the Americas was told by black narrators and viewed from an Afrocentric perspective. Further, *Changó, el gran putas* manages to accomplish what no other fictive work has: it provides a sense of the whole of the African diaspora in the Americas. The novel opens with an epic poem that recounts the fall from grace and exile of the *orisha* Changó, a deity in the YORUBA religion of NIGERIA and in Yoruba-derived religious traditions in the African diaspora (*see* RELIGIONS, AFRICAN, IN LATIN AMERICA AND THE CARIBBEAN). As a consequence of his own exile, Changó expels the human race from Africa and condemns them to the Middle Passage and slavery. Similarly, the novel recounts the struggles for freedom during colonial times, the HAITIAN REVOLUTION, the postcolonial fight for equality, and the civil rights struggles in the United States. Some of the best-known historical figures in black history appear as narrators or literary personae, among them BENKOS BIOHÓ, the sixteenth-century leader of a Colombian maroon community; Toussaint L'Ouverture, the Haitian Revolution's military leader; Aleijadinho, the eighteenth-century Brazilian sculptor; and the twentieth-century political thinker MALCOLM X.

In addition to writing fiction, Zapata Olivella has been a leading interpreter of racial and cultural *mestizaje* (cultural mixing in Latin America). However, unlike the proponents of racial democracy (the belief that racial mixture dilutes social tension in Latin America), Zapata Olivella views mestizaje as the form that oppressed groups have used to resist assimilation and genocide. In his 1990 biography, *¡Levántate mulato!* (Rise Up, Mulatto!, originally in French in 1987), Zapata Olivella writes: "America was blackened by the importation of Africans, not because of their black skin, but because of their resistance, their struggles against slavery, their joining forces with native Americans to fight against the oppressors."

Zapata Olivella also coordinated – in conjunction with ABDIAS DO NASCIMENTO and other black Latin Americans – the first Congress of Black Culture of the Americas, which took place in 1977 in Cali, Colombia (*see* PAN-AFRICANISM AND AFRO-LATIN AMERICANS). His most recent published work, titled *La rebelión de los genes: El mestizaje americano en la sociedad futura* (1997, The Revolt of the Genes: *Mestizaje* in the Future of American Societies), is an extensive essay that presents a historical and political analysis of mestizaje and its consequences for an increasingly globalized world.

Yvonne Captain

SEE ALSO

Middle Passage, The; Slavery in Latin America and the Caribbean; Civil Rights Movement; Harlem, New York; Cartagena de Indias, Colombia; Lisboa, Antônio Francisco ("Aleijadinho"); Martinique; Xangô; Toussaint L'Ouverture, François Dominique; Orishas; Myth of Racial Democracy in Latin America and the Caribbean: An Interpretation.

Africa

Zaramo, ethnic group of TANZANIA.

The Zaramo primarily inhabit coastal Tanzania in and around Dar es Salaam. They speak Swahili, a Bantu language. The term *Zaramo* refers both to the Zaramo people (or the Zaramo proper) and to a cluster of related peoples, including the KWERE, the Kaguru, and the Zaramo people themselves. The Zaramo people number around 400,000.

SEE ALSO

Bantu: Dispersion and Settlement; Dar es Salaam, Tanzania; Swahili Language.

Africa

Zebra, striped mammal native to Africa, smaller in size than the related horse and greatly resembling the wild ass in habit and form, having a short, erect mane, large ears, and a tufted tail. The stripes, which distinguish this animal from other members of the horse family, serve as protective coloration in its natural habitat. The chief enemies of the zebra are lions and hunters who kill zebras for their flesh and hide. Zebras can be trained to work in harness and are popular animals in zoos and circuses.

Three zebra species and several subspecies are generally recognized, chiefly according to variations in the arrangement of the stripes. The mountain zebra is the smallest species, averaging about 1.2 m (4 ft) high at the shoulders, and has a strong, muscular, and symmetrical body. It is silver white, striped with black markings that extend to every part of the body except the stomach and the inner part of the thighs. The markings on the head are brown, and the muzzle is a rich bay tan. The legs are short and wiry. Mountain zebras travel in small herds and inhabit the mountain ranges of SOUTH AFRICA. This species was formerly plentiful but has been decimated by intensive hunting.

Burchell's zebras travel in large herds and inhabit the central and eastern plains; the species is named after the British naturalist William John Burchell. They are pale yellow with broad, black stripes, generally interspersed with fainter markings called shadow stripes. The species has several variations; some have stripes down to the hooves, and the lower legs of others are solid white without any stripes. The Boers refer to all varieties of Burchell's zebra as *quaggas*. The true quaggas, however, were exterminated during the nineteenth century; they were darker in color than the zebra and striped only on the head, neck, and shoulders.

The largest species, Grévy's zebra, is named after the former French president Jules Grévy. It attains a height of about 1.5 m (5 ft) at the shoulders, and its stripes are narrow and numerous. Formerly plentiful and of wide range, this species now inhabits the arid plains of eastern Africa and is nearly extinct. **Scientific classification:** Zebras belong to the family Equidae. The mountain zebra is classified as *Equus zebra,* Burchell's zebra as *Equus burchelli,* the true quagga as *Equus quagga,* and Grévy's zebra as *Equus grevyi.*

SEE ALSO

Afrikaner; Lion.

Latin America and the Caribbean

Zeferina, black female leader of an 1826 slave revolt outside of Salvador, BAHIA, BRAZIL.

In the first half of the nineteenth century the northeastern part of BRAZIL witnessed a large number of slave revolts. Historians attribute the high incidence of slave rebellions at this time to the growth of the SUGAR industry, the intensified importation of African slaves, the fact that many of these slaves shared a common language and culture, and the increasing demands made of slave labor, among other factors. These conditions encouraged many slaves to run away and form isolated communities known as *quilombos*. Alone or in cooperation with the free black or enslaved populations, quilombo members planned and carried out rebellions against the slaveholding society. The insurrection led by Zeferina in December 1826 was just 1 of some 20 revolts that occurred in the northeastern state of Bahia between 1807 and 1835.

Zeferina was a member of the *Urubu* (Vulture) quilombo located just outside of BAHIA's capital, Salvador. With the assistance of other slaves, Zeferina and the Urubu quilombo made plans to invade the city and kill all of its white inhabitants on Christmas Day 1826. On December 16, however, a violent encounter between escaped slaves who were transporting food to the quilombo and a white farming family set the revolt into motion prematurely. In the following days slave hunters made several unsuccessful attempts to overthrow Urubu; after suffering some casualties, they joined forces with a small group of soldiers from Salvador and the Pirajá district, and attacked Urubu again. While many of the slave rebels carried knives and guns, Zeferina armed herself with a bow and arrows. She led a fierce counterattack in which some 50 blacks exchanged gunfire with the soldiers and assaulted them while intermittently yelling, "Death to whites! Long live blacks!" The colonial forces ultimately vanquished the quilombo, killing four blacks and taking ten others as prisoners, including Zeferina. Soldiers extolled her courage and prowess in battle. Upon seeing her, the provincial president Manoel Ignácio da Cunha Menezes called her a "queen." In the end nearly all of the other captives were returned to their masters, but Zeferina was sentenced to prison and hard labor.

The known personal history of Zeferina begins with the 1826 rebellion she spearheaded and ends with her interrogation and sentencing. As in the case of many slaves, her individual identity is shrouded in ambiguity. Historical documents indicate that after the incident Zeferina stated that the majority of the Urubu quilombo members were *Nagôs*, that is, members of the Yoruba ethnic group originating in the southwest parts of Nigeria and Benin. Religious artifacts found in the quilombo living quarters also testify to the Yoruban character of the Urubu quilombo. In particular, the color red found on much of the religious paraphernalia is associated with the African god of thunder and lightning, Shangó, who is also the ancestral king of the Yoruban kingdom of Oyo.

While women have long occupied an important leadership position as *mães de santos* (priestesses) in the Brazilian religion Candomblé, their role as quilombo community leaders during Brazil's long era of slavery has been discussed less often. As members of escaped slave communities, black women were occasionally required to take up arms against colonial forces in defense of their autonomy. In the struggle for freedom some women died anonymously and others escaped, their valiant efforts unrecorded. Zeferina is a symbol of the spirit with which so many slaves, both men and women, fought to achieve freedom in Brazil.

Aaron Myers

See Also

Maroonage in the Americas; Oyo, Early Kingdom of; Slave Rebellions in Latin America and the Caribbean; Salvador, Brazil.

Africa

Zenawi, Meles (b. May 9, 1955, Adwa, Ethiopia), prime minister of Ethiopia who was elected in 1995.

Meles Zenawi led the Ethiopian People's Revolutionary Democratic Front (EPRDF), which deposed the government of Haile Mariam Mengistu in 1991. After leading Ethiopia's transitional government, Zenawi won election as prime minister in 1995.

Born in Adwa in northern Ethiopia's Tigre Province, Zenawi was educated at the General Wingate School. In 1971 Zenawi began studying medicine at Addis Ababa University. After becoming active in the student political movement, which was agitating against the faltering regime of Emperor Haile Selassie I, he left the university to join the guerrilla fighters in the Ethiopian bush. A committed Marxist, Zenawi at first supported the regime that was headed by Haile Mariam Mengistu, which ousted Selassie in 1974.

However, Zenawi opposed Mengistu's use of brutal tactics to hold power. Along with other opponents of the Mengistu regime, Zenawi helped to found the Tigre People's Liberation Front (TPLF), which led a revolt in Tigre. By 1980, in alliance with the Eritrean People's Liberation Front (EPLF) (*see* Eritrea), the TPLF had driven out Mengistu's troops and controlled most of the Tigrean countryside. By 1989, with Zenawi in command, the TPLF controlled Tigre and was closing in on the Ethiopian capital of Addis Ababa. Zenawi helped found the Ethiopian People's Revolutionary Democratic Front (EPRDF) in 1989, an umbrella for the TPLF allies outside Tigre, to mobilize national support for what had so far been a regional movement. In early 1991 Zenawi became chairman of the supreme council of the EPRDF. He quickly distanced himself from his Marxist past and promised a more moderate approach that might gain international favor.

In May 1991 EPRDF forces took the capital shortly after Mengistu fled the country. Zenawi became the interim head of state. He quickly agreed to Eritrean independence and worked to develop the Ethiopian economy, which had been ruined after years of warfare and mismanagement under the Mengistu regime. He cut military spending, redistributed land, and fought to end government corruption. Zenawi still faced opposition, however, most notably from the Oromo Liberation Front, which withdrew from the EPRDF. In addition, some Ethiopians claimed that land distribution unfairly limited land ownership by former supporters of Selassie and Mengistu to one hectare (2.5 acres), while EPRDF supporters could own three hectares. In May 1998 Ethiopia and Eritrea became embroiled in a border dispute that continued in 1999. Ethiopia claimed that Eritrean forces occupied a part of northwestern Ethiopia. Zenawi responded to international calls for mediation of the dispute by requiring that Eritrea withdraw from the disputed area before Ethiopia would agree to negotiation.

Robert Fay

See Also

Addis Ababa, Ethiopia.

Latin America and the Caribbean

Zenón Cruz, Isabelo (b. 1939, Humacao, Puerto Rico), Afro-Puerto Rican writer, scholar, and professor of literature at the University of Puerto Rico, best known for his two-volume study *Narciso descubre su trasero: El negro en la cultura puertorriqueña*, published in 1974-1975. This study represents one of the first and more important attempts to analyze and discuss the complexities of race relations, racism, and prejudice in Puerto Rico.

Guided and inspired by the writings of Martinican political philosopher Frantz Fanon and American political activist Eldridge Cleaver, Isabelo Zenón Cruz defends the importance of African heritage in the formation of a Puerto Rican identity. *Narciso descubre su trasero* (Narcissus Discovers His Backside) questions the often accepted myth of racial harmony in the definition of a Puerto Rican identity, and presents extensive evidence of how racism and prejudice have always been part of Afro-Puerto Ricans' reality. It examines the historical, social, and cultural circumstances that have marginalized Afro-Puerto Ricans.

According to Zenón Cruz, the importance of Afro-Puerto Ricans has always been underestimated. To prove this he includes in his study a wide range of topics that he approaches with criticism and irony, using historical facts and anecdotes. In his extensive and comprehensive discussion of education, politics, language, the arts, religion, sports, and Puerto Rican folklore – to name a few topics – Zenón examines commonly accepted ideals. Another important contribution of Zenón's study is his inclusion and discussion of outstanding Afro-Puerto Rican figures in each one of these areas. The analysis of these examples serves as evidence of how prejudice is completely embedded in the way the black race is perceived in Puerto Rico. He also examines how racism is perpetuated in every aspect of the island's social and cultural life, and why it is even perpetuated by Afro-Puerto Ricans.

Zenón Cruz's study also denounces the blind spots of previous scholars, critics, poets, and writers who have ignored Afro-Puerto Rican contributions. His harsh critique addresses the apparent general indifference of the Puerto Rican left to questions of "race," especially that of the independence movement. For this reason his study was received with enthusiasm by some, but it was also dismissed and ignored by others. Nevertheless, in several of the island's newspapers it provoked a debate that had been almost nonexistent before the study's publication. Zenón Cruz exposed and addressed the taboos and complexities that permeate notions of race on the island.

In Zenón Cruz's version of the Greek myth, Narcissus discovers his behind rather than his face. This serves as a meaningful image of the ideology and politics concerning race relations in Puerto Rico. It brings to the surface many underlying truths, unveils the underestimation of African heritage and importance in Puerto Rico, confronts and questions official discourses, and plays a key role in the discussions about Afro-Puerto Rican identity.

Zenón Cruz also authored the book *El anhelo de la inmortalidad del alma en Unamuno*, and his works have been published in newspapers and magazines, including *Guajana*, *Educación*, *Llama*, *Humacao*, and *Ecos Grises*.

Mayda Grano de Oro

See Also

Cleaver, Eldridge Leroy; Martinique.

Africa

Zerma (also known as Djerma, Dyerma, Zabarma, Zaberma, Zabermawa, and Zarma), ethnic group of West Africa.

The Zerma primarily inhabit northern Burkina Faso and western Niger. Others live in northwestern Nigeria, northern Benin, Ghana, and Côte d'Ivoire. They speak a Nilo-Saharan language and are a subgroup of the Songhai people. Approximately 1.5 million people consider themselves Zerma.

See Also

Côte d'Ivoire; Languages, African: An Overview.

Africa

Zigua (also known as Zigula), ethnic group of Tanzania.

The Zigua primarily inhabit interior northeastern Tanzania. They speak a Bantu language. Approximately 400,000 people consider themselves Zigua.

See Also

Bantu: Dispersion and Settlement.

Africa

Zimbabwe, country in southern Africa that borders Zambia, Mozambique, South Africa, and Botswana.

The Zimbabwean plateau, bounded in the south by the Limpopo River, in the north by the Zambezi, and in the east by the eastern highlands and Chimanimani mountains, includes such natural wonders as Victoria Falls and the historic Matopos hills. It is also an area that has experienced three great waves of violence: the first as a result of the Zulu mfecane from South Africa; the second from colonial conquest; and the third during the war for independence. Land, the foundation of Zimbabwe's natural beauty, has been the issue that has most dramatically defined the country's history and politics.

Early History

Remains of *Homo sapiens rhodesiensis* found on the Zimbabwean plateau have been carbon-dated at 100,000 years old. But the first humans to leave behind more extensive records were the Khoikhoi, hunter-gatherers who produced thousands of rock paintings throughout Zimbabwe, and especially in the Matopos hills, between 2000 and 5000 years ago. Sometime between 200 B.C.E. and 500 C.E. Bantu-speaking agriculturists and herders using iron tools began migrating into the area, forcing the Khoikhoi north. Many of these groups spoke the Shona language, and by the tenth century Shona speakers were the most numerous people in the region.

After 1000 B.C.E. centralized states began to develop among the Shona as some groups monopolized the trade with Arabs from the coast of Mozambique. In the fourteenth century competition for trade in gold and ivory resulted in the creation of distinct empires. The first major empire was Great Zimbabwe (between 1250 and 1550), followed by the Torwa Empire under Khame. At about the same time the Munhumutapa Kingdom of the Mutapa, an expansionist trading state, emerged to the northeast. The Munhumutapa Kingdom also produced gold, dug from small surface deposits. The last Shona empire was that of Changamire, and those became known as the Rozvi, a confederation of tribute-paying chieftainships in the southwest. Although the empires and chieftainships differed in style of governance, all Shona groups believed that land was sacred, belonging to all people and being held only temporarily by the chief and elders.

In the early 1800s the violent upheavals known as the mfecane that followed the rise of the warrior-king Shaka in South Africa pushed new groups into Shona territory, leading to the eventual collapse of the southern Shona empires. The Nguni under Soshangane attacked the Shona at Manyika in the early 1820s. Two decades later the last emigrant Nguni group, the Ndebele under Mzilikazi, destroyed the Rozvi state in the southwest. The Ndebele incorporated local Shona inhabitants and established their own kingdom near present-day Bulawayo, in the area that became known as Matabeleland. The Ndebele kingdom was highly centralized, possessing an effective army led by senior chiefs under the command of the king, first Mzilikazi and later his son Lobengula. Both the Ndebele's gradual expansion and their periodic cattle raids increased tensions over land in Shona territory, or Mashonaland.

The Rhodesian Settlers

Until the late 1800s the only Europeans to venture into Matabeleland and Mashonaland were a few missionaries, including David Livingstone, and explorers. The first settlers came in 1890 when Cecil Rhodes sent nearly 200 farmers, artisans, miners, soldiers, doctors, and others – the so-called Pioneer Column – plus more than 300 policemen north from Johannesburg, under the flag of the British South Africa (BSA) company. Rhodes's objective was to find gold, expand British influence, and contain Afrikaner expansion. But the pioneers found little gold in Mashonaland – the surface deposits had been depleted at least 100 years earlier. Turning instead to farming and cattle ranching, the settlers fared so poorly for the first several years that they relied on trade with local Africans for foodstuffs. In order to secure better land for themselves, the settlers soon began forcing Africans into Tribal Reserves.

In Matabeleland land was scarcer than it had been in Mashonaland, and King Lobengula realized that Rhodes and the BSA company wanted to acquire the territory for settlers and prospectors. He turned to the British Crown for protection, but Britain approved of Rhodes's plan and gave a free hand to the BSA. Consequently, the BSA, using a cattle dispute as the pretext, invaded Matabeleland and defeated Lobengula in 1893. The imposition of new taxes and tribal reserves led to a rebellion against white rule in 1896-1897. Brutally suppressed, it was the last large-scale rebellion for nearly 70 years.

Offering scant mineral wealth, the Zimbabwean plateau initially attracted few white settlers. Those who did come, mostly from South Africa, sought unfettered access to the best possible land for farming and ranching. Settlers resented the BSA's intervention in land policies and challenged its supremacy. In 1923 the British held an all-white referendum in Southern Rhodesia, and the settlers voted to become a self-governing rather than company-run territory. This gave white Rhodesians more power to "resettle" Africans on Tribal Reserves (later called Native Reserves) and to impose in-kind taxes of cattle. The settlers also stole cattle outright. The 1930 Land Apportionment Act formally classified land according to race, with more than 50 percent of the land European and 30 percent African.

Although Africans bitterly resented the Native Reserves, other aspects of Rhodesian colonialism led to the emergence of African nationalism. The few educational opportunities available to Africans were usually religious or technical in nature. Mission schools taught humility and obedience, and the state school taught manual labor and minor artisan trades. Labor conditions and employment opportunities were also discriminatory. African wages were kept low and trade unions were prohibited in domestic service, mining, and agriculture, the three largest sectors of

African employment. Discontent first emerged in the African press, especially in the *Daily News* and the Roman Catholic *Moto*, and among the industrial labor unions that had not been banned. However, nationalist protests were sporadic and the leadership was often fragmented. The African National Congress, or ANC (distinct from the South African counterpart of the same name), founded in 1934, was often the mouthpiece for labor unions and individuals to voice their grievances. But the Rhodesian government, through censorship and the banning of undesirable organizations, firmly suppressed any more militant actions.

In the 1950s Britain gradually began to extricate itself from its colonies throughout Africa (*see* Decolonization in Africa: An Interpretation). In 1953 politicians in London, Pretoria, and Salisbury created the Central African Federation (also known as the Federation of Rhodesia and Nyasaland), uniting Southern and Northern Rhodesia and Nyasaland. Africans initially expressed ambivalence about the federation, but as it became evident that an "independent" federation would be more oppressive than British rule, their opposition grew. Under increasing pressure from African nationalists, the federation dissolved in 1963, with Northern Rhodesia and Nyasaland becoming independent Zambia and Malawi, respectively. The whites of Southern Rhodesia, much more numerous and prosperous than their kin to the north, chose a course of confrontation. Stridently opposed to making concessions to Africans, in 1964 Rhodesian Front Party leader Ian Smith became prime minister. Smith called a referendum on independence, and whites voted overwhelmingly for the Unilateral Declaration of Independence. The international community responded with moral condemnation and international sanctions. In independent Rhodesia, although whites comprised less than one-seventeenth of the total population, they held one-third of the land.

Chimurenga II: The War for Independence

Given the Rhodesian government's land policies, it is not surprising that the primary reason Africans fought for their independence was for land, the source of their livelihood as well as the sacred home of their ancestors. Traditional chiefs and spirit mediums played a vital role by asking the people to welcome

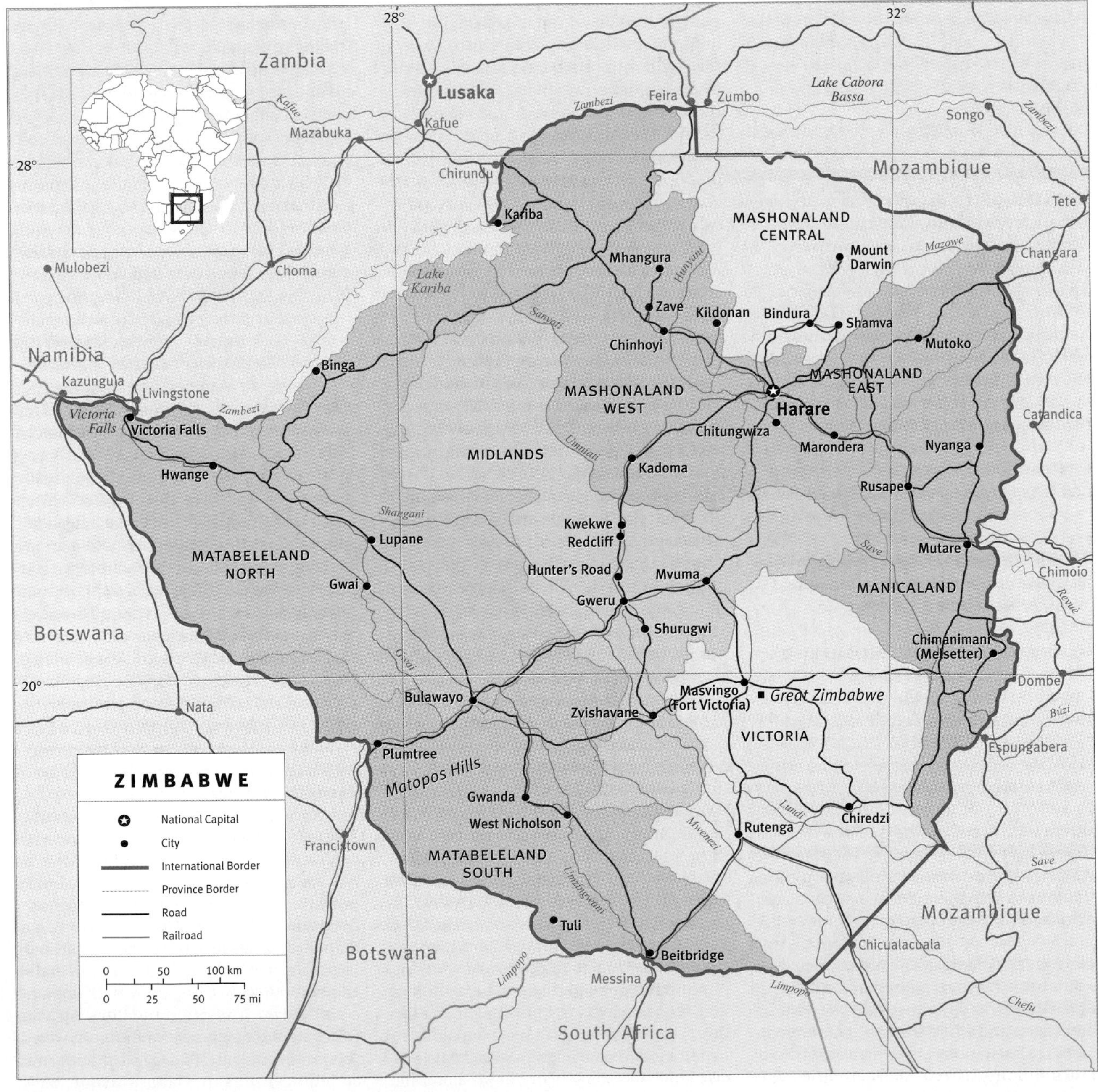

A woman sifts groundnuts at a village in Zimbabwe. An important ingredient in many African diets, groundnuts are primarily raised for sustenance, not export.
CORBIS/Hulton-Deutsch Collection

the nationalist soldiers as "sons of the soil" coming to reclaim the land for the people and their ancestors.

Initially peaceful, African nationalism became progressively militant as the Rhodesian government continued to force Africans onto Tribal Trust Lands. After the dissolution of the short-lived National Democratic Party, JOSHUA NKOMO formed the Zimbabwe African People's Union (ZAPU) in 1961. Two years later several leading Shona members of ZAPU broke away, charging that the party was Ndebele-dominated, to form the Zimbabwe African National Union (ZANU), under the leadership of Ndabaningi Sithole.

In 1964 ZANU and ZAPU began attacking white farms. Lacking popular support and military training, both parties soon recognized that they were no match for the Rhodesian military, and quickly adopted new strategies. ZANU began recruiting militants and politicizing the rural population, using force when necessary. ZAPU, by contrast, concentrated on building a large conventional force in camps in neighboring Zambia and ANGOLA. It was not until late 1972 that ZANU began launching concerted attacks. The war progressed slowly, as the divided nationalists sought to build popular support for their cause. The Rhodesian military, meanwhile, forced Africans into guarded villages, imposing a cordon sanitaire in the north to prevent the insurgents from crossing the border, and increased white and African conscription into the Rhodesian Security Forces. The Rhodesian government further fragmented the nationalist movements by negotiating with moderate opposition groups. Its position was bolstered by the state-controlled economy, centered on light manufacturing and agriculture, which fared remarkably well despite international sanctions.

The turning point came in 1975 with the independence of Mozambique. This galvanized the opposition groups and provided them with unhindered access to all of eastern Zimbabwe. The Rhodesian government's attempt to negotiate a peaceful compromise, providing for a political system with limited African rights, also failed. In 1977 ZANU and ZAPU reinvigorated their war effort. The number of ZANU insurgents operating in Zimbabwe jumped from approximately 3000 in 1977 to 10,000 in 1978, and the party, under the new leadership of ROBERT MUGABE, claimed to have "liberated" one-third of the country. Although both ZANU and ZAPU advocated socialism as well as national liberation, the former drew support from the Chinese and the latter from the Soviet bloc. ZAPU mounted sustained attacks with large regiments deploying heavy weapons from Eastern bloc countries, while ZANU pursued a classic hit-and-run guerrilla war.

The Rhodesian government responded to the growing strength of the independence forces by creating the pseudo-insurgent group MOZAMBICAN NATIONAL RESISTANCE (RENAMO) as well as the paramilitary Special Auxiliary Forces. But even as these groups pursued insurgents into neighboring states, the Rhodesian military grew weaker and more fragmented, and lost popular support. The Internal Settlement, in which the Rhodesian government convinced three prominent conservative opposition leaders to accept a transition government and limited constitutional reforms in 1978, failed to gain legitimacy among either African Zimbabweans or the international community. ZANU and ZAPU, now briefly joined as the Patriotic Front, boycotted the Internal Settlement and revived the war. By late 1979, at the cost of approximately 25,000 civilian lives – most of them black – the Rhodesian government agreed to negotiations with the Patriotic Front under British auspices.

INDEPENDENCE POLITICS

Zimbabwe became independent on April 18, 1980. In elections just prior to independence, Mugabe and ZANU captured 57 of the 80 African seats in parliament, with ZAPU

Despite the existence of opposition parties in Zimbabwe, evidenced in persuasive campaign posters, under Robert Mugabe the country has become virtually a one-party state. *Jason Lauré*

winning 20 seats. Mugabe became prime minister and, in a gesture of reconciliation, made Nkomo minister of home affairs. At independence Mugabe asked the country's whites to stay and contribute their wealth and skills to the construction of a prosperous Zimbabwe. Although the transition to independence was peaceful, it did not resolve many of the grievances that had originally sparked the war to overthrow white minority rule. In particular the inequitable distribution of land remained a source of tension.

Mugabe initially upheld many of the unpopular policies and practices of the Smith regime. The government jailed political opponents, censored the press, and gave extensive powers to the security forces. Mugabe also fired Nkomo after large caches of arms were found on ZAPU-owned farms. This action confirmed what many believed to be the mistreatment of ZAPU soldiers in the Zimbabwean army and the party during the elections, leading ZAPU soldiers and party members to take up arms. In 1982 these "dissidents" initiated a series of terrorist and criminal attacks in Matabeleland, although their exact goal was unclear and ZAPU officially distanced itself from the dissidents' activities. After six years of a low-intensity war in Matabeleland that resulted in at least 2000 civilian deaths, ZANU and ZAPU agreed to unite under the name ZANU-Patriotic Front (ZANU-PF). The Zimbabwe National Army (ZNA) also became heavily involved in the war in Mozambique, chiefly to protect the oil pipeline and transportation routes through Mozambique from RENAMO insurgents. As the war drained the Zimbabwean economy and became increasingly unpopular at home, the Zimbabwean government sponsored peace negotiations in the early 1990s, putting pressure on both RENAMO and Mozambique to end the war.

Since independence the Zimbabwean state has progressively become a centralized, de facto one-party regime, as President Mugabe has used patronage and parliamentary legislation to consolidate his own power. He has faced few serious challenges from the fragmented opposition. These groups are split among various personalities and interests, with parties such as the mainly white and agriculture-based Conservative Alliance of Zimbabwe, the upstart Zimbabwe Unity Movement, and the historic United African National Congress, all vying for popular support and represented by discontented politicians.

Mugabe's authoritarianism has been spared domestic and international criticism largely because of his popular appeal, especially in the rural areas, and the prosperous economy. Mugabe has built upon his cult of personality, using visits to communal lands (the previous Tribal Trust Lands) as media events to lash out at white farm owners and to trumpet government development projects. As a symbolic gesture toward promised land reform, in 1982 the government passed a law permitting women to own their own land. But most women in communal land are either not aware of the law or cannot afford to act upon it, and thus most land has remained in the hands of men. The government purchased additional lands, resettling approximately 70,000 families over the years. Despite the under-utilization of much of the land, by the late 1980s Zimbabwe had become self-sufficient in grain supplies, and many Zimbabweans saw real improvements in their standard of living. Conditions remained most difficult in the communal lands, which were often arid and barren, especially in the southern regions.

In the early 1990s widespread drought, combined with economic structural adjustment austerity measures, subjected many Zimbabweans to severe hardships. The government's structural adjustment program aimed to reduce government spending, particularly on defense, and to relax controls on prices, imports, and investments. It also led to the privatization of many state-run industries. Zimbabwe's national economy has long been diversified by African standards, being evenly divided among agriculture (tobacco, maize, and cotton), mining (gold, nickel, and asbestos), manufacturing (food processing and metals), and services. In the late 1990s the government sought to diversify further the agricultural export sector, especially into horticultural products, and to build its wildlife tourism industry. Zimbabwe is one of the few African countries in which elephants are abundant, and it received official clearance to export ivory.

Meanwhile, in 1997 Mugabe announced that he would appropriate more than 4.8 million hectares (12 million acres) of white-owned land and turn it over to landless blacks without compensation, despite the fact that these lands contain the most prosperous farms and employ large numbers of people. With the publication of a list of farms to be nationalized in 1998, the mostly white owners of large farms have become apprehensive about their future. Mugabe agreed to seek compensation for these landowners from international donors, and began to hint that the land reform package might be reduced. Meanwhile, in anticipation of the promised land redistribution, thousands of poor blacks began camping out on white-owned farms throughout Zimbabwe. The uncertainty over land rights threatened to stall the country's economic development. Amid growing social unrest, in 1998 Zimbabwe undertook a controversial military intervention to defend the government of the DEMOCRATIC REPUBLIC OF THE CONGO against an armed rebellion. The cost of this military operation, and the possibility that it might grow into a larger regional conflict, further threatened Zimbabwe's economic prosperity.

Eric Young

SEE ALSO

African Socialism; Colonial Rule; Elephant; Bantu: Dispersion and Settlement; Explorers in Africa Since 1800; Gold Trade; Ivory Trade; Smith, Ian Douglas; Johannesburg, South Africa; Pretoria, South Africa; Nationalism in Africa; Structural Adjustment in Africa; Tourism in Africa; Zambezi River; Christianity: Missionaries in Africa.

Africa

Zimbabwe (Ready Reference)

Official Name: Republic of Zimbabwe
Former Name: Rhodesia
Area: 390,759 sq km (about 150,873 sq mi)
Location: Southern Africa; borders SOUTH AFRICA, BOTSWANA, MOZAMBIQUE, and ZAMBIA
Capital: Harare (population 1,184,169 [1992 estimate])
Other Major Cities: Bulawayo (population 621,000), Chitungwiza (274,000), Gweru (124,700), Kwekwe (75,000), and Mutare (68,700) (1992 estimates)
Population: 11,044,147 (1998 estimate)
Population Density: 30 persons per sq km (about 76 persons per sq mi)
Population Below Age 15: 44 percent (male 2,439,907; female 2,397,761 [1998 estimate])
Population Growth Rate: 1.12 percent (1998 estimate)
Total Fertility Rate: 3.86 children born per woman (1998 estimate)
Life Expectancy at Birth: Total population: 39.16 years (male 39.12 years; female 39.19 years [1998 estimate])
Infant Mortality Rate: 61.75 deaths per 1000 live births (1998 estimate)
Literacy Rate (age 15 and over who can read and write in English): Total population: 85 percent (male 90 percent; female 80 percent [1995 estimate])
Education: Primary education in Zimbabwe is free and compulsory between ages 7 and 15. In the early 1990s approximately 2.4 million students were enrolled annually in primary schools and 657,000 in secondary schools. About 61,600 were enrolled in institutions of higher education, including a number of teachers' colleges and several agricultural and technical schools.
Languages: English is the official language. The most prevalent Bantu languages are Shona and Sindebele (the language of the Ndebele, sometimes called Ndebele).
Ethnic Groups: The bulk of Zimbabwe's population is formed by two major Bantu-speaking ethnic groups: the SHONA, who constitute 80 percent of the total population, and the NDEBELE (Matabele), who constitute about 19 percent of the total and are concentrated in the southwestern regions. The country also has small minorities of Europeans, Asians, and persons of mixed race.
Religions: Half of the population practices various syncretic religions, fusions of traditional African religions and Christianity. Approximately 25 percent are Christian, principally Roman Catholic or Anglican Communion; this number also includes many Protestant sects. About 24 percent practice traditional religions, and about 1 percent are Hindu or Muslim.
Climate: Although Zimbabwe lies in a tropical zone, its climate is moderated by high elevation. The average temperature is 16° C (60° F) in July, and 21° C (70° F) in January. Average rainfall is about 890 mm (35 in) in the High Veld and less than 610 mm (24 in) in most parts of the Middle Veld. The rainy season is from November to March.
Land, Plants, and Animals: Zimbabwe occupies part of the great plateau of southern Africa. Its most prominent feature is a broad ridge that runs southwest to northeast across the country at elevations of 1200 to 1500 m (4000 to 5000 ft), the High Veld. On either side of the ridge the land slopes downward, in the north to the ZAMBEZI RIVER and in the south to the Limpopo River. These areas are known as the Middle Veld. Along the eastern border is a mountain range. The land of Zimbabwe is primarily covered with savanna; a particularly lush grass grows during the moist summers. Animals include ELEPHANTS, HIPPOPOTAMUSES, LIONS, hyenas, CROCODILES, ANTELOPE, IMPALAS, GIRAFFES, and BABOONS.
Natural Resources: Mineral resources include coal, chromium ore, asbestos, gold, nickel, copper, iron ore, vanadium, lithium, tin, and platinum group metals.
Currency: The Zimbabwe dollar
Gross Domestic Product (GDP): $24.9 billion (1996 estimate)
GDP per Capita: $2200 (1996 estimate)
GDP Real Growth Rate: 8.1 percent (1996 estimate)
Primary Economic Activities: Agriculture (70 percent of the labor force, 40 percent of exports), mining (only 5 percent of employment and GDP, but 40 percent of exports), and manufacturing
Primary Crops: Tobacco, corn, cotton, wheat, coffee, sugar cane, and peanuts; cattle, sheep, goats, and pigs
Industries: Mining, steel, clothing and footwear, chemicals, food processing, fertilizer, beverage, transportation equipment, and wood products
Primary Exports: Agricultural products (especially tobacco), nickel metal, cotton, manufactures, gold, ferrochrome, and textiles
Primary Imports: Machinery and transportation equipment, other manufactures, chemicals, and fuels
Primary Trade Partners: European Union (especially United Kingdom, Germany, Italy), South Africa, Japan, United States, and Botswana
Government: Zimbabwe won independence from the United Kingdom on April 18, 1980. It is a parliamentary democracy. The executive branch is led by President Robert Gabriel Mugabe. He appoints a cabinet, which is in turn responsible to the legislative branch, the 150-member House of Assembly. Of these members, 120 are directly elected by popular vote to serve six-year terms; 12 are chosen by the president; 10 are traditional chiefs chosen by their colleagues; and 8 are chosen by provincial governors. The dominant political party, that of President Mugabe, is called the Zimbabwe African National Union-Patriotic Front (ZANU-PF).

Lisa Clayton Robinson

SEE ALSO

Bantu: Dispersion and Settlement; Harare, Zimbabwe; Mugabe, Robert.

Africa

Zinder, Niger, second-largest city of NIGER and the capital of the precolonial sultanate of Damagaram.

Located 908 km (567 mi) east of Niamey, Zinder was once a major center for the lucrative trans-Saharan trade. Overshadowed today by Niamey, Zinder remains an important commercial center, with an estimated population of 130,000.

Zinder was founded in the early sixteenth century. In the early nineteenth century Suleyman, a KANURI chief, founded the sultanate of Damagaram and made Zinder its capital. Though nominally a vassal of Bornu, Suleyman took advantage of the disruptive Bornu-Sokoto wars to expand Damagaram, and he established an alliance with TUAREG tribesmen, who controlled the important trans-Saharan trade routes to the north. Zinder's trade thrived under the protection of the strong Damagaram army and the Tuareg. In order to consolidate their power, Damagaram traded slaves for firearms. Zinder achieved its greatest prominence during the 1880s, when Damagaram renounced its allegiance to Bornu and challenged the Sokoto Empire.

FRANCE claimed Zinder in 1899, and after French campaigns to subdue the Tuareg disrupted the trans-Saharan trade during the first decade of the twentieth century, Zinder's economy began to decline. Although the French made Zinder the capital of the Niger colony in 1911, they moved the capital to Niamey in 1926. Today Zinder has regained economic vitality as a center for the region that produces Niger's important peanut and cotton crops.

Elizabeth Heath

SEE ALSO

Niamey, Niger; Sokoto Caliphate; Slavery in Africa; Trans-Saharan and Red Sea Slave Trade.

Africa

Zinza, ethnic group of TANZANIA.

The Zinza primarily inhabit northwestern Tanzania, on the southwestern shores of LAKE VICTORIA. They speak a Bantu language. Approximately 200,000 people consider themselves Zinza.

SEE ALSO

Bantu: Dispersion and Settlement.

Latin America and the Caribbean

Zobel, Joseph (b. 1915, Petit-Bourg, Martinique), Martinican writer and critic who portrays the life of the black underclass of Martinique, from whose ranks he comes.

After his schooling in Fort-de-France, Joseph Zobel moved to the poverty-stricken southern part of the island of MARTINIQUE. The result of Zobel's time among the peasants of Le Diamant is his first published novel, *Diab'la* (1946), a work that underscored the need for land reform by suggesting, not without some temerity, that those who work the land should own it. Although completed in 1942, the book was censured by the Vichy government, which occupied Martinique during World War II. A collection of Zobel's stories published just after the war, *Laghia de la mort* (1946), exemplified what could be called Martinican social realism, exposing the brutal existence of plantation workers.

Zobel's best-known work, the semiautobiographical, coming-of-age story *La rue cases-nègres* (1950; winner of the Prix des Lecteurs), explores different territory, recounting a young man's transition from the village to the city, from the peasantry to the intellectual class. Zobel's innovative use of Creole dialogue in this novel helped spark the CRÉOLITÉ literary movement that includes PATRICK CHAMOISEAU and RAPHAËL CONFIANT. Like many writers of his generation, Zobel flirted with a return to Africa.

In 1957 Zobel left France for DAKAR, SENEGAL, and in 1962 – in a newly independent Senegal under President Léopold Sédar Senghor – served as cultural advisor to the nascent Radio Senegal and helped establish and run the Sengalese Cultural Services. But Zobel grew disenchanted with Senghor's NÉGRITUDE-inspired ethnic nationalism. He returned to France, settling in the south, and published a collection of short stories, *Le soleil partagé* (1964), which promotes a model of racial reconciliation based on the values of the peasant class. With the advent of magical realism in the Caribbean, Zobel's brand of Balzacian social commentary fell decidedly out of fashion. The success of the film version of *La rue cases-nègres* (1983), directed by Euzhan Palcy, has led, however, to a positive reappraisal of his work in recent years.

Richard Watts

SEE ALSO

Nationalism in Africa; Senghor, Léopold Sédar.

Latin America and the Caribbean

Zouk, contemporary popular music of the French- and Creole-speaking Caribbean.

Like American RAP music and Jamaican REGGAE, zouk is the music of the descendants of African slaves in societies previously dominated by whites. The comparison between the genres, though, ends there. Sung in Creole and carried by an up-tempo dance rhythm, zouk is neither didactic nor explicitly political; it is in no way protest music. Rather, as its name implies ("zouk" is a Creole word first employed in MARTINIQUE that means "a party" or "to party"), zouk is a Carnivalesque music that celebrates Caribbean Creole culture, principally by drawing its lyrical themes from Creole folklore. Thanks to the sense of cultural pride (and, it should be noted, the urge to dance) that zouk fosters in its Creole-speaking audience, this festive music has become the most popular genre in the French overseas departments of Martinique and GUADELOUPE as well as in the neighboring islands of DOMINICA, ST. LUCIA, and HAITI. But zouk's popularity is not confined to the Caribbean sphere. In recent years zouk performers such as Kassav, Zouk Machine (led by three female vocalists), and Malavoi have developed substantial followings in Europe – and, in particular, in FRANCE – as well as in Africa.

Although zouk musicians generally steer clear of questions of racial and ethnic origins in their lyrics, they do evoke their African roots in the music. Zouk's rhythm, produced by traditional drums and, more recently, drum machines, has its source in the rhythm of the traditional West African drum or *tam-tam*. This influence can also be felt in zouk's musical predecessors: *gwo ka* (Creole for "large drum"), a traditional Guadeloupean drum music, and BIGUINE, the Martinican music of the 1940s and 1950s that is zouk's clearest musical forebear, both of which integrate elements of African drumming. Kassav, the most successful and influential of zouk bands, used the gwo ka in its earliest recordings, and the traditional rhythms of gwo ka can still be detected in most zouk songs.

But zouk's success can also be attributed to its integration of many contemporary musical styles, including JAZZ, FUNK, salsa, CALYPSO, *cadence-lypso* (from Dominica), and COMPAS direct (from Haiti). If there is a controversy surrounding zouk, it centers on this very point. According to zouk's detractors, the music has drifted too far from its roots and is no longer representative of Creole culture. This multiplicity of influences is seen by its fans as zouk's strongest point and, paradoxically, that which makes the music distinctly Caribbean. Zouk, like Caribbean culture, is nothing if not the creolization or mixture of American, European, and African cultural practices.

Richard Watts

SEE ALSO

Creoles; Salsa Music; Languages, Creole, in the Caribbean.

Africa

Zulu, the largest ethnic group in SOUTH AFRICA, with a population of approximately 6 million.

The Zulu are one of many southern African peoples belonging to the broader NGUNI linguistic group. Like other Nguni groups such as the XHOSA, the Zulu speak a Bantu language, and their ancestors are believed to have migrated into southern Africa sometime after the second century C.E. They settled in village communities, cultivated grains such as MILLET, and kept cattle, which became an important symbol of wealth. Also like other Nguni groups, the Zulu developed a distinct language well before they forged a collective identity or a centralized political structure. These did not emerge until the late eighteenth century, when competition for grazing lands and access to sources of ivory, an important trade commodity, fostered conflict among Nguni clans.

At that time only members of one Nguni clan identified themselves as Zulu, which was the name of one of the clan's founding ancestors. But not long after SHAKA became the clan chief in 1815, the Zulu began a campaign of conquest and expansion known as the MFECANE, which led to the incorporation of many other peoples. A brilliant military leader, Shaka soon built an army of more than 40,000 rigorously trained soldiers. Shaka also introduced several important military innovations, such as the short stabbing spear, which gave Zulu troops a distinct advantage over their adversaries. In a period of only ten years Shaka had built a kingdom – Zululand – that encompassed most of the area now known as Natal Province.

Shaka claimed absolute authority over his kingdom. His hierarchical leadership style was retained by subsequent Zulu rulers and later adopted by Inkatha, a twentieth-century Zulu political organization. In conquered territories Shaka appointed his own officials; any subjects who refused Shaka's overrule could be killed immediately. In addition, conquered peoples were expected to serve in the Zulu army, herd the king's cattle, and hunt elephants for ivory. Shaka consolidated his authority by conducting frequent cattle raids on neighboring groups, such as the Mpondo. A portion of the cattle was distributed to Shaka's chiefs and army officers to encourage their loyalty.

Despite these tactics, however, Shaka faced internal opposition, and in 1828 he was assassinated by his half brother DINGANE. But Dingane lacked Shaka's military acumen and fared poorly in battles against the expansionist Afrikaners (also known as Boers). Although the Zulu lost land to the Afrikaners during the mid-nineteenth century, they did not fall under European COLONIAL RULE until 1883, when Zululand was invaded by British troops.

As part of Great Britain's Natal Colony, Zululand was divided into 13 chiefdoms, and the Zulu king Dinuzulu was exiled. Missionaries encouraged the Zulu to forsake practices of ancestor worship in favor of Christianity. Zulu farmers initially profited from strong markets for maize in Durban and other rapidly growing cities, but government policies eventually alienated most Zulu farmland. Zulu men were consequently forced to migrate in search of wage labor, typically either in the gold mines or on sugar plantations. After the NATIONAL PARTY came to power in South Africa in 1948, its system of APARTHEID assigned all the country's Africans to one of ten "tribal" homelands (also known as Bantustans). The Zulu homeland was called KwaZulu and ruled by nominally independent "tribal" authorities.

In 1976 MANGOSUTHO GATSHA BUTHELEZI became the chief minister of KwaZulu. He began encouraging Zulu nationalism through the revived Inkatha Ya Ka Zulu, a Zulu cultural organization founded in 1928. A descendant of the nineteenth-century Zulu king CETSHWAYO, Buthelezi spoke out against apartheid, but his ethnic separatism and willingness to collaborate with the white-ruled South African government soon put him – and Inkatha's Zulu membership – at odds with antiapartheid groups such as the AFRICAN NATIONAL CONGRESS (ANC). During the 1980s and early 1990s the rivalry between the two groups often turned violent.

After Inkatha became an official political party in 1990 (the Inkatha Freedom Party, or IFP), it joined with far-right Afrikaner organizations to oppose democratic negotiations led by the ANC and the National Party, and Buthelezi pressed for a separate Zulu state. After the election of Nelson Mandela as president of postapartheid South Africa in 1994, the IFP pulled out of the South African Constitutional Assembly to protest the ANC government. Relations between the two parties remain contentious. In the former Zulu homeland, however, organizations such as the KwaZulu-Natal Arts and Culture Council are encouraging "nonpartisan" forms of Zulu nationalism.

Elizabeth Heath

SEE ALSO

Afrikaner; Antiapartheid Movement; Ivory Trade; Mandela, Nelson Rolihlahla; Inkatha Freedom Party; Christianity: Missionaries in Africa.

Latin America and the Caribbean

Zumbi (b. 1655?; d. November 20, 1695), legendary leader of the seventeenth-century *quilombo* (escaped slave colony) of Palmares in northeastern BRAZIL (*see* MAROONAGE IN THE AMERICAS).

Zumbi, the most vehement opponent of slavery in colonial Brazil, is closely linked with the settlement of Palmares, established by escaped slaves in Brazil's northeastern state of Alagoas. Escaped slaves first settled in this mountainous, forested region sometime between the end of the sixteenth century and the early years of the seventeenth century. Because of the abundance of palms, the settlement became known as Palmares. During the Dutch occupation of northeastern Brazil (1630-1654), Palmares received a large number of fugitive slaves and grew into a formidable, populous federation of villages covering a vast area of land from northern Alagoas to southern Pernambuco. Palmares' sophisticated fortifications and well-equipped defense force enabled it to resist repeated military incursions following the expulsion of the Dutch until it was finally conquered in 1694. The story of Zumbi is closely tied to Palmares, the largest and longest lasting quilombo in the history of the colonial Americas.

What little is known about Zumbi's early life is based on the personal records of a seventeenth-century priest named Antônio Melo, which have not been reliably documented. According to these sources, Zumbi was born in Palmares in 1655 and was captured that same year during a Portuguese attack on the quilombo. Zumbi was later placed under the care of Melo, who baptized him Francisco and taught him Portuguese, Latin, and other subjects. Research on Melo's written records indicates that in 1670, Zumbi ran away to Palmares.

Zumbi then began to appear in firsthand accounts of military missions sent by the Portuguese to destroy Palmares. Reports from a 1675-1676 campaign relate that Zumbi suffered a leg wound and describe him as "a black man of singular bravery, great spirit, and rare constancy." At this time Zumbi served as the war commander under GANGA ZUMBA, Zumbi's uncle and the leader of Palmares during the second half of the seventeenth century.

After being wounded in a 1677 attack, Ganga Zumba agreed to a peace treaty with the governor of Pernambuco the following year and, under its terms, relocated part of Palmares to the Cucaú Valley. According to official state documents, at this time Zumbi was part of the rebel faction that opposed the concession to colonial authorities. In 1680 he allegedly poisoned Ganga Zumba and became the new king of Palmares. Zumbi successfully spearheaded the defense of Palmares through 1694, when military units from São Paulo and the northeast vanquished the quilombo following a series of campaigns that lasted some two years.

Zumbi and a small band of his followers escaped during the final, 22-day-long battle. He avoided capture for more than a year until a member of his group disclosed his whereabouts to colonial forces, which ambushed and killed him on November 20, 1695. After Zumbi's death, colonial authorities publicly displayed his head in Pernambuco's capital, Recife. An alternate version of his death recounts that he and some 200 other residents of Palmares jumped off a cliff during the final battle rather than be re-enslaved.

Until recently the memory of Zumbi survived only in the oral histories of Afro-Brazilians. There are records of Zumbi being publicly celebrated by Bahian *afoxés* around the turn of the twentieth century and in an Afro-Brazilian festival in Alagoas in the 1930s. But during the 1970s this black hero began to gain much more recognition. Civil rights activism in the United States prompted a surge of black consciousness throughout Brazil and renewed interest in Afro-Brazilian history (*see* BLACK CONSCIOUSNESS IN BRAZIL). In 1978 the MOVIMENTO NEGRO UNIFICADO (United Black Movement) declared November 20 National Black Consciousness Day. On May 13, 1988, the centenary of the abolition of slavery in Brazil, Afro-Brazilians invoked

Zumbi during their protests of enduring discrimination and inequalities. In 1995 there were widespread observances of the tercentenary of Zumbi's death, including the first continental congress of blacks in São Paulo (Congreso Continental dos Povos Negros das Américas) and a march in the capital Brasília led by the Movimento Negro Unificado.

Such actions have helped make Zumbi a national hero, and Palmares a registered historical landmark. To many black Brazilians Zumbi symbolizes the ongoing Afro-Brazilian struggle for economic and political equality. In the words of Joel Rufino, president of the Palmares Foundation, a commission that organizes the annual celebration of Zumbi, "For us blacks, the example of Zumbi inspires our fight for justice and the right to be full-fledged citizens without fear and shame of our blackness."

Aaron Myers

See Also

Palmares: An African State in Brazil; Afoxés/ Blocos Afros; Abolition and Emancipation in Latin America and the Caribbean.

North America

Zydeco, the music of black Creoles in southwest Louisiana whose principal instruments are the accordion and the washboard.

Zydeco music, like the Louisiana cuisine gumbo, is an amalgamation of several cultural influences. It is rooted most strongly in French and African musical traditions, but Native American, German, and Spanish cultures have also informed its development. The history of settlement in Louisiana reveals how these various groups of people came together to forge the hybrid culture that spawned zydeco music.

Around 1700 several thousand Acadians who had been exiled from Nova Scotia by the British formed a French-speaking colony in Louisiana. They became known as Cajuns, a colloquialism for Acadians, and worked primarily as tenant farmers. Very few owned slaves, and they had a mutually influential relationship with the people of African descent, known as Creoles, who had been brought to Louisiana from other North American colonies or from the French- and Spanish-speaking Caribbean. These two ethnic groups, in turn, interacted with Native Americans and European immigrants. The sociocultural exchanges among these different ethnic groups during the late nineteenth century resulted in the emergence of two musical forms in the early twentieth century: zydeco and cajun.

Zydeco and cajun are closely related yet distinct musical forms. They have a similar instrumentation, including at least one fiddle, a guitar, and a button accordion backed by a bass and drums. Both zydeco and cajun are played in such contexts as nightclubs, picnics, and house parties, where people often dance as couples. Historian Barry Jean Ancelet explains that although both zydeco and cajun are bluesy, improvisational dance musics that speak of lost love and hard times, cajun music is smoother and emphasizes melody, while zydeco tends to be faster and more syncopated. Part of this rhythmic difference stems from the use in zydeco music ensembles of a corrugated sheet of metal worn over the shoulders like a vest that, when played with eating utensils, makes a raspy sound. In addition, even though zydeco and cajun musicians sing in both French Creole and English, there seems to be a greater prevalence of English lyrics in zydeco music.

The first commercial recordings of zydeco and cajun music were made during the late 1920s and early 1930s. In 1928 accordion player Joseph Falcon accompanied his wife, Cleoma, who sang lead vocals and played the guitar, on the earliest cajun music recording. The first black Creole to make a record was accordion player Amédé Ardoin, who, after performing with cajun fiddler Dennis McGee on a 1929 record, recorded his own songs in the early 1930s. In the late 1930s folklorists John and Alan Lomax made numerous recordings of early zydeco music for the Library of Congress, including the famed "Les haricots sont pas salés." The term *zydeco* is in fact a creolized pronunciation of the first two words of this song's title, which literally translates to "the snap beans ain't salty," but is used colloquially to convey the idea that "times are hard."

Many historians agree that Creoles were the first to pick up and master the button accordion, which became a staple of zydeco music. The accordion player widely recognized as the king of zydeco, Clifton Chenier, continued the legacy of Ardoin. Chenier emerged as a musician in the 1950s and pioneered the use of the piano accordion and brass horns, which replaced the fiddle, in zydeco music. His compositions were influenced by the sounds of rhythm and blues, soul, and blues music popular during the post-World War II period. Some of his better-known songs are "Black Gal" (1965), "Jambalaya" (1975), and "Country Boy Now" (1984), from his Grammy Award-winning album *I'm Here!* Two other major zydeco artists are accordionist Boozoo Chavis and singer Queen Ida. Though the bayou region of Louisiana continues to be the cradle of zydeco music, the genre is played along the Gulf Coast from Louisiana to Texas and is gaining national and international recognition.

Aaron Myers

See Also

Soul Music; World War II and African Americans; American Indians; Blues, The.

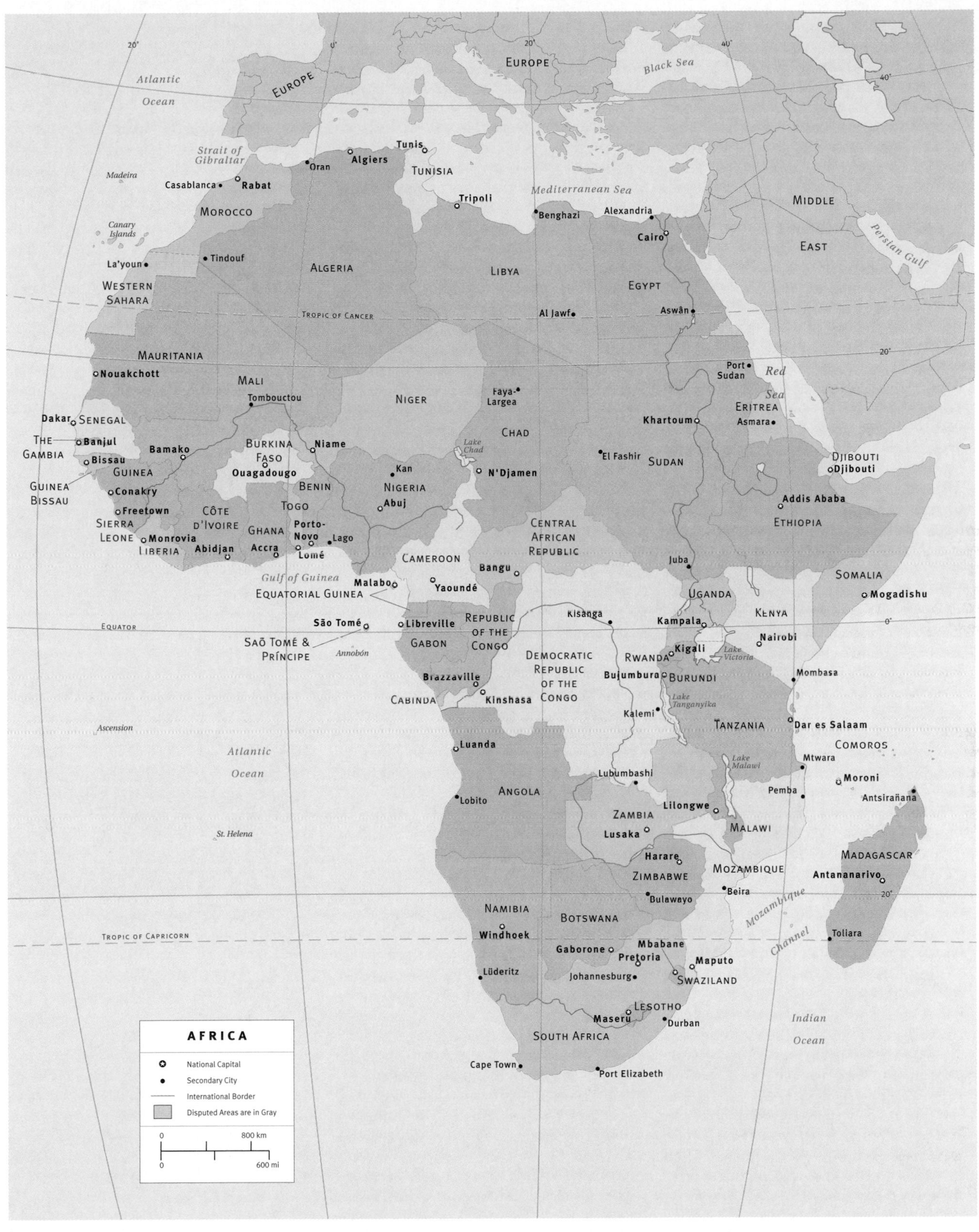
AFRICA
National Capital
Secondary City
International Border
Disputed Areas are in Gray
800 km
600 mi
Atlantic Ocean
Europe
Black Sea
Strait of Gibraltar
Madeira
Canary Islands
Casablanca
Rabat
Oran
Algiers
Tunis
Tunisia
Mediterranean Sea
Tripoli
Benghazi
Alexandria
Cairo
Middle East
Persian Gulf
Morocco
Tindouf
La'youn
Western Sahara
Algeria
Libya
Egypt
Aswān
Al Jawf
Tropic of Cancer
Mauritania
Nouakchott
Mali
Tombouctou
Niger
Faya-Largea
Port Sudan
Red Sea
Eritrea
Asmara
Khartoum
Dakar
Senegal
The Gambia
Banjul
Bissau
Guinea Bissau
Guinea
Conakry
Bamako
Burkina Faso
Ouagadougou
Niamey
Lake Chad
Chad
N'Djamen
El Fashir
Sudan
Djibouti
Addis Ababa
Ethiopia
Freetown
Sierra Leone
Monrovia
Liberia
Côte d'Ivoire
Abidjan
Ghana
Accra
Togo
Lomé
Benin
Porto-Novo
Lago
Nigeria
Kan
Abuj
Central African Republic
Bangu
Cameroon
Yaoundé
Gulf of Guinea
Malabo
Equatorial Guinea
Juba
Somalia
Mogadishu
Uganda
Kenya
Kampala
Nairobi
São Tomé
São Tomé & Príncipe
Annobón
Equator
Libreville
Gabon
Republic of the Congo
Kisangani
Democratic Republic of the Congo
Rwanda
Kigali
Lake Victoria
Bujumbura
Burundi
Mombasa
Brazzaville
Kinshasa
Cabinda
Kalemi
Lake Tanganyika
Tanzania
Dar es Salaam
Ascension
Luanda
Comoros
Mtwara
Moroni
Lake Malawi
Lubumbashi
Pemba
Antsirañana
Lobito
Angola
Zambia
Lilongwe
Lusaka
Malawi
St. Helena
Harare
Zimbabwe
Mozambique
Madagascar
Antananarivo
Beira
Bulawayo
Namibia
Windhoek
Botswana
Mozambique Channel
Tropic of Capricorn
Gaborone
Mbabane
Pretoria
Maputo
Toliara
Lüderitz
Johannesburg
Swaziland
Lesotho
Maseru
Durban
South Africa
Indian Ocean
Cape Town
Port Elizabeth

EUROPE
National Capital
Secondary City
International Border
400 km
300 mi
Greenland
Greenland Sea
Arctic Circle
Iceland
Reykjavik
Jan Mayen Island
Norwegian Sea
Faroe Islands
Shetland Islands
Orkney Islands
Hebrides
North Sea
Irish Sea
Ireland
Dublin
Belfast
Glasgow
Edinburgh
Aberdeen
Newcastle
Liverpool
United Kingdom
Cardiff
London
English Channel
Bay of Biscay
Norway
Bergen
Oslo
Trondheim
Narvik
Hammerfest
Sweden
Umeå
Gävle
Stockholm
Göteborg
Malmö
Finland
Oulu
Tampere
Helsinki
Gulf of Bothnia
Gulf of Finland
Russia
White Sea
Arkhangel'sk
St. Petersburg
Moscow
Tallinn
Estonia
Riga
Latvia
Lithuania
Vilnius
Minsk
Belarus
Gotland
Öland
Baltic Sea
Bornholm
Skagerrak
Denmark
Copenhagen
Rostock
Hamburg
Gdańsk
Vistula
Warsaw
Poznań
Poland
Berlin
Netherlands
Amsterdam
Germany
Rhine
Elbe
Odra
Brussels
Belgium
Bonn
Frankfurt
Luxembourg
Le Havre
Paris
Seine
Strasbourg
Munich
Danube
Prague
Czech Republic
Kraków
Slovakia
Vienna
Bratislava
Austria
Budapest
Hungary
L'viv
Ukraine
Kyyiv (Kiev)
Dnepr
Moldova
Chisinău
Odessa
Romania
Bucharest
Constanta
Black Sea
Nantes
Loire
France
Bordeaux
Marseille
Monaco
Bern
Switzerland
Liechtenstein
Slovenia
Ljubljana
Zagreb
Croatia
Bosnia & Herzegovina
Sarajevo
Belgrade
Yugoslavia
Varna
Bulgaria
Sofia
Venice
Po
Milan
San Marino
Italy
Adriatic Sea
Podgorica
Skopje
Macedonia
Istanbul
Tiranë
Albania
Thessaloníki
Greece
Aegean Sea
Turkey
Rome
Naples
Corsica
Sardinia
Tyrrhenian Sea
Ionian Sea
Pátrai
Athens
Crete
Sicily
Malta
Valletta
Tunis
Tunisia
Algiers
Algeria
Mediterranean Sea
Balearic Islands
Barcelona
Valencia
Andorra
Spain
Madrid
Bilbao
Porto
Portugal
Lisbon
Málaga
Gibraltar (U.K.)
Strait of Gibraltar
Morocco
10°W
0°
10°E
20°
30°
40°
70°
50°
40°

LATIN AMERICA AND THE CARIBBEAN
National Capital
Secondary City
International Border
0 800 km
0 600 mi
United States of America
Gulf of Mexico
North Atlantic Ocean
Caribbean Sea
Pacific Ocean
South Atlantic Ocean
Mexico City
Mexico
Havana
Cuba
Haiti
Dominican Republic
Puerto Rico
Jamaica
Kingston
Port-au-Prince
Santo Domingo
Lesser Antilles
Belize
Honduras
Guatemala
Tegucigalpa
San Salvador
El Salvador
Nicaragua
Managua
San Jose
Costa Rica
Panama
Caracas
San Cristóbal
Venezuela
Georgetown
Guyana
Paramaribo
Suriname
Cayenne
French Guiana
Bogotá
Cali
Colombia
Boa Vista
Mitu
Macapá
Quito
Ecuador
Guayaquil
Iquitos
Manaus
Fortaleza
Peru
Recife
Lima
Brazil
Salvador
Trinidad
Arequipa
La Paz
Lake Titicaca
Bolivia
Brasília
Sucre
Paraguay
Chile
Rio de Janeiro
Asunción
Florianópolis
Salto
Rosario
Uruguay
Santiago
Buenos Aires
Montevideo
Concepción
Argentina
Bahía Blanca
Puerto Montt
Comodoro Rivadavia
Stanley
Falkland Islands
Punta Arenas
Ushuaia
Magdalena R.
Negro R.
Japura R.
Amazon R.
Tapajós R.
Xingu R.
Tocantins R.
Ucayali R.
Paraná R.
90°
75°
60°
45°
30°
15°
0°

UNITED STATES OF AMERICA
National Capital
State Capital
Secondary City
State Border
International Border
0 800 km
0 500 mi
Canada
Mexico
Atlantic Ocean
Bahamas
Cuba
Havana
U.S.Naval Base
Ottawa
Montreal
Quebec
St. John
Toronto
Sudbury
Winnipeg
Regina
Vancouver
Tijuana
Monterrey
Tampico
Lake Winnipeg
Lake Superior
Lake Michigan
Lake Huron
Lake Ontario
Lake Erie
Missouri
Mississippi
Ohio
Colorado
Snake
Columbia
Rio Grande
WASHINGTON
Olympia
OREGON
Salem
CALIFORNIA
Sacramento
NEVADA
Carson City
IDAHO
Boise
MONTANA
Helena
UTAH
Salt Lake City
ARIZONA
Phoenix
WYOMING
Cheyenne
COLORADO
Denver
NEW MEXICO
Santa Fe
NORTH DAKOTA
Bismarck
SOUTH DAKOTA
Pierre
NEBRASKA
Lincoln
KANSAS
Topeka
OKLAHOMA
Oklahoma City
TEXAS
Austin
MINNESOTA
St. Paul
IOWA
Des Moines
MISSOURI
Jefferson City
ARKANSAS
Little Rock
LOUISIANA
Baton Rouge
WISCONSIN
Madison
ILLINOIS
Springfield
MISSISSIPPI
Jackson
MICHIGAN
Lansing
INDIANA
Indianapolis
KENTUCKY
Frankfort
TENNESSEE
Nashville
ALABAMA
Montgomery
OHIO
Columbus
GEORGIA
Atlanta
FLORIDA
Tallahassee
SOUTH CAROLINA
Columbia
NORTH CAROLINA
Raleigh
VIRGINIA
Richmond
WEST VIRGINIA
Charleston
PENNSYLVANIA
Harrisburg
Washington D.C.
MD.
Annapolis
DELAWARE
Dover
NEW JERSEY
Trenton
NEW YORK
Albany
CONN.
Hartford
R.I.
Providence
MASS.
Boston
VT.
Montpelier
N.H.
Concord
MAINE
Augusta
ALASKA
ARCTIC CIRCLE
Yukon
Tanana
Fairbanks
Anchorage
Homer
Juneau
Canada
Bering Sea
Aleutian Islands
Pacific Ocean
0 300 mi
HAWAII
Honolulu
Pacific Ocean
0 100 mi
45°
30°
20°
120°
105°
90°
75°
60°
140°
150°
160°
170°
155°
E 180° W

Select Bibliography

Abajian, James de T. *Blacks and their Contributions to the American West* (1974).

Abbott, D. "Revolution by Other Means," interview with Angela Davis, *New Statesman* 114 (14 August 1987): 16-17.

Abbott, Elizabeth. *Haiti: The Duvaliers and their Legacy* (1988).

Abdul-Jabbar, Kareem, with Mignon McCarthy. *Kareem* (1990).

Abenon, Lucien. *Petite histoire de la Guadeloupe* (1992).

Abernathy, Ralph David. *And the Walls Came Tumbling Down: An Autobiography* (1989).

Abrahams, R. G. *The Nyamwezi Today: A Tanzanian People in the 1970s* (1981).

Abrahams, Roger D. *Deep Down in the Jungle: Negro Narrative Folklore from the Streets of Philadelphia* (1964).

——. *Singing the Master: The Emergence of African American Culture in the Plantation South* (1992).

——. *Talking Black* (1976).

Abrahams, Roger, and John Szwed. *After Africa: Extracts from British Travel Accounts and Journals of the Seventeenth, Eighteenth and Nineteenth Centuries Concerning the Slaves, their Manners, and Customs in the British West Indies* (1983).

Abreu, Mauricio de. *Evolução urbana do Rio de Janeiro* (1987).

Abu-Lughod, Janet L. *Rabat: Urban Apartheid in Morocco* (1980).

Abu-Jamal, Mumia. *Live from Death Row* (1996).

Achebe, Chinua. *Hopes and Impediments: Selected Essays* (1988).

Adair, Gene. *George Washington Carver* (1989).

Adams, Barbara Eleanor. *John Henrik Clarke: The Early Years* (1992).

Adams, W. M., A. S. Goudie, and A. R. Orme. *The Physical Geography of Africa* (1996).

Adélaïde-Merlande, Jacques. *Delgrès, ou, la Guadeloupe en 1802* (1986).

Adenaike, Carolyn Keyes, and Jan Vansina, eds. *In Pursuit of History: Fieldwork in Africa* (1996).

Adjaye, Joseph K., and Adrianne R. Andrews, eds. *Language, Rhythm, and Sound: Black Popular Cultures into the Twenty-First Century* (1997).

"African-American Quilts: Tracing the Aesthetic Principles." *Clarion* 14, no. 2 (Spring 1989): 44-54.

"African Symbolism in Afro-American Quilts." *African Arts* 20, no 1 (1986).

"Afro-Brazilian Religion." Special issue of *Callaloo* 18, no. 4 (1995).

Agronsky, Jonathan. *Marion Barry: The Politics of Race* (1991).

Agorsah, E. Kofi, ed. *Maroon Heritage: Archaeological, Ethnographic, and Historical Perspectives* (1994).

Aguirre Beltrán, Gonzalo. *El negro esclavo en Nuevo España: La formación colonial, la medicina popular y otros ensayos* (1994).

Alagoa, E. J., F. N. Anozie, and Nwanna Nzewunwa, eds. *The Early History of the Niger Delta* (1988).

Albertson, Chris. *Bessie* (1972).

Algoo-Baksh, Stella. *Austin C. Clarke: A Biography* (1994).

Alie, Joe A. D. *A New History of Sierra Leone* (1990).

Allan D. Austin, ed. *African Muslims in Antebellum America: A Source Book* (1984).

Allen, Philip M. *Madagascar: Conflicts of Authority in the Great Island* (1995).

Alpert, Hollis. *The Life and Times of Porgy and Bess* (1990).

Alvarez Nazario, Manuel. *El elemento afronegroide en el español de Puerto Rico: Contribución al estudio del negro en América* (1974).

al-Amin, Jamil. *See* Brown, H. Rap.

The Amistad Case: The Most Celebrated Slave Mutiny of the Nineteenth Century, 2 vols. (1968).

Ammons, Kevin. *Good Girl, Bad Girl: An Insider's Biography of Whitney Houston* (1996).

Anderson, Jean Bradley. *Durham County: A History of Durham County, North Carolina* (1990).

Anderson, Jervis. *A. Philip Randolph: A Biographical Portrait* (1973).

——. *Bayard Rustin: Troubles I've Seen: A Biography* (1997).

Anderson, Marian. *My Lord, What a Morning: An Autobiography* (1956).

Andrews, Benny. *Between the Lines: 70 Drawings and 7 Essays* (1978).

ANDREWS, GEORGE REID. *Blacks and Whites in São Paulo, Brazil, 1888-1988* (1991).

ANDREWS, WILLIAM L. *The Literary Career of Charles W. Chesnutt* (1980).

——. *Sisters of the Spirit: Three Black Women's Autobiographies of the Nineteenth Century* (1986).

——. *To Tell a Free Story: The First Century of Afro-American Autobiography, 1760-1865* (1986).

ANDREWS, WILLIAM L., AND HENRY LOUIS GATES, JR., EDS. *The Civitas Anthology of African American Slave Narratives* (1999).

ANGELL, ROGER. *The Summer Game* (1972).

ANJOS, JOANA DOS. *Ouvindo historias na senzala* (1987).

ANTOINE, JACQUES CARMELEAU. *Jean Price-Mars and Haiti* (1981).

ANTOINE, RÉGIS. *La littérature franco-antillaise* (1992).

APARICIO, RAÚL. *Sondeos* (1983).

APPIAH, KWAME ANTHONY. *In My Father's House: Africa in the Philosophy of Culture* (1992).

APTHEKER, HERBERT. *American Negro Slave Revolts.* 6th ed. (1993).

——. *Nat Turner's Slave Rebellion* (1966).

——. *"One Continual Cry": David Walker's Appeal to the Colored Citizens of the World 1829-30: Its Setting and its Meaning, Together with the Full Text of the Third, and Last, Edition of the Appeal* (1965).

ARAUJO, EMANOEL, ED. *The Afro-Brazilian Touch: The Meaning of its Artistic and Historic Contribution.* Translated by Eric Drysdale (1988).

ARMAS, JOSÉ R. DE, AND CHARLES W. STEELE. *Cuban Consciousness in Literature: 1923-1974* (1978).

ARNOLD, A. JAMES. *Modernism and Negritude: The Poetry and Poetics of Aimé Césaire* (1981).

ASANTE, MOLEFI KETE. *The Afrocentric Idea* (1987).

——. *Afrocentricity* (1988).

——. *Kemet, Afrocentricity, and Knowledge* (1990).

ASCHENBRENNER, JOYCE. *Katherine Dunham: Reflections on the Social and Political Aspects of Afro-American Dance* (1981).

ASCHERSON, NEAL. *The King Incorporated: Leopold II in the Age of Trusts* (1963).

ASHBAUGH, CAROLYN. *Lucy Parsons: American Revolutionary* (1976).

ASHE, ARTHUR. *Days of Grace: A Memoir* (1993).

——. *A Hard Road to Glory: A History of the African-American Athlete* (1988).

AUSTERLITZ, PAUL. *Merengue: Dominican Music and Dominican Identity* (1997).

AUSTIN-BROOS, DIANE. *Jamaica Genesis: Religion and the Politics of Moral Orders* (1997).

AVERILL, GAGE. *A Day for the Hunter, A Day for the Prey* (1997).

AXELSON, ERIC. *Portuguese in South-East Africa, 1488-1600* (1973).

AYISI, RUTH A. "The Urban Influx." *Africa Report* (November-December 1989).

AYOT, H. OKELLO. *Historical Texts of the Lake Region of East Africa* (1977).

AZEVEDO, CELIA MARIA MARINHO DE. *Onda negra, medo branco: O negro no imaginario das elites, seculo XIX* (1987).

AZEVEDO, MARIO. *Historical Dictionary of Mozambique* (1991).

AZEVEDO, THALES. *Les élites de couleur dans une ville brésilienne* (1953).

BABB, VALERIE MELISSA. *Ernest Gaines* (1991).

BACELAR, JEFERSON AFONSO. *Etnicidade: Ser negro em Salvador* (1989).

BAER, HANS A., AND MERRIL SINGER. *African-American Religion in the Twentieth Century: Varieties of Protest and Accommodation* (1992).

BAILEY, PEARL. *Between You and Me: A Heartfelt Memoir of Learning, Loving, and Living* (1989).

——. *The Raw Pearl* (1968).

BAKER, DAVID. *The Jazz Style of Cannonball Adderley* (1980).

BAKER, HOUSTON A., JR. *Blues, Ideology, and Afro-American Literature: A Vernacular Theory* (1980).

BALANDIER, GEORGES. *Daily Life in the Kingdom of the Kongo: From the Sixteenth to the Eighteenth Century* (1968).

BALL, WENDY, AND TONY MARTIN. *Rare Afro-Americana: A Reconstruction of the Adger Library* (1981).

BALUTANSKY, KATHLEEN M., AND MARIE-AGNÈS SOURIEAU, EDS. *Caribbean Creolization: Reflections on the Cultural Dynamics of Language, Literature, and Identity* (1998).

BANDEIRA, MARIA DE LOURDES. *Territorio negro em espaço branco: Estudo antropológico de Vila Bela* (1988).

BAQUERO, GASTON. *Indios, blancos y negros en el caldero de América* (1991).

BARAKA, AMIRI. *The Autobiography of LeRoi Jones* (1984).

BARBOSA DEL ROSARIO, PILAR. *La obra de José Celso Barbosa.* 4 vols. (1937).

BARBOUR, DOUGLAS. *Worlds Out of Words: The SF Novels of Samuel R . Delaney* (1979).

BARFIELD, THOMAS J. *The Nomadic Alternative* (1993).

BARKER, DANNY. *A Life in Jazz* (1986).

BARNES, STEVE. "The Crusade of Dr. Elders." *New York Times Magazine* (October 15, 1989): 38-41.

BARNETT, ALAN W. *Community Murals: The People's Art* (1984).

BARNWELL, P. J., AND AUGUSTE TOUSSAINT. *A Short History of Mauritius* (1949).

BARRADAS, EFRAÍN. *Para leer en puertorriqueño: Acercamiento a la obra de Luis Rafael Sánchez* (1981).

BARREDA-TOMÁS, PEDRO M. *The Black Protagonist in the Cuban Novel* (1979).

BARROW, STEVE, AND PETER DALTON. *Reggae: The Rough Guide* (1997).

BASH, BARBARA. *Tree of Life: The World of the African Baobab* (1994).

BASIE, WILLIAM JAMES ("COUNT"), AS TOLD TO ALBERT MURRAY. *Good Morning Blues: The Autobiography of Count Basie* (1985).

"A Basis for Interracial Cooperation and Development in the South: A Statement by Southern Negroes." In *Southern Conference on Race Relations* (1942).

Bass, Charlotta Spears. *Forty Years: Memoirs from the Pages of a Newspaper* (1960).

Bastide, Roger, and Florestan Fernandes. *Relações raciais entre negros e brancos em São Paulo* (1955).

Baum, Robert M. *Shrines of the Slave Trade: Diola Religion and Society in Precolonial Senegambia* (1999).

Beach, David. *The Shona and their Neighbours* (1994).

Bearden, Jim, and Linda Butler. *Shadd: The Life and Times of Mary Shadd Cary* (1977).

Bearden, Romare, and Harry Henderson. *A History of African-American Artists from 1792 to the Present* (1993).

Beauford Delaney: A Retrospective (1978).

Bechkey, Allen. *Adventuring in East Africa* (1990).

Beckford, Ruth. *Katherine Dunham: A Biography* (1979).

Beckles, Hilary. *Afro-Caribbean Women and Resistance to Slavery in Barbados* (1988).

——. *Black Masculinity in Caribbean Slavery* (1996).

——. *Black Rebellion in Barbados: The Struggle against Slavery, 1627-1838* (1984).

——. *A History of Barbados: Amerindian Settlement to Nation-State* (1990).

——. *Natural Rebels: A Social History of Enslaved Black Women in Barbados* (1989).

——. *White Servitude and Black Slavery in Barbados, 1627-1715* (1989).

——, ed. *Inside Slavery: Process and Legacy in the Caribbean Experience* (1996).

Beckwourth, James P. *The Life and Adventures of James P. Beckwourth, Mountaineer, Scout and Pioneer and Chief of the Crow Nation of Indians.* Edited by T. D. Bonner (1965).

Bedini, Silvio. *The Life of Benjamin Banneker* (1971-1972).

Beeth, Howard, and Cary Wintz. *Black Dixie: Afro-Texan History and Culture in Houston* (1992).

Bego, Mark. *Aretha Franklin* (1989).

Behague, Gerard H., ed. *Music and Black Ethnicity: The Caribbean and South America* (1994).

Bell, Bernard. *The Afro-American Novel and its Tradition* (1987).

Bellegarde-Smith, Patrick. *In the Shadow of Powers: Dantès Bellegarde in Haitian Social Thought* (1985).

——. *Race, Class and Ideology: Haitian Ideologies for Underdevelopment 1806-1934* (1985).

Bell, Howard H. *Search for a Place: Black Separatism and Africa, 1860* (1969).

Bell, Malcom. *The Turkey Shoot: Tracking the Attica Cover-Up* (1985).

Benberry, Cuesta. *Always There: The African-American Presence in American Quilts* (1992).

Bennett, Lerone, Jr. *Before the Mayflower* (1962; revised ed., 1987).

Bennett, Norman. *Arab versus European: Diplomacy and War in Nineteenth-Century East Central Africa* (1986).

Bennett, Robert. "Black Episcopalians: A History from the Colonial Period to the Present." *Historical Magazine of the Protestant Episcopal Church* 43, no. 3 (September 1974): 231-45.

Benoît, Edouard. "Biguine: Popular Music of Guadeloupe, 1940-1960." In *Zouk: World Music in the West Indies,* ed. Jocelyne Guilbault (1993).

Benston, Kimberly, ed. *Speaking for You: The Vision of Ralph Ellison* (1995).

Bently, George R. *A History of the Freedmen's Bureau* (1955).

Berendt, Joachim. *The Jazz Book: From Rag-time to Fusion and Beyond.* 6th ed. (1992).

Berger, Phil. *Blood Season: Tyson and the World of Boxing* (1989).

Berlin, Ira. *Slaves without Masters: The Free Negro in the Antebellum South* (1974).

Bernabé, Jean, Patrick Chamoiseau, and Raphaël Confiant. *Eloge de la créolité / In Praise of Creoleness.* Translated by M. B. Taleb-Khyar (1993).

Bernd, Zila. *Introdução à literatura negra* (1988).

Bernsen, Charles. "The Fords of Memphis: A Family Saga." *Memphis Commercial Appeal* (July 1-4, 1990).

Bernstein, Iver. *The New York City Draft Riots: Their Significance for American Society and Politics in the Age of the Civil War* (1990).

Berrou, Raphael. *Histoire de la littérature haïtienne illustrée par les textes.* 3 vols. (1975-1977).

Berry, Chuck. *Chuck Berry: The Autobiography* (1987).

Berry, James. *Chain of Days* (1985).

Berry, Jason. *Amazing Grace: With Charles Evers in Mississippi* (1973).

Bertley, Leo W. *Canada and its People of African Descent* (1977).

Beyan, Amos J. *The American Colonization Society and the Creation of the Liberian State: A Historical Perspective, 1822-1900* (1991).

Bianco, David. *Heat Wave: The Motown Fact Book* (1988).

Bibb, Henry Walton. *Narrative of the Life and Adventures of Henry Bibb, an American Slave* (1849).

Bickerton, Derek. "The Language Bioprogram Hypothesis." *Behavioral and Brain Sciences* 7 (1984): 173-221.

Biebuyck, Daniel P., Susan Kelliher, and Linda McRae. *African Ethnonyms: Index to Art-Producing Peoples of Africa* (1996).

Birmingham, David, and Richard Gray. *Pre-Colonial African trade: Essays on Trade in Central and Eastern Africa before 1900* (1966).

Bishop, Jack. *Ralph Ellison* (1988).

"Black Clout in Clinton Administration." *Ebony* 48, no. 7 (May 1993): 60.

Black, Patti Carr, ed. *Something to Keep You Warm* (1981).

"Blacks in U.S. Foreign Policy: A Retrospective." *TransAfrica Forum* (1987).

"Black Women: Sisters Without Leaders." *Economist* (November 1, 1997): 31.

Blakely, Allison. *Blacks in the Dutch World: The Evolution of Racial Imagery in a Modern Society* (1993).

——. *Russia and the Negro: Blacks in Russian History and Thought* (1986).

Blanchard, Peter. *Slavery and Abolition in Early Republican Peru* (1992).

Bland, Randall W. *Private Pressure on Public Law: The Legal Career of Justice Thurgood Marshall* (1973).

Blancq, C. C. *Sonny Rollins: The Journey of a Jazzman* (1983).

Blassingame, John W., ed. *The Frederick Douglass Papers.* 4 vols. (1979-1991).

——. *The Slave Community: Plantation Life in the Antebellum South.* Rev. ed. (1979).

Blassingame, John W., and Mae G. Henderson, eds. *Antislavery Newspapers and Periodicals.* 5 vols. (1980).

Blesh, Rudi, and Harriet Janis. *They All Played Ragtime.* 4th ed. (1971).

Blier, Suzanne Preston. *African Vodun: Art, Psychology, and Power* (1995).

——. *The Royal Arts of Africa: The Majesty of Form* (1998).

Blight, David W. *Frederick Douglass' Civil War: Keeping Faith in Jubilee* (1989).

Bloch, Herman D. *The Circle of Discrimination: An Economic and Social Study of the Black Man in New York* (1969).

Bloch, M. *Placing the Dead: Tombs, Ancestral Villages, and Kinship Organization in Madagascar* (1971).

Bly, Nellie. *Oprah! Up Close and Down Home* (1993).

Boff, C., and L. Boff. *Introducing Liberation Theology* (1987).

Boggs, Victor. *Salsiology: Afro-Cuban Music and the Evolution of Salsa in New York City* (1992).

Bogle, Donald. *Blacks in American Films and Television: An Illustrated Encyclopedia* (1988).

——. *Dorothy Dandridge: A Biography* (1997).

——. *Toms, Coons, Mulattoes, Mammies, and Bucks : An Interpretive History of Blacks in American Films.* 3d ed. (1994).

Bolcom, William, and Robert Kimball. *Reminiscing with Sissle and Blake* (1973).

Bolland, O. Nigel. *A History of Belize: Nation in the Making* (1997).

Bolouvi, Lebene Philippe. *Nouveau dictionnaire étymologique afro-brésilien: Afro-brasilérismes d'origine Ewe-Fon et Yoruba* (1994).

Bongie, Chris. "The (Un)Exploded Volcano: Creolization and Intertextuality in the Novels of Daniel Maximin." *Callaloo* 17, no. 2 (Summer 1994): 627-42.

Bonilla, Adrián. "Conversación con Adalberto Ortiz." *Cultura: Revista del Banco Central del Ecuador* 6, no. 16 (1983): 189-96.

Boodoo, Ken I., ed. *Eric Williams: The Man and the Leader* (1986).

Boone, Graeme M., and James Clyde Sellman, "The Jook Joint: An Historical Note." Liner essay to *Quincy Jones, Q's Jook Joint* (1995).

Borders, William H. *Seven Minutes at the Mike in the Deep South* (1943).

Boskin, Joseph. *Sambo: The Rise and Demise of an American Jester* (1986).

Bourdillon, M. F. C. *The Shona Peoples: An Ethnography of the Contemporary Shona, with Special Reference to their Religion* (1987).

Bourne, M. "Bob, Baroque, the Blues: Modern Jazz Quartet." *Down Beat* 59, no.1 (January 1992): 24.

Bovill, E. W. *The Niger Explored* (1968).

Bowman, J. Wilson. *America's Black Colleges: The Comprehensive Guide to Historically and Predominantly Black 4-Year Colleges and Universities* (1992).

Bowman, Larry W. *Mauritius: Democracy and Development in the Indian Ocean* (1991).

Bowser, Frederick P. *The African Slave in Colonial Peru 1524-1650* (1974).

Boxer, C.R. *The Dutch in Brazil, 1624-1654* (1957).

——. *The Portuguese Seaborne Empire, 1415-1825* (1969).

Boyer, Jay. *Ishmael Reed* (1993).

Boykin, Keith. *One More River to Cross: Black & Gay in America* (1996).

Bozongwana, Wallace. *Ndebele Religion and Customs* (1983).

Bracey, John H., Jr., et al, eds. *Black Nationalism in America* (1970).

Bragg, George Freeman. *The History of the Afro-American Group of the Episcopal Church* (1968).

——. *The Story of the First Blacks: Absalom Jones* (1929).

Branch, Taylor. *Parting the Waters: America in the King Years: 1954-63* (1988).

Brandström, Per. "Who is Sukuma and Who is a Nyamwezi?: Ethnic Identity in West-Central Tanzania." In *Working Papers in African Studies* no. 27 (1986).

Brand-Williams, Oralandar. "Million Woman March: Black Women Vow to 'Act on Power,'" *Detroit News* (October 26, 1997).

Brathwaite, Edward Kamau. *Roots* (1993).

Brausch, Georges. *Belgian Administration in the Congo* (1961).

Brigham, David R. "Bridging Identities (The Works of Dox Thrash, Afro-American Artist)." *Smithsonian Studies in American Art* (Spring 1990).

Brisbane, Robert. *Black Activism: Racial Revolution in the U.S., 1954-70* (1974).

Bristow, Peggy, et al. *We're Rooted Here and They Can't Pull Us Up: Essays in African Canadian Women's History* (1994)

Britt, Stan. *Dexter Gordon: A Musical Biography* (1989).

Brode, Douglas. *Denzel Washington: His Films and Career* (1996).

Broderick, Francis L., August Meier, and Elliott M. Rudwick. *Black Protest Thought in the Twentieth Century.* 2d ed. (1971).

Brookshaw, David. *Race and Color in Brazilian Literature* (1986).

Broughton, Simon, Mark Ellingham, David Muddyman, and Richard Trillo. *World Music: The Rough Guide* (1994).

Broussard, Albert S. *Black San Francisco: The Struggle for Racial Equality in the West, 1900-1954* (1993).

Brown, A. Theodore, and Lyle W. Dorsett. *K.C.: A History of Kansas City, Missouri* (1978).

Brown, Claude. *Manchild in the Promised Land* (1965).

Brown, Diana DeGroat. *Umbanda: Religion and Politics in Urban Brazil* (1994).

Brown, Geoff, and Chris Charlesworth. *A Complete Guide to the Music of Prince* (1995).

Brown-Guillory, Elizabeth. "Alice Childress: A Pioneering Spirit," *Sage: A Scholarly Journal on Black Women* (Spring 1987): 104-9.

Brown, Henry. *Narrative of Henry Box Brown Who Escaped from Slavery Enclosed in a Box Three Feet Long and Two Wide, with Remarks upon the Remedy for Slavery* (1849).

Brown, H. Rap. *Die, Nigger, Die!* (1969).

Browning, Barbara. *Samba: Resistance in Motion* (1995).

Brown, Mervyn. *A History of Madagascar* (1995).

——. *Madagascar Rediscovered: A History from Early Times to Independence* (1978).

Brown, Ruth, with Andrew Yule. *Miss Rhythm: The Autobiography of Ruth Brown, Rhythm & Blues Legend* (1996).

Brown, Scott E. *James P. Johnson: A Case of Mistaken Identity* (1986).

Brown, Sterling A. "A Century of Negro Portraiture in American Literature." In *Black Insights: Significant Literature by Black Americans—1760 to the Present*, ed. Nick Aaron Ford (1971): 66-78.

Brown, Tony. *Black Lies, White Lies: The Truth According to Tony Brown* (1995).

Bruce, Dickson D., Jr. *Black American Writing from the Nadir: The Evolution of a Literary Tradition, 1877-1915* (1989).

Brundage, W. Fitzhugh, ed. *Under Sentence of Death: Lynching in the South* (1997).

Bryan, T. J. "The Published Poems of Helene Johnson," *Langston Hughes Review* 6 (Fall 1987): 11-21.

Bryant-Jackson, Paul, and Lois More Overbeck, eds. *Intersecting Boundaries: The Theater of Adrienne Kennedy* (1992).

Buckler, Helen. *Daniel Hale Williams: Negro Surgeon* (1968)

Buckley, Gail Lumet. *The Hornes: An American Family* (1986).

Bueno, Eva Paulino. *Resisting Boundaries: The Subject of Naturalism in Brazil* (1995).

Bugner, Ladislas, ed. *The Image of the Black in Western Art* (1976-).

Buhle, Paul. *C. L. R. James: The Artist as Revolutionary* (1988).

Bulhan, Hussein Abdilahi. *Frantz Fanon and the Psychology of Oppression* (1985).

Bullock, Penelope L. *The Afro-American Periodical Press, 1838-1909* (1981).

Buni, Andrew. *The Negro in Virginia Politics, 1902-1965* (1967).

Bunwaree, Sheila S. *Mauritian Education in a Global Economy* (1994).

Burckhardt, Titus. *Fez, City of Islam* (1992).

Burdick, John. *Blessed Anastacia: Women, Race and Popular Christianity in Brazil* (1998).

——. "The Spirit of Rebel and Docile Slaves: The Black Verson of Brazilian Umbanda." *Journal of Latin American Lore* 18 (1992): 163-87.

Burns, Khephra. "A Love Supreme: Ruby Dee & Ossie Davis." *Essence* (December 1994).

Busby, Mark. *Ralph Ellison* (1991).

Bush, Martin. *The Photographs of Gordon Parks* (1983).

Bustin, Edouard. *Lunda under Belgian Rule: The Politics of Ethnicity* (1975).

Butler, Addie Louise Joyner. *The Distinctive Black College: Talladega, Tuskegee and Morehouse* (1977).

Caamaño de Fernàndez, Vicenta. *El negro en la poesìa dominicana* (1989).

Cabrera Gomez, Jorge. *El Baobab* (1996).

Cabrera, Lydia. *Anaforuana: Ritual y simbolos de la iniciacion en la sociedad secreta* (1975).

——. *Anago: Vocabulario lucumi (el yoruba que se habla in Cuba)* (1957).

——. *Los animales en el folklore y la magia de Cuba* (1988).

——. *Cuentos negros de Cuba* (1972).

——. *Francisco y Francisca: Chascarrillos de negros viejos* (1976).

——. *La lengua sagrada de los nanigos* (1988).

——. *El monte, Igbo, Finda, Ewe orisha, vitti nfinda: (Notas sobre las religiones, la magia, las supersticiones y el folklore de los negros criollos y del pueblo de Cuba)* (1968).

——. *La Regla Kimbisa del Santo Cristo del Buen Viaje* (1977).

——. *Reglas de Congo: Palo Monte Mayombe* (1979).

——. *La sociedad secreta Abakua, narrada por viejos adeptos* (1959).

——. *Yemaya y Ochun (1974).*

Cagin, Seth, and Philip Dray. *We Are Not Afraid: The Story of Goodman, Schwerner, and Chaney and the Civil Rights Campaign for Mississippi* (1988).

Calcagno, Francisco. *Poetas de color* (1878).

Callaghan, Barry, ed. *The Austin Clarke Reader* (1996).

Calvo Ospina, Hernando. *Salsa! Havana Heat, Bronx Beat.* (1992).

Camargo, Oswaldo. *A razão da chama: Antologia de poetas negros brasileiros* (1986).

Caminha, Adolfo. *The Black Man and the Cabin Boy.* Translated by E. Lacey (1982).

Campbell, Elaine, and Pierrette Frickey, eds. *The Whistling Bird: Women Writers of the Caribbean* (1998).

Campbell, James T. *Songs of Zion: The African Methodist Episcopal Church in the United States and South Africa* (1995).

Campbell, Stanley W. *The Slave Catchers: Enforcement of the Fugitive Slave Law, 1850-1860* (1968).

Cannon, Steve, Tom Finkelpearl, and Kellie Jones. *David Hammons: Rousing the Rubble* (1991).

Cantarow, Ellen, and Susan Gushee O'Malley. "Ella Baker: Organizing for Civil Rights." In *Moving the Mountain: Women Working for Social Change* (1980).

Capeci, Dominic J., Jr. *The Harlem Riot of 1943* (1977).

Carby, Hazel V. *Reconstructing Womanhood: The Emergence of the Afro-American Woman Novelist* (1987).

Carew, Jan. *Fulcrums of Change: Origins of Racism in the Americas* (1988).

Carmichael, Stokely, and Charles V. Hamilton. *Black Power: The Politics of Liberation in America* (1992).

Carmichael, Trevor, ed. *Barbados: 30 Years of Independence* (1996).

Carner, Gary, ed. *The Miles Davis Companion: Four Decades of Commentary* (1996).

Caro, Timothy M. *Cheetahs of the Serengeti Plains: Group Living in an Asocial Species* (1994).

Carpenter, Bill. "Big Mama Thornton: 200 Pounds of Bugaloo." *Living Bluesletter* no. 106 (November 1992).

Carpentier, Alejo. *La música en Cuba* (1946).

——. *Obras Completas* (1983-).

Carr, Ian. *Miles Davis: A Biography* (1982).

Carroll, Patrick James. *Blacks in Colonial Veracruz: Race, Ethnicity, and Regional Development* (1991).

Carson, Clayborne. *In Struggle: SNCC and the Black Awakening of the 1960s* (1981).

Carvalho, José Jorge de, and Rita Laura Segato. *Shango Cult in Recife, Brazil* (1992).

Cash, Earl A. *John A. Williams: The Evolution of a Black Writer* (1975).

Cassidy, Frederic G. *Jamaica Talk: Three Hundred Years of the English Language in Jamaica* (1961).

Castellanos, Jorge, and Isabel Castellanos. *Cultura afrocubana: Las religiones y las lenguas*. 3 vols. (1992).

Castleman, Craig. *Getting Up: Subway Graffiti in New York* (1984).

Castor, Elie, and Raymond Tarcy. *Félix Eboué: Gouverneur et philosophe* (1984).

Castro, Ruy. *Chega de saudade : A história e as histórias da bossa nova* (1990).

Cayetano, Sebastian. *Garifuna History: Language and Culture of Belize, Central America and the Caribbean*. Rev. ed. (1997).

Centro de Articulação de Populações Marginalizadas. *The Killing of Children and Adolescents in Brazil*. Translated by Joscelyne Vera Mello (1991).

Chafets, Ze'ev. *Devil's Night and Other True Tales of Detroit* (1990).

Challenor, Herchelle Sullivan. "The Influence of Black Americans on U.S. Foreign Policy Toward Africa." *Ethnicity and U. S. Foreign Policy* (1981).

Chamberlain, Hope. "Against the System: Shirley Chisholm." In *A Minority of Members: Women in the U. S. Congress* (1973).

Chamberlain, Wilt. *The View From Above* (1991).

Chambers, Jack. *Milestones*. 2 vols. (1983-1985).

Chambers, Veronica. "The Essence of Essence." *New York Times Magazine* (June 18, 1995).

Chanan, Michael. *The Cuban Image: Cinema and the Cultural Politics in Cuba* (1985).

Chanock, Martin. *Law, Custom and Social Order: The Colonial Experience in Malawi and Zambia* (1985).

Chapelle, Tony. "Vanessa's Comeback." *The Black Collegian* (February 1995).

Chappell, Kevin. "The 3 Mayors Who Made it Happen." *Ebony* (July 1996): 66.

Charte de la révolution socialiste Malagasy Tous Azimuts (1975).

Charters, Samuel B. *The Bluesmen*. 2 vols. (1967-1977).

Cheney, Anne. *Lorraine Hansberry* (1984).

Chigwedere, Aeneas S. *Birth of Bantu Africa* (1982).

Chilton, John. *The Song of the Hawk: The Life and Recordings of Coleman Hawkins* (1990).

Chisholm, Shirley. *Unbought and Unbossed* (1970).

Chrisman, Robert, and Robert L. Allen, eds. *Court of Appeal: The Black Community Speaks Out on the Racial and Sexual Politics of Clarence Thomas vs. Anita Hill* (1992).

Christian, Barbara. *Black Feminist Criticism: Perspectives on Black Women Writers* (1985).

——. *Black Women Novelists: The Development of a Tradition, 1892-1976* (1980).

Christie, Iain. *Samora Machel: A Biography* (1989).

Christopher, A. J. *The Atlas of Apartheid* (1994).

Chucho Garcia, Jesus. *La diaspora de los Kongos en las Americas y los Caribes* (1995).

Church, Annette, and Roberta Church. *The Robert Churches of Memphis* (1975).

Clancy-Smith, Julia A. *Rebel and Saint: Muslim Notables, Populist Protest, Colonial Encounters: Algeria and Tunisia, 1800-1904* (1994).

Clairmont, Donald, and Dennis Magill. *Africville: The Life and Death of a Canadian Black Community*. Rev. ed. (1987).

Clarke, A.M. *Sir Constantine and Sir Hugh Wooding* (1982).

Clarke, Duncan. *The Art of African Textiles* (1997).

Clarke, George Elliott, ed. *Fire on the Water: An Anthology of Black Nova Scotian Writing*. 2 vols. (1991-1992).

Clark, Sebastian. *Jah Music* (1980).

Clark, Septima. *Echo in My Soul* (1962).

Clark, Septima, with Cynthia Stokes Brown. *Ready from Within: Septima Clark and the Civil Rights Movement* (1986).

Clash, M.G. *Benjamin Banneker, Astronomer and Scientist* (1971).

"Claude Albert Barnett." *New York Times* (August 3, 1967).

Clayton, Anthony. *The Zanzibar Revolution and its Aftermath* (1981).

Clay, William L. *Just Permanent Interests: Black Americans in Congress, 1870-1991* (1992).

Cobb, W. Montague. *The First Negro Medical Society: A History of the Medico-Chirurgical Society of the District of Columbia* (1939).

Cohen, David W., and Jack P. Greene. *Neither Slave nor Free: The Freedman of African Descent in the Slaves Societies of the New World Baltimore* (1972).

Cohen, Ronald, Goran Hyden, and Winston P. Nagan, eds. *Human Rights and Governance in Africa* (1993).

Cole, Herbert. *Christophe: King of Haiti* (1967).

Coleman, James W. *Blackness and Modernism: The Literary Career of John Edgar Wideman* (1989).

Coleman, Lucretia Newman. *Poor Ben: A Story of Real Life* (1890).

Coli, Suzanne M. *George Washington Carver* (1990).

Collier, Aldore. "Maxine Waters: Telling It Like It Is in L.A." *Ebony* (October 1992).

——. "Pointer Sisters Shed Old Look, Old Clothes to Reach New Heights." *Jet* (April 15, 1985): 58.

——. "Whatever Happened to the Nicholas Brothers?" *Ebony* (May 1985).

Collier, James Lincoln. *The Making of Jazz: A Comprehensive History* (1978).

Collins, L. M. *One Hundred Years of Fisk University Presidents* (1989).

Collins, R. *New Orleans Jazz: A Revised History: The Development of American Jazz from the Origin to the Big Bands* (1996).

Collins, Robert O. *The Waters of the Nile: Hydropolitics and the Jonglei Canal, 1900-1988* (1990).

Condé, Maryse, and Madelaine Cottenet-Hage, eds. *Penser la Créolité* (1995).

Cone, James H. *Martin and Malcolm and America: A Dream or a Nightmare* (1991).

Congress, Rick. *The Afro-Nicaraguans: The Revolution and Autonomy* (1987).

Conniff, Michael L. *Black Labor on a White Canal: Panama 1904-1981* (1985).

Conniff, Michael L., and Thomas J. Davis. *Africans in the Americas: The History of the Black Diaspora* (1994).

Connolly, Harold X. *A Ghetto Grows in Brooklyn* (1977).

Conrad, Robert Edgar, ed. *Children of God's Fire: A Documentary of Black Slavery.* (1983).

——. *The Destruction of Brazilian Slavery, 1850-1888* (1993).

Consentino, Donald J., ed. *Sacred Arts of Haitian Vodou* (1995).

Cook, David, and Michael Okenimpke. *Ngugi wa Thiong'o: An Exploration of His Writing,* 2d ed. (1997).

Coolidge, Christopher R. "Reply: Tolerance of Racial, Ethnic Jokes." In *ADS-L Digest* 22 (February 22, 1997).

Cooper, Gary. "Stage Coach Mary: Gun Toting Montanan Delivered U.S. Mail," as told to Marc Crawford in *Ebony* 14 (October 1959): 97-100.

Cooper, Ralph, with Steve Dougherty. *Amateur Night at the Apollo: Ralph Cooper Presents Five Decades of Great Entertainment* (1990).

Cooper, Wayne F. *Claude McKay: A Rebel Sojourner in the Harlem Renaissance: A Biography* (1987).

Coppin, Fanny Jackson. *Reminiscences of School Life, and Hints on Teaching* (1913).

Cordoba, Amir Smith, ed. *Vision socio-cultural del negro en Colombia* (1986).

Cornelius, Wayne A. "Spain: The Uneasy Transition from Labor Exporter to Labor Importer." In *Controlling Immigration: A Global Perspective,* ed. Wayne A. Cornelius, Philip L. Martin, and James F. Hollifield (1994).

Cornish, Dudley T. *The Sable Arm: Negro Troops in the Union Army, 1861-1865* (1956).

Cortés López, José Luis. *La esclavitud negra en la España peninsular del siglo XVI* (1989).

Cortner, Richard C. *A Mob Intent on Death: The NAACP and the Arkansas Riot Cases* (1988).

Cory, Hans H. *Sukuma Law and Custom* (1953).

Couffon, Claude. *René Depestre* (1986).

Counter, S. Allen. *North Pole Legacy: Black, White and Eskimo* (1991).

Courtney-Clarke, Margaret. *Ndebele: The Art of an African Tribe* (1986).

Covell, Maureen. *Historical Dictionary of Madagascar* (1995).

——. *Madagascar: Politics, Economics, and Society* (1987).

Cox, Harvey. *Fire From Heaven: The Rise of Pentecostal Spirituality and the Reshaping of Religion in the Twenty-First Century* (1995).

Craft, William, and Ellen Craft. *Running a Thousand Miles for Freedom; or, The Escape of William and Ellen Craft from Slavery* (1860; reprint ed., 1991.).

Creel, Margaret Washington. *A Peculiar People: Slave Religion and Community-Culture Among the Gullahs* (1988).

Crespo R., Alberto. *Esclavos negros en Bolivia* (1977).

Cripps, Thomas. *Making Movies Black: The Hollywood Message Movie from World War II to the Civil Rights Era* (1993).

——. *Slow Fade to Black: The Negro in American Film 1900-1942* (1977).

Crouchett, Lorraine J. *Delilah Leontium Beasley: Oakland's Crusading Journalist* (1990).

Cruise O'Brien, Donald. *The Mourides of Senegal: The Political and Economic Organization of an Islamic Brotherhood* (1971).

Cudjoe, Selwyn, ed. *Caribbean Women Writers: Essays from the First International Conference.* (1990).

——. *Resistance and Caribbean Literature* (1980).

Cullen, Countee. *My Soul's High Song: The Collected Writings of Countee Cullen, Voice of the Harlem Renaissance.* Edited by Gerald Early (1991).

Cullman, Brian. "Cheb Khaled and the Politics of Pleasure." *Antaeus* (Fall 1993).

Cuney-Hare, Maud. *Norris Wright Cuney: A Tribune of the Black People* (1995).

Cunningham, Carol, and Joel Berger. *Horn of Darkness: Rhinos on the Edge* (1997).

Curry, Leonard P. *The Free Black in Urban America, 1800-1850: The Shadow of the Dream* (1981).

Curtin, Philip D. *The Atlantic Slave Trade: A Census* (1969).

Cutler, John Henry. *Ed Brooke: Biography of a Senator* (1972).

Dabney, Virginius. *Richmond: The Story of a City* (1976).

Dabney, Wendell P. *Cincinnati's Colored Citizens: Historical, Sociological, and Biographical* (1926).

Dabydeen, David. "On Not Being Milton: Nigger Talk in England Today." In *The Routledge Reader in Caribbean Literature,* ed. Alison Donnell and Sarah Lawson Welsh (1996).

Dahl, Otto C. *Malgache et Maanjan: Une comparaison linguistigue* (1951).

DALFIUME, RICHARD M. *Desegregation of the U. S. Armed Forces: Fighting on Two Fronts, 1939-1953* (1969).

DALTON, NARINE. "The Maestros: Black Symphony Conductors are Making a Name for Themselves." *Ebony* (February 1989): 54-57.

DALY, VERE T. *A Short History of the Guyanese People* (1975).

DANCE, DARYL C. *Shuckin' and Jivin': Folklore from Contemporary Black Americans* (1978).

DANIELS, DOUGLAS HENRY. "Lester Young: Master of Jive." *American Music* 3 (Fall 1985): 313-28.

——. *Pioneer Urbanites: A Social and Cultural History of Black San Francisco* (1980).

DANIEL, WALTER C. *Afro-American Journals, 1827-1980: A Reference Book* (1982).

DASH, J. MICHAEL. *Edouard Glissant* (1995).

DASH, JULIE. *Daughters of the Dust: The Making of an African American Woman's Film* (1992).

DATES, JANNETTE L., AND WILLIAM BARLOW, EDS. *Split Image: African Americans in the Mass Media* (1990).

DATT, NORMAN. *Cheddi B. Jagan: The Legend* (1997).

DAVENPORT, M. MARGUERITE. *Azalia: The Life of Madame E. Azalia Hackley* (1947).

DAVIES, CAROL BOYCE, AND ELAINE SAVORY FIDO, EDS. *Out of the Kumbla: Caribbean Women and Literature* (1990).

DAVIS, ARTHUR P. *From the Dark Tower: Afro-American Writers, 1900-1960* (1974).

DAVIS, BENJAMIN O., JR. *Benjamin O. Davis, Jr., American: An Autobiography* (1991).

DAVIS, CHARLES T., AND HENRY LOUIS GATES, JR., EDS. *The Slave's Narrative* (1985).

DAVIS, CYPRIAN. *The History of Black Catholics in the United States* (1990).

DAVIS, DARIÉN J., ED. *Slavery and Beyond: The African Impact on Latin America and the Caribbean.*

DAVIS, DAVID BRION. *The Problem of Slavery in the Age of Revolution, 1770-1823.* 2d ed. (1998).

——. *The Problem of Slavery in Western Culture* (1966).

——. *Slavery and Human Progress* (1984).

DAVIS, H. P. *Black Democracy: The Story of Haiti* (1967).

DAVIS, JAMES J. "Entrevista con el dominicano Norberto James Rawlings." *Afro-Hispanic Review* (May 1987):16-18.

DAVIS, MICHAEL D. *Black American Women in Olympic Track and Field: A Complete Illustrated Reference* (1992).

DAVIS, RUSSELL. *Black Americans in Cleveland from George Peake to Carl B. Stokes, 1796-1969* (1972).

DAVIS, STEPHEN, AND PETER SIMON. *Reggae International* (1983).

DAVIS, THOMAS J. *A Rumor of Revolt: The "Great Negro Plot" in Colonial New York* (1985).

DAWKINS, WAYNE. *Black Journalists: The NABJ Story* (1993).

DAYAN, JOAN. "France Reads Haiti: An Interview with René Depestre." *Yale French Studies* 83: 136-153.

DEERR, NOEL. *The History of Sugar.* 2 vols. (1949-1950).

DELERIS, FERDINAND. *Ratsiraka: Socialisme et misère à Madagascar* (1986).

DELIUS, PETER. *A Lion Amongst the Cattle: Reconstruction and Resistance in the Northern Transvaal* (1996).

DEREN, MAYA. *Divine Horsemen: The Living Gods of Haiti* (1953).

DERRICOTTE, TOI. *The Black Notebooks: An Interior Journey* (1997).

DESMANGLES, LESLIE G. *The Faces of the Gods: Vodou and Roman Catholicism in Haiti* (1992).

DE WILDE, LAURENT. *Monk* (1997).

DIAWARA, MANTHIA. *African Cinema: Politics and Culture* (1992).

——, ED. *Black American Cinema* (1993).

DÍAZ AYALA, CRISTOBAL. *Música cubana del areyto a la nueva trova* (1981).

DIEDHIOUS, DJIB. "Paulin S. Vieyra a rencontré le cinéma africain." *Le Soleil* (December 27, 1982).

DILLON, MERTON L. *Benjamin Lundy and the Struggle for Negro Freedom* (1966).

DIOP, CHEIKH ANTA. *Nations nègres et culture: De l'antiquité Nègre-Egyptienne aux problèmes culturels de l'Afrique noire d'aujourd'hui.* 2d ed. (1965).

DITTMER, JOHN. *Black Georgia in the Progressive Era, 1900-1920* (1977).

——. *Local People: The Struggle for Civil Rights in Mississippi* (1995).

DIXON, WILLIE. *I Am the Blues: The Willie Dixon Story* (1989).

DOMÍNGUEZ ORTIZ, ANTONIO. "La esclavitud en Castilla durante la Edad Moderna." In *Estudios de historia social de España*, ed. Carmelo Viñas y Mey. 2 vols. (1952). Vol. II, pp. 369-427.

DONOVAN, NANCY, AND LAST, JILL. *Ethiopian Costumes* (1980).

DORSEY, CAROLYN. "Despite Poor Health: Olivia Davidson Washington's Story." *Sage: A Scholarly Journal on Black Women* (Fall 1985).

DORSEY, DAVID. "The Art of Mari Evans." In *Black Women Writers* (1984): 170-89.

DORSEY, THOMAS ANDREW. *Say Amen, Somebody* (1983).

DORSINVILLE, ROGER. *Jacques Roumain* (1981).

D'ORSO, MICHAEL. *Like Judgement Day: The Ruin and Redemption of a Town Called Rosewood* (1996).

DOUGLASS, WILLIAM. *Annals of the First African Church in the United States of America, Now Styled the African Episcopal Church of St. Thomas, Philadelphia* (1862).

DRAGO, EDMUND L. *Initiative, Paternalism, and Race Relations: Charleston's Avery Normal Institute* (1990).

DRAKE, SANDRA E. *Wilson Harris and the Modern Tradition: A New Architecture of the World* (1986).

DRAKE, ST. CLAIR. *Black Folk Here and There: An Essay in History and Anthropology.* 2 vols. (1987-1990).

DRAKE, ST. CLAIR, AND HORACE R. CAYTON. *Black Metropolis: A Study of Negro Life in a Northern City* (1945).

DRESCHER, SEYMOUR, AND STANLEY L. ENGERMAN, EDS. *A Historical Guide to World Slavery* (1998).

DRISKELL, DAVID. *Hidden Heritage: Afro-American Art, 1800-1950* (1985).

"Dr. Lillie M. Jackson: Lifelong Freedom Fighter." *Crisis* 82 (1975).

Drot, Jean-Marie. *Peintures et dessins, vaudou d'Haïti* (1986).

Duany, Jorge, and Peter Manuel. "Popular Music in Puerto Rico: Toward an Anthropology of Salsa." *Latin American Music Review* 5 (1984): 186-216.

Dubofsky, Melvyn, and Stephen Burwood, eds. *Women and Minorities During the Great Depression* (1990).

Du Bois, Shirley Graham. *His Day is Marching On: A Memoir of W. E. B. Du Bois.* (1971).

Du Bois, W. E. B. *Black Reconstruction in America* (1935).

——. *The Souls of Black Folk: Essays and Sketches* (1903).

Duffy, Susan. "Shirley Chisholm." *American Orators of the Twentieth Century,* ed. Barnard K. Duffy and Halford R. Ryan (1987).

Duggan, William, and John Civille. *Tanzania and Nyerere: A Study of Ujamaa and Nationhood* (1976).

Duggy, John. *Prince: An Illustrated Biography* (1995).

Dummett, Clifton O., and Lois Doyle Dummett. *Afro-Americans in Dentistry: Sequence and Consequence of Events* (1978).

Dunbar-Nelson, Alice. *Give Us This Day: The Diary of Alice Dunbar-Nelson,* ed. Gloria T. Hull (1984).

Duncan, John. "Negro Composers of Opera." *Negro History Bulletin* (January 1966): 79-80, 93.

Duncan, Quince. *Cultura negra y teologia* (1986).

——. *Dos estudios sobre diaspora negra y racismo* (1987).

Dundes, Alan, ed. *Mother Wit From the Laughing Barrel: Readings in the Interpretation of Afro-American Folklore* (1990).

Dunn, Richard S. *Sugar and Slaves: The Rise of the Planter Class in the English West Indies, 1624-1713* (1972).

Dunning, James Morse. *The Harvard School of Dental Medicine: Phase Two in the Development of a University Dental School* (1981).

Durham, Philip, and Everett L. Jones. *The Negro Cowboys* (1965).

Durix, Jean-Pierre. *Dictionary of Literary Biography* (1992).

Duster, Alfreda, ed. *Crusade for Justice: The Autobiography of Ida B. Wells* (1970).

Duster, Troy. *Backdoor to Eugenics* (1990).

Dynes, Wayne R., ed. *Encyclopedia of Homosexuality* (1990).

Edelman, Marian Wright. *The Measure of Our Success: A Letter to My Children and Yours* (1992).

Edreria de Caballero, Angelina. *Antonio Medina, el don Pepe de la raza de color* (1938).

Egerton, Douglas R. *Gabriel's Rebellion: The Virginia Slave Conspiracies of 1800 and 1802* (1993).

Ehret, Christopher, and M. Posnansky. *The Archaeological and Linguistic Reconstruction of African History* (1982).

Ehrlich, Walter. *They Have No Rights: Dred Scott's Struggle for Freedom* (1979).

Elders, Joycelyn. *Joycelyn Elders, M.D.: From Sharecropper's Daughter to Surgeon General of the United States of America* (1997).

Elias, João. *A impotencia da raca negra não tira da fraqueza dos brancos.* 2d ed. (1994).

Ellison, Ralph. *Romare Bearden: Paintings and Projections* (1968).

——. *Shadow and Act* (1964).

Ellsworth, Scott. *Death in A Promised Land: The Tulsa Race Riot of 1921* (1982).

Ely, Melvin Patrick. *The Adventures of Amos 'n' Andy: A Social History of an American Phenomenon* (1991).

Emecheta, Buchi. *Head Above Water* (1986).

Emery, Lynne Fauley. *Black Dance in the United States from 1619 to 1970* (1980).

Enciclopédia da música Brasileira: Erudita, folclórica, popular (1977).

Equiano, Olaudah. *Equiano's Travels: His Autobiography: The Interesting Narrative of the Life of Olaudah Equiano or Gustavus Vassa, the African.* Edited by Paul Edwards (1967).

Erlewine, Michael, et al, eds. *All Music Guide to Jazz: The Experts' Guide to the Best Jazz Recordings* (1996).

Erlmann, Veit, and Deborah Pacini Hernandez, eds. "The Politics and Aesthetics of Transnational Musics." Special issue of *World of Music* 35, no. 2 (1993).

Erstein, Hap. "Richards, Wilson Team Up on Prize Dramas." *Washington Times* (November 8, 1991): E1.

Estes, J. Worth. *The Medical Skills of Ancient Egypt* (1993).

Estupiñan Tello, Julio. *Historia de Esmeraldas* (1977).

Evans, Mari. *Black Women Writers (1950-1980): A Critical Evaluation* (1984).

Evers, Charles, and Grace Haskell, eds. *Evers* (1971).

Ewers, Traute. *The Origin of American Black English: Be-Forms in the HOODOO Texts* (1996).

Fabre, Michel. "The Last Quest of Horace Cayton." *Black World* 19 (May 1970): 41-45.

——. *The Unfinished Quest of Richard Wright.* Translated by Isabel Barzun (1973).

Fairclough, Adam. *To Redeem the Soul of America: The Southern Christian Leadership Conference and Martin Luther King, Jr* (1987).

Fair, Laura. "Dressing Up: Clothing, Class and Gender in Post-Abolition Zanzibar." *Journal of African History* 39 (1998): 63-94.

Fanon, Frantz. *Black Skin, White Masks.* Translation of *Peau noire, masques blancs* by Charles Lam Markmann (1967).

Farmer, James. *Lay Bare the Heart: An Autobiography of the Civil Rights Movement* (1985).

Farnsworth, Robert M. *Melvin B. Tolson, 1898-1966: Plain Talk and Poetic Prophecy* (1984).

Farrison, William Edward. *William Wells Brown: Author and Reformer* (1969).

Fehrenbacher, Don E. *The Dred Scott Case: Its Significance in American Law and Politics* (1978).

Feldman, Linda. "Norton Biography." *Christian Science Monitor* (March 31, 1992): 14:1

FERGUSON, JAMES. *Papa Doc, Baby Doc: Haiti and the Duvaliers* (1987).

FERGUSON, MOIRA. *Jamaica Kincaid: Where the Land Meets the Body* (1994).

FERGUSON, SHEILA. *Soul Food: Classic Cuisine from the Deep South* (1989).

FERRIS, WILLIAM, ED. *Afro-American Folk Arts and Crafts* (1983).

FERRIS, WILLIAM, AND BRENDA MCCALLUM, EDS. *Local Color: A Sense of Place in Folk Art* (1982).

FIELDS, BARBARA JEANNE. *Slavery and Freedom on the Middle Ground: Maryland During the Nineteenth Century* (1985).

FILHO, LUÍS VIANA. *O Negro na Bahia* (1988).

FITZGERALD, MARY ANN, HENRY J. DREWAL, AND MAYO OKEDIJI. "Transformation through Cloth: An Egungun Costume of the Yoruba." *African Arts* 28 (1995).

FLASCH, JOY. *Melvin B. Tolson* (1972).

FLEISCHER, NAT. *Black Dynamite: The Story of the Negro in the Prize Ring from 1782 to 1838* (1938).

FLETCHER, MARVIN E. *America's First Black General: Benjamin O. Davis, Sr.* (1989).

——. *The Black Soldier and Officer in the United States Army, 1891-1917* (1974).

FLETCHER, TOM. *One-Hundred Years of the Negro in Show Business* (1984).

FLINT, J. E. "Zanzibar 1890-1950." In *History of East Africa,* ed. Vincent Harlow and E. M. Chilver (1965).

FLOMENHAFT, ELEANOR, ED. *Faith Ringgold: A 25-Year Survey* (1990).

FLOYD, SAMUEL, ED. *Black Music in the Harlem Renaissance* (1990).

FLYNN, JOYCE, AND JOYCE OCCOMY STRICKLIN, EDS. *Frye Street and Environs: The Collected Works of Marita Bonner Occomy* (1987).

FOGEL, ROBERT W. *Without Consent or Contract: The Rise and Fall of American Slavery* (1989).

FOLEY, ALBERT S. *Bishop Healy: Beloved Outcaste* (1954).

FONER, ERIC. *Reconstruction: America's Unfinished Revolution, 1863-1877* (1988).

FONER, PHILIP. *Antonio Maceo* (1977).

——. *Black Panthers Speak* (1995).

——. *Blacks in the American Revolution* (1976).

——. *Organized Labor & the Black Worker 1619-1973* (1974).

——. *The Spanish-Cuban-American War and the Birth of U.S. Imperialism.* Vol. I (1962).

FONER, PHILIP, ED. *Black Socialist Preacher: The Teachings of Reverend George Washington Woodbey and his Disciple Reverend George W. Slater, Jr.* (1983).

FONER, PHILIP, AND RONALD LEWIS. *Black Workers: A Documentary History from Colonial Times to the Present* (1989).

FOOTE, JULIA. *A Brand Plucked From the Fire.* In *Spiritual Narratives,* ed. Henry Louis Gates Jr. (1988).

FORBES, JACK D. *Africans and Native Americans: The Language of Race and the Evolution of Red-Black Peoples* (1988).

FORBES, STEVEN. *The Baymen of Belize and How They Wrested British Honduras from the Spaniards* (1997).

FORMAN, JAMES. *The Making of Black Revolutionaries* (1985).

FOSTER, FRANCES SMITH. "Adding Color and Contour to Early American Self-Portraitures: Autobiographical Writings of Afro-American Women." In *Conjuring: Black Women, Fiction and Literary Tradition,* ed. Marjorie Pryse and Hortense J. Spillers (1985).

——. *Written By Herself: Literary Production by African American Women, 1746-1892* (1993).

FOUCHET, MAX POL. *Wifredo Lam.* (1976).

FOWLER, VIRGINIA. *Nikki Giovanni* (1992).

FRADY, MARSHALL. *Jesse: The Life and Pilgrimage of Jesse Jackson* (1996).

FRANCO, JOSÉ LUCIANO. *Apuntes para una historia de su vida.* 3 vols. (1951-1957).

FRANCO SILVA, ALFONSO. *La esclavitud en Sevilla y su tierra a fines de la edad media* (1979).

FRANKLIN, CHARLES LIONEL. *The Negro Labor Unionist of New York: Problems and Conditions among Negroes in the Labor Unions in Manhattan with Special Reference to the N.R.A. and Post-N.R.A. Situations* (1936).

FRANKLIN, JOHN HOPE. *The Free Negro in North Carolina, 1790-1863* (1943).

——. *From Slavery to Freedom: A History of Negro Americans* (1988).

——. *Race and History: Selected Essays, 1938-1988* (1989).

FRANKLIN, JOHN HOPE, AND AUGUST MEIER, EDS. *Black Leaders of the Twentieth Century* (1982).

FRANKLIN, VINCENT P. *The Education of Black Philadelphia: The Social and Educational History of a Minority Community, 1900-1950* (1979).

FRANK, RUSTY E. *Tap! The Greatest Tap Dance Stars and Their Stories, 1900-1955* (1990).

FRAZIER, E. FRANKLIN. "Durham: Capital of the Black Middle Class." In ALAIN LOCKE, ED. *The New Negro* (1925).

——. *On Race Relations: Selected Writings,* ed. Gilbert Edwards (1968).

FRAZIER, JOE, AND PHIL BERGER. *Smokin' Joe: The Autobiography of a Heavyweight Champion of the World, Smokin' Joe Frazier* (1996).

FREEDBERG, SYDNEY P. *Brother Love: Money, Murder, and a Messiah* (1994).

FRENCH, WILLIAM P. "Black Studies: Getting Started in a Specialty." *AB: Bookmans Weekly* (February 22, 1988): 737-41.

FREYRE, GILBERTO. *O Brasil em face das Africas negras e mesticas* (1963).

——. *The Masters and the Slaves: A Study in the Development of Brazilian Civilization.* Translation of *Casa grande e senzala* by Samuel Putnam (1986).

FREY, SYLVIA. *Water From the Rock: Black Resistance in a Revolutionary Age* (1991).

FRIEDEMANN, NINA S. DE. *Lengua y sociedad en el palenque de San Basilio* (1983).

——. *Ma ngombe: Guerreros y ganaderos en Palenque.* 2d ed. (1987).

——. *La saga del Negro: Presencia africana en Colombia* (1993).

FRIEDEMANN, NINA S. DE., AND ALFREDO VANIN, COMP. *Entre la tierra y el cielo: Magia y leyendas del Chocó* (1995).

FRIEDMAN, LAWRENCE J. *Gregarious Saints: Self and Community in American Abolitionism, 1830-1870* (1982).

FINLAYSON, IAIN. *Tangier: City of the Dream* (1992).

FOX, STEPHEN R. *The Guardian of Boston: William Monroe Trotter* (1970).

FOX, TED. *Showtime at the Apollo* (1983).

FRY, GLADYS-MARIE. *Stitched from the Soul: Slave Quilts from the Ante-Bellum South* (1990).

FREDERICKS, MARCEL, JOHN LENNON ET AL. *Society and Health in Guyana* (1986).

FUNARI, PEDRO PAUL A., MARTIN HALL, AND SIAN JONES, EDS. *Historical Archaeology: Back from the Edge* (1999).

FUNDAÇÃO CASA DE RUI BARBOSA. *O Abolicionista Rui Barbosa* (1988).

FUNKE, LEWIS. *The Curtain Rises: The Story of Ossie Davis* (1971).

FYFE, CHRISTOPHER. *Sierra Leone Inheritance* (1964).

GABBARD, KRIN, ED. *Representing Jazz* (1995).

GABRIEL, TESHOME. *Third Cinema in the Third World: The Aestheties of Liberation* (1982).

GADELII, KARL ERLAND. *Lesser Antillean French Creole and Universal Grammar* (1997).

GAINES, ERNEST. *Porch Talk with Ernest Gaines: Conversations on the Writer's Craft*, ed. Marcia Gaudet and Carl Wooton (1990).

GALEANO, EDUARDO. *Football in Sun and Shadow* (1998).

GAMBINO, FERRUCCIO. "The Transgression of a Laborer: Malcolm X in the Wilderness of America." *Radical History Review* 55 (Winter 1993): 7-31.

GAMBLE, DAVID. *The Wolof of Senegambia, Together with Notes on the Lebu and the Serer* (1967).

GANDY, SAMUEL LUCIUS. *Human Possibilities: A Vernon Johns Reader (1977).*

GANGITANO, LIA AND STEVEN NELSON, EDS. *New Histories* (1996).

GARCÍA, HORACIO, ED. *Pensamiento revolucionario cubano.* Vol. I (1971).

GARCÍA, JUAN. *Cuentos y décimas afroesmeraldeñas* (1988).

GARCÍA, JUAN MANUEL. *La Masacre de Palma Sola (Partidos, lucha política y el asesino del general): 1961-1963* (1986).

GARFINKEL, HERBERT. *When Negroes March: The March on Washington Movement in the Organizational Politics for FEPC* (1959).

GARROW, DAVID J. *Bearing the Cross: Martin Luther King, Jr., and the Southern Christian Leadership Conference* (1986).

——. *Protest at Selma: Martin Luther King, Jr., and the Voting Rights Act of 1965* (1978).

GASPAR, DAVID BARRY. *Bondmen and Rebels: A Study of Master-Slave Relations in Antigua* (1985).

GATES, HENRY LOUIS, JR. *Black Literature and Literary Theory* (1984).

——. *Colored People: A Memoir* (1994).

——. *Figures in Black: Words, Signs, and the Racial Self* (1992).

——. *Loose Canons: Notes on the Culture Wars* (1992).

——. *The Signifying Monkey: Towards A Theory of Afro-American Literary Criticism* (1988).

——. *Thirteen Ways of Looking at a Black Man* (1997): 155-79.

GATES, HENRY LOUIS, JR., ED. *Bearing Witness: Selections from African-American Autobiography in the Twentieth Century* (1991).

——, ED. *The Classic Slave Narratives* (1987).

——, ED. *Collected Black Women's Narratives: The Schomburg Library of Nineteenth-Century Black Women Writers* (1988).

GATES, HENRY LOUIS, JR., AND KWAME ANTHONY APPIAH, EDS. *Richard Wright: Critical Perspectives Past and Present* (1993).

——.*Gloria Naylor: Critical Perspectives Past and Present* (1993).

GATES, HENRY LOUIS, JR., AND NELLIE Y. MCKAY. *The Norton Anthology of African American Literature* (1997).

GATES, HENRY LOUIS, JR., AND CORNEL WEST. *The Future of the Race* (1996).

GATEWOOD, WILLARD B. *Aristocrats of Color: The Black Elite, 1880-1920* (1990).

GAVINS, RAYMOND. *The Perils and Prospects of Southern Black Leadership: Gordon Blaine Hancock, 1884-1970* (1977).

GAYLE, ADDISON, JR., ED. *The Black Aesthetic* (1971).

GAY, ROBERT. *Popular Organization and Democracy in Rio de Janeiro: A Tale of Two Favelas* (1994).

GEARY, LYNETTE G. "Jules Bledsoe: The Original 'Ol' Man River'." *Black Perspective in Music* 17, nos. 1, 2 (1989): 27-54.

GEIS, IMMANUEL. *The Pan-African Movement: A History of Pan-Africanism in America, Europe and Africa* (1974).

GELPÍ, JUAN. *Literatura y paternalismo en Puerto Rico* (1993).

GENOVESE, EUGENE D. *Roll, Jordan, Roll: The World the Slaves Made* (1974).

GEORGE, CAROL V. R. *Segregated Sabbaths: Richard Allen and the Emergence of Independent Black Churches 1760-1840* (1972).

GEORGE, NELSON. *Elevating the Game: Black Men and Basketball* (1992).

——. *Where Did Our Love Go?: The Rise and Fall of the Motown Sound* (1985).

GEORGE, NELSON, ET AL., EDS. *Fresh: Hip Hop Don't Stop* (1985).

GERBER, JANE S. *Jewish Society in Fez, 1450-1700: Studies in Communal and Economic Life* (1980).

GIBB, H.A.R. *Ibn Battuta: Travels in Asia and Africa 1325-1354* (1929).

GIBSON, BOB. *From Ghetto to Glory: The Story of Bob Gibson* (1968).

GIDE, ANDRÉ. *Travels in the Congo* (1962).

GILARD, JACQUES. "Crescencio ou don Toba? Fausses questions et vraies réponses sur le 'vallenato'." *Cahiers du monde hispanique et luso-brésilien, Caravelle* 48 (1987): 69-80.

GILL, GERALD R. "Win or Lose–We Win." In *The Afro-American Woman: Struggles and Images* (1978).

GILLESPIE, JOHN BIRKS ("DIZZY"), WITH AL FRASER. *Dizzy To BE, or Not . . . to BOP: The Autobiography of Dizzy Gillespie* (1979).

GILROY, PAUL. *There Ain't No Black in the Union Jack: The Cultural Politics of Race and Nation* (1991).

GIRAL, SERGIO. "Cuban Cinema and the Afro-Cuban Heritage." Interview by Julianne Burton and Gary Crowdus. In *Film and Politics in the Third World,* ed. John D. H. Downing (1987).

——. "Sergio Giral on Filmmaking in Cuba." Interview by Ana M. López and Nicholas Peter Humy. In *Cinemas of the Black Diaspora: Diversity, Dependence, and Oppositionality,* ed. Michael T. Martin (1995).

GIRVAN, NORMAN. *Poverty, Empowerment and Social Development in the Caribbean* (1997).

GLAZIER, STEPHEN D. *Marchin' the Pilgrims Home* (1983).

——, ED. *Perspectives on Pentecostalism: Case Studies from the Caribbean and Latin America* (1980).

GLEN, JOHN M. *Highlander: No Ordinary School, 1932-1962* (1988).

GLISSANT, EDOUARD. *Caribbean Discourse: Selected Essays.* Translated by J. Michael Dash (1989).

GOGGIN, JACQUELINE ANNE. *Carter G. Woodson: A Life in Black History* (1993).

GOINGS, KENNETH W. *Mammy and Uncle Mose: Black Collectibles and American Stereotyping* (1994).

GOLDBERG, JANE. "A Hoofer's Homage: John Bubbles." *Village Voice* (December 4, 1978).

GONZÁLEZ BUENO, GLADYS. "An Initiation Ceremony in Regla de Palo." In *AfroCuba: An Anthology of Cuban Writing on Race, Politics and Culture,* ed. Pedro Pérez Sarduy and Jean Stubbs (1993).

GONZÁLEZ DÍAZ, ANTONIO MANUEL. *La esclavitud en Ayamonte durante el Antiguo Régimen (siglos XVI, XVII y XVIII)* (1997).

GONZÁLEZ ECHEVARRIA, ROBERTO. *Myth and Archive: A Theory of Latin American Narrative* (1998).

——. *The Pride of Havana: The History of Cuban Baseball* (1999).

GONZALEZ-PEREZ, ARMANDO. *Acercamiento a la literatura afrocubana: Ensayos de interpretación* (1994).

GONZALEZ-WHIPPLER, MIGENE. *The Santeria Experience: A Journey into the Miraculous.* Rev. and exp. ed. (1992).

GOODHEART, LAWRENCE B., ET AL., EDS. *Slavery in American Society.* 3d ed. (1993).

GOODWIN, ANDREW, AND JOE GORE. "World Beat and the Cultural Imperialism Debate." *Socialist Review* 20, no. 3 (1990): 63-80.

GORDON, ALLAN M. *Echoes of Our Past: The Narrative Artistry of Palmer C. Hayden* (1988).

GORDON, P. "The New Right, Race, and Education." *Race and Class* 29, no. 3 (Winter 1987).

GOSNELL, HAROLD F. *Negro Politicians: The Rise of Negro Politics in Chicago* (1967).

GOURAIGE, GHISLAIN. *Histoire de la littérature haïtienne (de l'indépendance à nos jours)* (1982).

GOUREVITCH, PHILIP. *We Wish to Inform You that Tomorrow We Will Be Killed with Our Families: Stories from Rwanda* (1998).

GOURSE, LESLIE. *Unforgettable: The Life and Mystique of Nat King Cole* (1991).

GRANDA GUTIERREZ, GERMAN DE. *Estudios sobre un area dialectal hispanoamericana de poblacion negra: Las tierras bajas occidentales de Colombia* (1977)

GRANT, JOANNE. *Fundi: The Story of Ella Baker* (1981).

GRATIANT, GILBERT. *Fables créoles et autres récits* (1995).

GRAY, JOHN MILNER. *History of Zanzibar from the Middle Ages to 1856* (1962).

GRAY, RICHARD. *Black Christians and White Missionaries* (1990).

GREENBAUM, SUSAN. "A Comparison Between African-American and Euro-American Mutual Aid Societies in 19th-Century America." *Journal of Ethnic Studies* 19 (Fall 1991): 95-119.

GREENBERG, CHERYL LYNN. *"Or Does It Explode?": Black Harlem in the Great Depression* (1991).

GREENBERG, JACK. *Crusaders in the Courts: How a Dedicated Band of Lawyers Fought for the Civil Rights Revolution* (1994).

GREENE, LORENZO JOHNSTON. *Selling Black History for Carter G. Woodson* (1996).

GREENE, LORENZO JOHNSTON, GARY R. KREMER, AND ANTONIO F. HOLLAND. *Missouri's Black Heritage* (1993).

GREEN, TIM. *The Dark Side of the Game: The Unauthorized NFL Playbook* (1996).

GREGORY, DICK, WITH MARK LANE. *Up From Nigger* (1976).

GREGORY, DICK, WITH MARTIN LIPSYTE. *Nigger: An Autobiography* (1964).

GREGORY, PAYNE J., AND SCOTT C. RATZAN. *Tom Bradley: The Impossible Dream: A Biography* (1986).

GRENARD, STEVE. *Handbook of Alligators and Crocodiles* (1991).

GRIAULE, MARCEL. *Conversations with Ogotemmeli: An Introduction to Dogon Religious Ideas* (1965).

GROIA, PHILIP. *They All Sang on the Corner: A Second Look at New York City's Rhythm and Blues Vocal Groups* (1983).

GROSSMAN, JAMES R. *Land of Hope: Chicago, Black Southerners and the Great Migration* (1989).

GRUDIN, EVA UNGAR. *Stitching Memories: African-American Story Quilts* (1990).

GUERRERO, EDWARD. *Framing Blackness: The African American Image in Film* (1993).

GUILBAULT, JOCELYNE, WITH GAGE AVERILL, EDOUARD BENOÎT, AND GREGORY RABESS. *Zouk: World Music in the West Indies* (1993).

GUILLÉN, NICOLAS. *Martín Morúa Delgado: ¿Quién fue?* (1984).

GURALNICK, PETER. *Searching for Robert Johnson* (1989).

——. *Sweet Soul Music: Rhythm and Blues and the Southern Dream of Freedom* (1986).

GUTMAN, BILL. *The Harlem Globetrotters* (1977).

GUTMAN, HERBERT G. *The Black Family in Slavery and Freedom, 1750-1925* (1976).

GUY-SHEFTALL, BEVERLY, AND JO MOORE STEWART. *Spelman: A Centennial Celebration* (1981).

GUZMAN, JESSIE P. *Crusade for Civic Democracy: The Story of the Tuskegee Civic Association, 1941-1970* (1985).

HABEKOST, CHRISTIAN. *Verbal Riddim: The Politics and Aesthetics of African-Caribbean Dub Poetry* (1993).

HACKETT, ROSALIND. *Art and Religion in Africa* (1996).

HAIR, WILLIAM IVY. *Carnival of Fury: Robert Charles and the New Orleans Race Riot of 1900* (1976).

HALE, LINDSAY, "Preto Velho: Resistance, Redemption and Engendered Representations of Slavery in a Brazilian Possession-Trance Religion." *American Ethnologist* 24, no. 2 (1997): 392-414.

HALL, JACQUELYN DOWD. *Revolt Against Chivalry: Jessie Daniel Ames and the Women's Campaign Against Lynching* (1979).

HALL, MARGARET, AND TOM YOUNG. *Confronting Leviathan: Mozambique Since Independence* (1997).

HALL, RICHARD. *Stanley: An Adventurer Explored* (1974).

HALL, STUART. "Racism and Reaction." In *Five Views on Multi-Racial Britain* (1978).

HALL, STUART, AND BRAM GIEBEN, EDS. *Formations of Modernity* (1992).

HALL, STUART, AND MARTIN JACQUES, EDS. *New Times: The Changing Face of Politics in the 1990s* (1990).

HAMER, MARY. *Signs of Cleopatra: History, Politics, Representation* (1993).

HAMILTON, CHARLES V. *Adam Clayton Powell, Jr.: The Political Biography of an American Dilemma* (1991).

HAMILTON, HOLMAN. *Prologue to Conflict: The Crisis and Compromise of 1850* (1964).

HAMILTON, KENNETH MARVIN. *Black Towns and Profit: Promotion and Development in the Trans-Applachian West, 1877-1915* (1991).

HAMNER, ROBERT D, ED. *Critical Perspectives on Derek Walcott* (1993).

HANCHARD, MICHAEL GEORGE. *Orpheus and Power: The Movimento Negro of Rio de Janeiro and São Paulo, Brazil, 1945-1988* (1994).

HANDY, D. ANTOINETTE. "Conversations with Mary Lou Williams: First Lady of the Jazz Keyboard." *Black Perspectives on Music* 8 (Fall 1980): 195-214.

HANDY, WILLIAM C. *Father of the Blues: An Autobiography.* Edited by Arna Bontemps (1941).

HANSEN, EMMANUEL. *Frantz Fanon: Social and Political Thought* (1977).

HARDESTY, VON, AND DOMINICK PISANO. *Black Wings: The American Black in Aviation* (1983).

HARDY, CHARLES, AND GAIL F. STERN, EDS. *Ethnic Images in the Comics* (1986).

HARDY, GAYLE J. *American Women Civil Rights Activists: Biobibliographies of 68 Leaders, 1825-1992* (1993).

HARLAN, LOUIS R. *Booker T. Washington: The Making of a Black Leader, 1856-1901* (1972).

HARPER, MICHAEL S., ET. AL., EDS. *Chant of Saints: A Gathering of Afro-American Literature, Art, and Scholarship* (1979).

HARRINGTON, OLIVER. *Why I Left America and Other Essays* (1993).

HARRIS, FRED R., AND ROGER WILKINS, EDS. *Quiet Riots: Race and Poverty in the United States* (1988).

HARRIS, JESSICA B. *Iron Pots and Wooden Spoons: Africa's Gifts to New World Cooking* (1989).

HARRIS, MICHAEL. *The Rise of the Gospel Blues: The Music of Thomas Andrew Dorsey in the Urban Church* (1992).

HARRISON, ALFERDTEEN, ED. *Black Exodus: The Great Migration from the American South* (1991).

HARRISON, EARL. *The Dream and the Dreamer* (1956).

HARRIS, ROBERT. "Early Black Benevolent Societies, 1780-1830." *Massachusetts Review* 20 (Autumn 1979): 603-28.

HARRIS, WILLIAM HAMILTON. *Keeping the Faith: A. Philip Randolph, Milton P. Webster, and the Brotherhood of Sleeping Car Porters, 1925-37* (1977).

HARRIS, WILLIAM J. *The Poetry and Poetics of Amiri Baraka: The Jazz Aesthetic* (1985).

HARRIS, WILSON. *History, Fable, and Myth in the Caribbean and the Guianas* (1970).

HART, DAVID. *The Volta River Project: A Case Study in Politics and Technology* (1980).

HASKINS, JAMES. *Black Dance in America: A History through its People* (1990).

——. *Bricktop* (1983).

——. *Mabel Mercer: A Life* (1987).

——. *Pinckney Benton Stewart Pinchback* (1973).

HASKINS, JAMES, AND N. R. MITGANG. *Mr. Bojangles: The Biography of Bill Robinson* (1988).

HAYDEN, DOLORES. "Biddy Mason's Los Angeles, 1856-1891." *California History* 68 (Fall 1989): 86-99.

HAYDEN, TOM. *Rebellion in Newark: Official Violence and Ghetto Response* (1967).

HAYES, DIANA L. *And Still We Rise: An Introduction to Black Liberation Theology* (1996).

HAYGOOD, WIL. *King of the Cats: The Life and Times of Adam Clayton Powell, Jr.* (1993).

HAYNES, KARIMA A. "Mae Jemison: Coming in from Outer Space." *Ebony* 48, no. 2 (Dec. 1992):118.

HAYWOOD, HARRY. *Black Bolshevik: Autobiography of an Afro-American Communist* (1978).

HAZAEL-MASSIEUX, MARIE-CHRISTINE. "Le Criole aux Antilles: Evolutions et Perspectives." In Yacou Alain, ed., *Créoles de la Caraïbe: Actes du Colloque universitaire en hommage à Guy Hazael-Massieux, Pointe-à-Pitre, le 27 mars 1995* (1996): 179-200.

HEDGEMAN, ANNA ARNOLD. *The Trumpet Sounds: A Memoir of Negro leadership* (1964).

HEDRICK, JOAN. *Harriet Beecher Stowe: A Life* (1994).

HEILBUT, ANTHONY. *The Gospel Sound: Good News and Bad Times* (1971).

HELDMAN, MARILYN E., STUART MUNRO-HAY, AND RODERICK GRIERSON. *African Zion: The Sacred Art of Ethiopia* (1993).

HELG, ALINE. *Our Rightful Share: The Afro-Cuban Struggle for Equality, 1886-1912* (1995).

HELLER, PETER. *Bad Intentions: The Mike Tyson Story* (1989).

HELM, MCKINLEY. *Angel Mo' and Her Son, Roland Hayes* (1942).

HEMENWAY, ROBERT. *Zora Neale Hurston: A Literary Biography* (1980).

HEMPHILL, ESSEX, ED. *Brother to Brother: New Writings by Black Gay Men* (1991).

HENDERSON, ALEXA BENSON. *Atlanta Life Insurance Company: Guardian of Black Economic Dignity* (1990).

HENDERSON, HARRY, AND GYLBERT GARVIN COKER. *Charles Alston: Artist and Teacher* (1990).

Henson, Matthew A. *A Black Explorer at the North Pole 1866-1955* (1989).

Henze, Paul B. *The Defeat of the Derg and the Establishment of New Governments in Ethiopia and Eritrea* (1992).

Heuman, Gad, ed. *Out of the House of Bondage: Runaways, Resistance, and Marronage in Africa and the New World* (1986).

Heymount, George. "Blacks in Opera." *Ebony* (November 1981): 32-36.

Hidalgo Alzamora, Laura. "Del ritmo al concepto en la poesía de Preciado." *Cultura, Revista del Banco Central del Ecuador* 3, no.7 (May-August 1980): 102-19.

Higginbotham, A. Leon. *In the Matter of Color: The Colonial Period* (1978).

——. *Shades of Freedom: Racial Politics and Presumptions of the American Legal Process* (1996).

Higginbotham, Evelyn Brooks. *Righteous Discontent: The Women's Movement in the Black Baptist Church, 1880-1920* (1993).

Hill, Daniel G. *The Freedom Seekers: Blacks in Early Canada* (1981).

Hill, Donald. *Calypso Calaloo: Early Carnival Music in Trinidad* (1993).

Hill, Robert A., ed. *The Crusader.* 3 vols. (1987).

——. *The Marcus Garvey and Universal Negro Improvement Association Papers* (1983-1991).

Hine, Darlene Clark, ed. *Black Women in America: An Historical Encyclopedia.* 2 vols. (1993).

Hiro, Dilip. *Desert Shield to Desert Storm: The Second Gulf War* (1992).

Hirsh, Arnold R., and Joseph Logsdon. *Creole New Orleans: Race and Americanization* (1992).

Hirschorn, H. H. "Botanical remedies of South and Central America and the Caribbean: An Archival Analysis." *Journal of Ethnopharmacology* 4, no. 2 (1981).

Hochschild, Adam. *King Leopold's Ghost: A Story of Greed, Terror, and Heroism in Colonial Africa* (1998).

Hodges, LeRoy. *Portrait of an Expatriate: William Gardner Smith, Writer* (1985).

Hoffman, Frederick J., Charles Allen, and Carolyn R. Ulrich. *The Little Magazine: A History and a Bibliography* (1946).

Hoffman, Larry G. *Haitian Art: The Legend and Legacy of the Naïve Tradition* (1985).

Hoffmann, Léon-François. *Littérature d'Haïti* (1995).

Hofler, Robert. "Minority View: Seeing White, Being Black: Interview with Lou Gossett Jr." *Life* (March 1989).

Holanda, Aurélio Buarque de. "Teixeira e Souza." In *O Romance Brasileiro,* ed. Olivio Montenegro (1952).

Holdredge, Helen. *Mammy Pleasant* (1953).

Holloway, Joseph E., ed. *Africanisms in American Culture* (1990).

Holm, John. *Pidgins and Creoles.* 2 vols. (1988-1989).

Holt, Rackman. *Mary McLeod Bethune: A Biography* (1964).

Holway, John B. *Josh and Satch: The Life and Times of Josh Gibson and Satchel Paige* (1991).

Holyfield, Evander, and Bernard Holyfield. *Holyfield: The Humble Warrior* (1996).

hooks, bell, "Black is a Woman's Color." In *Bearing Witness: Selections from African-American Autobiography in the Twentieth Century,* ed. Henry Louis Gates Jr. (1991).

hooks, bell, and Cornel West. *Breaking Bread: Insurgent Black Intellectual Life* (1991).

Hope King, Ruby. *Education in the Caribbean: Historical Perspectives* (1987).

Horace, Lillian B. *"Crowned with Glory and Honor": The Life of Rev. Lacey Kirk Williams* (1978).

Horne, Gerald. *Communist Front? The Civil Rights Congress 1946-56* (1988).

Horton, Aimee Isgrig. *The Highlander Folk School: A History of its Major Programs, 1932-1961* (1989).

Hosher, John. *God in a Rolls Royce: The Rise of Father Divine: Madman, Menace, or Messiah* (1936).

Hosiasson, Jose. "Kid Ory." *New Grove Dictionary of Jazz* (1988).

House, Ernest R. *Jesse Jackson and the Politics of Charisma: The Rise and Fall of the PUSH/Excel Program* (1988).

Howat, Gerald. *Learie Constantine* (1975).

Howes, R. "The Literature of Outsiders: The Literature of the Gay Community in Latin America." In *Latin American Masses and Minorities: Their Images and Realities* (1987).

Howe, Stephen. *Afrocentrism: Mythical Pasts and Imagined Homes* (1998).

Hoyos, F. A. *A History from the Amerindians to Independence* (1978).

Huckaby, Elizabeth. *Crisis at Central High School: Little Rock, 1957-58* (1980).

Huggins, Nathan Irvin. *Harlem Renaissance* (1971).

Hughes, C. Alvin. "We Demand Our Rights: The Southern Negro Youth Congress, 1937-1949." *Phylon* 48, no. 1 (Spring 1987): 38-50.

Hull, Gloria T. *Color, Sex, and Poetry: Three Women Writers of the Harlem Renaissance* (1987).

Hunter-Gault, Charlayne. *In My Place* (1992).

Huntington, Richard. *Gender and Social Structure in Madagascar* (1988).

Hurd, Michael. *Black College Football, 1892-1992: One Hundred Years of History, Education, and Pride* (1993).

Hurley, Daniel. *Cincinnati, The Queen City* (1982).

Hurston, Zora Neale. "Hoodoo in America." *Journal of American Folklore* 44 (1931): 414.

——. *I Love Myself When I am Laughing...and Then Again When I am Looking Mean and Impressive: A Zora Neale Hurston Reader,* ed. Alice Walker (1979).

——. *Mules and Men* (1935).

Hutchinson, Earl Ofari. *Betrayed: A History of Presidential Failure to Protect Black Lives* (1996).

——. *Blacks and Reds: Race and Class in Conflict, 1919-1990* (1995).

IANNI, OCTÁVIO. *Escravidão e racismo.* 2d ed. (1988).

IHONVBERE, JULIUS O. *Economic Crisis, Civil Society, and Democratization: The Case of Zambia* (1996).

ILLINOIS STATE MUSEUM. *Healing Walls: Murals and Community, A Chicago History* (1996).

"Interview: Queen Mother Moore." *Black Scholar* 4 (March-April 1973): 47-55.

IOAKIMIDIS, DEMETRE. "Chu Berry." *Jazz Monthly* (March 1964).

IRVINE, CECILIA. "The Birth of the Kimbanguist Movement in Bas-Zaire, 1921." *Journal of Religion in Africa* 6, no. 1 (1974): 23-76.

ISICHEI, ELIZABETH. *A History of African Societies to 1870* (1997).

JACKSON, CARLTON. *Hattie: The Life of Hattie McDaniel* (1990).

JACKSON, KENNETH T., AND BARBARA B. JACKSON. "The Black Experience in Newark: The Growth of the Ghetto, 1870-1970." In *New Jersey Since 1860: New Findings and Interpretations,* ed. William C. Wright (1972).

JACKSON, LUTHER P. *Free Negro Labor and Property Holding in Virginia, 1830-1860* (1942).

JACKSON, REGINALD, WITH MIKE LUPICA. *Reggie* (1984).

JACKSON, RICHARD L. *Black Writers in Latin America* (1979).

JACOBS, DONALD M. *Antebellum Black Newspapers* (1976).

——. "David Walker: Boston Race Leader, 1825-1830." *Essex Institute Historical Collections* 107 (Jan. 1971): 94-107.

JACOBS, HARRIET. *Incidents in the Life of a Slave Girl, Written by Herself,* ed. Jean Fagan Yellin (1987).

JACOBSON, MARK. "When He Was King: Former Heavyweight Boxing Champ Larry Holmes." *New York* 30, no. 28 (July 28, 1997): 32-35.

JACQUES-GARVEY, AMY, ED. *Philosophy and Opinions of Marcus Garvey* (1923-1925).

JADIN, LOUIS. *Le Congo et la secte des Antoniens* (1961).

JAGAN, CHEDDI. *The West on Trial: My Fight for Guyana's Freedom* (1967).

JAMES, ADEOLA. *In Their Own Voices: African Women Writers Talk* (1990).

JAMES, C.L.R. *The Black Jacobins: Toussaint L' Ouverture and the San Domingo Revolution* (1963).

——. *A History of Pan-African Revolt* (1969).

JAMES, M. *Ten Modern Jazzmen: An Appraisal of the Recorded Work of Ten Modern Jazzmen* (1960).

"J. A. Rogers: Portrait of an Afro-American Historian." *Black Scholar* 6, no. 5 (January-February 1975): 32-39.

JASEN, DAVID A., AND TREBOR TICHENOR. *Rags and Ragtime: A Musical History* (1989).

JEFFREY, HENRY B., AND COLIN BABER. *Guyana: Politics, Economics, and Society: Beyond the Burnham Era* (1986).

JENKINS, MARK. *To Timbuktu* (1997).

JIMÉNEZ-ROMAN, MIRIAM. "Un hombre (negro) del pueblo: José Celso Barbosa and the Puerto Rican 'Race' towards Whiteness." *Centro de Estudios Puertorriqueños* (Spring 1996).

JIMENO, MYRIAM, AND MARÍA LUCIA SOTOMAYOR, LUZ MARÍA VALDERRAMA. *Chocó: Diversidad cultural y medio ambiente* (1995).

JOHNS, CHRIS. *Valley of Life: Africa's Great Rift* (1991).

JOHNSON, ABBY ARTHUR, AND RONALD MABERRY JOHNSON. "Charting a New Course: African American Literary Politics since 1976." In *The Black Columbiad: Defining Moments in African American Literature and Culture,* ed. Werner Sollors and Maria Diedrich (1994), pp. 369-81.

——. *Propaganda and Aesthetics: The Literary Politics of African-American Magazines in the Twentieth Century* (1991).

JOHNSON, CECIL, *Guts: Legendary Black Rodeo Cowboy Bill Pickett* (1994).

JOHNSON, DIANE. *Telling Tales: The Pedagogy and Promise of African American Literature for Youth* (1990).

JOHNSON, JOHN H., AND LERONE BENNETT, JR. *Succeeding Against the Odds* (1989).

JOHNSON, JAMES WELDON. *Black Manhattan* (1930).

——. Preface to *The Book of American Negro Poetry* (1922).

JOHNSON, RANDAL. *Cinema Novo x 5: Masters of Contemporary Brazilian Film* (1984).

JOHNSTON, J. H. "Luther Porter Jackson." *Journal of Negro History* (October 1950): 352-55.

JONAS, JOYCE. *Anancy in the Great House: Ways of Reading West Indian Fiction* (1991).

JONES, HOWARD. *Mutiny on the Amistad: The Saga of a Slave Revolt and its Impact on American Abolition, Law and Diplomacy* (1987).

——. "The Peculiar Institution and National Honor: The Case of the Creole Slave Revolt." *Civil War History* 21 (1975): 28-50.

JONES, JAMES H. *Bad Blood: The Tuskegee Syphilis Experiment* (1993).

JONES, JOYCE. "The Best Commerce Secretary Ever." *Black Enterprise* 26, no. 11 (1990).

JONES, RALPH H. *Charles Albert Tindley: Prince of Preachers* (1982).

JONES, TAD. "Professor Longhair." *Living Blues* 26 (March-April 1976): 16-29.

JORDAN, BARBARA, AND SHELBY HEARON. *Barbara Jordan: A Self-Portrait* (1979).

JOSEPH, CLIFTON. "Jump Up and Beg." *Toronto Life* (August 1996).

JOYCE, DONALD FRANKLIN. *Black Book Publishers in the United States: A Historical Dictionary of the Presses, 1817-1990* (1991).

——. *Gatekeepers of Black Culture: Black-Owned Book Publishing in the United States, 1817-1981* (1983).

JOYCE, PETER. *Anatomy of a Rebel: Smith of Rhodesia: A Biography* (1974).

JOYNER, CHARLES. *Down by the Riverside: A South Carolina Slave Community* (1989).

JULIEN, ISAAC. *Looking for Langston: A Meditation on Langston Hughes (1902-1967) and the Harlem Renaissance, with the Poetry of Essex Hemphill and Bruce Nugent (1906-1987)* (1992).

KAHAN, MITCHELL D. *Heavenly Visions: The Art of Minnie Evans* (1986).

KAPLAN, SIDNEY. "The Miscegenation Issue in the Election of 1864." In *American Studies in Black and White: Selected Essays, 1949-1989,* ed. Allan D. Austin (1991): 47-100.

KAPLAN, SIDNEY, AND EMMA NOGRADY KAPLAN. *The Black Presence in the Era of the American Revolution.* 2d ed. (1989).

KAPLAN, STEVEN. *The Beta Israel (Falasha) in Ethiopia: From Earliest Times to the Twentieth Century* (1992).

KARENGA, MAULANA. *The African American Holiday of Kwanzaa: A Celebration of Family, Community, and Culture* (1988).

——. *Introduction to Black Studies.* 2d ed. (1993).

KATZ, JONATHAN. *Resistance at Christiana: The Fugitive Slave Rebellion, Christiana, Pennsylvania, September 11, 1851: A Documentary Account* (1974).

KATZMAN, DAVID. *Before the Ghetto: Black Detroit in the Nineteenth Century* (1973).

KATZ, WILLIAM L. *Black People Who Made the Old West* (1992).

——. *The Black West* (1987).

KECKLEY, ELIZABETH. *Behind the Scenes; or, Thirty Years a Slave and Four Years in the White House* (1868).

KELLEY, ROBIN D. G. *Hammer and Hoe: Alabama Communists During the Great Depression* (1990).

KENNEDY, ADRIENNE. *People Who Led to My Plays* (1987).

KENNEDY, RANDALL. *Dred Scott and African American Citizenship* (1996).

——. *Race, Crime, and the Law* (1997).

KENNEY, WILLIAM HOWLAND. *Chicago Jazz: A Cultural History, 1904-1930* (1993).

——. "Jimmie Noone, Chicago's Classical Jazz Clarinetist." *American Music* 4 (1986): 145-58.

KENYATTA, JOMO. *Facing Mount Kenya: The Tribal Life of the Gikuyu* (1938).

KEPPEL, BEN. *The Work of Democracy: Ralph Bunche, Kenneth B. Clark, Lorraine Hansberry, and the Cultural Politics of Race* (1995).

KESSELMAN, LOUIS. *The Social Politics of FEPC: A Study in Reform Pressure Movements* (1948).

KESSLER, JAMES H. *Distinguished African American Scientists of the Twentieth Century* (1996).

KESTELOOT, LILYAN. *Black Writers in French: A Literary History of Negritude.* Translated by Ellen Conroy Kennedy (1991).

KEVLES, DANIEL. *In the Name of Eugenics: Genetics and the Uses of Human Heredity* (1985).

KHAZANOV, A. *Agostinho Neto* (1986).

KIM, AEHYUNG, AND BRUCE BENTON. *Cost-benefit Analysis of the Onchocerca Control Program (OCP)* (1995).

KINCAID, JAMAICA. *A Small Place* (1988).

KING, B. B., WITH DAVID RITZ. *Blues All Around Me: The Autobiography of B. B. King* (1996).

KING, BRUCE, ED. *West Indian Literature* (1979).

KING, CORETTA SCOTT. *My Life with Martin Luther King, Jr.* (1969).

KINGDON, ZACHARY, "Chanuo Maundu: Master of Makonde Blackwood Art." *African Arts* (Autumn 1996).

KIPLE, KENNETH F. *The Caribbean Slave: A Biological History* (1984).

KIRSH, ANDREA, AND SUSAN FISHER STERLING. *Carrie Mae Weems* (1992).

KIRWAN, ALBERT DENNIS. *John J. Crittenden: The Struggle for the Union* (1962).

KISKA, TIM. "CBS' Ed Bradley Recalls Childhood Days in Detroit." *Detroit News* (March 21, 1997) A, 2:2.

KITT, EARTHA. *Alone with Me* (1976).

——. *Thursday's Child* (1956).

KITWANA, BAKARI. *The Rap on Gangsta Rap: Who Run It? Gangsta Rap and Visions of Black Violence* (1994).

KLAPISCH, BOB. *High and Tight: The Rise and Fall of Dwight Gooden and Darryl Strawberry* (1996).

KLEHR, HARVEY. *The Heyday of American Communism: The Depression Decade* (1984).

KLEIN, HERBERT S. *African Slavery in Latin America and the Caribbean* (1986).

——. *The Middle Passage: Comparative Studies in the Atlantic Slave Trade* (1978).

——. *Slavery in the Americas: A Comparative Study of Virginia and Cuba* (1967).

KLEMENT, FRANK L. *The Copperheads of the Middle West* (1972).

KLEPPNER, PAUL. *Chicago Divided: The Making of a Black Mayor* (1985).

KLOTMAN, PHYLLIS RAUCH, ED. *Screenplays of the African American Experience* (1991).

KLOTS, STEVE. *Richard Allen* (1991).

KLUGER, RICHARD. *Simple Justice: The History of Brown v. Board of Education and Black America's Struggle for Equality* (1975).

KNAACK, TWILA. *Ethel Waters: I Touched a Sparrow* (1978).

KNIGHT, FRANKLIN. *The African Dimension in Latin American Societies* (1974).

——. *Slavery and the Transformation of Society in Cuba, 1511-1760: From Settler Society to Slave Society* (1988).

KNIGHT, GLADYS. *Between Each Line of Pain and Glory: My Life Story* (1997).

KOLCHIN, PETER. *American Slavery, 1619-1877* (1993).

KONCZACKI, Z. A. *The Economics of Pastoralism: A Case Study of Sub-Saharan Africa* (1978).

KOOK, HETTY, AND GORETTI NARAIN. "Papiamento." In *Community Languages in the Netherlands*, ed. Guus Extra and Ludo Verhoeven (1993): 69-91.

KORNWEIBEL, THEODORE, JR. *No Crystal Stair: Black Life and the Messenger, 1917-1928* (1975).

KOSTARAS, JAMES GEORGE. *Fez: Transformation of the Traditional Urban Environment* (1986).

KOSTARELOS, FRANCES. *Feeling the Spirit: Faith and Hope in an Evangelical Black Storefront Church* (1995).

KOTLOWITZ, ALEX. "A Bridge Too Far? Benjamin Chavis." *New York Times Magazine* (June 12, 1994).

KOTTAK, CONRAD P. *The Past and the Present: History, Ecology, and Cultural Variation in Highland Madagascar* (1980).

KOUSSER, J. MORGAN. *The Shaping of Southern Politics: Suffrage Restriction and the Establishment of the One-Party South, 1880-1910* (1974).

KRADITOR, AILEEN S. *Means and Ends in American Abolitionism: Garrison and his Critics on Strategy and Tactics, 1834-1850* (1989).

KREAMER, CHRISTINE M. *A Life Well Lived: Fantasy Coffins of Kane Quaye* (1994).

KREMER, GARY R., ED. *George Washington Carver in His Own Words* (1987).

KUREISHI, H. "Dirty Washing." *Time Out* (London) (November 14-20, 1985).

KUSMER, KENNETH. *A Ghetto Takes Shape: Black Cleveland, 1870-1930* (1976).

KUTZINKSI, VERA. *Sugar's Secrets: Race and the Erotics of Cuban Nationalism* (1993).

KWAMENAH-POH, M., J.TOSH, R. WALLER, AND M. TIDY, *African History in Maps* (1982).

LABELLE, MICHELINE. *Idéologie de couleur et classes sociales en Haïti.* 2d ed. (1987).

LABOV, WILLIAM. *Language in the Inner City: Studies in the Black English Vernacular* (1972).

LA GUERRE, JOHN GAFFAR. *Enemies of Empire* (1984).

LAMBERT, BRUCE. "Doxey Wilkerson is Dead at 88: Educator and Advocate for Rights." *New York Times* (June 18, 1993): D 16.

LANE, ANN J. *The Brownsville Affair: National Crisis and Black Reaction* (1971).

LANE, ROGER. *Roots of Violence in Black Philadelphia, 1860-1900* (1986).

LANNING, MICHAEL LEE, LT. COL. (RET.). *The African-American Soldier: From Crispus Attucks to Colin Powell* (1997).

LAPP, RUDOLPH M. *Blacks in Gold Rush California* (1977).

LAURINO, MARIA. "Sensitivity Comes From 'The Soles of the Feet.'" Interview with Anna Deveare Smith, *New York Newsday* (Feb. 23, 1994).

LAWLAH, JOHN W. "The President-Elect." *Journal of the National Medical Association* 55 (November 1963): 551-554.

LAWRENCE, ELIZABETH A. *Rodeo: An Anthropologist Looks at the Wild and the Tame* (1982).

LEAMAN, OLIVER. *Averroes and His Philosophy* (1988).

LEAVY, WALTER. "Howard University: A Unique Center of Excellence." *Ebony* (September 1985): 140-142.

——. "Is Tony Gwynn the Greatest Hitter in Baseball History?" *Ebony* (August 1997): 132.

LECKIE, WILLIAM. *The Buffalo Soldiers: A Narrative of the Negro Cavalry in the West* (1967).

LEEDS, ANTHONY, AND ELIZABETH LEEDS. *A Sociologia do Brasil Urbano (The Sociology of Urban Brazil).* Translated by Maria Laura Viveiros de Castro (1977).

LEE, JARENA. *The Life and Religious Experience of Jarena Lee* (1849). Reprinted in *Sisters of the Spirit: Three Black Women's Autobiographies of the Nineteenth Century.* Edited by William L. Andrews (1986).

LEEMING, DAVID. *James Baldwin: A Biography* (1994).

LEES, GENE. *Oscar Peterson: The Will to Swing* (1988).

LEFEVER, ERNEST W. *Crisis in the Congo: A United Nations Force in Action (1965).*

LEGUM, COLIN, AND GEOFFREY MMARI. *Mwalimu: The Influence of Nyerere* (1995).

LEMANN, NICHOLAS. *The Promised Land: The Great Black Migration and How It Changed America* (1991).

LEMARCHAND, RENÉ. *Political Awakening in the Belgian Congo* (1964).

LEÓN, ARGELIERS. *Del canto y el tiempo* (1984).

LEON, ELI. *Who'd a Thought It: Improvisation in African-American Quiltmaking* (1987).

LEONS, WILLIAM, AND ALLYN MACLEON STEARMAN. *Anthropological Investigations in Bolivia* (1984).

LEREBOURS, MICHEL PHILIPPE. *Haïti et ses peintres.* 2 vols. (1989).

LERNER, GERDA, ED. *Black Women in White America: A Documentary History* (1972).

LERNER, MICHAEL, AND CORNEL WEST. *Jews and Blacks: Let the Healing Begin* (1995).

LESLAU, WOLF, TRANS. *Falasha Anthology* (1954).

LESLIE, WINESOME J. *Zaire: Continuity and Political Change in an Oppressive State* (1993).

LEVINE, DONALD N. *Greater Ethiopia: The Evolution of a Multi-Ethnic Society* (1974).

LEVINE, LAWRENCE W. *Black Culture and Black Consciousness* (1977).

LEVINE, ROBERT M., AND JOSÉ CARLOS SEBE BOM MEIHY. *The Life and Death of Carolina Maria de Jesus* (1995).

LEWIS, DAVID LEVERING. *W. E. B. Du Bois: Biography of a Race* (1993).

——. *When Harlem Was in Vogue* (1981).

LEWIS, GORDON K. *Main Currents in Caribbean Thought: The Historical Experience of Caribbean Society and its Ideological Aspects, 1492-1900* (1983).

LEWIS, LANCELOT S. *The West Indian in Panama: Black Labor in Panama, 1850-1914* (1980).

LEWIS, MARVÍN A. *Ethnicity and Identity in Contemporary Afro-Venezuelan Literature: A Culturalist Approach* (1992).

LEWIS, MARY L. "The White Rose Industrial Association: The Friend of the Strange Girl in New York." *Messenger* 7 (April 1925): 158.

LEWIS, SAMELLA. *African American Art and Artists* (1990).

——. *The Art of Elizabeth Catlett* (1984).

LEWIS, SAMELLA, AND RICHARD POWELL. *Elizabeth Catlett: Works on Paper, 1944-1992* (1993).

LHAYA, PEDRO. *Juan Pablo Sojo, pasión y acento de su tierra* (1968).

LIBBY, BILL. *Goliath: The Wilt Chamberlain Story* (1977).

LICHTENSTEIN, GRACE, AND LAURA DANKNER. *Musical Gumbo: The Music of New Orleans* (1993).

LIEBENOW, J. GUS. *Colonial Rule and Political Development in Tanzania: The Case of the Makonde* (1971).

LIEB, SANDRA. *Mother of the Blues: A Study of Ma Rainey* (1981).

LIGHT, ALAN. "Curtis Mayfield: An Interview." *Rolling Stone* (October 28, 1993).

LINARES, OLGA. *Power, Prayer, and Production: The Jola of Casamance, Senegal* (1992).

LINCOLN, C. ERIC, AND LAWRENCE MAMIYA. *The Black Church in the African American Experience* (1990).

LINSLEY, ROBERT. "Wifredo Lam: Painter of Negritude." *Art History* 2, no. 4 (1988): 527-544.

LIPSKI, JOHN M. *The Speech of the Negros Congos of Panama* (1989).

LIPZITZ, GEORGE. *A Life in the Struggle: Ivory Perry and the Culture of Opposition* (1988).

LITVIN, MARTIN. *Hiram Revels in Illinois: A Biographical Novel about a Lost Chapter in the Life of America's First Black U.S. Senator* (1974).

LITWACK, LEON F. *Been in the Storm So Long: The Aftermath of Slavery* (1979).

——. *Trouble in Mind: Black Southerners in the Age of Jim Crow* (1998).

LITWACK, LEON F., AND AUGUST MEIER, EDS. *Black Leaders of the Nineteenth Century* (1988).

LIVINGSTON, JANE, JOHN BEARDSLEY, AND REGINIA PERRY. *Black Folk Art in America, 1930-1980* (1982).

LLERENA VILLALOBOS, RITO. *Memoria cultural en el vallenato* (1985).

LLEWELYN-DAVIES, MELISSA. *Some Women of Marrakech.* Videotape, Granada Television (1981).

LOCKE, ALAIN. *The New Negro* (1925).

LOCKE, MARY. *Anti-Slavery in America from the Introduction of African slaves to the Prohibition of the Slave Trade (1619-1808)* (1901).

LOCKE, THERESA A. "Willa Brown-Chappell, Mother of Black Aviation." *Negro History Bulletin* 50 (January-June 1987): 5-6.

LOCKHART, JAMES. *Spanish Peru, 1532-1560: A Social History* (1994).

LODER, KURT. "Bo Diddley Interview." *Rolling Stone* (February 12, 1987).

LOFTON, JOHN. *Denmark Vesey's Revolt: The Slave Plot that Lit a Fuse to Fort Sumter* (1983).

LOGAN, RAYFORD. *Howard University: The First Hundred Years, 1867-1967* (1969).

LOGAN, RAYFORD, AND MICHAEL R. WINSTON. *Dictionary of American Negro Biography* (1982).

LOMAX, ALAN. *Mister Jelly Roll: The Fortunes of Jelly Roll Morton, New Orleans Creole and Inventor of Jazz* (1973).

——. *The Land Where the Blues Began* (1993).

LONG, RICHARD. *The Black Tradition in American Dance* (1989).

LOOS, DOROTHY SCOTT. *The Naturalistic Novel of Brazil* (1963).

LOPES, HELENA T. *Negro e cultura no Brasil* (1987).

LOPES, JOSÉ SERGIO LEITE. "Successes and Contradictions in 'Multiracial' Brazilian Football." In *Entering the Field: New Perspectives on World Football,* ed. Gary Armstrong and Richard Giulianotti (1997).

LOTZ, RAINER, AND IAN PEGG, EDS. *Under the Imperial Carpet: Essays in Black History, 1780-1950* (1990).

LOVE, NAT. *The Life and Adventures of Nat Love, Better Known in the Cattle Country as "Deadwood Dick"* (1907; reprint ed., 1995).

LOVE, SPENCIE. *One Blood: The Death and Resurrection of Charles Drew* (1996).

LOVETT, CHARLES C. *Olympic Marathon: A Centennial History of the Games' Most Storied Race* (1997).

LOZANO, WILFREDO, ED. *La cuestión haitiana en Santo Domingo* (1992).

LUIS, WILLIAM. *Literary Bondage : Slavery in Cuban Narrative* (1990).

——, ED. *Voices from Under: Black Narrative in Latin America and the Caribbean* (1984).

LUMDSEN, I. *Society and the State in Mexico* (1991).

LUNDY, ANNE. "Conversations with Three Symphonic Conductors: Dennis De Couteau, Tania Leon, Jon Robinson." *Black Perspective in Music,* no. 2 (Fall 1988): 213-25.

LYNCH, HOLLIS R. *Black American Radicals and the Liberation of Africa: The Council on African Affairs, 1937-1955* (1978).

LYNCH, JOHN ROY. *Reminiscences of an Active Life: The Autobiography of John Roy Lynch.* Edited by John Hope Franklin (1970).

LYONS, LEONARD. *The Great Jazz Pianists: Speaking of Their Lives and Music* (1983).

MACDONALD, J. FRED. *Blacks and White TV: African Americans in Television Since 1948.* Rev. ed. (1992).

MACEO, ANTONIO. *El pensamiento vivo de Maceo: Cartas, proclamas, articulos y documentas.* Edited by José Antonio Portuondo (1960).

MACGAFFEY, WYATT. *Religion and Society in Central Africa: The BaKongo of Lower Zaire* (1986).

MACHARIA, KINUTHIA. *Social and Political Dynamics of the Informal Economy in African Cities: Nairobi and Harare* (1997).

MACKEY, NATHANIEL, ED. "Wilson Harris Special Issue." *Callaloo* (1995).

MACROBERT, IAIN. *The Black Roots and White Racism of Early Pentecostalism in the U.S.A.* (1988).

MAES-JELINEK, HENA, ED. *Commonwealth Literature and the Modern World* (1975).

MAGALHÃES, R., JR. *A Vida Turbulenta de José do Patrocínio* (1972).

MAGUBANE, VUKANI. "Graca Machel." *Ebony* (May 1997).

MAIN, MICHAEL. *Kalahari: Life's Variety in Dune and Delta* (1987).

MAIO, MARCOS CHOR. *A História do Projeto UNESCO: Estudos raciais e ciências sociais no Brasil* (1997).

MAIR, GEORGE. *Oprah Winfrey: The Real Story* (1994).

MAKEBA, MIRIAM, WITH JAMES HALL. *Makeba: My Story* (1988).

MALCOLM X, WITH ALEX HALEY. *The Autobiography of Malcolm X* (1964).

MALONE, JACQUI. *Steppin' on the Blues: The Visible Rhythms of African-American Dance* (1996).

MALTBY, MARC S. *The Origins and Early Development of Professional Football* (1997).

MANDELA, NELSON. *Long Walk to Freedom: The Autobiography of Nelson Mandela* (1994).

——. *The Struggle Is My Life: His Speeches and Writings Brought Together to Mark His 60th Birthday* (1978).

MANESS, LONNIE E. "The Fort Pillow Massacre: Fact or Fiction." *Tennessee Historical Quarterly* 48 (Winter 1986): 287-315.

MANGIONE, JERRE. *The Dream and the Deal: The Federal Writers' Project, 1935-1945* (1972).

MANLEY, ALBERT E. *A Legacy Continues: The Manley Years at Spelman College, 1953-1976* (1995).

MANNICK, A. R. *Mauritius: The Politics of Change* (1989).

MANUEL, PETER, ED. *Essays on Cuban Music: North American and Cuban Perspectives* (1991).

MANUEL, PETER, WITH KENNETH BILBY AND MICHAEL LARGEY. *Caribbean Currents: Caribbean Music from Rumba to Reggae* (1995).

MANUH, TAKYIWAA. "Diasporas, Unities, and the Marketplace: Tracing Changes in Ghanaian Fashion." *Journal of African Studies* 16, no.1 (Winter 1998).

MAPP, EDWARD. *Directory of Blacks in the Performing Arts* (1990).

MARCUS, HAROLD G. *A History of Ethiopia* (1994).

MARKMANN, CHARLES LAM. *The Noblest Cry: A History of the American Civil Liberties Union* (1965).

MARKOWITZ, GERALD E., AND DAVID ROSNER. *Children, Race, and Power: Kenneth and Mamie Clark's Northside Center* (1996).

MARQUIS, DONALD M. *In Search of Buddy Bolden: First Man of Jazz* (1978).

MARSHALL, RICHARD, ET. AL. *Jean-Michel Basquiat* (1992).

MARSH, J. B. T. *The Story of the Jubilee Singers with Their Songs* (1880; reprint ed., 1971).

MARTEENA, CONSTANCE HILL. *The Lengthening Shadow of a Woman: A Biography of Charlotte Hawkins Brown* (1977).

MARTÍ, JOSÉ. *Cuba, Nuestra América, los Estados Unidos* (1973).

——. *En los Estados Unidos* (1968).

MARTIN, ESMOND BRADLEY. *Zanzibar: Tradition and Revolution* (1978).

MARTIN, JAY, ED. *A Singer in the Dawn: Reinterpretations of Paul Laurence Dunbar* (1975).

MARTIN, MARIE-LOUISE. *Kimbangu: An African Prophet and His Church* (1975).

MARTIN, MICHAEL T., ED. *Cinemas of the Black Diaspora: Diversity, Dependence, and Oppositionality* (1995).

MARTIN, REGINALD. *Ishmael Reed and the New Black Aesthetic Critics* (1988).

——. "Total Life Is What We Want: The Progressive Stages of the New Black Aesthetic in Literature." *South Atlantic Review* (November 1986): 46-47.

MARTINS, LEDA MARIA. *A cena em sombras* (1995).

MARTIN, TONY. *Race First: The Ideological and Organizational Struggles of Marcus Garvey and the Universal Negro Improvement Association* (1986).

MASON, TONY. *Passion of the People? Football in South America* (1995).

MATORY, J. LORAND. *Sex and the Empire That Is No More: Gender and the Politics of Metaphor in Oyo Yoruba Religion* (1994).

MATTA, ROBERTO DA. *Carnivals, Rogues, and Heroes: An Interpretation of the Brazilian Dilemma.* Translated by John Drury (1991).

MATTHEWS, MARCIA M. *Henry Ossawa Tanner, American Artist* (1969).

MATTOSO, KATIA M. DE QUEIRÓS. *To Be a Slave in Brazil, 1550-1888.* Translated by Arthur Goldhammer (1994).

MAYNARD, OLGA. *Judith Jamison: Aspects of a Dancer* (1982).

MAZRUI, ALI A. *The Africans: A Triple Heritage* (1986).

MCADAM, DOUG. *Freedom Summer* (1988).

MCBROOME, DELORES NASON. *Parallel Communities: African Americans in California's East Bay, 1850-1963* (1993).

MCCABE, BRUCE. "Bringing the Streets to the Stage." *Boston Globe* (April 18, 1997): F 3.

MCCORMICK, RICHARD P. "William Whipper: Moral Reformer." *Pennsylvania History* 43 (January 1976): 22-46.

MCDONNELL, PATRICK, KAREN O'CONNELL, AND GEORGIA RILEY DE HAVENON. *Krazy Kat: The Comic Art of George Herriman* (1986).

MCDOWELL, ROBERT. "The Assembling Vision of Rita Dove." *Callaloo* 9 (Winter 1986): 61-70.

MCELVAINE, ROBERT S. *The Great Depression: America, 1929-1941* (1984).

MCFEELY, WILLIAM S. *Frederick Douglass* (1991).

MCGOWAN, CHRIS, AND RICARDO PESSANHA. *The Brazilian Sound: Samba, Bossa Nova, and the Popular Music of Brazil* (1991).

MCKIBLE, ADAM. "'These Are the Facts of the Darky's History': Thinking History and Reading Names in Four African American Tests." *African American Review* 28 (1994): 223-35.

MCKIVIGAN, JOHN R. *The War against Proslavery Religion: Abolitionism and the Northern Churches, 1830-1865* (1984).

MCLARIN, KIMBERLY J. *Native Daughter* (1994).

MCLENDON, JACQUELYN Y. *The Politics of Color in the Fiction of Jessie Fauset and Nella Larsen* (1995).

MCMILLAN, DELLA E. *Sahel Visions: Planned Settlement and River Blindness Control in Burkina Faso* (1995).

MCMURRY, LINDA O. *Recorder of the Black Experience: A Biography of Monroe Nathan Work* (1985).

MCNEIL, GENNA RAE. *Groundwork: Charles Hamilton Houston and the Struggle for Civil Rights* (1983).

MCPHERSON, JAMES M. *The Negro's Civil War: How American Negroes Felt and Acted During the War for the Union* (1965).

MEIER, AUGUST. "Introduction: Benjamin Quarles and the Historiography of Black America." In *Benjamin Quarles, Black Mosaic: Essays in Afro-American History and Historiography* (1989): 3-21.

——. *Negro Thought in America,1880-1915: Racial Ideologies in the Age of Booker T. Washington* (1963).

MEIER, AUGUST, AND JOHN H. BRACEY, JR. "The NAACP as a Reform Movement: 1909-1965." *Journal of Southern History* 49, no. 1 (February 1993).

MEIER, AUGUST, AND ELLIOTT RUDWICK. *Black History and the Historical Profession* (1986).

——. *CORE: A Study in the Civil Rights Movement, 1942-1968* (1973).

Melhem, D.H. "Dudley Randall: A Humanist View." *Black American Literature Forum* 17 (1983).

Mellafe R., Rolando. *La introducción de la esclavitud negra en Chile: Tráfico y rutas* (1984).

Menton, Seymour. *Prose Fiction of the Cuban Revolution* (1975).

Mercer, K. "Imagining the Black Man's Sex." In *Photography/Politics: Two,* ed. P. Holland et. al. (1987).

Mérian, Jean-Yves. *Aluísio Azevedo, Vida e Obra (1857-1913): O Verdadeiro Brasil do Século XIX* (1988).

Metcalf, George R. *Black Profiles* (1968).

Métraux, Alfred. "UNESCO and the Racial Problem." *International Social Science Bulletin* 2, no. 3 (1950): 384-90.

——. *Voodoo in Haiti* (1959).

Middleton, John, ed. *Encyclopedia of Africa South of the Sahara.* 4 vols. (1997).

Miles, Alexander. *Devil's Island: Colony of the Damned* (1988).

Miller, Errol. *Education for all: Caribbean Perspectives and Imperatives* (1992).

Miller, Floyd J. *The Search for a Black Nationality: Black Colonization and Emigration, 1787-1863* (1975).

Miller, Randall M., and John David Smith, eds. *Dictionary of Afro-American Slavery.* 2d ed. (1997).

Mills, Kay. "Maxine Waters: 'I Don't Pretend to Be Nice No Matter What . . . '." *The Progressive* (December 1993).

Miner, Horace. *The Primitive City of Timbuctoo* (1954).

Minnick-Taylor, Kathleen, and Charles Taylor II. *Kwanzaa: How to Celebrate It in Your Own Home* (1994).

Minority Rights Group, ed. *No Longer Invisible: Afro-Latin Americans Today* (1995).

Minter, William. *Apartheid's Contras: An Inquiry into the Roots of War in Angola and Mozambique* (1994).

Mintz, Sidney. *Sweetness and Power* (1985).

Mintz, Sidney, and Sally Price, eds. *Caribbean Contours* (1985).

MImanyara, Alfred M. *The Restatement of Bantu Origin and Meru History* (1992).

Moberg, Mark. *Myths of Ethnicity and Nation: Immigration, Work, and Identity in the Belize Banana Industry* (1997).

Models in the Mind: African Prototypes in American Patchwork (1992).

Moise, Claude. *Constitutions et luttes de pouvoir en Haiti (1804-1987)* (1988-1990).

Moisés, Massaud. *História da literatura Brasileira.* Vol. II (1989).

Moon, Elaine Latzman, ed. *Untold Tales, Unsung Heroes: An Oral History of Detroit's African American Community, 1918-1967* (1994).

Moorehead, Alan. *The White Nile* (1971).

Moore, Jesse Thomas. *A Search for Equality: The National Urban League, 1910-1961* (1981).

Moore, Joseph Thomas. *Pride Against Prejudice: The Biography of Larry Doby* (1988).

Moore, Robin. *Nationalizing Blackness: Afrocubanismo and Artistic Revolution in Havana, 1920-40* (1997).

Moore, Zelbert L. "Solano Trindade Remembered, 1908-1974." *Luso-Brazilian Review* 16 (1979): 233-38.

Morales, Florentino. "El poeta esclavo." *Conceptos* 2, no. 27 (December 1989): 2-3.

Moran, Charles. *Black Triumvirate: A Study of L'Ouverture, Dessalines, Christophe: The Men Who Made Haiti* (1957).

Mordecai, Pamela, and Betty Wilson, eds. *Her True-True Name* (1989).

Morell, Virginia. *Ancestral Passions: The Leakey Family and the Quest for Humankind's Beginnings* (1995).

Moreno Navarro, Isidoro. *Los cuadros del mestizaje americano: Estudio antropológico del mestizaje* (1973).

Morgan, Philip D. *Slave Counterpoint: Black Culture in the Eighteenth-Century Chesapeake and Lowcountry* (1998).

Morgan, Thomas L., and William Barlow. *From Cakewalks to Concert Halls: An Illustrated History of African American Popular Music from 1895-1930* (1992).

Morna, Colleen. "Graca Machel: Interview." *Africa Report* (July-August 1988).

Morris, Mervyn. "Louise Bennett." In *Encyclopedia of Post-Colonial Literatures in English.* Vol. I, ed. Eugene Benson and L. W. Conolly (1994).

Morris, Thomas D. *Free Men All: The Personal Liberty Laws of the North, 1780-1861* (1974).

Morrison, Toni. *Playing in the Dark: Whiteness and the Literary Imagination* (1992).

——, ed. *Race-ing Justice, En-gendering Power: Essays on Anita Hill, Clarence Thomas, and the Construction of Social Reality* (1992).

Morrow, Curtis. *What's A Commie Ever Done to Black People?: A Korean War Memoir of Fighting in the U.S. Army's Last All Negro Unit* (1997).

Morse, Stephen S. *Emerging Viruses* (1993).

Morsha, A. C. "Urban Planning in Tanzania at the Crossroads." *Review of Rural and Urban Planning in Southern and Eastern Africa* (1989): 79-91.

Mosby, Dewey F., Darrell Sewell, and Rae Alexander-Minter. *Henry Ossawa Tanner* (1991).

Moseley, Thomas Robert. "A History of the New York Manumission Society." Ph.D. Diss. University of Michigan, 1963.

Moses, Wilson Jeremiah. *Black Messiahs and Uncle Toms: Social and Literary Manipulation of a Religious Myth* (1982).

——. *The Golden Age of Black Nationalism: 1850-1925* (1978).

Mosquera, Gerardo. "Modernism from Afro-America: Wifredo Lam." In *Beyond the Fantastic: Contemporary Art Criticism from Latin America,* ed. Gerardo Mosquera (1996).

Moss, Alfred A., Jr. *The American Negro Academy: Voice of the Talented Tenth* (1981).

Mota, Ana Maritza de la. "Palma Sola: 1962," *Boletín: Museo de hombre dominicano* 14 (1980): 197-223.

Mott, Luiz. *Escravidão, Homossexualidade e Demonologia* (1988).

Mountoussamy-Ashe, Jeanne. *Viewfinders: Black Women Photographers* (1986).

Mudimbe-Boyi, Elisabeth. *L'oeuvre romanesque de Jacques-Stéphen Alexis : Une écriture poétique, un engagement politique* (1992).

Mudimbe, Valentin. *The Invention of Africa: Gnosis, Philosophy, and the Order of Knowledge* (1988).

Munford, Clarence. *Race and Reparations: A Black Perspective for the Twenty-First Century* (1996).

Munro-Hay, Stuart. *Aksum: An African Civilization of Late Antiquity* (1991).

Munro-Hay, Stuart, and Richard Pankhurst. *Ethiopia* (1995).

Munslow, Barry, ed. *Samora Machel, An African Revolutionary: Selected Speeches and Writings* (1985).

Murphy, Joseph M. *Working the Spirit: Ceremonies of the African Diaspora* (1994).

Murray, Pauli. *Dark Testament and Other Poems* (1970).

——. *Proud Shoes: The Story of an American Family* (1956).

——. *Song in a Weary Throat: An American Pilgrimage* (1987).

Musick, Phil. *Reflections on Roberto* (1994).

Myrdal, Gunnar. *An American Dilemma: The Negro Problem and Modern Democracy* (1944).

Nadel, Alan, ed. *May All of Your Fences Have Gates: Essays on the Drama of August Wilson* (1994).

Naison, Mark. *Communists in Harlem During the Depression* (1983).

Nalty, Bernard C. *Strength for the Fight: A History of Black Americans in the Military* (1986).

Nascimento, Abdias do. *Africans in Brazil: A Pan-African Perspective* (1992).

——. *Dramas para negros e prologo para brancos: Antologia de teatro negro-brasileiro.* (1961).

——. *Orixas: Os deuses vivos da Africa* (1995).

——. *O quilombismo: Documentos de uma militancia pan-africanista* (1980).

——. *Racial Democracy in Brazil, Myth or Reality?: A Dossier of Brazilian Racism.* Translated by Elisa Larkin do Nascimento; foreword by Wole Soyinka (1977).

——, ed. *O Negro revoltado* (1968).

Nash, Gary B. *Forging Freedom: The Formation of Philadelphia's Black Community, 1720-1840* (1988).

——. *Race and Revolution* (1990).

Navarrete, María Cristina. *Historia social del negro en la colonia: Cartagena, siglo XVII* (1995).

Navarro, Desiderio. *Ejercicios del criterio* (1988).

Neft, David S. *The Football Encyclopedia: The Complete History of Professional NFL Football, from 1892 to the Present* (1991).

Newby, I. A. *Black Carolinians: A History of Blacks in South Carolina from 1895 to 1968* (1973).

Newfield, Jack. *Only in America: The Life and Crimes of Don King* (1995).

Newman, Richard. *Words Like Freedom: Essays on African-American Culture and History* (1996).

——. *Lemuel Haynes: A Bio-bibliography* (1984).

——, comp. *Black Access: A Bibliography of Afro-American Bibliographies* (1984).

Newton, Huey P. *To Die for the People: The Writings of Huey Newton* (1972).

——. *War Against the Panthers: A Study of Repression in America* (1997).

"New Voice of the NAACP." Interview in *Newsweek* 46 (November 22, 1976).

Ngugi wa Thiong'o. *Decolonising the Mind: The Politics of Language in African Literature* (1986).

——. *Moving the Centre: The Struggle for Cultural Freedoms* (1993).

Nicolas, Armand. *Histoire de la Martinique.* 2 vols. (1996).

——. *La révolution antiesclavagiste de mai 1848 à la Martinique* (1967).

Nina Rodrigues, Raimundo. *Os Africanos no Brasil* (1977).

Nkomo, Joshua. *Nkomo: The Story of My Life* (1984).

——. *Zimbabwe Must and Shall be Totally Free* (1977).

Noble, Peter. *The Negro in Films* (1948).

Nobre, Carlos. *Mães de Acari: Uma história de luta contra a impunidade* (1994).

Noonan, John T. *The Antelope: The Ordeal of the Recaptured Africans in the Administrations of James Monroe and John Quincy Adams* (1977).

Norment, Lynn. "Vanessa L. Williams: On her Painful Divorce, the Pressures of Superstardom and her New Life as a Single Mom." *Ebony* (October 1997).

Norris, H. T. *The Berbers in Arabic Literature* (1982).

Norris, Jerrie. *Presenting Rosa Guy* (1988).

Northrup, Solomon. *Twelve Years a Slave: Narrative of Solomon Northrup, a Citizen of New York, Kidnapped in Washington City in 1841, and Rescued in 1853, from a Cotton Plantation near the Red River, in Louisiana* (1853).

Notcutt, Leslie A., and George C. Lantham. *The African and the Cinema: An Account of the Bantu Educational Cinema Experiment During the Period March 1935 to May 1937* (1937).

Notten, Eleonore Van. *Wallace Thurman's Harlem Renaissance* (1994).

Nugent, John Peer. *Black Eagle* (1971).

Nunn, John F. *Ancient Egyptian Medicine* (1996).

Nyerere, Julius K. *The Arusha Declaration: Ten Years After* (1977).

——. *Freedom and Socialism: Uhuru na Ujamaa: A Selection from Writings and Speeches, 1965-1967* (1968).

——. *Ujamaa: Essays on Socialism* (1971).

Oates, Stephen B. *The Fires of Jubilee: Nat Turner's Fierce Rebellion* (1975).

——. *To Purge This Land with Blood: A Biography of John Brown.* 2d ed. (1984).

Obadele, Imari. *America the Nation State: The Politics of the United States from a State-Building Perspective* (1988).

Ochs, Stephen J. *Desegregating the Altar: The Josephites and the Struggle for Black Priests, 1871-1960* (1970).

Ofcansky, Thomas, and Rodger Yeager. *Historical Dictionary of Tanzania* (1997).

Ogot, Bethwell A. *Africa and the Caribbean* (1997).

Ofíliam, José. *O Negro na Economia Mineira* (1993).

Olaniyan, Tejumola. *Scars of Conquest/Masks of Resistance: The Invention of Cultural Identities in African, African-American, and Caribbean Drama* (1995).

Oliver, Paul. *Songsters and Saints: Vocal Traditions on Race Records* (1984).

——, ed. *Black Music in Britain: Essays on the Afro-Asian Contribution to Popular Music* (1990).

Olson, James Stuart. *The Peoples of Africa: An Ethnohistorical Dictionary* (1996).

Olson, Sherry. *Baltimore: The Building of an American City*. Rev. and exp. ed. (1997).

Olwig, Karen Fog. *Cultural Adaptation and Resistance on St. John: Three Centuries of Afro-Caribbean Life.*

O'Meally, Robert G. *The Craft of Ralph Ellison* (1980).

Oodiah, Malenn. *Mouvement militant mauritien: 20 ans d'histoire (1969-1989)* (1989).

O'Reilly, Kenneth. *Nixon's Piano: Presidents and Racial Politics from Washington to Clinton* (1995).

Oriard, Michael. *Reading Football: How the Popular Press Created an American Spectacle* (1993).

Ormond, Roger. *The Apartheid Handbook: A Guide to South Africa's Everyday Racial Policies* (1985).

Orovio, Helio. *Diccionario de la música cubana: Biográfico y técnico* (1992).

Ortiz, Fernando. *Los bailes y le teatro de los negros en el folklore de cuba* (1951).

——. *Los instrumentos de la musica afrocubana*. 5 vols. (1952-1955).

——. *La música afrocubana* (1974).

——. *Los negros brujos* (1995).

——. *Wifredo Lam y su obra vista a traves de significados criticos* (1950).

Ortiz, Renato, "Ogum and the Umbandista Religion." In *Africa's Ogun: Old World and New*, ed. Santra Barnes (1989): 90-102.

Osofsky, Gilbert. *Harlem: The Making of a Ghetto: Negro New York, 1890-1930* (1971; revised ed., 1996).

Ospina, Hernando Calvo. *Salsa: Havana Beat, Bronx Beat* (1985).

Ossman, Susan. *Picturing Casablanca: Portraits of Power in a Modern City* (1994).

Otham, Haroub. *Zanzibar's Political History: The Past Haunting the Present?* (1993).

Otis, Johnny. *Upside Your Head!: Rhythm and Blues on Central Avenue* (1993).

Ottley, Roi. *The Lonely Warrior: The Life and Time of Robert S. Abbott* (1955).

Ottley, Roi and William Weatherby, eds. *The Negro in New York: An Informal Social History* (1967).

Owens, Thomas. *Bebop: The Music and its Players* (1995).

Pacini Hernández, Deborah. "The Picó Phenomenon in Cartagena, Colombia." *América Negra* 6 (December 1993): 69-115.

Painter, Nell Irvin. *Exodusters: Black Migration to Kansas after Reconstruction* (1986).

——. "Martin R. Delany: Elitism and Black Nationalism." In *Black Leaders of the Nineteenth Century*, ed. Leon Litwack and August Meier (1988): 148-171.

——. *Sojourner Truth: A Life, A Symbol* (1996).

Paiva, Eduardo Franca. *Escravos e libertos nas Minas Gerais do século XVIII: Estratégias de resistência através dos testamentos* (1995).

Palmer, Colin. *Slaves of the White God: Blacks in Mexico, 1570-1650* (1976).

Palmer, Richard. *Oscar Peterson* (1984).

Palmer, Robert. *Deep Blues* (1981).

Paquet, Sandra Pouchet. *The Novels of George Lamming* (1982).

Paris, Peter. *Black Religious Leaders: Conflict in Unity* (1991).

Park, Thomas K. *Historical Dictionary of Morocco* (1996).

Patterson, James T. *America's Struggle Against Poverty, 1900-1994* (1994).

Patterson, Orlando. *Freedom in the Making of Western Culture* (1991).

——. *The Ordeal of Integration: Progress and Resentment in America's "Racial" Crisis* (1997).

——. *Rituals of Blood: Consequences of Slavery in Two American Centuries* (1998).

Patterson, William. *The Man Who Cried Genocide: An Autobiography* (1971).

Paul, Joan, Richard V. McGhee, and Helen Fant. "The Arrival and Ascendance of Black Athletes in the Southeastern Conference, 1966-1980." *Phylon* 45, no. 4 (1984): 284-97.

Payne, Daniel A. *History of the African Methodist Episcopal Church*. Vol. I (1891; reprint ed., 1968).

Pease, Jane H., and William H. Pease. *They Who Would Be Free: Blacks' Search for Freedom, 1830-1861* (1974).

Penkower, Monty Noam. *The Federal Writers' Project: A Study in Government Patronage of the Arts* (1983).

Penvenne, Jeanne. *African Workers and Colonial Racism: Mozambican Struggles in Lourenço Marques, 1877-1962* (1997).

Pérez Sanjurjo, Elena. *Historia de la música cubana* (1986).

Perkins, Kenneth J. *Historical Dictionary of Tunisia* (1997).

Perkins, Linda M. *Fanny Jackson Coppin and the Institute for Colored Youth: A Model of Nineteenth-Century Black Female Educational and Community Leadership, 1865-1902* (1978).

Perlman, Janice. *The Myth of Marginality: Urban Poverty and Politics in Rio de Janeiro* (1973).

Pern, Stephen. *Another Land, Another Sea: Walking Round Lake Rudolph* (1979).

Perry, Bruce. *Malcolm: The Life of a Man Who Changed Black America* (1991).

Perry, Regina A. *Free Within Ourselves: African-American Artists in the Collection of the National Museum of American Art* (1992).

Peterson, Carla. *Doers of the Word: African-American Women Speakers and Writers in the North (1830-1880)* (1995).

Peterson, Kirsten Holst, and Anna Rutherford. *Chinua Achebe: A Celebration* (1991).

Peterson, Robert. *Only the Ball Was White: A History of Legendary Black Players and All-black Professional Teams* (1992).

Peters, Wallace, and Herbert M. Gilles. *Color Atlas of Tropical Medicine and Parasitology* (1995).

Pfaff, Françoise. *Conversations with Maryse Condé* (1996).

Phelps, J. Alfred. *Chappie: America's First Black Four-Star General: The Life and Times of Daniel James, Jr.* (1991).

Phelps, Timothy M., and Helen Winternitz. *Capitol Games: The Inside Story of Clarence Thomas and Anita Hill, and a Supreme Court Nomination* (1993).

Phillips, Christopher. *Freedom's Port: The African American Community of Baltimore, 1790-1860* (1997).

Picton, John, and John Mack. *African Textiles* (1989).

Pimpão, Álvaro Júlio da Costa. "José Basilio da Gama. Edição Comemorativa do Segundo Centenário." *Brasília* 2 (1942): 777-80.

Pino, Julio Cesar. *Family and Favela: The Reproduction of Poverty in Rio de Janeiro* (1997).

Pinto, Luiz de Aguiar Costa. *O Negro no Rio de Janeiro: Relações de raças numa sociedade em mudança* (1953).

Piven, Frances Fox, and Richard A. Cloward. *Poor People's Movements: Why They Succeed, How They Fail* (1977).

Placksin, Sally. *American Women in Jazz: 1900 to the Present: Their Words, Lives, and Music* (1982).

Placoly, Vincent. *Dessalines, ou, la passion de l'indépendance* (1983).

Plastow, Jane. *Ethiopia: The Creation of a Theater Culture* (1989).

Plato, Ann. *Essays: Including Biographies and Miscellaneous Pieces, in Prose and Poetry* (1841).

Platt, Anthony M. *E. Franklin Frazier Reconsidered* (1991).

Plowden, Martha Ward. *Olympic Black Women* (1996).

Pluchon, Pierre, and Louis Abenon, eds. *Histoire des Antilles et de la Guyane* (1982).

Poitier, Sidney. *This Life* (1980).

Polakoff, Claire. *Into Indigo: African Textiles and Dyeing Techniques* (1980).

Pollak-Eltz, Angelina. *Black Culture and Society in Venezuela (La Negritud en Venezuela)* (1994).

——. *La medicina popular en Venezuela* (1987).

——. *La religiosidad popular en Venezuela* (1994).

Porter, David L., ed. *Biographical Dictionary of American Sports: Basketball and Other Indoor Sports* (1989).

Porter, Dorothy B. "Maria Baldwin." *Journal of Negro History* (Winter 1952): 94-96.

Porter, James Amos. *Modern Negro Art* (1943).

Posada, Consuelo. *Canción vallenata y tradición oral* (1986).

Potash, Chris, ed. *Reggae, Rasta, Revolution: Jamaican Music from Ska to Dub* (1997).

Potter, David M. *The Impending Crisis, 1848-1861* (1976).

Poupeye, Veerle. *Modern Jamaican Art* (1998).

Povoas, Ruy do Carmo. *A linguagem do candomblé. Níveis sociolinguísticos de integração afro-portuguesa* (1989).

Powell, Colin L. *My American Journey* (1995).

Powell, Ivor. *Ndebele: A People and Their Art* (1995).

Powell, Richard J. *Black Art and Culture in the Twentieth Century* (1997).

——. *Homecoming: The Art and Life of William H. Johnson* (1991).

Powledge, Fred. *Free at Last? The Civil Rights Movement and the People Who Made It* (1991).

Prandi, J. Reginaldo. *Herdeiras do axé: Sociologia das religiões afro-brasileiras* (1996).

Prather, H. Leon. *We Have Taken A City: Wilmington Racial Massacre and Coup of 1898* (1984).

Prescott, Laurence E. *Candelario Obeso y la iniciación de la poesía negra en Colombia* (1985).

Price, Joe X. *Redd Foxx, B.S. (Before Sanford)* (1979).

Price-Mars, Jean. *La República de Haiti y la República Dominicana* (1958).

Price, Richard, ed. *Maroon Societies: Rebel Slave Communities in the Americas.* 3d ed. (1996).

Price, Sally, and Richard Price. *Maroon Arts: Cultural Vitality in the African Diaspora* (1999).

Pride, Charley. *Pride: The Charley Pride Story* (1994).

Primm, James Neal. *Lion of the Valley, St. Louis, Missouri* (1981).

Pruter, Robert. *Doowop: The Chicago Scene* (1996).

Pryse, Marjorie. "'Patterns Against the Sky': Deism and the Motherhood in Ann Petry's *The Street.*" In *Conjuring: Black Women, Fiction and Literary Traditions,* ed. Marjorie Pryse and Hortense Spillers (1985).

Quarles, Benjamin. *Black Abolitionists* (1969).

——. *The Negro in the American Revolution* (1961).

——. *The Negro in the Civil War (1953).*

Querino, Manuel. *The African Contribution to Brazilian Civilization.* Translated by E. Bradford Burns (1978).

——. *A Bahia de Outoura* (1955).

——. *Costumes africanos no Brasil* (1938).

——. *A raça africana e os seus costumes* (1955).

Quillen, Frank U. *The Color Line in Ohio* (1913).

Quilombhoje. *Criação crioula, nu elefante branco* (1987).

Quinn, Charlotte. *Mandingo Kingdoms of the Senegambia: Traditionalism, Islam, and European Expansion* (1972).

Quiroz Otero, Ciro. *Vallenato: Hombre y canto* (1982).

Rabinowitz, Howard N. *Race Relations in the Urban South, 1865-1890* (1996).

Ragan, Sandra L. et al, ed. *The Lynching of Language: Gender, Politics, and Power in the Hill-Thomas Hearings* (1996).

Rahier, Jean. *La décima: Poesía oral negra del Ecuador* (1987).

Rainwater, Lee. *Behind Ghetto Walls: Black Families in a Federal Slum* (1970).

Rajoelina, Patrick. *Quarante années de la vie politique de Madagascar, 1947-1987* (1988).

Rake, Alan. *Who's Who in Africa: Leaders for the 1990s* (1992).

Rakodi, Carole. *Harare: Inheriting a Settler-Colonial City: Change or Continuity* (1995).

Ramos, Arthur. *The Negro in Brazil* (1951).

Ramos Guedez, José Marcial. *El negro en Venezuela: Aporte bibliografico* (1985).

Rampersad, Arnold. *The Art and Imagination of W. E. B. Du Bois* (1990).

——. *Jackie Robinson: A Biography* (1997).

——. *The Life of Langston Hughes.* 2 vols. (1986-1988).

Ranvaud, Don. "Interview with Med Hondo." *Framework* (Spring 1978): 28-30.

Rap on Rap: Straight Up Talk on Hip Hop Culture. Compiled by Adam Sexton (1995).

Rasky, Frank. "Harlem's Religious Zealots." *Tomorrow* (Nov. 1949): 11-17.

Raper, Arthur F. *The Tragedy of Lynching* (1933).

Rawley, James A. *The Transatlantic Slave Trade: A History* (1981).

Ray, Benjamin. *African Religions: Symbol, Ritual, and Community* (1976).

Reader, John. *Africa: A Biography of the Continent* (1998).

Read, Florence. *The Story of Spelman College* (1961).

Redd, Lawrence N. *Rock Is Rhythm and Blues: The Impact of Mass Media* (1974).

Redkey, Edwin S. *Black Exodus: Black Nationalist and Back-to-Africa Movements, 1890-1910* (1969).

Redmon, Coates. *Come As You Are: The Peace Corps Story* (1986).

Rego, Waldeloir. *Capoeira Angola: Ensaio socio-etnografico* (1968).

Reid, Calvin. "Caught in the Flux." *Transition* (Spring 1995).

Reid, Ira de Augustine. *The Negro Immigrant: His Background, Characteristics, and Social Adjustment, 1899-1937* (1939).

Reis, João José. *Slave Rebellion in Brazil: The Muslim Uprising of 1835 in Bahia.* Translated by Arthur Brakel (1993).

"Religious Symbolism in African-American Quilts." *Clarion* 14, no. 3, (Summer 1989): 36-43.

Report of the National Advisory Commission on Civil Disorders (1968).

Render, Sylvia Lyons. *Charles W. Chesnutt* (1980).

Reswick, Irmtraud. *Traditional Textiles of Tunisia and Related North African Weavings* (1985).

Reynolds, Moira Davidson. *"Uncle Tom's Cabin" and Mid-Nineteenth Century United States: Pen and Conscience* (1985).

Ribeiro, René. *Religião e relações raciais* (1956).

Ribowsky, Mark. *Don't Look Back: Satchel Paige and the Shadows of Baseball* (1994).

Richards, Leonard L. *Gentleman of Property and Standing: Anti-Abolition Mobs in Jacksonian America* (1970).

Richardson, Joe M. *A History of Fisk University, 1865-1946* (1980).

Richardson, Michael, ed. *Refusal of the Shadow: Surrealism and the Caribbean.* Translated by Krzysztof Fijalkowski and Michael Richardson (1996).

Richmond, Merle. *Bid the Vassal Soar: Interpretative Essays on the Life and Poetry of Phillis Wheatley (ca. 1753-1784) and George Moses Horton (ca. 1797-1883)* (1974).

Rich, Wilbur C. *Black Mayors and School Politics: The Failure of Reform in Detroit, Gary, and Newark* (1996).

——. *The New Black Power* (1987).

Riley, James A. *The Biographical Encyclopedia of the Negro Baseball Leagues* (1994).

——. *Dandy, Day and the Devil* (1987).

Ringgold, Faith. *We Flew Over the Bridge: The Memoirs of Faith Ringgold* (1995).

Rishell, Lyle. *With A Black Platoon in Combat: A Year in Korea* (1993).

Ritchie, Carson. *Rock Art of Africa* (1979).

Ritz, David. *Divided Soul: The Life of Marvin Gaye* (1985).

Rivlin, Benjamin, ed. *Ralph Bunche: The Man and His Times* (1990).

Rivlin, Gary. *Fire on the Prairie: Chicago's Harold Washington and the Politics of Race* (1993).

Roberts, John Storm. *The Latin Tinge: The Impact of Latin American Music on the United States* (1979).

Roberts, A. D. "Tippu Tip, Livingstone, and the Chronology of Kazembe." *Azamoa* 2 (1967).

Roberts, Andrew. *A History of Zambia* (1976).

Roberts, A. "Nyamwezi Trade." In *Pre-colonial African Trade,* ed. R. Gray and D. Birmingham (1970).

Roberts, Martin. "'World Music' and the Global Cultural Economy." *Diaspora* 2, no. 2 (1992): 229-41.

Roberts, Randy. *Papa Jack: Jack Johnson and the Era of White Hopes* (1983).

Robeson, Paul. *Here I Stand* (1958).

Robeson, Susan. *The Whole World in His Hands: A Pictorial Biography of Paul Robeson* (1981).

Robinson, Donald. *Slavery in the Structure of American Politics, 1765-1820* (1971).

Robinson, Jackie, with Alfred Duckett. *I Never Had It Made* (1972).

Robinson, Jo Ann Gibson. *The Montgomery Bus Boycott and the Women Who Started It: The Memoir of Jo Ann Robinson* (1987).

Robinson, Jontyle Theresa, and Wendy Greenhouse. *The Art of Archibald J. Motley, Jr.* (1991).

Robinson, Ray, and Dave Anderson. *Sugar Ray* (1969).

Robinson, William H. *Phillis Wheatley and her Writings* (1984).

Rodman, Selden. *Renaissance in Haiti: Popular Painters in the Black Republic* (1948).

——. *Where Art is Joy: Haitian Art: The First Forty Years* (1988).

RODNEY, WALTER. *A History of the Guyanese Working People, 1881-1905.* (1981).

ROGERS, KIM LACY. *Righteous Lives: Narratives of the New Orleans Civil Rights Movement* (1993).

ROLLIN, FRANK A. *Life and Public Services of Martin R. Delany, Sub-assistant Commissioner, Bureau Relief of Refugees, Freedmen, and of Abandoned Lands, and Late Major 104th U.S. Colored Troops* (1868).

ROLLOCK, BARBARA. *Black Authors and Illustrators of Children's Books* (1988).

ROMAINE, SUZANNE. *Bilingualism* (1989).

RONDÓN, CÉSAR MIGUEL. *El libro de la salsa: Cronica de la música del Caribe urbano* (1980).

RO, RONIN. *Gangsta: Merchandizing the Rhymes of Violence* (1996).

ROSE, AL. *Eubie Blake* (1979).

ROSELLO, MIREILLE. *Littérature et identité créole aux Antilles* (1992).

ROSE, TRICIA. *Black Noise: Rap Music and Black Culture in Contemporary America* (1994).

ROSE, WILLIE LEE, ED. *A Documentary History of Slavery in North America* (1976).

ROSS, B. JOYCE. *J. E. Spingarn and the Rise of the NAACP, 1911-1939* (1972).

ROTH, DAVID. *Sacred Honor: A Biography of Colin Powell* (1993).

ROULHE, NELLIE C. *Work, Play, and Commitment: A History of the First Fifty Years, Jack and Jill of America, Incorporated* (1989).

ROUT, LESLIE B. *The African Experience in Spanish America, 1502 to the Present Day* (1976).

ROVINE, VICTORIA. "Bogolanfini in Bamako: The Biography of a Malian Textile." *African Arts* 30 (1997).

ROWELL, CHARLES H., AND BRUCE WILLIS. "Interview with Afro-Brazilian playwright and poet Luiz Silva Cuti." *Callaloo* 18, no. 4 (Fall 1996): 729-33.

RUEDA NOVOA, ROCÍO. *Zambaje y autonomía: La historia de Esmeraldas siglos XVI-XIX* (1990).

RUEDY, JOHN. *Modern Algeria: The Origins and Development of a Nation* (1992).

RUDWICK, ELLIOTT M. *Race Riot at East St. Louis, July 2, 1917* (1964).

RUFF, SHAWN STEWART. *Go the Way Your Blood Beats: An Anthology of Lesbian and Gay Fiction by African-American Writers* (1996).

RULE, SHEILA. "Fredi Washington, 90, Actress; Broke Ground for Black Artists." *New York Times* (June 30, 1994): D21.

RUSSELL, ROSS. *Bird Lives: The High Life and Hard Times of Charlie (Yardbird) Parker* (1973).

——. *Jazz Style in Kansas City and the Southwest* (1971).

RUSSELL-WOOD, A. J. R. *The Black Man in Slavery and Freedom in Colonial Brazil* (1982).

SACK, KEVIN. "A Dynamic Farewell from a Longtime Rights Leader." *New York Times* (July 29, 1997).

——. "Ex-Charlotte Mayor Earns Helms Rematch." *New York Times* (May 8, 1996): B10.

SAGINI, MASHAK M. *The African and the African American University: A Historical and Sociological Analysis* (1996).

SALEM, NORMA. *Habib Bourguiba, Islam and the Creation of Tunisia* (1984).

SALZMAN, JACK, DAVID LIONEL SMITH, AND CORNEL WEST, EDS. *Encyclopedia of African-American Culture and History.* 5 vols. (1996).

SAMKANGE, STANLAKE. *What Rhodes Really Said About Africans* (1982).

SAMMONS, JEFFREY T. *Beyond the Ring: The Role of Boxing in American Society* (1988).

SAMMONS, VIVIAN O. *Blacks in Science and Medicine* (1990).

SÁNCHEZ-BOUDY, JOSÉ. *Diccionario de cubanismos más usuales (Como habla el cubano).* 6 vols. (1978-1992).

SANDERSON, PETER. *Marvel Universe* (1995).

SANDOVAL, ALONSO DE. *De instauranda aethiopum salute - Un tratado sobre la esclavitud.* Translated by Enriqueta Vila Vilar (1987).

SAN MIGUEL, PEDRO. "The Dominican Peasantry and the Market Economy: The Peasants of the Cibao: 1880-1960." Ph.D. diss. Columbia University, 1987.

——. "The Making of a Peasantry: Dominican Agrarian History from the Sixteenth to the Twentieth Century." *Punto y Coma 2,* nos.1 and 2 (1990): 143-62.

SANTINO, JACK. *Miles of Smiles, Years of Struggle: Stories of Black Pullman Porters* (1989).

SANTOS, SYDNEY M. G. DOS. *André Rebouças e seu tempo* (1985).

SARTRE, JEAN-PAUL. "Orphée Noire." *Situations* 3 (1949): 227-86.

SATCHEL, LEROY. *Pitchin' Man: Satchel Paige's Own Story* (1992).

SATER, WILLIAM F. "The Black Experience in Chile." In *Slavery and Race Relations in Latin America,* ed. Robert Brent Toplin (1974).

SAUNDERS, A. C. *A Social History of Black Slaves and Freedmen in Portugal (1441-1555)* (1982).

SAVIANI, DERMEVAL, GERMAN RAMA, NORBERTO LAMARRA, INÉS AGUERRONDO, AND GREGÓRIO WEINBERG. *Desenvolvimento e educação na América Latina* (1987).

SAVOIA, RAFAEL. *Actas del Primer Congreso de Historia del Negro en el Ecuador y Sur de Colombia, Esmeraldas, 14-16 de octubre* (1988).

——, ED. *El Negro en la historia: Raices africanas in la nacionalidad ecuatorana* (1992).

SCARANO, JULITA. *Cotidiano e soli-dariedade: Vida diária da gente de cor nas Minas Gerais, século XVIII* (1994).

SCHAFFER, MATT, AND CHRISTINE COOPER. *Mandinko: The Ethnography of a West African Holy Land* (1980).

SCHARFMAN, RONNIE L. *"Engagement" and the Language of the Subject in the Poetry of Aimé Césaire* (1987).

SCHATZBERG, MICHAEL. *The Dialectics of Oppression in Zaire* (1988).

SCHEADER, CATHERINE. *Shirley Chisholm: Teacher and Congresswoman* (1990).

SCHIEFFELIN, BAMBI, AND RACHELLE DOUCET. "The 'Real' Haitian Creole: Ideology, Metalinguistics, and Orthographic Choices." *American Ethnologist* 21, no. 1 (1994): 176-200.

SCHNEIDER, JOHN J., AND D. STANLEY EITZEN. "Racial Segregation by Professional Football Positions,1960-1985." *Sociology and Social Research* 70, no. 4 (1986): 259-61.

SCHNEIDER, JOHN T. *Dictionary of African Borrowings in Brazilian Portuguese* (1991).

SCHREINER, CLAUS. *Música brasileira: A History of Popular Music and the People of Brazil.* Translated by Mark Weinstein (1993).

SCHUBERT, FRANK. *Black Valor: Buffalo Soldiers and the Medal of Honor, 1870-1898* (1997).

SCHULLER, GUNTHER. *Early Jazz: Its Roots and Musical Development* (1968).

——. *The Swing Era: The Development of Jazz, 1930-1945* (1989).

SCHWARTZMAN, MYRON. *Romare Bearden: His Life and Art* (1990).

SCHWARTZ-BART, SIMONE. *The Bridge of Beyond.* Translated by Barbara Bray. Introduction by Bridget Jones (1982).

SCHWARZ, ROBERTO. *Misplaced Ideas: Essays on Brazilian Culture* (1992).

SCOTT, KENNETH. "The Slave Insurrection in New York in 1712." *New York Historical Society Quarterly* 45 (January 1961).

SECRETAN, THIERRY. *Going into Darkness: Fantastic Coffins from Africa* (1995).

SENGHOR, LÉOPOLD SEDAR. *Liberté.* 5 vols. (1964-1993).

SERAILE, WILLIAM. *Voice of Dissent: Theophilus Gould Steward (1843-1924) and Black America* (1991).

SERELS, M. MITCHELL. *A History of the Jews of Tangier in the Nineteenth and Twentieth Centuries* (1991).

SHARP, WILLIAM FREDERICK. *Slavery on the Spanish Frontier: The Colombian Chocó, 1680-1810* (1976).

SHANNON, SANDRA G. *The Dramatic Vision of August Wilson* (1995).

SHAW, ARNOLD. *Honkers and Shouters: The Golden Years of Rhythm and Blues* (1978).

SHAW, DONALD L. *Alejo Carpentier* (1985).

SHERMAN, JOAN. *Invisible Poets: Afro-Americans of the Nineteenth Century.* 2d ed. (1989).

SHERMAN, RICHARD B. *The Case of Odell Waller and Virginia Justice, 1940-1942* (1992).

SHIELDS, JOHN C. "Phillis Wheatley." In *African American Writers,* ed. Valerie Smith (1991).

SHOCKLEY, ANN ALLEN. *Afro-American Women Writers, 1746-1933: An Anthology and Critical Guide* (1988).

SHOGAN, ROBERT, AND TOM CRAIG. *The Detroit Race Riot: A Study in Violence* (1964).

SHOMAN, ASSAD. *13 Chapters of a History of Belize* (1994).

SHUCARD, ALAN R. *Countee Cullen* (1984).

Sierra Leone: Twelve Years of Economic Achievement and Political Consolidation under the APC and Dr. Siaka Stevens, 1968-1980 (1980).

SILL, ROBERT. *David Hammons in the Hood* (1994).

SILVA, J. ROMÃO DA. *Luís Gama e suas poesias satíricas* (1981).

SILVERA, MAKEDA, ED. *The Other Woman: Women of Colour in Contemporary Canadian Literature* (1994).

SILVESTER, PETER. *A Left Hand like God: A History of Boogie-Woogie Piano* (1988).

SIMKINS, CUTHBERT O. *Coltrane: A Musical Biography* (1975).

SIMMONS, DIANE. *Jamaica Kincaid* (1994).

SIMO, ANA MARÍA. *Lydia Cabrera: An Intimate Portrait* (1984).

SIMMS, PETER. *Trouble in Guyana: An Account of People, Personalities, and Politics as They Were in British Guiana* (1966).

SIMPSON, DAVID IAN H. *Marburg and Ebola Virus Infections: A Guide for Their Diagnosis, Management, and Control* (1977).

SIMPSON, GEORGE EATON. *Black Religions in the New World.* (1978).

——. *The Shango Cult in Trinidad* (1965).

SIMS, JANET L. *Marian Anderson: An Annotated Bibliography and Discography* (1981).

SIMS, LOWERY STOKES. *Robert Colescott, A Retrospective 1975-1986* (1987).

SIMS, RUDINE. *Shadow and Substance: Afro-American Experience in Contemporary Children's Fiction* (1982).

SINGER, BARRY. *Black and Blue: The Life and Lyrics of Andy Razaf* (1992).

SINNETTE, ELINOR DES VERNEY. *Arthur Alfonso Schomburg, Black Bibliophile & Collector: A Biography* (1989).

SINNETTE, ELINOR DES VERNEY, W. PAUL COATES, AND THOMAS C. BATTLE, EDS. *Black Bibliophiles and Collectors: Preservers of Black History* (1990).

SITKOFF, HARVARD. *A New Deal for Blacks: The Emergence of Civil Rights as a National Issue.* Vol. I, *The Depression Decade* (1978).

SKIDMORE, THOMAS E. *Black Into White: Race and Nationality in Brazilian Thought* (1974; revised ed., 1993).

SLATER, LES. "What is Mas? What is Carnival? Profiling Carnival and its Origins." *Black Diaspora: A Global Black Magazine* (August 1997).

SLAUGHTER, THOMAS PAUL. *Bloody Dawn: The Christiana Riot and Racial Violence in the Antebellum North* (1991).

SMITH, ANNA DEVEARE. *Fires in the Mirror: Crown Heights, Brooklyn and Other Identities* (1993).

SMITH, BARBARA, ED. *Home Girls: A Black Feminist Anthology* (1983).

SMITH, CHARLES MICHAEL. "Bruce Nugent: Bohemian of the Harlem Renaissance." In *In the Life: A Black Gay Anthology,* ed. Joseph Beam (1986).

SMITH CÓRDOBA, AMIR. *Vida y obra de Candelario Obeso* (1984).

SMITH, IAN DOUGLAS. *The Great Betrayal: The Memoirs of Ian Douglas Smith* (1997).

SMITH-IRVIN, JEANNETTE. *Footsoldiers of the Universal Negro Improvement Association: Their Own Words* (1988).

SMITH, JESSIE CARNEY. *Black Academic Libraries and Research Collections: An Historical Survey* (1977).

——, ED. *Notable Black American Women.* 2 vols. (1992-1996).

SMITH, KEITHLYN B. *No Easy Pushover: A History of the Working People of Antigua and Barbuda, 1836-1994* (1994).

SMITH, KEITHLYN B., AND FERNANDO C. *To Shoot Hard Labour: The Life and Times of Samuel Smith, an Antiguan Workingman, 1877-1982* (1986).

SMITH, ROBERTA. "A Forgotten Black Painter Is Saved from Obscurity." *New York Times* (June 12, 1992): C18.

SMITH, RONNA. "Vida de Adalberto Ortiz." *Cultura: Revista del Banco Central del Ecuador* 6, no. 16 (1983): 99-118.

SMITH, S. CLAY, JR. "Patricia Roberts Harris: A Champion in Pursuit of Excellence." *Howard Law Journal* 29, no. 3 (1986): 437-55.

SMITH, WILLIAM E. "Commandments Without Moses: Abandoning His Principles, Sullivan Wants U. S. Firms to Pull Out." *Time* (June 15, 1987).

SNOWDEN, FRANK M., JR. *Before Color Prejudice: The Ancient View of Blacks* (1983).

——. *Blacks in Antiquity; Ethiopians in the Greco-Roman Experience* (1970).

SOLLORS, WERNER. *Amiri Baraka/LeRoi Jones: The Quest for a "Populist Modernism"* (1978).

——. *Neither Black nor White, Yet Both: Thematic Explorations of Interracial Literature* (1997).

——, ED. *Multilingual America: Transnationalism, Ethnicity, and the Languages of American Literature* (1998).

SOLOW, BARBARA L., ED. *Slavery and the Rise of the Atlantic System* (1991).

SOMJEE, SULTAN. *Material Culture of Kenya* (1993).

SOMMER, DORIS, *Foundational Fictions : The National Romances of Latin America* (1991).

SOTO, SARA. *Magia e historia en los "Cuentos negros": "Por que" y "Ayapa" de Lydia Cabrera* (1988).

SOUTHERN, EILEEN. *The Music of Black Americans: A History* (1983).

SOYINKA, WOLE. *The Burden of Memory, the Muse of Forgiveness* (1999).

——. *Myth, Literature, and the African World* (1976).

——. *The Open Sore of a Continent: A Personal Narrative of the Nigerian Crisis* (1996).

SPELLMAN, A. B. *Black Music: Four Lives* (1970).

SPINNER, THOMAS J., JR. *A Political and Social History of Guyana, 1945-1983* (1984).

SPIVAK, GAYATRI CHAKTAVORTY. *In Other Worlds: Essays in Cultural Politics* (1987).

SPOFFORD, TIM. *Lynch Street: The May 1970 Slayings at Jackson State College* (1988).

STAMPP, KENNETH M. *The Peculiar Institution: Slavery in the Ante-Bellum South* (1956).

STAM, ROBERT. *Tropical Multiculturalism: A Comparative History of Race in Brazilian Cinema and Culture* (1997).

STAM, ROBERT, AND RANDAL JOHNSON. *Brazilian Cinema.* Rev. and exp. ed. (1995).

STANLEY, HENRY MORTON. *In Darkest Africa; or, The Quest, Rescue and Retreat of Emin, Governor of Equatoria (1890).*

——. *Through the Dark Continent; or The Sources of the Nile around the Great Lakes of Equatorial Africa and Down the Livingstone River to the Atlantic Ocean* (1878).

ST. BOURNE, CLAIR. "The African-American Image in American Cinema." *Black Scholar* 21, no.2 (March-May 1990): 12 (8).

STEARNS, MARSHALL, AND JEAN STEARNS. *Jazz Dance: The Story of American Vernacular Dance.* Rev. ed. (1979).

STEIN, JUDITH E., ET AL. *I Tell My Heart: The Art of Horace Pippin* (1993).

STEIN, STEVE J. "Visual Images of the Lower Classes in Early Twentieth-Century Peru: Soccer as a Window to Social Reality." In *Windows on Latin America: Understanding Society through Photographs,* ed. Robert M. Levine (1987).

STEPAN, NANCY. *The Idea of Race in Science* (1982).

STEPHENS, THOMAS M. *Dictionary of Latin American Racial and Ethnic Terminology* (1989).

STEPTO, ROBERT B. "After Modernism, After Hibernation: Michael Harper, Robert Hayden, and Jay Wright." In *Chant of Saints: A Gathering of Afro-American Literature, Art, and Scholarship* (1979).

——. *From Behind the Veil: A Study of Afro-American Narrative* (1979)

STERLING, DOROTHY. *Black Foremothers: Three Lives* (1988).

——. *The Making of an Afro-American: Martin Robison Delany 1812-1885* (1971).

——. *We Are Your Sisters: Black Women in the Nineteenth Century* (1984).

STERN, YVAN. "Interview: Souleymane Cissé." *Unir Cinema* 23-24 (March-June 1986): 44-45.

STEVENSON, BRENDA, ED. *The Journals of Charlotte Forten Grimké* (1988).

STEVENS, PHILLIPS, JR. "Magic" and "Sorcery and Witchcraft." In *Encyclopedia of Cultural Anthropology,* ed. Melvin Ember and David Levinson (1996).

STEVENS, SIAKA. *What Life Has Taught Me* (1984).

STEWART-BAXTER, DERRICK. *Ma Rainey and the Classic Blues Singers* (1970).

STILL, JUDITH ANNE. *William Grant Still: A Bio-bibliography* (1996).

STILL, WILLIAM. *The Underground Railroad: A Record of Facts, Authentic Narratives, Letters, &c., Narrating the Hardships, Hair-breadth Escapes, and Death Struggles of the Slaves in Their Efforts for Freedom, as Related by Themselves and Others or Witnessed By the Author: Together with Sketches of Some of the Largest Stockholders and Most Liberal Aiders and Advisers of the Road* (1872).

STINSON, SULEE JEAN. *The Dawn of Blaxploitation: Sweet Sweetback's Baadasssss Song and its Audience* (1992).

STORY, ROSALYN M. *And So I Sing: African American Divas of Opera and Concert* (1990).

STRAUSS, NEIL. "Curtis Mayfield" (interview). *New York Times* (February 28, 1996).

STRAUS, NOEL. "Dorthy Maynor Berkshire Soloist." *New York Times* (August 10, 1939).

STOWE, HARRIET BEECHER. *Uncle Tom's Cabin: Authoritative Text. Backgrounds and Contexts* (Norton Critical Edition) (1994).

STREICKER, JOEL. "Policing the Boundaries: Race, Class and Gender in Cartagena, Colombia." *American Ethnologist* 22, no. 1 (1995), 54-74.

STUART, CHRIS, AND TILDE STUART. *Africa's Vanishing Wildlife* (1996).

——. *Chris and Tilde Stuart's Field Guide to the Mammals of Southern Africa* (1994).

STUCKEY, STERLING. *Slave Culture: Nationalist Theory and the Foundations of Black America* (1987).

SUGGS, HENRY LEWIS. *P. B. Young, Newspaperman: Race, Politics, and Journalism in the New South, 1910-1962* (1988).

SULLIVAN, PATRICIA. *Days of Hope: Race and Democracy in the New Deal Era* (1996).

SUMMERVILLE, JAMES. *Educating Black Doctors: A History of Meharry Medical College* (1983).

SUPER, GEORGE LEE, MICHAEL GARDEN, AND NANCY MARSHALL, EDS. *P. H. Polk: Photographs* (1980).

SUTTON, JOHN E. G. *Dar es Salaam: City, Port, and Region* (1970).

SUZIGAN, GERALDO. *Bossa nova: música, política, educação no Brasil* (1990).

SWEETMAN, DAVID. *Women Leaders in African History* (1984).

SWENSON, JOHN. *Stevie Wonder* (1986).

SYLVANDER, CAROLYN WEDIN. *Jessie Redmon Fauset, Black American Writer* (1981).

TARRY, ELLEN. *The Other Toussaint: A Modern Biography of Pierre Toussaint, a Post-Revolutionary Black* (1981).

TATE, CLAUDIA. *Domestic Allegories of Political Desire: The Black Heroine's Text at the Turn of the Century* (1992).

TAYLOR, FRANK. *Alberta Hunter: A Celebration in Blues* (1987).

TAYLOR, PATRICK. *The Narrative of Liberation: Perspectives on Afro-Caribbean Literature, Popular Culture, and Politics* (1989).

TAYLOR, QUINTARD. *The Forging of a Black Community: Seattle's Central District from 1870 through the Civil Rights Era* (1994).

TEIXEIRA, IVAN. *Obras poéticas de Basílio da Gama* (1996).

TENENBAUM, BARBARA A., ED. *Encyclopedia of Latin American History and Culture.* 5 vols. (1996).

"The Ten Most Beautiful Black Women in America (A Wide Range of External and Internal Beauty)." *Ebony* (July 1987).

TERRY, DON. "Hatcher Begins Battle to Regain Spotlight in Gary." *New York Times.* (May 6, 1991): A12.

TERRY, WALLACE, ED. *Bloods: An Oral History of the Vietnam War, by Black Veterans* (1984).

THOBY-MARCELIN, PHILIPPE. *Panorama de l'art Haïtien* (1956).

THOMAS, ANTONY. *Rhodes* (1996).

THOMAS, BETTYE COLLIER. "Harvey Johnson and the Baltimore Mutual United Brotherhood of Liberty, 1885-1910." In *Black Communities and Urban Development in America, 1720-1990: From Reconstruction to the Great Migration, 1877-1917*, ed. Kenneth L. Kusmer. Vol. IV, part 1 (1991).

THOMAS, BROOK. *Plessy v. Ferguson: A Brief History with Documents* (1997).

THOMAS, DAVID S. G. *The Kalahari Environment* (1991).

THOMAS, HUGH. *Cuba: The Pursuit of Freedom* (1971).

THOMPSON, FRANCESCA. "Final Curtain for Anita Bush." *Black World* 23 (July 1974): 60-61.

THOMPSON, LESLIE. *An Autobiography* (1985).

THOMPSON, ROBERT FERRIS. *Flash of the Spirit: African and Afro-American Art and Philosophy* (1983).

——. *Jean-Michel Basquiat* (1985).

THORNTON, J. MILLS III. "Challenge and Response in the Montgomery Bus Boycott of 1955-1956." *Alabama Review* 33 (1980): 163-235.

THORNTON, JOHN. *Africa and Africans in the Making of the Atlantic World: 1400-1800* (1998).

THORPE, EDWARD. *Black Dance* (1990).

THURMAN, HOWARD. *With Head and Heart: The Autobiography of Howard Thurman* (1979).

TIBBLES, ANTHONY, ED. *Transatlantic Slavery: Against Human Dignity* (1994).

TILLERY, TYRONE. *Claude McKay: A Black Poet's Struggle for Identity* (1992).

TIMBERLAKE, LLOYD. *Africa in Crisis: The Causes, the Cures of Environmental Bankruptcy* (1985).

TINGAY, PAUL, AND DOUG SCOTT. *Handy Guide: Victoria Falls* (1996).

TINHORAO, RAMOS JOSÉ. *Os Negros em Portugal: Uma presença silenciosa* (1988).

TIPPU TIP. *Maisha ya Hamed bin Muhammed el Murjebi, Yaani Tippu Tip, kwa Maneno Yake Mwenyewe.* Translated by W. H. Whitely (1966).

TOBIAS, CHANNING. "Autobiography." In *Thirteen Americans: Their Spiritual Biographies* (1953).

TOMKINS, CALVIN, "A Sense of Urgency." *New Yorker* (March 1989): 48-74.

TOOBIN, JEFFREY. *The Run of His Life: The People v. O. J. Simpson* (1996).

TOOP, DAVID. *Ocean of Sound: Aether Talk, Ambient Sound, and Imaginary Worlds* (1995).

TOPLIN, ROBERT BRENT. *The Abolition of Slavery in Brazil* (1972).

TORRENCE, RIDGELY. *The Story of John Hope* (1948).

TOUREH, FANTA. *L'imaginaire dans l'œuvre de Simone Schwartz-Bart: Approche d'une mythologie antillaise* (1986).

TOUSSAINT, AUGUSTE. *History of Mauritius* (1977).

TREXLER, HARRISON. *Slavery in Missouri, 1804-1865* (1914).

TREVISAN, JOÃO SILVERIO. *Perverts in Paradise.* Translated by Martin Foreman (1986).

TRUTH, SOJOURNER, AND OLIVE GILBERT, *Narrative of Sojourner Truth, a Northern Slave, Emancipated from Bodily Servitude by the State of New York, in 1828* (1850).

TURNBULL, COLIN M. *The Forest People* (1961).

TURNER, FREDERICK W. *Remembering Song: Encounters with the New Orleans Jazz Tradition.* Exp. ed. (1994).

TURNER, LORENZO DOW. *Africanisms in the Gullah Dialect* (1949).

TURNER, MARY. *From Chattel Slaves to Wage Slaves: The Dynamics of Labour Bargaining in the Americas* (1995).

——. *Slaves and Missionaries: The Disintegration of Jamaican Slave Society* (1982).

TUSHNET, MARK V. *The NAACP's Strategy Against Segregated Education, 1925-1950* (1987).

TUTTLE, WILLIAM M., JR. *Race Riot: Chicago in the Red Summer of 1919* (1970).

——, ED. *W. E. B. Du Bois* (1973).

TYGIEL, JULES. *Baseball's Great Experiment: Jackie Robinson and His Legacy* (1983).

UCHE, NENA. "Textiles in Nigeria." *African Technology Forum* 7, no. 2 (1994).

Ullman, Michael. *Jazz Lives: Portraits in Words and Pictures* (1980).

Ullman, Victor. *Martin R. Delany: The Beginnings of Black Nationalism* (1971).

Unesco General History of Africa. 8 vols. (1981-1993).

Urban, W. J. *Black Scholar: Horace Mann Bond 1904-1972* (1992).

Urquhart, Brian. *Ralph Bunche: An American Life* (1993).

Valdez Aguilar, Rafael. *Sinaloa: Negritud y olvido* (1993).

Van Deburg, William L. *New Day in Babylon: The Black Power Movement and American Culture, 1965-1975* (1992).

Vandercook, John W. *Black Majesty: The Life of Christophe, King of Haiti* (1934).

Van Sertima, Ivan. *Blacks in Science: Ancient and Modern* (1991).

——, ed. *African Presence in Early America* (1987).

——, ed. *African Presence in Early Europe* (1985).

——, ed. *Black Women in Antiquity* (1984).

Van Sertima, Ivan, and Runoko Rashidi, eds. *African Presence in Early Asia* (1988).

Vansina, Jan. *Les anciens royaumes de la savane: Les états des savanes méridionales de l'Afrique centrale des origines à l'occupation coloniale* (1965).

——. *Art History in Africa: An Introduction to Method* (1984).

——. *The Children of Woot: A History of the Kuba Peoples* (1978).

——. *Kingdoms of the Savanna* (1966).

——. *Oral Tradition as History* (1985).

——. *Paths in the Rainforests: Toward a History of Political Tradition in Equatorial Africa* (1990).

Van Tassel, David D., and John J. Grabowski. *Cleveland: A Tradition of Reform* (1986).

——. *The Encyclopedia of Cleveland History* (1987).

Varela, Beatriz. *El español cubano-americano* (1992).

Vasquez de Urrutia, Patricia, ed. *La democracia en blanco y negro: Colombia en los anos ochenta* (1989).

Vedana, Hardy. *Jazz em Porto Alegre* (1987).

Venet, Wendy Hammond. *Neither Ballots Nor Bullets: Women Abolitionists and the Civil War* (1991).

Verbeken, Auguste. *Msiri, roi du Garenganze: L' homme rouge du Katanga* (1956).

Verger, Pierre. *Bahia Africa Bahia: Fotografias* (1996).

——. *Bahia and the West African Trade, 1549-1851* (1964).

——. *Dieux d'Afrique; Culte des Orishas et Vodouns à l' ancienne côte des esclaves en Afrique et à Bahia, la baie de tous les saints au Brésil.*

——. *Ewe: Le verbe et le pouvoir des plantes chez les Yoruba* (1997).

——. *Flux et reflux de la traite des nègres entre le Golfe de Bénin et Bahia de todos os Santos, du XVIIè au XIXè siècle* (1968).

——. *Orixas: Deuses iorubas na Africa e no Novo Mundo* (1981).

——. *Retratos da Bahia, 1946 a 1952* (1980).

Verger, Pierre, and Jorge Amado. *Iconografia dos deuses africanos no candomblé da Bahia* (1980).

Vérin, Pierre. *The History of Civilization in North Madagascar.* Translated by David Smith (1986).

Vérin, Pierre, C. P. Kottack, and P. Gorlin. "The glottochronology of Malagasy speech communities." *Oceanic Linguistics* 8 (1970): 26-83.

Veríssimo, Inácio José. *André Rebouças através de sua auto-biografia* (1939).

Vestal, Stanley. *Mountain Men* (1937).

Vickery, Walter N. *Alexander Pushkin* (1970).

Vines, Alex. *Renamo: Terrorism in Mozambique* (1991).

Vitier, Cintio, and Fina García Marruz, eds. *Flor oculta de poesía cubana* (1978).

——. *Temas martianos* (1981).

Vlach, John Michael. *The Afro-American Tradition in the Decorative Arts* (1978).

Vogel, Arno. *A galinha-d'Angola: Iniciacão e identidade na cultura afro-brasileira* (1993).

Wade, Peter. *Blackness and Race Mixture: The Dynamics of Racial Identity in Colombia* (1993).

——. *Race and Ethnicity in Latin America* (1997).

Wagley, Charles., ed. *Race and Class in Rural Brazil.* 2d ed. (1963).

Wahlman, Maude Southwell. *Contemporary African Arts* (1974).

——. *Signs and Symbols: African Images in African-American Quilts* (1993).

Wakhist, Tsi Tsi. "Taking the Helm of the NAACP: The Ever-Ready Evers-Williams." *Crisis* 102 (May/June 1995): 14-19.

Waldman, Gloria F. *Luis Rafael Sánchez: Pasión teatral.* (1988).

Walker, Ethel Pitts. "The American Negro Theater." In *The Theater of Black Americans*, ed. Errol Hill (1987).

Walker, George E. *The Afro-American in New York City, 1827-1860* (1993).

Walker, James W. St. G. *The Black Loyalists: The Search for a Promised Land in Nova Scotia and Sierra Leone, 1783-1870* (1992).

Walker, Melissa. *Down from the Mountaintop: Black Women's Novels in the Wake of the Civil Rights Movement, 1966-1989* (1991).

Walls, William J. *The African Methodist Episcopal Zion Church: Reality of the Black Church* (1974).

Ward, William Edward. "Charles Lenox Remond: Black Abolitionist, 1838-1873." Ph.D. diss., Clark University, 1977.

Ware, Gilbert. *William Hastie: Grace Under Pressure* (1984).

Washington, Booker T. *Up From Slavery* (1901).

Washington, James M. *Conversations with God* (1994).

Watkins, Mel. *On The Real Side: Laughing, Lying, and Signifying. The Underground Tradition of African-American Humor* (1994).

Watson, Alan. *Slave Law in the Americas* (1989).

WATSON, DENTON L. *Lion in the Lobby: Clarence Mitchell, Jr.'s Struggle for the Passage of Civil Rights Laws* (1990).

WATTS, JILL. *God, Harlem U.S.A.: The Father Divine Story* (1992).

WEARE, WALTER B. *Black Business in the New South: A Social History of the North Carolina Mutual Life Insurance Company* (1973).

WEAVER, JOHN DOWNING. *The Brownsville Raid* (1970).

——. *The Senator and the Sharecropper's Son: Exoneration of the Brownsville Soldiers* (1997).

WEAVER, ROBERT C. "The Health Care of Our Cities." *National Medical Association Journal* (January 1968): 42-48.

WEBB, BARBARA J. *Myth and History in Caribbean Fiction: Alejo Carpentier, Wilson Harris, and Edouard Glissant* (1992).

WEBB, LILLIAN ASHCROFT. *About My Father's Business: The Life of Elder Michaux* (1981).

WEINBERG, KENNETH G. *Black Victory: Carl Stokes and the Winning of Cleveland* (1968).

WEINSTEIN, BRIAN. *Eboué* (1972).

WEINSTEIN, NORMAN. *A Night in Tunisia: Imaginings of Africa in Jazz* (1993).

WEISS, NANCY J. *Farewell to the Party of Lincoln: Black Politics in the Age of FDR* (1983).

——. *Whitney M. Young, Jr., and the Struggle for Civil Rights* (1989).

WELLS-BARNETT, IDA B. *On Lynchings: Southern Horrors; A Red Record; Mob Rule in New Orleans* (1969).

WESLEY, CHARLES H. *Charles H. Wesley: The Intellectual Tradition of a Black; Historian*, ed. James L. Conyers, Jr. (1997).

WESLEY, DOROTHY PORTER. "Integration Versus Separatism: William Cooper Nell's Role in the Struggle for Equality." In *Courage and Conscience: Black and White Abolitionists in Boston*, ed. Donald M. Jacobs (1993): 207-24.

WEST, CORNEL. *Beyond Eurocentrism and Multiculturalism* (1993).

——. *Black Theology and Marxist Thought* (1979).

——. *Keeping Faith: Philosophy and Race in America* (1993).

——. *Prophetic Reflections: Notes on Race and Power in America* (1993).

——. *Race Matters* (1993).

WEST, GUIDA. *The National Welfare Rights Movement: The Social Protest of Poor Women* (1981).

"What Martin Luther King Would Do Now about Drugs, Poverty and Black-Jewish Relations: Widow and Associates Tell How He Would Respond to Today's Burning Issues." *Ebony* (January 1991).

WHEAT, ELLEN HARKINS. *Jacob Lawrence, American Painter* (1986).

WHEELER, B. GORDON. *Black California: The History of African-Americans in the Golden State* (1993).

WHITE, ALVIN, "Let Me Tell You about My Love Affair with Florence Mills." *Sepia* 26, no. 11 (November 1977).

WHITE, TIMOTHY. *Catch a Fire: The Life of Bob Marley.* Rev. and enl. ed. (1998).

WHITE, WALTER F. *A Man Called White: The Autobiography of Walter White* (1948; reprint ed., 1995).

——. *Rope and Faggot: A Biography of Judge Lynch* (1929).

WHITFIELD, STEPHEN J. *A Death in the Delta: The Story of Emmett Till* (1988).

WHITING, ALBERT N. *Guardians of the Flame: Historically Black Colleges Yesterday, Today, and Tomorrow* (1991).

WHITMAN, MARK, ED. *Removing a Badge of Slavery: The Record of Brown v. Board of Education* (1993).

WHITTEN, NORMAN. *Black Frontiersmen: A South American Case* (1974).

——, ED. *Cultural Transformations and Ethnicity in Modern Ecuador* (1981).

WICKER, TOM. *A Time to Die* (1975).

WIENER, LEO. *Africa and the Discovery of America.* Vol. I (1920).

WIGG, DAVID. *And Then Forgot to Tell Us Why: A Look at the Campaign Against River Blindness in West Africa* (1993).

WIKRAMANAYAKE, MARINA. *A World in Shadow: The Free Black in Antebellum South Carolina* (1973).

WILKINS, ROY. *Standing Fast: The Autobiography of Roy Wilkins* (1982).

WILLIAMS, ELSIE A. *The Humor of Jackie Moms Mabley: An African American Comedic Tradition* (1995).

WILLIAMS, ERIC. *Capitalism and Slavery* (1944; reprint ed., 1994).

——. *Inward Hunger: The Education of a Prime Minister* (1969).

WILLIAMS, LORNA V. "Morúa Delgado and the Cuban Slave Narrative." *Modern Language Notes* 108, no. 2 (March 1993): 302-13.

——. *The Representation of Slavery in Cuban Fiction.* (1994).

WILLIAMS, MICHAEL W. *Pan-Africanism: An Annotated Bibliography* (1992).

WILLIAMSON, JANICE. *Sounding Differences: Conversations with Seventeen Canadian Women Writers* (1993).

WILLIAMSON, JOEL. *After Slavery: The Negro in South Carolina During Reconstruction, 1861-1877* (1965; reprint ed., 1990).

——. *The Crucible of Race: Black-White Relations in the American South Since Emancipation* (1984).

——. *New People: Miscegenation and Mulattoes in the United States* (1980).

WILLIAMS, PONTHEOLLA T. *Robert Hayden: A Critical Analysis of His Poetry* (1987).

WILLIAMS, ROGER. *The Bonds: An American Family* (1971).

WILLIS, SUSAN. "Crushed Geraniums: Juan Francisco Manzano and the Language of Slavery." In *The Slave's Narrative*, ed. Charles T. Davis and Henry Louis Gates, Jr. (1985).

——. *Specifying: Black Women Writing the American Experience* (1987).

WILLIS-THOMAS, DEBORAH. *Black Photographers, 1840-1940: An Illustrated Bio-Bibliography* (1985).

——. *An Illustrated Bio-Bibliography of Black Photographers, 1940-1988* (1989).

WILMER, VALERIE. "'Blackamoors' and the British Beat." In *Views on Black American Music*, no. 3 (1985-1988): 60-64.

WILSON, CHARLES REAGAN, AND WILLIAM FERRIS, EDS. *Encyclopedia of Southern Culture* (1989).

WILSON, MARY, WITH PATRICIA ROMANOWSKI AND AHRGUS JULLIARD. *Dreamgirl: My Life as a Supreme* (1986).

Wilson, William Julius. *The Bridge over the Racial Divide: Rising Inequality and Coalition Politics* (1999).

——. *When Work Disappears: The World of the New Urban Poor* (1996).

Winant, Howard. "Rethinking Race in Brazil." *Journal of Latin American Studies* 24 (1992): 173-92.

Winch, Julie. *Philadelphia's Black Elite: Activism, Accommodation, and the Struggle for Autonomy, 1787-1848* (1988).

Winks, Robin W. *The Blacks in Canada: A History* (1997).

Wippler, Migene González. *Santería: The Religion* (1982).

Woidek, Carl. *Charlie Parker: His Music and Life* (1996).

Wolfenstein, Eugene Victor. *The Victims of Democracy: Malcolm X and the Black Revolution* (1981).

Wolseley, Roland E. *The Black Press, U.S.A.* (1990).

Woodbridge, Hensley C. "Glossary of Names Found in Colonial Latin America for Crosses Among Indians, Negroes, and Whites." *Journal of the Washington Academy of Sciences* 38 (1948): 353-62.

Wood, Joe, ed. *Malcolm X: In Our Own Image* (1992).

Wood, Peter H. *Black Majority: Negroes in Colonial South Carolina from 1670 through the Stono Rebellion* (1974).

Wood, Peter H., and Karen C. C. Dalton. *Winslow Homer's Images of Blacks: The Civil War and Reconstruction Years* (1988).

Woodson, Carter G. "The Negroes of Cincinnati Prior to the Civil War." In *Free Blacks in America, 1800-1860,* ed. John Bracey, Jr. August Meier, and Elliot Rudwick (1971).

Woods, Sylvia. *Sylvia's Soul Food: Recipes from Harlem's World Famous Restaurant* (1992).

Woodward, C. Vann. *Origins of the New South: 1877-1913* (1951).

——. *Reunion and Reaction: The Compromise of 1877 and the End of Reconstruction* (1951; reprint ed. 1991).

——. *The Strange Career of Jim Crow* (1955).

Woolman, David S. *Stars in the Firmament: Tangier Characters, 1660-1960s* (1997).

Worcester, Kent. *C. L. R. James and the American Century, 1938-1953* (1980).

World Bank. *Mauritius Country Report* 4 (1988).

Wright, Giles R. *Afro-Americans in New Jersey: A Short History* (1988).

Wright, Lee Alfred. *Identity, Family, and Folklore in African American Literature* (1995).

Wright, Richard R., Jr. *The Negro in Pennsylvania, A Study in Economic History* (1969).

Wubben, Hubert H. *Civil War Iowa and the Copperhead Movement* (1980).

Wynes, Charles E. *Charles Richard Drew: The Man and the Myth* (1988).

Xavier, Ismail. *Allegories of Underdevelopment: Aesthetics and Politics in Modern Brazilian Cinema* (1997).

Yancey, Dwayne. *When Hell Froze Over: The Untold Story of Doug Wilder: A Black Politician's Rise to Power in the South* (1988).

Yau, John. "Please, Wait by the Coatroom: Wifredo Lam in the Museum of Modern Art." *Arts Magazine* 4 (1988): 56-59.

Yellin, Jean Fagan, and John C. Van Horne, eds. *The Abolitionist Sisterhood: Women's Political Culture in Antebellum America* (1994).

Yohe, Kristine A. "Gloria Naylor." In *The Oxford Companion to African American Literature,* ed. James David Hart and Phillip W. Leininger. 6th ed. (1995).

Young, Andrew. *An Easy Burden: The Civil Rights Movement and the Transformation of America* (1996).

——. *A Way Out of No Way: The Spiritual Memoirs of Andrew Young* (1994).

Young, Crawford. *Politics in the Congo: Decolonization and Independence* (1965).

Zangrando, Robert. *The NAACP Crusade Against Lynching, 1909-1950* (1980).

Zenón Cruz, Isabelo. *Narciso descubre su trasero: El negro en la cultura puertorriqueña.* 2d ed. (1975).

Zielina, Maria Carmen. *La africania en el cuento cubano y puertorriqueño* (1992).

Zinn, Howard. *SNCC: The New Abolitionists* (1965).